T5-DHW-746

Who's Who in the South and Southwest

Biographical Titles Currently Published by Marquis Who's Who

Who's Who in America

- Who's Who in America supplements:
  - Who's Who in America Classroom Project Book
  - Who's Who in America Index:
    Geographic Index, Professional Area Index

Who Was Who in America

- Historical Volume (1607-1896)
- Volume I (1897-1942)
- Volume II (1943-1950)
- Volume III (1951-1960)
- Volume IV (1961-1968)
- Volume V (1969-1973)
- Volume VI (1974-1976)
- Volume VII (1977-1981)
- Volume VIII (1982-1985)
- Index Volume (1607-1985)

Who's Who in the World

Who's Who in the East

Who's Who in the Midwest

Who's Who in the South and Southwest

Who's Who in the West

Who's Who in American Law

Who's Who of American Women

Who's Who in Finance and Industry

Who's Who in Frontiers of Science and Technology

Index to Who's Who Books

Directory of Medical Specialists

Who's Who in the South and Southwest®

Including Alabama, Arkansas, Florida, Georgia, Kentucky, Louisiana, Mississippi, North Carolina, Oklahoma, South Carolina, Tennessee, Texas, Virginia, West Virginia, Puerto Rico, the Virgin Islands, and Mexico

20th edition 1986-1987

MARQUIS
Who's Who

Macmillan Directory Division
3002 Glenview Road
Wilmette, Illinois 60091 U.S.A.

Library of Congress Catalog Card Number 50-58231
International Standard Book Number 0-8379-0820-5
Product Code Number 030411

Distributed in Asia by
United Publishers Services Ltd.
Kenkyu-Sha Bldg.
9, Kanda Surugadai 2-Chome
Chiyoda-Ku, Tokyo, Japan

Manufactured in the United States of America

Table of Contents

Preface

The twentieth edition of *Who's Who in the South and Southwest* represents our most recent effort to provide biographical information on men and women of distinction whose influence is concentrated in the southern and southwestern sectors of North America. Such individuals are of decided reference interest locally and, to an increasing degree, nationally.

The volume contains approximately 19,000 names from the region embracing Alabama, Arkansas, Florida, Georgia, Kentucky, Louisiana, Mississippi, North Carolina, Oklahoma, South Carolina, Tennessee, Texas, Virginia, West Virginia, Puerto Rico, and the Virgin Islands. Because of its own importance and its contiguity to the southwestern United States, Mexico is also covered in this volume. Reviewed, revised, and amended, the twentieth edition offers up to date coverage of a broad range of key individuals based on position or individual achievement.

The persons sketched in this volume represent virtually every important field of endeavor. Included are executives and officials in government, business, education, religion, the press, civic affairs, the arts, cultural activities, law, and other fields.

Most biographees have furnished their own data, thus assuring a high degree of accuracy. In some cases where individuals failed to provide information, Marquis staff members compiled the data through independent research. Such sketches are denoted by an asterisk. As in previous editions, biographees were given the opportunity to review prepublication proofs of their sketches to make sure they were correct.

The question is often asked, "How do people get into a Who's Who volume?" Name selection is based on one fundamental principle: reference value. Biographees of *Who's Who in the South and Southwest* can be classified in two basic categories: (1) persons who are of regional reference importance to colleagues, librarians, researchers, scholars, the press, historians, biographers, participants in business and civic affairs, and others with specific or general inquiry needs; (2) individuals of national reference interest who are also of such regional or local importance that their inclusion in the book is essential.

In the editorial evaluation that resulted in the ultimate selection of the names in this directory, an individual's desire to be listed was not sufficient reason for inclusion. Only occupational stature or achievement in a field within the southern or southwestern region of North America influenced selection.

Marquis Who's Who editors exercise the utmost care in preparing each biographical sketch for publication. Occasionally, however, errors do occur despite all precautions taken to minimize such occurrences. Users of this directory are requested to draw the attention of the publisher to any errors found so that corrections can be made in a subsequent edition.

The twentieth edition of *Who's Who in the South and Southwest* carries on the tradition of excellence established in 1899 with the publication of the first edition of *Who's Who in America.* The essence of that tradition is reflected in our continuing effort to produce reference works that are responsive to the needs of users throughout the world.

Board of Advisors

Marquis Who's Who gratefully acknowledges the following distinguished individuals who have made themselves available for review, evaluation, and general comment with regard to the publication of the twentieth edition of *Who's Who in the South and Southwest.* The advisors have enhanced the reference value of this edition by the nomination of outstanding individuals for inclusion. However, the Board of Advisors, either collectively or individually, is in no way responsible for the selection of names or for the accuracy of the information in this volume.

Dame Sonia Arova
Artistic Director
The State of Alabama Ballet

Edward J. Boling
President
The University of Tennessee

Betty E. Callaham
State Librarian
South Carolina

Frances T. Farenthold
Attorney
Houston, Texas

Maurice A. Ferre
Attorney
Miami, Florida

Robert A. Grasser
Executive Director
Central Alabama Regional Planning and Development Commission

Luis Herrera de la Fuente
Music Director
The Oklahoma Symphony Orchestra

John B. Hussey
Mayor
Shreveport, Louisiana

Joseph B. Johnson
President
Grambling State University

Hugh J. Morgan, Jr.
Chairman of the Board
Southern Natural Gas Company

Board of Nominators

Marquis Who's Who gratefully acknowledges the following distinguished individuals for their assistance with regard to the publication of the twentieth edition of *Who's Who in the South and Southwest.* As nominators, they have enhanced the reference value of this edition by the recommendation of outstanding persons from their respective states or local areas. The Board of Nominators, either collectively or individually, is in no way responsible for the final selection of names appearing in this volume, nor does the Board of Nominators bear responsibility for the accuracy or comprehensiveness of the biographical information or other material contained herein.

Ira M. Agricola
Executive Director
Hampton Roads Chamber of Commerce–Portsmouth Office
Portsmouth, Virginia

Gerald L. Bartels
Executive Vice President
Atlanta Chamber of Commerce
Atlanta, Georgia

Robert H. Booth
Executive Vice President
Greater Durham Chamber of Commerce
Durham, North Carolina

John A. Chapman
President
Charleston Regional Chamber of Commerce and Development
Charleston, West Virginia

Clyde A. Cole
President
Metropolitan Tulsa Chamber of Commerce
Tulsa, Oklahoma

Edward H. Cook
President
Oklahoma City Chamber of Commerce
Oklahoma City, Oklahoma

J. Mac Holladay
Executive Vice President
Trident Charleston Chamber of Commerce
Charleston, South Carolina

Ed Houlihan
President
Greater Lexington Chamber of Commerce
Lexington, Kentucky

Paul Latture, Jr.
Executive Vice President
Jackson Chamber of Commerce
Jackson, Mississippi

John A. Logan
President and General Manager
Lubbock Chamber of Commerce
Lubbock, Texas

Larry M. Malta
Former Executive Vice President
Hialeah Chamber of Commerce
Hialeah, Florida

Louis O. Miller, Jr.
Executive Vice President
Virginia Peninsula Chamber of Commerce
Hampton, Virginia

Don A. Newton
Executive Vice President
Birmingham Area Chamber of Commerce
Birmingham, Alabama

James O. Roberson
President
Louisville Chamber of Commerce
Louisville, Kentucky

Jack C. Smith
Executive Vice President
Roanoke Valley Chamber of Commerce
Roanoke, Virginia

Louie Welch
Former President
Houston Chamber of Commerce
Houston, Texas

Glenn E. West
Executive Vice President
The Greater Macon Chamber of Commerce
Macon, Georgia

Standards of Admission

The foremost consideration in selecting biographees for *Who's Who in the South and Southwest* is the extent of an individual's reference interest. Such reference interest is judged on either of two factors: (1) the position of responsibility held or (2) the level of significant achievement attained.

Admissions based on the factor of position include:

- Members of the U.S. Congress
- Federal judges
- Governors of states covered by this volume
- State attorneys general
- Judges of state and territorial courts of highest appellate jurisdiction
- Mayors of major cities
- Heads of major universities and colleges
- Heads of leading philanthropic, educational, cultural, and scientific institutions and associations
- Chief ecclesiastics of the principal religious denominations
- Principal officers of national and international business
- Others chosen because of incumbency or membership

Admission for individual achievement is based on objective qualitative criteria. To be selected, a person must have attained conspicuous achievement. The biographee may scarcely be known in the local community but may be recognized in some field of endeavor for noteworthy accomplishment.

Key to Information

❶ **FULTON, SAMUEL GARDNER** ❷ banker; ❸ b. Roanoke, Va., May 9, 1923; ❹ s. Oliver and Lorraine (Gardner) F.; ❺ m. Rachel Harrison, Dec. 24, 1946; ❻ children: Sallie Joe Fulton Potter, Walter James, Frances Ruth Fulton Palmer, Cecily Louise Fulton McBride. ❼ B.A., Furman U., 1944. ❽ Teller, Union Nat. Bank, Decatur, Ga., 1947-50, trust officer, 1950-57, v.p. trusts, 1957-65, pres., 1965—, chmn. bd., 1975—, also dir.; lectr. banking Decatur Jr. Coll., 1968—. ❾ Contbr. articles to profl. jours. ❿ Chmn. Decatur City Council, 1965-68, 71-74; bd. dirs. Salvation Army Home. ⓫ Served USNR, 1944-46; PTO. ⓬ Decorated Bronze Star; named Man of Yr., Decatur Jaycees, 1969; recipient Outstanding Alumnus award Furman U., 1976. ⓭ Mem. Am. Banker's Assn., AIM, Decatur Banker's League (pres. 1967-68, dir. 1970—), Phi Delta Theta. ⓮ Democrat. ⓯ Baptist. ⓰ Clubs: Decatur Country, Decatur Athletic. ⓱ Lodges: Masons, Shriners. ⓲ Avocations: golf, stamp collecting. ⓳ Home: 28 Hidden Hollow Rd Decatur GA 30032 ⓴ Office: Union Nat Bank 350 Peachtree St Decatur GA 30034

KEY

❶ Name
❷ Occupation
❸ Vital Statistics
❹ Parents
❺ Marriage
❻ Children
❼ Education
❽ Career
❾ Writing and special achievements
❿ Civic and political activities
⓫ Military record
⓬ Awards
⓭ Professional and association memberships
⓮ Political affiliation
⓯ Religion
⓰ Clubs
⓱ Lodges
⓲ Avocations
⓳ Home address
⓴ Office address

Table of Abbreviations

The following abbreviations and symbols are frequently used in this book.

*An asterisk following a sketch indicates that it was researched by the Marquis Who's Who editorial staff and has not been verified by the biographee.

A.A. Associate in Arts
AAAL American Academy of Arts and Letters
AAAS American Association for the Advancement of Science
AAHPER Alliance for Health, Physical Education and Recreation
AAU Amateur Athletic Union
AAUP American Association of University Professors
AAUW American Association of University Women
A.B. Arts, Bachelor of
AB Alberta
ABA American Bar Association
ABC American Broadcasting Company
AC Air Corps
acad. academy, academic
acct. accountant
accg. accounting
ACDA Arms Control and Disarmament Agency
ACLU American Civil Liberties Union
ACP American College of Physicians
ACS American College of Surgeons
ADA American Dental Association
a.d.c. aide-de-camp
adj. adjunct. adjutant
adj. gen. adjutant general
adm. admiral
adminstr. administrator
adminstrn. administration
adminstrv. administrative
ADP Automatic Data Processing
adv. advocate, advisory
advt. advertising
A.E. Agricultural Engineer (for degrees only)
A.E. and P. Ambassador Extraordinary and Plenipotentiary
AEC Atomic Energy Commission
aero. aeronautical, aeronautic
aerodyn. aerodynamic
AFB Air Force Base
AFL-CIO American Federation of Labor and Congress of Industrial Organizations
AFTRA American Federation TV and Radio Artists
agr. agriculture
agrl. agricultural
agt. agent
AGVA American Guild of Variety Artists
agy. agency
A&I Agricultural and Industrial
AIA American Institute of Architects
AIAA American Institute of Aeronautics and Astronautics
AID Agency for International Development
AIEE American Institute of Electrical Engineers
AIM American Institute of Management
AIME American Institute of Mining, Metallurgy, and Petroleum Engineers
AK Alaska
AL Alabama
ALA American Library Association
Ala. Alabama
alt. alternate
Alta. Alberta
A&M Agricultural and Mechanical
A.M. Arts, Master of
Am. American, America
AMA American Medical Association
A.M.E. African Methodist Episcopal
Amtrak National Railroad Passenger Corporation
AMVETS American Veterans of World War II, Korea, Vietnam
anat. anatomical
ann. annual
ANTA American National Theatre and Academy
anthrop. anthropological
AP Associated Press
APO Army Post Office
Apr. April
apptd. appointed
apt. apartment
AR Arkansas
ARC American Red Cross
archeol. archeological
archtl. architectural
Ariz. Arizona
Ark. Arkansas
ArtsD. Arts, Doctor of
arty. artillery
ASCAP American Society of Composers, Authors and Publishers
ASCE American Society of Civil Engineers
ASHRAE American Society of Heating, Refrigeration, and Air Conditioning Engineers
ASME American Society of Mechanical Engineers
assn. association
assoc. associate
asst. assistant
ASTM American Society for Testing and Materials
astron. astronomical
astrophys. astrophysical
ATSC Air Technical Service Command
AT&T American Telephone & Telegraph Company
atty. attorney
AUS Army of the United States
Aug. August
aux. auxiliary
Ave. Avenue
AVMA American Veterinary Medical Association
AZ Arizona

B. Bachelor
b. born
B.A. Bachelor of Arts
B.Agr. Bachelor of Agriculture
Balt. Baltimore
Bapt. Baptist
B. Arch. Bachelor of Architecture
B.A.S. Bachelor of Agricultural Science
B.B.A. Bachelor of Business Administration
BBC British Broadcasting Corporation
B.C., BC British Columbia
B.C.E. Bachelor of Civil Engineering
B. Chir. Bachelor of Surgery
B.C.L. Bachelor of Civil Law
B.C.S. Bachelor of Commercial Science
B.D. Bachelor of Divinity
bd. board
B.E. Bachelor of Education
B.E.E. Bachelor of Electrical Engineering
B.F.A. Bachelor of Fine Arts
bibl. biblical
bibliog. bibliographical
biog. biographical
biol. biological
B.J. Bachelor of Journalism
Bklyn. Brooklyn
B.L. Bachelor of Letters
bldg. building
B.L.S. Bachelor of Library Science
Blvd. Boulevard
bn. battalion
B.&O.R.R. Baltimore & Ohio Railroad
bot. botanical
B.P.E. Bachelor of Physical Education
br. branch
B.R.E. Bachelor of Religious Education
brig. gen. brigadier general
Brit. British, Britannica
Bros. Brothers
B.S. Bachelor of Science
B.S.A. Bachelor of Agricultural Science
B.S.D. Bachelor of Didactic Science
B.S.T. Bachelor of Sacred Theology
B.Th. Bachelor of Theology
bull. bulletin
bur. bureau
bus. business
B.W.I. British West Indies

CA California

CAA Civil Aeronautics Administration
CAB Civil Aeronautics Board
Calif. California
C.Am. Central America
Can. Canada, Canadian
CAP Civil Air Patrol
capt. captain
CARE Cooperative American Relief Everywhere
Cath. Catholic
cav. cavalry
CBC Canadian Broadcasting Company
CBI China, Burma, India Theatre of Operations
CBS Columbia Broadcasting System
CCC Commodity Credit Corporation
CCNY City College of New York
CCU Cardiac Care Unit
CD Civil Defense
C.E. Corps of Engineers, Civil Engineers (in firm's name only or for degree)
cen. central (To be used for court system only)
CENTO Central Treaty Organization
CERN European Organization of Nuclear Research
cert. certificate, certification, certified
CETA Comprehensive Employment Training Act
CFL Canadian Football League
ch. church
Ch.D. Doctor of Chemistry
chem. chemical
Chem.E. Chemical Engineer
Chgo. Chicago
chirurg. chirurgical
chmn. chairman
chpt. chapter
CIA Central Intelligence Agency
CIC Counter Intelligence Corps
Cin. Cincinnati
cir. circuit
Cleve. Cleveland
climatol. climatological
clin. clinical
clk. clerk
C.L.U. Chartered Life Underwriter
C.M. Master in Surgery
C.&N.W.Ry. Chicago & Northwestern Railway
CO Colorado
Co. Company
COF Catholic Order of Foresters
C. of C. Chamber of Commerce
col. colonel
coll. college
Colo. Colorado
com. committee
comd. commanded
comdg. commanding
comdr. commander
comdt. commandant
commd. commissioned
comml. commercial
commn. commission
commr. commissioner
condr. conductor
Conf. Conference
Congl. Congregational, Congressional
Conglist. Congregationalist
Conn. Connecticut
cons. consultant, consulting
consol. consolidated
constl. constitutional
constn. constitution
constrn. construction
contbd. contributed
contbg. contributing
contbn. contribution
contbr. contributor
Conv. Convention
coop. cooperative
CORDS Civil Operations and Revolutionary Development Support
CORE Congress of Racial Equality
corp. corporation, corporate
corr. correspondent, corresponding, correspondence
C.&O.Ry. Chesapeake & Ohio Railway
C.P.A. Certified Public Accountant
C.P.C.U. Chartered Property and Casualty Underwriter
C.P.H. Certificate of Public Health
cpl. corporal
CPR Cardio-Pulmonary Resuscitation
C.P.Ry. Canadian Pacific Railway
C.S. Christian Science
C.S.B. Bachelor of Christian Science
CSC Civil Service Commission
C.S.D. Doctor of Christian Science
CT Connecticut
ct. court
crt. center
CWS Chemical Warfare Service
C.Z. Canal Zone
d. daughter
D. Doctor
D.Agr. Doctor of Agriculture
DAR Daughters of the American Revolution
dau. daughter
DAV Disabled American Veterans
D.C.,DC District of Columbia
D.C.L. Doctor of Civil Law
D.C.S. Doctor of Commercial Science
D.D. Doctor of Divinity
D.D.S. Doctor of Dental Surgery
DE Delaware
dec. deceased
Dec. December
def. defense
Del. Delaware
del. delegate, delegation
Dem. Democrat, Democratic
D.Eng. Doctor of Engineering
denom. denomination, denominational
dep. deputy
dept. department
dermatol. dermatological
desc. descendant
devel. development, developmental
D.F.A. Doctor of Fine Arts
D.F.C. Distinguished Flying Cross
D.H.L. Doctor of Hebrew Literature
dir. director
dist. district
distbg. distributing
distbn. distribution
distbr. distributor
disting. distinguished
div. division, divinity, divorce
D.Litt. Doctor of Literature
D.M.D. Doctor of Medical Dentistry
D.M.S. Doctor of Medical Science
D.O. Doctor of Osteopathy
D.P.H. Diploma in Public Health
D.R. Daughters of the Revolution
Dr. Drive, Doctor
D.R.E. Doctor of Religious Education
Dr.P.H. Doctor of Public Health, Doctor of Public Hygiene
D.S.C. Distinguished Service Cross
D.Sc. Doctor of Science
D.S.M. Distinguished Service Medal
D.S.T. Doctor of Sacred Theology
D.T.M. Doctor of Tropical Medicine
D.V.M. Doctor of Veterinary Medicine
D.V.S. Doctor of Veterinary Surgery

E. East
ea. eastern (use for court system only)
E. and P. Extraordinary and Plenipotentiary
Eccles. Ecclesiastical
ecol. ecological
econ. economic
ECOSOC Economic and Social Council (of the UN)
E.D. Doctor of Engineering
ed. educated
Ed.B. Bachelor of Education
Ed.D. Doctor of Education
edit. edition
Ed.M. Master of Education
edn. education
ednl. educational
EDP electronic data processing
Ed.S. Specialist in Education
E.E. Electrical Engineer (degree only)
E.E. and M.P. Envoy Extraordinary and Minister Plenipotentiary
EEC European Economic Community
EEG Electroencephalogram
EEO Equal Employment Opportunity

EEOC Equal Employment Opportunity Commission
EKG Electrocardiogram
E.Ger. German Democratic Republic
elec. electrical
electrochem. electrochemical
electrophys. electrophysical
elem. elementary
E.M. Engineer of Mines
ency. encyclopedia
Eng. England
engr. engineer
engring. engineering
entomol. entomological
environ. environmental
EPA Environmental Protection Agency
epidemiol. epidemiological
Episc. Episcopalian
ERA Equal Rights Amendment
ERDA Energy Research and Development Administration
ESEA Elementary and Secondary Education Act
ESL English as Second Language
ESSA Environmental Science Services Administration
ethnol. ethnological
ETO European Theatre of Operations
Evang. Evangelical
exam. examination, examining
exec. executive
exhbn. exhibition
expdn. expedition
expn. exposition
expt. experiment
exptl. experimental

F.A. Field Artillery
FAA Federal Aviation Administration
FAO Food and Agriculture Organization (of the UN)
FBI Federal Bureau of Investigation
FCA Farm Credit Administration
FCC Federal Communication Commission
FCDA Federal Civil Defense Administration
FDA Food and Drug Administration
FDIA Federal Deposit Insurance Administration
FDIC Federal Deposit Insurance Corporation
F.E. Forest Engineer
FEA Federal Energy Administration
Feb. February
fed. federal
fedn. federation
FERC Federal Energy Regulatory Commission
fgn. foreign
FHA Federal Housing Administration
fin. financial, finance
FL Florida

Fla. Florida
FMC Federal Maritime Commission
FOA Foreign Operations Administration
found. foundation
FPC Federal Power Commission
FPO Fleet Post Office
frat. fraternity
FRS Federal Reserve System
FSA Federal Security Agency
Ft. Fort
FTC Federal Trade Commission

G-1 (or other number) Division of General Staff
Ga., GA Georgia
GAO General Accounting Office
gastroent. gastroenterological
GATT General Agreement of Tariff and Trades
gen. general
geneal. genealogical
geod. geodetic
geog. geographic, geographical
geol. geological
geophys. geophysical
gerontol. gerontological
G.H.Q. General Headquarters
G.N. Ry. Great Northern Railway
gov. governor
govt. government
govtl. governmental
GPO Governmental Printing Office
grad. graduate, graduated
GSA General Services Administration
Gt. Great
GU Guam
gynecol. gynecological

hdqrs. headquarters
HEW Department of Health, Education and Welfare
H.H.D. Doctor of Humanities
HHFA Housing and Home Finance Agency
HHS Department of Health and Human Services
HI Hawaii
hist. historical, historic
H.M. Master of Humanics
homeo. homeopathic
hon. honorary, honorable
Ho. of Dels. House of Delegates
Ho. of Reps. House of Representatives
hort. horticultural
hosp. hospital
HUD Department of Housing and Urban Development
Hwy. Highway
hydrog. hydrographic

IA Iowa
IAEA International Atomic Energy Agency

IBM International Business Machines Corporation
IBRD International Bank for Reconstruction and Development
ICA International Cooperation Administration
ICC Interstate Commerce Commission
ICU Intensive Care Unit
ID Idaho
IEEE Institute of Electrical and Electronics Engineers
IFC International Finance Corporation
IGY International Geophysical Year
IL Illinois
Ill. Illinois
illus. illustrated
ILO International Labor Organization
IMF International Monetary Fund
IN Indiana
Inc. Incorporated
ind. independent
Ind. Indiana
Indpls. Indianapolis
indsl. industrial
inf. infantry
info. information
ins. insurance
insp. inspector
insp. gen. inspector general
inst. institute
instl. institutional
instn. institution
instr. instructor
instrn. instruction
intern. international
intro. introduction
IRE Institute of Radio Engineers
IRS Internal Revenue Service
ITT International Telephone & Telegraph Corporation

JAG Judge Advocate General
JAGC Judge Advocate General Corps
Jan. January
Jaycees Junior Chamber of Commerce
J.B. Jurum Baccolaureus
J.C.B. Juris Canoni Baccalaureus
J.C.D. Juris Canonici Doctor, Juris Civilis Doctor
J.C.L. Juris Canonici Licentiatus
J.D. Juris Doctor
j.g. junior grade
jour. journal
jr. junior
J.S.D. Juris Scientiae Doctor
J.U.D. Juris Utriusque Doctor
jud. judicial

Kans. Kansas
K.C. Knights of Columbus
K.P. Knights of Pythias
KS Kansas

K.T. Knight Templar
Ky., KY Kentucky

La., LA Louisiana
lab. laboratory
lang. language
laryngol. laryngological
LB Labrador
lectr. lecturer
legis. legislation, legislative
L.H.D. Doctor of Humane Letters
L.I. Long Island
lic. licensed, license
L.I.R.R. Long Island Railroad
lit. literary, literature
Litt.B. Bachelor of Letters
Litt.D. Doctor of Letters
LL.B. Bachelor of Laws
LL.D. Doctor of Laws
LL.M. Master of Laws
Ln. Lane
L.&N.R.R. Louisville & Nashville Railroad
L.S. Library Science (in degree)
lt. lieutenant
Ltd. Limited
Luth. Lutheran
LWV League of Women Voters

m. married
M. Master
M.A. Master of Arts
MA Massachusetts
mag. magazine
M.Agr. Master of Agriculture
maj. major
Man. Manitoba
Mar. March
M.Arch. Master in Architecture
Mass. Massachusetts
math. mathematics, mathematical
MATS Military Air Transport Service
M.B. Bachelor of Medicine
MB Manitoba
M.B.A. Master of Business Administration
MBS Mutual Broadcasting System
M.C. Medical Corps
M.C.E. Master of Civil Engineering
mcht. merchant
mcpl. municipal
M.C.S. Master of Commercial Science
M.D. Doctor of Medicine
Md, MD Maryland
M.Dip. Master in Diplomacy
mdse. merchandise
M.D.V. Doctor of Veterinary Medicine
M.E. Mechanical Engineer (degree only)
ME Maine
M.E.Ch. Methodist Episcopal Church
mech. mechanical
M.Ed. Master of Education
med. medical
M.E.E. Master of Electrical Engineering
mem. member
meml. memorial
merc. mercantile
met. metropolitan
metall. metallurgical
Met.E. Metallurgical Engineer
meteorol. meteorological
Meth. Methodist
Mex. Mexico
M.F. Master of Forestry
M.F.A. Master of Fine Arts
mfg. manufacturing
mfr. manufacturer
mgmt. management
mgr. manager
M.H.A. Master of Hospital Administration
M.I. Military Intelligence
MI Michigan
Mich. Michigan
micros. microscopic, microscopical
mid. middle (use for Court System only)
mil. military
Milw. Milwaukee
mineral. mineralogical
Minn. Minnesota
Miss. Mississippi
MIT Massachusetts Institute of Technology
mktg. marketing
M.L. Master of Laws
MLA Modern Language Association
M.L.D. Magister Legnum Diplomatic
M.Litt. Master of Literature
M.L.S. Master of Library Science
M.M.E. Master of Mechanical Engineering
MN Minnesota
mng. managing
Mo., MO Missouri
moblzn. mobilization
Mont. Montana
M.P. Member of Parliament
M.P.E. Master of Physical Education
M.P.H. Master of Public Health
M.P.L. Master of Patent Law
Mpls. Minneapolis
M.R.E. Master of Religious Education
M.S. Master of Science
MS, Ms. Mississippi
M.Sc. Master of Science
M.S.F. Master of Science of Forestry
M.S.T. Master of Sacred Theology
M.S.W. Master of Social Work
MT Montana
Mt. Mount
MTO Mediterranean Theatre of Operations
mus. museum, musical
Mus.B. Bachelor of Music
Mus.D. Doctor of Music
Mus.M. Master of Music
mut. mutual
mycol. mycological
N. North
NAACP National Association for the Advancement of Colored People
NACA National Advisory Committee for Aeronautics
NAD National Academy of Design
N.Am. North America
NAM National Association of Manufacturers
NAPA National Association of Performing Artists
NAREB National Association of Real Estate Boards
NARS National Archives and Record Service
NASA National Aeronautics and Space Administration
nat. national
NATO North Atlantic Treaty Organization
NATOUSA North African Theatre of Operations
nav. navigation
N.B., NB New Brunswick
NBC National Broadcasting Company
N.C., NC North Carolina
NCCJ National Conference of Christians and Jews
N.D., ND North Dakota
NDEA National Defense Education Act
NE Nebraska
NE Northeast
NEA National Education Association
Nebr. Nebraska
NEH National Endowment for Humanities
neurol. neurological
Nev. Nevada
NF Newfoundland
NFL National Football League
Nfld. Newfoundland
N.G. National Guard
N.H. NH New Hampshire
NHL National Hockey League
NIH National Institutes of Health
NIMH National Institute of Mental Health
N.J., NJ New Jersey
NLRB National Labor Relations Board
NM New Mexico
N.Mex. New Mexico
No. Northern
NOAA National Oceanographic and Atmospheric Administration
NORAD North America Air Defense
NOW National Organization for Women
Nov. November
N.P.Ry. Northern Pacific Railway
nr. near
NRC National Research Council
N.S., NS Nova Scotia
NSC National Security Council
NSF National Science Foundation
N.T. New Testament
NT Northwest Territories
numis. numismatic

NV Nevada
NW Northwest
N.W.T. Northwest Territories
N.Y., NY New York
N.Y.C. New York City
NYU New York University
N.Z. New Zealand

OAS Organization of American States
ob-gyn obstetrics-gynecology
obs. observatory
obstet. obstetrical
O.D. Doctor of Optometry
OECD Organization of European Cooperation and Development
OEEC Organization of European Economic Cooperation
OEO Office of Economic Opportunity
ofcl. official
OH Ohio
OK Oklahoma
Okla. Oklahoma
ON Ontario
Ont. Ontario
ophthal. ophthalmological
ops. operations
OR Oregon
orch. orchestra
Oreg. Oregon
orgn. organization
ornithol. ornithological
OSHA Occupational Safety and Health Administration
OSRD Office of Scientific Research and Development
OSS Office of Strategic Services
osteo. osteopathic
otol. otological
otolaryn. otolaryngological

Pa., PA Pennsylvania
P.A. Professional Association
paleontol. paleontological
path. pathological
P.C. Professional Corporation
PE Prince Edward Island
P.E.I. Prince Edward Island (text only)
PEN Poets, Playwrights, Editors, Essayists and Novelists (international association)
penol. penological
P.E.O. women's organization (full name not disclosed)
pfc. private first class
PHA Public Housing Administration
pharm. pharmaceutical
Pharm.D. Doctor of Pharmacy
Pharm. M. Master of Pharmacy
Ph.B. Bachelor of Philosophy
Ph.D. Doctor of Philosophy
Phila. Philadelphia
philharm. philharmonic
philol. philological
philos. philosophical
photog. photographic
phys. physical
physiol. physiological
Pitts. Pittsburgh
Pkwy. Parkway
Pl. Place
P.&L.E.R.R. Pittsburgh & Lake Erie Railroad
P.O. Post Office
PO Box Post Office Box
polit. political
poly. polytechnic, polytechnical
PQ Province of Quebec
P.R., PR Puerto Rico
prep. preparatory
pres. president
Presbyn. Presbyterian
presdl. presidential
prin. principal
proc. proceedings
prod. produced (play production)
prodn. production
prof. professor
profl. professional
prog. progressive
propr. proprietor
pros. atty. prosecuting attorney
pro tem pro tempore
PSRO Professional Services Review Organization
psychiat. psychiatric
psychol. psychological
PTA Parent-Teachers Association
ptnr. partner
PTO Pacific Theatre of Operations, Parent Teacher Organization
pub. publisher, publishing, published
pub. public
publ. publication
pvt. private

quar. quarterly
q.m. quartermaster
Q.M.C. Quartermaster Corps.
Que. Quebec

radiol. radiological
RAF Royal Air Force
RCA Radio Corporation of America
RCAF Royal Canadian Air Force
RD Rural Delivery
Rd. Road
REA Rural Electrification Administration
rec. recording
ref. reformed
regt. regiment
regtl. regimental
rehab. rehabilitation
rep. representative
Rep. Republican
Res. Reserve
ret. retired
rev. review, revised
RFC Reconstruction Finance Corporation
RFD Rural Free Delivery
rhinol. rhinological
R.I., RI Rhode Island
R.N. Registered Nurse
roentgenol. roentgenological
ROTC Reserve Officers Training Corps
R.R. Railroad
Ry. Railway

s. son
S. South
SAC Strategic Air Command
SALT Strategic Arms Limitation Talks
S.Am. South America
san. sanitary
SAR Sons of the American Revolution
Sask. Saskatchewan
savs. savings
S.B. Bachelor of Science
SBA Small Business Administration
S.C., SC South Carolina
SCAP Supreme Command Allies Pacific
Sc.B. Bachelor of Science
S.C.D. Doctor of Commercial Science
Sc.D. Doctor of Science
sch. school
sci. science, scientific
SCLC Southern Christian Leadership Conference
SCV Sons of Confederate Veterans
S.D., SD South Dakota
SE Southeast
SEATO Southeast Asia Treaty Organization
sec. secretary
SEC Securities and Exchange Commission
sect. section
seismol. seismological
sem. seminary
s.g. senior grade
sgt. sergeant
SHAEF Supreme Headquarters Allied Expeditionary Forces
SHAPE Supreme Headquarters Allied Powers in Europe
S.I. Staten Island
S.J. Society of Jesus (Jesuit)
S.J.D. Scientiae Juridicae Doctor
SK Saskatchewan
S.M. Master of Science
So. Southern
soc. society
sociol. sociological
S.P. Co. Southern Pacific Company
spl. special
splty. specialty
Sq. Square
sr. senior
S.R. Sons of the Revolution

SS Steamship
SSS Selective Service System
St. Saint, Street
sta. station
stats. statistics
statis. statistical
S.T.B. Bachelor of Sacred Theology
stblzn. stabilization
S.T.D. Doctor of Sacred Theology
subs. subsidiary
SUNY State University of New York
supr. supervisor
supt. superintendent
surg. surgical
SW Southwest

TAPPI Technical Association of Pulp and Paper Industry
Tb Tuberculosis
tchr. teacher
tech. technical, technology
technol. technological
Tel.&Tel. Telephone & Telegraph
temp. temporary
Tenn. Tennessee
Ter. Territory
Terr. Terrace
Tex. Texas
Th.D. Doctor of Theology
theol. theological
Th.M. Master of Theology
TN Tennessee
tng. training
topog. topographical
trans. transaction, transferred
transl. translation, translated
transp. transportation
treas. treasurer
TV television
TVA Tennessee Valley Authority
twp. township
TX Texas
typog. typographical

U. University
UAW United Auto Workers
UCLA University of California at Los Angeles
UDC United Daughters of the Confederacy
U.K. United Kingdom
UN United Nations
UNESCO United Nations Educational, Scientific and Cultural Organization
UNICEF United Nations International Children's Emergency Fund
univ. university
UNRRA United Nations Relief and Rehabilitation Administration
UPI United Press International
U.P.R.R. United Pacific Railroad
urol. urological
U.S. United States
U.S.A. United States of America
USAAF United States Army Air Force
USAF United States Air Force
USAFR United States Air Force Reserve
USAR United States Army Reserve
USCG United States Coast Guard
USCGR United States Coast Guard Reserve
USES United States Employment Service
USIA United States Information Agency
USMC United States Marine Corps
USMCR United States Marine Corps Reserve
USN United States Navy
USNG United States National Guard
USNR United States Naval Reserve
USO United Service Organizations
USPHS United States Public Health Service
USS United States Ship
USSR Union of the Soviet Socialist Republics
USV United States Volunteers
UT Utah

VA Veterans' Administration
Va., VA Virginia
vet. veteran, veterinary
VFW Veterans of Foreign Wars
V.I., VI Virgin Islands
vice pres. vice president
vis. visiting
VISTA Volunteers in Service to America
VITA Volunteers in Technical Service
vocat. vocational
vol. volunteer, volume
v.p. vice president
vs. versus
Vt., VT Vermont

W. West
WA Washington (state)
WAC Women's Army Corps
Wash. Washington (state)
WAVES Women's Reserve, U.S. Naval Reserve
WCTU Women's Christian Temperance Union
we. western (use for court system only)
W. Ger. Germany, Federal Republic of
WHO World Health Organization
WI, Wis. Wisconsin
W.I. West Indies
WSB Wage Stabilization Board
WV West Virginia
W.Va. West Virginia
WY Wyoming
Wyo. Wyoming

YK Yukon Territory (for address)
YMCA Young Men's Christian Association
YMHA Young Men's Hebrew Association
YM & YWHA Young Men's and Young Women's Hebrew Association
Y.T. Yukon Territory
YWCA Young Women's Christian Association
yr. year

zool. zoological

Alphabetical Practices

Names are arranged alphabetically according to the surnames, and under identical surnames according to the first given name. If both surname and first given name are identical, names are arranged alphabetically according to the second given name. Where full names are identical, they are arranged in order of age—with the elder listed first.

Surnames beginning with De, Des, Du, however capitalized or spaced, are recorded with the prefix preceding the surname and arranged alphabetically, under the letter D.

Surnames beginning with Mac and Mc are arranged alphabetically under M.

Surnames beginning with Saint or St. appear after names that begin Sains, and are arranged according to the second part of the name, e.g. St. Clair before Saint Dennis.

Surnames beginning with Van, Von or von are arranged alphabetically under letter V.

Compound hyphenated surnames are arranged according to the first member of the compound. Compound unhyphenated surnames are treated as hyphenated names.

Parentheses used in connection with a name indicate which part of the full name is usually deleted in common usage. Hence Abbott, W(illiam) Lewis indicates that the usual form of the given name is W. Lewis. In such a case, the parentheses are ignored in alphabetizing. However, if the name is recorded Abbott, (William) Lewis, signifying that the entire name William is not commonly used, the alphabetizing would be arranged as though the name were Abbott, Lewis.

Who's Who in the South and Southwest

AANSTOOS, CHRISTOPHER MICHAEL, psychology educator; b. Saipan Island, U.S. Trust Ter., Apr. 4, 1952; s. Anthony Matthew and Frances Henrietta (Jambrick) A.; m. Rebecca Beryl Switzer, Aug. 6, 1977; 1 child, Megan Elizabeth. B.A., Mich. State U., 1974; M.A., Duquesne U., 1976, Ph.D., 1982. Instr. Pa. State U., McKeesport, 1979-82; asst. prof. psychology West Ga. Coll., Carrollton, 1982—; contracted researcher Pitts. Sch. Dist., 1979; manuscript reviewer Harcour, Brace, Jovanovich, N.Y., 1983, New Ideas in Psychology, 1984-85. Editor Exploring the Lived World, 1984, Jour. The Humanistic Psychologist, 1984—; cons. editor Jour. Metaphor and Symbolic Activity, 1985—, Phenomenological Psychology Jour., 1982; contbr. articles to profl. jours. Coordinator Fund Drive Am. Heart Assn., West Ga. Coll., 1985; vol. West Ga. Coll. Speakers Bur., 1983—. Faculty Research grantee West Ga. Coll., 1983-85. Mem. Am. Psychol. Assn. (exec. bd. divs. 24, 32), AAUP, Human Sci. Research Assn. (program chmn. 1984), Southeastern Psychol. Assn., Assn. Qualitative Research Psychology, Southern Soc. Philosophy Psychology, Phi Beta Kappa. Club: Chess Fedn. (West Ga.). Home: 101 Sims St Carrollton GA 30117 Office: Psy Dept West Ga Coll Carrollton GA 30118

AARON, CHARLES LYNN, JR., college chaplain, counselor; b. Memphis, Tenn., Aug. 3, 1956; s. Charles Lynn and Kathryn (Brewer) A.; m. Sandra Miller, May 25, 1985. B.A. magna cum laude, Lambuth Coll., Jackson, Tenn., 1978; M.S., Memphis State U., 1981; M.Div., Southern Meth. U., 1985. Pastor, Oakfield-Mt. Carmel United Meth. Ch., Jackson, 1976-79; social worker Northeast Mental Health Ctr., Memphis, 1980; dir. youth Emmanuel United Meth. Ch., Memphis, 1980-81; dir. residence hall Southern Meth. U., Dallas, 1984-85; chaplain, counselor Lambuth Coll., Jackson, 19—; chaplain intern Timberlawn Psychiatric Hosp., Dallas, 1983-84. Vol. counselor Memphis House, 1981. United Meth. Ch. scholar, 1982. Mem. Am. Assn. for Counseling and Devel., Assn. for Religious and Values Issues in Counseling, Omicron Phi Tau. Avocations: weight lifting; foreign langs.; guitar. Office: Lambuth Coll Jackson TN 38301

AARON, (HARRY) MICHAEL, psychologist, educator; b. Phila., Mar. 25, 1943; s. Bernard and Anne (Gelfand) A.; m. Anna Maria Arce, June 1, 1974; children—Michael, Kristina. B.S., Pa. State U., 1965; M.Ed., Our Lady of Lake Coll., 1972; M.S., East Tex. State U., 1977, Ph.D., 1977. Lic. psychologist, Tex. Ednl. counselor Concentrated Employment Program, San Antonio, 1971-73; counseling psychologist Lackland AFB, San Antonio, 1973-74; cons. Ariz. Dept. Econ. Security, Phoenix, 1978-79; lectr. II, U. N.Mex., Gallup, 1978-80; clin. psychologist McKinley County Community Mental Health Services, Gallup, 1979-80; cons. Tex. Rehab. Commn., Beaumont, 1979-80; clin. psychologist, supr. Mental Health-Mental Retardation S.E. Tex., Orange, 1980-83; asst. instr. psychology East Tex. State U., Commerce, 1975-77; sch. psychologist Dallas Ind. Sch. Dist., 1976-77, Gallup-McKinley County Sch. Dist., 1977-78; cons. psychologist Gallup Indian Med. Ctr., 1977-80; sch. psychologist Window Rock Sch. Dist. 8, Fort Defiance, Ariz., 1978-79; psychologist in pvt. practice, San Antonio, 1983—; lectr. U. Tex.-San Antonio, 1984—, Tex. Luth. Coll., Seguin, 1984—; cons. Alamo Area Rape Crisis Ctr., San Antonio State Hosp., Met. Health Dist., Jewish Family Services, San Antonio Free Clinic; mem. speakers bur. San Antonio Coalition for Children, Youth and Families, Mental Health Assn. San Antonio. Contbr. articles to profl. jours., column to newspaper. Bd. dirs. Family Outreach San Antonio, 1984-85; pres. bd. dirs. San Antonio Widowed Person's Service of Am. Assn. Ret. Persons, 1985—. Served to capt. U.S. Army, 1965-69, Vietnam. Recipient Community Service award Mental Health Assn., San Antonio, 1984; Service award San Antonio Coalition for Children, Youth and Families, 1983-84. Mem. Am. Psychol. Assn., Tex. Psychol. Assn., Bexar County Psychol. Assn. (chmn. job opportunity com. 1984-85), Psi Chi (pres. chpt. 1975-76). Democrat. Jewish. Avocations: autograph collection; woodworking. Home: 11719 Spring Rain San Antonio TX 78249 Office: 4203 Gardendale Suite C-107 San Antonio TX 78229

ABAGNALE, FRANK WILLIAM, JR., security company executive, lecturer; b. Bronx, N.Y., Apr. 27, 1948; s. Frank William and Paulette Noel (Anton) A.; m. Kelly Anne Welbes, Nov. 6, 1976; children—Scott, Chris, Sean. Student pub. schs., Houston. Pres., chief exec. officer Abagnale & Assocs., Houston, 1976—; also pub. speaker. Author: Catch Me If You Can, 1980; Green Book, 1982. Mem. Nat. Speakers Assn., Internat. Platform Assn. Republican. Roman Catholic. Home: PO Box 701290 Tulsa OK 74170

ABALOS, JOSE ALVAREZ, III, program evaluation specialist; b. Manila, July 25, 1948, came to U.S., 1976, naturalized, 1986; s. Jose Salinas and Josefina (Alvarez) A.; m. Barbara Jane Van Dusen, Jan. 28, 1979; children—Brian Joseph, David Francis. B.S. in Math., Philippine Coll. Arts and Trades, 1969; M.A. in Math. Edn., U. Philippines, 1973; Ph.D. in Ednl. Psychology, U. Hawaii, 1983. Instr. Pangasin State U., Philippines, 1969-73; sr. researcher Fund Assistance to Pvt. Edn., Philippines, 1974; asst. dir. Regional Sci. Teaching Ctr., Philippines, 1974-76; dir. research and devel. unit Philippine State U., 1974-76; evaluator and testing specialist Honolulu Sch. Dist., 1980-83; profl. assoc. East-West Ctr., Honolulu, 1981; evaluation specialist Palm Beach Sch. System, Fla., 1983—; cons. Honolulu Sch. Dist., 1981; research intern Northwest Regional Ednl. Lab., Oreg., 1980. Contbr. articles to profl. jours. Recipient award UNICEF, 1972; scholar U. Philippines, 1972, East-West Ctr., 1976-81; Nat. Inst. Edn. grantee, 1980. Mem. Am. Ednl. Research Assn., Fla. Ednl. Research Assn., U.S. Jaycees, Alpha Phi Omega (grand chancellor 1967-69). Avocations: tennis; running; guitar playing; jazz music. Home: 191 Bilbao St Royal Palm Beach FL 33411 Office: Palm Beach County Sch Bd 3323 Belvedere Rd W Palm Beach FL 33402

ABBASI, NUZHAT AZIZ, physician; b. Lahore, Pakistan, Aug. 15, 1952; came to U.S. 1973; d. Aziz Ahmed and Shafia A.; m. Ali M. Jafri, Aug. 25, 1979; 1 dau, Nazia Jafri. Pre-med. student, Govt. Coll., Karachi, Pakistan, 1965-67; M.B.B.S., Fatima Jinnah Med. Coll., Lahore, 1973. Diplomate Am. Bd. Internal Medicine. Intern St. Francis Hosp., Miami Beach, Fla., 1973-74; resident Prince George's Gen. Hosp., Cheverly, Md., 1974-76, chief med. resident, infectious disease fellow, 1976-77; emergency room physician, 1977-78; attending physician Kings County Hosp., Bklyn., 1978-80; clin. instr. Downstate Med. Ctr., Bklyn., 1978-80; practice internal medicine, North Miami Beach, Fla., 1980—. Mem. ACP, Dade County (Fla.) Med. Assn., Am. Soc. Internal Medicine. Office: 16200 NE 13th Ave North Miami Beach FL 33162

ABBEY, BRUCE JAMES, architect, educator; b. Burlington, Vt., May 18, 1943; s. Donald Lambert and Lillian (Bixby) A.; B.Arch., Cornell U., 1966; M.Arch., Princeton U., 1971; m. Linda Howard Rowe, Aug. 26, 1969; 1 son, Jason James. Vol., Peace Corps, Tunisia, 1966-69; asst. firm Michael Graves, Princeton, N.J., 1970-71; designer Geddes Brecher Qualls & Cunningham, Princeton, 1971-74; asst. prof. U. Va., Charlottesville, 1974-80, asso. prof. architecture, 1980-86, prof. architecture, 1986—, chmn. dept., 1981—; owner firm Bruce Abbey, 1977—. Prin. works include: Library Anaesthesia, U. Pa. Hosp., 1980, Hahn Residence addition, Ivy, Va., 1979. Home: 1336 Hilltop Rd Charlottesville VA 22903

ABBEY, NANCY CARROLL, ballet company director, choreographer, educator; b. Ann Arbor, Mich., Feb. 18, 1939; d. Raymond Edward and Amber Jean (Clark) Carroll; m. Stuart G. Abbey, Oct. 31, 1958; children—Michael Stuart, Marc Alan. Student U. Mich., 1956-64. Artistic dir. Tallahassee Ballet Co., 1977—; ballet instr. Cultural Arts Program, Ann Arbor, Mich., 1966-76, U. Mich., Ann Arbor, 1971-76, Hobart and William Smith Colls., Geneva, N.Y., 1976-77, Creative Dance Ctr., Sharon Davis Sch. Dance, Tallahassee, 1977—; dance injury cons. to Dr. Louis Kivi, Ann Arbor, 1973-74; musical comedy and opera choreographer U. Mich., Geneva Summer Theatre, others, 1970-77. Choreographer ballets Hansel and Gretel, 1978, Pas de Trois, 1979, Moonstone, 1980, Daisy Hill, 1982; The Seasons, 1984. Author: Dance Injuries: Their Prevention and Care, 1984. Mem. adv. com. Big Bend Very Spl. Arts Festival, Tallahassee, 1983-86. Mem. Cecchetti Council Am., State Dance Assn. Fla. Home: 3213 Del Rio Terr Tallahassee FL 32312

ABBOTT, HERSCHEL LEE, JR., lawyer; b. Little Rock, Sept. 4, 1941; s. Herschel Lee and Wanda Cathryn (Jones) A.; cert. U. Birmingham (Eng.), 1962; B.A., Tulane U., New Orleans, 1963, LL.B., 1966; m. Anne Elizabeth Hamilton, Dec. 21, 1963; children—Cathryn Boyd, Herschel Lee III. Asst. dean students Tulane U., 1965-66; assoc. prof. lit. Altus (Okla.) Jr. Coll., 1966-70; admitted to La. bar, 1966; lectr. bus. law Far East div. U. Md., Bien Hoa, Republic Vietnam, 1969-70; assoc. firm Jones, Walker, Waechter, Poitevent, Carrere & Denegre, New Orleans, 1970-73, partner, 1973—; mem. subcom. to revise La. Partnership Laws La. State Law Inst., 1975—. Mem. Bishop and Council Episcopal Diocese La.; bd. dirs. New Orleans Area Health Planning Council, 1974-81, 1st v.p., 1975, pres., 1976-77; trustee St. Martins Episcopal Sch., 1980—; bd. govs. Tulane Med. Ctr., 1984—; bd. dirs. Tulane U. Hosp., 1985—. Served to capt., USAF, 1966-70; Vietnam. Decorated Bronze Star medal, Cross of Galantry with Palm (Vietnam). Mem. New Orleans, La., Am. bar assns., Am. Law Inst., Omicron Delta Kappa, Kappa Delta Phi, Phi Sigma Alpha, Phi Delta Phi. Republican. Episcopalian. Clubs: Bienville, Stratford, Pickwick, Boston, So. Yacht, New Orleans Country, Plimsoll, City of Baton Rouge. Home: 6506 Oakland Dr New Orleans LA 70118 Office: Place St Charles 201 St Charles Ave New Orleans LA 70170

ABBOTT, ROBERT EARL, JR., city official; b. Dallas, Aug. 17, 1935; s. Robert Earl and Jane Ann (Hines) A.; B.S., Hardin Simmons U., 1960; M.Urban and Regional Planning, Va. Poly. Inst. and State U., 1970; D.P.A., NYU, 1979; 1 son, Mark Arthur. Sr. city planner City of Richmond (Va.), 1969-71; dir. mayors' council N. Hudson Council Mayors, Hudson County, N.J., 1971-73; exec. dir. Regional Planning Commn., Thomas Jefferson Planning Dist. Commn., Charlottesville, Va., 1973-78; cons. City of Charlottesville (Va.), 19798-80; sr. transp. planner City of Ft. Worth, 1981—; lectr. U. Va., U.S. Army Transp. Sch., Fed. Exec. Inst., Va. Commonwealth U., Va. Poly. Inst. and State U., North Tex. State U., Tex. A&M U., U. Tex.-Arlington. Served with AUS, 1960-62, 63-67. Mem. Am. Inst. Cert. Planners, Inst. Transp. Engrs., Am. Planning Assn., Tau Sigma Delta. Methodist. Lodge: Rotary. Home: 3739 Almazon Dr Dallas TX 75220 Office: City Hall Fort Worth TX 76102

ABBOTT, THOMAS BENJAMIN, educator; b. Atlasburg, Pa., June 27; s. Thomas Rankin and Emma Elizabeth (Behling) A.; B.A., Muskingum Coll., 1943; M.A., Case Western Res. U., 1948; Ph.D., U. Fla., 1957; m. Lee Margaret Parsons, Dec. 29, 1945; children—John P., Amy P. Dir. speech therapy programs RoseMary Home for Crippled Children, Cleve., 1948-49; asst. prof. speech Minn. Stat. Coll. at St. Cloud, 1949-53; instr. U. Fla. at Gainesville, 1955-57; lectr. U. So. Calif., Los Angeles, 1957-58; prof. Baylor U., Waco, Tex., 1958-63; prof. speech U. Fla. at Gainesville, 1963—, chmn. dept., 1978—; cons. Office Edn., 1966—; mem. adv. council Commr. Edn. Fla., 1969—. Bd. dirs. Fla. Easter Seal Soc., 1966—, pres., 1968-70; bd. dirs. Nat. Easter Seal Soc., 1979—. Served with AUS, 1943-45. Fellow Am. Speech-Lang. and Hearing Assn.; mem. Fla. Speech-Lang. and Hearing Assn. (pres. 1968-69), Speech Communication Assn., Nat. Council for Exceptional Children. Editorial cons. Jour. Speech and Hearing Disorders, 1966-69. Home: 1502 NW 31st St Gainesville FL 32605 Office: Dept Speech Univ Florida Gainesville FL 32611

ABBOTT, WILLIAM HAROLD, JR., micropaleontologist, diatomist; b. Atlanta, Mar. 23, 1944; s. William Harold Sr. and Mary Elizabeth (Casteel) A.; m. Eloise May Jones, Sept. 23, 1969; 1 child, John Casteel. B.S. in Geology, Ga. State U., 1969; M.S. in Geology, Northeast La. State U., 1970; Ph.D. in Geology, U. S.C., 1972. Cert. profl. geologist, Tex., S.C. Asst. prof. U. S.C., 1972-74; coastal plain geologist S.C. Geol. Survey, Columbia, 1974-80; sr. staff paleontologist Mobil Oil, Dallas, 1980—; research assoc. Baurch Inst., Columbia, S.C., 1974—. Editor: Neogene Stratigraphy, 1984; contbr. articles to profl. jours. Mem. Geol. Soc. of Am., Am. Assn. Petroleum Geologists, Soc. Econ. Paleontologists and Mineralogists (co-chmn. to chmn. diatom working group 1982, 83, 85—). Avocations: breeding Arabian horses; photography. Home: PO Box 1007 Midlothian TX 76065 Office: Mobil Exploration and Prodn PO Box 900 Dallas TX 75221

ABDEL-LATIF, ATA ABDEL-HAFEZ, cell and molecular biology educator; b. Ramallah, Jordan, Jan. 22, 1933; came to U.S., 1951, naturalized, 1963; m. Iris K. Graham, Sept. 10, 1957; children—Rhonda, David, Joseph, Rahdi. B.S. in Biology and Chemistry, DePaul U., Chgo., 1955, M.S. in Chemistry, 1958; Ph.D. in Biochemistry, Mt. Sinai Med. Research Found., Ill. Inst. Tech., 1963; postgrad. in Neurochemistry, U. Ill. Coll. Medicine, 1963-65, U. Nottingham Sch. Medicine, Eng., 1975-76. Research assoc. dept. psychiatry U. Ill., 1963-67; med. research scientist V, State Mental Health, State of Ill., 1963-67; assoc. prof. cell and molecular biology Med. Coll. Ga., Augusta, 1963-67, prof., 1974—; researcher, speaker in field. Contbr. articles to profl. pubs. NIH fellow, 1959-63; NIH grantee, 1965—; recipient Dreyfus SPL Found. Travel award Internat. Soc. Neurochemistry, 1971. Mem. Am. Soc. Biol. Chemists, Am. Physiol. Soc., Am. Soc. Pharmacology and Exptl. Therapeutics, Am. Soc. Neurochemistry, Internat. Soc. Neurochemistry, Soc. Exptl. Biology and Medicine, Internat. Soc. for Eye Research, Am. Chem. Soc., AAAS, Assn. Research in Vision and Ophthalmology, N.Y. Acad. Scis., Sigma Xi. Office: Med Coll Ga Augusta GA 30912

ABDUL-SABOOR, LONNIE, economic development executive, financial and management consultant; b. Chgo., Aug. 31, 1946; s. Lonnie and Minnie (Braboy) Sherman; m. Janet Carolyn Brown, Oct. 9, 1976; children—Jule, Karien, Rasheeda. B.A., Ottawa U., 1970; M.B.A., Atlatna U., 1977. Midwest regional admissions counselor Ottawa U. (Kans.), 1970-71; gen. mgr. Your Corp., Atlanta, 1974-77; dist. rep. Nat. Convience Store, Clarkston, Ga., 1977; sr. mgmt. cons. State of Ga., Atlanta, 1977-79; mgr. fin. programs Atlanta Econ. Devel. Corp., 1979—; corp. sec., treas. Atlanta Local Devel. Co., 1979—; pres. Universal Mgmt. & Acctg. Service, Inc., Atlanta, 1982—. Contbr. bus. articles to Muhammad Speaks Newspaper, 1976-77. Com. chmn. Atlanta Bus. League, 1979-83; chmn. pub. relations Oakland City Community Orgn., Atlanta, 1983; founder, exec. dir. Islamic Bus. Assn., Atlanta, 1983. Served with U.S. Army, 1971-73; Vietnam. Mem. Atlanta Urban Bankers Assn. Democrat. Home: 1101 Avon Ave SW Atlanta GA 30310 Office: Atlanta Econ Devel Corp 1350 N OMNI Internat Atlanta GA 30303

ABEL, RICHARD DENNIS, nurse; b. Gallipolis, Ohio, Jan. 23, 1945; s. Jesse Milford and Helen Louise (Wamsley) A. A.B., Marshall U., Huntington, W.Va., 1967; A.A.S., N.Mex. Jr. Coll., Hobbs, 1977. R.N., W.Va. Tchr., Wayne Jr. High Sch., W.Va., 1967-68; with Gen. Adjustment Bur., Athens, Ohio, 1968-70; head nurse orthopedics and gynecology Holzer Med. Ctr., Gallipolis, 1978—. Dir., Galleries of Interest, Point Pleasant, W.Va., 1982—. Served in USAF, 1971-75; Vietnam. Decorated Air Force Commendation Medal. Named Best Actor in a Musical Play, Mason County Galleries of Interest, 1981. Mem. Regional Nurses Assn. (treas.), Am. Legion, Zeta Beta Tau. Home: 311 7th St New Haven WV 25265 Office: 385 Jackson Pike Gallipolis OH

ABELOW, IRA MOSES, retired physical scientist, consultant; b. Bklyn., June 19, 1920; s. David and Sarah Abelow; m. Paula Brunner; children—Ralph, Eugene. B.A. in Sci., Bklyn. Coll., 1941; postgrad. NYU, 1950-51, Johns Hopkins U., 1958-61, George Washington U., 1969-70. Registered profl. engr., D.C. Acting process hand Merck & Co., Inc., 1946-51; chief process design br. U.S. Army Chem. Corps, Frederick, Md., 1964, chief bio detection and warning br., 1971-1981; cons. to instrument devel. and environ. firms, Bel Air, Md., 1981-85; now operates game preserve in W.Va. Contbr. articles to profl. jours. Patentee fluidized bed freezedrying. Served to 1st lt. C.E., U.S. Army, 1942-46, 51-53. Recipient Army Meritorious Civilian Service award, 1981. Mem. Am. Chem. Soc., Am. Def. Prepardness Assn., Sigma Xi. Jewish. Lodge: B'nai Brith. Home and office: Route 1 Box 437 Kearneysville WV 25430

ABELSON, MICHAEL AARON, management educator, scientist, consultant; b. Phila., Feb. 20, 1951; s. Leonard and Rita (Silow) A.; m. Sherry Lynn Iglesias, Nov. 25, 1972; children—Beth, Ellen. B.A., Pa. State U., 1972, M.B.A., 1980, Ph.D., 1981; M.A., Central Mich. U., 1975. Recreation therapist Phila. State Hosp., 1972-73; exec. dir. Crisis Center Inc., Mt. Pleasant, Mich., 1974-76; asst. prof. dept. mgmt. Tex. A&M U., College Station, 1981—; chmn. bd. dirs. Mich. Crisis Ctr. Services, Lansing, 1975-76; cons. various orgns. Author articles. Pres. Home Owners Assn., College Station, 1982-84. Recipient Disting. Teaching award Tex. A&M U., 1984-85. Mem. Acad. of Mgmt. (chmn. health care div. 1985—), Am. Psychol. Assn., Am. Inst. for Decision Scis. Office: Dept Mgmt Tex A&M Univ College Station TX 77843

ABERNATHY, DAVID MYLES, clergyman, producer; b. Connelly Springs, N.C., June 27, 1933; s. James William and Lorena Mae (Alexander) A.; m. Evelyn Diane Davis, Nov. 24, 1962 (div. Apr. 1970); m. 2d, Kathryn Lynn Fordham, Oct. 16, 1971; children—Marc Alexander, Chadwick Myles. A.B., High Point Coll., 1955; M.Div., Emory U., 1962; S.T.M., Union Theol. Sem. N.Y., 1964; Litt.D., Rust Coll., 1974; L.H.D., Tex. Wesleyan U., 1980. Ordained to ministry Methodist Ch., 1960. With Don Lee Network, Los Angeles, 1955-56; tutor asst., tutor Union Theol. Sem. N.Y., 1963-65; mem. adj. faculty Emory U., 1965-72; producer The Protestant Hour, Atlanta, 1959—; exec. dir. joint communications com. United Meth. Ch., Atlanta, 1974—; lectr. Emory U., U. Md., Meth. Coll., Lon Morris Coll., Pfeiffer Coll., Columbia Sem., Interdenominational Theol. Center, Atlanta U.; churchman in residence Candler Sch. Theology, 1985. Mem. adv. bd. Protestant Radio and TV Center. Served to capt. USAF, 1956-59. Recipient Clifford B. Scott award Sigma Phi Epsilon, 1953; C. L. Amos medal High Point Coll., 1955; Gold Mike award Far East Network, 1959; Ralph W. Sockman fellow TV, Radio and Film Commn., 1964-65; Gold medal Internat. Film and TV Festival, 1983; Bronze medal Internat. Film and TV Festival of N.Y., 1984; Angel award Religion in Media, 1984, 85; Peabody award, 1984. Mem. Nat. Acad. TV Arts and Scis., Broadcast Pioneers (life), Am. Film Inst., Internat. Communication Assn., Internat. Assn. Bus. Communicators, Internat. Platform Assn., Soc. Bibl. Lit., Am. Acad. Religion, ASCAP, Nat. Acad. Recording Arts and Scis., Pub. Relations Soc. Am., Am. Acad. Polit. and Social Sci., Authors League Am., Religious Pub. Relations Council, Sigma Phi Epsilon, Kappa Chi. Democrat. Methodist. Author: Hello Japan!, 1957; A Child's Guidebook to Rome, 1964; Ideas, Inventions and Patents (with Wayne Knipe), 1973; (with Norman Perrin) Understanding the Teaching of Jesus, 1983. Home: 935 Bream Ct NE Marietta GA 30067 Office: 159 Ralph McGill Blvd NE Suite 304 Atlanta GA 30365

ABERNATHY, EDWARD AUGUST, ophthalmologist; b. New Orleans, Feb. 18, 1947; s. Joseph Perry and Johanna Virginia (Christensen) A.; m. Faye Lynne Evans, May 29, 1969; children—Christian, Brooke. B.S., La. State U., 1969, M.D., 1973. Diplomat Am. Bd. Ophthalmology. Resident La. State U. Med. Ctr., New Orleans, 1973-76, asst. clin. instr. 1973-76, clin. instr., 1976-77, clin. asst. prof., 1977—. La. State U. Presdl. scholar 1968-69. Mem. La. State Med. Soc., La. Miss. O-O Soc., New Orleans Acad. Ophthalmology, Am. Acad. Ophthalmology, Phi Kappa Phi, Phi Eta Sigma, Alpha Omega Alpha. Avocations: boating; skiing; fishing. Office: 200 W Esplanade Ave Suite 604 Kenner LA 70065

ABERNATHY, HARRY HOYLE, JR., lawyer; b. Statesville, N.C., Mar. 28, 1925; s. Harry Hoyle and Pearl (Frazier) A.; B.S., Appalachian State U., 1950; LL.B., U. S.C., 1958, J.D., 1970; m. Elizabeth Bell, Aug. 31, 1948; children—Harry H., Donna Cooper. Tchr. public schs., Iredell County, N.C., 1953-54; salesman Bratgen & Kluge, 1954-55; adjuster Harleysville Mutual Ins. Co., Fayetteville, N.C., 1958-59; admitted to S.C. bar, 1958; sole practice law, Great Falls, S.C., 1959—; city atty., Great Falls, 1968—; bd. dirs. Lancaster-Chester County Public Defender's Corp. until 1982; pres. Chester County Pub. Defender's Corp., 1982-85, v.p., 1985—; bd. dirs. Palmetto Legal Services, Spartanburg, S.C. Pres., Great Falls United Fund, 1973-74. Served with USAAF, 1943-46, USAF, 1950-51. Mem. S.C. Bar Assn., Chester County Bar Assn. (pres. 1982—), S.C. City Atty.'s Assn., S.C. Librarians Assn., Phi Alpha Delta. Democrat. Methodist. Clubs: Masons, Scottish Rite, York Rite. Home: 20 Argonne St Great Falls SC 29055 Office: PO Box 488 Great Falls SC 29055

ABERNATHY, JOSEPH DUNCAN, data processing executive; b. Charlotte, N.C., May 25, 1944; s. Joel Leander and Carma Blaine (Arrowood) A.; Asso. in Communications, DeVry Tech. Inst., 1963; B.S., U. N.C., Charlotte, 1970; m. Phyllis Kay Weaver, Sept. 29, 1979; children by previous marriage—Christopher Scott, Kimberly Dianne; stepchildren—Jimmy, Sharon, Dean. Broadcast engr. Jefferson-Pilot Broadcasting Co., Charlotte, 1963-70; computer systems engr. Duke Power Co., Charlotte, 1970-73; mgr. data processing Jefferson Data Systems, Charlotte, 1973—; dir. mgmt. info. systems Jefferson-Pilot Communications Co., 1985—; pres. Freedom Automotive, Inc., Charlotte, 1979—; tchr. Central Piedmont Community Coll., Charlotte, 1973-74, Belmont (N.C.) Abbey Coll., 1977-78. Recipient Sigma Chi award, 1970. Mem. Carolina Honeywell User's Group, IBM Gen. Systems Users Group, Data Processing Mgmt. Assn. (past pres. Charlotte chpt.). Home: 5601 Sardis Rd Charlotte NC 28211 Office: 501 Archdale Dr Charlotte NC 28210

ABERNETHY, DEBORAH BENSON, personnel placement firm executive; b. Dalton, Ga., Mar. 4, 1953; d. James Henry and Robbie (Broome) Benson; m. James Elon Abernethy (div.); children—Lauren Marisa, Matthew Elon. B.S.H.E., U. Ga., 1974, Ed.M., 1983. Cert. tchr. home econs., Ga. Tchr. Paulding County High Sch., Dallas, 1974-80; personnel recruiter Premier Personnel, Atlanta, 1980-81; pres. Career Blazers, Inc., Atlanta, 1981—. Editor U. Ga. Yearbook, 1974. Mem. Atlanta C. of C., Am. Water Ski Assn. (asst. judge, asst. scorer 1978-80), Ga. Water Ski Fedn. (historian 1978-81), Phi Upsilon Omicron. Episcopalian. Avocations: collecting antiques; water and snow skiing; scuba diving. Home: 231 W Paces Ferry Rd Atlanta GA 30305 Office: Career Blazers Inc 3400 Peachtree Rd #715 Atlanta GA 30326

ABERSON, LESLIE DONALD, lawyer; b. St. Louis, May 30, 1936; s. Hillard and Adele (Wenneker) A.; m. Regene Jo Lowenstein, Oct. 16, 1960; children—Karen, Angie, Leslie. B.S., U. Ky., 1957, J.D., 1960. Bar: Ky. 1960, U.S. Dist. Ct. (we. dist.) Ky. 1964, U.S. Tax Ct. 1968, U.S. Supreme Ct. 1975. Assoc., Washer, Kaplan, Rothschild, Aberson & Miller, Louisville, 1963-65, ptnr., 1965—; dir. Bank of Louisville. Bd. dirs. Ky. Athletic Hall of Fame, 1965—, Jewish Hosp. Louisville, 1978—, Louisville Med. Research Found., 1975—, NCCJ; bd. dirs., past pres. B'rith Sholom Temple; bd. dirs., past v.p. Jewish Community Fedn. Louisville. Recipient Louis Cole Young Leadership award Louisville C. of C. Mem. Ky. Bar Assn., Louisville Bar Assn., Ky. Trial Lawyers Assn., Am. Trial Lawyers Assn., Louisville C. of C. (instl. rev. com.), U. Ky. Law Sch. Alumni Assn. (bd. dirs.). Home: 2306 Merrick Rd Louisville KY 40207 Office: 725 Marion E Taylor Bldg Louisville KY 40202

ABLON, ARNOLD NORMAN, accountant; b. Ft. Worth, July 12, 1921; s. Esir R. and Hazel (Dreeben) A.; B.S., La. State U., 1941; M.B.A., Northwestern U., 1942; m. Carol Sarbin, July 25, 1962; children—Jan Ellen, Elizabeth Jane, William Neal, Robert Jack. Lectr. accounting So. Methodist U., 1946-47; auditor Levine's Dept. Stores, 1947-49; accountant Peat, Marwick, Mitchell &

Co., 1946-47; sr. partner Arnold N. Ablon and Co., C.P.A.s, Dallas, 1949—; partner Troth & Ablon, investments; owner ANA Properties; dir. Ablon Enterprises, Inc., Hunsaker Truck Lease, Inc., 1st Continental Enterprises, Inc. Bd. dirs., past vice chmn. Greenhill Sch.; bd. dirs. St. Mark's of Tex. Sch.; past bd. dirs. Spl. Care Sch., June Shelton Sch.; bd. dirs., past v.p. Temple Emanu-El. Served as capt. F.A., AUS, World War II. Mem. Am. Inst. C.P.A.s, Tex. Soc. C.P.A.s, Nat. Assn. Accts. Mason (Shriner). Clubs: Dallas, Brookhaven, Chandler's Landing, Columbian, City, Engrs. Office: 3106 Republic Nat Bank Bldg Dallas TX 75201

ABLON, BENJAMIN MANUEL, accountant; b. Dallas, Feb. 12, 1929; s. Esir R. and Hazel (Dreeben) A.; B.B.A., So. Meth. U., 1948; M.B.A., Northwestern, 1949; LL.B., Harvard, 1956; m. Renee Angrist, Jan. 6, 1962 (div. Oct. 1969); 1 son, Edward Lawrence. Bar: Tex. 1956, D.C. 1957; lic. real estate broker. With tax rulings div. IRS, Washington, 1956-60; assoc. law firm, N.Y.C., 1960-62; accountant, tax mgr. Price Waterhouse & Co., N.Y.C., 1963-68; accountant, partner Arnold N. Ablon & Co., C.P.A.s, Dallas, 1968—. Served to lt. USAF, 1951-53. Mem. Am. Inst. C.P.A.s, Tex. Soc. C.P.A.s, State Bar Tex., Am. Assn. Attys.-C.P.A.s, Dallas Estate Planning Council, Beta Gamma Sigma. Contbr. articles to profl. jours. Home: 5917 Sandhurst St Dallas TX 75206 Office: Republic National Bank Bldg Dallas TX 75201

ABNEY, JOHN KYLE, family therapist, clergyman; b. Haynesville, La., Jan. 1, 1931; s. Wiley B. and Clayton (Ware) A.; m. Virginia Thomas, Jan. 11, 1953; children—Richard, Paul, John W., Katherine. B.A., Pasadena Coll., 1959; M.A., Columbia Pacific U., San Rafael, Calif., 1984, Ph.D., 1985. Ordained to ministry Ch. of Nazarene, 1961. Pastor Ch. of Nazarene, N.Mex., 1959-65, San Diego, 1965-70, Colorado Springs, Colo., 1970-76, Maryville, Tenn., 1976-80; dir., counselor, founder Christian Counseling Ctr., Maryville, 1979-83; family therapist Relationships, Inc., Oklahoma City, 1984—; cons. Girl's Home, Maryville, 1980-82; chaplain City Jail, Maryville, 1980-83. Inventor sermon wheel. Organizer Contact, Maryville, 1983; bd. dirs. Salvation Army, 1966. Served with USMC, 1951-54. Recipient Small Ch. Growth award Ch. of Nazarene, 1961; Community Service award Salvation Army, 1966; Community Service award Christian Counseling Ctr., 1983. Mem. Am. Assn. Counseling, Am. Assn. Sex Therapists, Tri-County Ministerial Assn. (pres. 1966 Community Star award 1966), Blount County Ministerial Assn. (pres. 1982). Republican. Avocations: fishing; art; scuba diving; treasure hunting. Office: Relationships Inc 301 NW 63d St Suite 140 Oklahoma City OK 73116

ABRAHAM, JACK HENRY, JR., real estate executive, horse breeder; b. Montgomery, Ala., Aug. 1, 1924; s. Jack Henry and Bertha (Sohval) A.; m. Rhoda Joyce Dreyfus; children—Diane, Jack, Edward. Student U. Ala., 1942, 45-48, Jones Law Sch., 1950; grad. U.S. Army Command and Gen. Staff Coll., 1963, USAF Air War Coll. Asst. purchasing agt. Rich's, Inc., Atlanta, 1948-49; founder Abraham Bros., Montgomery, Ala., 1950, sole owner, 1952—; owner thoroughbred horse farm; investment cons. Served to col. AUS, 1943-45. Mem. Res. Officers Assn. (life), Commerce Execs. Soc. (U. Ala.), Nat. Assn. Realtors. Jewish. Clubs: Standard, Capital City (Montgomery). Lodge: Lions (past pres., past dep. dist. gov.). Home: 3318 Stratford Ln Montgomery AL 36111 Office: 559 S Court St Montgomery AL 36104

ABRAHAMSON, ROYAL TED, civil engineer; b. Chgo., Oct. 21, 1930; s. Joseph I. and Frances L. (Unger) A.; m. Jan C. Cernohouz, Sept. 2, 1951; children—George W., Deborah A., Melody L., Steven J. A.A., Amarillo Coll., 1954; B.S.C.E., Tex. Tech U., 1957, B.B.A., West Tex. State U., 1963. Registered profl. engr., Tex.; registered pub. surveyor, Tex. Asst. traffic engr. City of Amarillo, Tex., 1957-64, traffic engr., 1964-72; prin. Abrahamson and Assocs., Amarillo, 1972—; chmn. Buffalo Lake Water Dist., Randall County, Tex., 1983—. Mem. Randall County Grand Jury, 1968; scoutmaster Liano Estacado council Boy Scouts Am., 1984, v.p. Eighty Scouts, Inc., 1986—. Served with M.C., U.S. Army, 1951-53. Recipient Silver Beaver award Boy Scouts Am., 1978, Vigil Order of Arrow award, 1978. Fellow ASCE, Inst. Transp. Engrs.; mem. Nat. Soc. Profl. Engrs. (pres., chpt. 1969-70), Am. Soc. Safety Engrs., Constrn. Specifications Inst. (pres. local chpt. 1982-83), Nat. Assn. Accident Reconstrn. Engrs., Nat. Forensic Ctr. Republican. Presbyterian. Club: Starlighters Dance (sec.-treas. 1965-74). Avocations: scouting; backpacking. Home: 3723 Wayne St Amarillo TX 79109 Office: Abrahamson & Assocs 211 W 8th Suite 536 Amarillo TX 79109

ABRAM, PATRICIA JEAN, securities company executive; b. Bangor, Maine, Dec. 15, 1951; d. Frank B. and Margaretta C. (Butler) A.; m. John H. Shorb, July 28, 1984. B.A., U. Maine, 1974; M.Ed., Ohio U., 1976. Student affairs coordinator U. Wis., Madison, 1976-78; asst. nat. sales mgr. ABT Mgmt. Inc., Palm Beach, Fla., 1979-81; v.p. mktg. Tax Deferred Capital, Palm Beach, 1981; mfrs. rep. Delta Foremost Chem., Memphis, 1981-82; mktg. specialist Lowry Fin. Services, North Palm Beach, Fla., 1982-84, v.p., 1984—. Editor, contbr.: Andersen on Mutual Funds, 1984. Mem. Am. Soc. Tng. and Devel. Avocations: scuba diving; racquetball; photography. Office: Lowry Fin Services Corp 701 N Federal Hwy North Palm Beach FL 33408

ABRAMS, CHARLES W., wholesale appliance company executive; b. 1919. With Union Nat. Bank, 1938-41; acct. W.W. Finley Co., 1947-48; with Lyon Frank Co., Little Rock, 1948—, now pres., also dir. Served with U.S. Navy, 1941-46. Office: Lyon Frank Co 65th St and Scott Hamilton Dr Little Rock AR 72214*

ABRAMS, EDWARD BENNETT, nurse; b. Chgo., Oct. 18, 1946; s. Abe Edward and Tillie (Witte) A.; m. Betty Mae Schoon, Mar. 14, 1970; children—Stephanie Dawn, Scott Edward. B.S. in Nursing, U. Ill.-Chgo., 1976; M.S., Am. Tech. U., 1983. Teaching asst. Rush U., Chgo., 1976-77; staff nurse Am. Internat. Hosp., Zion, Ill., 1977-78, VA Hosp., North Chicago, 1978-79; staff nurse U.S. Army, Ft. Huachuca, Ariz., 1979-81, nurse practitioner, Ft. Oro, Calif., 1981, adult nurse practitioner, Ft. Hood, Tex., 1981—. Coordinator pub. edn. Am. Cancer Soc., Killeen, Tex., 1982—. Mem. Assn. U.S. Army, Assn. Mil. Surgeons U.S., Oncology Nursing Soc., Internat. Assn. Nurses Cancer Care. Unitarian. Home: 5948-1 Wainwright Dr Ft Hood TX 76544 Office: Internal Medicine Clinic Darnall Army Hosp Ft Hood TX 76544

ABRAMS, ERWIN EDWARD, health care executive; b. Mpls., Sept. 3, 1941; s. Sam and Gertrude (Rojesky) A.; B.A., U. Minn., 1963; M.B.A., George Washington U., 1965; m. Phyllis L. Lehman, Aug. 25, 1963; children—Michael J., Stephen A. Adminstrv. resident Sinai Hosp., Balt., 1964-65; mem. adminstrv. staff Menorah Med. Center, Kansas City, Mo., 1969-75, sr. asso. dir., 1972-75; adminstr., exec. dir. Community Hosp. S. Broward, Hollywood, Fla., 1975-80; asst. v.p. Nat. Med. Enterprises, Tampa, Fla., 1980-82; v.p. devel. U.S. Health Corp., Clearwater, Fla., 1982-85; v.p. new bus. devel. Nat. Med. Enterprises, 1985—; instr. Penn Valley Community Coll., Kansas City, Mo., 1970-75; trustee Fla. League Hosps., 1976-82; mem. faculty Fla. Atlantic U., Boca Raton, 1977-80; pres., chmn. bd. Hospice Care, Inc., St. Petersburg, Fla., 1983—. Served as 2d lt. Med. Service Corps, USAR, 1965. Mem. Am. Coll. Hosp. Adminstrs., Am. Public Health Assn., Fedn. Am. Hosps., Fla. Hosp. Assn., George Washington U. Health Care Adminstrn. Alumni Assn. Home: 2843 Saber Dr Clearwater FL 33519 Office: 5201 W Kennedy Blvd Tampa FL 33609

ABRAMS, GLENN LEE, media executive; b. Harvey, Ill., Apr. 29, 1952; s. Walter and Ruth (Pressman) A.; m. Sandra Jo Willamon, Dec. 20, 1974; children—Ian Christopher, Shawn. Grad. Homewood-Flossmoor High Sch. (Ill.), 1970. Pres. Lee Abrams Music, Chgo., 1967-70; music dir. Bartell Broadcasting, Miami, 1970-71; program mgr. ABC-FM, Detroit, 1971-72; dir. Burkhart-Abrams, Atlanta, 1972—; cons. NBC radio network, MTV, N.Y.C., Brown U. radio sta., Providence; lectr. in field; record producer; co-host TV program. Office: Burkhart-Abrams Inc 6500 Riverchase Circle Atlanta GA 30328

ABRAMS, JEAN GARDNER, artist, educator; b. Braxton, Miss., Feb. 23, 1936; d. Ambros and Bonnie Catherine (Clark) Gardner; B.S. in Edn., Delta State U., Cleveland, Miss., 1964; M.A., U. Miss., 1968, M.F.A. in Painting, 1980; m. Joseph Robert Abrams, III, May 23, 1954; children—Catherine Jean, Robert Wade. Instr. art Miss. Delta Jr. Coll., Moorhead, 1968—, also art coordinator fine arts dept.; one-woman exhbns. include Miss. Delta Jr. Coll., 1963, Seymour Library, Indianola, Miss., 1964, Percy Library, Greenville, Miss., 1967, U. Miss., 1968, 80, Miss. Art Edn. Assn., 1968. Miss. Arts Festival, 1973, Greenwood Arts Festival, 1972, Central Delta Acad., 1973, Moorhead Library, 1974, Greenville First Fed. Savs. and Loan, 1974, Miss Art Colony travel shows, 1964, 65, 69, 70, 77, 82, U. Miss., 1964, 80, Delta State U., 1980, Miss. Arts Festival, 1967, 68, 73, Cleveland Crosstie, 1970-71, 75, 76, Miss. Art Assn. Jr. Coll. Faculty Exhibit, 1972, Mainstream Mall Gallery, Greenville, 1973, 74, 75, Miss. Artists Juried Exhbn., 1984, 85, Cottonlandia Competition, 1984, 85, 86; also Faculty exhibits; exhibiting artist Gulf South Galleries; represented permanent collections U. Miss., Newborn Center, Miss. Med. Center, Miss. Delta Jr. Coll., also pvt. collections. Sunday sch. tchr., mem. choir, dir. children's choir Second Baptist Ch., Indianola, Miss. Recipient award Monroe (La.) Ann., 1968, Miss. Nat. Watercolor Show, 1967, 68; hon. mention Cleveland (Miss.) Crosstie Festival, 1971, Holiday Arts Festival, McComb, Miss., 1974; 1st place in oils So. Contemporary Arts Festival, Greenville, Miss., 1966, 2d place in oils, 2d place in watercolor, 1968. Mem. Nat. (past Miss. chmn. tchr of art in higher edn.; state del. 1974-75), Miss. (past pres.) art edn. assns., Women's Caucus on Art, Miss. Jr. Coll. Art Tchrs. (past chmn.), Miss. Delta Jr. Coll. Faculty Assn. (past chmn.), Nat. Soc. Lit. and Arts, Miss. Art Assn., So. Watercolor Soc., Kappa Pi, Kappa Delta Pi, Delta Kappa Gamma (past membership chmn., past chpt. v.p.). Home: 500 Olive St Moorhead MS 38761 Office: Miss Delta Jr Coll Moorhead MS 38761

ABRAMS, KATHLEEN SHEA, public policy researcher, educator, administrator; b. Lackawanna, N.Y., Dec. 28, 1941; d. Edmond Joseph Shea and Mary Ann (Yerkovich) Shea; m. Harvey Alan Abrams, Mar. 13, 1968. B.A., Syracuse U., 1963; M. in Rehab. Counseling, U. Fla., 1964, Ph.D., 1980; M.A., U. Minn., 1968. Psychologist, Ypsilanti State Hosp., Mich., 1968-69; psychologist, instr. U. of Mich. Med. Ctr., Ann Arbor, 1969-72; counseling supr. Pre-Trial Intervention, Miami, Fla., 1973-75; psychology intern VA Hosp., Miami, 1978-79; research assoc. FAU-FIU Joint Ctr., North Miami, Fla., 1980-81, assoc. dir., 1981—; chmn. So. Fla. Regional Planning Council, Hollywood, 1981-82; mem. Fla. Coastal Adv. Commn. Tallahassee, 1981—; governing bd. So. Fla. Water Mgmt. Dist., West Palm Beach, 1983—; vice chmn. Fla. Keys Aqueduct Authority, Key West, 1984—. Contbr. articles to profl. jours. and mags. Producer, dir. 3 TV documentaries of Fla.'s environment, 1981—. Chmn. platform com. Dade Democratic Exec. Commn., Miami, 1973-75; vice chmn. Nat. Park System Adv. Bd., Washington, 1981-83; trustee Nat. Parks and Conservation Assn., Washington, 1983—. Office: FAU-FIU Joint Ctr Fla Internat U North Miami FL 33181

ABRAMS, LAURENCE, clinical psychologist; b. Boston, June 30, 1937; s. Aaron and Jeanette Marie (Shea) A.; m. Barbara C. Cameron, Feb. 10, 1982; children—Terrence, Lisabeth, Bradford, Laurence II. B.S., Wayne State U., 1959, M.A., 1963; Ph.D., U. Tex., 1964. Staff psychologist VA Hosp., Waco, Tex., 1964; staff psychologist Baylor Coll. Medicine and Tex. Research Inst. Mental Sci., Houston, 1964-66; chief child psychologist, assoc. dir. psychology tng. program, 1966-71; pvt. practice clin. psychology, Houston, 1971—; assoc. clin. prof. Baylor Coll. Medicine; mem. Tex. State Bd. Psychol. Examiners, 1984—; Gov.'s appointee Tex. Bd. of Examiners of Psychologists, 1983-89; cons. in field; condr. workshops on psychodrama, sudden infant death syndrome, families of schizophrenic patients, evaluation of hosps. in state system for children's service. Recipient Superior Performance award VA, 1964; U. Tex. scholar, 1962-63; Hogg Found. grantee, 1968, 71; Baylor Coll. Medicine grantee, 1968. Mem. Am. Psychol. Assn. (named One of Top 12 Psychodramatists in U.S. 1970, 71), Southwestern Psychol. Assn. (Tex. del. to exec. council), Tex. Psychol. Assn. (pres. 1982), Houston Psychol. Assn. (pres. 1977-78). Research, publs. in field. Home: 10922 Elmdale Houston TX 77070 Office: 1628 Fountain View Houston TX 77057

ABRAMSON, JERRY, city official. Mayor, City of Louisville. Office: 101 City Hall Louisville KY 40202*

ABRAMSON, JON STUART, pediatric infectious disease physician; b. Bklyn., Oct. 31, 1950; s. Herbert S. and Elaine (Scheller) A. B.A., Boston U., 1972; M.D., Bowman Gray Sch. Medicine, 1976. Diplomate Am. Bd. Pediatrics. Intern, resident N.C. Bapt. Hosp., Winston-Salem, 1976-79; fellow U. Minn., Mpls., 1979-81; asst. prof. pediatrics, researcher in pediatric infectious disease Bowman Gray Sch. Medicine, Winston-Salem, 1981—. Grantee Lederle Labs, 1982, NIH, 1984; research career devel. award, 1985. Beecham Labs grantee, 1982; recipient Proctor award, 1976. Fellow Am. Acad. Pediatrics, Am. Soc. Microbiology, So. Med. Soc., Am. Fedn. Clin. Research, Am. Assn. Immunologists, Soc. Pediatric Research. Jewish. Contbr. articles to profl. jours. Office: Bowman Gray Sch Medicine Winston-Salem NC 27103

ABRAMSON, SAMUEL RALPH, physician; b. Lafayette, La., Mar. 12, 1917; s. Nathan and Ula (Coronna) A.; m. Bella Nickerson Chappuis, Nov. 15, 1985; children by previous marriage—Darryl S. Turk, Robert Coronna, Suzanne Denise. B.S., U. Southwestern La., 1937; M.D., Tulane U., 1939. Diplomate Am. Bd. Family Practice. Intern, surg. resident Touro Infirmary, New Orleans, 1939-41; practice family medicine, Marksville, La., 1945-84; chief staff Marksville Gen. Hosp., 1973, 74. Past mem. Marksville Sch. Bd.; nat. bd. dirs. Am. Party U.S. Served with M.C., AUS, 1941-45; ETO. Recipient Overton Brooks award Am. Legion, 1966; Gen. Edn. Freedom award La. Farm Bur., 1966; commendation, Woodmen of the World, 1967. Mem. Pvt. Doctors Am., La. State Med. Soc. (del. ho. of dels.), Lafayette Parish Med. Soc. (pres.), So. Med. Assn. (life), Am. Legion. Roman Catholic. Lodges: K.C., Forty and Eight. Home: 310 N Sterling PO Box 90466 Lafayette LA 70509

ABRELL, JOSEPH KINDRED, professional football executive; lawyer; b. Freedom, Ind., July 24, 1934; s. Carl Calvin and Beatrice Mary (Kindred) A.; m. Judith Arlene Enlow, Aug. 9, 1959; children—Lisa T., Bradford E. A.B., Ind., U., 1960; M.A., Columbia U., 1966; J.D., U. Miami, 1976. Bar: Fla. 1976, D.C. 1977, U.S. Dist. Ct. (so. dist.) Fla., U.S. Ct. Appeals (5th and 11th cirs.) 1977. Reporter Terre Haute Star (Ind.), 1959; with Newsweek mag., Chgo., 1960-63; dir. pub. affairs Sta. WTVJ (CBS), Miami, 1972-84, news dir., 1969-72; v.p. Miami Dolphins; adj. prof. U. Miami Law Sch., 1976-77. Nat. trustee Nat. Acad. TV Arts Scis., N.Y.C., 1983-85; adviser U. Mo. Sch. of Journalism awards program, 1982-84; chmn. Fla. Gov.'s Cable TV Com. Served with USAF, 1953-57. CBS News fellow Columbia U., 1965-66; recipient Edward R. Murrow Documentary award, 1970; Emmy award (3), AP award, 1975-76; DuPont Columbia award, 1972; Am. Bar Gavel awards, 1972-80. Mem. Nat. Acad. TV Arts Scis. (past pres. Miami chpt.), Sigma Delta Chi (past pres.). Congregationalist. Clubs: Miami, University (Miami). Office: Miami Dolphins Ltd 4770 Biscayne Blvd Suite 1440 Miami FL 33137

ABRIEL, WILLIAM LEE, geophysicist; b. Syracuse, N.Y., Apr. 15, 1953; s. William Earl and Patricia Mary (Emerson) A.; m. Evangeline Greek, Apr. 25, 1981. B.S., Pa. State U., 1975, M.S., 1978. Geophysicist Chevron, New Orleans, 1978—. Contbr. articles to profl. jours. Active River Ridge Community Orgn. (La.), 1978. NASA research grantee, 1975. Mem. Soc. Exploration Geophysicists, Am. Assn. Petroleum Geologists, Southeastern Geophys. Soc., Sierra Club, Audubon Soc. Club: Round Table (New Orleans).

ABSHIRE, KYLE DEAN, optometrist; b. Jumping Branch, W.Va., June 1, 1941; s. Dee Bee and Ida (Charlton) A.; m. Margaret Whitaker, Aug. 3, 1974. B.S., Concord Coll., Athens, W.Va., 1963; O.D., So. Coll. Optometry, Memphis, 1966. Practice optometry, Orange Park, Fla., 1968—. Mem. code enforcement bd. Town of Orange Park (Fla.); pres. Clay County unit Am. Cancer Soc. Served to capt. U.S. Army, 1966-68. Mem. Am. Optometric Assn., Fla. Optometric Assn., Northeast Fla. Optometric Assn. (past pres.). Democrat. Baptist. Lodge: Rotary (Paul Harris fellow 1983, pres. Orange Park 1982-83).

ABSTON, DUNBAR, JR., parts distributor executive; b. Memphis, Jan. 26, 1931; s. Dunbar and Esther (Cook) A.; m. Constance Condon, Apr. 29, 1978; children—Lauri Abston Arnold, Dunbar, Linda Abston Larsen, Frank Norfleet; stepchildren—Selden Constance Early, Martha McKellar Early, William Cole Early, Elizabeth F. Early. A.B., Princeton U., 1953; M.B.A., Harvard U., 1955. Joined Parts, Inc., 1959—, with purchasing dept. to v.p., pres., 1972-79, chmn. bd., 1979—, sr. v.p. Parts Industries Corp., Memphis, 1979-81, pres., 1982-83, pres. and chief exec. officer, 1983—; pres. Tract-O-Land Plantation; dir. 1st Tenn. Nat. Corp., Data Communication Corp. Served to lt. USN, 1955-58. Baker scholar. Mem. Automotive Warehouse Distbrs. Assn. (past chmn.), Memphis Econ. Club (past pres.), Automotive Info. Council (past chmn.), Memphis Plough-Community Found. (past chmn.). Republican. Episcopalian. Home: 600 Shady Grove Rd Memphis TN 38119 Office: 601 S Dudley Memphis TN 38104

ACCARDO, JOSEPH JOHN, JR., writer, editor; b. Balt., July 7, 1936; s. Joseph John and Sue Marie (Carrano) A. A.B., U. Notre Dame, 1958. Reporter, television corr. UPI, Washington, 1959-61; news editor Cath. Standard, Washington, 1961; editor Nat. Acad. Scis., Washington, 1962-64; asst. editor Transport Topics, Washington, 1964-68; Washington editor Capitol Cities Corp., 1968-70; chief writer Burson-Marsteller, Washington, 1970; free-lance writer, editor, Arlington, Va. and Washington, 1970—. Editor World Conf. on Shell Structure, Nat. Acad. Scis., 1964; contbr. articles to mags., jours., newspapers; author: Teamsters All, 1976. Contact, Arlington County, 1981—. Meehan scholar, 1954, Georgetown U. Met. Area scholar, 1954. Mem. Nat. Press Club, Nat. Press Found. (charter sponsor) Home and office: PO Box 9700 Arlington VA 22209

ACKELL, EDMUND FERRIS, university president; b. Danbury, Conn., Nov. 29, 1925; s. Ferris M. and Barbara (Elias) A.; m. Carole M. Pryde, June 4, 1969. B.S., Holy Cross Coll., Worcester, Mass., 1949; D.M.D., Tufts U., 1953; M.D., Case Western Res. U., 1962; postgrad., U. Pa., 1955-57. Intern Bellevue Hosp., N.Y.C.; resident Meadowbrook Hosp.; practice medicine, specializing in oral and maxillofacial surgery; prof. medicine and dentistry U. Fla. Med. and Dental Sch., 1966-69; dean Sch. Dentistry, 1966-69, univ. v.p. health affairs, 1969-74; v.p. health affairs U. So. Calif., 1974-78; pres. Va. Commonwealth U., Richmond, 1978—; dir. Whittaker Corp., United Va. Bank. Served with USNR, 1943-46. Mem. AMA, ADA, Soc. Health and Human Values, Am. Public Health Assn., Va. Med. Assn., Va. Dental Assn., Richmond C. of C. (dir.). Clubs: Commonwealth, Country of Va. Home: 4700 Charmian Rd Richmond VA 23226 Office: 910 W Franklin St Richmond VA 23284

ACKER, DAVID DE PEYSTER, engineer, educator; b. Newark, Oct. 12, 1921; s. David De Peyster and Lillian Mulford (Gillmor) A.; m. Lillian Radcliff Work, Apr. 9, 1949; children—Suzanne Clark, Maritta Fairchild. B.S. in Mech. Engring., Rutgers U., 1948, M.S., 1950. Tool designer Wright Aero. Corp., Paterson, N.J., 1940-42; design engr. Am. Tool Engring. Co., N.Y.C., 1942; asst. to chief engr. Bright Star Battery Co., Clifton, N.J., 1945-46; instr. mech. engring. Rutgers U., 1948-51, Va. Polytech. Inst., summer 1950; with N.Am. Rockwell Corp., El Segundo, Calif., 1951-70, mem. sr. tech. staff, sr. v.p. research and engring., 1966-70; staff engr., dir. def. research and engring. Office Sec. Def., Washington, 1970-73; sr. mem. research staff, asso. dean adminstrn., prof. mgmt. Def. Systems Mgmt. Coll., Ft. Belvoir, Va., 1973—; instr., vis. lectr. UCLA, 1957-68; lectr. various univs. Served with AUS, 1942-45. Decorated Bronze Star medal, others; recipient Cert. of Merit Electronic Industries Assn., 1974, Outstanding Performance award Def. Systems Mgmt. Coll., 1975-81, Exceptional Performance award, 1982-85, Comdr.'s award for Civilian Service, 1986. Mem. ASME (chmn. exec. com. mgmt. div., 1973-74; mem. gen. engring. dept., policy bd. 1975-81, nat. membership devel. com. 1978-82; council on engring. 1981-83; recipient Centennial medal, other awards), Am. Soc. Engring. Edn., Soc. Mfg. Engrs. (grant bd. of award 1983-87, chmn. 1983-84), Sigma Xi. Presbyterian (elder). Author: Skill in Communication, a Vital Element in Effective Management, 1980; A History of the Defense Systems Management College; Center of Excellence in Acquisition Management Education and Research, 1986. Contbr. numerous articles to profl. lit. Home: 7723 Timon Dr McLean VA 22102 Office: Def Systems Mgmt Coll Fort Belvior VA 22060

ACKER, LINDA WEBSTER, business educator, accountant; b. Fayette, Ala., Jan. 26, 1943; d. Fred M. and Carrie Nell (Roberts) Webster; m. Joe D. Acker, Aug. 24, 1976; 1 child, Jim J. Shepherd. Instr., Brewer State Jr. Coll., Fayette, 1969—, chmn. div. bus., 1972-84; bus. edn. tchr. Berry High Sch., Ala., 1962-68; grad. tchg. asst. U. Ala., Tuscaloosa, 1968-69; acct. SRP Electronics, Inc., Fayette, 1984—; dir. Fayette TV Service Co. Pres. Music Study Club Fayette, 1981-83; mem. Progress Club II, Fayette, Exec. com. Fayette County Heart Assn., 1980. Mem. Ala. Bus. Edn. Assn., (pres. 1973-74, outstanding bus. educator Ala. 1980), So. Bus. Edn. Assn., Ala. Assn. Higher Edn. in Bus. (pres. 1976-77), Ala. Jr. Coll. Assn. (pres. bus. div. 1973-74), Ala. Acctg. Assn. (exec. bd. 1974-78), Delta Kappa Gamma, Alpha Xi (treas. 1981-83) Democrat. Methodist. Avocations: reading, needlepoint, swimming. Home: 2437 5th Ave NW Fayette AL 35555 Office: Brewer State Jr Coll 2631 Temple Ave North Fayette AL 35555

ACKER, NATHANIEL HULL, educational administrator; b. Manistee, Mich., July 29, 1927; s. Carmon Morell and Ava Cathryn (Keiser) A.; m. Mary Anne Brawley, June 6, 1951; children—Kristan, Nathaniel Hull, Amy. B.S., Miami U., Ohio, 1951. Sales rep. Procter & Gamble, Cin., 1951-53; with Mutschler Brothers Co., Nappanee, Ind., 1953-70, v.p., 1963-68; dir. Office Vol. Placement, Peace Corps, Chgo., 1970-71; assoc. dir. No. Region, New Delhi, India, 1971-72, exec. officer, 1972-73; dir. estate planning St. Lawrence U., Canton, N.Y., 1973-78; v.p. devel. Hampden-Sydney Coll., Va., 1978-84; dir. devel. Episcopal High Sch., Alexandria, 1984—. Mem. Lake Bluff Park Bd., Ill., 1965-68. Mem. Council for Advancement and Support of Edn. Sigma Alpha Epsilon. Club: Seabrook Island (S.C.). Home: 1200 N Quaker Ln Alexandria VA 22302 Office: Episcopal High Sch 1200 N Quaker Ln Alexandria VA 22302

ACKER, W. L. (LOU), security and protection professional; b. Amarillo, Tex., Mar. 24, 1937; s. Doyle and Jewel (Talley) A.; B.S. in Police Sci., Sam Houston State U., 1974; B.A. in History, U. Tex.-Dallas, 1985; m. Peggy Ann Thompson, Jan. 1, 1959; 1 son, Kelly Michael Kennedy. Dir. adminstrv. services bur. Dallas County Sheriffs Dept., 1965-76; chief campus police dept. North Lake Coll., Irving, Tex., 1977-84; ops. mgr. Network Security, Dallas, 1984—. Corp sec. Baruch Ha Shem Messianic Ministries. Served with AUS, 1955-57; maj. Tex. State Guard. Cert. protection profl., lic. peace officer, Tex. Confederate Hist. Inst. fellow; So. Hist. Assn. fellow; South Found. fellow. Mem. Internat., Tex. police assns., Tex. State Guard Assn., U.S. Armor Assn., State Def. Force Assn. U.S., Am. Soc. Indsl. Security, Internat. Assn. Chiefs of Police, Nat. Rifle Assn. (life), Hood's Tex. Brigade Assn., U.S. Horse Cavalry Assn., Order Ky. Cols., S.C.V. (3d lt. comdr. Tex. div. 1985, camp comdr. Gen. W.L. Cabell Camp 1983-84), Friends of Confederacy Soc. London, Confederate Alliance (Knight Class Order of Battle Flag), Mil. Order Stars and Bars (past comdr. Army of Trans-Miss.), Confederate High Command Internat. (col. cav.), Soc. Order of So. Cross, Clan Sutherland Soc. North Am., Am. Legion. Author: The Office of Sheriff in Texas, 1975. Home: 3502 Palm Dr Mesquite TX 75150 Office: Network Security Dallas TX

ACKER, WILLIAM MARSH, JR., U.S. district judge; b. Birmingham, Ala., Oct. 25, 1927; s. William Marsh and Estelle (Lampkin) A.; m. Martha Walters, 1957; children—William Marsh III, Stacey, Patricia. B.A., Birmingham So. Coll., 1949; LL.B., Yale U., 1952. Assoc. Graham, Bibb, Winge & Foster, Birmingham, 1952-57, Smyer, White, Reid & Acker, 1957-72, Dominick, Fletcher, Yeilding, Acker, Wood & Lloyd, Birmingham, 1972-82; U.S. dist. judge, No. Ala., 1982—. Del., Republican Nat. Conv., 1972, 76, 80; active Ala. Rep. Exec. Com. Address: 354 Federal Courthouse Birmingham AL 35203*

ACKERMAN, HELEN RUTH PENNER, psychologist; b. N.Y.C., Mar. 5, 1939; d. Isaac and Sylvia (Katz) Penner; m. Ross A. Ackerman, 1960; children—Eric, Ruth. B.A., Hofstra U., 1960; M.A., George Washington U., 1962; Ed.D., U. Md., 1967. Lic. psychologist, Fla., Md., New Hampshire. Psychiat. technician U. Md. Psychiat. Inst., Balt., 1960; psychology extern Springfield State Hosp., Sykesville, Md., 1961; tchr. Army Edn. Ctr., Bad Kissingen, W. Ger., 1961-63, lectr. U. Md. Schweinfurt Ctr., 1962-63; research psychologist Johns Hopkins U., Balt., 1965; asst. prof. Anne Arundel Community Coll., Arnold Md., 1968; psychologist Balt. County pub. schs., 1966-68, Mills Sch., Fort Lauderdale, Fla., 1968-69; cons. Hosp. Mgmt. and Planning Assocs., Miami, 1968-75; pvt. practice psychology, Ft. Lauderdale, 1975—; Md. psychol. cons. for Md. residents in Fla. institutions, 1979-83; psychol cons. Broward County (Fla.) pub. schs., 1980-83. U. Md. fellow, 1964-65. Trustee Ft. Lauderdale Am. Lung Assn.; active numerous Plantation (Fla.) civic orgns., local Jewish community affairs, local sch. support groups. Mem. Am. Psychol. Assn., Fla. Assn. Sch. Psychologists, SE Psychol. Assn., Md. Psychol. Assn., N.H. Psychol. Assn., Plantation C. of C. Contbr. numerous articles to profl. jours. Home: 5921 Almond Terr Plantation FL 33317 Office: 1020 SW 40th Ave Plantation FL 33317

ACKERSON, JON W., lawyer, state senator; b. Louisville, July 29, 1943; s. Louis E. and Sara M. (Romans) A.; B.A., U. Louisville, 1966; J.D., Ind. U., 1971; m. Patricia L. Ormerod, July 13, 1968; children—Brent Thomas, Marc Alan. Ptnr. firm Ackerson, Ackerson & Blandford; mem. Ky. Ho. of Reps., 1975-77, chmn. freshman Republican caucus; mem. Ky. Senate, 1977—. Active Jefferson County (Ky.) Metro United Way, Big Bros. and Big Sisters, Louisville. Mem. Ky. Bar Assn., Ind. Bar Assn., Jaycees. Republican. Roman

Catholic. Clubs: Toastmasters, Kiwanis. Office: 410 Burdorf Bldg 100 N 6th St Louisville KY 40202

ACKMAN, FREDRIC C(LARENCE), oil company executive; b. Oakland City, Ind., 1931; married. B.S., U. Okla., 1952. Exec. v.p. Exxon Corp., 1952-81; successively exec. v.p., chief operating officer, then pres., chief operating officer, now chmn. bd., pres., chief exec. officer Superior Oil Co., Houston, 1981—also dir.; dir. McIntyre Mines Ltd., Falconbridge Nickel Mines Ltd., Can. Superior Oil Ltd. Office: Superior Oil Co First City Bank PO Box 1521 Houston TX 77001

ACOCK, ALAN COLBY, educator; b. Trenton, N.J., June 7, 1944; s. George W. and Elizabeth (Shann) A.; m. Delores Antonia Haney, Dec. 10, 1964; children—Jorin, Peter, Gabriel, Anthony. B.A., Eastern Wash. U., 1966; M.A., Wash. State U., 1969, Ph.D. in Sociology, 1971. Research assoc. in gerontology U. So. Calif. Andrus Gerontology Ctr., 1971-74; assoc. prof. sociology U. So. Calif., Los Angeles, 1977-78, asst. prof. sociology, 1971-76; assoc. prof. sociology U. Okla., 1978-80; assoc. prof., grad. dir. sociology Va. Tech., Blacksburg, 1980-84; prof., grad. dir. sociology and rural sociology La. State U., Baton rouge, 1984—; cons. in field. Contbr. articles to profl. jours. Recipient E. Gordon Erickson award for grad. teaching excellence, Va. Tech., 1983, 84; Rueben Hill award for outstanding article in family theory, 1981. Mem. Am. Sociol. Assn., Nat. Council on Family Relations, So. Sociol. Soc., Southeastern Council on Family Relations. Avocations: soccer; stained glass. Office: Dept Sociology La State Univ Baton Rouge LA 70803

ACOSTA, HERNANDO, architect; b. Bogota, Columbia, July 23, 1928; came to U.S., naturalized, 1968; s. Lissandro and Merceds (Sanchez) A.; m. F. Margot Schroedel, Dec. 28, 1965; 1 son, Paul H. D.Arch. Nat. U. Colombia, 1954. Cert. Nat. Council Archtl. Registration Bd. Pres., ARK Ltd., Bogota, 1953-55; chief designer Rufus Nims, Architect, Miami, Fla., 1956-59; chief designer Robert B. Browne, Architect, Miami, 1959-66; ptnr. Irani & Acosta, Architects & Engrs., Miami, 1967-68; ptnr. Treister & Acosta, Architects, Miami, 1968-73; owner Hernando Acosta, Architects, P.A., Miami, 1973—; lectr. architecture Miami-Dade Community Coll. Mem., City of Miami Com. on Ecology and Beautification. Served as lt. Colombian Army, 1953-54. Mem. AIA, Fla. Assn. AIA, Sociedad Colombiana de Arquitectos Club: Coconut Grove Sailing. Designer award winning pub. housing in U.S. and Caribbean; award winning comml. bldgs. in Fla. Home: 2185 S Bayshore Dr Miami FL 33133 Office: 2890 SW 28th Terr Miami FL 33133

ACOSTA, MARGARET ANN, educator; b. Hanford, Calif., Jan. 23, 1946; d. Francisco Cordero and Tomasa (Reyes) A.; B.A., UCLA, 1971; M.Ed., U. Houston, 1973. Sch. tchr. Houston Ind. Sch. Dist., 1973-76, research asst. dept. research, evaluation and accreditation, 1981—; dir. ESSA Multicultural Bilingual Presch., Houston, 1976-78; program coordinator Tex. Family Inst., Houston, 1978-79, cons., 1978-79; supr. U. Houston Center for Study Teaching, 1979-81; cons. Internat. Yr. of Child, 1979. Bd. mem. Center for Human Devel., 1979, Houston Council Human Relations, 1978-79, Childrens Edn. and Devel. Center, Inc., 1976-79, Houston Area Womens Center, 1979. Doctoral student bilingual fellowship grantee, 1979. Mem. NEA, Nat. Assn. Bilingual Educators, Bilingual Edn. Students Orgn., Assn. Supervision and Curriculum Devel., Tex. Tchrs. Assn., Tex. Assn. Bilingual Educators. Democrat. Roman Catholic. Office: 3830 Richmond Ave Houston TX 77027

ACOSTA, URSULA, psychologist; b. Hannover, Ger., Jan. 14, 1933; came to U.S., 1954, naturalized, 1958; d. Johannes Karl and Irma (Ulrich) Schmidt; B.A., U. P.R., 1971, M.E., 1973; Ph.D. in Psychology, Gutenberg U., Mainz, W. Ger., 1979; m. Sebastian Acosta-Ronda, June 12, 1954; children—Johann, Dennis, Peter. Various occupations, 1954-66; instr., asst. prof., assoc. prof. psychology U. P.R., Mayaguez, 1973—; host public service TV program Changing Woman in a Changing World. Chairperson appeal bd. SSS. Mem. LWV (unit chair 1977-78), Am. Psychol. Assn., Psychol. Assn. PR. (chair ethics com. 1979-81). Active Puerto Rican Statehood Movement, founder PRP. Democrat. Co-author: Familias de Cabo Rojo (History prize Ateneo Puertor-riqueno de New York 1983); Cabo Rojo: Notas para su historia, 1985; contbr. articles to various jours. and newspapers. Office: U PR Mayaguez PR 00709

ACOSTA-RAMOS, JOSE, educator, educational consultant; b. Sabana Grande, P.R., Oct. 30, 1937; s. Atilano and Carlita (Ramos) Acosta; B.A., Inter Am. U., 1963; M.Public Health Edn., U. P.R., 1965; Ed.D., Lehigh U., 1978. Tchr. elem. and secondary schs. P.R. Public Instrn. Dept., 1958-64, sch. health supr., 1964-68; asst. supt. schs. Mayaguez (P.R.) Sch. Dist., 1969-78, 83-84, supt. schs., 1978; dir. curriculum design unit Puerto Public Inst. Dept., Hato Rey, P.R., 1979; asso. dean acad. affairs La Montana Regional Coll., Utuado, P.R., 1979-82, asst. prof. edn., 1979-83; asst. prof. ednl. adminstrn. U. P.R., Rio Piedras, 1983—, coordinator ednl. adminstrn. program, 1985—; prof. Inter Am. U., San German, P.R., part-time, 1972-76, 81—, U. P.R., Mayaguez, part-time, 1975, Bridgeport U.-P.R. Center, Mayaguez, part-time, 1978. Faculty rep. Harry S. Truman Scholarship Program, 1980-81; bd. dirs. Inst. Ednl. Scis., 1979—. Supreme Council 33d and Last Degree, Ancient Rite of Freemasonry scholar, 1974-76. Mem. NEA, Assn. Supervision and Curriculum Devel. (bd. dirs. 1985-86), Nat. Council Social Studies, P.R. Assn. Supervision and Curriculum Devel. (pres. 1985-86), P.R. Tchrs. Assn., Phi Delta Kappa. Club: Mason. Home: Rural Route 886 B333 Sabana Grande PR 00747 Office: Faculty Edn Grad Program U PR Rio Piedras PR

ACOSTA-RUA, GASTON JOSE, neurosurgeon; b. Cardenas, Cuba, Aug. 26, 1937; came to U.S., 1962, naturalized, 1969; m. Maria Victoria Pol; children—Gaston J., Fernando J., Antonio J. B.S., Trinitarios Coll., 1955; postgrad. Havana U. Med. Sch., 1960; M.D., Madrid U., Spain, 1963. Intern Marymount Hosp., Cleve., 1964-65; resident in surgery Fairview Gen. Hosp., Cleve., 1965-66; fellow in neurol. surgery Cleve. Met. Hosp., 1966-67; resident in neurosurgery Iowa U. Hosps., Iowa City, 1967-70, instr. neurosurgery, 1970-71; asst. neurosurgeon Kantonsspital Zurich, Switzerland, 1971; research assoc. Iowa U. Hosp., 1971-72; chief of neurosurgery St. Vincent's Med. Ctr., 1976-82, St. Luke's Hosp., 1977-82, 85—, Riverside Hosp., 1984—, Methodist Hosp., 1983—; mem. courtesy staff Baptist Med. Ctr., Meml. Hosp., Humana Hosp. Orange Park; mem. staff Nemours Children's Hosp., Cathedral Health and Rehab. Ctr.; cons. Fla. Dept. Profl. Regulation; dir. 1st Guaranty Bank and Trust Co. Internat. abstract editor Neurosurgery. Contbr. articles to profl. jours. Active Hispano-Am. Cultural Assn., Jacksonville C. of C. Fgn. Visitors Task Force. Mem. Duval County Med. Soc. (sec. 1985-86, v.p. 1986—, bd. dirs. 1982-85), Jacksonville Area Profl. Standards Rev. Orgn., Inc., (trustee 1977-78), Fla. Med. Assn. (ho. of dels. 1980—, health and edn. com. 1985—, Good Samaritan award 1985), Fla. Neurosurg. Soc. (bd. dirs. 1980-83, treas. 1983-85, pres.-elect 1985—), Assn. Brain Tumor Research (med. adv. council), ACS, Am. Assn. Neurol. Surgeons (joint socio-econ. com. 1982-85, med. practices com.), Council State Neurosurg. Socs., Congress Neurol. Surgeons, NE Fla. Health Agy. (governing bd., chmn. com. 1978-79), So. Neurosurg. Soc., AMA, Midwest Bio-laser Inst., Interam. Coll. Physicians and Surgeons. Clubs: Meninak, Univ., October, Fla. Yacht, Cuban-Am., St. Johns Dinner. Home: 4460 Ortega Forest Dr Jacksonville FL 32210 Office: Lyerly Neurosurg Group 2545 Riverside Ave Jacksonville FL 32204

ACOSTA-RUA, MARIA VICTORIA, child psychiatrist; b. Madrid, Spain, Nov. 28, 1939; came to U.S., 1964, naturalized, 1967; d. Antonio and Maria A. (Gimenez) Pol; m. Gaston J. Acosta-Rua, June 7, 1964; children—Gaston J., Fernando, Toney. B.D., St. Louis des Frncais Sch., Madrid, 1956; M.D., U. Madrid, 1963. Intern, Marymount Hosp., Cleve., 1966-67; resident Iowa U. Hosp., 1968-72; med. dir. St. Vincent's Children's Day Treatment Center for Emotionally Disturbed Children, Jacksonville, Fla., 1973-79; chief sect. child psychiatry Jacksonville Children's Hosp., 1974-75; psychiatric cons. Duval County Sch. System, 1974—, Full Yr. Head Start, Greater Jacksonville Econ. Opportunity, 1973-78; practice medicine, specializing in psychiatry, Jacksonville, 1973—; child psychiatry cons. Fla. Sch. for Deaf and Blind, St. Augustine, Fla., 1981-82; dir. Children's Unit, N.E. Fla. State Hosp., Macclenny, Fla., 1981—. Mem. AMA, Fla. Med. Assn., Duval County Med. Soc., Fla. Psychiatric Soc., Jacksonville Psychiatry Soc., Am. Orthopsychiatric Soc., Am. Group Psychotherapy Assn., Am. Psychiatric Assn., Am. Acad. Child Psychiatry. Roman Catholic. Address: 2323 Oak St Jacksonville FL 32204

ADAIR, ALLEN RAYMOND, criminalist; b. Montgomery, Ala., Sept. 19, 1945; s. John William and Ann (Ellis) A.; B.S. in Chemistry, U. Ala., 1968; M.S. in Criminal Justice, Auburn U., Montgomery, 1980; m. Carol Davis, May 31, 1970. Criminalist, Ala. Dept. Forensic Scis., Montgomery, 1972—; instr. Montgomery Police Acad.; speaker in field. Served with USAR, 1970-71. Mem. So. Assn. Forensic Scis. Episcopalian. Author papers on drug analysis. Home: 3248 N Colonial Dr Montgomery AL 36111 Office: 231 Montgomery St Montgomery AL 36103

ADAIR, CHARLES E., medical products distribution company executive; b. Birmingham, Ala., Dec. 26, 1947; s. Charles Watkins and Martha Edd (Chisenball) A.; m. Alice Virginia Barker, Jan. 31, 1970; children—Charles Thomas, Emily Elizabeth. Student, Vanderbilt U., 1966; B.S. in Acctg., U. Ala.-Tuscaloosa, 1970. C.P.A. Sr. acct. Haskins & Sells, Birmingham, 1970-73; chief fin. officer Durr-Fillauer Med. Inc., Montgomery, Ala., 1973-77, exec. v.p., 1977-81, pres., chief operating officer, 1981—. Served to sgt. U.S. Army, 1970. Mem. Fin. Execs. Inst., Am. Inst. C.P.A.'s Ala. Soc. C.P.A.'s. Home: 2431 Hermitage Dr Montgomery AL 36111 Office: Durr Fillauer Med Inc 218 Commerce St Montgomery AL 36192

ADAIR, HENRY, educational administrator. Supt. of schs. Montgomery County, Ala. Office: PO Box 1991 Montgomery AL 36192*

ADAIR, JOHN CLAY, petroleum company executive; b. Tonkawa, Okla., Aug. 20, 1933; s. Charles J. and Leona R. (Sexton) A.; m. Carole Joyce Ward, Nov. 20, 1955; children—Susan Elizabeth, Steven Clay, Robert Ward. B.S., U. Tulsa, 1956, M.B.A., 1965. Adminstrv. asst. Sinclair Research, Inc., Tulsa, 1953-63; economist Standard Oil Co. Ind., Tulsa, 1963-65; dept. head Gt. No. Oil Co., St. Paul, 1965-71; group v.p. Marion Corp., Mobile, Ala., 1971-85; pres. Marion Pipeline Co., Inc., Mobile, 1976-85; v.p. refining ops GAMXX Energy, Inc., 1985—. Served as capt. U.S. Army, 1956-57. Mem. Nat. Petroleum Refiners Assn., Am. Petroleum Inst., Mobile Area C. of C. Republican. Presbyterian. Club: Lake Forest Country (Daphne, Ala.). Home: 632 Tudor Ln W Mobile AL 36608 Office: PO Box 526 Theodore AL 36590

ADAIR, MANOI SMITH, business educator; b. Boswell, Okla., Dec. 8, 1927; d. Rowland Demcie and Bonnie Mae (Watson) Smith; m. Preston Lee Adair, Mar. 25, 1948; children—Karen Ruth, Sharon Kay. B.S., Okla. Bapt. U., 1950; M.Bus. Edn., U. Okla., 1958. Cert. profl. sec. With Okla. Bapt. U., Shawnee, 1955—, chmn. faculty, 1976-77, dir. European study tour, 1978, acting dean sch. bus. and adminstrn., 1981-82, 84-85, chmn. curriculum revision, 1982-83, assoc. prof. bus., 1969—; condr. workshops for secs. Mem. Nat. Bus. Edn. Assn., Okla. Bus. Edn. Assn., Southwestern Fedn. Adminstrv. Disciplines, S.W. Adminstrv. Services Assn., Profl. Secs. Internat., Delta Pi Epsilon, Kappa Delta Pi. Democrat. Baptist. Lodge: Eastern Star. Home: 4303 N Aydelotte Shawnee OK 74801 Office: Oklahoma Baptist University Shawnee Hall 116 Shawnee OK 74801

ADAMS, ALFRED GRAY, lawyer, real estate developer; b. Winston-Salem, N.C., Feb. 28, 1946; s. Carlton Noble and Elizabeth (Walker) A.; m. Linda Hinson, Apr. 4, 1970; children—Alfred Gray Jr., Amanda Laing. B.A., Wake Forest U., 1968, J.D., 1973. Bar: N.C. 1973. Ptnr. Van Winkle, Buck, Wall, Starnes & Davis, P.A., Asheville, N.C., 1973—; sec., dir. Greystone Properties, Inc., Asheville, 1983—. Assoc. editor Wake Forest Law Rev., 1972. Chmn. Buncombe County Tax Adv. Com., Asheville, 1983. James Mason scholar Wake Forest U., 1972. Mem. N.C. Bar Assn. (real property sect. vice chmn. 1982-83, chmn. 1983-84, writer, lectr. real property and future interests bar rev. course 1981-83, mem. real property curriculum adv. com. 1984—), ABA. Democrat. Presbyterian. Club: Biltmore Forest Country (golf com. 1984—), Rhododendron Royal Brigade Guards (Asheville) (capt. Ensign Class). Home: 21 White Oak Rd Asheville NC 28803 Office: Van Winkle Buck Wall Starnes & Davis PA 18 Church St PO 7376 Asheville NC 28807

ADAMS, ANNE MAYO, social worker; b. Cleve., Mar. 25, 1931; d. Edward L. and Kate S. (Hammond) Mayo; student Skidmore Coll., 1949-51; B.A. in Sociology, U. Wis., 1953; postgrad. Bridgewater State Tchrs. Coll., 1965-66; m. Charles B. Adams, Mar. 17, 1979; children by previous marriage—Michelle Morel, Jean Pierre Morel, Catherine Morel, Andre Morel. Social worker with aged, blind, disabled and children, Akron and Medina, Ohio, 1969-72; social worker, West Palm Beach, Fla., 1972-73; social worker adult protective service State of Fla., West Palm Beach, 1972-80, social and rehabilitative counsellor II, 1980—; public speaker in field; participant seminars in law, psychology and counselling techniques. Founder gerontology program Meml. Presbyn. Ch., West Palm Beach, 1982; mem. session, choir, Christian edn. com. Lakewood Congl. Ch.; mem. Fla. Council on Aging, 1984—. Mem. Fla. Assn. for Health and Social Services, Alpha Chi Omega. Republican. Club: Cotillion of Palm Beaches (pres.). Home: 2287 Carambola Rd West Palm Beach FL 33406 Office: Health and Rehabilitation Services State of Fla Unit II 2701 Lake Ave West Palm Beach FL 33405

ADAMS, BARBARA JEAN, painter, art educator; b. Plainfield, N.J., July 30, 1939; d. Robert and Georgeola (Whipple) Adams; m. H.C. Austin, Jr., Dec. 25, 1976. B.S. with high honors, Wheaton Coll., 1961; postgrad. Art Student's League, 1970-74, N.A.D., 1973-74. Tchr., Fine Arts Ctr., Camden, S.C., 1976-84, Sumter Gallery Art, S.C., 1976—; S.C. artist-in-residence S.C. Arts Commn., Columbia, 1982—. Chmn., Fanwood Environ. Commn., N.J., 1970-76; dir. Garden Club of S.C., 1983—; emergency med. tech. Bishopville Rescue Squad, S.C., 1982—. Named Woman of Yr., Scotch Plains Times, 1976; recipient Cert. of Distinction, Columbia Mus. Art, 1982. Mem. Art Students League (life), Guild of S.C. artists (v.p. 1983), Artists Equity, Allied Artists Am. (assoc. mem.), Artists Guild Columbia. Republican. Avocation: gardening. Home: 215 S Heyward St Bishopville SC 29010

ADAMS, BARRY KENT, government supervisor; b. Jacksonville, Fla., Feb. 11, 1948; s. Elbert Alpha and Agnes Marie (Harvey) A.; m. Mary Holly Clore, Jan. 26, 1975 (div. 1976); m. 2d, Carolyn Sue Greene, July 8, 1978. Student schools, Jacksonville. Aircraft foreman, Dept. Navy, Naval Air Sta., Jacksonville, Fla., 1971-75, foreman, 1975—. Served with U.S. Army, 1967-70. Recipient Meritorious Civilian Service award, Dept. Navy, 1982. Mem. Fed. Mgrs. Assn. (pres. 1981-84), Naval Air Sta. Assn. (v.p. 1983-85, nat. pres. 1985—). Democrat. Baptist. Lodge: Moose. Home: 3501 Cormorant Branch Ct Jacksonville FL 32217 Office: Naval Air Sta Roosevelt Blvd Jacksonville FL 32210

ADAMS, CAROLINE J. H., magazine sales manager; b. Dallas, June 15, 1951; d. Bill G. and Anita N. (Murrah) H. B.F.A., So. Methodist U., 1973. Office mgr., media planner Jim Leslie & Assocs., Dallas, 1973; continuity dir. Sta. KZEW-FM, Dallas, 1973-75; sec. Neiman-Marcus Co., Dallas, 1975-77; exec. sec. Harris Corp., Dallas, 1979-80; mgr. classified sales, circulation ADWEEK/Southwest Mag., Dallas, 1980—. Mem. Dallas Ad League, Am. Bus. Women's Assn. Republican. Methodist. Home: 5902 E University Blvd Dallas TX 75206 Office: ADWEEK 2909 Cole Ave Suite 115 Dallas TX 75204

ADAMS, CHARLES HERBERT, oil company executive; b. Elmira, N.Y., Dec. 18, 1929; s. Charles E. and Rhea M. (Hubbell) A.; m. Jacquelyn C. Cooper, Apr. 8, 1952; children—Charles, Patricia, Sally. B.A. in Geology, Cornell U., 1951. Geophysicist Cities Service Oil & Gas Corp., Tulsa, 1955-65, exploration mgr., 1965-69, gen. mgr., 1969-74, v.p. exploration and prodn., 1974-79, v.p. planning and tech., 1979-82, exec. v.p. exploration and prodn., 1982—. Served to lt. U.S. Navy, 1952-55. Mem. Am. Petroleum Inst., Soc. Exploration Geophysicists, Mid-Continent Oil and Gas Assn. Presbyterian. Office: Cities Service Oil & Gas Corp Cities Service Bldg Tulsa OK 74102

ADAMS, CLAUDIA NEFF, educator; b. Atlanta, July 10, 1921; d. Lawrence Wilson and Emmie (Knott) Neff; m. Alfred Bernard Adams, Jr., Dec. 28, 1942; children—Alfred Bernard, III, Tamara (Mrs. Carl Edward Dohn, Jr.), Carla (Mrs. William Huddleston York, Jr.). B.A. in Elem. Edn., Birmingham-Southern Coll., 1970; M.A. in Elem. Edn., U. Ala., 1974, also postgrad. Tchr. Locust Fork High Sch. (Ala.), 1970-73, Remlap Elem. Sch. (Ala.), 1974-75, Southeastern Elem. Sch., Remlap, co-editor Self-Study for Accreditation, 1976-77; mem. com. Right-to-Read Task Force, 1974-75; ret., 1985. Mem. NEA, Ala. Edn. Assn., Blount County Edn. Assn., Kappa Delta Pi. Home: 6051 Woodland Ave Pinson AL 35126 Office: Route 2 Box 888 Remlap AL 35133

ADAMS, DAMON R., city official; b. St. Louis, Mar. 29, 1948; s. William R. and Lois E. (Autry) A.; m. Carol A. Wilson, June 26, 1969; children—Stephen R., Glenn B., Philip S.; m. 2d, Valerie J. McCarthy, Mar. 11, 1982; children—Daniel R., Alex J., Nicholas. B.A., U. South Fla., 1970. C.P.A. Acct. various acctg. firms, St. Petersburg and Plant City, Fla., 1970-71; acct. City of Tampa, 1972; acct. Hillsborough County, Tampa, 1972-73; dep. fin. dir. City of Ft. Lauderdale (Fla.), 1973-78, dir. fin., 1978—. Mem. Mcpl. Fin. Officers Assn. U.S. and Can. (Fin. Reporting Achievement award 1977), Fla. Mcpl. Fin. Officers Assn. (pres. 1983-84), Am. Inst. C.P.A.s, Fla. Inst. C.P.A.s. Mem. Ch. of Christ. Home: 1525 NE 27th St Wilton Manors FL 33334 Office: City of Fort Lauderdale PO Box 14250 100 N Andrews Ave Fort Lauderdale FL 33302

ADAMS, DAVID ARTHUR, forestry educator; b. Lakewood, Ohio, Nov. 26, 1931. B.S. in Wildlife Conservation and Mgmt., N.C. State U., 1953, M.S. in Wildlife Conservation and Mgmt., 1957, Ph.D. in Plant Ecology, 1962. Waterfowl biologist N.C. Wildlife Resources Commn., 1955; chief naturalist N.C. Div. State Parks, 1957-59; curator N.C. State Mus., 1962-63; commr. N.C. Div. Comml. and Sports Fisheries, 1963-68; sr. staff mem. Nat. Council Marine Resources and Engrng. Devel., Exec. Office of Pres., 1968-69; pres. Coastal Zone Resources Corp., Wilmington, N.C. and v.p. Ocean Data Systems, Inc., 1969-76; asst. sec. for natural resources N.C. Dept. Natural Resources and Community Devel., Raleigh, 1976-78; vis. assoc. prof. N.C. State U., Raleigh, 1978-82, assoc. prof. depts. forestry and univ. studies, 1982—. Served to 1st lt. U.S. Army, 1953-55. Recipient N.C. Gov.'s Disting. Citizen award, 1968. Mem. Ecol. Soc. Am., Nat. Assn. Environ. Profls. (dir. 1980-85), Sigma Xi. Democrat. Methodist. Contbr. articles to profl. jours. Home: 7521 Haymarket Ln Raleigh NC 27609 Office: N C State U Dept Forestry Box 8002 Raleigh NC 27695

ADAMS, EENA J. CARLISLE, dietitian, educator; b. Mt. Hope, Kans.; d. Alfred George and Nora Agnes (Kissick) Carlisle; B.S. in Home Econs., Kans. State U., 1939; postgrad Ohio U., 1954-61; M.S. in Foods and Nutrition, 1970; m. Lawrence D. Adams, Dec. 11, 1940; children—Karen Jean Adams McCarthy, Maureen Janet Adams Mitchell. Tchr., Leonardville, Kans., 1939-40, Jane's Pvt. Sch., Front Royal, Va., 1949-52, Forestdale Sch., McCracken County, Ky., 1952-53, Jackson County and City Schs. (Ohio), 1953-68, Head Start, Jackson, 1965-68; grad. teaching asst. Kans. State U., Manhattan, 1969-70; asst. prof. home econs. Wayne (Nebr.) State Coll., 1970-76; asst. prof. home econs. and dietetics Morehead (Ky.) State U., 1976-82, coordinator energy mgmt. asst. program, 1979-80; cons. dietitian, 1980—. Mem. Front Royal (Va.) Recreation Council, Delta Kappa Gamma Annie Webb Blanton scholar, 1968. Mem. Am. Dietetic Assn. (registered dietitian), Nutrition Today Soc., Soc. Nutrition Edn., Am. Home Econs. Assn., Inst. Food Tech., Ohio Dietetic Assn., Ky. Dietetic Assn., Ohio Edn. Assn., Chi Omega, Delta Kappa Gamma (pres.), Alpha Lambda Delta. Home: Ka Mel Forms Beaver OH 45613 Office: Crique Side Apt 4 Morehead KY 40351

ADAMS, FRANCES GRANT, office procedures consultant; b. Springfield, Ill.; d. Daniel Harmon and Adah (Morris) Grant; A.B., U. Ill., 1960; student Ill. Wesleyan U., 1938-39, U. Miami, (Fla.), 1945, Am. Inst. Banking, 1959-60; m. Jack R. Adams, Oct. 24, 1945 (dec. 1975); children—Jack Richard, Jr., Alexander Beall, Frances Grant II. Sec., Ill. Senate, 1936; sec., bus. mgr. Wesleyan U. Ill., 1938-39; sec. to chief staff Flying Tng. Command, USAAF, 1951, personnel supr. U.S. Army Air Base, Ephrata and Moses Lake, Wash., 1941-42; job classification and adminstrv. survey analyst Canal Zone, 1942-44; sec. to comdr. USAF Res. Wing, Pitts., 1951-55; sec. to mayor City of Wheeling (W.Va.), 1955-59; sec. W.Va. Ho. of Dels., 1965-66, 77-78, 79-80; legis. aide W.Va. Senate, 1981—; mem. D.A.R., 1947—, state regent, 1986—, state chmn. by laws, 1983-86, nat. vice chmn. Service for vet. patients, 1968-71, editor W.Va. news, 1965-71, W.Va. state parliamentarian, 1979-80, dir. No. dist., 1980-83, state chmn. bylaws, 1983—; nat. chmn. pub. relations Nat. Soc. Women Descs. Ancient and Honorable Arty. Co., 1974-77; mem. Nat. League Am. Pen Women, 1949—, nat. 3d v.p., 1971-72, nat. rec. sec., 1966-68, nat. chmn. orgn., 1972-74, nat. chmn. commemorative endowment fund, 1976-80, W.Va. pres. 1980-82, nat. chmn. fin., 1982-84. Mem. Magna Charta Dames, Colonial Order of the Crown, Order of Washington, Phi Beta Kappa. Democrat. Presbyterian. Home: Route 1 Box 63 Elkins WV 26241

ADAMS, FRANCIS (FRANK) DONALD, electronics engineer, naval reserve officer; b. Pottsville, Pa., Sept. 23, 1943; s. Matthew and Frances Catherine (Guetling) A.; m. Jacqueline Irene Chapman, May 12, 1967; children—Donald Wayne, James Douglas, Deborah Marie. B.S.E.E., U. Miami, 1974; M.S.E.E., U. Central Fla., 1980, postgrad., 1984—. Cert. master instr. USAF. Electronics technician, instr. USAF Tech. Sch., Lackland AFB, Tex., 1966-70; airborne radar technician Homestead AFB, Fla., 1971-74; electronics engr. Naval Tng. Equipment Ctr., Orlando, Fla., 1974—, acquisition dir., project engr., 1974-81, electronics engr., software engr., computer resources cons., 1981—; commd. ensign USNR, 1979, advanced through grades to lt., 1983; Mem. Seminole County Local Sch. Adv. Com., 1982-83. Served with USAF, 1961-70, USAFR, 1971-79, USNR, 1979—. Decorated Army Commendation Medal; Fla. Engrng. Soc. scholar, 1973-74; Navy Long Term Tng. scholar, 1977-78. Named Outstanding Grad. Student of Yr., IEEE, 1978. Mem. U.S. Naval Inst., Winter Springs Civic Assn., Winter Springs C. of C., VFW, Sigma Xi, Tau Beta Pi, Eta Kappa Nu, Sigma Pi Sigma. Baptist. Home: 502 Murphy Rd Winter Springs FL 32708 Office: Naval Training Systems Ctr Code 251 Orlando FL 32813

ADAMS, GEORGE EMERY, mathematician, educator; b. Gary, Ind., Mar. 9, 1942; s. John Emery and Katherine Ellen (Cassiday) A.; B.A. in Math., Manchester Coll., 1963; M.A. (NSF fellow), U. Ill., 1967; postgrad. (univ. fellow) Fla. State U., 1969-71; postgrad. U. N.C.-Asheville, 1983-84, Clemson U., 1984-85; m. Elvira Elizabeth Bene, June 24, 1967; children—Robert Edward Lee, Kelly Elizabeth. Math. tchr. public schs., Cleve., 1963-66; asst. prof. math. Manchester Coll., N. Manchester, Ind., 1967-69, 71-72; prof. math. and computer sci. Montreat-Anderson Coll., Montreat, N.C., 1972-85, chmn. dept. math. and computer sci., chmn. div. natural sci.; teaching asst. Fla. State U., 1970-71; asst. prof. computer sci. Heidelberg Coll., Tiffin, Ohio, 1985—. Deacon, Montreat Presbyn. Ch., 1976-83. Recipient Tchr. of Year award, 1976, 78, 82. Mem. Math. Assn. Am., Am. Math. Assn. of Two-Yr. Colls. Republican.

ADAMS, GEORGE JAMES, financial executive; b. Hobart, Okla., Jan. 14, 1934; s. William T. and Nina Rae (Barkley) A.; m. Virginia Caswell, Sept. 3, 1956; children—Robert Wayne, Debora Sara Adams Barnes. Grad. Kemper Mil. Coll., 1951. Cert. consumer credit exec. With First Mercantile Corp., Wichita Falls, Tex., 1958—, sr. v.p., sec., mem. exec. com.; v.p. Broadway Life Ins. Co., Wichita Falls; dir. Paris Hide & Fur Co. Served to capt. USAF, 1954-58. Republican. Methodist.

ADAMS, HAZEL GREENLEE REDFEARN (MRS. PAYTON F. ADAMS II), retired educator; b. Monroe, N.C., Nov. 12, 1905; d. Ephraim Eugene and Rebecca (Laney) Redfearn; student Radford Coll., 1924; A.B., U. Ky., 1940, M.A., 1953; postgrad. U. Nebr., 1955; m. Payton F. Adams II, July 11, 1928; children—Payton F. III, Juliette Greenlee Adams Hawk. Elementary tchr. Larchmont Sch., Norfolk, Va., 1924-28, Winchester (Ky.) City Schs., 1943-53; supr. Clark County (Ky.) Schs., 1953-61; supr. student tchrs. Ky. Wesleyan Coll., 1945-48; instr. Wesleyan Coll., Macon, Ga., 1960; named asst. prof. edn. Dakota Wesleyan U., Mitchell, S.D., 1961, assoc. prof. edn. and psychology, 1961-70; assoc. prof. early childhood edn. Pfeiffer Coll., Misenheimer, N.C., 1970-77, adviser Student Edn. Assn., 1972-73. Chmn., Clark County Community Council, 1950-52, Clark County Recreation Bd., 1955-60; supr. Teen-Town, Winchester, 1954-60. Recipient Honor award State of Ky., 1960; mem. advisory council Southeastern Christian Coll. Mem. AAUP, AAUW, NEA, S.D. Edn. Assn., DAR (treas. chpt. 1974-80), Assn. Supervision Curriculum Devel., Assn. for Childhood Edn., Mitchell Bus. and Profl. Women, Nat. Trust Hist. Preservation, Ky. Hist. Soc., First Settlers Homemakers Club (family life chmn.), Albemarle Bus. and Profl. Women (pres. 1972-73), Assn. United Meth. Women, Phi Kappa Phi (pres. 1964-66), Delta Kappa Gamma (pres. 1964-66), Pi Gamma Mu. Methodist. Mem. Order Eastern Star. Clubs: Winchester Music, Daniel Boone Music; Winchester Hist., Nat. Hist., Ky. Hist., Christian Women's, Clark County Hosp. Aux.; Author: The Inimitable Educator: Robert E. Lee; contbr. to Elem. English Jour. Home: 136 College St Winchester KY 40391

ADAMS, IDA, librarian; b. Amsterdam, Ga., Jan. 13, 1930; d. Charlie and Flossie (Girvin) G.; m. Benjamin Franklin Adams, Aug. 16, 1963; 1 dau., Angela. B.S., Savannah State Coll., 1951; M.S.L.S., Syracuse U., 1956; A.M.D., Fla. State U., 1975, Ph.D., 1980. Tchr./librarian Jesup, Ga., 1951-53, Decatur County, Ga., 1953-55; cadet librarian Syracuse U., 1955-56; ref. documents, audio visual interlibrary loan librarian Syracuse U., 1956-65, asst. dir. libraries, 1965-78, Title III AIDP/LRC dir., 1978-81, interim dir. LRC, 1981-82; asst. dir. learning resources Fla. A&M U., Tallahassee, 1982—. Named to All Sports Hall of Fame, Savannah State Coll., 1973. Mem. ALA, Southeastern Library

Assn., Fla. Library Assn., NAACP, Urban League, Delta Sigma Theta. Democrat. Baptist. Club: Jack and Jill of Am. Office: PO Box 78 Fla A&M U Tallahassee FL 32307

ADAMS, JAMES BLACKBURN, state ofcl., former fed. govt. ofcl., lawyer; b. Corsicana, Tex., Dec. 21, 1926; s. Lynn and Florence (Blackburn) A.; student La. State U., 1944, Yale U., 1944-45; B.A., Baylor U., 1950, LL.B., 1949, J.D., 1969; m. Ione Winistorfer, Sept. 3, 1955; children—James Blackburn, Elizabeth, Martha. Bar: Tex., 1949, U.S. Supreme Ct. 1965. Asst. county atty. Limestone County, Tex., 1950; mem. Tex. Ho. of Reps., 1951; spl. agt. FBI, Seattle and San Francisco offices, 1951-53, supervisory spl. agt., Hdqrs., 1953-59, asst. spl. agt. in charge Mpls. field div., 1959-61, asst. chief personnel sect., 1961-65, chief personnel sect., 1965-71, exec. asst. to asst. to dir. adminstrn., Washington., 1971-72, spl. agt. in charge San Antonio div., 1972-74, asst. dir., head Office Planning and Evaluation, Washington, 1974, asst. to dir., 1974-78, asso. dir., 1978-79, ret., 1979; exec. dir. criminal justice div. Gov.'s Office, State of Tex., 1979-80, dir. Dept. Pub. Safety, 1980—; guest lectr. various U.S. and fgn. law enforcement, intelligence and bus. groups, 1974-79. Served with U.S. Army, 1945-46; PTO. Recipient numerous govt. achievement awards, 1953-79, Atty. Gen.'s award for Disting. Service, 1978; Nat. Intelligence Disting. Service medal, 1979. Mem. U.S. Supreme Ct. Bar, Tex. Bar Assn., Internat. Chiefs of Police Assn., Tex. Police Assn., Tex. Sheriff's Assn. Presbyterian. Lodge: Masons. Office: 5805 N Lamar Blvd Austin TX 78773

ADAMS, JOHN CARTER, JR., insurance executive; b. Williston, Fla., June 13, 1936; s. John Carter and Katharine Anna (Beall) A.; B.S. in Bus. Adminstrn., U. Fla., 1958; m. Leila Nora Johnson, Nov. 28, 1958; children—Julia Katharine, Ruth Anne. Agt., Pan Am. Ins. Co. 1958-59; acct. exec. Guy B. Odum & Co., Inc. 1959-63, v.p. 1963-66, exec. v.p. 1966-71, pres. 1971-76; pres. Jay Adams & Assocs., Inc. Daytona Beach, Fla., 1976—; chmn. bd. Heritage Fed. Savs. & Loan Assn., Daytona Beach; dir. Consolidated-Tomoka Land Co. Bd. visitors Embry-Riddle Aero. U., Daytona Beach, 1967-69, trustee, 1969—, mem. exec. com., 1972—, vice chmn. bd., 1981-82, chmn. exec. com., 1983; campaign chmn. Easter Seal Soc. 1969, trustee 1970-73, pres. 1972-73; bd. dirs. YMCA, Daytona Beach 1968-76, 78-81, treas. 1970, v.p. 1971-82, pres., 1983; 82; mem. Tourist Devel. Council, Volusia County, 1983—; mem. Halifax Area Advt. Authority, 1984-85; mem. Volusia County Bus. Devel. Corp., 1984—; gen. campaign chmn. United Way of Volusia County, Fla. 1977, pres. 1979, dir. 1976-84; mem. Civic League of Halifax Area, 1968—, bd. dirs., 1978—, chmn., 1983-84; mem. Com. of 100, 1962—, bd. dirs., 1968-74, pres., 1971-72. Served with USNR 1953-61. Recipient Disting. Service award Bd. visitors Embry-Riddle Aero. U. 1975; CHIEF award (Champion Higher Ind. Edn. in Fla.), Ind. Colls. and Univs. of Fla., 1973; Lou Fuchs Man of Yr. award Daytona Beach Area C. of C., 1985. Mem. Daytona Beach C. of C. (bd. govs. 1968-70, v.p. bus. and govt. 1970, pres. 1975, gen. fund drive chmn. 1984), Fla. C. of C. (bd. dirs. 1983—), Volusia County Insurors Assn., Fla. Assn. Ins. Agts. (bd. dirs. 1978-81), Nat. Assn. Casualty & Surety Agts. Democrat. Episcopalian. Home: 3 Riverside Circle Ormond Beach FL 32074 Office: 121 N Ridgewood Ave Daytona Beach FL 32014

ADAMS, JOHN MERLIN, librarian; b. Chgo., June 10, 1950; s. Merlin Jones and Esther Jane (Bohn) A.; m. Nancy Ileen Coultas, June 12, 1970; 1 dau., Arwen Lee. B.A., U. Ill., 1972. M.S., 1973. Grad. asst. U. Ill. Library, Champaign, 1972-73; br. librarian Los Angeles Pub. Library, 1973-75, librarian in philosophy dept., 1975-76; head readers services 1976-78; dir. Moline Pub. Library (Ill.), 1978-83; dir. Tampa-Hillsborough County Pub. Library System, Tampa, Fla., 1983—. Bd. dirs. Planned Parenthood, 1983-85. Mem. ALA, Fla. Library Assn. Lodges: Rotary. Home: 4708 Leona St Tampa FL 33629 Office: Tampa-Hillsborough County Pub Library 900 N Ashley St Tampa FL 33602

ADAMS, JOSEPH DAYTON, physicist; b. Carroll County, Ga., Oct. 6, 1938; s. Lewis Wilmer and Lois (Johnson) A.; m. Mary Ann Rutland, July 1961; children—Christopher, Suzanne, Lara, Keven. B.A., Berry Coll., 1960; M.S., Emory U., 1962; postgrad. Ga. Tech. Inst., 1967-70. Aerospace engr. NASA, Cleve., 1963-65; research physicist Naval Weapons Lab., Dahlgren, Va., 1965; sr. engr. Sperry Microwave Electronics, Clearwater, Fla., 1965-67; research scientist Ga. Inst. Tech., Atlanta, 1967-72; electronics engr. U.S. Army, Huntsville, Ala., 1972-73; sr. research scientist Ga. Inst. Tech., Atlanta, 1973—. Mem. IEEE, Am. Phys. Soc., Sigma Xi, Sigma Pi Sigma, Nat. Audubon Soc., Nat. Geog. Soc., Am. Forest Assn. Contbr. articles to profl. jours. Office: Ga Inst Tech GTRI-STL-MSD Atlanta GA 30332

ADAMS, KENNETH STANLEY, JR., energy company executive, football executive; b. Bartlesville, Okla., Jan. 3, 1923; s. Kenneth Stanley and Blanch (Keeler) A.; m. Nancy Neville, Oct. 26, 1946; children—Susan (Mrs. Thomas S. Smith), Amy (Mrs. Thomas A. Thompson), Kenneth Stanely III. Student, Menlo Coll., 1940-41, U. Kans., 1941-44. Chmn. bd. Adams Resources & Energy, Inc., Houston; v.p. Travel House of Houston; owner Bud Adams Ranches, KSA Industries, Inc., Houston Oilers, Inc., River Garden Farms, Southwest Lincoln-Mercury, Inc., Southwest Motor Leasing; adv. dir. First City Nat. Bank Houston, Am. Bank & Trust Co. Houston. Mem. exec. bd. Sam Houston Area council Boy Scouts Am.; trustee Profl. Football Hall Fame. Served with USNR, 1943-46. Named Houston Salesman of Year, 1960, Mr. Sportsman of 1961, Westerner of Year, 1969. Mem. Tex. Ind. Producers and Royalty Owners Assn., Ind. Petroleum Assn., Houston Assn. Petroleum Landmen, Houston Geol. Soc., Sigma Chi (named Significant Sig 1963). Clubs: River Oaks Country, Houston, Petroleum, 100 of Houston. Office: PO Box 844 Houston TX 77001

ADAMS, KENT MORRISON, lawyer; b. Houston, May 14, 1956; s. Duane Byron and Edith Marie (Giffen) A.; m. Joanne Catherine Brown, Dec. 30, 1981; 1 child, Mary Catherine. B.A. in Polit. Sci., George Washington U., 1978; J.D., La. State U., 1981. Bar: Tex. 1982, La. 1981, U.S. Ct. Appeals (5th cir.), U.S. Dist. Ct. (ea. and so. dists.) Tex. 1981, U.S. Dist. Ct. (we. dist.) La. 1983. Assoc. Brown and Adams, Beaumont, Tex., 1981-82, ptnr., 1985—; briefing atty. U.S. Dist. Ct., Beaumont, 1982-83; assoc. Benckenstein, Norvell, Bernsen and Nathan, Beaumont, 1983-85; instr. Lamar U., Beaumont, 1982-83. Del. Jefferson County Rep. Conv., 1984. Mem. ABA, Tex. State Bar Assn., Maritime Law Assn. U.S., Am. Soc. Law and Medicine, Def. Research Inst., Tex. Assn. Def. Counsel, La. State Bar Assn., Jefferson County Young Lawyers Assn. (v.p. 1985-86, bd. dirs. 1984-85). Presbyterian. Home: 3675 Long Ave Beaumont TX 77706 Office: Brown and Adams 395 N 11th St Beaumont TX 77702

ADAMS, LAMAR TAFT, physician; b. Hiawassee, Ga., Apr. 9, 1938; s. Cecil Taft and Julia Nadine (Wilson) A.; B.S., Wake Forest U., 1959; M.D., Bowman Gray Sch. Medicine, 1965. Intern, N.C. Bapt. Hosp., 1965-66, resident in internal medicine, 1966-69; staff physician VA Hosp., Mountain Home, Tenn., 1971-72; chief med.-surg. services Ga. Regional Hosp., Augusta, 1973-74; asst. prof., med. dir. physician's asst. tng. program Med. Coll. Ga., Augusta, 1974-75; practice medicine specializing in internal medicine, Monroe, Ga., 1975—. Served with USAF, 1969-71. Mem. Phi Rho Sigma. Baptist. Contbr. articles to med. jours. Home: Box 669 Monroe GA 30655 Office: Alcova St Monroe GA 30655

ADAMS, LARRY LEE, manufacturing company executive; b. Charlotte, Mich., Jan. 8, 1938; s. Donald Lyle and Mildred Marie (Keith) A.; m. Sharon Colleen Housler, Oct. 2, 1960; children—James F., Katherine E., Sarah M. B.S., Western Mich. U., 1963. Plant engr. Eaton Corp., Battle Creek, Mich., 1965-66, quality control mgr., 1966-70, engring. mgr., 1970-72, plant mgr., Sanford, N.C., 1972-77, div. mgr., Brazil, 1977-81; div. pres. Abex Corp., Winchester, Va., 1981—; dir. Eaton Corp., Brazil, 1977-81. Bd. dirs. United Fund, Winchester, 1983—; vice chmn. Lord Fairfax Community Coll. Found., 1983—; mem. Shenandoah Coll. Pres.'s Council, Winchester, 1983—; twp. trustee Battle Creek Twp., 1972. Boys Club of Am. fellow, 1981-83. Mem. Soc. Automotive Engrs. Republican. Club: Rotary. Home: 609 Bellview Ave Winchester VA 22601 Office: Abex Corp 2410 Papermill Rd Winchester VA 22601

ADAMS, LAWRENCE H., public utility executive; b. West Palm Beach, Fla., Feb. 11, 1927; s. Harry L. and Pauline (Kraynick) A.; m. Arminta Gregg, Oct. 27, 1951; children—Lawrence H., Ron, Thad. Student Purdue U., U. Miami; grad. advanced mgmt. program Harvard U. With Fla. Power & Light Co., Miami, 1949—. Mem. campaign cabinet United Way of Dade County (Fla.), 1976—; bd. dirs. Greater Miami chpt. Fellowship of Christian Athletes, 1976—, pres., 1980; mem. dinner com. NCCJ, 1977-84; mem. Hispanic Heritage Festival, 1977—, chmn., 1982; mem. exec. com. Fla. Meml. Coll. Adv. Council, 1980—; trustee Greater Miami United Way, 1981—; trustee U. Miami, 1973-76, 81-84, chmn. vis. com. on student life, 1982—; v.p. Orange Bowl Com., Miami, 1983—. Served to cpl. USAAF, 1944-46. Named Outstanding Businessman of Broward County, Broward Sales and Mktg. Assn., 1975; recipient Reubin O'D. Askew award Urban League Greater Miami, 1982, Community Excellence award Eastern Airlines Latin Adv. Council, 1982. Mem. Miami-Dade C. of C. (adv. council 1979—, membership chmn. 1980), Greater Miami C. of C. (vice chmn. for econ. devel. 1982—, chmn. Dade Clean Com., pres. elect). Baptist. Clubs: Kings Bay Yacht and Country, Am. Club in Miami, Miami, 200, Riviera Country, City Club of Miami. Office: Fla Power & Light Co PO Box 029311 Miami FL 33102

ADAMS, MARILYN LEE, nurse; b. Mechanicsburg, Pa., Sept. 14, 1940; d. Earl Wingert and Mary Jayne (Burger) Pyke; m. James Wesley Adams, Sept. 4, 1964; children—Timothy Allen, Pamela Sue. B.S. in Nursing, Messiah Coll., 1963. R.N., Pa., Ark. Staff nurse Harrisburg Hosp. (Pa.), 1963-64; nursing instr. Ark. Bapt. Hosp., Little Rock, 1964-67, neurosurg. nurse, 1969-74; rehab. staff nurse Central Bapt. Hosp., Little Rock, 1974-77; unit nursing supr. Ark. Rehab. Inst., Little Rock, 1977—; speaker, cons. in field. Author patient handbook, 1975. Leader Little Rock council Girl Scouts U.S., 1976-82. Ark. Regional Med. Program grantee, 1974. Mem. Assn. Practitioners in Infection Control (sec. 1980-83), Assn. Rehab. Nurses (charter), Harrisburg Hosp. Nursing Alumni, Ark. Quilters Guild. Republican. Baptist. Home: 3 Deerwood Dr Hensley AR 72065 Office: Arkansas Rehab Inst 12th and Marshal Sts Little Rock AR 72202

ADAMS, MITCHELL SCOTT, computer scientist; b. Miami, Fla., July 10, 1952; s. Joseph and Sheri (Hoffman) A.; B.S. in Computer Sci., Fla. Inst. Tech., 1976; m. Irene Alexis Adams, Feb. 25, 1978; children—Maegen Phyllis, Aria Danielle, Micah Ray. Systems analyst RCA, Cape Canaveral, Fla., 1976-77, DBA, Melbourne, Fla., 1977-78, Stromberg Carlson, Orlando, Fla., 1979-80; pres. Scott Adams, Inc., DBA Adventure Internat., Longwood, Fla. Democrat. Jewish. Club: Computer (pres.) (Orlando). Office: Box 3435 Longwood FL 32750

ADAMS, NORMAN ILSLEY, JR., physicist; b. Winthrop, Mass., Sept. 20, 1895; s. Norman Ilsley and Mabel Estelle (George) A.; B.A., Yale U., 1917, Ph.D., 1923; m. Genevieve A. Sloan, July 28, 1926; children—Norman Ilsley, Harry Bell. Engr. dept. devel. and research AT&T, N.Y.C., 1923-24; mem. faculty Yale U., New Haven, 1925—, prof. physics, 1944-64, prof. emeritus, 1964—; vis. prof. U. Idaho, 1964, U. Del., 1965, Central Wash. State Coll., 1967; cons. engr. in radio broadcasting, 1927—. Served as 2d lt., 301st Heavy Tank Bn., A.E.F., France, 1918; dir. Eatontown Signal Lab., Fort Monmouth, N.J., 1941-43; ret. rank lt. col. Registered profl. engr. (communications), Conn. Decorated Legion of Merit. Fellow Am. Phys. Soc.; mem. Res. Officers Assn., Ret. Officers Assn., Mil. Order World Wars, Order Lafayette, Gamma Alpha, Phi Beta Kappa, Sigma Xi. Republican. Episcopalian. Clubs: Appalachian Mountain; New Haven Lawn. Author: Principles of Electricity (with L. Page), 1931; Electrodynamics (with L. Page), 1940. Address: 6812 SW 35th Way Gainesville FL 32608

ADAMS, OSCAR WILLIAM, state justice; b. Birmingham, Ala., Feb. 7, 1925; s. Oscar William and Ella Virginia (Eaton) A.; m. Willa Ingersoll, Dec. 25, 1949 (dec.); children—Oscar William, III, Gail Ingersoll Adams Harden, Frank T. A.B., Talladega (Ala.) Coll., 1944; LL.B., Howard U., 1947. Bar: Ala. bar Practice in, Birmingham, 1947-80; partner firm Adams & Adams, 1980; asso. justice Supreme Ct. Ala., 1980—; past instr. Miles Coll. Sch. Law; bd. dirs. Lawyers Com. Civil Rights Under Law. Recipient Winner's award Talladega Coll.; award EEO Commn. Mem. Ala. Law Inst., Ala. Lawyers Assn. (award for outstanding public and profl. service), Nat. Bar Assn. (jud. council), Am. Trial Lawyers Assn., Omega Psi Phi, Phi Beta Boule. Democrat. Methodist. Clubs: Shriners, Elks. Home: 3531 Carter Hill Rd Montgomery AL 36111 Office: PO Box 218 Montgomery AL 36101

ADAMS, PAULETTE FREEMAN, nursing educator; b. Louisville, Oct. 22, 1942; d. Paul Logan and Mary Elizabeth (Osting) Freeman; m. Jerry Edward Adams, Aug. 1, 1964. B.S.N., Spalding U., 1964, M.A., 1974; Ed.D., U. Ky., 1985. Registered nurse. Staff/head nurse St. Joseph Hosp., Lexington, Ky., 1964-67; instr. St. Mary and Elizabeth Hosp., Louisville, 1967-68, St. Joseph Infirmary, Louisville, 1968-70, Norton's Hosp., Louisville, 1970-71, Jefferson Community Coll., Louisville, 1971-74; assoc. prof., asst. dean dept. nursing U. Louisville, 1974—; cons. Health Reach, Louisville, 1984—; presentor continuing edn. programs, Louisville, 1974—. Mem. Nurses Polit. Action, Louisville, 1983—; mem. Ky. Cancer Commn., 1979-81. Maternal child grantee Dept. Human Resources, Frankfort, Ky., 1978-80. Mem. Am. Nurses Assn., AAUP, Ky. Nurses Assn. (bd. dirs. 1983-85). Democrat. Roman Catholic. Avocations: gardening; raising roses. Office: U Louisville Sch Nursing Louisville KY 40292

ADAMS, RALPH WYATT, SR., university president, lawyer; b. Samson, Ala., June 4, 1915; s. Alfred E. and Eunice M. (Clements) A.; A.B., Birmingham-So. Coll., 1937; LL.B., U. Ala., 1940, LL.D., 1965, J.D., 1969; postgrad. U. Colo., 1958, George Washington U., 1960, Harvard U., 1981, Jesus Coll., Oxford U. (Eng.), 1983; m. Dorothy Kelly, Sept. 5, 1942; children—Ralph Wyatt, Kelly Clements (Mrs. James B. Allen, Jr.), Samuel. Bar: Ala. 1940, U.S. Supreme Ct. Atty., dep. supt. Ala. Dept. Ins., 1945-46; judge, Tuscaloosa, Ala., 1946-47; founder Acad. Life Ins. Co., Denver, 1957; tchr. life ins. U. Colo.; dep. dean, acting dean Air Force Law Sch., Air U., pres. Troy (Ala.) State U., 1964—; dir. Bankers Credit Life Ins. Co., Adams Life Ins. Co., 1st Ala. Bank of Troy, South Trust Bank of Montgomery. Former mem., chmn. State Personnel Bd. Ala., State Ins. Bd. Ala.; chmn. Ala. Oil and Gas Bd.; past mem. Presdl. Clemency Bd.; past commr. Edn. Commn. of States; past Ala. dir. Selective Service; past pres. Assn. Ala. Coll. and U. Pres.'s and Adminstrs.; past pres. Gulf South Conf.; trustee, vice chmn. Lyman Ward Mil. Acad., Camp Hill, Ala.; mem. appeal bd. U.S. Dept. Edn. Served to capt. USAAF, 1941-45; maj. gen. Res., also Ala. Air N.G. Recipient Silver Beaver award Boy Scouts Am.; Alumnus of Yr. award Birmingham-So. Coll., 1978; named to Ala. Acad. Honor, 1977, ICMS Newspaper Carrier Hall of Fame, 1979; Man of Yr., Troy, 1968, 75; First Citizen of Area, C. of C.; recipient Algernon Sydney Sullivan award. Mem. English Speaking Union (former nat. dir.), Am. Legion (state comdr., 1977-78), Mortar Bd., Phi Alpha Delta, Kappa Delta Pi, Pi Delta Phi, Kappa Phi Kappa, Phi Kappa Phi, Lambda Chi Alpha, Omicron Delta Kappa, Pi Tau Chi. Methodist. Clubs: Alexandria Civitan (past pres.), Army-Navy Country (Alexandria, Va.); Montgomery (Ala.) Country; Troy Country; Metropolitan, Cosmos (Washington). Lodges: Masons, Rotary. Home: President's Mansion Troy State U Troy AL 36081

ADAMS, RODERICK EDWIN, JR., clinical psychologist; b. Sanford, Fla., Sept. 8, 1953; s. Roderick Edwin and Edith (Miller) A.; m. Katrina Louise Marye, May 19, 1974; children—Daniel Eric, Elizabeth Marye, John Patrick. B.S. in Psychology, Northwestern State U. La., 1975; M.S., U. Mis.-Milw., 1977, Ph.D. in Clin. Psychology, 1979. Lic. psychologist, La. Coordinator children's services Region VI Mental Health-Mental Retardation Ctr., Greenwood, Miss., 1980-81; program dir. La. Spl. Edn. Ctr., Alexandria, 1981-82; clin. psychologist Central La. State Hosp., Pineville, 1982—; clin. psychologist Ctr. for Family and Individual Counseling, Alexandria, 1984—; cons. Family Counseling Agy., Alexandria, 1982-84, mem. profl. adv. com., 1985—. Contbr. articles to profl. jours. Mem. Am. Psychol. Assn. Home: 72 Rainbow Dr Pineville LA 71360 Office: Ctr for Family and Individual Counseling 3327 Jackson St Suite E Alexandria LA 71301

ADAMS, RONALD WAYNE, U.S. Army personnel service center administrator; b. Hannover, N.H., Apr. 2, 1938; s. Rodney Arthur and Myrtie (Godda) A.; m. Irene Rita Zimmerman, Sept. 24, 1958; children—Michael Wayne, Gary Dean. A.A., Armed Forces Inst., 1976. Joined U.S. Army, 1955, advanced through grades to sgt. maj., 1976; chief ops. sergeant Provost Marshal's Office, Ft. Bragg, N.C., 1972-75, provost marshal sgt. maj. 16th ABN Corps, 1976-77, law enforcement sgt. maj., 1977-78, sgt. maj. community life program 18th Airborne Corps, 1978-79, provost marshal sgt. maj. Western Command, Ft. Shafter, Hawaii, 1979-80; dir. Personnel Service Ctr., Ft. Bragg, N.C., 1981—; chmn. entertainment com. Non-Commd. Officers Club, 1983—. Mem. N.C. Sheriffs Assn., Spl. Forces Assn., Assn. U.S. Army (treas. 1977-78, chmn. renewal 1981-82, sec. 1983-84), Non-Commd. Officers Assn. Republican. Mem. Assembly of God Ch. Office: Personnel Service Ctr Fort Bragg NC 28307

ADAMS, RUSSELL ELLSWORTH, patent and trademark office executive; b. Phila., Apr. 20, 1948; s. Russell Ellsworth and Mabelle Emma (Root) A.; m. Patrivia Gale Smith, May 2, 1970 (div. Aug. 1984); children—Benjamin Russell, Jonathan Robert. B.S. in Physics, U. Fla., 1970. Primary examiner, U.S. Patent & Trademark Office, Arlington, Va., 1970—. Author: Reading Between the Lines, 1984. Editor: Barcode News, 1983—; East Coast editor: Business Software Mag., 1984-85; mem. software rev. bd. Info World, 1980-84. Contbr. numerous articles to mags. Recipient Bronze medal U.S. Dept. Commerce, 1983. Mem. IEEE Computer Soc., Patent & Trademark Office Soc. (chmn. history 1983-84), Recognition Technologies Users Assn. (chmn. industry 1985—). Democrat. Avocations: cooking; photography; video taping. Home: 3008 Mosby St Alexandria VA 22305 Office: US Patent and Trademark Office Crystal Plaza Arlington VA 22202

ADAMS, VINCENT DARREL, real estate executive, yacht broker; b. Rocky Mount, N.C., Mar. 30, 1927; s. Dennis Gilbert and Cora Ann (Becton) A.; m. Mary Lucille Mangum, Dec. 22, 1946; children—Mary Ann, Scott Dennis, Bethanie Mayo. B.S. in Civil Engring., The Citadel, 1952. Founder, owner Charleston Blue Print & Supply Co (S.C.), 1953-66, Charleston Yacht Sales, 1965-79, Adams Properties, Charleston, 1970—; dir. So. Bank & Trust Co., Charleston. Served with USN, 1944-46. Methodist. Clubs: Charleston Yacht, Charleston Cruising, Charleston Civil Engring. Home: 178 Hobcaw Dr Mount Pleasant SC 29464 Office: Charleston Mcpl Marina Lockwood Blvd Charleston SC 29401 also PO Box 757 Charleston SC 29402

ADAMS, WILLIAM L., petroleum products company executive; b. 1929. B.S., U. Kans., 1951; M.S., UCLA, 1956. With Amoco Co., 1956-81; v.p., 1975-81; exec. v.p. Champlin Petroleum Co., Fort Worth, 1981-82, pres., chief operating officer, 1982—, also dir. Office: Champlin Petroleum Co PO Box 7 Fort Worth TX 76101*

ADAMSON, DAN KLINGLESMITH, association executive; b. Vernon, Tex., Oct. 12, 1939; s. Earl Larkin and Edith (Klinglesmith) A.; B.A. in History, Southwestern U., Georgetown, Tex., 1962; m. Eva Diane Pope, Aug. 18, 1962; children—Larkin, Rebecca, Amy, Sarah. Sch. tchr., Jefferson County (Colo.), 1962-63; asst. to exec. sec., then gen. mgr. Soc. Petroleum Engrs., Dallas, 1964-79, exec. dir., 1979—, editor Jour. Petroleum Tech., 1967-72. Mem. adminstrv. bd. 1st United Meth. Ch., Richardson, Tex., 1980-83; mem. bd. James Bowie Elem. Sch. PTA, 1978-80, 81-82, Westwood Jr. High Sch. PTA, 1980-81, J.J. Pearce High Sch. PTA, 1981-82. Mem. Am. Soc. Assn. Execs., Council Engring. and Sci. Soc. Execs. Republican. Office: PO Box 833836 Richardson TX 75083

ADAMSON, J(OSEPH) RON, electronics company executive; b. Nashville, Aug. 30, 1940; s. Leslie C. and Mamie Adamson; m. Elizabeth Mary Layne, July 6, 1963 (dec. May 1983); children—Alan R., Lisa M.; m. Janette Kaye Phelps, Mar. 1, 1985. A.A.S., Community Coll Air Force, 1974; B.A., McKendree Coll., 1976; M.A., Webster Coll., 1977. Cert. quality engr. Joined U.S. Air Force, 1958; electronic technician, supr., 1958-71, master instr., instr. suprl Keesler AFB, Miss., 1971-75; recruiter, counselor, Louisville, 1975-78; ret., 1978; plant mgr. quality assurance supr. Aladdin Electronics, Smithville, Tenn., 1978-79; mgr. quality assurance AIE div. Vernitron, Nashville, 1979-85, dir. quality, 1986—. Mem. Am. Soc. Quality Control (sr.), Order Ky. Cols., Air Force Sgts. Assn. Home: 3979 Lawing Dr Nashville TN 37207 Office: 701 Murfreesboro Rd Nashville TN 37210

ADCOCK, DAVID LEE, educator, consultant; b. Cuero, Tex., July 3, 1945; s. Ocy Lee and Jewel D. (Stovall) A. A.A., Victoria Coll., 1965; B.S. in Social Sci., Tex. A&I U., 1967. Cert. tchr. in secondary edn., Tex.; tchr. spl. edn., Tex.; tchr. computer literacy, Tex. Tchr., spl. edn. coordinator John Marshall High Sch., San Antonio, 1967-72; spl. edn. tchr. Allen Jr. High Sch., Austin, Tex., 1973-76, behavioral specialist, 1977-80; spl. edn., social sci. tchr. O. Henry Jr. High Sch., Austin, 1980-83, tchr. spl. edn., computer literacy, 1984—; cons. Art Link Inc., Round Rock, Tex., 1983—. Author and presenter in field. Mem. Austin Assn. Tchrs. (Outstanding Tchr. award 1979), Northside Assn. Tchrs., Tex. Council Assn. Children with Learning Disabilities, Nat. Council Exceptional Children (presenter 1985), Tex. Council for Exceptional Children, NEA, Tex. State Tchrs. Assn., Assn. Spl. Edn. Tech., Tex. Computer Edn. Assn., MAD Ednl. Assocs. Edn. Assn. (computer cons. 1984—, bd. dirs.), Loca A.A. Found. (bd. dirs. 1978-85), O. Henry PTA, Austin Bird Club. Roman Catholic. Avocation: breeder of exotic parrots. Home: Route 3 Box 263 J Bastrop TX 78602 Office: O Henry Jr High Sch 2610 W 10th St Austin TX 78703

ADDISON, MARY JANE, clubwoman; b. Beaumont, Tex.; d. Henry Davis and Corinne (Carter) Pond; R.N., Jefferson Davis Sch. Nursing, 1945; m. Eugene Morse Addison, Mar. 10, 1946; children—Eugene Morse, Paul Davis. Mem. choir First Baptist Ch.; den mother Cub Scouts, 6 years, recipient Den Mothers award, 1961; pres. Huntsville (Tex.) PTA, 1955-56, v.p. dist. bd., 1956-57, state life mem. PTA, 1967; pres. Women's Missionary Union, First Bapt. Ch., 1965-68; chmn. heritage com. Mayor's Bicentennial Com., 1974-76; pres. Woman's Forum, Tex. Fedn. Womens Clubs, 1972-74, 80-81, named Woman of Year, 1974; life mem. Hosp. Aux., pres., 1971-72; bd. dirs. Sam Houston Mus., 1983—; active Walker County Hist. Commn., Tex. Hist. Found.; mem. Community Choir, Gilbert and Sullivan Soc.; chmn. Huntsville Beautification, 1979-84; mem. Beautify Tex. Council; pres. county chpt. Am. Cancer Soc., 1982-84. Decorated Grand Peiory of Am. Order St. John of Jerusalem, dame Knights Hospitaller. Mem. African Violet Soc. Am., Daus. Republic of Tex. (pres. Houston chpt. 1970-75, 79-81, state rec. sec. gen. 1973-75, state 1st v.p. gen. 1975-77, pres. gen. 1977-79, dir. 1979-81, mem. library bd. 1981-83, Alamo bd. 1983-85), DAR (regent Mary Martin Elmore Scott chpt. 1972-74, 82-86), Daughters Am. Colonists (regent Capt. John Utie chpt., state rec. sec. 1983-85, state 1st vice regent 1985-87 UDC (dist. chmn. 1981-84, pres. J.B. Gordon chpt. 1983-85, state historian 1984-86), Colonial Dames Am., Colonial Dames of XVII Century (organizing regent), Walker County Geneal. Soc., San Jacinto Mus. History Assn., Victorian Soc. (charter mem. Tex. chpt.), Tex. Hist. Assn., Tex. Acad. Family Practice (charter, parliamentarian 1983-85), Spain in Tex. Soc., Lone Star Hist. Assn. (state adv. com.), Am., Tex. (pres. 38th Dist. 1977-83) nurses assns., AMA, Tex., Tri-County (past pres.) med. auxs., Tex. Acad. Family Physicians (charter; state parliamentarian 1983-84), Nat. Soc. Magna Charta Dames, Daus of War of 1812. Clubs: Garden (past pres., chmn. city beautification com.); Univ. Women Sam Houston State U. (charter). Address: Huntsville TX 77340

ADKINS, BARBARA L., savings and loan association executive; b. Sugarland, Tex., Oct. 26, 1946; d. Thomas H. and Patricia M. Adkins. M.B.A., U. Dallas, 1982. With Pier 1 Imports, 1967-83, dir. European fin., 1973-76, mgr. mdse. stats., 1977, asst. to exec. v.p., 1977-78, merchandising systems analyst, 1979, real estate property mgr., 1980, real estate mgr. eastern U.S., 1981-83; v.p. Bright Banc, Tex., 1984—. Mem. Irving Tex. Mem. Irving Women's C. of C., Sigma Iota Epsilon.

ADKINSON, WILLIAM B., JR., telephone company executive, general contractor; b. Cornishville, Ky., Feb. 27, 1934; s. Willie B. and Nannie V. (Smith) A.; m. Shirley Ann Schulz, June 4, 1954; children—Cheryle Ann Chapline, Robert Joseph. Student U. Ky., 1959, Rollins Coll., 1966-67. Lineman So. Bell Telephone Co., Louisville, 1955-56, cable splicer, 1956-57, switching technician, Ky., Fla., 1958-64, engr., Orlando, Jacksonville, Fla., 1964-79, assoc. mgr., Jacksonville, 1979—; owner, mgr. Bill Adkinson Contractor, Jacksonville, 1975—; treas. C-Paw Inc., Palatka, Fla., 1982—. Author: Power Phobia-and Its Cure, 1984. Pres. San Jose Lake Assn., Jacksonville, 1970-84; pres. San Jose Civic Assn., 1980—; mem. Kings Trail Sch. Adv. Council, Jacksonville, 1980-84. Recipient Outstanding Leadership award Duval County Community Edn., 1982. Republican. So. Baptist. Avocations: Hunting; fishing; woodworking; auctioneer. Home: 7560 Old Kings Rd S Jacksonville FL 32217 Office: So Bell Telephone Co 21AA2 301 W Bay St Jacksonville FL 32202

ADLER, PATRICIA ANN, sociologist, educator; b. N.Y.C., Sept. 7, 1951; d. Benjamin Theodore and Judith Ann (Goldhill) Heller; m. Peter Adler, Aug. 20, 1972; children—Jori Ann, Brye Jacob. A.B. in Sociology summa cum laude, Washington U., St. Louis, 1973; M.A. in Sociol. Sci., U. Chgo., 1974; Ph.D. in Sociology, U. Calif.-San Diego, 1984. Instr. Tulsa Jr. Coll., 1981-83; research assoc. U. Tulsa, 1983-84; asst. prof., 1984-85; asst. prof. sociology Okla. State U., Stillwater, 1985—. Author: Wheeling and Dealing, 1985; (with others) The Social Dynamics of Financial Markets, 1984; (with others) The Sociologies of Everyday Life, 1980; also articles. U. Calif.-San Diego traineeship, 1978-81. Assoc. editor Social Problems Jour., 1984—, Jour. Urban Life, 1982—. Editor ann. series Sociol. Studies of Child Devel., 1984—. Mem. Am. Sociol. Assn., Soc. for Study Social Problems, Am. Soc. Criminology, Soc. for Study of Symbolic Interaction (publ. com. 1985-88, program chmn. 1984, 86), Phi Beta Kappa. Avocations: racquetball; aerobics; gardening; travelling. Office: Dept Sociology Okla State U 006 Classroom Bldg Stillwater OK 74078

ADLER, ROBERT, photographic company executive; b. N.Y.C., Dec. 25, 1906; s. Hyman and Freida (Byers) A.; student Ohio State U., 1925-27; m. Rosa Schuman, Aug. 5, 1933; 1 son, Michael Frederic. With advt., editorial depts. Cleve. Plain Dealer, 1927-32; advt. mgr. Lorain (Ohio) Times Herald, 1933-34; pub. Lorain Shopper, 1935-37; pub. Springfield (Ohio) Shopper, 1935-41; pub. Springfield Tabloid Times, Springfield Jour., 1939; owner Robert Adler Advt. Agy., Springfield, 1941-45; pres. Click Camera Shops, Inc., Springfield, 1945-63, Rapid Photo, Inc., Springfield, 1953-62, A & H Realty Co., Springfield; pres. Tru-Foto, Inc., Springfield 1953-64, now chmn. bd.; chmn. bd. Foto-Color Co., Dayton, Ohio, 1960—, Rapid Mail Co., Dayton, Tru-Foto, Inc.; chmn. bd. Progressive Industries Corp., Dayton; mem. adv. bd. Summit Bank, Tamarac, Fla. Mem. 4th Study Mission to Israel, 1957, Springfield Commn. Downtown Improvement Com., 1962; bd. dirs. Louis Calder Library, mem. bd. human resources U. Miami (Fla.) Med. Sch., also mem. vis. com.; pres. Retail Mchts. Council Springfield, United Jewish Appeal, Bonds for Israel; chmn. bd. So. Ohio Coll., 1967-74; bd. dirs. Springfield Devel. Council, Boy Scouts Am., Jr. Achievement, North Broward County Jewish Fedn., U. Miami Human Resources; mem. permanent vis. com. Louis Calder Med. Library; hon. chmn. A.D.L. Fla. One Thousand; nat. commr. Anti-Defamation League, also chmn. Fla. 1000 Soc. Fellows. Recipient David Ben Gurion award State of Israel Bonds, Leadership award Ft. Lauderdale Jewish Fedn. Mem. Springfield C. of C. (dir.), Wisdom Soc. Jewish (v.p. dir. temple). Clubs: Masons, Rotary, B'nai B'rith, Woodlands Country (bd. govs., award 1978) (Ft. Lauderdale). Author, producer, photographer: (films) Hong Kong Clicking, 1960, Israel, 1961. Home: 5719 Coco Palm Dr Fort Lauderdale FL 33319 Office: 4444 Lake Center Dr Dayton OH 45426

ADLER, SAM GUCKENHEIMER, JR., retired retail executive; b. Savannah, Aug. 2, 1925; s. Sam G. and Elinor (Grunsfeld) A.; children—Samantha Adler Dinsmore, Robert G. B.A., U. Pa., 1947. Asst. buyer exec. tng. program Bloomingdale's, N.Y.C., 1947-49; with retail fashion systems Spiegel's, Chgo., 1949-52; v.p., gen. mdse. mgr. Leopold Adler Co., Savannah, 1952-59; pres. and owner Leopold Adler Co. DBA Adler's for Quality, Savannah, 1960-85. Bd. dirs. and exec. com. St. Joseph's Hosp., Savannah, 1971—; mem. U.S. Trade Mission to Netherlands, 1963; past pres. Savannah Symphony Soc., hon. bd. dirs.; past vice chmn. Telfair Acad. Arts and Scis.; bd. dirs. Hilton Head Hosp., 1985—. Mem. Downtown Mchts. Assn. (past pres.), Shopping Ctr. Mchts. Assn. (past pres.), Savannah C. of C. (past dir.). Served with USN, 1943-45. Episcopalian. Clubs: Sea Pines, Spanish Wells (Hilton Head Island, S.C.); Chatham; First City. Office PO Box 13126 Savannah GA 31416

ADOLPHI, RONALD LEE, government official; b. Bremerton, Wash., Aug. 8, 1946; s. Robert L. and Margaret May (Hitland) A.; m. Sherry Lee Klepach, Oct. 5, 1968 (div. Jan. 1974), Celia Louise Fields, May 10, 1975; 1 adopted child, Christina. Lani. B.A. in Bus. Adminstrn., U. Wash., 1968; M.S. in Ednl. Adminstrn., Butler U., 1974; M.B.A., Syracuse U., 1976; grad. Indsl. Coll. Ph.D. in Mgmt., Calif. Coast U., 1986. Cert. cost analyst. Br. chief, capt. U.S. Army Fin. Sch., Indpls., 1972-73; fin. analyst Continental Steel Corp., Kokomo, Ind., 1973-74; fin. services officer Hdqrs. U.S. Army Pacific, Honolulu, 1974; fiscal specialist Office of Comptroller of Army, Washington, 1974-76; internat. economist Office Sec. of Def., Washington, 1976-82, asst. dir. for banking, 1982—; dir. Fin. Ctr. Fed. Credit Union., Indpls, 1972-74. Editorial bd. Armed Forces Comptroller Mag., 1979-83. Contbr. articles to profl. pubs. Fin. adviser St. John's Luth. Day Care Ctr., Alexandria, Va., 1983—; treas. St. John's Luth. Ch., Alexandria, 1978-80, sec., 1980-81, v.p. 1982-84, pres. 1984-86; chair fin. com. Nat. Luth. Assn. Scouters, 1983—, pres. 1980-82, sec., 1984-86; newsletter editor Capital Luth. Assn. Scouters, 1983-86, pres., 1977-80; chmn. protestant com. on scouting Nat. Capital Area council Boy Scouts Am., chmn. subcom. 1984-86. Served to capt. U.S. Army, Vietnam, lt. col. Res. Decorated Bronze Star with oak leaf cluster, Air medal, others; recipient Encased George Washington Honor medal Freedoms Found. at Valley Forge, 1964, Silver Beaver award Boy Scouts Am., 1979, Lamb award Luth. Council in USA, 1981, U.S. Treasury Dept. award for excellence in cash mgmt., 1985. Mem. Assn. Syracuse Army Comptrollers (1st v.p. 1978-83), Res. Officers Assn., Am. Econ. Assn., Am. Mgmt. Assn., Sr. Execs. Assn., Am. Soc. Mil. Comptrollers, Assn. Govt. Accts., Fed. Exec. Inst. Alumni Assn., Phi Theta Kappa, Beta Gamma Sigma. Republican. Avocations: travel, model trains, scouting and church activities. Home: 6028 Mayfair Ln Alexandria VA 22310 Office: Office Asst Sec of Def (Comptroller) Directorate for Banking The Pentagon Room 1A658 Washington DC 20301

ADREON, HARRY BARNES, architect; b. Norfolk, Va., July 18, 1929; s. Harry Barnes and Helen Rae (Medairy) A.; m. Beatrice Marie Rice, Dec. 27, 1952. B.S., Va. Poly. Inst. and State U., 1950, M.S., 1952; student, Internat. Law Sch., 1977-78. Registered architect, Va., Md. Prin. archtl. firm Cross & Adreon, Washington, 1961—. Mem. Washington Episcopal Diocesan Archtl. Commn., 1966—; Bd. dirs. Arlington YMCA, 1982—. Served as capt. USMCR, 1952-54. Recipient Design award Nat. Assn. Home Builders, 1965-66; award for architecture Washington Bd. Trade, 1965; Design award Bethesda-Chevy Chase C. of C., 1966, 67; Nat. Honor award Am. Inst. Steel Constrn., 1968. Mem. AIA (corporate mem., House and Home award 1966, 67, Honor award Middle Atlantic region 1967, Nat. Honor award 1968, commr./dir. D.C. Met. chpt. 1976-78, chmn. mcpl. procedures com. D.C. Met. chpt. 1975), Washington Bldg. Congress, Constrn. Specifications Inst. (profl. mem., pres. D.C. chpt. 1972-74, chmn. region, 2 awards com., Pres.'s plaque 1975, cert. specifications writer, continuing edn. coordinator 1980—), Arlington County C. of C., Tau Sigma Delta. Episcopalian (vestryman 1961-63, 67-69, 71-73). Club: Kiwanis (pres. 1983-84). Home: 4524 N 19th Rd Arlington VA 22207 Office: 950 N Glebe Rd Suite 140 Arlington VA 22203

ADSIDE, JOSEPH WILLARD, educator; b. Dublin, Ga., Jan. 29, 1934; s. Robert Sr. and Georgia (Robinson) A.; m. Bella Ferguson, Dec. 24, 1959; children—Marcus Keith, Malcom Kent, Arnelle Lynn. B.S., W.Va. State Inst., 1951; M.A., So. U., Baton Rouge, 1972; postgrad. U. Miami, Fla., 1974-75; Ph.D., Columbia Pacific U., 1983. Cert. tchr., Fla. Instr., team tchr. Mays Jr. High Sch., 1960-65, chmn. dept., 1966-71; tchr. Am. history Palmetto Sr. High Sch., 1972-82, 84—, sociology and psychology, 1983-84. Author: Attitudes toward Neighborhood in Sub-Communities, 1984. Contbr. articles to profl. publs. Bd. dirs. South Dade County Mental Health Assn., Miami, 1980-82; compaign worker Dade County Democratic Orgn., Miami, 1982; guest lectr. Bethel Afro-Am. Seminar, Miami, 1985; counselor Future Farmers Am., Miami, 1966. ABA fellow, 1965; U. Miami fellow, 1964-66; So. U. fellow, 1971. Mem. Am. Sociol. Assn., Nat. Council Social Studies, Smithsonian Instn., Assn. Afro-Am. History-Lit., Black Writers Assn. Baptist. Avocations: reading, hunting, fishing, writing, music. Home: 14940 SW 107th Ave Miami FL 33176 Office: Miami Palmetto Sr High Sch 118th St SW Miami FL 33156

AECHTERNACHT, STEPHEN MARK, orchestra administrator; b. Dallas, May 21, 1948; s. Albert Charles and Frances Ruth (Layton) A.; m. Claudia Nan Spessard, Aug. 13, 1983; 1 child, Martin. B.A. in Psychology, So. Meth. U., 1971, M.A. in Psychology, 1973; postgrad. in clin. psychology U. Tex. Health Sci. Ctr., 1975-76. Radio announcer WRR-FM, Dallas, 1970-78; instr. So. Meth. U., Dallas, 1974-76; store mgr. Sound Warehouse, Dallas 1976-78; regional mgr. PolyGram Records, Dallas, 1978-82; artistic adminstr. Houston Symphony Orch., Houston, 1982-84, dir. artistic ops., 1984—; instr. Rice U., Houston, 1982—; bd. dirs. New Music Forum of Houston, 1983—. Contbr. articles to profl. jours. Recipient Chevalier award Order of DeMolay, 1968, Gold Record PolyGram Records, 1983. Mem. AAUP, Psi Chi. Lodge: Order of DeMolay (Master Councilor 1965-66). Office: Houston Symphony Orchestra 615 Louisiana St Houston TX 77002

AFFLECK, MARILYN, sociologist, educator; b. Logan, Utah, July 1, 1932; d. Clark B. and Velda M. (Bryson) A.; children—Michelle Alisa, Kimberly Kay. B.A., U. Okla., 1954; M.A., Brigham Young U., 1957; Ph.D., UCLA, 1966. Asst. prof. Fla. State U., 1966-68; asst. prof. U. Okla.-Norman, 1968-71, assoc. prof. sociology, 1971—, asst. dean Grad. Coll., 1976-78, 80-82, interim dean Grad. Coll., 1978-79. Editor: Free Inquiry in Creative Sociology, 1984-86. Recipient AMOCO Good Teaching award U. Okla., 1974, Grad. Edn. Project award, 1978; NIMH fellow, 1963-65. Mem. Am. Sociol. Assn., Southwestern Social Sci. Assn., Okla. Sociol. Assn., Nat. Women's Studies Assn., South Central Women's Studies Assn. Democrat. Mormon. Office: Women's Studies U Okla Norman OK 73019

AFGAN, AGHA PERVAIZ, consultant, loss control representative; b. Lahore, Pakistan, Punjab, Pakistani, July 10, 1947; came to U.S., 1973, naturalized, 1977; s. Agha Mobin Khan and Shireen Naz; m. Shasta Kirmani, May 20, 1977; children—Nadia K., Izza K., Sarah K. Assoc. in Tech., Govt. Polytech. Inst., Hyderabad, Pakistan; Assoc. in Sci., Community Coll., Little Rock, 1978; B.S. in Indsl. Tech., So. Ill. U., 1979. Shift engr. Mehran Sugar Mills, Hyderabad, 1969-73; fuel specialist U.S. Air Force, Little Rock, 1975-80; risk mgmt. rep. St. Paul Ins. Co., Birmingham, Ala., 1980-84; loss control cons. So. Cons., Service, Atlanta, 1984—; adviser Safecomp: Loss Control Cons., Birmingham, 1985—. Author: (booklets) Research & Development Product Safety Program, 1983-84, Research & Development Fleet Safety Program, 1983-84, Evaluation Risk Management Activities Mining, Steel Bolt Manufacturing, 1983-84. Recipient Honor's Certificate, Miami Dade Community Coll., 1974. Mem. Amn. Soc. Safety Engrs. (v.p. 1983-84), Greater Birmingham Safety League, Am. Indsl. Hygiene Soc., N.S.C. Republican. Muslim. Avocations: swimming, table tennis, cricket, fishing, reading. Home: 69 Town Creek Apt Columbiana AL 35051 Office: PO Box 1124 Columbiana AL 35051

AGAPOS, ANGELO MICHAEL, financial economist, educator; b. Cleve., Oct. 28, 1932; s. Emmanuel Frank and Athena E. (Papadakis) A.; m. Sharon Lee McMahon, June 20, 1961; children—Emmanuel Michael, Catherine, John. B.S., Miami U., 1954, M.B.A., 1959; Ph.D., Case Western Res. U., 1967. Fin. adminstr. NASA, Lewis Research Ctr., Cleve., 1963-66; asst. prof. econs. Ohio U., Athens, 1966-69; prof. econs. and fin. U. New Orleans, 1969-84; prof., chmn. econs. and fin. U. South Ala., 1984—; bus. and banking cons.; dir. First Eastern Bank, New Orleans. Served to capt. USAF, 1954-57. Mem. Am. Econs. Assn., Fin. Mgmt. Assn. Office: U of South Alabama Mobile AL 36688

AGATHER, VICTOR NEILS, investment banker; b. Kalispell, Mont., Aug. 21, 1912; s. Alfons A. and Martha Bertha (Neils) A.; B.S., Georgetown U., 1934; M.B.A., Harvard U., 1936; m. Fifi O'Connor, Aug. 31, 1940; children—Merrilee, Anne, Neils, John. With Shields & Co., 1936-40; exec. v.p. La Consolidada, S.A., Mexico City, 1946-59; pres. Intercon, S.A., Mexico City, 1959—. Served to col. USAAF, 1940-45. Office: Intercon SA CV Monte Caucaso 915 4 Mexico 11000 Mexico

AGEE, STEVEN CRAIG, oil company executive; b. Wichita, Kans., May 23, 1953; s. John Edwin and Melba Lee (Adams) A.; m. Nancy Louise Lee, Jan. 8, 1977; children—Michael Steven, Kristen Lee. B.B.A., U. Okla., 1975; M.A. in Econs., U. Kans., 1979, Ph.D., 1981. Teaching asst. U. Kans., Lawrence, 1975-77, asst. instr., 1977-79, instr., 1979-81; asst. prof. Washburn U., Topeka, 1981-82; pres. XAE Corp., Oklahoma City, 1982—; econ. adviser Lee Energy Exploration Co., Oklahoma City, 1982—; dir. Enterprise Operating Co., Oklahoma City, Stonebridge Inn Assn., Snowmass, Colo. Mem. Am. Econ. Assn., Econ. History Assn., Oklahoma City C. of C. Clubs: Lifespace (Oklahoma City); Kickingbird Men's (Edmond, Okla.). Republican. Episcopalian. Office: XAE Corp 621 N Robinson Suite 490 Oklahoma City OK 73102

AGOR, WESTON HARRIS, management educator, consultant; b. Salamanca, N.Y., Dec. 30, 1939; s. Randall Walter and Ruth (Barrett) A.; m. Eliana Bauer, Aug. 20, 1963 (div. 1979); children—Lawrence, William. B.A., St. Lawrence U., 1961; M.P.A., U. Mich., 1963; Ph.D., U. Wis., 1969. Assoc. prof. U. Fla., Gainesville, 1971-73; exec. asst. to senate majority leader State of Mich., Lansing, 1973-75, spl. asst. to gov., 1976-78; prof., chmn. dept. bus. sch. U. Miami, Coral Gables, Fla., 1978-81; prof., dir. M.P.A. program U. Tex., El Paso, 1982—; asst. dir. Citizens Conf. State Legis., Kansas City, Mo., 1973; vis. prof. Ctr. for Pub. Policy Adminstrn. Calif. State U., Long Beach, 1981-82; pres. ENFP Enterprises, El Paso, 1982—. Author: Chilean Senate, 1971; Latin American Legislatures, 1971; Intuitive Management, 1984; The Logic of Intuition, 1986. Contbr. articles to profl. jours. Fellow Midwest Univs., Consortium, 1967-68, Danforth Found., 1980-86, Alden B. Dow Creativity Ctr. Resident, 1984. Fulbright grantee, Chile, 1963. Mem. Am. Soc. Pub. Adminstrn., Am. Polit. Sci. Assn., Tex. Assn. Schs. Pub. Affairs and Adminstrn. (treas. 1983-84), Greater Miami C. of C. (exec. dir. 1981). Republican. Avocations: tennis; music; sailing. Office: ENFP Enterprises 6022 Caprock #103 El Paso TX 79912

AGRICOLA, IRA M., association executive; b. Portsmouth, Va., Aug. 7, 1954; s. William Rudolph and Anne (Moore) A.; m. Belinda Cohoon, June 2, 1980; 1 child, Lindsay Ann. B.S., Va. Commonwealth U., 1976. Dir. therapeutic recreation Portsmouth Parks and Recreation, 1975-77, dir. spl. recreation, 1977-79; mgr. bus. and community affairs Portsmouth C. of C., 1979-83; dir. Portsmouth council Hampton Roads C. of C., 1983—. Bd. dirs. YMCA, High St. Ports, Va., 1984—; mem., ex-officio Portsmouth Port and Indsl. Com., 1984—. Recipient God and Country award Boy Scouts Am., 1968. Mem. Am. Assn. C. of C. Execs. Episcopalian. Lodge: Elks (trustee 1983). Avocations: swimming; running; football. Home: 409 Pennington Blvd P Portsmouth VA 23701 Office: PO Box 70 524 Middle St Mall Portsmouth VA 25705

AGRON, KATHERINE JONES, custom design company, gift basket company executive; b. Gastonia, N.C., Mar. 15, 1946; d. Laurence Graham and Laura M. (Ginn) Jones; m. Michael S. Agron, Dec. 15, 1971 (div. Nov. 1976); children—Candace De'Leslyn, Samantha Michelle. B.S., Averett Coll., 1976. Designer, Charlottesville, Va., 1971-76; instr. Piedmont Community Coll., Charlottesville, 1977-80; appraiser City of Charlottesville, 1977-80; owner Just Windows, Hilton Head Island, S.C., 1981—; pres. Basket Case Co., Hilton Head Island, 1985—. Mem. Hilton Head Home Builders, Hilton Head C. of C. Republican. Home: 119 Beckenham Hilton Head Island SC 29928 Office: Just Windows 14 Pope Ave PO Box 5552 Hilton Head Island SC 29928

AGUAR, CHARLES EDWIN, landscape architect, city planner, educator; b. Jacksonville, Ill., Mar. 29, 1926; s. Frank and Rose (Ornellas) A.; m. Berdeana Benson, June 8, 1947; children—David, Richard, Catherine, Daniel, Kenneth. B. Landscape Architecture, U. Ill., 1949; M. City Planning, 1950. Registered landscape architect, Ga. Chief planner St. Louis Plan Commn., 1952-55; exec. dir. Springfield/Sangamon County Plan Commn., Ill., 1955-60; prin. Aguar Jyring Whiteman Moser, Inc., Minn., 1960-70; assoc. prof. landscape architecture U. Ga., Athens, 1970-83, prof., 1983—, chmn. grad. landscape architecture program, 1982—; cons. Dept. Interior, U.S. Forest Service, Ga. Dept. Natural Resources, Minn. State Planning Agy., Minn. Hist. Soc., Minn. Dept. Natural Resources. Chmn. master plan com., charter bd. dirs. Northeast Ga. Nature Ctr., Inc., 1974—; trustee Ga. Conservancy, 1975-77, 81—. Served with USAAF, 1944-47; PTO. Named Environ. Educator of Yr., Sears, Roebuck and Co., Ga. Wildlife Fedn., 1975. Mem. Am. Inst. Cert. Planners, Am. Planning Assn., Council of Educators in Landscape Architecture. Democrat. Presbyterian. Lodges: Lions (Duluth, Minn.); Kiwanis (Athens); Masons (Champaign, Ill.). Contbr. chpts. to landscape books. Home: 715 Riverbend Pkwy Athens GA 30605 Office: Sch Environ Design U Ga 1 Landscape Architecture Bldg Athens GA 30602

AGUAYO-PERELES, JOAQUIN, lawyer, educator; b. Ponce, P.R., Oct. 7, 1949; s. Joaquin and Carmen (Pereles) Aguayo; m. Maria de los Angeles Pagan, Dec. 31, 1969; children—Joaquin III, Suzette M., Neshmayda M. B.B.A. cum laude, Inter-Am. U., 1974; J.D., Cath. U. (P.R.), 1977. Bar: P.R. 1978, U.S. Dist. Ct. P.R., 1978, U.S. Ct. Appeals (D.C. cir.) 1985, U.S. Supreme Ct. 1983, U.S. Tax Ct. 1985, U.S. Ct. Mil. Appeals 1985. Sole practice, Ponce, 1978-80; assoc. prof. Inter-Am. U., Ponce, 1978-80, World U., Ponce, 1978-80; trial lawyer Municipality of Ponce, 1979-80; atty. adviser Bd. Vet. Appeals, Washington, 1981—. Legal adviser Group Parents of Handicapped Children, 1978; basketball coach Springfield Youth Club, 1983—. Served with U.S. Army, 1968-70. Recipient Honor cert. Inter-Am. U., 1972; award for excellent achievement Bancroft-Whitney Co., 1976; Chmn.'s Commendation award Bd. Vet.'s Appeals, 1982, 83, 84, 85. Mem. P.R. Bar Assn., D.C. Bar Assn., Hispanic Bar Assn. Avocation: racquetball. Office: PO Box 2933 West Springfield VA 22152

AGUILAR, JOSE FUENTES, nurse; b. Iloilo, Philippines, May 29, 1952; came to U.S., 1983. S. Demetrio Magbanua and Josefina (Fuentes) A. B.S.N., Iloilo Doctors' Coll., 1975. R.N., Tex. With Iloilo Doctors' Hosp., 1976-83, supr. operating room-delivery room, 1979-81, supr. operating room-delivery room-ICU-recovery room, 1981-83, instr. nursing, clin. instr. operating room, inservice instr.-nursing service, 1978-83; nurse intensive CCU, Knapp Meml. Methodist Hosp., Weslaco, Tex., 1983-84, asst. head nurse intensive CCU, 1984—. Mem. Philippine Nurses Assn., Operating Room Nurses' Assn. of Philippines (sec. 1978-83), Iloilo Doctors' Coll. Alumni Assn. (pres. 1978-83), Am. Assn. Critical Care Nurses. Roman Catholic. Home: 610 Hospital Dr Tropicana B-6 Weslaco TX 78596

AGUIRRE, BENIGNO EMILIO, sociology educator; b. Trinidad, Las Villas, Cuba, Oct. 25, 1947; came to U.S., 1961, naturalized, 1970; m. Lauriece Chitwood; children—Carlos, Benigno E., Jr. B.A., Fla. State U., 1970; M.A. in Latin Am. Studies, Tulane U., 1972; Ph.D. in Sociology, Ohio State U., 1977. Mem. faculty Tex. A&M U., College Station, 1979, assoc. prof. sociology, 1985—; mem. faculty council Sterling C. Evans Library; research assoc. Disaster Research Ctr., Ohio State U., 1975-77. HEW fellow; Tex. A&M grantee, 1977-83, 81. Contbr. articles to profl. jours. Mem. team Com. Natural Disasters Nat. Research Council, 1982; cons. Family Violence Br., Tex. Dept. Human Resources, Austin, 1983. Mem. Sociol. Assn., Latin Am. Studies Assn., Nat. Council Family Relations, Soc. Study Social Problems, So. Sociol. Assn. Home: 1204 Goode St College Station TX 77840 Office: Dept Sociol Tex A&M Univ College Station TX 77843

AGUIRRE, NICOLAS, international trade executive; b. Quito, Ecuador, June 30, 1942; came to U.S., 1963, naturalized, 1979; s. Elias and Mariana (Armendaris) A.; m. Cheryl A. Reynolds, Aug. 30, 1969. Student Internat. Sch. Bus., NYU, 1972-73. With Am. Internat. Group, 1973-78, regional mgr. life ins. operation for Central Am., 1974-75, br. mgr. life ins. ops., Miami, Fla., 1975-78; founder, pres. Americas Internat. Trade and Investment Corp., Miami, 1978—; pres. U.S. Fedn. Export Mgmt. Companies, 1983-84; v.p. U.S. Fedn. Export Assns., 1984—; bd. dirs. Internat. Ctr. of Fla., 1981, 82, v.p., 1983—. Bd. dirs. SSS, 1984—, Hispanic Heritage Festival, 1984—, Council for Internat. Visitors, 1985; trustee Columbus 1992 Expo 500; chmn. Miami-Ibiza Sister Cities Program; hon. consul of Ecuador in Coral Gables; gov.'s appointee Bus. Adv. Council on Edn., State of Fla., 1985; pres. Bolivian Coordinating Council. Recipient Key to City of Coral Gables, 1981, Key to Dade County, 1984. Mem. Nat. Assn. Export Cos. (dir. 1984—), Fla. Exporters and Importers Assn. (pres. 1981, 82, bd. govs. 1983—), Greater Miami C. of C. (bd. govs. 1981, 82), Bolivarian Soc. of Miami (bd. dirs. 1983—). Democrat. Lodge: Rotary. Home: 717 Ponce de Leon Blvd Coral Gables FL 33134 Office: PO Box 450685 Miami FL 33145

AGUIRRE, ROBERT BERNAL, management consultant; b. San Antonio, May 14, 1950; s. Fernando Cervantes and Hortencia (Bernal) A.; m. Mary Elizabeth Ornelas, May 15, 1971; children—Jennifer, Adam. B.B.A., St. Mary's U., 1975. Div. controller Harry Tappan & Sons, San Antonio, 1975-77; asst. treas. Handy Andy, Inc., San Antonio, 1977-79; treas. Tex. Trust Co., San Antonio, 1979-81; pres. Falcon Food & Mgmt., San Antonio, 1981-85; self-employed corp. project coordinator and mgmt. cons., San Antonio, 1983—; chmn., pres. Concord Pub. Utility, San Antonio, 1984—, also dir.; mem. adv. bd. Franklin Mortgage Co., San Antonio, 1985—. Dir. Teresian Bd. Edn., San Antonio, 1982-84, pres., dir., 1985; v.p. Braun Station Homeowner's Assn., San Antonio, 1982-84. Roman Catholic. Avocations: photography; horseback riding; scuba diving. Home: 8611 Honiley St San Antonio TX 78250 Office: 221 W Poplar St San Antonio TX 78212

AHLBORN, ROBERT CHARLES, oil company executive; b. Berkeley, Calif., Aug. 9, 1944; s. Ernest J. and Margaret E. (Stephens) A.; m. Chammelia Deborah Adams, Feb. 3, 1969; children—Stephanie, Beth, Renae, Wendy, Becky, Adam, Rachel, Sarah, Bryan, Amy. B.S., Brigham Young U., 1969, M.S., 1973. Exploration geologist Exxon, 1973-78, Delta Drilling Co., Houston, 1978-79; pres. Carbonit Exploration, Houston, 1979-82, Diversified Energy Mgmt., Houston, 1985—; asst. to gen. mgr. Sandefer Oil and Gas Co., Houston, 1982-85. Contbr. articles to profl. publs. Served to capt. USMC, 1969-72, Vietnam. Mem. Am. Assn. Petroleum Geologists, Rocky Mountain Assn. Geologists, Houston Geol. Soc. Republican. Mormon. Home: 15103 Lakewood Forest Dr Houston TX 77070 Office: Diversified Energy Mgmt 1001 Fannin 2300 Houston TX 77070

AHLEN, JOHN WILLIAM, III, state official, scientist, educator; b. Oak Park, Ill., Jan. 4, 1947; s. John William and Helen Beatrice (Damaske) A.; m. Linda Sue Belton, Sept. 27, 1985; children—John William, Jenny Kristin. B.S. in Bioengring., U. Ill.-Chgo., 1969, Ph.D. in Physiology, 1974. USPHS bioengring. trainee, 1969-73; Ill. legis. sci. intern, 1973-74; staff scientist Ill. Legis. Council, Springfield, 1974-77, sr. staff scientist, 1978-82, asst. dir. sci. and tech., 1982-84; exec. dir. Ark. Sci. and Tech., Little Rock, 1984-85, pres., 1985—; vis. asst. prof. U. Ill., Urbana, 1977-78; adj. asst. prof. Sangamon State U., 1974-84, So. Ill. U. Sch. Medicine, Springfield, 1974-84; mem. Gov.'s Sci. and Tech. Task Force, 1977-78. Contbr. articles to profl. jours. NSF grantee, 1977-83. Mem. IEEE, ASME (v.p. pub. info. 1981-85), Sigma Xi. Congregationalist. Home: 1 Rook Pl Maumelle AR 72118 Office: Ark Sci and Tech Authority 200 Main St Suite 210 Little Rock AR 72201

AHLFELD, CHARLES EDWARD, nuclear industry executive; b. Peoria, Ill, Aug. 9, 1940; s. John Frederick and Kathryn Louise (Weisbruch) A.; m. Barbara Anne Slusher, Dec. 29, 1962; children—Judith Anne, Nancy Lynn, Sharon Leigh. B.S., U. Fla., 1962; M.S., Fla. State U., 1964, Ph.D., 1968. Grad. asst. Fla. State U., Tallahassee, 1962-67; research physicist E.I. duPont-Savannah River Lab., Aiken, S.C., 1967-75, staff physicist, 1975-78, research mgr., 1985—; asst. chief supr. E.I. duPont-Savannah River Plant, Aiken, 1978-81, chief supr., 1981-84, asst. dept. supt., 1984-85. Patentee in field. Chmn. sch. bd. St. Mary's Sch., Aiken, 1977; Active United Way, Aiken, 1982—. Mem. Am. Nuclear Soc. (sect. chmn. 1983-84, Cert. of Governance 1984), Am. Phys. Soc. Roman Catholic. Home: 340 Bordeaux Pl Aiken SC 29801 Office: EI du-Pont-Savannah River Lab Bldg 773-A Aiken SC 29801

AHLSTROM, RICHARD MATHER, oil company executive; b. Painesville, Ohio, Nov. 25, 1934; s. William McKinley and Janice (Mather) A.; A.B., Harvard U., 1956; exec. program Amos Tuck Sch. Bus. Adminstrn., 1974; m. Beverly Sowle, Apr. 6, 1957; children—Thomas Richard, Michael Christopher. With Diamond Shamrock Corp., Cleve., 1960—, treas. fgn. subs., 1964-65, mgr. adminstrn. chem. div., 1966-67, asst. treas. corp., 1968-71, treas. corp., 1971-76, v.p. fin. 1976-84, sr. v.p., chief fin. officer, 1984—; dir. Tex. Commerce Bank, Dallas. Bd. dirs. Dallas Theatre Ctr.; trustee Dallas Symphony Assn.; adv. bd. Ctr. Study Fin. Instns. and Markets, Cox Sch. Bus. So. Meth. U. Fellow Explorers Club; mem. Nat. Acctg. Assn., Fin. Execs. Inst., Ohio Archaeol. Soc. (chpt. dir.), SAR. Club: Bent Tree Country. Named Boss of Year, Am. Businesswomens Assn., 1971. Author: Indian Habitation of Lake County, Ohio, 1967; A Significant George Washington Discovery, 1975; Prehistoric Pipes, a Study of the Reeve Village Site, Lake County, Ohio, 1981. Office: Diamond Shamrock Corp 717 N Harwood St Dallas TX 75201

AHMAD, NASIHA, obstetrician/gynecologist; b. Dacca, Pakistan, Mar. 15, 1947; d. Syed Abu and Nasima (Khatun) Hamid; m. Syed Husain Ahmad; children—Mehdi, Zehra. H.S.C., U. Dacca (Pakistan), 1964, M.D., 1970. Intern, U. Dacca; resident in ob-gyn U. Dacca Med. Coll. Hosp.; resident Duke U., Durham, N.C., 1981-82; sr. resident dept. ob-gyn Tex. Tech. Sch. Medicine, Amarillo, 1982—. Mem. Am. Coll. Obstetricians and Gynecologists. Author numerous papers on fertility research. Office: Ob-Gyn Dept Tex Tech Sch Medicine 1400 Wallace Blvd Amarillo TX 79106

AHNER, RUSSEL OLIVER, seismological researcher; b. Ouaquaga, N.Y., Jan. 19, 1936; s. Russell Oliver and Thelma Elizabeth (Park) A.; m. Linda Rae Stage, Aug. 21, 1959; children—Joanne Loraine, Russel Oliver, Sandra Rae. B.A., Am. U., 1971. Teletype operator, data analyst Bendix Radio, Ft. Myers (Fla.) Radio Tracking Facility, 1960-61; seismic field team leader Geotech Corp., Garland, Tex., 1961-62, electronics technician, 1962; sr. seismic data analyst Blue Mountain Seisnol. Obs., Baker, Oreg., 1962-63, Uintah Basin Seismol. Obs., Vernal, Utah, 1963-66; researcher Seismic Data Lab., Alexandria, Va., 1966-71, research assoc., 1971-74; research assoc. Marine Scis. Inst., U. Conn., Groton, 1974-76; research assoc. Weston (Mass.) Obs., Boston Coll., 1976-80; sr. systems analyst ENSCO Inc., Indian Harbour Beach, Fla., 1980-81; sr. sci. programmer Teledyne Geotech, Indian Harbour Beach, 1981—; cons. Weston Obs., 1976, 80. Baseball umpire Little League and Stan Musial 1973—. Served with USAF, 1955-59. Mem. Am. Geophys. Union, Seismol. Soc. Am. Republican. Methodist. Co-editor: Quar. Bulletin of Seismicity of Northeastern U.S., 1975-79; contbg. author research reports. Home: 425 Penguin Dr Satellite Beach FL 32937 Office: 1300 Pinetree Dr Indian Harbour Beach FL 32937

AHRARI, MOHAMMED, political science educator, researcher, consultant; b. Hyderabad, India, Nov. 24, 1945; came to U.S., 1968; s. Mohammed

Hashmatullah and Sayyeda A.; m. Rheana Elizabeth Houser, Aug. 14, 1979. B.A., Eastern Ill. U., 1971, M.A., 1972; Ph.D., So. Ill. U., 1976. Grants specialist Jackson County Housing, Murpheesboro, Ill., 1977; vis. asst. prof. Eastern Ill. U., Charleston, 1977-79, Kean Coll. N.J., Union, 1980; asst. prof. polit. sci., East Carolina U., Greenville, 1980—; external research fellow World Acad. Devel. & Cooperation, College Park, Md., 1984—. Author: The Dynamics of Oil Diplomacy, 1980; OPEC The Failing Giant, 1985. Contbr. book revs. and articles to profl. jours. NEH fellow, 1979, 1984, 85. Mem. Am. Polit. Sci. Assn., Am. Soc. Pub. Adminstrn. (bd. dirs. Eastern N.C. 1980—), Petroleum Economists, Pi Sigma Alpha. Democrat. Muslim. Avocations: photography; racquetball; traveling. Home: 1108 W Wright Rd Greenville NC 27834 Office: Dept Polit Sci East Carolina U Brewster Hall Greenville NC 27834

AIKINS, SANDRA SUE, counselor; b. Temple, Tex., Dec. 31, 1944; d. John Arthur and Mary Madeline (Chapman) Gilley; m. Russell Dean Aikins Jr., July 29, 1978; stepchildren—Alexis, Bradley. A.A., Temple Jr. Coll., 1965; B.A., Baylor U., 1967; M.Ed., North Tex. State U., 1973. Licensed profl. counselor, cert. spl. edn. counselor, cert. ednl. supr., cert. tchr., Tex. Tchr. Hutcheson Jr. High Sch., Arlington, Tex., 1971-72; jr. high counselor, Everman Independent Sch. Dist., Tex., 1972-76; middle sch. counselor, Plano Independent Sch. Dist., Tex., 1976-85, counseling coordinator, 1985—; instr. Tarrant County Jr. Coll., Ft. Worth, 1972-76. Lectr. to various orgns., ch. groups. Vol., counselor trainer CONTACT Crisis Telephone Hotline, Arlington, 1973-76; vol. marriage and family counselor Galaxy Ctr., Garland, Tex., 1984; pvt. practice marriage and family counseling, Dallas, 1983-84; group leader for Neighborhood Support Group, 1st United Methodist Ch., Plano, 1984; mem. clinical adv. com. for Plano Crisis Ctr., 1985; mem. steering com. Plano War on Drugs. Mem. Am. Assn. for Counseling and Devel., Tex. Assn. for Counseling and Devel., Tex. Sch. Counselors Assn. (v.p. 1980-82, chmn. for interprofl. relations com. 1982-84), North Central Tex. Assn. for Counseling and Devel. (sec. 1981-82, program dir. 1982-83, awards chmn. 1979-80, hospitality chmn. 1983-84). Democrat. Avocations: travel; flower gardening; needlework; arts and crafts. Home: 3208 Rockbrook Dr Plano TX 75074

AIKMAN, ALBERT EDWARD, lawyer; b. Norman, Okla., Mar. 11, 1922; s. Albert Edwin and Thelma Annette (Brooke) A.; m. Shirley Barnes, June 24, 1944; children—Anita Gayle, Priscilla June, Rebecca Brooke. B.S., Tex. A&M U., 1947; LL.B. cum laude, So. Meth. U., 1948, LL.M., 1954. Bar: Tex. 1948, U.S. Supreme Ct. 1956. Staff atty. Phillips Petroleum Co., Amarillo, Tex., 1948-49; sole practice, Amarillo, 1949-53; tax counsel Magnolia Petroleum Co., Dallas, 1953-56; ptnr. firm Locke, Purnell, Boren, Laney & Neely, Dallas, 1956-71; sole practice, Dallas, 1972-81; sec., counsel Pickens Energy Corp., Dallas, 1981—. Served with inf. U.S. Army, 1943-45. Mem. ABA, Tex. Bar Assn., Dallas Bar Assn. Methodist. Contbr. articles in field to profl. jours.

AINBINDER, SEYMOUR, real estate consultant; b. Bklyn., July 10, 1928; s. Max and Sonia Rose (Alterman) A.; m. Rose Beatrice Cooper, Jan. 14, 1951; children—Michael Cooper, Jonathan Cooper. Student Rutgers U., 1955-56, Upsala Coll., 1957-58. Store mgr. S. Klein Dept. Stores, N.Y.C., 1947-60; v.p. Allied Dept. Stores, N.Y.C., 1960-72, Arlen Shopping Ctrs., N.Y.C. and Chattanooga, 1972-77; owner, mgr. Ainbinder Assocs., Houston, 1977-80; ptnr. Ainbinder Bramalea Co., Houston, 1980-82; real estate cons., owner Scads, Inc., Houston, 1982—; owner, mgr. Cards and Things, Houston, Scad's Gift Shop. Club: Westwood Country. Home: 1201 Hyde Park Houston TX 77006 Office: Scads Inc 800 Bell St Houston TX 77002

AIRY, SUBHASH C., pharmaceutical analytical chemist; b. New Delhi, India, Jan. 13, 1944; s. Ved Prakash and Santosh (Bhambi) A.; m. Saphla Meena Lall, Sept. 4, 1969; children—Shilpa, Alka. B.S. with honors, Kurukshetra U., (India), 1967, M.S., 1969; M.S., Eastern Mich. U., 1977; Ph.D., U. Mich., 1982. Chief chemist Liquid Glaze Inc., Lansing, Mich., 1970-74; clin. chemist St. Joseph Hosp., Ann Arbor, Mich., 1975-82; research assoc. A.H. Robins, Richmond, Va., 1982—; grad. teaching asst. Eastern Mich. U., U. Mich. Mem. Am. Chem. Soc., Am. Pharm. Assn., Acad. Pharm. Scis. Sigma Xi. Contbr. articles to profl. jours. Home: 100 Old Carrollton Rd Richmond VA 23236 Office: AH Robins 1211 Sherwood Ave Richmond VA 23220

AITKEN, PETER GIL, neurobiologist, photographer; b. N.Y.C., Mar. 7, 1947; s. Hugh Walter, Jr., and Laura Isabel (Tapia) A.; m. Kathryn Ann Conte, June 22, 1973; 1 son, Benjamin Joseph Tapia. B.S., U. Rochester, 1972; M.A., SUNY-Brockport, 1974; Ph.D., U. Conn., 1978. Lectr., Cornell U., Ithaca, N.Y., 1978-79; postdoctoral fellow Cornell U., 1979-82; asst. med. research prof. Duke U. Med. Ctr., Durham, N.C., 1982—; freelance photo-illustrator; reviewer profl. jours.; speaker profl. meetings. Recipient Individual Research Service award NIH, 1979-82; scholar Ansel Adams Photography Workshop, 1983. Mem. AAAS, Soc. Neurosci. Contbr. articles to sci. jours., photographs to artistic and comml. publs. Office: Box 3709N Duke University Medical Center Durham NC 27710

AJALAT, DICK S., dentist; b. Bklyn., Sept. 25, 1927; s. Saba D. and Mary B. (Curry) A.; m. Sybil Dawahare, Feb. 24, 1957; children—Stephen J., Mary Nell. B.S., Columbia U., 1951; D.D.S., Med. Coll. Va., Richmond, 1957. Pharmacist, Peoples Drug, Newport News, Va., 1951-57; dentist, Springfield, Va., 1957—. Author poetry; contbr. artist. Served with U.S. Coast Guard, 1946-48. Mem. ADA, Acad. Gen. Dentistry, Va. State Dental Assn. (del. 1981-85), No. Va. Dental Soc., Am. Acad. Cosmetic Dentistry, Fairfax County Dental Soc., Am. Legion, V.F.W. Club: Springfield Civic Assn. Avocations: Artist; lecturer. Home: 6115 Backlick Rd Springfield VA 22150

AJAX, MICHAEL FLEMING, physicist; b. Salt Lake City, May 8, 1936; s. William Theodore and Kathryn Ridley (Fleming) A.; B.S. in Physics and Math., U. Tex., El Paso, 1964, M.S. in Physics and Math., 1967; m. Shirley Ann Michels, Apr. 21, 1962; 1 dau., Deianira Ann. Instr. math. Edn. Center, Ft. Bliss, Tex., 1960-63, dir. evening program, 1963-67; asst. to dir. Kidd Meml. Seismic Obs. and Research Lab., U. Tex., El Paso, 1964-67; sr. research scientist applied physics div. S.W. Research Inst., San Antonio, 1967—; cons. in acoustics, noise prediction and control. Served in U.S. Army, 1955-59. Mem. Acoustical Soc. Am., ASME, Sigma Pi Sigma. Presbyterian. Author: Handbook for Noise Control at Gas Pipeline Facilities, 1977. Home: 6309 War Hawk Dr San Antonio TX 78238 Office: 6220 Culebra Rd San Antonio TX 78284

AKER, J. CALVIN, associate justice state supreme court; b. 1939. B.S., Eastern Ky. U.; J.D., U. Tenn. Bar: Ky. 1970. Sole practice, Vico, Ky., until 1976; ptnr. Aker & Rogers, Somerset, 1976-78; judge Ky. 28th Dist. Ct., Somerset, Ky., 1978-80; assoc. justice Ky. Supreme Ct., Frankfurt, 1980—. Office: Ky Supreme Ct Capitol Bldg Frankfurt KY 40601*

AKERS, GARY, artist; b. Pikeville, Ky., Feb. 22, 1951; m. Lynn Rita Keathley, Sept. 17, 1974; 1 child, Ashley Nicole. B.A., Morehead State U., 1972, M.A., 1974. Instr. art Menifee County Bd. Edn., Frenchburg, Ky., 1972-73; grad. teaching asst. Morehead State U., Ky., 1973-74, art instr., 1975; instr. art Kenton County Bd. Edn., Independence, Ky., 1974-76; artist Gary Akers Art Studio, Union, Ky., 1976—; condr. art workshops U. Evansville, Ind., 1982, Hopkinsville Art Assn., Ky., 1983, Boston Mills Artist Workshops, Peninsula, Ohio, 1984; watercolor demonstrator Owensboro Mus. Art, Ky., 1983. Contbr. articles to profl. jours. Fund raiser No. Ky. Easter Seal, 1981, Kendevelt #23, Cin., 1982, No. Ky. Easter Seal, 1983. Recipient Greenshields Found. grantee, 1976; Friends of Ky. Watercolor Soc. award, 1978; Top Merit award Ky. Watercolor Soc., 1983; Dale Meyers medal of honor So. Watercolor Soc., 1984. Mem. Am. Watercolor Soc. (Mario Cooper award 1984), So. Watercolor Soc. (Lee Printing award 1984), Ky. Watercolor Soc. (Top Merit award 1983), Ky. Heritage Artists. Home: 10100 Meiman Dr Union KY 41091

AKERS, JOHN NANCE, clergyman; b. Colorado Springs, Colo., Apr. 10, 1940; s. Byron Lionel and Lois Parke (Nance) A.; m. Anne Kathryn Wolfenden, June 15, 1968; 1 child, John Timothy. B.A., U. Colo., 1962; B.D., Columbia Theol. Sem., 1965, Th.M., 1968; Ph.D., U. Edinburgh, Scotland, 1973. Ordained to ministry Presbyterian Ch., 1965. Instr. of Bible, Belhaven Coll., Jackson, Miss., 1965-70; prof. Bible Montreat-Anderson Coll., Montreat, N.C., 1972-73, dean of coll., 1973-77; spl. asst. to Dr. Billy Graham, Billy Graham Evangelistic Assn., Montreat, 1977—; mem. exec. com., dir. Christianity Today, Inc., Carol Stream, Ill. Scholar Boettcher Found., 1958-62, Columbia Theol. Sem., 1965. Mem. Conf. Faith and History, Presbyn. Hist. Soc., Evangelical Theol. Soc. (pres. Southeastern region 1976-77). Republican. Avocations: antiques; mineralogy. Home: Box 1083 Montreat NC 28757 Office: Billy Graham Evangelistic Assn Box 937 Montreat NC 28757

AKERS, MONTE EDWARD, lawyer; b. Shattuck, Okla., June 27, 1950; s. Edward Eugene and Leona May (Bozarth) A.; m. Patricia LaVern Lankford, Aug. 15, 1981; 1 child, Nathan Edward. Student W. Tex. State U., 1968-71; B.A. in History, U. Tex.-Arlington, 1973; J.D., U. Houston, 1976. Bar: Tex. 1976. Asst. gen. counsel Tex. Dept. Water Resources, Austin, 1977-81; supr. land ops. lignite project Dow Chem. Co., Fairfield, Tex., 1981—. Contbr. articles to profl. jours. Pres. Freestone Living Arts Guild, Fairfield, 1984-86; v.p. Freestone County Hist. Commn., 1984-85; bd. dirs. Freestone County Animal Shelter, 1984. Recipient Alberta Williamson Scholarship award W. Tex. State Library, 1969; Fullbright & Jaworski Law Firm Scholarship award, 1976. Mem. Tex. Mineral Land Assn. (v.p. 1984-85), Order of Barons, Phi Delta Phi, Phi Alpha Theta. Democrat. Methodist. Home: PO Box 1001 Fairfield TX 75840 Office: Dow Chem Co 101 W Commerce Fairfield TX 75840

AKERS, PATRICIA LAVERN LANKFORD, lawyer; b. Dallas, Dec. 31, 1953; d. Eugene, Jr. and Frances LaVern (Pierce) Lankford; m. Monte Edward Akers, Aug. 15, 1981; 1 child, Nathan Edward. B.S. in Edn., U. Tex., 1977; J.D., St. Mary's U., San Antonio, 1979. Bar: Tex. 1980. Staff atty. Tex. Dept. Water Resources, Austin, 1980-81; sole practice, Fairfield, Tex., 1981—; atty. City of Fairfield, 1983—; staff atty. Heart of Tex. Legal Aid, Waco, 1982—; spl. county judge Freestone County, Fairfield, 1983—. Mem. City Planning Com., Fairfield, 1983—, City Sesquicentennial Com., 1984—; county coordinator Ferraro/Mondale Campaign, Freestone County, 1984; sec./treas. Dem. Coalition, 1984. Mem. ABA, Criminal Def. Lawyers Assn., State Bar Tex. (family law sect.), Fairfield C. of C., Gen. Fed. Women's Clubs (planning com.). Methodist. Club: Freestone Country (sec. 1982—). Home: PO Box 1001 Fairfield TX 75840 Office: PO Box 1091 552 E Commerce Fairfield TX 75840

AKERS, RONALD LOUIS, sociology educator; b. New Albany, Ind., Jan. 7, 1939; s. Charles Edward and Thelma Louise (Johnson) A.; m. Caroline Marie Rakes, June 20, 1958; children—Ronald Louis II, Tamara Noel, Levi Jeremiah. B.S. cum laude, Ind. State U., 1960; M.A. in Sociology, Kent State U., 1961; Ph.D., U. Ky., 1966. From asst. prof. to assoc. prof. sociology U. Wash., Seattle, 1965-72; prof. criminology Fla. State U., Tallahassee, 1972-74; prof., chmn. dept. sociology U. Iowa, Iowa City, 1974-80, U. Fla., Gainesville, 1980—; cons. NSF, Nat. Inst. Drug Abuse, Dept. Labor, PRC Pub. Mgmt., 1975-79, Koba Assoc., 1980—, Nat. Ctr. Juvenile Justice, 1984. Contbr. articles to profl. jours. Author: Deviant Behavior, 1973, 3d edit., 1985. Co-author: Law and Control in Society, 1975. Co-editor: Crime, Law, and Sanctions, 1978. Deacon, Westside Baptist Ch., Gainesville, 1983—, Downey Baptist Ch., Iowa, 1977-80; vice pres. Kanapha Home Owners Assn., Gainesville, 1984—. Boys Town Ctr. fellow, 1976-77; recipient Disting. Alumnus award in sociology U. Ky., 1980. Fellow Am. Soc. Criminology (pres. 1979, councilor 1972-80); mem. Am. Sociol. Assn. (chmn. criminology sect. 1979-80), So. Sociol. Soc. (exec. com. 1985—), Soc. for Study of Social Problems (chmn. com. on standards and freedom 1980-82). Democrat. Clubs: Maple Sugar Bluegrass, Soggy Bottom Bluegrass, Sante Fe Shade Tree Pickers (Fla.). Avocations: bluegrass and country music, Dobro player, song writer. Home: 8117 SW 90th Ln Gainesville FL 32608 Office: Dept Sociology U Fla Gainesville FL 32611

AKIN, RALPH HARDIE, JR., oil company executive, exploration geologist; b. Decatur, Ill., Oct. 18, 1938; s. Ralph Hardie and Darla (Sutterfield) A.; m. Joan Clements, Dec. 24, 1960 (div. Feb. 1972); m. Elaine Fleming, June 28, 1974; children—Laura Elizabeth, Michael Hardie, Jennifer Aimee, Julie Alicia. B.S. in Geology, Centenary Coll., 1960; M.S. in Geology, U. Tulsa, 1966. Cert. petroleum geologist, Okla., Tex. Computer operator Western Geophys. Co., Shreveport, La., 1960-62; geologist Apache Corp., Houston and Tulsa, 1962-67; exploration mgr. ADA Oil Co., Houston, 1967-70; v.p. T.C. Bartling & Assocs., Houston, 1971-76; pres. Akin Energy Corp., Houston, 1977—. Contbr. articles to profl. jours. Served to 1st lt. U.S. Army, 1960-61. Mem. Houston Geol. Soc., Am. Assn. Petroleum Geologists, Am. Assn. Petroleum Landmen. Republican. Methodist. Home: 11611 Windy Ln Houston TX 77024

AKINS, CHARLES WESLEY, ophthalmologist; b. Winona, Miss., Sept. 3, 1942; s. Charles Wesley and Mary Crow (Robinson) A.; m. Sherry Kay Drake, Dec. 27, 1966 (div. 1984); children—Charles, III, Melissa Kay, Todd Drake, Robin Scott. Student Miss. State U., 1960-63; M.D., U. Miss., 1967. Intern, Med. Coll. Va., 1967-68; resident Scott and White Clinic, Temple, Tex., 1971-74; practice medicine specializing in ophthalmology, Union City, Tenn., 1974—; disability examiner ophthalmology Dept. Human Services, Frankfort, Ky., 1979—, Tenn. Dept. Human Services, Nashville, 1985—; pres. med. staff Baptist Meml. Hosp., Union City, 1983—. Served to capt. USAF, 1968-71. Mem. AMA, Am. Acad. Ophthalmology, Tenn. Acad. Ophthalmology (sec.-treas. 1982-85), N.W. Tenn. Med. Assn., Tenn. Med. Assn. Methodist. Lodges: Rotary, Moose. Avocations: water sports; bee keeping; construction; old house restoration; cooking. Home: 804 E Main St Union City TN 38261 Office: 1407 Reelfoot Ave Union City TN 38261

AKISKAL, HAGOP SOUREN, psychiatric researcher, educator; b. Beirut, Jan. 16, 1944; came to U.S., 1969; s. Stephan Jacques and Vehanoushe Dickran (Bedrossian) A. M.D., Am. U. Beirut, 1969. Instr., U. Tenn., Memphis, 1972-73, asst. prof., 1973-77, assoc. prof., 1977-80, prof. psychiatry, dir. affective disorders program, 1980—, dir. med. student edn., 1974-78; research psychiatrist Sleep Disorders Ctr., Bapt. Meml. Hosp., Memphis, 1977—, assoc. dir. Sleep Disorders Ctr., 1983—; Eli Robins lectr. Washington U., 1980. Recipient Clin. Research award Am. Acad. Clin. Psychiatrists, 1981. Mem. AMA, Am. Psychiat. Assn., Soc. Biol. Psychiatry, Psychiat. Research Soc., Sleep Research Soc., Am. Psychopath. Assn. Office: 66 N Pauline St Suite 633 Memphis TN 38163

AKRIDGE, FRANCES HENDLEY GOODE, computer professional; b. Atlanta, Apr. 24, 1939; d. Abram and Katie Lois (Hasty) Goode; m. James Maxwell Elmo Akridge, June 9, 1962; 1 child, Karen. A.B. in Math., Huntingdon Coll., 1961; M.B.A. in Fin., Ga. State U., 1974. Computer programmer Johns Hopkins Applied Physics Lab., Silver Spring, Md., 1961-66; computer profl. Lockheed-Ga. Co., Marietta, 1966—. Mem. AIAA (sr.; mem. council 1983-85, sec. 1985-86), IEEE, Computer and Automated Systems Assn., Soc. Mfg. Engrs. (long range plan 1984-85), Assn. for Computing Machinery. Republican. Episcopalian. Home: 2468 MacLaren Circle Doraville GA 30360 Office: Lockheed-Ga Co D/87-16 Z/660 86 S Cobb Dr Marietta GA 30063

ALAIMO, ANTHONY A., federal judge; b. 1920; A.B., Ohio No. U.; J.D., Emory U. Admitted to bar, 1948; now chief judge U.S. Dist. Ct., So. Dist. Ga., Brunswick. Office: US District Court PO Box 944 Brunswick GA 31520*

ALANIZ, DAVID RAYMOND, chemical company executive; b. Corpus Christi, Tex., July 28, 1948; s. David J. and Elvira (Chavez) A. B.B.A., U. Tex., 1970. Asst. br. mgr. SBA, Corpus Christi, 1970-73; sr. fin. analyst Western Econ. Devel. Corp., San Francisco, 1973-74; regional dir., inter-govtl. and Congl. affairs U.S. Dept. Energy, Atlanta, 1974-81; dir. govt. affairs Law Engring. Co., Atlanta, 1981-83; pres., chief exec. officer PPM Can., Inc., Tucker, Ga., 1983—, also chmn. bd. dirs.; chmn. bd. Alaniz & Assocs., Atlanta, 1982—. Bd. dirs. Tennessee River Valley Assn., Decatur, Ala., 1982—; rep. Nat. Govs. Assn., Washington, Nat. Conf. State Legislators, Denver, So. Legis. Conf., So. Govs. Assn., So. States Energy Bd., Atlanta, S.W. Regional Energy Council, Dallas, 1983. Served with U.S. Army, 1971-72. Mem. Am. Chem. Soc., Pub. Affairs Council, Alpha Kappa Psi (life). Roman Catholic. Home: 1392 Churchill Way Marietta GA 30062 Office: PPM Can Inc 1875 Forge St Tucker GA 30084 also Continental Bank Bldg Suite 718 Boadelaide St W Toronto ON M5H 3P5 Canada

ALAR, JOHN, tobacco company executive. Pres., chief exec. officer, vice chmn. Brown & Williamson Tobacco Corp., Louisville. Office: Brown & Williamson Tobacco Corp 1600 W Hill St Louisville KY 40232*

ALAS, ROBERTO ANTONIO, general contractor; b. San Salvador, El Salvador, Jan. 28, 1935; came to U.S., 1980; s. Antonio Alas and Maria Luz Flores; m. Ana Maria Quinteros, Dec. 12, 1962; children—Jose Antonio, Ana Maria, Roberto. Civil Engr., Instituto Tecnologica de Monterrey (Mexico), 1959. Registered profl. engr., Fla. Prieto y Perla ingenieros Structural Engr., San Salvador, El Salvador, 1960-65; pres. Alas Ingenieros, San Salvador, 1965-78, Alas Conde SA de CV, San Salvador, 1978—; sec. Alas Condo Inc., Miami, 1980—; pres. Halcon Enterprises, Inc., Miami, 1981—. Home: 734 Benevento St Coral Gables FL 33146 Office: Halcon Enterprises Inc 1325 W 41st St 8 Hialeah FL 33012

ALBARADO, BILL JOE, physician; b. Kirbyville, Tex., July 7, 1946; s. Alcie I. and Emma Grace (Schrimpsher) A.; m. Mary L. Mize, Sept. 12, 1970. B.S., Lamar U., 1968; D.O., Coll. Osteo. Medicine & Surgery, Des Moines, 1972. Intern, Baylor Affiliated Schs. Medicine, Houston, 1972-73; practice medicine specializing osteo. medicine, Corpus Christi, Tex., 1973—; chmn. dept. obstetrics Corpus Christi Osteo. Hosp., 1982; chmn. dept. family practice Meml. Med. Ctr., Corpus Christi, 1983-84, mem. exec. com., 1983-84; physician Boys Club Boxing, Corpus Christi, 1981—, Corpus Christi Lighthouse for the Blind. Recipient plaque Boys Club. Mem. Tex. Osteo. Med. Assn., Am. Osteo. Med. Assn. Roman Catholic. Clubs: Trek Safaris (Fla.); A-Z Outfitters, Pan Am. Golf Assn., Gulf Coast Conservation, Ducks Unlimited. Avocations: fishing; hunting; golf. Office: 2222 Morgan St Suite 113 Corpus Christi TX 78405

ALBECK, STAN, basketball coach; b. Fairbury, Ill., May 17, 1931; s. Charles F. and Ruby M. A.; B.A., Bradley U., 1955; M.A., Mich. State U., 1957; m. Phyllis L. Mann, Dec. 11, 1952; children—Gary, Sheree, Jon and Roger (twins), Julie. Coach, Adrian Coll., No. Mich. U., Denver U.; coach profl. team, Denver; asst. coach profl. team, San Diego; asst. coach Ky. Colonels, Los Angeles Lakers; head coach Cleve. Cavaliers, San Antonio Spurs, N.J. Nets. Served with U.S. Army, 1952-54. Named to No. Mich. U. Hall of Fame, 1979, Bradley U. Hall of Fame, 1981; recipient Significant Sigaward Sigma Chi, 1983; named NBA Coach of Yr., Sporting News, 1981. Mem. Nat. Assn. Basketball Coaches. Lutheran. Author: Coaching Better Basketball. Office: PO Box 520 San Antonio TX 78292*

ALBERS, EDWARD JAMES, social studies educator, antique toy train collector; b. Centralia, Wash., July 6, 1922; s. Otto Johnson and Nell Genevieve Albers; m. Caroline Constance Cochran, July 30, 1944; 1 son, Edward James, Jr. Student Wash. State Coll., 1942, U. Ariz., 1949-51; B.A., U. Nebr.-Omaha, 1959; M.A., Rollins Coll., 1966. Cert. tchr., Fla. Pilot, U.S. Army Air Force, 1944, advanced through grades to maj., 1961, served command pilot SAC, ret., 1965. Tchr. Winter Park High Sch. (Fla.), 1966—, chmn. social studies dept., 1973—. Decorated Air Force Commendation medal; Yun-Hui medal, Chinese pilot wings. Mem. Am. Psychol. Assn., Fla. Tchrs. Assn., NEA, Orange County Tchrs. Assn., Nat. Geog. Soc., Aircraft Owners and Pilots Assn., Air Force Assn., Sigma Phi Epsilon. Democrat. Episcopalian. Clubs: Train Collectors Assn., Lionel Collectors Club Am. Office: 2100 Summerfield Rd Winter Park FL 32792

ALBERSTADT, WARREN EDWARD, real estate appraiser; b. New Orleans, Aug. 13, 1913; s. Philip and Elizabeth (Clement) A.; m. Eunice Bertha Keppler, Sept. 18, 1940; children—Kathleen Ann, Jill Beth, Beverly Jean. Student U. New Orleans, 1983, Our Lady of Holy Cross Coll., 1983. Self employed designer, builder, 1933-42; naval architect George Sharp & Co., N.Y.C., 1942-45; self employed designer, builder, owner Home Design Service, 1942-62; sr. real estate appraiser Central Appraisal Bur., New Orleans, 1962-80; owner New Thought Creations, New Orleans, 1981—; drummer, pianist, bassist. Co-founder, bd. dirs. Unity Ch. of Metairie (La.). Mem. Ind. Fee Appraisers Am., ASCAP. Lodge: Rotary (hon.). Composer numerous mus. compositions. Inventor games, action toys. Author books on designing, building, metaphysics. Home and Office: 430 Bellaire Dr New Orleans LA 70124

ALBERT, CARL, former congressman; b. McAlester, Okla., May 10, 1908; s. Ernest Homer and Leona Ann (Scott) A.; A.B., U. Okla., 1931; B.A., (Rhodes scholar), Oxford (Eng.) U., 1933, B.C.L., 1934, LL.D., Okla. City U., So. Meth. U.; m. Mary Harmon, Aug. 20, 1942; children—Mary Frances, David Ernest. Bar: Okla. 1935. Legal clk. FHA, 1934-37; atty., accountant Sayre Oil Co., Oklahoma City, 1937-38; with legal dept. Ohio Oil Co., Marshall, Ill., Findlay, Ohio, 1939-40; gen. practice law, Oklahoma City, 1938, Mattoon, Ill., 1938-39, McAlester, Okla., 1946-47; mem. 80th to 94th Congresses, 3d Okla. Dist., Dem. Whip, 1955-62; majority leader, 1962-71, speaker, 1971-76; Disting. vis. lectr. polit. sci. dept. U. Okla. Trustee, So. Meth. Univ. Served with AUS, 1941-46; PTO. Decorated Bronze Star medal; named to Okla. Hall Fame. Democrat. Methodist. Home: Route 2 McAlester OK 74501

ALBERTS, FRED LEE, JR., psychologist; b. Fairmont, W.Va., Nov. 15, 1949; s. Fred Lee and Evelyn Denise (McNeil) A.; B.A., U. South Fla., 1972, M.A., 1978; Ph.D., U. So. Miss., 1982; m. Kathryn Ann Henson, Apr. 6, 1979. Dir., sec., treas. The T Corp., Tampa, Fla., 1972-75; psychol. assoc. Theodore H. Blau & Assocs., Tampa, 1975-80; staff psychologist Psychol. Services, Pinellas County Schs., Clearwater, Fla., 1976-79; cons. psychologist, Hattiesburg, Miss., 1979-81; clin. psychol. intern Devereux Found., 1981-82; clin. psychologist, Tampa, Fla., 1982—; dir. Psychol. Seminars, Inc., Tampa. Mem. Am. Psychol. Assn., Nat. Acad. Neuropsychologists, Psi Chi. Democrat. Methodist. Patentee in field.

ALBERTSON, CHRISTOPHER ADAM, librarian; b. Oak Park, Ill., Dec. 10, 1951; s. Charles J. and Eve M. (Kosawick) A.; m. Sarah Ann Daugherty, Dec. 29, 1973; children—Julia, Stephanie, Matthew. Student, U. New Orleans, 1969-70; B.A. magna cum laude, U. Tex.-Arlington, 1972; M.L.S., N. Tex. State U., 1973. Cataloger, Orange (Tex.) Pub. Library, 1974-75, asst. librarian, 1975-79, city librarian, 1979-81; city librarian Tyler (Tex.) Pub. Library, 1981—. Mem. Am. Library Assn., Am. Soc. Pub. Adminstrn., Am. Mgmt. Assn., Am. Soc. Info. Sci., Tex. Library Assn. Presbyterian. Club: Rotary. Contbr. articles to profl. jours. Home: 3521 Bain Place Tyler TX 75701 Office: Tyler Pub Library 201 S College St Tyler TX 75702

ALBRECHT, KAY MONTGOMERY, learning center executive, administrator, educator; b. Lafayette, La., Jan. 29, 1949; d. Michael H. and Imogene (McCallum) M.; m. Larry Steven Albrecht, June 23, 1973. B.A., U. Southwestern La., 1970; M.S. in Child Devel., U. Tenn., 1972, Ph.D. in Family Studies, 1984. Head Start coordinator U. Tenn., Knoxville, 1972-74; instr. Incarnate Word Coll., San Antonio, 1976-77; instr. Southwest Tex. State U., San Marcos, 1977-80; tng. dir. Daybridge Learning Ctrs., Houston, 1984-85, v.p., 1985-86; v.p. Child Care Mgmt. Assocs., 1986—; founder Hearts Home Early Learning Ctrs., Inc., 1986—; cons. Adminstrn. for Children, Youth and Families, HEW, Washington, 1982-83; Author staff orientation manual and consumer curriculum guide, 1980, 85. Mem. Hayes County Child Welfare Bd. San Marcos, 1979-81; pres. bd. dirs. Big Bros.-Big Sisters, Knoxville, 1981-83; vol. cons. Head Start, San Marcos and Knoxville, 1978-84; mem. com. Mayor's Task Force on Children, Houston, 1985. Nat. Inst. Edn. fellow, 1982-83. Fellow Am. Psychol. Assn.; mem. Am. Home Econs. Assn. (treas. 1984-86), Nat. Assn. for Edn. Young Children, Nat. Council Family Relations, Houston Assn. Edn. Young Children (bd. dirs. 1984—), Democrat. Methodist. Avocations: water skiing; hiking; cooking; wild flower identification. Office: Child Care Mgmt Assocs 2211 Fry Rd Suite 177 Katy TX 77449

ALBRIGHT, DAPHNE GAIL, clinical psychologist; b. Nurnberg, Fed. Republic Germany, Oct. 3, 1952 (parents Am. citizens); d. Jack Alvin and Martha Elizabeth (Gilbert) A.; m. Mark Edward Dilley, Aug. 21, 1976 (div. 1982). B.S. in Math. and Psychology, Miss. U. for Women, 1972; M.S. in Social Psychology, Miss. State U., 1973; M.A. in Clin. Psychology, U. Ariz., 1975, Ph.D. in Clin. Psychology, 1977. Lic. psychologist, Calif., Ga. Psychol. intern Naval Hosp., Bethesda, Md., 1976-77, staff psychologist, Camp Pendleton, Calif., 1977-79; dir. psychol. services Capistrano by the Sea Hosp., Dana Point, Calif., 1979-85, Greenleaf Ctr., Inc., Valdosta, Ga., 1985—. Served to lt. comdr. USNR, 1976—. U.S. Navy scholar, 1975-76; traineeship NSF, 1972-73, NIMH, 1973-74. Mem. Am. Psychol. Assn., Western Psychol. Assn., S.E. Psychol. Assn., Ga. Psychol. Assn., Calif. State Psychol. Assn., Psychologists Affiliated with Pvt. Psychiat. Hosps. (sec.-treas. 1983-85, pres. 1985—). Office: Greenleaf Ctr Inc 2209 Pineview Dr Valdosta GA 31602

ALBRIGHT, JOHN RUPP, physics educator; b. Wilkes-Barre, Pa., June 10, 1937; s. John Rupp and Salome (Shettel) A.; m. Christina Lamson Bischoff, June 11, 1960 (div. 1982); children—Helen Jane Albright Black, Catherine Louise Albright Pottorff, John Rupp, III.; m. Elizabeth Helen Peters, Mar. 16, 1984. A.B., Susquehanna U., 1959; M.S., U. Wis.-Madison, 1961, Ph.D., 1964. Asst. prof. physics Fla. State U., Tallahassee, 1963-70, assoc. prof., 1970-78, prof., 1978—, assoc. chmn. physics dept., 1980-85. Author: (with others) Introduction to Atomic and Nuclear Physics, 1972. Contbr. articles to profl. jours. Sr. research fellow Sci. Research Council Gt. Britain, 1976; recipient Pres.'s Teaching award Fla. State U., 1980. Mem. Am. Phys. Soc., Am. Assn. Physics Tchrs., Theta Chi, Lionel Collectors Club Am. Lutheran. Home: Route

3 4060 Havana FL 32333 Office: Dept Physics Fla State U Tallahassee FL 32306

ALBRIGHT, RAY C., banker, state senator; b. Paint Rock, Ala., Feb. 28, 1934; married; 2 children. Mem. Tenn. Senate; mem. bd. Chattanooga Area Regional Council of Govts. Mem. Chattanooga Indsl. Devel. Bd.; bd. dirs. East Ridge Hosp.; chmn. Hamilton County Del.; mem. bd. St. John's Methodist Ch.; mem. Dirs. Roundtable of Clin. Edn. Center-S.E. Mem. Am. Inst. Banking. Republican. Clubs: Shriners, Optimist, Ruritan. Office: Room 317 War Memorial Bldg Nashville TN 37219*

ALBRIGHT, WAYNE HOHL, III, operational consultant; b. Reading, Pa., Aug. 5, 1944; s. Wayne Hohl and Lucille Galdys (Zechman) A.; m. Janet L. Baer, June 25, 1966; children—Jennifer N., Marcie L. B.B.A., Drexel U., 1968. With Rockwell Internat., Reading, 1966-70; cost mgr. chems. group Crompton & Knowles, Reading, 1970-73; corp. controller Sunny Slope Dairies, Inc., Spring City, Pa., 1973-75; controller Caron Internat., Reading, 1975-78; v.p. fin. Kruger Machinery Co., Saginaw, Mich., 1978-80; pres. W.H. Albright & Assocs., Inc., Venice, Fla., 1980—. Republican. Episcopalian. Club: Venice Sailing Squadron. Lodge: Masons. Office: 212 Parkview Dr Venice FL 33595

ALBRITTON, BOBBY GENE, area loss control consultant, safety engineer; b. Denco, Miss., Nov. 3, 1927; s. Buther Ellison and Hester Argyl (Hathorn) A.; m. Ada Carolyn Thompson, June 9, 1956; children—Robert Ellison, John Thompson, Vincie Caroline. B.S. in Indsl. Engring., 1954; M.B.A., Air Force Inst. Tech., 1959. Cert. safety profl.; cert hazardous materials mgr. Commd. 2d lt. U.S. Air Force, 1954, advanced through grades to maj., 1975, transport pilot, 1955-75, ret., 1975; safety engr. Am. Mut. Ins., Atlanta, 1975—. Mem. Chattahoochee Plantation Community Assn., Marietta, Ga., 1985—; mem. chancel choir Peachtree Presbyn. Ch., Atlanta, 1985—. Decorated D.F.C., Bronze Star, Air medal. Mem. System Safety Soc., Am. Soc. Safety Engrs. (pres. Ga. chpt. 1985—), Theta Xi. Republican. Home: 324 Rolling Rock Rd Marietta GA 30067 Office: Am Mut Ins Co 1 Executive Park NE Atlanta GA 30348

ALDERETE, JOSEPH FRANK, medical service adminstr., psychiatrist; b. Las Vegas, N.Mex., Sept. 10, 1920; s. Jose P. and Adela R. (Armijo) A.; B.S. in Chemistry and Biology, Tex. Western Coll., 1950; M.D., Nat. U. Mex., 1959; m. Christine Krajewski, June 24, 1964; children—Joseph Frank, Sarah A. Intern, USPHS Hosp., Balt., 1959-60; resident in psychiatry USPHS Hosp., Lexington, Ky., 1960-62; sr. resident in psychiatry U. Hosp., U. Okla. Sch. of Medicine, Oklahoma City, 1962-63; practice medicine specializing in psychiatry, Balt., 1963-65, Springfield, Mo., 1965-67, Atlanta, 1968—; staff psychiatrist USPHS Hosp., Balt., 1963-65; chief of psychiat. service U.S. Med. Center for Fed. Prisoners, Springfield, Mo., 1965-67; clin. and research fellow in electroencephalography Mass. Gen. Hosp.-Harvard, Boston, 1967-68; clin. instr. psychiatry Emory U. Sch. of Medicine, Atlanta, 1968-84, clin. asst. prof. medicine, 1984—; chief med. officer, hosp. dir. U.S. Penitentiary Hosp., Atlanta, 1968-78; asst. regional flight surgeon So. Dist., ARTCC, Atlanta, 1978—; evaluation sect. VA Hosp., Decatur, Ga., 1983—; psychiat. cons. to Student Health Office, Okla. State U., Stillwater, 1962-63, U.S. Fed. Reformatory, El Reno, Okla., 1962-63. Served with USAF, 1944-48, to capt. AUS, 1948-50. Mem. AMA, Am. Psychiat. Assn., Am. Soc. Clin. Hypnosis, So. EEG Soc., Am., Internat. acads. of law and psychiatry, Acad. of Psychosomatic Medicine, Atlanta Med. Soc., Clin. Soc. of USPHS, Phi Rho Sigma. Contbr. articles to profl. jours. Home: 4130 E Brockett Creek Ct Tucker GA 30084 Office: VA Hosp 1670 Clairmont Decatur GA

ALDERSON, CREED FLANARY, JR., financial services executive; b. Norton, Va., Nov. 21, 1933; s. Creed Flanary and Mary (Ford) A. B.S. in Commerce, U. Va., 1959; m. Nicola Dechurch, July 16, 1983; children—Robert Barney, Mary Anne. Vice pres., resident mgr. Dean Witter Reynolds, Ft. Lauderdale, Fla., 1974-79; 1st v.p., resident mgr. Smith Barney Harris Upham, Ft. Lauderdale, 1979—. Served with U.S. Army, 1952-55. Clubs: University (Miami, Fla.), Ocean Reef (Key Largo, Fla.); Boca Raton Hotel and Club (Fla.). Home: 5000 N Ocean Blvd Fort Lauderdale FL 33308 Office: 2780 E Oakland Park Blvd Fort Lauderdale FL 33306

ALDERSON, MARGARET NORTHROP, arts administrator, educator, artist; b. Washington, Nov. 28, 1936; d. Vernon D. and Margaret (Lloyd) Northrop; m. Donald Marr Alderson, Jr., June 4, 1955; children—Donald Marr III, Barbara Lynn Hennesy, Brian, Graham. Student George Washington U., 1954-55; A.A., Monterey Peninsula Jr. Coll., 1962. Staff, tchr. Galerie Jaclande, Springfield, Va. 1972-73; artist/tchr. Studio 7, Torpedo Factory Art Ctr., Alexandria, 1974—; tchr. Fairfax County Recreation, 1972-73, Art League Schs., Alexandria, 1978—; cons. in field; project supr. City of Alexandria for Torpedo Factory Art Ctr., 1978-83; ptnr. Soho Hubris Art Gallery (N.Y.), 1977-78; one woman shows at Way Up Gallery, Livermore, Calif., 1971, Lynchburg Coll. (Va.), 1978, Farm House Gallery, Rehobeth, Del., 1979, Art League Gallery, Alexandria, Va., 1980, Art League, 1986; exhibited in group shows at Art League Gallery, Alexandria, 1972—; represented in permanent collections Phillip Morse Collection, United Va. Bank, CSX Corp., Office U.S. Atty. Gen., Office of Ins. Gen. EPA, Aerospace Corp. Festival chmn. City Festival Cultural Arts, Livermore, Calif., 1971; bd. dirs., juror Cultural Alliance, 1982-85; bd. dirs. Torpedo Factory Art Ctr., 1978— mem. Partner's for Liveable Places, 1979—. Recipient 1st Place Awards in Watercolor, Art League, 1975, 76, 77, also numerous purchase awards. Mem. Va. Watercolor Soc. (pres. 1982, 1st place awards ann. exhibit 1980, 82), Potomac Valley Watercolorists (pres. 1978), Torpedo Factory Artists Assn. (pres. 1977-78), Springfield Art Guild (pres. 1977), Artists Equity, Am. Council on Arts, Am. Watercolor Soc., Am. Council of Univ. and Community Arts Ctrs., Nat. League Am. Pen Women, Am. Mgmt. Assn., Nat. Historic Trust. Republican. Home: 2204 Windsor Rd Alexandria VA 22307 Office: Torpedo Factory Art Ctr 105 N Union St Alexandria VA 22314

ALDRED, WILLIAM HERBERT, engineering company executive; b. Nashville, June 4, 1930; s. Herbert Gray and Dorothy (Graves) A.; B.E. in Civil Engring., Vanderbilt U., 1953; m. Dorothy Anne Cochran, Sept. 3, 1955; children—Lee Anne Aldred Maxfield, Tracey Carol. Asst. div. engr. Nashville, Chattanooga, and St. Louis R.R., 1953-57; design engr. City of Nashville, 1957-60; mgr. forms and scaffold dept. Encó Materials, Inc., Nashville, 1960-65; v.p. Howard, Nielsen, Aldred, Henry & O'Brien, Inc., Nashville, 1965-83; owner William Aldred & Assocs., Nashville, 1983—. Served as 1st lt. C.E., USAR, 1955-62. Mem. Nat. Soc. Profl. Engrs., ASCE, Am. Water Works Assn. Republican. Presbyterian. Club: Am. Saddle Horse Assn. Tenn. (former pres.). Office: 5205 Cochran Dr Nashville TN 37220

ALDREDGE, MARGARET RUFF, accountant; b. Conneaut, Ohio, Nov. 9, 1944; d. Paul Miller and Lydia Ruth (Zundel) Ruff; m. James William Aldredge, Feb. 17, 1979; children—Eric Zundel, Rachel Margaret. B.S. in Math., Wittenberg U., Springfield, Ohio, 1966; M.A.T., Emory U., 1970. Tchr., Lovett Sch., Atlanta, 1969-70, Cobb Schs., Marietta, Ga., 1970-71; distbr. Atlanta Newspapers, 1973-76; with Div. Family and Children's Services, Ga. Dept. Human Resources, Atlanta, 1977-84, sr. ops. analyst, 1980-84, also project mgr. child welfare info. system; acctg. officer controller's div. First Atlanta Corp. (First Wachovia), 1984-85, mgr. accounts payable, 1985—. Mem. coordinating com. food ministry Lutheran Ch. of Redeemer, Atlanta, 1982-84, mem. ch. council, 1984. NDEA fellow, 1967-69. Democrat. Home: 3288 Myrtle St Hapeville GA 30354 Office: First Atlanta Corp 2 Peachtree St Atlanta GA 30383

ALDRICH, CLARENCE KNIGHT, medical educator, psychiatrist; b. Chgo., Apr. 12, 1914; s. L. Sherman and Bessie A. (Knight) A.; m. Julie H. Murphy, Feb. 4, 1942; children—Carol Aldrich Barkin, Michael S., Thomas K., Robert F. B.A., Wesleyan U., 1935; M.D., Northwestern U., 1940. Diplomate Am. Bd. Psychiatry and Neurology. Intern, Cook County Hosp., Chgo., 1939-40; resident in psychiatry U.S. Marine Hosp., Ellis Island, N.Y., 1940-42; with USPHS, 1940-46; asst. prof. psychiatry U. Wis., Madison, 1946-47; asst., assoc. prof. psychiatry U. Minn., Mpls., 1947-55; prof. psychiatry U. Chgo., 1955-70, chmn. dept., 1955-64; prof., chmn. dept. psychiatry N.J. Coll. Medicine, 1969-73; prof. psychiatry and family medicine U. Va. Sch. Medicine, Charlottesville, 1973-84; vis. prof. psychol. medicine U. Edinburgh (Scotland), 1963-64. Bd. dirs. Child and Family Services Met. Chgo., 1956-63; chmn. profl. adv. com. Ill. Assn. Mental Health, 1964-67. Served to lt. comdr. USPHS, 1940-46. Recipient Centennial Disting. Alumnus award Northwestern U. Med. Sch., 1959. Erskine fellow U. Canterbury (N.Z.), 1971. Mem. Am. Psychiat. Assn., Am. Orthopsychiat. Assn., Am. Coll. Psychiatrists, Group for the Advancement of Psychiatry. Democrat. Club: Colonnade (Charlottesville). Contbg. author profl. publs. Home: 905 Cottage Ln Charlottesville VA 22903

ALDRICH, DOUGLAS FORD, information systems consultant; b. Troy, N.Y., July 18, 1951; s. Theodore Henry and Zelma Edith (Blackman) A.; A.A.S., Purdue U., 1971, B.S., 1974; M.B.A., Ind. U., 1978; m. Debra Ann Shipman, Feb. 6, 1971; children—Dara Jeanette, Amanda Lee, Ryan Douglas. With GTE Data Services, Ft. Wayne, Ind., 1970-72; programmer Lincoln Nat. Corp., Ft. Wayne, 1972-74; systems project leader Cummins Engine Co., Columbus, Ind., 1974-78; mgr. info. systems cons. Arthur Young Co., Dallas, 1978—, prin. mgmt. cons. group, 1982—, ptnr. Mgmt. Cons. Group, 1985—; instr. Ind. U.-Purdue U., Indpls., 1975-78; adj. prof. U. Dallas Grad. Sch. Bus., 1980-82, 83—, U. Tex. at Dallas Grad. Sch. Mgmt., 1982-83; speaker nat. seminar Computer Security Inst., Data Processing Security, Inc., also Am. Mgmt. Assn. Symposium on Computer Crime, Profl. Devel. Inst. Cert. data processor, data processing auditor. Mem. Assn. EDP Auditors, Assn. M.B.A. Execs. Home: 1700 Windsong Trail Richardson TX 75081 Office: 2121 San Jacinto Dallas TX 75221

ALDRICH, HENRY CARL, microbiology educator; b. Beaumont, Tex., Feb. 17, 1941; s. Carl Cecil and Berneice (Switzer) A.; m. Valerie Ann Clark, Sept. 1, 1962 (div. 1977); children—Clay Chapman, John Clark; m. 2d, Sylvia Ethel Coleman, Jan. 1, 1978. B.A., U. Tex., 1963, Ph.D., 1966. Asst. prof. botany U. Fla., Gainesville, 1966-71, assoc. prof., 1972-76, prof. microbiology and cell sci., 1977—. Mem. Mycol. Soc. Am. (pres.), Am. Soc. Cell Biology, Am. Soc. Microbiology. Democrat. Mem. United Ch. of Christ. Editor: (with J.W. Daniel) Cell Biology of Physarum and Didymium, 1982; (with W.J. Todd) Ultrastructure Techniques for Microorganisms, 1986.

ALDRIDGE, MELVIN DAYNE, engineering educator; b. Crab Orchard, W.Va., July 20, 1941; s. William Bert and Gladys Revelle A.; m. Nancy L. Dickinson, June 6, 1963; children—Kenrick Lee, Randal Jay. B.S.E.E. with high honors, W.Va. U., 1963; M.S.E.E., U. Va., 1965, D.Sc. E.E., 1968. Registered profl. engr. Electronic engr. NASA, 1963-68; from asst. prof. to assoc. prof. elec. engring., W.Va. U., Morgantown, 1968-76, prof., 1976-84, dir. W.Va. U. Energy Research Ctr., 1978-84; asst. dean for research, dir. engring. expt. sta. Auburn U., Ala., 1984—; cons. pvt. and govtl. orgns. Contbr. articles to profl. publs. Recipient Rufus A. West award, 1963; named Outstanding Young Engr. W.Va., 1977-78. Mem. IEEE (sr.), Am. Soc. Engring. Edn., Soc. Mining Engrs., Nat. Soc. Profl. Engrs. Baptist. Club: Rotary. Home: 254 Carter St Auburn AL 36830 Office: 108 Ramsey Hall Auburn U Auburn AL 36849

ALEWINE, JAMES WILLIAM, financial exec.; b. Williamston, S.C., Apr. 26, 1930; s. David Andrew and Ruby Mae (Moore) A.; B.A., Carolina Sch. Commerce, 1961; m. Bobbie Sue Crawford, June 18, 1949; children—David, Susan. With Daniel Internat. Corp., 1947—, mgr. internal audit, Greenville, S.C., 1970-72, adminstrv. mgr. M & M div., 1972-73, fin. adminstr., Jenkinsville, S.C., 1973-77, mgr. accounting M-E-T Group, Greenville, 1977-78, asst. treas., 1978—. Served with USN, 1952-55. Cert. internal auditor, S.C. Mem. Inst. Internal Auditors (pres. Palmetto chpt. 1975-76). Baptist. Clubs: Masons (past grand high priest, knight York grand cross of honour), Elks. Home: 2 Broad St Williamston SC 29697 Office: Daniel Bldg Greenville SC 29602

ALEXANDER, ALLEN FREDERICK, communications executive; b. Savannah, Ga., Sept. 28, 1948; s. Allen Lovette and Virginia Lee (Lightsey) S.; m. Diane Elizabeth Long, June 16, 1973; children—Brian Frederick, Alison Marie, Jeffrey David. A.B., U. Ga., 1969; postgrad. Columbia Sch. Bible and Missions, 1973-75. Info. dir. Columbia Bible Coll. (S.C.), 1975-77; communications and alumni dir. West Coast U., Los Angeles, 1978-79; exec. dir. mktg. communications U. So. Calif., Los Angeles, 1979-80; mgr. corporate communications Nantahala Power & Light Co., Franklin, N.C., 1980—. Bd. dirs. Macon County Cultural Arts Council, 1983—, Western N.C. Devel. Assn., Asheville, 1981—, Macon County Heart Assn., 1982—; pres. Greater Athens Young Republican Club (Ga.), 1968, Macon County Friends of the Library, 1983-84; bd. dirs. N.C. Energy and Aging Consortium, 1984—. Served to capt. USMC, 1969-73, maj. Res., 1973—. Mem. Pub. Relations Assn. Western N.C. (dir., founding pres. 1982-83), Franklin C. of C. (bd. dirs. 1984—, pres. 1985-86), Carolina Assn. Bus. Communicators (bd. dirs. 1984—). Baptist. Lodge: Gideons. Home: 87 Industrial Park Rd Franklin NC 28734 Office: Nantahala Power & Light Co PO Box 260 17 W Main St Franklin NC 28734

ALEXANDER, BILL J., oil recovery company executive; b. Wellington, Tex., Dec. 21, 1930; s. Alfred D. and Willie O. (Graham) A.; m. Carola D. Burns, Jan. 21, 1955; 1 dau., De-Ann. A.A. in Bus. Adminstrn., Frank Phillips Coll., 1957; postgrad. La. State U., 1974-77. Farmer, grain elevator operator, 1949-51; helper, Cabot Corp., Pampa, Tex., 1954-55; v.p., Beacon Supply Co., Pampa, 1955-74, also bd. dirs.; pres., chief exec. officer Dunham Cos., Baton Rouge, 1974-82; pres. CSI Energy Inc. Isubs. CS Industries), Baton Rouge, 1982—. Chmn. Central Br. bd. mgrs. YMCA, Baton Rouge, 1982, also mem. fin. and expansion coms. pres., mem. exec. bd. La. Edn. and Econ. Devel. Polit. Action Com.; exec. bd. Istrouma Area Council Boy Scouts Am., mem. trust fund and fin. coms.; chmn. comml. gifts div. United Way, Baton Rouge, 1981; mem. La. State U. Econ. Devel. Center Adv. Council, Baton Rouge, 1978-79; trustee, chmn. deacons, part time Sunday Sch. tchr. Broadmoor Baptist Ch., Baton Rouge. Served with USN, 1951-54. Mem. La. Assn. Bus. and Industry (personnel com. 1982, dir. 1983—). Clubs: Baton Rouge Country, Rotary (chmn. econ. devel. coms. Baton Rouge). Office: CSI Energy Inc 11017 Perkins Rd PO Box 80820 Baton Rouge LA 70898

ALEXANDER, CECIL ABRAHAM, architect; b. Atlanta, Mar. 14, 1918; s. Cecil Abraham and Julia (Moses) A.; m. Hermione Weil, Jan. 20, 1943 (dec. Oct. 1983); children—Therese, Judith, Douglas; m. Helen Eismann, Dec. 1. 1985. Student Ga. Inst. Tech., 1936; A.B., Yale U., 1940; student M.I.T., 1941; M.Arch., Harvard U., 1947. Partner Alexander & Rothschild, architects, Atlanta, 1949-58; chmn. bd. Finch, Alexander, Barnes, Rothschild & Paschal, Architects and Engrs., Inc., Atlanta, 1958-83; chmn. bd. A.S.D. Inc., interior design service; architect Ga. Power Bldg., 1st Nat. Bank (both Atlanta), Cin. Riverfront Stadium, Coca-Cola Internat. Hdqrs. Chmn. Atlanta Citizens Adv. Com. Urban Renewal, 1958-60; vice chmn. Atlanta Met. Planning Commn., 1962—; chmn. Ga. Fgn. Trade Zone Corp.; past vice chmn. Community Council, Atlanta, Ga. Mem. Mayor's Adv. Com. Race Relations, Nat. Citizens Com. Community Relations; chmn. Atlanta chpt. Am. Jewish Com., 1963; chmn. housing resources com. City of Atlanta; chmn. com. Yale Sch. Architecture; S.E. area chmn. adv. council Urban Am.; pres., founder Resurgens Atlanta; v.p. Atlanta Symphony Orch. Mem. Yale Nat. Alumni Bd., 1963; bd. dirs., exec. com. Clark Coll.; bd. dirs. Marist High Sch., Atlanta. Served to lt. co. USMCR, World War II. Decorated Air Medal, D.F.C. Recipient Brotherhood award NCCJ, 1964, 73. Fellow AIA (pres. Ga. 1957); mem. Atlanta C. of C. (dir.). Jewish (2d v.p. temple). Home: 2322 Mt Paran Rd Atlanta GA 30327 Office: The Equitable Bldg Suite 400 Atlanta GA 30303

ALEXANDER, CHARLES EDWARD, II, lawyer, fire truck manufacturer; b. Raleigh, N.C., Jan. 12, 1948; s. Douglas O. and Mary Louise (Baker) A.; m. Claria Gertrude Haines, Oct. 6, 1973; children—Edward Drummond, Martha Elizabeth Ledbetter, Douglas Campbell. B.A. with honors, N.C. State U., 1969; J.D., U. N.C., 1973. Bar: N.C. 1973, U.S. Dist. Ct. (ea. dist.) N.C. 1973. Staff atty. Nat. Assn. Attys. Gen., Raleigh, 1973-74; ptnr. Alexander, Monroe, Wyne and Atkins, Raleigh, 1974-83; U.S. bankruptcy trustee Eastern Dist. of N.C., 1975-78; owner, sec.-treas., gen. counsel Emergency Equipment, Inc., Raleigh, 1984—, also dir. Contbr. articles to profl. jours. Mem. SAR, Raleigh C. of C., N.C. Art Soc., Phi Kappa Phi, Delta Theta Phi. Republican. Episcopalian. Home: 1532 Carr St Raleigh NC 27608 Office: Emergency Equipment Inc 518 Pershing Rd Raleigh NC 27608

ALEXANDER, CHARLES KENNETH, JR., electrical engineer, educator; b. Amherst, Ohio, Aug. 4, 1943; s. Charles Kenneth and June Elaine (Carter) A.; m. Ruth Violet Elizabeth Wade, June 8, 1985; children—Christina, Tamara, Jennifer. B.S.E.E., Ohio No. U., 1965; M.S.E.E., Ohio U., 1967, Ph.D., 1971. Registered profl. engr. Ohio. Instr. elec. engring. Ohio U., 1967-71, asst. prof. elec. engring., 1971-72; assoc. prof. elec. engring. Youngstown (Ohio) State U., 1972-78, prof., 1978-80; prof., chmn. dept. elec. engring. Tenn. Tech. U., Cookeville, 1980—NASA summer faculty fellow Auburn U. Marshall Space Flight Ctr., 1973; cons. in field. Youngstown State U. Outstanding Prof. of Yr., 1978, Disting. Prof., 1977; research grantee. Mem. Ohio Solar Energy Assn., Am. Soc. Engring. Edn., IEEE, Sigma Xi, Tau Beta Pi, Eta Kappa Nu. Contbr. articles to profl. publs. Home: 1475 Pilot Dr Cookeville TN 38501 Office: Tennessee Technological U Electrical Engineering Dept Box 5004 Cookeville TN 38505

ALEXANDER, CHARLES THOMAS, optometrist; b. Jordan, Ky., Oct. 4, 1926; s. Jim Marshall and Grace Kathleen (Owens) A.; m. Dolores Marie Chaney, Apr. 3, 1949; children—Julia Marie, Charles David, Jim Marshall. O.D., So. Coll. Optometry, Memphis, 1950. Practice optometry, Scottsville, Ky., 1950—; pres. Ky. Bd. Optometric Examiners, 1970-74. Past scoutmaster Audubon council Boy Scouts Am.; mem. Scottsville Sch. Bd., 1962-74, v.p., 1970-74; past supt. Sunday Sch., Methodist Ch., Scottsville. Served to cpl. USAAF, 1944-46. Mem. Ky. Optometry Assn., Am. Optometry Assn., Beta Sigma Kappa, Sigma Alpha Sigma. Democrat. Lodges: Rotary (pres. local club 1959-60), Masons (master 1962-63). Avocations: hunting; fishing. Home and Office: PO Box 447 Scottsville KY 42164

ALEXANDER, DAVE ALMON, lawyer; b. Decatur, Ala., Dec. 28, 1915; s. Truman Hudson and Helen Elizabeth (Almon) A.; m. Jane Bagley, Feb. 1, 1958; children—Suzanne Alexander Silva, Sarah Almon, Dave A. B.A., Vanderbilt U., 1939, LL.B., 1942, J.D., 1969. Bar: Tenn. 1942. Sole practice, Franklin, Tenn., 1945—; dir. First Tenn. Bank. mem. Tenn. Gen. Assembly, 1945-47, floor leader, speaker pro tem, 1945-47. Mem. City Council, Franklin, 1951-52. Served as lt. comdr. USNR, 1942-45. Decorated Silver Star. Purple Heart. Mem. ABA (chmn. grievance com. 1951-52), Tenn. Bar Assn. (v.p. 1960-61, chmn. grievance com. 1960-61), Williamson County Bar Assn. (pres. 1960-61) Phi Beta Kappa. Phi Delta Phi. Sigma Nu. Democrat. Methodist. Club: Lions (pres.). Home: 1112 Franklin Rd Brentwood TN 37027 Office: Court Sq Alexander Bldg Franklin TN 37064

ALEXANDER, DIETRICH BIEMANN, JR., building components manufacturing and construction company executive; b. Greenwood, S.C., Aug. 28, 1902; s. Dietrich Biemann and Lillian (Malone) A.; B.C.E., The Citadel, 1922; LL.B., Woodrow Wilson Coll. Law, 1938; postgrad. Babson Inst., summers 1940-41; m. Merridy Wefing, Mar. 3, 1930; children—Dietrich Biemann III, Merridy Wefing (Mrs. Alexander Lloyd), Stanton Malone. Tchr., coach Thomas Indsl. Inst., De Funiak Springs, Fla., 1922-23; with Atlantic Steel Co., Atlanta, 1923-45, asst. sec.-treas. 1925-45; admitted to Ga. State bar, 1938; partner Mitchell & Alexander Lumber Co., Daytona Beach, Fla., 1945-49; chmn. bd., chief exec. officer Prefab Bldg. Components, Holly Hill, Fla., 1969—; pres. Alexander Constrn. Co., Holly Hill, 1969—; pres. Daytona Beach Builders Exchange, 1962. Mem. Daytona Beach Zoning Bd., 1947-50; mem. Recreation and Parks Adv. Council, Region IV, State of Fla., 1972—; pres. Daytona Community Chest, 1948; chmn. campaign com. Central Fla. council Boy Scouts Am., 1956-62; bd. visitors Embry-Riddle U., 1971—. Mem. Fla. Bldg. Material Dealers Assn. (pres. 1958-59), Daytona Beach C. of C. (v.p. 1953, dir. 1952-55), Daytona Beach Mchts. Assn. (dir. 1947-51), U.S. Navy League. Episcopalian (sr. warden 1962, vestryman 1954-62). Clubs: Kiwanis (pres. Daytona Beach, 1949), Piedmont Driving (hon. life mem.) (Atlanta); University of Volusia County (dir. 1963-68, pres. 1966), Halifax River Yacht, Daytona Beach Quarterback. Home: The Pendleton Club 1224 S Peninsula Dr Daytona Beach FL 32018 Office: 336 11th St Holly Hill FL 32017

ALEXANDER, HARRY JAMES, engineer; b. Rochester, N.Y., Aug. 12, 1947; s. William and Helen (Matheos) A.; B.C.E., Ga. Inst. Tech., 1970, M.S. S.E., 1974; postgrad. U. N.C., Chapel Hill, 1975-78; M.B.A., U. Tenn., 1985; m. Sharon Gail Smith, Dec. 12, 1969; children—Melissa, Pamela. Engr.-in-tng. State Highway Dept. Ga., Atlanta, 1971-72; project engr. John J. Harte Assos., Atlanta, 1973-75; sr. engr. Engring. Service Assos., Griffin, Ga., 1978-80, Bechtel Group, Inc., Houston and Oak Ridge, 1980-86; mgr. Oak Ridge ops. Advanced Scis., Inc., 1986—. Contbr. articles to profl. jours. Served with USPHS, 1969-71. Registered profl. engr. Ala., Fla., Ga., Miss., N.C., Tenn.; diplomate Am. Acad. Environ. Engrs. Mem. Am. Water Works Assn., Water Pollution Control Fedn., Ga. Soc. Profl. Engrs. (ethical practices com., 1980), Nat. Soc. Profl. Engrs., Tenn. Soc. Profl. Engrs. (ethical practices com. 1983-85, pres. Oak Ridge chpt. 1986—), Beta Gamma Sigma, Chi Epsilon, Chi Phi. Greek Orthodox. Lodges: Order of Ahepa, Kiwanis Internat. (com. chmn., Griffin, Ga. 1979-80), Masons, Lions Internat. (pres. Century club 1983-84) (Oak Ridge). Office: Advanced Scis Inc 107-F Jefferson Ave Oak Ridge TN 37830

ALEXANDER, JAMES ATWELL, poultryman; b. Stony Point, N.C. July 23, 1911; s. J. Will and Mary Emma (Alexander) A.; A.B. Davidson Coll., 1929, M.A., 1931; student Colo. Sch. Mines, 1930, postgrad. U. N.C., 1932-34 ; m. Anna Pauline Hill, Dec. 23, 1938; children—Mary Anna, Eva Pauline. Seismologist Shell Oil Co., Houston, 1931-40; owner, mgr. Alexander Poultry Farm, Stony Point, 1940—; dir. dirs. Alexander County Water Corp.; chmn. Alexander County Poultry Council, 1953-55, Catawaba Soil Conservation Dist. Suprs., 1949-51; mem. adv. com. poultry test, 1958—; mem. gen. bd. Northwestern Bank, 1971—. Mem. Bd. Commrs. Alexander County, 1950-54, Welfare Bd., 1952-54, Alexander County Planning Bd., 1969—; mem. N.C. State Bd. Agr., 1955—; mem. N.C. Gov's. Adv. Com. Nuclear Energy, 1957—, Gov.'s Council on Occupational Health, Gov.'s Council on Rehab.; chmn. Gov.'s Adv. Com. Agr., 1965—; mem. exec. com. Gov.'s Council for Econ. Devel. Mem. Fair Commn., Dixie Classic Fair, Winston-Salem, N.C. Bd. dirs. Alexander County Hosp.; exec. com. N.C. Agrl. Found., 1965—, v.p., 1967; adv. com. Sch. Agr. N.C. State U. Named Man of Year, Grange of Alexander County, N.C., 1957, Alexander County C. of C., 1967; N.C. Outstanding Farm Mgr., 1965; N.C. County Agrl. Agts. award, 1971, N.C. Commr. Agr. award, 1980; named to N.C. Poultry Hall Fame, 1976. Mem. N.C. Acad. Sci., N.W. N.C. Devel. Assn. (pres., chmn agrl. div. award 1969), C. of C. (dir.), N.C. Egg Mktg. Assn. (pres. 1961-62), N.C. Poultry Council (pres. 1963), N.C. Vocat. Agrl. Tchrs. Assn. (hon.), N.C. Agribusiness Council (exec. com.), Sigma Xi, Gamma Sigma Epsilon, Gamma Sigma Delta, Sigma Gamma Epsilon. Democrat. Lion (charter mem., zone chmn.). Home: Stony Point NC 28678

ALEXANDER, JAMES PATRICK, lawyer; b. Glendale, Calif., Oct. 14, 1944; s. Victor Elwin and Thelma Elizabeth (O'Donnell) A.; m. Jeanne Elizabeth Bannerman, June 10, 1967; children—Rene Leigh, Amy Lynne, A.B., Duke U., 1966, J.D., 1969. Bar: Ala. 1969. Assoc. law firm Bradley, Arant, Rose & White, Birmingham, Ala., 1969-75, ptnr., 1975—; adj. lectr. employment discrimination law U. Ala. Sch. of Law, 1981—; mem. adv. bd. div. paralegal studies Samford U. Mem. Birmingham Bar Assn., Ala. State Bar, ABA.

ALEXANDER, KENNETH EDWARD, financial executive; b. Columbia, Tenn., May 30, 1947; s. Edward Martin and Betty Jane (Green) A.; B.S. in Acctg. with honors, Tenn. Technol. U., 1969; m. Judy Elaine Woosely, Sept. 21, 1979; 1 dau., Jennifer Elaine. children by previous marriage—Gregory Ray, Sean Edward. With Haskins & Sells, N.Y.C., 1968; sr. mgr. audit Price Waterhouse & Co., Nashville, 1969-78; sr. v.p. fin. and adminstrn., mem. sr. mgmt. com. Fin. Instn. Services, Inc., Nashville, 1978—; treas., dir. Keckley Market Research, Bank Travel Clubs of Am., Inc., Highland Mktg. Group, Inc. Fin. Communications Network, Inc.; fin. officer, dir. Tenn. Radio Network, Inc., Ky. Network, Inc., S.C. Network, Inc. Pres. Tullahoma (Tenn.) Booster Club, 1980—, Big Orange Club, Tullahoma, 1980—; mem. audit com. United Way, 1975-78. Named hon. col., Tenn., also Tenn. squire; C.P.A. Mem. Am. Inst. C.P.A.s, Tenn. Soc. C.P.A.s, Fin. Execs. Inst. (dir.), Nat. Assn. Accts. (pres. Nashville chpt. 1980-81, nat. ops. com. 1982-84, outstanding member, Nashville 1973, 74, 77), Am. Mgmt. Assn., Planning Execs. Inst., Tenn. Tech. Alumni Assn., Alpha Kappa Psi, Sigma Iota Epsilon. Republican. Baptist. Clubs: U. Tenn. Presidents, Lakewood Country, Nashville Capitol; Richland Country. Office: 49 Music Sq W Nashville TN 37204

ALEXANDER, LAMAR, gov. Tenn.; b. Blount County, Tenn., July 3, 1940; B.A., Vanderbilt U.; J.D., N.Y. U., 1965; m. Leslee Kathryn Buhler, Jan. 4, 1969; children—Drew, Leslee, Kathryn, Will. Admitted to Tenn. bar, 1965; asso. firm Fowler, Rountree, Fowler and Robertson, Knoxville, Tenn., 1965; former law clk. U.S. Ct. Appeals for 5th Circuit, New Orleans; campaign coordinator for Howard Baker's U.S. Senate race, 1966; legis. asst. to U.S. Senator Howard Baker, Washington, 1967-69; exec. asst. to counselor in charge congressional relations White House, Washington, 1969-70; mgr. gubernatorial campaign of Winfield Dunn, Tenn., 1970; partner firm Dearborn & Ewing, Nashville, 1971-78; founder, co-chmn. Tenn. Citizens for Revenue Sharing, 1971; founder, 1st chmn. Tenn. Council on Crime and Delinquency, 1973; polit. commentator TV sta., Nashville, 1975-77; spl. counsel to Senate minority leader Howard Baker, 1977; gov. State of Tenn., Nashville, 1979—; state co-chmn. Appalachian Regional Commn., 1980-81; chmn. policy com. Republican Govs. Conf., 1980-81; vice-chmn. Pres.'s Com. Intergovtl. Relations, 1981—; chmn. So. Regional Edn. Bd., 1983. Mem. ABA, Phi Beta Kappa. Republican. Presbyterian. Office: Office of Gov State Capitol Bldg Nashville TN 37219

ALEXANDER, LOUIS, writer, educator; b. N.Y.C., Mar. 15, 1917; s. Louis I. and Gertrude (Seydel) A.; B.S. in Mktg., U. Newark, 1941; M. Letters in Journalism, U. Houston, 1961 m. Paulette Marlowe, Dec. 23, 1948 (div. Dec. 20, 1968); children—Kathryn, Marjory Lynn; m. 2d, Mildred Nootsie Crowe, Aug. 8, 1976. Reporter, county editor Houston Chronicle, 1947-57; free-lance writer for mags. and newspapers, 1957—; instr., then asst. prof. journalism U. Houston, 1954-82; corr. Wall Street Jour., 1959-75, Newsweek, 1964—, Nat. Pub. Radio, 1972-80; pres. All News Is Local, Inc., pubs. City-County News, Asheville, N.C.; dir. All-Media Properties, Inc., Houston. Mem. Bellaire Parks and Recreation Commn., 1957-60; mem. fin. subcom. Sch. Adv. Com., Bellaire, 1976-77; mem. citizens adv. bd. Met. Transit Authority, 1978-83. Served with USAAF, 1942-45; to capt. USAF, 1951-52; lt. col. Res. Decorated D.F.C., Air medal with three oak leaf clusters. Mem. Aviation/Space Writers Assn., Assn. Petroleum Writers, Am. Soc. Journalists and Authors, Nat. Conf. Editorial Writers, SCORE. Club: Press (Houston). Author: Beyond the Facts, 1975, 2d edit., 1982. Home: Old Charlotte Hwy Route 9 Box 1283 Asheville NC 28803

ALEXANDER, MARY LOUISE, educator; b. Ennis, Tex., Jan. 15, 1926; d. Emmett F. and Florence (Hill) Alexander; B.A., U. Tex., 1947, M.A., 1949, Ph.D., 1951. Instr., research asst. Genetics Found., U. Tex., Austin, 1944-51, postdoctoral research fellow, 1952-55, research scientist Genetics Found., 1962-68; postdoctoral fellow biology div. AEC, Oak Ridge, 1951-52; research asso. U. Tex.-M.D. Anderson Hosp. and Tumor Inst., Houston, 1956-58, asst. biologist, 1959-62; asso. prof. biology S.W. Tex. State U., San Marcos, 1967-69, prof., 1969—. Research cons. Brookhaven Nat. Lab., Upton, N.Y., 1955; research participant Oak Ridge Inst. Nuclear Studies, Tenn., 1951-77. Nat. Cancer Inst. fellow Inst. Animal Genetics, Edinburgh, Scotland, 1960-61. Mem. Genetics Soc. Am., Radiation Research Soc., Am. Soc. Human Genetics, Sigma Xi, Gamma Phi Beta, Phi Sigma, Alpha Epsilon Delta. Home: Hunter's Glen Route 2 Box 119 San Marcos TX 78666

ALEXANDER, MICHAEL WARREN, optometrist; b. Raleigh, N.C., Jan. 12, 1954; s. Ray Shirley and Mary Elizabeth (Andrews) A.; m. Libby Carol Cecil, Nov. 24, 1979; 1 child, Daniel Cecil. B.S., Western Carolina U., 1975; O.D., So. Coll. Optometry, 1980. With Alexander Optometric Clinic, Morganton, N.C., 1980-82; owner Optometric Office, Shelby, N.C., 1982—. Alternate bd. dirs. Western Carolina U. Alumni, Cullowhee, N.C., 1985—. Mem. Am. Optometric Assn., Catawba Valley Optometric Assn. (pres. 1984—), N.C. Optometric Exec. Council (liaison mem.), N.C. Optometric Assn. Democrat. Presbyterian. Lodge: Kiwanis (bd. dirs. 1985—). Home: 312 Circle View Dr Shelby NC 28150 Office: 111 N Lafayette St Shelby NC 28150

ALEXANDER, PATRICK BYRON, orchestra administrator; b. Texas City, Tex., May 11, 1950; s. Alvin Wesley and Mabel Bernice (Hovdahl) A.; m. Linda Graham, May 7, 1975. B.A. in Econs., George Mason Coll., U. Va., 1972. Publs. dir. George Mason U., Fairfax, Va., 1973-75, U. Okla. Health Services Ctr., Oklahoma City, 1975-78, Presbyn. Hosp. Inc., Oklahoma City, 1978-79; mng. dir. Okla. Symphony Orch., Oklahoma City, 1979—, also dir. Bd. dirs. Cimarron Opera Co., Ambassador's Concert Choir, Crown Heights Neighborhood Assn., Planned Parenthood of Okla. Kerr Found. fellow, 1981. Mem. Okla. Assn. Symphony Orchs. (dir.), Am. Symphony Orch. League, Oklahoma City C. of C. (cultural council). Office: Oklahoma Symphony Orch Inc 512 Civic Center Music Hall Oklahoma City OK 73102

ALEXANDER, PAUL MARION, training executive, consultant; b. Akron, Ohio, Aug. 21, 1927; s. George Dewey and Orpha Jane (Wagner) A.; m. Dora Jean Bee, Dec. 17, 1955; children—Geoffrey D., James C., Richard L. B.Sc. in Horticulture, Calif. State Poly. Coll., 1953; M.Sc. in Plant Pathology, Ohio State U., 1955, Ph.D. in Botany, 1958. Asst. prof., assoc. prof. Clemson U., S.C., 1958-69; dir. edn. Golf Course Supts. Assn. Am., Des Plaines, Ill., 1970-73; v.p. agronomy Sea Pines Co., Hilton Head Island, S.C., 1973-75; sr. agronomist sales Turf Chem. Firms, Shelby, Winston-Salem, N.C., 1975-79; v.p. golf ops. Sea Pines Co., Hilton Head Island, S.C., 1979-82; nat. tng. dir. Chem Lawn Services Corp., Atlanta, 1982—; agronomist U.S. Golf Assn., green sect., Chgo., 1969-70; cons., owner Grass Roots, Inc., Clemson, 1981—. Contbr. articles to profl. jours. Served to cpl. USMC, 1944-49, PTO. Mem. Am. Phytopath. Soc. (emeritus), Golf Course Supts. Assn. Am., Soc. Nematologists, Carolinas Golf Course Supts. Assn., S.C. Lawn and Turfgrass Council (bd. dirs. 1978-82). Club: Sertoma (silver honor award 1966-67). Avocations: fishing; stained glass design; counted cross stitch. Home: 9645 Loblolly Ln Roswell GA 30075 Office: ChemLawn Services Corp 5000 McGinnis Ferry Rd Alpharetta GA 30201

ALEXANDER, RUSSELL JAMES, oil company executive; b. Owasso, Okla., Oct. 20, 1922; s. Raymond Dolphin and Lena May (Poling) A.; m. Aldea Mary Carl, June 24, 1944; children—Alicia, Robert, Carl, Paul, Neal, Sarah, Nelson, David, Grant. B.S., U. Okla., 1951, M.S., 1952. Paleontologist, Chevron, Denver, 1952-78; staff geologist Tex. Pacific Oil Co., 1978-80; mgr. geology Sun Oil Co., 1980-81, South Ranch Oil Co., 1981; mgr. research Southwestern Energy Prodn. Co., Fayetteville, Ark., 1982—. Bd. dirs. Natrona County Sch., Casper, Wyo., 1967. Served to lt. (j.g.) USNR, 1944-46. Mem. Am. Assn. Petroleum Geologists, Rocky Mountain Assn. Geologists, Ft. Smith Geol. Soc. Republican. Avocations: fishing; boating. Home: 111 Crow's Roost Pl Rogers AR 72756 Office: Southwestern Energy Prodn Co PO Box 1827 Fayetteville AR 72702-1827

ALEXANDER, SANDRA CARLTON, educator, author, consultant, researcher; b. Warsaw, N.C., July 26, 1947; d. Willie G. Carlton and Annette (Robinson) C.; m. Rondal Graham Alexander, Sept. 6, 1970; children—Tonya, Derrick. B.S., N.C. A&T State U., 1969; M.A., Harvard U., 1970; Ph.D., U. Pitts., 1976; student U. Wis., Yale U., Columbia U. Instr. Allegheny Community Coll., 1972; instr. English, Coppin State Coll., Balt., 1973-74; assoc. prof. English, N.C. A&T State U., Greensboro, N.C., 1974—; dir. Triad Youth on the Move for the Humanities, NEH Youth Project, 1982. Bd. dirs. Greensboro YWCA; past pres. Greensboro Negro Bus. and Profl. Women's Club; active Parents Council. Danforth fellow, 1969; Woodrow Wilson teaching fellow, 1970; NEH grantee, 1977; Danforth assoc., 1978; recipient 3d prize Guilford County Writing Festival, 1980; Lady of Yr. award Greensboro Young Men's Club, 1982. Mem. South Atlantic MLA, Coll. Lang. Assn., Nat. Council Tchrs. English., Sigma Tau Delta, Kappa Delta Pi, Alpha Kappa Alpha. Democrat. Club: Nat. Assn. Bus. and Profl. Women. Author: (with Lillian Howell) The Color Me Black History Book, 1981; Peidmont Afro-American Humanists on Review, 1982; contbr. articles to profl. jours. Home: 4001 Hickory Tree Ln Greensboro NC 27406 Office: NC A&T State U 106 Crosby Hall Greensboro NC 27406

ALEXANDER, SHERRY LEE, broadcast journalist, educator; b. Miami, Fla.; d. Sol and Dee (Miller) A.; m. Keith Davidson, Apr. 20, 1973; children—Keith-Christopher, Alexandra-Star. B.A., U. Fla.; M.A., U. Miami (Fla.), 1970. Producer, reporter WPBT, Miami, Fla., 1970-74; asst. editor Miami Phoenix Weekly, 1974-75; adj. instr. Fla. Atlantic U., 1976-78; free lance writer/editor, Boston, 1978-80; prof. mass communication West Ga. Coll., Carrollton, 1980—; news advisor WWGC-FM/WGC-TV, 1980—. Mem. Radio-TV News Dirs. Assn., Mensa, Sigma Delta Chi. Author: Aussie-U.S. Slang Dictionary, 1977; Childsnatch: What Every Parent Should Know, 1979; Audible Delight: A Radio Lab Production Manual, 1981. Home: PO Box 134 Carrollton GA 30117 Office: West Ga Coll Carrollton GA 30118

ALEXANDER, THEODOR WALTER, emeritus German language educator; b. Vienna, Austria, Aug. 1, 1919; s. Gustav and Gisela (Rubel) A.; B.S., Tex. Tech. U., 1946, M.S., 1947; m. Beatrice Witte, Sept. 6, 1947; children—Richard Witte, Ronald Walter. Instr., Tex. Tech. U., Lubbock, 1947-53, asst. prof., 1954-58, assoc. prof., 1959-67, prof. German, 1968-84, prof. emeritus, 1984—; vis. assoc. prof. U. Tex., Austin, summer 1960. Served with AUS, 1941. Recipient Distinguished Teaching award Standard Oil (Ind.) Found., Inc., 1969. Mem. Modern Lang. Assn. Am., Am. Assn. Tchrs. German, South Central Modern Lang. Assn., Internat. Arthur Schnitzler Research Assn. Contbr. articles to profl. jours. Home: 3405 25th St Lubbock TX 79410

ALEXANDER, WELBORN EXCELL, JR., railroad executive; b. Lenoir, N.C., Feb. 12, 1941; s. Welborn Excell and Nancy Ellen (Thompson) A.; B.A., Duke U., 1963; postgrad. Baruch Sch. Bus. Adminstrn., CCNY; m. Patricia Carson Hutchins, June 8, 1963; children—Welborn Excell, III, Lucinda Carson. With sales dept. So. Ry. System, 1963-67; industry planning analyst N.Y. Central R.R., 1967-69; industry planning analyst, mgr. mktg., dir. mktg., asst. v.p. mktg., then v.p. mktg. Penn Central Transp. Co. to 1974-76; v.p. sales and mktg. planning Seaboard Coast Line/Louisville & Nashville R.R., 1976-78; sr. v.p. sales and mktg. Seaboard Coast Line Industries, Jacksonville, Fla., 1978-79, exec. v.p. sales and mktg., 1980-82; exec. v.p. sales and mktg. Seaboard System R.R., Jacksonville, 1983—, also dir.; dir. Flagship Bank of Jacksonville. Mem. Nat. Freight Transp. Assn., Am. Soc. Traffic and Transp., Phi Beta Kappa, Phi Delta Theta. Presbyterian. Clubs: Rotary, River, San Jose Country. Office: 500 Water St Jacksonville FL 32202

ALEXANDER, WESLEY MERLE, educator; b. Prairie Hill, Tex., Mar. 9, 1926; s. Lucian Merle and Dolly Madison (Fox) A.; B.Mus. with honors, Baylor U., 1949, B.S. in Physics with honors, 1952, M.Mus., M.S., 1953; Ph.D. magna cum laude, U. Heidelberg (W. Ger.), 1975; m. Mary Kathryn Stemm, Aug. 26, 1959; children—David Merle, Kathryn Jane, Sara Elizabeth, Matthew Lucian. Research acoustics engr. C.G. Conn, Ltd., 1953-54; asst. prof. physics Baylor U., 1954-56, asst. prof. 1967-75, asso. prof., 1975-78, prof., 1978—, dir. Inst. Environ. Studies, 1975—, dir. Glasscock Energy Research Center, 1979—; instr. physics, research electronics engr. Okla. State U., 1954-56; head astrochemistry sect. Goddard Space Flight Center NASA, 1959-66; research asso. space physics Temple U., 1966-67; pres. Am. Solar King, 1976-77; pres. AFS Research Corp., Waco, Tex., 1979-81, chmn. bd., 1981—; cons. solar energy. Mem. Environ. Commn. City Council of Waco, 1975—; asso. bd. dirs. World Hunger Relief, Inc. Served with USN, 1944-46, USNR, 1946-52, USAFR, 1952-58. Max Planck Institut fur Kernphysik fellow, 1972-73. Fellow Tex. Acad. Sci.; mem. AAAS, Internat. Commn. of Sci. Unions, Am. Assn. Physics Tchrs., Am. Geophys. Union, Am. Acoustical Soc., Tex. Acad. Sci., N.Y. Acad. Sci., Internat. Assn. Solar Energy, Sigma Xi, Sigma Pi Sigma. Presbyterian. Club: Rotary. Contbr. chpts. to books and articles in field to profl. jours. Home: 1208 Rio Vista Waco TX 76710 Office: Institute of Environmental Studies Baylor Univ Waco TX 76798

ALEXANDER, WILLIAM NEBEL, dentist, former army officer, educator; b. Pitts., May 22, 1929; s. William Harrison and Ida Margaret (Nebel) A.; m. Lorraine Michaela Berg, Nov. 29, 1958; children—Kathleen, Gregory, Christopher, Jeffrey, Steven. Student St. Vincent Coll., 1947-49; D.D.S., U. Pitts., 1953; cert. U. Pa., 1961; M.S. in Edn., Jackson State U., 1982. Diplomate Am. Bd. Oral Medicine. Commd. 2d lt. U.S. Army, 1952, advanced through grades to col., 1972; chief oral medicine service Letterman Army Med. Ctr., San Francisco, 1961-66, chief clinician, Kaiserslautern, W.Ger., 1966-69, comdg. officer, Vietnam, 1969-70, dir. gen. dental residency, Ft. Hood, Tex., 1970-74, dir., chmn. dental edn., Tacoma, 1974-78, ret., 1978; prof., dir. patient admissions U. Miss. Sch. Dentistry, Jackson, 1978—; cons. oral medicine; dental cons. Miss. State Dept. Edn., Jackson, 1980—. Co-editor: Problem Oriented Dental Record, 1980-81; contbg. author: Oral Health of the Elderly, 1983; author manual/clin. lab. medicine for dentists, 1980-81; video tape TMJ/MFPD Syndrome Diagnosis, 1977. Tchr. piloting U.S. Power Squadrons, San Francisco, Tacoma, 1965-78; co-chmn. parish council Christ the King Parish, Belton, Tex., 1971-83; usher-greeter St. Paul's Parish, Brandon, Miss., 1978—. Decorated Bronze Star, Legion of Merit. Fellow Am. Coll. Dentists, Am. Acad. Oral Medicine; mem. Internat. Assn. Dental Research, AAAS, Sigma Xi, Omicron Kappa Upsilon (pres. chpt. 1983), Phi Kappa Phi. Republican. Roman Catholic. Clubs: Presidio Yacht (San Francisco); Loyal Order of Boar. Home: 300 Forest Point Dr Brandon MS 39042 Office: U Miss Med Ctr 2500 MS State St Jackson MS 39216

ALEXANDER, WILLIAM VOLLIE, JR., congressman; b. Memphis, Jan. 16, 1934; s. William V. and Eulalia (Spencer) A.; student U. Ark., 1951-53; B.A., Southwestern at Memphis, 1957; LL.B. Vanderbilt U., 1960; 1 dau., Alyse Haven. Admitted to Tenn. bar, 1960, Ark. bar, 1963; law clk. to chief judge U.S. Dist. Ct., Memphis, 1960-61; asso. Montedonico, Bonne, Gilliland, Heiskell & Loch, Memphis, 1961-63; partner Swift & Alexander, Osceola, Ark., 1963-69; former dir. Osceola Riverport Authority; former commr. Arkansas Waterways Commn.; mem. 91st-97th Congresses from 1st Dist. Ark., chief dep. Democratic whip. Former bd. dirs. Osceola YMCA; East Ark. council Boy Scouts Am.; bd. dirs. Mississippi County YMCA, Southwestern at Memphis. Mem. Am. Acad. Polit. and Social Sci., Nat. Assn. Underwater Diving Instrs., Kappa Sigma, Phi Delta Phi. Episcopalian. Clubs: Masons, Rotary (pres., dir.). Office: Cannon House Office Bldg Washington DC 20515 also H-115 The Capitol Washington DC 20515

ALEXIADES, VASILIOS, mathematics educator; b. Xanthi, Greece, July 17, 1948; came to U.S., 1971, naturalized, 1983; s. Nikolaos and Anthy (Alexiadou) A.; m. Linda Susan Tobey, Oct. 28, 1972; children—Nikolas, Alexander, Anthy. B.A. in Math., U. Thessaloniki, Greece, 1971; M.S. in Math., St. Louis U., 1973; M.S. in Math., U. Del., 1976, Ph.D. in Math., 1977. Instr. U. Tex., Austin, 1977-78; asst. prof. U. Tenn., Knoxville, 1978-83, assoc. prof. math, 1983—; researcher Oak Ridge Nat. Lab., Tenn., 1982—, cons., 1980-81. Contbr. articles to profl. jours. Mem. Soc. for Indsl. and Applied Math. Office: Oak Ridge Nat Lab Bldg 9207A MS 2 Oak Ridge TN 37831

ALFONSI, MARTIN JOSEPH, data processing company executive; b. McKeesport, Pa., Apr. 2, 1943; s. Martin and Mary Ann (Gallo) A.; student Bucknell U., 1961, 63; B.S. in Bus. Adminstrn., U. Pitts., 1968; m. Kay Francis Drenik, Oct. 30, 1965; children—Joseph Martin, Sharyn Elizabeth. Procedure analyst U.S. Steel, Pitts., 1965-69; mgr. data processing Fayette County Schs., Uniontown, Pa., 1969-72; head data processing div. Allegheny Gen. Hosp., Pitts., 1972-75; co-founder Vector Group, Inc., Pitts., 1975, exec. v.p. Vector Group, Inc., Springfield, Va., 1975-82, also dir.; founder, pres. Methods Devel. Inc., Vienna, Va., 1982—. Asst. coach McLean Youth, Inc., Little League Football, 1980-84; bd. dirs. McLean Little League, 1980-82. Served with U.S. Army, 1962-65. Mem. Internat. Employees Benefit Found., Honeywell Users Group Small and Medium Systems (v.p. 1976-77). Roman Catholic. Club: McLean Hamlet Swim and Tennis. Author and installer Remote Entry Fortan, a computer system for high sch. students; author Mem. Record System, on-line computer system for labor unions, pension funds and health funds; author developer Padlock, security system for office word processing systems. Home. 1333 Vanetta Ln Vienna VA 22180 Office: Methods Devel Inc 111 Berry St Vienna VA 22180

ALFORD, BOBBY RAY, otolaryngologist, university administrator; b. Dallas, May 30, 1932; s. Bryant J. and Edith M. (Garrett) A.; m. Othelia Jerry Dorn, Aug. 28, 1953; children—Bradley Keith, Raye Lynn, Alan Scott. A.S. cum laude, Tyler Jr. Coll., 1951; postgrad. U. Tex., Austin, 1951-52; M.D. with honors, Baylor U., 1956. Diplomate Am. Bd. Otolaryngology. Intern Jefferson Davis Hosp., Houston, 1956-57; resident in otolaryngology Baylor U. Coll. Medicine, Houston, 1957-60; asst. prof., 1962-65, assoc. prof., 1965-66, program dir. residency tng., 1963—, prof. otolaryngology, chmn. dept. otolaryngology and communicative scis., 1967—, Olga Keith Wiess chair otolaryngology and communicative scis., 1981—, v.p., dean academic affairs, 1980-84, v.p., dean academic and clin. affairs, 1984—, Disting. Service prof., 1985—; mem. review panel Dept. HEW, 1965-68, NIH, 1977-80; chmn. sci. peer review com. Johnson Space Ctr., Houston, 1984—; mem. review panel Am. Inst. Biol. D-SP Scis., 1984—. Author: Neurological Aspects of Auditory and Vestibular Disorders, 1964. Chief editor Archives of Otolaryngology Jour., 1970-79. NIH fellow John Hopkins U., 1961-62. Fellow Am. Acad. Otolaryngology (pres. 1981), Am. Council Otolaryngology (pres. 1980-81), Am. Broncho-Esophagological Assn., ACS (bd. govs. 1977-82); mem. Am. Bd. Otolaryngology (pres. 1985). Mem. Christian Ch. Clubs: Doctor's (Houston), South Shore Harbor (League City), Tex. Corinthian Yacht (gov. 1978-80). Avocation: sailing. Office: Baylor Coll Medicine One Baylor Plaza Houston TX 77030

ALFORD, RANDALL LYNN, language and linguistics educator, consultant; b. Dallas, Mar. 20, 1953; s. Edward Jackson Alford and Bonnie Jean (Scoggins) Alford Williamson; m. Sylvia Elena Guarisco, Aug. 27, 1983. Sprachzeugnis, U. Innsbruck (Austria), summer 1971, Inst. European Studies, Vienna, Austria, summer 1976; B.A. in German, Tex. Tech U., 1975, M.A. in German, 1977; Ph.D. in Fgn. Lang. Edn., Fla. State U., 1982. Teaching fellow Tex. Tech U., Lubbock, 1975-77; tchr. O.D. Wyatt High Sch., Ft. Worth, 1977-79; teaching and research asst. Fla. State U., Tallahassee, 1979-80; asst. prof. applied linguistics and fgn. langs., dir. Lang. Inst., Fla. Inst. Tech., Melbourne, 1983—; cons. fgn. langs., ESL; edn. specialist Fla.-Colombia Ptnrs., Melbourne, 1984. Author: Foreign Language Curriculum and Materials Development, 1983. Interpreter Luth. Refugee Program, Melbourne, 1984; me. Fla. Senate campaign com., South Brevard County Dist. (Fla.), 1984. Named to Outstanding Young Men Am., U.S. Jaycees, 1983. Mem. Fla. Consortium of Multilingual Edn. (dir. 1984), Gulf Area Tchrs. ESL (exec. bd. 1983—, editor and pub. newsletter 1984), Am. Council on Teaching Fgn. Langs., Internat. TESOL, Fla. Fgn. Lang. Assn., Am. Assn. Depts. Fgn. Langs., Phi Kappa Phi, Phi Delta Kappa, Delta Phi Alpha (v.p. 1976-77), SAR. Republican. Baptist (deacon, dir. Sunday sch.). Office: Fla Inst Tech Lang Inst 150 W University Blvd Melbourne FL 32901

ALFORD, TERRY L., history educator; b. Mobile, Ala., Oct. 7, 1945; s. L.L. and Bess (Horne) A.; m. Jeanette Stewart, 1969; children—Jane, David, Cary. B.A., Miss. State U., 1966, M.A., 1967, Ph.D., 1970. Prof. history, trustee Students' Coll. of Arts and Scis., Washington, 1971-72; prof. history No. Va. Community Coll., Annandale, 1972—; guest curator, Lincoln Assassination Exhibit, Georgetown U. Library, Washington, 1985—. Author: Prince Among Slaves, 1977; This One Mad Act, 1985. Contbr. Dictionary of Afro-American Slavery, 1985. Contbr. articles to profl. jours. NEH fellow, 1978-79; recipient Key to City award Gloster, Miss., 1983. Mem. Manuscript Soc. (com. on pubs., replevin, 1982, 85), Orgn. Am. Historians, Soc. for Historians of Early Am. Republic. Research on John Wilkes Booth. Avocations: swimming; southern folklore; collecting historical documents and rare books. Office: Dept History No Va Community Coll 8333 Little River Turnpike Annandale VA 22003

ALFORD, WALTER HELION, telecommunications executive, lawyer; b. Atlanta, Apr. 10, 1938; s. Helion G. and Sarah M. (Smith) A.; m. Susanne K. Pichard, May 22, 1971; children—Walter Helion, Sarah E., P.K. Justin, Allison Smith. B.B.A., U. Ga., 1960; J.D., Emory U., 1962. Bar: Ga. 1962, Fla. 1965. Atty., So. Bell Tel.&Tel. Co., Atlanta, 1964, Jacksonville, Fla., 1964-67, Atlanta, 1967-68; atty. AT&T, N.Y.C., 1968-69; gen. atty. So. Bell Tel.&Tel. Co., Columbia, S.C., 1969-72, Miami, Fla., 1972-76, gen. solicitor, 1976-79, v.p. Fla. pub. affairs, 1979-82, v.p. Fla., 1982—; dir. Barnett Banks of Fla., Inc., Jacksonville. Bd. dirs. Fla. Council of 100, 1984—, Fla. Council Econ. Edn., 1984, United Way Dade County, 1984—, S. Fla. Health Action Coalition, Inc., 1982, Associated Industries Fla., 1982—; bd. govs. Greater Miami C. of C., 1982; mem. exec. com., bd. dirs. Fla. C. of C., 1982; exec. dir. Pub. Utilities Research Ctr., U. Fla., 1979—; trustee Fla. Ind. Coll. Fund, 1982—; mem. adv. bd. Salvation Army, Miami, 1982—, Lighthouse for the Blind, Miami, 1983—. Mem. Fla. Bar, Fla. Bar Found., Ga. Bar Assn. Clubs: Governors (Tallahassee); City (founding; bd. govs.), Miami, Bankers (Miami); Riviera Country (Coral Gables, Fla.). Office: 666 NW 79th Ave Room 666 Miami FL 33126

ALFORD, WILLIAM LUMPKIN, physicist; b. Albertville, Ala., Oct. 6, 1924; s. Bennett Allae and Emmie Sue (Lumpkin) A.; m. Ruth Wiggs, June 3, 1948; children—Linda Sue, Charles Alan, Lois Anne, John David, Barbara Jean. B.A., Vanderbilt U., 1948; M.S., Calif. Inst. Tech., 1949, Ph.D., 1953. Asst. prof. physics Auburn U., 1952-55, assoc. prof., 1955-58, prof., 1964-80, assoc. dean for research Sch. Arts and Scis., prof., 1980—; physicist U.S. Army Missile Comd., Redstone Arsenal, Ala., 1958-64. Served with AUS, 1943-46. Recipient Algernon Sydney Sullivan award Auburn U., 1985. Fellow Am. Phys. Soc. (Pegram award 1983), Phi Beta Kappa, Sigma Xi, Sigma Pi Sigma. Baptist. Club: Civitan (treas. 1957, v.p. 1966, pres. 1983). Contbr. articles to sci. jours. Office: Physics Dept Auburn U Auburn AL 36849

ALGER, BERNARD CARL, hospital administrator; b. Des Moines, Oct. 21, 1944; s. Carl Evert and Grace Patrica (Rambo) A.; m. Kathy Wall, Jan. 31, 1967 (div. 1977); children—Anjelicia, Stephen; m. Barbara Todd, July 22, 1978 (div. 1984); children—Heather, Karen; m. Cleta Jean Cogburn, Apr. 1985; 1 child, Cristin. B.A., Southwestern U., Georgetown, Tex., 1966; M.B.A., So. Methodist U., 1969; Ph.D., U. Iowa, 1973. Asst. adminstr. Presbyterian Hosp., Dallas, 1973-79; assoc. dir. Harris Hosp. Methodist, Ft. Worth, (now Harris Meth. Health System), 1979-80, sr. assoc. dir., 1980-82, sr. v.p., 1982-84, exec. v.p., 1984—. Author: Existing Methods of Resource Control in Non-Profit Hospitals, 1973; Hospital Resource Planning, 1975. Chmn. March of Dimes, Ft. Worth, 1979-81; mem. Tex. Govt. Effectiveness Program, Houston, 1981. Mem. South Area Ft. Worth C. of C. (chmn. 1981-83, exec. com. 1981-83), Am. Coll. Hosp. Adminstrs., Assn. Mental Health Adminstrs. (cert.), Am. Hosp. Assn. Republican. Methodist. Avocations: camping; running; stained glass; motorcycling; backpacking. Home: 3917 Ashbury St Bedford TX 76021 Office: Harris Methodist Health System 1325 Pennsylvania St Fort Worth TX 76104

ALGHITA, ADNAN JAFAR, land developer; b. Naiaf, Iraq, Oct. 1, 1944; s. Jafar K. Alghita and Zakia M. Husin. B.S. in Civil Engring., Baghdad U., 1966; M.S. in Structural Enging. Ga. Inst. Tech., 1971. Home builder, Baghdad, Iraq, 1966-69, Atlanta, 1971-76; land developer, exporter constrn. machinery, Atlanta, 1976—.

ALGINA, JAMES, educator, researcher; b. Bklyn., July 16, 1948; s. Joseph James and Eileen Mary (O'Rourke) A.; m. Elizabeth Silbert, Aug. 15, 1971; children—David James, Leah Catherine. B.A., U. R.I., 1971; Ed.D., U. Mass., 1976. Asst. prof. U. Ill., Chgo., 1975-76, U. Pitts., 1976-78; asst. prof. U. Fla., Gainesville, 1978-80, assoc. prof., 1980-83, assoc. prof., chmn. dept. foundations of edn., 1983-85, prof., chmn., 1985—. Editorial bd. Jour. Ednl. Psychology, 1979—; co-author: Introduction to Classical and Modern Test Theory, 1986; author articles. Mem. Ednl. Statisticians (pres. 1984-85), Am. Ednl. Research Assn., Nat. Council on Measurement in Edn., Am. Statis. Assn., Psychometric Soc., Soc. for Multivariate Exptl. Psychology. Office: 1403 Norman Hall Univ Fla Gainesville FL 32611

ALHADEFF, E(LLIOTT) RICHARD, lawyer; b. Mongomery Ala., Dec. 17, 1943; m. Meme Coleman, Aug. 31, 1964; 1 son, Mark C. B.S., U. Ala., 1965, LL.B., 1967; LL.M. in Taxation, U. Miami, 1974. Bar: Fla. 1967, Ala. 1967. Mem. Abbott Frumkes and Alhadeff, Miami Beach, Fla., 1970-77; mem. Broad and Cassel, Miami, Fla., 1977-84; mem. Arky, Freed, Miami, 1984-86, Stearns, Weaver, Miller, Weissler, Alhadeff & Sitterson, P.A., 1986—; former Assoc. town judge, Town of Surfside (Fla.); past chmn. 11th Jud. Circuit Unauthorized Practice of Law Com. Chmn. Miami Beach Planning Com.; past pres. Miami Beach Taxpayer's Assn.; pres. Friends of Bass Mus., 1983-85. Served to 1st lt. U.S. Army, 1968-70. Decorated Bronze Star medal. Mem. ABA, Fla. Bar Assn., Ala. Bar Assn., Miami Beach Bar Assn. (past pres.). Democrat. Club: Tiger Bay. Office: One Biscayne Tower Suite 2800 Miami FL 33131

ALLAIN, SUSAN COATS, television reporter, public relations executive; b. Daytona Beach, Fla., Aug. 15, 1951; d. Edwin Bryant and Mina Ruth (Cobb) C.; m. George Bert Allain, Jan. 21, 1971 (div. July 1976); 1 child, Christopher George. B.A., Northeast La. U., 1977. Anchor, news reporter, producer, documentary reporter KNOE-TV, Monroe, La., 1976-81, anchor, feature and entertainment reporter, pub. relations asst., 1984—; asst. dir. corporate pub. relations Century Telephone Enterprises, Inc., Monroe, 1981-83; dir. mktg., pub. relations and vol. services North Monroe Community Hosp., Monroe, 1983-84. Founder, pres. Friends of La. Purchase Gardens and Zoo, Inc., 1981-83; mem. Citizen's Com. for rededication Monroe Civic Center, 1982; bd. mem. Twin City Civic Ballet, 1980-81; mem. Northeast La. U. Alumni Bd., 1978-81; mem. adv. com. Northeast La. U. Reading Conf., 1981; entertainment chmn. Ouachita Riverfest, 1985; bd. dirs. Twin City Art Found.; sec.-treas. Northeast La. Arts Council; active Friends of Monroe Civic Center, Twin City Art Found. N.E. La Press Club scholar, 1976; recipient award Alpha Chi Alpha, 1977; award La. Associated Press Broadcasters, 1981. Mem. Am. Soc. Hosp. Pub. Relations, La. Hosp. Assn. Pub. Relations, Pub. Relations Assn. La., Monroe C. of C., N.E. La. U. Journalism Alumni (pres. 1978-81). Democrat. Baptist. Home: 6411 Mosswood Dr Monroe LA 71203 Office: PO Box 4067 Monroe LA 71211

ALLAIN, WILLIAM A., governor Mississippi ; b. 1928. Grad., U. Notre Dame; LL.B., U. Miss. Bar: Miss. 1950. Former asst. atty. gen. State of Miss., atty. gen., 1980-84, gov. Miss., 1984—. Office: Office of Gov PO Box 139 Jackson MS 39205

ALLARD, GILLES OLIVIER, geology educator; b. Rougemont, Que., Can., Dec. 12, 1927; s. Alcide and Jeanne (Favreau) A.; m. Bernadette Martineau, Sept. 27, 1952; children—Claude, Martine, Michel. B.A., U. Montreal, 1948, B.S., 1951; M.A. in Geology, Queen's U., 1953; Ph.D. in Geology, Johns Hopkins U., 1956. Exploration mgr. Chibougamau Mining and Smelting (Que.), 1955-58; asst. prof. geology U. Va., Charlottesville, 1958-59; prof. Centro de Aperfeicoamento e Pesquisas, Petrobras, Salvador, Brazil, 1959-64; vis. lectr. U. Calif.-Riverside, 1964-65; assoc. prof. U. Ga., Athens, 1965-69, prof., 1970—, acting head dept., 1969-70; cons. Que. Dept. Natural Resources, 1966—. Fellow Geol. Soc. Am., Mineralogical Soc. Am.; mem. Geol. Assn. Can., Mineralogical Assn. Can., Can. Inst. Mining and Metallurgy, Soc. Econ. Geologists, Am. Inst. Mining Engrs., Sociedade Brasileira de Geologia, Internat. Assn. Genesis of Ore Deposits, Ala. Geol. Soc., Ga. Geol. Soc., Carolina Geol. Soc., Sigma Xi. Roman Catholic. Club: Torch. Home: 225 Hampton Ct Athens GA 30605 Office: Dept Geology Univ Ga Athens GA 30602

ALLBRIGHT, KARAN ELIZABETH, guidance clinic administrator, psychologist, consultant; b. Oklahoma City, Okla., Jan. 28, 1948; d. Jack Gahnal and Irma Lolene (Keesee) A. B.A., Oklahoma City U., 1970, M.A.T., 1972; Ph.D., U. So. Miss., 1981. Cert. sch. psychologist, Ga.; cert. psychometrist, Ga. Psychol. technician Donald J. Bertoch, Ph.D., Oklahoma City, 1973-76; asst. adminstr. Parents' Assistance Ctr., Oklahoma City, 1976-77; psychology intern Burwell Psycho-ednl. Ctr., Carrollton, Ga., 1980-81; staff psychologist Griffin Area Psychoednl. Ctr., Ga., 1981-85; clinic dir. Sequoyah County Guidance Clinic, Sallisaw, Okla., 1985—; speaker, lectr. various orgns.; dir. workshops. Mem. Task Force to Prevent Child Abuse, Fayette County, Ga., 1984-85, Task Force on Family Violence, Spalding County, Ga., 1983-85; cons. Family Alliance (Parents Anonymous) Sequoyah County, Okla., 1985—. Named Outstanding Young Women in Am., 1980. Mem. Am. Psychol. Assn., Southeastern Psychol. Assn., Nat. Assn. Sch. Psychologists, Nat. Council for Exceptional Children, Ga. Psychol. Assn., Ga. Assn. Sch. Psychologists, Psi Chi, Delta Zeta (chpt. dir. 1970-72). Democrat. Presbyterian. Home: 2100 Brooken Hill Dr Apt 3-C Fort Smith AR 72903 Office: Sequoyah County Guidance Clinic 612 N Oak St Sallisaw OK 74955

ALLEN, BARBARA KIRKMAN, utility company executive; b. Asheville, N.C., July 23, 1931; d. Walter Alfred and Georgia Esmerald (Lewallen) Kirkman; m. Luke C. Allen, Jr., Sept. 9, 1949; 1 son, Michael Kirkman. With Carolina Power & Light Co., Raleigh, N.C., 1950—, mgr. adminstrv. services, 1979. Bd. dirs. N.C. Womens Forum; bd. deacon New Hope Baptist Ch., Raleigh; mem. J.J. Singers; mem. adv. bd. Wake County council Girl Scouts U.S.; mem. adv. council Women in Econ. Devel.; chairperson Acad. of Women, YWCA; bd. dirs. N.C. Community Colls., Wake County Council Aging; mem. N.C. Symphony Soc.; bd. assocs. Meredith Coll., mem. bd. friends of the coll.; bd. assocs. N.C. Child Advocacy Inst. Mem. Greater Raleigh C. of C. (mem. Mayor's com. of '85). Democrat. Club: Woman's of Raleigh (dir.). Office: 411 Fayetteville St PO Box 1551 Raleigh NC 27602

ALLEN, CHARLES MENGEL, judge; b. Louisville, Nov. 22, 1916; s. Arthur Dwight and Jane (Mengel) A.; m. Betty Anne Cardwell, June 25, 1949; children—Charles Dwight, Angela M. B.A., Yale U., 1941; LL.B., U. Louisville, 1943. Bar: Ky. 1944. Practiced in Louisville, 1947-55; asst. U.S. atty. for Western Dist. Ky., 1955-59; mem. firm Booth & Walker, Louisville, 1959-61; circuit judge 4th Chancery div. Jefferson County, 1961-71; dist. judge U.S. Dist. Ct., Louisville, 1971—, now sr. judge. Pres. Ky. Ry. Mus.; bd. dirs. Louisville Art Center; mem. Ky. Humane Soc., local chpt., Nat. Ry. Hist. Soc. Mem. Am., Fed., Ky., Louisville bar assns. Office: Room 252 US Courthouse Louisville KY 40202

ALLEN, CONNIE ANN, petroleum geologist; b. Norman, Okla., Jan. 5, 1947; d. Stanley Estes and Audrey Mae (Evans) Bland; m. Delmar Dwayne Allen, Dec. 26, 1965; children—Lance T., Shana E. B.S. in Geology, U. Ark., 1969. Computer geologist Cities Service Oil, Bartlesville, Tulsa, 1969-75; exploitation geologist Williams Exploration, Tulsa, 1975-77; devel. geologist Tex. Oil and Gas Corp., Oklahoma City, 1977-80; geologist Pacific Oil and Gas, Oklahoma City, 1980, Alpha Energy, Oklahoma City, 1980-83; pvt. practice geologist, Oklahoma City, 1983—. Mem. Am. Assn. Petroleum Geologists, Tulsa Geol. Soc. (treas. 1974-75, editor jour. 1976-77), Oklahoma City Geol. Soc. Democrat. Avocations: flying (pvt. pilot license); tennis; gardening; travel. Home: 1608 Leawood Dr Edmond OK 73034 Office: 426 NW 5th St Oklahoma City OK 73102

ALLEN, CONSTANCE OLLEEN, artist, Jewelry designer; b. Camphill, Ala., June 10, 1923; d. Alonza Evans and Sara Alvesta (Jones) Adcock; m. Byron Benjamin Webb, Oct. 12, 1947 (dec. Jan. 1975); children—Martha Ellen, Alan James, Deana Olleen; m. 2d, Walton Stanley Allen, Mar. 11, 1976. Student George Washington U., 1942-44. Pvt. tchr., Chickasha, Okla., 1969-74; instr. art U. Sci. and Arts Okla., Chickasha, 1974-75; owner, dir. The Studio Gallery, Chickasha, 1979—. One woman shows: Gilcrease Hills Art Gallery, Tulsa, 1973, 74, First Fed. Bank, Green Valley, Ariz., 1983, Pima Club, Green Valley, 1985; group shows include: Internat. Miniature Art Exhibit, Clearwater, Fla., 1976, Santa Cruz Valley Art Assn. Show, Tubac, Ariz., 1985. Recipient 1st place watercolor Anadarko Art Club, 1972; 1st place pastel Chickasha Art Guild, 1973; 1st place watercolor Lawton-Fort Sill Art League, 1978; Merit award Nat. Miniature Sch., 1976. Mem. Artists Equity Assn., Santa Rita Art League (pres. 1984-85), Santa Cruz Valley Art Assn., Arts and Crafts Club of Green Valley (v.p. 1986—). Democrat. Baptist. Club: Fortnighters (sec. 1977-78, pres. 1978-79). Avocations: gemology; lapidary; reading; traveling; sewing.

ALLEN, DAVID LEWIS, JR., journalist, photographer, public relations counsel; b. Hartsville, S.C., Nov. 1, 1954; s. David Lewis and Anna Divver (Vaughan) A.; m. Debra Kaye Wright, Sept. 12, 1982. B.A. cum laude, U. S.C., 1976, M.Mass. Communications, 1978. Reporter, photographer Darlington County Tribune, Hartsville, S.C., 1972-73; public info. specialist S.C. Land Resources Conservation Commn., Columbia, 1974-77, spl. cons., 1978; mng. editor Water and Pollution Control jour. U. S.C., Columbia, 1977-78, now chmn. edn. and membership coms., profl. advisor U. S.C. chpt. Pub. Relations Student Soc. Am. asst. dir. info. services Francis Marion Coll., Florence, S.C., 1978-79; asst. to dir. communications, assoc. editor S.C. Farmer, S.C. Farm Bur. Fedn., Columbia, 1979, 85; dir. communications, editor SCEA Emphasis, conv. coordinator S.C. Edn. Assn., Columbia, 1985—; tchr. short courses, lectr. public relations U. S.C. Mem. vol. tng. com. United Way of Midlands; past pres. Rosewood Community Council; chmn. pub. relations com. exploring div. Indian Waters council Boy Scouts Am. Recipient Info. award Am. Farm Bur. Fedn., 1980, 83, 84. Mem. Public Relations Soc. Am. (accredited; sec. S.C. chpt.), Greater U. S.C. Alumni Assn., S.C. Agrl. Council, Nat. Eagle Scout Assn. Methodist. Club: Spartanburg (S.C.) Ski. Home: 411 S Edisto Ave Columbia SC 29205 Office: 724 Knox Abbott Dr Cayce SC 29033

ALLEN, DAVID PRESTON, osteopathic physician, medical educator; b. Pearisburg, Va., Nov. 16, 1949; s. Robert Nevitt and Dorothy Ann (Sibold) A.; m. Maryann Letzo, Oct. 2, 1976; children—Charlotte, Gary, Kelly, Patrick. A.S. in Cytology, Marshall U., 1970, B.S., 1972; D.O., W.Va. Sch. Osteo. Medicine, 1978. Diplomate Nat. Bd. Examiners, Am. Osteo. Assn. Chief technologist, instr. cytotech. Cabell Huntington Hosp., W.Va., 1970-71; chief cytotechnologist Kings Daus. Hosp., Ashland, Ky., 1972-73; intern Doctors Osteo. Hosp., Erie, Pa., 1978-79; med. dir. Rainelle Med. Ctr., W.Va., 1979-80; gen. practice osteo. medicine, Rainelle, 1981—; assoc. prof. gen. practice W.Va. Sch. Osteo. Medicine, Lewisburg, 1984—. Med. dir. Western Greenbrier Ambulance Service, Rainelle, 1981; bd. dirs. Rainelle Voluntary Fire Dept., 1982, Lifeline, Lewisburg, 1984; mem. adminstrv. bd. Rainelle United Methodist Ch., 1983-84. Mem. Am. Osteo. Assn., Am. Coll. Gen. Practitioners in Osteo. Medicine and Surgery. Republican. Avocations: camping, fishing. Home: 908 Cadle Dr Rainelle WV 25962 Office: Allen Duncan & Minor PC 1102 Main St Rainelle WV 25962

ALLEN, DONALD LAVERN, automotive aftermarket company manager; b. Baxter Springs, Kans., Mar. 1, 1929; s. W. Tom and Helen Maleta (Parker) A.; m. Helen June Carter, June 26, 1954; children—Debra Ann, Kelli Sue. A.S. in Computer Sci., Mo. So. State Coll., 1974, B.S. in Mgmt. Tech., 1976. With materials mgmt. and inventory control dept. W.R. Grace & Co., Joplin, Mo., 1953-76, mgr. logistics control, Memphis, 1976-82, materials mgr. automotive jobbers distbrs., 1982—. Served with U.S. Army, 1950-53; Korea. Republican. Club: Colonial Country (Memphis). Lodge: Masons. Home: 6840 Aspenhill Dr Memphis TN 38134 Office: 263 Gayoso Ave Memphis TN 38103

ALLEN, EILEEN MARIE, science and computers educator; b. Corpus Christi, Tex., Oct. 9, 1946; d. William Lewis and Alice Estell (Farley) Dreyer; m. Jerry Don Allen, Aug. 7, 1966; children—Brian, Leah, Dawn. B.S. in Edn., Henderson State U., 1972, M.S. in Edn., 1975. Cert. secondary tchr. Neighborhood youth corps counselor OEO, Benton, Ark., summer 1972; tchr. Bismarck Pub. Schs. (Ark.), 1972—; cheerleader sponsor Bismarck High Sch., 1972-83, golf coach, 1983; instr. nuclear radiation instruments, 1983—. Com. mem. Ecology and Pollution Control for Edn., Little Rock, 1983; radiol. def. officer Office Emergency Service, Malvern, Ark., 1983—; mem. jr. bd. Conservation Dist. of Malvern, 1983-84; mem. Bismarck Fire Dept.; active Mothers Against Drunk Driving, Bismarck, 1983-84. Mem. NEA, Ark. Edn. Assn. (sect. instrn. and profl. devel.), Bismarck Edn. Assn. (pres. 1980-81, 83-84). Democrat. Methodist. Home: Route 1 Box 158 Bismarck AR 71929 Office: Bismarck Pub Schs Route 1 Bismarck AR 71929

ALLEN, ELMA LEITCH, educator, nutritional counselor; b. Raleigh, N.C., Nov. 20, 1948; d. John Campbell and Susan Letitia (Ashby) Leitch; m. James Michael Rawlings, Jan. 17, 1970 (dec. 1976); m. Charles William Allen, Jan. 22, 1977; children—John Gordon, Scott Edward. Student Oberlin Coll., 1966-68; B.A. in English Lit., Emory U., 1970; M.Edn. in Spl. Edn., U. Va., 1973; cert. in learning disabilities Va. Commonwealth U., 1976; postgrad. George Mason U., 1984-85. Cert. tchr., Va. Cottage program attendant Ga. Tng. Ctr., Chamblee, 1972; dir., tchr. custodian tng. program U. Va., Charlottesville, 1972-73; asst. exec. dir. Richmond Area Assn. for Retarded Children, Va., 1974-76; tchr. sch. systems, Albemarle County, Chesterfield County and Augusta County, Va., 1973, 76-77; diet counselor Diet Ctr., Inc., Tysons Corner, Va., 1983—; learning disabilities specialist Fairfax County Pub. Schs., Reston, Va., 1985; pvt. learning disabilities specialist, Reston, 1985—. Author poetry. Fellow Curry Meml. Sch. Edn. U. Va., 1972-73. Mem. NOW, AAUW (edn. area rep., newsletter editor, community rep.), YWCA, Freelance Cons. Assn., Reston Garden Club (chmn. publicity 1983-84, membership chmn. 1984-85, chmn. spl. events 1985—). Presbyterian. Club: Quota (Richmond). Avocations: needlework, aerobic dancing, reading.

ALLEN, FRANK ANTHONY, hospital administrator; b. St. Augustine, Fla., Aug. 4, 1953; s. Fredric Anthony and Ellen Toni (Sarris) A.; m. Patricia Michele Schneider, Feb. 28, 1981; children—Elizabeth Michele, Fredric Anthony. B.S., U. No. Fla., 1978, M.S., 1979. Adminstr. Union Gen. Hosp., Lake Butler, Fla., 1980, Holmes County Hosp., Bonifay, Fla., 1982-83; asst. adminstr. Beaches Hosp., Jacksonville Beach, Fla., 1980-81, Pembroke Pines Gen. Hosp., Fla., 1981-82; exec. dir. Heard Community Hosp., Franklin, Ga., 1983—; mem. council govt. relations Ga. Hosp. Assn., Atlanta, 1983—; bd. dirs. Fedn. Ga. Hosps., Atlanta, 1984—. Mem. Franklin Jaycees. Democrat. Greek Orthodox. Lodge: Lions. Avocations: golf; tennis; sailing. Home: 177 Glover Circle Newnan GA 32063 Office: Heard Community Hosp PO Box 218 Franklin GA 30217

ALLEN, FRED EDWIN, mailing list consultant; b. Mt. Pleasant, Tex., May 12, 1928; s. Claud E. and Lillie (Brownlee) A.; B.S., East Tex. U., 1949; m. Mildred Craghead, Mar. 19, 1955; 1 child, Linda. Nat. sales mgr. Royal Typewriter Co., N.Y.C., 1954-62; sales mgr. Bus. Equipment group Litton Industries, N.Y.C., 1962-66; founder, pres. List Mgmt., Inc. (div. Fairfield Communities Land Co. 1971). Rye, N.Y., 1966-73; founder, pres. Fred E. Allen, Inc., Mt. Pleasant, 1973—, now chmn. bd.; chmn. bd. Listfinder Corp., Am. Nat. Bank (all Mt. Pleasant). Vice chmn. bd. Titus County Meml. Hosp.; vice chmn. bd. dirs. East Tex. State U.; bd. dirs. Scottish Rite Found. Tex. Served with U.S. Army, 1952-54. Named Disting. Alumni East Tex. State U., 1985. Mem. Mailing List Industry Assn. (charter pres. 1970-72), Mailing List Mgrs. and Compilers Assn., Direct Mail Mktg. Assn., Tex. (dir.), East Tex. (pres.) Angus assns. Democrat. Methodist. Home: Spring Lake Estates Mount Pleasant TX 75455 Office: PO Box 1595 Mount Pleasant TX 75455

ALLEN, HERBERT, steel works exec.; b. Ratcliff, Tex., May 2, 1907; s. Jasper and Leona (Matthews) A.; B.S. in Mech. Engring., Rice Inst., 1929; m. Helen Daniels, Aug. 28, 1937; children—David Daniels (dec.), Anne (Mrs. Jonathan Taft Symonds), Michael Herbert. Engaged in miscellaneous research, 1929-31; chief engr. Abercrombie Pump Co., Houston, 1931-35; chief engr. Cameron Iron Works, Inc., 1935-41, v.p. engring. and mfg., 1942-50, v.p., gen. mgr., 1950-66, pres., 1966-73, chmn. bd., 1973-77, also dir.; dir. Tex. Commerce Bank. Bd. dirs. Houston Symphony Soc.; trustee emeritus William Marsh Rice U. Named Engr. of Year, San Jacinto chpt. Tex. Soc. Profl. Engrs.; Inventor of Yr., Houston Patent Atty. Assn., 1977; recipient Outstanding Engr. of Yr. award Rice U. Engring. Alumni, 1975, gold medal for distinguished service Assn. Rice U. Alumni, 1975; named to Nat. Acad. Engring., 1979. Registered profl. engr., Tex. Mem. ASME (hon. mem.), AIME, Am. Petroleum Inst., Houston Philos. Soc., Tex. Soc. Profl. Engrs., Houston Engring. and Sci. Soc., Newcomen Soc. N. Am., Tau Beta Pi. Episcopalian. Clubs: Ramada, River Oaks Country; Metropolitan (N.Y.C.); Petroleum, Houston, Bayou. Patentee in field. Home: 3207 Groveland Ln Houston TX 77019 Office: PO Box 1212 Houston TX 77251

ALLEN, HUGHIE J(ENNINGS), educational administrator, personnel services executive; b. Center, Tex., June 22, 1939; s. Willie Leroy Allen and Blanche Kathleen (Pilot) McClelland; m. Doris Fowler, Jan. 9, 1971; children—Claudia Raquel, Vincent Felipe. B.A. in Music, Tex. Coll., 1961; M.A. in Music, Stephen F. Austin U., 1970. Cert. tchr. all level music, elem., driver's edn., adminstr. Music tchr. Diboll Ind. Sch. Dist. (Tex.), 1961-66; elem. tchr. Lufkin Ind. Sch. Dist. (Tex.), 1966-74; asst. prin. West Orange-Cove Consol. Ind. Sch. Dist., Orange, Tex., 1974-80, elem. prin., 1980-83, dir. pupil/personnel services, 1983—. Bd. dirs. Job Services Employment Com., Orange, 1983; bd. dirs. United Fund, Orange, 1980-83, Lutcher Theatre for Performing Arts Adv. Bd., 1980-83; mem. adv. bd. YMCA, 1983; v.p. Orange County Tchrs. Credit Union Bd., 1983-84. Mem. Tex. Elem. Prin./Suprs. Assn. (lfe, coms.), Tex. Assn. Sch./Personnel Adminstrs., Assn. for Supervision and Curriculum Devel., PTA (life, hon., premier prin. 1982), Kappa Alpha Psi. Phi Delta Kappa. Democrat. Methodist. Club: Kiwanis. Office: West Orange-Cove Consol Ind Sch Dist PO Box 1107 Orange TX 77630

ALLEN, HUNTER SMITH, JR., lawyer; b. Sheffield, Ala., Mar. 10, 1946; s. Hunter Smith and Mary Ellen (Guthrie) A.; m. Sandra Fraley Shuford, Apr. 26, 1980. B.S., U. S.C., 1967, J.D., 1970. Bar: Ga. 1970, S.C. 1971, U.S. Dist. Ct. (no. dist.) Ga. 1970, U.S. Ct. Appeals (5th cir.) 1970, U.S. Ct. Appeals (11th cir.) 1982. Assoc. Swift, Currie, McGhee & Hiers, Atlanta, 1970-72; mem. Thomas Marvin Smith Jr., P.C., 1972-79; ptnr. Doster, Allen, King & Young, 1979—. Served with N.G., 1967-71. Mem. ABA, Ga. Bar Assn., Atlanta Bar Assn., Def. Research Inst., Ga. Assn. Hosp. Attys., Ga. Def. Lawyers Assn., Am. Soc. Law Medicine. Republican. Presbyterian. Clubs: Ansley Golf, Lawyers. Office: Doster Allen & King 230 Peachtree St NW Suite 2222 Atlanta GA 30303

ALLEN, JAMES HARRILL, emeritus ophthalmology educator, editor; b. Chattanooga, Jan. 31, 1906; s. George Henry and Mary Evelyn (Harrill) A.; m. Ruth Collin Sanford, Aug. 17, 1934; children—Mary Helen, George Sanford, John Robert. A.B., U. Tenn., 1926; M.S., U. Mich., 1930; M.S., U. Iowa, 1938. Diplomate Am. Bd. Ophthalmology. Intern, then resident U. Iowa Hosps., Iowa City, 1930-34; with U. Iowa, 1936-50, assoc. prof. ophthalmology, 1945-46, prof., 1946-50; prof. ophthalmology, Tulane U., 1950-71, chmn. dept., 1953-67, assoc. dean, med. dir. Tulane clinics, 1967-71, clin. prof. ophthalmology, 1971-76, prof. emeritus, 1976—; cons. in field; sr. surgeon Eye, Ear, Nose and Throat Hosp., 1950-51, Charity Hosp. New Orleans, 1950-71; chief eye service VA Hosp., 1971-76. Editor Jour. Survey Ophthalmology, 1962-68, cons. editor, 1968—; Jour. The Pen, 1977—. Mem. editorial adv. bd. Audio Digest in Ophthalmology, 1963-67, Annals of Ophthalmology, 1969—. Treas., Iowa Found. Advancement of Scis. Ophthalmology, 1946-50; chmn. Lighthouse for the Blind, New Orleans, 1971-81; bd. dirs. Gulf States Eye Surgery Found., 1950-60, So. Eye Bank, 1950-67, Info. Council of Americas, 1960—, Lighthouse for the Blind, 1962—. Served to lt. col. USAF, 1942-46. Recipient Beverly Meyers Nelson Achievement award, 1958. Mem. New Orleans Acad. Ophthalmology (pres. 1951-52), New Orleans Grad. Med. Assembly, New Orleans Neurol. Soc., Orleans Parish Med. Soc., La. State Med. Soc. (chmn. eye sect. 1961), La. Eye, Ear, Nose and Throat Soc., La.-Miss. Otolaryngological-ophthal. Soc. (pres. 1974-75), La. Ophthalmology Assn. (sec.-treas. 1975—), La. Physicians Guild, N.Y. Acad. Scis., So. Med. Assn., AMA (Gold medal 1970), Am. Acad. Ophthalmology and Otolaryngology (III v.p. 1960), Am. Ophthal. Soc., Am. Assn. Ophthalmology (ho. of dels. 1966-70, trustee 1970-76), Am. Soc. Microbiology, AAAS, Am. Physicians Guild, Aerospace Med. Assn., Assn. Mil. Surgeons, Assn. Research in Ophthalmology (chmn. 1960), Am. Assn. Physicians and Surgeons, Soc. Contemporary Ophthalmology (bd. dirs. 1969—; Gold medal 1973), Contact Lens Assn. Ophthalmologists (pres. 1972), Verhoeff Soc., Pan Am. Assn. Ophthalmology (asst. sec. 1952-74), Pan Am. Ophthal. Found. (pres. 1966-74), European Contact Lens Assn. Ophthalmologists, World Med. Assn., Internat. Contact Lens Assn. Opthalmologists (mem. exec. com. 1966-74) Internat. Council Ophthalmology, Physicians Edn. Network (chmn. 1977—), La. State Hi Twelve Assn. (pres. 1984-85), Gamma Rho, Theta Kappa Psi, Sigma Xi. Episcopalian. Clubs: Paul Morphy Chess, New Orleans Athletic, Hi Twelve, Pendennis, City New Orleans. Lodges: Masons, Shriners, Elks, Rotary. Home: 9104 Quince St New Orleans LA 70118

ALLEN, JAMES RICHARD, dentist; b. Louisville; s. John Matterson and Martha Kyle (Hendricks) A.; m. Harriet Gleen McCullough, Apr. 17, 1965; children—Richard Sean, Kristin Kyle. B.A., U. Louisville, 1961, D.M.D., 1965. Practice dentistry, Louisville, 1967—; chief dental services Kosair Hosp., Louisville, 1974-81; clin. instr. prosthodontics U. Louisville Dental Sch., 1974-80; founder, chief adminstr. Dentistry for the Handicapped, Louisville, 1977-82. Mayor, Indian Hills, Ky., 1980—; elder Presbyterian Ch. Served to capt. USNR, 1961—. Fellow Acad. Gen. Dentistry; mem. ADA, Louisville Dental Soc. (chmn. peer rev. 1981), Ky. Dental Assn. (state peer rev. 1982). Democrat. Home: 5403 Apache Rd Louisville KY 40207 Office: 2500 Hermitage Way Plantation Med Ctr Louisville KY 40222

ALLEN, JAMES RICKY, banker; b. Tallahassee, Ala., Mar. 17, 1952; s. James Henry and Evelyn Ruth A.; m. Laura Johnson, June 15, 1974. B.A., Auburn U., 1976. Office mgr. SunAmerica Corp. subs. Chem. Bank of N.Y., Columbus, Ga., 1976-77; br. mgr. Central Bank of the South, Auburn, Ala., 1977-84; asst. v.p. Farmers Nat. Bank, 1984—; instr. East Ala. chpt. Am. Inst. Banking. Bd. dirs. United Way Auburn, 1982—. Mem. Am. Inst. Banking. Lodges: Elks. (treas.) (Auburn-Opelika), Kiwanis. Home: PO Box 693 Auburn AL 36830 Office: 2085 E University Dr Auburn AL 36830

ALLEN, JANET SUE, university administrator; b. Fulton, Ky., Apr. 6, 1938; d. James Leonard and LaNette (Nelson) A. B.A., Murray State U., 1960, M.A., 1965; postgrad. U. Louisville, 1960-62. Tchr. biology Fulton City Schs. and Louisville Pub. Schs., 1962-67; buyer U. Louisville, 1967-80; mgr. purchasing Univ. Hosp. Louisville, 1980-82; dir. materials mgmt. Vanderbilt U., Nashville, 1982—. Vice pres. Middle Tenn. Regional Minority Purchasing Council, 1983—. Mem. Nat. Assn. Purchasing Mgmt., Nat. Assn. Ednl. Buyers. Democrat. Methodist. Home: 5244 Edmondson Pike Apt 124 Nashville TN 37211 Office: PO Box 7000 Sta B Nashville TN 37235

ALLEN, JEANNE SUITOR, real estate agy. exec.; b. Perryton, Tex., Oct. 23, 1934; d. Lonnie and Anna M. Suitor; student Tex. Tech U., 1955; m. Norman C. Allen, June 8, 1952; children—Cynthia, Lex. Asst. mgr. Neiman Marcus, 1957-58; asst. to pres. Sanger Harris, 1958-63; partner Allen Zarcaro Realty, Houston, 1978—, broker and v.p.; now pres. Allen Realty Assocs. Treas., Freeman Library Bd., 1967-72; mem. vestry St. Christopher Episcopal Ch.; chmn. United Way, Tex. Gulf Coast; bd. dirs. Coll. of Mainland real estate dept. Mem. Houston Bd. Realtors, Pasadena Bd. Realtors, Women's Council Realtors, Clear Lake C. of C., Houston Livestock Com. (life), Bay Civic Arts Mus. Home: 306 Crestwood St Seabrook TX 77586 Office: Allen Realty Assocs 1199 NASA One Houston TX 77058

ALLEN, JOANN LONG, real estate investment co. exec., artist; b. Laurens County, S.C., Nov. 25, 1932; d. Julius Vernon and Ruby Evelyn (Boland) Long; student Palmar Coll., 1964; B.A., Jacksonville U., 1970, M.A. in Math., 1974; m. Walter Gregory Allen, Jr., Oct. 12, 1952; 1 dau., Vivian JoAnn. With Colonial Properties, Inc., Jacksonville, Fla., 1965—, dir., 1970—, sec., 1970-76, sec., treas., 1976-79, v.p., 1979-85; bus. mgr. Allen Eye Clinic, 1985; group shows include: St. Augustine Art Assn., 1979—, Artists' Gallery, 1978—, Jacksonville U., 1980. Pres. Artists' Gallery, 1980; bd. dirs. Jr. Woman's Club Jacksonville, 1958-60, Garden Club Jacksonville, 1958, Duval County Hosp. Aux., 1960-61, Duval County Council Camp Fire Girls, 1973-75, Southside Women's Club, 1973-74, Empire Point Com. Council, 1976; mem. Mayor's Adv. Com. on Status of Women, 1978-79; art show judge Prudential Ins. Co., Jacksonville, 1981. Recipient various awards and hon. mentions for paintings and drawings. Mem. Jacksonville Symphony Guild, Jacksonville Art Mus., Arts Assembly, Friends of Fine Arts, Friends Jacksonville U. Library, Jacksonville U. Alumni Assn., St. Augustine Art Assn., Art League Jacksonville, Jacksonville Watercolor Soc. (1st v.p. 1985, chmn. ann. show 1985), Prevent Blindness Soc. Republican. Episcopalian. Clubs: Ponte Vedra, River. Home: 3739 Duval Dr Jacksonville Beach FL 32250 Office: 3116 Atlantic Blvd Jacksonville FL 32207

ALLEN, JOHN THOMAS, JR., lawyer; b. St. Petersburg, Fla., Aug. 23, 1935; s. John Thomas and Mary Lita (Shields) A.; m. Joyce Ann Lindsay, June 15, 1958 (div. 1985); children—John Thomas, III, Linda Joyce, Catherine Lee. B.S. in Bus. Adminstrn. with honors, U. Fla., 1958; J.D., Stetson U., 1961. Bar: Fla. 1961, U.S. Dist. Ct. (mid. dist.) Fla. 1962, U.S. Ct. Appeals (5th cir.) 1963, U.S. Supreme Ct. 1970. Assoc. Mann, Harrison, Mann & Rowe and successor Greene, Mann, Row, Stanton, Mastry & Burton, St. Petersburg, 1961-67, ptnr., 1967-74; sole practice, St. Petersburg, 1974; counsel Pinellas County Legis. Del., 1974; counsel for Pinellas County as spl. counsel on water matters, 1975—. Mem. Com. of 100, St. Petersburg, 1975—. Mem. ABA, Assn. Trial Lawyers Am., Acad. Fla. Trial Lawyers, Fla. Bar Assn., St. Petersburg Bar Assn., St. Petersburg C. of C., Beta Gamma Sigma. Democrat. Methodist. Lodge: Lions. Office: 4508 Central Ave Saint Petersburg FL 33711

ALLEN, JOHNNY MAC, journalist, communications educator; b. Burlington, Colo., Aug. 25, 1937; B.S., Central State U., Okla., 1978; M.S. in Journalism, U. Okla., 1979; Ed.D. in Higher Edn., Okla. State U., 1984; m. Mary Hughanne Maxwell, Feb. 15, 1974; children—Ammy Marc, Nicole Juliana. Program dir. Sta. KLOE-TV, Goodland, Kans., 1962-67, 68; public service dir. Sta. KBAT, San Antonio, 1967-68; program dir. Sta. KKAN, Phillipsburg, Kans., 1968; announcer, asst. prodn. dir. Sta. KTOK, Oklahoma City, 1969-71; music dir. Sta. KLEC, Oklahoma City, 1972-73; prodn., news dir. Sta. also Oklahoma City, 1973-77; chief announcer Sta. KWTV-TV, Oklahoma City, 1974—; instr. journalism U. Okla., Norman, 1979—, news mgr. Sta. KGOU-FM, 1979—; guest lectr. various civic groups, 1968—; contbg. photographer various publs. Rose State Coll., 1980-83, Oklahoma City Vocat. Tech. Dist., 1984—. Mem. subcom. Midwest City Tree Bd., 1981-82, co-chmn. Public Image Com., 1982-83; mem. govtl. affairs com., Del City, 1981-82. Served with U.S. Army, 1959-61. Recipient Bronze Derrick spl. achievement award Okla. chpt. Public Relations Soc. Am., 1980; Spl. Recognition award Alpha Epsilon Rho and Sta. KGOU, U. Okla., 1980. Mem. Ednl. Press Assn., Public Relations Soc. Am., Community Coll. Journalism Assn., Okla. Coll. Public Relations Assn., AAUP, Okla. Higher Edn. Alumni Assn. (dir. 1980—), Midwest City C. of C. (image com. 1981-82), Kappa Tau Alpha, Phi Delta Kappa (spl. achievement award U. Okla. chpt. 1980), Sigma Delta Chi. Author: The Aging Professor: The Graying of America, 1979; Technology and Communication, 1981; The Introduction of Telecourses, 1981; Marketing Higher Education: A Systems Analysis of One Two-Year School; Also weekly column for Del City News. Office: 6420 SE 15th St Midwest City OK 73110

ALLEN, LEE NORCROSS, school administrator, history educator; b. Shawmut, Ala., Apr. 16, 1926; s. Leland Norcross and Dorothy Herbert (Whitaker) A.; m. Catherine Ann Bryant, Aug. 24, 1963; children—Leland, Leslie. B.S., Auburn U., 1948, M.S., 1949; Ph.D. in History, U. Pa., 1955. From instr. to prof. Eastern Bapt. Coll., St. Davids, Pa., 1952-61; prof. history Samford U., Birmingham, Ala., 1961—, dean Howard Coll. Arts and Scis., 1975—. Active mem. Selective Service Draft Bd., 1982—; founder, exec. dir. Ala. Acad. Disting. Authors, 1982—. Served with U.S. Army, 1944-46. Recipient Citation of Merit, Am. Assn. State and Local History, 1970. Mem. Am. Hist. Assn., So. Hist. Assn., So. Bapt. Hist. Soc. Baptist. Lodge: Rotary (pres. 1969-70). Author: Sesquicentennial History...1819-1969, 1969; The First 150 Years: First Baptist Church, Montgomery, Ala.; 1829-1979, 1979; Born For Missions...1833-1983, 1984; Rings of Cooperation, 1984; From Many Streams; Meadow Brook Baptist Church, 1981-1985, 1985; Woodlawn Bapt. Ch., 1986. Home: 24 Pine Crest Rd Birmingham AL 35223 Office: Samford U Birmingham AL 35229

ALLEN, LEONARD J(ACKSON), educational administrator; b. Holden, W.Va., Sept. 19, 1950; s. Leonard and Ruth (Stepson) A. B.A., Marshall U., 1972, M.A., 1973; postgrad. W.Va. Coll. Grad. Studies, 1973-82. Cert. in elem.

edn., ednl. adminstrn., spl. edn., W.Va. Tchr. Kanawha County Schs., W.Va., 1972-75, curriculum specialist, 1975-79, elem. prin., 1979-84, dir. instrnl. services, 1984—; adj. asst. prof. W.Va. Coll. Grad. Studies, Institute, 1975—; cons. in field, 1975—; dir., cons. summer programs, 1978-79. Recipient Inst. for Leadership Effectiveness award Kanawha County Schs., 1983, Exemplary Sch. award W.Va. Dept. Edn., 1984. Mem. Assn. Supervision and Curriculum Devel., Nat. Assn. Elem. Sch. Prins., Am. Assn. Sch. Adminstrs., Phi Delta Kappa, Kappa Delta Pi. Democrat. Christian Scientist. Home: 802 Nease Dr Charleston WV 25312 Office: Kanawha County Schs 200 Elizabeth St Charleston WV 25311

ALLEN, LEWIS, JR., oil and gas operator, rancher; b. Hallettsville, Tex., Oct. 16, 1925; s. Lewis and Elma (Appelt) A.; B.A., U. Tex., 1949. Landman Deep Rock Oil Co., Tex. and La., 1950-54; ind. trader oil and gas properties, 1954—; rancher, South Central Tex., 1954—. Mem. Am. Assn. Petroleum Landmen, Tex. Ind. Producers and Royalty Owners Assn. (past dir., mem. state petroleum issues com.), Tex. SW cattle raisers assns., Ind. Cattlemen's Assn., Chi Phi. Methodist. Club: Petroleum (Houston). Home: 904 E 3d Hallettsville TX 77964 Office: PO Box 124 Hallettsville TX 77964

ALLEN, MATTHEW ROBERT, realtor; b. Chgo., Jan. 27, 1942; s. Matthew Paul and Frieda Edna (Selke) Fiertl; m. Diane Ross, June 30, 1961 (div. 1965). B.A., No. Ill. U., 1967; M.A., San Francisco State Coll., 1969. Cert. tchr. specializing in jr. coll. edn., Calif. Collector Comml. Discount Corp., Chgo., 1963-65; banker Exchange Nat. Bank, Chgo., 1965-67; lectr. in English, San Francisco State U., 1967-69; admissions officer, 1973-78; broker, salesman Century 21 InMan Realty Co., Ocala, Fla., 1980—. Democrat. Christian Scientist. Avocations: piano; swimming. Home: PO Box 562 Citrus Springs FL 32630 Office: Century 21 InMan Realty Co 2020 E Silver Springs Blvd Ocala FL 32670

ALLEN, PAMELA, pharmacist; b. Chillicothe, Ohio, July 17, 1947; d. Gilbert and Julia Ann (Kellhofer) A. B.S., Ohio State U., 1970. Registered pharmacist, Ohio, N.C. Staff pharmacist Grant Hosp., Columbus, Ohio, 1970-73, supr., 1973-78; dir. pharmacy Mount Carmel Hosp., Columbus, 1978-79; supr. Grant Hosp., Columbus, 1979-83; asst. dir. pharmacy Gaston Meml. Hosp., Gastonia, N.C., 1983—. Mem. Am. Soc. Hosp. Pharmacists, Ohio Soc. Hosp. Pharmacists, N.C. Soc. Hosp. Pharmacists. Vice pres. bd. dirs. Seal of Ohio Girl Scouts, 1975-78. Avocations: reading; boating; racquetball.

ALLEN, PETER MARTIN, geology educator; b. Chgo., Sept. 18, 1947; s. Simon and Marian (McCarthy) A.; m. Margaret Grinnan, May 19, 1979; children—Sarah, Maggie. B.A., Denison U., 1970; M.S., Baylor U., 1972; Ph.D., Southern Meth. U., 1977. Environmental planner, geologist Dept. Urban Planning, Dallas, 1972-78; asst. prof. geology Baylor U., Waco, Tex., 1978—; cons. in field. Contbr. numerous articles to profl. jours. Bd. dirs. Waco Symphony Orchestra, 1984-85. Recipient Biennial Urban Design award Dept. Housing and Urban Devel., 1975; Planning award Am. Inst. Planners, 1976. Fellow Inst. Study Earth and Man; mem. Geol. Soc. Am., Am. Planning Assn. Am. Water Resource Assn., Assn. Engring. Geologists (past chmn. Tex. sect.) Episcopalian. Club: Ridgewood Country (Waco). Home: 2611 Lake Air St Waco TX 76710 Office: Baylor U Dept Geology Waco TX 76798

ALLEN, PHILIP JAMES, clergyman; b. Termini, Palermo, Italy; Apr. 14, 1914; came to U.S., 1922, naturalized, 1927; s. Samuel and Santa (Grange) Alaimo; m. Dorothy Margaret Wiley, June 15, 1940; children—Kenneth Ray, Keith Roy. A.B., Ohio No. U., 1937; M.A., Northwestern U., 1940; M.Div., Garrett-Evangelical Theol. Sem., 1940; Ph.D., Am. U., 1954. Pastor Meth. Ch., Camden, Ohio, 1941-43; asst. prof. sociology U. Chattanooga, 1946-47; prof., chmn. dept. sociology Mary Washington Coll., U. Va., Fredericksburg, 1947-79; mem. State Bd. Welfare and Insts., 1971-74; sec. population adv. bd. U.S. Bur. Census, Washington, 1971-74. Editor: Pitirim Sorokin in Review, 1963; editor Am. Sociol. Forum, 1963—; contbr. articles to profl. jours. Pres. Ferry Farm Civic Assn., Stafford County, Va., 1958-59, Va. Council Family Relations, 1963-64. Served to capt. USAAF, 1943-46, ETO. Fellow Am. Sociol. Soc.; mem. Population Assn. Am., Nat. Council on Family Relations, AAAS, So. Sociol. Soc. Republican. Methodist. Republican. Home: 6529 Waterford Circle Sarasota FL 33583

ALLEN, RAY MAXWELL, college dean, educator; b. Memphis, Dec. 16, 1922; s. Harry Davis and Louise (Martin) A.; m. Julia Wellford, Apr. 3, 1948; children—Julia, Ray, Katherine. B.A., Rhodes Coll., 1944; B.D., Duke U., 1947, Ph.D., 1953. Dir. Memphis State U. Wesley Found., 1947-49; dir. Duke U. Meth. Student Movement, Durham, N.C., 1950-52; asst. prof. Wofford Coll., Spartanburg, S.C., 1953-56; prof. Lambuth Coll., Jackson, Tenn., 1956-63; dean, prof. Rhodes Coll., Memphis, 1963—. Office: Rhodes Coll 2000 N Parkway Memphis TN 38112

ALLEN, ROBERT BEN, state senator; b. Little Rock, June 9, 1925; s. George Mason and Josephine A. A.; m. Elois Kreth; children—Ben, David Kreth, Douglas Hamilton. Student Little Rock Jr. Coll., 1946, U. Ark., 1949. Mem. Ark. Ho. of Reps., 1959-65; mem. Ark. Senate, 1966—, pres. pro tem, chmn. revenue and taxation com., mem. rules com.; mem. Ark. legis. council; former asst. pros. atty. and asst. atty. gen.; former instr. Ark. Law Sch.; former instr. med. jurisprudence and pharm. jurisprudence U. Ark. Med. and Pharmacy Schs. Served with USN, World War II. Mem. ABA, Ark. Bar Assn., Kappa Alpha, Alpha Omicron. Democrat. Methodist. Office: Ark Senate State Capitol Little Rock AR 72201*

ALLEN, ROBERT RAY, research chemist, consultant; b. Potwin, Kans., Sept. 2, 1920; s. Jesse William and Blanche Ann (Corn) A.; m. Barbara Ruth Condell, Dec. 17, 1944; children—Judith, John, Susan, Jane, Sharon. B.S., Kans. State U., 1947, M.S., 1948, Ph.D., 1950. Analytical chemist Eagle Picher Lead Co., Joplin, Mo., 1940-42; research chemist Armour & Co., Chgo., 1950-56; prin. scientist Anderson Clayton Foods, Dallas, 1956-83; chemistry cons., McKinney, Tex., 1983—; vis. expert, Taiwan, 1984-85. Served to lt. USNR, 1942-46. Mem. Am. Oil Chemists Soc. (dir. 1967-69, v.p. 1969-70, pres. 1970-71; Bailey award 1983, Supelco award 1986), Phi Kappa Phi. Republican. Methodist. Patentee in field.

ALLEN, ROGER B., psychologist, educational consultant; b. Dallas, Mar. 23, 1945; s. Lamar and Lennie (Bownds) A.; m. Katherine L. Dossey, Nov. 30, 1969; 1 child, Lane McLendon. B.S., North Tex. State U., 1966; M.S., Okla. State U., 1968; Ph.D., Ariz. State U., 1977. Lic. psychologist, Tex. VISTA vol., W.Va., 1968-70; group counselor Salesmanship Boys Camp, Hawkins, Tex., 1970-71; rehab. counselor Tex. State Commn. of the Blind, Tyler, Tex., 1971-74; psychology intern VA and Good Samaritan Hosps., Phoenix, 1974-76; sch. counselor Williams AFB Sch., Chandler, Ariz., 1976; pvt. practice psychology, Tyler, 1977—; adj. instr. dept. psychology U. Tex.-Tyler, 1978—. Author: Common Sense Discipline: What to Say and Do When Children Misbehave, 1984. Charter sponsor Parents Anonymous, Tyler, 1982. Mem. Am. Psychol. Assn., Am. Assn. Counseling and Devel., Am. Mental Health Counselors Assn., East Tex. Psychol. Assn. Avocations: canoeing; woodworking. Home: 3331 Cameron Tyler TX 75701 Office: PO Box 130275 Tyler TX 75713

ALLEN, RONALD W., airline company executive; b. 1941. B.S., Ga. Inst. Tech. With Delta Airlines, Inc., Atlanta, 1963—, methods analyst, 1963-64, adminstrv. asst. personnel dept., 1964-66, dir. methods of tng., 1966-67, asst. v.p. adminstrn., 1967-69, v.p., 1969-70, sr. v.p. personnel, 1970-79, sr. v.p. personnel and adminstrn., 1979-83, pres., chief operating officer, 1983—, also dir. Office: Delta Airlines Inc Hartsfield Atlanta Internat Airport Atlanta GA 30320*

ALLEN, SARAH FRANCES, contractor; b. Tampa, Fla., Sept. 2, 1943; d. Ralph Walter and Allie Rebecca (Stafford) Overman; B.A., U. South Fla.; children—William Kennon, Heather. Founder, pres. Sarah Allen Homes, Inc., 1974—. Bd. dirs. Asolo Theater. Mem. Fla. Bd. Realtors, Sarasota-Manatee Contractors Assn., Nat. Assn. Home Builders, Fla. Assn. Home Builders, Sarasota Bd. Realtors, Fla. Bd. Realtors, DAR. Republican. Episcopalian. Home and Office: 1153 Lake House Cr #118 Sarasota FL 33581

ALLEN, SHEILA ANN, nurse; b. Denver, Sept. 6, 1954; d. Daniel Ray and Dorothy Mae (Landry) A. B.S., McNeese State U., 1976. R.N., La. Staff nurse Moss Regional Hosp., Lake Charles, La., 1976-78, asst. supr., 1978—; instr. Am. Heart Assn., Lake Charles, 1979-81; instr. Emergency Med. Services, Lafayette, La., 1980-82; R.N. advisor LPN Assn., Lake Charles, 1979-81. Sponsor Lake Charles Ballet Soc., 1982—, Foster Parents Plan, Warwick, R.I., 1979—. Mem. Am. Assn. Critical Care Nurses, Am. Soc. Evening and Night Nursing Suprs. Republican. Roman Catholic. Club: Newman (1st female pres. 1973). Author, photographer: Diabetes and You, 1976. Office: Moss Regional Hosp 1000 Walters St Lake Charles LA 70605

ALLEN, WILBUR COLEMAN, lawyer; b. Victoria, Va., Apr. 30, 1925; s. George Edward and Mary Lee (Bridgforth) A.; m. Frances Brockenbrough Gayle, Sept. 16, 1950; children—Frances Gayle Allen Fitzgerald, Wilbur Coleman, Robert Clayton, Edward Lefebvre, Courtney Bridgforth. B.A., U. Va., 1947, J.D., 1950. Bar: Va. 1949, D.C. 1954, U.S. Dist. Ct. (ea. and we. dists.) Va. 1951, U.S. Ct. Appeals 1950, U.S. Supreme Ct. 1954. Ptnr. Allen, Allen, Allen & Allen, Richmond, Va., 1950-69, pres., 1969—Served as lt. (j.g.) USN, 1942-45, PTO. Sunday Sch. supt. All Saints Episcopal Ch., Richmond, 1960-65, vestryman, 1964-68, 70-74, 80-83, sr. warden, 1967-68, chmn. stewardship com., 1980-81; bd. visitors Va. Commonwealth U., 1984-85, property com., 1984-85, audit com., 1984-85. Fellow Am. Coll. Trial Lawyers; mem. ABA, Assn. Trial Lawyers Am., Am. Judicature Soc., Va. State Bar, Va. Bar Assn., Va. State Bar Council, Va. Trial Lawyers Assn. (chmn. publicity com. 1968, chmn. spl. com. on ins. 1981), N.Y. State Trial Lawyers Assn., Richmond Bar Assn. (pres. 1979, outstanding contbn. award 1981). Clubs: Country of Va., Westwood (Richmond). Lodge: Rotary (pres. 1974-75, Rotarian of Yr. 1980). Home: 2 Gaymont Rd Richmond VA 23230 Office: Allen Allen Allen & Allen 1809 Staples Mill Rd Richmond VA 23230

ALLEN, WILLIAM JOSEPH, hospital administrator, health care consultant; b. Minden, La., Dec. 16, 1930; s. Lawrence Clyde and Vivian (Martin) A.; m. Louise Robinson, June 29, 1951; children—William Joseph, Catherine Louise, Andrew Martin. B.B.A., S.E. La. U., 1956, B.Music Edn., 1951; M.S. in Hosp. Adminstrn., Northwestern U., 1959. Exec. dir. Many Clinic and Hosp., La., 1963-66, Highland Hosp., Shreveport, La., 1966-76; adminstr. Truett-Baylor U. Med. Ctr., Dallas, 1976-80; exec. dir. Titus Meml. Hosp., Mt. Pleasant, Tex., 1980-84; adminstr. Gulf Pines Hosp., Port St. Joe, Fla., 1984—; trustee La. State Hosp. Bd., Baton Rouge, 1967-72; trustee Southeastern Hosp. Conf., Atlanta, 1963-65. Vice-chmn. Area Wide Health Planning Commn., Shreveport, 1968-76. Served with Med. Service, U.S. Army, 1954-56. Named Outstanding Civil Servant, State La., 1963-64. Mem. Am. Coll. Hosp. Adminstrs. Republican. Baptist. Club: Rotary. Avocations: brass instrumental music; church music. Office: Central Tex Rehab Ctr 1801 N 18th St Waco TX 76707

ALLEN-INSIGNARES, HARRIETTE BIAS, poet, educator; b. Savannah, Ga., Oct. 24, 1943; d. Caleb Harvey and Louise (Stokes) Bias; children—Tracy Marcette Allen, Heather Lenae Allen; m. 2d, Jorge Isaac Insignares, Feb. 1, 1982; 1 son, Eric. B.A., Fisk U., 1964; M.S., U. Wis.-Whitewater; Ph.D., Vanderbilt U., 1976-80. Tchr. kindergarten, English and phys. edn. Colegio Panamericano, Bucaramanga, Colombia, 1964-65; Spanish resource cons. Chgo. Bd. Edn., 1966-68; counselor, dir. tutorial ctr., U. Wis.-Whitewater, 1970-72; asst. prof. speech, U. Tenn., Nashville, 1977-80, dir. creative writing program, 1977-79; assoc. prof. communications Tenn. State U., Nashville, 1981—. Author: Genesis, 1976; Juba's Afro-American Folk Games, 1976; Juba's Jubilee, 1976. Mem. Mayor's Bicentennial Com., 1978-80; chmn. folk arts panel Tenn. Arts Commn., 1981—; poet Gov.'s Conf. on Women, 1976. Named state poet and arts advocate State of Tenn.; Ford Found. fellow, 1971, Am. Soc. Newspaper Editors fellow, 1982-83; Wis. Leadership grantee, 1968. Mem. Speech Communication Assn., Am. Theatre Assn., Nat. Assn. for Preservation and Perpetuation of Storytelling, S.E. Conf. English in the Two-Year Coll., Alpha Kappa Alpha, Pi Kappa Delta, Theta Alpha Phi. Club: Music City Chpt. of the Links, Inc. Editor Writer's Circle Mag., 1977-78; editor Black Families of Prisoners Research Project, 1975-76. Home: 812 Inverness Ave Nashville TN 37204 Office: Tenn State U 10th and Charlotte Sts Nashville TN 37203

ALLENSWORTH, THOMAS MIMMS, JR., dentist, naval officer; b. Hopkinsville, Ky., Apr. 6, 1931; s. Thomas Mimms and Bernice Lyon (Murray) A.; m. Jean Wimpy, July 25, 1955; children—Anne Alder, Walter Stephen, Paul Thomas. B.S. in Chemistry, U. Western Ky., 1953; D.M.D., U. Louisville, 1956; cert. Naval Dental Sch., 1963. Commd. lt. (j.g.) U.S. Navy, 1956, advanced through grades to capt., 1972; staff dental officer Naval Grad. Dental Sch., Bethesda, Md., 1967-72; dental instr. Naval Dental Sch., Bethesda, 1967-72; head dental dept. Naval Security Group Activity, Edzell, Scotland, 1972-76; dir. clin. services Naval Regional Dental Ctr., Charleston, S.C., 1976-80; head dental personnel Bur. Medicine and Surgery, Washington, 1980-83; comdg. officer Naval Dental Clinic, Pensacola, Fla., 1982—; dentist Presdl. staff, Camp David, Md., 1968-72; dental res. advisor Chief Naval Opera Washington, 1980-83. Active Boy Scouts Am., 1963-76. Lay reader, vestryman Episcopal Ch., various locations, 1963-65, 67-72, 76-80. Decorated Navy Commendation medal, Meritorious Service medal. Fellow Internat. Coll. Dentists; mem. ADA, Am. Acad. Gold Foil Operators, Acad. Operative Dentistry, West Central Dental Soc. (Ky.), Panhandle Fed. Dental Study Club, Delta Sigma Delta. Democrat. Avocations: sailing; fishing; bicycling; reading. Home: Quarters 20 Naval Air Sta Pensacola FL 32508 Office: Naval Dental Clinic Naval Air Sta Pensacola FL 32508

ALLGOOD, SAM S., corporate executive; b. 1926; married. B.S., La. State U., 1951. Tchr., 1951-55; sales staff Milwhite Mud, 1955-62; v.p. Grand Marien Service Inc., 1962-68; v.p. Tidewater Marine Service Inc., 1968-78, sr. v.p., 1978-79, exec. v.p., 1979—; sr. v.p. Tidewater Inc., New Orleans, 1977, now exec. v.p. Served with USN. Office: Tidewater Inc 1440 Canal St New Orleans LA 70112*

ALLISON, CHRISTOPHER FITZSIMONS, bishop; b. Columbia, SC, Mar. 5, 1927; s. James Richard and Susan Millikin (FitzSimons) A.; m. Martha Allston Parker, June 10, 1950; children—Christopher, James, Allston, John. B.A., U. South, 1949, D.D. (hon.), 1978; M. Div., Va. Theol. Seminary, 1952; D. Philosophy, Christ Ch., Oxford U., Eng., 1956; D.D. (hon.), Va. Theol. Seminary, 1981, Episc. Theol. Seminary, Lexington, Ky., 1981. Ordained priest Episcopal Ch., 1953; asst. prof. history U. South, Sewanee, Tenn., 1956-67; prof. ch. history Va. Theol. Seminary, Alexandria, 1967-75; rector Grace Ch., N.Y.C., 1975-80; bishop Diocese S.C., Charleston, 1980—. Author: Fear, Love and Worship, 1962; The Rise of Moralism, 1967; Guilt, Anger and God, 1972. Served as tech. sgt. Inf., AUS, 1945-47; Italy. Democrat. Clubs: E.Q.B. (pres. 1965-67) (Sewanee); Century Assn. (N.Y.C.). Office: Diocese of South Carolina PO Drawer 2127 Charleston SC 29403

ALLISON, DONALD CAMPBELL, computer science educator; b. Belfast, No. Ireland, June 5, 1938, came to U.S., 1979, naturalized, 1986; s. Henry Campbell and Margaret Elizabeth (Scott) A.; m. June Ann Fleming, Aug. 29, 1964; children—David, Kathryn, Andrew. B.S., Queen's U., Belfast, 1959, Ph.D., 1962. From lectr. to sr. lectr. computer sci. Queen's U., 1967-79; assoc. prof. Va. Poly. Inst. and State U., Blackburg, 1979—, head dept. computer sci., 1980—. Author: Pascal for Fortran Programmers, 1984. Contbr. articles to profl. jours. Mem. Assn. for Computing Machinery, IEEE Computer Soc. Avocation: walking. Office: Va Poly Inst and State U Computer Sci Dept Blacksburg VA 24061

ALLISON, HARRISON CLARKE, chemist, criminal justice educator; b. West Liberty, Ky., Nov. 4, 1917; s. Asher Owen and Florence Olivia (Davis) A.; m. Amy Lee Henry, Jan. 3, 1940 (div. 1946); 1 child, James L. (dec.); m. Jessie Hudson, Dec. 16, 1947; children—Anitia Charles, Nancy Zarczynski, Elizabeth, Sue Johnson. A.S., Cumberland Coll., 1937; A.B., Georgetown Coll., 1939; M.S., U. Ala., 1950. Mem. quality control staff Sylvania Electronics Products, Lexington, 1944-45; tchr. Marion Mil. Inst., Ala., 1947-50, 53—; lt. capt. Marion Police Dept., 1963-75. Author: Personal Identification, 1973. Co-author: Handbook Crime Scene Investigation, 1982. Editor: Fundamentals of Criminal Investigation, 1976. Chmn. Perry County Republican Com., Marion, 1964. Served to capt. U.S. Army, 1941-44. Named Profl. of Yr., Marion Mil. Inst., 1983. Fellow Am. Inst. Chemists, Am. Assn. Criminology; mem. Internat. Assn. Chiefs of Police, Internat. Assn. for Identification, Ala. Peace Officers Assn. Presbyterian. Avocations: reading; camping; collecting classical recordings. Home: 701 Moore St Marion AL 36756 Office: Marion Mil Inst Marion AL 36756

ALLISON, JOHN ROBERT, business administration educator; b. Waco, Tex., Apr. 6, 1948; s. Lloyd Burton and Mary LaBertha (Fulps) A.; m. Margo Lu Armstrong, Dec. 22, 1971; children—Sarah Marie, Jill Elaine, Eric Forrest. Student Tex. A&M U., 1966-69; J.D., Baylor U., 1972. Bar: Tex. 1972. Asst. prof. bus. law U. Tex., Austin, 1972-77, assoc. prof., 1977-81, prof., 1981-83, Mary John and Ralph Spence Centennial prof. bus. adminstrn., 1983—. Author: Business Law: Tex and Cases, 1978, alt. edit., 1979, 3d edit., 1985, 3d alt. edit., 1985; The Legal Environment of Business, 1984; Fundamentals of Business Law, 1984; editor-in-chief Am. Bus. Law Jour., 1983-85, mng. editor, 1981-83, articles editor, 1979-81; Bible tchr. Bannockburn Bapt. Ch., Austin, 1980—. Mem. State Bar Tex., Am. Bus. Law Assn. (best article award 1977; Holmes-Cardozo award 1985). Democrat. Home: 8616 Cameron Loop Austin TX 78745 Office: Dept Gen Business Univ Tex Austin TX 78712

ALLISON, KATHARINE POTTER, bookshop proprietor, conference coordinator; b. Ridgeway, Pa., Mar. 9, 1931; d. Guy Victor and Janet Jackson (Brew) Potter; m. Henry Vanmeter Herold, Sept. 18, 1948 (div. 1971); children—Rebecca, Janet, Van, David (dec.), Katharine, Robert; m. Brewster Sherman Allison, Mar. 23, 1977 (div. 1985). Founder, mgr. Christian Bookstore, Charlottesville, Va., 1971-73; typist Va. Research Group, Charlottesville, 1973-74; office mgr. Monroe Calculator Co., Charlottesville, 1974-75; founder pres., mgr. Quest Bookshop, Inc., Charlottesville, 1978—; founder, dir. Quest Inst., Charlottesville, 1984—; conf. coordinator. Sec., bd. dirs. Family Services, Inc., Charlottesville, 1972-73. Republican. Avocations: sewing; gardening. Office: Quest Bookshop 619 W Main St Charlottesville VA 22901

ALLISON, MARSHALL LORETZ, lawyer; b. Lavonia, Ga., Mar. 3, 1897; s. Thomas F. and Gertrude (Bost) A.; B.S., Young Harris Coll., 1915; m. Marion W. Willbanks, Aug. 27, 1919; 1 dau., Julia Carolyn Allison Urick. Bar: Ga. 1926, U.S. Supreme Ct. 1936. Practiced in Lavonia, 1926-36, city atty., 1926-36; asst. atty. gen. Ga., Atlanta, 1937-38, 38-41, 43-45; judge No. Jud. Circuit Ga., Lavonia, 1938; law asst. to chief justice Ga. Supreme Ct., 1941-42; pvt. practice law, Atlanta, 1945-53, Lavonia, 1953-81; apptd. mem. Jud. Council Ga., 1962-64. Trustee, Young Harris Coll., 1942—. Served with F.A., U.S. Army, World War I. Mem. ABA, Ga. Bar Assn., Bar Assn. No. Jud. Circuit Ga., Am. Legion (1st comdr.). Methodist. Lodge: Lion (1st pres.). Author: Compiled Opinions of Attorney General of Georgia, 1939-41, 1941-43. Address: 425 Branan Lodge Blairsville GA 30512

ALLISON, ROBERT DEAN, clinical physiologist; b. Farmersville Station, N.Y., Feb. 29, 1932; s. Robert Raymond and Alice Mary (Owens) A.; children—Robert, Emily, Margaret. B.A. in Biology, Hartwick Coll., 1954; student N.Y. Med. Coll., 1954, Gen. Electric Sci. fellow, 1957; M.S. in Physiology and Pharmacology, Wayne State U. Coll. Medicine, 1960, Ph.D., 1962. Cert. ind. lab dir., Tex., pvt. comml. pilot. Asst. fellow Mich. Heart Assn., Detroit, 1959-62; instr. dept. anesthesiology Grace Hosp., Detroit, 1961-62; staff physiologist Lovelace Found. for Med. Edn. and Research, Albuquerque, 1962-66; asst. prof. biology, U. N.Mex., 1965-66; chief cardiovascular physiology, lab. dir. Scott and White Clinic, Temple, Tex., 1966-73; assoc. prof., spl. lectr. La. State U., New Orleans, 1970—; research physiologist VA Med. Ctr., Temple, 1973-75; cons. Clin. Pathology Lab., Grand Prairie (Tex.) Community Hosp., 1978-80; pres. Dynamic Research Enterprises, Inc., Arlington, Tex., 1973—, Dynamic Health Care Services, 1979—; dir. N. Tex., Non Invasive Cardiovascular Lab., Arlington, 1973—; adj. assoc. prof. Southwestern Med. Sch., U. Tex., Arlington, 1976—; assoc. prof. Tex. Wesleyan Coll., 1976—; instr. BrookhavenColl., Dallas, 1982—; chmn. div. basic sci. and research Parker Coll., Irving, Tex., 1983—. Bd. dirs. Tex. Heart Assn.; active Vis. Scientist Program of N.Mex. Recipient Aesculupius award Tex. Med. Assn., 1967; Disting. Achievement award Tex. Heart Assn. Fellow Am. Geriatrics Soc.; mem. Am. Heart Assn. (fellow stroke council), Am. Physiol. Soc., Internat. Soc. of Nephrology, AMA (affiliate), Sigma Xi. Author numerous research papers, contbr. articles to profl. jours. Home: 1212 S Fielder St Apt B Arlington TX 76013

ALLISON, ROBERT JAMES, JR., oil company executive; b. Evanston Ill., Jan. 29, 1939; s. Robert James and Mary Susan (Rohrer) A.; B.S., Kans U., 1960; m Carolyn Jean Grother, June 17, 1961; children—Amy Elizabeth, Ann Mary, Jane Susan With Amoco Prodn Co. Okla. La. Kans. Tex., 1960-67, engr. Amoco Internat. Oil Co., Chgo. 1968-69; chief engr. Amoco Trinidad Oil Co., Port-of-Spain, 1970-71; advisor Amoco Iran Oil, Tehran, 1972-73 v.p. ops. Anadarko Petroleum Corp., Co., Houston, 1973-75, pres. dir., chief exec officer 1976—; dir. Pan Eastern Exploration Co., Panhandle Eastern Corp. Youghiogheny and Ohio Coal Co. Mem. Am. Petroleum Inst. Ind. Petroleum Assn. Am (dir. Mid-Continent Oil and Gas Assn. Soc. Petroleum Engrs. Presbyterian. Clubs: Petroleum. Houston. Champions Golf Lochinvar Golf (dir.). Office: PO Box 1330 Houston TX 77251

ALLISON, STEPHEN HAROLD, clinical psychologist, psychology educator; b. St. Louis, Sept. 14, 1954; s. Harold Gene and Joyce Ellen (Klausen) A.; m. Anne Renee Cagle, June 16, 1978; 1 child, Melody Anne. B.S. in Psychology, Abilene Christian U., 1976; M.A. in Theology, Fuller Theol. Sem., 1980, Ph.D. in Clin. Psychology, 1982. Lic. psychologist, Tex. Supr. clin. services Region II Mental Health Ctr., Hernando, Miss., 1982-83; instr. psychology Memphis State U., 1982-83; single adult minister Ch. of Christ at White Station, Memphis, 1981-83; exec. dir. Christian Psychol. Ctr., Tulsa, 1983-84; asst. prof. psychology, dir. psychol. services Abilene Christian U., Tex., 1984—; clin. psychologist Osborn and Assocs., Abilene, 1984—; lectr. in field. Contbr. articles to profl. jours. V.W. Kelley scholar, 1976. Mem. Abilene Psychol. Assn. (pres.-elect 1984—), Tex. Psychol. Assn., Southwestern Psychol. Assn., Am. Psychol. Assn., Christian Assocs. for Psychol. Studies, Tex. Assn. Coll. and Univ. Counseling Ctr. Dirs., Blue Key, Alpha Chi. Mem. Ch. of Christ. Avocations: racketball; jogging; gardening; reading. Office: Abilene Christian U Sta Box 8048 Abilene TX 79699

ALLISON, THOMAS GEORGE, exercise physiologist; b. McKeesport, Pa., July 8, 1946; s. George William and Helen (Toth) A.; m. Christine Faye Gricus, Aug. 6, 1971 (div. 1983); children—Thomas Forest, Benjamin James; m. Melanie Jane Cassell, Mar. 9, 1985. B.A., Princeton U., 1968; M.A., U. Pitts., 1976, M.P.H., 1978, Ph.D., 1978. Instr. math. and physics Serra Cath. High Sch., McKeesport, Pa., 1969-71, Central Cath. High Sch., Pitts., 1971-74; fellow U. Pitts., 1974-78; dir. Cardiac Ctr. and Wellness Ctr., Wheeling Hosp., W.Va., 1978—; instr. W.Va. No. Community Coll., Wheeling, 1978—; cons. stress mgmt., 1982—. Contbr. articles to profl. jours. and mags. Hon. chmn. MS Fund Drive, Wheeling, 1980. Named Track Coach of Yr., Tri-State Track Coaches Assn., Pitts., 1973. Mem. Am. Coll. Sports Medicine (cert. exercise program dir.), Wheeling Heart Assn. (pres. 1984—, bd. dirs. 1978—, chmn. research com. W.Va. affiliate 1983—). Republican. Presbyterian. Clubs: Oglebay Road Runners (pres. 1981-82) (Wheeling); Human Energy Running (pres. 1975-78) (Pitts.). Home: 27 Maple Ave Wheeling WV 26003 Office: Wheeling Hosp Inc Medical Park Wheeling WV 26003

ALLMAND, JAMES RUPERT, III, hotel executive; b. Houston, June 26, 1948; s. James Rupert and Marjorie Freeman (Ozborn) A.; m. Cynthia Johnson; 1 child Savanna Marie. A.A., N.Mex. Mil. Inst., 1968; B.A., U. Ariz., 1971; postgrad. Tulane U., 1983. With sales and mktg. Sea Pines Co., Hilton Head, S.C., 1973-75, Inns of the Ams., Inc. (now Pratt Hotel Corp.), Dallas, 1975-77; pres. Diners of the South, Jackson, Miss., Charter Properties, Inc., New Orleans, 1979—, Allmand Enterprises, Inc., Jackson, 1983—; owner Radisson Walthall Hotel. Bd. dirs. Arts Alliance of Jackson, Jackson Hotel Assn. Served to capt. USAR, 1973-79. Mem. Sigma Alpha Epsilon. Republican. Roman Catholic. Office: Radisson Walthall Hotel 225 E Capitol St Jackson MS 39201

ALLMAND, LINDA F., librarian; b. Port Arthur, Tex., Jan. 31, 1937; d. Clifton James and Jewel Etoile (Smith) A. B.A., N. Tex. State U., 1960; M.A., U. Denver, 1962. Clerical asst. Gates Meml. Library, 1953-55; library asst. Houston Pub. Library, 1955-58; children's librarian Denver Pub. Library, 1960-63; children's coordinator Anaheim Pub. Library, Calif., 1963-65; br. mgr. Dallas Pub. Library, 1965-71; instr. N. Tex. State U., Denton, 1967—; chief br. services Dallas Pub. Library, 1971-81; dir. Ft. Worth Pub. Library, 1981—; instr. Dallas County Community Coll., 1981; bldg. cons. Jacksonville Pub. Library, Tex., 1976-79, Haltom City Pub. Library, 1983—, Carrollton Pub. Library, 1979-81, Hurst Pub. Library, 1977-78, Dallas Pub. Library, 1974-80. Author: 1981-2000, Ft. Worth Public Library—Facilities and Long Range Planning Study, 1982; contbr. chpts. to books, articles to profl. jours. Bd. dirs. City of Dallas Credit Union, 1973-81; com. chmn. Goals for Dallas, 1967-69; mem. Forum Ft. Worth, 1983; bd. dirs. Sr. Citizen's Centers, Inc., 1982. Pilot Club of Port Arthur scholar, 1954; Library Binding Inst. scholar, 1958; recipient Disting. Alumnus award N. Tex. State U., 1983, Leadership Ft.

Worth, 1982-83. Mem. ALA, Tex. Library Assn. (pres. 1980-81, chmn. planning com. 1982-84, pres.-elect 1985; Librarian of Yr. 1984), Tarrant Regional Librarians Assn., Am. Mgmt. Assn., Dallas County Librarians Assn. (pres. 1968-69), Freedom to Read Found. Club: Zonta (bd. dirs. 1981—). Home: 701 Timberview Ct N Fort Worth TX 76110 Office: 300 Taylor St Fort Worth TX 76102

ALLPHIN, NYLEN LEE, JR., chemist; b. Laramie, Wyo., Feb. 25, 1937; s. Nylen Lee and Grace Phyllis (Hassell) A.; B.S., Brigham Young U., 1959; postgrad. U. Denver, 1960-61; Ph.D., U. Colo., 1964; m. Patricia Gail Adolf, Dec. 21, 1956; children—Nyla, Allan Lee, Eric Bruce, Kevin Dee, James Wayne, Owen Louis, Loreen, Darren, Susan, Andrew Nylen. Chemist, Marathon Oil Research Center, Denver, 1959-61; research chemist Chevron Research Co., Richmond, Calif., 1964-76; exec. v.p. Pearsall Chem. Corp., Houston, 1976-79; gen. mgr. Johann Haltermann, Ltd., Houston, 1979-81; pres. Lubritex, Inc., Houston, 1981-83, Allco Chem. Corp., Houston, 1983—; instr. chemistry U. Colo., 1961-64. Mem. Am. Chem. Soc., Am. Soc. Lubrication Engrs., Sigma Xi, Alpha Chi Sigma. Mormon (stake pres.). Contbr. articles to profl. publs. Patentee in field. Home: 12211 Coachman's Ln Pinehurst TX 77362 Office: 9391 Grogan's Mill Rd Woodlands TX 77380

ALMEIDA, JOSÉ AGUSTÍN, educator; b. Waco, Tex., Aug. 28, 1933; s. Jesse M. and Teodora (Mancillas) A.; B.A., Baylor U., 1961; M.A., U. Mo., 1964, Ph.D., 1967; m. Maritza Barros, Sept. 5, 1964; 1 child, José Rodolfo. Teaching asst. U. Mo., Columbia, 1961-66; instr. Baylor U., Waco, 1962-63; asst. prof. dept. Romance langs. U. N.C. Greensboro, 1966-77, asso. prof., 1977—, chmn. Latin Am. studies, 1979-81; vis. prof. Elmira (N.Y.) Coll., summer 1967; asst. prof. U. N.C. Greensboro and Guilford Coll. study abroad program, Cali, Colombia, summer 1973, Inst. in Middle Am., San Salvador, El Salvador, summers 1968, 69; cons. verbal-active teaching method Hampton Inst., 1976, 77, U. N.C. Charlotte, 1984; assoc. prof. Inst. in Spain, Madrid, summer 1980; lectr. First Internat. Conf. of Picaresque Lit., Madrid, 1976, 6th Conf. Internat. Assn. Hispanists, 1977, First Internat. Conf. on Lope de Vega, 1980, Nat. Symposium on Hispanic Theater, 1982. Active Common Cause, ACLU. Served with USAF, 1953-57. Nat. Endowment for Humanities fellow, 1970. Mem. MLA, S. Atlantic MLA, Am. Assn. Tchrs. Spanish and Portuguese, Internat. Assn. Hispanists, Cervantes Soc. Am., Sigma Delta Pi, Democrat. Roman Catholic. Author: (with Stephen C. Mohler and Robert R. Stinson) Descubrir y crear, 1976, 3d edit., 1985; La crítica literaria de Fernando de Herrera Madrid, Gredos, Herrera, 1976. Home: 1410 Valleymede Rd Greensboro NC 27410

ALMODOVÁR, ISMAEL, university president; b. San Germán, P.R., Apr. 14, 1932; s. Juan B. and Celia (Garcia) A.; B.Sc. magna cum laude, U. P.R., 1952; M.S. in Chemistry, Carnegie Inst. Tech., Pitts., 1958; Ph.D., Carnegie Mellon U., 1960; postdoctoral Brookhaven Nat. Lab., Upton, N.Y., 1962; postgrad. Grad. Sch. Law, U. PR., 1974; m. Magdaline Sosnoski, Jan. 6, 1964; children—John, Lisa, Andrew, Paul, Diana, Evelyn. Instr., U. P.R., Mayaguez, 1952-53, 55-60, asst. prof., 1960-62, asso. prof., 1962-67, prof. chemistry, 1967—; dir. nuclear sci. and tech. div. P.R. Nuclear Center, U. P.R., Mayaguez, 1960-62, dir. neutron diffraction program, 1963-65, dir. grad. studies, 1965-66, chmn. dept. chemistry, Rio Piedras, 1966-70, dean Coll. Natural Scis., 1970-74, dir. Center Energy and Environ. Research, 1976-77, pres., San Juan, 1977—; health scientist adminstr. div. research resources NIH, Bethesda, Md., 1974-75; cons. sci. programs P.R. Dept. Edn., 1967-70; instl. rep. Oak Ridge Asso. Univs., 1970-72, 75; mem. P.R. Bd. Examiners Practice of Chemistry, 1969-77, pres., 1976-77; mem. adv. com. marine affairs Nat. Assn. State Univs. and Land-Grant Colls., 1980-81; v.p. Assn. Caribbean Univs. and Research Insts., 1980—; peer evaluator NIH and NSF, Middle States Assn.; mem. Nat. Commn. Higher Edn. Issues, Am. Council on Edn., 1981; cons. Mem. adv. com. State Conservation Trust Fund, 1973-75; mem. tech. adv. com. Environ. Quality Bd. P.R., 1976-82; mem. Gov.'s Adv. Council on Energy, 1977-82, on Edn., 1978—, on Human Resources, 1978—; bd. regents Nat. Library Medicine, NIH, 1978-82; mem. adv. council to Sec. Army for ROTC; trustee UNICA Found. Served to 1st lt. U.S. Army, 1952-54; Korea. Mem. Am. Chem. Soc. (chpt. chmn. 1970—), Am. Inst. Chemists, Chemists Assn. P.R. (pres. 1968), Acad. Arts and Scis. P.R., P.R. Sci. Tchrs. Assn., Sigma Xi (chmn. chpt. 1962), Phi Kappa Phi. Contbr. numerous articles to sci. jours. Office: GPO Box 4984-G San Juan PR 00936

ALMON, RENEAU PEARSON, state justice; b. Moulton, Ala., July 8, 1937; s. Nathaniel Lee and Mary (Johnson) A.; B.S., U. Ala., 1959; LL.B., Cumberland Sch. Law Samford U., 1964; m. Deborah Pearson, June 27, 1974; children by previous marriage—Jonathan, Jason, Nathaniel; 1 stepson-Tommy Preer. Admitted to Ala. bar, 1964; judge 36th Jud. Circuit Ala., 1965-69, Ala. Ct. Criminal Appeals, 1969-75; justice Ala. Supreme Ct., Montgomery, 1975—. Mem. Am., Ala. bar assns. Office: Judicial Bldg 445 Dexter Ave Montgomery AL 36130

ALMOND, CARL HERMAN, thoracic and cardiovascular surgeon, educator; b. Latour, Mo., Apr. 1, 1926; m. Nancy Bewick Ginn, Dec. 9; children—Carrie Lucas, Callie Elliott, Carl Herman, Christopher Stanley. B.S. in Chemistry, Washington U., St. Louis, 1949, M.D., 1953. Diplomate Am. Bd. Surgery, Am. Bd. Thoracic Surgery. Intern, Los Angeles County Gen. Hosp., 1953-54; asst. resident surgery U. Mich., Ann Arbor, 1955-56; resent urolog. surgery Baylor U., Houston, 1958-59; resident thoracic, cardiovascular surgery UCLA, 1959; jr. clin. instr. surgery U. Mich., 1956-57, sr. clin. instr. surgery, 1957-58; asst. prof. surgery U. Mo. Sch. Medicine, Columbia, 1959-64, assoc. prof. surgery thoracic/cardiovascular, 1964-68, prof., chief thoracic/cardiovascular, 1968-77, prof. thoracic/cardiovascular surgery, 1978; prof., chmn. dept. surgery U. S.C. Sch. Medicine, 1978—; staff surgeon Univ. Hosp., Columbia, 1959-78, in thoracic/cardiovascular surgery, 1962-78, dir., 1968-77; house surgeon thoracic/cardiovascular surgery Brompton Hosp., London, 1961, Children's Hosp., U. So. Calif. Service, Los Angeles, 1962, Good Samaritan Hosp., 1962; dir. thoracic/cardiovascular surgery program VA Deans Hosp., Columbia, 1972-77; dir. thoracic/cardiovascular surg. programs Mo. State Chest Hosp., Mount Vernon, 1973-78; dir. gen. surgery residency tng. program Richland Meml. Hosp., Columbia, 1979—; vis. prof. cardiovascular surgery U. Geneva Hosp., 1973-74; cons. thoracic/cardiovascular surgery Elles Fischel Cancer Hosp., Columbia, 1976-78; mem. med. adv. panel FAA, 1970-75; mem. adv. com. Mo. Crippled Children Services, 1976-79, chmn., 1978; chmn. adv. com Republic Nat. Bank, Columbia; active United Way; mem. U.S. Commn. UNESCO, 1983-85. Washington U. Barnes Hosp. fellow, St. Louis, 1956; NIH fellow, London, 1961, UCLA, 1962. Fellow ACS (Mo. adv. com. 1970-77, S.C. credentials com. 1980—); mem. Internat. Cardiovascular Soc., Am. Assn. Med. Colls., Am. Assn. Thoracic Surgery (ethics com. 1976-78), Am. Coll. Cardiology, Am. Coll. Chest Physicians, Am. Heart Assn., AMA, Am. Soc. Artificial Internal Organs, Central Surg. Soc., Chest Club, Frederick A. Coller Surg. Soc., Marion S. DeWeese Surg. Soc., Soc. Surg. Chairmen, Soc. Med. Cons. Armed Forces (surg. adv. group Air Force, surg. team Vietnam 1967-68), Soc. Thoracic Surgeons, Southeastern Surg. Soc., So. Thoracic Surg. Assn., also local med. groups, Sigma Xi, Nu Sigma Nu, Sigma Chi. Lodge: Rotary. Contbr. 90 articles to profl. publs. Office: Dept Surgery U SC 3321 Med Park Rd Suite 300 Columbia SC 29203

ALMQUIST, SHARON GRIEGGS, librarian, musician; b. Kenmore, N.Y., Nov. 11, 1957; d. Thomas Mark and Dolores (Beneski) Grieggs; m. Arne John Almquist, May 15, 1982. B.A. in Music, SUNY-Buffalo, 1980, M.L.S., 1982, M.A. in Music, 1986. Grad. asst. music library SUNY-Buffalo, 1981-82, cataloger music, 1982-83; librarian music and media North Tex. State U., Denton, 1983—. German scholar Central Coll., 1975-76, Chinese, Spanish, French scholar Chautauqua Instn., 1976. Mem. Music Library Assn., Online Audiovisual Catalogers, Music Online Computer Library Ctr. Users Group, Am. Musicological Soc., Tex. Music Library Assn., North Tex. State U. Staff Assn. (pres. 1984-85). Avocations: tropical fish; walking; reading. Home: 501 Londonderry Ln #95 Denton TX 76205 Office: Willis Library Bibliographic Control Box 5188 Denton TX 76203

ALMY, EARLE (BUDDY) VAUGHN, JR., real estate executive; b. Fort Worth, July 29, 1930; s. Earle Vaughn and Minnye Ruth (Rounsaville) A.; m. Gorden Yetive McGowan, July 31, 1964 (div. 1967). B.S. in Animal Husbandry, Tex. Tech. U., 1952; postgrad., Am. Inst. Banking, 1956-62. Credit analyst First Nat. Bank, Fort Worth, 1956-62; dir. finance and poultry feed sales Burrus Feed Mills, Saginaw, Tex., 1963-69; pres., mgr. Almy and Co., Hurst, Tex., 1970-79, Granbury, Tex., 1979—; v.p., dir. Northeast Tarrant County Bd., Hurst, 1972-74; pres. Almy and Co. Realtors, Weatherford, Tex., 1973-78. Mem. Fort Worth Farm and Ranch Club; head usher Acton United Meth. Ch., Served with USAF, 1952-56. Sears Roebuck scholar, 1951. Mem. Nat. Assn. Realtors, Tex. Assn. Realtors, Granbury Bd. Realtors, Realtors Mktg. Inst., Nat. Farm and Land Inst., Tex. Farm and Land Inst., C. of C. Republican. Clubs: DeCordova Country, Pecan Plantation Country. Avocations: golf; hunting; fishing; boating; swimming. Home: Route 2 Box 65-1 PO Box 129 Granbury TX 76048

ALONSO, ANTONIO ENRIQUE, lawyer; b. Havana, Cuba, Aug. 31, 1924; came to U.S., 1959; J.D., U. Havana, 1946, Ph.D. in Humanities, 1952; postgrad. Fairleigh Dickinson U., 1968, Coll. St. Teresa, 1971, Iowa State U., 1973, Washington U., St. Louis, 1973; postgrad. Cuban-Am. Lawyers Program, U. Fla. Coll. Law, 1976; m. Daisy Ojeda, 1950; children—Margarita, Antonio, Henry, Jorge. Public defendant High Ct. of Las Villas Province (Cuba), 1946-49; tchr. Spanish lit. Valladares Acad., Cienfuegos, Cuba, 1948-52; ofcl. atty. Provincial Govt. Cuba, 1950-52; 1st undersec. of Treasury, Republic of Cuba, 1952-54; prof. tax law U. Jose Marti, Cuba, 1953-58; mem. Ho. of Reps., Congress Republic of Cuba, 1954-58; prof. criminal law U. Cienfuegos, 1958-60; editor stats. dept. Informes sobre Cuba, Miami, Fla., 1959-61; fin. columnist Agencia de Informaciones Periodisticas, Miami, 1963-69; dir. and lectr. Christian orientation 3d Summer Camp, YMCA, Miami, 1963-67; prof. public speech (Spanish), Inst. de Accion Social, Miami, 1964-65; prof. modern langs. dept. Coll. Saint Teresa, Winona, Minn., 1968-74, freshman adv., 1971-74, fgn. student adv., 1970-74, dir. Latin Am. area studies program, 1971-74; prof. grad. summer program Saint Mary's Coll., Minn., 1968-73; editor La Hacienda mag., Miami, 1974-81; admitted to Fla. bar, 1976. Recipient Nat. Order of Merit, Republic of Cuba, 1957; named Outstanding Citizen of Cienfuegos (Cuba), 1957; Ricardo Dolz award, 1947, Juan J. Remos award, 1985. Mem. ABA, Fla. Bar, Inter-Am. Bar Assn., MLA, Am. Assn. Tchrs. Spanish and Portuguese, Midwest Assn. Latin Am. Studies, Cath. U. Assn., Nat. Assn. Fgn. Student Affairs (grantee 1973), Fedn. Cuban Educators in Exile, Cuban Tchrs. in Exile, Cuban Soc. Internat. Law (nat. award 1946), AAUP, Acad. History of Cuba, N.W. Assn. Latin Am., Wis. Council Latin Americanists, Cuban Soc. Criminal Law, Fla. Bar, ABA, Inter-Am. Bar Assn., Sigma Delta Pi. Lodges: Kiwanis, Rotary, K.C. Author: Antonio Maceo. The Commandments of the Fatherland, 1954; Dynamic Budgets, 1956; Violation of Human Rights by the Government of Cuba, 1962; History of the Communist Party of Cuba, 1970; contbr. articles to publs. in Latin Am. and U.S. Home: 11125 SW 128 Ct Miami FL 33186 Office: 1699 Coral Way Suite 315 Miami FL 33145

ALONSO, IRMA GRACIELA TIRADO DE, economics educator, researcher; b. Cabo Rojo, P.R., May 26, 1941; d. Eladio and Dora (Concepcion) Tirado; m. Ivan Alonso, Jan. 5, 1973; children—Kevin, Nadeshka. B.A., U. P.R., 1963; M.A. 1966; Ph.D., U. York, Eng., 1969. Assoc. prof. U. P.R., San Juan, 1969-77, chmn. dept. econs., 1975-77; assoc. prof. econs. Fla. Internat. U., Miami, 1977—; cons. planning bd. Office of the Gov., San Juan, P.R., 1970-75. Author: Econometric Methods, 1981; co-author: Methodos Econometricos, 1981. Contbr. articles to profl. publs. Bd. dirs. ASPIRA of Fla., Miami, 1982-84. U. P.R. Scholar, 1966-69. Mem. Am. Econ. Assn., Miami Bus. Economists. Republican. Presbyterian. Avocation: gourmet cooking. Home: 10300 Coral Way Miami FL 33165 Office: Florida Internat U Dept of Econs Tamiami Trail Miami FL 33199

ALONSO, KENNETH BRAULIO, pathologist, educator; Tampa, Fla., Nov. 26, 1942; s. Braulio and Adelfa (Diaz) A.; m. Carmen Ann Gonzalez, June 24, 1967. A.B., Princeton U., 1964; M.D., U. Fla., 1968. Intern Riverside Hosp., Newport News, Va., 1968-69; resident U. Fla., Gainesville, 1969-70, Fitzsimmons Army Med. Ctr., Denver, 1971-73; chief resident pathology, 1973; chief pathology U.S. Army Regional Med. Lab., Atlanta, 1973-75; assoc. pathologist Bell-Meltzer Labs, East Point, Ga., 1975-76; dir. Lab Procedures South, Decatur, Ga., 1976-79; pathologist Henry Gen. Hosp., Stockbridge, Ga., 1979-84; dir. Lab Atlanta, Riverdale, Ga., 1984—; chief med. examiner Ga. Bur. Investigation, Decatur, 1985—; mem. adv. bd. Med. Lab. Observer, 1977—; assoc. prof. pathology Morehouse Sch. of Medicine, Atlanta, 1977—; v.p. Med. Research Found. Inc., Atlanta, 1982—. Contbr. articles to profl. jours. Served to maj. U.S. Army, 1970-75, Vietnam. Fellow ACP, Am. Soc. Clin. Pathologists, Coll. Am. Pathologists; mem. Soc. Nuclear Medicine, Am. Coll. Nuclear Physicians, Nat. Assn. Med. Examiners. Club: Internat. Wine and Food Soc. (Atlanta) (pres. 1985). Office: Lab Atlanta 203B Medical Way Riverdale GA 30274

ALOTTA, ROBERT IGNATIUS, historian, educator, writer; b. Phila., Feb. 26, 1937; s. Peter Philip and Jean (Sacchetti) A.; m. Alice J. Danley, Oct. 1, 1960; children—Peter Anthony, Amy Louise. B.A., LaSalle Coll., Phila., 1959; M.A., U. Pa., 1981; Ph.D., Temple U., 1984. With Triangle Publs., Phila., 1956-67, merchandising mgr. Inquirer div., 1959-63, mgr. customer service Inquirer-Daily News, 1963-66, new bus. coordinator Daily News, 1966-67; mgr. spl. projects Penn Central Transp. Co., Phila., 1967-72; dir. pub. infor. Phila. Housing Authority, 1972-81; asst. prof. communications Grand Valley State Coll., Allendale, Mich., 1981-84; asst. prof. communication Miss. State U., 1984—; exec. producer TV series The Kids Show, 1985—; scriptwriter radio series A Philadelphia Moment, 1982, Past/Prolog, 1976, other radio, TV series, 1969—; narrator radio series A Minute of Your Time, 1977-78, Author: Street Names of Philadelphia, 1975; Stop the Evil, 1978; Old Names and New Places, 1979; A Look at the Vice Presidency, 1981; Military Executions of the Union Army, 1861-1866, 1984; contbr. articles, book revs. to publs. Pres. Shackamaxon Soc., 1967—; mem. pres.'s council LaSalle Coll., 1976—. Served with Security Agy., AUS, 1960-61. Recipient Freedom Found. at Valley Forge awards, 1970, 73, 74, 76, Legion of Honor award Chapel of 4 Chaplains, 1975, Colonial Dames, DAR awards, 1976; Americanism award County Detectives Assn. Pa., 1977. Mem. Am. Name Soc. (trustee 1982-84), Council on Am.'s Mil. Past (bd. dirs. 1984—), Pub. Relations Soc. Am., Mil. History Inst., Orgn. Am. Historians, Am. Hist. Assn., Starkville C. of C., Pub. Relations Assn. Miss., Cross Keys, Sigma Delta Chi (bd. dirs. Golden Triangle chpt. 1984—), Tau Alpha Pi, Alpha Phi Omega. Clubs: Order Sons of Italy (trustee 1983-84), Marines Meml. (San Francisco); Nat. Press (Washington); Franklin Inn (Phila.). Home: 104 Hackberry Ct Starkville MS 39759-4310 Office: Miss State U PO Drawer PF Mississippi State MS 39762

ALPERIN, JACK BERNARD, physician; b. Memphis, June 19, 1932; s. Dave and Frances (Cohen) A.; student U. Tenn., 1951-57, M.D., 1957; m. Lynn Manaster, Feb. 14, 1960; 1 son, Bruce Charles. Intern, resident in medicine, fellow in hematology Michael Reese Hosp., Chgo., 1957-62; instr. internal medicine Chgo. Med. Sch., 1962-63; research fellow in hematology U. Tex. Med. Br., Galveston, 1963-65, mem. faculty, 1965—, asso. prof. internal medicine, 1969-83, prof., 1983—. Mem. Internat. Soc. Hematology, Am. Soc. Hematology, Am. Soc. Clin. Nutrition, Am. Fedn. Clin. Research, Am. Soc. Human Genetics, So. Soc. Clin. Investigation, Am. Assn. Blood Banks, AMA, AAUP, Am. Inst. Nutrition, Sigma Xi. Office: 422 Clin Scis Bldg U Tex Med Br Galveston TX 77550

ALPERT, BARNET IRWIN, osteopathic physician; b. Bklyn., Apr. 23, 1943; s. Morris and Esther (Kanes) A.; m. Patricia Plutchok, Aug. 15, 1965; children—Joyce Allyson, Teri Dawn. B.S., Bklyn. Coll., 1963; D.O., Chgo. Coll. Osteo. Medicine, 1967. Diplomate Am. Coll. Gen. Practitioners in Osteo. Medicine and Surgery. Intern, Interboro Gen. Hosp., Bklyn., 1967-68; gen. practice osteo. medicine, Miami, Fla., 1970—; mem. staff Westchester Gen. Hosp., 1972-73; Palmetto Gen. Hosp., 1971—, Baptist Hosp., 1981-84, Am. Hosp., courtesy staff Coral Reef Gen. Hosp. Trustee Med. Found. South Fla., 1984—. Served to capt. U.S. Army, 1968-73, Vietnam. Decorated Bronze Star. Mem. Assn. S.W. Dade Physicians (mem. liaison com. 1984—), Am. Coll. Gen. Practice in Osteo. Medicine and Surgery (trustee Fla. 1985—), Am. Osteo. Assn., Fla. Osteo. Med. Assn., Dade County Osteo. Med. Assn. Office: Dr Barnet I Alpert & Assocs PA 7745 W Flagler St Miami FL 33144

ALPHA, ROLAND ALAIN, architect, contractor; b. New Orleans, Jan. 17, 1947; s. Granville and Eleanor (Attaway) A.; m. Veralyn Rabalais, June 7, 1968; children—Jeffrey Scott, Katherine Yvette. B.A. in Architecture, Tulane U., 1969. Prin., Roland A. Alpha, Architect, AIA, River Ridge, La., 1979—. Recipient award La. Forestry, 1969. Mem. AIA, La. Architects Assn. Republican.

ALSTON, JERRY GORDON, college dean, vice president; b. Fulton, Ky., Nov. 12, 1937; s. D.E. and Sarah M. (Rushton) A.; m. Nancy Sue Lanier, Sept. 8, 1958; children—Leslie Sara, Kenneth Stuart. B.S., Murray State U., Ky., 1961, M.A., 1962; Ph.D. in Higher Edn. Adminstrn., So. Ill. U., 1969. Instr. Paducah Community Coll., Ky., 1965-67; asst. to pres. Lincoln Trail Coll., Robinson, Ill., 1969-70; dean of arts and scis. Lake Land Coll., Mattoon, Ill., 1970-74; dean instrn. Ill. Valley Coll., Oglesby, Ill., 1974-77; v.p., dean Lee Coll., Baytown, Tex., 1977—; cons. Concortium for Internat. Studies, Houston, 1983—, Inst. for Schs. of Future, N.Y.C., 1984—; speaker in field. Active Democratic Party, Tex. and Ill., 1967—; bd. dirs. Baytown Orch., 1980-82. Served to 1st. lt. U.S. Army, 1962-65. Fellow NDEA, 1967; named Outstanding Educator Am., Lake Land Coll., 1971, 72. Mem. Am. Assn. for Higher Edn., Baytown C. of C., Nat. Council Instrn., Phi Delta Pakka, Kappa Delta Pi. Clubs: Clear Lake Tennis Assn. (Houston). Lodge: Kiwanis. Avocations: reading; tennis; theatre; travel. Home: 4611 Gulfway Dr Baytown TX 77521 Office: Lee Coll PO Box 818 Baytown TX 77522

ALTENHOFF, NORMAN RICHARD, accountant; b. Chgo., May 30, 1934; s. Alexander and Beulah P. (Potts) A.; student Georgetown U., 1952-56; B.S. in Bus. Adminstrn., Roosevelt U., 1970, M.S., 1973; m. Erin Jane Alexander, Nov. 15, 1985; children—Alexander, Allison, Sherry, Kerry, Erin, Mikal. System engr. IBM, Chgo., 1964-67; div. comptroller First Nat. Bank of Chgo., 1967-73; mgmt. cons. Lester B. Knight & Asso., Inc., Chgo., 1973-76; v.p. Citizens Bancorp., Sheboygan, Wis., 1976-78; pres. Comml. Services Co., St. Petersburg, Fla., 1979—; instr. Grad. Sch. Bus., De Paul U., Chgo., 1975. Bd. dirs. St. Petersburg Opera Co. Served in USNR, 1956-58. Cert. data processor Data Processing Mgmt. Assn. Mem. Nat. Assn. Accts., St. Petersburg C. of C. Club: River Forest Tennis. Home: 4100 14th Way NE Saint Petersburg FL 33703 Office: 7901 4th St N Suite 303 Saint Petersburg FL 33702

ALTERMAN, ISIDORE, investment company executive. Chmn., treas. Alterman Investment Fund, Inc., Atlanta. Office: Alterman Investment Fund Inc 1218 Paces Ferry Rd Atlanta GA 30327

ALTIERI, PABLO IVAN, physician; b. P.R., May 16, 1943; s. Pablo Altieri and Monsita Nieto; M.D., U. P.R., 1967; m. Emma, June 2, 1967; children—Pablo Ivan, II, Mariemma. Intern, Univ. Hosp.-U. P.R. Med. Sch., 1967-68, resident, 1968-71; research fellow, clin. instr. Ohio State U., 1972-73; dir. cardiovascular lab. U. P.R. Med. Sch., 1975—, prof. medicine, 1975—, also faculty pres. Served with M.C., USAF, 1973-75. Mem. Am. Fedn. Clin. Research, Am. Heart Assn. (dir. P.R. chpt. 1975, Disting. Mem. 1975), AMA, Am. Soc. Electrophysiology. Roman Catholic. Club: Rotary (Humacao, P.R.). Office: PO Box 23134 U PR Sta Rio Piedras PR 00931

ALTMAN, CLINTON JESSE, JR., trucking company executive; b. Georgetown, S.C., Oct. 23, 1938; s. Clinton Jesse Altman and Margaret Ruth (Farris) Babson; m. Geraldine Barnes, Jan. 10, 1971 (div. 1980); children—Collin, Alycia. Student Trident Community Coll., 1964, Rice Bus. Coll., 1959-61, Wofford Coll., 1958-60. Mgr., sales rep. Bell Lines, Inc., Charleston, S.C., 1960-62; sales rep. Central Motor Line, Charleston, 1962-64; terminal mgr. R-C Motor Lines, Savannah, Ga., 1965-69, regional mgr., Charlotte, N.C., 1969-72; v.p., cons. Am. Delivery, Detroit, 1972-74; pres., chief exec. officer Atlanta Dispatch, 1974—; Altman Freight, Inc., Tallahassee, Fla., 1983—. Author, editor Red Coat Reporter mag., 1971, 72. Mem. Young Republicans, Charleston, 1966. Mem. Toastmasters Internat. (pres. 1966, named Speaker of Yr. 1966), Pensacola Traffic Club, West Atlanta Transp. Club (pres.), Mobile Traffic and Transp. Club, Panama City Transp. Club, Northeast Atlanta Transp. Club, Delta Nu Alpha. Methodist. Club: Fairington (Decatur, Ga.) (bd. dirs. 1980-84). Lodge: Rotary. Avocations: golf; fishing; karate; dancing. Home: 111 Tiburon Ct Decatur GA 30035 Office: Atlanta Dispatch & Distribution 2810 Regina Dr Atlanta GA 30318

ALTMAN, STEVEN, university president; b. Jacksonville, Fla., Oct. 24, 1945; s. I. Harold and Estelle A.; B.A., UCLA, 1967; M.B.A., U. So. Calif., 1969, D.B.A., 1975; m. Judy Ovadenko, Feb. 8, 1969. Asst. dean Sch. Bus., U. So. Calif., Los Angeles, 1969-72; asst. prof. Sch. Bus., Fla. Internat. U., Miami, 1972-75, assoc. prof. mgmt., 1975-84, prof. mgmt., 1984—, chmn. div. mgmt., 1972-77, asst. v.p. acad. affairs, 1977-78, assoc. v.p. acad. affairs, 1978-80, v.p. acad. affairs, 1981-85, provost, 1982-85; pres. Tex. A&I U., Kingsville, 1985—; labor arbitrator; cons. Mem. grad. council Embry Riddle Aero. U., 1974-76; bd. dirs. Internat. Ctr. of Fla., Internat. Health Council, Found. Excellence in pub. Edn., Inst. Human Service. Recipient gold medal Freedoms Found., 1971; named Outstanding Faculty mem. Fla. Internat. U., 1975; Labor Edn. award, 1982; named Spl. Master Fla. Pub. Employees Relations Commn., 1976-85. Mem. Am. Arbitration Assn., Indsl. Relations Research Assn., Acad. Mgmt., Am. Soc. Pub. Adminstrn., Am. Assn. Higher Edn., Internat. Personnel Mgmt. Assn., Soc. Profls. in Dispute Resolution, South Miami-Kendall C. of C. (pres.), Kingsville C. of C., Beta Gamma Sigma. Author numerous books; contbr. articles to profl. jours Office: Tex A&I U Campus Box 101 Kingsville TX 78363

ALTOBELLO, MILDRED FRANCES, realtor-associate; b. West Palm Beach, Fla., Mar. 3, 1953; d. Francis Anthony and Ethel Hamner (Martin) A. B.A., U. Ala., 1975; M.B.A., Samford U., 1977. Ter. mgr. Burroughs Corp., Miami, Fla., 1978-80; mgmt. trainee Coral Gables Fed. Savs. and Loan (Fla.), 1981; realtor-assoc. Keyes Co., Coral Gables, 1981—. Active, West Dade Jaycee Women, Miami, 1981, Coral Gables C. of C., 1978, Civic Opera Palm Beaches, 1969; chmn. Liturgical Co. U Ala., Tuscaloosa, 1973. Mem. Coral Gables Bd. Realtors (realtor-lawyer com., civic affairs com.), Sunset Jaycees, Coral Gables C. of C. Soc. Profl. Journalists, Women in Communications, Inc. Democrat. Roman Catholic.

ALTUS, PHILIP, physician; b. Troy, N.Y., Oct. 2, 1945; s. Harold R. and Cynthia J. (Chuckrow) A.; m. Muriel Ann Schoendorf, June 22, 1968; children—Stephen, Robert. A.B., U. Rochester, 1967; M.D., SUNY Upstate Med. Ctr., 1971. Diplomate Am. Bd. Internal Medicine. Intern, dept. medicine Upstate Med. Ctr., Syracuse, N.Y., 1971-72, asst. resident, 1972-73, sr. resident, 1975-76; asst. prof. medicine dept. internal medicine U. South Fla., Tampa, 1976-81, assoc. prof., 1981—, assoc. chmn. dept. internal medicine, 1984—; chief med. service Tampa Gen. Hosp., 1978—; cons. physician James Haley VA Hosp., Tampa, 1977—; chmn. residency selection com.; mem. exec. bd. Tampa Gen. Hosp. Contbr. articles to profl. jours. Bd. dirs. Congregation Rodeph Sholom, Tampa. Served to maj. USAF, 1973-75. Fellow ACP; mem. Fla. Med. Assn. (cons. editor Jour.), Hillsborough County Med. Assn., Assn. Program Dirs. of Internal Medicine, Southeastern U.S. Clerkship Coordinators, West Coast Acad. Medicine, Soc. for Research and Edn. Primary Care Internal Medicine. Club: Tampa Bay Bridge (pres.). Office: 12901 N 30th St Tampa FL 33612

ALUISE, JAMES ANTHONY, technological school administrator; b. Huntington, W.Va., Oct. 14, 1955; s. Albert James and Nancy Suzanne (Linsenmeyer) A. B.S. in Biol. Scis., B.S. in Med. Tech., Marshall U. Clk. Jellco Corp., Huntington, 1973-74; pharm. clk. St. Mary's Hosp., Huntington, 1974-78, med. technologist, 1978-85; sch. adminstr. Elkhart Inst., Huntington, 1985—. Active Big Bros. and Big Sisters, Birthright Inc.; pres. Huntington Ch. Basketball League, 1984-85. Recipient 5-Yr. award Big Bros. and Big Sisters, 1985. Mem. Am. Soc. Clin. Pathologists. Democrat. Roman Catholic. Lodge: K.C. (grand knight 1984—). Home: 1723 Woodward Terr Huntington WV 25705 Office: Elkhart Inst Tech 905 3d Ave Huntington WV 25701

ALUISE, JOHN JOSEPH, educator, orgnl. cons.; b. Huntington, W.Va., Nov. 14, 1942; s. Joseph Albert and Vanda (Citti) A.; B.S. in Acctg. (Presdl. scholar), Wheeling Coll., 1964; M.B.A., W.Va. U., 1967; Ph.D., U. N.C., 1982; m. Barbara Beavers, May 27, 1967; children—Joseph, Edward, Gina. Grad. research asst. W.Va. U., 1965-66, instr. mktg., 1967-69; with mktg. research, mgmt. tng. B.F. Goodrich, Akron, Ohio, 1969-72; mgmt. educator Akron City Hosp., 1973-77; dir. organizational devel. dept. family medicine U. N.C., Chapel Hill, 1977—; mgmt. cons.; vis. educator med. schs. and teaching hosps.; orgnl. cons. to acad. med. centers. Coach youth sports. Mem. Am. Soc. Tng. and Devel., Soc. Tchrs. of Family Medicine. Democrat. Roman Catholic. Author: Physician As Manager, 1980; contbr. articles on med. practice mgmt. to profl. publs. including Jour. Family Practice, Medical Dynamics, Family Medicine Rev., Family Medicine Seminars; contbr. workshops and papers to nat. confs. Home: 2452 Springview Trail Chapel Hill NC 27514 Office: Dept Family Medicine U NC Chapel Hill NC 27514

ALVAREZ, OSCAR ANTONIO, multinational company executive; b. Medellin, Colombia, Nov. 22, 1944; came to U.S., 1978, naturalized, 1983; s. Julio Cesar and Fabiola (Piedrahita) A.; m. Sonia Gutierrez de Pineres, Jan. 8, 1968; children—Juan Carlos, Sandra. B.Comm., U. Windsor (Ont., Can.), 1974, M.B.A., 1975. Export mgr. Steel Co. of Can., 1973-78; regional mgr.

Latin-Am., Rexnord Inc., Miami, Fla., 1978—; cons. internat. cos., law firms. Office: 7270 NW 12th St Suite 320 Miami FL 33126

ALVIG, OLAV HENRY, physician, radiologist, consultant in ultrasound and nuclear medicine; b. Oaklyn, N.J., Mar. 2; s. Margaret Louis (Kritschil) Alvig; m. Margaret Maney, May 18, 1961 (div. 1966); m. Mary Anne Burkhart, June 16, 1979; 1 child, Karl. A.A., U. Va., 1949; B.S., George Washington U., 1951, M.D., 1958. Diplomate Am. Bd. Radiology, Am. Bd. Quality Assurance and Utilization Rev. Intern Washington Hosp. Ctr., 1958-59, resident in gen. radiology, 1967-70; founder Old Dominion Med. Ctr., McLean, Va., 1958-66, Emergency Room Assocs. Cafritz Hosp., Washington, 1966-68; fellow in ultrasound Grady Hosp., Atlanta, 1978; chmn. dept. radiology Forsyth County Hosp., Cumming, Ga., 1979—, chief of staff, 1983; cons. ultrasound, 1981-82. Served to 1st lt. U.S. Army, 1951-54. Mem. Am. Coll. Nuclear Medicine, Am. Coll. Nuclear Physicians, Am. Inst. Ultrasound Medicine (sr.), Am. Coll. Radiology, AMA, Am. Coll. Med. Imaging. Lodge: Rotary. Avocation: coin collecting. Home: 116 Lakeview Circle Cumming GA 30130 Office: Forsyth County Hosp 133 Samaratin Dr Cumming GA 30130

AMAN, JOSEPH PAUL, mining company executive; b. Altoona, Pa., May 10, 1948; s. Charles Walter and Priscilla Louise (Moaba) A.; m. N. Dianne Bradley, June 14, 1970; children—Jennifer Lynn, Jarrod Paul, Michael Scott. B.S., Va. Poly. Inst. and State U., 1971. Supr. mining engring. Allied Chem. Co., Green River, Wyo., 1971-76; mine supt. Consolidation Coal Co., Bluefield, Va., 1977-80, mineproject mgr., 1980—. Dir., Va. Coal Council, 1982—. Served with Army NG, 1971-77. Mem. Va. Tech. Student Aid Assn., Richlands C. of C. (bd. dirs. 1986—). Independent. Baptist. Mailing Address: 525 Adams St Tazewell VA 24651 Home: 525 Adams St Tazewell VA 24651 Office: PO Box 890 Bluefield VA 24605

AMATANGELO, NICHOLAS S., financial printing company executive; b. Monessen, Pa., Feb. 12, 1935; s. Sylvester and Lucy A.; B.A., Duquesne U., 1957; M.B.A., U. Pitts., 1958; m. Kathleen Driscoll, May 16, 1964; children—Amy Kathleen, Holly Megan. Indsl. engr. U.S. Steel Inc., Pitts., 1959-61; indsl. engr. supr. Anaconda, N.Y.C., 1961-63; product mktg. mgr. Xerox Corp., N.Y.C., 1965-68; dir. mktg. MacMillan Co., N.Y.C., 1968-70; dir. product planning Philco-Ford Corp., Phila., 1970-72; pres. Bowne of San Francisco, Inc., 1972-79, Bowne of Houston, Inc., 1979-86, Bowne of Chgo., Inc., 1983—; instr. U. Pitts., 1959-61; asst. prof. Westchester Community Coll., N.Y.C., 1961-64, 70-72. Bd. dirs. San Francisco Boys Club, 1974-79, Boys Towns Italy, 1973-79, Alley Theatre, Houston, 1984—; mem. pres.'s council Houston Grand Opera, 1980-81. Served with U.S. Army, 1958-59, 61-62. Mem. Printing Industries Am. (dir.), Am. Soc. Corp. Secs., Am. Inst. Indsl. Engrs., Am. Soc. Tng. and Devel., Am. Mgmt. Assn. Pres. Assn. Clubs: Olympic (San Francisco); Houston, University, Forest (Houston); Economic, Executives (Chgo.). Contbr. articles to profl. jours. Office: 1200 Oliver St PO Box 70087 Houston TX 77007

AMATO, DOLORES ROSE, reading consultant; b. Newark, Nov. 7, 1941; d. Amelio and Carmela Amato; B.A., Caldwell Coll., 1963; M.A. in Reading, Keane State Coll., N.J., 1966; postgrad. Tex. So. U., 1976—. Elem. sch. tchr., Parsippany, N.J., 1963-66; nat. reading cons. Harcourt Brace-Jovanovich, N.Y.C., 1966-72; dir. reading K-12, Houston Ind. Sch. Dist., 1972-79; nat. reading cons. and author, Houston, 1979—. Recipient Outstanding Educator award Nat. Soc. Creative Intelligence, 1975. Mem. Internat. Reading Assn., Am. Bus. Women's Assn., Assn. Supervision and Curriculum Devel., Tex. Reading Assn., Gulf Coast Writer's Assn. Author: Frost Reading and Math Program, 1979; Spanish Reading Keys Basal Readers, 1978, 79; Reading is Fun Series and Workbooks for School and Home, 1982; Spanish Supplementary Readers, 1982; Enrich/Ohaus Comprehension Series, 1983; contbg. author: Reading Basics Plus, 1976, 80. Address: 1 Wind Poppy Ct The Woodlands TX 77381

AMATO, KENNETH ALAN, trailer leasing executive; b. N.Y.C., July 30, 1944; s. Vincent William and Pearl-Marie (Watts) A.; m. Susan Lorraine Conrad, Mar. 31, 1973; children—Karyn Elaine, Jeffrey Conrad. B.A. in English and bus., Parsons Coll., Fairfield, Iowa, 1966. Dist. mgr. Hertz Corp., Lexington, Ky., 1973-74, Jacksonville, Fla., 1974-76, Houston, 1976-78; regional v.p. Flexi-Van Corp., Atlanta, 1978-80; div. sales mgr. Gelco Corp. Trailer Leasing, Aglanta, 1980-83, div. mgr., 1983—. Served to lt. (j.g.) U.S. Navy, 1967-69. Mem. Ga. Motor Truck Assn. Republican. Episcopalian. Home: 95 Lake Top Ct Roswell GA 30075 Office: Gelco Trailer Leasing Inc 3169 Holcomb Bridge Rd Norcross GA 30071

AMAYA, HERMANN MIGUEL, electrical engineer; b. Bogota, Colombia, Sept. 29, 1945; s. Octavio and Sixta Tulia (Galarza) A.; m. Sylvia Ann Gonzalez, Dec. 19, 1981; B.S., Poly. Inst. N.Y., 1975. Mem. tech. staff Hughes Aircraft Co., Los Angeles, 1975-79, tech. rep. to U.S. Navy, 79; radar systems engr. automated test equipment systems and test program sets engr. Sperry Def. Systems, Clearwater, Fla., 1979—. Served with USAF, 1966-70. Mem. Aero Flying Club, Assn. Old Crows. Democrat. Roman Catholic. Office: PO Box 4648 MS 235 Clearwater FL 33518

AMBARDEKAR, RAJ, library administrator; b. Kurtade, Bombay, India, July 15, 1941; came to U.S. 1968, naturalized, 1975; s. Dattatray S. and Satyabhama (Sarpotdar) A.; m. Colleen Sue, Aug. 22, 1971. B.A. with honors U. Bombay, 1966, M.A., 1968; M.S., Ill. State U., Normal, 1970; M.L.S., U. Oreg., Eugene, 1971. Cert. librarian. Adminstrv. asst. U. Bombay, 1961-68; asst librarian Middle Ga. Coll., Cochran, 1971-77, asst. librarian, 1978-81, dir., 1981—; librarian Pulaski County Schs., Hawkinsville, Ga., 1977-78; chmn. Health Sci. Libraries Central Ga., Macon, 1983. Compiler handbook Roberts Meml. Library, 1983. Mem. Ga. Library Assn. (interlibrary loan round table 1980-81), Central Ga. Associated Libraries (sec.-treas. 1984), S.E. Library Assn., Phi Alpha Theta. Methodist. Lodge: Rotary (Cochran). Home: 809 Peacock St Cochran GA 31014

AMBROSE, JOHN AUGUSTINE, research chemist, educator, biochemical geneticist; b. Fort Dodge, Iowa, Feb. 15, 1923; s. Abraham E. and Josephine (Vega) A.; m. Edith Louise Brockman, June 27, 1964; 1 child, Dianne Louise. Student Marquette U., 1944-45, M.S., 1951; student U. Wis., summer 1947, 48; B.A., Johns Hopkins U., 1948; Ph.D. in Biochemistry and Microbiology, U. Miami, 1965. Research chemist Oreg. State U., 1951-52; research biochemist U. Chgo. Med. Sch., 1952-54, dept. physiol. chemistry Johns Hopkins U. Med. Sch., 1954-57; USPHS fellow Ind. U., 1958-60; research chemist Metabolic Disorders Lab., Ctr. for Disease Control, USPHS, Atlanta, 1964-65, chief Mental Retardation Lab., 1965-67, Chem. Genetics Lab., 1967-70, Biochem. Genetics and Metabolic Disorders Lab., 1970-72, Pediatric and Genetic Chemistry Lab., 1972-73, Genetic Chemistry Lab., 1973-74, research chemist Metabolic Disorders Lab., 1974-75, Nutritional Biochemistry Br., 1975-82, Metabolic Biochemistry Br., 1982-85, Spl. Activities Br., 1985—; dir. nat. and state health dept. multistate fluorometric and mental retardation workshops; cons. on mental retardation and chem. genetics. Recipient award Ga. Assn. for Retarded Children, 1971. Fellow Am. Inst. Chemists, Am. Pub. Health Assn., Internat. Biog. Assn., Nat. Acad. Clin. Biochemistry; mem. Am. Inst. Chemists, Am. Chem. Soc., Nat. Assn. Retarded Citizens, N.Y. Acad. Sci., Sigma Xi, Sigma Phi Epsilon. Contbr. articles to profl. jours. Home: 3552 Old Chemblee-Tucker Rd 3 Doraville GA 30340 Office: 1600 Clifton Rd NE Atlanta GA 30333

AMBROSE, J(OHN) HENRY, telecommunications manager, analyst; b. Memphis, Dec. 11, 1947; s. Henry and Lucy Jane (Hawkins) A.; m. Emma Kate Witherspoon, Apr. 7, 1979; children—John Henry, Jr., James Hampton. B.S. in Math. Coll. degree program Peace Corps, SUNY-Brockport, 1970; M.S. in Math. and Stats., U. Cin., 1975. Cert. secondary tchr., N.Y. Peace corps. vol. lectr. math. Kenyatta U. Coll., Nairobi, Kenya, 1971-73; staff specialist Ops. Research AT&T, N.Y.C., 1975-77, staff analyst statis. analysis, Basking Ridge, N.J., 1977-78; staff mgr. statis. analysis, ops. research Bell of Pa., Phila., 1978-81, staff mgr. revenue requirements, 1981-84; staff mgr. revenue requirement issues Bell Atlantic Network Services, Inc., Arlington, Va., 1984-85, dist. staff mgr. regulatory research, 1985—; teaching asst. U. Cin., 1973-75; adj. lectr. Sch. Bus. Adminstrn., Temple U., Phila., 1982, 83; instr. Bell System Sci. Sampling Course, Denver, 1977, 78, 83. Mem. Urban League, Phila. 1983-84. Mem. Am. Statis. Assn., Inst. Mgmt. Scis. (chpt. sec. 1981, chpt. seminar chmn. 1982-83), Alliance of Black Mgrs. Emory U. Alumni Assn., U. Cin. Alumni Assn., U. Cin. Black Alumni Assn. Democrat. Baptist. Clubs: Toastmasters. Avocations: photography; tennis; cycling; home computer. Office: Bell Atlantic Network Services Inc 1310 N Court House Rd Arlington VA 22201

AMBUHL, FRANK JERROLD, psychotherapist; b. Toronto, Ont., Can., Apr. 27, 1925 (parents U.S. citizens); s. Frank Frederick and Martha Lillian (Sasser) A.; m. Susan Tandy Durrett, Sept. 20, 1960; children—Elizabeth, Dan, Frank, Donald, Robert, Susanne, Tandy, Martha, Paul. B.A.Sc., U. Toronto, 1952; M.B.A., Harvard U., 1954; M. Div., Ch. Div. Sch., Berkeley, Calif., 1968; D.Min., Austin Presbyn. Sem., 1981. Lic. profl. counselor, Tex.; ordained priest Episcopal Ch., 1968. Vice pres. ops. Adminstrn. Services Internat., Monaco, 1959-63; assoc. rector St. Paul's Ch., Lubbock, Tex., 1968-70; priest-in-charge St. Stephen's Ch., Sweetwater, Tex., 1970-72, Holy Cross Episc. Ch., San Antonio, 1972-82; pvt. practice psychotherapy, San Antonio, 1980—; dir. Good Samaritan Ctr., San Antonio, 1980—; dir. counseling St. Mark's Episc. Ch., San Antonio, 1982—. Author: Enjoying Being Together, 1985; also newspaper articles, 1970—. Fellow Am. Assn. Pastoral Counselors; mem. Internat. Transactional Analysis Assn. (clin.), Am. Assn. Marriage and Family Therapists (clin.), Am. Assn. Sex Educators, Counselors, and Therapists. Republican. Club: Torch (San Antonio). Lodge: Masons. Avocations: photography; making reproductions of flintlock rifles and pistols; fishing; hunting; swimming. Home: 342 Maplewood San Antonio TX 78216 Office: 3030 Nacogdoches Suite 208 San Antonio TX 78217

AMBURGEY, LILLIAN WAYMACK, career counselor; b. Hopewell, Va., Feb. 2, 1917; d. William J. and Lillian (Davis) Waymack; m. William Martin Amburgey, Sept. 29, 1945; children—Leslie Ann Bryan, Stacy Lynn Person. B.A., William and Mary Coll., 1940; M.Ed., Va. Commonwealth U., 1959; Ed.D., Va. Poly. Inst. and State U., 1978. Profl. counselor, Va. Translator Spanish, Reynolds Metals Co., Richmond, 1940-44; sec. USF & G Ins. Co., Richmond, 1944-45; office mgr. Auto Club Va., Richmond, 1945-47; adminstfv. asst. Thalhimer Brothers, Richmond, 1947-52; tchr., counselor Collegiate Schs., Richmond, 1962-67, Henrico County Public Schs., Richmond, 1967-71; coordinator career planning and placement, prof. J. Sargeant Reynolds Community Coll., Richmond, 1971—; cons. Dept. Corrections, Staunton, Va., 1983, City Richmond, 1983, State Va., 1983. Tchr., River Rd. Bapt. Ch., 1952—. External examiner Va. Bd. Behavioral Scis., 1980-81; counselor supr. State of Va., 1978-83. Grantee Va. Dept. Vocat. Edn., 1982. Mem. Adminstv. Mgmt. Soc. (dir. 1978-86), Va. Coll. Placement Assn., Va. Counselors Assn., Chi Omega. Home: 9409 Bramall Rd Richmond VA 23229 Office: J Sargeant Reynolds Community Coll 1651 E Parham Rd Richmond VA 23228

AMELIA, THOMAS BAYARD, financial planning and leasing consultant; b. Balt., May 5, 1942; s. J. Donald and Elva N. Amelia; A.A., U. Balt., 1964, B.S., 1967; m. Elizabeth Jean Braden, June 6, 1964; children—Elizabeth Jean Kathleen Corrigan. Account mgr. IBM, Balt., 1967-75, product mgr., Washington, 1975-77; area dir. rail div. Itel Corp., Atlanta, 1977; v.p. Atlantic & Western Fin. Corp., Sanford, N.C., 1978-81, Atlantic & Western Ry. Co., Sanford, 1978-81; pres. Forest Corp. 1981-83; rep. Investment Mgmt. & Research, Inc., 1983—; pres. A&BP Ry. Co., 1983—. Registered rep. Nat. Assn. Securities Dealers, N.Y. Stock Exchange. Mem. Data Processing Mgmt. Assn., Nat. Assn. Shippers Adv. Bds., Internat. Assn. Fin. Planners, Am. Short Line R.R. Assn., Assn. Am. R.R.s, Car Officers Assn. Republican. Episcopalian. Clubs: Carolina Trace Country, Sherwood Forest, W. Lake Valley, Advocate of Balt. (dir. 1969-77). Home: 1626 Briarcliffe Dr Sanford NC 27330 Office: 600 SW Broad St Southern Pines NC 28387

AMELINCKX, FRANS CYRIEL, foreign language educator; b. St. Niklaas, Belgium, Sept. 23, 1932; came to U.S., 1961, naturalized, 1965; s. Leon Alberto Amelinckx and Josephine (Van Herwegen) Amelinckx Van Achter; m. Carol Bernice Cedar, June 19, 1959; children—Andrea, Alan, Andrew. Diploma de Contador, Underwood/Greg Coll., Caracas, Venezuela, 1956; B.S., No. State Coll., Aberdeen, S.D., 1964; M.A., U. Iowa, 1966, Ph.D., 1970. Acct.-controller Corrugadora de Carton, Maracay, Venezuela, 1955-61; asst. U. Iowa, Iowa City, 1964-69; asst. prof. U. Nebr., Lincoln, 1969-75, assoc. prof., 1975-83; prof. fgn. lang., head dept. fgn. lang. U. Southwestern La., Lafayette, 1983—. Editor: Travel, Quest, and Pilgrimage, 1978; editor Studies in Twentieth Century Lit., 1979-83. Contbr. articles to profl. jours. Served with Belgian Army, 1948-54, Korea. Recipient Disting. Teaching award U. Nebr., 1977, Maude Hommond Fling award U. Nebr., 1983; NDEA fellow U. Iowa, 1966-69; U. Nebr. Woods fellow, 1976; Camargo fellow, Cassis, France, 1976; U. Nebr. research fellow, Paris, 1979. Mem. Am. Assn. Tchrs. French (pres. Nebr. chpt. 1977-78), MLA, Association Culturelle de Louisiane (pres. 1984—), Société Chateaubriand, Société Théophile Gautier. Republican. Episcopalian. Lodge: Rotary (pres. So. La. Rotary Found. 1984—). Avocations: sailing; antique furniture. Office: U Southwestern La Lafayette LA 70504

AMES, CLINTON G., paper products manufacturing company executive; b. Norfolk, Va., 1922. Student Va. Poly. Inst., 1946. Pres. Inland Container Corp., Indpls., 1977—, former chief operating officer, chief exec. officer, 1979—; dir. Anderson Box Co., Temple Eastex Inc.; v.p., dir. El Morro Corrugated Box Corp.; pres. Ga. Kraft Co., 1982, chmn., 1983, also dir.; v.p. Time Inc. Mem. Am. Paper Inst. (dir.), Ind. C. of C. (dir.). Office: Georgia Kraft Co PO Box 1551 Rome GA 30161*

AMES, MICHAEL EINAR, school principal; b. Roswell, N.Mex.; s. David Cecil and Joyce Edith (Gigstad) A.; m. Dorothy June May; children—Halli, Julie, Amy Elizabeth. B.S.E., Ouachita Bapt. U., 1977; M.S.E., Ark. State U., 1980. Asst. activity dir. Am. Youth Activities, Weatherfield, Eng., 1966-69, youth activity dir., Winchester, Mass., 1974; food service Ouachita Bapt. U., Arkadelphia, 1974-77; resort coordinator So. Bapt. Conv., Cape Hatteras, N.C., 1977; tchr. Osceola Pub. Sch., Ark., 1978-79; prin. Horatio Pub. Sch., Ark., 1980-81; prin. Cotton Plant Pub. Sch., Ark., 1984-86, Calico Rock Pub. Sch., 1986—; chef in tng. Walt Disney World, Orlando, 1972-73; owner, mgr. Anchor Restaurant, Oscola, Ark., 1978-79, D.J. Nursery, Harrisburg, 1980—. Mem. Assn. Supervision and Curriculum Devel., Ark. Assn. Ednl. Adminstrn., Am. Assn. Sch. Adminstrs., Kappa Delta Pi, Phi Delta Kappa. Republican. Baptist. Club: Garden (chmn. 1984—). Avocations: Hunting; fishing; photography; canoeing; mountain climbing. Home: 403 Normal St Harrisburg AR 72432 Office: PO Box 226 Calico Rock AR 72519

AMESQUITA, CONNIE, human resources executive; b. Mathis, Tex. Aug. 20, 1942; d. Roman M. Carrasco and Manuela (Hernandez) C.; m. Phillip Amesquita, Feb. 3, 1963; 1 dau., Lisa Michelle. Student St. Mary's U., 1961-62, Our Lady of the Lake U., 1960-61. Chief clerk Met. Life Ins. Co., Burlington, Iowa, 1966; corr. USAA, San Antonio, 1968, tng. specialist, 1968-73, controller systems cons., 1978-79, sr. standards engr., 1972-78; mgr. work mgmt. Blue Cross/Blue Shield Tex., 1978-79; mgr. current claims systems Electronic Data Systems, Dallas, 1979; mgr. work mgmt. dept. J.C. Penney Life Ins. Co., 1979-82, dir. personnel, 1982, v.p. human relations, 1982—. Mem. Southwest Pension Conf., Dallas Personnel Assn., Inst. Indsl. Engrs., Bus. Forms Mgmt. Assn., Plano C. of C. Democrat. Roman Catholic. Office: J C Penney Life Ins Co 2425 N Central Expressway Richardson TX 75080

AMINI, BIJAN KHAJEHNOURI, technology company executive; b. Nice, France, Oct. 3, 1943; came to U.S., 1946; s. Ahmad and Georgianna Amini. B.S. in Physics, Carnegie Mellon U., 1962; M.S. in Aerospace Physics, Pa. State U., 1963, Ph.D., 1968. Lectr. UCLA, NASA, Pa. State U., 1968-73; sr. scientist Northrop Corp., 1968-71; pres., chief operating officer Armstrong Cork Co., Iran, 1976-79; sr. v.p. Gulf Interstate Corp., Houston, from 1981; now pres. Gulf Applied Research; dir. Gulf Applied Techs.; lectr. in field. Bd. dirs. Nat. Inst. Tech. and Applied Scis., Washington, 1978-81, Nat. Commn. on Indsl. Innovation, Inst. Tech. Devel. Mem. AIAA, ASME, AAAS, Sigma Xi. Office: Gulf Applied Techs 1233 W Loop South Houston TX 77027

AMIR-MOEZ, ALI REZA, mathematician, educator; b. Teheran, Iran, Apr. 7, 1919; s. Mohammad and Fatema (Gorgestani) A.-M.; B.A., U. Teheran, 1942; M.A., U. Calif. at Los Angeles, 1951, Ph.D., 1955. Came to U.S., 1947, naturalized, 1961. Instr. math. Teheran Tech. Coll., 1942-46; asst. prof. math. U. Idaho, 1955-56, Queens Coll., N.Y.C., 1956-60, Purdue U., 1960-61; asso. prof. U. Fla., Gainesville, 1961-63; prof. math. Clarkson Coll., Potsdam, N.Y., 1963-65, Tex. Tech U., Lubbock, 1965—. Author: Elements of Linear Space, 1961; (play) Kaleeheh & Demneh, 1962; Three Persian Tales, 1961, Matrix Techniques Trigonometry and Analytic Geometry, 1964; Mathematics and String Figures, 1966; Classes Residues et Figures ovec Ficelle, 1968; Extreme Properties of Linear Transformations and Geometry in Unitary Spaces, 1971; Elements of Multilinear Algebra, 1971; Linear Algebra of the Plane, 1973; contbr. articles to math. jours. on proper and singular values of linear operators and matrices. Served to 2d lt. Persian Army, 1936-38. Decorated Honor emblem Persian Royal Ct., medal Pro Mundi Beneficio Academia Brasileira de Ciencias Humanas. Mem. Am. Math. Soc., Math. Assn. Am., Sigma Xi, Pi Mu Epsilon. Office: Dept Math Texas Tech U Lubbock TX 79409

AMMA, ELMER L., chemistry educator, researcher; b. Cleve., Feb. 13, 1929; s. Martin and Mary Emma (Gnadt) A.; m. Marcia Bryant (div.); 1 child, Frances Kay; m. Anne Robinson McParland; children—Lara, Greg. B.S., Case Inst. Tech., 1952; Ph.D., Iowa State U., 1957. Research assoc. U. Pitts., 1957-59, asst. prof., 1959-65; assoc. prof. U. S.C., Columbia, 1965-70, prof. chemistry, 1970—; cons. Exxon Research, Linden, N.J., 1967-68. Recipient Russell award for research, U. S.C., 1970. Mem. Am. Chem. Soc. (S.C. Chemist of Yr. 1983, Stone award 1981), Am. Crystall. Assn., Am. Phys. Soc., Sigma Xi. Avocations: Farming, stock raising. Office: Chemistry Dept Univ SC Columbia SC 29208

AMMANN, LILLIAN ANN (NICHOLSON), plant company executive; b. Pearsall, Tex., June 20, 1946; d. Harvey Franklin and Annie Laura (Matthews) Nicholson; B.A. magna cum laude, Southwestern U., 1968; m. Jack Jordan Ammann, Jr., May 31, 1967; 1 son, William Erik. Inventory mgr. Kelly AFB, San Antonio, 1967-70; employment counselor Tex. Employment Commn., San Antonio, 1970-75; owner, operator Lillie's Lovely Little Gardens, San Antonio, 1975-77; owner, operator Lillie's Interior Landscapes, San Antonio, 1980-82, pres., 1982—; sec. Jack Ammann, Inc., 1983—; pres. Cas Mann Inc. doing bus. as Lillie's & Sherry's Plants & Pottery, San Antonio, 1977-80. Mem. North San Antonio C. of C., Nat. Assn. Self-Employed, Women in Bus., Interior Plantscape Assn., Nat. Council Interior Hort. Certification (charter mem., cert. interior horticulturist), San Antonio Interior Landscape Assn. (founder, immediate past pres.). Episcopalian. Author: Lillie's Lovely Little Gardening Book, 1976. Home: 603 Mauze San Antonio TX 78216 Office: 119 W Blanco Route 10 Box 82E San Antonio TX 78216

AMMARELL, JOHN SAMUEL, college president, former security services executive; b. nr. Reading, Pa., Mar. 21, 1920; s. John Samuel and Marie (Rothermel) A.; m. Florence Rebecca Althouse, June 27, 1942; children—John David, Robert Lynn. A.B., Muhlenberg Coll., 1941; postgrad. George Washington U., 1942-43. Spl. agt., asst. chief liaison FBI, Washington, 1942-54; asso. Gt. Am. Tchrs. Agy., Allentown, Pa., 1955-56; mgr. personnel, dir. security Air Products & Chems., Inc., Trexlertown, Pa., 1956-58; chmn. exec. com., dir. exec. v.p. Wackenhut Corp., Coral Gables, Fla., 1958-83, chmn. exec. com., dir., cons. to pres., 1983-85, dir., cons. to pres., 1985—; exec. v.p. Wackenhut Services, Inc., 1960-81, dir., 1960-83; pres., dir. Wackenhut Electronic Systems Corp., until 1983; pres. Newberry Coll. (S.C.), 1984—; former dir. Stellar Systems. Bd. dirs. Assoc. Industries Fla., 1966—. sec., 1968-69 treas., 1969-70, v.p., 1970-73, pres., 1973-74, chmn., 1974-75; bd. dirs. Greater Miami Citizens Crime Commn., 1975-84, pres., 1979-80. Trustee Newberry Coll., 1970-73, 74-85. Recipient Alumni Achievement award Muhlenberg Coll., 1971. Mem. Soc. Former Spl. Agts. FBI (pres. Pan Am. chpt. 1967-68), Com. Nat. Security Cos. (chmn. 1975-77). Am. Soc. Indsl. Security (chmn. pvt. security services council 1976-79), Lambda Chi Alpha, Omicron Delta Kappa, Phi Alpha Theta. Lutheran. Club: Country of Coral Gables. Lodges: Elks, Lions, Rotary. Home: 2104 Luther St Newberry SC 29108 Office: Newberry College Newberry SC 29108

AMMERMAN, DAN SHERIDAN, communications executive, actor, lecturer; b. Tyrone, Pa., June 10, 1932; s. Eugene Harry and Helen Leroy (Morrow) A.; m. Mary Teresa Graca, Jan. 10, 1953; children—Teresa Louise Saylor, Mark Alan. News dir., Sta. WVAM, Altoona, Pa., 1953-59; program dir. Sta. KGNC, Amarillo, Tex., 1959-66; news anchor Sta. KTRH, Houston, 1966-68; contbg. corr. CBS Radio, N.Y.C., 1966-68; news anchorman KTRK-TV, Houston, 1968-72, ABC-Radio, Houston, 1972-73; owner, chmn. Ammerman Enterprises, Inc., Houston, 1973—; dir. M-Bank Southwest, Houston, 1982—. Appeared as dr. who pulled bullet from J.R. Ewing in Dallas TV show; appeared in films including Local Hero and Red Alert. Served to 2d lt. U.S. Army, 1947-51, Korea. Named Big Brother of Yr., Big Bros. Amarillo, 1965; recipient Gabriel Found. award, Los Angeles, 1970, Headliners award Headliner Club, Austin, Tex., 1970, Houston Firefighters award, 1974. Mem. Vols. of Am. (nat. bd. dirs.). Republican. Roman Catholic. Clubs: Sugar Creek Country (Stafford, Tex.). Avocations: golf; acting. Office: Ammerman Enterprises Inc 4800 Sugar Grove Blvd 400 Stafford TX 77477

AMON, ANTON, soft drink company executive; b. Austria, Dec. 28, 1943; came to U.S., 1967; s. Anton Amon; m. Nelly Medina, Jan. 27, 1968; children—Yvonne, Jennifer. Diplom Ingenieur, U. A. Vienna, 1967; M.S. in Food Sci., Mich. State U., 1968, Ph.D. in Food Sci., 1970. Quality assurance mgr. Coca-Cola de Mex., Mexico City, 1975-77; mgr. mfg. quality assurance Central European div. Coca-Cola G.m.b.H., Fed. Republic Germany, 1977-81; v.p. Coca-Cola USA, Atlanta, 1981-83, sr. v.p., 1983—. Contbr. articles to profl. jours. Patentee in field. Trustee Am. Internat. Sch. of Dusseldorf, Fed. Republic Germany, 1979-80. Fulbright scholar, 1967. Mem. Inst. Food Technologists, Am. Chem. Soc., Austrian Inst. Food and Bio-Technologists (founding mem.; Achievement award 1984), Soc. Soft Drink Technologists, Sigma Xi. Roman Catholic. Club: Cherokee Town and Country (Atlanta). Avocations: skiing; racquetball. Office: Coca-Cola USA 310 North Ave Atlanta GA 30301

AMOS, CHARLES CLINTON, insurance company executive; b. Tucson, Sept. 3, 1940; s. Charles Cliff and Lucille Elizabeth (Pierce) A.; m. Joan Marie LaBelle, Feb. 2, 1962; 1 child, Jonathan Ashley. Student N.Mex. Mil. Inst., 1955-58, U. N.Mex., 1959-60, Boston U., 1969-70. C.P.C.U. Sales and field sales mgr. Employers Ins. of Wausau, Belmont, Mass. and Pitts., 1965-69; pres., chief exec. officer Henry J. LeBianc Ins. Agy., Inc., Fitchburg, Mass., 1969-74; pres., chief exec. officer Aanco Underwriters, Inc., St. Petersburg, Fla., 1972—, Aanco Ins. Services, Inc., Culver City, Calif., 1983—, , Pass-A-Grille Fishery, Inc., Countryside Insurors, Inc., St. Petersburg, 1981—; chmn. Flagship Mortgage Corp., Culver City, 1985—. sec.-treas. Blue Marlin, Inc., Clearwater, 1982-85, Cruising World Inc., St. Petersburg, 1983-85; pres. Latat Devel. Corp., 1985—, Lanay Constr., Inc., 1985—, Gulfport Mini-Storage, Inc., 1986—; instr. CPCU Soc. courses. Active Pinellas Assn. Retarded Children, Pinellas County Com. of 100, Fla. Gulf Coast Symphony; commr., chmn. Pinellas County Housing Authority, 1975-79. Served with Security Agy., U.S. Army, 1960-63. Named Agt. of Yr., Travelers Ins. Co., 1981; Nat. Sales Leader, Aetna Life Ins., 1978; other sales awards. Mem. Soc. C.P.C.U.s, Ind. Ins. Agts. Assn., Sales and Mktg. Execs. Democrat. Baptist. Clubs: Rotary, Pinellas County Com. of 100, Kappa Alpha Order. Lodge: Hon. Order Ky. Cols. Home: 300 Rafael Blvd NE Saint Petersburg FL 33704 Office: 1901 9th St N Saint Petersburg FL 33704

AMOS, CLIFFORD WILLIAM, fundraising executive; b. South Charleston, W. Va., Nov. 17, 1952; s. Ronald Brooks and Ruth Ann (Lucas) A.; m. Vickie Ann Richards, Apr. 16, 1977; children—Luke Finley, Rachel Frances. B.B.A., U. Cin., 1974; M. Div., New Orleans Bapt. Theol. Sem., 1981. Asst. mgr. Laynes Dept. Store, Loveland, Ohio, 1970-74, mgr. Gellers Dept. Stores, 1974-76, dist. mgr., 1977-78; mgr. Lamano Panno-Fallo Inc., New Orleans, 1978-80; dir. devel. New Orleans Bapt. Theol. Sem., 1981-83, v.p. devel., 1983—. Active New Orleans C. of C., 1982—. Avocations: furniture refinishing; karate. Home: 4217 Seminary Pl New Orleans LA 70126 Office: New Orleans Baptist Theol Sem 3939 Gentilly Blvd New Orleans LA 70126

AMOS, JOHN BEVERLY, insurance company executive, lawyer; b. Enterprise, Ala., June 5, 1924; s. John Shelby and Mary Helen (Mullins) A.; m. Elena Diaz-Verson, Sept. 23, 1945; children—John Shelby, II, Maria Teresa. Ed. U. Miami (Fla.), 1947, LL.D., 1979; J.D., U. Fla., 1949. Admitted to Fla. bar, 1949; pvt. practice, Fort Walton Beach, Fla., 1949-55; founder, 1955, since pres., chmn. bd., chief exec. officer Am. Family Life Assurance Co., Columbus, Ga.; pres., chmn. bd. Am. Family Corp. Past pres., Goodwill Industries, Columbus; past chmn. 3d Dist. Ga. Democratic Com.; trustee Morris Brown Coll., Atlanta, Roosevelt Warm Springs Found., Hughston Sports Medicine Found., Inc.; bd. visitors Boston U. Sch. Medicine, Walter F. George Coll. Law, Mercer U.; mem. pres.'s council Med. Coll. Ga.; mem. pres.'s adv. bd. Duke U.; bd. dirs. Metro Columbus Urban League; mem. exec. com. Hubert H. Humphrey Inst. Pub. Affairs, U. Minn.; chmn. Sch. of the Ams. Columbus Support Group, Inc., Fort Benning, Ga.; mem. Small Bus. Council Am.; mem. nat. com. Nat. Mus. Jewish History, Phila.; vice chmn. Nat. Bipartisan Polit. Action Com. Mem. Nat. Assn. Life Cos. (v.p.), NAM (bd. dirs.), Fla. Bar Assn. Roman Catholic. Clubs: Metropolitan (N.Y.C.); Pres.'s Club of U. Ga., Pres.'s

Club, Founder's Club of Med. Coll. of Ga., Big Eddy, Harmony (Columbus). Office: PO Box 1459 Columbus GA 31999

AMOS, MARVIN CYRIL, retired airline executive; b. Seymour, Ind., July 19, 1924; s. David Lawrence and Mary Eva (Hill) A.; B.A., Hanover (Ind.) Coll., 1949; m. Anne Addison, June 11, 1949; children—Patrick Marvin, Joanne Lee, Mark Addison, Judy Mitchell, Steven Lawrence. Edn. specialist RCA, Indpls., 1956-57; mgr. edn. and profl. placement, mgr. profl. placement and devel. Hotpoint div. Gen. Electric Co., Chgo., 1957-62; asst. to pres., dir. indsl. relations Wright Aero div. Curtiss-Wright Corp., Woodbridge, N.J., 1962-64; dir. planning and research, dir. personnel, v.p. personnel Eastern Air Lines, Inc., Miami, 1965-76, v.p. personnel and corporate adminstrn., 1976-78, sr. v.p. personnel and corporate adminstrn., 1978-84. Trustee Hanover (Ind.) Coll., from 1971, chmn. bldgs. and grounds com., from 1973; bd. dirs. Sanibel Moorings Assn., from 1975. Served with U.S. Army, 1943-46, 51-53. Named Alumnus of Yr., Hanover Coll., 1976. Mem. Greater Miami C. of C. Republican. Roman Catholic.

AMOS, TERRELL DEWEY, pharmacist, consultant pharmacist; b. Anniston, Ala., Feb. 21, 1956; s. Wyatt Edwin and Margaret Juanita (Shaw) A.; m. Barbara Jo Long, Nov. 4, 1982; 1 child, Michael Terrell. A.S., Gadsden State Jr. Coll., Ala., 1976; B.S. in Pharmacy, Auburn U., 1979. Registered pharmacist. Intern Peoples Hosp., Jasper, Ala., 1979; pharmacist, asst. mgr. Harco Drug, Inc., Bay Minette, Ala., 1979-82; pharmacist, mgr. Big B Drugs, Inc., Fort Payne, Ala., 1982-84, Harco Drug, Inc., Anniston, 1984—; cons. Prison Mgmt. Systems, Atmore, Ala., 1980-82. Big Brother, Big Bros. Am., Auburn, Ala., 1980-81; state del. Woodmen of the World, Mobile, Ala., 1985; scouting coordinator Boy Scouts Am., Anniston, Ala., 1985; priest, elder Ch. of Jesus Christ of Latter-day Saints, 1981, high priest, 1985, counselor in bishopric, 1985—. Mem. Ala. Pharm. Assn., Calhoun County Pharm. Assn., Kappa Psi (regent 1978-79). Republican. Lodge: Woodmen of the World (state del. 1985-87). Avocations: genealogy; swimming. Home: 1206 Merrimac Dr Oxford AL 36203 Office: Harco Super Drug 253 Route 2 Box 81A Oxford AL 36203

AMOSS, W. JAMES, JR., ocean freight transportation company executive; b. 1924; married. B.B.A., Tulane U., 1947. With Lykes Bros. Steamship Co., Inc., New Orleans, 1947—, v.p. traffic, 1967-70, exec. 1970-73, pres., chief operating officer, 1973-82, pres., chief exec. officer, 1982—, also dir.; dir. Hibernia Nat. Bank. Served with USN, 1945-46, 50-52. Office: Lykes Bros Steamship Co Inc Lykes Ctr 300 Doydras St New Orleans LA 70130*

AMSBARY, HARRY LOWELL, ophthalmologist; b. Gallipolis, Ohio, Jan. 13, 1949; s. Arthur Wayne and Gladys Eleanore (Steele) A.; m. Myla Jayne Hilligas, Jan. 1, 1972; children—Wayne Lowell, Kristine Diane. B.S., Ohio State U., 1970, M.D., 1973. Diplomate Am. Bd. Ophthalmology. Intern, St. Francis Gen. Hosp., Pitts., 1973-74; resident Mt. Sinai Hosp., Cleve., 1974-79; ophthalmologist Amsbary Eye Clinic, Gallipolis, 1977-79, Parkersburg Ophthal. Assocs., Inc., W.Va., 1979—; staff surgeon Camden-Clark Meml. Hosp., Parkersburg, 1979—, St. Joseph's Hosp., Parkersburg, 1979—. Fellow ACS; mem. Jaycees, C. of C. Republican. Baptist. Lodge: Lions. Avocations: skiing, camping. Home: Route 2 Box 236 Washington WV 26181 Office: POA Inc 2100 Dudley Ave Parkersburg WV 26101

ANASTI, JAMES ANTHONY, coroner; b. Fort Bragg, N.C., Apr. 29, 1945; s. Albert A. and Lillian L. (Morgan) A.B. Theol., Belmont Abbey Coll., Belmont, N.C., 1964. Mem. S.C. Hwy. Patrol, 1964-69; agt. S.C. Law Enforcement Div., Columbia, 1969-72; U.S. dep. marshall, Columbia, 1972-75; investigator 5th Jud. Cir. Ct., Columbia, 1975-76; chief dep. coroner Richland County, Columbia, 1976—. Pres. Oakwood Democratic Precinct Com.; chmn. Richland County Employees Grievance Com., 1982—; mem. Airport Commn., 1978—. Mem. S.C. Law Enforcement Officers Assn., S.C. Coroners Assn. Roman Catholic. Home: 5446 Pinestraw Rd Columbia SC 29206 Office: PO Box 192 Columbia SC 29202

ANASTOS, CHARLES HAROLD, architect; b. Brownsville, Tex., Feb. 15, 1954; s. Ray P. and Frances Elaine Anastos; B.Arch., Tex. Tech. U., 1979. Pres. Anastos Assocs., Inc. devel. cons. Marshall Co., Corpus Christi, Tex., 1979—. Vol., Big. Bros. Am.; bd. dirs. Corpus Christi Drug Abuse Council. Mem. AIA, Tex. Soc. Architects, Corpus Christi Issues Council, Corpus Christi C. of C., YMCA, Sigma Alpha Epsilon (past chpt. pres.). Republican. Methodist. Club: Corpus Christi Men's (v.p. 1981). Address: PO Box 3883 Corpus Christi TX 78404

ANDERS, MICHEAL JONES, human relations manager, consultant; b. Abilene, Tex., Aug. 15, 1947; s. Jones Lycurgus and Mary Frances (Diggs) A.; m. Patricia Elizabeth Taylor, Feb. 18, 1977; children—Christine Marie, Richard Dean. B.A., Howard Payne U., 1969; M.B.A., Pepperdine U., 1980. Adminstrv. aide Senator J.P. Ward, Austin, Tex., 1969-71; mgr. polit. campaigns, Austin, 1971-73; dir. personnel Continental Steel Co., Garland, Tex., 1973-77; regional personnel mgr. Dobbs/Lifesaver, Dallas-Fort Worth Airport, 1977-81; mgr. employee relations Harris Corp., Dallas, 1981—; lectr., cons. various Fortune 500 cos., 1983—. Author manual: Managers Sales Training, 1984. Served with Tex. Air N.C. Named Employer of Yr., Mental Health and Retardation Assn., Tex., 1979. Mem. Am. Soc. Tng. and Devel., Am. Mgmt. Assn. Lodges: Shrine, Scottish Rite. Avocation: Golf. Office: Harris Nat Accounts Div 16001 Dallas Pkwy Dallas TX 75248

ANDERSEN, JOHN, college administrator; b. Erding, Germany, Aug. 10, 1944; s. Gilford K. and Ellen M. Reeds; m. Sandra Ella Dorlac, Feb. 12, 1963; children—Dawn Marie, Kimberly Renee. A.A.S., Community College of the Air Force, 1980; B.S., Troy State U., 1984. Staff officer Elmendorf AFB, Anchorage, 1965-68; non-commd. officer in charge orthopedics, 1971-79; non-commd. officer in charge orthopedics Plattsburgh AFB Hosp. (N.Y.), 1968-71; non-commd. officer in charge orthopedic surgery Maxwell AFB Regional Hosp. (Ala.), 1979-82; program adminstr., supt. allied health dept. Community Coll. Air Force, Maxwell AFB, 1982—, also allied health program counselor. Editor: Fracture Line newsletter, 1983. Recipient Maxwell AFB Regional Hosp. Meritorious Service medal, 1982. Mem. Ala. Assn. Orthopedic Technologist (pres. 1984-85), Am. Assn. Orthopedic Technologists, Alpha Sigma Lambda, Gamma Beta Phi. Republican. Lutheran. Home: 3301 Covered Bridge Dr Montgomery AL 36116 Office: Community College of the Air Force Maxwell AFB AL 36112

ANDERSON, BRUCE CECIL, primary patent examiner, physics educator; b. St. Louis, Jan. 25, 1948; s. Cecil Elmer and Violet Barbara (Becker) A.; m. Linda M. Kacic, June 5, 1971 (div. 1977); children—Peter J., Lara J. B.S. in Physics, U. Mo.-Rolla, 1970; M.A. in Physics, Washington U., St. Louis, 1972. Tchr. physics Washington U., St. Louis, 1970-72; U.S. patent examiner U.S. Patent and Trademark Office, Dept. Commerce, Arlington, Va., 1972—; tchr. physics No. Va. Community Coll., Annandale, 1975-76 (part time). Mem. stewardship com. United Methodist Ch., Dale City, Va., 1985—, mem. fin. com., 1985—. Recipient numerous awards U.S. Patent and Trademark Office, 1973-86; Curators award U. Mo., 1969-70, numerous others. Fellow U.S. Patent Office Soc.; mem. Soc. Physics Students (sec., treas. 1970), Phi Kappa Phi, Sigma Phi Sigma. Avocations: baseball; football; history; science fiction; church related activities. Home: 13730 Langstone Dr Woodbridge VA 22193 Office: U S Patent and Trademark Office 2021 Jefferson Davis Hwy Arlington VA 22202

ANDERSON, BRUCE MORGAN, computer scientist, educator; b. Battle Creek, Mich., Oct. 8, 1941; s. James Albert and Beverly Jane (Morgan) A.; B.S. in Elec. Engring., Northwestern U., 1964; M.S. in Elec. Engring., Purdue U., 1966; Ph.D. in Elec. Engring. (NASA fellow), Northwestern U., 1973; m. Jeannie Marie Hignight, May 24, 1975; children—Ronald, Michael, Valerie, John, Carolyn. Research engr. Zenith Radio Corp., Chgo., 1965-66; asso. engr. Ill. Inst. Tech. Research Inst., Chgo., 1966-68; sr. electronics engr. Rockwell Internat., Downers Grove, Ill., 1973-75; computer scientist Argonne (Ill.) Nat. Lab., 1975-77; mem. group tech. staff Tex. Instruments, Dallas, 1977—; computer sci. lectr. U. Tex.-Arlington, U. Tex.-Dallas; adj. prof. computer sci. N. Tex. State U.; vis. indsl. prof. So. Meth. U.; computer systems cons. Info. Internat., Culver City, Calif., HCM Graphic Systems, Gt. Neck, N.Y.; computer cons. depts. geography, transp., econs., sociology and computer sci. Northwestern U., also instr. computer sci.; expert witness for law firm Burleson, Pate and Gibson. Mem. IEEE (chmn. Dallas sect. IEEE Computer Soc. 1984-85), Am. Assn. for Artificial Intelligence, Assn. Computing Machinery, Sigma Xi, Eta Kappa Nu, Theta Delta Chi. Contbr. articles to tech. jours. Home: 2716 Teakwood Ln Plano TX 75075 Office: Texas Instruments MS 238 PO Box 660246 Dallas TX 75266

ANDERSON, CAROL MCMILLAN, lawyer; b. Malone, Fla., Aug. 7, 1938; d. Fillmore Allen and Ernestine (Dickson) McMillan; m. Philip Sloan Anderson, Oct. 9, 1965; 1 dau., Courtney Beth. B.S., Fla. Atlantic U., 1969; J.D., Cumberland Sch. Law, 1971. Bar: Fla. 1971. Asst. U.S. atty. Office of U.S. Atty., Miami, Fla., 1971-74; ptnr. Anderson & Anderson, Ft. Lauderdale, Fla. 1974—. Chmn. Spring Flower Festival, Nova U., 1985; bd. dirs. Royal Dames Cancer Research. Recipient Alumnae Achievement award Katharine Gibbs Sch., Boston. Mem. ABA, Assn. Trial Lawyers Am., Fed. Bar Assn., Fla. Trial Lawyers, Fla. Bar, Broward County Bar Assn., Broward County Women Lawyers (v.p. 1981), Thousand Plus, Ft. Lauderdale Symphony Soc., Mus. Art, Gold Circle Nova U., Hospice Hundred. Club: Coral Ridge Yacht. Presbyterian. Home: Fort Lauderdale FL 33304 Office: Anderson & Anderson PA 1313 S Andrews Ave Fort Lauderdale FL 33316

ANDERSON, CHARLES ELWYN, manufacturing executive; b. Chgo., Aug. 28, 1929; s. Arthur Melcher and Ethel Teresina (Skoglund) A.; m. Lillian J. Anderson, Sept. 16, 1950; children—Gary, Kenneth, Kimberly, Lori. B.S. in E.E., U. Ill.-Urbana, 1950. Head dept. Hazeltine Corp., Commack, N.Y., 1950-66; dir. data systems Radiation, Inc., Melbourne, Fla., 1966-69; asst. to chmn. bd. Owen Steel Co., Inc., Columbia, S.C., 1969-83; gen. mgr. Winnsboro Plywood Co., Winnsboro, S.C., 1983—. Contbr. articles to profl. jours. Bd. dirs. Jr. Achievement Columbia, 1977—, pres., 1980-81; bd. dirs. United Way of Midlands, Columbia, 1979-82, Central Midlands Regional Planning Council, Columbia, 1981—, Central Midlands Devel. Corp., Columbia, 1982—. Recipient Achievement award Jr. Achievement, 1983. Mem. IEEE (sr.; chmn. computer group 1968-69), Am. Inst. Steel Constrn. (nat. chmn. safety and health com. 1972-82), Columbia C. of C. (v.p., dir. 1981—). Lodges: Rotary (Winnsboro); Masons. Home: 3701 Northshore Rd Columbia SC 29206 Office: Winnsboro Plywood Co Inc S Congress St PO Box 449 Winnsboro SC 29180

ANDERSON, DORIS EHLINGER, lawyer, editor; b. Houston, Dec. 1; d. Joseph Otto Ehlinger and Cornelia (Pagel) E.; m. Wiley Newton Anderson, Jr., Aug. 26, 1946; children—Wiley Newton III, Joseph Ehlinger. B.A., Rice U., 1946; LL.B., U. Tex., 1951, J.D., 1956; M.A. in Musicology, U. Okla., 1985. Bar: Tex. 1950. Assoc., Price, Guinn, Wheat & Veltmann, Houston, 1950-55; ptnr. Ehlinger & Anderson, Atty., Houston, 1955—; dir. Mus. Am. Architecture and Decorative Arts, Houston Bapt. U., 1980—. Parliamentarian, Harris County Flood Control Task Force; active Houston Ednl. Excellence Program, Preservation and Heritage, Docent at Bayou Bend, Mus. Fine Arts, Harris County, Heritage Soc., Harris County Hist. Soc., Am. Mus. Soc. and Nat. Trust, Alliance for Preservation, Ceramic Circle Am.; founder and dir. Liberty Belles and Beaux, Bayou Belles. Recipient YMCA's Outstanding Woman of Yr. award, 1982, 83. Mem. ABA, Tex. Bar Assn., Tex. Assn. Mus., Am. Assn. Mus., Decorative Arts Assn., Assn. State and Local History, Tex. Hist. Assn., Kappa Beta Pi. Episcopalian. Clubs: Sarah Lane Literary Soc., Duas. Republic Tex., San Jacinto Descs. (pres.). Editor: Houston, City of Destiny; contbr. articles to profl. jours. Home: 5556 Cranbrook Rd Houston TX 77056 Office: Houston Bapt U Mus of Am Architecture and Decorative Arts 7502 Fondren Rd Houston TX 77074

ANDERSON, E. KARL, lawyer; b. Huntington, W.Va., Mar. 30, 1931; s. Earle K. and Helen A.; m. Mary Elizabeth Williams, Nov. 13, 1953; children—Sharon E., Charles W. B.B.A., So. Meth. U., 1953, LL.B., 1960. Bar: Tex. 1960. Field service rep. Travelers Ins. Co., Dallas, 1956-57; claim mgr. Allstate Ins. Co., Dallas, 1958-63; sole practice, Dallas, 1963—; ptnr. Lastelick, Anderson & Hilliard, Dallas, 1968—. Served to 1st lt. USAF, 1954-56. Decorated Korean Service medal. Mem. ABA, Assn. Trial Lawyers Am., Tex. Trial Lawyers Assn., Dallas Trial Lawyers Assn. (dir.), Sigma Iota Epsilon, Delta Theta Phi. Republican. Presbyterian. Club: Dallas Country. Home: 3111 Drexel Dr Dallas TX 75205 Office: 1st Texas Bank 2608 Royal Ln Dallas TX 75229

ANDERSON, EDWARD MACKEY, geologist; b. Pottstown, Pa., Aug. 31, 1919; s. Harry Edward and Mary Kelso (Smith) A.; m. Janice Barnes Porter, Mar. 5, 1949; children—David Porter, Martha Barnes, Edward Mackey Jr., Sally Morton, Frederick Jason. B.A., Lafayette Coll., 1942. Geologist Tropical Oil Co., Bogota, Colombia, 1946-49; dist. geologist Am. Republics Corp., Houston, 1950-52, So. Union Gas, Dallas, 1952-54; chief geologist Aztec Oil and Gas Co., Dallas, 1954-61, v.p. exploration, 1961-73; sr. staff geologist Enserch Exploration, Inc., Dallas, 1973-77, chief geologist, 1977-84; dir. Geol. Info. Library of Dallas, 1970—; cons. in field. Communication chmn. Forest Hills Homeowners Assn., Dallas, 1985—. Served to lt. USN, 1942-46. Decorated Bronze Star. Mem. Am. Assoc. Petroleum Geologists, Dallas Geol. Soc. (pres. 1969-70, life), Phi Gamma Delta. Presbyterian. Club: U.S.S. Little Assn. (Dallas) (sec. treas. 1983—). Home: 8155 Santa Clara Dr Dallas TX 75218 Office: 111 E Irving Blvd Suite 406 Irving TX 75060

ANDERSON, FRANK WALTER, JR., bookstore executive; b. Birmingham, Ala., Sept. 28, 1921; s. Frank Walter and Margaret (Rasmussen) A.; m. Jose Dillon; 1 child, Julie; m. Helen Turner; children—Lisa, Carl. B.A., Birmingham So. Coll., 1946; M.A., U. N.C., 1948, Ph.D., 1951. Coll. instr. Birmingham So. U., U.N.C., Am. U., 1941-42, 1949-52, 1971; Editor Air U. Rev., Montgomery, Ala., 1951-61; historian NASA, Washington, 1961-80; bookseller Bookshelf Inc., Norcross, Ga., 1980—. Author: Orders of Magnitude, 1975, 80. Editor: Great Flying Stories, 1958. Contbr. articles to profl. jours. Served with USAF, 1942-46. Episcopalian. Avocation: woodworking. Home: 381 Engle Dr Tucker GA 30084 Office: Bookshelf Inc 5345 Jimmy Carter Blvd Norcross GA 30093

ANDERSON, FRANKLIN ROOSEVELT, plastic processing executive; b. Phenix City, Ala., Dec. 6, 1936; s. Charlie and Annie Lee (Wright) A.; m. Susie Ruth Powell, Aug. 31, 1973. M.B.A., Harvard U., 1971. With Hough Area Devel. Corp., Cleve., 1968-75, chief exec. officer, exec. dir., 1971-75; pres., chief exec. officer Custom Molders, Inc., Durham, N.C., 1977—. Chmn. Durham County Black Republicans, 1982—; mem. exec. com. Durham County Rep. Com., 1982-83. Served with USAF, 1954-58. Mem. Soc. Plastic Engrs. Baptist. Office: PO Box 15296 Durham NC 27704

ANDERSON, GEORGE ROSS, JR., federal judge; b. Anderson, S.C., Jan. 29, 1929; s. George Ross and Eva Mae (Pooler) A.; B.Comml. Sci., Southeastern U., 1949; postgrad. George Washington U., 1949-51; LL.B., U. S.C., 1954; m. Dorothy M. Downie, Dec. 2, 1951; 1 son, G. Ross. Mem. identification div. FBI, Washington, 1945-47; clk. to U.S. Senator Olin D. Johnston, Washington 1947-51, Columbia, S.C., 1953-54; admitted to S.C. bar, 1954; individual practice law, Anderson, S.C., 1954-79; U.S. dist. judge Dist. of S.C., Greenville, 1980—. Bd. dirs. Salvation Army, 1968, YMCA, 1968-79, Anderson Youth Assn., 1978-80. Served with USAF, 1951-52. Fellow Internat. Acad. Trial Lawyers (dir. 1979-81), Internat. Soc. Barristers; mem. S.C. Bar Assn. (dir. 1977-80, past circuit v.p.), Am. Bar Assn., Assn. Trial Lawyers Am. (bd. govs. 1969-71), S.C. Trial Lawyers Assn. (v.p. 1970-71, pres. 1971-72), Ga. Trial Lawyers Assn., Am. Assn. Forensic Scientists. Democrat. Baptist. Asst. editor U. S.C. Law Rev., 1953-54. Office: PO Box 2147 Anderson SC 29622

ANDERSON, GERALD BENTON, educator; b. Milw., Feb. 24, 1925; s. William Thomas and Helen Elvira (Merrell) A.; student Oberlin Coll., 1945-46; A.B., DePauw U., 1948; postgrad. Western Res. U., 1948-49; M.Ed., Coll. William and Mary, 1964, C.A.G.S. in Edn., 1979, postgrad. in higher edn., 1979—; M.S. in Personnel Adminstrn., George Washington U., 1967, M.A. in Edn., 1975, Ed.S., 1976; C.A.S. in Ednl. Adminstrn., Old Dominion U., 1978; m. Margaret Lee Walke, Apr. 11, 1953; children—Bradford Lee, Brice Tilden, Margaret Ellen. Served as enlisted man U.S. Navy, 1942-46, commd. ensign, 1949, advanced through grades to lt. comdr., serving 1949-56, 62, 68-72; head recruting br., Manpower div., Naval Res. and Tng. Dept., Fifth Naval Dir., Norfolk, Va., 1968-72; ret., 1977; social worker A, Social Service Bur., City Portsmouth (Va.), 1956; mgmt. trainee Sears Roebuck Co., Inc., Norfolk, Va., 1956-57; tchr. public schs., Portsmouth, 1957-58; contract specialist C.E., U.S. Army, Ft. Norfolk, Norfolk, 1958-59; personnel asst. Naval Ammunition Depot, St. Juliens Creek, Portsmouth, 1959, placement asst., 1959-62, personnel staffing specialist, 1962-64; employee devel. officer Naval Supply Center, Norfolk, 1964-66; head Employment/Employee Relations and Services Sect., Indsl. Relations Br., Naval Air Systems Command Rep., Atlantic, Norfolk, 1966-68, prin. classifier, 1972-73, sr. classification specialist, 1973-74, sr. staffing specialist, 1974, staff edn. and curriculum mgmt. specialist Fleet Tng. Center, 1974—. Mem. Am. Soc. Tng. and Devel. (pres. Southeastern Va chpt. 1980), Res. Officers Assn. U.S., Naval Res. Assn., Ret. Officers Assn., Nat. Soc. for Performance and Instrn., Nat. Geog. Soc., U.S. Naval Inst., D.A.V., V.F.W. (post comdr. 1982-84), Beta Theta Pi, Phi Delta Kappa. Methodist. Clubs: Toastmasters (pres. chpt. 1964), Kiwanis. Home: 601 Nansemond St Portsmouth VA 23707 Office: Fleet Tng Center Naval Sta Norfolk VA 23511

ANDERSON, HAYWARD SULLIVAN, educator; b. Thomasville, Ga., Nov. 30, 1920; s. Walter and Leroy (McCloud) A.; B.S., Savannah (Ga.) State Coll., 1946; B.S., Northwestern U., 1949; M.B.A., NYU, 1952; D.B.A. (Univ. doctoral research fellow 1957-58), Harvard U., 1961; m. Althea Mayme Williams, Mar. 19, 1966. Asst. prof. bus. W.Va. State Coll., Institute, 1953-56; prof. bus. adminstrn. Savannah State Coll., 1959-69, 73—, chmn. div., 1959-69; prof. bus. Jackson (Miss.) State Coll., 1969-72, chmn. div., 1969-72, dean Sch. Bus. and Econs., 1972. Mem. Ga. adv. council SBA, 1969; bd. dirs. Jackson Nat. Bus. League, 1970-72; bd. dirs. Jackson Urban League, 1972; bd. dirs. Savannah Area Minority Contractor Assn., 1976-78, chmn. bd., 1978; mem. adv. bd. dirs. YWCA, 1976-81; mem. Chatham County-Savannah Met. Planning Commn., 1977-82. Served to 1st lt. U.S. Army, 1943-46, 50. Mem. Am. Accounting Assn., Am. Mktg. Assn., AAUP (pres. local chpt. 1967-69, mem. exec. com. Ga. conf. 1968-69), Harvard Bus. Club Atlanta, So. Bus. Adminstrn. Assn. (exec. com. 1972-73), Savannah Area C. of C. (bus. task force 1977-80), Phi Delta Kappa. Mailing Address: PO Box 3655 Savannah GA 31414

ANDERSON, HELEN SHARP, civic worker; b. Ennis, Tex., June 10, 1916; d. John H. and Eula (King) Sharp; A.B., U. Tex., 1937; m. Thomas Dunaway Anderson, Feb. 21, 1938; children—John Sharp, Helen Shaw, Lucille Streeter. Mem. Mt. Vernon Ladies Assn. of the Union, vice regent, 1967—, regent, 1982—; bd. dirs. Nat. Cathedral Assn., Washington, 1971-75, also mem. various spl. coms.; mem. Garden Club Am., 1945—, zone vice-chmn., 1959-62, nat. dir., 1975-77, nat. v.p., 1977-79, nat. chmn. long-range planning, 1979-80; bd. dirs. Japan Am. Soc. Houston, 1974-78; mem. fine arts adv. com. U. Tex., Austin, 1963—; chmn. Jr. Gallery, Mus. Fine Arts, Houston, 1953-54, docent, 1964-70; bd. dirs. Houston and Harris County council Girl Scouts U.S.A., 1966-67, Sheltering Arms, 1964-67; bd. dirs. Harris County Heritage Soc., 1963-65, v.p., 1965-66; mem. River Oaks Garden Club, Houston, 1945—, pres., 1958, 59; mem. coms. Christ Ch. Cathedral, Houston; mem. Houston Jr. League. Republican. Episcopalian. Clubs: Sulgrave (Washington); River Oaks Garden (Houston); Assembly; Bolero. Address: 3925 Del Monte Dr Houston TX 77019

ANDERSON, HENRY BARRY, fire chief, educator; b. Columbia, S.C., Sept. 26, 1952; s. Henry Wilson and Margie Elizabeth (Martin) A.; m. Kathi Marlene Sheppard, Apr. 19, 1973 (div. Feb. 1976); m. Cynthia Jean Moore, Aug. 7, 1977; 1 child, Lauren Nicole. Student Midlands Inst. Tech., Columbia, 1970-71; student various fire service classes S.C. Fire Acad., 1971-75, S.C. Criminal Justice Acad., 1976, 79, Internat. Assn. Arson Investigators, 1977, Rugers U., 1978, Wateree Dive Sch., 1980. Firefighter West Columbia Fire Dept., S.C., 1971-72, engr., 1972-74, lt., 1974-76, capt., 1976, asst. chief, 1976-81, chief, 1981—; instr. S.C. Fire Acad. Mem. Internat. Assn. Arson Investigators (pres. S.C. chpt. 1982—), S.C. State Fire Chiefs Assn. (com. chmn. 1984-85), Lexington County Fire Chiefs (sec. 1983-85), S.C. State Firemen's Assn. Lodge: Masons. Avocations: drag racing; yardwork. Home: 121 Ivyfield Rd Columbia SC 29169 Office: West Columbia Fire Dept PO Box 4044 West Columbia SC 29171

ANDERSON, HERMAN LEROY, bishop, African Methodist Episcopal Zion Church; b. Wilmington, N.C.; s. Felix Sylvester and Bessie Bernice (Bizzell) A.; m. Ruth Rosetta Rogers, July 6, 1946; children—Deborah Anderson Kareem, Herman L., Derrick R. B.S., Tuskegee Inst., 1943; B.Div., Hood Theol. Sem., Salisbury, N.C., 1959; D.Div. (hon.), Livingstone Coll., Salisbury, 1980. Pastor, St. James A.M.E. Zion Ch., Ithaca, N.Y., 1959-62, Soldiers Meml. A.M.E. Zion Ch., Salisbury, N.C., 1962-72, Broadway Temple A.M.E. Zion Ch., Louisville, 1972-76; gen. sec. A.M.E. Zion Ch., Charlotte, N.C., 1976-80, bishop, 1980—. Co-author: Churches and Church Membership, 1980. Bd. dirs. World Meth. Council; trustee Livingstone Coll. Served with USNR, 1944-46. Mem. Congress Nat. Black Churchmen (dir. 1984—). Address: African Methodist Episcopal Zion Church 5700 Barrington Dr Charlotte NC 28215*

ANDERSON, HOWARD PALMER, state senator; b. Crystall Hill, Va., May 25, 1915; B.A., Coll. William and Mary, 1940; LL.B., U. Richmond, 1948; m. Mildred Graham Webb. Bar: Va. 1948. Former FBI agt.; practice law, Halifax, Va., 1950—; mem. Va. Ho. of Dels., 1958-71, Va. State Senate, 1972—. Trustee, Patrick Henry Meml. Found.; mem. Halifax County Sch. Bd., 1952-57. Served with USNR, World War II. Mem. Va. Bar Assn., Halifax County Bar Assn., U. Richmond Law Sch. Assn., Halifax County C. of C., Am. Legion, VFW. Baptist. Clubs: Masons, Sportsman (Halifax). Office: PO Box 847 Halifax VA 24558

ANDERSON, J. C., JR., university dean. Dean, U. S.C. at Sumter. Office: U SC at Sumter 200 Miller Rd Sumter SC 29150*

ANDERSON, JACK OLAND, college president emeritus; b. Mich., Aug. 5, 1921; s. Seymour and Laura (Fox) A.; student Ferris State Coll.; B.S., Central Mich. U., 1948; M.A., U. Mich., 1950; Ed.D., Mich. State U., 1962. Tchr. pub. schs., Mich., 1949-59; asst. instr. Mich. State U., 1959-62; dir. edn. Lansing (Mich.) Bus. Inst., 1963-65; exec. dir. Lockyear Bus. Coll., 1965-66; acad. dean Detroit Coll., 1966-69; pres. Bristol (Tenn.) Coll., from 1969, now pres. emeritus, bd. dirs.; chmn. bd. dirs., mem. Sullivan County Vocat. Adv. Com.; past-chmn. region IV proprietary sch. coordinating council U.S. Dept. Edn. mem. task force com. vocat.-bus. and industry project U. Tenn. Coll. Vocat.-Tech. Edn. Mem. Tenn. Pub. Service Council; past mem. bd. adminstrn. First Bapt. Ch., Bristol; past mem. exec. com. Appalachian Regional Community Health Assn.; mem. Bristol Power Bd. Served to capt. U.S. Army, 1942-46. Mem. Assn. Ind. Colls. and Schs. (mem., past chmn. research com.), Tenn. Bus. Coll. Assn. (past pres. and dir.), Southeastern Bus. Coll. Assn. (past pres. and dir.), Sullivan County Hist. Assn., Bristol Hist. Assn., Rocky Mount Hist. Soc., Bristol Humane Soc., Bristol C. of C. (past dir., chmn. congressional action 1979, chmn. econ. impact subcom. of coal com.). Baptist. Club: Country of Bristol. Lodges: Bristol Rotary (dir., chmn. Dist. 757 Rotary Found.), Elks. Address: PO Box 757 Bristol TN 37621

ANDERSON, JAMES CARL, energy information specialist, speaker and writer; b. Gainesboro, Tenn., Oct. 22, 1931; s. James Bedford and Lola Betty (Loftis) A.; m. Mary Ann Roselli, July 3, 1965 (div. Aug. 1976); children—Kimberly Ann, Michael Stuart. B.S., Tenn. Tech. U., 1954; M.Ed., U. Colo., 1962. Cert. flight instr. Exhibits mgr. Oak Ridge Inst. Nuclear Studies, 1957-66; staff asst. energy devel. Dept. of Commerce, State of Wash., Olympia, Wash., 1966-69; tng. coordinator Combustion Engring., Inc., Windsor, Conn., 1969-75; TV support activities NUS Corp., Rockville, Md., 1970-73; speaker, energy info. specialist, lectr. Oak Ridge Assoc. Univs., 1976—. Mem. Republican Nat. Comm., 1976—. Served as 1st lt., Signal Corps, U.S. Army, 1954-56. Mem. Am. Nuclear Soc., Phi Delta Kappa. Lodge: Toastmasters (past pres., area gov. and dist. gov.). Home: 214 N Purdue St Apt 308 Oak Ridge TN 37830 Office: Oak Ridge Associated Universities PO Box 117 Oak Ridge TN 37830

ANDERSON, JAMES WILSON, banker; b. Scottsboro, Ala., Mar. 16, 1946; s. James Clyde and Kate Audrey (Ledbetter) A.; m. Sheila Elaine Guinn, Sept. 18, 1971; children—Lori Leigh, Blake Guinn. Diploma Grad. Sch. Banking of the South, La. State U., 1975; A.S., Snead State Jr. Coll., 1977; B.S., Jacksonville State U., Ala., 1979. With People's State Bank, Grant, Ala., 1969-76, cashier, 1973-76; asst. v.p. Citizens Bank of Talladega, Ala., 1976-79, sr. v.p., 1979-82, exec. v.p., 1982-83; corp. v.p. AmSouth Bank, N.A., Talladega, 1983—. Mem. citizens adv. com. Talladega Sch. Bd., 1984; mem. Talladega Indsl. Devel. Bd., 1983—; mem. com. United Way, Talladega, 1985—; bd. dirs. Assn. for Retarded Citizens, Guntersville, Ala., 1971-72, treas., 1970-71. Served with USAF, 1964-69, PTO. Recipient spl. award State Senate of Ala., 1983. Mem. Ala. Cattleman's Assn. Baptist. Club: Alpine Bay Country. Lodge: Lions (v.p. 1981-84, pres. 1984—). Home: 113 Brookview Dr PO Box 522 Talladega AL 35160

ANDERSON, JANICE CAROLYN, nurse, cardiac sonographer; b. Savannah, Ga., Aug. 27, 1939; d. James Carswell and Lois Elizabeth (Robbins) Milligan; m. James Mixon Anderson, Sr., Sept. 5, 1959; children—James Mixon, Joseph, Jill. Diploma nursing U. Sch. Nursing, Augusta, Ga., 1966;

B.S., Med. Coll. Ga., 1977. Staff nurse U. Hosp., Augusta, Ga., 1966; staff nurse coronary care unit St. Joseph Hosp., Augusta, 1967, head nurse coronary care unit, 1968, adminstrv. supr. coronary care unit, 1969-73, nurse instr. coronary care tng. program, 1970-73; nurse coordinator Augusta area cardiovascular facility Univ. Hosp., Augusta, 1972-73; inservice ednl. instr., coordinator continuing nursing edn. Hosp. and Clinics, Med. Coll. Ga., Augusta, 1973-75; cardiovascular nurse cons. Meml. Hosp. Washington County, Sandersville, Ga., 1974-75; cardiovascular nurse clinician Paul E. Cundey, Jr., M.D., cardiologist, Augusta, Ga., 1975—. Chmn. nursing edn. com. Am. Heart Assn., Ga. affiliate, 1973-74; bd. dirs. Am. Heart Assn., Ga. affiliate, Richmond County unit, 1973—, co-chmn. high blood pressure com. Recipient Bronze Service medallion, Ga. affiliate, Am. Heart Assn., 1971, Silver Service medallion, 1973, Gold Service medallion, 1975. Mem. Am. Heart Assn., Am. Soc. Echocardiography. Home: 3410 Sutton Pl Augusta GA 30906 Office: 1003 Chafee Ave Augusta GA 30904

ANDERSON, JAY ROBERT, computer co. exec.; b. Mpls., July 26, 1946; s. John Robert and Barbara Ann (Bessesen) A.; student public schs.; m. Sandra Marie Lons, July 4, 1972. Tech. support engr. Data 100 Corp., Washington, 1971-72; sales rep. Mohawk Data Co., Washington, 1972-73; sr. sales rep. Pertec Computer Co., Washington, 1973-77; br. mgr. Tesdata Systems Co., Washington, 1977-78; sales mgr. Nixdorf Computer Corp., Arlington, Va., 1979-81; v.p. Terminals Unltd., Inc., 1981-83; nat. sales mgr. Forte Data Systems, Vienna, Va., 1983—. Served with USMC, 1964-68; Vietnam. Decorated Purple Heart. Mem. Data Processing Mgmt. Assn., Data Entry Mgmt. Assn., VFW, DAV. Home: 12211 Jennell Dr Bristow VA 22013 Office: 301 Maple Ave W Vienna VA 22013

ANDERSON, JOHN WILLIAM, corporation research director; b. Lexington, Ky., Feb. 7, 1946; s. John and Ethel Kathleen (Wallace) A.; m. Karen Sue Cahoon, Nov. 2, 1968; 1 dau., Sara. B.S. in Bus. Adminstrn., Eastern Ky. U., 1968. Indsl. engr. Blue Bell Inc., Lenoir, N.C., 1973-76, Mayaguez, P.R., 1976-78, indsl. engring. mgr., Morehead City, N.C., 1978-84, dir. research, 1984—. Deacon, 1st Presbyterian Ch., Morehead City. Served to capt. U.S. Army, 1968-72. Decorated Bronze Star, Air Medal. Mem. Am. Inst. Indsl. Engrs. Republican. Club: Rotary. Home: 19 Wheaton Circle Greensboro NC 27406 Office: care Blue Bell PO Box 21488 Greensboro NC 27420

ANDERSON, KENNETH HARTLEY, geologist; b. Carthage, Mo., Mar. 28, 1923; s. Frank O. and Madoline A. (Aurelia) A.; B.A., Drury Coll., 1951; postgrad. Mo. Sch. Mines, 1953-54. Cartographic engr. Central Topographic div. Dept. Interior, Rolla, Mo., 1951; subsurface geologist Mo. Geol. Survey, Rolla, 1951-54; party chief Egyptian-Am. Oil Co., Cairo/Alexandria, 1954-56; research geologist Pan Am. Petroleum, Midland, Tex. and Libya, 1956-58; party chief Petrobras, Brazil, 1958-60; chief subsurface geology and oil and gas Mo. Geol. Survey, Rolla, 1960-81; sr. devel. geologist Coastal Oil & Gas, Amarillo, Tex., 1981—; cons. in field. Served with USAAF, 1943-46. Mem. Am. Assn. Petroleum Geologists, Soc. Mining Engrs. of AIME, Panhandle Geol. Soc., Assn. of Mo. Geologists, Sigma Xi. Democrat. Presbyterian. Club: Optimist. Contbr. articles to profl. jours. Home: 3113 Surf Dr Amarillo TX 79110 Office: PO Box 1332 Amarillo TX 79189

ANDERSON, KIM EDWARD, manufacturing company executive; b. Okarche, Okla., Nov. 6, 1950; s. Kermit E. and Zeta F. (Crawfords) A.; m. Rebecca Cogwell, May 29, 1976; children—Kristin Lain, Courtney Lynn. B.S., East Central U., 1972; M.S., Okla. U., 1973, Ph.D., 1986. Cert. hazard control mgr., cert. hazardous material mgr. Engr., Okla. Health Dept., Ada, 1971-72; indsl. hygienist Johnson Space Ctr., NASA, Houston, 1973-74; supr. indsl. hygienist U.S. Dept. Labor, Little Rock, 1974-78; corp. dir. environ. safety and health A.O. Smith Corp., Milw., 1978—; asst. prof. U. Ark., 1976—, U. Central Ark., Conway. Author: Fundamentals of Industrial Toxicology, 1981. Contbr. articles to profl. jours. Mem. clean air com. Am. Lung Assn., Little Rock, 1980; mem. com. hazardous waste Conv. Commn. 83, bd. dirs., v.p., chmn. Ark. Fedn. Water Air Users Soc., Little Rock, 1983—. Recipient Skylab Achievement award Johnson Space Ctr., NASA, 1973, Environ. Merit award Okla. Health Dept., 1972; named Ark. Safety Profl. of Yr., 1984; grantee EPA, 1980-82, USPHS, 1972-73; Okla. Frontiers Sci. scholar, 1972-73. Mem. Am. Soc. Safety Engrs. (pres. Ark. chpt. 1982-83), Am. Indsl. Hygiene Assn. (mem. toxicology com. 1978-81, workroom environ. exposure level com. 1979-81), Am. Indsl. Hygiene Assn. (sec. Gulf Coast sect. 1973, pres. Ark. sect. 1979), Am. Welding Soc. (co-chmn. safety health com. 1980-81), Ark. State C. of C. (chmn. safety and health com.). Republican. Methodist. Avocations: athletics; tennis. Office: A O Smith Corp PO Box 23974 Milwaukee WI 53223

ANDERSON, LARRY EMMETT, vocational guidance counselor; b. Roanoke, Va., July 18, 1942; s. James Emmett and Beulah Mae (Duncan) A.; m. Brenda Kay Dillon, June 11, 1966; 1 son, Larry Emmett. A.B., Marshall U., 1966; M.A., W.Va. U., 1969; postgrad. W.Va. U., 1969-72, Marshall U., 1972-76. Tchr., Stoco Jr. High Sch., Besoco, W.Va., 1966-67; counselor Stratton Jr. High Sch., Beckley, W.Va., 1967-72; career edn. coordinator Raleigh County Schs., Beckley, 1972-76; vocat. guidance counselor Raleigh County Vo-Tech Ctr., Beckley, 1976—. Mem. W.Va. State Adv. Council Voct. Edn., 1980; cons. career edn. Mem. NEA, W.Va. Edn. Assn., W.Va. Personnel and Guidance Assn. Home: Route 2 Box 126B Beckley WV 25801 Office: 410 1/2 Stanaford Rd Beckley WV 25801

ANDERSON, MARTHA JEAN, genealogical publisher, researcher; b. Columbus, Ga., Dec. 8, 1933; d. Ocie Dee and Mary W. (Curlee) Smith; m. James Cornelius Anderson, Aug. 12, 1950; children—Melanie Delane Anderson Knight, Susan Denise Anderson Hancock, Teresa Jean, James Kelly. Student Perry Bus. Sch., 1957-59. Sec., receptionist Sta. WTRP, LaGrange, Ga., 1959-60, program dir., 1960-72, comml. writer sales, 1972-74, mgr., 1974-81; owner, pub. Family Tree, Geneal. Books & Supplies, LaGrange, 1981—. Columnist LaGrange Daily News, 1979-84. Bd. dirs. Am. Heart Assn., Am. Cancer Soc., United Fund. Recipient Dist. Award of Merit, Boy Scouts Am., 1975. Mem. Ga. Geneal. Soc., LaGrange C. of C. (pres. women's div.), Ala. Geneal. Soc., West Central Ga. Geneal. Assn. (bd. dirs. 1983—). Democrat. Methodist. Avocations: needlework, free lance writing. Home: 100 Shamrock Dr LaGrange GA 30240 Office: Family Tree 109 Bull St LaGrange GA 30240

ANDERSON, MICHAEL ANTON, oil field production equipment company sales account representative, custom home builder; b. Galveston, Tex., June 10, 1957; s. Bernard Anton and Joyce Elaine (Hersey) A.; m. Gay Lynn Hoffman, Aug. 20, 1983. B.B.A., U. Tex., 1980. Sales rep. Bethlehem Steel Corp., Houston, 1980-84, Red Man Pipe & Supply Co., Houston, 1984—. Mem. U. Tex. Ex-Students Assn., U. Tex. Coll. Bus. Adminstrn. Century Club. Republican. Roman Catholic. Clubs: Eldorado Country. Avocations: golf; water skiing. Home: 54 N Watertree Ln The Woodlands TX 77380 Office: Red Man Pipe & Supply Co 12941 Interstate Hwy 45 N Suite 408 Houston TX 77060

ANDERSON, NANCY KATHERINE, food company official, career development consultant; b. Mpls., Apr. 17, 1948; d. Robert V. and Kathleen M. (Kanz) A.; m. Gordon V. Wein, Feb. 14, 1985. Student Cardinal Stritch Coll., Milw., 1966-69; B.S. in Psychology, George Washington U., 1979; M.P.A., U. Colo., 1982. Trainer, career cons. GAO, Washington, 1970-80; prin., career cons. Nancy K. Anderson & Assocs., Denver, 1980-83; mgr. mgmt. devel. Anderson Clayton Foods, Dallas, 1983—. Author articles in field. Sec.-treas., bd. dirs. Prestonwood Green Condo Assn., 1984-86; chair women's adv. bd. to Comptroller Gen. U.S., 1977-79; mem. EEO adv. council GAO, 1977-78. Recipient EEO award Comptroller Gen., 1977; cert. of merit GAO, 1978, 79; others. Mem. Am. Soc. Tng. and Devel. (award 1984), Dallas Personnel Assn., Nat. Assn. Female Execs. Avocations: tennis; scuba diving; softball; bicycling; filmmaking. Home: 5300 Keller Springs Rd Suite 1075 Dallas TX 75248 Office: Anderson Clayton Foods 12221 Merit Dr Dallas TX 75251

ANDERSON, NEIL MARTIN, management consultant; b. Boone, Iowa, May 2, 1937; s. Wilbert Martin and Leona Jeannette (Larson) A.; B.A. with distinction. U. Iowa; m. Barbara Gordon Nall, June 11, 1960; children—Keith Gordon, Sally Wadsworth. Actuarial asst. Nat. Life & Accident Ins. Co., Nashville, 1959-62, asst. actuary, 1962-65, 2d v.p., assoc. actuary to v.p. and chief actuary individual ins. div., 1965-75, sr. v.p., chief actuary, 1975-79; sr. v.p. NLT Corp., Nashville, 1979-80, exec. v.p., also dir., 1980-84; v.p. Tillinghast, Nelson & Warren, Atlanta, 1984—; pres. Tillinghost & Co., Atlanta, 1986—. Fellow Soc. Actuaries; mem. Am. Acad. Actuaries, Southeastern Actuaries Club (past pres.). Lutheran. Home: 1075 Brookhaven Sq Atlanta GA Office: 3340 Peachtree Rd NE Suite 2000 Atlanta GA 30026

ANDERSON, R. LANIER, judge; b. Macon, Ga., Nov. 12, 1936; s. Robert L. and Helen Anderson; m. Nancy Briska, Aug. 18, 1962; children—Robert, William Hilliar, Browne McIntosh. A.B. magna cum laude, Yale U., 1958; LL.B., Harvard U., 1961. Judge U.S. Ct. Appeals, 11th Cir., Macon, 1979—. Address: PO Box 977 Macon GA 31202*

ANDERSON, REBECCA SHEIDLER, mathematics educator, computer consultant; b. Mansfield, Ohio, Nov. 21, 1944; d. Robert Guy and Helen Bartholomew Sheidler; m. Robert Wayne Anderson, Nov. 27, 1981; children by previous marriage—Steven Nolte, Christopher Nolte. B.A., Miami U., Oxford, Ohio, 1966; postgrad. Hillsborough Community Coll., 1980-81, U. South Fla., 1981—. Tchr., Shroder Jr. High Sch., Cin., 1966-68, Anderson High Sch., Cin., 1968-70, West Milford High Sch., 1978-80; tchr., curriculum coordinator Tomlin Jr. High Sch., Plant City, Fla., 1980—; v.p. Mgmt. Internat. Resources, Brandon, Fla., 1981—; pres. Anderson Assocs., Brandon, 1981—. Mem. State Tchrs. Assn., Tampa C. of C. Republican. Presbyterian. Home: 3066 Wister Circle Valrico FL 33594 Office: PO Box 1520 Brandon FL 33511

ANDERSON, RICHARD LOREE, mathematician, educator; b. North Liberty, Ind., Apr. 20, 1915; s. George W. and Mabel (Schrader) A.; m. Mary E. Turner, Jan. 31, 1946; children—Kathryn Hart, William Bayard. A.B., DePauw U., 1936; M.S., Iowa State Coll., 1938, Ph.D., 1941. Mem. faculty dept. stats. N.C. State U., Raleigh, 1941-66, assoc. prof. 1945-50, prof., 1951-66; research mathematician Princeton U., 1944-45; prof. stats. Purdue U., Lafayette, Ind., 1950-51; research prof. stats. U. Ga., Athens, 1966-67; prof. dept. stats. U. Ky., Lexington, 1967-80, chmn. dept., 1967-79, asst. to dean Coll. Agr., 1980-85; v.p. Statis. Consultants, Inc., 1985—; mem. econ. research adv. com. U.S. Dept. Agr., 1965-68; cons. various def., govt. instns., 1955-67, Internat. Math. and Stats. Libraries, 1970—; vis. prof. U. Umea, Sweden, 1977, Indian Statis. Inst., 1977. Mng. editor Statis. Theory and Method Abstracts, 1958-67. Author: (with T.A. Bancroft) Statistical Theory in Research, 1952. Mem. editorial bd. Communications in Stats., 1972-85. Contbr. articles to profl. jours. Grantee Ford Found. 1958, U. Cairo 1969. NSF vis. lectr. 1954-65. Fellow Am. Statis. Assn. (mem. census adv. com. 1972-77, chmn. com. 1977, dir., 1976-78, chmn. com. stats. and environ. 1979-81, pres. 1983), Inst. Math. Stats. (mem. council 1955-57, 62-64), AAAS (sect. U 1979); mem. Biometric Soc. (pres. Eastern N.Am. region 1966). Internat. Statis. Inst., Phi Beta Kappa, Sigma Xi, Phi Kappa Phi, Gamma Sigma Delta. Home: 3349 Braemer Dr Lexington KY 40502

ANDERSON, ROBERT AEIKER, college administrator; b. Winfield, W.Va., July 22, 1927; s. Jerome Waldo and Mae (Aeiker) A.; m. Charlotte Ann Thomas, Aug. 2, 1952; children—Robert Thomas, Stephen Phillip, Nancy Dianne. Student Duke U., 1945-46; B.A., Marshall U., 1951, M.A., 1954; Ed.D., Nova U., 1979. Tchr., coach Winfield High Sch., W.Va., 1951-57, prin., 1957-60; asst. prin. Stonewall Jackson High Sch., Charleston, W.Va., 1960-62; prin. Cocoa High Sch., Fla., 1962-66; dir. maintenance and transp., Brevard County Sch. Bd., Titusville, Fla., 1966-68; dean collegewide student services, Brevard Community Coll., Cocoa, 1968—. Trustee Wuesthoff Meml. Hosp., Rockledge, Fla., 1978-85; bd. dirs. Brevard United Way, Cocoa, 1973-85, Community Services Council, Cocoa, 1983-85; councilman City of Rockledge, 1968-72; mem. sch. bd. Brevard County, 1972-84. Served with U.S. Army, 1946-47. Recipient Fla. State 4-H award, 1975, Marshall U. Alumni award, 1982. Mem. Fla. Assn. Community Colls., Fla. Assn. Coll. Registrars and Admissions Officers, So. Assn. Coll. Registrars and Admissions officers, Am. Assn. Coll. Registrars and Admissions Officers. Democrat. Presbyterian. Lodges: Rotary, Masons, Shriners, Internat. Order Foresters. Avocations: sports; gardening. Home: 1292 St Andrews Dr Rockledge FL 32955 Office: Brevard Community College 1519 Clearlake Rd Cocoa FL 32922

ANDERSON, ROBERT CLETUS, university administrator; b. Birmingham, Ala., July 18, 1921; s. Allie Cletus and Dana Beatrice (Hilliard) A.; B.S., Auburn U., 1942; M.A., U. N.C., 1948; Ph.D., NYU, 1950; m. Evalee R. Pilgrim; children—Margaret Campbell, William Robert. Research asst. U. N.C., 1946-47; asst. to dean N.Y. U., 1948-50; dir. Grad. Sch., Memphis State U., 1950-53; exec. assoc. So. Regional Edn. Bd., Atlanta, 1953-55, assoc. dir., 1955-57, dir., 1957-61; exec. v.p. Auburn U. Research Found., 1961-65; v.p. research, prof. sociology U. Ga., Athens, 1965-84, Univ. prof., spl. asst. to pres., 1984—; pres. U. Ga. Research Found., 1978-84. Mem. Surgeon Gen.'s Cons. Group on Med. Edn., 1958-59; mem. edn. adv. com. W.K. Kellogg Found., 1960-64; mem. Joint Council on Ednl. Telecommunications, 1961-70, v.p., 1965-67; dir. Nat. Conf. on the Future of Univ. Research, 1984. Served with U.S. Army, 1942-46. Decorated Purple Heart. Mem. AAAS, Nat. Acad. Univ. Research Adminstrs. (pres. 1985—), N.Y. Acad. Sci., Am. Assn. Higher Edn., Nat. Coalition for Sci. and Tech. (adv. bd.), Nat. Council Univ. Research Adminstrs. (exec. com. 1982-85), Nat. Conf. Advancement Research (exec. com. 1980-84), Soc. Research Adminstrs. (editorial bd.), Phi Kappa Phi, Alpha Tau Omega, Alpha Kappa Delta, Kappa Delta Pi, Omicron Delta Kappa, Phi Delta Kappa. Home: 110 Holmes Ct Athens GA 30606 Office: Old College U Ga Athens GA 30602

ANDERSON, ROBERT LEE, forest pathologist; b. Monmouth, Ill., Nov. 28, 1944; s. Clifford D. and Donna M. (Hoffman) A.; m. Martha Jane Montgomery, June 29, 1968; children—Rodney, Janette. B.S., U. Mo., 1968, M.S., 1969; postgrad. U. Nev., 1969-70. Spl. project forester Mo. Dept. Conservation, Columbia, 1972-74; plant pathologist U.S. Dept. Agr. Forest Service, St. Paul, 1974-77, methods application coordinator, Delaware, Ohio, 1977-78, supervisory plant pathologist, mgr. Resistance Screening Ctr., Asheville, N.C., 1978—. Co-pres. P.T.A., 1982; Sunday Sch. supt. Assembly of God Ch., 1982. Served to capt. USAF, 1969-72. Recipient Merit award Mo. Dept. Conservation, 1972; Merit award U.S. Forest Service, 1978, Outstanding Achievement award, 1981, Merit award, 1983; N.C. P.T.A. Oak Leaf award, 1983; named Civil Servant of Yr., Fed. Employees Bd., 1975. Mem. Soc. Am. Foresters, Forest Farmer Assn., Am. Phytopath. Assn., Xi Sigma Pi, Gamma Sigma Delta. Mem. Assembly of God Ch. Contbr. articles to profl. jours. Home: Route 3 Box 2680 Arden NC 28704 Office: 200 Weaver Blvd Asheville NC 28806

ANDERSON, ROBERT WAYNE, nursing home administrator; b. Huntsville, Ala., Feb. 11, 1946; s. Clinton Carter and Pearl M. (Flatt) A.; m. Gwendelin Scudder, June 28, 1969; 1 child, Rachael Louellen. Student George Washington U., 1967, U. Ill.-Chgo., 1964-65, U. Md., 1967, Chulalonghorn U., Bangkok, 1968; B.A., Harding U., 1977. Clk. cost acctg. Am. Maize, Roby, Ind., 1965-66; purchasing agt. Cosden Oil and Chem., Calumet City Ill., 1969-71; asst. mgr. office Harts Bakery, Memphis, 1977-79; adminstr. Care Ctr. Mgmt. Co., Memphis, 1979—; cons. in field. Mem. steering com. Project Life, 1983-84; mem. com. ARC. Served with U.S. Army, 1966-69. Mem. Am. Coll. Health Care Adminstrs., Tenn. Health Care Assn. (edn. com. 1982-83), Am. Health Care Assn., Nat. League Nurses, VFW, NEA. Mem. Ch. Christ. Avocations: artistry; woodworking; bass fishing. Office: Mid City Care Ctr 1428 Monroe St Memphis TN 38104

ANDERSON, RONALD KENT, nurse; b. Jacksonville, Fla., July 25, 1952; s. James Elias II and Dortha Helen (Brannen) A. A.A., Fla. Jr. Coll., 1974; B.S., Atlantic Christian Coll., Wilson, N.C., 1979. R.N., Fla. critical care nurse Bapt. Med. Ctr., Jacksonville, 1979—. Expert witness legal matters, 1984—. Recipient Service award Bapt. Med. Ctr., 1985. Mem. Fla. Nurses Assn., Am. Nurses Assn., Am. Assn. Critical Care Nurses, Sigma Theta Tau. Democrat. Baptist. Lodge: DeMolay. Avocations: aerobics; music; dance; gemology; hunting. Office: Bapt Med Ctr 800 Prudential Dr Jacksonville FL 32207

ANDERSON, SCARVIA BATEMAN, psychologist, educator; b. Balt., Aug. 12, 1926; d. Samuel Harrison Bennett and Juliette R. (Bateman) Anderson; m. John S. Helmick, Jan. 8, 1983. B.S. in English and Math., Miss. State U., 1945; M.A. in Psychology, Vanderbilt U., 1951; Ph.D. in Psychology, U. Md., 1955. Tchr., Nashville City Schs., 1945-51; research psychologist Naval Research Lab., Washington, 1951-55; with Edn. Testing Service, Princeton, N.J., 1956-77, sr. v.p., 1977-82; cons., prof. psychology Ga. Inst. Tech., Atlanta, 1982—. Author: The Profession and Practice of Program Evaluation, 1978; Encyclopedia of Educational Evaluation, 1975. Editor: book on edn. testing, 1983. Contbr. articles to profl. jours. Fulbright fellow, 1955-56. Fellow Am. Psychol. Assn.; mem. Evaluation Research Soc. (past pres.), Am. Ednl. Research Assn., Nat. Council Measurement Edn. (past dir.), Internat. Council Psychologists, Sigma Xi, Kappa Mu Epsilon, Ansley Golf Club, Sea Pines Club. Republican. Episcopalian. Avocations: golf; needlework; writing. Home: 1243 Colony House 145 15th St NE Atlanta GA 30361 Office: Sch Psychology Ga Inst Tech Atlanta GA 30332

ANDERSON, TERRY DALE, manufacturing company official; b. Galesbury, Ill., Feb. 3, 1945; s. Richard Lloyd and Mary Climons (Simmons) A.; m. Sandra Smith, May 6, 1977; children—Donna D., David D. B.S. in Electronics, Bradley U., 1968. Supr., Johnson & Johnson MSDP, Chgo., 1968-70, planning mgr., 1970, dept. mgr., 1971, asst. engring. mgr. Baby Products div., Park Forest South, Ill., 1971-73, supt., 1973-74, mgr. package engring., Piscataway, N.J., 1976-80, mgr. engring. projects, 1976-81, nat. energy coordinator, 1977-81, mgr. packaging engring., 1980-81; group mgr. packaging equipment design and devel. Frito-Lay, Inc., Dallas, 1982-83, sect. mgr. packaging equipment implementation, 1983—. Active United Fund. Mem. Assn. Energy Engrs., Am. Mgmt. Assn., N.J. Assn. Energy, Pi Kappa Alpha. Democrat. Baptist. Home: 123 Red Oak Ln Flower Mound TX 75028 Office: 7929 Brook River Dr Dallas TX 75247

ANDERSON, THOMAS JEROME, educational administrator, orchestra conductor; b. Atlanta, Feb. 28, 1943; s. Farris Furman and Suzelle (Bergren) A.; children—Scott Thomas, Kristen Sue. B.A., Duke U., 1965; Mus.M., Fla. State U., 1967, Ph.D., 1977. Chmn. div. fine arts DeKalb Coll., Clarkston, Ga., 1971—; condr. DeKalb Symphony Orch., Clarkston, 1979—. Mem. Met. Assn. for Performing Arts, Inc. (pres., dir. 1984—). Home: 4305 Lehaven Circle Tucker GA 30084 Office: DeKalb Symphony Orch 555 N Indian Creek Dr Clarkston GA 30021

ANDERSON, THOMAS LEE, clinical psychologist; b. Dallas, Dec. 22, 1952; s. Cecil Hall and Winnie Maude (Hargrove) A. B.S., Tex. A&M U., 1974; M.A., Stephen F. Austin State U., 1980; Ph.D., U. Miss., 1984. Lic. psychol. examiner, Tenn. Head Start cons., Oxford, Miss., 1980-82; commd. 2d lt. U.S. Army, 1982, advanced through grades to capt., 1982; intern in psychology Beaumont Army Med. Ctr., El Paso, Tex., 1982-83; chief psychology service Moncrief Army Hosp., Ft. Jackson, S.C., 1984—. U.S. Army scholar 1980-82. Mem. Am. Psychol. Assn., Am. Soc. Clin. Hypnosis, S.C. Soc. Clin. Hypnosis. Republican. Methodist. Lodge: Shriners. Avocations: photography, skiing, racquet sports, flying. Home: 308 Greengate Dr Columbia SC 29223 Office: Community Mental Health Service PO Box 193 Moncrief Hosp Ft Jackson SC 29207

ANDERSON, THOMAS PHILLIP, city official; b. Honolulu, Jan. 21, 1950; s. Howard T.E. and Josephine (Valek) A.; m. Mary Carmen Morera, Dec. 23, 1972; children—Scott Anthony, Cliff Howard. B.S. in Bus. Adminstrn., Fla. Atlantic U., 1972. Export sales adminstr. Sandria Corp., Ft. Lauderdale, Fla., 1972-74, Sylvan Ginsbury, Ltd., Teaneck, N.J., 1974-75; bus. mgr. Zool. Soc. Broward County, Ft. Lauderdale, 1976; purchasing agt. Fla. Dept. Health and Rehab. Services, Ft. Lauderdale, 1977-82; purchasing supr. City of Boca Raton (Fla.), 1982—. Mem. Nat. Assn. Purchasing Mgmt. (cert. purchasing mgr.), Nat. Inst. Govtl. Purchasing, Fla. Assn. Govt. Purchasing Officers, Phi Kappa Phi, Phi Theta Kappa. Republican. Lutheran. Office: City of Boca Raton 201 W Palmetto Park Rd Boca Raton FL 33432

ANDERSON, THOMAS WAYNE, mgmt. engr.; b. Montgomery, Ala., Dec. 10, 1946; s. Orville Lynn and Ann Leona (Kennedy) A.; B.Indsl. Engring., U. Fla., 1970; m. Catherine Lee Sullivan, Mar. 15, 1969; children—Melissa Joy, Heather Lee. Systems rep. computer div. RCA, Tallahassee, 1970-71: dir. mgmt. systems engring. U. Fla., Gainesville, 1971-75; dir. mgmt. engring. Sarasota (Fla.) Meml. Hosp., 1975-77; dir. mgmt. systems engring. Bapt. Med. Centers, Birmingham, Ala., 1977-78; dir. systems devel. U. Ala. Hosps., Birmingham, 1978—. Served with USN, 1966. Recipient Coll. Engring. Service Key, 1970. Mem. Am. Inst. Indsl. Engrs. (L.J. Turaville Achievement award 1970, speaker confs. 1975, 79), Hosp. Mgmt. Systems Soc. (speaker conf. 1977), Am. Hosp. Assn. Democrat. Baptist. Collaborator: Changing Patterns of Psychiatric Inpatient Care in a University General Hospital, 1975; co-author: A Study of Components of Nursing Job Satisfaction, 1977. Home: 637 Wilderness Rd Pelham AL 35124 Office: 619 S 19th St Birmingham AL 35233

ANDERSON, WILLIAM BANKS, JR., ophthalmologist, educator; A.B., Princeton U., 1952; M.D., Harvard Med. Sch., 1956. Diplomate Am. Bd. Ophthalmology (bd. dirs. 1985—). Intern, Duke U. Med. Ctr., Durham, N.C., 1956-57; resident in ophthalmology, 1959-62; asst. prof. ophthalmology Duke U. Sch. Medicine, 1962-67, assoc. prof. ophthalmology, 1967-76, prof. ophthalmology, 1976—; staff. Duke U. Med. Ctr., 1962—, Durham VA Hosp., 1962—, Oteen VA Hosp., 1976—, Durham County Gen. Hosp., 1977—. Served with M.C., U.S. Army, 1957-59. Fellow ACS (adv. council ophthalmol. surgery 1977-82), Am. Acad. Ophthalmology (bd. councillors 1983-85, bd. dirs. 1985—); mem. Am. Ophthal. Soc., Assn. Research in Vision and Ophthalmology, Am. Assn. Ophthalmology, N.C. Soc. Ophthalmology (past pres.), Undersea Med. Soc., N.C. Med. Soc., Durham-Orange County Med. Soc., AMA, Aerospace Med. Assn., Pan Am. Assn. Ophthalmology, Retina Soc. Office: Dept Ophthalmology Duke U Med Ctr Durham NC 27710

ANDERSON, WILLIAM CLIFTON, veterinarian; b. Ft. Worth, Mar. 6, 1951; s. Dan J. and Frances S. (Smith) A.; m. Marilynn S. Conine, July 26, 1980. B.S., Tex. A&M U., 1974; postgrad. U. Philippines, 1975-77; D.V.M., U. Mo., 1980. Owner, Haltom City Animal Hosp. (Tex.), 1980—; owner, veterinarian N.E. Animal Hosp., North Richland Hills, Tex., 1983—; adj. prof. Tex. Wesleyan Coll. Mem. Tex. Vet. Med. Assn., AVMA. Methodist. Home: 5809 Diamond Oaks Dr S Fort Worth TX 76117 Office: 5705 E Belknap St Fort Worth TX 76117

ANDERSON-CHANDLER, URSULA KELLY, nurse; b. Pitts., July 14, 1944; d. Bernard Andrew and Ursula Mary (O'Hara) Meisner; m. John Karl Anderson, Aug. 26, 1967 (div. Feb. 1974); m. 2d, John Taylor Chandler, June 14, 1975. B.S.N., Carlow Coll., 1966; postgrad. Duke U., 1966-67; M.S.N., Cath. U. Am., 1974, doctoral candidate, 1986—. Clin. specialist critical care George Washington U. Med. Ctr., 1974-75; critical care nursing instr. The Arlington (Va.) Hosp., 1975-78; coordinator cardiac rehab., 1978-81; asst. prof. grad. cardiovascular nursing Cath. U. Am., Washington, 1981—. Vol. pet therapist The Arlington Animal Rescue League. HEW trainee, 1972-74. Mem. Am. Assn. Critical Care Nurses, Am. Nurses Assn., Am. Heart Assn., No. Va. Heart Assn. (bd. dirs. 1976-81) meritorious service award 1980), Nursing Alumnae Assn. Cath. U. Am. (bd. dirs. 1984—), Sigma Theta Tau. Roman Catholic. Club: The Flying Crows (Washington).

ANDREASON, GEORGE EDWARD, univ. adminstr.; b. Seattle, July 4, 1932; s. Alfred M. Andreason and Alberta (Brewer) Andreason Thompson; B.S. in Bus. Adminstrn., Tex. Wesleyan U., Ft. Worth, 1960; M.P.A. (Ford. Found. scholar), Ind. U., 1966; Ph.D., Clayton U., St. Louis, 1979; m. Carolyn A. McKown, June 30, 1973; 1 son, Paul Edward. Program analyst U.S. Army, Washington, 1963-64; asst. chief mgmt. analysis div. FAA, Ft. Worth, 1964-67, chief mgmt. analysis div., Oklahoma City, 1968-70, exec. officer, 1970-71; mgmt. cons. Dept. Transpo., 1966-67; asst. dir. IRS, Denver, 1971-72, asst. regional commr. adminstrn., Dallas, 1972-74, dist. dir., Denver, 1974, asst. dir. dir., St. Louis, 1974-76; dir. adminstrv. services McLennan Community Coll., Waco, Tex., 1976-77; v.p. bus. and adminstrn. U. Mary Hardin-Baylor, Belton, Tex., 1977-80, exec. v.p., 1980—; partner McGregor Assos., bus. and mgmt. cons., McGregor, Tex. Served with USN, 1951-55. Recipient Career Edn. award FAA and Nat. Inst. Public Affairs, 1965. Fellow Nat. Inst. Public Affairs; mem. Am. Soc. Public Adminstrn., Personnel and Mgmt. Assn., Nat. Coll. and Univ. Bus. Officers, So. Assn. Coll. and Univ. Bus. Officers, Belton C. of C. Baptist. Clubs: Rotary (Belton); Masons (master McGregor 1977, Tex. dist. dep. grand master 1980) (McGregor and Ft. Worth). Home: PO Box 181 McGregor TX 76657 Office: U Mary Hardin-Baylor MHB Station Belton TX 76513

ANDRES, PAUL ANTHONY, insurance executive, investment adviser; b. Tulsa, Feb. 7, 1928; s. Paul Hall and Helen (Ardizzone) A.; student Georgetown U., 1946-47, U. Wis., 1947; B.A. in Journalism, U. Okla., 1950; postgrad. Washington U. 1951; B.A. in Geology, Oklahoma City U., 1957; m. Ann Simmons Alspaugh, July 24, 1954 (div. Jan. 1963); children—Holly Antoinette, Louis Howard, Paul Anthony; m. Deena Anderson, May 30, 1964; 1 son, Kevin Michael. Info. asst. pub. relations dept. Southwestern Bell Telephone Co., Oklahoma City, 1950-51, gen. info. supr., gen. info. dept., St. Louis, 1951-52; dir., editor, pres. Paul Andres Publs., Inc., 1953-62; pres., dir. Adcraft Mail of Okla., Inc., 1957-62; v.p. Cunningham, Andres & Co., Inc., Oklahoma City, 1958-62; gen. mgr. Paul Andres Realty to 1962; v.p. Sey-Co

Products Co., Inc., Van Nuys, Calif., 1963-72; dir. Robert Bye Assocs., Houston, 1972-80, ASK Realty, 1972—; partner Andres & Schildhauer, Cons., 1975—; pres. Andres Fin. Corp., 1981—. Served from 2d lt. to capt. USAF, 1952-53. C.L.U.; chartered fin. cons. Mem. Nat. Assn. Securities Dealers, Nat., Houston assns. life underwriters, Tex. Real Estate Commn., New Eng. Life Leaders Assn. (life mem. Hall of Fame), Million Dollar Round Table, Internat. Assn. Fin. Planners. Club: Pine Forest Country. Home: 14630 Carolcrest Dr Houston TX 77079 Office: Suite 200 Three Riverway Houston TX 77056-1967

ANDRESS, TONY D., petroleum company executive; b. 1937; B.S., Tex. Tech. Coll., 1961. Prodn. engr. Celanese Chem. Co., 1961-65; asst. pres., then v.p. Premier Oil Refining Co., 1965-67; pres., dir. LaJet Petroleum Co., Abilene, Tex., 1976—. Address: PO Box 5198 Abilene TX 79608*

ANDREW, DAVID ROBERT, mathematics educator; b. Wink, Tex., Nov. 10, 1935; s. Robert Augustus and Gussie Wilma (Oyler) A.; m. Catherine Ann Vige, Aug. 30, 1958; children—Robert Craig, Lisa Lenore, David Harold. B.S., U. Southwestern La., 1958; M.S., Iowa State U., 1959; Ph.D., U. Pitts., 1961. Asst. prof. math. U. Southwestern La., Lafayette, 1961-64, assoc. prof., 1964-66, prof., 1966—, head dept. math., 1969-75, dean Coll. Scis., 1975-86; cons. Minn. Sch. Math. and Sci. Teaching Project., 1965-68; dir. Profl. NSF Summer Conf. for Math. Tchrs., 1967, 68, NSF Summer Inst. for Math. Tchrs., 1974; bd. dirs. Gulf South Research Inst., 1980-83. Contbr. articles to profl. publs. Bd. dirs. Episcopal Sch. La., Cade, 1980-82. Woodrow Wilson Found. fellow, 1958-59; Iowa State Research Found. fellow, 1958-59; Andrew Mellon Found. fellow, 1959-61. Mem. AAAS, Math. Assn. Am., Nat. Council Colls. Arts and Scis., La. Acad. Sci., La. Council Deans of Arts, Scis. and Humanities (chmn. 1985), Blue Key (faculty adviser 1974-84), Phi Kappa Phi. Avocations: swimming, hiking. Home: 412 Kim Dr Lafayette LA 70503 Office: U Southwestern LA Box 43290 Lafayette LA 70504

ANDREW, LLOYD B., JR., chemical company executive; b. Joliet, Ill., Nov. 30, 1923; s. Lloyd Brummond and Elizabeth (Frick) A.; m. Frances Burdett, Dec. 31, 1948; children—Joyce, Cindy, Lloyd B. III. Student, Ill. Inst. Tech., 1944-46; B.S.M.E. with distinction, Purdue U., 1948; M.S.M.E., La. State U., 1956. Process engr. Phillips Petroleum, Oklahoma City, 1948-50, Borger, Tex., 1950-51; with Ethyl Corp., 1951—, gen. mgr. VisQueen div., Baton Rouge, 1963-68, dir. fin. relations parent co., Richmond, Va., 1968-74, v.p. fin. relations, 1974-81, v.p., treas., 1981-83, sr. v.p., treas., 1983-84, exec. v.p., dir., 1984—, mem. exec. com., 1985—. Served with USAAC, 1942-44; ETO. Decorated D.F.C., Air medal with 4 oak leaf clusters. Mem. Nat. Investor Relations Inst. Republican. Methodist. Clubs: Wall St. (N.Y.C.); Downtown (Richmond); Kiwanis. Home: 103 Roslyn Hills Dr Richmond VA 23229 Office: PO Box 2189 Richmond VA 23217

ANDREWS, ANTHONY PARSHALL, anthropology educator, archaeologist; b. Washington, Aug. 23, 1949; s. Edward Wyllys and Ann (Wheeler) A.; m. Barbara McClatchie, Sept. 13, 1979; 1 child, Julian. B.A. in Anthropology magna cum laude, Harvard U., 1973; M.A., U. Ariz., 1976, Ph.D., 1980. Asst. prof. anthropology Hamilton Coll., Clinton, N.Y., 1980-81; asst. prof. anthropology New Coll. of U. South Fla., Sarasota, 1981-85, assoc. prof., 1985—; archaeology researcher Mex., Central Am. Research grantee Nat. Geog. Soc., Instituto Nacional de Antropología e Historia (Mex.), U. South Fla. Research Council. Mem. Am. Anthrop. Assn., Soc. Am. Archaeology, Sociedad Española de Estudios Mayas, Sociedad Mexicana Antropologia. Author: (with E.W. Andrews) A Preliminary Study of the Ruins of Xcaret, Quintana Roo, Mexico, 1975; (with Antonio Benavides) Ecab. Poblado y Provincia del Siglo XVI en Yucatán, 1979; Maya Salt Production and Trade, 1983; contbr. articles to profl. jours. Home: 7932 Westmoreland Dr Sarasota FL 34243 Office: Div Social Scis New Coll U South Fla Sarasota FL 34243

ANDREWS, ARLENE BOWERS, social policy consultant, social work educator; b. Ft. Leonard Wood, Mo., Dec. 6, 1950; d. Rhudar Erby and Elfriede Else (Traeger) Bowers; m. Stuart Murray Andrews, May 22, 1976; children—Brook, Emily. B.A., Duke U., 1972; M.S. in Social Work, U. S.C., 1974. Cert. social worker. Dir. research and evaluation Social Policy div. Office of Gov., Columbia, S.C., 1974-77; exec. dir. Council on Child Abuse and Neglect, Inc., Columbia, 1977-78, Sistercare, Inc., Columbia, 1981-83; lectr. Coll. Social work, U. S.C., Columbia, 1983—; ptnr. Social Policy Resource Assocs., Columbia, 1984—; organizational cons. various human service agys., Columbia, 1979—; design cons., S.C., 1982-83. Co-author: (tng. manual) Teaching Children to Resist Sexual Assault, 1985. Contbr. articles to profl. jours. Bd. dirs. Sistercare, Inc.; mem. Joint Legis. Com. on Children, S.C. Gen. Assembly, 1983—; co-founder S.C. Coalition Against Domestic Violence and Sexual Assault. Mem. Am. Psychol. Assn., Nat. Assn. Social Workers, Phi Beta Kappa. Quaker. Avocations: wilderness camping. Home: 3921 Verner St Columbia SC 29204 Office: Social Policy Resource Assocs PO Box 8514 Columbia SC 29202

ANDREWS, BETHLEHEM KOTTES, research chemist; b. New Orleans, Sept. 18, 1936; d. George Leonidas and Anna Mercedes (Russell) Kottes; B.A. with honors in Chemistry, Newcomb Coll., Tulane U., 1957; m. William Edward Andrews, May 9, 1959; children—Sharon Leslie, Keith Edward. Chemist wash wear investigation, So. Regional Research Center, Sci. and Edn. Adminstrn., Dept. Agr., New Orleans, 1958-63, research chemist wash wear investigation, cotton textile chemistry lab., 1968-70, research chemist spl. products research, cotton textile chemistry lab., 1976-83, sr. research chemist cotton chem. reactions research, 1983-85, lead scientist textile finishing chemistry research, 1985—; scientist-supr. Grace King High Sch. Lab. Tech. Tng. Program; U.S. del. ISO Meeting on Textiles, 1984. Recipient outstanding professionalism citation New Orleans Fedn. Businessman's Assn., 1977, Disting. Service award in med./sci. category, 1983, named Women of Yr. award in profl. category, 1978; La. Heart Assn. grantee, 1957. Mem. Am. Chem. Soc., Am. Assn. Textile Chemists and Colorists (exec. com. on research), Fiber Soc., Phi Beta Kappa, Sigma Xi, Phi Mu. Democrat. Roman Catholic. Clubs: P.E.O., Southern Yacht. Contbr. chpts. to books, articles to sci. jours.; patentee. Office: So Regional Research Center Agrl Research Service Dept Agr 1100 Robert E Lee Blvd New Orleans LA 70124

ANDREWS, CHARLES HAYNES, college dean, educator; b. Waycross, Ga., Nov. 30, 1937; s. Charles Haynes and Louise Rebecca (McQuaig) A.; m. Susan B. Gahan, Aug. 29, 1961 (div. 1973); m. Lorraine Lynn, Aug. 24, 1974; children—Charles Haynes, William Edward. A.B., Mercer U., 1960; Ph.D. in Econs., Vanderbilt U., 1967. Assoc. prof. Stetson U., DeLand, Fla., 1964-73; dean Sch. Bus., Mercer U., Macon, Ga., 1978—; dir. Bank South Macon, Inc.; mem. Ga. Commn. on State Growth Policy, 1983-84. Author: The Economic Performance of the Compania de Acero del Pacifico, 1970. Commr. Macon Housing Authority, 1984—. Fellow Woodrow Wilson Found., 1960-61, Earhart Found., 1961-62; fgn. area fellow Ford Found., 1963-64. Mem. Am. Econ. Assn., So. Econ. Assn., So. Bus. Adminstrn. Assn., Phi Kappa Phi, Delta Sigma Pi. Methodist. Club: Kiwanis. Home: 121 Wesley Ann Ct Macon GA 31210 Office: Mercer Univ 1400 Coleman Ave Macon GA 31207

ANDREWS, EDWIN EVERTS, prosthodontist, forensic odontologist; b. Syracuse, N.Y., July 30, 1934; s. George Bouton and Marie (Buggeln) A.; B.S., Syracuse U., 1956; D.M.D., Fairleigh Dickinson U., 1963; M.Ed., Central State U., 1976; m. Patricia Ann McCarthy, Nov. 27, 1963; 1 son, Mark Robert. Intern Upstate Med. Center, Syracuse, 1963-64; resident in prosthetics N.Y. U., 1964-66; practice prosthetics, Syracuse, 1966-72; chief maxillofacial prosthetics State Univ. Hosp. Upstate Med. Center, Syracuse, 1967-72; asst. prof. maxillofacial prosthodontist U. Mo. Sch. Dentistry, Kansas City, 1972-73; asso. prof., chmn. maxillofacial prosthetics U. Okla. Coll. Dentistry, Oklahoma City, 1973-77; pvt. practice prosthodontics and maxillofacial prosthetics, Oklahoma City, 1977—; attending maxillofacial prosthetics U. Hosp, Children's Meml. Hosp, 1973, Presbyn. Hosp., 1976—, Health Scis. Center, courtesy staff Mercy Health Ctr., 1982—, O'Donoghue Rehab. Inst., 1982—; cons. VA Hosp, Oklahoma City, Muskogee, Okla., 1973—, Okla. Office of Chief Med. Examiner, 1974—, FAA, 1974—, Okla. State Bur. Investigtors, 1982—. Served USAF, 1956-58. Res. Diplomate Am. Bd. Prosthodontics, Am. Bd. Forensic Odontology. Fellow Am. Coll. Prosthodontists, Am. Acad. Forensic Scis., Am. Acad. Maxillofacial Prosthetics, Acad. Internat. Dental Studies, Midwest Acad. Prosthodontics; mem. ADA, Am. Prosthodontic Soc. (chmn. nomenclature com. 1983—), Am. Soc. Forensic Odontology, Fedn. Prosthodontic Orgns., Internat. Reference Orgn. in Forensic Medicine and Scis., Okla. State Dental Assn., Oklahoma County (Okla.) Dist. Dental Soc. Home: 16 Oakwood Dr Oklahoma City OK 73121 Office: 1117 N Shartel Ave Oklahoma City OK 73103

ANDREWS, HARVEY WELLINGTON, medical laboratory executive; b. Stowe Twp., Pa., Sept. 9, 1928; s. Robert W. and Theresa R. (Reis) A.; B.B.A. cum laude, U. Pitts., 1952; M.B.A., Harvard U., 1957; m. Jane Garland, Aug. 9, 1969; children—Marcia Lynne, Glynis Susann, Elizabeth Jane. With Gen. Electric Co., Syracuse, N.Y., 1952-55, Scovill Mfg. Co., Waterbury, Conn., 1957; comptroller Alcon Labs., Inc., Ft. Worth, 1958-61, comptroller, treas., 1961-65, v.p. finance, 1964-68; founder, pres. Medimation, Inc., Ft. Worth, 1968—, also dir.; dir. Med. Scis. Computer Corp., First's Clin. Labs., Tex. Commerce Bank, Ft. Worth, Hereford Med. Labs., Dalworth Med. Labs.; founder, dir. Tarrant Health Maintenance Orgn., Inc.; founder, dir., Tarrant Health Protection Plan, Inc., 1978—. Bd. dirs. Fort Worth Opera Assn. Served with AUS, 1946-48. Mem. AAAS, Am. Acad. Polit. and Social Scis., Ft. Worth C. of C., Soc. Advancement Mgmt., TCU Pres.'s Roundtable Assn., Order Artus, Scabbard and Blade, Sigma Alpha Epsilon. Lutheran. Clubs: Rotary, Masons (32 deg.), Golden Eagle Assn., Colonial Country, Century II, Met. Knife and Fork. Home: PO Box 1786 3124 Chaparral Ln Fort Worth TX 76101 Office: 800 5th Ave Fort Worth TX 76104

ANDREWS, JAMES AUDUBON, dentist; b. Wadesboro, La., June 28, 1926; s. Brown Brumfield Andrews and Hildegarde Margarite (Pflanze) Boudreaux; m. Lois Helen Harpster, Sept. 13, 1978; children—Richard Michael, Kimberly Winslow. B.A., Southeastern U., Hammond, La., 1948; D.D.S., Loyola U. of South, New Orleans, 1958. Salesman N.Y. Life Ins. Co., Baton Rouge, 1949-52; mgr. grocery store, Ponchatoula, La., 1952-53; pres. Inst. Cosmetic Dentistry, Covington, La., 1965—. Author: Andrews Bridge System, 1976, Andrews System Laboratory Guide, 1977. Patentee in field. Served with Maritime Service, 1944-46. Fellow Royal Soc. Health, Acad. Gen. Dentistry; mem. ADA, Am. Acad. Gnathologic Orthopedics (bd. dirs.). Republican. Club: La. Crozat Study (pres., founder, 1984). Avocations: sketching; hunting; golf; fishing. Home: 315 Royal Dr Slidell LA 70460 Office: 639 W Cavsaway Approach Mandeville LA 70448

ANDREWS, JANET A.C., librarian, consultant; b. Hamilton AFB, Calif., Mar. 7, 1953; d. Edward McIntyre and Janet (Johnson) Andrews. B.S. in Biology, Grove City (Pa.), Coll. 1976; M.L.S., Rutgers U., N.J., 1978; postgrad. Nova U., Ft. Lauderdale, Fla., 1983—. Cert. profl. librarian, N.J. Instr., asst. librarian Westminster Coll., New Wilmington, Pa., 1978-80; head adult services Clark (N.J.) Pub. Library, 1980-81; tech. services librarian, Winter Park (Fla.) Pub. Library, 1982—. Contbr. articles to publs. Mem. ALA, Fla. Library Assn. (vice chmn. collection devel. caucus 1986), Theta Alpha Phi, Episcopal Honor Soc. Republican. Club: University (Winter Park) Lodge: Order Eastern Star. Office: Winter Park Pub Library 460 E New England St Winter Park FL 32789

ANDREWS, JESSIE (BALDWIN) MATSON, educator, retired government official; b. Omaha, July 18, 1904; d. William Arthur and Elizabeth M. (Bratt) Baldwin; student Grinnell Coll., 1922-25; A.B., U. Nebr., 1926; postgrad. U. Utah, 1945-47; children—John Hanthorn (dec.), Joanne Sandra; m. Tedford G. Andrews, Sept. 4, 1982. Writer, Omaha Daily Jour. Stockman, 1926-30; syndicate writer Corn Belt Farm Dailies, 1930-34; state dir. women's div. Iowa Emergency Relief Adminstrn., 1934-40; Iowa dir. women's and profl. projects WPA, Archives Security, Air Force, 1942; faculty mem. U. Utah, 1945-46; tchr. Guam, Mariannas Islands, 1946-47; coordinator women's activities St. Paul CD, 1951-70; tchr. So. Cross Christian Sch., Miami, Fla., 1971-72; substitute tchr. Charlotte and Lee County Schs. Former comdr. Ramsey County Cancer Soc.; founder St. Paul Council Human Relations, 1948; former chmn. Nat. Thanksgiving Day Assn.; past v.p. public affairs Soroptimist Fedn. Ams.; life mem. past pres. St. Paul Club. State chmn. Luther W. Youngdahl campaign for gov., 1949-50. Recipient cert. of merit Gov. of Minn., 1961, 70, 14 awards on retirement. Mem. Bus. and Profl. Women's Assn. (v.p.), VFW Aux., Nat. Assn. Ret. Govt. Profl. Employees, Inter-Club Council (founder 1944, pres. 1948-49), Internat. Platform Assn., PEO, Waterways Civic Assn., Theta Sigma Phi, Alpha Phi, Gamma Alpha Chi. Clubs: Soroptimists, Toastmistress (founder 1st St. Paul and Peace River clubs), R-R Investment, River Forest Cultural Exchange (Ft. Myers). Home: 1729 Inlet Dr Waterway Estates North Fort Myers FL 33903

ANDREWS, MARK EDWIN, III, oil and gas exploration company executive; b. Houston, June 1, 1950; s. Mark Edwin and Lavone (Dickensheets) A.; m. Elizabeth Quay, June 28, 1975; children—Elizabeth Quay, Mark Edwin IV. B.A., Harvard U., 1972, M.B.A., 1975. Vice-pres. corp. fin. Rotan Mosle Inc., N.Y.C., 1975-80; pres., chmn. bd. Am. Exploration Co., N.Y.C., 1980—; dir. Ancon Oil and Gas, Inc., Houston, 1968—. Mem. Rockefeller U. Council, N.Y.C. Republican. Episcopalian. Clubs: River, Links, Knickerbocker (N.Y.C.); Fishers Island Country (N.Y.); Bayou, Houston Country, Houston, Athletic of Houston (Houston). Office: Am Exploration Co 535 Madison Ave New York NY 10022

ANDREWS, MARY SUE, community relations administrator; b. Chattanooga, Sept. 26, 1940; d. Olen and Aileen (Cooper) Vardaman; student So. Meth. U., 1974-79; m. James Wortham Andrews, 1961; children—Haydon Willson, Jeffery Sterling, Daniel Walter. Various secretarial positions, 1958, 60-69; public relations asst. Atlantic Richfield Co., Dallas, 1969-79; public relations rep., Dallas, 1979—. Mem. exec. com. Sch. Vol. Program, Dallas, 1973—; mem. Women's Center Dallas, 1975—; adv. com. Arts Magnet High Sch., Dallas, 1979—, sec. Employer's Affirmative Action Com., Dallas, 1974-79; mem. bus. com. Vol. Center, 1981—; mem. selection com. City Arts Program, 1982; mem. urban info. service adv. Council Dallas Pub. Library; mem. adv. Council Ctr. Non-Profit Mgmt.; mem. adv. Council Women and Their Work, Austin; Program advisor Tex. Energy Edn. Program; mem. steering com., advisor Nat. Energy Edn. Program, Reston, Va. mem. Dallas Bus. Vol. Council, 1981—; bd. dirs. Shakespeare Festival of Dallas, 1984-86, Tex. Conservation Corps, Austin, 1984—. Mem. Public Relations Soc. Am., Dallas Advt. League (dir. 1978-79), LWV, Dallas Hist. Soc. Home: 2311 Spring Hill Dr Dallas TX 75228 Office: PO Box 2819 Dallas TX 75221

ANDREWS, MICHAEL A., U.S. Congressman; b. Houston, Feb. 7, 1944. B.A., U. Tex., 1967; J.D., So. Methodist U., 1970. Law clk. for U.S. Dist. Judge, 1971-72; asst. dist. atty. Harris County, Tex., 1972-76; sole practice law, Houston, 1976—; mem. 98th Congress from 25th Dist., Tex. Address: Room 1039 Longworth House Office Bldg Washington DC 20515*

ANDREWS, MICHAEL CURTIS, public relations specialist; b. Columbus, Ohio, Oct. 22, 1949; s. Michael Frank and Helen W. (Baker) A.; m. Dorothy Ann Andrews; 1 child, Michael George. Student U. Hawaii, 1967; B.S. in Radio and TV, Syracuse U., 1971. Dir. prodn. WHEN Radio, Syracuse, N.Y., 1972-74; program dir. WRGI Radio, Naples, Fla., 1974-75; asst. gen. mgr. Sterling Communications, Naples, Fla., 1976-76; program dir. WFBL Radio, Syracuse, N.Y., 1976-77; dir. comml. prodn. and promotion WFLA AM & FM, Tampa, 1977-81; dir. pub. relations The Shrine of N.Am. and Shriners Hosps., Internat. Shrine Headquarters, Tampa, 1981—. Mem. exec. com. Univ. Tampa Bd. Counselors, 1983—; bd. dirs., vice chmn. pub. relations com. ARC, Tampa, 1984-85. Mem. Tampa C. of C. (chmn. internal promotions council 1985), Pub. Relations Soc. Am. (bd. dirs.), Internat. Assn. Bus. Communicators, Am. Soc. Hosp. Mktg. and Pub. Relations (mem. Tampa area council), Sigma Phi Epsilon. Clubs: Masons, Shriners. Office: 2900 Rocky Point Dr Tampa FL 33607

ANDREWS, RICHARD FRANCIS, ins. agy. exec., kennel exec.; b. N.Y.C., Sept. 19, 1936; s. William R. and Mary J. (O'Neil) A.; B.S., Fordham U., 1958; m. Barbara Fripp, Nov. 9, 1969; 1 son, Gordon. Vice pres. James A. Kennedy Co., Inc., Miami, Fla., 1961-67; pres. Andrews & Co., Inc., Miami, 1967—; pres. Dick Andrews, Inc., greyhound racing kennel, Miami, 1971—; guest lectr. and instr. for Dade County Public Safety Dept. Served to capt. U.S. Army, 1958-60. Finished 1st and 2d Irish-Am. Classic greyhound race, 1979, finished 1st, 1970. Mem. Best Recommended Ins. Adjusters, Nat. Assn. Ind. Adjusters, South Fla. Claimsmen Assn., Nat. Greyhound Assn. Roman Catholic. Jewelry recoveries include Brasher Doubloon for Yale U. Sterling Mus., 1968 and Katherine the Gt. silver collection, 1972.

ANDREWS, ROBERT VINCENT, engineering science educator, engineering consultant; b. Portland, Oreg., July 4, 1916; s. Merrill Grover and Mildred Gertrude (Snelling) A.; m. Marjorie Louise Kibbe, July 11, 1942. B.S., Oreg. State U., 1938; M.S. Tex. A&M U., 1940, Ph.D., 1952; postgrad. Harvard U., MIT, 1942. Registered profl. engr., Ohio, Tex. Chem. engr. Tidewater Assoc. Oil Co., Martinez, Calif., 1938-40; from instr. to prof. chem. engring. Tex. A&M U., College Station, 1938-55; research and design engr. Monsanto Chem. Co., Anniston, Ala., 1948-49; design and constrn. engr. Hanford Works, Gen. Electric Co., Richland, Wash., 1951-52; dean engring., dir. Lamar Research Ctr., Lamar U., Beaumont, Tex., 1955-61; dean engring. Trinity U., San Antonio, 1961-76; trustee S.W. Research Inst., San Antonio, 1968—; engring. cons., San Antonio, 1960—. Contbr. articles to tech. jours. Served to maj. USAF, 1942-46. Mem. Am. Inst. Chem. Engrs., Tex. Soc. Profl. Engrs. (pres. Bexar chpt. 1967-68, dir. 1984—, Engr. of Yr. 1967). Democrat. Methodist. Avocations: swimming; hiking; travel. Home: 114 Medford Dr San Antonio TX 78209 Office: Trinity U 715 Stadium Dr San Antonio TX 78284

ANDREWS, SUSANNAH SMITH, clinical and consulting psychologist; b. Jackson, Miss., Mar. 15, 1949; d. Sydney Allen and Frances Smith Darden (Witty) S.; m. Kent Walter Andrews, Aug. 14, 1976; children—Nathan Walter, Erik Sydney. A.B., Vassar Coll., 1970; M.S., San Jose State U., 1973; Ph.D., Calif. Sch. Profl. Psychology, San Diego, 1975. Lic. psychologist Miss., Calif. Child and family worker Child and Family Clinic and Counseling Ctr., San Jose (Calif.) State U., 1970-72, Peninsula Children's Ctr., Palo Alto, Calif., 1970-72; psychotherapist, psychologist Family Services Assoc., San Diego, 1973-74; intern, post-doctoral fellow Mercy Hosp., San Diego, 1974-75; dir. research and program evaluation, dir. day treatment and srs. program San Luis Obispo (Calif.) Mental Health, 1976-80; pvt. practice clin. and cons. psychology, Gulfport, Miss., 1980—; cons. staff Gulf Coast Community Hosp., Hancock Gen. Hosp., co-founder Inst. Life Enrichment: Wellness Ctr. mem. faculty U. So. Miss. Bd. dirs., co-founder Anred (Anorexia Nervosa and Related Eating Disorders), San Luis Obispo, 1979—; condr. workshops, lectr. Rape Crisis Ctr.; cons. Shelter for Battered Women; dir. psychology Sand Hill Hosp., Gulfport, 1984-85; mem. cons. staff Gulfport Meml., Garden Park, Biloxi Regional hosps. Mem. Miss. Psychol. Assn., Calif. Psychol. Assn., Am. Psychol. Assn. Democrat. Episcopalian. Contbr. articles to profl. jours.; columnist Practical Psychology: What's On Your Mind?, Tupelo (Miss.) N.E., Miss. Daily Jour.; composer several songs. Home: 757 E Scenic Dr Pass Christian MS 39571 Office: 3106 11th St Gulfport MS 39501

ANDREWS, WILLIAM COOKE, physician; b. Norfolk, Va., June 7, 1924; s. Charles James and Jean Curry (Cooke) A.; A.A., Princeton U., 1946; M.D., Johns Hopkins U., 1947; m. Elizabeth Wight Kyle, Nov. 10, 1951; children—Elizabeth Randolph, William Cooke, Susan Carrington. Intern, N.Y. Hosp., 1947, resident in ob-gyn, 1948-50, 52-53; practice medicine specializing in ob-gyn, Norfolk, Va., 1953—; asst. in ob-gyn Cornell U. Med. Sch., 1948-50, 52-53; mem. attending staff Med. Center Hosp.; mem. vis. staff DePaul Hosp.; prof. ob-gyn Eastern Va. Med. Sch., Norfolk, 1975—, pres. faculty senate, 1976-77; mem. fertility and maternal health drugs adv. com FDA, 1980-82, chmn., 1982-83. Chmn. Bicentennial Commn., City of Norfolk, 1969-71; commr. Community Facilities Commn., 1971-73, chmn., 1973-81; bd. dirs. Va. League Planned Parenthood, 1966-68; pres. Norfolk chpt. Planned Parenthood, 1966-68, vice-chmn. nat. med. com., 1980-82, chmn. nat. med. com., 1983-84. Served with M.C., USN, 1950-52. Named hon. officer Order Brit. Empire, 1967. Diplomate Am. Bd. Ob-Gyn. Fellow Am. Coll. Obstetricians and Gynecologists, Am. Gynec. and Obstet. Soc., Am. Assn. Obstetricians and Gynecologists; mem. Am. Fertility Soc. (dir. 1970-73, pres. 1977), Med. Soc. Va., Norfolk Acad. Medicine, Va., Tidewater obstetrical and gynecol. socs., Continental Gynecol. Soc., So. Med. Assn., AMA, South Atlantic Assn. Obstetricians and Gynecologists, Norfolk C. of C. (chmn. armed forces com. 1966-68, v.p. 1968-69, pres. 1970), Internat. Fedn. Fertility Socs. (asst. treas. 1974-77, pres. 1983—), Navy League U.S. (pres. Hampton Roads council 1968-70, nat. dir. 1970-74), English Speaking Union U.S. (pres. Norfolk-Portsmouth br. 1964-66), Planned Parenthood Fedn. Am. (cons. nat. med. com. 1975—). Presbyterian. Club: Norfolk Yacht and Country (commodore 1966). Contbr. articles to profl. jours. Home: 929 Graydon Ave Norfolk VA 23507 Office: 903 Medical Tower Norfolk VA 23507

ANDREWS, WILLIAM HENRY, clergyman, school psychologist; b. Decatur, Ga., May 4, 1929; s. John Edward and Semite Rebecca (Hall) A. B.S., U. Ga., 1953, M.Ed., 1969, Ed.S., 1972; A.B., Ga. State U., 1963; M.S. in Edn., Baylor U., 1968; B.D., So. Baptist Sem., 1956, M.Div., 1969; Th.M., Luther Rice Sem., 1971, Th.D., 1973, D.Ministry, 1982. Ordained to ministry Bapt. Ch., 1956. Pastor 1st Bapt. Ch., Danielsville, Ga., 1956-61, County Line Bapt. Ch., Douglasville, Ga., 1962-67, 71-75, New Ga. Bapt. Ch., Dallas, 1968-71, 1st Bapt. Ch., Damascus, Ga., 1984—; evangelist Bill Andrews Assocs., Blakely, Ga., 1976-84; sch. psychologist Early County Bd. Edn., Blakely, 1977-85; moderator Tallapoos Bapt. Assn., Dallas, 1969-71. Mem. Am. Assn. Pastoral Counselors, So. Bapt. Religious Edn. Soc. Republican. Lodge: Masons (sr. deacon 1959-60). Avocations: hunting; fishing; stamp collecting. Home: 417 N Main St Blakely GA 31723 Office: First Bapt Ch of Damascus PO Box 227 Blakely GA 31723

ANDUIZA, FRANCISCO ARMANDO, pharmaceutical company sales representative; b. Havana, Cuba, Aug. 26, 1957; came to U.S., 1962; s. Francisco Armando and Carmen Maria (Gonzalez) A. A.A., Miami Dade Community Coll., 1980, A.Gen. Studies, 1980, emergency technician cert., 1981; cert. Respiratory Therapy Inst., 1982. Cert. arterial blood gas analysis technician, Fla. Respiratory care equipment technician Mercy Hosp., Miami, Fla., 1978-79; respiratory care therapist Victoria Hosp., Miami, 1980-82, Am. Heart Assn. Spanish CPR inservice educator, 1980-82; dir. respiratory care program Foster Med. Home Health, Dania, Fla., 1982-83; mktg./sales rep. Travenol Labs., Miami, 1983—; asst. site coordinator Am. Heart Assn./Health Fare Com., Miami, 1981-83, site coordinator, 1983; mem. com. Run For Heart, Am. Heart Assn., 1983—. Mem. rescue disaster team Metro Fire Dept., Miami, 1981; com. mem. Victoria Hosp. Credit Union, 1982. Mem. Am. Assn. Respiratory Care, Fla. Soc. Respiratory Therapy, Am. Heart Assn., Am. Lung Assn., Internat. Soc. Clin. Lab. Tech., ARC, Phi Theta Kappa. Republican. Roman Catholic. Home: 525 NW 72 Ave Apt 204 Miami FL 33126 Office: Travenol Labs Inc 1705 NW 79 Ave Miami FL 33126

ANGEL, HATTIE LAVERNE, music company executive; b. Memphis, Mar. 12, 1952; d. Alvaughn and Hattie Ethel (Gordon) Dean; m. Juan Ricardo Angel, Feb. 14, 1975 (div. Apr. 1982); 1 son, Juan Ricardo. B.A., So. Ill. U., 1982. Sec., Music Factory, Inc., Memphis, 1973-76; tax examiner IRS, Memphis, 1975-76; claims clk. Social Security Adminstrn., Memphis, 1976-78; corp. dir., adminstr. Al Green Music, Inc., Memphis, 1978—; v.p., 1978—; pres., treas. Angel's Acctg. Service, Memphis, 1980-84; sec. Lee County Publ. Co., Memphis, 1983-84; cons. Concert Bookings, Inc., Birmingham, 1983—. Spl. dep. Shelby Spl. Deputies Assn., 1983; assoc. Nat. Urban League, 1983; mem. econ. and devel. com. City Hall. Recipient Outstanding Achievement award Social Security Adminstrn., 1976, Outstanding Performance award IRS, 1975. Mem. NAACP. Home: 2311 Marble Ave Memphis TN 38108 Office: Al Green Music Inc PO Box 9485 Memphis TN 38118

ANGEL, RITA DUNHAM, insurance agency executive, construction company executive; b. Pikeville, Tenn., May 23, 1948; d. Raymond Hargis and Catherine Evella (Evans) Dunham; m. Richard Dewayne Foley, Jan. 1968 (div.); 1 child, Heather Lee; m. Roy Joe Angel, Nov. 18, 1977. Student Middle Tenn. State U., 1966-68, U. Ariz., 1974-75. Cert. and lic. in property and casualty ins.; cert. in fed. crop insurance. Ins. agt. Associated Gen. Agy. Inc. of Chattanooga, Pikeville br., 1975—, br. mgr., 1978—, asst. v.p., 1979—; fin. advisor, investor, v.p. Angel Constrn. Co., 1977—. Bd. dirs. VanBuren County Fair and Horseshow Assn., Spencer, Tenn., 1985; contestant sponsor Tenn. Miss T.E.E.N. Pageant, Nashville, 1985; mem. Bledsoe County Agr. Council, Pikeville, 1985. Mem. Insurors of Tenn., Nat. Assn. Crop Ins. Agts., Bus. Profl. Women's Orgn. (sec. 1980-81), Nat. Fedn. Ind. Bus. Democrat. Baptist. Avocations: gardening; writing poetry; boating. Office: Associated Gen Agy of Pikeville City Hall St Pikeville TN 37367

ANGEL, STEVEN MICHAEL, lawyer; b. Frederick, Md., Sept. 19, 1950; s. Charles Robert and Laura Emily (Holland) A.; m. Joan Comproni, Dec. 7, 1972 (div. May 1975); m. Constance McCarthy, Apr. 24, 1981; children—Michael Sean, James Curtis. B.S., U. Md., 1972; J.D., Oklahoma City U., 1976; LL.M., George Washington U., 1979. Bar: Okla. 1976, Tex. 1981, U.S. Dist. Ct. Md. 1977, U.S. Dist. Ct. (no. dist.) Tex. 1979, U.S. Dist. Ct. (we. dist.) Okla. 1981, U.S. Dist. Ct. (we. dist.) Tex 1981, U.S. Ct. Claims 1981, U.S. Ct. Appeals (5th, 10th, and 11th cirs.) 1981, U.S. Ct. Appeals (D.C. cir.) 1983, U.S. Supreme Ct. 1984. Field atty. NLRB, Balt., 1976-79; supervising trial atty. Fed. Labor Relations Authority, Dallas, 1979-80; mem. Hughes & Nelson, Oklahoma City and San Antonio, 1980—. Articles editor Oklahoma City U. Law Rev., 1976, 77. Contbr. articles to profl. jours. Recipient cert. Spl.

Confidence in Labor, Law Tex. Bd. Legal Specialization, 1982; various awards Oklahoma City U., 1975, 76; Spl. Achievement cert. Fed. Labor Relations Authority, 1980. Mem. ABA, Assn. Trial Lawyers Am., Okla. Bar Assn., Okla. Trial Lawyers Assn., State Bar Tex., Tex. Trial Lawyers Assn., Phi Delta Phi. Democrat. Baptist. Home: 4506 Karen Dr Edmond OK 73034 Office: Hughes & Nelson 5801 N Broadway Extension Suite 302 Oklahoma City OK 73118

ANGELINI, JOHN MICHAEL, artist, writer; b. N.Y.C., Nov. 18, 1921; s. Andrew and Rose (Dragone) A.; children by previous marriage—Maria, J. Michael, David; m. Elisabeth V. Erne, Mar. 5, 1971; children—Kenneth, Daniel. cert. fine arts Newark Sch. Fine and Indsl. Arts, 1948; postgrad. spl. studies, Italy, 1961. Design cons., art dir. Berles Carton Co., Inc., Paterson, N.J., 1950-79; contbg. editor N.J. Music & Arts Mag., 1971-77, also adv. bd. Exhibited 21 one man shows including N.Y. Cultural Ctr., N.Y.C., 1970, Nabisco World Hdqrs., Hanover, N.J., 1978; represented in permanent collections Morgan Guaranty Trust Co., N.Y., Yunich Collection, N.Y.C., AT&T Long Lines Div., N.J., Morris Mus., Morristown, N.J., Paterson (N.J.) Pub. Library; illustrator articles Am. Artist, Palette Talk, N.J. Art/Form; featured on cover Prizewinning Watercolors Book II; subject of interview and painting demonstration Cable TV, N.Y. and N.J., 1978; included in Watercolor '86 (book). Author: The North Light Art Competition Handbook, 1986. Mem. regional and nat. art juries. Served in U.S. Army, 1942-46. Recipient medal of Honor, Audubon Artists, 1963, Nat. Arts Club, N.Y.C., 1963, N.J. Watercolor Soc., 1964; named Artist of Yr. State of N.J., 1974. Mem. Allied Artists Am. (editor newsletter), Audubon Artists Inc. (past membership com.), Am. Watercolor Soc., N.J. Watercolor Soc. (past treas.). Presbyterian. Home: 12603 Pecan Tree Dr Hudson FL 33562

ANGLE, SHARON ANN, retail executive; b. Fairland, Okla., Sept. 8, 1946; d. Bernie and Thelma Louise (Wilmoth) Pennington; cert. Paralegal Inst. Ariz., 1979; student N.E. Okla. A&M Coll., Miami, 1980-82; 1 son, David Scott. Service rep. Gen. Telephone Co., Belvidere, Ill., 1968-69, bus. office supr., 1969; sec. to dir. adult edn. Rock Valley Community Coll., Rockford, Ill., 1970-73; legal sec. Hall, Stockwell & Wooley, Miami, 1975; legal asst. law firm Garrette & Stockwell, Miami, 1976-84; cert. legal asst. T. Logan Brown, Miami, 1983—; sec. Ray Son, Inc., Miami, 1980—, Maverick Enterprises, 1980—, As-Tech Oil Producers Inc., 1983; owner, operator Wallpapering Unltd., The Classic Touch, interior design accessories, 1984—. Mem. adv. bd. N.E. Okla. A&M Coll., 1980—. Club: Hi-Noon Bus. and Profl. Women's (pres. 1979-80). Home: 410 5th St SE Miami OK 74354 Office: 122 N Main St Miami OK 74354

ANGLIN, ANTOINETTE TRACY, organist, choirmaster, educator; b. Pine Bluff, Ark., June 7, 1953; d. William Noel and Margaret Rozelle (Herron) Tracy; m. Kim Woods Corbet, Dec. 27, 1975 (div. 1984); m. John Henry Anglin, Nov. 17, 1984. B.Mus., Henderson State U., 1975; M.Mus., North Tex. State U., 1978, D.M.A., 1984. Teaching fellow North Tex. State U., 1977-81; organist, choirmaster Oakhurst Presbyn. Ch., Fort Worth, 1978-81; instr. U. Tex.-Arlington, 1983, 85, Mt. View Coll., Dallas, 1981-84; organist, choirmaster East Dallas Christian Ch., Dallas, 1981-84, St. Luke's in Meadow Ch., Fort Worth, 1985; staff curriculum devel. Brookhaven Coll., Dallas, 1980. Contbr. articles to profl. jours. Trinity Found. scholar, 1971-75; winner Ark. Am. Guild Organists Competition, 1976. Mem. Am. Guild Organists, Soc. Music Theory, Am. Musicol. Soc., Coll. Music Soc., Am. Choral Dirs. Assn., Pi Kappa Lambda, Delta Omicron. Presbyterian. Home: 2917 Princeton 21 Fort Worth TX 76109 Office: St Lukes in Meadow 4301 Meadowbrook Dr Fort Worth TX 76103

ANGLIN, BETTY LOCKHART, artist, educator; b. Greenwood, S.C., Apr. 23, 1937; d. Malcolm Mabry and Dorothy (Roessler) Lockhart; m. Ernie LaRue Anglin, June 10, 1957; children—Nancy Louise, Malcolm Lawrence. B.A., Coll. William and Mary, 1972. Instr., Hampton Arts and Humanities, Va., 1967-73, Cecil Rawls Mus., Courtland, Va., 1973—; tchr. Trinity Lutheran Sch., Newport News, Va., 1972—; adj. prof. Christopher Newport Coll., Newport News, 1975—. One woman shows include Va. Wesleyan Coll., 1972, Peninsula Arts Assn., Newport News, 1972, Arts Internat. Gallery Ltd., Norfolk, Va., 1973, 74, Virginia Beach Arts Ctr., 1973, 74, Kirn Meml. Library, Norfolk, 1976, Jr. League of Hampton Rds. Hdqrs., 1981, Coliseum Mall, Hampton, Va., 1982, Mary Immaculate Hosp., 1983, Jr. League Offices, Newport News, 1983, Village Gallery, Newport News 1983; exhibited in numerous group shows, Va.; represented in permanent collections Hampton Sch. System, City of Hampton, Tenneco, Va. State Fair Collection, Cecil Rawls Mus., Peninsula Arts Assn., Riverside Hosp., City of Stoney Creek, Va., others. Work appears in numerous publs. Active Hidenwood Presbyn. Ch., Newport News. Recipient numerous awards and prizes. Mem. Peninsula Arts Assn., Hampton Arts and Humanities, Va. Mus., Chrysler Mus., Virginia Beach Arts Assn., Tidewater Artists, Va. Watercolor Soc., P.E.O., DAR, On The Hill Arts and Crafts Co-op, Alpha Delta Kappa. Home: 213 Parkway Dr Newport News VA 23606 Office: Christopher Newport Coll 50 Shoe Ln Newport News VA 23606

ANGOTTI, CATHERINE MARIE, nutritionist; b. Arlington, Va., Nov. 9, 1946; d. Frank William and Catherine Jeannette (Kolakoski) Poos; B.S., James Madison U., 1968; R.D., Med. Coll. Va., 1969; grad. Va. Poly. Inst. and State U., 1975; m. John Joseph Angotti, Sept. 15, 1973; 1 child, Heather Jeannette. Home economist Washington Gas Light Co., 1968; clin. dietitian Fairfax Hosp., Fairfax, Va., 1969-73; pvt. practice as nutrition cons., Alexandria, Va., 1972—; nutrition cons. Manassas (Va.) Manor Nursing Home, 1973-74, Bio-Tech., Inc., Falls Church, Va., 1977-78; nutrition surveyor JWK Internat., Annandale, Va., 1980-81; nutrition cons. NASA, Washington, 1977—; pres. Nutrition Cons., Inc., 1980—. Del. for Va. Dietetic Assn. to Va. Council on State Legis., 1974-76; mem. Com. for Pub. of Regional Diet Manual, 1971-73. Food Service Execs. awards scholar, 1967; Mem. Am. Dietetic Assn. (named outstanding Young Dietitian of Yr. 1975, Va. rep. on third party reimbursement 1984—), Va. Assn. Allied Health Profls. (bd. dirs. 1974-79, bd. dirs. 1975-77), Cons. Nutritionists (Va. state coordinator 1976-79), D.C. Dietetic Assn., Va. Dietetic Assn. (exec. bd. 1974-76, 82—, nominating com. 1984-86, co-chmn. licensure com. 1984—, mem. nat. polit. action com., registered lobbyist 1985-86), No. Dist. Dietetic Assn. (exec. bd. 1970—, treas. 1980-82, pres. elect 1982-83, pres. 1983-84, chmn. nominating com. 1977-78 1984-85), Fairfax County Nutrition Com., Nat. Assn. Female Execs., Soc. for Nutrition Edn. Democrat. Roman Catholic. Contbr. articles to profl. jours. Home: 2727 Oak Valley Dr Vienna VA 22180 Office: 10721 Main St Suite 1400 Fairfax VA 22030

ANGUIZOLA, GUSTAVO A., political science educator, author; b. Panama City, Panama, Feb. 29, 1928; B.A., U. Evansville, 1948; M.A., Ind. U., 1950, Ph.D., 1953; M.S., Mich. State U., 1953; postgrad. Am. Sch. Classics, Athens, Greece, 1964, Stanford U., 1975. With U.S. Dist. Engrs. Corps, C.Z., 1941-44; prof. econs. and govt., chmn. dept. Morris (S.C.) Coll., 1960-61; prof. Latin Am. history and govt., chmn. dept., N.C. State U., Elizabeth City, 1961-62; vis. prof. Latin Am. instns. N.Y. State U., 1961, 62; asst. prof. history polit. sci. Purdue U., 1963-66; assoc. prof. history polit. sci. Chgo. State U., 1967-68; research prof. history polit. sci. U. Tex., Arlington, 1966—, co-founder Mesoamerica Ctr. Spl. asst. to mayor Chgo. for Pan Am. Games, 1959; mem. adv. bd. Am. Security Council. Recipient grand prize, gold medal Sesquicentennial Commn. for Panama Canal, 1953; Hays-Mundt award, 1953; Fulbright-Hays award, 1964-65; NSF grantee, 1975; decorated Medal of Merit, U.S. Pres. Mem. Am., So., European, Nat. hist. assns., AAUP, Conf. Latin Am., Western Social Sci. Assn., Am. Security Council, Tex. Commn. Minorities, Hispanic Assembly (vice chmn.), Council Inter-Am. Security, Instituto Panamericano de Geografia e Historia, Interam. Soc., Classical Soc. Clubs: Westerners (Ft. Worth); Maverick; Dallas Republican Men's. Author: Violation of Human Rights and Civil Liberties in Panama, 1977, 78; Isthmian Political Instability: 1821-1976, 1976, 77; Philippe Bunau-Varilla: The Man Behind the Panama Canal, 1980. Home: 920 Appleton Arlington TX 76010 also 2909 W Logan Blvd Chicago IL 60647 Office: Box 19488 U Texas Station Arlington TX 76019 also PO Box 2138 Panama City Panama

ANNIS, LAWRENCE VINCENT, forensic clinical psychologist; b. Augusta, Ga., Dec. 28, 1946; s. Lawrence Vincent Sr. and Betty (Allen) An.; m. Kathy Ann Kirkwood, June 12, 1971 (div. 1973); m. Christy Adde Baker, Aug. 23, 1982. Lic. clin. psychologist, Fla. Behavior specialist Gracewood State Sch., Augusta, 1980-81; clin. dir. Youth Enrichment Services, Lumberton, N.C., 1982-83; clin. psychologist Fla. State Hosp., Chattahoochee, 1981-82, 83-84, internship dir., 1984—; supervising psychologist Corrections Mental Health Inst., Chattahoochee, 1984—; forensic cons. various corrections agys., 1985—. Contbr. chpts. to books, articles to profl. jours. Served to lt. comdr. USN, 1969-86. Mem. Am. Psychol. Assn., S.E. Psychol. Assn., Am. Assn. for Correctional Psychology, Internat. Council Psychologists. Avocations: running; sailing. Office: Corrections Mental Health Inst Chattahoochee FL 32324

ANNULIS, JOHN THOMAS, mathematics educator; b. Cin., Nov. 13, 1945; s. John James and Vivian Marie (Jaeger) A.; m. Elizabeth Bruce, Jan. 25, 1969; children—Laura Elizabeth, Leah Catherine. B.A., Grand Valley State Coll., 1966; M.A., U. N.Mex., 1968, Ph.D., 1971. Asst. prof. math. U. Wis.-Whitewater, 1971-72; asst. prof. math. U. Ark.-Monticello, 1972-75, assoc. prof., 1975-81, prof., 1981—, head dept. math., 1979-82, head dept. math. and physics, 1982—. Contbr. articles to profl. jours. Named Disting. Alumnus, Grand Valley State Coll., 1985. Mem. Math. Assn. Am., Ark. Council Tchrs. Math. Avocations: gardening; reading. Home: 150 Hutchinson Dr Monticello AR 71657 Office: Dept Math and Physics U Ark Science Center Monticello AR 71657

ANSARI, MEGILL SHAKIR, company owner; b. Tuskegee, Ala., May 11, 1957; s. John Thomas and Ethel Mae (Mims) P.; m. 1975. Student Vocat. Nursing, So. Vocat. Coll., 1975-76, Tuskegee Inst., 1977-79, Troy State U. (Ala.), 1981, Federated Tax Service, Chgo., 1983-85, N.Am. Sch. Animal Sci., 1982-83, Atlanta Sch. Med. Assts., 1984, Internat. Corr. Schs., 1984-85; Songwriter, Tuskegee, 1980-83; home care nurse, Tuskegee, 1982; author, songwriter Sweet Musicman Products, Tuskegee, 1981-83; music reporter Troy State U. newspaper, 1982; editor Sweet Musicman Songwriters, Tuskegee, 1981-83; Sec. Air Force R.O.T.C., 1982—. Author: Confine Love, 1986. Scoutmaster Tuskegee Housing Dept., 1980-83; sustaining mem. Republican Nat. Com., 1984. Mem. Am. Film Inst., Nat. Writer's Union, C.of C. U.S. Author: (book of poems) Loneliness is my Only Friend, 1983 It Is I, 1984; Barroom, 1983; (novel) The First Time, 1984. Home: Rural Route 3 Box 1045 Tuskegee AL 36083

ANSLEY, D'ARCY MELL, nurse, management consultant; b. Wharton, Tex., Jan. 18, 1947; s. William Allen and Annie Lee (Border) A. B.S. in Nursing, U. Tex., 1969; M.B.A., U. St. Thomas, 1983. Registered nurse. Adminstrv. coordinator Tex. Inst. Rehab., Houston, 1973-74; ednl. coordinator St. Luke's Episcopal Hosp., Houston, 1974-79, asst. dir. nursing edn., 1979-81; dir. critical care services Hermann Hosp., Houston, 1981-84; v.p. Affiliate Hosp. Systems, Houston, 1984—; clin. instr. U. Tex. Med. Sch., Houston, 1981—; faculty assoc. U. Tex. Nursing Sch., Houston, 1984—, Tex. Women's U., 1985—.Com. mem. Am. Heart Assn., Houston, 1976-81, ARC, Houston, 1982-84. Named Outstanding Mgr., Adminstrn.-Hermann Hosp., Houston, 1983. Mem. Am. Orgn. Nurse Execs., Tex. Hosp. Assn., Assn. Houston Nursing Adminstrs. (bd. dirs. 1984—), Alpha Delta Pi. Avocations: snow skiing; tennis; water skiing.

ANSLEY, SHEPARD BRYAN, lawyer; b. Atlanta, July 31, 1939; s. William Bonneau and Florence Jackson (Bryan) A.; m. Boyce Lineberger, May 9, 1970; children—Anna Rankin, Florence Bryan. B.A., U. Ga., 1961; LL.B., U. Va., 1964. Bar: Ga. 1967. Assoc., Carter, Ansley, Smith & McLendon, Atlanta, 1967-73, ptnr., 1973-84, of counsel, 1984—; dir. DeKalb Fed. Savs. & Loan Assn.; chmn. bd. dirs. Sodamaster Co. Am. Bd. dirs. Jour. Pub. Law Emory U., 1961-62. Mem. vestry St. Luke's Episcopal Ch., Atlanta, 1971-74; treas., mem. exec. com., bd. dirs. Alliance Theatre Co., Atlanta, 1974-85; trustee Atlanta Music Festival Assn., Inc., 1975—, Atlanta Preservation Ctr., Inc. Served to capt. U.S. Army, 1965-67. Mem. ABA, Ga. Bar Assn., Atlanta Bar Assn., Atlanta Lawyers Club, Am. Coll. Mortgage Attys. Clubs: Piedmont Driving, World Trade (Atlanta).

ANSLEY-DIXSON, ELIZABETH GLEN, business skills development lecturer, facilities planner; archivist; b. Moultrie, Ga., Dec. 7, 1948; d. Campbell Wallace and Elizabeth Nadeene (Darbyshire) Ansley. B.A. in English, Mercer U., 1970; M.L.S., Emory U., 1973. Admissions counselor Montreat-Anderson Jr. Coll., Montreat, N.C., 1970-71; librarian Middle Ga. Regional Libraries, Macon, 1971-72; dir. adult services Methodist Home, Macon, 1975-76; head librarian Ga. Acad. for Blind, Macon, 1977; library, computer research services, archives, learning resource and devel. ctr. supr. Ga. Power Co., Atlanta, 1977-84; pres. Prompt Cons. Group, 1985—; assoc. Metrics Research Corp., 1983—; nat. project mgr. Edison Electric Inst. speaker, cons. Active Jr. League Winston-Salem, Inc., 1976—; del. White House Conf. Libraries and Info. Services, 1979; vice-chair Library Services Constrn. Act, 1983-84; mem. adv. council Ga. Dept. Edn., 1980-84; membership com. Atlanta Arts Festival Council, 1982-84; pres. Friends of the Library, Inc., 1973-77; adv. bd. Image Film Video Ctr., 1983-84. Mem. Spl. Libraries Assn. (chair nat. com.), ASTD (mem. expo. com.), Info. Industry Assn. Ga. Library Assn., Winston-Salem Consoma Soc. (bd. dirs.). Republican. Presbyterian. Club: Ansley Golf. Author producer 6 films/videotapes on library and archives subjects.

ANTHONY, BERYL FRANKLIN, JR., congressman; b. El Dorado, Ark., Feb. 21, 1938; s. Beryl Franklin and Oma Lee (Roark) A.; B.S., U. Ark., 1961, J.D., 1963; m. Sheila Foster, Aug. 4, 1962; children—Alison, Lauren. Admitted to Ark. bar; asst. atty. gen. Ark., 1964-65; dep. pros. atty. Union County, 1966-70; pros. atty. 13th Jud. Dist. Ark., 1971-76; legal counsel Anthony Forest Products Co., El Dorado, 1977; pvt. practice, El Dorado, 1977—; mem. 96th-97th Congresses from 4th Dist. Ark.; pres. Ark. Pros. Attys. Assn., 1975; dir. Union Fidelity Savs. and Loan Assn., El Dorado. Recipient Outstanding Young Man award El Dorado Jaycees, 1973. Mem. Ark. Bar Assn., Ark. Forestry Assn. (sec., dir. 1977). Democrat. Episcopalian. Office: 213 Cannon House Bldg Washington DC 20515

ANTHONY, CHARLES JOSEPH, accountant; b. Joplin, Mo., Oct. 23, 1916; s. Ben L. and Blanche M. (Bloomer) A.; m. Catherine Louise Ball, Aug. 22, 1940; children—Sarah Catherine, Charles Thomas, Cheryl Ann. Student Rice U., 1934-35; B.S. in Commerce, So. Meth. U., 1938; M.B.A., Northwestern U., 1939. C.P.A., Tex. Asst. prof. acctg. So. Meth. U., Dallas, 1939-40; prof. acctg. Butler U., Indpls., 1940-44; with Arthur Andersen & Co., Houston, Dallas, 1944-79, ptnr., 1954-79; prof. acctg. N. Tex. State U., Denton, 1979-81; cons. Trustee, Nat. Benevolent Assn. of Christian Chs., St. Louis, 1964—. Recipient Elijah Watts Sells Silver medal Am. Inst. C.P.A.s, 1939; Outstanding Com. Chmn., Tex. Soc. C.P.A.s, 1969-70. Mem. Am. Inst. C.P.A.s, Tex. Soc. C.P.A.s, Dallas C. of C. Clubs: City, Masons (32 deg.), Shriners. Contbr. articles to profl. jours. Home: 7238 Mimosa Ln Dallas TX 75230 Office: 5600 Interfirst Plaza Dallas TX 75265

ANTHONY, GRETCHEN WILHELMINA HAUSER, architect, consultant on accessibility for disabled; b. Mpls., Nov. 13, 1936; d. Theodor Emmanuel and Margrete Alice (Norman) Hauser; m. John Duncan Anthony, June 17, 1961 (div. Jan. 1980); children—Caitlin Anharad, Ian David. Student Pa. State U., 1954-59; B.Arch., U. Mich., 1961. Registered profl. architect, Pa. Draftswoman, designer Todd & Giroux AIA, Rochester, N.Y., 1961-62, Michaell DeAngelis AIA, Rochester, 1962-63, John M. Puskar AIA, Pitts., 1963-66; ptnr. Puskar & Anthony, Pitts., 1968-70; self-employed architect, 1970—, Fairmont, W.Va., 1974—; cons. Washington County Planning Commn., Pa., 1966-67, 1970-73. Draftswoman, designer and specifications writer on variety of construction and remodeling projects. Organizer, past pres. Marion County High Spirit MS Com., Fairmont, W.Va., 1975—; del. Gov. of W.Va. Conf. on Handicapped Individuals, Charleston, 1976; alt. White House Conf. on Handicapped Individuals, 1976; mem. W.Va. Adv. Council on Edn. of Exceptional Children, Charleston, 1978-81; organizer Handicapped United of W.Va., Fairmont, pres., 1982—; bd. dirs. greater W.Va. chpt. Nat. M.S. Soc., Charleston, 1983—; vice chmn. consumer adv. com. Clarksburg Dist. div. W.Va. Vocat. Rehab., 1983—; trustee Coordinating Council for Ind. Living, Morgantown, W.Va., 1984—; mem. consumer adv. com. W.Va. Client Assistance Program, Charleston, 1984—. Avocations: reading; knitting. Home and office: Access Unltd 6 Diana Dr Fairmont WV 26554

ANTHONY, LANCE COLEMAN, marketing research firm executive; b. Columbus, Ga., Nov. 20, 1947; s. Noel Mercer and Mable Irene (Brookins) A.; B.A., Columbus Coll., 1970; M.A., Stephen F. Austin State U., 1972. Founder L.C.A. Enterprises, Inc., Phenix City, Ala., 1978—, pres., chief exec. officer, 1978—. Mem. Mktg. Research Assn., Am. Mktg. Assn. Democrat. Baptist. Lodge: Masons, (master), K.T., DeMolay (sr.). Home: 1408 14th Ct Phenix City AL 36867 Office: PO Box 3050 Phenix City AL 36868

ANTHONY, RAY TAYLOR, department store executive; b. Cleveland, Okla., June 16, 1913; s. Charles Ross and Lutie Lillian (Mauldin) A.; m. Claudia Chesnut Bettis, Feb. 1, 1940; children—Claudia Raye, Carol Gaye, Linda June, Lutie C., Ray Bettis. B.S. in Bus. Adminstrn., U. Okla., 1934. Salesman C.R. Anthony Co., Oklahoma City, 1934-38, mdse. mgr. shoes, 1938-44, traffic mgr., 1945-52, dir., 1949—, office mgr., treas., 1952-55, v.p., treas., 1955-72, chmn. bd., 1972—; dir. Citizens Nat. Bank & Trust Co., 1976—; Pres. Community Council Central Okla., 1975-77; pres. Better Bus. Bur., 1977-79. Chmn. Areawide Health Planning Orgn., 1969-72; bd. dirs. Oklahoma City YMCA, pres., 1982-83; bd. dirs. Okla. State Fair Bd., Oklahoma City Appeals Rev. Bd.; pres. United Way, 1983; trustee Okla. Zool. Soc. Served with USAAF, 1944-45. Decorated Air Medal, D.F.C. Mem. Fin. Execs. Inst., Oklahoma City C. of C. (v.p.). Democrat. Mem. Disciples of Christ. Clubs: Oklahoma City Golf and Country, Quail Creek Country, Petroleum, Econ., Whitehall, Lions (pres. 1950-51). Home: 6901 Avondale Dr Oklahoma City OK 73116 Office: 701 N Broadway Oklahoma City OK 73102

ANTHONY, RAYFORD GAINES, chemical engineering educator, researcher, consultant; b. Abilene, Tex., Dec. 26, 1935; s. Oscie Eldredge and Lila Vinita (Sherrill) A.; m. Jo-Ann Turnbough, Jan. 17, 1959; children—Kathryn Margaret, Elizabeth Renee'. B.S., Tex. A&M U., College Station, 1958, M.S., 1962; Ph.D., U. Tex., 1966. Registered profl. engr., Tex. Asst. research engr. Petroleum Chem. Co., 1958-60; research engr. Sun Oil Co., Dallas, summer 1964; asst. prof. chem. engring. dept. Tex. A&M U., College Station, 1966-69, assoc. prof., 1969-74, prof., 1974—; cons. Celanese Chem. Co., Corpus Christi, 1978—. Author: (with C.D. Holland) Fundamentals of Chemical Reaction Engineering, 1979. Contbr. articles to profl. jours. Patentee in field. Bd. dirs. Bluebonnet council Girl Scouts U.S., 1974-76. Served as 2d lt. USAR, 1958. Recipient Outstanding Teaching award Standard Oil Found. 1970. Mem. Am. Inst. Chem. Engrs. (area chmn. nat. program com. 1980-82, dir. fuels and petrochem. div. 1985—; Pub. award 1980, 82), Am. Chem. Soc., S.W. Catalyst Soc. (chmn. 1983-84), Tau Beta Pi. Methodist. Lodges: Masons, Lions. Avocation: reading. Office: Tex A&M U Chem Engring Dept College Station TX 77843

ANTHONY, ROBERT ARMSTRONG, lawyer; b. Washington, Dec. 28, 1931; s. Emile Peter and Martha (Armstrong) A.; m. Ruth Grace Barrons, Feb. 7, 1959; 1 son, Graham Barrons; m. 2d, Joan Patricia Caton, Jan. 3, 1980; 1 son, Peter Christopher Caton. B.A., Yale U., 1953; B.A. in Jurisprudence (Rhodes scholar), Oxford (Eng.) U., 1955; J.D., Stanford U., 1957. Bar: Calif. 1957, N.Y. 1971, D.C. 1972. Assoc. Pillsbury, Madison & Sutro, San Francisco, 1957-62, Kelso, Cotton & Ernst, San Francisco, 1962-64; assoc. prof. law Cornell U., 1964-68, prof., 1968-75; chief counsel U.S. Office Fgn. Direct Investments, Dept. Commerce, Washington, 1972-73, dir., 1973; chmn. Adminstrv. Conf. U.S., Washington, 1974-79, cons., 1968-71, 82-84; ptnr. McKenna, Conner & Cuneo, Washington, 1979-82; sole practice, Washington, 1982-83; prof. law George Mason U., 1983—; lectr. Acad. Am. and Internat. Law, Southwestern Legal Found., Dallas, summers 1967-72; mem. Pres.'s Inflation Program Regulatory Council, 1978-79; mem. Fairfax County (Va.) Rep. Com., 1984—; mem., chmn. panel U.S. Dept. Edn. Appeal Bd., 1981-83; cons. Internat. Law Inst., 1984—. Bd. dirs. Marin Shakespeare Festival, San Rafael, Calif., 1961-64, Nat. Ctr. for Adminstrv. Justice, 1974-79; commr. Sausalito (Calif.) City Planning Commn., 1962-64. Mem. ABA, D.C. Bar, State Bar Calif., Am. Law Inst., Stanford Law Soc. Washington (pres. 1982). Clubs: Cosmos. Contbr. articles to legal jours. Home: 2011 Lorraine Ave McLean VA 22101 Office: George Mason U Sch Law 3401 N Fairfax Dr Arlington VA 22201

ANTHONY, ROBERT HOLLAND, department store chain executive; b. Oklahoma City, Okla., May 15, 1948; s. Guy Mauldin and Christine (Holland) A.; B.S. in Econs., Wharton Sch., U. Pa., 1970; M.Sc. in Econs., London Sch. Econs., 1971; M.A., Yale U., 1973; M.P.A. in Public Adminstrn., John F. Kennedy Sch. of Govt., Harvard U., 1977; m. Nancy Bargo, May 25, 1975; children—Elizabeth Bargo, Christine Holland, Suzanne Mauldin, Katherine Beeler. Salesman, C.R. Anthony Co., Oklahoma City, 1963-74, dir. employee benefit plans, 1975-80, chmn. pension and profit sharing trust, 1976-86, asst. to pres., 1978-80, v.p., 1979-80, pres., 1980—, also dir.; staff economist U.S. Ho. of Reps. Com. on Interior and Insular Affairs, 1972; asst. to adminstr., staff economist Okla. Gov.'s Office of Community Affairs & Planning, 1973-74; econ. cons. U.S. Library of Congress, 1975; dir. Liberty Nat. Bank, Oklahoma City, Okla. Med. Enterprises. Councilman, City of Oklahoma City, 1979-80, vice mayor, 1980; bd. dirs. Oklahoma County Council for Mentally Retarded Children, 1974-79; bd. dirs. central br. YMCA, Oklahoma City, 1977-79, E. Side br. YMCA, 1981—; mem. adminstrv. bd. 1st Meth. Ch., Edmond, Okla., 1976-77, Crown Heights Meth. Ch., Oklahoma City, 1978—; trustee Okla. Sci. and Arts Mus., 1978-81, Okla. City Zoo, 1979-80, Oklahoma City U., 1981—; commr. Oklahoma City Convs. and Tourism Commn., 1979-80; trustee Oklahoma City Econ. Devel., Found. 1982—; mem. Gov.'s Adv. Bd. on Productivity, 1982-84; vice chmn. Okla. Centennial Planning Div., 1982—; bd. dirs. Leadership Oklahoma City, 1982—, Com. of 100, 1984—; mem. exec. bd. Wharton Sch., 1985—. Served to capt. USAR, 1966-78. Mem. Econ. Club of Okla. (dir. 1981—), Beta Gamma Sigma. Club: Oklahoma City Men's Dinner. Home: 3605 N McKinley Oklahoma City OK 73118 Office: CR Anthony Co 701 N Broadway Oklahoma City OK 73102*

ANTHONY, THOMAS NILE, real estate, investment and insurance company executive; b. East Liverpool, Ohio, Oct. 25, 1935; s. Norman H. and Jane (Gessford) A.; student Ohio U., 1954-57; diagnostic X-ray degree U. Western Pa., 1958; children—Thomas N., Matthew D., Stephen G., Christopher T., Mark A. Sales rep. Warren Teed, Inc., Jamestown, N.Y., 1958-61; mgr. sales IBM, Jamestown, 1961-65; brokerage rep. Conn. Gen. Ins. Co., Miami, 1965-67; asst. to pres. Cockaigno, Inc., Jamestown, 1964-65; mgr. Md. Life Ins. Co., Miami, 1967-69; pres. Thomas Anthony Assos., Inc., Ft. Lauderdale, Fla., 1969—; pres. Hollywood Meml. Gardens; dir. Atlantic Telephone Equipment Co. Pres. Ft. Lauderdale Community Service Council, 1973-77; bd. dirs. Help on Wheels, 1973-77; bd. dirs., pres. Adv. Council Transp. for Sr. Citizens; bd. dirs. Emergency Family Housing Center; bd. dirs., v.p. Star of David Meml. Gardens; bd. dirs., mem. exec. com. Broward County Health Planning and Rehab. Council, pres., 1978—; mem. Broward County Drug Abuse Council; mem. Broward County Estate Planning Council; bd. dirs. Govt. Adv. Council Health Rehab. Services, Tenn. Adv. Council Manpower, Hospice of Broward, Inc., 1980; chmn. Coll. for Human Services, 1980; mem. ADOC, So. Fla. State Hosp. Broward County Assn. Life Underwriters. Republican. Lutheran. Clubs: Tower, Tennis, Le Club Internat., Touchdown, Marian Bay, Coral Ridge Country, Player's, Elks. Office: 5100 N Federal Hwy Fort Lauderdale FL 33308

ANTOINE, WINNIE VANCE, educational administrator; b. Panola County, Tex., July 1, 1941; d. James and Vera (Reagan) Vance; B.S., Wiley Coll., 1962; M.Ed., Prairie View A&M Coll., 1970; postgrad. U. Santa Clara, 1972-73, Northwestern U., 1974-75, La. Inst. Tech., 1974-75, So. U., 1974-75, East Tex. State U., 1975-76, U. Houston, 1979-80; m. Roland L. Antoine, Aug. 24, 1963; children—Roland L., Carmen Nicole. Tchr., Shreveport, La., 1963-71; guidance counselor, Shreveport, 1971-73; parish coordinator Title I math., Shreveport, 1973-78; prin. Northside Elem. Sch., Shreveport, 1978—; mem. adv. bd. Security Nat. Bank. Chmn. Ebony Fashion Fair, Shreveport, 1978-80; bd. dirs. St. John's Sch., 1977-78, Caddo-Bossier Day Care Ctr. Mem. Assn. Supervision and Curriculum Devel., Nat. Assn. Elem. Sch. Prins., La. Assn. Supervision and Curriculum Devel., NEA, La. Assn. Educators, Caddo Assn. Elem. Sch. Prins., Nat. Council Tchrs. of Math., Caddo Prins. Assn. (pres.), Joint Adminstrs. Club, Caddo-Bossier Urban League, Silhouette of Kappa Alpha Psi, Alpha Kappa Alpha. Democrat. Roman Catholic. Clubs: Wiley Alumni, Shreveport's Links (corr. sec.). Home: 3217 Lawden St Shreveport LA 71103 Office: 2000 Northside Dr Shreveport LA 71107

ANTOKOLETZ, JUANA CANABAL, psychologist; b. Havana, Cuba, Aug. 21, 1938; came to U.S., 1961; d. Pedro and Consuelo (Villanueva) Canabal; m. Elliott Antokoletz, May 28, 1972; 1 child, Eric. D.Psychology, Universidad Santo Tomas Villanueva, Havana, 1968; Ph.D., St. John's U., 1970. Lic. psychologist, profl. sch. psychologist. Psychologist, Madonna Heights Residential Treatment Ctr., Huntington, N.Y., 1962-70, Bd. Coop. Ednl. Services, Nassau County, N.Y., 1970-73; chief psychologist Puerto Rican Family Inst., N.Y.C., 1973-76; postdoctoral tng. in psychotherapy Adelphi U., 1976; psychologist AISD, Austin, Tex., 1977—; pvt. practice psychology, Austin, 1982—. Author articles. Mem. Am. Psychol. Assn., NEA, Capital Area Psychol. Assn. (newsletter editor 1985—). Avocations: writing; travel. Home: 2802 Horseshoe Bend Cove Austin TX 78704 Office: AISD 6016 Dillard Circle Austin TX 78752

ANTON, LAURENCE HARVEY, automotive warehouse executive; b. Ft. Worth, May 24, 1946; s. Charles and Shirley (Ginsberg) A.; m. Harriet Linda

Hamill, Apr. 7, 1968; children—Jennifer Lynn, David Barnett. B.A., Tex. Christian U., 1968. With Big 4 Automotive, Ft. Worth, Tex., 1968—, ops. mgr., 1974, pres., 1976—; pres. Scotty's & All-Pro, 1978; dir., mem. loan com. Tex. Am. Bank-West Side, 1982—. Chmn., Tex. Christian U. Alumni Fund, 1981; bd. dirs. Inst. Human Fitness, Tex. Coll. Osteo. Medicine. Recipient Northwood Inst. Auto. Replacement Ednl. award, 1983. Mem. Automotive Warehouse Distbr. Assn. (1st vice chmn., exec. com.), Young Pres.'s Orgn., Automotive Wholesalers of Tex., Automotive Service Industry Assn. Jewish. Clubs: Ft. Worth (fin. com.), Colonial Country, Shady Oaks Country. Office: 512 S Jennings St PO Box 1696 Fort Worth TX 76101

ANTONELLI, GEORGE ANTHONY, university dean, educator; b. DuQuoin, Ill., Oct. 6, 1941; s. George Joseph and Mary (Cizauskas) A.; m. Eileen Bond, Apr. 17, 1966; 1 child, George Andrew. B.A., So. Ill. U., 1963, Ph.D., 1972; M.A., U. Wis., 1968. Tchr.-intern high sch., Beaver Dam, Wis., 1967-68; tchr. high sch., West Bend, Wis., 1968-69; instr. So. Ill. U., Carbondale, 1969-72; from asst. prof. to assoc. prof. U. N.C.-Charlotte, 1972-83; dean, prof. U. Ark., Pine Bluff, 1983—; cons. Dept. Edn., Raleigh, N.C., 1977-83, Little Rock, 1983—. Mem. editorial bd. profl. jours. Mem. child adv. council Exceptional Children's Agy., Charlotte, 1980-83; pres., bd dirs. Am. Lung Assn.-Metrolina, 1980-82; bd. dirs. Jefferson County United Way, 1983—. Served with USNR, 1965-71. Recipient Leadership award Assn. Teaching Educators, 1981-85, Vol. of Yr. award Am. Lung Assn., 1982-83; Service award Am. Assn. Coll. Tchr. Edn. Mem. Assn. Tchr. Educators (exec. bd., Service award 1984, 85), Assn. Middle Sch. Adminstrs. (exec. bd.), Kappa Delta Pi (pres., v.p., service award 1981, 85), Phi Delta Kappa (pres., v.p., Service award 1977). Lodge: Rotary Internat. Home: 18 Mockingbird Ln Pine Bluff AR 71603

ANTONY, MOSS LEON, ophthalmologist; b. Albuquerque, Nov. 1, 1937; s. Moses Leon and Marie Louise (Speckels) A.; m. Gayle Allison Houston, June 16, 1962 (div. 1983); children—Brent Houston, Allison Marie, Charlotte Granville. Student Tulane U., 1955-56, Tex. A&M U., 1957-59; M.D., Baylor U., 1963. Diplomate Am. Bd. Ophthalmology. Intern, Charity Hosp. of La., New Orleans; resident in ophthalmology Eye, Ear, Nose and Throat Hosp., Tulane U., New Orleans; practice medicine specializing in ophthalmology Eye Care/Surg. Assocs. of New Orleans, 1967—. Served to capt. USAF, 1964-69. Fellow ACS, Am. Acad. Ophthalmology; mem. New Orleans Acad Ophthalmology (pres. 1981-83), La. Ophthalmology Assn. (pres. 1978-82), Contact Lens Assn. Ophthalmologists, Orleans Parish Med. Soc., La. State Med. Soc., Phi Kappa Phi. Republican. Episcopalian. Clubs: Windsor, Quin, New Orleans Tennis, Alphine (New Orleans). Home: 3101 Prytania St New Orleans LA 70115 Office: Eye Care/Surg Assocs New Orleans 3525 Prytania St New Orleans LA 70115

ANTOS, JOHN JEFFREY, electric company executive; b. Chgo., Jan. 13, 1949; s. Frank J. and Estelle (Petko) A.; m. Lana Ethelyn Uryasz, Feb. 12, 1978; 1 child, Emily Marie. B.S. in Bus. Adminstrn., U. Ill., 1971; M.B.A., U. Chgo., 1976. Lic. real estate broker, Tex., Fla.; cert. mgmt. acct., fin. planner. Asst. sales mgr. Southwestern Co., Nashville, 1968-73; pres. Antos & Assocs., Chgo., 1973-75; fin. analyst Marsh & McLennan, Chgo., 1975-77; sr. cons. W.A. Golomski & Assocs., Chgo., 1977-79; mgmt. cons., real estate developer, Chgo. and Fla., 1980-84; controller, treas. Hi-Line Electric Co., Dallas, 1984—, also dir.; instr. grad. acctg. Roosevelt U., Chgo. Founder, pres. Young Execs. Club, Chgo., 1974-77; co founder Republican Assocs., Chgo., 1978. Mem. Nat. Assn. Accts., Am. Soc. Quality Control, Tex. Arts Alliance, 500 Inc., Assn. Corp. Growth. Office: 2121 Valley View Rd Dallas TX 75234

ANZEK, LOUIS MICHAEL (MICHAEL ST. JOHN), radio programming executive; b. Huntsville, Ala., Oct. 13, 1951; s. Michael Joseph and Sadie Elizabeth (Citrano) A.; m. Leisa Ann McBrayer, Jan. 24, 1975; children—Louis Christopher, Jamie Michelle. B.A. in Psychology, Vanderbilt U., 1973. Music dir., asst. program dir., Sta. WERC AM-FM, 1973-76; program dir. Sta. WMPS, Memphis, 1976-77; program dir. Sta. WTIC-FM, Hartford, Conn., 1977; v.p. programming Sta. WWKX, Gallatin, Nashville, Tenn., 1978-84; v.p., gen. mgr. Sta. WYHY, 1985—; cons. Stas. WKXC, Chattanooga, WAHR, Huntsville, others. Bd. dirs. Summer Acad., Gallatin, Tenn.; co-commr. Gallatin Midget Football Assn. Mem. Nat. Assn. Broadcasters, Nat. Radio Broadcaster's Assn. Roman Catholic. Club: Gallatin Lions.

APARICIO, HENRY RAYMOND, securities broker; b. Tampa, Fla., July 9, 1939; s. Henry C. and Irene Z. A.; m. Peggy L. Abshier, June 29, 1969; children—Ashley, Nicolas. B.S., U. So. Miss., 1962; postgrad. U. Valencia, Spain, 1961, U. Fla., 1963. Mgr., Dole Internat., Tampa, 1968-71; computer div. mgr. Xerox Corp., New Orleans, 1972-79; with Harger-Aparicio-Prejean, Metairie, La., 1979—, sr. v.p., 1986—; sr. prin. Internat. House of New Orleans World Trade Ctr. Named Jr. C. of C. Most Outstanding Man of the Yr. 1966; One of Outstanding People City of New Orleans, 1983. Mem. La. Real Estate Securities and Syndication Inst. (dir., officer), Nat. Assn. Realtors, Jefferson Bd. Realtors. Methodist. Clubs: Big Gold, Beach, Rotary. Contbr. in field. Home: 28 Waverly Pl Metairie LA 70003 Office: Suite 116 3500 N Causeway Blvd Metairie LA 70002

APEL, EDWIN ARTHUR, consulting engineer; b. Gatesville, Tex., Dec. 24, 1927; s. Albert Karl and Lizzie A.; B.S. in Civil Engring., Tex. A&M U., 1952; m. Valla Gene Medart, Dec. 23, 1949; children—Edwin Michael, Sharon Sue, Barry Charles, Kenneth Lynn, Richard Gayle. Project engr. H.B. Zachry Co., San Antonio, 1952-54; design engr. Joe J. Rady & Co., Ft. Worth, 1954-62; exec. v.p. Rady & Assocs., Inc., Ft. Worth, 1962-74; propr. Edwin A. Apel, Cons. Engrs., Ft. Worth, 1974—; pres. Wani, Apel & Assocs., Ft. Worth, 1980—; sec., treas., dir. Dallas Mint, Inc., Arlington, Tex., 1981—; dir. Star Worth, Inc. Served with U.S. Army, 1946-47. Mem. Nat. Soc. Profl. Engrs. (pres. Ft. Worth chpt. 1974-75), Tex. Soc. Profl. Engrs. (chmn. chpt. activities com. 1975-76), Water Pollution Control Fedn. Republican. Baptist. Club: Petroleum (Ft. Worth). Home: 1809 Ridgeside Dr Arlington TX 76013 Office: 1062 Forest Ave Fort Worth TX 76112

APINIS, JOHN, chemist; b. Katvari, Latvia, Mar. 20, 1933; came to U.S., 1949, naturalized, 1954; s. Augusts and Marta (Gravelsins) A.;m. Johnnie Verena Burden, Feb. 6, 1960. B.S., Clemson U., 1960. Apprentice, Am. Thread Co., Willimantic, Conn., 1951-52, Leiss Velvet Mfg. Co., Willimantic, 1952-53; asst. plant chemist Burlington Industries, Wake Finishing Co., Raleigh, N.C., 1960-65, plant chemist, 1965-75, mgr. dept. dyeing, 1975-76, tech. coordinator, 1976—. Served with AUS, 1953-55. Mem. Am. Assn. Textile Chemists and Colorists. Clubs: Elks, Rotary (v.p. 1963-64, pres. 1964-65, dir. 1963-66), Raleigh Music, Questers (v.p. 1977-78, pres. 1978-79), Raleigh Clemson Alumni (pres. 1976-77). Research in textile color computer and chromosorter. Home: 5400 Alpine Dr Raleigh NC 27609 Office: Box 61168 Neuse Br Raleigh NC 27661

APLIN, CHARLES O'NEAL, ednl. administrator; b. Birmingham, Ala., June 14, 1943; s. Sam O'Neal and Rebecca Lee A.; A.A., Wallace Community Coll., 1967; B.S., Troy State U., 1969; M.Ed., U. West Fla., 1974; Ed.S., Fla. State U., 1976, Ed.D., 1979; m. Edith Joy Hardwick, Dec. 13, 1968; children—Michelle Leigh, Kevin O'Neal. Bookkeeper, Aplin's TV Service, Eufaula, Ala., 1961-67; tchr., chmn. math. dept. Ft. Walton Beach (Fla.) High Sch., 1969-83; math. program coordinator Okaloosa County Schs. (Fla.), 1983—; adj. asst. prof. math. Troy State U., 1980—; adj. assoc. prof. math. and edn. St. Leo Coll., 1981—. Named Ft. Walton Beach High Schs. Tchr. of Yr., 1980. Mem. Nat. Council Tchrs. Math., Assn. Supervision and Curriculum Devel., Fla. Council Tchrs. Math., Phi Kappa Phi, Phi Delta Kappa. Democrat. Baptist. Club: Masons. Home: 516 Justine Ave Fort Walton Beach FL 32548 Office: 120 Lowery Pl Fort Walton Beach FL 32548

APONTE, GONZALO ALFREDO, architect; b. San Juan, P.R., Apr. 23, 1948; s. Gonzalo and Mary Elsa (Otero) A.; m. Aileen Ellen Gotstein, May 26, 1973; 1 child, Alfredo Gonzalo. B.Arch., Ga. Inst. Tech., 1972. Registered architect, P.R., Tex. Project architect Guillermety, Ortiz & Assocs., San Juan, 1973-74, Acme Constructors, Inc., San Juan, 1975-76, Augur & Assocs., Inc., Dallas, 1977-78, RYA Architects, Inc., Dallas, 1978-79, H.J. Chris, Architects, Inc., Dallas, 1979-81; pres. Aponte & Assocs., Architects, Dallas, 1981—, A & A Imports, Inc., Dallas, 1981—; v.p. Empresas A & A Corp., San Juan, 1974—. Mem. site task force Landmark Com., City of Dallas, 1983—. Mem. AIA, Tex. Soc. Architects, Colegio de Arquitectos de P.R., N.Tex. Ga. Tech. Alumni Assn., Phi Eta Sigma. Office: 4508 Shady Hill Dr Dallas TX 75229

APPELBAUM, ALAN Z., securities executive; b. Jersey City, June 3, 1947; s. David D. and Tillie (Milstein) A.; m. Terri Lynn Siegel, Nov. 16, 1979; children—Shane Alexander, David Alan. B.A., Jersey City State Coll., 1968. History tchr. pub. schs., Bayonne and Jersey City, 1969-73; sr. v.p., dir. mktg. J.B. Hanauer, North Miami Beach, Fla., 1973-82; v.p., br. mgr. Paine Webber, 1982-83; pres. A.F. Best Securities, Ft. Lauderdale, Fla., 1983—. Jewish.

APPERSON, WILLIAM EUGENE, physician; b. Albemarle County, Va., July 3, 1910; s. Eugene Revercomb and Loula Temple (Robertson) A.; m. Ellen Cosby Carter, Oct. 29, 1938; children—William Eugene, Margaret Ellen Apperson Mayo. M.D., U. Va., 1935. Med. and surg. resident U. Va. Hosp., 1935-37; mem. staff Blue Ridge Hosp., Charlottesville, Va., 1937-50; instr. internal medicine U. Va. Hosp., 1940-50; dir. Tb Control Program, Va. Dept. Health, 1950-81; part-time med. cons. Va. Dept. Health, Richmond, 1981—. Recipient Douglas Southall Freeman award, 1969; Va. Pub. Health award, 1978. Mem. Am. Thoracic Soc., Am. Coll. Chest Physicians, AMA, Va. Med. Soc., Richmond (Va.) Acad. Medicine. Republican. Episcopalian. Home: 905 Pine Ridge Rd Richmond VA 23226

APPERT, ROBERT ALBERT, surgeon; b. Neenah, Wis., Nov. 15, 1944; s. Richard Joseph and Mary Lou (Stirn) A.; m. Jennifer Jansen, June 3, 1967 (div. 1983); children—Amy Elizabeth, Betsy Lynn, Gregory Cameron. B.S., U. Wis., 1966; M.D., Albany Med. Coll., 1971. Diplomate Am. Bd. Orthopedic Surgeons. Intern, Albany Med. Ctr. Hosp. (N.Y.), 1971-72, resident in surgery, 1972-76; instr. Albany Med. Coll., 1971-76; ptnr. Carolina Clinic, Inc., Wilson, N.C., 1976—; mem. staff Wilson Meml. Hosp.; dir. Peoples Bank & Trust Co., Wilson. Bd. dirs. Wilson County ARC, 1977-79; trustee Greenfield Acad., 1980-83. Fellow Am. Acad. Orthopedic Surgeons; mem. AMA, Wilson County Med. Soc., N.C. Orthopedic Soc. Republican. Episcopalian. Home: 3402 Wescott Dr Wilson NC 27893 Office: 1700 S Tarboro St Wilson NC 27895

APPLE, JOHN BOYD, elevator company executive; b. Dallas, Jan. 27, 1935; s. John Frank and Vaneta Margaret (Lafollette) A.; m. Carl Ann Graham, Mar. 14, 1958; children—Jane Anne, Julia Graham, John Boyd. B.S. in Geology, So. Meth. U., 1957. Salesman, Hunter-Hayes Elevator Co., Dallas, 1959-64, sales mgr., 1964-68, v.p. sales, 1968-71; zone mgr. Dover Elevator Co., Dallas, 1971-74, regional mgr., 1974-77; v.p. mktg. elevator div. Dover Corp., Memphis, 1977-81, pres., 1981-85; pres., chief exec. officer Dover Elevator Internat., Memphis, 1985—; dir. Nat. Elevator Industry Inc. Served to 1st lt. USAF, 1957-59. Republican. Episcopalian. Clubs: Chickasaw Country, Summit. Home: 2296 Kimbrough Woods Pl Memphis TN 38138 Office: Dover Elevator Internat 6750 Poplar Ave Suite 419 Memphis TN 38138

APPLE, ROBAH WARREN, JR., music educator; b. Danville, Va., Aug. 19, 1955; s. Robah Warren and Mabel Irene (Gwynn) A.; m. Nancy Louise Speakman, Aug. 12, 1984. Student Acad. Music, Vienna, Austria, 1977-78; Mus.B., N.C. Sch. Arts, 1977; Mus.M., Eastman Sch. Music, 1979, Mus.D., 1981. Prof. music Mitchell Coll., Statesville, N.C., 1982-85, U. S.C.-Aiken, 1985—. Editor of music scores, 1985. Mem. Am. Guild Organists, Coll. Music Soc., Am. Musicol. Soc., Music Tchrs. Nat. Assn., N.C. Music Tchrs. Assn. Avocations: record collecting; church laywork. Home: 105 Springhill Ct North Augusta SC 29841 Office: U SC 171 University Pkwy Aiken SC 29801

APPLEGATE, KENNETH CHARLES, health care administrator; b. Alliance, Ohio, June 29, 1944; s. Orville B. and Sara Jane (Thornburg) A.; m. Michele Wilkes, Sept. 6, 1982. B.S., Calif. Western U., 1981; postgrad. bus. adminstrn. Calif. Coast U., 1981-84. Coordinator emergency services Washington Clinic, 1967-68; asst. dir. respiratory services Fairfax Hosp., Falls Church, Va., 1969-72, dir. cardiopulmonary services, 1972-80, dir. life support services, 1980—; adj. prof. Geneva Coll., Beaver Falls, Pa., 1976—. NSF grantee, 1978. Mem. Nat. Soc. Cardiopulmonary Technology (dir. 1980-85), Am. Assn. Respiratory Therapy, Am. Mgmt. Assn., Greater Washington Soc. Cardiopulmonary Tech. Republican. Clubs: Kenwood Golf and Country (Bethesda, Md.). Lodge: Masons. Office: Fairfax Hosp 3300 Gallows Rd Falls Church VA 22046

APPLEGATE, WALTER VAN, export trading company executive, industrial psychology consultant; b. Willoughby, Ohio, July 18, 1928; s. Van Buren and Grace (Bay) A.; m. Lee Paxton, June 1, 1979; children—Cynthia, Shelly, Sharon. B.S., Ohio State U., 1952; M. Mil. Art and Sci., U.S. Army Command and Gen. Staff Coll., 1967; M.A., St. Mary's U., San Antonio, 1982. Commd. 2d lt. U.S. Army, 1952, advanced through grades to lt. col., 1970; bn. comdr., Vietnam, 1968-69; non commd. officer tng. dir. Pentagon, Washington, 1969-70; ret., 1970; exec. v.p. mktg. Ross Industries, Midland, Va., 1970-79; pres., chmn. Lord & Applegate, San Antonio, 1979—; pres. Intercontinental Network for Trade, Inc. Decorated Legion of Merit. Mem. N.Am. Soc. Adlerian Psychologists, Am. Mgmt. Assn., Tex. Assn. Mex.-Am. C. of C. (sec. 1983-84), San Antonio Mex.-Am. C. of C. (chmn. 1983). Republican. Office: INT PO Box 29334 Dallas TX 75209

APPLEGATE, YVONNE HOYLMAN, social worker; b. Marmet, W.Va., Nov. 10, 1940; d. Marshall James and Naomi Adele Hoylman. B.A., W.Va. U., 1962; M.A., Ind. U., 1964; Ph.D., Smith Coll., 1982. Cert. clin. social worker, Fla. Social worker VA, Indpls., 1964; social worker for adoptions, Children's Home Soc., Daytona Beach, Fla., 1964-66; social worker group home for adolescent girls Cath. Service Bur., Miami, Fla., 1966-72; social worker Pinellas County Schs., St. Petersburg, Fla., 1977—; also pvt. practice social work. Kroger scholar, 1958-59; W.Va. U. bd. govs. grantee, 1960, 61, 62; Indpls. Welfare Bd. scholar, 1962-63; VA grantee, 1963-64; NIMH grantee, 1972-75. Mem. Nat. Assn. Social Workers (cert.), Internat. Assn. Pediatric Social Work (editor jour.), Smith Coll. Alumni Assn. Democrat. Methodist. Author: The Narcissism of the Borderline Patient, 1982. Office: 1015 10th Ave N Saint Petersburg FL 33705

APPLEMAN, BUFORD MARION, mgmt. cons. co. exec.; b. Fullerton, Calif., May 20, 1925; s. Milford Harold and Bessie Amelia (Olson) A.; A.A., Fullerton Jr. Coll., 1948; B.B.A., U. Tex., 1950; m. Virginia H. Maufrais, Apr. 28, 1946; children—Vicki, Susan. Indsl. engr., service mgr., dist. sales mgr. Tex. Foundries, Lufkin, 1950-62; mgr. asphalt sales Douglas Oil Co., Los Angeles, mgr. corp. planning, 1962-66; asst. to pres. Challenge-Cook Bros., Los Angeles, 1966-67; mgr. nat. account sales Taylor Machine Co., Louisville, Miss., 1967-68; v.p. leasing and maintenance contracts Crane Carrier Corp., Tulsa, 1968-74; prin. Appleman & Assos., Tulsa, 1974—; pres. Appleman Profit Systems, Inc., San Antonio, 1978—; cons. ready-mix concrete and concrete products industries. Served with USAAF, 1943-46; ETO. Mem. Nat. Ready Mixed Concrete Assn., Tex. Aggregates and Concrete Assn. (chmn.). Republican. Methodist. Home: 3427 Hunters Circle San Antonio TX 78230

APPLETON, FELIX GEORGE, dentist; b. Lawrenceburg, Tenn., July 21, 1924; s. Felix Columbus and Flora Belle (McGee) A.; m. Nadean Cary, Sept. 20, 1953; children—Gregory Scott, Bryan Cary, Betsey Carol. B.A., U. Tenn., 1949; D.D.S., U. Tenn.-Memphis, 1957. Bacteriologist East Tenn. Bapt. Hosp., Knoxville, 1949-53; gen. practice dentistry, London, Tenn., 1957-69, Fort Worth, 1969—. Contbr. articles to profl. jour. City Commr. City of Loudon, Tenn., 1963; chmn. City and County Planning Commns., Loudon, 1964-68; mem. Tellico Regional Planning Commn. Loudon, 1967; organizer Patriotic Youth Day, Loudon, 1968. Served with USNR, 1942-46, ETO. Decorated Purple Heart. Fellow Am. Acad. Forensic Sci.; mem. ADA, Tex. Dental Assn., Fort Worth Dental Soc. (pres. 1985—), Am. Soc. Forensic Odontology. Republican. Mem. Ch. of Christ. Lodge: Rotary (pres. Loudon 1961). Home: 5801 Diamond Oaks Dr N Fort Worth TX 76117 Office: 7600 Glenview Dr Fort Worth TX 76118

APTON, RALPH JULIUS, investment adviser, business and financial consultant; b. Cologne, Ger., Oct. 16, 1930; came to U.S., 1935, naturalized, 1940; s. Adolph A. and Erna (Neu) A.; B.A., U. Chgo., 1950, M.B.A., 1954; m. Renate Sickinger, Dec. 30, 1959; children—Kory Kim, Keith Jerrard. Fgn. trade and investment asst. AID, Dept. State, Washington, 1954, asst. indsl. analyst, New Delhi, 1955-57, dep. regional tech. aids coordinator for Latin Am., Mexico City, 1957-59; dep. exec. sec. Pres. Task Force for Fgn. Econ. Assistance, Washington, 1960-61; chief mgmt. analysis br. Bur. for Latin Am. Affairs, Washington, 1962; devel. loan officer, Quito, Ecuador, 1963-65, AID del. to Ecuadorian Hwy. Transp. Com., 1963-65; chief pre-investment loans Inter-Am. Devel. Bank, Washington, 1966-76; real estate operator; pres. Apton Investment Adviser, Inc.; regional v.p. Corp. Fin. Assos. for Va.-Md.-D.C.; chmn., treas. Tack N'Teake Ltd., 1978-80; trustee Stonewall Farm; radio-TV guest fin. commentator; instr. U.S. Dept. Agr. Grad. Sch. Mem. Fairfax County Republican Com. Mem. Am. Fin. Assn., Am. Mktg. Assn., U.S. C. of C., Fairfax County C. of C., Psi Upsilon. Clubs: U. Chgo. of Washington; River Bend Country (Va.); Quito Golf and Tennis. Home: 9610 Beach Mill Rd Great Falls VA 22066 Office: 1318 Vincent Pl McLean VA 22101 also 1050 17th St NW Washington DC

ARABIE, DOROTHY TRIPP, nurse; b. Nichols, N.Y., Feb. 12, 1935; d. Norman R. and Mamie Ethel (Wilhelm) Tripp; m. Norman L. Miller, Feb. 12, 1954 (div. Sept. 1968); children—Glenn R., Faith A. Miller Castille, Christopher L., John D.; m. Francis Blanchard (dec. Jan. 1978); m. Emmett J. Arabie, Aug. 15, 1981. L.P.N., T.H. Harris Vocat.-Tech. Sch., 1968; A.Nursing, La. State U., 1976; student U. So. La., 1973-74; B.S. St. Joseph's Coll., Windham, Maine, 1985. Hosp. cert. critical care. Housekeeping aide Fayetteville (Ark.) Hosp., 1951, Mercy Hosp., Durango, Colo., 1953; lic. practical nurse Charity Hosp., Lafayette, La., 1968; lic. practical nurse Lourdes Hosp., Lafayette, 1968-76, nurse CCU, 1976-78, nurse, shift dir., 1978—. Mem. Nat. League Nursing, Quality Assurance Assn. (sec. 1978-82), Oncological Nursing Soc. (chmn. publicity chpt.), VFW Aux., Women's Bowling Congress. Democrat. Roman Catholic. Club: African Violet. Home: Route 1 Box 159 Youngsville LA 70592 Office: Our Lady of Lourdes Hosp 611 Saint Landry St Lafayette LA 70506

ARAFA, ABDEL-MONIEM SAYED, food scientist; b. Cairo, Sept. 11, 1944; came to U.S., 1969; s. Sayed M. and Fawzeia M. (Nassif) A.; m. Fatimah N. Abdel-Haleem, Mar. 17, 1969; children—Eman-Amy, Sallwa-Sally, Hoda-Dede. B.Sc. with highest distinction, Ain-Shams U., Cairo, 1967, M.Sc., 1973; Ph.D., Miss. State U., 1975. Lectr., Ain-Shams U., 1967; research asst. Miss. State U., State College, 1972; faculty U. Fla., Gainesville, 1976-83, assoc. prof. poultry products and meat tech., 1981-83; assoc. prof. food sci. Faculty Agr., King Saud U., Riyadh, Saudi Arabia, 1984—; vis. assoc. prof. food sci. U. Riyadh (Saudi Arabia), 1981-82. Recipient Research award Am. Egg Bd., 1981. Mem. Am. Soc. Microbiology, Inst. Food Technologists, Poultry and Egg Inst. Am., Poultry Sci. Assn., Fla. Acad. Sci., Moslem Scientists and Engrs. Contbr. articles to profl. jours.

ARAMBULA, JOHN, municipal official; b. Dolores, Tex., Feb. 4, 1935; s. Jose M. and Apolonia (Rodriguez) A.; m. Elva Rodriguez, Feb. 24, 1957; children—Mary Cynthia, John Jr., Joseph R., Norma Jean, Jeffrey Dean, Elva Suzanne. B.S. in Physics, St. Mary's U., San Antonio, 1967. Asst. sec., engring Motorola Inc., Phoenix, 1973-75; asst. mgr. accident prevention Tex. Atty. Gen. Office, Austin, 1975-79; dir. bus. mgmt. Dept. Human Resources, State of Texas, 1979-81; occupational safety specialist U. Tex.-Austin, 1981-83; program mgr. City of Austin, 1983—, assoc. v.p. pub. employee sect., 1983-86, v.p. pub. employee sect., 1986—; chmn. adv. com. Community Safety Program, Austin, 1985—. Patentee in field. Served as sgt. USMC, 1954-57. Mem. Tex. Safety Assn. (bd. dirs. 1985—), Am. Soc. Safety Engrs., Employers' Safety Forum (founder, chmn. 1983-85, plaque 1985), Republican. Mem. Unity Ch. nat. youth regional coordinator 1978-82. Home: 5800 Thames Dr Austin TX 78723 Office: City of Austin PO Box 1088 Austin TX 78767

ARANA, ORLANDO ANTONIO, surgeon; b. Matanzas, Cuba, May 20, 1925; s. Francisco Manuel and Rita Maria A.; B.S., Matanzas Inst., 1942; M.D., Havana U., 1951; m. Suelena Maria Sires, July 14, 1958; children—Orlando, Silvia, Cynthia Lynn, Anthony Kerwin, Kassandra Lena, Ashley Marie. Intern, Marymount Hosp., Cleve., 1963-64; resident in surgery St. Francis Hosp., Miami Beach, Fla., 1964-65; resident in surgery Mt. Sinai Hosp., Miami Beach, 1965-68, chief surg. resident, 1967-68; practice medicine specializing in surgery, Miami, 1968—; staff Coral Gables Hosp., Miami, 1972—, chief of surgery, 1977-78; staff Victoria Hosp. Diplomate Am. Bd. Surgery. Fellow A.C.S., I.C.S.; mem. AMA, Fla. Med. Assn., Dade County Med. Assn., Fla. Assn. Gen. Surgeons, Royal Soc. Medicine (affiliate). Republican. Roman Catholic. Office: 1830 NW 7th St Miami FL 33125

ARANDA, ARMANDO ARTURO, land surveying firm executive; b. San Antonio, Sept. 28, 1931; s. Pedro R. and Sara E. (Martinez) A.; m. Alice Salinas, June 10, 1954 (div. 1955); m. Ventura Garcia; children—Anna, Maria Elena, Armando, Rosa, Esther, Yolanda. Registered public surveyor. Pres. Tex. Surveyors Assn., San Antonio, 1979-80, pres., 1980-81; dir., pres. Aranda, Inc., San Antonio, 1974—; dir. VIA Metropolitan Transit, San Antonio. Chmn. Handicapped Boy Scouts, 1977-80; sec. Internat. Right of Way Assn., 1983-85; bd. dirs. sr. community services, 1980-84, Womens Shelter, 1980-84; mem. exec. bd. Democrats; mem. United Way. Recipient Silver Beaver award Boy Scouts Am., 1974, Wood Badge award, 1978. Mem. Tex. Surveyors Assn., Am. Congress on Mapping (pres.), Nat. Fedn. Ind. Businessmen Assn. (pres.) Club: St. Stephens Mens, Holy Name Soc. Avocation: reading. Home: 2222 Beechaven Dr San Antonio TX 78207 Office: Aranda Inc 434 S Main Ave Suite L102 San Antonio TX 78204

ARANDA, MIGUEL ANGEL, surgeon, educator; b. Chihuahua, Chih, Mexico, Nov. 25, 1939; s. Miguel and Rebeca Aranda; student English Lang. Inst., Ann Arbor, Mich., 1957; M.D. with honors, U. Chihuahua, 1964; m. Bertha Lucia Vargas, Oct. 31, 1964; children—Berta Miriam Irais, Rebeca Cristina Isabel, Miguel Angel, Jorge Xavier, Alejandro Manuel. Trained in legal medicine, Mexico City, 1971, aerospace medicine, 1972; prof. legal medicine Sch. Law, U. Chihuahua, 1965—, prof. legal medicine Med. Sch., 1972-77, assoc. prof. surgery, 1968-77; head teaching dept. Univ. Hosp., 1974-77, jr. surgeon men's surgery service, 1972-77; asst. prof. clin. gastroenterology, 1974-76, asst. prof. clin. path. neurology, 1974-75; vis. prof. U. Ill. Med. Center, Chgo., 1975; dean (dir.) Clinic Sanatorio Mederno, Chihuahua City. Served with Instituto Regional, 1948-56. Fellow Internat. Coll. Surgeons, mem. Asociación de Médicos Egresados de la Universidad Autónoma de Chihuahua, Asociación Mexicana de Cirugía General, Colego Nacional de Medicina Psicosomática, Civil Aviation Med. Assn., Aerospace Med. Assn., Asociación Latino Americana de Medicina de Aviación y del Espacio, Asociación Mexicana de Medicina de Aviación y del Espacio, Sociedad de Cirugía del Hospital Juárez, Soc. of Forensic Medicine and Criminology of Chihuahua. Roman Catholic. Club: Country of Chihuahua. Contbr. articles to profl. jours. Home: 1400 26th St Chihuahua Chihuahua Mexico Office: 510 Bolivar St Chihuahua Chih Mexico

ARAUZ, CARLOS GASPAR, city official; b. Havana, Cuba, Jan. 6, 1949; came to U.S., 1960, naturalized, 1974; s. Agnelio Alejandro and Mariana (Rodriguez) A.; B.S., Loyola U., Los Angeles, 1970; M.S., Ga. Inst. Tech., 1975, postgrad., 1975—. Bacteriologist, Emory U. Hosp., Atlanta, 1970-72; research psychologist Atlanta Regional Commn., 1973-74; dir. personnel City of College Park (Ga.), 1974-75; indsl. psychology cons. Lockheed Ga. Co., Marietta, 1976; asst. dir. human resources City of Miami, 1976-81, spl. asst. to city mgr., 1981-82; bur. chief labor relations/personnel adminstrn. City of Orlando, Fla., 1982-85; dir. personnel and labor relations City of Corpus Christi, 1985-86; dir. personnel City of Phoenix, 1986—; cons. govt. and industry. Bd. dirs. New World Bicultural Generation, Inc. Mem. Internat. Personnel Mgmt. Assn. (young personnel profl. award N. Ga. 1975; pres. N. Ga. chpt. 1976, S. Fla. chpt. 1978, v.p. So. region 1979-80, pres. So. region 1980-81), Am. Soc. Personnel Adminstrn., Fla. Public Personnel Assn., Internat. City Mgmt. Assn., Nat. Pub. Employer Labor Relations Assn., Tex. Pub. Employer Labor Relations Assn., S.E. Psychol. Assn., Sigma Xi. Roman Catholic. Club: Lake Arrowhead Yacht and Country. Office: City of Phoenix 251 W Washington St Phoenix AZ 85003

ARBIB, JOHN A., construction company executive; b. Lawrence, N.Y., Sept. 18, 1924; s. Robert Simeon and Edna (Henry) A.; student Pa. State Coll., 1942-43, Ala. Poly. Inst., 1943, Columbia U., 1946-47; m. Leonore Grandlinger, June 5, 1949; children—John Paul, Peter Laurence, Diane Lynn. Partner, Robert S. Arbib & Co., N.Y.C., 1946-57; pres. Arbib Building Corp., Margate, Fla., 1958-62; pres. Custom Craft Homes of So. Fla., Inc., Boca Raton, 1962-65; v.p. VR Corp., Hallandale, Fla., 1965-68; v.p. Royal Palm Beach Colony Inc., Hallandale, 1968-72, St. Petersburg, Fla., 1971-72; v.p., gen. mgr. Pinebrook Bldg. Corp., Pembroke Pines, Fla., 1972-76; v.p. Pasadena Homes, Inc., gen. mgr. Pinebrook div., 1976—; pres. Home Owners Warranty Corp. of South Fla., 1974-76, v.p., 1977-81, dir., 1981—; dir. Home Owners Warranty Corp., Washington, 1974-80, mem. exec. com., 1979-80. Pres., Lakeville Estates, N.Y. Civic Assn., 1953-54; mem. Fla. Sec. Edn. Constrn. Industry Adv. Com., 1980—; mem. Fla. Condominium Commn., 1972—; mem. Gov.'s Econ. Adv. Com., 1980-81. Bd. dirs. Ft. Lauderdale Symphony Orch. Assn., 1981—, v.p., mem. exec. com., 1983—; bd. dirs. Progress for Dade County, Fla., 1973—, Broward County Urban League, 1980—; vice-chmn. Fla.

Housing Fin. Agy., 1980—, chmn., 1983; mem. Broward County Bd. Rules and Appeals, 1975-81, mem. exec. com., 1979-81. Served with AUS, 1943-46; ETO. Named Builder of Month, Gen. Electric Corp., Oct. 1971. Mem. Builders Assn. S. Fla. (dir. 1966—, pres. 1973; Pres.'s award 1975, Builder of Year 1976), Fla. Home Builders Assn. (dir. 1969—, area v.p. 1973, sec. 1977, treas. 1978, pres. 1980, Fla. Builder of Yr. 1984), Nat. Assn. Home Builders (dir. 1970—, chmn. bus. mgmt. com. 1975-76, vice chmn. consumer affairs com. 1977, resolutions com. 1979-81, nat. v.p. 1981-82, planning com. 1982—, mortgage fin. com. 1982—, chmn. state and local housing fin. agys. com. 1983—, exec. com. Conf. Housing Agy. Chmn. and Commrs. 1983—), Constrn. Council Fla. (pres. 1975, dir. 1974-82). Democrat. Unitarian (dir. 1965-70), pres. Ft. Lauderdale ch. 1969). Home: 5561 SW 8th St Plantation FL 33317 Office: PO Box 8360 Pembroke Pines FL 33024

ARCAND, ROSALIE, insurance official; b. Okmulgee, Okla., Feb 7, 1926; d. John Russell and Susan Ethel (Polk) Barksdale; m. Napoleon Jackson Arcand, Jr., Aug. 28. 1943; children—Sharron Louise, John Michael, Tani Marie, Neal Jay, Anita Renee. A.S. in Property Claims Law, Am. Ednl. Inst., 1981. Claims supr. Poe & Assocs., Tampa, Fla., 1964-81; property claims examiner Whiting Nat. Services, Tampa, 1981—. Mem. Ins. Women Tampa (pres. 1976-77), Bus. and Profl. Women Tampa (corr. sec. 1983-84), Fla. Assn. Ins. Women (dir. 1983-84), Nat. Assn. Ins. Women, Downtown Tampa Bus. and Profl. Women (dir. 1980-84), Republican. Methodist. Home: 812 Monaco Dr Tampa FL 33612 Office: Whiting Nat Services Inc PO Box 2938 Tampa FL 33601

ARCE-CACHO, ERIC AMAURY, engineer, consultant; b. Morovis, P.R., Sept. 24, 1940; s. Eduardo and Celia Arce-Cacho; m. Carmen Ruth Gonaalez, Nov. 19, 1960; children—Eric Edmaury, Ruth Dagmar. Student, Coll. Engring., Myz, P.R., 1960, U.S. Air Force Adminstrn. Sch., 1963; M.A. in Econs., InterAm. U., Bay, P.R., 1972; M.A., Ch. of God Sch. of Theology, 1985. Registered profl. engr., P.R. Intercept control tech. Dept. Defense, San Juan, P.R., 1963-77; safety engring. cons., Bay, 1978-80; solar energy cons., safety engr. Solar Devices, Inc., San Juan, 1980—; cons., researcher Energy Saving Equipment Inc., Bay, 1980—; dir. World Vocat. Sch. Missioneries, San Juan; dir., founder Internat. Recreational Areas. Author: (poems) Soledad, 1979. Editor articles. Safety and security counselor Neighborhood Community Ctr., Bay, 1984. Mem. Am. Soc. Safety Engrs. Clubs: Community (Fort Buchanan, P.R.), Gulf Course. Avocations: paso fino horse riding. Home: C-17 Forest Hills Flamboyan Bay PR 00619

ARCENEAUX, GEORGE, JR., judge; b. New Orleans, May 17, 1928; s. George and Louise (Austin) A.; B.A., La. State U., 1949; LL.B., Am. U., 1957; m. Mary Elizabeth Martin, Aug. 17, 1954; children—Mary Elizabeth, George III, Robert Martin. Program dir. Radio Sta. KCIL, Houma, La., 1949; state editor Daily Advertiser, Lafayette, 1949-50; legis. asst. Senator Allen J. Ellender, Washington, 1952-56, adminstrv. asst., 1957-60; bar: La. 1959; practiced in Houma, 1960-79; mem. firm Duval, Arceneaux, Lewis & Funderburk, 1960-79; U.S. dist. judge Eastern Dist. La., New Orleans, 1979—. Chmn., Houma-Terrebonne Regional Planning Commn., 1963-69. Served with AUS, 1950-51. Mem. Am., La., Terrebonne Parish (pres. 1964-65) bar assns., C. of C. (dir. 1963, pres. 1966-67). Methodist. Clubs: Internat. House (New Orleans); Univ. (Washington); Rotary (dir. 1963, pres. 1966, dist. gov. 1971-72, internat. dir. 1981-83, v.p. 1982-83). Home: 500 Camp St New Orleans LA 70130 Office: 500 Camp St New Orleans LA 70130

ARCHER, BILL, congressman; b. Houston, Mar. 22, 1928; married; 5 children. Student, Rice U., 1945-46; B.B.A., LL.B. with honors, U. Tex. Bar: Tex. bar. Pres. Uncle Johnny Mills, Inc., 1953-61; rancher, bus. exec.; partner firm Harris, Archer Parks & Graul, Houston, 1968-71; mem. 92d-99th Congresses from 7th Dist. Tex.; mem. Banking and Currency Com., 1971-72, Ways and Means Com., from 1973; Ad Hoc Com. on Energy. Mem. Hunters Creek Village (Tex.) City Council, 1955-62, also mayor pro tem.; mem. Tex. Ho. of Reps., 1966-70, Republican Task Force on Energy and Resources, 1971-72. Served with USAF, 1951-53. Mem. Tex., Houston bar assns., Phi Delta Phi, Sigma Alpha Epsilon (Houston Man of Year 1968). Roman Catholic. Club: Rep. Chowder and Marching. Office: 1135 Longworth House Office Bldg Washington DC 20515

ARCHER, CARL MARION, oil and gas co. exec.; b. Spearman, Tex., Dec. 16, 1920; s. Robert Barton and Gertrude Lucille (Sheets) A.; student U. Tex., Austin, 1937-39; m. Peggy Garrett, Aug. 22, 1939; children—Mary Frances, Carla Lee. Pres., Anchor Oil Co., Spearman, 1959—, Carl M. Archer Farms, Spearman, 1960—; gen. mgr. Speartex Grain Co., Spearman, 1967—, Speartex Oil & Gas Co., 1974—; dir. Panhandle Bank & Trust Co., Borger, Tex. Chmn. County Democratic Com., 1969—. Mem. Tex. Grain Dealers Assn., Ind. Royalty Owners and Producers Assn., Nat. Grain Dealers Assn., Am. Petroleum Landmen Assn., Nat., Tex. bankers assns. Mem. Ch. of Christ. Clubs: Perryton, Borger Country, Amarillo. Home: 304 S Endicott Spearman TX 79081 Office: 514 Collard St Spearman TX 79081

ARCHER, EARNEST RICHARD, management educator, consultant; b. Watkinsville, Ga., Mar. 10, 1934; s. Jessie Jewell and Mertie Marie (Townsend) A.; m. Sally Ann Rachels, July 6, 1958; children—Richard Wesley, Stephen Cabot, Stuart Keith. B.S. cum laude, North Ga. Coll., 1958; M.B.A., U. Ga., 1969, Ph.D., 1971. Registered profl. engr., S.C. Sr. indsl. engr Deering-Milliken, Gaffney, S.C., 1958-63; plant mgr. Burlington Industries, Lafayette, Ga., 1963-66; dir. engring., internal cons. Phila. & Reading, Lynchburg, Va., 1966-68; instr. U. Ga., Athens, 1969-71; asst. prof. mgmt. Ga. Coll., Milledgeville, 1971-72; prof. Winthrop Coll., Rock Hill, S.C., 1972—; cons. Herald Pub. Co., Rock Hill, S.C., 1975—, Art Printing Co., Rock Hill, 1979—, Town of Hilton Head, 1985—, Homelite/Textron, Charlotte, N.C., 1984—, Mirafi Inc., Charlotte, 1984—. Author Quality of Work Life Measurement System (region V Am. Soc. Personnel Adminstrs. Outstanding Personnel Practitioner award 1979), Comparable Worth/Competitive Worth Job Evaluation and Performance Appraisal System, 1982; also articles, chpts. Mem. task force Dept. Commerce, Washington, 1967-68; key communicator Rock Hill Sch. Dist., 1982—; chmn. bd. Salvation Army, Rock Hill, 1985—; chmn. Rock Hill City Council's Race Relations Com., 1981-82; bd. dirs. Rock Hill Econ. Devel. Bd., 1985—. Served to sgt. U.S. Army, 1951-54; Korea; to 1st lt. U.S. Army, 1958-59. Recipient Disting. Prof. award Winthrop Coll., 1978, Disting. Prof. prize Winthrop Alumni Assn., 1978. Mem. Nat. Soc. Profl. Engrs. (chpt. pres. 1983-84, Disting. Service award 1984), Am. Soc. Personnel Adminstrs. (chpt. pres. 1980-81, Disting. Service award 1981, Nat. Outstanding Prof. award 1977, 78), Am. Mgmt. Assn., Am. Inst. Indsl. Engrs., Rock Hill Area C. of C. (chmn. task force 1980-81), Phi Kappa Phi (Excellence in Teaching award 1981), Beta Gamma Sigma. Methodist. Lodges: Lions (pres. local club 1976-77), Kiwanis. Avocations: real estate investments; watercolor painting; book collecting; gardening. Home: 1621 Stonehill Pl Rock Hill SC 29730 Office: Winthrop Coll Oakland Ave Rock Hill SC 29733

ARCHER, LYNN ANN, college administrator; b. Woodward, Okla., Feb. 23, 1957; d. Billy Lynn and Donna Dee (Johnson) Wilson; m. Philip Ray Archer, Sept. 2, 1983. B.S., West Tex. State U., 1979, M.Ed., 1981. Cert. profl. counselor, Tex. Dir. continuing edn. Frank Phillips Coll., Borger, Tex., 1979—; sec.-treas., co-owner Archer, Inc., Spearman, Tex., 1984—. Bd. dirs., ednl. chmn. Am. Cancer Soc., Hutchinson County, Tex., 1979—; Sunday sch. instr. United Methodist Ch., Spearman, 1985. Mem. Tex. Assn. Community Service and Continuing Edn. (bd. dirs. 1984—), Am. Assn. Counseling and Devel., Am. Soc. Tng. and Devel., Tex. Jr. Coll. Tchrs. Assn., Nat. Council on Community Services and Continuing Edn., Tex. Assn. Continuing Edn. Adminstrs., Borger C. of C. Republican. Avocations: teaching aerobic dance; square dancing. Home: 321 S Barkley Spearman TX 79081 Office: Frank Phillips Coll PO Box 5118 1101 Roosevelt Borger TX 79007

ARCILESI, WILLIAM RICHARD, JR., distributing company executive; b. Spruce Pine, N.C., July 6, 1956; s. William Richard and Martha Adele (Sparks) A.; m. Linda Joyce Adkins, Sept. 11, 1982. B.A. magna cum laude in Bus. Adminstrn., Queens Coll., Charlotte, N.C., 1977, M.B.A., 1981. With inventory control dept. Iveys Corp., Charlotte, 1972-74, with accounts receivable dept., 1975-76; asst. credit mgr. Mitchell Distbg. Co., Charlotte, 1977-78, asst. sales adminstr., 1978-79, mktg. mgr., 1979—; cons. Jordan Air, Charlotte, 1983—, Saber Aviation, Charlotte, 1982—; mem. cons. bd. Tyche Co., Charlotte, 1983—; actor, model Jan Thompson Agy., Charlotte, 1976—; prof. mktg. Queens Coll. Bd. dirs. Charlottetowne Players, 1983—, Spanish Am. Cultural Soc., Charlotte, 1977-80; TV auction coordinator, bd. dirs. Boystown of N.C., Charlotte, 1983-84; mem. fund raising com. Nature Mus. and Discovery Pl., Charlotte, 1976-82. Mem. World Future Soc., Internat. Thespian Soc., Screen Actor's Guild, Assn. Equipment Distbrs. Republican. Baptist. Clubs: NCSL, Sounds of Am. Home: 7435 Ashfield Ct Charlotte NC 28226 Office: Mitchell Distbg Co 3535 N Graham PO Box 32156 Charlotte NC 28232

ARD, HAROLD JACOB, library administrator; b. Herrick, Ill., Aug. 26, 1940; s. Jacob S. and Hazel Elizabeth (Taylor) A.; m. Erma J. Chapman, Jan. 30, 1960 (div. 1974); children—Teri Ann, Mark Alan. B.S. in Edn., Ill. State U., 1962, M.S. in Psychology, 1964; M.S. in L.S., Rosary Coll., 1968. Materials cons. Decatur (Ill.) pub. schs., 1962-64; head librarian Barrington (Ill.) Pub. Library, 1964-68; exec. librarian Arlington Hts. (Ill.) Meml. Library, 1968-72; library dir. Jackson (Miss.) Met. Library System, 1972-77; assoc. dir. Rowland Med. Library, U. Miss. Med. Ctr., Jackson, 1978-84; mgr. bus. sci. and tech. depts. Ft. Worth Pub. Library, 1985—; library cons.; lectr. in field. Mem. ALA, Tex. Library Assn., Med. Library Assn., Southeastern Library Assn., Beta Phi Mu. Methodist. Club: Rotary. Contbr. articles to profl. jours. Home: 1320 Pinehurst Dr Fort Worth TX 76134 Office: 300 Taylor St Fort Worth TX 76102

ARDOIN, KENNETH ALLEN, pharm. co. exec.; b. Alexandria, La., Dec. 15, 1942; s. Francis Allen and Mary Elizabeth (Edwards) A.; B.S. in Econs., U. Southwestern La., 1964; cert. Baylor U., 1974; m. Mary Annette Butler, July 22, 1967; children—Brett Allen, Scott David, Michelle Annette. Med. service rep. Roerig div. Pfizer Inc., Little Rock, 1969, hosp. mgr., New Orleans, 1969-71, dist. mgr., Chgo., 1971-77, Dallas, 1977-82, state govt. relations mgr., 1982—; mem. La. Drug and Therapeutic Adv. Bd., 1983—. Coach, Little League, Little Rock and Chgo., 1966-76; coach baseball YMCA, Dallas, 1977—; coach soccer, Dallas, 1977—; chmn. Dallas Mayor's Neighborhood Adv. Council, 1983—; state advisor U.S. Congl. Adv. Bd., 1982—; chmn. polit. info. Far North Dallas Homeowners Coalition, 1982—; vice chmn. civil service bd. City of Dallas, 1983—; pres. Highlands North Homeowner's Assn., 1983—; group chmn. Keep a Clean Dallas, 1984—; mem. host com. Republican Nat. Conv., 1984. Named Dist. mgr. of Yr., 1972. Mem. Tex. Pharm. Assn., Colo. Pharm. Assn., Ark. Pharm. Assn., N.Mex. Pharm. Assn., La. Pharm. Assn., Mo. Pharm. Assn., Dallas C. of C., Richardson C. of C., North Dallas C. of C., Am. Security Council, Internat. Platform Assn., Nat. Legis. Services and Security Assn., U. Southwestern La. Alumni Assn. (gov. 1982—, pres. Dallas chpt. 1982—), Pharm. Mfrs. Assn. (La. chmn. 1983—), Mgrs. Advisory Bd., V.P. Council (1981). Roman Catholic (parish adv. council 1979, mem. choir). Clubs: Dallas N. Soccer Assn., St. Theresa's Mens (pres. 1968-69), All Saints Mens (pres. 1979—). Home: 16306 Fallkirk St Dallas TX 75248

ARDOYNO (DORR), DOLORES, opera company administrator; b. Moble, Ala., Sept. 23; d. William John and Kathryn Cecelia (Hickey) A.; student Webster Coll., 1939-41, Springhill Coll., 1944, St. Louis U., 1944-45, Loyola U., Los Angeles, 1951-52; m. Donald Dorr, Apr. 29, 1971. Asst. prodn. coordinator western div. ABC-TV, Hollywood, Calif., 1950-54; head radio/TV, Whitlock, Swigart & Evans Advt. Co., New Orleans, 1956-59; owner, dir. PR Service New Orleans, 1960-68; dir. public relations New Orleans Opera, 1968-71; gen. mgr. Opera/South, Jackson, Miss., 1971-80; gen. mgr. Baton Rouge Opera, 1981-85; mgr. New Orleans Summer Pops, 1960-66. Democrat. Roman Catholic. Home and Office: Rt 1 Box 414 Coden AL 36523

AREND, JOHN R., chemical company executive; b. 1931. With legal dept. Conoco Inc., 1961-64; v.p. internat. mktg. Conoco Plant Food Group, 1964-71; v.p. Williams Cos., 1971-76; pres. Internat. Chem. Co., Tulsa, 1976—, also dir. Office: Internat Chem Co 1887 E 71st St Tulsa OK 74136

AREY, DEWELL FRANKLIN, JR., architect; b. Mountain Home, Ark., Nov. 25, 1941; s. Dewell Franklin and Josie Corine (Marshall) A.; student U. Ark., 1960-62, 64-66; div.; children—Dewell Franklin III, Randall C., Susan N., Rhonda L. Individual practice architecture, 1970—; pres. The Arey Group, P.A., Architects, North Little Rock, Ark., 1979—; pres. Developers Southwest, Inc.; sec. Mgrs. Southwest, Inc.; prin. works include Baseline Elem. Sch., Little Rock, 1974, Pul. County Spl. Sch. Dist. Adminstrn. Bldg., 1975, Westside Elem. Sch., Cabot, Ark., 1978, Central Bapt. Ch., North Little Rock, 1980, Middle Sch., Waldron, Ark., 1981, Upper Elem. Sch. and Jr. High Sch., Clarksville, 1985. Cert. Nat. Council Archtl. Registration Bds. Mem. Constrn. Specifications Inst., Am. Arbitration Assn. Baptist. Club: Sertoma. Office: 817 McCain Blvd North Little Rock AR 72116

ARIAS-ARIAS, RAMON, economics educator; b. Manzanillo, Oriente, Cuba, Apr. 19, 1921; s. Ramon Arias Garcia and Maria De Los Milagros Arias-Alvarez; m. Anais della Concepcion Roca, July 7, 1946; children—Anais Milagros, Ramon Salvador, Fernando Salvador, Salvador Luis. Student Fordham U., 1939; Doctor en Ciencias Commerciales, U. Havana, 1945; postgrad. La. State U., 1965-66. C.P.A., Cuba. Pres., Arias Corp., Manzanillo, Cuba, 1942-60; treas. Malvango Cattle Co., 1947-60; mng. ptnr. Cudeza Rice Farms, 1957-60; exec. asst. to Pres. Tagaropulos, Panama, 1961-64; exec. v.p. Fed. Meat of P.R., Inc., San Juan, 1965; asst. dir. Manzanillo Profl. Sch. Bus., Cuba, 1952-57; mem. faculty John C. Calhoun State Community Coll., Decatur, Ala., 1966—, chmn. bus. div., 1969-82, prof. Spanish, 1966—, prof. econs., 1972—. Mem. Ala. del. White House Conf. Small Bus., 1979—. Recipient First Faculty External Contbns. to Community and Sch. award Calhoun Community Coll., 1981. Mem. Calhoun Edn. Assn., Ala. Assn. Higher Edn. in Bus. (pres. 1977-78). Roman Catholic. Club: Decatur Country. Lodge: KC. Home: 1505 Curtis Dr SE Decatur AL 35601 Office: PO Box 2216 Decatur AL 35602

ARMAN, ARA, civil engineering educator, university official; b. Istanbul, Turkey, Sept. 12, 1930; came to U.S., 1955; s. Hayg and Mary Ann (Papazian) A.; m. Claudia Catherine Carr, Nov. 30, 1963; children—Eric H., Mitchell M. B.S.C.E., U. Tex., 1955, M.S.C.E., 1956. Dist. lab. engr. La. Dept. Transp., Baton Rouge, 1956-60, soil design engr., 1960-63; asst. prof. civil engring. La. State U., Baton Rouge, 1963-67, assoc. prof., 1967-70, prof., 1970—, asst. dir. engring research, 1965-76, chmn. dept. civil engring., 1976-80, assoc. dean Coll. Engring., 1980—; dir. La. Transp. Research Ctr., 1986—; mem. U.S.-USSR Tech. Exchange Com. Mem. various East Baton Rouge/Parish County coms., local civic assns. Mem. ASCE, ASTM, Nat. Acad. Scis., Transp. Research Bd., La. Engring. Soc., Am. Rd. and Transp. Builders Assn., Internat. Soc. for Soil Mechanics and Found. Engring., Sigma Xi, Tau Beta Pi, Phi Kappa Phi. Mem. Armenian Apostolic Ch. Contbr. numerous articles on geotech. engring. to profl. jours. Home: 1148 Verdun Dr Baton Rouge LA 70810 Office: Coll Engring La State U Baton Rouge LA 70810

ARMAND, RAUL ARTURO, pharmaceutical company executive; b. Havana, Cuba, Feb. 18, 1953; came to U.S., 1960; s. Raul Jesus and Yvette (Duany) A. B.S., Fla. State U., 1975. Mktg. rep. Gillette Corp., Miami, Fla., 1976-78; dermatol. rep. Bristol Myers, 1978—, mem. Pres.'s council, 1985—. Mem. Fla. State U. Mktg. Club. Home: 10207 SW 20th Terr Miami FL 33165

ARMAND, RUTH HALL, ret. counselor; b. Mansfield, La., Dec. 8, 1915; d. Guy Bridges and Mary (Christian) Hall; A.A., Dodd Coll., 1935; B.S., La. Poly. Inst., 1937; M.Ed., Northwestern State U. La., 1958, postgrad., 1969-75; m. Lawrence B. Armand June 1948; children—Lawrence B., James Hall. Home mgmt. supt. FHA, Avoyelles, La., 1938-46; home demonstration agt. La. Extension Service, Avoyelles, 1946-48; tchr. home econs. Avoyelles Parish Sch. System, 1948-71, reading specialist, 1971-76, guidance counselor, 1976-79, Marksville Sr. High Sch., 1959-79. Chief RADEF decontamination Avoyelles Parish CDA, 1966—; tng. officer, 1975—. Mem. Am., La. personnel and guidance assns., Am., La. (La. Sr. High Counselor of Year 1978-79) assns. sch. counselors, Am., La. vocat. counselors assns., Avoyelles Guidance Assn. (pres. 1977-79), Rapides Ladies Golf Assn. (tournament chmn. 1984), Alpha Delta Kappa (pres. chpt. 1963-65). Democrat. Baptist. Club: Rapides Golf and Country. Home: 721 Washington St S Marksville LA 71351

ARMENTROUT, DARYL RALPH, civil engineer; b. Greeneville, Tenn., Apr. 6, 1942; s. James Ralph and Nola Flora (Brobeck) A.; m. Mary Rose Carmichael, July 19, 1969; children—Rose, Michael. Student Grace Coll., 1960-62; B.S., U. Tenn., 1965, Ph.D., 1981; M.S., Va. Poly. Inst., 1968. Registered profl. engr., Tenn. Prodn. engr. Humble Oil & Refining Co., New Orleans, 1965-66; civil engr. TVA, Knoxville, 1968-74, chief, engring. services, 1974-77, asst. to mgr., 1977-85, chief procurement quality assurance, 1986—. Sr. exec. fellow John F. Kennedy Sch. Govt., Harvard U., 1983. Fellow ASCE; mem. U.S. Com. Large Dams, Nat. Soc. Profl. Engrs., Nat. Mgmt. Assn., Tenn. Soc. Profl. Engrs., Tech. Soc. Knoxville C. of C., Sigma Xi, Phi Kappa Phi, Tau Beta Pi, Chi Epsilon. Presbyterian. Contbr. articles to profl. jours. Home: 1117 Burning Tree Ln Knoxville TN 37923 Office: 400 W Summit Hill Dr W6 C134 Knoxville TN 37902

ARMENTROUT, DAVID PAUL, clin. psychologist; b. Columbus, Ohio, Apr. 15, 1945; s. Chester Way and Edith (Kissel) A.; B.S., U. Tenn., 1967, M.A., 1969, Ph.D., 1973; m. Glenna Jane Faidley, Sept. 13, 1969; children—Sean David, Darren Paul, Shannon Stacey. Staff psychologist Dede Wallace Mental Health Center, Nashville, 1972-75; pain unit dir. Truman Meml. VA Hosp., also asst. prof. U. Mo. Med. Sch., Columbia, 1975-79; dir. behavioral sci., asso. prof. family medicine Oral Roberts U. Med. Sch., Tulsa, 1979—. NIH fellow, 1967-68; VA trainee, 1968-72. Mem. Am. Psychol. Assn., Internat. Soc. Study Pain, Am. Pain Soc. (charter), Okla. Psychol. Assn., Tulsa Psychol. Assn., Full Gospel Businessmen's Assn. Presbyterian. Author papers in field. Home: 7718 S 230th E Ave Broken Arrow OK 74012 Office: 7306 S Lewis St Tulsa OK 74136

ARMENTROUT, JOHN ROBERT, construction company executive; b. Charleston, W.Va., Apr. 15, 1947; s. Lewis Hamilton and Marianne Frances (Dorsey) A.; student Va. Poly. Inst. and State U., 1967-68, Va. Commonwealth U., 1970; m. Carol Louise Stansfield, Jan. 30, 1971; 1 dau., Jennifer Elizabeth. Estimator mgr., corp. sec. United Insulation, Inc., Richmond, 1975-78, pres., 1978—; dir. Phoenix Harbor Corp. Chmn. Fluvanna County Econ. Devel. Commn.; bd. dirs. Va. Mental Health Assn. Mem. Am. Inst. Plant Engrs., ASHRAE, Va. Insulation Contractor's Assn., Met. Astrological Research Soc. Republican. Presbyterian. Club: Richmond Engrs. Home: RFD 2 PO Box 176 Palmyra VA 22963 Office: PO Box 15118 Richmond VA 23227

ARMEY, RICHARD KEITH, U.S. congressman; b. Cando, N.D., July 7, 1940; s. Glen Forest and Marion (Gutschlog) A.; m. Susan Byrd; children—Kathryn, David, Chip, Scott. B.A., Jamestown Coll., 1963; M.A., U. N.D., 1964; Ph.D., U. Okla., 1968. Faculty econs. U. Mont., 1964-65; asst. prof. W.Tex. State U., 1967-68; asst. prof. Austin Coll., 1968-72; assoc. prof. North Tex. State U., 1972-77, chmn. econs. dept., 1977-83; U.S. congressman 26th Dist. Tex., 1985—. Recipient Disting. Fellow award Fisher Inst. Mem. Southwestern Social Scis. Assn. Address: 514 Cannon House Office Bldg Washington DC 20515

ARMINANA, RUBEN, university administrator, educator; b. Santa Clara, Cuba, May 15, 1947; came to U.S., 1961; s. Aurelio Ruben and Olga Petrona (Nart) A.; m. Maria Gertrudis Nunez, July 2, 1977; children—Cesar A. Martino, Maria G. Martino. A.A., Hill Jr. Coll., 1966; B.A., U. Tex., 1968, M.A., 1970; Ph.D., U. New Orleans, 1983; postgrad. Inst. of Applied Behavioral Scis., Nat. Tng. Labs., 1971. Nat. assoc. dir. Phi Theta Kappa, Canton, Miss., 1968-69; dir. ops. and tng. Inter-Am. Ctr., Loyola U., New Orleans, 1969-71; adminstrv. analyst City of New Orleans, 1972, adminstrv. analyst and organizational devel. and tng. cons., 1972-78; anchor and reporter part time STA. WWL-TV, New Orleans, 1973-81; v.p. Commerce Internat. Corp., New Orleans, 1978-83; exec. asst. to sr. v.p. Tulane U., New Orleans, 1983-85, assoc. exec. v.p., 1985—; TV news cons., New Orleans, 1981—; lectr. Internat. Trade Mart, New Orleans, 1983—, U.S. Dept. Commerce, New Orleans. Co-author: Hemisphere West-El Futuro, 1968; co-editor: Colloquium on Central America-A Time for Understanding, Background Readings, 1985. Bd. dirs. Com. on Alcoholism and Substance Abuse, 1978-79, SER, Jobs for Progress, Inc., 1974-82, Citizens United for Responsive Broadcasting, Latin Am. Festival Com; dir., bd. advisors Sta. WDSU-TV, 1974-77; mem. League of United Latin Am. Citizens, Mayor's Latin Am. Adv. Com., Citizens to Preserve the Charter, Met. Area Com., Mayor's Com. on Crime. Kiwanis scholar, 1966; Books scholar, 1966. Mem. Am. Econ. Assn., Assn. of Evolutionary Econs., Am. Polit. Sci. Assn., AAUP, Latin Am. C. of C. (founding dir. New Orleans and River Region 1976-83), Phi Theta Kappa, Omicron Delta Epsilon, Sigma Delta Pi, Delta Sigma Pi. Democrat. Roman Catholic. Club: Cuban Profl. Avocation: mask collecting. Office: 218 Gibson Hall Tulane Univ New Orleans LA 70118

ARMSTRONG, DANIEL WAYNE, chemistry researcher, consultant, writer, educator; b. Ft. Wayne, Ind., Nov. 2, 1949; s. Robert Eugene and Nila Louise (Koeneman) A.; m. Linda Marilyn Todd, June 11, 1972; children—Lincoln Thomas, Ross Alexander, Colleen Victoria. B.S., Washington and Lee U., 1972; M.S. in Chem. Oceanography, Tex. A&M U., 1974, Ph.D. in Chemistry, 1977. Prof., Bowdoin Coll., Brunswick, Maine, 1978-79, Georgetown U., Washington, 1980-83; prof., head analytical chemistry Tex. Tech U., Lubbock, 1983—. Grantee Research Corp., 1979, Petroleum Research Fund, 1979, NSF, 1981; research grantee Whatman Corp., 1981, Dept. Energy, 1984, Dow Chem., 1985, 86, NIH, 1986. Mem. Am. Chem. Soc., Sigma Xi, Phi Lambda Upsilon. Host Univ. Forum Radio Show, Washington, 1981-83; author film, radio shows; contbr. articles to profl. publs. Office: Dept Chemistry Tex Tech Univ Lubbock TX 79409

ARMSTRONG, DAVID LOVE, lawyer, attorney general of Kentucky; b. Hope, Ark., Aug. 6, 1941; m. Carol Burress, 1963; 1 child, Bryce Shannon. B.S., Murray State U., 1966; J.D., U. Louisville, 1969; postgrad. Coll. Trial Advocacy Harvard U. Law Sch., 1972, U. Nev., 1973. Bar: Ky. 1969. Ptnr. Turner, McDonald & Armstrong, Louisville, 1969-76; commonwealth atty. City of Louisville, 1976-83; atty. gen. State of Ky., 1983—; asst. prosecutor Police Ct., 1969-71; judge Juvenile Ct. Jefferson County, Ky., 1971-73; hearing officer Louisville Jefferson County Bd. Health. Chmn. fund raising Brooklawn Home, Louisville. Mem. Ky. Commonwealth Attys. Assn. (pres.), Nat. Dist. Attys. Assn. (sec.), ABA. Recipient Fleur de Lis award City of Louisville, 1973; Outstanding Achievement award Nat. Assn. County Ofcls., 1977. Address: Jefferson Hall of Justice 2d Floor Louisville KY 40202*

ARMSTRONG, ELMER E., accountant; b. Monmouth, Ill., Dec. 20, 1904; s. Elmer Ellsworth and Alice (Logan) A.; A.A., Kansas City Jr. Coll., 1921; student Centenary Coll., 1942-43; grad. Internat. Acctg. Soc., 1944; m. Ruth Marie Dale, July 25, 1925; children—Dale E., Lenora Ann (Mrs. Steve Cowel). Mem. editorial staff Kansas City Jour., 1920-22, Kansas City Kansan, 1922-25; editor Alva Record, Okla., 1922; account specialist Burroughs Adding Machine Co., 1925-45; with Smith, Cole, Armstrong & Filipowski, and predecessor, C.P.A.s, Shreveport, La., 1945—, sr. partner, 1952—; treas. Honor Oil Co., Inc., Shreveport, 1951—. Lectr. advanced acctg. Centenary Coll. of La., 1950-52, So. States Acctg. Conf., Savannah, Ga., Conf. Lawyers and C.P.A.s, U. Miss. at Hattiesburg, 1951; dean Shreveport Sch. Theology, 1968-78. Mem. NCCJ, Shreveport, 1968—, dir. Speakers Bur., 1969—, chmn. Brotherhood Week, 1972; chmn. Shreveport Housing Authority, 1967-79; mem. lay adv. council Perkins Sch. Theology, So. Meth. U., Dallas. Bd. dirs. Mental Health Assn. N.W. La., 1975-76. E.E. Armstrong Elderly Service Ctr. named in his honor Shreveport Housing Authority, 1980. C.P.A., La., Okla., Tex. Mem. Soc. La. C.P.A.s (pres. Shreveport 1967-68), Am. Inst. C.P.A.s, Shreveport C. of C., Internat. Platform Assn., Am. (dist. treas.), Shreveport (v.p. 1970-71) rose socs., Nat. Writers Club. Methodist (steward; dir. adult tchrs. 1963-66; dist. dir. adult ministries Shreveport dist. 1968—, lay del. La. Annual Conf. 1975, 77). Clubs: Shreveport Petroleum, Univ. Kiwanis (treas. 1952-56, dir. 1969-71, Shreveport), Toastmasters (dist. gov. 1952). Home: 1402 Audubon Pl Shreveport LA 71105 Office: Smith Cole Armstrong & Filipowski 800 Lane Bldg Shreveport LA 71101

ARMSTRONG, JOHN DALE, lawyer; b. Petersburg, Va., Dec. 7, 1918; s. William Davis and Ethel Kathryn (Walter) A.; B.S. in Bus. Adminstrn., U. Fla., 1941; LL.B., U. Va., 1948; LL.M. in Taxation, N.Y. U., 1951; m. Geneva Pratt, Aug. 3, 1951; children—Dale Armstrong James, William Taylor. Admitted to N.Y. bar, 1949, Fla. bar, 1950; asso. firm Cadwalader, Wickersham & Taft, N.Y.C., 1948-49; asso. firm Shutts & Bowen, Miami, 1949-50; trial atty. Office Regional Counsel, IRS, Phila., 1951-56; asso. firm Mershon, Sawyer, Johnston, Dunwoody & Cole, Miami, 1956-60, partner, 1960—. Mem. S. Fla. Coordinating Council, from 1979; pres. Estate Planning Council of Greater Miami, 1970-71; chmn. planning and program com. U. Miami Ann. Tax Conf., 1960-79; treas., bd. dirs. Sch. Vol. Program; chmn. bd. mgrs. S.W. YMCA, 1970-71, now bd. dirs. Served to col., Transp. Corps, AUS, 1941-46. Decorated Bronze Star. Mem. Am. Law Inst., Am. Bar Assn. (past chmn. regional liaison com., sect. taxation), Fed. Bar Assn., N.Y. Bar, Fla. Bar (chmn. tax sect. 1962-63), Mil. Order World Wars (comdr. Miami chpt.), Res. Officers Assn. (life), Miami C. of C. (trustee). Democrat. Christian Scientist. Clubs: Miami; Riviera Country. Office: 1600 Southeast First Nat Bank Bldg Miami FL 33131

ARMSTRONG, LUCILLE M., educator; b. Marlin, Tex., Feb. 11, 1931; d. Osie Hugh and Beverly Etta (Carter) McGruder; m. Allen Earl Armstrong, Sept. 6, 1955; children—Marian Kathleen Pryor, Charlotte Yvonne, Carol Allenette. B.S., Paul Quinn Coll., 1952; M.Ed., U. Tex.-El Paso, 1976. Payroll clk. Prairie View A&M U., 1952-55; elem. sch. tchr. El Paso (Tex.) Ind. Sch. Dist., 1968—, Hart Elem. Sch., El Paso, 1983—. Mem. Mark White for Gov. El Paso County Steering Com. Named West Area Tchr. of Yr., El Paso Ind. Sch. Dist., 1973-74. Mem. Internat. Reading Tchrs. Assn., NEA, Assn. Childhood Edn., Tex. State Tchrs. Assn., El Paso Tchrs. Assn., Hart Sch. Parent-Tchr. Assn., Zeta Phi Beta. Democrat. Baptist. Lodge: Order Eastern Star.

ARMSTRONG, MARTHA ALLEN, painter, photographer; b. Brunswick, Ga., July 15, 1935; d. Luther Stanton and Ruby Ellen (Woods) Allen; m. Thomas G. Armstrong, Mar. 24, 1956; 1 dau., Melissa Woods. Student Converse Coll., 1953-56, Heatherly Sch. Fine Art, London, 1967-69. One-woman shows: 3221 Gallery, Houston, 1981, La. Gallery, Houston, 1981, McMurtrey Gallery, Houston, 1981, 82, Donnell Library Center N.Y. Pub. Library, 1984; group shows include: Ogunquit (Maine) Art Ctr., 1958, 60, 62, 63, Hudson Valley Art Assn., White Plains, N.Y., 1958, 59, 66, Mamaroneck Artists Assn. (N.Y.), 1965, 66, Royal Inst., London, 1967, 68, Summer Salon, London, 1967, 68, 69, Royal Acad., London, 1968, Fedn. Brit. Artists, London, 1968, Royal Soc. Portrait Painters, London, 1968, 69, Covo De Iongh Gallery, Houston, 1977, Mus. Fine Arts, Houston, 1978, 83, U. Houston, 1979, 83, Houston Ctr. for Photography, 1983, 84, Midtown Art Center, 1983; works represented in permanent collections. Chmn. bd. Cultural Arts Council Houston, 1983, pres., 1982, v.p., 1981, bd. dirs., 1979—; mem. adv. bd. Houston Ctr. for Photography, 1983; mem. Jr. League Houston; chmn. ann. TV art auction Channel 8, 1978; trustee Contemporary Arts Mus., 1978-80, Houston Grand Opera, 1975-80; mem. Mayor's Com. Arts Awards, 1984. Work documented in Archives of Am. Art, Smithsonian Instn. Mem. Artists Equity, Houston Ctr. Photography, Asia Soc. (trustee 1979-83). Episcopalian. Home: 2420 Brentwood Houston TX 77019

ARMSTRONG, MARY DEMILLE MCLEOD, publicity administrator; b. Boston, May 22, 1911; d. Frank Fenwick McLeod and Emma Laura (King) McLeod Cushman; m. William J. Armstrong, June 17, 1944 (div. 1951). Cert., The Citadel, 1955; student Coll. of Charleston, 1972, 73, 78, 80, 81. Personnel supr. Curtiss Wright, Caldwell, N.J., 1942-43; Charleston mgr. World Travel Carolina Motor, Charlotte, 1957-58; art dir. Camp Interlachen, Croyden, N.H., summer 1959; part-time sec. Charleston, 1960-65; pub. relations dir. The Charleston Mus., 1963-67; publicity, exec. sec. Coll. Prep, Charleston, 1968-70; artist Charleston Artist Guild, 1967, 68, 69, 70. Contbr. articles to newspapers. Pres., Charleston Symphony Women's Assn., 1961-62; historian First Scots Presby. Ch., Charleston, 1979-80; membership chmn. Charleston Natural History Soc., 1981-82. Recipient Award of Merit, ARC, 1948-49; Outstanding Publicity award Community Chest, 1949. Avocations: writing, painting, reading, crafts, bicycling, gardening. Home: 1668 Pearlott St Charleston SC 29407

ARMSTRONG, PRINCE WINSTON, mathematics educator; b. Montgomery, Ala.; d. John Henry and Frankie Lee (Madison) Winston; m. Willie Clifford Armstrong, Dec. 23, 1960; children—Kim Élise, Jada Lea. B.S., Ala. State U., 1958; M.S., Atlanta U., 1959; D.Ed., U. Okla., 1972. Instr. Spelman Coll., Atlanta, 1959-60; asst. prof. math. Albany State Coll., Ga., 1960-61; asst. prof. So. U., Baton Rouge, 1962-67, assoc. prof., 1971—; vis. prof. Atlanta U., summers 1961, 62; cons. Tchr. Core, Baton Rouge, 1974, 75, United Methodist Career Day, Baton Rouge, 1984; evaluator Black Experience Group, Baton Rouge, 1984, 85; researcher Am. Cancer Soc., Baton Rouge, 1983—. Mem. supt. adv. com. East Baton Rouge Parish, 1982—; v.p. Scotlandville Magnet Sch. PTO, Baton Rouge, 1983-84. Atlanta U. fellow 1959; So. U. fellow, 1970-72; named Math. Tchr. of Yr., So. U. Math. Club, 1982, 83, 84, 85. Mem. Nat. Council Tchrs. Math., Math. Assn. Am., Phi Delta Kappa (historian, sec.), Pi Mu Epsilon (adviser), Alpha Kappa Mu, Beta Kappa Chi. Democrat. Avocations: reading; fishing; gardening. Home: 4205 Alief Dr Baker LA 70714 Office: So U Baton Rouge LA 70813

ARMSTRONG, ROBERT LAURENCE, philosophy educator; b. Bayonne, N.J., Apr. 6, 1926; s. Robert L. and Mary Agnes (Klein) A.; m. Betty Burnett, Sept. 14, 1960; children—Benjamin, Marianne. B.A., Antioch Coll., 1951; M.A., Roosevelt U., 1954; Ph.D., U. Calif.-Berkeley, 1962. Instr. U. Nev., 1962-64, asst. prof. 1964-67; assoc. prof., chmn. philosophy and religious studies, U. West Fla., 1967-70, prof., chmn., 1970-76, prof., chmn. dept. art, philosophy, and religious studies, 1976—. Served with USN, 1944-46. Mem. Am. Philos. Assn., So. Soc. Philosophy and Psychology, Fla. Philos. Assn., Phi Kappa Phi. Democrat. Author: Metaphysics and British Empiricism, 1970; contbr. articles to profl. jours. Home: 6118 Bougainvilla Circle Pensacola FL 32504 Office: Dept Art Philosophy and Religious Studies U W Fla Penascola FL 32514

ARMSTRONG, THOMAS RICHARD, business executive, systems electrical engineer; b. Pitts., June 13, 1939; s. Thomas Vincent and Florence Margaret (Gilliland) A.; m. Gloria Stewart, July 8, 1977; adopted children—Angie, Christina. B.E.E., Cornell U., 1962; M.S., Carnegie Inst. Tech., 1963; Ph.D., Carnegie Mellon U., 1968. Staff engr. Honeywell, Inc., St. Petersburg, Fla., 1968-73, sr. staff engr. Aerospace div., 1976-77; sr. design engr. Paradyne Corp., Largo, Fla., 1973-76, mgr. systems engring., 1977-80, dir. product planning, 1980—. Named to Computer Industry Hall of Fame, 1982. Mem. IEEE, Tau Beta Pi, Eta Kappa Nu. Club: Aero Flying (pres.). Patents, publs. in engring. field. Home: 1674 Sheffield Dr Clearwater FL 33546 Office: Paradyne Corp 8550 Ulmerton Rd Largo FL 33540

ARMSTRONG, WALTER PRESTON, JR., lawyer; b. Memphis, Oct. 4, 1916; s. Walter Preston and Irma Lewis (Waddell) A.; m. Alice Kavanaugh McKee, Nov. 3, 1949; children—Alice Kavanaugh, Walter Preston. A.B., Harvard U., 1938, J.D., 1941; D.C.L. (hon.), Southwestern at Memphis, 1961. Bar: Tenn. 1940. Practiced in Memphis, 1941—; assoc. Armstrong, Allen, Braden, Goodman, McBride & Prewitt, and predecessors, Memphis, 1941—, ptnr., 1948—; mem. Tenn. Commn. for Promotion Uniformity of Legis. in U.S., 1947-67. Author articles in field. Mem. Tenn. Hist. Commn., 1969-80; pres. bd. edn. Memphis City Schs., 1956-61; mem. Tenn. Higher Edn. Commn., 1967-84, chmn., 1974-75. Served from pvt. to maj. AUS, 1941-46. Hon. French consul, 1978-86. Fellow Am. Bar Found. (sec. 1960-62), Am. Coll. Trial Lawyers; mem. ABA (ho. of dels. 1952-75), Tenn. (pres. 1972-73), Memphis and Shelby County, Inter-Am., Internat. bar assns., Tenn. Bar Found. (chmn. 1983-84), Assn. Bar City N.Y., Am. Law Inst., Am. Judicature Soc., Nat. Conf. Commrs. on Uniform State Laws (pres. 1961-63), Harvard Law Sch. Assn. (sec. 1957-58), Order of Coif, Phi Delta Phi, Scribes (pres. 1960-61), Omicron Delta Kappa. Home: 1530 Carr Ave Memphis TN 38104 Office: One Commerce Sq Memphis TN 38103

ARNAUD, PHILIPPE, immunologist; b. Saint-Etienne, France, Mar. 30, 1935; came to U.S., 1975; s. Leonce Jules and Louise Aimee (Vial) A.; B., Acad. Lyons, 1952; M.D., U. Lyons (France), 1969; Ph.D., Med. U. S.C., 1977; m. Marie Laure Boigues du Rozet, July 8, 1961; children—Laurent Pierre, Eric Alexandre, Jean Christophe. Intern, Med. U. Lyons, 1956-64, resident, 1964-66, instr., 1966-70, asst. prof., 1970-75, chef de travaux, 1975; vis. asst. prof. Med. U. S.C., 1975-77, assoc. prof. basic and clin. immunology, from 1979, now prof. mem. sci. council Institut Pasteur, Lyons, Societe Francaise de Medecine Fonctionnelle, Paris. Served with French Army, 1962-64. Postdoctoral fellow Societe Medicale de Hopitaux de Lyons, 1974, Fondation de l'Industrie Pharmaceutique pour la Recherche, 1975, Mem. AAAS, Societe de Chimie Biologique, Am. Fedn. Clin. Research, Am. Assn. Immunologists, Am. Soc. Human Genetics, Electrophoresis Soc. Clubs: Snee Farm Country (Mt. Pleasant, S.C.); Societe Francaise Humanitati (Charleston, S.C.). Author: Human Alphal-Antitrypsin, 1983; editor: (with others) Electrophoresis 81, 1981; Marker Proteins of Inflammation, 1984; mem. editorial bd. Electrophoresis, Jour. Immunogenetics, Analytical Biochemistry; contbr. articles to profl. jours. Home: 1127 Daffodil Ln Mount Pleasant SC 29464 Office: Dept of Immunology Medical University of South Carolina Charleston SC 29425

ARNAUDO, PATRICIA SUSAN ALEXANDER, government official; b. Peoria, Ill., Jan. 3, 1943; d. Barton and Marian Francis (Gordon) Alexander; B.A., U. Mich., 1964, M.P.A., 1965, doctoral student, 1970-71; m. David Lloyd Arnaudo, Apr. 30, 1966; 1 dau., Juliet Gordon. Program analyst HEW, 1966-69; research assoc. cons. firm, 1969-70; program developer D.C. Mayor's Office, 1970-75; sr. program analyst HUD, Washington, 1975-76, dep. dir. project mgmt. div., chief sect. 8 mgmt. br., 1976-78, dir. existing housing div., 1979-81, dep. dir. Office of Indian Housing, 1981, acting dir. Office Indian Housing, 1982-85. Active Hopkins House, Housing Coalition, Olde Town Civic Assn., Consumer Affairs Commn. (all Alexandria, Va.). Recipient cert. of spl. achievement HUD, 1977, cert. of merit, 1979, cert. of superior service, 1980, 85; recipient planning award City of Alexandria. Mem. Nat. Assn. Housing and Redevel. Officers, Am. Soc. Pub. Adminstrn. Episcopalian. Contbr. articles to profl. jours. Home: 413 S Fairfax St Alexandria VA 22314 Office: HUD 451 7th St SW Washington DC 20410

ARNETT, EDWARD MCCOLLIN, chemistry educator; b. Phila., Sept. 25, 1922; s. John Hancock and Katherine Williams (McCollin) A.; m. Sylvia Gettmann, Dec. 10, 1970; children—Eric, Brian; stepchildren—Elden, Byron, Colin Gatwood. B.S., U. Pa., 1943, M.S., 1946, Ph.D., 1949. Research dir. Max Levy and Co., Phila., 1949-53; asst. prof. Western Md. Coll., Westminister, 1953-54, assoc. prof., 1954-55; research fellow Harvard U., Cambridge, Mass., 1955-57; asst. prof. chemistry U. Pitts., 1957-61, assoc. prof., 1961-64, prof., 1964-80; R. J. Reynolds Corp. prof. Duke U., Durham, N.C., 1980—; vis. lectr. U. Ill., 1963; vis. prof. U. Kent, Canterbury, Eng., 1970; dir. Pitts Chem. Info. Ctr., 1967-70; mem. adv. bd. Petroleum Research Fund, 1968-71; mem. com. on chem. info. NRC, 1969-71. DuPont fellow, 1948-49; Guggenheim fellow, 1968-69; Mellon Inst. adj. sr. fellow, 1964-80; Inst. Hydrocarbon Chemistry sr. fellow, 1980. Fellow AAAS; mem. Am. Chem. Soc. (James Flack Norris award 1977, Pitts. award Pitts. chpt. 1976, Petroleum Chemistry award 1985), Nat. Acad. Scis., The Chem. Soc., Sigma Xi, Phi Lambda Upsilon. Author papers in field.

ARNETT, GERSON LUCAS, systems engineer; b. Franklin, Ga., Apr. 16, 1939; s. Lonnie B. and Ethel Loette (Lucas) A.; m. Martha Clementine Arnett, Dec. 21, 1958; children—Stanley Gerson, Anthony Scott. B.Indsl. Mgmt., Ga. Inst. Tech., 1963; M.B.A., George Washington U., 1966; postgrad. Ga. State U., 1970-73. Systems analyst U.S. Dept. Health, Atlanta, 1959-62; systems engr. IBM, Atlanta, 1967-77, sr. systems engr., 1977—. Contbr. articles to profl. jours. Pres., W. Nancy Creek Civic Assn., Atlanta, 1979-80. Served to lt. USN, 1963-66. Republican. Baptist. Home: 1265 W Nancy Creek Dr Atlanta GA 30319 Office: IBM 219 Perimeter Center Pkwy Suite 111 Atlanta GA 30346

ARNETT, ROBERT KENNETH, urologist; b. Huntington, Tex., May 21, 1919; s. Ralph Clint and Minnie Day (Welch) A.; student Stephen F. Austin State Coll., 1937-39; student U. Tex., 1939-40, M.D., 1943; m. Alice June Holton, July 27, 1946; children—Lizabeth Len Arnett Medford, Robert Kenneth, Darwin Philip. Intern, Hermann Hosp., Houston, 1943-44, resident in surgery and urology, 1944-45, 48, 49; practice medicine specializing in urology, Lufkin, Tex., 1950—; voting rep. Am. Bd. of Med. Specialties, 1974-77; dir. Home Savs. and Loan Assn. of Lufkin, 1959—, First City Nat. Bank-Lufkin, 1968—. Mem. Angelina County Planning Bd., 1951; mem. Lufkin Ind. Sch. Dist. Bd. Edn., 1957-75, pres., 1960-61. Served to capt. M.C., U.S. Army, 1946-47. Diplomate Am. Bd. Urology. Mem. Angelina County Med. Soc., AMA, Tex. Med. Assn., So. Med. Assn., Am. Urol. Assn., S. Central sect. Am. Urol. Assn., Tex. Assn. Genito-Urinary Surgeons. Baptist. Home: 714 Pine Tree Ln Lufkin TX 75901 Office: 1113 Ellis Ave Lufkin TX 75901

ARNOLD, CARROLL ANNE WALCUTT, nurse; b. Paris, Ky., Apr. 29, 1954; d. Hardin Owsley and Cecele Christine (Smith) Walcutt; m. Richard Wood Arnold, Feb. 22, 1976; 1 child, Richard Wood Jr. A. in Nursing, Midway Coll., 1975; student in Psychology, St. Joseph's Coll., 1985—. Staff nurse, evening supr. U. Ky. Med. Ctr., Lexington, 1976-77; office mgr. Arnold, M.D., Cynthiana, Ky., 1977—; obstetric nurse Humana Corp., Lexington, 1983—. Dir. Woman's Missionary Union, Cynthiana Bapt. Ch., 1982-86, tchr. Sunday sch., 1978-85, mem. choir, 1978-85; mem. Harrison County Fine Arts Council, 1980-85. Recipient Woman of Achievement award YMCA, 1982; fellow U. Ky. Mem. Midway Coll. Alumni Assn. (named Miss Midway Coll. 1975), Ky. Nurse's Assn., Am. Nurse's Assn., Colonial Dames, Phi Theta Kappa. Democrat. Clubs: DAR (def. chmn. 1979-81, Good Citizenship award 1975, 1st alt. nat. conv. 1980), Harrisa County Women's Club (fine arts chmn. 1978-80, 1st v.p. 1981-83), Harrison Hosp. Aux. (pres. 1979-80). Home: 312 E Pike St Cynthiana KY 41031 Office: 300 E Pleasant St Cynthiana KY 41031

ARNOLD, DANIEL CALMES, financial executive; b. Houston, Mar. 14, 1930; m. Beverly Bintliff; children—Mrs. Randy Helms, Mrs. Tom Martin, Steven Arnold. B.B.A., U. Tex.-Austin, 1951, L.L.B., 1953. Assoc. Vinson & Elkins, Houston, 1953-83; chmn. bd., pres., dir. First City Bancorp. Tex., Inc., Houston, 1983—; dir. Visa, U.S.A., Inc. Bd. dirs. Harris County Hosp. Dist., 1962-69, chmn. 1963-69; bd. dirs. Tex. Med. Ctr., Inc., Baylor Coll. Medicine; bd. dirs. Houston-Harris County chpt. ARC, chmn. 1970-72; chmn. bd. dirs. Met. Transit Authority Harris County, Tex., 1980-84. Mem. ABA, Tex. Bar Assn., Houston Bar Assn., Assn. Res. City Bankers. Methodist. Office First City Bancorp Texas Inc 1001 Fannin St Houston TX 77002

ARNOLD, DOUGLAS ALAN, architect; b. Paragould, Ark., Sept. 14, 1951; s. Thomas Earl and Melba Mae (Thompson) A. B.Arch., U. Ark., 1974. Registered architect, Ark., Mo, Okla., Tenn.; cert. energy auditor, Ark. Apprentice Little-Maddox & Standefer Architects, Jonesboro, Ark., 1974-76; assoc. Brackett & Assocs., Jonesboro, 1976-77, Brackett-Krennerich & Assocs., Jonesboro, 1977-78; project architect Arnold & Stacks Architects, P.A., Jonesboro, 1978-82, corp. dir., 1982—. Chmn. United Way, Jonesboro, 1976; treas. Craighead County Com. for new Ark. Constn., 1980; bd. dirs. Jonesboro YMCA, 1974-76, March of Dimes, 1981-83. Mem. Nat. Trust for Historic Preservation, AIA, Am. Planning Assn., Council Ednl. Facilities Planners Internat., Jonesboro Jaycees (dir. 1980-82), Greater Jonesboro C. of C. Methodist. Lodges: Elks, Kiwanis (dir. 1981-83). Home: 728 W Cherry St Jonesboro AR 72401 Office: Arnold & Stacks Architects PA 527 W Washington Ave PO Box 69 Jonesboro AR 72401

ARNOLD, GARY STEPHEN, real estate and foundation executive; b. 1954; m. June Elizabeth Borg, Sept. 1, 1979; 2 children. Student Ga. Inst. Tech., 1972-74; B.A., Georgetown U., 1977. Ptnr., dir. So. Woodlands, Atlanta, 1978-81; exec. v.p. Southfield Petroleum, Hattiesburg, Miss., 1980-82, vice chmn. bd., 1980-82; SE ptnr. Albritton Devel., Dallas, 1983—; cons. Hallum-Arnold Found., Atlanta, 1980—, chmn. bd. govs., 1983—. Mem. adminstrv. bd. Northside Methodist Ch., Atlanta; cons. fund raising activities Lovett Sch., Atlanta. Mem. Nat. Assn. Indsl. and Office Parks, Urban Land Inst., Atlanta C. of C. Republican. Clubs: Georgian, Capital City (Atlanta). Office: Albritton Devel 3101 Tower Creek Pkwy Suite 200 Atlanta GA 30339

ARNOLD, GLEN ELDRED, management consultant; b. Shreveport, La., Nov. 4, 1931; s. Eulice Eldred and Myrtle Elizabeth (Comalander) A.; student La. Tech. U., 1949-52; B.S. in Acctg., Centenary Coll., La., 1960; postgrad. So. Meth. U., 1970; m. Delores Nickels, Aug. 15, 1952; children—David Bruce, James Rendall. Plant acct. Ark. La. Gas Co., Shreveport, La., 1955-56, jr. engr. trainee, 1956-57, asst. supr. gen. accounting dept., 1957-59; traveling auditor So. Union Gas Co., Dallas, 1960-62, methods engr., 1962-63, data systems analyst, 1963-65, compensation mgr., 1965-69; corp. dir. personnel Great Southwest Corp. and subs.'s Six Flags, Inc. and GSC Devel. Corp., Arlington, Tex., 1969-72; sr. prin. with Hay Assocs., mgmt. cons.'s, Dallas, 1972—; instr. Eastfield Jr. Coll., Dallas, 1973-76. Served to sgt. U.S. Army, 1953-54. Mem. Am. Soc. Personnel Adminstrn., Dallas Personnel Assn., Am. Mgmt. Assn. (guest lectr. 1966—), Kappa Alpha, Omicron Delta Kappa, Pi Kappa Delta. Republican. Baptist. Office: 12700 Park Central Dallas TX 75251

ARNOLD, JASPER HENRY, III, banker; b. Temple, Tex., June 30, 1944; s. Jasper Henry and Clara Imogene (Alsup) A.; m. Daphne Chiarulli, July 14, 1973; children—Charlotte, Jasper. B.B.A., U. Tex., 1968, M.B.A., 1969; D.B.A., Harvard U., 1975. Research asst. Harvard Bus. Sch., Boston, 1971; asst. treas. Bankers Trust Co., N.Y.C., 1974-76; sr. v.p. First City Nat. Bank of Houston, 1976—; dir. First City Fin. Corp. Bd. dirs. Houston Youth Symphony and Ballet, Art League of Houston; bd. dirs. Mayor's Telephone Reassurance, 1977-80; sector chmn. Houston Festival, 1980, 81, 82. Served with USMC, 1965-71. Republican. Methodist. Clubs: Houston, Harvard Bus. Sch. of Houston. Contbr. articles in field to profl. publs. Home: 5659 Del Monte Houston TX 77056 Office: First City Nat Bank 1001 Main St Houston TX 77002

ARNOLD, JOHN R., university dean. Dean, U. S.C. at Lancaster. Office: U SC at Lancaster Hubbard Dr Lancaster SC 29720*

ARNOLD, LOUIS WALKER, clergyman; b. Garrard County, Ky., Jan. 17, 1914; s. Edward Lawrence and Texie Bell (Agee) A.; m. Jessie Arnold; children—June Louise Arnold Parker, Sue Ann Arnold True. Student So. Baptist Sem., Louisville, 1942; D.D., Pioneer Theol. Sem., 1953; student U. Ky., 1955; D.Litt., Colonial Acad., 1956. Ordained to ministry Bapt. Ch., 1933; pastor Fellowship Bapt. Ch., Lexington, Ky., 1950-57, Central Bapt. Ch., Cin., 1945-47; flying pastor, preaching from airplane over powerful PA system; fgn. missionary; radio preacher on network stas.; evangelist; owner Arnold Publs., Nicholasville, Ky., 1965—; past pres. Blue Grass Bible Inst., Internat. Fellowship Fundamentalists. Ky. Col., Hon. Commr. Agr., Ky., Hon. Dep. Sheriff, Jessamine County, Adm., Cherry River Navy (W.Va.). Author: Way of Revival, 1947; God's Message for This Hour, 1964; Israel: Countdown to Eternity, 1985; The Legend of Old Faithful, 1986; Beyond the Rapture, 1986. Composer numerous gospel songs. Contbr. articles to religious publs. Home and Office: 2440 Bethel Rd Nicholasville KY 40356

ARNOLD, LUCILLE EDNA COCKRIEL, medical group administrator; b. Indpls., Oct. 14, 1926; s. George W. and Cleo A. (DuChemin) C.; student Purdue U., 1944-46, Ind. U., 1946-48; m. William Arnold, June 22, 1947; 1 son, Tab. With Foster Bros., Weber, Toledo, 1957-59; gen. bookkeeper, fin. bookkeeper Ind. Bank, Ft. Wayne, Ind., 1965-68; tchr. Payne (Ohio) Elem. Sch., 1966-68; bus. mgr. Pediatrics Assocs., Hollywood, Fla., 1970-77; adminstr. Internal Medicine Assocs. of Hollywood (Fla.), 1977—; dir. Prudential Bank Fla.; med./bus. cons. Mem. Am. Coll. Med. Group Adminstrs., Med. Group Mgmt. Assn., Fla. Med. Group Mgmt. Assn. (past treas., pres. 1984), Page A Computer Users Group (pres. 1985). Club: Order Eastern Star. Office: Internal Medicine Assos of Hollywood 750 S Federal Hwy Hollywood FL 33020

ARNOLD, PETER VAUGHN, aviation, marine and civil engineering consultant; b. Gardner, Mass., May 1, 1933; s. Elsworth Vaughn and Lois Arelia (Nichols) A.; B.C.E., New Eng. Coll., 1959; m. Geraldine Ann Avellar, June 6, 1953; children—Deborah Lee, Kevin Vaughn. Engr., Morrison Knudsen & G.A. Fuller Co., 1959-61; gen. mgr. Astro Technology, Mountain View, Calif., 1961-65; contract adminstr. Nat. Accelorator Labs., Stanford, Calif. and Batavia, Ill., 1965-72; pres. Constellation Aeros., Tallahassee, 1961—, also Admiralty Marine Service, Tallahassee. Mem. CAP, Coast Guard Aux. Served with USCG, 1951-59. Mem. U.S. Naval Inst., Am. Boat and Yacht Council, Fla. Engrs. Soc., Nat. Soc. Profl. Engrs., ASCE, Soc. Mil. Engrs., Soc. Naval Architects and Marine Engrs., Sigma Phi Delta. Clubs: Moose, Masons. Patentee in field. Home: 655 Conner Blvd Tallahassee FL 32301 Office: 1024 East Park Ave Tallahassee FL 32301

ARNOLD, RICHARD SHEPPARD, judge; b. Texarkana, Tex., Mar. 26, 1936; s. Richard Lewis and Janet (Sheppard) A.; children—Janet Sheppard, Lydia Palmer; m. Kay Kelley, Oct. 27, 1979. B.A. summa cum laude, Yale U., 1957; J.D. magna cum laude, Harvard U., 1960. Bar: D.C. 1961, Ark. 1960. Practiced in Washington, 1961-64, Texarkana, 1964-74; law clk. to Justice Brennan, Supreme Ct. U.S., 1960-61; assoc. Covington & Burling, 1961-64; partner Arnold & Arnold, 1964-74; legis. sec. Gov. of Ark., 1973-74, staff coordinator, 1974; legis. asst. Senator Bumpers of Ark., Washington, 1975-78; judge U.S. Dist. Ct. Eastern and Western Dists. Ark., 1978-80, U.S. Ct. Appeals 8th Circuit, Little Rock, 1980—; part-time instr. U. Va. Law Sch., 1962-64; mem. Ark. Constl. Revision Study Commn., 1967-68. Case editor: Harvard Law Rev., 1959-60; contbr. articles to profl. jours. Gen. chmn. Texarkana United Way Crusade, 1969-70; pres. Texarkana Community Chest, 1970-71; mem. overseers com. Harvard Law Sch., 1973-79; candidate for Congress 4th Dist. Ark., 1966, 72; del. Democratic Nat. Conv., 1968, Ark. Constl. Conv., 1969-70; chmn. rules com. Ark. Dem. Com., 1968-74, mem. exec. com., 1972-74; mem. Com. on Legis. Orgn., 1971-72; trustee U. Ark., 1973-74. Mem. Am. Law Inst., Cum Laude Soc., Phi Beta Kappa. Episcopalian. Home: 3901 Cedar Hill Rd No 5 Little Rock AR Office: US Court of Appeals PO Box 429 Little Rock AR 72203

ARNOLD, VERNA ALINE, college administrator; b. Haskell, Tex., Apr. 7, 1931; d. Bert W. and Juanita (Brooks) Marchbanks; m. Walter Eugene Arnold, Sept. 6, 1969; B.B.A., N. Tex. State U., 1975, M.B.A., 1976, Ph.D., 1978. Adminstrv. asst. Baylor U. Med. Center, 1960-66; adminstr. Ennis Mcpl. Hosp., 1966-70; instr. mgmt. and mktg. N. Tex. State U., Denton, 1975-78, asst. prof., 1978—, exec. asst. to chancellor, 1982—; mgmt. cons. to health instns. Chmn., United Way, 1969, 81. Mem. Acad. Mgmt., Am. Hosp. Assn., Soc. Advancement Mgmt., Tex. Hosp. Assn., Southwestern Fedn. Adminstrv. Disciplines, Beta Gamma Sigma, Sigma Iota Epsilon, Phi Theta Kappa, C. of C. Baptist. Contbr. articles to profl. jours. Office: NT Station PO Box 13737 Denton TX 76203

ARNOULT, ELDEN BREWER, JR., petrophysicist; b. New Orleans, Sept. 4, 1942; s. Elden Brewer and Rita Caroline (Zimmer) A.; m. Patricia Ann McFaull, Aug. 13, 1966; children—Nicole Marie, Elden Brewer III, Andrea Christine, Christopher Patrick. Student U. New Orleans, 1960-62; B.S. in Geology, Tulane U., 1965. Field jr. engr. Schlumberger Well Service, Gretna, La., 1966-67; log analyst GTS Corp., New Orleans, 1967-73; petrophysicist Shell Oil Co., New Orleans, 1973-74; mgr. geol. ops. GTS Corp., New Orleans, 1974-76; geol. systems coordinator Amoco Prodn., Tulsa, 1976-79, chmn. digital well log standards com., 1977-79; sr. petrophysicist La. Land and Exploration Co., New Orleans, 1979—. Author: Quality control in Well Log Digitization, 1968; Detection and Evaluation of Fractures from Well Logs, 1980. Contbr. articles to profl. jours. Republican precinct leader, New Orleans, 1972; bd. govs. concerned Reps. of ward 9, 1970, area subcoordinator, 1964. Mem. Soc. Profl. Well Log Analysts, Am. Assn. Petroleum Geologists. Roman Catholic. Club: Paradise Manor Country (River Ridge, La.). Avocations: softball; fishing; stamp and rock collecting; church work. Lodge: K.C. Home: 9716 Dart St River Ridge LA 70123 Office: La Land and Exploration Co PO Box 60350 New Orleans LA 70160

ARNOULT, KENNETH MAURICE, biomedical electronic technician; b. New Orleans, Jan. 16, 1946; s. William Joseph and Blanche Rita (Dickinson) A.; m. Patricia Ann Hattier, Aug. 1, 1970; children—Kenneth Jr., Cecile. Assoc. in Sci., Delgado Coll., 1967. Electronic technician Electro Med. Co., New Orleans, 1967-68, Tulane Med. Sch., New Orleans, 1968-69; electronic technician Ochsner Found. Hosp., New Orleans, 1969-71, biomed. technician, 1971-76, dir. biomed. dept., 1976—. Mem. So. Biomed. Instrumentation Assn. (charter), La. Soc. Biomed. Equipment Technicians of La. Hosp. Assn. (charter). Roman Catholic. Avocations: Cars; fishing; boating; target shooting. Office: Ochsner Found Hosp 1516 Jefferson Hwy New Orleans LA 70121

ARONIN, PATRICIA ANNE, neurosurgeon; b. N.Y.C., Feb. 24, 1948; d. Stanley Michael and Anne Marie (Metzger) A. A.B., Manhattanville Coll., 1969; M.S. in Biochemistry, U. N.C., 1974, M.D., 1975. Diplomate Am. Bd. Neurologic Surgery. Intern in gen. surgery NCMH, Chapel Hill, 1976-77, resident in neurosurgery, 1977-81, fellow in neuropathology, 1976, fellow in neuro-oncology, 1978-79; fellow in pediatric neurosurgery Children's Hosp. Med. Ctr., Cin., 1982; clin. asst. pediatric neurosurgery Hosp. for Sick Children, Toronto, Ont., Can., 1982; practice medicine specializing in pediatric neurosurgery, Birmingham, Ala., 1983—; chief pediatric neurosurgery The Children's Hosp., Birmingham, 1985—; asst. prof. div. neurosurgery U. Ala., Birmingham, 1983—. Mem. Congress Neurol. Surgeons, Nathan Womack Surg. Soc., Gordon S. Dugger Neurosurg. Soc., Acad. Pediatrics. Roman Catholic. Home: 3057 Old Stone Dr Birmingham AL 35243 Office: Div Neurosurgery U Ala University Station Birmingham AL 35223

ARONOVITZ, SIDNEY M., U.S. district judge; b. Key West, Fla., June 20, 1920; s. Charles A. and Ethel (Holtsberg) A.; m. Elinore Richman, Mar. 24, 1943; children—Elaine, Tod, Karen. B.A., U. Fla., 1942, J.D., 1943. Atty., vice mayor City of Miami, Fla., 1965; city commr. Miami, 1962-66; U.S. dist. judge So. Fla., Miami, 1976—. Mem. ABA, Am. Judicature Soc., Fla. Bar Assn., Dade County Bar Assn. Office: PO Box 013069 Miami FL 33101*

AROVA, SONIA, dancer, educator; b. Sophia, Bulgaria, June 20, 1928; came to U.S., 1954; d. Albert and Rachel (Melemedon) A.; m. Job Sanders (div.); m. Thor Sutowski, Mar. 11, 1965; 1 dau., Ariane. B.F.A. with honors, Paris Conservatory of Fine Arts, 1940. Ballerina, Met. Ballet, Eng., 1944, Internat. Ballet, Eng., 1945, Ballet Rambert, Eng., 1947, Ballet Champs-Elysee, France, 1947, Am. Ballet Theatre, N.Y.C., 1953; dir. Nat. Ballet of Norway, Oslo, 1965-70, Hamburg Opera Ballet (Ger.), 1970-71, San Diego Ballet, 1971-76; guest ballerina Royal Ballet, London, 1963, Komaki Ballet, Tokyo, 1952, Chgo. Opera Ballet, 1960-64, Australian Ballet, Melbourne, 1963-64; prof.

dance Ala. Sch. Fine Arts, Birmingham, 1976. Winner World Championship of Dance, Paris, 1939; decorated knight First Order (Norway), 1970. Office: State of Ala Ballet PO Box 55566 Birmingham AL 35205

ARRINGTON, BILL CHARLES, pharmacist; b. Marlow, Okla., Nov. 10, 1953; s. Charles A. and Margaret Jane (Stone) A.; m. Danielle Suzanne Taylor, Aug. 1, 1976. B.S. in Pharmacy, S.W. Okla. State U., 1977. Registered pharmacist. Staff pharmacist Stillwater Med. Ctr., Okla., 1977-79, dir. pharmacy, 1979—; advisor I.V. Tng. Manual for Nursing, 1982. Mem. Am. Pharm. Assn., Am. Soc. Hosp. Pharmacists, Okla. Soc. Hosp. Pharmacists, Cowboy Country Jaycees. Democrat. Mem. First Christian Ch. Avocations: flying, travel. Office: Stillwater Med Ctr 1323 W 6th St Stillwater OK 74074

ARRINGTON, CAROLYN RUTH, education executive; b. Parkersburg, W.Va., May 20, 1942; d. Robert Ray and Grace (Emrick) Dotson; m. Wayne Vernon Arrington; children—Kevin Ray, Kemp Gray, Korey Shay. A.A., Ohio Valley Coll., 1962; B.A., Fairmont State Coll., 1964; M.A., W.Va. U., 1966; supr. cert. Marshall U., 1970. Tchr., Greenbrier Bd. Edn., Lewisburg, W.Va., 1964-68; supr. Mason County Bd. Edn., Point Pleasant, W.Va., 1968-70; media specialist Kanawha County Bd. Edn., Charleston, W.Va., 1970-71; dir. fed. program W.Va. Dept. Edn., Charleston, 1971—; cons. in field. Author numerous poems. Developer workshop materials. Treas. Kanawha Family and Children Ctr., Charleston, 1980. SEA fellow U.S. Dept. Edn., 1984. Mem. Assn. Ednl. Communications and Tech. (pres. 1979-80; Edgar Dale award 1975, Spl. Service award 1982), W.Va., Ednl. Media Assn. (pres. 1975-76). Lodge: Zonta (pres.-elect 1980). Avocations: fishing; camping. Office: WVa Dept Edn 1900 Washington St Room B 252 Charleston WV 25305

ARRINGTON, JOHN LESLIE, JR., lawyer; b. Pawhuska, Okla., Oct. 15, 1931; s. John Leslie and Grace Louise (Moore) A.; grad. Lawrenceville Sch., 1949; A.B., Princeton U., 1953; LL.B., Harvard U., 1956, LL.M., 1957; m. Elizabeth Anne Waddington, July 21, 1956 (div. Jan. 1972); children—Elizabeth Anne, John Leslie III, Winifred Louise, Katherine Moore; m. 2d, Linda Vance Mullendore, 1972. Admitted to Okla. bar, 1956; with Huffman Arrington Kihle Gaberino & Dunn, and predecessor firms, Tulsa 1957—, partner, 1961—; chmn. bd. Woodland Bank Tulsa. Recipient Jr. award for service to profession Tulsa County Bar Assn., 1962; named Outstanding Young Man, Tulsa Jr. C. of C., 1963. Mem. Okla., Tulsa County (pres. 1970), Am., Fed. Energy bar assns., Motor Carrier Lawyers Assn., Am. Soc. Internat. Law, Harvard Law Sch. Assn. Okla (pres. 1961) Phi Beta Kappa. Republican. Episcopalian (vestryman). Clubs: Tulsa, Southern Hills Country, Princeton (pres. 1964-65) (Tulsa); Princeton (N.Y.C.). Home: 2136 E 26th Pl Tulsa OK 74114 Office: 1000 ONEOK Plaza Tulsa OK 74103

ARRINGTON, RICHARD, mayor; b. Livingston, Ala., Oct. 19, 1934; A.B., Miles Coll., 1955; M.S., U. Detroit, 1957; Ph.D. in Zoology, U. Okla., 1966. Asst. prof. Miles Coll., 1957-63, prof. from 1966, counselor, 1962-63, dir. Summer Sch., acting dean, 1966-67, dean, 1967-70; exec. dir. Ala. Center for Higher Edn., 1970-79; mayor City of Birmingham (Ala.), 1979-83, 83-87; mem. Birmingham City Council, 1971-75. Office: Office of Mayor 710 20th St N Birmingham AL 35203

ARSENAULT, ANZIA KUBICEK, educator, ballet teacher, choreographer; b. Amsterdam, N.Y., Nov. 25, 1926; d. Edward and Helen Mildred (Hoffman) Kubicek; m. Ralph Lincoln Arsenault, Mar. 7, 1947; 1 son, Keith Lawrence. Grad. high sch., N.Y.C. Dancer, singer, actress Provincetown Playhouse, Greenwich Village, N.Y.C., 1943-46; dancer Gluck Sandors' Ballet In Time, N.Y.C., 1943-53; dancer, singer Broadway musicals Louisiana Lady, Gay New Orleans, N.Y.C., 1945-47; founder, tchr. Anzia's Sch. Ballet, Tampa, Fla., 1954-76; founder, tchr. Tampa Ballet Arts, 1976— 1960-63, Tampa Civic Ballet, 1964; artistic dir. Tampa Ballet, 1964-84, artistic dir. emeritus, 1984—, bd. dirs., 1964-84; choreographer numerous ballets, 1963—; ballet tchr., program dir., U. Tampa, 1975—. Recipient U. Tampa Pres.'s Gold medal of honor, 1984; Recognition award Mayor of Tampa, 1984. Mem. Chorus Equity Soc., Southeastern Regional Ballet Assn. (bd. dirs. 1979-81), State Dance Assn. Fla. (bd. dirs. 1984—), Nat. Assn. Regional Ballet. Methodist. Home: 3620 S Hubert Ave Tampa FL 33609 Office: Tampa Ballet/Tampa Ballet Arts U of Tampa Box 95F Tampa FL 33606

ARTERBURN, JAMES GREGORY, radiologist; b. Blandville, Ky., July 3, 1942; s. William Henry and Mary Mona (Rials) A.; m. Wynemia Wheeler, Aug. 1, 1970. B.A., Murray State U., 1964; M.D., U. Louisville, 1971. Diplomate Am. Bd. Diagnostic Radiology, Am. Bd. Nuclear Medicine. Intern, Tampa Gen. Hosp., Fla., 1971-72; resident in radiology U. South Fla., Tampa, 1973-76; radiologist Community Hosp., Mayfield, Ky., 1976-77, Palms of Pasadena Hosp., St. Petersburg, Fla., 1978-85, Lake Seminole Hosp., Seminole, Fla., 1978—; clin. asst. prof. radiology U. South Fla., Tampa, 1981—; instr. med. sonography Hillsborough Community Coll., Tampa, 1984—. Contbr. articles to profl. jours. Trustee Palms of Pasadena Hosp., 1984-85; pres. Paradise Island Civic Assn., Treasure Island, Fla., 1984-85, Fla. West Coast Radiology Soc., 1981-82. Recipient Outstanding Diagnostic Radiology Resident award E.I. DuPont Co., 1976. Mem. AMA, Am. Coll. Radiology, Am. Coll. Nuclear Physicians, Fla. Med. Assn., Pinellas County Med. Assn. Democrat. Avocations: tennis; snowskiing; powerboating; personal computing; breeding registered beefcattle. Home: 10112 Tarpon Dr Treasure Island FL 33706 Office: RA Castillo MD and Assocs PA 1609 Pasadena Ave S Saint Petersburg FL 33707

ARTHUR, ALLEN A., public relations counsel, writer; b. Ft. Scott, Kans., Jan. 24, 1920; s. Louis R. and Mary J. (Allen) Divilbiss. B.S. cum laude, U. So. Calif., 1952. Promotion dir. U. So. Calif., 1955-57; exec. mgr. San Diego Conv. and Tourist Bur., 1957-58; ind. counsel in pub. relations, Los Angeles and San Francisco, 1958-83; dir. advt. Crowell-Collier Broadcasting Corp., 1961; dir. univ. relations/spl. projects U. So. Calif., Los Angeles, 1974-76; pub. relations counsel, 1976—. Assoc. mem. Calif. Republican Central Com., 1965-76. Mem. Am. Philatelic Soc., Am. Theatre Organ Soc., Internat. Wine and Food Soc., Soc. Wine Educators, Les Amis Du Vin, Les Grand Crus, Am. Wine Soc., Wine and Food Soc. Tulsa (founder 1983), Blue Key, Alpha Kappa Psi, Beta Gamma Sigma, Alpha Delta Sigma, Alpha Phi Omega, Alpha Tau Omega. Presbyterian.

ARTHURS, DARREL RAY, industrial construction company official; b. Rl Reno, Okla., Mar. 16, 1947; s. Ronald Zoren and Gwen (Garvin) A.; m. Beth Ann Howell, Apr. 18, 1975; children—David Bryan, Angela Marie, Mandy Dee Ann. Student Northeastern State U., 1966-68. Mgr. purchasing Barnard & Burk, Baton Rouge, 1976-78; material control mgr. Foster Wheeler Corp., Venezuela, 1978-81; mgr. procurement Merit Indsl. Construction Co., Baton Rouge, 1982—. Served with USMC, 1968-70. Mem. Assoc. Bldg. Contractors. Republican. Lodges: Elks. Home: 2105 Stonewood Baton Rouge LA 70816 Office: Merit Indsl Constructors Baton Rouge LA 70810

ARTIS, GREGORY DWIGHT, lawyer, pharmaceutical consultant; b. Columbus, Ohio, July 8, 1952; s. Willie J. and Eloise I. (Smith) A.; m. Fredi Kay Johnson, Mar. 13, 1976; children—Kierstian D., Bethany S., Gregory Dwight Jr. B.S. in Pharmacy, Ohio State U., 1976; J.D., Emory U., 1982. Registered pharmacist, Ohio, Ga. Bar: Ga. 1982. Pharmacist, Thrift Drug Co., Atlanta, 1976-78, Eckerd Drugs, Atlanta, 1978-82; assoc. Smith, Cohen, Ringel, Kohler & Martin, Atlanta, 1982-84; atty. So. Bell, Atlanta, 1984—. Bd. dirs. Urban League, Columbus, 1974-75; mem. steering com. Progressive Alliance, Atlanta, 1985. Recipient D. Robert Owen award Emory U., 1982, coach, Mugel Moot Court Tax Team, Moot Court Directorate, Coach of Yr., 1982, semi-finalist mem. Giles Sutherland Regional Moot Court Patent Team, 1982. Mem. ABA, Gate City Bar Assn. (exec. com. 1985-86, asst. sec. 1986—), State Bar Ga., Atlanta Bar Assn., Nat. Order Barristers. Avocation: travel. Office: So Bell Telephone and Telegraph Co 675 W Peachtree St NE Atlanta GA 30375

ARVOLD, ORRIN WAYNE, architect, consultant; b. Chgo., Nov. 19, 1945; s. Omer Bernard and Jean Madeliane (Lindahl) A.; m. Bridget Anne Beilstein, May 31, 1969; children—Erica, Trina. B. Arch., Miami U., Oxford, Ohio, 1968. Registered architect, Va., Ill. Architect intern A.M. Kinney & Assocs., Cin., 1968-70; archtl. designer Holabird & Root, Chgo., 1971-72, architect assoc., 1972-76; prin. Orrin W. Arvold & Assocs., Blacksburg, Va., 1978-83; project mgr. Va. Poly. Inst. and State U., Blacksburg, 1983—; pres. Architects Alliance, Blacksburg, 1984—. Active Montgomery County Planning Commn. (Va.), 1984, 85, Va. Citizens Planning Assn., Richmond, 1984, 85; campaign sector coordinator Blacksburg United Fund, 1985. Mem. AIA, Sigma Tau Delta. Lodge: Kiwanis (lt. gov. 1984-85). Home: 43 Indian Meadow Dr Blacksburg VA 24060 Office: Architects Alliance Inc 200 N Main St Blacksburg VA 24060

ASCHERMAN, TOMMY MARVIN, insurance company executive; b. Orlando, Fla., Nov. 26, 1937; s. Frank Joseph and Marion (Kersey) A.; m. Noreen Hammond, Oct. 26, 1956 (div. 1967); 1 child, Tommy Marvin, II; m. Sharon Samuel, May 10, 1976; 1 child, Shelly Michelle. Student in Fire Protection, Tex. A&M U., 1971, in Audio Metric Tech., Fla. Tech. Coll., 1974, in Chem. Hazards, U. N.C., 1975. Lt. Tampa Fire Dept., Fla., 1979-63; safety dir. Shell Oil Co., New Orleans, 1963-73; sr. loss control cons. Hartford Ins. Co., Houston, 1973-81, Alexander & Alexander of Tex., Inc., Houston, 1982—. Recipient Service award Brevard Bd. County Commrs., 1976, Peabody Internat., 1982. Mem. Am. Soc. Safety Engrs., Tex. Safety Assn., Nat. Safety Council. Home: 9515 Water Park Ct Houston TX 77086 Office: Alexander & Alexander of Tex Inc 5851 San Felipe Houston TX 77027

ASH, CLARKE BENEDICT, newspaper editor; b. Mankato, Minn., Oct. 19, 1923; s. Benedict S. and Mary V. (Clarke) A.; m. Agnes McCarty, Feb. 2, 1957; children—David Jones, Eric, James, Jennifer. B.S. in Bus. Adminstrn., U. Dayton, 1949. Reporter Dayton (Ohio) Daily News, 1949-53; asst. pub. relations dir. Columbia Gas System, N.Y.C., 1953-59; assoc. editor Miami (Fla.) News, 1959-76, Palm Beach Post, West Palm Beach, Fla., 1976—. Served to capt., USAAF, 1943-46. Mem. Am. Soc. Newspaper Editors, Fla. Soc. Newspaper Editors. Democrat. Roman Catholic. Office: Palm Beach Post PO Drawer T West Palm Beach FL 33402

ASH, DAVID WILLIAM, geophysicist; b. Stamford, Conn., Jan. 29, 1953; s. Arnold William and Elsa (Spiess) A.; m. Frances Muriel Edmonds, Aug. 17, 1974 (div. July 1984); children—Melanie Frances, Timothy McGregor. B.S. in Geophys. Engring., Colo. Sch. Mines, 1975. Geophysicist, Union Oil Co. Calif., Anchorage, Alaska, 1975-78; cons. John F. Partridge, Casper, Wyo., 1978-80; sr. geophysicist Marathon Oil Co., Casper, 1980-81, Mapco Oil & Gas Co., Billings, Mont., also Tulsa, 1981-85, CNG Producing Co., Tulsa, 1985—. Mem. Soc. Exploration Geophysicists, Am. Assn. Petroleum Geologists, Tulsa Geol. Soc. Inc., Geophys. Soc. Tulsa, Mont. Geol. Soc., Billings Geophys. Soc. Avocations: skiing; working on automobiles. Office: CNG Producing Co 705 South Elgin Tulsa OK 74101-2115

ASH, GARRETT OSBORNE, furniture retail company executive, importer; b. Washington, Nov. 12, 1943; s. Willard Osborne and Louise (Van Ormer) A.; m. Susan Joan Rablen, Aug. 9, 1966 (div. Apr. 1979); children—Andy, Allison; m. 2d, Jill Karen Gottermeyer, Aug. 29, 1981; 1 son, Alex. B.S.B.A., U. Fla., 1965. With Rablen West Interiors Inc., Stuart, Fla., 1970—, owner, 1976—. Bd. zoning adjustment, Martin County, Fla., 1978. Served to capt. U.S. Army, 1965-70. Decorated Bronze Star. Mem. Nat. Home Furnishing Assn., Sigma Alpha Epsilon. Republican. Lutheran. Office: Rablen West Interiors Inc 3718 SE Ocean Blvd Stuart FL 33494

ASH, GERALD W., state senator; b. Clarksburg, W.Va., June 3, 1939; M.S.J., W.Va. U.; m. Michele Emilie Linn; 1 dau., Elisabeth Linn. Dir. community relations Monongalia Gen. Hosp., Morgantown, W.Va.; mem. W.Va. Senate from 15th Dist., 1980—, chmn. small bus. com., vice chmn. pub. inst. Mem. exec. com. W.Va. Dem. Party. Served with AUS. Mem. VFW. Lodge: Rotary. Office: State Capitol 1800 Washington St E Charleston WV 25305

ASHBURN, SARAH JO, school administrator; b. Graham, Tex., 1939; d. Harold and H. Jo (Bryson) Heard; m. Pat Ashburn, 1956; children—Steve, Lisa, Robert, Denise. B.S., West Tex. State U., 1963, M.A., 1966; Ed.D., Am. U., 1976. Tchr. pub. schs., Colo.; social worker pub. schs., Va.; support tchr. Ithaca (N.Y.) schs., 1973-74; ednl. researcher Nat. Pub. Service Research Inst., Washington, 1974-76; research and evaluation dir. Galveston (Tex.) schs., 1978-81, exec. dir. curriculum and instruction, 1982-83, asst. supt. for curriculum and instrn., 1983—. Mem. Assn. Supervision and Curriculum Devel., Tex. Assn. Sch. Adminstrs., Am. Psychol. Assn., Phi Delta Kappa. Republican. Methodist. Research in pupil performance, spl. ednl. needs in pub. schs. Office: PO Drawer 660 Galveston TX 77550

ASHBY, JOHN EDMUND, JR., marketing executive; b. Dallas, Mar. 5, 1936; s. John Edmund and Lillian Eloise (Cox) A.; B.B.A., U. Tex., 1957; m. Martha Caroline Isabel de Larios, June 25, 1975; children—Nancy Suzanne Robertson, Shelley Bickham, Elizabeth Ann, Vicki Suzanne Anderson, Dana Elizabeth Strickland. Salesman, IBM, Corpus Christi, 1959-63, San Antonio, 1963-64; mktg. mgr. St. Louis Recognition Equipment Inc., Dallas, 1964-67, v.p. mktg. N.Am., Japan, 1967-81; exec. v.p. Teknekron Fin. Systems, 1981—. Served with USMCR, 1957-59. Recipient Sales award IBM, 1964. Mem. Sales and Mktg. Execs. Inc. (award 1961), Beta Theta Pi. Republican. Presbyn. Club: Royal Oaks Country. Home: 3429 Cornell Ave Dallas TX 75205

ASHBY, RONALD BRYAN, auto parts company executive; b. Dallas, Mar. 12, 1948; s. Joe Ben and Bonnie Belle (Cooner) A.; m. Mary Jason Sanders, June 26, 1971; children—Elizabeth Sybil, Ronald Bryan. B.F.A., Tex. Christian Univ., 1970. Owner, gen. sales mgr. Ashby Automotive Warehouse, Inc., Dallas, 1970—. Bd. dirs. Dallas County Community Coll. Dist.; active Park Cities Family League, Park Cities Hist. Soc. Mem. Automotive Service Industry Assn., Young Execs., Sales Exec. Club, Jr. Chamber Commerce, Delta Tau Delta. Republican. Baptist. Clubs: Dallas Country, Chaparral. Home: 3808 Stanford St Dallas TX 75225 Office: Ashby Automotive Warehouse Inc 2601 Swiss Ave Dallas TX 75204

ASHCRAFT, HUGH G., JR., supermarket company executive; b. 1919. B.S., Washington and Lee U. With R.S. Dickson & Co., 1954—, v.p., 1957—; v.p., sec. Ruddick Corp., Charlotte, N.C.; with Harris-Teeter Super Markets, Charlotte, 1955—, now pres., chief exec. officer, also dir. Office: Harris-Teeter Super Markets Inc 4017 Chesapeake Dr Box 33129 Charlotte NC 28233*

ASHCRAFT, RONALD EUGENE, jewelry company executive; b. Hertha, Kans., Oct. 1, 1936; s. Willis Vaughn and Fannie Mae (Archer) A.; A.A., Pueblo Coll., 1956; B.Mus.Ed., U. Colo., 1958; cert. in diamonds Gemological Inst. Am., 1970; m. Joy Hill, Dec. 29, 1974; 1 son, Brian Eugene; 1 dau. (by previous marriage), Julie. Tchr. pub. schs., Monte Vista, Colo., 1958-59, Denver-Adams County, 1960-63, Denver-Ashcraft Piano Studios, 1960-69; engaged in piano sales and service, Denver, 1963-69, Dallas, 1969-72; owner, pres. Ronald Ashcraft Assos., Inc., Dallas, 1973—. Served with U.S. Army, 1959. Mem. Diamond Dealers Club N.Y., Jewelers Bd. Trade (asso.). Clubs: Park Cities Rotary, Brookhaven Country, University, Dallas Knife and Fork. Office: 5710 LBJ Freeway Suite 230 Dallas TX 75240

ASHE, CAROLYN HENLEY, business educator, management consultant; b. Belton, Tex., Feb. 13, 1947; d. Adolphus Isaac and Alva Evelyn (Weaver) Henley; m. Roy L. Ashe, Feb. 11, 1975; 1 dau., Alva Madelaine. B.B.A., N. Tex. State U., 1969, M.B.A., 1971; Ed.D., U. Houston, 1983. Teaching fellow Sch. Bus. Adminstrn., N. Tex. State U., Denton, 1969-70; with bookkeeping dept. So. Union Gas Co., Galveston, Tex., 1970-72; fin. analyst comml. loan dept. U.S. Nat. Bank, Galveston, 1972-74; instr., mgmt. coordinator Galveston Coll., 1974-76; prof., coordinator mgmt. devel. dept. San Jacinto Coll., Pasadena, Tex., 1976-83; prof. Coll. Bus., Prairie View A&M U., Prairie View, Tex., 1983-84; cons. in field; pres. Ashe and Assocs. Mem. Nat. Assn. Mgmt. Educators, Am. Soc. Tng. and Devel., Nat. Bus. Edn. Assn., Assn. Info. Systems Profls., Tex. Bus. Edn. Assn., Delta Pi Epsilon, Delta Sigma Theta. Republican. Methodist. Office: Ashe & Assos 4151 Southwest Freeway Houston TX 77027

ASHINGTON-PICKETT, MICHAEL DEREK, construction company executive; b. London, Oct. 11, 1931; s. Edward Robert and Mary Dorothy (Trewhella) Ashington-Pickett; came to U.S., 1965, naturalized, 1971; Civil and Structural Engring. degrees London U., 1956; m. Sandra Helen Smart, Nov. 20, 1976; children—Mary Hillary, Michael Derek II, Claire Amanda. Constrn. mgr. various firms in Eng., 1956-63; pres. So. Precast Holdings, London, Eng., 1963-65, Ashington-Pickett Constrn. Co., Inc., Orlando, Fla., 1965-83; pres. Ashington-Pickett, Selmer Devel. Co. Inc.; sr. v.p. Selmer Corp. Country Side Properties, Inc., Orlando, 1972-78; chmn. Orlando Constrn. and Licensing Bd., 1974-82, bd. dirs., 1978-80; lectr. for Brit. Council, 1963-65; chmn. Mid-Pac, 1982. Served as officer Brit. Army, 1950-52; Korea. Recipient Disting. Service award Orange County Bicentennial Commn., 1976; cert. of merit Comité National des Vins de France; named Builder of Yr., 1981, companion Order of Beaujolais. Mem. home builders assns. Am. (dir.), Mid-Fla. (pres., dir.; Disting. Service award 1973), Fla. (life dir., Builder of Yr. award 1981), Orlando C. of C. (dir., v.p.), Orlando Jaycees, Chaine de Rotisseurs, Order de Mondial. Presbyterian. Club: Citrus. Lodge: Kiwanis. Kiwanis, Citrus. Home: 1307 Montcalm St Orlando FL 32806 Office: PO Box 19044 Orlando FL 32814

ASHLER, PHILIP FREDERIC, international trade consultant; b. N.Y.C., Oct. 15, 1914; s. Philip and Charlotte (Barth) A.; m. Jane Porter, Mar. 4, 1942 (dec. 1968); children—Philip Frederic, Robert Porter, Richard Harrison; m. Elise Barrett Duvall, June 21, 1969; stepchildren—Richard Edward Duvall, Jeffries Harding Duvall.B.B.A. cum laude, St. John's Coll., 1935; M.B.A., Harvard U., 1937; postgrad. Indsl. Coll. Armed Forces, 1956; Sc.D. (hon.), Fla. Inst. Tech., 1969; LL.D. (hon.), U. West Fla., 1969. Enlisted U.S. Marine Corps, 1932; commd. ensign U.S. Navy, 1938, advanced through grades to rear adm., 1959; dir. Office of Small Bus., Dept. Def., Washington, 1948-51; mem. joint staff Joint Chiefs of Staff, Washington, 1957-59; ret., 1959; dir. devel. Pensacola Jr. Coll., 1960-68; vice chancellor adminstrn. State Univ. System Fla., Tallahassee, 1968-70, exec. vice chancellor, 1970-75; treas. State of Fla., 1975-76, also ins. commr., state fire marshal; advisor for econ. devel. to gov. of Fla., 1977; sec. of commerce, 1977-79; pres. Philip F. Ashler & Assocs., Tallahassee, internat. trade and devel., 1979—; chmn. bd. Mfrs. Internat. Trade Corp., Tampa, The Cambridge Group Internat., Tallahassee; dir. U.S. Fidelity and Guaranty Co., Balt., Fidelity & Guaranty Life Ins. Co., Balt., Lewis State Bank, Tallahassee; rep. NATO Sci. Session, W.Ger., 1973; mem. Inter-Am. Congress on Psychology, Bogota, Colombia, 1974; guest lectr. U. Belgrade (Yugoslavia), 1973; mem. Dist. Export Council, U.S. Dept. Commerce, 1978—; mem. services policy adv. com. U.S. Trade Rep. Office, Exec. Office of Pres., 1980-85. Mem. Fla. Edn. Council, 1967-68, Fla. Council of 100, 1976—; commr. from Fla., Edn. Commn. of States, 1967-68; mem. legis. adv. council So. Regional Edn. Bd., 1966-68; chmn. Fla. Civil Def. Adv. Council, 1966-69; mem. State Bd. Ind. Colls. and Univs. Fla.; mem. Fla. State Officers Compensation Commn., 1980—; mem. Select Council on Post-High Sch. Edn., 1967-68; chmn. bd. Fla. Council Internat. Devel.; mem. Fla. Ho. of Reps., 1963-68; treas. Internat. Cardiology Found., 1973-78; founding chmn. bd. Tallahassee Symphony Orch., 1980-81; mem. Fla. Econ. Devel. Adv. Council, 1979—; bd. dirs. Fla. Heart Assn., 1963—, chmn., 1969-71; chmn. Fla. Med. Liability Ins. Commn., 1975-76; bd. dirs. Am. Heart Assn., 1971-76, LeMoyne Art Found., Tallahassee, Tallahassee Meml. Hosp., Internat. Cardiology Fedn., Geneva, 1974-78. Decorated Bronze Star with Combat V; recipient Kiwanis Internat. Disting. Service award, 1965, Am. Heart Assn. Disting. Service award, 1965, 71, Disting. Achievement medal Am. Heart Assn., 1975, St. Petersburg Times Legis. award, 1967. Mem. Nat. Assn. Ins. Commrs. (vice chmn. exec. com. 1976, chmn. com. valuation bonds and other securities 1975-76), Fla. C. of C. (chmn. internat. bus. com., dir.), Internat. C. of C. (U.S. council internat. bus. 1979—), S.E. U.S.-Japan Assn. (chmn.), Kappa Delta Pi. Democrat. Episcopalian (lay reader). Mason (32 deg., Shriner), Rotarian. Clubs: Governor's, Fla. Econs., Capital City Tiger Bay (bd. chmn.) (Tallahassee); Curzon House (London). Office: 2115 E Randolph Circle Tallahassee FL 32312 also 11 Riad Sultan Kasbah Tangier Morocco

ASHLEY, DAVID JOHN, author; b. London, Dec. 12, 1950; came to U.S., 1972; s. John Macpherson Ashley and Jill Elizabeth (Bayliss) Clarke; m. Barbara Lynne Renchkovsky, Aug. 12, 1978. B.A. with honors, U. York, Eng., 1972; Ph.D., U. Pitts., 1978. Asst. prof. sociology U. Louisville, 1979-85. Author: (with others) Sociological Theory, 1985. Contbr. articles to profl. jours. Mem. Am. Sociol. Assn. Home: 1009 Falconwood Louisville KY 40222

ASHLOCK, JAMES ALLEN, minister; b. Flint, Mich., Aug. 10, 1955; s. James Andrew and Lowanda June (Proctor) A.; m. Mary Beth Wood, Aug. 20, 1977; children—Sarah Elizabeth, Jason Ashlock. B.S., Freed-Hardeman Coll. Ordained minister Church of Christ, 1977. Minister, Church of Christ, Bay, Ark., 1977—; tchr. Ch. of Christ Coll., Paragould, Arks., 1984. Author publs. in field. Named Outstanding Young Men Am., 1981, 83; recipient Cert. Appreciation Freed-Hardeman Coll., 1977, Outstanding Service award, 1977; Appreciation award Soc. Disting. High Sch. Students, 1984. Mem. Crowleys Ridge Acad. (plaque 1983), Am. Philatelic Soc. Republican. Avocations: stamp collecting; hiking; swimming; fishing. Home: 222 Central Box 159 Bay AR 72411

ASHMORE, HENRY L(UDLOW), educational association executive; b. Tallahassee, 1920; m. Clarice Langston, 1946; children—Randan L., Jerri. B.A.E. with honors, U. Fla., 1942, M.A.E., 1948, D.Ed., 1950. Prin., St. Marks Sch., 1946-57; coordinator student teaching Ga. So. Coll., 1950-54; pres. Pensacola Jr. Coll. (Fla.), 1954-64; pres. Armstrong State Coll., Savannah, Ga., 1964-82; assoc. exec. dir. commn. on colls. So. Assn. Colls. and Schs., Atlanta, 1982-84, interim exec. dir. commn. on colls., 1985—. Trustee Candler Hosp., Savannah; bd. dirs. Am. Cancer Soc.; mem. Ga. Heart Assn., advisor, bd. dirs. Better Bus. Bur.; mem. Nat. council Boy Scouts Am. Mem. Am. Assn. State Colls. and Univs. (chmn. nat. com. on cultural programs), Ga. Assn. Colls. and Univs. (pres.), So. Assn. Colls. and Schs. (former chmn. commn. on admission to membership, commn. on colls., former mem. exec. council commn. on colls.). Baptist. Author: Hypocrisy in Academia?, contbr. articles to profl. jours. and newspapers. Home: PO Box 52066 Atlanta GA 30355

ASHTON, JAMES PRESTON, educational administrator, clergyman; b. Alexandria, Va., Feb. 4, 1942; s. James Ashton; m. Doris P. Ashton; children—Gisele Diggs, Kimberly. B.S. in Math., St. Augustine's Coll., 1965; M.Ed., George Mason U., 1978; postgrad. Cath. U. Am., 1980, Va. Union U., 1983—. Ordained to ministry Baptist Ch. Tchr. math. Alexandria pub. schs., 1966-72; rep./cons. D.C. Health Pubs., Lexington, Mass., 1973-78; tchr. math. Richmond pub. schs., Va., 1978-80; supr. Va. Dept. Edn., Richmond, 1981—; cons. in field. Contbr. articles to profl. jours. Recipient Project of Month award Alexandria Jaycees, 1968. Mem. NAACP, Phi Delta Kappa. Democrat. Baptist. Avocations: carpentry; jogging; drama; literature. Home: 7911 Frye Rd Alexandria VA 22309 Office: Va Dept Edn PO Box 60 Richmond VA 23216-2060

ASHTON, SAMUEL COLLIER, research company executive; b. Hohenwald, Tenn., Sept. 26, 1922; s. Arch Will and Lula Earl (Collier) A.; m. Rita Jane Anderson, Oct. 18, 1947; 1 son, Craig Collier. B.S.E.E., U.S. Naval Acad., 1945. Head, Cryogenic Lab., Texaco Co., Long Beach, Calif., 1947-48; asst. dir. fin., bus. and facilities Stanford Research Inst., 1948-59; corp. v.p. Research Triangle Inst., Research Triangle Park, N.C., 1959—. Served with USN, 1942-47. Mem. Am. Preparedness Assn. Republican. Episcopalian. Club: Hope Valley Country (Durham, N.C.).

ASHTON, THOMAS WALSH, investment banker; b. Rochester, N.Y., May 11, 1929; s. Charles Edward and Marie Margaret (Walsh) A.; B.S., U.S. Mil. Acad., 1952; M.B.A., Harvard U., 1957; m. Frances E. Hickey, May 16, 1953; children—Lucy M., Mary B. Ashton Anders, Monica H., William T.; m. 2d, Mary K. Joy, Dec. 20, 1978. Assoc. corp. fin. Eastman Dillon Union Securities, N.Y.C., 1957-61, gen. partner, 1967-69; asst. v.p. Harris Upham & Co., N.Y.C., 1961-67; v.p. duPont Glore Forgan, Inc., N.Y.C., 1971-73; sr. v.p. ABD Securities Corp., N.Y.C., 1973-75; fin. cons. Am. Cancer Soc. of N.Y.C., East West Group Inc.; pres. Peninsular Investments, Treasure Island, Fla., 1977—; cons. Dept. Commerce, 1971. Chmn. parent's council Smith Coll., 1974-76. Served with AUS, 1946-48, 52-55. Mem. Soc. Harvard Engrs. and Scientists (gov. 1974-75), West Point Soc. N.Y. (dir. 1971-75). Republican. Clubs: Army and Navy (Washington); Seminole Lake Country (Seminole, Fla.). Office: 150 153d Ave Madeira Beach FL 33708

ASHWORTH, WILLIS LOUIS, stockbroker, mutual fund manager; b. Birmingham, Ala., Aug. 30, 1939; s. Willis Louis and Glenda (Collins) A.; m. Margaret Rodgers As (div.); children—Philip Rodgers, Margaret Collins. B.S., Am. U., 1966. Stockbroker, mut. fund mgr. Paine, Webber, McLean, Va., 1980—. Mem. Internat. Game Fishing Assn., Mercedes Benz Motor Club. Avocations: deep sea fishing; travel; hunting. Home: 11820 Stuart Mill Rd Oakton VA 22124 Office: Paine Webber Jackson Curtis Greensboro Dr McLean VA 22102

ASHY, STEVE M., building materials company executive; b. Lafayette, La., Nov. 23, 1953; s. Doug E. and Claire (Moss) A.; m. Debra Ann Billeaud, July 1, 1977; children—Lauren, Steven. B.S. in B.A., U. Southwestern La., 1975. Notary pub., 1976. With Doug Ashy Bldg. Materials, Inc., Lafayette, 1971—, exec. v.p., 1980—. Bd. dirs. Better Bus. Bur. Mem. Acadian Home Builders, La. Bldg. Materials Dealers (dir.). Office: 4950 Johnston St Lafayette LA 70508

ASKEW, MARY FRANCES, educator; b. Eufaula, Ala., Oct. 31, 1921; d. Emmett Tyler and Frances Perry (Warr) Brown; B.S., Troy State U., 1962; M.S., Auburn U., 1964, postgrad., 1972-73; postgrad. Ga. State U., 1979; m. William Henry Askew, III, 1945; 1 child, William Henry Askew, IV. Tchr. Ft. Rucker (Ala.) Elem. Sch., 1963-69; tchr. Ft. Benning (Ga.) Dependents' Schs., 1969-72, reading specialist, 1979—. Night Circle pres. Women of the Ch., First Presbyn. Ch., Phenix City, Ala.; den mother Cub Scouts, Eufala and Ft. Benning; active Girl Scouts, 4 yrs.; 1st v.p. Ft. Benning PTA, 1977-78; past pres. Barbour County Dist. PTA, Eufala PTA. Mem. Ala. Hist. Assn., Ga. Hist. Soc., NEA, Ga. Assn. Educators, Benning Edn. Assn. (pres. 1976-77, 83-84), Internat. Reading Assn. (pres. Muscogee County Reading Council 1978-79), Ga. Reading Assn., Ala. Reading Assn., East Ala. Geneal. Soc., Old Muscogee County Geneal. Soc., Russell County Hist. Commn., Eufaula Heritage Assn., Phenix City Preservation Soc., Chattahoochee Valley Assn. Children with Learning Disabilities (dir.), Ga. Assn. Children with Learning Disabilities, Nat. Assn. Children with Learning Disabilities, Nat. Registrar Children of Confederacy (chpt. organizing pres.), L.S. Raiford Soc. (organizer, pres. 1973-79), Children Am. Revolution, Daus. Am. Colonists, DAR, Children of Confederacy (Ala. dir.), UDC (pres. Russell County 1971-81, Jefferson Davis Gold medal for dedicated service 1980), Eufaula Bus. and Profl. Women's Assn. (pres.), Friends Confederate Naval Mus., Kappa Delta Pi. Presbyterian. Editor profl. studies. Home: 212 N Randolph Ave Eufaula AL 36027 Office: 300 First Division Rd Fort Benning GA 31905

ASPIRAS, VICTORINA ORILLE, dentist, educator; b. Philippines, Dec. 23, 1939; came to U.S., 1965; d. Modesto M. and Segunda (Quero) Orille; m. Dionisio F. Aspiras, July 29, 1964; children—Dionisio O., Catherine O. B.S. U. of East, Manila, 1958, D.M.D., 1963; M.S. in Edn., Nova U., Ft. Lauderdale, Fla., 1979. Practice gen. dentistry, Philippines, 1963-65; prof., dir. dental assisting program So. Coll., Orlando, Fla., 1976—; cons. Assn. Ind. Colls. and Schs., Washington, 1984-85; mem. adv. com. Dental Hygiene Program, Valencia Community Coll., 1978-85. Sec. Fil-Am. Club, Orlando, 1984, v.p. internat. affairs, 1985. Named Outstanding Faculty Mem., So. Coll., 1978. Mem. ADA, Orange County Dental Soc., Nova U. Alumni Assn. Roman Catholic. Club: Bally Health and Racquet (Orlando). Home: 5541 Bellewood St Orlando FL 32806 Office: Southern Coll 5600 Lake Underhill Dr Orlando FL 32807

ASTENEH-ASL, ABOLHASSAN, civil engineering educator; b. Tabriz, Iran, Jan. 7, 1948; came to U.S., 1978; s. Ebrahim and Sahineh Asteneh-Asl; m. Mehry Adrangi, Oct. 11, 1973; children—Kaveh, Cyrus. M.S. in Civil Engring., Tehran Poly., Iran, 1969; M.S. in Structures, U. Mich., 1979, Ph.D., 1982. Structural engr. Nava Co., Iran, 1973-76; ptnr. Dillon Constrn. Co., Iran, 1976-80; research asst. U. Mich., Ann Arbor, 1979-82; asst. prof. U. Okla., Norman, 1982—; structural cons. Oklahoma City, 1982—. Contbr. articles to profl. jours. U. Mich. fellow, 1980. Mem. ASCE, Earthquake Engring. Research Inst., Am. Inst. Steel Constrn., Am. Soc. Engring. Edn., Nat. Civil Engring. Honor Soc. Office: U Okla 202 W Boyd Room 334 Norman OK 73019

ASTIGARRAGA, JOSE IGNACIO, lawyer; b. Habana, Cuba, July 20, 1953; came to U.S., 1960, naturalized 1974; s. Jose Agustin and Carolina (Vila) A.; m. Nancy Louise Upchurch, Aug. 11, 1979. A.A., Miami Dade Community Coll., 1973; B.B.A. summa cum laude, U. Miami, 1975; J.D. magna cum laude, 1978. Bar: Fla. 1978, U.S. Dist. Ct. (so. dist.) Fla. 1978, U.S. Ct. Appeals (5th and 11th cir.) 1981. Chief bailiff Dade County Juvenile and Family Ct., Miami, Fla., 1972-74; law clk.-bailiff 11th Judicial Cir., Miami, 1974-77; with firm Steel, Hector & Davis, Miami, 1978—, ptnr., 1984—; adminstrv. hearing officer Dade County Schs. Bd., Miami, 1982—; adj. faculty U. Miami Sch. Law, Coral Gables, Fla., 1980-81. Contbr. article to Dade County Young Lawyers Manual, 1980. Chmn. Biotech Task Force Greater Miami C. of C., 1984—; mem. health care task force Beacon Council of Dade County, 1984, bus. task force Am. Heart Assn., Miami, 1984. Hispanic affairs com. C. of C. of Greater Miami, 1984; dir. Leadership Miami, 1984; bd. dirs. Miami Children's Hosp., 1985—, Bealon Council Dade County, Inc.; legal counsel Cuban Mus. Arts and Culture, 1985—. Named Harvey T. Reid Scholar U. Miami Sch. Law, 1975-78, Leonard T. Abess Scholar, U. Miami, 1974-75. Mem. U. Miami Sch. Law Alumni Assn. (bd. dirs. 1981—), Fla. Bar Assn. (sec. civil procedure rules com. 1979-84), ABA (mem. uniform comml. code com., 1984—, litigation sect. 1984—), Dade County Bar Assn., Cuban-Am. Bar Assn., Greater Miami C. of C. (bd. govs.). Office: Steel Hector & Davis 4000 Southeast Fin Ctr Miami FL 33131-2398

ASTLER, VERNON BENSON, physician; b. Wyoming, Ohio, Sept. 5, 1925; s. Vernon Wolfert and Blanche (Benson) A.; student Miami U., 1943-45; M.D., Temple U., 1949; M.S., U. Mich., 1953; m. Louise Menge, Aug. 9, 1949 (div.); children—Kim Louise, Kristy Lee, Douglas Vernon; m. Diane Rosacker, Dec. 31, 1969 (div.). Diplomate Am. Bd. Surgery. Intern, Univ. Hosp., Ann Arbor, Mich., 1949-50, resident, 1950-57; practice medicine specializing in surgery, Boynton Beach, Fla., 1958—; mem. staff Bethesda Hosp., Boca Raton Hosp., Doctors Hosp., Lake Worth, Fla., Delray Beach Community Hosp.; past mem. Fla. Bd. Med. Examiners, pres., 1971-73; mem. Fla. Council of 100. Served with M.C., AUS, 1953-55. Fellow ACS, Southeastern Surg. Congress; mem. Am. Hosp. Assn. (com. on physicians 1974-76), Fla. Med. Assn. (gov. 1971-84, pres. 1975-76), Frederick A. Coller Surg. Soc., AMA, Delray Beach C. of C., Sigma Nu, Phi Chi. Clubs: Little (Gulfstream, Fla.); Sapphire Valley Country (N.C.); Quail Ridge Tennis (Boynton Beach, Fla.); Pine Tree Country, Masons, Shrine, Kiwanis. Home: 4253 Gleneagles Boynton Beach FL 33436 Office: Med Arts Center 2800 S Seacrest Blvd Boynton Beach FL 33435

ATCHESON, MARION MACK, synthetic fuels and engineering consultant; b. Graham, Tex., July 28, 1920; s. Frank and Bess (Barton) A.; m. Marianne McLane, Dec. 13, 1946; children—Thomas Gavin (dec.), James Barton (dec.). B.S. in Chem. Engring., Tex. Tech. Coll., 1942. Registered profl. engr. Engr. research devel. dept. Elliott Co., Jeannette, Pa., 1946-49; process engr. El Paso Natural Gas Co. (Tex.), 1949-53, chief design engr., 1953-55, asst. v.p., 1974-80, also exec. v.p. affiliates El Paso, El Paso Coal Co., Fuel Conversion Co., Mesa Resource Co., 1976-80; dir. El Paso Coal Co., Mesa Resource Co., 1976-80; chief engr. subs. El Paso Products Co., 1956-59, asst. operating mgr., 1959-60, mgr. engring. and petrochem. devel., 1961-64, exec. engr., 1964-65, v.p. engring. constrn., Odessa, Tex., 1965-72, dir., 1966-72, dir. engring. constrn. Synfuels div., 1972-74, v.p. affiliate Fuel Conversion Co., 1972-76, dir., 1972-80; pres. Atcheson & Assocs., Inc., El Paso, 1980—; pres. Engrs. of El Paso, Inc., 1983—. Served with C.E., U.S. Army, 1942-46. Named Disting. Engr., Tex. Tech. U., 1975. Mem. Am. Inst. Chem. Engrs. Home and office: 3000 Stone Edge El Paso TX 79904

ATCHLEY, BEN, state senator; b. Knoxville, Tenn., June 30, 1930; married; 2 children. Grad. U. Tenn. Mem. Tenn. Gen. Assembly, Nashville, Senate Republican Leader; rep. NEL Equity Services Corp. Mem. Mt. Olive Exec. Com.; Tenn. Senate v. chmn. for Am. Legis. Exchange Council; elder, bd. dirs. Graystone Presbyn. Ch. Served with USNR, 1948-58. Mem. New Eng. Life Leader's Assn., Nat. Assn. Life Underwriters (pres. Knoxville chpt. 1971-72), Am. Coll. Life Underwriters (C.L.U.), Nat. Assn. Charter Life Underwriters (v.p. Knoxville chpt. 1972-73), Knoxville Gen. Agts. and Mgrs. Assn. (pres. 1966-67). Club: Optimist of South Knoxville (pres. 1966; Disting. Pres. award Optimist Internat. 1967; trustee scholarship fund 1972-74), SAR. Lodges: Masons, Shriners. Office: Tenn Senate Room 313 War Meml Bldg Nashville TN 37219*

ATCHLEY, BILL LEE, university president; b. Cape Girardeau, Mo., Feb. 16, 1932; s. William Cecil and Mary (Bicket) A.; B.S. in Civil Engring., U. Mo.-Rolla, 1957, M.S., 1959; Ph.D., Tex. A&M U., 1965; m. Pat Limbaugh, Aug. 1954; 3 children. From asst. prof. to prof. engring. mechanics U. Mo.-Rolla, 1957-75; prof., dean Coll. Engring., W.Va. U., Morgantown, 1975-79; pres. Clemson (S.C.) U., 1979—; cons. Systems Cons. Inc.; chmn. Gov. W.Va. Commn. Energy, Economy and Environment, 1975; sci. and tech. adviser to Senate and Ho. of Dels. W.Va., 1976; mem. W.Va. Bd. Registration Profl. Engrs.; sci. and tech. adviser to Gov. Mo., 1972-75, to Gov. W.Va., 1975-79; W.Va. gov.'s rep. to U.S. Govs. Commn. on Energy, 1979; energy advisor to Gov. S.C., 1980; mem. Gov.'s Council on Alcohol Fuels; mem. fed. fossil energy adv. com. Dept. Energy; mem. sports com. USIA; bd. dirs. Kelwynn; trustee S.C. Research Authority. Served with AUS, 1952-54. Ford Found. fellow; recipient Disting. Service award Rolla Bicentennial Com., 1975; Outstanding Civilian Service medal Dept. Army, 1984. Registered profl. engr., Mo., W.Va. Mem. Nat. Govs. Conf., Am. Soc. Engring. Edn., ASCE, Nat. Soc. Profl. Engrs., Assn. Colls. and Univs., Am. Inst. for Pub. Service, Nat. Soc. Profl. Engrs., S.C. Energy Forum, Newcomen Soc. N.Am., Future Farmers Am. (hon.), Sigma Nu, Phi Kappa Phi (hon.), Beta Sigma Gamma (hon.), Gamma Sigma Delta (hon.). Methodist. Author papers in field. Office: Office of Pres Clemson U PO Box 992 Clemson SC 29631

ATKINS, C(ARL) CLYDE, judge; b. Washington, Nov. 23, 1914; s. C. C. and Marguerite (Criste) A.; m. Esther Castillo, Jan. 18, 1937; children—Julie A. Landrigan, Carla A. Schulte (dec.), Carl Clyde. Student, U. Miami, Fla., 1931-32; LL.B., U. Fla., 1936, J.D., 1967; LL.D., Barry Coll., Miami Shores, 1966, Biscayne Coll., Miami, 1970. Bar: Fla. bar 1936. Practice in, Stuart, 1936-41, Miami, 1941-66; partner firm Walton, Lantaff, Schroeder, Atkins, Carson & Wahl (and predecessors), 1941-66; U.S. dist. judge So. dist. Fla., 1966—, chief judge, 1977-82, sr. judge, 1983—; founder-trustee Lawyers Title Guaranty Fund, 1948—, treas., 1963-66; mem. Nat. Commn. for Rev. of Anti-trust Laws and Procedures, 1978-79. Contbr. articles to profl. jours. Pres. St. Augustine Diocesan Union Holy Name Societies, 1950-51, Miami Archdiocesan Council Cath. Men, 1959-70. Recipient Outstanding Cath. award NCCJ, 1959. Jud. fellow Am. Coll. Trial Lawyers; mem. ABA (ho. of dels. 1960-66, 79-80), Dade County Bar Assn. (pres. 1953-54), Fla. Bar (bd. govs. 1954-59, pres. 1960-61), Nat. Conf. Fed. Trial Judges (chmn. exec. com. 1975-77, del. Jud. Adminstrn. Council 1979-82), Tau Kappa Alpha, Phi Kappa Tau, Phi Alpha Delta. Clubs: Kiwanis (past dir. Miami), Miami, Coral Gables Country. Office: PO Box 013009 Miami FL 33101

ATKINS, CHARLES EDWARD, JR., orthodontist; b. Birmingham, Ala., July 9, 1941; s. Charles Edward and Louise Swann (Smith) A.; m. Elizabeth Drew Crouch, May 26, 1971; children—Susanne, Trey, Lindsey. Student U. Ala., 1959-63; D.M.D., U. Ky., 1967, cert., 1979. Family dentist in pvt. practice, Columbus, Miss., 1970-77, orthodontist, 1979—. Served as lt. comdr. USN, 1967-69. Mem. ADA, Miss. Dental Assn., So. Soc. Orthodontists, Am. Assn. Orthodontists, N.E. Miss. Dental Soc., Republican. Episcopalian. Club: Exchange (pres. 1985—) (Columbus). Lodges: Masons, Shriners, Sertoma (pres. 1976). Avocations: whitewater canoeing and rafting. Office: 300 Hospital Dr Columbus MS 39701

ATKINS, CHARLES SHANE, safety and training coordinator, city official; b. Gaffney, S.C., June 29, 1945; s. Max Laban and Margaret (Rowe) A.; m. Jacquelyn Marrow Petty, Nov. 22, 1975; children—Christy Michelle Green, Lindsay Blake. Student U. S.C., 1964, Lee Coll., 1966. Buyer and scheduler Eastex Packaging, Charlotte, N.C., 1967-73; mgr. Little Rock Enterprises, Charlotte, 1973-75; driver Thurston Motor Line, Charlotte, 1975-78; technician Emergency Med. Services, Spartanburg, S.C., 1978-79; safety and tng. coordinator City of Spartanburg, 1979—; state instr. emergency med. services S.C. Dept. Health and Environ. Control, Columbia, 1979—; cons. Safety Manual for Municipalities, 1985. State Constable S.C., Columbia, 1983; bd. dirs. Spartanburg, chpt. ARC, 1981-82; chmn. adv. com. Spartanburg Tech. Coll., 1985-86; bd. dirs. S.C. Occupational Safety Council, 1986—. Served with U.S. N.G., 1969-74. Recipient Occupational Advancement award Spartanburg Tech. Coll., 1983; named Outstanding Mgmt. Services Employee, City of Spartanburg, 1984. Mem. Am. Soc. Safety Engrs. (pres. Piedmont chpt. 1985-86), S.C. C. of C. (com. mem. 1981—), Nat. Safety Council, Spartanburg Bass Anglers Club (charter pres. 1980), Bass Anglers Sportsman Soc. Democrat. Baptist. Lodge: Masons. Avocations: fishing; golf; snow skiing. Home: 300 Seven Oaks Ln Spartanburg SC 29301 Office: City of Spartanburg City Hall 145 Broad St Spartanburg SC 29301

ATKINS, RODNEY LAMAR, librarian; b. East St. Louis, Ill., Mar. 15, 1955; s. Jessie and Ocie (Anthony) L.; m. Yvonne Turner, Oct. 20, 1979; children—Paul J., Paula J. B.A. in History, No. Ill. U., 1977; M.S. in L.S., Atlanta U., 1978. Reference, circulation librarian Wiley Coll., Marshall, Tex., 1978-81, library dir., 1981; circulation media services librarian Tyler Pub. Library (Tex.), 1981—, dir. Black History Month Programming, 1983—; asst. pastor Houston Temple Ch. of God in Christ, Tyler, 1983; project chmn. Black History Month Com., Tyler, 1983-84. Recipient Minister of Year award Tyler Rose Bud Civitan Club, 1983; grantee Tex. Com. for Humanities, 1983; named Outstanding Citizen of Marshall, Alpha Phi Alpha, 1980; appreciation award Negro Bus. and Profl. Women's Club, Tyler, 1984. Mem. ALA, Tex. Library Assn., Phi Beta Sigma. Democrat. Office: Tyler Pub Library 201 South College St Tyler TX 75702

ATKINS, SAMUEL JAMES, III, banker; b. Wichita Falls, Tex., 1944. B.S., U. Okla., 1968; M.B.A., Harvard U., 1970. Petroleum engr. Shell Oil Co., 1965-68; with Republicbank Dallas NA, 1970—, loan rep. and banking officer petroleum and minerals div., 1971-72, asst. v.p. petroleum and minerals div., 1972-74, v.p., 1974-75, v.p., group mgr., 1975-78, sr. v.p. petroleum and minerals div., 1977, sr. v.p., gen. mgr., 1978-80, sr. v.p., div. mgr. region corp. banking, 1980-81, exec. v.p. petroleum minerals dept., 1981—, exec. dir. RepublicBank Energy Banking Group, 1982—; dir. Republic Venture Group. Office: Republicbank Dallas NA 310 N Ervay St Dallas TX 75201

ATKINSON, BILL, designer; b. Utica, N.Y., Feb. 22, 1916; s. J. Harry and Elizabeth Anne (Woolfenden) A.; m. Sylvia Small, 1940; children—Lynn, Gail; m. Jeanne Marie Pagnucco, 1969; stepchildren—Robert, Rachael. B. Arch.-/Landscape Arch., Cornell U., 1940; postgrad., New Sch. Social Research, 1965, Sch. Visual Arts, N.Y.C., 1966. Spl. asst. to Eero Saarinen, Bloomfield Hills, Mich.; research engr. Chrysler Corp., Detroit, 1942-46; pres., designer Bill Atkinson Ltd., N.Y.C., 1974—, Atkinson Internat., Ltd., 1983—; dir. Glen Mfg. Co., Milw.; cons. to bd. trustees R.I. Sch. Design. Set designer, Metro-Goldwyn Meyer, 1938-39; draftsman/designer, Architects Edward Stone, Phillip Goodwin, N.Y.C.; designer, renderer, Architects McKim, Meade & White, N.Y.C.; pvt. practice architecture, design, Bloomfield Hills, 1946-49; fashion designer, 1950-70; designer, V.P. Glen of Michigan, N.Y.C.; photographer: book series Time-Life, N.Y.C., 1971; designer career apparel, Amtrak, N.Y.C., St. Louis, Washington, 1972; originator, designer: Hilton Hotel's Rainbow Concept, N.Y.C., St. Louis, Beverly Hills, Calif., 1973. Co-winner Rome Collaborative in Architecture, 1937; recipient numerous awards including Designer of Yr. award Sports Illustrated, Corduroy Council awards, Made in U.S.A. award for Am. Sportswear, 1965 awards Am. Retailers, Coty award for Am. fashion, 1978, Am. Design award Leather Industries Am., 1979; Flying Colors Fashion award, 1980; winner Silver Medal del Amo Internationale Invitational Competition for Sculpture and Fashion for Yr. 2000. Mem. Council Am. Fashion Designers, Cornell U. Alumni Assn., Sch. Visual Arts Alumni Assn., New Sch. Social Scis. Alumni Assn.

ATKINSON, BRUCE ERROL, physician; b. Greenwood, Miss., Dec. 21, 1946; s. Errol Ward and Mabel (Blackwell) A.; B.S., U. Miss., 1968, M.D. magna cum laude, 1971; m. Sandra Faye Parkinson, Dec. 27, 1969; 1 son, George Michael. Intern, Parkland Meml. Hosp., Dallas, 1971-72; resident in internal medicine Univ. Hosp., Jackson, Miss., 1972-75, chief resident, 1974-75; practice medicine specializing in internal medicine, Amory, Miss., 1975—, Tupelo, Miss., 1979-80. Bd. dirs. Miss. Found. for Med. Care, Inc., 1983—; adult leader Boy Scouts Am., 1982-84. Diplomate Am. Bd. Internal Medicine. Chmn. deacons 1st Baptist Ch., Amory, 1977-78. Fellow A.C.P.; mem. Miss. Med. Assn. (jud. council 1977-83), Miss. Soc. Internal Medicine (pres. 1979-83), Amory-North Monroe County C. of C. (dir. 1983—). Club: Rotary. Home: Route 2 Box 343-A Amory MS 38821 Office: PO Box 119 Amory MS 38821

ATKINSON, GARY RAY, educational administrator, educator; b. Roanoke, Va., Dec. 1, 1945; s. William Ray and Gertrude Safronia (Brewer) A.; m. Brenda Faye Barksdale, Aug. 23, 1968; children—Hunter Barksdale, Ashley Elizabeth. B.A., U. Va., Charlottesville, 1968, M.Ed., 1972, Ed. D., 1976. French tchr. Roanoke pub. schs., 1968-74; field rep. Am. Inst. Fgn. Study, Roanoke, 1974-75; asst. regional dir. U. Va.-Roanoke, 1975-78, regional dir., 1978—; cons. sch. systems and instns. higher learning; cons. tng. programs, govt., bus., industry. Bd. dirs. U. Va. Sch. Edn. Found., 1976-79, 81-84, exec. com. 1979, 81; bd. dirs. Roanoke Valley div. Am. Heart Assn., 1981-84, Coll. Health Scis. Roanoke Valley, 1982-84, Western Region Consortium for Continuing Higher Edn., 1978—. Recipient Dean's award Sch. Edn., U. Va., 1975; Service award Am. Heart Assn., 1982, 83. Mem. Nat. Univ. Continuing Edn. Assn., Lychnos Soc., Phi Delta Kappa, Pi Delta Phi, Phi Sigma Kappa. Democrat. Methodist. Office: 2103 Electric Rd SW Roanoke VA 24018

ATKINSON, HAROLD WITHERSPOON, utilities consultant, real estate broker; b. Lake City, S.C., June 12, 1914; s. Leland G. and Kathleen (Dunlap) A.; B.S. in Elec. Engring., Duke, 1934; M.S. in Engring., Harvard U., 1935; m. Pickett Rancke, Oct. 6, 1946; children—Henry Leland, Harold Witherspoon. Various positions in sales, engring. Cambridge Electric Light Co. (Mass.), 1935-39, 46-73, asst. mgr. power sales dept., 1946-49, gen. mgr., 1957-73, dir., 1959-84, exec. v.p., 1972-73; mgr. Pee Dee Electric Membership Corp., Wadesboro, N.C., 1939-46; gen. mgr. Cambridge Steam Corp., 1951-73, v.p., 1959-73, dir. 1955-84. Chmn., Cambridge Traffic Bd., 1962-73; pres. Cambridge Center Adult Edn., 1962-64; v.p. Cambridge Mental Health Assn.; chmn. allocations com. Greater Boston United Community Services, 1971-72; chmn. Cambridge Commn. Services, 1955-56; adv. bd. Cambridge Council Boy Scouts Am.; mem. corp., chmn. camping com. Cambridge YMCA, 1964-71; chmn. Cambridge chpt. ARC, 1969-71; trustee of trust funds Town of Harrisville, N.H., 1978-83; treas. North Myrtle Beach Citizens Assn., 1982-84. Served from pvt. to capt. AUS, 1942-45. Registered profl. engr., Mass. Mem. IEEE (sr.), Mass. Soc. Profl. Engrs., Elec. Inst. (pres. 1971), Harvard Engring. Soc., Cambridge C. of C. (pres. 1957-58). Newcomen Soc. N.Am., Phi Beta Kappa, Tau Beta Pi, Pi Mu Epsilon. Clubs: Cambridge Boat (treas. 1962-65), Cambridge (pres. 1972-73); Carolina Golf; Bay Tree Golf; Plantation; Civitan (pres. Wadesboro 1940-41); Rotary (v.p.). Home: 705 Holloway Circle N North Myrtle Beach SC 29582 Office: PO Box 533 North Myrtle Beach SC 29597

ATKINSON, HARRISON B., trading company executive; b. Farmville, Va., July 22, 1914; m. Shirley B. Atkinson, Mar. 23, 1985; 1 child, Kim Hodges. Pres., H.B. Atkinson Co., Vienna, Va., 1947—, Vienna Properties, 1970—; chmn. bd. dirs. Atlantic Pacific Trading Inc., Vienna, 1983—; dir. Atkinson Tile Co., Vienna. Served with USN, 1939-47. Mem. Christian Fellowship Ch. Club: Washington Golf and Country (Arlington, Va.). Address: 2122 Galloping Way Vienna VA 22180

ATKINSON, PAUL PHILLIP, art dealer; b. Chgo., Nov. 28, 1924; s. Roy Richard and Violet Henrietta (Robellaz) A.; m. Nancy James, May 13, 1950; 1 child, Katherine Jane. Student Northwestern U., 1948, U. Chgo., 1948-50; UN exchange student, France, 1948. Travel writer Chgo. Tribune, 1948-49; market researcher Chgo. Am., 1950-53; art dealer James-Atkinson Ltd., Houston, 1953—; U.S. rep. English painting Newman & Cooling Ltd., Eng., 1970—. Contbr. articles to newspapers. Served with U.S. Army, 1943-46, ETO. Decorated Croix de Guerre avec Palme, Silver Battle Star. Republican. Presbyterian. Club: Winter (Lake Forest, Ill.). Avocations: painting; drawing. Home: 1601 S Shepherd #105 Houston TX 77109

ATKINSON, REGINA ELIZABETH, medical social worker; b. New Haven, May 13, 1952; d. Samuel and Virginia Louise Griffin; B.A., U. Conn., Storrs, 1974; M.S.W., Atlanta U., 1978. Social work intern Atlanta Residential Manpower Center, 1976-77, Grady Meml. Hosp., Atlanta, 1977-78; med. social worker, hosp. coordinator USPHS, Atlanta, Palm Beach County (Fla.) Health Dept., West Palm Beach, 1978-81; dir. social services Glades Gen. Hosp., Belle Glade, Fla., 1981—; instr. Palm Beach Jr. Coll.; participant various work shops, task forces. Vice pres. Community Action Council South Bay, 1978-79. Whitney Young fellow, 1977; USPHS scholar, 1977. Mem. Nat. Assn. Black Social Workers, Nat. Assn. Social Workers, Soc. for Hosp. Social Work Dirs., Fla. Public Health Assn., Fla. Assn. Health and Social Services, Glades Area Assn. for Retarded Citizens. Home: 525 1/2 SW 10th St Belle Glade FL 33430 Office: 1201 S Main St Belle Glade FL 33430

ATKINSON, ROBERT P., bishop, Episcopal Church; b. Washington, Nov. 16, 1927; s. William Henry and Anna A.; m. Rosemary Clemence, Aug. 8, 1953. B.A., U. Va., 1950; B.D., Va. Theol. Sem., 1953, D.D., 1973. Rector, Ch. of Fairmont, 1955-58, W. Va. Bd. Examining Chaplains, 1958-62; chmn. BEC, 1958-64; rector Calvary of Memphis, 1964-73; bishop, co-adjutar, W. Va., 1973-76; bishop of W. Va., Charleston, 1976—. Address: Episcopal Ch 1608 Virginia St E Charleston WV 25311*

ATKINSON, WILLIAM JAMES, JR., internist; b. Mobile, Ala., July 4, 1917; s. William J. and Gertrude (Smith) A.; m. Glenda E. Street, Oct. 29, 1949; children—Glenda Street, Regina Creswell, William James. B.A., Amherst Coll., 1939; M.D., U. Pa., 1943; M.S. in Internal Medicine, St. Louis U., 1949. Intern, Phila. Gen. Hosp., 1943-44; resident in medicine St. Louis City Hosp., 1946-48; resident in cardiology St. Louis U., 1948-49; practice medicine specializing in internal medicine and cardiology, Mobile, Ala., 1949—; mem. staff U. South Ala. Med. Ctr. Hosp., Mobile Infirmary, Providence Hosp.; chmn. bd. Diagnostic and Med. Clinic P.A., 1973—; clin. assoc. prof. medicine U. Ala., 1964—; clin. assoc. prof. medicine U. South Ala., 1973—. Served as capt. M.C., AUS, 1944-46. Decorated Bronze Star. Diplomate Am. Bd. Internat. Medicine, Am. Bd. Cardiovascular Disease. Fellow ACP, Am. Coll. Cardiology, Am. Coll. Chest Physicians; mem. Am. Heart Assn., Ala. Heart Assn. (chmn. bd. 1956), AMA, Am. Soc. Clin. Pharmacology and Therapeutics, Mobile C. of C. Republican. Episcopalian. Clubs: Rotary, Mobile Country, Mobile Yacht. Home: 3965 Byronell Ct Mobile AL 36609 Office: 1217 Government St Mobile AL 36604

ATTAL, GENE (FRED EUGENE), hosp. exec.; b. Austin, Tex., Oct. 6, 1947; s. Sam Arthur and Olga (Johns) A.; B.J. with spl. honors (NDEA fellow in langs. 1968-69), U. Tex., 1970; M.S. (Internat. fellow 1972), Columbia U., 1972; m. Marsha Ablah, July 26, 1970; children—Christopher, Allison, Anne. Public relations exec. Westinghouse Electric Corp., 1972-75; dir. public relations and devel. Seton Med. Center, Austin, 1975—; exec. dir. The Seton Fund; mem. faculty U. Tex. Recipient Telstar Excellence in Communication award, annually 1978-81. Mem. Am. Soc. Hosp. Public Relations (regional dir.), Tex. Soc. Hosp. Public Relations (pres. 1981). Greek Orthodox. Club: Lost Creek Country. Home: 1201 Constant Springs Dr Austin TX 78746 Office: 1201 W 38th St Austin TX 78705

ATTANASI, EMIL DONALD, economist, planning commissioner; b. Newark, July 5, 1947; s. Dominick Joseph and Katherine (Cavitch) A.; m. Diana Elizabeth Frank, Aug. 29, 1969; children—Jennifer, Katherine, Marie. B.A. in Math. magna cum laude, Evangel Coll., 1969; M.A. in Econs., U. Mo., 1971, Ph.D., 1972. Economist, U.S. Geol. Survey, Reston, Va., 1972—; mem. faculty George Mason U., Fairfax, Va., 1979-80; commr. Vienna Town Planning Commn., 1983—; lectr. U.S. Congl. Fellows, Washington, 1982. Contbr. articles to profl. jours.; co-editor spl. jour. issues of procs. of Mineral Economics Symposium, 1980-83. Trustee Fairfax Assembly of God, 1980—; trustee, bd. dirs. Key to Life Assembly of God, McLean, Va., 1977-78. U. Mo. fellow, 1969-72. Mem. So. Econ. Assn. (jour. referee), Am. Econ. Assn., Am. Inst. Mining Engrs., Omicron Delta Epsilon (treas. 1971-72). Office: US Geol Survey Nat Ctr MS 920 Reston VA 22092

ATTAWAY, GEORGE C., tax consultant; b. San Angelo, Tex., Nov. 26, 1935; s. Gambrell Cranfil and Mary Opal (Gossett) A.; m. Virginia Ann Eaves, Sept. 10, 1957; children—Kerri Lin Attaway Allahverdi, Vicki Ann, Dana Kaye Attaway Martin. Assoc. B.A., Angelo State U., 1954; B.S., Hardin-Simmons U., 1958; LL.B., LaSalle Sch. Law, 1969. Cons. engr. Pritchard & Abbott, Ft. Worth, 1957-63; cons., ptnr. Mizell, Carruth & Bradford, Dallas, 1963-74; pres., chmn. bd. dirs. Ad Valorem Tax Cons., Inc., Dallas, Lewisville, Tex., 1974—; co-owner Attaway-Bush Enterprises, Justin, Tex., 1982-83; ptnr. ATC Investment Co., Lewisville, Tex., 1981—; co-owner Precious Cargo Pub. Co., Denton, Tex., 1983—, Attaway Enterprises, Denton, 1982—; advisor Tex. Senate Com. Urban Edn., Austin, 1970-71. Author: Cutter's Magic, 1984. Pres., Argyle Sch. Bd. Argyle, Tex., 1969-71; asst. leader Girl Scouts Am., Denton County, Tex., 1970-73; deacon So. Bapt. Assn., Dallas, 1967. Served with U.S. Army ROTC, 1956-58. Mem. Am. Quarter Horse Assn., Tex. Quarter Horse Assn., Nat. Cutting Horse Assn., Petroleum Accts. Soc. N.Am., Tex. Mid-Continent Oil and Gas Assn., Tex. Assn. Assessing Orgns., Kans. Producers Assn. Baptist. Home: 916 Chasewood St Denton TX 76205 Office: Ad Valorem Tax Cons Inc 560 W Main St Suite 202 Lewisville TX 75067

ATTAWAY, WILLIAM HAROLD, hospital administrator; b. Shreveport, La., Jan. 23, 1932; s. Alonzo Clifton and Opal (Anderson) A.; m. Melba R. Wild, Oct. 14, 1962; children—Raymond Bret, Aaron Craig, William Todd. B.S., La. Tech. U., 1955; M.A., Central Mich. U., 1977. Lab. dir. Matagorda Gen. Hosp., Bay City, Tex., 1959-74, asst. adminstr., 1974-79, adminstr., 1979—. Author: A Guide to Diagnostic Microbiology. Served with U.S. Army, 1955-57. Mem. Am. Hosp. Assn., Tex. Hosp. Assn., Am. Soc. Clin. Pathologists (cert. med. technologist), SAR, Sons of Republic of Tex., Sons of Confederate Vets. Republican. Methodist. Avocations: tennis; equestrics; skiing; swimming; jogging. Home: 1 Pheasant Run Bay City TX 77414 Office: Matagorda Gen Hosp 1115 Ave G Bay City TX 77414

ATTURA, GEORGE MARCELLO, engineering company executive; b. Rome, Feb. 9, 1923; came to U.S., 1928; s. Joseph John and Lucy (Guidoni) A.; m. Irma Carmela Nobilio, May 24, 1947; children—Clare, Barbara, Joseph, Joan. B.E.E., Manhattan Coll., 1943; postgrad. Harvard U., 1943, MIT, 1944; M.E.E., NYU, 1950. Engr., Fairchild Camera & Instrument Co., 1947-48; dir. research Servomechanisms Inc., 1948-49; founder, gen. mgr., chief engr. Indsl. Control Co., Rockledge, Fla., 1949—; prof. CCNY, 1955-58. Served to lt. (j.g.), USNR, 1943-46. Mem. Inst. Naval Engrs., Sigma Xi. Roman Catholic. Author: Magnetic Amplifier Engineering, 1959; patentee in field. Home: 846 Malibu Ln Indialantic FL 32903 Office: Indsl Control Co 3100 Pineda Ave Rockledge FL 32955

ATWATER, BARBARA BRENT, lawyer, private investigator, real estate broker; b. Greensboro, N.C., Sept. 2, 1949; d. Robert Nathaniel and Julia Brent (Byrum) Atwater-Teague. B.A. in Art, B.A. in Creative Writing, Hollins Coll., 1969; B.S. in Art Edn., U. N.C., 1968; J.D., Wake Forest U., 1983. Profl. fashion model for Chanel, Yves St. Laurent, Ralph Lauren, Halston, Bill Blass, N.Y.C. and Atlanta; pres., owner Realty Services Renovation and Constrn. Co., Atlanta, 1972-78; owner, pres. Lit'l House Farms, Inc., Southern Pines, N.C., 1969—; real estate broker, N.C., 1972—; real estate sales agt., Ga., 1972—; dir. pub. relations Solar Energy Industries, Washington, 1975; cons., market analyst Johnstown Properties, Atlanta, 1978-79; pvt. practice law (domestic relations litigation). Winston Salem, N.C., 1983—; Dir. pub. relations Atlanta Humane Soc., 1978-79, Med. Aux., 1979-81; bicentennial dir. City of Burlington (N.C.), 1972-76. Named Woman of Yr., Atlanta Task Force on Youth, Atlanta, 1972; Outstanding Woman of N.C., 1974. Mem. ABA, Acad. Trial Lawyers, Women Bus. Owners of Southeast (founding bd. dirs. 1979), N.C. Thorobred Breeders Assn., Am. Horse Show Assn., N.C. Hunter-Jumper Assn. Clubs: Ocean Reef (Key Largo, Fla.); Moore County Hounds (Southern Pines, N.C.); Capital City (Raleigh, N.C.). Carolina Sailing. Painting accepted for permanent collection N.C. Mus. Home: Lit'L House Farms 808 W Willowbrook Dr Burlington NC 27215

AU, CHI-KWAN EDMUND, theoretical physics educator, researcher; b. Macao, Portuguese Colony, Jan. 21, 1946; came to U.S., 1968; s. Po-Chun and Yuet-Ho (Wong) A.; m. Bernadette Bit-Mi Tsui, July 31, 1970; children—Irene, Banjamin. B.Sc. with 1st class honors, Hong Kong U., 1968; M.A., Columbia U., 1970, Ph.D., 1972. Research assoc. U. Ill., Urbana, 1972-74, Yale U., 1974-75; asst. prof. physics/astronomy U. S.C., Columbia, 1975-79, assoc. prof., 1979-84, prof., 1985—; vis. asst. prof. physics Columbia U., summers 1976-78; mem. Inst. for Theoretical Physics, Santa Barbara, Calif., 1981; hon. lectr. Hong Kong U., 1981-82. Recipient Smithsonian Summer Visitor's award Harvard-Smithsonian Obs., 1982, 83, 84, award in sci. and engring. research U. So. Calif. Edn. Found., 1985. Mem. Am. Phys. Soc. Contbr. articles to physics jours. Office: Dept Physics U SC Columbia SC 29208

AUBURN, MARK STUART, university educator, administrator; b. Cin., Dec. 9, 1945; s. Norman Paul and Kathleen (Montgomery) A.; m. Sandra Korman, Jan. 25, 1969; children—David Andrew, Benjamin Max Joseph. B.S. in Math. magna cum laude, U. Akron, 1967, B.A. in English magna cum laude, 1967; A.M. in English, U. Chgo., 1968, Ph.D. in English with honors, 1971. Asst. prof., then assoc. prof. English, Ohio State U., Columbus, 1971-83, assoc. vice provost and sec. Coll. Arts and Scis., 1980-83; prof. English, dean Coll. Arts and Scis., Ark. State U., Jonesboro, 1983-85; v.p. for planning and mgmt. support U. Ark. System 1985—; adj. prof. English, U. Ark., Fayetteville, 1986—; cons.-evaluator North Central Assn., 1985—; cons. Nat. Assessment Ednl. Progress, 1985, Pa. State U., 1985 Winthrop Rockefeller Found. and Ark. Dept. Edn., 1984, U. Maine, Farmington, 1985, U. Conn., 1983, div. research programs NEH, 1979-82, 84, U. Tex., Dallas, 1979, Ohio U., Athens, 1979. Author: Sheridan's Comedies: Their Contexts and Achievements, 1977; co-author: Drama through Performance, 1977; also numerous revs. and essays in scholarly publs. Editor: Marriage a la Mode, 1981. Mem. Ohio Humanities Council, 1981-83; coll. coordinator United Way, Ark. State U., 1984; host Great Decisions series Sta. KASU-TV, Jonesboro, Ark., 1984; trustee Focus, Inc., Jonesboro, 1984—, v.p., 1985—; trustee Ark. Endowment for Humanities, 1983—, v.p., 1986—. Recipient grants and fellowships Am. Philos. Soc., 1972, Ohio State U., 1972, 73, 75, 76, 78, 80, NEH, 1984. Mem. Coll. English Assn. Ohio (exec. com.), AAUP, Am. Soc. for 18th Century Studies, Am. Soc. for Theatre Research, Midwest Modern Lang. Assn., MLA, S.W. MLA, Phi Delta Kappa, Phi Kappa Phi. Unitarian-Universalist. Lodge: Rotary (chmn. fgn. group study exchange com. Jonesboro 1983-85). Home: 1012 Shamrock Dr Little Rock AR 72207 Office: Univ of Ark 1201 Mc Almont St Little Rock AR 72203

AUCHINCLOSS, CLAIROISE ANN, electronics company executive; b. West Plains, Mo., June 1, 1929; d. William Ernest and Vivian (Butler) Willard; m. Angus John Auchincloss, Aug. 1, 1952 (div. 1973); children—John Angus, Debra Ann, William Bruce, Jamie Scott. B.A., Calif. State Coll., 1970; M.Ed., U. Ariz., 1972. Dir., Area Agy. on Aging, Jasper, Tex., 1974-75; planning cons./planner Equal Opportunity Commn. of S.E. Tex., Port Arthur, 1975-76; regional planner Tex. Dept. Human Resources, Beaumont, 1976-79; coordinator Community Care for the Elderly, United Way of Dade, Miami, Fla., 1979-80; dir. pub. services Link to Life Industries, Inc., Ft. Lauderdale, Fla., 1980-81, v.p. community relations, 1981—; acting v.p. CAAPS Enterprises, Inc., Miramar, Fla., 1982—; cons. Mem. Nat. Assn. Female Execs. Democrat.

AUFDEMORTE, THOMAS BRUCE, oral pathologist, educator; b. Borger, Tex., July 25, 1950; s. Bruce Hugo and Mary Nell (May) A.; m. Haroldene Hamm, Nov. 24, 1971; children—Christy Marie, Lori Ann. B.S., W. Tex. State U., 1972; D.D.S., U. Tex. Health Sci. Ctr. San Antonio, 1977. Cert. Nat. Bd. Dental Examiners; lic. Tex. Bd. Dental Examiners; diplomate Am. Bd. Oral Pathology. Fellow in oral pathology U. Tex. Health Sci. Ctr. San Antonio, 1977-78, resident gen. pathology, 1978-80, resident oral pathology, 1978-81, asst. instr., 1977-80, instr., 1980-81, asst. prof., 1981-84, assoc. prof. pathology and surgery, 1984—; mem. med.-dental staff Med. Ctr. Hosp., San Antonio, 1977—, Audie Murphy VA Hosp., San Antonio, 1977—. Contbr. articles to profl. jours. Inventor appliance for treatment erosive mucous membrane lesions. Cons. Am. Cancer Soc., 1980—, Mended Hearts Assn., 1980, SW Research Inst., 1981; alumni vol., recruiting program W. Tex. State U., 1984. Fellow Am. Acad. Oral Pathology (mem. fin. com. 1984); mem. ADA, Am. Soc. Clin. Pathologists, Am. Assn. Dental Research, Internat. Assn. Oral Pathologists, Alpha Chi, Beta Beta Beta, Omicron Kappa Upsilon. Episcopalian. Avocations: photography, autosports. Office: U Tex Health Sci Ctr Dept Pathology 7703 Floyd Curl Dr San Antonio TX 78284

AUFDERHEIDE, KEITH HARLAN, chemistry educator; b. Dayton, Ohio, Feb. 11, 1954; s. Eugene John and Maxine Lamar (Heller) A.; m. Sandra Lynch; 1 child, Seth Joseph. B.S., Wilmington Coll., 1976; Ph.D., Miami U., Oxford, Ohio, 1980. Asst. prof. chemistry Oglethorpe U., Atlanta, 1980-84, assoc. prof., 1984—. NSF postdoctoral assoc., 1980. Mem. Am. Chem. Soc., Sigma Xi. Contbr. articles to profl. jours. Office: Oglethorpe U 4484 Peachtree Rd NE Atlanta GA 30319

AUKLAND, ELVA DAYTON, educator; b. Arlington, Va., Apr. 25, 1922; d. William A. and Helen Gertrude (Rollins) Dayton; A.B. cum laude, Wheaton Coll., 1943; M.S., U. Minn., 1946; m. Merrill Forrest Aukland, June 18, 1949; children—Bruce Michael, Duncan Dayton, Rebecca Elizabeth. Teaching asst. U. Minn., 1943-46; instr. botany Ohio Wesleyan U., Delaware, 1946-49; instr. zoology and microbiology Ohio U., Athens, 1949-50; bacteriologist E.R. Squibb & Sons, New Brunswick, N.J., 1951-53; tchr., chmn. sci. dept. Washington-Lee High Sch., Arlington, 1962-78; tchr. T. C. Williams High Sch., Alexandria, Va., 1978—, biology coordinator, 1980—; dir. Insect Zoo, Smithsonian Instn., 1972; dir. Va. Sci. Talent Search, 1980-82. Commr., Arlington Parks and Recreation Commn., 1971-77; mem. Environ. Improvement Commn., Arlington County, 1977-83; bd. dirs. No. Va. Conservation Council. Named Outstanding Tchr. Sci. and Math., Washington Acad. Sci., 1966. Mem. Am. Inst. Biol. Scis., Va. (Outstanding Tchr. 1975), Va. Jr. (dir.) acads. sci., Nat. Sci. Tchrs. Assn., NEA, So. Edn. Assn., Va. Edn. Assn. (task force on quality in edn. 1983—), Am. Chem. Soc., Wilderness Soc., Audubon Soc., Delta Kappa Gamma, Phi Theta Kappa. Editor sci. tchrs. sect. Va. Jour. Sci., 1971-76. Home: 2412 N Columbus St Arlington VA 22207

AULBACH, GEORGE LOUIS, property investment company executive; b. York, Pa., July 9, 1925; s. George A. and Mary N. (Goulden) A.; m. Gertrude Frisby, June 24, 1949; children—Jeanne, Cynthia, Patricia, Kathleen, Barbara. B.S. in Civil Engring., Villanova U., 1945. Registered profl. engr., Pa., Ga. Successively field engr., estimator, chief engr., project mgr., exec. v.p., pres. R.S. Noonan, Inc., York, Pa., 1946-63, pres., chief exec. officer R.S. Noonan, Inc. and Noonan Engring. Corp., York, 1963-72; pres. systems building div. McCrory-Sumwalt, Columbia, S.C., 1972-76; pres., chief exec. officer Laing Properties, Inc., Atlanta, 1976—; dir. Laing Properties plc, London. Pres. adminstrv. bd. Straight, Inc., Atlanta, nat. bd. dirs., St. Petersburg, Fla.; chmn. bd. dirs. PRIDE, Atlanta. Served to lt. (j.g.) USN, 1943-46. Mem. Nat. Soc. Profl. Engrs., Ga. Soc. Profl. Engrs. Roman Catholic. Clubs: Cherokee Town and Country, Commerce, World Trade, Georgian (all Atlanta). Office: 5780 Peachtree-Dunwoody Rd NE Suite 500 Atlanta GA 30342

AULICK, CHARLES MARK, computer science educator; b. Vero Beach, Fla., July 25, 1952; s. Donald Loraine and Frances Louise (Smith) A.; m. Nona Ann Sewell, Mar. 5, 1983; 1 stepdau., Amber Rae Bentrup. Student Fla. Technol. U., 1970-72; B.S. in Math., Stetson U., 1975; M.S. in Applied Math., Fla. State U., 1977; Ph.D. in Computer Sci., Duke U., 1981. Grad. asst. Fla. State U., 1976-77; instr. math. Stetson U., 1977-78; grad./research asst. Duke U., 1978-81; asst. prof. math. and computer sci. La. State U., Shreveport, 1981—. Order of AHEPA scholar, 1970; Fla. State U. fellow, 1975. Mem. Assn. for Computing Machinery, Soc. for Indsl. and Applied Math., IEEE Computer Soc., Omicron Delta Kappa. Republican. Baptist. Office: 8515 Youree Dr Shreveport LA 71115

AULSTON, MELVIN DOUGLAS, educator; b. Norfolk, Va., Feb. 14, 1940; s. Robert and Emily (Dickins) A.; 1 son, Melvin Douglas. B.S., Norfolk State U., 1964; M.A., U. Conn., 1970, Ph.D., 1972. Tchr., athletic dir. Robert L. Vann High Sch., Ahoskie, N.C., 1964-69; instr. U. Conn., Storrs, 1970-71; vice prin. Edwin Smith High Sch., Storrs, 1971-72; asst. dir. coop. extension service U. Conn., 1972-75; asst. registrar Norfolk (Va.) State U., 1975-79, asst. prof. sch. mgmt., 1979—. Mem. Chesapeake Civic League. Recipient Cert. of Appreciation, Norfolk State U., 1983. Mem. Nat. Assn. Secondary Sch. Prins., Council for Exceptional Children, C. of C., Phi Delta Kappa. Democrat. Baptist. Club: Princess Anne Keglers. Lodge: Elks. Home: 2001 Buckland Ave Chesapeake VA 23324 Office: 911 B St Chesapeake VA 23324

AULT, MARVIN BELL, association executive; b. Cin., Dec. 20, 1920; s. Charles Henry and Anna Mae (Bell) A.; m. Ruth Andrews, Sept. 25, 1943; 1 dau., Cynthia Brooke Ault Frakes. B.S. in Bus., Miami U., Oxford, Ohio, 1942; postgrad. Harvard U. Bus. Sch., 1944; M.A. in Indsl. Relations, U. Cin., 1978. Indsl. engr. Procter & Gamble Co., Cin., 1942, mfg. engr., 1945-50, 53-59, mfg. ops. mgr., 1959-74, mgr. indsl. relations, 1974-79; v.p. indsl. relations research Employers Assn. of Fla., Orlando, 1980—. Active Orange-Osceola County Pvt. Industry Council. Served to lt. U.S. Navy, 1942-45, 50-53. Named Buckeye of Yr., 1983. Mem. Am. Soc. Personnel Adminstrn., Personnel Assn. Central Fla., Indsl. Relations Research Assn. Presbyterian. Clubs: Sweetwater Country, Sabal Point Country (Orlando). Home: 166 Duncan Trail Longwood FL 32779 Office: Employers Assn Fla PO Box 68 Marjland FL

AUSTIN, ARTHUR CONVERSE, clergyman, missionary; b. N.Y.C., June 9, 1911; s. Alva Carlos and Ada Florence (Stevens) A.; m. Esther Naoma Plank, Jan. 1, 1933; children—Dorothy Orilla, Edith Nell, Ada Marie, Arthur Converse, Isabelle Joan. Student Moody Bible Inst., summer 1955, U. Md., 1963-64. Archtl. designer, Zephyrhills, Fla., 1945-53; ordained to ministry Apostolic Meth. Ch., Christian and Missionary Alliance; ofcl. worker, evangelist S.E. dist. Christian and Missionary Alliance, 1951-53; missionary Far East Broadcasting Co., Okinawa, Korea, 1957-72, Eastern U.S. rep., 1973-83, semi-ret., Zephyrhills, 1983—. Charter mem. Republican Presdl. Task Force. Designed and built radio stas. in Far East; designed rec. studio in Bolivia. Address: PO Box 576 Zephyrhills FL 34283

AUSTIN, CARL CHRYSLER, writer, clergyman; b. Riverton, N.J., Apr. 10, 1909; s. Carl C. and Edna Grey Howard (Schertzer) A.; m. Sarah Louise Lockard, Dec. 7, 1940 (dec. 1984). Student Princeton U., 1931. Sr. market research asst. Lever Bros. Co., Cambridge, Mass., 1938-43; dir. mktg. research Chicopee Mfg. Co., 1943-45, Nat. Biscuit Co., N.Y.C., 1945-48; pvt. cons. Mgmt. and Mktg. Counsel, Newark, 1948-65; condr. mgmt. seminars in U.S. and overseas under State Dept. and for Comité Internat. de l'Organization Scientifique de Geneva, 1955-62; owner Carl C. Austin Bible Found. Dir. CD Harding Twp.; minister Internat. Order St. Luke, 1975. Mem. Am. Mktg. Assn. (dir. N.Y.), Council Internat. Progress in Mgmt. (dir.), Nat. Indsl. Conf. Bd. Club: Morristown (N.J.) Men's. Author: The Christian Bible, 1981; The Keys of the Kingdom, 1983; The Broken Chalice, 1985. Home: 229-A Canal Ln Whispering Pines NC 28327

AUSTIN, CHARLES JOHN, university president; b. Cin., Nov. 28, 1934; s. Charles D. and Catherine (Shields) A.; B.S. summa cum laude, Xavier U., 1956; M.S., U. Colo., 1969; Ph.D., U. Cin., 1972; m. Mary Carroll Nurre, June 4, 1955; children—Mary Lynn, Charles, Christopher, Andrew, Carroll Jane. Systems analyst, programmer Proctor & Gamble Co., Cin., 1957-60; data processing mgr., mgmt. analyst HEW, Washington, 1960-66; computer center dir., prof. dept. preventive medicine U. Colo. Med. Ctr., 1967-69; prof. dept. hosp. adminstrn. Xavier U., Cin., 1970-72; study dir. Commn. on Edn. for Health Adminstrn., Washington, 1972-74; dean grad. studies Trinity U., San Antonio, 1974-78; v.p. Ga. So. Coll., Statesboro, 1978-82; pres. East Tex. State U., Commerce, 1982—. Served with U.S. Army, 1957-58. Fellow Am. Pub. Health Assn.; mem. Tex. Assn. Grad. Schs. (pres.), Conf. So. Grad. Schs. (dir.). Clubs: Rotary, Torch. Author: The Politics of National Health Insurance, 1975; Information Systems for Hospital Administration, 1979, 2d edit., 1983; contbr. articles to profl. jours. Home: PO Box 3001 ET Sta Commerce TX 75428 Office: East Tex State U Commerce TX 75428

AUSTIN, CONRAD NELSON, mathematics educator, counselor, consultant; b. Charlotte, N.C., July 22, 1938; s. Kenneth and Ollie Vee (Conrad) A.; m. Mary Alice Roberts, June 3, 1962; children—Michael Nelson, Kenneth William. A.A. in Elec. Engring., Mars Hill Jr. Coll., 1958; B.A. in Math., Edn., Pfeiffer Coll., 1962; M.Ed. in Counseling, U. N.C.-Greensboro, 1984. Nat. cert. counselor; cert. counselor and tchr., N.C. Math. tchr. N.C. Pub. Schs., Albermarle, 1962-65; student actuary Pilot Life Ins. Co., Greensboro, 1965-82; math. tchr. Greensboro Schs., 1982-83; counseling intern Guilford Tech. Community Coll., Jamestown, N.C., 1983-84, instr., counselor, 1984—; owner C. Austin For Counseling, Greensboro, 1984—. Author wellness course: Fitness Framers, 1984. Vice chmn. precinct Democratic Party, Greensboro, 1975-76; del. to county conv. Guilford County, 1970; cub and scoutmaster Gen. Green council Boy Scouts Am., Greensboro, 1969-84. Recipient Dist. Award of Merit Boy Scouts Am., 1975, Conservation award, 1971. Mem. Alliance for Invitational Edn., Am. Assn. of Counseling and Devel., So. Assn. Coll. Student Affairs. Methodist. Clubs: Greensboro Running (bd. dirs. 1976-78). Lodge: Optimist Internat. Avocations: music, crafts, exercise. Home: 3713 Parkwood Dr Greensboro NC 27403 Office: Guilford Tech Community Coll PO Box 309 Jamestown NC 27282

AUSTIN, DAN, dean; b. DeKalb County, Ala., Aug. 24, 1929; s. William J. and Edwina (Murphy) A.; m. Myra Sue Emmett, Jan. 14, 1951; 1 child, Deborah Elaine Austin Land. B.S. in Edn., Jacksonville U., 1964, M.S. in Edn., 1971. Tchr., Etowah County Bd. Edn., Gadsden, Ala., 1964-65, Anniston City Bd. Edn., Ala., 1965-66; faculty Ayers State Tech. Coll., Anniston, 1966-67, dean of instrn., 1967—. Served as sgt. U.S. Army, 1951-53. Mem. Dean's Assn. Ala. (pres. 1969-70, treas. 1972-74). Democrat. Baptist. Avocations: photography; camping; gardening. Home: 600 E 11th St Jacksonville AL 36265

AUSTIN, DAVID STEPHEN, coal contract specialist; b. Bristol, Tenn., Aug. 30, 1956; s. David Arthur and Zulla Eloise (Roop) A.; m. Susan Goble, July 21, 1979; 1 son, Aaron Stephen. B.S. in Bus. Adminstrn., U. Tenn., 1978; M.B.A. in Fin., Va. Poly. Inst. and State U., 1980. Mgmt. intern, asst. contract adminstr. Amax Coal Co., Indpls., 1980-81, contract adminstr., 1981-82, contract analyst spl. projects, 1982-83; sr. coal contract analyst System Fuels, Inc., New Orleans, 1983—. Designer computer model. Mem. Soc. Advancement of Mgmt., Exec. Forum, Gamma Beta, Phi Kappa Phi, Beta Gamma Sigma. Republican. Mem. Christian Ch. Club: Key (Bristol). Home: 6124 Palton St New Orleans LA 70113 Office: System Fuels Inc Box 61532 New Orleans LA 70161

AUSTIN, RHEA COCHRAN, librarian; b. Dallas, July 6, 1938; d. William Rhea and Dorothy (Shaw) Cochran; m. Richard Stephen Austin, Aug. 21, 1965; children—Patricia Louise. B.A., So. Meth. U., 1959, M.A., 1961; M.S., Cath. U. Am., 1982. Teaching asst. So. Meth. U., Dallas, 1959-60; tchr. Dallas Ind. Sch. Dist., 1960-61, Highland Park Ind. Sch. Dist., Dallas, 1961-64; asst. prof. Centenary Coll. La., Shreveport, 1964-65; adminstrv. aide Overseas Edn. Fund of LWV, Washington, 1969; librarian ISC Inc., Vienna, Va., 1984-85. Mem. home econs. adv. com. Arlington County Pub. Schs., 1983—. NDEA grantee, 1961, 62. Mem. ALA, Va. Library Assn., D.C. Library Assn., Phi Beta Kappa, Pi Delta Phi, Alpha Lambda Delta. Episcopalian. Home: 4848 27th St N Arlington VA 22207 Office: OAO Corp 7500 Greenway Center Greenbelt MD 20770

AUSTIN, ROBERT CRAFT, manufacturing company executive; b. Portland, Oreg., Mar. 21, 1933; s. Ernest Campbell Edward and Minnie Olive (Craft) A.; 1 son, Craig Randall. Patent draftsman firm Buckhorn, Blore, Klarquist & Sparkman, Portland, 1959-63; project engr. Cranston Machinery Co., Portland, 1963-65, C. Tennant Sons & Co. of N.Y., Warren, Ohio, 1965-67, EPI and Reid Strutt Co., Portland, 1967-68; service engr. Lamb Grays Harbor Co., Hoquiam, Wash., 1968-69; tech. dir. Weld-Loc Systems, Inc., Alliance, Ohio, 1969-83; pres. PFD, Inc., Jacksonville, Fla., 1983—. Chmn. bd. dirs. Berlin Reservoir (Ohio) Property Owners Assn., 1975-78. Served with U.S. Army, 1953-59. Mem. Soc. Plastics Engrs. (sr. mem.). Republican. Methodist. Designer prodn. systems for manufacture of extruded plastic strapping. Office: 2260 University Blvd N Apt 87B Jacksonville FL 32211

AUSTIN, ROBERT EUGENE, JR., lawyer; b. Jacksonville, Fla., Oct. 10, 1937; s. Robert Eugene and Leta Fitch A.; B.A., Davidson Coll., 1959; J.D., U. Fla., 1964; m. Jayne Talley, Dec. 28, 1964; children—Robert Eugene, George Harry Talley. Admitted to Fla. bar, 1965, U.S. Supreme Ct. bar, 1970, D.C. bar, 1983; legal asst. Fla. Ho. Reps., 1965; asso. firm Jones & Sims, Pensacola, Fla., 1965-66; partner firm Warren, Warren & Austin, Leesburg, Fla., 1966-68; partner firm McLin, Burnsed, Austin & Cyrus, Leesburg, 1968-77, Austin & Burleigh, Leesburg, 1977-81; individual practice law, Leesburg, 1981—; asst. state atty., 1972; mem. Jud. Nominating Commn. 5th Dist. Fla., 1979-83, mem. grievance com., 1981-83. Chmn. Lake dist. Central Fla., Boy Scouts Am.; asst. dean. Leesburg deanery Episcopal Diocese of Central Fla., 1981; trustee Fla. House, Washington, 1979—; U. Fla. Law Ctr. Served to capt. U.S. Army, 1959-62. Mem. Acad. Fla. Trial Lawyers, Am. Arbitration Assn., Am. Bar Assn., Am. Judicature Soc., Am. Law Inst., Assn. Trial Lawyers Am., Def. Research Inst., Fla. Bar (bd. govs.), Def. Research Inst., Nat. Inst. Trial Advocacy, Fed. Bar Assn., Lake County Bar Assn., Roscoe Pound Am. Trial Found., Kappa Alpha, Phi Delta Phi. Democrat. Clubs: Timuquana Country (Jacksonville); University (Orlando, Fla.). Home: 6300 N Silver Lake Dr Leesburg FL 32748 Office: 900 N 14th St PO Box 1930 Leesburg FL 32748

AUSTIN, ROBERT REID, sales executive; b. Altus, Okla., Aug. 25, 1953; s. William and Virginia (Reid) A.; m. Elizabeth Elaine Holland, Apr. 2, 1982. B.S. in Mktg., Okla. State U., 1976. Gen. mgr. Austins Men's Wear, Ponca City, Okla., 1976-77; dir. helicopter mktg. Nordam, Tulsa, 1978-80; pres. Helicomb Internat., Tulsa, 1981—. Southwestern Life Ins. scholar, 1975. Mem. Am. Helicopter Soc., Helicopter Assn. Internat., Soc. Advanced Material Process Engrs., Leadership Tulsa, Sigma Alpha Epsilon (pres. 1975). Clubs: Rotary, Jaycees. Home: 2128 E 187th St Tulsa OK 74104 Office: 6956 E 13th St Tulsa OK 74112

AUSTIN, SHIRLEY JEAN BOYKIN, management consultant; b. Troy, Ala., Feb. 8, 1949; d. Robert D. and Lousie (Grider) Boykin; B.A. in Indsl. Psychology, U. Central Fla., Orlando, 1976; M.S. in Mgmt., Rollins Coll., Winter Park, Fla., 1981; m. William T. Austin, Feb. 25, 1967; children—Stephen, Keith. Personnel asst. United Parcel Service, Atlanta, 1970; with mktg. dept. Am. Can Co., Cin., 1974; personal banker II, Sun 1st Nat. Bank, Orlando, 1977-79; asst. v.p., community reinvestment coordinator, loan officer Ameri-First Fed. Savs. and Loan Assn., Orlando, 1979-81; mgr. Orlando Minority Bus. Devel. Ctr.-Boone, Young & Assocs., 1981—; mem. adv. com. fin. program Valencia Community Coll. Pres. bd. dirs. Met. Orlando Urban League, 1981-83; bd. dirs. United Way Orange County, 1981, mem. budget rev. team, 1981-82; mem. Statewide Black Coalition, 1979-82; mem. community housing resource bd., fair housing div. HUD, 1980-81; regional sec. Nat. Urban League, 1981-83. Recipient Community Service award United Way Orange County, 1977-81, Citizen of Yr. award, 1981. Mem. Nat. Assn. Female Execs., Am. Bus. Women's Assn., NAACP, Orlando Area C. of C. Alpha Kappa Alpha. Office: 132 E Colonial Dr Suite 211 Orlando FL 32801

AUSTIN, STUART RICHARDSON, JR., nurse educator; b. Rahway, N.J., Nov. 7, 1941; s. Stuart R. and Elizabeth (Marshall) A.; m. Lois Ritter, Oct. 10, 1963; children—Gayle, Gretchen, Elise. R.N., Westchester Sch. Grasslands Hosp., Valhalla, N.Y., 1963; B.S. in Nursing, U. Buffalo, 1971, M.A. in Nursing Edn., 1972. R.N., N.Y. Staff nurse Grasslands Hosp., 1963-64, Phelps Meml. Hosp., North Tarrytown, N.Y., 1964, Avery Tng. Sch., Valhalla, 1964-65; head nurse Bronx State Hosp., (N.Y.), 1965; staff nurse Phelps Meml. Hosp., 1965-66; charge nurse Naval Hosp., Phila., 1966-68; instr. Naval Sch. Health Scis., San Diego, 1972-76; charge nurse U.S. Naval Hosp., Guam, Marianas Islands, 1979-78; area coordinator Naval Hosp., Great Lakes, Ill., 1978-81, coordinator nursing edn., Charleston, S.C., 1981-83, advisor operational readiness tng. com., 1982—, head edn. and tng., 1983—. Served to comdr. U.S. Navy. Vice pres. Cherry Hill Civic Assn., Goose Creek, S.C., 1982, pres. 1983. Decorated Nat. Def. Medal, 1966, Meritorious Unit Commendation, 1966-68. Mem. Am. Nurses Assn., Am. Heart Assn. Republican. Baptist. Office: PO Box 492 Naval Hosp Charleston SC 29408

AUSTIN, THOMAS NELSON, banker, lawyer; b. Athens, Ga., Oct. 7, 1945; s. William Delaus and Gladys (McDaniel) A.; m. Mary Ellen Holbrook, June 9, 1968; children—Ellen Sherman, Lydia Erwin. B.A. in Journalism cum laude, U. Ga., 1966, M.A. in Polit. Sci., 1968; J.D., 1975. Bar: Ga. 1975, U.S. Dist. Ct. (mid. dist.) Ga. 1975, U.S. Ct. Appeals (5th cir.) 1976, U.S. Ct. Appeals (11th cir.) 1981. Asst. city atty. Columbus Consol. Govt., Ga., 1976-82; asst. v.p. Columbus Bank & Trust, 1982—. Author: Perceptions of Reapportionment in the Georgia General Assembly, 1968. Fellow Phi Beta Kappa, Phi Kappa Phi; mem. Ga. Bar Assn. (young lawyers dist. rep. 1979-82), ABA. Republican. Presbyterian. Clubs: Columbus Country, Columbus Lawyers, Breakfast. Avocations: Victorian English literature and culture; modern southern writers; tennis; art; travel. Home: 1615 18th Ave Columbus GA 31901 Office: PO Box 1384 Columbus GA 31902

AUSTIN, TOM NOELL, tobacco company executive; b. Greeneville, Tenn., May 11, 1916; s. Clyde Bernard and Felice (Noell) A.; student UCLA, 1936; B.A., U. Tenn., 1937; m. Emily Donaldson, Nov. 19, 1938; children—Tom Noell, Merrily (Mrs. Charles L. Teasley, Jr.), Jay Donaldson, Richard Lyon. Shipping clk. Douglas Tobacco Co., 1937; with Austin Co., Inc., Greeneville, 1940—, v.p., 1944-48, pres., 1948-70, chmn. bd., 1970—; dir. Carolina & Northwestern Ry., Commerce Union Corp., Commerce Union, Greeneville; v.p. Unaka Co., Greeneville, Austin Carolina Co., Kinston, N.C., Mullins Leaf Tobacco Co. (S.C.); mem. Ky. and Tenn. Dist. Export Council. Trustee Tusculum Coll.; mem. devel. council U. Tenn. Mem. Young Pres. Orgn., Chief Execs. Forum, Phi Gamma Delta, Omicron Delta Kappa. Clubs: Elks, Exchange (Greeneville). Home: RFD 7 Greeneville TN 37743 Office: Austin Co Inc Hall and Willis St Greeneville TN 37743

AUTHEMENT, RAY, college president; b. Chauvin, La., Nov. 19, 1929; s. Elias Lawrence and Elphia (Duplantis) A.; m. Barbara B. Braud, June 1, 1950; children—Kathleen Elizabeth, Julie Ann. B.S., U. Southwestern La., 1950; M.S., La. State U., 1952; Ph.D., 1956. Instr. La. State U., Baton Rouge, 1952-56; asso. prof. McNeese State Coll., Lake Charles, La., 1956-57, U. Southwestern La., 1957-59, prof. math., from 1959, acad. v.p., 1966-73, pres., 1973—; vis. prof. U. N.C., Chapel Hill, 1962-63. Mem. Downtown Devel. Com. Lafayette, 1972—; mem. La. Bicentennial Commn., 1973, Lafayette Bicentennial Commn., 1973, Econ. Devel. Com., Lafayette, 1973, Sch. Bd. Fatima Parish, Lafayette, 1963-65; bd. dirs. United Way, Lafayette, 1973, U. Southwestern La. Found., 1967; trustee Lafayette Gen. Hosp., 1981—; mem. bd. advisers John Gray Inst., 1982—, St. Joseph Sem., 1967; bd. dirs., mem. council trustees Gulf South Research Inst.; mem. Commn. Colleges So. Assn. Colls., 1981-83. Mem. AASA, Lafayette C. of C. (dir. 1983—), Blue Key, Phi Kappa Phi, Kappa Mu Epsilon, Sigma Pi Sigma, Phi Kappa Theta. Roman Catholic. Club: Rotary. Home: PO Drawer 41008 USL Station Lafayette LA 70504 Office: U Southwestern La Office of Pres Lafayette LA 70504

AUTRY, BILLY EDWARD, building company executive; b. San Antonio, Tex., Nov. 29, 1956; s. Aubrey Jack and Doris Ann (Noyes) A.; m. Lynn Ann Knowles, Dec. 15, 1984. B.A., St. Mary's U., 1980, M.A. in Pub. Adminstrn., 1983. Cert. secondary tchr. in polit. sci. and English, Tex. Ins. specialist United Services Auto. Assn., San Antonio, 1974-77; adminstrv. asst. Louis P. White

Co., San Antonio, 1974-83; sales rep. Pella Products, San Antonio, 1983-85; sales mgr., co-founder J.J. Parkes Div. Anderson Windows, San Antonio, 1985, dir. 1985—; builder Woodlake Builders, San Antonio, 1985; sales cons. Hawthorne Mfg., San Antonio, 1984—. Author: de Tocqueville and Reagan: Similarities in Power, 1983. Mem. San Antonio Exec. Com., Texas, 1984-86; del. Tex. State Dem. Conv., 1984; precinct chmn. San Antonio Dem. party, 1984. Mem. Polit. Sci. Majors Assn. (founding mem. 1977, pub. relations dir.), Am. Polit. Sci. Assn., San Antonio House Builders Assn., Pi Sigma Alpha (v.p. 1979-80), Delta Epsilon Sigma, Lambda Chi Alpha. Avocations: photography; motorcycling. Office: 5920 Misty Glen San Antonio TX 78247

AUTRY, OTIS, educator; b. Beggs, Okla., June 22, 1923; s. James Paul and Laura B. (Jeffries) A.; B.S. magna cum laude, Langston U., 1950; M.S., Okla. State U., 1958; M.S., Purdue U., 1963; NSF fellow various univ. summer sessions, 1957-58, 58-65; m. Loeveta Cole, Aug. 28, 1948; children—Charron Autry Eckwood, Otis LeNere, Arven Damon. Machinist, Puget Sound Navy Yard, Bremerton, Wash., 1943; sci. tchr. Douglas High Sch., Bartlesville, Okla., 1950-56; tchr. biology, chemistry and advanced placement biology, chmn. sci. dept. Booker T. Washington High Sch., Tulsa, 1958—; del. NEA convs. Bd. mgmt. Hutcherson br. YMCA, 1976—; bd. dirs. Bd. Christian Edn. of Christ Temple C.M.E. Ch., 1967-80, pres. usher bd., 1979—. Served with AUS, 1943-46. Named Okla.'s Outstanding Biology Tchr., 1963; recipient Good Guy award Sta. KRMG, 1963, Okla. Industry award, 1963, Outstanding Service award Langston U., 1979; mem. Honor Roll of Month, Tulsa Tribune, 1963. Mem. Tulsa Sci. Tchrs. Assn. (past pres.), Tulsa Edn. Assn. (pres. elect 1968), Okla. Sci. Tchrs. Assn., Okla. Edn. Assn. (del. assembly), NEA, Tulsa Classroom Tchrs. Assn. (del.), Nat. Assn. Biology Tchrs., Tulsa City Dist. Tchrs. Assn. (past pres.), Nat. Sci. Tchrs. Assn., Phi Delta Kappa, Phi Sigma, Alpha Phi Alpha. Democrat. Methodist. Revision cons. biology textbooks. Home: 2116 N Boston Pl Tulsa OK 74106 Office: 1631 E Woodrow Pl Tulsa OK 74106

AUTRY, TED DUANE, petroleum executive; b. Heryetta, Okla., Oct. 31, 1940; s. Wilbur Garfield and Fannye Jeanette (Turnbull) A.; m. Judith Irene West, Jan. 26, 1963; children—Dawni J., Steven W., Julie K. B.S. in Petroleum Engring., Tulsa U., 1962, M.S. in Petroleum Engring., 1963; postgrad. La. State U., 1967-68; cert. U. Va. Exec. Program, 1982. Dist. engr. Amoco Prodn. Co., Lafayette, La., 1970-74, mgr. prodn. research, Tulsa, 1980—, regional engring. mgr. Amoco Internat. Oil Co., Chgo., 1974-78, mgr. engring., 1978-79, mgr. ops. coordination, 1979-80. Mem. Soc. Petroleum Engrs., Am. Petroleum Inst. Republican. Baptist. Address: 6310 S Richmond Tulsa OK 74136

AUVENSHINE, ANNA LEE BANKS, educator; b. Waco, Tex., Nov. 27, 1938; d. D.C. and Lois Elmore Banks; m. William Robert Auvenshine Dec. 21, 1963; children—Karen Lynn, William Lee. B.A., Baylor U., 1959, M.A., 1968, Ed.D., 1978; postgrad. Colo. State U., 1970-71, U. No. Colo., 1972. Tchr. math. and English, Lake Air Jr. High Sch., Waco Ind. Sch. Dist., 1959-63, Ranger (Tex.) Ind. Sch. Dist., Ranger High Sch., 1964, Canyon (Tex.) Ind. Sch. Dist., Canyon Jr. High Sch., 1964-66; instr. English, Baylor U., 1963; tchr. math. Canyon Ind. Sch. Dist., Canyon High Sch., 1968-70; tchr. math. and English, St. Vrain Sch. Dist., Erie (Colo.) High Sch., 1970-71; tchr. English and reading Thompson Sch. Dist., Loveland (Colo.) High Sch., 1971-72; instr., reading program dir. Ranger Jr. Coll., 1972-84, chmn. humanities div., 1978-82; tchr. math. Hillsboro High Sch., 1984-85, adminstr. Hillsboro Ind. Sch. Dist., 1985—. Trustee, Ranger (Tex.) Ind. Sch. Dist., 1979-84, v.p. bd. trustees, 1980-82, pres., 1982-84; community chmn., publicity chmn., troop leader Ranger Girl Scout Assn., 1974-77; sec. Eastland County Heart Assn., 1975-77; ch. sch. supt. First United Meth. Ch., Ranger, 1979-81, organist, 1974-77, mem. adminstrv. bd., 1979-84. Recipient cert. of appreciation Tex. Jr. Coll. Tchrs. Assn., 1979. Mem. Internat. Reading Assn., Assn. Supervision and Curriculum Devel., Tex. Assn. Sch. Adminstrs., Tex. Assn. for Gifted and Talented, Ranger PTA (parliamentarian 1978-79), Ranger Jr. Coll. Faculty Orgn. (pres. 1980-81), Baylor Alumni Assn. (life), Delta Kappa Gamma (pres. Gamma Delta chpt. 1986—, achievement award 1980). Methodist. Clubs: 1947 (pres. 1977-78) (Ranger); Baylor Bear (Waco). Home: 412 Corsicana St Hillsboro TX 76645 Office: Hillsboro Ind Sch Dist Box 459 Hillsboro TX 76645

AVANT, DAVID ALONZO, JR., realty company executive, photographer; b. Tallahassee, Apr. 11, 1919; s. David Alonzo and Fenton Garnett (Davis) A.; B.A., U. Fla., 1940; M.A., Cornell U., 1941; postgrad. Sch. Modern Photography, N.Y.C., 1946, Winona (Ind.) Sch. Photography, 1951; B.A., Fla. State U., 1958; m. Anne Leigh Wilder, Nov. 22, 1961 (div. Mar. 4, 1976); children—David Alonzo III, Eugenia Tatum Davis. Instr. art Fla. State U., Tallahassee, 1946-47; partner, owner, color portrait photographer L'Avant Studios, Tallahassee, 1947—; partner Avant Offices & Apts., Tallahassee, 1953—, Avant Tree Farms, Tallahassee, 1964—; dir. Indian Hills Estates, Tallahassee br. Fla. Fed. Savs. & Loan, 1961-81. Pres. Old St. Augustine (Fla.) Estates, 1968; chmn. Armed Forces Day Tallahassee, 1958; bd. dirs. Salvation Army; curator Joshua Davis House. Served to lt. col., USAAF, 1941-68. Named Am. Territorial Krewe Chief and Andrew Jackson XI, Springtime Tallahassee Festival, Tallahassee Sesquicentennial Com., 1974. Mem. U.S. Navy League (v.p. 1975-76), Tallahassee Jaycees (dir.), Profl. Photographers Assn. Am. (Master of Photographery cert. 1964), Am. Soc. Photographers, (dir.), Fla. Photographers' Assn. (dir.), Fla. Public Relations Assn. (dir., Gold award 1966), Tallahassee Art League (pres. 1954), New Eng. Hist. and Geneal. Soc. (trustee), Tallahassee Camellia Club (pres. 1953-54 68-69), Soc. Cincinnati of Md., Nat. Geneal. Soc. (regional rep. council), Tallahassee SAR (pres. 1957-58, 76-77, 77-78), Order of First Families Va., Order Founders and Patriots Am., Soc. Colonial Wars, Order Loyalists and Patriots, Soc. Descs. Colonial Clergy, Jamestowne Soc., Soc. War of 1812, S.R., Flagon and Trencher, Mil. Order World Wars, Mil. Order Fgn. Wars, Order Stars and Bars, Sons Confederate Vets., (comdr.), Huguenot Soc. S.C., St. Andrew's Soc. Tallahassee. (dir.). Democrat. Methodist (steward, trustee ch.). Rotarian. Author: (with others) More Money Selling Portraits, 1956; Tallahassee Sesquicentennial Pageant, 1974; Florida Pioneers and Their Alabama, Georgia, Carolina, Maryland and Virginia Ancestors, 1974. Some Southern Colonial Families, Vols. 1, 2. Contbr. articles to profl. photog. jours., genealogical jours. Pub. Illustrated Index, J. Randall Stanley's History of Gadsen County, 1948; Like a Straight Pine Tree, 1971; Professional Raccoon Trapping, 1979; The Davis-Wood Family of Gadsden County, Florida, 1979; editor: My Tallahassee, 1982. Home: 2312 Don Patricio Dr Tallahassee FL 32304 Office: PO Box 1711 Tallahassee FL 32302

AVANT, GAYLE, political science educator; b. Mercedes, Tex., Aug. 23, 1940; s. George Clarence and Winnie Lela (Bagley) A.; m. Patricia Kay Coalson, Sept. 1, 1970; children—Samantha, Celia. B.A., U. Tex., 1962; M.A., U. N.C., 1965, Ph.D., 1969. Devel. officer AID/State Dept., Washington, 1966-68; asst. prof. Miami U., Oxford, Ohio, 1968-70; assoc. prof. polit. sci. Baylor U., Waco, Tex., 1970—; cons. Learner Based Accountability System, 1984—, Region 12 Edn. Service Ctr. Author: (with Hugh Davis Jr.) The U.S. Constitution in School, 1984; En Extremis, 1976. Vice pres., bd. dirs. Tex. Cultural Alliance, Dallas, 1983—. Mem. Centex Pub. Adminstrn. Assn. (program chmn. 1982—), Southwest Social Sci. Assn., Tex. City Mgrs. Assn., Tex. Council for Social Studies, Am. Polit. Sci. Assn. Baptist. Lodge: Lions. Office: Polit Sci Dept Baylor U Waco TX 76798

AVELLA, WILLIAM R., real estate company executive; b. 1936. B.A., CUNY, 1961, M.B.A., 1965. With Black-Clawson, 1957-61, Internat. Bus. Machines Corps., 1961-69, Levitt & Sons., Inc., 1969-73; v.p. Larwin Group Inc., 1973-74; with Dell Labs., Inc., 1977-78; sr. v.p. Gen. Devel. Corp., Miami, 1974-77, pres., chief exec. officer, 1978, chmn. bd., dir., 1980—. Address: Gen Devel Corp 1111 S Bayshore Dr Miami FL 33131*

AVERBUCH, PHILIP FRED, physician; b. Bklyn., Nov. 28, 1941; s. Murray and Dorothy (Budelglass) A.; m. Judy Rosenberg, June 14, 1967; children—Amy Lynne, Robert Neil. Intern, Hosp. Joint Diseases, N.Y.C., 1967-68, resident in orthopedic surgery, 1968-72; practice medicine, specializing in orthopedic surgery, Tamarac, Fla., 1974—; staff Univ. Community Hosp., 1974—, chief surgery, 1975-77, asst. chief of staff, 1977-79, chief of staff, 1979-81, dir. phys. medicine, 1974—; chief of surgery Margate Gen. Hosp., 1976-78, dir. phys. medicine, 1974-79. Trustee Nora U., Univ. Community Hosp. Served to maj., MC, U.S. Army, 1972-74. Diplomate Am. Bd. Orthopedic Surgery. Fellow Am. Acad. Orthopedic Surgeons, ACS, Internat. Coll. Surgeons; mem. AMA, Eastern Orthopedic Soc., Fla. Med. Assn. Jewish. Office: 7301 N University Dr Tamarac FL 33321

AVERY, CHARLOTTE KAY GRUBB, nurse; b. West Helena, Ark., Jan. 28, 1955; d. Charles Glenn and Anna Gwen (Hill) Grubb; m. Robert David Avery, June 28, 1985; 1 stepchild, Kathryn Elizabeth. R.N., U. Ark.-Monticello, 1980. Home health nurse Ark. State Health Dept., Chicot County, 1977-78; staff nurse Demmott-Chicot Meml. Hosp., Ark., 1978-80; clin. nurse III St. Vincent's Infirmary, Little Rock, 1980—. Mem. Neurol. Nurses Assn. (pres. Ark. chpt. 1983-85). Baptist. Avocations: cross-stitch; sewing; painting; gardening; hunting; hiking; skiing. Home: Route 1 Box 117 Eudora AR 71640

AVERY, HENRY, management consultant; b. Boston, Oct. 6, 1919; s. Henry P.D. and Mary Ellen (Mitchell) A.; m. Mary Ruth Halverson, 1947; children—Cynthia, Deborah, Eric, Sarah. S.B., MIT, 1941. Bus. devel. mgr. Cabot Corp., Boston, 1946-57; gen. mgr. Pitts. Coke & Chem., 1957-60; exec. v.p., dir. Pitts. Chem. Co., 1960-66; group v.p. chem. div. U.S. Steel, Pitts., 1966-68, v.p. plastics div., 1968-78; v.p. devel. Koch Industries, Boston, 1979-81; pres. Avery Bus. Devel. Services, Ponte Vedra Beach, Fla., 1981—; cons., dir. Macrochem, Woburn, Mass.; dir. Pane/Graphic, West Caldwell, N.J. Served to maj. U.S. Army, 1941-46. Decorated Legion of Merit, Medal of Valor, Italian Govt.; recipient Bronze Beaver award MIT, 1976. Mem. Comml. Devel. Assn. (pres. 1974-75), Pitts. C. of C. Clubs: Duquesne (Pitts.), Downtown. Avocations: golf; swimming. Home: 2506 Saint Michel Ct Ponte Vedra Beach FL 32082 Office: Avery Bus Devel Services 80 Bacon St Waltham MA 02154

AVES, HELENA SOPHIA, petroleum computer company executive; b. Buenos Aires, Argentina, Oct. 21, 1950; came to U.S., 1957; d. Edward Leon and Nora Winifred (Hankinson) Swiderski; m. Christopher James Aves, Sept. 18, 1976; 1 child, Alexandra Wendy. B.A., Rutgers U., 1971; M.A., Columbia U., 1973, M.Philosophy, 1974, Ph.D., 1976; M.B.A., U. Dallas, 1979. Sr. exploration geologist Mobil Oil Corp., Dallas, 1976-79; pres. Helchris Assocs., Dallas, 1978—; v.p. PetCom Systems, Inc., Dallas, 1981—. Contbr. articles to profl. publs. Mem. Am. Assn. Petroleum Geologists, Soc. Ind. Profl. Earth Scientists, Zonta, Sigma Xi. Roman Catholic. Avocations: classical music; modern and classic art; reading. Office: PetCom Inc 14001 Dallas Pkwy Suite 400 Dallas TX 75240

AVINGER, JUANITA HUNT, educator; b. Brownwood, Tex., Jan. 4, 1920; d. Benjamin Franklin and Laura Peachie (Chrane) Hunt; B.S. in Edn., Tex. Technol. U., 1955, M.S. in Edn., 1960; postgrad. U. Tex., Austin, 1970-71; Ed.D., Baylor U., 1974; m. William Herschel Avinger, Aug. 26, 1939; children—James Herschel, John Ross. Elem. tchr. Lubbock (Tex.) Ind. Sch. Dist., 1955-66; asst. prof. Abilene (Tex.) Christian U., 1966-73, asso. prof., 1973-78, prof. edn., 1978—, prof. reading, dir. reading clinic; cons. Right to Read, Tex. Ind. Sch. Dists. of Anson, Stamford, Abilene, Edn. Service Center Region XIV, Ginn Pub. Co. Named Tchr. of Yr., Abilene Christian U., 1971. Mem. Tex. Tchrs. Assn., Tex. Assn. Profs. of Reading, Tex. Assn. Improvement of Reading, Internat. Reading Assn. (cons. nat., state, regional, local workshops, mem. Big Country Council, Tex. Council speaker nat conf. 1982), Tex. Assn. Gifted and Talented, Phi Delta Kappa, Phi Kappa Phi, Phi Delta Kappa, Kappa Delta Pi, Delta Kappa Gamma (scholar, 1969-74). Democrat. Mem. Chs. of Christ. Club: Faculty Wives of Abilene Christian U. Researcher in field; editor DISTAR III, Sci. Research Assos. Home: 910 Harwell Abilene TX 79601 Office: Abilene Christian U 1600 Campus Cts Abilene TX 79601

AVINGER, WILLIAM HERSCHEL, education professor, director graduate studies; b. Brownwood, Tex., Aug. 26, 1915; s. Willie Barnard and Dora Ethel (Hutcherson) A.; m. Ora Juanita Hunt, Aug. 26, 1939; children—James Herschel, John Ross. B.A., Howard Payne Coll., 1937; M.A., U. Tex.-Austin, 1943; Ed.D., Tex. Tech. U., 1965. Tchr., prin. Coleman (Tex.) Pub. Schs., 1937-43; prin. Coleman (Tex.) High Sch., 1943, Marfa (Tex.) High Sch., Electra (Tex.) High Sch., 1947; supt. schs. Electra, Tex., 1947, Plainview, Tex., to 1953; dir. pupil personnel services, Lubbock, Tex., 1954-65; prof. edn. Abilene Christian U., 1966—, now dir. grad. studies in edn. Named Tchr. of Year, Abilene Christian U., 1982-83. Mem. Tex. Assn. Sch. Adminstrs. (mem. coll. adv. com. 1978—), Tex. Profs. Ednl. Adminstrn., Am. Assn. Sch. Adminstrs., Nat. Orgn. Legal Problems of Edn. Mem. Ch. of Christ. Club: Kiwanis. Home: 910 Harwell St Abilene TX 79601 Office: Box 7914 ACU Sta Abilene TX 79699

AVRIGIAN, HARRY CASPAR, industrial management executive; b. Phila., Nov. 23, 1921; s. Harry Toros and Nevart A.; diploma in indsl. moblzn. U.S. Staff Coll., 1961; diploma city and county planning and plan implementation U. Mo., 1976; m. Bernice Bess, May 15, 1943; children—Barry, Brian, Diane. Machinist Nat. Def. Tng. Inst., Phila., 1938-40; Baldwin Locomotive Works, Eddystone, Pa., 1940-41; armament machinist Empire Ordnance Co., Phila., 1941-42; indsl. mgmt. cons., 1948-69; with Western States Exploration, Inc., Salt Lake City, 1972—, chief exec. officer, chmn. bd., 1975-79; chief exec. officer, chmn. bd. Am. Fuel & Power Corp., 1980—; cons. UN Habitat and Human Settlement Found., Nairobi, Kenya. Active SCORE program SBA, 1970-72. Served with U.S. Army, 1942-45; ETO. Mem. U.S. Indsl. Council, Am. Chem. Soc., Am. Soc. Metals, Soc. Automotive Engrs. Episcopalian.

AWALT, MARILENE KAY, educational administrator; b. Mineral Wells, Tex., Mar. 20, 1942; d. Pat O. T. and Mary Lee (Curry) Morse; m. H. Mike Awalt, Aug. 25, 1962; children—Stacy (dec.), Bradley. B.S., Tex. Wesleyan Coll., 1966; M.S. in Edn., Baylor U., 1972; candidate Ph.D., George Peabody Coll., Vanderbilt U. Cert. tchr., prin., supr. Elem. tchr. San Antonio Pub. Schs., 1966, LaVega Pub. Schs., Waco, Tex., 1966-68; with reading clinic Baylor U., Waco, 1969-70; tchr. reading Franklin Spl. Schs. (Tenn.), 1970-71, first grade tchr., 1971-80, asst. prin., 1980-85, prin., 1985—. Mem. adv. council for tchr. cert. and edn. Tenn. State Sch. Bd., 1977—. Tenn. spl. scholar, 1983-84. Mem. Middle Tenn. Council Insternat. Reading Assn., Internat. Reading Assn., Assn. Supervision and Curriculum Devel., Tenn. Assn. Supervision and Curriculum Devel.(pres. 1986-87), Delta Kappa Gamma (pres. Rho chpt.). Baptist. Co-author Religious Christian Day Sch. Curriculum, 1978; author: Study Book for 6-8 Year Olds, 1980; chmn. for revision elem. cert. State of Tenn. Office: Franklin Elem Sch Cannon St Franklin TN 37064

AXELRAD, SYLVIA ROSEN, real estate broker; b. Phila., June 15, 1912; d. Samuel Daniel and Dora (Friedman) R.; student pub. schs., Miami, Fla.; m. Jack Harry Axelrad, Feb. 14, 1932 (dec.); children—Moise, Samuel, David, Sandra. Real estate broker Sylvia Axelrad, Houston, 1937—. Licensed real estate broker, Tex., 1978. Home: 5500 N Braeswood St Apt 181 Houston TX 77096 Office: PO Box 35817 Houston TX 77235

AXNICK, NORMAN WALTER, federal government health official; b. Milw., Mar. 23, 1933; s. Walter and Hattie Marie (Rose) A.; m. Caroline Dendy, Apr. 12, 1958; 1 son, Ron V. B.S., U. Wis., 1955, M.S., 1956; postgrad. U. Minn., 1961. With Ctrs. for Disease Control, USPHS, Atlanta, 1956—, dir. office program planning and evaluation, 1969—. Pres. CDC Fed. Credit Union, 1977-80. Recipient commendation award Ctrs. for Disease Control, 1975. Mem. Am. Pub. Health Assn., Sigma Xi. Episcopalian. Home: 2694 Shetland Dr Decatur GA 30033 Office: 1600 Clifton Rd NE Atlanta GA 30333

AYAD, AHMED MOHAMED, physician; b. Alexandria, Egypt, Jan. 8, 1951; came to U.S., 1978; m. Salwa Awny, 3 children. M.B.Ch.B., U. Alexandria, 1970, M.D., 1975. Diplomate Am. Bd. Internal Medicine. Rotating intern Univ. Hosps., Alexandria, 1976-77; gen. practice medicine Sidi-Bel-Abbes Gen. Hosp., 1977-78; house physician Wheeling Hosp., W.Va., 1979; intern in internal medicine St. Barnabas Med. Ctr., Livingston, N.J., 1979-80, resident in internal medicine, 1980-82; chief resident dept. internal medicine, 1981-82; fellow in gastroenterology Tulane Med. Sch., New Orleans, 1982-84; practice medicine specializing in gastroenterology, Jacksonville, Fla., 1984—; mem. staff Bapt. Hosp., Meth. Hosp., Meml. Hosp., Humana Hosp. of Orange Park, Riverside Hosp., St. Vincent's Med. Ctr., St. Luke's Hosp., Beaches Hosp. Mem. ACP, Am. Gastroenterology Assn.

AYAD, JOSEPH MAGDY, psychologist; b. Cairo, Egypt, May 21, 1926; s. Fahim Gayed and Victoria Gabour (El-Masri) A.; came to U.S., 1949, naturalized, 1961; B.A. in Social Scis., Am. U., Cairo, 1946; M.A. in Clin. Psychology (Univ. scholar), Stanford U., 1952; Ph.D. in Clin. Psychology (Univ. scholar), U. Denver, 1956; m. Widad Fareed Bishai, May 29, 1954; children—Fareed Merritt, Victor Maher, Michael Joseph, Mona Elaine. Lectr., Fitzsimmons Army Hosp., Denver, 1953-54; staff psychologist Cons. Psychol. Services, Denver, 1954-55; psychologist, Denver, 1956-57, High Plains Neurol. Center, Amarillo, Tex., 1957—. Pres. JMA Cattle Co., Amarillo, 1973—; v.p., treas. Filigon Inc., Amarillo, 1962-75, pres., 1976—; cons. psychologist Tex. Dept. Pub. Welfare. Mem. profl. adv. bd. Amarillo Mental Health Assn., 1968-69. Mem. Amarillo Child Welfare Bd., 1961-63; area chmn. U. Denver Fund Raising Campaign, 1963; mem. profl. adv. bd. St. Paul's Meth. Ch. Sch. for Children with Learning Disabilities, Amarillo, 1969-70. Recipient Grad. Sr. award in Philosophy Am. U. at Cairo, 1946. Mem. Am. Psychol. Assn., Internat. Assn. Applied Psychology, Am. Assn. Marriage and Family Counselors, Am. Nat. Cattlemen's Assn., Potter-Randall County (Tex.) Psychol. Soc. (pres. 1974). Presbyn. Club: Amarillo Country. Contbr. articles to profl. jours. Home: 4239 Erik St Amarillo TX 79106 Office: 2301 W 7th St Amarillo TX 79106

AYCOCK, HUGH D., diversified metals company executive; b. 1930. With Nucor Corp., Charlotte, N.C., 1954—, div. shop supt., 1956-57, div. sales mgr., 1957-64, div. gen. mgr., 1964-65, v.p. steel div., 1965-84, pres., 1985—. Served with USN, 1950-54. Office: Nucor Corp 4425 Randolph Rd Charlotte NC 28211

AYCOCK, ROBERT, plant pathology educator; b. Lisbon, La., Dec. 23, 1919; s. Seaborn Jesse and Mary Amanda (Hightower) A.; m. Elsie Johnson, Nov. 1, 1941; children—Nancy Aycock Metz, Paula Suzanne Aycock King. B.S., La. State U., 1940; M.S., N.C. State Coll., 1942; Ph.D., N.C. State U., 1949. Assoc. plant pathologist S.C. Agrl. Exptl. Sta., 1949-55; assoc. prof., prof. plant pathology N.C. State U., Raleigh, 1955-60, prof. plant pathology and hort. sci., 1960-73, prof., head dept. plant pathology, 1973—. Served with M.C., AUS, 1942-46. Fellow Am. Phytopathol. Soc. (pres. 1976); mem. N.C. Assn. Plant Pathologists and Nematologists. Democrat. Presbyterian. Lodge: Torch. Editor-in-chief Phytopathology, 1970-72; contbr. articles to profl. jours. Home: 2001 Manuel Dr Raleigh NC 27612 Office: PO Box 5397 NC State U Raleigh NC 27650

AYENI, BABATUNDE JUNAID, petroleum engineering educator, researcher; b. Lagos, Nigeria, May 29, 1954; came to U.S., 1977; s. Shittu Ayoade and Alhaja Lutifat (Ottun) A.; m. Flora Olubunmi, Dec. 23, 1978; children—Tina Abisola, Louis Olanrewaju, Lawrence Adewale. B.S. in Petroleum Engring., U. Southwestern La., 1980, M.S. in Petroleum Engring., 1981, Ph.D. in Stats., 1984. Cert. engr., La. Teaching and research asst., lectr. U. Southwestern La., Lafayette, 1980-84; asst. prof. Southern U., New Orleans, 1984—, acting dir. tech. program, 1985—. Fed. Govt. Nigeria scholar, 1977, 82. Mem. La. Engring. Soc., Soc. Petroleum Engrs., La. Acad. Sci., Am. Statis. Assn., Math. Assn. Am., Nat. Soc. Profl. Engrs., Pi Mu Epsilon, Phi Eta Sigma, Epsilon Beta Pi. Home: PO Box 29591 New Orleans LA 70189 Office: Southern Univ 6400 Press Dr New Orleans LA 70126

AYERS, HARRY BRANDT, editor, publisher, columnist; b. Anniston, Ala., Apr. 8, 1935; b. Harry Mell and Edel Olga (Ytterboe) A.; m. Josephine Ehringhaus, Dec. 10, 1961; 1 dau., Margaret. B.A. in History, U. Ala.-Tuscaloosa, 1959. Polit. writer The Raleigh Times (N.C.), 1959-61; Washington corr. Bascom Timmons Bur., Washington, 1961-63; mng. editor The Anniston Star (Ala.), 1963-69, editor, pub., 1969—; dir. Nat. News Council, N.Y.C., 1981-84. Trustee, Talladega Coll. (Ala.), 1972—, 20th Century Fund, 1985—, Ctr. for Excellence in Govt., 1985—; bd. dirs. So. Ctr. for Internat. Studies, Atlanta, 1979—, Bd. Fgn. Scholarships, Washington, 1981-84; mem. Council Fgn. Relations, N.Y.C., 1983—. Named Disting. Journalism Grad., U. Ala., 1967; recipient Human Relations award Am. Jewish Com., 1977; Green Eyeshade award Sigma Delta Chi, 1985. Fellow Nieman Found.; mem. Ala. Press Journalism Found. (founding pres. 1969), Am. Soc. Newspaper Editors, So. Newspaper Pubs. Assn. (dir. 1981—). Democrat. Episcopalian. Clubs: Metropolitan (Washington), Relay House (Birmingham, Ala.). Mem. adv. bd. Inside Story, Pub. Broadcasting System, N.Y.C., 1981-85; co-editor: You Can't Eat Magnolias, 1972; co-author: A Bicentennial Portrait of the American People, 1975; 1977 Inaugural Book President Carter, 1977; Dixie Dateline, 1983. Home: 1 Booger Hollow Anniston AL 36201 Office: Anniston Star 216 W 10th St Anniston AL 36201

AYOUB, MAHMOUD AMIN, industrial engineering educator; b. Cairo, Jan. 1, 1942; m. Amira Deif, Jan. 26, 1967; children—Shahinaz, Nader. B.S., Cairo U., 1964; M.S., Tex. Tech. U., 1969, Ph.D., 1971. Asst. prof. indsl. engring. N.C. State U.-Raleigh, 1971-73, assoc. prof., 1973-79, prof., 1979—; cons. govt. and industry. Office: Dept Indsl Engring NC State U Raleigh NC 27650

AYOUB, SAM, retired soft drink company executive, finance company executive; b. Tantah, Egypt, Dec. 24, 1918; s. Youssef and Basima A.; m. Louisa Elmasry, May 8, 1948. B.B.A. in Fin., Hofstra U., 1964; postgrad. Advanced Mgmt. Program, Harvard U., 1967. Mgr. State Bank of Ethiopia, 1945-55, Ethiopia Air Lines, 1955-58; treas. Coca-Cola Export Co., 1971-72, v.p., 1972-76; v.p., treas. Coca-Cola Co., Atlanta, 1976-77, sr. v.p., then pres. Coca-Cola Middle East, 1977-80, exec. v.p. gen. ops., 1980-81, sr. exec. v.p., chief fin. officer, 1981-84; co-chmn. Citadel Group Inc.; dir. Roses Stores, Inc., Cousins Properties, Inc., Digital Transmissions Systems, Inc. Elder North Ave. Presbyterian Ch.; mem. Atlanta dist. Council Dept. Commerce; dir., past chmn. Ga. Dept. Industry and Trade; chmn. So. Ctr. Internat. Studies; hon. chmn. World Trade Club Atlanta. Recipient service award Ga. Bus. and Industry Assn., 1980, Gov.'s Internat. award, 1981; IBM fellow, 1981. Mem. Egypt/U.S. C. of C. (vice chmn.). Clubs: Capital City, World Trade. Office: 3400 Peachtree Rd NE Atlanta GA 30326

AYRES, MARY ANN, management consultant; b. Ardmore, Okla., May 19, 1949; d. Deward Earl and Verna Mae (Toups) Bannister; student Oscar Rose Jr. Coll., 1978, U. Okla., 1981—; children—Brandon Joseph, Rebecca Ann. Bookkeeper, Webbs Office Supply, Ardmore, 1968; asst. mgr. Beneficial Fin. Co., Dallas, 1969-73; apt. reservationist U. Okla. Housing Programs, 1977-80, mgr., 1980-84; small bus. cons., wholesale broker Shaklee Corp., 1984—. Chairperson, Norman (Okla.) Fair Housing Resource Bd., 1981-82; charity fundraiser; civic vol. Recipient Pres.'s Leadership award, 1981, Disting. Service award, 1984. Mem. Assn. Coll. and Univ. Housing Officers, S.W. Assn. Coll. and Univ. Housing Officers (state dir.), U. Okla. Managerial Staff Assn. (sec. 1982-83), Boulder Hot Tub Assn. (co-founder). Clubs: Trosper Archery, Okla. State Archery Assn. (sec. 1980-81), Fellowship of Robin Hood, Tapa Nu Keg. Home: PO Box 34 Luther OK 73054

AYRES, ROBERT MOSS, JR., university president; b. San Antonio, Sept. 1, 1926; s. Robert Moss and Florence (Collett) A.; student Tex. Mil. Inst., 1944; B.A., U. of South, 1949; postgrad. Oxford (Eng.) U., 1949; M.B.A., U. Pa., 1952; D.C.L., U. of South, 1974; m. Patricia Ann Shield, Sept. 10, 1955; children—Robert Atlee, Vera Patricia. With Kidder, Peabody & Co., Phila., N.Y.C., 1950-53; with Dittmar & Co., San Antonio, 1952-53; pres., dir. Russ & Co., Inc., San Antonio, 1953-73; sr. v.p., dir. Rotan Mosle Inc., San Antonio, 1973-77; pres. U. South, Sewanee, Tenn., 1977—; former allied mem. N.Y. Stock Exchange, Am. Stock Exchange. Past pres. Asso. Alumni U. of South; past pres. bd. dirs. Bexar County chpt. ARC; past pres. bd. trustees Tex. Mil. Inst.; trustee, past chmn. bd. regents U. of South; past pres. Coll. Athletic Assn., So. Colls. and Univs. Union; trustee Brother's Bro. Found.; mem. exec. council Episcopal Ch., also mem. nat. and world mission com.; bd. dirs. Inst. European Studies, Presiding Bishop's Fund World Relief, Alfalit, Internat. Served with USN, 1944-46, lt. Res., 1949-60. Mem. San Antonio Soc. Fin. Analysis (past pres.), Securities Industries Assn. (past mem. governing council), Investment Bankers Assn. Am. (past chmn. Tex. group)., Nat. Assn. Securities Dealers (past mem. dist. com.), Young Pres.'s Orgn., Order of Alamo, Tex. Cavaliers, Argyle, Sigma Alpha Epsilon. Episcopalian (mem. exec. bd. diocese W. Tex.; vestryman). Clubs: San Antonio German, San Antonio Country, San Antonio. Office: University of the South Sewanee TN 37375

AYTCH, ANNAS, college dean, mathematics educator, researcher; b. Pine Bluff, Ark., July 3, 1943; d. Mack and Josephine Virginia (Hudson) Aytch; m. Rosemary Holmes, Dec. 18, 1966; children—Rosanna, Annary, Dawnnamaria, Samuell. B.S. U. Ark.-Pine Bluff (formerly Ark. A&M and N. Coll.), 1965; M.A., U. Pitts., 1968, Ph.D., 1973. Assoc. instr. math. U. Pitts., 1969-71, program coordinator math. univ. community ednl. program, 1971-77, asst. prof. math., 1973-77, asst. to grad. dean, 1975-77; assoc. dean Ala. A&M U. Grad. Sch., Normal, 1978-83, grad. dean, 1983—; exec. com. Conf. of So. Grad. Schs., 1983—; cons. Dept. Edn., Washington, 19. Author: Algebra is Easy, Thesis and Report Writing, 1973. Editor Grad. Informer Newsletter, 1982—. Chmn. bd. dirs. Pitts. Sch. Bible, 1972-76; exec. sec. Ala. Coalition on Post-Secondary Edn., Birmingham, 1978; pres. PTA, Huntsville, Ala., 1979; mem. adv. bd. Huntsville Sch. Bd. for Middle Schs., 1979; chmn. United Negro Coll. Fund Drive, Huntsville, 1980. U. Buhl Found. fellow, 1981; U. Pitts. math. dept. fellow, 1967. Mem. Ala. Grad. Deans (sec., exec. com. 1983—), Deans of Black Grad. Schs. (sec., treas. 1981—), Am. Math. Soc., Sigma Xi,

Beta Kappa Chi. (pres. 1964-65). Avocations: financial planning and investments. Office: Grad Sch Ala A & M U Normal AL 35762

AZRIKAN, JOEL, educational specialist; b. Bklyn., Feb. 22, 1948; s. Milton and Zelda (Cohen) A.; m. Laura Joanne Haytas, June 17, 1974; children—Melissa Yvette, Sara Rochelle. A.A., Miami-Dade Community Coll., 1968; B.A., Fla. Atlantic U., 1970; M.S., Barry U., 1974. Elem. tchr. Dade County Pub. Schs., Miami, Fla., 1970-83, ednl. specialist, 1983—; adj. prof. Nova U., Miami, 1982-83; cons. Fla. Dept. Edn., Tallahassee, 1975-77, 83—. Contbr. articles to profl. jours. City activist Davie Town Council, Fla., 1982-84. Mem. Am. Assn. for Counseling and Devel., Fla. Assn. for Counseling and Devel., Phi Delta Kappa (pres. 1982-83). Avocations: tennis; boating; fishing. Office: Dade County Pub Schs 1450 NE 2d Ave Miami FL 33132

BAAL, ROBERT G., real estate company executive; b. N.Y.C., July 5, 1928; s. Robert A. and Louise B. (Beisler) B.; m. Ruth E. Kohl, Apr. 8, 1961; children—Robin, Robert K., Perri Ann. B.A. in Mktg. and Econs., Bates Coll., Lewiston, Maine. Vice pres., dir. sales NBC Radio Network, N.Y.C.; v.p., gen. sales mgr. Sta. TVAR, Inc., Westinghouse Broadcasting, N.Y.C.; v.p. brokerage sales Walter Etling Co. Realtors, Miami; prin., exec. v.p. Sisler-Baal, Inc., Miami; prin., dir. Asset Mgmt. Systems, Inc., GCB Mgmt. Co. Chmn. bd. Sta. WPBT, Channel 2 Pub. TV. Served with AUS, 1952. Mem. Soc. Indsl. Realtors, Nat. Assn. Indsl. and Office Parks, Urban Land Inst., Indsl. Assn. Dade County (dir.), Greater Miami C. of C. Lutheran. Office: 7235 Corporate Ctr Dr Miami FL 33126

BAAMONDE, JOSEPH, JR., pharm. co. exec.; b. Tampa, Fla., Aug. 31, 1944; s. Joseph and Lupe (Randon) B.; B.A., Parsons Coll., 1972; m. Judith Frisk, June 9, 1973; children—Jennifer Judith, John Joseph. With Mallinckrodt, Inc., Brandon, Fla., 1973—, regional sales mgr. S.E. region, 1978—; dist. sales mgr. Wallace Labs. Inc.; pres. Baval Med Cons. Inc. Pres., Lutheran Churchmen of Salem Luth. Ch., Peoria, Ill., 1977; pres. bd. edn. Immanuel Luth. Ch. Sch., Brandon; pres. Luth. Laymen's League, Immanuel Luth. Ch. Named Mgr. of Yr., Mallinckrodt, Inc., 1978, 81, Wallace Labs., 1980-81. Mem. Am. Mgmt. Assn., Profl. Pharm. Mfrs. Reps. Assn. (v.p. Peoria 1976-77), Theta Chi. Republican. Address: 1306 Brandonwood Dr Brandon FL 33611

BAASCH, HAROLD DAVID, hospital corporation public relations administrator; b. Mayaguez, P.R., Aug. 31, 1948; s. David Henry and Iva Nellie (Munson) B.; m. Evonne Lindquist, Dec. 20, 1970. B.A., Columbia Union Coll., Takoma Park, Md., 1971; M.Div., Andrews U. Sem., Berrien Springs, Mich., 1974; diploma bus. and mgmt. LaSalle Extension U., Chgo., 1976. Ordained to ministry Seventh-day Adventist Ch., 1977. Assoc. pastor Seventh-day Adventist Ch., Cin., 1971-72, pastor chs., Reynoldsburg and Lancaster, Ohio, 1975-78; dir. pub. relations Columbia Union Coll., 1978-81; dir. pub. relations Adventist Health System/Sunbelt, Orlando, Fla., 1981—, editor Sunbelt Healthview, 1982—, speech writer for corp. pres., 1982—; chmn. Sunbelt Advt. Agy., Orlando, 1982—. Mem. Pub. Relations Soc. Am., Am. Soc. Hosp. Pub. Relations. Lodge: Rotary (Altamonte Springs/Forest City, Fla.). Office: Adventist Health System/Sunbelt 2400 Bedford Rd Orlando FL 32803

BABB, DONALD QUENTIN, entomologist; b. Dalton, Ga., Oct. 11, 1950; s. Quentin Marion and Dot (Ford) B.; A.S., Dalton Jr. Coll., 1970; B.S. in Entomology, U. Ga., 1972; m. Judy Ann Kinnett, Aug. 17, 1971; 1 dau., Fawn Yonah; m. 2d, Betty Joan Bailey. Research staff U.S. Dept. Agr., summer 1972; Fla. mgr. Stephenson Chemicals Co., Orlando, 1972-73; agent U. Ga. Extension Dept., Rome, 1973; inspector Ga. Dept. Agr., Atlanta, 1973-74; tng. and tech. dir. Met. Exterminating Co., College Park, Ga., 1974-75; pres. Babb Exterminating Co., Douglasville, Ga., 1975-83; pres. Babb Christmas Tree Farm, Dalton, Ga., 1983—. Mem. Am. Entomol. Soc., Jaycees. Democrat. Baptist. Lodge: Kiwanis. Home: Route 1 Armachee GA 30105 Office: 2098 Fairburn Dr Douglasville GA 30135

BABB, THOMAS JACKSON, marketing educator, consultant; b. Hertford, N.C., July 26, 1930; s. Everett Duke and Irene Virginia (Layden) B. B.S., Bob Jones U., 1952; M.S., U. Tenn., 1958; Ph.D., Ohio State U., 1981; postgrad. Pa. State U., 1963-64, U.S.C., 1967, W.Va. U., 1972-73. Mfr.'s agt., 1956-58; instr. Mich. Tech. U., Houghton, 1958-61; prof. mktg. West Liberty (W.Va.) State Coll., 1961—; chmn. dept. gen. bus. and mktg., 1967—; cons. in field. Served with USN, 1952-56. NSF fellow, summer 1967; Am. Risk and Ins. Assn. fellow, 1969. Mem. Am. Mktg. Assn., Am. Vocat. Assn., W.Va. Vocat. Assn., Mountain State Econs. Assn., Delta Sigma Pi. Republican. Episcopalian. Home: 207 Eastview Dr West Liberty WV 26074 Office: West Liberty Coll 236 Main Hall West Liberty WV 26074

BABER, WILBUR H., JR., lawyer; b. Shelby, N.C., Dec. 18, 1926; s. Wilbur H. and Martha Corinne (Allen) B.; B.A., Emory U., 1949; postgrad. U. N.C., 1949-50, U. Houston, 1951-52; J.D., Loyola U., New Orleans, 1965. Admitted to La. bar, 1965, Tex. bar, 1966; practice law, Hallettsville, Tex. Served with U.S. Army. Mem. Am., La., Tex. bar assns., La. Engring. Soc., Tex. Surveyors Assn. Methodist. Club: Rotary. Office: PO Box 294 Hallettsville TX 77964

BACHI, MICHAEL MARIO, artist, educator; b. Genoa, Italy, Mar. 1, 1920 (parents Am. citizens); s. Angelo Luigi and Alcisa (Cardinale) B.; B.A., Oklahoma City U., 1951; M.F.A., U. Okla., 1953, postgrad., 1953; postgrad. Southeastern State Coll., Durant, Okla., 1954, Instituto de Allende, San Miguel De Allende, Gt., Mexico, 1964; m. Mable Naomi Baker, Apr. 5, 1947. Tchr. art McAlester (Okla.) Jr. and Sr. High Schs., 1953-56; prof., head dept. art Rio Grande (Ohio) Coll., 1956-57; asst. prof. art Wis. State Coll., Superior, 1957-60; asst. prof. art Chadron (Nebr.) State Coll., 1960-62; prof. art Central State U., Edmond, Okla., 1962—, mem. faculty governance com., 1968-69, mem. faculty senate, 1969-70, 76-77, 79-80; exhibited in one man shows: Henson Gallery, Yukon, Okla., 1966, Pioneer Mus. Art Ctr., Woodward, Okla., 1986. Ballet Theatre Sch., Oklahoma City, St. Paul's Cathedral, Oklahoma City, 1968; exhibited in group shows: Philbrook Mus., Tulsa, 1953, Okla. U. Show at Forum Gallery, N.Y.C., 1954, Tweed Gallery, Duluth, Minn., 1959, galleries in Superior, Wis., 1958, Norman, Okla., 1963, Yukon, 1966, Oklahoma City, 1967, Faculty Show, Okla. Sci. and Arts Found., 1965, Okla. Painting and Sculpture Biennial, 1971, Balcony Art Gallery, Oklahoma City, 1971, Faculty Art Show, Central State U. Mus. Art, Edmond, Okla., 1986; executed mural Midland Coop. Supermarket, Superior, 1959; tchr. watercolor Okla. Sci. and Art Found. Faculty, 1965-66. Mem. Gov.'s Council on Arts and Humanities, 1966. Served with USAAF, 1941-45. Decorated Bronze Star with five clusters. Mem. Contemporary Art Found. Oklahoma City, Nat. Graphics Council, So. Graphics Council, AAUP (exec. com. local chpt.), Kappa Pi, Delta Phi Delta. Democrat. Home: 3700 Mason Hills Dr Edmond OK 73034

BACHMAN, JOHN ANDREW, JR., engineer; b. Washington, Apr. 26, 1926; s. John Andrew and Margaret Eleanor (Hauf) B.; B.Aero. Engring., Ga. Inst. Tech., 1951; m. Mary Irene Dougherty, Dec. 27, 1952; children—Barbara Lee (dec.), Robert J., John D., Thomas A., Lisa Marie. Jr. engr. Boeing Co., Seattle, 1951-52; aerodynamist Chase Aircraft Co., Trenton, N.J., also Fairchild Aircraft Co., Hagerstown, Md., 1953-54; engring. cons. Washington area, 1955-57; staff engr. Honeywell Inc., Mpls. and Washington, 1957-68; regional mgr. Ground Transp. div. LTV Corp., Washington, 1968-73; with Mitre Corp., McLean, Va., 1973-77; dept. head Unified Industries Inc., Alexandria, Va., 1977-81, Riverside Research Inst., Arlington, Va., 1981-83; prin. Bachman Assocs., 1983—. Active Boy Scouts Am., 1938-72. Served with USNR, 1944-46. Assoc. fellow AIAA (sect. council 1976-78); mem. ASME, Am. Def. Preparedness Assn., Transp. Research Bd., Washington Area Ry. Engring. Soc., Air Force Assn. Episcopalian. Author publs. in field. Home: 205 Yoakum Pkwy Apt 626 Alexandria VA 22304 Office: PO Box 9768 Alexandria VA 22304

BACHNER, JOHN PHILIP, business consultant; b. Boston, Nov. 8, 1944; s. Barnard and Bertha (Bellar) B.; A.B., Harvard, 1966; m. Marcia L. Davis, Aug. 7, 1966; children—Barnard David, Lissa Suzanne. Screenplay writer Screen Presentations, Inc., film prodn. co. Washington, 1967-68; account exec. Hoffman Assocs., Inc., Silver Spring, Md., 1968-71; pres. Bachner Communications, Inc., communications-mktg. co., Silver Spring, 1971—; pres. Bachner Mgmt. Systems, multiple assn. mgmt. co. Silver Spring, 1973—; exec. dir. Cons. Engrs. Council of Met. Washington, Silver Spring, 1971—, Property Mgmt. Assn. Met. Washington, Silver Spring, 1973—, Washington Area Council Engring. Labs., Silver Spring, 1975—, Property Mgmt. Assn. Am., Silver Spring, 1979—; exec. dir. Assn. Soil, Found. Engrs., Silver Spring, 1973—; chmn. bd. Constrn. Industry Tech., Inc., Silver Spring, 1973—. Exec. dir. Spruce Knob Assn., Silver Spring, 1975—; pres. Most for the Lease, 1982—; v.p. Lodzarend, Inc., 1982—. Author: Marketing and Promotion for Design Professionals, 1977; writer 25 motion pictures; contbr. numerous articles to profl. publs., popluar mags. Home: 9206 Sterling Montaque Dr Great Falls VA 22066 Office: 8811 Colesville Rd Silver Spring MD 20910

BACK, KURT WOLFGANG, sociologist, educator; b. Vienna, Austria, Oct. 17, 1919; came to U.S., 1938, naturalized, 1943; s. Paul L. and Thekla E. (Fuchs) B.; m. Mary Louise Vincent, Oct. 18, 1969; 1 son, Allan T. B.A., NYU, 1940; M.A., UCLA, 1941; Ph.D., MIT, 1949. Statistician, Aberdeen Proving Ground, 1946; asst. study dir. Research Ctr. for Group Dynamics, 1946-49; social sci. analyst Bur. of Census, 1949-51; research assoc. Columbia U., 1951-53, U. P.R., 1953-56, Conservation Found., 1955-58; research assoc. prof. U. N.C., 1956-59; assoc. prof. Duke U., Durham, N.C., 1959-62, prof. sociology and psychiatry, 1962—, James B. Duke prof. sociology, 1976—, chmn. dept. sociology, 1976-81. Served with AUS, 1943-46. Recipient Helen L. Deroy award Soc. for Study Social Problems, 1956; Competition for Plans in TV Research award, 1961; Burgess award Nat. Council Family Relations, 1961; NIH spl. research fellow, 1967-68, 73-74. Mem. Am. Sociol. Assn., Am. Psychol. Assn., Am. Assn. for Pub. Opinion Research, So. Soc. for Pub. Opinion Research (pres. 1983-84), Population Assn. Am., AAAS (chmn. sect. K 1978-79), Soc. Exptl. Social Psychology, So. Sociol. Soc., Sociol. Research Assn. (pres. 1981-82). Author: (with Festinger and Schachter) Social Pressures in Informal Groups, 1951; (with Hill and Stycos) The Family and Population Control, 1959, Slums, Projects and People: Social Psychological Problems of Relocation in Puerto Rico, 1962, Beyond Words: The Story of Sensitivity Training and the Encounter Movement, 1972; editor; contbr. Social Psychology, 1977; In Search of Community Groups and Social Change, 1978; The Life Course: Integrative Theories and Exemplary Populations, 1980. Home: 2735 McDowell St Durham NC 27705 Office: Dept Sociology Duke U Durham NC 27706

BACKELS, JOHN STEVEN, counselor; b. Corona, Calif., Jan. 19, 1955; s. John Franz and Mary Beatrice (Stevens) B.; m. Kelsey Susan Kime, May 30, 1982; 1 child, Adam K. B.A. in Psychology, U. Va., 1976; M.Ed., James Madison U., 1978. Lic. profl. counselor, Va. Dir. Parks and recreation City of Clifton Forge, Va., 1976-77; evening counselor Bluefield State Coll., W.Va., 1979-80; dir. counseling Averett Coll., Danville, Va., 1980—; pvt. practice profl. counseling, Danville, 1983—. Bd. dirs. Mental Health Assn. Danville-Pittsylvania County, 1983—; vol. counselor Mental Health Assn. Danville-Pittsylvania County, 1980-83; vol. Big Bros. of Danville-Pittsylvania County, 1982-84; mem. licensure com. Va. Bd. Lic. Profl. Counselors, 1983. Mem. Va. Counselors Assn. (bd. dirs., chpt. pres.), Va. Coll. Personnel Assn. Club: Danville Canoe (editor 1983-84, dir. 1981-83). Avocations: skiing; outdoor activities; athletics. Address: Averett Coll 420 W Main St Danville VA 24541

BACKELS, KELSEY KIME, college counselor; b. Roanoke, Va., Apr. 26, 1954; d. Robert Wilberforce and Gladys Patricia (Sobol) Kime; m. John Steven, May 30, 1982; 1 child, Adam Kime. B.S. in Psychology, James Madison U., 1976, M.Ed. in Counselor Edn., 1978. Lic. counselor, Va.; nat. cert. counselor. Dir. student activities, resident supr. Averett Coll., Danville, Va., 1978-79, dir. career counseling and placement, 1979—; pvt. practice counseling, Danville, 1984—. Vice pres., rape counselor Domestic Violence Emergency Services, Danville, 1981—; bd. dirs. Danville 70001 Program, 1983-84. Mem. Am. Assn. for Counseling and Devel., Va. Counselors Assn., Am. Coll. Personnel Assn., Va. Coll. Personnel Assn. (4-yr. pvt. coll. dir. 1984—). Avocations: racquetball; snow-skiing; reading. Office: Averett Coll 420 W Main St Danville VA 24541

BACKMAN, CARL A., education educator, university administrator; b. Apr. 24, 1941; m. Ingrid M. Hakansson, July 4, 1964; children—Carla M., Linda M., Cynthia E. B.S. in Edn., Northeastern U., 1963, M.Ed., 1967; Ph.D. in Edn., Syracuse U., 1969. Tchr. math. Central Jr. High Sch., Quincy, Mass. Pub. Sch. System, 1963-66; instr. Coll. Edn., Syracuse U., 1967-69; asst. prof. Coll. Edn., U. West Fla., Pensacola, 1969-73, assoc. prof., 1973-78, prof., 1978—, asst. chair, 1977-78, chair dept. elem. edn. and secondary edn., 1978-82, acting dean Coll. Edn., 1982-83, dean, 1983—; cons. and lectr. in field. Author: Objectives Tests for Mathematics One, 1974. Co-author: Random House Mathematics Program, 1976—; Introduction to Concepts of Geometry, 1971. Editor of books in field. Contbr. articles, chpt. to profl. jours. and books. Columnist numerous newspapers. NSF grantee, 1966; NDEA fellow, 1966-69; recipient Research and Creative Activities award, 1975, Research Project award U. West Fla., 1981-82. Mem. Am. Assn. Colls. for Tchr. Edn. (chief instl. rep., task force on tchr. cert. 1983-85), Assn. for Supervision and Curriculum Devel., Assn. Tchr. Educators (com. on standards and performance 1983—), Tchr. Edn. Council for State Colls. and Univs., Soc. Professors Edn., Nat. Council Tchrs. Maths., Research Council for Diagnostic and Prescriptive Math., So. Council Tchr. Edn., Fla. Assn. Colls. Tchr. Edn. (pres. 1985—), Fla. Assn. Tchr. Educators, Fla. Assn. Staff Devel., Fla. Council Tchrs. Math., Escambia County Council of Tchrs. of Math., West Fla. Citizens Com. on Pub. Edn. (v.p. 1985-86), Phi Delta Kappa (pres. 1981-82, exec. bd. 1982-85), Phi Kappa Phi, Kappa Delta Pi. Home: 11604 Clear Creek Dr Pensacola FL 32514 Office: U West Fla Coll Edn Pensacola FL 32514

BACKSTROM, JAMES ARTHUR, JR., lawyer, federal prosecutor; b. McKeesport, Pa., Nov. 12, 1952; s. James A. and Anna Maxine (Omler) B. B.S. with distinction in Speech, Northwestern U., 1973; J.D., U. Pa., 1976. Bar: Pa. 1976, D.C. 1977, U.S. Supreme Ct. 1980, Tex. 1986. Law clk. FPC, Washington, 1976; trial atty. U.S. Dept. Justice, Phila., 1976-79, spl. asst. Office of Ops., Antitrust Div., Washington, 1979-81, chief Dallas Office, 1982—; spl. asst. U.S. atty., Phila., 1981-82; instr. Atty. Gen.'s Advocacy Inst., Washington, 1979. Trustee Ctr. for Law and Social Policy, Washington, 1975; active ACLU. Served to lt. JAGC, USNR, 1983—. Named Outstanding Young Man of Am., U.S. Jaycees, 1983. Mem. Dallas Bar Assn. (antitrust and trade regulation sect. 1982-83, mem. council 1982—), State Bar Tex. (mem. council antitrust and trade regulation sect. 1984—). Lutheran. Office: US Dept Justice 1100 Commerce St Room 8C6 Dallas TX 75242

BACON, DOUGLAS EUGENE, geologist; b. Boone, Iowa, June 11, 1925; s. Raymond H. and Lola M. (Adams) B.; m. Emily Jane Coghlan, Oct. 15, 1949; children—S. Douglas, Robert M., Barbara S. Bacon McKeithen. B.S., U. Ark., 1948, M.S., 1949. Geologist, Atlantic Refining Co., Wichita, Kans., 1949-52, dist. geologist, Bismarck, N.D., 1952-55, asst. to chief geologist, Dallas, 1955-56, dist. geologist, Houston, 1956-60; cons. geologist, Houston, 1960-70; ptnr. Bock & Bacon Oil Co., Houston, 1970—; cons. geologist; rancher. Chmn. phys. com., dir. YMCA, 1967-75; mem. Meadowbrook Civic Club, 1957. Served with USMC, 1943-46. Mem. Am. Assn. Petroleum Geologists (dist. rep., cert.), Am. Inst. Petroleum Geologists (cert.), Crude Club (dir., pres.), Am. Geophys. Inst., Am. Geol. Inst., Soc. Ind. Profl. Earth Scientists (chpt. v.p., dir., cert.), Houston Geol. Soc., So. Tex. Geol. Soc. Methodist (dir.). Contbr. chpt. in book. Lodge: Lions.

BACON, RICHARD F., motor transportation company executive; b. La Harpe, Kans., Jan. 13, 1927; s. Frank E. and Helen M. (Alderman) B.; m. Betty Anne Buchanan, Aug. 18, 1950; children—David, Dan, Randall. B.B.A., So. Meth. U., 1950; postgrad. in transp. mgmt. Stanford U., 1969. Supt. ops. M&D Motor Freight Lines, Inc., Dallas, 1950-57; supt. terminals Mchts. Fast Motor Lines, Inc., Abilene, Tex., 1957-62, v.p. ops., 1962, exec. v.p., 1968-72, pres., 1972—; exec. v.p. Mchts. Inc., 1976, pres., 1977—, also dir.; dir. First Nat. Bank Abilene, West Tex. Utilities Co. Chmn. bd. trustees St. Paul Meth. Ch.; mem. exec. com. Tex. Research League. Served with USN, 1945-46; USAF, 1950. Mem. West Tex. C. of C. (nat. affairs com., exec. com.), Middlewest Motor Freight Bur. (bd. dirs.), Abilene C. of C. (chmn. legis. com.), Am. Trucking Assn., Tex. Motor Transp. Assn. (dir., exec. com.).

BADER, MARK BRUCE, legal educator; b. Bridgeport, Conn., Dec. 27, 1946; s. Philip and Lillian (Islovitz) B.; m. Sandra Fay Wolf (div. 1982); 1 dau., Rachel Barrett. B.B.A., U. Miami (Fla.), 1968; postgrad. U. Tex.-Austin, 1968-70; J.D., So. Meth. U., 1974. Bar: Tex. 1974. Assoc., Herndon, Girard, Smith, Kolodey, Dallas, 1974-76; ptnr. Pailet & Bader, Dallas, 1976-80; of counsel Bard and Graves, Houston, 1980-82; ptnr. Ryerson & Bader, Houston, 1983-83; asst. prof. legal studies U. Tex., Austin, 1980—; cons. in field. Bd. dirs. Jewish Community Council of Austin, 1982-83; sec./treas. Am. Friends of Wilton Park, 1980-82. Named Outstanding Prof., Phi Eta Sigma, 1981; CBA Found. teaching award, 1982; Tex. Ex-Students Assn. Outstanding Teaching award, 1983; Utmost mag. best prof., 1981, 82, 83; Inst. for Constructive Capitalism fellow, 1983. Mem. ABA, Tex. Bar Assn., Union Avocats des Internationale, Am. Bus. Law Assn. Author: (with Bill Shaw) Amendment of the Foreign Corrupt Practices Act, 1983; Jurisdictional No Man's Land, The American Foreign Trade Zone, 1983; contbr. articles to profl. jours. Home: 1707 Spylass St Apt 53 Austin TX 78746 Office: GSB 4-138 U Tex Austin TX 78712

BADO, EDUARDO, television executive; b. Mayaguez, P.R., Oct. 15, 1950; s. Eduardo and Isabel Bado; m. Alice A. Barreto, Jan. 27, 1974; children—Eduardo Jose, Ivan Eduardo, Carlos Eduardo. B.A. in Polit. Sci., U. P.R., 1973; M.S. in Communications, U. Bridgeport (Conn.), 1978. Coordinator edn. program dept. Labor Govt. P.R., 1973-79; gen. mgr. WORA-TV, Mayaguez, 1979—; mktg. con. P.R. Realty. Recipient Citizen of Yr. award Jr. Chamber Internat., 1980, 81; Top Mgmt. award Sales and Mktg. Execs. Internat., 1982. Mem. C. of C. Western P.R. (dir.), N.Y. Acad. Scis., Assn. for Ednl. Communications and Tech., Jr. Chamber Internat. Clubs: Deportivo del Oeste, Casino de Mayaguez. Lodge: Lions (sec., v.p., zone chmn.). Home: Toledo 75 Urb Belmonte Mayaguez PR 00708 Office: Box 901 Mayaguez PR 00709

BADRE, ALBERT Y(USUF), economics educator; b. Merjayoun, Lebanon, Apr. 25, 1912; came to U.S., 1960; s. Nasib Badre and Afifé Badre Haddad; m. Lily Badr, Aug. 14, 1938; children—Sami, Ramsey, Nasib, Leila, Maria. B.B.A., Am. U. Beirut, 1934; M.A. in Econs., U. Iowa, 1948, Ph.D., 1950. Asst. prof. econs. Am. U. Beirut, 1938-48, assoc. prof., 1948-53, prof., 1953-63; prof. U. Iowa, Iowa City, 1963-66, So. Ill., U., Carbondale, 1966-73; pres. Beirut U. Coll., 1973-83; vis. prof. econs. Agnes Scott Coll., Atlanta, 1983—; cons. in field; mem. planning and devel. bd. Govt. Lebanon, Beirut, 1953-60; mem. council econ. advisers to Pres. Lebanon, 1955-60; head Middle East unit UN Secretariat, 1957-58, chief economist UN, Congo, 1960-63. Author: National Income of Lebanon, 1955; Manpower and Oil in Arab Countries, 1960; (with Simon Siksek) Economic Development and the Role of the U.S., 1966. Pres. UN Assn., Carbondale, 1973-74; elder First Presbyterian Ch., Carbondale. Decorated knight Order of the Cedar (Lebanon). Mem. Internat. Statis. Inst. (life), Am. Econ. Assn., Econometric Soc. Clubs: Cosmos (Washington); Berkeley Country (Atlanta). Lodges: Elks, Masons.

BAEDECKER, PHILIP ACKERMAN, chemist; b. East Orange, N.J., Dec. 19, 1939; s. Harold John and Audrey Sarah (Ackerman) B.; m. Mary Josephine LaFuze, Jan. 2, 1966; 1 dau., Cheryl Elise. B.S., Ohio U., 1961; M.S., U. Ky., 1964, Ph.D., 1967. Research assoc. MIT, Cambridge, 1967-68; asst. research chemist UCLA, 1968-73, asst. prof. in residence, 1970-71; research chemist. U.S. Geol. Survey, Reston, Va., 1974-81, chief, br. analytical chemistry, 1981—. Bd. dirs. Reston Community Players, pres. 1978-79; bd. dirs. Friends of Reston Community Center, pres. 1979-80. Haggin fellow, 1963-64; Murrill fellow, 1964-65; Tenn. Eastman fellow, 1965-66; NSF fellow, 1966. Mem. Am. Chem. Soc., Meteoritical Soc., AAAS, Sigma Xi. Home: 11314 Handlebar Rd Reston VA 22091 Office: Mail Stop 923 US Geol Survey Reston VA 22092

BAER, BEN KAYSER, cotton merchant; b. Charleston, W. Va., June 26, 1926; s. Frank Adler and Helen (Kayser) B.; m. Eleanor Hirsch, Nov. 5, 1953; children—Julie Ann, Ben, Frank Edward. B.A., Phillips Exeter Acad., 1944; A.B., Princeton U., 1948; LL.B., Yale U., 1950. Ptnr. Campbell, McClintic & Jones, Charleston, 1950-57; chmn. bd. Allenberg Cotton Co., Memphis, 1965—, N.Y. Cotton Exchange, 1983; pres. Am. Cotton Shippers, 1974, So. Cotton Shippers, Memphis, 1970. Served with USNR, 1944-46. Mem. Phi Beta Kappa. Jewish. Home: 5026 Greenway Rd Memphis TN 38117 Office: Allenberg Cotton Co PO Box 154 Memphis TN 38101

BAER, TOMMY PERCY, lawyer; b. Berlin, Germany, Aug. 4, 1938; s. Bernhard and Lucie (Hirsch) B.; m. Margret A. Gogliormella, Feb. 27, 1967 (div. Feb. 1981); children—Dahlia R., Jason B.; m. 2d, Elizabeth T. Shull, Mar. 21, 1981. J.D., Georgetown U., 1963; B.A., U. Richmond, 1960. Bar: Va. 1963. Law clk. U.S. Dist. Ct. (ea. dist.) Va., 1963-64; asst. U.S. atty. Ea. Dist. Va., 1964-67; ptnr. Horwitz, Baer & Neblett, Richmond, 1967-74, Baer & Neblett, 1974—. Bd. dirs. NCCJ, Richmond; vice chmn. B'nai B'rith Internat. Membership Cabinet; mem. Gov.'s Adv. Com. on Volunteerism; mem. Henrico County Democratic Com., 1981-83. Recipient Young Leadership award B'nai B'rith Internat., 1978. Mem. Henrico County Bar Assn. (pres. 1984-85) Richmond Criminal Bar Assn. (co-founder), Phi Beta Kappa, Omicron Delta Kappa. Lodge: B'nai B'rith (internat. v.p. 1984—). Home: 1617 Swansbury Dr Richmond VA 23233 Office: 2907 Hungary Spring Rd Richmond VA 23228

BAESLER, SCOTTY, city official. Mayor, City of Lexington, Ky. Office: 200 E Main St Lexington KY 40507*

BAGBY, RICHARD JULIAN, radiologist; b. Banner Elk, N.C., July 18, 1940; s. Wesley Marvin and Ila Paunee (Rigsby) B.; m. Nancy Ellen Shea, Aug. 14, 1965; children—MaryKatherine, Julia Ellen. B.A., Emory U., 1962, M.D., 1966. Intern, Emory U., Atlanta VA, Grady Meml. Hosp., 1966-67; resident in diagnostic radiology Emory U., 1969-71; fellow in med. journalism Northwestern Medill Sch. Journalism, 1963; fellow in pathology Mayo Clinic, 1964; fellow in psychiatry Menninger Found., 1965; gen. vascular radiology fellow Emory U., 1971-72; radiologist Morgan, Hiatt, Hines, Culbert & March, P.A., Winter Park, Fla., since 1972—; staff Winter Park Meml. Hosp., Brookwood Community Hosp. Bd. dirs. central chpt. Am. Heart Assn., 1983-85; founder Human Crisis Council, 1981, pres., 1981-82; bd. dirs. Local Health Council East Central Fla., Inc., 1982-84; bd. dirs. United Fund, 1976, Northeast Orange County Community Mental Health Bd., 1980-82, Health Systems Agy. Orange County, 1980-82. Served to capt. USAF, 1967-69. Mem. AMA, Fla. Med. Assn. (del. 1984-85), Orange County Med. Assn. (exec. com. 1979—, pres. 1985), So. Med. Assn., Am. Coll. Radiology, Radiol. Soc. North Am., Soc. Nuclear Medicine, Am. Coll. Med. Imaging, Central Fla. Ultrasound Soc. (pres. 1983-84), Soc. Aerospace Medicine, Central Fla. Radiol. Soc. (founder 1982, pres. 1983-84), Sigma Chi, Eta Sigma Psi, Phi Rho Sigma, Phi Chi. Clubs: Winter Park Racquet; Orlando Country. Avocations: long distance running (Boston marathon 1981, 82, 84); canoeing; kayyaking; long distance swimming.

BAGBY, WILLIAM RARDIN, lawyer; b. Grayson, Ky., Feb. 19, 1910; s. John Albert and Nano (Rardin) B.; A.B., Cornell U., 1933; LL.B., U. Mich., 1936; postgrad. Northwestern U., 1946-47; m. Elizabeth Hinkel, Nov. 22, 1975; 1 son from previous marriage, John Robert. Bar: Ky. 1937, Ohio 1952. Practiced in Grayson, 1937-43; city atty. Grayson, 1939-41, judge, 1941-43; pub. Enquirer, Grayson, 1937-43; counsel U.S. Treasury, 1946-54; practice law, Lexington, Ky. 1954—; prof. law U. Ky., 1956-57. Chmn., Lexington-Fayette County Bd. Adjustment, 1964—; trustee Bagby Music Lovers' Found., N.Y.C., 1963-67; trustee, counsel Ephraim McDowell Cancer Research Found., 1980—; gen. counsel Headley-Whitney Mus., 1975-83; bd. dirs. Bluegrass Trust for Hist. Preservation, 1973-79. Served as lt. USNR, 1944-46. Mem. ABA, Ky., Ohio bar assns., Kappa Sigma, Democrat. Episcopalian. Clubs: Rotary, Iroquois Hunt, Keeneland, Spindletop; Wichita Country. Home: 228 Market St Lexington KY 40508 Office: First Nat Bldg Lexington KY 40507

BAGGERLY, EVERETT ELZY, finance company executive; s. Newton and Sarah Elizabeth (Ferguson) B.; A.B., Goddard Coll.; M.Ed., Wayne State U., also Edn. Specialist; m. Bonnie M. Barnette, Mar. 1, 1969; children by previous marriage—Edward E., Timothy M. Salesman, sales mgr., collector, collection mgr. P.F. Collier & Son, Inc., N.Y.C., 1933-38; collector, collection mgr., credit mgr., operations mgr., dist. mgr. CIT Corp., N.Y.C., 1939-53, gen. mgr., pres. Island Interprises, Inc., Okinawa, 1949-51; mng. dir. Micronesia Nav. Co., Micronesia Metal & Equipment Co., Inc., Trust Ty. of Pacific Islands, 1953-56; owner, pres. Micronesia Investment Co., Guam, Marianas Islands, 1956-59; gen. operations mgr., v.p., cons. urban problems Ford Motor Credit Co., Dearborn, Mich., 1959-71; owner Eastern Calif. Investment Co., pres. Micronesia Investment Co., Inc., owner Everett E. Baggerly Ins. Agy., Victorville, Calif., 1973-74; v.p. adminstrn. Freightliner Credit Corp., Portland, Oreg., 1974-78; gen. mgr. Stewart & Tunno Inc., Portland, 1978-80. Chmn. Tax Appeal Bd., Guam, Bd. Equalization, 1957-59; adv. council SAC, 1950-59; mem. Oreg. Wages and Hours Commn., 1975-80; treas. Dem. Party of Oreg., 1977-83. Mem. bd. advisors City and Country Sch., Bloomfield Hills, Mich., 1961-69. Trustee, v.p. Childrens Internat. Summer Village, 1964-70. Served to capt. USAAF, 1943-45. Mem. Am. Mgmt. Assn., Soc. for Advancement Mgmt., Internat. Soc. Gen. Semantics (v.p., dir.), Am. Legion, People to People, C. of C. (dir.), Am. Humanistic Psychol. Assn., Am. Indsl. Bankers Assn. (dir.), Ops. Research Soc. Am. Clubs: Elks, Kiwanis (pres. 1979-80), City, Internat., Royal Rosarian (Knight). Home: 1978 Wolf Laurel Dr Sun City Center FL 33570 also 19 Cove Rd Wilmot Creek Newcastle ON Canada

BAGGETT, DURWARD AUGUSTUS, physician; b. Smackover, Ark., Dec. 30, 1924; s. David A. and Thelma (Collins) B.; B.S., U. Tex., 1949, M.D., U. Tex.-Galveston, 1959; m. Vadis Dale Park, Apr. 7, 1946; children—Mary Ann Baggett McGuffin, David D. Chemist, Cities Service Refining Corp., Lake Charles, La., 1949-51; research chemist Dow Chem. Co., Freeport, Tex., 1951-55; intern Brackenridge Hosp., Austin, 1959-60; family practice as physician and surgeon, Austin, 1960—; chief of staff Brackenridge Hosp., 1976. Served with USNR, USMCR, 1942-46. Diplomate Am. Bd. Family Practice. Fellow Am. Acad. Family Physicians; mem. AMA, Tex. Med. Assn. (council ann. sessions), Travis County Med. Assn., Tex. Acad. Family Physicians (pres.), Travis County Acad. Family Physicians (pres. 1966), Sigma Xi, Phi Theta Kappa. Baptist. Clubs: Masons (32 deg.), Shriners. Patentee in chem. field. Home: Austin TX Office: 1313 Red River Suite 126 Austin TX 78701

BAGGS, LEAH L. BATES (MRS. LINTON DANIEL BAGGS, JR.), civic worker; b. Franklinville, N.Y.; d. William Henry and Arlie Mae (Bozworth) Bates; A.B., Barnard Coll., 1922; student spl. courses various univs.; m. Linton Daniel Baggs, Jr., Oct. 1, 1926; children—Joan Bates (Mrs. Herbert A. McKenzie, Jr.), Linton Daniel III. Hon. bd. dirs. Macon Community Concert Assn., 1968—, pres., 1959-64; bd. dirs. Middle Ga. Camellia Soc., v.p. Macon Grand Opera Assn., 1954—; vice regent Ga. div. Magna Charta Dames, 1968-70, regent, 1970-72; hon. state regent Daus. Am. Colonists, 1962, nat. chmn. colonial heritage com., 1962-64; com. chmn. Ga. br. Sons and Daus. of Pilgrims Soc., 1954-55. Mem. AAUW, Ga. Soc. Mayflower Descs. (corr. sec. 1960-62), Pilgrim John Howland Soc., D.A.R., Middle Ga. Hist. Soc. (charter mem.). Am., Ga., Middle Ga. (dir. 1974—), S.C. camellia socs., Nat. Trust for Historic Preservation, Sigma Alpha Iota. Presbyterian. Clubs: Barnard Coll. (v.p. 1967-72), Morning Music (pres. 1951-53), Atlanta Music, Capitol City Atlanta (Atlanta); Idle Hour Country (Macon, Ga.). Home: 1137 N Jackson Springs Rd Macon GA 31211

BAGGS, WILBUR JAMES, JR., gynecologist; b. Balt., Nov. 10, 1919; s. Wilbur James and Evelyn Thistle (McCoy) B.; B.A., U. Richmond, 1940; M.D., Med. Coll. Va., 1943; m. Jessie Joyner, Nov. 17, 1980; children by previous marriage—Beverly Lynn, Barbara Denise. Intern, Charity Hosp. La., New Orleans, 1944; resident Norfolk (Va.) Gen. Hosp., 1946-47, Charity Hosp. La., 1947-50; practice medicine specializing in gynecology, New Orleans, 1950, Newport News, Va., 1951—. Served with USN, 1944-46. Diplomate Am. Bd. Ob-Gyn. Fellow A.C.S.; mem. Am. Acad. Thermology, Soc. Study Breast Disease, Med. Soc. Va., Newport News Med. Soc. (pres. 1968). Episcopalian. Club: James River Country (Newport News). Office: 328 Main St Newport News VA 23601

BAGLEY, MARK LEE, engineering company excutive; b. Dearborn, Mich., June 13, 1958; s. Tolly Pierson and Patricia Ann (Mandefield) Booker. B.S., Ind. State U., 1981. Cert. in radiol. safety, Ala. Safety engr. J.M. Foster Inc., Clairton, Pa., 1980-81; safety dir. So. div. J.M. Foster Inc., Alcoa, Tenn., 1981-82; area supt. Foster, Correct & Sargent, Birmingham, Ala., 1982—; pres. M.L. & B. Safety Engring., Cons., Cropwell, Ala., 1983—; cons. in field. Contbr. articles to profl. jours. Active Baptist Med. Ctr. Found., Birmingham, 1984, Annual Antique Show, 1985, Big Brothers Greater Birmingham, 1985. Mem. Nat. Safety Mgmt. Soc., Am. Soc. Safety Engrs., Nat. Fire Protection Assn., Nat. Safety Council, Sigma Mu. Republican. Methodist. Avocations: flying, mountain climbing; skiing. Home: Route 1 Box 46 Logan Martin Lake Cropwell AL 35024 Office: Foster Correct & Sargent PO Box 540 Fairfield AL 35064

BAGLEY, ROBERT GILBERT, fire chief; b. South Norfolk, Va., Dec. 11, 1930; s. James Clark and Corrine (White) B; m. Peggy Poplin, Nov. 17, 1956; 1 child, Jocelyn Page. Student Purdue U., Old Dominion U., U. Md., Coll. William and Mary. With Chesapeake Fire Dept., Va., 1950—, fire chief, 1970—. Mem. Chesapeake Transp. Safety Commn., 1970—; bd. dirs. Tidewater Emergency Med. Service, 1972-80; local advisor U.S. Selective Service System, 1971-75. Served with U.S. Army, 1952-54. Mem. Chesapeake Firemen's Assn. (past pres.), Tidewater Firemen's Assn. (past pres.), Chesapeake Better Bus. Bur., Hampton Roads C. of C. (vice chmn. bd. dirs. 1984—), Va. Fire Chiefs Assn. (exec. bd. 1965-75), Police Assn. Va., Southeastern Assn. Fire Chiefs, Internat. Assn. Fire Chiefs, Internat. Assn. Arson Investigators, Nat. Fire Protection Assn. Club: Tenn. Squires. Lodges: Moose, Masons, Shriners. Home: 1403 Freeman Ave Chesapeake VA 23324 Office: Chesapeake Fire Dept 304 Albemarle Dr Chesapeake VA 23320

BAGLEY, SONTAG (SONNY), management company executive, publisher, editor; b. Cross, S.C., Feb. 24, 1942; s. Joseph Edward and Catherine Elizabeth (McCabe) B.; m. Joanne Elaine LaPorte, Apr. 11, 1963; children—Michael, Vincent. B.S. in Acctg., U. S.C., 1964. Acctg. clk. 1st Nat. Bank Balt., 1964-68; dir. fin. ops. Mil. Arms Inc., Miami, Fla., 1968-70; with CIA, McLean, Va., 1970-73; pres. Ramsay, Inc., Fayetteville, N.C., 1973-76; gen. mgr. Auto Plaza, Gadsden, Ala., 1978-79; pres. Sonny Bagley Mgmt. Group, Gadsden, 1979—; editor, pub. Bagley's Law, 1983; editor Automobile Dealer Info. Report, 1983. Republican. Mormon. Author: Sharp Axes, Dancing Bears, 1982, C-4 Plastic Explosives, A Manual, 1972; (under name Rollo Byrnes) Staying Out, Staying Cold, 1974. Office: Airport Rd Gadsden AL 35901 also PO Box 177 Gadsden AL 35902

BAGWELL, CECIL RAY, economics and political science educator; b. Slaton, Tex., Dec. 4, 1929; s. James Cecil and Mildred (Marsh) B.; m. Bonnie Shamburger, Aug. 24, 1951; children—Rebecca Lynne, David Ray. B.A., Baylor U., 1950; M.S., East Tex. State U., 1964; postgrad. U. Tex.-Tyler, 1978-80. Owner Ray Bagwell Rose Nursery, Tyler, 1951-62; tchr. Tyler Ind. Schs., 1963-67; instr. Tyler Jr. Coll., 1967-76, dept. chair, 1971-81, div. dir., instr., 1982—. Precinct chmn. Smith County Democratic Party, Tyler, 1960—. Mem. Tex. Jr. Coll. Tchrs. Assn., Phi Delta Kappa. Baptist. Avocation: gardening. Home: Route 1 Box 626 Tyler TX 75708 Office: Tyler Jr Coll PO Box 9020 Tyler TX 75711

BAGWELL, JOHN CLAUDE, medical oncologist; b. Rochester, Minn., Feb. 20, 1939; s. John S. and Elwyn (Hatchett) B.; m. Betsy Monroe, Dec. 28, 1965 (dec. 1982); children—Wendy Elizabeth, Andrew Monroe. Student Baylor U., 1956-60, M.D., 1966; B.S., So. Meth. U., 1962. Diplomate Am. Bd. Internal Medicine (Hematology and Oncology). Intern, Vanderbilt U. Med. Ctr., Nashville, 1966-67, resident, 1967-68; resident Parkland Meml. Hosp., Dallas, 1970-72; practice medicine specializing in oncology, sr. ptnr. med. oncology group, Dallas, 1974—; attending physician Baylor Med. Ctr., Presbyn. Hosp., Dallas; dir. oncology unit Baylor U. Med. Ctr., Dallas; clin. prof. U. Tex. Southwest Med. Sch. Vice pres., treas., bd. dirs. Shakespeare Festival of Dallas, 1978—. Served to maj. U.S. Army, 1968-70. Decorated Bronze Star. Mem. ACP, Tex. Soc. Med. Oncology, Tex. Club Internists, Dallas County Med. Soc. (dir.), AMA, Am. Soc. Clin. Oncology, Alpha Omega Alpha. Presbyterian. Clubs: Chandlers Landing Yacht, Tower (Dallas). Home: 712 N Washington Dallas TX 75246 Office: 3500 Gaston Dallas TX 75246

BAGWELL, NOEL REESE, JR., lawyer; b. Clarksville, Tenn., Oct. 3, 1955; s. Noel Reese and Henrietta (Smith) B.; m. Susan Kay Perrine, June 7, 1981; children—Noel Reese III, Holly Perrine. B.S., Austin Peay State U., Clarksville, 1977; J.D., Samford-Cumberland Sch. Law, 1980. Bar: Tenn. 1980, U.S. Dist. Ct. (mid. dist.) Tenn. 1980, U.S. Supreme Ct. 1984. Sr. ptnr. Bagwell, Bagwell, Parker, Riggins & Kennedy, Clarksville, 1980—; counsel Maples, Stacey and Assocs., Inc., So. Pub. Co. Stuart Calvarsina Enterprises, Inc., So. Computers Inc. (all Clarksville). Mem. Fed. Bar Assn., ABA, Tenn. Bar Assn., Montgomery County Bar Assn., Montgomery County Assn. Criminal Def. Lawyers (pres. 1982-83), Assn. Trial Lawyers Am., Tenn. Trial Lawyers Assn. (life), Tenn. Assn. Criminal Def. Lawyers, Nat. Assn. Criminal Def. Lawyers, Lawyers Involved for Tenn. Republican. Baptist. Club: Clarksville Country. Home: 1721 Merrywood Dr Clarksville TN 37043 Office: Bagwell Bagwell Parker Riggins & Kennedy 116 S 2d St Clarksville TN 37041

BAHN, GILBERT SCHUYLER, mechanical engineer; b. Syracuse, N.Y., Apr. 25, 1922; s. Chester Bert and Irene Eliza (Schuyler) B.; B.S., Columbia U., 1943; M.S. in Mech. Engring., Rensselaer Poly. Inst., 1965; Ph.D. in Engring., Columbia Pacific U., 1979; m. Iris Cummings Birch, Sept. 14, 1957 (dec.); 1 son, Gilbert Kennedy. Chem. engr. Gen. Electric Co., Pittsfield, Mass., 1946-48, devel. engr., Schenectady, 1948-53; sr. thermodynamics engr. Marquardt Co., Van Nuys, Calif., 1953-54, research scientist, 1954-64, research cons., 1964-70; engring. specialist PRC Kentron, Inc., Hampton, Va., 1970—. Mem. JANNAF Performance Standardization Working Group, 1966—, thermochemistry working group, 1967-72; propr. Schuyler Tech. Library, 1952—. Active Boy Scouts Am., 1958-78. Served to capt. USAAF, 1943-46. Recipient Silver Beaver award Boy Scouts Am., 1970. Registered profl. engr., N.Y., Calif. Mem. ASME, Am. Chem. Soc., Spl. Libraries Assn., Combustion Inst. (sec. western states sect. 1957-71), Soc. for Preservation Book of Common Prayer. Episcopalian (vestryman 1968-70). Author: Reaction Rate Compilation for the H-O-N System, 1968; Blue and White and Evergreen: William Byron Mowery and His Novels, 1981; Oliver Norton Worden's Family, 1982. Founding editor Pyrodynamics, 1963-69; proceedings editor Kinetics, Equilibria and Performance of High Temperature Systems, 1960, 63, 67; contbr. articles to profl. jours.; discoverer free radical chem. species diboron monoxide, 1966. Home: 615 Brandywine Dr Newport News VA 23602 Office: 3221 N Armistead Ave Hampton VA 23666

BAHNER, THOMAS MAXFIELD, lawyer; b. Little Rock, Nov. 26, 1933; s. Carl Tabb and Catharine (Garrott) B.; B.S., Carson Newman Coll., 1954; B.D., So. Bapt. Theol. Sem., 1957; J.D., U. Va., 1960; m. Sara Minta McIntyre, Sept. 28, 1957; children—Maxfield Tabb, Minta Susan, Margaret Catharine. Bar: Va., Tenn. 1960. Assoc., Kefauver, Duggan and McDonald, Chattanooga, 1960-62; ptnr. Duggan, McDonald and Bahner, Chattanooga, 1962-64, Chambliss, Bahner Crutchfield Gaston & Irvine, Chattanooga, 1964—. Mem. adv. com. civil rules Tenn. Supreme Ct., 1982—, mem. bd. profl. responsibility, 1982—, chmn. fin. com., 1984—. Pres. United Cerebral Palsy Greater Chattanooga, 1966-67; mem. allocations steering com. United Fund Greater Chattanooga, 1970—, vice chmn. com., 1972-73; bd. dirs. Chattanooga Council Alcoholism, 1964-65, Team Evaluation Center Inc., Chattanooga, 1965-70, Chattanooga Symphony, 1978-81; bd. dirs. Orange Grove Sch. and Center for Retarded, Chattanooga, 1962—, pres., 1973-75, chmn., 1975-76; mem. Hamilton County Sch. Bd., 1969-74; mem. adv. bd. Carson-Newman Coll., Jefferson City, Tenn., 1969—, trustee, sec., 1975-81, 83—, chmn. bd., 1983—; mem. Tenn. and Am. Sch. Bds. Assn. Recipient Disting. Alumni award Carson-Newman Coll., 1984. Fellow Am. Bar Found., Tenn. Bar Found.; mem. Chattanooga Bar Assn. (pres. 1969-70), Tenn. Bar Assn. (lectr. 1965, bd. govs. local bar conf. 1969-71, bd. govs. 1975—, pres. 1980-81), ABA, Va. State Bar, Tenn. Def. Lawyers Assn., Assn. Past Pres. Chattanooga Bar Assn., Am. Judicature Soc., So. Conf. Bar Pres. (chmn. 1980-81), Estate Planning Council (dir. 1971-72), Baptist (deacon). Clubs: Mountain City, Walden, Signal Mountain Golf and Country. (Chattanooga). Home: 718 Parsons Ln Signal Mountain TN 37377 Office: 1000 Tallan Bldg Two Union Sq Suite 1000 Chattanooga TN 37402

BAHR, EDWARD RICHARD, musician, educator, performer; b. N.Y.C., Apr. 4, 1941; s. C. Charles and M. Virginia (Rich) B.; m. Jane Ann Hartsell, June 15, 1963; children—David, Brian. B.M. in Music Edn. with distinction, Eastman Sch. Music, Rochester, N.Y., 1964, M.Mus. in Edn., 1965; D.Mus. Arts in Performance, U. Okla., 1980. Tchr., Mt. Greylock Regional High Sch., Williamstown, Mass., 1965-68; instr. music Fredonia State U., N.Y., 1968-73; lectr. music Central State U., Edmond, Okla., 1974-81; asst. prof. music Troy State U., Ala., 1981-83; assoc. prof. music Delta State U., Cleveland, Miss., 1983—. Solo euphonium player Westchester Pops Band, White Plains, N.Y., 1955-65; euphoniumist Eastman Wind Ensemble, 1963-65; 1st trombonist Berkshire Symphony Orch., 1965-68; trombonist, euphoniumist White Eagle Band, Dunkirk, N.Y., 1968-73; asst. condr. 1st trombonist Erie (Pa.) Philharm. Orch., 1968-73; soloist 1st trombone Okla. State Fair Concert Band, 1980, 81; 1st trombonist Montgomery Symphony Orch. (Ala.), 1981-83; Bach Festival Music, Rochester, Montgomery Performing Arts Ballet Orch., Ice Capades, Ice Follies, Chorus Line and Annie musicals; condr. St. Mark's Episcopal Ch. Choir, Edmond, Okla.; lectr., music competition adjudicator; editor record revs. Internat. Trombone Assn. Jour., 1975—. Home: 13 Memorial Dr Boyle MS 38730 Office: Box 3256 Dept Music Delta State U Cleveland MS 38733

BAIER, RONALD ANTON, structural engineer; b. Flushing, N.Y., Sept. 7, 1943; s. Anton and Margaret (von der Heydt) B.; B.E. in Civil Engring., City Coll. N.Y., 1967; M.E., U. Fla., 1970. Assembly and test engr. Boeing Co., Cocoa Beach, Fla., 1967-69; field engr. Pitts. Testing Lab., Miami, Fla., 1970-71; design engr. Alpine Engineered Products Inc., Pompano Beach, Fla., 1971-72, Arthur L. Bromley, cons. engr., Ft. Lauderdale, Fla., 1972-74, Jenkins & Charland, cons. engrs., Ft. Lauderdale, 1974; pvt. practice cons. structural engring., Ft. Lauderdale, 1974—; v.p. Southeastern Engring. Testing Lab., 1973—; constrn. mgr. Roof Structures, Inc., Ft. Lauderdale, 1976-77; dir. structural engring. Craven, Thompson & Assocs., Ft. Lauderdale, 1977; prin. Herbert M. Schwartz & Assos., Cons. Engrs., Miami, 1978—. Registered profl. engr., Fla., N.Y. Mem. ASCE (asso.), Fla. Engring. Soc., Am. Concrete Inst., Nat. Soc. Profl. Engrs., Mensa. Republican. Roman Catholic. Home: 1750 NW 3rd Terr 208C Ft Lauderdale FL 33311

BAILES, (ORAL) JACK, book store executive; b. Nettie, W.Va., July 16, 1910; s. Theodore and Mary (Shawver) B.; m. Lois Jones, Apr. 12, 1976. Student, Vocat. Sch., 1934-35, Blairs Bus. Coll., 1936. Asst. golf profl. Lakewood Country Club, Hendersville, N.C., 1934; owner Second Hand Store, St. Petersburg, Fla., 1935, Hotel, Colorado Springs, Colo., 1936, Gift/Shop/Antiques, Eureka Springs, Ark., 1937-58, Jack Bailes Books, Eureka Springs, 1959—. Democrat. Mem. Ch. Christ. Avocations: golf; traveling; photography; woodworking; painting. Home: 66 Mountain St PO Box 150 Eureka Springs AR 72632 Office: Jack Bailes Books PO Box 150 Eureka Springs AR 72632

BAILEY, ANN KATHLEEN, counselor, consultant; b. Conroe, Tex., Feb. 25, 1946; d. Emory Drayton and Ferne Louise (Morrison) Mahan; m. Philip Morris Bailey, Aug. 7, 1965; 1 child, Jay Morris. B.A., So. Methodist U., 1967; M.Ed., Wayne State U., 1974; Ph.D., North Tex. State U., 1985. Tchr. elem. schs. Dallas Ind. Sch. Dist., 1967-72, Arlington Ind. Sch. Dist., Tex., 1976-81; counselor, The Counseling Ctr., Arlington, 1982—; cons. Arlington Cancer Treatment Ctr., 1983-86, Jr. League of Arlington, 1981—. Named Tchr. of Yr., Butler Elem. Sch., Arlington, 1980. Mem. Tex. Assn. Counseling and Devel., Am. Assn. Counseling and Devel., Nat. Bd. Cert. Counselors. Democrat. Methodist. Avocations: weaving; skiing; painting; swimming. Home: 1433 Crownhill Dr Arlington TX 76012 Office: The Counseling Ctr 1304 W Abrams St Arlington TX 76012

BAILEY, BEN F., III, citrus grower; b. Valdosta, Ga., Aug. 15, 1944; s. Ben and Virgil (Howard) B.; children—Ryan, Erin. B.S., Fla. State U., 1966. Pres., Central Groves Corp., Vero Beach, Fla., 1979—; chmn. bd. Indian River Citrus League, 1981-83, pres., 1979-81; bd. dirs., v.p. Fla. Citrus Mut., 1977-78; mem. Indian River Grapefruit Com., 1972-73, 75-77; mem. adv. council Sen. Hawkins, Congressmen Nelson and Lewis. Trustee, Fla. House, Washington; bd. dirs Seminole Boosters, Inc.; chmn. major bus. United Way; vice chmn. Parks, Planning and Zoning Commn.; mem. bldg., long range planning com. Indian River Meml. Hosp. Served with USAR, 1966-73. Republican. Baptist. Club: 100 of Indian River County (pres.); Riomar Bay. Home: 1415 43d Ct Vero Beach FL 32960 Office: PO Box 2069 Vero Beach FL 32960

BAILEY, BENNY RAY, health care administrator, state senator; b. Price, Ky., Nov. 16, 1944; s. Viola (Tackett) B.; m. Celestine Little, June 9, 1963; m. 2d, Nikki Rieck, June 30, 1973; children—Glenn, Benny Ray, Chet, Steven. A.A., Alice Lloyd Coll., 1964; B.A., Pikeville Coll., 1966; M.S., Ind. State U., 1968; Ph.D., Ohio U., 1972. Tchr. Floyd County pub. schs., Prestonsburg, Ky., 1966-67; dean Alice Lloyd Coll., Pippa Passes, Ky., 1968-71; exec. dir. E. Ky. Health Services, Hindman, 1972—; mem. Ky. Senate, 1979—. Address: Route 1 Box 102A Hindman KY 41822

BAILEY, CARL F., telephone company executive; b. 1930. B.S./B.A., Auburn U., 1952. Asst. v.p. Ala. area AT&T, 1955-68, exec. asst., 1968-71; with South Central Bell Telephone Co., Birmingham, Ala., 1968—, asst. to pres. corp. holding, 1971, gen. mgr. ops., 1972-76, v.p. customer facility services, 1976-77, v.p., 1977-80, exec. v.p. corp. affairs, 1980, pres., chief exec. officer. Address: South Central Bell Telephone Co PO Box 771 Birmingham AL 35201*

BAILEY, CAROLYN FAULKNER, computer programmer; b. Troy, Ala., Nov. 6, 1942; d. Martin C. and Sylvania (Knotts) Faulkner; B.S. in Computer Sci. and Mgmt., U. Ala., 1980; M.S. in Personnel Mgmt., Troy State U., 1982; postgrad. Auburn U., 1982—. Staff asst. Air War Coll., Maxwell AFB, Ala., 1970-74, editorial asst., asso. programmer, 1974-75; computer technician Air Force Data Systems Design Center, Gunter AFB, Ala., 1975—; planner, organizer, dir. ednl. seminars, workshops for women, 1979—; investment and fin. mgmt. cons., 1970—; data elements mgr., dir. Med. Systems, 1980—. Vol. counselor Montgomery Area Mental Health, 1979—; bd. dirs. El Matador Condo Assn., 1983-85. Mem. LWV, AAUW (dir.), Federally Employed Women (past pres.), Cottage Hill Hist. Assn., U. Ala. Alumni Assn., Okaloosa Island Improvement Assn., Alpha Xi Delta, Beta Gamma Phi. Episcopalian. Contbr. articles to various publs. Home: 3503 Castle Ridge Rd Montgomery AL 36116 Office: Turner Bldg Gunter Air Force Station AL 36114

BAILEY, CHARLES WILLIAMS, III, realtor, electrical engineer; b. Spartanburg, S.C., July 26, 1925; s. Charles W. and Katherine F. (Ford) B.; B.E.E., Clemson U., 1947; M.E.E., N.C. State U., 1949; m. Dorothea Theresa Lamb, Feb. 5, 1960; children—Elizabeth Mary, Susan Margaret, Charles Williams IV. Asst. prof. elec. engring. The Citadel, S.C., 1949-51; design engr. Westinghouse Electric Corp., Balt., 1951-54; sales engr. Mpls. Honeywell, Charlotte, N.C., 1954-55; v.p. M.N. Weir & Sons, Inc., Pompano Beach, Fla., 1955-58; asst. to gen. mgr. Arvida Corp., Miami, 1958-61, asst. to pres., 1961-63; v.p. Arvida Realty Sales, Inc., Miami, 1963-71; pres. Bailey & Casey, Inc., Miami, 1971—; v.p. Bailey & Casey Mgmt. Co., apt. developers; developer apt. units, Pompano Beach, 1969-76; active real estate sales, Sweden, Belgium, Eng., Holland, Luxembourg. Served with U.S. Army, 1944-46. Mem. Am. Soc. Appraisers (pres. S. Fla. chpt. 1966-67), Nat. Assn. Rev. Appraisers, Fla. Assn. Mortgage Brokers, Bldg. Owners and Mgrs. Inst. Internat., Inst. Real Estate Mgmt., Nat. Inst. Farm and Land Brokers, Miami Bd. Realtors, Fla. Assn. Realtors, Internat. Real Estate Fedn. Republican. Presbyterian. Clubs: Key Biscayne Yacht, Key Biscayne Beach; Univ. (Miami), Miami, 200 Club, Bankers. Inventor underwater breathing electronic device. Contbr. articles to profl. jours. Office: 1220 AmeriFirst Bldg Miami FL 33131

BAILEY, DANNY GALE, college counselor, educator; b. Paintsville, Ky., Feb. 7, 1947; s. Andrew Lowell and Lorraine (Ferguson) B.; m. Charlene Gaye Boyd, Aug. 26, 1972. B.S., U. Ky., 1968, M.S., 1971; M.A., Morehead State U., 1983, M. Higher Edn., 1983. Tchr. agr. and forestry Johnson County Bd. Edn., Paintsville, 1969; extension agt. Cooperative Extension Service, Paintsville, 1969-70; tchr. agriculture and horticulture Franklin County Bd. Edn., Frankfort, Ky., 1970-73; coordinator spl. services, asst. prof. Ashland Community Coll., Ky., 1973-79, counselor, assoc. prof., 1979—; mem. grad. curriculum com. Morehead State U., 1982—, coll. commn. vis. com. So. Assn. Colls. Schs., 1981—. Chmn. Ashland Area Consumer Fair, 1975-77, Boyd County Community Chest 1977-78. Served to maj. U.S. Army Res., 1969—. Recipient Outstanding Young Educator award Frankfort Jaycees, 1973, Maj. Gen. Benjamin J. Butler Community Relations award U.S. Army Res., 1979, Disting. Alumnus award U. Ky. Coll. Agr., 1981, Mem. Eastern Ky. Assn. Counseling and Devel. (pres. 1981-82, 85—), Ky. Assn. Counseling and Devel. (bd. dirs. 1981-82, 85—), Ky. Assn. Res. Officers Am. (v.p. chpt. 1985—), Alpha Zeta, Phi Delta Kappa, Coll. Personnel Assn. Ky. Democrat. Baptist. Avocations: running; reading; basketball; travel. Home: 3712 Greenbriar Rd Ashland KY 41101 Office: Ashland Community Coll 1400 College Dr Ashland KY 41101

BAILEY, FREDERICK EUGENE, industrial polymer chemist, researcher, educator; b. Bklyn., Oct. 8, 1927; s. Frederick Eugene and Florence (Berkeley) B.; m. Mary Catherine Lowder, May 7, 1979. A.B., Amherst Coll, 1948; M.S., Yale U., 1950, Ph.D., 1952. With Union Carbide Corp., South Charleston, W.Va., 1952—, sr. chemist, 1952, group leader, 1959, asst. dir. research devel., 1962, mgr. market research, 1969, sr. research scientist, 1971—; adj. prof. chemistry Marshall U., 1975—; adj. prof. chem. engring. W.Va. Coll. Grad. Studies, 1980—; chmn. Gordon Research Conf. Polymer, 1972, 1984. Fellow AAAS, N.Y. Acad. Scis., Am. Inst. Chemists (cert. chemist); mem. Am. Chem Soc. (chmn. div. polymer chemistry 1976—, chmn., councillor 1978—), Am. Phys. Soc., Soc. Rheology. Republican. Episcopalian. Clubs: Williams (N.Y.), Charleston Tennis. Author: Poly (Ethylene Oxide), 1976; assoc. editor Urethane Chemistry, Am. Chem Soc. Symposium Series, 1981, editor series Initiation of Polymerization, 1984; co-editor Coulombic Interactions in Macromolecules, 1986; contbr. articles to tech. publs.; patentee in field. Office: Union Carbide Tech Ctr PO Box 8361 South Charleston WV 25303

BAILEY, JACK BENNETT, healthcare management executive; b. Celina, Tenn., Aug. 29, 1940; s. Jack Marcom and Lockie Marie (Reed) B.; m. Lyla French, Oct. 19, 1968; children—Mark Bennett, Caroline Jennings. B.S., Tenn. Tech. U., 1969. C.P.A., Tenn. Mem. audit staff Ernst & Ernst, Nashville, 1969-72; controller, audit mgr. Hosp. Corp. Am., Macon, Ga. and Nashville, 1972-74; asst. regional mgr. Humana Inc., Mobile, Ala., 1974-80; exec. dir. Hospital de la Tour, Geneva, Switzerland, 1980-82; adminstr. Springhill Hosp., Mobile, Ala., 1982-83; pres. Spectra Profl. Search, Atlanta, 1983-84; dir. Internat. Healthcare Mgmt., Inc., 1984—; chmn. bd. dirs. Jack B. Bailey & Assocs., Atlanta, 1983—. Bd. dirs. Springhill Hosp., Mobile, Ala., 1982-83. Served with AUS, 1958-61. Ky. Col. Mem. Am. Inst. C.P.A.s, Tenn. Soc. C.P.A.s, Healthcare Fin. Mgmt. Assn., Am. Coll. Hosp. Adminstrs. Democrat. Episcopalian. Home: 140 Valley Cove Atlanta GA 30338 Office: Internat Healthcare Mgmt Inc 140 Valley Cove Atlanta GA 30338

BAILEY, JACK CLINTON, research entomologist; b. Austin, Tex., Aug. 10, 1936; s. Landrum Littlepage and Ella Mae (Sanders) B.; m. Maybell Abernathy, July 22, 1961; children—Clinton, Brian. B.S., Tex. A&M U., 1959; M.S., Miss. State U., 1965, Ph.D., 1967. Jr. entomologist Tex. A&M Expt. Sta., Westaco, Tex., 1959-63; research technician U.S. Dept. Agr., Agrl. Research Service, Mississippi State, Miss., 1963-67, research entomologist, Stoneville, Miss., 1967—; adj. assoc. prof. entomology Miss. State U., 1968-83. Scouting coordinator Boy Scouts Am. Mem. Entomol. Soc. Am., Miss. Entomol. Assn., Ga. Entomol. Soc., Kans. Entomol. Soc. Baptist. Lodge: Lions (Leland, Miss.) (pres. 1973-74). Contbr. articles to profl. jours. Office: PO Box 225 Stoneville MS 38776

BAILEY, JAMES LOVELL, conservationist, former state official; b. Portland, Tenn., Dec. 18, 1907; s. James Johnson and Annie May (Lovell) B.; student Bowling Green U., 1925, Middle Tenn. State Tchrs. Coll., 1926-29, Western Ky. State Coll., 1929-30, George Washington U., 1931-33, U. Tenn., 1938-41; m. Fairrelle Brown, June 1, 1940 (dec. Dec. 1976); 1 dau., Annie Elizabeth (Mrs. Richard Genung); m. Hester W. Brown, Apr. 29, 1979; 3 stepchildren. With U.S. Bur. of Census, 1930-32, U.S. Dept. of Agr., 1933-37; with Tenn. Dept. Conservation, Nashville 1937-76, dir. ednl. service, 1957-76; organized 1st soil conservation dist. in Tenn., 1940; mem. Tenn. Conservation Commn., 1978-85, sec., 1980—. Pres. Davidson County (Tenn.) chpt. Muscular Dystrophy Assn., 1957; mem. garden com. Tenn. Bot. Gardens and Fine Arts Center, Nashville, 1969—; mem. Vol. State Coll. Adv. and Devel. Council, 1976—; charter mem., bd. dirs. Tenn. Environ. Council, 1970-77, life mem., 1977—; bd. dirs. Tenn. Beautiful, 1972; trustee West Coast Christian Corp. Served with USNR, 1942-45. Recipient awards including Cartter Patten award Tenn. Conservation League, 1963, Key Man award Conservation Edn. Assn., 1967, Gov.'s Conservationist of Year award, 1971, silver seal Nat. Council State Garden Clubs, 1973, Forestry Recognition award Soc. Am. Foresters, 1976; cert. of appreciation Nat. Resources Socs. Tenn., 1982; citation Hort. Soc. Davidson County, 1983. Fellow Soil Conservation Soc. Am. (pres. Tenn. council chpts. 1961, regional rep., conservation history com.); meritorious service award 1985; mem. Middle Tenn. Conservancy Council, East Tenn. Edn. Assn., Nat. Assn. Conservation Edn. and Publicity (pres. 1949), Conservation Edn. Assn. (life), Highland Rim (dir.) Hist. Soc., Dickson County Hist. Soc.; Nat. Wildlife Fedn., Tenn. Assn. Preservation Antiquities, Nat. Trust for Historic Preservation, Bowen Campbell House Assn. (v.p.), Common Cause, Tenn. Fedn. Garden Clubs Inc. (life). Mem. Ch. of Christ. Club: Nashville Torch (pres. 1963-64). Author: Our Land and Our Living, 1940. Assoc. editor Tenn. Conservationist, 1959-72, editor-in-chief, 1972-76, editor emeritus, 1976—. Home: Route 2 Box 102 White Bluff TN 37187

BAILEY, JAMES RUDY, JR., religious administrator; b. Murray, Ky., Sept. 3, 1946; s. James R. and Georgia E. B.; m. Judy V. Spivey, Dec. 25, 1968; children—Angela Hope, April Dawn. Student Draughons Bus. Coll., 1968-69, Murray State U., 1970-72. Sales cons. Met. Ins. Co., Paducah, Ky., 1970; clk., parts man, blueprint reader TVA, Knoxville, Tenn., 1971-72; ptnr., operator Rudy's Body Shop, Murray, Ky., 1972-74; gen. mgr. body shop and service dept. North City Ford Co., Madisonville, Ky., 1974-76; tchr., Sunday sch. supt., adminstrv. asst. Madisonville Christian Sch., Madisonville (Ky.) Baptist Temple, 1976-81; minister fin. and adminstrn. Martinsburg (W.Va.) Christian Acad., Shenandoah Bible Bapt. Ch., 1981-85; supt. Maj. Fla. Enterprises, Inc., 1985—; cons. Dupont Refinish Tng. Ctr. Found. Econ. Edn. Served in USMC, 1964-68.

BAILEY, JOE DAN, contact lens manufacturing company executive; b. Quanah, Tex., Oct. 8, 1932; s. Joe Curtis and Ellen Marie (Cox) B.; m. Mary Jane Smith, June 20, 1955; children—Mary Christine Bailey Vaughan, Anna Kathryn Bailey Sullivan, Theodore Curtis, Shirley Rebecca, Joseph Allen. B.S.,

Tex. Tech U., 1957. Cert. Nat. Bd. Contact Lens Examiners. With Anderson-Clayton, Inc., 1957-59, Santa Fe Industries, 1960-65, Mead Corp., Lubbock, Tex., 1965-67, Union Corp., Little Rock, 1967-71; pres. Bailey-Smith Corp., Little Rock, 1972—; v.p., sec., dir. Precision Bus. Computors, Little Rock, 1982—; v.p., sec., dir. Data World, Inc., Little Rock, 1982—; pres. Product Devel. Consortium, Inc., Little Rock, 1981—; clin. instr. dept. ophthalmology U. Ark. Med. Scis. Campus, Little Rock. Fellow Contact Lens Soc. Am.; Contact Lens Mfrs. Assn. (dir.), C. of C., Kappa Sigma. Roman Catholic. Clubs: Rotary, Serra; Country (Little Rock). Office: PO Box 3038 Little Rock AR 72203

BAILEY, (JOHN) LARRIE, investment advisor; b. Weston, W.Va., Mar 2, 1934; s. John W. and Carrie Elizabeth (Given) B.; A.B., U. S.C., 1955; M.A. in Polit. Sci., W.Va. U., 1966; m. Joyce Kennedy, Oct. 15, 1966; children—John Kennedy, David Cleveland, Anne Joyce. Tchr., Lost Creek (W.Va.) High Sch., 1960-62; mem. W.Va. Ho. of Dels., 1960-62; stockbroker Parker-Hunter, Inc., Clarksburg, W.Va., 1969-71; pres. Bailey & Assocs., Inc., Fairmont, W.Va., 1971-76; treas. State of W.Va., 1976-85; investment advisor, 1985—. Served as officer USN, 1956-59. Recipient Meritorious Service award W.Va. N.G., 1981. Mem. Nat. Assn. State Treas. pres. 1984), Naval Res. Assn., Res. Officers Assn. (v.p. for navy, marine corps and coast guard 1967-68), Navy League, S.R. (pres. W.Va. Soc.), Phi Kappa Sigma. Democrat. Baptist. Lodges: Elks, Shriners. Home and office: 5 Jo Harry Rd Fairmont WV 26554

BAILEY, JOY HAFNER, university program administrator, psychologist, educator; b. Weehawkin, N.J., Aug. 15, 1928; d. Elmar William and Fern (Williams) Hafner; children—Kerry, Jan, Leslie, Liza, Annie Laurie, Kristin. B.A., Austin Coll., 1974; M.S., East Tex. State U., 1975, Ed.D., 1977. Counselor, instr. East Tex. State U., 1976-80; dir. spl. services acad./counseling program Ga. State U., 1980—, asst. prof. devel. studies; pvt. practice marriage and family therapy. Mem. Am. Psychol. Assn., Am. Assn. Marriage and Family Therapists, Psi Chi. Office: Box 649 GA State U Atlanta GA 30303

BAILEY, K. E., petroleum pipeline company executive; b. 1942. B.S., Mo. Sch. Mines, 1946. With Continental Pipe Line, 1964-66, Yellowstone Pipeline, 1966, Continental Pipeline, 1966-73; with Williams Pipe Line Co. Inc., Tulsa, Okla., 1973—, pres., 1980—, also dir. Office: Williams Pipe Line Co One Williams Ctr Tulsa OK 74101*

BAILEY, LUTHER CARROLL, industrial company executive; b. Techumpsy, Okla., Mar. 2, 1951; s. Denzil Woodfer and Marjorie Louise (Melot) B.; m. Martha Jane Becton, June 26, 1971; children—Jennifer, Amanda. Student Gulf Coast Coll., 1970-71, Tech. Tech. U., 1969-72. With Bailey Boiler Works, Inc., Lubbock, Tex., 1967—, now v.p., boiler and steam engr. Served with USAR, 1970-76. Republican. Methodist. Address: 3505 83d Dr Lubbock TX 79423

BAILEY, ROBERT FREDERICK, manufacturing company executive; b. Corsicana, Tex., Oct. 29, 1943; s. O'Connor and Carleen Alice (Trower) B.; m. Martha Elizabeth Irwin, Dec. 21, 1965; children—Ashley Alaine, Caroline Elizabeth. B.B.A., N. Tex. State U., 1966. Sr. sales rep. Scott Paper Co., Dallas, 1966-68; area mgr. Gen. Electric-Silicone, Houston, 1968-71, market devel. specialist, Waterford, N.Y., 1971-75; sales and mktg. mgr. Compo Industries, Waltham, Mass., 1975-79; gen. mgr., dir. Plastics Concepts, Inc., Houston, 1979-82; dir. internat. ops. Kerite Co. subs. Harvey Hubbell, Houston, 1982—; dir. Plastics Concepts, Inc., Houston, Leather Concepts, Houston, 1980-83; cons. Ludlow Corp., Freemont, Ohio, 1980-82, Monkey Grip Rubber Co., Dallas, 1979-81. Co-chmn. Klein United Methodist Activity Com., Houston, 1977; sub-chmn. Klein High Sch. Booster, Houston, 1982. Named Top Salesman, Scott Paper Co., 1967. Mem. Soc. Plastic Engrs., Am. Mgmt. Assn., Plastic Suppliers Assn., Soc. Petroleum Engrs. Republican. Methodist. Home: 7607 Feliciana Ln Spring TX 77379 Office: The Kerite Co 2650 Fountainview 200 Houston TX 77057

BAILEY, ROBERT LEE, JR., sheriff, county official; b. Huntington, W.Va., Oct. 7, 1939; s. Robert Lee and Pearl (Ferguson) B.; m. Carol Joyce Schill, Dec. 1, 1961; children—Lisa Diann, Robin Lee. B.S., Marshall U., 1970, M.A., 1972; student Nat. Sheriffs Acad., Quantico, Va., 1981. Dep. sheriff Cabell County, Huntington, W.Va., 1964-68, parole officer State W.Va., Charleston, 1968-69; tchr., coach Huntington East High Sch., 1970-81; sheriff, treas. Cabell County, Huntington, 1981—. Served with USMC, 1958-61. Recipient George Van Zant award Jaycees Huntington, 1981-82. Mem. W.Va. Sheriffs Assn. (pres. 1983), Internat. Asn. Chiefs Police, Nat. Sheriffs Assn., Internat. Narcotic Enforcement Officers Assn., Marine Corps League, Am. Legion, DAV. Democrat. Baptist. Lodges: Elks, Moose. Avocation: fishing. Home: 2127 Washington Ave Huntington WV 25704 Office: Cabell County Sheriffs Dept 8th St and 4th Ave Huntington WV 25701

BAILEY, ROBERT LESLIE, insurance company manager; b. Atlanta, Oct. 9, 1938; s. Earl L. and Florence (Carlos) B.; student Ga. State U., 1957-60; m. Lorrie Wade, July 26, 1964; 1 dau., Tonya. With Wausau Ins. Cos., 1959—, claims adjuster, then liability and compensation examiner and supr., Atlanta office, to 1976, liability claim mgr., Orlando, Fla., 1976—; lectr. in field; mem. Regular Arbitration Ins. Co., Atlanta, 1974-76; chmn. Orlando Spl. Arbitration Com., 1959—; mem. Adv. Com. for Ins.-Legal Activities, Atlanta, 1972-74; mem. adv. com. Ga. Workers Compensation Com., 1974-76; mem. Ga. Gov.'s Adv. Com. on No-Fault Impact on Ins. Rates, 1970; instr. time mgmt. techniques to industry personnel; speaker bus. and motel assns. on liability and security problems. Author guides on pub. liability exposure for constrn. industry. Mem. Orlando Claim Assn., Atlanta Claim Assn., Orlando Claim Mgrs. Council. Republican. Baptist. Club: Toastmasters (pres. Druid Hills 1971). Home: 687 Blairshire Circle Winter Park FL 32792 Office: 1040 Woodcock Rd Orlando FL 32814

BAILEY, RUTH HILL (MRS. A. PURNELL BAILEY), foundation executive; b. Roanoke, Va., Sept. 17, 1916; d. Henry Palmer and Carolyn Ruffin (Andrews) Hill; B.S. in Edn., Longwood Coll., Farmville, Va., 1939; postgrad. Ecumenical Inst., Jerusalem, 1979; m. Amos Purnell Bailey, Aug. 22, 1942; children—Eleanor Carol Bailey Harriman, Anne Ruth Bailey Page, Joyce Elizabeth Bailey Richardson, Jeanne Purnell Bailey Dodge. High sch. tchr. in Va., 1939-48; tour dir. to Europe and Middle East, 1963-73; syndicated columnist family newspaper, 1954-70; exec. sec. Nat. Methodist Found., Arlington, Va., 1979—; pres. Va. Conf. Bishop Cabinet Wives, United Meth. Ch., 1963-64; pres. Richmond (Va.) Ministers Wives, 1965-66; chmn. bd. missions Trinity United Meth. Ch., McLean, Va., 1975-79, adminstrv. bd., 1971—; life mem. United Meth. Women. Div. sec. United Givers Fund, 1964-65; sec. bd. dirs. N.T.M., 1981—. Recipient Staff award Bd. Higher Edn. and Ministry, United Meth. Ch., 1976, Chaplain Ministry award, 1981. Clubs: Country of Va., Jefferson Woman's. Home: 7815 Falstaff Rd McLean VA 22102 Office: 1835 N Nash St Arlington VA 22209

BAILEY, SCOTT FIELD, bishop; b. Houston, Oct. 7, 1916; s. William Stuart and Tallulah (Smith) B.; B.A., Rice U., 1938; postgrad. U. Tex. Law Sch., 1938-39; M.Div., Va. Theol. Sem., 1942, D.D., 1965; S.T.M., U. of South, 1953, D.D., 1965; m. Evelyn Williams, Dec. 11, 1943; children—Louise (Mrs. Allen C. Taylor), Nicholas, Scott Field, Sarah (Mrs. Hugh A. Fitzsimons III). Ordained to ministry Episcopal Ch., 1942; pastor in Waco, Lampasas, San Augustine, Nacogdoches, Austin, Tex., 1942-51; asst. to bishop of Tex., 1961-64; suffragan bishop of Tex., 1964-75; coadjutor bishop of West Tex., 1976-77, bishop of West Tex., 1977—. Sec. ho. of bishops Episcopal Ch., 1967—, exec. officer Gen. Conv., 1973-77. Served as chaplain USNR, World War II. Fellow Coll. of Preachers; mem. Phi Delta Theta. Home: 2422 Toftrees Dr San Antonio TX 78209 Office: PO Box 6885 San Antonio TX 78209

BAILLIE, MARY HELEN, accounting company executive; b. Clio, S.C., Aug. 18, 1926; d. Paul Clydus and Laurie (Easterling) Orr; grad. Carolina Bus. Coll., 1946; children—William Sinclair, Carol Anderson. Controller, George I. Clarke, Inc., Atlanta, 1953-57, DuBose Reed Constrn. Co./W. Carroll DuBose, Inc., Ft. Lauderdale, Fla., 1970-74; asst. controller H.B. Fuller Co., Ft. Lauderdale, 1975-76; owner M.H. Baillie & Assocs., Inc., Ft. Lauderdale, 1977—. Mem. sign adv. bd. City of Ft. Lauderdale; bd. dirs. Women in Distress, 1984—; mem. Broward County Commn. on Status of Women, 1984—, mem. Leadership Broward, 1985. Mem. Nat. Accts. Assn. (dir. 1977-79, dir. spl. activities 1979—), Fla. Accts. Assn. (dir. 1977-79, sec. 1977-79), Ft. Lauderdale C. of C. (dir. 1979—), Internat. Assn. Fin. Planners. Republican. Clubs: Women's Execs. (dir. 1978-80, treas. 1978-80), Ft. Lauderdale Country, Le Club Internat. Home: 3471 NE 17th Terr Fort Lauderdale FL 33334 Office: MH Baillie & Assos Inc Suite 208 2801 E Oakland Park Blvd Fort Lauderdale FL 33306

BAILLIO, O. DALLAS, JR., library official; b. Shreveport, La., Feb. 16, 1940; s. O. Dallas and Edna Oden (Hartsfield) B.; m. Jimmie Les Dawson, Mar. 14, 1964; children—Emily Rene, Nancy Amy. B.S., La. Tech. U., 1962; M.S., U. So. Calif., 1970, La. State U., 1971. Library dir. Withers Public Library, Bloomington, Ill., 1972-76, Mobile (Ala.) Public Library, 1977—. Served to capt. USAF, 1963-70. Mem. ALA, Ala. Library Assn. (pres. 1980-81), S.E. Library Assn. Presbyterian. Home: 1569 McIntyre Dr Mobile AL 36618 Office: 701 Government St Mobile AL 36602

BAINBRIDGE, RUSSELL BENJAMIN, JR., oil and gas property management executive, consultant; b. Chgo., Feb. 24, 1945; s. Russell Benjamin, Sr. and Mary (Hudson) B.; m. Nancy H. Ferguson, Nov. 13, 1982. B.A. in Philosophy, Duquesne U., 1968; M.S. in Geology, Iowa State U., 1976; M.B.A. in Fin., DePaul U., 1980. Instr., Iowa State U., Ames, 1975-76; banking assoc. Continental Ill. Bank, Chgo., 1976-81; v.p. Penn Square Bank, Oklahoma City, 1981-82; sr. v.p. Union Bank and Trust, Oklahoma City, 1982-85; pres., chief exec. officer TCO Mgmt., Inc., Oklahoma City, 1985—, also dir. Mem. governing bd. Okla. Mus. of Art Assocs., Oklahoma City, 1984—. Mem. AAAS, Am. Assn. Petroleum Geologists. Office: Trust Co of Okla 1001 NW 63rd St Oklahoma City OK 73116

BAINES, ROBERT EMMETT, consultant; b. Poughkeepsie, N.Y., Dec. 29, 1922; s. Robert and Laura Anna (Briggs) B.; m. Kathryn Rose Feagin, Sept. 4, 1949; children—Robert Ellis, Jack Clifford, Lawrence Arthur. B.A. in Math., So. Meth. U., 1949. Mgr. actuarial Republic Nat. Life Ins. Co., Dallas, 1950-53, asst. actuary, 1953-56, asst. v.p., programming, 1956-61, v.p. in charge data processing, 1962-73; with Consol. Am. Life Ins. Co., Jackson, Miss., 1973—, adminstrv. v.p., 1973-76, sr. v.p. adminstrn., dir., 1976-84, pres., chief exec. officer, dir., 1984-85; cons., 1985—. Served with USN, 1943-46. Mem. Actuaries of Southwest. Methodist. Lodge: Lions (Jackson, Miss.). Home: 4605 Nordell Dr Jackson MS 39206 Office: 8930 Livenshire Dr Dallas TX 75238

BAIR, ANNA WITHERS, educator, musician; b. Mayodan, N.C., Aug. 12, 1916; d. Percy Lawson and Lydia Lucile (Williamson) W.; A.B. cum laude, Salem (N.C.) Coll., 1936, Mus.B. cum laude, 1937; postgrad. Royal Sch. Ch. Music, Eng., summer 1962; M.A., DePaul U., Chgo., 1969; postgrad. Duke U., 1967, Coll. William and Mary, 1969-72; m. Clifford Edwin Bair, June 16, 1938; children—Anna Elizabeth, Mary Ellen, Lucile Withers. Mem. music faculty Salem Coll., 1937-39; organist Home Moravian Ch., Winston-Salem, N.C., 1937-38, 40; organist, choir dir. Christ Moravian Ch., Winston-Salem, N.C., 1943-48, Calvary Moravian Ch., Winston-Salem, 1948-53; choir master-organist St. Mary's Epis. Ch., High Point, N.C., 1955-64, St. Paul's Epis. Ch., Edenton, N.C., 1965-69, Cann Meml. Epis. Ch., Elizabeth City, N.C., 1983-86; mem. fine arts faculty Coll. of Albemarle, Elizabeth City, N.C., 1965-81, chmn. dept. fine arts, 1972-81; vis. scholar U. N.C., Chapel Hill, summer 1980; pvt. tchr. piano and organ, 1943-86. Mem. Edenton Hist. Commn., 1978-83. Named Outstanding Tchr., Coll. of Albemarle, 1973, 75; Elizabeth City Musician of Yr., 1975; Nat. Endowment Humanities grantee, 1974. Mem. Am. Guild Organists (assoc.), Nat. Soc. Colonial Dames Am., Nat. Trust for Historic Preservation, Wachovia Hist. Assn., Pasquotank Hist. Assn., Delta Kappa Gamma. Democrat. Moravian. Contbr. articles to Dictionary of North Carolina Biography, 1980, 86—.

BAIR, RONALD LEHMAN, human relations counselor; b. Williamsport, Pa., Jan. 1, 1937; s. Clyde Donald and Marjorie Lenore (Bendle) B.; student Temple U., 1954-55, Ursinus Coll., 1955-56; B.D., Christian Congl. Div. Sch., 1964; Th.D., Zion Theol. Sem., 1969; m. Sandra Ann Adams, Apr. 6, 1974; children—Ronald Lehman, Kevin J., Guy D., Jimmy, Janell, Jeremy, Jonas. Exec. dir. Consulting Center, Williamsport, Pa., 1965-72; exec. dir. Christian Counseling Center, West Palm Beach, Fla., 1972—; staff psychologist Palm Beach County, Fla., 1977-80; adminstrv. asst., sr. counselor Urban League Palm Beach County, 1980—; pvt. practice psychotherapist, West Palm Beach, 1969-82, human relations counselor, 1982—. Bd. dirs. Project Rescue, Inc., 1979—, Nova U., 1979-82; mem. Community Housing Resource Bd., Palm Beach County. Diplomate Am. Bd. Examiners in Pastoral Counseling. Mem. Am. Psychotherapy Assn., Am. Counseling Assn., Nat. Psychol. Assn., Am. Ministerial Assn., Nat. Acad. Family Therapists and Counselors, Assn. Christian Marriage Counselors, Nat. Acad. Counselors and Family Therapists, Internat. Assn. Clin. Christian Counselors, Order St. Luke the Physician. Republican. Mem. Christian Ch. Club: Elks. Author: (with H.E. Lindsay) Clinical Hypnosis, 1969. Editor, Observer, 1974—, Graymatter, 1978—. Home: 1401 20th Ave N Lake Worth FL 33460 Office: PO Box 2436 Brass Bldg West Palm Beach FL 33402

BAIRD, C. BRUCE, lawyer, consultant; b. DeLand, Fla., Apr. 18, 1935; s. James Turner and Ethelyn Isabelle (Williams) B.; m. Barbara Ann Fabian, June 6, 1959 (div. Dec. 1979); children—C. Bruce, Jr., Robert Arthur, Bryan James; m. Byung-Ran Cho, May 23, 1982; children—Merah-Iris, Haerah Violet. B.S. in M.E., U. Miami, 1958; postgrad UCLA, 1962-64; M.B.A., Calif. State U., 1966; J.D., Am. U., 1971. Bar: Va. 1971, U.S. Dist. Ct. (ea. dist.) Va. 1971, D.C. 1973, U.S. Dist. Ct. D.C. 1973, U.S. Ct. Appeals (4th cir.) 1974, U.S. Supreme Ct. 1975. Research engr. Naval Ordnance Lab., Corona, Calif., 1961-67; aerospace engr. Naval Air Systems Command, Washington, 1967-69; cons. engr. Bird Engring. Research Assts., Vienna, Va., 1969-71; prof. Def. Systems Mgmt. Coll., Ft. Belvoir, Va., 1982; spl. asst. for policy compliance USIA Voice of Am., Washington, 1983-84; cons. Booz, Allen & Hamilton, Inc., Bethesda, 1975-82, IBM, Bethesda, Md., 1984. Contbr. articles to profl. jours. Inventor computer-based communications systems for the gravely handicapped. Bd. govs. Sch. Engring. U. Miami, 1957; trustee Galilee United Meth. Ch., Arlington, Va., 1983—. Mem. Assn. Trial Lawyers Am., Soc. Gen. Systems Research, Sigma Alpha Epsilon. Republican. Home and Office: 2728 Sherwood Hall Ln Alexandria VA 22306

BAIRD, HAYNES WALLACE, pathologist; b. St. Louis, Jan. 28, 1943; s. Harry Haynes and Mary Cornelia (Wallace) B.; B.A., U. N.C., 1965, M.D., 1969; m. Phyllis Jean Tipton, June 26, 1965; children—Teresa Lee, Christopher Wallace, Kelly Wallace. Intern, N.C. Meml. Hosp., Chapel Hill, 1969-70, resident in pathology, 1970-72, chief resident in pathology, 1972-73; asso. pathologist Moses H. Cone Meml. Hosp., Greensboro, N.C., 1973—; practice medicine, specializing in pathology Greensboro, 1973—; clin. asst. prof. U. N.C., Chapel Hill, 1978—; clin. lectr. chemistry U. N.C., Greensboro, 1973—. Bd. dirs. Greensboro unit Am. Cancer Soc., 1980-81. Diplomate Am. Bd. Pathology. Fellow Coll. Am. Pathologists (ho. of dels. 1983-85); mem. AMA, So. Med. Assn., Am. Soc. Cytology, Am. Soc. Clin. Pathologists, Internat. Acad. Pathology, N.C. Med. Soc., Guilford County Med. Soc., N.C. Soc. Pathologists (sec.-treas. 1977-79), Greensboro Acad. Medicine. Methodist. Home: 2805 New Hanover Dr Greensboro NC 27408 Office: 1200 N Elm St Greensboro NC 27401

BAIRD, JAMES AVERY, SR., petroleum geologist; b. Chillicothe, Ohio, Aug. 3, 1928; s. Earl Cunningham and Mabel (Avery) B.; 1 child, James Avery Jr. B.A., Ohio State U., 1949, B.S., 1956. Geologist various cos., Tex., La., 1955-84; sr. exploration geologist Western div. Santa Fe Minerals, Lafayette, La., 1984—; cons. geologist Santa Fe Minerals, Lafayette, 1984. Contbr. articles to profl. jours. Scoutmaster Harlem Council Boy Scouts Am., 1952-53. Served with U.S. Army, 1951-52. Mem. Am. Assn. Petroleum Geologists (cert., del. 1972—), Am. Inst. Profl. Geologist (cert., chmn. membership La. chapt. 1968), Lafayette Geol. Soc., Houston Geol. Soc., Ducks Unltd., Nat. Rifle and Pistol Club, La. Trappers and Alligators Assn., Acadiana Racing Pigeon Combine, Internat. Treasure Hunting Soc., Nat. Geog. Soc., Lafayette Racing Pigeon Club, Swampbuster Lab Kennel, Wild Bird Duck Camp, Black Powder Rendevous, Am. Wildlife Fedn. (environ. com.), Tng. and Field Trial Labradors, Audubon Soc., Baton Rouge Mus. Geosci. (charter), Hunting Retriever Club, Power Squadron, U.S.C.G. Aux. Club: Kabar Knife (charter). Republican. Presbyterian. Office: Santa Fe Minerals Inc Div Santa Fe Internat 301 Kaliste Saloom Rd Lafayette LA 70508

BAIRD, JOHN EDWARD, mental health administrator; b. Seattle, May 22, 1922; s. John Morris and Mary Evelyn (Daniels) B. B.A., U. So. Calif., 1947; M.S., Va. Commonwealth U., 1975; postgrad. Coll. of William and Mary, 1977; Sc.D. (hon.), U. Rome, 1967. Cert. counseling psychotherapist, rehab. counselor, chem. dependence counselor, Ga. Coordinator rehab. VA, Hampton, Va., Dublin, Ga., Hot. Springs, S.D., 1970-84; group therapist Ridgeview Inst., Smyrna, Ga., 1985—; assoc. dir. Ridgeview Counseling Ctr., Atlanta, 1985; cons. in field. Contbr. articles to profl. jours. Mem. Republican Nat. Com., Washington, 1983; founding trustee Ronald Reagan Trust, Washington, 1985. Served with USAAF, 1942-44. Recipient George Washington Honor medal Freedoms Found., 1957; Alexander Hamilton award Am. Soc. Securities Dealers, 1958. Mem. Soc. Behavioral Medicine, Am. Assn. Counseling and Devel., Am. Mental Health Counselors Assn., Am. Rehab. Counselors Assn. Methodist. Club: Ponte Vedra Beach (Fla.). Avocations: sailing; travel. Home: Roswell GA

BAIRD, WILLIAM DAVID, history educator; b. Oklahoma City, July 8, 1939; s. Everette W. and Faye (Shinn) B.; m. Brenda Jane Tacker, Nov. 24, 1961; children—Angela, Anthony. A.A., George Washington U., 1959; B.A., Central State U., Okla., 1962; M.A., U. Okla., 1964, Ph.D., 1969. Asst. prof. history U. Ark.-Fayetteville, 1968-72, assoc. prof., 1972-77, prof., 1977-78; prof. history Okla. State U., 1978—, head dept. history, 1978-84. Mem. Western Hist. Soc., Am. Hist. Assn., Orgn. Am. Historians. Democrat. Mem. Ch. of Christ. Club: Rotary. Author: Peter Pitchlynn: Chief of the Choctaws, 1970; Medical Education in Arkansas, 1879-1978, 1978; The Quapaw Indians: A History of the Downstream People, 1980. Home: 4902 Country Club Dr Stillwater OK 74074 Office: 502 MS Okla State U Stillwater OK 74078

BAKAS, SERGIO S., architect; b. Havana, Cuba, June 2, 1957; came to U.S. 1960, naturalized 1961; s. James and Ida Israelit Bakas. B.Arch., Tulane U., 1980, M.B.A., 1980. Registered architect. Vice pres. Arquitectonica Internat. Corp., Coral Gables, Fla., 1980—; mem. Shoreline Devel. Review Bd., Miami, 1985—. Mem. AIA, Constrn. Specifications Inst., Nat. Trust for Hist. Preservation, Beta Gamma Epsilon, Zeta Beta Tau (treas. 1978-79). Avocations: music, photography. Home: 3139 SW 27 Ave 3 Coconut Grove FL 33133 Office: Arquitectonica Internat Corp 4215 Ponce De Leon Blvd Coral Gables FL 33146

BAKER, ALICE ANN, exercise physiologist, exercise educator; b. Durant, Okla., Oct. 25, 1946; d. Finis Cortez and Alice Joyce (Hamilton) Baker; m. John Arthur Dailey, Nov. 23, 1985. B.A. in Music, U. Okla., 1968; M.S., North Tex. State U., 1985. Cert. fitness instr. Am. Coll. Sports Medicine. Piano tchr. Dallas Ind. Sch. Dist., 1969-71; music tchr. Houston Ind. Sch. Dist., 1971-75; mail order adminstr. Neiman-Marcus, Dallas, 1978-81; exercise physiologist Tex. Instruments, Dallas, 1984—, Internat. Athletic Club of Dallas, 1985—; owner, pres. Alice Ann Baker Exercise: Therapeutic Conditioning, Dallas, 1980—; cons. Region 10 Edn. Service Ctr., Dallas, 1985, RepublicBank, Dallas, 1985; exec. producer and creator exercise video on therapeutic conditioning Warner Amex Community Services Channel, Dallas, 1984-85; research paper presented conf. AAHPERD, Cin., 1986. Active mem. Dallas Mus. Art League, Dallas Symphony Orchestra League. Mem. Assn. for Fitness in Bus., Am. Coll. Sports Medicine, Kappa Alpha Theta. Republican. Methodist. Avocations: piano, sewing, needlework, gardening. Home: 4020 Holland Ave #102 Dallas TX 75219

BAKER, ANITA DIANE, lawyer; b. Atlanta, Sept. 4, 1955; d. Byron Garnett and Anita (Swanson) B. B.A. summa cum laude, Oglethorpe U., 1977; J.D. with distinction, Emory U., 1980. Bar: Ga. 1980. Assoc. Hansell & Post, Atlanta, 1980—. Mem. ABA, Atlanta Bar Assn., Ga. Bar Assn., Order of Coif, Phi Alpha Delta, Phi Alpha Theta, Alpha Chi, Omicron Delta Kappa, Atlanta Hist. Soc. Baptist. Notes and Comments editor Emory Law Jour., 1979-80. Office: Hansell & Post 56 Perimeter Center E 5th Fl Atlanta GA 30346

BAKER, ARNOLD BARRY, economist; b. N.Y.C., Feb. 3, 1946; s. Max Michael and Sue (Feingold) B. B.A. in History, Va. Poly. Inst., 1968; M.A., in Econs., 1970, Ph.D., 1972. Spl. asst. to undersec. for monetary affairs U.S. Dept. Treasury, Washington, 1977-79; sr. cons. Atlantic Richfield Co., Los Angeles, 1979-82; mgr. planning info. analysis Arco Exploration Co., Dallas, 1983; mgr. strategic planning Arco Oil and Gas Co., Dallas, 1983—. Contbr. articles to profl. jours., chpt. to book. Mem. Am. Econ. Assn., Dallas Economists Club, Nat. Assn. Bus. Econs., Internat. Assn. Energy Econs. Clubs: Exchange, Lancers. Avocation: jogging. Office: Arco Arco and Gas Co Box 2819 Dallas TX 75221

BAKER, BAXTER LEE, SR., school psychologist; b. Brewton, Ala., Feb. 6, 1951; s. Ollie Baxter and Mary Ann Baker; m. Ivey Ruth Liles, Dec. 27, 1979; 1 child, B. Lee. A.S., Jefferson Davis State Jr. Coll., 1971; B.S., Auburn U., 1974; M.S., Jacksonville State U., 1975; Ph.D., U. Ala., 1983. Lic. profl. counselor. Counselor Indian program Escambia County (Ala.) Schs., 1975-77, sch. psychologist, 1978—; grad. asst. U. Ala., 1977-78, teaching asst., summers 1979-81; cons. edn. for Ala. Dept. Edn. and local sch. dists. Elder, First Presbyterian Ch., Brewton. Named to Outstanding Young Men Am., U.S. Jaycees, 1977. Mem. Ala. Assn. Sch. Psychologists, Ala. Edn. Assn., Ala. Assn. Counseling and Devel., Am. Assn. Counseling and Devel., Am. Sch. Counselor Assn., Escambia County Assn. Retarded Citizens, Escambia County Mental Health Assn., Nat. Assn. Sch. Psychologists, NEA, Kappa Delta Pi, Psi Chi. Office: PO Box 644 Brewton AL 36427

BAKER, BILL RYAN, dental educator; b. Denton, Tex., Jan. 26 1930; s. Bailey R. and Callie (Smith) B.; m. Virginia Mann, June 7, 1952; children—Bill Ryan (dec.), Lela, John, Nancy. B.S., Baylor U., 1950, D.D.S., 1953; M.S.D., Ind. U., 1963. Gen. practice dentistry, Victoria, Tex., 1955-56; commd. capt. U.S. Air Force, 1956, advanced through grades to col., 1970; chmn. dept. gen. dentistry USAF Med. Ctr., Tex., 1970-74; ret., 1974; mem. faculty U. Tex. Health Sci. Ctr. Dental Sch., San Antonio, 1974—, profl. dental diagnostic sci., 1976—, prof. pathology, 1976—, prof. dental hygiene, 1980—. Author: Oral Diagnosis, Oral Medicine and Treatment Planing, 1984; contbr. articles to profl. jours. Fellow Am. Acad. Oral Pathology, Am. Coll. Dentists, Acad. Gen. Dentistry; mem. Orgn. Tchrs. Oral Diagnosis (pres. 1980-81), Am. Assn. Dental Schs. (officer), ADA, Omicron Kappa Upsilon. Democrat. Presbyterian. Avocations: Reading; photography; travel. Home: 224 Park Hill Dr San Antonio TX 78212 Office: Dental Diagnostic Sci U Tex Health Sci Ctr 7703 Floyd Curl Dr San Antonio TX 78284

BAKER, BRAD, computer company executive; b. Detroit, Dec. 19, 1959; s. Clarence Walter and Shirley Elaine (Kostoff) B. A.A., Manatee Jr. Coll., 1981; B.S., Nova U., 1983. Pres., chief exec. officer Computer Centre Inc., Venice, Fla., 1977-85, Tech:Time Inc., Venice, 1981—. Author newspaper column, 1984-85. Vice pres., Venice Friends of Library, 1985; bd. dirs., Grace Meth. Ch., Venice, 1985. Mem. Data Processing Mgmt. Assn., Mensa, Com. of 100, Sarasota C. of C., Venice Area C. of C. (v.p. 1985), Manatee Jr. Coll. Alumni Bd. (v.p. 1985). Republican. Methodist. Lodge: Masons. Avocation: flying. Office: Tech:Time Inc 917 S Tamiami Trail Nokomis FL 33555

BAKER, CLIFFORD CORNELL, state educational administrator; b. Gadsden, Ala., Dec. 29, 1929; s. Joe and Bessie (Fluker) B.; m. Helen Clancy, Aug. 26, 1953 (dec. June 1976); 1 child, Angelia Denise; m. Alma Jean Bibb, Dec. 29, 1978; children—Edward, Chequita. B.S., Ala. State U., 1954, M.Ed., 1956; postgrad. U. Ala.-Tuscaloosa, 1967-69; D.Ed., Auburn U., 1973. Tchr., then prin. Bunche High Sch., Anadalusia, Ala., 1954-61; prin. Woodson High Sch., Andalusia, 1961-70; asst. prof. Auburn U., Ala., 1973-75; assoc. prof. Ala. State U., Montgomery, 1975-76; asst. state supt. edn. Ala. Dept. Edn., Montgomery, 1976—, dir. profl. services, 1978—. Active Cleveland Ave. br. YMCA Century Club, Montgomery, Montgomery County Democrats, 1985-86. Served to cpl. U.S. Army, 1950-52; Korea. Recipient Ednl. Leadership award Ala. A&M U., 1976; Ednl. Leadership award Tuskegee Inst., 1981; Outstanding Alumnus award Ala. State U., 1984. Mem. Am. Assn. Sch. Adminstrs., Phi Delta Kappa (Service award 1979), Sigma Phi Boule (Sir Archon of Phi chpt. 1985-86), Kappa Alpha Psi (chpt. bd. dirs., So. Leadership award 1968). Baptist. Lodge: Masons (master). Avocations: travel; golf; reading; gardening. Home: 3529 Suwanee Dr Montgomery AL 36108

BAKER, DANIEL RICHARD, computer systems consultant; b. Rostock, Denmark, Mar. 19, 1932; came to U.S., 1936, naturalized, 1945; s. Arthur and Molly (Needman) B.; student Tufts Coll., 1949-51; B.A., Bklyn. Coll., 1957; postgrad. Fairleigh Dickinson U., 1961-64; postgrad. in math. Am. U., 1968; m. June Ellin Nebenzahl, Oct. 2, 1960; children—David Charles, Jill Alison. Tchr. math. N.Y.C. Public Schs., 1958-59; computer programmer Systems Devel. Corp., Paramus, N.J., 1959-61; programmer analyst ITT, Paramus, 1961-64; sr. mathematician Melpar Corp., Falls Church, Va., 1964-65; systems analyst Wolf Research & Devel. Corp., Badensburg, Md., 1965-66, Aries Corp., McLean, Va., 1966-68; sr. systems analyst N.Am. Rockwell Corp., Roslyn, Va., 1968-70; pres. Baker & Baker Data Assos., Fairfax Station, Va., 1970—; real estate broker; permanent group leader Dale Carnegie Sales Courses. Vol.

ann. fund campaign Tufts Coll., 1976—. Served with AUS, 1954-55. Mem. No. Va. Bd. Realtors (multilist com., Million Dollar Sales Club), Va. Assn. Realtors (dir. 1977-80, 83—), Nat. Assn. Realtors, Am. Soc. Cybernetics, Silvanus Packard Soc. Club: Washington Tufts (v.p. 1975). Office: 7310 Craftown Rd Fairfax Station VA 22039

BAKER, DAVID HAROLD, JR., real estate company executive; b. Atlanta, Oct. 24, 1950; s. David Harold and Ruth Elizabeth (Isakson) B. B.B.A. in Acctg., Ga. So. U., 1973, M.B.A. in Mktg. Mgmt., 1975; grad. Dale Carnegie Inst., 1985. Acct., U.S. Postal Service, Atlanta, 1975-76; sales mgr. Coldwell Banker Realtors, Atlanta, 1977-83, Mobil Land Mktg., Inc., Atlanta, 1983—. Backer, Alliance Theatre Co., Atlanta, 1985. Named to Hall of Fame and Pres. Club, Coldwell Banker Realtors, 1982, Recruiter of Yr., Sales and Mktg. Council, 1983-84, Nat. Sales Mgr. of Yr., Nat. Home Builders Assn., 1984. Mem. Sales and Mktg. Council (bd. dirs., vice chmn. 1985—, sec. 1984-85, membership chmn. 1984-85), Atlanta Bd. Realtors, Nat. Assn. Realtors. Avocations: bicycling; physical fitness; scuba diving; theater; travel. Office: One Concourse Pkwy Suite 755 Atlanta GA 30328

BAKER, EDITH PEARL, nursing educator; b. Westmoreland County, Pa., June 6, 1943; foster parents John Henry and Edna Rachel (Suckau) Gerstner, Jr.; m. Rayburn Donald Baker, Jr., Mar. 10, 1973 (div.); children—Jason John, Jonas Reade. Diploma nursing Columbia Hosp., 1965; B.S.N., Goshen Coll., 1970; M.S.N., U. Tex.-Arlington, 1980; M.A. in Pub. Service, Tarleton State U., 1984. Staff nurse Columbia Hosp., Pitts., 1965-66; float nurse Deaconess Hosp., Buffalo, 1966-67, Valley Hosp., Ridgeway, N.J., 1967-68; staff nurse Goshen Gen. Hosp. (Ind.), 1968-70; coll. health nurse Goshen Coll., 1968-69; pub. health nurse Allegheny County Health Dept., Pitts., 1970-72; staff nurse U.S. Air Force Nurse Corps, 1972-74; pub. health nurse II San Diego County Health Dept., 1974-75; instr. Tarleton State U., Stephenville, Tex., 1976—, Migrant Health Program, Ft. Morgan, Colo., summers 1983, 84, Granbury Gen. Hosp., Tex., summer 1985, Baylor Med. Ctr., Dallas, summer 1985, El Centro Coll., Dallas, summer 1985. Bd. dirs. Am. Cancer Soc., Stephenville, 1976-77; instr./trainer Am. Heart Assn., Stephenville/Ft. Worth, 1976—. Served to capt. USAF, 1972-74. Mem. Tex. Nurses Assn., Am. Nurses Assn. Republican. Presbyterian. Home: 912 Old Hico Rd PO Box 355 Stephenville TX 76401 Office: Tarleton State U T-338 Tarleton Sta Stephenville TX 76401

BAKER, EDWARD GEORGE, retired mechanical engineer; b. Freeport, N.Y., Oct. 20, 1908; s. Edward George and Mary (Dunham) B.; m. Mary Louise Freer, Feb. 7, 1931; children—Edward Clark, Marna Larson, Ellen Freer (Mrs. George W. Lewis), John Durrin, Bruce Robert. B.A., Columbia Coll., 1930, M.A., 1931, Ed.D., 1938. Assoc. prof. math. Newark Coll. Engring., N.J., 1930-42; mem. tech. staff Am. Bur. Shipping, N.Y.C., 1942-73. Author: First Course in Mathematics, 1942. Contbr. articles on marine engring. to profl. jours. Pres. Nutley (N.J.) Symphony Soc., 1939-41; chmn. zoning bd. of adjustment, Pine Knoll Shores, N.C., 1979-84. Recipient Order of Long Leaf Pine award State of N.C., 1982. Mem. Am. Math. Soc., ASME, Soc. Naval Architects and Marine Engrs., N.Y. Acad. Sci., Phi Beta Kappa. Republican. Episcopalian. Home: 106 Carob Ct Pine Knoll Shores Route 3 Morehead City NC 28557

BAKER, ELIZABETH RENWICK, physician, educator; b. Washington, Sept. 24, 1949; d. Ralph Parr and Frances Elizabeth (Renwick) B. A.B., Duke U., 1971, M.D., 1975. Diplomate div. reproductive endocrinology Am. Bd. Ob-Gyn. Resident in ob-gyn Duke Med. Ctr., Durham, N.C., 1975-79; fellow in reproductive endocrinology and infertility Med. U. S.C., Charleston, 1979-81, clin. instr., 1980-81; asst. prof. ob-gyn Milton S. Hershey Med. Ctr., Hershey, Pa., 1981-86; assoc. prof. ob-gyn U. S.C. Sch. Medicine, Columbia, 1986—. Mem. Duke Med. Alumni Exec. Council, 1978-84, pres., 1985-86. S.C. State grantee, 1980-81. Fellow Am. Coll. Ob-Gyn; mem. AMA, Newberry County Med. Soc., S.C. Med. Assn., Bayard Carter Soc., Am. Fertility Soc., Internat. Fedn. Fertility Socs., So. Med. Assn. Republican. Presbyterian. Clubs: DAR, Children of Confederacy, Hershey Racquet. Contbr. articles to profl. jours. Home: 1905 Main St Newberry SC 29108 Office: Ob-Gyn U SC Med Sch 2 Medical Park Columbia SC 29203

BAKER, GARY HUGH, lawyer; b. Broken Arrow, Okla., Nov. 18, 1947; s. Theodore Roosevelt and Maxine Gladys (Smittle) B.; m. Karen Louise DeLong, Aug. 29, 1970; 1 child, Katherine Elizabeth. B.A. with highest honors, U. Okla., 1970; J.D., U. Chgo., 1973. Bar: Okla. 1973, U.S. Dist. Cts. (no., we. and ea. dists.) Okla. 1973, U.S. Ct. Appeals (10th cir.) 1975. Assoc. Conner, Winters, Ballaine, Barry & McGowen, Tulsa, 1973-79, ptnr., 1979-81; ptnr. Baker, Hoster, McSpadden, Clark & Rasure, Tulsa, 1981—; dir. Legal Service of Eastern Okla., Tulsa, 1980-84. Mem. Citizen's Coalition for Community Devel., Tulsa, 1980. Mem. Tulsa County Bar Assn. (sec. 1981, Outstanding Young Lawyer award 1979), Tulsa County Young Lawyers Assn. (chmn. 1979), Okla. Bar Assn. (banking Com. 1981—). Home: 1718 E 30th St Tulsa OK 74114 Office: Baker Hoster McSpadden Clark & Rasure 800 Kennedy Bldg Tulsa OK 74103

BAKER, GORDON NEWTON, library media specialist; b. Atlanta, June 30, 1954; s. Howard Franklin and Mary Ina (Newton) B. A.A., Clayton Jr. Coll., 1973; B.S. in Edn., Valdosta State Coll., 1975; M.L.S., Atlanta U., 1978, specialist in library service diploma, 1981. Tchr., librarian Griffin-Spalding Schs., Griffin, Ga., 1975-76; tchr. Clayton County Schs., Jonesboro, Ga., 1976-77; pub. services librarian Clayton Jr. Coll., Morrow, Ga., 1979—; library/media specialist Clayton County Schs., Jonesboro, 1977—; library cons. Meadow Creek Acad., McDonough, Ga., 1982; 6th dist. chmn. Ga. Library/Media Dept., Decatur, 1979, treas., 1980-82, pres., 1982-83, exec. sec., 1983—; mem. Area IV media com. Ga. Dept. Edn., 1983. Co-author: Study Guide for TCT for Media Specialists, 1983. Vice pres. Kilpatrick P.T.A., Jonesboro, Ga., 1979-80. Mem. ALA, Am. Assn. Sch. Librarians, Ga. Library Media Dept. (conf. coordinator 1980, 86, William E. Patterson service award 1986), Ga. Library Assn., Clayton County Library/Media Assn. (treas. 1978-79, pres. 1979-81), Clayton County English Lang. Arts Council (pres. 1979-80), Ga. Council Media Orgns. (steering com. joint conf. com. 1988), Beta Phi Mu, Sigma Alpha Chi. Republican. Methodist. Home: 32 Daniel Dr Stockbridge GA 30281 Office: Edwin S Kemp Elementary Sch 10990 Folsom Rd Hampton GA 30228

BAKER, IRA LEE, journalist, former educator; b. Fairwood, Va., Sept. 5, 1915; s. Joseph Franklin and Celia (Blackburn) B.; B.A., Wake Forest Coll., 1936; M.A., Columbia U., 1952; postgrad. U. Ill., U. Wis., U. Tenn., Syracuse U.; M.Sc. in Journalism, U. Ill., 1963. Instr. English, N.C. State Coll., Raleigh, 1946-50, asst. extension editor State Coll. Extension Service and mng. editor Extension Farm-News, 1950-51; head journalism dept. Furman U., Greenville, S.C., 1951-65; assoc. prof. journalism and English, High Point (N.C.) Coll., 1965-68; prof. journalism East Carolina U., Greenville, 1968-80, prof. emeritus, 1983—, columnist, mem. editorial staff Communication: Journalism Education Today, 1977—; corr. Religion News Service, 1953—; prof. Wingate Coll., 1980-83; permanent advisor S.C. Collegiate Press Assn. Publicity chmn. Wake County council N.C. Symphony Orch., 1947-51; active Raleigh Music Club, Raleigh Little Theatre, 1946-51, Greenville Little Theater, 1951—; mem. alumni council Wake Forest Coll., 1964; relationships chmn. Pitt County council Boy Scouts Am., 1975; del. S.C. Republican Conv., 1958; chmn. bd. deacons 1st Baptist Ch., China Grove, N.C., 1982-84; historian Rowan County Bapt. Assn., N.C., 1984-85. Served with USAAF, 1942-44. Recipient Scholastic Pioneer award Nat. Scholastic Press Assn., 1970; named Distinguished Newspaper Adviser, Nat. Council Coll. Publs. Advisers, 1973. Mem. Am. Assn. Coll. and Univ. Profs. (v.p. Furman U. chpt.), Am. Assn. Tchrs. Religious Journalism, Assn. Ednl. Journalism (state dir.), S.C. Press Assn., Nat. Council Coll. Publs. Advisers (membership chmn. dist. III 1967-68), Pub. Relations Soc. Am. (asso.), S.C. Assn. Coll. Publs. Advisers (pres. 1957—), South Atlantic Modern Lang. Assn., Pitt County (N.C.) Hist. Soc., (publicity chmn.) SAR, Sigma Delta Chi, Tau Kappa Epsilon, Alpha Phi Gamma (nat. pres. 1968-70). Lodge: Rotary (China Grove) (dir. 1981-82, editor Rotary Log). Co-author: Modern Journalism, 1961; mem. adv. bd. Student Writer; chmn. adv. bd. Cerebral Palsy News of S.C.; mem. bd. editors Scholastic Mag.; mem. book reviewing staff Greensboro News, 1960, Richmond News Leader, 1975; editor The Collegiate Journalist; contbr. book revs. to Raleigh News and Observer, 1968—, Richmond (Va.) News Leader, 1974—, also articles to Ency. So. Bapts., 1958. Lodge: Rotary (editor 1981—). Home: 106 Stevens St China Grove NC 28023

BAKER, JAMES NEWSOM, orthodontist; b. McKenzie, Tenn., Nov. 14, 1949; s. Roy Newsom and Janie Nelson (Mullen) B.; m. Beverly Anne Brown, Feb. 14, 1976. B.S., Bethel Coll., 1970; D.D.S., U. Tenn.-Memphis, 1972, M.S. in Orthodontics, 1974. Pvt. practice orthodontics, Maryville, Tenn., 1974—. Mem. ADA, Am. Assn. Orthodontists, Maryville C. of C. Republican. Methodist. Club: Kiwanis. Avocations: Snow skiing; sailboat racing; backpacking; photography. Home: Route 1 Box 334 Louisville TN 37777 Office: 1618 Smoky Mountain Hwy Maryville TN 37801

BAKER, JESSE KIRKLAND, oil company executive; b. Houston, Aug. 9, 1941; s. Dillard W. and Mary (Thomas) B.; m. Catherine Theresa Daigle, July 25, 1970; children—Mary Rose, Katie. B.A., U. Tex., 1964; J.D., So. Methodist U., 1969. Vice pres. Charter Internat. Oil Co., Houston, 1972-79, Multi Mineral Corp., Houston, 1979—; dir. Nat. Council of Synthetic Fuels Production. Mem. Nat. Cattlemans Assn., Am. Mining Congress, Rocky Mountain Oil and Gas Assn., Tex. Bar Assn., Tex. and S.W. Cattle Raisers Assn., Tejas Vaqueros, Kappa Sigma, Phi Delta Phi. Methodist. Home: 3112 Mid Lane Houston TX 77027 Office: 8441 Gulf Freeway Houston TX 77017

BAKER, JOSEPHINE L. REDENIUS, civic worker, retired army officer; b. Oceanville, N.J., Aug. 31, 1920; d. Jacob and Josephine (Palmer) Redenius; student Columbia U., 1948-49, L.I.U., 1957-58, George Washington U., 1947-48; M.A. in Journalism, Am. U., 1963; L.H.D. (hon.), Temple U., 1964; postgrad. St. Charles Sem., 1978-81; M.Div., Eastern Bapt. Theol. Sem., 1984, postgrad., 1985—; m. Milton G. Baker (dec. 1976). Enlisted as pvt. WAAC, 1943, advanced through grades to lt. col. U.S. Army, 1963; intelligence officer atomic installations throughout U.S. and Can., 1943-53; asst. in Office Chief of Staff, Army Forces Far East, Japan, 1954-56; public info. officer Office Chief of Info., Washington, 1958-61; chief Women's Army Corps Recruiting, U.S. Army, 1962-66; info. liaison officer U.S. Army, 1966-67, ret., 1967; dir. public relations and devel. Valley Forge Mil. Acad. and Jr. Coll., Wayne, Pa., 1967-70, dir. found., 1970—; pres. Intercounty Trading Co., Inc., Surfside, Fla., 1976-80, Potential Gift Shop & Boutique, Ardmore, Pa., 1979-82; pres. dirs. Surf Club Apts., Inc., 1977-79, treas., dir., 1983-86. Bd. dirs. Republican Women of Pa., Freedom Valley council Girl Scouts U.S.A., 1970-76, St. Anna's Home for Women, Phila., 1984—, Opera Guild Miami (Fla.); pres. found., bd. dirs. Chapel of St. Cornelius the Centurian, Wayne, Pa., 1976—; mem. aux. Miami Heart Inst. Decorated Legion of Merit, U.S. Army Commendation medal with 1st oak leaf; recipient Pa. Meritorious Service medal; Disting. Alumnus, Am. U., 1969. Mem. Pub. Relations Soc. Am., Am. Personnel and Guidance Assn., Am. Coll. Personnel Assn., Nat. Vocat. Guidance Assn., Am. Sch. Counselors Assn., Am. Legion Aux., Ret. Officers Assn., Assn. U.S. Army (Anthony J. Drexel Biddle medal 1968), Army-Navy Union, Assn. Measurement and Evaluation in Guidance, Emergency Aid of Pa., Pa. Med. Missionary Assn. (dir. 1984—), Am. Legion, Mil. Order World Wars, La Boutique des Huit Chapeaux et Quarante Femmes, Women in Communications, AAUW, Hospice Assn. Dade County. Episcopalian. Clubs: Acorn, St. David's Golf, Surf, La Gorce Country. . Address: Tower House 920 Eagle Rd Wayne PA 19087 also Surf Club Apts 9133 Collins Ave Surfside FL 33154

BAKER, JULIAN CRAWFORD, pharmacist; b. Hawkins, Wis., Jan. 8, 1933; s. Julian Cedric and Gudrun (Nygaard) B.; m. Patricia Elizabeth Sullivan, June 14, 1958 (div. 1976); children—Michael Julian, Martin Roy; m. Faye Henry Bowling, Jan. 8, 1982. A.D. in Biology, Ga. Southwestern Coll., 1956; B.S. in Biology and Chemistry, Valdosta State Coll., 1958; B.S. in Pharmacy, Auburn U., 1961. Intern and staff pharmacist Clifton's East Albany Pharmacy, Ga., 1961-65; cons. pharmacist Fryers Pharmacy, Blakley, Ga., 1965-67, Menomonie Pharmacy, Wis., 1967-69, Dunn County Hosp., Menomonie, 1969-70; dir. pharmacy Cherry Hosp., Goldsboro, N.C., 1970—; sec.-treas. B-C Clinic Pharmacy, Inc., Goldsboro, 1980—; pres. Pegasus Enterprises, Goldsboro, 1975—. Served to 2d lt. CAP, Goldsboro, 1974. Served with USN, 1951-55. Fellow Am. Soc. Cons. Pharmacists; mem. Am. Soc. Hosp. Pharmacists, N.C. Soc. Hosp. Pharmacists, N.C. Pharmacy Assn., Am. Soc. for Pharmacy Law, Aircraft Owners and Pilots Assn., Lutheran. Lodge: Elks. Avocations: flying; golf; photography. Home: 2004 Rose St Goldsboro NC 27530 Office: Cherry Hosp Pharmacy Dept Box 81 Goldsboro NC 27530

BAKER, KERRY ALLEN, proprietary drug company executive; b. Selmer, Tenn., Sept. 21, 1949; s. Austin Clark and Betty Ann (Brooks) B.; B.I.E., Ga. Inst. Tech., 1971; M.B.A., Ga. State U., 1973. With dept. law State of Ga., 1971-73; commd. 2d lt. U.S. Army, 1973, advanced through grades to capt., 1977; assembly and transport platoon leader 1st 12th Lance F.A., Ft. Sill, Okla., 1973-74; adminstrv. officer weapons dept. F.A. Sch., Ft. Sill, 1974-77; instr. logistics br. weapons dept., Ft. Sill, 1977; div. engr. N.W. Ga. div. Gold Kist Inc., Ellijay, Ga., 1977-80; sr. mfg. engr. Plough, Inc., Memphis, 1980-82, mgr. indsl. engring., 1983—. Decorated Order of St. Barbara. Mem. Am. Inst. Indsl. Engrs., Am. Mgmt. Assn., Soc. Advancement Mgmt., Am. Inst. Plant Engrs., Soc. Am. Mil. Engrs., Scabbard and Blade, Sigma Phi Epsilon, Pi Delta Epsilon, Alpha Phi Omega. Baptist. Club: Masons. Home: 3548 Evening Light Dr Bartlett TN 38134 Office: 3030 Jackson Ave Box 377 Memphis TN 38151

BAKER, LENOX DIAL, JR., cardiothoracic surgeon, business executive; b. Durham, N.C., Nov. 18, 1941; s. Lenox Dial and Virginia (Flowers) B.; m. Frances Watt, Aug. 24, 1963; children—Sarah Flowers, Margaret Watt, Carol Lenox, Katherine Dial. Student Davidson Coll., 1959-61; B.A., Johns Hopkins U., 1963, M.D., 1966. Diplomate Am. Bd. Surgery, Am. Bd. Thoracic Surgery. Resident in surgery U. Pitts., 1966-72; asst. chief surgery Med. Ctr. for Fed. Prisoners, Springfield, Mo., 1972-73; chief surgery Indian Health Service, Talihina, Okla., 1973-74; adj. prof. biomedical engring. Ariz. State U., Tempe, 1974-75; cardiothoracic surgeon Ariz. Vascular Surgeons, Phoenix, 1975-79, Surg. Specialists, Inc., Norfolk, Va., 1979—; chmn. bd. Impra, Inc., Tempe, 1974—; dir., chmn. profl. relations com. Blue Cross/Blue Shield of Va., Richmond, 1985—; exec. com., chmn. patient care com. Med. Ctrs. Hosps., Norfolk, 1985—; mem. nat. council Johns Hopkins Med. Sch., Balt., 1985—. Contbr. articles to profl. jours. Served to comdr. USPHS, 1972-74. Am. Heart Assn. grantee, 1975-76. Fellow ACS; mem. So. Surg. Assn., Soc. Thoracic Surgeons, So. Thoracic Surg. Assn., Am. Heart Assn. (pres. Tidewater affiliate 1985—). Club: Yacht & Country (Norfolk). Avocations: tennis; skiing. Home: 7446 N Shore Rd Norfolk VA 23505 Office: Surg Specialists Inc 400 W Brambleton Ave Norfolk VA 23510

BAKER, MARGIE SPARKMAN, government agency official; b. Leon, Ky., Jan. 28, 1943; d. Frank and Lora Jane (Allen) Sparkman; student No. Va. Community Coll., 1975-77, George Washington U., 1977-79; B.A. in Sociology, Columbia Coll. Arts and Scis., 1979; m. Richard L. Baker, Nov. 21, 1962; 1 dau., Cheri Michelle, Various secretarial and adminstrv. positions U.S. Dept. Def. and U.S. Dept. Agr., Washington area, 1961-69; staff asst. to dep. for programs Am. Revolution Bicentennial Adminstrn., Washington, 1969-75; mgmt. analyst Office of Surface Mining and Reclamation Dept. Interior, Washington, 1978; adminstrv. asst. to legal counsel, Commn. on Accident at Three Mile Island, Washington, 1979; program analyst Mine Safety and Health Adminstrn., U.S. Dept. Labor, Arlington, Va., 1979—. Recipient Sustained Superior Performance award Commn. on Three Mile Island, Outstanding Achievement award and Sustained Superior Performance award Mine Safety and Health Adminstrn. Mem. Nat. Assn. Female Execs., Federally Employed Women, Am. Fedn. Govt. Employees (steward local 12). Home: 6826 Stoneybrooke Ln Alexandria VA 22306 Office: Wilson Blvd Arlington VA 22203

BAKER, MARTIN CHARLES, transportation auditing and consulting executive, investor; b. Montreal, Que., Can., July 2, 1944; came to U.S., 1964; s. Walter J. and Mary E. (McDonald) B.; student U. Minn., 1963-64; B.S., La. Tech. U., 1969; postgrad. S. Tex. Coll. Law, 1973; m. Jean V. Robson, June 1, 1977; children—Robson McDonald, Danielle Jean. Sales exec. Sperry Univac, Houston, 1969-74; exec. v.p. SSA Cos., Houston, 1974-79; pres., chief exec. officer Kona Tech. Corp., Houston, 1979—, Silver Beach Partnership-Kona Contractors Inc., Kona Mgmt. Services, Inc., 1982—, Kona Investments, 1982—. Clubs: Orgn. Pirates Beach Property Owners Assn. (pres.), Galveston County. Home: Route 4 Box 147 V 4 Galveston TX 77551 Office: 4000 Dover St Houston TX 77087

BAKER, MARY ALICE, communication educator, consultant; b. Stuart, Okla., Sept. 9, 1937; s. James Roy and Emma M. (Bird) B. B.S., U. Okla., 1959, M.A. in Speech, 1966; Ph.D. in Communication, Purdue U., 1983. Speech and debate tchr. Southeast High Sch., Oklahoma City, 1959-65; instr. Eastern Ill. U., Charleston, 1966-69; assoc. prof. Lamar U., Beaumont, Tex., 1966-75, 78—, dir. forensics, 1969—. Contbr. articles to profl. jours. David Ross fellow, 1977; Regents' Merit prof. Lamar U., 1984. Mem. Tex. Speech Communication Assn. (regional rep. 1978—), Speech Communication Assn. Am., Tex. Assn. Coll. Tchrs. (regional v.p. 1985—), Tex. Forensics Assn. (pres. 1974), Internat. Communication Assn., Zeta Phi Eta, Alpha Delta Pi. Democrat. Episcopalian. Avocations: reading; politics; travel. Home: 3720 Laurel St Apt 16 Beaumont TX 77707 Office: Lamar U Dept Communication Beaumont TX 77710

BAKER, NEWTON CHARLES, newspaper executive; b. West Fork, Ark., Jan. 27, 1925; s. Hobert and Martha Isabell (Hann) B.; m. Geraldine McClelland, May 22, 1947; 1 child, Cynthia Anne. Grad. Prairie Grove High Sch., Ark. Printer, Enterprise, Prairie Grove, 1940-41, 46-51; prodn. dir. Daily Phoenix, Muskogee, Okla., 1951—. Chmn. Muskogee War Meml. Park, 1979—; vice chmn. United Way, Muskogee, 1972—; adviser Indian Capital Vocat.-Tech. Sch., Muskogee High Vocat.-Tech. Sch. Served with USN, 1941-45. Recipient Legion Honor award Internat. DeMolay, 1975, Quality Control award Rochester Inst. Tech., 1982. Mem. Am. Newspaper Pubs. Assn., Digital Equipment Corp. Users Group, Muskogee C. of C. (chmn. crime control 1981—). Republican. Avocations: antique clock collecting and repair; golf; fishing. Home: 2830 N Country Club Rd Muskogee OK 74403 Office: 214 Wall St Muskogee OK

BAKER, PAUL, theatre consultant, director; b. Hereford, Tex., July 24, 1911; s. William Morgan and Retta (Chapman) B.; student U. Wis., 1929; B.A., Trinity U., Waxachie, Tex., 1932, D.F.A. (hon.), 1958; M.F.A., Yale U., 1939; D. Humanities (hon.), Tex. Christian U., 1978; student of Elsie Fogarty, Central Sch. Speech, London, 1932; studied, observed theatre in Eng., Germany, Russia, Japan; m. Sallie Kathryn Cardwell, Dec. 21, 1936; children—Robyn Cardwell, Retta Chapman, Sallie Kathryn. Chief entertainment br. spl. services div., ETO, 1944-45; prof. drama, chmn. dept. Baylor U., 1934-63; dir. Dallas Theatre Ctr., from 1959; prof. drama, chmn. dept. Trinity U., San Antonio, 1963-77; organized S.W. Summer Theatre, Waco, 1939, also built theatre inside Waco Hall, Baylor U., 1939; designed Studio I, Baylor U., 1942; dir. exptl. prodn. Othello, 1953; co-designer Weston Theatre addition to Baylor Theatre, 1954; dir. A Different Drummer, Baylor U. and CBS-TV, 1955, Hamlet with Burgess Meredith and Charles Laughton, Baylor Theatre, 1956, Journey to Jefferson, Theatre des Nations, Paris, France, 1964 (recipient Spl. Jury Prize for season); promoted bldg., founding Frank Lloyd Theatre in Dallas, 1959, also establishment permanent sch. and repertory co. for Am. in Dallas, 1959; mem. Tex. Fine Arts Commn., 1967-68; design cons. Taylor Theater, Trinity U.; mem. Ad Hoc Com. on Profl.-Ednl. Theater Relationships; co-organizer, dir. Arts Magnet High Sch., Booker T. Washington Sch., Dallas Ind. Sch. Dist., 1975-79. Bd. govs. Am. Playwrights Theater. Served to maj. AUS, 1943-45; ETO. Decorated Legion of Merit; Rockefeller Found. fellow, 1937-39, 41, 46, 59; recipient Rodgers and Hammerstein award for outstanding theatrical contbn. in Southwest, 1961; Disting. Alumnus award Trinity U., 1978; others. Mem. Nat. Theatre Conf. (pres. 1958-62), S.W. Theatre Conf. (pres. 1956), ANTA (dir. 1967-68). Am. Ednl. Theatre Assn., Tex. Inst. Letters. Presbyn. (past elder). Author: Integration of Abilities, 1972; contbr. chpts. in books. Home: RFD 1 Box 181 Waelder TX 78959

BAKER, PAUL LAWRENCE, mathematics and computer science educator; b. Champaign, Ill., Sept. 23, 1943; s. James Gerard and Geneva Earl (Lloyd) B.; m. Nancy Rose Robertson, July 23, 1966; children—Ginger Rose, Genevieve Aileen. B.S. in Math., U. N.C., 1965, M.A., 1967; Ph.D., U. Del., 1976; M.Div., Hood Theol. Sem., 1980. Prof. math. Naval Acad. Prep. Sch., Newport, R.I., 1970-75, Livingstone Coll., Salisbury, N.C., 1975-82; prof. math and computer sci. Catawba Coll., Salisbury, 1982—, dir. acad. computer ctr., 1982—; math. programming cons. Impact Tech. Group, Salisbury, 1981—, documentation and tech. writer, 1982-84, artificial intelligence cons., 1984—; systems analyst Diversified Acad. Services, Chapel Hill, 1984—; cons. in field. Author: An Approximation to Linear Algebra, 1979; author software documentation manuals. Dir. prison ministry Rowan Coop. Christian Ministries, Salisbury, 1977-80; counselor Yokefellows Prison Ministry, Salisbury, 1977—; community service vol. Bur. Corrections, Raleigh, N.C., 1980—; mem. Gov.'s Prison Adv. Com., Salisbury, 1981-83. Served to lt. USN, 1965-75. Mem. Inst. Ch. Renewal (coordinator), Math. Assn. Am., N.C. Council Tchrs. Math., Nat. Council Tchrs. Math., Assn. Ednl. Data Systems. Democrat. Lutheran. Clubs: Luth. Ch. Men (Salisbury) (v.p. 1985), Christian Singles (advisor). Home: Route 13 Box 196 Salisbury NC 28144 Office: Catawba Coll Acad Computer Ctr Salisbury NC 28144

BAKER, PAUL MANUEL AVILES, land use and development planner, consultant; b. Washington, Sept. 2, 1955; s. Bruce Arnold and Dolores Joyce (Aviles) B. Student Coll. William and Mary, 1973-75; B.S. in Zoology, U. Wis.-Madison, 1980; M.Planning, Sch. Architecture, U. Va., 1984. Environ. scientist HDR, Inc., Alexandria, Va., 1981-83; research analyst Labat-Anderson, Inc., Arlington, Va., 1983-84; land planner Patton, Harris, Rust & Assocs., Fairfax, Va., 1984; mktg. cons. Consumer Health Services, Alexandria, 1985; pres. Baker, Owen Assocs., Cons. Group, Arlington, 1983—. Co-author various environ. impact statements. Mem. Alexandria Environ. Policy Commn., 1981-84. Mem. Am. Inst. Cert. Planners, Am. Planning Assn. (teller com. 1985), AAAS, Am. Inst. Biol. Scis., Ecol. Soc. Am. Episcopalian. Club: U.S. Swimming (Washington). Avocations: sailing; swimming; bicycle racing. Home: 1002 N Columbus St Alexandria VA 22314 Office: Baker Owen Assocs PO Box 12312 Arlington VA 22209

BAKER, ROBERT HART, conductor, composer; b. Bronxville, N.Y., Mar. 19, 1954; s. Lee and Jeanne (Sacher) B.; A.B. cum laude, Harvard Coll., 1974; M.Mus., Yale U., 1976, M.M.A., 1978. Music dir. and condr. Bach Soc. Orch., Cambridge, Mass., 1972-74, Conn. Philharm. Orch., Greenwich, 1974—; music dir., condr. Youth Symphony Orch. N.Y., 1977-81, Danbury (Conn.) Little Symphony, 1978-81, Putnam Symphony Orch., Brewster, N.Y., 1979-81; asst. condr. Festival of Two Worlds, Spoleto, Italy, 1979-83; music dir., condr. Asheville (N.C.) Symphony Orch., 1981—; mem. faculty choral singing SUNY, Purchase, 1977-78, oboe Horace Mann Sch., 1979-81; faculty U. N.C., Asheville, 1981-83; condr. St. Louis Philharm. Orch., 1982—; music dir., condr. York (Pa.) Symphony, 1983—. Recipient Harvard Council on Arts award, 1974, McCord Book prize Harvard U., 1974, Composition award Nat. Fedn. Music Clubs, 1975, Yale Sch. Music Alumni Assn. prize, 1978, Composition Commn. award Conn. Commn. on Arts, 1978. Mem. ASCAP (programming award 1981), Internat. Double Reed Soc., Am. Inst. Verdi Studies, Greenwich Arts Council, Am. Symphony Orch. League Condr.'s Guild, Ernest Bloch Soc., Stamford Musicians Assn. Clubs: Harvard N.Y.C., Yale N.Y.C. Composer: Tombling Day Songs, 1979 (for mezzo-soprano Betty Allen); Baroque music editor Vanguard Records, London, 1970-78; contbg. editor Record Rev. Mag., 1978-79. Home: 129 Evelyn Pl Asheville NC 28801 Office: PO Box 2852 Asheville NC 28802

BAKER, ROBERT WILLIAM, security consultant; b. Pittsburg, Feb. 5, 1944; s. Eugene R. and Viola Baker; divorced; children—Robert, Donna, Julie. B.S. in Law Enforcement Corrections, U. Nebr., 1971; M.A. in Criminal Justice, Wash. State U., 1979. Commd. airman basic U.S. Air Force, 1961, advanced through grades to capt., 1975, ret. 1982; safety and security mgr. Apple Computer, Carrollton, Tex., 1982-83; corp. security mgr. Digital Switch Corp., Richardson, Tex., 1984-85; cons., Dallas, 1985—. Disaster chmn. ARC, McKinney, Tex., 1982—; civil def. dir. Collin County Govt., McKinney, 1984—. Mem. Am. Soc. Indsl. Security, Am. Soc. Safety Engrs., Nat. Mgmt. Assn., Soc. Former Air Force OSI Agts. Home: 17490 Meandering Way #1204 Dallas TX 75252

BAKER, RONALD MARSHAL, microbiologist, educator; b. Oak Park, Ill., June 27, 1952; s. Ivan Alexander and Margaret (Bednarska) B.; m. Julia Lynn Blick. B.S. in Biology, Ill. State U., 1974; med. tech. cert. St. Anne's Sch. Med. Tech., 1976; M.S. in Biology and Microbiology, U. West Fla., 1982. Microbiologist St. Joseph's Hosp., Bloomington,Ill., 1976-80; research asst., teaching asst. U. West Fla., Pensacola, 1980-82, vis. instr. microbiology, 1982-83; co-investigator Fla. Sea Grant Coll., Pensacola, 1982-83, research asst., 1983—; asst. dir. Pensacola Br. Lab., Fla. Dept. Health and Rehab. Services. Mem. Am. Soc. Microbiology, Am. Soc. Clin. Pathologists, Sigma Xi, Phi Sigma.

BAKER, STANLEY EUGENE, college administrator, mathematics, chemistry educator; b. Oneida, Ky., July 3, 1944; s. Delbert and Margaret Alice (House) B.; m. Virginia Sue Powell, June 14, 1975. A.A. in Math./Sci., Sue Bennett Coll., 1965; B.A. in Math. Sci., Berea Coll., 1967; M.A. in Edn., Union Coll., 1970; postgrad. studies in Higher Edn., U. Ky., 1982-84. Cert. secondary math. and sci. tchr. Tchr. jr. high math., sci. Hazel Green High Sch., Ky., 1967-69; tchr. math., sci. London High Sch., Ky., 1969-70; bus. mgr. Sue Bennett Coll., London, 1970-72, registrar, bus. mgr., 1974—, assoc. prof.

math., chemistry, 1974—; tchr. jr. high math., sci. East Bernstadt Schs., Ky., 1972-74; free-lance photographer, 1968—. Author ednl. computer programs, 1983-85. Coach, judge Corbin Optomist Club Speech Contest, Ky., 1971-75, coach London Optomist Club Speech Contest, Ky., 1976-77; registrar selective service system Sue Bennett Coll., 1974-75. Recipient Sue Bennett Coll. Trustees award, 1983; named to Outstanding Young Men Am., Jaycees, 1978. Mem. Am. Chem. Soc., Ky. Assn. Student Fin. Aid Adminstrn., Ky. Assn. Coll. Registrars and Admissions Officers, Phi Kappa Phi, Kappa Delta Pi, Pi Alpha (Berea Coll.). Democrat. Baptist. Avocations: photography; computer programming; radio-controlled aircraft. Home: 112 Corbin Mobile Home Park Corbin KY 40701 Office: Sue Bennett College London KY 40741

BAKER, STANLEY RYAN, clinical psychologist, consultant; b. Cleve., May 16, 1947; s. Harold and Phyllis Marie (Ryan) B.; m. Linda Bonnie Leeman, June 12, 1974 (div. 1986). B.A. in Psychology, John Carroll U., 1969; M.S. in Clin. Psychology, U. Wis.-Milw., 1972, Ph.D. in Clin. Psychology, 1975. Psychologist, Lee Mental Health Ctr., Ft. Myers, Fla., 1975-76, research dir., 1976-82; pvt. practice psychology, Ft. Myers, 1982—; cons. in field. Chmn. agy. rev. budget com. United Way Lee County, 1983—. Recipient Outstanding Com. Chmn. award United Way of Lee County 1984. Mem. Am. Psychol. Assn., Fla. Psychol. Assn. Club: Ft. Myers Sail (vice commodore 1975-78). Lodge: Rotary. Avocations: sailing; photography; music. Home: Rural Route 1 Box 484-E Fort Myers FL 33905 Office: 2221 1st St Suite D Fort Myers FL 33901

BAKER, WILFRED EDMUND, ballistics engineer; b. Balt., Jan. 3, 1924; s. Walter Ernest and Alice Lillian (Prince) B.; m. Isabel Catherine Brady, Aug. 3, 1947; children—Isabel C., Kathleen A., Wilfred E. Jr., Barbara A., Quentin A., Lesley C. B.E. in Engring., Johns Hopkins U., 1943, M.S. in Engring., 1949, D. Engring., 1958. Instr. Johns Hopkins U., 1946-49; ordnance engr., sect. head U.S. Army Ballistics Research Lab., 1949-61; prin. devel. engr. AAI Corp., 1961-64; sect. mgr. Southwest Research Inst., San Antonio, 1964-72, inst. scientist, 1972-84; pres. Wilfred Baker Engring., 1984—; tchr. grad. level short courses; cons. in field. Author: Explosions in Air, 1973; Similarity Methods in Engineering Dynamics, 1973; Explosion Hazards and Evaluations, 1983; contbr. articles to tech. publs. Served with USN, 1943-46. Fellow ASME; assoc. fellow AIAA; mem. Sigma Xi. Clubs: Woodlawn Sailing, Austin Yacht, Johns Hopkins. Home and Office: 218 E Edgewood Pl PO Box 6477 San Antonio TX 78209

BAKER, WINDA LOUISE (WENDY), social worker; b. Suwannee County, Fla., July 16, 1952; d. Austin Sidney Baker and Jessie Mae (Williams) Baker Jones; B.A. in Theology, Berkshire Christian Coll., 1974. Clk.-typist State of Fla., Tallahassee, 1974-76; cashier Tallahassee-Eastern Theatres, 1975-76; field rep. Commn. Human Relations, 1976-77; asst. to dir. retirement living, sec., receptionist Advent Christian Village, Dowling Park, Fla., 1977-79, admissions counselor, social worker, after 1979, multi-purpose worker, 1980; geriatric care worker Advent Christian Village, Dowling Park, Fla., 1983-85, med. transcriptionist, 1985, advt. sales staff, 1986—. Vol. ARC and Assoc. Charities, 1977—; founder Suwannee County Overeaters Anonymous, Live Oak, Fla., 1982. Mem. Suwannee County Mental Assn., Assn. Informed Travelers, Christian Fin. Planning, Inc., Cheeks Sch. Gymnastics Alumni. Republican. Advent Christian. Home: PO Box 4355 Dowling Park FL 32060

BAKER-VANCURA, ANNA, ballet dancer, director, educator; b. Springfield, Ohio, Aug. 29, 1945; d. Howard and Florence (Porter) Miller; m. Barry Jack VanCura, Aug. 18, 1979; children—Anamarie, Anthony, Victoria. Student Dayton Ballet Sch., 1957-64, Sch. Nat. Ballet, Washington, 1964-65, George Washington U., 1964-65, Chgo. City Coll., 1969-70. Soloist, ballerina Ruth Page Internat. Ballet, Chgo., 1965-74; founder, dir., ballerina Ballet Midwest, Chgo., 1977-84; dir. Nat. Acad. Dance, Champaign, Ill., 1979-81; mem. dance faculty U. Ill., Champaign-Urbana, 1979-81, also dance exhbns., 1981; dir. Chattanooga Ballet, 1984—; founder DuPage Dance Acad., Elmhurst, Ill., 1972; resident choreographer Hinsdale Opera Theatre, Ill., 1978-79; co-founder Friends of Ballet Midwest, Youngstown, Ohio, 1983, Chattanooga Ballet Guild, 1984; dance panelist Ohio Arts Council, Columbus, 1984-87. Guest choreographer Rondo Ballet (Ill. Arts Council award 1978), 1978. Ill. Arts Council scholar, Ford Found. scholar, 1964-65. Mem. Nat. Assn. Regional Ballet, Southeastern Regional Ballet Assn., Assn. Ohio Dances Cos., Am. Coll. Dance Assn., Assn. Ill. Dance Cos., Chgo. Friends of Am. Ballet Theatre. Buddhist. Home: 4126 Mountain Creek Rd Apt 5 Chattanooga TN 37415 also 1915 S 59th Ave Cicero IL 60650

BAKES, PHILIP JOHN, JR., lawyer, airline executive; b. Little Rock, Mar. 6, 1946; s. Philip John and Theresa B.; m. Priscilla C. Smith, June 19, 1977; children—Tia, Justin. B.A. magna cum laude, Loyola U., Chgo., 1968, J.D. magna cum laude (Sheldon fellow), Harvard U., 1971. Bar: Ill. 1971, D.C. 1975. Assoc. firm Devoe, Shadur & Krupp, Chgo., 1972-73; asst. spl. prosecutor Watergate Spl. Prosecution Force, Washington, 1973-74, asst. chief counsel Senate Subcom. on Adminstrv. Practice and Procedures, Washington, 1974-77; spl. counsel Senate Antitrust Subcom., Washington, 1977; gen. counsel CAB, Washington, 1977-79; dep. campaign mgr. Kennedy for Pres., 1979-80; sr. v.p. Tex. Air Corp., Houston, 1980-82; exec. v.p., chief operating officer Continental Air Lines, Houston, 1982-84, pres., 1984—; mem. adv. com. govtl. relations Am. Enterprise Inst. Mem. D.C. Bar Assn., Ill. Bar Assn. Office: PO Box 4607 Houston TX 77210-4607*

BALA, MANI, pathologist, army officer; b. Madras, India, Sept. 16, 1944, came to U.S. 1968, naturalized, 1979; s. P. Muthuswamy and Subbalakshmi Mahalingam; m. Padma Suriyanarayanan, Feb. 16, 1972; children—Priya, Venkat, Reka. Grad., Hans Raj Coll., 1962; M.B.B.S., All India Inst. of Med. Scis., New Delhi, 1967. Diplomate Am. Bd. Pathology, diplomate Am. Bd. Dermatopathology. Resident in gen. surgery Wayne State U., Detroit, 1968-72; resident in pathology Grant Hosp., Chgo., 1972-73, Mt. Sinai Hosp., Chgo., 1973-77; commd. maj. U.S. Army Med. Corp., 1977, advanced through grades to col., 1985; chief of pathology, U.S. Army Hosp., Ft. Stewart, Ga., 1977-81; fellow, staff mem. Armed Forces Inst. of Pathology, Washington, 1981-82; asst. chief dept. of pathology Darnall Army Hosp., Ft. Hood, Tex., 1982—. Decorated Army Commendation medal. Fellow Coll. Am. Pathologists, mem. Am. Soc. Clin. Pathologists, Ill. Med. Soc., Chgo. Med. Soc. Hindu. Home: 13 Mighty Oak Ln Killeen TX 76541 Office: Darnall Army Hosp Fort Hood TX 76544

BALD, MARGARET, librarian; b. Pitts., Sept. 3, 1913; d. Edmond James and Margaret (Siemon) Bald; A.B., Asbury Coll., 1934; B.S., Carnegie Inst. Tech., 1935. Asst. Carnegie Library, Pitts., 1935-37; asst. librarian Carnegie Steel Corp., 1937-40; asst. Pasadena Pub. Library, 1940-44; various positions U.S. Navy Dept., 1944-48; librarian Bob Jones U., Greenville, 1948—. Mem, Am., S.C. library assns. Home: Bob Jones Univ Greenville SC 29614

BALDRIDGE, THOMAS MCINTYRE, real estate developer; b. Nashville, June 17, 1953; s. Thomas Eugene and Martha Warner (McIntyre) B.; m. Lynn Overton, Sept. 22, 1978 (div. May 1979); m. Melinda Moore Milam, Aug. 1984. B.A., Vanderbilt U., 1977. Buyer, Lord & Taylor, N.Y.C., 1977-79; v.p. Sports Industries of Am., Nashville, 1979-82; exec. v.p. Commerce Group, Nashville, 1983—; pres. Baldridge Properties, 1982—; exec. v.p. B and L Devel., Nashville, 1983—. Mem. Republican Nat. Com. Mem. Nashville C. of C., Vanderbilt U. Alumni Assn. Club: Cumberland (Nashville).

BALDUCCI, ROXANNE, educator, coach; b. Fitchburg, Mass., June 25, 1955; d. Joseph Abraham and Rachel Ann (LeBlanc) B. B.S., U. Mass., Amherst, 1977, 78; M.Ed., Pan Am. U., 1980. Head swim coach Greenfield YMCA (Mass.), 1977-78; tchr. health, head swim coach Edinburg (Tex.) Sch. Dist., 1978—. Dir. Learn to Swim program Edinburg Recreation Dept. 1982-83. Mem. Tex. Tchrs. Assn., NEA, Am. Swim Coaches Assn., Tex. Intercollegiate Swim Coaches Assn., U.S. Swimming Assn. Republican. Roman Catholic. Home: 615 S Sugar Rd Apt 65 Edinburg TX 78539 Office: Edinburg High Sch 801 E Canton Rd Edinburg TX 78539

BALDWIN, BONNIE CREASEY, nurse; b. Roanoke, Va., Jan. 16, 1949; d. Marshall Bernice and Cynthia Marie (Leftwich) C.; m. Richard Kyle Baldwin, Aug. 26, 1972; children—Annick Marie, Stephen Kyle, William Preston. B.S., Med. Coll. Va., 1972. Staff nurse burn unit Med. Coll. Va., Richmond, 1970-72, Norfolk Gen. Hosp., Va., 1973-74; dir. infection control Virginia Beach Gen. Hosp., Va., 1974—. Contbr. articles to profl. jours. Active Nat. Trust Hist. Preservation, Washington, 1985, Smithsonian Assocs., Washington, 1985. Mem. Assn. Practitioners Infection Control, Va. Assn. Practitioners Infection Control. Methodist. Avocations: furniture refinishing; antiques; playing the accordion and guitar. Office: Virginia Beach Gen Hosp 1060 1st Colonial Rd Virginia Beach VA 23454

BALDWIN, GEORGE ALEXANDER DAVISON, JR., oil company executive; b. Shreveport, La., Apr. 16, 1956; s. George Alexander and Melba Yvonne (Warr) B.; m. Jean Anne Murphy, Mar. 11, 1978; children—Mary Kathleen, Molly Kristen. B.S. in Petroleum Engring., 1978. Registered profl. engr., La. Petroleum engr. I, Arkla Exploration Co., Shreveport, 1978-80, petroleum engr. II, 1980; project engr. Core Labs., Inc., Dallas, 1980-81; petroleum engr. Majestic Energy Corp., Shreveport, 1981-82, v.p. engring., 1982-85; mgr. acquisitions and engring. Templeton Energy, Inc., Houston, 1985—. Mem. Soc. Petroleum Engrs., Nat. Soc. Profl. Engrs., La. Engring. Soc., Tex. Soc. Profl. Engrs., Tau Beta Pi, Pi Epsilon Tau. Democrat. Methodist. Home: 4018 Haven Pines Dr Kingwood TX 77345 Office: Templeton Energy Inc PO Box 1414 Houston TX 77251

BALDWIN, JOAN (JODY) BOLLING, lobbyist; b. Norton, Va., Aug. 31, 1930; d. Henry C. and Nelle E. (Mann) Bolling; A.B., Hollins (Va.) Coll., 1953; M.A., U. Va., 1955; m. Donald Winston Baldwin, Nov. 16, 1957; children—Winston Monroe, Elizabeth Bolling, Alan Henry. Sec. to asst. register of copyrights Library of Congress, Washington, 1955-59; mem. profl. staff U.S. Senate Republican Policy Com., 1959-62; press and research asst. to Senator Len B. Jordan of Idaho, 1962-64; research asst. Rep. Nat. Com., 1964; polit. researcher James N. Juliana Assocs., Washington, 1965-69; legis. asst. to Senator James B. Pearson of Kans., 1969-71; spl. asst. to asst. sec. HEW, 1971-73; dep. staff dir. and editor Legis. Notice, Senate Rep. Policy Com., 1973-85, dep. editor 1984 Rep. platform; ptnr. United Internat. Consultants, 1985—. Del., Va. Rep. Conv., 1973, 80; pres. Alexandria (Va.) Rep. Women's Club, 1965-66; 2d v.p., 1st v.p. Alexandria Jr. Women's Club, 1963-64; treas. The Twig, 1968-69. Mem. Chi Omega. Anglican. Clubs: Capitol Hill; Senate Staff; Belle Haven Country (Alexandria). Office: Suite 600 1800 Diagonal Rd Alexandria VA 22314

BALDWIN, LEE JAMES, psychologist; b. Sioux Falls, S.D., Aug. 12, 1959; s. Robert Lester and Jean (Lincoln) B. B.S., Central Mo. State U., 1980, M.S., 1982. Assessment counselor Dept. Social Services, Appleton City, Mo., 1982-83; clin. psychologist Fulton State Hosp., Mo., 1983-84; outpatient therapist Shawnee Mental Health Ctr., Coal Grove, Ohio, 1984—; police instr. Ohio Peace Officer Basic Tng. Program, Ironton, 1985; cons. Callaway County Hospice, Fulton, 1984. Big Bro., Warrensburg, Mo., 1978-79. Mem. Am. Psychol. Assn. (assoc.), Assn. for Advancement of Psychology. Baptist. Avocations: Volleyball; jogging; listening to music. Home: 347 Etna St Russell KY 41169 Office: Shawnee Mental Health Ctr 225 Carlton Davidson Ln Coal Grove OH 45638

BALDWIN, WILLIAM RUSSELL, optometrist, university dean; b. Danville, Ind., July 29, 1926; s. Edward Claire and Letha Verona (Russell) B.; m. Honey Esther Fisher, Aug. 16, 1947; children—Linda Marie Smith, Leslie Ann Baldwin Bloom. B.S., Pacific U., 1949, O.D., 1951; M.S., Ind. U., 1956, Ph.D., 1964; L.H.D. (hon.), New Eng. Coll. Optometry, 1982. Practice optometry, Beech Grove, Ind., 1951-54; dir. optometry clinic Ind. U., Bloomington, 1959-63; dean Coll. Optometry, Pacific U., Forest Grove, Oreg., 1963-69; pres. New Eng. Coll. Optometry, Boston, 1969-79; dean U. Houston, 1979—. Author: (with C.R. Schick) Corneal Contact Lenses, Fitting Procedures, 1962; (with others) The Refractive State of the Eye, 1969. Mem. exec. com. Republican Central Com., Washington County, Oreg., 1963-69; chmn. arts, scis. div. Ind. Reps., 1962-63; chmn. Vellore India Hosp. Fund Drive, 1959-61; mem. men's adv. council Bloomington Hosp., 1959-63. Recipient Disting. Alumni Service award Ind. U., 1977, Gold Medal award Beta Sigma Kappa, 1968, Pres.'s medal New Eng. Coll. Optometry, 1977. Fellow AAAS; mem. Nat. Research Council Com. Vision of Nat. Acad. Scis., Am. Optometric Assn., Assn. Schs. Colls. Optometry (chmn. internat. optometric edn.), Am. Acad. Optometry (chmn. sect. on edn.), Sigma Xi. Lodge: Rotary. Office: U Houston Coll Optometry 4901 Calhoun Houston TX 77004

BALE, DONALD CHARLES, publisher; b. Madison, S.D., Aug. 20, 1937; s. Burtes Donald and Eleanor Maude (Schmidt) B. B.A., State U. S.D., 1959; M.S., Columbia U., 1960. Writer KELO-TV, Sioux Falls, S.D., 1962; pres., owner Bale Books & Bale Publs., New Orleans, 1963—. Author: Complete Guide for Profitable Coin Investing and Collecting, 1963. Contbr. articles to profl. jours. Recipient Customer Service award Krause Publs., 1983. Mem. Phi Beta Kappa. Methodist. Avocation: numismatics. Office: PO Box 2727 New Orleans LA 70176

BALENTINE, ROBERT CHAPMAN, mathematician; b. Poteau, Okla., Dec. 29, 1934; s. Fred Roosevelt and Eula Ruth (Chapman) B.; B.S., Baylor U., 1957; postgrad. Tex. A&M U., 1957-58, 60; m. Patsy Lee Byrum, June 30, 1962 (div. Aug. 1971); children—David Michael, Timothy Charles. Mathematician, Army Ballistic Missile Agy., Redstone Arsenal, 1958-61, NASA Johnson Space Center, Hampton, Va., 1961-62, NASA, Huntsville, Ala., 1962—, Hubble Space Telescope software mgr., 1979—. Baptist. Home: 336 Jack Coleman Dr NW Huntsville AL 35805 Office: EE61 Marshall Space Flight Center Huntsville AL 35812

BALES, JOHN WAYLAND, mathematics educator; b. Cameron, Tex., Oct. 12, 1943; s. Loyie McKimm and Zula Mae (Adams) B. B.A., U. Tex., 1965, M.A., 1967; Ph.D., Auburn U., 1975. Research assoc. Applied Research Labs., Austin, Tex., 1966-70; vis. instr. La. State U., Baton Rouge, 1975-76; asst. prof. math. Tuskegee Inst., Ala., 1976-82, assoc. prof., 1982—; adj. asst. prof. Auburn U., Ala., 1984. Pres., Opelika Interclub Council, 1984-85. Mem. Am. Math. Soc., Nat. Council Tchrs. Math., Pi Mu Epsilon. NASA fellow, summers 1979, 80. Club: Opelika Civitan (pres. 1984-85; Service award 1982). Avocations: hunting; fishing; hiking; gardening. Office: Tuskegee Inst Tuskegee AL 36088

BALFANZ, ROBERT DON, automobile repair service executive; b. Evanston, Ill., Nov. 29, 1951; s. William R. and Eunice Nora (McGraw) B. B.A., Northeastern Ill. U., 1973. Owner, operator Corvette Clinic, Dallas, 1979—, Corvette Salvage, Dallas, 1982—; presenter seminars. Columnist, corr. Keepin' Track of Vettes mag., Spring Valley, N.Y., 1976—. Mem. Nat. Inst. Automotive Service Excellence (cert. master auto technician), Chili Appreciation Soc. Internat. (judge ann. world championship chili cookoff 1980—). Lodges: Masons, Shriners. Office: Corvette Clinic Suite 12 9709 Miller Rd Dallas TX 75238

BALILES, GERALD L., governor of Virginia; b. Stuart, Va., July 8, 1940. B.A., Wesleyan U., 1963; J.D., U. Va., 1967. Bar: Va. 1967, U.S. Supreme Ct. 1971. Asst. atty. gen. of Va., 1967-72, dep. atty. gen., 1972-75, atty. gen., 1982-86; gov., Va., 1986—; mem. Va. Ho. of Dels., mem. appropriations com., 1978-82, com. corp. ins. and banking, 1976-82, com. conservation and natural resources, 1979-82; formerly ptnr. Lacy and Baliles, Richmond; chmn. Joint House-Senate Ins. Study Com., 1977-79; Legal Drafting Sub-Com., State Water Study Commn., 1977—; vice chmn. Joint House-Senate Com. on Nuclear Power Generation Facilities, 1977-79; co-chmn. 3rd Dist. Com. Virginians for Bonds Campaign, 1977. Mem. Richmond Bar Assn., Va. Bar Assn. (exec. com. 1979), ABA (environ. quality com., natural resources law sect. 1973—, environ. control com., corp., banking and bus. law sect. 1974—), Va. State Bar (chmn. environ. quality com. 1975-77). Office: Office of the Governor 3d Floor Capitol Bldg Richmond VA 23219*

BALIN, DONNA FAYE, geologist; b. Hampton, Va., July 5, 1956; d. Henry Stanley and Fayrene Timm (Timm) B. B.S. summa cum laude, U. Tex.-Auston, 1978. Exploration geologist Houston Oil & Minerals Corp., 1978-80; geologist U.S. Geol. Survey, Menlo Park, Calif., 1980-81; Amoco Oil Co., Denver, summer 1983; Amoco found. fellow U. Ariz., Tucson, 1982-83; NSF grad. fellow U. Cambridge, Eng., 1983—. Contbr. articles to profl. publs. Getty Oil Co. scholar, 1977-78, Grad. Tuition scholar U. Ariz., 1982-83; recipient Overseas Research Student award U. Cambridge, 1983—, Cambridge Chancellor's Bursary award, 1983-84. Fellow: Geol. Soc. London, Cambridge Philos. Soc.; mem. Am. Assn. Petroleum Geologists, Sierra Club, Phi Beta Kappa, Phi Kappa Phi. Club: Servas. Avocations: running, general athletics, camping. Home: 127 Claywell San Antonio TX 78209 Office: U Cambridge Dept Earth Scis Downing St Cambridge CB2 3EQ England

BALINT, LEE DUGGAR, insurance adjuster; b. Hosford, Fla., June 9, 1930; d. James Adelbert and Nezzie (Mosley) Duggar; m. John Steve Balint, June 5, 1948; children—Donald Steve, Daniel Lynn. Student Massey-Draughon Bus. Coll., Montgomery, Ala., 1947-48. Cert. profl. ins. woman Ins. Inst. Am.; lic. ins. adjuster, Ala. Sec., Montgomery County Sch. System (Ala.), 1947, State of Ala., Montgomery, 1948-49; sec. Al Levy's Dept. Store, Montgomery, 1949, Paul Smith Gen. Ins. Agy., Montgomery, 1950-51; claims sec. various ind. adjusters, Montgomery, 1952-65; claim sec., cashier Md. Casualty Co., Montgomery, 1966-72; claim sec., workers compensation ins. adjuster Crawford and Co., Montgomery, 1973-80; workers compensation claim adjuster Collier Cobb & Assocs., Montgomery, 1981-82; workers compensation claim rep. Great Am. Ins. Co., Montgomery, 1982—. Vol., bd. dirs. Arthritis Found., Montgomery, 1969—. Mem. Ins. Women of Montgomery (treas. 1965; Claims Person of Yr. 1978, Ins. Woman of Yr. 1983), Montgomery Claims Assn. (Claims Person of Yr. 1980), Am. Bus. Women's Assn., Atlanta Claims Assn., Ala. Claims Assn., Workers Compensation Claims Assn. Presbyterian. Home: 738 Karen Rd Montgomery AL 36109

BALL, ARDELLA PATRICIA, library science educator; b. Nashville, Dec. 15, 1932; d. Otis Hugh and Mary Ellen (Staples) Boatright; m. Wesley James Ball, Aug. 28, 1957; children—Wesley James, Roderick Lynn, Wesleyn Lynette, Patrick Wayne. A.B., Fisk U., 1953; M.S. in L.S., Atlanta U., 1956; postgrad. St. Louis U. Cataloger Ala. A.&M. Coll., Huntsville, 1957-59; sr. cataloger St. Louis U., 1960-65; cataloger Savannah Pub. Library (Ga.), 1965-68; cataloger Armstrong State Coll., Savannah, 1968-74, instructional devel. librarian, 1974-77, library media instr., 1977—. Mem. LWV, NAACP, PTA (life), Ga. Library Assn., Southeastern Library Assn., Ga. Library Media Dept; Coastal Ga. Library Assn. Ch. Christ Contbrs. course manuals in library media. Office: 1935 Abercorn Extension Armstrong State College Savannah GA 31406

BALL, CARROLL RAYBOURNE, anatomist, medical educator, researcher; b. Leakesville, Miss., Oct. 11, 1925; s. Marvin Hugh and Elizabeth (Hillman) B.; m. Jannie Vee Brooks, Sept. 5, 1947 (dec. 1954); children—Hugh Brooks, Peter Stephen; m. 2d, Sally Ann Montgomery, Mar. 22, 1963 (div. 1976); children—1 dau., Lou Ellen. Student Millsaps Coll., 1942-44; B.A., U. Miss., 1947, M.S., 1948, Ph.D., 1963. Instr. Duke U., 1948-51. Grad. asst. in zoology U. Miss., Oxford 1946-48, instr. anatomy Med. Sch., 1962-63, asst. prof., 1963-66, assoc. prof., 1966-71, prof., 1971—; instr. anatomy Med. Sch., W.Va. U., 1951-57; asst. prof. biology U. So. Miss., 1957-60. Pres. Jackson Civil War Round Table, 1983-84; v.p. Magnolia chpt. Nat. Assn. Watch and Clock Collectors, 1980-82. Served to lt. comdr. USNR, 1944-71; PTO. NIH predoctoral trainee, 1960-63; Miss. Heart Assn. grantee, 1963-66. Mem. Am. Assn. Anatomists, Soc. Exptl. Biology and Medicine, Am. Assn. Pathology, So. Assn. Anatomy, Miss. Acad. Sci., Hattiesburg Jr. C. of C. (sec. 1959-60), Order of First Families of Miss., Sigma Xi, Alpha Epsilon Delta, Theta Nu Sigma, Beta Beta Beta (pres. 1947-48), Omicron Delta Kappa, Pi Kappa Alpha (sec. 1943-44). Methodist. Contbr. numerous articles to nat. and internat. sci. jours. Home: 905 Pinehurst Pl Jackson MS 39202 Office: Dept Anatomy U Miss Med Ctr 2500 N State St Jackson MS 39216

BALL, DOLORES ANITA, educator; b. Limestone County, Tex., Sept. 19, 1940; d. Thomas Coleman and Grace Estelle (Spruiell) Taylor; B.A., Baylor U., 1962, M.S., 1979; m. Jimmy Wayne Ball, Sept. 1, 1961 (div.); children—Randal Wayne, Kristi D'Ann Ball Burkett. Tchr. Bell's Hill Elem. Sch., Waco, Tex., 1962-63, LaVega Intermediate Sch., Bellmead, Tex., 1963-67, Kaiser Elem. Sch., Ypsilanti, Mich., 1968-69, Marlin (Tex.) Elem. Sch., 1974-75, Riesel (Tex.) Elem. Sch., 1975-80; ednl. diagnostician, supr. Hill County Enrichment Program, Hillsboro, Tex., 1980-85; spl. edn. tchr. Midway High Sch., Waco, Tex., 1985—. Mem. Assn. Tex. Profl. Educators. Republican. Baptist. Home: 600 Rolling Hills Dr Hewitt TX 76643 Office: Midway High Sch 9101 Woodway Dr Waco TX 76610

BALL, HELEN MARIE, communications consultant; b. San Antonio, Dec. 10, 1938; d. George Fred and Helen (Smith) Franz; student public schs.; m. Davis Frederick Ball, Jan. 13, 1972; children—Scott Wade, Elizabeth Ann. Sec., 1959-66; tech. editor computer field Randolph AFB, Tex., 1966-71, advt. copywriter recruiting, 1971-75, EEO officer, 1975-80, personnel mgmt. specialist, 1980-82; tng. cons., 1979—; owner Ball Diversified, San Antonio; mem., 1st vice chmn. Randolph-Brooks Credit Union. Recipient various govt. performance awards. Author publs. in field. Home: 2330 Nashwood Dr San Antonio TX 78232 Office: ATC/PA Randolph AFB TX 78150

BALL, MARGARET ANGEL ROGERS, carpet corporation executive; b. Highlands, N.C., May 3, 1925; d. Jamie Newton and Sarah Maude Delena (Keener) Rogers; m. James Aaron Ball, Aug. 20, 1944; children—James Aaron, Ronald Winston, Randal Newton, Angela Sharon. Grad. in Acctg., Herrin Sch. Bus., Dalton, Ga., 1944. Sec.-treas. Ball Carpet Industries, Inc., Dalton, 1972-75, sec. Ball Internat. Equipment, Inc., Dalton, 1982—, pres. Ball of Ga. Inc. (formerly Carpet Central Ltd.), 1976—. Active PTA, 1952—, pres. local unit, 1954-60, dist. dir., 1962-66, state v.p./legis. chmn. 1968-74, state sec., 1982—; trustee Ga. PTA Birney Endowment Fund, 1980-82; bd. dirs. Dalton-Whitfield Day Care Ctrs., 1976-82; co-chmn. Citizens' Com. on Day Care in Whitfield and Murray counties, 1984—; area rep. World Trade Council, Chattanooga/Dalton Area, 1982—; div. 8 account exec. Dalton United Way, 1983; state sec. Ga. Legis. Forum, Atlanta, 1983—. Named Hon. Life Mem., 1958, also Hon. Founder, Ga. PTA, 1960, Parent of Year, Valley Point Elem./High Schs., Dug Gap Elem. Sch., 1960-74; recipient Outstanding Service award Dalton-Whitfield County Day Care Ctrs., 1982, Outstanding Citizen award, 1980. Mem. Dalton-Whitfield C. of C. (diplomat club, chmn. fed. govt. com. 1984), Network Floor Covering Women (bd. dirs., charter), Carpet Capitol Toastmasters (communicator editor 1983—), Ladies Aux. of Ga. Sheriffs Assn. (Cherokee Estates chpt.), LWV (bd. dirs., edn. chmn. Dalton Area 1980—). Democrat. Club: Lenna Judd Women's (2d v.p. Dalton 1980-84). Home: 2479 Dug Gap Rd SW Dalton GA 30720 Office: Ball of Ga Inc 310 Holiday Ave CRI Bldg Dalton GA 30720

BALL, PATRICIA GAIL, public relations executive, instructor, consultant; b. Roanoke, Va., Jan. 19, 1951; d. Wilmer and Betty Ball. B.S., Radford Coll., 1971; M.S., U. Tenn., 1973, Ed.D., 1976. Asst. prof. U. Tenn., Knoxville, 1976-78; dir. Appalachian Ctr. for Ednl. Equity, 1977-78; dir. office pub. affairs City of Knoxville, 1978-83; dir. mktg. and pub. relations Park West Hosp., Knoxville, 1983—. Contbr. articles profl. jours. Mem. leadership Knoxville com. C. of C.; bd. dirs. Dogwood Arts Festival, Greater Knox Council for Arts; trustee Dulin Gallery Art. Recipient Career Woman of Yr. award Am. Bus. and Profl. Women, 1978; Mortar Bd. Faculty award for outstanding accomplishment, 1976. Mem. Assn. Women in Psychology, Exec. Women's Assn., Internat. Assn. Bus. Communicators, State Tech. Inst. Knoxville. Contbr. articles to profl. jours.

BALLANTINE, THOMAS AUSTIN, JR., judge; b. Louisville, Sept. 22, 1926; s. Thomas Austin and Anna Marie (Pfeiffer) B.; m. Nancy A. Armstrong, June 10, 1953; children—Thomas A., Nancy Adair, Brigid A., Joseph A. Student, Northwestern U., 1944-46; B.A., U. Ky., 1948; J.D., U. Louisville, 1954. Bar: Ky. bar 1954. Asso. firm McElwain, Dinning, Clarke & Winstead, Louisville, 1954-64; dep. commr. Jefferson Circuit Ct., 1958-62; commr. Jefferson Fiscal Ct., 1962-64; judge Jefferson Circuit Ct., 1964-77, U.S. Dist. Ct., Western Dist. Ky., 1977—; instr. U. Louisville Law Sch., 1969-75. Bd. dirs. Louisville Urban League, 1958-64, chmn., 1963-64; dir. NCCJ, 1960-65, Health and Welfare Council, 1969, Louisville Theatrical Assn., 1970. Mem. Louisville Bar Assn., Ky. State Bar. Democrat. Roman Catholic. Club: Pendennis. Home: 48 Hill Rd Louisville KY 40204 Office: 247 USPO and Courthouse Louisville KY 40202

BALLANTYNE, ROBERT HUBBARD, psychologist, educator, consultant; b. Kansas City, Mo., Aug. 2, 1932. Lic. psychologist N.C. Assoc. prof. Duke U., Durham, N.C., 1962—, dir. admissions, dir. inst. research and asst. to the pres. for planning, 1964-73; Fulbright Hayes prof. Ministry of Edn., Nicosia, Cyprus, 1973-74; vis. adj. faculty U. N.C., Chapel Hill, from 1973, N.C. State U., from 1979, N.C. Central U., from 1982; pres. Counseling and Psychology Consulting Service, Durham, 1978—. Mem. Am. Psychol. Assn., Am. Assn. Counseling and Devel. Office: 213 W Duke Bldg Duke U Durham NC 27708 also: Counseling & Cons Service 1809 Chapel Hill Rd Durham NC 27707

BALLARD, EDWARD BROOKS, landscape architect; b. Lexington, Mass., Jan. 25, 1906; s. Walter Clark and Clara Abbie (Bigelow) B.; m. Mina Louise McCormick, Dec. 20, 1947; 1 son, Robert Clark. A.B., Harvard Coll., 1927;

M.L.A., Harvard U., 1933. Asst. to editor Horticulture Mag., Boston, 1930; landscape architect, assoc. recreation planner, assoc. field coordinator Nat. Park Service, Springfield, Boston and Cambridge, Mass., 1933-36, Washington, 1937-39; exec. sec. Nat. Parks Assn., Washington, 1940-42; spl. rep. Nat. Recreation Assn., N.Y.C., 1946-47; asst. dir. Md. Dept. Forests and Parks, Annapolis, 1947-48; supt. Cumberland Falls State Park, Corbin, Ky., 1948-49; prin. landscape architect Pa. Bur. Parks, Harrisburg, 1949-52; landscape architect Office Chief of Engrs., U.S. Dept. Army, Washington, 1952-58, chief mil. project site planning, 1958-74; mng. landscape architect Miller, Wihry & Lee, Washington, 1975-80; cons. on mktg. profl. services to govt. agys., 1982-84. Served to capt. U.S. Army, 1942-46. Fellow Am. Soc. Landscape Architects (emeritus; pres. Potomac chpt. 1961-62, trustee 1964-67, nat. sec.-treas. 1967-71, nat. archivist 1972-76, sec.-treas. council of fellows 1976-78); mem. Internat. Fedn. Landscape Architects (U.S. rep.; mem. com. transl. tech. terms 1979—), Fairlington Civic Assn. (pres. 1954-55), Broyhill Crest Citizens Assn. (pres. 1961-62), Annandale Community Council (sec. 1959-60, chmn. 1963-65), Harvard Sch. Design Assn., Am. First Day Cover Soc., Va. Wildflower Preservation Soc. (chmn. nominating com. 1984-85, pres. Potowmack chpt. 1985-86), Delta Upsilon. Home and office: 3913 Longstreet Ct Annandale VA 22003

BALLARD, JAMES ALAN, geophysicist; b. Rockingham, N.C., Aug. 13, 1929; s. William Douglas and Deborah Anne (Jones) B.; B.S., U. N.C., 1953, M.S., 1959, Ph.D., 1979; m. Betsy Lee Bowie, Dec. 27, 1953; children—William Mark, Robert Clay, Joel Bowie, Mary Eleanor. Geophysicist, Ind. Exploration Co., Houston, 1953-54; oceanographer U.S.N. Hydrographic Office, Suitland, Md., 1959-62, supervisory oceanographer, Oceanographic Office, Washington, 1962-75; research oceanographer, Naval Ocean Research and Devel. Activity, Nat. Space Tech. Labs., Miss., 1976-78, geophysics programs mgr., 1978—; tech. adv. Md. Geol. Survey, 1974-75. Trustee, Prince Georges County (Md.) Public Schs., 1965-69. Served with AUS, 1954-56. Mem. Soc. Exploration Geophysicists, Southeastern Geophys. Soc., Am. Geophys. Union, Potomac Geophys. Union, Sigma Xi. Presbyterian. Clubs: Toastmasters, Picayune Band Boosters. Contbr. articles to profl. jours. Home: 1520 4th Ave Picayune MS 39466 Office: Naval Ocean Research and Devel Activity Nat Space Tech Labs Station MS 39529

BALLARD, ROBERT WILLIAMS, III, structural engineer; b. Greensboro, N.C., Mar. 6, 1953; s. Robert Williams and Emily (Marie Rhodes) B.; m. Deborah Lee Baldwin, June 20, 1981; children—Ryan Lane, Ashley Lauren. Student Guilford Tech. Inst., 1971-73; B.S. cum laude, N.C. State U., 1979. Registered profl. engr., N.C. Engr. in tng. Civil Engring. & Applied Research, Raleigh, N.C., 1980, Bigger & Agnew Inc., Engrs., Raleigh, 1980; jr. engr. Lasater-Hopkins Engrs., Raleigh, 1981-83; structural engr. DSA Group, Inc., Raleigh, 1983-86, head structural dept., Winston-Salem, N.C., 1986—. Served with USAF, 1973-76. Mem. ASCE (assoc.), Tau Beta Pi, Chi Epsilon. Baptist. Club: Wolfpack. Home: 217 Rosehaven Dr Raleigh NC 27609 Office: 1033 Wade Ave Suite 120 Raleigh NC 27605

BALLENGEE, BERT H., utility company executive; b. Trinidad, Colo., 1924; married. B.B.A., U. Tex., 1948. Salesman, Southwestern Life Ins. Co., 1948-49; with Southwestern Pub. Service Co., 1949—, chief clk., 1952-57, personnel mgr., 1957-62, dir. dept., 1962-72, dir. fin., asst. sec., 1972-73, v.p. fin., 1973-79, exec. v.p., 1979-82, pres., chief operating officer, 1982—, also dir. Office: Southwestern Pub Service Co PO Box 1261 Amarillo TX 79170

BALLENTINE, GEORGE DERRILL, civil engineer; b. White Rock, S.C., Nov. 11, 1936; s. William Franklin and Mae Belle (Lindler) B.; m. Carolyn Sue Gearhart, Dec. 16, 1959 (div. Nov. 12, 1969); children—Christopher Mark, Kelly Marie. B.S. in Civil Engring., U. S.C., 1958; M.S., Purdue U., 1965; Ph.D. in Civil Engring., U. Tex., 1973. Registered profl. engr., S.C. Commd. 2d lt. USAF, 1958, advanced through grades to lt. col., 1976, ret., 1980; programs officer Hdqrs. Command, Bolling AFB, D.C., 1965-69; dep. base civil engr., Osan Air Base, Korea, 1969-70; research engr., then dir. Air Force Civil Engring. Lab., Kirtland AFB, N.Mex. and Tyndall AFB, Fla., 1973-80; dir. dams and reservoirs safety State S.C. Land Resources Commn., Columbia, 1980—. Decorated Meritorious Service medal, Air Force Commendation medal. Mem. ASCE. Methodist. Contbr. numerous articles to publs. Home: Route 5 Box 367 Chapin SC 29036 Office: 2221 Devine St Suite 222 Columbia SC 29205

BALLI, GIORGIO, architect, builder; b. Lima, Peru, Jan. 19, 1937; came to U.S., 1971, naturalized, 1978; s. Decimo and Leonor (Yacuzzi) B.; m. Rosario Maria Verme, July 14, 1962; children—Giorgio Luigi, Fabrizio, Francesco. Architect, Universidad Nacional de Ingenieria, Peru, 1960. Registered architect. Ptnr. Balli & Canepa Architects, Lima, 1960-70; with G.R.V., Los Angeles, Miami, Fla., 1971-73; ptnr. Krome Devel. Co., Miami, 1973-75; sole practice, Miami, 1975—; bd. dirs. Architect Rev. Bd., Coral Gables, Fla., 1985—; guest critic U. Miami, 1983—. Prin. works include Ch. of the Epiphany, 1985; also numerous residences. Bd. dirs. Cocoplum Civic Assn., Coral Gables, 1983—, Architectural Rev. Bd. City Coral Gables, 1985—. Recipient Second place and Three Hon. Mentions City Beautiful award Coral Gables C. of C. 1985, Grand prize Aurora award Southeast Builders Conf. 1982, 85, Residential Design award Dist. Council Pueble Libre, 1961, 66, First Prize Multi Family Bldg. Design award Coll. Architects 1969. Mem. AIA, Fla. Assn. Architects, Constrn. Industry License Assn. Roman Catholic. Avocation: painting. Office: 9835 Sunset Dr Suite 209 Miami FL 33173

BALLIETT, JOHN WILLIAM, business consultant b. Rochester, N.Y., Sept. 10, 1947; s. Charles G. and Burnetta E. Balliett; B.S. in Physics, Grove City (Pa.) Coll., 1969; postgrad. U. Rochester; m. Betsy Jane VanPatten, Jan. 25, 1969; 1 dau., Noelle Elizabeth. Engr., Eastman Kodak Co., Rochester, 1969-70; with Tropel Inc., 1970-74, mktg. mgr., 1973-74; co-founder, exec. v.p., dir. Quality Measurement Systems Inc., Penfield, N.Y., 1974-77; pres. QMS Internat. Inc., Penfield, 1976-77; v.p. parent co. EG&G, 1977-78; pres. Balliett Assos., Inc. (sold to Charter One, Inc. 1981), Sarasota, Fla., 1978-81, Charter One, Inc., 1981—, mktg. and cons., devel. and hotel mgmt. co., Sarasota, 1981—, Shore Lane Devel. Corp., 1981—; bus. cons., Sarasota, 1978—. Patentee optical and measurement systems. Home: 1404 Westbrook Dr Sarasota FL 33581 Office: 1390 Main St Suite 1006 Sarasota FL 33577

BALLTRIP, EWELL HERMAN, journalist, publisher; b. Harlan, Ky., May 27, 1950; s. Ewell Lloyd and Beatrice Nancy (Meadors) B.; m. Kathy Mills, July 23, 1978; children—Andrew Lee, Amanda Beth. B.A. in Journalism and Polit. Sci., Baylor U., 1972. Reporter-writer, Harlan Daily Enterprise, 1972-73, assoc. editor, 1973-79, editor, 1979-85, pub., 1985—; former contbg. writer McGraw-Hill World News, N.Y.C., Ky. Bus. Ledger, Louisville. Recipient awards for polit. commentary, news reports, feature reports, editorals Ky. Press Assn., 1972-78, 1980-82; news report citations AP Mng. Editors Assn., 1974, 79. Democrat. Baptist (deacon). Past contbr. to Coal Age mag. Home: PO Box 1212 Harlan KY 40831 Office: Harlan Daily Enterprise Box E Harlan KY 40831

BALNICKY, ROBERT GABRIEL, clergyman; b. Elizabeth, N.J., Apr. 18, 1922; s. Harry and Irene (Sawicky) B.; m. Annette Virginia Hawkins, Dec. 24, 1977; children by previous marriage—Richard Ozzie, Barbara Gail. Student Pensacola Jr. Coll., 1949, Emory U., 1950, Columbia Theol. Sem., Decatur, Ga., 1952; B.Min., M.Min., Internat. Bible Inst. and Sem., Orlando, Fla., 1979, D.D., 1980, D.Min., 1985. With Merck & Co., Rahway, N.J., 1939-42; pastor Troy (N.C.) Presbyn. Ch., 1952-55, 1st Presbyn. Ch., Ocean Drive Beach, S.C., 1955-56, McCutchen Meml. Ch., Union, S.C., 1956-60, Fairfield Presbyn. Ch., Pensacola, Fla., 1960-64; founder, pastor Trinity Bible Ch., Pensacola, 1964-70; pastor Inskip Presbyn. Ch., Knoxville, Tenn., 1970-72; founding pastor Grace Presbyn. Ch., Knoxville, 1973-74; pastor Handsboro Presbyn. Ch., Gulfport, Miss., 1979-81; interim pastor Berean Presbyn. Ch., New Orleans, 1982-83; chmn. Ch. Devel. Commn., Evang. Presbyn. Ch., 1982-85; dir. communications, dir. family services Salvation Army, New Orleans, 1983-85; chaplain Pay Cash Wholesale Grocery, 1972-74; chaplain coordinator La. World Expn., 1984; counseling center dir. Christian Broadcasting Network, Inc., Knoxville, 1975-76; coordinator chaplaincy New Orleans Fire Dept., 1985—; chaplain New Orleans Fire Fighters Assn. and New Orleans Fire chief's Assn., 1985—; pres. Robert G. Balnicky Evang. Assn., Inc.; pres. Union County (S.C.) Ministers Assn., 1957; chmn. Enoree Presbytery Com. Evangelism, 1956-60; mem. com. evangelism S.C. Synod, 1956-60; chmn. bd. dirs. Pensacola Youth for Christ; bd. dirs. Fla. Alcohol-Narcotics, Inc., Fla. United Christian Action, Inc.; mem. adv. bd. Community Action Program, Am. Security Council. Lt. col., chaplain Fla. CAP, 1965-70; dep. wing chaplain Tenn. CAP, 1970-74, dep. chaplain S.E. Region CAP, 1974-82; chaplain S.W. regional staff CAP, 1982—. Served as aviation machinist's mate, flight engr. 1st class USN, 1942-49. Recipient Four Chaplains citation Chapel Four Chaplains, Phila., 1960; Meritorious Service award CAP 1973, Exceptional Service award, 1982; Grover Loening Aerospace award, 1974, Paul E. Garber award 1981, Vol. of Yr. award New Orleans City Welfare Dept. Emergency Services, 1984. Mem. Am. Legion (state chaplain S.C. 1956-58, post comdr. 1953-54; grad. Am. Legion Coll., Indpls. 1954; mem. nat. press assn.; chmn. S.C. religious emphasis com. 1956-58, mem. nat. comdr.'s flying squadron; mem. Century Club 1954-55), 40 and 8 (grand aumonier S.C.; state chaplain 1957-59, aumonier nat., nat. chaplain 1959-60; local chaplain 1961-70), Navy League, World Ministry Fellowship (pres. 1966-68), Mil. Chaplains Assn. (life), Nat. Assn. Evangs., Fellowship of Fire Chaplains, Firefighters for Christ, Fellowship of Christian Fighters, Internat. Order St. Luke the Physician. Club: Masons (32 deg.). Address: PO Box 57435 New Orleans LA 70157

BALOGH, JAMES MICHAEL, geologist; b. Riverdale, Md., Aug. 30, 1948; s. James Jr. and Ruth Margaret (Teti) B.; m. Char Dahlgren, Dec. 8, 1984. B.S. in Geology, U. Tex., 1972. Geologist, REB Petroleum Co., Houston, 1975-79; area geologist INEXCO Oil Co., Houston, 1979-80; div. geologist Exchange Oil & Gas Corp., Houston, 1980-85; sr. geologist Transco Joint Ventures, 1985—. Mem. Houston Symphony Chorale, 1979-83. Mem. Am. Assn. Petroleum Geologists. Avocations: buying and selling antiques; remodeling houses. Office: Transco Energy Co PO Box 1396 Houston TX 77215002

BALOGH, JOSEPH DAVID, retired automobile manufacturing company executive; b. Detroit, Mar. 12, 1930; s. Joseph and Mary Ann (Koska) B.; m. Mary Caroline Ladd, Dec. 16, 1949; children—Celeste Jeanine, Constance Denice. Grad. Coll. Advanced Traffic, Detroit, 1954; student Henry Ford Community Coll., 1957-62, Washtenaw Community Coll., 1975. Traffic supr. Ford Motor Co., Dearborn, Mich., 1959-68; gen. mgr. Fleak Carloading Co., Chgo., 1968; traffic rep. fin. and ins. subs. Ford Motor Co. Dearborn, 1968-78, traffic rep. Climate Control div., Plymouth, Mich., 1978-82. Chmn. food services Chelsea (Mich.) Community Fair, 1973; instr. med. self-help course Office C.D., Wyandotte, Mich., 1963; mem. Chelsea Village Planning Commn., 1974-77. Served with USMC, 1947-50. Mem. Motor City Traffic Club, Coll. Advanced Traffic Detroit Alumni Assn. (pres. 1982). Methodist (treas. 1963). Lodge: Moose. Home: 22239 Breezeswept Ave Port Charlotte FL 33952

BALSLEY, IROL WHITMORE (MRS. HOWARD L. BALSLEY), educator; b. Venus, Nebr., Aug. 22, 1912; d. Sylvanus Bertrand and Nanna (Carson) Whitmore; B.A., Nebr. State Coll., Wayne, 1933; M.S., U. Tenn., 1940; Ed.D., Ind. U., 1952; m. Howard Lloyd Balsley, Aug. 24, 1947. Tchr. high schs., Osmond and Walthill, Nebr., 1934-37; asst. prof. Ind. U., 1942-49; lectr. U. Utah, 1949-50, Russell Sage Coll., 1953-54; prof. office adminstrn. La. Tech. U., 1954-65, also head dept. office adminstrn., 1963-65; prof. bus. edn. Tex. Tech. U., 1965-72, prof. edn., 1972-75; prof. adminstrv. services U. Ark., Little Rock, 1975-80, prof. emeritus, 1980—; adj. prof. Hardin-Simmons U., Abilene, Tex., 1980-81; coordinator USAF clk.-typist tng. program Pa. State U., 1951, instr., head office tng. sect. TVA, 1941-42; editorial asst. South-Western Pub. Co., 1940-41. Mem. Adminstrv. Mgmt. Soc., Nat. Collegiate Assn. Secs. (co-founder, past pres., nat. exec. sec. 1976-81), Pi Lambda Theta, Delta Pi Epsilon (past nat. sec.), Beta Gamma Sigma, Phi Delta Kappa, Pi Omega Pi, Sigma Tau Delta, Alpha Psi Omega, Delta Kappa Gamma. Author: (with Wanous) Shorthand Transcription Studies, 1968; (with Robinson) Integrated Secretarial Studies, 1963; (with Wood and Whitmore) Homestyle Baking, 1973; Century 21 Shorthand, Vol. I, 1974, (with Robert Hoskinson) Vol. II, 1974; Self-Paced Learning Activities for Century 21 Shorthand, Vol. I, 1977; High Speed Dictation, 1980. Address: 6501 15th Ave W Bradenton FL 33529

BALSLEY, PHILIP ELWOOD, singer; b. Augusta County, Va., Aug. 8, 1939; s. Henry Elwood and Marjorie Walden (Fielding) B.; m. Wilma Lee Kincaid July 21, 1962; children—Gregory Statler, John Marklev, Leah Marie. Grad. high sch. 1956. Mem. Statler Bros. singing group; treas. Statler Bros. Prodns., Inc., 1973—, Am. Cowboy Music Co., Inc., 1973—; dir. Happy Birthday USA, Inc., 1970. Recipient 3 Grammy Awards. Mem. Country Music Assn. (9 awards), AFTRA. Presbyterian.

BALTHROPE, WILLIAM DUNBAR, music systems executive; b. San Antonio, Dec. 10, 1939; s. Charles W. and Mary V. (Edmiston) B.; m. Sue Hardy, Sept. 1, 1960; children—Charles W., Brett H. B.B.A., So. Meth. U., 1961. Sales mgr. Muzak Systems of San Antonio, 1961-68, pres., owner, 1968—; dir. First City Bank, Windsor Park. Mayor, City of Alamo Heights (Tex.), 1981—; alderman, 1975-81; trustee Southwest Tex. Meth. Hosp.; past pres. Christman Clearing Bur., 1968, Conopus Club, 1974, Cambridge Elem. PTA, 1972; past vice chmn. YMCA, 1972-73. Methodist. Clubs: Tex. Cavaliers, Order of Alamo, San Antonio German, San Antonio County, Argyle. Office: 4242 N Panam Expressway San Antonio TX 78208

BANDER, NORMAN ROBERT, communications and information management consultant; A.B., Dartmouth Coll., 1954; postgrad. Harvard U., Columbia U., U. Pa., N.Y. U. Former sales research dir. Benton & Bowles, Inc., N.Y.C.; media program research dir. Lennen & Newell, Inc., N.Y.C.; dir. mktg., test analysis Gillette Co., Boston; dir. creative communication evaluation and advt. research J. Walter Thompson Co., N.Y.C.; pres. AdTracks and Bander & Assocs., Malvern, Pa., 1968-78, Sarasota, Fla., 1978—. Served as clin. psychologist M.C., AUS, 1954-56. Mem. Am. Mktg. Assn. Clubs: Dartmouth, Yale (N.Y.C.). Author studies on mktg. and advt. effectiveness, consumer behavior and public opinion. Office: PO Box 190 Sarasota FL 33578

BANE, GILBERT WINFIELD, fisheries biology administrator; b. San Diego, Calif., Dec. 11, 1931; s. Gilbert W. and Eva (Chaffin) B.; m. Anneka Wright. B.S., San Jose State U., 1954; M.S., Cornell U., 1959, Ph.D., 1963. Scientist, dir. Internat. Am. Tropical Tuna Com., 1955-58; cruise scientist Star-Kist Foods, Chana, 1959-61; fisheries dir. U. P.R., Mayaguez, 1963-65; asst. prof. U. Calif.-Irvine, 1965-69; asst. prof. L.I. U., St. Francis Coll., Maine; environ. studies dir. U. N.C., Wilmington, 1975-81; dir. Coastal Fisheries La. State U., Baton Rouge, 1981—, prof. marine scis., 1982—. Author books; contbr. numerous articles in field to profl. jours. Named Disting. Scientist, Orange County Hist. Soc., 1967, Profl. Fisheries Oceanographer, Am. Fisheries Soc., 1971; recipient Disting. Citizen award N.C. Office Marine Affairs, 1979. Fellow Explorers Club, Danforth Soc.; mem. Am. Soc. Ichthyologists and Herpetologists, Am. Fisheries Soc., Am. Soc. Mammals, Am. Soc. Zoology, Sigma Xi, Phi Kappa Phi. Office: Coastal Fisheries Inst Louisiana State U Baton Rouge LA 70802

BANE, JOHN WARD, lawyer; b. Hampton, Va., Dec. 21, 1944; s. Wista Frederick and Edna (Gardner) B.; m. Denise Elora Ford, Sept. 27, 1968 (div. Aug. 1983); 1 child, Gregory Charles. B.A. in Am. History, Coll. William and Mary, 1967, J.D., 1973. Bar: Va. 1974, U.S. Dist. Ct. Va. (ea. dist.) 1974, U.S. Ct. Appeals (4th cir.) 1974. Cons. civil rights U.S. Dept. Justice, Norfolk, Va., 1970-73; law clk. to Commonwealth Atty., Hampton, Va., 1972-73; sole practice, Hampton, 1974—; mem. joint legis. sub-com. revision Va. Med. Malpractice Laws, Richmond, 1984—. Author: Juvenile Offenders Manual for Police, 1972. Bd. dirs. Hampton Boys' Club. Served to capt. U.S. Army, 1968-70, Vietnam. Decorated Combat Infantryman's Badge; recipient Gary Joel Hirsh Meml. award, 1973. Mem. Hampton Bar Assn. (bd. dirs. 1981-82), Am. Legion (state legis. chmn. 1978-79), Va. State Bar, Am. Trial Lawyers Assn. (co-chmn. sect. on radiation litigation 1985), Va. Trial Lawyers Assn., Peninsula Econ. Devel. Council (exec. com.), Phoebus Civic Assn. (v.p., legis. chmn.), Res. Officers Assn., Phi Delta Phi (pres. 1973), Theta Delta Chi (pres. 1967). Home: 20 Thimble Shoals Ct Hampton VA 23664 Office: 55 W Queensway Hampton VA 23669

BANISTER, CYNTHIA CAROLYN, nurse, program administrator; b. Blytheville, Ark., Aug. 22, 1951; d. Billy Myron and Evelyn Merle (Ashley) Banister. Assoc. in Applied Scis., Nursing, Pan Am. U., Edinburg, Tex., 1971. R.N., Tex. Staff nurse Cameron County Health Dept., San Benito, Tex., 1971-74, Cameron County Health Dept., Harlingen, Tex., 1974-79; nurse supr. Pub. Health Region 8, Harlingen, 1979-83; adminstr. tech. programs Tex. Dept. Health, Austin, 1984—mem. Health Adv. Council Tex. Migrant Council, Rio Grande Valley, Tex., 1983—. Mem. ARC, West Cameron County chpt., 1974-84; mem. Hyde Park Bapt. Ch., Austin. Recipient Cert. of Appreciation, Vol. Services in Community, Tex. Dept. Health, 1982. Mem. Tex. Pub. Health Assn., U.S.-Mex. Border Health Assn. Office: Texas Dept Health Immunization Div T 401 1100 W 49th St Austin TX 78756

BANKS, BROOKSHER LEIGH, drycleaning executive; b. Little Rock, July 10, 1953; s. Brooksher T. and Thelma (Bleidt) B.; m. Rhonda Elder, Aug. 2, 1975; children—Melissa Faye, Matthew Leigh. B.B.A., Baylor U., 1975. C.P.A., Ark. Staff acct. Russell Brown and Co. (now Arthur Young and Co.), Little Rock, 1975-76, sr. acct., 1977; exec. v.p. Fashion Park Cleaners, Inc., North Little Rock, Ark., 1977—. Deacon, Park Hill Bapt. Ch., pres. sanctuary choir; adv. council Thunderbird dist. Boy Scouts Am.; pres., bd. dirs. North Little Rock unit Am. Cancer Soc.; sec. North Little Rock Hosp. Commn.; mem. community adv. bd. Meml. Hosp. Mem. Am. Inst. C.P.A.s, Internat. Fabricare Inst., Assn. Interior Decor Specialists, Ark. Soc. C.P.A.s, Cert. Master Cleaners Ark., Central Ark. Execs. Assn. (bd. dirs.) (pres.-elect). Baptist. Club: Rotary (treas. 1982-83) (North Little Rock). Home: 3801 Lochlane North Little Rock AR 72116 Office: 3723 JFK Blvd North Little Rock AR 72116

BANKS, RICHARD AUSTIN, insurance company executive; b. Glendale, Calif., June 18, 1928; s. Sydney Allen and Audrey Manifold B.; A.A., Glendale Coll., 1949; student UCLA, 1949-50; m. Laverne Hall, Apr. 27, 1963; children—Brenda Kay, Lori Lynn. With Am. Nat. Ins. Co., 1953—, regional dir., Calif., 1969-74, v.p., asst. dir., Galveston, Tex., 1974-76, exec. v.p., dir. combination agys., 1976—; dir. Am. Nat. Property and Casualty. Securities Mgmt. Research, Commonwealth Life & Accident Ins. Co. Active Boy Scouts Am. Served with U.S. Army, 1950-52. Republican. Episcopalian. Club: Galveston Country. Home: 2878 Dominique Galveston TX 77551 Office: Am National Ins Co Galveston TX 77550*

BANKS, WILLIAM LOUIS, JR., biochemistry educator, consultant; b. Paterson, N.J., Mar. 25, 1936; s. William Louis and Martha Elizabeth (Roughgarden) B.; m. Sharon Ruth Hazelton, Aug. 1, 1965; 1 dau., Heather. B.S., Rutgers U., 1958; M.S., Bucknell U., 1960; Ph.D., Rutgers U., 1963. Asst. prof. Med. Coll. Va., Richmond, 1965-69; assoc. prof. Med. Coll. Va.-Va. Commonwealth U., Richmond, 1969-74, co-dir. Cancer Ctr., 1974-83, prof. biochemistry and surgery, 1974—; co-dir. Massey Cancer Ctr. Mem. pub. edn. com. Va. div. Am. Cancer Soc., bd. dirs. Richmond unit. Served to capt. USAF, 1963-65. Recipient 22 outstanding prof. awards Med. Coll. Va.-Va. Commonwealth U., 1970-83; named Hon. Texan, 1978; Alfred P. Sloan Found. faculty scholar, 1975-76; Johnson & Johnson predoctoral fellow, 1962-63; recipient cert. of appreciation USAF, 1965. Mem. AAAS, Am. Assn. Cancer Research, AAUP, Am. Inst. Nutrition, N.Y. Acad. Scis., S.E. Cancer Research Assn., Va. Acad. Sci., Am. Assn. Cancer Edn., Am. Chem. Soc., Soc. for Exptl. Biology and Medicine, Sigma Xi, Rho Chi. Contbr. articles to sci. and ednl. publs., chpts. to sci. books. Office: Box 37 MCV Station Richmond VA 23298

BANKS, WILLIE IVORY, educational administrator; b. Couchwood, La., Oct. 3, 1934; s. Dock Ivory and Cassana Berniece (Jack) B.; B.S., So. U., 1972, M.Ed., 1977; postgrad. in gen. adminstrv. leadership George Peabody Coll. for Tchrs.; Ed.D., Vanderbilt U., 1984; children—Ivory Donnel, Sean V. Enlisted U.S. Navy, 1955, advanced through grades to chief petty officer, 1968; served in Vietnam, ret., 1975; tchr. schs., Crowley, La., 1977-78; guidance counselor, Greensburg, La., 1978-84; asst. dir. student personnel services Baton Rouge Vocat. Tech. Inst., 1984—. Mem. Ednl. Leadership Assn. (comprehensive), Am. Vocat. Assn., Nat. Assn. Black Sch. Educators, Fleet Res. Assn., Mensa, Am. Legion, Kappa Kappa. Democrat. Baptist. Home: 1689 78th Ave Baton Rouge LA 70807 Office: 3250 N Acadian Thruway Baton Rouge LA 70805

BANKSTON, DAMON B., corporate executive; b. 1927; married. B.S., La. State U., 1948. Gulf Coast sales mgr. Baroid div. Nat. Lead Corp., 1948-58; with Tidewater Inc., New Orleans, 1958—, v.p., 1959-67, exec. v.p., 1967-79, sr. exec. v.p., from 1979, now pres., chief operating officer, also dir.; dir. Offshore Marine Service Assn., Employers Info. Service. Served with USN, 1945-46. Office: Tidewater Inc 1440 Canal St New Orleans LA 70112*

BAÑOS, JOSÉ LUIS, banker, lawyer; b. New Orleans, Aug. 25, 1918; s. Jose Rodrigo and Julia (Sussman Del Olmo) B.; B.B.A., Tulane U., 1939, LL.B., 1946; m. Catherine Dunbar Bensabat, June 20, 1947; children—Catherine Baños Eustis, Julia Banos Poitevent, Margot Baños Jones, José Luis, George. Mem. staff dept. fgn. banking Whitney Nat. Bank of New Orleans, 1946-49, asst. mgr., 1949-53, mgr., 1953-59, v.p., 1959-83; counsel Jones, Walker, Waechter, Poitevent, Carrere & Denegre, 1983—; pres. White-LaFourche, Inc., Thibodaux, La. Past chmn. pres. council, trustee St. Mary's Dominican Coll.; bd. dirs. City of New Orleans Delgado Albania Plantation Commn., Internat. Trade Mart; past bd. dirs. New Orleans Philharm. Soc.; mem. exec. com., past pres. Internat. House; vice chmn. planned gifts com. Tulane U.; past pres. bd. Sociedad Española. Served to lt. comdr. USN, 1941-46. Decorated Knight comdr. Order Isabel la Catolica (Spain); knight grand cross Mil. and Hospitaller Order St. Lazarus of Jerusalem; Knight Sovereign Mil. Order Malta; knight comdr. Equestrian Order of Holy Sepulchre of Jerusalem. Mem. Am., La. bar assns., Am. Inst. Banking, New Orleans C. of C. (past sec.-treas., exec. com., dir.), Phi Delta Theta. Clubs: Boston, Pickwick, Plimsoll, New Orleans Country, Southern Yacht, Bayou Country, Wyvern. Home: 9 Richmond Pl New Orleans LA 70115 Office: Place St Charles 201 St Charles Ave New Orleans LA 70170

BANZHAF, CLAYTON HARRIS, retired financial executive; b. Buffalo, Dec. 24, 1917; s. Joseph Maximilian and Elizabeth (Harris) B.; M.B.A., U. Chgo., 1954; m. Dolores J. Gavins, Dec. 30, 1962; children by previous marriage—Barbara A. (Mrs. Thomas T. Grimmett), Debra R. (Mrs. Stephen T. York), William Clay. With Sears, Roebuck & Co., 1936-81, trainee, Buffalo, retail auditor, Phila., 1939-41, retail controller, Washington, 1946-48, Pitts., 1949-50, wage and salary adminstr. nat. personnel dept., Chgo., 1951-57, corp. asst. treas., 1958-60, sr. asst. treas., Chgo., 1961-74, treas., 1975-76, v.p., treas., 1976-81, ret., 1981; pres., chief exec. officer, dir. Sears Roebuck Acceptance Corp., Wilmington, 1963-72, dir., 1972-80; former treas. Sears Internat. Finance Co., Sears Roebuck Overseas Inc., Sears Roebuck de Puerto Rico S.A., Seraco Enterprises Inc., Fleet Maintenance Inc., Lifetime Foam Products Inc., Terminal Freight Handling Co., Tower Ventures, Inc.; former asst. treas. other Sears subsidiaries; former dir. Homart Devel. Co., Banco de Credito Internacional S.A., Lake Shore Land Assn. Inc., Sears Overseas Finance N.V., Curaçao, Western Forge Corp., Colorado Springs; chmn. audit com. Barclays Am. Corp., Charlotte, N.C. Mem. exec. bd. Chgo. Area council Boy Scouts Am., 1963-68, mem. adv. bd., 1969-81; mem. bus. adv. council Coll. Bus. Adminstrn., U. Ill., Chgo. Circle, 1979-81; bd. dirs. Council for Community Services, Chgo., 1975-77, United Way Met. Chgo., 1977-81; trustee Elmira (N.Y.) Coll., 1975-81. Served to maj. AUS, 1941-45. Mem. Financial Execs. Inst. (pres. Chgo. chpt. 1972-73, nat. dir. 1975-78, mem. exec. com. 1976-77, v.p. Midwest area 1977-78), U. Chgo. Alumni Assn. (Exec. Program, Grad. Sch. Bus., dir. 1966-67, v.p. 1968, pres. 1969, mem. alumni council Grad. Sch. Bus. 1969, pres. 1972-75), C. of C. U.S. (com. on banking and monetary policy 1967-72, com. on banking, monetary and fiscal affairs 1972-74), AIM (pres. council, fellow), Am. Assembly Collegiate Schs. Bus. (accreditation mem.), AMA (com. allied health edn. and accreditation). Republican. Presbyterian. Mason. Clubs: Hound Ears, Sara Bay Country, Long Boat Key, Medinah Country. Home: 5270 Gulf of Mexico Dr Long Boat Key FL 33548 also 259 Evergreen Box 188 Hounders Club Blowing Rock NC 28605

BAPTIE, CHARLES, photographer, printer, publisher; b. Munhall, Pa., Mar. 13, 1914; s. Charles and Constance B.; m. Joan Pratt, Jan. 1, 1970; 1 son by previous marriage, Ronald. Photographer, Trans World Airways, Pitts., 1933-34, Capital Airlines, Washington, 1935-45; freelance photographer, Annandale, Va., 1945—; illustrator numerous books; owner, operator Charles Baptie Studios, Annandale, 1945—; cons. graphic arts. Mem. Photog. Soc. Am. (asso.), Nat. Press Club, Nat. Photographers Assn. Author: (with Ollie Atkins) Camera on Assignment, 1958; (with Hope Ridings Miller) Great Houses of Washington, D.C., 1970; (with Jack Lloyd) How to Play Baseball; (with Margaret MacBeth Seiler) Mid the Hills of Pennsylvania, 1980; The Steel Valley, 1982; Capital Airlines a Nostalgic Flight into the Past, 1984; picture editor 16-vol. United States History, 1963—; photo illustrator Guest House of the Presidents (Eleanor Lee Templeman), 1980. Office: 4124 Village Ct Annandale VA 22003

BARACH, JEFFREY ALVAN, management educator; b. N.Y.C., Aug. 15, 1934; s. Alvan L. and Frederica P. (Barbour) B.; m. Katarina Roth (div. 1982); 1 son, Jeffrey Alvan. A.B. cum laude, Harvard U., 1956, M.B.A., 1961, D.B.A., 1967, postgrad. individual studies program, 1977. Tech. writer Honeywell Corp., Phila., 1956-58; account exec., copywriter Renner, Inc., Phila., 1958; tech. writer Teleregister Corp., Stanford, Conn., 1959; research asst. Harvard U. Bus. Sch., 1961-62; asst. prof. Tulane U. Sch. Bus., 1965-68, assoc. prof.

mgmt., 1968-85, prof., 1986—; mktg. and mgmt. cons., New Orleans, 1965—. Mem. Met. Crime Commn. of New Orleans, recipient extraordinary service award, 1978; mem. Friends of Audubon Zoo. Recipient Detur prize Harvard Coll., 1953; Wissner award Tulane U., 1979, 82; Ford Found. grantee, 1962-63. Mem. AAUP, Acad. Mgmt., Soc. for Bus. Ethics, Beta Gamma Sigma. Clubs: New Orleans Yacht, Krewe of Bacchus. Author: Individual, Business and Society, 1977; contbr. articles on mktg. and mgmt. to profl. jours. Office: Sch Bus Tulane U New Orleans LA 70118

BARBANEL, SIDNEY MANUEL (SID), medical instruments manufacturing company executive; b. Savannah, Ga., Mar. 5, 1936; s. Leon and Ann M. (Kramer) B.; student U.S. Naval Acad., 1956, Coll. Charleston, 1957-58; B.A., Oglethorpe U., 1960; m. Anne Matthias, Mar. 16, 1961; children—Amy Laura, Bonnie Lynne. Salesman, Dun & Bradstreet, Inc., 1960-64; Purdue Frederick Co., Atlanta, 1964-68, Medtronic, Inc., Atlanta, 1968-69; So. div. mgr. sales and mktg. Cordis Corp., Atlanta, 1969-74; mgr. ARCO Med. Products Co. subs. Atlantic Richfield Corp., Pitts., 1974-76; exec. v.p. sales Intermedics Inc., Freeport, Tex., 1976—; v.p. Intermedics Intraocular, Inc., 1976-78; pres. Intermedics Pacemakers Inc., 1981-83, Ram Cons. Co., 1983—; chmn., pres., chief exec. officer Cardio-Pace Med., Inc., 1983—; lectr. in field. Bd. visitors Oglethorpe U., 1979. Served with USN, 1954-56. Named to Pres.'s Club, Medtronic, Inc., 1969, Loyalty Club, Oglethorpe U., 1978; recipient cert. Ga. Heart Assn., 1972. Mem. Assn. Advancement Med. Instrumentation, Am. Mgmt. Assn., N.Am. Soc. Pacing and Electrophysiology. Sales and Mktg. Execs., Citadel Devel. Found., James Edward Oglethorpe Soc. Club: Masons. Office: 2265 River Valley Dr West Columbia TX 77486

BARBARA, BARBARA S(UE), real estate research firm executive; b. Detroit, Mar. 14, 1953; d. Donald Edward and Susan Elizabeth (Sonda) Niemeyer; m. William D. Barbara, Oct. 11, 1975. B.S. in Journalism, Okla. State U., 1975; M.S. in Tech., U. Houston, 1983. Reporter, Daily O'Collegian, Okla. State U., Stillwater, 1971-74, editor-in-chief, editorial editor, 1975; intern reporter Tulsa Tribune, 1974; reporter Daily Ardmoreite, Ardmore, Okla., 1975; asst. info. officer Okla. State U., Stillwater, 1975-76; media specialist energy extension service Pa. State U., University Park, 1976-78; program mgr. energy extension service U. Houston, 1978-79, assoc. dir. energy extension service, 1979-81; sr. assoc. Rice Ctr., Houston, 1982-85, dir. research, 1985—; editor Pa. Aggregates Assocs., Harrisburg, Pa., 1976-78. Author, editor numerous research documents, 1982—; editor numerous newsletters, radio spots, 1976—. Adviser pub. relations Child Devel. Council Centre County (Pa.), 1978; mem. adv. bd. Energy and Home Improvement Fair, Houston, 1981. Co-prin. investigator Nat. Credit Union Mgmt. Assocs., Cleve., 1981-82. Mem. Assn. M.B.A. Execs., Houston C. of C. (communications adv. com. 1982—), Am. Soc. Engring. Edn. (chmn. publicity com. regional conf. 1981-82), Sigma Delta Chi. Office: Rice Ctr 9 Greenway Plaza Suite 1900 Houston TX 77046

BARBER, CHARLES EDWARD, journalist; b. Miami, Fla., Oct. 30, 1939; s. James Plemon and Margaret Katherine (Grimes) B.; A.A., Santa Fe Community Coll., 1971; m. Judith Margaret Tuck, May 28, 1960; children—Janet Lynn, Christopher Edward. Prodn. mgr. dept. student publs. U. Fla., Gainesville, 1966-68, ops. mgr., 1968-70, asst. dir., 1970-72, dir., 1972-73, dir. div. publs., 1974; prodn. mgr. State Univ. System Press, Gainesville, 1975-76; pres., gen. mgr. Campus Communications, Inc., Gainesville, 1976—; cons. in field. Mem. citizens adv. council Stephen Foster Elem. Sch., Gainesville, 1973-77; mem. Friends of Five, 1975-77, Friends of Library, 1975-77; chmn. book com. Fla. State Prison, 1973—; bd. dirs. Gainesville High Sch. Band Boosters, 1978-79, 83-84, treas., 1984; key communicator Alachua County Sch. Bd., 1980—; spl. registered dep. sheriff Alachua County Sheriff's Dept., 1979—; mem. gifted students boosters Howard Bishop Middle Sch., 1980-82; dir. Howard Bishop Band Boosters, 1980-82; mem. pres.'s council U. Fla., 1978—; mem. Leadership Gainesville, 1979; pack com. chmn. Cub Scouts Am., 1977-78. Served with USCGR, 1957-65. Recipient Nat. 1st Place for Editorial Writing, Hearst Found., 1965, Service award Santa Fe Community Coll., 1982; named nation's most disting. bus. adv. to coll. press, 1978; Cert. of Appreciation, Big Bros. and Big Sisters of Gainesville, 1984; Addy award Gainesville Advt. Fedn., 1986. Mem. Am. Advt. Fedn., Am. Newspaper Pubs. Assn., Associated Collegiate Press, Assn. for Edn. in Journalism and Mass Communications, Coll. Newspaper Bus. and Advt. Mgrs. (dir. 1981), Fla. Scholastic Press Assn. (newspaper judge 1981—), Fla. Newspaper Advt. and Mktg. Execs. (chmn. edn. com.), Fla. Press Found., Fla. Press Assn., Fla. Press Club, Alligator Press Council (moderator 1979), Gainesville Advt. Fedn., (dir. 1979-80), Internat. Newspaper Fin. Execs., Internat. Newspaper Fin. Assn., Internat. Newspaper Advt. and Mktg. Execs., Internat. Newspaper Promotion Assn., Coll. Media Advisers, Retail Grocers Assn. Fla., So. Univ. Newspapers (dir. 1980—), Fla. Retail Fedn., Printing Industries Fla., Gainesville Area C. of C. (com. of 100), Alligator Alumni Assn. (dir. 1980—), Soc. Profl. Journalists-Sigma Delta Chi (treas. No. Fla. chpt. 1972-75), Alpha Phi Gamma. Democrat. Baptist (chmn. bd. deacons 1978, ch. moderator 1981-85). Clubs: Red Herring, Alachua Health and Fitness. Lodge: Kiwanis. Adv. editor Fla. Quar., 1973-74; contbr. articles to profl. jours. Home: 4205 NW 21st St Gainesville FL 32605 Office: PO Box 14257 Gainesville FL 32604

BARBER, JOHN CLARK, consultant; b. Liberty, N.C., Jan. 6, 1925; s. Yates Middleton and Emily Lucille (Clark) B.; m. Francene King, June 16, 1951; children—John Clark, Lewis Williams. B.S., N.C. State U., 1950, M.S., 1951; Ph.D., U. Minn., 1961. Research forester Southeastern Forest Expt. Sta., Asheville, 1951-52, Macon, Ga., 1952-57, project leader seed, nursery and genetics research, 1957-64; project leader Inst. Forest Genetics, So. Forest Expt. Sta., Gulfport, Miss., 1964-67; br. chief Timber Mgmt. Research forest genetics and timber related crops U.S. Dept. Agr., Forest Service, Washington, 1967-71, asst. to dep. chief research, 1971-72, dir. So. Forest Expt. Sta., New Orleans, 1972-76, assoc. dep. chief state and pvt. forestry, Washington, 1976-80; exec. v.p. Soc. Am. Foresters, Bethesda, Md., 1980-85; cons. renewable natural resources, 1985—. Served with U.S. Army, 1943-46. Recipient Disting. Alumnus award N.C. State U., 1982. Fellow Soc. Am. Foresters (award 1977); mem. Internat. Poplar Commn., N.Am. Forestry Commn., Internat. Union Forestry Research Orgns., Am. Forestry Assn., Forest Farmers Assn., Soil Conservation Soc. Am., Sigma Xi.

BARBER, PAUL, sales executive; b. Leapwood, Tenn., Jan. 22, 1945; s. Deward R. and Demova A. (Sewell) B.; m. LaVona Kay Bannon, Jan. 29, 1966; m. 2d, Vickie Lynn Christopherson, July 18, 1981. B.S. in B.A., U. Tenn.-Knoxville, 1972. With The Stereo Center, Knoxville, 1969-77, E.P. Turner & Assoc., Atlanta, 1977-81, Hi-Tek Mktg., Chgo., 1981-82, Landmark Sales Co., Atlanta, 1982-83; S.E. regional sales mgr. Commodore Bus. Machines, Atlanta, 1983—. Served with USAF, 1965-69, Air N.G., 1969-83. Mem. Jaycees, Delta Nu Alpha. Club: Sertoma. Home: 570 Tahoma Dr Atlanta GA 30338 Office: 1200 Wilson Dr Westchester PA 19380

BARBOUR, WILLIAM H., JR., U.S. district judge; b. 1941. B.A., Princeton U., 1963; J.D., U. Miss., 1966; postgrad. NYU Sch. Law, 1966. Individual practice, with firm Henry, Barbour & DeCell, Yazoo City, Miss., 1966-83; youth counselor Yazoo City Cts., 1971-82; U.S. dist. judge So. Miss., Jackson, 1983—. Office: PO Box 2247 Jackson MS 39225-2247

BARBREY, WATSON THOMAS, pharmacist; b. Greenville, S.C., May 30, 1952; s. Charles Gray and Annie Lou (Waddell) B.; m. Rebecca Ann Raines, July 19, 1975; children—Jonathan Ashley, Marianna Raine, Austin-Gray Thomas. B.S. in Microbiology, Clemson U., 1974; B.S. in Pharmacy, Med. U. S.C., 1978. Registered pharmacist, S.C. Intern pharmacy Miller Liggett, Charleston, S.C., 1975-76; intern pharmacy Revco Discount, Charleston, 1976-78, pharmacist, 1978-79; med. rep. Hoffmann-Larouche, Nutley, N.J., 1979—. Mem. S.C. Soc. Hosp. Pharmacists, S.C. Pharm. Assn. (bd. dirs. 1982—, v.p. 1984—, chmn. profl. affairs com. 1984—, awards com., nominating com., bldg. and grounds com. 1984—, chmn. continuing edn. com. 1984—, mem. polit. action com. 1982—), Acad. Nursing Home Pharmacists in S.C., Am. Soc. Hosp. Pharmacy, Pee Dee Pharm. Assn. (sec.-treas. 1980-82, 84, legis. dinner chmn. 1984, membership chmn. 1980-82, 84). Baptist. Lodge: Rotary. Avocations: softball; golf; tennis; working with teenagers. Home: 2707 Andover Rd Florence SC 29501 Office: Hoffmann-LaRoche Inc 240 Kingsland Nutley NJ 07110

BARCENAS, CAMILO GUSTAVO, physician; b. Managua, Nicaragua, Sept. 18, 1944; came to U.S., 1969; s. Camilo and Margarita (Levy) B.; M.D., U. Nicaragua, 1968; m. Aurora Cardenas, Dec. 22, 1969; children—Margarita, Marcela, Camilo. Diplomate Am. Bd. Internal Medicine. Intern, Managua (Nicaragua) Gen. Hosp., 1967-68, Mt. Sinai Hosp., U. Conn., 1969; resident internal medicine Baylor Coll. Medicine, Houston, 1970-72; chief resident St. Luke's Episcopal Hosp., Houston, 1971; chief resident VA Hosp., Houston, 1972; fellow nephrology U. Tex. Health Sci. Center, Dallas, 1972-74; practice medicine specializing in internal medicine, Dallas, 1974-76, Houston, 1976—; chief home dialysis unit VA Hosp., Dallas, 1974-75, chief hemodialysis unit, 1975; chief nephrology sect. St. Luke's Episcopal Hosp., Houston, 1976—; asst. prof. medicine U. Tex. Health Sci. Center, Dallas, 1974-75; clin. asst. prof. medicine Baylor Coll. Medicine, Houston, 1976-79, clin. asso. prof., 1979-85, clin. prof., 1985—. Gen. sec. Juventud Social Christiana, 1968. Fellow A.C.P.; mem. Internat. Soc. Nephrology, Houston Soc. Internal Medicine, Am. Soc. Nephrology, Harris County Med. Soc., Tex. Med. Assn., Colegio Medico Nicaraguense. Roman Catholic. Contbr. articles on nephrology to med. jours. Office: 6720 Bertner St Houston TX 77030 also 9197 Winkler St Bldg D Houston TX 77017

BARD, JAMES W., physician, dermatologist; b. New London, Wis., Mar. 12, 1934; s. Everett K. and Gertrude (Chapiewsky) B.; m. Elaine D. Winter, Sep. 14, 1957; children—Paul, Stephen. M.D., Med. Coll. Wis., 1958. Diplomate Am. Bd. Dermatology. Intern, Yale-New Haven Hosp., 1958-59; resident in dermatology Mayo Clinic, 1962-65; sect. head Lexington Clinic, Ky., 1965—; dir. Lexington Clinic, 1976—, v.p., 1980-85, pres., 1985—. Contbr. articles to profl. jours. Exhibited in group shows Ky. Photographers, 1983. Served to capt. U.S. Army, 1959-62. Recipient Humanitarian service award AMA, 1971. Fellow Am. Acad. Dermatology; mem. Noah Worcester Dermatol. Soc. (sec., treas. 1981—), Cin. Dermatol. Soc. (pres. 1985-86), Ky. Dermatol. Soc. (pres. 1977-78). Lodge: Rotary. Avocation: photography. Office: Lexington Clinic 1221 S Broadway Lexington KY 40504

BARDEN, ROBERT CHRISTOPHER, psychology educator, psychologist; b. Richmond, Va., June 7, 1954; s. Elliott Hatcher and Jane Elizabeth Cole (Ferris) B. B.A. summa cum laude, U. Minn., 1976, Ph.D. in Clin. Psychology, 1982; postgrad. U. Calif.-Berkeley, 1977. Lic. psychologist, Tex. Project dir. NSF, 1978-79; intern in psychology Minn. State Prison, 1980, VA Med. Ctr., Stanford Med. Ctr., Palo Alto, Calif., 1980-81; asst. prof. psychology So. Meth. U., Dallas, 1981—; dir. psychology Tex. Craniofacial Inst., Dallas, 1983—; pvt. practice psychology, Dallas, 1982—. Recipient Young Scholar award Found. for Child Devel., 1981-82; research award Tex. Craniofacial Inst., 1983; Minn. Gov.'s Internship awardee, 1978; Eva Miller Social Sci. fellow, 1978-79; NIMH fellow, 1976-77, 77-78. Mem. Am. Psychol. Assn., Soc. for Research in Child Devel., Midwestern Psychol. Assn., Southwestern Psychol. Assn., U.S. Profl. Tennis Assn., Phi Beta Kappa, Sigma Xi. Club: Sierra.

BARDENWERPER, WILLIAM BURR, lawyer; b. Milw., Jan. 12, 1952; s. H. William and Dorothy W. B.; m. Gail Smith, Apr. 11, 1959. B.A., U. Va., 1974; J.D., U. Louisville, 1977. Bar: Ky. 1978, Wis. 1985, U.S. Dist. Ct. (western dist.) Ky. 1978. Assoc. Marlin M. Volz, Louisville, 1977-78; counsel, dir. intergovtl. affairs Jefferson County, Louisville, 1978-84; mem. Rice, Porter & Seiller, Attys., 1984—; chmn. operating co. Louisville Gardens. Vice chmn. bd. Wesley Community House. Cons. to ABA, 1980-82. Recipient Disting. Service award U. Louisville Sch. Law, 1977. Mem. ABA, Wis. Bar Assn., Ky Bar Assn., Louisville Bar Assn. (award of merit 1980). Republican. Episcopalian. Editor-in-chief Louisville Lawyer mag. Home: 122 Southampton St Louisville KY 40223 Office: 22d Floor Meidinger Tower Louisville KY 40202

BARDIN, CHARLES ANDREW, insurance company executive; b. Tampa, Fla., Sept. 25, 1940; s. Charles Newton and Helen (Campbell) B.; m. Wanda Carter, June 13, 1964; children—Christopher, Andrew. C.L.U. Detective, Tampa Police Dept., 1962-68; agy. mgr. Bankers Life Ins. Co. Iowa, Atlanta, 1968—. Contbr. articles to profl. jours. Bd. trustees Asbury Theol. Sem., Wilmore, Ky., 1978—; mem. adminstrv. bd. Roswell United Methodist Ch. (Ga.), 1978—. Mem. Nat. Assn. Life Underwriters, Am. Soc. C.L.U.s. Democrat. Lodges: Kiwanis (pres. 1973), Masons, Shriners. Home: 740 Hunterhill Ct Roswell GA 30075 Office: Eight Piedmont Center Suite 300 Atlanta GA 30305

BARDON, JACK IRVING, psychologist, consultant, educator; b. Cleve., Oct. 24, 1925; s. Isador and Rose (Greene) B.; m. Carla Helene Wininger, Sept. 12, 1948; children—Janet, Ruth. B.A., Western Res. U., 1949; M.A., U. Pa., 1951, Ph.D., 1956. Diplomate Am. Bd. Examiners in Psychology. Sch. psychologist Princeton (N.J.) Schs., 1952-60; assoc. prof. Rutgers U., New Brunswick, N.J., 1960-63, prof., 1963-74, chmn. dept. ednl. psychology, 1968-73, prof., Grad. Sch. Applied and Profl. Psychology, 1974-76, co-dir., 1974; Excellence Found. prof. edn. and psychology U. N.C., Greensboro, 1976—. Served with U.S. Army, 1944-46. Fulbright sr. research scholar, N.Z., 1979. Mem. Am. Psychol. Assn. (disting. service award div. sch. psychology 1976, disting. contbns. to applied psychology as profl. practice 1981), Am. Orthopsychiat. Assn. (dir. 1981-84), Am. Assn. Counseling and Devel., Council Exceptional Children, Sigma Xi. Author: (with Virginia C. Bennett) School Psychology, 1974; contbr. articles to profl. jours. Home: 902 Greenwood Dr Greensboro NC 27410 Office: Curry Bldg U NC-Greensboro Greensboro NC 27812

BARE, RONALD KENT, medical clinic administrator; b. Washington, Aug. 24, 1948; s. John Creston and Roberta Ann (Kent) B.; m. Angela Jackson, Feb. 5, 1977; children—Erin Kimberly. B.S., Jacksonville U., 1974; M.A., Pepperdine U., 1978. Asst. adminstr. Riverside Clinic, Jacksonville, Fla., 1972-78, chief adminstrn., 1978—. Chmn. bd. dirs. Young Life, Inc., 1977-78; bd. dirs. Fellowship Christian Athletes, 1979-81; chmn. bd. dirs. Hyde Park Bapt. Ch., 1980-84, Jerry Drace Evangel. Assn., 1982-83. Fellow Am. Coll. Med. Group Adminstrs.; mem. Med. Group Mgmt. Assn. (state pres. 1980), Fla. Med. Group Mgmt. Assn. (pres. bd. dirs. 1980). Baptist. Home: 4361 Savannah Ave Jacksonville FL 32210 Office: 2005 Riverside Ave Jacksonville FL 32204

BARED, PABLO ROLANDO, construction executive; b. Havana, Cuba, Nov. 17, 1960; came to U.S., 1960; s. Jose and Ofelia (Santeiro) B. B.B.A. in Internat. Fin. and Mktg., U. Miami (Fla.), 1982. Heating, ventilation and air conditioning designer Ferendino Grafton Spillis Candella, Miami, 1978-79; project mgr. Bared & Co., Miami, 1979-82, internat. cons., 1982—; v.p. overseas div. Harvesters Group, Inc., Miami, 1982—; cons. Art Gathering, Miami, 1982—. Mem. Latin Builders Assn., ASHRAE, S. Fla. Builders Assn., Am. Builders and Contractors, Am. Mktg. Assn., Nat. Home Builders Assn. Republican. Roman Catholic. Clubs: Jockey, Ocean Reef Yacht (Miami). Home: 1525 Sarria Ave Coral Gables FL 33146 Office: Harvesters Group Inc 7845 NW 56 St Miami FL 33166

BAREFOOT, HYRAN EUVENE, college administrator, educator, minister; b. Mantee, Miss., Jan. 14, 1928; s. James Lee and Martha Caroline (Martin) B.; m. Joyce Lynn Camp, Nov. 24, 1949; children—Judy Barefoot Thomas, June Barefoot Dark, Jane Barefoot Hunter. B.A., Miss. Coll., 1949; B.D., New Orleans Bapt. Theol. Sem., 1952, Th.D., 1955; postdoctoral U. N.Mex., 1965-66, Bapt. Theol. Sem., 1971. Asst. prof. religion Union U., Jackson, Tenn., 1957-60; asst. prof. N.T., So. Bapt. Theol. Sem., Louisville, 1960-62; prof. religion Union U., 1962—, chmn. dept. religion, 1966-75, chmn. div. humanities, 1972-75, v.p. acad. affairs, 1975—, acad. dean; pastor Liberty Bapt. Ch., Calhoun, La., 1946-49, Goss Bapt. Ch., Miss., 1949-52, Hebron Bapt. Ch., New Hebron, Miss., 1952-55, First Bapt. Ch., Crowley, La., 1955-57, Woodland Bapt. Ch., Brownsville, Tenn., 1957-60, 66-75. Recipient Tchr. of Yr. award Union U., 1967, Disting. Faculty award, 1973. Mem. Assn. So. Bapt. Colls. (sec. 1984-85). Club: Jackson Rotary. Avocations: antique furniture refinishing; hunting; fishing. Home: 1232 Hollywood Jackson TN 38301 Office: Union U Jackson TN 38305

BARFIELD, BOURDON REA, diversified investor; b. Amarillo, Tex., Oct. 28, 1926; s. Bourdon Ivy and Oliver Rea (Eakle) B.; B.B.A., U. Tex., 1951; m. Carolyn Grissom, Jan. 4, 1951; children—Deyanne, Amanda, Bourdon Ivy, John Callaway. Vice pres. Barfield Corp., Amarillo, 1951-57, pres., 1957—; dir. Mr. Burger Inc.; pres. Pembrooke Corp., Amarillo, 1969—, Guaranty Mortgage Corp., Amarillo. Mem. Durett Scholarship Com. Amarillo Pub. Schs., 1951—; area chmn. Crusade for Freedom, 1957; pres. Amarillo Symphony Orch., 1959-61; chmn. Citizens' Action Program, Amarillo, 1961-63; mem. exec. com. U. Tex. Dads' Assn., 1975—; mem. dist. Democratic Congressional Campaign Com., 1962-65, chmn., 1969; bd. dirs. Dallas Civic Opera, 1962, St. Andrew's Day Sch., Amarillo, 1962, Family Service Inc., Amarillo, 1969, Amarillo Art Center, 1972—; chmn. bd. dirs. Amarillo Pub. Library, 1963. Recipient Young Man of Year award Jr. C. of C., 1960, award of Honor Downtown Amarillo Unltd. for Redevel. Work., 1966. Mem. Amarillo (pres. 1961), U.S. (dir. civic devel. com. 1960) chambers commerce, Jovian, 49ers, Beta Theta Pi. Episcopalian (lay reader, vestryman 1958-61). Clubs: Amarillo Country, Palo Duro. Lodges: Masons (32d deg.), Rotary. Home: 3201 Ong St Amarillo TX 79109 Office: 1620 Tyler St Amarillo TX 79105

BARFIELD, ROBERT F., university administrator, mechanical engineer; b. Thomaston, Ga., Feb. 8, 1933; s. Jason Malcome and Nettie Lee Barfield; m. Marion Janelle Neill, June 25, 1953 (div. Jan. 1980); children—Kimberly Faith, Robert Frederick; m. 2d, Sara de Saussure Davis, Nov. 27, 1981 (div. Jan. 1983). B.M.E., Ga. Inst. Tech., 1956, M.S.M.E., 1958, Ph.D., 1965. Registered profl. engr., Ala., Ga. Preliminary design engr. AiResearch Corp., Los Angeles, 1957-58; asst. prof. Ga. Tech. Inst., Atlanta, 1958-65; corp. mech. engr. Thomaston Mills Corp. (Ga.), 1965-67; assoc. prof. mech. engring. U. Ala., University, 1967-71, prof., 1971—, chmn. Thermal/Fluid Scis. div., 1973-76, 77-80, dean Coll. Engring., 1982—; vis. prof. Kabul, Afghanistan, 1963; prof., chmn. mech. engring. dept. U. Petroleum and Minerals, Dhahran, Saudi Arabia, 1971-73; sr. advisor, chief party (acting dir.) Shiraz Tech. Inst. (Iran), 1975-77; advisor faculty engring. U. Jordan, Amman, 1981, Yamouk U., Jordan, 1986, King Saud U., Sauid Arabia, 1983—. Recipient Disting. Service award U. Ala., 1980, Student Govt. Assn. commendation, 1981; commendation Imperial Orgn. for Social Services (Iran), 1976; fellow NSF, 1962-63, E.I. Dupont, 1964, Am. Soc. Engring. Edn./NASA, 1967-68; grantee NASA, 1968-69, 70-71, 74-75, 77-79, 79-81, 81-83, NSF, 1969-70, 69-71. Fellow ASME (faculty advisor 1978-83); mem. Am. Soc. Engring. Edn. (chmn. internat. div. 1982-84), Nat. Soc. Profl. Engrs., Ala. Acad. Sci., Ala. Commn. on High Tech., Sigma Xi. Presbyterian. editor faculty research reports Marshall Space Flight Ctr., NASA/Am. soc. Engring. Edn. Research Program. Office: U Ala PO Box 1968 University AL 35486

BARFIELD, W. LOWRY, jewelry company executive; b. 1927. Student Miss. State U., 1951; LL.B., South Tex. Law Sch., 1945. With Tex. Natural Petroleum Co., 1955-57, Kirby Petroleum Co., 1951-55, 57-59; with Gordon Jewelry Corp., Houston, 1959—, sr. v.p., sec., treas., exec. v.p., dir., 1981-85, vice chmn., chief fin. officer, 1985—. Served with USMC, 1945-46. Office: Gordon Jewelry Corp 821 Fannin St Houston TX 77002*

BARGEON, HERBERT ALEXANDER, JR., writer; b. Fayetteville, N.C., May 23, 1934; s. Herbert Alexander and Violet (Geilfuss) B.; B.S. in Bus. Adminstrn., U. Va., 1956; LL.B., U. Fla., 1968; m. Gail Freer, Mar. 14, 1963; children—Herbert Alexander III, Violet Gail. Bar: Fla., D.C. Pres., chmn. bd. Royal Poinciana Playhouse, Palm Beach, Fla., 1973-81. Served to 2d lt. AUS, 1957. Mem. Am. Bar Assn. Republican. Presbyterian. Home: Barker's Creek Rural Route 2 Box 145AA Whittier NC 28789

BARGHOORN, TERESA JOAN LA CROIX, librarian, adult education instructor; b. Boston, May 29, 1925; d. Joseph Alfred and Eva Marie (St. John) La Croix; m. Elso Sterrenberg Barghoorn, July 21, 1953 (div.). B.S., Simmons Coll., 1947; M.S., U. Houston, 1969. Tchr. Concord Acad. (Mass.), 1961-62; adminstrv. asst. Harvard Bus. Sch., Cambridge, Mass., 1963; adminstrv. asst. U. Houston, 1964-67; tchr. Houston Ind. Sch. Dist., 1967-68; head sci. dept. Clear Creek Ind. Sch. Dist., League City, Tex., 1969-78, librarian, 1978—; adult edn. instr. San Jacinto Coll., Pasadena, Tex., 1979—. Contbr. articles to profl. jours. NSF fellow, 1967, 68-69. Mem. ALA, Tex. Library Assn., U.S.-Chinese People's Friendship Assn., AAUW (edn. fellow 1978-79; community affairs com. 1982, newsletter editor 1983), Delta Kappa Gamma, Kappa Kappa Iota. Home: 10514 Seaford St Houston TX 77089 Office: League City Intermediate Sch 2451 E Main St League City TX 77573

BARK, JOSEPH PAUL, dermatologist, writer, medical media expert, consultant; b. Canton, Ohio, Feb. 18, 1946; s. William Edward and Mildred M. (Gresser) B.; m. Linda Shoemaker, June 12, 1971; B.S., U. Akron, 1968; M.D., U. Ky., 1972. Diplomate Am. Bd. Dermatology. Intern, Med. Coll. Ga. Hosp., 1972, resident, 1973-76; practice medicine specializing in dermatology, Lexington, Ky., 1976—; creator Medically Speaking on PM Mag., 1976, Ask the Doctor, WKYT-TV, Lexington; resident dermatologist Bob Braun Show, 1981—, Doctor to Doctor, KMOX Radio, St. Louis; med. commentator 27 News First, WKYT-TV, Lexington; creator radio show, 1981; med. cons. news program, 1982—; cons. media relations Key Pharm. Co.; guest lectr. Med. Coll. Ga. Author: Skin Secrets; contbr. Ob-Gyn World mag., Consultant mag., other profl. publs. Bd. dirs. Am. Cancer Soc., Lexington Philharm. Orch. Mem. Am. Acad. Dermatology (chmn. task force on news liaison, pub. relations com.), AMA, Ky. Med. Assn., Royal Soc. Medicine, So. Med. Assn., Internat. Soc. Pediatric Dermatologists, Cin. Dermatol. Soc., Ky. Dermatol. Soc., Am. Cryosurg. Soc., Am. Med. Writers Assn., Writers Club Am., Physician's Jour. Club, Undersea Med.Soc. Home: 428 Fayette Park Lexington KY 40508 Office: 1401 Harrodsburg Rd Suite A-500 Lexington KY 40504

BARKER, JOHN FRANKLIN, state government official; b. Lockport, N.Y., Nov. 26, 1941; s. B. Franklin, Jr., and Aletha Marie (Barney) B.; m. Louisa Penick Brandon, July 17, 1968; children—Benjamin Brandon, John Graham. A.B., Harvard U., 1963; A.B., M.A. (Lazard fellow), Corpus Christi Coll., Cambridge U., Eng., 1973. Legis. asst. to U.S. Sen. Thomas J. McIntyre of N.H., 1965-67; aide to Pres. Lyndon B. Johnson, 1967-68; spl. asst. to Watergate spl. prosecutors Archibald Cox and Leon Jaworski, 1973-75; dir. public and congl. affairs U.S. Privacy Commn., 1976-78; press sec. to Gov. Bill Clinton of Ark., 1979-80; pres., chmn. bd. Research Assocs., Inc., Little Rock, 1980-85; exec. dir. State Mgmt. Audit and Rev. Commn., 1985—; pub. Ark. Report and Legis. Record. Chmn. bd. Elizabeth Mitchell Children's Center, 1981-82, Ark. Repertory Theater, 1979; bd. dirs. Ark. Heart Assn.; bd. dirs. KLRE-FM. Democrat. Episcopalian. Club: Little Rock. Contbr. numerous articles to mags. and newspapers. Home: 5134 P St Little Rock AR 72207 Office: 1300 Tower Bldg Little Rock AR 72201

BARKER, STEPHEN GERALD, lawyer; b. Ary, Ky., Oct. 2, 1953; s. Talmon D. and Eliza (Grigsby) B.; m. Sharon Francis, Aug. 29, 1974; children—Stephanie, Sara Kimberly. B.S. in Forestry, U. Ky., 1975, J.D., 1980. Bar: Ky. 1980, U.S. Dist. Ct. (ea. dist.) Ky. 1980. News anchorman Sta. WKYH-TV, Hazard, Ky., 1972-73; dist. conservationist Soil Conservation Service, U.S. Dept. Agr., Manchester, Ky., 1975-77; ptnr. Barker & Allen, Hazard, 1980-85; sole practice, Hazard, 1985—; asst. gen. counsel 1st Fed. Savs., Hazard, 1981-84, gen. counsel, 1985—; master commr. Perry Cir. Ct., Hazard, 1982—; dir., gen. counsel Novation Land Co., Hazard, 1982—. Mem. ABA, Perry County Bar Assn. (pres. 1981—), Ky. Bar Assn., Assn. Trial Lawyers Am. Democrat. Baptist. Home: Duane Mountain Bulan KY 41722 Office: 600 High St Suite 203 PO Box 860 Hazard KY 41701

BARKER, WILLIAM ONICO, state senator, funeral director; b. Reidsville, N.C., Nov. 6, 1934; m. Lucy Mae Lovell. B.A. in Acctg., Va. Poly. Inst.; grad. Ky. Sch. Mortuary Sci. Lic. funeral dir. Mem. Va. Senate, 1980—. Mem. Danville YMCA; bd. dirs. Danville chpt. ARC, Danville Meml. Hosp., Hughes Meml. Home and Nat. Tobacco Textile Mus. Served with U.S. Army, 1957-60; Korea. Republican. Baptist. Office: Va Senate Gen Assembly Bldg 9th and Broad Sts Richmond VA 23219*

BARKLEY, HENRY BROCK, JR., research and development executive; b. Raleigh, N.C., Apr. 5, 1927; s. Henry Brock and Thelma Maurine (Dutt) B.; m. Edith Sumner Stowe, June 24, 1950; children—Margaret Susan, Henry Brock, Jane Stowe. Student U. N.C., 1944-45; B.S., U.S. Naval Acad., 1949; B.S. in E.E., U.S. Naval Postgrad. Sch., 1954, M.S. in E.E., 1955. Supr. space power sect. Bendix, Ann Arbor, Mich., 1962-63; chief reactor div. Lewis Research Center, NASA, Sandusky, Ohio, 1963-73; asst. gen. mgr., dir. power reactors EG&G Idaho, Inc., Idaho Falls, 1973-81; mgr. internat. bus. Babcock & Wilcox Co., Lynchburg, Va., 1981-83, mgr. 205 plant project services, 1983—; dir. Devel. Workshop, Inc., Idaho Falls, 1977-81; IEEE disting. lectr. in S.Am. and C.Am., 1984. Bd. dirs. Sandusky (Ohio) Concert Assn., 1965-73; chmn. Huron (Ohio) sch. levy campaigns, 1970. Served to lt. comdr. USN, 1949-61. Mem. Am. Nuclear Soc., IEEE, Am. Guild Organists. Presbyterian. Home: 1216 Norvell House Ct Lynchburg VA 24503 Office: PO Box 10935 Lynchburg VA 24506

BARKLEY, LAURA ESTELLE, counselor; b. San Antonio, June 16, 1958; d. Robert Webster and Maria Estella (Garcia) B. B.S., Corpus Christi State U., 1979; M.S., Tex. A&I U., 1982. Cert. secondary tchr., Tex.; lic. counselor, Tex. Counselor, Tex. A&I U., Kingsville, 1982—; internat. student adviser, test supr. Student Orgn., Kingsville. Mem. Am. Assn. for Counseling and Devel., Nat. Assn. Fgn. Student Advisers, Tex. Assn. for Counseling and Devel., Gulf Coast Assn. Counseling and Devel., Tex. Assn. Coll. and Univ. Student

Personnel Adminstrs. Avocation: dancing. Home: 305 W St Peters St San Diego TX 78384 Office: Tex A&I U Campus Box 112 Kingsville TX 78363

BARKMAN, KEVIN PAUL, marketing manager; b. Omaha, Mar. 12, 1954; s. Richard David and Sharon Ann (Ling) B.; m. Margaret Cheryl Dulion; 1 child, Michelle Sharon. B.S., U. Central Fla., 1976. Sales rep. Copytronics, Orlando, Fla., 1976-77; nat./internat. travel trade sales mgr. Ringling Bros. Barnum and Bailey Circus World, Entertainment div. Mattel Toys, Orlando, 1977-80; v.p. adminstrn. United Med. Corp., Orlando, 1980—. Active Indsl. Devel. Council, Fla. Citrus Sports Assn.; bd. dirs. U. Central Fla. Knight's Boosters, Alumni Assn. Mem. Am. Mktg. Assn., Am. Mgmt. Assn., Pub. Relations Council Fla. Hosp. Assn.

BARKSDALE, ARLEN O'NEIL, investment and development company executive; b. San Diego, Apr. 8, 1945; s. Earlie Nathaniel and Carmen Pauline (Wilson) B.; A.A., Weatherford Coll., 1967; B.S., U. Tex., Arlington, 1969; M.A., Rice U., 1971, Ph.D., 1972; m. Ruby Diane Haynes, June 3, 1966; children—Julie Elisabeth, Shane Arlen. Prodn. planner Aerospace div. LTV, Grand Prairie, Tex., 1967; lab. technician, materials research Bell Helicopter, Ft. Worth, 1968; ops. mgr. silicon mfg. Tex. Instruments, Sherman, 1973-77; chmn. bd., chief exec. officer Cory Enterprises, Inc. (d.b.a. Sealcrest Homes), Weatherford, Tex., 1977—; chmn. bd. Tex. & So. Quarter Horse Jour., 1979-80; chmn. bd., chief exec. officer Lanier Machine Works, Inc., 1980-82; owner Barksdale Orchards, 1975-82, Hytec Engring., 1974—. Served with USAF, 1963-65. AEC spl. fellow, 1969-72; NDEA fellow, 1972-73; U. Tex. grantee, 1967-79. Mem. Am. Phys. Soc., C. of C., Tex. Quarter Horse Assn., Am. Forestry Assn., Smithsonian Instn., AAAS, Phi Beta Kappa, Sigma Xi. Clubs: Lions, DeMolay. Contbr. articles to profl. jours. Office: 1744 W Division Arlington TX 76012

BARKSDALE, ETHELBERT COURTLAND, educator; b. Arlington, Tex., Apr. 9, 1944; s. E.C. and Marjorie M. Barksdale; B.A., U. Tex., Arlington, 1965; M.A., Ohio State U., 1968, Ph.D., 1971. Lectr., U. Calif., Irvine, 1971-72; asso. prof., chmn. dept. German and Slavic langs. and lits. U. Fla., Gainesville, 1972—. NDEA fellow, 1965-68. Mem. Am. Assn. Advancement Slavic Studies, MLA. Mem. Christian Ch. Author: The Dacha and the Duchess, 1974; Cosmologies of Consciousness, 1980; Daggers of the Mind, 1979. also articles. Home: 1333 S Pecan St Arlington TX 76010 Office: 261 ASB Univ Fla Gainesville FL 32611

BARKSDALE, JAMES L., air freight company executive. Exec. v.p., chief operating officer Fed. Express Corp. Office: 2990 Airways Blvd Memphis TN 38194

BARKSDALE, RICHARD DILLON, engineering educator, consultant, researcher; b. Orlando, Fla., May 2, 1938; s. William Spruil and Lucile (Dillon) B.; m. Bonnie Alice McClung, Nov. 16, 1962; children—Cheryl Lynn, Richelle Denise. A.S., So. Tech. Inst., Marietta, Ga., 1958; B.C.E., Ga. Inst. Tech., 1962, M.S., 1963; Ph.D., Purdue U., 1965. Registered profl. engr., Fla., Ga., S.C., N.C., Tenn., Ala., La. Spl. lectr. So. Tech. Inst., 1958-60; asst. prof. civil engring. Ga. Inst. Tech., 1965-69, assoc. prof., 1969-75, prof., 1975—; v.p. Soil Systems Inc., Marietta, 1972-79; dir. Geotech. Research Inc., Marietta, 1973-79. Co-pres. Briarcliff High Sch. Boosters Club, 1983-84, Briarcliff High Sch. PTA, 1985-86. Recipient Ga. Engring. Soc. award, 1962; Am. City Aid to Edn. award, 1962; NSF grantee. Mem. ASCE (recipient Norman medal 1978; pres. Ga. sect., chmn. nat. com. on structural design of roadways), Internat. Soc. Soil Mechanics and Founds., Phi Kappa Phi (pres. Ga. Tech. chpg. 1979). Republican. Baptist. Club: Apalachee Sportsman (pres. 1974—). Contbr. articles to profl. jours. Home: 1306 Christmas Ln NE Atlanta GA 30329 Office: Sch Civil Engring Ga Inst Tech Atlanta GA 30332

BARLAR, LARRY JOE, import-export company executive; b. Pulaski, Tenn., Dec. 28, 1935; s. Woodrow W. and Willa M. (Blair) B.; B.S., Columbia U., 1953; M.B.A., U. Tenn., 1959; m. Norma J. Wilkerson, Dec. 8, 1953; children—Sheri Jo, Kristopher, Norman. Salesman, IBM, Nashville, 1957-61; cons. Lockheed Corp., Atlanta, 1961-70; pres., chief exec. officer Barlar Internat., Dallas, 1970—. Served to 1st lt. USMCR, 1954-57. Home: 2714 Lakeview Ln Carrolton TX 75006 Office: Box 814702 Dallas TX 75381

BARLOW, DANIEL LENOX, educator; b. Elizabeth, Pa., June 24, 1926; s. Walter J. and Ruth Elizabeth (Lenox) B.; B.A., Franklin Coll., 1947; M.Div., Colgate-Rochester Div. Sch., 1950; M.A., Ariz. State U., 1965, Ed.D., 1970; postgrad. Purdue U., Cin. U., 1975; m. Wilma Mae Jackson, June 1, 1947; children—Dana Scott, Brett Robin. Ordained to ministry Bapt. Ch., 1950; pastor Trinity Bapt. Ch., Toledo, 1950-53, 1st Bapt. Ch., Brookings, S.D., 1953-55, Pricehill Bapt. Ch., Cin., 1955-59, Mt. Auburn Bapt. Ch., Cin., 1960-61, Ch. of Savior, Mesa, Ariz., 1961-64; assoc. prof. humanities Miami-Dade Jr. Coll., Miami, Fla., 1965-66; assoc. dean students Santa Fe Jr. Coll., Gainesville, Fla., 1966-68; dean S.W. Va. Community Coll., Richlands, Va., 1968-74; therapist, sch. cons. Dearborn Mental Health Center, Lawrenceburg, Ind., 1974-76; owner Dana Robin Assocs., personnel cons., Florence, Ky., 1976-77; asst. mgr. Dutch Pantry Restaurant, 1977-78; prof. edn. Liberty Bapt. Coll., Lynchburg, Va., 1978—. Author: Educational Psychology: The Teaching-Learning Process, 1985. Mem. Assn. for Supervision and Curriculum Devel., Assn. Tchr. Educators Va., Assn. Tchr. Educators Nat., Phi Delta Kappa, Kappa Delta Pi. Republican. Baptist. Home: PO Box 367 Rustburg VA 24588 Office: Liberty Baptist College PO Box 21276 Lynchburg VA 24506

BARLOW, THOMAS JAMES, industrial corporation executive; b. Houston, June 22, 1922; s. Thomas Jefferson and Dorothy (James) B.; B.S., Tex. A&M U., 1943; postgrad. Harvard U., 1962; m. Billye Louise Sears, May 31, 1944; children—Lance, Lynne. Trainee, Western Cottonoil Co., Abilene, Tex., 1946-47, asst. gen. mgr., 1948-49; constrn. engr. San Joaquin Cottonoil Co., Bakersfield, Calif., 1948; supt. Western Cotton Products Co., Phoenix, 1949-50; prodn. mgr. Nile Ginning Co., Minia, Egypt, 1950-56; prodn. engr. Anderson, Clayton & Co., Houston, 1956-57, v.p., 1961-66, pres., chief exec. officer, 1966-76, chmn. bd.-chmn. exec. com., chief exec. officer, 1976—, also dir.; dir. Central Southwest Corp., Hughes Tool Co. Served from ensign to lt. USNR, World War II; PTO. Mem. Houston C. of C. (dir. at large 1940—), Tex. A&M U. Assn. Former Students (council). Tex. Research League. Clubs: River Oaks Country, University (Houston). Home: 35 Willowend St Houston TX 77024 Office: Anderson Clayton & Co First Internal Plaza 1100 Louisiana Houston TX 77001*

BARLOW, W. P., JR., lawyer; b. Washington, July 29, 1945; s. W.P. and Elaine Virginia (Zweifel) B.; m. Kathryn L. Prescott, June 13, 1977; 1 child, Ashley Prescott. B.A., U. Wis., 1967; J.D., Marquette U., 1970. Bar: Wis. 1970, Tex. 1981, U.S. Dist. Ct. (no. and so. dist.) Tex. 1981, U.S. Dist. Ct. (ea. and we. dist.) Wis. 1970, U.S. Ct. Appeals (5th, 7th, 11th cirs.), 1971. Assoc., Ames, Riordan, Crivello & Sullivan, Milw., 1970-74; sr. ptnr. Barlow, Russo & Felker, Milw., 1974-78, Dallas, 1978-83; sr. ptnr. Barlow & Lippe, Dallas, 1983-84; pres. W.P. Barlow Jr., P.C., Dallas, 1984—; dir. 1st Nat. Group, Houston, 1983—; chmn. bd. dirs. 1st Savs. & Loan, Burkburnett, Tex., 1983—; dir. 1st Nat. Bank, Tom Bean, Tex., 1st Life Ins. Co., Dallas, Nat. Indemnity Co., Cisco, Tex. Mem. Shakespeare Festival, Mus. Fine Arts, Historic Preservation League, Dallas, 1978—; mem. Friends of Pub. Library, Dallas, 1983—; bd. dirs. Tex. Spl. Olympics, Austin, 1983—, Nat. Interfrat. Conf., Indpls., 1985—. Served to lt. comdr. USN, 1971-74. Sequoyah fellow Am. Indian Sci. and Engring. Soc., 1985. Mem. ABA, Fed. Bar Assn., Assn. Trial Lawyers Am., Am. Judicature Soc., Tex. Trial Lawyers Assn., Tex. Bar Assn., Dallas Bar Assn., Dallas Trial Lawyers Assn., Houston Bar Assn. Houston Trial Lawyers Assn., Fellowship Christian Athletes, Sigma Tau Gamma (bd. dirs. 1972-84, pres. 1978-80, Ellsworth C. Dent award 1967), Sigma Tau Gamma Found. (bd. dirs., pres. 1984—; Wilson C. Morris award 1982, Marvin M. Millsap award 1983), Delta Theta Phi, Alpha Epsilon Rho. Clubs: Lincoln City, Energy, Dallas (Dallas). Home: 9502 Bill Browne Ln Dallas TX 75243 Office: 8080 N Central Expressway 13th Fl Lock Box 13 Dallas TX 75206

BARNA, GABRIEL GEORGE, research company executive; b. Budapest, Hungary, Mar. 13, 1946; came to U.S., 1972, naturalized, 1985; s. George and Eva (Kaposy) B.; m. Betty Louise Collier, May 23, 1971; children—Andrew, Adrienne. B.Sc. in Chemistry with honors, McGill U., Montreal, Can., 1968, Ph.D., 1973. Mem. tech. staff, central research Tex. Instruments, Dallas, 1972-83, sect. mgr., sr. mem. tech. staff, 1983—. Contbr. articles to profl. jours.; patentee in field. Mem. Am. Chem. Soc., Electrochem. Soc., Sigma Xi. Clubs: Texins Camera (v.p. 1975-77); Texins Flying (pres. 1982-85). Avocations: flying; sailing. Office: TX Instruments PO Box 225621 M/S 3618 Dallas TX 75265

BARNARD, ANTHONY CHARLES LANGRISH, university administrator, educator; b. Birmingham, Eng., Apr. 30, 1932; came to U.S., 1958, naturalized, 1965; s. George L. and Florence V. (Gould) B.; m. Barbara Douglass Blackburn, June 6, 1964; children—Lisa, Carol. B.Sc., U. Birmingham, Eng., 1953, Ph.D., 1957, D.Sc., 1974; M.B.A., U. Ala. in Birmingham, 1979. Research physicist Assoc. Elec. Industries, Adermaston, Eng., 1956-58; postdoctoral fellow U. Iowa, Iowa City, 1958-60; from instr. to asst. prof. physics Rice U., Houston, 1960-65; mgr. physics dept. IBM Sci. Ctr., Houston, 1965-68; from assoc. prof. to prof. U. Ala. in Birmingham, 1968—, chmn. dept. computer and info. scis., 1972-78, from asst. to assoc. v.p., 1979-84, dean grad. sch., 1984—. Mem. Am. Phys. Soc., Assn. Computing Machinery, Sigma Xi, Beta Gamma Sigma, Phi Kappa Phi, Omicron Delta Epsilon. Home: 3037 Westmoreland Dr Mountain Brook AL 35223 Office: U Ala in Birmingham 511 University Ctr University Station Birmingham AL 35294

BARNARD, D. DOUGLAS, JR., congressman; b. Augusta, Ga., Mar. 20, 1922; s. D. Douglas and Lucy (Burns) B.; B.A., Mercer U., 1943, LL.B., Walter F. George Sch. Law, 1948; m. Naomi Elizabeth Holt, Dec. 15, 1946; children—Pamela, Lucy, D.Douglas, III. Exec. v.p. Ga. R.R. Bank, 66-76; exec. sec. Gov. Carl E. Sanders, 1963-66; mem. Ga. Bd. Transp., 1966-76; mem. 95th-97th Congresses from 10th Ga. Dist. Deacon, First Bapt. Ch., Augusta; chmn. Richmond County (Ga.) Dem. Exec. Com., 1955-60; mem. State Dem. Exec. Com., 1963-66; bd. dirs. Augusta Boys Club; trustee Mercer U. Served with Fin. Corps, U.S. Army, 1943-45. Named Outstanding Man of Year, Augusta, 1957. Mem. Augusta C. of C., Phi Delta Theta, Phi Alpha Delta. Office: 236 Cannon House Office Bldg Washington DC 20515

BARNARD, FRANCES FLYNN, civic worker; b. Fort Worth, Tex., Sept. 16, 1938; d. Elgate Daniel and Effie Danella (Ross) Hitch; B.S.R., Tex. Wesleyan U., 1975; postgrad. Tex. Christian U., 1975-77; m. Doyle Graves Flynn, June 12, 1958 (dec.); children—Stehlin, Shari, Shareese, Shawn; m. 2d, William Gene Barnard, Aug. 13, 1979. Employment developer City of Fort Worth, 1978-80; exec. dir. Am. Med. Consumers, Fort Worth, 1977-80; field dir. Circle T council Girl Scouts U.S.A., Fort Worth, 1980-81; cons. women's affairs; devel. specialist, Cassata Learning Center, 1981-82; bd. dirs. Widowed Persons Services, 1978-80; mem. task force Area 5 Health Systems Agy. Mem. Assn. Girl Scout Exec. Staff, AAUW, Am. Soc. Tng. and Devel., Widowed Persons Services, Hospice Assn., Alpha Kappa Delta. Roman Catholic. Democrat. Club: Order Eastern Star. Home: 6513 Armando St Fort Worth TX 76133

BARNES, ANDREW EARL, newspaper editor; b. Torrington, Conn., May 15, 1939; s. Joseph and Elizabeth (Brown) B.; B.A., Harvard U., 1961; m. Marion Otis, Aug. 26, 1960; children—Christopher Joseph, Benjamin Brooks, Elizabeth Cheney. Reporter, bur. chief Providence Jour., 1961-63; from reporter to edn. editor Washington Post, 1965-73; met. editor, asst. mng. editor St. Petersburg (Fla.) Times, 1973-75, mng. editor, 1975-84, editor, pres., 1984—; pres. Fla. Trend, 1985—; dir. Times Pub. Co. Bd. dirs. Poynter Inst., Congl. Quar. Served with USAR, 1963-65. Alicia Patterson fellow, 1969-70. Mem. Am. Soc. Newspaper Editors, AP Mng. Editors Assn., Fla. Soc. Newspaper Editors (pres. 1980-81). Home: 4819 Juanita Way S Saint Petersburg FL 33705 Office: 490 1st Ave S Saint Petersburg FL 33731

BARNES, BENJAMIN SHIELDS, JR., banker; b. Dothan, Ala., Jan. 26, 1919; s. Benjamin Shields and Ruth Graham (Blue) B.; m. Bettye Osborne Withers, Apr. 2, 1948; children—Julia Lee Reid, Elizabeth Randylyn French, Carole Ostborne Beason, Bettye Graham Malcolm. B.S., U. Ga., 1941; postgrad. Rutgers U., 1950-52, Harvard U., 1968. With Atlantic Refining Co., 1941; with First Nat. Bank Atlanta, 1946—, asst. cashier, 1948-50, asst. v.p., 1950-54, v.p., 1954-67, exec. v.p., dir., 1967-75, vice chmn. bd., 1975-78, exec. v.p., dir. First Atlanta Holding Corp., 1970-75, vice chmn. bd., 1975-78, pres., dir. First Atlanta Internat. Corp., 1971-78, chmn. bd. London Interstate Bank Ltd., 1975-78, dir., 1970-78; chmn. bd., dir. First Bank Savannah, Ga., 1978—; vice chmn. bd. Munich Am. Reassurance Co.; dir. Atlanta Gas Light Co. Served to lt. USNR, 1941-46; PTO. Recipient Disting. Service award Baylor Sch. Alumni Assn., 1969; Disting. Alumnus award U. Ga. Coll. Bus. Adminstrn. Alumni Assn., 1972. Mem. Chi Phi. Presbyterian. Clubs: Marshwood at the Landings, Oglethorpe, Chatham (Savannah), Capital City (Atlanta). Home: 6 Blackbeard Ln The Landings on Skidaway Island Savannah GA 31411 Office: First Bank of Savannah 136 Bull St Savannah GA 31401

BARNES, CARNELL MARTIN, psychologist, marriage and family therapist; b. Odell, Okla., May 12, 1933; d. Carval Anderson and Roberta (Hamil) Martin; B.S., Southeastern Okla. State U., 1963, M.S., 1966; Ph.D. in Marriage and Family Counseling, Tex. Woman's U., 1982; children—James Wayne, Joe Bill, Jerry Bob Barnes. Tchr. vocat. home econs., Maud, Okla., 1963-64, Bokchito, Okla., 1964-67, Spurger, Tex., 1967-68, Winnie, Tex., 1968-72; tchr. learning disabilities, Wise County, Tex., 1972-73; counselor spl. edn., Mesquite, Tex., 1973-76, asso. sch. psychologist, 1976-77, coordinator appraisals, 1977-78, coordinator spl. edn. counseling, 1978-79; marriage and family counselor, Dallas, 1978—. Cert. tchr., Okla., Tex.; cert. counselor, Tex.; lic. psychologist, Ark.; lic. profl. counselor, Tex. Mem. Am. Assn. Marriage and Family Therapy (clin. mem.), Am. Assn. for Counseling and Devel., Tex. Council on Family Relations, Am. Psychol. Assn. Home: 1625 South Pkwy Mesquite TX 75149

BARNES, CORNELIUS WHITE, geologist; b. New Orleans, July 22, 1956; s. James William and Aylmer Virginia (White) B.; m. Debra Gail Hudspeth, June 3, 1978; 1 child, Megan Elizabeth. Student, Tulane U., 1974-75, U. New Orleans, 1975, 76; B.S. in Geology, La. State U., 1978. Geologist, petroleum geologist Texaco, Inc., New Orleans, 1978-82; sr. geologist, area geologist ANR Prodn. Co., Jackson, Miss., 1982—. Bd. dirs. Treasure Cove Homeowners Assn., Madison, Miss., 1983-84, pres., 1984—; deacon bldg. use Pear Orchard Ch., Ridgeland, Miss., 1984, deacon, chmn. fin. com., 1985. Mem. Am. Assn. Petroleum Geologists, Soc. Econ. Paleontologists and Mineralogists, Miss. Geol. Soc. (program chmn. 1983-85, continuing edn. coordinator 1984-85), New Orleans Geol. Soc. (chmn. sch. info. com. 1980-82). Republican. Presbyterian. Avocations: basketball, softball, hunting, fishing, gardening. Home: 3007 Tidewater Circle Madison MS 39110 Office: ANR Prodn Co 111 Capitol Bldg Suite 400 Jackson MS 39201

BARNES, DANIEL WALTER, pharmacist; b. Oklahoma City, June 12, 1953; s. Walter and Mildred Barnes; m. Elizabeth Ann Thomason, Aug. 16, 1974; 1 child, Gina Elizabeth. B.S. in Pharmacy, Southwestern Okla. State U., 1976. Registered pharmacist, Okla. Intern pharmacist Edmond Meml. Hosp., Okla., 1976-77; staff pharmacist Moore Mcpl. Hosp., Okla., 1978-81, South Community Hosp., Oklahoma City, 1977-81, pharmacy supr., 1981-82, dir. pharmacy, 1982-83, dir. pharmacy, risk mgmt., and materials mgmt., 1985—; adj. faculty Southwestern Okla. State U.-Weatherford, 1982—, Okla. U., Oklahoma City, 1983—. Mem. Okla. Soc. Hosp. Pharmacists (dist. chmn. 1983-84, treas. 1984—), Am. Soc. Hosp. Pharmacists, Okla. Pharm. Assn. Home: 1209 NE 18th Ct Moore OK 73160 Office: South Community Hosp 1001 SW 44th St Oklahoma City OK 73109

BARNES, DENISE RENE, psychology educator, psychotherapist; b. Washington, Mar. 24, 1954; d. Henry Joseph and Doris Louise (Williams) B. B.A. magna cum laude, Mt. Holyoke Coll., 1976; M.A., Adelphi U., 1978, Ph.D., 1980. Lic. practicing psychologist, N.C. Clin. asst. prof. U. N.C., Chapel Hill, 1980-82, asst. prof., 1983—; adj. prof. Duke U., Durham, N.C., 1981—. Contbr. articles to profl. jours. Contbr. chpt. to Assessment Strategies in Behavior Modification, 1982. Postdoctoral fellow Duke U. Med. Ctr., 1982-83, adj. sr. fellow, 1983. Mem. Am. Psychol. Assn. (mem. minority fellowship adv. com.), Gerontological Soc. Am. Avocations: horseback riding; yard work; collecting art and antiques. Office: U NC Davie Hall Dept Psychology Chapel Hill NC 27514

BARNES, JAMES E., energy industry executive; b. Ponca City, Okla. Student U. Tex.; B.S. in Indsl. Engring. Mgmt., Okla. A & M U., 1957; A.M.P., Harvard U., 1970. With Conoco, 1956-83, gen. mgr. natural gas and gas products dept., 1965-70, v.p. corp. purchasing, 1970-75, v.p. supply-trading, 1975-78, v.p. supply-transp., 1978-80, exec. v.p. petroleum products N.Am., 1980-83; sr. exec. v.p., chief operating officer Mapco Inc., Tulsa, 1983-84, pres., chief exec. officer, 1984—, also chmn. bd. dirs.; dir. Kansas City So. Industries, Inc., Vista Chem. Co., BancOkla. Corp. Bd. govs. Okla. State U.; active Boy Scouts Am.; bd. dirs. Tulsa Opera; trustee Philbrook Art Ctr. Mem. Am. Petroleum Inst. (bd. dirs.), Responsible Govt. for Am. Found. (bd. dirs.), Nat. Coal Assn. (bd. dirs., exec. com.), Tex. Mid-Continent Oil and Gas Assn., Internat. Inst. Strategic Studies, Okla. State U. Alumni Assn., Houston Farm and Ranch Club, Met. Tulsa C. of C. (bd. dirs., exec. com. steering com., Com. of 200). Clubs: Southern Hills Country, Summit, Tulsa Golf, Golf of Okla. (bd. govs.). Address: Mapco Inc 1800 S Baltimore Ave Tulsa OK 74119

BARNES, JEAN, jewelry company executive, management consultant, mortgage broker; b. Beaver Falls, Pa., Aug. 7, 1923; d. Sam and Clara (Jerome) Deltino; m. Bruce Barnes, Mar. 11, 1947 (dec. 1971); children—Louise, Pamela, Karen, Kimberly. Former mem. June Taylor Dancers; sales mgr. Empire Crafts, Newark, N.Y., 1951-61; pres., founder Tammey Jewels, Inc., Indpls., 1961—, cons., 1985—; dir. Barnes Enterprise, Satellite Beach, Fla. Writer sales weekly The Jean Barnes Newsletter. Mem. Pres. Reagan's Task Force, Washington, 1982-85. Recipient Speaker of Yr. award Sertoma Club, 1978; numerous recruiting and mgmt. awards Empire Crafts Corp., 1951-61; named Lt. col. State of Ga., 1975. Mem. Nat. Direct Selling Assn. (pres.'s council 1965—), Order Ky. Cols. Republican. Avocations: dancing pool; swimming; cooking; yachting. Home: 725 Beach St Satellite Beach FL 32937 Office: Tammey Jewels Inc 745 Beach St Satellite Beach FL 32937

BARNES, JOHN ANDERSON, marketing executive; b. Quanah, Tex., Nov. 13, 1946; s. John Lynder and Emma Lorice (Anderson) B.; student Tex. Tech. U., 1965-69; m. Dana McCaleb, May 22, 1971; children—Kevin Anderson, John Kelly, Kimberly. Dir. membership W. Tex. C. of C., Abilene, 1975-80; pres. J-Bar-D Mktg. Inc., Abilene, 1980—, also dir.; fin. cons., owner Barnes & Assocs. Crusade chmn. Am. Cancer Soc., 1980, pres., 1981-82. Recipient Am. Cancer Soc. Pub. Edn. award, 1974. Mem. Abilene C. of C., Am. Entrepreneur Assn., Tex. Tech. U. Ex-Students Assn. (dist. rep. 1983—). Baptist. Clubs: Abilene Jaycees, Lions Tex. Tech Red Raiders (bd. dirs. 1983—). Home: 62 Augusta St Abiline TX 79606 Office: PO Box 3301 Abilene TX 79604

BARNES, JOHN R., gas company executive; b. 1944; married. B.B.A., Southwestern State U., 1966; M.B.A., U. Tulsa, 1971. Acctg. mgr. Sun Oil Co., 1966-71; mgr. fin. planning Samsonite Corp., 1971-73; v.p., treas. Aztec Oil & Gas, 1973-76; pres., chief operating officer Dorchester Gas Corp., Dallas, 1976—, also dir. Office: Dorchester Gas Corp 5735 Pineland Rd Dallas TX 75231*

BARNES, MAGGIE LUE SHIFFLETT (MRS. LAWRENCE BARNES), nurse; b. nr. Red Mud, Tex., Mar. 29, 1931; d. Howard Eldridge and Sadie Adilene (Dunlap) Shifflett; student Cogdell Sch. Nursing, 1959-60; Western Tex. Coll., 1972-76, grad. Meth. Hosp. Sch. Nursing, Lubbock, Tex., 1975; B.S. in Nursing, W. Tex. State U., 1977; m. T.C. Fagan, Jan. 1950 (dec. Feb. 1952); 1 son, Lawayne L.; m. 2d, Lawrence Barnes, Sept. 2, 1960. Floor nurse D.M. Cogdell Meml. Hosp., Snyder, Tex., 1960-64, medication nurse, 1964-76, asst. evening supr., 1976-78, charge nurse, after 1973, evening nursing supr., until 1980; nursing supr. Scurry, Borden, Mitchel, Fisher, Howard Counties, West Central Home Health Agy., Snyder, 1980-83; supr. Root-Meml. Hosp., 1983—; regional coordinator home health services Beverly Enterprises, 1983—; supr. emergency room Foot Meml. Hosp. Den mother Cub Scouts Am., Holliday, Tex., 1960-61; mem. PTA, Snyder, Tex., 1960-69; adv. Sr. Citizens Assn.; mem. Tri-Region Health Systems Agency, 1979—; mem. adv. bd. Scurry County Diabetes Assn., 1982—. Mem. Vocat. Nurses Assn. Tex. (mem. bd. 1963-65, div. pres. 1967-69), Emergency Dept. Nursing Assn. Apostolic Faith Ch. (sec., treas. 1956-58). Home: Route 1 Box 9B Hermleigh TX 79526

BARNES, MICHAEL DUANE, architect; b. Kansas City, Mo., June 30, 1954; s. Henry Delbert and Deloris Jean (Henrion) B.; m. Candice Kay Anderson, Aug. 10, 1974; children—Juliette, Gabriel. B.Arch., U. Kans., 1974; M.Arch., Va. Poly. Inst., 1978. Ordained minister Assemblies of God Ch., 1985. Owner Design Build Firm, Blacksburg, Va., 1976-78; architect Pentecost & Assocs., Virginia Beach, Va., 1978-79; architect, owner Warner & Barnes, Virginia Beach, 1979—; ptnr. W&B Real Estate Investment Properties Virginia Beach, 1985—. Author: 3-Hand Monte, 1983, Pulsating Symbols, 1983. Vice pres. Full Gospel Businessman's Fellowship Internat., Virginia Beach, 1984—; dir. Youth Fellowship Group, Norfolk, Va., 1979-84. Mem. AIA, Am. Soc. Magicians, Internat. Brotherhood Magicians (local chpt. pres. 1983-84, 1st place award sleight of hand 1983, 3d place award comedy stage 1983), Suffolk Builders Assn. (pres. 1981-84). Republican. Mem. Assembly of God Ch. Avocations: fishing; magic; photography. Home: 3704 S Queensgrove Circle Virginia Beach VA 23452 Office: Warner & Barnes Architects 1611 Lynnhaven Pkwy Suite 200 Virginia Beach VA 23452

BARNES, RANDOLPH CHRISTOPHER, industrial engineer; b. N.Y.C., May 9, 1953; s. Frederick Woodruff and Annette Marie (Corradi) B. B.Bus. Mgmt. summa cum laude, Ft. Lauderdale Coll., 1981. Staff indsl. engr., group leader Participate Mgmt. Program adminstarn. Motorola Communications, Ft. Lauderdale, Fla., 1977—. Served with USN, 1973-78. Mem. Am. Inst. Indsl. Engring., Am. Mgmt. Assn. Republican. Roman Catholic. Office: 8000 W Sunrise Blvd Room 103 Fort Lauderdale FL 33313

BARNES, ROBERT VERTREESE, JR., masonry contractor executive; b. Dallas, Oct. 7, 1946; s. Robert Vertreese and Doris Corinne (Haffen) B.; m. Deborah Dee Brown, May 31, 1968; children—Robert V. III, John David, Leslie Shannon. B.S. in Indsl. Tech., E. Tex. State U., 1976. Salesman, Sears, Roebuck and Co., Dallas, 1965-66, dept. mgr., 1967-69; estimator Dee Brown Masonry, Inc., Dallas, 1970-75, contract adminstr., 1976-77; v.p. Cardinal Masonry Co., Houston, 1978-79; v.p. Dee Brown Masonry, Inc., Houston, 1980-84, exec. v.p., 1985—; v.p. Dee Brown, Inc. 1980-84, exec. v.p., 1984—; v.p. Shiloh Investment Co. Pres. Katy Youth Soccer Assn., 1980, 81; dir. Whiterock Chs. Athletic Assn., 1972-77; chmn. Bricklayers Health and Welfare, 1983-85; trustee Bricklayers Pension Fund, 1983-85; warden St. Cuthberts Episcopal Ch., 1985—. Mem. Assoc. Masonry Contractors Tex. (pres. 1983, sec./treas. 1981, 82), Assoc. Masonry Contractors Houston (pres. 1982, 83, v.p. 1981), Am. Subcontractor Assn. (v.p. 1982, 83, dir. Houston 1982-85, also mem. nat. coms.), Dallas Exec. Assn., Mason Contractors Assn. Am. (contract research com. 1982-83), Houston C. of C., Northwest Houston C. of C., Delta Sigma Pi. Republican. Episcopalian. Clubs: Dallas Athletic, Country (Dallas). Office: PO Box 28335 Dallas TX 75228

BARNES, THOMAS JEFFERSON, JR., pharmacist; b. Baxley, Ga., June 23, 1926; s. Thomas Jefferson Sr. and Merle Fenton (Johnson) B.; m. Barbara Lynn Tollison, Dec. 12, 1954; children—Barbara Karen Barnes Yonchak, Mark Tollison, Jane Ellen. B.S.Pharmacy, U. Ga., 1949. Lic. pharmacist, Ga. Pharmacy intern Roy G. Williams Drug, Macon, Ga., 1949-50; pharmacist employee Barnes Drug Store, Baxley, 1950-59, owner, pres., 1959-82, Barnes Prescription Shop, 1974-82; ptnr. Barnes Drug Store, Baxley, 1982—, Barnes Prescription Shop, 1982—; cons. in field. Mem. sch. bd. Appling County Schs., Baxley; mem. city council City of Baxley; mem. Appling County Bd. Health. Served with USN, 1944-46. Mem. Appling County C. of C. (past bd. dirs., past pres.), Ga. Pharm. Assn., Nat. Assn. Retail Pharmacists, Am. Pharm. Assn. Baptist. Lodge: Lions (sec. 1950s). Avocations: fishing; hunting; golfing. Home: 805 Lackawanna St Baxley GA 31513 Office: Barnes Drug Store 110 N Main St PO Box 126 Baxley GA 31513

BARNETT, BERNARD HARRY, lawyer; b. Helena, Ark., July 13, 1916; s. Harry and Rebecca (Grossman) B.; student U. Mich., 1934-36; J.D., Vanderbilt U., 1940 ; m. Marian Spiesberger, Apr. 9, 1949; 1 son, Charles Dawson. Admitted to Ky. bar, 1940; pvt. practice, Louisville, 1940-42; asso. firm Woodward, Dawson, Hobson & Fulton, 1946-48; partner firms Bulitt, Dawson & Tarrant, 1948-52, Greenebaum, Barnett, Wood & Doll, 1952-70, Barnett & McConnell, 1972, Barnett, Greenebaum, Martin & McConnell, 1972-74, Barnett, Alagia, Greenebaum, Miller & Senn, 1974-75, Barnett & Alagia, 1975—; dir. Cook United, Inc., Fuqua Industries, Inc., Hasbro Industries, Inc., Triton Group Ltd. Mem. adv. group Joint Com. on Internal Revenue Taxation, U.S. Congress, 1953-55, Com. on Ways and Means, U.S. Ho. of Reps., 1956-58. Chmn., Louisville Fund, 1952-53; mem. nat. exec. com., nat. campaign cabinet United Jewish Appeal, 1959—, nat. chmn., 1967-71; chmn. Louisville United Jewish Appeal, 1968-69. Mem. Louisville and Jefferson County Republican Exec. Com., 1954-60; chmn. Ky. Rep. Finance Com., 1955-60. Trustee Spalding Coll., Louisville, 1975-82, Norton Gallery and Sch. Art, 1980—, Benjamin N. Cardozo Sch. Law, 1979—, Ford's Theatre, 1981—. Served as lt. USNR, 1942-45. Mem. ABA, D.C., Ky., Louisville bar assns. Home: 575 N Lake Way Palm Beach FL 33480 Office: 5th Ave Bldg 444 S 5th St Louisville KY 40202

BARNETT, CRAWFORD FANNIN, JR., physician; b. Atlanta, May 11, 1938; s. Crawford Fannin and Penelope Hollinshead (Brown) B.; student Taft Sch., 1953-56, U. Minn., 1957; A.B. magna cum laude, Yale U., 1960; postgrad. (Davison scholar) Oxford (Eng.) U., 1963; M.D. (Trent scholar), Duke, 1964; m. Elizabeth McCarthy Hale, June 6, 1964; children—Crawford Fannin III, Robert Hale. Intern internal medicine Duke U. Med. Center, Durham, N.C., 1964-65, resident, 1965; resident internal medicine Wilmington (Del.) Med. Center, 1965-66; dir. Tenn. Heart Disease Control Program, Nashville, 1966-68; practice medicine specializing in internal medicine, Atlanta, 1968—; mem. staff Crawford Long, Northside, Grady Meml., Doctors Meml., West Paces Ferry, Piedmont, hosps. (all Atlanta); mem. teaching staff Vanderbilt Med. Center, Nashville, 1966-68, Crawford Long Meml. Hosp., 1969—; clin. instr. internal medicine, dept. medicine Emory U. Med. Sch., Atlanta, 1969—. Vice pres., dir. Preferred Equities Corp., 1970—. Bd. govs. Doctors Meml. Hosp., 1971-80; bd. dirs. Atlanta Speech Sch., 1976-80, Historic Oakland Cemetery, 1976-84, So. Turf Nurseries, 1977—, Tech Industries, 1978—. Served as surgeon USPHS, 1966-68. Fellow Am. Geog. Soc.; mem. Am. Fedn. Clin. Research, Council Clin. Cardiology, Am., Ga., Atlanta med. assns., Am., Ga. heart assns., Am., Ga. socs. internal medicine, Am. Assn. History Medicine, Ga., Atlanta (dir. 1976—) hist. socs., Ga., Nat. Trust for Historic Preservation, Internat. Hippocratic Found. Soc. (Greece), Faculty of History of Medicine and Pharmacy Worshipful Soc. Apothecaries of London, Atlanta Com. on Fgn. Relations (chmn. exec. com.), So. Council Internat. and Public Affairs, Newcomen Soc., Atlanta Clin. Soc., Victorian Soc. Am. (bd. advisers Atlanta chpt. 1971—), Mensa, Gridiron, Phi Beta Kappa. Episcopalian. Clubs: Piedmont Driving, Yale (dir. 1970-74), Nine O'Clocks (Atlanta); Pan Am. Doctors (Hidalgo, Mex.). Contbr. articles to profl. publs. Home: 2739 Ramsgate Ct NW Atlanta GA 30305 Office: 3250 Howell Mill Rd NW Atlanta GA 30327

BARNETT, ISAAC, safety and driver education educator; b. South Boston, Va., Apr. 1, 1928; s. Alexander and Lottie (Lipscomb) B.; m. Dorothy Prince, Dec. 27, 1977. B.S., N.C. A&T State U., 1948, M.S., 1960; Ed.D., Mich. State U., 1970. Instr., N.C. A&T State U., Greensboro, 1948-60, asst. prof., 1960-68, prof. safety and driver edn., chmn. dept., 1970—; asst. Eastern Mich. U., Ypsilanti, 1969-70; cons. Mich. Dept. State, Lansing, 1974-77. Recipient Outstanding Contbns. to Safety award N.C. Driver Traffic Safety Edn. Assn., 1971; Disting. Service to Safety award Nat. Safety Council, 1984. Fellow Am. Acad. Safety Educators (v.p. 1984—); mem. Am. Soc. Safety Engrs. (exec. com. 1981—), Phi Delta Kappa. Avocations: bowling, tennis. Home: 5213 Hicone Rd McLeansville NC 27301 Office: NC A&T State U 1601 E Market St Greensboro NC 27411

BARNETT, JOHN BIGHAM, III, lawyer, banker; b. Monroeville, Ala., Apr. 12, 1952; s. John Bigham Jr. and Annie Maud (Hayles) B.; m. Rebecca Lewis, July 26, 1975; 1 child, Courtney. B.A., Birmingham So. U., 1974; J.D. magna cum laude, Cumberland U., 1983. Bar: Ala. 1983, U.S. Dist. Ct. (so. dist.) Ala. 1984. Sec. Barnett Ins. Agy., Monroeville, 1977—; v.p. Monroe County Bank, Monroeville, 1978-79, also dir.; ptnr. Barnett, Bugg & Lee, Monroeville, 1983—. Editor in chief Am. Jour. Trial Advocacy, 1981. Chmn. Monroe County Cancer Soc. Crusade, 1984. Mem. Monroeville C. of C. (pres. 1975), Kappa Alpha Order I (Phi chpt.). Methodist. Lodge: Rotary. Home: 401 S Mount Pleasant St Monroeville AL 36460 Office: Barnett Bugg & Lee Hines St PO Box 278 Monroeville AL 36461

BARNETT, JOHN MONROE, III, association administrator; b. Spartanburg, S.C., Apr. 1, 1950; s. John Monroe, Jr. and Grace Elizabeth (McKehan) B.; m. Alice Maxine Vila, Dec. 22, 1972; 1 dau., Rachel Jean. B.A. in Pub. Adminstrn. and Polit. Sci., U. North Fla., 1975. Asst. mgr. North Fla. chpt. Nat. Elec. Contractors Assn., Jacksonville, 1975-82, exec. dir., 1982—. Mem. Jacksonville Apprenticeship Assn. (pres. 1983—), Master Electricians Assn. (sec. 1982-83). Republican. Office: Nat Elec Contractors Assn 1295 Gulf Life Dr #19 Jacksonville FL 32207

BARNETT, LEWIS BRINKLEY, biochemistry educator; b. Lexington, Ky., Jan. 29, 1934; s. Brinkley Bobbitt and Harriett Theresa (Kinne) B.; m. Charlotte Alta Barnes, Nov. 1, 1956; children—Elizabeth Ann Barnett Notess, William, Charles, Catherine. B.S. in Chemistry, U. Ky., 1955; M.S., U. Iowa, 1957, Ph.D. in Biochemistry, 1959. NSF postdoctoral fellow U. Wis., Madison, 1959-61; Am. Heart Assn. advanced postdoctoral fellow U. Utrecht (Netherlands), 1961-63; asst. prof. biochemistry Va. Poly. Inst. and State U., Blacksburg, 1963-67, assoc. prof., 1967—, asst. dean Coll. Arts and Scis., 1984—. Chmn. Montgomery County PTA, 1971-73; mem. Blacksburg Planning Commn., 1969—, chmn., 1974, 79. NIH fellow, 1957-59. Mem. Am. Soc. Biol. Chemists, Am. Chem. Soc., Va. Acad. Sci., AAUP (pres. Va. conf. 1973-74), Phi Beta Kappa (pres. Va. Tech. chpt. 1982-83), Omicron Delta Kappa, Phi Lambda Upsilon, Sigma Xi (pres. Va. Tech. chpt. 1972-73). Presbyterian. Club: Am. Contract Bridge League (dir.). Contbr. articles to biochem. jours. Home: 303 Overlook Dr Blacksburg VA 24060 Office: College of Arts & Sciences Va Poly Inst and State U Blacksburg VA 24061

BARNETT, NED BEATTY, marketing executive, author; b. Cleve., Oct. 2, 1951; s. Richard Graham and Elaine Dolores (Beatty) B.; m. Mary Ann Lines, June 4, 1972; 1 son, Michael Andrew. A.B. with honors, U. Ga., 1973; postgrad. U. S.C., 1975-79. Spl. copywriter Provident Life and Accident Ins. Co., Chattanooga, 1973-74; editor S.C. Econ. Trends Mag., S.C. State Devel. Bd., Columbia, 1974-75; dir. pub. info. and acting dir. coll. relations Midlands Tech. Coll., Columbia, 1975-77; dir. pub. relations and mktg. Lexington County Hosp., West Columbia, S.C., 1977-80; adj. prof. Middle Tenn. State U., Murfreesboro, 1982-83; dir. pub. relations and mktg. communications Consortium Southeastern Assns., 1982-83; v.p. pub. relations and mktg. Corporate Learning Center, div. Diversified Services, Inc., subs. Tenn. Hosp. Assn., Nashville, 1982-83; regional marketing mgr. Republic Health Corp. of Dallas, Nashville, 1983—; v.p. pub. relations, consumer affairs and mktg. Tenn. Hosp. Assn., Nashville, 1980-83; cons. Holston Valley Hosp. and Med. Center, Kingsport, Tenn., 1983, Red Bank Community Hosp., Red Bank, Tenn., 1983, Unicoi County Hosp., Erwin, Tenn., 1983. Mem. pub. relations com. Middle Tenn. Diabetes Assn., 1981-82, bd. mem., 1981-82; mem. pub. relations com. Middle Tenn. Heart Assn., 1980-81; pub. relations advisor United Way Nashville, 1981-82; pub. relations dir. Lexington County Heart Assn., 1977-80. Recipient Gold Quill Writer of Yr. award Chattanooga Assn. Bus. Communicators, 1974; Art Dir. of Yr. award Kimberly-Clark, 1975; Addy award Ad Club, 1975; Publs. award So. Indsl. Devel. Council, 1976, Nation's Sch. Report, 1976; Wally awards Carolinas Hosp. Pub. Relations Soc., 1978, 79; MacEachern awards Acad. Hosp. Pub. Relations, 1980, 81, 82, 83; Gold award United Way, 1981-82; Meritorious Service award Tenn. Hosp. Assn., 1982; Gold award Allied Hosp. Assn. Pub. Relations Dirs., 1983. Mem. Pub. Relations Soc. Am. (sec. Nashville chpt. 1982), Am. Soc. Hosp. Pub. Relations (edn. com. 1980-83, co-chmn. 1982-83), Acad. Hosp. Pub. Relations, Carolinas Hosp. Pub. Relations Soc. (dir. 1979), Middle Tenn. Diabetes Assn. (mem. 1981-82, pub. relations com. 1981-83), Sigma Delta Chi-Soc. Profl. Journalists. Clubs: Lions (publicity com. chmn. Nashville chpt. 1981-82, chpt. sec. 1982-83); Internat. Plastic Modelers Soc. (editor quarterly jour. 1977-78, nat. sec. 1978-80). Author: Communications Guide, 1982; Basic Guide to Hospital Public Relations, 2d edit., 1984; also articles in profl. jours. Home: 3518 Wood Bridge Dr Nashville TN 37217 Office: Republic Health Corp 976 Murfreesboro Rd Suite 29 Nashville TN 37217

BARNETT, PATRICIA (TRICIA) ANN, public relations director; b. Culver City, Calif., Jan. 25, 1956; d. Howard Taft and Sarah Beatrice (Ross) Barnett. B.J., U. Tex., 1978. Program specialist Dallas C. of C., 1978-79, communications specialist, 1979-81; mgr. pub. relations Trailways, Inc., Dallas, 1981-82, dir. pub. relations, 1982-85; account exec. Keller Crescent, 1985—. Mem. Women in Communications, Pub. Relations Soc. Am., U. Tex.-Ex's. Office: Keller Crescent PO Box 619028 Dallas TX 75261

BARNETT, RICHARD CHAMBERS, historian, educator; b. Davenport, Fla., Apr. 27, 1932; s. Jones Richard and Helen June (Chambers) B.; m. Betty May Tribble, Oct. 18, 1957; children—Amelia Carlton, Colin Warwick. B.A., Wake Forest Coll., 1953; M.Ed., U. N.C., 1954, Ph.D., 1963. Instr., acting chmn. dept. social sci. Gardner-Webb Coll., 1956-58; instr. dept. history Wake Forest U., Winston-Salem, N.C., 1961-62, asst. prof., 1962-67, assoc. prof., 1967-76, prof., 1976—, chmn. dept. history, 1968-75, 1983—, acting dean grad. sch., 1979. Pres. Winston-Salem/Forsyth PTA, 1969-71; bd. mgrs. N.C. PTA, 1971-73, exec. com., 1972-73, life mem.; adv. com. N.C. Bd. Edn., 1973-76. Served with AUS, CIC, 1954-56. Southeastern Inst. Medieval and Renaissance Studies fellow, summer 1974. Mem. Am. Hist. Assn., AAUP, Carolinas Symposium Brit. Studies (pres. 1979-80), So. Conf. Brit. Studies (exec. com.), N.Am. Conf. Brit. Studies, Danforth Assocs. Contbg. author history and polit. sci. vols., also articles and book revs. Home: 2130 Royall Dr Winston-Salem NC 27106 Office: Wake Forest U Dept History Winston-Salem NC 27109

BARNETT, RONALD DAVID, agronomist, educator; b. Texarkana, Ark., Nov. 20, 1943; s. Herman Clark and Agnes Margaret (Nolte) B.; m. Pamela Powell, Nov. 4, 1961; children—Penny, Brad, Amy. B.S.A., U. Ark., 1965, M.S., 1968; Ph.D., Purdue U., 1970. Plant breeder, genetist U. Fla., Quincy, 1970—, asst. prof. agronomy, 1970-75, assoc. prof., 1975-83, prof., 1983—. Mem. Am. Soc. Agronomy, Crop Sci. Soc. Am., Am. Genetic Assn., AAAS, Council Agrl. Sci. and Tech. Baptist. Lodge: Rotary (pres. 1975-76). Contbr. chpt. in books, articles in field to sci. jours. Home: Rt 2 Box 186 Quincy FL 32351 Office: Univ of Fla Route 3 Box 4370 Quincy FL 32351

BARNETTE, SHEILA CLUGGISH, micropaleontologist; b. Newark, Ohio, Nov. 26, 1946; d. Earl Edward and Wanza Marie (Harris) C.; m. George Nelson Barnette, Aug. 27, 1970; 1 child, Matthew Jared. B.A. cum laude, Ohio State U., 1968. Micropaleontologist Texaco, Houston, 1969-76, Cities Service Oil Co., Houston, 1976-80; staff micropaleontologist Sohio Petroleum Co., Houston, 1980—. Mem. Soc. Econ. Paleontologists and Mineralogists (gulf coast sect.-Soc. Econ. Paleontologists and Mineralogists, sec. 1980-81), Am. Assn. Petroleum Geologists, Houston Geol. Soc., N. Am. Micropaleontological Soc. Republican. Methodist. Avocations: fossil; rock and mineral collecting; reading; travel; antique glass. Home: 2915 Tory Hill Ln Sugar Land TX 77478 Office: Sohio Petroleum Co 9401 Southwest Freeway Houston TX 77074

BARNEY, CHARLES LESTER, petroleum company executive; b. Shreveport, La., Nov. 4, 1925; s. Lester K. and Ruby Lee (Weeks) B.; B.S., Petroleum Engr., La. State U., 1949; m. Frances Jenkins, Oct. 13, 1944; children—Jerry, Charles, Merilyn. Ops. mgr. Mobil Can., 1966-66; gen. mgr., exploration and producing Mobil Germany, 1966-70; producing mgr. Mobil Internat., 1970-71, planning mgr., 1971-72, mgr., acquisitions and concessions, 1972-74; corp. producing mgr. Mobil, 1974-75; v.p. drilling and prodn. Superior Oil Co., Houston, 1975-78, sr. v.p., prodn., sales, mfg. and planning, 1978-81, also dir.; chmn. bd., chief exec. officer McIntyre Mines Ltd., Can., 1979; chmn. bd., dir. Can. Superior Oil Ltd.; pres., chief exec. officer Mark Producing Inc., Houston, 1981—. Served with USN, 1945-46. Mem. Soc. Petroleum Engrs., Mid-Continent Oil and Gas Assn. Episcopalian. Office: 675 Bering Dr Houston TX 77057

BARNHARDT, ZEB ELONZO, JR., lawyer; b. Winston-Salem, N.C., Dec. 28, 1941; s. Zeb Elonzo and Katie Sue (Taylor) B.; m. Jane Elizabeth Black, June 19, 1965; children—Daniel Black, Kathleen Martin. A.B., Duke U., 1964; J.D., Vanderbilt U., 1969. Bar: N.C. 1969. Assoc. Womble, Carlyle, Sandridge & Rice, Winston-Salem, 1969-75, ptnr., 1975—; lectr. continuing legal edn. seminars. Mem. alumni-admissions com. Duke U., 1970-72; adv. bd. Salvation Army, Winston-Salem, 1973-85, chmn. 1979-80; bd. dirs. Little Theatre Winston-Salem, 1979-85, treas., 1981-82, v.p., 1983-84, pres., 1984-85; mem. Winston-Salem Found. com., 1975-84, vice-chmn., 1979-80, chmn., 1983-84; bd. dirs. Industries for Blind, Winston-Salem, 1973-85, vice chmn., 1983-84, chmn., 1985; bd. dirs. Goodwill Industries, Winston-Salem, 1973-80, Leadership Winston-Salem, 1984—; trustee High Point Coll., 1984—. Served to lt. USNR, 1964-66. Mem. N.C. Bar Assn., Forsyth County Bar Assn., ABA, Am. Judicature Soc., Winston-Salem Jaycees (life, pres. 1973, Young Man of Yr. 1974), N.C. Jaycees (regional dir. 1974-75, legal counsel 1975-77), Greater Winston-Salem C. of C. (dir. 1973-74), Forsyth County Duke Alumni Assn. (Disting. Alumnus award 1979). Democrat. Methodist. Club: Forsyth Country. Lodge: Rotary. Home: 932 Kenleigh Circle Winston-Salem NC 27106 Office: 2400 Wachovia Bldg 301 N Main St Winston-Salem NC 27111

BARNHART, RICHARD DEE, computer science educator, consultant; b. Everett, Wash., Feb. 3, 1944; s. Dee Barnhart and Mary Margaret (Herd) Beasley; m. Kathleen Faye Strobel, Sept. 4, 1965; children—Jonathan, Christine. B.S., Whitworth Coll., 1966; M.S., U. Idaho, 1968, Ph.D., 1972. Math. prof. Bryan Coll., Dayton, Tenn., 1971-78; computer programmer KMC Co., Knoxville, Tenn., 1978-80, data processing mgr., 1980-82; software developer Mgmt. Software, Knoxville, 1982-83; assoc. prof. math. and computer scis. Liberty U., Lynchburg, Va., 1984—. Mem. Am. Math. Soc., Math. Assn. Am. Baptist. Avocations: renovating old houses; playing piano; listening to jazz and classical records. Office: Liberty U PO Box 20000 Lynchburg VA 24506

BARNHILL, DONALD EUGENE, air force officer; b. Zeigler, Ill., Aug. 8, 1922; s. Oscar Bennet and Melinda Ellen (Bullard) B.; m. Billie Deane Meshew, Nov. 22, 1940; children—Donald E. Jr., Terry Lynn, Michael J., Kimberly K., Mary Jo, Margaret A., Patricia A. Student So. Ill. U., 1939-41; D.D.S., Washington U., St. Louis, 1952. Diplomate Am. Bd. Dentistry. Dental comdr. U.S. Air Force, advanced through grades to col., 1971; served as dental comdr., tng. dir. U.S. Air Force Regional Hosp., Carswell AFB, Tex., 1972-76, 79-84, U.S. Air Force Med. Ctr., Scott AFB, Ill., 1976-79; ret., 1984. Contbr. articles to profl. jours. and numerous tng. manuals. Active in numerous civic and profl. orgns. Mem. ADA (cons. 1974-78). Republican. Roman Catholic. Club: Ridgley Country. Avocations: hunting; fishing. Home: 3817 Misty Meadow Fort Worth TX 76133

BARNHILL, MICHAEL EDWARD, geologist, consultant; b. Dothan, Ala., Apr. 22, 1956; s. Charles Edward and Mary Frances (Campbell) B.; m. Edith Grace Tyler, Nov. 12, 1983; children—Mia Campo, Tyler Edward. B.S., U. Ala., 1979; postgrad. U. Houston, 1980-81, Northeastern U., 1981-83. Geologist, Hunt Energy Corp., Houston, 1979-81, John D. Clay Exploration, Monroe, La., 1981-84; researcher Coal Research Lab., Monroe, 1983-84; geologist Ergon Exploration, Monroe, 1984—; head coal researcher Northeast La. U., Monroe, 1983-84. Mem. Am. Assn. Petroleum Geologists, Shreveport Geol. Soc., Houston Geol. Soc., Soc. Econ. Paleontologists and Mineralogists, Sigma Gamma Epsilon. Republican. Methodist. Club: Chess (Monroe). Avocations: camping; fishing; canoeing. Home: 31 Colonial Dr Monroe LA 71203 Office: Ergon Exploration PO Box 4761 Monroe LA 71211

BARNHILL, SCOTT ANDREW, law engineering testing company executive, consulting engineer; b. Norfolk, Va., July 15, 1953; s. Fabian Andrew and Regina Evelyn (Nelson) B.; m. Laurel Ennis, Sept. 18, 1983. B.S., Coll. William and Mary, 1975; M.S., Va. Poly. Inst., 1978. Registered profl. engr., Va., N.C. Project engr. Law Engring. Testing Co., Virginia Beach, Va., 1978-81, engring. dept. mgr., Chesapeake, Va., 1981-82, mgr. Norfolk office, 1982—; guest lectr. Coll. William and Mary, Williamsburg, Va., 1980. Mem. ASTM, ASCE (assoc.), Soc. Am. Mil. Engrs., City of Chesapeake C. of C., Greater Hampton Roads C. of C. Republican. Baptist. Office: Law Engring Testing Co 2220 Paramount Ave Suite 106 Chesapeake VA 23320

BARNS, DORETHA MAE CLAYTON, librarian, orgn. exec.; b. Fairmont, W.Va., Nov. 28, 1917; d. Sylvester Richard and Della Pearl (Morgan) Clayton; A.B., Fairmont State Coll., 1939; M.A., W.Va. U., 1940; B.S. in L.S., Western Res. U., 1947; m. William Derrick Barns, Sept. 3, 1947. Tchr., librarian Wetzel County (W.Va.) Schs., 1940-41, Preston County Schs., 1944-46; teaching fellow dept. English, W.Va. U., 1941-43, sec. to dean grad. sch., 1942-44, cataloguer library, 1947-48; dir., Internat. relations chmn. LWV W.Va., 1969—, 2d v.p., 1981-83. Bd. dirs. W.Va. affiliate Council of Internat. Programs, 1975—. Mem. Women's Internat. League for Peace and Freedom, Kappa Delta Pi, Nu Alpha Phi. Republican. Mem. Soc. Friends. Club: Order Eastern Star. Author: An Outline of the West Virginia Merit System, 1957; West Virginia's Interest in Foreign Trade, 1971; International Services Available to West Virginia Businesses, 1980. Home: 512 Beverly Ave Morgantown WV 26505

BARNUM, OTIS RAY, physician, consultant; b. Guymon, Okla., Apr. 16, 1951; s. Phillip R. Barnum and Jewel M. (Gross) Darnell; m. Cindy Marie Von Bargen, Nov. 25, 1983; children—Keely Lauren, Aaron Rider. B.S., U. Okla., 1973; D.O., Kansas City Coll. Osteopathic Medicine, 1977. Resident in internal medicine Tulane Sch. Medicine, New Orleans, 1977-80; chief resident USPHS Hosp., New Orleans, 1980; gen. practice medicine, Guymon, 1981—; dir. intensive care unit Meml. Hosp., Guymon, 1982—, dir. cardiac rehab., 1982—, dir. med. edn., 1982—; med. advisor Tex. County Heart Assn., Okla., 1983—. Profl. del. Hosp. Planning Com., Guymon, 1983-85. Served to lt. comdr. USPHS, 1977-80. Mem. AMA, So. Med. Assn., Nat. Am. Osteopathic Assn., Okla. Osteopathic Assn. (v.p. northwest dist. 1983), Am. Diabetes Assn. Republican. Methodist. Avocation: photography. Home: 1903 Blue Sage Dr Guymon OK 73942 Office: Meml Specialty Clinic 524 Medical Dr Guymon OK 73942

BARNWELL, JAMES CECIL, JR., business forms company executive; b. Honolulu, Hawaii, Jan. 9, 1948; s. James C. and Robin (Barth) B.; m. Sara Alice Lowe, Aug. 15, 1969 (div. Nov. 20, 1979); 1 son, Andrew Price. Student Kennesaw Coll., 1966, U. Ga., 1966-69. Sales mgr. Hammett Realty, Marietta, Ga., 1971-74; sales mgr. Pulte Home Corp., Atlanta, 1974-78; v.p., chmn. Phoenix Bus. Forms, Inc., Atlanta, 1978—. Ga. Republican party del., 1978. Named Mgr. of Yr., Pulte Home Corp., 1976-77. Served with U.S. Army, 1969-71; Vietnam. Mem. Am. Mgmt. Assn., Internat. Bus. Forms Assn. Home: 3149 Terrace Dr Marietta GA 30066 Office: Phoenix Bus Forms Inc 5599 New Peachtree Rd Atlanta GA 30341

BARON, IRA SAUL, accountant, management and tax consultant; b. Bklyn., Nov. 8, 1948; s. Morris and Janet (Loeb) B.; B.A., U. Fla., 1971. Corp. controller Community Newspapers Corp., Miami, 1971-72; v.p. Nat. Funding Corp. Am., Miami, 1971-72; mng. ptnr. Baron, Melnick & Powell, P.A., Gainesville, Fla., 1973—; v.p., chief exec. officer, dir. Hemochek Corp., Gainesville, 1984—; treas. Future tech Industries, Inc., Gainesville, 1985—; dir. Baron-Johnson, Inc., Gainesville Personnel Services, Inc., Aerofleet Corp., ARPA Brokerage, N.V. Active Ronald McDonald House of Gainesville; trustee Temple Shir Shalom of Gainesville, Mem.Internat. Assn. Fin. Planners, Am. Acctg. Assn., Gainesville Bd. Realtors, Alachua County Humane Soc., Gainesville C. of C., Com. of 100. Republican. Club: Heritage of Gainesville. Home: Spanish Grant Alachua FL 32601 Office: PO Box 14036 Gainesville FL 32604

BARON, SAMUEL, microbiologist, virologist, educator, consultant, researcher; b. Bronx, N.Y., July 27, 1928; s. Harry and Gertrude (Lipnick) B.; m. Phyllis Goodman, Feb. 4, 1951; children—Steven, Clifton, Jeffrey, Jonathan, Jody Lynn. B.A., NYU, 1948, M.D., 1952. Intern, Montefiore Hosp., Bronx, N.Y., 1952-53; postdoctoral virology research fellow U. Mich., Ann Arbor, 1953-55; virology sect., div. biol. standards, NIH, Bethesda, M.d., 1957-60; sr. surgeon Nat. Inst. Allergy and Infectious Diseases, NIH, Bethesda, 1960-67, med. dir., head. sect. cellular lab., 1968-75; prof. and chmn. dept. microbiology U. Tex., Galveston, 1975—. Recipient Henry L. Moses award USPHS, 1956, Meritorious Service award, 1970; Disting. Service award U. Tex. Med. br., 1978, Leone award, 1985; Equal Employment award NIH, 1975. Mem. Am. Assn. Immunologists, Soc. Exptl. Biology and Medicine, Am. Soc. Microbiology, Assn. Med. Sch. Microbiology Chmn., Soc. Gen. Microbiology, Sigma Si. Editor: Interferon Symposium, Medical Microbiology. Contbr. articles to profl. jours.

BARONDESS, SHIRLEY SPIEGEL, public relations executive, consultant; b. Vineland, N.J., Aug. 11, 1929; d. Jacob David and Mary (Opachinsky) Spiegel; m. Stuart H. Barondess, Apr. 1, 1955; children—David Paul, Mark Adam. Student Temple U., 1947-51. Asst. v.p. Terry Corp. of Va., Virginia Beach, 1969-74; pub. relations cons. Pembroke Realty & Ins. Agy., Inc., 1974-76; dir. pub. relations Star-Cross Corp., Virginia Beach, 1976-81; cons. pub. relations, 1982—; dir. consumer pub. relations Omni Devel. Corp. Va., Virginia Beach, 1982-84; coordinator for devels. of local builders, 1984—. Past v.p. Point O View PTA; bd. dirs. Council of Civic Orgns.; mem. Norfolk (Va.) Civic Chorus, Norfolk Symphony Orch. Aux.; mem. Va. Beach Commn. on Arts and Humanities; mem. Virginia Beach Bicentennial Commn.; bd. dirs. Virginia Beach Neptune Festival; past pres. Cath. Family and Children's Services of Tidewater; bd. dirs. Russell House, Inc., Mother Seton House, Inc. Recipient award Virginia Beach unit Am. Cancer Soc., 1968-83; award Cath. Family and Children's Services, 1975, 76, 78. Mem. Pub. Relations Soc. Am., Virginia Pub. Relations Soc., Hampton Roads Pub. Relations Soc., Tidewater Builders Assn. Jewish. Home: 100 Conference Ct Virginia Beach VA 23462

BAROODY, TERRANCE ARTHUR, furniture manufacturing company executive; b. Buffalo, N.Y., Jan. 4, 1938; s. Thomas Asa and Florence Rose (Welch) B.; m. Lorraine Belluomo, Aug. 30, 1968; children—Eden Ann, Terrance Adam. B.B.A., Georgetown U., 1959. Account exec. Dean Witter Reynolds, Phila., 1960-63, F.I. Dupont, Honolulu, 1963-68; ptnr. Fells & Baroody, N.Y.C., 1968-76; chief exec. officer Baroody Spence Furniture Industries Inc., Orange Park, Fla., 1976—. Patentee structural tee joint. Mem. Devel. Com. West Windosr Twp., Princeton Junction, N.J., 1973-76. Served with U.S. Army, 1959-65. Mem. Summer and Casual Furniture Mfrs. Assn. (dir. 1982—). Republican. Roman Catholic. Home: 2127 Foxwood Dr Orange Park FL 32073 Office: Baroody Spence Furniture Industries Inc 234 C Indsl Loop Orange Park FL 32073

BAROODY, THOMAS EDWARD, chemical company executive; b. Richmond, Va., Nov. 12, 1944; s. Edward Saliba and Ruth Catherine (Sleyman) B.; m. Vicki Lynn, Aug. 23, 1980; children—Edward Thomas, David William. B.Civil Engring., Rensselaer Poly. Inst., 1967; M.S. in Civil Engring., U. Mo., 1969. Sr. staff engr. Amax Iron Ore Corp., N.Y.C., 1973-75; sr. project engr. indsl. minerals Amax Inc., Greenwich, Conn., 1975-78, project mgr. indsl. minerals, 1978-80; mgr. engring. Amax Phosphate, Inc., Lakeland, Fla., 1980, dir. bus. planning and devel., 1980-82; v.p. Amax Chem. Corp., Lakeland, 1983—. Mem. Soc. Mining Engrs., Iron and Steel Soc., Am. Inst. Mining Engrs., Am. Inst. Chem. Engrs., Nat. Maritime Hist. Soc. Republican. Roman Catholic. Club: Imperialakes Country (Lakeland). Home: 4504 Sugartree Dr E Lakeland FL 33803 Office: Amax Chem Corp 402 S Kentucky Ave Lakeland FL 33801

BARR, GARY STANLEY, oral and maxillofacial surgeon; b. Bklyn., Jan. 7, 1946; s. Samuel and Seena (Moss) B.; m. Barbara Ann Bass, Aug. 26, 1967 (div. 1984); children—Geoffrey, Adam. Student SUNY-Buffalo, 1963-66; D.M.D., U. Pa., 1970; postgrad. Coll. Medicine and Dentistry N.J., 1972-76. Diplomate Am. Bd. Oral and Maxillofacial Surgery. Pvt. practice in oral and maxillofacial surgery, New Braunfels, Tex., 1976—. Contbr. articles to profl. jours. Served to capt. USAF, 1970-72. Fellow Am. Assn. Oral and Maxillofacial Surgeons, Am. Dental Soc. Anesthesiology; mem. ADA, New Braunfels C. of C. Jewish. Lodge: Rotary. Avocations: tennis; jogging; music. Home: 950 Moonglow New Braunfels TX 78130 Office: 705 Landa St New Braunfels TX 78130

BARR, JAMES HOUSTON, III, lawyer; b. Louisville, Nov. 2, 1941; s. James Houston and Elizabeth Hamilton (Pope) B.; m. Sara Jane Todd, Apr. 16, 1970; 1 child, Lynn Jamison. Student U. Va., 1960-63, U. Tenn., 1963-64; B.S.L., J.D., U. Louisville, 1966. Bar: Ky. 1966, U.S. Ct. Appeals (6th cir.) 1969, U.S. Supreme Ct. 1971, U.S. Ct. Mil. Appeals 1978. Law clk., Ky. Ct. Appeals, Frankfort, 1966-67; asst. atty. gen. Ky., Frankfort, 1967-71, 1979-82; asst. U.S. atty. U.S. Dept. Justice, Louisville, 1971-79, 1983—; asst. dist. counsel U.S. Army C.E., Louisville, 1982-83. Served to lt. comdr. USNR, 1967-81, to lt. col. USAR, 1981—. Mem. Fed. Bar Assn. (pres. Louisville chpt. 1975-76, Younger Fed. Lawyer award 1975), Ky. Bar Assn., Louisville Bar Assn., Soc. Colonial Wars. Republican. Episcopalian. Clubs: Pendennis, Louisville Boat, Filson (Louisville). Home: 218 Choctaw Rd Louisville KY 40207 Office: US Atty 211 US Courthouse Louisville KY 40202

BARR, MARLEEN SANDRA, English educator; b. N.Y.C., Mar. 1, 1953; d. George and Roslyn B. B.A., SUNY-Albany, 1974; M.A., U. Mich., 1975; Ph.D., SUNY-Buffalo, 1979. Asst. prof. English, Va. Poly. Inst., 1979—; Fulbright lectr. Universität Düsseldorf (W.Ger.), 1983-84. NEH grantee, 1980; recipient Pedagogy award from Women's Inst. for Freedom of the Press, 1982. Mem. MLA, Sci. Fiction Research Assn., Soc. Utopian Studies, Popular Culture Assn. Contbr. articles to profl. jours. Office: Dept English Va Poly Inst Blacksburg VA 24061

BARR, RAYMOND ARTHUR, music history educator; b. Pitcairn, Pa., Jan. 1, 1932; s. David Russell and Myrtle Jean Barr. B.S. in Music Edn., Pa. State U., 1953; M.S. in Music Edn., U. Wis., 1961, Ph.D. in Musicology, 1968. Tchr. vocal music Connellsville High Sch., Pa., 1953-58; tchr. music Scotland Sch., Chambersburg, Pa., 1958-60, Arnold High Sch., Wiesbaden, Germany, 1963-64; prof. music history SUNY-Geneseo, 1968-71; prof. music history U. Miami, Coral Gables, Fla., 1971—; music dir. Meth. Ch., South Miami, Fla., 1971—. Contbr.: Groves Dictionary of Music and Musicians, 6th edit., 1980. Recipient Dankstipendium, German Acad. Exchange Program, Berlin, 1962-64, SUNY grantee, W.Ger., 1970. Mem. Am. Musciol. Soc. (pres. so. chpt. 1979-81), Coll. Music Soc. (pres. so. chpt. 1981-83), Phi Mu Alpha (gov. 1980—). Democrat. Avocations: tennis; chess. Home: 5840 SW 57th Ave Miami FL 33143 Office: Sch of Music U Miami Coral Gables FL 33124

BARR, RICHARD STUART, management science educator; b. Austin, Tex., Sept. 3, 1943; s. Howard Raymond and Margaret (Pressler) B.; B.S. in Elec. Engring., U. Tex., Austin, 1966, M.B.A., 1972, Ph.D., 1978. Assoc. dir. Coll.

of Bus. Computer Center, U. Tex., Austin, 1968-72; exec. v.p. Analysis, Research and Computation, Inc., Austin, 1975-76; asst. prof. mgmt. sci. and computers So. Meth. U., Dallas, 1976-80, assoc. prof., 1980—; assoc. prof. ops. research and engring. mgmt., 1984—; pres. Orion Systems, Inc.; cons. Dept. Treasury, Dept. Agr., Dept. Health and Human Services; vis. fellow Dept. Treas., 1977-78; vis. scholar Princeton U., 1984. Recipient Research Excellence award So.Meth.U. Sch. Bus., 1980, Outstanding Grad. Instr. award, 1983. Mem. Assn. Computing Machinery, Inst. Mgmt. Scis., Math. Programming Soc., Ops. Research Soc. Am. Contbr. articles to profl. jours. Home: 6812 Velasco Dallas TX 75214 Office: So Meth U Sch Engring and Applied Scis Dallas TX 75275

BARRENTINE, JIMMY LLOYD, clergyman, missions administrator; b. MaGee, Miss., Oct. 4, 1946; s. Jim David and Mary Christine (Nations) B.; m. Joan Winifred Turnage, Sept. 8, 1967; children—Daniel Wayne, Jenifer Renee. B.A., Miss. Coll., Clinton, 1969; M. Divinity, Southwestern Bapt. Theol. Sem., Ft. Worth, 1972. Ordained clergyman Southern Baptist Ch., 1966. Pastor, Myrtle Springs Bapt. Ch., Hooks, Tex., 1972-75; pastor Fgn. Mission Bd., So. Bapt. Conv., Paraguay, 1975-82; dir. missions Ouachita Baptist Assn., Polk and Sevier counties, Ark., 1982-84; exec. dir. Bowie Bapt. Assn., New Boston, Tex., 1984—. Home: 103 Meadow Dr New Boston TX 75570 Office: Bowie Baptist Assn 412 Hwy 8 N New Boston TX 75570

BARRERA, ALFREDO BEN, business executive; b. Laredo, Tex., July 14, 1939; s. Alfredo Canales and Mary (Salinas) B.; m. Barbara Anne Brandes, Aug. 29, 1964; children—Lise Anne, Alfred III, Alessandra, Tessa. B.S., Oreg. State U., 1962. Sales mgr. Gen. Internat., Laredo, 1965-66; project planner Paul Garza & Assocs., Laredo, 1966-70; dir. regional planning South Tex. Devel. Council, Laredo, 1970-76; pres./mgr. Al Barrera Corp., Laredo, 1976—; dir. Ceramica Lampasos S.A., Mex.; sales cons. Ceramica Estructural Mexicana S.A., 1983—; dir. Republic Rio Gran de Mus., Laredo, 1977—; comdg. officer U.S. Naval Res., Laredo, 1967-77, 83-84. Author: Regional Parks and Recreation, 1973; Regional Historical Site Development, 1973; Regional Land Use Plan, 1974. Pres. Laredo Hist. Soc., 1977—; active City of Laredo Archtl. Rev. com., 1978—; chmn. City of Laredo Planning Commn., 1980-83; chmn./commr. Aztec Dist. Council Boy Scouts Am., 1971. Served to lt. USN, 1962-65. Recipient Civic Achievement award Laredo City Council, 1983. Mem. Am. Inst. Planners, Assn. Am. Geographers, Naval Res. Assn.; charter mem. Am. Inst. Cert. Planners. Republican. Roman Catholic. Office: PO Box 1910 100 Corpus Christi St Laredo TX 78041

BARRETT, CAROLYN JEAN HARTZ, nutritionist, educator; b. Oceanside, N.Y., July 22, 1947; d. Ernest William and Marguerite Lawrence (Sagendorph) Hartz; m. George Warren Barrett, Jr., Nov. 1, 1980; 2 children. B.S. in Biol. Health, Pa. State U., 1970; M.S. in Dietetics and Nutrition, U. Kans., 1972; M.P.H. in Nutrition, Tulane U., 1977. Intern U. Kans. Med. Ctr., Kansas City, 1971; pediatric nutritionist Frances Stern Nutrition Ctr., Boston, 1972-74; pub. health nutritionist Project Hope, Natal, Brazil, 1974-76; head nutrition sect. Div. for Disorders of Devel. and Learning U.N.C., Chapel Hill, 1977—, adj. asst. prof. dept. nutrition Sch. Pub. Health, 1980—; clin. instr. dept. pediatrics Sch. of Medicine, 1977—. Mem. Am. Dietetic Assn., Nutrition Today Soc., N.C. Dietetic Assn., Project Hope Alumni Assn., Penn State Alumni Assn., Alpha Omicron Pi. Methodist. Club: Durham-Chapel Hill Ski and Sports. Contbr. reviews, book chptrs. to profl. works in field. Home: Route 5 Storybook Farm Chapel Hill NC 27514 Office: DDDL BSRC 22OH Univ NC Chapel Hill NC 27514

BARRETT, CHARLES DAVID, technical services executive; b. Clay Center, Kans., Jan. 22, 1951; s. John Marion and Mary Ann (Sandwith) B.; m. Janet Gwen Searles; 1 child, Amy Christine. A.A.S., Tidewater Community Coll., Va., 1981. Dept. mgr. Comptek Tech. Services Inc., Virginia Beach, Va., 1976—. Served with USN, 1970-76. Avocations: reading; outdoor sports. Home: 1621 Wildwood Dr Virginia Beach VA 23454 Office: Comptek Tech Services Inc 596 Lynnhaven Pkwy Virginia Beach VA 23452

BARRETT, EDWARD, geologist; b. West Frankfort, Ill., Jan. 26, 1921; s. Edward and Margaret Wilhelmina (Stefan) B.; student So. Ill. U.; B.S., U. Nebr., 1948; m. Valerie Louise Horvat, Jan. 14, 1957; children—Monica Lisa, Jeb Elia. Sr. geologist Conoco, Oklahoma City, 1948-70; v.p. Duplin Corp., Oklahoma City, 1970-78; pres. Monjeb Minerals, Inc., Oklahoma City, 1978-81, exec. v.p., 1981-83. Vice mayor City of Warr Acres (Okla.), 1959-67, mayor, 1967-69. Served with USAAF, 1942-45. Fellow AAAS, Geol. Soc. Am.; mem. Phi Beta Kappa, Sigma Xi, Sigma Gamma Epsilon. Contbr. in field. Home: 5705 N MacArthur Blvd Oklahoma City OK 73122 Office: Fifty-Six Expressway Pl 5601 NW 72d St Suite 300 Oklahoma City OK 73132

BARRETT, JAMES EMMETT, insurance company executive; b. Omaha, May 30, 1923; s. John C. and Elizabeth M. (Wilson) B.; LL.B., Creighton U., 1948; m. Mary Ann Forsyth, Oct. 20, 1944; children—Mary Margaret Barrett Slye, Susan Elizabeth Barrett Kozlowski, Joanne Barrett Gates, James Emmett. Admitted to Nebr. bar, 1948; with Mut. of Omaha Ins. Co., 1948—, v.p., 1959-65, exec. v.p., 1965—; vice chmn. bd. dirs. Tele-Trip Co., Inc., Omaha, 1964—; dir. Companion Life Ins. Co., N.Y.C. Mem. Greater Washington Bd. Trade; pres.'s council Creighton U.; founding pres., dir. U.S. Phys. Edn. and Sport Devel. Found.; trustee Behrend Found., Washington; trustee Nat. Capital chpt. Nat. Multiple Sclerosis Soc., chmn., 1973-78, nat. conf. chmn., 1976; bd. dirs. The Heights Sch., Washington, 1974-78; bd. dirs. Marymount Coll. of Va., Arlington; trustee Am. U., Washington; bd. govs. USO, Inc., chmn. exec. com., 1977-78, pres., 1978-82; v.p. USO of Met. Washington; dir. USO Met. N.Y., USO Central Md. Served as officer, inf., AUS, World War II; ETO. Decorated chevalier de grace Ordre Souverain Militaire et Hospitalier de St. Thomas d'Acre (Rome); recipient Community Service award Sales and Mktg. Execs. Washington, 1978; Hope Chest award Nat. Multiple Sclerosis Soc., 1980; Four Seasons award, 1981; D.C. Community Service award, 1981; named to Hall of Fame, Infantry Officer Candidate Sch., 1982; Bess Goodman Humanitarian award, 1982; Disting. Service award Nat. Assn. Health Underwriters, 1984; Presdl. summer jobs award, 1984; Honor award Fleet Res. Assn., 1984. Mem. Health Ins. Assn. Am. (dir. 1966-68; nat. health care programs com.; chmn. task force vets. affairs), Am., Fed., Nebr. bar assns., Nebr. Soc. Washington (pres. 1962), HEROES, Inc. (charter), C. of C. U.S. (health care com. 1974-79, 84—), Washington Inst. Fgn. Affairs, Nat. Assembly of Nat. Voluntary Health and Social Welfare Orgns. Inc. (colleague 1979-82), Delta Theta Phi, Alpha Sigma Nu. Clubs: F Street Capitol Hill, Met. (Washington). Home: Old Post Farm Route 2 Box 206A Edinburg VA 22824 Office: 1700 Pennsylvania Ave NW Washington DC 20006

BARRETT, JOHN RICHARD, lawyer; b. N.Y.C., Nov. 26, 1928; m. Marie Louise Barrett; children—William, Brian. B.A. cum laude, Notre Dame U., 1952; J.D., U. Va., 1955. Bar: Va. 1955, Fla. 1957, U.S. Dist. Ct. (so. dist.) Fla. 1961, U.S. Supreme Ct. 1972, U.S. Ct. Appeals (5th and 11th cir.) 1981. Legal asst. to chief judge N.Y. Ct. Appeals, 1955-56; corp. counsel Gen. Aniline & Film Corp., N.Y.C., 1957; mcpl. judge City Miami (Fla.), 1959-63; city atty. Miami, 1963-66; sr. ptnr. Barrett & Rogers, P.A. and predecessor, Miami, 1974—; chmn. grievance com. Fla. Bar 1967-70. Mem. administrv. bd. trustees, gen. counsel St. Thomas U., 1981—; bd. dirs. Greater Miami Philharmonic Soc., Inc., 1968-69; mem. diocesan bd. edn. Roman Cath. So. Diocese, 1967-71; v.p. bd. dirs. Miami Chamber Symphony, 1982—; trustee Miami Country Day Prep. Sch., 1981—. Mem. ABA (antitrust com., adminstrv. law com.), Fla. Bar Assn. (chmn. grievance com. 1967-70), Dade County Bar Assn. (med. professions liaison com.), Fed. Bar Assn., Am. Judicature Soc., Am. Judges Assn., Fla. Bar Found. Office: 100 N Biscayne Blvd 7th Fl Miami FL 33132

BARRETT, KENNETH RICHARD, telephone company executive, investments firm executive; b. New Orleans, May 4, 1952; s. Glenn Burdette and Maude Marie (Gregory) B.; m. Doreen Ann Curet, Nov. 30, 1979 (div. Sept. 1985); children—Chad William, Dawn Michelle. B.B.A., U. Houston, 1974. Computer attendant S. Central Bell, New Orleans, 1974—; pres., founder BCD Investments, Violet, La., 1982—. Sustaining mem. Republican Nat. Com., 1981—. Recipient Presdl. Achievement award Rep. Party, 1980, Project Life award Sta. WWL-TV, New Orleans, 1968. Mem. Communications Workers Am. (exec. bd. local chpt. 1974-79, Outstanding Mem. award 1977, Outstanding Steward award 1980), Nat. Wildlife Fedn., Northshore Animal League, Tenn. Squires Club. Roman Catholic. Lodge: Kiwanis. Avocations: football; baseball; bowling; golf; tennis. Home: PO Box 617 2817 Reunion Dr Violet LA 70092 Office: S Central Bell Co 6767 Bundy Rd New Orleans LA 70140

BARRETT, LARRY JAMES, real estate management company executive; b. Fayetteville, N.C., July 15, 1943; s. James Chalmus and Nancy Estelle (Parham) B.; m. Carol Sottile, Aug. 10, 1968; children—Brantlee Sottile, Francis Chalmus, Allison Estelle. B.S., U. S.C., 1965. Cert. property mgr. Account exec. News & Observer, Raleigh, N.C., 1965-69; gen. mgr. Pastime Amusement Co., Charleston, S.C., 1969-72; exec. v.p. Rental Property Mgmt. Co., Charleston, 1972—; cons. The Beach Co., Charleston, 1972—. Chmn. Isle of Palms (S.C.) Recreation Com., 1982—; mem. Isle of Palms Planning Commn., 1982—; treas. Sullivan Island (S.C.) PTA, 1981-83; v.p. Stella Maris Sch. Bd., Mt. Pleasant, S.C., 1979-81; coach youth baseball and football, Mt. Pleasant, 1970—. Mem. Inst. Real Estate Mgmt. (pres. S.C. chpt. 1982), Nat. Assn. Realtors, Greater Charleston Bd. Realtors, Southeastern Assn. HUD Mng. Agts. Democrat. Roman Catholic. Clubs: Exchange (Charleston); Sport Fishing, Beach Combers (Isle of Palms). Home: 296 Forest Trail Isle of Palms SC 29451 Office: Rental Property Mgmt Inc 10-A Courthouse Sq Charleston SC 29401

BARRINGER, PAUL BRANDON, II, lumber company executive; b. Sumter, S.C., Aug. 22, 1930; s. Victor Clay and Gertrude (Hampton) B.; B.S., U. Va., 1952; postgrad. George Washington U., 1954; m. Merrill Underwood, May 27, 1957; children—Merrill U., Victor Clay, Ann Hampton. With Human Relations Lab., Washington, 1954; with Coastal Lumber Co., Weldon, N.C., 1954—, pres., treas., dir., 1967—; 1st v.p., dir. exec. com. State Record Co., Columbia, S.C., 1966—, Gulf Pub. Co., Biloxi, Miss., 1967; dir. Sun Pub. Co., Newberry Pub. Co., Branch Corp., Wilson, N.C., Branch Banking & Trust Co., State Printing Co., Columbia Newspapers Inc., State Telecasting Co. Inc. Trustee, mem. exec. com. Louisburg Coll.; trustee Brandon Ednl. Found.; mem. St. Catherine's bd. govs., Richmond, Va.; mem. Pres.'s Task Force Internat. Pvt. Enterprise, 1983—. Served with USAF, 1952-54. Mem. Young Pres. Orgn. (chmn. rebel chpt.), N.C. Forestry Assn. (dir.), NAM (dir.), N.C. Forestry Found., Zeta Psi, Sigma Delta Psi, Lambda Chi. Episcopalian. Clubs: Sea Pines Plantation, Summitt, Chockoyotte Country, Farmington Country, Augusta Athletic, Downtown. Home: Country Club Rd Weldon NC 27890 Office: PO Box 829 Weldon NC 27890 also Coastal Lumber Co Elm St Extension Weldon NC 27890

BARRINGTON, BRUCE DAVID, corporate executive; b. Chgo., Apr. 9, 1942; s. Arthur Richard and Lorene Cora (Powell) B.; B.S. in Math., Bradley U., 1964; m. Gayle Marguerite Wilcoxen, June, 1970; children—Arthur Richard, II, Kenneth Alan, Paige Marguerite. Systems analyst Caterpillar Tractor Co., Peoria, Ill., 1965-67; mgr. hosp. systems devel. McDonnell Douglas Automation Co., Peoria, 1967-73; founder, dir. HBO & Co., Atlanta, 1973-83; mng. ptnr. Barrington Group; owner Hawk's Cay Resort; chmn. Barrington Systems, Inc., Barrington Aviation Inc., dir. Internat. Food Equipment Inc. Trustee Bradley U.; bd. dirs. Pine Crest Sch. Named Centurian Disting. Alumnus Bradley U., 1985. Clubs: Country of Peoria; Lighthouse Point (Fla.) Yacht and Racquet, Adios Golf, Boca Raton Country, Country of Coral Springs. Office: 150 E Sample Rd Suite 200 Pompano Beach FL 33064

BARRITT, EVELYN RUTH BERRYMAN, nurse, educator, university dean; b. Detroit, Sept. 4, 1929; d. George C. and Ruby (Mathews) Berryman; A.A., Graceland Coll., 1949; diploma Independence (Mo.) Sanitarium and Hosp. Sch. Nursing, 1952; B.S., Ohio State U., 1956, M.A., 1962, Ph.D., 1971; m. Ward LeRoy Barritt, Oct. 28, 1951; 1 dau., Kelli Jo. Asst. instr. nursing Atlantic City Hosp., 1952-53; staff nurse Shore Meml. Hosp., Somers Point, N.J., 1953-54, Ohio State U. Hosp., Columbus, 1954-55; instr. White Cross Hosp., Columbus, 1955-57; assoc. dir. nursing service Riverside Meth. Hosp., Columbus, 1957-64; asst. exec. dir. Ohio Nurses Assn., Columbus, 1964-65; dean Capital U. Sch. Nursing, Columbus, 1965-72; dean Coll. Nursing U. Iowa, Iowa City, 1972-80, prof. nursing, 1972-80; dean, prof. Sch. of Nursing, U. Miami (Fla.), 1980—. Mem. Am., Ohio (pres. dist. 1966-68), Iowa nurses assns., Nat. League Nursing, Graceland Coll. Alumni Assn., Am. Assn. Higher Edn., Am. Assn. Colls. Nursing (pres. 1976-78), Independence Hosp. Sch. Nursing Alumnae Assn., Iowa, Johnson County women's polit. caucuses. Author: Florence Nightingale: Her Wit and Wisdom, 1975; contbr. articles to profl. jours. Address: 15001 SW 69th Ct Miami FL 33124

BARRON, DEMPSEY J., state senator; b. Andalusia, Ala., Mar. 5, 1922; s. Jessie Carl and Minnie (Brown) B.; m. Louverne Hall, Jan. 27, 1952; children—Stephen D., Stuart J. B.S., Fla. State U.; J.D., U. Fla. Atty. firm Barron, Redding, Boggs & Hughes, 1954—; owner D-Bar ranch.; Mem. Fla. Ho. of Reps., 1956-60; mem. Fla. senate, 1960—, pres. pro tem, 1967-68, pres., 1975-76. Served with USN, 1942-47; PTO, ETO. Mem. Panama City-Bay County C. of C., Fla. Bar, ABA, Nat. Soc. State Legislators. Methodist. Named one of 10 outstanding mems. Fla. legislature by press, 1957-83. Home: 2311 Magnolia Dr Panama City FL 32407 Office: PO Box 1638 Panama City FL 32401

BARRON, JOHN MARSHALL, spice company executive; b. New Marshfield, Ohio, May 19, 1912; s. Joseph Cephus and Nettie (Stewart) B.; m. Evelyn Joan McRill, Mar. 1, 1961; children—Patricia, Virginia, Karen, Beverly, Allona. Student Mountain State Coll., 1930-32; B.B.A., Ohio U., 1933. Tchr., New Marshfield High Sch., 1933-34; sales mgr. F.J. Beasley Co., Athens, Ohio, 1934-38; sales and advt. mgr. David Kirk Sons Co., Findlay, Ohio, 1938-47; dist. mgr. Woolson Spice Co., Toledo, 1947-61, v.p. sales, also dir., 1961-66; sales mgr. Baker Importing div. and Mut. Spice div. Hygrade Food Products, Detroit, 1966-69; account exec. Frank Tea and Spice Co., Cin., 1969-74, v.p., sales mgr., dir. Spicecraft, Inc., St. Louis, 1974-84; v.p., sales mgr. Colonial Spice Co., Bklyn., 1984—; v.p., sales mgr. Dorothy Dawson's Foods, Inc., Jackson, Mich., 1984—. Sec.-treas. New Marshfield, Bd. Edn., 1935-38. Served to lt. comdr. USNR, World War II; tire and gasoline rationing officer half of Island of Oahu (Hawaii), 1943, 44. Mem. Res. Officers Assn. U.S., Am. Legion. Baptist. Lodges: Masons, Scottish Rite, Shriners, Kiwanis, Sertoma (pres. 1940-41). Home: 3011 SE Aster Lane Condo 806 Stuart FL 33497

BARRON, JOHN WILLARD, pharmaceutical company executive, pharmacist; b. Marksville, La., Jan. 7, 1931; s. Estine and Theresa (Brouillette) B.; m. Carmel Clair Newton, Sept. 23, 1951; children—Brenda Joan, John Mark, David Lawrence. B.S. in Pharmacy, Loyola U., New Orleans, 1952, Pharm.D., 1982. Registered pharmacist, La. Co-owner, Profl. Pharmacy, Baton Rouge, 1959-64; med. service rep. Burroughs Wellcome Co., Alexandria and Lafayette, La., 1964-69, dist. sales mgr., 1969-71, sales mgr. Wellcome Diagnostics div., 1971-73, dir. Wellcome Diagnostics div., 1975—. Served to capt. Med. Service Corps, U.S. Army, 1952-59. Mem. Am. Mktg. Assn., Bio-Med. Mktg. Assn. (dir. 1983), La. Pharmacists Assn. Republican. Roman Catholic. Home: 1607 Greenleaf St Apex NC 27502 Office: 3030 Cornwallis Rd Research Triangle Park NC 27709

BARRON, ORAN JAMES, JR., rancher; b. Athens, Tex., May 29, 1916; s. Oran James and Mavit (Hardin) B.; student U. Ariz., 1933, Tex. Western U., 1934-35; m. Eleonora Prudence Swenson, Feb. 20, 1942; children—Oran James III, Helen Mavit (Mrs. Ronald Day), Amanda Hope (Mrs. Kevin Coyle). Owner Spur Hdqrs. Ranch, Spur Tex., 1946—; pres. Caprock Telephone Co. Inc., Spur 1955—, Tongue River Ranch Corp., 1978—; dir. Swenson Land & Cattle Co., N.Y.C., 1959-78. Mem. Tex. Water Resources Research Adv. Com., 1968-71; mem. Tex. Brush and Range Improvement Com., 1969—; mem. Tex. Agrl. Water Com., 1972—, pres., 1973—; chmn. Beef Devel. Task Force, 1974-77; mem. Gov.'s Agribus. Adv. Com., 1979-82. Chmn. Dickens County (Tex.) Bd. Edn., 1956-78; pres. Dickens County Water Control and Improvement Dist. 1, 1962-70; dir. Tex. Exptl. Ranch Com., 1958—. Served to maj. AUS, 1941-45. Decorated Bronze Star with oak leaf cluster; recipient Cert. of Appreciation, Range Tng. Program, Tex. Christian U.; Gerald W. Thomas award for outstanding agriculturist Tex. Tech. U., 1975; named Man of Yr. in service to agr. in Tex., Progressive Farmer, 1981. Mem. Am. Soc. Animal Sci., Am. Soc. Range Mgmt. (Outstanding Range Man award Tex. sect. 1972), Tex. Cattle Feeders Assn. (dir. 1967-82, treas. 1972-73, 1st v.p. 1974-75, pres. 1976-77), Nat. Cattlemen's Assn. (dir. 1974-78, Spl. Breed award 1984), Nat. Livestock and Meat Bd. (dir. 1975-82), Am. Simmental Assn. (hon. life). Club: Block and Bridle (hon. mem. 1967). Address: Route 1 Spur TX 79370

BARRON, RAYMOND FRANK, financial services executive; b. Clifton, N.J., June 5, 1925; s. Joseph Arthur and Lydia Emily (Pojar) B.; m. Lee Ainsworth, Dec. 30, 1950; children—Raymond Ainsworth, Christie Lee. Student Albany Bus. Coll., 1941-42, Sienna Coll., 1946-49, Seton Hall U., 1951-52; B.B.A., Rutgers U., 1954. Cert. fin. planner. Regional mgr. Hayden Stone, Miami Beach, Fla., 1959-62; mgr. Thomson, McKinnon, Miami Shores, Fla., 1962-78; v.p., mgr. Dean Witter Reynolds, Miami Shores, 1978—; cons. trust dept. Little River Bank, Miami, 1962-71, Miami Shores 1st Nat. Bank, 1962-73. Bd. dirs. YMCA, North Miami, Fla., 1965-67. Served to 1st lt. USAF, 1942-46. Mem. Coll. Fin. Planning (exam. supr. 1977-78), Internat. Assn. Fin. Planners. Republican. Episcopalian. Club: Miami Shores Country. Lodge: Masons. Home: 14351 S Biscayne River Dr Miami FL 33161 Office: Dean Witter Reynolds Inc 9600 NE 2d Ave Miami Shores FL 33138

BARROW, LEE G(ORDON), music educator; b. Atlanta, Jan. 7, 1952; s. J. Gordon and Janie Rae (Cook) B.; m. Cathy Anne Mickle, Sept. 18, 1971. Mus.B., Samford U., 1974; Mus.M., Fla. State U., 1979; postgrad. U. Miami, 1981—. Asst. prof., dir. music program South Ga. Coll., Douglas, 1979—; dir. Douglas Community Chorus, 1979—; dir. Douglas Community Theatre, 1981—, pres., 1982-83. Mem. Am. Choral Dirs. Assn., Coll. Music Soc., Ga. Assn. Music Theorists, Ga. Music Educators Assn., Music Educators Nat. Conf., Pi Kappa Lambda. Baptist. Club: Douglas Music. Dir., music dir. numerous mus. theatre prodns. Office: Music Dept South Ga Coll Douglas GA 31533

BARROW, THOMAS DAVIES, oil and mining company executive; b. San Antonio, Dec. 27, 1924; s. Leonidas Theodore and Laura Editha (Thomson) B.; m. Janice Meredith Hood, Sept., 16, 1950; children—Theodore Hood, Kenneth Thomson, Barbara Loyd, Elizabeth Ann. B.S., U. Tex., 1945, M.A., 1948; Ph.D., Stanford U., 1953; grad. Advanced Mgmt. Program, Harvard U., 1963. With Humble Oil and Refining Co., 1951-72, regional exploration mgr., New Orleans, 1962-64, exec. v.p., dir. Esso Exploration, Inc., 1964-65, dir. 1965-72, sr. v.p., 1967-70, pres., 1970-72; sr. v.p. dir. Exxon Corp., N.Y.C., 1972-78; chmn., chief exec. officer Kennecott Corp., Stamford, Conn., 1978-81; vice chmn. Standard Oil Co. (Ohio), 1981-85, also dir. mem. Commn. Natural Resources, NRC, 1973-78, com. phys. scis. and math., 1983—; dir. Tex. Commerce Bankshares, Am. Gen. Corp., Cameron Iron Works, McDermott Internat., Inc. Trustee Woods Hole Oceanographic Instn., 20th Century Fund-Task Force on U.S. Energy Policy; trustee Am. Mus. Natural History, Stanford U.; bd. dirs. Baylor Coll. Medicine, Tex. Med. Ctr.; chmn. bd. dirs. Houston Grand Opera, 1985—. Served with USNR, 1943-46. Recipient Disting. Achievement award Offshore Tech. Conf., 1973; Disting. Engring. Grad. award U. Tex., 1970, Disting. Alumnus award, 1972, Disting. Grad. Sch. Geol. Scis., 1985; named Chief Exec. of Yr. in Mining Industry, 1979. Fellow N.Y. Acad. Scis.; mem. Nat. Acad. Engring., Am. Mining Congress (bd. dirs. 1978-85, vice chmn. 1984-85), Am. Assn. Petroleum Geologists, Geol. Soc. Am., Internat. Copper Research Assn. (dir.), Nat. Ocean Industry Assn. (dir.), AAAS, Am. Soc. Oceanography (pres. 1970-71), Am. Geophys. Union, Am. Petroleum Inst., Am. Geol. Soc., Sigma Xi, Tau Beta Pi, Sigma Gamma Epsilon, Phi Eta Sigma, Alpha Tau Omega. Episcopalian. Clubs: Clove Valley; Houston Country; Petroleum; Ramada; River Oaks Country. Home: 911 Briar Ridge Dr Houston TX 77057 Office: 1010 Lamar Suite 400 Houston TX 77002

BARRY, HELEN BRYANT, psychotherapist, hynotherapist; b. Baden, N.C., July 9, 1918; d. Walter Royce and Ola Myrtle (Johnson) Bryant; m. John Andral Barry, Jr., Aug. 4, 1942; children—Ann Royce Barry Wright, Mary Helen Barry Siegling. B.A., Winthrop Coll., 1935; M.A., Furman U., 1954; Ph.D., Internat. Grad. U., Leysin, Switzerland, 1976. Prof. psychology Belmont Coll., Nashville, 1960-65; chmn. dept. psychology Baptist Coll., Charleston, S.C., 1965-83; practice clin. psychology, Sullivan's Island, S.C., 1983—. Author: Royston, 1984. Contbr. articles to profl. jours. Mem. Am. Psychol. Assn., Am. Assn. Marriage and Family Therapy, Am. Soc. Clin. Hypnosis, Soc. Clin. and Exptl. Hypnosis, AAAS. Democrat. Baptist. Avocations: writing, speaking, reading sketching. Home and Office: 2907 Marshall Blvd Sullivan's Island SC 29482

BARRY, MARY EILEEN, fashion merchandising educator, consultant; b. Hartford, Conn., Nov. 13, 1931; d. Richard Joseph and Mary Eleanor (Mahoney) B. B.S. in Home Econs. and Econs., St. Joseph Coll., 1953; M.S. in Retailing, N.Y. U., 1954; Ed.D. in Vocat. Edn.-Distributive Edn., Temple U., 1974. Buyer G. Fox & Co., Hartford, 1956-69; fashion merchandising coordinator Pa. State U.-Scranton, 1969-73; assoc. prof. consumer affairs dept. Auburn (Ala.) U., 1973—, cons. world prodn. and distbn. textiles and apparel; book and manuscript reviewer; mem. fiber, textiles and apparel panel, com. on tech. and internat. econ. and trade issues Office of Fgn. Sec., Nat. Acad. Engring.; mem. NRC Commn. on Engring. and Tech. Systems, 1980-82; mem. bus. research adv. com. Bur. Labor Stats., Dept. Labor, 1980—; expert witness Consumer Product Safety Commn., 1983. Mem. Assn. Coll. Profs. Textiles and Clothing (chairperson com. pub. relations 1980-84, chairperson overall program nat. meeting 1980), Acad. Internat. Bus., World Future Soc. Contbg. author: Know Your Merchandise, 1981; contbr. articles to profl. publs. Home: Route 3 Box 287 Dadeville AL 36853 Office: Dept Consumer Affairs Sch Home Econs Auburn U Auburn AL 36849

BARRY, RICHARD FRANCIS, III, newspaper publisher; b. Norfolk, Va., Jan. 18, 1943; s. Richard F. and Mary Margaret (Perry) B.; B.A., LaSalle Coll., 1964; J.D., U. Va., 1967; m. Carolyn Ann Kennett. Aug. 7, 1965; children—Carolyn Michelle, Christopher David. Bar: Va. 1967. Assoc. firm Kaufman & Canoles, Norfolk, 1967-71, ptnr., 1972-73; corp. sec. Landmark Communications, Inc., Norfolk, 1973-74; pres., gen. mgr. Roanoke (Va.) Times & World-News, 1974-76, The Virginian-Pilot and The Ledger-Star, Norfolk, 1976-78, exec. officer, pub., 1983—; pres., dir. Landmark Communications, Inc., Norfolk, 1978—; dir. Greensboro News Co., Times-World Corp., Telecable Corp. Bd. dirs. Norfolk State U. Found., Chrysler Mus.; pres. United Way of South Hampton Roads, 1984—. Mem. Am. Newspaper Pubs. Assn., (govt. affairs com.), 1978—. Office: 150 W Brambleton Ave Norfolk VA 23510

BARTELS, GEORGE THOMAS, physician, obesity researcher; b. Wilmington, Del., Jan. 14, 1954; s. George William and Helen Anna (MacFarland) B.; m. Susan Elizabeth Haney, July 27, 1979; children—Elizabeth, Laura Paige. A.B. in Psychology, U. N.C., 1975; M.D., Duke U., 1978. Intern Tallahassee Regional Med. Ctr., 1979, resident, 1979-80; med. dir. Bartels Clinic, Garner, N.C., 1981—; mem. staff Wake Med. Ctr., Raleigh, N.C., Raleigh Community Hosp. Mem. AMA (Physician's Recognition award 1983), Am. Soc. Bariatric Physicians, N.C. Med. Soc., Wake County Med. Soc., Am. Acad. Family Physicians, Phi Beta Kappa, Alpha Epsilon Delta. Presbyterian. Office: Bartels Clinic 1201 Aversboro Rd Garner NC 27529

BARTELS, GERALD LEE, association executive; b. Omaha, Dec. 28, 1931; s. Emil Frank and Mable Anna (Denker) B.; children—Susan Bartels Reid, Jeri Bartels Blair. B.A. cum laude, Midland Coll., 1953. Cert. chamber exec. Dir. publicity Wittenberg U., Springfield, Ohio, 1955-56; Eastern projects mgr. Harry Krusz & Co., Lincoln, Nebr., 1956-59; gen. mgr. St. Paul Area C. of C., 1959-63; exec. v.p. Greater Macon C. of C., Ga., 1963-65; pres. Shrimp Boats, Inc., Macon, 1965-67; exec. v.p. Greater Greenville C. of C., S.C., 1967-76, Jacksonville C. of C., Fla., 1976-83, Atlanta C. of C., 1983—. Bd. dirs. Pendleton Manor, Inc., Greenville. Served with U.S. Army, 1953-55. Recipient Gov. Nebr.'s award 1982; named Man of Yr., Greenville Downtown Council, 1975, Elks Club, 1978. Mem. Am. C. of C. Execs. (chmn. 1982-83), So. Assn. Chamber Execs., Fla. C. of C. Execs. (dir. 1979-82), Ga. C. of C. Execs. (dir. 1985-87), S.C. C. of C. Execs. (pres. 1971). Episcopalian. Clubs: Commerce, Poinsett. Lodge: Rotary. Office: Atlanta C of C 1300 Omni Internat S Atlanta GA 30303

BARTELT, MARTIN WILLIAM, mathematics educator, researcher; b. Bklyn., Apr. 4, 1941; s. George William and Nellie (Petersen) B.; m. Gay Helen Penfield, Jan. 23, 1965; children—Andrew, Margaret. B.A., Hofstra U., 1963; M.A., U. Wis., 1965, Ph.D., 1969. Asst. prof. Rensselaer Poly. Inst., Troy, N.Y., 1969-75; vis. asst. prof. U. R.I., Kingston, 1973-74; asst. to assoc. prof. Christopher Newport Coll., Newport News, Va., 1975-83, prof., 1983—. Contbr. articles to Jour Approximation Theory, others. Mem. Am. Math. Soc. Home: 465 Winterhaven Dr Newport News VA 23606 Office: Christopher Newport College 50 Shoe Ln Newport News VA 23606

BARTH, ALF OTTO, architect, city official; b. Risor, Norway, Aug. 5, 1921; s. Haakon Hjalmar and Emilie (Evensen) B.; came to U.S., 1929, naturalized, 1943; B.Arch. with honors, U. Fla., 1953; m. Mary Jayne Ingram, Apr. 28, 1951; children—Kathleen Elizabeth, Paul Haakon. Architect, dir. sch. planning Polk County, Fla., 1956-60; assoc. dir. sch. planning Dade County, Fla., 1960-64; coordinating architect Orange County (Fla.) Schs., 1964-65; architect in charge Charles W. Cole & Son, South Bend, Ind., 1966; chief architect Dade County, 1968-79; prin. architect Metro Transit Authority, Dade County, 1979-81; chief bldg. ofcl. City of Coral Gables (Fla.), 1982—; cons. architect, 1956—; prin. works include Oakland Elementary Sch., Haines City, Fla., 1960;

Sanctuary for Grace Luth. Ch., Winter Haven, Fla., 1960, ednl. bldg., 1967; addition Redeemer Luth. Ch., Miami Shores, Fla., 1961; Immanuel Luth. Ch., Tavernier, Fla., 1967; ednl. bldg. Concordia Luth. Ch., Miami, 1966. Chmn. Dade County Archtl. Selection Com., 1968-74, Dade County Archtl. Certification Com., 1974-79; mem. S. Fla. Bldg. Ofcls. Council. Bd. dirs. Eastridge Retirement Village, Miami, 1963-64; mem. Dade County Transit Advisory Com., 1974-79. Served with USNR, 1943-46; U.S. Army, 1947-50. Mem. AIA (dir. local chpt. 1964), Nat. Council Archtl. Registration Bds., Am. Arbitration Assn., Am. Pub. Works Assn., Gargoyle (historian), Phi Kappa Phi. Lutheran (chmn. trustees 1961-65). Lodges: Masons, Odd Fellows. Home: 7581 SW 58th St Miami FL 33143 Office: 405 Biltmore Way Coral Gables FL 33134

BARTHELEMY, SIDNEY JOHN, mayor; b. New Orleans, Mar. 17, 1942; s. Lionel and Ruth (Fernandez) B.; m. Michaele Thibodeaux, 1968; children—Cherrie Ann, Bridget, Sidney Jr. Student Epiphany Apostolic Jr. Coll., 1960-63; B.A., St. Joseph Sem., 1967; M.S.W., Tulane U., 1971. Adminstrv. asst. CEP, 1967-69; dir. Parent-Child Ctr., Family Health Inc., 1969-71; tutor-counselor coordinator labor edn. Urban League of New Orleans, 1969-72; dir. social service Parent Child Devel. Ctr., 1971-72; dir. Dept. Welfare, New Orleans, 1972-74; asst. dir. Urbinvolve Program, Xavier U., 1974—; mem. La. State Senate, 1974-78; councilman at large New Orleans City Council; mayor City of New Orleans, 1986—. Mem. Orleans Parish Democratic Exec. Com. Recipient Community Service award Desire Community Ctr., La. Women's Polit. Caucus Achievement award, Outstanding Black Achievement award. Mem. Family Service Soc. Roman Catholic. Office: Office of Mayor 1300 Perdido St Room 2E10 New Orleans LA 70112*

BARTLETT, MICHAEL SHOFNER, pharmaceutical company executive consultant; b. Shelbyville, Tenn., Nov. 22, 1954; s. Ottie and Emily Johnston (Shofner) B. B.S. in Biology, Middle Tenn. State U., 1977, B.S. in Agr., 1977, postgrad. in Bus. Adminstrn., 1978-79. Supr. quality assurance Swan Drugs div. CMC, Inc., Smyrna, Tenn., 1978-79, asst. mgr. quality assurance, 1979-80, mgr. quality assurance, 1980-81; supr. quality assurance Key Pharms., Inc., Miami, Fla., 1981-82, prodn. mgr., 1982—; cons. Orgn. of Quality Assurance Depts., 1981—. Mem. Am. Soc. Quality Control (regional dir. 1983, exec. com. 1982, govt. com. 1982), Kappa Alpha. Republican. Methodist. Club: Nat. Grotto. Home: PO Box 69-3431 Miami FL 33169 Office: Key Pharms Inc 50 NW 176th St Miami FL 33167

BARTLETT, STEVE, congressman; b. Los Angeles, Sept. 19, 1947; m. Gail Coke, 1969; children—Allison, Courtney, Brian. B.A., U. Tex., 1971. Businessman; mem. 98th Congress from 3d Dist. Tex., mem. exec. com. Rep. study com., co-chmn. edn. policy task force, ranking Rep. select edn. subcom. Mem. Dallas City Council, 1977-81; mem. Bd. Dental Health Programs. Mem. North Dallas C. of C., Neighborhood Housing Services of Dallas, Birthright, Inc. Republican. Office: 1233 Longworth House Office Bldg Washington DC 20515

BARTLEY, DAVID ANTHONY, electronics executive; b. Connellsville, Pa., Apr. 5, 1946; s. Anthony Eugene and Dorothy Charlotte (Hilliard) B.; m. Anna Luralene Smith, June 25, 1969 (div. Nov. 1977); 1 child, Marva Joanna. Student bus. adminstrn. Alderson-Broaddus Coll., 1964-65, Fairmont State Coll., 1965-66. Mech. designer Tex. Instruments Co., Dallas, 1966-70; sales rep. Multi-Plate Co., Inc., Dallas, 1970-74, v.p., gen. mgr., 1974-81, pres., 1981—. Mem. Ctr. Entrepreneurial Mgmt., Am. Mgmt. Assn., Am. Electronics Assn., Dallas C. of C. Republican. Lutheran. Office: 2362 Lu Field Rd Dallas TX 75229

BARTLEY, JERALD HOWARD, remote sensing exploration, independent oil operator, geologist; b. Springtown, Tex., Nov. 25, 1913; s. Hugh Thomas and Emma (Johnson) B.; m. Bernice Odelia Lonsdorf, Jan. 6, 1946; children—Bruce Howard, Steven Charles, Ann Marie. B.S. in Geology, U. Tex., 1937, postgrad., 1938. Geologist, U.S. Geol. Survey, 1937-38, Tex. U. Lands, Midland, 1938-49; cons. geologist, ind. oil operator, Midland, 1949—; exec. v.p., chief geologist Tex. Am. Oil Corp., Midland, 1955-66; ptnr. Autograph Driltime Corp., Midland, 1961-66, Broxson-Bartley Ins. Agy., Midland, 1966-69; v.p., dir. Pacific Union Gas Co., Midland, 1961-66, Western Oil Shale Corp., Midland, 1964-72. Patentee in field. Served to lt. USNR, 1942-46. Mem. Am. Assn. Petroleum Geologists, Soc. Ind. Profl. Earth Scientists, Ind. Petroleum Assn. Am., Mid-Continents Oil and Gas Assn., Tex. Ind. Producers and Royalty Owners Assn., Tex. Acad. Sci. Republican. Roman Catholic. Home: 1705 W Illinois St Midland TX 79701 Office: 300 W Wall Suite 1300 Midland TX 79701

BARTOLINI, R. PAUL, librarian; b. Ladd, Ill., July 21, 1920; s. Romeo and Ersilia (Galletti) B.; m. Myrtle J. File, Dec. 31, 1942; children—Richard Paul, David R., William F., Mary T. B.S., Ill. State U., 1942, U. Ill., 1946, M.S., 1947. Coordinator adult services Free Library of Phila., 1953-56; asst. city librarian ext. services Milw. Public Library, 1956-65; dir. Lake County (Ind.) Public Library, 1965-79, Public Library of Knoxville-Knox County, Tenn., 1979—. Served with U.S. Army, 1942-46. Mem. ALA, Southeastern Library Assn., Tenn. Library Assn., Am. Soc. Public Adminstrn., Kans. Library Assn. (past pres.), Wis. Library Assn. (past pres.). Republican. Roman Catholic. Clubs: Rotary, Italian-Am. Soc. Knoxville. Home: 7140 Dan Rose Ln Knoxville TN 37920 Office: 500 W Church Ave Knoxville TN 37902

BARTON, ALAN RAYMOND, utility executive; b. West Haven, Conn., Feb. 6, 1925; s. Alan Raymond and Edith Beatrice (Muicahy) B.; student Ga. Inst. Tech., 1944; B.Mech. Engring., Tulane U., 1946; B.E.E., Auburn U., 1948; M.B.A., U. Ala., 1979; m. Peggy Finneran, Feb. 11, 1952 (dec. Apr. 1980); children—Alan, Mary Rae, Elizabeth, William. With Ala. Power Co., Birmingham, 1948-80, v.p., 1964-69, sr. v.p., 1969-75, exec. v.p., 1975-80, also dir.; pres. Miss. Power Co., Gulfport, 1980—, also dir.; dir. Served to lt. (j.g.) USNR, 1943-47. Mem. IEEE. Roman Catholic. Office: Mississippi Power Co Gulfport MS 39501

BARTON, ALEXANDER JAMES, ecologist, educator, naval officer; b. Mt. Pleasant, Pa., May 9, 1924; s. Paul Carnahan and Barbara (Eggers) B.; B.S., Franklin and Marshall Coll., 1946; M.S., U. Pitts., 1957; m. Arlene Florence Arment, Oct. 6, 1945; children—Sandra, Lynne, Alexander James III. Herpetologist, Highland Park Zool. Gardens, Pitts., 1946-52; instr. biology Stony Brook (N.Y.) Sch., 1952-63, dir. admissions and fin. aid, 1957-63; profl. asst. NSF, Washington, 1963-65, profl. asso., 1965-70, program dir. sci. and engring. edn., 1970—; extended mil. furlough serving as capt. U.S. Navel Reserve, naval mem. OSD staff revising Res. Officers' Personnel Mgmt. Act, 1981-83; adj. asst. prof. biology C.W. Post Coll., Brookville, N.Y., 1961-63; dir. Savannah (Ga.) Natural History Mus., 1957; chmn. Fed. Interagency subcom. Environ. Edn., 1980-81; chmn. U.S. planning com., mem. U.S. delegation UN Conf. on Environ. Edn., Tbilisi, USSR, 1977; cons. sci. books Doubleday & Co., 1962-64. Scoutmaster Allegheny County council Boy Scouts Am., Pitts., 1947-52, mem. nat. adv. com., 1950-54, mem. exec. council Suffolk County council, 1957-63; mem. Internat. Com. on Endangered Reptiles and Amphibians, 1967-74. Pres., Arlington Rose Found., 1970-71. Served to capt. USNR, 1943-45, 81-83. Fellow Explorers Club; mem. Acad. Ind. Scholars (charter mem.), Potomac Rose Soc. (1st v.p. 1972-73, pres. 1974-75, dir. 1976—, gold medal 1983), Am. Rose Soc. (vice director Colonial dist. 1985—, 1971-72, cons. rosarian 1970—, chmn. nat. long-range planning com. 1973-75; accredited rose show judge 1970-77, life judge 1978—, gen. chmn. nat. conv. 1981, outstanding dist. judge award 1983, Silver Honor medal, 1984 dir. 1985—), Assn. Admissions Officer Ind. Secondary Schs. (pres. 1959-62), Am. Inst. Biol. Sci., Ecol. Soc. Am., others. Presbyn. (deacon 1946—, lay preacher 1954-65, tchr. adult bible class 1964-68). Contbr. numerous articles, papers to profl. publs.

BARTON, CARL JOSEPH, cons.; b. Mansfield, Ohio, June 9, 1935; s. John J. and Sophia A. B.; B.E.E.; M.B.A.; M.Engring.; D.Engring.; m. Marianne Patrick, Nov. 26, 1959; children—Amy, John J. II, C. Bart II, Jennifer. Systems engr. process control IBM, 1963-69; chmn., pres. Systems Cons. Corp., Beaumont, Tex., 1969-70; v.p., dir. Asso. Computer Services, Inc., Houston, 1970-71; cons. Sybron/Taylor, Beaumont, 1971-83, Bailey, Beaumont, 1983-85; pres. SCC Systems, 1983—; dir. Internat. Tech. Inst., Pitts., 1976—, Mgmt. Insts. Unlimited, Beaumont, 1978—, Congress Internat. Tech., Pitts., 1976—. Served with Signal Corps, U.S. Army, 1958-59. Recipient Literary Gold medal Freedom Found., 1955. Mem. Leadership Beaumont, Eta Kappa Nu. Roman Catholic. Home: 120 Stratton Ln Beaumont TX 77707 Office: 120 Stratton Ln Beaumont TX 77707

BARTON, JOE LINUS, congressman; b. Waco, Tex., Sept. 15, 1949; s. Larry Linus and Bess Wynell (Buice) B.; m. Janet Sue Winslow, Jan. 31, 1970; children—Bradley Linus, Alison Renee, Kristen Elizabeth. B.S. in Indsl. Engring., Tex. A&M U., 1972; M.S. in Indsl. Adminstrn., Purdue U., 1973. Asst. to v.p. Ennis Bus. Forms, Tex., 1973-81; fellow White House Fellows, Washington, 1981-82; cost control cons. ARCO, Dallas, 1982-84; mem. 99th Congress from Tex. Chmn. Republican Energy and Environ. Task Force, 1985. Mem. Assn. Former Students Tex. A&M U. (councilman at large 1985). Republican. Methodist. Avocation: tennis. Office: 1017 Longworth House Office Bldg Washington DC 20515

BARTON, NELDA ANN LAMBERT, nursing home administrator; m. Harold Bryan Barton, May 11, 1951 (dec. 1977); children—William Grant (dec.), Barbara Lynn, Harold Bryan Jr., Stephen Lambert, Suzanne. Student Western Ky. U., 1947-49; grad. Norton Meml. Infirmary Sch. Med. Tech., 1950; postgrad. Cumberland Coll., 1978. Registered med. technician Am. Coll. Clin. Pathologists, Ky., 1950-52; nursing home adminstr. Ky. Bd. Licensure for Nursing Home Adminstrs., Frankfort, Ky., 1979—; chmn. bd. dirs. Tri County Nat. Bank, 1985—; mem. Corbin Deposit Bank Exec. Com., 1982-84; mem. Fed. Council Aging, 1982—; pres., chmn. bd. Health Systems Inc., Barton and Assocs. Inc., Hazard Nursing Home, Inc., Williamsburg Nursing Home, Inc., Corbin Nursing Home, Inc., Barbourville Nursing Home, Inc., Key Distbg. Inc., Whitley Whiz. Inc. Bd. dirs. Leadership Ky., 1984—; v.p. Southeastern Ky. Rehab. Com., 1981—; mem. devel. bd. Cumberland Coll., 1981—; mem. Fair Housing Task Force City of Corbin, 1980-83, Ky. Mansions Preservation Found. Inc., Corbin Community Devel. Com., 1970-83, adv. com. City of Corbin, 1960-72; parliamentarian Ky. Mothers Assn., 1970—; cub scout den mother, 1965-67; pres. Corbin Central Elem. P.T.A., 1963-65, vice chmn. 9th dist. P.T.A., 1958-59; Republican nat. committeewoman for Ky., 1968—; vice-chmn. Rep. Nat. Com., 1984—; sec.-treas. Nat. Rep. Inst. Internat. Affairs, 1984—. Mem. Am. Coll. Nursing Home Adminstrs., Ky. Assn. Health Care Facilities (legis. com. 1980—), Ky. Assn. Nursing Home Adminstrs. (bd. dirs., polit. action com. 1979—), Ky. Med. Aux. (chmn. health edn. com. 1975-77), Am. Health Care Assn., Ky. Commn. on Women, Women's Aux. So. Med. Assn. (Ky. counselor), Whitley County Med. Aux. (pres. 1959-60), Aux. Ky. Med. Assn., Ky. C. of C. (bd. dirs. 1983—). Avocations: fishing; oil painting. Home: 1311 7th St Rd Corbin KY 40701

BARTON, PHILIP WAYNE, lawyer, negotiator, arbitrator, educator; b. Jacksonville, Ark., s. David Monroe and Ruby (Akridge) B.; 1 child, Christy Suzanne. B.A., Henderson State U., 1977; J.D., U. Ark., 1979. Bar: Ark. 1980, U.S. Dist. Ct. (ea. dist.) Ark. 1980, U.S. Ct. Mil. Appeals 1980. Personnel dir. Brandon Industries, Lake Hamilton, Ark., 1975-77; labor research assoc. John T. Lavey, Little Rock, 1978-80; labor lawyer, arbitrator Ark. Power and Light Co., Little Rock, 1980; labor lawyer XVIII Airborne Corps, Fort Bragg, N.C., 1980-84; asst. prof. Grad. Sch., Websters U., Pope AFB, N.C., 1982—; labor lawyer Communication Electronics, Fort Monmouth, N.J., 1984-85; adj. faculty Meth. Coll., Fayetteville, N.C., 1981, Fayetteville Tech. Inst., 1981—, Campbell U., Buies Creek, N.C., 1982-83. Sponsor Big Bros. Am., 1982-83; active Little Rock Jaycees, Young Democrats, Hot Springs, Ark. Served with U.S. Army, 1980—. Recipient Disting. Mil. Grad. award Henderson State U., 1977; Army Achievement medal for Grenada, 1983, Meritorious Service medal for labor law, 1984. Mem. Am. Trial Lawyers Assn., Ark. Bar Assn., Delta Theta Phi (vice chancellor 1977-78, spl. mem.'s award 1978). Republican. Baptist. Office: 1413 Gen Lee Fayetteville NC 28305

BARTON, THOMAS DONALD, lawyer, educator; b. Lincoln, Nebr., July 1, 1949; s. Donald Walter and Dorothy Louise (Farlin) B.; m. Sharon Lee Foster, July 26, 1980. B.A., Tulane U., 1971; J.D., Cornell U., 1974; Ph.D., Cambridge (Eng.) U., 1982. Bar: N.Y 1974. Assoc. Harris, Beach & Wilcox, Rochester, N.Y., 1974-76; asst. prof. W.Va. U. Coll. Law, Morgantown, 1978-80, assoc. prof., assoc. dean acad. affairs, 1982-84, prof., 1984—. Active Morgantown Bd. Zoning Appeals, 1983—; bd. dirs. W.Va. Tax Inst., 1978-80; cons. W.Va. State Elections Commn., 1979. NEH fellow, 1979; recipient Gustavus Hill Robinson award, 1974; W.D.P. Carey Exhbn. prize, 1972. Mem. Phi Beta Kappa, Phi Sigma Delta, Delta Alpha Pi. Contbr. articles to profl. jours. Office: WV U Coll Law Morgantown WV 26505

BARTOW, GENE, athletic director; b. Browning, Mo., Aug. 18, 1930; s. T.I. and Almeda (Gooch) B.; m. Ruth Huffine, Dec. 24, 1952; children—Mark, Murry, Beth. B.S. in Edn., N.E. Mo. State U., 1952; M.A., Washington U., St. Louis, 1957. Head basketball coach Central Mo. State U., 1961-64, Valparaiso U., Ind., 1964-70, Memphis State U., 1970-74, U. Ill., Urbana, 1974-75, UCLA, 1975-77; dir. athletics, coach U. Ala., Birmingham, 1977—. Served with U.S. Army, 1952-54. Democrat. Methodist. Club: Rotary. Author: Winning Basketball, 1978. Home: 2636 Creekview Birmingham AL 35226 Office: University Station Birmingham AL 35294*

BASANDA, NICK J(OHN), equipment company executive; b. East Chicago, Ind., Dec. 10, 1917; s. John and Julia (Hamnik) B.; m. Gladys R. Walker, July 28, 1940; children—Julie Ann, Lynn. Student pub. schs., Paw Paw, Mich. Job. supt. Laird Constrn. Co., Battle Creek, Mich., 1939; job. supt., office engr. Reinhart & Donovan Co., Oklahoma City, 1940-45; pres., gen. mgr. Basanda Constrn. Co., 1945-60; pres., gen. mgr. UEC Equipment Co., 1960-77, pres., chmn. bd., 1980-82, chmn. bd., 1982—; pres., chmn. bd. UEC Industries, Inc., 1977-80, chmn. bd., 1982—; pres., chmn. bd. UEC Mfg. Co., 1977-80 Mem. Internat. Trade Club, Soc. for Advancement Mgmt., Utility Equipment Dealers Assn., Power and Communications Assn. Republican. Roman Catholic. Clubs: Petroleum, Quail Creek Golf and Country. Lodges: Rotary. Home: 1523 Camden Way Oklahoma City OK 73116 Office: 341 NW 122d St Oklahoma City OK 73156

BASDEN, SHARON JANE, business educator; b. Little Rock, Dec. 24, 1946; d. Merle T. and Jane Elizabeth (Orr) B.; m. Gary T. Frankenfield, July 22, 1972. B.B.A., Tex. Wesleyan U., 1970; M.B.E., North Tex. State U., 1976; Ed.D., Memphis State U., 1985. Instr. Lowe Career Coll., Houston, 1977-80; grad. teaching asst. Memphis State U., 1981-83; instr. Coll. Mainland, Tex. City, Tex., 1984, Tarrant County Jr. Coll., Ft. Worth, 1984—; cons. computer instr. Bauder Fashion Coll., Arlington, 1985—. Vol. tutor Child Guidance Ctr., Ft. Worth, 1984—; counselor Women's Shelter, Memphis, 1983. Mem. Am. Bus. Communication Assn., Tex. Jr. Coll. Tchrs. Assn., Nat. Bus. Edn. Assn., Phi Kappa Phi, Delta Phi Epsilon, Beta Sigma Phi. Democrat. Baptist. Avocation: snow skiing. Office: Tarrant County Jr Coll Box 120 South Campus Fort Worth TX 76119

BASH, FRANK NESS, astronomer, educator; b. Medford, Oreg., May 3, 1937; s. Frank Cozad and Kathleen (Ness) B.; m. Susan Martin Fay, Sept. 10, 1960; children—Kathryn, Lee. B.A., Willamette U., 1959; M.A., Harvard U., 1962; Ph.D., U. Va., 1967. Asst. prof. dept. astronomy U. Tex., Austin, 1969-73, assoc. prof., 1973-81, prof., 1981—, chmn. dept. astronomy, 1982—, W.D. Blunk Meml. prof., 1983, Edmonds Regent prof., 1985—. Author: Astronomy, 1977; also articles. Mem. Am. Astron. Soc., Internat. Astron. Union, Internat. Sci. Redio Union, Phi Kappa Phi. Club: Town and Gown (Austin). Home: 4507 Balcones Dr Austin TX 78731 Office: U Tex Astronomy Dept Austin TX 78712

BASHOR, RONALD LESLIE, dentist, pharmacist, air force officer; b. Kansas City, Mo., Apr. 5, 1949; s. John Leslie and Lucille Adel (Hyke) B.; m. Mary Elizabeth Enslen, May 11, 1974; children—Brian, Becky. B.S. in Pharmacy, U. Mo., 1972, D.D.S., 1976; grad. Air Command and Staff Coll., 1984. Commd. 2d lt. U.S. Air Force, 1975, advanced through grades to maj., 1980; gen. dentist, Blytheville AFB, Ark., 1984—, pharmacy cons., 1984—; cons. Kansas City Drug Abuse Com., 1975. Asst. organizer Miss. County Spl. Olympics, Blytheville, 1985—. Decorated Air Force Commendation medal. Mem. Am. Pharm. Assn., Am. Soc. Hosp. Pharmacists, ADA, Acad. Gen. Dentistry, Assn. Mil. Surgeons U.S. Clubs: IPMS (v.p. 1976-79) (Abilene, Tex.); Air Force Mus. Found. (Wright-Patterson AFB). Avocations: scuba diving; traveling. Office: PSC 1 Box 4664 Blytheville AR 72317

BASHORE, ROBERT LEROY, college administrator; b. Lebanon County, Pa., Feb. 18, 1936; s. LeRoy W. and Mae M. (Weidner) B.; m. Joy Kittredge Wackerbarth, June 27, 1964; children—Scott W., Robert S. A.A., York Coll. of Pa., 1959; B.A., Defiance Coll., 1962; M.S., Radford U., 1971; Ed.D., Va. Poly. Inst. and State U., 1979. Dist. exec. Blue Ridge Council Boy Scouts Am., Roanoke, Va., 1962-69; counselor Central Va. Community Coll., Lynchburg, 1970-73, fin. aid adminstr., 1974-75, dir. admissions and student services, 1975-80, dean student services, 1980-85, 85. Chmn. Campbell County Sch. Bd., Rustburg, Va., 1981-82, mem., 1979—; mem. Regional Magnet Sch. Bd., math. and sci., Lynchburg, 1985—; chmn. Central Va. Career Fair, 1975—; chmn. Central Dist. Boy Scouts Am., Lynchburg, 1984—. Recipient Dist. Award of Merit, Boy Scouts Am., 1985; mem. Nat. Staff Jamboree, Nat. Council Boy Scouts Am., 1981, 85; Gen. Electric fellow, 1971. Mem. Am. Assn. Coll. Admissions and Registrars, Va. Assn. Student Personnel Adminstrs., So. Va. Regional Sch. Bd. Assn. (pres.-elect Charlottesville 1985-86), Phi Delta Kappa (exec. com. 1984—, rep. to Testing Service 1981—). Republican. Presbyterian. Avocations: Snow skiing; reading; golf; travel. Home: 105 Wellington Dr Lynchburg VA 24502 Office: Central Va Community Coll 3506 Wards Rd Lynchburg VA 24502

BASKAR, JOHN F(REDERICK), pathobiologist, biomedical researcher; b. Madras, India, July 17, 1936; came to U.S., 1964, naturalized, 1976; s. David V. Dhyriam and Leelavathy Jane Savarus; m. Nirmala Adhilingham, May 3, 1969. B.S., U. Madras, 1959; M.S., Howard U., 1967; Sc.D., Johns Hopkins U., 1975. Asst. Madras Secretariat, 1960-64; grad. teaching asst. Howard U., Washington, 1964-67; sr. technician Microbiol. Assocs., Inc., Bethesda, Md., 1967-69; NIH postdoctoral research fellow in reproductive physiology Harvard U. Med. Sch., Boston, 1975-77, research assoc., 1977-78; research assoc. Cancer Research Ctr., U. N.C.-Chapel Hill, 1978-84, research asst. prof., 1984—. John Hopkins U. scholar, 1971-75; Nat. Inst. Child Health and Human Devel. grantee, 1980—. Mem. AAAS, Am. Soc. for Microbiology, N.Y. Acad. Scis., Sigma Xi. Contbr. numerous articles to profl. publs.; biomed. research on effect of cytomegalovirus on embryonic devel. Office: Cancer Research Ctr U NC Chapel Hill NC 27514

BASKERVILLE, CHARLES ALEXANDER, geologist; b. Jamaica, N.Y., Aug. 19, 1928; s. Charles H. and Annie M. (Allen) B.; m. Susan Platt, July 5, 1979; children—Mark Dana, Shawn Allison, Charles Morris. B.S., CCNY, 1953; M.S., NYU, 1958, Ph.D., 1965. Cert. geologist, Maine, cert. profl. geologist, Ind. Asst. civil engr. N.Y. State Dept. Transp., Babylon, 1953-66; prof. engring. geology CUNY, 1966-79, dean sch. gen. studies, 1970-79, prof. emeritus; project research geologist U.S. Geol. Survey, 1979—; cons. IBM, Madigan-Hyland Engrs., Consol. Edison Co. N.Y.C., others. Active com. for minority participation in the geosciences U.S. Dept. Interior, 1972-75; panelist Grad. Fellow Program, NSF; chmn. Minority Grad. Fellowship Program, 1979-80; active U.S. Nat. com. Tunneling Tech., chmn. subcom. edn. and tng., active nat. research council. Recipient Founders Day award NYU, 1966; 125th Anniversary medal City Coll., 1973; award for excellence in engring. geology Nat. Consortium Black Profl. Devel., 1978. Fellow Geol. Soc. Am. (com. on minorities in geoscis.); mem. N.Y. Acad. Scis., Geol. Soc. Washington, Am. Inst. Profl. Geologists, Assn. Engring. Geologists (rep. to nat. bd. dirs. 1973-74, chmn. N.Y.-Phila. sect. 1973-74), Internat. Assn. Engring. Geology, Yellowstone-Bighorn Research Assn., Sigma Xi. Office: US Geol Survey 922 National Center Reston VA 22092

BASKIN, CHARLES RICHARD, physical scientist; b. Houston, Mar. 6, 1926; s. Charles Todd and Bessie Emma (Heilig) B.; B.S. in Civil Engring., La. State U., 1953; m. Peggy June Holden, Dec. 31, 1952; children—Richard Karl, Sheila Frances. Design engr. City-Parish Dept. Pub. Works, Baton Rouge, 1953-57; city engr. City of Plaquemine (La.), 1957-58; sect. head, asst. chief engr. Tex. Bd. Water Engrs., Austin, 1958-62; asst. chief engr. Tex. Water Commn., Austin, 1962-65; asst. chief engr. and chief engr. Tex. Water Devel. Bd., Austin, 1965-77; dir. data and engring. services div. Tex. Dept. Water Resources, Austin, 1977-83; spl. asst. Office of Asst. Dir. Info. Systems, U.S. Geol. Survey, Reston, Va., 1983—. Chmn., Tex. Mapping Adv. Com., 1968-83, Tex. Natural Resources Info. System Task Force, 1972-83; mem. Non-Fed. Adv. Com. on Water Data for Public Use, 1970-83; chmn. Water Data Coordination Task Force, Interstate Conf. on Water Problems, 1975-83. Served with U.S. Army, 1944-47; p.o.w. Recipient John Wesley Powell award U.S. Geol. Survey, 1972; registered profl. engr., La., Tex. Mem. Phi Kappa Phi, Tau Beta Pi, Chi Epsilon, Phi Eta Sigma, Sigma Tau Sigma. Adventist (elder). Contbr. articles to profl. jours. Home: 1330 Quail Ridge Dr Reston VA 22094 Office: 801 National Ctr US Geol Survey Reston VA 22092

BASKIND, FRANK RONALD, social work educator; b. Queens, N.Y., May 27, 1945; s. Haskel Thomas and Angelina Frances (Sarcona) B.; m. Patricia Anne Browne, B.A., Fordham U., 1967; M.S.W., U. Conn.-West Hartford, 1971; Ph.D., U. Conn., 1978. Regional coordinator Helpline Central Conn., Plainville, 1970-72; social worker Big Brother, Big Sisters, New Haven, Conn., 1973-78; marriage and family counselor pvt. practice, Conn., 1976-80; adj. prof. Union for Experimenting Colls. and Univs., Cin., 1981-84; assoc. prof. social work South Conn. State Coll., New Haven, 1972-80; dir. social work program U. Tenn., Knoxville, 1980-85; asst. dir. staff devel. and tech. assistance Grad. Sch. Social Work Countinuing Social Work Edn. U. Tenn., Knoxville, 1983-84; cons. Smoking Cessation Assn., Knoxville, 1982-85; staff devel. trainer Dept. Social Services, S.C., 1982-83, Sch. Social Work, Knoxville, 1981-85. Author: Defining Generalist Social Work Practice, 1984. Contbr. articles to profl. jours. Mem. allocations com. United Way, Knoxville, 1982-85; mem. child abuse review team Dept. Human Services, Knoxville, 1982-85; mem. social services adv. council Dept. Human Services, Knoxville, 1984-85, Edn. Bd. Sacred Heart Sch., Knoxville, 1982-84. Served to lt. comdr. USAR, 1967—, Vietnam. Decorated Bronze Star, Army Achievement medal. NIMH scholar, 1970-71. Mem. Nat. Assn. Social Workers (Social Service Agency of Year award 1983), Council on Social Work Edn., Acad. Certified Social Workers (sec. Conn. chpt. 1979-80, treas. Tenn. chpt. 1982-84, pres. elect 1985); Phi Delta Kappa, Phi Kappa Phi. Club: Social Service (Knoxville) (treas. 1981-82, pres. 1982-83). Avocations: Gardening; jogging; youth league coaching.

BASLER, WAYNE GORDON, glass manufacturing executive, consultant; b. Cedar Rapids, Iowa, Aug. 16, 1930; m. Betty Jean Lawrence, June 27, 1953; children—Eric, Janelle, Peter. B.S. in Ceramic Engring., Iowa State U., 1953. With Ford Motor Co., 1960-72; dir. tech. devel. Guardian Industries, Detroit, 1972-77; pres. AFG Industries, Inc., Kingsport, Tenn., 1977—. Served to 1st lt. USAF, 1954-56. Republican. Presbyterian. Office: AFG Industries Inc 1400 Lincoln St Kingsport TN 37660

BASS, BOB, professional basketball team executive. Gen. mgr. San Antonio Spurs, NBA. Office: Care San Antonio Spurs Hemis Fair Arena PO Box 530 San Antonio TX 78292

BASS, CORNELIUS GRAHAM, oil jobber exec.; b. Latta, S.C., May 28, 1918; s. Howard H. and Sarah (Carmichael) B.; B.S. in Bus. Adminstrn., U. S.C., 1940; m. Ann Blair, May 23, 1942 (div. Jan. 1976); children—Ann Blair (Mrs. James E. Crowder, III), Cornelius Graham. With The Latta Cotton Co., 1940-41; asst. mgr. Dilmar Oil Co., Latta, 1941-42; mgr. Santee Oil Co., 1945-47, sec.-treas., 1947-71, v.p., 1971—, gen. mgr., 1947—; partner, gen. mgr. S & P Tire Co., Kingstree, S.C., 1949-80; sec.-treas., gen. mgr. Services, Inc., Kingstree, 1950-71; pres. Warsaw Mfg. Co., Kingstree, 1958-63; pres. Bass Farms, Inc., Latta, 1963—; pres. Santee Broadcasting Co., Inc. (radio sta. WDKD), 1965-69, treas., 1970-75; pres. Kingstree Indsl. Devel. Corp., 1958—, Sunrise, Inc., 1976-81, SUNUP, Inc., 1976-81, Airport Beverage Corp., 1976—, TAB Enterprises, Inc., 1973-81; sec.-treas. King's Tree Inn, Inc., 1967-70, v.p., 1980—. Mem. Williamsburg Planning Commn., 1967—; chmn. Williamsburg County Bd. Edn., 1957-62. Served with AUS, World War II. Decorated Bronze Star. Mem. Kingstree C. of C. (v.p. 1956-58), S.C. Oil Jobbers Assn. (pres. 1954-55). Moose (past gov. Kingstree). Clubs: Kingstree Country (pres.), Optimists (past pres.), Lions (past pres.). Home: US 52 N Kingstree SC 29556 Office: Santee Oil Co Inc Hwy 52 N Kingstree SC 29556

BASS, DAVID LOREN, artist; b. Conway, Ark., July 19, 1943; s. Deward Clark Bass and Gillian Henrietta (Oliver) Bass Carter. B.S.Edn., Ark. State Tchrs., Coll., 1965; student Aspen Sch. Contemporary Art, summer 1964; M.F.A., U. N.C.-Greensboro, 1975; postgrad. U. N.C., Chapel Hill, summer 1974. Tchr. 7th-8th grades Met. Schs. Nashville and Davidson County, Tenn., 1965-67; tchr. 7th-12th grades U.S. Def. Dept., Kenitra, Morocco, 1967-73; artist, Greensboro, N.C., 1975—; artist-in-residence Washington and Lee U., Lexington, Va., 1976; curator Peter Agostini sculpture exhbn. DuPont Art Gallery, Lexington, 1976; cons. Waterworks Gallery, Salisbury, N.C., 1983; dir. United Arts Council, Greensboro, 1978-80, Ctr. for Creative Arts, Greensboro, 1978-80, Green Hill Ctr. for N.C. Art, Greensboro, 1977-80, 83—. One man shows include: Theater Art Gallery, High Point, N.C., 1977, 82, Asheville Art Mus., 1980, Recent Works, 1985; group shows include: Southern Realism, Miss. Mus. Art, Jackson, 1980, Biennial Exhbn. Piedmont Painting, Mint Mus., Charlotte, N.C., 1983; Contemporary Art Acquisitions, Equitable Gallery, N.Y.C., 1984. Bd. dirs. O. Henry Festival, Greensboro, 1985. Fellow Corp. Yaddo, Saratoga Springs, N.Y., 1978, 81, 84. Ossabaw Island Project,

Ga., 1979, Va. Ctr. for Creative Arts, Sweetbriar, 1978. Mem. Greenhill Ctr. for N.C. Art, Southeastern Ctr. for Contemporary Art, Weatherspoon Art Gallery, Artists' Choice Mus., N.C. Arts Soc. (adv. council 1981-83). Address: 1401 Roanoake Dr Greensboro NC 27408

BASS, HAROLD FRANKLIN, JR., political science educator; b. Corpus Christi, Dec. 4, 1948; s. Harold Franklin and Bettye Jane (Sparkman) B.; m. Carol Ann Watson, Jan. 8, 1972; children—Jessica Marie, Franklin Sparkman. B.A., Baylor U., 1971; M.A., Vanderbilt U., 1974, Ph.D., 1978. Instr. polit. sci. Ouachita Baptist U., Arkadelphia, Ark., 1976-78, asst. prof., 1978-83, assoc. prof., 1983—, chmn. dept., 1979—. Author: (with others) Presidents and their Parties: Leadership or Neglect, 1984. Mem. editorial bd. Ark. Polit. Sci. Jour., 1983—. Named Outstanding Faculty Mem., Ouachita Bapt. U. Student Senate, 1978-79, 83-84; Moody Research grantee Lyndon Baines Johnson Found., 1975; research grantee Harry S Truman Library Inst., 1975. Mem. Am. Polit. Sci. Assn., So. Polit. Sci. Assn., Ark. Polit. Sci. Assn. (exec. com.), AAUP, Ctr. for Study of Presidency, Arkadelphia C. of C., Alpha Kappa Psi, Sigma Phi Epsilon. Baptist. Club: Arkadelphia Country. Avocations: Golf; racquetball. Home: 828 N Park Dr Arkadelphia AR 71923 Office: Ouachita Baptist U Dept Polit Sci Arkadelphia AR 71923

BASS, LESLIE RANDOLPH, JR., merchant, magistrate, fire administrator; b. Rocky Mount., N.C., Feb. 23, 1939; s. Leslie Randolph and Sadie (Matthews) B.; m. Rebecca Ann Jones, Nov. 26, 1959; children—Leslie R. III, Daniel A., Rebecca E. Student East Carolina U., 1957-60, Nashville Tech. U. Fire chief Fire Dept., Nashville, N.C., 1979—; Peoples Bank. bd. dirs. Nashville, Nashville Town Bd. Recipient Fireman of Yr. award Nashville Fire Dept. Democrat. Baptist. Home: 415 E Green St Nashville NC 27856 Office: LR Bass & Son 223 W Washington St Nashville NC 27856

BASS, LINDA JEAN, optometrist; b. Mitchel AFB, N.Y., Apr. 23, 1951; d. Harry Lee and Frances Jean (Bartoletti) B.; m. R. Gerry Miller, May 23, 1983. Student U. Ga., 1969-72; B.S. in Physiol. Optics, U. Ala., Birmingham, 1977, O.D., 1979. Resident in primary care optometry So. Coll. Optometry, Memphis, 1980, clin. faculty, 1980-82; staff optometrist Bay Pines VA Med. Ctr., Fla., 1982-85, chief optometry sect., 1985—; adj. faculty Pa. Coll. Optometry, Phila., 1982—, U. Houston Coll. Optometry, 1984—; cons. in field. Contbr. articles to profl. jours. Recipient Preceptor of Yr. award Pa. Coll. Optometry, 1985; Found. Edn. and Research scholar, 1977; named one of Outstanding Young Women Am., 1980. Fellow Am. Acad. Optometry; mem. Am. Optometric Assn., Fla. Optometric Assn., Pinellas County Soc. Optometry, Nat. Assn. VA Optometrists. Office: Bay Pines VA Med Ctr Bay Pines FL 33504

BASS, PATRICIA FARR, insurance executive; b. New Orleans, Mar. 24, 1942; d. Robert and Anne Mae (Allbritton) Farr; m. Charles W. Bass, Jan. 1, 1973 (div. Sept. 1978); 1 son, Samuel Patrick. B.S., Miss. Coll., Clinton, 1964; postgrad. Life Office Mgmt. Assn., 1967-80. Cert., Nat. Assn. Ins. Women. Exec. sec. Anaheim Community Hosp., (Calif.), 1964-65; chief underwriter Dixie Nat. Ins. Co., Jackson, Miss., 1965-76, asst. v.p. claims, 1976—. Asst. editor: Today's Insurance Woman, 1979-80. Vol. ARC, 1960—, vice chmn. Central Miss. chpt., Jackson, 1970-83; sec. Parents without Ptnrs., Jackson, 1980—, exec. v.p., 1981-83, regional sec., 1982-84, dir. pub. relations, 1983. Named Vol. of Month, VA Ctr. Jackson, 1980; Single Parent of Yr., Parents without Ptnrs., 1982; YWCA Outstanding Woman Achiever, 1984. Mem. Ins. Women of Jackson (pres. 1972-73, 83-84, sec. 1971-72; Ins. Woman of Yr. 1976, Claimswoman of Yr. 1981-82). Baptist. Office: Dixie Nat Life Ins Co PO Box 22587 Jackson MS 39205

BASS, RAY DEAN, state highway director, engineer consultant; b. Slocomb, Ala., Dec. 19, 1933; s. Alexander Bell and Ellie (Warr) B.; m. Clara Nell Smith, Dec. 21, 1957; children—Elizabeth, Thomas, Joan. B.C.E., Auburn U., 1959. Registered profl. engr. County engr.; contractor W. O. Smith Constrn. Co., Montgomery, Ala., 1965-67; county engr. Montgomery County (Ala.), 1967-71; state hwy. dir. Ala. Hwy. Dept., Montgomery, 1971-79, 83—; cons., engr. Monn-Bass, Inc., Tuscaloosa, Ala., 1981-83. Served with U.S. Navy, 1951-54. Mem. Am. Soc. Profl. Engrs., Nat. Assn. County Engrs. Democrat. Methodist. Home: Route 2 Box 424AA Montgomery AL Office: Ala Hwy Dept 11 S Union St Montgomery AL 36130

BASS, ROY WADE, company official; b. Marion, Ky., June 3, 1949; s. Raymond H. and Iva N. (Cooper) B.; m. Janet G. MaCurdy, June 1, 1979; 1 dau., Tara Miller. A.S. in Mech. Engring., U. Evansville, 1972; B.S. in Indsl. Mgmt., Purdue U., 1974; M.B.A., Mercer U., Atlanta, 1983. With Babcock & Wilcox Co., Mt. Vernon, Ind. and Lynchburg, Va., 1967-78, sr. engr., 1978; asst. to site quality assurance mgr. Brown & Root, Inc., Houston, 1978-79, corp. quality assurance audit mgr., 1979-80; S.E. region quality assurance mgr. Impell Corp., Atlanta, 1981—; conf. presenter. Mem. Am. Soc. Quality Control (cert.), Am. Nuclear Soc. Lodge: Elks. Office: Impell Corp 333 Research Ct Technology Park Norcross GA 30092

BASS, STEVEN FRANCIS, safety engineer, insurance executive; b. Shelbyville, Tenn., Feb. 17, 1952; s. Sion D. and Corinne (Simmons) B.; m. Brenda Ann Roberson, Oct. 31, 1981; B.S., Middle Tenn. State U., 1973, B.S., 1975; M.B.A., Embry-Riddle Coll., 1982. Cert. safety profl. Loss control advisor Fireman's Fund Ins., Nashville, 1975-83; loss control supr., Memphis, from 1983; now with John Deere Ins. Co., Marietta, Ga. Del. Tenn. Safety Congress, Nashville, 1982—. Mem. Am. Soc. Safety Engrs. (exec. adv. com. 1984, safety award chmn. 1985), Nat. Safety Mgmt. Soc., Am. Mgmt. Assn., Clubs: Antique Airplane Assn., Exptl. Aircraft Assn., Aircraft Owners Pilots Assn. Republican. Methodist. Avocations: flying; antique aircraft. Home: 4935 Condor Pl NE Marietta GA 30066 Office: John Deere Ins Co PO Box 669171 Marietta GA 30066

BASYE, SUZANNE STOVER, interior designer; b. Wilkensburg, Pa., May 16, 1926; d. Luther Heilman and Dorothy (Flack) Stover; m. Paul E. Basye, May 7, 1946 (div. 1979); children—Lee, Jayne. Student Syracuse U., 1944-46; M.F.A., Fla. Atlantic U., 1956; postgrad. U. Tenn., 1968-69, U. Mont., 1952-54, Fla. State U., 1962-68, U. Fla., 1959-62. Cert. in Bus., Art, Early Childhood Elem. Edn., Fla. With data computer dept. Internat. Bus. Machines, Syracuse, N.Y., 1942-46; owner, designer Sooki Children's Clothing, Auburn, N.Y., 1948-51; co-owner Sch. House Tea Room, Auburn, 1951-53; dir. art, chmn. early edn. dept. Hillsboro County Day Sch., Hillsboro Beach, Fla., 1955-68; interior designer Suzanne Interiors, Ft. Lauderdale, Fla., 1972—. Bd. dirs. Henderson Clinic, Ft. Lauderdale, 1958-69, Broward County Libraries, 1960-66. Mem. Nat. Tchrs. Assn., Classroom Tchrs. Assn., Kappa Kappa Gamma. Club: Le Playa Rosa (Jalisco, Mexico). Home: 2575 S Ocean Blvd Highland Beach FL 33431

BATCHELDER, DRAKE MILLER, lawyer; b. Indpls., Dec. 12, 1941; s. Keith Drake and Anna (Miller) B.; m. Hallie Boucher Walker, Aug. 22, 1964; children—Brian, Michael, David. B.S. in Indls. Engring., U. Fla., 1965, J.D. with honors, 1969. Bar: Fla. Assoc. Mershon, Sawyer, Johnston, Dunwody & Cole, Miami, 1969-71; ptnr. Rimes, Greaton, Murphy & Batchelder, Ft. Lauderdale, Fla., 1971-79, English, McCaughan & O'Bryan, Ft. Lauderdale, 1979—. Editor U. Fla. Law Rev., 1969. Trustee Fla. Oaks Sch. Bd., Ft. Lauderdale, 1981—, chmn. sch. bd., 1985—; trustee St. Thomas Aquinas Found., Ft. Lauderdale, 1982—. Mem. Broward County Bar Assn. (pres. young lawyers sect. 1973-74), Fla. Bar NE 3d Ave govs. 1974-78, 79-84, chmn. merit retention commn. 1981-82), Ft. Lauderdale C. of C. (chmn. task force 1981-82). Democrat. Roman Catholic. Clubs: Touchdown (pres. Ft. Lauderdale 1980-81), Lauderdale Yacht, Lago Mar Country. Home: 2620 Castilla Isle Fort Lauderdale FL 33301 Office: 100 NE 3d Ave Suite 1100 Fort Lauderdale FL 33301

BATEMAN, C. FRED, educational administrator. Supt. of schs., Chesapeake, Va. Office: PO Box 15204 Chesapeake VA 23320*

BATEMAN, DOTTYE JANE SPENCER, Realtor; b. Athens, Tex.; d. Charles Augustus and Lillie (Freeman) Spencer; student Fed. Inst., 1941-42, So. Meth. U., Dallas Coll., 1956-58; m. George Truitt Bateman, 1947 (div. Apr. 1963); children—Kelly Spencer, Bethena; m. 2d, Joseph E. Lindsley, 1968. Sec. to state senator, Tyler, Tex., 1941-42; sec. to pres. Merc. Nat. Bank, Dallas, State Fair of Tex., Dallas, 1942-48; realtor, broker, Garland, Tex., 1956—; co-partner Play-Shade Co.; appraiser Asso. Soc. Real Estate Appraiser; auctioneer, 1963—; developer Stonewall Cave, 1964—, Guthrie East Estates, 1984—; Pres., Central Elementary Sch. PTA, 1955-56, Bussey Jr. High PTA, 1956-57; den mother Cub Scouts Am., 1957-59; chmn. Decent Lit. Com., 1956-58; chmn. PTA's council, 1958; dir. Dallas Heart Assn., 1960, local chmn., 1955-57, county chmn., 1957-60; spl. dir. Henderson County Red Cross, 1945; local chmn. March of Dimes, 1961-63; mem. Dallas Civic Opera Com., 1963-64; mem. homemaker panel Dallas Times Herald, 1955-74. Named Outstanding Tex. Jaycee-Ette Pres., 1953, hon. Garland Jay-Cee-Ette, 1956, hon. Sheriff, Dallas County, 1963; headliner Press Club Awards dinner, 1963-68, 84. 84. Mem. Garland Bd. Realtors, Greater Dallas Bd. Realtors (chmn. reception com., past dir., mem. comml.-investment div., mem. make Am. better com. 1973-78, mem. beautify Tex. council 1977-78, 84, by-laws com. 1977-78), Auctioneers Assn., Internat. Real Estate Fedn., Soc. Prevention Cruelty to Animals, Dallas Women's (project chmn.), Garland (chmn. spl. services com. 1955-56) chambers commerce, Tex. Hist. Soc., Dallas Hist. Soc., Henderson County Hist. Soc., 500, Inc., Consejo Internacional De Buena Vecindad, Delphian Study Club, Eruditis Study Club, D.A.R. (Daniel McMahan chpt.). Christian Scientist. Clubs: Garland (past v.p., pres.), Tex. (past treas., ofcl. hostess) Jaycee-Ettes, Garland Fedn. Women's (past pres.), Garland Garden, Trinity Dist. Fedn. Women's (past pres.), Pub. Affairs Luncheon, Dallas Press (dir. 1973-74), chmn. house com. 1973-74, chmn. hdqrs. com. 1973-74). Home: 6313 Lyons Rd Garland TX 75043 Office: 5518 Dyer St Dallas TX 75206

BATEMAN, HERBERT HARVELL, congressman; b. Elizabeth City, N.C., Aug. 7, 1928; s. Elbert E. and Edna (Buffkin) B.; m. Laura Ann Yacobi, May 29, 1954; children—Herbert H., Laura Margaret. B.A., Coll. of William and Mary, 1949; LL.B., Georgetown U., 1956. Bar: Va. Tchr., Hampton High Sch. (Va.), 1949-57; law clk. justice U.S. Ct. Appeals (D.C. cir.), 1956-57; assoc. Jones, Blechman, Woltz & Kelly, Newport News, Va., 1957-82; mem. Va. State Senate, 1968-82; mem. 98th Congress from 1st Va. Dist., 1982—; mem. Va. Joint Legis. Audit and Rev. Commn., 1974-82; mem. Va. Peninsula Ports Authority, 1968-72, Study Commn. on Va. Jud. System, 1970-72, Study Commn. on Pub. Sch. Fund Allocation; legal counsel U.S. Jaycees, 1965, pres. Va. Jaycees, 1961-62. Served to 1st lt. USAF, 1951-53. Recipient Disting. Service award Hampton Rds. Jaycees. Mem. ABA, Va. Bar Assn., Newport News Bar Assn., Am. Judicature Soc., Am. Legion. Republican. Office: 1 518 Longworth Bldg Washington DC 20515

BATEMAN, WILLIAM ALBERT, forensic engineer; b. Amarillo, Tex., Aug. 27, 1931; s. Elbert Oren and Alta Selma (Nowlin) B.; m. Darlene Mulherin, Nov. 27, 1953; children—June Bateman Coburn, Susan Gay, William A., Clay Alan. A.S., Amarillo Coll., 1951; B.S. in Mech. Engring., U. Tex., 1954. Registered profl. engr. Tex., Calif.; cert. safety profl., forensic engr., hazard control mgr. Various positions Shell Oil Co., 1954-79; pres. W.A. Bateman Cons., Midland, Tex., 1979—. Mem. Nat. Soc. Profl. Engrs., Tex. Soc. Profl. Engrs., Am. Soc. Safety Engrs. (various offices Permian Basin chpt.), Nat. Acad. Forensic Engrs. (charter), System Safety Soc. (sr.) Republican. Baptist. Avocations: micro computers; stained glass. Home: 3613 Jordan Ave Midland TX 79707 Office: PO Box 10196 Midland TX 79702

BATES, BERT POPE, nurse; b. Pinehurst, N.C., July 25, 1953; d. John Patrick and Clara Elizabeth (Byrd) Pope; children—Eric Quinn, Scarlet Marie. Lic. practical nurse cert. Sandhills Community Coll., 1973, A.S. in Nursing, 1983. Charge nurse Sandhills Nursing Ctr., Pinehurst, 1977-78; mem. recovery room staff S.W. Miss. Regional Med. Ctr., McComb, 1978-80; head nurse Manor Care of Pinehurst, 1983-85; staff nurse emergency dept. Central Carolina Hosp., Sanford, N.C., 1985—. Democrat. Presbyterian. Home: Route 1 Box 136A Cameron NC 28326 Office: Central Carolina Hosp 1135 Carthage St Sanford NC 27330

BATES, CAROL HENRY, musicologist; b. Chgo., Aug. 31, 1944; d. Carl F.H. and Helga Irmgard (Bender) Henry; m. William Henry Bates, Aug. 25, 1971; 1 child, Stephen Henry. B.Mus. in Piano, Wheaton Coll., Ill., 1965; M.Mus. in Musicology, Ind. U., 1968, Ph.D. in Musicology, 1978. Asst. prof. Houghton Coll., N.Y., 1969-71; vis. instr. U. West Fla., Pensacola, 1972; teaching assoc. U. S.C., Columbia, 1978—. Editor: Elizabeth Jacquet de la Guerre: Pieces de clavecin, 1985. Ind. U. fellow, 1968; research grantee, Ind. U., 1973; travel grantee, NEH, 1985. Mem. Am. Musicological Soc., Pi Kappa Lambda. Republican. Home: 108 Dale Valley Rd Columbia SC 29223

BATES, DONALD HARRY, construction company executive; b. Henry County, Iowa, Dec. 18, 1933; s. Bernard Max and Anna May (Wilson) B.; m. Janice Irene Rowe, July 15, 1956 (div. 1977); children—Diana, Kenneth, Barbara, David; m. Johanna Stevenson, June 9, 1978. Student Iowa Wesleyan Coll., 1952-53, 64. Sales mgr. Mix-Mill, Inc., Iowa and Kans., 1964-68; dist. mgr. Butler Mfg. Co., Nebr., N.D. and S.D., 1969-72; field sales mgr. Quonset div. Stran-Steel, Houston, 1972-76; gen. sales mgr. Ruth Berry Pump div. Daniel Industries, 1976-78; v.p., gen. mgr. Bernard Johnson Builders, 1978-79; div. mgr. IBS div. Bertram Smith, Inc., 1979—, v.p., 1983—. Served with U.S. Army, 1953-55. Mem. Internat. Maintenance Inst., Am. Concrete Inst. Republican. Methodist. Office: Bertram Smith Inc 9125 Airport Blvd Suite B-2 Houston TX 77061

BATES, FRED WESTERMAN, consulting geologist, engineer; b. New Haven, Aug. 19, 1911; s. Clifford Whitman and Katharine (Westerman) B.; m. Katharine Woodward Smith; children—Marc, Barbara, Laura, Martha, Sarah. B.S. in Engring., Princeton, 1933; postgrad. in petroleum geology U. Okla., 1934-35. Registered prof. engr., Tex. La. Seismologist, Amerada Petroleum Co., Tulsa, 1933-34; dist. geologist Conoco Oil Co., Ponce City, Okla., 1935-37; ptnr. Bates & Cornell, Lafayette, La., 1937-39, Fred W. Bates & Assoc., 1939—; rep. at pub. hearings La. Dept. Conservation; panelist Am. Arbitration Assn.; dir. emeritus 1st Nat. Bank of Lafayette. Mem. Am. Assn. Petroleum Geologists (cert.), Lafayette Geol. Soc. Office: Bates & Assoc Box 51789 Lafayette LA 70505

BATES, GEORGE WILLIAM, obstetrician, gynecologist, educator; b. Durham, N.C., Feb. 15, 1940; s. George W. and Lillian M. (Streete) B.; m. Susanne Rayburn, Oct. 18, 1969; children—Jonathan Rayburn, Jeffrey William, Robert Wiser. B.S., U. N.C., 1962, M.D., 1965; S.M., MIT, 1984. Diplomate Am. Bd. Ob-Gyn. Intern, U. Ala., Birmingham, 1965; resident ob-gyn U. N.C., 1966-70; prof., chmn. ob-gyn U. Tenn., Knoxville, 1972-76; fellow reproductive endocrinology U. Tex., Dallas, 1976-78; prof. U. Miss. Med. Ctr., Jackson, 1978-86; dean Coll. Medicine, Med. U. S.C., 1986—. Served to maj. USAF, 1970-72. Morehead scholar, 1958; NIH research trainee, 1976-78; Sloan fellow, 1983; recipient Henry Fordham award, 1966; named Prof. of Yr., U. Miss., 1980. Mem. AMA., Soc. Gynecol. Investigation, Am. Fertility Soc., Endocrine Soc., AAAS. Contbr. articles to profl. publs. Office: 171 Ashley Ave Charleston SC 29425

BATES, HAMPTON ROBERT, JR., pathologist; b. Roanoke, Va., Feb. 1, 1933; s. Hampton Robert and Mary Mildred (Crowder) B.; B.S., Roanoke Coll., 1953; M.D., Med. Coll. Va., 1957; m. Carole Harrison Young, Apr. 12, 1958; children—Hampton Robert III, Catherine Louise. Intern, Med. Coll. Va. Hosp., Richmond, 1957-58, resident in pathology, 1958-63; practice medicine specializing in pathology and nuclear medicine, Richmond, 1963—; pathologist Johnston-Willis Hosp., Chippenham Hosp.; v.p. Clin. Lab. Consultants, Inc., Richmond, 1976—; forensic pathologist Richmond Met. Area, 1959—. Diplomate Am. Bd. Pathology, Am. Bd. Nuclear Medicine, Nat. Bd. Med. Examiners. Fellow Coll. Am. Pathologists (life), Am. Soc. Clin. Pathologists; mem. Med. Soc. Va., Richmond Acad. Medicine, Swedish Pathol. Soc. (corr.). Episcopalian. Club: Diogenes. Contbr. articles on descriptive, exptl. and forensic pathology to med. Jours. Home: 641 Mobrey Dr Richmond VA 23236 Office: 7101 Jahnke Rd Richmond VA 23225

BATES, HAROLD MARTIN, lawyer; b. Wise County, Va., Mar. 11, 1928; s. William Jennings and Reba (Williams) B.; m. Audrey Rose Doll, Nov. 1, 1952 (div. Mar. 1978); children—Linda, Carl. m. Judith Lee Farmer, June 23, 1978. B.A. in Econs., Coll. William and Mary, 1952; LL.B., Washington and Lee U., 1961. Bar: Va. 1961, Ky. 1961. Spl. agt. FBI, Newark and N.Y.C., 1952-56; tech. sales rep. Hercules Powder Co., Wilmington, Del., 1956-58; practice law, Louisville, 1961-62; sec.-treas., dir., house counsel Life Ins. Co. of Ky., Louisville, 1962-66; practice law, Roanoke, Va., 1966—; sec., dir. James River Limestone Co., Buchanan, Va., 1970—; sec. Eastern Ins. Co., Roanoke, 1984—. Pres., Skil, Inc., orgn. for rehab. Vietnam vets., Salem, Va., 1972-75. Served to cpl. U.S. Army, 1946-47, PTO. Mem. Va. Bar Assn., Roanoke Bar Assn., William and Mary Alumni Assn. (bd. dirs. 1972-76), Soc. Former Spl. Agts. of FBI (chmn. Blue Ridge chpt. 1971-72). Republican. Presbyterian. Home: 2165 Laurel Woods Dr Salem VA 24153 Office: Dominion Bank Bldg Suite 1213 Roanoke VA 24011

BATES, JOHN WESLEY, JR., drilling company executive; b. Spirit Lake, Iowa, Sept. 9, 1919; s. John Wesley and Caroline (Colcord) B.; B.A., Dartmouth Coll., 1941; grad. U.S. Naval Air Sch., 1942; m. Avilla Hinckley-Brooks, Oct. 2, 1967; children—Heather, Belinda, Melanie, Laurie. Pres. B & B Drilling Co., Odessa, Tex., 1946-55; pres. Reading & Bates Offshore Drilling Co., Tulsa, 1955-67, chmn. bd., chief exec. officer, 1967—; dir. 1st Nat. Bank & Trust Co., Tulsa. Southwestern Bell Telephone Co. Mem. adv. bd. sch. bus. U. Okla.; bd. dirs. Tulsa Psychiat. Found.; chmn. Tulsa Airport Authority. Served with Air Corps. USN, 1941-45. Republican. Episcopalian. Office: 3800 1st Pl Tulsa OK 74103*

BATES, LESTER LEE, III, lawyer; b. Columbia, S.C., Oct. 1, 1959; s. Lester Lee, Jr. and Gertrude (Lomas) B. B.S. in Fin., U. S.C., 1979; J.D., Washington and Lee U., 1982; postgrad. U. Ga., 1983. Bar: S.C. 1983, U.S. Dist. Ct. S.C. 1983, U.S. Ct. Appeals (4th cir.) 1983. Exec. dir. Law Research Ctr., Columbia, 1982-83; ptnr. Bates & Bates, Columbia, 1984—; dir. Capital Syndication Group, 1983—. Mem. ABA, S.C. Bar Assn., S.C. Trial Lawyers Assn. Republican. Baptist. Office: Bates & Bates 1511 Richland St Columbia SC 29201

BATES, RALPH JAMES, furniture retailer; b. Eldorado, Ark., May 19, 1925; s. Arvin Everitt and Francis (Bogey) B.; m. Mary Lou Hall, Nov. 10, 1961; children—Melodi Dawn, Ralph James; 3 stepsons—Lynn and Glynn (twins), Ben Oliver. Student U. Houston, 1947; Trinity U., 1948, Stephen F. Austin U., 1960. Foreman machine shop Brown Root Inc., Houston, 1951-53; salesman Sears Roebuck & Co., Houston, 1953-54; br. mgr. Electrolux Corp., Houston and Austin, Tex., 1954-59; owner, operator Bates Sewing Ctr., Nacogdoches, 1959-65; pres., chief exec. officer Good Housekeeping Furniture Appliance Inc., Nacogdoches and Lufkin, 1965—; dir. Southside Nat. Bank, Nacogdoches; program installer/computer broker Balco, Nacogdoches, 1979—. Mem. Piney Woods Country Club. Served with USN, 1943-46; Pacific. Mem. Southwest Furniture Assn., Nacogdoches C. of C. Democrat. Methodist. Home: 410 Fairway Dr Nacogdoches TX 75961 Office: Good Housekeeping Furniture Appliance Inc 2219 South St Nacogdoches TX 75961 also 1508 S 1st St Lufkin TX

BATES, ROBERT EDWARD, dental educator; b. Sedalia, Mo., Apr. 10, 1938; s. Robert Edward and Goldia Mae (Smith) B.; m. Sarah Ann Smith, Sept. 1, 1959 (div. 1984); children—Edward, James, Jean; m. Carol Marie Stewart, Feb. 9, 1985. B.S., Central Mo. State U., 1960; D.D.S., U. Nebr., 1970, M.S., 1977. Biochemist, Harris Labs., Lincoln, Nebr., 1960-70; gen. practice dentistry, Lincoln, 1970-74; prof. dentistry U. Nebr.-Lincoln, 1974-84, U. Fla.-Gainesville, 1984—; cons. VA Hosp., Lincoln, 1977-84, Shands Hosp., Gainesville, 1984—. Contbr. articles to profl. jours. Recipient Outstanding Teaching award U. Nebr., 1979. Mem. ADA, Am. Assn. Dental Schs., Am. Pain Soc., Internat. Assn. for Study of Pain, Am. Equilibrium Assn., Omicron Kappa Upsilon. Episcopalian. Avocations: car racing; aviation; car restoration. Home: 10922 NW 11th Ave Gainesville FL 32606 Office: Coll Dentistry U Fla Gainesville FL 32610

BATES, WILLIAM HENRY, JR., music educator, organist; b. Brownwood, Tex., Jan. 12, 1943; s. William Henry Bates and Hazel Elizabeth (Harp) Stuard; m. Carol Jennifer Henry, Aug. 25, 1971; 1 child, Stephen Henry. B.Mus., Howard Payne Coll., 1966; B.A., 1966; M.Mus., Ind. U., 1968, D.Mus., 1978. Instr., asst. prof. U. West Fla., Pensacola, 1969-78; assoc. prof. U. S.C., Columbia, 1978—; organ recitalist, 1968—; organ cons., 1969—. Mem. Am. Guild Organists (dean, 1973-75, 80-81), Am. Musicological Soc., Pi Kappa Lambda. Republican. Home: 108 Dale Valley Rd Columbia SC 29223

BATES-NISBET, (CLARA) ELISABETH, lawyer, school administrator, piano teacher, poet, songwriter; b. Houston, Dec. 4, 1902; d. William David and Kate Broocks (Arnall) Bates; B.A., U. Tex., 1938; M.A., U. Houston, 1941; LL.B., South Tex. Sch. Law, 1937. Tchr. pub. schs., Houston, 1923-49, prin., 1950-73, ret. prin. James Arlie Montgomery Elementary Sch.; admitted to Tex. bar, 1937; tchr. piano. Houston, 1928—. Life mem. chancellor's council U. Tex., Austin, Tex. Congress Parents and Tchrs. Mem. State Bar Tex., Houston Bar Assn., Tex. Tchrs. Assn. (life), Ex-Students Assn. U. Tex. at Austin (life), Tex. Geneal. Soc., Magna Charta Dames (organizing charter mem. East Tex. Colony 3d vice regent courier Round Table Tex. div. 1962-66), Tex. Hist. Assn. (patron, life), Colonial Dames XVII Century (registrar Col. John Alston chpt., mem. nat. com. on Am. history), Alston-Williams-Boddie-Hillard Soc. N.C., Colonial Order Crown, San Augustine County Hist. Soc. (charter), San Jacinto Descs., Inc., Daus. Republic Tex. (organizing charter mem. Ezekial Cullen chpt., rec. sec. gen., compiler and editor annuals 1963-65, state 2d v.p. gen., chmn. orgn. 1965-67, state chmn. Kate Broocks Bates award hist. research Tex. 1976-85), Officers Gen. Club, Soc. Descs. Charlemagne, D.A.R. (Tejas chpt. regent 1966-68, mem. nat. coms.), Soc. Descs. Knights of Order of Garter, Plantagenet Soc., Daus. Am. Colonists (organizer charter mem. LaSalle chpt.), U.D.C., Sovereign Colonial Soc. Ams. Royal Descent, Dames of Ct. of Honor, Daus. of Founders and Patriots of Am., Freedoms Found. Valley Forge (Houston women's chpt.), Internat. Platform Assn., Smithsonian Instn., Bates Family of Old Va. Assn., Jamestowne Soc. (organizing gov. 1st Tex. co. 1982), Delta Kappa Gamma (Eta Delta chpt. 1st v.p. 1966-68, life mem.), Nat. Soc. Poets. Founder perpetual endowment for Kate Harding Bates Parker Fund for Library of Daus. Republic Tex. at the Alamo, also co-founder with Kate Harding Bates Parker perpetually endowed PresI. scholarship in law, history, govt. or music U. Tex. at Austin, and Kate Broocks Bates award for research in Tex. history Daus. Republic Tex.; founder Kate Harding Bates Parker Award Fund for Jr. Historians orgn. of Tex. Hist. Assn., Emma Broocks Arnall perpetual endowment Okla. U., Norman, maj. perpetual endowment for Coll. Fine Arts, U. Tex. honoring her mother Kate Broocks Bates and her children, endowment culminating in the naming of Kate Broocks Bates Recital Hall founder perpetual endowment for San Jacinto Mus. Assn., honoring her great-grandfather, John Pelham Border, soldier at Battle of San Jacinto. Address: 2305 Woodhead St Houston TX 77019

BATEY, SHARYN REBECCA, clinical psychiatric pharmacist, pharmacy consultant; b. Nashville, Apr. 19, 1946; d. Robert Thomas and Sue (Alred) B. B.S. in Pharmacy, U. Tenn., 1969, Pharm.D., 1975; M.S. in Pub. Health, U. S.C., 1984. Registered pharmacist, Tenn., S.C. Hosp. pharmacist Vanderbilt Hosp., Nashville, 1969-71, VA Hosp., Beckley, W.Va., 1971-72, Gainesville, Fla., 1972-73, Battle Creek, Mich., 1973-74; hosp. pharmacy resident VA Hosp., Memphis, 1974-76; psychopharmacy resident Menninger Found., Topeka, 1976-77; clin. pharmacist William S. Hall Psychiat. Inst., Columbia, S.C., 1977-82; asst. prof. U. S.C. Coll. Pharmacy, Columbia, 1977-83, asst. prof. Sch. Medicine, 1981-83, assoc. prof. Coll. Pharmacy and Sch. Medicine, 1983—; chief clin. pharmacy services and ednl. programs William S. Hall Psychiat. Inst., Columbia, 1982—; clin. drug research/drug devel. fellow U. N.C. and Burroughs Wellcome, Research Triangle Park, N.C., 1983-84; pharmacist cons. NIMH, Bethesda, Md., 1982-84, Burroughs Wellcome, Research Triangle Park, 1984—, Health Care Fin. Adminstrn., Balt., 1985—. Author slide/audio programs Psychotropic Medication Education Program, 1978. Contbr. articles on psychopharmacology to profl. jours. Recipient Significant Achievement award Am. Psychiat. Assn., 1980, Sci. award Am. Psychiat. Assn., 1981. Mem. Am. Pub. Health Assn., Am. Assn. Coll. Pharmacy, Am. Coll. Clin. Pharmacy, Am. Soc. Hosp. Pharmacists (chmn. edn. and tng. working group of psychopharmacy spl. interest group 1983-85, chmn.-elect 1985-86, chmn. 1986-87), Southeastern Soc. Hosp. Pharmacists. Avocations: travel; reading. Home: PO Box 11092 Columbia SC 29211 Office: William S Hall Psychiat Inst PO Box 202 Columbia SC 29202

BATRA, SUBHASH KUMAR, textile and nonwoven technology and fiber science educator and researcher, consultant; b. Bannu, India (now Pakistan), Oct. 4, 1935; s. Hira N. and Mukandi Bai (Banga) B. B.S. in Textiles, Delhi U., 1957; S.M., MIT, 1961, S.M. in Mgmt., Sloan Sch. Mgmt., 1977; Ph.D. in Mechanics, Rensselaer Poly. Inst., 1966. Trainee, spinning dept. Delhi (India) Cloth Mills, 1955-56; supr. Ahmedabad (India) New Cotton Mill No. 2, 1957-68; research asst. MIT, Cambridge, 1959-61, research engr., 1961-62, research assoc., 1970-77; grad. asst. Rensselaer Poly. Inst., Troy, N.Y., 1962-66; sr. scientist Battelle Meml. Inst., Columbus, Ohio, 1966-70; assoc. prof. dept. textile materials and mgmt. Sch. Textiles, N.C. State U., Raleigh, 1977-84, prof. dept. textile engring. and sci., 1984—; cons. Kendall Research Lab., Lexington, Mass., 1975, Data Packaging Corp., Cambridge, 1975, Johnson and Johnson, New Brunswick, N.J., 1976, World Bank, Washington,

1975-77, Avtex Fibers Inc., Front Royal, Va., 1978, Monsanto Triangle Park (N.C.) Devel. Center, Inc., 1979-83, Exxon Chem. Co., Baytown, Tex., 1981. Chmn. Gordon Research Conf. on Fiber Sci., 1985. Fellow Textile Inst., Am. Acad. Mechanics; mem. ASME (chmn. textile industries div. 1983—, sec.-treas. 1978-82), Fiber Soc. Buddhist. Contbr. articles to profl. publs.

BATROUNEY, GEOFFREY DAVID, manufacturing company executive, political consultant; b. Melbourne, Australia, Feb. 28, 1954; came to U.S., 1975; s. David and Mary Elizabeth (Gilchrist) B.; m. Nancy Katherine Ablan, Jan. 4, 1976; children—David Charles Geoffrey, Nicholas John Geoffrey, James Gregory.Student in econs. U. Melbourne, 1972-75; B.Sc. in Polit. Sci., U. Wis., 1978. James C. Hagerty fellow Ctr. for Study Presidency, N.Y.C., 1978-79, counsellor to pres., 1979-80, mem. nat. adv. council, 1980—; dir. research Republican Party Wis., Madison, 1979-80; dep. dir. Nat. Inst. Advanced Studies, Washington, 1980-81; v.p. the Co. Store, Inc., Gillette Industries Inc., LaCrosse, Wis., 1982-84; mgr. analysis, new markets Kayser-Roth Hosiery Inc. div. Gulf & Western Industries, Inc., 1984—; cons. Rep. Party Wis. Senate and Assembly caucuses, 1980—; polit. cons. to various corps., polit. action coms. Mem. Com. on Fed. Contracting Practices, Washington, 1980-81. Mem. Inst. World Affairs (Milw. citizens cabinet on U.S. fgn. policy), Am. Council Young Polit. Leaders, Heritage Found. (nat. resource bank 1981—). Republican. Mem. Antiochian Eastern Orthodox Christian Ch. Club: Melbourne Cricket. Home: 4507 Radnor Dr Greensboro NC 27410 Office: Kayser-Roth Hosiery Inc 2306 W Meadowview Rd PO Box 77077 Greensboro NC 27407

BATSON, STEPHEN WESLEY, university administrator, consultant strategic planning and educational law; b. Wilmington, N.C., Aug. 20, 1946; s. John Thomas and Mildred (Pritchard) B.; m. Kathleen Lawless, Apr. 11, 1985. B.A., Mercer U., 1970; M.Ed., Ga. Coll., 1974, Ed.S., postgrad. U. Ga., 1978-84. High sch. tchr., adminstr. several schs., Ga., 1970-75; headmaster John Hancock Acad., Sparta, Ga., 1975-76; sci. chmn. Tattnall Sq. Acad., Macon, Ga., 1976-78; middle sch. coordinator Jefferson Sch. System (Ga.), 1978-79; asst. v.p. for acad. affairs Ga. So. Coll., Statesboro, 1979-82; asst. to pres., dir. planning East Tex. State U., Commerce, 1982—. Bd. dirs. Ga. Jr. Acad. Sci., 1979-81, exec. dir., 1981-82; planning cons. So. Regional Edn. Bd., Atlanta, 1983. Contbr. articles in field to profl. jours. Active Dallas Zool. Soc., 1982—; co-chmn. United Way campaign, Commerce, 1984. Named Bulloch County Leader, Ga. Power Leaders of Tomorrow Program, 1980, Outstanding Young Alumnus, Ga. Coll., 1981. Mem. Nat. Orgn. for Legal Problems in Edn., Assn. for Instl. Researchers, Nat. Assn. Secondary Sch. Prins., Soc. for Coll. and U. Planning, Tex. Acad. Sci., Commerce C. of C. (disting. community service award 1984), Am. Mensa, Phi Delta Kappa. Lodge: Kiwanis (bd. dirs., pres. Commerce). Office: Office of Planning East Tex State U Commerce TX 75428

BATTEN, FRANK, newspaper publisher, broadcaster; b. Norfolk, Va., Feb. 11, 1927; s. Frank and Dorothy (Martin) B.; A.B., U. Va., 1950; M.B.A., Harvard U., 1952; m. Jane Neal Parke; children—Frank, Mary, Dorothy. Asst. sec., treas., v.p., dir., Norfolk Newspapers, Inc., 1952-54; chmn. bd., chief exec. Landmark Communications, Inc., Norfolk, 1967—; pub. Norfolk Virginian-Pilot, Norfolk Ledger-Dispatch, 1954—, Portsmouth Star, 1954—; chmn. Greensboro (N.C.) Daily News, Greensboro Record, 1965—, WTAR Radio, KNTV, KLAS-TV, Roanoke Times and World-News, Tele Cable Corp.; dir. Capital-Gazette Newspapers, Inc., Annapolis, Md.; bd. dirs. Assoc. Press, 1975—, 1st vice chmn., 1979-81, chmn. bd., 1981—; chmn. Newspaper Advt. Bur., 1972-74. Chmn. 1957 Internat. Naval Rev., Hampton Roads, Va.; pres. Norfolk Area United Fund, 1964; former vice chmn. State Council Higher Edn. for Va.; chmn. bd. Old Dominion U., 1962-70; trustee Hollins Coll., 1969-75; trustee U.S. Naval Acad. Found.; past trustee U. Va. Grad. Bus. Sch. Sponsors, SNPA Found. Served with U.S. Mcht. Marine, World War II, later officer USNR. Recipient Norfolk's First Citizen award, 1966. Mem. Norfolk C. of C. (pres. 1961), Am. Press Inst. (dir.), Sigma Delta Chi. Episcopalian. Clubs: Princess Anne Country, Norfolk Yacht. (Norfolk). Office: 150 W Brambleton Ave Norfolk VA 23510*

BATTEN, JAMES KNOX, newspaperman; b. Suffolk, Va., Jan. 11, 1936; s. Eugene Taylor and Josephine (Winslow) B.; B.S., Davidson Coll., 1957; M.P.A., Princeton U., 1962; m. Jean Elaine Trueworthy, Feb. 22, 1958; children—Mark Winslow, Laura Taylor, Taylor Edison. Reporter, Charlotte (N.C.) Observer, 1957-58, 62-65; corr. Washington bur. Knight Newspapers, 1965-70; editorial staff Detroit Free Press, 1970-72; exec. editor Charlotte (N.C.) Observer, 1972-75; v.p. Knight-Ridder Newspapers, Inc., Miami, Fla., 1975-80, sr. v.p., 1980-82, pres., 1982—. Trustee Davidson Coll. (N.C.), U. Miami (Fla.). Served with AUS, 1958-60. Recipient George Polk Meml. award for regional reporting, 1968; Sidney Hillman Found. award, 1968. Methodist. Office: One Herald Plaza Miami FL 33101

BATTEN, JAMES WILLIAM, educator; b. Goldsboro, N.C., Aug. 5, 1919; s. Albert LeMay and Lydia Annie (Davis) B.; A.B., U. N.C., 1940, M.A., 1947, Ed.D., 1960: postgrad. Columbia U., 1942; D.C.A., U. Ariz., 1982; m. Sara Magdalene Storey, June 1, 1945. Tchr., Glendale High Sch., Kenly, N.C., 1940-41, Wilmington Jr. Coll., 1946-47; tchr., coach Princeton (N.C.) High Sch., 1947-50; prin. Micro (N.C.) High Sch., 1950-58; teaching fellow, narrator Morehead Planetarium, Chapel Hill, N.C., 1958-60; prof. edn. E. Carolina U., Greenville, N.C., 1960—, chmn. dept. secondary edn., 1967—, also asst. dean Sch. Edn. Active in civic affairs. Served to lt. comdr. USNR, 1941-46. Mem. NEA, N.C. Assn. Educators (chpt. pres. 1961-62), Nat. Sci. Tchrs. Assn., AAAS, Assn. for Supervision and Curriculum Devel., Phi Delta Kappa (pres. 1961-62), Horace Mann League (pres. 1975-77), Nat. Soc. Study of Edn., Am. Ednl. Research Assn., N.C. Lit. and History Assn., N.C. Assn. for Research in Edn., South Atlantic Philosophy Edn. Soc., Kappa Delta Pi (counselor 1967-74). Democrat. Baptist (deacon). Lion (pres. 1949-51). Author: Our Neighbors in Space, 1962, rev. edit., 1969; Research as a Tool for Understanding, 1965; Stars, Atoms, and God, 1968; (with J. Sullivan Gibson) Soils, 1970, rev. edit., 1977; Understanding Research, 1970, rev. edit., 1972; Human Perspectives in Educational Research, 1973; Rumblings of a Rolling Stone, 1974; Procedures in Educational Research, 1975, rev. edit., 1978; Developing Competencies in Educational Research, 1981, revised edit., 1984; Research in Education, 1986. Contbr. numerous articles to profl. jours.

BATTIN, (ROSABELL HARRIET) RAY, psychologist, audiologist; b. Rock Creek, Ohio; d. Harry Walter and Sophia (Boldt) Ray; A.B., U. Denver, 1948; M.S., U. Mich., 1950; Ph.D., U. Fla., 1959; postgrad. U. Miami (Fla.) Sch. of Medicine, 1957, U. Iowa, 1958; m. Tom C. Battin, Aug. 24, 1949. Instr. in speech pathology U. Denver, 1949-50; audiologist Ann Arbor (Mich.) Sch., 1950-51; audiologist Houston (Tex.) Speech and Hearing Center, 1954-56; dir. speech pathology-psychology Hedgecroft Hosp. and Rehab. Center, Houston, 1956-59; audiologist with Drs. Guilford, Wright and Draper, Houston, 1959-63; pvt. practice in psychology, audiology and psycholinguistics, Houston, 1959—; clin. instr. dept. otolaryngology U. Tex. Sch. Medicine, Galveston, 1964-80; dir. of audiology vestibulography and speech pathology lab. Houston Ear Nose and Throat Hosp. Clinic, 1963-73; adj. clin. instr. U. Houston, 1981—; lectr. The First Word program Sta. KUHT-TV, 1959; guest lectr. to various workshops and schs., 1959—. Lic. psychologist and healthcare provider, audiologist and speech pathologist, Tex. Recipient Gold award for Ednl. Exhibit, Am. Acad. Pediatrics, 1969. Fellow Am. Speech and Hearing Assn. (profl. services bd. 1967-70, com. on pvt. practice 1971-74), World Acad. Inc.; mem. Acad. Pvt. Practice in Speech Pathology and Audiology (pres. 1968-70), Am. Psychol. Assn., Tex. Speech and Hearing Assn. (v.p. 1968), Cleft Palate Assn., Tex., Houston psychol. assns., Acad. of Aphasia, Internat. Assn. of Logopedics and Phoniatrics, Am. Auditory Soc., Orthopsychiat. Assn., Am. Biofeedback Soc., Tex. Biofeedback Soc., Harris County Biofeedback Soc. (pres. 1984—), Sigma Alpha Eta. Author: (with C. Olaf Haug) Speech and Language Delay, 1964; Vestibulography, 1974; Private Practice: Guidelines for Speech Pathology and Audiology, 1971; editor (with Donna R. Fox) Private Practice in Audiology and Speech and Language Pathology, 1978; contbg. author: Seminars in Speech, Language, Hearing (Northern); Auditory Disorders in School Children (Roeser and Downs); Current Therapy of Communications Disorder (Perkins); contbr. articles in field to profl. jours.; author (with Irvin A. Kraft) The Dysynchronous Child (film), 1971; editor Jour. Am. Acad. Pvt. Practice in Speech Pathology and Audiology, 1981-85. Home: 3837 Meadow Lake Ln Houston TX 77027 Office: Battin Clinic 3931 Essex Ln Houston TX 77027

BATTLE, BETTY RUTH, educator; b. Miami, Fla., Nov. 13, 1940; d. Willie Frank and Lealer (Marshall) Garrison; B.A., U. Miami, 1981; m. James Otis Battle, Sr.; children by previous marriage—Elaine, Samuel. Sec., Liberty City Ch. of Christ, Miami, 1973—; editor, pub. Christian Women at Work mag., Miami, 1981—; tchr. journalism and English, Dade County (Fla.) Public Schs., 1981—. Mem. Sigma Delta Chi. Mem. Churches of Christ. Author booklets. Home: 1425 NW 56th St Miami FL 33142

BATTLE, COLIN, business educator, college administrator, consultant; b. Havana, Cuba, Feb. 15, 1944; came to U.S., 1960; s. Joseph E. and Graciela (Primo) B.; m. Donna Raye Manor, May 26, 1978; children—Kerk, Ryan, Tracy, Stephanie. B.B.A., U. Fla., 1967; M.S. in Acctg., U. Mass., 1969; M.B.A., 1971; Ed.D., Fla. Atlantic U., 1982. Instr. Champlain Coll., Burlington, Vt., 1969-71; staff auditor Price Waterhouse & Co., Miami, Fla., 1971-72; prof. acctg. Broward Community Coll., Ft. Lauderdale, Fla., 1972-73, chmn. dept. bus. adminstrn., 1972-75, div. dir., 1976—; adj. prof. Fla. Internat. U., Miami, 1974-75; cons. Am. Council on Edn., Fla. Dept. Edn., others. Author publs. in field. Mem. adv. edn. com. Fla. Real Estate Commn., Orlando, 1983; adv. mem. Atlantic Vocat. Sch., Margate, Fla., 1980-82, Broward County Coordinating Council, 1975-80; cons. Community Service Council, Ft. Lauderdale, 1975, 77. Fla. Dept. Edn. grantee, 1975, 76, 83, 84; recipient Cert. of Service Fla. Bus. Edn. Assn., 1975, 1977. Mem. Fla. Assn. Community Colls. (v.p. 1976-77, 82-83), Fla. Assn. Acctg. Educators. Episcopalian. Club: Broward Elite Swim Team/USS (pres. Ft. Lauderdale 1981-82). Avocations: boating; fishing. Office: Broward Community Coll 1000 Coconut Creek Blvd Coconut Creek FL 33066

BATTLES, RODNEY LAMAR, hospital administrator; b. Gadsden, Ala., Dec. 25, 1959; s. Fred Lamar and Grace (Langston) B.; m. Cathy Sue Steed, Sept. 29, 1984. A.S., Snead State Coll.; B.S., U. Ala. Asst. adminstr. Atlanta Hosp. and Med. Ctr., 1983, Paul B. Hall Regional Med. Ctr., Paintsville, Ky., 1983; interim adminstr. Electria Meml. Hosp., Tex., 1983; adminstr. Grant County Hosp., Williamstown, Ky., 1984—; seminar speaker in field. Mem. Am. Coll. Hosp. Adminstrs., Am. Hosp. Assn., Ky. Hosp. Assn., Williamstown C. of C. Baptist. Lodge: Rotary. Office: Grant County Hosp 238 Barnes Rd Williamstown KY 41097

BATTON, KENNETH DUFF, EDP administrator; b. Greenwood, S.C., May 30, 1942; s. Roy L. and Heppie Duff (Mayson) B.; B.S., Mankato State U., 1970; m. Deborah Dean Solsaa, Feb. 14, 1965; children—James Stanislaus, Michele Dean. EDP programmer operator Josten's, Inc., Owatonna, Minn., 1964-65; programmer, analyst, sr. analyst Mankato (Minn.) State U., 1965-70; EDP mgr. Associated Coll. Central Kans., 1971-72; EDP mgr. U. Va., Charlottesville, 1973-74; sr. mgr. U. Va. Med. Center, 1975-77; systems cons. Glen Raven Mills (N.C.), 1977; sr. asso. PRC Data Services Co., McLean, Va., 1977-78; dep. project mgr. Computer Center, Exec. Office of Pres., Washington, 1978; project mgr. Alaska Fed. Data Processing Center, Anchorage, for PRC Govt. Info. Systems, McLean, Va., 1978-83, mgmt. analyst NASA Hdqrs., 1983-84, data base adminstr. NASA Sci. and Tech. Info. Ctr., 1984-85; prin. cons. govt. info. Systems Prince George's County, Md., 1985—; instr. computer sci. colls. Mem. Data Processing Mgmt. Assn. (chpt. pres. 1977—). Republican. Home: Route 4 Greenwood SC Office: 1500 PRC Dr McLean VA 22102

BAUBLITZ, FREDERICK ULRICH, optometrist; b. Wyanet, Ill., Aug. 17, 1915; s. Fred Ulrich and Garnett Bessie (Faul) B.; m. Victoria Elizabeth Jackson, July 8, 1937; 1 child, Jacquelin B. Grogan. B.S. in Optometry, Ohio State U., 1941, O.D., 1976. Diplomate Am. Acad. Optometry. Pvt. practice optometry, Martinsville, Va., 1947—; mem. State Bd. Examiners in Optometry, Richmond, Va., 1965-75. Pres. Cathedral Choir of Martinsville and Henry County, Va., 1954-59, 61-62; chmn. Health Systems Agy. Sub-Area Council, Southwest Va., 1979-82. Mem. Am. Acad. Optometry (pres. 1977, 78), Nat. Acads. Practices (mem. optometric sect.), Am. Optometric Assn. (hon. life), Va. Optometric Assn. (dir. optometric edn. 1965-71, pres. 1974, Optometrist of Yr. 1968), So. Council Optometrists (chmn. optometric edn. 1968-71), Optometrist of the South 1969). Mem. Christian Ch. (Disciples of Christ). Lodge: Rotary (pres. 1974). Avocations: woodworking; furniture design and gardening. Office: 904 Brookdale Rd Martinsville VA 24112

BAUCHMOYER, MADELEINE ANNE, nurse, educator; b. Los Angeles, Feb. 19, 1945; d. William Frederick and Dorothy Rose (Dalton) Muller; B.S. in Nursing, Catholic U. Am., 1966; M.Ed., U. Miami (Fla.), 1973; M.Nursing, La. State U., 1980, Ph.D. in Ednl. Research, 1986; children—Regina Louise, Karl Celby, Kenneth Garrett. Nurse clinician Miami VA Hosp., 1970; mem. faculty Miami-Dade Community Coll., 1970-73, U. Miami Med. Sch., 1973-75; dir. nursing, coordinator health care program U. Miami, 1973-75; mem. faculty Nicholls State U., Thibideaux, La., 1976-78, La. State U. Sch. Nursing, New Orleans, 1978-80; asst. prof. nursing U. Southwestern La. Coll. Nursing, Lafayette, 1980-86, dir. ednl. mobility track 1982—; cons. quality assurance, research and evaluation Univ. Med. Ctr., 1986—, symposia participant. Reader mass St. Jules Roman Catholic Ch., Lafayette, 1982—; ann. judge Internat. Sci. and Engring. Fair, Office of Naval Research, 1982—; state coordinator Navy Sci. Awards, Regional Sci. Fairs, 1983—. Served as officer Nurse Corps, USNR, 1964-69; capt. Res. Navy scholar, 1964-66. Mem. Am. Council Nurse Researchers, Am. Nurses Assn., Nat. League Nursing, AAUP, Am. Ednl. Research Assn., Nat. Council on Measurement in Edn., Mental Health Assn. Lafayette, Res. Officer Assn. (past chpt. v.p.), Naval Res. Assn., Southwestern La. Arts Council, Spring Fiesta Hist. Assn., Sigma Theta Tau. Republican. Club: Univ. Women's. Office: PO Box 12435 Rosslyn VA 22209

BAUCOM, TERRY MYERS, bookstore executive; b. Roanoke, Va., Mar. 4, 1956; d. Lewis Edward Myers and Betty (Ferris) Brown; m. Ralph Denny Baucom, Aug. 7, 1975 (div. Jan. 1983). Student Roanoke Coll., 1974-76. Collection corr. Sears Roebuck & Co., Roanoke, 1974-80; office mgr. Century Communications, Vinton, Va., 1980-82; ptnr. B&D Buyer Service, Roanoke, 1982—; bd. dirs. Rovacon SF Inc., Salem, Va., 1983-84, mem. adv. bd., 1984—. Editor comic book The Baroness and The Duke, 1984. Recipient Cert. of Appreciation, Rovacon SF Inc., 1984. Democrat. Lutheran. Avocation: panelologist. Home: 3514 Williamson Rd NW Roanoke VA 24012 Office: B&D Buyer Service 3514 Williamson Rd NW Roanoke VA 24012-7623

BAUCUM, ROBERT CLAYTON, medical center administrator, pharmacist; b. Natchez, Miss., Aug. 28, 1953; s. Benjamin Clayton and Ina Jaunette (Crain) B.; m. Gina Marie Rambin, Nov. 28, 1981. B.S. in Pharmacy, Northeast La. U., 1975; M.B.A., La. State U.-Shreveport, 1984. Registered pharmacist, La. Pharmacist Lewis Pharmacies, Shreveport, 1975-78, Medic Pharmacies, Shreveport, 1978-79; registered pharmacist Willis Knighton Med. Ctr., Shreveport, 1979-83, fin. staff, 1984-85, dir. materials mgmt., 1985—; mgr., pharmacist South Shreveport Pharmacy, 1983-84. Mem. La. Pharmacist Assn., North La. Soc. Hosp. Pharmacists, La. State U.-Shreveport M.B.A. Assn. Mem. Ch. of Christ. Avocations: reading; running; tennis. Home: 142 Albany Ave Shreveport LA 71105 Office: Willis Knighton Med Ctr 2600 Greenwood Rd Shreveport LA 71103

BAUDENDISTEL, JOSEPH MATHIAS, air force officer, civil engineer; b. Tinker AFB, Okla., Mar. 9, 1956; s. Richard Henry and Rosalie Anne (Dresner) B.; m. Cindy Kay Ridge, June 9, 1979. B.S. in Civil Engring., U.S. Air Force Acad., 1977; postgrad. Squadron Officer Sch., 1981, Air command and Staff Coll., 1986. Commd. 2d lt. U.S. Air Force, 1977, advanced through grades to capt., 1981; instr. pilot T-37, 81 Flying Squadron, Vance AFB, Enid, Okla., 1978-80; acad. instr. pilot T-37, 71 Student Squadron, Vance AFB, 1980-82; aircraft comdr. KC-135, 509 Air Refueling Squadron, Pease AFB, Portsmouth, N.H., 1982-85; instr. pilot, flight comdr. T-38, 86 Flying Tng. Squadron, Laughlin AFB, Del Rio, Tex., 1985—. Head coach Aquatic Club, Enid, 1977-78; co-head coach Portsmouth Aquatic Club, 1982-84; pres. Booster Club, Portsmouth High Sch. Swim Team, 1984; dir. N.H. High Sch. Swimming, 1983-85. Decorated Air Force Commendation medal with oak leaf cluster. Roman Catholic. Avocation: aquatics. Home: 109 Garden Crest Del Rio TX 78840 Office: 86 Flying Tng Squadron Del Rio TX 78843

BAUER, DAVID FRANCIS, statistics educator; b. Lehighton, Pa., Apr. 13, 1940; s. Luther Franklin Bauer and Grace Barron (Gregory) Flickinger; m. Margaret Knandel, Aug. 28, 1965; children—Lillian G., Sarah M. B.S. in Edn., East Stroudsburg State U., Pa., 1963; M.S., Ohio U., 1965; Ph.D., U. Conn., 1970. Instr. math. Denison U., Granville, Ohio, 1965-66; assoc. mem. tech. staff Bell Labs., Holmdel, N.J., 1966-67; asst. prof. stats. U. Del.-Newark, 1970-74; asst. prof. math. sci. Va. Commonwealth U., Richmond, 1974-78, assoc. prof., 1978—. Contbr. articles to profl. jours. Pres., v.p., treas. Glen Ridge-Rivermont Civic Assn., Richmond, 1976-81. NDEA fellow, 1967-70. Mem. Am. Statis. Assn., Math. Assn. Am., Inst. Math. Statis. Presbyterian. Avocations: golf; reading; travel. Home: 8507 Rivermont Dr Richmond VA 23229 Office: Va Commonwealth U 1000 W Main St Richmond VA 23284

BAUER, ERNEST, atmospheric scientist; b. Vienna, Austria, Mar. 24, 1927; s. Robert and Frederika (Gross) B.; m. Marion Correa, June 1, 1959; children—Eric J., Sharon L. B.A., Cambridge U., Eng., 1947, Ph.D., 1950. Postdoctoral fellow Nat. Research Council, Ottawa, Ont., Can., 1950-52; research assoc. Courant Inst., NYU, N.Y.C., 1952-54, 55-57; asst. prof. physics U. N.B., Fredericton, Can., 1954-55; prin. scientist AVCO Research & Advanced Devel., Wilmington, Mass., 1957-59; staff scientist physics Philco-Ford Corp., Newport Beach, Calif., 1959-65; mem. research staff Inst. Def. Analyses, Alexandria, Va., 1965—; instr. math. and physics NYU, 1953-54, 55-57, Cath. U. Am., Washington, 1968-69, CCNY, 1969-70; mem. tech. adv. com. Internat. Air Pollution Adv. Bd., U.S. Can. Internat. Joint Commn., 1985; cons. NASA, 1979-82. Contbr. articles to profl. jours. Asst. scoutmaster Nat. Captial Area council Boy Scouts Am., 1974-77; mem. Citizens Adv. Com. on Wastewater Treatment Plants, Montgomery County, Md., 1979—; trustee Carderock Springs Elem. Sch., Bethesda, Md., 1968-70. Scholar, Selwyn Coll., Cambridge U., 1947. Fellow Am. Phys. Soc.; mem. Am. Geophys. Union, AIAA (various tech. coms.), Sierra Club (exec. com. Washington group 1981-83, chmn. outings com. 1984-85). Club: Toastmasters (various offices Silver Spring 1978-85). Avocations: outdoor recreation; gardening; ecology; nature. Home: 8109 Fenway Rd Bethesda MD 20817 Office: Inst for Def Analyses 1801 N Beauregard St Alexandria VA 22311

BAUER, JANE ELIZABETH, resort manager; b. Enid, Okla., June 5, 1931; d. Richard Herman and Rena Callista (Stanton) Gengelbach; m. Robert Ivan Bauer, Mar. 18, 1977; children—Janice Elaine, Jay Douglas, Jill Annette. Student Mo. Western State Coll., 1949-50; degree in social sci. Wichita State U., 1982. Clk., Hirsch Bros., St. Joseph, Mo., 1949-51; mem. staff inventory control dept. Quaker Oats, St. Joseph, Mo., 1951-52; IBM operator, gen. office worker Gen. Motors Parts Dept., Wichita, Kans., 1955-56; supr. care or treatment dept., Sedgwick County, Wichita, 1967-75, child custody investigator, 1975-80, adminstrv. aide, 1980-83; mgr. Crestview Recreational Vehicle Ctr., Buda, Tex., 1983—; v.p., treas. J-R Assocs. Mem. Epsilon Sigma Alpha. Republican. Office: Exit 200 I 35 Buda TX 78610

BAUER, JOHN PETER, business executive; b. Fuerth/Bavaria, Germany, Nov. 14, 1925; s. August and Agnes (Rosenfeld) B.; m. Mimi Orozco, Apr. 19, 1975; 1 child, August; children by previous marriage—Steven, David. B.S., M.B.A., NYU. Vice pres. BNS Internat. Sales Corp., 1955-64; pres. Bauer Internat. Corp., N.Y.C., 1964-70, Bauer Industries, Inc., N.Y.C., 1964-70; pres. Basic Food Internat., Inc., Global Food Corp., Fort Lauderdale, 1974—; hon. consul Guatemala. Author: The Chicken War; Trade Policy of the EEC; Foreign Policy with Agricultural Exports. Bd. govs. Weitzmann Inst., Tel Aviv; bd. dirs. Boys Club Am., Fort Lauderdale, Fla. Served with U.S. Army, 1943-45. Decorated Bronze Star medal; Weitzmann Inst. grantee Latin Trade Am. Inst. Mem. Am. Meat Inst., Poultry and Egg Inst., World Trade Council. Clubs: Le Club Internat., Lago Mar Beach, Tower (Fort Lauderdale, Fla.); Marco Polo, Harmony (N.Y.C.); Bankers (Miami). Office: 1300 SE 17th St Fort Lauderdale FL 33316

BAUER, JOSEPH DART, accountant; b. Norfolk, Va., July 22, 1946; s. Leonard Joseph and Muriel Ursula (Gibbons) B.; m. Iona Kathleen Eddlemon, Nov. 25, 1971; 1 dau., Staci. Student U. Ala., 1970-71; B.B.A., U. Tex.-Arlington, 1972; M.Profl. Acctg., U. Tex.-Austin, 1975; postgrad. North Tex. State U., 1980. C.P.A., Ga., Tex., Okla. Staff auditor Price Waterhouse & Co., Atlanta, 1972-74; sr. tax acct. Arthur Andersen & Co., Dallas, 1976-79; tax mgr. Arthur Young & Co., Dallas, 1979-81; tax ptnr. Hupp, Thompson, Crain, Hardon & Bauer, Wichita Falls, Tex., 1981—. Served with USAF, 1965-69. Mem. Am. Inst. C.P.A.s, Ga. Soc. C.P.A.s, Okla. Soc. C.P.A.s, Tex. Soc. C.P.A.s, North Tex. Oil and Gas Assn., Council Petroleum Accts. Socs. Club: Rotary. Baptist. Home: 2418 Bryan Glen Wichita Falls TX 76308 Office: Hupp Thompson et al 1100 Wichita Tower Wichita Falls TX 76301

BAUER, RICHARD HENRY, psychology educator, researcher; b. Garrison, N.D., Oct. 5, 1939; s. Richard and Martha (Sayler) B. B.A. in Psychology, B.A. in Sociology, U. Mont., 1963, M.A., 1965; Ph.D., U. Wash., 1970. Instr. U. Mont., Missoula, 1964-65, U. Houston, 1970-72; research asst. U. Wash., Seattle, 1965-70; postdoctoral fellow UCLA, 1972-77; asst. prof. Kans. State U., Manhattan, 1977-81; asssoc. prof. Middle Tenn. State U., Murfreesboro, 1981—; cons. NSF, Washington, various book publishers, 1980—. Editor profl. jours., 1979—. Contbr. articles to profl. jours. Served with U.S. Army, 1957-59. Predoctoral grad. trainee USPHS, 1963-65, trainee NSF, 1966-70; fellow NIMH, 1972-77, grantee, 1975-77. Fellow Internat. Acad. Research in Learning Disabilities (mem. membership com. 1983—); mem. Am. Psychol. Assn., N.Y. Acad. Sci., Soc. Neurosci., Sigma Xi, others. Avocation: fishing. Office: Dept Psychology Middle Tenn State Univ PO Box 87 Murfreesboro TN 37132

BAUER, SYDNEY MEADE, lawyer; b. Seguin, Tex., Sept. 18, 1957; s. Sydney Moore and Dorothy Meade (Bruns) B.; m. Ann Thompson, Dec. 18, 1982. B.B.A., U. Tex., 1979, J.D., 1982. Bar: Tex. 1982. Assoc., Cox & Smith, San Antonio, 1983—; mem. Pro-Bono Law Project, San Antonio, 1983—. Mem. steering com. John Connally Presdl. Campaign, Guadalupe County, Tex., 1980; mem. exec. heart club Am. Heart Assn., San Antonio, 1984. Mem. ABA (real estate financing com. 1985—), Tex. Bar Assn., San Antonio Bar Assn., State Bar Tex. (constn. com. 1985—), Tex. Exes. Alumni Assn., Pi Kappa Alpha (pres. 1978-79), Phi Delta Phi. Republican. Episcopalian. Office: Cox & Smith 600 NBC Bldg San Antonio TX 78205

BAUGH, JOEL EASTWOOD, JR., architect; b. Washington, Oct. 1, 1946; s. Joel Eastwood and Hazel (Waller) B.; m. Sharon McGourin, May 1, 1970; children—Robert Paul, Alison Christine. B.Arch., U. Fla., 1972. Registered architect, Fla. Architect, Schwab & Twitty, Palm Beach, Fla., 1973-75, David L. Leonard, Deland, Fla., 1978-79; asst. sch. planner Volusia County Sch. Bd., 1975-77; ptnr. Leonard & Baugh, Deland, 1979—. Mem. code enforcement bd. City of Deland, 1985. Served to sgt. USMC, 1964-68; Vietnam. Mem. AIA. Republican. Methodist. Avocations: bodybuilding; skydiving; reading. Office: Leonard & Baugh Architects PA 512 W New York Ave Deland FL 32720

BAUGH, JOHN, linguistics and anthropology educator, researcher; b. Bklyn., Dec. 10, 1949; s. John G. and Barbara G. Baugh; m. Charla Larrimore; 1 child, Chenoa Trout-Baugh. B.A., Temple U., 1972; M.A., U. Pa., 1976, Ph.D., 1979. Trustee, Ctr. Applied Linguistics, Washington, 1983-86; chmn. Am. Linguistics Research Inst., Inc., Austin, Tex., 1985. Author: Black Street Speech: Its History, Structure and Survival, 1983; editor: (with J. Sherzer) Language in Use: Readings in Sociolinguistics, 1984. Am. Council Learned Socs. grantee, 1980; Ford Found. fellow, 1982. Mem. Linguistic Soc. Am., Am. Dialect Soc., Am. Anthropol. Assn., Nat. Council Tchrs. of English, Congress for Coll. Composition and Communication. Avocation: sailing. Office: U Tex Dept Linguistics Austin TX 78712

BAUGH, JOHN FRANK, wholesale company executive; b. Waco, Tex., Feb. 28, 1916; s. John Frank and Nell (Turner) B.; student U. Houston, 1934-36; m. Eula Mae Tharp, Oct. 3, 1936; 1 dau., Barbara. With A&P Food Stores, Houston, 1932-46; owner, operator Zero Foods Co., Houston, 1946-69; chmn. bd. Sysco Corp., Houston, 1969—, also dir.; adv. dir. Bank of Houston; dir. First City Nat. Bank, Houston, Valero Energy Corp. Bd. dirs. Bapt. Found. Tex.; founding trustee Houston Bapt. U.; chmn. trustees Bapt. Ch., 1966—, chmn. deacons, 1954-55. Clubs: Univ., Petroleum, Lakeside Country (Houston); Quail Creek Country (San Marcos, Tex.). Lodge: Rotary. Home: 11111 Wickdale Dr Houston TX 77024 Office: Sysco Corp 1177 W Loop S Houston TX 77027

BAUGHAM, LEONARD ANDREW, surgeon; b. Atlanta, Nov. 21, 1949; s. Lloyd Edward and Lenora Ellen (McMillim) B.; m. Ila Annette Evans, Oct. 17, 1982; children—Leonard Andrew. B.S., Davidson Coll., 1971; M.D., Med. Coll. Ga., 1975. Intern, Charlotte Meml. Hosp., 1975-76, resident, 1878-82; gen. surgeon Wilks Gen. Hosp., North Wilkesboro, N.C., 1982—, chief surgery, 1983. Mem. Wilks County Health Coalition. Served with U.S. Army, 1976-78. Mem. ACS. Republican. Baptist. Club: Elks (North Wilkesboro, NC). Home: Route 1 Box 118-E North Wilkesboro NC 28659 Office: Box 876 North Wilkesboro NC 28659

BAUGHN, ROBERT ELROY, microbiology educator; b. Chanute, Kans., Jan. 31, 1940; s. Berryman Thomas and Oella Louise (Smith) B.; B.S., The Citadel, 1963; M.S. (USPHS fellow), U. Tenn., 1966; Ph.D. (NIH fellow), U. Cin., 1975; M.B.A., Houston Bapt. U., 1980; m. Myra Donell Phillips, Dec. 12, 1965; children—Heather Lynne, Brenna Gayle. Microbiologist, Hutcheson Meml. Tri-County Hosp., Ft. Oglethorpe, Ga., 1969-71, Parkridge Hosp., Chattanooga, 1971; instr. dept. dermatology and dept. microbiology and immunology Baylor Coll. Medicine, 1975-77, asst. prof., 1977-83, assoc. prof., 1983—. Mem. sch. bd. St. Mark's Episcopal Day Sch., Houston, 1978-81; vestryman St. Mark's Ch., 1983-85. Served as capt. AUS, 1967-69. Mem. Am. Soc. Microbiology, Am. Assn. Immunologists, Am. Soc. Clin. Pathology, Undersea Med. Soc., Reticuloendothelial Soc., Sigma Xi. Editorial bd. Infection and Immunity, 1985-87. Contbr. articles to profl. jours. Home: 11003 Atwell Dr Houston TX 77096 Office: Dept Infectious Diseases VA Hosp Bldg 211 2002 Holcombe Houston TX 77211

BAUKNIGHT, CLARENCE BROCK, wholesale and retail company executive; b. Anderson, S.C., May 14, 1936; s. John Edward and Theodosia (Brock) B.; m. Harriet League, June 29, 1959; children—Harriet League, Clarence Brock. B.S., Ga. Inst. Tech., 1958. Dist. mgr. Wickes Corp., and predecessor, Atlanta, 1960-65; exec. v.p. Builder Marts Am., Inc., Greenville, S.C., 1965-70, pres., chief exec. officer, 1970—, dir.; chmn. bd. Aid-in-Mgmt. Tel-Man, Inc., Greenville; dir. Ins. Mgmt. Services, Greenville, Parks Lumber Co., Gainesville, Ga., Robert L. Head Lumber Co., Blairsville, Ga., Atkin Harper Lumber Co., Asheville, N.C., Bivens Builder Mart, Pickens, S.C., Builderway of Fla. and Tex., Jacksonville, Fla., Thompson Lumber Co., Memphis, Jim White Lumber Co., Bay City, Mich. Mem. nat. adv. bd. Ga. Inst. Tech.; mem. policy adv. bd. Joint Ctr. Urban Studies Harvard U., MIT; trustee Buncombe St. United Meth. Ch. Mem. Indsl. Mgmt. Soc., Chief Execs. Orgn., Phi Delta Theta. Clubs: Greenville Country; Poinsett (Greenville); Wildcat Cliffs, Highlands Country (Highlands, N.C.). Lodges: Masons; Shriners. Home: 111 Rockingham Rd Greenville SC 29607 Office: Builder Marts of Am PO Box 47 Greenville SC 29602

BAUM, ALVIN JOHN, JR., optometrist, professional clown; b. Birmingham, Ala., June 25, 1918; s. Alvin John and Mildred (Fox) B.; m. Ruth Virginia Marks, Sept. 4, 1943 (div. 1966); children—Barbara, Joanne; m. Charlene Ballingee Wall, Feb. 26, 1971; children—Teddie, Leslie, Robert Jr., Jefferson, Lance. O.D., Pa. Coll. Optometry, 1941. Cert. optometrist, Va. Practice optometry specializing in contact lenses, Richmond, Va., 1945—. Contbr. articles to profl. jours. Life mem. Tuckahoe Vol. Rescue Squad, Richmond, 1975; mem. USCG Aux., 1942-78 (past comdr. Flotilla 34, 1945) Richmond, 1978; pres. Va. Citizens Band Communicators, Richmond, 1985. Served with USCG, 1942-45. recipient Service award USAF aux. CAP, Va., 1973. Mem. Clowns Am. Internat. (nat. dir. 1974-84, cert. of recognition 1980), USCG Past Comdrs. Assn., Richmond Optometric Soc. (past pres. 1950). Republican. Jewish. Club: Virginia Alley 3 (pres. 1950-60). Avocations: Professional clown; citizens band communications assisting police control. Home: 3802 Lake Hills Rd Richmond VA 23234 Office: Clown Assn Richmond 4000 Hull St Richmond VA 23224

BAUM, ROBERT JAMES, educator; b. Chgo., Oct. 19, 1941; s. Adam and Jean (TerMeer) B. B.A., Northwestern U., 1963; Ph.D., Ohio State U., 1969. From asst. prof. to prof. philosophy Rensselaer Poly. Inst., 1969-81; dir. ethics and values in sci. and tech. program NSF, 1974-76; dir. Human Dimensions Ctr., Rensselaer Poly. Inst., 1976-81; prof. and chmn. dept. philosophy U. Fla., Gainesville, 1981—, dir. Ctr. Applied Philosophy, 1981—. Served with U.S. Peace Corps, 1965-67. Mellon fellow Aspen Inst., 1977; recipient Disting. Service award NSF, 1975. Mem. Am. Philos. Assn., Philosophy Sci. Assn., Soc. Study Profl. Ethics. Author: Philosophy and Mathematics, 1974; Logic, 1975, 81; Ethics and the Engineering Curriculum, 1981; editor: Ethical Arguments for Analysis, 1973, 77; co-editor Bus. and Profl. Ethics Jour., 1980—; series editor Advanced Studies in Professional Ethics. Office: Dept Philosophy U Fla Gainesville FL 32611

BAUMAN, CHARLES EDWARD, informations systems executive; b. Tacoma, Aug. 9, 1950; s. Austin Carl and Marilyn Cecelia (Mulderig) B.; m. Dottie Jean Rodgers; children—Melissa, Melanie. A.S. in Computer Sci., Thomas Nelson Community Coll., 1968-70; B.S. in Mgmt., Golden Gate U., 1974, M.B.A., 1976; Air Command and Staff Coll. diploma Air U., 1983. Sr. programmer analyst Computer Scis. Corp., San Diego, 1974-76; site systems analyst Honeywell Info. Systems, McLean, Va., 1976; chief command and control plans Hdqrs. Tactical Air Command, Langley AFB, Va., 1976-81, dir. tactical air mission mgmt., 1981-85, dep. comdr. tactical systems, 1985—; chmn. Air Force Civilian Awards Bd., 1983—; command rep. Air Force Info. Systems Career Program, Randolph AFB, Tex., 1984-85; council mem. Air Force Tng. and Devel. Panel, 1983-85. Newport News rep. Va. Baptist Children's Home, Salem, 1985. Served with USAF, 1970-74. Recipient Outstanding Young Men of Am. award Jaycees, 1980, 85. Mem. Armed Forces Communications and Electronics Assn. Bapt. Clubs: RX7 of Am. (Calif.), Z of Am. (N.J.). Avocations: sports cars; golf; automobile racing; music. Home: 124 Daphne Dr Yorktown VA 23692 Office: Hdqrs 1912 Info Systems Support Group Tactical Systems Langley AFB VA 23665

BAUMAN, EDWARD JOSPEH, company executive; b. Lorain, Ohio, Jan. 7, 1925; s. Henry Elmer and Clara (Haehner) B.; m. Vivien Kelley; children—Jeff, Kim, Jim. B.S. in Mech. Engring., Purdue U., 1950. Div. pres. Hicks-Ponder div. Blue Bell, Inc., El Paso, Tex., 1976-78; exec. v.p. Red Kap Industries div. Blue Bell Inc., Nashville, 1978-79; pres., 1979-82; pres., chief operating officer Blue Bell, Inc., Greensboro, N.C., 1982-83, pres., chief exec. officer, 1983—, dir.; dir. 1st Union Corp., Charlotte, N.C., AAMA, Arlington, Va., Piedmont Industries, Greensboro. Mem. Old Greensborough, Greensboro Devel. Com. Clubs: Country, Greensboro City (Greensboro).

BAUMAN, ROBERT POE, physicist; b. Jackson, Mich., May 8, 1928; s. Chester E. and M. Victoria (Poe) B.; m. Edith Jane Gerkin, Aug. 27, 1949; children—Katherine Jane, David Gordon, Jeffrey Allen, Alice Victoria. B.S., Purdue U., 1949, M.S., 1951; Ph.D., U. Pitts., 1954. From instr. to assoc. prof. chemistry Poly. Inst., Bklyn., 1954-67; tech. staff Bell Telephone Labs., Murray Hill, N.J., summer, 1966; prof. physics U. Ala., Birmingham, 1967—, chmn. dept., 1967-73, dir. project on tchg., learning, U. Coll., 1975-78; vis. fellow Joint Inst. Lab. Astrophysics, Boulder Colo., 1980-81; assoc. counselor Ala. Jr. Acad. Scis., 1970-73. Pres. Birmingham Civic Chorus, 1974-75; mem. Bethpage (N.Y.) Bd. Edn., 1965-67, pres., 1965-66. Mem. Am. Phys. Soc., Am. Assn. Physics Tchrs. (pres. 1983), Coblentz Soc. (past pres.), Ala. Acad. Scis. (vice chmn., v.p., 1968-70). Author: Absorption Spectroscopy, 1962; Introduction to Equilibrium Thermodynamics, 1966. Office: Physics Dept University of Alabama Birmingham AL 35294

BAUMANN, DEAN ROBERT, petroleum geologist; b. Algoma, Wis., May 14, 1957; s. Elmer and Elmyra (Sell) B.; m. JoAnn Mary Zirbel, June 12, 1976; children—Aaron Michael, Nathaniel Dean, David Elias. B.S. in Geology, U. Wis.-Oshkosh, 1979; M.S. in Geology, So. Ill. U., 1982. Geologist, White Pine Copper Co., Mich., 1979; prodn. geologist Sun Prodn. div. Sun Co., Longview, Tex., 1981-83, exploration geologist Sun Exploration div., Dallas, 1983—. Recipient James Vedder Meml. award Geology Dept. U. Wis.-Oshkosh, 1979. Mem. Am. Assn. Petroleum Geologists, Dallas Geol. Soc., Phi Kappa Phi. Republican. Clubs: Geology (pres. 1978-79), U. Wis. (Oshkosh). Avocations: photography; woodworking; gardening. Office: Sun Exploration and Prodn Co 8150 N Central Expressway Dallas TX 75221

BAUMANN, JOHN, printing company financial executive, consultant; b. Phila., May 23, 1948; s. Francis Albert and Rita (Manning) B. B.S., Fla. State U., 1970, M.B.A., 1976. Intern acct. Deloitte Haskins and Sells, N.Y.C., 1969, Miami, Fla., 1970; staff acct. IBM, White Plains, N.Y., 1970-71, Keller Industries, Miami, Fla., 1971-72; corp. auditor Knight-Ridder News, Miami, 1972-73; fin. analyst FMC Corp., Lakeland, Fla., 1976-77; sr. internal auditor DWG Corp., Miami, 1977-78; corp. controller Haff-Daugherty Graphics, Inc., Miami, 1979—, trustee employees retirement plan and trust, 1983—, corp. asst. sec., 1985—; cons. fin. planning, taxes. Campaign treas. Bill Porter for City Commr., South Miami, Fla., 1980, Bill Porter for Mayor, 1984, 86; sec.-treas. Dade County Fla. State U. Seminole Boosters, 1981-82, pres., 1982—; chmn. Fla. State U. Found. Dade County Bd., 1981—. Mem. Republican Nat. Com., Fla. State U. Alumni Assn. (life), Greater Miami C. of C. (sustaining), Hist. Assn. South Fla., Christopher Columbus High Sch. Alumni Assn., Fla. State U. Found. Pres.'s Club, Alpha Kappa Psi (life; v.p. Housing Found., Inc., Tallahassee 1984—). Home: 5740 SW 46 Terr Miami FL 33155 Office: Haff-Daugherty Graphics Inc PO Box 490 950 SE 8th St Hialeah FL 33011

BAUMANN, RICHARD BERNARD, association executive; b. Sheboygan, Wis., June 11, 1946; s. Bernard E. and Mildred L. (Steffen) B.; m. Maj-Charlotte C. Lindblom, Oct. 19, 1971; Diploma, Concordia Coll., Milw., 1966; B.A., Carthage Coll., Kenosha, Wis., 1968; M.A., U. Wis.-Milw., 1974; postgrad. Goethe Inst., Hong Kong. Tchr. English, Luth. Middle Sch., Kowloon, Hong Kong, 1968-69; research officer/analyst, dept. supr. Luth. World Fedn./World Service, Hong Kong, 1969-72; assoc. planner Mental Health Planning Council, Milw., 1974-79; dir. community ops. Am. Heart Assn. Wis., Milw., 1979-82; dir. fund raising and field services Am. Heart Assn. Fla., St. Petersburg, 1982—; research cons. Action Com. Against Narcotics, Hong Kong, 1970-71. Bd. dirs. Swedish Am. Hist. Soc. Wis., vice chmn., 1979-82. Mem. Nat. Soc. Fund Raising Execs. Lutheran. Lodge: Vasa Order Am. (vice chmn. local lodge 1978-79). Home: PO Box 681 Saint Petersburg FL 33731 Office: 810 63d Ave N PO Box 42150 Saint Petersburg FL 33742

BAUMER, DAVID LEE, economics educator, lawyer, antitrust consultant; b. Columbus, Ohio, Apr. 28, 1949; s. Elmer Frederick and Virginia Catherine B.; m. Joan Leslie Malinas, May 23, 1976; children—Erik, Paul. B.A. cum laude, Ohio U., 1971; J.D. cum laude, U. Miami, 1979; Ph.D. in Econs., U. Va., 1980. Bar: N.C. 1980. Economist, Nat. Milk Producers Fedn., Washington, summer 1975, U.S. Dept. Agr., Washington, summers 1976-78; asst. prof. dept. econs. and bus. N.C. State U., Raleigh, 1978—; antitrust cons.; expert witness antitrust cases involving dairy industry. Earhart fellow, 1975; Thomas Jefferson Found. fellow, 1976; J.M. Olin fellow in Law and Econs., 1976-79; NSF grantee. Mem. Am. Econ. Assn., Agrl. Econ. Assn., ABA, N.C. State Bar. Republican. Contbr. articles to profl. publs. Home: 1307 College Pl Raleigh NC 27605 Office: NC State Univ Dept Econs and Bus 220 Patternson Hall Raleigh NC 27695

BAUMGARDNER, JAMES LEWIS, educator; b. Bristol, Va., Jan. 26, 1938; s. John Richard and Roxie Katherine (Lewis) B.; A.A., Bluefield Jr. Coll., 1957; B.A., Carson-Newman Coll., 1959; M.A., U. Tenn., Knoxville, 1964, Ph.D., 1968; children—Ellen Lorena, James Michael. Asst. prof. history Carson-Newman Coll., Jefferson City, Tenn., 1964-67, asso. prof., 1967-73, prof., 1973—, chmn. history-polit. sci. dept., 1974—; ordained to ministry Baptist Ch., 1955. Interim mem. Jefferson County (Tenn.) Bd. Sch. Commrs., 1978. Served with U.S. Army, 1959-62. Mem. Am. Hist. Assn., Acad. Polit. Sci., Orgn. Am. Historians, So. Hist. Assn., So. Bapt. Hist. Soc., Phi Alpha Theta. Contbr. articles to learned jours. Office: Box 1929 Carson-Newman Coll Jefferson City TN 37760

BAWUAH, KWADWO, economics and business educator; b. Kumasi, Ashanti, Ghana, June 13, 1946; came to U.S., 1969; s. Yaw Acheampong and Abena Achiaa; m. Elizabeth Adjei; children—Nana A., Sabrina Y., Edwina A. B.A., Bethany Coll., 1972; M.B.A., Eastern Ill. U., 1973, M.A., 1974; Ph.D., Va. Poly Inst. and State U., 1980. Instr., then asst. prof. Ky. State U., Frankfort, 1977-81; asst. prof. S.C. State Coll., Orangeburg, 1982-84; assoc. prof. econs and bus. Va. State U., Petersburg, 1984—; cons. in field. Contbr. articles to profl. publs. Kellog fellow, 1979. Mem. Am. Econ. Assn., Nat. Econ. Assn., Delta Tau Delta. Republican. Roman Catholic. Lodge: K.C. Office: Va State U Box 515 Petersburg VA 23803

BAXLEY, WILLIAM JOSEPH, state lieutenant governor; b. Dothan, Ala., June 27, 1941; s. Keener and Lemma Dorcas (Rountree) B.; m. Lucy Richards; 1 son, Louis. B.S., U. Ala., 1962, LL.B., 1964. Bar: Ala. 1964. Law clk. Ala. Supreme Ct., 1964-65; mem. firm Lee & McInish, Dothan, 1966; dist. atty. 20th Jud. Circuit Ala., 1966-71; atty. gen. State of Ala., 1971-79; ptnr. Baxley, Beck, Dillard & Dauphin, Birmingham, Ala., 1979-83; lt. gov. State of Ala., 1983—. Bd. dirs. Dothan Boys Club. Served with USAF, 1965-66. Mem. Houston County Bar Assn. (pres. 1969), United Comml. Travelers, Kappa Sigma, Alpha Kappa Psi, Phi Alpha Delta. Democrat. Methodist. Lodges: Masons; Shriners; Elks; Eagles; Woodmen of World. Office: Office of Lt Gov Suite 725 Ala State House Montgomery AL 36130

BAXTER, TURNER BUTLER, ind. oil operator; b. Dermott, Ark., Mar. 13, 1922; s. Robert Wiley and Sallie Hollis (Murphy) B.; B.B.A., U. Tex., 1947; M.B.A., Pepperdine U., Los Angeles, 1976; m. Pauline Taylor Bond, June 7, 1947; children—David Bond, Paula Taylor. With Rio Grande Nat. Life Ins. Co., Dallas, 1947-67, sr. v.p., 1963-67; engaged in investments, 1967-75, 79—; independent oil operator, 1979—; pres. Shelby Office Supply Inc., Dallas, 1975-79. Pres. Dallas Health and Sci. Museum, 1953-56; adv. bd. Dallas Community Chest Trust Fund, 1976—; v.p. Circle Ten council Boy Scouts Am., 1970-74. Served with USAAF, 1943-46. Recipient Silver Beaver award Boy Scouts Am., 1968. Mem. Salesmanship Club Dallas. Methodist. Clubs: Kiwanis (pres. 1966), Dallas Country, Petroleum (Dallas). Home: 5815 B E University Dallas TX 75206 Office: PO Box 297 Dallas TX 75221

BAYAZITOGLU, YILDIZ YONDEMLI, mechanical engineering educator; b. Sivas, Turkey, July 27, 1945; came to U.S., 1967; d. Fikri Ahmet and Kadriye (Gunay) Yondemli; m. Yildirim Omer Bayazitoglu, July 29, 1967; children—Ozgur Kaya, Yavuz Mert, Cengis Koont. B.S., Middle East Tech. U. (Turkey), 1967; M.S., U. Mich., 1969, Ph.D., 1974. Registered profl. engr., Tex. Asst. prof. med. engring. Middle East Tech. U., 1973-74; vis. asst. prof. U. Houston, 1975-76; asst. prof. Rice U., Houston, 1977-80, assoc. prof., 1980—; vis. prof. Imperial Coll., U. London, 1983—. NSF grantee, 1977-81. Mem. ASME. Contbr. articles to profl. jours. Office: Mech Engring Dept Rice U Houston TX 77251

BAYER, ALAN EVERETT, sociology educator; b. Webster, Mass., May 3, 1939; s. J. Otto and Doris (Carver) B.; B.S., Pa. State U., 1961; M.S., Fla. State U., 1963, Ph.D., 1965; m. Carolyn A. Reeves, Aug. 3, 1963; children—Karen, Lisa. Research assoc. Nat. Acad. Scis., Washington, 1965-67; research scientist Am. Insts. Research, Palo Alto, Calif., 1967-68; assoc. dir. research Am. Council on Edn., Washington, 1968-73; prof., chmn. sociology Fla. State U., 1973-80; prof., head dept. sociology Va. Tech. U., 1982—; vis. fellow Boys Town Research Center, Omaha, 1980-82. Mem. Am. Sociol. Assn., Am. Ednl. Research Assn., Nat. Council on Family Relations, Soc. Social Studies of Sci., Assn. Study of Higher Edn. Co-author: Human Resources and Higher Education, 1970; The Power of Protest, 1975. Home: 1902 Lacy Ln Blacksburg VA 24060 Office: Dept Sociology Va Tech U 24061

BAYER, KAREN ELAINE, educator; b. Tulsa, Sept. 24, 1950; d. Kenneth Charles and Vivian (Smith) B. B.S. in Edn. and Psychology, James Madison U., 1975; M.Ed. in Edn., George Mason U., 1985. Cert. tchr. emotional disturbed, mentally retarded and learning disabled, Va. Tchr. mentally retarded Fairfax County Pub. Schs., Va., 1976-81, tchr. learning disabled, 1981—, mem. spl. edn. curriculum team for computer applications, 1985; also condr. inservices for classroom mgmt. and new tchr. tng. Decorated U.S. Army Commendation medal; recipient commendation Fairfax County Sch Bd., 1984. Mem. NEA, Va. Edn. Assn. (del. state convs.), Fairfax Edn. Assn., Council Exceptional Children, Va. Psychol. Assn., Kappa Delta Pi. Avocations: U.S. Army. Office: Crestwood Elementary Sch 6010 Hanover Ave Springfield VA 22150

BAYNARD, MILDRED MOYER (MRS. ROBERT S. BAYNARD), former business executive, civic worker; b. Lincoln, Nebr., May 10, 1902; d. Charles Calvin and Flora (Harter) Moyer; student Sullins Coll., 1921, U. So. Calif., 1922; B.A., U. Nebr., 1925; m. Robert S. Baynard, May 24, 1927; 1 son, Lester B. Tchr. public schs., Lincoln, 1926-27, Crescent City, Fla., 1925-26; sec. Venice Land Co., Inc., 1949-69; sec. Fla. Bridge Co., 1960-68; partner Ind. Parking, 1965-72; v.p. Venice-Nokomis Bank, Venice, Fla., 1947-63, dir., 1947-63; pres. Venice Land Co., 1969-72. Mem. Fla. State Dist. Welfare Bd., 1948-52; pres. bd. dirs. YWCA, 1953-56; Fla. chmn. Nat. Soc. Prevention Blindness, 1957-60, bd. dirs., 1960-67, v.p., 1963-66; nat. v.p., pres. Fla. Soc. Prevention Blindness, 1958-64, v.p., 1967-68, also mem. Fla. exec. com., hon. life mem.; dir. Center for Blind, 1956; pres. Suncoast div. Arthritis Found. Inc., 1966-67; mem. nat. voter adv. bd. Nat. Security Council; pres. North Ward PTA, 1938; sec. St. Petersburg (Fla.) Woman's Club, 1945-46; corr. sec. St. Margaret's Guild, St. Thomas Episcopal Ch., St. Petersburg; Democratic precinct committeewoman, 1936. Recipient Outstanding Citizen's award Pinellas County Commn., 1964, Sarah Schwab Deutsch award, 1978. Mem. Stuart Soc., St. Petersburg Hist. Soc., Mus. Fine Arts, All Childrens Hosp. Guild, U. Nebr. Alumni Assn. (dir. Fla. Gulf Coast), Museum of Fine Arts, Nat. Soc. for Lit. and Arts, Am. Council World Freedom, Nat. Taxpayers Union, DAR, Conservative Caucus, Nat. Conservative Found. Delta Gamma (province officer 1950-56, conv. chmn. 1964, Cable award 1964, Shield award 1973, house corp. 1969—, hon. fellow found. 1974—). Clubs: Sorosis; Rotary Ann (pres. Venice 1962); Yacht of St. Petersburg, Panhellenic, Women's, Interlock (sec. 1942-44) (St. Petersburg, Fla.); Venice Nokomis Woman's (life). Mem. editorial adv. bd. Florida Lives. Home: 627 Brightwaters Blvd NE Saint Petersburg FL 33704

BAZEN, DAPHNE PORTER, nurse; b. Loris, S.C., June 2, 1939; d. Burris Herbert and Naomi Grace (Stevens) Porter; m. Borie Edward Bazen, Mar. 29, 1959; children—Barry Edward, Lesli Maria. A.S. in Nursing, Florence-Darlington Tech. Coll., 1975; B.S. in Nursing, Med. U. S.C., 1984. R.N., S.C. Grad. nurse intern McLeod Meml. Hosp., Florence, S.C., 1975-76, staff nurse, 1976-78; head nurse CCU, McLeod Regional Med. Ctr., Florence, 1978—, instr. basic cardiac life support, 1978-79; mem. nurses' continuing edn. com. for S.C.; vol. S.C. Heart Assn., Columbia, 1979-84; instr. basic electrocardiography course Pee Dee chpt. Area Health Edn. Com., Florence, 1979-80. Named Employee of Yr., Active Med. Staff McLeod Regional Med. Ctr., 1984; McLeod Meml. Med. Aux. scholar Florence-Darlington Tech. Coll., 1975. Mem. Am. Assn. Critical Care Nurses (pres. Pee Dee chpt.), Am. Nurses Assn., S.C. Nurses Assn. (del. 1985), Pee Dee Nurses Assn., Sigma Theta Tau. Republican. Baptist. Lodge: Civitan. Avocations: bicycling; reading; sewing. Home: 1708 Winthrop Dr Florence SC 29501 Office: McLeod Regional Med Ctr 555 E Cheves St Florence SC 29501

BEACH, ROBERT OLIVER, II, computer executive; b. Washington, June 25, 1932; s. Oliver Fairmont and Aldora (Stone) B.; student George Washington U., 1950-51, 57-62; m. Allie A. Lamb, Aug. 14, 1976; children by previous marriage—Patricia Ann, Robert Edward, Michael Oliver, John Roger. With Engring. Research Corp., 1951-52; design engr. Nems-Clarke, 1952-55; project engr. Frederick Research Corp., 1955-59; project mgr. Am. Machine & Foundry Co., 1959-62; pres., founder SAID, Inc., Falls Church, Va., 1962—, Systems, Analyses, Instrumentation & Devel., 1977—; pres. Quick Copy, Inc., 1972—, Air Parcel Delivery, Inc., 1974—; real estate broker; comml. airplane pilot; cons. mktg. and fin.; v.p. Interstate Service Corp.; high sch. faculty adv. devel. data processing curriculum, 1971. Mem. Falls Church Bicentennial Commn., 1975—. Cert. data processor; cert. systems profl.; cert. air taxi capt. Mem. Data Processing Mgmt. Assn., UNIVAC Users Assn., Aircraft Owners and Pilots Assn., Falls Church C. of C., Mensa. Club: Optimist (charter). Home: 1300 N Tuckahoe St Falls Church VA 22046 Office: 417 W Broad St Falls Church VA 22046

BEACHAM, WOODARD DAVIS, physician, emeritus educator; b. McComb, Miss., Apr. 10, 1911; s. Woodard D. and Ida (Felder) B.; B.A., U. Miss., 1932; B.S., 1933; M.D., Tulane U., 1935. Intern, Charity Hosp. of La., New Orleans, resident in obstetrics and gynecology, sr. vis. surgeon, 1948-74, cons., 1975—; prof. clin. gynecology and obstetrics Tulane U. Sch. Medicine, 1949-81, prof. emeritus, 1981—; obstetrician and gynecologist So. Bapt. Hosp., pres. staff, 1961, now hon. staff; past pres. surg. staff Charity Hosp., New Orleans; cons. Beacham Meml. Hosp. Magnolia, Miss., Dieu Sisters Hosp., New Orleans, Methodist Hosp.; hon. staff Tulane U. Hosp., New Orleans; practice medicine specializing in obstetrics and gynecology, 1940-74, in gynecology, 1975—; chmn. internat. relations com. 10th World Congress Gynecology and Obstetrics; pres. Beacham Corp., 1964-79. Mem. adminstrv. bd., fin. com. Carrollton Meth. Ch. Recipient A.C.S. med. records prize, 1943; Spl. award So. Bapt. Hosp., 1979. Diplomate Am. Bd. Obstetrics and Gynecology. Fellow A.C.S. (gov. as rep. obstet., gynecol. sect. AMA 1955-60, gov. as rep. Am. Gynecol. Soc. 1961-63; med. devices com. 1985—, past pres. La. chpt.), Am. Gynecol. Soc. (council 1959, 60), Am. Assn. Obstetricians and Gynecologists (com. on maternal welfare 1960, v.p. 1970-71), Am. Coll. Obstetricians and Gynecologists (first pres., liaison com. with Internat. Fedn. Gynecology and Obstetrics 1973-84, chmn. president's group, Disting. Service award 1976, com. on devel. 1985—), Am. Gynecol. and Obstet. Soc.; mem. ACP (emeritus), So. Gynecol. and Obstet. Soc. (pres. 1967), Am. (chmn. sect. obstetrics and gynecology 1957-58), So. (chmn. sect. on obstetrics 1949, mem. council 1961-63, gen. chmn. arrangements ann. meeting 1972, 2d v.p. 1972, 1st v.p. 1973, Disting. Service award 1975) med. assns., Internat. House New Orleans (founder; dir. 1974—, exec. com. 1977—), Internat. Trade Mart, C. of C., New Orleans Mus. Art, New Orleans Tourist and Conv. Commn., La., Orleans Parish med. socs., New Orleans Grad. Med. Assembly (past pres.), New Orleans Gynecol. and Obstet. Soc. (past pres.), Conrad G. Collins Obstetric and Gynecologic Soc. Tulane U. (1st pres.), Central Assn. Obstetricians and Gynecologists (asst. sec. 1950-52), U. Miss. Alumni Assn. (dir. 1962-65, past pres. New Orleans; named to Hall of Fame 1976), Philippine Obstet. and Gynecol. Soc. (hon.), AAAS, Assn. Profs. Gynecology and Obstetrics, Peruvian (hon.), Paraguayan (hon.) obstet. and gynecol. socs., Tulane Med. Alumni Assn. (sec. 1971-73, v.p. 1974-75, pres. 1976-77), Tulane Med. Ctr. Hosp. Aux. (life), Sigma Xi, Alpha Omega Alpha, Phi Chi (grand presiding sr., nat. pres. 1970-73, trustee 1973-84), Beta Theta Pi. Methodist (chmn. pastor-parish relations com. 1980, chmn. trustees, 1980, chmn. adminstrv. bd. 1981). Clubs: Plimsoll, Circumnavigators, Tulane Green Wave, Tulane Emeritus Author: (with Robert J. Crossen and Dan W. Beacham) Synopsis of Gynecology (5th edit.), (with Dan W. Beacham) 6th edit., 1963, 7th edit., 1967, 8th edit., 1972, 9th edit., 1977, 10th edit., 1982; editor for gynecology and obstetrics Stedman's Med. Dictionary, 23d edit.; contbr. to publs. in field. Home: 504 Alverton Ct Jackson MS 39208

BEACHLEY, CHARLES EDWARD, JR., surgeon; b. Nutley, N.J., Feb. 25, 1924; s. Charles Edward and Ruth Edna (Baitzell) B.; A.B., Johns Hopkins, 1943; M.D., Harvard, 1947; m. Joan Elizabeth Nichols, Apr. 3, 1948 (div.); children—Charles Edward III, Ann (Mrs. Lynn Patrick Martin), Holly Gail (Mrs. Russell Brear), Pamela Ruth; m. Linda Kay Callendar, June 23, 1984. Intern U. Pitts. Med. Center, 1947-48; resident in surgery N.Y. U. Bellevue Med. Center, 1948-53; pvt. practice gen. surgery, Mt. Lebanon, Pa., 1955-57, Paris, Tex., 1957—. Served with USAF, 1953-55. Diplomate Am. Bd. Surgery. Fellow A.C.S.; mem. Community Concert Assn. Paris (Tex.), Phi Beta Kappa, Omicron Delta Kappa, Pi Delta Epsilon, Alpha Tau Omega. Episcopalian. Club: Masons. Home: 2940 Briarwood Dr Paris TX 75460 Office: 2850 Lewis Ln Paris TX 75460

BEACROFT, PERCIVAL THOMAS, real estate executive, lawyer; b. Freeport, Tex., Apr. 21, 1935; s. Percival Thomas and Pollye (Maddox) B.; B.A., So. Meth. U., 1957, J.D., 1960; cert. internat. law U. London, Eng., 1962. Bar: Tex. 1960. Lawyer Chase Manhattan Bank, N.Y.C., 1965-67; legal counsel Ashley Famous Agy., N.Y.C., 1967-69; pres., owner Beacroft Real Estate Inc., N.Y.C., 1968-78, Freeport, Tex., 1978—; pres. R.E.L. Stringfellow Interests, Freeport, 1971—. Bd. dirs. Jefferson Davis Assn., Houston, 1976—, Tex. Hist. Found., Austin, 1980—. commr. Freeport Planning Commn., 1974-75; adv. dir. Brazoria County Mus., Angleton, Tex., 1982—. Recipient Jefferson Davis medal United Daus. of Confederacy, Richmond, Va., 1977, 78, Am. State and Local History Preservation award Ms., 1980. Mem. Tex. Bar Assn. Republican. Episcopalian. Clubs: University (Houston); New Orleans Athletic. Avocations: history; restorations. Office: R E L Stringfellow Interests 225 Park Ave Freeport TX 77541

BEADLES, JOHN KENNETH, biologist, educational administrator; b. Alva, Okla., Sept. 22, 1931; s. Joseph Haven and Ellen Amanda (Applebee) B.; m. Sharon Kay Ruch, Dec. 18, 1955; children—Kristi, John David. B.S., Northwestern State Coll., 1957; postgrad. Phillips U., 1959, U. Okla., summers 1960-61; M.S., Okla. State U., 1962, Ph.D., 1965. Tchr. sci. Alva (Okla.) pub. schs., 1957-62; grad. research asst. Okla. State U., Stillwater, 1963-64, grad. research trainee, 1964-65; asst. prof. biology Ark. State U., State University, 1965-66, prof. biology, chmn. dept. biol. scis., 1968-84, dean Grad. Sch., 1984—; prof., researcher, advisor U.S.AID program Okla. State U., Ethiopia, Africa, 1966-68; fish disease cons. Trustee Jonesboro United Way, 1975-80, 83—, chmn. survey and admissions com., 1975-80; mem. Crowley's Ridge Devel. Council, Bd. Drug and Alcohol Abuse, 1972-73; mem. Jonesboro YMCA bldg. and expansion com., 1978. Served with USN, 1950-54. U.S. Soil Conservation Service, grantee, 1975-78; Ark. Game and Fish Commn. grantee, 1979-80; U.S. C.E. grantee, 1972-78; Ark. Eastman Co. grantee, 1974-75; Al C. Young Assocs. Tulsa Inc. grantee, 1981-82. Mem. Am. Fisheries Soc., Southwestern Assn. Naturalists, Am. Soc. Ichthyologists and Herpetologists, Ark. Acad. Sci. (pres. 1981-82), Sigma Xi. Baptist. Lodge: Rotary (pres. 1978-79, dist. gov. 1985-86). Contbr. articles to profl. jours. Home: 1111 Thrush Rd Jonesboro AR 72401 Office: Grad Sch PO Box 60 State University AR 72467

BEAIRD, CHARLES T., publisher; b. Shreveport, La., July 17, 1922; s. James Benjamin and Mattie Connell (Fort) B.; B.A., Centenary Coll., 1966; Ph.D. in Philosophy, Columbia, 1972; m. Carolyn Williams, Feb. 6, 1943; children—Susan Beaird McCormick, Marjorie (Mrs. M. Buie Seawell, Jr.), John B. Vice pres., asst. gen. mgr. J.B. Beaird Corp., Shreveport, 1946-57; cons. oil and investments, Shreveport, 1957-59; pres. Beaird-Poulan Inc., Shreveport, 1959-73; chmn. bd. Beaird-Poulan div. Emerson Electric Co., 1973-76; pres., pub. Shreveport Jour., 1976—; dir. Fed. Res. Bd. Dallas, 1972-78, dep. chmn., 1973-78; adj. prof. Centenary Coll., Shreveport, 1969—. Mem. Caddo Parish Police Jury, 1956-60. Chmn. Caddo Parish Republican Exec. Com., 1952-56. Bd. suprs. So. U. La., 1975-76; bd. dirs. Woodrow Wilson Nat. Fellowship Found., Princeton, N.J., 1975-78. Served to capt. USMCR, 1943-46. Clubs: Shreveport, Shreveport Country, Univ. (Shreveport). Office: PO Box 31110 Shreveport LA 71130

BEAL, FRANK BRADLEY, textile executive; b. Lincolnton, N.C., July 2, 1946; s. Edgar Frank and Anna Louise (McGinnis) B.; m. Rebecca Kiser, Feb. 15, 1969. B.S. in Textile Tech., N.C. State U., 1968. Mgr. indsl. engring. West Point Pepperel, LaGrange, Ga., 1968-72, Nat. Spinning Mills, Whiteville, N.C., 1973; plant mgr. Hanes Knitwear, Galax, Va., 1973-81; apparel mgr. Washington Mills, Mayodan, N.C., 1981-83; v.p. mfg. Standard Knitting Mills, Knoxville, Tenn., 1983—. Bd. dirs. United Way LaGrange, 1971; chmn. Sheltered Workshop, Indsl. Adv. Com., Galax, 1980. Mem. Assn. Textile Indsl. Engrs., Nat. Knitwear Mfg. Assn., Jaycees. Lodges: Lions, Elks, Masons (32 deg.), Shriners.

BEALE, KAREN BOSTICK, hospital nursing and management control administrator; b. Big Spring, Tex., May 14, 1947; d. William Carroll and Bertha Lee (Tonn) Bostick; m. William Ruffin Beale, Jr., June 23, 1967; children—Ronda Sue, William Bryan, Kimberly Lyn. R.N., Our Lady of Lake, 1979; cert. psychiat. nursing, Parkland Hosp., 1979; cert. EKG supr., Univ. Med. Coll., 1985; cert. clin. supr., Earl K. Long Hosp., 1985. Psychiat. staff nurse Parkland Hosp., Baton Rouge, 1979-80, psychiat. unit dir., 1980-82; central supply dir. Greenwell Springs Hosp., La., 1982—, infection control dir., 1982—, EKG dir., 1983—. Pres. Goodwood Elem. Sch. PTA, Baton Rouge, 1974-76; leader Girl Scouts U.S.A., Baton Rouge, 1973-77; Panther pushers Woodlawn High Sch., Baton Rouge, 1983—; supr. Gray Ladies Clinic, Goodwood Elem. Sch., Baton Rouge, 1970-76. Democrat. Baptist. Avocations: swimming; walking; skiing; reading. Office: Greenwell Springs Hosp PO Box 549 Greenwell Springs LA 70739

BEALL, KENNETH SUTTER, JR., lawyer; b. Evanston, Ill., Aug. 9, 1938; s. Kenneth Sutter and Helen Canton (Koenig) B.; B.A., Washington and Lee U., 1961, LL.B., 1963; m. Blair Hamilton Bissett, May 23, 1975; children—Kevina Anne, Hunter Bissett, Baret Bissett. Admitted to Fla. bar, 1964; mem. firm, dir. Gunster, Yoakley, Criser & Stewart, P.A., Palm Beach, Fla., 1964—. Chmn. Palm Beach County (Fla.) Environ. Control Hearing Bd., 1970—; bd. dirs. Palm Beach Habilitation Center, Whitehall Found., Inc. Served with USMCR, 1963-69. Mem. ABA, Palm Beach County Bar Assn., Fla. Bar, Fed. Bar Assn. (pres. chpt. 1979-80). Democrat. Roman Catholic. Clubs: Everglades, Bath and Tennis, Sailfish (Palm Beach). Home: 744 Island Dr Palm Beach FL 33480 Office: Phillips Point Suite 500 700 S Flagler Dr West Palm Beach FL 33401

BEAM, CHARLES GRIER, motor transportation executive; b. Cherryville, N.C., Jan. 15, 1906; s. Charles Lefter and Nancy (Carpenter) B.; m. Lena Sue Brawley, June 14, 1936; children—Joel V., Linda Sue. Student, Brevard Coll., 1927-29; B.S., N.C. State U., 1931. Owner, Beam Trucking Co., Cherryville, 1933-37; pres., dir., chief exec. officer, mem. exec. com. Carolina Freight Carriers Corp., Cherryville, 1937—, now chmn. bd. Mem. Gaston County Bd. Commrs., 1951-77, chmn. bd., 1960-77; trustee Brevard Coll., Gaston Coll.; past dir. Children's Home Soc. of N.C., Inc. Named Cherryville Citizen of Yr., 1979; named to N.C. State Agr. Hall of Fame, 1980; recipient Disting. Alumnus award N.C. State U., 1980; Service to Mankind award Gaston County Sertoma Club, 1980; Am. Truck Hist. Soc. award as founder of trucking industry, 1980. Mem. N.C. Motor Carriers Assn. (past pres., dir.), Am. Trucking Assn. (bd. govs. 1965—). Democrat. Methodist. Clubs: Masons, Shriners, Lions. Home: Route 4 Sunbeam Rd Cherryville NC 28021 Office: PO Box 697 Cherryville NC 28021

BEAM, FRANK LETTS, communications corporation executive; b. Mount Vernon, Ohio, Apr. 10, 1942; s. James Alfred and Margaret Adele (Rudin) B. B.S.B.A., Northwestern U., Evanston, 1964. With advt. dept. ITT Bell and Gossett, Morton Grove, Ill., 1961-62; exec. trainee Leo Burnett Co., Chgo., 1964-65; acct. exec. Young and Rubicam, Chgo., 1965-67; prin., founder Frank L. Beam Co., Chgo., 1967-80; founder, pres. Beam Communications, Key Biscayne, Fla., 1981—; dir., vice chmn. Tousley Bixler, Indpls.; v.p. MR Group, Inc., Key Biscayne, 1985—. Author: Effects of the Inner Six Outer Seven on Damlier-Benz ATG, 1961. Co-founder Key Biscayners for Responsive Govt., 1985; mem. steering com. Rep., 1972. Mem. Broadcast Pioneers, Nat. Assn. Broadcasters, Internat. Radio and T.V. Soc. Presbyterian. Clubs: Chig. Yacht; Key Biscayne Yacht. Avocations: boating; music; photography. Home: 201 Crandon Blvd Key Biscayne FL 33149 Office: Beam Communications Corp 50 W Mashta Dr Key Biscayne FL 33149

BEAMER, ROBERT KEITH, physician; b. Sandusky, Ohio, Sept. 18, 1947; s. Robert William and Anna Ruth (Bechtel) B.; m. Kristina Marie Miller; Aug. 3, 1976; children—Robert Lawrence, Kristy Ann. B.S., Ohio State U., 1969; D.O., Kirksville Coll. of Osteo. Medicine, 1973. Cert. gen. family practice, 1981, utilization rev. and quality assurance, 1985. Gen. practice medicine, Pinellas Park, St. Petersburg, Fla., 1976—; physician advisor Met. Gen. Hosp., Pinellas Park, 1985—; med. dir. Good Samaritan Nursing Home, St. Petersburg, 1984—. Served to capt. U.S. Army, 1974-76, Korea. Fellow Am. Coll. of Utilization Rev. Physicians; mem. Am. Osteo. Assn., Fla. Osteo. Med. Assn., Pinellas Park C. of C., Sigma Sigma Phi. Lutheran. Avocations: golf; scuba diving; swimming. Home: 12831 Lois Ave Seminole FL 33542 Office: 6251 Park Blvd Pinellas Park FL 33565

BEAN, ALAN LAVERN, former astronaut, artist; b. Wheeler, Tex., 1932; s. Arnold Horace and Frances (Murphy) B.; m. Leslie Brelsford, July 15, 1982; children—Clay, Amy. B.S. in Engring. with disting. Engr. honors, U. Tex., 1955; Naval Test Pilot Sch., Patuxent River, Md., 1960; Doctorates (hon.), Tex. Wesleyan Coll., U. Akron; art student St. Mary's Coll., Md., 1962; Mus. Fine Arts' Alfred C. Glassell Sch. Art, 1977, other. Commd. ensign U.S. Navy, 1955, advanced through ranks to capt., 1969; served on Jet Attack Sqadron 44, Jacksonville, Fla., 1956; selected astronaut NASA, 1963; lunar module pilot Apollo 12, man's 2d lunar landing (4th man on moon), 1969; spacecraft comdr. Skylab Mission II, 59-day, 24,400,000 mile, world record setting flight, 1973; comdr. backup spacecraft joint Am-Russian Apollo-Soyus Test Project, 1975; chief ops., tng., astronaut office, 1978-81; ret.; now artist; one-man show, Ft. Worth, 1983, Meredith Long Gallery, Houston, 1984. Decorated 2 Navy Disting. Service Medals, 2 NASA Disting. Service Medals. Recipient Robert J. Collier Trophy, 1973, Yuri Gagarin Gold Medal, 1973, numerous other nat., internat. honors; holder 11 world records in space, astronautics.

BEAN, FRANK DAWSON, JR., sociology educator; b. Harlan, Ky., May 20, 1942; s. Frank Dawson and Alta Louzana (Scott) B.; m. Carolyn P. Boyd, Jan. 4, 1975; children—Alan McDavid, Deborah Scott, Peter Justin, Michael Franklin. Student Oberlin Coll., 1960-62; B.A., U. Ky., 1964; M.A., Duke U., 1965, Ph.D., 1970. Asst. prof. sociology, U. Tex., Austin, 1968-71, assoc. prof., 1972-78, prof., 1978—, dept. chmn. since 1978—; asst. prof. Ind. U., Bloomington, 1971-72. Recipient numerous research grants. Mem. Am. Sociol Assn., Population Assn. Am., So. Sociol. Soc., Sociol. Research Assn., Southwestern Social Sci. Assn. Lutheran. Editor: (with H.Y. Tien) Comparative Family and Fertility Research, 1974; (with W.P. Frisbie) The Demography of Racial and Ethnic Groups, 1978. Office: Dept Sociology U Tex Austin TX 78712

BEAN, FRANK WILSON, soft drink marketing executive, lawyer, advertising and public relations executive; b. Bloomington, Ill., Jan. 14, 1940; s. Wilson Rosemond and Beatrice (Mill) B.; m. Joyce Travis Whitsel, June 11, 1960; children—Brenton Sewell, Kimberly Whitsel. B.S., U. Fla., 1962, M.A. in Journalism and Communication, 1963; J.D., Woodrow Wilson Coll. Law, 1983. Bar: Ga. Ga. Supreme Ct., Ga. Appeals Ct., U.S. Dist. Ct. (no. dist.) Ga. 1984. Staff rep. pub. relations Coca-Cola Co., Atlanta, 1968-72, services mgr. pub. relations, 1972-76; mgr. corp. sport sponsorships Coca-Cola Export Corp., Atlanta, 1976-79, mgr. internat. sports, 1980—; instr. DeKalb Community Coll. (Ga.), 1975-78. Adv. com. U. Fla., 1978-81; notary pub. at-large, State of Ga., 1983-87. Served to capt. USAF, 1963-67. Recipient Golden Eagle award CINE, 1980. Mem. Pub. Relations Soc. Am. (accredited), Atlanta Jaycees (v.p. 1968-74), Alpha Delta Sigma, Pi Kappa Alpha. Republican. Episcopalian. Club: Capital City (Atlanta). Home: 275 Forrest Lake Dr NW Atlanta GA 30327 Office: Coca-Cola Co PO Box 1734 NAT 10 Atlanta GA 30301

BEAN, GLYNIS JANE, telecommunications company manager, marketing researcher; b. Concord, Mass., Nov. 18, 1956; d. Leonard Arthur Matthew and Lucille Catherine (Meuse) B. B.A., U. Mass., 1978; M.A., Temple U., 1981, Ph.D., 1983. Instr. Temple U., Phila., 1979-81, Curry Coll., Milton, Mass., 1981-82; mktg. research analyst Arkwright-Boston Ins., Waltham, Mass., 1983; staff mgr. So. Bell, Atlanta, 1984—; cons. in field. Contbr. articles to profl. jours. Mem. fund-raising Scottish Rite Children's Hosp., Atlanta, 1983-84, Atlanta Symphony Orch., 1986. Grantee, U. Mass., 1978, Temple U., 1981. Mem. Am. Psychol. Assn., Am. Mktg. Assn., Soc. for Advancement Social Psychology, Atlanta Lawn Tennis Assn. Republican. Home: 2071-D Lake Park Dr Smyrna GA 30080 Office: So Bell 20V93 SBC 675 W Peachtree St Atlanta GA 30375

BEAN, ROBERT BEVERIDGE, zoologist; b. Oak Park, Ill., Feb. 7, 1933; s. Robert Anderson and Janet (Beveridge) B.; m. Joan Ellen Alderson, May 20, 1954; children—Pamela, Janet, Ellen. Student, U. Fla., Fla. So. Coll. Animal keeper Chgo. Zool. Park, Brookfield, Ill., 1956-61; with Resources Research, Lakeland, Fla., 1961-63; staff asst. zool. dept. Busch Gardens, Tampa, Fla., 1963-64; curator animals, asst. dir. Jimmy Morgan Zoo, Birmingham, Ala., 1964-67; zool. dir., zoo mgr. Anheuser-Busch Gardens, Tampa, Fla., 1967-71, gen. mgr., Tampa, 1971-74; dir. Louisville Zool. Gardens, 1974—. Trustee Wild Animal Propagation Trust; bd. dirs. Am. Assn. Zool. Parks and Aquariums, 1985—. Mem. Fla. Wildlife Exhibitors Criteria Com. Served with Armed Forces, 1953-55. Recipient Edward H. Bean award, cert. of appreciation for service in futherance conservation of fish and wildlife resources State of Fla. Mem. Louisville C. of C. Lodge: Rotary. Home: 1615 Windsor Pl Louisville KY 40204 Office: Louisville Zool Garden PO Box 37250 Louisville KY 40233

BEAN, RUSSELL OWEN, comptroller, accountant; b. W. Palm Beach, Fla., Feb. 14, 1948; s. Harold Earle and Sibyl (Pool) B.; m. Joyce Dillingham, July 26, 1968; 1 child, Robert Edward. A.A., Palm Beach Jr. Coll., 1967; B.A., Fla. Atlantic U., 1969. Office mgr. Al Packer Ford, West Palm Beach, Fla., 1973-77; comptroller Schumacher Buick, West Palm Beach, 1977—, corp. sec., 1977—. Avocations: computer programming. Home: 293 Oneida Terr Wellington FL 33414 Office: Schumacher Buick 3031 Okeechobee Blvd West Palm Beach FL 33414

BEARD, BARBARA JERALDINE, building manager; b. Ascalon, Ga., Dec. 13, 1935; d. Waymon Dural and Frances Lucille (Smith) Wilkerson; m. Alfred Lawrence Beard, Oct. 2, 1956; children—Kenneth Wayne, Kimberly Renee. Student South Oklahoma City Jr. Coll., 1983. Bookkeeper Ackerman Advt., Oklahoma City, 1965-72, Chandelle, Oklahoma City, 1972-76; asst. mgr. United Founders Life, Oklahoma City, 1976-78; bldg. mgr. Northwest Investors, Oklahoma City, 1978-80, Univ. Real Estate, Oklahoma City, 1980-83, Nat. Capital Real Estate Trust, Oklahoma City, 1983—. Pres. Bldg. Owners Mgrs. Assn. Methodist. Avocations: Writing poetry; reading; bowling. Home: 6012 Broadmoor Oklahoma City OK 73132 Office: United Founders Tower 5900 Mosteller Dr Oklahoma City OK 73112

BEARD, EUGENE MONK, law enforcement official; b. Moultrie, Ga., Dec. 27, 1931; s. Thomas Valentine and Matilda (Monk) B.; m. Lillian Christine Roberts, June 21, 1957; children—Eugene Monk Jr., Cynthia Lee, James Bryan. Sheriff, Colquitt County, Moultrie, Ga. Served with U.S. Army, 1950-52. Mem. Ga. Sheriffs Assn. (sec./treas. 1984—). Office: Court House Colquitt County Main St Moultrie GA 31768

BEARD, JACOB THOMAS BARRON, JR., mathematics educator; b. Jacksonville, Fla., Nov. 29, 1940; s. Jacob Thomas Barron and Mamie (Green) B.; m. Marjorie Elizabeth Pybas, Dec. 29, 1961; children—Elizabeth Michelle, Katherine Ann. B.S., Tenn. Tech. U., 1962, M.S., 1967; Ph.D., U. Tenn., 1971. Mathematician, TVA, Chattanooga, 1962-65; asst. prof. U. Tex., Arlington, 1971-76, assoc. prof., 1976-79; vis. assoc. prof. Emory U., Atlanta, 1978-79; chmn. math. and computer sci. Tenn. Tech. U., Cookeville, Tenn., 1979-81, prof. math., 1979—; vis. prof. U. Tenn., 1984-85. Mem. Am. Math. Soc., Soc. Indsl. and Applied Math., Math. Assn. Am., AAUP, Sigma Xi. Contbr. research articles to various publs. Office: Box 5132 Tenn Tech U Cookeville TN 38505

BEARD, JOHN HARVEY, exploration company executive; b. Pike City, Ark., Apr. 18, 1928; s. William Alexander and Nobia Gertrude (Head) B.; m. Delores Griffiths, Aug. 1949 (div. 1974); children—John Raymond, Nathan Lee, Rachel Johnell, Denise Louise, Morgan Louis; m. 2nd Laurel June McCarthy, Mar. 1974. B.S., U. Utah, 1957, M.S., 1959. Teaching asst. U. Utah, Salt Lake City, 1957-59; geologist Carter Oil Co., Salt Lake City, 1959-61, Humble Oil & Refining Co., Denver, 1961-62, Humble Prodn. and Research, Houston, 1962-63; geologist, micropaleontologist Humble Oil & Refining, Denver, 1963-66; sr. research geologist Exxon Prodn. Research Co., Houston, 1966-70, sr. research specialist, Houston, Singapore, 1970-72, Houston, 1972-74, Houston, 1975-79, Esso Prodn. Research, Bordeaux, France, 1974-75, Houston, 1974-75; sr. exploration geophysicist Exxon Co. U.S.A., Houston, 1979-81; exec. v.p., stockholder Zenith Exploration Co., Inc., Houston, 1981—; dir., stockholder Kiowa Exploration, Houston; pres., stockholder, incorporator StrataVision Energy Inc., Houston, 1985—. Co-author (with others) The University of Kansas Paleontological Contribution-Article 62, 1975. Contbr. articles to profl. jours. Served with USN, 1945-49. Mem. Am. Assn. Petroleum Geologists (cert., author bull. 1968-69, 82), Soc. Exploration Geophysicists, Houston Geol. Soc., Geophys. Soc. Houston, Soc. Econ. Paleontologists and Mineralogists. Republican. Baptist. Avocations: fishing, golf. Home: 14135 Cardinal Ln Houston TX 77079 Office: Zenith Exploration Co Inc 10497 Town and Country Way Houston TX 77024

BEARD, MYRON JOSEPH, psychologist; b. Sante Fe, N.Mex., Feb. 14, 1947; s. Myron J. and Ava (Wertz) B.; m. Linda M. Fischer, Jan. 8, 1977. B.A., So. Methodist U., 1968; M.A., N.Mex. Highlands U., 1976; Ph.D., North Tex. State U., 1982. Lic. psychologist, Tex. Dir. Adventure Trails, Dallas, 1975-77, Salesmanship Club, Dallas, 1977-78; staff psychologist Lubbock Mental Health Mental Retardation, Tex., 1982-83; clin. dir. Crossroads Counseling Ctr., Lubbock, 1983—. Treas., High Plains Assn. Marriage Family Therapy, Lubbock, 1985. Mem. Am. Psychol. Assn., Am. Assn. Pastoral Counseling (profl. affiliate), Assn. Couples for Marriage Enrichment (cert. leader), Interpersonal Communication Programs (cert. leader), Assn. Health Service Providers. Baptist. Avocations: camping; skiing; golf; racquetball; backpacking. Home: 3617 55th St Lubbock TX 79413 Office: Crossroads Samaritan Counseling Ctr Inc 5313 50th St Bldg B Lubbock TX 79414

BEARDEN, LISA JEAN, counselor educator, consultant; b. Oak Ridge, Jan. 15, 1955; d. Joseph Reuben and Doris Jean (Donovan) B. B.A., U. S.C., 1977, M.Ed., 1979; Ph.D., U. Ala., 1984. Research asst. Univ. Affiliated Facilities, Columbia, S.C., 1978; counselor William S. Hall Psychiat. Inst., Columbia, 1979; grad. asst. U. Ala., Tuscaloosa, 1981-82; counselor Vets. Upward Bound, University, Ala., 1982-84; instr. psychology Shelton State Community Coll., Tuscaloosa, 1984; asst. prof. counselor edn. Auburn U., Ala., 1984—, faculty advisor edn. council, 1984—. Mem. editorial bd. Ala. Assn. for Counseling and Devel. Quar., 1985—. Author: Vocational Training for Developmentally Disabled Adults, 1978. Contbr. articles to profl. jours. Sunday sch. tchr. 1st Baptist Ch., Auburn. Mem. Nat. Rehab. Assn. (chmn. policy and procedure com. S.E. region 1985—), Nat. Rehab. Counseling Assn., Am. Assn. for Counseling and Devel., Assn. for Counselor Edn. and Supervision, Mid-South Ednl. Research Assn., Ala. Rehab. Counseling Assn. (bd. dirs. 1984—), Kappa Delta Pi. Republican. Avocations: water skiing; needlework; riflery. Home: 305 Cherry Dr Auburn AL 36830 Office: Auburn U 2014 Haley Ctr Auburn University AL 36849

BEARDSWORTH, DONALD EUGENE, college president; b. Clinton, Iowa, Jan. 2, 1921; s. Arthur E. and Hazel M. (Higgins) B.; student Northeastern State Coll., Tahlequah, Okla., 1939-41; m. Janyce Estelle McDorman, Feb. 3, 1968; children—Donald Eugene, Jerry Lee, Mary Carol Beardsworth Anderson. Vice pres., cashier Comml. Bank, Muskogee, Okla., 1946-52; v.p. Bank of N.Mex., Albuquerque, 1952-54; pres. Citizens Bank, Albuquerque, 1962-66, LSI/Draughon Sch. Bus., Oklahoma City, 1967-72, Nettleton Bus. Coll., Omaha, 1972-73; pres., chmn. bd., chief exec. officer Internat. Bus. Colls., El Paso, Tex., Las Cruces and Alamogordo, N.Mex., Lubbock, Tex. and Albuquerque; mem. proprietary adv. council Region VI, Office Edn.; dir. Tex. Commerce Bank, Border City; real estate and ins. agt., Albuquerque, 1955-62. Mem. City Council Muskogee, 1950-52; bd. mgrs. Thomason Gen. Hosp., El Paso, 1983—. Served with AUS, 1943-46. Mem. Southwestern Comml. Schs. Assn. (pres. 1977—), Tex. Assn. Pvt. Schs. (dir., pres. 1980-81), Nat. Assn. Ind. Colls. and Schs., N.Mex. Assn. Pvt. Schs. (bd. dirs.), Tex. Tchrs. Assn., Nat. Rehab. Assn., Okla. Writers Guild, Am. Legion, Phi Sigma Epsilon. Democrat. Methodist. Clubs: El Paso, El Paso Internat., Kiwanis (pres. High-land-Albuquerque 1960, pres. El Paso 1983-84). Editor N.Mex. Realtor, 1962-63. Home: 9001 McFall St El Paso TX 79925 Office: 6501 Boeing Bldg I Suite 200 El Paso TX 79925

BEARY, THOMAS JOSEPH, III, broadcast electronics engineer, consultant; b. Port Chester, N.Y., Nov. 23, 1943; s. Thomas Joseph and Mary Irene (Torpey) B.; children—Mary Elizabeth, Michael Joseph. B.A., St. Louis U., 1975. Systems engring. technician Sunair Electronics, Ft. Lauderdale, 1981-82; chief engr. Belleville Broadcasting, (Ill.), 1982-83; staff engr. United Press Internat. Service Co., Miami and Dallas, 1983—; cons. in field. Mem. IEEE (sr.; chmn. pub. relations St. Louis 1982-83), Soc. Broadcast Engrs., Am. Radio Relay League. Roman Catholic. Club: Optimists Internat. (chmn. youth activity 1981) (Cahokia, Ill.). Home: PO Box 140927 Coral Gables FL 33114 Office: United Press Internat Service Co Suite 201 2081 Hutton Dr Dallas TX 75006

BEASLEY, ERNEST WILLIAM, JR., endocrinologist; b. Atlanta, May 7, 1924; s. Ernest William and Arrinda Elizabeth (Eidson) B.; M.D., Georgetown U., 1949; m. Ann Lee Jeffreys, July 1, 1950; children—Janet Ann, Ernest William III, Mary Elizabeth, Barbara Elaine. Intern, Walter Reed Hosp., Washington, 1949-50; resident in internal medicine VA Hosp.-Grady Meml. Hosp.-Emory U. Hosp., Atlanta; practice medicine specializing in family practice, Atlanta, 1955-65, in internal medicine, Atlanta, 1966-75, in endocrinology, Atlanta, 1975—; chief endocrinology and metabolism Ga. Bapt. Med. Center; asso. dept. internal medicine Emory U.; cons. endocrinology Crawford Long Hosp. of Emory U.; cons. Ga. Assn. Retarded Children, 1955-65; dir. Diabetes Assn. Atlanta, 1976. Served with AUS, 1943-45, M.C., U.S. Army, 50-52. Diplomate Am. Bd. Internal Medicine, Sub-Bd. Endocrinology, Am. Bd. Family Practice. Mem. A.C.P. Med. Assn. Atlanta, Med. Assn. Ga., AMA, Am. Soc. Internal Medicine, Am. Diabetes Assn. Methodist. Club: Cherokee Country. Address: 478 Peachtree St NE Atlanta GA 30308

BEASLEY, MARY SHARMAN, educator; b. Roanoke, Va., Sept. 2, 1944; d. William Howard and Ann (Waddell) Beasley, Jr. Student Lindenwood Coll., 1963-64; B.A., U. Tex., 1966; M.L.A., So. Meth. U., 1981; postgrad. Sorbonne, Paris, 1967. Tchr., Dallas Ind. Sch. Dist., 1966-71, Richardson (Tex.) Ind. Sch. Dist., 1971-72; with Congressman Wright Patman's Office, Washington, 1972-73; legal asst. Morgan, Lewis & Bockius, Washington, 1973-74; asst. adminstr. Fina Found., Fina Oil Co., Dallas, 1974-76; instr., coordinator El Centro Coll., Dallas, 1976-83. Mem. Dallas Soc. for Crippled Children, 1981-83; bd. dirs. 500, Inc., 1968-72, Le Circle Français, 1971-72, Dallas Civic Music, 1971-81, Dallas Civic Ballet, 1971-78; v.p. Friends of the Met, 1978-80. Recipient Past Pres. award, 500, Inc., 1971. Mem. Tex. Jr. Coll. Assn., Dallas Jr. Coll. Assn., Dallas Hist. Soc., Dallas Symphony, Dallas Theatre Ctr. Women's Guild, Tex. U. Alumni Assn. Republican. Presbyterian. Clubs: Cotillion (v.p. assemblage 1969-70), Brook Hollow Golf, Argyle. Contbr. articles to profl. jours. Address: 4132 Druid St Dallas TX 75205

BEASLEY, MODENA JAMES, nursing executive; b. Cedar Creek, Tex., July 12, 1934; d. H.B. and Jessie Gertrude (Watson) James; m. John O'Bert Beasley, Sept. 4, 1959; children—John O'Bert III, Lisa, Laura. Diploma John Peter Smith Hosp. Sch. Nursing, 1954; B.S. in Nursing Edn., Tex. Wesleyan U., 1955; M.S., U. Tenn., 1977. Relief supr. John Peter Smith Hosp., Fort Worth, 1954-55; staff nurse Meth. Hosp., Lubbock, Tex., 1955-57; instr. East Tenn. Bapt. Hosp., Knoxville, 1957-62, dir. nursing edn., 1962-72, asst. v.p. nursing, 1983—; instr. Cumberland Coll., Middlesboro, Ky., 1974-76, Walters State Community Coll., Morristown, Tenn., 1976-77; asst. prof. Lincoln Meml. U., Harrogate, Tenn., 1977-83. Contbr. articles to profl. jours. Mem. Am. Hosp. Assn., Tenn. Hosp. Assn. Democrat. Presbyterian. Avocations: reading; writing; gardening. Office: East Tenn Bapt Hosp Blount Ave Knoxville TN 37918

BEASLEY, THURMOND, dentist, anesthesiologist; b. New Albany, Miss., Dec. 30, 1943; s. Dock and Ella (Jones) B.; m. Ethel Marietta Stewart; children—Veroniaa Joe, Thomas Becwith, Richard Calldwell. B.S., Jackson State Coll., 1965; D.D.S., Meharry Med. Coll., 1971; Anesthesiologist, Harvard U., 1974. Practice dentistry, Tupelo, Miss., 1974—; anesthesiologist Union County Gen. Hosp., New Albany, Miss., 1974—. Chmn. Union County Polit. Action Com., New Albany, 1979—; deacon Watson Grove Baptist Ch., New Albany, 1976; bd. dirs. Three Rivers, Pontotoc, Miss., 1983, Lift Inc. Named Man of Yr., Lift Inc., 1984. Fellow Am. Dental Soc. Anesthesiologists; mem. ADA, Miss. Dental Assn. (sec.-treas. polit. action com. 1978-83), Miss. Dental Soc. (pres. 1982, chmn. 1984—), Nat. Dental Assn. Democrat. Lodges: Masons, Elks, Henry Hampton.

BEATLEY, CHARLES EARLE, JR., city official; b. Urbana, Ohio, May 17, 1916; s. Charles Earle and Alice Elizabeth (Carson) B.; m. Marjorie Perry, Nov. 10, 1945; children—Elizabeth, Christopher, Timothy. B.A., Ohio State U., 1938, M.B.A., 1947. Capt. United Airlines, 1943-76; mayor City of Alexandria, Va., 1967-76, 79-85; owner, operator Warrenton Air Park Inc., Va., 1977—. Pres. Seminary Hill Citizens Assn., 1955-58, Minnie Howard Elem. Sch. PTA, 1961; commr. No. Va. Transp. Commn., 1966-76, 79—, chmn., 1984; mem. Alexandria City Council, 1966-76, Va. Airport Authority, 1977-80, Va. Aviation Commn., 1980—; bd. dirs. Washington Met. Area Transit Authority, 1970-72, 74-76, 79—, No. Va. Park Authority, 1970-72. Mem. Air Line Pilots Assn. (1st v.p. 1955-57), Capital Airlines Assn. (pres. 1981), Met. Washington Council Govts. (dir. 1967-76, chmn. health and environ. protection policy com. 1972-73, pres. 1972), Va. Mcpl. League (chmn. urban sect. 1979-80, mem. exec. com. 1979-80). Democrat. Presbyterian. Home: 4875 Maury Ln Alexandria VA 22304 Office: Warrenton Air Park Inc Warrenton VA 22186

BEATRÍZ, DULCE, artist; b. Havana Cuba, Mar. 17, 1931; came to U.S. 1960, naturalized 1970; d. José Mariá and Dulce Amelia (Moreno de Ayala) Hernández; m. Leonardo Beatríz, Mar. 30, 1959. Grad. Tchr.'s Coll., Havana, 1949; M.A. in Music, Conservatory Peyrellade, Havana, 1953; M.F.A., San Alejandro, Havana, 1955. First tech. dir. Cuban dept. fine arts, prof. drawing and painting, mem. judging bd. City Hall, Havana, 1956-59. Exhibited in 61 one-man shows, more than 150 group shows; represented in permanent collections in N.Am., Central Am., S.Am., Europe. Recipient Hall of Fame Internat. award for painting and sculpture Hispanic Internat. Research Inst., New York, 1971, Internat. award Honor Al Merito, 1974, Royal Order of Isabel La Católica decoration for painting and sculpture, Spain, 1983, Gold Keys, Dade County, Fla., 1983; travel prize San Alejandro, Havana, 1956, Gold medal Havana City Hall, 1956, commendation City of Miami, 1970; Lincoln-Marti nat. award Dept. HEW, 1971; named Eminent Alumna, Conservatory Peyrellade, Havana, 1953; hon. ambassador, Dade County, Fla., 1977. Fellow Royal Soc. Arts, London, 1977; mem. Hispania Nostra, Spain, 1978, Circulo de Cultura Panamericana, 1978. Republican. Roman Catholic.

BEATTIE, WILLIAM JOHN, III, foundry executive; b. St. Louis, Nov. 18, 1933; s. William John and Mary Ellen (Chipley) B.; student Washington U., St. Louis, 1951-54, Tex. Christian U., 1958-61; m. Rebecca Sue Czeschin, July 11, 1970; children—William, Ann, Todd, Chad, David. Engring. supr. Emerson Electric Co., St. Louis, 1966-69; asst. mktg. mgr. Meyer Labs. Inc., Maryland Heights, Mo., 1969-70; v.p., gen. mgr. Forecast, Inc., Kirkwood, Mo., 1970-74; pres. St. Charles Aluminum Casting Co. (Mo.), 1974-78; v.p. ops. Mfr.'s Brass & Aluminum Foundry, Inc., 1979-80; v.p. ops. BALCAR, Inc., Dallas, 1980-82; pres. Beattie Aluminum Foundry Co., 1983—. Planning and zoning commr. City of St. Charles, 1976-79; bd. dirs. Boys Club St. Charles, 1975-79; planning and zoning commr., City of Carrollton, Tex., 1981—. Served with USAF, 1954-56; Korea. Mem. Am. Foundrymen's Soc., Am. Soc. Metals, Sigma Chi. Republican. Presbyterian (deacon, elder). Club: Rotary. Home: 2308 Evergreen Dr Carrollton TX 75006 Office: 1408 Hutton Dr Carrollton TX 75006

BEATTY, GWEN FAYE, petroleum geologist; b. Newton, N.C., June 14, 1946; d. Ray Von and Elizabeth M. (Cain) B. A.A., St. Petersburg Jr. Coll., 1973; B.A., U. South Fla., 1975; M.S., U. Fla., 1977. Project geologist Gulf Oil Corp., Lafayette, La., 1979-85; geologist Chevron, U.S.A., Lafayette, 1985—. Mem. Am. Assn. Petroleum Geologists, Lafayette Geol. Soc., Assn. Women Geoscientists (co-vice chmn. 1983-84), Sierra Club (bd. dirs. Lafayette 1984-85), Gulf Employee's Club (bd. dirs. 1984—). Avocations: camping; hiking; backpacking; canoeing; cooking. Office: Chevron USA 900 E University Ave Lafayette LA 70503

BEATTY, JERRY ALFRED, entertainment director; b. Roanoke, Va., July 14, 1947; s. Alfred Maurice and Gladys Odell (Manning) B. B.A. in English, Bridgewater Coll., 1969; M.F.A. in Theatre, Catholic U., 1973. Cert. tchr., Va. Theatre dir. Roanoke City Schs., Va., 1969-70, Alexandria City Schs., Va., 1972-80; exec. dir. Fairfax Arts Council, Alexandria, 1982-83; conv. mgr. Am. Theatre Assn., Washington, 1984-85; entertainment dir. U.S. Dept. Def., Bamberg, Ger., 1985—; pres., founder Seaport Players, Inc., Alexandria, 1975-80; local arrangements chmn. Southeastern Theatre Conf., Arlington, Va., 1982-83. Adjudicator One Act Play Festival, Washington, 1982, Arlington, Va., 1983. Mem. Am. Theatre Assn., Alpha Psi Omega, Pi Delta Epsilon. Democrat. Avocations: travel; reading. Home: 3453-A S Stafford St Arlington VA 22206 Office: Morale Support Activities Music & Theatre USMCA Bamberg APO NY 09139

BEATTY, JOYCE W., counselor; b. Cheraw, S.C., d. Henry J. and Essie M. (Windham) Eddings; m. Ray Von Beatty, Jr.; children—Jeff, Johnna, David. B.S., Pembroke State U., 1978; M.A., East Carolina U., 1980; postgrad. Nova U., 1985—. Counselor, St. Paul's High Sch., N.C., 1980; dir. counseling and testing Robeson Tech. Coll., Lumberton, N.C., 1981—. Co-pres. PTA, J.P. Moore Middle Sch., Lumberton, 1979; mem. Lumberton Mayor's Com. for Handicapped, 1985; bd. dirs. Woodside Pool, Inc., 1972-83; den mother Boy Scouts Am., 1972-73. Mem. N.C. Assn. Counsling and Devel. (chpt. pres. 1983-84; plaque 1985), N.C. Coll. Personnel Assn., N.C. Assn. Women Deans, Adminstrs. and Counselors, Am. Assn. Counseling and Devel., Alpha Chi, Psi Chi. Home: 2519 Roberts Ave Lumberton NC 28358 Office: Robeson Tech College PO Box 1420 Lumberton NC 28359

BEATTY, RAY VON, university administrator, psychology educator; b. Fayetteville, N.C., Oct. 8, 1942; s. Ray Von and Elizabeth (Cain) B.; m. Caron Apple, Sept. 27, 1964 (div.); m. Joyce Eddings, June 10, 1977; children—Jeff, Holly, Johnna, David. B.S., Pembroke State U., 1965; M.Ed., U. N.C., 1966, Ph.D., 1974. Registered practicing counselor, marital and family therapist, nat. cert. counselor, cert. clin. mental health counselor, sch. psychologist III. Dir. guidance Asheboro City Schs., N.C., 1967-68; counselor U. N.C., Chapel Hill, 1968-72; dir. counseling, assoc. prof. psychology Pembroke State U., 1972—; employees asst. program counselor Human Affairs, Inc., Atlanta, 1984—; counselor N.C. Prison System, 1974-78; pvt. practice counseling, 1974—; social security disability determination evaluator, Raleigh, N.C., 1975-76. Contbr. articles to profl. jours. Pres. Jr. High Sch. PTA, Lumberton, N.C., 1980; bd. dirs. Presbyterian Family Life Inst., 1984; dir. tng. Contact Crisis Line Counseling Service, Lumberton, 1983. Recipient Outstanding Adminstr. award Pembroke State U., 1983, Yr. Book Dedication, 1983. Mem. N.C. Bd. Registered Practicing Counselors, Am. Psychol. Assn., N.C. Assn. for Specialists in Group Work (pres. 1984—), N.C. Mental Health Counselors Assn. (pres. 1985—), N.C. Coll. Personnel Assn. (newsletter editor 1984—), N.C. Assn. Counseling and Devel. (exec. council 1983—). Avocation: sports. Office: Pembroke State U Pembroke NC 28372

BEATTY, SAMUEL ALSTON, justice Ala. Supreme Ct.; b. Tuscaloosa, Ala., Apr. 23, 1923; s. Eugene C. and Rosabelle (Horton) B.; B.S. in Commerce and Bus. Adminstrn., U. Ala., 1948, J.D., 1953; LL.M., Columbia U., 1959, J.S.D., 1964; m. Maude Applegate, Jan. 19, 1949; children—Rosa Beatty Lord, Eugene A. Admitted to Ala. bar, 1953; pvt. practice, Tuscaloosa, 1953-56; mem. faculty U. Ala. Law Sch., 1955-70, prof. law, 1963-70, asst. dean, 1969-73; vis. prof. law U. Cin. Law Sch., 1966-67; asso. dir. Ala. Defender Project, 1967-70; dean, prof. law Mercer U. Law Sch., 1970-72, adj. prof., 1972-74; v.p., trust officer First Nat. Bank & Trust Co., Macon, Ga., 1972-74; asst. atty. gen., chief civil div. State of Ala., 1974; partner firm Henley & Beatty, Tuscaloosa and Northport, Ala., 1975-76; asso. justice Ala. Supreme Ct., 1976—; adj. prof. U. Ala. Grad. Sch., 1975—; speaker, lectr. in field. Served to maj. USAAF, 1942-45; PTO. Decorated Air medal with 9 oak leaf clusters. Mem. Am. Bar Assn., Ala. Bar Assn., Tuscaloosa County Bar Assn., Montgomery County Bar Assn., Nat. Orgn. Legal Problems Edn., Am. Legion, Farrah Order Jurisprudence, Order Coif, Phi Alpha Delta. Democrat. Methodist. Club: Gridiron (U. Ga.). Contbr. articles to legal jours.

BEATTY-DESANA, JEANNE WARREN, cytogenetics service association executive; b. Tuscaloosa, Ala., Sept. 18, 1920; d. William Charles and Anna Belle (Rice) Warren; B.S., U. Ala., Tuscaloosa, 1946; M.S. (fellow), Emory U., 1952; cert. tutorial-human cytogenetics U. Chgo., 1972; m. Alvin V. Beatty, May 23, 1951 (dec.); m. 2d, James A. DeSana, May 28, 1970; children—Susan Warren Beatty, Jane Warren Beatty. Research assoc. biology dept. Emory U., Atlanta, 1952-70; dir. cytogenetics services Ga. Retardation Center, Atlanta, 1970—; adj. assoc. prof. biology Ga. State U., Atlanta, 1972—; cons. Fernbank Sci. Center, DeKalb County, Ga., 1975—; cons. cytogenetics Scottish Rite Hosp., Atlanta, 1979—; mem. Genetics Task Force, State of Ga., 1978, 79, Biosafety com. Ga. Inst. Tech., 1980—; mem. nat. com. Cytogenetics Proficiency testing HEW, Center for Disease Control, 1978-79. Recipient Profl. of Yr. award Assn. Retarded Citizens, Atlanta, 1979, Outstanding research award (with A.V. Beatty), Assn. SE Biologists, 1960, 63, 64, Outstanding Achievement award Emory U. Women's Club, 1956, Sigma Xi Research award Emory U., 1955. Atomic Energy grantee (with A.V. Beatty), 1952-70. Mem. Atlanta Genetics Soc. (dir. 1971-81, chmn. 1973-75, 1978-80), AAAS (mem. S.E. sect. adv. com. 1978-79), Assn. S.E. Biologists, Ga. Conservancy (dir. 1968-71), Am. Soc. Human Genetics (program com. Atlanta meeting 1973), Mammalian Cell Genetics Soc. Contbr. articles to profl. publs. Home: 122 Greenwood Dr Box 601 Cumming GA 30130 Office: Ga Retardation Center Cytogenetics Sect 4770 N Peachtree St Atlanta GA 30338

BEATY, SALLY KEITH CARROLL, cultural organization administrator; b. San Diego, Sept. 23, 1945; d. George Frank and Ruth Louise (Theus) Carroll; m. Wade David East, Jan. 24, 1967 (div. July 1977); 1 child, David Ponder; m. Daniel Joseph Beaty, Mar. 18, 1980; stepchildren—Eric, Brent, Scott, Craig. Mus.B., La. State U., 1967; Mus.M., Baylor U., 1970; M.L.S., U. Tex., 1978. Spl. events coordinator Armstrong Browning Library, Baylor U., Waco, Tex., 1970-73; voice instr. McLennon Community Coll., Waco, 1973, U. Nev., Las Vegas, 1974; music librarian Stephen F. Austin State U., Nacogdoches, Tex., 1978-82, music appreciation lectr., 1983; exec. dir. MUSECOMP, Nacogdoches, 1984—; instr. voice and piano, Waco, Las Vegas, Nacogdoches, 1973-77, 84; sect. chmn. grants, spl. projects com. Fine Arts Soc. Tex., 1981—; chmn. music com. Spring Arts Festival, Stephen F. Austin State U., 1983-84; piano clinician Piano Guild, Temple, Tex., 1982, 85. Compiler: Browning Music, 1973. Assoc. editor jour. The Direction Line, 1977-78. Editor newsletter Tex. Quarter Notes, 1978-82. Precinct del. Nacogdoches Democratic Party, 1984; chorus mem. Nacogdoches Community Chorus, 1981; soloist New Music Ensemble, Nacogdoches, 1980-81; charter mem., sec. Tex. Libertarian Party, Waco, 1970-73. La. State U. scholar 1964-67. Mem. Nev. Music Tchrs. Assn. (newsletter editor 1974-77), Am. Musicological Soc., Am. Soc. U. Composers, Las Vegas Music Tchrs. Assn., Music Library Assn., Music Tchrs. Nat. Assn., Pi Kappa Lambda. Club: U. Profl. Women's Orgn. Avocations: jogging; reading; yard work. Home: 830 Sarah Ann Nacogdoches TX 75961 Office: MUSECOMP 830 Sarah Ann Nacogdoches TX 75961

BEAUCHAMP, JAMES HARRY, lawyer; b. Stillwater, Okla., Sept. 19, 1942; s. Raymond O. and Helen Ruth (Pennington) B.; m. Frances Reams, Sept. 1, 1943; children—Gregory, Colleen, John. B.S., Okla. State U., 1965; J.D., Tulane U., 1968. Bar: Ohio 1968, U.S. Supreme Ct. 1976, Okla. 1978, U.S. Dist. Ct. (we. dist.) Okla. 1971, U.S. Dist. Ct. (so. dist.) Ohio, U.S. Ct. Appeals (6th cir.) 1974, U.S. Ct. Appeals (10th cir.) 1978, U.S. Dist. Ct. (no. dist.) Okla. 1980, U.S. Dist. Ct. (ea. dist.) Okla., 1984, U.S. Tax Ct. Assoc., Bieser, Greer & Landis, Dayton, Ohio, 1971-77, Miller, Dollarhide & Beauchamp, 1978-79; spl. counsel Profl. Investors Corp., 1980-81; sole practice, Tulsa, 1981-85; prin. McDaniel & Beauchamp, Tulsa, 1985—. Served to capt. U.S. Army, 1969-70. Recipient Am. Jurisprudence award, 1977. Mem. Okla. Bar Assn., Tulsa Bar Assn., ABA. Author: What if Karen Quinlan Had Lived in Oklahoma?Office: Suite 922 4500 S Garnett Tulsa OK 74146

BEAUCHAMP, JEFFERY OLIVER, mechanical engineer; b. Alice, Tex., Jan. 19, 1943; s. Charles Kirkland and Lila Arminda (Calk) B.; B.S. in Mech. Engring., U. Houston, 1969, M.S. in Mech. Engring., 1973; m. Toni Ramona Nobler, Sept. 7, 1963. Mech. designer Great Lakes Petroleum Service, Houston, 1963-64; mech. engr. Elliott Co. div. Carrier Corp., Houston, 1964-68; research asst. U. Houston, 1968-70; mech. design chief engr. Mallay Corp., Houston, 1970-74; project mgr. Fluor Engrs. & Constructors, Houston, 1974-78; pres. INTERMAT Internat. Materials Mgmt. Engrs., Houston, 1978—; cons. in field; speaker, lectr.Bd. dirs. Houston Dist. Export Council, Dept. Commerce; pres. Leadership Houston Assn., 1985-86; pres. Sci. Engring. Fair of Houston, Inc., 1983-84. Registered profl. engr., Tex. Mem. Nat., Tex. (Outstanding Young Engr. 1974) socs. profl. engrs., Am., Tex. cons. engrs. councils, Engrs. Council Houston (past pres.), ASME, Profl. Engrs. in Pvt. Practice, Houston C. of C. (internat. bus. and small bus. coms.), Inst. Internat. Edn., Common Cause, Houston Mus. Fine Arts, Los Angeles County Mus., Smithsonian Assos., Sigma Xi, Phi Kappa Phi, Pi Tau Sigma. Contbr. articles to profl. jours. Home: 2636 Albans Rd Houston TX 77005 Office: 11 Greenway Plaza Suite 1404 Houston TX 77046

BEAUCHAMP, JERRY JAY, insurance company executive; b. Coleman, Tex., Apr. 7, 1932; s. Joe Burleson and Stella (Needham) B.; m. Clara Mae Walker, Sept. 17, 1954; children—Sharon Beauchamp Shaw, Teri Beauchamp Chance, Joe R., Carla, Mary Ann. Student San Antonio Coll., 1955, Tex. U., 1961, NYU, 1960, Vanderbilt U., 1985. Vocat. counselor San Antonio State Hosp., Tex., 1954-63; dir. pub. relations Dyer Real Estate Ctr., 1958-63; owner, operator State Farm Ins. Agy., San Antonio, 1964—; res. dep. constable Bexar County, Tex., 1985—. Contbr. articles to profl. jours. Mem. Presdl. Republican Task Force, 1984-85; campaign treas. Com. to Elect Commr. Bob Lee, Bexar County, 1985; mem. Bexar County Judge Vision 2000 Task Force; v.p. San Antonio State Hosp. Vol. Council, 1985—; pres. bd. dirs. East Central Ind. Sch. Dist., 1978—; life mem. (hon.) PTA; Dem. candidate Dist. 119 Tex. Ho. of Reps., 1986. Recipient Hidalgo de Bexar award County Commrs Ct., 1980, Citation, Mayor City of San Antonio, 1983; Cert. of Appreciation, Tex. Legisl., 1984. Mem. San Antonio Psychiat. Technician Assn. (pres. 1967-69), Town East Bus. and Profl. Assn. (pres. 1976-79), Southeast Econ. Devel. Assn. (bd. dirs. 1979-82), Tex. Bank (bd. dirs.), Tex. Sch. Bd. Assn. (bd. dirs.), Nat. Sch. Bd. Assn. (legis. com.), Bexar Fedn. Sch. Bds., State Farm Ins. Agts., Tex. Sheriffs Assn. Baptist. Lodge: Rotary (pres. 1979, bd. dirs. 1982—). Avocations: charter boat operator; car wash business. Home: 4708 Pecan Grove San Antonio TX 78222 Office: State Farm Ins Agy 1736 South W W White Rd San Antonio TX 78220

BEAUDREAU, DAVID EUGENE, dentist; b. Plummer, Idaho, May 30, 1929; s. Arthur Thurston and Ada (Olmstead) B.; m. Leah LaVerne Hardin, Dec. 17, 1950; children—Gary, Brian, Ron. D.D.S., U. Wash., 1954; M.S. in Dentistry, U. Pa., 1965; D.Sc. (hon.), Georgetown U., 1981. Asst. prof., chmn. U. Pa. Dental Sch., Phila., 1968; prof., chmn. Med. Coll. Ga., Augusta, 1968-72, assoc. dean., 1972-76; dean Georgetown U. Sch. Dentistry, Washington, 1977-81; gen. practice dentistry, Evans, Ga., 1981—. Author Atlas of Fixed Prosthesis, 1975. Sect. editor to profl. jours. Mem. adv. bd. D.C. Hosp., 1977; mem. deans council VA, Washington, 1977. Served to lt. USN, 1954-56. Recipient Outstanding Alumnus award U. Wash. Sch. Dentistry, 1983. Fellow Am. Coll. Dentistry, Internat. Coll. Dentists; mem. Acad. Restorative Dentistry, Acad. Crown and Bridge, Am. Equilibration Soc., Nat. Acads. Practice. Republican. Presbyterian. Avocations: woodworking; model railroading; skiing; water sports. Home: 4356 Deerwood Ln Evans GA 30809 Office: 4250 Washington Rd PO Box 335 Evans GA 30809

BEAUFAIT, FREDERICK W(ILLIAM), civil engineering educator; b. Vicksburg, Miss., Nov. 28, 1936; s. Frank W. and Eleanor Chambliss (Haynes) B.; m. Lois Mary Erdman, Nov. 27, 1964; children—Paul Frederick, Nicole. B.Sc., Miss. State U., 1958; M.Sc., U. Ky., 1961; Ph.D., Va. Poly. Inst., 1965. Engr., L.E. Gregg & Assocs., Lexington, Ky., 1959-60; vis. lectr. civil engring. U. Liverpool (Eng.), 1960-61; prof. civil engring. Vanderbilt U., Nashville, 1965-79; prof., chmn. dept. civil engring. W.Va. U., Morgantown, 1979-83, assoc. dean Coll. Engring., 1983—; vis. prof. civil and structural engring. U. Wales-Cardiff, 1975-76; cons. in field. Vice chmn. stewardship com. 1st Presbyterian Ch., Morgantown, 1982, elder, 1983-85, mem. long-range planning com., 1985—; deacon Southminster Presbyn. Ch., Nashville, 1968-69, elder, 1971-73, 78-79, clk. of session, 1971-73; bd. dirs. Presbyn. Campus Ministry, Nashville, 1972-78, treas., 1972-75, pres., 1976-78; mem. citizens adv. com. Met. Sch. System, Nashville, 1978-79. Mem. ASCE, Am. Concrete Inst., Am. Soc. Engring. Edn., Morgantown C. of C. (chmn. county-wide sewerage com.), Chi Epsilon, Tau Beta Pi. Co-author: Computer Methods of Structural Analysis, 1970; author: Basic Concepts in Structural Analysis, 1977. Home: 488 Rebecca St Morgantown WV 26505 Office: Coll Engring WVa U Morgantown WV 26506

BEAVER, AUBREY JOE, customs officer; b. Burkburnett, Tex., Nov. 22, 1936; s. Homer W. and Tillie E. (Jacobs) B.; m. Jo Ann Freeman, Jan. 9, 1959; children—Melissa Marie, David Wayne, Carrie Eddith. B.S. in E.E., U. Okla., 1972. Test technician Martin Marietta, Denver, 1959-61; field engr. RCA, N.J., 1962; field engr. Collins Radio Co., Dallas, 1963-66; elec. engr. Tex. Instruments, Dallas, 1972-74; customs officer U.S. Customs Service, El Paso, Tex., 1974—. Bd. dirs. Christian Schs. of El Paso, 1983—. Served with USN, 1955-59. Mem. Internat. Narcotics Enforcement Officer Assn., Airborne Law Enforcement Officers Assn. Republican. Mem. Ch. of Christ. Home: 3121 E Glen Dr El Paso TX 79936 Office: 6812 Northrop Dr El Paso TX 79925

BEAVER, MARTHA SCOTT, newspaper art critic; b. Union Point, Ga., July 22, 1920; d. John Abbott and Annie Louise (Guill) Scott; m. Alfred Thomas Beaver, Feb. 5, 1942 (dec. 1972); 1 child, Angela Beaver Mack. A.B. in Journalism, U. Ga., 1941, postgrad. in art, 1966-70; postgrad. in stone sculpture, U. Karlsruhe, Fed. Republic Germany, 1955. Women's editor Daily Times, Gainesville, Ga., 1960-63; prof. art and journalism Brenau Coll., Gainesville, 1963-70; instr. art history and drawing U. S.C., Conway, 1966-70; exec. editor The Star, Marion, S.C., 1972-74; art critic, columnist The State, Columbia, 1974—. Contbr. articles on art to newspapers. Founding mem. Animal Protection League, Columbia, 1977—. Recipient numerous awards for excellence in art criticism and pub. service including Art Guilds awards, 1980, awards for Outstanding Service in Arts, 1981-85, Best Arts Writer, High Mus., Atlanta, 1982. Mem. Nat. League Am. Pen Women, Am. Contract Bridge League (jr. master), Nat. Trust for Historic Perservation, Sigma Delta Chi. Republican. Presbyterian. Avocations: animals; playing bridge. Home: 414 Sedgefield Dr Columbia SC 29210 Office: Columbia Newspapers Inc George Rogers Blvd Columbia SC 29202

BEAVER, PAUL JAMES, geologist, consultant; b. Eureka Springs, Arks., Aug. 28, 1924; s. Harold J. and Celia A. Beaver; m. Lillie Greene, Dec. 23, 1945; children—Paula Beaver Dennis, Patricia F. Beaver Skakon, Sylvia A. Beaver Schneider. B.S., Tex. Tech U., 1948. Geologist Cities Service Oil Co., Midland, Tex., 1948-55; dist. geologist, div. geologist Sunray Dx Oil Co., Calgary, Alta., Can. and Midland, Tex., 1955-76; geol. cons., Denver, 1970-73, Houston 73-76, 79—; chief geologist Home Petroleum Corp., Houston, 1976-79. Mem. Am. Assn. Petroleum Geologists, Houston Geol. Soc., Assn. Profl. Engrs., Geologists and Geophysicists of Alta., Rocky Mountain Assn. Geologists. Republican. Baptist. Club: Houston. Avocation; golf.

BEAZLIE, FRANK SMOOT, JR., urologist; b. Newport News, Va., Sept. 24, 1919; s. Frank Smoot and Mary Margaret (McConaghy) B.; m. Edith Irene Crawford, Mar. 6, 1948; children—Thomas, Margaret, Frances. B.S., Washington and Lee U., 1940; M.D., U. Va., 1943. Diplomate Am. Bd. Urology. Intern, U. Va., 1944-45, resident, 1945-51; practice medicine specializing in urology, pres., founder Hampton Rds. Urology Clinic, Inc., Newport News, Va., 1951—. Served to lt. M.C., USNR, 1944-46. Fellow ACS; mem. AMA, Am. Urol. Assn., So. Med. Assn., Med. Soc. Va., Va. Urol. Soc. (past pres.), Newport News Med. Soc. (past pres.), Pi Kappa Alpha. Episcopalian. Club: James River Country (Newport News). Contbr. med. articles to profl. jours. Office: 610 Thimble Shoals Blvd Newport News VA 23606

BEBOUT, DON GRAY, geologist; b. Monesson, Pa., Jan. 23, 1931; s. William Gray Bebout and Esther (McCurdy) Campbell; m. Lois Joan Heinzerling, Feb. 2, 1952; children—Beth Ann, Gray Edward, Martin Earl. B.Sc., Mt. Union Coll., 1952; M.Sc., U. Wis.-Madison, 1954; Ph.D., U. Kans., 1961. Research geologist Exxon Prodn. Research, Houston, 1960-72; research scientist Bur. Econ. Geology, Austin, Tex., 1972-78, sr. research scientist, 1981—; lectr. Dept. Geol. Sci., U. Tex., Austin, 1972-78; dir. research La. Geol. Survey, Baton Rouge, 1978-81; prof. geology La. State U., Baton Rouge, 1978-81; cons. in field. Author: (with Loucks) Stuart City Trend-South Texas, 1974. Editor: (with Scholle and Moore) Carbonate Depositional Environments, 1983. Contbr. articles to profl. publs. Served with U.S. Army, 1954-56. Recipient medal of merit Alta. Soc. Petroleum Geologists, 1969. Fellow Geol. Soc. Am.; mem. Am. Assn. Petroleum Geologists, Soc. Econ. Paleontologists, and Mineralogists (pres. gulf coast sect. 1984-85). Home: 3304 Bridle Path Austin TX 78703 Office: Bur Econ Geology U Tex Austin Univ Sta Box X Austin TX 78713

BEBOUT, EVELYN JUNE, government executive, lecturer; b. Anadarko, Okla., June 8, 1930; d. Leon Abriel Niles and Maude Irene (Gilliam) N.; m. Arthur Odell Andrews, Mar. 22, 1950 (div.); children—Roger Leon, Leslie David. B.L.S., U. Okla., 1973; M.S. in Systems Mgmt., U. So. Calif., 1979. With U.S. Air Force, 1958-83, maintenance specialist, inventory mgmt. specialist, logistics mgmt. specialist; supply systems analyst Sec. of Def., Falls Church, Va., 1983—. Vol. Sta. WAMU-Pub. Radio. Recipient Meritorious Civilian award, 1978. Mem. AAUW, Soc. Logistics Engrs. Club: Toastmistress. Home: 11811 S 28th St Arlington VA 22202 Office: Sec of Def Skyline #3 Suite 1506 Falls Church VA 22041

BECAN-MCBRIDE, KATHLEEN ELIZABETH, medical and cytogenetic technology educator; b. Houston, Feb. 24, 1949; d. Frank Ernest and Dorothy C. (Sturm) B.; m. Mark Anerson McBride, July 11, 1970; children—Patrick Becan, Jonathan Aaron. B.S. in Biology, U. Houston, 1971, M.Ed. in Allied Health, 1973, Ed.D. in Higher Edn. Adminstrn., 1977. Med. technologist St. Luke's Hosp., Houston, 1971-73; instr. med. br. U. Tex., Galveston, 1973-75, Houston Community Coll., 1975-77; asst. dir. med. and cytogenetic tech. U. Tex.-Houston, 1977-79, asst. prof., 1977-79, dir., assoc. prof., 1979—; instructional cons. Pvt. Industry Council, Houston, 1982-85, Peace Corps, Houston, 1984, ITT, Houston, 1985—; ednl. research cons. Am. Soc. for Med. Tech., Houston, 1977-79, 83-84; ednl. cons. La. State Bd. Regents, Baton Rouge, 1985. Author: Textbook of Clinical Lab Sciences, 1982; (with others) Phlebotomy Handbook, 1984; contbr. articles and monographs to Med. Lab. Scis. jour., chpts. to books; editor med. jours. Mem. adv. bd. for health occupation, adv. bd. com. for edn. evaluation Houston Ind. Sch. Dist., 1985—. Grantee U. Tex., Peace Corps, Pvt. Industry Council, Tex. Edn. Agy., ITT. Named one of Outstanding Young Women Am., 1979-82, 84. Mem. Am. Soc. Med. Tech. (coms. chmn.), Tex. Soc. for Med. Tech. (chmn. coms.), Houston Soc. Clin. Pathologists, Tex. Soc. Allied Health Professions (bd. dirs. 1981-82, pres. 1984, 85), Am. Soc. Clin. Pathologists (research and devel. com. 1983—, cert.), Clin. Lab. Mgmt. Assn., Zonta Internat. Exec. Bus. and Profl. Woman's Orgn., Alpha Mu Tau, Omicron Sigma. Democrat. Episcopalian. Avocations: tennis; jogging; soccer coaching; piano. Home: 3806 Marlowe St Houston TX 77005 Office: U Tex Health Sci Ctr PO Box 20708 Houston TX 77225

BECERRIL, MARY FOWLER, nursing educator; b. Dallas, Dec. 9, 1943; d. Isaac Odell and Josie Lee (Coffer) Fowler; m. Luis Espinoza Becerril, Dec. 19, 1973; 1 son, Joseph Luis. B.S., Tex. Woman's U., 1965, Ph.D., 1985; M.S., Boston U., 1969. Instr., Tex. Woman's U., Dallas, 1966-67, asst. prof., 1973-74; staff nurse medicine Parkland Hosp., Dallas, 1965; staff nurse pediatrics Bapt. Hosp., Beaumont, Tex., 1965-66; staff nurse psychiatry, pediatrics Children's Med. Ctr., Dallas, 1967; staff nurse pediatrics St. Paul Hosp., Dallas, 1967-68, maternal child clin. specialist, 1970-73; instr. pediatrics Meth. Hosp. Sch. Nursing, Dallas, 1969-70; sch. nurse Dallas Ind. Sch. Dist., 1978-79; assoc. prof. Dallas Bapt. Coll., 1979—; instr. CPR, Am. Heart Assn., 1980-84. Prison ministry vol. Beverly Hills Ch. of Dallas, 1972—. Mem. Am. Nurses Assn. Republican. Club: Woman's of Dallas Bapt. Coll. (historian 1982-83). Home: 3302 Texas Dr Dallas TX 75211 Office: Dept Nursing Dallas Bapt Coll 7777 W Kiest Blvd Dallas TX 75211

BECHANAN, WILLIAM BRYAN, electric utility executive; b. Hodgenville, Ky., Oct. 18, 1925; s. Lucien Bryan and Ruby Jane Bechanan; B.S. in Elec. Engring., U. Ky., 1949; m. Ann L. Goins, May 10, 1947; children—Gary, Karen. Asst. v.p. Ky. Utilities Co., Lexington, then v.p., now pres.; v.p. Old Diminion Power Co., now pres.; dir. 1st Security Nat. Bank, Electric Energy, Inc., Ohio Valley Electric Corp. Mem. IEEE. Office: Old Dominion Power Co One Quality St Lexington KY 40507

BECHTEL, MICHEL JOSEPH, geologist, oil company executive; b. New Orleans, Sept. 26, 1948; s. Joseph Poirson and Marie Therese (Barbier) B.; m. Mary Lynn Geiger, Jan. 23, 1970; children—Sherri Monique, Nicole Elise, Renee Christine. B.S. in Earth Scis., La. State U., 1970; M.S. in Petroleum Geology, U. New Orleans, 1974. Geologist Amoco Prodn. Co., New Orleans, 1970-73, U.S. Geol. Survey, Metairie, La., 1974-77; exploration geologist Ocean Drilling and Exploration, New Orleans, 1977-80; v.p. Weaver Exploration, Houston, 1980-84; pres. Bechtel Exploration, Houston, 1984—; dir. Energy Resource Assocs., Houston, Wallace Operating Co., Houston. Mem. Republican. Presdl. Task Force, 1984—. Mem. Am. Assn. Petroleum Geologists, New Orleans Geol. Soc. Avocations: hunting, fishing, stamp collecting. Office: Bechtel Exploration Co 3050 Post Oak Blvd Suite 1740 Houston TX 77056

BECK, DONALD FRANK, health care financial consultant; b. Toledo, Oct. 6, 1942; s. Frank L. and Virginia D. (Lesniewicz) B.; m. Andrea K. Najarian, May 29, 1965; children—Leslie Ann, Marjorie Marie, Donald Raymond. B.B.A., U.Toledo, 1970, M.B.A., 1975. C.P.A., Ohio, Miss., Tenn., Ill. Internal auditor Med. Coll. Ohio, Toledo, 1971-76; asst. controller Toledo Hosp., 1976-78; cons. TriBrook Inc., Chgo., 1977-78; hosp. controller Hosp. Corp. of Am., Nashville, 1978-79; controller Meth. Hosps. at Memphis, 1979-81; pres. D.F. Beck & Assocs., Memphis, 1981—; exec. dir. Physicians Health Plan of Tenn.; lectr. in field; adj. prof. acctg. Owens Coll., Perrysburg, Ohio, 1975-77; lectr. in health care fin. U. Miss. grad. program in healthcare adminstrn., 1982—. Mem. Am. Coll. Hosp. Adminstrs., Healthcare Fin. Mgmt. Assn., Nat. Writers Assn., Tenn. Hosp. Assn., Toastmasters Internat., Assn. MBA Execs., Republican. Beta Gamma Sigma. Club: K.C. Author: Basic Hospital Financial Management, 1980; Principles of Reimbursement in Healthcare, 1983. Mem. editorial bds. Healthcare Supr., So. Hosps., Hosp. Topics, Topics in Hosp. Pharm. Mgmt.; contbr. articles to hosp. jours. Home: 5327 Wilton St Memphis TN 38119 Office: 4515 Poplar Ave Suite 202 Memphis TN 38117

BECK, DONALD THOMAS, public affairs and community relations executive; b. Bowling Green, Ky., July 1, 1942; s. Kirby Thomas and Ida Mildred (McCown) B.; m. Patricia Lee Richmond, July 27, 1963; children—Barbara Susan, Clinton Vance, Zachary Grier. A.A., Alan Hancock Jr. Coll., Santa Maria, Calif., 1963; B.A. in Communications, Mich. State U., 1969; M.A. in Communications, U. Denver, 1973. Chief community relations U.S. Air Force, Andrews AFB, Md., 1973-75, dir. info., Udorn, Thailand, 1975-76; chief internal info. Pacific Air Forces, Hickam AFB, Hawaii, 1976-79; dir. pub. affairs U.S. Air Force Eastern Space and Missile Ctr., Patrick AFB, Fla., 1979-80; dir. customer-pub. relations Martin Marietta Aerospace Co., Cape Canaveral, Fla., 1980-83; dir. community relations Lockheed Space Ops. Co., Titusville, Fla., 1983—. Mem. Brevard County Civilian-Mil. Community Relations Council, Fla., 1980—; bd. dirs. Jr. Achievement-Fla., East Coast, 1982—; chmn. Gt. Indian River Raft Race, Titusville, 1984. Recipient Community Achievement award Canaveral Council Tech. Socs., 1983, Silver Snoopy award NASA Astronaut Corps, Kennedy Space Ctr., 1985. Mem. Space Coast Pub. Relations Assn. (pres. 1983), Air Force Assn. (pres. Cape Canaveral chpt. 1983-84, v.p. Fla. chpt. 1984-85; Nat. Programming award 1984, Man of Yr. award 1984), Cocoa Beach Area C. of C. (bd. dirs. 1984—). Avocations: golf; fishing. Office: Lockheed Space Ops Co 3880 S Washington Ave Titusville FL 32780

BECK, EARL RAY, history educator; b. Junction City, Ohio, Sept. 8, 1916; s. Ernest Ray and Mary Francis (Helser) B.; A.B., Capital U., 1937; M.A., Ohio State U., 1939, Ph.D., 1942; m. Marjorie Lois Culbertson, Nov. 7, 1944; children—Ann, Mary Sue. Instr., Capital U., Columbus, Ohio, 1942-43, Ohio State U., Columbus, 1946-49; asst. prof. Fla. State U., Tallahassee, 1949-52, assoc. prof., 1952-60, prof. history, 1960—, chmn. dept. history, 1967-72, assoc. chmn. grad. studies, 1982—; vis. faculty U. Ky., Lexington, 1948, La. State U., 1955, Tulane U., 1959, Duke U., Durham, N.C., 1968. Served with U.S. Army, 1943-46. Mem. Am. Hist. Assn., So. Hist. Assn. (chmn. European history sect. 1983-84), German Studies Assn., Soc. Spanish and Portuguese History, Conf. Group Central European History, Com. for Study of History of Second World War. Democrat. Presbyterian. Author: Verdict on Schacht, 1955; Death of the Prussian Republic, 1959; Contemporary Civilization, 1959; On Teaching History in Colleges and Universities, 1966; Germany Rediscovers America, 1968; A Time of Triumph and of Sorrow - Spanish Politics during the Reign of Alfonso XII, 1874-1885, 1979; Under the Bombs: The German Home Front, 1942-45, 1986. Office: Dept of History Fla State Univ Tallahassee FL 32306

BECK, GEORGE PRESTON, anesthesiologist, educator; b. Wichita Falls, Tex., Oct. 21, 1930; s. George P. and Amanda (Wilbanks) B.; B.S., Midwestern U., 1951; M.D., U. Tex., 1955; m. Constance Carolyn Krog, Dec. 22, 1953; children—Carla Elizabeth, George P., Howard W. Intern, John Sealy Hosp., 1955-56; resident anesthesiology Parkland Meml. Hosp., Dallas, 1959-62, vis. staff, 1964—; practice medicine, specializing in anesthesiology, Lubbock, Tex., 1964—; chief staff Meth. Hosp., Lubbock, 1967-68; asst. prof. anesthesiology Southwestern Med. Sch., Dallas, 1962-64, asst. clin. prof., 1964-71, asso. clin. prof. anesthesiology U. Tex. Med. Br. at Galveston, 1971—; pres. Gt. Plain Ballistics Corp., 1967—. Pres. found. bd. Tex. Tech U., 1972—. Served with USAF, 1956-59. Diplomate Am. Bd. Anesthesiology. Fellow Am. Coll. Anesthesiologists; mem. Am., Tex. (pres. 1974) socs. anesthesiologists, Tex., Lubbock County med. socs., Lubbock Surg. Soc. (pres. 1969). Lutheran (pres. ch. council 1965-66, pres. congregation 1965-66). Author: The Ideal Anesthesiologist, 1960; Mnemonics as an Aid to the Anesthesiologist, 1961; Anterior Approach to Sciatic Nerve Block, 1962. Inventor Beck Airway Airflow Monitor. Home: 4601 W 18th St Lubbock TX 79416 Office: PO Box 16385 Lubbock TX 79490

BECK, JAMES L., agricultural lending service executive; b. Badin, N.C., July 6, 1933; s. Lytle Patrick and Thelma (Tadlock) B.; m. Frances Riggins, Aug. 25, 1950 (dec. 1972); children—Katherine Beck Smith, Charles P.; m. Peggy Jean Welch, June 7, 1972; children—Wesley L., Lisa G. Student Wingate Coll., 1954-55; B.S. in Agronomy, N.C. State U., 1958. Br. mgr. Piedmont Prodn. Credit Assn., Monroe, N.C., 1967-68; mgr. Fed. Land Bank Assn. of Monroe, 1968-70; pres. Fed. Land Bank Assn. of Winston-Salem, N.C., 1970-71, Farm Credit Service of Asheville, N.C., 1971-75; regional v.p. Farm Credit Banks of Columbia (S.C.), 1975-76; pres. Farm Credit Service of Lakeland, Fla., 1976—. Past dir. Lakeland Symphony Orch. Served with U.S. Army, 1950-54. Mem. Am. Soc. Agronomy. Methodist. Clubs: Lakeland Yacht and Country, Rotary (past pres. and dir. Lakeland South), Wingate Lions (past pres.). Home: 4630 Kings Point Ct Lakeland FL 33803 Office: 1005 N Lake Parker Ave Lakeland FL 33805

BECK, MELVIN LOYD, biology educator, geneticist; b. Mena, Ark., Mar. 22, 1945; s. Raymond Walter and Annis Marie (McKee) B.; m. Meriwether Colbert Reaves, May 14, 1977; 1 child, Christopher Loyd. B.S., Ark. Poly. Coll., 1967; Ph.D., U. Ark., 1974. Instr. dept. biology Memphis State U., 1974-77, asst. prof., 1977-81, assoc. prof., 1981-85, prof., 1985—, coordinator grad. studies and research, 1983—. Served to capt. Chem. Corps, U.S. Army, 1967-69. NDEA Title IV fellow U. Ark., 1970-73. Mem. Soc. Study Evolution, Am. Genetic Assn., Am. Soc. Ichthylogists and Herpetologists, Sigma Xi, Phi Beta Kappa. Contbr. articles to profl. jours. Office: Dept Biology Memphis State U Memphis TN 38152

BECK, NANCY MANN MCCONNICO (MRS. EARL CRAFTON BECK, JR.), civic leader; b. Memphis, Aug. 31, 1931; d. John Davis and Pauline (Hilton) McConnico; grad. So. Sem. and Jr. Coll., 1949; m. Dean Carlton DuBois, Aug. 19, 1951 (div. Nov. 1963); children—Denise Hilton, Dean Carlton; m. 2d, Earl C. Beck, Jr., Jan. 31, 1971; 1 son, John Harrington. Asst. buyer, sportswear John Gerber Co., Memphis, 1950-51; fashion coordinator J. Hilton McConnico, Designer, Memphis, 1963-65; buyer, mgr. Bridal Salon, Goldsmiths, Memphis, 1965-70, French Room, 1970-71; v.p. Beck Distbg. Co., 1970-73; v.p. Crittenden Fine Arts Bd., 1977—; chmn. Children's Art Day, Memphis, 1976-78; chmn. Women's coordination Billy Graham Crusade, Crittenden County, 1978; sec.-treas. Rivertown Devels., Inc., v.p., 1981—. Press relations Hunter Lane for mayor, 1967; bd. dirs., v.p. Memphis Symphony League, pres., 1980-81; mem. Memphis Arts Council, Memphis Woman's Exchange; mem. bd. Memphis Orchestral Soc.; chmn. Memphis Symphony Ball; mem. vol. council, bd. dirs. Am. Symphony Orch. League; mem. president's adv. bd. So. Sem., Buena Vista, Va.; trustee So. Sem. Jr. Coll., Buena Vista. Recipient nat. award Children's Arts Day-Am. Symphony Orch. League. Episcopalian. Clubs: Town and Country Garden (pres.) (Hughes, Ark.), Josephine Circle (past pres.) (Memphis). Home: Casa Lorraine Plantation Hughes AR 72348

BECK, WILLIAM HAROLD, JR., lawyer; b. Clarksdale, Miss., Aug. 18, 1928; s. William Harold and Mary (McGaha) B.; m. Nancy Cassity House, Jan. 30, 1954; children—Mary, Nancy, Katherine. B.A., Vanderbilt U., 1950; J.D., U. Miss., 1954. Bar: Miss. 1954, La. 1960. Atty., Clarksdale, Miss., 1954-57; asst. prof. Tulane U., 1957-59; ptnr. Foley Judell Beck Bewley Martin & Hicks, New Orleans, 1959—. Served to capt., AUS, 1951-53. Mem. ABA, La. Bar Assn., Miss. Bar Assn., SAR, Sons Colonial Wars. Office: 535 Gravier St New Orleans LA 70130

BECK-BRAKE, CANDYCE LYNNE, exploration geologist; b. Williamsport, Pa., Sept. 10, 1958; d. Jay Alvin and Doris Marcella (Bower) Beck; m. Christopher French Brake, May 29, 1982. B.S., Pa. State U., 1980; M.A., Rice U., 1981. Exploration geologist Shell Western Exploration and Prodn., Houston, 1981—. Mem. Am. Assn. Petroleum Geologists (jr. mem.). Mem. Disciples of Christ Ch. Avocations: ballet; sewing; piano. Home: 15207 Barbarossa Dr Houston TX 77083 Office: Shell Western Exploration and Production Box 527 Houston TX 77001

BECKELHEIMER, CHRISTINE ELIZABETH CAMPBELL, nurse; b. Oak Hill, W.Va., Sept. 6, 1916; d. Charles Earl and Macie Avis (Boothe) Campbell; diploma in nursing Somerset Hosp., Somerville, N.J., 1938; B.S. in Nursing Edn., Hunter Coll., 1954; M.A. in Nursing Service Adminstrn., Tchrs. Coll. Columbia U., 1959, profl. diploma, 1961, postgrad, 1961-65; m. Joseph Howard, June 6, 1941 (dec.); 1 dau., Mary Elizabeth; m. 2d, Harry Abrahamsen, Oct. 10, 1943; 1 dau., Cherri Georgette; m. 3d, Robert Ernest Beckelheimer, Jan. 18, 1980. Staff nurse obstetrics Somerset Hosp., 1939; staff nurse Goldwater Meml. Hosp., Welfare Island, N.Y.C., 1939-40, research nurse, 1940-41; staff nurse St. Vincent's Hosp., N.Y.C., 1941-43; lab. asst. Am. Cyanamid Co., Bound Brook, N.J., 1943; charge nurse Paul Kimball Hosp., Lakewood, N.J., 1943-44; staff nurse to head nurse Pinewald Hosp., Bayville, N.J., 1944-46; staff nurse Morrisania City Hosp., Bronx, N.Y., 1946-49, head nurse, 1949-50, clin. instr., 1950-54; instl. insp. Dept. Hosps. City of N.Y., 1954-58; supr. edn. City Hosp., Elmhurst, N.Y., 1958-60, research asst. Fedn. of the Handicapped, 1962-63; research asso. Yeshiva U. Lincoln Hosp., N.Y.C., 1963-64; asst. coordinator exchange grad. nurse program St. Luke's Hosp., N.Y.C., 1964-65, asst. dir. nursing service inservice edn., 1966-67; cons. research and hosp. nursing service Nat. League Nursing, N.Y.C., 1968-70, acting dir. research (cons.), 1970-71; assoc. prof. nursing W.Va. Inst. Tech., 1971-73, chmn. dept. nursing, 1973-75; coordinator patient care Raleigh Gen. Hosp., Beckley, W.Va., 1975-78, dir. hosp. inservice, 1978-79. USPHS Nurse Research fellow, 1961-63; USPHS grantee, 1965-66. Mem. Am., W.Va. nurses assns., Am., N.Y.C. public health assns., N.Y. Acad. Scis., Aerospace Med. Assn., Tchrs. Coll. Nurses Alumni Assn., Hunter Coll. Alumni Assn., Pi Lambda Theta, Kappa Delta Pi, Am. Legion Aux., DAR, UDC (past pres. W.Va. div.), Fayette County Hist. Soc., Genealogy Soc. Fayette and Raleigh Counties, Wittenfort Long Rifles, Mountaineer Flintlock Rifles, Rosicrucian Order. Author: Cristabel Manalacor of Veltakin, 1970; The Cruachan and the Killane, 1970; The Mortal Immortals, 1971; The Golden Olive, 1972; The Bride of Kilkerran, 1972. Home: 213 Washington Ave Oak Hill WV 25901

BECKER, JOSEPH ALBERT, laboratory administrator; b. Ft. Worth, Nov. 8, 1941; m. Sandy Kay Becker; children—Stephen, Joseph, Brandon, David, Dawn, Lisa. A.S., U. Tampa, 1968; B.A., Ottawa U. (Kans.), 1980; M.A. in Health Care Adminstrn., Columbia Pacific U., 1983, Ph.D. in Health Care Adminstrn., 1984. Staff technologist Med. Ctr. Hosp., Punta Gorda, Fla., 1964-66, supr. blood bank, 1966-68, supr. microbiology, 1968-73; supr. microbiology St. Joseph's Hosp., Port Charlotte, Fla., 1973-74; supr. microbiology Med. Ctr. Hosp., Punta Gorda, 1974-78, asst. chief technologist, 1978-80, adminstrv. dir. lab., 1980—, blood bank chmn., 1983—. Campaign chmn. Republican candidate in Charlotte County, Fla., 1968. Served with USN, 1959-62. Recipient Employee of Month award Med. Ctr. Hosp., 1980; Fla. Soc. Am. Med. Tech. Cert. of Appreciation, 1982. Mem. Fla. Soc. Am. Med. Tech. (dir. 1982-83, Gulf coast dist. dir. 1982-83), Am. Med. Technologists, Am. Soc. Med. Technologists, Am. Bd. Bioanalysis, Clin. Lab. Mgmt. Assn., Fla. Soc. Med. Technologists, Nat. Cert. Agy. Contbr. articles to profl. jours. Address: Med Center Hosp 809 E Marion Ave 25130 Punta Gorda FL 33950

BECKETT, TERRY S., political consultant, pollster; b. Orlando, Fla., Dec. 15, 1953; d. Eugene and Patricia (Hoage) Savoca; m. William Albert Beckett, Aug. 25, 1979. B.S., Rollins Coll., 1975. Adminstrv. aide, mem. exec. staff Office of Gov., Tallahassee, Fla., 1981-82; campaign mgr. Batchelor Congress Campaign, Orlando, 1982; Fla. campaign dir. Askew Presdl. campaign, Orlando, 1984; Fla. campaign dir. Hart Presdl. campaign, Orlando, 1984, La. campaign dir., Baton Rouge, 1984; campaign mgr., cons. Batchelor Legis. campaign, Orlando, 1984; sr. assoc. Kitchens & Assocs., Orlando, 1985—. Democrat. Avocation: tennis. Home: 3411 Marston Dr Orlando FL 32806 Office: Kitchens & Assocs 5384 Hoffner Rd Orlando FL 32812

BECKHAM, GERALD GIST, educational administrator; b. Denison, Tex., Nov. 8, 1934; s. Walter C. and Treva (Gist) B.; m. Wanda Jean Wells, July 25, 1958; children—Elizabeth Karron. B.S., East Tex. State U., 1956, M.S., 1965; postgrad. U. Houston, 1966-75, U. Colo., 1961, U. No. Colo., 1974. Tchr., Bellaire High Sch. (Tex.), 1958-70; asst. prin. Lincoln Jr.-Sr. High Sch., 1970-75; prin. Houston Night High Sch., 1975-76; dir. bus. and office edn. Houston Ind. Sch. Dist., 1976-83; prin. Bells Elem. Ind. Sch. Dist., 1983—. Active Sharpstown Civic Assn. Served with U.S. Army, 1956-58. Named Outstanding Young Educator of Houston, Houston Jr. C. of C., 1968. Mem. Tex. Elem. Prins. Assn., Greater Houston Bus. Edn. Assn. (pres. 1962-63), Houston Tchrs. Assn. (pres. 1967-68), Tex. Classroom Tchrs. Assn. (exec. bd. 1969-70), Tex. Tchrs. Assn. Dist. IV (exec. bd. 1968-72), Houston Profl. Adminstrs. (exec. bd. 1970-83, v.p. 1980-81), Tex. Bus. Edn. Assn. (pres. 1982-83), NEA, Nat. Bus. Edn. Assn., Crosstimbers Land Owners Assn. Democrat. Baptist.

BECKHAM, GERALD WAYNE, association executive; b. Louisville, Ky., Sept. 20, 1946; s. Chester Earl and Doris Victorine (Hatcher) B.; m. Dallas Katrena Henderson, July 17, 1971; children—Chesa Kristina, Wendy Sheree. B.A., Western Ky. U., 1975. Sales rep. Servomation Corp., Atlanta, 1975-77; exec. dir. United Way Warren County, Bowling Green, Ky., 1977-82, United Way Ouachita, Inc., Monroe, La., 1982—. Served with USN, 1965-69, Vietnam. Named to Hon. Order Ky. Cols., 1978. Mem. Ch. of Christ. Lodge: Rotary. Home: 1908 John Circle Monroe LA 71201 Office: 1401 Hudson Ln Suite 227 Monroe LA 71201

BECKHAM, WILLIAM A., bishop, Episcopal Church; b. Columbia, S.C., Apr. 29, 1927; s. Francis Morgan and Maud Elizabeth (Guthrie) B.; m. Harriet Louise Wingate, Dec. 17, 1948. B.S., U. S.C., 1951; M.Div., Va. Theol. Sem., 1954, D.D., 1980. Rector, Trinity Edgefield, S.C., 1954-56; asst. sec. Conv. of Our Savior Ch., Trenton, S.C., 1956-63; priest-in-charge Union & Calvin Glenn Springs, 1957-58; archdeacon Upper S.C., 1964-79; bishop of S.C., 1979—. Address: The Episcopal Ch PO Box 1789 Columbia SC 29202*

BECKWITH, HENRY HOPKINS, construction company executive; b. Jacksonville, Fla., Oct. 18, 1935; s. Francis Judd and Marian (Hopkins) B.; m. Patricia Stonis, Apr. 30, 1960 (div. 1970); m. Madeleine Elmore, Mar. 15, 1971; children—Henry Hopkins Jr., Kathryn Ann, Michael E. Ingram, Thomas D. Ingram. B.S., Fla. So. Coll., 1959. Project mgr. Henley & Beckwith, Jacksonville, Fla., 1954-61; v.p. Tompkins-Beckwith, Jacksonville, 1965, exec. v.p., 1972, pres., 1978, chmn. bd., pres., 1985—; dir. Fla. Nat. Banks of Fla., Turknett-MPS Engrs., Am. Surety & Casualty Co. Democratic candidate Fla. Ho. of Reps., 1962; bd. dirs. State Bd. Social Welfare, Fla., 1966-68, Fla. State Community Coll. Coordinating Bd.; 1981-83; mem. council the Fla. Sch. of Arts, 1985; pres. Gator Bowl Assn., 1985. Served with U.S. N.G., 1957-63. Named Man of Vision, Nat. Soc. to Prevent Blindness, Jacksonville, 1980; recipient Top Mgmt. award Sales and Mktg. Execs. of Jacksonville, 1983. Mem. Fla. Council of 100, ASME, ASHRAE, Am. Nuclear Soc., Mech. Contractors Assn. Am., Nat. Constructors Assn., TAPPI. Democrat. Episcopalian. Club: Capt. Jacksonville Quarterback. Lodge: Rotary (pres. Jacksonville 1978-79, dist. gov. 1982-83). Avocations: hunting; fishing. Office: Tompkins-Beckwith Inc 2160 McCoys Blvd Jacksonville FL 32204

BECKWITH, RICHARD WENDELL, leasing company executive; b. Greene, N.Y., Feb. 8, 1943; s. Wendell D. and Lois Lee (Taylor) B.; m. Ruby Gates, Sept. 1, 1962; children—Rebecca, Richard Wendell, Randy, Ruby Allyn. B.S. in Gen. Engring., U. Omaha, 1965; J.D., Woodrow Wilson Law Sch., Atlanta, 1968, LL.M., 1969; B.S. in Theology, Lee Coll., Cleveland, Tenn., 1983. Cert. estimator gen. constrn. Am. Soc. Estimators; cert. purchasing mgr. Nat. Assn. Purchasing Mgrs.; lic. gen. contractor, Fla. Controller, constrn. supt. WCB Assocs., 1969-78; dir. constrn. Cardinal Industries, Columbus, Ohio, 1978-79; engring. instr. Columbus Inst. Tech. (Ohio), 1979-80; engring. mgr. Aide Engring., Paradise Steam Plant, Ky., 1981; purchasing agt. M&M, Mars Co., Cleveland, Tenn., 1982—. Assoc. pastor, counselor Cedar Valley Christian Fellowship, 1982—; regional bd. dirs. Christian Def. League. Served with AUS, 1962-68. N.Y. State Regents scholar, 1961. Mem. ASCE, Nat. Holstein Breeders Assn., Tenn. Holstein Breeders Assn., John Birch Soc., Assn. Christian Attys. Republican. Home: RFD 1 Riceville TN 37370 Office: 3500 Peerless Rd Cleveland TN 37311

BECNEL, ALBERT THOMAS, ednl. adminstr.; b. Taft, La., June 24, 1916; B.S. in Vocat. Edn., La. State U., Baton Rouge, 1939; grad. Command and Gen. Staff Sch.; M.Ed. in Guidance, Adminstrn. and Supervision, Nicholls State U., Thibodaux, La., 1968; married, 2 children. Tchr., supr. St. John Parish Schs., Reserve, La., 1939-64, supt. schs., 1964—; mem. supt.'s adv. council La. State Bd. Edn. Chmn. Reserve Charity to Birth Defects March Dimes Fund, 1964-84. Served to maj. AUS, 1942-46. Mem. La. Assn. Sch. Supts., South Central La. Supts. Assn. La. Assn. Sch. Execs., La. Tchr. Assn., NEA, La. Edn. Assn., Nat. Assn. Ret. Persons, Phi Delta Kappa. Lodge: KC. Home: PO Box 191 134 W 1st St Reserve LA 70084 Office: PO Box AL W 10th St Reserve LA 70084

BEDDOW, JERRY TIPTON, telecommunications executive; b. Dallas, Mar. 11, 1946; s. Gerald Burke and Joyce Loretta (Mackey) B.; m. Linda Gayle Hatfield, June 16, 1967; children—Melinda, Meredith. B.A., So. Meth. U. Supr. Tex. Instruments, Dallas, 1968-76, br. mgr., 1976-78; v.p. mfg. Honeywell, Dallas, 1978-83, v.p. ops., 1983—; cons. in field. Recipient Honeywell Advanced Dir.'s award 1983. Mem. Am. Mgmt. Assn., Soc. Advancement Mgmt. Republican. Baptist. #2509 Teakwood Plano TX 75075 Office: Honeywell Inc 4401 Beltwood Pkwy S Dallas TX 75234

BEDEIAN, ARTHUR GEORGE, business educator; b. Davenport, Iowa, Dec. 22, 1946; s. Arthur and Varsenick (Donjoian) B.; m. Lynda L. Kennon, June 29, 1968; children—Katherine Nicole, Thomas Arthur. B.B.A., U. Iowa, 1967; M.B.A., Memphis State U., 1968; D. Bus. Adminstrn., Miss. State U., 1973. Instr. Mgmt. Miss. State U., Mississippi State, 1969-71; asst. prof. Ga. So. Coll., Statesboro, 1971-73; adj. asst. prof. Boston U., 1973-74; Edward L. Lowder prof. mgmt. Auburn (Ala.) U., 1974-85; Ralph and Kacoo G. Olinde prof. mgmt. La. State U., 1985—. Served with USAR, 1968-73. Fellow Acad. Mgmt. (bd. govs. 1979-81); mem. Inst. Decision Scis. (nat. council), Southeastern Inst. Decision Scis. (pres. 1978-79), So. Mgmt. Assn. (pres. 1982-83), Am. Sociol. Assn., Beta Gamma Sigma, Delta Mu Delta. Armenian Apostolic. Lodge: Elks. Author: Organizations: Theory and Analysis, 2d edit., 1984; Management, 1986; editor Jour. of Mgmt., 1977-79. Home: 838 High Plains Ave Baton Rouge LA 70810 Office: Dept of Mgmt La State U Baton Rouge LA 70830

BEDELL, GEORGE CHESTER, university administrator; b. Jacksonville, Fla., May 13, 1928; s. Chester and Edmonia (Hair) B.; children—George Chester, Frank Moor, Nathan Gale; m. Elizabeth Reed, Jan. 22, 1983. B.A., U. of South, 1950; B.D., Va. Theol. Sem., 1953; M.A., U. N.C., 1966; Ph.D., Duke U., 1969. Ordained priest Episcopal Ch. Parish priest, Lake City, Panama City and Tallahassee, Fla., 1953-64; asst. prof. religion Fla. State U., Tallahassee, 1967-73, assoc. prof., 1973-74, courtesy assoc. prof., 1974—; dir. humanities and fine arts State U. System Fla., 1971-72, dir. personnel and faculty relations, 1972-76, assoc. vice chancellor, 1976-77, exec. asst. to chancellor, dir. pub. affairs, 1977-79, vice chancellor, 1979-80, interim chancellor, 1980-81, exec. vice chancellor, 1981—; historiographer Episc. Diocese of Fla., 1968-76. Author: Kierkegaard and Faulkner: Modalities of Existence, 1972; Religion in America, 1975, 2d edit., 1983. Mem. Tallahassee City Park Bd., 1972-76, chmn., 1974-76; mem. Leon County Democratic Exec. Com., 1970-74; trustee Jessie Ball du Pont Religious, Charitable and Ednl. Fund, 1985—; dir. Big Bend Health Plan, Inc., 1974-75. Arthur N. Morris fellow, 1964-67; Duke-Danforth fellow, 1965-67. Mem. Am. Acad. Religion (mng. editor Studies in Religion 1972-76). MLA, Soc. Sci. Study of Religion. Office: 210 Collins Bldg Tallahassee FL 32301

BEDELL, LEONARD A., diversified financial services executive; b. Beeville, Tex., Feb. 7, 1945; s. Peter Bryce and Katherine (Dromgoole) B.; 1 son, William Lee. A.A., Del Mar Coll., 1966; B.B.A. in Acctg., Tex. A&I U., 1968; C.P.A., Tex. Audit mgr. Arthur Andersen & Co., Houston, 1968-76; dir. fin. reporting Am. Gen. Life Ins. Co., Houston, 1976-79; prin. Kenneth Leventhal & Co., Houston, 1979-81; ptnr., exec. v.p., investor relations and sales HOU-TEX Land & Cattle, Houston, 1981-82; fin. cons. Houston, 1982; pres. real estate services Commonwealth Fin. Group, Houston, 1982—; cons. W.A. Daniel Oil & Gas, 1981—. Campaign chmn. Ralph Russell Professorship Endowment, Tex. A&I U., 1982—. Mem. Mortgage Bankers Assn., Assn. Corp. Growth (dir. 1980-82), Am. Inst. CPAs, Tex. Soc. C.P.A.s (dir. 1982), Tex. A&I U. Alumni Assn. (dir. 1983—). Republican. Methodist. Clubs: Houstonian, Heritage. Office: Commonwealth Fin Group 2223 W Loop S Suite 700 Houston TX 77027

BEDFORD, MADELEINE ALANN PECKHAM, civic worker; b. Ontario, Calif., Jan. 25, 1910; d. Allen Lewis and Madeleine (Elliott) Peckham; A.B., U. Calif. at Berkeley, 1930, M.A., 1937; LL.D. (hon.), Tex. Christian U., 1973; m. Charles Francis Bedford, Dec. 30, 1930; children—Madeleine Alann, Frances Ellen, Charlotte Jean. Supr. tchr. tng. and counseling, in charge testing Univ. High Sch., U. Calif. at Berkeley, 1931-38; tchr. English to fgn. born San Leandro (Calif.) Evening Schs., 1931-38. Treas., Tarrant County Day Care Assn., 1953-54; pres. Ft. Worth and Tarrant County council Camp Fire Girls, 1961-63, pres. nat. council, 1965-68; pres. Ft. Worth Lit. Council, 1963-65; v.p. Tarrant County United Fund and Community Council, 1963-66, mem. exec. com. bd. dirs., 1963—, chmn. speakers tours film div. United Way Met. Tarrant County, 1973, chmn. planning and research div., 1973-75, v.p., 1973-75, chmn. Community Services Div., pres. Ft. Worth chpt. Am. Field Service, 1964-66; chmn. budget sub-com. United Fund, 1959-68; sec. Tex. United Community Services, 1968-70, v.p., 1970-73, pres., 1973-75, hon. chmn. bd., 1975—; mem. Mid-Am. Regional Vol. Task Force United Way Am., 1973-75, Tex. rep. for UNICEF, 1969—; mem. gov's. steering com. White House Conf. on Children and Youth, 1970, chmn. task force com. for Tex. on internat. relations, 1970; chmn. Met. div. Crusade of Hope campaign, 1970; chmn. Mayor's Council on Youth Opportunity, Fort Worth, 1971-72; chmn. Tarrant County Task Force Aging, 1972-74; fin. and sec. social services adv. com. Tex. Dept. Pub. Welfare, 1974-75, chmn. com., 1975-76; bd. dirs., mem. advisory council adult basic edn. Tarrant County chpt. ARC, 1966-69; bd. dirs. United Cerebral Palsy Tarrant County, pres., 1976-77, chmn. bd., 1977—; v.p. United Cerebral Palsy of Tex., 1978, pres., 1983-85, chmn. bd., 1985—; mem. coordinating bd. United Cerebral Palsy Assn. Am., 1983—; bd. dirs. Tarrant County Community Action Agy., Tarrant County Community Council, Tex. Social Welfare Assn., Community Trust Met. Tarrant County, 1982—, Girls Club Am., Ft. Worth YWCA, 1982— mem. com. on nat. agy. support United Way Am., 1975-78; mem. Child Care '76, Tarrant County; trustee Assn. for Grad. Edn. and Research North Tex., 1971-74, 78—, Tex. Christian U., 1975—, Tex. Coll. Osteo. Medicine Found., 1980—, Sch. Social Work Found., U. Tex., Austin, 1981—; bd. dirs. Ft. Worth Epilepsy Assn., 1982—, Nat. Conf. Social Welfare, 1976-80, Dallas/Ft. Worth Airport Chaplaincy Bd., 1983—, Ft. Worth Girls Club, 1979—, YWCA, 1982—; bd. visitors Add-Ran Coll., Tex. Christian U., 1971-77; mem. Housing Rehab. Project for Ft. Worth, 1975-79; mem. corp. bd. UNICEF, 1981—; mem. fin. assistance adv. council Tex. Dept. Human Resources, 1981—; pres. Women's Haven Tarrant County, 1978-81; bd. dirs. Tarrant Area Community of Chs., 1983—, pres., 1984—; mem. nat. bd. dirs. Girls Clubs Am., 1982—; bd. dirs. Family Services, 1982—, v.p., 1983—; pres. bd. dirs. Family Service Assn., 1985—. Recipient Board (pres. Ft. Worth chpt. 1983—), award Camp Fire Girls, 1961, Wo-He-Lo award, 1968; award of Excellence for Outstanding Leadership and Service Tarrant Co. Community Council, 1964, Civic award First Lady Ft. Worth Altrusa, 1966; Hercules award, planning and research div. United Way Met. Tarrant County, 1977; award for service to Tex. Christian U. students, 1982, award for human services Sertoma Club, 1983, Royal Purple award Tex. Christian U. Alumni Assn., 1983. Mem. Ft. Worth Lecture Found., Ft. Worth C. of C. (pvt. enterprise com. 1983—), Council on World Affairs (pres. 1984—), Internat. Good Neighbor Council, DAR, Mortar Board (pres. Ft. Worth Chpt. 1983—), Phi Beta Kappa (pres. Ft. Worth 1958-59), Alpha Chi Omega, Pi Sigma Alpha. Episcopalian. Club: Ft. Worth Woman's (past pres. history sect.). Home: 7 Westover Rd Fort Worth TX 76107

BEDSOLE, ANN SMITH, state senator; b. Selma, Ala., Jan. 7, 1930; divorced; children—Mary Martin Riser, John Martin; m. M. Palmer Bedsole, Jr.; 1 child, Loraine. Student U. Ala., Denver U.; LL.D. (hon.), Mobile Coll., 1984. Mem. Ala. Ho. of Reps., 1978-82, Ala. Senate, 1982—. Presdl. elector, 1972; del. Rep. Conv., 1964, 72, 84; state chmn. Ala. Bus. Consortium for Gifted and Talented, 1984—; bd. dirs. Nat. Kidney Found. Ala., Inc.; trustee Perdue Hill-Claiborne Historic Preservation Found., Huntingdon Coll. Named First Lady of Mobile, 1972; recipient Presdl. citation Springhill Coll., 1974, Outstanding Contemporary Ala. Woman award Ala. Women's Polit. Caucus, 1981. Mem. Ala. Bus. and Profl. Women (trustee). Jr. League. Methodist. Club: Mobile United. Avocations: farming; scuba diving. Office: State Legislature PO Box 16642 Mobile AL 36626

BEEBE, E(DWARD) RICK, psychologist; b. Los Angeles, Jan. 26, 1944; s. Edward Richard and Jean (Elford) B.; m. Marnie Bankson, June 13, 1969; 1 child, Kelzie Elford. B.A. with honors, Carroll Coll., 1966; M.Ed., U. Vt., 1968; Ed.D., Ind. U., 1972. Lic. psychologist, Pa., W.Va. Psychologist, Bedford Mental Health, Pa., 1972-75; exec. dir. Family Service Assn., Chico, Calif., 1975-76; dir. counseling Salem Coll., W.Va., 1976-79; pvt. practice psychology, Clarksburg, W.Va., 1979—; forensic cons. Weston Hosp. and State of W.Va., 1980—. Contbr. articles to profl. jours. Bd. dirs. Big Bros./Big Sisters of Harrison County, Clarksburg, 1984—. Ind. U. fellow, 1969-70. Mem. Am. Psychol. Assn., W.Va. Psychol. Assn. Avocation: farming. Office: 101 Stoneybrooke Rd Clarksburg WV 26301

BEEBE, MIKE, lawyer, state senator; b. Amagon, Ark., Dec. 28, 1946; s. Lester Kendall and Meadean Louise (Quattlebaum) B.; m. Ginger Croom, Mar. 2, 1979; 1 child, Kyle. B.A., Ark. State U., 1968; J.D., U. Ark., 1972. Bar: Ark. Ptnr. Lightle, Beebe, Raney & Bell, Searcy, Ark., 1972—; mem. Ark. Senate, 1982—. Editor-in-chief U. Ark. Sch. Law. Trustee Ark. State U., Jonesboro, 1974-79, chmn. bd. trustees, 1977-79; bd. dirs. Ark. chpt. Nat. Multiple Sclerosis Soc.; chmn. Central Ark. Gen. Hosp., Searcy, 1985-86. Mem. Ark. Trial Lawyers Assn. (outstanding trial lawyer award 1982), Ark. Mcpl. League (dist. service award 1985), Searcy C. of C. Democrat. Episcopalian. Avocation: golf. Office: Lightle Beebe Raney & Bell 211 W Arch St Searcy AR 72143

BEECH, GOULD MEANS, journalist, social activist; b. Montgomery, Ala., May 5, 1913; s. James L. and Lida (Means) B.; m. Mary Adair Foster, Sept. 11, 1935; children—Mary Adair Finger, Edward Gould. A.B. in Journalism, U. Ala., 1934; postgrad. U. N.C., 1936-37; M.A., U. S. Ala., 1976. Editor Montgomery Advertiser, Ala., 1940-42, So. Farmer, Montgomery, 1946-48; mgr. radio Sta. KSOX, Harlingen, Tex., 1948-52; exec. asst. Mayor of Houston, 1953-57; self-employed real estate investor, Houston, Magnolia Springs, Ala., 1958—; campaign strategist, ghost writer Gov. Jim Folsom, Senators Lister Hill and John Sparkman, Ala., Mayor Roy Hofheinx, Sch. Bd. Mem. Mrs. Charles E. White, former Congresswoman Barbara Jordan, others in Tex. Contbr. editorials and news stories to profl. jours. Served to maj. U.S. Army, 1942-46. Democrat. Episcopalian. Avocation: counseling. Home: River Route Box 24 Magnolia Springs AL 36555 Office: Gould Beech & Assocs Realtors 9219 Katy Freeway Suite 100A Houston TX 36555

BEEKER, DANIEL EDWARD, geophysicist; b. Bloomington, Ind., Nov. 18, 1949; s. Emmet Richard and Phyllis Irene (Davis) B.; m. Viola Welchman, June 25, 1951; children—Andria, Dawn, Patrick, Rachael, Eva. B.S., N.Mex. Inst. Mining and Tech., 1980. Engring. technician Argonne Nat. Lab., 1978-79; geophysicist Gulf Oil Co., Oklahoma City, 1980-82; dist. geophysicist Donald C. Slawson Oil Producer, Oklahoma City, 1982-86; cons. geophysicist, 1986—. Served with USN, 1970-76. Mem. Am. Physics Soc., Soc. Exploration Geophysicists, Am. Assn. Petroleum Geologists. Home and Office: 212 Dripping Springs Dr Edmond OK 73034

BEELER, NICKI JAN, nurse; b. Ranger Tex., Sept. 24, 1950; d. Ben E. and Dortha B. (Hightower) Blitch; m. Allen Wayne Beeler, Dec. 28, 1979; children—Jeffrey Allen, Jenna Beth. B.S. in Nursing, U. Tex., 1972, M.S. in Nursing, 1975. R.N., Tex. Instr. Brackenridge Hosp. Sch. Nursing, Austin, Tex., 1974-76; staff nurse Brackenridge Hosp., Austin, 1976-77; staff nurse Parkland Meml. Hosp., Dallas, 1977-79, instr. nurse internship, 1979-80; nursing instr. Paris Jr. Coll., Tex., 1980-82; nursing adminstr. McCuistian

Regional Med. Ctr., Paris, 1980—. Chmn. fund raising March of Dimes, Cooper, Tex., 1985. Mem. Tex. Hosp. Assn., Tex. Soc. Hosp. Nursing Service Adminstrs., Exec. Women of Paris. Mem. Ch. of Christ. Home: Route 1 Box 223 A 10 Cooper TX 75432 Office: McCuistion Regional Med Ctr 865 DeShong Paris TX 75460

BEER, PETER HILL, U.S. district judge; b. New Orleans, Apr. 12, 1928; s. Mose Haas and Henret (Lowenburg) B.; B.B.A., Tulane U., 1949, LL.B., 1952; LL.M., U. Va., 1986; m. Roberta Webb, 1953; (div. 1982); children—Kimberly Beer Bailes, Kenneth, Dana Beer Long-Innes. Bar: La. 1952. Successively asso., ptnr., sr. ptnr. firm Montgomery, Barnett, Brown & Read, New Orleans, 1955-74; judge La. Ct. Appeal, 1974-79; U.S. dist. judge Eastern Dist. La., New Orleans, 1979—; vice chmn. La. Appellate Judges Conf.; mem. state-fed. com. Jud. Conf. U.S., 1984—. Bd. mgrs. Touro Infirmary, New Orleans, 1969-74; exec. com. Bur. Govtl. Research, 1965-69; chmn. profl. div. United Fund New Orleans, 1966-69; mem. New Orleans City Council, 1969-74, v.p., 1972-74. Served to capt. USAF, 1952-55. Decorated Commendation medal, Bronze Star. Mem. ABA (ho. dels), Fed. Bar Assn., La. Bar Assn. Jewish. Clubs: Nat. Lawyers, So. Yacht. Home: 5855 Bellaire Dr New Orleans LA 70124 Office: US Dist Court Chambers C-206 New Orleans LA 70130

BEEUWKES, LAMBERT BAER, broadcast sta. mgmt. cons.; b. Balt., May 6, 1907; s. John Christian and Elizabeth (Baer) B.; grad. Balt. Poly. Inst., 1926; student Johns Hopkins U., 1926-28; m. M. Eleanor Byerly, Oct. 14, 1936; 1 son, Foster L. Aero. constrn. and exptl. design aircraft Ford-Stout, Fokker, Glenn L. Martin, 1928-35; radio sta. mgmt. and constrn. stas. KYW, WXYZ, WROV, WDAS, WLAW, Mich. Radio Network MBS, NBC, 1936-70; sales dir. NBC Radio Network, 1970-72; personal mgr. The Lone Ranger, 1942-45. Inventor retractable wing, boundary layer laminar flow control; pioneer broadcast techniques such as telephone giveaway, continuous news program, guarantee sales compensation. Address: 4596 Mountain Creek Dr Roswell GA 30075

BEGGS, MARILYN SUE, mental health counselor; b. Chattanooga, May 11, 1947; d. Prince A. and Anne B. (Cowart) Snow; m. James Randy Beggs, Sept. 24, 1977. B.A., Ga. State U., 1979, M.Ed., 1985. Adminstrv. asst. Grady Meml. Hosp., Atlanta, 1968-76; supr. Peat, Marwick, Mitchell & Co., Atlanta, 1980-84; pvt. practice mental health counseling, Stone Mountain, Ga., 1985—; group leader Ga. Council on Child Abuse, Atlanta, 1985—. Mem. Am. Assn. for Counseling and Devel., Ga. Mental Health Assn., Endometriosis Assn. (co-founder Atlanta chpt., pres. 1984—), Alpha Lambda Delta. Home and Office: 482 Maid Marion Ln Stone Mountain GA 30087

BEGLEY, CARL EDWARD, psychologist; b. Springfield, Ky., Nov. 4, 1928; s. William Woodson and Jenny May (Logsden) B.; m. Mary Anaise Lanter, Jan. 25, 1958; children—Catherine, Joseph, Ellen. B.S., U. Ky., 1951, M.A., 1956, Ph.D., 1961. Lic. psychologist, Fla.; diplomate Am. Bd. Profl. Psychology. Intern Dept. Psychology U. Louisville, 1956-57; psychol. asst. Child Guidance, Lexington, Ky., 1957-59; sr. psychologist Ky. State Hosp., Danville, 1959-61; chief psychologist Mental Health Clinic, Jacksonville, Fla., 1961-68; part time psychologist Child Guidance Clinic, Jacksonville, 1968-71; pvt. practice psychology, Jacksonville, 1971—. Contbr. articles to profl. jours. Sec. Fla. State Bd. Examiners in Psychology, 1979. Mem. Am. Psychol. Assn., Fla. Psychol. Assn. (pres. Northeast Fla. chpt. 1984), Sigma Xi. Roman Catholic. Home: 1962 Largo Pl Jacksonville FL 32207

BEIER, ROSS CARLTON, research chemist, educator; b. Portage, Wis., Dec. 27, 1946; s. Carl August and Jean Marie (Buzzell) B.; m. Janet Mary Bauknecht, July 27, 1974; children—Joshua Carlton, Samuel Robert. B.S. in Chemistry and Math., U. Wis.-Stevens Point, 1969; Ph.D. in Organic Chemistry, Mont. State U., 1980. Research chemist Nat. Cotton Pathology Research Lab., College Station, Tex., 1979-80; research chemist Vet. Toxicology and Entomology Research Lab., College Station, 1980—; vis. mem. grad. faculty Tex. A&M U., College Station, 1982—; participant profl. confs. Contbr. chpts. to books, articles to profl. jours. Served with U.S. Army, 1969-72. Recipient Rudy Johansson Teaching award Mont. State U., 1975. Mem. Am. Chem. Soc. (div. agrochems., agr. and food chemistry, organic chemistry, analytical chemistry), Am. Soc. Mass Spectrometry, N.Y. Acad. Scis. Republican. Avocations: wood carving; photography. Office: Vet Toxicology and Entomology Lab F&B Rd PO Drawer GE College Station TX 77841

BEIGHLEY, PEGGY JEAN, educator; b. Natchez, Miss., Aug. 19, 1930; d. Lawrence K. and Lottie M. (Klar) Murray; m. Paul S. Beighley, Dec. 21, 1959; children—Paul S., Lynn Karen. B.A., U. S.W. La., 1951; M.A., U. So. Miss., 1954; postgrad. U. N.D., 1964. Tchr., Jennings (La.) Elem. Sch., 1951-52, Natchez (Miss.) City Pub. Sch., 1952-55, Escambia County Sch., Pensacola, Fla., 1955-57, USAF Dependent's Sch., Yokoto, Japan, 1957-58, Ramstein, Ger., 1958-60, Savage (Md.) Elem. Sch., 1960-61, Westwood Terrace Elem. Sch., San Antonio, 1967—. Mem. Tex. State Tchrs. Assn. (life), NEA, Northside Ind. Tchrs. Assn. Democrat. Baptist. Office: 7615 Bronco Ln San Antonio TX 78227

BEIL, RICHARD O., human resources consulting company executive, consultant; b. Oklahoma, Okla., May 8, 1927; s. Mahlon R. and Ida N. (Wheeler) B.; m. Anna Louisa Thurlow, Aug. 18, 1950; children—Nancy, Richard, Jr., Katherine. B.A. in Personnel Psychology, U. Okla., 1951, postgrad. 1952. Personnel mgr. Marco Chem. Co., Ft. Worth, 1955-56; ednl. services coordinator Gen. Dynamics Corp., Ft. Worth, 1956-61; gen. supr. tng. Thiokol Chem. Corp., Brigham City, Utah, 1961-64; owner R.O. Beil Assoc., Tremonton, Utah, 1964-65; tng. coordinator City Pub. Service, San Antonio, 1965-83; pres. Human Resources Cons. Services, Universal City, Tex., 1983—; cons. San Antonio Ind. Sch. Dist., 1976-78; instr. St. Phillips Coll, San Antonio, 1973-77; mem. Blue Ribbon Task Force, Austin, Tex., 1978-79, Pres's. Adv. Council for Tech. Edn., Washington, 1963. Author: Customers Are People, 1971; Our Telephone Customers, 1969. Author, editor: Math and Physics Handbook, 1958. Ednl. dir. Christian Ch. (Disciples of Christ), San Antonio, 1969-79; deacon Community Christian Ch., San Antonio, 1979, elder, 1980-83, 85-87, chmn. bd., 1983. Served to Pfc. USAAF, 1945-47. Named Hon. Citizen New Orleans, 1976; recipient Award of Appreciation Boy Scouts Am., 1973. Mem. ASTD (nat. v.p., treas. 1977-78, regional v.p. 1975-76, v.p. spl. interests 1973-74, Sparkplug award, 1958, Torch award 1975). Democrat. Lodge: Elks. Avocations: hunting, fishing, watersports, woodworking. Home: 14503 Plumwood St San Antonio TX 78233 Office: Human Resources Cons Services PO Box 2515 Universal City TX 78148

BEILER, THEODORE WISEMAN, chemistry educator; b. Meadville, Pa., Apr. 29, 1924; s. Irwin Ross and Eva Kelsey (Crates) B.; m. Dorthea Ann Brush, Sept. 1, 1951; 1 child, Theodore Donald. B.S., Allegheny Coll., 1948; M.A., Harvard U., 1950, Ph.D., 1952. Research chemist NIH, Bethesda, Md., 1951-53; prof. chemistry, chmn. Stetson U., DeLand, Fla., 1953—; vis. prof. U. Fla., 1956, Duke U., 1979-80; Fulbright lectr. U. Panjab, Lahore, Pakistan, 1962-63; cons. Floral Greens Internat., DeLeon Springs, Fla., 1975-80. Mem., former chmn. Environ. Control Bd., Volusia County, Fla., 1974—. Served to sgt. U.S. Army, 1943-46. Mem. Am. Chem. Soc. (councilor 1968—), Div. Chem. Edn., Phi Beta Kappa, Sigma Xi, Omicron Delta Kappa. Democrat. Presbyterian. Club: Gem and Mineral of DeLand (pres. 1981-82, editor 1983—). Avocations: lapidary; photography; hiking; silversmithing. Home: 813 Oak Tree Ter DeLand FL 32724 Office: Stetson U Woodland Blvd DeLand FL 32724

BEIMAN, IRVING HARRY, JR., psychologist, consultant; b. Birmingham, Ala., Oct. 31, 1946; s. Irving Harry and Martha (Leland) B.; m. Abbie Willard, June 15, 1968 (div. Dec. 1977); m. Cinthia Shelnutt, June 19, 1981 (separated). B.A., Auburn U., 1968; M.A., U. Ill., 1972, Ph.D., 1973. Lic. psychologist, Ga., N.C. Asst. prof. U. Ga., Athens, 1973-80; organizational cons. Farr Assocs., Greensboro, N.C., 1980-83; pres. IB Assocs., Greensboro, 1983—. Contbr. chpts. in books, articles on stress mgmt., meditation and behavioral medicine to profl. jours. Cons. Champaign Police Dept. Probation Office, Ill., 1971-73, Juvenile Detention Home, Athens, Ga., 1975. Served to capt. MSC, U.S. Army, 1973. NIMH fellow, 1968-69; VA trainee, 1969-71; NIMH trainee, 1972-73. Mem. Am. Psychol. Assn. Democrat. Methodist. Avocations: wellness; holistic health; physical conditioning; camping. Home and Office: IB Assocs 4051 Blumenthal Rd Greensboro NC 27406

BEKER, GISELA U., artist; b. Zoppot, Ger.; came to U.S., 1956. Student The Kunst-Institut, Rostock, E.Ger.; pupil of Rudolf Krohl. Solo shows include Bodley Gallery, N.Y., 1973, Women's Bldg., Los Angeles, 1973, Mus. Art, Huntsville, Ala., 1974, Tower Gallery, Southampton, N.Y., 1974, Arts and Sci. Ctr., Baton Rouge, 1975, Wilkes Coll., Pa., 1975, Tower Gallery, 1975, NYU, 1976, Everson Mus., Syracuse, 1976, Tower Gallery, 1976, Wilkes Coll., 1976, G. Sander Fine Art, Daytona Beach, Fla., 1985; represented in permanent collections of Chrysler Mus., Norfolk, Va., New Orleans Mus. Art, Aldrich Mus., Ridgefield, Conn., Fine Art Ctr., Nashville, Okla. Art Ctr., Oklahoma City, Everson Mus., Syracuse, Palm Spring Mus., Calif., Long Beach Mus., Calif., Mus. Art, Huntsville, Ala., Arts and Sci. Ctr., Baton Rouge, Phoenix Art Mus., Mus. Art, Lodz, Poland, others; exhibited in group shows at Jersey City Mus., 1973, Nat. Acad. N.Y., 1973, State Capitol Mus., Olympia, Wash., 1973, Fairleigh Dickenson U., 1973, U. Portland, 1974, Central Wyo. Mus. Art, Casper, Northeastern Okla. A&M Coll., 1974, Rosenberg Library, Galveston, Tex., 1974, Mus. Modern Art, Paris, 1974, 20th Salon de Thouars, France, 1974, Marathon Mus., Warsau, Wis., 1974, Hoyt Inst. Fine Arts, Pa., 1974, Spring Arbor coll., Mich., 1975, LaSalle Coll. Union, Phila., 1975, Pensacola Art Ctr., Fla., 1975, Art Ctr., Richmond, Ind., 1975, Jesse Beser Mus., Alpena, Mich., 1976, Bronx Mus. Art, 1976, Charles and Emma Frye Mus., Seattle, 1976, Watkins Inst., Nashville, 1976, Louisville Sch. Art, 1977, Cayuga Mus. History and Art, Auburn, N.Y., 1977, Tower Gallery, 1977, others. Contbr. articles to profl. jours.

BELANGER, SHERRY GALE, hospital nursing administrator; b. Paragould, Ark., Feb. 19, 1943; d. Eugene and Jean (Parkin) Coffel; children—Tanya, Rocky, Tina; m. N.R. Belanger, June 18, 1983. A.S. with honors, Delta Coll., 1971. R.N., La., Mich., Ark., Tex. Asst. dir. nursing Lawrence Meml. Hosp., Walnut Ridge, Akr., 1976-79; dir. nursing AMI-Randolph County Med. Ctr., Pocahantas, Ark., 1979-81, AMI-Riverside Community Hosp., Bossier City, La., 1981-83, AMI-Citizens Gen. Hosp., Houston, 1983—. Bd. dirs. Black River Vocat. Tech. Sch., Walnut Ridge, 1977-81, La. Nursing Service Adminstrs., 1979-81, Shreveport Nursing Service Adminstrs., 1979-81. Fellow Assn. Houston Area Nursing Service Adminstrs.; mem. Greater Houston Hosp. Council, Ptnrs. for Profit, Ladies Aux. Cape Conroe. Methodist. Avocations: water skiing; ceramics; antiques. Home: 1102 Lakeview Dr Montgomery TX 77356 Office: AMI-Citizens Gen Hosp 7407 N Freeway Houston TX 77076

BELARMINO, ROSALINA YU, nurse; b. Cavite, Philippines, Oct. 20, 1956; d. Carlos Lim and Marcy (Buenaventura) Yu; m. Benjamin Castro Belarmino, Oct. 17, 1981; 1 dau., Ruby Anne. Student, U. Santo Tomas, Manila, 1973-74; B.S. Nursing, St. Jude Coll., Manila, 1978. Nurse aide Coronado (Calif.) Hosp., 1980, med./surg. nurse, 1980-81; intravenous therapist Meth. Hosp., Phila., 1982; mem. trauma team staff Univ. Hosp., Jacksonville, Fla., 1983—. Tchr.'s aide Most Precious Blood Roman Cath. Ch., Chula Vista, Calif., 1980. Democrat. Office: Univ Hosp Jacksonville 655 W 8th St Jacksonville FL 32209

BELCHER, FORREST RENFROW, management consultant; b. Tulsa, Mar. 5, 1922; s. John Cheslow and Sarah Blanche (Renfrow) B.; student Okla. State U., 1939-42, Okla. U., 1944; B.A. in Psychology, U. Tulsa, 1947, M.A. in Psychology, 1949; postgrad. in psychology U. Houston, 1950-52; m. Betty Dings, June 2, 1943; children—Forrest Ray, Gail, Michael, Lynne. With Amoco Prodn. Co., 1948-69, employee relations supr., Houston, 1955-57, tng. and devel. cons., Tulsa, 1957-69; mgr. tng. and devel. Standard Oil Co. Indiana, Chgo., 1970-78; pvt. practice mgmt. cons., Tulsa, 1978—; pres. Mega Cons., Inc., Tulsa, 1981—; adj. prof. Okla. State U.; gen. chmn. First Internat. Tng. and Devel. Conf., Geneva, 1972; chmn. First Inter Am. Tng. Conf., Caracas, Venezuela, 1971; cons., speaker First S.E. Asia Tng. Conf., Manila, 1974; cons. in field, Eng., Mex., Peru, Venezuela, 1982-83; speaker in field; founder, chmn. Woodlands Group, a tng. and devel. think tank. Served with inf. U.S. Army, 1942-45; ETO. Decorated Purple Heart. Mem. Am. Soc. Tng. and Devel. (life; pres. 1970, Gordon M. Bliss Meml. award 1979), Am. Assn. Humanistic Psychology, U. Tulsa Alumni Assn., Internat. Platform Assn. Democrat. Unitarian. Author booklet: How to Form a National Training Society, 1971; contbr. articles to profl. jours. Home and Office: 10 Lookout Ln Diamond Head Sand Springs OK 74063

BELCHER, GARY PAUL, information systems director, education management educator; b. Buffalo, Dec. 16, 1947; s. Clifford William and Myrtle Marie (Wittman) B.; m. Vanessa Natallie Mangini, Oct. 31, 1970; children—Derek, David, Valerie. B.A. in Math., SUNY-Buffalo, 1969, M.A. in Stats., 1973; Ph.D. in Stats., George Washington U., 1984. Computer specialist Def. Systems Mgmt. Coll., Ft. Belvoir, Va., 1971-78, sr. computer systems analyst, 1978-83, info. systems dir., prof. acquisition mgmt., 1983—. Coach, Prince William Soccer Inc., Woodbridge, 1982—; mem. spl. interest group U. Computer Ctr. Mgmt. Served with U.S. Army, 1970-72. NDEA fellow, 1969-70; recipient Joint Service Commendation medal Def. Systems Mgmt. Coll., 1972. Mem. Am. Statis. Assn. Avocations: soccer; running; golf. Office: Def Systems Mgmt Coll Bldg 209 Fort Belvoir VA 22060

BELCHER, JAMES MICHAEL, periodontist; b. Kansas City, Kans., July 23, 1947; s. Milton Parks and Nina Sylvia (Schwab) B.; m. Carolyn Sue Siegel, May 8, 1976 children—Christopher, Jennifer. B.A. in Biochemistry, U. Kans., 1969; D.D.S., U. Mo.-Kansas City, 1973, cert. in periodontology, 1976. Practice dentistry specializing in periodontology, Lakeland, Fla., 1976—; dir. FCA Investment Corp., Orlando Computer Corp. Author: Immunology and Periodontal Disease, 1975; Data Base Systems for Periodontics, 1985. Bd. dirs. Girls Club of Lakeland; chmn. Thunderbird dist. council Boy Scouts Am. Mem. Am. Acad. Periodontology, ADA, Fla. Dental Assn., West Coast Dental Assn., Polk County Dental Assn. (pres. elect), Polk County Dental Study Club Assn., Fla. Acad. Practice Mgmt., Phi Kappa Sigma, Phi Psi Republican. Roman Catholic. Lodge: Kiwanis (bd. dirs.). Home: 4313 Forest Hill Dr Lakeland FL 33803 Office: James Belcher 215 Imperial Blvd Lakeland FL 33803

BELCHER, KENNETH NELSON, pharmacist; b. Birmingham, Ala., Aug. 19, 1952; s. Wilburn Nelson and Margaret Frances (Wood) B.; m. Debra Lynn Smith, Dec. 22, 1972; 1 child, Jeffrey Kenneth. B.S. in Pharmacy, Samford U., 1975. Pharmacist, Big B Drugs, Birmingham, 1975-84; owner, pharmacist Hyatt's Pharmacy, Addison, Ala., 1984—. Pianist, Friendship United Methodist Ch., Gardendale, Ala., 1974-83, bd. dirs., 1978-83; active Parent Tchr. Orgn., Addison, 1985; asst. coach Youth Baseball, Gardendale, 1984, coach, Addison, 1985. Optimist Club scholar, 1970. Mem. Ala. Pharm. Assn., Cullman County Pharm. Assn. Democrat. Baptist. Avocations: tennis; fishing; quail hunting; church work; piano. Home: PO Box 85 Addison AL 35540 Office: Hyatt's Pharmacy Route 1 Box 209 Addison AL 35540

BELCHER, SARAH ELLEN, nurse; b. Saltville, Va., Oct. 10, 1956; d. James Grayson and Martha Brown (Patton) Wilson; m. Charles Edward Belcher, Sept. 26, 1981. B.S.N. with honors, U. Tenn.-Knoxville, 1981. R.N., Tenn., Va. R.N. team leader Meml. Hosp., Chattanooga, 1981—, mem. patient care com., 1983—. Republican. Methodist. Home: 5611 Landrum Dr Ooltewah TN 37363 Office: Meml Hosp 2500 Citico Ave Chattanooga TN 37404

BELCHER, WILLIAM ALVIS, rancher, veterinarian; b. Del Rio, Tex., Aug. 25, 1918; s. Clifton C. and Willie (Cochran) B.; D.V.M., Tex. A. and M. U., 1943; postgrad. Mich. State U., Colo. State U.; m. Hazel Arledge, Sept. 8, 1937; children—Willie Ellen Langham, Madge Elizabeth Belcher Keys. Gen. practice vet. medicine, Crystal City, Tex., 1943-46; rancher, Brackettsville, Tex., 1946—; owner, operator Shirley Commn. Co.-Ft. Worth Stockyard, 1956-59; area veterinarian Tex. Animal Health Commn., 1965—; 1st v.p. Del Rio Wool and Mohair Co., 1950—; chmn. bd. dirs. San Antonio br. Dallas Fed. Res. Bank. County chmn. Screw Worm Eradication Program, 1961—; veterinarian in charge Tex. Screw Worm Program; Mem. AVMA, Tex. S.W. cattle raisers assn., Tex. Sheep and Goat Raisers Assn. (dir.), Tex. Angus Assn. (dir.). Address: PO Box 588 Bracketville TX 78832

BELDEN, DAVID LEIGH, professional association executive; b. Mpls., Jan. 9, 1935; B.G.E., U. Omaha, 1961; M.S.I.E., Stanford U., 1963, Ph.D., 1969; disting. grad. Indsl. Coll. Armed Forces, 1973; m. Lois Marion Lind, June 14, 1956; children—Richard Alan, Grant David. Enlisted in U.S. Air Force, 1954, commd. 2d lt., 1956, advanced through grades to col., 1973; instr. air. nav. Air Tng. Command, 1956-61; chief indsl. engring. br. and chief prodn. div. Air Force Plant Rep. Office, Lockheed Missile & Space Co., Sunnyvale, Calif., 1964-67; exec. officer 553d Reconaissance Squadron, Thailand, 1969-71; asst. prof. mgmt. sci. Air Force Inst. Tech., 1971-72; procurement mgmt. Office Sec. Air Force, Washington, 1973-76; ret., 1976; exec. dir. Inst. Indsl. Engrs., Norcross, Ga., 1976—, pres. Peninsula (Calif.) chpt., 1967-68, dir. aerospace div., 1972-73; adj. prof. U. Md. Far East Div., 1969-70; asso. prof. George Washington U., 1974-76. Decorated Legion of Merit, Meritorious Service medal, others; registered profl. engr., Calif. Fellow Inst. Indsl. Engrs.; mem. Am. Assn. Engring. Socs., Council Engring. and Sci. Soc. Execs. (pres. 1984-85), Am. Soc. Assn. Execs., Ga. Soc. Assn. Execs., Council Indsl. Engring., Am. Soc. Engring. Edn., Australian Inst. Indsl. Engrs. (hon.), Japan Mgmt. Assn. (hon. assoc.), Brit. Instn. Prodn. Engrs. (hon., life), Alpha Pi Mu, Tau Beta Pi. Republican. Club: Dunwoody Country. Contbr. numerous articles to profl. jours. Home: 1870 Baynham Dr Dunwoody GA 30338 Office: 25 Technology Park/Atlanta Norcross GA 30092

BELEW, DAVID OWEN, JR., U.S. district judge; b. Ft. Worth, Mar. 27, 1920; s. David Owen and Mazie Despard (Erskine) B.; B.A., U. Tex., 1946, LL.B., 1948; m. Marjorie Dale Mitchell (dec.); children—Marjorie Dale Belew Cordray, Susan Elizabeth Belew Arnoult, David Mitchell. Admitted to Tex. bar, 1948; practice with father, Ft. Worth, 1948-49; asst. U.S. atty. No. Dist. Tex., 1949-52; partner firm Cantey, Hanger, Gooch, Munn & Collins, Ft. Worth, 1952-79; U.S. dist. judge No. Dist. Tex., 1979—. Served with AUS, 1942-45. Decorated Silver Star, Purple Heart (3). Mem. Am. Bar Assn., Fed. Bar Assn., State Bar Tex., Ft. Worth-Tarrant County Bar Assn. (pres. 1970). Home: 4447 Crestline Rd Fort Worth TX 76107 Office: 201 US Courthouse Fort Worth TX 76102

BELEW, JOE DUNCAN, government relations director; b. Johnson City, Tenn., May 26, 1949; s. Henry Carr and Anne Grainger (Harrison) B.; m. M. Elaine Bunn, June 21, 1980. A.B. in Journalism, U. Ga., 1972. Asst. press sec. to U.S. Senator Herman Talmadge, Washington, 1972-75; freelance polit. cons., Atlanta, 1975-77; press sec. to U.S. Rep. Doug Barnard, Jr., Washington, 1977-79, exec. asst., 1979-84; v.p. govt. relations Consumer Bankers Assn., Washington, 1984—. Recipient Leadership Ga. award, 1978; Internat. Bus. fellow Ga. World Congress Inst., 1984. Mem. U. Ga. Alumni Assn. (chmn. Washington 1980). Democrat. Methodist.

BELEW, THOMAS EUGENE, musical instrument retailer, musician; b. Paris, Tex., Jan. 29, 1948; s. Eugene Maxwell and Gladys Emogene (Bolin) B. B.B.A. in Mktg., North Tex. State U., 1970. Pres., gen. mgr. Belew Music Co., Paris, Tex., 1970—; organist, choirmaster Central Presbyterian Ch., Paris, 1977—. Treas. Paris Downtown Devel. Assn., 1982—; co-founder Paris Motet Choir, 1981—; pres. Paris Community Concert Assn., 1974-76; mem. Paris Mcpl. Band, 1965—. Recipient award of merit Nat. Fedn. Music Clubs, 1971. Mem. Nat. Assn. Music Mchts., Choristers Guild, Am. Guild English Handbell Ringers, Am. Guild Organists (exec. com. Dallas 1977-79), Phi Mu Alpha Sinfonia. Lodge: Greater Paris Rotary (dir. 1978-80, Disting. Service award internat. 1977). Home: 3175 Clark Ln Paris TX 75460 Office: Belew Music Co 218 Bonham St Paris TX 75460

BELFIGLIO, VALENTINE JOHN, political science educator; b. Troy, N.Y., May 28, 1934; s. Edmond Liberato and Mildred Elizabeth (Sherwood) B.; B.S., Union U., 1956; M.A., U. Okla., Norman, 1967, Ph.D., 1970; 1 son by previous marriage, Valentine Edmond. Grad. asst., instr. U. Okla., 1967-70; asso. prof. polit. sci. Tex. Woman's U., Denton, 1970—. Reviewer textbooks in internat. politics Holbrook Press, Boston, 1973-75. Served with USAF, 1959-67. Decorated knight Order of Merit (Italy); recipient Guido Dorso prize in research U. Naples, Italy, 1985; Tex. Woman's U. Instl. Research grantee, 1973-74, 76-77; postdoctoral fellow Republic of South Africa, 1976; Nat. Endowment for Humanities grantee, 1978. Mem. Internat. Studies Assn. (sec.-treas. region 1974-76), Am. Polit. Sci. Assn., AAUP, MENSA, Kappa Psi. Democrat. Roman Catholic. Author: The United States and World Peace, 1971; American Foreign Policy, 1979; Italian Experience in Texas, 1983. Contbr. numerous articles on internat. relations, Asian politics to profl. jours. Home: 704 Camilla Ln Garland TX 75040 Office: Box 23974 Tex Woman's U Denton TX 76204

BELIN, JACOB CHAPMAN, paper company executive; b. DeFuniak Springs, Fla., Oct. 28, 1914; s. William Jacob and Addie (Leonard) B.; m. Myrle Fillingim, Nov. 28, 1940; children—Jacob Chapman, Stephen Andrew. Student, George Washington U., 1935-38. Dir. sales St. Joe Paper Co., Fla., 1949-56, v.p., 1956-68, pres., dir., 1968—; v.p., dir. St. Joseph Land & Devel. Co., Jacksonville Properties, Inc., Wakulla Silver Springs; pres., dir. St. Joe Container Co.; chmn. bd., dir. New Eng. Container Co.; dir. St. Josaph Tel. & Tel. Co., Talisman Sugar Corp. Bd. dirs. Nemours Found., Alfred I. duPont Found.; trustee Edward Ball Wildlife Found., Estate of Alfred I. DuPont. Mem. Kappa Alpha. Baptist. Clubs: Elks, Rotary. Office: St Joe Paper Co PO Box 190 Port Saint Joe FL 32456

BELIVEAU, MARTHA OATES, business education educator; b. Gastonia, N.C., Sept. 25, 1944; d. Grady and Helen (White) Oates; m. Paul Roland Beliveau, May 27, 1977. B.S., We. Carolina U., 1967; M.A., 1969; Ed.S., Ga. State U., 1981. Cert. tchr., Ga. Sec. to Congressman B. Whitener, Washington, 1965; instr. Haywood Tech. Inst., Clyde, N.C., 1967-68; instr. Gaston Coll., 1968-73; adminstrv. asst. Pilot Internat. Hdqrs., Macon, Ga., 1973; instr. Macon Jr. Coll., 1973-75; asst. prof., coordinator bus. edn. Clayton Jr. Coll., 1975-82, asst. prof., 1982—; communications cons. Mem., Mid-Ga. Symphony Guild. Mem. AAUW, Assn. Info. Systems Profls., Am. Vocat. Assn., Ga. Vocat. Assn., Nat. Bus. Edn. Assn., So. Bus. Edn. Assn., Ga. Bus. Edn. Assn., Delta Pi Epsilon. Lutheran (mem. Southeastern Synod ch. ext. com., mem. ch. council, fin. chmn.). Contbg. author: Business Writing: Concepts and Applications, 1983. Home: 732 Valley Trail Macon GA 31204 Office: Clayton Jr Coll Bus Edn Morrow GA 30260

BELK, IRWIN, mcht., former state senator; b. Charlotte, N.C., April 4, 1922; s. William Henry and Mary Leonora (Irwin) B.; student Davidson Coll., U. N.C., 1946; m. Carol Grotnes, Sept. 11, 1948; children—William, Irene Belk Miltimore, Marilyn Bryan, Carl. Trained in mdse. field since childhood; chmn. bd. Monroe Hardware Co.; pres. Belk Fin., Belk Credit, Belk Leasing; v.p., dir. Belk Group of Stores, Charlotte; chmn. bd. P.M.C., Inc., Raleigh, N.C.; v.p. Belk Stores Services, Inc., Charlotte; dir. First Union Nat. Bank, Stonecutter Mills, Spindale, N.C., Fidelity Bankers Life Ins. Co., Richmond, Va., Adams-Millis Corp.; Lumbermen's Mut. Casualty Co. Bd. dirs. Belk Found. Mem. N.C. Ho. of Reps., 1959-60, 61-62; N.C. state senator, 1960-61, 63-66; mem. N.C. Legislative Council, 1963-64, Legislative Research Commn., 1965-66; del. Nat. Democratic Conv., 1956, 60, 64, 68, 72; Democratic nat. committeeman, 1969-72. Mem. finance com., trustee U. N.C., Charlotte; trustee, mem. finance com. Queens Coll.; dir. Bus. Found. N.C.; mem. ho. of dels., local dir. Am. Cancer Soc.; bd. dirs. N.C. Med. Adv. Council U. N.C.; past pres. Carolinas Carrousel; bd. dirs. Charlotte Opera Assn. (mem. finance bd.), Hist. Found. Presbyn. and Reformed Chs.; bd. assos. Mars Hill Coll., Campbell Coll.; bd. advisers Chowan Coll.; mem. adv. council Wingate Coll.; bd. govs. U. N.C., Chapel Hill; bd. assos. Meredith Coll.; bd. counselors Erskine Coll.; bd. dirs., past pres. N.C. Soc. Prevention Blindness; bd. dirs. Bus. Found. N.C., Ednl. Found., Inc. (both Chapel Hill); mem. bd. Wake Forest U. Sch. Bus. Served as sgt., 8th Air Force, World War II. Named One of 10 Outstanding Young Men in Charlotte, 1954, 55, 56, 57. Mem. N.C. Mchts. Assn. (past pres., state dir.), Charlotte C. of C. (dir.), Charlotte Mchts. Assn., Kappa Alpha, Delta Sigma Pi. Presbyn. (past deacon, elder; past pres. men's council Synod of N.C.). Mason (shriner), Lion (past dist. gov.). Clubs: Executives (dir., past pres.), Charlotte Country, Myers Park Country, Charlotte City (Charlotte); Union League, Sky (N.Y.C.). Office: 308 E 5th St Charlotte NC 28201

BELK, THOMAS MILBURN, corporate executive; b. Charlotte, N.C., Feb. 6, 1925; s. William Henry and Mary Leonora (Irwin) B.; B.S. in Mktg., U. N.C., 1948; m. Katherine McKay, May 19, 1953; children—Katherine Belk Morris, Thomas Milburn, Jr., Hamilton McKay, John Robert. With Belk Stores Services, Inc., 1948—, pres., 1980—; dir. NCNB Corp., Mut. Savs. & Loan Assn., Bus. Devel. Corp. of N.C. Bd. dirs. Mecklenburg County council Boy Scouts Am., Presbyn. Home at Charlotte; bd. dirs. YMCA, pres., 1978, 79; gen. chmn. Shrine Bowl of Carolinas, 1963-64, United Appeal, 1959; past pres. United Community Services; trustee Charlotte Community Coll. System, 1958-65, Montreat-Anderson Coll., 1964-68, St. Andrews Presbyn. Coll., Laurinburg, N.C., 1967-71, Crossnore (N.C.) Sch., Inc., Davidson (N.C.) Coll., 1974—, Endowment Fund, 1975-78, Presbyn. Hosp., Charlotte; trustee U. N.C., Charlotte, 1975-85, chmn., 1981-85. Served to lt. (j.g.), USN, 1943-46. Named Young Man of Year, Jr. C. of C., 1960, Man of Year, Charlotte News, 1962, Tarheel of Week, Raleigh News & Observer, 1964, Man of Year, Delta Sigma Pi, 1962. Mem. Charlotte C. of C. (chmn. 1977), N.C. Citizens for Bus. and Industry (past pres.), Central Charlotte Assn. (pres. 1965-66), Mountain Retreat Assn. (past chmn. bd. trustees). Democrat. Clubs: Charlotte City (bd. dirs., pres. 1986—), Charlotte Country, Quail Hollow Country, Country of

N.C., Biltmore Forest, Grandfather Golf and Country. Lodges: Rotary; Masons; Shriners. Home: 2441 Lemon Tree Ln Charlotte NC 28211 Office: 308 E 5th St Charlotte NC 28202

BELL, BRYAN, real estate, oil investment exec., educator; b. New Orleans, Dec. 15, 1918; s. Bryan and Sarah (Perry) B.; B.A., Woodrow Wilson Sch. Public and Internat. Affairs, Princeton U., 1941; M.A., Tulane U., 1962; m. Rubie S. Crosby, July 15, 1950; children—Rubie Perry Bell Gosnell, Helen Elizabeth, Bryan, Beverly Saunders, Barbara Crosby. Pres., Tasso Plantation Foods, Inc., New Orleans, 1945-66; ptnr. 5 Bell Oil Cos., New Orleans, 1962—, also 12 apt. complexes, The Bell-Drumm Co., New Orleans, 1970—; pres. Bell & Assos., Inc., New Orleans, 1970—; gen. ptnr. Walnut St. Venture Capital; instr. econs. of real estate devel. Sch. Architecture. Entrepreneurship Univ. Coll. Tulane U., New Orleans, 1967—. Mem. Garden Dist. Assn., 1964—; bd. dirs. United Fund for Greater New Orleans Area, 1964-71, pres., 1968-69; chmn. Human Talent Bank Com., New Orleans, 1969—. Mem. City Planning Commn., New Orleans, 1956-58; bd. dirs. Met. Area Com., 1968—, pres., 1975—; bd. dirs. Bur. Govtl. Research, 1966—, pres., 1971—; chmn. com. Met. Leadership Forum, 1969—; mem. bd. New Orleans Area Health Council, 1966-70; bd. dirs. Tulane-Lyceum, 1947-51, Family Service Soc., 1951-58, pres., 1956-58; bd. dirs. St. Martin's Protestant Episcopal Sch., 1964-68, Metairie Park Country Day Sch., 1967-71; bd. dirs. Trinity Episc. Sch., chmn., 1958-68; chmn. Trinity Christian Community, 1975—; bd. dirs. Christian Spirit of '76 Com., Fedn. Chs., 1975—, pres., 1984, named Layman of Year, 1977; bd. dirs. Alton Ochsner Meml. Found., 1983—. Served to 1st lt. AUS, World War II. Recipient Weiss Brotherhood award NCCJ, 1983. Mem. New Orleans C. of C., Princeton Alumni Assn. La. (pres. 1962-63), Fgn. Relations Assn. Democrat. Episcopalian (vestry 1960—, jr. warden 1968-70, sr. warden 1970-72, sr. counsellor 1975—). Clubs: Internat. House, Boston, New Orleans Lawn Tennis, Wyvern, Lakeshore, Pickwick. Address: 1331 3d St New Orleans LA 70130

BELL, CARL JOSEPH, psychologist, consultant; b. Batchtown, Ill., July 22, 1922; s. Elbie Columbus and Minnie Louise (Cockrell) B.; m. Grace Rita Glynn, Nov. 21, 1948; children—Christopher, Geraldine, Maureen. B.S., Ill. State U., 1949, M.S., 1950, postgrad., 1964-67. Lic. psychologist, Fla. Pvt. practice psychology, Iowa, Ill., Ga., Fla., 1950-83; cons. Uganda, East Africa, 1983—; pres. Iowa Council Exceptional Children, Des Moines, 1953; co-founder Sheldered Workshop, Davenport, Iowa, 1956; pres. Mental Health Ctr., Bloomington, Ill., 1970. Author: Kindergarten Syllabus, 1967; Learning Disability, 1969. TV shows Learning Disability, 1971. Served to maj. U.S. Army, USAR, 1942-82. Mem. Am. Psychol. Assn., Iowa C. of C. (chmn. econs. course 1960-62), Res. Officers Assn. (pres. 1959). Republican. Roman Catholic. Lodge: Kiwanis. Avocation: artist. Home and Office: 54 Osborne Ave Kenner LA 70065

BELL, CECELIA LOUISE, librarian; b. New Orleans, July 10, 1959; d. Thomas Alvin and Barbara Jean (Trapp) B. B.S., Miss. State U., 1981; M.L.S., U. So. Miss., 1982. Asst. librarian Univs. Ctr. Library, Jackson, Miss., 1982—; summer intern Miss. Library Commn., 1980; grad. asst. Sch. Library Sci., U. So. Miss., 1981-82. Miss. State U. pres.'s scholar, 1980-81. Mem. ALA, Miss. Library Assn. Presbyterian. Home: 615-H Hampton Circle Jackson MS 39211 Office: Universities Center Library 3825 Ridgewood Rd Jackson MS 39211

BELL, CLARENCE ELMO, state senator; b. Camden, Ark., Feb. 1, 1912; s. Joseph Dudley and Dona (Massengale) B.; A.B., Ouachita Bapt. U., 1934; M.A., U. Ark., 1940; m. Hope Raney, Aug. 16, 1936; children—Joseph Dudley, Beverly (Mrs. William Kinneman), Barbara (Mrs. Richard Blaine). High sch. prin., coach, Parkin, Ark., 1935-39; coach, Marked Tree, Ark., 1939-40; supt. schs., Parkin, 1941-63; with Ark. La. Gas Co., Little Rock, 1963—, dir., 1972—. Named Layman of Yr. in Edn., Ark., 1972; Conservationist of Yr., Ark., 1966. Rotarian.

BELL, DAVID PAIGE, hospital administrator; b. Gallipolis, Ohio, June 7, 1944; s. Hollie Paige and Hortense Pearl (Hogue) B.; B.S. in Pharmacy, W. Va. U., 1968; M.B.A., W. Va. Coll. Grad. Studies, 1973; Ph.D., Ohio U., 1979; m. Roberta Ann Steel, June 10, 1967; 1 dau., Robin Ann. Cert. compensation profl. Am. Compensation Assn. Pharmacist, Rogers Pharmacy, Morgantown, W. Va., 1965-69; mgr. Cohen Drug Stores, Charlestown, W. Va., 1969-72; dir. pharmacy service, Camden Clark Hosp., Parkersburg, W. Va., 1972-78, dir. human resources, 1978-85; dir. human resources St. Joseph's Hosp., Parkersburg, W.Va., 1985—; faculty Parkersburg Community Coll.; cons. in field. Mem. W.Va. Adv. Com. Pharmacy Consultants. Named W.Va. Hosp. Pharmacist of Year, 1977. Fellow Am. Soc. Cons. Pharmacists; mem. Am. Soc. Personnel Adminstrs., W. Va. Soc. Hosp. Pharmacists (pres. 1977—), Am. Soc. Hosp. Pharmacists, Am. Soc. Hosp. Personnel Adminstrs., Am. Coll. Health Execs., Parkersburg-Marietta Assn. Personnel Adminstrs. (pres. 1981), Res. Officers Assn., Am. Mgmt. Assn., Phi Delta Kappa, Phi Kappa Phi, Delta Sigma Rho, Phi Kappa Sigma. Lodge: Rotary (sec.). Home: 4500 10th Ave Vienna WV 26105 Office: St Joseph's Hosp 19th St and Murdoch Ave Parkersburg WV 26102

BELL, DELLA PEARL, mathematics educator; b. Beaumont, Tex., May 5, 1942; d. Elijah and Signora (Allen) Domoneck; m. Robert Lee Alfred Bell, June 21, 1969; children—Alfreda, Brian. B.S., Lamar U., 1963; M.Ed., U. Tex., 1968, Ph.D., 1974; postgrad. Tex. A&M U., 1972, U. Houston, 1984. Cert. math. and English tchr., Tex. Tchr. math. Franklin Jr. High Sch., Port Arthur, Tex., 1963-66, Austin and Lincoln High Sch., Port Arthur, 1966-67, 68-71; teaching asst. U. Tex., Austin, 1973-74; asst. prof. math. Tex. So. U., Houston, 1974-79, assoc. prof., 1979—; coordinator Blacks and Math. Program, Houston, 1977—; cons. Houston Ind. Sch. Sch. Dist., 1985. Alpha Kappa Alpha scholar, 1959; grantee NSF, 1967-68; faculty research grantee Tex. So. U., 1981, 82, 83; recipient Disting. Faculty Mem. of Yr. award Student Govt. Assn., Tex. So. U., 1985. Mem. Math. Assn. Am., Nat. Council Tchrs. of Math., Assn. for Women in Math., Nat. Tech. Assn., Pi Lambda Theta, Phi Kappa Phi. Democrat. Methodist. Avocations: reading; working problems; traveling. Office: Tex So U 5100 Cleburne St Houston TX 77004

BELL, DENISE PRICE, physician; b. Chgo., Aug. 3, 1954; d. Theodore Roosevelt and Ollie (Pierson) Price; m. William Richard Bell, Aug. 21, 1976; 1 son, Sean Julian. B.A., Fisk U., 1976; M.D., Meharry Med. Coll., 1980. Resident internal medicine Hubbard Hosp., Nashville, 1980-83; staff physician Matthew Walker Health Ctr., Nashville, 1983—; instr. Am. Cancer Soc., Nashville, 1979-80. Mem. ACP (assoc.), Am. Med. Student Assn., Phi Beta Kappa, Alpha Omega Alpha, Beta Kappa Chi. Democrat. Presbyterian. Office: Matthew Walker Health Ctr 1501 Herman St Nashville TN 37208

BELL, H. JENKINS, clergyman. Bishop, Church of God in Christ, S.C. Office: Ch of God in Christ PO Box 6118 Knoxville TN 37914*

BELL, HARRY SATCHER, farm bureau federation executive; b. Greenwood, S.C., Nov. 11, 1927; s. Harry DeVaughan and Floriede (Satcher) B.; m. Jean Arthur Hall, Sept. 28, 1954; children—William DeVaughan, James Arthur, Harry Satcher, Harriett Jean. Student Clemson U., 1945; B.S. in Acctg., U.S.C., 1950. Teller, Ridge Banking Co., Ridge Spring, S.C., 1950-51, teller, br. office mgr., Johnston and Ridge Spring (S.C.), 1953-60; farmer, Ward, S.C., 1960-71; pres. S.C. Farm Bur., Columbia, 1971—, pres. affiliates, 1971—; 1st v.p., dir., mem. exec. com. So. Farm Bur. Life Ins. Co., Jackson, Miss., 1972—; dir., mem. exec. com. So. Farm Bur. Casualty Ins. Co., Jackson, 1971—; dir. Am. Farm Bur. and Affiliates, Park Ridge, Ill. Treas. Johnston Presbyterian Ch. (S.C.); mem. S.C. Water Resources Commn., Columbia, 1967-85. Served to 2d lt. USAF, 1951-53. Mem. Am. Farm Bur. Fedn. (v.p. 1986—), Am. Legion. Home: Route 1 Ward SC 29166 Office: SC Farm Bur 724 Knox Abbott Dr Cayce SC 29033

BELL, HENRY NEWTON, III, lawyer; b. Temple, Tex., Mar. 5, 1941; s. Henry Newton and Mildred (Smith) B.; B.B.A., U. Tex., 1965; J.D., Baylor U., 1968; m. Pamela Roberts, July 25, 1964; children—Regina Eleanor, Henry Newton. Bar: Tex. bar 1970, U.S. Ct. Mil. Appeals. Practice law, Austin, Tex., 1970—; sr. trial counsel Comfort Supply, Inc., Austin, 1973—; owner Bell Ranches, Bastrop and Burleson Counties, Tex.; oil operator. Lobbyist various spl. interest groups; judge Internat. Moot Ct. Competition, U. Tex. Sch. Law, 1980; bd. dirs. First Meth. Ch., Bastrop, Tex., 1980. Served with QMC, U.S. Army, 1968-70. Decorated Bronze Star; recipient cert. of Honor, Tex. Dept. Agr., 1974. Mem. Internat. Bar Assn., Fed. Bar Assn., ABA, Tex. Bar Assn., Am. Judicature Soc., Assn. Am. Trial Lawyers, SAR (sec. 1979), Sons Republic of Tex. (v.p. 1981), SCV, Phi Delta Phi. Democrat. Methodist. Home: PO Box H Bastrop TX 78602 Office: Suite 214 300 E Huntland Dr Austin TX 78752

BELL, JAMES CARLTON, aero-mech. engr., aerospace mfg. co. exec.; b. Jefferson, Pa., Sept. 12, 1933; s. James Carlton and Geraldine Lora (Pryor) B.; B.S. in Engring. Sci., Cleve. State U., 1957; m. Roberta K. Keller, Sept. 10, 1955; children—Robert J., Gary L., Ronald K., Lora J. Research and devel. engr. in aero-mech. programs Goodyear Aerospace Corp., Akron, Ohio, 1957-60, project engr., 1960-68, engring. group leader of electromech. antenna systems, 1964-70, program mgr. electromagnetic pulse simulator systems, 1968-72, engring. rep., 1971-72; asst. chief engr. seal systems devel. Bell Aerospace Co., New Orleans, 1972-73, chief engr., 1973—. Mgr. div. United Fund Campaign, 1969-70; baseball commr. Plantation Athletic Club, 1980—; La. dir. Dizzy Dean Baseball, 1981—. Recipient Top Producer Campaign award YMCA, 1971, 72. Mem. AIAA (nat. tech. com.), Soc. Naval Architects and Marine Engrs., Lighter Than Air Soc. Methodist. Contbr. articles on various structural design systems to tech. jours. Patentee in field. Home: 3710 Rue Michelle New Orleans LA 70114 Office: 13800 Gentilly Rd New Orleans LA 70189

BELL, LEWIS CLAY, economics educator, administrator; b. New Dorp, S.I., N.Y., Mar. 29, 1928; s. Samuel Virgil and Ruth Bell; m. Dolores Eva Bell, Dec. 12, 1951; children—Brent, David, Daniel. B.A. in Econs., Berea Coll., 1953; postgrad. Emory U., 1953-54; Ph.D. in Econs., U. Ky., 1957. Research asst. Bur. Bus. Research, U. Ky., 1954-55, research assoc., 1956-57; asst. dir. purchases Commonwealth Ky., 1957, dir., purchases, 1957-60; assoc. prof. U. Miss., 1960-63, assoc. prof. econs., econs. research analyst, 1963-64, prof. econs., sr. research analyst, 1964, prof. econs., 1964-65; dir. Tax Research Ctr., prof. econs. Western Ky. U., 1965-66, dir. Tax Research Ctr., Office of Research and Services, prof. econs., 1966-68; prof. econs. fiscal cons. to W.Va. Legis., 1968-70; dir. legis. fiscal studies, prof. econs. W.Va. U., 1969-70, prof. econs., 1970-78, dir. grad. programs econs., prof. econs., 1978-83, prof. econs., 1983—, exec. dir. W.Va. Council Econ. Edn., 1985—. Author: (with D.H. McKinney) The Role of Third-Structure Taxes in the Highway-User Tax Family, 1968. Contbr. articles to profl. jours., chpt. to book. Mem. Ky. Efficiency Task Force, 1966-68; Ky. col.; Adv. Sch. Bonds Com., Morgantown, W.Va., 1971; treas. Support Our Schs., Morgantown, 1971. Mem. Am. Econ. Assn., Nat. Tax Assn., Tax Inst. Am., So. Econs. Assn. W.Va. Tax Inst. (pres. 1973), Phi Kappa Phi, Beta Gamma Sigma, others. Democrat. Christian Scientist. Lodge: Rotary (pres. 1983-84). Home: 1287 Colonial Dr Morgantown WV 26505 Office: Coll Bus Econs W Va U Morgantown WV 26506

BELL, LUCILLE LOWERY, nurse-anesthetist; b. Jacksonville, Fla., Apr. 6, 1924; d. Benjamin and Mary Lowery; student Edward Waters Coll., 1939-41; diploma Brewster Hosp. Sch. Nursing, 1942; grad. anesthesia Cook County Hosp., 1947. Sec., treas. Fed. Duval Enterprises, Inc., Jacksonville, 1957; founder Nightengale Home Nursing Care Class, Inc., Jacksonville, 1975; nurse, counselor Greater Jacksonville Econ. Opportunity Program. Bd. dirs., trustee Mt. Ararat Convalescent Home; bd. dirs. YWCA, Jacksonville. Certified in psychiat. nursing Fla. Bd. Health; recipient Distinguished Service citation Fla. div. Am. Cancer Soc., 1966. Mem. Am. Nurses Assn., LWV, Chi Eta Phi (charter). Baptist.

BELL, MARY E. BENITEAU, accountant; b. San Antonio, Dec. 20, 1937; d. Thomas Alfred and Mary Elizabeth (McMurrain) Beniteau; B.B.A., Baylor U., 1959; M.B.A., U. Tex., 1960; m. William Woodward Bell, May 31, 1969; children—Susan Elizabeth, Carol Ann. Teaching asst. U. Tex., Austin, 1959-60; prin. Deloitte, Haskins & Sells, C.P.A.s, Dallas, 1960-69; county auditor Brown County, Tex., 1972-78; pvt. practice acctg., Brownwood, Tex., 1969—; acct. Brownwood Regional Hosp. Women's Aux., 1969—. Mem. bus. and audit com. Baptist Gen. Conv. of Tex., 1985—. Named Outstanding Com. Chmn., Dallas chpt. C.P.A.s, 1968-69; C.P.A., Tex. Mem. Brownwood C. of C. (dir. 1979-82, sec.-treas. 1981-82), Tex. Soc. C.P.A.s (dir. 1979-82, trustee ednl. found. 1981—, sec.-treas. 1982-84, pres. 1984—), Am. Inst. C.P.A.s, Am. Soc. Women Accts., Am. Woman's Soc. C.P.A.s, Abilene Soc. C.P.A.s (dir. 1984-85, C.P.A. of Yr. 1984-85), AAUW, Pi Beta Phi, Baylor U. Alumni Assn. (dir. 1979-82). Clubs: Brownwood Woman's (pres. 1980-81), Rotary Ann of Brownwood (pres. 1983-84), Baylor U. Hankamer Sch. Bus. Alumni Bd. Home: PO Box 1564 Brownwood TX 76804 Office: 109 N Fisk St Brownwood TX 76801

BELL, NOEL JAMES, electrical engineer; b. Salem, Mo., Feb. 8, 1946; s. Noah Edgar and Melba Maxine (Counts) B.; m. Beverly Rea Lloyd, May 16, 1981; children—Noel James, Jennifer Lynn. B.S. in Elec. Engring., U. Mo., Rolla, 1968; M.S., Duke U., 1973, Ph.D., 1977. Telecommunications engr. IBM, Research Triangle Park, N.C., 1968-77, computer systems analyst, Cape Canaveral, Fla., 1977-81, system engr., Manassas, Va., 1981-82; engring. analyst, research scientist Mitre Corp., McLean, Va., 1982—; lectr. George Mason U., Fairfax, VA., 1984—. Mem. Sigma Xi, Tau Beta Pi, Eta Kappa Nu. Home: Route 1 Box 43 Delaplane VA 22025 Office: Mitre Corp W193 1820 Dolley Madison Blvd McLean VA 22102

BELL, RICHARD, state supreme court associate justice; b. 1920. B.S., Presbyterian Coll.; LL.B., Emory U. Bar: Ga. 1950. Assoc. justice Ga. Supreme Ct., Atlanta, 1982—. Office: Georgia Supreme Ct State Jud Bldg Atlanta GA 30334*

BELL, RICHARD EUGENE, grain company executive; b. Clinton, Ill., Jan. 7, 1934; s. Lloyd Richard and Ina (Oglesby) B.; B.S. with honors, U. Ill., 1957, M.S., 1958; m. Maria Christina Mendoza, Oct. 22, 1960; children—David Lloyd, Stephen Richard. Internat. economist Dept. Agr., Washington, 1959-60, dir. grain div., 1969-72; agrl. attache Am. embassies in Ottawa, Can., Brussels, and Dublin, Ireland, 1961-68; asst. sec. agr. internat. affairs and commodity programs, 1973-77; pres. Riceland Foods Inc., Stuttgart, Ark., 1977—; pres., dir. Commodity Credit Corp., also Fed. Crop Ins. Corp., 1975-77; exec. sec. President's Agrl. Policy Com., 1976-77; rep. Internat. Wheat Council, London, 1970-77; adv. World Food Conf., Rome, 1974. Recipient Disting. Service award Dept. Agr., 1975. Mem. Christian Ch. (Disciples of Christ). Home: 2001 Beumer St Stuttgart AR 72160 Office: Riceland Foods Inc 2120 Park Ave PO Box 927 Stuttgart AR 72160

BELL, RONNIE MICHAEL, contract negotiator/administrator; b. Canton, Ga., May 17, 1947; s. Roy Harold and Lassie Inez (Millwood) B.; m. Tanya Trimble, Sept. 11, 1970; children—Gretchen, Rebecca. Student, Ga. Inst. Tech., 1964-68; B.A., Ga. State U., 1969, Lee Coll., 1971; M.A., Ohio State U., 1973. Music dir. Frebis Ave. Ch. of God, Columbus, Ohio, 1971-73, Tremont Ave. Ch. of God, Greenville, S.C., 1973-75; choral dir. Lookout Valley High Sch., Chattanooga, 1975-79; research analyst TVA, Chattanooga, 1979-80, supr. contract services, 1980—. Mem. Cleveland (Tenn.) Civic Chorus, 1970-71, Greenville Civic Chorale, S.C., 1974-75; mem. Chattanooga Pub. Schs. music curriculum devel. com., 1976; bd. dirs. East Chattanooga Community Choir, 1976, 78; dir. music Woodmore Ch. of God, 1982—. Mem. Nat. Assn. Ch. Musicians for the Ch. of God (organizer, 1st pres. chpt.), Nat. Mgmt. Assn., Nat. Contract Mgmt. Assn., Music Educators Nat. Conf., Mensa, Alpha Gamma Chi. Republican. Home: 4307 Tee Pee Dr Chattanooga TN 37406 Office: TVA 1120 Chestnut Street Tower II Chattanooga TN 37401

BELL, THOMAS EUGENE, risk management, safety engineer; b. Moline, Ill., Aug. 9, 1949; s. Milton Eugene and Alta Marie (Porter) B.; B.S., Mich. State U., 1971; m. Lorene Ann Ames, Feb. 1, 1969; children—Tommy, Jessica-Rae Marie. Safety rep. U.S. Fidelity and Guaranty Ins., East Lansing, Mich., 1971-73; sr. loss prevention rep. Royal Globe Ins., Southfield, Mich., 1973-77; corp. mgr., dir. loss prevention and control ARA Services, Inc., Phila., 1977-81; dir. risk mgmt. Donham Oil Tool Co., Dallas, 1981-85; risk, safety officer City of Carrollton, Tex., 1985—. Cert. safety profl. Mem. Am. Soc. Safety Engrs., Nat. Safety Mgmt. Soc., Internat. City Mgmt. Assn., Pub. Risk/Ins. Mgmt. Assn., Risk/Inc. Mgmt. Soc. Home: 1837 Chamberlain Carrollton TX 75007 Office: 1341 W Mockingbird Ln Donham Oil Co Dallas TX 75247

BELL, THOMAS ROWE, natural gas transmission company executive; b. Chattanooga, Feb. 26, 1928; s. Joseph Sumner and Hattie Bush (Rowe) B.; m. Agnes Louise Slaughter, Dec. 29, 1956; children—Bush A., Thomas Rowe, Mary E., David L. B.S. in Bus., U. Tenn., 1950. With E. Tenn. Natural Gas Co., 1950—, dir. sales devel., asst. treas., 1959-64, v.p., 1964-72; pres. Knoxville, 1973—; chmn. mgmt. com. Knoxville Internat. Energy Expn., 1979—. Bd. dirs. Webb Sch.; past pres. Met. Knoxville YMCA. Served with AUS, 1950-52. Mem. Am. Gas Assn., Ind. Natural Gas Assn., So. Gas Assn. (dir.), Tenn. Gas Assn. (past pres.), Sigma Phi Epsilon. Presbyterian. Office: 8200 Kingston Pike PO Box 10245 Knoxville TN 37919

BELLAMY, JEANNE, journalist, banker; b. Bklyn., Nov. 15, 1911; d. Donald Lamont and Ethel Park (Houston) Bellamy; student Barnard Coll., 1928-29; A.B., Rollins Coll., 1933; Ph.D. (hon.), Biscayne Coll., 1975; m. John Turner Bills, Jan. 30, 1942. Reporter, Miami (Fla.) Tribune, 1935-37; staff writer Miami Herald, 1937-58; sr. editorial writer, 1958-73; chmn. bd. Sun Bank Midtown, Miami; 1973-77; dir. Sun Bank of Miami, 1977-82; commentator Sta. WGBS, 1962-63; moderator We Want to Know, Sta. WLBW-TV, 1961-63. Mem. Miami-Dade Water and Sewer Authority, 1975-80; mem. governing bd. So. Fla. Water Mgmt. Dist., 1979-83; bd. dirs. Nat. Audubon Soc., 1963-71; trustee Biscayne Coll., 1976-82, Rollins Coll., 1977-80; vestryman St. Stephen's Ch., 1975-78; trustee Fairchild Tropical Garden, Coral Gables, 1961—, pres., 1977-82; bd. dirs. Fla. chpt. Nature Conservancy, 1983—, WPBT-TV, 1984—. Recipient ann. awards Fla. Bar, 1959, 62; Jose Marti Journalism award, 1966; Thomas Barlour medal for conservation Fairchild Tropical Garden, 1984. Mem. Fla. Soc. Editors (pres. 1962), Hist. Assn. So. Fla., Greater Miami Opera Assn., Vizcayans, Women in Communications, Greater Miami C. of C. (pres. 1977-78), Soc. Woman Geographers, Kappa Alpha Theta. Episcopalian. Author: Taming the Everglades, 1947; Newspapers of America's Last Frontier, 1952; Communism: What It Means to You, 1961. Home: 2718 Segovia St Coral Gables FL 33134

BELLER, HARRY EDWARD, orthopaedic surgeon; b. N.Y.C., Sept. 16, 1905; s. Max and Anna (Mezeritsky) B.; m. Maysie Y. Yates, Aug. 28, 1946; children—Alexander, Linda Childs. Student Columbia U., 1922-24; M.D., L.I. Coll. Medicine, 1928. Diplomate Am. Bd. Orthopaedic Surgery. Intern, Englewood (N.J.) Hosp., 1928-29, Beth El Hosp., Bklyn., 1929; resident Kennedy Hosp., Memphis, 1946-47, Univ. Hosp., Augusta, Ga., 1948-49; asst. in surgery Kings County Hosp. div. L.I. Med. Coll., Bklyn, 1930-42; orthopaedic surgeon, neurosurgeon, gen. surgeon, Jewish Hosp. and Beth-El Hosp., Bklyn., 1930-42; asst. prof. orthopaedic surgery Ga. Sch. Medicine, Augusta, 1948-49; clin. assoc. prof. U. Miami Med. Sch., Fla., 1950-81; mem. staff Jackson Meml. Hosp., Mercy Hosp., Variety Hosp., Cedars of Lebanon Hosp. Served to maj. M.C., U.S. Army, 1942-46. Fellow A.C.S., Internat. Coll. Surgeons; assoc. Royal Soc. Medicine; mem. Acad. Orthopaedic Surgery. Home: 1010 Persian Ln Sebastian FL 32958

BELLER, RONALD E., university president; b. Cin., Oct. 4, 1935; s. Ervin Charles and Marion Helen B.; B.E.E., U. Fla., 1957; M.B.A., Kent State U., 1966; Ph.D., U. Fla., 1971; m. Judith Anne Cline, Feb. 13, 1970; children—Julia, Deborah, Lee Anne, Bradley, James, Elizabeth, Ronald. Head budgeting services, asst. prof. hosp. adminstrn. Hillis Miller Health Center, U. Fla., 1970-71; spl. asst. to pres. U. S. Ala., Mobile, 1972-74, dean fin. and adminstrn., 1974-77; provost for adminstrn. Va. Commonwealth U., Richmond, Va., 1977-79; exec. v.p., 1979-80; pres. E. Tenn. State U., Johnson City, 1980—. Vice chmn. Emergency Med. Service Council of Forsyth County, N.C., 1971-72; mem. personal health services com. Forsyth County Health Planning Council, 1971-72; chmn. Task Force on Orgn., Mobile Mental Health Center, 1973-74, chmn. Task Force on Drug Abuse Program, 1974-76; mem. adv. council 5th Dist. of City Council, City of Richmond, Va., 1977-79. Mem. Am. Public Health Assn., Acad. Mgmt., Am. Assn. Med. Colls., Phi Kappa Phi, Beta Gamma Sigma. Presbyterian. Clubs: Kiwanis, Rotary. Contbr. articles to profl. jours. Office: E Tenn State U Johnson City TN 37614

BELLI, GREGORY CHARLES, bilingual educator; b. Paterson, N.J., Nov. 16, 1951; s. Barth John and Mary Louise Emma (Roth) B.; m. Leslie Ann Box, Feb. 17, 1979; 1 child, Michael Christopher. B.S., Georgetown U., 1973; M.A., Fla. Atlantic U., 1979. Cert. tchr., Fla. Tchr. ESOL, Delray Beach, Fla., Palm Beach County Schs., 1976—, bilingual elem. tchr., 1976-79, bilingual coordinator, 1979-80, parental involvement coordinator ESEA, Title I/ECIA Chpt. 1979-80, parental involvement coordinator ECIA Chpt. I Basic and Migrant Programs, 1980-83, coordinator ESEA Title VII bilingual, 1983—. Mem. Blue Key, Phi Delta Kappa, Alpha Phi Omega. Roman Catholic. Home: 208 S Swinton Ave Delray Beach FL 33444

BELLOMO, SALVATORE JOHN, transportation engineer; b. Somerville, N.J., June 10, 1941; s. Angelo and Pearl B.; m. Janice Catherine Lorah, June 22, 1963; children—Diane, Douglas, Carryn. B.S. in Planning Engring., Rutgers U., 1963; M.C.E., Cath. U., 1967, D.Engring., 1971. Registered profl. engr., D.C., Md., N.J., Pa., Va., Calif., Del. Research asst. Rutgers U., 1959-63; sect. mgr., project mgr., asst. project mgr. Alan M. Voorhees & Assocs., Inc., McLean, Va., 1963-72, v.p., 1972-78; pres. BKI Assocs., Inc., Vienna, Va., 1978-82, Bellomo-McGee Inc. (BMI), Vienna, 1982—; assoc. professorial lectr. George Washington U., 1971-75, professorial lectr., 1975—; professorial lectr. U. Va., 1978; adj. prof. U. Md., 1978; U.S. del. Soviet Union Transp. Recipient James Laurie Prize, ASCE, 1983. Fellow ASCE (chmn. urban transp. div.), Inst. Transp. Engrs.; mem. Am. Inst. Certified Planners, Am. Planning Assn., Sigma Xi. Club: Lake of the Woods (Orange County, Va.). Contbr. articles in field to profl. jours. Home: 9528 Rockport RD Vienna VA 22180 Office: 901 Follin Ln Suite 220 Vienna VA 22180

BELLOMO, VINCENT ANTHONY, personnel executive, consultant; b. Astoria, L.I., N.Y., Apr. 29, 1928; s. Fedele and Virginia Rose (Bonerba) B.; m. Virginia Harriet White, Feb. 5, 1949; children—Valerie Sue, Randy Vincent. B.S. in Bus. and Econs., Rollins Coll., 1974; M.P.A., U. Okla., 1976. Tech. instr. aircraft engine maintenance USAF Civilian, Chanute AFB, Ill. 1952-55; employee utilization officer U.S. Air Force, Chanute AFB, Ill., 1955-58, civilian personnel dir., Plattsburgh AFB, N.Y., 1958-63, supr. personnel mgmt. specialist Hdqrs. 8th Air Force, Westover AFB, Mass., 1963-70, civilian personnel dir., Patrick AFB, Fla., 1970-83; tchr. pub. adminstrn. and mgmt. Rollins Coll., Patrick AFB br., 1979-82; personnel dir. City of Cocoa Beach, Fla., 1984—; cons. mgmt., personnel adminstrn., pub. adminstrn., Satellite Beach, Fla., 1982—. Councilman City of Satellite Beach, Fla., 1979-82, vice mayor, 1981-82. Served with USAF, 1948-52. Recipient Meritorious Civilian award Air Force Systems Command, Patrick AFB, Fla., 1975. Mem. Brevard County Profl. Mgrs. Assn., Brevard Personnel Assn., Omicron Delta Epsilon, Alpha Sigma Lambda. Democrat. Roman Catholic. Lodges: Lions (tailtwister 1954-58), K.C. (lectr. 1954-58). Avocations: model bldg.; carpentry; auto mechanics; reading; swimming. Home: 580 Teakwood Ave Satellite Beach FL 32937 Office: City of Cocoa Beach Personnel Dept 2 S Orlando Ave Cocoa Beach FL 32931

BELLOT, FRANK MARTIN, realty company executive; b. Cross City, Fla., July 9, 1943; s. Gordon Wade and Allene Frances (Smoak) B.; m. Darlin Dee Boak (div. 1976). Grad. Fla. Barber Coll., 1961; grad. Realtor Inst., 1982. Owner, operator Bellot's Barber Shop, 1961-78; salesman Montgomery Real Estate Co., 1978-80; real estate broker, owner Bellot Realty, Inc., Inverness, Fla., 1980—; mortgage broker; chmn. Multiple Listings Service, Citrus County Bd. Realtors, Inc. Mem. Citrus County Mosquito Control Bd., 1970-74; v.p. Earth Beautiful Found., 1981—. Served with USAR, 1963-69. Mem. Nat. Assn. Realtors, Fla. Assn. Realtors, Citrus County C. of C. (com. of 100), Realtor Honor Soc. Democrat. Clubs: Citrus Shrine. Lodges: Elks, Masons, Shriners, Moose. Home: PO Box 351 Inverness FL 32651 Office: Bellot Realty Inc 209 W Main St Inverness FL 32650

BELMONT, WILLIAM ROBERT, economist, corporation executive, consultant; b. Chgo., Oct. 24, 1927; s. Hiram Francis and Margaret B. (Faye) Woosley; m. Bernice Theresa Pietrucha, Apr. 10, 1948; children—Marcia Valerie Belmont Stengel, Gregory Steven. A.B., DePaul U., 1952; M.A., George Washington U., 1954, Ph.D., 1968. Econ. adv. Central Bank Nigeria, Lagos, 1964-66; assoc. prof., Bradley U., Peoria, Ill., 1966-75; econ. adv. GSA Fed. Govt., Washington, 1975-77; economist, v.p. McCabe-Belmont Assocs., McLean, Va., 1977-80; economist, pres. ETC, Inc., Rockville, Md., 1980—. Served with USN, 1945-46. Postdoctoral fellow George Washington U., 1954-57, Am. Assembly Collegiate Schs. of Bus., 1975-77; postdoctoral grantee Ford Found., 1962, HEW, 1970. Mem. Am. Econ. Assn., Nat. Economists Club, Am. Statis. Assn., Nat. Soc. Rate Return Analysts, Omicron Delta Epsilon (pres. 1957-58). Democrat. Club: Regency Racquet (McLean). Home: 1800 Old Meadow Rd 221 McLean VA 22102 Office: ETC Inc 6241 Executive Blvd Rockville MD 20852

BELSKY, MARTIN HENRY, university legal research administrator, law educator, lawyer; b. Phila., May 29, 1944; s. Abraham and Fannie (Turnoff) B.; m. Kathleen Waits, Mar. 9, 1985. B.A. cum laude, Temple U., 1965; J.D.

cum laude, Columbia U., 1968; cert. of study Hague (Netherlands) Acad. Internat. Law, 1968; diploma in criminology Cambridge (Eng.) U., 1969. Bar: Pa. 1969, Fla. 1983, U.S. dist. ct. (ea. dist.) Pa. 1969, U.S. Ct. Appeals (3d cir.) 1970, U.S. Supreme Ct. 1973. Chief asst. dist. atty. Phila. Dist. Atty.'s Office, 1969-74; assoc. Blank, Rome, Klaus & Comisky, Phila., 1975; chief counsel U.S. Ho. of Reps., Washington, 1975-78; asst. adminstr. NOAA, Washington, 1979-82; dir. Ctr. for Govtl. Responsibility, assoc. prof. law U. Fla. Holand Law Ctr., 1982—; faculty adv. Environ. Law Soc., Jessup Internat. Moot Ct. Team and Pre-Law Soc. (all at U. Fla.); bd. advs. Ctr. Oceans Law and Policy; mem. corrections task force Pa. Gov.'s Justice Commn., 1971-75; adv. task force on cts. Nat. Adv. Commn. on Criminal Justice Standars and Goals, 1972-74; mem. com. on proposed standard jury instrns. Pa. Supreme Ct., 1974-81; lectr. in law Temple U., 1971-75; mem. faculty Pa. Coll. Judiciary, 1975-77; adj. prof. law Georgetown U., 1977-81. Chmn. Phila. council Anti-Defamation League, 1975, mem. D.C. bd., 1977-78, now mem. nat. leadership Council. Stone scholar and Internat. fellow Columbia U. Law Sch.; pres. Gainesville Jewish Appeal; vice chmn. Gainesville ACLU; bd. dirs. Gainesville LWV. Mem. Phila. Bar Assn. (chmn. young lawyers sect. 1974-75), Pa. Bar Assn. (exec. com. young lawyers sect. 1973-75), ABA (del. young lawyers sect. exec. bd. 1973-75), Fla. Bar Assn., Fed. Bar Assn., Am. Judicature Soc., Nat. Dist. Attys. Assn., Am. Soc. Internat. Law, Am. Arbitration Assn., Temple U. Liberal Arts Alumni Assn. (v.p. 1971-75), Sword Soc. Jewish. Club: B'nai B'rith (v.p. lodge 1973-75). Author: (with Steven H. Goldblatt) Analysis and Commentary to the Pennsylvania Crimes Codes, 1973; Handbook for Trial Judges, 1976; contbr. articles to legal publs.; editor-in-chief Jour. Transnat. Law, Columbia Law Sch., 1968, now bd. dirs. Office: Center for Govtl Responsibility U Fla Holland Law Center Gainesville FL 32611

BELTRAN, EUSEBIUS JOSEPH, bishop; b. Ashley, Pa., Aug. 31, 1934; s. Joseph C. and Helen Rita (Kozlowski) B. Ed., St. Charles Sem., Overbrook, Pa. Ordained priest Roman Cath. Ch., 1960; consecrated bishop, 1978, pastor chs. in, Atlanta and Decatur, Ga., 1960; notary, then vice officialis Atlanta Diocesan Tribunal, 1960-62; vice chancellor Archdiocese Atlanta, 1962; officialis Archdiocesan Tribunal, 1963-74; pastor chs. in, Atlanta and Rome, Ga., 1963-66; vicar gen. Archdiocese of Atlanta, 1971-78; pastor St. Anthony's Ch., Atlanta, 1972-78; bishop of, Tulsa, 1978—; mem. com. liturgy Nat. Conf. Cath. Bishops; also com. for Am. Coll., Louvain, Belgium; bd. regents Conception Sem.; bd. dirs. St. Gregory's Coll., Shawnee, Okla. Mem. Equestrian Order Holy Sepulchre, NCCJ. Club: K.C. Home: 2151 N Vancouver St Tulsa OK 74127 Office: 820 S Boulder St PO Box 2009 Tulsa OK 74101*

BELVIN, ANNA NEWELL, hospital administrator, mental health executive, consultant; b. DeKalb, Miss., July 12, 1950; d. Thomas Tatum and Mildred Mae (Hammack) Newell; children—Kenneth Brad, John David. B.S.N., U. Miss.-Jackson, 1972; M.S., U. So. Miss., 1983. Lic. nurse, Miss. Psychiat. nursing supr. Weems Mental Health Ctr., Meridian, Miss., 1973-74, dir. inpatient services, 1975-76, aftercare coordinator, 1976-79, clin. specialist aftercare clinic, 1979-82; nursing adminstr. East Miss. State Hosp., Meridian, 1979-82; psychiat. coordinator Laurelwood Psychiat. Ctr., Meridian Regional Hosp., 1983-84, dir. psychiat. services Laurelwood Psychiat.-Recovery Ctr., 1984-85, hosp. adminstr., 1985—; mem. cons. staff dept. staff devel. East Miss. State Hosp., Meridian, 1975; mem. faculty continuined edn. Meridian Jr. Coll., 1977-78; cons. in field, including to Office Ct. Monitor, State Ala., 1981-82, Nat. Commn. Human Service Workers, Columbia, S.C., 1983-84; mem. faculty, cons. U. So. Miss., Hattiesburg, 1983, 85. Recipient Leadership award U. So. Miss., 1984. Mem. Miss. Community Mental Health and Mental Retardation Council (exec. com. 1978-79), sec.-treas. 1979-80, pres. 1981-82, Miss. Mental Health and Mental Retardation Achievement award 1983), Soc. Dirs. Nursing Service, Am. Nurses Assn. (cert. nursing adminstr.), Miss. Nursing Assn., Mental Health Assn., Sigma Theta Tau. Baptist. Home: Route 1 Box 638 Meridian MS 39301 Office: Laurelwood Psychiat/Recovery Ctr Hwy 39 N Meridian MS 39303

BELVIN, M. T., JR., energy company executive; b. 1924. B.S., Tex. A&M U., 1948. With United Energy Resources Inc., 1949-74; pres. United Tex. Transmission Co. subs. United Energy Resources Inc., Co., Houston, 1974—, also dir. Office: United Tex Transmission Co 711 Louisiana Houston TX 77001*

BEMPORAD, SANDRA SMITH, respiratory therapist; b. Denver, May 30, 1943; d. Carl D. and Ruth O. Smith; m. David Sherman (div. Mar. 1975); children—Jaca, Aaron; m. Jack Bemporad, Nov. 21, 1978. Student, U. Colo., 1961-63, Del Mar Coll., 1971-73. Asst. tech. dir. respiratory therapy Spohn Hosp., Corpus Christi, Tex., 1971-73; coordinator critical care Med. City Hosp., Dallas, 1974-78, coordinator pulmonary rehab., 1981—; dir. dept. Carrollton Hosp., Dallas, 1978-80. Mem. Am. Assn. Respiratory Therapists, Tex. Soc. Respiratory Therapists, Better Breathing Clubs, Am. Lung Assn. Jewish. Home: 6514 Royal Dallas TX 75230 Office: Med City Hosp 7777 Forest Ln Dallas TX 75230

BENAFIELD, JAMES WELDON, mayor, investments and farming executive; b. Coy, Ark., July 5, 1927; m. Anita Carr (div.); children—Dawne Benafield Vandiver, Shannon; m. 2d, Dena Vanloon, Oct. 25, 1973; 1 stepson, Doug Vanloon Grad., Little Rock Jr. Coll. (now U. Ark.-Little Rock), 1948; B.S.E., U. Central Ark., Conway, 1950. Pres., Benafield Cos.; owner Benafield Farms, Charleston, Miss., 1984—; pres. J.W. Benafield Co., Little Rock, 1984—; dir. Am. Transp. Corp., Conway, Savers Fed. Savs. and Loan Assn. Mayor, City of England (Ark.), 1967-74, City of Little Rock, 1983—. Sec. Ark. Democratic Party, 1967-76; bd. dirs. Econ. Opportunities Agy., Little Rock; bd. dirs. Little Rock Advt. and Promotion Commn.; visitors U. Ark., Little Rock; chmn. Ark. Racing Commn. Mem. Soybean Assn., Greater Little Rock C. of C., Ark. State C. of C. (dir.). Methodist. Office: J W Benafield Co 212 Center St 12th Floor Little Rock AR 72201

BENAVIDES, YOLANDA ANNA CORTEZ, school counselor; b. San Antonio, Dec. 27, 1951; d. Gumesindo Trejo and Luz (Cantu) Cortez; m. David Paul Benavides Sr., Dec. 22, 1973; children—Idalia Ivanna, David Paul, Beatriz Bianca. B.A., Our Lady of the Lake Coll., 1972; M.A., U. Tex.-San Antonio. Cert. elem. tchr., cert. counselor, Tex. Elem. tchr. Harlandale Ind. Sch. Dist., San Antonio, 1972-75, Title 1 resource tchr., 1975-79, sch. counselor, 1979—; conf. presenter Tex. Edn. Agy., Austin, 1983; panel presenter Title VII Bilingual Counseling, San Antonio, 1985; workshop presenter Harlandale Fed. Program Parent Adv. Council, San Antonio, 1982. Precinct conv. del. Democratic Com., San Antonio, 1984. Our Lady of Lake Coll. grantee and scholar 1969-72. Mem. Tex. State Tchrs. Assn., NEA, Tex. Assn. Counseling and Devel. (conv. com. 1984-85), Am. Assn. Counseling and Devel., S. Tex. Assn. Counseling and Devel. (conf. com. 1984), San Antonio Bowling Assn., Am. Bowling Assn., Sigma Zeta, Alpha Mu Gamma. Roman Catholic. Avocations: reading; bowling; exercise; tennis; travel. Home: 161 Tommins San Antonio TX 78214 Office: Harlandale Ind Sch Dist 102 Genevieve San Antonio TX 78285

BENCE, ALFRED EDWARD, geochemist, researcher; b. Saskatoon, Sask., Can., Aug. 30, 1940; came to U.S., 1962; s. Alfred Henry Bence and Vera Borland; m. Linda Ruth Johnson, Jan. 19, 1966 (div. 1981); 1 child, Carolyn Elizabeth. B.Engring. in Geology, U. Sask., Can., 1962; M.A. in Geology, U. Tex., 1964; Ph.D. in Geochemistry, MIT, 1966. Research fellow Calif. Inst. Tech., Pasadena, 1966-68; asst. prof. SUNY, Stony Brook, 1968-71, assoc. prof., 1971-74, prof., 1974-80; research assoc. Exxon Prod. Research, Houston, 1980-82; sr. research assoc. Exxon Minerals, Houston, 1982—; vis. prof. Australian Nat. U., 1974-75, 1978-79; dir. undergrad. studies SUNY, Stony Brook, 1977-80; mem. Lunar and Planetary Rev. Panel, NASA, Houston, 1978-80, constrn. adv. panel, 1977-79. Assoc. editor: Proceedings Fifth Lunar and Planetary Science Conf., 1974; contbr. articles to profl. jours. Prin. investigator Apollo Program, NASA, 1970-80, Deep Sea Drilling Project, NSF, 1973-80, Earth Sciences, NSF, 1969-74; NASA award for Excellence, 1984. Mem. Geochemical Soc. (councilor 1983-86), Am. Geophysical Union (assoc. editor 1977-80) Microbeam Analysis Soc., Am. Assn. of Petroleum Geologist. Avocations: flying; camping. Home: 703 Tanglewood Dr Friendswood TX 77546 Office: Exxon Prodn Research Co PO Box 2189 Houston TX 77252

BENDA, CHARLES JEFFERSON, JR., architect; b. Hilo, Hawaii, Feb. 16, 1927; s. Charles Jefferson and Eleanor (Rose) B.; B.A., Fla. State U., 1952; m. Nancy Carlton Tribble, Aug. 19, 1950. Cons., architect Fla. Dept. Edn., Tallahassee, 1960-66; architect firm Charles J. Benda, Tallahassee, 1966-69, Odom Benda Assos., Tallahassee, 1969-71; now owner Charles Benda Assos., Tallahassee; prof. Coll. Architecture, Fla. A&M U.; cons. architect U.S. AID, Survey of Njala U. Coll., Sierra Leone, West Africa. Mem. Council Ednl. Facility Planners, Internat., 1969. Served with AUS, 1945-47. Recipient Gov.'s Design award, 1981. Mem. Bldg. Research Inst., AIA (award for excellence 1979, 80, 81), Sigma Nu. Democrat. Elk. Clubs: St. Mark's Yacht, Apalachee Bay Yacht. Home: 1700 Kathryn Dr Tallahassee FL 32308 Office: Charles Benda Assos Architects 2416 Old St Augustine Rd Tallahassee FL 32301

BENDELIUS, ARTHUR GEORGE, engineer, consulting firm executive; b. Passaic, N.J., May 21, 1936; s. Arthur Leopold and Lydia Ella (Flach) B.; B.E., Stevens Inst. Tech., 1958, M.M.S., 1966; m. Virginia Brown, June 21, 1958; children—Linda Ellen, Bonnie Sue, Heidi Ann. Engr. firm Syska & Hennessey, N.Y.C., 1958-60; engr. firm Parsons, Brinckerhoff Quade & Douglas, Inc., N.Y.C., 1960-62, asst. dept. head, 1963-68, dept. head, 1968-70, project mgr., 1970-73, regional mgr., Atlanta, 1973-76, asst. v.p., 1976-78, v.p., 1978-82, sr. v.p., 1982—; engr. Nat. Biscuit Co., N.Y.C., 1962-63; condr. seminars, moderator forums in computer usage and environ. design. Pres. Brookside Home Sch. Orgn., Westwood, N.J., 1972-73; co-v.p. Dunwoody (Ga.) Band Booster Club, 1975-76, co-pres., 1976-77. Named Atlanta Engr. of Yr. in Pvt. Practice, 1978; Harold R. Fee Alumni award, 1978; registered profl. engr., N.Y., N.J., Minn., Ga., Fla., Tex., Ala., Ky., N.C., S.C., Miss., Tenn., La., Ark., Okla., Utah, Md., Ohio; lic. pilot. Fellow Soc. Am. Mil. Engrs. (nat. dir. 1983—, pres. Atlanta post 1978-79); mem. Nat., Ga. (dir. 1976-78) socs. profl. engrs., Nat. Council Engring. Examiners (cert.), Ga. Engring. Found. (dir. 1977—, sec. 1979, v.p. 1980, pres.-elect 1981, pres. 1982-83), N.Y. Assn. Cons. Engrs. Computer Group Inc. (chmn. com. mech. advi. 1967-71), Stevens Alumni Assn. (fund agt. 1970—), ASME, ASHRAE (chmn. tech. com. 1975-79, research promotion com. 1980-82), Brit. Tunnelling Soc., Electric Railroaders Assn., Aircraft Owners and Pilots Assn., Ga. Conservancy, Atlanta C. of C., Sigma Nu (pres. alumni assn. 1966-70, comdr. 1971-73). Lutheran. Club: Atlanta City, Ansley Golf, Atlanta Stevens (pres. 1974—). Co-author Tunnel Engineering Handbook, 1982. Contbr. articles to profl. jours. Home: 1220 Witham Dr Dunwoody GA 30338 Office: 148 International Blvd Atlanta GA 30303

BENDER, JOHN HENRY (JACK), JR., editor, cartoonist; b. Waterloo, Iowa, Mar. 28, 1931; s. John Henry and Wilma (Lowe) B.; m. Mary P. Henderson; children—Thereza, John IV, Anthony. B.A., U. Iowa, 1953; M.A., U. Mo., 1962; postgrad. Art. Inst. Chgo., Washington U., St. Louis. Art. dir., asst. editor Commerce Pub. Co., St. Louis, 1953-58; editor Florissant Reporter, 1958-61; editorial cartoonist Waterloo Courier, 1962-84, assoc. editor, 1975—, sports editor, 1983-84; art. dir., editor Alpha VII Corp., Tulsa, 1984—; sports cartoons Baseball Digest Mag., U. Iowa, others. Author: Pocket Guide to Judging Springboard Diving; (with Dick Smith) Inside Diving; (with Ed Gagnier) Inside Gymnastics. Served with USAF, 1954-56, now col. Res. Recipient Best Editorial award Mo. Press Assn., 1960; Grenville Clark Editorial Page award, 1968, Freedoms Found. award, 1969, 71, 75. Mem. Assn. Am. Editorial Cartoonists, Nat. Cartoonists Soc., Sigma Chi. Office: 6105 S Peoria St A124 Tulsa OK 74136

BENDER, MIRIAM LATTA, learning disabilities cons.; b. Washington, Mar. 13, 1908; d. William Richard and Jennie Latta (Polson) Rodenberger; A.B., Washington U., St. Louis, 1929; M.S., U. Wis., 1942; cert. in phys. therapy Mayo Clinic, 1948; Ph.D. in Spl. Edn., Purdue U., 1971; m. Howard Walter Bender, Mar. 2, 1957 (div. Sept. 1966). Tchr. East St. Louis (Ill.) High Sch., 1929-42; commd. 2d lt. U.S. Army, 1943, advanced through grades to capt., 1946; phys. therapy officer, 1943-46; chief phys. therapist Jefferson Barracks VA Hosp., St. Louis, 1946-50; served to lt. col. U.S. Air Force; phys. therapy officer U.S. Air Force, 1951-67, ret., 1967; ednl. therapist Purdue U. Achievement Center for Children, Lafayette, Ind., 1968-69, motor devel. specialist, 1970-71, asst. prof., dir. clin. services, 1972-73; asso. prof., evaluator learning analysis center Ga. So. Coll., Statesboro, 1973-81; cons. in field. Recipient Children's Friendship award Ga. Assn. Sch. Psychologists, 1982. Mem. Council for Exceptional Children, Assn. for Children with Learning Disabilities, Am. Phys. Therapy Assn., Ret. Officers Assn., P.E.O. Republican. Presbyterian. Author: Bender-Purdue Reflex Test and Tng. Manual, 1976. Home: 205 Circle Dr Statesboro GA 30458 Office: Ga So Coll Statesboro GA 30458

BENDURE, LEONA JENSEN, pianist, educator; b. Springtown, Tex., Sept. 27, 1912; d. James Daniel and Nettie Mae Folley Jensen; B.M. (Scholar), U. Kans., 1934, B.M.E. (Scholar), 1937; postgrad. Midwestern U., Wichita Falls, Tex., 1966-67; m. Lloyd Kenneth Bendure, Aug. 14, 1938 (dec. 1971); children—Lorene Joan Bendure Teed, Donald Wesley. Tchr. music edn., Gove, Kans., 1937-38; tchr. piano, Lawton, Okla., 1943—; bd. dirs. Lawton Symphony Soc., dir. childrens' concerts; pianist Meth. Youth camp, 1934-36; instrumental in addition of elem. music to pub. sch. curriculum, Lawton, 1957-58. Mem. Citizens Edn. Council, Lawton, 1956-58; 3d v.p. Lawton's Woman's Forum, 1974-75, bd. dirs., 1976-79, 2d v.p., 1975-76, fine arts chmn., 1970-71, dir. fine arts and crafts dept., 1981-82. Friends in Council scholar, Theodore Presser scholar, Howard Taylor scholar. Mem. Nat. Piano Guild, AAUW (chmn. Ednl. Found.), Okla. Music Tchrs. Assn. (pres. Lawton 1969-70), Nat. Assn. Music Tchrs., Mu Phi Epsilon (Scholar), Pi Kappa Lambda. Methodist (mem. Commn. on Missions). Club: Entre Nous (historian).

BENEDETTI, ROBERT REED, political science educator, college administrator; b. San Francisco, Dec. 31, 1942; s. Narciso Joseph and Lucille Gertrude (Schmoll) B.; m. Susan Jean Napier, Aug. 12, 1967; 1 child, Susan Elizabeth. B.A., Amherst Coll., 1964; postgrad. Union Theol. Sem., 1964-65; M.A., U. Pa., 1967, Ph.D., 1975. Lectr., teaching asst. U. Pa., 1966-68; tutor New Coll., U. South Fla., Sarasota, 1970-71, asst. prof., 1971-78, assoc. prof. polit. sci., 1978-84, prof., 1985—, chmn. div. social scis., 1981-83, provost 1984—. Contbg. author: Florida and its Governments, 1980. Active Sarasota County Civic League, Sarasota Inst. Lifetime Learning. Fellow Rockefeller Found., 1964-65, Kent/Danforth Found., 1968-75; recipient Disting. Teaching award New Coll., 1980. Mem. Am. Polit. Sci. Assn., So. Polit. Sci. Assn., Midwest Polit. Sci. Assn., Fla. Polit. Sci. Assn. (past pres.). Republican. Episcopalian. Home: 546 47th St Sarasota FL 33580 Office: New Coll U South Fla Sarasota FL 34243

BENEDICT, MARILYN FISK, psychologist; b. San Antonio, Feb. 20, 1950; d. Ellsworth William and Doris Rosalie (Scanlan) Fisk; m. Ronnie Howard Benedict, Mar. 27, 1982; 1 child, Bret Colin. A.A., San Antonio Coll., 1970; B.A., U. Tex., 1972; M.S., East Tex. State U., 1980, postgrad., 1985—. Lic. counselor, Tex., Nat. Bd. for Cert. Counselors. Social worker III, Dept. Human Resources, Dallas, 1975-79; police officer Dallas Police Dept., 1979—, police psychologist, investigator, 1982—; counselor Eastfield Community Coll., part-time 1980-81; instr. Dallas Police Acad., 1983—. Vol. Tex. Dept. Human Resources, Austin, 1975. U. Tex. scholar, 1971. Mem. Am. Assn. Suicidology, Tex. Police Officers Assn., Dallas Police Assn., Am. Assn. for Counseling and Devel., Alpha Delta Phi. Roman Catholic. Avocations: police olympics. Office: Psychol Services Dallas Police Dept 8700 Stemmons Suite 352 Dallas TX 75247

BENEDICT, NORMAN VINCENT, construction management and cement and concrete products consultant; b. Phila., Aug. 27, 1920; s. August G. Sarah E. (Burbage) B.; m. Valerie Ann Loucks, Dec. 24, 1945; children—Thomas William, Suzan Grace. B.S.E.E., Purdue U., 1947, postgrad. in indsl. engring., 1946-47; diploma commerce Northwestern U., 1954, M.B.A., 1955. Assoc. prof. indsl. tech. Purdue U., 1950-55; indsl. engr. Inland Steel Co., East Chicago, Ind., 1947-48; constrn. project engr. E. I. duPont de Nemours, East Chicago, 1948-49; assoc. prof. indsl. tech., head dept. Purdue U., Hammond, Ind., 1950-55; supr. staff services Core Labs., Dallas, 1955-58; mgmt. cons. Peat, Marwick, Mitchell & Co., Dallas, 1958-60; corp. planner LTV, Dallas, 1961-62; asst. to controller Gen. Dynamics, Fort Worth, 1962-64; budget and cost acctg. mgr. Tex. Industries, Dallas, 1964-70, asst. to exec. v.p., 1971-84; cons. constrn. mgmt. and cement and concrete products industries, also thermal mass housing cons., 1985—; lectr. mgmt. Tex. Christian U., Fort Worth, 1961-64, U. Tex., Arlington, 1972-75; cons. to constrn. firms for Tex. Industries, 1964-84. Scoutmaster, Boy Scouts Am., East Chicago; mem. Smoke Abatement Council, East Chicago, 1948-50; pres. Dallas chpt. Submarine Vets. World War II. Served as officer USN, 1941-45, 52-54. Named Disting. Student, Purdue U., 1947. Mem. Soc. Advancement Mgmt. (past chpt. pres.), Assn. Iron and Steel Engrs., Am. Mgmt. Assn., Planning Execs. Inst., IEEE, Masonry Soc., ASHRAE, Scabbard and Blade, VFW, Phi Sigma Kappa, Alpha Phi Omega. Republican. Episcopalian. Contbr. articles to profl. jours. Home: 7240 Fenton Dr Dallas TX 75231 Office: 7240 Fenton Dr Dallas TX 75231

BENEFIELD, BRUCE, manufacturing company executive; b. Danville, Va., Dec. 16, 1927; s. William G. and Lessie Lee (Arrington) B.; B.S., U. Miami (Fla.), 1951; M.S., Air Force Inst. Tech., 1964; Ph.D., Harvard U., 1968; m. Barbara Jean Goodell, Dec. 15, 1951; children—Bruce, Brian Scott, Bradley Stuart. Commd. 2d lt., U.S. Air Force, 1951, advanced through grades to col., 1973, ret., 1973; dir. fin. TRW, Inc., Washington, 1973-79, v.p. electronics and def., 1980—. Mem. Am. Assn. Accts., Assn. Govt. Accts., Nat. Contract Mgmt. Assn., Nat. Indsl. Security Assn. (trustee), Clubs: George Town, Washington Golf and Country, Harvard Bus. Sch. Home: 3009 N Edison St Arlington VA 22207 Office: 1000 Wilson Blvd Suite 2600 Arlington VA 22209

BENEL, DENISE C.R., human factors specialist; b. Brockton, Mass., Aug. 26, 1950; d. John Reynolds and Anita Clare (Phaneuf) Roan; m. Russell Andrew Benel, Nov. 22, 1969; children—Deirdre Reynolds, Wesley John. B.A., Trinity U., 1975; M.A., U. Ill., 1979, postgrad. 1979. Grad. research and teaching asst. dept. psychology Trinity U., San Antonio, 1975-76; traineeship and grad. research asst. U. Ill., Urbana, 1976-79, grad. research asst., 1978-79, grad. teaching asst., 1979; with Essex Corp., Alexandria, Va., 1980—, project mgr. for projects with consumer product safety commn. and prin. investigator for 2 small bus. innovative research projects, 1984—. Contbr. articles to jours., chpts. to books. USPHS fellow, 1976-79. Mem. Human Factors Soc., Potomac Human Factors Soc. Avocation: antique collecting. Home: 8603 Buckboard Dr Alexandria VA 22308 Office: Essex Corp 333 N Fairfax Alexandria VA 22314

BENFER, NEIL ALFRED, technical writer, editor, oceanographer; b. Lewisburg, Pa., Sept. 16, 1920; s. John Walton and Elva Elizabeth (Kline) B.; m. Mary Alice Fertich, Apr. 26, 1947; children—Neil, Carol Ann, Susan Lee, Brian Arthur. B.S., Bucknell U., 1948; M.S., Pa. State U., 1951. Oceanographer U.S. Navy Hydrographic Office, Suitland, Md., 1951-56; soil sci. editor U.S. Soil Conservation Service, Beltsville, Md., 1956-57; earth scis. editor McGraw-Hill Ency. Sci. and Tech., Charlottesville, Va., 1957-62; tech. writer, editor U.S. Coast and Geodetic Survey, 1963-65, U.S. Environ. Sci. Services Adminstrn., Washington, 1965-70; gen. physical scientist NOAA, U.S. Dept. Commerce, Washington, 1970-80. Editor: Natural Disaster Survey Series, Professional Paper Series, San Fernando, Calif., Earthquake of Feb. 9, 1971 (3 vols.), U.S. Ocean Policy in 1970s. Served with U.S. Army, 1942-45, ETO. Recipient Bronze medal Dept. Commerce, 1980. Mem. Geol. Soc. Am., Assn. Earth Sci. Editors. Republican. Baptist. Address: 1815 Meadowbrook Heights Rd Charlottesville VA 22901

BENINI, painter; b. Imola, Italy, Apr. 17, 1941; came to U.S., 1977; s. Paolo and Ida Benini; m. Lorraine Frances Link; children from previous marriage—Christopher, Elisa. Liceo Classico, Bologna, Italy, 1956, Evalc Assisi cum laude, 1958. Mgmt. positions with various firms, 1959-67; mng. ptnr. Green & Assoc., Grand Bahama, 1968-72; chmn. Space Bahamas Ltd., 1973-76; painter, solo exhibitions in numerous museums, galleries, pub. instns., insts., univs., 1965—; exhibited in group shows Charleston Heights Arts Ctr., Las Vegas, 1985, Landmark Ctr., Orlando, Fla., Jacksonville U., Fla., Daytona Beach Community Coll., Fla., 1985; lectr. in visual arts. Served with Italian Army, 1960-63. Named Kiwanis Man of Yr., 1970-71. Researcher in visual arts, 1977—. Studio: 3488 Lake Harney Circle Oviedo FL 32765

BENITEZ, MAURICE M., bishop, Episcopal Church; b. Washington, Jan. 23, 1928; s. Enrique M. and Blossom (Compton) B.; m. Joanne Dossett, Dec. 18, 1949. B.S., U.S. Mil. Acad., 1949; B.D., U. of South, 1958, D.D., 1973. Priest-in-charge St. James Ch., Lake City, Fla., 1958-61; canon resident St. John's Cathedral, Jacksonville, Fla., 1961-62; rector Grace Ch., Ocala, Fla., 1962-68; rector ch., San Antonio, 1968-74; exec. bd. fin. dept., trustee U. of South, 1969; dep. Gen. Conv. Episc. Ch., 1970-73, 79; regent U. of South, 1973-79; bishop of Tex., 1980—. Served to capt. USAF, 1949-55. Address: 520 San Jacinto St Houston TX 77002*

BENJAMIN, DON CARLOS, JR., educator; b. Barksdale AFB, La., Mar. 14, 1942; s. Don C. and Edith M. (Beltz) B. B.A., St. Bonaventure U., 1964; M.A., Cath. U. Am., 1969; Ph.D., Claremont Grad. Sch., 1981. Tchr. counselor Salpointe Cath. High Sch., Tucson, 1968-69; tchr., dept. chmn. Mt. Carmel High Sch., Los Angeles, 1969-72; lectr. theology Mt. St. Mary Coll., Los Angeles, 1975-76; acting dir. Carmelite Retreat and Edn. Center, Los Angeles, 1976-78; lectr. Grad. Sch. Theology, U. St. Thomas, Houston, 1980-83; lectr. religious studies Rice U., Houston, 1978—; Scanlon vis. scholar in religious studies U. Houston, 1986. Mem. Soc. Bibl. Lit., Cath. Bibl. Assn. Author: Deuteronomy and City Life, 1983; contbr. articles to profl. jours. Office: Dept Religious Studies Rice Univ PO Box 1892 Houston TX 77251

BENJAMIN, EDWARD BERNARD, JR., lawyer; b. New Orleans, Feb. 11, 1923; s. Edward Bernard and Blanche (Sternberger) B.; B.S., Yale U., 1944; J.D., Tulane U., 1952; m. Adelaide Wisdom, May 11, 1957; children—Edward Wisdom, Mary Dabney, Ann Leith, Stuart Minor. Admitted to La. bar, 1952, since practiced in New Orleans; partner Jones, Walker, Waechter, Poitevent, Carrere & Denegre; chmn. bd. Starmount Co., Greensboro, N.C.; mem. adv. bd. CCH Estate and Fin. Planning Service. Trustee Hollins Coll.; vice chmn. bd. trustees Southwestern Legal Found.; mem. Tulane Tax Inst., past chmn. program com.; pres. Internat. Acad. Estate and Trust Law, 1976-78; chancellor Episcopal Diocese of La.; vestryman, chancellor Trinity Episcopal Ch., New Orleans. Served to 1st lt. U.S. Army, 1943-46. Mem. ABA (sec. taxation sect. 1967-68, council 1976-79, real property, probate and trust law sect. council 1978-81), La. Bar Assn. (chmn. sect. taxation 1959-60), New Orleans Bar Assn., Am. Law Inst., La. Law Inst., Am. Coll. Probate Counsel (bd. regents 1980—, sec. 1983-84, v.p. 1984-85, pres. 1986-87), Am. Coll. Tax Counsel, La. Law Inst. Clubs: New Orleans Country, Greensboro Country, So. Yacht, New Orleans Lawn Tennis, Petroleum. Editor in chief Tulane Law Rev., 1951-52. Home: 1837 Palmer Ave New Orleans LA 70118 Office: Place St Charles 201 St Charles Ave New Orleans LA 70170

BENJAMIN, MAYNARD HENRY, association executive, computer consultant; b. Petersburg, Va., Jan. 6, 1951; s. Willis and Erica (Kraske) B.; m. Carol Baber, June 23, 1973. B.S. in Bus. Adminstrn., Va. Poly. Inst., 1973; M.S. in Adminstrn., George Washington U., 1977. Sr. cons. Arthur Young & Co., Washington, 1977-79; dir. northeast ops. Cexec, Inc., McLean, Va., 1978-80; mgr. Syscon Corp., Washington, 1980-81; mgr. industry services Am. Assn. Equipment Lessors, Arlington, Va., 1981-83; v.p., treas. Envelope Mfg. Assn., Arlington, Va., 1984—; dir. M.H. Benjamin, Inc., Alexandria, Network Resources Inc., Washington, Recognition Systems Inc., Washington; dir. Fin. Mgmt. Roundtable, Washington, 1984—. Contbr. articles to profl. jours. Served to capt. U.S. Army, 1973-77. Mem. Greater Washington Soc. Assn. Execs., Am. Soc. Assn. Execs., Associated Info. Mgrs. Republican. Baptist. Avocations: fly fishing; skiing; hunting; sailing. Home: 821 Wolfe St Alexandria VA 22314 Office: Envelope Mfrs Assn Am 1300 N 17th St Suite 1520 Arlington VA 22209

BENKERT, KYLE GRANT, architect, city planner, real estate developer; b. Chgo., June 17, 1931; s. Ernst August and Helen (Limerick) B.; student Amherst Coll., 1949-51; A.B. cum laude, Harvard U., 1953; postgrad. Princeton U., 1958-59; B.Arch. with honors, U. Pa., 1960, M.City Planning, 1960, M.Arch., 1961; m. Adrienne Lee Hurley, Apr. 19, 1958; children—Adrienne Joan, John Hurley, Mark Grant, Helen Keith, Paul David, John Christopher. Office mgr. Ernst A. Benkert, Architect, Winnetka, Ill., 1955-57; job capt. Morton Salt Bldg. firm Graham, Anderson, Probst & White, Chgo., 1957-58; head central area sect. gen. plan Chgo. Dept. Planning, 1961-66; prin. Kyle G. Benkert & Assocs., Architects & Planners Chgo., 1966-86, Columbus, N.C., 1973-81; vis. critic lectr. U. Ill., 1962-66, Hunter Coll., 1965. Bd. dirs. Chgo. Commons Assn., 1968-72. Served with USCGR, 1953-55. Mem. Nat. Council Archtl. Registration Bds. Roman Catholic. Clubs: Arts (Chgo.); Red Fox Country (Tryon, N.C.). Prin. work includes: plan for City of Chgo., I.C. air rights, plan for Chgo. bicentennial exhbn., 1963-64, design and devel. Lake Hinsdale, Willowbrook, Ill., 1970, 73, Larrabee Ct., Lincoln Park, Chgo., 1971-83, Morgan Chapel Village, Columbus, 1974-77, Liberty Sq., Spartanburg, S.C., 1980-83, Patriots Point Master Plan, Charleston Harbor, S.C., 1982-83, Chatham Manor, Buffalo Grove, Ill., 1984-86. Home and office: PO Box 1 Columbus NC 28722

BENNETT, BETTY BESSE, librarian; b. Omaha, Feb. 18, 1921; d. Gordon Stanley and Besse Harriet (Amos) Bennett; B.A., Mcpl. U. Omaha, 1942; B.S. in L.S., U. Ill., 1943; M.A., U. Iowa, 1948; M.L.S., Tex. Woman's U., 1960. Asst. documents librarian U. Iowa Library, Iowa City, 1943-50; reference and documents librarian Kans. State Tchrs. Coll. Library, Pittsburg, 1950-57, reference librarian, archivist, 1957-67; reference and research librarian Stephen

F. Austin State U. Library, Nacogdoches, Tex., 1967-72, govt. documents librarian, 1972—. Resource cons. Gov.'s Conf. on Libraries, Austin, Tex., 1974; mem. ad hoc com. on superceded documents U.S. Govt. Printing Office, 1985. Exec. dir. Westminster Presbyn. Ch. Telephone Reassurance Program for Elderly Shut-ins, 1977-81. Mem. ALA (state document classification com. 1974-76, state documents task force), Tex. Library Assn. (chmn. govt. documents round table 1975-76), Southwestern Library Assn., Tex. Assn. Coll. Tchrs., Nacogdoches Friends of the Library, Alpha Xi Delta. Presbyn. (clk. of session 1967-81, ruling elder 1975—). Office: Stephen F Austin State U Library Nacogdoches TX 75962

BENNETT, BOBBIE JEAN, state official; b. Gwinnett County, Ga., July 13, 1940; d. William Claude and Clara Maude (Nichols) Holcome; B.B.A. magna cum laude, Ga. State U., 1973; 1 dau., Terri Lynne. With Ga. State Merit System, Atlanta, 1960—, sr. acct., 1967, asst. div. dir., 1968-70, fiscal officer, 1970-74, div. dir., 1975-78, asst. dep. commr., 1978—. Mem. Internat. Personnel Mgmt. Assn., Ga. Fiscal Mgmt. Council, Ga. Council Personnel Adminstrn., State and Local Govt. Benefit Assn., Nat. Assn. Deferred Compensation Adminstrs., Beta Gamma Sigma, Phi Kappa Phi, Beta Alpha Psi. Democrat. Home: 2072 Malabar Dr NE Atlanta GA 30345 Office: 200 Piedmont Ave Atlanta GA 30334

BENNETT, CHARLES EDWARD, congressman; b. Canton, N.Y., Dec. 2, 1910; s. Walter James and Roberta Augusta (Broadhurst) B.; A.B., U. Fla., 1934, J.D., 1934; H.H.D. (hon.), U. Tampa, 1950; LL.D. (hon.), Jacksonville U., 1972; m. Jean Bennett; children—Bruce, James, Lucinda. Admitted to Fla. bar, 1934, practiced in Jacksonville, until 1949; mem. 81st-99th congresses from 3d Fla. Dist., mem. armed services com., chmn. seapower subcom. Mem. Fla. Ho. of Reps., 1941. Bd. dirs. Boys' Home, ARC, Tb Assn. Council Social Agys., Multiple Sclerosis Assn. Served from pvt. to capt., inf., AUS, 1942-47; New Guinea and Philippines, including guerrilla fighting in Luzon. Decorated Silver Star, Bronze Star; Philippine Legion of Honor and Gold Cross; French Legion of Honor; recipient Cert. of Merit, Freedoms Found., 1951, 56, Good Govt. award, Jr. C. of C., 1952, Good Citizenship gold medal Nat. SAR, 1959. Mem. DAV, VFW, Fla. Bar, Am. Legion, Fleet Res. Assn. (hon.), Jacksonville Bar Assn., Jr. C. of C. (pres. 1939). Democrat. Mem. Disciples of Christ Ch. (elder). Club: Mason. Author: Laudonniere, 1964; Settlement of Florida, 1967; Congress and Conscience, 1970; Southernmost Battlefields of the Revolution, 1970; Three Voyages, 1974; Florida's "French" Revolution, 1982; also hist. papers. Office: 2107 Rayburn House Office Bldg Washington DC 20515

BENNETT, CLARK EUGENE, psychologist; b. Wyalusing, Pa., Apr. 12, 1924; s. Clark E. and Frances M. (Boyd) B.; m. Shirley Jean Bowen, Apr. 3, 1948; children—Gene Paul, Jon Bruce, Jay Alan. B.A., Harpur Coll., 1954; M.A., Furman U., 1962. Apprentice tool maker IBM, Endicott, N.Y., 1942-46, machinist, 1946-48; program dir. Boys Club of Greater Endicott, 1948-54; exec. dir. Cherokee County Boys Club, Gaffney, S.C., 1955-56, social worker, 1955-56; asst. supt. John de la Howe Sch., McCormick, S.C., 1956-63; psychologist, therapist Alexander Children's Ctr., Charlotte, N.C., 1963—. Contbr. author: Creating Environments for Troubled Children, 1980. Served to cpl. U.S. Army, 1943-45. Decorated Purple Heart, Bronze Star; recipient Friend of Children award N.C. Child Care Assn., 1981, Profl. of Yr. award Mecklenburg County Mental Health Assn., 1982. Mem. Am. Psychol. Assn., N.C. Psychol. Assn., Mecklenburg Psychol. Assn., Nat. Register Practicing Psychologists. Presbyterian. Lodge: Lions (numerous awards, offices). Avocations: reading; family; sports; travel. Home: 300 Meadowbrook Rd Charlotte NC 28211 Office: Alexanders Children's Ctr PO Box 220632 Charlotte NC 28222

BENNETT, DELLA MAE, ednl. adminstr.; b. Goliad, Tex., Nov. 15, 1919; d. George and Lucy Francis (Perryman) McDow; B.S., Prairie View A&M U., 1950, M.S., 1953; postgrad. Tex. A&I U., 1961, U. Houston, 1977; m. Sidney E. Bennett, Apr. 14, 1952; 1 dau., Carrie Nell. Tchr., Vidauri, Tex., 1940-42; tchr. math. and sci. Goliad (Tex.) Ind. Sch. Dist., 1946-80, 4th grade tchr., 1982—, dir. Emergency Sch. Aid Act, 1980—. Youth sponsor Minnehulla Bapt. Ch., 1970; county youth sponsor Goliad, Victoria and Calhoun Inst. Youth; sponsor Mt. Zion Dist. Youth, 1982—; bd. dirs. Goliad County Hosp., 1981. Mem. NEA, Tex. Tchrs. Assn. Democrat. Club: Order Eastern Star (matron Sunlight Chpt. 23). Home: 604 E Pearl St Goliad TX 77963 Office: 600 Church St Goliad TX 77963

BENNETT, FRANK WILLIAM, psychologist; b. Orange, Tex., Sept. 1, 1948; s. David and Edna Mae (Goldfine) B. B.S., Tulane U., 1970; M.S., North Tex. State U., 1971, Ph.D., 1979. Lic. psychologist, La. Psychologist, Tyche Inc., Delhi, La., 1979—; adj. prof. psychology Northeast La. U., Monroe, 1984—; cons. Assn. for Retarded Citizens, Monroe, 1981—, Ouachita Pastoral Counseling Ctr., West Monroe, La., 1982—. Contbr. articles to profl. jours. Mem. Am. Psychol. Assn., Southwest Psychol. Assn. Office: Tyche Inc 203 Rancher St Delhi LA 71232

BENNETT, G(EORGE) KEMBLE, JR., industrial and management systems engineering educator, consultant; b. Jacksonville, Fla., Apr. 2, 1940; s. George K. and Murla E. (Weeks) B.; m. Cindy E. Bull, June 25, 1966 (div. 1978); children—Russell William, Paige E.; m. 2d Jill Alison McMaster, June 5, 1982. B.S., Fla. State U., 1962; M.S., San Jose State U., 1968; Ph.D., Tex. Tech U., 1970. Profl. engr., Fla. Assoc. engr. Martin Co., Orlando, Fla., 1962-63; math. analyst Lockheed Research Labs., Palo Alto, Calif., 1963-66; asst. dir. Computer Ctr., Tex. Tech U., Lubbock, 1966-69; vis. scientist NASA Manned Spacecraft Lab., Houston, 1969-70; asst. prof. indsl. engring. Va. Poly. Inst., Blacksburg, 1970-73; prof., chmn. indsl. and mgmt. systems engring. U. South Fla., Tampa, 1973—; logistics engring. cons. to Honeywell Avionics. Active Fla. Fleet Five. Mem. Am. Soc. Engring. Edn., Inst. Indsl. Engrs. (Fla. West Coast Engr. of Year 1979, 82), The Inst. Mgmt. Scis., Tau Beta Pi, Phi Kappa Phi. Republican. Methodist. Assoc. editor IIE Transactions; tech. editor Logistics Spectrum; contbr. articles to nat. and internat. jours. Home: PO Box 768 Seffner FL 33584 Office: Dept Indsl Engring Univ South Fla Tampa FL 33620

BENNETT, HAROLD CLARK, clergyman, religious organization administrator; b. Asheville, N.C., July 30, 1924; s. Charles C. and Emily H. (Clark) B.; student Asheville Biltmore Jr. Coll., 1946, Mars Hill Coll., 1946-47; B.A., Wake Forest U., 1949; postgrad. Duke U. Div. Sch., 1949-51; Div.M., So. Bapt. Theol. Sem., 1953; LL.D. (hon.) Stetson U., 1968; D.D. (hon.), Campbell U., 1982, Wake Forest U., 1985; m. Phyllis Jean Metz, Aug. 17, 1947; children—Jeffery Clark, John Scott, Cynthia Ann Bennett Howard. Clk., FBI, Washington, 1942-43; ordained to ministry Baptist Ch., 1948; pastor Glen Royal Bapt. Ch., Wake Forest, N.C., 1948-51; chaplain Ky. State Reformatory, LaGrange, 1951-53, Ky. Woman's Prison, 1951-53; pastor Westpoint (Ky.) Bapt. Ch., 1952; asst. pastor First Bapt. Ch., Shreveport, La., 1953-55; pastor Beech St. Bapt. Ch., Texarkana, Ark., 1955-60; supt. new work Sunday Sch. Dept., Sunday Sch. bd., So. Bapt. Conv., Nashville, Tenn., 1960-62; interim pastor Little West Fork Bapt. Ch., Hopkinsville, Ky., 1960, Two Rivers Bapt. Ch., Nashville, 1962; sec. met. missions home mission bd. So. Bapt. Conv., Atlanta, Ga., 1962-65; dir. missions div. Bapt. Gen. Conv. Tex., Dallas, 1965-67; exec. sec., treas. Fla. Bapt. Conv., Jacksonville, 1967-79, So. Bapt. Conv., Nashville, 1979—. Mem. adv. council Fla. State Alcoholism, 1973-78; trustee Fla. Meml. Coll., Miami, 1967-74. Served with USN Air Corps, 1942-45. Named Ky. Col. Mem. Assn. of Bapt. State Exec. Secs. (pres. 1978-79), Assn. of Bapt. State Conv. Ch. Bond Plans (pres. 1978-79), Fla. Bapt. State Bd. Missions (sec. 1967-79), Am. Bible Soc. (gov.), Religion in Am. Life (dir.). Lodge: Rotary. Author: Reflections of Faith, 1983; contbr. numerous articles to religious publs.; compiler: God's Awesome Challenge, 1980. Home: 202 Long Valley Rd Brentwood TN 37027 Office: 901 Commerce St Nashville TN 37203

BENNETT, HARRIET COOK, social worker, educator; b. Telfair County, Ga., Aug. 3, 1945; d. Harry A. and Amy H. Cook; B.A., LaGrange (Ga.) Coll., 1967; M.S.W., U. Ga., Athens, 1969; postgrad. Tulane U., 1970; m. Fredrick E. Bennett, Jr., June 6, 1971; children—Amy, Andrew. Med. social reviewer state rev. team, Dept. Family and Children Services, Atlanta, 1969-71; social worker/instr. U. Mo. Med. Center, Columbia, 1971-73; social worker Easter Seal Rehab. Center, Tampa, Fla., 1978-79, Children's Home Society Fla., St. Petersburg, 1984—; dir. LaPetite Acad., Tampa, 1980, tchr. kindergarten, 1981-84; vol. cons. Desenzano, Italy, 1976-78. Vol. fundraiser Nat. Kidney Found., Arthritis Found. Lic. clin. social worker. Mem. Northdale Civic Assn., Nat. Assn. Social Workers, Acad. Cert. Social Workers, Hillsborough County PTA. Methodist. Home: 16006 Honeysuckle Pl Tampa FL 33624

BENNETT, IVAN STANLEY, counselor; b. Harrisburg, Pa., Jan. 27, 1949; s. Ivan Frank and Audrey (Poley) B.; student Butler U., 1967-69; B.A., Thomas More Coll., 1972; M.Ed., Xavier U., 1974; m. Susan Lee Elliott, Aug. 3, 1974; children—Jonathan Lee, Jason Charles, Joseph Wesley. Tchr., Covington (Ky.) Ind. Sch. Dist., Job Preparation Center, 1973-75; coordinator Scott St. Job Preparation Center, Covington, 1975-76; mgr.-coordinator Greenup St. Job Preparation Center, Covington, 1976-77; mgr. Greenup St. Job Preparation Sch., 1977-78; dir. admissions and release No. Ky. State Vocat. Tech. Sch., Covington, 1978-80; sr. counselor Holmes High Sch., Covington, 1980-84; dir. pupil personnel/coordinator spl. programs Walton-Verona Sch. Dist. (Ky.), 1984-85, asst. prin., 1985—; mem. tchr. adv. com. Dist. Speakers Bur. Chmn., Com. for Sch. Dropouts, 1974-75; chmn. Alternative Sch. Adv. Com., 1975-76; mem. Juvenile Delinquency Task Force, Ky. Adv. Commn., 1975-76, Regional Council on Substance Abuse, 1975-76, Kenton County Manpower Adv. Com., 1976-77, No. Ky. Adv. and Resources Council for Teenage Parents, 1975-78. Cert. tchr. and guidance counselor, Ky., Ohio. Mem. Am. (So. region br. assembly, dir. 1981—), Ky. (cert. of appreciation; pres. 1980), No. Ky. (cert. of appreciation) personnel and guidance assns., Ky. Assn. Sch. Adminstrs., Lambda Chi Alpha. Republican. Lutheran (ch. council 1984—). Home: 6766 McVille Rd Burlington KY 41005 Office: Walton Verona Bd Edn Box 167 Walton KY 41094

BENNETT, JANE DYER, savings and loan executive; b. Cornelia, Ga., Oct. 13, 1949; d. Odell Buford and Joyce G. (Jenkins) Dyer; m. Alva David Bennett, Sept. 13, 1970; 1 child, Karen. B.S. in Edn., U. Ga., 1971, M.Ed., 1976. Tchr. Gwinnett County Bd. Edn., Lawrenceville, Ga., 1971-74; resource specialist Hall County Bd. Edn., Gainesville, 1974-78, tchr., 1981-83; research dir. Home Fed. Savs. & Loan, Gainesville, 1983, v.p., dir. planning and devel., 1983—. Active First Baptist Ch., Gainesville, 1974—; fundraiser United Way, Gainesville, 1983—, Gainesville Jr. Coll., 1985. Named Tchr. of Yr., Snellville Middle Sch., Ga., 1973. Mem. Gainesville C. of C., Fin. Mgrs. Soc., Planning Execs. Inst. Office: Home Fed Savs Bank of Ga 104 Green St PO Box 1418 Gainesville GA 30503

BENNETT, JOHN HENRY, controller, public accountant; b. Glens Falls, N.Y., Dec. 31, 1947; s. John Henry and Teri Loretta (Moculski) Bennett; m. Joan Karen Tedeschi, Feb. 16, 1975; 1 son, Nicholas Anthony. A.B. in Polit. Sci., Ga. State U., Atlanta, 1970; M.B.A., Savannah (Ga.) State Coll., 1982. C.P.A., Ga. Clk., acct. State Hwy. Dept. Ga., Atlanta, 1969-72; fin. mgr. State Crime Commn., Atlanta, 1972-74; fin. dir. Coastal Area Planning, Devel. Commn., Brunswick, Ga., 1974; controller Sea Island Co., Ga., 1975—; C.P.A. sole practioner. St. Simons Island, Ga., 1983. Mem. Internat. Assn. Hospitality Accts. (cert. hospitality acct. exec.), Am. Inst. C.P.A.s, Ga. Soc. C.P.A.s. Roman Catholic. Club: Exchange (St. Simons Island) (treas. 1976-77). Office: Sea Island Co Cloister Pl Sea Island GA 31561

BENNETT, JOHN PRICE, state agency administrator; b. Richmond, Va., May 11, 1947; s. Bradford Sherwood and Lenoah Arminta (Long) B.; m. Claudia Jean Adams, June 14, 1969; children—Zachariah Price, Rebecca Adams. B.A., Coll. William and Mary, 1969; M.Ed., Va. Commonwealth U., 1972; Ed.D., No. Ill. U., 1980. Phys. edn. tchr. Henrico County Pub. Schs., Richmond, 1969-74; supr. health, phys. edn. and driver edn. Hanover County Pub. Schs., Va., 1974-76; instr. health and phys. edn. dept. No. Ill. U., DeKalb, 1976-81; asst. prof. health and phys. edn. dept. George Mason U., Fairfax, Va., 1981-85; asst. dir. health, phys. edn., safety and sports N.C. Dept. Pub. Instrn., Raleigh, 1985—. Contbr. articles to profl. jours. Recipient Teaching Excellence award No. Ill. U., 1980. Mem. AAHPERD (Disting. Leader award 1982, Spotlight on Achievement award 1984), Omicron Delta Kappa, Theta Delta Chi. Avocations: guitar; harmonica; singing; participating in and teaching sports and dance. Home: 1314 Hampton Valley Rd Cary NC 27511 Office: Dept Public Instrn Div Health Phys Edn Safety and Sports Education Bldg Raleigh NC 27603

BENNETT, JONATHAN LEE, safety engineer; b. Union City, Tenn., Jan. 4, 1957; s. Charles Franklin and Martha Lu (Templeton) B.; m. Brenda Juanita Williams, Nov. 28, 1981; 1 child, Ashley Leigh. B.S. in Occupational Safety and Health, Murray State U., 1979. Loss control rep. Hewitt, Coleman and Assocs., Greenville, S.C., 1979-82; safety coordinator Container Corp. of Am., Brewton, Ala., 1982-84; safety and security dir. W.F. Hall Printing Co., Augusta, Ga., 1984-85; safety coordinator Container Corp. Am., Brewton, Ala., 1985—. Mem. Am. Soc. Safety Engrs., Nat. Safety Mgmt. Assn. Republican. Baptist. Avocations: golf; hunting; tennis. Home: 102 Glen Rd Brewton AL 36426 Office: Container Corp Am Brewton Timber Div Brewton AL 36426

BENNETT, KATHERINE ANN, cosmetics co. exec.; b. Alexandria, La., Dec. 12, 1939; d. Charles D. and Esther V. (Whaley) Ward; student Cambridge U., 1960, Mercer U., 1976-77; m. Preston G. Bennett; children—Kerry D. Wolfe, Michael W. Wolfe. Sec. treas. Yellow-Cab Co., Inc., Alexandria, 1962-70; dist. sales mgr. Avon Products, Inc., Atlanta, 1970-75, mgmt. assoc. 1975-77, div. sales mgr., 1977—. Loaned exec. United Way Campaign, Atlanta. Mem. Nat. Assn. Female Execs. Republican. Roman Catholic. Office: PO Box 105541 Atlanta GA 30348

BENNETT, LARRY THOMAS, real estate developer; b. Decatur, Ala., Sept. 14, 1952; s. Thomas Andrew and Alice Eloise (Riethmaier) B.; m. Deborah Lynn Herndon, Feb. 1, 1975; 1 son, Christopher Thomas. B.S. in Bus. Adminstrn. and Mgmt., Auburn U., 1976, M.B.A., 1976. Dist. mgr., area mgr., regional mgr. Mgmt. Enterprises, Inc., Atlanta, 1976-78, v.p., 1978-79, exec. v.p., 1979-80; pres. Calibre Mgmt., Inc., Atlanta, 1980-81; pres. Calibre Co. Ga., Inc., Atlanta, 1981—. Mem. Nat. Assn. Homebuilders, Atlanta Apt. Owners and Mgrs. Assn., Assn. Grad. Bus. Students, Cobb County C. of C. Methodist. Home: 2239 Rolland St Marietta GA 30062 Office: 5600 Roswell Rd Suite 200 Prado W Atlanta GA 30342

BENNETT, LEEMAN, football coach; b. Paducah, Ky., June 20, 1938; B.S., U. Ky., 1961. Asst. coach U. Ky., 1961-62, 65, U. Pitts., 1966, U. Cin., 1967-68, U.S. Naval Acad., 1969, St. Louis Cardinals, 1970-71, Detroit Lions, 1972, Los Angeles Rams, 1973-76; head coach Atlanta Falcons, 1977-82, Tampa Bay Buccaneers, 1985—. Address: Tampa Bay Buccaneers 1 Buccaneer Pl Tampa FL 33607*

BENNETT, LOWELL HOWARD, lawyer, health care systems executive, former government official; b. Charleston, S.C., Feb. 22, 1913; s. Henry William Benjamin and Chloe Ann (Howard) B.; m. Marian Clae Brown, June 5, 1941; 1 dau., Marian Clae. A.B. cum laude, Fisk U., 1935; postgrad. Grad. Sch. U. Chgo., J.D., 1950; L.H.D., Allen U., 1964. Bar: Minn. 1950. Field sec. Fisk U., Nashville, 1935-39; Julius Rosenwald fellow Grad. Sch. U. Chgo., 1939-41, Law Sch., 1947-50; dir. Avery Inst., Charleston, 1941-44; regional dir. USO, Kansas City, Mo., 1944-45; field dir. Am. Council on Race Relations, 1945-47; mem. Hall, Smith and Hedlund, Mpls., 1950-57; ptnr. Hall, Smith, Hedlund, Bennett, Juster, Forsberg and Merlin, Mpls., 1955-57, Hall, Smith, Hedlund et al, Mpls., 1960-63; judge Minn. State Ct., Mpls., 1957-60; apptd. prin. asst. to dep. asst. sec. Dept. Def., Washington, 1965-69, dep. asst. sec. def. for civil rights and equal opportunity, 1969-71; chmn. bd., pres. Magnolias Nursing and Convalescent Center, Pensacola, Fla., 1975—; v.p., dir. Community Convalescent Center, Mobile, Ala., 1979—; cons. GAO, Washington, 1973-74. Exec. sec. Mayor's Biracial Council, Charleston, 1942-44; v.p. Progressive Democratic Party of S.C., Charleston, 1943-44; mem. Alumni Senate U. Chgo., 1964-66; exec. com. United Bd. Coll. Devel., Atlanta, 1983; bd. dirs. Escambia Govt. Study Comm., 1986; organizer and 1st exec. sec. Negro Community Council, Charleston, 1941-44; mem. exec. bd. dirs. Chgo. Council Against Racial and Religious Discrimination, Chgo., 1949-51; pres. Mpls. br. NAACP, 1956-56; bd. dirs., pres. Mpls. Urban League, 1960-61; bd. dirs., exec. com. Hennepin County Community Chest (United Way), Mpls., 1957-63; mem. fgn. relations com., adv. council Dem. Nat. Com., 1957-61; mem. state central com. and 5th dist. com. Minn. Dem. Farmer Labor Party, Mpls., 1956-63. Mem. ABA, Hennepin County Bar Assn., Minn. State Bar Assn., Nat. Bar Assn., Am. Soc. Pub. Adminstrn., Alumni Assn. of Law Sch. U. Chgo. (bd. dirs. 1974-80), Pensacola Area C. of C. (pvt. industry council and edn. task force 1983), Phi Beta Kappa. Methodist. Clubs: Ambassador, Executive (Pensacola). Office: Magnolias Nursing and Convalescent Center 600 W Gregory St Pensacola FL 32501

BENNETT, MARSHALL GOODLOE, JR., state official, lawyer; b. Lexington, Miss., Dec. 25, 1943; s. Marshall G. and Tavia (Childress) B.; m. Shirley Shelton, July 15, 1963; children—Steven, Elizabeth, Russell. B.A., U. Miss., 1965, J.D., 1967. Bar: Miss. 1967, U.S. Supreme Ct. 1971. Exec. dir. Miss. Crime Commn., Jackson, 1967-68; asst. atty. gen. State of Miss., Jackson, 1970-72, 74-79; asst. dist. atty. 7th Dist., State of Miss., Jackson, 1972-74; adminstrv. asst. to gov. State of Miss., Jackson, 1980-81; chmn., commr. Miss. Workmen's Compensation Commn., Jackson, 1981—; ptnr. Peters, Royals, Bennett, & Jackson, 1972-74. Pres. Nat. Soc. Prevent Blindness, Jackson, 1984-85, So. Workers Compensation Adminstrs., Atlanta, 1984; treas., bd. dirs. State YMCA, Jackson, 1980; bd. dirs. Community Trust Found. Miss., Jackson, 1985. Served to capt. U.S. Army, 1968-70. Mem. Jackson Young Lawyers Assn. (sec. 1972), Miss. State Bar Assn. Democrat. United Methodist. Home: 933 Briarfield Rd Jackson MS 39211 Office: Miss Worker's Compensation Commn 1428 Lakeland Dr Jackson MS 39216

BENNETT, MAX LEON, judge; b. Kingsville, Tex., May 6, 1938; s. Roy Chilton and Zachie Ford (Dunahay) B.; student Tex. A&I U., 1956-57; B.A., Baylor U., 1960, J.D., 1962; m. Betty Joyce Trapp, Dec. 23, 1961; children—Catherine, Susan. Bar: Tex. 1962. Atty., Humble Oil and Refining Co., Corpus Christi, Tex., 1962-65; practiced in Corpus Christi, 1965—; partner Howard, McDowell, Bennett and Cartwright, 1973-75; judge Nueces County Ct. at Law, 1974-78, 319th Jud. Dist. Ct., 1979—; instr. in law adult edn. Del Mar Coll., Corpus Christi, 1971-72. Bd. dirs. Corpus Christi Boys Club, 1973—, pres., 1975—; bd. dirs. Coastal Bend Youth City, 1982—; mem. devel. council Baylor U., 1973—. Fellow Internat. Acad. Trial Judges, Tex. Bar Found.; mem. Tex., Nueces County (pres. 1968-69) trial lawyers assns., Nueces County Bar Assn. (dir. 1972-74), Coastal Bend Baylor Alumni Club (pres. 1972-73), Baylor U. Alumni Assn. (dir. 1978—). Author: Criminal Proceedings in County Courts in Texas. Office: Nueces County Courthouse Corpus Christi TX 78401

BENNETT, RAYMOND TERRY, lawyer; b. Muskogee, Okla., July 3, 1945; s. Raymond H. and Barbaranelle (Standfield) B.; m. Kay Camille Liverman, June 17, 1967; children—Brian, Tiffany. A.B., Coll. William and Mary 1967, J.D. (Disting. Mil. grad., Army ROTC scholar) Wake Forest U., 1970. Bar: N.C. 1970, Ky. 1974, U.S. Dist. Ct. (we. dist.) Ky. 1976, U.S. Ct. Mil. Appeals 1970, U.S. Sup. Ct. 1973, U.S. Ct. Appeals (6th cir.) 1982. Law clk. to Atty. Elkin, N.C., 1969-70; ptnr. Skeeters and Bennett, Radcliff, Ky., from 1974, now city atty. City of Radcliff; prof. bus. law U. Md., 1972-73, Elizabethtown Community Coll., 1978-81. Served to capt. JAGC, U.S. Army, 1970-74. Asst. Sunday Sch. dir. and bus. moderator Stithton Bapt. Ch.; mem. Ky. Public Health Task Force on Alcoholism and Alcohol, 1976-79; coach Peanut League and Little League Baseball, 1977—, North Hardin Little League Basketball, 1978—; mem. adv. bd. Elizabethtown Community Coll., 1979—; hon. mem. Boy Scouts Am., Ky. Sheriffs Assn. Recipient Am. Jurisprudence award, 1970; Am. Legion Excellence award, 1970; hon. Ky. Col., 1969; Disting. Service award Jaycees, 1976, Radcliff C. of C., 1978, others, including mil. decorations. Mem. ABA, Am. Judicature Soc., Ky. State Bar (ho. of dels. 1983—, chmn. elect local govt. sect.), Hardin County Bar Assn. (v.p. 1980), Eta Sigma Phi. Democrat. Assoc. editor Wake Forest Law Rev., 1969-70. Clubs: Jaycees, Rotary (Radcliff). Office: 550 W Lincoln Trail Blvd Radcliff KY 40160

BENNETT, RICHARD EDWIN, shopping center executive; b. Oshkosh, Wis., July 29, 1943; s. Richard Howell, Jr. and Dorothy Coroline (Brain) B.; student U. Wis., 1961-63, 67-68; m. Priscilla Kowalski, Nov. 25, 1967; children—Richard Howell, Jean Ann, Carol Ann. Asst. mgr. Robert Hall Clothes, Janesville, Wis., 1968-69; v.p., gen. mgr. Bennett Industries, Inc., St. Petersburg, Fla., 1969-72, dir., 1969—; asst. mgr., then mgr. W.T. Grant Co., Mt. Dora, Fla., 1972-76; asst. gen. mgr. Rouse Co., Tampa (Fla.) Bay Center, 1976-78, v.p., gen. mgr. Charlottetown Mall (now Outlet Sq.), Charlotte, N.C., 1978-82; dir. property mgmt. Mgmt. Resource Services, Inc., Greensboro, 1982-84; gen. mgr. Shannon Mall, Atlanta, 1984-86; adv. Union City Devel. Authority; partner Bennett & Assocs., 1982—; Atlanta regional mgr. Cadillac Fairview Shopping Ctrs. (U.S.) Ltd., 1986—. Served with AUS, 1963-66. Lic. real estate broker, Inst. Real Estate Mgmt. Mem. South Fulton C. of C., Atlanta C. of C. (Southside devel. task force), Internat. Internat. Council Shopping Centers. Home: 4539 Cherie Glen Trail Stone Mountain GA 30083 Office: 2050 Lawrenceville Hwy Decatur GA 30033

BENNETT, RICHARD HOWELL, JR., former sales executive; b. Chgo., Aug. 10, 1916; s. Richard Howell and Beatrice (Schiebel) B.; student U. Ill., 1935-37; m. Dorothy Caroline Brain, Dec. 28, 1940; children—Carol Ann Bennett Matenaer, Richard Edwin, Dorothy Marion Bennett Shope. Buyer coll. textbook dept. Wilcox & Follett, Chgo., 1937-42; salesman Bauer-Black, Oshkosh, Wis. and Detroit, 1942-47; salesman, dist. mgr., regional mgr., nat. sales mgr. U.S. Time Corp., N.Y.C., 1947-54; gen. sales mgr. Amity Leather Products, West Bend, Wis., 1954-64; mdse. coordinator Am. Optical Co., Boston, 1964-65; nat. sales mgr. Bentley Lighter Corp., N.Y.C., 1965-69; Fla. regional mgr. Garrity Industries, Inc., Stamford, Conn., 1969—; chmn. bd. Bennett Industries, Inc., Naples, Fla., 1969—; v.p., cons. Meeker Co., Joplin, Mo., 1976-77, Bruce Shope Enterprises, 1977-81. Mem. Fed. Wholesale Druggists Assn., Nat. Assn. Tobacco Distbrs., Nat. Assn. Chain Drug Stores, Mawanda Assn. of U. Ill., Delta Alpha Epsilon. Clubs: Boston Skating, Glades Country (Naples). Home: 180 Harrison Rd Glades Apt G-4 Naples FL 33962

BENNETT, ROBERT MCARN, automobile dealer; b. Cheraw, S.C., Apr. 13, 1932; s. Russell Evans and Mary Ella (Gandy) B.; m. Mary Murray Paulling, Aug. 1, 1953; children—Robert McArn, D. Paulling, J. McCauley. Student, Duke U., 1950-52; A.B., U. S.C., 1954. Pres., Bennett Motor Co., Cheraw, 1954—; v.p. Russell Bennett Chevrolet-Buick-Mazda, Rockingham, N.C., 1973—; dir. 1st Fed. Savs. & Loan; adv. mem. 1st Citizens Bank & Trust. Ruling elder, clk. First Presbyterian Ch., Cheraw; trustee Pee Dee Presbytery, U. S.C. Mem. Chevrolet Dealer Council, Oldsmobile Dealer Council, Buick Dealer Council, Jr. C. of C. (past pres.). Clubs: Cheraw Country (past pres.), Country of N.C., So. Pines, Palmetto (Columbia, S.C.) Home: 409 Greene St Cheraw SC 29520 Office: Bennett Motor Co PO Box 231 Hwy 9 W Cheraw SC 29520

BENNETT, ROLLAND LEE, academic librarian, genealogical researcher; b. Lansing, Mich., Feb. 24, 1926; s. Chester Earl and Mary Marie (Knight) B.; m. Mary Esther Guiles, Aug. 8, 1953; children—Sanford E., Leland G. B.A., Greenville Coll., 1952; M.A., Western Mich. U., 1958, M.S.L.S., 1963. Dir. Coopersville High Sch. Learning Ctr. (Mich.), 1963-68; reference librarian Ruby E. Dare Library, Greenville Coll. (Ill.), 1968-74; acad. librarian Morrison-Kenyon Library, Asbury Coll., Wilmore, Ky., 1974—, dir. library service, 1974-81, acquisition librarion, 1981—. Mem. Hist. Commn. Free Methodist Ch. N.A., 1968-82. Served with U.S. Army, 1944-46. Mem. Ky. Edn. Assn., Ky. Library Assn., Jessamine County Hist. Soc. (sec.), Washington County Hist. Soc., Ky. Hist. Soc., Soc. Genealogists. Democrat. Club: Scriberious Ten (Wilmore). Poetry published in numerous magazines. Home: 139 Lowry Ln Wilmore KY 40390 Office: Morrison Kenyon Library Asbury Coll Wilmore KY 40390

BENNETT, SOLON ANTHONY, city official; b. Chgo., Sept. 21, 1922; s. Anthony Constantine and Anna C. (Damofli) B.; B.S., Ill. Inst. Tech., 1951, postgrad., 1951-52; postgrad. Ariz. State U., 1957-65; m. Loretta J. LaValley, June 3, 1958; children—Leslie Anne, Christopher Solon, Stephen Anthony. Mem. mfg. engring. staff Internat. Harvester Co., Chgo., 1945-52; mem. purchasing mgmt. staff Garrett Corp., Phoenix, 1952-67; dir. purchasing State of Ariz., Phoenix, 1967-68, Overhead Door Corp., Dallas, 1968-71; dir. purchasing City of Austin (Tex.), 1971—; instr. U. Tex., 1974—, Austin Community Coll., 1975—; mem. Joint Fed., State and Local Govt. Adv. Panel on Procurement and Supply, 1975-77; mem. adv. com. on pub. purchasing and materials mgmt. U. Tex., 1974—; chmn. mkt. adv. com. Austin Community Coll., 1975—. Served with USAAF, 1944-45. Mem. Nat. Inst. Govtl. Purchasing (dir. 1975—, pres. 1982; cert. pub. purchasing officer), Inst. Purchasing and Supply Gt. Britain (v.p. 1983), Nat. Assn. Purchasing Mgmt. (Profl. Devel. Person of Yr. award 1979, cert.), Nat. Contract Mgmt. Assn. (cert.), Am. Prodn. and Inventory Control Soc. Sect. editor Aljian's Purchasing Handbook, 4th edit., 1982. Home: 4201 Endcliffe Dr Austin TX 78731 Office: City of Austin Mcpl Bldg Austin TX 78767

BENNETT, STEPHANIE MITCHELL, college president; b. Albuquerque, Jan. 19, 1941; d. Claude Stephen and Alma Nelle (Cashion) Mitchell; 1 child, Brendan T. B.A., U. N.Mex., 1963, M.A., 1966; Ph.D., U. Iowa, 1973. Instr. Loretto Heights Coll., Denver, 1967-68; asst. prof. Albion Coll., Mich., 1968-76; dean Westhampton Coll., U. Richmond, Va., 1976-84; pres. Centenary Coll., Hackettstown, N.J., 1984—; pres. So. Assn. Colls. for Women, 1981-82; state coordinator Va. Women Adminstrs. Program, 1983-84; bd. dirs., exec. com. Va. Women's Cultural Hist. Project, Richmond, 1983-84. Author filmstrip series Am. Invention and Ingenuity, 1968. Contbr. articles and book revs. to profl. jours. Pres. Maymont Vol. Guild, Richmond, 1980-81. Ford Found. fellow, 1963-65, Earhart Found. fellow, 1974, NEH summer fellow, 1975, program grantee Xerox, IBM, 1978. Mem. Am. Studies Assn., Assn. for Study Higher Edn. Episcopalian. Avocation: hiking.

BENNETT, TERRY RANDOLPH, dentist; b. Erick, Okla., July 31, 1950; s. Lowell A. and Veneda R. (Brooks) B.; m. Kathleen A. Kauffman, Aug. 22, 1971; children—Amy Denise, Megan Rae, Chase Alan. B.S., Okla. State U., 1972; D.M.D., U. Louisville, 1977. Pvt. practice dentistry, Cleveland, Okla., 1977—. Deacon, First Christian Ch., Cleveland, 1981—. Named Man of Yr., Beta Sigma Phi, Cleveland, 1981. Mem. ADA, Okla. Dental Assn. (house del. 1982-84), Am. Orthodontic Soc., Am. Straight Wire Orthodontic Soc., Cleveland Jaycees (v.p. 1981-82). Republican. Lodge: Rotary. Avocations: snow skiing; tennis; golf; photography. Home: Route 1 Box 18B Cleveland OK 74020 Office: PO Box 590 Cleveland OK 74020

BENNETT, VELA LEE, educator; b. Gadsden, Ala., May 3, 1918; d. Alto Velo and Eloise (Frost) Lee; m. Daniel Dozier Bennett, Sept. 25, 1940; children—Daniel D., Alto Lee. B.S., U. Ala., 1939; postgrad. U. Tenn., 1975. Cert. tchr., Ala., Tenn. Tchr. Bearden Jr. High, Knoxville, Tenn., 1957-81, Knoxville Catholic High Sch., 1981-83. Vol. E. Tenn. Children's Hosp., Knoxville, Med. Library, Knoxville, Knoxville Symphony Orchestra, U. Tenn. Theater, Knoxville. Named Outstanding Tchr. Knoxville Pub. Schs., 1980. Mem. NEA, Nat. Council of Math. Tchrs., Tenn. Edn. Assn., DAR, Knoxville Exec. Club, Delta Kappa Gamma, Alpha Gamma Delta, P.E.O. Democrat. Methodist. Avocations: reading, cooking, travel. Home: 5607 N Century Ct Knoxville TN 37919

BENNETT, WAYNE MICHAEL, dentist; b. Brookline, Mass., Feb. 23, 1946; s. Robert and Shirley (Malenbaum) B.; m. Susan Ann Walz, Apr. 8, 1970; children—Kimberly Ann, Brian Christopher. A.B., U. N.C., 1967; D.M.D., Med. U. S.C., 1971. Pvt. practice dentistry, Longwood, Fla., 1973—; team dentist Orlando Renegades, Minn. and Orlando Twins; cons. Dept. Profl. Regulation, Tallahassee, 1980—. Pres. bd. dirs. Easter Seals Soc. Orange, Osceola, and Seminole Counties, Orlando, Fla., 1977-78; bd. dirs. Fla. Citrus Bowl, Orlando, 1979—; mem. Fla. Gov.'s Council Phys. Fitness and Sports, Tallahassee, 1981-85. Served to capt. U.S. Army, 1971-73. Mem. Acad. Sports Dentistry (charter founder), ADA, Fla. Dental Assn., Ctr. Dist. Dental Soc., Orange County Dental Soc. (dir. pub. relations 1978). Democrat. Club: Rotary (Seminole County) (bd. dirs. 1985—). Avocations: golf; photography. Office: 840-C State Rd 434 N Altamonte Springs FL 32714

BENNETT, WILLIAM SABIN, III, operations analyst, educator; b. Rawlins, Wyo., Mar. 20, 1923; s. William Sabin Bennett, Jr. and Alice Elinor (Downer) McCord; m. Grace Marion Hayes, Mar. 2, 1945; children—Arthur, William IV, Gale, Linda, Deborah, Susan. B.A., Williams Coll., 1946; M.A., Duke U., 1947; Ph.D., Am. U., 1965. Group leader Los Alamos Sci. Lab., N.Mex., 1951-53, 69-76, study chmn. Ops. Research Office, Johns Hopkins U., Bethesda, Md., 1955-60; project leader SRI Internat., Menlo Park, Calif., 1961-69, 77; sr. assoc. Los Alamos Tech. Assocs., 1978-79; staff mem. Inst. for Def. Analyses, Alexandria, Va., 1979-84; mem. faculty Southampton Acad., Courtland, Va., 1985. Contbr. articles, reports to profl. pubs. Pres. Los Alamos Humanities Council, 1976. Served with USN, 1943-45, PTO. Fellow AAAS; mem. Ops. Research Soc. Am., Inst. Mgmt. Scis., N.Y. Acad. Scis., Am. Statis. Assn., Phi Beta Kappa, Sigma Xi, Sigma Pi Sigma. Avocations: travel, computers. Home: 419 Shands Dr Courtland VA 23837 Office: Southampton Acad 320 Old Plank Rd Courtland VA 23837

BENNINGTON, RICHARD ROY, business educator, researcher, author; b. Marion, Va., May 17, 1945; s. Roy Alfred and Virginia (Eastridge) B.; m. Barbara Winn, Dec. 28, 1971 (div. 1983); 1 child, Sarah. B.A., Emory and Henry Coll., 1967; M.B.A., Va. Poly. Inst. and State U., 1969; Ed.D., U. Ga., 1974. Tchr. bus. Averett Coll., Danville, Va., 1969-72; head bus. sch. High Point Coll., N.C., 1975—, prof. bus., 1981—, coordinator home furnishings mktg. program, 1983—; bus. adv. com. Guilford Tech., Jamestown, N.C., 1980—. Author: Furniture Marketing, 1985; also articles. Recipient Outstanding Grad. Research award U. Ga., 1976. Mem. High Point C. of C. (small bus. com.), Delta Mu Delta (faculty advisor 1975—), Phi Kappa Phi, Delta Pi Epsilon, Kappa Delta Pi, Sigma Mu. Methodist. Clubs: Positive Single Connection (steering com.), Toastmasters. Avocations: golf; collecing soda pop bottles and advertising; antiques; refinishing furniture. Home: 1216 Guilford Ave High Point NC 27262 Office: High Point Coll 933 Montlieu Ave High Point NC 27262

BENOIT, KENNETH ROGER, composer, conductor, music librarian; b. Coral Gables, Fla., Oct. 12, 1952; s. Albert Harvey and Mary (Mosca) B.; m. Barbara Gale Rogers, Apr. 3, 1982. A.A., Miami-Dade Community Coll., 1972; B.A., U. West Fla., 1974; M.Mus., U. Miami, 1978; M.Sc., Fla. State U., 1979. Music librarian Miami-Dade Pub. Library (Fla.), 1979-84. Asst. condr. North Miami Community Concert Band (Fla.), 1982-84. Composer: Symphony No. 1 in G Minor, 1976; Requiem, 1978; String Quartet in A Minor, 1978; Missa brevis in F Major, 1982; Suite No. 2 for Piano, 1984; Gestures, 1984; String Quartet No. 2, 1984; Model Impressions for Chamber Ensemble, 1985; Evolution, 1985; Hill Songs, 1986; Air, 1986. Mem. ASCAP, Am. Soc. Univ. Composers, Am. Symphony Orch. League, Condrs. Guild. Democrat. Methodist. Home: 1475 NE 111th St Apt 109 Miami FL 33161

BENSKI, RAYMOND, physician, educator; b. Bridgeport, Conn., Sept. 18, 1931; s. Casimir Francis and Margaret (Phelke) B.; m. Sandra Laputz, Sept. 5, 1964; children—Bradley Raymond, Pamela Ann. B.S. in Pharmacy, U. Houston, 1954; M.D., U. Tex., 1962. Diplomat Am. Bd. Family Practice. Intern Green Hosp., San Antonio, 1962-63; owner, physician Family Clinic P.A., Nederland, Tex., 1963—; chief staff Mid Jeff Hosp., Nederland, 1969, 80; co-dir. U. Tex. FPC Residency Program, Port Arthur, Tex., 1981-82; clin. assoc. prof. U. Tex., Port Arthur, 1982—. Committeeman, Republican Party of Tex., Austin, 1980—; del. Rep. Nat. Conv., Detroit and Dallas, 1980-84; regional dir. Phil Gramm for Senate, Beaumont, Tex., 1984. Served to capt. M.C., U.S. Army, 1954-69. Mem. Jefferson County Med. Soc., Tex. Med. Assn., AMA, Tex. Acad. Family Physicians, Am. Acad. Family Physicians, VFW, Am. Legion. Republican. Episcopalian. Lodges. Masons, Shriners. Avocations: stamp collecting; personal computers. Home: 927 30th St Nederland TX 77627 Office: Family Clinic PA 1323 South 27th St Nederland TX 77627

BENSON, BETTY JONES, educator; b. Barrow County, Ga., Jan. 11, 1928; d. George C. and Bertha (Mobley) Jones; B.S. in Edn., N. Ga. U., Dahlonega, 1958; M.Ed. in Curriculum and Supervision, U. Ga., Athens, 1968, edn. specialist in Curriculum and Supervision, 1970; m. George T. Benson; children—George Steven, Elizabeth Gayle, James Claud, Robert Benjamin. Tchr. Forsyth County (Ga.) Bd. Edn., Cumming, 1956-66, curriculum dir., 1966—; asst. supt. for instrn. Forsyth County Schs., 1981—. Active Alpine Center for Disturbed Children; chmn. Ga. Lake Lanier Island Authority; mem. N. Ga. Coll. Edn. Adv. Com., Ga. Textbook Com.; adv. Boy Scouts; Sunday sch. tchr. 1st Baptist Ch. Cumming. Mem. NEA, Ga. Assn. Educators (dir.), Nat., Ga. (pres.) assns. supervision and curriculum devel., Assn. Childhood Edn. Internat., Bus. and Profl. Women's Club, Internat. Platform Assn., Ga. Future Tchrs. Adv. Assn. (pres.), HeadStart Dirs. Assn., Forsyth County Hist. Soc. Home: Route 1 Box 12 Cumming GA 30130 Office: 101 School St Cumming GA 30130

BENSON, DON GEHR, JR., palynologist; b. Houston, Sept. 3, 1940; s. Don Gehr and Patricia (Shamblin) B.; m. Katherine Mae Adams, Oct. 27, 1962; children—Patricia Lynn, Elizabeth Lea. B.S., Tulane U., 1962; Ph.D., U. Va.-Charlottesville, 1965; M.S., Va. Poly. Inst., 1975. Asst. prof. biology La. State U., Baton Rouge, 1965-67, Va. Poly. Inst., Blacksburg, 1967-72; paleontologist Texaco, Inc., New Orleans, 1975-78; sr. staff palynologist Amoco Prodn. Co., New Orleans, 1978—. Contbr. articles to profl. jours. Mem. Am. Assn. Stratigraphic Palynologists (pres.-elect), Am. Assn. Petroleum Geologists, Soc. Econ. Paleontologists and Mineralogists, New Orleans Geol. Soc., Nat. Rifle Assn., La. Shooting Assn., Sigma Xi (Andrew Fleming award 1965). Republican. Methodist. Club: Southwest Gun (McComb, Miss.). Avocations: competitive shooting; gunsmith. Office: Amoco Prodn Co PO Box 50879 New Orleans LA 70150

BENSON, HARRY EDDIE, agricultural extension service manager; b. Port Arthur, Tex., Dec. 13, 1925; s. William H. and Eddie Arkie (Rhea) B.; A.B.S., Lamar Jr. Coll., 1947; B.S., U. Houston, 1953; m. Mary Nell Harwell, Aug. 20, 1949; children—Elizabeth Ann Benson-Smith, David Harwell. Estimator prodn. man Gulf Printing Co., Houston, 1952-59, prodn. mgr., 1959; typographer Naylor Type 1962-84, Mats, Houston, 1959-60; estimator prodn. man Webb Printing Co., Houston, 1960, Western Lithograph Co. Tex., Houston, 1960-61; buyer Tenneco Inc., Houston, 1961-67, purchasing rep., 1967-72, mgr. corp. procurement, 1972-75, mgr. purchasing and forms adminstrn., 1975-82; publ. services mgr. Tex. Agrl. Extension Service, College Station, 1982—; instr. in forms adminstrn. North Harris County; instr. graphic communications Main Campus U. Houston. Pres. Oak Forest Civic Club, 1963-64; v.p. Nottingham Civic Club, 1965-66; precinct committeeman Harris County Rep. party, 1964, chmn. Neighbor to Neighbor fund drive, 1965-66, dir. public relations, 1966-69, mem. public relations com., 1969-70, del. county/dist. and state conv., 1962-84, alt. del. Rep. nat. conv., 1964; advisory com. Houston Ind. Sch. Dist. Office Edn., Printing Tech. Dept., San Jacinto Coll.; edn. com. Printing Industries of Gulf Coast; graphic communications career edn. council Tex. Edn. Agency; mem. adv. council for program standards in graphics Am. Vocat. Assn.; participant project bus. Jr. Achievement; adv. council Pittsburg (Kans.) State U. Sch. Printing. Recipient Ben Franklin award, Houston Printing Week Com., 1974; named Graphic Communicator of Yr., Graphic Communication Council of Houston, 1979. Mem. Purchasing Mgmt. Assn. Houston (local bd. dirs. 1976-79, newsletter editor, co-chmn. publicity Dist. II), Bus. Forms Mgmt. Assn. Houston (pres. 1977-79, v.p. internat. of Dist. II, internat., Region II, local outstanding mem. of year 1976-77, outstanding mem. of year Dist. II 1977-78, internat., 1978-79), Houston Litho Club, Internat. Graphic Arts Edn. Assn., Graphic Arts Tech. Found., Nat. Assn. Printing Buyers (organizing dir.), Tex. Assn. Bus., Nat. Composition Assn. Methodist. Clubs: Masons, KT, Shriners. Contbr. articles to publs., 1951-82; conf. speaker, 1976. Home: 13930 Barryknoll Ln Houston TX 77079 Office: 102 Reed McDonald Bldg College Station TX 77843

BENSON, JAMES MICHAEL, management consultant; b. Tampa, Fla., Jan. 6, 1947; s. Hilton Rollins and Betty Jo (Alderman) B.; m. Connie Cope, Dec. 20, 1968; children—Michelle, Heather, James Michael, Jr. B.A., U. South Fla., 1970. Mgr. customer service Systams Corp., Tampa, 1967-73; v.p. Fails & Assocs., Tampa, 1973-80; sr. v.p. Cheezem Devel. Corp., St. Petersburg, Fla., 1980-81; pres. Mancon Assocs., Tampa, 1981-83, Focus Cons. Group, Tampa; chief exec. officer Inst. Mgmt. Execs., Tampa, 1983—. Contbr. articles to profl. jours. Mem. Am. Soc. Tng. and Devel., Assoc. Gen. Contractors, Assoc. Builders and Contractors, Petroleum Equipment Inst., C. of C. Republican. Mem. Ch. of Christ. Lodge: Rotary. Avocation: public speaking. Office: Inst Mgmt Excellence PO Box 290062 Temple Terrace FL 33687

BENSON, NETTIE LEE, history educator; b. Arcadia, Tex., Jan. 15, 1905; d. Jasper William and Vora Ann (Reddell) B. Student Tex. Presbyn. Coll., 1922-24; B.A., U. Tex., Austin, 1929, M.A., 1935, Ph.D., 1949. High sch. tchr., Monterrey, Mex., 1925-27; public sch. tchr., Sinton, Tex., 1927-28, Hartley, Tex., 1930-31; high sch. tchr., Ingleside, Tex., 1932-41; librarian Latin Am. collection U. Tex., Austin, 1942-75, prof. Mexican history, 1962—, prof. library sci., 1964-75; Latin Am. Coop. Acquisition Project agt. N.Y. Public Library and Steebert-Hafner, Inc., 1960-62; pres. Seminar Acquisition Latin Am. Library Materials, 1970-71, Internat. Congress Mexican Studies, 1972; mem. task force on libraries Info. Resources Internat. Edn., Am. Council Edn., 1974. Recipient S.W. Council on Latin Am. Studies award for distinction in scholarship and teaching, 1968-69; Disting. Service award Conf. Latin Am. History, Am. Hist. Assn., 1976, Capt. Alonso de Leon medal Nuevo Leon Soc. History, Geography and Stats., 1974, Disting. Alumni award U. Tex., Austin, 1981; Nettie Lee Benson Collection named by U. Tex. bd. regents, 1975; decorated Order of Aztec Eagle (Mex.). Fellow Tex. Hist. Assn.; mem. Am. Hist. Assn., Conf. Latin Am. Studies, Latin Am. Studies Assn., Sigma Delta Pi, Phi Alpha Theta, Pi Kappa Alpha. Democrat. Presbyterian. Author: La Diputacion provincial y el federalismo mexicano, 1955; Mexico and the Spanish Cortes 1810-1822, 1968. Translator: The United States versus Porfirio Diaz, 1964. Mem. editorial bd. Hispanic Am. Hist. Rev., 1974-80. Contbr. articles to profl. jours. Home: 2834 Shoal Crest St Austin TX 78705

BENSON, RONALD EDWARD, state humanities program executive, clergyman, educator; b. Pine Ridge, S.D., June 19, 1936; s. Edward William, Jr., and Mary Jewett (Mixter) B.; m. Donna Kathryn Ellis, Mar. 30, 1956; children—Ronald Edward, Paul Louis, Kathryn Mary. B.A., Mich. State U., 1958, Ph.D., 1970; M.Div., Drew U., 1961. Ordained to ministry United Methodist Church, 1961. Pastor, Wesley United Meth. Ch., Warren, Mich., 1961-67; asst. prof. philosophy McKendree Coll., Lebanon, Ill., 1970-71; asst. prof. philosophy Ohio No. U., Ada, 1971-73, assoc. prof., 1973-80, prof., 1980-82; pres., exec. dir. Ga. Endowment for the Humanities, Emory U., Atlanta, 1980—, vis. prof. philosophy, Emory U., 1981, adj. prof. philosophy, 1982—. Citizens' adv. council Warren Consol. Schs., vice-chmn. steering com., 1963-66; exec. com. and bd. dirs. West-Central Ohio Health Systems Agy., Lima, 1976-77; mem. exec. com., sec. bd. dirs., trustee NW Ohio Hospice Assn., Toledo, 1978-80; apptd. to Statewide Health Coordinating Council, advisory to State Health Planning and Devel. Agy., Ohio Dept. Health, 1976-80, chmn. com., 1977-80. Mem. Soc. Health and Human Values, Am. Philos. Assn., Ga. Adult Edn. Assn., Ga. Hist. Soc. Contbr. articles in field to publs. Home: 3683 Toxaway Ct Atlanta GA 30341 Office: 1589 Clifton Rd NE Emory Univ Atlanta GA 30322

BENSON, STANLEY HUGH, librarian; b. Sparta, Ill., Oct. 1, 1930; s. Edward Hugh and Laurence (Sanders) B.; B.S., So. Ill. U., 1951; B.D., Southwestern Bapt. Theol. Sem., 1956, Th.D., 1964; M.L.S., U. Tex.-Austin, 1965; Ph.D., U. Okla., 1979; m. Sara Elizabeth Collins, Dec. 28, 1959; children—Andrew, Raymond. Library asst. Tex. Christian U., 1959-61; head librarian Ky. So. Coll., 1964-68, Gardner-Webb Coll., 1968-69, Berry Coll., 1969-71; head librarian Okla. Bapt. U., Shawnee, 1971—, dir. Mabee Learning Center, 1976-85; dir. library services Carson-Newman Coll., Jefferson City, Tenn., 1985—; instr. library sci. and religion, part-time 1964—. Lilly Endowment fellow Am. Theol. Library Assn., 1963. Mem. ALA, Okla. Library Assn., Assn. Coll. and Research Libraries (pres. Okla. chpt. 1983). Baptist. Home: Route 1 Box 34 New Market TN 37820 Office: Carson-Newman Coll Library Jefferon City TN 37760

BENSTOCK, GERALD MARTIN, uniform manufacturing executive; b. Bay Shore, N.Y., May 7, 1930; s. David Lewis and Jane M. B.; m. Joan Kline, Nov. 18, 1951; children—Susan, Wendy, Michael, Peter. B.S., N.Y. U., 1951. Formerly v.p. Superior Surg. Mgf. Co., Inc., Seminole, Fla., now chmn. bd., pres., chief exec. officer; lectr. in field. Author articles in field. Pres. United Jewish Appeal, Fedn. Jewish Philanthropies, 1965-79; dir. Com. of 100 of Pinellas County. Mem. Textile Rental Services Assn., Am. Hotel Assn., Am. Hosp. Assn., Assn. Contamination Control. Home: 3126 Tiffany Dr Belleair Beach FL 33535 Office: Superior Surg Mfg Co Inc Seminole Blvd at 110th Terr Seminole FL 33542

BENT, DEVIN, political scientist, educator, consultant; b. Washington, Apr. 7, 1940; s. Donn N. and Gail J. (Jones) B.; m. Judith Gold, Oct. 11, 1967; children—Jennifer, John. B.A., George Washington U., 1965; Ph.D., Columbia U., 1974. Asst. prof. polit. sci. Jersey City State Coll., 1969-76; fellow in polit. sci. U. Wis.-Madison, 1976-77; spl. asst. to mayor City of Atlanta, 1977-78; coordinator pub. adminstrn. James Madison U., Harrisonburg, Va., 1978—; assoc. sci. Idaho Nat. Engring. Lab., Idaho Falls, 1980; cons. Office of Chief of Staff U.S. Army, Washington, 1983—. Contbr. articles to profl. jours. Co-pres. Anthony-Seeger P.T.A., Harrisonburg, 1980; tchr. Schs. Without Walls, Atlanta, 1978. Ford Found. fellow, 1972, NEH, 1977; recipient Commander's award U.S. Army, 1982. Mem. Am. Polit. Sci. Assn., Am. Soc. Pub. Adminstrn. Home: 320 Franklin St Harrisonburg VA 22801 Office: Polit Sci Dept James Madison U Harrisonburg VA 22807

BENT, HENRY ALBERT, chemist, educator; b. Cambridge, Mass., Dec. 21, 1926; s. Henry Edward and Florence Elizabeth (Demo) B.; m. Asenath Anne McKnight, Aug. 19, 1959; children—Brian Edward, Elizabeth Graves. A.B., Oberlin Coll., 1949; Ph.D., U. Calif.-Berkeley, 1952. Instr. phys. chemistry U. Conn., Storrs, 1952-55; research fellow, prof. inorganic chemistry U. Minn., Mpls., 1955-69; prof. phys. chemistry N.C. State U., Raleigh, 1969—. Author: The Second Law, 1965; Chemical Thermodynamics, 1981; contbr. articles to profl. jours. Served with USN, 1944-46. Fellow AAAS, mem. Am. Chem. Soc., Am. Phys. Soc., Phi Beta Kappa, Sigma Xi. Democrat. Office: NC State U Chemistry Dept Dabney Hall Raleigh NC 27695

BENTLEY, CLARENCE EDWARD, savings and loan association executive; b. Ranger, Tex., Oct. 9, 1921; s. Clarence Edward and Rosa Estelle (Bryant) B.; student McMurry Coll., Abilene, Tex., 1939-42; m. Gloria Gill, Oct. 9, 1943; children—Jon, Kitty, Perry. Pres., Abilene Savs. Assn., 1944-77, Southwestern Group Fin. Co., Houston, 1976-77; pres. United Savs. Assn. Tex., Houston, 1977-80, chmn. bd., 1980—; chmn. United Fin. Mortgage Co., Dallas; dir. Kaneb Services Inc., Investors Mortgage Ins. Co., Boston; past dir. Fed. Home Loan Bank, Little Rock. Pres. Abilene Indsl. Found., 1970, United Fund Abilene, 1962; mem. bd. Tex. State Hosps., 1962-64; mem. Tex. Fin. Commn., 1964-76, chmn., 1971. Served with USAAF, 1942-43. Recipient Outstanding Citizen award City of Abilene, 1964, Disting. Alumnus award McMurry Coll., 1971. Mem. Nat. Savs. and Loan League (pres. 1970-71), Tex. Savs. and Loan League (pres. 1970-71), Abilene C. of C. (pres. 1964). Episcopalian. Clubs: Abilene Country (pres. 1951); Preston Trails Golf (Dallas). Contbr. articles to profl. publns. Home: 52 Rue Maison Abilene TX 79605 Office: 5251 Westheimer St Houston TX 77056

BENTLEY, CLAUDE EUGENE, banker; b. Virgie, Ky., May 29, 1951; s. Smith and Maggie (Belcher) B.; m. Neva Mae Baker, July 5, 1969; children—Donald Eugene, Scottie Ruben. Student Ky. Bus. Coll., 1972; A.A., U. Ky.-Lexington, 1976. Asst. v.p. Pikeville Nat. Bank (Ky.), 1980-81, v.p., 1981—; 1st class mine foreman Ky. Dept. Mines, Pikeville, 1983. Founder, Pikeville Area Coal Expo, 1983—; pres. Dorton Little League, 1979-80. Served with U.S. Army, 1971-73. Named Banker Advocate of Year, SBA, 1983. Mem. Ky. Bankers Assn., Am. Bankers Assn. (cert. comml. lending officer), Knott-Perry-Letcher Coal Operators Assn., Harlon County Coal Assn. Republican. Baptist. Clubs: Rotary. Lodges: Masons, Shriners. Home: PO Box 822 Pikeville KY 41501 Office: Pikeville Nat Bank PO Box 2947 Pikeville KY 41501

BENTLEY, DIANE KAY, word processing consultant; b. Wichita, Kans., Nov. 30, 1943; d. Ralph Franklin and Betty Jane (Hemsworth) Garrett; m. Philip Robert Bentley, Apr. 5, 1963; children—Cheryl Elaine, Shawn Philip. Student Butler County Community Jr. Coll., 1967, Wichita State U., 1972, 76. With bookkeeping dept. Kans. State Bank, Wichita, 1960-62; sec. Ranson & Co., Inc., Wichita, 1962-64, Vickers Refining Co., Wichita, 1964-66; owner The Letter Shop, Haysville, Kans., 1966-75; exec. asst. Ranson & Co., Inc., 1975-80; owner Bentley & Assocs., Tulsa, 1980—; owner, ptnr. Satellite Office Systems, Tulsa, 1983-84; tchr. typing, shorthand, word processing; adj. instr. Tulsa Jr. Coll.; lectr., cons. in field; mem. steering com. S.W. Computer Conf., Tulsa, 1982, 83, S.W. Bus. and Equipment Show of Tulsa, 1983-85. Mem. office systems adv. com. Tulsa Jr. Coll., 1983-87; mem. word processing sec. adv. com. Tulsa County Vocat.-Tech.; dist. del. Kans. Republican State Conv., 1976. Mem. Assn. Info. Systems Profls. (charter pres. 1982-84), Okla. Word Processing Assn. (Assn. Info. Systems Profl. regional rep. 1986—), Adminstrv. Mgmt. Soc. (dir.). Mem. Christian Ch. Home and Office: 2518 S 96 E Place Tulsa OK 74129

BENTLEY, DONNA ANDERSON, psychology educator, writer; b. Pontiac, Mich., Aug. 2, 1930; d. Albin Theodore and Hazel (Morrill) Anderson; m. Edward Allen Bentley, Nov. 23, 1957; 1 son, John Edward. B.A., Wayne State U., 1957; M.Ed., U. Tenn., 1966; Ph.D., Ga. State U., 1979. Writer, Oakland Press, Pontiac, 1952-54; mem. pub. relations staff Chrysler Corp., 1956-57; corr. McGraw-Hill World News, 1958-67; asst. prof. psychology Dalton (Ga.) Jr. Coll., 1967—. Mem. Am. Psychol. Assn., Am. Ednl. Research Assn., Eastern Ednl. Research Assn., Community Coll. Social Sci. Assn., Delta Kappa Gamma. Republican. Episcopalian. Writer, account exec. Ga. Jour.; contbr. articles to profl. jours. and popular mags. Home: 615 Miller St Dalton GA 30720 Office: Dalton Junior Coll Dalton GA 30720

BENTLEY, ERNEST LYNNWOOD, clergyman, coll. recruiter; b. Lauderdale County, Tenn., Nov. 28, 1914; s. Kenneth Oscar and Lula Dean (Miller) B.; student U. Tenn., 1945-60; m. Martha Lynne Caldwell, Dec. 12, 1943; children—Pearl Dean, Ernest Lynnwood, Elizabeth Anne. Ordained to ministry Ch. of Christ, 1949; insp. Procter & Gamble Wolf Creek Ordnance Plant, Milan, Tenn., 1940-44; safety insp. Ford, Bacon & Davis, Inc., Oak Ridge, 1944-45; safety engr. Tenn. Eastman Corp., Oak Ridge, 1945-47, Union Carbide Corp., Oak Ridge, 1947-76; ret., 1976; field rep. East Tenn. Sch. Preaching and Missions, Knoxville, 1977-80; field rep. Tenn. Bible Coll., Cookeville, 1980—. Recipient Disting. Service award, Tenn. Bible Coll., 1981; cert. safety profl. Mem. Am. Soc. Safety Engrs., Am. Indsl. Hygiene Assn. Home: 8305 S Burchfield Dr Oak Ridge TN 37830 Office: Tennessee Bible College Box 865 Cookeville TN 38501

BENTLEY, FRED DOUGLAS, JR., lawyer; b. Marietta, Ga., Aug. 27, 1955; s. Fred Douglas and Sara Tom (Moss) B.; m. Patricia Ann Foster, Dec. 17, 1983. B.B.A. in Acctg., U. Ga., 1977; J.D., Emory U., 1980. Bar: Ga. 1980, La. 1983, U.S. Ct. Appeals (11th cir.) 1982, U.S. Dist. Ct. (no. dist.) Ga. 1982, U.S. Ct. Appeals (5th cir.) 1983, U.S. Dist. Ct. (ea. and mid. dists.) La. 1983. Ptnr. Bentley & Bentley, Marietta, 1980-83; assoc. Phelps, Dunbar, Marks, Claverie & Sims, New Orleans, 1983—; faculty Phillips Jr. Coll., Metaire, La., 1983. Dist. rep. Republican Party Big Shanty Dist., Kennesaw, Ga., 1982-83. Recipient Jour. Cup award Atlanta Constn. Newspaper, 1973; Outstanding Young Men of Am. award Jaycees, 1981. Mem. ABA, Ga. State Bar Assn., La. State Bar Assn., Fed. Bar Assn., Cobb County Bar Assn., Ga. Trial Lawyers Assn., Assn. Trial Lawyers Am., New Orleans Assn. Def. Counsel, Cobb County C. of C. (trustee 1982-83), Phi Delta Phi. Republican. Roman Catholic. Lodge: Rotary (New Orleans). Home: 3411 Vincennes Pl New Orleans LA 70125 Office: Claverie & Sims 30th Floor Texaco Ctr 400 Poydras St New Orleans LA 70130

BENTLEY, JAMES ARTHUR, JR., ophthalmologist; b. Nashville, Dec. 20, 1942; s. James Arthur and Beulah Martha (Thompson) B.; m. Nancy Gene Higginbotham, June 8, 1968; children—James Arthur III, Frederick Lanham. B.A., Vanderbilt U., 1964; M.D., 1969. Diplomate Am. Bd. Ophthalmology. Pvt. practice ophthalmology, Dallas, 1976—, Kaufman, Tex., 1980—; assoc. clin. prof. U. Tex. Health Sch. Ctr., 1983—. Served to capt. USAF, 1970-72. Mem. AMA, Tex. Med. Assn., Dallas Acad. Ophthalmology, Am. Acad. Ophthalmology and Otolaryngology, Am. Intraocular Implant Soc. Republican. Methodist. Club: Dallas Country. Home: 4224 Caruth Dallas TX 75225 Office: 8210 Walnut Hill Ln Suite 109 Dallas TX 75231

BENTLEY, JAMES ROBERT, association curator; b. Louisville, Feb. 14, 1942; s. Francis Getty and Katharine Elizabeth (Wescott) B.; B.A., Centre Coll. Ky., 1964; M.A., Coll. William and Mary, 1971. Research asst. Colonial Williamsburg (Va.), 1966-68; asst. to curator Filson Club, Louisville, 1964-65, curator, 1968-83, sec., 1972-84, acting dir., 1983-84, dir., 1984; dir. G.R. Clark Press, Louisville; mem. adv. com. to photograph archives U. Louisville, 1971-72; mem. Hist. Zoning Task Force Louisville and Jefferson County, 1971-73; mem. hist. protection and preservation com. Bd. Aldermen Louisville, 1972-73; commr. Hist. Landmarks and Preservation Dists. Commn., Louisville, 1973-79. Mem. SAR (registrar 1970—, library com.), Ky. Soc. Mayflower Descs. (historian, librarian 1970-78, gov. 1978-84, dep. gov. gen. 1981—, 5 generation project com. 1979—), Ky. Soc. Colonial Wars (councillor 1971-76, registrar 1976—), Jeffersontown Hist. Soc. (dir. 1972-73, v.p. 1974-76, pres. 1976-78), Soc. Am. Archivists, Manuscript Soc., Nat. Trust Historic Preservation, Hist. Homes Found. Louisville, Vt. Hist. Soc. (life), New Eng. Hist. Geneal. Soc., English Speaking Union, Nat. Geneal. Soc. (life), Vt. Geneal. Soc., Ind. Hist. Soc., Vt. Old Cemetery Assn., Louisville Hist. League, Alden Kindred Am., Soc. Stukely Westcott Descs., Edmund Rice 1638 Assn., Soc. Descs. Robert Bartlett of Plymouth Colony, Order Ky. Cols., Sigma Chi. Episcopalian. Clubs: Pendennis (Louisville), Filson (life). Editor, pub. Ky. Genealogist, 1979—. Home: 3621 Brownsboro Rd Louisville KY 40207 Office: 1310 S 3d St Louisville KY 40208

BENTLEY, JOSEPH OLIVER, JR., software service company executive; b. Sylacauga, Ala., June 22, 1954; s. Joseph Oliver and Mary Virginia (Roberson) B.; m. Vicki D. Buckley, Mar. 22, 1980. B.S., U. Ala.-Tuscaloosa, 1972-76, M.A., 1977. C.P.A., Ala., Tex. Staff acct. Ernst & Whinney, Houston, 1977-79; supr. Arthur Young & Co., Birmingham, Ala., 1979-82; exec. v.p. Sofsearch Internat., Inc., San Antonio, 1982-84; project controller Infomart, Dallas, 1984—. Mem. Am. Inst. C.P.A.s, Nat. Assn. Accts., Tex. Soc. C.P.A.s, Ala. Soc. C.P.A.s. Republican. Baptist. Office: 2100 Stemmons Freeway Dallas TX 75207

BENTON, ARTHUR LOUIS, criminal justice assessment center director; b. Geneva, Ohio, June 30, 1927; s. Benjamin F. and Marian (Pratt) B.; m. Michiko

Kondo, Dec. 20, 1958; children—Terrence, Sandra Jean Benton Nichols. B.S., Mont. State U., 1964, M.Ed., 1964; Ph.D., Am. Univ., 1971. Lt. col. Corps of Engrs. U.S. Army, 1945-68; chief of tng. and devel. Army Topographic Command, Washington D.C., 1968-70; chmn. dept. health and human services U. Maine, Bangor, 1970-76; project dir. So. Regional Edn. Bd., Atlanta, 1976-79; dir. Criminal Justice Assessment Ctr., Miami-Dade Community Coll., Miami, Fla., 1984—; prin. Benton Enterprises, Inc., Monticello, Ga., 1979—. Author: Human Services Credentialing, 1976. Contbr. articles to profl. jours. Inventor photogrammetric gunfire position system. Treas. Jasper County Bus. Assn., Monticello, 1980-83; v.p. Turtle Cove Property Owner's Assn., Monticello. 1983-84. Recipient Honors medallion Univ. Md., 1962, Legions of Merit, 1967, 68, Nobel Order of Crown, King of Thailand, 1965. Mem. Nat. Assn. Human Service Educators (founder), Am. Psychologist Assn., Nat. Rifle Assn., Nat. Vocat. Guidance Assn., Monticello C. of C. (v.p. 1980-83), Phi Kappa Phi. Home: 8901 NW 15th Ct Pembroke Pines FL 33024 Office: Miami-Dade Community Coll 11380 NW 27th St Miami FL 33167

BENTON, CATHY CALLIHAN, educator; b. Elizabethtown, N.C., Oct. 19, 1953; d. Curtis Eugene and Jewel (Medlin) Callihan; m. James Gerrin Benton, Feb. 28, 1981; children—James Gerrin, Catherine Connor. B.S. in Elem. Edn., East Carolina U., 1976. Tchr. Pitt County Sch., Greenville, N.C., 1977-82, Sampson County Sch., Harrells, N.C., 1982—. Dir. day camp Pines of Carolina Girl Scouts Am., 1981. Mem. N.C. Assn. Educators (rep. 1984-85), NEA, Am. Bus. Women's Assn., N.C. Council Tchrs. Math. Democrat. Baptist. Avocations: water skiing; interior decorating. Home: PO Box 2008 Elizabethtown NC 28337

BENTON, CURTIS DUDLEY, JR., ophthalmologist; b. Columbus, Ga., Apr. 28, 1921; s. Curtis Dudley and Evelyn Jane (Millspaugh) B.; m. Lucille Margaret McCann, Nov. 14, 1947; children—Janet Margaret, Dudley James. B.S., U. Calif.-Berkeley, 1942; M.D., Emory U., 1945. Diplomate Am. Bd. Ophthalmology. Author: Spectacles for Aphakia, 1966. Organizer com. for early identification of children with learning disabilities Broward County Sch. Bd., Fort Lauderdale, Fla., 1975—. Served with U.S. Army. Mem. Broward County Med. Assn., Fla. Med. Assn., Am. Acad. Ophthalmology, Fla. Soc. Ophthalmology, Broward County Ophthal. Soc. Republican. So. Baptist. Clubs: Lauderdale Yacht; Coral Ridge Country. Avocations: golf; travel; writing. Home: 1802 E Las Olas Blvd Fort Lauderdale FL 33301 Office: Drs Benton & Mcann P A 1800 E Las Olas Blvd Fort Lauderdale FL 33301

BENTON, PAMELA GAIL TART, nurse; b. Greensboro, N.C., July 1, 1955; d. William Bruce and Mary Bell (Gregory) Tart; m. Randall George Benton, Sept. 6, 1975; 1 child, Nathan Bryant. Cert. practical nursing, Wilkes Community Coll., 1975; cert. operating room tech., Bowman Gray Sch. Med., 1978. Operating room technician, lic. practical nurse, N.C. Bapt. Hosp., Winston-Salem, 1977-79; operating room technician, lic. practical nurse Duke U. Hosp., Durham, N.C., 1979-80, sterile process coordinator, 1980-84, sterile process chief, 1984-85, asst. dir. sterile process, 1985—. Mem. N.C. Assn. Hosp. Central Service Personnel (bd. dirs. 1982-84), Am. Soc. Hosp. Central Service Personnel. Avocations: camping; doll making; hiking; refinishing. Office: Duke U Med Ctr PO Box 3820 Durham NC 27710

BENTRUP, HENRY DANIEL, JR., systems analyst; b. Memphis, Sept. 22, 1944; s. Henry Daniel and Ada Smalling (Goodpasture) B.; m. Helen Patricia Boyd, July 4, 1976; children—Benjamin Boyd, Keith Henry, Carl Stephen, Samuel Sigrist, Christina Rose. B.A., George Peabody Coll. for Tchrs., 1972; M.P.A., Tenn. State U., 1986. Programmer/analyst Vanderbilt U., Nashville, 1967-73; info. systems analyst 4 for environ. health services Tenn. Dept. Health and Environment, Nashville, 1973—. Bd. dirs. Nashville chpt. UN Assn., 1982—, v.p. program, 1982-85, treas., 1986—. Mem. Assn. Computing Machinery, Spl. Interest Group on Computers and Soc. Mem. Disciples of Christ Ch. Home: 426 Rosebank Ave Nashville TN 37206 Office: Customs House 4th Floor 701 Broadway Nashville TN 37219

BENTSEN, LLOYD, U.S. senator; b. Mission, Tex., Feb. 11, 1921; s. Lloyd M. and Edna Ruth (Colbath) B.; m. Beryl Ann Longino, Nov. 27, 1943; children—Lloyd M. III, Lan, Tina. LL.B., U. Tex., 1942. Bar: Tex. 1942. Practice law, McAllen, Tex., 1945-48, judge, Hidalgo County, Tex., 1946-48; mem. 80th to 83d congresses from 15th Tex. Dist.; pres. Lincoln Consol., Houston, 1955-70; U.S. Senator from Tex., 1971—, mem. fin., environment and public works coms., intelligence com., also Congl. joint econ. com.; chmn. Dem. Senatorial Campaign Com. Served to maj. USAAF, 1942-45. Decorated D.F.C., Air Medal with 3 oak leaf clusters. Home: Houston TX Office: Room 703 Hart Senate Office Bldg Washington DC 20510 also 4026 Fed Bldg 515 Rusk St Houston TX 77002 also 912 Fed Bldg Austin TX 78701 also Earle Cabell Bldg Room 7C30 Dallas TX 75242

BENTZ, EDWARD JOSEPH, JR., energy and transportation management consulting firm executive; b. N.Y.C., May 17, 1945; m. Carole. B.S. in Physics, Rensselaer Poly. Inst., 1966; vis. fellow Rockefeller Inst., 1966-67; M. Phil., Yale U., 1969, Ph.D., 1971. Danmark-Amerika Fondet George C. Marshall fellow Neils Bohr Inst., Copenhagen, 1971-72; vis. fellow USSR Acad. Scis., 1972, mem. tech. staff David Sarnoff Research Center, RCA, Princeton, N.J., 1972-74; mem. policy staff EPA, Washington, 1974-77; Congl. fellow U.S. Senate com. Commerce, sci. and transp., Washington, 1976-77; dir. impact analysis Presidential-Congl. Nat. Transp. Policy Study Commn., Washington, 1977-79; exec. dir. Presidential-Congl. Nat. Alcohol Fuels Commn., Washington, 1979-80; pres. E.J. Bentz & Assocs., Inc., Springfield, Va., 1980—. Mem. N.Y. Acad. Scis., Transp. Research Bd. Va. Acad. Scis., Soc. Govt. Regulatory Economists, Sigma Xi, Sigma Pi Sigma. Author books; contbr. articles to profl. jours. Office: EJ Bentz & Assocs Inc 7915 Richfield Rd Springfield VA 22153

BENTZEL, CHARLES HOWARD, business executive; b. Balt., July 30, 1926; s. Reece Emory and Idel Burton; B.A., U. Balt., 1952, B.S., 1962; D.Comml. Sci., London Inst. Applied Research, 1973; m. Wandalee Baer, July 27, 1947; children—Brent, Alan, Leslie. Vice pres., chief fin. officer Roblin Industries, Inc., N.Y.C., 1968-69; v.p., dir. fin., controller ITT and subs., N.Y.C. and abroad, 1969-76; v.p., chief fin. officer Trane Co., Wis., 1976-79, Iscott, Trinidad, 1980-82; pres., chief exec. officer Severance Ref. Lab., San Antonio, 1982—, also dir.; dir. Data Terminals Corp. Bd. dirs. YMCA, Wis., 1976-79. Mem. Internat. Assn. Fin. Execs. Insts. (dir.), Brazilian Fin. Execs. Inst. (hon., life mem.), Fin. Execs. Inst., Am. Acctg. Assn., Nat. Assn. Accts., Internat. Treas. Assn. Republican. Clubs: N.Y. Athletic, Marco Polo, Fair Oaks Golf and Country, Plaza, Ariel House; Masons (Md., Argentina, Brazil). Contbg. author: The Modern Accountants Handbook, 1973. Home: 28637 Dapper Dan Boerne TX 78006 Office: 601 N Frio San Antonio TX 78207

BENVENISTE, MARILYN B., lecturer, public speaking consultant; b. Atlanta, July 27, 1940; d. Irving and Rose (Silver) Berkowitz; m. Morris Benveniste, Apr. 7, 1963; children—Mark, Marshall, Melissa. B.S. in Edn., U. Ala.-Tuscaloosa, 1962. Tchr., Atlanta pub. schs., 1962-63; co-dir. Assertiveness Tng. Inst., Atlanta, 1977-78; pub. speaking cons., Atlanta, 1978—; spl. asst. on coll. relations to pres. Kennesaw Coll., Marietta, Ga., 1983-84; chmn. Leadership Cobb, 1984-85. cons., lectr. in field. Author, trainer: Gaining Awareness Through Education, 1979; author: Put the Lid on Pot, 1978; author/producer slide show: Pot The Quiet Persuader, 1979, Kennesaw Coll., A Place for All Seasons, 1983. Sec. Atlanta Jewish Community Ctr., 1979-81, v.p., 1981-83; pres. Alpha Omega Dental Aux., 1972-73; v.p. Brandeis Women's Com., 1968-70; pres. Temple Sinai Women's Com., Atlanta, 1972-74; bd. dirs. chpt. Am. Cancer Soc., Straight, Inc. Recipient Young Leader award Jewish Welfare Bd., 1976, Leadership Ga., 1982, Leadership Atlanta, 1981; Tribute to Women nominee YMCA, 1985. Mem. Am. Soc. Tng. and Devel., Atlanta Women's Network, Cobb C. of C., Nat. Speakers Assn., Leadership Ga. (trustee), AAUW. Clubs: B'nai B'rith Women, Women's Am. ORT, U. Ala. Alumni Assn. Home: 14 Heards Overlook Ct NW Atlanta GA 30328 Office: PO Box 420123 Atlanta GA 30342

BENZINGER, RAYMOND BURDETTE, lawyer, educator; b. Pitts., Apr. 29, 1938; s. William Patrick and Margaret Ellen (Depp) B.; B.S., Carnegie-Mellon U., 1962; J.D., Georgetown U., 1971, LL.M., 1973; m. Patricia Ann Kate, May 22, 1971; children—Raymond Howard, Susan Rae. Admitted to D.C. bar, 1971, Va. bar, 1971, U.S. Ct. of Claims bar, 1972, Pa. bar, 1972, U.S. Dist. Ct. D.C. bar, 1971, U.S. Supreme Ct. bar, 1976, West Dist. Pa. bar, 1978, Eastern Dist. Va. bar, 1980; trial atty. civil div. U.S. Dept. Justice, Washington, 1972-77; vis. prof. law Internat. Sch., Law, Arlington, Va., 1977-78; prof. law George Mason U., Arlington, 1978-83, Cath. U. Am. Sch. Law, Washington, 1983—; mem. speakers bur. Georgetown U., Washington, 1970—. Mem. Va. Trial Lawyers Assn., Arlington County Bar Assn., Delta Theta Phi (dep. vice chancellor 1977—, Nat. Outstanding Law Prof. award 1978). Bus. editor: Law and Policy in Internat. Bus., 1970-71. Home: 5509 Ivor St Springfield VA 22151 Office: 2009 N 14th St Suite 105 Arlington VA 22201

BERANEK, JUDITH SPURLOCK, Spanish language educator; b. Gainesville, Fla., Aug. 31, 1941; d. Alvin Harold and Merry Louise (Carter) Spurlock; m. John Russell Beranek, June 22, 1968. B.A., U. Fla., 1963, Ph.D., 1966. Cert. Spanish and Portuguese tchr., Fla. Asst. prof. Spanish, U. South Fla., Tampa, 1966-68; prof. Palm Beach Atlantic Coll., West Palm Beach, Fla., 1968—, registrar, 1969-70, chmn. fgn. langs. dept., 1970—, head div. humanities, 1984—. Mem. Commn. on Status of Women, Palm Beach County, 1973-83, chmn., 1979-80. Woodrow Wilson Hon. fellow, 1963. Mem. South Atlantic MLA, Phi Beta Kappa, Kappa Delta. Democrat. Baptist. Club: Jr. League of Palm Beaches. Avocations: woodworking; water sports. Home: 113 Summa St West Palm Beach FL 33405 Office: Palm Beach Atlantic Coll 1101 S Olive Ave West Palm Beach FL 33401

BERARDO, FELIX MARIO, sociology educator, researcher; b. Waterbury, Conn., Feb. 7, 1934; s. Rocco and Maria Berardo; m. Donna Hodgkins; children—Marcellino A., Benito A. B.A., U. Conn., 1961; Ph.D., Fla. State U., 1965. Asst. prof. sociology Wash. State U., 1965-69; assoc. prof. U. Fla., 1969-72, prof., 1973-85, chmn. dept., 1985—. Served with USAF, 1952-56. Mem. Am. Sociol. Assn., Rural Sociol. Soc., Nat. Council Family Relations, So. Sociol. Soc., Gerontol. Soc. Am., Phi Beta Kappa, Phi Kappa Phi, Alpha Kappa Delta. Roman Catholic. Author: (with F. Ivan Nye) The Family: Its Structure and Interaction, 1973; contbr. numerous chpts., articles to profl. publs.; editor: (with F. Ivan Nye) Emerging Conceptual Frameworks in Family Analysis, 1966, 2d edit., 1981; assoc. editor Internat. Jour. Sociology of the Family, 1970—, Family Coordinator, 1971-75, Social Forces, 1976-79, Death Edn., 1979—; assoc. editor Jour. of Marriage and Family, 1972-75, 82—, editor, 1976-81; editorial adv. bd. Population Research and Policy Rev., 1980—, Sage Family Studies Abstracts, 1981—; guest editor spl. issue Jour. Marriage and Family, 1971, Family Coordinator, 1972, Annals of Am. Acad. Polit. and Social Sci., 1982; Death Studies, 1985; referee profl. jours. Office: Dept Sociology U Fla Gainesville FL 32611

BERBARY, MAURICE SHEHADEH, physician, mil. officer, hosp. adminstr., educator; b. Beirut, Lebanon, Jan. 14, 1923; s. Shehadeh M. and Marie K. Berbary; came to U.S., 1945, naturalized, 1952; B.A., Am. U., Beirut, 1943; M.D., U. Tex., 1948; M.A. in Hosp. Adminstrn., Baylor U., 1970; diploma Army Command and Gen. Staff Coll., Leavenworth, Kan., 1963, Air Force Sch. Aerospace Medicine, 1964, Army War Coll., Carlisle, Pa., 1969; m. Bruennhild Hepp; children—Geoffrey Maurice, Laura Marie. Intern, Parkland Meml. Hosp., Dallas, 1948-49, resident in obstetrics and gynecology, gen. surgery and urology, 1949-53; resident in obstetrics and gynecology Walter Reed Army Hosp., Washington, 1955-57; fellow in obstetric and gynecologic pathology Armed Forces Inst. Pathology, Washington, 1959-60; practice clin. medicine in obstetrics and gynecology, 1953-—; capt. M.C., U.S. Army, 1952, advanced through grades to col., 1968; chief dept. obstetrics and gynecology U.S. Army Hosp., Ft. Polk, La., 1957-59, Womack Army Hosp., Ft. Bragg, N.C., 1960-62; div. surgeon 1st inf. div., Ft. Riley, Kans., 1963-64, 3d. Armored div., Germany, 1964-65; corps surgeon, V. Corps, Germany, 1965-67; corps surgeon 24th Army Corps, S. Vietnam Theater of Operation, 1970; comdr., hosp. adminstr. U.S. Army Hosp., Teheran, Iran, 1954-55; comdr. hosp. group complex, Vietnam, 1969-70; command surgeon U.S. Armed Forces Command and U.S. Army South, U.S. C.Z., Panama, 1970-73; comdr. 5th Gen. Hosp., U.S. Army, Stuttgart, West Germany, 1973-77, Munson Army Hosp., Ft. Leavenworth, Kans., 1977-81, William Beaumont Army Med. Ctr., Ft. Bliss, Tex., 1981-83; ret., 1983; vis. lectr. obstetrics and gynecology pathology Duke U. Med. Center, Durham, N.C., 1960-62; clin. instr. obstetrics and gynecology U. Kans. Med. Center, Kansas City, 1963-64; instr. 5th Army NCO Acad., Fort Riley, Kans., 1963-64. Decorated Legion of Merit with three oak leaf clusters, Bronze Star medal, Army Commendation medal. Diplomate Am. Bd. Obstetrics and Gynecology. Fellow A.C.S., Am. Coll. Obstetricians and Gynecologists; mem. AMA, Assn. of Mil. Surgeons, Soc. of U.S. Army Flight Surgeons, Am. Coll. Health Care Execs., Internat. Platform Assn., Am. Hosp. Assn., N.Y. Acad. Scis., Dallas County Med. Soc., Tex. State Med. Assn. Mason (32 deg.). Home: 7923 Abramshire Ave Dallas TX 75231

BERCHTOLD, PAUL, manufacturing company executive, contractor, mechanical engineer; b. Mercer, Pa., May 19, 1931; s. Oscar and Bertha M. Berchtold; children by previous marriage—Steven, Robert, Lynn. B.S., Case Western Res. U. 1955. Registered profl. mech. engr. Constrn. supt. KREBS-Calkins, Inc., Elyria, Ohio, 1952-63; gen. sales mgr. Foster Thornberg Co., Huntington, W.Va., 1963-66; pres. Standard Enterprises, Inc., South Charleston, W.Va., 1972—; pres. Country Club Village, Inc., South Charleston, 1972—; dir. H. & K Knitting Factory, Ltd., Continental Textiles, Ltd. Mem. Presdl. Task Force; 2d. lt. CAP, W.Va. wing. Served to tech. sgt. USMC, 1948-51. Recipient Blue Flame award Elyria Jr. C. of C., 1961; Devel. award Lorain County (Ohio), 1956. Mem. Solar Research Inst., Constrn. Specifications Inst., Internat. Garment Mfrs., Caribbean Assn. Indsl. Commerce, Jr. C. of C., Nat. C. of C., Kanawha Valley Bd. Realtors, Aircraft Owners and Pilots Assn., Nat. Sales Exec. Club (v.p., 1965), Cherry River Navy (adm. 1979). Presbyterian. Lodge: Masons. Office: PO Box 8745 South Charleston WV 25303

BERDANIER, CAROLYN DAWSON, foods and nutrition educator, administrator, researcher; b. East Brunswick, N.J., Nov. 14, 1936; d. Frederick H.C. and Mabelle (Virginia McNiven) Dawson; m. Charles Reese Berdanier, Aug. 10, 1957; children—Lynnette, Charles, Robert. B.S., Pa. State U., 1958; M.S., Rutgers U., 1963, Ph.D., 1966. Therapeutic dietitian St. Peters Hosp., New Brunswick, N.J., 1960-61; research asst. Rutgers U., 1961-63, grad. research fellow, 1963-66; postdoctoral fellow Rutgers U., 1966-67; research nutritionist Nutrition Inst. U.S. Dept. Agr., Beltsville, Md., 1968-75; asst. prof. nutrition U. Md., College Park, 1970-75; assoc. prof. biochemistry and medicine U. Nebr., Omaha, 1975-77; prof., head dept. foods and nutrition Coll. Home Econs., U. Ga., Athens, 1977—; mem. review panel in human nutrition U.S. Dept. Agr. Competitive Grants Program, 1978, 79, 81. Recipient Ga. Nutrition Council award for Outstanding Contbns. to Research in Human Nutrition, 1982; Lamar Dodd award for research, 1984; NIH fellow, 1966-67. Fellow Am. Inst. Chemists; mem. N.Y. Acad. Scis., AAAS, Soc. Exptl. Biology and Medicine, Am. Inst. Nutrition, Am. Home Econs. Assn., Endocrine Soc., Am. Soc. Clin. Nutrition, Sigma Xi, Gamma Sigma Delta, Phi Kappa Phi. Mem. editorial bd. Jour. Nutrition, 1977-81; contbr. articles to profl. jours.

BERDECIA, LUIS ANTONIO, educator; b. Barranquitas, P.R., Mar. 17, 1939; s. Enrique and Maria (Rodriguez) B.; B.A. in Secondary Edn., U. P.R., 1966; M.A. in Higher Edn., N.Y. U., 1969; m. Irma Falcon, Apr. 24, 1965; children—Irma Maricelli, Luis Antonio, Rafael Enrique. Elem., jr. and sch. high sch. tchr., Barranquitas, 1960-68, tchr. evening schs., 1964-70; zone. supr. English, Naranjito, P.R., 1968-69, 69-75; tchr. English, Job Corps, Aibonito, P.R., 1969; gen. supr. English, P.R. Dept. Edn., 1975-76; instr. English and edn. part-time Inter Am. U., Barranquitas Regional Coll., 1971-76, instr. English and linguistics, 1976-78, asst. prof., 1978—. Mem. NEA, Bilingual Edn. Assn., Tchrs. Assn. P.R., TESOL, Alumni Assn. N.Y. U., Nat. Wild Life Assn. Roman Catholic. Address: A-5 San Cristobal Barranquitas PR 00618

BERESFORD, JOHN CLINTON, demographer; b. St. Paul, Mar. 11, 1930; s. Howard Clinton and Vivian Alexis (Brand) B.; m. Nancy Harris, Mar. 29, 1951; children—Alison, J. Roderic. B.A., Antioch Coll., 1951; M.A., U. Mich., 1952. Demographer U.S. Bur. Census, Washington, 1958-69; founder, pres. DUALabs, Arlington, Va., 1969-82; pres. DUAL-Comm Inc., 1982-86; statistician U.S. Bur. Census, Washington, 1986—; dir. Donnes Pour le Developpment. Served with U.S. Army, 1953-55. Fellow AAAS; mem. Population Assn. Am., Am. Statis. Assn., Am. Sociol. Assn. Home: 1317 Alexandria Ave Alexandria VA 22308 Office: US Bar Census Dept Commerce Washington DC 20233

BEREZANSKY, RICHARD FABIAN, safety engineer; b. New Brunswick, N.J., Apr. 10, 1948; s. Nicholas Peter and Lillian Catherine B.; B.S. in Mgmt., Embry Riddle U., Daytona Beach, Fla., 1970; m. Donna Milchanoski, June 12, 1971; 1 son, Nicholas A. Sr. loss control rep. Allstate Ins. Co., Murray Hills, N.J., 1971-73; dir. safety ins. and claims Hermann Forwarding Co., New Brunswick, 1973-75; dir. safety and security Tose Inc., Bridgeport, Pa., 1975-76; dir. safety, security and claims William H.P. Inc./Burgmeyer, Phila., 1976-79; mgr. safety distbn. systems div. Ryder Systems Inc., Miami, Fla., 1979-86; dir. safety scheduled Truckways, Rogers, Ark., 1986—. CPR, 1st aid instr. Am. Heart Assn., ARC; cert. hazard control mgr.; dist. chmn. N.J. First Aid Council, 1977-79. Mem. Am. Soc. Safety Engrs., Am. Soc. Indsl. Security, Nat. Fire Protection Assn., Nat. Assn. Chiefs of Police, Am. Trucking Assn. (safety planning com. pvt. carrier conf. and common carrier conf.). Republican. Roman Catholic. Home: 1205 S 13th St Rogers AR 72756 Office: 2600 Hwy 102 W Rogers AR 72757

BERG, RICHARD ALAN, clinical neuropsychologist, researcher; b. Albany, N.Y., Mar. 30, 1953; s. Gunter A. and Sylvia (Falkow) B. B.A., SUNY-Buffalo, 1974; M.A., U. Houston, 1976, Ph.D., 1980. Lic. psychologist, W. Va., Tenn. Staff psychologist St. Jude's Children's Research Hosp., Memphis, 1980-84; dir. assessment service W. Va. Med. Ctr., Charleston, 1984—. Co-author: Interpretation of the H-R Battery, 1981; contbr. chpts. to books, articles to profl. jours. Active Am. Cancer Soc., Memphis, 1983-84, Alzheimer's Disease Support Group, Charleston, 1985. Nat. Cancer Inst. Research grantee, 1980-84. Fellow Nat. Acad. Neuropsychologists (sec. 1984, Outstanding Contbn. award 1983); mem. Internat. Neuropsychol. Soc., Am. Psychol. Assn., W. Va. Psychol. Assn. Avocations: photography; sailing; skiing; computer programming. Office: W VA U Med Ctr Dept Behavioral Medicine PO Box 2867 Charleston WV 25330

BERG, THOMAS, development corporation executive; b. Sparta, Wis., Dec. 28, 1914; m., Nov. 13, 1937; children—Barbara, James Richard. B.S.E.E., U. Wis., 1937. Elec. engr. Gen. Electric Co., Schenectady, 1937-46; owner, pres. Arcway Equipment Co., Phila., 1946-58, Airco Welding Products div., 1958-68; pres., chief exec. officer Friedrich Refrigeration Co., N.Y.C., 1968-75, also dir.; pres. Ray Ellison Devels. Inc., San Antonio, 1975-81; v.p., dir. Ellison Industries, San Antonio, 1981—; instr. Rensselear Poly. Inst., Troy, N.Y., 1937-48; chmn. bd., dir. Jim Berg Publs. Inc.; chmn. bd., pres., dir. J.E.T. Properties, Inc.; dir. 1st Nat. Bank, San Antonio, Universal Bookbindery Inc.; v.p. Wylain Inc., Dallas; v.p., dir. Crutcher Resources Corp., Houston. chmn. bd. dirs. Southwest Research Inst., San Antonio. Chmn. bd. trustees City Pub. Service Bd. San Antonio, 1973-78; bd. dirs. Myasthenia Gravis Soc., 1982—; bd. dirs., v.p. San Antonio Soc. Prevention Blindness; founder Skills Tng. Center, San Antonio, 1971. Honored by City of San Antonio for pub. service, 1978. Mem. Am. Welding Soc. (life), Am. Inst. Elec. Engrs. (former dir.), Greater San Antonio C. of C. (dir.), North San Antonio C. of C. Presbyterian. Clubs: San Antonio Country, Argyle, Plaza, University, City, St. Anthony. Lodge: Rotary (dir.). Honored front cover Iron Age mag., 1967; author: Move Up to a Job in Welding, 1967; developer universal jeep welding system. Office: PO Box 5250 San Antonio TX 78201

BERGEN, HOWARD SILAS, JR., chemical and plastics executive; b. St. Louis, Apr. 4, 1921; s. Howard S. and Marion Leonie (Broyer) B.; Carol, July 8, 1983; children—Lisa T., Laurie A., Bruce H., Patricia A. B.S. in Chem. Engring., Washington U., St. Louis, 1942. Engaged in plasticizer devel. Monsanto Co., St. Louis, 1946-55, field sales specialist, 1955-57, product mgr. plasticizers, 1957-64, dir. sales, 1964-67, sales dir. functional fluids, 1967-68, bus. dir. functional fluids, 1968-70, bus. dir. splty. products, 1970-76; pres. Shintech, Inc., Houston, 1976-77; gen. mgr. resins Ga.-Pacific Corp., Atlanta, 1978-80, v.p., 1981--. Contbr. articles to profl. lit. Served to capt. USAF, 1942-46. Mem. Am. Chem. Soc., Soc. Plastics Industry, Paper Industry Mgmt. Assn., Pulp Chem. Assn. (exec. com.), Formaldehyde Inst. (exec. com.), Sigma Xi, Alpha Chi Sigma. Baptist. Club: Atlanta Athletic. Home: 4615 Gray Wood Trace Norcross GA 30092

BERGER, ARTHUR JOEL, lawyer; b. Cleve., Nov. 21, 1947; s. Henry and Edith (Hirshkowitz) B.; m. Andrea Celeste Knobler, June 15, 1969; children—Jeffrey David, Michael Daniel. B.A. with honors in Polit. Sci., Case Western Res. U., 1969; M.A. in Polit. Sci., U. Pa., 1971; J.D., U. Miami, 1974. Bar: Fla. 1974, U.S. Ct. Appeals (5th cir.) 1975, 81, U.S. Ct. Appeals (11th cir.) 1981, U.S. Dist. Ct. (so. dist.) Fla. 1977, U.S. Supreme Ct. 1978. Asst. atty. gen. State of Fla., 1975-78; asst. state atty. 11th Jud. Cir. Fla., Miami, 1978—. Mem. ABA, Fla. Bar Assn., Assn. Trial Lawyers Am., Soc. Bar and Gavel, Phi Alpha Theta, Phi Alpha Delta (past justice Rasco chpt.; Outstanding Active Mem. Rasco chpt. 1973). Democrat. Jewish. Home: 13389 SW 114th Terr Miami FL 33186 Office: 1351 NW 12th St 6th Floor Miami FL 33125

BERGER, RITA ROSE, educator; b. Bronx, N.Y., Jan. 1, 1925; s. Jack Maurice and Helene (Abrevaya); B.Ed., U. Miami, 1949; M.A., U. South Fla., 1973; m. Nathaniel Leah Berger, Sept. 29, 1949; 1 son, Carl Franklin. Tchr., North Miami (Fla.) Christian Ch., 1960-61, East Zephyrhills (Fla.) Elem. Sch., 1962-63; tchr. spl. edn. Polk County, Fla., 1965-67, tchr., 1967-73, reading tchr., 1973-81, tchr. learning disabled Rochelle Elem. Sch., Lakeland, 1981—; reading tchr. Plant City (Fla.) campus Hillsborough Community Coll., 1974-75; sec.-treas. Nate's Bike and Mower Sales and Service, Inc., Lakeland, Fla., 1973—; West area dir. Polk Edn., 1970-71; sec. Polk County Schs. Title I Dist. Parent Adv. Council, 1980-81; sales assoc. Prepaid Legal Services Fla., Inc., 1983—. Vol. counselor Billy Graham Crusade, Miami; altar worker First Assembly of God Ch., Lakeland. Recipient award for meritorious service United Negro Coll. Fund, 1977; cert. in elem. edn., reading, and secondary social studies, also adminstrn. and supervision, specific learning disabilities, and gifted edn., Fla. Mem. Internat. Reading Assn. (treas., del. Gen. Assembly), Fla. Reading Council (life), Assn. Children with Learning Disabilities, Polk Edn. Assn. (chmn. human relations com.), Fla. Teaching Profession (mem. conf. on exceptional edn.), NEA, Assn. Supervision and Curriculum Devel., Fla. Assn. Supervision and Curriculum Devel., Nat. Assn. Female Execs., Internat. Platform Assn. Kappa Delta Pi. Republican. Pentecostal. Home: 811 Arietta Dr Auburndale FL 33823 Office: 1728 E Edgewood Dr Lakeland FL 33803

BERGER, STEVEN R., lawyer; b. Miami, Fla., Aug. 23, 1945; s. Jerome J. and Jeanne B. B.; m. Francine Blake, Aug. 20, 1966; children—Amy, Charlie. B.S., U. Ala., 1967, J.D., 1969. Bar: Fla. 1969, U.S. Dist. Ct. (no. dist.) Fla. 1969, U.S. Dist. Ct. (so. dist.) Fla. 1971, U.S. Ct. Appeals (5th cir.) 1971, U.S. Supreme Ct. 1972, U.S. Ct. Claims 1977, U.S. Ct. Appeals (11th cir.) 1981. Assoc., W. Dexter Douglass, Tallahassee, 1969-71; assoc. William R. Dawes, Miami, 1971; ptnr. Carey, Dwyer, Cole Selwood & Bernard, Miami, 1971-81; sole practice, Miami, 1981—; mem. faculty Nat. Appellate Advocacy Inst., Washington, 1980; vice chmn. bench-bar adv. com. 4th Dist. Ct. Appeals, 1985—. Chmn. City Miramar Planning Bd., 1975-76. Mem. ABA (vice chmn. app. practice com. litigation sect. 1981-83, chmn. 5th cir. subcom. appellate practice com. 1978-81), Tallahassee Bar Assn., Am. Judicature Soc., Fla. Bar (appellate ct. rules com. 1974-76, 84), Kendall-South Miami Dist. Bar Assn., Dade County Def. Bar Assn., Fla. Def. Lawyers Assn., Def. Research Inst., Am. Arbitration Assn. Contbr. articles to legal jours.; editorial bd. Trial Advocate Quar. Address: 8525 SW 92d St Miami FL 33156

BERGER, VERNON EDWARD, geologist; b. San Antonio, Oct. 29, 1950; s. Lawrence A. and Virginia Mae (Ripps) B.; m. Margaret Eva Hera, Dec. 20, 1975; children—Andrea Kristin, Madelene Nicole. B.S. in Geology, Lamar U., 1975. Dist. geologist U.S. Forest Service, Watford City, N.D., 1976-77, staff geologist, Atlanta, 1977-80; geologist Tetra Tech Inc., Houston, 1981-82, Transco Exploration Co., Houston, 1982—. Served with U.S. Army, 1969-71, Vietnam. Recipient Cert. of Merit, U.S. Forest Service, 1980. Mem. Am. Assn. Petroleum Geologists. Avocations: backpacking, woodworking, reading. Home: 2935 Cotton Stock Sugarland TX 77479 Office: Transco Exploration Co 2800 Post Oak Blvd Houston TX 77251

BERGER, WILLIAM ERNEST, newspaper publisher; b. Ferris, Ill., June 6, 1918; s. William George and Ethel (Nelson) B.; student Carthage Coll., 1935-38; m. Jerry June Barnes, Feb. 26, 1943; children—William Edward, Barbara, John Jeffrey. Newspaper editor and pub., Hondo, Tex., 1946-65, 81—; commr. Tex. Water Rights Commn., Austin, 1965-69; pres. Assoc. Tex. Newspapers, Inc., 1957—; pres. South Tex. Press, Inc., Hondo, 1979—; owner Sta. KRME Hondo, 1969—. Treas., Medina Meml. Hosp., Hondo, 1962-64. Del., Tex. Democratic Conv., 1962, 64, 66, 68, Nat. Dem. Conv., 1968. Served with AUS, 1942-46. Mem. Tex. Press Assn. (pres. 1963), South Tex. Press Assn. (pres. 1954), Sigma Delta Chi (chpt. treas. 1967-69). Methodist. Clubs: Headliners, Lions (Hondo past pres.); Nat. Press (Washington).

BERGERON, VILLERE PAUL, architect; b. Lockport, La., May 19, 1932; s. Villere P. and Eva M. (Delaune) B.; children—Greg, Stephanie. B.Arch., La. State U., 1955; postgrad. U. Wis.-Milw., 1959-60, Rice U., 1985—; grad. officer's career course Command and Gen. Staff Coll., 1977. Lic. architect, Tex., La., Fla. Architect various archtl. firms, Thibodaux, La., 1957-59, Milw.,

1959-61, Houston, 1962-74; regional mgr. Archtl. & Engring. Co., Houston, 1974-80; prin. V.P. Bergeron, Architect, Houston, 1981—. Served to maj. M.I., USAR, 1955-79. Recipient Sch. Design award Am. Assn. Sch. Bd. Adminstrn., 1968. Mem. Nat. Council Archtl. Registration Bds., Am. Legion, AIA, Tex. Soc. Architects. Roman Catholic. Office: 2807 Buffalo Speedway Suite 302 Houston TX 77098

BERGIN, J. C., oil machinery company executive; b. 1928. With Republic Supply Co., Oklahoma City, 1948—, pres., chief exec. officer, 1980—, also dir. Office: Republic Supply Co 4200 Perimeter Center Dr Oklahoma City OK 73112*

BERGUSON, ROBERT JENKINS, artist, educator; b. Blossburg, Pa., Dec. 6, 1944; s. Robert Albert and Isabelle (Jenkins) B.; m. Marjorie Sue West, Apr. 13, 1968; children—Benjamin West, Cody Jenkins. A.A. in Humanities, Social Scis., Corning Community Coll., 1964; B.A., U. Iowa, 1967, M.A., 1968, M.F.A., 1970. From asst. prof. to prof. art Sch. Art and Architecture, La. Tech. U., 1970—. One man shows include Corning Community Coll., N.Y., 1968, U. Iowa, Iowa City, 1969, Visual Arts Ctr. Gallery, La. Tech. U., Ruston, 1972, 73, 79, U. Southwest La., Lafayette, 1978, Lauren Rogers Library Art Mus., Miss., 1978, Alexandria City Mus., La., 1978, Delta State U., Cleveland, Miss., 1979, Jackson Mcpl. Art Gallery, Miss., 1979, Meridian Mus. Art, Miss., 1979, Nichols State U., Thibodeaux, La., 1980, Northeast La. U., Monroe, 1980, Craft Alliance, Shreveport, La., 1980, Delgado Community Coll., New Orleans, 1984, Bolton Gallery La. State U., Alexandria, 1984, Bry Art Gallery, Northeast La. U., 1985, Abercrombie Gallery McNeese U., Lake Charles, La., 1985; exhibited in group shows at Contemporary Arts Ctr., New Orleans, 1983, 84, Corning Community Coll., 1982, Weatherspoon Art Gallery, U. N.C., 1981, and many others; represented in permanent collections Norfolk Mus. Arts and Scis., Va., U. N.D., Grand Forks, U. Iowa, Blossburg Meml. Library, Pa., La. Tech. U., Lincoln-Davies, Ind., Chattanooga, Delta State U., Cleve., and many others. Mem. Coll. Arts Assn., Contemporary Art Ctr., Mus. Modern Art, Southeast Ctr. for Contemporary Art. Republican. Presbyterian. Avocations: jogging; coaching sports for children. Home: 1211 Robinette Dr Ruston LA 71270 Office: Sch Art and Architecture La Tech U Ruston LA 71272

BERING, NORMAN JOSEPH, II, retail hardware store executive; b. Houston, July 16, 1949; s. August Charles III and Lottie (Hutton) B.; B.Jour., U. Tex., 1973; m. Kelly Ann Mulligan, June 2, 1973; children—Blakely Edith, Bevin Ann. Vice-pres. Bering Home Center, Inc., Houston, 1973—; chmn. bd. Handy Hardware Wholesale, Inc., 1980—. Mem. Nat. Retail Hardware Assn., Nat. Home Center Inst. Republican. Baptist. Office: 6102 Westheimer Houston TX 77057

BERKELEY, EDMUND, JR., archivist, educator; b. Charlottesville, Va., Apr. 1, 1937; s. Edmund and Dorothy A. Berkeley; m. Elizabeth Makaritis, June 9, 1963; children—Maria Randolph, Edmund III. B.A., U. South, 1958; M.A. in Am. History, U. Va., 1961. Prep. sch. tchr., 1961-63; asst. archivist Archives div. Va. State Library, 1963-65; sr. asst., asst. curator Manuscripts div. U. Va., Charlottesville, 1965-69, univ. archivist, 1970—, curator manuscripts, 1970-76, records adminstr., 1976—; assoc. prof. Coll. Arts and Scis., 1976—; cons. U. Ga. Library, George C. Marshall Library, SUNY-Stony Brook. Nat. Hist. Publs. Commn. grantee. Fellow Soc. Am. Archivists (council 1977-81); mem. Mid-Atlantic Regional Archives Conf., Orgn. Am. Historians, Am. Assn. State and Local History, Va. State Hist. Records Adv. Bd. Episcopalian. Editor: Autographs and Manuscripts: A Collector's Manual, 1978; author, editor articles in profl. jours. Home: 2403 Bennington Rd Charlottesville VA 22901 Office: U Va Library Manuscripts Dept Charlottesville VA 22903-2498

BERKELEY, FRANCIS LEWIS, JR., retired archivist; b. Albemarle County, Va., Apr. 9, 1911; s. Francis Lewis and Ethel (Crissey) B.; B.S., U. Va., 1934, M.A., 1940; m. Helen Wayland Sutherland, June 12, 1937. Tchr. Va. pub. schs., 1934-38; asst. curator manuscripts U. Va. Library, Charlottesville, 1938-41, curator and univ. archivist, 1946-63, asso. librarian, 1957-63, sec. of Rector and Visitors, 1953-58, exec. asst. to pres., 1963-74, archivist emeritus, prof. emeritus, 1974—; council Inst. Early Am. History and Culture. Fulbright research fellow U. Edinburgh, 1952-53; Guggenheim fellow U. London, 1961-62; sec. of navy adv. com. on naval history, 1958-83. Trustee Thomas Jefferson Meml. Found.; mem. adv. com. Papers of Thomas Jefferson, Papers of James Madison, Papers of George Washington; mem. Va. Com. on Colonial Records, 1955-71, Va. Commn. on Hist. Records, 1976—. Served with USNR, 1942-46; capt. ret. Fellow Soc. Am. Archivists; mem. Am. Antiquarian Soc., Mass., Va., (v.p. 1970-78, trustee 1979-82), other hist. socs., Colonial Soc. Mass., Walpole Soc., Raven Soc., Phi Beta Kappa, Omicron Delta Kappa. Democrat. Episcopalian. Clubs: Colonnade (Charlottesville); Century (N.Y.). Editor and compiler: Dunmore's Proclamation of Emancipation, 1941; Annual Reports on Historical Collections, University of Virginia Library, 1945-50, with cumulative indexes, 1945, 50; Jefferson Papers of the University of Virginia, 1950; Papers of John Randolph of Roanoke, 1950; John Rolfe's True Relation. 1951; Introduction to Thomas Jefferson's Farm Book, 1953. Editorial bd. Va. Quar. Rev., 1961-74. Contbr. to Dictionary of Biography, Ency. Brit., Collier's Nat. Am. Cyclopedia; and other reference works. Home: 1927 Thomson Rd Charlottesville VA 22903

BERKMAN, HAROLD WILLIAM, management educator, educational administrator; b. Bklyn., Feb. 22, 1926; s. Abel A. and Rose F. (Garfinkel) B.; m. Muriel Siegel, Feb. 3, 1950; children—Gary Keith, Karen A. B.B.A., U. Ga., 1949; M.B.A., St. John's U., 1969, Ph.D., 1971. Pres. Hastings and Berwick, Ltd., N.Y. and Conn., 1960-69; sr. ptnr. Halmor Mgmt. Co., N.Y.C., 1960-77; adj. prof. bus. C.W. Post Ctr., L.I.U., Greenvale, N.Y., 1969; assoc. prof., 1970-75, prof., 1975-77; exec. v.p., dir. Acad. Mktg. Sci., Miami, 1971—; dir. exec. and spl. programs U. Miami (Fla.), 1977-80, prof. bus. mgmt. orgn., 1977—, assoc. dean Sch. Bus. Adminstrn., 1980—; vis. prof. mgmt. M.B.A. program N.Y. Inst. Tech., 1976; vis. prof. mktg. St. John's U., 1971. Served to staff sgt. U.S. Army, 1944-46; ETO. Danforth fellow, 1976-82; recipient Meritorious Service award Fedn. Jewish Philanthropies, 1963-64; ann. mktg. award Bus. Adminstrn. Soc. St. John's U., 1969; Outstanding Faculty Scholar of Yr. award C.W. Post, Sch. Bus., 1974; Significant Writing Activity award Sch. Bus. Adminstrn., U. Miami, 1978, Excellence in Published Writing award, 1979, World Mktg. Congress award, 1983. Mem. Acad. Mktg. Sci. (Disting. Service award 1972, Leadership award 1979), Am. Mktg. Assn., So. Mktg. Assn., So. Mgmt. Assn., Acad. Internat. Bus., Beta Gamma Sigma, Delta Mu Delta, Delta Sigma Pi (Service award, 1970). Jewish. Author: The Human Relations of Management, 1974; (with J.J. Young) The Human Relations of Management: Cases and Issues, 2d edit., 5th printing, 1980; (with J. Young) Contemporary and Classical Readings in Human Relations, 1975; (with Armandi and Barbera) Marketing Update, 1977; (with Ivan R. Vernon) Perspectives in International Business, 1979; (with C.C. Gilson) Advertising Today: Concepts and Strategies, 1980; (with C.C. Gilson) Consumer Behavior: Concepts and Strategies, 2d edit., 1981; (with Armandi and Barbera) Organizational Behavior: Contemporary and Classical Readings, 1982; Consumer Behavior: Concepts and Strategies (with C.C. Gilson), 3d edit., 1986; (with V.V. Bellur) Readings in Marketing Management, 1986; (with V.V. Bellus and Law) Readings in Advertising, 1986; contbr. numerous articles to profl. jours. Home: 5882 SW 105th St Miami FL 33156 Office: 321 Jenkins Bldg Sch Bus U Miami Coral Gables FL 33124

BERKOWITZ, PAUL HOWARD, medical supply distributing company executive; b. Cleve., July 16, 1949; s. Sam and Evelyn (Pollack) B.; m. Cindy Louise Nordin, June 23, 1973 (div. Jan. 1979). Student U. Fla., 1967-69; B.S., U. Miami, 1971; postgrad. Sch. Dentistry, U. Md., 1972-74. Med. rep. Warner Chilcott Co., Morris Plains, N.J., 1974-78; dist. mgr. Junc Products Co., Cin., 1978-81; med. distbr. Dow Corning Wright Co., Arlington, Tenn., 1981—; cons. Dade County Hosps., Miami, 1981—. Mem. Alpha Epsilon Pi Alumni Assn. Miami, Democrat. Jewish. Club: Palm Bay (Miami). Lodge: B'nai B'rith. Home: 11118-1 SW 132d Pl Miami FL 33186

BERLAND, NANCY WINNIK, psychologist; b. Milw., Feb. 11, 1949; d. Norvall Oscar and Betty Jane (Feldman) Winnik; m. Lincoln Lewis Berland, June 12, 1971; children—Matthew, Nicole. B.A., U. Wis.-Madison, 1971; Ph.D., Washington U.-St. Louis, 1975. Lic. psychologist, Wis., Ala. Pvt. practice psychology, Milw., 1975-82; psychologist Curative Workshop, Milw., 1976-77, Mt. Sinai Hosp., Milw., 1978-82, U. Ala., Birmingham, 1982-84; psychologist, dir. Ctr. for Eating Disorders, Birmingham, 1985—, cons. in nutrition, 1984; lectr. Cardinal Stritch, Milw., 1976-78. Mem. Birmingham PTA. Mem. Am. Psychol. Assn., Ala. Psychol. Assn., Birmingham Regional Psychol. Assn. Avocation: tennis. Home: 3421 Brookwood Trace Birmingham AL 35223 Office: Ctr Eating Disorders Inc 404 Ambulatory Care Ctr Brookwood Med Ctr Birmingham AL 35209

BERLIN, BARRY N., investment counselor; b. Martinsville, Va., Dec. 6, 1954; s. Theodore and Zelda (Berlin). B.S., U. Va., 1977; M.B.A., Northwestern U., 1978. Chartered fin. analyst. Econ. analyst, v.p. First Nat. Bank Tulsa, 1978-82; counselor Wachovia Bank, Winston-Salem, N.C., 1983—; council examiners Inst. Chartered Fin. Analysts, Charlottesville, Va., 1984—. Participant Leadership Tulsa, 1982; trustee Temple Israel, Tulsa, 1981-82; com. co-chmn. Leadership Winston-Salem, 1984—; founder, chmn. Jewish Young Adults Tulsa, 1980-81. Fellow N.C. Soc. Fin. Analysts (dir.); mem. U. Va. Alumni Okla. (treas., founder 1982). Republican. Club: Bachelors (Winston-Salem). Avocations: amatuer potter; golf; triathlete.

BERLIN, JACOB BORIS, psychotherapist; b. N.Y.C., Apr. 16, 1924; s. Alexander and Martha (Aranow) B.; m. Anne Wright Morris, Apr. 26, 1947; children—Alexander, Ralph, Christopher, Letitia, Deborah. A.B., Harvard U., 1950; M.S.P.H., U. N.C., Chapel Hill, 1951; M.Div., Va. Theol. Sem., 1960; M.A., U. S.C., 1975. Lic. marriage and family counselor, Ga.; ordained to ministry, Episcopal Ch., 1960. Sanitarian, Near East Found., Iranian area, 1951-57; vicar St. Andrew's Episcopal Ch., Pasadena, Md., 1960-64, St. Anne's Episcopal Ch., Damascus, Md., 1964-69; assoc. dir. pastoral Counseling Ctrs. of Augusta (Ga.), 1969-73; asst. prof. Sch. Nursing, Med. Coll. Ga., 1973-75; dir. St. Paul's Counseling Service, Augusta, 1975—; assoc. rector St. Paul's Episcopal Ch., Augusta, 1975—. Pres., Augusta Area Mental Health Assn., 1976-77; bd. dirs. Sr. Citizens Council, Augusta, 1975-76, Augusta Players, 1969-72, Housing Authority Adjudication Ct., Richmond County, 1973-75. Served with U.S. Army, 1942-45. Named Hon. Citizen of Sarlat, the Dordogne, France in recognition of service as OSS agt. with French resistance in World War II, 1985. Mem. Am. Assn. Pastoral Counselors (diplomate), Am. Assn. Marriage and Family Therapy. Office: 605 Reynolds St Augusta GA 30901

BERLIN, JEROME CLIFFORD, lawyer, accountant, real estate developer; b. N.Y.C., Aug. 23, 1942; s. Benjamin R. and Muriel (Weintraub) B.; B.S. Bus. Adminstrn., U. Fla., 1964; J.D., U. Fla., 1968; student U. Exeter (Eng.), 1967; m. Gwen Tischler, July 30, 1977; children—Bret Jason, Sharon Nichole, Ashley Lauren. Accountant, Peat, Marwick, Mitchell & Co., Houston, 1968-69; mem. law firm Jerome C. Berlin, Miami, Fla., 1969-71; pres. Sterling Capital Investments, Inc., Miami, 1971-80; pres., chief operating officer The Robino-Ladd Co., Miami, 1974-80; pres., chief exec. officer Inprojet Corp., Miami, 1978-80; ptnr. Schwartz and Nash, P.A., Miami, 1980-82; pres. Verdi Capital Corp., 1979; dir. Enterprise Bank, Miami. Chmn., Dade County Zoning Appeals Bd., 1971-73; chmn. bd. Signature Gardens, 1984—, Deux Michel; bd. overseers Hebrew Union Coll., N.Y.C., 1983; bd. dirs. Democratic Nat. Com., also mem. fin. council; chmn. regional bd. Anti-Defamation League, chmn. Soc. Fellows; chmn. Fla. Thousand; mem. Fla. Internat. Banking Com.; mem. planning bd. Miami Children's Hosp.; mem. South Miami Hosp. Assos.; mem. exec. bd. Project Newborn, Miami; bd. dirs. Temple Beth Am, Miami; bd. dirs. Juvenile Diabetes Assn. C.P.A., Fla., Tex. Mem. Am. Inst. C.P.A.s (nat. bd. dirs.), Fla. Inst. C.P.A.s, Tex. Soc. C.P.A.s, Am. Bar Assn., Fla. Bar Assn., Am. Assn. Atty.-C.P.A.s. Jewish. Home: 5425 SW 92d St Miami FL 33156

BERLOWE, FREDERIC HERMAN, industrial engineer; b. N.Y.C., Aug. 16, 1930; s. Phillip and Mae (Palmet) B.; m. Sondra Satz, Dec. 27, 1959; children—Amanda Joy, Laura Jane, Peter Emerson. B.S. in Indsl. Engring., U. Miami, 1952. Registered profl. engr., Fla. Engr. product design, layout Miami Window, Ludman Corp., Miami, 1952-54; engr. mech. contractors Hill-York, Dublin Co., Miami, 1955-60; mech. designer Brown and Sells, Coral Gables, Fla., 1960-63; tchr. mech. engring. and refrigeration Miami Dade Community Coll., 1961-62, U. Miami, Coral Gables, 1960-63; pres. Frederic H. Berlowe Assocs., Inc. Coral Gables, 1963—; village engr. Va. Gardens, Fla., 1964-72. Mem. Nat. Soc. Profl. Engrs. (sr.), Fla. Engring. Soc. (sr.), ASHRAE (sr.), Nat. Acad. Forensic Engrs. (diplomate), Nat. Fire Protection Assn. Lodge: Masons. Avocations: reading; horseback riding; hunting; boating; woodworking. Office: 420 S Dixie Hwy Suite 2R Coral Gables FL 33146

BERMAN, MARGO RENEE, advertising executive; b. Jersey City, July 8, 1947; d. Jack H. and Blanche (Bram) Breitbart; m. Jack Robert Berman, June 25, 1978. Mus. B., U. Miami (Fla.), 1971, M.Music, 1974, postgrad., 1977. Cert. tchr., Fla. Program host, producer Sta. WLRN-FM, 1977-78; copywriter, Ellman's, Atlanta, 1978-79; advt. supr. Mktg. Services, Hollywood, Fla., 1980-81; writer, account exec. WWJF, Fort Lauderdale, Fla., 1981, WKQS, Fort Lauderdale, 1981-82; producer, copywriter, dir. Hume, Smith, Mickelberry, Miami, Fla., 1982-83; sr. copywriter, dir., producer The Ad Team, North Miami Beach, Fla., 1983-84; prin. Madison Ave. Advt. Co., Inc., Miami Beach, 1984—, Margo Berman Creative Services, North Miami Beach, 1985—; lectr. in field; judge Miami Herald Cannes Awards, 1984, Nat. Clarion awards, 1986. Author TV and radio commls.: Miami Citizens Against Crime, 1982. Recipient Bronze award Internat. Film Festival of N.Y., 1982, Nat. Advt. Agy. Network, 1982; Bronze Telly award TV Commls. Festival, 1982; 1st place Angel award Fla. Advt. Fedn., 1982; John Caples award for Fla. Power & Light comml., 1983; Andy awards for Hilton Resort print campaign, 1983, Fla. Power & Light print ad, 1983, Pantry Pride Supermarkets radio campaign, 1983; Clarion award for Security First Fed. radio spot, 1985; Addy awards for numerous radio and campaign spots, 1985; Mem. Women in Communications (profl. advisor 1982-83, rec. sec. Miami 1984-85, hist. 1985-86), Nat. Acad. TV Arts and Scis. (judge Chgo. 1983), Miami Advt. Fedn., Phi Kappa Phi, Sigma Alpha Iota. Home: 3351 NE 164 St North Miami Beach FL 33160 Office: Margo Berman Creative Services 1869 NE 163 St North Miami Beach FL 33162

BERMELLO, GUILLERMO RUIZ, publishing company executive; b. Camaguey, Cuba, Apr. 16, 1918; s. Claudio C. and Amparo A. (Ruiz) B.; came to U.S., 1960, naturalized, 1969; Degree in Pub. Accounting, U. Havana (Cuba), 1949, Dr.Comml. Scis., 1952, Doctor in Laws, 1957; m. Martha Guardia, Sept. 11, 1949; 1 son, Willy A. Pvt. practice accounting and law, Havana, 1949-58; justice Nat. Ct. of Accounts, Havana, 1959-60; pvt. practice accounting, Miami, Fla., 1961-65; exec. v.p., gen. mgr. Editorial Am., S.A., Virginia Gardens, Fla., 1966-75; pres. Bermello Consulting Inc. Mem. Am. Accounting Assn. Roman Catholic. Club: Coral Gables Country. Home: 726 Santander Ave Coral Gables FL 33134 Office: 55 Almeria Ave Coral Gables FL 33134

BERNAL, ERNESTO MARROQUIN, educational administrator; b. San Antonio, July 9, 1938; s. Ernest M. and Herlinda G. (Marroquin) B.; B.A., St. Mary's U., San Antonio, 1960; M.Ed., Our Lady of Lake U., San Antonio, 1964; Ph.D., U. Tex., Austin, 1971; m. Carmen Tafolla, June 29, 1979; children—Ann Elizabeth, Sean Michael, Cielos (dec.), Marilinda. Tchr., then asst. prin. Keystone Sch., San Antonio, 1960-66; instr., then asst. prof. edn. St. Mary's U., 1966-71; dir. bilingual early elem. program S.W. Ednl. Devel. Lab., Austin, Tex., 1971-74; asso. prof. bicultural bilingual studies U. Tex., San Antonio, 1974-78; profl. asso. Ednl. Testing Service, 1978-79; pres. Creative Ednl. Enterprises, Inc., Austin, 1980-83; coordinator Zone 2 Bilingual Multifunctional Support Ctr., Calif. State U., Fresno, 1983-84; prof. tchr. edn. Calif. State U., San Bernardino, 1984—; nat. adv. council Gifted Students Inst. Research and Devel., Nat. Clearinghouse Bilingual Edn., 1980; recipient citation merit Nat./State Leadership Tng. Inst. Gifted and Talented, 1974. Mem. Am. Ednl. Research Assn., Am. Psychol. Assn., Council Exceptional Children, Evaluation Research Soc., Nat. Soc. Study Edn., Nat. Assn. Bilingual Edn. Democrat. Author articles, reports in field.

BERNARD, ALAN LEROY, management and political consultant; b. Webster City, Iowa, Apr. 13, 1953; s. Emerson LeVay and Belva F. (Myers) B.; m. Kay Ellen Erickson, Aug. 11, 1979; 1 child, Joshua. B.S. in Polit. Sci., Drake U., 1975, J.D., 1980. Bar: Iowa 1980. County program adminstr. Iowa Democratic party, Des Moines, 1976; chmn. Iowa Dem. Central Com., 1978-79; pres. Bernard & Assocs., Des Moines and Orlando, Fla., 1979—; exec. v.p. Mid Continent Small Bus. United, Kansas City, Mo., 1980-83, Fla. Nurserymen and Growers Assn., Orlando, 1983-85. Author: Small Business: The Economic Engine, 1982. Mem. Am. Soc. Assn. Execs., Fla. Soc. Assn. Execs., Nat. Assn. Exhbn. Mgrs. Democrat. Lutheran. Home: 8559 Pomelo Tree Ln Orlando FL 32819 Office: 7600 Dr Phillips Blvd Suite 126 Orlando FL 32819

BERNARD, JAMES DONALD, dermatologist; b. Neptune, N.J., Dec. 15, 1938; s. Donald Joseph and Myrtle Marite (Boyd) B.; m. Tommie Lou Lowrey, May 31, 1969; B.S., Ariz. State U., 1961; D.O., U. Health Scis. Coll. Osteo. Medicine, Kansas City, Mo., 1969. Diplomate Am. Osteopathic Bd. Dermatology. Intern Phoenix Gen. Hosp., 1969-70; resident in dermatology Detroit Osteo. Hosp., 1970-73; practice osteo. medicine specializing in dermatology, Atlanta, 1973—; chief of staff Ga. Osteo. Hosp., Atlanta, 1979-80. Served to 1st lt. MC, USAR, 1964-71. Fellow Am. Osteo. Coll. Dermatology (pres. 1977-78, sec.-treas. 1979—); mem. Am. Osteo. Assn., Ga. Osteo. Med. Assn. (pres. 1982-83). Ex officio mem. Am. Osteo. Bd. Dermatology, 1979—. Republican. Roman Catholic. Lodges: Civitan, K.C. Avocations: swimming; tennis. Home: 4330 Idlewood Ln Tucker GA 30084 Office: 4480 Covington Hwy Suite A Decatur GA 30035

BERNARD, ROBERT SCALES, applied physicist; b. Conway, S.C., Mar. 5, 1946; s. Henri Joseph and Bettye (Scales) B. B.S., Miss. State U., 1969, Ph.D., 1981; M.S., Stanford U., 1971. Staff mem. Sandia Labs., Albuquerque, 1969-73; research physicist Waterways Experiment Sta., Vicksburg, Miss., 1973—. Contbr. articles to profl. jours. Recipient Hamilton Watch award Hamilton Watch Co. 1968, Cert. Achievement, U.S. Army, 1976. Mem. Am. Phys. Soc., AIAA. Avocations: music; distance running; backpacking; motorcycling. Home: 115 Bellwood Dr Vicksburg MS 39180 Office: Waterways Experiment Sta WESHS-R PO Box 631 Vicksburg MS 39180

BERNARD, SPENCER THOMAS, lieutenant governor; b. Rush Springs, Okla., Feb. 5, 1915; s. Cicero Edgar and Gertrude (Sperling) B.; m. Vivan Opal Dorman, Aug. 3, 1935; 1 dau., Kay Ann Bernard Jones. Farmer, rancher, Rush Springs, Okla.; pres. Bernard Enterprises; mem. Okla. Ho. of Reps., 1960-78, speaker pro tempore, until 1978, vice-chmn., then chmn. soil and water resources com., vice chmn. house rules com.; now lt. gov., State of Okla., 1978—; v.p. Mid-Continent Farmers Coop. Mem. Cattlemen's Assn., Farmers Union. Democrat. Mem. Ch. of Christ. Club: Lions (past pres.). Home: Box 158 Rush Springs OK 73082 Office: 211 State Capitol Oklahoma City OK 73105

BERNAU, SIMON JOHN, mathematics educator; b. Wanganui, N.Z., June 12, 1937; came to U.S., 1969; s. Ernest Henry Lovell and Jessie Ella Mary (Mason) B.; m. Lynley Joyce Turner, Aug. 11, 1959; children—Nicola Ann Bernau Cohn, Sally Jane. B.Sc., U. Canterbury, Christchurch, N.Z., 1958, M.Sc., 1959; B.A., Cambridge U., Eng., 1961, Ph.D., 1964. Lectr. U. Canterbury, 1964-65, sr. lectr., 1965-66; prof. math. U. Otago, Dunedin, N.Z., 1966-69; assoc. prof. U. Tex.-Austin, 1969-76, prof., 1976-85; prof., head dept. math. Southwest Mo. State U., 1985—. Contbr. articles to profl. publs. Mem. Am. Math. Soc., London Math. Soc. Avocations: running, hiking.

BERNAY, BETTI (MRS. J. BERNARD GOLDFARB), artist; b. N.Y.C.; d. David Michael and Anna Gaynia (Bernay) Woolin; grad. costume design Pratt Inst., 1946; student Nat. Acad., N.Y.C., 1947-49, Art Students League, N.Y.C., 1950-51; m. J. Bernard Goldfarb, Apr. 19, 1947; children—Manette Deitsch, Karen Lynn. One-man shows at Galerie Raymond Duncan, Paris, France, Salas Municipales, San Sebastian, Spain, Circulo de Bellas Artes, Madrid, Spain, Bacardi Gallery, Miami, Fla., Columbia (S.C.) Mus., Columbus (Ga.) Mus., Galerie Andre Weil, Paris, France, Galerie Hermitage, Montecarlo, Monaco, Casino de San Remo (Italy), Galerie de Arte de la Caja de Ahorros de Ronda, Malaga, Spain, Centro Artistico, Granada, Spain, Circulo de la Amistad, Cordoba, Spain, Galerie Andre Weil, Paris, France, Studio Gallery H, N.Y.C., Walter Wallace Gallery, Palm Beach, Fla., Museo Bellas Artes, Malaga, Spain, Harbor House Gallery, Miami Beach, Fla., Crystal House Gallery, Miami Beach, Fla., Internat. Gallery, Jordan Marsh, Miami, Fontainebleau Gallery, Miami Beach, Fla., Carriage House Gallery, Miami Beach; exhibited in group shows at Painters and Sculptors Soc., Jersey City (N.J.) Mus., Salon de Invierno, Museo Malaga, Spain, Salon des Beaux Arts, Cannes, France, Nat. Acad. Gallery, N.Y.C., Salon des Artistes Independants, Paris, Salon des Artistes Francais, Paris, Salon Populiste, Paris, Salon de Otono, Madrid, Spain, Salamagundi Club, N.Y.C., Nat. Assn. Painters and Sculptors Spain, Madrid, Phipps Gallery, Palm Beach, Fla., Lever House, N.Y.C., Knickerbocker Artists, N.Y.C., Artists Equity, Hollywood (Fla.) Mus., Nat. Arts Gallery, N.Y.C., Springfield (Mass.) Mus., ACA Gallery, N.Y.C., Argent Gallery, N.Y.C., Nat. Acad. Gallery, N.Y.C., Gables Art Gallery, Miami, Gibralter Internat. Art Exhbn., Gault Gallery Cheltenham, Phila., Century Gallery, Miami, Fla., Met. Mus. and Art Center, Miami, Lord & Taylor Gallery, N.Y.C., Pageant Gallery, Galerie 99 (both Miami), Rosenbaum Gallery, Palm Beach, Fla., Planet Ocean, Jockey Club Art Gallery (both Miami); represented in permanent collections at Museo de Malaga, Circulo de la Amistad, Cordoba, Spain, I.O.S. Found., Geneva, Switzerland, Columbia (S.C.) Mus., others. Recipient Medal for artistic merit City of N.Y., Sch. Art Leagues, N.Y.C.; Prix de Paris, Raymond Duncan, 1958; others. Mem. Nat. Assn. Painters and Sculptors Spain, Nat. Assn. Women Artists, Societe des Artistes Francais, Societe des Artistes Ind., Fedn. Francais des Societes d'Art Graphique et Plastique, Artists Equity, Am. Artists Profl. League, Women's Caucus for Art, Profl. Artists Guild, Nat. Soc. Lit. and the Arts, Am. Fedn. Art, South Fla. Shell Club. Address: 10155 Collins Ave Bal Harbour FL 33154

BERND, DAVID LEMOINE, health system administrator; b. Milw., Mar. 3, 1949; s. Robert L. and Betty J. B.; m. Helen M. Menge, Mar. 15, 1976; children—Kelly Elizabeth, Jason LeMoine, Jeffrey David. B.A. in History, Coll. William and Mary, 1971; M.H.A., Med. Coll. Va., 1973. Adminstrv. asst. Norfolk Gen. Hosp. (Va.), 1972-73, asst. adminstr., 1974-79, adminstr., 1979—; pres. Med. Center Hosps., Norfolk, 1983-85; exec. v.p., Chief operating officer Alliance Health System, 1985—; exec. bd. Mut. Fed. Savs. and Loan. Bd. dirs. Big Bros. of Am., Norfolk, 1973-83, 83—. Mem. Am. Coll. Hosp. Adminstrs. (Young Adminstr. of Yr. award 1984), Med. Coll. Va. Alumni Soc., Alumni Assn. of Dept. Health Adminstrn. of Med. Coll. Va. (pres. 1984-85). Office: Kroger Exec Ctr Bldg 18 Suite 202 Norfolk VA 23502

BERNHARDT, HARVEY EVAN, pathologist, educator; b. Bronx, N.Y., July 27, 1944; s. Harry and Gertrude (Solomon) B.; m. Regina Therese Wakin, Sept. 30, 1967; children—Wesley Joseph, Monica Denise, Harrison Bradley. B.S., Queens Coll. CUNY, 1964; M.D., U. Louisville, 1968. Diplomate Am. Bd. Pathology. Intern, Jackson Meml. Hosp., Miami, 1968-69; resident in pathology Los Angeles County Harbor Gen. Hosp., 1969-71, Mt. Sinai Hosp., Miami, Fla., 1973-74; dir. clin. labs. Univ. Hosp., Jacksonville, Fla., 1974-76; pathologist Meth. Hosp., Jacksonville, 1976-79; chief exec. officer Am. Med. Labs., Jacksonville, 1979-81; chmn. dept. pathology, dir. clin. labs. Jacksonville Gen. Hosp., 1981—; med. dir. Smith Kline Biosci. Labs., Jacksonville, Fla.; clin. assoc. prof. U. Fla. Med. Sch., 1975—; adj. prof. U. North Fla., 1982—. Bd. dirs. Duval County Republican Exec. Com., 1974-76. Served to lt. comdr. USNR, 1971-73. Mem. AMA (Physicians Recognition award 1973, 76, 80, 85), Fla. Soc. Pathology (Alfred L. Lewis award 1974), Duval County Med. Soc. (Beals award 1978), Fla. Med. Assn., Coll. Am. Pathologists, Internat. Acad. Pathologists, Assn. Clin. Scientists, Am. Soc. Clin. Pathologists. Jewish. Contbr. articles to profl. jours. Office: 4901 Richard St Jacksonville FL 32207

BERNHARDT, JOHN BOWMAN, banker; b. Norton, Va., Aug. 7, 1929; s. Claude Bowman and Mabel (Dixon) B.; B.A., U. Va., 1954. LL.B., 1957; postgrad. Rutgers U., 1967; m. Ada Nuckels, Aug. 29, 1952; children—Jared B., J. Carter. Exec. v.p. Va. Nat. Bank, Norfolk, 1969-79, pres., 1980-83; exec. v.p. Va. Nat. Bankshares, 1972-79, pres., 1980-83; vice chmn. bd. Sovran Fin. Corp. Sovran Bank, N.A., 1984—; dir. Dominion Resources Inc., Va. Electric and Power Co. Trustee Eastern Va. Med. Sch. Found.; past pres. United Way; chmn. Greater Hampton Roads Orgn.; mem. Va. Fuel Converson Authority. Mem. Va. Bankers Assn. (pres. 1979). Res. City Bankers, Hampton Rds. Maritime Assn., Am. Bankers Assn. (dir. 1985—), Hampton Roads C. of C. (vice chmn. bd.). Presbyterian. Clubs: Norfolk Yacht and Country, Harbor (Norfolk); Cedar Point (Suffolk, Va.). Home: 8020 Quail Hollow Cedar Point Suffolk VA 23433 Office: 1 Commercial Pl Norfolk VA 23510

BERNHARDT, ROBERT LINN, III, mathematics educator and administrator; b. Salisbury, N.C., Apr. 28, 1939; s. Robert Linn and Edna (Hethcox) B.; m. Norma Lee Woosley, June 21, 1961 (div. 1974); 1 child, Lydian Lee; m. Judy Ruth Hayes, Feb. 15, 1975; 1 stepchild, William H. Brande, Jr. B.S. in Math., U. N.C., 1961, M.A., 1964; Ph.D., U. Oreg., 1968. Asst. prof. U. N.C.-Greensboro, 1968-74; asst. prof., assoc. prof. Chgo. State U., 1974-83, chmn. dept., 1977-83; prof., chmn. dept. math. East Carolina U., Greenville, N.C., 1983—. Contbr. articles to profl. jours. Recipient Outstanding Tchr. award. Chgo. State U., 1976. Mem. Am. Math. Soc., Math. Assn. Am., N.C. Council Tchrs. Math., Sigma Xi. Avocation: Music, record collecting. Address: 1808 Forest

Hills Dr Greenville NC 27834 Office: Dept Math East Carolina U Greenville NC 27834

BERNIUS, PAUL STEPHEN, construction company official; b. N.Y.C., Jan. 9, 1944; s. Paul S. and Florence P. (O'Meara) B.; B.A., St. Francis Coll., N.Y.C., 1965; M.A. in Human Resource Devel., New Sch. Social Research, 1975; m. Maureen McLaughlin, Feb. 15, 1975; children—Paul Stephen, Megan McLaughlin. With personnel dept. Standard Oil Co. Calif., 1967-72; dir. personnel adminstrn. and employee relations Sea-Land Service, Inc., Menlo Park, N.J., 1972-83; dir. organizational devel. Hilti, Inc., Tulsa, 1983-84, dir. compensation and indsl. relations, 1984-85, v.p. human resources, 1985—. Served with USMCR, 1965-70. Mem. Am. Soc. Tng. and Devel. Republican. Roman Catholic. Address: 10 Spring Creek Ln Broken Arrow OK 74014

BERNSTEIN, JOSEPH, lawyer; b. New Orleans, Feb. 12, 1930; s. Eugene Julian and Lola (Schlemoff) B.; B.S., U. Ala., 1952; LL.B., Tulane U., 1957; m. Phyllis Maxine Askanase, Sept. 4, 1955; children—Jill, Barbara, Elizabeth R, Jonathan Joseph. Clk. to Justice E. Howard McCaleb of La. Supreme Ct., 1957; admitted to La. bar, 1957; asso. firm Jones, Walker, Waechter, Poitevent, Carrere & Denegre, 1957-60, partner, 1960-65; gen. practice New Orleans, 1965—. Past pres. New Orleans Jewish Community Ctr., Met. New Orleans chpt. March of Dimes. Trustee New Orleans Symphony Soc.; past mem. adv. council New Orleans Mus. Art; past nat. exec. com. Am. Jewish Com. Served to 2d lt. AUS, 1952-54. Mem. Am., La., New Orleans bar assns., Phi Delta Phi, Zeta Beta Tau. Democrat. Jewish. Home: 3119 Prytania Ave New Orleans LA 70115

BERRY, ARNOLD JOEL, anesthesiologist, educator; b. Nashville, Aug. 28, 1948; s. Lester and Mamie Rebecca (Lebed) B.; m. Loraine Mendel, June 28, 1970 (div.); children—Michael, Jeremy. A.B., Emory U., 1970; M.D., U. Pa., 1974. Diplomate Am. Bd. Anesthesiology. Intern, Hosp. U. Pa. Phila., 1974-75, resident in anesthesiology, 1975-77, research fellow in anesthesiology, 1977-78; practice medicine specializing in anesthesiology; asst. prof. anesthesiology Emory U., Atlanta, 1978-84, assoc. prof., 1984—; lectr. in field. Mem. Am. Soc. Anesthesiologists, Internat. Anesthesia Research Soc., AMA, Ga. Soc. Anesthesiologists, Soc. Cardiovascular Anesthesiologists, Phi Beta Kappa, Alpha Omega Alpha. Contbr. articles in field to profl. jours. Office: Dept Anesthesia Emory Univ Hosp Atlanta GA 30322

BERRY, BETTYE FOSTER, nursing educator; b. Birmingham, Ala., Jan. 12, 1935; d. Jim and Effie Mae (White) Foster; 1 child, Adrienne. B.S., Tuskegee Inst., 1961; M.S., Ind. U., 1965; Ed.D., U. Ala., 1981. Registered nurse, Ala. Instr. Albany State Coll., Ga., 1963-67; asst. prof. Tenn. State U., Nashville, 1967-69; supervisory nurse Meharry Med. Coll., Nashville, 1969-71; project dir. Lawson State Community Coll., Birmingham, Ala., 1971-75, chmn., 1977—; dir. nursing service Roosevelt Health Ctr., Birmingham, 1975-77; sec. Western Mental Health Dept. Bd. Dirs., Birmingham, 1976. Mem. Law Dames Support Assn. Inc., Miles Coll., Birmingham, 1981—; mem. Ctr. for Aging, Birmingham, 1981-83. Mem. Am. Nurses Assn., Nat. League Nursing, Kappa Delta Pi, Alpha Kappa Alpha. Democrat. Roman Catholic. Club: Jack and Jill. Avocations: reading; gardening. Home: 3115 Altaloma Dr Vestavia Hills AL 35216 Office: Lawson State Community Coll 3060 Wilson Rd Birmingham AL 35221

BERRY, CHARLES MARVIN, oil company executive; b. Minden, La., Mar. 4, 1939; s. Fred Howard and Nobie O'dell (Craine) B.; m. Glenna Mae Lindsey, Feb. 18, 1966; children—David Walter, Kimberley Renae, Michelle Alyse. B.S. in M.E., U. Houston, 1963. Prodn. engr. Continental Oil Co., Midland, Tex., 1963-69; chief engr. McRae Oil Corp., Houston, 1969-74; v.p., dir. McRae Consol. Oil & Gas., Houston, 1974-84; mgr. ops. Lear Petroleum Corp., Houston, 1984-85; chief ops. officer D-I Energy, Inc., Houston, 1986—. Served with Army N.G., 1964-69. Mem. Soc. Petroleum Engrs., Ind. Petroleum Assn. Am., La. Assn. Producers and Royalty Owners, Tex. Ind. Producers and Royalty Owners. Republican. Methodist. Clubs: Champions Golf, Wimbledon Racquet, Athletic of Houston. Home: 6214 Rolling Water Dr Houston TX 77069 Office: 625 Paragon Ctr One 450 Gears Rd Houston TX 77067

BERRY, FRANCIS CLIFFORD, engineer; b. Selma, Ala., Sept. 1, 1924; s. Robert Clifford and Fannie (Scoggin) B.; m. Mary Jacqueline Meeks, Sept. 3, 1944; children—Judith Ann, Alice Jane. B.S. in Elec. Engring., U. Ala., 1950. Lic. profl. engr. Ala., Calif. With Chgo. Bridge & Iron Co., various locations, 1950—, nondestructive engring. coordinator, AMC Ltd. subs., Scotland, 1979-81, engr. research and devel. and spl. projects, Houston, 1981—; cons. and lectr. in field. Served with U.S. Mcht. Marine, 1941-45. Mem. ASME, Am. Welding Soc., Pressure Vessel Research Com. (subcom. chmn.), Welding Research Council, Am. Soc. Nondestructive Testing (sec., treas., v.p., pres., chmn. bd.), Tau Beta Pi. Democrat. Presbyterian. Lodge: Masons. Contbr. articles to profl. jours. Home: 3754 Brookwood Rd Birmingham AL 35223

BERRY, JAMES D., banker; b. Sapulpa, Okla., June 23, 1921; s. James D. and Gertrue (Morrow) B.; m. Mary Evelyn Irby, Oct. 16, 1946; children—Beverly, James D., Robert Neil. B.S., U. Okla., 1943; grad., Rutgers U. Grad. Sch. Banking, 1959, Harvard U., 1963. With Am. Nat. Bank, Sapulpa, 1932-50, asst. v.p., 1948-50; with Republic Nat. Bank, Dallas, 1950-74, sr. v.p., 1961-63, exec. v.p., later vice chmn. bd.; pres. Republic Tex. Corp., Dallas, 1974-77, chmn. bd., chief exec. officer, 1977-85, chmn. bd., 1985—; dir. Dynalectron Corp., Taylor Pub. Co., Alexander & Alexander Services, Inc., RepublicBank Dallas, Indsl. Properties Corp. Bd. govs. Dallas County chpt. ARC; bd. dirs. Dallas Summer Musicals. Served to capt. AUS, 1943-46. Mem. Inter-frat. Council, Scabbard and Blade, Beta Theta Pi. Lodges: Masons (33 degree), Shriners. Office: RepublicBank Corp Ervay and Pacific Dallas TX 75201

BERRY, JANE WYPLER, employee relations executive; b. Boston, Feb. 16, 1943; d. Alfred Robert and Frances Emery Wypler; B.A., Cornell U., 1965; M.P.A., So. Meth. U., 1976; m. Robert Reed, Oct. 4, 1980. Personnel adminstr. employee relations City of Dallas, 1969-75; corp. benefits adminstr. Tex. Instruments, Dallas, 1976; mgmt. trainer Equitable Gen. Ins. Co., Ft. Worth, 1977; adminstr. response program United Way, Dallas Council on Alcoholism, 1979-82; pres. Employee Assistance Resource Tex., Inc., 1982—; mem. faculty Summer Inst. Alcohol Studies, U. Tex., Austin, 1980, 83, Tex. Tech. Med. Sch. Inst., 1981. Mem. Am. Soc. Tng. and Devel., Delta Delta Delta. Republican. Unitarian. Home: 2429 Heathercrest Dr Arlington TX 76018

BERRY, KENNETH WAYNE, sheriff's deputy, retail sporting goods store executive; b. Houston, Nov. 28, 1948; s. S.B. and Rose Mary (Kelly) B.; 1 child, Christopher Wayne. Grad. Total Data Processing Course, Manpower Bus. Sch., Houston, 1971, VA Hosp. Police Tng. Ctr., 1971; A.A., Houston Community Coll., 1974; cert. Harris County Sheriff's Dept. Acad., 1975; B.S. in Criminal Justice, U. Houston, 1976; specialized tng. Houston Police Acad., 1979, 84, Harris County Sheriff's Dept. Acad., 1977, 78, FBI Nat. Acad., 1984. Cert. advanced and instr. Tex. Commn. Law Enforcement Officer Standards and Edn. Policeman, VA Hosp., Little Rock, Ark., 1971-73; spl. agt. So. Pacific R.R., Houston, 1973-75; mem. Harris County Sheriff's Dept., Houston, 1975—, patrol sgt., 1978-79, patrol lt., 1979-81, jail capt., 1983-84, patrol capt., 1981—; dist. comdr. Law Enforcement Bur. Active Big Bros. of Houston, 1973-77. Served to sgt. USAF, 1966-70, Vietnam. Recipient Commondation award V.A. Hosp., 1971, numerous other appreciation awards from civic groups and law enforcement agencies. Mem. Sheriff's Assn. Tex., Nat. Orgn. Black Law Enforcement Execs., Harris County Dep. Sheriff's Assn. Roman Catholic. Lodge: Masons. Avocations: Fishing; hunting; archery; boating; skiing. Office: Harris County Sheriff's Dept 1301 Framklin Houston TX 77002

BERRY, MICHAEL FRANCIS, lawyer; b. Miami, Fla., May 7, 1945; s. Frank M. and Marguerite (Hawkins) B.; children—David Marion, Rebecca Leigh. B.S. cum laude, Fla. So. U., 1977; J.D., Stetson U., 1980; M.B.A., Nova U., 1984. Bar: Fla. 1981. Ptnr. Sullivan, Sullivan, LaJoie & Thacker, Vero Beach, Fla., 1981—. Mem. Jacksonville Bar Assn., Fla. Bar Assn., Am. Trial Lawyers Assn., ABA. Republican. Home: 400 18th St Apt A-7 Vero Beach FL 32960 Office: 1601 20th St Vero Beach FL 32961

BERRY, MICHAEL JAMES, physical chemist, research and development company executive, consultant, researcher, writer; b. Chgo., July 17, 1947; s. Bernie Milton and Irene Barbara (Lentz) B.; m. Julianne Elward, Apr. 28, 1967 (div. 1982); children—Michael James, Jennifer Anne; m. Patricia Gale Hackerman, July 7, 1984. B.S. in Chemistry, U. Mich., 1967; Ph.D., U. Calif.-Berkeley, 1970. Asst. prof., assoc. prof. dept. chemistry U. Wis.-Madison, 1970-76; mgr. photon chem. dept. Allied Chem. Corp., Morristown, N.J., 1976-79; Robert A. Welch prof. chemistry dir. Rice Quantum Inst., Rice U., Houston, 1979—; pres. Antropix Corp., 1982—; dir. Laser Applications Research Inst. HARC, 1984—; cons. in field. Recipient Fresenius award, 1982, research grantee NSF, Dept. Def., Welch Found., Research Corp.; tchr.-scholar Dreyfus Found., 1974-76; Alfred P. Sloan Found. fellow, 1975-76; named One of Best New Generation of Men and Women Under 40 Who Are Changing Am., Esquire Register, 1984. Guggenheim Found. fellow, 1981-82. Mem. Am. Chem. Soc. (award in pure chemistry 1983), Am. Phys. Soc., Optical Soc. Am., AAAS, AIAA, Houston Philos. Soc., Am. Soc. Photobiology, Materials Research Soc. Contbr. writings to sci. publs.; patentee. Home: 378 Litchfield Ln Houston TX 77024 Office: Dept Chemistry Rice U PO Box 1892 Houston TX 77251

BERRY, ROBERT LYON, ophthalmologist; b. Little Rock, Jan. 27, 1947. B.S., U. Ark., 1970; M.D., U. Ark.-Little Rock, 1977. Diplomate Am. Bd. Ophthalmology. Tech. engr. Aluminum Co. Am., Ark., 1970-73; intern, Baptist Med. Ctr., Little Rock, 1977-78; resident in ophthalmology Tulane Med. Sch., New Orleans, 1979-80, chief resident, 1980-81; practice medicine specializing in ophthalmology, Little Rock, 1982—; mem. staff F.H. Roy, M.D., P.A., active staff Bapt. Med. Ctr.; courtesy staff St. Vincents, Doctors, and Univ. Hosps. Mem. Am. Acad. Ophthalmology, Am. Intra Ocular Implant Soc., Am. Soc. Contemporary Ophthalmologists, Ark. Ophthalmology Soc., Keratorefractive Soc. Office: F Hampton Roy MD PA 1000 Med Towers Bldg Little Rock AR 72205

BERRY, ROY LEE, oil company executive; petroleum geologist; b. Fullerton, Calif., Oct. 2, 1933; s. Charles Roy and Alice Faye (Morton) B.; m. Sandra Glassman, Aug. 21, 1954; children—Mark V., Teresa A., Curtis R. B.S., U. N.Mex., 1956; postgrad. U. Calif.-Berkeley, 1969; Bus. Devel., Emory U., 1975. Registered geologist, Calif. Geologist, Humble Oil Co., New Orleans, 1959-63; supvr. geology Oasis Oil Co., Tripoli, Libya, 1963-71; geologist area Continental Oil Co., N.Y.C., 1971-75; mgr. exploration Conoco (U.K.) Ltd. div. Conoco Inc., London, 1975-81, area mgr. internat. exploration Conoco Inc., Houston, 1982—. Served to capt. USMC, 1956-59. Mem. Am. Assn. Petroleum Geologists (ho. of dels. 1978-81), Houston Geol. Soc. Republican. Clubs: Roehampton (London) (tennis com. 1979-81); Westside Tennis (Houston). Avocations: history; gardening; tennis. Home: 11615 Manor Park Dr Houston TX 77077 Office: Conoco Inc 600 N Dairy Ashford Rd Suite 3036 Oasis Houston TX 77077

BERRY, SARA MATHEWS, insurance company executive; b. Macon, Ga., Jan. 3, 1937; d. Robert Vinson and Mamie Celestia (Draper) Mathews; m. Ernest Floyd Berry, Jr., Aug. 11, 1957. Student, Mercer U., 1955-56. C.P.C.U. With Ins. Co. N.Am., Macon, 1955—, supr., 1958-64, dept. head, 1964-81, dir., 1981—, mem. corp. employee adv. bd. to pres., Phila., 1978. Loaned exec. United Way, Macon, from 1970, div. leader, account exec., to 1978. Mem. Soc. C.P.C.U.s (sec./treas. Macon sub-chpt. 1981-82), Ins. Women of Macon (pres. 1975, Woman of Year 1975), Middle Ga. Hist. Soc., Macon C. of C. Mem. Ch. of Christ. Clubs: Metropolitan Dinner, Macon Little Theatre. Office: Ins Co NAm 201 2d St Macon GA 31213

BERRY, STANLEY KEITH, economist, consultant; b. Little Rock, Nov. 22, 1951; s. Chase Stanley and Arminta Jane (Nichols) B.; m. Susan Gail Rummel, Dec. 29, 1979; 1 child, Laura Elizabeth. Student Vanderbilt U., 1969-70, Ph.D. in Econs., 1979; B.A. in Math., Hendrix Coll., 1973. Instr. Vanderbilt U., Nashville, 1976-77; asst. prof. Hendrix Coll., Conway, Ark., 1977-79; chief economist Ark. Pub. Service Commn., Little Rock, 1979—; cons. Ill. Atty. Gen., Springfield, 1982. Contbr. articles to profl. jours. Recipient Math. Sci. award Renselaer Inst., 1968; Earhart fellow, 1975-76; Vanderbilt U. assistantship, 1975-76. Mem. Am. Econ. Assn., So. Econ. Assn., Western Econ. Assn. Methodist. Lodge: Rotary. Avocations: jogging; reading. Home: 146 White Oak Ln Little Rock AR 72207 Office: Ark Pub Service Commn 1000 Center St Little Rock AR 72203

BERRY, WILLIAM WILLIS, public utility executive; b. Norfolk, Va., May 18, 1932; s. Joel Halbert and Julia Lee (Godwin) B.; m. Elizabeth Wall Mangum, Aug. 23, 1958; children—Elizabeth Preston, William Godwin, John Willis. B.S. in Elec. Engring., Va. Mil. Inst., 1954; M.C., U. Richmond, 1964. Registered profl. engr., Va. Engr., Gen. Electric Co., Schenectady and Pittsfield, N.Y., 1954-55; with Va. Electric & Power Co., Richmond, 1957—, mgr. electric ops., 1971-73, v.p. div. ops., 1974-76, sr. v.p. comml. ops., 1976-77, exec. v.p., 1978-80, pres., 1980-85, chmn., 1985—; dir. Ethyl Corp., Sovran Fin. Corp. Trustee Union Theol. Sem.; bd. visitors Va. Commonwealth U.; elder 1st Presbyterian Ch., Richmond, 1976—. Served with AUS, 1955-57. Clubs: Commonwealth, Country of Va. Home: 6601 Three Chopt Rd Richmond VA 23226 Office: Va Electric & Power Co PO Box 26666 Richmond VA 23261

BERRY CABÁN, CRISTOBAL SANTIAGO, educator; b. Aguadilla, P.R., Jan. 9, 1953; s. Charles William and María de Lourdes (Cabán) Berry; m. Kathryn C. Brue; children—Anna Katya, Anthony Wilson. B.A., Colegio Universitario Sagrado Corazón, Santurce, P.R., 1974; M.A., Marquette U., 1976; Ph.D. (fellow), U. Wis., 1981. Tchr., curriculum developer Milw. Pub. Schs., 1975-77; faculty, adminstr. U. Wis., Milw., 1977-81; research fellow The Latino Inst., Reston, Va., 1982; cons., Washington, 1982-84; pres. Atlantic Resources Corp., 1985—; lectr. George Mason U., 1983—. Editor P.R. Jour., Washington, 1982; author: Aromaliris, 1973; editor: Hispanics in Wisconsin, 1981; contbr. articles to profl. and popular jours. Fellow Am. Psychol. Assn.; mem. Am. Hist. Assn., Am. Sociol. Assn., Nat. Assn. Bilingual Edn. Roman Catholic. Office: PO Box 3322 Reston VA 22090

BERRYHILL, HENRY LEE, JR., research marine geologist; b. Charlotte, N.C., Nov. 6, 1921; s. Henry Lee and Viola Estelle (Johnston) B.; m. Louise Randall Russell, Sept. 13, 1947; children—Stuart Randall, Keith Courtney. B.S. in Geology, U. N.C., 1947, M.S. in Geology, 1949. Research geologist U.S. Geol. Survey, Washington, 1948-53, New Philadelphia, Ohio, 1953-55, San Juan, P.R., 1955-59, Denver, 1959-62, chief Rocky Mountain Region Publs. Unit, Denver, 1963-65, research marine geologist, Denver, 1965-67, chief Gulf of Mexico-Caribbean Region, Marine Geologic Studies, 1967-70, chief Nat. Marine Program, 1970-73, coordinator Marine Geologic Studies, Gulf of Mexico, 1974, chief Corpus Christi office (Tex.), 1982-85; advisor in marine geology Centre for Earth Sci. Studies, India, 1980—. Chmn. Coastal Bend Group, Sierra Club, 1981-82. Served with USAF, 1942-45. Decorated D.F.C., Air medal with three oak leaf clusters; recipient Superior Performance award U.S. Geol. Survey, 1969. Fellow Geol. Soc. Am.; Mem. Am. Assn. Petroleum Geologists, Soc. Econ. Paleontologists and Mineralogists. Episcopalian. Author: Geology of Belmont County, Ohio, 1963; Geology of the Ciales Quadrangle, Puerto Rico, 1965; Upper Pennsylvania and Lower Permian Rocks, Washington Area, Pennsylvania, 1971; The World Wide Search for Petroleum Offshore for the Quarter Century, 1947-72, 1973; Seismic Models of Late Quaternary Facies and Structure, Northern Gulf of Mexico, 1985; contbr. numerous papers to geol. publs. Home: 213 Rosebud Corpus Christi TX 78404 Office: US Geological Survey PO Box 6732 Corpus Christi TX 78411

BERRYHILL, JAMES JEFFERY, naturopathic physician; b. Atlanta, July 9, 1943; s. Orrie Henry and Ruth Laura (Lewis) B.; m. Cheryl Diane Francisco, Nov. 8, 1965; children—James Jay, Sabrina Breccia. Student Emory U., 1962; A.B., Ga. State U., 1966, M.G.A., 1973; N.D., Coll. Natural Therapeutics, 1976; Ph.D. in Psychology, Addison State U., 1976. Dir., Ga. Accident Control Program, 1968-70; community planner DeKalb County, Ga., 1971-72; dir. community improvement City of Decatur, Ga., 1972-74; resource planner U.S. Dept. Interior, 1974-77; dir. Naturopathic Inst., Inc., Atlanta, 1977—; mem. Ga. Bd. Naturopathic Examiners, 1980-82. Pres. So. Bicycle League, 1975-76. Served with C.E., U.S. Army, 1965-68. Decorated Purple Heart; Legion of Valor (Vietnam). Fellow Soc. Nutrition and Preventive Medicine, Internat. Naturopathic Assn.; mem. Am. Holistic Health Scis. Assn., Alternative Med. Assn., Ga. State Naturopathic Assn. (pres. 1978-82). Unitarian. Club: League Am. Wheelmen (life). Editor Freewheelin' Bicycle Mag., 1974-78. Office: 1787 Lavista Rd NE Atlanta GA 30345

BERRYMAN, HUGH EDWARD, physical anthropology educator; b. Paris, Tenn., May 20, 1949; s. W.C. and Vannie (Fagan) B.; m. Treva Ann Griffith, Aug. 14, 1971; children—Johnathan Fagan, Jessica Doran. B.S., U. Tenn., 1973, M.A., 1975, Ph.D., 1981. Instr. pathology U. Tenn. Ctr. Health Scis., Memphis, 1980—, instr. clin. lab. scis., 1982—, dir. Shelby County Morgues, 1980—; adj. prof. anthropology Memphis State U., 1982—; cons. Tenn. Med. Examiner. Gluck Bros. scholar, 1971-72; U. Tenn. Nat. Alumni Assn. fellow, 1977-78; Hilton A. Smith fellow, 1977-78. Mem. Am. Assn. Phys. Anthropology, Soc. Am. Archeology, Am. Anthrop. Assn., Tenn. Anthrop. Assn., Southeastern Archeol. Soc., Am. Acad. Forensic Scis., Sigma Xi (assoc.), Phi Kappa Phi. Republican. Mem. Ch. of Christ. Contbr. articles to profl. jours. Office: 858 Madison Ave Memphis TN 38163

BERRYMAN, JAMES CLEO, religion and philosophy educator; b. Russellville, Ark., Sept. 28, 1935; s. Henry Cleo and Corrine (Swearengen) B.; m. Mary Anne Pierce, Aug. 5, 1961; children—James Andrew, Cathryn Anne. B.A., Ouachita Bapt. U., 1957; B.D., Southwestern Bapt. Sem., 1960, Th.D., 1964. Vice pres. Book Nook Inc., Ft. Worth, 1958-63; dir. sem. extension Southwestern Sem., Ft. Worth, 1959-62; prof. religion and philosophy Ouachita Bapt. U., Arkadelphia, Ark., 1964—; vis. prof. St. Johns Sem., Little Rock, 1967, Henderson State U., Arkadelphia, So. Bapt. Sem., Louisville, 1984. Chmn. Central Ark. Devel. Council, Benton, 1970-80; treas., producer Arkadelphia Community Theatre, 1978—; founder, chmn. Festival Two Rivers, Arkadelphia, 1975-84. Civitan Internat. Found. fellow 1983. Recipient Internat. Honor Key award Civitan Internat., 1979, 83; named Outstanding Faculty Mem., Ouachita Bapt. U. 1971. Mem. Am. Acad. Religion, Assn. Bapt. Tchrs. Religion (sec., treas. 1972-82), Ark. Philos. Assn. (pres. 1984—). Democrat. Baptist. Club: Civitan Internat. (pres. 1982-83) (Birmingham). Avocations: needlepoint; reading.

BERRYMAN, KARAN ANN, librarian; b. Cuthbert, Ga., June 26, 1956; d. John Robert and Wilda (Fowler) B.; A.A. cum laude, Andrew Coll., 1975; B.S. with high honors, Auburn U., 1977; M.S.L.S., U. N.C., Chapel Hill, 1979. Dir. library services Andrew Coll., Cuthbert, 1980-84; head reference services Flagler Coll., St. Augustine, Fla., 1984—. Mem. ALA, Southeastern Library Assn., Ga. Library Assn., Muscogee County Geneal. Soc., Carroll County Geneal. Soc., Thronateeska Heritage Found., Phi Kappa Phi, Phi Theta Kappa. Home: PO Box 234 Cuthbert GA 31740 Office: Flagler Coll Library Saint Augustine FL 32084

BERSIA, JOHN CESAR, editor, publisher, political risk/public affairs consultant; b. Orlando, Fla., Nov. 23, 1956; s. Alfred and Rose-Marie (Idromasia) B.; m. Lucia Maryl Baez, Dec. 27, 1985. B.A. in Polit. Sci. and French, U. Central Fla., 1977; M.A. in Govt., Georgetown U., 1979; M.S. in Pub. Info. Adminstrn., Am. U., 1980; M.Sc., in Internat. Relations and Polit. Economy, London Sch. Econs., 1981. Distbr. Dexter Press Inc., Orlando, 1975-77; intern, analyst U.S. Dept. Labor, Washington, 1978-79; cons., staff assoc. Am. U., Washington, 1979-80; editor, cons. Global Perspectives and Transnational Studies Assn., Orlando, 1981-83; pres. Global Perspectives Research Group Inc., Casselberry, Fla., 1983—; dir. Transnational Studies Assn., Orlando, 1982—; ind. assoc. Cons. Capacities Group Inc., Cold Spring Harbor, N.Y., 1983—; coordinator U.S. A.I.D. Seminar, Winter Park, Fla., 1984—. Author: Directory of Community Resources: Orlando, 1983. Editor-in-chief Global Perspectives: An Interdisciplinary Jour. Internat. Relations, 1982—. Contbr. articles to profl. jours. Active Orlando Sci. Ctr., 1978—, Central Fla. Police Benevolent Soc., Winter Park, 1983—, Council Arts and Scis., Orlando, 1984—; vol. Mid-Fla. Council Internat. Visitors, Winter Park, 1983—, bd. dirs., 1985—. Named to Outstanding Young Men Am., Jaycees, 1978. Mem. Am. Polit. Sci. Assn., Acad. Polit. Sci., COSMEP: Internat. Assn. Ind. Pubs., London Sch. Econs. Soc., Am. Friends London Sch. Econs., Phi Kappa Phi, Omicron Delta Kappa. Roman Catholic. Avocations: canoeing; boating; marksmanship; hiking; travel. Home: 2825 Salisbury Blvd Winter Park FL 32789 Office: Global Perspectives Research Group Inc 1398 E Semoran Blvd Casselberry FL 32707

BERT, CLARA VIRGINIA, home economics educator, administrator; b. Quincy, Fla., Jan. 29, 1929; d. Harold C. and Ella J. (McDavid) B. B.S., Fla. State U., 1950, M.S., 1963, Ph.D., 1967. Cert. tchr., Fla.; cert. pub. mgr. Home econs. tchr. Union County High Sch., Lake Butler, Fla., 1950-53, Havana High Sch., Fla., 1953-65; cons. research and devel. Fla. Dept. Edn., Tallahassee, 1967-75, sect. dir. research and devel., 1975-85, program dir. home econs. edn., 1985—; cons. Nat. Ctr. Research in Vocat. Edn., Ohio State U., 1978; field reader U.S. Dept. Edn., 1974-75. Author/editor booklets. U.S. Office Edn. grantee, 1976, 77, 78. Mem. Am. Home Econs. Assn. (state treas. 1969-71), Am. Vocat. Assn., Fla. Vocat. Assn., Am. Vocat. Edn. Research Assn. (nat. treas. 1970-71), Nat. Council Family Relations, Am. Ednl. Research Assn., Kappa Delta Pi, Omicron Nu (chpt. pres. 1965-66), Delta Kappa Gamma (pres. 1974-76), Sigma Kappa (pres. corp. bd.), Fla. State U. Alumni Assn. (bd. dirs. home econs.). Club: Havana Golf and Country. Office: Fla Dept Edn Knott Bldg Tallahassee FL 32301

BERTAGNE, ROBERT GABRIEL, oil company executive; b. Marseille, France, Mar. 17, 1931; came to U.S., 1950, naturalized, 1931; s. Jean Baptiste and Marie Louise (Guibert) B.; m. Marlene Georgette Strong, Apr. 28, 1956 (div. 1977); m. Elia Rakotomalala, June 15, 1984; children—Allen, Michael. B.S. in Math. and Physics, Aix-Marseille U., 1949. Geophysicist to mgr. Continental Oil Co., Houston, 1955-74; v.p. Tex. Pacific, Dallas, 1974-77; internat. coordinator Houston Oil and Minerals, Houston, 1974-80; v.p. Wainoco Internat., Houston, 1980-82, pres. Marex Petroleum Corp., Houston, 1982—; cons. Rutherford Oil Co., Houston, 1982—, Pennzoil, Houston, 1982—; petroleum adviser, cons. to fgn. govts. Participant, Republican Party Com., Houston, 1984. Served with U.S. Army, 1951-53. Mem. Am. Assn. Petroleum Geologists, Soc. Exploration Geophysicists. Roman Catholic. Club: Heritage (Houston). Avocation: foreign travel. Home and Office: 204 E Cowan Dr Houston TX 77007

BERTELSMAN, WILLIAM ODIS, judge; b. Cin., Jan. 31, 1936; s. Odis William and Dorothy (Gegan) B.; m. Margaret Ann Martin, June 13, 1959; children—Kathy, Terri, Nancy. B.A., Xavier U., 1958; J.D., U. Cin., 1961. Bar: Ky. bar 1961. Law clk. firm Taft, Stettinius & Hollister, Cin., 1960-61; mem. firm Bertelsman & Bertelsman, Newport, Ky., 1962-79; judge U.S. Dist. Ct. Eastern Dist. Ky., Covington, 1979—; instr. Coll. Law U. Cin., 1965-72; city atty., prosecutor, Highland Heights, Ky., 1962-69. Contbr. articles to profl. jours. Served to capt. AUS, 1963-64. Mem. No. Ky. C. of C. (pres. 1974, dir. 1969-77), Ky. Bar Assn. (bd. govs. 1978-79), Am. Bar Assn., Campbell County Bar Assn. Republican. Roman Catholic. Club: Optimist. Home: 78 W Vernon Ln Fort Thomas KY 41075 Office: 700 Scott St Covington KY 41012

BERTRAND, GRACE ANN LOOTEN, nurse; b. Jefferson City, Mo., July 18, 1956; d. Elroy Joseph and Gladys Velma (Bernskoetter) Looten; m. Charles Neal Bertrand, June 14, 1980; children—Jeremy Joseph, Elizabeth Sue. A.D. in Applied Sci., Lincoln U. Sch. Nursing, 1977; student Christian Teaching Ctr., 1980. Sales clerk, seamstress, fabric cons. Fabricland, Jefferson City, Mo., 1969-71; bakery personnel Schult's, Jefferson City, 1971-74; nurse's asst. St. Mary's Health Ctr., Jefferson City, 1974-77; R.N. orthopedics-surgery, 1977-78; R.N., Charity Hosp., Lafayette, La., 1978, Lafayette Gen. Hosp., 1979-80, nursing care services Upjohn Health Care Services, Lafayette, 1980-82; pvt. duty nurse registrar All Paramed. Procedures, Lafayette, 1983—; participant phys. assessment series U. Mo.-Columbia, 1978. Editor: About the Last Days, 1981; composer secular, scriptural and religious songs, 1975—. Supporter La Leche League, 1981—, Natural Childbirth, 1979—, Midwifery: Natural Family Planning, 1979—. Recipient Citizenship award VFW, Jefferson City, 1970; scholarship award Am. Bus. Women's Assn., 1974-76, Cheeseborough Ponds, Inc., 1975-76; cert. of Recognition, Mo. Sch.-Coll. Relations Commn., 1974; cert. of achievement Central Mo. State U., 1974. Mem. Am. Bus. Women's Assn. (com. 1982-83). Home: 908 Amilcar Blvd Lafayette LA 70501 Office: PO Box 2293 Lafayette LA 70502

BERTRAND, VIRGINIA ROOS, oil company executive; b. Shreveport, La., Dec. 28, 1953; d. Henry Kahn and Sybil (Friedenthal) Roos; m. Benedict Byron Bertrand, Nov. 26, 1977; children—Aimee Elizabeth, Rebecca Noel. B.A., Northeast La. U., 1975; postgrad. La. State U., Oxford U., Eng., 1975. Tng. asst. Exxon Coal USA, Inc., Houston, 1975-77, adminstrv. asst., 1977-80, assoc. tng. analyst, 1980-84, safety, manpower, tng. analyst, 1984—. Mem. Hear-Say Orgn. for Hearing Impaired, Houston, 1975—; panelist Houston Pub. Library, 1978—. Mem. Am. Soc. Tng. Devel., Am. Vocat. Assn., Northeast La. U. Alumni Assn. (bd. dirs. 1977), AAUW, Phi Mu (editor newsletter 1978). Republican. Roman Catholic. Avocations: cross stitch; cooking; writing; sewing. Home: 3626 Riverwood Park Dr Kingwood TX 77345 Office: Exxon Coal USA Inc PO Box 2180 Room 1230F Dresser Tower Houston TX 77252-2180

BERTSCH, GARY KENNETH, political science educator, researcher, consultant; b. Vallejo, Calif., June 8, 1944; s. Gideon and Freda (Hepper) B.; m. Joan Elizabeth Brubacher, Feb. 29, 1964; children—Dawn, Todd, Jason. B.A., Idaho State U., 1966; M.A., U. Oreg., 1968, Ph.D., 1970. Vis. prof. U. Zagreb, Yugoslavia, 1969-70; Sandy Beaver prof. polit. sci. U. Ga., Athens, 1970—; vis. prof. nat. security affairs Air U., Dept. Def., Maxwell AFB, Ala., 1981-82; Fulbright prof. politics U. Lancaster, Eng., 1984-85. Author books, including East-West Strategic Trade and the Atlantic Alliance, 1983; Power and Policy in Communist Systems, 1985; also numerous articles. Editor: National Security and Technology Transfer, 1983. Recipient numerous awards for teaching U. Ga., 1970—, professorial chair for disting. teaching, 1982—; numerous research grants, 1970—. Mem. Am. Polit. Sci. Assn., Internat. Studies Assn. Home: 218 Fortson Dr Athens GA 30006 Office: U Ga Dept Polit Sci Athens GA 30602

BERUBE, MICHAEL EDWARD, nursing administrator; b. St. Johnsbury, Vt., Dec. 26, 1946; m. Edward Ludger and Leona Oberlin (LaChance) B.; m. Maryann Phalen Foster, Feb. 4, 1967; 1 child, Marilee. Assoc. Nursing, Castleton State Coll., 1970; B.S. in Nursing, U. Fla., 1975, M.Nursing, 1977. Staff nurse VA, Gainesville, Fla., 1971-73, charge nurse, 1973-74, head nurse, nurse supr., 1974-79, asst. chief nursing service, Castle Point, N.Y., 1979-81, assoc. chief nursing service, Little Rock, 1981-83, chief nursing service, 1983—; adj. assoc. prof. U. Ark., Little Rock, 1984—; adj. asst. prof. Harding U., Searcy, Ark., 1984—. Served to maj. USAR. Mem. Am. Nursing Assn., Ark. State Nursing Assn., Ark. Soc. Hosp. Nursing Service Dirs., Am. Legion, Sigma Theta Tau. Republican. Roman Catholic. Avocations: sailing; golf. Home: 5 Royal Ct Little Rock AR 72211 Office: John L McClellan Meml Vets Hosp 4500 W 7th St Little Rock AR 72205

BERUMEN, JAVIER ANTONIO, mechanical engineer; b. Chihuahua, Mex., June 11, 1950; came to U.S., 1956; s. Ricardo Alberto and Rita (Lechuga) B.; m. Emilia Munoz, Aug. 6, 1982; children—Valerie Y., Lisa Y. B.S.M.E., U. Tex.-El Paso, 1973. Registered profl. engr., Tex. Mech. engr. El Paso Natural Gas Co., 1974-75; design engr. Gen. Instrument Corp., El Paso, 1976-77; mech. engr. White Sands Missile Range (N.Mex.), 1977-81; sr. mech. engr., directorate of engring. and housing, engring. planning and services div., design branch Ft. Bliss, El Paso, 1981—. Recipient Farah Scholarship Found. scholarship, 1969; letter of appreciation White Sands Missile Range, 1979. Mem. Am. Soc. Mil. Engrs. Home: 10209 Maxwood St El Paso TX 79925 Office: EPSD Bldg 1165 Fort Bliss TX 79916

BESHEAR, STEVEN L., state official; b. Dawson Springs, Ky., Sept. 21, 1944; A.B., U. Ky., 1966, J.D., 1968. Admitted to N.Y. bar, 1969, Ky. bar, 1971; asso. firm White and Case, N.Y.C., 1968-70, firm Harbison, Kessinger, Lisle & Bush, Lexington, Ky., 1971-75; partner firm Beshear, Meng and Green, Lexington, 1976-79; atty. gen. State of Ky., 1979-83, lt. gov., 1983—; mem. Ky. Ho. of Reps. from 76th dist., 1974-79. Mem. Fayette County Bar Assn., Ky. Bar Assn., Am. Bar Assn., Phi Beta Kappa, Phi Delta Phi, Omicron Delta Kappa, Order of Coif. Bd. editors Ky. Law Jour., 1967-68. Office: Office of Lt Gov State Capitol Frankfort KY 40601

BESOM, ROBERT DODDS, museum director; b. Olean, N.Y., May 9, 1943; s. Donald Guest and Henrietta Evelyn (Dodds) B.; m. Patsy Ann McCrary, Sept. 26, 1980; 1 child, Lela Jane. B.A., U. Nebr., 1966; M.A., U. Ark., 1972, Ph.A., 1977. Research asst. U. Ark. Library, Fayetteville, 1971, archivist, 1975-77; archtl. surveyor Capitol Zoning Commn., Little Rock, 1978; historian Ark. Hist. Preservation Program, Little Rock, 1979, Old State House Mus., Little Rock, 1980, dir. Shiloh Mus., Springdale, Ark., 1980—; cons. Hist. Preservation Assn. Contbr. articles to profl. jours. Commr. Ark. Sesquicentennial Celebration Commn., Little Rock, 1982—. Served to 1st lt. inf. U.S. Army, 1977-79. Mem. Ark. Archivists Records Mgrs., Ark. Hist. Assn. (bd. dirs. 1983—), Ark. Museums Assn., Ozark Soc., Washington County Hist. Soc. (bd. dirs. 1983-85). Lodge: Kiwanis. Home: 15 North West Fayetteville AR 72701 Office: Shiloh Mus 118 W Johnson Springdale AR 72764

BESSON, TAUNEE SUE SNYDER, career planning executive, columnist; b. Pitts., Sept. 12, 1946; d. Garvin Walter and Lillian (Pantall) Snyder; m. Lawrence George Besson, Jan. 6, 1968; children—Amber Lynn, Teal Lorraine. B.S. in Bus. Adminstrn., Pa. State U., 1967. Buyer J.C. Pennys, N.Y.C., 1969-75; dept. mgr. Sanger Harris, Dallas, 1975-77; dir. employment Women's Ctr., Dallas, 1977-79; columnist Dallas Times Herald, 1984—, Nat. Bus. Employment Weekly, 1985—; pres. Career Dimensions, Dallas, 1979—. Author: (workbook) The Lifespace Process, 1984. Moderator TV series Getting the Job You Want, 1985. Trainer United Way Agys., 1983—; speaker Mental Health Assn.; pres. bd. dirs. Women's Ctr. of Dallas, 1985. Recipient Woman of Yr. award Alpha Gamma Delta, 1983. Mem. Am. Soc. Tng. and Devel. Office: Career Dimensions 11520 N Central Expressway Dallas TX 75243

BEST, FREDERICK NAPIER, artist, designer; b. Macon, Ga., Jan. 17, 1943; s. John Frederick and Sara (Napier) B.; m. Rebecca Alice Freeman, Apr. 6, 1974; children—Eric Jonathan, Emily Anne. Student Auburn U., 1961-64; B.A., Birmingham So. Coll., 1969; Artist Birmingham News, 1969; design dept. mgr. Dampier-Harris, Alabaster, Ala., 1970-78; model designer Rust Engring., Birmingham, 1978-81; owner, mgr. Best Finesse Studio, Leeds, Ala., 1981—; design instr. Jefferson State Jr. Coll., Birmingham, 1981—. Contbr. articles to profl. jours. Recipient award of honor Birmingham Advt. Club, 1982. Mem. AIA (profl. affiliate), Am. Inst. Design and Drafting, Am. Engring. Model Soc. (bd. dirs. 1984—), Internat. Plastic Modeler's Soc., Nat. Forensic Ctr. Methodist. Avocations: writing; hiking; reading. Home and Office: Best Finesse Studio R1-B901C Leeds AL 35094

BESTHOFF, SYDNEY J., III, drug store company executive. Chmn., pres. K & B, Inc., New Orleans. Office: K & B Inc K & B Plaza Lee Circle New Orleans LA 70130*

BETHEA, BARRON, lawyer, state legislator, elec. hardware mfr.; b. Birmingham, Ala., May 20, 1929; s. Malcolm and Wilma (Edwards) B.; student U. of South, 1948-50; B.S., U. Ala., 1952, LL.B., 1953. Admitted Ala. bar, 1953; practiced in Birmingham, 1953-54; founder Barron Bethea Co., Inc., elec. hardware mfrs., Birmingham, 1957, pres., sec., treas. 1957—. Mem. Ala. Democratic Exec. Com., 1958-62—; mem. Ala. Ho. of Reps., 1962—. Mem. mgmt. bd. Five Points YMCA, 1962—. Served as 1st lt. USAF, 1954-56. Mem. Ala. State Bar, Birmingham Bar Assn., Asso. Industries Ala., Birmingham C. of C., Scabbard and Blade, Phi Gamma Delta, Phi Alpha Delta. Methodist. Elk. Home and Office: 1625 Carolina Ave Bessemer AL 35020

BETHEA, WILLIAM LAMAR, JR., lawyer; b. Dillon, S.C., June 2, 1940; s. William Lamar and Lillie (Hotchkiss) B.; m. Margaret McInnis, June 23, 1962 (div. Mar. 1977); children—William Lamar, Margaret Amanda; m. 2d, Paula Mikell Harper, Aug. 12, 1977. A.B., Newberry Coll., 1962; J.D. magna cum laude, U. S.C., 1969. Bar: S.C. 1969, U.S. Dist. Ct. S.C. 1969, U.S. Ct. Appeals (4th cir.) 1974, U.S. Supreme Ct. 1981. Assoc., Harvey Battey & Bethea, P.A., and predecessors, 1969-71, ptnr., 1971-81; prin. Bethea Jordan & Griffin, P.A., Hilton Head Island, S.C., 1981—, sr. ptnr., 1981—; dir. Citizens & So. Corp., Citizens & So. Nat. Bank S.C. Chmn. bd. trustee Hilton Head Hosp.; trustee, chmn. acad. affairs and faculty liaison com. U. S.C.; trustee U. S.C. Bus. Partnership Found., Drug Sci. Found. Served with USMCR, 1958-63, USMC, 1963-66. Mem. ABA, Beaufort County Bar Assn. (pres.), Hilton Head Island Bar Assn. (past pres.), Am. Judicature Soc., Am. Land Devel. Assn., Communities Assn. Inst., Urban Land Inst., Order Wig and Robe, Phi Beta Kappa, Phi Alpha Delta (Outstanding Scholastic Achievement award 1969). Episcopalian. Clubs: Gamecock, U. S.C. Alumni. Lodge: Masons. Home: 3 Gray Fox Ln Hilton Head Island SC 29228 Office: PO Box 5666 Hilton Head Island SC 29938

BETTERSWORTH, JOHN KNOX, history educator, writer; b. Jackson, Miss., Oct. 1909; s. Horace Greely and Annie McConnell (Murphey) B.; B.A. magna cum laude, Millsaps Coll., 1929; Ph.D., Duke U., 1937; m. Ann L. Stephens, Oct. 28, 1943; 1 child, Nancy Elizabeth Bettersworth Underwood. Instr., Jackson (Miss.) Central High Sch., 1930-35; grad. fellow Duke U., 1935-37, vis. prof., summer 1940; vis. instr. Asheville (N.C.) Normal, summer 1937; instr. history Miss. State U., Mississippi State, 1937, asst. prof., 1938-42, assoc. prof., 1945-48, prof., 1948-79, head dept. history and govt., 1948-61, dir. Social Sci. Research Center, 1950-60, assoc. dean for liberal arts Sch. Arts and Sci., 1956-61, acad. v.p., 1961-66, acad. v.p. and dean faculty, 1966-69, spl. cons. to pres., 1977-79, prof., v.p. and dean faculty emeritus, 1978—; text editor Miss. Hist. Commn., 1948-68; chmn. Miss. Research Clearing House, 1953-55; pres. So. Conf. Deans Faculty and Acad. Vice Pres.'s, 1967-68. Pres., Mississippians for ETV, 1972-73; founding pres. Friends of the Arts in Miss., 1978-80; trustee Miss. Dept. Archives and History, 1955—; chmn. Miss. Hist. Preservation Rev. Bd., 1979-81. Served as lt. (j.g.) USNR, 1942-45 (instr. Naval Indoctrination Sch., Tucson). Fellow Internat. Inst. Arts and Letters; mem. Miss. Hist. Soc. (dir. 1953—, v.p. 1955-56, pres. 1961-62), Am., So. hist. assns., Phi Beta Kappa, Omicron Delta Kappa, Phi Kappa Phi, Phi Alpha Theta, Alpha Tau Omega. Democrat. Episcopalian. Club: Starkville Rotary (pres. 1951-52). Author: Confederate Mississippi, The People and Policies of a Cotton State in Wartime, 1943; People's College: A History of Mississippi State, 1953; People's University: The Centennial History of Mississippi State, 1980; Mississippi: A History, 1959; Mississippi in the Confederacy: As They Saw It, 1961; Your Old World Past, 1960; Mississippi: Yesterday and Today, 1965; This Country of Ours, 1965; New World Heritage, 1968; Your Mississippi, 1975; South of Appomattox, 1959; contbg. author: A History of Mississippi, 1973; Mississippi Heroes, 1980; Mississippi: The Land and the People, 1981; contbr. articles to profl. publs.; founder, pub. The Miss. Quar., editor, 1946-56. Home: 401 Broad St Starkville MS 39759 Office: Drawer B Mississippi State MS 39762

BEU, MARJORIE JANET, music director; b. Elgin, Ill., Nov. 22, 1921; d. Herman Henry and Hattie Belle (Beverly) B.; B.M., Am. Conservatory Music, 1949; B.M.Ed., 1949, M.M.Ed., 1953; advanced cert. No. Ill. U., 1969; D.Ed., U. Sarasota, 1979. Music tchr. Sch. Dist. 21, Wheeling, Ill., 1961-64; music and fine arts coordinator, 1964-68, asst. supt. instrn., 1968-79; minister of music United Meth. Ch., Sun City Center, Fla., 1980—; dir. Kingo Point Community Chorus, 1984—; pres. Council Study and Devel. Ednl. Resources, 1971-79. Pres., Wheeling Community Concerts Assn.; dir. Community Chorus; pres. Sun City Center Concert Series. Mem. NEA, Am. Guild Organists and Choir Dirs., Music Educators Nat. Conf., Assn. Supervision and Curriculum Devel., Ill. Edn. Assn., Ill. Council Gifted, No. Ill. Assn. Ednl. Research, Evaluation and Devel. (pres.), Mu Phi Epsilon, Phi Delta Kappa (sec. N.W. Suburban Cook County chpt.), Delta Kappa Pi (pres. alumni chpt.). Home: 610 Fort Duquesna Dr Sun City Center FL 33570

BEUERLEIN, SISTER JULIANA, hospital administrator; b. Lawrenceburg, Tenn., June 19, 1921; d. John Adolph and Sophia (Held) B. R.N., St. Joseph's Sch. Nursing, Chgo., 1945; B.S. in Edn, DePaul U., 1947; M.S. in Nursing Edn, Marquette U., 1954; postgrad., St. Louis U. Operating room supr. St. Joseph's Hosp., Alton, Ill., 1945-48; dir. sch. of nursing and nursing service Providence Hosp., Waco, Tex., 1948-56; dir. sch. nursing and nursing service St. Joseph's Hosp., Chgo., 1956-62, asst. administr., 1962-63; adminstrv. asst. St. Mary's Hosp., Evansville, Ind., 1963-65, adminstr., 1965-73, pres. governing bd., 1965-73; adminstr. St. Joseph Hosp., Chgo., 1973-81, pres. governing bd., 1973-75; adminstr. St. Thomas Hosp., Nashville, 1981—: Mem. governing bd. St. Vincent's Hosp., Indpls., 1969-73; mem. governing bd. St. Mary's Hosp., Milw., 1974-75, chmn., 1978-79; mem. governing bd. Providence Hosp., Southfield, Mich., 1975-78, chmn. governing bd., 1977-78; mem. Chgo. Health Systems Agy., 1976-79; mem. governing bd. DePaul Community Health Center, Bridgeton, Mo., 1980—; chmn. bd. dirs. St. Vincent Hosp., Birmingham, Ala.; mem. Hubbard Hosp., Nashville; mem. Am. Hosp. Assn. Commn. on Nursing, 1980—. Fellow Am. Coll. Hosp. Adminstrs. (com. on elections); mem. Cath., Tenn. hosp. assns. Address: 4200 Harding Rd Nashville TN 37205

BEUTEL, PAUL WAYNE, performing arts administrator; b. Houston, June 29, 1950; s. Vernon William and Gertrude Clara (Drews) B. B.S., U. Tex., 1972, M.A., 1979. Entertainment writer Austin Am.-Statesman, Tex., 1975-78; mng. editor Austin Mag., 1980; mgr. publicity and promotion U. Tex. Performing Arts Ctr., Austin, 1980-85; mgr. programming and mktg. Paramount Theatre, Austin, 1985—; bd. dirs. Zachary Scott Theatre, Austin, 1980—; adv. bd. KTVV-TV, Austin, 1982-83. Contbr. articles to profl. jours. Founding editor Austin Arts and Leisure mag., 1979. Mem. Austin Circle of Theatres, 1979—; lifetime mem. U. Tex. Longhorn Singers, 1984. Recipient Best Actor in a Musical award Austin Circle of Theatres, 1982. Mem. Internat. Soc. Performing Arts Adminstrs. (editor 1984—), Theta Xi. Methodist. Office: Paramount Theatre 713 Congress Ave Austin TX 78701

BEVERLY, MONA RUTHERFORD, educational administrator; b. Bristol, Va., May 21, 1949; d. Stanley Carlisle and Mona Elizabeth (Thomas) R.; m. Dan Beverly, Sept. 10, 1973. B.S., East Tenn. State U., 1971, M.A., 1973; postgrad. U. Tenn., 1981—. Cert. tchr., Tenn. Tchr., Bristol Sch., Tenn., 1971-73, Knox County Bd. Edn., Knoxville, 1973-84; evaluator Career Ladder Program, State of Tenn., Nashville, 1984—; instr. U. Tenn., Knoxville, 1984—. Mem. MLA, South Atlantic Modern Lang. Assn., Nat. Council Tchrs. English, Mensa, Phi Kappa Phi. Home: 312 Peterson Rd Knoxville TN 37922 Office: Career Ladder Office Dept Edn 111 Cordell Hall Bldg Nashville TN 37219

BEVILL, TOM, lawyer, congressman; b. Townley, Ala., Mar. 27, 1921; s. Herman and Fannie Lou (Fike) B.; B.S., U. Ala., 1943, LL.B., 1948; LL.D. (hon.), 1981; m. Lou Betts, June 24, 1943; children—Susan B., Donald H., Patricia Lou. Ala. Bar: 1949. Practiced in Jasper, Ala., 1949-1967; past mem. Ala. Ho. of Reps.; mem. 90th-99th congresses from 4th Ala. Dist. Mem. ABA, Ala. Bar Assn., Walker County Bar Assn. (pres. 1954-55) Am., Judicature Soc. Office: 2302 Rayburn House Office Bldg Washington DC 20515

BEVILLE, ROSE WARREN, medical school administrator, researcher; b. Richmond, Va., Mar. 13, 1940; d. Maynard Warren and Bessie Virginia (Edwards) Berryman; children—William Warren Beville; Robert Berryman, William Joseph Berryman. A.B., Randolph Macon Woman's Coll., 1962. Labor. mgr. Med. Sch., Tulane U., New Orleans, 1965-72, lab. adminstr., 1972-78, research asst., 1978-81, research assoc., 1981—. Contbr. articles to profl. jours. Recipient Mayor's Civic award, 1982. Mem. AAUW, Kappa Alpha Theta, La. Nature Ctr. Episcopalian. Avocations: foreign travel; antiques; gardening. Home: 7020 Bamberry St New Orleans LA 70126 Office: Tulane U Med Sch 1430 Tulane Ave New Orleans LA 70112

BEVIS, HERBERT ANDERSON, engineering educator and consultant; b. Perry, Fla., Sept. 28, 1929; s. Herbert Urlin and Virginia Thomas (Anderson) B.; m. Cotella Marie Ingle, Aug. 24, 1952; children—John Herbert, Gerald Clayton. B.C.E., U. Fla., 1951, M.S., 1952; M.S., U.S. Naval Postgrad. Sch., Monterey, Calif., 1958, Ph.D., 1963. Diplomate Am. Acad. Environ. Engrs.; registered profl. engr., Fla., Tex.; cert. health physicist. Commd. health officer, USPHS, 1952, advanced through grades to dir. grade, 1979, sanitary engr., N.Y.C., 1952-53, Washington, 1953-55, Cin., 1955-56, Monterey, Calif., 1956-58; chief ionizing program Tex. State Dept. Health, Austin, 1958-61; teaching asst. dept. civil engring. U. Fla., Gainesville, 1961-63, assoc. prof. and grad. coordinator dept. environ. engring. scis., 1964-74, prof. and vice chmn. environ. engring. dept., 1974-81, asst. dean Coll. Engring., 1978-79, assoc. dean Coll. Engring., 1981—; propr., cons., dir. Water and Air Research, Inc., Gainesville. Asst. scoutmaster North Fla. council Boy Scouts Am., 1965-71, scoutmaster, 1971-73, troop com., 1973-76; mem. Alachua County Fin. Com., 1977; bds. dirs. United Way, Civitan Regional Bloodbank. Served with USPHS, 1952—. Named Tchr. of Year, Coll. Engring. U. Fla., 1977. Fellow Fla. Engring. Soc., Am. Pub. Health Assn.; mem. Nat. Soc. Profl. Engrs., Am. Soc. Engring. Edn., Water Pollution Control Fedn., ASCE, Indsl. Hygiene Assn., Health Physics Soc., Assn. Environ. Engring. Profs., Sigma Xi, Tau Beta Pi, Phi Kappa Phi, Omicron Delta Kappa. Democrat. Methodist. Club: Civitan Internat. (Gainesville). Author: Stream Sanitation in Florida, 1954; contbr. articles to profl. jours.; author script, lectr. tech. films. Home: 3414 NW 7th Pl Gainesville FL 32607 Office: Coll Engring Univ Fla Gainesville FL 32611

BEVIS, ROBERT ALLEN, cable TV executive; b. Tallahassee, July 3, 1937; s. Albert Myers and Grace Vivian (Ellis) B.; student U. Fla., 1955-58; m. Jacqueline Mary Steiner, May 16, 1975; children—William Allen, Robert Jon Wayne Newell (stepson). Photo-optical engr. RCA Service Co., Cape Kennedy, Fla., 1958-68, Technicolor Corp., Cape Kennedy, 1968-69; chief engr. Communicable div. Southland Communications Inc., 1969-74, gen. mgr., 1974-79, dir. nat. ops., 1979—. Pres. City of Cocoa Beach (Fla.) Bus. Improvement Council, 1975—; treas. Cocoa Beach Police Cadets, 1976—. Mem. Soc. Cable TV Engrs. (sr.), Fla. Cable TV Assn. (pres. 1978—, chmn. bd. dirs.), So. Cable TV Assn. (sec.-treas. 1984), Cape Kennedy Area C. of C. Republican. Methodist. Clubs: Optimists (life)(pres. chpt. 1976-77, disting. pres. 1977-78, Optimist of Year 1975-76), Elks (disting. citizen award 1976, 82). Office: Southland Communications Inc 210 Center St Cape Canaveral FL 32920

BEYLE, THAD LEWIS, political science educator, consultant; b. Syracuse, N.Y., May 11, 1934; s. Herman Carey and Madelon (McCulloch) B.; m. Patricia Fae Cain, Nov. 14, 1934; children—Carey, Jeffrey Lewis, Jonathan West, Aimee Maurine. A.B., Syracuse U., 1956, A.M., 1960; Ph.D., U. Ill., 1963. Asst. prof. polit. sci. Denison U., Granville, Ohio, 1963-64; faculty fellow Office of the Gov. of N.C., Raleigh, 1964-65; research assoc. Study of Am. States, Duke U., Durham, N.C., 1965-67; asst. prof. polit. sci. U. N.C., Chapel Hill, 1967-69, assoc. prof., 1969-76, prof., 1976—; dir. Ctr. for Policy Research Nat. Gov.'s Assn., 1974-76, sr. research fellow, 1978-84; chmn. bd. dirs. N.C. Ctr. for Pub. Policy Research, 1980—. Mem. Am. Polit. Sci. Assn., Midwest Polit. Sci. Assn., So. Polit. Sci. Assn., Am. Soc. for Pub. Adminstrn. Democrat. Co-editor: Planning and Politics, 1969; The American Governor in Behavioral Perspective, 1972; Politics and Policy in North Carolina, 1975; Being Governor, 1983; editor: State Government, 1985; Gubernatorial Transitions, 1985; Gubernatorial Re-elections, 1986.

BHAGAT, PRAMODE KUMAR, engineering educator, researcher; b. Ranchi, India, Oct. 7, 1944; came to U.S., 1965; s. Basant Lal and Shanta (Jaiswal) B.; m. Asha Jaiswal, June 15, 1973; 1 child, Rahul. B.Tech., India. Inst. Tech., 1965; M.S.E.E., U. Cin., 1966; Ph.D., Ohio State U., 1972. Project engr. Systems Research Labs., Dayton, Ohio, 1966-67; research assoc. Ohio State U., Columbus, 1972-73; research assoc. U. Ky., Lexington, 1973-74, asst. prof., 1974-80, assoc. prof. engring., 1980—; prin. engr. E-Systems Melpar Div., Falls Church, Va., 1985—; vis. scientist Air Force Materials Labs., Dayton, 1982-83; design fellow NASA, Houston, summer 1977; cons. NASA, Houston, 1984—, Wright Patterson AFB, Dayton, 1983—. Inventor, patentee limb volume system, (NASA cert. 1980). Mem. IEEE, Am. Soc. Engring. Edn., ASME. Office: Wenner Gren Research Lab Rose St Lexington KY 40506

BHALLA, MADHU BALA, physician; b. Agra, U.P., India, May 21, 1944; came to U.S., 1968; d. Gopal Singh and Brij Rani (Kakkar) Sarin; m. Vinod K. Bhalla, May 29, 1966; children—Niti, Jyoti, Varun Kumar. B.Sc., St. John's Coll., Agra, UP, India, 1962; M.B.B.S., S.N. Med. Coll., Agra, 1966; M.S. in Anatomy, U. Ga., 1972. Rotating intern S.N. Med. Coll., Agra, U.P., India, 1966; ob-gyn housemanship K.E.M. Hosp., Poona, India, 1967-68; postdoctoral fellow U. Ga., Athens, 1968-71; rotating intern Crawford W. Long Hosp., Atlanta, 1972-73; resident ob-gyn Ga. Bapt. Hosp., Atlanta, 1973-74; fellow in family planning Med. Coll. Ga., Augusta, 1974-75, resident ob-gyn, 1975-78; practice medicine specializing in ob-gyn, Augusta, 1978—; mem. med. staff Univ. Hosp., Augusta, 1978—, mem. D.R.G. review com., 1984; mem. med. staff St. Joseph Hosp., Augusta, 1978—, mem. infectious control com., 1980. Recipient Merit award in med. jurisprudence and toxicology S.N. Med. Coll., Agra, India, 1965; Good Samaritan award St. Joseph Hosp., Augusta, 1983—; postdoctoral fellow NIH Grant, U. Ga., Athens, 1968. Jr. fellow Am. Coll. Ob-gyn; mem. Ob-gyn Soc. Augusta. Office: 2320 Wrightsboro Rd Augusta GA 30904

BHATTACHARYYA, SHANKAR PRASHAD, electrical engineering educator; b. Rangoon, Burma, June 23, 1946; came to U.S., 1967, naturalized, 1985; s. Nil Kantha and Hem Nalini (Mukherjee) B.; m. Carole Jeanne Colgate, Feb. 10, 1971 (div. Oct. 1985); children—Krishna Lee, Moha Dev, Sona Lee; m. Supriya Goswami, Dec. 14, 1985. B. Tech., Indian Inst. Tech., 1967; M.S. in Elec. Engring., Rice U., 1969, Ph.D., 1971. Asst. prof. Fed. U., Brazil, 1971-72, assoc. prof., 1972-76, prof., 1976-80, chmn. elec. engring., 1978-80; prof. Tex. A&M U., College Station, 1984—. Contbr. articles to profl. jours. Nat. Research Council resident research fellow NASA, 1974-75; NSF grantee, 1983—. Mem. IEEE (control system soc. assoc. editor 1985—), Soc. Indsl. and Applied Math. Home: 2803 Normand College Station TX 77840 Office: Tex A&M U Dept Elec Engring College Station TX 77843

BIBEAU, DENISE NOELLA, human resources executive; b. Manchester, N.H., Jan. 18, 1955; d. Andre Aime and Rita Noella (Poirier) Lavigne; m. Ronald Michael Bibeau, Oct. 4, 1974; 1 child, Lauren Marie. B.A. in Bus. Adminstrn., U. So. Fla., 1984. Personnel mgr. Indian Head Casket Co., Inc., Nashua, N.H., 1975-80; div. tng. adminstr. Steak N' Shake, Inc., Tampa, Fla., 1981-84; mgr. human resources Pick-Kwik Food Stores, Inc., Clearwater, Fla., 1985—. Mem. Am. Soc. Tng. and Devel., Retail Grocers Assn. Fla. (personnel and human resources 1985—), Am. Soc. Personnel Adminstrn., Am. Mgmt. Assn. Republican. Roman Catholic. Avocations: tennis; boating; racquetball. Home: 9337 Rustic Pines Blvd Seminole FL 33542 Office: Pick-Kwik Food Stores Inc 3165 McMullen-Booth Rd Clearwater FL 33518

BICE, DAVID ALLEN, writer, publishing company executive; b. Danbury, Conn., Aug. 12, 1940; s. Ray and Gunhild Christina (Olander) B.; m. Patty Jo Adkins, July 29, 1959 (div. Apr. 1985); children—Penny, Cheryl, Daniel, Jeffrey, Richard. B.S. in Edn., W.Va. State Coll., 1963; M.A. in History, Marshall U., 1967. Cert. tchr., W.Va. Tchr., Kanawha County Schs., Charleston, W.Va., 1963-79; instr. W.Va. Coll. Grad. Studies, Institute, 1978-79; pres. Jalamap Publs., South Charleston, W.Va., 1983—; cons. in field. Author: The Pringle Tree, 1977; A Panorama of West Virginia, 1979; 2d edit., 1985; The Legend of John Henry, 1980; Mad Anne Bailey, 1980; A Panorama of Florida, 1982; West Virginia and the Appalachians, 1983; A Panorama of Tennessee, 1984. Contbr. articles to newspapers and mags. Recipient Outstanding Contbn. to Geog. Edn. award Nat. Council for Geography, 1980. Mem. South Charleston C. of C., Greater Kanawha Valley C. of C. Republican. Home: PO Box 8917 South Charleston WV 25303 Office: Jalamap Publications Inc 601 D St South Charleston WV 25303

BICKETT, GARRY RICHARD, marketing executive; b. Charlotte, N.C., Apr. 8, 1955; s. George Leslie Jr. and Ruby Violet (Cieutat) B.; m. Kathy Denise Knight, Oct. 28, 1978; 1 son, Jonathan Leslie. A.B. in Journalism, U. N.C., 1977. Pub. relations coordinator Carowinds Theme Park, Charlotte, 1977-78, mgr. pub. relations, 1978-82, mgr. advt. and pub. relations, 1982-84, dir. mktg., 1984—. Mem. Pub. Relations Soc. Am., Travel and Tourism Research Assn., Southeastern Tourism Soc. Republican. Roman Catholic. Office: PO Box 240516 Charlotte NC 28224

BICKEY, DANIEL, manufacturers representative; b. Bridgeport, Conn., Feb. 8, 1946; s. Daniel and Mary (Cashavelly) B.; B.S. in Bus. Adminstrn., Concord Coll., Athens, W.Va., 1972; m. Cynthia Jane Morrison, Aug. 8, 1967; children—Matthew Daniel, George David, Bronwen Drew, Melissa Diane. Salesman, Burroughs Corp., 1972-74, Gould, Inc., 1975-76; founder, 1977, since pres. Mine Power Systems, Inc., mfrs. rep. indsl. batteries, Beckley, W.Va.; pres., owner Mine Battery Service Inc.; instr. Beckley Coll. (W.Va.); mem. steering com. U.S. Senatorial Bus. Adv. Bd.; cons. in field. Recipient various sales awards. Mem. Nat. Fedn. Ind. Bus., Am. Security Council. Democrat. Club: Mabscott-Pleasant Hills Lions (dir. 1980-81). Home: 201 Millstone Dr Beckley WV 25801 Office: 107 George St Beckley WV 25801

BICKHAM, ALAN DEMINT, petroleum geologist; b. Shreveport, La., July 3, 1961; s. Billy Jack and Margaret Ann (Demint) B.; m. Cynthia Pease Pamplin, May 10, 1985; 1 child, Kristy Pamplin. B.S., Centenary Coll., 1983. Exploration geologist Fortune Gas and Oil Co., Shreveport, La., 1983—. Mem. Am. Assn. Petroleum Geologists, Shreveport Geol. Soc., Sigma Gamma Epsilon (pres. 1982-83). Republican. Office: Fortune Gas and Oil Inc 504 Mid-South Tower Shreveport LA 71101

BICKNELL, KENT, financial service company executive; b. Atlanta, Ga., Nov. 17, 1945; s. Hunter and Martha Doris (Kent) B.; B.B.A., Baylor U., 1968; m. Carolyn Holloway, Apr. 24, 1976; children—Jordan Kent, Wilson Terrell, David Carroll. Salesman, Fidelity Union Life Ins. Co., Waco and Dallas, 1967-70; propr. Kent Bicknell & Assocs., Dallas, 1972-73; founder, 1973, since chmn., chief exec. officer Balanced Fin. Corp., Dallas; chmn., chief exec. officer Balanced Fin. Adv. Corp., Balanced Fin. Securities Corp., Balanced Fin. Venture Corp., Balanced Fin. Mortgage Corp.; vice chmn. Banc Am. Savs. Assn.; pioneer in devel. fee compensated objective fin. planning; dir. MSD Systems, Inc., Am. Tract Soc.; tchr. fin. seminars. Served with AUS, 1971. Cert. fin. planner. Mem. Security Dealers Assn., Internat. Assn. Fin. Planners (dir. local chpt.), Nat. Assn. Securities Dealers. Conservative. Evang. Christian. Club: East Dallas Rotary (program chmn. 1977). Office: 8333 Douglas Ave Dallas TX 75225

BICKNESE, GUNTHER, German language educator, translator; b. Gütersloh, West Germany, Feb. 16, 1926; came to U.S., 1955; s. Ernst F. K. and Emma W. F. (Reinking) B.; m. Gisela Marietta Eppe, Aug. 26, 1957; children—Karsten, Mark E., Ralf. Ph.D., Philipps U., Marburg, W. Germany, 1953. Asst. prof. German, Southwestern U., Memphis, 1960-63; assoc. prof. Millersville State U., Pa., 1963-66, dir. Jr. Yr. in Marburg program, 1963-66; assoc. prof. Agnes Scott Coll., Decatur, Ga., 1963-70, prof. German, 1970—, chmn. dept., 1969—. Author: Elementary German, 3d edit., 1976; Hier und Heute (German Reader), 1983; Travelog for young readers, 1957; translator: A Private Treason (novel), 1981. Mem. Am. Assn. Tchrs. of German, Am. Council on Teaching of Fgn. Langs. Home: 4101 Spartan Ln Stone Mountain GA 30083 Office: Agnes Scott College College Ave Decatur GA 30030

BIDDLE, ALBERT G. W., trade association executive; b. Tulsa, Aug. 14, 1930; s. Albert G. W. and Margaret (Brubeck) B.; m. Stephanie Greher, Mar. 7, 1974; children—Albert G. W., Lisa F., James, Alexandra. B.S., U.S. Mil. Acad., 1952. Cons., Booz, Allen & Hamilton, Chgo., 1957-61; dir. diversification H. I. Thompson, Los Angeles, 1961-62; dir. corporate planning Mattel Inc., Los Angeles, 1962-64; pres. Biddle & Assocs., Los Angeles, 1964-68, Decision Resources Corp., Los Angeles, 1968-72, Computer and Communications Industry Assn., Arlington, Va., 1972—; founder, dir. Corp. for Open Systems Internat., Alexandria, Va., 1985—; dir., chmn. Esnet, Inc., Washington, 1983—; mem. U.S. Council World Communications Yr., Washington, 1982—; advisor Office of Tech. Assessment, U.S. Congress, Washington, 1980—; mem. adv. com. ind. sector to sec. Dept. Commerce, Washington, 1982—. Served to 1st lt. U.S. Army, 1952-55; Korea. Decorated Bronze Star. Republican. Episcopalian. Club: Republican (Washington). Home: Great Falls VA 22006 Office: Computer & Communications Industry Assn 1500 Wilson Blvd Arlington VA 22209

BIDDLE, ERIC HARBESON, JR., lawyer; b. Bryn Mawr, Pa., Feb. 10, 1928; s. Eric Harbeson and Katharine Clover (Rogers) B.; A.B. cum laude (scholar), Harvard U., 1950; J.D., George Washington U., 1977; m. Mary Churchill, 1948 (div.); 1 son, Michael C. Soviet Area intelligence officer CIA, Washington and overseas, 1951-60; contract negotiator Smith Kline & French Labs., Phila., 1960-61; editor and estimator Bechtel Corp., San Francisco, 1961-64; insp. govt. programs OEO and ACTION, Washington, 1969-80; admitted to Va. bar, 1979, D.C. bar, 1980; individual practice law, Arlington, Va., 1980—; cons. fed. grants and program audits. Served as officer USNR, 1951-71. Mem. Va. Bar Assn., D.C. Bar Assn., Am. Bar Assn., Fed. Bar Assn., Assn. Trial Lawyers Am., Inter-Am. Bar Assn., Am. Immigration Lawyers Assn. Anglican. Club: Harvard (D.C.). Office: 2251 N Vermont St Arlington VA 22207

BIELFIELD, BRUCE ROBERT, stock brokerage account executive, lawyer; b. Terre Haute, Ind., Jan. 12, 1951; s. Robert Walter and Ruby Evelyn (Baker) Bielfield; m. Sandra J. Bergmann, Feb. 28, 1981; 1 dau., Kira Beth. B.S. in Econs. and Polit. Sci., Ind. State U., 1972; J.D., U. Miami, 1976. Bar: Fla. 1976. Lic. real estate, ins. agent. Lifeguard, water safety instr., Terre Haute, Ind., 1969-76; profl. musician Mass. Assembly, Terre Haute, 1966-71; sr. acct. exec. Merrill Lynch, Miami, Fla., 1976—; mem. med. malpractice bd., Miami, 1976—; speaker. Mem. Fla. Bar Assn., Exec. Club, Pres.'s Club. Mem. United Ch. of Christ. Club: Roundtable of the Light Ctrs. (Miami). Composer: Little Star, 1972; The Gingerbread Age (sr. div. Poet award). Office: Merrill Lynch 8840 SW 136 St Miami FL 33176

BIELKE, SHELDON PETER, apparel company executive; b. Shakopee, Minn., Aug. 11, 1946; s. Peter William and Laverne Emma (Kaneiss) B.; m. Victoria Elma Belanger, Aug. 23, 1966; children—Morgan, Holly. Student Mankato State Tchrs. Coll., 1964-66; B.A., U. Minn., 1968. Cert. air traffic controller, Hawaii. Air traffic controller FAA, Mpls., 1969-70; project mgr. J. C. Henning Constrn. Co., Eden Prairie, Minn., 1970-72; salesman Munsingwear, Inc., Mpls., 1972-80; v.p. Monarch Hosiery Mills, Inc., Burlington, N.C., 1980-85; internat. sales mgr. Munsingwear, Inc., Mpls., 1980-85; chief exec. officer, v.p. Bitches Britches, Inc., Burlington, N.C., 1980—; govtl. aide Island of Nevis. Bd. dirs. Civic Arts and Drama Club, Alamance County, N.C., 1981-82, Condominium Homeowners Assn., Burlington, N.C., 1983-84 Seco of Nevis, 1984—; sponsor AID, Caribbean Islands, GOP Victory Fund, 1984. Served with USN, 1968-70. Mem. Fed. Aviation Assn. (air traffic controller 1968—). Republican. Lutheran. Clubs: Toastmaster (Mpls.); Men's Apparel (Charlotte, N.C.); St. Paul Pass Hunt (Elbow Lake, Minn.). Home: 60 Spotted Sandpiper Land's End Emerald Isle NC 28557

BIERCE, CAROL ANNE HOOVER, computer software specialist; b. Pensacola, Fla., Jan. 30, 1954; d. Ralph Alwin Hoover, Jr. and Hazel Floyce (Warren) Roberts; B.A. in Math. with highest distinction, U. North Fla., 1975, B.A.E. with highest distinction, 1976, M.B.A., 1979; m. Daniel Ambrose Bierce, Oct. 17, 1975; 2 sons, Adam Anthony, Joseph Alexander. Programmer, Sav-A-Stop, Inc., Orange Park, Fla., 1975-76; with City of Jacksonville (Fla.), 1976—, sr. application analyst, 1980-82, asst. computer systems officer, asst. tech. dir., 1982—; project leader water and electric computer services, tech. support; cons. for Jacksonville Software Devel. Corp. Mem. Assn. M.B.A. Execs., Nat. Assn. Female Execs., Riverside-Avondale Preservation Soc., Fla. Epilepsy Found., Phi Theta Kappa, Pi Mu Epsilon. Democrat. Episcopalian. Home: 1624 Cherry St Jacksonville FL 32205 Office: City Hall 220 E Bay St Jacksonville FL 32202

BIERING, ISABEL MARY, librarian; b. Helotes, Tex., July 7, 1929; d. Nestor and Guadalupe (Quintero) Trevino; m. Vernon J. Biering, July 3, 1976 (div. 1985). B.A., Incarnate Word Coll., 1961; M.L.S., Our Lady of the Lake U., 1970; postgrad. U. Tex., 1977, 79, 83, 84, U. London, 1978. Tchr., Sisters of Charity of Incarnate Word Sch., San Antonio, 1946-61; prin. Our Lady of Refuge Sch., Eagle Pass, Tex., 1961-65; librarian San Antonio Pub. Library, 1966-68, San Antonio Ind. Sch. Dist., 1968-71; librarian, assoc. prof. bus. communications San Antonio Coll., 1971—. Mem. AAUP (chpt. pres. 1982-84), Tex. Library Assn., Bexar Library Assn., Cath. Library Assn., Delta Kappa Gamma (pres. 1986-88). Home: PO Box 100373 San Antonio TX 78201 Office: San Antonio Coll Library 1001 Howard St San Antonio TX 78284

BIERMACHER, KENNETH WAYNE, lawyer; b. Hartford, Conn., Oct. 15, 1953; s. Donald David and Ethel Pearl (Biermacher) Lawton; m. Bonnie Louise Gordon, May 26, 1975; children—Carl Joseph II, Matthew Robert. B.S. summa cum laude, U. New Haven, 1976; J.D. with honors, Drake U., 1979. Bar: Iowa 1980, Tex. 1985, U.S. Dist. Ct. (so. dist.) Iowa 1980, U.S. Dist. Ct. (no. dist.) Iowa 1981, U.S. Ct. Appeals (8th cir.) 1981, U.S. Supreme Ct. 1983, U.S. Dist. Ct. (no. dist.) Tex. 1984, U.S. Dist. Ct. (ea. and we. dists.) Tex. 1985, U.S. Ct. Appeals (5th cir.) 1985. Assoc. Whitfield, Musgrave, Selvy, Kelly, Eddy, Des Moines, 1980-84, Geary, Stahl & Spencer, P.C., Dallas, 1984—; lectr. Iowa Defense Counsel Assn. Annual Mtg., 1982, Des Moines Area Community Coll. Legal Asst. Program, 1981-82, Human Resources Forum, Am. Electronics Assn., 1985; legal research asst. Iowa State Bar Assn. Com. on Study Fed. Rules Evidence, 1982; chmn. spl. com. on Friends of Moot Ct. Drake Law Sch. Bd. Counsellors, 1983-84. Editor (handbook, guide) Energy and Nat. Resources Guide for Iowa, 1979. Adv. U. New Haven Law Enforcement Explorers Post Boy Scouts Am., 1975; coach Johnston Sr. High Sch. Mock Trial Teams, Iowa, 1984; del. Polk County Republican Conv., Des Moines, 1980, Iowa Republican State Convention, 1980. Recipient Academic Scholarship U. New Haven, 1973-76; semi-finalist Midwest Regional Moot Ct. Competition, 1979. Mem. ABA (subcom. on fraudulent and deceptive trade practices sect. tort and ins. practice 1985-86), Iowa State Bar Assn. (mem. Young Lawyer Sect. ethics com. 1981, law schs. panel com. 1982, law-related edn. com. 1983-84), Polk County Bar Assn., Def. Research Inst., Iowa Defense Counsel Assn., Am. Trial Lawyers Assn., Iowa Assn. Trial Lawyers (founding dir., chmn. Drake U. Law Sch. student bd. dirs., 1978-79, ex-officio mem. bd. dirs. 1978-79), Dallas Bar Assn. (mock trial com., law in changing soc. com. 1985, speech com. 1985-86), State Bar Tex., Dallas Assn. Young Lawyers (liaison with other profls., fed. opinions com. 1985), Order of Barristers, Alpha Chi (vice chmn. Conn. chpt. 1975-76). Baptist. Home: 1100 Princeton Dr Richardson TX 75081 Office: Geary Stahl & Spencer PC 2800 One Main Pl Dallas TX 75250

BIERMAN, DON EDWARD, geographer, educator; b. Kowel, Poland, July 24, 1931; s. Marion Chester and Natalja (Nikolajev-von Nolde) B.; came to U.S., 1949, naturalized, 1955; A.B. in Govt., George Washington U., 1963, M.A. in Geography, 1966; Ph.D. in Geography, Mich. State U., 1970; postgrad. in Transp. Northwestern U., Evanston, Ill., 1972; m. Marilyn Marie Brown, June 18, 1955. Asst. prof. geography U. Louisville, 1970-73, chmn. dept. geography, 1972-73, asso. prof., 1973-79, prof., 1979—, dir. Soviet studies, 1976—. Tutor St. Peter's Coll. U. Oxford (Eng.), 1974. Served with AUS, 1952-54; Korea. Decorated Bronze Star medal. Mem. Am. Assn. Advancement Slavic Studies, Assn. Am. Geographers, Am. Soc. Traffic and Transp. (examiner 1973—), Transp. Research Forum. Author: The Oder River: Transport and Economic Development, 1973. Contbr. articles to profl. jours. Office: Geography Dept U of Louisville Louisville KY 40292

BIERSCHENK, ROMAN FRED, banker; b. Lindsay, Tex., Feb. 13, 1921; s. Joe and Mathilda (Koelzer) B.; m. Ruth M. Vinson, Dec. 26, 1941; children—Cecelia Ann, Edward R., Rosemary, William J., Frederick V., John T. Student Tex. Bus. Coll., 1939-40. Asst. sec.-treas. Nat. Farm Loan Assn., Belton, Tex., 1940-47; acct. Southeastern Transit Co., 1947-49; asst. cashier Temple Nat. Bank (Tex.), 1949-50, asst. v.p., 1950-63, v.p., 1963-76, comptroller, 1976—, sr. v.p., 1978-80; exec. v.p. InterFirst Bank, Temple, 1980—. Cubmaster, dist. committeeman, dist. Cub leader Boy Scouts Am., 1953-73. Recipient Catholic Scouters award Diocese of Austin, 1962. Roman Catholic. Lodge: KC.

BIERSDORF, WILLIAM RICHARD, research scientist, educator; b. Salem, Oreg., Sept. 27, 1925; s. Edgar Alvin and Gale Irene (Tidland) B.; B.S., Wash. State U., 1950, M.S., 1951; Ph.D. (Univ. fellow), U. Wis., 1954; m. Rosa Kucera, Feb. 18, 1966; children—James Anthony, William Robert. Exptl. psychologist Walter Reed Army Inst. Research, Washington, 1954-67, acting head dept. psychophysiology, 1966-67; asso. prof. ophthalmology Ohio State U., 1967-78, asso. prof. biophysics, 1970-78; prof. ophthalmology U. South Fla., 1978—; health sci. officer Tampa VA Hosp., 1978—; mem. Visual Scis. Study Sect., NIH, 1971-76. Served with U.S. Army, 1944-46; ETO. Decorated Bronze Star; Nat. Eye Inst. grantee, 1969-80; VA grantee, 1980—. Mem. Assn. Research in Vision and Ophthalmology, Internat. Soc. Clin. Electrophysiology Vision, AAAS, Am. Psychol. Assn. Research, publs. in field of vision research; co-editor: Procs. XVIth Symposium Internat. Soc. for Clin. Electrophysiology Vision, Tokyo, 1979. Office: VA Hosp 13000 N 30th St Tampa FL 33612

BIGDA, RICHARD JAMES, chemical engineer; b. Detroit, May 15, 1930; s. John Joseph and Ernestine Florence (Tweddle) B. B.S.Ch.E., Wayne State U., 1952; M.S.Ch.E., M.S.I.E., U. Mich., 1957. Research engr. Shell Chem. Co. div. Shell Oil Co., Deer Park, Tex., 1952-53; refinery engr. Exxon, Baytown, Tex., 1957-58; tech. mgr. Wyandotte Chem. Internat. (Mich.), 1958-67; asst. to pres. Helmerich & Payne, Inc., Tulsa, 1967-68; pres., cons. engr. Richard J. Bigda & Assocs., 1968—; pres. Technobyte Inc.; prof. engring. Okla., Tex. univs. Co-chmn. Presdl. Reelection Com. Tulsa County, 1972, Rep. State committeeman, 1973-75, chmn. presdl. reception com., 1974; mem. Indian com. Philbrook Art Ctr. Served with Chem. Corps, U.S. Army, 1953-55. Mem. Okla. Soc. Profl. Engrs. (chmn. Tulsa chpt. 1980-81), Am. Inst. Chem. Engrs., AAAS, Nat. Soc. Profl. Engrs., Am. Chem. Soc., Tau Beta Pi. Club: Philbrook Friends of Indian Art (pres.) Author profl. publs. Home: 6732 S Columbia Ave Tulsa OK 74136 Office: Richard J Bigda & Assocs 6216 S Lewis Ave Tulsa OK 74136

BIGGER, MORTON, JR., oil company executive; b. Dallas, Feb. 9, 1924; s. Morton, Sr. and Mildred (Lowrey) B.; m. Anita Byrde Craddock, Dec. 27, 1947 (div. 1967); children—Mildred Anne Bigger Nixon, Margaret Morton Bigger Tarrance, Carolyn Byrde Bigger Peck; m. Catherine Rhody, Sept. 30, 1967. Student Washington and Lee U., 1942-43, Kenyon Coll., 1943-44; B.S., U. Tex., 1947. Geologist, Chevron Oil Co., New Orleans, 1947-49; asst. to v.p. Republic Nat. Gas Co., Dallas, 1949-51; v.p. subs. Union Oil Co. of Calif., Trucial Coast, Africa, Norway, 1966-75; v.p. Transcontinental Oil Corp., Shreveport, La., 1975-80; sr. v.p. Latham Exploration Co., Shreveport, 1981-83; pres. Atakora Corp., Shreveport, 1980—; petroleum cons., Dallas, 1951-66, Shreveport, 1980-81. Served with U.S. Army, 1943-44. Decorated chevalier l'Ordre Nationale du Dahomey, 1972. Mem. Am. Assn. Petroleum Geologists, Shreveport Geol. Assn., West Tex. Geol. Assn., Dallas Geol. Soc., Sigma Gamma Epsilon. Republican. Presbyterian. Clubs: Shreveport Country, Les Ambassadeurs (London). Avocations: hunting; golf; painting. Home: 939 Oneonta St Shreveport LA 71106 Office: Atakora Corp Suite 924 Am Tower Shreveport LA 71101

BIGGERS, NEAL BROOKS, JR., U.S. district judge; b. Corinth, Miss., July 1, 1935; s. Neal Brooks and Sara (Cunningham) B.; m. Jo Ann, 1970; 1 child, Sherron. B.A., Millsaps Coll., 1956; J.D. cum laude, U. Miss., 1963. Sole practice law, Corinth, 1963-68; pros. atty. Alcorn County, 1964; dist. atty. 1st Jud. Dist. Miss., 1968-75; cir. judge, 1975-84; U.S. dist. judge No. Miss., Oxford, 1984—. Contbr. articles to profl. jours. Office: PO Box 1238 Oxford MS 38655-1238*

BIGGS, GLENN, banker; b. Eldorado, Tex., June 10, 1933; s. Bennie Austin and Clara Francis B.; m. Ann Carolyn, July 29, 1955; children—Barry, Brian. B.A., Baylor U., 1956. Asst. mgr. Abilene C. of C. (Tex.), 1956-59; ptnr. Millerman & Millerman, Abilene, 1959-65; exec. aide to speaker Tex. Ho. of Reps., 1965-68; pres. Nat. Western Life Ins. Co., Austin, 1968-70; pres., chmn. bd. First Nat. Bank, San Antonio, from 1970; chmn. exec. com. Interfirst Bank, San Antonio; dir. Interfirst Corp., Dallas, Kans. Gas & Electric Co., Wichita. Chmn. bd. dirs. City Pub. Service, San Antonio; pres. Met. Hosp., San Antonio; trustee Baylor U., Waco, Tex., Baylor Med. Ctr., Dallas; mem. Gov.'s Select Com. on Higher Edn. Mem. Tex. Bankers Assn. Baptist. Clubs: Oak Hills Country (San Antonio). Office: City Public Service Board 145 Navarro St San Antonio TX 78296

BIGGS, NANCY GENE, educator; b. Memphis, Sept. 28, 1923; d. Raynor H. and Genevieve (Tarrant) Chisholm; B.S., Memphis State U., 1961, M.A., 1962, Ed.D., 1969; m. Jack Clayton Biggs, Jan. 21, 1965; children—Charles C. Shoaf III, Raynor G. Shoaf, Robert J. Burnett, John A. Burnett. Tchr., Memphis City Schs., 1961-71, math. cons., 1971—. Recipient Woman's award Memphis State U., 1961. Mem. Nat. Council Tchrs. Math., Nat. Council Suprs. Math. (1st v.p., 1981—), Assn. Supervision and Curriculum Devel., Tenn. Math. Tchrs. Assn., Memphis Area Council Tchrs. Math., Delta Kappa Gamma (pres. Alpha Lambda chpt.). Republican. Baptist. Clubs: Stage Set, Gavel (sec., 1981), Twentieth Century (pres. 1980—), Quota (pres. Memphis, 1977-78). Editor 9 books for individualized math. Home: 1330 Brookfield Memphis TN 38119 Office: Memphis City Schs Room 254 2597 Avery Memphis TN 38112

BIGGS, THOMAS HOWARD, exploration geologist; b. Front Royal, Va., Apr. 10, 1949; s. Robert Mumford and Katherine (Howard) B. B.S. in geology, B.A. in history, Va. Poly. Inst. and State U., 1972; M.S. in geology, U. Ga., 1982. Cert. profl. geologist, Va. Geologist, Va. Div. Mineral Resources, Charlottesville, 1972-76; lab. instr. Dept. Geology, U. Ga., Athens, 1976-78; project geologist U.S. Bur. Mines, Denver Fed. Ctr., 1978; corp. staff geologist U.S. Gypsum Co., Chgo., 1979-80; geologist, geology mgr. Bartlett Energy Exploration, Inc., Abingdon, Va., 1980-83; geologist U.S. Energy Devel. Corp., Buffalo, 1984—. HEW grantee, 1979. Mem. Am. Assn. Petroleum Geologists, Va. Oil and Gas Assn., Am. Inst. Profl. Geologists, Va. Tech Alumni Assn., Highty-Tighty Alumni Assn. Methodist. Contbr. articles to profl. jours.

BIGLER, BERNARD PHILIP, history educator; b. Coral Gables, Fla., July 15, 1952; s. Charles Everest and Bernice Olga (Reins) B.; m. Linda Lee Mimms, Oct. 16, 1982. B.A., James Madison U., 1974, M.Ed., 1976; M.A., Coll. William and Mary, 1984. Cert. tchr., Va., Md. History tchr. Fairfax County Pub. Schs., Fairfax, Va., 1975-82; historian Arlington Nat. Cemetery, Va., 1983-85; high sch. history tchr. Montgomery County Schs., Rockville, Md., 1985—; tchr., counselor Gov.'s Sch. for Gifted and Talented, Blacksburg, Va., 1985. Author: (ednl. simulation) The Electors, 1980. Vice chmn. Coll. Republicans, Harrisonburg, Va., 1973-74; sustaining mem. Rep. Party, 1973—. Am. Studies scholar Coll. William and Mary, 1982-83; Fulbright scholar, Netherlands, 1981; recipient cert. of Achievement, The Old Guard, 1985, cert. of Appreciation, U.S. Secret Service, 1985; cert. of commendation Va. State Dept. Edn., 1985. Mem. Lincoln Group of Washington, No. Va. Assn. Historians, Wayland Hist. Soc. (pres. 1973-74), James Madison Leadership Soc., Phi Alpha Theta (historian 1973-74), Kappa Delta Pi. Roman Catholic. Avocation: competitive running in marathons, including Boston Marathon, 1979, N.Y.C. Marathon, 1980, 82, 83. Home: 5120 Portsmouth Rd Fairfax VA 22032 Office: Bethesda-Chevy Chase High Sch 4301 East West Hwy Bethesda MD 20814

BILGER, HANS RUDOLF, electrical and computer engineering educator; b. Singen, Germany, May 17, 1935; came to U.S., 1962; s. Martin and Elisabeth (Wenz) B.; m. Edda Luise Goenner, Oct. 8, 1958; children—Martin, Eva, Monika, Burkhard, Andrea. Ph.D., U. Basel, Switzerland, 1961. Research assoc. U. Basel, 1961-62, U. Ill., Urbana, 1962-63; asst. prof. elec. and computer engring Okla. State U., Stillwater, 1963-68, assoc. prof., 1968-75, prof., 1975—; research assoc., vis. scientist Argonne Nat. Lab., Ill., 1965-67; research fellow Calif. Inst. Tech., Pasadena, 1973-74; prof. associe U. des Sciences, Montpellier, France, 1976-78; research assoc. Nuclear Research Ctr., Karlsruhe, Fed. Republic Germany, 1970-71. Contbr. articles to profl. publs. Patentee in field. Mem. AAUP, Sigma Xi, Eta Kappa Nu. Roman Catholic. Avocations: sailing; chess. Home: 417 N Donaldson Stillwater OK 74075 Office: 310 ES Okla State U Stillwater OK 74078

BILIRAKIS, MICHAEL, lawyer, congressman, business executive; b. Tarpon Springs, Fla., July 16, 1930; s. Emmanuel and Irene (Pikramenos) B.; m. Evelyn Miaoulis, Dec. 27, 1959; children—Emmanuel, Gus. B.S. in Engring., U. Pitts., 1959; student, George Washington U., 1959-60; J.D., U. Fla., 1963. Diplomate; cert. coll. tchr., Fla., Fla. 1964. Atty., small businessman, Pinellas and Pasco Counties, Fla., 1968—; mem. 98th Congress from 9th Dist. Fla. Mem. Republican Task Force on Social Security; founder, charter pres. Tarpon Springs Vol. Ambulance Service; dir. Greek Studies program U. Fla.; bd. devel. Anclote Manor Psychiat. Hosp. Served to sgt. USAF, 1951-55. Named Citizen of Yr. for Greater Tarpon Springs, 1972-73. Mem. Am. Legion (comdr. 1977-79), VFW, Air Force Assn., Greater Tarpon Springs C. of C. (past pres., dir.), Pinellas C. of C. (gov.), West Pasco Bar Assn., Am. Judicature Soc., Fla. Bar Assn., Gator Boosters, Phi Alpha Delta. Lodges: Masons; Shriners; Tarpon Springs Rotary; Elks; Eastern Star; White Shrine of Jerusalem. Office: 319 Cannon House Office Bldg Washington DC 20515

BILLHOFER, BETTE PHELPS, woodworking machinery company executive, graphic designer; b. Jackson, Miss., Jan. 3, 1946; d. William T. and Betty (Howard) Phelps; m. Rolf D. Billhofer, Feb. 17, 1973; children—Steffan Heinz, Belmont Claire. B.A., Belhaven Coll., 1968; postgrad. Miss. U., 1971—. Art tchr. Jackson Pub. Schs. (Miss.), 1968-71, Clarksdale City Schs. (Miss.), 1972-73, Pearl City Schs., (Miss.), 1974-78; v.p. R.D. Billhofer Co., Jackson, Miss., 1978—. Mem. DAR, 99s Women's Pilot Assn., Kappa Pi. Republican. Episcopalian. Club: Jackson Yacht. Painter of murals Crippled Children's Hosp., Whitfield State Mental Hosp. and Pearl City Schs. Home: 5249 Wayneland Dr Jackson MS 39211 Office: PO Box 20307 Jackson MS 39209

BILLICK, L. LARKIN, advertising agency executive; b. Des Moines, Sept. 15, 1948; s. Lyle Larkin and Florence (Carlson) B.; m. Kathryn Rose Gildner, Aug. 14, 1971; children—Kelly Lynne, Brett Larkin. B.S., U. Kans., 1970; grad. Inst. Bank Mktg., U. So. Calif., La. State U., 1978. Group ins. trainee Bankers Life Co., Des Moines, 1970-71; nat. advt. rep. Stoner Broadcasting Co., Des Moines, 1971-74; advt. account supr. Mid-Am. Broadcasting, Des Moines, 1974-75; dir. pub. relations and mktg. Iowa Bankers Assn., Des Moines, 1975-77; asst. v.p., advt. mgr. corp. staff Marine Banks, Milw., 1977-79, v.p. advt., 1979-81; pres. Edwards-Billick Fin. Mktg. Group, Milw., 1981-82; sr. v.p. mktg. University Savings Assn., Houston, 1982-84; mgmt. supr. W.B. Donner Advt., Houston, 1984—; dir. Grad. Inst. Bank Mktg., La. State U., 1978-79. Chmn. communications Milw. County Performing Arts Ctr., 1978-79; advt. and promotion cons. to polit. candidates; chmn. communications council United Performing Arts Fund Milw., 1978-79; dist. coordinator State Del. for Jimmy Carter, 1972-80; chmn. communications com. Milw. County council Boy Scouts Am., 1979-80. Recipient numerous advt. and pub. relations awards. Mem. Bank Mktg. Assn. (chmn. nat. advt. conf. 1979, advt. council 1980-81), Am. Bankers Assn. (mem. nat. mktg. conf. com. 1980), Am. Advt. Fedn. (pub. service com. 1980-81), Am. Mktg. Assn., Milw. Advt. Club (v.p. fin. 1979-81, dir. 1981-82), Tex. Savings and Loan League (mem. mktg. com. 1983-84). Democrat. Roman Catholic. Home: 20619 Hannington Ln Katy TX 77450 Office: 2900 Weslayan Houston TX 77027

BILLINGHAM, RUPERT EVERETT, biology educator, biologist, researcher; b. Warminster, Eng., Oct. 15, 1921; s. Albert Everett and Helen Louise (Green) B.; m. Jean Mary Morpeth, Mar. 29, 1951; children—John David, Peter Jeremy, Elizabeth Anne. B.A., Oriel Coll., Oxford (Eng.) U., 1943, M.A., 1947, D.Phil., 1950, D.Sc., 1957; D.Sc. (hon.), Trinity Coll., Hartford, Conn., 1965. Lectr. dept. zoology U. Birmingham (Eng.), 1947-51; research fellow Brit. Empire Cancer Campaign, hon. research assoc. dept. zoology Univ. Coll. London, 1951-57; mem. Wistar Inst. Anatomy and Biology, Phila., 1957-65; prof. zoology, U. Pa., 1958-71; prof., chmn. dept. med. genetics and dir. Henry Phipps Inst., Sch. Medicine, U. Pa., 1965-71; prof., chmn. dept. cell biology and anatomy U. Tex. Health Sci. Center at Dallas, 1971—. Served to lt. Royal Navy, 1942-46. Recipient Alvarenga prize Coll. Physicians of Phila., 1963, Hon. award Am. Assn. Plastic Surgeons, 1964, Frederick Lyman Adair award Am. Gynecol. Soc., 1971. Fellow Royal Soc. of London, Am. Acad. Arts and Scis.; mem. Am. Assn. Immunologists, N.Y. Acad. Scis., Transplantation Soc. (pres. 1974-76), Internat. Soc. for Immunology of Reprodn. (pres. 1983-86). Contbr. sci. articles to profl. jours. Home: 6181 Preston Haven Dr Dallas TX 75230 Office: Dept Cell Biology and Anatomy Univ Tex Health Sci Center Dallas 5323 Harry Hines Blvd Dallas TX 75235

BILLINGS, ANSIL DONALD, college administrator; b. Vernon, Tex., Sept. 23, 1936; s. Melford Ray and Louise Dorothy (Frank) B.; m. Jerre L. Hale, Mar. 2, 1966; children—Kerri L. Billings Crow, Kelli Dawn. B.S. in Acctg. magna cum laude, Bethany Nazarene Coll., 1969; M.S. in Mgmt. cum laude, Case Western Res. U., 1978. Sr. auditor Blue Cross of N.E. Ohio, Cleve., 1969-71; bus. mgr. Luth. Med. Ctr., Cleve., 1971-73; controller St. Vincent Charity Hosp., Cleve., 1973-74, dir. fin., 1974-77, sr. v.p., 1977-81; v.p. fin. affairs Bethany Nazarene Coll., Okla., 1981—. Contbr. articles to profl. jours. Bd. dirs. Okla. State Nazarene Student Ctr., Stillwater, 1973—. Fellow Hosp. Fin. Mgmt. Assn. (pres. 1980-81); mem. Nat. Assn. Coll. and Univ. Bus. Officers, Bethany C. of C. (pres. 1984). Republican. Mem. Ch. of the Nazarene. Lodge: Kiwanis (v.p. 1985). Avocations: fishing; sports. Home: 7510 NW 39 St Bethany OK 73008 Office: Bethany Nazarene Coll 6729 NW 39 Expressway Bethany OK 73008

BILLINGS, CLARENCE DAVID, university dean, finance educator; b. Stella, Mo., Apr. 13, 1943; s. Clarence Emmett and Christina Marie (Clary) B.; m. Nancy Ann Carter, Dec. 14, 1963; children—John David, Amanda Gayle. B.S., Southwest Mo. State U., 1965; Ph.D., U. Mo., 1969. Cost analyst U.S. Army, Washington, 1968-70; asst. prof. fin. U. Ga., Athens, 1970-75, assoc. prof. fin., 1975-81, coordinator grad. bus., 1976-81; prof. fin., dean Sch. Adminstrv. Sci., U. Ala., Huntsville, 1981—; trustee Grad. Mgmt. Admission Council, Princeton, N.J., 1981-82. Editor State and Local Govt. Rev., 1975-81. USPHS fellow, 1966-68; recipient Meritorious Service medal U.S. Army, Washington, 1970. Mem. Am. Econ. Assn., Nat. Tax Assn., Am. Inst. Decision Scis., So. Econ. Assn., So. Bus. Adminstrn. Assn., Beta Gamma Sigma. Methodist. Lodge: Rotary. Home: 706 Corlett Dr SE Huntsville AL 35802 Office: Sch Adminstrv Sci U Ala Huntsville AL 35899

BILLINGS, JOHN PHILIP, management executive; b. Madison, Wis., Sept. 16, 1941; s. Frederick Perry and Helen Elizabeth (Johnson) B.; B.A., Tex. Christian U., 1966; m. Carrie Jane Hudson, Aug. 24, 1962; 1 son, John Philip. Asst. dir. safety programs Dallas County chpt. ARC, 1968-69, dir. programs Galveston (Tex.) County chpt., 1970-71; dir. personnel and tng. Sparkman Hillcrest Ambulance Co., Dallas, 1969-70; dir. spl. programs, fin. and adminstrn. Gulf Coast Regional Mental Health/Mental Retardation Center, Galveston, 1971-74, exec. dir., 1974-82; v.p., chief operating officer The Browser Corp., 1983—. Served with USNR, 1960-63. Recipient County Achievement award Nat. Assn. Counties, 1975, Liberty Bell award Jr. Bar Assn., 1979, Gold award Am. Psychiat. Assn., 1980; Braniff fellow, 1968-70. Mem. Nat. Council Community Mental Health Centers, Mental Health Assn., Assn. Retarded Citizens, Assn. Med. Rehab. Dirs., Assn. Mental Health Adminstrs., Tex. Corrections Assn., Phi Alpha Theta, Phi Sigma Alpha. Clubs: Elks, Rotary, Masons. Author articles in field. Home: Blue Heron Friendswood TX 77546 Office: 3111 S Maine Pearland TX 77581

BILLINGSLEA, WILLIE DEAN, association executive; b. Atlanta, Nov. 25, 1937; d. Willie Lee and Emma Lou (Montgomery) Moore; student Blayton Sch. Acctg., 1956-58, Ga. State U., 1967, 74, 77; m. Grady Lee Billingslea, June 28, 1958; children—Grady Lee, Dynite Darlene, Willie DeMoore. Sec., Met. Atlanta Assn. for the Blind, 1958-69; clerical mgr. Phyllis Wheatley br. YWCA, Atlanta, 1969-70; adminstrv. services supr. Community Council of Atlanta Area, 1970-75; bus. mgr. Gate City Day Nursery Assn., Atlanta, 1975—; field office mgr. Westat Research Inc., Rockville, Md., 1975; field staff coordinator Belden Asso., Dallas, 1972, 73, 76. Chmn. human relations com., Atlanta chpt. Continental Socs., 1979-80; troop membership chmn. Boy Scouts Am., Atlanta, 1976; sec. Benjamin E. Mays High Sch. PTA, 1981-82, membership chmn., 1983-84; citizenship chmn. Atlanta Council PTAs; sec. bd. dirs. Atlanta Police Athletic League; fin. officer Fulton Flight, CAP. Mem. NAACP (dir. 1974), Atlanta LWV, Am. Bus. Women Assn., Nat. Soc. Pub. Accts., Chi Mu Epsilon. Baptist. Office: 2080 Cascade Rd SW Atlanta GA 30311

BILLS, ROBERT E(DGAR), emeritus educator; b. Nutley, N.J., Dec. 15, 1916; s. Willis Minard and Leah Catherine (Condit) B.; m. Annie Tarleton Carley, Dec. 22, 1944; children—Mary Ann Bills Niles, Leah Catherine Bills Hawkins. B.S., Western Ky. U., 1938; M.A., U. Ky., 1946; Ed.D., Columbia U, 1948. Tchr. sci. Breathitt County (Ky.) Bd. Edn., 1938-42; tchr. Anchorage Bd. Edn. (Ky.), 1943-44, prin., 1944-5; critic tchr. sci. U. Ky. Coll. Edn., 1945-46, faculty Coll. Arts and Scis., 1948-56, asst. prof. psychology, 1948-52, assoc. prof., 1952-56, chmn. div. biol. scis., 1950-51; prof. psychology, chmn. dept. Auburn U., 1956-61; prof. ednl. psychology U. Ala., 1961-69, research prof. edn., 1969-79, research prof. emeritus, 1979—, asst. dean research, 1961-63, interim dean Coll. Edn., 1963-65, dean, 1965-69, dean emeritus, 1979—; mem. council psychol. resources of South So. Regional Edn. Bd., 1953-56; chmn. Ky. Bd. Examiners Psychologists, 1954-56; vis. prof. U. Fla., 1953, 54, Mich. State U., 1956, U. Wash., 1963; lectr. in field. Bd. dirs. Southeastern Ednl. Corp., 1966-67; sec. Ala. Coalition for Better Edn., 1969-70, pres., 1971-72. Served with U.S. Army, 1943-44. Recipient Outstanding prof. award Coll. Edn. U. Ala., 1979; Ednl. Press Assn. award for disting. contbn. to ednl. journalism, 1982. Fellow Am. Psychol. Assn. (sec.-treas. div. 1963-66), Mid-South Edn. Research Assn. (v.p. 1978, pres. 1979), Assn. Supervision and Curriculum Devel. (dir. 1962-64), Sigma Xi, Kappa Delta Pi, Psi Chi, Phi Delta Kappa. Author: Education for Intelligence or Failure?, 1982; contbr. chpts. to books, articles in field to profl. jours. Home: 55 N Blackwater Ln Key Largo FL 33037

BILYEA, DAVID LOGAN, osteopathic surgeon, medical educator; b. Kirksville, Mo., June 15, 1929; s. George and Cleo (Fritz) B.; m. Carolyn O. Dornoff, July, 1951; children—Kathryn Bilyea-Harmon, Cynthia Bilyea McKenney, Richard. Student, Westminister Coll., 1947-49; D.O., Kirksville Coll., 1949-53. Diplomate Am. Osteo. Bd. Surgery. Intern, Lakeview Hosp., Milw., 1953-54; gen. practice medicine, Louisiana, Mo., 1954-66; resident in gen. surgery Grandview Hosp., Dayton, Ohio, 1966-69; fellow in pulmonary medicine Ingham Med. Hosp., Lansing, Mich., 1969-70, resident in thoracic and cardiovascular surgery, 1970-72; mem. staff, cons. thoracic and cardiovascular surgery Ft. Worth Osteo. Med. Ctr., 1972—; assoc. prof. surgery Tex. Coll. Osteo. Medicine, Ft. Worth, 1972-85, chief dept. surgery, 1973-75. Mem. Health Planning Council Tex., 1980-83; mem. Tex. Osteo. Polit. Action Com., 1982—; bd. dirs. Tex. Heart Assn., 1979-80. Fellow Am. Coll. Osteo. Surgeons, Phi Delta Theta. Republican. Mem. Disciples of Christ. Lodges: Odd Fellows, Elks. Avocations: gardening; personal computers; travel. Home: 6420 Landsdale St Fort Worth TX 76116 Office: TCOM Surgical Assocs 901 Montgomery St Fort Worth TX 76107

BILZERIAN, PAUL ALEC, real estate executive; b. Miami, Fla., June 18, 1950; s. Oscar A. and Joan I. (Barrie) B.; B.A., Stanford U., 1975; M.B.A., Harvard U., 1977; m. Terri L. Steffen, Sept. 17, 1978; children—Dan, Adam. Asst. dir. World Data Analysis Center, Stanford, Calif., 1974-75; treasury asso. Crown Zellerbach Corp., San Francisco, 1977-78; chmn. bd. Internat. Broadcasters, Inc., Seminole, Fla., 1978-79; exec. v.p. Nat. Bus. Enterprises, Inc., Sacramento, 1979-82; pres. So. Bus. Enterprises, Inc., St. Petersburg, Fla., 1982—, also dir.; pres. Bicoastal Oil & Gas Corp., Sacramento, Calif., 1984—; dir. Southbay Hardware Co., Inc. (all St. Petersburg). Served to 1st lt. U.S. Army, 1968-71. Decorated Bronze Star. Club: Harvard Bus. Sch. Home: 1914 Carolina Ave NE Saint Petersburg FL 33703 Office: 1264 S Tamiami Trail Osprey FL 33559 also 7919 Folsom Blvd Suite 250 Sacramento CA 95826

BINGHAM, BARRY, editor; b. Louisville, Feb. 10, 1906; s. Robert Worth and Eleanor (Miller) B.; m. Mary Clifford Caperton, June 9, 1931; children—Worth (dec.), Barry, Sarah, Jonathan (dec.). Eleanor (Mrs. Rowland Miller). Student, Middlesex Sch., Concord, Mass., 1921-23; A.B. magna cum laude, Harvard U., 1928; LL.D., U. Ky., Kenyon Coll., Bellarmine Coll., Ind. U., Spalding Coll., Edgecliff Coll.; Litt.D., U. Louisville, U. Cin., Centre Coll., Alfred U., Berea Coll. With Courier-Jour. and; Louisville Times Co., 1930—, editor, pub., 1945-71, chmn. bd., 1971—; chmn. bd. WHAS, Inc., Standard Gravure Corp. Trustee Berea Coll., 1938-76; trustee Nat. Portrait Gallery; bd. overseers Harvard U.; dir. Asia Found.; chmn. Internat. Press Inst., 1964-66; hon. life mem. Chief of mission to France, ECA, 1949-50; Nat. chmn. Vols. for Stevenson-Kefauver, 1956. Served to comdr. USNR, 1941-45. Decorated comdr. Order Brit. Empire; comdr. Legion of Honor; recipient Sullivan award U. Ky.; William Allen White Journalism award U. Kans.; Roger W. Straus award NCCJ. Mem. English-Speaking Union U.S. (chmn. bd. trustees 1974-77). Democrat. Episcopalian. Clubs: River Valley, Wynn-Stay, Louisville Country, Jefferson (Louisville); Century Assn. Home: Glenview KY 40025 Office: Courier-Journal and Times Louisville KY 40202

BINGHAM, ELIZABETH ELLIOTT, librarian; b. Butler, Ala., June 29, 1948; d. James Howard and Emogene (Shamburger) Elliott; m. Clifton O. Bingham, Jr., Apr. 16, 1965 (div. Mar. 1977); 1 son, Clifton O. B.S., La. State U.-Baton Rouge, 1970, M.S., 1971. Reference librarian East Baton Rouge Parish Library, 1970-74, head mid-city br., 1974-75, head adult services, 1975—. Contbr. articles to profl. jours. HEW fellow, 1975. Mem. Am. Library Assn. (pres. Jr. Mem. Round Table 1979-80), La. Library Assn. (treas. 1979-80, recipient Mid-Career award 1983), Southeastern Library Assn. Democrat. Presbyterian. Clubs: Altrusa Internat., Jr. League (Baton Rouge); Found. for Hist. La. Home: 402 Stanford Ave Baton Rouge LA 70808 Office: E Baton Rouge Parish Library 7711 Goodwood Blvd Baton Rouge LA 70806

BINGHAM, R(OBERT) GORDON, educational administrator; b. Evanston, Ill., Jan. 26, 1942; s. Robert Gordon and Betty Sue (Stripp) B.; m. Lucinda Elise Petersen, June 12, 1965; children—Christopher Robert, Matthew Kimball. B.A., Middlebury Coll., 1964; M.A., Northwestern U., 1967. Lectr. econs. Lake Forest Coll., Ill., 1966-67; dir. student aid Union Coll., Schenectady, N.Y., 1967-69, asst. to pres., 1969-72; dean students Hamilton Coll., Clinton, N.Y., 1972-81; headmaster Forsyth Country Day Sch., Lewisville, N.C., 1981—. Contbr. articles to profl. jours. Bd. dirs. Little Theatre, Winston-Salem, N.C., 1982—. Erhart Found. fellow 1964-65, 65-66. Mem. Nat. Assn. Ind. Schs., N.C. Assn. Ind. Schs. Lodge: Rotary. Office: Forsyth Country Day Sch 5501 Shallowford Rd Lewisville NC 27023

BINGHAM, SALLIE, writer, playwright, educator; b. Louisville, Jan. 22, 1937; d. Barry and Mary (Caperhon) B. B.A. magna cum laude, Radcliffe Coll., 1958. Mem. faculty U. Louisville, 1977—, tchr. advanced playwrighting, 1985—. Author: (plays) Milk of Paradise, 1980, The Wall Between, 1983, Couvade, 1983, Paducah, 1985; (novel) After Such Knowledge, 1959; (novella and short stories) The Touching Hand, 1968; (short stories) The Way It Is Now, 1972. Contbr. stories to anthologies and mags. Guest fiction editor Mademoiselle mag., 1958; book editor Louisville Courier Jour., 1982—. Founder The Am. Voice, Ky. Found. for Women, 1985; bd. dirs. Spalding U., Louisville, 1984—, Maryhurst Sch., 1985—. MacDowell Colony fellow, 1979, 81, 82, 84; Ossabaw Found. fellow, 1980; Yaddo fellow, 1980, 83; Va. Ctr. Creative Arts fellow, 1980, 82. Mem. Nat. Book Critics Circle (dir. 1982—). Office: Heyburn Bldg Suite 1215 4th and Broadway Louisville KY 40202

BINGMAN, HARRY DAVID, geology educator; b. Richardson, W.Va., Mar. 15, 1921; m. Eleanor Frances Smith, June 21, 1942; children—Harry David III, Stephen Michael. A.B., Marietta Coll., 1948; M.A., W.Va. U., 1964; postgrad. Rice U. Tchr. Wirt County High Sch., Elizabeth, W.Va., 1948-50, Parkersburg High Sch., W.Va., 1950-59; dir. Wood County Planetarium, Parkersburg, 1959-64; instr. W.Va. U.-Parkersburg Ctr., 1965-72; instr., div. chmn. Parkersburg Community Coll., 1972—. Served as sgt. U.S. Army, 1942-46. Mem. W.Va. Acad. Sci., Nat. Assn. Geology Tchrs., Soc. Econ. Paleontologists and Mineralogists, Ohio Valley Gem and Mineral Assn. (pres. 1976-78), Phi Delta Kappa. Republican. Lodges: Mason, Elks. Avocations: boating; mineral and fossil collecting; music. Home: 2702 Harrison Ave Parkersburg WV 26101 Office: Dept Sci Parkersburg Community Coll Route 5 Box 167A Parkersburg WV 26101

BINKLEY, JAMES EDGAR, dentist; b. Hennessey, Okla., July 27, 1931; s. Floyd Halie and Faye Sincle (Keller) B.; m. Shirley Kathleen Weeks, Jan. 24, 1953; children—Kathleen Ann, James Michael. Student U. Okla., 1949-53; D.D.S., Kansas City Western Dental Coll., U. Mo., 1957. Gen. practice dentistry, Hennessey, 1957-58, 60—. Officer Hennessey Sch. Bd., 1961-66; mem. Republican Nat. Com.; former deacon 1st Christian Ch. Served to capt. U.S. Army, 1953-60. Recipient Service award Seoul Orphanage, Korea, 1959. Mem. ADA, Okla. Dental Assn., Northwest Dist. Dental Assn., Okla. Wildlife Fedn., U. Okla. Alumni Assn. (life mem.), Hennessey C. of C. (founding mem., 1st sec.-treas.), U.S. Golf Assn., Nat. Rifle Assn. Clubs: Hennessey Golf and Country (charter mem.); Bella Vista Golf and Country (Ark.); Fishing of Am. Lodges; Mason (32 degree), Order Eastern Star. Avocations: golf; fishing; hunting; coin collecting. Home: 214 E 3d St Hennessey OK 73742 Office: Binkley Dental Clinic 120 E Oklahoma Ave Box 265 Hennessey OK 73742

BINNING, BETTE FINESE (MRS. GENE HEDGCOCK BINNING), athletic assn. ofcl.; b. Brandon, Man., Can., Sept. 20, 1927 (father Am. citizen); d. Henry Josiah and Beatrice Victoria (Harrop) Ames; grad. Brandon Collegiate, 1944; student Brandon, U., 1944-46; m. Gene Hedgcock Binning, May 3, 1952; children—Gene Barton, Barbara Jo, Bradford Jay. Exec. sec. to mgr. Gardner-Denver Co., Denver, 1950-52; mem. age group swimming com. Amateur Athletic Union U.S., 1966-68, 70-72, women's swimming com., 1968-69, 72—, age group swimming objectives subcom., 1970-71, del. conv., 1971, 72, 73, 74, 75, 76, 77, 79, 80; Okla. state chmn. age group swimming Amateur Athletic Union, 1966-68, 70-72, chmn. women's swimming com., 1968-69, 72-79, mem. Okla. exec. bd. for all amateur sports, also registration com., 1971-79; mem. U.S. Olympic com., 1972-80; nat. dir. swimming records, 1972-81; U.S. rep. to records com. Amateur Swimming Assn. Ams., 1975-83, dir. records com., 1975-83; dir., sec. records com. Union Amateur de Natacion de las Americas, 1979-83; tech. ofcl. Pan Am. Games, Mexico City, 1975, San Juan, P.R., 1979; ofcl. XXI Olympiad, Montreal, Que., Can., 1976. Team capt. YMCA fund drives, 1966-78; active Community Chest, Cancer, Muscular Dystrophy fund drives, Okla. Horse Shows. Mem. Kiwanis Ladies, Youth Study Club (treas. 1971-72). Presbyn. Clubs: Kerr-Mcgee Swim (dir. 1968-75), Quail Creek Golf and Country, Oklahoma City Ski (Oklahoma City); La Quinta Golf (Calif.); Vail Athletic (Colo.). Home: 3101 Rolling Stone Rd Oklahoma City OK 73120

BIOLCHINI, ROBERT FREDRICK, lawyer; b. Detroit, Sept. 22, 1939; s. Alfred and Erma V. (Barbatti) B.; A.B., U. Notre Dame, 1962; LL.B., George Washington U., 1965; m. Frances Lauinger, June 5, 1965; children—Robert F., Douglas C., Frances E., Tobin M., Thomas A., Christine M. Bar: Okla. 1965. Mich. 1965. Assoc. Doerner, Stuart, Saunders, Daniel & Anderson, Tulsa, 1968-71, partner, 1971—; dir. Pennwell Pub. Co., Lawrence Electronics Inc., Valley Nat. Bank, Bank of Jackson Hole, Bank of Lakes, Centrifugal Casting, Inc.; mem. Lloyds of London; judge Okla. Ct. Appeals, 1981—. Bd. dirs., sec. Tulsa Ballet Theatre, 1974-85; pres. Monte Cassino Sch., 1970-78; pres. Thomas Gilcrease Mus., 1976-78, dir. emeritus; mem. alumni senate U. Notre Dame, adv. council law sch., 1982—; bd. dirs. Tulsa United Way, 1986—. Served as capt. AUS, 1965-67. Roman Catholic (chmn. parish council 1973-74). Clubs: Tulsa, So. Hills County, Notre Dame of Tulsa (pres.). Home: 1744 E 29th St Tulsa OK 74114 Office: 1000 Atlas Life Bldg Tulsa OK 74103

BIRCHER, EDGAR ALLEN, lawyer, manufacturing company executive; b. Springfield, Ohio, Apr. 28, 1934; s. John Clark and Ethel Ann B.; m. Jean Ann Berry, Aug. 24, 1957 (div. Apr. 1976); m. 2d, Lavinia Camille Brock, Sept. 30, 1978; children—Douglas, Stephen, Todd, Karen. B.A., Ohio Wesleyan U., 1956; J.D., Ohio State U., 1961. Bar: Ohio 1962, Tex. 1973. Assoc., Fuller, Seney Henry & Hodge, Toledo, 1962-64; with Cooper Industries, Inc., Houston, 1964—, v.p., gen. counsel, 1977—. Bd. dirs. Houston Urban Affairs Corp. Served to capt. USAF, 1956-59. Mem. ABA, Tex. Bar Assn., Ohio Bar Assn., Houston Bar Assn., Am. Corp. Counsel Assn., Machinery and Allied Products Assn. (law council), Phi Delta Theta, Phi Delta Phi. Clubs: Houston; Bob Smith Yacht (Galveston, Tex.).

BIRCHETT, JO ANN, government official; b. Emporia, Kans., Feb. 19, 1944; d. Clarence Othel and Wilma Jane (Young) B. B.S., Tex. A&I U., Kingsville, 1967. Cooperative edn. student NASA-Johnson Space Center, Houston, 1963-67, computer programmer, data analyst, 1967—. Mem. Fed. Women's Program com., 1979-81. Mem. AIAA, Am. Fedn. Govt. Employees (women's coordinator 1980-81, treas. 1981—), Nat. Mgmt. Assn. Democrat. Mem. Christian Ch. Home: Route 2 Box 2222 7510 Sunflower St Pearland TX 77584 Office: NASA Johnson Space Center Houston TX 77058

BIRCHFIELD, MARY EVA, retired librarian; b. Sarasota, Fla., Mar. 8, 1909; d. Benjamin Franklin and Mary Charlotte (Farnbach) McCall; m. William Otto Birchfield, Dec. 5, 1933; children—William, Benjamin, Hal, James. B.S. in Physics, Fla. State Coll. for Women, 1929; M.S., Fla. State U., 1961, M.S. in L.S., 1963. Cert. tchr. Tchr., Lafayette County, Mayo, Fla., 1930-61; librarian Fla. State U., Tallahassee, 1963-77. Compiler bibliographies: Consolidated Catalog of League of Nations Publications Offered for Sale, 1976, Complete Reference Guide to United Nations Sales Publications, 1946-1978, 1982. Pres. PTA, Mayo, 1940-42. NSF study awardee, 1958-60. Mem. Phi Kappa Phi, Kappa Delta Pi, Delta Kappa Gamma, Beta Phi Mu. Democrat. Baptist. Home: 125 Westridge Dr Tallahassee FL 32304

BIRCHUM, DONALD GENE, SR., supermarket chain executive; b. Norman, Okla., Dec. 18, 1930; s. Joseph Wesley and Vada Lee (Southerland) B.; B.F.A. in Advt., Okla. U., 1953; m. Betty Marie Kegler, Nov. 10, 1961 (dec. May 1982); 1 child, Donald Gene. Asst. advt. prodn. mgr. H.E. Butt Grocery Co., Corpus Christi, Tex., 1957-62, advt. mgr., family center div., 1969-71, corporate advt. mgr., 1971-85; owner, operator Birchum Advt. Cons., 1986—. advt. mgr., grocery div. Gulf-Mart Inc., San Antonio, 1962-68. Served as 1st lt. USAF, 1954-56. Named hon. adm. Tex. Navy. Mem. Corpus Christi Advt. Fedn., South Tex. Press Assn., U.S. Power Squadron (nat. com. audio visual aids 1978—, dist. 21 sec. 1980-81), Corpus Christi Power Squadron (sec. 1974-76, editor, art dir. Gulf Breeze 1974-78), N.Am. Cruiser Assn. (pub. relations chmn.), Am. Power Boat Assn., Alpha Delta Sigma, Phi Delta Theta. Episcopalian. Club: Bay Yacht. Illustrator, cartoonist Ensign mag. U.S. Power Squadrons, 1975—. Home: 518 Evergreen Dr Corpus Christi TX 78412 Office: 807 N Upper Broadway Corpus Christi TX 78408

BIRD, DANIEL WOODROW, JR., state senator, lawyer; b. Bland, Va., Dec. 26, 1938; m. Barbara Joan McEldowney; children—Virginia, Woodrow, Benjamin. B.S., Va. Poly. Inst. and State U.; LL.B., Washington and Lee U. Mem. Va. Senate, 1976—; spl. counsel Va. Atty. Gen.'s Office; mem. Mountain Security Savs. & Loan Assn. Served to capt. U.S. Army. Mem. Wythe Farm Bur., Wytheville-Wythe-Bland C. of C., Va. Bar Assn., ABA, Va. Trial Lawyers Assn., Va. Poly. Inst. Alumni Assn. (dir.), Phi Kappa Alpha, Phi Alpha Delta, Omicron Delta Kappa. Democrat. Methodist. Club: Golden Infield. Lodges: Rotary (del. internat. edn. study), Lions (past pres.). Office: Va Senate Gen Assembly Bldg 9th and Broad Sts Richmond VA 23219*

BIRD, ESTHER JANE, psychotherapist; b. Indpls., Jan. 17, 1945; d. James Dwire and Margaret Esther (Brunson) Rees; m. Milton Bird, June 4, 1966 (div. May 1978); children—Andrew Milton, Laura Esther; m. John Leslie Ellis, July 31, 1982; stepchildren—John Leslie Ellis, Jr., Christopher William. B.A., Hanover Coll., 1966; M.A., U. Houston-Clear Lake, 1978. Psychotherapist, dir. biofeedback treatment Wetcher Clinic, Houston, 1978—; dir. Crisis Mgmt. Service, 1985—; resource coordinator Wetcher Wellness System, Houston, 1984—; speaker Mental Health Assn. Houston and Harris County, 1978—. Mem. Am. Assn. Marriage and Family Therapy (clin.), Am. Psychol. Assn. (assoc.), Am. Group Psychotherapy Assn. (assoc.), Soc. Behavioral Medicine, Biofeedback Soc. Am., Am. Running and Fitness Assn. (Nat. Achievement award 1983). Republican\ Presbyterian. Clubs: Bay Area Running (Clear Lake); Wolfpack Bicycle (Friendswood, Tex.); Bay Area Triathletes (Nassau Bay, Tex.). Avocations: triathlons; bicycle touring; masters running; sewing. Home: 1214 Saxony Ln Nassau Bay TX 77058 Office: Wetcher Clinic 16902 El Camino Real 2C Houston TX 77058

BIRD, FRANCIS MARION, lawyer; b. Comer, Ga., Sept. 4, 1902; s. Henry Madison and Minnie Lee (McConnell) B.; A.B., U. Ga., 1922, LL.B., 1924; LL.M., George Washington U., 1925; LL.D. (hon.), Emory U., 1980, U. St. Andrews, 1982; m. Mary Adair Howell, Jan. 30, 1935; children—Francis Marion, Mary Adair Bird Kennedy, Elizabeth Howell Bird Hewitt, George Arthur. Admitted to Ga. bar, 1924, D.C. bar, 1925; since practiced in Atlanta, with U.S. Senator Hoke Smith, 1925, individual practice, 1930-45, Bird & Howell, 1945-59, Jones, Bird & Howell, 1959-82, now Alston & Bird, 1982—; served as part-time U.S. referee in bankruptcy, 1945-54; spl. asst. to U.S. atty. gen. as hearings officer Nat. Selective Service Act; mem. commn. for preparation plan of govt. City of Atlanta and county area; mem. permanent rules com. Ga. Supreme Ct.; chmn. Ga. Bd. Bar Examiners, 1954-61; mem. Permanent Editorial Bd. Uniform Comml. Code, 1962-77, Fed. Jud. Conf., 5th Circuit, 1962-81, 11th Circuit, 1981—; chmn. Met. Atlanta Commn. on Crime and Juvenile Delinquency, 1969-70. Former Ga. co-chmn. Tech-Ga. Devel. Fund; trustee Young Harris Coll., U. Ga. Found., Atlanta Lawyers Found., Interdenomnl. Theol. Center; trustee, past mem. exec. com. Emory U. Recipient Distinguished Service citation U. Ga. Law Sch., Alumni Achievement award George Washington U., 1965; Pres.'s award Assn. Pvt. Colls. and Univs. Ga., 1979. Fellow Am. Bar Found.; mem. Am. Judicature Soc. (past dir.) Am. Law Inst. (council 1949-82, now emeritus mem., past chmn. com. on membership), Am., Ga. (past pres.), Atlanta (past pres.; Distinguished Service award 1977), bar assns., Assn. Bar City N.Y., Atlanta C. of C. (past pres., Atlanta Civic Service award 1957), U. Ga. Alumni Assn. (past pres., certificate of merit 1952), Sigma Chi, Phi Kappa Phi, Phi Delta Phi. Methodist. Clubs: Peachtree Golf, Piedmont Driving, Capital City, Lawyers of Atlanta (past pres.), Atlanta Athletic (past pres.), Kiwanis (Atlanta); Augusta (Ga.) Nat. Golf. Home: 89 Brighton Rd NE Atlanta GA 30309 Office: 1200 Citizens and So Nat Bank Bldg Atlanta GA 30335

BIRD, FRANK EDWARD, JR., educational institute administrator; b. Netcong, N.J., Dec. 19, 1921; s. Frank Edward and Virginia (Goebel) B.; m. Esther Savidge, Nov. 6, 1948; children—Frank Edward, Susan Bird Arnold, Bille Bird Baird, David, Johnny. B.S., Albright Coll., Reading, Pa., 1950; postgrad. NYU, 1956-57. Supr. safety Lukens Steel, Coatesville, Pa., 1953-68; dir. engring. services Ins. Co. N.Am., Phila., 1968-71; exec. dir. Internat. Safety Acad., Macon, Ga., 1971-73; pres. Internat. Loss Control Inc., Atlanta, 1973—. Author: Damage Control, 1966; co-author: Management Guide to Loss Control, 1974, Loss Control Management, 1976, Practical Loss Control Leadership, 1985. Patentee in field. Chmn. safety Chester County Council Boy Scouts, Phila., 1955-64; mem. instrn. tng. bd. ARC, Phila. regional officer 1965-71; pres. Chester County Safety Council, 1958-71. Served with USN, 1942-46. Recipient Gold award Royal Soc. Prevention of Accidents, Eng., Pub. Service award U.S. Dept. Interior, 1971; named Optimist of Yr., 1967. Fellow Am. Soc. Safety Engs.; mem. Ind. Occupational Prevention Assn. Ont. (hon. life), Can. Soc. Safety Engrs. (hon.), Soc. Systems Safety Soc. Methodist. Home: Centerhill Church Rd Loganville GA 30249 Office: Internat Loss Control Inst Hwy 78 PO Box 345 Loganville GA 30249

BIRD, GAYLE L., interior designer; b. New Orleans, Jan. 26, 1947; s. Francis J. Lajaunie and Marie E. Lajaunie Folse; m. Thomas Bird, Feb. 10, 1976. Student LaSalle Coll., 1970. Owner, pres. Gayle Bird Interiors, Ltd., New Orleans, 1975—; mem. La. State Licencing Bd. for Interior Design, 1985—. Contbr. articles to various mags. Mem. com. Opera Guild, New Orleans, 1984, Overture to the Culture Season, New Orleans, 1985, Soc. Prevention Cruelty to Animals, New Orleans, 1985; mem. adv. com. Kidney Found., New Orleans, 1985; chmn. antique show Delta Ballet, New Orleans, 1985. Named 1 of ten Best Dressed Women in New Orleans, Men of Fashion, 1985; Alfa awards (3) Interior Design, 1985. Mem. Am. Soc. Interior Design (Outstanding Service award 1984), Fashion Group New Orleans (asst. regional dir. 1984—). Clubs: Opera, Ballet (New Orleans). Home: 1702 Valence St New Orleans LA 70130 Office: Gayle Bird Interiors Ltd 1820 St Charles Ave Suite 204 New Orleans LA 70130

BIRD, ROSALINA MONES, nurse; b. Puelay, Villasis, Philippines, Dec. 30, 1952; came to U.S. 1978; d. Emeterio Duatin and Isabel S. (Sansano) Mones; m. Stephen Alistair Bird, May 7, 1982; children—Ian Christopher, Samuel Edward. B.S. in Nursing, U. of East Meml. Med. Ctr., Manila, R.N., Fla. ICU nurse Polymedic Gen. Hosp., Rizal, Philippines, 1974-78; telemetry nurse Mt. Sinai Med. Ctr., Miami Beach, Fla., 1978-79, surg. ICU nurse, 1979—. Mem. United Ch. of Christ. Home: 900 NE 72d Terr Miami FL 33138

BIRD, WENDELL RALEIGH, lawyer; b. Atlanta, July 16, 1954; s. Raleigh Milton and R. Jean (Edwards) B.; m. Celia Ann Reed, Dec. 22, 1978; 1 child, Courtenay Asheton. B.A. summa cum laude, Vanderbilt U., 1975; J.D., Yale U., 1978. Bar: Ga. 1978, Calif. 1981, Fla. 1982, Ala. 1980, U.S. Supreme Ct. 1983, U.S. Ct. Appeals (4th, 5th, 8th, 9th, 11th cirs.). Law clk. to judge U.S. Ct. Appeals (4th cir.), Durham, N.C., 1978-79, U.S. Ct. Appeals (5th cir.), Birmingham, Ala., 1979-80; atty. Parker, Johnson, Cook & Dunlevie, Atlanta, 1982—; adj. prof. Emory U. Law Sch., Atlanta, 1985—; lectr. Washington Non-Profit Tax Conf., 1982, 84, 85. Bd. govs. Council for Nat. Policy, Washington, 1983—; pres. Rutherford Inst. Ga., Atlanta, 1983—; bd. dirs. Transnat. Assn. Christian Schs., Dallas, 1985—; mem. nat. adv. council Nat. Civil Liberties Legal Found., Milw., 1983—. Author: Home Education and Constitutional Liberties, 1984. Bd. editors Yale Law Jour., 1977-78. Recipient Egger prize Yale U., 1978. Mem. ABA, Assn. Trial Lawyers Am., Atlanta Bar Assn., Phi Beta Kappa. Republican. Baptist. Office: Parker Johnson Cook & Dunlevie Suite 700 1275 Peachtree St NE Atlanta GA 30309

BIRDSONG, ROBIN LEA, bottling company marketing executive; b. Atlanta, Apr. 8, 1956; d. Roy Neese and Barbara Ann (Martin) B. B.S., Centenary Coll. Tchr. of gifted and talented, Shreveport, La., 1978-81; mktg. rep. Burroughs Corp., Shreveport, 1981-82, Procter & Gamble, Shreveport, 1982-84, Pepsi Cola Bottling Group, San Antonio, 1984—; rep. Communispond, Dallas, 1984. Mem. Chi Omega. Republican. Methodist. Home: 4000 Horizon Hill #2307 San Antonio TX 78229 Office: Pepsi Cola Bottling Group 6100 NE Loop 410 San Antonio TX 78218

BIRDWELL, JAMES EDWIN, JR., banker; b. Chuckey, Tenn., Apr. 22, 1924; s. James Edwin and Mary Eleanor (Earnest) B.; m. Marilyn Margaretta Gibson, Dec. 20, 1949; children—James Edwin, III, Amy Eleanor, Todd Gibson. A.B., Tusculum Coll., 1949; M.A., Vanderbilt U., 1951. Tchr., coach Doak High Sch., 1948-50; field rep. 3d Nat. Bank, Nashville, 1951-52; trainee Va. Nat. Bank, 1957, v.p., from 1962; chmn., pres. First Am. Bank, Clinton, Tenn., 1973-84; vice chmn. First Am. Nat. Bank, Knoxville, Tenn., 1984—. Commr. bldgs and grounds Va. Beach, Va., 1970-72; dir. Daniel Arthur Rehab. Ctr., Oak Ridge, 1974—; dir. Oak Ridge Hosp., 1976—; v.p. Roane Anderson Econ. Council, 1976—; chmn. Clinton Port Authority, 1978—; mem. exec. com. Melton Hill Regional Indsl. Authority, Clinton, Tenn., 1978—; mem. Anderson County Tax Adv. Bd., 1978—; mem. Indsl. Devel. Bd. Anderson County, 1978—. Served with USNR, 1942-46, 52-57. Decorated Air medal. Mem. Am. Bankers Assn., Tenn. Bankers Assn., Robert Morris Assocs., Bank Adminstrn. Inst., Bank Mktg. Assn. Republican. Methodist. Clubs: Oak Ridge Country, Civitan, LeConte. Office: First Am Nat Bank Knoxville TN

BIRKELAND, BRYAN COLLIER, lawyer; b. Hibbing, Minn., May 29, 1951; s. Lionel Owen and Peggy Jean (Smith) B.; m. D.J. Loras, Jan. 5, 1974; children—Brett Holton, Blair Leigh, Blake Owen. Student, Washington and Jefferson Coll., 1969-70; B.A. with high honors, U. Tex., 1973, J.D. with honors, 1975. Bar: Tex. 1976; ptnr. Jackson, Walker, Winstead, Cantwell & Miller, Dallas, 1982—. Moody Found. grantee, 1971. Mem. ABA, State Bar Tex., Dallas Bar Assn., Rocky Mountain Legal Found., Order of Coif, Phi Beta Kappa, Phi Kappa Phi, Delta Sigma Rho, Tau Kappa Alpha. Presbyterian. Home: 4106 Amherst Dallas TX 75225 Office: 6000 Interfirst Plaza Dallas TX 75202

BIRKENSTEIN, LILLIAN RAY (MRS. GEORGE ULMAN BIRKENSTEIN), ornithologist; b. Phila., Oct. 9, 1900; d. Morris and Stella (Schloss) Rosenzweig; B.A. (coll. scholar), Wellesley Coll., 1922; student U. Pa., 1920-21, Northwestern U., 1936-37, Instituto Allende (Mexico), 1951-55, Academia Hispana-Americana (Mexico), 1960-68; m. George Ulman Birkenstein, Sept. 2, 1922; children—Dorothy (Mrs. Jose Vidargas), Jean (Mrs. Atlee Washington). Pres., Anker-Holth Mfg. Co., Port Huron, Mich., 1944-51; researcher local Spanish and tribal Indian names of Mexican birds, 1952—; vol. librarian, San Miguel Allende, 1954-64, tchr. ornithology Institute Allende, San Miguel Allende, 1973; Mexican rep. one common Spanish name project Smithsonian Tropical Inst. in Panama, 1981; del. 11th Iberoam. Congress of Ornithology, Vera Cruz, Mex., 1983. Bd. dirs. Public Library San Miguel Allende, 1954-67, Hot Breakfasts for Sch. Children, San Miguel, 1957-61. Mem. San Miguel Allende Audubon Soc. (founder 1967, pres. 1967-71, dir. 1971—), Am. Soc. Mfg. Engrs. (hon. life), Am. Ornithologists Union, Cooper Ornithol. Soc., Linnaean Soc., Wilson Ornithol. Soc., Cornell Lab. Ornithology, Mexican Natural History Soc. (dir. 1972—), Mexican Ornitholog. Soc. (dir.), Internat. Com. for Bird Preservation (treas. Mexican sect. 1968—), Women's Aux. AIME (hon.). Clubs: San Miguel Allende Garden (1st v.p. 1971—); Golf Malanquin. Author: Native Names of Mexican Birds, 1981. Contbr. articles to various publs. Home: Tenerias 45 San Miguel Allende Guanajuato Mexico

BIRNE, CINDY FRANK, advertising representative; b. Chgo., Nov. 13, 1956; d. Gordon D. and Paula (Feldman) Frank; m. Robert E. Birne, June 27, 1981. B.A., Ohio State U., 1979. Creative coordinator Point-Communications div. Tracy-Locke Advt., Dallas, 1983; asst. to Tex Schramm, pres. of Dallas Cowboys, 1984, sales and advt. rep. Dallas Cowboys, 1985—. Active Ohio campaign Ronald Reagan for Pres., 1980-81. Club: Press (Dallas).

BIRSTEIN, SEYMOUR JOSEPH, aerospace scis. co. exec.; b. N.Y.C., May 1, 1927; s. Harry D. and Golde (Lenoff) B.; B.A. in Chemistry, N.Y. U., 1947; M.S. in Phys. Chemistry, Mont. State U., 1948; postgrad. Bklyn. Poly. Inst., 1949-50, Cornell U., 1953; div.; 1 dau., Diane. Research chemist Airco, Murray Hill, N.J., 1949-50; br. chief Air Force Cambridge Research Labs., Bedford, Mass., 1951-76; pres. SJB Assos., Inc., Atlanta, 1977—. Fellow Am. Inst. Chemists; mem. Am. Chem. Soc., Am. Meteorol. Soc., Sigma Xi. Contbr. articles to profl. jours. Patentee in field. Home and office: 7354 Cardigan Circle Atlanta GA 30328

BISBEE, DAVID GEORGE, lawyer; b. Council Bluffs, Iowa, June 7, 1947; s. George Kimball and Margaret Ruth (McMurry) B.; m. Rita Ann Bentley, May 21, 1981; children—Michael, Christopher, Tyler. Student Iowa State U., 1965-67; B.A., Augusta Coll., 1973; J.D., U. Ga., 1975. Bar: Ga. 1975, U.S. Dist. Ct. (no. dist.) Ga. 1976, U.S. Ct. Appeals (5th cir.) 1978, (11th cir.) 1981. Assoc. Troutman, Sanders, et al, Atlanta, 1975-81; ptnr. Bisbee, Parker & Rickertsen, Atlanta, 1981—; seminar lectr. Nat. Bus. Inst., Georgetown U. Contbg. editor Norton Bankruptcy Law and Practice. Contbr. articles to legal jours. Served to capt. inf. U.S. Army, 1968-72. Mem. ABA (subcom. on internat. insolvencies of bus. bankruptcy com.), Am. Bankruptcy Inst., Atlanta Bankruptcy Bar Assn. (bd. dirs. 1980—), Order of Coif. Republican. Methodist. Home: 926 Plymouth Rd Atlanta GA 30306 Office: Bisbee Parker & Rickertsen 400 Candler Bldg Atlanta GA 30303

BISCHOFF, FREDERICK CHRISTOPHER, III, accountant; b. Walhalla, S.C., Oct. 1, 1941; s. Frederick Christopher and Kathleen (Kay) B. B.B.A., Ga. State U., 1966; B.S. (hon.), Ohio Christian U., 1968. Market devel. mgr. Grizzard Advt., Atlanta, 1966-71; v.p. Leedy Enterprises Inc., Atlanta, 1971-72; acct. APAC-GA Inc., Atlanta, 1973—. Active Fulton County Young Republicans, Atlanta, 1964-68. Methodist. Club: Ponte Vedra (Fla.). Avocations: Photography; travel. Home: 3495 Old Plantation Rd NW Atlanta GA 30327 Office: APAC-GA Inc 3111 Port Cobb Dr Smyrna GA 30080

BISHARA, MAKRAM, educational administrator, real estate broker; b. Luxor, Egypt, May 20, 1935; came to U.S., 1969, naturalized, 1967; s. Aziz and Maria Paulus (Abd-El-Mesia) B.; m. Nabila Abd Alla Fam, Apr. 25, 1965; children—Tarek, Steve. B.S., Alexandria U., Egypt, 1958, M.S., 1962; Ph.D., Cairo U., Egypt, 1966; Ed.S., Peabody Coll., 1972; Ed.S., U. S.C., 1982, Ed.D., 1984. Sr. researcher Ministry of Agr., Cairo, 1962-69; sci. and math tchr. Richland Dist. I, Columbia, S.C., 1969-70; sci. tchr. Mullins Dist II, S.C., 1970-75, prin., drug edn. coordinator, 1975—, PET observer, 1983—; broker-in-charge Bishara Realty, Mullins, 1979—. Author: Rice Field Insects and Their Control, 1966; Recruitment, Selection and Interviewing of Teachers in South Carolina, 1982; Job Perception of Public School Superintendent in South Carolina, 1984. Editor: Physician Desk Reference on Drug Abuse Control, 1972. Contbr. articles to profl. publs. Coordinator, Marion County Drug Edn. Program, 1971-72. Recipient Anti-Pollution award EPA, 1973. Mem. Nat. Assn. Secondary Sch. Prins., S.C. Assn. Secondary Sch. Prins., Nat. Bd. Realtors, Marion County Bd. Realtors (program chmn. 1982-83). Democrat. Baptist. Lodge: Lions. Avocations: reading; electronics; swimming. Home: 1321 Horseshoe Rd Mullins SC 29574 Office: Prin Mullins High Sch Mullins SC 29574

BISHKO, JAY RICHARD, anesthesiologist; b. Cleve., July 6, 1949; s. Maurice Jerome and Lillian Jean (Green) B.; m. Adrienne Carol Litt, Aug. 7, 1971; children—Jack Aron, Emily Rose. B.S. cum laude, U. Mich., 1971; M.D., Case Western Res. U., 1975. Intern, U. Mich., Ann Arbor, 1975-76; resident in anesthesiology, U. Fla., Gainesville, 1976-78, fellow in anesthesiology, 1978-79; fellow in cardiovascular anesthesia, U. Ala., Birmingham, 1979; ptnr. Lanier Park Anesthesia Group, Gainesville, Ga., 1979—. Vol. Am. Cancer Soc., Gainesville Ballet Co., Elachee, Quinlan Art Assn.; fundraiser Brenau Coll., Gainesville. Recipient award Am. Cancer Soc. Mem. AMA, Med. Assn. Ga., Am. Soc. Anesthesiologists, Ga. Soc. Anesthesiologists, Hall County Med. Soc., Internat. Anesthesia Research Soc. Club: Kiwanis. Home: 2590 Cove Rd Gainesville GA 30506 Office: 644 Lanier Med Pkwy Gainesville GA 30501

BISHOP, ALFRED CHILTON, JR., lawyer; b. Alexandria, Va., Oct. 3, 1942; s. Alfred Chilton and Margaret (Marshall) B.; divorced; 1 son, Alfred Chilton III; m. 2d Catherine Ann Keppel, May 17, 1980. B.A. with distinction, U. Va., 1965, LL.B., 1969; LL.M. in Taxation, Georgetown U., 1974. Bar: N.Y. 1970, U.S. Ct. Appeals (2d cir.), 1970, U.S. Tax Ct. 1971, U.S. Ct. Claims 1971, D.C. 1977. Assoc. Shearman and Sterling, N.Y.C., 1969-70; assoc. trial atty., Office of Chief Counsel IRS, Washington, 1970-74, sr. trial atty., 1974-80, sr. technician reviewer, 1980-81, br. chief, 1981—. Recipient Am. Jurisprudence award 1968, 1968. Mem. ABA (tax sec.), D.C. Bar Assn., Sr. Exec. Service Candidate Network (v.p. 1980-81, pres. 1981-82, dir. 1983), Sr. Exec. Assn., Phi Delta Phi. Episcopalian. Home: 7523 Thistledown Trail Fairfax Station VA 22039

BISHOP, BRUCE BENNINGTON, oil company executive; b. Columbus, Ohio, Nov. 26, 1938; s. Myron Clayton and Lillian Mae (McNabb) B.; B.S. in Bus. Adminstrn., Calif. Western U., 1980, M.Human Resource Devel., 1980; m. Donna Jean Snedeker, May 15, 1982; children—Bradley Alan, Jeffrey Scott, Renee Christine. With Ohio Bell Telephone Co., 1956-80, mgr. orgn. devel. and managerial effectiveness, until 1980; mgr. orgn. devel. Cities Service Co., Tulsa, 1980-82, dir. employee relations, 1982—; cons. in field. Served with USMCR, 1957. Mem. Am. Soc. Tng. and Devel., Nat. Orgn. Devel. Network. Republican. Methodist. Lodges: Masons, Shriners. Home: 4106 E 103d St Tulsa OK 74137 Office: PO Box 300 Tulsa OK 74102

BISHOP, CHARLES EDWIN, economist, university president; b. Campobello, S.C., June 8, 1921; s. Fred and Hattie Bess (Wall) B.; B.S., Berea Coll., 1946; M.S., U. Ky., 1948; Ph.D. (Farm Found. fellow 1948-49), U. Chgo., 1952; m. Dorothy Anderkin, Feb. 13, 1943; children—Susan Ann, Mary Catherine, Charles Edwin. Research asst. agrl. econs. U. Ky., 1947-48; research assoc. in econs. U. Chgo., 1949-50; mem. faculty N.C. State U., 1950-70, prof. agrl. econs., 1956-70, head dept. agrl. econs., 1957-65, head dept. econs., 1965-66. William N. Reynolds disting. prof., 1957-70; v.p. U. N.C., Chapel Hill, 1966-70, exec. dir. Agrl. Policy Inst., 1960-66; chancellor U. Md., College Park, 1970-74; pres. U. Ark., Fayetteville, 1974-80. U. Houston System, 1980—; vis. prof. U. Va., 1961-63; cons. U. Agraria, Lima, Peru, 1961-65; mem. Nat. Com. Agrl. Policy, Nat. Planning Assn., 1958-70; agrl. bd. Nat. Acad. Scis., 1963-68; mem. sci. adv. com. to sec. agr., 1962-68; mem. Nat. Manpower Adv. Com., 1962-68, exec. dir. Nat. Adv. Com. on Rural Poverty, 1966-67; mem. food adv. com. Pres. Nixon's Cost of Living Council, 1972; mem. Pres.'s adv. com. White House Conf. on Balanced Nat. Growth and Econ. Devel., 1978; mem. com. on vet. med. edn. So. Regional Edn. Bd., 1974; trustee Farm Found., 1968-78; bd. dirs. Winthrop Rockefeller Found., 1975-78; co-chmn. bd. dirs. Nat. Rural Ctr., 1975-79; mem. Pres.'s Commn. on Agenda for Eighties, 1980; bd. dirs. Resources for Future, 1980—, Houston Industries, 1983—. Mem. Am. Agr. Econ. Assn. (pres. 1967-68), Am. Econ. Assn., Internat. Assn. Agrl. Econs., Alpha Zeta, Phi Kappa Phi, Gamma Sigma Delta. Co-author. Introduction to Agricultural Economic Analysis, 1958. Home: 1505 South Blvd Houston TX 77027 Office: Office of Pres U Houston Houston TX 77004

BISHOP, EUGENE E., food service company executive. With Morrison Inc., Mobile, Ala., 1947—, sr. v.p., 1968, then exec. v.p., pres., chief operating officer, 1979-81, pres., chief exec. officer, 1981—, also dir. Office: Morrison Inc PO Box 160266 Mobile AL 36625*

BISHOP, GENE HERBERT, banker; b. Forest, Miss., May 3, 1930; s. Herbert Eugene and Lavonne (Little) B.; B.B.A., U. Miss., Oxford, 1952. With First Nat. Bank, Dallas, 1954-69, sr. v.p., chmn. sr. loan com., 1963-68, exec. v.p., 1968-69; past pres., dir. SBIC subs. First Dallas Capital Corp.; pres. Lomas & Nettleton Fin. Corp., Dallas, 1969-75, Lomas & Nettleton Mortgage Investors, Dallas, 1969-75; chmn. bd., chief exec. officer Mercantile Nat. Bank, Dallas, 1975-79, MCorp, Dallas, 1975—; dir. Lomas & Nettleton Fin. Corp., Lomas & Nettleton Mortgage Investors, Anderson Industries, Inc., S.W. Airlines Co., Republic Fin. Services, Inc., Gulf Broadcast Co. Bd. govs. Dallas Symphony Assn.; bd. dirs. Dallas Citizens Council, Dallas Council World Affairs; Southwestern Med. Found., State Fair Tex.; exec. bd. Maguire Oil and Gas Inst.; mem. devel. com. Children's Med. Center; trustee So. Meth. U. Served to 1st lt. USAF, 1952-54. Mem. Assn. Res. City Bankers, Tex. Bankers Assn. Methodist. Clubs: Dallas Petroleum, Terpsichorean, Idlewild, Brook Hollow Golf. Office: PO Box 225415 Dallas TX 75265

BISHOP, GEORGE DAVID, psychology educator; b. South Haven, Mich., May 30, 1949; s. Rex. R. and Lillian Carlene (Bidwell) B.; m. Jane Andrew, June 9, 1973; one son, one dau. B.A., Hope Coll., 1971; M.S., Yale U., 1973, Ph.D., 1976. Research psychologist Walter Reed Army Inst. of Research, Washington, 1975-79; asst. prof. psychology Am. U. Cairo, 1979-81, U. Tex-San Antonio, 1981—. Contbr. articles to profl. jours., chpt. to book. Served to capt. U.S. Army, 1975-79. Grantee U. Tex., 1982, Am. U. in Cairo, 1980. Mem. Am. Psychol. Assn., Soc. Psychol. Study Social Issues, Southwestern Psychol. Assn., Soc. Personality and Social Psychology. Episcopalian. Office: U Tex-San Antonio Div Behavioral and Cultural Scis San Antonio TX 78285

BISHOP, KATHLEEN ANN, customer service, education and communication consultant, professional speaker; b. Pueblo, Colo., Dec. 10, 1947; d. Jerome H. and Iona L. (Bird) B.; m. Larry Douglas Hawkins, Dec. 31, 1972. A.A., Brookdale Community Coll., N.J., 1971; B.A. in English, Stockton State Coll., 1974; M.A., Century U., Calif., 1982. Accredited records technician. Supr. med. records dept. Fla. Med. Ctr., Ft. Lauderdale, 1980; med. records adminstr. Henderson Mental Health Ctr., Ft. Lauderdale, 1980-81; instr. Sheridan Vo-Tech Ctr., Hollywood, Fla., 1981-84; edn. cons. Shared Med. Systems, Hollywood, 1984-85; tng. cons. Bishop Neill & Assocs., Plantation, Fla., 1984—. Author: Getting Out of Your Own Way: A Guide to Successful Living for the Unassertive, 1984; also articles. Mem. Nat. Speakers Assn., Fla. Speakers Assn. (sec. 1984-85, pres. 1985-86), Women in Communications, Am. Soc. for Tng. and Devel. Club: Toastmasters (treas. 1984-85). Avocations: aerobics; reading; movies. Home: 1960 SW 81st Way Davie FL 33324 Office: 712 SW 42d Ave Plantation FL 33317

BISHOP, PATRICIA JOY, mechanical engineering educator; b. Anchorage, July 12, 1949; d. Robert L. and Claudia J. (Baker) Bishop. B.S.E., U. Central Fla., 1971; M.S. in M.E., Purdue U., 1972, Ph.D., 1976. Registered profl. engr., Fla. Research asst., fellow Purdue U., West Lafayette, Ind., 1971-76; asst. prof. Clemson (S.C.) U., 1976-78; asst. prof. U. Central Fla., Orlando, 1978-83, assoc. prof. mech. engring., 1983—. Mem. Gov.'s Task Force Indsl. Energy Conservation, 1981-82; mem. adv. com. Orlando Pub. Works Commn.; coordinator, lectr. many energy edn. workshops for pub. and pvt. schs.; co-dir. SEEK Conf. Recipient Young Engring. of Yr. award Soc. Central Fla., 1980. NSF undergrad. research fellow, 1970; ASHRAE fellow, 1971; David Ross fellow, 1972. Mem. ASME (chmn. profl. devel., chmn. energy systems nat. com., sect. chmn.), Nat. Soc. Profl. Engrs. (Young Engr. of Yr. nat. award 1984), Fla. Engring. Soc. (Young Engr. of Yr. award 1984), Am. Soc. Engring. Edn., Sigma Xi, Pi Tau Sigma, Tau Beta Pi. Office: Dept Mech Engring Central U Fla Orlando FL 32816

BISHOP, PETER CRAIG, sociology educator; b. Orlando, Fla., Dec. 20, 1944; s. George Washington and Kathleen Virginia (Keane) B.; m. Luetta Rose Bishop, Nov. 7, 1982; children—D'Ann, Kathleen. B.A., St. Louis U., 1968; M.A. in Sociology, Mich. State U., 1972, Ph.D., 1974. Asst. prof. Ga. So. Coll., Statesboro, 1973-76; assoc. prof. U. Houston-Clear Lake, 1976—, chmn. studies of the future, 1982—; pres. Tex. Council of Faculty Governance Orgns., Austin, 1983-85; bd. dirs. Tex. Econ. and Demographic Assn., 1985—. Mem. strategic planning com. Houston C. of C., 1984—. Recipient U. Houston Clear Lake City Piper award, 1980. Mem. Am. Sociol. Assn., AAUP. Avocation: sailing. Home: 3817 Youpon LaPorte TX 77571 Office: U Houston Clear Lake 2700 Bay Area Blvd Houston TX 77058

BISHOP, REITA JANE, educator, coach; b. Hartselle, Ala., Dec. 21, 1956; d. James Edward and Ila Jo (Wallace) B. B.S., Samford U.; M.A., U. Ala.-Birmingham. Clk. typist U.S. Govt., Ft. Meade, Md., 1976-78, Birmingham, 1979; supr. dining room Cpt D's, Birmingham, 1978-79; with Southeastern Bible Coll., Birmingham, 1979-83, coach, asst. dean students, 1981-83, intramural dir., 1979-83; instr. phys. edn., coach Reinhardt Coll., Waleska, Ga., 1983—, dir. student activities, 1983—. Baptist. Office: Southeastern Bible Coll 2901 Pawnee Ave Birmingham AL 35256

BISHOP, ROBERT KALMAN, pharmacist, consultant; b. Miami, Jan. 31, 1942; s. William Taylor and Helen (Robey) B.; m. Susan Hicks, Apr. 11, 1964 (div. 1977); children—Lesa Ann, Bradley Scott. B.S. in Chemistry, U. Ky., 1965, B.S. in Pharmacy, 1968, Ph.D., 1969. Pharmacist Northland Pharmacy, Kansas City, 1969-74; asst. dir., pharmacist Children's Mercy Hosp., Kansas City, 1974-79; store mgr., pharmacist Revco DS Inc., Kansas City, 1979-83; pharmacist-in-charge Eckerd's Pharmacy, Dallas, 1983—; cons. pharmacist Dallas County Nursing Home, Dallas, 1984—. Editor newsletter Children's Mercy Hosp. News, 1979. Patentee in field. Served to 1st lt. U.S. Army, 1960-61. Grantee Hoffman LeRoche, Inc., 1983, Kappa Psi Aux., 1967; Rho Chi scholar, 1968. Mem. Am. Pharm. Assn., Tex. Pharm. Assn., Dallas County Pharm. Assn., Kappa Psi Alumni Assn. (v.p. 1981-82, Man of Yr. 1983), Mo. Pharm. Assn. (state conv. chairperson 1983). Republican. Lutheran. Avocations: tennis, karate, sailing. Home: 8110 Skillman St Apt 3071 Dallas TX 75231 Office: Eckerds Inc 9780 Walnut St Dallas TX 75243

BISHOP, ROBERT WHITSITT, lawyer; b. Atlanta, Jan. 7, 1949; s. James Clarence and Dorothy Davis (Whitsitt) B.; m. Cynthia Graham, Aug. 23, 1970; children—Jessica Levesque, Joshua Davis, Amanda Joyce. Student, Duke U., 1966-68; B.A. with high distinction, U. Ky.-Lexington, 1973; postgrad. George Washington U., 1973-74; J.D., U. Ky., 1976. Bar: Ohio 1976, Ky. 1981. Mem. Squire, Sanders & Dempsey, Cleve., 1976-80, Barnet & Alagia, Louisville, 1980-84; ptnr. Greenebaum, Young, Treitz & Maggiolo, Louisville, 1984—; founder, dir., officer Indoor Soccer of Louisville Inc., (The Louisville Thunder), 1984—, Central Indoor Soccer League, 1984. Author: The Interdict. Bd. dirs., mem. personnel and fin. coms. Louisville Central Community Ctrs. Inc., 1985. Mem. ABA, Ky. Bar Assn., Ohio Bar Assn., Louisville Bar Assn., Cleve. Bar Assn., Order of the Coif, Phi Beta Kappa, Sigma Alpha Epsilon. Avocations: mountain and rock climbing, soccer, creative writing. Home: 13108 Settlers Point Trail Prospect KY 40059 Office: Grenebaum Young Treitz & Maggiolo 27th Floor First National Tower Louisville KY 40202

BISHOP, SID GLENWOOD, union ofcl.; b. Gladehill, Va., Nov. 11, 1923; s. Clarence Glenwood and Lillian Helen (Onks) B.; grad. U.S. Naval Trade Sch., 1942; certificate in coll. labor relations Concord Coll., Athens, W.Va., 1961; m. Margaret Lucille Linkous, June 6, 1947. Telegraph operator Virginian R.R., 1946-47, C & O R.R., 1947-62; local chmn. Order R.R. Telegraphers, 1960-62, gen. chmn. C & O-Virginian R.R.'s, 1962-68; 2d v.p. Transp-Communication Employees Union, St. Louis, 1968-69; v.p. communication-transp. div. Brotherhood Ry. and Airline Clks., Rockville, Md., 1969-73, asst. internat. v.p., 1973—; mem. subcom. Labor Research Adv. Council, Dept. Labor, 1975, mem. com. on productivity, tech., growth Bur. Labor Statistics, 1975-77. Served with USN, 1941-46. Mem. AFL-CIO, Canadian Labor Congress, Hunting Hills Home Owners Assn. Democrat. Clubs: Chantilly Nat. Golf and Country, VFW. Lodges: Elks, Masons, Royal Arch Masons, K.T., Shriners. Home: 5211 Chukar Dr SW Roanoke VA 24014 Office: 3140 Chaparral Dr SW Suite C-100 Roanoke VA 24018

BISHOP, THOMAS RAY, mech. engr.; b. Hutchinson, Kans., Oct. 26, 1925; s. Orren E. and Myrtle (Dale) Bish; student California (Pa.) State Tchrs. Coll., 1947-48; B.S., U. Houston, 1953; postgrad. U. Wash., 1960-61; grad. Alexander Hamilton Bus. Inst., 1972; m. Mary Lou Nesmith, Sept. 1, 1951 children—Thomas Ray II, Frances Joann. Research engr. Boeing Co., Seattle, 1953-64, research engr. Apollo program, 1964-69; asst. chief engr. Product div. Bowen Tools, Inc., Houston, 1969-75, chief engr., 1975-77, chief engr. research and devel., 1977—; asso. ABC Mech. Engr. Cons. Precinct committeeman King County (Wash.) Democratic Com., 1960. Served with USMCR, 1944-46. Decorated Purple Heart; named Engr. of Year, Boeing Aerospace Co., 1966; recipient Excellence in Engring. citation A.I.S.I., 1975. Registered profl. engr., Ala., La., Tex. Mem. Tex. Soc. Profl. Engrs. Unitarian. Mason. Contbr. articles to profl. jours.; patentee oil field equipment field. Home: 2202 Viking Dr Houston TX 77018 Office: 2429 Crockett St Houston TX 77007

BISSETT, WILLIAM F., metals company executive. Pres. Huntington Alloys, Inc., W.Va. Office: Huntington Alloys Inc Huntington WV 25720

BISSETTE, SAMUEL DELK, artist; b. Wilson, N.C., Aug. 10, 1921; s. Zachariah Coye and Annie Wright (Rice) B.; student public schs., various coll. courses; m. Ruby Graham Raynor, Sept. 8, 1943; children—Judy Sabra, David Coye. With Peoples Fed. Savs. and Loan Assn., Wilmington, N.C., 1939—, pres., chief exec. officer, 1959-77, chmn. bd., 1973—, dir., 1954—; visual artist, 1972—; one-man exhbns. include: FDIC Gallery, Washington, 1978, St. John's Mus. Art, Wilmington, N.C., 1974, 81, 84, Raleigh Civic Center, 1977, Kinston (N.C.) Art Center, 1974, Wilkes Art Mus., North Wilkesboro, N.C., 1980; group show: 82d Ann. U.S. Open Watercolor Exhbn., N.Y.C., 1982, N.C. Mus. Art, 1978; commd. by Wachovia Bank to execute 40 paintings Portrait of North Carolina, 1976; originated mosaic murals for Belk-Beery Co., Wilmington, 1979; originated exhbn. N.C. Circa 1900, 1984-87; traveling tour N.C. Mus., 1984-87; trustee N.C. Mus. Art, Raleigh, 1980-85; chmn. N.C. Artists Exhbn., 1979. Served with USAAF, 1941-45. Mem. Am. Watercolor Soc. (assoc.), N.C. Watercolor Soc. (v.p. 1980), N.C. Art Soc. (dir. 1974-82), St. John's Mus. Art (pres. 1973-74). Republican. Baptist. Clubs: Cape Fear (pres. 1978), Cape Fear Country, Carolina Yacht (Wilmington). Address: 1939 S Live Oak Pkwy Wilmington NC 28403

BISTLINE, FREDERICK WALTER, JR., lawyer; b. Lakeland, Fla., Sept. 30, 1950; s. Frederick W. and Carolyn Mary (Stansell) B.; m. Rabun Huff, Mar. 18, 1972. B.A., Emory U., 1972; J.D., Boston U., 1975. Bar: N.Y. 1976, Tex. 1979. Assoc. firm White & Case, N.Y.C., 1975-79; assoc. firm Johnson & Swanson, Dallas, 1979-81, ptnr., 1981—; guest lectr. Internat. Fin. Seminar, U. Tex. Sch. Law, 1980; lectr. in field; condr. seminars in field. Chmn. bd. dirs. Oak Tree Village Homeowners Assn., 1982-83; pres. Boston U. Law Alumni Class of 1975. Mem. ABA (sect. internat. law), Am. Soc. Internat. Law, Assn. Internationale des Jeunes Avocats, Internat. Law Assn. Contbr. articles to profl. jours. Address: 4800 Interfirst Two Dallas TX 75270

BISWAS, MRINMAY, engineering educator, consultant, researcher; b. Calcutta, India, Sept. 6, 1939; came to U.S., 1963, naturalized, 1973; s. Manindra K. and Menoka (Sarkar) B.; m. Susana Banawa Martinez, Dec. 27, 1966; children—Sorojini Judith, Meghdut Robert, Monoroma Abigail. B.Tech., Indian Inst. Tech., 1961; M.C.E., U. Va., 1965, Ph.D., 1970. Registered profl. engr., N.Y., Tex., N.C. Project engr. URS/Madigan Praeger, N.Y.C., 1968-74; lead engr. Stone & Webster Engring. Corp., N.Y.C., 1974-77; prin. engr. Ebasco Services, Inc., N.Y.C., 1977-79; assoc. prof. civil engring. Tex. A&M U., College Station, 1979-82; assoc. research engr. Tex. Transp. Inst., College Station, 1979-82; assoc. prof. civil engring. Duke U., Durham, N.C., 1983—, also dir. Transp. and Infrastructure Research Center, dir. undergrad. studies; researcher, cons. Grantee Tex. Hwy. Dept., Fed. Hwy. Adminstrn., 1981, USAF, 1983. Mem. ASCE, Am. Concrete Inst., ASTM, Structural Stability Research Council, Sigma Xi (transp. research bd., bridge constrn. com.). Contbg. author profl. jours. Office: Civil Engineering Dept Duke U Durham NC 27706

BITNER, GARY E., publicist; b. Lake Forest, Ill., June 4, 1953; s. John Ensign and Beverly Ann (Johnson) B. B.S. in Journalism, U. Fla. Account exec. Hank Myer Assocs., Miami, Fla., 1975-77; staff writer Ft. Lauderdale (Fla.) News, 1977-78; supr. pub. relations Marriott Corp., Washington, 1978-80; pres. G. Bitner Pub. Relations, Ft. Lauderdale, 1980—. Mem. pub. relations adv. council U. Fla., Gainesville, 1983—; bd. dirs. United Way of Broward County, Twig House Inc. Recipient Disting. Service award Kids in Distress, Inc., 1983. Mem. Second Century Broward, Leadership Broward, Execs. Assn. Ft. Lauderdale, Downtown Council. Home: 1312 SW 19th St Fort Lauderdale FL 33315 Office: Gary Bitner Pub Relations Inc 1330-B SE 4th Ave Fort Lauderdale FL 33316

BITZER, BETTY RICHMOND, nurse; b. Hinton, W.Va., Apr. 25, 1935; d. Clarence Mathew and Katheryn Richmond (Via) R.; m. Emory West Bitzer, Jr., July 14, 1956; children—Mary Bitzer Hutsenpillar, John West; m. Bob Hutsenpillar, May 23, 1982; children by previous marriage—David McNeil, Shonet Marie. R.N., U. Va., 1956. Emergency room nurse St. Joseph's Hosp., Tampa, Fla., 1956-58, recovery nurse, 1958-60; pvt. duty nurse, Tampa, 1960-72, Orlando, Fla., 1972-73; nurse oncology Univ. Community Hosp., Tampa, 1973-79; nurse, asst. supr. med.-surgery Summers County Hosp., Hinton, 1979—. Author: Medical Technology Handbook, 1958-60. Fla. state head med. tech Dr.'s Aux. Assn., Ocala, Fla., 1958-59. Mem. Am. Nurses Assn., Fla. Nurses Assn. Episcopalian. Home: 101 1/2 Main St Hinton WV 25951 Office: Summers County Hosp PO Box 940 Terrace St Hinton WV 25951

BIVINS, BETTY TEEL, cattle company executive; investor; b. Amarillo, Tex., Oct. 2, 1919; d. Bernard Peyton and Louise (Green) Teel; student Amarillo Coll., 1937-38, U. Tex., 1938-39; B.B.A., U. Okla., 1940; m. Lee T. Bivins, May 5, 1945; children—Lee Bivins II, Miles Teel, Thomas Peyton, Mark Ernest. With Hagy, Harrington & Marsh, 1941-45; pres. Exell Cattle Co., Amarillo, 1972—, Pioneer Realty Co., Amarillo, 1972—; dir. First Nat. Bank, Amarillo, First Amarillo Bancorp, Inc. Pres., Jr. League; v.p. Amarillo Area Found.; mem. Symphony Bd., Art Center Bd., Discovery Center Bd., Lone Star Ballet Group, Tex. Art Alliance Bd., Tex. Assn. Museums Found.; mem. exec. com. Panhandle Plains Mus.; bd. dirs. St. Andrew's Episcopal Ch. Day Sch.; jr. warden Episcopal Ch., mem. standing com. Diocese N.W. Tex.; active various community drives. Named Woman of Yr., Beta Sigma Phi, 1966. Office: PO Box 708 Amarillo TX 79105

BLACK, CREED CARTER, newspaper publisher; b. Harlan, Ky., July 15, 1925; s. Creed Carter and Mary (Cole) B.; m. Mary C. Davis, Dec. 28, 1947 (div. 1976); children—Creed Carter, Steven D., Douglas S.; m. Elsa Goss, Dec. 9, 1977. B.S. with highest distinction and honors in Polit. Sci., Northwestern U., 1949; M.A., U. Chgo., 1952. Reporter Paducah (Ky.) Sun-Democrat, 1942-43, 46; editor Daily Northwestern, 1947; copy editor Chgo. Sun-Times, 1949, Chgo. Herald-Am., 1950; editorial writer Nashville Tennessean, 1950-57, exec. editor, 1957-59; v.p., exec. editor Savannah (Ga.) Morning News and Savannah Evening Press, 1959-60, Wilmington (Del.) Morning News and Evening Jour., 1960-64; mng. editor Chgo. Daily News, 1964-68, exec. editor, 1968-69; asst. sec. for legislation HEW, 1969-70; editor Phila. Inquirer, 1970-77; chmn. bd., pub. Lexington (Ky.) Herald & Leader, 1977—. Served with 100th Inf. Div. AUS, World War II; ETO. Decorated Bronze Star; recipient Northwestern U. Alumni medal, 1973. Mem. Am. Newspaper Pubs. Assn., So. Newspaper Pubs. Assn. (treas. 1986), Am. Soc. Newspaper Editors (dir.; pres. 1983), Nat. Conf. Editorial Writers (pres. 1962), Sigma Delta Chi, Kappa Tau Alpha, Lambda Chi Alpha. Methodist. Clubs: Lexington Country, Lafayette, Greenbrier Golf (Lexington). Home: 1932 Blairmore Rd Lexington KY 40502 Office: Lexington Herald & Leader Main and Midland Sts Lexington KY 40507

BLACK, DANIEL HUGH, educator; b. Arab, Ala., July 4, 1947; s. Lehmon Ray and Lillian Geneve (Divine) B.; B.S., U. Ala., Tuscaloosa, 1970; M.Ed., Ala. A&M U., 1976; Ph.D., Vanderbilt U., 1981. Social studies tchr., dept. chmn. Grissom High Sch., Huntsville, Ala., 1970—. Mem. NEA, Ala. Edn. Assn., Huntsville Edn. Assn., Nat. Council Social Studies, Ala. Hist. Assn., Phi Delta Kappa. Home: 1229 Willowbrook Dr Huntsville AL 35802 Office: Virgil I Grissom High School Bailey Cove Huntsville AL 35802

BLACK, DANNY EARL, dentist; b. Enid, Okla., Feb. 27, 1944; s. Earnest Earl and DeVerle Nora (Holland) B.; m. Cindy Lynn Smith, July 29, 1966; children—Michelle, Matthew, Braden. A.S., Amarillo Jr. Coll., 1964; B.S., West Tex. State U., 1966; postgrad. Sch. Dental Medicine, U. Pa., 1970. Rotating dental internship VA, Clarksburg, W.Va., 1970-71; staff dentist, St. Cloud, Minn., 1971-77; staff dentist VA Med. Ctr., Amarillo, Tex., 1977-81, acting chief, 1981, staff dentist, 1981—. Dir. Citywide Christian Movie Promotion, St. Cloud, 1972. U. Pa. Scholar 1966-70. Mem. ADA, Beta Beta Beta, Alpha Chi. Avocations: trap shooting; target shooting. Home: 4013 Pinehurst Dr Amarillo TX 79109 Office: VA Med Ctr 6010 Amarillo Blvd W Amarillo TX 79106

BLACK, DORIS JEAN, dentist; b. Washington, July 31, 1950; d. James Edward and Margaret Ella (Burton) B.; m. Stephen Curtis Shackelford, Aug. 21, 1971 (div. 1976); m. David Francis Collins, Apr. 7, 1977; 1 child, Wendy Lee. B.A. in Math., Longwood Coll., 1972; D.D.S., U. N.C., 1981. Intern, Indian Health Service, Tahlequah, Okla., 1980; chmn. dental dept. Coastal Carolina Community Coll., Jacksonville, N.C., 1981—; dental assoc. Anderson & Slack, P.A., Swansboro, N.C., 1981—. Recipient Lynchnos award Longwood Coll., Farmville, Va., 1970, Internat. Coll. Dentists Outstanding Achievement award, 1981; N.C. Dental Found. fellow, U. N.C. Sch. Dentistry, 1980. Mem. ADA, Coastal Carolina Dental Soc., Onslow County Dental Soc. (pres. 1983-84), N.C. Dental Soc., Kappa Delta Pi, Pi Mu Epsilon, Omicron Kappa Upsilon. Republican. Baptist. Avocations: fishing; sewing; boating. Home: 1 Creek Side Wood Hubert NC 28539 Office: Coastal Carolina Community Coll 444 Western Blvd Jacksonville NC 28540

BLACK, JOHN ROY, JR., independent oil operator, developer, rancher; b. Corsicana, Tex., May 17, 1924; s. John Roy and Thelma Katherine (Nored) B.; m. Jayne Kingston, Oct. 17, 1948 (div. Mar. 1977, remarried 1983); children—John Roy III, Robert Carlton. Student Tex. U., 1942, 44-46. Active in oil exploration; owner, operator Mercury Oil Co., Dallas, 1952—. Served with USAAF, 1942-44. Mem. Ind. Producers Assn. Am., Tex. Ind. Producers and Royalty Orgn., Mid-Continent Oil and Gas Assn., Am. Petroleum Inst., Phi Gamma Delta. Presbyterian. Club: Dallas. Lodge: Elks. Office: 1712 Commerce St Suite 800 Dallas TX 75201

BLACK, JUDITH STANFIELD, personnel firm executive; b. Dayton, Ohio, Jan. 21, 1948; d. David O. and Helen V. (Lewis) Stanfield; m. Alan P. Quinn, Mar. 6, 1967 (div. Mar. 1973); children—John Theodor, Kevin Lee; m. Fred A. Black, Sept. 30, 1978. B.S. in Bus., Ind. U. Southeast, 1975. C.PA., Ind., Va. With Deloitte, Haskins & Sells, Greensboro, N.C., Boston and Manchester, N.H., 1975-78, Daniel, Skinnell & Co., C.P.A.s, Lynchburg, Va., 1979-81; controller Indsl. Products Co., Lynchburg, 1982; auditor Carolina Power & Light Co., Raleigh, N.C., 1982; controller Personnel Pool of Raleigh-Durham, Inc., Research Triangle Park, N.C., 1983—. Mem. Am. Inst. C.P.A.s, Nat. Assn. Accts. Quaker. Office: Personnel Pool of Raleigh-Durham Inc PO Box 13158 Research Triangle Park NC 27709

BLACK, KRIS SUSAN LYNN, marketing company executive; b. Ladysmith, Wis., Sept. 19, 1950; d. Bruce Roger and Christine Mae (Sweet) Black. A.A. with honors, Bakersfield Coll.; postgrad., Phoenix Coll. Asst. mgr. jewelry dept. K Mart, Rapid City, S.D., 1965-68; beauty titlist, actress, model, tchr. Patricia Stevens, Phoenix, 1968-72; dir. nat. promotions Buck Owens Internat., Bakersfield, Calif., 1972-76; dir. internat. mktg. K.B. Properties, Dallas, 1976-78; v.p. Wynn Investments, Dallas, 1978—; pres. Sunflower Mktg., Dallas, 1982—; cons. CBI Labs., Aloe Labs. of Tex., 1979—, Richard Simmons, 1983, March of Dimes, 1976; dir. mktg. Colibri Skin Care, Dallas, 1984—. Narrator, actress, writer, dir. various videos. Recipient Cert. Achievement award U.S. Army, 1970, Dept. Fish and Game, 1974. Roman Catholic. Lodges: Order Long Local Pine, Ky. Cols. (hon.) Avocations: horseback riding; water sports; singing. Office: Sunflower Mktg 13140 Coit 301 Dallas TX 75240

BLACK, NORMAN WILLIAM, judge; b. Houston, Dec. 6, 1931; s. Dave and Minnie (Nathan) B.; m. Berne Rose Efron, Feb. 21, 1959; children—Elizabeth Ann, Diane Rebecca. B.B.A., U. Tex., Austin, 1953, J.D. (Frank Bobbitt scholar 1954), 1955. Bar: Tex. 1955. Law clk. to Houston judge, 1956, asst. U.S. atty., Houston, 1956-58, pvt. practice, 1958-76, U.S. magistrate, 1976-79; U.S. dist. judge So. Dist. Tex., Houston, 1979—; adj. prof. South Tex. Coll. Law. Served with AUS, 1955-56. Mem. Fed. Bar Assn., State Bar Tex., Houston Bar Assn., Houston Philos. Soc. Office: 515 Rusk Ave Suite 10501 Houston TX 77002

BLACK, RIKKI ROAN, university facilities administrator; b. Monroe, La., Jan. 4, 1956; s. Lonnie Roy Black, Jr. and Mazie Nell (Roan) Black Winters; m. Elizabeth Ann Funderburk, Nov. 27, 1982. B.F.A., La. Tech. U., 1978. Mem. staff spl. projects La. Tech. U., Ruston, 1979-80, dir. assembly ctr., 1980-81, dir. facilities, 1981—, chmn. facilities planning, 1980—, mem. faculty senate, 1981-84; cons. arena planning Lamar U., Ark. State U.; mem. evaluation com. Cajun Dome U. Southwest La., 1982. Mem. Am. Plant Engrs., Internat. Assn. Auditorium Mgrs., Nat. Entertainment and Campus Activities Assn. Democrat. Southern Baptist. Avocations: duck and quail hunting; boating. Home: Route 1 Box 290-93 Ruston LA 71270 Office: Louisiana Tech U PO Box 3042 Ruston LA 71270

BLACK, ROBERT PERRY, banker; b. Hickman, Ky., Dec. 21, 1927; s. Burwell Perry and Veola (Moore) B.; m. Mary Rives Ogilvie, Oct. 27, 1951; children—Patty Rives, Robert Perry. B.A., U. Va., 1950, M.A., 1951, Ph.D., 1955. Part-time instr. U. Va., 1953-54, research assoc. Fed. Res. Bank, Richmond, Va., 1954-55, assoc. economist, 1956-58, economist, 1958-60, asst. v.p., 1960-62, v.p. 1962-68, 1st v.p., 1968-73, pres., 1973—; asst. prof. U. Tenn., 1955-56; lectr. U. Va., 1956-57; mem. Gov.'s Adv. Bd. Revenue Estimates, 1976—. Contbr. articles to profl. jours. Mem. adv. bd. Central Richmond Assn.; trustee Collegiate Schs., also past chmn.; bd. dirs. Richmond Eye Hosp.; trustee Richmond Meml. Hosp., E. Angus Powell Endowment for Am. Enterprise, 1980—; past pres. United Way Greater Richmond; bd. dirs., mem. exec. com., chmn. fin. com. Downtown Devel. Unltd., chmn. adv. com. Ctr. for Banking Edn. Va. Union U., 1977-79; bd. dirs., mem. exec. com. Central Va. Ednl. TV Corp., 1979-82; bd. dirs. Blue Cross and Blue Shield of Va., mem. fin. and audit com. 1983—, mem. pub. info. and mktg. com., 1984—; mem. adv. bd. ctr. advanced studies U. Va., 1985—. Served with AUS, 1946-47. Recipient George Washington Honor medal award Freedoms Found. Valley Forge, 1978. Mem. Am. and So. Econ. Assn., Am. Fin. Assn., Richmond Soc. Fin. Analysts, Am. Inst. Banking, Raven Soc., Phi Beta Kappa (past pres. Richmond chpt.), Beta Gamma Sigma, Alpha Kappa Psi, Kappa Alpha. Methodist. Club: Country of Va. (bd. dirs. 1980-85, v.p. 1981-83, chmn. fin. com. 1981-83, pres. 1983-85). Office: Fed Res Bank 701 E Byrd St Richmond VA 23219

BLACK, SAMUEL HAROLD, educator; b. Lebanon, Pa., May 1, 1930; s. Harold William and Beatrice Irene (Steckbeck) B.; student Hershey Jr. Coll., 1948-50; B.S., Lebanon Valley Coll., 1952; postgrad. U. Pa., 1952-54; M.S., U. Mich., 1958, Ph.D., 1961; m. Elisabeth Martha Zandveld, Aug. 16, 1961; children—Vicki Ann, Alisa Jo. NSF fellow Tech. U., Delft, Netherlands, 1960-61; instr. U. Mich., Ann Arbor, 1961-62; asst. prof. Baylor Coll. Medicine, Houston, 1962-67, asso. prof., 1967-71; asso. prof. Mich. State U., East Lansing, 1971-73, prof., 1973-75; prof., head dept. med. microbiology and immunology, Tex. A&M U., College Station, 1975—, asst. dean for curriculum and undergrad. med. edn. Coll. Medicine, 1985—; lectr. U. Houston, 1964-66; vis. prof. Swiss Fed. Inst. Tech., Zurich, 1969-70. Served with M.C., U.S. Army, 1954-56. Recipient Alumni Assn. citation Lebanon Valley Coll., 1981; Faculty Disting. Achievement award in teaching Tex. A&M U., 1982. Fellow Am. Acad. Microbiology; mem. Am. Soc. Microbiology, Am. Soc. Cell Biology, Soc. for Gen. Microbiology, Electron Microscope Soc. Am., Soc. for Invertebrate Pathology. Home: 1205 King Arthur Circle College Station TX 77840 Office: Dept Med Microbiology and Immunology Coll of Medicine Tex A&M Univ College Station TX 77843

BLACK, SUSAN HARRELL, judge; b. Valdosta, Ga., Oct. 20, 1943; d. William H. and Ruth Elizabeth (Phillips) Harrell; m. Louis Eckert Black, Dec. 28, 1966. B.A., Fla. State U., 1964; J.D., U. Fla., 1967. Bar: Fla. 1967. Asst. state atty. 4th Jud. Circuit Fla.; asst. gen. counsel City of Jacksonville, Fla.; judge County Ct. of Duval County, Fla.; judge 4th Jud. Circuit Ct. of Fla.; U.S. dist. judge Middle Dist. Fla., Jacksonville, 1979—; former mem. faculty Nat. Jud. Coll., Reno. Mem. adv. bd., former trustee Jacksonville Hosp. Ednl. Program; mem. Jacksonville Council Citizen Involvement; trustee Law Sch. U. Fla. Mem. Am. Bar Assn., Fla. Bar Assn., Jacksonville Bar Assn., Conf. Circuit Judges (former chmn. edn. com., dean New Judges Coll.). Episcopalian. Office: 311 W Monroe St Jacksonville FL 32202

BLACK, THOMAS MORCOMBE, lawyer; b. Nashville, Sept. 23, 1935; s. Thomas and Edith Marion (Morcombe) B.; m. Ann Marie Sammons, Apr. 18, 1964; children—Thomas Morcombe Jr., Robert Samuel, Ann Marie. B.A., U. of South, 1958; J.D., Vanderbilt U., 1963. Bar: Tenn. 1963, U.S. Dist. Ct. (mid. dist.) Tenn. 1965, U.S. Ct. Appeals (6th cir.) 1966. Law clk. Tenn. Supreme Ct., Nashville, 1963-64; assoc. firm Gracey, Buck, Maddin & Cowan, Nashville, 1964-72; ptnr. firm Stewart & Black, Madison, Tenn., 1972—. Mem. Nashville Bar Assn. (sec.-treas. 1972-73, bd. dirs. 1974), Tenn. Bar Assn., ABA. Democrat. Episcopalian. Clubs: Madison Optimists; Barristers of Nashville (pres. 1972-73). Home: 1506 Saunders Ave Madison TN 37115 Office: Stewart & Black 223 Madison St Madison TN 37115

BLACK, WILLIAM BRUCE, chemist; b. Indpls., Feb. 25, 1923; s. Paul and Vivian Love (Rothgeb) B.; B.A. in Chemistry, U. Va., 1950, M.S. in Organic Chemistry (Philip Francis duPont research fellow 1952-53), 1953, Ph.D. in Organic Chemistry (duPont postgrad. fellow 1953-54), 1954; m. Marie Christoffersen, Sept. 20, 1945; children—Linda Bruce Black Willson, John Christopher. Research chemist Chemstrand Research Corp., Decatur, Ala., 1954-59, Chemstrand Research Center, Inc., Research Triangle Park, N.C., 1959-69; with Monsanto Textiles Co., Pensacola, Fla., 1969-84, sr. group leader, 1969-80, sr. fellow, 1980-84; owner Photography by Black, Pensacola, 1971—. Served to 1st lt. USAAF, 1943-46. Decorated Air medal; recipient President and Visitors prize U. Va., 1954. Mem. Am. Chem. Soc., Fiber Soc., Pensacola Artists, Sigma Xi. Presbyterian. Author, patentee in field. Co-editor: High-Modulus Wholly Aromatic Fibers, 1973; Stress-Induced Crystallization, Part II, 1979. Home and office: 2300 N Whaley Ave Pensacola FL 32503

BLACKBURN, JAMES ROSS, JR., business executive, airline pilot; b. Lakeland, Fla., Feb. 28, 1930; s. James Ross and Esther Louise (Flagle) B.; student Davidson Coll., 1948-49; B.B.A., U. Miami, 1953, postgrad., 1968-69; m. Joyce Gaynelle Green, Aug. 29, 1960; children—Linda Marie, Lisa Joyce. Pilot, Eastern Air Lines, 1957—, capt., 1969—; mktg. cons. Comrex Corp., 1967-72; pres. Surete Ltd., 1973; pres. J.R. Blackburn & Assocs., 1974-76; pres. Blackburn Assocs., Inc., Miami, Fla., 1977-81; pres., chief exec. officer Aerodynetics Corp., 1981—, chmn. bd., 1985—; Mem. steering com., mem. chmn.'s com. U.S. Senatorial Bus. Adv. Bd., Washington, 1980-83; co-founder (with Pres. Ronald Reagan) Republican Presdl. Task Force, 1981—; mem. Rep. Senatorial Inner Circle, Washington, 1983—. Served to 1st lt. USAF, 1953-57. Mem. Air Line Pilots Assn., First Flight Soc., AMS/Oil Dealers Assn., Geneal. Soc. Greater Miami (past treas.), Internat. Platform Assn., Am. Hall Aviation History (founding mem.) Quiet Birdmen, Greater Miami Aviation Assn., Nat. Aero. Assn., Soc. So. Families, Fla. Soc. SAR, SCV (past comdr.), Nat. Rifle Assn. (life), Mil. Order Stars and Bars, Sigma Chi. Baptist. Clubs: Masons; U.S. Senatorial (Washington); Country of Coral Gables. Home: 10745 S W 53d Ave Miami FL 33156

BLACKBURN, KATIE TAGGART, mathematics educator, researcher; b. Lynchburg, Va., July 6, 1942; d. Norval Alfred and Mary Fay (Dougherty) Taggart; 1 child, Ian. B.S., George Peabody Coll., 1963; M.S., U. Wis.-Madison, 1965; cert. advanced study U. Chgo., 1976; Ph.D., U. Tenn., 1983. Tchr. math. John Sevier Sch., Kingsport, Tenn., 1964-66, Lavergne Sch., Berwyn, Ill., 1972-74, Kenwood High Sch., Chgo., 1974-77; asst. prof. math. Tusculum Coll., Greeneville, Tenn., 1977-81; chairperson math., dept. developmental studies U. Ga., Athens, 1983-84; assoc. prof. math. edn. East Tenn. State U., Johnson City, 1984—; dir. Horizons for Jr. Scholars, Johnson City, 1985. Contbr. revs. and articles to profl. jours. Hilton A. Smith fellow, 1982. Mem. Am. Edn. Research Assn., Na. Council Tchrs. Math., Phi Delta Kappa, Kappa Delta Pi, Pi Lambda Theta, Delta Kappa Gamma. Avocations: white water rafting, square dancing. Office: Dept Curriculum and Instrn East Tenn State U Johnson City TN 37614

BLACKBURN, ROBERT MCGRADY, bishop; b. Bartow, Fla., Sept. 12, 1919; s. Charles Fred and Effie Frances (Forsythe) B.; m. Mary Jeanne Everett, Nov. 16, 1943 (dec. May 1977); children—Jeanne Marie (Mrs. Ramon Cox), Robert M., Frances Lucille; m. Jewell Haddock, Sept. 9, 1978. B.A., Fla. So. Coll., 1941; M.Div., Emory U., 1943, LL.D., 1973; D.D. (hon.), LaGrange Coll., 1961. Ordained to ministry Methodist Ch., 1943; pastor United Methodist Ch., Boca Grande, Fla., 1943-44; asso. pastor First Methodist Ch., Orlando, Fla., 1946-48, Mt. Dora, Fla., 1948-53, DeLand, Fla., 1953-60, Jacksonville, Fla., 1960-68, sr. pastor, Orlando, 1968-72; bishop United Methodist Ch., Raleigh, N.C., 1972-80, Va. Conf., 1980—; Mem. program council United Methodist Ch., 1963-72; del. to Meth. Gen. Confs., 1968, 70, 72. Trustee Emory U., Randolph-Macon Coll., Randolph-Macon Woman's Coll., Randolph-Macon Acad., Va. Wesleyan, Shenandoah Coll. and Conservatory of Music, Ferrum Coll., Wesley Sem. Served as chaplain U.S. Army, 1944-46. Home: 10610 Baypines Ln Richmond VA 23233 Office: 4016 W Broad St Richmond VA 23230

BLACKMAN, BRUCE ALLEN, electrical engineer; b. Weleetka, Okla., Dec. 21, 1919; s. George C. and Ruby (Hamilton) B.; B.S., Okla. State U., 1941, M.S., 1955; m. Dorothy Atterberry, July 1, 1945; children—Barry, Susan. Instr. mech. engring. Okla. State U., Stillwater, 1946-48; research engr. Dowell Inc., Tulsa, 1948-53, Well Surveys, Inc., Tulsa, 1953-60; project engr. Otis Engring. Corp., Dallas, 1960-62; devel. engr., sect. leader Halliburton Co., Duncan, Okla., 1962-69, sect. supr., 1969-80, asst. mgr. elec. research, 1980-83. Served to 1st lt. Signal Corps AUS, 1941-46, to capt., 1950-52. Registered profl. engr., Okla. Mem. IEEE, Eta Kappa Nu. Home: 1924 Parkview St Duncan OK 73533 Office: Blackman Consult 1924 Parkview Duncan OK 73533

BLACKMAN, JOHN GORDON, JR., investment banker; b. Nashville, Nov. 2, 1947; s. John Gordon Sr. and Eleanor Anne (Bailey) B. B.A., Vanderbilt U., 1970; M.B.A., U. N.C., 1972. Chartered fin. analyst. Securities analyst, asst. treas. Nat. Life & Accident Ins. Co., Nashville, 1972-81; asst. v.p. securities NLT Corp., Nashville, 1981-82, treas., 1982-83; asst. v.p. Equitable Securities Corp., Nashville, 1983—. Mem. Nashville Soc. Fin. Analysts (pres. 1981-82). Republican. Baptist. Club: Cumberland (Nashville). Avocations: stereo equipment, tennis. Office: Equitable Securities Corp First American Ctr 25th floor Nashville TN 37328

BLACKMAN, MURRAY, rabbi; b. N.Y.C., Nov. 18, 1920; s. Maxwell and Sarah (Levy) B.; B.S.S., Coll. City N.Y., 1940; B.H.L., Hebrew Union Coll., 1945, M.H.L., 1949, D.D., 1974; Ph.D., Walden U., 1975; m. Martha Dora Mecklenburger, Aug. 31, 1947; children—Michael Simon, Margaret Jo, Barbara Sarah. Rabbi, 1949; asst. rabbi Temple B'nai Jeshurun, Newark, 1949-50; rabbi Temple Concord, Binghamton, N.Y., 1950-51, Barnert Temple, Paterson, N.J., 1953-56; sr. rabbi Rockdale Temple, Cin., 1956-67; rabbi St. Thomas (V.I.) Synagogue, 1967-70, Temple Sinai, New Orleans, 1970—. Spl. lectr. edn. Hebrew Union Coll., Cin., 1962-67; instr. comparative religion Coll. of V.I., 1967-70; spl. lectr. history La. State U., Baton Rouge, 1971-75; assoc. prof. U. New Orleans, 1974—; instr. Loyola U., New Orleans, 1980—. Chmn. Cin. Jewish Community Relations Com., 1966-67; interfaith chmn. Greater New Orleans United Fund, 1971; mem. adv. council New Orleans council Boy Scouts Am., 1971-73; mem. Mayor's Job Force for Vets. Com., 1970-72; mem. Am. Jewish Com., Central Conf. Am. Rabbis; chmn. community relations com. Jewish Welfare Fedn., New Orleans, 1971-79; pres. New Orleans Rabbinical Council, 1973-78; mem. exec. bd. Central Conf. Am. Rabbis, 1978-82; mem. exec. bd. Nat. Jewish Community Relations Adv. Council, N.Y.C., 1975—, vice chmn., 1976-81; exec. bd. La. State Com. for Humanities, 1975-80, Willowood Home for Jewish Aged, 1977-82, La. Renaissance, Religion and the Arts, 1977-82; nat. chmn. Joint Commn. on Jewish Edn., Union Am. Hebrew Congregations-Central Conf. Am. Rabbis, 1982—; trustee Union Am. Hebrew Congregations, 1982—, exec. bd. Southwest Council, 1982—. Served with USNR, 1951-53. Mem. Adult Edn. Assn. U.S., Soc. Israel Philatelists, Southwest Assn. Reform Rabbis (pres. 1978-80), Phi Delta Kappa. Author: A Guide to Jewish Themes in American Fiction 1940-80, 1981. Home: 1408 Frankfort St New Orleans LA 70122 Office: 6227 St Charles Ave New Orleans LA 70118

BLACKMORE, JAMES DOUGLAS, public relations and advertising executive; b. Acushnet, Mass., Dec. 7, 1946; s. James Howard and Clotilda (Perry-Ponte) B.; student Southeastern Mass. Technol. Inst., 1966, U. Tex., Austin, 1970-73; m. Sharon Cramer, Aug. 18, 1973. Pres., Blackmore Agy., Austin, 1969-73; announcer Sta. KTBC, Austin, 1970; exec. dir. Austin USO, 1970-73; dir. public relations Tex. Pacific Oil Co., Inc., Dunigan Tool & Supply Co., Inc., Dallas, 1973-81; pres., founder Blackmore Public Relations, Inc., 1981—; vis. lectr. S.W. Tex. State U., 1975, U. Tex., Austin, Arlington, Dallas; adj. prof. communications U. Tex., Arlington, 1983—; adj. prof. public relations So. Meth. U., 1982—; mem. curriculum study com. public relations and journalism Sch. Communication, U. Tex., Austin, 1980. Served with USAF, 1966-70. Recipient Excellence in Graphics award Ga.-Pacific, 1974, award of graphic recognition Internat. Papers, 1974, 75. Mem. Tex., La. Mid-Continent oil and gas assns., Okla. Petroleum Council, Am. Petroleum Inst., Aviation Space Writers Assn., Assn. Petroleum Writers (assoc.), Internat. Assn. Bus. Communicators (Rookie Editor of Year 1974), Public Relations Soc. Am. (accredited mem.; accreditation chmn. North Tex. 1978, dir. 1979—, pres. 1981, Southwest Jud. Rev. Panel 1985-86), Dallas/Ft. Worth Bus./Profl. Advt. Assn. (dir.), Dallas Ad League. Clubs: Dallas Press (gen. chmn. Gridiron Show 1978); Arlington City. Editor: TP Voice, Dunigan Diary, 1973-81. Contbr. articles to profl. jours. Producer, NET-PBS TV Spl., Christmas Folk, 1971. Home and Office: 2505 Pecan St Grand Prairie TX 75050

BLACKSTOCK, VIRGINIA LEE LOWMAN (MRS. LEROY BLACKSTOCK), civic worker; b. Bixby, Okla., July 2, 1917; d. Joseph Arthur and Winifred (Lundy) Lowman; student Tulsa Coll. Bus., 1935-37; m. Leroy Blackstock, Dec. 29, 1939; children—Vincent Craig, Priscilla Gay (Mrs. Richard S. Kurz), Birch Lee, Lore Anne (Mrs. Dwight Mitchell), Trena Jan (Mrs. Frank Dale). Legal sec. law firm, Tulsa, 1937-41. Chmn. program Internat. Students in Tulsa, 1955-65; mem. Tulsa Council Camp Fire Girls, 1963-66; mem. youth com. Tulsa Philharmonic Soc., 1969-70; now mem. women's assn.; pres. Eliot Elementary P.T.A., 1961-62, Edison High Sch. P.T.A., 1971-72; mem. Tulsa Opera Guild. Co-chmn. Democratic precinct No. 132, 1960-67. Mem. Tulsa County Bar Aux. (pres. 1954-55, sec. 1962-63, chaplain 1966-67). Baptist. Clubs: Summit, Petroleum. Home: 7213 S Atlanta St Tulsa OK 74136

BLACKTON, FRANK, industrial engineer; b. Los Angeles, Dec. 29, 1927; s. James Stuart and Evangeline (Russell) B.; m. Josephine Reeves, Nov. 4, 1951; 1 son, Frank Reeves. Student, Ga. Inst. Tech., 1951, Atlanta Law Sch., 1951, Lockheed Emory Mgmt. Inst., Emory U., 1980. Gen. indsl. engr. Lockheed Ga. Co., Marietta, 1955-72, mfg. bid and proposal coordinator, 1972-78, mfg. engr., dept. mgr., 1979-81, planning dept. mgr., 1981-83, mfg. tech. engring. specialist, 1983, space shuttle SRB, 1984—; cons. Lockheed Aircraft Corp., Burbank, Calif., 1982, 83. Patentee computer assisted mfg. advanced composites. Sustaining mem. Republican party, 1981. Served with USNR, 1943-46; PTO. Recipient written commendations for effort Lockheed Aircraft Corp., 1982, 83. Mem. Am. Inst. Indsl. Engrs. (sr., sec. 1971—), Soc. Advancement Materials-Process Engring., Soc. Mfg. Engrs. (sr.), Nat. Mgmt. Assn., AIAA. Mem. Christian Ch. (Disciples of Christ). Club: Peachtree Toastmaster (Atlanta) (pres. 1961-62). Home: 3426 Raymond Dr Doraville GA 30340 Office: Lockheed Ga Co D/4111 ZN 71 86 S Cobb Dr Marietta GA 30063

BLACKWELL, WILLIAM ERNEST, insurance company executive; b. Rocky Mount, N.C., Apr. 1, 1932; s. Rosser Ira and Ellen Wimberley (Wilkinson) B.; m. Elizabeth Ann Levitan, Feb. 22, 1973; children—Scott, Tracy. B.S., Davidson Coll., 1954; M.B.A., U. N.C., 1958. Chartered fin. analyst. Security analyst Jefferson Standard Life Ins. Co., Greensboro, N.C., 1958-66, asst. treas., 1966-69, 2d v.p., 1969-81; v.p. Jefferson-Pilot Corp, Greensboro, 1981-83, sr. v.p., 1984—; dir. Jefferson Pilot Communications, Charlotte, N.C., Jefferson Pilot, Greensboro, Jefferson Standard, Greensboro. Served to cpl. U.S. Army, 1954-56. Mem. Inst. Chartered Fin. Analysts, N.C. Soc. Fin. Analysts, N.C. Security Traders Assn., Nat. Investor Relations Inst. Home: 1106 Hammel Rd Greensboro NC 27408 Office: Jefferson-Pilot Corp PO Box 21008 Greensboro NC 27420

BLACKWOOD, LYNN CARSON, JR., clinical child psychologist, child development research scientist; b. Burlington, N.C., Dec. 7, 1949; s. Lynn Carson and Ann Louise (Diffee) B.; M. Lori Ann Alphin, May 5, 1984; 1 child by previous marriage, John Lynn. B.A., U. N.C., 1972, Ph.D., 1976. Lic. clin. psychologist, Va. Intern, Nat. Naval Med. Ctr., Bethesda, Md., 1976-77; commd. ensign U.S. Navy, 1972, advanced through grades to lt. comdr., 1981; clin. psychologist Marine Corps Devel. and Edn. Command, Quantico, Va., 1977-79; clin. child psychologist Naval Hosp., Portsmouth, Va., 1979-81; ret., 1981; child psychologist inpatient child unit Eastern Va. Med. Authority, Community Mental Health Ctr. and Psychiat. Inst., Norfolk, 1981-83, co-dir. Infancy Devel. Ctr., 1983—, clin. supr. grad. students, 1981—; asst. prof. Eastern Va. Med. Sch., Norfolk, 1981—. Mem. Norfolk Com. for Prevention of Child Abuse, 1981—. Grantee in field. Mem. Am. Psychol. Assn., Soc. Research in Child Devel., Internat. Assn. Infant Mental Health, Va. Psychol. Assn., Va. Acad. Clin. Psychologists, Phi Beta Kappa, Psi Chi. Methodist. Club: Elizabeth Manor Golf and Country (Portsmouth, Va.). Avocations: golf; basketball; swimming; sculpting; singing. Office: Community Mental Health Ctr and Psychiat Inst PO Box 1980 Norfolk VA 23708

BLAGG, DONALD EUGENE, psychologist; b. Gary, Ind., Jan. 18, 1952; s. Worick Donald and Bonnie Jean (Douthitt) B.; m. Susan Lynn Schmitz, May 17, 1975; children—Eric Donald, Kyle Eugene. B.S., Ind. State U., 1975, M.S. Ed., 1977; Ed.D., U. Ga., 1982. Lic. psychologist, Ga. Coordinator psychol. services Chattahoochee-Flint CESA, Americus, Ga., 1981—; instr. dept. psychology Ga. Southwestern Coll., 1982—; psychologist in pvt. practice Psycho Diagnostics, Inc., Americus, 1985—; psychologist Middle Ga. Psycho-edn. Ctr., Macon, 1981; psychologist, cons. Macon County Tng. Ctr., Montezuma, 1985. Sec. career counseling Ft. Valley Meth. Ch., 1984-85. Served with USMC, 1971-73. Mem. Am. Psychol. Assn., Nat. Assn. Sch. Psychologists, Ga. Assn. Sch. Psychologists (pres.). Lodge: Lions (pres. 1984-85). Avocations: golf; running; skiing. Home: Route 3 418 Christopher Circle Fort Valley GA 31030 Office: Paul Stephens Sch Reid 54 Warner Robbins GA 31088

BLAIR, BOBBY CHARLES, chemical engineer; b. Arcadia, Kans., Sept. 21, 1941; s. Charles Warren and Hazel Louise (Wyckoff) B.; B.S. in Chem. Engring., Okla. State U., 1964; M.B.A., U. Tulsa, 1969. With Phillips Petroleum Co., 1964—, mktg. research engr., Bartlesville, Okla., 1974-77, mktg. and tech. analyst, 1977-80, mining chems. project dir., Bartlesville, 1980-85; gas sales specialist, 1985—. Wentz Found. Service scholar. Mem. AIME, Natural Gas Assn. Okla., Soc. Mining Engrs., Phi Theta Kappa, Sigma Tau. Republican. Mem. Christian Ch. (Disciples of Christ). Co-inventor, patentee high speed fibrillation process. Home: 4200 Beacon Ct Bartlesville OK 74003 Office: 6C3 HS&L Bartlesville OK 74004

BLAIR, MARTHA FITCH, health services administrator, nurse coordinator; b. Boleyn, Ky., July 31, 1940; d. Chester and Mae (Coburn) Fitch; m. James P. Blair, Dec. 31, 1957; children—Kenneth Darrel, Sheila Kaye Blair Sergent. B.S. in Nursing, Berea Coll. (Ky.), 1963; M.A. in Edn., Union Coll., Barbourville, Ky., 1976. Asst. instr. pub. health nursing, Berea Coll., 1963-66; instr. publ. health nursing Appalachian Regional Hosp., Harlan, Ky., 1966-67; nurse cons. Ky. State Health Dept., Frankfort, 1968-77; instr. practical nursing Wise County Vocat. Sch. (Va.), 1977-78; nursing instr. S.E. Community Coll., Cumberland, Ky., 1978-79; dir. health services Mountain Trails Health Plan, Harlan Ky., 1978—; nurse coordinator Cumberland Valley Dist. Health Dept., Manchester, Ky., 1983—; cons. family planning Daniel Boone Clinic, Harlan, 1970-74; coordinator childbirth classes M.T.H.P., Inc., Harlan, 1976-78; mem. State Task Force Health Edn., 1982-84. Health editor Health Notes newsletter, 1978—, participant health films. Former pres. Emphysema Anonymous chpt., Harlan; former sec. Harlan County Mental Retardation Assn., Council So. Mountains, Berea, Ky.; mem. White House Conf. Youth, 1966. Recipient Cert. Appreciation, Pine Mountain chpt. Jaycees, 1974, Cardinal chpt. March of Dimes, Somerset, Ky., 1979; Life Saver award Ky. Cancer Soc., Louisville, 1979-80; Cert. of Appreciation, Western Ky. U., Bowling Green, 1981. Mem. Ky. Nursing Assn. (dist. pres. 1968-70), Ky. Pub. Health Assn., Soc. Pub. Health Educators (sec. 1981-82), Lodge: Lioness (Harlan). Home: PO Box 421 Harlan KY 40831

BLAIR, ROBERT CHARLES, educator; b. Bethesda, Md., Feb. 25, 1952; s. Ira W. and Arlene (Bross) B.; m. Dorcas Catherine Campbell, June 17, 1972; 1 child, Justin Tyler. B.A. in Biology, Bridgewater Coll., 1974; M.A. in Ednl. Adminstrn., Va. Poly. Inst. and State U., 1986. Tchr. Fauguier Pub. Schs., Warrenton, Va., 1974-76, Frederick County Pub. Schs., Winchester, Va., 1976—; adj. prof. Lord Fairfax Community Coll., Middletown, Va., 1985—. Author: Photographic Calibration, 1982. NSF grantee. Mem. NEA, Frederick County Edn. Assn., Va. Edn. Assn., Shenandoah Photog. Soc., Phi Delta Kappa. Avocations: photography; computer programming; landscaping; sailing. Home: 4990 Wythe Ave Stephens City VA 22655 Office: James Wood High Sch 1313 Amherst St Winchester VA 22601

BLAIR, ROBERT RUSH, oil company executive; b. Rawlins, Wyo., Sept. 22, 1928; s. James Scott and Ellen Scott (Rush) B.; B.S., Okla. State U., 1950; m. Carine Naveau de la Hault, Apr. 28, 1967; 1 dau., Tracy Catherine. With Sinclair Oil Corp., various locations, 1950-70, product coordinator Eastern Hemisphere, Brussels, 1964-67, gen. mgr., Algiers, 1967-70; v.p. Delhi Internat. Oil Corp., Dallas, 1970—, v.p., dir. Delhi Pacific Minerals Corp., Dallas, 1970—, exec. v.p. Delhi Internat. Oil Corp., Dallas, 1979-81; chmn. bd., pres. CINCO Drilling Co., 1979-81; pres. Magnolia Exploration Co., 1981—. Served with AUS, 1951-53; Korea. Registered profl. engr., Tex. Mem. Ind. Petroleum Assn. Am., Am. Petroleum Inst., Australian Petroleum Exploration Assn. (dir.), Soc. Petroleum Engrs., Am. Inst. Mgmt., Am. C. of C. in Australia, Australian Am. Assn. Methodist. Clubs: Dallas Petroleum, Northwood, Commerce South Australia, South Australian Cricket Assn., University, Half Moon (Montego Bay, Jamaica). Home: 4506 Kelsey Rd Dallas TX 75229 Office: 2 Energy Sq Suite 440 Dallas TX 75206

BLAIR, STEVEN NOEL, biomedical scientist, public health educator, consultant; b. Mankato, Kans., July 4, 1939; s. Bernard Samuel and Wilma Edith Faye (Fisher) B.; m. Jane Marie Pottberg, Apr. 10, 1965; children—Max Earl, Ann Marie. B.A., Kans. Wesleyan U., 1962; M.S., Ind. U., 1965, P.E.D., 1968. Instr. Kans. Wesleyan U., Salina, 1963-64; instr. U. S.C., Columbia, 1966-75, prof., 1975-86; vis. sr. research scholar Stanford U. Sch. Medicine, Palo Alto, Calif., 1978-80; dir. epidemiology Inst. Aerobics Research, Dallas, 1980—; cons. occupational health promotion programs. Named Health

Educator of Yr., S.C. Assn. Health Edn., 1982; recipient Bronze Service Medallion, S.C. Heart Assn.; S.C. Assn. Health, Phys. Edn., Recreation and Dance scholar. 1981. Fellow Am. Coll. Sports Medicine, Council on Epidemiology of Am. Heart Assn., Am. Acad. Phys. Edn.; mem. AAAS, Am. Pub. Health Assn., Soc. Behavioral Medicine, Soc. Epidemiologic Research, Human Biology Council. Democrat. Methodist. Contbr. articles to profl. jours. Home: 9316 Windy Crest Dr Dallas TX 75243 Office: Inst for Aerobics Research 12200 Preston Rd Dallas TX 75230

BLAIS, MARK ALAN, psychologist, educator; b. Barre, Vt., Nov. 24, 1956; s. Leo J. and Earlene (Shannon) B. B.S., SUNY-Cortland, 1979; M.A., Towson State U., 1981; postgrad. Nova U., 1984—. Instr., Towson State U., Balt., 1980-81, Community Coll., Burlington, Vt., 1982-84; psychologist Howard Mental Health, Burlington, 1981-84. Contbr. articles to profl. jours. Recipient Psychology Faculty award Towson State U., 1981. Mem. Am. Psychol. Assn. (assoc.), Eastern Psychol. Assn., Vt. Psychol. Assn. Avocations: poetry, sports. Home: 3367 College Ave 104B Fort Lauderdale FL 33314 Office: Nova U Dept Psy Program 3301 College Ave Fort Lauderdale FL 33314

BLAIS, ROGER NATHANIEL, physics educator, researcher, consultant; b. Duluth, Minn., Oct. 3, 1944; s. Eusebe Joseph and Edith Seldena (Anderson) B.; m. Mary Louise Leclerc, Aug. 2, 1971; children—Christopher Edward, Laura Louise. B.A. in Physics and French, U. Minn., 1966; Ph.D. in Physics, U. Okla., 1971; cert. in computer programming Tulsa Jr. Coll., 1981; cert. in bus. UCLA, 1986. Registered profl. engr., Okla. Instr. physics Westark Community Coll., Ft. Smith, Ark., 1971-72; asst. prof. physics and geophys. scis. Old Dominion U., Norfolk, Va., 1972-77; asst. prof. engring. physics U. Tulsa, 1977-81, assoc. prof., 1981—, assoc. dir. Artificial Lift Projects. Contbr. articles to profl. jours. Mem. Am. Phys. Soc., AAAS, Am. Geophys. Union, Nat. Soc. Profl. Engrs., AAUP, Soc. Petroleum Engrs., Instrument Soc. Am., N.Y. Acad. Sci., Iron Wedge Soc., Phi Beta Kappa, Sigma Xi, Sigma Pi Sigma, Tau Beta Pi. Home: 5348 E 30th Pl Tulsa OK 74114-6314 Office: Physics Dept U Tulsa 600 S College Ave Tulsa OK 74104-3189

BLAKE, CARLTON EARLON, insurance agency executive; b. Lowell, Mass., Jan. 27, 1920; s. Chester Arthur and Annie May (Holman) B.; m. Ruby Lee Henry, May 30, 1941 (div.); 1 son, Robert Earlon; m. 2d, Virginia Lee Lucas, Nov. 15, 1947; children—Richard Carlton, Susan Elaine Blake Erwin. Student Bentley Coll., Boston, 1939-40, George Washington U., 1945-47; C.L.U., Am. Coll., Bryn Mawr, Pa., 1953, chartered fin. cons., 1984. Salesman, Phoenix Mut. Life Ins. Co., Washington, 1944-68; pres. Blake Ins. Agy., Inc., McLean, Va., 1968—; choral dir. numerous churches, Washington and no. Va., 1944—. Author: Descendants of Jasper Blake, 1980; composer anthems and cantata. Served with U.S. Army, 1943. Mem. No. Va. Assn. Life Underwriters (pres. 1968-69), Am. Soc. C.L.U.s (pres. No. Va. chpt. 1976-77), DAV (life). Presbyterian (deacon). Clubs: SAR, Nat. Geneal. Soc. Lodge: Masons (32 deg.). Office: Blake Ins Agency Inc PO Box 49 McLean VA 22101

BLAKE, CECILE CARTEE, investor relations company executive; b. Paducah, Ky., Mar. 26, 1938; d. Walter Edward and Charlene (Peck) Cartee; m. Glenn A. Blake, Feb. 20, 1965; children—Glynnis, Mitchell, Kyle, Amy. B.A. in Math., U. St. Thomas, 1980; M.S. in Biometry, U. Tex., 1982, Ph.D. in Biometry, 1985. Clin. chemist M.D. Anderson Hosp., Houston, 1959-60; dir. research and devel. Hycel Inc., Houston, 1960-65; prin. Frequency Forecasting, Houston, 1985—; v.p. McCormick & Pryor, N.Y.C., 1985—; statis. cons. AID, Washington, 1984—, Pan-Am. World Health Orgn., 1984—. Mem. Am. Statis. Soc., Nat. Inst. Investor Relations. Club: Glenbrook Valley Investment (pres. 1966-67) (Houston). Avocations: bicycling, sewing, reading. Home and office: 2004 Wroxton Rd Houston TX 77005

BLAKE, ELIAS, JR., college president; b. Brunswick, Ga., Dec. 13, 1929; s. Elias and Ruth B.; m. Mona Williams, June 13, 1963; children—Michael, Elias Ayinde. B.A., Paine Coll., 1951; M.A., Howard U., 1954; Ph.D., U. Ill., 1960; LL.D. (hon.), Paine Coll., 1983. Asst. prof. Howard U., Washington, 1959-66; Southeastern dir. dir. Upward Bound-Inst. in Services to Edn., 1966-67; pres. Inst. Service to Edn., Washington, 1969-77; pres. Clark Coll., Atlanta, 1977—; chmn. Nat. Adv. Com. on Black Higher Edn. and Black Colls. and Univs. Active Leadership Ga. Served with U.S. Army, 1951-53. Recipient Outstanding Tchr. award Coll. Liberal Arts, Howard U., 1964; Meritorious Achievement award Tenn. State U., 1981; Disting. Service award Ohio State U., 1983. Mem. Carnegie Found. Advancement Teaching, Assn. Pvt. Colls. and Univs. Ga. (chmn.), Assn. Equal Opportunity in Higher Edn. (vice chmn.). Methodist. Club: Kiwanis. Office: James P Brawley Dr Atlanta GA 30314

BLAKE, JAMES FREDERICK, JR., naval logistician; b. Hillsborough, N.C., Nov. 21, 1933; s. James Frederick and Alpha (Snipes) B.; B.S., U. N.C., 1955; M.S. in Mgmt., Rensselaer Poly. Inst., 1967; postgrad. Naval War Coll., 1973-74, Harvard Bus. Sch., 1972; m. Barbara Lee Darkis, Mar. 24, 1956; children—James Frederick, III, Susan Lynn. Commd. ensign U.S. Navy, 1955, advanced through grades to capt., 1976, ret., 1978; mgr. logistics sci. dept. group CACI Inc., Arlington, Va., 1978—. Decorated Navy Commendation medal (2). Club: Harvard Bus. Sch. (Washington). Methodist. Home: 7930 Bayberry Dr Alexandria VA 22306 Office: 1815 N Fort Myer Dr Arlington VA 22209

BLAKE, RUTHEL LOIS, media specialist; b. Fruitland Park, Fla., Aug. 1, 1938; d. John Samuel and Eva Beatrice (Thompson) B. B.S., Fla. A&M U., 1960; postgrad. Nova U., 1981, Fla. State U., 1985. Librarian Dade County Pub. Schs., Miami, Fla., 1960-63, Queens Borough Pub. Library, Jamaica, N.Y., 1963-65, N.Y.C. Pub. Schs., Queens, 1966-68, D.C. Pub. Schs., Washington, 1968-71; media specialist Palm Beach County Schs., West Palm Beach, Fla., 1972-80, Broward County Pub. Schs., Fort Lauderdale, Fla., 1982—; sch. liaison cons. Queens Borough Pub. Library, Jamaica, 1964-65; mem. library evaluation team Dunbar High Sch., Fort Meyers, Fla., 1962; cons. U.S. Govt. Emergency Sch. Asst. Program, Fla., 1970-71. Mem. Fla. Assn. Media Educators, Broward County Assn. Media Specialists, Fla. A&M U. Alumni Assn., Urban League Fla., LWV, Palm Beach House Condominium Assn., Phi Delta Kappa, (treas. 1968-69), Alpha Kappa Alpha, Alpha Beta Alpha. Democrat. Methodist. Clubs: Willing Workers (pres. 1954-56), Fla. A&M U. Boosters. Avocations: writer; pianist; tennis; bridge; travel. Office: South Broward High Sch 1901 N Federal Hwy Hollywood FL 33020

BLAKE, STANFORD, lawyer; b. Detroit, Sept. 13, 1948; s. Morris and Betty (Yaffe) B.; m. Ellen Perkins, Mar. 5, 1978; children—Cary, Brandon, Stephanie. B.S., U. Fla. 1970; J.D., U. Miami, 1973. Bar: Fla. 1973, U.S. Dist. Ct. (so. dist.) Fla. 1973, U.S. Supreme Ct. 1980, U.S. Ct. Appeals (5th and 11th cirs.) 1981. Asst. pub. defender Dade County, Miami, Fla., 1973-78; ptnr. Todd, Rosinek & Blake, Miami, 1978-84, Rosinek & Blake, Miami, 1984-86, Law offices of Stanford Blake, 1986—. Chmn. Jr. Maccabiah Games S. Fla., Miami, 1984—; chmn. Dade County Outstanding Citizen award, 1986. Mem. ABA, Fla. State Bar Assn. (grievance com.), Fed. Bar Assn., Nat. Assn. Criminal Def. Lawyers, Fla. Criminal Def. Attys. Assn. (pres. 1982-83), so. Miami Kendall Bar Assn. (pres. 1984—). Lodge: B'nai B'rith (pres. 1980-81). Democrat. Jewish. Home: 7810 SW 164th St Miami FL 33157 Office: Law Offices of Stanford Blake 9200 S Dadeland Blvd Suite 617 Miami FL 33156

BLAKELY, LAWRENCE ELDON, audio consultant; b. Winfield, Kans., Sept. 9, 1941; s. James Earl and Lucille Margaret (Hall) B.; m. Melody-Andreasen, Apr. 21, 1984. Student U. Colo. Musical instrument and electronic equipment repairman Dodge Music, Dodge City, 1957-59; communications chief U.S. Army Nat. Guard, 1960-67; repairman Noggle Radio and TV, Dodge City, 1961; bookkeeping supr. Fidelity State Bank, Dodge City, 1962-63; owner House of Sound, Dodge City, 1963-65; record producer Decima Records, Dodge City, 1964-65; rec. engr. Sunset Sound Recorders, Hollywood, Calif., 1966-68; pres. Animated Audiophonics Inc., Hollywood, 1968; pres. Integra Corp., Glendale, Calif., 1969-73; mktg. dir. DBX Inc., Newton, Mass., 1973-78; pres. Blakely Cons. Group, Inc., Framingham, Mass., 1978-86; mng. dir. Audio Media Research, Decatur, Miss., 1986—. Author: Cameo Dictionary of Creative Audio Terms, 1978; Audio Almanac, 1979; Audio Measurements, Their Importance and How to Make Them, 1982; Understanding Power Amplifiers, 1985. Contbr. articles to profl. jours. Recipient Regional and State Music Festival award State of Kans., 1957, 58, 59; Rec. Engr. for Soundtrack Album from Walt Disney's Jungle Book and a Happy Birthday Party Grammy nominee, 1967. Mem. Nat. Acad. Rec. Arts and Scis., Audio Engring. Soc., Am. Music Conf., Bd. Industry Pres. Nat. Assn. Music Merchants, Creative Audio and Music Electronics Orgn. (pres., co-founder). Address: Route 2 Box 408 State Blvd Extension Meridan MS 39305

BLAKENEY, ROGER NEAL, educator, psychologist; b. Deatur, Tex., Sept. 16, 1939; s. C.B. and Flora M. (McAnelly) B.; B.S. in Psychology, Tex. A&M U., 1964; M.A. in Indsl. Psychology, U. Houston, 1967, Ph.D. in Indsl. Psychology, 1969; m. Jennifer; children—Christopher Alan, Benjamin G. wife Jenifer, daughter of Mr & Mrs Jerry Witte. Teaching fellow dept. psychology U. Houston, 1965-68, instr. mgmt., 1968-69, asst. prof. behavioral mgmt. sci., 1969-72, dir. masters program, 1970, coordinator Human Resources Center, 1971-72, assoc. prof. behavioral mgmt. sci., 1972-74, assoc. prof. organizational behavior and mgmt. Coll. Bus. Adminstrn., 1974—, dir. exec. devel. program, 1985—; indsl. psychology intern Exxon U.S.A., 1967-68; adj. prof. Houston Bapt. U., 1978-1984; pres. Blakeney & Assocs., 1972—, Organizational Tech., Inc., 1973-78; dir. Self-Dimensions, Inc., 1983—. cons. to various govt., labor and bus. orgns. Served with AUS, 1960-62. Mem. Am., Southwestern, Tex., Houston psychol. assns., Am., Southwestern acads. mgmt., Internat. Transactional Analysis Assn., Sigma Xi, Beta Gamma Sigma, Alpha Kappa Delta, Alpha Zeta, Sigma Iota Epsilon. member of Editorial Board of Transactional Analysis Journal Author: (with E.C. Bell) Building Effective Local Unions; Course XV of the Labor Education Program of District 37 United Steelworkers of America, 1972, Advanced Leadership: Course XIII of the Labor Education Program of District 37 United Steelworkers of America, 1972; Introduction To Management By Objectives, 1974; Developmental Supervision: Performance Review and Career Planning with Dan & Billie Duncan; That Special Person is Me, 1983; I Have the Power, 1983; Early Start, 1984. Editor: (with M.T. Matteson and D.R. Domm) Contemporary Personnel Management, 1972; (with D.R. Domm, R.W. Scofield and M.T. Matteson) The Individual and the Organization: A book of readings, 1971; Current Issues in Transactional Analysis, 1977; contbg. author: Certificate in Management Accounting Review, 1978; editorial bd. Transaction Analysis Jour.; contbr. articles to profl. publs. Office: Dept Mgmt U Houston University Park Houston TX 77004

BLAKLEY, JOHN CLYDE, administrator; b. Bogota, Colombia, Sept. 14, 1955; came to U.S., 1964; s. Arthur C. and Dorothy M. (Balcome) B.; m. Jean M. Padden, May 21, 1983. B.S., U. Miami, 1977, M.S.Ed., 1979. Mgr., adminstrv. asst. U. Miami Student Union, Coral Gables, Fla., 1977-79; mgr. Aladdins Castle, Inc., South Miami, Fla., 1979-80; adminstrv. mgr., cons. Lexow & Brackins, C.P.A.s, Hollywood, Fla., 1981-84; firm adminstr., Cons. Lexow, Brackins, Koffler, Hollywood, 1985—; pres. Miami Apple Users Group, 1983; cons. YMCA, 1983. Chmn., Multiple Sclerosis Project Dance Marathon, Coral Gables, 1977-79; coordinator United Way Miami, 1975-79. Recipient Whitten award Assn. Coll. Unions, 1977; Outstanding Leadership award C. of C., 1973; Outstanding Vol., United Way, 1975. Mem. Assn. Coll. Unions Internat. (chmn. region 6, 1975-77), Assn. Acctg. Adminstrs., Fla. Inst. C.P.A.s, U. Miami Young Alumni Assn. (dir., pres.). Clubs: Hurricane. Home: 11531 SW 98th St Miami FL 33176 Office: Lexow Brackins Koffler CPAs 2611 Hollywood Blvd Hollywood FL 33020

BLANCHARD, DALLAS ANTHONY, sociology and anthropology educator, consultant, minister; b. Mobile, Ala., Aug. 6, 1933; s. Dallas Anthony and Georgia Van (Bethune) B.; m. Betty Jean Taylor, Sept. 14, 1956 (div. Nov. 1973); 1 child, Barclay Elizabeth; m. Glenda Fay Hendrix, Feb. 26, 1974; 1 child, Sharon Lynne. A.B., Birmingham-So. Coll., 1956; M.Div., Vanderbilt U., 1960; Ph.D., Boston, U., 1973. Ordained to ministry United Methodist Ch, 1956. Minister, United Meth. Ch., Ala., 1951—; assoc. prof. sociology, anthropology U. West Fla., Pensacola, 1969—; pres. Bytesize, Inc., Pensacola, 1984—; leadership cons. various C.s of C., 1982—. Prin. investigator documentary film, 1982. Mem. commn. Ala. Civil Rights, Mobile, 1964-68; mem. exec. com. Escambia County Democrats, Pensacola, 1975-76. Served as airman 1st class USAF, 1953-54. Mem. Am. Sociol. Assn., So. Sociol. Soc., Internat. Conf. Sociology of Religion, Religious Research Assn., Soc. Sci. Study of Religion. Home: 11542 Clear Creek Drive Pensacola FL 32514 Office: Univ West Fla Pensacola FL 32514

BLANCHARD, RICHARD EMILE, sr., personnel services executive, consultant; b. Thompson, Conn., July 13, 1928; s. Lionel A. and Bernadette L. (Jolicoeur) B.; m. Lorraine Patricia Lachapelle, July 3, 1954; children—Michele Blanchard Womack, Richard E., Danielle, Marie Blanchard Oser, Robert Allen, Janine Theresa. B.S. in Biology, Providence Coll., 1952; postgrad. U. Conn. Sch. Law, West Hartford, 1952-53. Chemist, Charles Pfizer Co., Inc., N.Y.C., 1953-56, med. salesman, 1956-60, coll. relations mgr., 1960-63, personnel mgr., 1963-67; dir. manpower and orgn. devel. Sky Chef div. Am. Airlines, N.Y.C., 1967-70; dir. manpower ARA Services, Inc., Phila., 1970-72; v.p., 1972-76; v.p. personnel Jerrico, Inc., Lexington, Ky., 1976-78; pres. Career Mgmt., Inc., C.M. Temporary Services, Lexington, 1978—; cons. personnel services. Mem. adv. bd. Lexington Tech. Inst., U. Ky. Small Bus. Devel. Ctr., Excepticon Workshop, Inc.; mem. adv. bd. Community Coll. div. U. Ky.; v.p. Bluegrass Ednl. Work Council, 1980—; mem. Lexington-Fayette Jobs Tng. Planning Council; bd. dirs. Bluegrass Pvt. Industry Council, 1979—, Jr. Achievement Ky., 1982—. Served with USN, 1946-48. Mem. Ind. Temporary Services Assn., Am. Soc. Personnel Assocs. (past pres. N.Y. chpt.), Ky. Assn. Temporary Services (pres.), Sales Mktg. Assn. Lexington (pres.), Sales Mktg. Execs. Internat. (dist. dir. 1985—), Nat. Assn. Temporary Services. Republican. Roman Catholic. Clubs: Big Elm Country, Lafayette. Lodge: Rotary. Home: 628 Tally Rd Lexington KY 40502 Office: Career Mgmt Inc 340 Legion Dr CM Temporary Services Suite 14 Lexington KY 40504

BLANCHARD, ROBERT TREAT, petroleum co. exec.; b. Boston, Mar. 31, 1937; s. James A. Blanchard II and Cornelia Williams Sullivan; grad. Kimball Union Acad., Meriden, N.H., 1956; B.S. cum laude, Fla. Atlantic U., 1968; grad. Advanced Mgmt. Program, Harvard U., 1982; m. Mary E. Corbin, Sept. 1, 1962; children—Jill A., Stephanie A. Mgmt. trainee Union Oil Co. of Calif., 1961-66; supply rep. Phillips Petroleum Co., Bartlesville, Okla., 1968-74; with La Gloria Oil & Gas Co., subs. Tex. Eastern Corp., Houston, 1974—, exec. v.p., 1978—. Served with USNR, 1959-61. Mem. Ind. Refiners Assn. Am. (dir. 1977-80). Republican. Office: 2911 Trail Lodge Dr Kingwood TX 77339

BLANCHARD, URANIE DANET, banker; b. St. Thomas, V.I., Jan. 7, 1942; d. Pierre Mederic and Marie Lucina (Ledee) Danet; student pvt. schs., St. Thomas; m. Edward Blanchard, June 23, 1959; children—Jean Louis, Suzanne Patricia. Exec. sec. Chase Manhattan Corp., St. Thomas, 1961-64, personnel asst., 1965-67, personnel officer, 1968-74, staff human resources officer, Miami, V.I. and Eastern Caribbean region, 1974-78, human resources mgr. Caribbean region, 1978-85, v.p., 1985—. Home: 6530 SW 48th St Miami FL 33155 Office: PO Box 012439 1000 Miami Ctr Miami FL 33101

BLANCHE, FRED A., JR., judge; b. Baton Rouge, Jan. 18, 1921; s. Fred A. and Amy (Moran) B.; m. Polly Pepper, Dec. 27, 1942; children—Fred A., Elizabeth April (dec.), Lauren, Robert Vincent. B.S., La. State U., 1941, LL.B., 1948. Bar: La bar 1948, U.S. Supreme Ct. bar 1948. Practice law, Baton Rouge; judge La. Dist. Ct. 19th Jud. Dist., 1960-69, 76-77, La. Ct. of Appeal 1st Circuit, 1969; now assoc. justice Supreme Ct. of La. Bd. deacons First Presbyn. Ch. Mem. La. State Law Inst., La. Jud. Coll. (bd. govs.), La. State Bar Assn., La. Dist. Judges Assn. (past pres.), Baton Rouge Power Squadron, Am. Legion, East Baton Rouge Parish Jr. Bar Assn. (past pres.), Kappa Alpha Alumni Assn. Democrat. Presbyterian. Office: Supreme Ct of Louisiana 301 Loyola Ave New Orleans LA 70112

BLAND, EDWIN CLINTON, JR., air traffic controller; b. Woodbridge, Va., May 30, 1933; s. Edwin Clinton and Marguerite (Stanley) B.; m. Joan Barbara Lohr, June 28, 1952; children—Wanda Leah, Sandra Lynn, G. Martin. B.A., Shepherd Coll., 1976. With FAA, 1957—, tng. instr., 1970-73, area supr., 1973-75, area officer, 1975-79, area mgr., 1979-81, asst. air traffic mgr., (all Leesburg, Va.), 1981-84, asst. air traffic mgr. Washington Nat. Tower, 1984—; tng. instr. Washington Community Coll., 1970-73. Pres., Toppettes Drum and Majorette Corp, Manassas, Va., 1964-65; mem. Prince William County Hist. Commn. (Va.), 1978-85. Democrat. Methodist. Lodge: Loom (Leesburg). Home: 10206 Baltusrol Ct Oakton VA 22124 Office: Washington Nat Tower FAA Washington DC 20001

BLAND, JAMES THEODORE, JR., lawyer; b. Memphis, June 16, 1950; s. James T. and Martha F. (Downen) B.; m. Pattie Martin, Apr. 12, 1974. Student, U. Tenn., 1968-69; B.B.A. magna cum laude, Memphis State U., 1972, J.D., 1974. Bar: Tenn. 1975, U.S. Tax Ct. 1976, U.S. Supreme Ct. 1983. C.P.A., Tenn. Law student trainee IRS, Memphis, 1974-75, estate tax atty., 1975-76; assoc. Armstrong, Allen et al., Memphis, 1976-81, ptnr., 1981—. Mem. Am. Assn. Attys.-C.P.A.s, Tenn. Soc. C.P.A.s, ABA, Memphis and Shelby County Bar Found. (pres. 1983), Fed. Bar Assn. (1st v.p. 1985), Tenn. Young Lawyers Conf. (pres. 1984), Beta Alpha Psi, Phi Kappa Phi, Beta Gamma Sigma, Delta Theta Phi. Home: 3557 Shirwood Ave Memphis TN 38122 Office: Armstrong Allen et al 1900 One Commerce St Memphis TN 38103

BLAND, JOSEPH THOMAS, JR., hospital administrator; b. Panama City, Fla., Nov. 4, 1947; s. Joseph Thomas and Anna Lavada (Adams) B.; m. Patricia Louise Sumrall, June 16, 1967; children—Tracye Celeste, Amy Louise. B.S. in Acctg., N.E. La. U., 1970. Acct., Jefferson Davis Meml. Hosp., Natchez, Miss., 1972-73, controller, 1973-74; asst. adminstr. Montfort Jones Meml. Hosp., Kosciusko, Miss., 1974-76, adminstr., 1976—. Served to maj. U.S. Army, 1970—. Mem. Am. Coll. Hosp. Adminstrs., Central Hosp. Council (Pres. 1982-84). Democrat. Baptist. Lodge: Lions (pres. 1984-85). Avocations: hunting, fishing, jogging. Home: Route 2 Box 115Y Kosciusko MS 39090 Office: Montfort Jones Meml Hosp Hwy 12 W Box 677 Kosciusko MS 39090

BLAND, ROBERT BUFORD, English studies educator, consultant; b. Guthrie, Okla., Apr. 19, 1933; s. Forrest and Amy (Green) B.; m. Aileen Louise Gunning, Mar. 29, 1953; children—Janet Kathleen Mathes, Cheryl Amy Alexander. B.A., Central Okla. State U., 1958, M.Teaching, 1960; Ed.D., Highland U., 1976. Tchr. pub. schs., Depew and Woodward, Okla., 1958-60, 67-69; pastor Depew Ch. of God, 1958-60, Shattuck Ch. of God, Okla., 1967-68, Amorita Community Ch., Okla., 1972-73; English prof. Northwestern Okla. State U., Alva, 1969-73; English prof., registrar Toccoa Falls Coll., Ga., 1973-75; assoc. prof. English and edn. Gulf-Coast Bible Coll., Houston, 1960-67, 75-85, Mid-Am. Bible Coll., Oklahoma City, 1985—. Contbr. articles to religious jours. Served as cpl. U.S. Army, 1953-55. Mem. Nat. Council Tchrs. of English, Christianity and Lit., Kappa Delta Pi. Home: 10304 Primrose Ln Oklahoma City OK 73159 Office: Mid-Am Bible Coll 3500 SW 119th St Oklahoma City OK 73170

BLANDFORD, SISTER MARGARET VINCENT, infirmary executive; b. Lebanon, Ky., Oct. 27, 1920; d. John Martin and Mary Lyda (O'Daniel) B.; R.N., St. Joseph's Sch. Nursing, 1941; B.S. in Nursing Edn., Spalding Coll., 1952; postgrad. Sloan Inst. Hosp. Adminstrn., Cornell U., 1962. Asst. adminstr. St. Joseph's Hosp., Lexington, Ky., 1949-54; adminstr. St. Vincent Infirmary, Little Rock, 1955-61, pres., chief exec. officer, chmn. bd., 1971—; hosp. coordinator Hosps. of Sisters of Charity, Nazareth, Ky., 1961-71; chmn. bd. govs. Am. Health Congress, 1971-72; mem. exec. com. Ark. Regional Med. Program; mem. U.S. Cath. Health Conf., 1974-77; mem. med. morals com. Diocese of Ark., 1973-76; bd. dirs. Our Lady of Peace Hosp., Louisville, 1973-79; dir. Worthen Bank & Trust Co., 1974-86. Bd. dirs. United Way Pulaski County, 1978, Central Ark. Radiation Therapy Inst., 1974-82. Central Ark. Health Systems Agy., 1980-83; v.p. chpt. NCCJ, 1972-82, pres., 1982—. Named Woman of Yr., Greater Little Rock, 1960; recipient A. Allen Weintraub award, 1980; 100 Ark. Women of Achievement award, 1980, Humanitarian award Ark. Council on Brotherhood NCCJ, 1985; named Ark. Citizen of Yr., March of Dimes, 1986. Fellow Am. Coll. Hosp. Adminstrs.; mem. Am. Hosp. Assn. (ho. of dels. 1984—, mem. regional adv. bd. 1984), Ark. Conf. Cath. Hosps. (pres. 1957-59), Little Rock Hosp. Council (pres. 1960-61), Cath. Health. Assn. (sec. bd. trustees 1961-65, dir. 1966-71, pres. 1971-72), Ark. Hosp. Assn., Ark. (dir. 1978), Little Rock, (exec. com. 1978-82, 84—), Met. (dir. 1978) chambers commerce. Contbr. article to profl. jour. Home: 5800 A St Little Rock AR 72201 Office: St Vincent Infirmary Two St Vincent Circle Little Rock AR 72205

BLANFORD, GEORGE EMMANUEL, physics and astronomy educator; b. Lebanon, Ky., Sept. 16, 1940; s. George Emmanuel and Catherine Josephine (Hardesty) B.; m. Juliane Maney, Aug. 7, 1971 (div. 1981); children—Elizabeth Braznell, Peter Emmanuel. B.A., Cath. U. Am., 1964; M.S., U. Louisville, 1967; Ph.D., Washington U., St. Louis, 1971. Resident research assoc. NASA Johnson Space Ctr., Houston, 1973-75; postdoctoral fellow Lunar Sci. Inst., Houston, 1975; asst. prof. U. Houston-Clear Lake, 1975-78, assoc. prof. physics and astronomy, 1978—. Contbr. articles to profl. jours. Recipient Spl. Recognition award NASA, 1979. Mem. AAAS, Am. Assn. Physics Tchrs., Am. Geophys. Union, Am. Astron. Soc., Am. Phys. Soc. Democrat. Roman Catholic. Clubs: J.S.C. Bicycle (pres. 1982-84); League Am. Wheelman. Avocations: bicycling; scuba diving; photography; gardening. Office: U Houston-Clear Lake 2700 Bay Area Blvd Houston TX 77058

BLANK, A(NDREW) RUSSELL, lawyer; b. Bklyn., June 13, 1945; s. Lawrence and Joan B.; children—Adam, Marisa. Student U. N.C., 1963-64; B.A., U. Fla., 1966, postgrad. Law Sch., 1966-68; J.D., U. Miami, 1970. Bar: Ga. 1971, Fla. 1970. Diplomate Am. Bd. Trial Advocacy (advocate). Law asst. Dist. Ct. Judge, Atlanta, 1970-72; sole practice law, Atlanta, 1972—. Mem. pub. adv. com. Atlanta Regional Commn., 1972-74. Recipient Merit award Ga. Bar Assn., 1981. Ga. Bar Assn., Ga. Trial Lawyers Assn., Fed. Assn. Atlanta, Lawyers Club Atlanta, ABA, Am. Trial Lawyers Assn., Fla. Bar Assn., Nat. Bd. Trial Advocacy (civil trial specialist). Address: 405 Bainbridge Dr Altanta GA 30327

BLANK, ANITA MARIE, educator, coach; b. Columbia, Pa., Feb. 3, 1942; d. Thomas Metzger and Harriet Wolf (Rannels) B. B.S., Tufts U., 1964; M.S., Smith Coll., 1971. Cert. tchr., Tex. Tchr. sci. and phys. edn. Sedgwick Jr. High Sch., West Hartford, Conn., 1964-67; assoc. prof. Colby Jr. Coll., New London, N.H., 1967-70; tchr. phys. edn., volleyball coach McCallum High Sch., Austin, Tex., 1971—; co-dir. Colbytown Camp, New London, N.H., summers 1965, 67. Mem. NEA, Tex. Tchrs. Assn., Austin Assn. Tchrs., AAHPERD. Home: 5702 Ave F Austin TX 78752 Office: McCallum High School 5600 Sunshine Dr Austin TX 78756

BLANKENSHIP, DAVID BRUCE, real estate and investment executive, educator; b. Lubbock, Tex., Feb. 19, 1949; s. Wesley B. and Maxine Olson (Wiese) B.; m. Cheryl Hope Hedges, June 20, 1969; children—Brian David, Kevin Bruce. B.A., Tex. Tech U., 1971; M. Internat. Mgmt., Am. Grad. Sch. Internat. Mgmt., 1972. Mgr., Am. Express Internat. Banking Corp., Okinawa, Japan, 1972-73, dist. mgr., Taichung, Taiwan, 1973, Subic Bay, Philippines, 1973-74, credit officer, N.Y.C., 1974-75, London, 1975-76, asst. mgr., New Delhi, 1975-76, credit officer, N.Y.C., 1976-77, London, 1977-78; v.p. Blankenship Developments, Inc., Lubbock, Tex., 1978—; instr. dept. econs. Tex. Tech U., Lubbock, part-time, 1978-80; dir. Bank of West, Lubbock. Bd. dirs. Lubbock Cultural Affairs Com., 1980-83, Friends of the Library/Southwest Collection, Tex. Tech. U. Mem. Lubbock C. of C. (mem. internat. trade com. 1979—), Internat. Council Shopping Ctrs., Nat. Assn. Bus. Economists, Mensa. Lodge: Rotary. Office: PO Box 5246 Lubbock TX 79417

BLANKENSHIP, EARL RANDOLPH, JR., architect; b. Lynchburg, Va., Mar. 1, 1956; s. Earl Randolph and Eliza (McDaniel) B. B.Arch., U. Va., 1978. Registered architect, Va. Draftsman, J. Everette Fauber, Jr., FAIA, Lynchburg, 1974-78, Frank Folsom Smith, AIA, Charlottesville, Va., 1978; project architect Odell Assocs. Inc., Richmond, Va., 1978-84; sr. architect Va. Power, Richmond, 1984-85; dir. architecture Strategic Design Group, Richmond, 1985—. Adviser youth group St. Paul's Episcopal Ch., Richmond, 1983—. Mem. AIA, Va. Mus., Va. Hist. Soc., Nat. Trust Hist. Preservation, U. Va. Alumni Assn., Delta Tau Delta. Republican. Avocations: tennis; piano; ante-bellum house renovation; travel. Home: 2324 E Marshall St Richmond VA 23223

BLANKENSHIP, JAMES ROBERT, JR., marketing executive; b. Paducah, Ky., Aug. 8, 1941; s. James Robert and Nell (Mitchell) B.; m. Icle Elain, July 1, 1964; children—Susan Elain, Mary Nell. Student, U. Ala.-Tuscaloosa, 1959-61. Draftsman Army Ballistic Missile, Huntsville, Ala., 1960, Brown Engring. Co., 1961-64; supr. Trans-Data Inc., Huntsville, 1964-66; elec. designer SCI Inc., Huntsville, 1966-75; designer Monsanto, Guntersville, 1975-80; fed. mktg. dir. Copy Right Enterprises, Inc., Huntsville, 1980—. Mem. Assn. of Info. Systems Profls. (dir.), Jaycees. Mem. Ch. of Christ. Lodge: Lions (chpt. pres. 1978-79, dept. dist. gov. Ala. 1979-80). Home: 1700 Palmer St Guntersville AL 35976 Office: Copy Right Enterprises Inc 7920 Charlotte Dr Suite 1 Huntsville AL 35802

BLANKENSHIP, JO ANN FORBES, nursing coordinator; b. Elizabethton, Tenn., Dec. 18, 1939; d. William Milburn and Florence Anna (Oxendine) Forbes; m. George Wallace Blankenship, Sr., Aug. 10, 1963; 1 child, George Wallace, Jr. B.S. in Nursing, East Tenn. State U., 1984. Cert. operating room nurse, Tenn. Charge nurse Carter County Hosp., Elizabethton, 1960-61; staff nurse VA, Johnson City, Tenn., 1961-79, head nurse, 1979-81, supervision coordinator, 1981—. Mem. Tri-Cities Assn. Operating Room Nurses (pres., bd. dirs. 1981—), Tenn. Nurses Assn., Am. Nurses Assn. (cert. in nursing adminstrn.), State of Franklin Assn. Operating Room Nurses. Democrat.

Methodist. Avocations: reading; traveling; crafts. Home: Route 8 Box 363 Johnson City TN 37601 Office: VA Mountain Home TN 37684

BLANKENSHIP, LINDA MANLEY, safety engineer; b. Knoxville, Tenn., Mar. 1, 1939; s. Hal Clinton and Katherine (Lee) Manley; married (div. 1972); children—D. Lynn Spruill, Frank C. Spruill, III; m. John Guy Blankenship, June 6, 1978. B.A., U. Tenn., 1976; M.P.H. in Environ., Occupational Health and Safety, 1983. Process safety analyst Martin Marietta Energy Systems, Inc., Oak Ridge, 1978-84, safety engr., 1984—; mem. chem. sect. and off-the-job safety standing com. Nat. Safety Council, Chgo., 1985—; conv. speaker on off-the-job injury econs. Nat. Safety Congress, Chgo., 1984, Western N.Y. Safety Conf., Buffalo, 1985, Tenn. Safety Congress, Nashville, 1985. Mem. Am. Soc. Safety Engrs. (pres. East Tenn. 1985-86, vice pres. 1984-85, sec. 1983-84, tech. session chmn. 1984, Safety Profl. of Yr. award 1985). Club: Martin Marietta Energy Systems Toastmasters (Oak Ridge). Avocations: reading; travel; bridge. Home: 101 Umbria Lane Oak Ridge TN 37830 Office: Martin Marietta Energy Systems Inc Y-12 Plant Bldg 9706-1 MS-1 Oak Ridge TN 37831

BLANKENSHIP, LYTLE HOUSTON, wildlife research scientist, educator; b. Campbellton, Tex., Mar. 1, 1927; s. Sidney Young and Amanda Elizabeth (Judd) B.; m. Margaret Lee Luecke, July 30, 1954; children—Terry Lynn, Kerry Jon, Jerry Alan, Sheri Ann. B.S., Tex. A&M U., 1950; M.S., U. Minn., 1952; Ph.D., Mich. State U., 1956. Cert. wildlife biologist. Game biologist Mich. Dept. Conservation, Lansing, 1954-56; research biologist Minn. Div. Game & Fish, St. Paul, 1956-61, U.S. Fish & Wildlife Service, Tucson, 1961-69; research scientist Caesar Kleberg wildlife program Tex. A&M U., Nairobi, Kenya, 1969-72; prof., research scientist Tex. Agrl. Expt. Sta., Uvalde, 1972—; cons. World Bank in Kenya, Orgn. Am. States in Dominican Republic; vis. lectr. Univ. Dar es Salaam, Tanzania, 1978; workshop cons. for U.S. Fish and Wildlife Service to India, 1981, 82. Contbr. numerous articles to profl. jours. Trustee, Uvalde Community Christian Sch. Wildlife Mgmt. Inst. grantee, 1950-51; Mich. State U. fellow; People-to-People program fellow, 1968. Mem. The Wildlife Soc. (internat. affairs com. 1971-86, pres. 1986—, Outstanding Service award Tex. chpt.), Wildlife Disease Assn., East African Wildlife Soc., Wildlife Soc. South Africa, Audubon Soc. Council for Agrl. Science and Tech., Sigma Xi. Democrat. Baptist. Clubs: Uvalde Lions, Lions Internat. (dist. gov. 1981-82), Uvalde County Aggie, Uvalde Band and Choir Booster (pres. 1974-75). Home: Batesville Star Route Box 979 Uvalde TX 78801 Office: Tex A&M Univ 1619 Garner Field Rd Uvalde TX 78801

BLANKSTEEN, MERRILL, savings and loan executive, economist; b. Springfield, Mass., Dec. 1, 1953; s. Saul C. and Carolyn H. (Alexander) B.; m. Christina N. Salo, Aug. 2, 1980; children—Melissa, Anthony. B.A., Fla. Atlantic U., 1974, M.A., 1975. Economist, Gen. Services Adminstrn., Washington, 1975; corp. planning analyst AmeriFirst Fed. Savs. and Loan, Miami, Fla., 1976-81, div. v.p., economist, 1981—. Mem. Gov.'s Econ. Adv. Com., Tallahassee, Fla., 1981-84; mem. tech. adv. com. United Way, Miami, 1982; pvt. sector vol. Area Agy. on Aging, Miami, 1984—. Mem. Miami Bus. Economists Assn. (pres. 1984-85), South Fla. Econ. Soc., Nat. Assn. Bus. Economists, Am. Econs. Assn. Home: 901 NE 74 St Miami FL 33138 Office: AmeriFirst Fed Savs and Loan 1 SE 3 Ave Miami FL 33131

BLANTON, FRED, JR., lawyer; b. Muscle Shoals, Ala., July 2, 1919; s. Fred and Mary (Covington) B.; A.B., Birmingham-So. Coll., 1939; J.D., U. Va., 1942; postgrad. U. Ala., summer 1946; postgrad. U. Mich., 1951; LL.M. in Taxation, U. Ala., 1979; m. Mercer Potts McAvoy, Aug. 11, 1962. Bar: Ala. 1946. Pvt. practice law, Birmingham, Ala., 1946-48; prof. Dickinson Sch. Law, Carlisle, Pa., 1948-49; vis. prof. law U. Ala., Tuscaloosa, summer 1949; asst. prof. law U. Va., Charlottesville, 1949-51; asso. firm Martin & Blakey, Attys., Birmingham, 1951-54; pvt. practice law, Birmingham, 1954-83, Gardendale, Ala., 1983—. Served with USNR, 1942-46. Mem. Ala. Bar Assn. Republican. Episcopalian. Contbr. articles to profl. jours. Home: 1912 KC DeMent Ave Fultondale AL 35068 Office: PO Box 15 Fultondale AL 35068

BLANTON, HOOVER CLARENCE, lawyer; b. Green Sea, S.C., Oct. 13, 1925; s. Clarence Leo and Margaret (Hoover) S.; J.D., U. S.C., 1953; m. Cecilia Lopez, July 31, 1949; children—Lawson Hoover, Michael Lopez. Admitted to S.C. bar, 1953; since practiced in Columbia; mem. firm Whaley & McCutchen, 1953-66, Whaley, McCutchen, Blanton & Richardson, 1967-72, Whaley, McCutchen, Blanton & Dent, 1973-74, Whaley, McCutchen & Blanton, 1974-81, Whaley, McCutchen, Blanton & Rhodes, 1981—; bd. dirs. Legal Aid Service Agy., Columbia, chmn., 1972-73. Gen. counsel S.C. Republican Party, 1963-66; pres. Richland County Rep. Conv., 1962; del. Rep. State Convs., 1962, 64, 66, 68, 70, 74. Bd. dirs. Midlands Community Action Agy., Columbia, vice chmn., 1972-73; mem. Gov.'s Legal Services Adv. Council, 1976-77; mem. Commn. on Continuing Legal Edn. for Judiciary, 1977-84, named lifetime mem., 1984. Served with USNR, 1942-46, 50-52. Mem. S.C. Bar (mem. ho. of dels. 1975-76, chmn. fee disputes bd. 1977-81), Am., Richland County (pres. 1980) bar assns., S.C. Def. Trial Attys. Assn., Am. Bd. Trial Advocates, Def. Research Inst., Assn. Ins. Attys. (state chmn. 1971-77, 80—, exec. council 1977-80), Phi Delta Phi. Baptist (deacon). Club: Toastmasters (pres. 1959). Assoc. editor S.C. Law Quar. Home: 3655 Deerfield Dr Columbia SC 29204 Office: 1414 Lady St Columbia SC 29201

BLANTON, JACK SAWTELLE, oil company executive; b. Shreveport, La., Dec. 7, 1927; s. William Neal and Louise (Wynn) B.; B.A., U. Tex., 1947, LL.B., 1950; m. Laura Lee Scurlock, Aug. 20, 1949; children—Elizabeth Louise (Mrs. Peter Staub Wareing), Jack Sawtelle, Eddy Scurlock. Bar: Tex. 1950. With Scurlock Oil Co., Houston, 1950—, v.p., 1956-58, pres., 1958—, dir., 1956—; v.p. Eddy Refining Co.; dir. Quanex Corp., Southwestern Bell Telephone Co., Tex. Commerce Bank N.A. Trustee, vice chmn. exec. com. Meth. Hosp.; past chmn. bd. trustees St. Luke's United Meth. Ch., Houston. Named Houston's outstanding young man of year, 1960. Mem. Tex. Mid-Continent Oil and Gas Assn. (past pres.), Houston C. of C. (life), Sons Rep. of Tex. (past pres. San Jacinto chpt.). Sam Houston Meml. Assn., Nat. Tennis Assn., U.S. Lawn Tennis Assn., Am. Petroleum Inst. (dir.). Tex. Ind. Oil Producers and Refiners. Ex-Students Assn. U. Tex. (past pres.). Delta Kappa Epsilon, Phi Delta Phi, Phi Alpha Delta. Clubs: Houston (past pres.), River Oaks Country (Houston). Office: Houston Club Bldg Houston TX 77002*

BLANTON, JAMES CLEVELAND, JR., insurance company executive; b. Nichols, S.C., June 9, 1930; s. James Cleveland and Emma Vincia (Hooks) B.; m. Catherine Porter Hamilton, Oct. 31, 1953; children—James Cleveland, Alfred H., A. Clarke, Catherine, Clifton M. B.A., U. S.C., 1955; LL.B., Miss. Coll. Sch. Law, 1959. Bar: Miss. 1960. Chief investigator U.S. Refugee Program, Frankfurt, Germany, 1955-57; exec. trainee Allstate Ins. Co., Jackson, Miss., 1957-62; with legal dept. Carolina Casualty Ins. Co., Jacksonville, Fla., 1962-69, pres., dir., 1970—; chmn. bd. dirs. Comml. Gen. Agy., Jacksonville, 1970—; chmn. bd. dirs., pres. Transp. Claims Service, 1981—; dir. S.E. Bank; bd. dirs. Fla. Ins. Council, 1978-79. Trustee Jacksonville Symphony Assn., 1978-80, pres., 1978-80; trustee Bartram Sch., Jacksonville, 1975-83; active Jacksonville C. of C., mem. com. of 100. Mem. Miss. Bar Assn., ABA, Am. Bar Assn. Fedn., Ins. Counsel, Internat. Assn. Ins. Counsel, Fla. Ins. Council. Republican. Episcopalian. Clubs: Fla. Yacht, River, Ponte Vedra, Meninak. Author: Businessmen's Guide to Insurance, 1981; Truckers' Liability Claims, 1984. Home: 3919 Baltic Ave Jacksonville FL 32210 Office: Carolina Casualty Ins Co PO Box 2575 Jacksonville FL 32203

BLANTON, JOE, supermarket company executive; b. 1908. With Publix Super Markets Inc., Lakeland, Fla., 1930—, v.p., 1954-73, pres., chief operating officer, 1973—, also dir. Office: Publix Super Markets Inc 2040 George Jenkins Blvd Lakeland FL 33802*

BLANTON, JOHN RALSTON, oil executive, rancher, businessman, banker; b. Pineland, Tex., Sept. 14, 1935; s. Ralph Ralston and Sally B. (Richardson) B.; m. Sally Sappington, Sept. 9, 1959 (div. 1983); children—Bryan, Brent, Whitney. B.A. in Geology, Tex. Christian U., 1960. Pres., Hughes-Blanton, Inc., 1970-81, Trojan Drilling & Operating Co., Inc., Dallas, 1981—, U.S. Operating, Inc., Dallas, 1982—; dir. Northway Nat. Bank, Richardson Nat. Bank, Northway BancShares. Assoc. Dallas Mus. Fine Arts; mem. found. for N.Am. Wild Sheep, Game Conservation Internat., Summer Music Guild, Fellowship Christian Athletes, YMCA, 500, Inc., Tex. and SW Cattle Breeders Assn., N. Tex. Simmetal Assn. (dir. 1977). Served with Air N.G., 1959-65. Mem. Chief Exec. Round Table, Internat. Assn. Drilling Contractors, N.Tex. State U. Pres. Council. Republican. Methodist. Clubs: Dallas Gun, Dallas Woods and Water, Dallas Safari (dir. 1978-80), Ducks Unlimited. Home: 4207 Windsor Pkwy Dallas TX 75205 Office: 5950 Berkshire Ln #300 Dallas TX 75205

BLANTON, ROBERT D'ALDEN, anthropology and history educator; b. Gastonia, N.C., Jan. 4, 1943; s. Buford Webb and Naomi (Gibson) B. A.A., Mars Hill Coll., 1961; B.S., Appalachian State U., 1963, M.A., 1967; postgrad. U. Colo., U. Americas, Mex., U. Guadalajara, Mex. Assoc. prof. anthropology and history Gaston Coll., Dallas, N.C., 1969-75, prof., 1975—, dept. chmn., 1975—, study tours dir., 1978—. County chmn. Am's. 400th Anniversary Com., Gaston County, 1984—, Friendship Force of N.C., 1983-84; bd. dirs. Schiele Mus., 1982—, Am. Field Service, Gastonia, 1981—; active Gaston County Democratic com., 1980—. Named Outstanding Educator, Gaston Coll., 1980. Mem. N.C. Assn. Educators, N.C. Archaeol. Soc., Pi Gamma Mu. Baptist. Avocations: gardening; weight-lifting; swimming; cycling. Home: 1640 S New Hope Rd Gastonia NC 28054 Office: Social Sci Dept Gaston Coll Dallas NC 28034

BLASING, TERENCE JACK, bioclimatologist; b. Waukesha, Wis., Dec. 16, 1943; s. Jack Lester and Alice Marie (Granger) B.; m. Carolyn Birch, Nov. 4, 1967; children—Jill Marie, Keith Malcolm. B.S., U. Wis.-Madison, 1966, M.S., 1968, Ph.D., 1975. Research assoc. Lab. Tree-Ring Research, U. Ariz., Tucson, 1971-77; research assoc. Environmental Scis., Oak Ridge Nat. Lab., 1977-84, mem. research staff, 1984—; adj. asst. prof. geography dept. U. Tenn., 1981—. Mem. Appalachian Zool. Soc., Am. Meteorol. Soc., Am. Geophys. Union, Sigma Xi. Methodist. Lodge: Masons. Contbr. articles to profl. jours. Home: 1145 Lovell View Dr Knoxville TN 37922 Office: Bldg 1505 PO Box X ORNL Oak Ridge TN 37830

BLASINGAME, ELBERT GENE, insurance agency executive; b. Galena Park, Tex., Feb. 17, 1942; s. Elbert Gee and Letha Robelle (Casey) B.; m. Patricia Ella Thompson, May 8, 1976; children—Ricky Quin, Herbert William, Suzanne Elayne, Mark Wayne, Judith Gayle, Katherine Sue. Student San Jacinto Coll., 1961-64. Police officer City of Galena Park, 1965-67, city of Jacinto City (Tex.), 1964-65; rate clk. Ryder Truck Lines, 1961-64, 67-74; traffic mgr. Jefferson Chem. Co., Houston, 1974-75; owner, mgr. Blasingame Ins. Agy., Houston, 1975—. Mem. Mem. Ind. Ins. Agts. Am., Ind. Ins. Agts. Tex., Ind. Ins. Agts. Houston, Nat. Fedn. Ind. Businessmen, North Channel C. of C. (founding bd. dirs., 1st v.p.), Jacinto City C. of C. (pres. 1983-84), Aircraft Owners and Pilots Assn. Democrat. Baptist. Clubs: Rotary, Masons, Gideons. Office: 1210 Holland Ave Houston TX 77029

BLASINGAME, WILBUR BURNARD, physician; b. Cin., Jan. 3, 1913; s. James Henry and Bennie (Fields) B.; m. Naomi Gillette, Oct. 26, 1943, (div. 1946); 1 child, James Edward. Grad. Kirksville Coll. of Osteo. Medicine, 1937; D.O. U. Ga., 1970. Diplomate Am. Bd. of Osteo. Medicine; lic. in medicine and surgery, Ga. Gen. practice medicine, Cordele, Ga., 1937—; mem. U. of Ga. Med. C.M.E. Program, Augusta, 1970—; mem. staff Sumpter Regional Hosp. C.M.E., Americus, Ga., 1980—; trustee Scottish Rite Childrens Hosp., Atlanta, 1978—, Ga. Ednl. Found., Macon, Atlanta, 1980—. Deputy sheriff Crisp County Sheriff Dept., Cordele, 1981—; mem. Salvation Army Service Unit, Macon, 1984. Mem. Psi Sigma Alpha, Alpha Tau Sigma (pres. 1937). Lodges: Scottish Rite (33 deg., Temple trustee 1974—), Shriners (ambassador 1974—), Jesters, Masons (33 deg.). Avocation: bass fishing. Home and Office: 411 6th St S Cordele GA 31015

BLASIUS, JACK MICHAEL, aluminum company executive; b. Atlanta, Feb. 29, 1932; s. Arthur George and Jessie Lee (Pate) B.; B.S. Indsl. Mgmt. and Accounting, U. Ala., 1954, M.B.A. in Mktg., 1957; m. Sybil Claire Watkins, Oct. 12, 1957; children—Michael Stribling, Kimberly Anne. Successively indsl. salesman, area sales mgr., nat. mgr. foundry ingot products Kaiser Aluminum Corp.; pres., gen. mgr. Batchelder-Blasius, Inc., Spartanburg, S.C., 1966—, also dir.; partner LBE Investment Co., Consol. Investments, Inc. (both Spartanburg); dir. Whitehead Leasing Corp., Atlanta, Charles Batchelder Co., Botsford, Conn., Statewide Waste Oil & Chem. Corp., Spartanburg, 1st Nat. Bank, Spartanburg. Mem. Spartanburg City Council; exec. dir. Spartanburg YMCA; scholarship donor Clemson U.; trustee Spartanburg Day Sch.; bd. dirs. Spartanburg Girls' Home, Doctors Meml. Hosp., Spartanburg, Jr. Achievement, Spartanburg; mem. chmn.'s com. U.S. Senatorial Bus. Adv. Bd.; mem. Republican Inner Circle; mem. pres.'s club Wofford Coll., Spartanburg; mem. trustee's club Spartanburg Methodist Coll.; mem. founders club U. Ala., Tuscaloosa; mem. thousand club Ga. Inst. Tech., Atlanta. Served with U.S. Army; ETO. Mem. Soc. Die Casting Engrs., Am. Foundryman Soc., Inst. Scrap Iron and Steel, Aluminum Recycling Assn., Aluminum Recycling Assn. (dir., v.p., chmn. govt. liaison com.), Spartanburg Devel. Assn., Spartanburg C. of C. (dir.), U. Ala. Alumni Assn. Republican. Presbyterian. Clubs: Rotary (dir.), Spartanburg Country, Piedmont (Spartanburg); Atlanta Athletic, Ansley Golf (Atlanta); Founder's. Home: 8891 Greenville Hwy Spartanburg SC 29304 Office: Batchelder Blasius PO Box 5503 Spartanburg SC 29304

BLASSICK, JOHN EDWARD, architect, executive; b. Evanston, Ill., Nov. 27, 1935; s. Jack A. and Helen Katherine (Haisman) B.; m. Barbara Mae McDoniel, Sept. 1, 1957; children—John, Jr., Kenneth Allan, Susie Katherine Irene. B.Arch., U. Ill., 1958. Registered architect, Wis., Fla., Ga. Designer Knodle & Baucon, Beloit, Wis., 1958-64; designer, architect Flad & Assocs., Madison, Wis., 1964-68, architect, project mgr., 1968-79; pres. Flad & Assocs., Gainesville, Fla., 1979—. Mem. Exchange Club, Madison, 1970-79. Recipient Honor award for design Bell System, 1975. Mem. AIA (Honor Award Design 1968, 1976, Merit Award Design 1974). Lutheran. Club: Gator Golf Booster. Avocations: golf; fishing. Home: 6424 SW 37th Way Gainesville FL 32608 Office: Flad & Assocs Fla Inc 3300 SW Archer RD Gainesville FL 32608

BLATT, SOLOMON, JR., U.S. district judge; b. Sumter, S.C., Aug. 20, 1921; s. Solomon and Ethel (Green) B.; m. Carolyn Gaden, Sept. 12, 1942; children—Gregory, Sheryl Blatt Hooper, Brian. A.B., U. S.C., 1941, LL.B., 1946. Ptnr. firm Blatt & Fales, Barnwell, S.C., 1946-71; U.S. dist. judge S.C., Charleston, 1971—. Office: PO Box 835 Charleston SC 29402*

BLAU, ZENA SMITH, sociology educator; b. N.Y.C., Aug. 4, 1922; d. Joseph and Lena K. Smith; m. Peter M. Blau, Aug. 7, 1948 (div. 1968); 1 dau., Pamela L. A.B., Wayne State U., 1943, M.S.W., 1946; Ph.D., Columbia U., 1957. Asst. prof. U. Ill. Med. Center-Chgo., 1957-65; sr. research scientist Inst. Juvenile Research, Chgo., 1965-75; assoc. prof. Northwestern U., 1969-74; prof. Ritchmond Coll., CUNY, 1975-76; prof. sociology U. Houston, 1976—, chmn. dept. sociology, 1976-79. HEW Social and Rehab. Adminstrn. grantee, 1967-72; Tex. Dept. Human Resources grantee, 1977-79. Mem. Am. Sociol. Assn., Am. Gerontol. Soc., Sociologist for Women in Soc., Soc. for Study Social Probelms. Author: Old Age in a Changing Society, 1973, 2d edit., Aging in a Changing Society, 1981; Black Children/White Children: Competence, Socialization and Social Structure, 1981; contbr. articles to profl. jours. Office: Dept Sociology U Houston University Park Houston TX 77004

BLAYLOCK, MABRY GENE, tutor; b. Hammon, Okla., Apr. 17, 1927; s. Charles Jasper and Dollie B. B.A. in Letters, U. Okla., 1952, M.A. in Spanish, 1953. U. Okla. press fellow, Norman, 1953-54, athletic dept. tutor, 1953-55; profl. tutor, Norman, 1954—. Author: How to Study and Like It, 1973. Contbr. articles to profl. jours. Democrat. Mem. Phi Beta Kappa. Paraplegic, 1941—. Home and Office: 702 Normandie Dr Norman OK 73072-3224

BLAYNEY, KEITH DALE, university administrator, consultant; b. Anamosa, Iowa, Feb. 8, 1937; s. Darrell Price and Evelyn Mae (Thompson) B.; m. Joyce Ann Bryan, Sept. 14, 1958 (div. 1978); children—Michael Bryan, Steven Price. B.Sc., U. Iowa, 1959, M.S., 1961, Ph.D., 1966. Adminstr. U. Ala. Hosps., Birmingham, 1969-71; dean Sch. Community and Allied Health U. Ala., Birmingham, 1971—; hosp. adminstr., cons. to China Project HOPE, 1983—. Contbr. articles to profl. jours. Hon. bd. dirs. Xian Med. U., People's Republic of China, 1984. Served to 1st lt. USAF, 1961-64. Recipient 50th Anniversary commendation AMA, 1978; Am. Soc. Allied Health Professions fellow, 1984. Fellow Am. Coll. Hosp. Adminstrs. Unitarian. Avocation: fishing. Office: U Ala Sch Community and Allied Health University Station Birmingham AL 35294

BLAZER, JOHN ALLISON, marriage and family counselor; b. Nashville, Apr. 18, 1930; s. John Payne and Henryetta (Rowland) B.; B.S., Coll. William and Mary, 1959; M.S., Va. Commonwealth U., 1960; Ph.D., Free Protestant Episcopal U., 1962. Staff psychologist Mental Health Clinic, Bristol, Va., 1963-64; sr. clin. psychologist Mental Health Clinic, Savannah, Ga., 1964-74; dir. Savannah Testing Service, 1974-78; dir. Marriage and Family Counseling Center, Madison, Tenn., 1978—; cons. in field. Served with USMC, 1948-53. Decorated Purple Heart. Lic. profl. counselor, Va., social worker, Md.; cert. profl. marriage counselor; diplomate Am. Bd. Examiners in Psychotherapy. Mem. Am. Assn. Sex Educators, Counselors and Therapists, Am. Group Psychotherapy Assn., Am. Personnel and Guidance Assn., Am. Psychotherapy Assn., Nat. Psychol. Assn. Editor: Psychology, 1962-79; editorial advisor: Education, 1970—; cons. editor Educators and Psychologists Press, 1970—; editorial bd. Instructional Psychology, 1973—. Office: 1994 Gallatin Rd N Suite 301 Madison TN 37115

BLEDSOE, MARGARET ANN, occupational therapist, educator, consultant; b. Burbank, Calif., Feb. 18, 1952; d. William Terrell and Doris Ella (Goulding) B. A.A. in Gen. Edn., Pierce Jr. Coll., 1975; B.S. in Occupational Therapy, San Jose State U., 1977; M.S., La. Tech. U., 1984; M.A. in Psychology, Human Relations and Supervision. Registered occupational therapist, La. Occupational therapist Children's Hosp. and Med. Ctr., Oakland, Calif., 1981-82; pvt. practice cons., San Mateo, Calif., 1981-82; instr. N.E. La. U., Monroe, 1982-84; data collector Western Psychol. Services, Los Angeles, 1984; administrv. asst. Ouachita Community Action Program, Monroe, 1984-85; staff occupational therapist Garden Sullivan Rehab. Ctr., San Francisco, 1979-80, Garden Sullivan Learning and Devel. Program, 1979-82; occupational therapist cons. Daniel Webster Elem. Sch., Daley City, Calif., 1981-82. Ednl. scholar Calif. Found. Occupational Therapy, 1981. Mem. Am. Occupational Therapy Assn. (vice chmn. nat. student com. 1977, chmn. 1978-80, sgt.-at-arms rep. assembly 1980—, rep. for Calif. 1985-87), Occupational Therapy Assn. Calif. (sec. Golden Gate chpt. 1979, co-chmn. state conf. 1981), Ctr. for Study of Sensory Integration Dysfunction, Am. Soc. Tng. and Devel., Am. Assn. Counseling and Devel., Gamma Beta Phi. Republican. Avocations: travel; entertaining.

BLEDSOE, RUTH ERLENE, dept. store exec.; b. Oklahoma City, May 21, 1935; d. Clayton Eschol and Dollie Marie (Bradbury) Ellis; A.A., Oklahoma City Southwestern Coll., 1980; student Oklahoma City Sch. Banking and Bus.; divorced; children—Ivan Gene, Rebecca Diane, William Travis. With John A. Brown, Oklahoma City, 1968-80, accounts payable and import mgr., 1969-80; asst. accounts payable mgr. Neiman-Marcus, Dallas, 1980-82; accounts payable mgr. Dillard Corp., Little Rock, 1982—. Mem. Internat. Female Execs. Club, Oklahoma City Internat. Assn. (chmn. reception com. 1979), Internat. Trade Assn. Democrat. Mem. Pentecostal Holiness Ch. Home: 2400 McCain Blvd #1117 North Little Rock AR 72116 Office: 900 W Capitol St Little Rock AR 72203

BLEIMANN, KARL RICHARD, steel company executive; b. Siegen, W. Germany, Aug. 19, 1934; came to U.S., 1969; s. Friedrich and Irmgard (Kaufmann) B.; m. Rena J. Eggert, Aug. 21, 1964; children—Gregor, Joern, Tino. M.S., Clausthal U., W. Germany, 1959. Asst. supt. meltshop Stahlwerke Bochum, W. Germany, 1959-66; supt. meltshop Edelstahlwerke Witten, W. Ger., 1967; supt. meltshop Georgetown Steel Corp., Georgetown, S.C., 1969-70; asst. v.p. Korf Industries, Charlotte, N.C., 1970-78, exec. v.p. engring. Korf Technologies, Inc., Charlotte, N.C., 1978-79; pres. Korf & Fuchs Systems, Inc., Salisbury, N.C., 1979—. Mem. Assn. Iron and Steel Engrs., AIME, Nat. Geog. Soc., Roman Catholic. Club: Raintree Country. Home: 8201 Eagles Point Ct Charlotte NC 28105 Office: PO Box 379 Salisbury NC 28144

BLEIMANN, ROBERT LESLIE, project design and management consultant, researcher; b. N.Y.C., Aug. 27, 1947; s. J. Les. and Lois Catherine (Meier) B. B.A., Muhlenberg Coll., 1969; M.A., Lehigh U., 1970; Ph.D., U. Coll., London, Eng., 1975; CE credits USDA Grad. Sch., Washington, 1979. Cons., Orkand Corp., Silver Spring, Md., 1977; research assoc. Kramer Assocs., Washington, 1978-79, Koba Assocs., Washington, 1979-81; project mgr. Assn. Schs. and Colls. of Optometry, Washington, 1981-83; project mgr., coordinator research programs Am. Optometric Assn., Washington, 1983-85; sr. analyst Advanced Scis., Inc., Washington, 1985—; cons. RL Bleimann & Assocs., Arlington, Va., 1985—; cons. in field. Author articles, reports. Ticket taker Kennedy Ctr. for Performing Arts, Washington, 1977-84; mem. Arena Stage Assocs., Washington, 1984-85; team capt. USTA/Volvo League, No. Va., 1983-85. Named Fgn. Assoc. Mem. Royal Inst. Internat. Affairs, London, 1972. Mem. Am. Polit. Sci. Assn., Policy Studies Orgn. Presbyterian. Clubs: Ski, Badminton (Washington). Avocations: tennis; biking; theatre; classical music and opera. Home: 1600 S Joyce St Apt A-802 Arlington VA 22202

BLEND, STANLEY LOUIS, lawyer; b. Dallas, June 28, 1942; s. Jake and Henrietta (Boronstein) B.; m. Linda Freedman, Dec. 26, 1965; children—Michael Louis, Sheila Renee. B.A., Tulane U., 1964; J.D. cum laude, U. Houston, 1967; LL.M. in Taxation, Georgetown U., 1970. Bar: Tex. 1967. Mem. staff Office Chief Counsel, IRS, 1967-72; mem. Oppenheimer, Rosenberg, Kelleher & Wheatley, Inc., San Antonio, 1972—; dir. Summit Bank of San Antonio. Pres., treas., v.p. Jewish Fedn. San Antonio. Mem. Fed. Bar Assn. (pres. San Antonio chpt.), U. Houston Law Alumni Assn. (pres. San Antonio chpt.), State Bar Tex. (mem. council sect. taxation), ABA, San Antonio Bar Assn., Tex. Bar Assn. Contbr. articles to profl. jours. Home: 16427 Axis Trail San Antonio TX 78232 Office: Suite 620 711 Navarro San Antonio TX 78232

BLEVINS, GARY LYNN, architect, real estate broker; b. St. Charles, Ark., Feb. 17, 1941; s. Franklin Monroe and Frances Pauline (Breland) B.; B.S. in Architecture, U. Tex., 1964, B.Arch., 1969; M.B.A., So. Meth. U., 1974; postgrad. U. Tex., Dallas, 1975-76. Draftsman, Omniplan Architects, Dallas, 1969-70; project mgr. STB Architects, Dallas, 1970-71; designer Architectonics, Inc., Dallas, 1971-72; architect Envirodynamics, Inc., Dallas, 1973-75; architect/real estate broker Gary L. Blevins Co., Dallas, 1975-77, Trammell Crow Co., Dallas, 1977-83; pres. Gary L. Blevins AIA, Dallas, 1983—, Gable Cos., Dallas, 1983—; v.p., mgr. Farr Constrn. Co., Inc., Dallas, 1983-85; instr. El Centro Coll., 1981—. Served with USN, 1964-67; Vietnam. Registered architect, Tex., Fla.; lic. real estate broker, Tex.; cert. Nat. Council Archtl. Registration Bds., Constrn. Specifications Inst. Mem. AIA, Tex. Soc. Architects, Am. Planning Assn., Constrn. Specifications Inst., Nat. Assn. Realtors, Tex. Assn. Realtors, Greater Dallas Bd. Realtors, Dallas Mus. Fine Arts, Dallas Classic Guitar Soc., The 500, Dallas Symphony Assn. So. Meth. U. M.B.A. Assn., U.S. Tennis Assn., Tex. Tennis Assn., Dallas Tennis Assn. Republican. Methodist. Clubs: Exchange; POR Racquet. Home: 1026 Tranquilla Dallas TX 75218 Office: 2650 Lombardy Suite N Dallas TX 75220

BLEVINS, LOWELL ERWIN, engineer; b. Seymour, Mo., May 8, 1941; s. Orville Franklin and Blanche (Silvey) B.; m. Diane McKeel, June 15, 1962 (div. 1975); 1 child, Christopher; m. Sharon Sue Stone, Jan. 11, 1980. B.S., U. Okla., 1964; M.S., Western Mich. U., 1976. Registered profl. engr., Mich. Traffic engr. Gen. Telephone of Mich., Maskegon, 1970-75, supr. planning engr., 1975-79, sr. math. analyst, Stamford, Conn., 1980-83, sr. engr. Telecommunications System Ctr., Vienna, Va., 1983—. Served to capt. USAF, 1962-69. Mem. Am. Statis. Assn., Mensa. Avocations: gardening; amateur radio; beer making. Home: 13772 Vint Hill Rd Nokesville VA 22123 Office: GTE Telecommunications System Ctr 8330 Old Courthouse Rd Vienna VA 22180

BLEVINS, MELVIN LEE, physician; b. South Pittsburg, Tenn., Aug. 12, 1948; s. Robert Lee and Dorothy (Durham) B.; m. Betty Wright, Sept. 2, 1967 (div. 1978); 1 child, Michael; m. Jo Ann Minturn, Oct. 15, 1978; children—Jefry, Justin, Patrick. B.A., Vanderbilt U., 1969; M.D., U. Tenn., 1972. Intern Baptist Meml. Hosp., Memphis, 1973; physician, ptnr. in gen practice medicine, Smithville, Tenn., 1974—; owner, ptnr., administr. Doctor's Hosp., Smithville, 1982—, ptnr. ER Services, Smithville, 1985—. Mem. AMA, Am. Acad. Family Practice, Tenn. Med. Assn., Southern Med. Assn. Republican. Avocations: golfing; snowskiing; scuba diving. Office: 102 W Church St Smithville TN 37166

BLEVINS, MERRILL MAYHALL, consultant, former foreign service officer; b. Somerset, Ky., June 9, 1916; s. David Blucher and Nellye (Mayhall) B.; m. Esther Merriam, Sept. 14, 1946 (dec. 1968); children—Karen Lee, Katheryn Mary Anne; m. 2d, Susan Patricia Groom, Mar. 24, 1972. A.B., U. Ky., 1938; postgrad. U. Chgo., summer 1961. Personnel mgr. War Dept., 1940; joined U.S. Fgn. Service, 1947; asst. attché, Brussels, also The Hague, Luxembourg, 1947-48; econ. commr. Office Spl. Rep. for ECA, 1948-49; assigned Dept. State, 1949-51; attaché, Bonn, Germany, 1951-52, Bern, Switzerland, 1952-54, New Delhi, India, 1954-55; 1st sec., consul, Canberra, Australia, 1956-60; fgn. affairs officer Dept. State, 1961-65; U.S. dep. rep. to food agys. FAO, UN, Rome, 1965-68; ret., 1968; spl. asst. to asst. dir.-gen. for adminstrn. and fin. FAC,

Rome, 1968-71, protocol officer, chief protocol, 1972-79; cons., Alexandria, Va., 1979—; adminstr. Va. Trust Historic Preservation; asst. for presdl. visits abroad Dept. State, 1962-63; asst. to sec. Dept. Interior, 1964-65; sec.-gen. Internat. Symposium on Water Desalination, 1964-65. Served to capt. USAAF, 1942-46. Decorated Air medal with palm, Purple Heart; recipient Meritorious Service award Dept. Interior, 1965; named Ky. col., 1955. Mem. Diplomatic and Consular Officers Ret., Res. Officers Assn. of U.S., RAF Assn. London, SAR, Soc. of the Lees of Va., George Washington's Fire Engine Co., Delta Tau Delta, Pi Sigma Alpha, Phi Mu Alpha. Episcopalian. Club: Caterpillar (London). Home: Alexandria House Apt 510 400 Madison St Alexandria VA 22314 also Via Nicolo Paganini 7 00198 Rome Italy

BLEVINS, PHILLIP K., plastic surgeon, educator; b. Parmleysville, Ky., Mar. 30, 1942; s. Guy Kimble and Marie (Guffey) B.; student Berea Coll., 1959-61; A.B., U. Ky., 1963, M.D., 1967; m. MaryJo McDaniel, July 2, 1977. Intern, Univ. Hosp., Lexington, Ky., 1967-68; resident in gen. surgery Harvard surg. service Boston City Hosp., 1968-75; resident in plastic surgery U. Miss., 1975-77; asst. prof. surgery U. Ky. A.B. Chandler Med. Center, Lexington, 1977—; mem. staff St. Joseph Hosp., Good Samaritan Hosp., VA Hosp., Shriner's Hosp., Univ. Hosp., dir. Peoples State Bank, Monticello, Ky. Served with M.C., USN, 1969-71. Decorated U.S. Navy Commendation medal with V; medal of honor 1st class (Republic of Vietnam); recipient cert. appreciation Vietnam Ministry of Health, 1970; diplomate Am. Bd. Surgery, Am. Bd. Plastic Surgery. Fellow A.C.S., Southeastern Surg. Soc.; mem. AMA, N.Y. Acad. Scis., Fayette County Med. Soc., Ky. Med. Assn., Cleft Palate Assn., Ky. Soc. Plastic and Reconstructive Surgeons, Am. Burn Assn. Republican. Episcopalian. Club: Ky. Civil War Roundtable. Home: 3204 Pepperhill Rd Lexington KY 40502 Office: 1725 Harrodsburg Rd Lexington KY 40504

BLIGH, THOMAS JOSEPH, ophthalmic products manufacturing company executive; b. Bklyn., July 16, 1948; s. Henry Francis and Frances Beverly (Herbert) B.; m. Elaine Patricia Clark, Mar. 18, 1972; children—Thomas Christopher, Brian Patrick. B.A., Fairfield U., 1970; M.B.A. with distinction, N.Y. Inst. Tech., 1977. Sr. sales exec. Xerox Corp., Woodbury, N.Y., 1971-78; account exec. Forum Corp., Boston, 1978-79; ops. mgr. Pepsi Cola Mgmt. Inst., Purchase, N.Y., 1979; asst. to pres. Am. Hydron Co., Woodbury, N.Y., 1979-80, dir. mktg., 1980-81, dir. sales, 1982; v.p. mktg. CILCO, Inc., Huntington, W.Va., 1982—; cons. in bus., Rockville Center, N.Y., 1980-82; adj. prof. Adelphi U., 1981-82. Dad's Club scholar, 1966; Kiwanis scholar, 1966. Mem. Assn. MBA Execs., Fairfield Alumni Assn., Am. Soc. Tng. and Devel., Delta Mu Delta. Republican. Roman Catholic. Club: K.C. Home: 2 Pine Hills Dr Huntington WV 25705 Office: CILCO Inc 1616 13th Ave Huntington WV 25717

BLILEY, THOMAS JEROME, JR., congressman; b. Chesterfield County, Va., Jan. 28, 1932; s. Thomas J. and Carolyn F. B.; m. Mary Virginia Kelley, June 22, 1957; children—Mary Vaughan, Thomas Jerome III. B.A., Georgetown U., 1952. Pres. Joseph W. Bliley Funeral Home, 1972-80; mem. Congress from Va.; Vice-mayor Richmond City Council, 1968-70, mayor, 1970-77; past bd. dirs. Nat. League Cities; past pres. Va. Municipal League. Past bd. dirs. Crippled Children's Hosp., St. Mary's Hosp.; bd. visitors Va. Commonwealth U. Served with USN. Republican. Roman Catholic. Office: 214 Cannon House Office Bldg Washington DC 20515

BLITCH, JAMES BUCHANAN, architect; b. Charleston, S.C., Sept. 2, 1923; s. Norman Henry and Louise (Buchanan) B.; m. Hilda Goodspeed Mouledoux, Nov. 24, 1945; children—James Buchanan, John Crandell, Ronald Buchanan, Judith Ann (dec.), Courtney Ann, David Alan, Leslie Anne, Lisl Maria. B.Arch., Tulane U., 1950. Owner J. Buchanan Blitch & Assocs., 1958-66; pres. J. Buchanan Blitch & Assoc., Inc., 1966-78; chmn. Blitch Architects, Inc., New Orleans, 1978—; vis. lectr. U. Southwestern La. Sch. Architecture; archdiocesan cons. on facilities for aged. Prin. works include Vatican Pavilion, other New Orleans World's Fair structures; homes for aged, religious, med. and ednl. facilities throughout Gulf South.; contbg. author: Housing for a Maturing Population, Urban Land Inst. Pres. adv. council Jesuit High Sch.; mem. bd. Holy Cross High Sch.; Trustee Assoc. Catholic Charities, St. Mary's Dominican Coll., Schimek Meml. Eye Found.; pres. St. Elizabeth's Home for Girls, East Jefferson Hosp. Found.; chmn. Abita Springs Planning Commn.; pres. St. Tammany Parish Hist. Soc.; mem. panel of arbitrators Am. Arbitration Assn. Served with USNR, 1943-45. Recipient 23 honor awards for design Nat. Guild for Religious Architecture, Gulf States region AIA, Am. Planning Assn., La. Architects Assn.; Named papal Knight of Holy Sepulchre New Orleans Archdiocesan Order of St. Louis. Fellow A.I.A. (regional dir. nat. com. on architecture for health); mem. La. Architects Assn. (pres.), New Orleans C. of C., New Orleans Constrn. Industry Assn. (trustee). Republican. Roman Catholic. Clubs; Lotus, Empire. Pioneer devel. regional archtl. design prins., passive energy conservation procedures. Home: Ahmeek Plantation Abita Springs LA 70420 Office: 1070 Saint Charles Ave New Orleans LA 70130

BLITCH, RONALD BUCHANAN, architect; b. New Orleans, May 14, 1953; s. James Buchanan and Hilda Goodspeed (Mouledoux) B. B. Arch. magna cum laude, U. Notre Dame, 1976. Lic. architect. Architect Blitch Architects, Inc., New Orleans, 1970—, pres., 1977—. Bd. dirs. St. Elizabeth's Home, New Orleans, 1982—, Holy Cross Sch., New Orleans, 1984—, East Jefferson Hosp. Found., Metairie, La., 1985—, Rotary Internat., 1985—. Mem. La. Architects Assn. (bd. dirs. 1979-83, honor award 1980, 84, 85, honor award of excellence 1982, 84, 85), AIA (sec. New Orleans chpt. 1983-85, newsletter editor; honor award 1984, 85, honor award of excellence 1985, 86), Nat. Council Archtl. Registration Bds., Greater New Orleans Execs. Assn. (dir. 1978—), Tau Beta Pi, Tau Sigma Delta. Republican. Roman Catholic. Clubs: Notre Dame (pres. 1984-85), Mercedes Benz (bd. dirs. 1982-83), Serra (trustee 1984-85). Home: 4430 Palmyra St New Orleans LA 70119 Office: Blitch Architects Inc 757 St Charles Ave New Orleans LA 70130

BLOCH, MILTON JOSEPH, museum administrator; b. Bronx, N.Y., Apr. 1, 1937; s. Seymore Jerome and Evelyn Joliet (Foltz) B.; m. Mary E. Lynn, June 2, 1962; 1 dau., Kimberly Dacia B.Indsl. Design, Pratt Inst., 1958; M.F.A., U. Fla., 1961. Head art dept. Lake-Sumter Community Coll., Leesburg, Fla., 1961-63; dir. Pesacola (Fla.) Art Center, 1964-65, Mus. of Sci. and History, Little Rock, 1966-68, Monmouth (N.J.) Mus., 1968-76, Mint Mus., Charlotte, N.C., 1976—. Editor: Southeastern Mus. Conf. Jour., 1978—. Served with U.S. Army, 1958-61. Mem. Southeastern Mus. Conf., Am. Assn. Mus., N.C. Mus. Assn. Home: 1824 Asheville Pl Charlotte NC 28203 Office: 501 Hempstead Pl Charlotte NC 28207

BLOCK, FARRIS FREDERICK, public relations consultant, lecturer; b. Port Neches, Tex., July 20, 1924; s. Martin Edison and Adelle (Garrison) B.; m. Delores Jean Allen, May 22, 1948; children—Renee Ann, George, David. B.A., Tex. A&M U., 1948; postgrad. U. Zurich, 1948; M.A., U. Houston, 1963. Editor, Port Neches Chronicle (Tex.), Athens Daily Rev. (Tex.), Midcounty Rev. (Nederland, Tex.), 1948-54; dir. info. U. Houston, 1954-77, exec. dir. univ. relations, 1977-84; lectr. pub. relations and journalism; pub. relations cons. non-profit instns. Served to lt. col. USAR, 1943-77; CBI. Decorated Silver Star, Bronze Star, Battle Star (3). Recipient Midcounty Jr. C. of C. Outstanding Young Man award, 1953; U. Houston Excellence award, 1976. Mem. Press Club Houston (past pres.), Soc. Profl. Journalists (past pres. Houston chpt.), Pub. Relations Soc. Am. (past pres. Houston chpt.), Council for Advancement Higher Edn., Houston C. of C. (communications com.). Democrat. Unitarian. Club: Waterwood Country. Author: History of Texas Newspapers Prior to 1836, 1963. Home: 4369 Faculty Ln Houston TX 77004 Office: Univ Houston Sch Communication University Park Houston TX 77004

BLOCK, JACK, judge; b. Newark, Sept. 2, 1926; s. William and Rose (Englander) B.; m. Shirley Greenberg, Dec. 21, 1947; children—Bart William, Russell David, Keith Isaac, Wendy Ann. J.D., U. Miami, 1949. Sole practice law, Miami, Fla., 1949-84; dir. Bank of Fla., mem. council City of South Miami (Fla.), 1958-60, mayor, 1968-84; mcpl. judge City of South Miami, 1962-66, assoc. mcpl. judge, 1966-68; judge Dade County Ct., 1985—. Recipient numerous certs. of appreciation from civic and profl. assns. Mem. Fla. Bar Assn., Am. Legion. Democrat. Jewish. Club: Alumni Gridders U. Miami. Lodges: K.P., Elks, Moose. Office: 10710 SW 211th St Miami FL 33189

BLOCK, JOHN BRADFORD, physician; b. Louisville, Oct. 27, 1933; s. Edward Joseph and Cecilia Ann (Ford) B.; A.B., Bellarmine Coll., 1955; M.A., U. Louisville, 1959, M.D., 1966; M.S., U. Cin., 1969; m. Mary Juanita Slack, June 11, 1960; children—John Gregory, Brian Christopher. Intern, Piedmont Hosp., Atlanta, 1966-67; resident in occupational medicine U. Cin., 1967-69; practice medicine specializing in occupational medicine; med. dir. Union Carbide, South Charleston, W.Va., 1969-71; med. cons. Ky. Dept. Health, 1971-73, Dept. Labor, 1973-79; corp. med. dir. Cin. Milacron, 1979-82, U.S. Postal Service, 1982-83; med. dir. U.S. Steel, Fairfield, Ala., 1983-84, Am. Hoechst, Spartanburg, S.C., 1984—; asst. prof. U. Louisville, 1973—; guest faculty U. Ky., 1973—. Served with U.S. Army, 1955-57. Diplomate Am. Bd. Preventive Medicine. Recipient Norvin Green Meml. prize U. Louisville Med. Sch., 1966, Cleveland Acad. award, 1966; Distinguished Service award Ky. Dental Assn., 1977. Fellow Am. Acad. Occupational Medicine, Am. Coll. Preventive Medicine, Am. Occupational Med. Assn., So. Med. Assn., Royal Soc. Health; mem. Pan Am. Med. Assn., Occupational Med. Assn., AMA, Ala. Med. Assn., Jefferson County Med. Soc., Alpha Epsilon Delta, Psi Chi. Democrat. Roman Catholic. Club: Filson. Contbr. articles to med. jours. Home: 211 Winfield Dr Spartanburg SC 29302 Office: PO Box 599 Fairfield AL

BLOCK, RICHARD ALLEN, publisher; b. N.Y.C. June 30, 1935; s. Wesley Steele Jr. and Helen Frances (O'Neill) B.; m. Gwendolyn Marie Joubert, Dec. 8, 1978; 1 stepson, Michael E. Denning Jr. B.A. cum laude, Washington and Lee U., 1957; M.S. in Edn., L.I. U., 1961. Cert. prin., N.Y. Vice pres. So. Offshore Safety & Supply Inc., Houma, La., 1972-75, Internat. Logistics Inc., Houma, 1975-76; ops. mgr. Offshore Services & Transp. Inc., Lafayette, La., 1976-78, Gerald P. Hebert Enterprises, Houma, 1980; pub. Marine Edn. Textbooks, Houma, 1970—; cons. marine edn. Served to 1st lt. U.S. Army, 1957-59. Recipient Ship Safety Achievement award Nat. Safety Council, 1975. Episcopalian. Avocation: boating. Office: Marine Edn Textbooks 124 N Van Ave Houma LA 70363-5895

BLOCKER, KENT ROBERT, mental health counselor; b. Arlington, Va., Aug. 12, 1946; s. Jack Snead and Bonita Irene (Riefenstahl) B.; m. Ellen Espy, Apr. 17, 1971; 1 child, Whitney Ellen. B.A., U. Va., 1968; M.A., Miami U., Ohio, 1971, doctoral candidate, 1971; cert. health care adminstrn. U.S. Army Acad. Health Scis., 1978. Cert. Nat. Bd. Cert. Counselors; cert. Nat. Acad. Clin. Mental Health Counselors; lic. psychol. examiner; lic. profl. counselor; cert. Am. Bd. Clin. Biofeedback. Practice psychology Human Resources, Inc., Nashville, 1973-74; psychol. examiner and asst. grant coordinator Central State Psychiat. Hosp., Nashville, 1971-75; successively dir. acute services, consulation dir., grant writer, outpatient dir., clin. dir. C.E.D. Mental Health Ctr., Gadsden, Ala., 1975—; founder, dir. Stress Control Services, Gadsden, 1982—; profl. cons. Am. Cancer Soc., 1981—. Pub., editor-in-chief ALMHCA newsletter, 1979-82. Contbr. articles to profl. jours. Editor column The Clin. Psychologist, 1979-82. Bd. dirs. The Shelter, Inc., Gadsden, 1977—, Anchor, Inc., Gadsden, 1976—; pres. Etowah County Council Community Services, 1980-82, mem., 1975—; v.p. Etowah County Mental Health Assn., 1978-80; mental health rep. Area IV Health Systems Agy., 1977-83. Served to maj. USAR, 1968—. Mem. Am. Assn. Counseling and Devel., Ala. Assn. Counseling and Devel., Am. Mental Health Counselors Assn., Ala. Mental Health Counselors Assn., Biofeedback Soc. Am., Am. Acad. Behavioral Medicine, Phobia Soc. Am. Baptist. Lodge: Kiwanis. Avocations: reading; tennis. Home: 525 Country Club Rd Gadsden AL 35901 Office: Stress Control Services 1507-B Rainbow Dr Gadsden AL 35901

BLOMQUIST, HARRY LAURENTZ, JR., natural gas company executive; b. Kenedy, Tex., 1929. B.S., U. Tex., 1952. With Texaco Inc., 1952-66; with Coastal Corp., Houston, 1966—, v.p., 1968-74, exec. v.p., 1974-75, pres., 1975-85, also dir. Office: Coastal Corp 9 Greenway Pl Houston TX 77046*

BLONKVIST, CARL LEONARD, management consultant; b. Pampa, Tex., Mar. 12, 1937; s. Brent Gustave and Louise (Powers) B.; B.S., Tex. Tech. U., 1960; M.B.A., Columbia U., 1965; m. Kaye Treadaway, Sept. 8, 1961; children—Bradford. Design engr. machinery div. Cabot Corp., Pampa, 1961, sr. indsl. engr., 1962-63; with Booz Allen & Hamilton, Dallas, 1965—, sr. v.p., 1978—, mng. officer, Dallas, 1976—; dir. ALD Corp.; U.S. Sec. Def. appointee def. adv. com. women in the services, 1978-80. Bd. dirs. Dallas Civic Opera, Internat. Trade Council, N. Tex. Planning Assn. Mem. Am. Inst. Indsl. Engring., Am. Prodn. and Inventory Control Assn., Inst. Mgmt. Cons. Republican. Presbyterian. Club: T-Bar-M. Contbr. articles to profl. jours. Home: 5121 Tanbark St Dallas TX 75229 Office: 1700 One Dallas Centre Dallas TX 75201

BLOODWORTH, ALBERT WILLIAM FRANKLIN, lawyer; b. Atlanta, Sept. 23, 1935; s. James Morgan Bartow and Elizabeth Westfield (Dimmock) B.; A.B. in History, French, Davidson (N.C.) Coll., 1957; J.D. magna cum laude with first honors, U. Ga., 1963; m. Elizabeth Howell, Nov. 24, 1967; 1 child, Elizabeth Howell. Asst. dir. alumni, pub. relations Davidson Coll., 1959-60; admitted to Ga. bar, 1962, U.S. Supreme Ct. bar, 1971; partner firm Hansell & Post (formerly Hansell, Post, Brandon & Dorsey), Atlanta, 1963-84; ptnr. firm Bloodworth & Nix, Atlanta, 1984—. Mem. Vol. Counsel to organized crime com. Commn. on Crime, Juvenile Delinquency Metropolitan Atlanta, 1965-67; asst. sec., counsel Metropolitan Found. Atlanta, 1968-76. Bd. dirs. Atlanta Presbytery, Inc., 1974-78; trustee Synod of the Southeast, Presbyn. Ch. U.S.A., 1982—, Big Canoe Chapel (Ga.), 1983—. Served to 1st lt., Intelligence Corps, AUS, 1957-59. Recipient Outstanding Student Leadership award Student Bar Assn. U. Ga., 1963, Jessie, Dan MacDougal Scholarship award U. Ga. Found., 1963. Fellow Am. Coll. Probate Counsel; mem. Am., Atlanta bar assns., State Bar Ga., Lawyers' Club Atlanta, Atlanta Estate Planning Council, Phi Beta Kappa, Phi Kappa Phi, Omicron Delta Kappa, Alpha Tau Omega (chpt. pres. 1957), Phi Delta Phi (pres. chpt. 1963, Grad. of Year for S.E. award 1963). Presbyterian. (elder). Clubs: Capital City, Sphinx, Gridiron. Home: 3784 Club Dr NE Atlanta GA 30319 Office: 706 Monarch Plaza 3414 Peachtree Rd NE Atlanta GA 30326

BLOOM, EUGENE CHARLES, physician; b. Tupelo, Miss., June 3, 1933; s. Robert Harold and Anna Esther (Kronick) B.; m. Joan Ellen Margoles, July 22, 1956; children—Marjorie Wynne Bloom Albert, Stacey Joy, Robin Hilary. Student Emory U., 1951-55, U. Fla., 1955-56; M.D., U. Miami, 1960. Intern, Cook County Hosp., Chgo., 1960-61; resident in internal medicine Jackson Meml. Hosp., 1961-63; resident in gastroenterology Coral Gables VA Hosp., 1963-64; research fellow dept. medicine, div. gastroenterology U. Miami (Fla.) Sch. Medicine, 1964-65, research scientist, 1964-66, instr. medicine, 1964-74, clin. asst. prof. medicine, 1974—; gen. practice medicine, Miami, 1966—; mem. staff Baptist Hosp. Miami, sec.-treas. med. staff, 1979-80, chief of staff, 1980-82. Bd. dirs. Miami Jewish Vocat. Service. Served to capt. M.C., U.S. Army, 1963-67; Vietnam. Recipient Iron Arrow, U. Miami, 1974. Mem. AMA, So. Med. Assn., Fla. Med. Assn., Dade County Med. Assn. (alt. del. Fla. Med. Assn. 1974), U. Miami Med. Alumni Assn. (chmn. Dade County chpt. 1972-75, nat. pres. 1975-77), Gen. Alumni U. Miami (dir. 1973-77), Fla. Gastroent. Soc., Greater Miami Jewish Fedn. (chmn. physicians div. 1979-80), Alpha Omega Alpha, Omicron Delta Kappa. Democrat. Jewish. Club: King's Bay Yacht and Country. Contbr. articles to profl. jours. Office: 9045 SW 87 Ct Miami FL 33176

BLOOM, EUGENE HAROLD, retail executive; b. Emporia, Va., Dec. 17, 1918; s. David and Rose Hazel (Rosenthal) B.; m. Betty Rose Davis, Feb. 5, 1944; children—Stephen Davis, Diane Bloom McCabe. Student Va. Poly. Inst., 1936-38, U. Richmond, 1938-39. With Bloom Brothers Inc., Emporia, 1940—, pres., 1969—; dir. 1st Nat. Bank, Emporia Fed. Savs. & Loan Assn. Pres., Greenville Meml. Hosp., 1958—; treas. Temple Emanu-El, Weldon, N.C., 1977—. Served to capt. U.S. Army, 1942-46. Decorated Silver Star, Bronze Star, Purple Heart with cluster; named #1 Citizen, Emporia Book Club, 1983; Outstanding Grad., Greensville County High Sch., 1983; recipient Outstanding Community Service award Greenville Meml. Hosp. Employees, 1980; Israel Solidarity award Israel Bond Campaign, 1974-75. Mem. Va. Retail Mchts. Assn. (dir.), Emporia C. of C. (past pres.), Am. Legion (comdr. 1981-83). Democrat. Club: Emporia Country (past pres.). Lodges: Lions (past pres.), Masons, Shriners, Woodmen of the World. Home: 313 Laurel St Emporia VA 23847 Office: 419 Halifax St Emporia VA 23847

BLOOM, FRANCIS JAMES (HANK), mayor, cookware, china and crystal wholesale executive; b. Palmyra, Mo., Nov. 23, 1918; s. James Theodore and Edith Zelma (Browning) B.; B.J., U. Mo., 1941; m. Ruby Joyce Burroughs, June 6, 1942; children—Michael Theodore, Sherra Jacque Bloom Johnson, Linda Lee Bloom Fort, Cathey, Jim Ed. Reporter, Hannibal (Mo.) Courier Post, 1941-42, 45-46; reporter San Antonio Express, 1946-48; commd. 2d lt., U.S. Army, 1942, advanced through grades to lt. col., 1964; ret., 1964; with Gen. Motors Corp., Detroit, 1964-65; v.p. Saladmaster Corp., Dallas, 1965-84; v.p. Masterguard Corp., Dallas, 1984—; pres. Pantego Indsl. Devel. Corp.; mayor Town of Pantego (Tex.), 1981—. Vice chmn. Tarrant County Arson Abatement Commn.; bd. dirs. S.E. div. Crimestoppers. Served with AUS, 1942-45, 48-64. Decorated Croix de Guerre, Bronze Star with V. Mem. Tarrant County Council Mayors, Direct Sales Assn., Arlington C. of C. (dir.), Tex. Mcpl. League, Sigma Delta Chi. Editor Saladmaster News, 1967—. Lodge: Lions (charter pres. 1982-83, zone chmn. 1983—). Office: 131 Howell St Dallas TX 75207

BLOOM, HAROLD EDWARD, marketing executive; b. N.Y.C., May 4, 1946; s. Sidney and Rose B.; B.B.A., U. Miami, 1968; M.B.A., City U. N.Y., 1971; m. Ellen T. Friedman, July 14, 1973; children—Allison, Robert. Project dir. Monar Market Planning, N.Y.C., 1968-71; asst. tech. dir. Grey Advt., N.Y.C., 1971-73; market research mgr. ITT Continental Baking, Rye, N.Y., 1973-74; mgr. consumer research Coca-Cola, Atlanta, 1973-78; dir. market research Pillsbury Co., Mpls., 1978-79; dir. market research STP Corp., Ft. Lauderdale, Fla., 1979-82; pres. Cons. in Mktg. Research, Inc., Coral Springs, Fla., 1982-84; v.p. Tupperware Home Parties, Orlando, Fla., 1984—. Mem. Am. Mktg. Assn., Am. Mgmt. Assn. Home: 400 Beech Tree Ln Longwood FL 32779 Office: PO Box 2353 Orlando FL 32802

BLOOM, HOWARD CECIL, executive search firm executive; b. Cleve., Oct. 14, 1942; s. Myer M. and Ruth (Rudnick) B.; m. Joyce Weinberg, Sept. 5, 1966; children—Cathy, Kenneth. B.S. in Mktg., Miami U., Oxford, Ohio, 1961-64. Sales, advt. Bloom Bros. Supply, Chesterland, Ohio, 1964-70; nat. account sales Apeco Corp., Dallas, 1970-74; account exec. Salesworld, Inc., Dallas, 1974-79; account exec. Wright Bergquist & Assocs., Dallas, 1979-81; pres. Howard C. Bloom, Inc., Dallas, 1981—. Mem. Tex. Assn. Personnel Cons., Miami U. Alumni Club Dallas. Lodge: Masons. Office: Howard C Bloom Inc 12201 Merit Dr Dallas TX 75251

BLOOMINGBURG, LARRY WAYNE, optometrist; b. Lafayette, Ind., Aug. 9, 1951; s. Wendell Hall and Mary Elizabeth (Dunham) B.; m. Debra Lynne Collins, Mar. 26, 1977; children—Amy Lynne, Katie Lynne. A.A., Freed-Hardeman Coll., 1971; B.S., So. Coll. Optometry, 1975, O.D., 1975. Asst. dir. Visual Perception Ctr., Hendersonville, Tenn., 1975-76; gen. practice optometry, Henderson, Tenn., 1977—. Assoc. editor (newspaper) Nat. Optometric Student Rev., 1973-75. Chmn. bd. dirs. Mid-South Youth Camp, Henderson, 1982-84; mem. F-H C Devel. Council, Henderson, 1979-82, Chester County Literacy Council, Henderson, 1985—. Named Tenn. Col., Gov. Winfield Dunn, 1974; recipient Gold Key Internat., So. Coll. Optometry, 1975. Mem. Am. Optometric Assn., Tenn. Optometric Assn., Middle Tenn. Optometric Soc., NW Tenn. Optometric Soc., Chester County C. of C. (pres. 1973-75). Mem. Ch. of Christ. Lodges: Civitan (sec.-treas. 1978-79), Rotary. Home: 538 Johnson Circle Henderson TN 38340 Office: PO Box 367 114 A S Cason St Henderson TN 38340-0367

BLOSSER, JAMES JOSEPH, lawyer; b. Ft. Wayne, Ind., Mar. 27, 1938; s. Walter and Sara Blosser; m. Judy Harwood; m. 2d, Nancy Wood; children—Jay Bentley, Gretchen Ann, Whitney Ann, Jamie Sloan, Bailey Wood. B.B.A., U. Miami, 1960, J.D., 1965. Bar: Fla., N.Y. With firm English, McCaughan & O'Bryan, Ft. Lauderdale, Fla., 1965-86, adminstrv. ptnr., until 1986; with Ruden, Barnett, McClosky, Schuster & Russell, P.A., Ft. Lauderdale, 1986—. Pres. Stranahan House Restoration Project, Ft. Lauderdale, 1983-84, Broward County Community Found., 1985—; bd. dirs. Ft. Lauderdale Symphony Orch. Assn., 1983. Served with U.S. Army, 1961-62. Mem. ABA, Fla. Bar Assn., Broward County Bar Assn., Ft. Lauderdale-Broward County C. of C. (pres. 1984). Club: Lauderdale Yacht (commodore 1983-84). Home: 19 S Victoria Park Rd Fort Lauderdale FL 33301 Office: Ruden barnett McClosky Schuster & Russell PA Box 1900 Fort Lauderdale FL 33301

BLOSSOM, DEANNA ELIZABETH, pharmacist; b. Urbana, Ohio, Aug. 31, 1957; d. Robert Dean and Sara Joan (Brown) Woodruff; m. Jeffrey Edward Blossom, July 4, 1981; children—John Darren, Andrew Dand. B.S. in Pharmacy, U. Toledo, 1980. Registered pharmacist, Ohio, Fla. Pharmacist Oak Pharmacy, Inc., Toledo, 1977-81, Kahler Pharmacy, Toledo, 1982-84, Eckerd Drug, Vero Beach, Fla., 1984—. Vol. March of Dimes, Maumee, Ohio, 1983. Mem. Ohio State Pharm. Assn., Nat. Assn. Retail Druggists, Indian River Pharm. Assn., Toledo Acad. Pharmacy (bd. dirs. 1984), Lambda Kappa Sigma. Republican. Roman Catholic. Lodge: Order Eastern Star. Avocations: sailing; needlework. Home: 752 S Fischer Circle Sebastian FL 32958

BLOUET, BRIAN WALTER, geography educator; b. Darlington, Eng., Jan. 1, 1936; came to U.S., 1966, naturalized, 1982; s. Raymond Walter and Marjorie Hannah Blouet; m. Olwyn Mary Salt, July 30, 1970; children—Andrew, Helen, Amy. B.A. with honors, U. Hull, Eng., 1960, Ph.D., 1964. Lectr. U. Sheffield, Eng., 1964-69; vis. assoc. prof. U. Nebr., Lincoln, 1966-67, assoc. prof., 1969-75, prof., 1975-83, chmn. dept. geography, 1976-81, dir. Ctr. Gt. Plains studies, 1979-83; head dept. geography Tex. A&M U., College Station, 1983—. Author: The Story of Malta, 1967, 72, 76, 81; editor: (with M.P. Lawson) Images of the Plains, 1975, (with O.M. Blouet) Latin America, 1981, Origins of Academic Geography in the United States, 1981. Served with Royal Air Force, 1955-57. Fellow Royal Geog. Soc., Ctr. Gt. Plains Studies; mem. Assn. Am. Geographers. Office: Tex A&M U Dept Geography College Station TX 77843

BLOUNT, WILLIAM HOUSTON, company executive; b. Union Springs, Ala., Jan. 3, 1922; m. Frances Dean. Student, U. Ala., Advanced Mgmt. program, Harvard U. Ptnr. Blount Bros. Corp., Montgomery, Ala.; pres. Southeastern Sand & Gravel Co., Tallassee, Ala., also dir.; v.p. So. Cen-Vi-Ro Pipe Corp., Birmingham; with Vulcan Materials Co., Birmingham, 1957—, exec. v.p. constrn. materials group, 1970-77, pres., 1977—, chief operating officer, 1977-79, chief exec. officer, 1979—, also dir.; mem. exec. com., mem. fin. com.; dir. Blount, Inc., Montgomery, Protective Corp., Birmingham, First Ala. Bancshares, Inc., Montgomery, First Ala. Bank of Birmingham. Mem. Ala. Safety Council; pres. Birmingham Area council Boy Scouts Am., 1977-79, 79; active Jr. Achievement of Jefferson County; bd. trustees YWCA; chmn. ann. awards dinner Nat. Conf. Christians and Jews, 1982; active Am. Cancer Soc.; gen. chmn. United Way Drive, 1975; gen. chmn. ann. fund drive Jr. Achievement, 1981; Ala. chmn. US Olympic Com.'s fund raising drive; active Canterbury United Methodist Ch., Mountain Brook, Ala. Served with Air Corps USN, 1943. Mem. Birmingham Area C. of C. Clubs: Mountain Brook Country (Ala.); Shoals Creek; Linville Golf (N.C.); Willow Point Country, Chgo.; River (N.Y.C.); Relay House, The Club. Office: Vulcan Materials Co 1 Metroplex Dr Birmingham AL 35209

BLOUNT, WINTON MALCOLM, construction and manufacturing company executive; b. Union Springs, Ala., Feb. 1, 1921; s. Winton Malcolm and Clara B. (Chalker) B.; student U. Ala., 1939-41; L.H.D., Judson Coll., 1967; Dr. Humanities, Huntingdon Coll., 1969; LL.D., Birmingham-So. Coll., 1969. D.C.L., Southwestern U., 1969; D.Sc., U. Ala., 1971; D.Pub. Service, Seattle-Pacific Coll., 1971; m. Mary Katherine Archibald, Sept. 12, 1942; children—Winton Malcolm III, Thomas A., S. Roberts, Katherine Blount Miles, Joseph W. Pres., chmn. bd. Blount Bros. Corp., Montgomery, Ala., 1946-68; postmaster gen. U.S., Washington, 1969-71; chmn. exec. com. Blount, Inc., 1973—, chmn. bd., chief exec. officer, 1974—; dir. Union Camp Corp., Munford Inc. Chmn. Ala. Citizens for Eisenhower, 1952; Southeastern dir. Nixon-Lodge, 1959-60. Bd. dirs. United Appeal Montgomery; bd. dirs. Montgomery YMCA, also life mem.; former trustee So. Research Inst.; trustee U. Ala., Southwestern U.; bd. visitors Air U., Maxwell AFB, 1971-73; mem. adv. council U.S. Army Aviation Mus., Ft. Rucker, Ala. Served with USAAF, 1942-45. Named one of four Outstanding Young Men Ala., 1956; Man of Year, Montgomery, 1961; recipient citation for disting. service to City of Montgomery, 1966; Ct. Honor award Montgomery Exchange Club, 1969; Nat. Brotherhood award NCCJ, 1970; Silver Quill award Am. Bus. Press, 1971; Golden Plate award Am. Acad. Achievement, 1980; non-mem. award Outstanding Achievement in Constrn., The Moles, 1980. Mem. Am. Mgmt. Assns. (trustee). Bus. Council. Conf. Bd., NAM (Golden Knight Mgmt. award Ala. Council 1962). U.S. C. of C. (nat. pres. 1968). Ala. C. of C. (pres. 1962-65), Newcomen Soc. N.Am. Presbyterian (deacon). Rotarian. Home: Route 10 Box 43 Vaughn Rd Montgomery AL 36116 Office: Blount Inc Box 949 4520 Executive Park Montgomery AL 36192*

BLOUNT, WINTON MALCOLM, III, construction executive; b. Albany, Ga., Dec. 14, 1943; s. Winton M., Jr., and Mary Katherine (Archibald) B.; m. Lucy Dunn, June 6, 1970; children—Winton M. IV, Katherine Stuart, William, Judkins. B.A., U. of South, 1966; M.B.A., U. Pa., 1968. With Blount Bros., Montgomery, Ala., 1968-73, project mgr., 1972-73; with Mercury Constrn. Corp., Montgomery, 1973-77, pres., 1975-77; chief exec. officer, chmn. bd. Benjamin F. Shaw Co., Wilmington, Del., 1977—, also pres., chief operating officer Blount Internat., Ltd., Montgomery, 1980-83, pres., 1983-85, chief exec. officer, 1983—, chmn., 1985—; dir. Blount, Inc., Dunn Constrn. Co., First Ala. Bank Montgomery, N.A. Bd. dirs. Ala. Pub. Affairs Research Council, 1979-81, Ala. C. of C., 1980-83, Episcopal High Sch., Alexandria, Va., Huntingdon Coll., Montgomery, Montgomery Acad., Montgomery C. of C., Tukabatchee Area council Boy Scouts Am., 1980-83, YMCA; mem. fin. com. Ala. Republican. Com., 1980-82; bd. visitors Coll. Commerce and Bus. Adminstrn., U. Ala. Mem. Young Pres. Orgn., NAM (bd. dirs.), Ala. C. of C. (bd. dirs.), Men of Montgomery (bd. control, bus. com. arts), Beavers, Moles. Beavers. Office: PO Box 4577 Montgomery AL 36195

BLOWERS, JAMES VERNON, operations research analyst, mathematician; b. Rochester, N.Y., Aug. 13, 1946; s. Vernon Alvin and Eula Lee (Maddox) B.; m. Anne Louise Seiler, Aug. 23, 1969; 1 child, Aaron T. B.A. in Math. magna cum laude, U. Rochester, 1968; Ph.D. in Math., Northwestern U., 1972. Ops. research analyst Letterkenny Army Depot, Chambersburg, Pa., 1975-76, 7th Signal Command, Ft. Ritchie, Md., 1976-78, U.S. Army Logistics Ctr., Ft. Lee, Va., 1978—; part time math. instr. St. Leo Coll., Ft. Lee, 1980-83, part time adj. prof. Fla. Inst. Tech., Ft. Lee, 1982-84. Author jour. articles. Served to 1st lt. USAF, 1972-75. NDEA Title IV fellow, 1968. Mem. Am. Math. Soc., Math. Assn. Am., Ops. Research Soc. Am. (assoc.), Assn. for Computing Machinery (assoc.), Richmond Astron. Soc. Unitarian Universalist. Avocations: recreational mathematics, astronomy, computers, running, composing piano music. Home: 4600 Wraywood Ave Chester VA 23831 Office: Ops Analysis Directorate US Army Logistics Ctr ATCL-OMM Fort Lee VA 23801

BLUE, MARTS DONALD, research physicist, consultant; b. Des Moines, Iowa, Feb. 4, 1932; s. Marts D. and Marie (Gengler) B.; divorced; children—Marie Faith, Molly Anne, Stephen Douglas, Timothy Leigh. B.S., Iowa State U., 1952, M.S., 1953, Ph.D., 1956. Scientist Honeywell, Inc., Mpls. 1957-63, dept. mgr., 1967-69, sci. attache, Brussels, Belgium, 1969-71, program mgr., Lexington, Mass., 1972-74; prin. research scientist Ga. Inst. Tech., Atlanta, 1974—; cons. to various corps., firms and agys. Contbr. articles to profl. jours. Inventor silicon ultraviolet radiation detector. Fulbright fellow U. Paris, 1956-57. Mem. Am. Phys. Soc., Sigma Xi. Avocations: playing piano; collecting prints. Home: 1818 Ashborough Circle Marietta GA 30067 Office: Research Inst Ga Inst Tech Baker Bldg Atlanta GA 30332

BLUFORD, GUION STEWART, JR., astronaut, aerospace engineer; b. Phila., Nov. 22, 1942; s. Guion Stewart and Lolita Harriet (Brice) B.; m. Linda Mae Tull, Apr. 7, 1964; children—Guion Stewart, James Trevor. B.S. in Aerospace Engring., Pa. State U., 1964; M.S. in Aerospace Engring., Air Force Inst. Tech., 1975, Ph.D., 1978; D.Sc. (hon.), Fla. A&M U., 1983. Joined U.S. Air Force, advanced through grades to col.; served in Vietnam; staff devel. engr. Air Force Flight Dynamics Lab., Wright-Patterson AFB, Ohio; dep. for advanced concepts, aeromechanics div., br. chief aerodynamics and airframe br.; astronaut candidate, 1978-79; mission specialist space shuttle flight crews, 1979—, mem. Orbiter Challenger's 3d flight, 1983, 9th flight, 1985. Recipient Mervin E. Gross award Air Force Inst. Tech., 1974; Meritorious Service award USAF, 1978; Disting. Nat. Scientist award Nat. Soc. Black Engrs., 1979; Group Achievement award NASA, 1980, 81; Disting. Alumni award Pa. State U., 1983; Astronaut Pilot Wings, USAF, 1983. Home: 16439 Brookvilla Dr Houston TX 77059 Office: Johnson Space Ctr NASA Houston TX 77058

BLUHM, GEORGE CHARLES, soil conservation specialist, government administrator; b. Grand Rapids, Minn., May 24, 1940; s. Howard Christian and Hattie Elizabeth (Woodley) B.; m. Karen Therese Keil, Aug. 25, 1962; children—Jennifer Jo, Tanya Lee. B.S. with honors, Wash. State U., 1963; postgrad. in meteorology Pa. State U., 1963-64; M.S. in Atmospheric Scis., U. Wash., 1972. With Soil Conservation Service, Dept. Agr., 1967—, planning engr., Spokane, Wash., 1976-78, asst. dir. program evaluation, Washington, 1978-80; dir. integrated resources info. system, Washington, 80-83, chief data base tech. br. info. resources mgmt. div., Washington, 1983, dir. West Regional Tech. Ctr., 1983—. Served to capt. USAF, 1963-67, to lt. col. Air N.G., 1968-83. Decorated Air Force Achievement medal; recipient Outstanding Performance award Dept. Agr., 1976, cash award, 1977; Collens award USAF, 1982. Mem. Am. Soc. Agrl. Engrs., Soil Conservation Soc. Am., Soc. Am. Foresters, Nat. Assn. Conservation Dists., Sigma Xi, Tau Beta Pi, Sigma Tau. Lutheran. Lodge: Elks. Contbr. articles to profl. publs. Home: 8421 Damian Ct Annandale VA 22003

BLUM, UDO, botany educator; b. Ludenscheid, Westphalia, Germany, Nov. 29, 1939; s. Gerhard and Lydia B.; m. Mary Ann Schriefer, Aug. 25, 1968; children—Amy, Nicole. B.A., Franklin Coll., 1962; M.A., Ind. U.-Bloomington, 1965; Ph.D., U. Okla., 1968. Vis. asst. prof. U. Okla., Norman, 1968-69; asst. prof. N.C. State U., Raleigh, 1969-75, assoc. prof., 1975-80, prof. botany, 1980—. U.S. Dept. Agr. grantee, 1981-86. Mem. Bot. Soc. Am., Internat. Soc. Biometeorology, Ecol. Soc. Am., Brit. Ecol. Soc., Assn. Southeastern Biologists, N.C. Acad. Sci., Sigma Xi. Office: NC State U Dept Botany Box 7612 Raleigh NC 27695

BLUMBERG, EDWARD ROBERT, lawyer; b. Phila., Feb. 15, 1951. B.A. in Psychology, U. Ga., 1972; J.D., Coll. William and Mary, 1975. Bar: Fla., 1975, U.S. Dist. Ct. Fla., 1975, U.S. Ct. Appeals, 1975, U.S. Supreme Ct., 1979; cert. civil trial adv. Nat. Bd. Trial Advocacy. Assoc., Knight, Peters, Hoeveler, Pickle, Niemoeller & Flynn, Miami, Fla., 1976-78; assoc. Goldfarb, Deutsch & Blumberg, Miami, 1976-78; ptnr. Deutsch & Blumberg, P.A., Miami, 1978—; adj. prof. U. Miami Sch. Paralegal Studies. Mem. Dade County Bar Assn., Assn. Trial Lawyers Am., Acad. Fla. Trial Lawyers. Office: 100 N Biscayne Blvd 28th Floor Miami FL 33132

BLUMENTHAL, DANIEL SENDER, medical educator; b. St. Louis, May 26, 1942; s. Herman T. and Eleanore G. B.; m. Janet M. Berstein, June 7, 1968; children—Rebecca, Jeffrey. B.A., Oberlin Coll., 1964; M.D., U. Chgo., 1968. Diplomate Am. Bd. Pediatrics. Intern, Charity Hosp., New Orleans, 1968-69, resident, 1970-72; med. epidemiologist Ctrs. for Disease Control, 1972-75; asst. prof. Emory U. Sch. Medicine, 1975-80; assoc. prof. dept. community medicine and family practice, Morehouse Sch. Medicine, 1980-85, prof., chmn. dept., 1985—. acting chmn. dept., 1982-85; mem. Nat. Adv. Council Maternal, Fetal and Infant Nutriton, U.S. Dept. Agr., 1979-82; med. cons. Job Corps, U.S. Dept. Labor, 1975-82. Bd. dirs. ACLU, 1983—. Served with USPHS, 1972-75. Mem. Am. Pub. Health Assn., Am. Acad. Pediatrics, Am. Soc. Tropical Medicine and Hygiene, Assn. Tchrs. Preventive Medicine (mem. found. bd.), Ambulatory Pediatric Assn., others. Contbr. articles to profl. jours. Home: 445 Clifton Rd Atlanta GA 30307 Office: 720 Westview Dr Atlanta GA 30310

BLUM-WEST, STEPHEN ROBERT, marketing research company executive; b. Oak Ridge, Dec. 3, 1951; s. Paul James and Olie Marie (Wright) West; m. Dina Lubar Blum, Nov. 10, 1979; children—Reston, Michelle. B.A., U. Tenn., 1972; M.A., Ill. State U., 1974; Ph.D., U. Va., 1980. Asst. prof. sociology Radford U., Va., 1978-83; sr. project dir. Southeastern Inst. Research, Richmond, Va., 1983-85; gen. mgr. Mid-Atlantic Research, Inc., 1985—. Contbr. articles to profl. publs. Mem. Am. Mktg. Assn., Am. Sociol. Assn., So. Sociol. Soc. Avocations: photography, racquetball, tennis. Home: 741 Keppel Dr Newport News VA 23602 Office: Mid Atlantic Research Inc 161-A John Jefferson Sq Williamsburg VA 23186

BLUNK, FIDELIS, TV producer, director; b. Louisville, July 7, 1922; s. Frank M. and Abbie Beatrice (Chester) B.; m. Jean Rigo, May 29, 1948 (dec. 1978); children—Linda, Christopher, Julia; m. Patricia Speiss, June 21, 1980. B.A., Columbia U., 1943. TV dir. NBC, N.Y.C., 1948-59; film/TV producer/dir. Picture House, N.Y.C., 1959-72; audiovisual dir. Nassau County Govt., N.Y., 1973-80; sr. producer/dir. Instructional TV, U. Louisville, 1981—. Active CAP, Actors Theatre Louisville, Louisville Ballet Assn., 1980—; chmn. speakers bur. Starwish Found. Served as lt. (j.g.) USN, 1943-46. Mem. Indsl. TV Assn., Soc. Motion Picture and TV Engrs., Aircraft Owners and Pilots Assn. Roman Catholic. Clubs: Aero of Louisville, Falls City Pilots Assn. Contbr. articles to profl. jours. Home: 8504 Bambi Way Louisville KY 40214 Office: Univ Louisville Instructional Comm Center Louisville KY 40292

BLY, LARRY ROBERT, advertising executive; b. Balt., Oct. 17, 1947; s. Beverly Clydus and Mickie (McGlothan) B. Student Monroe Bus. Coll. Announcer, disc jockey Sta. WHBG, Harrisonburg, Va., 1966-68, Sta. WHBG, Harrisonburg, 1970-71, Sta. WWWW, Detroit, 1971, Sta. WROV, Roanoke, Va., 1971-73; network announcer AFKN, Seoul, Korea, 1969-70; owner, pres. System 4 Advt. Agy., Roanoke, 1973—; staff announcer Sta. WBRA-TV, Roanoke; co-host, owner/creator Cookin' Cheap TV show, 1980—. Advisor Valley United Way, Roanoke, 1979, Jr. League Roanoke Valley; mem. Family Services Roanoke, 1983. Served with U.S. Army, 1968-70. Mem. Advt. Fedn. Roanoke Valley (dir. 1983-86, treas. 1985-86). Mem. Disciples of Christ. Home: 5320 Spencer Dr Roanoke VA 24018 Office: System 4 Advertising Agy Inc 526 W Campbell Ave Roanoke VA 24016

BLYTHE, ARDVEN LOUIS, engineering research analyst; b. Pitts., July 25, 1934; s. Ardven Maurice and Ruth Eleanor (Fichter) B.; m. Jonne Muriel Renner, May 2, 1956; children—James, Marjory, Dyana, Cheryl. B.S., Tex. A & M U., 1963; M.S., Ohio State U., 1970; postgrad. Nova U., 1981-84. Program control officer, pilot USAF, Wright-Patterson AFB, Ohio, 1956-68; dir. ops. research projects Sperry Univac, St. Paul, 1969-73; prin. systems analyst Teledyne Brown Engring., Huntsville, Ala., 1973-80; mem. research staff Riverside Research Inst., Huntsville, Ala., 1980-83; sr. engr./project mgr. Triad Microsystems Inc., Huntsville, 1983—; adj. faculty Fla. Inst. Tech. Pres., North Ala. chpt. Aviation Hall of Fame. Served to capt. USAF, 1956-68, col. USAFR. Decorated D.F.C., Air Medal, Bronze Star. Mem. Inst. Indsl. Engrs., Inst. Mgmt. Scis., Phi Kappa Phi, Tau Beta Pi, Alpha Pi Mu. Lutheran. Club: Sertoma Internat. (chpt. officer 1974-80). Contbr. articles to profl. jours. Home: 7814 Haven St Huntsville AL 35802 Office: 555 Sparkman Dr Suite 636 Huntsville AL 35805

BOACKLE, TERESA LARUSSA, pharmacist; b. Birmingham, Ala., July 15, 1956; d. Frank Paul and Mary Ann (Marino) LaRussa; m. Charles C. Boackle, Oct. 3, 1980. B.S. in Pharmacy, Samford U., 1980. Registered pharmacist, Ala., Fla. Pharmacist Big B Drugs, Birmingham, 1980-81, Revco Drugs, Pensacola, Fla., 1981-82, K-Mart, Birmingham, 1982—. Mem. Am. Pharm. Assn., Ala. Pharm. Assn., Lambda Kappa Sigma. Republican. Roman Catholic. Home: 5125 Stratford Rd Birmingham AL 35243 Office: K-Mart Pharmacy 3000 Montgomery Hwy Pelham AL 35124

BOARD, GENE ALAN, publisher; b. Fairmont, W.Va., Aug. 7, 1947; s. Lawrence Dalton and Ada Lucile (Boyles) B.; m. Janielu Ball, Dec. 20, 1970; children—David Alan, Lydia Jane, Jonathan Andrew. A.B., Fairmont State Coll., W.Va., 1972. Dist. mgr. Field Enterprises Ednl. Corp., Fairmont, W.Va., 1973-75; co-founder, co-pub. Your Bull. Bd., Fairmont, 1975—. Served with U.S. Army, 1967-70, Vietnam. Mem. Marion County C. of C., Epsilon Pi Tau, Kappa Delta Pi. Republican. Baptist. Avocations: Bible study; computer programming; photography. Home: 1702 Morgantown Ave Fairmont WV 26554 Office: Photo Craft 2616 Fairmont Ave Ext Fairmont WV 26554

BOARDMAN, WILLARD HARLOW, cardiologist; b. Dundee, N.Y., Jan. 6, 1922; s. Warren Milton and Lulu B. (Covert) B.; m. Jean Elizabeth Moore, Oct. 13, 1956; children—Lori Ann, Lisa Allyn, Lynn Amy. M.D., U. Buffalo, 1944. Diplomate Am. Bd. Internal Medicine. Intern, E.J. Meyer, Buffalo, 1944-45, resident in cardiology, 1945-46, 49-50, 51-52; resident in internal medicine, fellow in cardio-vascular diseases U. Buffalo, 1951-52; practice medicine specializing in cardiology, Lancaster, N.Y., 1953-56, Orlando, Fla., 1956—. Active Com. 100, Orlando, 1978—. Served to capt. M.C., AUS, 1946-47, 53. Fellow Am. Coll. Cardiology, Am. Coll. Chest Physicians; mem. ACP, Central Fla. Cardiology Group (pres. 1974—), Am. Heart Assn. Presbyterian. Office: 500 E Colonial Dr Orlando FL 32803

BOATMAN, RALPH HENRY, JR., health educator; b. Carlinville, Ill., Apr. 20, 1921; s. Ralph Henry and Mildred Elizabeth B.; m. Helen Weaver, June 11, 1943; children—Cynthia Anne Boatman Laughey, Elizabeth Wade Boatman Batton. B.S. in Edn., So. Ill. U., 1943; M.P.H., U.N.C.-Chapel Hill, 1947, Ph.D., 1954. Chmn. health edn. and health sci. depts. So. Ill. U., Carbondale, 1947-54; dir. community health Tuberculosis Inst. of Chgo. and Cook County, Chgo., 1954-60; asst. prof. U. Ill., 1955-60; prof. health edn., dir. Office Allied Health Scis. and Continuing Edn., Div. Health Affairs, U.N.C., Chapel Hill, 1960—, chmn. health edn. dept. Sch. Pub. Health, 1961-69; cons. WHO, HEW. Served with USNR, USPHS Res., 1950—. Decorated D.F.C., Air medal; USPHS fellow, 1946-47; WHO fellow, 1966. Mem. Soc. Pub. Health Educators (pres.), Am. Soc. Allied Health Professions (pres.), N.C. Pub. Health Assn. (pres.), Am. Pub. Health Assn. Lodges: Kiwanis, Lions, Elks. Contbr. articles to profl. jours. Home: 231 Flemington Rd Chapel Hill NC 27514 Office: Miller Hall O28H Univ NC Chapel Hill NC 27514

BOATNER, ROY ALTON, state senator; b. Durant, Okla., Nov. 9, 1941; s. Frank and Minnie Ola B.; B.S., Southeastern Okla. State U., 1965, M.Ed., 1973; m. Winona Wlaker, Oct. 13, 1967; children—Rhonda, Alton. Office mgr. Snak Bar Inc., Dallas, 1964-65; credit rep. Ford Motor Credit Co., Dallas, 1965-66; adjustor Am. Road Ins. Co., Dallas, 1966-67; prin. Achille (Okla.) High Sch., 1967-70; mem. Okla. Ho. of Reps. 1970-74, Okla. Senate, 1974—. Democrat. Baptist. Office: 105 N 3d St Durant OK 74701

BOB, MATTHEW REGIS, exploration geologist; b. Passaic, N.J., Mar. 30, 1957; s. Regis Paul and Joan Francis (Steel) B. B.A., St. Louis U., 1979; M.S. in Geology, Memphis State U., 1981. Geologist, Tiaga Resources, Calgary, Alta., Can., 1979—; exploration geologist Union Oil Co. of Calif., Houston, 1981—. Mem. Am. Assn. of Petroleum Geologists, Houston Geol. Soc., Soc. Profl. Well Log Analysts. Roman Catholic. Avocations: backpacking; canoeing; spelunking. Office: Union Oil Co of Calif 4615 Southwest Freeway Houston TX 77027

BOBICK, J. BRUCE, art educator, painter; b. Indiana, Pa., Oct. 25, 1941; s. John J. and Helen T. (Wingard) B.; widower; children—Bridget, Bryna. B.S. in Art Edn., Indiana U. of Pa., 1963, M.Ed., 1967; M.F.A., U. Notre Dame, 1968. Art tchr. pub. schs., Ford City, Pa., 1963-64, Indiana, 1964-67; from asst. to assoc. prof. art Western Ill. U., 1968-76; from assoc. prof. to prof. art West Ga. Coll., 1976—, chmn. art dept., 1979—. One man shows include: W.Va. U., Morgantown, 1971, Ill. State Mus., Springfield, 1974, Image South Gallery, Atlanta, 1978, 81, Delta State U., Cleveland, Miss., 1981, Savannah Coll. of Art and Design, Ga., 1982, Am. Cultural Ctr., U.S. Embassy, Brussels, 1984; group shows include: Springfield Art Mus., Mo., 1968, 69, 71, 73, 75, 77, Pa. Acad. Fine Arts, Phila., 1969, Nat. Watercolor Exhbns., Laguna Beach, Calif., 1969, 71, 72, 79, Oakland Art Mus., Calif., 1970, Los Angeles, 1973, 77, Palm Springs, Calif., 1973; represented in permanent collections: Ill. State Mus., Springfield, Mount Mercy Coll., Cedar Rapids, Iowa, Augustana Coll., Rock Island, Ill., Western Ill. U., Macomb, Laura Musser Art Mus., Muscatine, Iowa, Springfield Art Mus., Mo. (Purchase award 1975), Peat, Marwick, Mitchell & Co., Chgo. (Purchase award 1978), Albany Mus. Art, Ga. (Purchase award 1981). Mem. Nat. Watercolor Soc., Ga. Watercolor Soc. (bd. dirs. 1979—). Office: Dept Art West Ga Coll Carrollton GA 30118

BOBO, ELIZABETH ANNE, accountant; b. Columbia, S.C., Nov. 19, 1956; d. William and Elizabeth Susan (Hutto) B. B.S., U. S.C., 1978. Tax specialist Peat, Marwick, Mitchell & Co., Dallas, 1979-81; acct. Gov. Clements Campaign, Dallas, 1978-79; oil and gas tax acct. Enserch Exploration, Inc., Houston, 1982-84; oil and gas financialist Harrison Interests, Ltd., Houston, 1984—. Mem. NOW, Jr. League of Houston, Delta Delta Delta. Republican. Clubs: Cotillion, 500 Inc. Office: Harrison Interests Ltd 520 Post Oak Blvd Suite 600 Houston TX 77027

BOCK, JOHN LOUIS, architect; b. Richmond, Va., Aug. 17, 1945; s. Paul Hevener and Byrd (Johnson) B.; m. Carol Ann Chiocca, Feb. 5, 1983. Student Va. Poly. Inst., 1963-65; B.S., Richmond Profl. Inst., 1968. Draftsman, G. Richard Brown, Architect, 1964-66; project capt. J. Henley Walker, Jr., Architect, 1966-69; tchr. mech. drawing Chesterfield County Schs., 1969-70; project architect J. Henley Walker, Jr., Architect, 1970-76, Harry S. Cruickshank, Architect, Richmond, 1976-77, Edward F. Sinnott & Son, Architect, Richmond, 1977-78; v.p., sec. Ernie Rose, Inc., Architects, Richmond, Va., 1978—, also dir. Mem. Constrn. Specifications Inst. (dir. Richmond chpt. 1981, v.p. chpt.; award 1981, 83), Ducks Unltd. (chmn. Mechanicsville chpt. 1983—, nat. sponsor 1983-85). Episcopalian. Home: 1721 Shady Grove Rd Mechanicsville VA 23111 Office: 110 N Jefferson St Richmond VA 23220

BOCKHAUS, JAMES HOWARD, manufacturing company executive; b. Keokuk, Iowa, Feb. 25, 1939; s. Howard Burton and Mary Irene (Zimmerman) B.; A.B. cum laude, Harvard Coll., 1960; M.S., Syracuse U., 1968; m. Nancy Jean Beattie, July 7, 1965; children—Kimberly Kristen, Jay Bradford. With Gen. Electric Co., Fairfield, Conn., 1960-75, mgr. European mfg. automation ops., 1970-72, mgr. strategic planning cons., 1973-75; dir. corp. strategy devel. Internat. Paper Co., N.Y.C., 1975-77; v.p. corp. planning LTV Corp., Dallas, 1977-81; chmn., bd., pres. ATEC Internat. Inc., Arlington, Tex., 1981—. Trustee, Dallas Ballet Assn., 1978—, Shakespeare Festival of Dallas, 1983—; bd. dirs. Citizens Found. Syracuse, 1967-68. White House fellow, 1968-69. Mem. N. Am. Soc. Corp. Planning (past pres. Dallas-Ft. Worth chpt.), Planning Execs. Inst. (past pres. Dallas-Fort Worth chpt.), Assn. Corp. Growth, White House Fellows Assn. Republican. Presbyterian. Clubs: City (Dallas); Gt. Southwest Golf (Arlington). Home: 5351 Spring Meadow Dr Dallas TX 75229 Office: 1227 Corporate Dr Arlington TX 76011

BOCKIAN, HERBERT HAROLD, psychiatrist, consultant; b. Jersey City, Oct. 14, 1927; s. Abraham and Eva (Skner) B.; m. Natalie Paula Fink, Aug. 15, 1958; children—Phyllis, David, Barry, Steven. A.B., Columbia Coll., 1950; M.A., U. Miami, 1955; M.D., U. Tenn., 1960. Diplomate Am. Bd. Psychiatry and Neurology. Intern, St. Thomas Hosp., Nashville, 1960-61; resident in psychiatry Vanderbilt U. Hosp., Nashville, 1961-63, resident in child psychiatry, 1963-65; dir. adolescent service Middle Tenn. Mental Health Inst., Nashville, 1965-67; staff child psychiatrist Dade County Children's Psychiat. Ctr., Miami, 1967-73; clin. dir. Bristol Regional Mental Health Ctr. (Tenn.), 1974-82; practice medicine specializing in psychiatry, Bristol, 1962—; cons. Southwestern State Hosp., Marion, Va., 1982—; clin. assoc. prof. psychiatry Quillen-Dishner Coll. Medicine, East Tenn. State U., Johnson City, 1976—; mem. attending staff Bristol Meml. Hosp., 1974—. Served with USN, 1946-47. USPHS research fellow, 1958-59; recipient Charles C. Verstaendig award U. Tenn. Coll. Medicine, 1960. Mem. Am. Psychiat. Assn., So. Med. Assn., Tenn. Med. Assn., S.W. Va. Med. Soc., Upper East Tenn. Psychiat. Soc., Sullivan County Med. Soc. Democrat. Jewish. Home: 6 Yorkshire-Middlebrook Bristol TN 37620 Office: 1601 Bluff City Hwy Bristol TN 37620

BODDEKER, EDWARD WILLIAM, III, retired architect; b. Houston, Mar. 22, 1929; s. Edward William and Ruth Margaret (Cook) B.; B.Arch., Tex. A. and M. U., 1951; m. Salee Boddeker; 1 child, Mark Montagne. Architect, MacKie & Kamrath, architects, Houston, 1960-63; architect Manned Spacecraft Center, NASA, Clear Lake, Tex., 1963-82 project design mgr., 1963-65, master planner, 1965-67, head master planning sect., 1967-68, head archtl. civil sect., engring. div., 1968-76, head facilities programs sect., 1976-77, chief facilities planning office, 1977-81, spl. asst. for facilities planning, 1981-82, ret., 1982. Bd. dirs., treas. Clear Creek Basin Authority, 1972-74. Served to 1st lt. Army Security Agy., AUS, 1952-54. Recipient Apollo and Skylab Achievement awards NASA, also NASA Gemini, Apollo, Skylab, Lunar Landing Team, Apollo Soyuz Test Project, Space Shuttle group achievement awards. Registered architect, Tex. Mem. AIA, Tex. Soc. Architects. Home: 13915 Grosvenor Houston TX 77034

BODDY, WALLACE ALMON, tire company executive; b. Columbus, Ga., Jan. 23, 1929; s. Clovis Almon Boddy and Capitola Brunice (Whatley) Duke; m. Virginia Webb, Apr. 3, 1955; children—Cheryl Evelyn, Vance Wallace, Mark Gordon, Craig Sherwood. Student So. Coll., Collegedale, Tenn., 1946-47, 47-48, U. Ga., 1949. Mgr. dealer sales Pa. Tire Co., Atlanta, 1949-57, nat. sales mgr., Mansfield, Ohio, 1957-67; nat. fleet mgr. Oliver Tire and Rubber Co., Emeryville, Calif., 1967-71; nat. sales mgr. AMF Voit, Inc., Santa Ana, Calif., 1971-72; pres. Boddy Enterprises, Inc., Atlanta, 1972—. Mem. Pres.'s Com. on Small Bus., 1980, Better Bus. Bur. Atlanta, 1973-83. Contbr. articles to profl. jours. Mem. Nat. Tire Dealers and Retreaders Assn., Adventist Services and Industries, C. of C. U.S., Northwest Businessmen's Assn., Nat. Fedn. Ind. Bus. Republican. Seventh-day Adventist. Home: 6039 Shallow Wood Ct Douglasville GA 30135 Office: Boddy Enterprises Inc 1395 Howell Mill Rd NW Atlanta GA 30318

BODEY, GERALD PAUL, physician, medical research administrator, educator; b. Hazleton, Pa., May 22, 1934; s. Allen Z. and Marie F. (Smith) B.; A.B. magna cum laude, Lafayette Coll., 1956; M.D., Johns Hopkins U., 1960; m. Nancy Louise Wiegner, Aug. 25, 1956; children—Robin Gayle, Gerald Paul, Sharon Dawn. Intern, Osler Med. Service, Johns Hopkins Hosp., Balt., 1960-61, resident, 1961-62; clin. assoc. Leukemia Service, Nat. Cancer Inst., 1962-65; resident U. Wash., Seattle, 1965-66; asst. prof. medicine U. Tex. System Cancer Center, M.D. Anderson Hosp. and Tumor Inst., Houston, 1966-72, assoc. prof., 1972-75, assoc. internist dept. developmental therapeutics, 1972-75, prof., internist, 1975—, dep. head, 1975-76, med. dir. Cancer Clin. Research Center, 1977-81; asst. prof. medicine U. Tex. Health Sci. Center, Houston, 1969-72, assoc. prof. medicine, 1972-75, prof. medicine, 1975-81, prof. pharmacology, 1976—, clin. prof. Dental Br., 1977—; adj. asst. prof. microbiology Baylor Coll. Medicine, Houston, 1969-73, clin. asst. prof. medicine dept. medicine, 1969-73, adj. assoc. prof. medicine, 1973-75, adj. prof. microbiology, immunology and medicine, 1975—; chief chemotherapy and infectious diseases dept. developmental therapeutics M.D. Anderson Hosp., 1971-83, chief infectious disease, dept. internal medicine, 1983—; cons. to Brooke Army Med. Center, Ft. Sam Houston, Tex., 1971—, preventive medicine div., biotech. splty. teams Manned Spacecraft Center, Houston, 1970-71, Wilford Hall USAF Med. Center, Lackland AFB, Tex., 1975—, Commn. for Devel. of Comprehensive Cancer Care Center, Republic of Panama; mem. Collaborative Cancer Treatment Research Program, Pan Am. Health Orgn.; chmn. various symposia on antibiotic and antitumor therapy, 1978—; cons. mem. orphan products product devel. initial rev. group FDA, 1984—. Served with USPHS, 1962-66. Henry Strong Denison fellow, 1958-60; diplomate Am. Bd. Internal Medicine (subspltys. oncology, infectious diseases). Fellow ACP, Royal Coll. Medicine, Am. Coll. Clin. Pharmacology, Royal Soc. for Promotion of Health; mem. Infectious Disease Soc. Am., Am. Soc. Microbiology, Am. Soc. Hematology, Am. Soc. Clin. Oncology, Am. Assn. Cancer Research, Internat. Soc. Chemotherapy, Internat. Assn. for Study of Lung Cancer, Am. Soc. for Pharmacology and Exptl. Therapeutics, Assn. for Gnotobiotics, Am. Fedn. Clin. Research, AAAS, Johns Hopkins Med. Assn., Houston Acad. Medicine, AMA, Tex. Med. Assn. (mem. com. Cancer adv. panel 1984—), Harris County Med. Soc., Academia Peruana de Cirugía of Peru (hon. mem.), Sociedade Brasileira de Cancerologia (hon. mem.), Phi Beta Kappa, Sigma Xi. Presbyterian. Contbr. chpts., articles and abstracts on oncology and infectious diseases to med. books; editorial bd. Antimicrobial Agts. and Chemotherapy, 1975-77, 81—, Leukemia Research, 1977—, Jour. Soviet Oncology, 1979—, Cancer Research, 1982—, Jour. Clin. Oncology, 1982—, Today's Therapeutic Trends, 1982—. Office: MD Anderson Hosp 6723 Bertner Houston TX 77030

BODIE, ALPHONSO R., diversified company executive; b. Sneads, Fla., Sept. 29, 1952; s. O.H. and Ann N. Bodie; m. Cristy L. McCullough, May 24, 1978; children—Alicia, Michelle, Kelly. B.S.B.A. in Acctg., U. Miami (Fla.), 1972. Account exec. Met. Life Ins. Co., Coral Gables, Fla., 1973-76; account mktg. rep. IBM, Coral Gables, 1976-84, staff instr., Dallas, 1984—; career counselor Dade County Pub. Schs., Miami, 1980-83. Pres. Dade County North Central Adv. Bd., 1975; advisor Jr. Achievement, 1977-82; mem. Leadership Miami, 1983—. Recipient Advisor of Yr. award Jr. Achievement, 1978. Mem. Phi Beta Sigma (v.p. 1973-74). Democrat. Baptist.

BODIFORD, WILLIAM DANIEL, manufacturer representative; b. Hillsboro, Tex., Nov. 12, 1924; s. William Lewis Bodiford and Alva Aline (Swint) Bodiford Blacklock; m. Nellie Marie Newton, Sept. 13, 1942; children—Lewis Wayne, Debra Lynn. Salesman Tru-Ade Bottling Co., Ft. Worth, 1946-50; salesman Terrell Supply Co., Ft. Worth, 1950-69; salesman Gentec Hosp. Supply, San Francisco, Calif., 1969-80, Gentec Health Care, Inc., San

Francisco, 1980-82, dir., 1981-82; salesman Whittaker Gen. Med., Richmond, Va., from 1982; now mfr.'s rep. Served to sgt. USAAF, 1942-45; ETO. Decorated Air medal with 4 oak leaf clusters. Named Salesman of Yr., Gentec Hosp. Supply, 1978, recipient Top Producer award, 1975. Republican. Baptist. Lodge: Masons.

BODNAR, LOUIS JOSEF, lawyer, author; b. Vilshofen, Bavaria, Germany, Aug. 18, 1945; came to U.S., 1958, naturalized, 1967; s. Steven Michael and Angela Teresia (Gyorke) B.; divorced; children—Louis Josef II, Angela Suz Suzanne. B.S. in Bus. Adminstrn., Okla. State U., 1969; J.D., Okla. U., 1972; LL.M. in Internat. and Comparative Law, Georgetown U., 1985. Bar: Okla. 1972, U.S. Supreme Ct. 1977. Ptnr. Miller & Spencer, Oklahoma City, 1972-77, Bodnar Williams & Boren, Oklahoma City, 1977-83, Bodnar & Armstrong, Oklahoma City, 1983-84; sole practice, Oklahoma City and Washington, 1984—; chief exec. officer Fin. Group, Ltd., Oklahoma City and Tampa, Fla., 1982; chmn. bd. 1st Nat. Bank, Willow, Okla., 1983; dir. Bank of Granite, 1st State Bank of Blanchard, 1st Nat. of Tipton. Author: Fazenda, 1983; Woman in White, 1984; Letters, 1985; Sunbelt, 1985. Chmn. Cancer Crusade, Oklahoma City, 1982; mem. Republican Senatorial Com., 1983; mem. council Nat. Conservative Polit. Action Com., 1982-83. Named among Top 20 Real Estate Lawyers, Brokers Mag., 1978. Mem. Okla. Bar Assn. Methodist. Club: Young Men's Dinner (Oklahoma City). Office: 1200 N Walker Ave Suite 601 PO Box 54971 Oklahoma City OK 73154

BODNER, EMANUEL, industrial scrap metals recycling company executive; b. Houston, July 25, 1947; s. Eugene and Eve (Pryzant) B.; B.B.A., U. Tex., Austin, 1969; m. Jennifer Leigh Holt, Sept. 13, 1981; children—Jessica Elyse, Jeremiah. Vice pres. Bodner Metal & Iron Corp., Houston, 1969—. Bd. dirs. Cy-Champ Utility Dist., 1978-79, Tex. Rehab. Commn., 1985—, Tex. Council on Disabilities; mem. Tex. Legis. Council, Citizens Adv. Commn. Study of Vocat. Rehab., 1970-72; mem. removal of archtl. barriers com. Tex. Rehab. Assn., 1971; mem. handicapped access program task force Tex. Dept. Human Resources, 1978-79; mem. Tex. Gov.'s Com. Employment of Handicapped, also vice-chmn. employment devel. subcom., 1981-82; mem. New Leadership Exec. Com., State of Israel Bonds, 1984. Mem. Inst. Scrap Iron and Steel (nat. public relations com., nat. fgn. trade com.; dir. Gulf Coast chpt. 1977-84, chmn. chpt. public relations com. 1978-85, editor Gulf Coast Reporter 1978-85, 2d v.p. Gulf Goast chpt. 1986—, chmn. membership com. 1986—), Ex-Students Assn. U. Tex., Houston C. of C., Alpha Epsilon Pi (life). Jewish. Clubs: Masons (32 deg.), Shriners. Office: 3660 Schalker Dr Houston TX 77026

BODNER, MICHAEL SIMON, physicist, computer scientist; b. Bklyn., Apr. 4, 1948; s. Nathan and Marsha (Wasser) B.; m. Bernice Joy Blumenreich, Apr. 11, 1970 (div. Sept. 1983); chidren—Sacha, Zachary. B.S., Bklyn. Coll., 1969; M.S., St. Johns U., 1972, Ph.D., 1975. Physics tchr. Stuyvesant High Sch., N.Y.C., 1973-74; physics prof. St. Johns U., Jamaica, N.Y., 1974-75, Erie Community Coll., Orchard Park, N.Y., 1975-79; vis. scientist NASA, Houston, 1979-80; sr. v.p. research and devel. Comnet Inc., Houston, 1981-85; dir. research and devel. Bodner, Hutchins & Assocs. Inc., Houston, 1985—; cons. Traffic Central Inc., Houston, 1980—, TWA, Kansas City, Mo., 1981-82, Comnet Inc., Houston, 1983-84, Bank Am., San Francisco, 1985—; vis. scientist NASA, 1978-79, speaker Nat. Computer Conf. Anaheim, Calif., 1978. Talk show guest WGR, Radio, Buffalo, 1978-79, KULF Radio, Houston, 1980; TV show guest, San Antonio, 1983. N.Y. State Regents scholar 1964; named one of Outstanding Young Men Am. 1983. Mem. Am. Phys. Soc., N.Y. Acad. Sci., IEEE, Am. Assn. Physics Tchrs., AAAS. Jewish. Avocations: cinema; science fiction; jazzercize; writing. Home: 7627 Cambridge Houston TX 77054 Office: Bodner Hutchins & Assocs Inc 2300 Old Spanish Trail #2105 Houston TX 77054

BODRON, ELLIS BARKETT, JR., lawyer, former state legislator; b. Vicksburg, Miss., Oct. 25, 1923; s. Ellis Barkett and Helen (Kenaan) B.; B.A., U. Miss., 1946, LL.B., 1946; m. Jane Workman, July 30, 1960; children—Helen Estelle, Lawrence Ellis. Admitted to Miss. bar; individual practice law, 1947-49; mem. firm Bodron, Nichols & Levy, 1949-53; mem. firm Bodron & Nichols, 1954-57, firm Ramsey & Bodron (now Ramsey, Bodron, Robinson, Andrews & Yoste), 1976-83, Bodron & Yoste, 1983—; mem. Miss. Ho. of Reps., 1948-51; mem. Miss. Senate, 1952-83, chmn. fin. com., 1961-83; officer, dir. Vicksburg Enterprises, 1967—, Gulf Health Enterprises, Pascagoula, Miss., 1977—, Shady Lawn Corp., Vicksburg, 1978—, Hill City Enterprises, Vicksburg, 1979—, Compere's Nursing Home, Inc., Jackson, Miss., 1979—; dir. Deposit Guaranty Nat. Bank. Former trustee All Saints Sch. Mem. ABA, Miss. Bar Assn., Warren County Bar Assn., Am. Health Care Assn., Miss. Health Care Assn., Phi Delta Phi, Phi Eta Sigma, Omicron Delta Kappa, Phi Kappa Alpha. Office: 701 Clay St Vicksburg MS 39180

BOE, MYRON TIMOTHY, lawyer; b. New Orleans, Oct. 30, 1948; s. Myron Roger and Elaine (Tracy) B. B.A., U. Ark., 1970, J.D., 1973; LL.M. in Labor, So. Methodist U., 1976. Bar: Ark. 1974, Tenn. 1977, U.S. Ct. Appeals (4th, 5th, 6th, 7th, 8th, 9th, 10th, 11th cirs.) 1978, U.S. Supreme Ct. 1978. City atty. City of Pine Bluff, Ark., 1974-75; sec.-treas. Ark. City Atty. Assn., 1975; labor atty. Weintraub-Dehart, Memphis, 1976-78; sr. ptnr. Rose Law Firm, Little Rock, 1980—. Author: Handling the Title VII Case Practical Tips for the Employer, 1980. Contbr. book supplement: Employment Discrimination Law, 2nd edit., 1983. Served to 2d lt. USAR, 1972-73. Recipient Florentino-Ramirez Internat. Law award, 1975. Mem. ABA (labor sect. 1974—, employment law com. 1974—), Ark. Bar Assn. (sec., chmn. labor sect. 1978-81, ho. of dels. 1979-82, Golden Gavel award 1983), Def. Research Inst. (employment law com. 1982—), Ark. Trial Lawyers Assn., Ark. Bd. Legal Specialization (sec. 1982-85, chmn. 1985—). Office: Rose Law Firm 120 E Fourth Little Rock AR 72201

BOEHLER, HURLEY KIRCHMAN, pilot; b. Montgomery, Tex., Oct. 17, 1918; s. Fritz J. and Ethel M. (Turner) B.; 1 dau. from previous marriage—Barbara Ann; m. Maria Cristina Pinero, June 30, 1966 (div. 1976); 1 son, Terry. Student U. Ala., 1944. Lic. comml. pilot. Mechanic, Johnson Chevrolet Co., 1936-39; with Civil Service, Kelly, Fla., 1940-43, Barsdall Oil Co., 1945-50; corp. pilot Standard Oil Co., 1950-77; mgr., pilot Eagle Aviation, Tulsa, 1977-80; mgr., test pilot Iliff Aircraft Co., Tulsa, 1980—; aviation cons.; aircraft insp.; ground inst. Tulsa, Voteck; flight instr. Tulsa N. Airport, 1950-77. Served with USAAF, 1943-45. Mem. Christian Motorcycle Assn., Exptl. Aircraft Assn. Baptist. Clubs: Cactus, Masons. Inventor in field; Tulsa Aviation Booster Day named for him.

BOEHM, C. J., state official. Treas., State of Va., Richmond. Office: 101 N 14th St PO Box 6H Richmond VA 23215*

BOEHM, JOHN FRANCIS, oil company executive; b. St. Louis, Nov. 5, 1926; m. Lois Jeanne Byrne, Jan. 27, 1951; children—Nancy, John, Robert, Thomas. Salesman, Quaker State Oil Refining Corp., Standard Oil Co. (Ind.); sales mgr. R.J. Brown Co., St. Louis, 1957-59; div. mgr. Valvoline Oil Co., Cin., 1959-67, v.p. sales, Ashland, Ky., 1968-69, exec. v.p., 1970-71, pres., Ashland and Lexington, Ky., 1971—, group v.p. Ashland Petroleum Co., 1974—; dir. First Security Nat. Bank & Trust Co., Lexington. Bd. dirs. Ky. Alcoholism Council, U. Ky. Hosp., Ky. Diabetes Found., United Way; mem. exec. bd. Bluegrass council Boy Scouts Am.; mem. adv. bd. Lexington Community Coll.; mem. council suprs. U. Ky. Med. Ctr.; trustee Midway Coll., Ky. Served with USN, 1944-46. Mem. Lexington Bluegrass C. of C. (bd. dirs.). Home: 969 Warrenton Circle Lexington KY 40502 also 1975 Nogales Way Palm Springs CA 92262 Office: 3499 Dabney Dr Lexington KY 40509

BOEHM, MARY MAGDALENE, interior designer, space planning consultant; b. Bluffton, Ohio, June 23, 1944; d. Marvin George and Martha Leoda (von Stein) B. B.S. in Interior Design, U. Cin., 1967. Designer, Taylor Designs, Cin., 1967-68, Space Design/Interior Architecture, Cin., 1968-74, Caudill, Rowlett, Scott, Houston, 1974-76; head dept. interior design Klein Partnership, Houston, 1977-80; propr. Boehm Design Assocs., Houston, 1980—; expert witness Tex. Health Facilities Commn.; tchr. interior design Jewish Community Ctr., Cin., 1968. Recipient Hexter award Hexter Corp., 1969, 76; Burlington House award Burlington House Corp., 1974; Nat. award Inst. Bus. Designers, 1974. Mem. AIA (assoc.), Tex. Soc. Architects, Preservation Alliance, Neartown Civic Assn. Contbr. articles on interior design to profl. jours. and newspapers.

BOEKE, EUGENE H., JR., construction executive; b. Birmingham, Ala., Oct. 7, 1925; s. Eugene Herman and Lillian (Rogers) B.; m. Joy Weller, Aug. 11, 1951. B.S. in Architecture, Ga. Inst. Tech., 1949. Engr., Beers Constrn. Co., Atlanta, 1949-51, supt., 1951-55, gen. supt., 1955-59, project mgr., 1959-70, v.p., 1970—; dir. Bon Enterprises, Tulsa. Active Boy Scouts Am. Served with U.S. Army, 1943-46. Recipient Silver Beaver award from Boy Scouts Am., 1975. Fellow Am. Concrete Inst.; mem. Reinforced Concrete Research Council. Baptist. Club: Gombe Soc. Home: 3039 Westminster Circle Atlanta GA 30327 Office: 70 Ellis St Atlanta GA 30303

BOELCSKEVY, BENCE DAVID, physiologist; b. Gyongyos, Hungary, Oct. 1, 1944; s. Laudislaus Zoltan and Soja (Jovanovic) deB.; came to U.S., 1950, naturalized, 1956; B.S., W.Liberty State Coll., 1969; M.S., Ohio State U., 1971, Ph.D., 1976; m. Susan Patricia Metcalf, June 1, 1968. Quality assurance profl. Ross Labs., Columbus, Ohio, 1971-74; asst. prof. physiology W.Va. Sch. Osteopathic Medicine, Lewisburg, 1976-78, asst. dean clin. tng., 1978-79, asst. to pres., 1979—; exec. v.p. W.Va. Sch. Medicine Found., 1981—; pres. BDB Electronic Cons., 1979—. Treas. Greenbrier County Public Sewer Dist. 1, 1981—. Mem. Soc. Tchrs. Family Medicine, Am. Soc. Quality Control, Digital Equipment Computer Users Soc., BMW Car Club Am. (nat. pres. 1978-81, ambassador-at-large 1981—). Episcopalian. Office: 400 N Lee St Lewisburg WV 24901

BOERTIEN, HARMON S., linguistics educator, researcher, educational administrator; b. Yakima, Wash., Oct. 4, 1936; s. Seine and Ethel (Terpstra) B. B.A., U. Wash., 1958, M.A., 1966; Ph.D., U. Tex., 1975. Instr., Tex. A&M U., Kingsville, 1966-70; asst. instr. U. Tex., Austin, 1970-72, 74-75, vis. asst. prof., summer 1977; asst. prof. U. Houston, 1975-81, assoc. prof. linguistics, 1981—, grad. dir. English, 1982—. Mem. editorial bd. Jour. of Linguistic Assn. S.W. Contbr. articles to linguistics jours. Served with U.S. Army, 1959-61. Recipient Grantmanship Workshop award NEH, 1982; U. Houston grantee, 1976; U. Tex. fellow, 1972-74. Mem. Am. Dialect Soc., Linguistic Assn. S.W., Linguistic Soc. Am. Home: 1808 Morse St Houston TX 77019 Office: Dept English U Houston Univ Park Houston TX 77004

BOGAEV, LEONARD ROCKLIN, physician; b. Phila., Sept. 27, 1928; s. Harry A. and Vera Ethel (Rocklin) B.; B.A., Princeton, 1950; M.D., U. Pa., 1954; m. Rosa Lee Ayres, Oct. 1, 1957; children—Susan, Keith Richard, Douglas, Christopher. Intern U. Pa. Hosp., 1954-55; resident in urology, surgery U. Va. Hosp., Charlottesville, 1955-59; practice medicine specializing in urological surgery, Jonesboro, Ark., 1959—; chief of staff St. Bernard's Hosp., Jonesboro, 1974-76; pres. Bogaev & Williams Urology Clinic Profl. Assn., Jonesboro, 1972—; asst. clin. prof. U. Ark. Med. Center. Served with USNR, 1959-61. Diplomate Am. Bd. Urology. Fellow A.C.S.; mem. Am. Urol. Assn., Ark. Soc. Urologists (pres. 1975), Memphis-Shelby County (Tenn.) Urol. Soc., Ark. State Soc., AMA, Craighead-Poinsett Med. Soc., Phi Beta Kappa, Alpha Omega Alpha. Republican. Methodist. Elk. Home: 906 Pinecrest St Jonesboro AR 72401 Office: One Medical Plaza 303 E Matthews Jonesboro AR 72401

BOGAR, CHRISTINE BARBARO, university counselor; b. Neptune, N.J., Mar. 10, 1954; d. Louis and Gretchen (Gabler) Barbaro; m. Craig Thomas Bogar, June 5, 1976. B.A., Wheaton Coll., Norton, Mass., 1976; M.A., U. Md., 1980. Cert. counselor. Resident counselor Mount Ida Coll., Newton Center, Mass., 1976-77; assignments officer Trenton State Coll., N.J., 1978; resident dir. U. Md., College Park, 1978-79, grad. asst., 1979-80; program coordinator Newcomb Coll., New Orleans, 1980-82; counselor Loyola U., New Orleans, 1982—; vol. Battered Women's Program, New Orleans, 1981-83. Mem. Am. Coll. Personnel Assn. (state membership chmn. 1981-85, nat. membership com. 1983-85), Am. Assn. Counseling and Devel., So. Assn. Coll. Student Affairs, La. Coll. Personnel Assn. (pres. 1984-85). Office: Loyola U 6363 St Charles Ave New Orleans LA 70118

BOGDAL, PHILLIP, landscape architect; b. Syracuse, N.Y., Sept. 16, 1949; s. John Frank and Sophie (Kuznia) B.; m. Nidia Paula Echegaray, Aug. 4, 1982; 1 child, Sofia. B.Environ. Sci., SUNY-Syracuse, 1972, B.Landscape Architecture cum laude, 1973. Landscape architect Edward D. Stone, Jr. and Assocs., Ft. Lauderdale, Fla., 1973—, office mgr., Houston, 1978-80, ptnr., Ft. Lauderdale, 1983—; landscape architect Duryea & Wilhelmi, Inc., Syracuse, 1975-76. Chief planner Mayor's City Beautification Team, Ft. Lauderdale, 1977-78. Recipient 2d place award Hwy. Beautification Competition, Knight Found., 1977. Mem. Am. Soc. Landscape Architects. Avocations: real estate investment, historical preservation, travel, painting, running. Office: Edward D Stone Jr & Assocs PA 1512 E Broward Blvd #110 Fort Lauderdale FL 33301

BOGDANSKY, JOHN JOSEPH, marketing executive; b. Chgo., Sept. 1, 1938; s. Joseph and Julia (Walkonis) B.; m. Joann May Cesky, Feb. 4, 1960; children—John Edward, James Brian. B.S. in Chem. Engring., Northwestern U., 1967. Dist. mgr. BASF Corp., Chgo., 1961-69; pres. Tamite Industries, Inc., 1969-78; sr. mktg. rep. Nat. Gypsum Co., 1978-80; mktg. mgr. J & J Cons., Miami, Fla., 1980—; cons. in field. Active Miami Lakes Civic Assn. Mem. Soc. Plastics Engrs., Am. Mktg. Assn., Delta Sigma Pi. Developed plastisol coatings and molding materials.

BOGER, LAWRENCE LEROY, university president; b. DeKalb County, Ind., Sept. 26, 1923; s. Lester Elmer and Lazeal (Witt) B.; B.S., Purdue U., 1947; student Harvard, U. Chgo.; M.A., Mich. State U., 1948, Ph.D., 1950; m. Frances June Wilbur, Sept. 2, 1945; children—Richard Lee, Judith Ann. Faculty dept. agrl. econs. Mich. State U., 1948-77, beginning as instr., successively asst. prof., asso. prof. 1948-54, prof., head dept., 1954-69, dean coll. Agr. and Natural Resources, 1969-76, univ. provost, 1976-77; pres. Okla. State U., Stillwater, 1977—; cons. U.S. Crop Reporting Service, Dept. Agr., 1953-56, cons. Bur. Census and Statis. Reporting Service, 1965-68; cons. village devel. program for Pakistan govt., Ford Found., 1957, 64, 67; cons. programs econ. assistance Nat. U. of Colombia, S.Am., Kellogg Found., 1959; mem. Nat. Com. on Use of Electronic Data Processing in Farm Mgmt.; dir.-at-large Central Bank for Coops., FCA, 1967-71; mem. joint univ. adv. com. U. Nigeria, 1965-68; mem. Spl. Commn. on Land Use Planning, 1971—; chmn. Gov.'s Oil and Gas Task Force, 1973; del. White House Conf. on Nutrition, 1969, Chgo. Foothills Conf. on Inflation, 1974, Pres.'s Conf. on Inflation, Washington, 1974; mem. Blue Ribbon Com. on Recommendations on Maximizing U.S. Farm Exports, 1980; trustee Nat. 4-H Council, 1981—; mem. Gov.'s Council Sci. and Tech., 1983—; mem. bd. sci. and tech. for internat. devel. NRC, 1984—; mem. Benedum panel on agr. W.Va. U., 1984. Chmn. Commn. on County Govt. Personnel Edn. and Tng., 1982—; bd. dirs. State Fair Okla., Omniplex; trustee Scroggs Scholarship Found., Inc., Okla. Health Scis. Found. Mem. Am. Econ. Assn., Am. Agrl. Econs. Assn. (v.p. 1960-61), Internat. Assn. Agrl. Econs. (Am. council), Am. Statis. Assn., Mid-Am. State Univs. Assn. (chmn. council 1980-81), Okla. C. of C. (dir.), Oklahoma City C. of C. (dir.), Stillwater C. of C. (dir.), Blue Key, Sigma Xi, Alpha Zeta, Omicron Delta Kappa, Pi Mu Epsilon, Phi Kappa Phi. Home: 1600 N Washington Stillwater OK 74075 Office: Office of Pres Oklahoma State U 107 Whitehurst Hall Stillwater OK 74078

BOGER, RICHARD LEE, ins. broker; b. Lafayette, Ind., Oct. 1, 1946; s. Lawrence Leroy and Frances June (Wilbur) B.; m. Harriet Owen, Apr. 6, 1974; children—Owen Richard, Burke Lawrence. B.A., U. Mich.-Ann Arbor, 1968; postgrad. U. Pa., 1977, Ill. State U., 1981. C.P.C.U.; cert. assoc. risk mgr. Mgmt. trainee Mich. Nat. Corp., Lansing, Mich., 1968, dept. supr., econ. analyst, 1968-71; loan officer Export-Import Bank of U.S., Washington, 1971-72; v.p., ins. broker Frank B. Hall Co. of Ga. Inc., Atlanta, 1972-82; co-founder, chmn. Boger & Reid, ins. brokers, Atlanta, 1982—; guest lectr. Emory U., U. Ga., Ga. State U., Am. Mgmt. Assn. Advisor, Jr. Achievement, 1968-69; chmn. adv. council Ga. State U. Inst. Internat. Bus., 1979-82; mem. Peach Bowl Com., 1980-81. Eagle Scout awardee, 1960. Mem. Atlanta C. of C. (vice-chmn. internat. task force 1980-82), Ga. C. of C. (mem. internat. council 1974-79), Ga. Internat. Trade Assn., Ga. Soc. CPCUs, U. Mich. Alumni Assn., Delta Tau Delta. Clubs: U. Mich. of Atlanta, Capital City, World Trade of Atlanta. Home: 495 Arden St at Argonne NW Atlanta GA 30305 Office: 2951 Piedmont Rd NE Atlanta GA 30305

BOGGS, CORINNE C. (LINDY), congresswoman; b. Brunswick Plantation, La.; grad. Sophie Newcomb Coll.; m. Thomas Hale Boggs (dec.); children—Barbara (Mrs. Paul Sigmund), Thomas Hale, Corinne (Mrs. Steven V. Roberts). Active numerous civic activities; elected to 93d Congress from 2d La. dist. in spl. election to fill vacancy caused by death of husband, 1973, elected to 94th-99th congresses, chmn. joint com. Bicentennial arrangements, 1975-76, mem. com. on appropriations, 1977—, subcom. on energy and water devel., subcom. on housing and urban devel. and ind. agys., subcom. on legis. br.; mem. Select Com. on Children, Youth and Families, chairperson Task Force on Crisis Intervention. Past pres. Women's Nat. Democratic Club, Dem. Congl. Wives' Forum, Congl. Club; active numerous Dem. events including inaugural balls Pres. Kennedy and Pres. Johnson; chairwoman Dem. Nat. Conv., 1976. Bd. regents Smithsonian Instn., 1976-77, regent emeritus, 1980—bd. dirs. La. Council Music and Performing Arts, Am. Revolution Bicentennial Adminstrn.; chairwoman Commn. Bicentenary of U.S. Ho. Reps.; Ho. speaker's designee Commn. Bicentennial of U.S. Constitution. First woman to receive Veterans of Fgn. Wars Congl. Medal of Honor. Mem. Nat. Soc. Colonial Dames, League Women Voters. Roman Catholic. Address: Rayburn House Office Bldg Rm 2353 Washington DC 20515

BOGGS, DEIRDRE POSTE, safety engineer; b. Yonkers, N.Y., May 9, 1950; d. Albert Gaeton and Dorothea (Acito) Poste; m. Clifford Paul Senkpiel, Sept. 16, 1972 (div. 1981); m. Billy Ray Boggs, May 5, 1983; stepchildren—Robert Eugene, Amy Marie. B.A., Knox Coll., 1972. Adminstrv. asst. Computer Centre, Inc., Chgo., 1972-73; data processing administrv. asst. Little Company of Mary Hosp., Evergreen Park, Ill., 1973-78; purchasing agt. Wheelock Lovejoy, Bridgeview, Ill., 1978-81; asst. dir. personnel Chisholm Trail Constrn., Ft. Worth, 1981-82; safety coordinator Vecta Contract, Grand Prairie, Tex., 1982—. Mem. Tex. Safety Assn., Am. Soc. Safety Engrs. Republican. Avocations: reading; music; swimming; dancing. Office: Vecta Contract Inc 1800 S Great Southwest Pkwy Grand Prairie TX 75053

BOGGS, GEORGE TRENHOLM, lawyer; b. Charleston, S.C., Apr. 17, 1947; s. Edwin and Laura (Blair) B.; m. Emilie Louise von Thelen, Sept. 6, 1975; children—George T., Blair M. A.B., Princeton U., 1969; J.D., U. Va., 1974. Bar: Va. 1974, D.C. 1975. Tchr., Taft Sch., Watertown, Conn., 1969-71; mem. Dickstein, Shapiro, Morin, Washington, 1974—, ptnr., 1980—. Mem. ABA, Va. Bar Assn. Republican. Episcopalian. Clubs: Gibson Island, Wilmington, City Tavern. Editor: (with John M. Paxman) The United Nations: A Reassessement, 1973.

BOGGS, WILLIAM BRADY, quality engineering consultant; b. Atlanta, Nov. 15, 1943; s. William Brady and Callie Kathleen (Jordan) B.; m. Rebecca Lynn Taunton, Feb. 26, 1966; children—Jason Alan, Brian Daniel. B.S. in Physics, Ga. Inst. Tech., 1965; M.S., Fla. State U., 1970, M.B.A., 1971; postgrad N.C. State U., 1979-80; diploma in Bible and Doctrine, Berea Sch. of Bible, 1985. Cert. quality engr. Am. Soc. Quality Control. Radar systems analyst Calspan Corp., Buffalo, 1972-74; sect. head research systems engring. BASF Corp. (formerly Am. Enka Co.), Enka, N.C., 1974-78, mgr. research systems engring., 1978-82, research staff statistician, 1982-83, engring. staff statistician, 1983—; pres. Alpha Quality Services, Inc., Candler, N.C., 1985—. Contbr. papers to profl. conf. Sr. comr. Royal Rangers outpost 46 Christian ministry for boys, Asheville, 1984-85, sect. comdr. Gt. Smoky Mountain sect. N.C. dist., 1986—. Served to capt. U.S. Army, 1965-68. Mulliken fellow, 1968-70; Fla. State U. fellow, 1970-71. Mem. Am. Soc. Quality Control, Am. Statis. Assn., Tau Beta Pi, Phi Kappa Phi, Sigma Pi Sigma, Pi Eta Sigma, Sigma Iota Epsilon, Beta Gamma Sigma. Mem. Assembly of God. Clubs: Full Gospel Businessmens Fellowship (treas. 1980, sec. 1981-82); Frontiersman Camping Fraternity N.C. Avocations: photography; camping. Home: Route 2 Box 391-A Candler NC 28715 Office: BASF Corp Am Enka Co Enka NC 28728

BOGHETICH, ANTONIO, lawyer; b. Milano, Italy, Apr. 20, 1954; came to U.S., 1956, naturalized, 1960; s. Luigi and Arlette (Trevis) Bogazinavich de la Boghetich; m. Jilene Kay Milligan, May 29, 1976; children—April Michelle, Travis Luigi, Cody Kyle. Student, N. Central Coll., 1971; B. Bus., So. Methodist U., 1975, J.D., U. Okla. 1978. Bar: Tex. 1978, U.S. Dist. Ct. (so. dist.) Tex. 1979, Okla. 1980, U.S. Dist. Ct. (we. dist.) Okla. 1980. Assoc. McConnico Gregg & Jones, Houston, 1978-80; atty., v.p. Liberty Nat. Bank & Trust Co, Oklahoma City, 1980—; adj. prof. Oklahoma City Community Coll., 1981—; comml. underwriting com. Liberty Mortgage Co., Oklahoma City, 1982—; lectr. Oklahoma Bar Assn. Continuing Legal Edn., Am. Inst. Banking, Okla., 1981—. Author: How to Handle Garnishment and I.R.S. Tax Levies, 1984. Bd. dirs. Oklahoma City Food Bank, 1980—, exec. com. 1982—; state vice chmn. U.S. Olympic Com., Okla., 1980—; team capt. and prodn. award winner YMCA campaign, 1985; chmn. benevolence bd., mem. exec. com. Mayflower Ch., 1986—. Recipient Officer Call award Liberty Nat. Corp. 1981, 83, 84, Goal Setting award, 1982, 83; Okla. Credit Mans Cert. of Appreciation, 1982-83; Cert. of Appreciation, Credit Womens Assn. 1982. Mem. Okla. Bar Assn. (banking law sect.), Tex. Bar Assn., ABA (corp., banking and bus. law sect.) Phi Delta Phi. Republican. Clubs: Greens Country Woodlake Racquet (Oklahoma City). Office: Liberty Nat Bank & Trust Co 100 N Broadway Oklahoma City OK 73125

BOGUE, ERNEST GRADY, educator; b. Memphis, Dec. 9, 1935; s. Emery Grady and Ardell (Wiseman) B.; m. Linda Young; children—Karin, Michele, Barrett, Sara, Michael. B.S., Memphis State U., 1957, M.A., 1965, Ed.D., 1968. Asst. v.p. acad. affairs Memphis State U., 1971-74; fellow in acad. adminstrn. Am. Council on Edn., Washington, 1974-75; assoc. dir. acad. affairs Tenn. Higher Edn. Com., Nashville, 1975-80; chancellor La. State U., Shreveport, 1980—. Author: The Enemies of Leadership, 1985. Contbr. articles to profl. jours. Bd. dirs. Norwela council Boy Scouts Am., Shreveport, 1980—, Shreveport Opera Bd., 1981-84, United Way, Shreveport, 1983—. Served to capt. USAF, 1958-61. Mem. Shreveport C. of C. (dir. 1980-83), Am. Assn. State Coll. and Univs., So. Assn. Colls. and Schs. (chmn. personnel tng. com.), Phi Delta Kappa, Omicron Delta Kappa. Mem. Church of Christ. Avocations: racquetball; tennis; playing French Horn. Address: La State Univ 8515 Youree Dr Shreveport LA 71115

BOHANON, RICHARD LEE, United States bankruptcy judge; b. Oklahoma City, Feb. 9, 1935; s. Luther Lee and Marie Frances (Swatek) B.; m. Margaret Jane Herrmann, Aug. 12, 1959; children—Christopher, David, Philip. A.B., Dartmouth Coll., 1957; LL.B., Oklahoma U., 1960; LL.M. in Comparative Law, NYU, 1962. Bar: Okla. 1960, U.S. Supreme Ct. 1972. Mem. firm Bohanon & Barth, Oklahoma City, 1964-79, Andrews, Davis, Legg, Bixler, Milsten & Murrah, Oklahoma City, 1979-82; U.S. bankruptcy judge Western Dist. Okla., Oklahoma City, 1982—. Bd. govs. Nat. Conf. Bankruptcy Judges, 1985—. Democrat. Roman Catholic. Club: Oklahoma City Golf and Country. Avocations: squash; golf; skiing. Home: 1611 Westminster Pl Oklahoma City OK 73120 Office: US Bankruptcy Ct US Courthouse Oklahoma City OK 73102

BOHN, BARBARA ANN, laboratory director; b. St. Louis, Nov. 24, 1943; d. Arthur John Joseph and Eleanor Caroline (Kinsman) B. B.S. in Med. Tech., Loyola U., New Orleans, 1965; M.B.A., Old Dominion U., 1984. Med. technologist Broward Gen. Med. Ctr., Ft. Lauderdale, Fla., 1965-66; microbiologist Duke U. Hosp., Durham, N.C., 1966-71; tech. lab. coordinator Harvard Community Health Plan, Cambridge, Mass., 1971-77; tech. lab. dir. Louise Obici Meml. Hosp., Suffolk, Va., 1977—, planning analyst, chmn. Diagnosis Related Group task force, 1983—; bd. dirs., sec. Edmarc, Inc., Suffolk, 1985—, also dir. Mem. adv. bd. Western Tidewater Area Health Edn. Com., 1983—. Mem. Am. Soc. Clin. Pathologists (assoc.; program chmn. workshops Boston 1977), Clin. Lab. Mgmt. Assn. (fin. chmn. 1983), Hosp. Purchasing Service (pres. lab. com. 1983), Beta Beta Beta. Avocations: Piano, tennis, poetry, gardening. Home: 1420 Planters Dr Suffolk VA 23434 Office: Obici Hosp Lab 1900 N Main St Suffolk VA 23434

BOHN, PHILLIP DUDLEY, appraiser; b. Wheeling, W.Va., Feb. 28, 1948; s. William Dudley and Phyllis Abegail (Arn) B.; m. Sharon Lee McAninch, July 26, 1980; children—Amy Lynn Smith, Rollin Phillip. B.S., Washington and Jefferson Coll., 1974; diploma computer sci. Wheeling Coll. Commerce, 1971. Tax appraiser I, W.Va. State Tax Dept., 1973-83, tax appraiser II, 1983—. Mem. Wheeling Jaycees (pres. 1978-79, sec., dir., state dir., internal v.p., Outstanding Regional Dir. 1979-80, Outstanding Young Man Am. 1979, 80, internat. senator 1983). Lutheran. Lodges: Elks, Masons, Shriners. Home: 11 Ark Ave Wheeling WV 26003

BOHN, WILLIAM CHANLER, radio electronics merchant marine officer; b. Ithaca, N.Y., June 29, 1921; s. William Christian and Alida (Chanler) B.; m. Helen Louise Reary, Dec. 17, 1953; children—Cynthia Nancy, Peter Willoughby. Student YMCA Trade Sch., N.Y.C., 1941-42, Harvard U., 1946-48. Audio engr. ABC, N.Y.C., 1951-52; owner, engring. designer Bohn Music Systems Co., 1952-58; dir. tech. info. Indsl. Acoustics Co., Inc., Bronx, N.Y., 1958-59; audio-acoustic cons., owner mgr. Hi-Fi Doctor Service, N.Y.C., 1959-80; radio electronics officer U.S. Merchant Marine, N.Y.C., 1977—. Served to lt. U.S. Mcht. Marine, 1942-46, 48-50. Decorated Meritorious Service medal. Mem. Acoustical Soc. Am., Audio Engring. Soc., AAAS, Am. Inst. Physics, IEEE, AIAA, Am. Radio Assn., Vet. Wireless Operators Assn., Soc. Wireless Pioneers, Am. Radio Relay League, N.Y. Acad. Scis. Club: Camden

(Maine) Yacht. Host, writer radio program The Art of High Fidelity, 1958-59; contbr. articles to mags. Office: Am Radio Assn 26 Journal Sq Suite 1501 Jersey City NJ 07306

BOHORFOUSH, JOSEPH GEORGE, physician; b. Birmingham, Ala., Dec. 20, 1907; s. George and Susan (Joseph) B.; A.B., Vanderbilt U., 1929, M.D., 1933; m. Agravene Meshad; children—David, William. Intern Hillman Hosp., Birmingham, 1933-34; resident Waverly Hills (Ky.) Sanatorium, 1934-35; asst. med. dir. Lake View Sanatorium, Madison, Wis., 1936-41; med. dir. Jefferson Sanatorium, Birmingham, 1946-47; instr. medicine U. Ala. Med. Coll., 1946-48; chief profl. services VA Hosp., Memphis, 1947-51; asst. prof. medicine U. Tenn., Memphis, 1947, 51; clin. prof. medicine Med. Coll. Ga., 1951-60; chief medicine VA Hosp, Augusta, Ga., 1951-60. Served as maj. M.C., AUS, 1941-45; col. M.C. ret. Diplomate Am. Bd. Internal Medicine, Am. Bd. Pulmonary Diseases. Fellow A.C.P., Am. Coll. Chest Physicians; mem. AMA, Am. Thoracic Soc., So. Med. Assn., Ret. Officers Assn. Home: 1300 Beacon Pkwy Birmingham AL 35209

BOHROFEN, TOMMY MICHAEL, electric utility company executive; b. Sherman, Tex., Jan. 19, 1948; s. William Homer and Martha Elizabeth (Cooper) B.; m. Barbara Elizabeth Wilson, Sept. 22, 1967; children—Michael Brent, Amy Dawn. B.A. in Bus. Adminstrn., Central State U., Edmond, Okla., 1972. Sales cons. Okla. Gas & Electric, Oklahoma City, 1970-76, sr. sales cons., 1976-77, consumer energy cons., 1977-78, consumer energy adviser 1978-79, coordinator energy mgmt., 1979-81, mgr. energy services, 1981—; lectr. in field; seminar leader in energy. Chmn. accountability program Oklahoma City Pub. Schs., 1977, chmn. instructional mgmt. program, 1978; bd. dir. Oklahoma City All Sports Assn., 1982—; active YMCA. Recipient Award of Honor, Oklahoma City Bicentennial Commn., 1976, Cert. of Achievement in Okla. energy policy Okla. Dept. Energy, 1978, also numerous awards for service from civic orgns. Mem. Southwestern Hombuilding Assn. (bd. dirs.), Sales and Mktg. Execs., Fellowship Christian Athletes, Okla. Electric League, Apt. Assn. Central Okla., Refrigeration Service Engrs. Soc., Oklahoma City Execs. Assn., Friendship Park Raider Athletic Assn. (pres. 1978-79). Republican. Lodge: Order Demolay. Home: 10325 Ranchwood Manor Dr Oklahoma City OK 73139Office: Oklahoma Gas and Electric 321 N Harvey Oklahoma City OK 73101

BOILLIN, MARION ELIZABETH CAMP, draftsman, artist; b. Granger, Tex., Aug. 15, 1916; d. Joseph Hedden and Leta Mary (Cooke) Camp; B.S., Tex. Women's U., 1936. With supts. office Houston Public Sch. System, 1937-42, substitute art tchr., 1946; asst. bursar U. Houston, 1947-48; comml. artist Citizens Newspaper and Gulf States Advt. Agy., Houston, 1948-51; with Transco Energy Co. (formerly Transco Pipe Line Corp.), Houston 1951-82, sr. geol. draftsman, 1974-82; land analysis drafting promotional brochures Ind. Research Assocs., 1970-73; work in permanent collection Houston Pub. Library; designer, calligrapher awards. Republican. Baptist. Home: 5611 Spellman St Houston TX 77096 Office: Transco Energy Co PO Box 1396 Houston TX 77251

BOKLAGE, CHARLES EDWARD, medical educator; b. Louisville, Aug. 25, 1944; s. George Charles and Mary Mildred (Buckman) B.; m. Sharon Ann Sias, 1964 (div. 1971); children—Leah, Anna; m. Diana Marie Hartwig, 1972 (div. 1977); children—Lara, Kelly; m. Cecilia Moore, Dec. 29, 1978; children—Peyton, Georgia. A.B. summa cum laude, Bellarmine Coll., 1965; Ph.D., U. Calif.-San Diego, 1972. Research assoc. Kans. State U., 1972-75, instr., 1973-74, vis. asst. prof., 1974-75; fellow in med. genetics, biostats., neurobiology, and devel. psychology U. N.C., Chapel Hill, 1975-78; asst. prof. microbiology and genetics East Carolina U. Sch. Medicine, Greenville, 1978-85, assoc. prof., 1985—, dir. genetics program, 1982—. Bellarmine Coll. Pres.'s scholar, 1961-65; NSF fellow, 1964-65, 65-70; NIH trainee, 1970-72. Mem. Internat. Soc. for Twin Studies (founding mem.), Am. Soc. Human Genetics, Internat. Neuropsychology Soc., Soc. for Neuroscis., N.C. Assn. Med. Genetics, Sigma Xi. Contbr. articles to profl. jours. Home: 1103 E Rock Spring Rd Greenville NC 27834 Office: Brody Bldg East Carolina U Sch of Medicine Greenville NC 27834

BOLAND, LOIS WALKER, former mathematician and computer systems analyst; b. Newton Center, Mass., Sept. 14, 1919; d. Charles Nelson and Nell Flora (Kruse) Walker; m. Ralph Montrose Boland, June 2, 1943; children—Charles Montrose, William Ralphs (dec.), Ann Helen Boland Garner. B.S., Stetson U., 1940; grad. fellow U. Ala., 1940-41; postgrad. U. Fla., 1948, 51-52, U. Mich., 1958, 65, U. Colo., 1966, 68. Elec. engring. draftsman Tampa Ship Corp., Fla., 1943-46; math. tchr. Plant High Sch., Tampa, 1947-50; mathematician/computers, data reduction div. Patrick AFB, Fla., 1951-54; mathematician, computer supr. data reduction div. White Sands Missile Range, N.Mex., 1954-63; ops. research analyst Peterson AFB, Colo. Springs, Colo., 1963-78, ret., 1978. Author: AUPRE Computer Program Manual, 1963, 77; Askania Photheodolite Computer Manual, 1956; editor Q-Point mag., 1966. Elected mem. Democratic exec. com. Volusia County, Fla., 1984—; mem. bell choir First Baptist Ch., DeLand, Fla., 1981—, mem. ch. choir, 1979—. Pioneer mathematician Pioneer Group White Sands Missile Range, 1985; math. fellow U. Ala., 1940-41. Mem. Math. Assn. Am. (emeritus), Am. Math. Soc., AAUW (pres. DeLand 1984—), Mensa, Am. Contract Bridge League. Clubs: Halifax, Lake Beresford Yacht. Avocations: writing; pianist; travel; duplicate bridge; swimming. Home: PO Box 215 Cassadaga FL 32706

BOLAND, THOMAS EDWIN, banker; b. Columbus, Ga., July 8, 1934; s. Clifford Edwin and Helen Marjorie (Robinson) B.; m. Beth Ann Campbell, May 23, 1959; children—Susan Ann, T. Edwin, Student Emory U., 1952-54; B.B.A., Ga. State U., 1957; postgrad. Stonier Grad. Sch. Banking, Rutgers U., 1964-66; Advanced Mgmt. Program Emory U., 1972. With 1st Nat. Bank Atlanta, 1954—, v.p., 1968-71, group v.p., 1972-73, sr. v.p., 1974-78, exec. v.p., 1979—, chief adminstrv. officer, 1981—; also exec. v.p., chief adminstrv. officer 1st Atlanta Corp., 1981—; v.p. 1st Atlanta Internat. Corp., 1979—; exec. v.p. First Wachovia Corp., 1986—; dir. 1st Nat. Bank Atlanta, First Atlanta Corp., First Atlanta Mortgage Corp., First Atlanta Leasing, First Nat. Building Corp., First Nat. Bank of Dalton, Tharpe & Brooks, Inc., First Family Fin. Services, Inc.; mem. investment com. Minbanc Capital Corp., Washington, 1978—. Trustee Atlanta Bapt. Coll., 1970-72; trustee, treas. Ga. Bapt. Found., 1980—, also mem. investment and endowment coms.; bd. visitors Emory U., 1982; mem. exec. bd. Atlanta Area council Boy Scouts Am., 1982; mem. Pres.'s council Mercer U., Macon, Ga., 1980—. Served with AUS, 1957. Named Salesman of Yr., Atlanta Sales and Mktg. Execs. Club, 1968. Mem. Am. Bankers Assn. (cert. comml. lender, bank card com. 1964-66), Robert Morris Assocs. (security dealers relations com. 1974-75, Atlanta area chmn. 1979—, chmn., dir. Eastern group Southeastern chpt. 1981—, pres., dir. so. chpt. 1982, mem. policy div. council 1982—, chmn. policy div. council 1984—, nat. dir. 1984—), Ga. State U. Alumni Assn. (dir. 1979—, mem. exec. com., pres. 1985-86). Club: Cherokee Town and Country (Atlanta). Office: PO Box 4148 Atlanta GA 30302

BOLCH, BEN WILSMAN, financial company executive; b. Danville, Ill., Aug. 22, 1938; s. Carl E. and Juanita (Newton) B.; m. Anne Whisnant, Aug. 24, 1961; 1 dau., Suzanne Elisabeth. B.B.A., Emory U., 1960, M.A., 1962; Ph.D. in Econs., U. N.C., 1966. Mem. faculty Vanderbilt U., Nashville, 1966-80, prof. econs., until 1980, chmn. econs. dept., 1978-80; chief fin. officer Racetrac Petroleum, Inc., Atlanta, 1980-83; chmn. bd. Bolch Group, Inc., Atlanta, 1983—. Univ. fellow Emory U., 1961-62; Ford Found. fellow, 1965-66. Mem. Am. Econ. Assn., Am. Statis. Assn. Club: Willow Springs (Atlanta). Author: Practical Business Statistics, 1968; Multivariate Methods for Business and Economics, 1974. Home 9855 Trace Valley Atlanta GA 30338

BOLCH, CARL EDWARD, JR., lawyer, corporation executive; b. St. Louis, Feb. 28, 1943; s. Carl Edward and Juanita (Newton) B.; m. Susan Bolch; children—Carl, Allison, Natalie. B.S. in Econs., U. Pa., 1964; J.D., Duke U., 1967. Bar; Fla. 1967. Chmn. bd., chief exec. officer Racetrac Petroleum, Inc., Atlanta, 1967—. Edition editor: Close Corporations, 1967. Mem. ABA, Fla. Bar Assn., Soc. Ind. Gasoline Marketers (dir.). Office: Suite 100 2625 Cumberland Pkwy Atlanta GA 30339

BOLDEN, ALJERNON JOHN, dentist, public health official; b. Richmond, Va., Apr. 25, 1951; s. Charles and Eunice Virginia (Hunter) Miller; m. Jacquelyn Anderson Bolden, Aug. 14, 1982; 1 dau., Janee' Tharese. B.A., Boston U., 1973; D.M.D., Tufts U., 1976; M.P.H., Harvard U., 1980. Cons., research assoc. Newark Beth Israel Hosp., 1976-77; pvt. practice dentistry, East Orange, N.J., 1977-78; dental dir. Whittier Street Health Ctr., Boston, 1977-81, Fulton County Health Dept., Atlanta, 1981—; field cons. Mexican Health Care Council, Mexico City, 1980; mem. adv. com. Mass. Minority Council on Alcoholism, Boston, 1980-81; cons., lectr. Action for Boston Community Council, 1980-81; mem. health service adv. com. Head Start, Atlanta, 1982-83. Contbr. articles to profl. jours. Vice pres. J.H. Lockett Choir, College Park, Ga., 1982; mem. Friendship Chorale, 1983; mem. New Temple Singers, St. Paul A.M.E. Ch., Cambridge, Mass., 1975-81. Recipient J. Stoke award Fulton County Health Dept., 1983. Mem. ADA, Am. Pub. Health Assn., Ga. Dental Assn., Mass. Pub. Health Assn., Alpha Omega, Omega Psi Phi. Home: 611 Camelot Dr College Park GA 30349 Office: Dental Dept Fulton County Health Dept 99 Butler St Atlanta GA 30349

BOLDT, DONALD BERNARD, manufacturing company executive, educator; b. Waterloo, Iowa, June 8, 1934; s. Jurgen B. and Bess L. (Wylam) B.; m. Wilma Maxine Robinson, June 12, 1955; children—David W., John F., Thomas E. B.S. in Chem. Engring. with honors, U. Iowa, 1957; postgrad. U. Utah, 1959; M.B.A. with honors (Baker fellow), Harvard U., 1962. Mng. dir. Kawneer Co. Pty. Ltd. subs. Amax, Inc., Sydney, New South Wales, Australia, 1965-69, chmn. Mackamax Aluminum Ltd. subs. Amax, Inc., Runcorn, Cheshire, Eng., 1969-72; group v.p. Neptune Internat. Corp., Atlanta, 1972-79, also dir.; pres. Wall Lenk Corp., Kinston, N.C., 1979—; lectr. Sch. Bus. East Carolina U., Greenville, N.C., 1981—. Pres. Jr. Achievement of Lenoir County, N.C., 1981-82; bd. dirs. Lenoir County United Way, 1982—; mem. Lenoir County Devel. Commn. Served as 1st lt. USAF, 1957-60. Mem. Lenoir County Mfrs. Assn. (pres. 1982), Lenoir C. of C. (v.p. 1982-84), Tau Beta Pi, Phi Lambda Upsilon, Omicron Delta Kappa, Sigma Iota Epsilon, Beta Gamma Sigma. Presbyterian. Clubs: Kinston Country; Am. Nat. (Sydney). Home: 1700 Greenbriar Rd Kinston NC 28501 Office: PO Box 3349 Kinston NC 28501

BOLEN, BOB, mayor of Fort Worth, retail merchant; b. Chgo., Apr. 10, 1926; s. Milford Louis and Beatrice (Pinkerton) B.; m. Frances Dolores Ciborowski, May 3, 1953; children—Rickey, Bobby, Randy, Ronny, Terri Ann; 1 foster child, Don Crosby. B.S. in Bus. Adminstrn., Tex. A&M U., 1948. Mgr., McCrory's Variety Stores, Syracuse, N.Y., 1948-51, Fort Worth, 1951-52; owner, operator Toy Palace, 1952, Bob Bolen's Inc., Fort Worth, 1952—; mayor City of Fort Worth, 1982—; dir. Altamesa Nat. Bank, Fort Worth, Summit Bancshares, Inc., Fort Worth. Mem., former chmn. Dallas/Fort Worth Internat. Airport Bd.; bd. dirs. March of Dimes; hon. chmn. bd. dirs. Casa Manana; active Friends of Youth of YMCA; elder Westminister Presbyterian Ch., Fort Worth. Served with USN, 1944-46. Recipient Man of Yr. award B'nai B'rith, 1984, Fort Worth Civic award Fort Worth Civic Assn., 1985. Mem. Tex. Mcpl. League (2d v.p.), Nat. League Cities (chmn. transp. and communications steering com.). Lodge: Rotary. Avocation: golf. Office: Office of Mayor City of Fort Worth 1000 Throckmorton St Fort Worth TX 76102

BOLEN, TERRY LEE, optometrist; b. Newark, Ohio, Sept. 16, 1945; s. Robert Howard and Mildred Irene (Hoover) B.; B.S., Ohio U., 1968; postgrad. Youngstown State U., 1973; O.D., Ohio State U., 1978; m. Debbie Elaine Thompson, Mar. 23, 1985. Quality control inspector ITT Grinnell Corp., Warren, Ohio, 1973, jr. quality control engr., 1974; pvt. practice optometry, El Paso, Tex., 1978-80, Dallas, 1980-81, Waco, Tex., 1981—, Hewitt, Tex., 1983—; bd. dirs. Am. Optometric Found., 1975-77; nat. pres. Am. Optometric Student Assn., 1977-78; pres. El Paso Optometric Soc., 1980. Vol. visual examiner, Juarez, Mex., 1979—; chmn. Westside Recreation Center Adv. Com., El Paso, 1979. Served to lt. USN, 1969-72. Recipient public service award, City of El Paso, 1980. Mem. Am. Optometric Assn., Tex. Optometric Assn., Optometric Assn. (clin. assoc. Optometric Extension Program Found. 1978—), Heart of Tex. Optometric Soc. (sec.-treas. 1984-85, pres.-elect 1986), North Tex. Optometric Soc., Epsilon Psi Epsilon (pres., 1977-78). Republican. Mem. Christian Ch. (Disciples of Christ). Club: Lions (3rd v.p. Coronaco Club, El Paso 1980, service award, 1978, 79, pres. Hewitt club 1985, v.p. W. Tex. Lion's Eye Bank, El Paso 1980). Home: 316 Chapman Rd Hewitt TX 76643 Office: 512 Hewitt Dr Hewitt TX 76643

BOLGE, GEORGE STEPHEN, museum director, exhibition design consultant; b. Trenton, N.J., Feb. 14, 1942; s. George R. and Grace M. (Rago) B.; m. Elizabeth Ann Stover, July 14, 1967 (div. 1983); 1 dau., Ann Elyse. B.A. and B.S., Rutgers U., 1964; M.A., NYU, 1967; Ph.D. (hon.), Nova U., 1986. Asst. curator ancient art Bklyn. Mus. Art, 1966-67; exec. dir. Mus. Art, Inc., Fort Lauderdale, Fla., 1970—; exhbn. cons. Fort Lauderdale Hist. Soc., 1978-79. Editor: (catalog) The Graphic Work of Renoir, 1975; author: (catalogs) Leon Kroll, 1980, Italian Art, 1981, Matta, 1983. Mem. Fort Lauderdale Community Appearance Bd., 1982, Fort Lauderdale Downtown Devel. Council, 1982—; bd. dirs. Broward County Arts Council, 1982, Art in Pub. Places, Broward County, 1982. Served to lt. USNR, 1967-69. Nat. Trust Hist. Preservation fellow, 1966. Mem. Fla. League Arts (dir. 1970-72), Fine Art Mus. Dirs. Assn. (state exec. com. 1982), Am. Assn. Mus., Coll. Art Assn. Democrat. Roman Catholic. Office: One E Las Olas Blvd Fort Lauderdale FL 33301

BOLGER, ROBERT JOSEPH, trade association executive; b. Phila., Aug. 9, 1922; s. Harold Stephen and Edna (Adams) B.; B.S., Villanova U., 1943; postgrad. Northwestern U., 1945-46, U. Pa., 1946-47, U. Geneva, 1948-49; Pharm.D. (hon.), Mass. Coll. Pharmacy, 1983; m. Helen Siegfried, May 22, 1954; children—Robert, Mary T., Cynthia A., Ann M., Catherine B., David A. Salesman, Container Corp., Phila., 1947; sales supr. Kraft Food Co., Phila., 1949-52; overseas mgr., dir. retail relations Smith, Kline & French Labs., Phila., 1952-62; asst. to exec. v.p. Nat. Assn. Chain Drug Stores, Inc., Arlington, Va., 1962-67, pres., 1967—. Bd. dirs. Am. Found. Pharm. Edn., Nat. Council Patient Info. and Edn.; bd. dirs. Nat. Drug Trade Conf., pres., 1974, 82; bd. dirs. Alexandria Hosp. Served to lt. comdr., USNR; PTO. Decorated Air medal; named Man of Year Cosmetic and Toiletry sect. United Jewish Appeal, 1972; Chain Exec. of Year, Chain Drug Rev., 1979; recipient Council of Overseers award L.I. U., 1982. Mem. Am. Pharm. Assn., Com. of 100, U.S. C. of C., Central Council Nat. Retail Assns. (chmn.), Am. Retail Fedn. (dir.), Nat. Assn. Retail Druggists, Am. Pharm. Assn., Am. Soc. Assn. Execs. (key industry assns. com.). Clubs: Belle Haven Country (Alexandria); Metropolitan (N.Y.C.); Seaview Country (Absecon, N.J.). Contbr. articles to trade publs. Home: 7705 Maid Marian Ct Alexandria VA 22306 Office: PO Box 1417-D49 Alexandria VA 22313

BOLGER, THOMAS JAMES, human resources executive; b. N.Y.C., Oct. 13, 1950; s. Martin John and Katherine (Flatley) B.; m. Susan Mary Regan, Sept. 15, 1979; children—Kaitlin, Daniel. B.B.A., Baruch Coll., 1972; M.B.A., Pace U., 1974. Personnel mgt. trainee Chase Manhattan Bank, N.Y.C., 1972-73; compensation specialist AMF Inc., White Plains, N.Y., 1973-77; mgr. compensation Pepsico, Purchase, N.Y., 1977-79, div. employee relations mgr., 1979-83; dir. human resources Communications Industries, Dallas, 1983—. Republican. Roman Catholic. Avocations: baseball; racquetball; track; antique restoration. Home: 5719 Richwater Dr Dallas TX 75252 Office: Communications Industries 3811 Turtle Creek Blvd Dallas TX 75219

BOLIN, ALPHA E., JR., manufacturing executive; b. Madison, Ill., Mar. 4, 1927; s. Alpha E. and Cynthia B. (Putnam) B.; B.S. in Elec. Engring., Am. Inst. Engring. and Tech., Chgo., 1952; m. Shirley J. Wiseman, Jan. 7, 1956; children—Janis A., Nancy Jo, Donald A. Elec. engr. Wagner Electric Co., St. Louis, 1952-59; dir. research and devel. Precision Trans-Chgo., 1959-60; chief engr. Dowzer Electric Co., Mt. Vernon, Ill., 1960-63; founder VanTran Electric Corp., Waco, Tex., 1963, chmn. bd., pres., 1963—; sr. partner B & K Properties, Waco, Tex.; dir. Central Nat. Bank, Waco. Active Am. Cancer Soc., 1967-69; bd. dirs. Woodway Boys Club, 1975—, McLennan County Better Bus. Bur. Served with U.S. Army, 1945-47. Mem. NAM, Nat. Elec. Mfrs. Assn., Am. Hist. Soc., Waco Creative Art Center, Hist. Waco Soc., Nat. Trust Hist. Preservation, Nat. Pilots Assn. Clubs: Woodland West Country (dir.); Vandalia (Ill.) Country; Lancers (Dallas); Lakewood Tennis and Country, Brazos (Waco). Home: 425 Whitehall Rd Waco TX 76710 Office: 7711 Imperial Dr PO Box 20128 Waco TX 76702

BOLING, EDWARD JOSEPH, university president; b. Sevier County, Tenn., Feb. 19, 1922; s. Sam R. and Nerissa (Clark) B.; B.S. in Accounting, U. Tenn., 1948, M.S. in Statistics, 1950; Ed.D. in Ednl. Adminstrn., George Peabody Coll. Vanderbilt U., 1961; m. Carolyn Pierce, Aug. 8, 1950; children—Mark Edward, Brian Marshall, Steven Clark. With Wilby-Kinsy Theatre Corp., Knoxville, Tenn., 1940-41, Aluminum Co. Am., 1941-42; instr. statistics U. Tenn., 1948-50; research statistician Carbide & Carbon Chem. Corp., Oak Ridge, 1950, supr. source and fissionable materials accounting K-25 plant, 1951-54; budget dir. Tenn., 1955-59, commr. finance and adminstrn., 1959-61; v.p. U. Tenn., 1961-70, pres., 1970—. Dir. N.Am. Philips Corp., Signal Cos., Genex Corp., United Foods, Inc., CSX Corp., Home Fed. Savs. Bank Tenn., Swan's. Mem. So. Regional Edn. Bd., 1957-61, 70—, exec. com., 1974-75; mem. Edn. Commn. of States, 1970-83; trustee, chmn. Am. Coll. Testing Program; mem. Nat. Govs. Conf. Good Will Tour to Brazil and Argentina, 1960. Mem. com. on taxation Am. Council on Edn. Served with AUS, 1943-46; ETO. Mem. Am. Statis. Assn., Assn. Higher Edn., Nat. Assn. Land-Grant Colls. (com. on financing higher edn.), Am. Coll. Pub. Relations Assn. (trustee, chmn. com. taxation and philanthropy), Am. Council on Edn., Knoxville C. of C. (dir.), Am. Legion, L.Q.C. Lamar Soc., Phi Kappa Phi (Scholarship award 1947), Beta Gamma Sigma (charter pres. Alpha chpt. 1948), Phi Delta Kappa, Omicron Delta Kappa, Beta Alpha Psi. Democrat. Club: Univ. Author: (with D. A. Gardiner) Forecasting University Enrollment, 1952; Methods of Objectifying The Allocation of Tax Funds to Tennessee State Colleges, 1961. Home: 940 Cherokee Blvd Knoxville TN 37919

BOLING, FREDRICK WILLIAM, surgeon; b. Edmond, Okla., Nov. 11, 1926; s. Fredrick William and Florence Chloe (Hargrave) B.; m. Wilma Lee Cave, June 4, 1950; children—Paul Fredrick, Amy Lou Boling Blassingame, David Charles, Mark Edwards. A.A., Northwestern Okla. A&M Coll., 1947; postgrad. Central State U., Edmond, Okla., 1947-48; D.O., Univ. Health Scis.-Coll. Osteo. Medicine, Kansas City, Mo., 1952. Diplomate Am. Acad. Osteo. Surgeons. Intern, Gleason Hosp., Larned, Kans., 1958-59; resident Fremont Hosp., Riverton, Wyo., 1960-65; chief dept. surgery Commerce Med. Surg. Ctr., Tex., 1969-76, Fairfax Meml. Hosp., Okla., 1977—. Fellow Am. Acad. Osteo. Surgeons; mem. Am. Osteo. Assn., Okla. Osteo. Assn. Democrat. Methodist. Lodges: Lions, Masons. Avocations: golf, organist, creative writing, hunting. Home: 623 S 6th St Fairfax OK 74637 Office: PO Box 483 Fairfax OK 74637

BOLING, HAROLD EDWARD, software company executive, consultant; b. Portsmouth, Ohio, June 17, 1939; s. Andrew Edward and Ruth Lucille (Stratton) B.; m. Virginia Lee Lowman, Dec. 27, 1962; children—Constance, Edward. B.S. in Bus. and Edn., Va. Commonwealth U., 1974; postgrad. U. Ark., 1978-79. Registrar, Wesleyan U., Middletown, Conn., 1968-70, Va. Commonwealth U., 1970-75; pres. Edn. Data Mgmt., Richmond, Va., 1975-77; registrar U. Ark., Little Rock, 1977-79; dist. sales mgr. Westinghouse Info. Service, Richardson, Tex., 1979-83; dist. sales mgr. Info. Assocs., Inc., Richardson, 1984—, v.p., Plano, Tex., 1984—; owner Am. Internat. Computer Systems, Inc., Plano, Tex., 1981—; bd. dirs. Universal Algorithms, Inc., Portland, Oreg., 1983—. Author, coordinator workshop On-Line Registration and Data Base Mgmt., 1979. Mem. adv. council Salvation Army, Athens, Ohio, 1965-67; coach YMCA Basketball, 1979, 1980-81; scoutmaster Boy Scouts Am., 1980-82, mem. council, 1980-82. Recipient Super Salesman award Internat. Computer Programs, 1982-83; Cert. of Appreciation, So. Assn. Coll. Registrars and Admissions Officers, 1985. Republican. Methodist. Office: Information Assocs Inc 840 E Central Pkwy Plano TX 75074

BOLING, JEWELL, ret. govt. ofcl.; b. Randleman, N.C., Sept. 26, 1907; d. John Emmitt and Carrie (Ballard) Boling; student Women's Coll., U. N.C., 1926, Am. U., 1942, 51-52. Interviewer, N.C. Employment Service, Winston-Salem, Asheboro, 1937-41; occupational analyst Dept. Labor, Washington, 1943-57, placement officer, 1957-58, employment service adv., 1959-61, occupational analyst, 1962, employment service specialist counseling and testing, 1963-69, manpower devel. specialist, from 1969. Recipient Meritorious Achievement award Dept. Labor, 1972. Mem. AAAS, N.Y. Acad. Scis., Am. Assn. Counseling and Devel. (profl. mem. nat. vocat. guidance assn.), Am. Rehab. Counseling Assn. (archivist 1964-68), Assn. Measurement and Evaluation in Guidance, Assn. Humanistic Psychology, Smithsonians, Sierra Club, Internat. Platform Assn., Audubon Naturalist Soc., Planetary Soc., Nat. Capital Astronomers (editor Star Dust 1949-58), Nature Conservancy. Author: Counselor's Handbook, 1967; Counselor's Desk Aid, Eighteen Basic Vocational Directions, 1967; Handbook for New Careerists in Employment Security, 1971. Contbr. articles to profl. pubs. Address: Route 2 Box 176 Randleman NC 27317

BOLING, JOHN CARL, computer software company executive, statistical and computer software educator; b. Parkersburg, W. Va., Mar. 2, 1949; s. John Lafayette and Anne Mildred (Brown) B.; m. Kathleen Marie Haaser, Aug. 24, 1974; children—Jonathan, Todd, Michelle, B.S., Va. Tech. 1971, M.A., 1973; Ph.D. U. Tenn., 1979. Faculty Va. Tech., Blacksburg, 1973-74; mgr. statis. cons. U. Tenn. Computing Ctr., Knoxville, 1976-78; statistician TVA, Knoxville, 1978-80; adj. faculty U. Tenn., Knoxville, 1978-80; dir. SAS Inst., Cary, N.C., 1980—; dir. Va. Tech. Alumni Assn., Blacksburg, 1978—; stat. cons. Knoxville Orthopedic Clinic, 1978-80. Contbr. articles on video, computer based and instructional computer software tng. Served to staff sgt. USAR, 1974-80. Named Outstanding Young Men in Am., Jaycees, 1978. Mem. Am. Statis. Assn., Internat. TV Assn., Phi Kappa Phi, Phi Eta Sigma, Omicron Delta Kappa. Republican. Methodist. Avocations: running; racquetball; tennis; golf. Home: 103 Deer Park Ln Cary NC 27511 Office: SAS Inst PO Box 8000 Cary NC 27511

BOLINGER, CLAYTON DANIEL, management evaluator, project engineer; b. Knoxville, Tenn., Mar. 15, 1946; s. Clayton Armstrong and Ruth LeVena (Hale) B.; m. Martha Ann Hayes, Mar. 2, 1974; children—Sarah Nicole, Hannah Danielle, Jessica Ruth. B.S.E.E., U. Tenn., 1968. Registered profl. engr., Tenn. Engring. aide Tenn. Valley Authority Design, Knoxville, 1966-68, elec. engr., 1968-83, mgmt. evaluator, 1983—. Com. mem. Tenn. Valley Authority Credit Union, 1985—; bd. govs. Vol. Blind Industries, Morristown, Tenn., 1984—; sustaining mem. Republican Nat. Com., 1983—; steering com. Combined Fed. Campaign, 1984—. Served to capt. USAF, 1968-72, Tenn. Air N.G., 1984—. Grantee U.S. ROTC, 1967-69; recipient Electronics Honor award USAF, 1968. Mem. IEEE, Tenn. Soc. Profl. Engrs., Soc. Am. Mil. Engrs., U. Tenn. Alumni Club Band, Tau Beta Pi. Republican. Baptist. Lodge: Lions (pres. 1983—). Avocations: public speaking, eyesight conservation work. Home: 4317 Ventura Dr Knoxville TN 37938 Office: Tenn Valley Authority Office Gen Mgr 400 Summit Hill Knoxville TN 37902

BOLINGER, JOHN C., JR., management consultant, gas company executive; b. Knoxville, Tenn., Feb. 12, 1922; s. John C. and Elsie Marie (Burkhart) B.; m. Helen McCallie, Jan. 26, 1944; children—Janet, Robert, John. B.S. in Fin., U. Tenn., 1943; M.B.A., Harvard U., 1947. Asst. sec. Lehigh Coal and Navigation Co., Phila., 1947-49, asst. to pres., 1949-50, v.p., 1950-54; asst. to pres. Mississippi River Corp., St. Louis, 1954-57, exec. v.p., 1963-67; pres., dir. East Tenn. Natural Gas Co., Knoxville, 1957-61, Tenn. Bank & Trust Co., Houston, 1961-63; pres. Mississippi River Transmission Corp., 1963-67; pres., dir. Tenn. Natural Resources, Inc. (name formerly Tenn. Natural Gas Lines, Inc.), chmn., 1976—; chmn., dir. Nashville Gas Co., 1973—, pres., 1973-83; vice chmn., dir. Piedmont Natural Gas Co., Charlotte, N.C., 1985—; mgmt. cons., Knoxville, 1967—; dir. Mo. Pacific R.R., 1963-67, Nashville br. Fed. Res. Bank, 1976-81, Aladdin Industries, Inc., Home Fed. Savs. & Loan, Knoxville, Consol. Freightways Inc., Palo Alto, Calif., Gen. Shale Products Corp., Johnson City, Tenn.; vis. lectr. Coll. Bus., U. Tenn., 1970-79. Served to capt., inf., U.S. Army, 1943-46. Decorated Purple Heart, Bronze Star; Croix de Guerre (France). Presbyterian (elder). Clubs: Cherokee Country (Knoxville); Cumberland, City, Belle Meade Country (Nashville); Lost Tree (North Palm Beach, Fla.). Home: 1400 Kenesaw Ave SW Knoxville TN 37919 also 1000 Lake House Dr S Lost Tree Village North Palm Beach FL 33408 Office: 814 Church St Nashville TN 37203

BOLLUM, KEITH CHARLES, bookstore executive; b. Alexandria, Minn., June 11, 1950; s. Rolf Lewis and Alice Miriam (Persson) B.; m. Janet Lynn Erickson, June 3, 1972; 1 child, Justin Keith. B.A. in History, N.D. State U., 1972; postgrad., Moorhead State U., 1973. History tchr. Victoria Edn. Dept., Melbourne, Australia, 1973-75, Onamia Pub. Schs., Minn., 1977-78, Ne-Ah Shing Sch., Mille Lacs Reservation, Minn., 1978-79; book store propr. Muse Book Shop, DeLand, Fla., 1980—; pres. Helikon Books, Inc., DeLand. Sec. West Volusia Hist. Soc., DeLand, 1983-84, dir., 1985—; trustee DeLand Library Adv. Bd., 1985. Mem. Am. Booksellers Assn. Democrat. Home: 626 N Palmetto DeLand FL 32720 Office: Muse Book Shop 112 S Woodland Blvd DeLand FL 32720

BOLNER, CLIFTON JOSEPH, manufacturing company executive; b. San Antonio, Tex., July 30, 1928; s. Joe and Josephine (Grandjean) B.; B.S., Tex. A&M U., 1949; m. Rosalie Richter, Jan. 20, 1949; children—Tim, Mike, Deb, Cindy, Bev, Chris, Mary. Partner, Bolner's Grocery & Meat Market, San Antonio, 1949-55; pres. Bolner's Fiesta Products, Inc., San Antonio, 1955—;

dir. Exchange Nat. Bank, Kelly Field Nat. Bank. Pres., Cath. Family and Children Services, San Antonio, 1968-69; chmn. fin. com. San Antonio Archdiocese, 1978-79; chmn. annual awards dinner NCCJ, 1974; bd. dirs. San Antonio Symphony Soc., 1973—, San Antonio Mus. Assn., 1973—, Opera Superman, 1975—, San Antonio Muscular Dystrophy Assn., 1975—, San Antonio Right to Life Com., 1981—; mem. devel. bd. Incarnate Word Coll., 1974—; San Antonio Cath. rep. NCCJ, 1978—; adv. bd. St. Mary's U., 1981—. Served to 1st lt. USAF, 1950-52. Recipient Archbishop Furey Outstanding award medal, 1969; Disting. Alumni award Central Cath. High Sch., 1979; Cath. Brotherhood award NCCJ, 1982 Mem. Oblate Asso., Assn. Holy Family Guilds. Roman Catholic. Clubs: KC, San Antonio Serra Vocation, Italo Am. Young Men's, St. Paul's Men's, Soc. of Mary Assos. Home: 110 W Lynwood St San Antonio TX 78212 Office: 426 Menchaca St San Antonio TX 78207

BOLT, BRENDA ANNE, nurse; b. West Point, Ga., July 6, 1944; d. Wallace Berry and Burnie Sue (Mitchell) B. R.N., St. Margaret Hosp., Montgomery, Ala., 1965. Commd. 2d lt. U.S. Army, 1967, advanced through grades to capt., 1971; mem. operating room staff George H. Lanier Hosp., Valley, Ala., 1965-67; asst. operating room supr., 1969-70, operating room, recovery room supr., 1984—; operating room supr. U.S. Army 17th Field Hosp., Viet Nam, 1968-69; instr. Fort Leonard Wood Army Hosp., Mo., 1970-72; mem. operating room staff 2d Gen. Hosp., Landstuhl, Fed. Republic Germany, 1972-74; supr. infection control central material service, Martin Army Hosp., Fort Benning, Ga., 1974-77; operating room supr. Keller Army Hosp., West Point, N.Y., 1977-79; operating room central material service supr. Wurzburg Army Hosp., Fed. Republic Germany, 1979-82; head nurse, same day surgery Madigan Army Med. Ctr., Tacoma, Wash., 1982-84. Decorated Nat. Def. medal, Army Commendation medal with three oak leaf clusters. Mem. Operating Room Nurses Assn. Democrat. Roman Catholic. Avocations: softball; skiing; camping; reading; gardening. Home: 1007 S Jenning Ave Lanett AL 36863 Office: George H Lanier Meml Hosp 4800 48th St Valley AL 36854

BOLTE, CHARLES CLINTON, printing and graphic arts consultant; b. Marshall, Mo., Jan. 8, 1945; s. Harry Ben and Laura Louise (Barnhill) B.; m. Mary Elizabeth Tomaszewski, Sept. 2, 1973; children—Nicole Alison, Lauren Ann. B.I.E., Ga. Inst. Tech., 1967; M.B.A., U. Va., 1972. Mktg. rep. W.R. Grace and Co., Columbia, Md., 1972-74; engrng. mgr. William Byrd Press, Richmond, Va., 1974-76, exec. dir., 1976-79, v.p. research and devel., 1979-84; printing and graphic arts cons., 1984—; mem. exec. devel. program faculty Printing Industries Am.; chmn. research and techno-econ. forecasting coms. Graphic Arts Tech. Found.; chmn., co-chmn. several graphic arts confs. Contbr. articles to profl. jours. Vestryman, Episc. Ch. of Redeemer, Richmond, Va., 1981-83. Served to 1st lt. U.S. Army, 1968-71. Decorated Commendation medal. Mem. Am. Inst. Indsl. Engrs. (sr., past dir. graphic arts div.), Word Processing Assn. Richmond (dir.). Club: Granite Recreation (past pres.). Contbr. articles to profl. jours. Office: American Business Consultant Box W Chambersburg PA 17201

BOLTON, ELIZABETH B., educator; b. Milton, Fla., Oct. 20, 1938; d. Clyde and Verna (Lundy) Bass; m. James M. Post, May 9, 1982; 1 child by previous marriage—Elaine. B.S., U. Fla., 1959; M.A., U. South Fla., 1971; Ph.D., Fla. State U., 1975. Sec. Tex. Instruments, Dallas, 1961; tchr. pub. schs., Fla., Tenn., 1962-69; instr. City Ctr. for Learning, St. Petersburg, Fla., 1969-71; instr. dept. vocat. and adult edn. Coll. Edn., U. South Fla., Tampa, 1971-73; grad. asst. in career edn. Fla. State U., 1974-75; coordinator joint doctoral program in adult edn. Va. Poly. Inst. and Va. Commonwealth U., 1977-80; coordinator ops. Richmond Area Coop. Doctoral Programs in Adult Edn., 1979-80; asst. prof. adult edn. Va. Poly. Inst. and State U., 1975-80; assoc. prof. and extension specialist Fla. Coop. Extension Service, U. Fla., Gainesville, 1980—; cons. and lectr. in field. Contbr. articles to profl. jours. Recipient numerous grants. Mem. Adult Edn. Assn., Am. Ednl. Research Assn., Am. Home Econs. Assn., Am. Soc. Tng. and Devel. (dir. 1981-82), Am. Vocat. Assn., Assn. Vol. Action Scholars, Commn. of Profs. of Adult Edn., Fla. Vocat. Assn., Univ. Assn. Women Faculty, Va. Adult Edn. Assn. (exec. bd. 1979), Va. Social Sci. Assn., LWV, Historic Gainesville, Inc., Alachua County Hist. Soc., Phi Delta Kappa. Office: Univ Fla 3033 McCarty Hall Gainesville FL 32611

BOLTON, JOSEPH COLLIER, JR., art gallery and frame serice company executive; b. Harrisburg, Pa., Aug. 7, 1936; s. Joseph Collier and Grace Elizabeth (Nauss) B. B.A., Gettysburg Coll., 1959; postgrad. Temple U., 1962. Mgr. Howard Johnson Restaurants, Harrisburg, 1959-60; promotion dir. Sta. WTPA-TV, Harrisburg, 1960-62; asst. dir. advt. Bd. of Publ., Lutheran Ch. Am., Phila., 1962-63; adminstrv. asst. Ugite Gas Co., Malvern, Pa., 1963-65; Phila. dist. mgr. Pa. Blue Shield, 1965-76; owner, pres. The Frame Factory, Fort Lauderdale, Fla., 1976—. Vice pres. Breakwaters Homeowners Assn., Fort Lauderdale, 1985—. Mem. Bus. and Profl. Group (pres. 1981-83), English-Speaking Union, Pompano Beach C. of C.. Club: Lago Mar Beach (Fort Lauderdale). Lodges: Masons (32 deg.), Robert Burns. Home: 2005 SE 26th Terr Fort Lauderdale FL 33316 Office: Frame Factory and Gallery 1744 E Commercial Blvd Fort Lauderdale FL 33334

BOLTON, MIMI DUBOIS, artist, writer; b. Gravlotte, Alsace-Loraine, France, Dec. 12, 1902; came to U.S., 1902, naturalized, 1907; d. Paul and Anna DuBois; m. George W. Bolton. Student Marquette U., 1924. One man shows include Balt. Mus., DuBose Gallery, Houston, Alexandria Mus., La., Anglo-Am. Mus., Baton Rouge, Johnson-White Gallery, New Orleans. Represented in permanent collections at Alexandria Mus., Gloria-Laguna Mus., Corcoran Mus., Washington. Author: Merry-Go-Round Family, 1954 (Jr. Literary award); Karlas Reise Mit Dem Katussell, 1955; Wilhamina's Inheritance, 1984. Home and Office: 1404 Twisted Oak Ln Baton Rouge LA 70810

BOLTON, WILLIS LLOYD, librarian; b. Atlanta, Aug. 25, 1933; s. Robert L. and Eva (Davis) B. A.B., Clark Coll., 1956; M.S., Atlanta U., 1968, Specialist in Library Service, 1976. Tchr., Atlanta Pub. Schs., 1958-68; librarian Profl. Library Atlanta, 1968-74; coordinator Atlanta Pub. Schs., 1974-76; resource librarian Area III Office, Atlanta, 1976—. Trustee, Allen Temple African Methodist Episcopal Ch., 1963—, bass soloist sr. choir, 1964—; mem. Atlanta U. Community Chorus, 1964—. UCLA fellow, 1974. Mem. Citizen Action Program, Ga. Library Assn., ALA, Phi Delta Kappa.

BOMAR, PORTIA HAMILTON, psychoanalyst, psychotherapist; b. Cleve., July 19; d. Charles Brooks and Marian (Clements) Goulder; m. William P. Bomar, July 1, 1966. B.A., U. Mich., 1923; M.A., Columbia U., 1932; Ph.D., 1940; postgrad., Oxford U., 1923-25. Pvt. practice psychoanalysis and psychotherapy, N.Y.C., 1930-58; dir. teaching clinic Columbia-Presbyn. Med. Ctr., 1942-50; assoc. prof. psychology U. Coll., U. Richmond, 1964-66; mem. faculty Southwestern Grad. Sch. Banking, So. Meth. U., Dallas, from 1975; lectr. U. Tex., Austin, from 1968. Author: When 'Mid This Glory I Was Young, 1980; also articles in profl. jours. Bd. dirs. Child Study Ctr., Ft. Worth, from 1974, Ft. Worth Zool. Assn., from 1974, Tarrant County Mental Health Assn., 1974-76, Hist. Soc. Tarrant County, from 1968, Casa Manana, Ft. Worth, 1975-76; active Human Relations Commn. Ft. Worth, 1968-71. Fellow Am. Psychol. Assn.; mem. Psychical Research Found. (bd. dirs.), Corp. Eye Inst., Retina Found., Chi Omega. Clubs: Ft. Worth, Rivercrest Country; Univ. of Sarasota, Woman's of Sarasota. Home: 888 Blvd of the Arts Sarasota FL 33577

BOMBAUGH, KARL JACOB, research scientist; b. Johnstown, Pa., Dec. 29, 1922; s. Anthony and Elizabeth Margaret (Kosmatin) B.; U.S. Army cert. completion Ala. Poly. Inst., 1944; B.S., Juniata Coll., 1947; m. Martha Heisey, Feb. 20, 1943; children—Dianne Lee, Marcia Lynn, Karl David, Keith Daniel. Analytical devel. chemist E. I. DuPont de Nemours, Linden, N.J., 1947-53; devel. group leader Am. Cyanamid Co., Avondale, La., 1953-58; sr. research scientist Spencer Chem. Co., Merriam, Kans., 1958-64; mgr. application research Mine Safety Appliances, Pitts., 1964-66; v.p. Waters Assos., Inc., Framingham, Mass., 1966-71, also dir.; pres., founder Chromatec, Inc., Ashland, Mass., 1971-73; sr. scientist Tracor, Inc., Austin, Tex., 1973-75; prin. scientist Radian Corp., Austin, 1975—; cons. Varian Assos.; fellow on Pres.'s Council, Am. Inst. Mgmt., 1968-75; dir. cooperative internat. environ. study, Yugoslavia, 1977—. Bd. dirs. N.E. Johnson County (Kans.) YMCA, 1960-64, East Suburban Pitts. YMCA, 1964-65; elder Village Presbyn. Ch., Prairie Village, Kans., 1958-64; chmn. archtl. control com. River Point Estates, Comal County, Tex., 1976—. Served with U.S. Army, 1943-46. Mem. Am. Chem. Soc., Instrument Soc. Am. (sr.), ASTM (affiliate; tech. program chmn. 1966-70, chmn. Com. E-19 1970-74, since chmn. emeritus, award for appreciation 1974). Contbr. chpts., numerous articles to profl. publs.; editorial adv. bd. Jour. Chromatograph Sci., 1969-74, CRC Handbook Chromatography, 1972—. Home: 7301 West Rim Austin TX 78731 Office: 8500 Shoal Creek Blvd PO Box 9948 Austin TX 78766

BOMBOY, PAMELA KIRK, librarian, educator; b. Meadville, Pa., May 24, 1949; d. David Andrew and Lois Claire (Slack) Kirk; m. Barry Joseph Bomboy, Feb. 11, 1972; children—Erin Elizabeth, Joseph David. B.S. in Edn., Shippensburg U., 1970; M.S. in L.S., U. Pitts., 1972; M.S. in Edn., Va. Commonwealth U., 1980. Tchr., Butler Area Pub. Schs., Butler, Pa., 1970-71, Harlan County Pub. Schs. (Ky.), 1973-75, Good Shepherd Sch., Richmond, Va., 1979-82; librarian Ringgold Area Pub. Schs., Monongahela, Pa., 1973-74, Henrico County Pub. Library, Richmond, 1975-77, Chesterfield County Pub. Schs. (Va.), 1982—. Book reviewer Sch. Library Jour. Rec. sec., librarian Henrico County Hist. Soc., Richmond, 1978—. Elva B. Smith scholar Sch. Library and Info. Scis., U. Pitts., 1972. Mem. ALA (Putnam Pub. Group award 1985), NEA, Alpha Delta Kappa (pres. Gamma chpt.), Beta Phi Mu. Methodist. Clubs: National Story League (mem. program com. 1983-84, rec. sec. 1984—) (Richmond, Va.); Clowns of America (Richmond, Va.). Performs as Pistachio, clown and storyteller. Home: 6 Narrowridge Rd Richmond VA 23231 Office: Chesterfield County Pub Schs Chesterfield VA 23832

BONAVENTURA, RICHARD JOSEPH, software engineer; b. Portland, Maine, Mar. 18, 1947; s. Joseph Anthony and Estelle Louise (LaRou) B.; m. Robin Polk Jones, July 16, 1977; children—Patrick James O'Reilly, Leslie Ann. B.A., U. Maine, 1969. Systems programmer IBM, White Plains, N.Y., 1969-70; grad. asst. U. Ariz., Tucson, 1970-72; math. instr. U. Maine, Portland, 1973-74; systems programmer Arlington Trust Co., Methuen, Mass., 1974-77; sr. systems engr. Four-Phase Systems, Tulsa, 1977—. Den leader Indian Nations council Boy Scouts Am., 1982—. Mem. Phi Beta Kappa, Phi Kappa Phi. Democrat. Roman Catholic. Avocations: stamp collecting; jogging. Home: 13222 E 40th Pl Tulsa OK 74134 Office: Four-Phase Systems Inc 10830 E 45th St Tulsa OK 74135

BOND, JOHN ADIKES, lawyer; b. Jamaica, N.Y., Jan. 14, 1955; s. John Lionel Alexander and Avis Ann (Adikes) B. B.A., U. Miami (Fla.), 1975, J.D., 1978; data processing cert. Prospect Hall Coll., 1982. grad. Ctr. Bilingual and Multicultural Studies, Cuernavaca, Mex., 1983. Bar: Fla. 1979, U.S. Supreme Ct., 1985. Polit. pub. relations cons., 1976-79; editor, pub. Beach Jour., Miami Beach, Fla., 1978-79, Atlantic Jour., Miami Beach, 1979; developer, mktg. dir. Atlantis, The Water Kingdom, Hollywood, Fla., 1979-82; practice law, Hollywood, Fla., 1979—; adj. prof. journalism Nova U., Ft. Lauderdale, 1979-80; pub. relations cons., 1980—. Del. Young Democrats of Am. Conv., 1977; v.p. Dade County Young Dems., 1979; v.p. Hollywood Dem. Club, 1981; mem. Broward County Dems., Exec. Com., 1980-82. Mem. Fla. Bar Assn., Broward County Bar Assn., Pub. Relations Soc. Am. (dir.), Profl. Assn. Diving Instrs. (awarded Master Instructor, 1985), Sierra Club (newsletter editor 1980-82), Mensa (newsletter editor 1983), ACLU, U.S. Chess Fedn. Sigma Delta Chi. Roman Catholic. Contbr. articles to profl. jours. Office: N Perry Airport #16 7501 Pembroke Rd Pembroke Pines FL 33023

BOND, JOSEPH FRANCIS, textile company executive; b. Troy, N.Y., Feb. 17, 1927; s. John A. and Catherine (Waters) B.; B.B.A., Siena Coll., Loudonville, N.Y., 1950; m. Jane A. Powers, Oct. 4, 1952; children—Joseph Francis, Mary Marcia, John Matthew, Mary Louise. With Behr-Manning, Inc., Troy, 1950-57; with Gen. Electric Co., 1957-60, Gen. Aniline & Film Corp., Rensselaer, N.Y., 1960-62; controller Macmillian, Inc., 1963-67, v.p., 1966-67, sr. v.p. fin., 1967-68, exec. v.p., dir., 1968-75; v.p., treas. Cone Mills Inc., Greensboro, N.C., 1975-79, exec. v.p., treas., 1979-84, vice chmn., treas., 1984—, also dir.; dir. No. region Wachovia Bank & Trust Co. Bd. dirs. Greensboro United Way, 1976-78, Cerebral Palsy Sch., Greensboro, 1978-79; bd. regents Inst. Mgmt. Acctg., 1976-79. Served with USNR, 1945-46. Mem. Fin. Execs. Inst. (dir. 1980-83), Am. Mgmt. Assn., Nat. Assn. Accts., Greensboro C. of C. (dir. 1979—), N.C. Textile Found. (dir. 1979—), Am. Textile Mfg. Inst. (chmn. econ. policy com. 1985-86). Club: Greensboro Country. Home: 2805 Lake Forest Dr Greensboro NC 27408 Office: 1201 Maple St Greensboro NC 27405

BOND, JULIAN, state senator, civil rights leader; b. Nashville, Jan. 14, 1940; s. Horace Mann and Julia Agnes (Washington) B.; B.A., Morehouse Coll., 1971; m. Alice Louise Clopton, July 28, 1961; children—Phyllis Jane, Horace Mann, Michael Julian, Jeffrey Alvin, Julia. A founder Com. Appeal for Human Rights, 1960, exec. sec., 1961; a founder Student Nonviolent Coordinating Com., 1960, communications dir., 1961-66; reporter, feature writer Atlanta Inquirer, 1960-61, mng. editor, 1963; mem. Ga. Ho. of Reps. from Fulton County, 1965-75, Ga. Senate, 1975—; barred from house because of Vietnam statements, 1966; U.S. Supreme Ct. ruled his Constl. rights were violated, 1966. Chmn. bd. So. Elections Fund; pres. So. Poverty Law Center. Bd. dirs. So. Conf. Edn. Fund, NAACP; mem. Robert Kennedy Meml. Fund, Highland Research and Edn. Center. Mem. So. Corr. Reporting Racial Equality Wars, Phi Kappa (hon.). Author poems, articles. Address: 361 West View Dr SW Atlanta GA 30310

BOND, LESLIE ANN BEARD, psychologist; b. Muskogee, Okla., July 17, 1946; d. Charles E. and Martha G. Beard; B.S., Northeastern U., Tahlequah, Okla., 1968; M.A. (EPDA grad. fellow 1969-70), U. Okla., 1970, Ph.D., 1976; m. Patterson Bond, Aug. 6, 1977; children—Austin Patterson, Lindsay Ann. Clin. psychologist, program dir. Austin (Tex.) State Hosp., 1974-79; clin. cons. Inpatient Psychiat. Hosp. and Drug Treatment Program, Tulsa, 1980-81; pvt. practice, Austin, 1978-81, Tulsa, 1981—; cons. to community service, hosp., theology programs, womens growth ctr., Okla. Methodist Youth and Counseling Services. Bd. dirs. Domestic Violence Intervention Services, 1984-85, Womens Treatment Ctr., 1984, Tulsa Council on Alcoholism, 1985-86; mem. adv. bd. Jr. League, Tulsa. Mem. Am. Psychol. Assn. (core trainer clin. psychology internship), Capital Area Psychol. Assn. (a founder 1973, exec. bd. 1978-79), Tex. Psychol. Assn., Okla. Psychol. Assn., Tulsa Psychol. Assn., Tulsa County Bar Aux. (exec. bd. 1981-84). Republican. Episcopalian. Address: 1214 E 17th Pl Tulsa OK 74120

BOND, LEWIS HONYMAN, banker; b. Ashport Tenn.; July 31, 1921; s. Lewis H. and Ruth (Bowman) B.; B.S. in Petroleum Engring., U. Okla., 1947; m. Le Kathrin Ozbirn, June 7, 1947; children—Kathrin, Susan Lee, Jane Ann. Petroleum engr. Stanolind Oil & Gas Co., 1947-52; petroleum engr. Ft. Worth Nat. Bank, 1952-53, asst. v.p., petroleum engr., 1953-54, v.p., petroleum engr., 1954-59, pres., dir., 1959-72; chmn. bd., chief exec. officer Ft. Worth Nat. Bank, also Ft. Worth Nat. Corp., 1972-74, Tex. Am. Bancshares Inc., 1974—; dir., mem. exec. com. State Res. Life Ins. Co., Millers Ins. Group, Ft. Worth; class A dir. Fed. Res. Bank, 11th dist.; mem. adv. council 11th Fed. Dist., 1972-74. Former trustee Austin Coll., Ft. Worth Country Day Sch.; bd. dirs. North Tex. Commn., pres., 1975; bd. dirs. Tex. Christian U. Research Found., Southwestern Expn. and Fat Stock Show; past trustee Saint Joseph Hosp.; mem. devel. bd. U. Tex.-Arlington. Mem. Ft. Worth C. of C. (past pres., bd. dirs.), Assn. Res. City Bankers (dir. 1975-78, com. govt. relations 1985-86), Am. Bankers Assn., Tex Bankers Assn. (past v.p., mem. legislative com.), Tex. Research League (dir., mem. adv. com., treas. 1973-74, vice chmn. 1975-76, chmn. 1976—). Newcomen Soc. (Ft. Worth com.). Pi Kappa Alpha. Tau Beta Pi, Sigma Tau. Presbyterian (elder). Clubs: Ft. Worth, Exchange (past pres.), Shady Oaks, Century II, Rivercrest Country, City Mid-day, University (N.Y.C.). Home: 429 Rivercrest Dr Fort Worth TX 76107 Office: PO Box 2050 Fort Worth TX 76101*

BOND, RICHARD MICHAEL, police chief; b. Atlanta, Nov. 18, 1947; m. Dorothy McBride, Sept. 27, 1969; children—Paige, Carla, Clay. B.S., Ga. State U., 1974, M.P.A., 1977. Sgt., Atlanta Police Dept., 1969-77; maj. Cobb County Sheriff Dept., Marietta, Ga., 1977-80; chief of police Americus Police Dept., Ga., 1980—; chmn. tng. standards com. Ga. Peace Officer Standards and Tng. Council, Atlanta, 1984-85; mem. Ga. Jail Standards Tech. Adv. Task Force, 1979; mem. Ga. Crime Commn., 1980; mem. Ga. Criminal Justice Co-ordinating council, 1981-85. Served with USN, 1965-69. Recipient Larry E. Quinn award Ga. State U., 1973. Mem. Ga. Assn. Chiefs of Police (pres. 1984-85), Internat. Assn. Chiefs of Police, Internat. City Mgmt. Assn., Nat. Criminal Justice Assn., Peace Officer Assn. Ga. Episcopalian. Lodge: Kiwanis. Home: 2008 Rose Ave Americus GA 31709 Office: Americus Police Dept 119 S Lee St Americus GA 31709

BONDINELL, STEPHANIE, educational administrator; b. Passaic, N.J., Nov. 22, 1948; d. Peter, Jr. and Gloria Lucille (Burden) Honcharuk; m. Paul Swanstrom Bondinell, July 31, 1971; 1 child, Paul Emil. B.A., William Paterson Coll., 1970; M.Ed., Stetson U., 1983. Cert. elem. educator, Fla.; guidance counselor, grades K-12, Fla. Tchr., Blommingdale Bd. Edn., N.J., 1971-80; edn. dir. Fla. United Methodist Children's Home, Enterprise, 1982—. Sec. adv. com. Deltona Jr. High Sch., Fla., 1984—; sec. Deltona Jr. PTA, 1982. Academic scholar Becton, Dickinson & Co., N.J., 1966; N.J. State scholar, 1966-70; named girls state rep. Am. Legion, N.J., 1966; recipient Vol. Service award Volusia County Sch. Bd., Deland, 1985. Mem. Am. Assn. for Counseling and Devel., Assn. for Curriculum Devel., Council for Exceptional Children, Div. for Learning Disabilities, Fla. Personnel and Guidance Assn., N.J. Edn. Assn., Deltona Civic Assn. Republican. Avocations: painting; creative writing; dancing. Home: 1810 W Cooper Dr Deltona FL 32725 Office: Fla United Methodist Childrens Home Enterprise FL 32725

BONDOUX, JEAN, geophysicist; b. Paris, Jan. 31, 1926; came to U.S., 1957, naturalized, 1963; s. Francis and Marie-Louise Bondoux; m. Simone J. Gantoy, June 21, 1947; children—Martine Marie Bondoux Gibbons, Francis Jean. B.S., B.S.B.A., SUNY; B.A. in Natural Sci., Thomas Edison State Coll. N.J.; M.B.A., U. Houston, Clear Lake City, 1978, M.S. in Phys. Scis., 1981. Seismologist/geophysicist Rogers/Ray Geophys., Houston and overseas, 1956-66; in various tech. managerial and cons. positions in geophysics and computer sci., U.S., Can., 1966-79; staff geophysicist Amoco Prodn. Co., Houston, 1979-81; geophysicist Santa Fe Energy, Houston, 1982-83; chmn., chief exec. officer Aquarius Resources, Inc., Houston, 1983—; cons. geophysics, computer sci. Served with French Paratroopers, 1952-55; Vietnam. Mem. Soc. Exploration Geophysicists, Am. Assn. Petroleum Geologists, Alumni Assn. U. Houston (charter). Republican. Roman Catholic. Research and publs. in geophysics; instrumental in discovery of oil and gas in Libya, Saudi Arabia, Egypt, 1960-65; pioneer in digital seismic recording and computer processing of seismic data; developer advanced tech. for oil and gas exploration in carbonate reservoirs. Home: 12151 Maple Rock Dr Houston TX 77077 Office: 11200 Westheimer Suite 600 Houston TX 77042

BONDURANT, ALBERT WINANS, geologist; b. Baton Rouge, Apr. 4, 1955; s. Albert G. and Helen C. (Hopper) B., Jr.; m. Lynn Marie Acosta. B.S. in Geology, La. State U., 1973-77; postgrad. U. Southwest La., 1983—. Geol. asst. La. State Mineral Bd., Baton Rouge, 1975-77; geologist Gulf Oil, Houma, La., 1977-78, Colo. Interstate Gas, Colorado Springs, 1978-80; prodn. geologist Superior Oil, Lafayette, La., 1980-81; sr. exploration geologist Tenneco Oil, Lafayette, 1981-82; pvt. practice geologist, Lafayette, 1982-85; cons. geologist Performance Exploration Co., Lafayette, 1985—. Vol. Lafayette Parish 4H Clubs, 1983—. Mem. Am. Assn. Petroleum Geologists, Lafayette Geol. Soc., Soc. Econ. Paleontologists and Mineralogists, Republican. Episcopalian. Club: Petroleum (Lafayette). Home: 97 Avery Dr Youngsville LA 70592 Office: Performance Exploration Co PO Box 51774 Lafayette LA 70505

BONDURANT, JOSEPH E., business executive; b. 1929; married. B.S. in E.E., Ga. Inst. Tech., 1957. Herd tester Dairy Herd Imperial, 1947-48; jr. engr. Union Carbide Corp., 1957; engr. Gulf States Utilities Co., Beaumont, Tex., 1957-67, supr. scheduling, 1965, div. engr., 1967-69, operating supr., 1969-71, mgr. Lake Charles div., 1971-75, v.p., 1975-78, sr. v.p., 1978-79, exec. v.p. ops., 1979-84, exec. v.p. adminstrv. and tech. services, 1984—. Served with USMC, 1948-53. Office: Gulf States Utilities Co PO Box 2951 Beaumont TX 77704

BONDURANT, LEO HORACE, engineering services company executive, consultant; b. Wisner, La., Sept. 18, 1935; s. Leo and Maxine Marie Fichte, Feb. 27, 1960; children—Michele Marie Bondurant Read, Pamela Renee. B.S. in Chem. Engring., La. Tech. U., 1957. Registered profl. engr., Tex., La. Engr. Universal Oil Prodn. Co., Des Plaines, Ill., 1957-69; plant mgr. Quaker State Oil, Newell, W.Va., 1969-74; v.p. refining Sunland Refining Corp., Bakersfield, Calif., 1974-77; pres. Foster Wheeler Mgmt. Ops., Ltd., USA, Houston, 1977—, also dir.; past dir. 1st Nat. Bank, Chester, W.Va. Pres. Cypresswood Homeowner's Assn., Spring, Tex., 1979; bd. dirs. ARC, East Liverpool, Ohio, 1976. Recipient Energy Conservation award So. Calif. Gas Co., 1976. Mem. Am. Inst. Chem. Engrs., Nat. Petroleum Refiners Assn. (panelist 1976), Am. Petroleum Inst. (sec. com. tng. 1975, 76). Republican. Methodist. Club: Stockdale Country. Avocations: reading; traveling. Home: 3907 Snag Ln Spring TX 77388 Office: Foster Wheeler Mgmt Ops Ltd USA 3535 Sage Rd Houston TX 77056

BONER, WILLIAM H., congressman; b. Nashville, Feb. 14, 1945. B.A., Middle Tenn. State U., 1967; M.A., George Peabody Coll., 1969; grad., YMCA Night Law Sch., 1978. Tchr., coach Trevecca Nazarene Coll., 1969-71; sr. staff asst. Mayor's Office, Nashville, 1971-72; dir. public relations First Am. Nat. Bank, 1972-76; mem., Tenn.; Ho. of Reps., 1970-72, 74-76; mem., Tenn.; State Senate, 1976-78; mem. 96th-98th Congresses from 5th Tenn. Dist. Office: Room 107 Cannon House Office Bldg Washington DC 20515

BONGAERTS, EDUARD, JR., machinery manufacturing executive, engineer; b. Weeze, North Rhine, Germany, Aug. 29, 1944; came to U.S., 1980; s. Eduard, Sr. and Dorothea (Kuck) B.; m. Ute Schroeter, Oct. 16, 1977; children—Anna-Fee, Lena-Joy. Engr., Technicum, Dusseldorf, 1973. Draughtsman, Australian Iron & Steel, Sydney, 1963-67; drawing checker Demag Pty, Johannesburg, South Africa, 1967-68; project engr., mgr. Siempelkomp GmbH, Krefeld, Fed. Republic Germany, 1968-79; v.p. ops. Aumund Internat. Inc., Atlanta, 1980—, also dir. Mem. Soc. Mining Engrs., TAPPI. Office: Aumund Internat Inc 2030 Powers Ferry Rd Atlanta GA 30339

BONHAM-YEAMAN, DORIA, business law educator; b. Los Angeles, June 10, 1932; d. Carl Herschel and Edna Mae (Jones) Bonham Emanuel; widowed; children—Carl Q., Doria Valerie-Constance. B.A., U. Tenn., 1953, J.D., 1957, M.A., 1958; Ed.S. in Computer Edn., Barry U., 1984. Instr. bus. law Palm Beach Jr. Coll., Lake Worth, Fla., 1960-69; instr. legal environment Fla. Atlantic U., Boca Raton, 1969-73; lectr. bus. law Fla. Internat. U., North Miami, 1973-83, assoc. prof. bus. law, 1983—. Editor: Anglo-Am. Law Conf., 1980; Developing Global Corporate Strategies, 1981; editorial bd. Attys. Computer Report, 1984-85, Jour. Legal Studies Edn., 1985—. Contbr. articles to profl. jours. Bd. dirs. Palm Beach County Assn. for Deaf Children, 1960-63; mem. Fla. Commn. on Status of Women, Tallahassee, 1969-70; mem. Broward County Democratic Exec. Com., 1982—; pres. Dem. Women's Club Broward County, 1981; mem. Marine Council of Greater Miami, 1978—, Service award, 1979. Recipient Faculty Devel. award Fla. Internat. U., Miami, 1980; grantee Notre Dame Law Sch., London, summer 1980. Mem. Am. Bus. Law Assn., No. Dade C. of C., Am. Acctg. Assn., AAUW (pres. Palm Beach County 1965-66), Alpha Chi Omega (alumnae chpt. pres. 1968-71), Tau Kappa Alpha. Episcopalian. Office: Fla Internat Univ North Miami FL 33181

BONIFAZI, STEPHEN, chemist; b. Hartford, Conn., Oct. 31, 1924; s. Camillo and Carrie (Mortensen) B.; B.S., Trinity Coll., Hartford, 1947; postgrad. Okla. U., 1943-44, Rensselaer Poly. Inst., 1955-58; m. Joan Rose Dunlop, Dec. 19, 1959; 1 dau., Karen Stephanie. Sr. chemist Pratt & Whitney Aircraft Co., East Hartford, Conn., 1950-56, supr. chemistry, 1956-58, project chemist, West Palm Beach, Fla., 1958-63, gen. supr. chemistry, 1963-78, fuels and lubricants specialist, 1978—. Served with inf. AUS, 1943-45; ETO. Decorated Bronze Star medal. Mem. Am. Chem. Soc., Am. Soc. Lubrication Engrs., Internat. Assn. for Hydrogen Energy, ASTM, Coordinating Research Council, Sigma Pi Sigma. Contbr. articles to sci. jours. Home: 516 Kingfish Rd North Palm Beach FL 33408 Office: Box 2691 West Palm Beach FL 33402

BONIOL, EDDIE EUGENE, leasing and investment executive; b. Port Arthur, Tex., Sept. 14, 1931; s. Willie Bernice and Leila Evelina (Chase) B.; diploma in acctg. Tyler Comml. Coll., 1949; student Baylor U., 1955-56, La. Coll., 1956, SUNY, 1981—; m. Marguerite Faye Aguillard, Feb. 5, 1966; children—Joe Ed, Mark Eugene, Liesl Michelle. Various positions Bus. Services Group Comml. Credit Co., Balt., 1959-73, area dir., 1970-73; freelance mgmt. cons. Dallas, 1973; v.p. Tex. Western Fin. Corp., Dallas, 1974-76; asst. v.p. Citicorp Bus. Credit Inc., Dallas, 1976-78; v.p. fin. and adminstrn., also chief fin. officer Superior Iron Works & Supply Co. Inc., Shreveport, La., 1978-80; sr. v.p., chief fin. officer Latham Resources Corp., 1980-81; pres. Decca Leasing Corp., Shreveport, 1981—, Med. Bus. Services, Inc., Shreveport, 1982—; cons. in field. Trustee La. Coll., Pineville, 1983. Served with USN, 1950-53. Cert. credit analyst, credit and fin. analyst. Republican. Baptist. Clubs: East Ridge Country, University. Lodge: Lions. Office: 610 Texas Suite 307 Shreveport LA 71136

BONJEAN, CHARLES MICHAEL, foundation executive, sociology educator; b. Pekin, Ill., Sept. 7, 1936; s. Bruno and Catherine Ann (Dancey) B. B.A., Drake U., 1957; M.A., U. N.C., 1959, Ph.D. in Sociology, 1963. Mem. faculty U. Tex., Austin, 1963—, Hogg prof. sociology, 1974—, chmn. dept. sociology,

1972-74; exec. assoc. Hogg Found., Austin, 1974-79, v.p., 1979—; sociology editor Chandler Pub. Co., 1967-73, Crowell Pub. Co., 1973-77, Dorsey Press, 1979—; mem. council Inter-Univ. Consortium Polit. and Social Research, 1972-75; mem. steering com. Council Social Sci. Jour. Editors, 1975-81; v.p. Conf. Southwest Founds., 1985-86, pres., 1986-87. Recipient Howard Odom award U. N.C., 1963, Teaching Excellence award U. Tex. Students Assn., 1965, Alumni Disting. Service award Drake U., 1979; Sigma Delta Chi scholar, 1957. Mem. Am. Sociol. Assn. (chmn. orgns. and occupations sect. 1983-84, career of disting. scholarship award com. 1981-84, chmn. 1982-84, council 1985—), Southwestern Sociol. Assn. (pres. 1972-73), Southwestern Polit. Sci. Assn., Phi Beta Kappa. Co-author: Sociological Measurement, 1967; co-editor: Blacks in the United States, 1969; Planned Social Intervention, 1969; Community Politics, 1971; Political Attitudes and Public Opinion, 1972; The Idea of Culture in the Social Sciences, 1973; Social Science in America, 1976; The Mexican Origin: People in the United States, 1984; editor Social Sci. Quar., 1966—; cons. editor Am. Jour. Sociology, 1974-76; contbr. articles to profl. jours. Home: 16310 Clara Van Tr Austin TX 78734 Office: WCH 310A U Tex Austin TX 78712

BONNER, JACK WILBUR, III, psychiatrist; b. Corpus Christi, Tex., July 30, 1940; s. Jack Wilbur and Irldene (Turner) B.; m. Myra Lynn Taylor; children—Jack Wilbur IV, Katherine Lynn, Shelley Bliss. A.A., Del Mar Coll., 1960; B.A. with honors, U. Tex., 1961, M.D., 1965. Diplomate Am. Bd. Psychiatry and Neurology. Intern, U. Ark. Med. Ctr., Little Rock, 1965-66; resident in psychiatry Duke U. Med. Ctr., Durham, N.C., 1966-69; clin. assoc. prof. psychiatry U. Tex. Med. Sch. at San Antonio, 1970-71; assoc. in psychiatry Highland Hosp. Div., Duke U. Med. Ctr., Asheville, N.C., 1971, asst. prof., 1972-80, staff psychiatrist, 1971-72, dir. outpatient services, 1972-75, med. dir., 1975-81; asst. clin. prof. psychiatry Duke U. Med. Ctr., Durham, 1982—; med. dir. Highland Hosp., Asheville, 1975—, chmn. bd., 1981—, chief exec. officer, 1981—. Cons., Asheville VA Hosp., 1974-78; teaching staff Bexar County Hosp., San Antonio, 1970-71; med. staff Highland Hosp., 1971—; cons. staff St. Joseph Hosp., Asheville, 1980—, Meml. Mission Hosp. of Western N.C., Inc., Asheville, 1980—; bd. dirs. Western N.C. Med. Peer Rev. Found., Inc., 1975-78; examiner Am. Bd. Psychiatry and Neurology; mem. Nat. Anorexia Adv. Council, 1978—; mem. Gov.'s Task Force on Mental Health, 1979-80; bd. dirs. N.C. Inst. Medicine, 1984—; pres., chmn. bd. Highland Clinic P.A., 1980—, Highland Found., 1980—; trustee La Amistad Found., Maitland, Fla., 1985—. Served to maj. M.C., USAF, 1969-72. Fellow Am. Coll. Psychiatrists, Am. Psychiat. Assn., So. Psychiat. Assn.; mem. N.C. Neuropsychiat. Assn. (coms.; pres. 1982-83), Buncombe County Med. Soc. (coms.; dir. 1982—, pres. 1983), N.C. Med. Soc. (coms.), So. Med. Assn. (chmn. sect. neurology and psychiatry 1981-82), Nat. Assn. Pvt. Psychiat. Hosps. (coms.), Central Neuropsychiat. Hosp. Assn. (pres. 1983-84), Am. Group Psychotherapy Assn., AMA, AAAS, Phi Theta Kappa. Editorial reviewer So. Med. Jour., 1978-84; contbr. articles to profl. jours. Home: 125 Patton Mountain Rd Asheville NC 28804 Office: PO Box 1101 Highland Hosp Asheville NC 28802

BONNER, MARGIE WILLIAMS, educator, counselor; b. Jacksonville, Ala., Apr. 3, 1944; d. Jerret, Jr. and Lucille (Franklin) Williams; m. Robert Bonner, Jr., June 20, 1981; 1 child, Vanessa Marie. B.S., Tuskegee Inst., 1966; Tchr.'s cert. Jacksonville State U., 1970, M.S., 1975. Tchr., Heflin Tng. Sch., Ala., 1966-67, Cleburne County Elem. Sch., Heflin, 1967-70; tchr., asst. dir. Jacksonville Day Care, Ala., 1971-72; tchr. Jacksonville High Sch., 1972-80; counselor Jacksonville Elem. Sch., 1980-83; counselor, tchr. Jacksonville High Sch., 1983—; counselor Youth Conservation Corps, Talladega, Ala., summer 1978, Ft. McClellan, Ala., summer 1979. Mem. Jacksonville City Planning Bd., 1978—. Recipient Merit cert. Dept. Agr., 1979. Mem. Jacksonville Edn. Assn. (past pres.), Ala. Edn. Assn., NEA, Am. Assn. for Counseling and Devel., Delta Kappa Gamma, Phi Delta Kappa. Democrat. Methodist. Club: Officers Wives (Ft. McClellan). Avocations: reading, music, travel. Home: 1607 Fairway Circle Jacksonville AL 36265 Office: Jacksonville High Sch N Pelham Rd Jacksonville AL 36265

BONNER, ZORA DAVID, petroleum company executive; b. San Antonio, Feb. 23, 1919; m. Dorothy Shaw, Feb. 28, 1942; children—David Calhoun, Julie Ann. B.S. in Chem. Engring., U. Tex., 1941. With Gulf Oil Corp., after 1941, former pres., chief exec. officer, Houston, also dir.; vice chmn. Tesoro Petroleum Corp., 1980—. Mem. nat. bd. dirs. Jr. Achievement; mem. adv. council Engring. Found., U. Tex., Austin. Served to lt. comdr. USN, 1941-46. Recipient Disting. Grad. award, Disting. Engring. Grad., U. Tex., 1968. Mem. Am. Petroleum Inst. (dir.). Clubs: Petroleum, Giraud, Dominion Country (San Antonio); Ramada (Houston). Address: 8700 Tesoro Dr San Antonio TX 78286

BONNEY, CLARA ANN, computer analyst; b. Gloucester, Mass., Dec. 11, 1946; d. Oliver William and Anna Josephine (Anderson) B. Assoc.Sci., Middlesex Community Coll., 1968; B.S., Suffolk U., 1974, M.Pub. Adminstrn., 1977. Pub. info. and program dir. Epilepsy Soc. Mass., Boston, 1973-75; research intern Boston Fin. Commn., 1976-77; staff asst. for spl. projects Boston Housing Authority, 1977-80; computer systems analyst Fla. Internat. U. Sch. of Hospitality Mgmt., Miami, Fla., 1980—, adj. instr. dept. math. and computer sci., spring 1984, 85, adj. lectr., spring 1986. Researcher: Your Mass Government, 1977, biography Gavin, 1980; author resource book: A Resource Guide to State and Philanthropic Grants Information, 1978. Mem. Mass. Gov.'s Planning Council (Conf.-Developmentally Disabled), Boston, 1972-73, Downtown Ministries Task Force on the Needs of Poor, Boston, 1976-78; bd. dirs. Hill House-Beacon Hill, Boston, 1979-81. Suffolk U. grad. fellow, 1976. Mem. Assn. Computing Machinery, Am. Soc. Pub. Adminstrn., Suffolk U. Presdl. Search Com. (alumni rep. 1980), Suffolk U. Alumni Assn. Republican. Office: Fla Internat U Tamiami Trail Miami FL 33199

BONNEY, HAL JAMES, JR., judge; b. Norfolk, Va., Aug. 27, 1929; s. Hal J. and Mary (Shackelford) B.; m. Marie McBee, July 4, 1963 (div. 1979); children—David James, John Wesley. B.A., U. Richmond, 1951, M.A., 1953; J.D., Coll. William and Mary, 1969. Instr. Norfolk public schs., 1951-61; supt. Douglas MacArthur Acad., 1961-67; practiced law, 1969-71; law clk. U.S. Dist. Ct., 1969; prof. U. Va., 1964-71, Coll. William and Mary, 1969-71; U.S. bankruptcy judge, Norfolk, 1971—. WTAR radio tchr. Wesleymen Bible class, 1962—; Treas. Wesleymen Found., Inc., Billy Graham Crusades, 1974-76. Recipient S.A.R. Good Citizenship medal; U. Richmond Gold medal. Mem. Am. Bar Assn., Nat. Conf. Bankruptcy Judges (pres. 1983), Va. State Bar, Norfolk, and Portsmouth Bar Assn., Nat. Film Soc., Am. Film Inst., Phi Alpha Theta, Pi Sigma Alpha, Phi Alpha Delta. Methodist. Clubs: Masons, Shriners. Home: 1357 Windsor Point Rd Norfolk VA 23509 Office: 408 US Court House Norfolk VA 23501

BONNEY, ROGER EARL, transportation executive, consultant; b. Norfolk, Va., Jan. 20, 1933; s. Guy and Goldie Lou (Sanderlin) B.; m. Eva Lou Ferebee, Aug. 31, 1957; children—Roger Earl, Nancy Lynn. B.S., Va. Poly. Inst., 1955; D.M.S. (hon.), 1955. Treas. Bonney Motor Express, Inc., Norfolk, Va., 1957-70, chmn. bd. dirs., Atlanta, 1983—; pres. Trailer Service & Refrigeration Co., Virginia Beach, Va., 1970—; dir. Bonney Van Line, Inc., Tequesta, Fla., Ingram Pharmacy, Inc., Virginia Beach; cons. various ltd. partnerships, Virginia Beach, 1981—. Chmn. bd. trustees Scott Meml. United Methodist Ch., 1976—. Served to 1st lt. U.S. Army, 1955-57. Recipient S. Barron Segar award Norfolk Acad., 1951. Home: 2492 Haversham Close Virginia Beach VA 23454 Office: Trailer Service & Refrigeration Co 516 S Military Hwy Virginia Beach VA 23464

BONNYMAN, GEORGE GORDON, mining company executive; b. Knoxville, Tenn., Oct. 22, 1919; s. Alexander and Frances (Berry) B.; B.S., Princeton U., 1941; m. Isabel Fouche Ashe, May 20, 1942; children—Isabel Ashe Bonnyman Stanley, George Gordon, Anne Berry Bonnyman Lippincott, Alexander Ashe, Brian Andrew. With Blue Diamond Coal Co., Knoxville, 1945—, asst. gen. mgr., gen. mgr., pres., 1953-70, chmn. bd., 1970-74, pres., chmn., 1974—. Served as capt. F.A., AUS, World War II. Decorated Silver Star, Bronze Star with oak leaf cluster, Purple Heart. Mem. Princeton Engring. Soc., Soc. Mining Engrs., AIME, Tau Beta Pi Assn. Home: 6633 Sherwood Dr Knoxville TN 37919 Office: Blue Diamond Coal Co PO Box 10008 Knoxville TN 37919

BONTOS, GEORGE EMMANUEL, physician; b. Alton, Ill., Dec. 7, 1924; s. Emmanuel Anthony and Lillian (Saris) Bontozlakis; B.A., U. Chgo., 1949; M.D., U. Athens (Greece), 1968; m. Athena M. Teregis, Sept. 21, 1952; children—E. Christopher, Elizabeth Ann. Research asso. Chgo. State Hosp., 1969; intern Wheeling (W.Va.) Hosp., 1970-71, resident, 1971-73; practice medicine specializing in family medicine, Wheeling, 1973—; sr. attending Wheeling Hosp., Ohio Valley Med. Center; sr. attending staff, instr. dept. family practice, chief dept. family practice Wheeling Hosp.; plant physician Wheeling-Pitts. Steel Corp. Bd. dirs. Wheeling chpt. ARC, 1975, Health Plan Upper Ohio Valley, Vis. Nurses Assn. Ohio County, 1976. Served with U.S. Army, 1945-46; Korea. Diplomate Am. Bd. Family Practice. Fellow Am. Acad. Family Physicians, Am. Geriatrics Soc.; mem. AMA (Recognition award 1975, 78, 80, 82, 85), So. Med. Assn., W.Va. Med. Assn., Ohio County Med. Soc. (pres. 1985), Ohio County Found. Med. Care, Pan-Cretan Assn. Republican. Greek Orthodox. Lodges: Masons (32d degree), Jesters, Scottish Rite, Shriners. Home: 160 Oakmont Rd Wheeling WV 26003 Office: 2427 Warwood Ave Wheeling WV 26003

BOOCKHOLDT, JAMES LEE, accountancy educator, consultant; b. Selma, Ala., Feb. 28, 1945; s. James Howard and Hazel (Maddox) B. B.A., Rice U., 1968, M.E.E., 1968; M.B.A., U. Pa., 1971; Ph.D., U. Ala.-Tuscaloosa, 1977. C.P.A., Tex. Acct. Arthur Andersen & Co., 1971-73; controller Trinity Forge, Inc., 1973-75; assoc. prof. accountancy U. Houston, 1978—. Served to lt. USNR, 1968-70. Mem. Am. Inst. C.P.A.s, Assn. Computing Machinery, Am. Inst. Decision Scis., Am. Acctg. Assn., Am. Mensa. Author: Cost Accounting for Managerial Planning, Decision Making and Control, 1982. Contbr. articles to profl. jours. Home: 1440 Arlington Houston TX 77008 Office: Dept Accountancy and Taxation U Houston-University Park Houston TX 77004

BOOHER, DIANNA DANIELS, author, writing consultant; b. Hillsboro, Tex., Jan. 13, 1948; d. Alton B. and Opal (Schronk) Daniels; m. Daniel T. Booher, June 23, 1967; children—Jeffrey, Lisa. B.A., North Tex. State U., 1970; M.A., U. Houston, 1979. Cert. tchr., Tex. Tchr. Pampa Ind. Schs., Tex., 1975-77, Cy-Fair Ind. Schs., Houston, 1979, N. Harris County Coll., Houston, 1978-80; pres. Booher Writing Cons., Houston, 1980—; cons. IBM, Dresser Industries, Allied Corp., Exxon, Tenneco, Pennzoil. Author: Not Yet Free, 1981; RAPE, 1981 (ALA Best Young Adult Book award 1981); Making Friends With Yourself and Other Strangers, 1982; Would You Put That in Writing?, 1983; Send Me A Memo, 1984; Love, 1985, others. Mem. Am. Soc. Tng. and Devel., Phi Kappa Beta. Baptist. Office: Booher Writing Cons 12215 Moorcreek Dr Houston TX 77070

BOOK, JOHN KENNETH, retail store owner; b. Hillsboro, Ill., June 26, 1950; s. Vern Ray Book and Pearl Iva (Foster) Book Alford; Asso. in Acctg., Ky. Bus. Coll., 1974. Laborer, Lexington (Ky.) Army Depot, 1968-70; machine operator A.O. Smith, Mt. Sterling, Ky., 1971-72; laborer Irvin Industries, Lexington, 1973-75; owner Kenny's Signs & Bus. Services, Winchester, Ky., 1977—. Democrat. Office: Winn Ave PO Box 840 Winchester KY 40391

BOOKER, PHILIP, JR., social work and criminal justice educator; b. Norfolk, Va., May 30, 1946; s. Philip and Sarah Ann (Dixon) B.; m. Jarmilia Parks, Dec. 30, 1976; children—Felicia, Denitra, Philip, III. B.S. in Social Work, East Carolina U., 1972, M.S.W., U. Louisville, 1974; M. Pub. Affairs, Ky. State U., 1977. Counselor, Va. Probation and Parole Bd., Richmond, 1973; asst. dir. treatment Bur. Corrections, Frankfort, Ky., 1974-77; dir. social work Ky. State U., Frankfort, 1980-83, asst. prof., 1983—, chmn. social work and criminal justice, 1983-85; recreational coordinator William Byrd Community Ctr., Richmond, Va., 1973; counselor Fed. Probation Parole Bd., Louisville, 1974; lectr. Spaulding Coll., Louisville, 1975; cons. Ashland Coll., Ohio, 1983-84. Author: Pre-Retirement Education, 1980; Mary McLeod Bethune, 1985. Coach, YMCA, Frankfort, 1975-79. Named hon. Ky. col., 1979, Capt. of Belle of Louisville, 1979; grantee Dept. Human Resources, 1978, Council on Higher Edn., 1979. Mem. Council on Social Work Edn., Nat. Assn. Social Work, Ky. Assn. Social Work Educators, Democrat. Mem. Pentecostal Ch. Home: 506 Williamsburg Rd Frankfort KY 40601 Office: Ky State U E Main St Frankfort KY 40601

BOOKER, TERRI JO, nurse; b. Tuscumbia, Ala., Apr. 1, 1953; d. Bobby Jo and Emma Frances (Curtis) Akers; m. Carl Edward Booker, Oct. 21, 1969; children—Chris, Carla, Brad. L.P.N., Northeast Miss. Jr. Coll., 1975; emergency med. tech. Muscles Shoals Tech. Coll., 1982; intermediate emergency med. tech. Northwest Ala. Jr. Coll., 1983. Registered emergency med. tech., Miss. Circuit clk. Tisomingo County Ct. House, Iuka, Miss., 1971-72; nurse Tishomingo County Hosp., Iuka, 1975-77; teamster Peter Kewiet Co., Paden, Miss., 1978-79; ceramic instr. Basement Ceramics, Iuka, 1979-80; florist Country Cottage Flowers, Iuka, 1980-82; nurse Pickwick Manor Nursing Home, Iuka, 1981-82; emergency room nurse Tishomingo County Hosp., 1982—. Leader, Girl Scouts U.S.A., Iuka, 1978-82; CPR, first aid instr. ARC, Iuka. Democrat. Baptist. Club: Eastport Homemakers (Iuka). Lodge: Order Eastern Star (Star Point).

BOOKIN-WEINER, JEROME BRUCE, history educator, educational administrator; b. Louisville, Ky., June 21, 1946; s. Robert H. and Jane (Lasner) W.; m. Muriel R. Zober, July 25, 1976 (div. 1980); m. Hedy E. Bookin, Mar. 27, 1983. B.A., Dickinson Coll., 1968; diploma, Bourguiba Inst., Tunis, Tunisia, 1972; M.A., Columbia U., 1970, M.Phil., 1974, Ph.D., 1976. Vol., Peace Corps, Rabat, Morocco, 1972-73; asst. prof. history, coordinator internat. programs Old Dominion U., 1976-82, dir. Ctr. for Internat. Programs, assoc. prof. history, 1982—; dir. Extended Tchr. Insts. Middle East Studies, 1981-83; dir. Group Project in Africa, 1983; dir. Group Project in Israel and Egypt, 1984; exec. dir. Va. Ctr. World Trade, 1984—; exec. sec. Southeast Regional Middle-East and Islamic Studies Seminar, 1977—. Sec., World Affairs Council Greater Hampton Roads (Va.), 1978-80, dir., 1980-82, pres., 1982—. NCAA postgrad. scholar, 1968; Kappa Nu grad. fellow, 1968. Mem. Am. Hist. Assn., Middle East Studies Assn., Internat. Studies Assn. Jewish. Lodge: Rotary. Contbr. articles to profl. jours. Home: 1325 Westover Ave Norfolk VA 23507 Office: Center for Internat Programs Old Dominion U Norfolk VA 23508

BOOM, GLENN LEONARD, petroleum distribution company executive; b. Sacramento, Calif., Aug. 9, 1926; s. Leonard Archer and Dorothy Dam B.; m. Sally Streeter, May 18, 1951; children—Susan, Michael, Douglas, Judith. B.A., U. Calif.-Berkeley, 1946; postgrad. Syracuse U., 1967-68. With Shell Oil Co., various locations, 1946-78; pres. Delta Oil Co., Bay Minette, Ala., 1978-85; v.p. mktg. Berwick Bay Oil Co., Inc., Morgan City, La., 1985—; dir. First Nat. Bank Mobile, Rojo Stores Inc., Retail Info. Systems Inc. Bd. dirs. Contact Helpline, Mobile, Ala., 1978—, Shores Alcohol Recovery Program. Served to capt. USNR, 1944-75. Mem. U.S. Naval Inst., Naval Res. Assn., Ala. Oilmen's Assn. Republican. Episcopalian. Clubs: Masons, Shriners. Home: PO Box 303 Montrose AL 36559 Office: PO Box 90 Mobile AL 36507

BOONE, DORIS RUTH ESTILL, accountant; b. Ft. Worth, Tex., July 27, 1916; d. Everett and Bethena (Grammer) Estill; m. Jack Landrine Boone, Jan. 18, 1952. Student Baylor U., 1934-36; B.S. in Commerce, Tex. Christian U., 1950, M.B.A., 1957. C.P.A., Tex. Clk., U.S. Civil Service, Washington, Phila. and Ft. Worth, Tex., 1942-55; acct. Miller Truck Line, Ft. Worth, 1955-60; pvt. practice acctg., Ft. Worth, 1957-81; pres., Ruth Estill Boone, A Profl. Corp., Ft. Worth, 1981—; instr. acctg. Tex. Christian U., Ft. Worth, 1952-65. Sec., Travis Ave. Baptist Ch., 1937-41. Mem. Am. Soc. Women Accts. (chpt. pres. 1958-59), Tex. Soc. C.P.A.s (chpt. sec. 1962-64), Am. Acctg. Assn., Am. Inst. C.P.A.s. Lodge: Order Eastern Star. Address: 6068 Wrigley Way Fort Worth TX 76133

BOONE, HARRY LINDSAY, JR., wholesale distributor; b. Portsmouth, Va., Feb. 5, 1950; s. Harry Lindsay and Martha Elizabeth (Richardson) B.; m. Patricia Mc Cain, Aug. 13, 1983; children—Glyn, Lauren, Melanie. A.A.S., Tidewater Community Coll., 1976. With Boone Distbg. Co., Inc./Pet Supplies, Inc., Portsmouth, Va., 1969—, v.p., office mgr., 1976-85; owner Dirty Harry's Gun Shop, Portsmouth. Mem. Portsmouth Democratic Exec. Com., 1975-77. Served with USMCR, 1969-75, capt. Va. State Guard. Recipient Recognition award, Portsmouth Clean Community Commn., 1979-84. Mem. Nat. Food Dealers Assn., Tidewater Food Dealers Assn., Sons Confederate Vets. (past comdr. camp), Nat. Rifle Assn. (mem. endowment), N-S Skirmish Assn., Mil. Order Stars and Bars, Wise Food Distbrs. Assn., Direct Store Delivery Assn., Confederate Alliance Officer Corps, Order of Battleflag, Friends of Confederacy Soc., SCV (life), Dixie Club, Am. Pistol and Rifle Assn., Nat. Assn. Federally Lic. Firearms Dealers. Mem. So. Nat. party. Episcopalian. Club: KP. Home: Hobhouchin Manor Route 2 Box 872 Smithfield VA 23430

BOONE, JAMES LEROY, JR., industrial education educator; b. Houston, May 15, 1923; s. James Leroy and Mora Evelyn (Waddell) B.; m. Lillian Vorpahl, May 18, 1944; 1 son, James Leroy, III. B.S., Tex. A&M U., 1947, M.Ed., 1948, Ed.D., 1966. Tchr., trainer Laredo (Tex.) Jr. Coll., 1948-50, dir. Vocat. Sch., 1950-52; instr., asst. prof., assoc. prof. indsl. edn. Tex. A&M U., College Station, 1952-69, head dept. indsl. edn., 1969-77, prof. indsl. edn., 1977—. Mem. Tex. Adv. Council Tech.-Vocat. Edn., 1971-77; trustee Brazos County (Tex.) Sch. Bd., 1960-70; mem. Brazos County Hist. Survey Commn., 1967—. Served to col. AUS, 1943-46. Decorated Legion of Merit; recipient Faculty Disting. Achievement award Tex. A&M U., 1965. Mem. Nat. Assn. Indsl. and Tech. Tchr. Educators (pres. 1981), Am. Vocat. Assn., Am. Indsl. Arts Assn., Am. Council Indsl. Arts Tchr. Edn., Res. Officers Assn. U.S., Iota Lambda Sigma, Phi Kappa Phi, Phi Delta Kappa. Methodist. Contbr. articles to profl. jours. Home: Route 5 Box 852 College Station TX 77840 Office: Dept Indsl Edn Tex A and M U College Station TX 77843

BOONE, LESLIE SPEARMAN, educator; b. W. Palm Beach, Fla., July 18, 1930; d. Robert Ewell and Zonise (Wood) Spearman; B.A., U.S. Fla., Tampa, 1975, M.Ed., 1981; m. Floyd E. Boone, June 3, 1950; children—Zonise Jeanette Boone Swanson, Robert Edward, William Gordon. Head Start tchr. Manatee County (Fla.), 1967-75, head tchr. Bradenton (Fla.) Center, 1973-75; kindergarten tchr. Orange Ridge Elementary Sch., Bradenton, 1975—. Sunday sch. tchr. Trinity United Methodist Ch., Bradenton, 1958-78; instr. swimming, social worker ARC; active local PTA, Girl Scouts, Heart Fund. Mem. UDC, DAR, Nat. Soc. Colonial Dames of the XVII Century, Alpha Delta Kappa (pres. 1984-86). Democrat. Club: Sons of Norway. Home: 2611 26th Ave Dr W Bradenton FL 33505 Office: 400 30th Ave W Bradenton FL 33505

BOONE, RICHARD WINSTON, lawyer; b. Washington, July 19, 1941; s. Henry Shaffer and Anne Catherine (Huehne) B.; m. Jean Knox Logan, Dec. 17, 1966; children—Elizabeth Anne, Richard Winston, Jr., Katheryn Jeanne. B.A. with honors, U. Ala., 1963; J.D., Georgetown U., 1970. Bar: Va. 1970, U.S. Ct. Claims 1975, U.S. Ct. Appeals (D.C. cir.) 1970, U.S. Ct. Appeals (2d cir.) 1973, U.S. Ct. Appeals (4th cir.) 1972, U.S. Supreme Ct. 1974. Ptnr. Carr, Jordan, Coyne & Savits, Washington, 1977-81; shareholder, dir. Wilkes, Artis, Hedrick & Lane, Washington, 1981-84; pres. Richard W. Boone, P.C., Arlington, Va., 1984—. Served to capt. USAR, 1964-67. Mem. Am. Soc. Hosp. Risk Mgrs., Am. Soc. Hosp. Attys., Def. Research Inst., D.C. Def. Lawyers Assn., Va. Trial Lawyers Assn., ABA, Fed. Bar Assn., Assn. Trial Lawyers Am., Barristers. Avocations: model railroading. Home: 1949 Hopewood Dr Falls Church VA 22043 Office: 2020 N 14th St 210 Arlington VA 22201

BOONE, ROBERT LEE, educational administrator; b. Carthage, Miss., Sept. 21, 1945; s. Burton and Betty (Johnson) B.; m. Rita Watts, Dec. 18, 1976; children—Kyoko, Marshand, Devin. A.A., Coahoma Jr. Coll., 1965; B.S., Jackson State U., 1967; M.Ed., Delta State U., 1973. Tchr., Wilson Elem. Sch., Grenada, Miss., 1967-68, Leake County Schs., Carthage, Miss., 1968-73; counselor Copiah County Schs., Crystal Springs, Miss., 1973-81; prin. Hazlehurst High Sch., Miss., 1981—. Mem. Leake County Democratic Com., Carthage, 1968-73; mem. Star Adv. Bd. Adult Edn., Carthage, 1968-71; mem. Head Start, Friends of Children, Carthage, 1970-72. Mem. Jackson State U. Alumni Assn. (v.p. Copiah County chpt. 1984—), NEA, Miss. Assn. Educators, Hazlehurst Assn. Educators, Nat. Assn. Secondary Sch. Prins., Miss. Assn. Sch. Adminstrs. Baptist. Clubs: Hazlehurst High Sch. Band Booster, Hazlehurst High Sch. Athletic Booster. Avocations: fishing; reading. Home: 429 Monticello St Hazlehurst MS 39083

BOORTZ, NEAL A., JR., lawyer, columnist, radio commentator; b. Bryn Mawr, Pa., Apr. 6, 1945; s. Neal A. and Mary F. (Lucas) B.; m. Donna Crousen, Aug. 11, 1973; 1 dau., Laura Dawn. Student in journalism Tex. A&M U., 1963-67; J.D., John Marshall Law Sch., Atlanta, 1977. Bar: Ga. 1977, U.S. Dist. Ct. (11th dist.) Ga. 1977. Talk show host Sta.-WRNG, CBS Radio, Atlanta, 1969-80; sole practice, Atlanta, 1977—; daily commentator WGST Radio, Atlanta. Columnist, local newspaper. Mem. ABA, Assn. Trail Lawyers Am., Ga. Trial Lawyers Assn., State Bar Ga., Decatur-DeKalb Bar Assn. Lodge: Elks. Home: 2454 Empire Forest Dr Tucker GA 30084 Office: 3537 Habersham at Northlake Tucker GA 30084

BOOTH, ALEX, religious institute administrator; b. Warfield, Ky., Oct. 24, 1924; s. Alex Lunsford and Emma (Kyle) B.; m. Beatrice Thompson, Oct. 5, 1947; children—Carolyn, Daniel, Ellen Gayle, Allen, Gary. B.A., King Coll., Bristol, Tenn., 1951; M.Div., Southeastern Bapt. Theol. Sem., Wake Forest, N.C., 1959; D.D., Gardner-Webb, Boiling Springs, N.C., 1983. Ordained to ministry So. Baptist Ch., 1950. Pastor Cedar Fork Bapt. Ch., Yates Assn., Durham, N.C., 1957-59; pastor Spence Bapt. Ch., Md., 1959-61, Round Hill Bapt. Ch., Union Mills, N.C., 1961-64; mem. faculty Fruitland Bapt. Bible Inst., Hendersonville, N.C., 1964—, dean, 1965-74, dir., 1974—. Pres. Henderson County Mental Health Assn., 1973-74; mem. Henderson County Bd. Edn., 1973—. Mem. So. Bapt. Adult Edn. Assn. (pres.). Lodge: Rotary (past dir.). Office: Fruitland Bapt Bible Inst Hendersonville NC 28739

BOOTH, CYNTHIA LYNN, athletic trainer; b. Oak Hill, W.Va., Oct. 12, 1955; d. William Hobart and Sarah Frances (Kerby) Booth. B.S., W.Va. U., 1978; M.S., U. Kans., 1982. Cert. athletic trainer. Women's athletic trainer U. Kans., Lawrence, 1980-83; clin. asst. Morgantown Phys. Therapy Assocs. (W.Va.), 1983—. Mem. W.Va. Athletic Trainers Soc. (sec. 1983—). Roman Catholic. Home: 907 Dudley Ave Morgantown WV 26505

BOOTH, DOUGLAS WADE, utility company executive; b. Atlanta, 1924; married. B.S.E.E., U. Ala., 1947. With Gen. Electric Co., 1947-50, W.T. Dabney Furniture Co., 1950-52; with Duke Power Co., Inc., Charlotte, N.C., 1952—, v.p. mktg., 1965-71, sr. v.p. retail ops., 1971-76, exec. v.p., 1976-82, pres., chief operating officer, dir., 1982—. Office: Duke Power Co Inc 422 S Church St Box 33189 Charlotte NC 28242

BOOTH, HILDA EARL FERGUSON, clinical counselor, Spanish educator; b. Pinehurst, N.C., Aug. 14, 1943; d. Arthur C. and Edna Estelle (Henry) Ferguson; m. Thomas Gilbert Booth, Oct. 25, 1966. A.A., Montreat-Anderson Coll., 1963; B.A., Pembroke State U., 1965; M.S., Valdosta State U., 1985. Spanish instr. Community Coll., Lake City, Fla., 1983—; clin. counselor Columbia Counseling, Lake City, Fla., 1985—; dir. women FORSPRO (Spain), Coral Gables, Fla., 1984—; emergency services staff Mental Health, Lake City, 1985—. Pres. Protestant Women of Chapel, Nfld., Can., 1969, Church Women United, Lake City, 1976; deacon First Presby. Ch., Lake City, 1976—, chmn. bd. deacons, 1982, elder 1985. Mem. Am. Psychol. Assn., Inter-Am. Soc. of Psychology, Am. Assn. for Counseling and Devel., Am. Legion. Democrat. Avocations: painting, swimming, traveling, cycling, guitar, reading. Home: Rt 1 Box 319 Lake City FL 32055 Office: Columbia Counseling Ctr PO Box 2818 Lake City FL 32055

BOOTH, JOHN ROBERT, pharmaceutical executive; b. Greenville, Miss., Jan. 29, 1947; s. Robert Elmo and Mary Kathryn (Shearer) B.; m. Julia Hall, Aug. 23, 1970; children—Katie, Brian, Brad. B.S. in Pharmacy, U. Miss., 1970. Registered pharmacist, Miss. Pharmacist, mgr. Thompson Drugs Inc., Grenada, Miss., 1970-73, Chaney's Pharmacy Inc., Greenwood, 1973; sr. profl. sales rep. Parke Davis and Co., Detroit, 1973-80; pres., founder Gen. Generics Inc., Oxford, Miss., 1980—. Dir. Lafayette County Assn. Retarded Citizens. Mem. Miss. Pharmacists Assn., Nat. Pharm. Alliance, Nat. Drug Assn., Ole Miss Pharacy Alumni Assn. (dir.). Baptist. Clubs: Grenada County Jaycees (pres. 1971); Kiwanis (Grenada fin. chmn. 1978-81, Grenada Kiwanian of Yr. 1979, 80). Home: PO Box 510 Oxford MS 38655 Office: General Generics Inc PO Box 510 Oxford MS 38655

BOOTH, JUNE MARTIN, physical education educator; b. Pleasantville, N.J., Sept. 25, 1936; d. William David and Kathryn Adele (Wells) Martin; m. Albert James Booth, Dec. 26, 1959 (div. 1964). B.S., Trenton State Coll., 1958; M.S., Glassboro State Coll., 1972. Tchr., Ocean City High Sch., N.J., 1958-61, Atlantic City High Sch., N.J., 1961-65; tchr. Mainland Regional High Sch., Linwood, N.J., 1966-75; assoc. prof., tennis coach Northwestern U., Evanston, Ill., 1975-79; assoc. prof. health, phys. edn. Sweet Briar Coll., Va., 1979—, athletic dir., 1979-83; cons. alcoholism Stockton State Coll., 1983—; lectr. in field. Hostess, Dem. Nat. Conv., Atlantic City, 1964. Mem. Va. Athletic Assn., N.J. Athletic Assn., AAUP, AAHPERD, Ill. Assn. Intercollegiate Athletics for Women, Intercollegiate Tennis Coaches Assn. Address: Sweet Briar Coll PO Box 28 Sweet Briar VA 24595

BOOTH, ROBERT H., association executive. Pres., Durham C. of C., N.C. Office: Durham C of C 201 N Roxbury St Durham NC 27701*

BOOTH, WILLARD CLAUDE, speech communication educator; b. Chefoo, China, Apr. 4, 1926; s. William Claude and Elsie (Harrod) B.; m. Rowena Alexandra Boutwell, July 21, 1971; 1 son, Robert Allen. B.A., U. Mich., 1949; M.A., 1951; Ph.D., U. So. Calif., 1959. Speech supr. Whittier (Calif.) City Schs., 1951-54; asst. prof. speech S.W. Tex. State U., San Marcos, 1954-60; assoc. prof., dir. speech edn. Calif. State Coll., Chico, 1961-69; assoc. prof., chmn. speech communication George Peabody Coll., Nashville, 1969-76; prof., chmn. speech communication Delta State U., Cleveland, Miss., 1976—. Bd. dirs. Cleveland Community Theater, Clarksdale Community Theater, Greenville Community Theater. Served with AUS, 1943-47. Ford Found. scholar, 1951-53; Danforth grantee, 1960-61. Mem. Speech Communication Assn., Assn. Communication Adminstrn., Internat. Platform Assn. Mem. Disciples of Christ Ch. Home: 501 S Court St Cleveland MS 38732 Office: Box 3137 Delta State U Cleveland MS 38733

BOOTHE, BUNAH ANGLE, insurance executive; b. Wirtz, Va., Mar. 26, 1924; d. John Aaron and Ola Ethel (Flora) Angle; m. Claude O. Boothe, Sept. 25, 1944. Cert. Ins. Inst. Am., 1978. Cert. profl. ins. woman. Clk. typist Charles Lunsford Sons and Izard, Roanoke, Va., 1957-58; dept. mgr. Life of Roanoke subsidiary Lunsford's, 1958-60; comml. lines policy processor Charles Lunsford Sons & Izard, Inc. (now Chas. Lunsford Sons & Assocs. and Frank B. Hall & Co. Va., Inc.), Roanoke, 1960-64, supr. comml. lines, 1974-83, casualty technician comml. lines, 1983—. Mem. Nat. Assn. Ins. Women (pres. local chpt. 1981-83), Am. Bus. Women's Assn. Republican. Mem. Ch. of Brethren.

BOOTHE, LEON ESTEL, university administrator; b. Carthage, Mo., Feb. 1, 1938; s. Harold Estel and Merle Jane (Hood) B.; m. Nancy Janes, Aug. 20, 1960; children—Cynthia, Diana and Cheri (twins). B.S. (Curators' scholar), U. Mo.-Columbia, 1960, M.A., 1962; Ph.D. in History, U. Ill., 1966. Tchr. history Valparaiso (Ind.) High Sch., 1960-61; asst. prof. history U. Miss., Oxford, 1965-68, assoc. prof., 1968-70; assoc. prof. history George Mason Coll. (now U. Va.), Fairfax, 1970-73, prof. history, 1973-80, assoc. dean coll., 1970-71, dean, 1971-72, dean Coll. Arts and Scis., 1972-80; provost, v.p. acad. affairs Ill. State U., Normal, 1980-82, acting pres., 1982; pres. No. Ky. U., Highland Heights, 1983—; dir., mem. exec. com. Greater Cin. Consortium Colls. and Univs. Adv. bd. Cin. Council World Affairs; Bd. dirs. Wesley Found., Fairfax County and McLean County chpts. ARC, McLean County Heart Assn., McLean County United Way, NCCJ; mem. No. Ky. Bicentennial Exec. Com.; mem. adv. bd. Kids Helping Kids; mem. Met. Bd. YMCA No. Ky. NEH postdoctoral fellow, 1967-68; scholar Diplomat Seminars U.S. Dept. State. Mem. Soc. Historians for Am. Fgn. Relations, McLean County Assn. Commerce and Industry, No. Ky. C. of C., Sigma Rho Sigma, Omicron Delta Kappa, Phi Alpha Theta, Phi Delta Kappa. Democrat. Methodist (pres. governing bd.). Lodges: Rotary; Masons. Home: 1 University Dr Highland Heights KY 41076 Office: office of Pres No Ky Univ Highland Heights KY 41076

BOOTLE, WILLIAM AUGUSTUS, retired judge; b. Colleton County, S.C., Aug. 19, 1902; s. Philip Lorraine and Laura Lilla (Benton) B.; A.B., Mercer U., 1924, LL.B., 1925, LL.D., 1982; m. Virginia Childs, Nov. 24, 1928; children—William Augustus, Ann, James C. Bar: Ga. 1925. Practiced in Macon, 1925—; U.S. dist. atty. Middle Ga. Dist., 1929-33; mem. firm Carlisle & Bootle, 1933-54; acting dean Law Sch., Mercer U., 1933-37, part-time prof. law, 1926-37; judge U.S. Dist. Ct. for Middle Dist. Ga., Macon, 1954-81, sr. judge, 1972-81, ret., 1981. Trustee, Mercer U., 1933—, chmn. exec. com., 1941-46, 48-53; trustee Walter F. George Sch. Law Found., 1961—, v.p., 1963-65, pres., 1965-66. Recipient Disting. Alumnus award Mercer U., 1971. Mem. Phi Alpha Delta, Phi Delta Theta. Republican. Baptist. Clubs: Masons, Shriners, Civitan (pres. 1936). Office: Federal Bldg and US Courthouse Macon GA 31202

BOOZER, JOHN CALVIN, JR., hospital manager; b. Newberry, S.C., Oct. 11, 1953; s. John Calvin and Mary Vanessa (Mills) B. B.S., U.S.C., 1974, M.Ed., 1978. Clin. counselor S.C. Dept. Mental Health, Columbia, 1975-78; project mgr. S.C. Commn. Alcohol/Drugs, Columbia, 1978-82; risk mgr. Providence Hosp., Columbia, 1982—. Mem. Am. Soc. Safety Engrs., Nat. Fire Protection Assn., Am. Hosp. Assn. Soc. for Hosp. Risk Mgrs., S.C. Hosp. Assn. Soc. for Hosp. Risk Mgrs., Phi Beta Kappa. Avocations: playing piano, fitness, home carpentry and remodeling, bicycling. Home: 2509 Burney Dr Columbia SC 29205

BOQUER, ANTONIO JAMES, JR., commercial diving company executive; b. Manila, Dec. 28, 1947; came to U.S., 1977, naturalized, 1984; s. Antonio Maria and Casimira James (Vasquez) B.; B.S. in Bus. Mgmt., Loyola U., 1969, postgrad. in bus. adminstrn., 1974-77; m. Margaret Hernandez, Dec. 6, 1969; children—Dorethea Margaret, Marie Michelle, Monica Anne. Asst. mktg. dir. Hitachi-Union, Inc., Manila, 1969-70; sales mgr. Excellence Mktg., Manila, 1970-71; mgr. dealer sales Gen. Electric (Philippines), Inc., Paranaque, 1971-74; pres., gen. mgr. Sagisag Sales, Inc., Makati Philippines, 1974-77; v.p., mgmt. cons. Boquer and Assocs., New Orleans, 1977-78; mktg. dir. Harry Hebert Homes, Lafayette, La., 1979-82; sales mgr. Dondi Housing Corp., 1982-84; v.p. mktg. and sales Magna Communications Corp., Lafayette, 1984; purchasing mgr., adminstrv. asst. Am. Oilfield Divers, Inc., Broussard, La. 1984—; mktg. cons., media buyer thrifty Way Pharmacies of La., Abbeville, 1984—. Chmn. publicity 4th of July celebration Town of Erath (La.), 1981-84, pres., 1983. Recipient Disting. Service award Dozier Elem. Sch., Erath, 1983. Mem. La. Home Builders Assn. (chmn. publicity 23d Ann. Conv. 1980, cert. of appreciation 1980, Big Spike award 1982), Nat. Assn. Home Builders (Mktg. Dir. of Yr. award 1981), Acadian Home Builders Assn. (media cons. 1980—, mem. blueprints bd. 1984, cert. of merit 1980), La. Assn. Profl. Insulators (charter), Advt. Club of Acadiana. Lodge: K.C.

BORCHELT, MERLE LLOYD, electric utility company executive; b. Mercedes, Tex., Jan. 4, 1926; s. George Cornelius and Pauline Caroline (Lange) B.; m. Virginia Mae Gullatt, Aug. 3, 1947; children—Lawrence Frederick, Linda Diane, Mark Randall. B.S. in Elec. Engring., La. Tech. U., 1949; postgrad., Westinghouse Advanced Electric Utility Program, 1958, Harvard U. Advanced Mgmt. Program, 1983. Registered profl. engr., Tex. With Central Power & Light Co., Corpus Christi, Tex., 1949—, gen. mgr. fuels-systems planning, 1975-77, v.p., 1977-79, exec. v.p., chief engr., 1979-81, pres., chief exec. officer, 1981—, dir. Chmn. United Way of Coastal Bend, 1982. Served with USN, 1943-45. Mem. IEEE (pres. Corpus Christi chpt.), Edison Electric Inst. (dir.), Tex. Atomic Energy Research Found. (dir.), South Tex. C. of C. (exec. bd. 1980—), South Tex. Found. Econ. Edn., Tex. Assn. Taxpayers, Assn. Electric Cos. Tex. (dir. 1980—). Lutheran. Clubs: Corpus Christi County, Town, Nueces. Office: Central Power & Light Co 120 N Chaparral St Corpus Christi TX 78401

BORDERS, ELIZABETH ACOSTA, architect; b. El Paso, Tex., Oct. 14, 1949; d. Salomon Acosta Baylon and Betsy Ruth (Horner) Acosta; m. James Buchanan Borders IV, Oct. 16, 1976; 1 child, James Buchanan V. B. Arch., Tulane U., 1973. Lic. real estate broker, La. Architect Inmobiliaria Del Norte, Juarez, Mex., 1974; sole proprietor, mgr. Tianguis Imports, New Orleans, 1975-80; architect Maison Blanche Co., New Orleans, 1979-81; architect, v.p. Architects Internat., New Orleans, 1982—; cons., New Orleans, 1975—. Prin. works include La Placita Restaurant, Tijuana, Mex., Weekend Residences, Pontchatoula, La. Bd. dirs. Lower Garden Dist. Assn., New Orleans, 1984—; pres. Coliseum Place Condominiums, 1984—. Mem. Architects Internat., Rainbow Cottage Inc., Nat. Assn. Female Execs. Roman Catholic. Clubs: Contemporary Art Ctr. (New Orleans), Women in Mainstream (New Orleans). Avocations: painting; reading; travel. Home: 1629 Coliseum Pl Unit 5 New Orleans LA 70130 Office: 1629 Coliseum Pl Unit 4 New Orleans LA 70130

BOREN, DAVID LYLE, senator; b. Washington, Apr. 21, 1941; s. Lyle H. and Christine (McKown) B.; m. Molly Shi, Dec. 1977; children—David Daniel, Carrie Christine. B.A. summa cum laude, Yale, 1963; M.A. (Rhodes scholar), Oxford (Eng.) U., 1965; J.D. (Bledsoe Meml. prize as outstanding law grad.), U. Okla., 1968. Bar: Okla. 1968. Asst. to dir. liaison Office Civil and Def. Moblzn., Washington, 1960-62; propaganda analyst Soviet affairs USIA, Washington, 1962-63; mem. Speakers Bur., Am. embassy, London, Eng., 1963-65; mem. residential counseling staff U. Okla., 1965-66; practiced in, Seminole, 1968-74; mem. Okla. Ho. of Reps., 1966-74; gov., Okla., 1975-79; mem. U.S. Senate from Okla., 1979—. Chmn. govt. dept. Okla. Baptist U., 1969-74. Del. Democratic Nat. Conv., 1968, 76. Named U.S. Army ROTC Disting. Mil. Grad.; One of 10 Outstanding Young Men in U.S. U.S. Jaycees, 1967. Mem. Assn. U.S. Rhodes Scholars, Order of Coif, Phi Beta Kappa, Sigma Delta Rho, Phi Delta Phi. Methodist. Club: Yale of Western Okla. Home: 2369 S Queen St Arlington VA 22202 also Seminole OK 74868 Office: 452 Russell Senate Office Bldg Washington DC 20510

BOREN, JAMES ERWIN, artist; b. Waxahachie, Tex., Sept. 26, 1921; s. John Darrell and Fannie (Goodwin) B.; m. Mary Ellen Selvidge, July 30, 1949; children—Nancy, John D. B.F.A., Kansas City Art Inst., 1950, M.F.A., 1951. Art instr. St. Mary Coll., Xavier, Kans., 1951-53; freelance artist, Anchorage, 1953-56; concept illustrator Martin-Marietta Co., Denver, 1956-65; art dir. Nat. Cowboy Hall of Fame, Oklahoma City, 1965-69; artist, Clifton, Tex., 1969—. Served with USN, 1942-45. Recipient Gold medal in watercolor category Cowboy Artists of Am. ann. art show, 1968, 69, 70, 71, 76, 77, 78, 79, 80, 83, 84, Gold medal in other media category, 1972, Silver medal, 1972, 73, 77, 80, 81, Silver award in drawing category, 1971, 75, 77, Gold medal in water solubles, 1985, Best of Show award, 1985. Mem. Cowboy Artists Am. (sec. treas. 1969-70, v.p. 1978-79, pres. 1973-74, 79-80), Western Heritage Sale, Grand Central Art Gallery. Republican. Avocations: travel; photography. Home and Office: PO Box 533 Clifton TX 76634

BOREN, JAMES LEWIS, JR., lawyer, insurance company executive; b. Portland, Tenn., Sept. 15, 1928; s. James Lewis and Carolyn Duval (Moore) B.; m. Carolyn Prewitt, Oct. 27, 1961; 1 dau., Dudley Prewitt; B.A., Vanderbilt U., 1950, LL.B., 1953. Bar: Tenn. 1953. Staff atty. Mid-South Title Co., Inc., Memphis, 1953-56, sec.-treas., 1956-63, v.p., 1963-67, exec. v.p., 1967-73, pres., 1973-78; pres., chief exec. officer Mid-South Title Ins. Corp., Memphis, 1978-85, chmn., chief exec. officer, 1985—. Pres., chmn. United Way of Greater Memphis, 1974, 75; pres., chmn. Memphis/Mid South chpt. Am. Diabetes Assn., 1977-78. Served with USAF, 1951-53. Mem. ABA, Tenn. Bar Assn., Memphis-Shelby County Bar Assn., Am. Judicature Soc., Am. Land Title Assn. (pres. 1980-81), Tenn. Land Title Assn. (pres. 1966-67). Presbyterian. Clubs: University, Rotary (pres. Memphis 1969-70). Address: PO Box 432 Memphis TN 38101

BORGARD, JOHN HENRY, university administrator; b. Chgo., Mar. 5, 1938; s. Clemens Florian and Eleanor (Handtke) B.; m. Peggy Jo Garrison, Aug. 14, 1970; 1 child, Matthew. A.B., Marquette U., 1960, M.A., 1964; Ph.D., Loyola U., 1974. Asst. to dean sch. bus. Loyola U., Chgo., 1964-65, dir. summer sessions, 1966-70, centennial dir., 1968-70; asst. dean Va. Commonwealth U., Richmond, 1971—. Mem. Richmond Pub. Sch. Bd., 1985—. Awardee Nat. Acad. Advising Assn. Mem. Acad. Affairs Adminstrs. (pres. 1982-83), Am. Coll. Personnel Assn. (pres. commn. 1982-83), Am. Assn. Higher Edn. Roman Catholic. Home: 3310 Gloucester Rd Richmond VA 23227 Office: Va Commonwealth U 900 Park Ave Richmond VA 23284

BORGES, MYRNA, pediatrician; b. Caguas, P.R., Jan. 2, 1951; d. Rosali and Maria E. (Perez) Borges. B.S. magna cum laude in Sci., Cath. U. of P.R., 1973, M.D., 1977. Pediatric resident Caguas Regional Hosp., 1977-80, staff pediatrician Caguas City Hosp., 1980; mem. med. staff Coffee Gen. Hosp., Douglas, Ga., 1983—; practice medicine specializing in pediatrics, Douglas, 1983—; cons. in adolescent medicine Caguas City Hosp., 1982-83, Am. Cancer Soc., Caguas, 1982—. Fellow Inter Am. Coll. of Physicians and Surgeons; mem. AMA, Coffee County Med. Soc., P.R. Med. Assn. Roman Catholic. Home: Hill House Apts D-2 Douglas GA 31533 Office: PO Box 671 Caguas PR 00626

BORGESON, EARL CHARLES, law librarian, educator; b. Boyd, Minn., Dec. 2, 1922; s. Hjalmar Nicarner and Dohris (Donaldson) B.; B.S. in Law, U. Minn., 1947, LL.B., 1949; B.A. in Law Librarianship, U. Wash., 1950; m. Barbara Ann Jones, Sept. 21, 1944; children—Barbara Gale, Geoffrey Charles, Steven Earl. Librarian, Harvard U. Law Sch. Library, 1952-70; asso. dir. Stanford U. Libraries, 1970-75; asso. law librarian Los Angeles County Law Library, 1975-78; prof., law librarian So. Meth. U., Dallas, 1978—; lectr. UCLA Grad. Sch. Library Sci., 1975-78; adj. prof. Tex. Womens U., 1979-80; cons. Am. Assn. Law Libraries, Am. Bar Found., Asia Found. Served with USNR, 1943-46. Mem. Am. Assn. Law Libraries. Home: 2801 Binkley Apt 102 Dallas TX 75205 Office: Underwood Law Library So Methodist Univ Dallas TX 75275

BORIE, BERNARD SIMON, physicist, educator; b. New Orleans, June 21, 1924; s. Bernard S. and Ruth L. B.; m. Martine Descamps, May 2, 1957 (div., 1963); children—Kathleen, Marianne. B.S., U. of SW La., 1944; M.S. in Physics, Tulane U., 1949; Ph.D. in Physics, MIT, 1956. Sr. scientist Oak Ridge Nat. Lab., 1953-85; prof. U. Tenn.-Knoxville, 1969—; vis. prof. Cornell U., 1971-72; U. Calif.-Berkeley, 1980. Served to lt. USNR, 1943-45. Fulbright fellow U. Paris, 1956-57. Fellow AAAS; mem. Am. Crystallographic Assn., AIME, Am. Soc. Metals. Contbr. numerous articles to profl. jours.

BORISH, IRVIN MAX, optometrist, educator; b. Phila., Jan. 21, 1913; s. Max and Rose (Gimson) B.; m. Beatrice Evelyn Silver, June 28, 1936; 1 dau., Frances Borish Goldman. Student Temple U., 1930-31, Ill. Inst. Tech., 1935-36; O.D., No. Ill. Coll. Optometry, 1934, D.O.S., 1935; LL.D., Ind. U., 1968; D.Sc. (hon.) Pa. Coll. Optometry, 1975; D.O.S. (hon.), So. Calif. Coll. Optometry, 1984; D.Sc. (hon.), SUNY, 1984. Diplomate Am. Acad. Optometry; lic. optometrist, Ill. Instr. to prof. No. Ill. Coll. Optometry, 1935-43; dir. No. Ill. Eye Clinic, 1935-43; practice optometry, Kokomo, Ind., 1944-72; vis. lectr. Ind. U., 1955-64, part-time prof., 1965-72, prof., 1972-83; Benedict prof. optometric practice U. Houston, 1983—. Bd. dirs., pres. Kokomo Art Assn., 1950-72; bd. dirs. Civic Music Assn., Kokomo Civic Theatre, both 1950-72. Recipient Alumni Scholarship award No. Ill. Coll., 1934; Benjamin Franklin award SUNY, 1976. Mem. So. Council Optometry (Disting. Service award 1975), Ind. Optometric Assn. (Disting. Service award 1975), Am. Optometric Found. (Silver medal 1972) Am. Acad. Optometry (hon. life, William Feinbloom award 1985), Am. Optometric Assn. (Apollo award 1968), AAUP. Democrat. Jewish. Clubs: Rotary. Author: Clinical Refraction; (with Clifford Brooks) Systematic System of Opthalmic Dispensing; contbr. numerous articles to profl. jours.; patentee, inventor in field. Home: 4520 Rockwood Dr Houston TX 77004 Office: Coll Optometry U Houston Suite 2146 Houston TX 77004

BORKAN, WILLIAM NOAH, inventor, entrepreneur; b. Miami Beach, Fla., Apr. 29, 1956; s. Martin Solomon and Annabelle (Hoffman) B.; B.S.E.E., Carnegie Mellon U., 1977; Ph.D., Sussex Coll. Tech., 1979. Tech., Dominicks' Radio & TV Co., Miami Beach, 1971-74; computer programmer Mt. Sinai Hosp., Miami Beach, 1973-74; chief studio engr. WGMA, Hollywood, Fla., 1973-74; disc. jockey WBUS-FM, Miami Beach, 1974; chief recording engr. Dukoff Recording Studios, Miami, 1974-75; rec. studio design and constrn. TSI, Hollywood, Fla., 1975-77; chief design engr. Lumonics Co., Miami, 1974; lab. tech. Carnegie-Mellon U.; founder, gen. mgr. Tech. Electronics Co., Pitts., 1976; pres. Borktronics Co. Miami, 1974-84; cons. specialist in neurobiometrics St. Barnabas Hosp., N.Y.C., 1978-84; rec. studio designer FXL Studios, Sunrise, Fla., 1978; pres., chief exec. officer Electronic Diagnostics, Inc., 1978-83, NeuroMed, Inc., 1980—; mem. coll. curricular coms. E.E. Dept. Grantee Carnegie Corp. and Carnegie Mellon U. Mem. ASHRAE, Assn. Energy Engrs., Soc. Automotive Engrs., Assn. Advancement Med. Instrumentation, AAAS, N.Y. Acad. Scis., Audio Engring. Soc. Author publs. in field; patentee multielectrode catheter for spinal cord stimulation, energy monitor and control system, others. Home: 3364 NE 167th St North Miami Beach FL 33160 Office: 5000 Oakes Rd Fort Lauderdale FL 33314

BORKMAN, THOMASINA SMITH, sociology educator, researcher, consultant; b. Boise, Idaho, Oct. 3, 1936; d. Babe Adam and Irene (Leppala) Stunz; m. John Borkman, Aug. 10, 1967 (div. 1972); m. Placidus O. Ekwueme, June 7, 1984. Student drama U. Wash., 1954-56; B.A. in Sociology magna cum laude, Occidental Coll., Los Angeles, 1958; M.A. in Sociology, Columbia U., 1959, Ph.D., 1969. Human factors specialist System Devel. Corp., N.J., 1959-63; research sociologist Fountain House Found. (Halfway house), N.Y.C., 1963-64; project dir. Alameda County Blood Pressure Study, Calif. Dept. Pub. Health, Berkeley, 1964-67; pub. health analyst Kidney Disease Control Program, USPHS, Arlington, Va., 1967-69, vis. research fellow Nat. Inst. on Alcohol Abuse and Alcoholism, Rockville, Md., 1978-80; asst. prof. sociology Catholic U. Am., Washington, 1969-74; assoc. prof. George Mason U., Fairfax, Va., 1974—; cons. Hypertension Detection and Follow-Up Program, Georgetown U. Med. Div., Washington, 1972, R.A. Becker Inc., N.Y.C., 1973, 75, Divine Word Missionaries, Empirical Research, Inc.; mem. adv. coms. Nat. Heart and Lung Inst., 1975, Nat. Conf. on Emotional Stress and Heart Disease, 1975, Nat. Heart, Lung and Blood Inst., NIH, 1974-76, Internat. Health Resource Consortium, 1976-77, Am. Heart Assn., 1977-78, Nat. Council on Aging, Nat. Inst. on Alcohol Abuse and Alcoholism, State of Calif. Alcohol Programs, 1985. NIMH predoctoral fellow, 1963; grantee Cath. U., 1970-71, NIMH, 1972-73, George Mason U. Found., 1977. Mem. Am. Sociol. Assn., Assn. Voluntary Action Scholars, D.C. Sociol. Soc., Nat. Women's Health Network, Sociologists for Women in Soc., So. Sociol. Soc.,Common Cause, Alpha Kappa Delta, Sigma Epsilon Sigma, Zeta Phi Eta. Democrat. Contbr. numerous articles to profl. jours. Office: George Mason U 4400 University Dr Fairfax VA 22030

BORLAUG, NORMAN ERNEST, agricultural scientist; b. Cresco, Iowa, Mar. 25, 1914; s. Henry O. and Clara (Vaala) B.; B.S. in Forestry, U. Minn., 1937, M.S. in Plant Pathology, 1940, Ph.D. in Plant Pathology, 1941; Sc.D. (honoris causa), Punjab (India) Agrl. U., 1969, Royal Norwegian Agrl. Coll., 1970, Luther Coll., 1970, Kanpur U. (India), 1970, Uttar Pradesh Agrl. U. (India), 1971, Mich. State U., 1971, Universidad de la Plata (Argentina), 1971, U. Ariz., 1972, U. Fla., 1973, Universidad Católica de Chile, 1974, Universität Hohenheim, Germany, 1976, U. Agrl. Lyallpur, Pakistan, 1978; L.H.D., Gustavus Adolphus Coll., 1971; LL.D. (hon.), N.Mex. State U., 1973; m. Margaret G. Gibson, Sept. 24, 1937; children—Norma Jean (Mrs. Richard H. Rhoda), William Gibson. With U.S. Forest Service, 1935-36, 37, 38; instr. U. Minn., 1941; microbiologist E.I. DuPont de Nemours, 1942-44; research scientist in charge wheat improvement Coop. Mexican Agrl. Program, Mexican Ministry Agr.-Rockefeller Found., Mexico, 1944-60; asso. dir. assigned to Inter-Am. Food Crop Program, Rockefeller Found., 1960-63; dir. wheat research and prodn. program Internat. Maize and Wheat Improvement Center, 1964-79, asso. dir. Rockefeller Found., 1964-82; cons., collaborator Instituto Nacional de Investigationes Agricolas, Mexican Ministry Agr., 1960-64; cons. FAO, North Africa and Asia, 1960; ex-officio cons. wheat research and prodn. problems to govts. in Latin Am., Africa, Asia. Mem. Citizen's Commn. on Sci., Law and Food Supply, 1973-74, Commn. Critical Choices for Am., 1973—, Council Agr. Sci. and Tech., 1973—; dir. Population Crisis Com., 1971; asesor especial Fundacion para Estudios de la Poblacion A.C., Mexico, 1971—; mem. adv. council Renewable Natural Resources Found., 1973—; Presdl. commn. World Hunger, 1978-79. Recipient Distinguished Service awards Wheat Producers Assns., and state govts. Mexican States of Guanajuato, Queretaro, Sonora, Tlaxcala and Zactecas, 1954-60; Recognition award Agrl. Inst. Can., 1966, Instituto Nacional de Tecnologia Agropecuaria de Marcos Juarez, Argentina, 1968; Sci. Service award El Colegio de Ingenieros Agronomos de Mexico, 1970; Outstanding Achievement award U. Minn., 1959, E.C. Stakman award, 1961, named Uncle of Paul Bunyan, 1969; recipient Distinguished Citizen award Cresco Centennial Com., 1966; Nat. Distinguished Service award Am. Agrl. Editors Assn., 1967; Genetics and Plant Breeding award Nat. Council Comml. Plant Breeders, 1968; Star of Distinction, Govt. of Pakistan, 1968; citation and street named in honor Citizens of Sonora and Rotary Club, 1968; Internat. Agronomy award Am. Soc. Agronomy, 1968; Distinguished Service award Wheat Farmers of Punjab, Haryana and Himachal Pradesh, 1969; Nobel Peace prize, 1970; Diploma de Merito, El Instituto Tecnologico y de Estudios Superiores de Monterrey (Mexico), 1971; medalla y Diploma de Merito Antonio Narro, Escuela Superior de Agricultura de la U. de Coahuila (Mexico), 1971; Diploma de Merito, Escuela Superior de Agricultura Hermanos Escobar (Mexico), 1973; award for service to agr. Am. Farm Bur. Fedn., 1971; Outstanding Agrl. Achievement award World Farm Found., 1971; Medal of Merit, Italian Wheat Scientists, 1971; Service award for outstanding contbn. to alleviation of world hunger 8th Latin Am. Food Prodn. Conf., 1972; Bernardo O'Higgins award Govt. Chile, 1974; Presdl. medal of Freedom (U.S.), 1977; Hilal-I-Imtiaz award, Pakistan, 1978; numerous other honors and awards from govts. ednl. instns., citizens groups. Hon. fellow Indian Soc. Genetics and Plant Breeding; mem. Nat. Acad. Sci., Am. Soc. Agronomy (1st Internat. Service award 1960, 1st hon. life mem.), Am. Assn. Cereal Chemists (hon. life mem., meritorious service award 1969), Crop Sci. Soc. Am. (hon. life mem.), Soil Sci. Soc. Am. (hon. life mem.), Sociedad de Agronomia do Rio Grande do Sul Brazil (hon.), India Nat. Sci. Acad. (fgn.), Royal Swedish Acad. Agr. and Forestry (fgn.), Academia Nacional de Agronomia y Veterinaria (Argentina); hon. academician N.I. Vavilov Acad. Agrl. Scis. Lenin Order (USSR.). Address: Centro Internacional de Mejoramiento de Maiz y de Trigo Apartado Postal 6-641 Londres 40 Mexico City 6 Mexico

BORMAN, FRANK, former astronaut, airline executive; b. Gary, Ind., Mar. 14, 1928; s. Edwin Borman; B.S., U.S. Mil. Acad., 1950; M.Aero. Engring., Calif. Inst. Tech., 1957; grad. USAF Aerospace Research Pilots Sch., 1960; grad. Advanced Mgmt. Program, Harvard Bus. Sch., 1970; m. Susan Bugbee; children—Frederick, Edwin. Commd. 2d lt. USAF, advanced through grades to col., 1965, ret., 1970; assigned various fighter squadrons, U.S. and Philippines 1951-56; instr. thermodynamics and fluid mechanics U.S. Mil. Acad., 1957-60; instr. USAF Aerospace Research Pilots Sch., 1960-62; astronaut With Manned Spacecraft Center, NASA, until 1970; command pilot on 14 day orbital Gemini 7 flight, Dec. 1965, including rendezvous with Gemini 6; command pilot Apollo 8, 1st lunar orbital mission, Dec. 1968; sr. v.p. ops. Eastern Air Lines, Inc., Miami, Fla., 1970-74, exec. v.p., gen. ops. mgr., 1974-75, pres., chief exec. officer, 1975—, chmn. bd., 1976—. Recipient Disting. Service award NASA, 1965; Collier Trophy. Nat. Aeros. Assn., 1968. Address: Eastern Air Lines Inc Miami International Airport Miami FL 33148

BORMASTER, JEFFREY STEVEN, chemical dependency counselor; b. Pittsburg, Kans., July 4, 1947; s. Sam Bormaster and Ruth (Berman) Kottler. B.S. in Edn., U. Tex., 1970, M. Ed., 1974. Tchr. Oklahoma City Pub. Schs., 1970-73; edn. cons., Austin, Tex., 1974-82; prin. Lake Travis high sch., Austin, 1982-84; exec. dir. Groveland Ctr. for Treatment Alcohol and Drug Dependency, Austin, 1984—; coordinator S.W. Tchrs. Ctrs., U.S. Office Edn., 1979; cons. Regional Edn. Service Ctr. XIII Author: Talking, Listening, Communicating, 1978; Counseling, Consulting, 1980. Okla. State U. NSF grantee, 1971. Mem. Assn. Supervision and Curriculum Devel., Phi Delta Kappa. Home: 8409 Ardash Ln Austin TX 78759

BORNMAN, LAURA KATHLYN, college nursing program coordinator; b. Cin., Apr. 24, 1950. B.S., Tex. Woman's U., 1973, M.S., 1980. Staff nurse Children's Med. Ctr., Dallas, 1973-76, asst. head nurse, 1976-78; instr. El Centro Coll., Dallas, 1978-85, coordinator vocat. nursing program, 1985—. Author pediatric curriculum Navarro Coll., 1984. Contbg. author: Nursing Care of Children and Families Workbook. Mem. Nat. League Nursing, Tex. League Nursing, Assn. Advancement Assoc. Degree Nursing (recruitment chmn. 1984-85), Am. Nurses Assn., Tex. Nursing Assn., Sigma Theta Tau. Avocations: photography; needlepoint. Office: El Centro Coll Health Occupations Div Main and Lamar Dallas TX 75202

BORNSTEIN, JOAN LEVINE, organization administrator, educator; b. N.Y.C., May 24, 1930; d. Abraham and Gertrude (Rifkin) Levine; m. Jacob George Bornstein, Aug. 3, 1952; children—David (dec.), Rachelle, Jonathon, Avram. B.A., Bklyn Coll., 1952; M.Ed., U. Miami, 1967, Ph.D., 1984. Tchr., coordinator pilot project for culturally disadvantaged children, Miami, Fla., 1964-65; ptnr., pres. The Learning Workshop, Miami, 1977—; dir. of edn. Easter Seal Soc., Dade County, Fla., 1969—, asst. dir., 1983—. Tchr., dir. religious sch., Miami, 1952—; mem. Community Com. for Devel. Handicaps and Retardation; mem. Central Agy. for Jewish Edn. Named Outstanding Employee, Fla. Easter Seal Soc., 1973. Mem. Assn. for Children with Learning Disabilities, Nat. Soc. for Autistic Children, Council for Exceptional Children, Dade County Pub. Sch. Diagnostic and Learning Resources, Assn. for Curriculum and Supervision Devel., Phi Delta Kappa. Author: Outline for Remediation of Problem Areas for Children with Learning Disabilities, 1972; Eye Movement Patterns in Dyslexic Children, 1980. Home: 8440 SW 84th Terr Miami FL 33143 Office: 1475 NW 14th Ave Miami FL 33125

BORNSTEIN, RITA JOYCE, university executive; b. N.Y.C., Jan. 2, 1936; d. Carl and Florence (Gates) Kropf; m. Allen Bornstein, Sept. 1963, (div. 1979); children—Rachel, Mark. B.A. in English, Fla. Atlantic U., 1970, M.A., 1971; Ph.D., U. Miami, 1975. Tchr., adminstr. Dade County Pub. Schs. (Fla.), 1971-75; dir. Fed. Ednl. Equity Projects dept. edn. U. Miami, Coral Gables, 1975-81, adj. assoc. prof. dept. ednl. leadership and instrn., 1978—, dir. found. and corp. relations, 1981-82, asst. v.p. for devel., 1982-85, v.p. for devel., 1985—. Recipient Sojourner Truth award NOW, 1979. Mem. Council for Advancement and Support of Edn., Am. Assn. Higher Edn., Am. Ednl. Research Assn. Democrat. Author: Freedom or Order: Must We Choose?, 1976; Title IX Compliance and Sex Equity: Definitions, Distinctions, Costs and Benefits, 1981; contbr. articles to profl. jours. Office: PO Box 248073 University of Miami Coral Gables FL 33124

BOROCHOFF, CHARLES ZACHARY, business executive; b. Atlanta, Apr. 11, 1921; s. Isadore and Pauline (Reisman) B.; LL.B., Atlanta Law Sch., 1941; m. Ida Dorothy Sloan, Jan. 11, 1942; children—Lynn (Mrs. Myles Jarrett Gould), Toby Ann (Mrs. Jeffrey Bernstein), Jean Sue (Mrs. Mark Shapiro),

Lance Mark. Exec. v.p. So. Wire & Iron Works, Atlanta, 1936-63; owner, pres. Borochoff Realty, Atlanta, 1954—, Designs Unlimited, Inc., Atlanta, 1964—, Scottdale Enterprises, Atlanta, 1972—. Mem. High Museum of Art, 1955—, NCCJ, 1967—, Planned Parenthood, 1970—; mem. Nat. UN Day Program Com., 1977, 78, 79; trustee Atlanta Playhouse, 1971—, A.A. Synagogue; spl. advisor Am. Security Council Found.; lt. col. a.d.c. Gov.'s Staff, 1975-80. Mem. Am. Mgmt. Assn. (presdl. club), Dekalb C. of C. (mem. exec. devel. com. 1975), Nat. Retail Wholesale Furniture Assn., Internat. Home and Furniture Reps. Assn., UN Assn. U.S.A., Nu Beta Epsilon. Club: Atlanta Music. Lodges: Masons, Shriners, B'nai B'rith. Home: 3450 Old Plantation Rd NW Atlanta GA 30327 Office: 3451 Church Scottdale GA 30079

BOROCHOFF, IDA SLOAN, real estate agent, art gallery executive; b. Havana, Cuba, July 29, 1922; d. Louis and Eva (Bistrick) Sloan; m. Charles Borochoff, Jan. 11, 1942; children—Lynn Gould, Jean Shapiro, Toby Bernstein, Lance Mark. Student U. Ga., 1939-40, Ga. State U., 1940; diploma Chgo. Sch. Interior Decorating, 1966; student Allegro Sch. Ballet, 1948-54; diploma Newspaper Inst. Am. Vice pres. Designs Unltd. Inc., Atlanta, 1964—; pres. Sloan Borochoff Gallery, Atlanta, 1970—; lectr. Metro Ednl. Service, Atlanta, 1974-84, lectr., tchr. Emory U. Community Edn., Ga. Inst. Tech.; cable TV producer, 1984-85, Caber award 1985. Mem. adv. bd. Am. Security Council, Washington, 1984-85; chmn. Atlanta Playhouse Theatre Ltd., 1973—; bd. dirs. Atlanta Ballet, 1950-57; chmn. Am. Heart Assn., 1980-84. Mem. Nat. Fedn. Local Cable Programmers, Women in Film (co-editor newsletter 1984), UN Assn., Atlanta Hist. Soc., Women's C. of C (chmn. fine arts com. 1977-78). Clubs: Atlanta Writers, Atlanta Music. Lodge: B'nai B'rith (pres. chpt. 1975). Avocations: Artist; author; TV producer, host. Home: 3450 Old Plantation Rd NW Atlanta GA 30327 Office: Designs Unlimited Inc 733 Glendale Rd Scottsdale GA 30079

BORUM, OLIN HENRY, realtor, former government official; b. Spencer, N.C., Nov. 3, 1917; s. Oscar Henry and Marjorie Mae (Leigh) B.; B.S., U. N.C., 1938, M.A., 1947, Ph.D., 1949; postgrad., teaching fellow U. Md., 1940-41; m. Beatrice Star Comulada, Nov. 14, 1944; children—Pamela Leigh, Robin Olin, Denis Richard. Research chemist E.I. duPont de Nemours & Co., Phila. Lab., 1949-50; interim research asst. prof. Cancer Research Lab., U. Fla., 1950; instr., asst. prof. chemistry U.S. Mil. Acad., 1952-55; research adminstr. U.S. Army Chem. Corps Research and Devel. Command, Washington, 1956-60; research adminstr. U.S. Army Materiel Command, Washington, 1964-76; realtor assoc. Unique Properties, Alexandria, Va., 1974-79; realtor, assoc. broker The J. Edwards Co., Inc., Alexandria, 1979-82; prin. broker Olin H. Borum Realty, 1982-86; tchr. chemistry U. Va., Arlington, Va., 1966-68; teaching fellow U. Md., 1940-41; grad. asst., teaching fellow U. N.C., 1946-49. Adult scouter Nat. Capital Area council Boy Scouts Am., 1964-75, unit commr., 1968-75; sec. Mt. Vernon (Va.) Civic Assn., 1965-66; mem. Com. of 33 (nat. adv. group Nat. Sojourners, Inc.), 1962-71, chmn., 1969-71. Nat. trustee Nat. Sojourners, Inc., 1971-73. Served from 2d lt. to maj. AUS, 1941-46; as maj. USAF, 1951-56, lt. col., 1960-64. Recipient Certificate of Achievement Dept. Army, 1971. Fellow Am. Inst. Chemists; mem. Am. Chem. Soc., Phi Beta Kappa, Sigma Xi. Presbyn. Mason (K.T., Shriner). Contbr. articles to profl. jours. Home: 9002 Volunteer Dr Alexandria VA 22309 Office: 6641 Backlick Rd Springfield VA 22150

BORUM, RODNEY LEE, trade association executive; b. nr. High Point, N.C., Sept. 30, 1929; s. Carl Macy and Etta (Sullivan) B.; m. Helen Marie Rigby, June 27, 1953; children—Richard Harlan, Sarah Elizabeth. Student U. N.C., 1947-49; B.S., U.S. Naval Acad., 1953. Design-devel. engr. Gen. Electric Co., Syracuse, N.Y., Cape Kennedy, Fla., 1956-58, missile test condr., Cape Kennedy, 1958-60, mgr., ground equipment engr., 1960-61, mgr. Eastern Test Range Engring., 1961-65; adminstr. Bus. and Def. Services Adminstrn., U.S. Dept. Commerce, 1966-69; pres. Printing Industries of Am., Inc., Arlington, Va., 1969—, also mem. exec. com., dir.; gov. Comprint Internat.; dir. Inter-Comprint Ltd., Strangers Cay, Ltd.; sec. Graphic Arts Show Corp.; founding trustee Graphic Arts Edn. and Research Trust Fund; bd. dirs. Graphic Arts Council N.Am.; mem. edn. council bd. dirs. Graphic Arts Tech. Found. Bd. dirs. United Fund, Brevard County, Fla., 1963—, v.p., 1964-65; exec. council Cub Scouts Am., 1965; bd. dirs. Brevard Beaches Concert Assn., 1964; Republican candidate Fla. Ho. of Reps., 1960. Served to 1st lt. USAF, 1953-56. Named Boss of Yr., Jaycees, 1965; recipient Bausch and Lomb sci. award; award Am. Legion. Mem. U.S. Naval Inst., U.S. Naval Acad. Alumni Assn., Phi Eta Sigma. Methodist. Clubs: Columbia Country, City Tavern. Home: 4008 Glenrose St Kensington MD 20895 Office: 1730 N Lynn St Arlington VA 22209

BOSLET, GEORGE J., banker; b. N.Y.C., June 28, 1921; s. George J. and Marie Boslet; m. Carol B. Nalen, June 6, 1953 (div.); children—Mark G., Christopher P., Drew G., Claudia M. B.S., Fordham U., 1943; M.B.A., NYU, 1955. With Irving Trust Co., N.Y.C., 1945-78; sr. v.p. Barnett Bank, Miami, Fla., 1978—. Served with AUS, 1943-45. Home: 16571 Blatt Dr Fort Lauderdale FL 33326 Office: 800 Brickell Ave Miami FL 33131

BOSSAK, ERIC SCOTT, healthcare company executive; b. N.Y.C., Jan. 29, 1943; s. Hilfred Norman and Gertrude (Tannenbaum) B.; m. Doris Ellen Applebaum, Mar. 26, 1970; children—Brian Hugh, Kerry Jay. B.I.E., Ga. Inst. Tech., 1965, M.S.I.E., 1967. Prodn. planner Fairchild Semiconductor Mt. View, Calif., 1967-68, mktg. analyst, 1968-69; prin. Kurt Salmon Assocs., Atlanta, 1969-75; regional mgr. Medicus Systems Corp., Atlanta, Washington, 1975-77; sr. assoc. CDP Assocs., Washington, 1977, regional mgr., Atlanta, 1978, v.p., 1979; v.p. Interstate Health Mgmt., Inc., Atlanta, 1979-83; exec. v.p., gen. mgr. Interstate Health Mgmt., 1983-86; v.p. ops. Health Corp., Inc., 1984-86; pres. Paragon Health Mgmt., Inc., 1986—. Mem. Ga. Inst. Human Nutrition (bd. advisors), Hosp. Mgmt. Systems Soc. Democrat. Jewish. Office: Paragon Health Mgmt 365 Northridge Rd Suite 160 Atlanta GA 30338

BOSSIER, ALBERT LOUIS, JR., shipbuilding company executive; b. Gramercy, La., Nov. 29, 1932; s. Albert Louis and Alba Marie (Dufrense) B.; B.S., La. State U., 1954, B.S. in Elec. Engring., 1956; J.D., Loyola U., New Orleans, 1971; m. Jo Ann Decedue, Jan. 11, 1958; children—Albert Louis III, Brian, Donna, Steven. With Avondale Shipyards, Inc., New Orleans, 1957—, elec. supt., 1961-67, gen. plant supt., 1967-69, v.p. prodn. ops., 1969-72, exec. v.p., 1972-78, pres., 1978—. Bd. dirs. Better Bus. Bur. of New Orleans. C. of C. of New Orleans and River Regions. Served as 1st lt. Signal Corps, AUS, 1956. Registered profl. engr., La. Mem. ABA, La. Bar Assn., Am. Welding Soc., Navy League of U.S. (pres. Greater New Orleans council 1981-83). Club: Propeller (New Orleans). Office: PO Box 50280 New Orleans LA 70150

BOST, JANE MORGAN, psychologist; b. Corpus Christi, Aug. 20, 1953; d. Clayton Aquilla and Eleanor (Hoving) M.; m. David Edward Bost, June 16, 1984. B.S., Okla. State U., 1976, M.S., 1980, Ph.D., 1984. English tchr. Perry High Sch., Okla., 1976-78; acad. advisor Okla. State U., Stillwater, 1980-82, staff therapist, 1982-83; counseling psychology intern Tex. A&M U., College Station, 1983-84; counselor students Southwestern U., Georgetown, Tex., 1984—. Contbr. articles to profl. jours. Mem. Am. Psychol. Assn., Tex. Psychol. Assn., Capitol Area Psychol. Assn., Am. Assn. Counseling and Devel., Assn. Profl. Devel. in Applied Behavioral Studies (sec. chpt. 1982), Phi Delta Kappa, Phi Kappa Phi. Republican. Methodist. Avocations: hiking; photography; reading; artwork. Office: Southwestern U Georgetown TX 78626

BOSTIC, TERRANCE ALLEN, lawyer; b. Huntington, W.V., May 30, 1948; s. Edsel Arnold and Bonnie L. (Thomas) B.; m. Cathi Ashley Shaffer, Apr. 24, 1982; children—Robert Chad, Teryn Ashley. B.A., Our Lady of the Lake U., 1975; J.D., U. Miami, 1980. Bar: Fla. 1980, U.S. Dist. Ct. (no., so., middle dists.) Fla. 1980, U.S. Ct. Appeals (5th and 11th cirs.) 1980. Law clk. U.S. Dept. Justice Organized Crime and Racketeering Strike Force, Miami, Fla., 1978-80; asst. U.S. states atty. Dept. of Justice, Washington, 1980-82; asst. minority counsel U.S. Senate Permanent Subcom. on Investigations, Washington, 1982-83; assoc. Trenam, Simmons, Kemker, Scharf, Barkin, et al., Tampa, Fla., 1983—. Served with USAF, 1971-74. Mem. Fla. Bar Assn., ABA, Assn. Trial Lawyers Am. Democrat. Episcopalian. Office: Trenam Simmons Kemker et al 111 Madison Ave Tampa FL 33601

BOSTON, WILLIAM CLAYTON, JR., lawyer; b. Hobart, Okla., Nov. 29, 1934; s. William Clayton and Dollie Jane (Gibbs) B.; B.S., Okla. State U., 1958; LL.B., U. Okla., 1961; LL.M., N.Y. U., 1967; m. Billie Gail Long, Jan. 20, 1962; children—Kathryn Gray and William Clayton. Admitted to Okla. bar, 1961; asso. firm Mosteller, Fellers, Andrews, Snider & Baggett, Oklahoma City, 1962-64; partner firm Feller, Snider, Baggett Blankenship & Boston, 1968-69; partner firm Andrews, Davis, Legg, Bixler, Milsten & Murrah, Oklahoma City, 1969—. Past trustee Nichols Hills Meth. Ch., 1976-79; pres. Ballet Oklahoma Inc., 1975, 76, trustee, 1975—; past v.p., bd. dirs. Art Council Oklahoma City, 1977-80; chmn. bd. trustees Okla. Found. for the Humanities. Served with U.S. Army, 1954-56. Mem. Fed., Am., Okla., Oklahoma County bar assns., Phi Kappa Tau, Delta Theta Phi. Republican. Methodist. Contbr. articles to profl. publs. Home: 1701 Camden Way Nichols Hills OK 73116 Office: 500 W Main Oklahoma City OK 73102

BOSWELL, CELIA COLE, public relations practitioner, consultant; b. Spartanburg, S.C., Mar. 23, 1933; d. James Anderson Cole and Eula Blanche (Zimmerman) C.; m. Kenneth Boyd Boswell, Apr. 10, 1976; 1 dau. Margaret Gettle Washburn. B.A. with honors, Winthrop Coll., 1953; postgrad. Emory U., NYU, U. Ga. Examinations specialist Ga State Merit System, Atlanta, 1962-67; dir. pub. info. Ga. Dept. Family and Children Services, Atlanta, 1967-72; dir. pub. relations and info. Ga. Dept. Human Resources, Atlanta, 1972—; mem. Gov.'s Task Force Roosevelt-Warm Springs Inst. for Rehab., 1980, Gov.'s Task Force on Internships and Fellowships, 1982. Ga. Area Emmy award nominee, 1980-81. Mem. Pub. Relations Soc. Am. (govt. sect. bd. dirs. 1977-82, sect. chmn. 1983, S.E. dist. treas. 1982, bd. dirs. Ga. chpt. 1979-81, v.p. Ga. chpt. 1985, pres. Ga. chpt. 1986, presdl. citation 1983, Phoenix award Ga. soc. 1984, Silver anvil award 1985), Ga. Soc. Cert. Pub. Mgrs. Methodist. Office: 878 Peachtree St NE Room 529 Atlanta GA 30309

BOSWELL, GARY TAGGART, electronics company executive; b. Ft. Worth, Dec. 24, 1937; s. David W. and Marjory (Taggart) B.; B.A., Tex. Christian U., 1958, M.S., 1965; postgrad. San Diego State Coll., 1960-61; m. Margaret Ruth Yelvington, Sept. 8, 1957; children—Michael David, Margaret McQuiston, Susannah Ruth. Scientist U.S. Govt., White Sands (N.M.) Missile Range, 1958-59; research engr. Gen. Dynamics, San Diego, 1959-60; programmer Bell Helicopter, Hurst, Tex., 1960-63; sect. head Collins Radio Co., Dallas, 1963-68; mgr. software devel. Tex. Instruments, Inc., Austin, 1968-72; mgr. ASC (Advanced Sci. Computer) Marketing, 1973-75, mgr. ASC div., 1975-76, mgr. computer systems, 1976-80, mgr. global positioning systems, 1980-81, mgr. TI engrng. systems, 1981-83, v.p. equipment group, mgr. intelligent systems div., 1983—. Mem. Am. Nat. Fortran Standards Com., 1970-74. Mem. Assn. Computing Machinery, Snipe Class Internat. Racing Assn. Club: White Rock Sailing. Designer several Fortran Compliers. Winner Western Hemisphere Snipe championship, 1970, also other maj. regattas. Home: 9221 Clover Valley Dr Dallas TX 75243 Office: PO Box 405 Lewisville TX 75067

BOSWELL, KENNETH BOYD, county official; b. Statesboro, Ga., Mar. 9, 1938; s. Boyd E. and Ruby Dell (Rushing) B.; m. Celia Anne Cole, Apr. 10, 1976; children by previous marriage—Janice Marie, Kenneth Boyd, Laura Dell, Amy Lynn. A.B.J., U. Ga. Reporter Augusta (Ga.) Chronicle, 1963-64, asst. city editor, 1964-65, state editor, 1964, govt. affairs reporter, 1965-68, enterprise reporter, 1968-69; govt. affairs reporter Athens (Ga.) Daily News, 1969-70; gen. assignment reporter, county govt. reporter Atlanta Jour., 1970-75; info. officer Fulton County Dept. Info., Atlanta, 1975-83, pub. relations officer, 1983—. Served with Security Agy., U.S. Army, 1956-59. Mem. Public Relations Soc. Am. Baptist. Office: Fulton County Adminstrn 165 Central Ave SW Atlanta GA 30303

BOSWORTH, FRANK MALING, III, architect; b. Washington, Feb. 13, 1946; s. Frank Maling, Jr. and Avalon Anna (Robertson) B.; 1 child, Christopher Maling. B.S., Rensselaer Poly. Inst., Troy, N.Y., 1971, B.Arch., 1972. Registered architect, Fla. Designer, v.p. King Melody Assocs., Clearwater, Fla., 1972-76; prin. Frank M. Bosworth, Architect, Inc., 1976-83; v.p., ops. mgr. C.E. Maguire FL, Inc., Clearwater, 1983—. Mem. Com. 100, Pinellas County, Fla., 1985—; mem. adv. bd. Pinellas Vocat. and Tech. Sch., 1977-80. Recipient Aurora award S.E. Builders Congress, 1983. Mem. Constrn. Specifications Inst. Home: 1858 Venetian Point Dr Clearwater FL 33515 Office: CE Maguire FL Inc 1002 S Fort Harrison Ave Clearwater FL 33516

BOTT, GEORGE FREDRICK, clergyman, former naval officer, residential developer; b. Horseshoe Bend, Idaho, Sept. 20, 1926; s. Edward Homer and Nellie Mae (Reynolds) B.; m. Marian Nettie Housley, Feb. 2, 1948 (div. Sept. 1971); 1 dau., Kimberly Anne; m. Harriet Claire Grayson, Apr. 15, 1973; 1 child, Jonathan Edward. B.A., N.W. Nazarene Coll., Nampa, Idaho, 1952, Th.B., 1953; B.D., San Francisco Theol. Sem., 1960, Th.D. (residency), 1963. Investigator, Liberty Mut. Ins. Co., 1954-58; chaplain San Quentin Prison, 1959-60; ordained to ministry Presbyterian Ch., 1960; enlisted in U.S. Navy, 1943, commd. lt. (j.g.), 1960, advanced through grades to lt. comdr., 1966; various assignments as chaplain, 1960-81; served on USNS Barrett, USS Everglades, USS Eldorado, USS Mt. McKinley; assignments include 1st Marine Aircraft Wing, Okinawa, Japan, 1975-76; ret., 1981; pres. Bott and Hughes Enterprises, Inc., Pensacola, Fla., 1983—; interim and supply pastor Presbytery of Fla., 1982—. Grantee Lilly Found., 1958; scholar San Francisco Theol. Sem., 1960. Mem. Am. Legion. Republican. Author: The Robinson-McClusky Descendants, 1969.

BOTTA, JOSE ANGEL, JR., engring. co. exec.; b. Santiago de Cuba, Cuba, Aug. 27, 1937; came to U.S., 1961, naturalized, 1966; s. Jose Angel and Carmen Rosa (Llarch) B.; B.S. in Metall. Engring., Mo. Sch. Mines and Metallurgy, 1965; m. Maria Del Carmen Alvarez, May 11, 1961; children—Maria Del Carmen, Jose Angel. Cadet engr. Koppers Co., Inc., Pitts., 1965-66, engr., 1966-67, sr. staff engr., 1967-74; gen. mgr. Complejo Metalurgico Dominicano, Santo Domingo, 1974-76; export mgr. S.A. Person, Inc., Pitts., 1976; pres. Siderurgical Services Corp., Miami, Fla., 1976—. Mem. Am. Iron and Steel Engrs., Am. Soc. Metals, Am. Security Council Found., U.S. Congressional Adv. Bd., Nat. Rifle Assn., Conservative Caucus Found., Washington Legal Found. Roman Catholic. Contbr. articles to profl. jours.; patentee continuous casting of steel. Home and Office: 1733 SW 103d Pl Miami FL 33165

BOTTOMLEY, LEROY NEALL, dentist; b. Greeneville, Tenn., June 11, 1932; s. Virgil R. and Elizabeth (Raitt) Bottomley; m. Marilyn Eileen Downs, June 11, 1961; children—Leroy Neall, Robert Charles. D.D.S., U. Tenn., 1954. Pvt. practice dentistry, Orlando, Fla., 1957—. Served to capt. USAF, 1954-56. Home: 124 Lake Rena Dr Longwood FL 32750 Office: 2316 Hillcrest St Orlando FL 32803

BOUCHER, FREDERICK C., congressman, lawyer; b. Abingdon, Va., Aug. 1, 1946; s. Ralph E. and Dorothy (Buck) B. B.A., Roanoke Coll., 1968. Ptnr. Boucher & Boucher, Abingdon, Va., mem. Va. Gen. Assembly, 1975-79, 79-80; mem. 98th-99th congresses from Va. 9th Dist.; mem. com. on judiciary, com. on sci. and tech., com. on edn. and labor, mem. select com. on aging, 1983—; dir. First Va. Bank, Damascus. Recipient Disting. Service award Va. Highlands Community Coll., Abingdon; Dedicated Leadership award Va. Park and Recreation, 1985; named Outstanding Young Businessman, Abingdon Jaycees, 1975; Jimmy Doolittle fellow Air Force Aerospace Edn., 1983. Democrat. Methodist. Office: 428 Cannon House Office Bldg Washington DC 20515

BOUCHILLON, JOHN RAY, educational consultant, real estate executive; b. Covington, Ga., Sept. 3, 1943; s. John Ray and Mary Reid (Death) B.; m. Martha Jo Logue, Dec. 18, 1965; children—Trey, Monica, Beth. B.A., LaGrange Coll., 1965; M.Ed., Ga. Coll., 1969. Tchr. chemistry Baldwin County, Milledgeville, Ga., 1965-71, career coordinator, 1971-72; dir. career edn. Liberty County, Hinesville, Ga., 1972-75; career edn. cons. Ga. Dept. Edn., Atlanta, 1975—; chmn. career edn. adv. com. Ga. So. Coll., Statesboro, 1972-73; dir.-at-large guidance div. Ga. Vocat. Assn., Atlanta, 1976; sec.-treas. Ga. Vocat. Guidance Assn., 1976, pres., 1979. Co-editor: (newsletter) Ga. Pupil Personnel, 1975; editor: (newsletter) Ga. Personnel and Guidance, 1977-78; mem. editorial bd. Jour. Career Edn., 1978-80, Future Mag., 1978. Mem. Ga. Sch. Counselors Assn. (long-range planning com.). Democrat. Methodist. Avocations: photography; woodworking. Home: 4276 Village Green Circle Conyers GA 30208 Office: Ga Dept Edn 205 Butler St SE Atlanta GA 30334

BOUCK, DAVID WILLIAM, consulting engineering corporation executive; b. Corning, N.Y., Sept. 26, 1949; s. Harold Jacob, Jr., and Frances Lorraine (Barker) B.; m. Nancy Louise Lumpkin, June 27, 1981. Student U. Tenn., 1967-70; B.S. in Civil Engring., U. Central Fla., 1971, M.S. in Environ. Engring., 1973. Student engr. Martin-Marietta Aerospace Div., Orlando, Fla., 1967-68; project mgr. to v.p. and dir. civil/environ. engring., Dawkins & Assocs. Inc., Cons. Engrs., Orlando, 1971-82; prin. Blount, Sikes, Bouck & Rockett, Inc., Cons. Engrs., Winter Park, Fla., 1982—. Active Orlando Leadership Council, 1978—. Registered profl. engr., Fla., Ga. Mem. Nat. Soc. Profl. Engrs., ASCE, Fla. Engring. Soc., Water Pollution Control Fedn., Fla. Pollution Control Assn., Am. Water World Assn., Orlando C. of C. Contbg. author to various tech. books and jours. including Civil Engineering, Water & Wastes Engineering. Office: 1199 N Orange Ave Orlando FL 32804

BOUCOUVALAS, MARCIE, adult learning educator; b. Boston, Mar. 22, 1947; d. Stellios Efstathios and Georgia (Foundas) B.; m. Nicholas Gregory Gianourakos, May 17, 1970; 1 child, Anastasia Starr Boucouvalas-Gianourakos. B.S., Boston State Coll., 1968; M.Ed., Boston U., 1971; Ph.D., Fla. State U., 1980. Social worker Roxbury Neighborhood House, Boston, 1966; research assoc. Postgrad. Med. Inst., Boston, 1968-71; program info. coordinator Bd. Health Columbia, S.C., 1971-72; human resources devel. staff Dept. Corrections, Columbia, 1972-76; editor Career Edn. Ctr., Fla. State U., Tallahassee, 1978; tutor, cons. Adult Pub. Sch., Charlottesville, Va., 1978-79; freelance editor, Tallahassee, 1979-80; asst. prof. adult learning Va. Poly. Inst. and State U., No. Va. Grad. Ctr., Falls Church, 1980—. Field editor Jour. Transpersonal Psychology, 1981—; author: Interface: Lifelong Learning and Community Education, 1979; Adult Education in Greece, 1986; contbr. articles to profl. jours. Counselor, trainer Contact-help, Columbia, S.C., 1972-76; rape educator YWCA, 1975-76. Recipient disting. acad. service award Phi Delta Kappa, 1985, Golden Key award, 1986. Mem. Am. Assn. Adult and Continuing Edn. (head commn. on status of women 1977-78; head adult psychology 1980-83; recipient Service awards 1978, 82), Commn. on Profs. Adult Edn. (co-chmn. task force on internat. adult edn. 1984—), Va. Assn. Adult and Continuing Edn., Met. Washington Area Assn. Adult and Continuing Edn., Am. Soc. Tng. and Devel., Am. Psychol. Assn., Transpersonal Psychology Interest Group, Assn. Transpersonal Psychology (field editor jour.), World Future Soc., Internat. Assocs. in Adult Edn., Psi Chi. Fla. State U. fellow, 1977; Kellogg exchange prof., Eng., 1984. Greek Orthodox. Avocations: Music, dancing, ice skating. Office: Va Poly Inst and State U No Va Grad Ctr 2990 Telestar Ct Falls Church VA 22042

BOUDREAU, ALBERT HENRY, aerospace engineer, writer; b. Manchester, Conn., May 14, 1942; s. Albert H. and Pauline L. (Doucett) B.; m. Sheila M. McDonald, June 27, 1964; children—Joseph Patrick, Robert Joseph. B.S.A.E., St. Louis U., 1963; M.S.A.E., U. Tenn., 1969. Aerospace engr. Aro Inc., Arnold Air Force Sta., Tenn., 1963-81; tech. mgr. U.S. Air Force, Arnold Air Force Sta., 1981—. Pres., Catholic Evangelism Inc.; capt. CAP. Mem. AIAA, Air Force Assn., Exptl. Aircraft Assn. Roman Catholic. Author: The Born-Again Catholic, 1980. Home: Route 1 Box 51A Tullahoma TN 37388 Office: AEDC/DOFAR Arnold Air Force Station TN 37389

BOUDREAUX, CHARLES JOSEPH, food company executive, thoroughbred breeder; b. Longview, Tex., Dec. 18, 1935; s. Percy Joseph and Ollie Lorraine (Smith) B.; m. Wilhelmina J.E.B. Van Heck, Feb. 15, 1958; children—Caroline, Pamela, Francine, Steven. B.B.A., North Tex. State U., 1962. C.P.A., Tex. Sr. auditor Peat, Marwick Mitchell & Co., C.P.A.s, Dallas, 1962-65; chief acct. Steakley Bros. Chevrolet, Dallas, 1965-66; plant controller Wynnewood Products Co., Jacksonville, Tex., 1966-70; v.p. fin. Gen. Aluminum Corp., Carrollton, Tex., 1970-75; asst. v.p. fin. John E. Mitchell Co., Dallas, 1975—; v.p.-sec./controller Jimmy Dean Cos., Dallas, owner, operator Wilhelmina Originals House of Couture, Dallas, Served with USN, 1954-58. Mem. Am. Inst. C.P.A.s, Tex. Soc. C.P.A.s, Beta Gamma Sigma. Republican. Roman Catholic. Clubs: Holly Lake Ranch Golf (Hawkins, Tex.); Brookhaven Country (Dallas); St. Rita's Men's (treas. 1974). Home: 4546 Thunder Rd Dallas TX 75234 Office: Jimmy Dean Cos 1341 W Mockingbird Ln Suite 1100E Dallas TX 75247

BOUDREAUX, WARREN LOUIS, bishop; b. Berwick, La., Jan. 25, 1918; s. Alphonse Louis and Loretta Marie (Senac) B. Student, St. Joseph's Sem., Benedict, La., 1931-36, Notre Dame Sem., New Orleans, 1937, 42, LL.D., 1963, Grand Sem. de St. Sulpice, Paris, France, 1938-39; J.C.D., Catholic U. Am., 1946; D.D.; hon., Pope John XXIII, 1962. Ordained priest Roman Catholic Ch., 1942; asst. pastor, Crowley, La., 1942-43; vice chancellor Diocese of Lafayette, La., 1946-54, officialis, 1949-54; Vicar gen., 1957-61, aux. bishop., 1962-71; pastor St. Peter's Ch., New Iberia, La., 1954-71; bishop of Beaumont, Tex., 1971-77, bishop of Houma-Thibodaux, La., 1977—; dean New Iberia Deanery, 1954-71; Vice pres. S.W. La. Registry Newspaper, 1957-75; Mem. New Iberia Community Relations Council, 1963-71, U.S. Bishops Liturgical Commn., 1966-70, U.S. Bishop's Louvain Coll. Commn., 1970-76; imem. adv. council U.S. Cath. Conf., 1969-73; chmn. liaison com. Nat. Conf. Cath. Bishops, 1972-75, mem. liturgy commn., 1975—, mem. com. on canon law, 1975-78; state chaplain K.C. State of Tex., 1975-77; nat. moderator Marriage Encounter in U.S.A., 1975-77; mem. La. Cath. Conf., 1977—, La. Interch. Conf., 1977—. Bd. dirs. S.W. Ednl. Devel. Lab., Iberia Paris Youth Home, Consolata Home for Aged, New Iberia; Pres. Archdiocesan Conf. Chancery Ofcls. Archdiocese New Orleans, 1950-51, bd. dirs., 1952-55. Address: PO Box 9077 Houma LA 70361

BOUGHTON, JAMES KENNETH, instrument engineer, educator; b. Akron, Ohio, Mar. 22, 1922; s. James Arthur and Louise (Smith) B.; student U. Akron, 1940-42; B.S. in Elec. Engring., Ill. Inst. Tech., 1944; M.S., Lamar Coll. Tech., 1968; Ph.D. candidate Columbia Pacific U.; m. Evelyn Frances Robottom, Feb. 10, 1945; children—Steven Kent, Susan Lynn, Lisa Jean, Jeffrey Leigh. With Goodyear Tire and Rubber Co., 1942-77, machine designer, Akron, 1951, atomic supt. elec. and instrument maintenance, 1953-60, mgr. engring., Beaumont, Tex., 1960-77; sr. instrument engr. Stubbs Overbeck & Assos., Beaumont, 1977—; sec.-treas. Westbury Mgmt. Group, Inc., 1983—; assoc. prof. Lamar U., Beaumont, 1977—; ptnr. Vantec Inc., Cons. Engrs.; instr. U. Akron, 1947-49. Mem. cultural affairs com. Lamar U., 1968—; active Beaumont Symphony, Lamar Philharm. Orch. Served to lt. comdr. USNR, 1942-45, 51-53; PTO. Recipient Goodyear Patent award, 1974. Registered profl. engr., Ohio. Mem. IEEE, Beaumont C. of C. Republican. Episcopalian (sr. warden 1970-71). Club: Pinewood Country (Pinewood Estates, Tex.). Patentee tire bldg. machines, prodn. counters and controls. Home: Route 9 Box 485 Sour Lake TX 77659 Office: Lamar U Beaumont TX 77710

BOULDIN, RICHARD HINDMAN, mathematics educator; b. Florence, Ala., Feb. 23, 1942; s. Morris Nelson and Jo (Stine) B.; m. Sandra Martin, Aug. 30, 1970; children—Laura, Mark. B.S., U. Ala., 1964; M.S., U. Chgo., 1966; Ph.D., U. Va., 1968. Instr. U. Va., Charlottesville, 1968-69; asst. prof. U. Ga., Athens, 1969-73, assoc. prof., 1973-82, prof., 1982—. Author: Mathematics with Applications, 1985; Calculus with Applications, 1985; also articles. Recipient Summer Teaching stipend Coll. Arts and Scis., U. Ga., 1980, Spl. Sandy Beaver Teaching award, 1984. Mem. Am. Math. Soc. Republican. Avocations: studying economics; investments and real estate. Home: 1091 Hickory Hill Dr Watkinsville GA 30677 Office: U GA Math Dept Athens GA 30602

BOULTER, ELDON BEAU, U.S. congressman from Texas; b. El Paso, Tex., Feb. 23, 1942; m. Rosemary Rutherford; children—Rebecca, Matthew, Elizabeth. B.A., U. Tex., 1965; J.D., Baylor U., 1968. Briefing atty. Supreme Ct. Tex., 1968-69; chmn. ethics com. Lubbock Bar Assn., 1973-74; Republican precinct capt., 1978-79; lectr. Amarillo Bar Inst., 1980; mem. Amarillo City Commn., 1981-83; mem. 99th U.S. Congress from 13th dist. Tex., 1985—. Mem. ABA, Amarillo Bar Assn., Tex. Assn. Def. Counsel. Office: US House of Reps Office House Members Washington DC 20515*

BOULTINGHOUSE, DANIEL FRANK, architect; b. Corpus Christi, Tex., Jan. 3, 1944; s. Avery Leland and Alma Lefay (Martin) B.; A.A., Del Mar Coll., 1964; B. Arch., U. Tex., 1969; m. Nancy Sharon Miller, June 8, 1968; 1 dau., Wanza Lefay. Mem. staff Brooks, Barr, Graeber & White, Austin, Tex., 1968-69, Jack Rice Turner & Assocs., Corpus Christi, 1969-72; assoc. Turner, Rome, Cotten & Assocs., Corpus Christi, 1972-76; v.p. Turner, Rome, Boultinghouse, McAllen, Corpus Christi and Laredo, Tex., 1976-83; pres. Boultinghouse & Assocs., Architect, 1983—. Mem. adv. com. Tex. State Tech. Inst.; mem. City of McAllen Housing Bd. of Appeals, 1977—; bd. dirs. McAllen Housing Services Inc., McAllen Citizens League; mem. exec. bd. Leadership McAllen Inc.; mem. dist. bd. of location and bldgs. United Meth. Ch.; adv. bd. South Tex. Children's Heart Inst. Recipient Featherlite Design Competition award, 1968. Mem. Tex. Soc. Architects, AIA, Sphinx. Methodist. Club: Rotary. Home: 2208 Westway St McAllen TX 78501 Office: 998 Kerria Suite 111 McAllen TX 78501

BOUNDS, LAURENCE HAROLD, gas company executive; b. Newcastle, Wyo., Feb. 15, 1922; s. James Henry and Blanche Agnes (McKay) B.; B.S., Simpson Coll., 1943; postgrad. Columbia, 1943; m. Dorothy May Bostrom, Nov. 20, 1965; 1 stepchild, Allen J. McDowell. With comptroller dept. Kemper

Ins., Chgo., 1947-51; sec.-treas. W & J Constrn. Co., 1951-64; auditor Roosevelt Hotel, Jacksonville, Fla., 1964-66; v.p., sec., dir. Western Natural Gas Co., Jacksonville, 1966—. Served to lt. USNR, 1942-46. Mem. Navy League, Jacksonville Symphony Assn., Alpha Tau Omega. Episcopalian. Clubs: St. Simons Island; Tournament Players (Ponte Vedra, Fla.); MG Classics (Jacksonville). Home: 6926 Bakersfield Dr Jacksonville FL 32210 Office: 2960 Strickland St Jacksonville FL 32205

BOUNDS, SARAH ETHELINE, historian, educator; b. Huntsville, Ala., Nov. 5, 1942; d. Leo Deltis and Alice Etheline (Boone) B.; A.B., Birmingham-So. Coll., 1963; M.A., U. Ala., 1965, Ed.S., 1971, Ph.D., 1977. Tchr. social studies Huntsville City Schs., 1963, 65-66, 71-74; instr. history N.E. State Jr. Coll., Rainsville, Ala., 1966-68; instr. history U. Ala., Huntsville, 1975, 78-80, 85-86; dir. Weeden House Mus., Huntsville, 1981-82; asst. prof., supr. student tchrs. U. North Ala., Florence, 1978; residence hall advisor, dir. univ. housing U. Ala., 1963-65, 68-71. Mem. Huntsville Hist. Soc., Hist. Huntsville Found., Ala. Hist. Assn., Ala. Assn. Historians, Assn. Tchr. Educators, Ala. Assn. Tchr. Educators, Nat. Council Tchrs. Social Studies, Ala. Personnel and Guidance Assn., NEA, Huntsville Edn. Assn., AAUW, Alpha Delta Kappa (pres. Ala. sect.), Kappa Delta Pi, Phi Alpha Theta. Methodist. Club: Pilot. Home: 1100 Bob Wallace Ave SE Huntsville AL 35801

BOURGEOIS, MARTHA L., nurse; b. Calsbad, N. Mex., Feb. 1, 1939; d. Roy A. Simmons and Mary Ruth (Powell) Die; m. Warren R.E. Bourgeois, Jr., July 3, 1955; children—Warren III, Christopher M., Michelle M. A.S. with honors, Miss. Gulf Coast Jr. Coll.-Jeff Davis Campus, Gulfport, 1983. R.N., Miss., Calif., La. Adminstrv. asst. Tulane U. Sch. Medicine, New Orleans, 1965-79; personnel mgr. Halter Marine Inc., Pearlington, Miss., 1979-80; staff nurse Meml. Hosp., Gulfport, Miss., 1983, Gulf Coast Community Hosp., Biloxi, Miss., 1984, Humana Hosp., New Orleans, 1985—. Editorial asst. monograph La. Tumor Registry, 1979. Mem. ANA, Miss. Nurses Assn. Democrat. Roman Catholic. Home: 419 Waveland Ave Waveland MS 39576

BOURGUIGNON, ROGER LUCIEN, orthopedic surgeon; b. Coquilhatville, Belgian Congo, Jan. 31, 1930; came to U.S. 1967; s. Gustave Christophe and Lucienne Madeleine (Grandjean) B.; m. Renée Georgette De Coen, Apr. 9, 1953; children—Dominique, Beatrice, Denis, Valerie. B.S., M.D., Université Libre de Bruxelles, Belgium, 1954. Diplomate Am. Bd. Orthopedic Surgeons. Hosp. physician, chief of service Govt. of Belgian Congo, 1954-60; physician Union Minière du Haut-Katanga, 1961-63; resident in orthopedic surgery Orange Meml. Hosp., Orlando, Fla., 1968-72; practice medicine specializing orthopaedic surgery, Orlando Clinic (Fla.), 1972—; mem. staff Orlando Regional Med. Ctr., Humana Hosp. Lucerne. Mem. Am. Acad. of Orthopedic Surgeons, Société Française de Chirurgie Orthopédique et Traumatologique. Roman Catholic. Office: Orlando Clinic 1723 Lucerne Terr Orlando FL 32806

BOURKE, WILLIAM OLIVER, metals company executive; b. Chgo., Apr. 12, 1927; s. Robert Emmett and Mabel Elizabeth (D'Arcy) B.; m. Elizabeth Philbey, Sept. 4, 1970; children—William, Judy, Andrew, Edward. B.S.C., DePaul U., 1951. Asst. gen. sales mgr. Studebaker Corp., South Bend, 1952-56; exec. v.p. Ford Motor Co., Dearborn, Mich., 1956-80; pres., chief operating officer Reynolds Metals Co., Richmond, Va., 1981—; dir. Dart & Kraft, Inc., Abex Corp., Robertshaw Controls Co. Served to 1st lt. M.I., U.S. Army, 1944-48. Clubs: Commonwealth (Richmond); Farmington Country (Charlottesville, Va.). Office: 6601 W Broad St Richmond VA 23261

BOURLAND, HOMER LLOYD, retired air force officer, medical service executive; b. Vernon, Tex., July 16, 1922; s. Elijah and Mary Blanche (Ashley) B.; m. Betty Frances Bullen, Apr. 1, 1944; children—Nancy Carol, Thomas Jeffrey, Priscilla Angelique. Student Rice U., 1946-47, U. Houston, 1956-57. Joined U.S. Army Air Corps as pvt., 1940, advanced through grades to col., ret., 1975; pres., chief exec. officer Zee Med. Services div. Bourland Enterprises, Inc., San Antonio, 1975—. Pres. Melbert Bible Class Travis Park Meth. Ch., San Antonio, 1985. Decorated D.F.C., Air medal with 3 oak leaf clusters. Mem. Am. Soc. Safety Engrs., Res. Officers Assn., 20th Air Force Assn., 73d Bomb Wing Assn. Republican. Methodist. Avocations: reading; boating; walking. Home: 14210 Cradlewood St San Antonio TX 78233 Office: Zee Med Service PO Box 33008 5419 Brewster San Antonio TX 78233

BOURN, FRED EXZELL, JR., acct.; b. Jackson, Miss., Jan. 10, 1945; s. Freddie Exzell and Hallie Marion (Bass) B.; B.B.A., U. Miss., 1966, M. Public Accountancy, 1967; m. Rebekah Jane Toland, June 12, 1966; children—Fred Exzell III, Jenny Rebekah. Asst. acct., sr. acct., supervising sr. acct. Peat, Marwick, Mitchell & Co., Jackson, 1966-67; partner Smith, Bourn & Co., Jackson, 1970-71, Bourn Crowell & Co., Jackson, 1971-72, Tann, Bourn, Brown & Co., and predecessor firms, Jackson, 1972-80; pres. Colonial Corp., Jackson and Mendenhall, Miss., 1975—, Bourn Western Investments Inc., 1981—, Western World Devel. Inc., Jackson and Angel Fire, N.Mex., 1981—, Bourn & Assocs., Jackson, 1983—. Mem. fin. com. U.S. senatorial campaign M. Dantin, 1978; treas. city commr. campaign, Jackson, 1980-81; deacon Bapt. Ch. C.P.A., Miss. Mem. Am. Inst. C.P.A.s, Miss. Soc. C.P.A.s. Home: 1110 Briarwood Dr Jackson MS 39211 Office: 213 Highland Village Jackson MS 39211

BOURNE, DOUGLAS JOHNSTON, natural resource company executive; b. Tulsa, Mar. 18, 1923; s. Alva Fountain and Evabel (Johnston) B.; B.S. in Chem. Engring., U. Okla., 1943; postgrad. Harvard U. Grad. Sch. Bus., 1966; m. Hilda Hess, Feb. 28, 1944; children—Laurie Douglas Bourne Widman, Janalee Bourne McDonald. Asst. chemist Sulphur div. Duval Corp., Orchard, Tex., 1946-47, process engr., chief metallurgist, plant supt. Potash div., Carlsbad, N.Mex., 1948-58, dir. research, v.p. research and planning. v.p. mktg., Tucson, 1959-72, exec. v.p., Houston, 1972-77, pres., 1977-80, pres., chief exec. officer, 1980-83, chmn., chief exec. officer, 1983—; pres. Duval Sales Corp., Houston, 1968-75; group mgmt. v.p. Pennzoil Co., Houston, 1975-77; dir. Anderson, Greenwood & Co., Pennzoil Co. Served to lt. (j.g.) USNR, 1943-46. Mem. Sulphur Inst. (dir., past chmn.), Potash and Phosphate Inst. (dir., chmn.), Am. Mining Congress (dir.). Clubs: River Oaks Country, Marco Polo, University. Office: 700 Milam PO Box 2967 Houston TX 77001

BOUSTANY, FREM FREM, JR., physician, wholesale bakery exec.; b. Lafayette, La., May 7, 1928; s. Frem Frem and Beatrice (Joseph) B.; B.S., Tulane U., 1948, M.D., 1950; m. Angell FaKouri, Jan. 6, 1957; children—Deborah, Jennifer, Stephanie. Intern, Charity Hosp., New Orleans, 1950-51, resident, 1951-54; practice medicine specializing in ob-gyn, Crowley, La., 1958-69; v.p. Huval Baking Co., Lafayette, 1950-70, pres., 1970-76, chief exec. officer, 1976—; dir. Flowers Industries, Inc., Thomasville, Ga., La. Bank & Trust Co., Crowley, City Savs. Bank & Trust Co., DeRidder, La. Bd. dirs. Lafayette Boys Club, 1972-75, Jr. Achievement, 1972-76; v.p. United Giver's Fund, Lafayette, 1974-78, bd. dirs., 1970-78. Served with M.C., USAF, 1954-56. Mem. AMA, La. Med. Soc., Am. Bakers Coop. (past chmn., pres.), Am. Bakers Assn., So. Bakers Assn. (gov.), Am. Inst. Baking, Bakers Ambassadors Assn. (pres.). Democrat. Roman Catholic. Clubs: Bayou Bend Country, Crowley Town (Crowley); Lafayette Town, City, Krewe of Gabriel, Krewe of Zeus, Order of Troubadours (Lafayette); Camelot (Baton Rouge); K.C. Home: 200 Oakwater Dr Lafayette LA 70503 Office: Huval Baking Co Box 2339 Lafayette LA 70502

BOUTWELL, WALLACE KENNETH, JR., business executive; b. Newton, Miss., Jan. 7, 1939; s. W. Kenneth and Elizabeth (Wilson) B.; m. Jean Youngblood, Aug. 13, 1961; children—Jennifer, Jeffrey, Julie. B.S., Miss. State U., 1961; M.S., N.C. State U., 1963; Ph.D., 1965. Systems analyst Office of Sec. Def., 1965-68; assoc. prof. agrl. econs. U. Fla., 1969; dir. budgeting, 1970; dir. planning and budgeting State Univ. System Fla., 1970-73, vice-chancellor, 1973-75; co-founder, pres. MGT Am., mgmt. cons., Tallahassee, 1975—; co-founder, chmn. bd. Capital Health Plan (HMO), Tallahassee, 1979—; cons. to govt. and univs. Mem. Fla. Edn. Council, 1976-77, Fla. Council on Handicapped, 1983. Served to capt. U.S. Army, 1965-67. Recipient citation Fla. Bd. Regents, 1975. Home: 3431 Cedar Ln Tallahassee FL 32312 Office: 2425 Torreya Dr Tallahassee FL 32303

BOUVIER, JOHN ANDRE, JR., lawyer, investment counselor, business executive; b. nr. Ocala, Fla., May 16, 1903; s. John Andre and Ella (Richardson) B.; student Davidson Coll., 1922-24; A.B., U. Fla., 1926, J.D., 1929; M.B.A., Northwestern U., 1930; D.L.H., Windham Coll., 1977; D.Com., Ft. Lauderdale Coll., 1985; m. Helen A. Schaefer, June 6, 1928 (dec. July 1983); children—Helen Elizabeth (Mrs. William Spencer), John Andre III, Thomas Richardson; m. 2d, Barbara A. Carney, Feb. 12, 1984. Admitted to Fla. bar, 1929, pvt. practice, Gainesville, 1929, Miami, 1930—, specialist corp., real estate, probate law, cons.; gen. counsel Patterson & Maloney, Ft. Lauderdale; chmn. bd., pres. Pantex Mfg. Corp. (Delaware), 1958-60; pres. Pantex Mfg. Corp. (Can.), 1958-60; chmn. exec. com. Permutit Co.; chmn. bd. Prosperity Co. div., vice chmn. bd. Ward Industries Corp.; pres. Nat. Leasing Inc., Miami; pres. West Kingsway, Inc., 1952-73, East Kingsway, Inc., 1952-73, South Kingsway, Inc., 1952-73; now pres. Knight Manor #1, Inc., Knight Manor #2, Inc., South Central Manor, Inc.; pres. Knaust Bros., Inc., West Coxsackie, N.Y., 1960-64, chmn., 1964-65; pres. K-B Products Corp., Hudson, N.Y., 1960-64, chmn., 1960-65; pres. Farm Industries, Inc., Iron Mtn. Atomic Storage Vaults, Inc.; v.p., sec. Miami Service Co., 1956-73, pres., chmn., 1973—; sec. 50th St. Heights, Inc., Dade Constrn. Co., Miami, Karen Club Apt. Hotel, Ft. Lauderdale, 1951-67; dir. Ocean 1st Nat. Bank; dir., exec. com. Landmark Banking. Commr. Dade County council Boy Scouts Am.; chmn. Malecon Com. Dade County; dir. Syracuse Govtl. Research Bur., Inc.; mem. Nat. Def. Exec. Res. Planning council Zoning Bd. Miami. Bd. trustees Parkinson Rehab., Diagnostic and Research Inst.; vice chmn. Nat. Parkinson Found.; pres. Ella R. Bouvier Fund; bd. dirs. Boys Club. Mem. Internat. Platform Assn., Am. Ordnance Assn., Am. Judicature Soc., Am., Florida, Dade County, Broward County bar assns., N.A.M. (conservation of renewable natural resources com.), Mfrs. Assn. of Syracuse (dir.), Miami, Auburn civic music assns., Cayuga Mus. History and Art, Am. Acad. Polit. Sci., Scottish Am. Soc., C. of C., Sigma Chi. Presbyn. (trustee, chmn., elder). Mason (Shriner), Elk, Rotarian. Clubs: Civitan (dir.), Miami Beach Rod and Reel, Surf, Riviera Country, Skaneateles Country; Tower; Ponte Vedra; Washington Lawyers, Capitol Hill. Author monographs, newspaper articles in field. Home: 608 Intracoastal Dr Fort Lauderdale FL 33304 also Lenoir Turnpike Blowing Rock NC 28605 Office: PO Box 7254 Fort Lauderdale FL 33338

BOVE, ANNETTE DEMARIA, cosmetics company executive, consultant; b. Paterson, N.J., Nov. 15, 1943; d. Joseph Emanuel and Sarah Corrine (Pratt) DeM.; m. Terence John Bove, Apr. 19, 1965 (div. 1970); 1 child, Tracey Ann. Student U. Miami, 1961-63. Exec. asst. Southeast Investment Corp., Miami, Fla., 1969-85; owner, operator So. Cosmetics, Inc. (franchise of Caswell-Massey), 1985—. Republican. Roman Catholic. Office: Southern Cosmetics Inc Caswell-Massey of the Falls 8888 Howard Dr #385 Miami FL 33176

BOWDEN, ANN, librarian, educator; b. East Orange, N.J., Feb. 7, 1924; d. William and Anna Elisabeth (Herrstrom) Haddon; B.A., Radcliffe Coll., 1948; M.S. in L.S., Columbia U., 1951; Ph.D., U. Tex., Austin, 1975; m. Edwin T. Bowden, June 12, 1948; children—Elisabeth Bowden Ward, Susan Turner Bowden, Edwin Eric Bowden; m. 2d, William B. Todd, Nov. 23, 1969. Cataloger, reference asst. Henry L. Stimson Collection, Yale U., 1948-53; manuscript cataloger Rare Book Library, U. Tex., 1958-59, rare book librarian, 1959-60, librarian Humanities Research Center, 1960-63, Acad. Center, 1963, sr. lectr. Sch. Library and Info. Sci., 1964—; dir. films and recs. Austin Public Library, 1963-65, coordinator adult services, 1965-67, asst. dir., 1967-71, dep. dir., 1971-77, asso. dir., 1977—. Chmn. bd. trustees AMIGOS Bibliog. Council, Inc., Dallas, 1980-81, vice chmn., 1979-80; chmn. AMIGOS '85 Plan; bd. dirs. Tex. Info. Exchange, Inc., Houston, 1977-78. Served with USMC Women's Res., 1944-46. Mem. ALA (chmn. membership com. 1968-72, regional membership com. 1972-74, mem.-at-large governing council 1975-79), Assn. Coll. and Research Libraries (chmn. rare book and manuscript sect. 1975-76, chmn., nominating com. 1979-80), S.W. Library Assn. (state chmn. nat. endowment for humanities Southwestern libraries project 1974-75), Tex. Library Assn. (chmn. publs. com. 1965-71, chmn. intellectual freedom com. 1972-74, mem. steering com. Tex. libraries and public policy 1977-78), Kappa Tau Alpha, Phi Kappa Phi. Club: Grolier. Assoc. editor: Papers of the Bibliographical Soc. Am., 1967-81; editor: Maps and Atlases, 1978, T.E. Lawrence/Fifty Letters: 1921-35, 1962; contbr. articles in field to profl. publs. Home: 2109 B Exposition Blvd Austin TX 78703 Office: 800 Guadalupe St Austin TX 78701 Mailing Address: Box 2287 Austin TX 78768

BOWDEN, BONNER BOYD, petroleum geologist, petroleum engineer; b. Wichita Falls, Tex., Sept. 18, 1947; s. Bonner Boyd and Mildred Pearl (Booher) B.; m. Julia Lyn Crary, Feb. 25, 1978; children—Kirsten Marie, Bonner Benjamen. B.S. in Geology, U. Kans., 1970; postgrad. So. Meth. U., 1971, Kearney State Coll., 1972. Prodn. geologist Kans.-Nebr. Gas Co., Hastings, Nebr., 1973-76, reservoir engr., 1973-76; exploration geologist CIG Exploration, Amarillo, Tex., 1976; dist. geologist Grace Petroleum Corp., Oklahoma City, Okla., 1976-79; geologist Lario Oil & Gas Co., Wichita, Kans., 1979-80; sr. geologist Kaiser-Francis Oil Co., Tulsa, 1980—. Contbr. author Selected Oil and Gas Fields of the Texas Panhandle, 1977. Supporting mem. Tulsa Philharm. Soc., 1985—. Mem. Am. Gas Assn. (res. analyst, del. 1975), Panhandle Geol. Soc. (editor newsletter 1976), Am. Assn. Petroleum Geologists, Tulsa Geol. Soc., Okla. City Geol. Soc. Presbyterian. Avocations: electronics; photography; camping.

BOWDEN, DELLE AVARY, hospital administrator, consultant; b. Grenada, Miss., Apr. 5, 1942; d. John Willis and Onnie Dell (Lowrimore) Avary; m. Ronald Edmund Davis, Nov. 22, 1959 (div. July 1969); children—Ronald Edmond, Margaret Elizabeth; m. Lowell Wayman Bowden, Dec. 29, 1984. Student, U. So. Miss., 1957; Assoc. nursing, Jones Jr. Coll., 1975; B.S.N., William Carey Coll., 1981; postgrad., Ark. State U., 1985. R.N. Staff nurse Jones County Community Hosp., Laurel, Miss., 1970-75; newborn intensive care U. Miss. Med. Ctr., Jackson, 1975-76; dir. nursing Mediplex Inc., Jackson, 1976-78; hosp. supr. Humana Doctors Hosp., Jackson, 1978-80; dir. nursing Humphreys C. Meml. Hosp., Belzoni, Miss., 1980-83; asst. adminstr. Ark. Meth. Hosp., Paragould, 1983—; self-employed cons., Miss., 1979-82; adviser legal standards com. Ark. State Bd. Nursing, Little Rock, 1983-84; adviser Delta Vocat. Tech. Practical Nursing Sch., Jonesboro, Ark., 1983—. with adult edn. dept. Belzoni chpt. ARC, 1982; mem. speakers bur. Am. Cancer Soc., Jackson, 1980-83. Mem. Soc. Hosp. Pub. Relations (bd. dirs. Jackson 1983), Sigma Theta Tau. Democrat. Episcopalian. Avocation: theater. Home: 4410 Randall Rd Paragould AR 72450 Office: Ark Meth Hosp 900 W Kingshighway Paragould AR 72450

BOWDEN, ROBERT HENRY, chemical engineer; b. Russellville, Ark., Oct. 28, 1921; s. George Raymond and Jennie (Dillon) B.; m. Zoe Eleanor Brandau, Nov. 15, 1947; children—Sharon Ann, Sally Elizabeth. B.S. in Chem. Engring., Tex. A&M U., 1943; M.S. in Chem. Engring., U. Tex., 1945. Instr. applied math. U. Tex., Austin, 1943-44; refinery engr. Mobil Oil Co., 1945-64, planning analyst, 1964-65, chief engr. Mobil Oil Barbados Ltd., 1979, tech. supr., Beaumont, Tex., 1966—. Republican. Episcopalian. Club: Bus. and Profl. Men's. Home: 1340 Woodpark Ln Beaumont TX 77706 Office: PO Box 3311 Beaumont TX 77704

BOWDRE, PAUL REID, police officer, paramedic, consultant; b. N.Y.C., Aug. 27, 1958; s. Philip Ross and Inge Elenore (Eckert) B. B.S., Western Carolina U., 1981; cert. in Social Gerontology, U. N.C.-Asheville, 1981; postgrad. Profl. Studies, Coll. Boca Raton, Fla., 1985—. Research asst. Mo. Gerontology Inst., Columbia, 1981-83; asst. swim coach U. Mo., Columbia, 1981-83, teaching asst. Dept. Sociology, 1982-83; pub. safety officer North Palm Beach Dept. Pub. Safety, Fla., 1983-85; nat. and olympic swim coach Federcion Nacional de Natacion, Guatemala, May-Aug. 1984; police officer Town of Palm Beach, 1985—; cons. in field. Author: (with others) Death & Dying: In-Home Care-A Teaching Curriculum, 1983, Safety: In-Home Care-A Teaching Curriculum, 1983. Contbr. articles to profl. publs. Asst. scoutmaster Troop 132 Gulf Stream council Boy Scouts Am., 1981-84; trustee North Palm Beach Police and Fire Pension Bd., 1984-85. Research grantee Sigma Xi, 1981. Mem. Nat. Eagle Scout Assn., Am. Soc. Criminology, Midwest Sociol. Soc. (student dir. 1981-82), Am. Sociol. Assn. (regional newsletter reporter 1982-83), Geronto. Soc. Am. (Biol. scis. sect. com. member 1983), Alpha Kappa Delta, Sigma Phi Omega. Democrat. Baptist. Home: 9628 Begonia St Palm Beach Gardens FL 33410 Office: Palm Beach Police Dept 360 S County Rd Palm Beach FL 33480

BOWEN, DUDLEY HOLLINGSWORTH, JR., district judge; b. Augusta, Ga., June 25, 1941; s. Dudley Hollingsworth and Edna (Maury) B.; m. Madeline Martin, Aug. 14, 1963; children—Laura Madeline, Anna Maury. A.B. in Fgn. Langs., U. Ga., 1964, LL.B., 1965. Bar: Ga. 1965. Sole practice, Augusta, 1968-72; bankruptcy judge So. Dist. Ga., 1972-75; ptnr. firm Dye, Miller, Bowen & Tucker, Augusta, 1975-79; U.S. dist. judge So. Dist. Ga., Augusta, 1979—; tchr. seminars; panelist Atlanta Bar Assn., S.C. Bar, Inst. Continuing Legal Edn., 1976-78; dir. Southeastern Bankruptcy Law Inst., 1976—. Served to 1st lt., inf., U.S. Army, 1966-68. Decorated Army Commendation medal. Mem. ABA, State Bar Ga. (chmn. bankruptcy law sect. 1977). Presbyterian. Address: PO Box 2106 Augusta GA 30903

BOWEN, ELIZABETH ANN, sports company executive; b. Beaumont, Tex., Nov. 18, 1950; d. James Willie and Bobbie Jean (Harrison) B.; B.S. in Recreation, Lamar U., 1975, B.S. in Phys. Edn., 1977. Cert. water safety instr., Tex.; cert. scuba diver, Tex. Coach, tchr. West Hardin High Sch., Saratoga, Tex., 1980—; founder, dir. Youth Sports Enterprises, Silsbee, Tex., 1979—. Pres. Silsbee Little Dribbler Basketball Assn., 1978-80; active ARC; Swim instr. Youth Sports Softball Assn.; camp counselor; swim team coach, swimming instr. Recipient Golf Scholarship Sabine Area Men's Golf Assn., 1970; Winner Golf Championship Tex. Commn. on Inter-scholastic Athletics for Women, 1971. Mem. Tex. High Sch. Girls' Coaches Assn., Assn. Tex. Profl. Educators, Aircraft Owners and Pilots' Assn., Phoenix Soc. of Lamar U. Author: Collection of Moonster Fables for Children, 1983.

BOWEN, JOHN METCALF, pharmacologist, toxicologist, educator; b. Quincy, Mass., Mar. 23, 1933; s. Loy J. and Marjorie (Metcalf) B.; m. Jean Alma Schmidt, Dec. 26, 1956; children—Mark John, Richard Kelley. D.V.M., U. Ga., Athens, 1957; Ph.D., Cornell U., Ithaca, 1960. Assoc. prof. Kans. State U., Manhattan, 1962-63; post-doctoral fellow Emory U., Atlanta, 1963; assoc., then prof., U. Ga., Athens, 1963—, assoc. dean, dir. veterinary med. expt. sta., 1976—; cons. Veterinary Med. Ctr., Washington, 1978—. Mem. Am. Veterinary Med. Assn., Soc. Neuroscis., Am. Soc. Pharmacology, Exptl. Therapeutics. Office: College of Veterinary Medicine U Ga Athens GA 30602

BOWEN, JUDY WILLIAMS, speech and language pathologist; b. Atlanta, Mar. 30, 1939; s. Leslie Spencer and Jewell Winifred (Ivey) Williams; B.A., Mercer U., 1961; M.Ed., Emory U., 1964; m. Henry Horace Bowen, Feb. 21, 1965; children—Susan Elizabeth, Sally Winifred. Speech pathologist DeKalb County Bd. Edn., Decatur, Ga., 1963-65, Atlanta Speech Sch., 1963-65, Central State Hosp., Milledgeville, Ga., summer 1966, Clarke County Bd. Edn., Athens, Ga., 1966-68, Wilkes County Bd. Edn., Washington, Ga., 1977—; cons. in field; mem. Title 1 adv. council Washington-Wilkes Middle Sch., 1979-80, program chmn. Parent-Tchr. Group. Bd. dirs. Friends of Savannah River, 1976-78; v.p. prodns. Washington Little Theater Co., 1977, bd. dirs., 1977, 83—; v.p. Fidelis Sunday Sch. class 1st Baptist Ch., Washington, 1979, pres., 1980-81; pres. Washington-Wilkes Primary Sch. Parent-Tchr. Group, 1977-78. Cert. speech/lang. pathologist, Ga. Mem. Am. Speech and Hearing Assn. (cert. clin. competence), Ga. Speech and Hearing Assn. (sec. 1967-68), DAR, Phi Mu. Home: 202 Water St Washington GA 30673 Office: Wilkes County Bd Edn PO Box 279 Washington GA 30673

BOWEN, LAWRENCE HOFFMAN, chemistry educator, researcher; b. Lynchburg, Va., Dec. 20, 1934; s. Charles Wesley and Eleanor (Hoffman) B. B.S. in Chemistry, Va. Mil. Inst., 1956; PH.D. in Phys. Chemistry, MIT, 1961. Teaching asst. MIT, Cambridge, 1956-58, research asst., 1958-61; asst. prof. chemistry N.C. State U., Raleigh, 1961-65, assoc. prof. chemistry, 1965-70, prof. chemistry, 1970—. Served with U.S. Army, 1961. Recipient Jackson-Hope medal, 1956; Gen. Electric Co. Grad. fellow, 1958. Mem. Am. Chem. Soc., AAUP, Am. Phys. Soc., Sigma Xi. Contbr. chpts. to books, articles to profl. jours. Office: Dept Chemistry Box 8204 NC State U Raleigh NC 27695

BOWEN, MICHAEL LEE, lawyer; b. Sellersville, Pa., Apr. 4, 1951; s. Walton Rayburn and Elizabeth (Holly) B.; m. Laura Morgan, Aug. 1, 1981; children—Ashley Elizabeth, Kelly Amanda. Student Muhlenberg Coll., 1969-72; B.A., Fla. Atlantic U., 1975; J.D., Nova U., 1982. Bar: Fla. 1982, U.S. Dist. Ct. (mid. dist.) Fla. 1983, U.S. Ct. Appeals (11th cir.) 1983. Head teller, mgr. Flagler Nat. Bank, West Palm Beach, Fla., 1974-76; sales rep. Bernard Food Industries, Inc., Evanston, Ill., 1976-79; cert. legal intern Broward County Pub. Defender, Ft. Lauderdale, Fla., 1982; asst. pub. defender Brevard County Pub. Defender, Titusville, 1983-85; mem. firm Cianfrogna, Telfer, Evans & Reda, Titusville, 1985—. Regional dir. Young Republicans, eastern Pa., 1971-72. Lic. pvt. pilot. Mem. Fla. Bar Assn., ABA (drunk driving com. 1983-84), Fla. Pub. Defenders Assn. Republican. Roman Catholic. Office: 308 Julia St Titusville FL 32796

BOWEN, PAUL HENRY, JR., lawyer; b. Troy, Ohio, Sept. 28, 1948; s. Paul Henry, Sr. and Dorathy Jane (Winters) B.; m. Linda Margaret Mary Eisenhart, Mar. 2, 1974. B.A., Pa. State U., 1970; J.D., U. Pitts., 1973. Bar: Pa. 1973, Fla. 1978, U.S. Dist. Ct. (mid. dist.) Fla. 1978, U.S. Ct. Appeals (5th cir.) 1984, U.S. Supreme Ct. 1983. Assoc., Vernon David, P.A., Winter Garden, Fla., 1980-81, Swann & Haddock, P.A., Orlando, Fla., 1981-85, Trenam, Simmons, Kemker, Scharf, Barkin, Frye & O'Neill, P.A., Tampa, Fla., 1985—. Precinct capt. to re-elect Mayor Frederick of Orlando, 1984. Served to capt. JAGC, USAF, 1975-80. Mem. ABA, Assn. Trial Lawyers Am., Acad. Fla. Trial Lawyers. Democrat. Methodist. Lodge: Kiwanis (citizenship com.). Home: 2625 Watrous Ave Tampa FL 33629

BOWEN, RALEIGH L., Democratic national committeeman, retired soldier; b. Sherman, Tex., Dec. 27, 1911; s. Alexander A. and Dixe Lee (Powel) B.; student Wiley Coll., 1932-35, U. Md., 1959-62; B.A., Northeastern Okla. State U, now postgrad.; m. Pearl E. Soloman, Aug. 21, 1941. Enlisted as pvt. U.S. Army, 1942, advanced through grades to master sgt., 1962; with 92d Inf. Div., Italy, World War II, later served in Korea, ret., 1962; food service dir. U. Md., Princess Anne, 1962-73; now with Leake Industries, Inc., Tulsa. Steward, chmn. bd. trustees, treas. Bee Be C.M.E. Ch., Muskogee, Okla.; mem., past chmn. Met. Planning Comm., City of Muskogee; mem. Democratic Nat. Com., 1955—; sec. Muskogee County Bicentennial Com., 1975-76. Mem. Internat. Platform Assn., Northeastern Okla. State U. Alumni Assn., Lost Bridge Village Community Assn., Am. Assn. Ret. Persons, Md. Classified Employees Assn., Am. Legion, Armed Forces Communications and Electronics Assn., C. of C., Kappa Alpha Psi (life). Methodist. Mason (32 deg., Shriner), Elk. Home: 2705 W Broadway Muskogee OK 74401

BOWEN, W. J., gas company executive; b. Sweetwater, Tex., Mar. 31, 1922; s. Berry and Annah (Robey) B.; m. Annis K. Hilty, June 6, 1945; children—Shelley Ann, Barbara Kay, Berry Dunbar, William Jackson. B.S., U.S. Mil. Acad., 1945. Petroleum engr. Delhi Oil Corp., Dallas, 1949-57; v.p. Fla. Gas Co., Houston, 1957-60, pres., Winter Park, Fla., 1960-74; chmn., chief exec. officer Transco Energy Co., Houston, 1974—, chmn., 1976—; dir. Crown Zellerbach Corp., Newpark Resources Inc., S.W. Bancshares, Inc. Chmn. Houston Clean City Commn.; bd. dirs. YMCA, Houston, Houston Mus. Fine Arts. Served with AUS, 1945-49. Mem. Am. Gas Assn. (bd. dirs.), U.S. Mil. Acad. Assn. Grads. (bd. dirs.), Am. Petroleum Inst. (bd. dirs.), Delta Kappa Epsilon. Presbyterian. Office: PO Box 1396 Houston TX 77251

BOWER, BRENDA BLEVINS, bookstore executive; b. Worth, W. Va., Aug. 11, 1942; d. Frank G. and Frances W. Blevins; m. Robert B. Bower, July 3, 1959; 1 child, Christopher B. B.B.A., Roanoke Coll. Asst. dept. mgr. Advance Stores Inc., Roanoke, Va., 1959-61; acctg. Allstate Ins., Roanoke, 1961-62; accts. mgr. Berry & Dail, Salem, Va., 1962-63; corp. acctg. George Summers Atty., Salem, 1968-73; mgr. retail ops. Roanoke Coll., Salem, 1973—. Recipient Govs. Merit award State of W. Va., 1959. Mem. Va. Coll. Stores Assn. (treas., pres. elect 1985), Va. Assn. P.T.A.s, Jr. Womens Club, Heritage Garden Club, Am. Bus. Women, Delta Mu Delta. Republican. Methodist. Office: Roanoke Coll Bookstore High St Salem VA 24153

BOWER, E. BRUCE, banking executive. Pres., dir., chief operating officer Fla. Nat. Banks of the Florida, Inc., Jacksonville. Office: Fla Nat Banks of the Florida 214 Hogan St Jacksonville FL 32201*

BOWERS, CAROLYN SUE, interior designer, education administrator, educator; b. Keyser, W.Va., Jan. 8, 1947; d. Philip Riley and Edna Frances (Porter) Baker; m. Clifford E. Bowers, Sr., Sept. 1984. B.A. with honors, Berea Coll., 1968; M.A. with honors in Curriculum Devel. and Instrn., U. Chgo., 1969; M.A. with honors in Adminstrn., San Francisco State U., 1978; B.F.A. with distinction in Environ. Design, Calif. Coll. Arts and Crafts, 1980. Instr. English Berea Coll. (Ky.), 1969; tchr./curriculum devel. Jefferson Sch. Dist., Lexington, Ky., 1969-72; curriculum cons. Total Reading Pub. Co., Moraga, Calif., 1974-75; tchr., program coordinator, librarian Brandeis Hillel Day Sch., San Francisco, 1973-76; project coordinator Jefferson Elem. Sch. Dist., Daly City, Calif., 1976-79; assoc. firm, sr. designer/project mgr., studio dir. Hunter/Miller & Assocs., Alexandria, Va., 1980—. Environ. Design scholar Calif. Coll. Arts and Crafts, 1980. Mem. ASID (com. co-chmn. 1984—), Phi Kappa Phi, Kappa Delta Pi, Alpha Sigma Chi, Pi Lambda Theta, Phi Delta

Kappa; assoc. mem. Illuminating Engring. Soc. Am. Republican. Presbyterian. Office: Hunter/Miller & Assocs 225 N Fairfax St Alexandria VA 22314

BOWERS, ELLIOTT TOULMIN, university president; b. Oklahoma City, Aug. 22, 1919; s. Lloyd and Enah (McDonald) B.; B.S., Sam Houston State U., 1941, M.A., 1942; Ed.D., U. Houston, 1959; m. Frances Marie Handley, May 29, 1940; children—Linda Lu (Mrs. Charles Rushing), Cynthia Ann (Mrs. Paul Kimmell). Dir. music Huntsville High Sch., 1937-42; mem. faculty Sam Houston State U., 1946—, v.p. univ. affairs and dean of students, 1964-70, acting pres., 1963-64, pres., 1970—; dir. First Nat. Bank, Huntsville, Tex. Mem. Tex. Criminal Justice Council; bd. dirs. Sam Houston Area council Boy Scouts Am., Salvation Army, Am. Cancer Soc.; pres. bd. Wesley Found., 1962-63. Served with USAAF, 1943-46. Mem. Assn. Higher Edn., Huntsville C. of C. (past pres.), SAR, Alpha Phi Omega, Kappa Delta Pi, Phi Mu Alpha. Clubs: K.T., Masons. Office: Office of President Sam Houston State U Huntsville TX 77341

BOWERS, HUGH RUSSELL, oil company executive; b. Kingsville, Tex., Sept. 21, 1938; s. Hugh and Georgie Mae (White) B.; m. Ryn Rhea, Sept. 1, 1962; children—Barton Rhea, Brian Russell. B.A., Rice U., 1961, B.S. in Chem. Engring., 1962; postgrad. exec. program Stanford Bus. Sch., 1980. Research engr. Petro-Tex Chem., Houston, 1962-63, process design engr., 1964-67, prodn. supt., 1968-72, dir. engring., 1975-80, v.p. mktg. and supply, 1981, pres., 1982-84; v.p. chems. Tenneco Oil, 1984—; regional mgr. Rollins Environ. Services, Houston, 1973-74. Deacon Second Baptist Ch., Houston. Mem. Am. Inst. Chem. Engrs., Am. Mgmt. Assn., Houston C. of C., Harris County Heritage Soc., Houston Zoological Soc. Clubs: Forum, Houston City, Fondren Tennis, Petroleum (Houston). Patentee purification of hydrocarbons.

BOWERS, MARIANNE, clergywoman; b. Lafayette, Ind., Feb. 5, 1919; d. Gilbert Melville and Mary Frances (Montgomery) Wilson; m. Carl Eugene Bowers, June 19, 1964 (dec.); children by previous marriage—Frederick Kelly, Deborah Kelly Kivisels, Karen Kelly Wootton. B.S., Purdue U., 1940; grad. Unity Ministerial Sch., Unity Village, Mo., 1980. State exec. sec. Tex. Lic. Vocat. Nurses Assn., Austin, 1964-66; employment counselor Tarrant Employment Agy., Austin, 1966-68; owner, mgr. Horizons Unltd., Austin and San Antonio, 1968-72; with bus. devel., mktg., pub. relations depts. First Nat. Bank, Harlingen, Tex., 1973-76; exec. officer Rio Grande Apt. Assn., 1976-78; ordained to ministry Unity Ch., 1980; minister Unity of San Angelo, Tex., 1980—. Mem. Assn. Unity Chs., Internat. New Thought Alliance, AAUW, Scriveners, Nat. Assn. Female Execs., Internat. Platform Assn., Alpha Lambda Delta, Delta Rho Kappa, Chi Omega. Address: PO Box 1221 San Angelo TX 76902

BOWERS, MARY NANCE, educator, educational cousultant-counselor; b. Choctaw, Okla., July 16, 1923; d. W.E. and Bertha (Kint) Nance; m. William Russell Bowers, Sept. 25, 1953; children—James Nance, Jeannette Lynn Bowers Queen. B.S. in Elem. Edn., Okla. Baptist U., 1961; M.S. in Guidance and Counseling, U. Okla., 1964; postgrad. Central State U., Edmond, Okla., 1969. Cert. tchr. elem. edn., spl. edn., elem. counselor, learning disabilities. Tchr. 1st grade, counselor learning disabilities and edn. mentally handicapped Shawnee Pub. Sch., Okla., 1961-68, elem. tchr., 1981-82; child guidance specialist Okla. Health Dept., Oklahoma City, 1968-81. Mem. Am. Assn. for Counseling and Devel., Southwestern Psychol. Assn., NEA, Okla. Edn. Assn. Avocations: ceramics; oil painting; gardening. Home: Route 2 Box 86 Shawnee OK 74801

BOWERS, MICHAEL JOSEPH, state official; b. Commerce, Ga., Oct. 7, 1941; s. Carl Ernest and Janie Ruth (Bolton) B.; m. Bette Rose Corley, June 8, 1963; children—Carl Edward, Bruce Edward, Michelle Lisa. B.S., U.S. Mil. Acad., 1963; M.S., Stanford U., 1965; M.B.A., U. Utah, 1970; J.D., U. Ga., 1974. Commd. capt. U.S. Air Force, 1963; served in W. Ger., 1963-70; asst. atty. gen. State of Ga., Atlanta, 1974-81, atty. gen., 1981—; mem. bd. govs. State Bar Ala., Atlanta, 1981—. Mem. Lawyers Club Atlanta, Decatur/Dekalb Bar Assn. Democrat. Methodist. Lodge: Kiwanis (Atlanta). Home: 817 Allgood Rd Stone Mountain GA 30083

BOWERS, WILLIAM MARVIN, III, nurse; b. Atlanta, Jan. 21, 1950; s. William Marvin and Frances Blanche (Salmond) Bowers, Jr.; m. Dorothy Ann Coble, Feb. 18, 1973 (div. 1979); m. Linda Sandusky, Nov. 9, 1979; 1 dau., Ashley Lynne. B.S. in Nursing, Western Carolina U., 1976; cert. emergency med. tech. Southwestern Tech. Coll., 1979. R.N., N.C. Salesman, Bowers Furniture Co., Atlanta, 1968-71; emergency room technician C.J. Harris Hosp., Sylva, N.C., 1971-76; dir. activities and social services Skyland Care Ctr., Sylva, 1976-78; asst. dir. nursing Hemlock Nursing Home, Waynesville, N.C., 1978-79; charge nurse Smoky Mountain Area Mental Health, Dillsboro, N.C., 1979-83, nurse clinician, 1983—; 1st aid nurse Western Carolina U. Bands, 1976-77; nurse/emergency med. technician Jackson County Sheriff's Dept., Sylva, 1981—; fire safety and personal safety intervention instr. N.C. Health Care Facilities. Recipient Eagle Scout award N.E. Ga. council Boy Scouts Am., 1967, God and Country award, 1968; Ga. Boys State, Am. Legion Post, 1967; Ga. Gov.'s Council, Office of Gov., 1967; cert. of appreciation Smoky Mountain Mental Health, 1981. Mem. N.C. Emergency Med. Technicians Assn., Nat. Assn. Emergency Med. Technicians. Kappa Kappa Psy (Epsilon Lambda chpt.), Nat. Hon. Band Frat. Democrat. Presbyterian. Club: Nat. Rifle Assn. Home: PO Box 722 Sylva NC 28779 Office: Amelia Bauer-Kahn Psychiatric Unit Angel Community Hosp White Oak and Riverview Sts Franklin NC 28734

BOWES, KENNETH EBERLE, advertising executive; b. Montreal, Que., Can., May 16, 1937; s. David Proctor and Corine (Eberle) B.; came to U.S., 1943, naturalized, 1955; B.S., Fla. State U., 1959; m. Mary Priscilla Mohlhenrich, Aug. 10, 1958; children—Kenneth William, Douglas Proctor, Ann Eberle. Advt. writer Atlanta Gas Light Co., 1959-66; with Liller Neal Battle & Lindsey, Atlanta, 1966-72, v.p., 1969-72; pres. Bowes/Hanlon Advt., Atlanta, 1972—; chmn. bd. govs. Trans-World Advt. Agy. Network, Auric Group, Inc., Bowers/Hanlon/Yarbrough Pub. Relations, Inc., George & Marcus Communications, Inc. Bd. dirs. Kidney Found. Ga., Atlanta Area council Boy Scouts Am., Hub Family Crisis Ctr., Callanwolde Fine Arts Ctr.; pres. Ga. Youth and Family Network; v.p. Mountain Shadow Civic Assn. Mem. Ga. C. of C., Friends of the Alphabet. Republican. Mem. Moravian Ch. Clubs: Druid Hills Golf, Toastmasters. Home: 5290 Antelope Ln Stone Mountain GA 30087 Office: 3925 Peachtree Rd NE Atlanta GA 30319

BOWIE, JAMES DWIGHT, radiologist; b. Sentinel, Okla., Oct. 25, 1941; s. Loyd William and Nelda Lucille (Tatum) B.; m. Maria Anna Borgo, May 4, 1968; children—Christine Angela, Catherine Anne. B.A., U. Okla., 1963, M.D., 1967. Diplomate Am. Bd. Radiology. Intern, Chelsea Naval Hosp., Boston, 1967-68; resident in radiology U. Chgo., 1971-74; instr., asst. then assoc. prof. dept. radiology, 1974-79; assoc. prof. dept. radiology Duke U. Med. Ctr., Durham, N.C., 1979—, chief ultrasound sect., 1979—, asst. prof. dept. ob-gyn, 1980—. Served with M.C., USN, 1967-71. Mem. Radiol. Soc. N.Am. (cert. of merit 1977, 78, 79), Assn. Univ. Radiologists. Contbr. articles to profl. jours., chpts. to texts.

BOWLER, JOSEPH, JR., portrait artist; b. Forest Hills, N.Y., 1928; s. Joseph and Catherine Louise (Bowdish) B.; m. Marilyn Carscallen Crang, June 16, 1950; children—Jolyn Louise, B. Brynne Bowler Wakefield. Commd. portraits include: Presdl. Candidates' Wives, McCall's Mag., 1968, Ladies' Home Jour. cover portrait Rose Kennedy, Saturday Evening Post cover Julie and David Eisenhower, 1972; Good Housekeeping Mag. portraits of Pearl S. Buck, Lee Radziwill, Jackie Onassis, Ladies Home Jour. portraits of Senator Edward Kennedy, Caroline Kennedy, Duchess of Windsor; Time Mag. covers of Gen. DeGaulle, Ali McGraw, Pres. Nixon. Address: 9 Baynard Cove Rd Hilton Head Island SC 29928

BOWLES, FRANCES MARIE, business executive; b. Paducah, Ky., Feb. 5, 1938; d. Jesse Raymond and Anna Lou (Varnell) Walker; student Murray State U., 1955-57; m. James Everette Bowles, July 9, 1973; children—Robert Wayne, Michael Ray, Benjamin Earl. Collection correspondent, office supr. Sears Roebuck & Co., Paducah, 1957-65; credit mgr. Jeans Dept. Store, Paducah, 1965-67; mgr., estimator Slay Plumbing & Heating, Paducah, 1967-72; office mgr. Amick & Helm C.P.A., Madisonville, Ky., 1972-74; mgr. Arch Mgmt. Corp., Madisonville, 1974-83, exec. asst. to pres. of affilated cos., 1974-83; owner, operator Sebiee Dock, Nat. Testing Labs., 1983—. Vol. United Way, Madisonville, Cancer Soc., Madisonville; pres. Democratic Women's Club of Hopkins County; mem. Ky. Bd. Housing, Bldgs. and Constrn. Mem. Nat. Sec. Assn. (v.p. Madisonville chpt. 1974, pres. 1976—), Nat. Assn. Exec. Secs., Nat. Assn. Female Execs., Madisonville C. of C. (bd. dirs., exec. com. for leadership). Baptist. Home: 1061 Parkwood St Madisonville KY 42431 Office: PO Box 88 38 W Arch St Madisonville KY 42431

BOWLES, JOANN FAYE DANIELS, registered nurse; b. Dayton, Ohio, June 23, 1948; d. Arland Wilmer and Juanita Delores (Hood) Daniels; m. Larry Dean Bowles, Feb. 10, 1973; children—Scott Alan, Kevin Lee. A.A.S., Sinclair Community Coll., 1973. Registered profl. nurse, Ohio, La. Charge nurse VA Ctr., Dayton, Ohio, 1968-80, Grandview Hosp., Dayton, 1980-82; nurse Pendleton Meml. Meth. Hosp., New Orleans, 1982—; cons. Home Health Care, Inc., Slidell, La., 1982—. Mem. Am. Assn. Critical Care Nurses, Am. Nurses Assn., Phi Beta Kappa. Democrat. Roman Catholic. Club: Daus. of Isabella (v.p. Dayton, 1979—). Author, editor (slide-tape) Recruitment Film for PMMH, 1983. Office: Pendleton Meml Meth Hosp 5620 Read Blvd New Orleans LA 70127

BOWLING, MARY ALICE, nurse administrator, educator, consultant; b. Chattanooga, Aug. 2, 1945; d. John Thomas and Pauline (Nolton) Murray; m. George Henry Bowling, Oct. 27, 1973; children—Lutricia Joy, Michael George. B.S. in Nursing, Tuskegee Inst., 1971. R.N., Tenn. Instr. nursing Cleveland State Community Coll., Tenn., 1971-73, 78-81; primary care nurse Whitney M. Young Health Ctr., Albany, N.Y., 1973-74; family nurse practitioner Chattanooga-Hamilton County Health Dept., Chattanooga, 1976-83; coordinator infection control and in-service Metropolitan Hosp., Chattanooga, 1983-84, asst. dir. nursing, 1984-85, dir. quality assurance 1985—. Mem. health adv. bd. dirs. Chattanooga-Hamilton County Head Start Program, 1975-78; task force mem. Youth Edn. for Living, Chattanooga, 1977-78, profl. adv. bd. dirs. OMNI Home Health Care, Chattanooga, 1982-83, Assocs. Home Health Care, Chattanooga, 1983—; tchr. Ministers' Wives, Chattanooga, 1982-84; asst. sec. United Presbyterian Women, Chattanooga, 1985—; elder, choir dir. Presbyn. Ch. of Reconciliation. Mem. Bus. and Profl. Women Club (membership chmn. 1979-81). Home: 8224 Cicero Trail Chattanooga TN 37421 Office: Metropolitan Hosp 511 McCallie Ave Chattanooga TN 37402

BOWMAN, JANE BELKNAP, genealogist, librarian; b. Atlanta, Ind., July 14, 1923; d. Ruel Kendall and Inez Jane (Caudle) Belknap; m. Ezra Alva Bowman, Dec. 2, 1944; children—Alan Alva, John Ezra, Ruel Arnold. B.S. in Edn., Pa. State Coll.-Millersville, 1947; M.S. in L.S., Syracuse U., 1957. Cert. librarian/media specialist. Librarian, Capt. Jack Jr. High Sch., Mt. Union, Pa., 1954-57; librarian/media specialist Long Beach Schs. (Calif.), 1957-79; genealogist Los Angeles Pub. Library, 1965-80; genealogist Harrison County (W.Va.), West Milford, 1980—; vol. librarian Louis A. Johnson VA Hosp., Clarksburg, W.Va., 1981—. Author: Before the Bowman Boys, 1976; contbr. articles to profl. jours. Served with USNR, 1942-45. Life mem. NEA, ALA, Nat. Ret. Tchrs. Assn., Nat. Geneal. Soc., Ross County Geneal. Soc.; mem. DAR (regent Clarksburg 1983—), U.S. Daus. of 1812 (chaplain local chpt. 1983-84), Order of Crown of Charlemagne, Magna Charta Dames, AAUW, Daus. Am. Colonists (W.Va. state librarian 1984—). Republican. Methodist. Lodge: Order Eastern Star. Home: PO Box 206 West Milford WV 26451

BOWMAN, JOHN KEITH, petroleum geologist; b. Macon, Ga., Aug. 14, 1959; s. Jimmy Lawton and Merrill Ann (Lipford) B.; m. Eugina Ann McPherson, Oct. 7, 1983; 1 child, Jenna Daniel. Assoc. Sci., Macon Jr. Coll.; B.S., Ga. Southwestern Coll.; M.S. in Geology, U. So. Miss. Electrician, Macon, summers 1972-80; tchr. Perkinston Jr. Coll., Miss., 1982-83; cons. geologist Simo Oil Corp., Dallas, 1985—; research scientist Atlantic Richfield, Lafayette, La., 1984-85. Miss. Mineral Resource Inst. grantee, 1983-84. Mem. Am. Assn. Petroleum Geologists (jr.), Dallas Geol. Soc. Republican. Methodist. Avocations: skiing, reading. Home and Office: 1120 Park Ave #151 Dallas TX 75006

BOWMAN, JOHN THEODORE, ophthalmologist; b. Orange, N.J., Nov. 7, 1942; s. George Klyne and Eleanor May (Potts) B.; m. Maryann Hale, May 26, 1979; children—Jefferson Theodore, Jennifer Teal. B.S., Baylor U., 1964; Ph.D., U. Tex.-Austin, 1970; M.D., U. Tex.-San Antonio, 1975. Diplomate Am. Bd. Ophthalmology, Nat. Bd. Med. Examiners. Research and teaching assoc. U. Ga., Athens, 1970-71; intern U. Okla. Hosps., 1975-76; resident U. Okla. Hosps.-Dean A. McGee Eye Inst., 1976-79; practice medicine specializing in ophthalmology Eastern Okla. Eye Clinic, Inc., Tahlequah, 1979—; cons. Indian Health Service, Tahlequah, 1979—; clin. asst. prof. ophthalmology U. Okla. Med. Sch., Oklahoma City, 1982—. Chmn. fund raising campaign Cherokee Nat. Hist. Soc., Tahlequah, 1985. Fellow Am. Acad. Ophthalmology; mem. AMA, Okla. State Med. Assn., Tri-County Med. Soc. (pres. 1984-85), Okla. State Soc. Eye Surgeons and Physicians (bd. dirs. 1982—). Republican. Mem. Ch. of Christ. Avocations: tennis; ranching; collecting Indian art. Home: Route 3 Box 407 Tahlequah OK 74464 Office: Eastern Okla Eye Clinic Inc 201 Harris Circle Tahlequah OK 74464

BOWMAN, KARL FREDERICK, veterinary surgeon, educator; b. Indpls., Mar. 6, 1953; s. Harold Edward and Sally Ann (Merica) B.; m. Gale Marie Gilbert, Sept. 3, 1976; children—Karl Frederick, Brooks Edward. B.S. in Vet. Sci. and Medicine with honors, Mich. State U., 1974, D.V.M. with honors, 1976; M.S. in Large Animal Surgery and Medicine, Auburn U., 1981. Diplomate Am. Coll. Vet. Surgeons. Intern large animal clinic Auburn U. Sch. Vet. Medicine, 1976-77, resident in large animal surgery, 1977-79; resident in large animal surgery New Bolton Ctr., Sch. Vet. Medicine, U. Pa., 1979-81; instr. dept. large animal surgery and medicine Sch. Vet. Medicine, Auburn (Ala.) U., 1977-79; veterinarian Del. Harness Racing Commn., Brandywine Raceway, Wilmington, 1980-81; asst. prof. equine surgery dept. food animal and equine medicine Vet. Teaching Hosp., Sch. Vet. Medicine, N.C. State U., Raleigh, 1981—, chief surg. services, 1981-84. Recipient Autotutorial Excellence award AVMA, 1977, 79. Mem. AVMA, Am. Coll. Vet. Surgeons, Omega Tau Sigma, Sigma Xi, Tri Beta, Phi Zeta. Episcopalian. Contbr. numerous articles to profl. jours.; editorial rev. bd. Vet. Surgery, 1984; author autotutorial programs on equine surgery and medicine. Office: Sch Vet Medicine NC State U 4700 Hillsborough St Raleigh NC 27606

BOWMAN, NED DAVID, medical administrator; b. Chattanooga, July 15, 1948; s. Ned Turner and Charlotte (Bramlett) B.; stepson Charlotte Bramlett; B.S., U. Tenn., 1971, postgrad., 1971-81; M.B.A., Vanderbilt U., 1982; m. Linda Carol Eggers, Sept. 18, 1970; children—Bob, Jean, Beth, Scott, Ben. Adminstr., pres. Ancillary Physicians Services, Oak Ridge, 1971—; pres. Bowman & Assos., Inc.; cons. med. adminstrn. Mem. Oak Ridge Human Resources Bd., 1975; co-chmn. substance abuse com. Anderson County Health Council, pres., 1980-81; adv. com. vocat. edn. Oak Ridge city schs., 1977; bd. dirs. E. Tenn. Detoxification and Rehab. Inst., Knoxville; treas. UN Com. Oak Ridge, 1977, 81. Recipient certs. of appreciation City of Oak Ridge, Oak Ridge City Schs. Mem. AAAS, UN Assn. U.S., Soc. Advancement Mgmt. (certificate appreciation 1975, v.p. 1975), Oak Ridge C. of C. (past dir.), N.Y. Acad. Sci., Med. Group Mgmt. Assn. (pres. Tenn. chpt.), Am. Coll. Med. Group Adminstrs., Tenn. Med. Group Mgmt. Assn. Nat. Fedn. Interscholastic Ofcls. Assn., Tenn. Conservation League, Orthopedics Overseas. Mem. Ch. of Jesus Christ of Latter-day Saints. Lodge. Rotary. Basketball ofcl. Home: 502 Delaware Ave Oak Ridge TN 37830 Office: 145 E Vance Rd Oak Ridge TN 37830

BOWMAN, RICHARD FREDERICK, banker; b. Evanston, Ill., Jan. 16, 1952; s. Donald Wallace and Elizabeth Mary (Hauser) B.; m. Mary Jane Sweeney, May 10, 1975. A.B., Coll. William and Mary, 1972. C.P.A., Va.; chartered bank auditor. Staff acct. A.M. Pullen & Co., Richmond, Va., 1972-73; sr. acct. Laventhol & Horwath, Norfolk, Va. and Washington, 1973-75; v.p., controller First Va. Banks, Inc., Falls Church, 1975—; instr. Am. Inst. Banking. Bd. dirs. Laurel Mews Condominium Assn., 1980—, Arlington County Indsl. Devel. Authority, 1982—. Mem. Am. Inst. C.P.A.s. Home: 6705-E Washington Blvd Arlington VA 22213 Office: 6400 Arlington Blvd Falls Church VA 22046

BOWMAN, ROBERT DALE, architect, tenor; b. Mt. Sterling, Ohio, May 30, 1947; s. Avery Elton and Ruby Mildred (Boyd) B.; B.Arch., Ohio State U., 1970; postgrad. Memphis State U., 1974-75; student in opera N.C. Sch. Arts, 1977; m. Joyce D. Bowman; 1 son, Marc Anthony. Asso., Harold S. Schofield, Architect, Columbus, Ohio, 1967-68, Granzow and Guss, Architects, Columbus, 1968-70, George Kontogiannis and Assos., Columbus, 1970-72, Heery and Heery, Architects and Engrs., Atlanta, 1972-73; univ. architect Memphis State U., 1974-75; prin. Robert D. Bowman, Archtl. Cons., Sarasota, 1975, 76-77; project mgr., archtl. designer Coker Design Assos., Bradenton, Fla., 1977—; partner, archtl. prin. Environ. Designers Collaborative, Bradenton, 1977-82; project mgr., architect Gee and Jenson, Engrs., Architects and Planners, Inc., Bradenton, 1982—; asst. project architect DMJM/Kidde, Cairo, 1982; debut in opera as Sid el Kar in Desert Song, Springfield (Ohio) Civic Opera, 1971; mem. Dayton (Ohio) and Toledo (Ohio) opera assns., 1971-72; appeared in various musical prodns., including leading role as Vakula, the Blacksmith in Am. premiere of Tchaikovsky's Christmas Slippers, Asolo Opera, Sarasota, 1973, role of Tom in The Bishop's Ghost's world premiere, So. Opera Theatre, Memphis, 1975; with Internat. Opera Center, Zurich, Switzerland, 1975; bd. dirs. Inter-City Opera Co.; artistic advisor Community Concert Assn., Sarasota. Active local Democratic coms. Recipient Civic Beautification award City of Sarasota, 1976; award for design playground equipment Alcoa Aluminum, 1965; Tenn. Opera Studies fellow, 1974-75. Author: Solar Energy in South Florida, 1981; research on solar and passive energy, 1977-81. Home: 3500 Elconquistador Pkwy #351 Bradenton FL 33507 Office: 1010 Manatee Ave W Bradenton FL 33505

BOWRON, EDGAR PETERS, museum adminstr., art historian; b. Birmingham, Ala., May 27, 1943; s. James Edgar Bowron and Dorothy (Peters) Lowles; B.A. in English Lit., Colgate U., 1965; M.A. in History of Art, Inst. Fine Art, N.Y. U., 1969, also cert. mus. tng., 1969, Ph.D., 1979; m. Lornagrace Thomas Grenfell, Aug. 20, 1966 (div. 1981); children—James Edgar III, Clara Beatrice, St. John Grenfell. Lectr. dept. edn. Met. Mus. of Art, 1969-70; registrar Mpls. Inst. Arts, 1970-73; curator and baroque art Walters Art Gallery, Balt., 1973-78; adminstrv. asst., curator of Renaissance and baroque art Nelson Gallery Atkins Mus., Kansas City, Mo., 1978-81; dir. N.C. Mus. Art, Raleigh, 1981—; mem. faculty Peabody Inst., Johns Hopkins U., 1974-78. Ford Found. fellow, 1967-69, Nat. Endowment for Arts fellow, 1975-76; Am. Acad. Rome grantee, 1979—. Mem. Coll. Art Assn., Am. Soc. 18th Century Studies, Assn. Art Mus. Dirs. Episcopalian. Co-author: The J. Paul Getty Collection, 1972; author: Renaissance Bronzes in the Walters Art Gallery, 1978; Pompeo Batoni (1708-87), 1982; Pompeo Batoni and his British Patrons, 1982; editor: Selected Writings of Anthony M. Clark: Studies in Eighteenth-Century Roman Painting, 1981; The North Carolina Museum of Art: Introduction to the Collections, 1983; Anthony M. Clark, Pompeo Batoni, 1985; contbr. to exhbn. catalogues and numerous profl. publs. Office: NC Museum of Art 2110 Blue Ridge Blvd Raleigh NC 27607

BOWSER, WILLIAM LEE, consulting service executive; b. Roanoke, Va., June 5, 1954; s. Cleveland, Jr. and Eva Lee (McGinley) B.; m. Diane Laverne Wright, Sept. 6, 1975; children—Brian McGinley, Phillip Altizer. B.S. in Mgmt., Va. Poly. Inst. and State U., Blacksburg, 1976; M.B.A., Va. Poly. Inst. and State U., Fairfax, 1985. Contracting officer U.S. Govt., various locations, 1976-79; sr. contract adminstr. CACI Inc., Arlington, Va., 1979-82, mgr. contracts, 1982-84; dir. contracts Presearch Inc., Fairfax, 1984-85, sec., treas., 1984—, v.p. fin. and adminstrn., 1985—, also dir. Author: Competitive Procurement, 1983; also articles and seminar materials. Campaigner Young Republicans, Washington, 1980, 84. Fellow Nat. Contract Mgmt. Assn. (cert. profl. contracts mgr.); mem. Am. Mgmt. Assn., Fairfax C. of C., U.S. Navy League, Alpha Kappa Psi. Baptist. Avocations: golf; tennis; fishing. Home: 500 Montpelier Dr Stafford VA 22554 Office: Presearch Inc 8500 Executive Park Ave Fairfax VA 22031

BOX, BENTON HOLCOMB, university dean; b. Norfield, Miss., Jan. 31, 1931; s. James Alexander and Lola Gay (Holcomb) B.; student Southeastern La. U., 1949-51; B.S., La. State U., 1957, M.F., 1959; D.F., Duke U., 1967; m. Sallie Yates, Feb. 10, 1952; children—Benton Holcomb, John William, Janice Ellen Box Bishop. Research asso. dept. forestry and specialist Coop. Extension Service, La. State U., Baton Rouge, 1957-60, asst. prof., 1960-67, asso. prof., 1967-69, specialist Coop. Extension Service, 1969-72; exec. v.p. So. Forest Inst., Atlanta, 1972-77; forestry cons., Atlanta, 1977-78; dean Coll. Forest and Recreation Resources, Clemson (S.C.) U., 1978—. Served with USAF, 1951-55. NSF grantee; named Disting. Alumnus, Sch. Forestry, Duke U., 1980. Mem. Soc. Am. Foresters, S.C. Forestry Assn., Am. Forestry Assn., Forest Farmer Assn., Nat. Recreation and Park Assn., S.C. Recreation and Park Soc., Assn. State Coll. and Univ. Forestry Research Orgns. (exec. com.), So. Appalachian Research-Resource Mgmt. Coop. (chmn.). Baptist (deacon). Club: Sertoma (pres. Clemson 1981-82). Contbr. articles to profl. jours. Office: Coll Forest and Recreation Resources Clemson U Clemson SC 29631

BOX, DON D., cement company executive, financial consultant; b. Dumas, Tex., Aug. 30, 1950; s. Cloyce Kennedy and Fern Virginia (Cunningham) B. B.A., U. Pa., 1973; B.S. in Econs., Wharton Sch., 1973; M.B.A., So. Meth. U., 1974. Dir. mktg. refined petroleum products OKC Corp., Dallas, 1974-76, v.p. corp. devel., 1976-81, dir., 1981—; pres. Box Engring., Inc., Dallas, 1982—, Mecca Cement Co., Dallas, 1982—. Active, Dallas Civic Opera. Mem. 100 Club Dallas, Tex., Inc., Tex. Assn. Bus. Brokers, Wharton Alumni Assn. Club: Brook Hollow Golf (Dallas).

BOX, THOMAS MORGAN, management consultant, educator; b. Cleve., July 12, 1937; s. Bert William and Margaret Kathryn (Williams) B.; m. Barbara Jean Grden, Nov. 25, 1961; children—Anne Louise, Valerie Morgan, Thomas Morgan. B.S. in Math., U. Tulsa, 1977, M.B.A., 1979. Mgr. prodn. and inventory Kirby Bldg. Systems, Houston, 1968-69; v.p., div. mgr. Riverside Industries, Tulsa, 1969-72; v.p. ops. Braden Steel, Tulsa, 1972-80; sr. v.p. Southwest Tube Mfg., Tulsa, 1980-84; ptnr. Webb Shirley and Box, Tulsa, 1984—; instr. U. Tulsa, 1979—. Vol. United Way, 1977, Walk for Mankind, 1978. Served with USMC, 1956-59. Nat. Merit Scholar, 1955; John Huntington Found. grantee, 1956. Mem. Am. Mktg. Assn. (bd. dirs. Tulsa Chpt.), Inst. Indsl. Engrs., Am. Inst. for Decision Scis., Acad. of Mgmt. Roman Catholic. Condr. research in field. Home: 4304 E 83d St Tulsa OK 74137 Office: 320 S Boston Tulsa OK 74103

BOYD, CLARENCE ELMO, surgeon; b. Leesville, La., Nov. 2, 1911; s. Isaac C. and Ada Lee (Stakes) B.; B.A., U. Tex., 1932, M.D., 1935; m. Emma Sims, Aug. 13, 1937; children—Charles E., Marjorie E., Frances A., James E. Intern, Charity Hosp., New Orleans, 1935-36; resident North La. San. (now Doctors Hosp.), Shreveport, La., 1936-37; gen. practice medicine, Shreveport, 1937-42, specializing in gen. surgery, 1942—; founder, sr. mem. C.E. Boyd Clinic, Shreveport, 1942—; vis. surgeon Drs. Hosp., Shreveport, 1937—, founding dir., 1959, chmn. bd., 1959-80, med. dir., 1959—; jr. vis. surgeon Charity Hosp. (now La. State U. Med. Ctr.), 1937-42; sr. vis. surgeon Confederate Meml. Hosp., Shreveport, 1942—; clin. asst. prof. surgery La. State U. Postgrad. Sch. Medicine, 1957-67, La. State U. Sch. of Medicine, Shreveport, 1967—; teaching faculty Am. Bd. Abdominal Surgeons, 1967; chief surgeon La. and Ark. Ry. Co. Employees' Hosp. Assn. to 1967; founding dir. Shreveport Bank & Trust Co., 1954—, chmn. investment com., 1954-78, chmn. bd. dirs., 1961—. Sponsors com. Shreveport United Fund, 1962-66. Dir. Vols. Am., 1950-58, chmn. bd., 1955-57; trustee Pub. Affairs Research Council, La., 1959-79; nat. adv. bd. We, The People, 1964-82. Diplomate Internat. Bd. Proctology. Fellow ACS, Internat. Coll. Surgs., Southwestern Surg. Congress, Am. Soc. Abdominal Surgeons (founder 1959, pres. 1966-67, chmn. com. preparing audio-visual postgrad. program on diseases of gall bladder, teaching faculty 1962, Gold medal 1962, Disting. Service award 1986), mem. AMA (chmn. surg. sect. 1965, 67, alt. del. sect. council on surgery 1972-78, mem. surg. council 1972-78, del. 1978-79, Recognition award 1966-69, 70-72, 73-75, 76-78, 79-81, 82-84), La. (chmn. pub. policy and legislative com. 1954-57, chmn. surg. sect. 1957, 4th dist. councilor 1959-66, del. 1945-59, v.p. 1967-68, chmn. com. on hosps. 1968-71), Shreveport (pres. 1956, 1st chmn. med. progress 1957-59, Gold medal 1956-57), med. socs., Am. Cancer Soc. (dir. Caddo br. 1952-59, vice chmn. bd. 1957-58), Surg. Assn. La., Am. Mastology Assn., So. Med. Assn. (asso. Councilor 1959-68), Pan Pacific Surg. Assn., Am. Assn. Physicians and Surgeons (del., mem. chmn. 1960-72, pres. La. chpt. 1972-73). Episcopalian (vestryman, Gold Medal Bible Class 1965). Clubs: Rotary (pres. Cedar Grove, Shreveport, 1940-41, founder and chmn. com. of student loan fund 1942—), Masons (32 deg.), Shriners. Contbr. articles to profl. jours. Research on operative cholangiography, local hernioplasty with immediate ambulation; producer color film on cholangiogram, 1960. Home: 401 Delaware St Shreveport LA 71106 Office: 1128 Louisiana Ave Shreveport LA 71101

BOYD, DANNY DOUGLASS, marriage and family counselor, financial counselor; b. Olustee, Okla., Oct. 18, 1933; s. Robert and Juanita Henrietta (Crawford) B.; B.A. magna cum laude, Abilene Christian U., 1954; M.A. in Linguistics, U. Tex., Arlington, 1976; C.L.U.; chartered fin. cons.; m. Mary Ann Thomas, Jan. 25, 1953; children—Robert Lee, Rebecca Dyann Boyd McCully, Scott Thomas, Douglas Dean. Minister Chs. of Christ, Ardmore,

Okla., 1954-56, Velma, Okla., 1956-57, Cisco, Tex., 1958-60, Utrecht, Netherlands, 1960-65, Wilmington, Del., 1965-69, Dallas, 1969-71; v.p. Nat. Comp Assocs., Dallas, 1972-77; marriage and family counselor Adaptive Counseling Assocs., Dallas, 1977—; fin. counselor CIGNA Ind. Fin. Services Co., 1979—; founder Chair of Bible, Cisco Jr. Coll., 1959. Bd. dirs. Skyline High Sch. PTA, 1971; intervenor for integrated neighborhoods fed. dist. ct. desegregation suit, Dallas, 1977. Mem. N. Dallas C. of C., Dallas chpt. Am. Assn. C.L.U.s., Internat. Assn. Fin. Planning, Am. Assn. Counseling and Devel. Republican. Office: 600 E Las Colinas Blvd Suite 1400 Irving TX 75039

BOYD, GILBERT H., geologist, consultant; b. Chattanooga, Tenn., Mar. 3, 1926; s. Gilbert Herschel and Mathel N. (Martin) B.; m. Jo Ann Boring, Aug. 4, 1956; children—Gilbert Edwin, Sarah Elizabeth. B.S., U. Tenn., 1951, M.S., 1955. Cert. profl. petroleum geologist. Instr., asst. prof. U. Tenn., Martin and Knoxville, 1954-56; devel. geologist Texaco, New Orleans, 1956-58; petroleum geologist Hunt Oil Co., Dallas, 1958-66; regional mgr. exploration Sun Oil Co., Dallas, Shreveport, La., 1966-70; cons. petroleum, geology sole practice, Houston, 1970. Served with USN, 1944-45. Mem. Am. Assn. Petroleum Geologists. Republican. Episcopalian. Home: 414 Kickerillo Ct Houston TX 77079

BOYD, JOSEPH ARTHUR, JR., chief justice Fla. Supreme Ct.; b. Hoschton, Ga., Nov. 16, 1916; s. Joseph Arthur and Esther (Puckett) B.; grad. Piedmont Coll., LL.D., 1963; J.D., U. Miami, 1948; LL.D., Western State U., 1981; m. Ann Stripling, June 6, 1938 children—Joanne (Mrs. Robert Goldman), Betty Jean (Mrs. David Jala), Joseph, James, Jane. Bar: D.C. 1973, N.Y. 1982. City atty., Hialeah, Fla., 1951-58; commr. Dade County, 1958-68, vice mayor, 1967; chmn. Dade County Commn., 1963; dir. Fla. Assn. County Commrs., 1964-68; justice Fla. Supreme Ct., Tallahassee, 1969—, chief justice, 1984—. Trustee Piedmont Coll. Served with USMCR, 1943-46; PTO. Decorated Japanese Occupation medal with one star; recipient Top Hat award for advancing status of women Nat. Bus. and Profl. Women's Clubs, 1967. Mem. ABA, Fla., D.C., Hialeah-Miami Springs (pres. 1955), Tallahassee bar assns., Hialeah-Miami Springs (pres. 1956), Tallahassee chambers commerce, Am. Legion (state comdr. 1953), V.F.W., Soc. of Wig and Robe, Pi Kappa Psi, Phi Alpha Delta. Baptist. Lodges: Masons, Shriners, Lions, Elks, Moose. Office: Supreme Ct Bldg Tallahassee FL 32304

BOYD, JOSEPH AUBREY, communications company executive; b. Oscar, Ky., Mar. 25, 1921; s. Joseph Ray and Relda Jane (Myatt) B.; m. Edith A. Atkins, May 13, 1942; children—Joseph Barry, Joel Edd. S.B. in Elec. Engring., U. Ky., 1946, M.S., 1949; Ph.D., U. Mich., 1954. Instr., then asst. prof. elec. engring. U. Ky., 1947-49; mem. faculty U. Mich., 1949-62, prof. elec. engring., 1958-62, asso. dir., then dir., 1958-60, dir., 1960-62; exec. v.p. Radiation Inc., Melbourne, Fla., 1962-63, pres., 1963-72; exec. v.p. electronics Harris Corp., Cleve., 1967-71, exec. v.p. ops., 1971-72, pres., dir., 1972—, chmn., 1978—; Cons. Inst. for Def. Analyses, 1956—, Nat. Security Agy., 1957-62; spl. cons. to (Army Combat Surveillance Agy.), 1958-62; mem., chmn. adv. group electronic warfare Office Dir. Def. Research, Engring., Def. Dept., 1959-61, cons., 1959—. Contbr. articles to profl. jours. Fellow IEEE; mem. Assn. U.S. Army, Armed Forces Communications and Electronics Assn. (pres. 1971, 72), AAAS, Sigma Xi, Eta Kappa Nu, Tau Beta Pi. Baptist. Office: Harris Corp Melbourne FL 32919

BOYD, LEONARD DAVIS, consulting engineer; b. Horry, S.C., Feb. 1, 1943; s. Leston Sherwood and Ruth Fayette (Gore) B.; m. Elizabeth Ann Sellers, Oct. 13, 1962; children—Lauren Davis, Leah Rachelle. B.S. in Chem. Engring., Clemson U., 1966. Registered profl. engr., Tex. With Gulf Oil Corp., 1966-79, project chmn. Enex, Inc., Houston, 1980—; pres., dir., 1980—. Mem. Tex. Soc. Profl. Engrs., Tex. Realtors. Home: 3306 Village Oaks Kingwood TX 77339 Office: PO Box 52355 Houston TX 77052

BOYD, MARY ANN, psychotherapist; b. Bakersfield, Calif., Dec. 22, 1934; d. Augustus Lee and Clara Mary (Walling) Thomas; m. Danny Douglass Boyd, Jan. 25, 1953; children—Robert Lee, Rebecca Dyann Boyd McCully, Scott Thomas, Douglas Dean. B.A. summa cum laude, U. Tex.-Arlington, 1980, M.S. in Social Work, 1981. Cert. social worker; lic. profl. counselor, Tex.; nat. cert. counselor. Counselor Human Potential Ctr., Dallas, 1978-79, Adaptive Counseling Assocs., Dallas, 1979—; lectr. Effective Parenting, Dallas Parks and Recreation Dept., 1983—; missionary Chs. of Christ, Utrecht, Netherlands, 1960-65. Pres. Birdie Alexander Elem. Sch. PTA, Dallas, 1974-75. Mem. Nat. Assn. Social Workers, Am. Assn. Counseling and Devel., Am. Mental Health Counselors Assn., Alpha Chi, Alpha Delta Mu. Republican. Avocations: walking; singing; travel. Office: Adaptive Counseling Assocs 652 Shadowcrest Ln Coppell TX 75019

BOYD, MARY OLERT, lawyer, educator, journalist; b. Holland, Mich., Aug. 28, 1930; d. Frederick H. and Sarah (Klooster) Olert; m. Joseph M. Boyd, Jr., Dec. 29, 1953; children—Andrew Martin, David Alexander, Martha Lucile. B.A., Hope Coll., 1952; postgrad. Johns Hopkins Med. Sch., 1952-53, Am. U., 1953-54, Sch. Law Vanderbilt U., 1955-56; J.D., Memphis State U., 1977. Bar: Tenn. 1977, U.S. Dist. Ct. (we. dist.) Tenn. 1977, U.S. Ct. Appeals (6th cir.), 1982. Tchr. schs. Nashville, Dyer County, and Dyersburg, Tenn., 1954-61; legal asst. Joseph M. Boyd, Jr., Dyersburg, 1965-74; ptnr. firm Boyd and Boyd, 1977—; asst. dist. atty. Dyer County (Tenn.), 1980—; head Child Support Div. for 29th Jud. Cir., Dyer and Lake County (Tenn.); instr. bus. law and other paralegal courses, Dyersburg State Community Coll., 1977—; free-lance writer, Dyersburg, 1961—. Chmn. Dyer County Democratic Party, 1979-83. Recipient Labor prize Memphis State Law Sch., 1977. Mem. ABA (family law sect.), Tenn. Bar Assn. (chmn. family law sect. 1985—), Dyer County Bar Assn. (pres. 1982-83), Tenn. Jaycettes (pres. 1961-62). Methodist. Club: Dyersburg Woman's (pres. 1964-65). Contbr. photos and articles to Memphis Press-Scimitar and other newspapers; contbr. articles to profl. jours. and popular mags. Home: 607 Troy Ave Dyersburg TN 38024 Office: Dyer County Court House Dyersburg TN 38025

BOYD, RICHARD ALFRED, state superintendent education; b. Coshocton, Ohio, July 4, 1927; s. Lester Stephenson and Opal Irene (King) B ; m. Marye Joanne McPherson, Aug. 29, 1953; children—Lynne, Julie, Michael, Stephanie. B.S. in Edn., Capital U., 1951, D.H.L. (hon.), 1984; M.A., Ohio State U., 1958; Ed.D., U. Akron, 1970. Research assoc. U. Akron, Ohio, 1968-70; asst. supt. Warren City Schs., Ohio, 1970-71, supt., 1971-75; project dir. Commn. Pub. Sch. Personnel Policies of Ohio, Warren, 1971; supt. Lakewood Pub. Schs., Ohio, 1975-84; state supt. edn. Miss. Dept. Edn., Jackson, 1984—. Contbr. articles to profl. jours. Trustee Jr. Achievement of Warren and Cleve., 1970-84, U. for Young Ams., Cleve., 1982-84; pres. Trumbull County Community Chest, Warren, 1973-75; bd. dirs. Bar Assn. Greater Cleve., 1983-84. Served with USN, 1945-46. Recipient Outstanding Educator award Ohio PTA, 1979; Educator of Yr. award Council Exceptional Children, 1981; Outstanding Contbn. to Adult Edn. award Ohio Assn. Adult Educators, 1983; Exec. Educator 100 award N.Am.'s Top 100 Sch. Execs., 1984. Mem. Am. Assn. Sch. Adminstrs. (exec. com. 1983-86), Buckeye Assn. Sch. Adminstrs. (pres. 1981-82), Nat. Assn. Accreditation Tchr. Edn. (exec. com. 1984—), Council Chief State Sch. Officers. Episcopalian. Home: 60 Eastbrooke Jackson MS 39216 Office: State Dept of Edn PO Box 771 Jackson MS 39205

BOYD, ROBERT EDWARD LEE, II, mechanical engineer; b. Wheeling, W.Va., Nov. 12, 1914; s. Robert E. Lee and Mary (Bachtler) B.; m. Julia Eleanor Beal, Jan. 1, 1938; children—Mary Eleanor Boyd Eads, Barbara Ann Boyd Hall, Robert E. Lee, III. A.B. in Physics, Kenyon Coll., 1936. With Westinghouse Co., 1937-38; mech. contractor, 1939; with Houston Lighting and Power Co., 1940-42; heat pump contractor, 1946-48; with Airtemp Corp., 1948-51, contractor, 1951-53; with Eleromode Corp., 1953-57; tech. dir. Edwin L. Wiegand Co., Pitts., 1957-66; engring. cons. climate control div. Singer Co., Auburn, N.Y., 1966-71; asso. prof. air-conditioning tech. State U. N.Y. Coll., Alfred, 1971-74; asso. tech. dir. Sheet Metal and Air Conditioning Contractors' Nat. Assn., Vienna, Va., 1974-76; sr. mech. engr. NAHB (Nat. Assn. Home Builders) Research Found., Inc., Rockville, Md., 1976-78, ret., 1978. Contbr. numerous articles on heating and air conditioning application engring. to trade and profl. pubs.; patentee in field. Served to 1st lt. C.E., AUS, 1942-46. Fellow ASHRAE; mem. Engrs. Joint Council, Engrs. of Distinction, Am. Assn. Ret. Persons, Phi Beta Kappa, Tau Kappa Alpha. Home: 413 Brewers Creek Ln Carrollton VA 23314

BOYD, WILLIAM CLARK, lawyer; b. Edom, Tex., Jan. 8, 1940; s. Fred W. and Annice H. Boyd; m. Linda Capps, June 15, 1963; children—William Clark, Standford Scott. B.S. in Math., Tex. Tech U., 1962; postgrad. U. N.Mex., 1962-63; J.D., U. Houston, 1968. Bar: U.S. Dist. Ct. (so. dist.) Tex. 1968, U.S. Dist. Ct. (we. dist.) Tex. 1973. Data analyst T.S.I., White Sands, N.Mex., 1962-64; aerospace technologist NASA, Houston, 1964-68; assoc. Woodard Hall & Primm, Houston, 1969-72; ptnr. Patterson Boyd Lowery & Aderholt, Houston, 1972—. Trustee Tex. Tech. U. Mem. Houston Bar Assn. (dir. 1974-75, liaison 1981-82), State Bar Tex. (dir. 1979-82), ABA, Phi Delta Theta. Presbyterian. Club: Kiwanis (Houston). Office: 2101 Louisiana Houston TX 77002

BOYD, WILLIAM DOUGLAS, JR., library science educator, clergyman; b. Pulaski, Tenn., Dec. 15, 1929; s. William Douglas and Lula May (Scott) B.; m. Margaret Woolfolk, July 16, 1966; 1 child, Julia Woolfolk. B.A., Rhodes Coll., 1952; B.D., Union Theol. Sem., N.Y.C., 1955; Th.M., Princeton Theol. Sem., 1958; M.L.S., Ind. U., 1972, Ph.D., 1975. Ordained to ministry, 1956. Pastor First Presbyn. Ch., Mt. Pleasant, Tenn., 1956-63; asst. pastor Ind. Presbyn. Ch., Birmingham, Ala., 1963-67; asst. law librarian Ind. U., Bloomington, 1972-73; asst. prof. library sci. U. So. Miss., Hattiesburg, 1973-77, assoc. prof., 1977—; reviewer pub. library program NEH, 1978. Translator: (L. Buzás) German Library History 800 1945, 1986. Contbr. articles to profl. jours. Recipient Algernon Sydney Sullivan award Rhodes Coll., 1952. Mem. SAR, (sec. Miss. 1985—), Tenn. Library Assn. (vice-chmn. trustees and friends sect. 1962-63), ALA, Miss. Library Assn., Am. Assn. Adult and Continuing Edn., Miss. Inst. Arts and Letters, Presbytery of Miss., Mil. Order Stars and Bars, Omicron Delta Kappa, Beta Phi Mu. Democrat. Club: Hattiesburg Country. Home: 104 Lee Circle Hattiesburg MS 39401 Office: U So Miss Hattiesburg MS 39401

BOYDSTUN, JACKSON BENJAMIN, architect; b. Natchitoches, La., Feb. 5, 1908; s. Benjamin Kendall and Eunice Augusta (Hargis) B.; grad. high sch.; m. Bernice Erline Hill, Apr. 19, 1930; children—Nelwyn (Mrs. Dan W. Poole, Jr.), Betty Sue (Mrs. Stuart Carpenter), Jackson Benjamin, David H. Constrn. supervising engr. constrn. firms, 1936-46; archtl. assoc. Barron, Hienberg & Brocato, architects, Alexandria, La., 1947-50; self-employed as architect, Natchitoches, 1960—; dir., chmn. bd. J. B. Boydstun & Assocs., Inc. Mem. Constrn. Legislative Council La., 1970-72; trustee First Meth. Ch., Natchitoches. Served with AUS, World War II. Mem. AIA, Am. Legion (comdr. 1945-46), La. Architects Assn. Democrat. Mason (Shriner). Prin. archtl. works include Marthaville Phys. Edn. and Auditorium, St. Matthew High Sch., Elementary Sch. Library, Allen High Sch. Classroom Bldg., Goldonna High Sch. Auditorium and Classroom Bldg., Robeline Phys. Edn. and Classroom Bldg., Conv. Center-Hodges Garden, ch. bldg. for Ch. of Nazarene, Natchitoches, La., apt. bldg. and two shopping centers, Natchitoches. Author: (novel) On the Wings of Truth. Home and Office: 410 Stephens Ave Natchitoches LA 71457

BOYER, JOE L., university president. Pres. Miss. Valley State U., Itta Bena, Miss. Office: Miss Valley State U Itta Bena MS 38941

BOYER, JOHN CLOYD, plastic co. exec.; b. Littlefield, Tex., Oct. 20, 1929; s. Robert McKinley and Viola Ann (Aucutt) B.; grad. high sch.; m. Imogene Alsup, June 3, 1949; children—John Larry, Patricia Boyer Neal. Pres., Thermo Plastics Corp., Ft. Worth, 1964—. Mem. Soc. Plastic Engrs. Republican. Methodist. Home: 3501 N Beach St Fort Worth TX 76111 Office: 4101 Hahn St Haltom City TX 76117

BOYKIN, MARY JONES, nursing administrator; b. Columbia, S.C., Mar. 9, 1948; d. Jim Bob and Jessie Bell (Watts) Jones; m. Eddie Boykin, Jr., May 1, 1971; children—Ginger Renee, Darrell Timothy. B.S. in Nursing cum laude, N.C. Central U., 1983, postgrad., 1985; A.D., U. S.C., 1975. R.N., N.C. Nurses' asst. Richland Meml. Hosp., Columbia, 1966-67, L.P.N., 1968-75; staff nurse Duke U. Med. Ctr., Durham, N.C., 1975-80, nursing supr., 1980-85, asst. dir. nursing, 1985—, career counselor intern, 1985. Mem. Am. Assn. Critical Care Nurses, Nat. Employment Counselors Assn., Nat. Vocat. Guidance Assn., Am. Assn. Counseling and Devel., Nat. Soc. for Autistic Children, Am. Mental Health Counseling Assn., Nat. Assn. Female Execs., Durham Adoption Support Group (vlpl. 1983—). Democrat. Baptist. Avocations: camping; sightseeing; traveling; reading; cooking. Home: 5802 Sandstone Dr Durham NC 27713 Office: Duke U Med Ctr PO Box 3714 Durham NC 27710

BOYLE, JOHN ALOYSIUS, JR., biochemist, educator; b. New Orleans, Nov. 5, 1950; s. John Aloysius and Frances Rose (Coniglio) B.; m. Carolyn Ann Redding, May 26, 1973; 1 son, Alan Patrick. B.S., U. New Orleans, 1972; postgrad. Vanderbilt U., 1972-73; Ph.D., Duke U., 1978. Postdoctoral assoc. Yale U., 1978-79; assoc. prof. dept. biochemistry Miss. State U., 1979—. NIH trainee, 1972-78; recipient Merck award, 1972; Am. Chem. Soc. award, 1972; Sigma Xi young researcher award, 1985; Gamma Sigma Delta research award, 1985. Mem. Am. Chem. Soc., Am. Soc. Microbiology, AAAS, Sigma Xi. Roman Catholic.

BOYLE, TERRENCE W., U.S. district judge; b. 1945. B.A., Brown U., 1967; J.D., Am. U., 1970. Minority counsel housing subcom., banking and currence com. U.S. Ho. of Reps., 1970-73; legis. asst. U.S. senator J. Helms, 1973; ptnr. law firm LeRoy, Wells, Shaw, Hornthal & Riley, Elizabeth City, N.C., 1974-84; U.S. dist. judge, Fayetteville, N.C., 1984—; lectr. Wake Forest Law Sch. Mem. 1st Jud. Dist. Bar Assn. (sec.-treas. 1982-83, v.p. 1983-84). Office: PO Box 1148 Fayetteville NC 28302*

BOYLE, WALTER D(OUGLAS) L(ONG), construction company executive, consultant; b. East Orange, N.J., Mar. 24, 1924; s. Harold Lauren and Alma Jane (Long) B.; m. Elizabeth Ann Peterson, Mar. 27, 1953 (div.); children—Harold Lauren, Douglas Kane, Walter Douglas Long, Jr., Janna Cecile; m. 2d Joan Riley Buehler, July 4, 1965; children—Carl Buehler, Jay Wight Buehler, Martin Buehler. B.A., U. Calif.-Berkeley, 1946; postgrad. Law Sch., Cornell U., 1946-47, Oliver Wendell Holmes Inst., 1954-55. With real estate dept. W.T. Grant, N.Y.C., 1947-59; pres. Central Mercantile, Chgo., 1959-72; exec. search and tng. dir. Tex. Refinery Corp., Ft. Worth, 1973-75; asst. to pres. Consol. Cos., Cleve., 1975—; pres. Southeastern Roof Cons. Ltd., Advance, N.C., 1978—; pres., R.H. Macy Shopping Ctr. Assocs., Mission, Kans., 1957; cons. E&K Roof Systems Ltd., Jackson, Tenn., 1983-84. Author: Corporate Roof Maintenance, 1979. Vice chmn. Erie Philharmonic Orch. (Pa.), 1955; fund raiser and vol. YMCA, Gary, Ind., Chgo., Kansas City, Mo., 1948-49, 56. Served with USMC, 1942-45, to capt., 1950-53. Recipient Mr. Goodyear award Consol. Cos., 1981, 83; named World Wide Volume Leader, 1976, 77, 78, 79, 80, 81, 84; named to N.C. AAU All-Star Swimming Team, 1978; nat. YMCA swimming freestyle record holder. Mem. Winston-Salem Engrs. Club, Million Dollar Club Cleve., N.C. Pub. Schs. Maintenance Assn. (adv. council, Raleigh 1979-84). Episcopalian. Clubs: YMCA Bus. (Winston-Salem), Bermuda Run Country, Tar Heel Masters Swim (Charlotte). Home: 104-106 Tifton Dr Bermuda Run NC 27006 Office: Southeastern Roof Cons Box 511 Advance NC 27006

BOYLES, HARLAN EDWARD, state official; b. Lincoln County, N.C., May 6, 1929; s. Curtis E. and Kate S. Boyles; student U. Ga., 1947-48; B.B.A. in Acctg., U. N.C., 1951; m. Frankie Wilder, May 17, 1952; children—Mrs. G.E. Ferrell, Lynn Boyles Freeman, Harlan Edward. Corp. tax auditor N.C. Dept. Revenue, 1951-56; exec. sec. N.C. Tax Rev. Bd., 1956-76; treas. State of N.C., 1977—; mem. Council of State; mem. mcpl. securities rulemaking bd. SEC, 1975-77. Mem. adv. com. Raleigh Salvation Army; chmn. Local Govt. Commn., dep. treas. and sec., 1960-76; chmn. State Banking Commn., Tax Rev. Bd.; mem. State Bd. Edn., State Bd. Community Colls., N.C. Capital Bldg. Authority, Capital Planning Commn., others. C.P.A., N.C. Mem. N.C. Assn. C.P.A.'s, Nat. Assn. State Auditors, Comptrollers and Treasurers (treas., exec. dir.), Raleigh C. of C. (dir.), N.C. State Employees Assn. Democrat. Presbyterian (deacon, elder, treas., clk.). Clubs: N.C. Young Dems., Rotary (dir.), Execs. of Raleigh (dir.). Office: 325 N Salisbury St Albemarle Bldg Raleigh NC 27611

BOYLES, JAMES EDWARD, industrial engineer; b. Houston, Aug. 15, 1929; s. Lester Tucker and Hazel Viola (Montgomery) B.; B.S., Tex. A&M U., 1951; m. Martha Faye Brannen, Oct. 20, 1957; children—William, Johnna. Home builder, Houston, 1955; indsl. engr. Reed Roller Bit Co., 1956-60; indsl. engr. W.K.M. Valve div. A.C.F. Industries, Houston, 1960-66, head indsl. engring. dept., 1966-69, mgr. indsl. engring., 1970-73, mgr. mfg. engring., 1973-74; mgr. indsl. engring. and prodn. planning and control, casting facility TRW/Mission Mfg. Co., Houston, 1974-76, mgr. mfg. casting facility, 1976-77, prodn. supt., 1977-79, plant mgr. casting facility, 1979-80; mgr. indsl. engring. Fluid Control div. F.M.C. Corp., Houston, 1980-81; mgr. mfg. Tapco Internat., unit of Gen. Signal, Houston, 1981-85; cons. engr. Boyles and Assocs., Houston, 1985—; lectr. U. Houston. Served to capt. USAF, 1952-54, now lt. col. Res. Registered profl. engr., Tex. Mem. Am. Inst. Indsl. Engrs. (pres.; nat. gen. conf. chmn. 1969), Res. Officers Assn., Air Force Assn., Armed Forces Communications and Electronics Assn., Tex. Soc. Profl. Engrs., Nat. Mgmt. Assn. Home: 2923 Shadowdale St Houston TX 77043 Office: PO Box 19884 Houston TX 77024

BOYNTON, ELIZABETH JORDAN, planner, requirements representative; b. Liberty, Tex., Oct. 26, 1937; d. Curt Max and Ruby Elizabeth (Enloe) Jordan; m. Frank Ellis Boynton, May 1, 1982. B.B.A., U. Tex., 1959, M.B.A., 1964. Cert. secondary tchr., Tex. Tchr., Flour Bluff High Sch., Corpus Christi, 1959, Brazosport High Sch., Freeport, Tex., 1959-61; instr. U. Tex., Austin, 1961-62; market support rep. IBM, Dallas, 1962-67, edn. planning rep., 1967-70, product edn. mgr., Austin, 1970-74, product mktg. program mgr., Franklin Lakes, N.J., 1974-75, internat. market requirements program mgr., Franklin Lakes, 1975-79, applications devel. mgr., Austin, 1979-82, sr. planner, Austin, 1982-83, planning and requirements rep., Irving, 1983—. Mem. Am. Soc. Tng. and Devel., Delta Pi Epsilon. Methodist. Avocations: travel; photography; spectator sports. Office: IBM Corp 225 JW Carpenter Freeway Irving TX 75062

BOYS, G(EORGE) WARING, JR., investment company executive; b. Charlotte, N.C., June 12, 1938; s. George W. and Muriel (Dole) B.; m. Elizabeth Carpenter, May 4, 1968; 1 child, Elizabeth. B.S., N.C. State U., 1960; postgrad. NYU, 1962-63. Account exec. Smith Barney, N.Y.C., 1962-70; v.p. Loomis, Sayles & Co., Boston, 1970-77; pres. G. Waring Boys Co Inc., Asheville, N.C., 1977—.

BOYT, PATRICK ELMER, farmer, real estate executive; b. Liberty, Tex., Sept. 22, 1940; s. Elmer Vernon and Kathleen (Nelson) B.; B.S. in C.E., U. Tex., 1963; m. Elizabeth Ruth Jefferson, June 16, 1962; children—Jefferson Elmer, Mark Cecil. Owner, mng. partner P.E. Boyt Farms; pres. Boyt Realty Co.; dir. First State Bank, Liberty, 1978—, Beaumont State Bank, 1969-78, Farm Credit Banks of Tex., 1986—. Bd. dirs. Beaumont Art Mus., 1973—, Devers Ind. Sch. Dist., 1974—, Am. Rice Growers, 1974—; mem. Tex. Commn. for Arts, 1978-81; bd. dirs. Kersting Meml. Hosp., 1976-83; supr. Lower Trinity Soil and Water Conservation Dist., 1972—. Mem. Am. Brahman Breeders Assn., Tex. Rice Improvement Assn. (dir.), Coastal Cattlemen's Assn. (dir.), Tex. and Southwestern Cattleraisers Assn. (dir.), Am. Quarter Horse Assn., Tex. Arts Alliance. Democrat. Presbyterian. Home and Office: Box 575 Devers TX 77538

BOZARTH, ROBERT STEPHEN, lawyer; b. Glendale, Calif., May 21, 1945; s. Marion Farrell and Elna Josephine (Haynes) B.; m. Marsha Ketcham, June 8, 1968; children—Howard Austin, Robert Belden. B.S., U. Va., 1967, J.D., 1975. Bar: Va. 1975. Law clk. Supreme Ct. Va., Richmond, 1975-76; assoc. McDonald & Crump, P.C., Richmond, 1976-81; assoc. counsel law div. Lawyers Title Ins. Corp., Richmond, 1982—. Vol. referee, coach Three Chopt Youth Soccer League, Richmond, 1981-83. Served to lt. USN, 1969-73. Mem. Va. Bar Assn., Richmond Bar Assn. Republican. Episcopalian. Club: Ridgetop Recreation Assn. Home: 1103 E Durwood Crescent Richmond VA 23229 Office: PO Box 27567 6630 W Broad St Richmond VA 23261

BOZONELOS, JAMES ANGELO, insurance company executive; b. Peru, Ill., July 14, 1937; s. Angelo Peter and Helen Ann (Orzechowski) B.; m. Sally Ann LePage, Dec. 29, 1956; children—Gregory James, Michelle Ann Bozonelos Lauletta, Mariellen E. Grad. pvt. sch., Peru, Ill. C.L.U. Sales rep. Rockford Life Ins. Co., Rockford, Ill., 1958-60, sales mgr., 1960-61, dist. mgr., Havana, Ill., 1961-73; v.p., sec., Rockford, Ill., 1974-81; dir. mgmt. tng. Liberty Nat. Life Ins. Co., Birmingham, Ala., 1982—; chmn. tng. com. Life Ins. Mktg. and Research Assn., 1981-82; dir. Southeastern Tng. Assn., 1985-86. Chmn. Mason County unit Am. Cancer Soc., Havana, Ill., 1972-73; tng. officer, Explorer Scouts, Birmingham, Ala., 1983-85. Served with USN, 1954-58. Decorated Commendation, U.S. Navy, 1957. Mem. Southeastern Tng. Dirs. Assn. (chmn. 1984-85, Accomplishment award 1985), Am. Soc. for Tng. and Devel. (pres. 1981-82), Gen. Agts. and Mgrs. Assn. (v.p. 1979-80), Nat. Assn. Life Underwriters, Am. Soc. C.L.U.S. Democrat. Roman Catholic. Club: Altadena Valley Country (Birmingham). Lodge: K.C. (grand knight 1972-73). Office: Liberty Nat Life Ins Co 2001 3d Ave S Birmingham AL 35233

BRABHAM, LEWIS CORNELIUS (NEIL), JR., engineering executive; b. Olar, S.C., July 2, 1929; s. Lewis C. and Mildred (Cook) B.; m. Sylvia Bash Estes, Aug. 22, 1952; children—Edward, Mary Elizabeth. Student U. S.C., 1946-47; Registered profl. engr., Fla. Electronics and elec. engr. Dixie Radio Supply, Columbia, S.C., 1952-55, DuKane Corp., St. Charles, Ill., 1955-58, Goddard Electronics, West Palm Beach, Fla., 1958-65, Adair & Brady Engrs., West Palm Beach, 1965-76; v.p., sec., ptnr. Brabham, Debay & Assocs., West Palm Beach, 1976—. Mem. West Palm Beach Bd. Adjustments and Appeals; past chmn. Fla. Hotel/Motel Ad-Hoc Fire Code Com.; vice chmn. Fla. Bd. Bldg. Codes and Standards; chmn. Palm Beach County Fire Code Com. Served with USN, 1947-53. Mem. Nat. Soc. Profl. Engrs., Fla. Engring. Soc., Elec. Council Fla. (past pres. East Coast chpt.), Constrn. Specifications Inst. (past pres. Palm Beach County). Democrat. Presbyterian. Home: 3217 Vincent Rd West Palm Beach FL 33405 Office: Brabham Debay & Assocs 2725 N Australian Ave West Palm Beach FL 33407

BRABSON, LEONARD ALLISON, obstetrician, gynecologist; b. Knoxville, Tenn., Apr. 22, 1948; s. Paul Hasson and Katherine Marie (Basham) B.; m. Sharon Bradley, June, 1968 (div. Mar. 1975); 1 son, Leonard Allison; m. Pamela Herron, Apr. 1975 (div. Mar. 1982); 1 stepson, Bryant Herron; 1 dau., Amanda Megan; m. Gail Martin, Aug. 22, 1982. B.S., U. Tenn., 1969; M.D., U. Tenn.-Memphis, 1973. Diplomate Am. Bd. Ob-Gyn. Intern, U. Tenn. Hosp., Knoxville, 1973-74, resident ob-gyn, 1974-77, vol. teaching faculty, 1977—; practice medicine specializing in ob-gyn, Knoxville, 1977—; mem. staff St. Mary's Med. Ctr., chmn. dept. ob-gyn, 1984-85; mem. staff Univ. Hosp. Mem. AMA, Am. Coll. Ob-Gyn, Am. Assn. Gynecologic Laparascopists, Am. Soc. Clin. Hypnosis, Tenn. Med. Assn., Knoxville Acad. Medicine (pres. —E— club 1982), E. Tenn. Ob-Gyn Soc. (pres. 1982), Am. Fertility Soc.; Cybele Soc., Royal Soc. Medicine. Methodist.

BRABSON, MAX LAFAYETTE, health care executive; b. Otto, N.C., Dec. 9, 1926; s. John Miller and Mary Elizabeth (McDowell) B.; m. Kathryn Louise Rice, Sept. 22, 1951; children—Mary Kathryn, Max L. B.S., U. Ga., 1950; M.H.A., Washington U., St. Louis, 1958. Adminstr., Middle Ga. Hosp., Macon, 1965-68, Americus-Sumter Co. Hosp., (Ga.), 1968-69; v.p. Charter Med. Corp., Macon, 1969-76; pres. Health Care Mgmt. Co., Columbus, Ga., 1976-77; pres., chief exec. officer Med. Ctr., Columbus, 1977—; dir. Fedn. Am. Hosps., Inc., 1970-75; mem. hosp. adminstrs. devel. program Cornell U., Ithaca, N.Y., 1961. Mem. adv. bd. dirs. Ret. Sr. Vol. Program, Columbus, 1977-81; bd. dirs. United Way, Inc., Columbus, 1979—, Blue Cross Blue Shield Ga.-Columbus, 1978—. Served to lt. col. USAR, 1944-61; PTO. Mem. Am. Coll. Hosp. Adminstrs., Ga. Hosp. Assn. (chmn. council on fin. Atlanta, 1982-83), Columbus C. of C. (bd. dirs. 1979-81). Club: Exec. of Columbus (pres. 1982-83). Lodge: Kiwanis (Columbus). Home: Route PO Box 19A Cataula GA 31804 Office: Med Center PO Box 951 Columbus GA 31994

BRADBURY, ROSANNE BROWN, speech/language pathologist; b. Norfolk, Va., Jan. 10, 1944; d. Melvin Dillard and Mattye Marie (Cox) Brown; B.S., U. Ga., 1968, M.Ed., 1971; m. Steve Banker, Aug. 24, 1962 (div.); m. Luke Lindley Bradbury, Dec. 13, 1974 (div.); children—Steve Bunker, Amy Bunker Hurtado. Speech pathologist Barrow County Schs., Winder, Ga., 1968-69, Madison County schs., Danielsville, Ga., 1969-70, Hall County Schs., Gainesville, Ga., 1971-72, Hope Haven Sch. for Retarded Children, Athens, Ga., 1972-73, Buford (Ga.) City Schs., 1973-75, Duval County Bd. Pub. Instrn., Jacksonville, Fla., 1975-79, Orange County Public Schs., Orlando, Fla., 1979—. Sallie Maude Jones scholar, U. Ga., 1966-68; USPHS grad. fellow, 1970-71. Mem. Am. Speech and Hearing Assn. (cert. of clin. competence), Duval Tchrs. United (faculty rep. 1977-79), Delta Zeta, Zeta Phi Eta, Kappa Delta Pi, Phi Kappa Phi. Mem. Disciples of Christ. Clubs: Order Eastern Star, Order Amaranth, Lotus Shrine Guild, U.S.S. Yosemite Wives (pres. 1977), U.S.S. Sarsfield Wives (pres. 1975). Editor, Speakeasy, Speech and Language Newsletter, 1982—. Home: 606 David St Winter Springs FL 32708 Office: 434 N Tampa Ave Orlando FL 32801

BRADEN, DANA DANIELLE, lawyer; b. Detroit, June 8, 1951; d. William A. and Marjorie L. (Badertscher) B. B.A., Mich. State U., 1973; J.D., Detroit Coll. Law, 1977; postgrad. U. Miami Law Sch., Fla., 1979-81. Bar: Mich. 1977, Fla. 1978. Asst. bank mgr. Community Nat. Bank, Pontiac, Mich., 1973-76;

asst. trust officer Genesee Bank, Flint, Mich., 1976-78; trust officer Sun Banks of Fla., Orlando, 1978-79; assoc. Storms Krasny et al, Melbourne, Fla., 1979, Raymond & Dillon, P.C., West Palm Beach, Fla., 1979-81; sole practice, West Palm Beach, 1981-85; prin. Braden & Shane, P.A., West Palm Beach and Ft. Lauderdale, Fla., 1985—. Author monthly newsletter Current Developments in the Taxation of Ins., 1982—. Republican precinct del., 1972; 2d vice-chair Rep. party Oakland County, Mich., 1972; bd. dirs. Big Bros./Big Sisters Brevard County, Fla., 1978. Joseph S. Burak scholar, 1977. Mem. Mich. Bar Assn., Fla. Bar Assn., ABA, Martin County Estate Planning Council (co-founder). Co-founder Planned Giving Council Palm Beach County, pres., 1982—. Congregationalist. Home: 4000 Shelley Rd S West Palm Beach FL 33407 Office: Suite 319 Forum III 1655 Palm Beach Lakes Blvd West Palm Beach FL 33401

BRADFORD, JACKIE, management executive; b. Hahira, Ga., Aug. 13, 1940; s. Olan Jackson and Leona Ruth (Pack) B.; m. Mary Ann Sellers, Feb. 29, 1964; 1 dau., Renee. B.A., David Lipscomb Coll., 1966; M.Ed., Ga. State U., 1971. With Pioneer Realty, Lawrenceville, Ga., 1982-83; owner, dir. Atlanta Superstar Sports Camps, 1978-83; cons. OSP, 1978-83; v.p., head basketball coach Greater Atlanta Christian Schs., 1968-83; v.p. sales Marathon Health Internat., Newport Beach, Calif., 1983—; cons. Christian schs.; lectr. Named Coach of Yr., State of Ga., 1971, 72, 77, Atlanta Tipoff Club, 1971, 72, 77. Mem. Ga. Athletic Coaches Assn. (v.p. 1981-83, dir. 1974-83). Clubs: Rotary (dir.), Atlanta Tipoff (pres. 1975-77, dir. 1971-83). Author: Spartan Diet-Basketball Players Handbook, 1981. Home: 1164 Sweetwater Cir Lawrenceville GA 30245 Office: PO Box 732 Suite 12 Lawrenceville GA 30246

BRADFORD, JAMES RONALD, nursing administrator; b. Swanton, Ohio, Mar. 23, 1938; s. Ronald and Estella (Jordan) B.; m. Rachel Carolyn Langford; children—Spencer, Stacey. B.S.N., Fla. State U., 1971; M.Nursing, U. Fla.-Gainesville, 1974. Cert. nursing adminstr. advanced. Dir. nursing Athens Community Hosp., Tenn., 1974-75; dir. nursing Carlsbad Regional Med. Ctr., N.Mex., 1975-77, West Volusia Meml. Hosp., Deland, Fla., 1977—. Pres. Am. Cancer Soc., West Volusia chpt., Deland, 1985-86. Served with U.S. Army, 1961-63. Mem. Fla. Soc. Hosp. Nursing Service Adminstrs. (pres. 1984-85). Republican. Baptist. Avocations: photography; carpentry. Home: 300 Raymore Ave Deland FL 32720 Office: West Volusia Meml Hosp Box 509 Deland FL 32720

BRADFORD, JAY TURNER, insurance executive, state legislator; b. Little Rock, Apr. 30, 1940; s. Turner and Chrystal (Jacobs) B.; m. Sue Beard, Aug. 28, 1960; 1 dau., Chrystal. B.A., Henderson Coll., 1963. Cert. ins. counselor. Ins. agt. Metropolitan Life Co., Pine Bluff, Ark., 1963-65, McLellan Ins. Co., Pine Bluff, 1968-76; pres. Bradford-Madding-Scallion-Eddins Inc., Pine Bluff, 1976—; pres. Pine Bluff Ins. Exchange, 1976—. Alderman, City of Pine Bluff, 1981-82; mem. Ark. State Senate, 1983—; mem. State of Ark. Revenue and Tax Com., 1983—. Named Boss of Yr., Southeast Ark. Ins. Women, 1975. Mem. Soc. Ins. Agts. (cert. ins. counselor), Ind. Ins. Agts. Ark. (treas. 1981—), Subiaco Alumni Assn. (pres. 1977). Democrat. Episcopalian. Lodge: Pine Bluff Civitan (pres. 1967). Office: Bradford-Madding-Scallion-Eddins 801 E 8th PO Box 836 Pine Bluff AR 71611

BRADFORD, MICHAEL LEE, consulting chemical engineering firm executive; b. Jackson, Ohio, July 18, 1942; s. Meredith Elmo and Doris Jean (Shear) B.; m. Patricia Gayle Guay, Mar. 16, 1968; children—Charles Shear, Christine Marie. B.S., Ohio U., 1964; M.S., Northwestern U., 1965. Process design engr. Ethyl Corp., Baton Rouge, 1965-73; chief process engr. G.R. Stucker & Assocs., Inc., Baton Rouge, 1973-77; founder, pres. M.L. Bradford Engrs., Inc., Baton Rouge, 1977—; mgr. process engring. Jacobs Engring. Group, Baton Rouge, 1982—. Grad. fellow Northwestern U., 1964-65. Mem. Am. Inst. Chem. Engrs. Democrat. Roman Catholic. Home: 11924 Fairhaven Dr Baton Rouge LA 70815 Office: Jacobs Engring 2155 Sorrel Ave Baton Rouge LA 70802

BRADFORD, TUTT S., publisher; b. Columbia, S.C., Apr. 30, 1917; s. Tutt S. and Zula (Bowen) B.; student Wofford Coll., 1934; m. Elizabeth Hendley, June 30, 1941; children—Nancy, Debbie. Pub. Cleve. Daily Banner, 1948-51; asst. to pres. Gen. Newspapers, 1951; pub. Bristol (Va.) Herald Courier, 1951-55, Maryville (Tenn.) Alcoa Daily Times, 1955-85. Pres. Blount County Indsl. Devel. Bd., 1970-72. Mem. bd. Audit Bur. Circulations, 1967-72; mem. devel. council U. Tenn., 1980-83; bd. dirs. Maryville Coll., 1974-79, 81—, Knoxville Symphony, Dulin Art Gallery, Bus. Trust for Art, Blount Indsl. Bd., Tenn. Tech. Found. Served with AUS, 1943-45; ETO. Recipient Disting. Service award Bristol Jr. C. of C., 1952, Maryville-Alcoa Jr. C. of C., 1958, 73. Mem. So. Newspaper Pubs. Assn. (dir. 1968-70), Blount County C. of C. (pres. 1960). Lodge: Kiwanis (pres. Maryville 1967). Home: 1901 Westwood St W Maryville TN 37801 Office: 307 E Harper St Maryville TN 37801

BRADFORD, WILLIAM DALTON, pathologist, educator; b. Rochester, N.Y., Nov. 2, 1931; s. William Leslie and Lenora Dee (Dalton) B.; m. Anne Bevington Harden, July 8, 1961; children—Scott Harden, Lisa Graham. B.A., Amherst Coll., 1954; M.D., Western Res. U., 1958. Diplomate Am. Bd. Pediatrics, Am. Bd. Anatomic Pathology. Intern in pathology Boston Children's Med. Ctr., 1958-59, resident in pediatrics, 1959-61; teaching fellow pathology Harvard Med. Sch., 1963-64; asst. prof. pathology Duke U., Durham, N.C., 1966-70, assoc. prof., 1970-81, prof., 1981—, assoc. dean, 1970-71, 74-78, 84—, dir. pediatric pathology, 1966—. Pres., Durham YMCA, 1978, bd. dirs., 1976-83. Served to lt. comdr. USN, 1961-63. Recipient Golden Apple award Student Med. Assn., 1969; Layman of Yr. award YMCA, 1974, 78, Mead Johnson fellow, 1963-64. Mem. Internat. Acad. Pathology, Am. Assn. Pathologists, Soc. Pediatric Research, Group for Research in Pathology Edn., Soc. Pediatric Pathology. Methodist. Office: Box 3712 Duke U Med Ctr Durham NC 27710

BRADHAM, DOUGLAS DONALDSON, health services researcher, educator; b. Roanoke, Va., June 20, 1950; s. Ingram Donaldson and Estelle Elizabeth (Huff) B.; m. Renee Lavern Ferree, June 5, 1971; children—Douglas Page, Stefan Ryan. A.B., U. N.C., 1972, M.P.H., 1975, M.A. in Econs., 1982, Dr.P.H., 1981. With Office of Chief Med. Examiner, State Bd. Health, Chapel Hill, N.C., 1972-75; assoc. dir. Agassiz Health Systems, East Grand Forks, Minn., 1975-78; research asst. health adminstrn. dept. Sch. Pub. Health, U. N.C., Chapel Hill, 1978-81; asst. prof. Coll. Medicine and Coll. Pharmacy, U. Fla., Gainesville, 1981-85, asst. dir. Ctr. for Health Policy Research, 1983-85; asst. prof. Coll. Pub. Health, U. South Fla., Tampa, 1986—; cons. VA, 1983—, Blue Cross of Fla., 1983—. Contbr. articles to profl. jours. Elder, Grace Presbyterian Ch., Gainesville, 1982-85, v.p., 1982-84, pres., 1984-85; bd. dirs., sec. North Central Fla. Planned Parenthood, 1982-84. Research grantee Fla. Dept. Health and Rehab. Services, 1981-85, U.S. Dept. MHS, Blue Cross/Blue Shield of Fla., 1983-85, Fla. Hosp. Cost Containment Bd., 1984—, Robert Wood Johnson Found., 1985—. Mem. Am. Econs. Assn., Am. Rural Health Assn., Am. Pub. Health Assn., Fla. Pub. Health Assn., U. N.C. Sch. Pub. Health Alumni Assn. Avocations: sailing; landscaping; golf. Home: 3225 NW 25th Ave Gainesville FL 32605 Office: Coll Pub Health U South Fla 13301 N 30th St MHH-104 Tampa FL 33612

BRADISH, WARREN ALLEN, internal auditor, operations analyst, management consultant; b. Adrian, Mich., June 9, 1937; s. Calvin Gamber and Florence Helen (Schulze) B.; m. Setsuko Arimatsu, May 18, 1959 (div.); children—Donna, John, Bradly, Jacqueline; m. 2d, Roberta Mary Kalil, Sept. 26, 1969. B.A. in Bus. Adminstrn. summa cum laude, St. Leo Coll., 1977; M.A. in Bus. Mgmt., Central Mich. U., 1980. Registered pvt. detective, Ga. Enlisted in U.S. Army, 1956, comd. officer, advanced through ranks to maj., 1976, intelligence officer, ret., 1976; edn. and tng. officer, State of Ga., 1977; mgmt. cons. Gov's office, Ga., 1977-80, dir. investigations Sec. State, 1980-82, dir. surveillance, specialized investigative services, 1982-83; internal auditor/ops. analyst Ga. Dept. Revenue, 1983—. Decorated Bronze Star. Mem. Am. Soc. Indsl. Security, Ga. Peace Officers Assn., Internat. Narcotic Enforcement Officers Assn., Nat. Assn. Chiefs of Police, Spl. Forces Decade Assn., Disabled Vets. Am., Ga. Assn. Security Personnel, Sigma Iota. Home: 4180 Will Lee Rd College Park GA 30349

BRADLEY, DAVID GILBERT, religion educator; b. Portland, Oreg., Sept. 1, 1916; s. Rowland Hill and Edith (Gilbert) B.; m. Gail Soules, Mar. 19, 1940 (dec. 1982); 1 child, Katherine Ann Bradley Johnson; m. Lorene Lutz Greuling, Dec. 27, 1984. A.B., U. So. Calif., 1938; postgrad. Drew Theol. Sem., 1938-39; B.D., Garrett Theol. Sem., 1942; M.A., Northwestern U. (Ill.), 1942; Ph.D., Yale U., 1947; postgrad. Sch. Oriental and African Studies, U. London, 1955-56. Asst. prof., chaplain Western Md. Coll., Westminster, 1946-49; asst. prof. dept. religion Duke U., Durham, N.C., 1949-59, assoc. prof., 1959-70, prof., 1970—; mem. faculty Garrett Sem., summer 1960, U. Va., Charlottesville, summer 1969, U. N.C., Chapel Hill, fall 1970; mem. So. Calif.-Ariz. Conf. Meth. Ch., 1939-51, N.C. Conf. United Meth. Ch., 1951-81. Author: A Guide to the World's Religions, 1963; Circles of Faith, 1966; The Origins of the Hortatory Materials in the Letters of Paul, 1977; also book revs. and articles. Mem. Sr. Screening Com. Fulbright-Hays in Religion, 1966-68; active civic groups, Durham. Gt. Religious Fund grantee to South and East Asia, 1969-70. Mem. Am. Soc. Study Religion (editor newsletter 1973—), AAUP, Am. Acad. Religion (program chmn. 1958, pres. so. sect. 1963-64), Assn. Asian Studies, N.C. Tchrs. Religion, Soc. Internat. Devel. (sec./treas. Research Triangle chpt. 1983-84). Democrat. Home: 2414 Perkins Rd Durham NC 27706 Office: Duke U Box 4735 Durham NC 27706

BRADLEY, JOHN HILTON, waste management company executive; b. Manila, May 12, 1936; s. Noble James and Amelia Mary (Langley) B.; student Pomona Coll., 1953-54, Am. U., 1965-66; B.S., U.S. Mil. Acad., 1958; grad. Army Command and Gen. Staff Coll., 1968; M.A., Rice U., 1970; m. Ann Marie Summa, Feb. 4, 1961; children—James Noble, Susan Paige, JohnHilton, Thomas Joseph. Commd. 2d lt. U.S. Army, 1958, advanced through grades to lt. col., 1971; dir. bicentennial activities U.S. Mil. Acad., 1973-77; dep. dir. plans, tng. and security, Ft. Leavenworth, Kans., 1977-78; ret., 1978; div. v.p. mgmt. devel. Browning Ferris Industries Inc., Houston, 1979—; chmn. Tex. Gov.'s Adv. Com. Mgmt. Tng., 1980. Pres., Ft. Leavenworth Mus. Assn., 1977-78; mem. West Point Mus. and Memorialization Bd., 1973-77; recorder, West Point Am. Revolution Bicentennial Com., 1973-77; speaker in field of mil. history, career of Douglas Mac Arthur. Decorated Bronze Star, Air medal, Meritorious Service medal (2), Army Commendation medal (2); Vietnamese Gallantry Cross. Mem. Am. Soc. Tng. and Devel., Am. Public Works Assn., Nat. Solid Waste Mgmt. Assn., Army Athletic Assn., Assn. Grads. U.S. Mil. Acad. Roman Catholic. Author: The Second World War: Asia and the Pacific, 1978; West Point and the Hudson Highlands in the American Revolution, 1976. Office: 14701 St Marys St Houston TX 77079

BRADLEY, JOHN M(ILLER), JR., forestry consulting firm executive; b. Birmingham, Ala., Mar. 20, 1925; s. John Miller and Frances Watkins (Davis) B.; m. Isabella Elmore, Feb. 14, 1953; children—John M. III, I. Jocelyn. Student U. Ala.-Tuscaloosa, 1941-42, 46-47; B.S. in Math., Samford U., 1948; B.S. in Forestry, U. Calif.-Berkeley, 1949; M.F., Yale U., 1950. Laborer, smoke chaser U.S. Forest Service, summers 1941, 47; foreman, project supt. U.S. Park Service, Yellowstone Nat. Park, 1948-49; founder/pres. So. Timber Mgmt. Service, Birmingham, 1950-63; chmn., pres. Resource Mgmt. Service, Birmingham, 1963—; mem. adv. com. on state and pvt. forestry Sec. Agr., Washington, 1972-76; U.S. del. 8th World Forestry Congress, Jakarta, Indonesia, 1975; mem. univ. council com. on forestry and environ. studies Yale U., 1985—; dir. Pamlico Corp., Contbr. articles on forestry to profl. jours. Pres., Search Found., Washington, 1971—; bd. dirs. Red Mountain (Sci.) Mus. Soc., Birmingham, 1976-84, pres., 1976-78; bd. dirs. Birmingham Hist. Soc., 1975-84, pres., 1977-79; bd. dirs. Red Mt. Museum, Birmingham, 1976-84, chmn., 1978-83; deacon Briarwood Presbyn. Ch., Birmingham. Mem. Soc. Am. Foresters (chmn. nat. conv. 1986), Assn. Cons. Foresters (sr. v.p. 1972-74, pres. 1974-76), Ala. Forestry Assn. (bd. dirs. 1985—, named to Hall of Fame 1984), Ala. Com. So. Timber Study, Newcomen Soc. U.S., Tau Beta Pi. Clubs: Birmingham Country, Inverness Country, The Club (Birmingham). Lodge: Rotary (Birmingham). Home: 5006 Applecross Rd Birmingham AL 35243 Office: Resource Mgmt Service Inc PO Box 43388 4650 US Hwy 280 E Birmingham AL 35243

BRADLEY, LAURENCE ALAN, clinical psychologist; b. Cleve., Sept. 13, 1949; s. Irving and Jeanne (Weil) B.; m. Gifford Weary, Dec. 28, 1974 (div. 1979); m. Elizabeth Wrenn, Oct. 3, 1981; children—Sean C. Sullivan, Samantha A.W. Sullivan. B.A. in Psychology, Vanderbilt U., 1971, Ph.D., 1975. Clin. intern Duke U. Med. Ctr., Durham, N.C., 1975-76; asst. prof. U. Tenn., Chattanooga, 1976-77, Fordham U., Bronx, N.Y., 1977-80; asst. prof. Bowman Gray Sch. Med., Winston-Salem, N.C., 1980-82, assoc. prof., 1982—, adminstrv. head, sect. on med. psychology, 1981—; adj. assoc. prof. U. N.C.-Greensboro, 1983—. Editor: (with others) Medical Psychology: Contributions to Behavioral Medicine, 1981; Coping with Chronic Disease: Research and Applications, 1983. Robert Wood Johnson Found. research grantee, 1983. Fellow Soc. for Personality Assessment; mem. Am. Psychol. Assn., Internat. Assn. Study of Pain, Am. Pain Soc., Sigma Xi, Phi Beta Kappa. Democrat. Avocations: whitewater rafting; skiing; cinema. Home: 2016 Gaston St Winston-Salem NC 27103 Office: Sect Med Psychology Bowman Gray Sch Medicine Winston-Salem NC 27103

BRADLEY, MARTHA WASHINGTON NUTTER, educator; b. East St. Louis, Ill.; d. Cecil Grafton and Mabel (Hunt) Nutter; m. George Washington Bradley, Feb. 20, 1960. B.S. in Edn., U. Va., 1951, M.Ed., 1960; diplome de la langue Française, Alliance Française, Paris, 1958; Ph.D. (NDEA fellow), Syracuse U., 1967. Tchr. elem. sch., East St. Louis, 1951-53, Long Beach, Calif., 1953-54, U.S. Army Dependent Schs., Europe, 1954-59, 60-61; reading cons. public schs., Fredericksburg, Va., 1961-62; instr. U. Va. Sch. Gen. Studies, 1962-63; asst. prof. edn. E. Tenn. State U., Johnson City, 1967-70, asso. prof. edn., 1970-76, prof., 1976—, chmn. univ. publs. com., 1979-80, chmn. univ. acad. honor day com., 1980-81, bd. dirs. Christian Student Fellowship, 1978-80; faculty adv. Student NEA, 1968-71. Trustee, George and Martha Washington Bradley Found., 1968-81, Johnson City, 1968-83, U. Va. Edn. Found., 1983—; bd. dirs. Sister City Town Affiliation, Johnson City, 1971—, 2d v.p., 1972-76; mem. Robert Young Cabin com. City of Johnson City, 1975-85; vol. service nat. appointee VA, 1973-80; bd. dirs. Appalachian Dist. council Girl Scouts U.S., 1978-79, U. Va. Edn. Found., 1983—. Mem. Nat. (life), Tenn., East Tenn. (pres. East Tenn. State U. unit 1977-78) edn. assns., Conf. English Edn. (evaluator com. to evaluate documents 1968—), Nat. Council Tchrs. English, DAR (chmn. service for vet. patients Tenn. 1971-74, 76-77, chpt. vice regent 1974-77, regent 1977-80, pres. Tenn. regents' club 1978-79, chpt. dir. 1980-83, chpt. mag. advt. chmn. 1980—), Daus. Am. Colonists (regent 1985—, chmn. Tenn. ann. assembly 1985), Internat. Reading Assn. (upper East Tenn. council research chmn. 1969-70), Bus. and Profl. Women's Club (chmn. nominating com. Tenn. fedn. 1972-73; dist. dir. 1974-75, fin. chmn. 1976-77, treas. 1977-78, local chmn. personal devel. com. 1969-70, local pres. 1971-72, 2d v.p. 1972-73; local chmn. by-laws com. 1973-75, chmn. young careerist com. 1975-76, legis. com. 1976-79), Am. Ednl. Research Assn., Nat. Soc. Study of Edn., AAUW (publicity chmn. 1968-70, corp. del. 1976-79, br. pres. 1976-80), Unaka Rock and Mineral Soc. (pres. 1969-70), Friends of the Reece Mus. (mem. edn. com. 1973-75), So. Garden Soc. (charter), Assn. for Preservation Tenn. Antiquities, Mensa (East Tenn. proctor 1975-79), Phi Kappa Phi (life, charter pres. East Tenn. State U. chpt. 1970-72), Kappa Delta Pi (life, counselor Zeta Iota chpt. 1968-80; Honor Key 1983), Delta Kappa Gamma (1st v.p. 1972-74), Phi Delta Kappa (life). Mem. Christian Ch. (pres. Women's council 1970-72, edn. com. 1970-82, bequest com. 1983—, missions com. 1982—, dir. Bible sch. 1971-73). Clubs: Wednesday Morning Music (yearbook com. 1971-74, chmn. Music Week com. 1974—), E. Tenn. State U. Women's Faculty (co-chmn. book com. 1969-70), v.p. 1971-72, pres. 1972-73). Office: Box 20110A East Tenn State U Johnson City TN 37614

BRADLEY, MATTHEW HENRY, III, cardiologist; b. Akron, Ohio, Aug. 7, 1926; s. Matthew Henry and Margot (Williams) B.; B.S., Kent State U., 1947; M.D., Ohio State U., 1951; m. Marian Young, July 1, 1950; children—Sandra Baden, Matthew, Kathleen, Laura. Intern, U.S. Naval Hosp., Pensacola, Fla., 1951-52; resident VA Hosp., Milw., 1955-58, U.S. Naval Sch. Aviation Medicine, Pensacola, 1952-53; practice medicine specializing in internal medicine and cardiology, Miami, 1958—; pres. med. staff, dir. Miami Heart Inst., also v.p., trustee; FAA med. examiner; dir. Bay Shore Bank of Fla., Sanifoam, Inc., Costa Mesa, Calif. Served with USNR, 1951-55. Fellow ACP, Am. Coll. Cardiology, Am. Coll. Chest Physicians; mem. AMA, Fla. Med. Assn., Dade County Med. Assn., Flying Physicians Assn., Vol. Physicians Vietnam. Contbr. articles to profl. jours. Home: 184 Park Dr Bal Harbour FL 33154 Office: 1160 Kane Concourse Miami Beach FL 33154

BRADLEY, NOLEN EUGENE, JR., personnel executive, educator; b. Memphis, Nov. 29, 1925; s. Nolen Eugene and Anice Pearl (Luther) B.; B.S., Memphis State U., 1951, M.A., 1952; Ed.D., U. Tenn., 1966; m. Eloise Mullins, Jan. 7, 1947; children—Sharon (Mrs. Brabson), Diana (Mrs. Wiley M. Rutledge), Nolen Eugene III, David Lee. Instr. polit. sci. Memphis State U., 1951-52; tchr. English, Messick High Sch., Memphis, 1952-56; asst. dean admissions Memphis State U., 1956-64; dir. State Agy. for Title I, Higher Edn. Act 1965, Div. Continuing Edn., U. Tenn., 1966-70; dean instrn. Vol. State Community Coll., Gallatin, Tenn., 1970-78; tutor, ednl. cons., 1978-79; personnel asst. Hoeganaes Corp., Gallatin, 1979-80, personnel mgr., 1980-82; dir. personnel Music Village U.S.A., Inc., Hendersonville, Tenn., 1984—. Served with AUS, 1944-46. Mem. Am. Assn. Sch. Adminstrs., Tenn. Adult Edn. Assn., Tenn. Edn. Assn., Omicron Delta Kappa, Pi Delta Epsilon, Phi Delta Kappa, Phi Kappa Phi. Baptist (deacon 1966—). Lion. Home: 907 Harris Dr Gallatin TN 37066

BRADLEY, RUNDY, financial analyst; b. Los Angeles, Apr. 26, 1952; s. Thomas Arthur and Dorothy Louise (McCracken) B. B.S. in Econs., U. Pa., 1974; M.B.A., Harvard Bus. Sch., 1977. Prin., Fayez Sarofim & Co., Houston, 1977—. Mem. Houston Soc. Fin. Analysts. Republican. Baptist. Club: Harvard Bus. Sch. (Houston). Avocations: swimming; skiing. Home: 5203 Memorial Dr Houston TX 77007 Office: Fayez Sarofim & Co Two Houston Ctr Suite 2907 Houston TX 77010

BRADLEY, S(HIRLEY) RAY, author, editor, engineer, consultant; b. Ottowa, Ill., Oct. 12, 1926; s. Walter E. and Mary A. (Kinkade) B.; m. Fay E. Gross, July 16, 1955; children—Gordon J., Bonnie E., Morgan D., Robyn S. Student U. Louisville, 1956, U. Ala., 1971, U. Tenn., 1976-78. Author/editor def. industries, 1955-66; author/editor, trainer NASA, Huntsville, Ala., 1966-73; quality assurance engr./trainer Nuclear Power Industry, TVA, Knoxville, 1973-83, cons. quality assurance engr., 1983—. Former pres. Ed. White Jr. High Sch., Huntsville. Mem. Nat. Mgmt. Assn., Am. Soc. Quality Control. Editor: IEEE mag. Home: 316 Hardwick Dr Knoxville TN 37923

BRADLEY, STERLING GAYLEN, university dean, biomedical research educator, consultant; b. Springfield, Mo., Apr. 2, 1932; s. Benn and Lora (Brown) B.; m. Lois Evelyn Lee, May 13, 1951 (div. 1973); children—Don, Evelyn, John, Phillip; m. 2d, Judith Schneider Bond Bradley, July 24, 1974; 1 son, Kevin. B.A., B.S., Southwest Mo. State U., 1950; M.S., Northwestern U., 1952, Ph.D., 1954. Instr. biology Northwestern U., Evanston, Ill., 1954; postdoctoral research trainee U. Wis.-Madison, 1954-56; instr., asst. prof., then assoc. prof. microbiology U. Minn., Mpls., 1956-63, prof. microbiology, 1963-68; prof., chmn. microbiology and immunology Va. Commonwealth U., Richmond, 1968-82, assoc. dir. Massey Cancer Ctr., 1982—, dean basic scis., 1982—; cons. Mpls. VA Hosp., 1961-68, Upjohn Co., 1960-68, E.R. Squibb & Sons, 1969-74. Pres., Sherwood Park Assn., 1983-84; chief pamunkey nation YMCA Indian Guides, 1982-83. Fogarty Ctr. sr. internat. fellow, 1978; recipient Charles Porter award Soc. Indsl. Microbiology, 1983. Fellow Va. Acad. Sci., AAAS; mem. Am. Acad. Microbiology, Am. Assn. Immunologists, Am. Soc. Microbiology (treas. 1985—), Soc. Toxicologists, Soc. Exptl. Biology and Medicine. Methodist. Contbr. articles to profl. jours. Home: 1324 Brookland Pkwy Richmond VA 23227 Office: MCV Sta Box 110 Richmond VA 23298

BRADLEY, THOMAS AUGUSTUS, communications educator; b. Danville, Va., Mar. 5, 1939; s. Augustus and Annie (Leake) B.; B.S., The Citadel, 1961; M.A., U. N.C., 1971; m. Patsy Jean Griswold, Aug. 27, 1967; children—Patricia Jean, Thomas Augustus. Tchr., media specialist Richland Dist. I Sch. System, Columbia, S.C., 1965-82; tchr. math. and sci. St. Peter's Sch., 1982-83; instr. communications U. S.C., Columbia, 1983—, Columbia Jr. Coll., 1984—; ednl. cons. Distinctive Ednl. Ctr., Columbia, 1983—; tutor Epworth Children's Home, Columbia, 1985—. Mem. adminstrv. bd. St. Mark United Meth. Ch., 1980-81; active United Way, YMCA Indian Guides. Served with U.S. Army, 1961-64. Mem. Palmetto State Tchrs. Assn., U. N.C. Alumni Assn., Assn. Citadel Men. Club: Garden Dale Swim and Racquet. Office: Columbia Jr Coll 3810 Main St Columbia SC 29203

BRADLEY, WILLIAM, optometrist, researcher; b. Kalamazoo, Mich., June 2, 1954; s. James Lewis and Thelma Mae (Brock) Rohrer; m. Milena Stekly, Dec. 14, 1974 (div. Nov. 1981); 1 dau., Cassandra; m. 2d, Sara Denice Click, Nov. 2, 1982. B.S., Ohio State U., 1976, O.D., 1978, M.S., 1978. Optometrist, Downtowner Eye Clinic, Mobile, Ala., 1978-81; practice optometry, Mobile, 1981—; mem. council on sports vision Bausch & Lomb, 1979-83, research fellow, 1977. Recipient Pride of Mobile award Jaycees, 1980; Optometric Recognition award Am. Optometric Assn., 1981, 84. Mem. Better Vision Inst., Am. Optometric Assn., Optometric Extension Program, Beta Sigma Kappa. Republican. Methodist. Home: 111 Cherry Circle Daphne AL 36526 Office: 3480-B Bel Air Mall Mobile AL 36606

BRADLEY, WILLIAM ARTHUR, state official, educational counselor; b. N.Y.C., Dec. 20, 1940; s. Clarence Dexter and Cleo Ruth (Gabriel) B.; m. Susie Kimball Pierce, May 7, 1966; 1 child, Heather Louise. A.A., St. Petersburg Jr. Coll., Fla., 1967; B.A., U. South Fla., 1969, M.A., 1971. Cert. tchr., vocat. rehab. counselor, Fla. Vocat. rehab. counselor State of Fla., Tampa, 1971-78; vocat. evaluator Hillsborough County Schs., Tampa, 1978-81, coordinator learning lab., 1981-84; exec. dir. region 17 coordinating council for adult and community edn. State of Fla., Tampa, 1984—, mem. vocat. evaluation adv. com., 1982—; mem. gen. adv. com. for vocat. edn. Hillsborough County Pub. Schs. Named Counselor of Yr., Hillsborough region, State of Fla., 1983. Mem. Am. Vocat. Assn., Fla. Vocat. Assn., Hillsborough Vocat. Assn., Fla. Council Adminstrs., Fla. Assn. of Deaf, Tampa C. of C. (mem. legis. task force 1984—), Tampa Artifact Soc., Tampa Gem and Mineral Soc. Republican. Avocations: artifact and fossil collecting; raising orchids; mineral collecting. Home: 1722 Ryan Dr Lutz FL 33549 Office: Regional Coordinating Council PO Box 22127 Tampa FL 33630

BRADLEY, WILLIAM LUTHER, manufacturing company sales executive; b. Nashville, Nov. 18, 1927; s. Maud and Elizabeth (Nelms) B.; m. Faye Marie Satterwhite, Nov. 23, 1926; children—Patricia Lynn, Barbara Elise, William Luther. Student, U. Houston, 1949-50. Purchasing agt. N.O. Nelson Co., Houston, 1950-56; sales rep. Bridgeport Brass Co., Houston, 1956-62; ind. mfrs.' rep., Houston, 1962-65; asst. to nat. sales mgr. Sunroc Corp., Glen Riddle, Pa., 1965-66, Eastern regional sales mgr., 1966-72, Mid-Am. regional sales mgr., Old Hickory, Tenn., 1972—; speaker at sales meetings and seminars; selection and tng. sales reps. Vol., Tenn. Mus. Fine Arts, Cheekwood in Nashville. Served with USN, 1944-48; PTO. Mem. Sigma Xi. Roman Catholic. Home and office: 545 Westport Dr Old Hickory TN 37138

BRADSHAW, CHARLES MARSHALL, physician; b. Springtown, Tex., Dec. 14, 1938; s. Joseph Kenton and Iris (Carter) B.; B.A., Tex. Tech U., 1961; M.D., U. Tex., 1965; m. Judy Cole, Nov. 22, 1966; children—Damon Robert, Lloyd Kenton; m. Louise Milke; 1 dau., Amy Louann. Intern, Meth. Hosp. of Dallas; gen. practice medicine, Crosbyton, Tex., 1966-69, Lubbock, Tex., 1969-70; resident dept. neurology, psychiatry U. Tex. Med. Br., Galveston, 1970-73; pvt. practice medicine specializing in psychiatry, neurology and clin. EEG, Fort Worth, 1970—; pres., co-dir. EEG Services, Inc., 1975—; chief psychiatry All Saints Hosp., 1984—, co-dir. Sleep Ctr., 1985—; mem. staffs various hosps. Served with USAF. Diplomate Am. Bd. Psychiatry and Neurology. Mem. AMA, Am. Med. EEG Assn. (pres. 1983-84), Tex. Med. Assn., So. EEG Soc., Tarrant County Med. Soc., Central Neuropsychiat. Assn., Ft. Worth Neurosci. Soc. (pres. 1986), Manic Depressive Assn. (dir. 1983—). Club: Fort Worth Internists. Office: Suite 722 1550 W Rosedale St Fort Worth TX 76104

BRADSHAW, COUNCIL FOY, pharmacist, consultant, educator; b. Lenoir, N.C., Apr. 30, 1938; s. Julius Foy and Virginia Onzelle (Cowan) B.; m. Velma Rene Tyre, Sept. 24, 1960; children—Theresa Onzelle, Zina Foye, John Council. B.S. in Pharmacy, U. N.C., 1961; postgrad. East Carolina U., 1981—. Pharmacist New River Pharmacy, Jacksonville, N.C., 1961-62, Taylor Drug Co., Washington, N.C., 1962-68; dir. pharmacy Edgecombe Gen. Hosp., Tarboro, N.C., 1968-85, asst. adminstr. ancillary services, 1971-78; dir. pharmacy Heritage Hosp. of Tarboro, 1985—; instr. nursing pharmacology Edgecombe Tech. Coll., Tarboro, 1984—. Active Washington and Tarboro Jaycees, 1967-75; high sch. referee. Mem. Am. Soc. Hosp. Pharmacists, N.C. Soc. Hosp. Pharmacists (pres. 1974-75). Republican. Episcopalian. Avocations: hunting; woodworking. Home: 905 Saint Andrew St Tarboro NC 27886 Office: Heritage Hosp 111 Hospital Dr Tarboro NC 27886

BRADSHAW, GLORIA CHARLIESE, media specialist, librarian; b. Loris, S.C., Oct. 9, 1936; d. Charlie Henry and Janie (Best) Johnson; m. George Washington Bradshaw, Jr., Sept. 16, 1961; 1 son by previous marriage, James Christopher. B.S., S.C. State Coll.-Orangeburg, 1959; M.S.L.S., N.C. Central U., 1970. Librarian, New Bethel Sch., Woodruff, S.C., 1959-61, Terrell's Bay Sch., Centenary, S.C., 1961-62, Finklea Sch., Loris, 1962-71; tchr. Green Sea

High Sch., S.C., 1971-74; librarian Main St. Elem. Sch., Conway, S.C., 1974-75, Conway High Sch., 1975—. Sec., Bayboro Community Polit. Orgn., Loris, 1972. Recipient Homemakers award Horry County Extension Homemakers, 1983. Mem. ALA, S.C. Assn. Sch. Librarians (regional coordinator), Waccamaw Library Assn. (pres.). Democrat. Methodist. Club: Horry County Extension Homemakers. Lodge: Order Eastern Star. Home: Route 3 Box 314 Loris SC 29569 Office: Conway High Sch Box 39 Conway SC 29526

BRADSHAW, HOWARD HOLT, management consulting company executive; b. Phila., Feb. 28, 1937; s. Howard Holt and Imojeen (Campbell) B.; m. Loretta Warren Sites, Aug. 13, 1982; children by previous marriage—Elaine Allen, Howard Holt. B.A., Yale U., 1958; postgrad., Duke U., 1958-60. Cert. mgmt. cons. Western Electric Co., various locations, 1960-68; head behavioral scis. cons. Celanese Fibers Co., Charlotte, N.C., 1968-71; pres. Orgn. Cons., Inc., Charlotte, 1972—; cons. in field. Author: Personal Power, Self Esteem and Performance, 1983; The Management of Self Esteem, 1981. Contbr. articles to profl. jours. Regional chmn. Constl. Party of Pa., Harrisburg, 1964-66; pres. Coordinated Planning League, Inc., Charlotte, 1972-74. Recipient cert. of appreciation Charlotte Police Dept., 1969, Mecklenburg County Com., 1970. Mem. Inst. Mgmt. Cons., Am. Psychol. Assn., Soc. Indsl. and Organizational Psychology, Am. Soc. Tng. and Devel., Orgnl. Devel. Network. Republican. Presbyterian. Home: 3031 Arundel Dr Charlotte NC 28209 Office: Orgn Cons 1913 Charlotte Dr Charlotte NC 28203

BRADSHAW, JOHN W., management consultant; b. N.Y.C., June, 1931; s. Walter J. and Maude Bradshaw; m. Elizabeth Tucker Pierce, Oct. 12, 1957; children—Margaret A., John E., Christopher P. B.S., Cornell U., 1953. Dir. employee relations GTE, Stamford, Conn., 1957-74; v.p. Rust Engring., Birmingham, Ala., 1974-76; v.p. Boyden Assocs., Houston, 1977-82, Lamalie Assocs., Houston, 1983; sr. v.p. Paul R. Ray & Co., Houston, 1983—; vis. lectr. U. Ala., Rice U., Clarkson U. Grad. Bus. Sch. Served to 1st lt. USAF, 1954-57. GTE fellow Pres. Exec. Interchange, Washington, 1971-72. Mem. Cornell Univ. Alumni Assn. Republican. Episcopalian. Club: Houston Racquet. Home: 14919 LaCosta Ln Houston TX 77079 Office: 1010 Lamar Houston TX 77002

BRADY, PEGGY JOE, oil company executive, consultant; b. Grimsley, Tenn., May 24, 1941; d. Paul Earl and Daisy Elease (Demonbreun) Stults; m. Robert Collins Whited, Oct. 9, 1959 (dec. July 1975); children—Paula Diane, Robert Wayne, Wesley Dale (dec.); m. James Dexter Brady, Mar. 10, 1984. A.B., U. Tenn., 1972-73. Insp. Colonial Mfr., Jamestown, Tenn., 1957-60; clk. Frisch's, Inc., Dayton, Ohio, 1960-64, Tenn. Dept. Pub. Health, Nashville, 1967-69; acct. Tenn. Dept. Safety, Nashville, 1969-73; service rep. IRS, Nashville, 1973-74; pvt. practice acctg., Crossville, Tenn., 1977-79; exec. asst. Vol. Energy, Inc., Crossville, 1979-82; corp. officer H. Stone Well Service, Inc., Crossville, 1982—; owner Brady Enterprises; cons. to oil and gas industries. Bd. dirs. Community Action Services Cumberland County; counselor Wautauga council Boy Scouts Am., 1968-69; advisor Am. Inst. for Cancer Research, 1984-85. Mem. Tenn. Oil and Gas Assn., Nat. Assn. Female Execs., Internat. Platform Assn. Lodge: Order Eastern Star. Office: Harold Stone Well Service Inc Hwy 127 PO Box 2768 Crossville TN 38555 also Brady Enterprises Hwy 127 PO Box 2646 Crossville TN 38555

BRADY, ROBERT THOMAS, mail order company financial executive; b. Glen Ridge, N.J., May 16, 1947; s. Thomas Laurence and Marjorie Winnifred (Sultzer) B.; children—Erik Paine, Caroline Alice. B.S. in Commerce, U. Va., 1969. Staff auditor, sr., mgr. Arthur Andersen & Co., Boston, 1969-78; dir. fin. mgmt. Am. Tourister, Inc., Warren, R.I., 1978-80; controller, v.p. fin. The Stuart McGuire Co. Inc., Salem, Va., 1980-82, sr. v.p. fin. and adminstrn., treas., 1982-84, exec. v.p., treas., 1984—, also pres. subs. MarkeTechs. Mem. Am. Inst. C.P.A.s, Va. Soc. C.P.A.s. Office: 115 Brand Rd Salem VA 24156

BRADY, SCOTT THOMAS, civil engineer; b. Fulton County, Ga., Apr. 4, 1956; s. Thomas Reid and Margaret Elizabeth (Muckenfuss) B.; m. Gloria Ann Carroll, June 24, 1978. B.C.E., Ga. Inst. Tech., 1977, M.S.C.E., 1978. Registered profl. engr., Tenn., Ga., Ala., Fla. Assoc. geotech. engr. Froehling & Robertson, Inc., Greenville, S.C., 1978-80; civil engr. TVA, Knoxville, 1980-82; dir. engring., sr. geotech. engr. Hill-Staton Engrs., Inc., Columbus, Ga., 1982-84; v.p. Delta Assocs., Inc., Sarasota, Fla., 1984—. Adv. bd. Musuclar Injuries and Skeletal Diseases Found., 1979—. Named Outstanding Vol., Muscular Injuries and Skeletal Diseases Found., 1983. Mem. ASCE (assoc.). Office: 420 Braden Ave Suite 202 Sarasota FL 34243

BRADY, WILLIAM MILNER, oil company executive, geophysicist; b. Mex., Nov. 26, 1945; came to U.S., 1947; s. William Connolly and Kathryn (Annis) B.; m. Ruth Annette Hartmann, Sept. 18, 1970 (div.). Student, U. So. Calif., 1962-64, U. Mich., 1964-65; B.S. in Geology, U. Tex., 1969; postgrad. UCLA, 1974-76. Geophysicist, Eltres/Richard Brewer & Assocs., 1978-80; gen. ptnr. Alpine Resources, Tex., 1980-85, Ashton Resources Ltd., Houston, 1983—; cons. Katana Belize Ltd., Denver, 1982-85, D&S Belize Ltd., Calgary, Can., 1982-85, Fairfield Indsl. Belize, Houston, 1978-80, Basic Resources Ltd., N.Y.C., 1973-78. Patentee in field. Mem. Am. Assn. Petroleum Geologists, Soc. Am. Inventors. Clubs: St. Anthony (San Antonio); Soc. War 1812 (New Orleans). Office: PO Box 218431 Houston TX 77084

BRAGG, G., computer company executive; b. 1932. B.S. in Bus. Adminstrn., Pepperdine U., 1954; postgrad. U. So. Calif., UCLA, Free U. Berlin. With N.Am. Rockwell, 1959-71; self-employed, 1971-73; with Collins Radio, 1973-74; v.p. corp. devel. Memorex Corp., 1974-81; pres. Telex Computer Products Inc., Tulsa, 1981—, also dir.; group v.p. Telex Corp. Office: Telex Computer Products Inc 6422 E 41st St Tulsa OK 74135

BRAGG, ROBERT LLOYD, psychiatrist; b. Jackson, Miss., Nov. 3, 1916; s. Jubie Barton and Anna Amelia (Smith) B. B.S., Fla. A&M U., 1936; M.A., Boston U., 1938; M.D., Columbia U., 1952; M.P.H., Harvard U., 1955. Diplomate Am. Bd. Psychiatry and Neurology. Intern, USPHS Hosp., S.I., 1952-53; gen. physician Bur. Indian Affairs, S.D., 1953-54; resident in preventive medicine N.Y.C. Health Dept., 1955-56; resident in psychiatry Medfield State Hosp., Harding, Mass., 1956-57, Mass. Gen. Hosp., Boston, 1957-60; asst. prof. psychiatry Harvard U. Med. Sch. at Mass Gen. Hosp., 1960-73; prof. psychiatry, vice chmn. for psychiat. edn., assoc. dean for spl. projects U. Miami (Fla.), 1973—; cons. Wellesley Pub. Sch. System (Mass.), 1960-73. Contbr. articles on psychol. disability and effects of hysterctomy to med. jours. Served to capt. U.S. Army, 1941-46. Grantee NIMH, 1960-73, 74-83. Fellow Am. Psychiat. Assn., Am. Pub. Health Assn.; mem. South Fla. Psychiat. Soc., Fla. Med. Assn., Dade County Med. Assn. Democrat. Congregationalist. Home: 1199 NW 88th St Miami FL 33150 Office: U Miami Sch Medicine Dept Psychiatry D-29 PO Box 016960 Miami FL 33101

BRAHM, NANCY CARTER, pharmacist; b. Borger, Tex., Jan. 27, 1953; d. Everett Lewis and Margaret Elizabeth (Chapman) Carter; m. Richard Alan Brahm, Mar. 20, 1976; children—Rebecca Elizabeth, Matthew Alan. B.S. in Pharmacy, U. Houston, 1975. Registered pharmacist, Tex. Chief pharmacist Metro Pharmacy, Inc., Houston, 1976-78; mng. pharmacist Avalon Drug Co., Houston, 1978-83; staff pharmacist Walgreens, Houston, 1983—; cons. Crisis Hotline, Houston, 1976-77, R. Hartgraves, M.D., Houston, 1978-83. Interim sec. Spring Branch Woods Civic Assn., Houston, 1983. Mem. Tex. Pharm. Assn., U.S. Judo Assn., Psi Chi. Republican. Presbyterian.

BRAIN, WALLACE THOMAS, JR., printing company executive; b. Warren, Ohio, June 11, 1945; s. Wallace Thomas and Helen Ann B.; m. Janet Ann von Behren, Aug. 24, 1973; children—Kevin Wallace, Kristin Jane, Scott Thomas, Melissa Ann. Student, Ohio State U., 1963-67, Youngstown State U., 1967-69. With computer ops. dept. Packard Electric Corp., Warren, 1968-69; co-owner Diversified Products, Ashtabula, Ohio, 1970-71; pres., chief exec. officer Suncolor Graphics, Inc., Pompano Beach, Fla., 1971—. Served with USNR, 1963-69. Mem. Nat. Assn. Printers and Lithographers, Internat. Assn. Printing House Craftsmen (past pres.), Printing Industry of South Fla., Entrepreneurs Club Broward County (past pres.), Pompano Beach Jaycees (past pres.). Republican. Presbyterian.

BRAINARD, HARRY GRAY, retired economics educator; b. Rochester, N.Y., Aug. 16, 1907; s. Harry Cummings and Anna (Conner) B.; m. Elizabeth McEvoy, July 10, 1936. B.S., U. N.C., 1930, M.S., 1931; Ph.D., U. Ill., 1935. Asst. prof. The Citadel, Charleston, S.C., 1935-37; prof., head dept. econs. So. Ill. U., Carbondale, 1937-46; prof. Mich. State U., East Lansing, 1946-74, prof. econs. emeritus, 1974, acting head, dept. econs., 1960, 61; economist Dept. Labor, Washington, 1937, Office Price Adminstrn., Washington, 1942-45, War Dept., 1945, Research Div. Gen. Hdqrs., Japan, 1946; vis. prof. U. N.C., Chapel Hill, 1946, 1979, U. Ariz., Tucson, 1962, Old Dominion U., Norfolk, Va., 1979-80; lectr. George Washington U., 1944; acting dir. Bur. Bus. Econ. Research, 1966; cons. Agy. Internat. Devel. Contract Ministry Edn., Turkey, 1967-69, Appropriations Com. U.S. House Reps., 1951, 52, Air War Coll., Maxwell AFB Ala., 1964, Naval War Coll., Newport, R.I., 1965. Author: International Economics and Public Policy, 1954; Economics in Action, 1959; International Economic Relations, 1972 (in Turkish). Contbr. chpts. to books, articles to profl. jours. Mem. quota com. Mich. United Fund, Lansing, 1956-67. Recipient Disting. Service Commendation U.S. Naval War Coll., 1965-66. Mem. Midwest Econs. Assn. (pres. 1965-66), Am. Econs. Assn., Beta Gamma Sigma, Delta Upsilon. Democrat. Episcopalian. Avocations: photography; travel. Home: 43 Oakwood Dr Chapel Hill NC 27514

BRAINARD, JAYNE DAWSON, club woman; b. Amarillo, Tex., Nov. 1; d. Bill Cross and Evelyn (McLane) Dawson; A.B., Oklahoma City U., 1950; m. Ernest Scott Brainard, Nov. 26, 1950; children—Sydney Jane, Bill Dawson. Sec.-treas. E.W. Brainard, Inc.; v.p. J.T. Cattle Co.; guardian Camp Fire Assn., 1960-65; vol. N.W. Tex. Hosp. Aux., 1960-63; state chmn. Am. heritage DAR, 1963-67, vice regent chpt., 1963-66, regent, 1966-68, state historian Tex. soc., 1967-70, state chmn. marshalls Tex. soc., 1967-70, 73-76, nat. vice chmn. marshal com., 1969-79, Tex. rec. sec., 1970-73, vice regent Tex. soc., 1976-79, state regent Tex. Soc., 1979-82, state parliamentarian Tex. Soc., 1982-85, mem. state organizing com., 1967-70, mem. by-law revision com., 1974-75, Tex. conf. chmn., 1975, 78, nat. vice chmn. motion picture commn., 1971-74, Tex. chmn. State Regents Project, 1973-76, mem. state speakers staff, 1973—, nat. chmn. State Regents dinners, 1980-81, pres. chpt. Regents' club, 1974, state vice chmn. nat. def., 1973-76, state mem. fin. com., pres. Nat. Vice Regents Club, 1977-78, mem. Nat. Officers' Club, 1979—, area rep. nat. speakers staff, 1977-85, pres. state officers club, 1980-81, organizing pres. Children of Am. Revolution, 1963-66, state chmn., mem. Nat. Chmns. Assn., 1980—; organizing regent Daus. Am. Colonists, 1972-75, state chmn. radio-TV com., 1975—, state chmn. Yorktown Bicentennial Club, 1981; bd. pres. AAUW, 1963-65, mem. state library com., 1967-69; sec.-treas. group League of Democratic Women, 1964; pres. Amarillo Republican Women's Club, 1968, v.p., 1972, pres., 1973; pres. Panhandle Geol. Soc. Aux., 1959; pres. Speaking of Living Study Club, 1962-63, 77-78, sec., 1974-75; pres. Starlighters Dance Club, 1963-64; bd. dirs., chmn. pub. relations Amarillo Little Theater; chmn. leaders assn. Amarillo Camp Fire Council, Inc., 1964-69, 75—, pres. bd. dirs., 1977-78; mem. steering com. Nat. Library Week, Amarillo, 1964-68; bd. dirs. Amarillo Fine Arts Council, 1966-68, Amarillo Heart Assn., 1972-73; pres. Amarillo Little Theatre, 1968-69; mem. Revitalize Amarillo Com., vol. St. Anthonys Hosp. Recipient medal of appreciation SAR, 1975, Martha Washington award, 1982. Profl. registered parliamentarian. Mem. U.D.C., United Daus. of 1812 (regent 1979, state chmn. 1984—), Nat. Assn. Parliamentarians (pres. unit 1980-81, v.p. 1985-86), Daus. Colonial Wars, Internat. Platform Assn., Amarillo Art Alliance, Amarillo Symphony Guild, Amarillo Geneal. Soc. (pres. adv. bd. 1982-84, nat. chmn. 1984-86), St. Anthony's Hosp. Aux. (vol.), Nat. Soc. So. Dames. Editor: Texas Society DAR Cookbook, 1972; Texas Daughters Revolutionary Ancestors, 4 vols., 1975. Home: 2119 S Lipscomb St Amarillo TX 79109 Office: Box 1101 Amarillo TX 79105

BRAITHWAITE, JAMES ROLAND, music educator, organist; b. Boston, Feb. 28, 1927; s. James Arthur and Ina Payne (Miller) B.; m. Drina Stewart, Sept. 4, 1960; children—Elisa Diane, Roland Alexander. Mus.B., Boston U., 1948, M.A., 1950, Ph.D., 1967. Prof. music Talladega Coll., Ala., 1952—, program dir., 1967-74, head music dept., 1969-76, chmn. humanities div., 1967-71, dean, 1974-81, 83-84. Mem. editorial com. Administration of a Curriculum Experiment. Contbr. articles to profl. jours. Bd. dirs. Health Systems Agy., Gadsden, Ala., 1976-82. Served with U.S. Army, 1950-52. NEH fellow, 1985. Mem. Am. Guild Organists, Am. Musicol. Soc., AAUP, Phi Mu Alpha, Pi Kappa Lambda. Democrat. Episcopalian. Avocation: jogging. Home: 706 W Battle St Talladega AL 35160 Office: Talladega Coll 627 W Battle St Talledga AL 35160

BRAME, JOSEPH ROBERT, III, lawyer; b. Hopkinsville, Ky., Apr. 18, 1942; s. Joseph Robert and Atwood Ruth (Davenport) B.; m. Mary Jane Blake, June 11, 1966; children—Rob, Blake, Virginia, John. B.A., Vanderbilt U., 1964; LL.B., Yale U., 1967. Bar: Ky. 1968, Va. 1968. Assoc., McGuire, Woods & Battle, Richmond, Va., 1967-72, ptnr., 1972—; lectr. in field. Mem. adv. bd. Salvation Army, Richmond, 1980—; bd. dirs. Am. Vision, Atlanta, Clearinghouse for Edn. Choice, N.C.; troop com. chmn. Robert E. Lee council Boy Scouts Am., Richmond, 1980—. Mem. ABA, Va. State Bar (chmn. sect. A 3d dist. com.), Va. Bar Assn., Def. Research Inst., Christian Legal Soc. Republican. Presbyterian. Contbr. articles to profl. jours. Office: 1 James Center Richmond VA 23219

BRAMLETT, JAMES LAWRENCE, computer company executive, consultant; b. Belzoni, Miss., Sept. 15, 1947; s. Leffel and Mavis Ozzell (Upchurch) B.; m. Susan Darlene Bailey, Oct. 5, 1980; 1 son, James Lawrence. B.S., U. So. Miss., 1976. Tchr. pub. schs., Marion County, Miss., 1970-71; operating mgr. Valve Mart, Hattiesburg, Miss., 1975-76; sr. programmer Anchor Wire, Goodlettsville, Tenn., 1976-78; mgr. systems programming Faber-Castell, Lewisburg, Tenn., 1978-79; data processing mgr. United Way, Nashville, 1979-81; dir. data processing Fischer Ednl. Systems, Nashville, 1981—; cons. Standard Candy Co., Nashville, 1983. Served to sgt. USAF, 1971-75. Mem. Data Processing Mgmt. Assn., Nashville Jaycees (pres. 1978-79), Kappa Mu Epsilon. Democrat. Episcopalian. Home: 8300 Sawyer Brown Rd Apt D-305 Nashville TN 37221 Office: Fischer Ednl Systems 2 Internat Plaza Suite 910 Nashville TN 37217

BRANAN, CAROLYN BENNER, accountant, lawyer; b. Wiesbaden, Fed. Republic Germany, Mar. 7, 1953; came to U.S., 1958; d. Huebert Harrison and Kathryn Wilfreda (Diggs) Benner; m. Robert Edwin Branan, Oct. 3, 1981. B.A. in Philosophy, U. S.C., 1973, J.D., 1976. Bar: S.C. 1977, U.S. Dist. Ct. S.C. 1977, U.S. Ct. Appeals (4th cir.) 1977; C.P.A., N.C. Sole practice law, Columbia, S.C., 1977-79; mgr. Deloitte Haskins & Sells, Charlotte, N.C., 1979—; cons. Gov.'s Bus. Council Task Force on Infrastructure Financing, 1983. Contbr. articles to profl. jours. Mem. exec. com., v.p., chmn. budget com. Charlotte Opera Assn., 1981—; exec. com., chmn. 1st and 2d ann. funding campaigns N.C. Opera, 1982—; exec. com. mayor's study com. Performing Arts Ctr., Charlotte, 1983—; mem. adv. council, chmn. performing arts Springfest, Charlotte, 1982—; fin. chmn. Opening of New Charlotte Transit Mall, 1984-85; bus. adv. council Queens Coll., Charlotte, 1984—. Mem. ABA (chmn. important devels. regulated pub. utilities tax sect. 1984—), N.C. Bar Assn., S.C. Bar Assn., Charlotte Estate Planning Council, Nat. Assn. Accts. (bd. dirs., dir. profl. devel., dir. community affairs 1979-84), N.C. Assn. C.P.A.s, Founders Soc. of Charlotte Opera Assn. (life). Episcopalian. Club: Charlotte City. Home: 530-A N Poplar St Charlotte NC 28202 Office: Deloitte Haskins & Sells 2100 So Nat Ctr Charlotte NC 28202

BRANCH, GARY LEO, college president, consultant; b. Birmingham, Ala., Sept. 25, 1942; s. Leo Frank and Mable (Tibbet) B.; m. Janis Dianna Miller, Nov. 1, 1945; children—Gary Leo, Tracy Dianna. B.S., U. Ala., 1965, M.A., 1967; LL.D., Livingston U., 1981. Counselor to men, U. Ga., Athens, 1967-68; asst. dir. student affairs Floyd Jr. Coll., Rome, Ga., 1970-71; assoc. dean student affairs Troy State U. (Ala.), 1971-75, dean enrollment and counseling services, 1975-78; pres. Brewer State Jr. Coll., Fayette, Ala., 1979-81; pres. James H. Faulkner State Jr. Coll., Bay Minette, Ala., 1981—; cons. services in higher edn. Mem. Ala. Postsecondary Policy Adv. Com.; mem. Regional Employment and Tng. Adv. Council; pres. Fayette County Heart Assn.; chmn. Troy Recreation and Day Care Bd.; chmn. sustaining membership drive for Pike County, Ala. council Boy Scouts Am. Named Outstanding Young Man Fayette County, 1980. Mem. Nat. Assn. Student Personnel Adminstrs., So. Coll. Personnel Assn., Am. Assn. Collegiate Registrars and Admissions Officers, So. Assn. Collegiate Registrars and Admissions Officers, Ala. Assn. Collegiate Registrars and Admissions Officers, Ala. Council Jr. and Community Coll. Presidents, Ala. Jr. and Community Coll. Assn. (pres.-elect 1984-85), Ala. Assn. Coll. Adminstrs. (pres.-elect 1984-85), Bay Minette C. of C. (bd. dirs.), North Baldwin County Ministerial Assn. (pres. 1983), Omicron Delta Kappa (nat. editor The Circle 1978-80, Meritorious Service award 1979, Disting. Service Key 1980), Delta Chi. Mem. Assembly of God. Home: College Dr Bay Minette AL 36507 Office: Faulkner State Jr Coll Hwy 31 S Bay Minette AL 26507

BRANCH, JOSEPH, state justice; b. Enfield, N.C., July 5, 1915; s. James C. and Laura (Applewhite) B.; LL.B., Wake Forest Coll., Winston-Salem, N.C., 1938; LL.D., Campbell U., 1981; m. Frances Jane Kitchen, Dec. 7, 1946; children—Jane Branch, James C. Admitted to N.C. bar, 1937; individual practice law, Enfield, 1938-45; partner firm Dunn and Johnson, Enfield, 1945-66; asso. justice Supreme Ct. N.C., 1966—, chief justice, 1979—; dir. Enfield Savs. and Loan Assn., Peoples Bank and Trust Co., Enfield; atty., dir. Halifax Mut. Fire Ins. Co. Mem. N.C. Gen. Assembly, 1947-53; legis. counsel to govs. N.C., 1957, 65; chmn. Halifax County Democratic Party, 1957-63; del. Dem. Nat. Conv., 1956; trustee Wake Forest U., 1966-68, 71-73, 75-77, 79-80, chmn., 1970-71; trustee Wesleyan Coll., Rocky Mount, N.C.; deacon Enfield Bapt. Ch. Served with U.S. Army, 1943-45. Recipient Alumni Service award Wake Forest U. Sch. Law, 1971; Distinguished Service citation Wake Forest U., 1974, Carroll Wayland Weathers Disting. Alumnus award, 1980. Mem. N.C., Wake County, Halifax County bar assns., N.C. State Bar. Clubs: Enfield Lions (past pres.), Masons. Office: PO Box 1841 Raleigh NC 27602

BRANCH, WILLIAM TERRELL, urologist; b. Paragould, Ark., Dec. 7, 1937; s. William Owen and Mary Rose (Dempsey) B.; B.S. (hon.), Ark. State U., 1963; B.S., U. Ark., Little Rock, 1966, M.D., 1971; m. Mary Fletcher Cox, Dec. 11, 1965; 1 dau., Ashley Tucker. Adminstrv. asst. mental retardation planning State Ark., Little Rock, 1964-66; intern U. So. Fla. Sch. Medicine, Tampa, 1971-72, surg. resident, 1972-73, urology resident, 1973-76, chief resident, 1975-76; practice medicine specializing in urology, Tampa, 1976—; clin. assoc. prof. U. South Fla. Sch. Medicine, Tampa, 1976—, adv. com. Suncoast Telecommunications Systems; cons. urology Tampa VA Hosp., 1977—; credentials com. St. Joseph's Hosp. of Tampa; co-chmn. surgery, mem. exec. com. Meml. Hosp., Tampa, 1978—, chief of staff, 1982-84; vice-chief urology Tampa Gen. Hosp., 1978-80, chief urology, 1980-82; mem. Profl. Health Care Found., Tampa, 1978—; mem. adv. bd. for West Coast of Fla., Glendale Fed-Savs. and Loan Assn., 1983-85; mem. adv. bd. Beneficial Savs. Bank, Tampa, 1985—. Mem. Priorities 21st Century Com., Tampa, 1981—, Tampa Bd. Ballet, 1980; bd. dirs., mem. exec. com. United Way of Tampa; trustee Meml. Hosp. of Tampa; med. adv. bd. Nat. Kidney Found. of Fla. Named Outstanding Intern, U. South Fla. Sch. Medicine, 1971-72. Diplomate Am. Bd. Urology. Fellow ACS (credentials com. Dist. 4 Fla. 1981—, exec. com. Fla. chpt. 1984—); mem. Am. Urol. Assn., Royal Soc. Medicine (London), AMA (Physicians Recognition award 1977, 80, 83, 85, physician research and evaluation panel 1984-85), Fla. Urol. Soc. (Milton Copeland award 1976, mem. exec. council 1979-81), Hillsborough County Med. Assn. (treas. 1981, exec. council 1979-81, sec. 1983-84, treas. polit. action com. 1984), Fla. Med. Soc. (Cons. editor jour., council on health care fin. 1981-82, del. 1981; chmn. com. bus. and industry 1981), Greater Tampa C. of C. (bd. govs. 1982—, named Tampa Super Star 1983), Tampa Hist. Soc., Tampa Horse Show Assn. (bd. dirs. 1984—). Clubs: University, Yacht and Country (bd. govs. 1984—), Ye Mystic Krewe of Gasparilla, Centre (Tampa). Home: 909 Golfview St Tampa FL 33609 Office: 2919 Swann St Suite 303 Tampa FL 33609

BRAND, EDWARD CABELL, mail order company executive; b. Salem, Va., Apr. 11, 1923; s. William F. and Ruth (Cabell) B.; m. Shirley Hurt, June 20, 1964; children—Sylvia, Richie, Liza, Miriam, John, Edward, Marshall, Caroline. Grad. Va. Mil. Inst., 1944; student seminars Harvard Bus. Sch., 1966-69, U. Va. Grad. Sch. Bus., 1966-69. Econ. analyst Intelligence Office, Berlin Mil. Govt., 1944-47; with State Dept., Europe, 1947-49; with Ortho-Vent Shoe Co. (now Stuart McGuire Co.), Salem, Va., 1949—, sales mgr., 1949-52, v.p., 1953-62, pres., 1962—, chmn. bd., chief exec. officer, 1973—; pres. Brand Edmonds Assocs. Advt., Salem, 1956-66, chmn. bd., 1962-81; dir. First Va. Bank Roanoke W., Salem, First Va. Banks, Inc., Falls Church, Va. Pres., Total Action Against Poverty in the Roanoke Valley, 1965—; bd. dirs. The Woodlands Conf. (Tex.), 1981—; bd. advisers Inst. Socioecon. Studies; mem. exec. council Conf. Bd.; mem. Roanoke Valley Council on Community Services; mem. Commn. on Block Grants, Commonwealth of Va., 1982—. Served to capt. U.S. Army, 1944-47. Decorated Bronze Star medal; recipient Good Citizen of Yr. award Salem/Roanoke County C. of C., 1979; Nat. VISTA award, 1980. Mem. Direct Selling Assn. (past dir., Hall of Fame award), Am. Mgmt. Assn. (mem. pres. assn.), Direct Mail Mktg. Assn., Chief Execs. Assn., C. of C. U.S., Newcomen Soc. N.Am., Young Pres.' Orgn. (past bd. dirs.), U.S. Assn. of Club of Rome, Archaeol. Soc. Va., Roanoke Valley Hist. Soc. Presbyterian. Clubs: Roanoke Country, Hunting Hills Country (Roanoke, Va.). Home: 701 W Main St Salem VA 24153 Office: Stuart McGuire Co Inc 115 Brand Rd Salem VA 24156

BRAND, JOHN HANS, oil company executive, consultant; b. Vienna, Austria, May 1, 1923; came to U.S., 1938, naturalized, 1943; s. Max Leopold and Margaret Stephanie (Herliczka) B.; m. Martha Elizabeth Rutland, June 26, 1946 (dec. 1979); children—James R., Deborah Brand Fainstein, David B.; m. Martha Jo Godwin, Mar. 15, 1980. Student NYU, 1940-42; J.D., Northwestern U., 1949; M.Theol., So. Meth. U., 1953. Sr. pastor North Tex. Conf. United Meth. Ch., Dallas, 1949-69; v.p. Birkman & Assocs., Houston, 1969-76; dir. orgn. and human resources Warren-King Oil & Gas, Houston, 1976-80; cons. Western Co. N.A., Ft. Worth, 1982, Grand Bancshares, Dallas, 1984—. Author weekly column Sherman Democrat, 1983-84. Chmn. Child Welfare Bd., Sherman, Tex., 1955-56, United Fund, Carrollton, Tex., 1962-63; mem. City Council, Whitesboro, Tex., 1983—; founder CONTACT-Dallas, 1969; mem. Texoma council Boy Scouts Am., 1958-59. Served to sgt. U.S. Army, 1943-45, ETO. Decorated Purple Heart. Recipient Book of Golden Deeds, Dallas Exchange Club, 1969; Founder's Plaque CONTACT-Dallas, 1970. Mem. Phi Alpha Delta. Lodge: Rotary (dir. 1982-83). Avocations: scuba, marathon running, writing. Home: 208 E Main St Whitesboro TX 76273

BRAND, MARY GUILBERT, librarian; b. Oak Park, Ill., Mar. 26, 1936; d. Jacob and Maisie (Guilbert) Brand. B.L.S., Fla. State U., 1960, postgrad., 1960-64. Cert. sch. and jr. coll. librarian, Fla. Reference librarian V.I., Library, St. Thomas, 1967-69; librarian Hebrew Acad., Miami Beach, Fla., 1970-83; Temple Sinai, North Miami Beach, Fla., 1982—; evening coordinator Riverside Meml. Chapel, Miami Beach, 1982—; cons., researcher to children's author Donald J. Sobol, Miami, Fla., 1980—. Author newsletter The Jewish Bibliophile, 1976-81; editor newsletter Jewish Hist. Soc. South Fla., 1979-83. Mem. Assn. Jewish Libraries (nat. treas. 1979-81, editor conv. proc. 1976-79, South Fla. chpt. 1976-83), ALA, Am. Soc. Notaries (membership chmn.). Republican. Christian Scientist. Home: 2301 Collins Ave 1415A Miami Beach FL 33139

BRAND, VIVIAN JUANITA, bookstore manager; b. Albertville, Ala., June 29, 1934; d. William Marion and Berta Annie Jane (Aldridge) Goggans; m. J.B. Brand, Oct. 19, 1957; children—Rodney Jay, Lisa Gaye, William Bart. Cert. secretarial acct. Alverson Draughon Bus. Coll., Birmingham, 1954. Bookkeeper, Morgan Electric Supply, Gadsden, Ala., 1954-55; billing clk., sec. Gadsden AF Depot, 1955-58; typist Sand Mountain Pub., Albertville, 1968-77; coll. bookstore mgr., central receiving clk. Snead State Jr. Coll., Boaz, Ala., 1977—. Den mother Chocolocco council Boy Scouts Am., 1964-71; scout leader North Ala. council Girl Scouts U.S.A., 1968-73; Sunday Sch. tchr. Second Bapt. Ch., Boaz, 1963-68; dir. girls aux. First Bapt. Ch., Boaz, 1974-80. Mem. Edn. Support Personnel Orgn., NEA. Club: T.O.P.S. (pres. 1965-68). Avocations: needlework; sewing. Office: Office: Snead State Jr Coll Walnut St Boaz AL 35957

BRANDE, SCOTT, geology educator; b. Altoona, Pa., May 23, 1950; s. Harold and Selma (Stein) B. B.S. in Biology-Geology, U. Rochester, 1972; M.S. in Geology, Calif. Inst. Tech., 1974; Ph.D. in Geology, SUNY-Stony Brook, 1979. Asst. prof. geology U. Ala., Birmingham, 1979-85, assoc. prof., 1985—; faculty Dauphin Island Sea Lab. (Ala.), 1980—. Vice chmn. Ala. State Textbook Com., 1983. Grantee, Miss.-Ala. Sea Grant Consortium, 1980, 81, 82. Mem. Paleontol. Soc., Geol. Soc. Am., AAAS, Sigma Xi. Office: Geology Dept Physical Sciences Room 214 Univ Ala Birmingham AL 35294

BRANDEN, J.P., architect; b. Warren, Ohio, Jan. 5, 1948; s. Frederick and Vivian (Stube) B.; m. Martha Alley, Aug. 26, 1972; children—Laura Louise, Mary Virginia. B.Arch. with honors, N.C. State U. Sch. Design, 1971; M.B.A., Fla. Atlantic U., 1981. Registered architect, N.C., Fla. Designer Wilber, Kendrick, Workman & Warren Architects, Charlotte, N.C., 1971-72; designer, assoc. Beemer Harrell, AIA Architects and Cons., Hickory, N.C., 1973-82; assoc., office mgr. James C. Buie, Architects, Tampa, Fla., 1982—; adj. prof. Catawba Valley Tech. Inst., Hickory, 1981, Gardener Web Coll., Newton, N.C., 1982. Designer, craftsman stained glass window Phila. Luth. Ch., 1976. Developer computer programs. Rec. sec. Buckhorn Elem. Sch. PTA, Brandon, Fla., 1985; mem. housing com. Catawba County Council on Aging, Hickory,

1975-77; co-chmn. bldgs. and properties com. of camping com. Presbytery of Concord, Statesville, N.C., 1980-82. Recipient regional TV coverage of passive solar design for multi-family housing Farmers Home Adminstrn., 1976. Mem. AIA (N.C. and Fla. chpts., 1st place award team captain for sand castle design competition Fla. chpt. 1985), Am. Arbitration Assn. (arbiter). Republican. Presbyterian. Avocations: Photography, travel, real estate development. Home: 811 Arch McDonald Dr Dover FL 33527 Office: James C Buie Architects 100 S Ashley Dr Suite 770 Tampa FL 33602

BRANDENBURG, ROBERT FAIRCHILD, JR., lawyer, business executive; b. Oklahoma City, Mar. 6, 1938; s. Robert Fairchild and Lorraine (Harkey) B.; m. Heidi Harper, Sept. 28, 1962; children—Robert Fairchild III, John Harper, Adam Charles. B.A., U. Okla., 1961, J.D., 1966. Bar: Okla. 1966, U.S. Dist. Ct. (we. dist.) Okla. 1968, U.S. Tax Ct. 1969, U.S. Ct. Appeals (10th cir.) 1972, U.S. Ct. Claims 1977. Sole practice, Norman, Okla., 1968-75; ptnr. Floyd, Brandenburg, Rogers & Willis and predecessors, Norman, 1975—; pres. Brandenburg Enterprises, 1970—, also dir.; pres., dir. Cumberland Heights, Inc., 1973-77, Robert F. Brandenburg, Jr. Atty. at Law P.C., 1979—; instr. dept. continuing edn. U. Okla., 1978; co-trustee John B. Brandenburg Trust, 1971—. Bd. dirs., mem. exec. com. Norman Alcohol Info. Ctr., Inc., 1972—, past pres., sec.; trustee Okla. Resource Found. for Alcoholism & Chem. Dependency, 1975—, vice chmn., chmn.; pres., dir. Southwest Inst. Human Relations, Inc., 1978—; dir. Phi Delta Theta Ednl. Found., Inc., 1982—, Phi Delta Theta Endowment Fund, 1982—; vestryman St. Michael's Episcopal Ch., Norman, 1976-78, 83—. Served to lt. USNR, 1961-70. Mem. ABA, Okla. Bar Assn., Cleveland County Bar Assn., Nat. Assn. Bond Lawyers, Phi Alpha Delta. Republican. Securities. Address: 116 E Main St Norman OK 73069

BRANDIMORE, STANLEY ALBERT, holding company executive, lawyer; b. Highland Park, Mich., Aug. 20, 1927; s. Albert James B. and Genevieve (McCormick) Weideman; m. E. Kennedy Greene, Dec. 27, 1952; children—Venessa Brandimore Lund, Darrell Stanley. B.B.A. in Acctg., U. Miami, Fla., 1954, J.D., 1957. Bar: Fla. 1957, U.S. Supreme Ct. 1968. Instr., lectr. acctg. U. Miami, 1954-57; atty. Fla. Pub. Service Com., Tallahassee, 1957-59, Fla. Power Corp., St. Petersburg, 1959-63, asst. gen. counsel, 1963-68, v.p., gen. counsel, 1968-75, sr. v.p., gen. counsel, 1975-83; exec. v.p., gen. counsel Fla. Progress Corp., St. Petersburg, 1983—. Served with USN, 1945-48, 50-52. Mem. St. Petersburg Bar Assn. (treas. 1964-65), Fla. Bar Assn., ABA, St. Petersburg C. of C. Democrat. Clubs: Suncoasters; Tiger Bay, Presidents (St. Petersburg); Treasure Island Tennis and Yacht (Fla.). Home: 8573 42d Ave N Saint Petersburg FL 33709 Office: Fla Progress Corp 270 1st Ave S PO Box 33042 St Petersburg FL 33733

BRANDON, DOUG, state senator; b. Aug. 23, 1932; m. Elizabeth Riggs, 1958; 4 children. B.A., U. Ark; grad. Command and Gen. Staff Sch. Former mem. Ark. Ho. of Reps., chmn. legis. council, joint budget com., revenue and taxation com.; mem. Ark. Senate, 1980—; owner, mgr. Brandon Furniture Co. Dem. nominee U.S. Congress, 1978; bd. dirs. Ark. Children's Hosp.; mem. Am. Legion. Mem. Nat. Home Furnishing Bd., Inst. Politics and Govt. Democrat. Lodge: Kiwanis. Office: Ark Senate State Capitol Little Rock AR 72201

BRANDON, ELVIS DENBY, JR., financial planner; b. Sheridan, Ark., Nov. 28, 1927; s. Elvis Denby and Hazel Ion (Davidson) B.; m. Helen Holt Deupree, Apr. 25, 1953; children—Elvis Denby III, Raymond Wilson. B.A., Rhodes Coll., Memphis, 1950; M.A., Duke U., 1952. C.L.U., C.F.P., ch. F.C. Fin. planner, pres., registered prin. Denby Brandon Orgn., Inc./Branco Planning Co., Inc., Memphis, 1952—; chmn. Brandon Underwriting Specialists, Inc., Memphis, 1969—; mem. adj. faculty Coll. Fin. Planning, Memphis, 1982-84; lectr. in fin. planning; dir. Internat. Bd. Standards and Practices of CFPS. Author: A New Beginning, 1979. Bd. dirs. Monroe Harding Children's Home, Nashville, 1982-84; elder, tchr. A.W. Dick meml. class Second Presby. Ch., Memphis. Named Young Man of Yr., Memphis Jaycees, 1953. Mem. Inst. Cert. Fin. Planners Internat. Assn. Fin. Planning (registered), Am. Soc Chartered Life Underwriters, Soc. Fin. Planning Practitioners (charter), Econ. Club Memphis, Phi Beta Kappa. Club: Racquet (Memphis), Rotary (Memphis). Home: 5711 The Forest Gate Rd Memphis TN 38119 Office: Denby Brandon Orgn Inc 3100 Walnut Grove Rd #501 Memphis TN 38111

BRANDON, GERALD GLEN, hospital administrator, educator; b. Wichita, Kans., Feb. 26, 1947; s. Glen Alfred and Anne (Dugi) B.; m. Kathryn Ann Lamberty, June 8, 1974; children—Christopher Eric, Melissa Nicole. B.A. cum laude, St. Mary's U., 1969; M.S., U. So. Calif., 1978. Commd. health care logistics officer U.S. Army, 1969, advanced through grades to capt., 1978; health facility project officer, Washington, 1978-82; buyer Brackenridge Hosp., Austin, 1981-82, dir., 1982-84, coordinator supply and distbn., 1984-86; dir. material mgmt. Peninsula Gen. Hosp. Med. Ctr., Salisbury, Md., 1986—; instr. Park Coll., Parkville, Mo., 1980-85. Technician camera and audio Catholic Diocese of Austin and Trinity Broadcasting Network, 1985—. Baseball coach Balcones Little League, Austin, 1982-83. Republican. Roman Catholic. Lodge: Lions. Avocations: music; sports; cooking.

BRANDON, MARY JANE HOWARD, lawyer, social worker; b. New Orleans, Sept. 19, 1944; d. Victor Charles and Mildred Eileen (Neal) Howard; B.A., Southwestern at Memphis, 1966; M.S.W., U. Tenn., 1968; J.D., Loyola U., New Orleans. Social worker Head Start program City of Memphis, 1965; dir. adoptions St. Peter Home for Children, Memphis, 1968-71; dir. social services Ednl. Research & Treatment Center, New Orleans, 1971-77; social worker in pvt. practice, 1975-77; chief social worker Hope Haven-Madonna Manor, New Orleans, 1977-80. Trustee, fin. sec. First Unitarian Ch., New Orleans; mem. Children's com. Mental Health Assn.; bd. dirs. Parents Anonymous; pres. adv. bd. Adult Group Homes, 1982-83. NIMH fellow, 1966-68. Mem. Nat. Assn. Social Workers, Acad. Cert. Social Workers, La. Assn. Bd. Cert. Social Workers, Nat. Soc. Autistic Children, Am. Orthopsychiat. Assn., Am. Group Psychiat. Assn., Interam. Bar Assn., Am. Soc. Internat. Law, Am. Bar Assn., Assoc. Cath. Charities. Republican. Roman Catholic. Home: 1418 8th St New Orleans LA 70115

BRANDON, ROBERT ALAN, insurance executive; b. Havana, Cuba, June 14, 1933; s. David Phillip and Marta (Torok) B.; m. Joy Kane, Feb. 17, 1957 (div. 1967); children—Steven G., Todd A., Garry M., Brandon; m. Marianne Rothberg, Apr. 11, 1968; stepchildren—Michelle Green, Marisa Levy. B.A., U. Havana, 1954. Exec. v.p. R.A. Brandon & Co., Inc., Coral Gables, Fla., 1954-57; exec. v.p. Agencia de Tractores y Equipos S.A., Havana, 1957-60; pres. R.A. Brandon & Co., Inc., Coral Gables, 1960—; dir. Miami Fed. Savs. and Loan Assn. Mem. Million Dollar Roundtable, (life), 10 Million Dollar Forum, Top of the Table (life), Nat. Assn. Health Underwriters (life; Nat. Quality award 1983). Home: 9440 Old Cutler Ln Journeys End Coral Gables FL 33156 Office: 217 Aragon Ave Coral Gables FL 33134

BRANDT, HENRY, psychologist, counselor; b. Edmonton, Alta., Can., July 4, 1916; came to U.S., 1919, naturalized, 1943; s. Heinrich and Elizabeth (Schilling) B.; m. Eva Lillian Morway, Jan. 20, 1940 (dec. 1982); children—Richard Paul, Elizabeth Brandt Blanchard, Suzanne Marie; m. Marcella LaVonne Noret McKillip, July 3, 1983. B.A., Houghton Coll., 1947; M.A. in Clin. Psychology, Wayne State U., 1949; Ph.D. in Marriage and Family, Cornell U., 1952. Lic. psychologist, Mich. Dean of men Houghton Coll., N.Y., 1952-54; marriage and family counselor, Detroit, 1954-68; prof. counseling Trinity Sem., Chgo., 1952-68; lectr. mission bds., all religious denominations, 1968—; counselor, prof., lectr., Singer Island, Fla. Author: Six Talks on Family Living, 1958; Keys to Better Living for Parents, 1958; Building a Christian Home, 1960; Happy Family Life, 1963; You and Your Job, 1966; Build a Happy Home With Discipline, 1965; The Struggle for Peace, 1965; When a Teen Falls in Love, 1965; Balancing Your Marriage, 1966; Christians Have Troubles, Too, 1968; Successful Marriage, 1974; Personal Growth, 1974; Successful Parenthood, 1974; I Want to Enjoy My Children, 1975; I Want My Marriage to be Better, 1976. Mem. Am. Psychol. Assn. Republican. Baptist. Avocations: sailing; tennis; raquetball; golf; hiking. Home and Office: 5380 N Ocean Dr Riviera Beach FL 33404

BRANDT, JOE ANN MARIE, clinical psychologist; b. Mpls., Jan. 8, 1952; d. Henry Aimar and Estelle Ann (Smith) B.; m. William Arthur Dickinson, Apr. 4, 1981. B.A., U. Ga., 1974; Ph.D., U. Ark., 1979; postdoctoral fellow U. Ala. Med. Ctr., 1978-80. Lic. clin. psychologist Nat. Register Health Care Providers. Clinician, Western Ark. Counseling Ctr., 1975-77; mem. interdisciplinary team in adolescent medicine U. Ala. Med. Ctr., 1978-79; intern U. Ala. Med. Ctr., 1978-79, instr., 1979-80, postdoctoral fellow, 1979-80, learning disability trainee, 1980; clin. psychologist, co-owner, operator Savannah (Ga.) Psychol. Cons.; mem. staff St. Joseph's, Broad Oaks, Meml. hosps.; cons. Candler Hosp.; mem. psychiat. inpatient services State Health Planning Agy. Active, Citizens for Clean Air, Ga. Conservancy, Sierra Club, Bethesda Home for Boys, Hist. Savannah, NOW. Recipient letter of recognition U. Ark., 1975. Mem. Am. Psychol. Assn., Ga. Psychol. Assn., Coastal Assn. Lic. Psychologists, Assn. Advancement Psychology, Assn. Women Psychologists, Am. Soc. Clin. Hypnosis. Roman Catholic. Home: 729 Dancy Ave Savannah GA 31419 Office: 1 St Joseph's Profl Plaza 11706 Mercy Blvd Savannah GA 31419

BRANHAM, MACK CARISON, JR., theological seminary president, clergyman; b. Columbia, S.C., Apr. 20, 1931; s. Mack Carison and Laura Pauline (Sexton) B.; m. Jennie Louise Jones, Dec. 17, 1953; children—Kenneth Gary, Charles Michael, Keith Robert, Laurie Lynn. B.S., Clemson U., 1953; M.Div., Luth. Theol. So. Sem., 1958, S.T.M., 1963; M.S., George Washington U., 1968; Ph.D., Ariz. State U., 1974. Ordained to ministry Lutheran Ch., 1958; pastor Providence-Nazareth Luth. Parish, Lexington, S.C., 1958-59; commd. 2d lt. U.S. Air Force, 1953, advanced through grades to col., 1959; ret., 1979; adminstrv. asst., registrar Luth. Theol. So. Sem., 1979-81, v.p. adminstrn., 1981-82, pres., 1982—; instr., counselor. Decorated Bronze Star, Legion of Merit. Mem. Am. Assn. Marriage and Family Therapy. Club: Rotary. Editor Air Force Chaplain newsletter, 1974-77. Office: 4201 N Main St Columbia SC 29203

BRANNEN, ARTHUR O'HAGAN, real estate development executive; b. Atlanta, Oct. 16, 1950; s. Jesse Ewell and Patricia J. (O'Hagan) B. B.S. in Indsl. Mgmt., Ga. Inst. Tech., 1973. Supt. Holder Constrn. Co., Atlanta, 1973-76, project mgr., 1976-77; constrn. mgr. Jim Wilson & Assocs., Montgomery, Ala., 1976-78; dir. constrn. Southcoast, Inc., Tampa, Fla., 1979-81; pres. Brannen Devel. Co., Atlanta, 1981—. Served with USCG, 1969-75. Mem. Delta Sigma Pi. Roman Catholic. Clubs: Kiwanis, (pres. 1983-84), Toastmasters (Sandy Springs). Office: Brannen Devel Co 2700 Cumberland Pkwy Atlanta GA 30339

BRANNEN, STEPHEN JOSHUA, agricultural educator; b. Glennville, Ga., Oct. 19, 1925; s. Henry Lonnie and Ellen Finer (Guy) B.; m. Ruth Edge, June 8, 1948; children—Rita Hatcher, Carolyn Sanders. B.S.A., U. Ga., 1950, M.A., 1952; Ph.D., N.C. State U., 1966. Instr. Ga. Dept. Edn., Greensboro, 1950; asst. county agt. County Extension Office, Cordele, Ga., 1950-51, Swainsboro, Ga., 1952-53; economist Coop. Extension Service, Athens, Ga., 1953-61; chmn. dept. agrl. econs. U. Ga., Athens, 1961—. Served with U.S. Army, 1944-46. Recipient Disting. Teaching award Agrl. Alumni Assn., 1967. Mem. Internat. Assn. Agrl. Economists, Am. Agrl. Econs. Assn., Farm Mgrs. and Rural Appraisers Assn., Ga. Agrl. Econ. Assn., So. Agrl. Econ. Assn., Am. Soc. Agr. (pres. Ga. chpt. 1980). Home: Route 1 Box 101 Watkinsville GA 30677 Office: Dept Agrl Econs U Ga Athens GA 30602

BRANNON, J. BRUCE, oil and gas leasing landman; b. Tulsa, July 26, 1947; s. James Barton and Eloise Nadean (Bruce) B.; m. Hilda Ann Mouton, Oct. 6, 1982; children—James Allen, Jenifer Diana. B.B.A., Tex. Christian U., 1971; postgrad. in bus. mgmt. U. S.W. La., 1977-78. Cert. petroleum landman, La. Landman, Hawthorne Oil & Gas, Lafayette, La., 1980-81, Lavino Oil & Gas, 1981-82; pres. 3-B Brokerage, Lafayette, La., 1982—. Lt. Scott Police Dept. Res. Mem. Am. Assn. Petroleum Landmen, Lafayette Assn. Petroleum Landmen. Club: Lafayette Optimist (pres. 1984). Home: PO Box 1232 Scott LA 70583 Office: 3-B Brokerage Co 110 Travis St Suite 105 Tri-Key Bldg Lafayette LA 70505

BRANSCOM, WILLIAM JAMES, bank holding company executive; b. Roanoke, Va., Nov. 29, 1926; s. George Alexander and Georgia Douglas (Firestone) B.; m. Dorothy Jean Larson, Mar. 24, 1951; children—Dorothy Diane, Georgia Kay Branscom Carter, Joel Robert, William Eric. B.A. in Econs., Roanoke Coll., 1950; M.B.A. in Fin., U. Pa., 1952; cert. in comml. banking Stonier Grad. Sch. Banking, 1963. Trainee cashier's dept. First Nat. Exchange Bank, Roanoke, 1954, trainee investment div., 1954, security analyst investment div., 1954-57, asst. cashier investment div., 1957-58, asst. v.p. investment div., 1958-59, sr. v.p. investment div., 1959-73; sr. v.p., treas. fin. group Dominion Bankshares Corp., Roanoke, 1973—; instr. Va. Bankers Sch. Bank Mgmt., Charlottesville, 1973-83. Bd. dirs. Va. Fuel Conversion Authority, 6 yr. appointment by gov., Richmond, 1980—; dir., treas. Greater Roanoke Valley Devel. Found., 1971—; chmn. Roanoke Valley Savs. Bonds Com., 1965—; bd. dirs. Roanoke Valley chpt. ARC, 1985; trustee Evergreen Burial Park, Roanoke, 1966—; mem. Botetourt County Planning Commn., Botetourt County Bd. Zoning Appeals. Served to 1st lt. U.S. Army, 1952-54. Clubs: Botetourt Country (Fincastle, Va.); Jefferson (Roanoke, Va.). Avocations: farming; horses; traveling; foreign languages. Office: Dominion Bankshares Corp 213 S Jefferson St PO Box 13327 Roanoke VA 24040

BRANTLEY, ALICE VIRGINIA SINGER (MRS. EDWARD FITZROY BRANTLEY), civic worker; b. Muncie, Ind.; d. Harry Dwight and Dessa (Slater) Singer; student Muncie Conservatory Music, 1912-20, Met. Sch. Music, 1920-22; studied harp with Louise Schelschmidt Koehne, Indpls., 1917-22, Henriette Renie, Paris, France, 1922-26, 50; m. Edward Fitzroy Brantley, Sept. 19, 1956. Concert debut, Paris, 1925; mem. Septuor Renie, 1923-26; concerts in Paris, N.Y.C., Chgo., Ft. Wayne, Indpls., St. Petersburg, Fla., 1920-63, with Alice Singer Trio, St. Petersburg, 1933-56; performed with St. Petersburg Symphony, Jacksonville (Fla.) Symphony, Tampa (Fla.) Philharmonic, Fla. Philharmonic, 1950-66; radio program WSUN, St. Petersburg, 1933. Ambassador, People-to-People Goodwill Mission from St. Petersburg to Europe and Middle East, 1960, to Soviet Union and satellites, 1965; mem. Fla. Art Commn., 1964-67; v.p. Suncoast Goodwill Industries, 1965-69, v.p. Aux. Guild, 1965-66; mem. St. Anthony's Hosp. Guild, 1961—, Children's Home Soc., 1963—, Suncoast Heart Assn., 1966; chmn. Queen of Hearts Ball, St. Petersburg, 1968; Heart Sunday chmn., 1963; asst. treas. Fla. Suncoast Opera Guild, 1981-84; bd. dirs. Pinellas County Mental Health Assn., Mound Park Hosp. Aux., All Children's Hosp. Guild. Recipient Renie Harp award Paris, 1926, citation Radio Sta. WDAE, Tampa, 1965; named Princess of Royal Ct., St. Petersburg Heart Assn., 1963, Queen of Hearts, 1967; Contessa of Yr., Suncoast Opera Guild, 1970. Mem. Fla. Philharmonic Soc. (charter pres. 1954), Chamber Music Soc. (charter pres. 1966-68), Bel Canto (charter 1956), St. Petersburg opera assns., Fla. Art Council (charter 1963), Lions Club Aux. (past pres.), Soroptimist Internat. (pres. St. Petersburg 1962-63), St. Petersburg Hist. Soc., Mus. Fine Arts.

BRANTLEY, HASKEW HAWTHORNE, JR., mfg. co. exec., state senator; b. Birmingham, Ala., Sept. 28, 1922; s. Haskew Hawthorne and Maggie Lee (Hicks) B.; B.A., Ga. Tech. U., 1948; m. Miriam Laughlin, Sept. 11, 1948; children—Jacquelyn, Lynn, Susan, David. Pres., Indsl. Vulcanizing Co., Brantley Coatings Co., Haskew Brantley Co., Alpharetta, Ga.; v.p. govt. mktg. Panafax Corp., Alpharetta. Mem. Ga. Ho. of Reps., 1966-74, Ga. Senate, 1975—. Served with U.S. Navy, 1943-46, 50-53. Republican. Episcopalian. Patentee in field. Office: PO Box 605 Alpharetta GA 30201*

BRANTLEY, HELEN THOMAS, psychologist, clinical educator; b. Palmerton, Pa., Jan. 29, 1942; d. Francis Clyde and Elizabeth Emily (Jennings) Thomas; m. John Croft Brantley, June 15, 1963; children—Elizabeth Ann, John Thomas. B.A., Duke U., 1963, Ph.D., 1973. Lic. psychologist, N.C. Research assoc. Duke U., Durham, N.C., 1974-77; postdoctoral fellow U. N.C., Chapel Hill, 1978, research asst. prof., 1978-79, asst. prof., 1979-81, clin. asst. prof., 1984—; practice clin. psychology, Chapel Hill, 1981—; cons. in field. Contbr. articles to profl. jours. Mem. Orange County Commrs. Spl. Task Force, Chapel Hill, 1983; mem. adv. bd. YMCA, Chapel Hill, 1985. NIMH grantee, 1980; Spencer Found. grantee, 1980. Mem. Am. Psychol. Assn., N.C. Psychol. Assn. N.C. Assn. Advancement of Psychology, Phi Beta Kappa, Psi Chi. Home: 635 Totten Pl Chapel Hill NC 27514 Office: 109 Conner Dr 204 Chapel Hill NC 27514

BRANTLEY, PHOEBE FRANCES, ballet director, choreographer; b. Hastings, Nebr., Mar. 2, 1926; d. Louis Damron Kinney and Helen Cook Batham; m. Joseph Patton Brantley III, June 15, 1944 (dec. Aug. 6, 1964); children—Joseph Patton IV, John Bretton, David Wightman. Student George Washington U. With Washington Ballet, 1940-44; artistic dir. La. Ballet, Baton Rouge, 1976—, also choreographer. Mem. Southwest Regional Ballet Assn. (pres. 1981-82). Republican. Episcopalian. Home: 5845 Glenwood Dr Baton Rouge LA 70806 Office: Louisiana Ballet 1765 Dallas Dr Baton Rouge LA 70806

BRANTON, SANDRA SHELBY, state official; b. Little Rock, Apr. 22, 1944; d. Eagle Chinook and Martha (Branch) Shelby; m. John S. McIntosh, Oct. 16, 1964 (div. May 1970); Herman H. Branton, Jr.; 1 child, John Sanders. B.S. in Elec. Engring. Tech., U. Ark., 1981, postgrad. in engring. mgmt., 1985—. Elec. maintenance supr. intern Alcoa Corp., Bauxite, Ark., 1981-82, material expeditor/planner relief, 1983-85, also writer, tchr. elec. and instruments apprentice programs, 1981-84; tech. transfer program mgr. Ark. Sci. and Tech. Authority, Little Rock, 1986—. Active Ark. Polit. Action Com., Bauxite Charities. Ben Hogan scholar, 1980. Mem. IEEE (I COMP pres. 1985—). Home: 9521 Kling Rd Mabelvale AR 72103 Office: Ark Sci and Tech Authority 200 Main St Suite 210 Little Rock AR 72201

BRAR, CANDACE JEAN, speakers bureau administrator; b. Mexico, Mo., Dec. 24, 1933; d. Nolan Daniel Ross and Helen Anna (Willis) May; m. Balbir Singh Brar, Jan. 30, 1959 (div. 1972). A.A., Southwest Bapt. Coll., Bolivar, Mo., 1953; B.A., Ouachita Bapt. U., Arkadelphia, Ark., 1955; M.R.E., Southwestern Baptist Theol. Sem., 1957. Baptist student union dir. Fresno State and City Colls., 1957-60; youth dir., Fort Worth, also McLean, Va., 1955-60; clerk stenographer U.S. Army Engr. Ctr., Fort Belvoir, Va., 1961-62; exec. sec. IBM, Corp., Arlington, Va., 1963-66, McLendon Theatres, Dallas, 1974-76; pres., owner Celebrity Speakers Bur., Nashville, 1979—. Editor: An Illustrator's Music City, 1984. Recipient Tng. award for Religious Leadership, Order Eastern Star. Mem. Nashville Area C. of C. (membership com., music industry com.), Hotel Sales Mgmt. Assn. (bd. dirs. 1982-83), Meeting Planners Internat., Nat. Speakers Assn. (mem. ethics com. 1980—), Tenn. Soc. Assn. Execs. (mem. pub. relations com., trade show com.), Country Music Assn., India Assn. Nashville. Avocations: reading; people watching; painting; crafts, creative design. Office: Celebrity Speakers Bur 50 Music Square W Suite 405 Nashville TN 37203

BRASEL, VERGIL LEON, process quality engineer; b. Wartburg, Tenn., Sept. 8, 1937; s. Claude Leighton and Mildred (Heidle) B.; m. Rena Joyce Strutton, Oct. 10, 1959. B.S., Carson-Newman Coll., 1961; postgrad. U. Tenn., 1970-75. Tchr. pub. high schs. Morgan County Sch. System, Wartburg, 1961-62, 64-67; process quality engr. nuclear div. Martin Marietta Energy Systems, Inc., Oak Ridge, 1967—. Sch. commr.-at-large Morgan County Bd. Edn., Wartburg, 1982—. Served with U.S. Army, 1962-64. Mem. Am. Soc. Quality Control (cert. quality engr.). Baptist. Lodges: Masons, Scottish Rite, York Rite, Shriners, Elks. Home: Route One Wartburg TN 37887 Office: Martin Marietta Energy Systems Inc PO Box Y Oak Ridge TN 37830

BRASHER, JERRY WAYNE, sports and medical company executive; b. Baton Rouge, June 10, 1954; s. Tallie John and Bertha Mae (Shanks) B. A.S. in Design Tech., Hinds Jr. Coll., 1976, A.A. in Engring., 1978; B.S. in Indsl. Engring., Miss. State U., 1980. Product engr. Cameron Iron Works, Houston, 1980-81, systems engr., 1981-82, indsl. engr., 1982-83; pres. GALACTI Sports/Med. Industries, Baton Rouge, 1983—. Served with U.S. Army, 1972-74. Named lifetime canoeer 1st Armored Div. Arty. Mem. Tex. Soc. Profl. Engrs., Am. Inst. Indsl. Engrs., Soc. Mfg. Engrs., Am. Soc. Metals, Iron and Steel Soc., Tau Beta Pi, Alpha Pi Mu, Phi Kappa Phi, Phi Theta Kappa. Inventor optical distance finder, force converter, force positioner. Home: PO Box 15689 Baton Rouge LA 70895 Office: GALACTICA Sports/Med Industries PO Box 15689 Baton Rouge LA 70895

BRASHIER, EDWARD MARTIN, waste mgmt. exec.; b. New Iberia, La., Sept. 30, 1954; s. Martin Lee and Ann Elizabeth (Bosier) B.; A.S., Jones Jr. Coll., 1974; B.S., U. Miss., 1976; cert. environ. profl.; m. Debbie Warren, July 12, 1974; children—Shannon Elise, Edward Martin II, and Joseph Lee II (twins). Safety engr. Fla. Machine & Foundry Co., Jacksonville, Fla., 1976-77; lab. technician Union Carbide Corp., Woodbine, Ga., 1977-78; research chemist Nilok Chemicals, Inc., Memphis, 1978-79; tech. mgr. Chem. Waste Mgmt. Co., Emelle, Ala., 1979-82; tech. dir. Am. Environ. Protection Corp., Jacksonville, 1982-83; tech. mgr. Stablex Corp., Rock Hill, S.C., 1983—. Mem. Am. Chem. Soc., Am. Soc. Safety Engrs., Instrument Soc. Am., Am. Indsl. Hygiene Assn., Am. Water Works Assn., ASME. Methodist. Home: 1425 River Oaks Ct Rock Hill SC 29731

BRASWELL, ROBERT NEIL, scientist, engineer, computer scientist; b. Boaz, Ala., July 23, 1932; s. Homer Winston and Gladys Irene (Wright) B.; m. Wynona Chambers, Apr. 17, 1954; children—John Robert, Jefferson Monroe. B.S. in Engring., U. Ala., 1957, M.S., 1959; Ph.D., Okla. State U., 1964; postgrad. U. Fla., 1975-76. Registered profl. engr., Fla. Engr., Bell Telephone, Hughes Aircraft, U.S. Post Office Dept., VA; dir. systems engring. Teledyne, Huntsville, Ala., 1959-64; prof., chmn. indsl. and systems engring. dept. U. Fla., 1964-72; tech. dir. Air Force Systems Command, Eglin AFB, Fla., 1971-82, dir. computer scis. Armament div., 1982—; adj. prof. engring. U. Fla., 1973—. Served with USAF, 1950-53. Mem. AIAA, Am. Soc. Engring. Edn., Inst. Indsl. Engrs., IEEE, Ops. Research Soc. Am., Jaycees (pres.), C. of C., Tau Beta Pi, Omicron Delta Kappa, Pi Mu Epsilon, Phi Kappa Phi, Chi Alpha Phi, Alpha Pi Mu, Phi Theta Kappa, Theta Tau, Sigma Tau. Democrat. Baptist. Clubs: Univ., Com. of 100, Krewe of Bowlegs. Lodge: Rotary. Contbr. articles to profl. jours. Home: 804 Tarpon Dr Fort Walton Beach FL 32548 Office: AD/KR Eglin AFB FL 32542

BRATTEN, THOMAS ARNOLD, lawyer, cons. engr.; b. Dayton, Ohio, Sept. 11, 1934; s. Samuel Arnold and Helen Jeannette (Wonderly) B.; m. Glenna Mary Bratten, Apr. 20, 1963; children—Charles, Christina, Thomas. M.E. U. Cin., 1957; J.D., Chase Coll., Cin., 1968. Bar: Ohio, 1968, Fla., 1968, U.S. Supreme Ct., 1972; cert. Nat. Bd. Trial Advocacy; diplomate Nat. Acad. Forensic Engrs. Engr. in tng. Gen. Motors Corp., 1953-57, test engr., 1957-59, project engr., 1963-68, sr. project engr., 1968; design engr. Pratt & Whitney Aircraft, 1959-61; gen. mgr. Auto-Technia, Inc., 1961-63; with Pub. Defender's Office, 1968-75, chief trial atty., 1970-72, chief Capital div., 1972-75; ptnr. Campbell, Colbath, Kapner & Bratten, West Palm Beach, Fla., 1969-72; prin. Bratten & Harris, P.A., West Palm Beach, 1973—; spl. master, 1973—; faculty Nat. Inst. trial Advocacy, U. Fla., 1978—; nat. panel arbitrators Am. Arbitration Assn., 1970-78. Mem. Palm Beach County Republican Exec. Com., 1971-80, county campaign chmn., 1974. Mem. Fla. Bar Assn. (exec. com. criminal law sect. 1978-81), Acad. Fla. Trial Lawyers, Assn. Trial Lawyers Am., Palm Beach County Bar Assn., Fla. Engring. Soc., Soc. Automotive Engrs., Pi Tau Sigma. Author: Criminal Lawyers Trial Notebook, 1977; Florida Criminal Procedure, 1981. Inventor, holder 6 U.S. and 9 fgn. patents. Home: 8623 Thousand Pines Ct West Palm Beach FL 33411 Office: 319 Clematis St Suite 700 Comeau Bldg West Palm Beach FL 33401

BRATTON, JAMES HENRY, JR., lawyer; b. Pulaski, Tenn., Oct. 9, 1931; s. James Henry and Mabel (Shelley) B.; B.A., U. of South, 1952 B.A. Oxford U. (Eng.), 1954, M.A., 1978; LL.B., Yale U., 1956; m. Alleen Sharp Davis, Oct. 15, 1960; children—Susan Shelley, James Henry III, Margaret Alleen. Admitted to Tenn. bar, 1956, Ga. bar, 1957; practice in Atlanta, 1956—; mem. firm Smith, Gambrell, Russell, and predecessors, 1956—; vis. lectr. law U. Ga., 1967—; adj. prof. Emory Law Sch., 1984—Bd. dirs. Churches Homes for Bus. Girls, 1970—, Protestant Welfare and Social Service, Atlanta, 1960—; mem. council Christian Council of Met. Atlanta, 1966—; trustee Ga. chpt. Multiple Sclerosis Soc., 1984—, U. of South, 1984—, Trust Fund for Sibley Park, 1985—; pres. Peachtree Heights West Civic Assn., 1985—. Fellow Ga. Bar Found.; mem. Am. Law Inst., Am. (chmn. standing com. on aero. law 1977-79), Ga. (founding chmn. environ. law sect. 1970-71), Atlanta, Internat. bar assns., Am. Judicature Soc., Yale Law Sch. Assn. (exec. com. 1976-80), Gridiron Secret Soc., Phi Beta Kappa. Democrat. Methodist. Clubs: Lawyers, Burns, Old Warhorse Lawyers (Atlanta). Contbr. articles to profl. jours. Home: 63 N Muscogee Ave NW Atlanta GA 30305 Office: 1st Atlanta Tower Atlanta GA 30383

BRAUER, HARROL ANDREW, JR., TV executive; b. Richmond, Va., Oct. 17, 1920; s. Harrol Andrew and Bertie (Gregory) B.; B.A., U. Richmond, 1942; LL.D. (hon.), Christopher Newport Coll.; m. Elizabeth Anne Hill, May 18, 1946; children—Harrol Andrew III, William Lanier, Gregory Hill. Chief announcer, program dir., account exec. various radio stas. in Va., 1939-42, 45-49; asso. WVEC radio, Hampton, Va., 1949-78; v.p., dir. sales Sta. WVEC-TV, Hampton, 1953-82; v.p. Peninsula Cable Corp., 1966-82; dir. Peninsula Broadcasting Corp. Pres., Hampton Community Chest, 1951-52; crusade chmn. Peninsula unit Am. Cancer Soc., 1960—. Mem. Hampton Sch. Bd., 1963—, vice chmn., 1964-68, chmn., 1968-70; bd. dirs. YMCA, Va. U.S.O.; bd. dirs., vice chmn. Va. Pub. Telecommunications Council; chmn. bd. trustees Hampton Roads Ednl. TV Assn., 1965-70; chmn. bd. Va. Pub. Telecommunications, 1985; rector Christopher Newport Coll., 1976-82. Served from midshipman to lt. USNR, 1942-45. Recipient Disting. Service medallion Christopher Newport Coll.; award NCCJ, Disting. Citizen award City of

Hampton. Mem. Hampton Retail Mchts. Assn. (past pres., dir.), Jamestowne Soc., Peninsula C. of C. (past dir.), Broadcast Pioneers, Sigma Alpha Epsilon. Episcopalian (vestryman). Clubs: Commonwealth; Indian Creek Yacht and Country; Town Point; Peninsula Executive's (past pres., dir.), Kiwanis (past dir., pres., lt. gov.); James River Country; Hampton Yacht. Home: 35 N Boxwood St Hampton VA 23669

BRAUN, WARREN L(OYD), communications engineer; b. Postville, Iowa, Aug. 11, 1922; s. Karl William and Cornelia (Muller) B.; student Valparaiso Tech. Inst., Capitol Radio Engring. Inst., 1953; B.S.E.E., Valparaiso Inst., 1985; 8y m. Lillian Carol Stone, May 24, 1942; children—Warren (dec.), Dikki Carol. Chief engr. WKEY, 1941, WSVA, 1941; E.S.M.W.T.P. sect. head, 1942-45; charge installation stas. WSIR, WTON, WJMA, WSVA-FM, WJZ-TV, WSVA-TV, Blue Ridge TV cable facilities, 1945-55; gen. mgr. WSVA-AM-FM-TV, 1964-65; pres. Com Sonics, Inc., Research and Devel. Labs., Warren Braun, cons. engrs., Shenandoah Devel. Corp. Panel 4 mem. TV allocations study orgn.; mem. FCC coms., 1961-63; del. Internat. Deliberations at Interim Conf. of CCIR, 1962; mem. FCC-C-TAC Com., panels 1 and 8; v.p. Market Dimensions, Inc., 1965-71. Bd. dirs. Salvation Army, 1961-73. Chmn. Harrisonburg-Rockingham County Recreation Study Commn., 1963-66; mem. Va. Air Pollution Control Bd., 1966-73, mem. Va. State Water Bd., 1974-82, chmn., 1977-78; mem. Va. Citizens Com. for Outdoor Planning, 1964-69; chmn. Upper Valley Regional Park Authority, 1966-69, dir., 1969-82; mem. Dist. Export Council, chmn. nat. conf., 1985; mem. Air Pollution Control Task Force; mem. Va. Far East Trade Mission, 1972, 77, 81; mem. Ohio River Sanitation Commn., 1974-82, chmn., 1978-80; mem. bd. Tb and Thoracic Soc., Va. state seal chmn., 1967—. Bd. dirs. Va. Cultural Laureate Found., 1976—; mem. bd. Hunter McGuire Sch.; mem. bd., mem. exec. com. Sta. WVPY-TV, ednl. sta.; mem. bd. advisors council Sch. Bus., James Madison U., also mem. adv. council Entrepreneurial Ctr. Registered profl. engr. Va., S.C. Recipient Jefferson Davis medal U.D.C., 1961; named outstanding engr. of year Va. Soc. Profl. Engrs., 1965; man of year Harrisonburg and Rockingham County, 1965; Internat. award Am. Soc. Engring., 1969; Rietzke Nat. award, 1972; named PSI Exec. of Yr., 1983; Harrisonburg and Rockingham Businessman of Yr., 1985. Fellow Audio Engring. Soc. (bd. dirs. 1962), Internat. Consular Acad.; mem. IEEE, Soc. Motion Picture and TV Engrs., Acoustical Soc. Am., Nat. Soc. Profl. Engrs., Va. Soc. Profl. Engrs. (mem. bd. and exec. com. 1964-65, chpt. pres. 1963-64, Distinguished Service award 1973), Va. Assn. Professions (charter, regional v.p. 1970-73, pres. 1974—), Va. C. of C. (chmn. world trade com. 1968-82, dir. 1973—, v.p. 1975—), Harrisonburg C. of C. (chmn. bus. relations com. 1959-61, mem. bd. 1961-66, pres. 1964), ESOP Assn. Am. (dir. 1979—, pres. 1985), Soc. Cable Television Engrs. (chpt. pres. 1973, nat. dir. 1972), Internat. Broadcaster Soc. (corp. mem.), ASTM. Lutheran. Lodge: Elks. Address: PO Box 1106 Harrisonburg VA 22801

BRAUTIGAM, DANIEL CORY, foundry executive, writer, educator; b. Shelby County, Ohio, Feb. 10, 1918; s. Ervin D. and Mary (Cory) B.; m. Beulah Arlene Clay, Oct. 9, 1937; children—Marian Nelle Brautigam Desch, Albert Clay, John Philip. A.B., DePauw U., 1939; postgrad. U. Ill. M.Ed., Wittenberg U., 1965. Tchr. English, high sch., Catlin, Ill., 1939-42; foundryman Sidney Aluminum Products (Ohio), 1942-48, supt., 1948-67, personnel dir., 1967-69; instr. bus. mgmt. Wittenberg U., Springfield, Ohio, 1969-71; supt. Quincy Foundry div. Warren Tool, Quincy, Ohio, 1971-83; operator Tropics Aquarium, Pemberton, Ohio, 1968-80; free-lance fiction writer, Lavonia, Ga., 1983—. Rector scholar DePauw U., 1935-39. Republican. Author: Tropical Fish For Fun and Profit, 1982. Home: Route 1 Box 307 Lavonia GA 30553

BRAVERMAN, HOWARD LEE, hospital administrator; b. Passaic, N.J., Nov. 15, 1946; s. Samuel and Lillian (Lazerowitz) B.; m. Mollie E. Goldstein, June 8, 1969; children—Joshua, Marc, Robyn. B.A., Rutgers U., 1968; M.H.A., Tulane U., 1975. Lic. nursing home administr. and registered sanitarian. Environ. health cons. N.J. Dept. Health, Trenton, 1968-69; asst. dir. East Jefferson Gen. Hosp., Metairie, La., 1975-77; administr. St. Charles Gen. Hosp., New Orleans, 1977-79; exec. dir. New Orleans Home for Jewish Aged, 1979-82, B'nai B'rith Home and Hosp., Memphis, 1982—; adj. faculty Tulane U., New Orleans, 1975—, George Washington U., Washington, 1982—. Bd. dirs. Vis. Nurse Assn., Memphis, 1982—, treas., 1985. Named one of Outstanding Young Men of Am. U.S. Jaycees, 1978. Served to capt. U.S. Army, 1969-73, Vietnam. Mem. Am. Coll. Hosp. Administrs., Am. Coll. Health Care Administrs., Tenn. Assn. Homes for Aging (pres.-elect 1984—), Am. Assn. Homes for Aging (del. 1985), Tenn. Health Care Assn. (legis. com. 1985), Tenn. Hosp. Assn. (long-term care panel 1983—). Avocations: golf; woodworking; reading; sports. Home: 8210 Pine Creek East Germantown TN 38138 Office: B'nai B'rith Home and Hosp 131 North Tucker Memphis TN 38104

BRAVERMAN, ROBERT CARL, environmental control equipment company official; b. Passaic, N.J., Sept. 23, 1935; s. Robert Thomas and Rose C. (Salern) B.; m. Beverly Greaves, Aug. 30, 1958; 1 dau., Chris Ann. B.S. in Indsl. Engring. and Mgmt., Fairleigh Dickinson U., 1958; M.S. in Indsl. Mgmt., Purdue U., 1959. Regional sales mgr. Westinghouse Electric Co., Buffalo, 1964-66, sales mgr., 1966-68, corp. mktg. cons., Pitts., 1968-70, strategic planning mgr. indsl. group, 1970-73; corp. devel. mgr. Am. Air Filter Co., Louisville, 1973-75, corp. advt. and pub. relations mgr., 1974-78, corp. mgr. mktg. and communications, 1978-80, mktg. and sales mgr. environ. control div., 1980-84, gen. corp. sales mgr., 1984—. Served with USMCR, 1956-60. Mem. Pub. Relations Soc. Am., ASHRAE, U.S. C. of C., N.Am. Soc. Corp. Planning. Republican. Presbyterian. Clubs: Louisville Boat (Louisville); Press, University (Chgo.). Office: 215 Central Ave Louisville KY 40208

BRAXTON, HERMAN HARRISON, physician; b. Almanance County, N.C., Nov. 13, 1906; s. James Guy and Nette E. (Guthrie) B.; A.B., U. N.C., 1928; M.D., Johns Hopkins, 1932; m. Anne Norfolk Grimm, June 22, 1935; children—Herman Harrison II, Elizabeth Anne. Mem. house staff Duke Hosp., 1932-33, White Plains (N.Y.) Hosp., 1933-34; gen. practice medicine, Chase City, Va., 1934—; mem. staffs Community Meml. Hosp., South Hill, Va., Southside Community Hosp. Farmville, Va., local med. dir. Nat. Found.; med. examiner Mecklenburg County, 1947—; surgeon So. R.R.; bd. dirs. Chase City Indsl. Devel. Corp.; mem. adv. bd. Fidelity Nat. Bank. Mem. local bi-racial commn., 1965—. Mem. Chase City Town Council, 1955-63. Recipient Outstanding Citizenship award Chase City Jaycees, 1968; Service to Mankind award Mecklenberg Sertoma Club, 1975. Fellow Am. Acad. Family Practice (charter); mem. Va. Med. Soc., A.M.A., Chase City C. of C. (past pres., named Citizen of Yr. 1985), Phi Beta Kappa. Episcopalian. Clubs: Lions (past pres., zone chmn.); Mecklenburg Country (past pres.). Home: 440 Walker St Chase City VA 23924 Office: Chase City Med Clinic 946 N Main St Chase City VA 23924

BRAXTON, HERMAN HARRISON, JR., lawyer; b. Durham, N.C., May 15, 1936; s. Herman Harrison and Anne (Grimm) B.; A.B. in Polit. Sci., U. N.C., 1958; J.D., U. Va., 1961; m. Patricia Gail Galway, June 26, 1965; children—Herman Harrison III, Grace Anne, William Marshall. Admitted to Va. bar, 1961; ptnr. Willis, Braxton, Ashby & Bass, Fredericksburg, 1965—; commonwealth atty. City of Fredericksburg, 1974-82. Pres. Fredericksburg chpt. Va. Mus. Fine Arts, 1970-72. Served to capt. JAGC, USAF, 1961-64. Recipient disting. service award Fredericksburg Jr. C. of C. Mem. Fredericksburg C. of C. (pres. 1972-73), Va. Bar Assn., 15th Jud. Circuit Bar Assn., Fredericksburg Area Bar Assn. (pres. 1980), Pi Kappa Alpha, Phi Alpha Delta. Episcopalian. Home: 1204 Charles St Fredericksburg VA 22401 Office: 315 William St Fredericksburg VA 22401

BRAY, BUN BENTON, JR., association executive; b. Siler City, N.C., Nov. 7, 1911; s. Bun Benton and Berta Mae (Phillips) B.; m. Sadie Marie Shelton, June 20, 1936; children—Donna Marie, Bonnie Patricia. A.B., U. N.C., 1933, postgrad., 1935. Dir. research N.C. Manpower Council, 1939-42; dir. field ops. U.S. Bur. Employment Security-Labor, 1946-50; spl. asst. to Sec. of Navy, Washington, 1950-54; dep. dir. manpower mgmt. Dept. Def., 1954-58; staff dir. Manpower subcom. Ho. of Reps., Washington, 1958-72; exec. dirs. Fed. Mgrs. Assn., 1972—; lectr. in field. Editor Fed. Mgrs. Quar. Mag., 1983—. Pres. Fairfax County Fedn. Civic Assns., Va., 1956-57, Fairfax County PTA, 1961-62; vice chmn. bd. trustees Jump Found., Washington, 1980—. Served to lt. comdr. USN, 1942-46, ETO. Recipient award Washington-Evening Star, 1962. Mem. Phi Beta Kappa. Democrat. Baptist. Lodge: Rotary. Avocations: Gardening; tennis. Home: 6628 Van Winkel Dr Falls Church VA 22044 Office: Fed Mgrs Assn 2300 S 9th St Arlington VA 22204

BRAZDA, FREDERICK WICKS, pathologist; b. New Orleans, Dec. 17, 1945; s. Fred George and Helen Josephine (Wicks) B.; student U. Chgo., 1962-64; B.S. cum laude, Tulane U., 1966; M.D., La. State U., 1970; m. Margaret Mary Hubbell, Sept. 8, 1973; children—Geoffrey Frederick, Gretchen Marie, Gregory Paul. Intern, then resident in pathology La. State U. div. Charity Hosp., New Orleans, 1970-75; asso. pathologist Hotel Dieu Hosp., New Orleans, 1975-83, dir. Sch. Med. Tech., 1976-83; assoc. med. dir. Am. Bio-sci. Labs., New Orleans, 1983-84, Smith Kline Bio-sci. Labs., New Orleans, 1985—; cons. St. Tammany Parish Hosp., Covington, La., Riverside Hosp., Franklinton, La, 1976-84; asst. clin. prof. pathology and med. tech. La. State U. Med. Center. Diplomate Am. Bd. Pathology. Mem. AMA, Am. Soc. Clin. Pathologists, Coll. Am. Pathologists, Am. Assn. Clin. Chemistry, So. Med. Assn., La. Med. Soc., La. Pathology Soc., Orleans Parish Med. Soc., Greater New Orleans Pathology Soc., La. Civic Service League, Friends of City Park, Friends of Zoo, Friends of Symphony, New Orleans Mus. Art, Les Amis du Vin, Phi Beta Kappa, Alpha Omega Alpha, Phi Beta Pi. Democrat. Roman Catholic. Home: 6525 Argonne Blvd New Orleans LA 70124 Office: 2025 Gravier St Suite 140 New Orleans LA 70112

BRAZIEL, JAMES HARRISON, III, anesthesiologist; b. Lyons, Ga., June 13, 1950; s. James Harrison and Martha Nelle (Flanders) B.; B.S. in Pharmacy, U. Ga., 1974; M.D., Med. Coll. Ga., 1978; m. Debran Keith Taylor, June 24, 1978. Intern, Med. Coll. Ohio, Toledo, 1978-79; resident in anesthesiology Med. Coll. Ga., Augusta, 1979-81, clin. instr., 1981-82, asst. prof., 1982-83; staff anesthesiologist Northeast Ala. Regional Med. Center, Anniston, 1983—. Mem. Am. Soc. Anesthesiologists, Ga. Soc. Anesthesiologists, Ala. Soc. Anesthesiologists, Internat. Anesthesia Research Soc., AMA, Phi Delta Chi, Theta Kappa Psi. Mem. Christian Ch. Home: 1707 Cherry Circle Anniston AL 36201 Office: Dept Anesthesiology NE Ala Regional Med Center Anniston AL 36201

BRAZIL, WILLIAM OSCAR, college dean; b. Hot Springs, Ark., Nov. 4, 1934; s. Leonard A. and Gertrude W. (Cole) B.; m. Carolyn Wellborn, Nov. 30, 1963; children—William W., Caroline W. Student Henderson State U., 1952-56; B.B.A., U. Ark., 1956, M.A., 1963; postgrad. Sanford U., 1966, Fla. State U., 1969, U. Scranton, 1976. Dean students Young Harris Coll., Ga., 1963-69; headmaster Madison Acad., Fla., 1973-81; dean students North Fla. Jr. Coll., 1981—, also instr. history, 1969-73. Mem. Fla. Assn. Student Fin. Aid Adminstrs., So. Assn. Student Fin. Aid Adminstrs., So. Assn. Collegiate Registrars and Adminstrn. Officers, Fla. Assn. Collegiate Registrars and Admissions Officers, Fla. Council Ind. Schs. (state bd. dirs. 1979-81). Republican. Episcopalian. Club: South Ga. Hunter/Jumper Assn. (pres. 1979-81). Lodge: Masons. Avocations: antiques; horses. Home: 617 N Court St Quitman GA 31643 Office: North Fla Jr Coll Turner Davis Dr Madison FL 32340

BREARD, BENJAMIN ALLEN, art dealer; b. Dallas, July 4, 1946; s. Jack Hendricks Breard and Kathleen (Herrell) Byrne; m. Janice Platt, June 14, 1974; children—Angela Kathleen, Benjamin Allen Jr. B.S. in Journalism, Northwestern U., 1969; M.S. in Photojournalism, Syracuse U., 1971. Owner, dir. The Afterimage Gallery, Dallas, 1971—. Bd. dirs. The Allen Street Gallery, Dallas, 1983—. Mem. Am. Booksellers Assn., Assn. Internat. Photography Art Dealers Inc. Republican. Mem. Evangelical Ch. Avocations: photography; music; bird watching; gardening. Home: 19 Merrie Circle Richardson TX 75081

BREAUD, STEPHEN MARON, surgeon; b. Pitts., Feb. 12, 1952; s. P.M. and Amy (Hebert) B.; m. Rebecca Eleanor Butler, June 19, 1982; 1 child, Alec Butler. B.S. in Zoology, La. State U., 1974, M.S., 1975, M.D., 1979. Diplomate Am. Bd. Ophthalmology. Resident in ophthalmology U. Ala. Eye Found., Birmingham, 1979-82; fellow in retina and vitreous surgery Eye Found Hosp., Birmingham, 1983-84, U. Cologne, Fed. Republic Germany, 1983-84; practice medicine specializing in retina and vitreous surgery, Baton Rouge, 1984—; asst. clin. prof. U. Ala. 1984-85. Fellow Am. Acad. Ophthalmology; mem. AMA, So. Med. Assn., East Baton Rouge Med. Assn., Vitreous Soc., C. of C. (med. com. 1985—). Republican. Roman Catholic. Home: 428 Woodstone Dr Baton Rouge LA 70808 Office: 7341 Jefferson Hwy Baton Rouge LA 70806

BREAUX, HELEN ISABEL, religious administrator; b. Westwego, La., July 13, 1934; d. John Paul and Adelaide Isabel (Cooke) Breaux. B.S. in Edn., Loyola U. New Orleans, 1970; M.R.E., Notre Dame Sem., 1973, D.R.E., 1970. Entered Sisters of Our Lady of Mt. Carmel, Roman Catholic Ch., 1953; Sisters Christian Community, 1975; tchr. various schs., 1955-69; dir. Religious Edn., Our Lady of Prompt Succor Parish, Westwego, La., 1970-74; asso. dir. Office Religious Edn., Archdiocese of New Orleans, 1975-82; adminstr. Annunciation Inn, New Orleans, 1983—; commr.-in-charge Ward 14, Precinct 25, New Orleans, 1978—. Organist, chairperson liturgy com. St. Rita Ch., New Orleans. Recipient award for service Our Lady of Prompt Succor Parish, 1974; recipient Key to City of Westwego, 1974, 81. Mem. Nat. Cath. Educators Assn., Assn. for Supervision and Curriculum Devel., Nat. Assn. Ch. Personnel Adminstrs., Nat. Council Diocesan Dirs. Religious Edn., Religious Edn. Assn., U.S. Hist. Assn., Assn. Mgmt. Elderly Housing, New Orleans Mus. Art, St. Vincent de Paul Soc. Democrat. Club: K.C. Aux. One of several editors for religion text series, 1976-81. Home: 2719 1/2 Pine St New Orleans LA 70125 Office: 1220 Spain St New Orleans LA 70117

BREAUX, JOHN BERLINGER, congressman; b. Crowley, La., Mar. 1, 1944; s. Ezra H., Jr. and Katherine (Berlinger) B.; B.A. in Polit. Sci., U. Southwestern La., 1964; J.D., La. State U., 1967; m. Lois Gail Daigle, Aug. 1, 1964; children—John Berlinger, William Lloyd, Elizabeth Andre, Julia Agnes. Admitted to La. bar, 1967; partner Brown, McKernan, Ingram & Breaux, 1967-68; legis. asst. to Congressman Edwin W. Edwards, 1968-69, dist. asst., 1969-72; mem. 92d-99th Congresses from 7th Dist. La., mem. select com. on outer continental shelf, mem. com. on mcht. marine and fisheries, com. on pub. works and transp., policy and steering com.; chmn. subcom. on fisheries and wildlife conservation and environ., House whip-at-large 99th Congress; Congl. del. World Food Conf., 1974. Mem. Dem. Research Orgn.; La. chmn. March of Dimes, 1974-75. Recipient Am. Legion award. Moot Ct. finalist La. State U., 1966. Mem. La., Acadia Parish bar assns., Internat. Rice Festival Assn. (dir.), Crowley Jr. C. of C., La. Jr. C. of C., Nat. Blue Key Honor Soc., Pi Lambda Beta, Phi Alpha Delta, Lambda Chi Alpha. Democrat. Office: 2113 Rayburn House Office Bldg Washington DC 20515

BREAUX, LAWRENCE DAVID, optometrist; b. Houma, La., July 12, 1956; s. Lloyd Joseph and Verla (LeBoeuf) B.; m. Sharon Gail Carpenter, July 28, 1979; children—Jennifer, Celeste. B.S., La. State U., 1977; O.D., So. Coll. Optometry, 1981. Staff Contact Lens Clinic, Franklin, La., 1981-82; pvt. practice optometry Family Vision Clinic, Houma, La., 1982—. Bd. dirs. Am. Cancer Soc., 1984—; mem. Terre Vonne Parish Sch. Bd., 1984—. Fellow Am. Coll. Optometric Physicians; mem. La. Assn. Optometry, Am. Optometric Assn. Democrat. Roman Catholic. Lodge: Lions (v.p. 1982—). Avocations: music; fishing; hunting. Home: 218 Central Ave Houma LA 70360 Office: Family Vision Clinic 3 Professional Dr Houma LA 70360

BREAUX, LONNIE MICHAEL, architect; b. Abbeville, La., Apr. 1, 1951; s. Ralph Joseph and Anna Louise (Meaux) B.; m. Patricia Ann Ford, June 2, 1973; children—Heather Rene, Christopher Michael, Joshua Michael. B.Arch., U. Southwest La., 1975. Registered architect, La., Tex. Architect L. P. Manson, Baton Rouge, 1976-83, Thompson, Washer, Baton Rouge, 1983-84; hosp. architect Scott and White Hosp., Temple, Tex., 1984—; prin. Lonnie M. Breaux & Assocs., Temple, 1985—. Team leader March of Dimes, Temple, 1985. Mem. AIA, Tex. Architects Soc., Nat. Council Archtl. Registration Bds. Republican. Roman Catholic. Lodge: Lions. Avocations: skiing; rose gardening; hunting. Office: Scott and White Meml Hosp 2401 S 31st St Temple TX 76502

BRECHIN, JOHN BRYCE, III, management consultant; b. Beaumont, Tex., Dec. 3, 1926; s. John Bryce and Carlyse (Bliss) B.; B.B.A., U. Tex., 1951; postgrad. U. Houston, 1952-53, Lamar U. Continuing Edn. Program, 1972-74; m. Jane Alice Hodges, Apr. 8, 1951; children—John B. IV, Heidi Lynn, Jamie Leigh, Mark Andrew. Solicitor, Newtex S.S. Lines, Houston, 1951; traffic mgr. oil tool div. Cameron Iron Works, Houston, 1951-54; traffic mgr., mfg. plant buyer Moncrief-Lenoir Mfg. Co., Houston, 1954-57; gen. mgr. Rioco Oil Co., Beaumont, 1957-60; pres. Ranger Ind. Oil Corp., Winnie, Tex., 1960-82; mgmt. cons., 1982—; lectr. drilling fluids Lamar U. Oil and Gas Drilling Inst., 1975. Active Boy Scouts Am., 1967—, camping chmn., 1969-79, tng. chmn., 1980-84, mem. council com., 1964-84, recipient Dist. Merit award, 1973, Vigil of Honor, 1977, Silver Beaver award, 1979. Mem. Soc. Petroleum Engrs., Internat. Platform Assn., AIME. Episcopalian (tchr. 1966-68, 84—, mem. bishop's com. 1967, troop com. 1985—). Clubs: Rotary, Optimists. Patentee drilling fluids additives. Home: 213 Westview Dr Sealy TX 77474 Office: PO Drawer A Sealy TX 77474

BRECKENRIDGE, JAMES, religion educator; b. St. Louis, June 30, 1935; s. Vance Newman and Elsa Schuarte (Breckenridge) Newman Breckenridge; m. Linda Faye Smit, June 21, 1969; children—Bonnie Lin, Rebecca Jane. B.A., Biola Coll., 1957; B.D., Calif. Bapt. Theol. Sem., 1960; M.A., U. So. Calif., 1965, Ph.D., 1968. Lectr., Am. Bapt. Sem. of West Covina (Calif.), 1967-74, Calif. Poly. Coll.-Pomona, 1969-74, U. Redlands (Calif.), spring 1972; prof. religion Baylor U., Waco, Tex., 1974—. Served to capt. USAR, 1958-66. Mem. Am. Acad. Religion, Collectors of Religion on Stamps, Phi Kappa Phi. Baptist. Contbr. religious articles to profl. publs. Home: 1300 N 62d St Waco TX 76710 Office: Baylor U Tidwell Bldg B 27 Waco TX 76798

BREEDEN, JUDY COBB, insurance agent; b. Lake Charles, La., Apr. 26, 1943; d. Thomas William and Beatrice B. Cobb; m. Richard Dean McCullor, Sept. 7, 1963 (div. June 1966); m. Marvin Lee Breeden, Nov. 9, 1970; 1 son, Kevin Dean McCullor. Student McNeese State Coll., 1959-60; grad. Ins. Inst. Am., 1978. Gen. ins. office duties Ratliff & Myers Ins., Lake Charles, 1960-63; office mgr., servicing agt. Atkinson/Kaylor Agy., Pensacola, Fla., 1963-67; office mgr., servicing agt. Aaron Topek Ins. Agy., 1967-72; office mgr. Cravens, Warren & Co., Houston, 1972-78, Woodlands br. mgr. Cook Cravens Warren & Co., 1978-81; owner Breeden & Assocs., Woodlands, Tex., 1981—. Mem. Am. Bus. Womens Assn. (Woman of Yr. award Conroe charter chpt. 1983), Nat. Ind. Ins. Agts. Assn., Cert. Ins. Counselors Soc., Ind. Ins. Agts. Assn. Tex., Profl. Ins. Agts. Tex., Conroe C. of C., South Montgomery County C. of C. Republican. Club: Panorama Country (Conroe). Office: 1717 Woodstead Ct Suite 101 Woodlands TX 77380

BREEDING, GARNETT MONROE, JR., insurance agent; b. Moody, Tex., Oct. 17, 1932; s. Garnett Monroe and Mildred Eunice (Thompson) B.; m. Anita Jeanne Merchant, June 1, 1954; children—Charles Alan, Scott Monroe, Elizabeth Ann. Student U. Tex.-Arlington, 1965, Pensacola Jr. Coll., 1970-71. Clk., Glo Cleaning System, Dallas, 1950-51; sales clk. R.B. George Equipment Co., Dallas, 1951-53; asst. instr. naval sci. Santa Rosa County Sch. System, Milton, Fla., 1972-76; agt. N.Y. Life Ins. Co., N.Y.C., 1977—. Bd. dirs. West Fla. Heart Assn., Pensacola, 1974-75; Mem. exec. bd. Pvt. Industry Council Okaloosa/Walton/Santa Rosa, 1983-84; adv. bd. Locklin Vo-Tech Ctr., Milton, 1983-84, Downtown Redevel. Commn., Milton, 1983-84; pres. Progressive Milton Assn. 1982. Served with USN, 1953-72. Decorated Navy Achievement medal, 1968-69. Mem. Million Dollar Round Table, Pensacola Assn. Life Underwriters (dir. 1977-81), Santa Rosa County C. of C. (pres. 1983). Democrat. Methodist. Club: Kiwanis (pres. 1983-84). Lodge: Masons. Home: 922 Lakeside Dr Milton FL 32570 Office: NY Life Ins Co Courthouse Sq Prof Mall 3B Milton FL 32570

BREHONY, KATHLEEN ANN, clinical psychologist; b. Newark, May 23, 1949; d. James Luke and Mary Catherine (Kelly) B. B.A., Cath. U. Am., 1973; M.S., Va. Tech. Coll., 1977, Ph.D., 1981. Lic. psychologist, Va. Mgr. Arthur Young & Co., Washington, 1981-82; asst. prof. Va. Tech. Inst. and State U., Blacksburg, 1982-84; psychologist Counseling Ctr., Roanoke, Va., 1984—; v.p. Media Works, Roanoke, 1983—; staff psychologist Community Hosp. Ctr. Women's Health, Roanoke, 1984—. Editor: (with others) Marketing Health Behaviors, 1984; editorial bd. Jour. Women and Therapy, 1985. Contbr. chpt. to book. Mem. task force on battered women Council Community Services, Roanoke, 1984-85; mem. First Friday, Roanoke, 1981—. Va. Tech. Inst. scholar, 1976-77. Mem. Am. Psychol. Assn., Nat. Women's Studies Assn., Southeastern Psychol. Assn. (Research award 1978), Va. Psychol. Assn., Psi Chi (certs. of excellence in research 1978, 79). Democrat. Roman Catholic. Avocations: Fiction writing; music; photography; tennis. Home: 339 King George Ave Roanoke VA 24016 Office: Counseling Ctr 3144 Brambleton Ave Roanoke VA 24018

BREIT, WILLIAM, economist, educator, mystery writer; b. New Orleans, Feb. 13, 1933; s. Murray and Sylvia (Shor) B. B.A., U. Tex., 1955, M.A., 1956; Ph.D., Mich. State U., 1961. Asst. prof. La. State U., Baton Rouge, 1961-63, assoc. prof., 1964-65; assoc. prof. U. Va., 1965-70, prof., 1970-83; E.M. Stevens disting. prof. econs. Trinity U., San Antonio, 1983—. Author: (with others) The Antitrust Penalties, 1976; Murder at the Margin, 1978; The Academic Scribblers; 1982; The Fatal Equilibrium, 1985. Recipient Phi Beta Kappa book prize, 1977. Mem. So. Econ. Assn. (v.p. 1980-81, pres. 1985—), Mystery Writers Am., Am. Econ. Assn. Club: Cosmos. Avocations: philately; Abyssinian cats. Home: 438 E Hildebrand San Antonio TX 78212 Office: Trinity U 715 Stadium Dr San Antonio TX 78284

BREITBURG, EMANUEL, zooarchaeologist, anthropologist, consultant; b. Munich, W.Ger., Mar. 12, 1949; came to U.S., 1949, naturalized, 1955; s. Moise and Rosa (Zelekovich) B. B.A., U. Cin., 1973; postgrad. U. Tenn., 1974-75, So. Ill. U., 1984—; M.A., Vanderbilt U., 1983. Archaeol. aide U. Tenn., 1973; field asst. Clinch River Breeder Reactor, 1973-74; phys. anthropologist Tellico Archaeol. Project, 1974-75; zooarchaeologist Tenn. Div. Archaeology, Dept. Conservation, 1976-79; research zooarchaeologist Ctr. Archaeol. Investigations, So. Ill. U., Carbondale, 80, research asst., 1984—; cons. zooarchaeologist Chattanooga Regional Anthropol. Assn., Middle Cumberland Archaeol. Soc., Tenn. Div. Archaeology, 1979—; adj. curator Cumberland Mus. and Sci. Ctr., 1983-84; vis. scientist in anthropology U. Cin., 1984. Workum scholar, tuition grantee, 1968-73. Mem. Am. Assn. Phys. Anthropologists, Am. Anthropol. Assn., Soc. Am. Archaeology, Soc. Hist. Archaeology, Tenn. Anthrop. Assn., Sigma Xi. Contbr. articles to profl. jours.

BREITHAUPT, JAMES FREDERICK, labor and business law educator; b. Oneida, N.Y., May 11, 1939; s. Alton Brooks Parker and Mildred (Rhoades) B.; m. Wanda Hamalea Youngblood, Mar. 20, 1982. B.A., U. Miami (Fla.), 1962; LL.B. cum laude, Syracuse U., 1965, J.D., 1968. Bar: N.Y. 1965, Fla. 1970. Asst. title atty. Lawyers Title Ins. Co., Winter Haven, Fla., 1969-70; asst. prof. law U. Fla., Gainesville, 1970-71; owner, broker Alligator Realty, Gainesville, 1972-80; asst. prof. labor and bus. law Auburn U., Montgomery, Ala., 1981—; instr. real estate Santa Fe Community Coll., Gainesville, 1971-76. Served to lt. col. USAFR, 1966—. Mem. Bus. Law Tchrs. Assn., Res. Officers Assn. (life), Air Force Assn. (life), VFW, Nat. Rifle Assn. (life), Order Coif, Phi Kappa Phi, Gamma Beta Phi. Baptist. Lodge: Elks. Contbr. articles to profl. jours. Office: Sch Bus Auburn Univ Montgomery AL 36104

BREITHAUPT, ROBERT HOWARD, portrait photographer; b. Vicksburg, Miss., May 3, 1944; s. William Edward and Ruth Virginia (Smith) B.; m. Ruby Lynn McElroy, June 30, 1963 (div. 1968); 1 dau., Kimberly Lynn; m. 2d, Lynda Irene Street, Dec. 25, 1969. Staff announcer Sta. WGVM-(AM-FM), Greenville, Miss., 1958-62; Chief announcer, dir. campus radio U. So. Miss.-Hattiesburg, 1962-68; announcer Sta. WTUF-, Mobile, Ala., 1963-64; program dir., news dir. Fortenberry Broadcasting Corp., Columbia and Hattiesburg, Miss., 1964-68; assoc. editor Sosland Pub. Co., Kansas City, Mo., 1968-75; mgr., photographer Beckers of Dadeland, Inc., Miami, Fla., 1976-82; co-owner, ptnr., pres. Photography by Robert-Thomas, Inc., Miami, 1982—. Mem. Profl. Photographers Am., Inc. (Honor Print Merit award 1983), Southeastern Profl. Photographers, Inc. (Honor Print Merit award 1982), Profl. Photographers Fla. (Honor Print Merit award 1982), South Fla. Profl. Photographers Guild. Club: Kendall Bus. and Profl. Lodge: Moose. Contbr. photog. work to profl. publs. Home: 11760 SW 176th St Miami FL 33177 Office: 12588 N Kendall Dr Miami FL 33186

BREMERMANN, HERBERT JOHN, JR., insurance executive; b. New Orleans, Dec. 9, 1922; s. Herbert John and Hilda Marie (Lemarie) B.; m. Mary Gibson Parlour, Feb. 14, 1950; children—Eve P., Herbert John, III. A.B., Tulane U., New Orleans, 1944, LL.B., 1949. Spl. agt. FBI, 1949-53; with Black, Rogers & Co., 1953-56, Md. Casualty Co., 1956-82; successively resident v.p., v.p. casualty div.; v.p. mktg. div. Md. Casualty Co., 1973-75, exec. v.p., 1975-76, pres., chief exec. officer, Balt., 1976—, chmn. bd., 1979—; vice chmn. bd., dir. Am. Gen. Corp., Houston, 1982—; chmn. bd. Life & Casualty Ins. Co. Tenn., 1982—, Nat. Life & Accident Ins. Co., 1982—; sr. chmn. Am. Gen. Corp., Nashville; chmn., chief exec. officer Gulf Life Ins. Co.; dir. Md. Nat. Corp., 3d Nat. Bank, 3d Nat. Corp., Nashville. Mem. pres.'s council Tulane U.; bd. dirs. Assn. Ind. Colls. in Md. Served to capt. USMC, 1943-46. Named Oustanding Alumnus Tulane U. Sch. Law, 1977. Mem. Ins. Info. Inst. (dir.), Am. Ins. Assn. (dir.), Nashville C. of C. (dir.). Clubs: Balt. Country (Balt.); Belle Meade Country; Center, Balt. City, Md. (Balt.); Cumberland, Nashville

City (Nashville). Home: 3704-Q Estes Rd Nashville TN 37215 Office: Nat Life & Accident Ins Co Am Gen Ctr Nashville TN 37250

BRENNAN, CIARAN BRENDAN, accountant, independent oil producer; b. Dublin, Ireland, Jan. 28, 1944; s. Sean and Mary (Stone) B.; B.A. with honors, Univ. Coll., Dublin, 1966; M.B.A., Harvard U., 1973; M.S. in Acctg., U. Houston, 1976. Auditor, Coopers & Lybrand, London, 1967-70; sr. auditor Price Waterhouse & Co., Toronto, Ont., Can., 1970-71; project acctg. specialist Kerr-McGee Corp., Oklahoma City, 1976-80; controller Cummings Oil Co., Oklahoma City, 1980-82; chief fin. officer Red Stone Energies Ltd., 1982; chief fin. officer Leonoco, Inc., 1982—, JKJ Supply Co., 1982—, dir., cons. numerous small oil cos.; mem. adj. faculty Okla. City U., 1977—; vis. faculty Central State U., 1977—. Mem. Inst. Chartered Accts. England and Wales, Inst. Chartered Accts. Can., Inst. Chartered Accts. in Ireland, Tex., Okla. socs. C.P.A.s, Am. Acctg. Assn., Petroleum Accts. Soc., Inter-Am. Acctg. Assn. Democrat. Roman Catholic. Club: Irish (Oklahoma City); Summerfield Racquet. Contbr. articles to profl. jours. Home: 6029 NW 55th St Oklahoma City OK 73122

BRENNAN, JAMES JOSEPH, mechanical engineering educator; b. Hot Springs, Ark., Apr. 2, 1924; s. James J. and Cynthia Anne (Straw) B.; m. Lolan S. Schroeder, June 25, 1949; children—Juli A. Brennan Davis, Cynthia A. Brennan Becker, James Joseph. B.S.E.E., Iowa State Coll., 1945; postgrad. Columbia U., 1949-52; M.S.I.E., U. Ark., 1963; Ph.D., U. Tex., 1972; postgrad. Tex. A&M U., 1980. Diplomate Nat. Acad. Forensic Engrs. Patent examiner U.S. Patent Office, Washington, 1947-48; engr. U.S. Naval Supply Research and Devel. Facility, Bayonne, N.J., 1948-53; dir. indsl. devel. Hot Springs C. of C., 1954-56; indsl. engr. Ark. Indsl. Devel. Commn., Little Rock, 1956-58; plant engr. elec. organ div. Baldwin Piano Co., Fayetteville, Ark., 1958-60; asst. prof. indsl. engring. U. Ark., Fayetteville, 1960-65; research assoc. U. Ark. Med. Ctr., Little Rock, 1962-64; instr. mech. engring. U. Tex., Austin, 1966-68; assoc. prof. Lamar U., Beaumont, Tex., 1968-73, prof., 1974—, head indsl. engring. dept., 1979-80; pres. Brennan Engring. Co., Beaumont, 1977—; cons. Nat. Clay Pipe Mfrs. Assn., 1953-54, Cherokee Molded Products Co., Ft. Smith, Ark., 1960-63, Levingston Shipbuilding Co., Orange, Tex., 1969-73, Beaumont Refinery, Mobil Oil Corp., 1974-76. Served as ensign USN, 1943-46. NSF faculty fellow, 1965-66. Mem. Nat. Soc. Profl. Engrs., Tex. Soc. Profl. Engrs., ASME, Am. Soc. for Quality Control (pres. Sabine subsect. East Tex. chpt. 1976), ASTM (sec. com. on tech. aspects of product liability litigation 1981-82, chmn. statis. group 1950, mem. various coms.), Nat. Safety Council, Am. Inst. Indsl. Engrs. (dir. Austin chpt. 1967), Am. Soc. Safety Engrs., Sigma Xi, Alpha Pi Mu, Pi Tau Sigma. Home: 2441 Liberty St Beaumont TX 77702 Office: PO Box 10032 Lamar U Beaumont TX 77710

BRENNAN, JOHN SULLIVAN, clothing company executive; b. Harvey, Ill., July 12, 1952; s. Thomas Vincent Joseph and Helen Marie (Howard) B.; m. Peggy Ann Florence, Nov. 2, 1979; step-children—Michael B. Justice, Melissa Ann Justice. B.A., Northwestern U., 1974; cert. profl. selling skills Xerox Corp., 1979. Line supr. distbn. Levi Strauss & Co., 1975-77, area mgr. distbn., Florence, Ky., 1977-79, sales rep., Madisonville, Ky., 1979-83, account mgr., Virginia Beach, Va., 1983—. Recipient Outstanding Sales Achievement award Levi Strauss & Co., 1980, $5 Million award, 1982, 5 Yr. Service award, 1982. Club: Men's Apparel.

BRENNAN, ROBERT J., shipping company executive; married. B.B.A., Loyola U., 1950. With Lykes Bros. Steamship Co. Inc., New Orleans, 1942—, various traffic mgr. positions various divs. UK, Mediterranean, asst. tonnage controller, 1964-66, tonnage controller, asst. v.p., 1966-70, v.p. traffic, 1970-74, sr. v.p., 1974-76, exec. v.p., 1976—. Office: Lykes Bros Steamship Co Inc 300 Poydras St Lykes Ctr PO Box 53068 New Orleans LA 70153*

BRENNER, SAUL, political science educator, lawyer; b. Bklyn., Oct. 9, 1932; s. Harry and Sylvia (Berman) B.; m. Martha Judith Funt, Dec. 25, 1966; children—Daniel, David. B.A., Bklyn. Coll., 1954, M.A., 1963; LL.B., Columbia U., 1959; Ph.D., NYU, 1970. Bar: N.Y. 1959. Practice law, N.Y.C., 1959-65; instr. U. N.C., Charlotte, 1965-68, asst. prof., 1968-80, assoc. prof., 1980—. Bd. dirs. N.C. Hebrew Acad., Charlotte, 1969-85. Served with U.S. Army, 1954-56, 61. NSF grantee, 1970, 73; NEH grantee, 1980; So. Regional Edn. Bd. grantee, 1980. Mem. Am. Polit. Sci. Assn., So. Polit. Sci. Assn., Midwest Polit. Sci. Assn. Democrat. Jewish. Contbr. articles to profl. jours. Home: 329 Ridgewood Ave Charlotte NC 28209 Office: Polit Sci Dept U of NC Charlotte NC 28223

BRENTNALL, LYNN COLLINS, management consulting institute executive; b. West Palm Beach, Fla., Oct. 19, 1948; d. William Arnold and Lorna (Holt) Collins; m. Edward Merritt Brentnall, June 20, 1970. B.S., West Ga. Coll., 1966; M.A., Ga. State U., 1975, Ph.D., 1979. Instr. Pace Acad., Atlanta, 1973-77; grad. instr. Ga. State U., Atlanta, 1975-78; psychologist's asst. Drs. Janus & Martin, Atlanta, 1977-79; indsl. psychologist Inst. for Mgmt. Improvement, 1979—, v.p., gen. mgr., West Palm Beach, Fla., 1984—; guest lectr. U. Tenn., Chattanooga, 1983—. Vol. Jr. League Atlanta, 1975-79. Recipient Dean's award Ga. State U., Mem. Am. Psychol. Assn., Southeastern Psychol. Assn., Am. Soc. for Tng. and Devel., Nat. Soc. for Performance Instrn. Avocations: biking; needlepoint. Office: Inst Mgmt Improvement 400 Australian Ave Suite 200 West Palm Beach FL 33401

BRESLAV, JONATHAN, sales executive; b. New Haven, Jan. 1, 1936; s. Walter and Florence Sophie (Ullman) B.; m. Diana Dorothy Paris, Aug. 21, 1965; children—Alison, Gordon. B.A., Yale U., 1957; M.B.A., So. Ill. U., 1977. Asst. to gen. sales mgr., regional mgr. Hertz Corp., N.Y.C., 1959-73; gen. mgr. U.S. Fleet Leasing, St. Louis, 1973-74; v.p., gen. mgr. GelCar div. Gelco Corp., St. Louis, 1975-80; area sales mgr. Avis Car Leasing, Miami, 1980—. Served with U.S. Army, 1958-61. Mem. Am. Arbitration Assn., Beta Sigma Gamma. Club: Pine Crest Fathers (pres. 1984-85). Office: 1100 NW 72d Ave Suite 200 Miami FL 33126

BREST, ALEXANDER, television executive, consulting engineer; b. Boston, Nov. 4, 1894; s. Simon and Sarah (Rosenthal) B.; children—Paul Andrew, Peter Ronald. B.S., MIT, 1916; D.Civil Law (hon.), Jacksonville U., 1974. Registered profl. engr., land surveyor, Fla. San. engr. Fla. Bd. Health, 1919-21; asst. prof. civil engring. U. Fla., Gainesville, 1921-23; sec.-treas. Duval Engring. & Contracting Co., Jacksonville, Fla., 1923-72; founder, pres., treas. WTLV Channel 12, Jacksonville, 1954—; cons. engr. Harbor Engring., 1975—; dir. Flagship Banks, WesJax Corp. Bd. dirs. Mus. Arts and Scis., 1973—, St. Vincent's Hosp., 1979—; mem. No. Fla. council Boy Scouts Am.; trustee Jacksonville U., 1954—; founder, trustee Alexander Brest Planetarium, 1973. Served to lt. col. C.E., U.S. Army, 1942-45. Decorated Legion of Merit; recipient Disting. Service award Fla. Assn. Colls., 1982; Disting. Citizen award Boy Scouts Am., 1983. Mem. ASCE (life; World War II award 1945), Fla. Road Builders Assn. (life), Asphalt Contractors Assn. Fla. (hon. life). Jewish. Club: River of Jacksonville (dir.). Lodge: Shriners, Jesters. Office: WTLV Channel 12 PO Box TV 1212 1020 E Adams St Jacksonville FL 32231

BRETT, THOMAS RUTHERFORD, judge; b. Oklahoma City, Oct. 2, 1931; s. John A. and Norma (Dougherty) B.; B.B.A., U. Okla., 1952, LL.B., 1957, J.D., 1971; m. Mary Jean James, Aug. 26, 1952; children—Laura Elizabeth Brett Tribble, James Ford, Susan Marie Brett Crump, Maricarolyn. Bar: Okla. 1957. Asst. county atty. Tulsa, 1957; mem. firm Hudson, Hudson, Wheaton, Kyle & Brett, Tulsa, 1958-59, Jomes, Givens, Brett, Gotcher, Doyle & Bogan, 1969-79; U.S. dist. judge No. Dist. Okla., Tulsa, 1979—. Bd. regents U. Okla., 1971-78; mem. adv. bd. Salvation Army; trustee Okla. Bar Found. Served to col. JAG, USAR, 1953-81. Fellow Am. Coll. Trial Lawyers, Am. Bar Found.; mem. ABA, Okla. Bar Assn., Tulsa County Bar Assn., Am. Judicature Soc., U. Okla. Coll. Law Alumni Assn. (dir.), Phi Alpha Delta, Order Coif. Democrat. Office: 333 W 4th St Room 4-508 Tulsa OK 74103

BREWER, FRANKLIN DOUGLAS, research entomologist, educator; b. Electric Mills, Miss., Sept. 25, 1938; s. Olen B. and Meredith (Woodruff) B.; m. Mary Carol Ward, May 27, 1966; children—Douglas Alexander, Olen Andrew, Kelly Crisler. B.S., Miss. Coll., 1960; M.S., U. So. Miss., 1963; Ph.D., Miss. State U., 1970. Grad. fellow biology dept. U. So. Miss., Hattiesburg, 1961-63; instr. biology dept. Miss. U. for Women, 1964-66; acting instr., microbiology dept. Miss. State U., Mississippi State, 1966-67, research asst. entomology dept., 1967-70, research assoc. biochemistry dept., 1970-71; research entomologist Agrl. Research Service, U.S. Dept. Agr., Stoneville, Miss., 1971-84, Boll Weevil Research Lab., 1984—; adj. asst. prof. entomology Miss. State U. Com. mem. Pack 1, Delta council Boy Scouts Am., Leland, Miss.; active Leland PTA. Recipient service award U.S. Dept. Agr., 1982. Mem. Entomol. Soc. Am., Miss. Entomol. Assn., Sigma Xi, Phi Kappa Phi, Gamma Sigma Delta, Beta Beta Beta, Alpha Epsilon Delta. Presbyterian. Club: Deer Creek Town and Racquet. Lodge: Lions. Contbr. articles to profl. jours. Home: 103 Peninsula Dr LeLand MS 38756 Office: PO Box 225 Stoneville MS 38776

BREWER, NORMA JANE, vocational educator; b. Birmingham, Ala., Apr. 10, 1928; d. Arthur Melville and Nellie May (Stine) Bruce; m. Leo Ira Louie Brewer, Dec. 19, 1950 (div. June 1972); children—Arthur Bruce, Barbara Janet, Leo Ira Louie, William David. B.S., U. Montevallo, 1950; M.S.Ed., Troy State U., 1970; Ed.D., Auburn U., 1978. Tchr. Pasadena City Schs., Tex., 1950-51, Jefferson County Bd. Edn., Birmingham, 1955-57, Montgomery Community Action Com., Ala., 1968-69; reading specialist Rehab. Research Found., Draper Prison, Speigner, Ala., 1970-74; research assoc. Ala. Dept. Edn., Montgomery, 1976-77, coordinator curriculum and instrn. Skills Tng. and Edn. Program, 1982—; research assoc. Auburn U., Ala., 1977-78; assoc. prof. secondary edn. Northwestern State U., Natchitoches, La., 1978-80; region V coordinator La. Dept. Edn., Lake Charles, 1980-82; mem. Ala. Taskforce on Curriculum Devel., 1982-85, State Adv. Council for Vocat. Edn., La., 1980-82; chmn. Region V Adv. Com. on Vocat. Edn., Baton Rouge, 1980-82. Mem. Montgomery County Democratic Com., 1972-73; pres. Ala. Democratic Women, 1970-72; legis. chmn. Ala. IWV, 1965-70; com. chmn. Montgomery Mental Health, 1970-71; sec. Ala. Mental Health, 1970-71; site com. chmn. Wetumpka Beautification Com., Ala., 1985. Recipient Disting. Performance award Nat. Alliance Bus., 1985. Mem. Am. Soc. Tng. and Devel., Manpower Tng. and Devel., Am. Vocat. Assn., Phi Delta Kappa. Democrat. Presbyterian. Club: Civitan (com. chmn. 1985), Montgomery Singles. Avocations: art; reading; collecting antiques. Home: 106 N Bridge St Wetumpka AL 36092 Office: Skills Tng and Edn Program Bell Bldg Suite 700 Montgomery AL 36103

BREWER, PHILIP WARREN, civil engineer; b. Hagerstown, Md., Dec. 18, 1923; s. J. Chester and Ruth (Emmert) B.; m. Elizabeth Marvel Wynn, Aug. 29, 1947; children—Dorothy Wynn, Bruce Douglas. B.S., U. Md., 1945. Hydraulic engr. Water Resources Br., U.S. Geol. Survey, College Park, Md., 1945-47; designing engr. Wash. Suburban San. Commn., Hyattsville, Md., 1947-53; san. engr., civil engr. Bur. Yards and Docks, Dept. Navy, Washington, 1953-68, head spl. design Naval Facilities Engring. Command, 1968-73, chief civil engr., 1973-80. Bd. dirs. Madison County Wildlife Assn. Registered profl. engr., Vt. Clubs: Monument River Sportmen's Assn. (Houlton, Maine); Ruritan (Wolftown, Va.). Lodge: Lions. Episcopalian. Home: Rural Route 1 Box 66-C Madison VA 22727

BREWER, STANLEY EUGENE, librarian; b. Glendale, Calif., Feb. 24, 1944; s. William S. and Bonnie (Engler) B. B.A. in History, Okla. State U., 1966; M.L.S., U. Okla., 1967. Asst. social sci. librarian U. Houston Library, 1970-72, history and polit. sci. librarian, 1972-74; librarian Gulf Oil Corp., Houston, 1974-82, head librarian, 1982-86; library supr. Chevron USA, Inc., Houston, 1986—. Served to 1st lt. U.S. Army, 1967-69. Decorated Bronze Star. Mem. Spl. Libraries Assn. (chmn. petroleum and energy resources div. 1981-82), ALA, Mensa. Methodist. Contbr. articles to profl. jours. Office: 1301 McKinney St Houston TX 77010

BREWER, WILLIAM WALLACE, dentist; b. Anadarko, Okla., July 17, 1937; s. Wallace and Daisey Edna (Dean) B.; m. Harriet Ann Hackett, Dec. 21, 1958; children —Brian, Shelley. A.Sc., Eastern Okla. A&M U., 1958; B.A., Central State Coll., 1960; D.D.S., U. Tenn., 1968. Pvt. practice dentistry, Oklahoma City, 1968—. Fellow Acad. Gen. Dentistry (pres. Okla. chpt. 1973); mem. Okla. Dental Assn., ADA, Assn. Mil. Surgeons U.S., Res. Officers Assn., U. Tenn. Coll. Dentistry Alumni Assn. (trustee 1983—), Registered Artists of Okla. (bd. govs. 1979-85, pres. 1984—), Democrat. Methodist. Club: Lions (pres. N.W. Oklahoma City 1983-84, Zone Chmn. Okla. 1984-85). Avocations: running; quail hunting; flying. Home: 8232 NW 114th St Oklahoma City OK 73132 Office: 4400 NW 63rd St Oklahoma City OK 73116

BREWTON, BENJAMIN COY, JR., vocational technical school administrator; b. May 3, 1929, Claxton, Ga.; s. Benjamin Coy, Sr. and Fleta (Durden) B.; m. Hortense Newsome, Mar., 1951; children—Benjamin Coy, III, Teresa Ann, William Dewey, Tina Marie. B.S. in Edn., Ga. Southern U., 1950; M. in Edn., U. Ga., 1965, postgrad., 1970. Indsl. arts instr. Richmond County Bd. Edn., Augusta, Ga., 1951-60, diversified coop. tng. coordinator, 1960-63, asst. dir. area vocat./tech. sch., 1963-66; dir. area vocat./tech. sch. Bibb County Bd. Edn., Macon, Ga., 1966—. Trustee Ga. Indsl. Home, Macon, 1979—, ARC, 1980—. Mem. Nat. Assn. Educators, Ga. Assn. Educators, Am. Vocat. Assn., Huguenot Soc. Am., Kappa Delta Pi, Phi Kappa, Phi Delta Kappa, Iota Lambda Sigma. Baptist. Lodge: Lions (pres. 1978). Home: 2460 Alandale Dr Macon GA 31211 Office: Macon Area Vocat Tech Sch 330 Macon Tech Dr Macon GA 31206

BREYER, ARTHUR WILLIAM, III, safety manager; b. N.Y.C., Aug. 5, 1940; s. Arthur William, Jr. and Lillian Bernice (Ostrom) B.; B.A. in Psychology, Stetson U., DeLand, Fla., 1964. Cert. hazard control mgr. Safety adv. Boeing Co., Kennedy Space Center, Fla., 1968-72; exec. officer OSHA, Washington, 1972-74; indsl. occupational safety and health mgr. Eastern Space and Missile Center, Patrick AFB, Fla., 1974—; cons. in field. Served with U.S. Army, 1964-66. Mem. Am. Soc. Safety Engrs. (chpt. pres. 1977-78), Vets. of Safety, Assn. Fed. Safety and Health Employees. Republican. Methodist. Home: 340 S 11th St Cocoa Beach FL 32931

BRIAN, ALEXIS MORGAN, JR., lawyer; b. New Orleans, Oct. 4, 1928; s. Alexis Morgan and Evelyn (Thibaut) B.; B.A. in Sociology, La. State U., 1949, J.D., 1956; M.S. in Psychology, Trinity U., 1954; m. Elizabeth Louise Graham, Mar. 17, 1951; children—Robert Morgan, Ellen Graham. Admitted to La. bar, 1956; asso. firm Deutsch, Kerrigan & Stiles, New Orleans, 1956-60, partner, 1961-79; sr. partner firm Brian, Simon, Peragine, Smith & Redfearn, New Orleans, 1979-80, counsel, 1980-82; sr. ptnr. Fawer, Brian, Hardy & Zatzkis, New Orleans, 1982—; mem. legal adv. council Ams. United for Separation Ch. and State, 1977—. Mem. com. on bds. So. Bapt. Conv., 1969, mem. exec. bd. New Orleans Bapt. Assn., 1958-63, sec. trustees, 1967-70. Asst. scoutmaster local troop Boy Scouts Am., 1963-72. Trustee New Orleans Bapt. Theol. Sem., 1961-74, v.p., 1966-68, pres., 1968-74; bd. dirs. Goodwill Industries, 1968—, v.p., mem. exec. com., 1975-77, mem. adv. bd., 1978; bd. dirs. New Orleans Bapt. Theol. Sem. Found., 1972-81, Inter-Varsity Christian Fellowship, 1974—; bd. dirs. Trinity Christian Community, 1970-78, treas., 1977-78. Served with USAF, 1951-55. Named Boss of Year, New Orleans Legal Secs. Assn., 1966. Mem. ABA (tort and ins. practice sect., constrn. industry forum and fidelity and surety coms.), La. Bar Assn. (asst. examiner admissions com.), New Orleans Bar Assn., Internat. Assn. Ins. Counsel (fidelity and surety com.), La. Assn. Def. Counsel, Def. Research Inst., Am. Arbitration Assn. (panel of arbitrators 1970—), Internat. House, La. Civil Service League, La. State U. Found., Upper Carrollton Neighborhood Assn. (v.p. 1976-77), Phi Delta Phi, Theta Xi. Baptist (deacon; trustee; tchr.; lay preacher). Home: 1738 S Carrollton Ave New Orleans LA 70118 Office: 2355 Pan-Am Life Center 601 Poydras St New Orleans LA 70130

BRICE, DONALD A., hydrogeologist; b. Covington, Ky., May 22, 1958; s. Trinnie A. and Emiko (Watanabe) B. B.S. in Geology, Denison U., Granville, Ohio, 1981; M.S. in Geology, U. Ky., 1985. Geologist, Continental Labs., Oklahoma City, Okla., 1981-82; geol. Cons. Petroleum Ventures, Ltd., Florence, Ky., 1983—; research asst. U. Ky.-Lexington, 1983-85; hydrogeologist Geraghty & Miller, Inc., Oak Ridge, 1985—. Pianist, Crittenden Christian Ch., Ky., 1983; telethon vol. U. Ky., 1985. Lamoreaux geology scholar, 1980. Mem. Soc. Econ. Paleontologists and Mineralogists, Am. Assn. Petroleum Geologists (jr.), Geol. Grad. Student Assn. (teaching asst. rep. 1984). Club: U. Ky. Tae Kwan Do (Lexington) (v.p. 1985). Home: 231 W Fairview Rd Oak Ridge TN 37830 Office: 140 E Division Rd Oak Ridge TN 37830

BRICE, LEE ALLAN, pharmacist; b. Miami, Fla., May 23, 1953; s. Anton Melvin and Lillian (Craft) B.; m. Barbara Jean Flynn, Aug. 4, 1984. B.S. in Pharmacy, U. Fla., 1976. Registered pharmacist, Fla., Ga. Pharmacist Walgreen Drugs, Miami, 1976-78, chief pharmacist, 1978-81; chief pharmacist Walgreen Drugs, Jacksonville, Fla., 1981-84; pharmacist, owner, operator Medicine Shoppe, Jacksonville, 1984—; owner, v.p. Blanding Med. Ctr. Pharmacy, Orange Park, Fla., 1985—. Mem. Am. Pharmacy Assn., Fla. Pharmacy Assn. Republican. Methodist. Avocations: racquetball; photography. Home: 2202 Burpee Dr W Jacksonville FL 32210 Office: Medicine Shoppe 3993 University Blvd Jacksonville FL 32216

BRICKELL, EDWARD ERNEST, JR., school superintendent; b. Norfolk, Va., June 22, 1926; s. Edward Ernest and Rosa Willie (Babb) B.; m. Nancy Dunn Brickell; children—Dennis Sean, Heidi Josette, Todd Beatty. B.A., Coll. of William and Mary, 1950, advanced cert. sch. adminstrn., 1970, Ed.D., 1973; M.A., U. Chgo., 1952. Tchr., coach, prin. South Norfolk (Va.) Pub. Schs., 1951-61, supt. schs., 1961-62, Franklin (Va.) Pub. Schs., 1962-65; asst. to pres. Coll. of William and Mary, 1965-66; dir. secondary edn., asst. supt. schs. Virginia Beach (Va.) City pub. schs., 1966-68, supt. schs., 1968—; Prof. Nat. Acad. Sch. Execs.; chmn. Tidewater Supts., 1972-77; mem. State Supts. Adv. Council.; Mem. Drug Focus Com. of Virginia Beach, 1970—. Bd. dirs. Big Bros. Virginia Beach, Gen. Hosp. of Virginia Beach, United Community Fund; former chmn. bd. trustees Tidewater Community Coll.; Trustee Bayside Hosp.; rector, bd. visitors Coll. William and Mary. Served with USAAF, 1944-46. Recipient First Citizen award South Norfolk, 1958, Service to Scouting award, 1969; named Va. Ednl. Adminstr. of Year, 1973. Mem. N.E.A. (life), Nat., Va. assns. sch. adminstrs., Va. Assn. Sch. Execs., Va. Congress Parents and Tchrs. (life), Quill and Scroll, Phi Beta Kappa, Phi Delta Kappa (award for contbn. to edn. 1970), Kappa Delta Pi, Phi Kappa Phi. Methodist. Club: Rotarian. Home: 129 67th St Virginia Beach VA 23451 Office: Princess Anne Station PO Box 6038 Virginia Beach VA 23456

BRICKER, JOHN ALEXANDER, JR., bank executive; b. Houston, Dec. 3, 1951; s. John Alexander and Lucy (Quinby) B.; m. Diane Elaine Wende, Sept. 15, 1973. B.A. in Econs., U. Tex.-Austin, 1973; postgrad. Magdalen Coll., Oxford, Eng., 1973-74; M.B.A., Harvard U., 1976. Asst. treas. Morgan Guaranty Trust Co., N.Y.C., 1976-79; asst. v.p. Republic Bank Dallas, N.A., 1979-80, v.p., 1980-82, sr. v.p., 1982—. Clubs: Lakewood Country, Tex., Crescent. Home: 8811 Windy Terr Dr Dallas TX 75231 Office: Pacific at Ervay Sts Dallas TX 75202

BRICKER, WILLIAM HAROLD, mfg. exec.; b. Detroit, Jan. 29, 1932; B.S. in Agr., Mich. State U., 1953, M. Hort., 1954; m. Doris Arlene Bricker, Apr. 30, 1955. With Diamond Shamrock Chem. Co., Dallas, 1969—, v.p. biochems., 1969-72, pres., 1973-74, v.p. Diamond Shamrock Corp., 1973-74, chief operating officer, 1974-75, pres., 1975-76, chief exec. officer, 1976-79, chmn. bd., 1979—; dir. Norfolk & Western Ry. Co., LTV Corp., Interfirst Corp., AMF Corp. Bd. govs., adv. com. Dallas Symphony Mus.; bd. dirs. Am. Petroleum Inst., Tex. Research League; mem. communications com. Dallas Citizens Council; mem. Dallas Mus. Fine Arts, ARC, bus. adminstrn. and devel. council Tex. A&M U. Mem. Soc. Chem. Industry, Conf. Bd., Dallas Petroleum Club. Clubs: Union (Cleve.); Preston Trail Golf, Brook Hollow, Tower (bd. govs.). Office: Diamond Shamrock Corp 717 N Harwood St Dallas TX 75201

BRICKLE, JUDITH HERRMANN, appliance manufacturing company personnel manager; b. Evansville, Ind., Nov. 19, 1940; d. Edwin Frederick and Anna Zerilda (Fridy) Herrmann; B.S., Northwestern U., 1962; 1 dau., Anne Elizabeth. Asst. to advt. mgr. Fortune Mag., Boston, 1962; editorial asst. Am. Pharm. Assn., Washington, 1962; asst. editor Nat. Def. Transp. Assn., Washington, 1962-63; freelance writer, Washington, 1963-70; women's editor No. Va. Sun, Arlington, 1970-71; copy editor Evansville (Ind.) Courier, 1971-72; sr. writer Keller Crescent Co., Evansville, 1972-77; supr. creative programs Gen. Electric Advt., Louisville, 1977-82; mgr. employee programs Gen. Electric major appliance bus. group, 1982—. Mem. Advt. Club Louisville, Mensa. Home: 10604 Linn Station Rd Louisville KY 40223 Office: Appliance Park 3 #232 Louisville KY 40225

BRIDEAU, THOMAS MATTHEW, university administrator; b. Detroit, Feb. 28, 1953; s. David Raymond and Carol Jean (Tassie) B.; m. Jane Marie Piersante, July 30, 1983. Russian Lang. cert., Def. Lang. Inst., Monterey, Calif., 1971; B.S., Central Mich. U., 1978, M.A., 1984. Spl. edn. tchr. Birch Run Area Schs., Mich., 1979-80; residence hall dir. Central Mich. U., Mount Pleasant, 1980-84; area coordinator residence life Tulane U., New Orleans, 1984—. Coach Mount Pleasant Little League Assn., 1978-84; participant Big Bros. Orgn., Mount Pleasant, 1981-82, New Orleans, 1985—. Served with USAF, 1971-74. Decorated Air medal. Mem. Nat. Assn. for Student Personnel Adminstrs., Am. Assn. for Counseling and Devel., S. Atlantic Assn. for Coll. and Univ. Residence Halls. Avocations: fishing; camping; guitar; photography; wood burnings/drawing. Home: 27 McAlister Dr New Orleans LA 70118 Office: Dept Univ Housing Tulane U New Orleans LA 70118

BRIDGES, DEANNA, counselor; b. Indiahoma, Okla., July 8; d. Arthur A. and Vera O'Nita (Riggs) Prince; m. Don Ray Tucker, Dec. 18, (div. Jan. 1979); m. Hayden Ray Bridges, June 6, 1981; children—Lori Dee, Hoyt Arthur. A.A., Cameron U., Lawton, Okla., 1965; B.A., S.W. State Coll., Weatherford, Okla., 1966; M.Ed., Okla. U., 1979. Cert. Nat. Bd. Cert. Counselors. Tchr., Snyder Pub. Sch., Okla., 1966-67; tchr. Indahoma Pub. Sch., 1967-72, counselor, 1973-81; counselor Great Plains Area Vo-Tech, Lawton, Okla., 1981—. Mem. Okla. Assn. Counseling and Devel. (pres. 1985-86, Counselor of Yr. award SW region 1983), Am. Assn. Counseling and Devel., Great Plains Vocat. Edn. Assn., Am. Vocat. Assn., Youth Advocacy Council, Delta Kappa Gamma (chpt. pres. 1986). Home: Box 107 Route 1 Indiahoma OK 73552 Office: 4500 W Lee Blvd Lawton OK 73501

BRIDGES, EDWIN CLIFFORD, state official; b. Greenville, S.C., Oct. 18, 1945; s. Henry A. and Elizabeth (Bruce) B.; m. Martha Callison, Aug. 31, 1967; children—Sarah, Mary, Abigail. B.A., Furman U., Greenville, S.C., 1967; M.A., U. Chgo., 1969, Ph.D., 1981. Tchr. Social Studies J.E. Beck & J.L. Mann High Sch., Greenville, S.C., 1968-70; hist. resources cons. Ga. Dept. Natural Resources, Atlanta, 1973-75; instr. Ga. Inst. Tech., Atlanta, part-time, 1973-75; asst. to dir. Ga. Dept. Archives and History, Atlanta, 1976-78, asst. dir., 1981-82; dir. Ala. Dept. Archives and History, Montgomery, 1982—, chmn. State Records Commn., County Records Commn.; coordinator Ala. Hist. Records Adv. Bd.; chmn. Gov.'s Mansion Adv. Bd. Mem. Com. for Humanities in Ala., Ala. Hist. Commn. Author: (with others) Georgia Signers of the Declaration of Independence, 1981. Mem. Soc. Am. Archivists, So. Hist. Assn., Nat. Assn. Govt. Archives and Records Adminstrs. (treas. 1980-85). Home: 3336 Wiley Rd Montgomery AL 36106 Office: State of Ala Dept Archives and History 624 Washington Ave Montgomery AL 36130

BRIDGES, JERRY GENE, personnel specialist; b. Ardmore, Okla., Aug. 7, 1930; s. A.C. Franklin and Geneva Jo (Heron) B. B.S.B.A., East Central U., Okla., 1960. Adminstrv. trainee Conoco, Ardmore, Okla., 1960, analyst, 1960-72, coordinator personnel devel., Oklahoma City, 1972—; also cons. Mem. Okla. Safety Council (bd. dirs. 1983—, planning com. 1984-85), Okla. Soc. to Prevent Blindness (adviser 1983—), Am. Petroleum Inst. (Gulf Coast tng. com.), Nat. Safety Council, Am. Soc. Safety Engrs. Democrat. Methodist. Avocations: public speaking; hunting; fishing. Home: 6001 N Brookline Oklahoma City OK 73112 Office: 3817 NW Expressway Oklahoma City OK 73112

BRIDGES, JESSE LEON, financial holding company executive; b. Lincoln, N.C., Feb. 16, 1929; s. Jesse Lee and Myrtle (Wilson) B.; m. Margaret Moss, Oct. 18, 1958; children—Susan A., Glenn L. Mgr. United Credit Corp., Spartanburg, S.C., 1952-55; founder, pres. Security Fin. Corp., Spartanburg, 1955—, chmn. bd., 1983—. Served with USN, 1948-52. Address: 106 Fernbrook Circle Spartanburg SC 29302 also 341 Fernandina St Fort Pierce FL 33449

BRIDGES, WILLIAM TURNER, state official; b. Prentiss, Miss., Aug. 27, 1932; s. C. Bryant and Luna (Russell) B.; m. Bonita Spence, June 25, 1961; children—Spence, Chad. B.S., U. So. Miss., 1968. Mgr. Prentiss Elec. Co., Miss., 1951-59; bus. mgr. Jeff Davis County Schs., Prentiss, 1960-68; auditor State Dept. Edn., Jackson, Miss., 1969-72, food distbn. dir., 1972—. Area dir. ARC-Jeff Davis County, Prentiss, 1954; sec.-treas. Civitan Club, Prentiss, 1962, sec.-records award, 1962. Recipient Charter Mem. award Covington-Jeff Davis Baptist Assn., Prentiss, 1961. Mem. Nat. Assn. State Agys. for Food Distbn., Am. Sch. Food Service Assn., Miss. Sch. Food Service Assn. Democrat. Baptist. Home: 56 Terrapin Hill Rd N Brandon MS 39042 Office: Miss Dept Edn PO Box 771 Jackson MS 39205

BRIDGES, WORTH TALMADGE, JR., dentist; b. Hickory, N.C., May 29, 1928; s. Worth Talmadge Sr. and Florrie Jane (Jeffcoat) B.; m. Ethel Lawing, Aug. 23, 1953; children—Melissa Bridges Caldwell, Sherri Leigh. B.S., Wake Forest U., 1954; D.M.D., U. Louisville, 1959. Lic. dentist. Pvt. practice dentistry, Shelby, N.C., 1959, Mooresville, N.C., 1960—. Mem. Lowrance Hosp. Corp., Mooresville. Served as dental technician USN, 1946-51. Mem.

Alexander-Iredell County Dental Soc. (sec.-treas. 1962-63, pres. 1972-73), N.C. Dental Soc., ADA, N.C. Southeast Analgesic Soc. (charter, chmn. 1972), VFW. Republican. Baptist. Lodges: Masons (32 degree); Shriners. Home: 781 Pinewood Circle Mooresville NC 28115 Office: 213 S Broad St Mooresville NC 28115

BRIDGFORTH, RICHARD BASKERVILLE, JR., tobacco company executive; b. Kenbridge; Va., Jan. 3, 1925; s. Richard Baskerville and Elizabeth (Cunningham) B.; m. Nancy Dickinson, June 12, 1948; children—Richard Baskerville, III, Andrew Dickinson, Robert Manson, Nancy Hatton, John Cunningham. Student, Va. Mil. Inst., 1942-43, Cornell U., 1943-44, U. Va., 1946-48. Vice pres. Internat. Planters Corp., 1949-56; also dir.; pres. G.R. Garrett Co., 1958-61; v.p. Dibrell Bros., Inc., Danville, Va., from 1961, later pres., now chmn. bd., chief exec. officer, also dir.; dir. Bank Va. Co., Richmond.; Chmn. Nat. Tobacco and Textile Museum, Danville. Trustee, mem. exec. com. Meml. Hosp., Danville; trustee Averett Coll., Colgate Darden Grad. Sch. Bus., U. Va., Charlottesville. Served with USMC. Mem. Tobacco Assn. U.S. (gov.). Presbyterian. Clubs: Commonwealth (Richmond); Danville Golf. Office: 512 Bridge St Danville VA 24541

BRIER, DANIEL LEWIS, hosiery company executive, real estate executive; b. Queens, N.Y., Dec. 29, 1932; s. Frederick and Teresa (Gluck) B.; B.S.T.E., Lowell Tech. Inst., 1954; M.B.A., U. Fla., 1956; postgrad. N.Y. U., 1958-60; m. Lynn E. Freeman, June 15, 1957; children—Frederick Nathan, Phillip David. Instr. engring. U. Fla., 1954-56; mktg. mgr. Tropical Delicacies, 1956-57; mktg. cons. Werner Mgmt. Cons., 1958-59, dir. mktg. services, 1960-61; pres. Chemo Products, Inc. of Crompton Co., Inc., N.Y.C., 1961-63, dir. corp. market planning, 1964-65; asst. to pres. B.V.D. Co., Inc., N.Y.C., 1965, chief exec. officer The Alligator Co., 1966, dir. textile mfg. Knitwear group, 1967-69; pres. Corp. Planners, Inc., 1970, Brookdale Securities, Inc. and predecessor firm, N.Y.C., 1971-74; pres., dir. Rudin & Roth, Inc., Lincolnton, N.C., 1975—; exec. v.p., chief operating officer Silverstein Properties, Inc., N.Y.C., 1981-82; former mem. N.Y., Pacific and Am. stock exchanges. Mem. Village of East Rockaway (N.Y.) Planning Commn., 1965-66. Served with USAR, 1956-64. Mem. UN Day Com., Am. Arbitration Assn., Real Estate Bd. N.Y., Nat. Assn. Hosiery Mfrs. (dir., chmn. tech. com. 1984—), Alpha Kappa Psi, Pi Lambda Phi. Clubs: Catawba Country (Newton, N.C.); Ocean Reef (Key Largo, Fla.); Hounds Ears (Blowing Rock, N.C.). Contbr. articles to profl. jours., chpts. in books. Office: PO Box 160 Lincolnton NC 28092 also 384 Fifth Ave New York NY 10018

BRIGGS, DICK DOWLING, JR., physician, educator; b. Electric Mills, Miss., Jan. 28, 1934; s. Dick Dowling and Anita (Carnathan) B.; m. Susan Hunt Davis, June 20, 1959; children—Adrienne Davis, Dick Dowling III, Daniel Roth. B.S. in Chemistry, U. of South, 1956; M.D., Washington U., 1960. Diplomate Am. Bd. Internal Medicine. Intern, U. Ala. Hosp., Birmingham, 1960-62, resident in internal medicine, 1964-65, chief resident, 1965-66; mem. faculty U. Ala. Med. Sch., Birmingham, 1965—, prof. medicine, 1972—, dir. div. pulmonary and critical care medicine, dept. medicine, 1971—, vice-chmn. dept. medicine, 1981—; dir. med. edn. pulmonary lab., also respiratory therapy Carraway Methodist Med. Ctr., Birmingham, 1968-71; cons. Birmingham VA Hosp. Chmn. claims com. U. Ala.-Birmingham Liability Ins. Trust. Served to capt. USAF, 1962-64. Baker scholar, 1952-56, Danforth scholar, 1956-60; grantee Nat. Heart, Lung and Blood Inst., 1972-77. Fellow ACP, Am. Coll. Chest Physicians (pres.-elect 1983-84); mem. Am. Soc. Internal Medicine, Am. Thoracic Soc., AMA, Assn. Am. Med. Colls., So. Med. Assn., Med. Assn. Ala., Jefferson County Med. Soc., Soc. Medica de Santiago (hon.), Phi Beta Kappa. Episcopalian. Clubs: Mt. Brook Swim and Tennis, The Club, Relay House, Ala. Tennis Assn. (pres. 1968-69). Author numerous papers in field. Office: Pulmonary Division University of Alabama Medical School University Station Birmingham AL 35294

BRIGGS, WARREN MARSHALL, foundation executive; b. St. Paul, June 30, 1923; s. Charles William and Lois Ione (Johnson) B.; m. Gloria Gardner Clancy, Dec. 29, 1945; children—Warren Marshall, Sandra Lynne. Student U. Minn., 1940-42; B.S., U.S. Mil. Acad., 1945; M.A., Columbia U., 1954. Vice pres., then pres. Alger-Sullivan Co., Century, Fla., 1957-72; pres. Health Care Found. Bapt. Hosp., Pensacola, Fla., 1975—; dir. Fla. Nat. Bank, Pensacola. Mem. Fla. Ho. of Reps., 1968-70; mayor City of Pensacola, 1977-78; Republican candidate U.S. Congress, 1978-80; pres. Pensacola Mus. Art, 1984, 85; bd. dirs. Rayburn-Dirksen Inst. Applied Politics U. West Fla. Served to maj. USAF, 1945-57. Recipient Liberty Bell award Fla. Bar, 1973; Good Govt. award Jaycees, 1972. Mem. U.S. Navy League (dir., state pres. outstanding Pensacola council 1982). Episcopalian. Home: 3361 Palermo Rd Pensacola FL 32503 Office: 1000 W Moreno St Pensacola FL 32501

BRIGHT, EDGAR ALLEN GORDON, JR., mortgage banker, retail executive; b. New Orleans, Jan. 14, 1929; s. Edgar Allen Gordon and Ethel (Fox) B.; m. Marion Earling, May 8, 1954; children—Edgar Allen Gordon, Hollis E., Timothy P., Elinor S. B.S., Yale U., 1951. Registered rep. Tullis Craig & Bright, 1954-57; account exec. Merrill Lynch Pierce Fenner & Smith, New Orleans, 1957-64; with Standard Mortgage Corp., New Orleans, 1964—, pres., 1975—, also chmn., Atlanta; chief exec. officer Computerland Stores, various locations, 1979—. Chmn. bd. trustees Tulane U. Bus. Sch.; trustee Dillard U. Served with U.S. Army, 1951-53. Roman Catholic. Office: 300 Plaza One Shell Sq New Orleans LA 70139

BRIGHT, HARVEY R., oil producer; b. Muskogee, Okla., Oct. 6, 1920; s. Christopher R. and Rebecca E. (Van Ness) B.; m. Mary Frances Smith, May 27, 1943 (dec. Apr. 1971); children—Carol (Mrs. James B. Reeder), Margaret (Mrs. Jerry R. Petty), Christopher R., Clay Van Ness; m. Peggy Braselton, Dec. 15, 1972. B.S., Tex. A. and M. U., 1943. Partner Bright & Co. (oil producers), Dallas; chmn. bd. E. Tex. Motor Freight Lines, Inc., So. Trust & Mortgage Co., Trinity Savs. and Loan Assn.; dir. Dallas Market Center Co., Republic Nat. Bank, Reynolds Penland Co., Southwestern Pub. Service Co., Republic of Tex. Corp., Mass. Mut. Life Ins. Co. Bd. dirs. Dallas Citizens Council; chmn. bd. Children's Med. Center, Dallas. Served with AUS, World War II. Home: 4500 Lakeside Dr Dallas TX 75205 Office: 2355 Stemmons Bldg Dallas TX 75207

BRIGHTBILL, L. O., III, bank holding company executive; b. Fairmont, W.Va., June 20, 1936; s. L.O., Jr., and Mary (Smith) B.; m. Ruth Conley, Aug. 5, 1961; children—Mark, Amy, Ann (twins), Cynthia. B.S. in Indsl. Mgmt., W.Va. U., 1960; grad. Southwestern Grad. Sch. Banking, 1971, Advanced Mgmt. Program, Harvard U., 1975. Mem. installment loan dept. Tex. Am. Bank, Ft. Worth, 1964-67, mem. comml. loan dept., 1967-69, asst. v.p., 1969-72, v.p., 1972-73; v.p., liaison officer Tex. Am. Bancshares, 1972-73. sr. v.p., 1973-75, exec. v.p., 1975-76, pres., chief exec. officer Tex. Am. Bank, Dallas, 1976-80, pres. Tex. Am. Bancshares, Inc., Ft. Worth, 1980—; dir. Tex. Am. Bancshares, Tex. Am. Bank, Ft. Worth, Tex. Am. Investment Mgmt., Am. AgCredit Corp. Bd. dirs. Rotary Club; Arts Council, 1983, Boy Scout Found., 1983; trustee U. Dallas, 1983; bd. dirs., United Way, 1983. Mem. Assn. Res. City Bankers, Am. Inst. Banking, Newcomen Soc. N.Am. Roman Catholic. Clubs: Exchange, Fort Worth, River Crest Country, Century II. Office: PO Box 2050 Fort Worth TX 76113

BRILL, EDWARD TOBIAS, oil company executive, consultant; b. Washington, May 20, 1950; s. Daniel H. and Charlotte (Lobel) B.; m. Diane Shor, June 11, 1972; children—Joshua Ethan, Jessica Ruth. B.S. in Geology and Physics, U. Rochester, 1972, M.S. in Geology and Physics, 1973; M.B.A., Wharton Bus. Sch., 1979. Corporate planning mgr. Cities Service Co., Tulsa, 1979-80, mgr. internat. planning and budget, Houston, 1980-82; dir. internat. econs. Conoco, Inc., Houston, 1982-84, mgr. strategic planning, 1984—; pres. Brill Co., Houston, 1983—. Treas. Jewish Community North, Spring, Tex., 1983-84. Served to lt. USNR, 1973-81. Recipient NROTC Gold Medal, DAR 1973; named Distinguished Grad., U.S. Naval Acad. Alumni Assn., 1973; NROTC scholar, 1969; Public Policy fellow, Wharton Bus. Sch., 1978. Mem. Assn. Internat. Petroleum Petroleum Negotiators, Assn. Petroleum Geologists, Corp. Planning Soc. N. Am., Nat. Assn. Bus. Economists, Meml. Northwest Houston Apple Users Group. Avocations; reading; home computers; tennis. Home: 8118 Teakwood Forest Dr Spring TX 77319

BRILLHART, DAVID WINTHROP, banker; b. Bethlehem, Pa., Jan. 9, 1925; s. David H. and Elizabeth L. (Lehr) B.; B.S., U.S. Mil. Acad., 1946; M.B.A., N.Y. U., 1960; m. Joan Jeffris, Mar. 5, 1948; children—Jeff, Sally, Jon. Vice pres. Morgan Guaranty Trust Co., N.Y.C., 1954-72; exec. v.p. S.E. First Nat. Bank of Miami (Fla.), 1972-76; pres., chief exec. officer 1st Bancshares of Fla., Inc., Boca Raton, 1977-79; chmn. David Brillhart and Assocs., Miami, 1979—; dir. Independence Bancorp, Perkasie, Pa., Unionbank, Bethlehem, Pa., Constrn. Spltys., Inc., Cranford, N.J., AmeriTravel Internat., Inc., Miami, Fla., Miami Nat. Bank. Served to capt. AUS, 1946-54. Mem. N.Y. Soc. Security Analysts, AIM, Am. Mgmt. Assn. Clubs: Standard, Miami, Coral Reef Yacht (Miami). Home: 5401 SW 98 Terr Miami FL 33156 Office: 5900 SW 73d St Miami FL 33143

BRINDLEY, HANES H., JR., orthopedic surgeon; b. New Orleans, May 18, 1943; s. Hanes H. and Julia Martha (Barton) B.; m. Rolinda Lois Russell, June 24, 1965; children—Hanes H. III, Barton Russell. B.A., U. Tex., 1965, M.D., 1972. Intern, U. Tex. Med. Br., Galveston, 1972-73; resident in surgery Campbell Clinic, Memphis, 1973-77; staff surgeon dept. surgery, div. orthopedics Scott & White Clinic, Temple, Tex., 1980—. Served with USN, 1977-79.

BRINEGAR, JERRY LEE, pastoral psychotherapist; b. Hamburg, Iowa, May 1, 1943; s. W.A. and Gladys Lenore (Geyer) B.; m. Carleen Deanna Fisher, June 11, 1967 (div. 1979), m. Meg Workman, Apr. 19, 1981; children—Keily Mitchell, Autumn Fawn, Kyffon Joseph Lee. B.A. cum laude, Central Meth. Coll., Fayette, Mo., 1970; M.Div., Emory U., 1973, postgrad., 1976-78. Lic. marriage and family therapist, Ga., N.C.; cert. police instr. in stress mgmt. and crisis intervention. Ordained to ministry, 1971; police officer, Atlanta, 1972-76; pastor Splice Creek Meth. Ch., 1966-67, Armstrong-Higbee United Meth. Ch., 1967-70, Elizabeth United Ch., 1970-72, Dahlonega Presbyn. Ch., 1981, Nacoochee Presbyn. Ch., Sautee, Ga., 1981—; pvt. practice psychotherapy Mountain People's Clinic, Hayesville, N.C., 1979-81; exec. dir., clin. supr. Family Counseling Service, Athens, Ga., 1977-79; police stress instr. Ga. Police Acad., 1975—; dir. New Beginnings Counseling Service, Sautee, 1981—. Chmn. Athen's Presbytery Peace and Justice Com., 1982-86; Nacoochee Presbytery Peace Task Force, 1982-83; pres. N. Ga. Citizens Opposed to Paraquat Spraying, 1983; mem. N. Ga. campaign SANE. Served with USN, 1962-66; Vietnam. Mem. Am. Assn. Marriage and Family Therapists (clin. supr.). Am. Assn. Pastoral Counselors. Author: Breaking Free, 1985. Address: Route 1 PO Box 87 Sautee GA 30571

BRINKER, PAUL ALBERT, economics educator; b. Pitts., Feb. 14, 1919; s. William Herman and Elizabeth Sophia (Kauffmann) B.; m. Dorothy Amelia Roberts, June 27, 1949; children—Barbara, Marilyn. B.A., U. Pitts., 1939, M.A., 1940; Ph.D., Pa. State U., 1948. Instr. Miami U., Oxford, Ohio, 1942; asst. prof. U. Vt., Burlington, 1946-47; from asst. prof. to prof. U. Okla., Norman, 1947—; research asst. Exxon Inc., Tulsa, 1952-53. Author: Poverty, Manpower and Social Security, 1976, 2d edit., 1982. Served with USAF, 1942-45. Home: 1309 Melrose Norman OK 73069 Office: U Okla 307 W Brooks Norman OK 73019

BRINKHAUS, ARMAND J., lawyer, state senator; b. Nov. 7, 1935; student U. Southwestern La., Springhill Coll., Mobile, Ala.; LL.B., Loyola U., New Orleans; m. Margaret Bellemin. Practiced in Sunset, La.; mem. La. Ho. of Reps., 1968-76, La. Senate, 1976—. Mem. St. Landry (La.) Parish Library Bd.; bd. dirs. S.W. La. Rehab. Center. Mem. Am. Bar Assn., La. Bar Assn., Am. Trial Lawyers Assn., Am. Judicature Soc., Nat. Rice Growers Assn., St. Landry Cattlemen's Assn., La. Farm Bur., Woodman of World. Democrat. Roman Catholic. Clubs: KC, Lions, Elks. Address: PO Drawer E Sunset LA 70584*

BRINKLEY, CHARLES ALEXANDER, geologist; b. Moody, Tex., Oct. 3, 1929; s. Jess Daniel and Vera Allene (Anderson) B.; student Temple Jr. Coll., 1947-48; B.S. in Geology, Midwestern State U., 1957; M.S. in Geology, Pa. State U., 1960; m. Jeraldine Athalene Skeeter, June 18, 1952. Checker, stock mgr. A & P Tea Co., Temple and Waco, Tex., 1947-50; office asst. John M. Mouser, ind. oil operator, Wichita Falls, Tex., 1957; grad. asst. Pa. State U., 1957-59; geologist Texaco, Inc., New Orleans and Jackson, Miss., 1959-70, dist. geologist, 1970-72, dist. stratigrapher, 1972-75; regional geologist Gen. Crude Oil Co., Houston, 1975-77, exploration mgr. West Gulf dist. 1977-79; exploration mgr. (West Gulf) Mobil-GC Corp., 1979; exploration mgr./chief geologist Maralo, Inc., Houston, 1979-85; ind. petroleum geologist, Kingwood, Tex., and Houston, 1985—. Served with USN, 1950-54. Fellow AAAS; mem. Am. Assn. Petroleum Geologists (cert., v.p. div. profl. affairs 1980-82), Soc. Econ. Paleontologists and Mineralogists, Am. Inst. Profl. Geologists (cert.), New Orleans Geol. Soc., Houston Geol. Soc., Miss. Geol. Soc., West Tex. Geol. Soc., Internat. Airline Passengers Assn. Baptist. Clubs: Houston, Maxim, Midland Petroleum. Home and Office: 3015 Redwood Lodge Dr Kingwood TX 77339

BRINSMADE, LYON LOUIS, lawyer; b. Mexico City, Feb. 24, 1924 (parents Am. citizens); s. Robert Bruce and Helen (Steenbock) B.; student U. Wis., 1940-43; B.S., Mich. Coll. Mining and Tech., 1944; J.D., Harvard, 1950; m. Susannah Tucker, June 9, 1956 (div. 1978); children—Christine Fairchild, Louisa Calvert; m. 2d, Carolyn Hartman Lister, Sept. 22, 1979. Bar: Tex. 1951. Assoc. Butler, Binion, Rice, Cook & Knapp, Houston, 1950-58, ptnr. in charge internat. dept., 1958-83; ptnr. in charge internat. dept. Porter & Clements, Houston, 1983—. Bd. dirs. Houston br. English-Speaking Union of U.S., 1972-75. Served with AUS, 1946-47. Mem. Am. (chmn. com. on internat. investment and devel., sect. internat. law and practice 1970-76, mem. council 1972-76, 81-82, vice chmn. 1976-79, chmn.-elect 1979-80, chmn. 1980-81, co-chmn. com. on Mex. 1982—), Internat., Inter-Am. (co-chmn. sect. on oil and gas law, com. on natural resources 1973-76), Houston bar assns., State Bar Tex. (chmn. internat. law com. 1970-74, mem. council sect. internat. law 1975-78), Am. Soc. Internat. Law, Houston World Trade Assn. (sec., dir. 1967-70, chmn. legis. com.), Houston C. of C. (chmn. legis. subcom. internat. business com. 1970-72), Houston Com. on Fgn. Relations, S.A.R., Allegro of Houston, Sigma Alpha Epsilon. Episcopalian. Clubs: Houston, Houston Athletic, Harvard (Houston). Home: 1700 Main St The Beaconsfield Houston TX 77002 Office: 3500 Republic Bank Ctr Houston TX 77002

BRINSON, DANIEL FRANKLIN, artist, pipeline company technician; b. Coosa County, Ala., Sept. 23, 1939; s. Albert D. and Lorena M. (Huett) B.; student Nat. Radio Inst., 1973, RCA, 1975; m. Brenda J. Harrell, Sept. 11, 1958; children—Juanita J., Frankie J., Albert E., Brenda Celiece, Roger E., Charles D. Field rep. Equifax Services, Jacksonville and Palatka, Fla., 1962-65; asst. plant supt. bldg. maintenance Cairo Pickle Co. (Ga.), 1966; ops. technician Plantation Pipeline Corp., Atlanta, 1966—; owner Dan Brinson & Assocs., Douglasville, Ga., part-time, 1977—; represented in permanent collection Roddenbery Meml. Library, Cairo, Ga., Douglas County Library, Douglasville; cons. in graphic arts, leather art, genealogy. Founder, pastor Christian Patriots Mission, Inc., Douglasville, 1982—. Served with U.S. Army N.G., 1956-65. Mem. Internat. Entrepreneurs, John Birch Soc., Terrell Soc. Am. (sec. 1984—), Nat. Taxpayers Union (field rep.). Baptist. Home and Office: 5115 Hwy 5 PO Box 1354 Douglasville GA 30133

BRINSON, DONALD EDWARD, data processing executive; b. Ponca City, Okla., Sept. 6, 1953; s. Merwyn Glen and Mildred Colleen (Good) B.; B.S. in Math., U. Okla., 1980. With Sta. KGOU, Norman, Okla., 1971-73; lab. instr. ELS Lang. Center, Norman, 1972-74; computer programmer Oscar Rose Jr. Coll., Midwest City, Okla., 1974-78; systems programmer Okla. Tax Commn., Oklahoma City, 1978-80; dir. computer center Rose State Coll., Midwest City, 1980-85; systems specialist Hertz Corp., Oklahoma City, 1985—; cons. Organizer, activities coordinator Single Adult Persons, 1977-79. Mem. Assn. Computing Machinery, Hewlett-Packard Internat. Users Group (pres. Central Okla. Regional Users Group 1982-83). Methodist. Club: Order of Foresters. Home: 308 Draper Dr Midwest City OK 73110 Office: Hertz Corp 5601 Northwest Expressway Oklahoma City OK 73132

BRINSON, ROBERT FRANCIS, JR., history/geography educator; b. Montegomery, Ala., Oct. 28, 1943; s. Robert Francis and Margie Elizabeth (Durden) B.; m. Caryl Ann Dieringer, Dec. 18, 1967. B.A., Fla. State U., 1966, M.A., 1967. Instr. St. Johns River Jr. Coll., Palatka, Fla., 1967-69; instr. history and geography Santa Fe Community Coll., Gainesville, Fla., 1969—. Author: (with Dykes) Study Guide for Modern World History, 1981. Home: 5500 SW 35th Dr Gainesville FL 32608 Office: Santa Fe Community Coll 3000 NW 83rd St Gainesville FL 32602

BRION, DENIS JOLY, legal educator, consultant; b. Decatur, Ill., Jan. 24, 1939; s. Maurice Joseph and Mary Mildred (Joly) B. B.S. in Engring., Northwestern U., 1961; J.D., U. Va., 1970. Bar: D.C., 1971, Va. 1971, U.S. Dist. Ct. D.C. 1971, U.S. Ct. Appeals (D.C. cir.) 1971. Washington sr. counsel RCA Global Communications, Inc., 1974-75; asst. prof. law Coll. William and Mary, Williamsburg, Va., 1975-78; asst. prof. Washington and Lee Law Sch., Lexington, Va., 1978-80, assoc. prof., 1980—; vis. assoc. prof. Boston Coll. Law Sch., 1984-85; cons. U.S. Dept. Energy, John Muir Inst., Va. Assn. Counties, Va. Mcpl. League. Mem. Va. Wetlands Study Com., 1971-72, Va. State Water Control Bd., 1972-76. Served to lt. USN, 1964-67. Mem. ABA, Am. Soc. Legal Hist., Selden Soc. Contbr. numerous articles to profl. jours. Office: Washington and Lee Sch Law Lexington VA 24450

BRISCOE, JOHN ALLEN, oil company executive, horse rancher; b. Hutchison, Kans., Mar. 8, 1949; s. Carrol Dean and Meryle Modell (French) B.; m. Teresa Briscoe; children—John Robert, Melissa. B.S., Okla. State U., 1971. Geologist, Cities Service Oil Co., Midland, Tex., 1971-74; sr. geologist Standard Oil Co. of Ohio, Oklahoma City, 1974-77; geologist Davis Oil Co., Tulsa, 1977-79; v.p., exploration mgr. Post Petroleum Co., Regency Co., Oklahoma City, 1979-82; pres. MPV Energy Corp., Briscoe Investments Co., Oklahoma City, 1982—; ptnr. Briscoe, Chevankia, Schachle & Traweek Ranch, Janco Oil Co., Oklahoma City, 1980—. Mem. Am. Assn. Petroleum Geologists, Oklahoma City Geol. Soc., Am. Quarter Horse Assn., Republican. Episcopalian. Home: 3609 Rena Dawn Ln Edmond OK 73034 Office: Suite 110 One Western Plaza 5500 N Oklahoma City OK 73118

BRISOLARA, ASHTON, alcoholism and drug abuse committee executive; b. New Orleans, Sept. 14, 1924; B.S. Maxima cum laude, Springhill (Ala.) Coll., 1952; M.Ed., Loyola U., New Orleans, 1960; certificate Yale, 1961, Columbia, 1961; m. Geri Martin, Mar. 12, 1961; children—Sharon, Anne Marie, Joanne, Janet. Tchr., St. Joseph's High Sch., Metuchen, N.J., 1943-46, St. Joseph's Novitiate, Metuchen, 1946-47, St. Willibrord High Sch., Montreal, Que., Can., 1947-48, McGill Inst., Mobile, Ala., 1948-50, St. Joseph High Sch., 1950-52, St. Stanislaus Coll., Bay St. Louis, Miss., 1952-54, St. Francis de Sales High Sch., Houma, La., 1954-55, Cor Jesu High Sch., New Orleans, 1954-55, St. Aloysius High Sch., Vicksburg, Miss., 1957-59, St. Aloysius High Sch., New Orleans, 1959-61; vocat. counselor high schs. and colls. in La., Miss., Ala. and Fla., 1955-57; exec. dir. Com. on Alcoholism and Drug Abuse for Greater New Orleans, Inc., 1961—; cons. VA Hosp., New Orleans, 1978—, New Orleans Adolescent Hosp., 1982—, VA Med. Ctr. Aftercare Unit, 1981—. Spl. lectr. dept. health and phys. edn. La. State U., New Orleans, 1961-74; pres. faculty La. Inst. Alcohol Studies, Baton Rouge, 1964-67, spl. lectr., 1966—, faculty, 1972—; faculty New Orleans Police Acad., 1961-74; lectr. So. U. of New Orleans, 1962—, Charity Hosp. Sch. Nursing, 1963—; staff Alcoholism Treatment Service, S.E. La. Hosp., Mandeville, 1965—; lectr., faculty Jefferson Parish (La.) Tng. Acad., Sheriff Dept., 1973; lectr. div. continuing edn. U. Miss., 1974; mem. exec. com. Blue Ridge (N.C.) Inst. So. Community Service Execs., 1964—, pres., 1975; lectr., group discussion leader Southeastern Alcoholism Clinic, 1965-73; faculty S.C. Sch. Alcohol Studies, 1975; faculty Fla. State Sch. Alcohol Studies, U. Miami, Fla. Technol. Inst., Orlando, 1965-73; hon. capt. New Orleans Police Dept., 1964, spl. officer, 1969—; dep. sheriff Hancock County, Miss., 1969-72; faculty Southeastern Sch. Alcohol Studies, U. Ga., Athens, 1966—; faculty dept. psychiatry and neurology Tulane U. Sch. Medicine, 1968—, adj. asso. prof. dept. health services adminstrn., 1971—; faculty, sect. leader Utah Sch. on Alcoholism and other Drug Dependencies, U. Utah, 1971—; vis. prof., cons. U. So. Miss., 1973—; faculty Southwestern Sch. Alcohol Studies, U. Ariz., 1975—; asso. dir., faculty Deep South Sch. Alcohol and Drug Studies, Centenary Coll., Shreveport, La., 1974, dir., 1975—; cons. DePaul Community Mental Health Center, New Orleans, 1969-72, N.I.A.A.A. occupational br., 1972-73, N.W. Fla. Mental Health Center, Panama City, Fla., 1972-75, Gulf Coast Mental Health Center, Gulfport, Miss., 1973—, S.W. La. Edn. and Referral Center, Inc., Lafayette, 1963; bd. mem. La. Inst. Alcohol Studies, 1964-67; staff Mid-South Exec. Devel. Program, 1972—; mem. council of agencies bd. mgmt. Alcohol and Drug Problems Assn. N. Am.; community cons. Nat. Council on Alcoholism, N.Y.C. Mem. profl. advisory com. Social Welfare Planning Council, New Orleans; speaker, lectr. various univs. and orgns. Author: Handbook for Handling the Alcoholic Employee, 1978. Contbr. articles to profl. publs. Home: 4013 Cleary Ave Metairie LA 70002 Office: 3314 Conti St 2d floor New Orleans LA 70119

BRISTOW, WILLIAM EDWARD, blood center administrator; b. Paris, Tex., Apr. 21, 1937; s. William Robert and Lela O'Dena (Crosby) B.; m. Linda Sue Hardee, July 19, 1958; children—Michael Alan, Sharon Kay. Student, Paris Jr. Coll., 1955-56, N. Tex. State U., 1957-58, Baylor Med. Ctr. Sch. Med. Technologists, 1958-59. Blood Bank technologist Wadley Blood Ctr., Dallas, 1959-67, blood bank lab. supr., 1967-70, adminstrv. and tech. dir., 1970-82, adminstr., 1982; exec. dir. Stewart Blood Ctr., Tyler, Tex., 1983—; mem. blood service delivery system research project com. Tex. Area V Health Systems Agy., 1982; mem. adv. com. Kilgore Jr. Coll., 1985-86; mem. blood utilization com. U. Tex. Health Ctr., Tyler, 1985-86. Mem. Am. Soc. Clin. Pathologists, Am. Assn. Blood Banks (mem. clearinghouse lifeline com. 1983-87, chmn. com. exhibits 1980-86, cons. task force on chief exec. officer forums 1983-84, ad hoc com. to coordinate annual meeting 1980-87), South Central Assn. Blood Banks (pres., exec. bd. 1983-84), Club: Tyler (Tex.) Petroleum. Author: BBright! A Computerized Blood Bank Data System, 1978; Development of a Multifaceted Education Program, 1982. Office: 815 S. Baster Ave Tyler TX 75701

BRITAIN, PERRY G., energy services company executive; b. 1925. B.S.E.E., U. Tex.-Austin, 1949. Vice-pres., engr. Dallas Power and Light Co., 1949-72; pres. Tex. Utilities Service, Inc., 1972-81, chmn. bd., chief exec. officer, 1981; pres. Tex. Utilities Fuel Co., 1974—, chief exec. officer, chmn. bd., 1981; with Tex. Utilities Co., 1974—, exec. v.p., now pres., chmn. Address: Tex Utilities Co 2001 Bryan Tower Dallas TX 75201*

BRITAN, SCOTT STEVEN, lawyer; b. Chgo., Oct. 5, 1956; s. Jack and Reva Britan. B.A., U. Miami, 1978, J.D., 1981. Bar: Fla. 1981, U.S. Dist. Ct. (so. dist.) Fla. 1982. Assoc., Steven M. Falk, P.A., Miami, 1981—. Pres. Dade County Young Democrats. Mem. ABA, Assn. Trial Lawyers Am., Acad. Fla. Trial Lawyers, Dade County Bar Assn., Zeta Beta Tau (mem. alumni bd.). Lodge: B'nai B'rith (v.p. South Dade council).

BRITT, ANN ROBERTSON, educational administrator; b. Rocky Mount, N.C., May 21, 1948; d. Leon Whitfield and Virginia (Lancaster) Robertson; m. Morris F. Britt, Apr. 24, 1976. Certificat d'etudes, U. Poitiers, La Rochelle, France, 1966; student Meredith Coll., Raleigh, N.C., 1966-68; B.A. in French, U. N.C., 1970; M.Ed. in French, U. N.C.-Greensboro, 1975; Ph.D. in Adminstrn. Higher Edn., Duke U., 1981. Dean women, asst. dean students High Point (N.C.) Coll., 1974-75; grad. asst. for dir. grad. studies, Duke U., Durham, N.C., 1976-78; dir. devel. Meredith Coll., 1978-80; dir. devel. Charlotte (N.C.) Country Day Sch., 1980-82; exec. dir. Community Sch. Arts, Charlotte, 1982—. Recipient award Council Advancement and Support of Edn., 1984. Mem. Kappa Delta Pi, Pi Delta Phi, Kappa Kappa Gamma. Democrat. Presbyterian. Club: Zonta. Contbr. articles to profl. jours. Home: 5805 Sharon Rd Charlotte NC 28210 Office: Community School of Arts 200 West Trade St Charlotte NC 28202

BRITT, JUDITH ROWE, safety engineer; b. Hartsville, S.C., Nov. 5, 1959; d. Edgar Riley and Dorothy (Hine) R.; m. Timothy Marshal Britt, Aug. 2, 1980. B.S., Clemson U., 1981; postgrad. U. Miami, Fla., 1981-82, U. S.C., 1983-84. Loss control rep. Kemper Ins. Group, Ft. Lauderdale, 1981-82, So. Underwriters, Coral Gables, Fla., 1982-83; loss control technician Lumbermen's Mutual, Columbia, S.C., 1983-84; loss control rep. Utica Nat. Ins., Atlanta, 1984—. Mem. Am. Soc. Safety Engrs. (sec. 1984), Ins. Loss Control Assn., Gamma Sigma Sigma. Republican. Methodist. Lodge: Civitans. Avocations: travel; reading. Office: Utica Nat Ins Group 47 Perimeter Ctr NE Atlanta GA 30346

BRITT, SAM GLENN, artist, educator; b. Ruleville, Miss., Sept. 26, 1940; s. Sam A. and Hazel (Griffith) B.; m. Linda Newsome; children—Linda Alison, Glenn, Steve. B.F.A., Memphis Acad. Arts, 1964; M.F.A., U. Miss., 1964-66. Grad. asst. U. Miss., Oxford, 1964-66; mem. faculty Delta State U., Cleveland, Miss., 1967—, assoc. prof. art 1980—; instr. area painting and drawing, workshops. One man shows include: Bryant Galleries, Jackson, Miss., 1982, Union Planters Nat. Bank Gallery, Memphis, 1984; group shows include: Gallery III, Roanoke, Va., 1983, Hinds Jr. Coll., Raymond, Miss., 1985;

executed mural Winterville Mounds, 1968; represented in permanent collections Union Planters Nat. Bank, Delta State U. Ednl. Bldg., Delta State U. Library. Recipient Nat. Small Painting award, Hadley, Pa., 1974, Best in Show award Crosstie Arts Festival, Cleveland, Miss., 1979. Avocations: running; jogging; swimming; raquetball; coaching youth baseball. Office: Delta State U Box 3236 Cleveland MS 38733

BRITT, W. EARL, federal judge; b. McDonald, N.C., Dec. 7, 1932; s. Dudley H. and Martha Mae (Hall) B.; student Campbell Jr. Coll., 1952; B.S., Wake Forest U., 1956, J.D., 1958; m. Judith Moore, Apr. 17, 1976; children—Clifford P., Mark E., Elizabeth C. Admitted to N.C. bar, 1958; practiced law, Fairmont, N.C., 1959-72, Lumberton, N.C., 1972-80; judge U.S. Dist. Ct. Eastern Dist. N.C., 1980—, now chief judge; Trustee, Southeastern Community Coll., 1965-70, Southeastern Gen. Hosp., Lumberton, 1965-69, Pembroke State U., 1967-72; bd. govs. U. N.C. Served with U.S. Army, 1953-55. Mem. Am. Bar Assn., N.C. Bar Assn. Baptist. Office: PO Box 27504 Raleigh NC 27611

BRITTAIN, PERRY GEORGE, electric utility company executive; b. Center, Tex., Mar. 10, 1925; s. Zack B. and Donnie (Matthews) B.; B.S., U. Tex., 1949; m. Martha Nelle Black, Dec. 30, 1945; children—Jennifer Margaret, Martha Katharine. With Dallas Power & Light Co., 1949-72, v.p. engring., purchasing, 1968-72; exec. v.p. Tex. Utilities Services Inc., 1972-73, pres., 1973-81, chmn. bd., chief exec., 1981-84; exec. v.p. Tex. Utilities Co., 1974-81, pres., 1981-83, chmn. bd., chief exec., 1983—; pres. Tex. Utilities Generating Co., 1974-81, chmn. bd., chief exec., 1981-84; pres. Tex. Utilities Fuel Co., 1974-81, chmn. bd., chief exec., 1981—; chmn. bd., chief exec. Tex. Utilities Mining Co., 1984—; chmn. bd. Basic Resources Inc., 1983—, Chaco Energy Co., 1983—. Trustee Tech. Edn. Research Center, 1978-84; ; bd. dirs. Ctr. for Occupational Research and Devel., 1980-86. Served with USAAF, 1943-46. Recipient Disting. Grad. award U. Tex. Coll. Engring., 1976. Registered profl. engr., Tex. Mem. IEEE, Tex. Soc. Profl. Engrs. (Engr. of Yr. award 1977), Edison Electric Inst. (bd. dirs. 1984—). Office: Tex Utilities Co 2001 Bryan Tower Dallas TX 75201

BRITTON, GARY LINN, dentist; b. Tulsa, May 8, 1947; s. Guy J. and Mildred I. (Gurney) B.; m. Frances T. Kempster, July 9, 1971; children—Susan D., Carrie K., Sarah E. B.S., Okla. State U., 1968; D.D.S., U. Mo.-Kansas City, 1972. Gen. practice dentistry, Yukon, Okla., 1974—. Served to capt. U.S. Army, 1972-74. Mem. ADA, S. Central Dist. Dental Assn. (past pres. 1980-81, pres. elect 1985-86), Okla. Dental Assn., Delta Sigma Delta (life). Republican. Roman Catholic. Lodges: Kiwanis (pres. 1977-78), K.C. (sec. 1982-83). Avocations: golfing; oil painting. Office: 401 Vandament Ave Suite 101 Yukon OK 73099

BRITTON, LEONARD, educational administrator. Supt. of schs., Dade County, Fla. Office: 1410 NE 2d Ave Miami FL 33132*

BRITTON, THOMAS CALHOUN, federal judge; b. Shanghai, China, Mar. 13, 1919; came to U.S., 1937; s. Thomas Cotton and Ruth (Yeager) B.; m. Lois A. Peterson, June 15, 1950; 1 child, Thomas Calhoun Jr. B.A., Yale U., 1942, LL.D., 1948. Bar: Conn., U.S. Dist. Ct. Conn., Fla., U.S. Dist. Ct. (no. and so. dists.) Fla., U.S. Supreme Ct., U.S. Ct. Appeals (5th cir.) 1948, U.S. Ct. Appeals (11th cir.) 1982. Assoc., E. F. Brigham, Miami, Fla., 1948-53; ptnr. Britton, Hodges & Hyman, Miami, 1953-57; county atty. Dade County, Fla., Miami, 1957-71; sr. ptnr. Schults and Bowen, Miami, 1971-75; judge U.S. Bankruptcy Court, Miami, 1975—, chief judge, 1969—. Served to lt. USNR, 1942-46. Set world record for swimming 400 yard relay, 1942. Mem. Fla. Bar, Phi Beta Kappa. Republican. Baptist. Office: US Bankruptcy Court 51 Sw First Ave Miami FL 33130

BROAD, MORRIS N., savings and loan executive; b. Burlington, Vt., Apr. 11, 1935; s. Shepard and Ruth (Kugel) B. B.B.A., U. Miami, 1956. Chmn. bd., chief exec. officer Am. Savs. and Loan Assn. of Fla., Miami Beach, 1965—. Trustee U. Fla. Found.; mem. founders council Fla. Internat. U.; mem. citizens bd. and law and econ. council U. Miami; mem. adv. bd. and planning com. St. Francis Hosp.; dir. Dade Safety Council; trustee So. Fla. Council Boy Scouts Am.; founder, trustee Mt. Sinai Med. Center of Greater Miami; mem. adv. council Barry Coll.; trustee Nova U. Served with U.S. Army, 1951-58. Recipient Humanitarian award B'nai B'rith. Office: Am Savs and Loan Assn 17801 N 2d Ave Miami FL 33139

BROADHURST, NORMAN NEIL, foods company executive; b. Chico, Calif., Dec. 17, 1946; s. Frank Spencer and Dorothy Mae (Conrad) B.; B.S., Calif. State U., 1969; M.B.A., Golden Gate U., 1975; m. Victoria Rose Thomson, Aug. 7, 1976; 1 son, Scott Andrew. With Del Monte Corp., San Francisco, 1969-76, product mgr., 1973-76; product mgr. Riviana Foods, Inc., div. Colgate Palmolive, Houston, 1976-78; new products brand devel. mgr. foods div. Coca Cola Co., Houston, 1978-79, brand mgr., 1979-82, mktg. dir., 1982-83; v.p. mktg. Beatrice Foods, Chgo., 1983—. Chmn., Cystic Fibrosis Youth Soccer, 1982. Mem. Am. Mgmt. Assn., Am. Mktg. Assn. Clubs: Toastmasters Internat. (past chpt. pres.), Houston Met. Racquet.

BROADWAY, ANGELA SHARON, lawyer; b. Charleston, S.C., Sept. 22, 1957; d. Reid Archie and Althea (Sineath) Broadway. B.S., Med. U. S.C., 1980; J.D., U. S.C., 1983. Bar: S.C. 1983. Law clk. Law Office Donald Rothwell, Columbia, part-time, 1981-82; assoc. Law Office Wheeler M. Tillman, Charleston, S.C., 1983—. Mem. ABA, S.C. Bar Assn., Charleston County Bar Assn., Charleston Women Lawyers Assn., S.C. Trial Lawyer's Assn., Phi Delta Phi. Home: 1082 Meader Ln PO Box 935 Mount Pleasant SC 29464 Office: Law Offices Wheeler M Tillman Suite 202 Post-Courier Bldg 6296 Rivers Ave North Charleston SC 29418

BROADWELL, DEBRA CHRISTINE, nursing educator, administrator; b. Greenwood, S.C., Oct. 31, 1949; d. Wayne Carvile and Nadine (Dixon) B. B.S., Med. U. S.C., 1971; M.Nursing, Emory U., 1975; Ph.D., Ga. State U., 1983. Cert. enterostomal therapist. Staff nurse Emory U. Hosp., Atlanta, 1971-73, nurse clinician, 1973-74, program dir. enterostomal therapy ednl. program, 1975-84, assoc. prof. Sch. Nursing, 1984—; mem. adv. com. Digestive Disease Edn. and Info. Clearinghouse, NIH, Bethesda, Md., 1982-84; mem. service and rehab. com. Am. Cancer Soc., N.Y.C., 1982-85. Contbr. chpt. to book, articles to profl. jours.; editor: Principles of Ostomy Care, 1982. Mem. Internat. Assn. for Enterostomal Therapy (pres. 1981-85), Am. Nurses Assn., Sigma Theta Tau. Methodist. Home: 998 Williams Mill Rd NE Atlanta GA 30306 Office: Sch Nursing Emory U Altanta GA 30322

BROCK, CHARLES RUSSELL, food company executive, consultant main event marketing; b. Dearborn, Mich., Nov. 1, 1954; s. Lester Copeland and Geraldine (Dameron) B.; m. Patricia Davidson, Mar. 19, 1977; children—Anna Ruth, Katherine Rachel. B.A. in Mktg., U. Ga., 1976. Sales rep. Procter and Gamble, Jacksonville, Fla., 1976-77, dist. field rep., 1977-78, unit mgr., 1978-83; regional sales mgr., Frito Lay, Jacksonville, 1983-84, assoc. mktg. mgr., Atlanta, 1984-85, regional sales mgr., 1985—; cons. main event mktg. Mem. Grocery Mfrs. Retail Assn. Republican. Avocations: black belt; tae kwon do. Home: 4124 Manor House Dr Atlanta GA 30062

BROCK, JAMES GERALD, author, petroleum consultant; b. New Orleans, May 11, 1951; s. Gerald Edward and Carmen Marie (Ehninger) B.; B.S. in Elec. Engring., U. New Orleans, 1975; M.B.A., U. Tex., 1983; m. Jannye Bristow, Aug. 1, 1981; children—Heath, Amy, Roxanne. From technician to adminstr. Schlumberger Well Services Co., 1973-79; sales coordinator, dist. mgr., tng. adminstrn. Welex div. Halliburton Corp., Houston, 1979-83; cons. well analysis, computer anaylsis. Author: Analyzing Your Logs, Vols. I, II, III. Dir. disaster services shelter New Orleans chpt. ARC, 1969-79. Mem. Am. Mgmt. Assn., Am. Soc. Tng. and Devel., Soc. Profl. Well Log Analysts, Soc. Petroleum Engrs., U.S. Chess Fedn. Republican. Presbyterian. Home: 1729 Rose Rd Tyler TX 75701 Office: PO Box 6238 Tyler TX 75711

BROCK, JOYCE LAWTON, lawyer; b. N.Y.C., Sept. 7, 1948; d. Vasco Lawton and Rita (Castagna) B.; m. Robin L. Hitchcock, Dec. 30, 1981. B.A., Cornell U., 1965; J.D., U. S.C., 1978. Bars: S.C. 1978, U.S. Dist. Ct. S.C. 1981, U.S. Ct. Appeals (4th cir.) 1982. Asst. atty. gen. S.C. Atty. Gen., Charleston, 1978-81; ptnr. Durban & Brock, Charleston, 1981-82, Brock & Settlemyer, Charleston, 1982-83; sole practice, Charleston, 1983-84; ptnr. Brock & Hitchcock, Charleston, 1984—. Chmn. Cornell Alumni Assn. Secondary Sch. Com., 1978-80. Recipient Outstanding Work award Am. Jurisprudence Soc., 1976. Mem. S.C. Bar Assn. (mem. ethics adv. com. 1981—), Charleston County Bar Assn., Am. Trial Lawyers Assn., ABA, S.C. Hist. Soc., Carolina Arts Assn., Order Wig and Robe. Club: Long Room. Home: 12 Wentworth St Charleston SC 29401 Office: Brock & Hitchcock 31 Broad St Charleston SC 29401

BROCK, KARENA DIANE, ballerina educator, choreographer; b. Los Angeles, Sept. 21, 1942; d. Orville DeLoss and Sallie Alice (Anderson) Brock; m. John Robert Carlyle, III. grad. Barstow sch., Kansas City, Mo. Dancer, David Lichine Concert Group, Los Angeles, 1959-61, Netherlands Nat. Ballet Co., Amsterdam, 1962; mem. corps Am. Ballet Theatre, N.Y.C., 1963-68, soloist, 1968-73, prin. ballerina, 1973-79; artistic dir., prima ballerina Savannah (Ga.) Ballet Co., 1979-85; founder, artistic dir., Hilton Head Dance Theatre and Sch., S.C., 1985—; guest artist Miami (Fla.) Civic Ballet, Macon (Ga.) Civic Ballet, Tampa (Fla.) Civic Ballet, U. Ill. Ballet Co., Champaign, San Jose (Calif.) Civic Ballet, Ballet de San Juan, P.R., Gala Ballet, Amarillo (Tex.) Civic Ballet, Maywood Ballet Co., Phila., U. Wis., Milw. Civic Ballet, Stars of Am. Ballet, various TV shows; guest artist White House, 1966, 69; tchr. master classes Radford (Va.) Coll., U. Louisville, U. Tampa; staff tchr. Bklyn. Coll.; mem. faculty SUNY, Purchase; guest tchr. Walnut Hill Sch., Boston. Savannah Ballet, Cleve. Ballet. Office: 7 Bow Circle Hilton Head SC 29928

BROCK, LOUIS MILTON, JR., engineering educator, researcher; b. Davenport, Iowa, Apr. 16, 1943; s. Louis Milton and Mary Elizabeth (Creech) B.; m. Carolyn Starbuck Pratt, July 22, 1972. B.S., Northwestern U., 1966, M.S., 1967, Ph.D., 1972. Draftsman Black and Veatch, Kansas City, Mo., 1962; research technician Gen. Dynamics/Convair, San Diego, 1963-64, Sargeant-Welch Co., Skokie, Ill., 1964, Am. Can Co., Barrington, Ill., 1965; asst. prof. engring. mechanics U. Ky., Lexington, 1971-76, assoc. prof., 1976-81, prof., 1981—; cons. McDonnell Douglas Corp., Huntington Beach, Calif., 1972-74, Compusport, Inc., Ocala, Fla., 1983—. Mem. editorial bd. Jour. Engring. Mechanics, 1983-85. Contbr. articles to profl. jours., 1973—. Active Sloane for Gov. Campaign, Lexington, 1983. Recipient Research award U. Ky. Research Found., 1977; NSF grantee, 1972, 79, 84; U.S. Navy/Am. Soc. Engring. Edn. fellow, 1983, 85. Mem. ASME, ASCE (chmn. com. elasticity 1983-85), AAUP (pres. chpt. 1978, 83, pres. conf. 1984-86), Sigma Xi. Avocations: hiking; classical music; reading history. Home: 133 Sycamore Rd Lexington KY 40502 Office: U Ky Dept Engring Mechanics 00461 Lexington KY 40506

BROCK, RAY LEONARD, JR., state justice; b. McDonald, Tenn., Sept. 21, 1922; s. Ray Leonard and Ila Venore (Bailey) B.; student U. Tenn., 1940-43, U. Colo., 1945-46; LL.B., Duke U., 1948; m. Juanita Addabelle Barker, Sept. 18, 1944; children—Ila Raye, Elaine Rose, Karen Denise. Bar: Tenn. 1948. Practiced in Chattanooga, 1948-63; judge Chancery Ct. of Tenn., 1963-74; justice Supreme Ct. Tenn., 1974—. Served with U.S. Army, 1943-44. Mem. Tenn., Chattanooga bar assns., Am. Judicature Soc., Tenn. Trial Lawyers Assn. Democrat. Mem. Pilgrim Congregational United Ch. Christ. Club: Big Orange. Office: 300 Supreme Ct Bldg Nashville TN 37219

BROCKERT, JOSEPH PAUL, government executive, philatelic consultant; b. Tipp City, Ohio, Sept. 17, 1954; s. Paul Edwin and Mary (Aten) B.; m. Deborah Sue Schaefer, Apr. 10, 1976; children—Jonathan Andre, Jason Anthony. B.S. in Journalism, Ohio U., 1975. Sr. editor Linn's Stamp News, Sidney, Ohio, 1976-84; sr. stamp program specialist U.S. Postal Service, Washington, 1984—; coordinator Citizens' Stamp Adv. Com., 1985—. Author: Basic Knowledge for the Stamp Collector, 1978 (silver medal Am. Philatelic Soc. 1979). Publicity chmn. Gunston Elem. PTA, Va., 1985. Mem. Mensa. Roman Catholic. Avocations: music; stamp collecting; photography; film study. Office: US Postal Service Hdqrs L'Enfant Plaza Washington DC 20260

BROCKETT, OSCAR GROSS, theater educator, writer; b. Hartsville, Tenn., Mar. 18, 1923; s. Oscar Hill and Minnie Dee (Gross) B.; m. Lenyth Rose Spenker, Sept. 4, 1951 (dec. Jan., 1979); 1 dau., Francesca Lane. B.A., Peabody Coll., 1947; M.A., Stanford U., 1949, Ph.D., 1953. Instr. English, U. Ky., 1949-50; asst. instr. Stanford (Calif.) U., 1950-52; asst. prof. drama Stetson U., 1952-56; asst. prof. theater U. Iowa, 1956-59, assoc. prof., 1959-63; prof. theater Ind. U., Bloomington, 1963-76, Disting. prof., 1976-78; dean Coll. Fine Arts, U. Tex., Austin, 1978-80, Leslie Waggener prof. drama and fine arts, 1981—; DeMille prof. drama U. So. Calif., Los Angeles, 1980-81. Served with USNR, 1943-46. Recipient medallion of Honor, Theta Alpha Pi, 1977. Fulbright fellow, Eng., 1963-64; Guggenheim fellow, 1970-71. Fellow Am. Theatre Assn. (award of Merit 1979; pres. 1975-76); mem. Am. Soc. Theatre Research (exec. com. 1974-79), MLA, Speech Communications Assn. Democrat. Episcopalian. Author: The Theatre, an Introduction, 1964, 4th edit., 1979; Plays for the Theatre, 1967, 4th edit., 1984; History of the Theatre, 1968, 4th edit., 1982; Perspectives on Contemporary Theatre, 1971; Century of Innovation, 1973; The Essential Theatre, 1976, 3d edit., 1984; World Drama, 1983; contbr. articles to profl. jours. Office: Dept Drama U Tex Austin TX 78712

BROCKWAY, DONALD LEE, research biologist; b. Palo Alto, Calif., Sept. 5, 1939; s. Maywood Laverne and Mildred Camille (Choate) B.; m. Mary Ann Merzenich, Dec. 27, 1961; children—Kathryn Marie, Teresa Ann, David William. B.S. in Fisheries, Oreg. State U., 1962, M.S. in Fisheries, 1963; Ph.D. in Fisheries, U. Mich., 1972. Biologist, Fed. Water Pollution Control Adminstrn., Athens, Ga., 1968-72; research biologist EPA, Athens, 1972—. Nutrilite Found. scholar, 1960; Fed. Water Pollution Control Adminstrn. fellow, 1963-68. Mem. Am. Fisheries Soc., Ga. Conservancy, Audubon Soc., Nat. Wildlife Fedn., Sierra Club, Sigma Xi. Roman Catholic. Lodge: K.C. Home: 255 Rollingwood Dr Athens GA 30605 Office: Athens Environ Research Lab EPA College Station Rd Athens GA 30613

BRODERICK, GRACE NOLAN, physical scientist, management analyst, lawyer; b. Niagara Falls, N.Y.; d. Emmett Robert and Edna Alice (Burnett) Nolan; m. Francis Byrne Broderick, Aug. 5, 1959; 1 child, Grace Margaret. B.A., U. Buffalo, 1947; M.A., Brigham Young U., 1950; J.D., Georgetown U., 1956. Export clk., translator Carborundum Co., Niagara Falls, N.Y., 1947-48; asst. in geology Brigham Young U., Provo, Utah, 1948; asst. in mineralogy Pa. State U., University Park, 1950-52; geologist U.S. Geol. Survey, Washington, 1952-67; physical scientist U.S. Bur. of Mines, Washington, 1967—, acting research coordinator, 1970, mining econs. commodity specialist, 1970-78, state liaison officer W.Va., 1978-79, asst. to chief of State Mineral Info. Program, Washington, 1979-82, mgmt. analysis staff, 1982—. Mem. adv. bd. Victims of Violence Program, Arlington, Va., 1982-83. Recipient Spl. award U.S. Bur. of Mines, 1970—, Spl. Achievement Group award, 1981. Mem. Am. Inst. Profl. Geologists, Am. Assn. Petroleum Geologists, Am. Inst. of Mining, Metall. and Petroleum Engrs., Geol. Soc. of Washington, Phi Delta Gamma, Sigma Delta Epsilon, Kappa Beta Pi, Delta Phi Alpha. Home: 4141 N Henderson Rd Arlington VA 22203 Office: US Bur Mines 2401 E St NW Washington DC 20241

BROERSMA, SYBRAND, physics educator; b. Harlingen, The Netherlands, Sept. 20, 1919; came to U.S., 1947, naturalized, 1957; s. Jacob and Johanna (Zwanenburg) B. Candidaats, Leiden U., 1939, Doctoraal, 1941; Ph.D., Delft Inst. Tech., 1947. Grad. asst. U. Leiden, 1939-40, Delft U., 1940-46; Internat. Exchange fellow Northwestern U., Evanston, Ill., 1947; research assoc. Columbia U., N.Y.C., 1947; instr. U. Toronto (Ont., Can.), 1948; prof. exptl. physics U. Indonesia, 1949-51; asst. prof. physics Northwestern U., 1952-58; prof. physics U. Okla., Norman, 1959—; adj. prof. materials research U. Tex., Dallas, 1967-70. NSF grantee, 1956-68. Mem. Am. Phys. Soc., Netherlands Phys. Soc., European Phys. Soc. Contbr. articles to profl. jours.; author: Elementary Physics Laboratory Manual, 1963; Magnetic Measurements on Organic Compounds, 1947. Office: Dept Physics Univ Okla Norman OK 73019

BROESCHE, SUSAN JANE, language arts educator, coach; b. Brenham, Tex., June 8, 1950; d. Jerome P. and Elnora Mary (Goldberg) Stanley; m. Marcus Lee Broesche, Nov. 29, 1968. A.A., Blinn Coll., 1976; B.S., Tex. A&M U., 1977; M.L.S., Sam Houston State U., 1979. Cert. tchr., Tex. Kindergarten spl. edn. resource tchr., Brenham Ind. Sch. Dist., 1977-80; jr. high sch. lang. arts tchr., coach Burton Ind. Sch. Dist. (Tex.), 1980—; organizer, sponsor Burton Council Jr. High Students, 1983—. Bd. dirs. Brazos Valley Mental Health and Mental Retardation, 1984—; sec. edn. Am. Luth. Ch. Women, Burton, 1981-82, pres., 1984—. Tex. A&M Mothers' Club scholar, 1977. Mem. Tex. Classroom Tchrs. Assn. (also local), Tex. Assn. Community Schs., Tex. High Sch. Coaches Assn., Burton Elem. PTO, Sam Houston State U. Alumni Assn. Democrat. Lutheran. Home: PO Box 75 Burton TX 77835 Office: Burton Ind Sch Dist PO Box 37 Burton TX 77835

BROGDON, BYRON GILLIAM, physician, educator; b. Ft. Smith, Ark., Jan. 22, 1929; s. Paul Preston and Lela Florence (Gilliam) B.; m. Barbara Walkow Schreiber, June 23, 1978; 1 son, David Pope; stepchildren—William Schreiber, Diane Schreiber. B.S., U. Ark., 1951, B.S.M., 1951, M.D., 1952. Intern, Univ. Hosp., Little Rock, 1952-53, resident, 1953-55; resident in radiology N.C. Bapt. Hosp., Winston-Salem, 1955-56; asst. prof. radiology U. Fla., 1960-63; assoc. prof. radiology and radiol. scis., radiologist-in-chief div. diagnostic radiology Johns Hopkins U. and Hosp., 1963-67; prof., chmn. dept. radiology U. N.Mex., 1967-77; prof. radiology U. South Ala, Mobile, 1978—, chmn. dept., 1986—, asst. dean for continuing med. edn., 1981—. Served to maj. USAF, 1953-60. Recipient Disting. Alumnus award U. Ark., 1978. Fellow Am. Coll. Radiology (pres. 1978-79); mem. Am. Roentgen Ray Soc. (2d v.p. 1979-80), So. Radiol. Conf. (pres. 1967-68), Radiol. Soc. N.Am., Soc. Pediatric Radiology, Assn. Univ. Radiologists (pres. 1973-74, Gold medal 1985), Soc. Chmn. Acad. Radiol. Depts. (sec.-treas. 1969-70), AMA (recipient Physician-Speaker award 1979), Sigma Xi, Alpha Omega Alpha, Sigma Chi. Club: Bienville. Author: Opinions, Comments and Reflections on Radiology, 1982; contbr. numerous articles to med. jours. Office: Dept Radiology U South Ala Med Ctr 2451 Fillingim St Mobile AL 36617

BROHAMER, RICHARD FREDERIC, psychiatrist; b. Rockford, Ill., Nov. 9, 1934; s. Joseph C. and Marthe Marie (Ringuette) B.; Ph.B., U. Detroit, 1960; M.D., U. Fla., 1964; postgrad. basic tng. diving medicine Internat. Underwater Explorers Soc., 1973, Advanced Tng. Diving Medicine, 1974; m. Shirley Ruth Noble, June 22, 1956; children—Richard Frederic II, Renee Marie, Rory Christopher. Intern Duval Med. Center, Jacksonville, Fla., 1964-65; resident psychiatry U. Fla., 1965-68; practice medicine specializing in psychiatry, Fort Lauderdale, Fla., 1968—; mem. staffs Broward Gen., Coral Ridge, North Beach, North Ridge hosps., Imperial Point Med. Center; chmn. dept. psychiatry Imperial Point Hosp., 1975-80, Holy Cross Hosp., 1981—. Research fellow tropical medicine La. State U., Costa Rica, 1963, Central Am., 1968. Served with USAF, 1954-58; Korea. Diplomate Am. Bd. Psychiatry and Neurology. Mem. AMA (pres. student chpt. 1961-64), So. Fla., Broward County (Fla.) med. assns., Am., Fla., Broward County psychiat. socs., Undersea Adventurers, Internat. Soc. Diving Medicine. Republican. Roman Catholic. Home: 3200 NE 38th St Fort Lauderdale FL 33308 Office: 3035 E Commercial Blvd Fort Lauderdale FL 33308

BROHARD, ELLEN BRADY, educator; b. Ashland, Va., Aug. 11, 1942; d. Patrick L. and Effie B. Brady; B.S. in Bus. Edn., Longwood Coll., 1963; M.S. in Vocat. Tech. Edn., Va. Poly. Inst./State U., 1975; m. Thomas L. Brohard, Feb. 10, 1967; children—Bill, Mark. Bus. edn. tchr. Fairfax County Schs., George Marshall High Sch., Falls Church, Va., 1963-68; bus. edn. tchr., coordinator Fairfax County Adult Edn., Falls Church, 1969-74; secretarial sci. program head, asst. prof. No. Va. Community Coll., Loudoun Campus, 1974—, coordinator coop. edn. and coordinated internship, 1981—; reviewer Choice, ALA, 1982. Asst. soccer coach; mem. PTA, 1978—; sec. Cub Scouts, 1978—; mem. fund raising com. Soccer League, 1979, Pee Wee League, 1979. Mem. Nat. Bus. Edn. Assn., So. Bus. Edn. Assn., Internat. Platform Assn., Bus. and Profl. Women's Club, Longwood Coll. Alumni Assn. (co-chmn.). Methodist. Home: Route 2 Box 218F Leesburg VA 22075 Office: 1000 H F Byrd Hwy Sterling VA 22170

BROKAW, C(HARLES) FORREST, JR., public relations specialist; b. Shawnee, Okla., Sept. 5, 1928; s. Charles Forrest and Bernice Evelyn (Scott) B.; B.J., Woodbury Coll., Los Angeles, 1949; B.C.A., Dallas Bapt. Coll., 1976; m. JoNell Louise Foster, Aug. 27, 1950; children—Charles Forrest III, Nancy Beth Brokaw Turner, Linda Susan Brokaw Waldron. News dir. Sta. KVOO-AM-TV, Tulsa, 1956-61; city hall reporter Tulsa Tribune, 1954; news dir. Sta. KELI, Tulsa, 1961-65, account exec., 1965-68, news dir., 1968-72; gen. mgr. Sta. KIXZ, Amarillo, Tex., 1972-74; asst. mgr. Sta. KTRN, Wichita Falls, Tex., 1974-75; external relations cons.-media Sun Oil Co., Dallas, 1975-76; regional pub. relations mgr. Sun Co., Tulsa, 1976-80; dir. pub. affairs Sun Pipe Line Co., Tulsa, 1980-82; area pub. relations mgr. Sun Refining & Mktg. Co., 1982—. Served with AUS, 1946-48. Mem. Pub. Relations Soc. Am. (chpt. pres. 1984), Sigma Delta Chi (pres. Tulsa chpt. 1960). Clubs: Tulsa Press (pres. 1972). Home: 1523 S Madison Ave Tulsa OK 74120 Office: 908 S Detroit St Tulsa OK 74012

BROMBERG, ALAN ROBERT, lawyer, educator, writer; b. Dallas, Nov. 24, 1928; s. Alfred L. and Juanita (Kramer) B.; A.B., Harvard, 1949; J.D., Yale, 1952; m. Anne Ruggles, July 26, 1959. Admitted to Tex. bar, 1952, U.S. Tax Ct. bar, 1959; asso. firm Carrington, Gowan, Johnson, Bromberg and Leeds, Dallas, 1952-56; atty. and cons., 1956-76; of counsel Jenkens & Gilchrist, 1976—; part-time lectr. Law Sch., So. Methodist U., Dallas, 1955-56, vis. asst. prof. law, 1956-57, asst. prof. law, 1957-58, asso. prof., 1958-62, prof. law, 1962—, univ. disting. prof. law, 1983—, chmn. law curriculum com., 1961-72, trustee retirement plan, 1967-70, faculty rep. bd. trustees, 1969-70, 74, mem. exec. com. faculty senate, 1968-70, mem. presdl. search group, 1971-72; faculty adviser Southwestern Law Jour., 1958-65; sr. fellow Yale U. Law Faculty, 1966-67; vis. prof. Stanford U. Law Sch., 1972-73; lectr. in field; adv. bd. U. Calif. Securities Regulation Inst. Counsel Internat. Data Sytems, Inc., 1961-65, sec., dir. 1963-65; mem. Tex. Legis. Council Bus. and Commerce Code Adv. Com., 1966-67. Sec., mem. bd. dirs. Community Arts Fund, 1963-73; gen. atty. Dallas Mus. Contemporary Arts, 1956-63. Bd. dirs. Dallas Theater Center, 1955-73, life mem., 1973—, sec., 1957-66, finance com., 1957-65, mem. exec. com., 1957-70, v.p., trustee endowment fund, 1974—. Served as cpl. M.I., AUS, 1952-54. Mem. Am. Bar Assn. (mem. com. commodities, com. partnerships; mem. com. fed. regulation of securities), Dallas Bar Assn. (chmn. com. on uniform partnership act 1959-61, mem. library com. 1981--), State Bar Tex. (com. corp. law revision, 1957—, mem. com. on securities and investment banking 1957—, chmn. 1965-69, mem. com. on information of corp. banking and bus. law sect. 1961-69, mem. council of sect. 1963-69, vice chmn. 1965-67, chmn. 1967-68, reporter com. on revision of penal code 1967-70, com. on partnership 1974—, chmn. 1979—), Am. Law Inst., Southwestern Legal Found., AAUP (exec. com. So. Methodist U. chpt. 1962-63; chmn. acad. freedom and tenure com. 1968-70, 71-72). Author: (with Byron D. Sher) Cases and Materials on Texas Partnerships, 1958, supplemented 1960; Supplementary Materials on Texas Corporations, 1959, rev. 1965, 71; Partnership Primer-Problems and Planning, 1961; Materials on Corporate Securities and Finance—A Growing Company's Search for Funds, 1962, rev. 1965; Securities Fraud and Commodities Fraud, Vol. 1, 1967, Vol. 2, 1970, Vol. 3, 1973, Vol. 4, 1977, Vol. 5, 1982, supplements pub. annually; Crane and Bromberg on Partnership, 1968; Corporate Organizational Documents and Securities—Forms and Comments, rev. edit., 1976. Contbr. numerous articles and revs. to law and bar jours. Adv. editor Rev. Securities Regulation, 1969—, Securities Regulation Law Jour., 1973—, Jour. Corp. Law, 1976—; ednl. publs. adv. bd. Matthew Bender & Co., 1977—, chmn., 1981—. Office: So Meth U Law Sch Dallas TX 75275 also 2200 Inter First One Dallas TX 75202

BRONFMAN, EDGAR MILES, distillery executive; b. Montreal, Que., Can., June 20, 1929; s. Samuel and Saidye (Rosner) B. Student, Williams Coll., 1946-49; B.A., McGill U., 1951. Chmn. adminstrv. com. Joseph E. Seagram & Sons, Inc., 1955-57, pres., 1957-71; chmn., chief exec. officer; pres. Distillers Corp.-Seagrams Ltd., Montreal, 1971-75; now chmn., chief exec. officer Seagram Co. Ltd.; chmn., dir. Clevepak Corp., Gulfstream Land and Devel. Corp.; dir. Am. Technion Soc., Internat. Exec. Service Corps; hon. trustee Bank N.Y. Bd. dirs. Citizens Com. for N.Y.C., Interracial Council for Bus. Opportunity; mem. com. Weizmann Inst. Sci.; exec. bd. govs. N.Y. councils Boy Scouts Am.; trustee Mt. Sinai Hosp., Sch. Medicine and Med. Center, Salk Inst. Biol. Studies; trustee, pres. Samuel Bronfman Found.; founding mem. Rockefeller U. Council; pres. World Jewish Congress; mem. exec. com. Am. Jewish Congress, Am. Jewish Com.; mem. nat. commn. Anti-Defamation League, B'nai B'rith. Mem. Center for Inter-Am. Relations, Council Fgn. Relations, Hundred Year Assn. N.Y., United Jewish Appeal, Fedn. Jewish Philanthropies, Com. for Econ. Devel., Nat. Urban League, Fgn. Policy Assn., Bus. Com. for Arts, Inc.

BRONIS, STEPHEN J., lawyer; b. Miami, Fla., Feb. 23, 1947; s. Larry and Thelma (Berger) B.; m. Jan Louise Perkins, Jan. 1, 1984; children—Jason Michael, Tyler Adam. B.S. in Bus. Adminstrn., U. Fla., 1969; J.D., Duke U., 1972. Bar: Fla. 1972, D.C. 1973, U.S. Dist. Ct. (so. dist.) Fla. 1973, U.S. Ct. Appeals (5th cir.) 1977, U.S. Supreme Ct. 1978, U.S. Ct. Appeals (11th cir.) 1981. Asst. pub. defender 11th Jud. Cir. Fla., Miami, 1972-75; ptnr. Rosen & Bronis, P.A., Miami, 1975-77, Rosen, Portela, Bronis, et al., Miami, 1977-82, Bronis & Potela, P.A., Miami, 1982—; Nat. Inst. Trial Attys. faculty Cardoza Law Sch., 1985, U. N.C. Sch. Law, 1986. Contbr. articles to profl. jours. Recipient Am. Jurisprudence award Bancroft-Whitney Co., 1972; cert. of Appreciation Fla. Shorthand Reporters Assn., 1984; Outstanding Service award Fla. Criminal Def. Attys. Assn., 1981. Mem. Fla. Criminal Def. Attys. Assn. (pres. 1980-81), Am. Bd. Criminal Lawyers (v.p. 1981-82), Assn. Trial Lawyers Am. Nat. Criminal Def. Attys. Assn., Calif. Attys. Criminal Justice, Acad. Fla. Trial Lawyers (criminal law sect. dir.). Democrat. Home: 9201 SW 69th Ct Miami FL 33156 Office: Bronis & Portela PA 1395 Coral Way Miami FL 33145

BRONZINI, MICHAEL STEPHEN, transportation researcher, civil engineer, educator; b. Johnstown, Pa., Aug. 21, 1944; s. Stephen Joseph and Lillian Elmina (Hill) B.; m. Blanche Marie Laposata, Dec. 30, 1967; children—Jennifer Marie, Mary Susan, Megan Jane. B.S. with distinction, Stanford U., 1967; M.S., Pa. State U., 1969, Ph.D., 1973. Registered profl. engr., Pa. Research asst. Pa. Transp. Inst., Pa. State U., University Park, 1967-72; asst. prof. civil engring. Ga. Inst. Tech., Atlanta, 1973-75; sr. assoc. CACI, Inc., Arlington, Va., 1975-78; assoc. dir. Transp. Ctr., U. Tenn., Knoxville, 1978-82, assoc. prof. civil engring., 1978-83, dir. Transp. Ctr., 1983—, prof., 1983—; transp. cons. to pvt. bus. and govt. agys. Mem. Transp. Research Forum (pres. 1982), ASCE, Inst. Transp. Engrs., Transp. Research Bd., Soc. for Computer Simulation, Permanent Internat. Assn. Navigation Congresses, AAAS, Am. Road and Transp. Builders Assn., Sigma Xi, Tau Beta Pi, Chi Epsilon. Contbr. articles on transp. systems, planning, engring., opns., econs. and edn. to profl. jours. Office: 357 S Stadium Knoxville TN 37996

BROOKMAN, RICHARD ROBERT, pediatrician, educator; b. Paterson, N.J., Oct. 28, 1944; s. Paul Robert and Alice Elizabeth (Hauserman) B.; m. Barbara Ann Lewis, June 27, 1970; children—Sean Gavin, Lara Nikol, Mandi Page. A.B., Franklin and Marshall Coll., 1965; M.D., Tufts U., 1969. Diplomate Am. Bd. Pediatrics. Intern, Montefiore Hosp., Bronx, N.Y., 1969-70, resident in pediatrics, 1970-72; chief pediatrics Naval Regional Med. Clinic, Washington, 1972-74, fellow adolescent medicine, 1974-75; instr. pediatrics, div. adolescent medicine U. Cin. Adolescent Clinic, 1975-76; asst. prof. pediatrics, asst. dir. adolescent clinic Children's Hosp., Cin., 1976-80; assoc. prof. pediatrics, dir. Adolescent Health Service, Med. Coll. Va./Va. Commonwealth U., Richmond, 1981—; author; researcher, cons. Active Richmond Youth Services Commn., 1982—, Va. State Sch.-Age Parents Com., 1983—. Served with USNR, 1972-74. Mem. Soc. Adolescent Medicine, Am. Acad. Pediatrics, Am. Pub. Health Assn. Author: Pediatric and Adolescent Gynecology Case Studies, 1981; contbr. articles to profl. jours., chpts. to books. Office: PO Box 151 Med Coll Va Sta Richmond VA 23298

BROOKS, CAROLYN SAULS, insurance company executive; b. Lyons, Ga., Aug. 13, 1941; d. Rema T. and Annie Mae (Mayes) Sauls; m. Charles A. Brooks, Apr. 23, 1966; m. Robert L. Young, Nov. 11, 1959 (div. 1962); 1 dau., Lisa Carol. Cert., Boland Draughn Bus. Sch., Savannah, Ga., 1959. Cert. Ins. Inst. Am., 1977. Ins. clk. Ben Rice Ins., Atlanta, 1966-70, Charles Parrott & Assocs., Athens, Ga., 1970-73; ins. agt. Bill Johnson Ins., Columbia, SC., 1973-76, Edens Real Estate & Ins., Columbia, 1976-82; owner, pres., mgr. Carleton Co., Inc., Columbia, 1982—. Advisor Richland Sch. Dist. I-Columbia High Sch., 1982, 83. Mem. Columbia Assn. Ins. Women (pres. 1981-82, Ins. Woman of Yr. 1981), Columbia Network Female Execs., Ind. Ins. Agts. Columbia (exec. bd. 1979-83), Nat. Assn. Ins. Women, Columbia C. of C. (sec. area council 1982, 83), Ind. Ins. Agrs. Columbia, Beta Sigma Phi. Baptist. Lodge: Order Eastern Star. Home: 242 Mariners Row Columbia SC 29210 Office: Carleton Co Inc 8 Diamond Ln Columbia SC 29210

BROOKS, DAVID VICTOR, lawyer; b. Sendai, Japan, May 22, 1948; came to U.S., 1951, naturalized, 1975; s. David Kenneth and Mary Victoria (Gooding) B.; m. Deborah Ann Gary, Nov. 14, 1970 (div. 1983); m. Mary Bonnie Kemp, July 7, 1984; children—Meredith Maxwell, Heather Branan. B.A. with high honors, N.C. State U., 1974; J.D., U. N.C., 1977. Bar: N.C. 1977, U.S. Ct. Mil. Appeals 1978, U.S. Dist. Ct. (ea. dist.) N.C. 1980. Sr. trial atty. Naval Legal Service Office, Pearl Harbor, Hawaii, 1977-78; tort claims atty., Norfolk, Va., 1978-80; assoc. Maupin, Taylor & Ellis, P.A., Raleigh, N.C., 1980-84, ptnr., 1984-85; chmn. N.C. Indsl. Commn., 1985—; cons. Capital Assoc. Industries, Raleigh, 1982-85. Bd. dirs. Mid-State Safety Council, Henderson, N.C., 1983—; gen. counsel N.C. Republican Party, Raleigh, 1983-85; dist. commr. Boy Scouts Am., Raleigh, 1981—. Served to capt. USMC, 1966-72, Vietnam; to lt. comdr. USN, 1977-80. Decorated Navy and Marine Corps medal, Bronze Star, Purple Heart. Mem. ABA, N.C. Bar Assn., Am. Soc. Safety Engrs., Wake County Bar Assn., VFW. Republican. Roman Catholic. Lodge: Lions. Home: 208 Trinity Woods Dr Raleigh NC 27605 Office: NC Indsl Commn Dobbs Bldg 213 N Salisbury St Raleigh NC 27611

BROOKS, HENRY WELLS, III, seismic analyst; b. Butler, Ga., June 18, 1955; s. Henry Wells and Melba Joyce (Gloss) B.; m. Lori Ann Robertson, Mar. 17, 1984; 1 child, Henry Mitchell. B.S., Auburn U., 1979. Research asst. Auburn U., Ala., 1979; trainee seismologist Seismograph Service, Tulsa, 1980-81, seismic surveyor, 1981-82, field crew mgr., 1982-84, seismic analyst, 1984—. Mem. Am. Assn. Petroleum Geologists (jr.). Democrat. Avocations: collecting Indian artifacts; geological field work; football; softball. Home: 27228 E 82nd St Broken Arrow OK 74014

BROOKS, JACK BASCOM, congressman; b. Dec. 18, 1922; s. Edward Chachere and Grace Marie (Pipes) B.; m. Charlotte Collins; children—Jack Edward, Katherine Inez, Kimberly Grace. Admitted to Tex. bar, 1949; mem. Tex. Legislature, 1946-50; mem. 83d-89th Congresses from 2d Tex. dist., 90th-98th Congresses from 9th Tex. dist. Col. USMCR ret. Home: 1029 East Dr Beaumont TX 77706 Office: Rayburn House Office Bldg Washington DC 20515

BROOKS, JAMES E., JR., police chief; b. Macon, Jan. 17, 1948; s. James and Gladys (Freeman) B. Student Ga. Mil. Coll., 1973; A.A. in Criminal Justice, Macon Jr. Coll., 1977; B.S. in Criminal Justice, Ga. Coll., Milledgeville, 1981, M.P.A., 1982. Trooper Ga. State Patrol, Madison, 1971-73; asst. foreman Bassett Furniture Co., Macon, 1973-74; salesman Clance-Chapman Chrysler Plymouth, Macon, 1974; airport police capt. Lewis B. Wilson Airport, Macon, 1974-81, asst. aviation dir., 1981; asst. chief adminstrv. officer City of Macon, 1981-83, chief of police, 1983—. Coordinator Macon Airshow, Ga. State Fair Assn.; elder, chmn. youth council and other com. and clubs local ch.; developer security programs Wesleyan Coll., Albany Airport Police; chmn. Child Sex Abuse Task Force; vice chmn. adv. com. Middle Ga. Law Enforcement Tng. Ctr.; mem. exec. bd. Ga. Policy Acad., Central Ga. council Boy Scouts Am.; trustee United Way; bd. dirs. Muscular Dystrophy Assn.; mem. adv. bd. Regional Police Acad.; mem. steering com. Macon Cherry Blossom Fest.; mem. Middle Ga. Council Boy Scouts Am.; mem. law enforcement coordinating com. Fed. Middle Dist. Ga.; mem. enforcement com. Clean Community Comm., adminstrv. govt. access channel com.; past mem. Leadership Macon. Served with USMC, 1967-71. Recipient cert. of appreciation, Adopt-a-Sch. Program, Gamma Beta Phi, Ga. Burglar and Fire Alarm Assn., Inc., Downtown Council of Greater Macon C. of C., Macon Tracks Running Club, VFW. Mem. Ga. Mcpl. Assn. (pub. safety com., community service com., state patrol interstate com., cert. of appreciation), Ga. Assn. Chiefs of Police, Internat. Assn. chiefs of Police, Internat. City Mgmt. Assn. Clubs: Macon Exchange, Bibb County Exchange (Officer of Yr. award 1983). Home: 6628 Fran Dr Macon GA 31206

BROOKS, JEFFREY MARTIN, accountant; b. Charlotte, N.C., Oct. 14, 1958; s. Jack M. and Margaret Anne (Reap) B.; m. Kim Marie Whitaker, Sept. 26, 1981. B.S.B.S. in Acctg., East Carolina U.; M.S. in Econs. candidate N.C. State U. Staff acct. Ernst & Whinney, Raleigh, N.C., 1981-82; acctg. mgr. Browning-Ferris Industries, Raleigh, 1982-83; small bus. fin. and EDP cons., Garner, N.C., 1981-83; systems engr. Data Gen. Corp., Charlotte, 1983-85; co-founder, sr. v.p., chief operating officer Aero-Byte Info. Systems, Charlotte, 1985—. Precinct chmn. local Republican Com.; del. N.C. Rep. Conv., 1982. Participant AAU Nat. Amateur Swimming Trials, 1975. Mem. Nat. Assn. Accts., Am. Acctg. Assn., Nat. Soc. Pub. Accts., Am. Mgmt. Assn., Raleigh C. of C., Garner C. of C., Zebulon C. of C. Presbyterian. Home: 3200 Pendleton Ave Charlotte NC 28210 also 1906 Simpkins Rd Raleigh NC 27603 Office: PO Box 10038 Charlotte NC 28212

BROOKS, JERRY CLAUDE, textile company official; b. College Park, Ga., Apr. 23, 1936; s. John Bennett and Mattie Mae (Timms) B.; B.S., Ga. Inst. Tech., 1958; m. Peggy Sue Thornton, Feb. 26, 1961; children—Apryll Denise, Jerry Claude, Susan Vereen. Safety engr. Cotton Producers Assn., Atlanta, Ga., 1959-64, dir. safety and loss control, 1964-70; dir. corporate protection Gold Kist, Inc., Atlanta, 1970-81; corp. safety dir. J. P. Stevens & Co., Inc., Greenville, S.C., 1981-84, dir. corp. safety and security, 1984-86, dir. health and safety, 1986—; instr. Ga. Safety Inst., Athens, Ga., 1971-81; mem. faculty Greenville TEC. Bd. dirs. Ga. Safety Council, Ga. Soc. Prevention of Blindness. Served with AUS, 1958-59. Mem. Am. Soc. Safety Engrs. (chpt. pres. 1968-69, regional v.p. 1974-76), Nat. Safety Council (gen. chmn. agrl. chem. sect. 1969-70, gen. chmn. textile sect. 1985-86), So. Safety Conf. (pres. 1973), Am. Soc. Indsl. Security, Ga. Bus. and Industry Assn. (bd. govs.; Outstanding Mem. 1981). Mason, Rosicrucian. Club: Exchange (pres. 1969-70; Book of Golden Deeds award 1981) (Lithonia, Ga.). Home: 222 Rusty Ln Easley SC 29640 Office: Box 2850 Greenville SC 29602

BROOKS, LESLIE ERNEST, retired marketing research consultant, company executive; b. Pensacola, Fla., May 15, 1907; s. Leslie Ernest and Frederica (Loftin) B.; m. Dorothy Jayne Whitehead, June 4, 1938; children—Robert Leslie, Patricia Ruth. Student, U. Tulsa, 1926-27, U. Chgo., 1928, Tulsa Law Sch., 1929-30, Columbia U., 1934, U. Calif.-Berkeley, 1938. Reporter, Tulsa Tribune, 1925-26, asst. telegraphy editor, 1926, Sunday editor, 1927, city editor, 1928-29; owner Sand Springs Leader, 1930-31; copywriter Batten, Barton, Durstine & Osborn, Inc., N.Y.C., 1934; founder, owner Advt. Engrs., Inc., Tulsa, 1936-79; pres. Leslie Brooks & Assocs., Inc., Tulsa, 1940-85, Acquisition Cons., Tulsa, 1968—; research cons., 1968—. Chmn., Right-to-Work Com. for Okla.; former chmn. bd. trustees Oklahomans for Right to Work, recipient Oustanding Performance award, 1968. Recipient Outstanding Service award Nat. Right to Work Legal Def. Found., 1983; Disting. Service award Okla. Petroleum Council, 1971; Disting. Service award, Engrs. Soc. Tulsa, 1976-77, 1980; Silver Link Award of Merit, Pub. Relations Soc. Am., 1983; Disting. Service award Okla.-Kans. Oil and Gas Assn., 1983. Mem. Engrs. Soc. Tulsa (pres.), Am. Mktg. Assn. (chpt. pres. 1953), Am. Statis. Assn. (pres. 1956), Am. Petroleum Inst., Pub. Relations Soc. Am., Okla. Animal Protection League, United Humanitarians, Inc. (pres.). Republican. Christian Scientist. Clubs: Tulsa Knife and Fork (pres.), Utica 21 The Tulsa (Tulsa). Office: 2410 E 38th St Tulsa OK 74105

BROOKS, LESLIE GENE, association executive; b. Fletcher, Okla., June 15, 1936; s. Frank and Ethel Earlene (Spears) B.; m. Nancy Carman, Aug. 15, 1970; 1 son, Steven. B.A. in Piano, Okla. Bapt. U.; M.A., Ph.D. in Music Adminstrn., U. Okla. Dept. chmn. Cameron State U., Lawton, Okla., 1962-69, Midwestern State U., Wichita Falls, Tex., 1969-75, U. Ark., Little Rock, 1975-77; nat. exec. sec. Am. Choral Dirs. Assn., Lawton, 1977—, nat. conv. chmn., 1973. Mem. Internat. Choral Music (sec.-gen. 1982—), Music Tchrs. Nat. Assn. (nat. choral chmn. 1971-73, chmn. music in higher edn. 1974-75), Internat. Fedn. Choral Music. Democrat. Baptist. Home: 912 NW 41st St Lawton OK 73505 Office: Am Choral Dirs Assn 502 SW 38th St PO Box 6310 Lawton OK 73506

BROOKS, LINDA YVONNE, university dean; b. Andalusia, Ala., Feb. 21, 1944; s. Jesse Carl and Mittie Edna (Huggins) B. B.A., Abilene Christian U., 1966; M.Ed., Auburn U., 1973, Ed.D., 1975. Tchr., Stone Jr. High Sch., Huntsville, Ala., 1967-69; tchr. Madison Acad., 1969-73, GACS, Norcross, Ga., 1979-80; div. chmn. L.B.W. State Jr. Coll., Andalusia, 1975-77; mgr. Word Book-Childcraft, Panama City, Fla., 1977-79; chmn. dept. English, Faulkner U., Montgomery, Ala., 1980-81, chmn. div. humanities, 1981-82, chmn. div. edn., 1982-84, acad. dean, 1984—. Mem. Phi Delta Kappa. Mem. Ch. of Christ. Avocations: reading; hiking; cooking; traveling.

BROOKS, LORENZO, city police official; b. Huntsville, Ala., Sept. 9, 1942; s. Fred Dan and Amanda J. (Reed) B.; m. June R. Allison, June 11, 1983; children—Lori L. Brooks, Malcolm L. Allison. A.S., Palm Jr. Coll., 1978; B.A. in Criminal Justice, Fla. Atlantic U., 1981. With Mercer-Wenzel Dept. Store, 1962, Coleman Funeral Home, 1963; with Delray Beach Police Dept. (Fla.), 1963—, police lt., adminstrv. asst., 1974-77, capt. detectives, 1977-79, capt. spl. services, 1979-80, capt. patrol, 1980-81, capt. adminstrn., 1981-84, capt. staff services div., 1984—; instr. criminal justice Palm Beach Jr. Coll. Continuing Edn., Lake Worth, Fla., 1975-81. Active Delray Beach Police Benevolent Assn., 1965—; bd. dirs. South County Drug Abuse Found., Delray Beach, 1980—, South County Mental Health Assn., 1980—; mem. credit com. Delray Beach Employees Credit Union, 1981—; trustee Mt. Olive Bapt. Ch., Delray Beach, 1981—; mem. City Delray Beach Civil Service Bd., 1977-79, sec., 1977-78, chmn., 1979. Served with USAF, 1960. Mem. Nat. Orgn. Black Law Enforcement Execs., Fraternal Order Police. Lodge: Masons. Home: Apt A-104 825 Egret Circle Delray Beach FL 33444 Office: Delray Beach Police Dept 200 S W 1st St Delray Beach FL 33444

BROOKS, MICHAEL ZANE, civil engineer; b. Anniston, Ala., Oct. 5, 1949; s. William L. and Margaret Jane (Casey) B.; m. Cynthia Ann Martin, Aug. 2, 1975; children—Jon Michael, William Martin, Mary Katherine. B.S. in Civil Engring., U. Ala., 1975, M.S., 1983. Registered profl. engr. and land surveyor, Ala., Fla., Miss. Design engr. Almon Assocs., Inc., Tuscaloosa, Ala., 1975-80, project mgr., 1980-82, assoc., 1982-83; design engr. Flood Engrs.-Architects-Planners, Jacksonville, Fla., 1983—; instr. math. dept. Fla. Jr. Coll., Jacksonville. Served with U.S. Army, 1970-72. Mem. Am. Soc. Civil Engrs., Water Pollution Control Fedn., Ala. Soc. Profl. Land Surveyors. Republican. Presbyterian. Home: 5602 Clifton Ave Jacksonville FL 32211 Office: PO Box 8869 Jacksonville FL 32211

BROOKS, PATRICK, mathematics educator; b. Norton, Va., Sept. 25, 1954; s. James Pledger and Manila Victoria (Powers) B. B.A. in Math., Clinch Valley Coll., 1976; M.A. in Edn., Murray State U., 1984. Cert. tchr. in math. and French, Ky. Loan adjustor First Nat. Exchange Bank, Appalachia, Va., 1976; math. instr. Wise County Sch., Va., 1976-78; mgr. trainee CIT Fin. Services, Appalachia, 1978-79; salesman Ward's Mobile Homes, Coeburn, Va., 1979; teaching asst. Murray State U., Ky., 1983-84; math instr. Fayette County Schs., Lexington, Ky., 1979-83, 84—, faculty forum rep., 1982-83, 84-85; tchr. del. Ky. Tchr. Recognition Conf., 1985. Vol. coach YMCA, Lexington, 1984-85, Bryan Station Sr. High, Lexington, 1984-85; judge Fayette County Math. Bowl, Lexington, 1980-85, Thelma Beeler Speech Tournament, Lexington, 1982-83, Western Ky. Fgn. Lang. Festival, Murray, 1983-84; faculty rep. PTSA, Fayette County Schs., 1983-85. Mem. Nat. Council Tchrs. Math., Fayette County Edn. Assn. (bldg. rep. 1982-83), Math. Assn. Am., Bryan Station Parent Student Tchr. Assn., Ky. Council Tchrs. Math., Lexington Council Tchrs. Math., Euclidean Math. Club, Phi Delta Phi, Pi Mu Epsilon, Mu Alpha Theta. Lodge: Kiwanis. Avocations: fishing; reading; bowling. Home: Route 3 Box 796 Wise VA 24293 Office: Bryan Station Sr High Sch Edgeworth Dr Lexington KY 40505

BROOKS, PHILIP BARRON, retired accountant; b. N.Y.C., Apr. 20, 1914; m. Betty R. Ralston; children—Richard L., Michael B., Philip J., Jeffrey R. A.B. cum laude, Rider Coll., 1935. C.P.A., N.J., N.Y. Pvt. practice pub. acctg., Montclair, N.J., 1937-67; founder, chmn. bd., chief exec. officer Bank of Bloomfield (N.J.), 1972-74; past pres. Surf Club Apts., Inc., Surfside, Fla.; past treas., dir. Computer Spltys. Corp., Palisades Park, N.J.; founder, ret. dir. Garden State Title Ins. Co., Montclair; founder, ret. pres., chief exec. officer TransJersey Bancorp.; founder, ret. dir. Garden State Mortgage Agy., Inc., Montclair, N.J.; dir. Nortek, Inc., Providence, Christenson & Gutmann, San Francisco; formerly lectr. tax subjects; panel mem. Am. Arbitration Assn. Former trustee, treas. Youth Employment Service Montclair, Montclair Urban Coalition, 1968-71; trustee emeritus Rider Coll.; former trustee Montclair Community Hosp. Recipient Disting. Alumnus award Rider Coll., 1974. Mem. Fla., N.J., socs. C.P.A.s. Am. Inst. C.P.A.s, Rider Coll. Alumni Assn. (nat. pres. 1965-67, past trustee), Grand Jury Assn. Essex County, N.J. Hosp. Assn., Montclair C. of C. (dir., pres. 1966-69, past trustee), N.J. Hist. Soc., U.S. Croquet Assn., Zeta Beta Tau. Clubs: Spring Lake Bath and Tennis, Spring Lake Golf, Green Gables Croquet (pres. 1984), La Gorce Country, Com. of One Hundred (dir.) (Miami, Fla.); Surf (treas., bd. govs.) (Surfside, Fla.); One Hundred (former trustee, treas.) (Montclair); N.Y. Athletic; Elks (past exalted ruler). Home: Surf Club Apts Surfside FL 33154

BROOKS, REX DWAIN, lawyer; b. Blanchard, Okla., Feb. 2, 1937; s. Berry Wilson and Edith Bane (Byers) B.; m. Norma Newton, May 16, 1964; 1 dau., Elizabeth Ann. B.B.A., U. Okla., 1965, J.D., 1967. Bar: Okla. 1967, U.S. Dist. Ct. (we. dist.) Okla. 1974, U.S. Sup. Ct. 1977, U.S. Ct. Apls. (10th cir.) 1978. Assoc., Elliot, Woodard and Rolston, 1967-68; atty. Md. Casualty Co., Oklahoma City, 1968-74; sole practice, Oklahoma City, 1974—. Served with U.S. Army, 1960-62. Mem. ABA, Oklahoma County Bar Assn., Okla. Bar Assn., Okla. Heritage Assn., Assn. Trial Lawyers Am., Okla. Trial Lawyers Assn. Democrat. Baptist. Address: 2323 N Indiana St Oklahoma City OK 73106

BROOKS, ROBERT TERYL, JR., physician; b. Moncla, La., Feb. 18, 1934; s. Robert Teryl and Lily (Moncla) B.; m. Helen Claire Martin, Aug. 17, 1957; children—Martin Teryl, Katherine Sue. B.S., Tulane U., 1955, M.D., 1958. Diplomate Am. Bd. Urology. Intern, San Diego Naval Hosp., 1958-59; resident urology Bethesda Naval Hosp., 1959-60, resident gen. surgery, 1960-61, resident urology, 1961-63; urologist Portsmouth Naval Hosp. (Va.), 1963-68, chief urology, 1967-68; urologist Jefferson Hosp., Pine Bluff, Ark., 1968—, chief staff, 1976-77, chief surgery, 1984-85; clin. instr. urology U. Ark. Med. Center, 1968-77, asst. clin. prof., 1978—. Bd. dirs. United Way, 1974-76, Jefferson Prep. Sch., 1975-78, 78-81, Fifty for the Future, 1980-83, Nat. Bank Commerce, 1980—; elder First Presbyn. Ch., 1974-79, 81-86; mem. Area Health Edn. Center Adv. Bd., 1978—. Served from lt. to comdr. USN, 1958-68. Mem. AMA, Am. Urol. Assn., ACS, Ark. Med. Soc., Ark. Urol. Soc. (pres. 1979-80), Jefferson County Med. Soc. (v.p. 1975). Contbr. articles to profl. jours. Office: 1801 W 40th St Suite 1-B Pine Bluff AR 71603

BROOKS, SAMUEL ROBERT, III, lawyer; b. Arlington, Va., Dec. 18, 1950; s. Samuel Robert and Ruth Jean (Heasley) B.; m. Barbara Kristine Miller, Nov. 23, 1971 (div. Mar. 1983); m. Linda Bender, July 1, 1983; children—Samuel Robert IV, Jeremy Rogers. B.S., U.S. Coast Guard Acad., 1972; J.D., Am. U., 1980. Bar: Ala. 1980, Miss. 1981, U.S. Dist. Ct. (so. dist.) Ala. 1981, U.S. Dist. Ct. (so. dist.) Miss. 1981, U.S. Ct. Appeals (5th cir.) 1981, U.S. Ct. Appeals (11th cir.) 1981, U.S. Ct. Mil. Appeals, 1983, U.S. Ct. Claims. 1984, U.S. Ct. Appeals (fed. cir.) 1985. Sole practice, Mobile, Ala. and Pascagaula, Miss., 1980—. Served to lt. USCG, 1968-82. Mem. ABA, Assn. Trial Lawyers Am., Ala. Trial Lawyers Assn., Miss. Trial Lawyers Assn. Home: 1318 Polaris Dr Mobile AL 36609 Office: Suite 502 900 W American Circle Mobile AL 36609

BROOKS, WANDA NELL, nurse administrator; b. Daingerfield, Tex., Nov. 27, 1931; s. Melvin L. and Opal (White) Puckett; m. Olan O. Brooks, Feb. 6, 1954; children—Deborah, Karen. Diploma in nursing Northwestern State U., Natchitoches, La., 1953, B.S.N., 1959, M.S.N., 1975. From staff nurse to supr. VA Med. Ctr., Shreveport, La., 1954-75; asst. chief nurse VA Med. Ctr., New Orleans, 1976-77; dir. nursing service VA Med. Ctr., Bonham, Tex., 1977-79, VA Med. Ctr., Hampton, Va., 1979-83, VA Med. Ctr., Jackson, Miss., 1983—. Recipient Spl. Performance award VA, 1980, Spl. Performance award, 1981, commendation, 1983. Mem. Assn. Nurse Adminstrs., Univ. Med. Ctr. Honor Soc., Sigma Theta Tau. Democrat. Mem. Ch. of Christ. Avocations: sewing; smocking; quilting. Home: 47 Sunline Dr Brandon MS 39042 Office: VA Med Ctr 1500 E Woodrow Wilson Jackson MS 39216

BROOKSHIRE, ROBERT GORDON, computer analyst, political science educator; b. Colorado Springs, Colo., Oct. 27, 1950; s. Joe Grady and Gloria Belle (Davies) B.; m. Cathy Leigh Agrin, July 29, 1973; 1 child, Bethany Rose. B.A., U. Ga., 1972; M.A. in Edn., Ga. State U., 1978; Ph.D., Emory U., 1982. Research programmer North Tex. State U., Denton, 1981-84, mgr. acad. computing services, 1984—, asst. prof. polit. sci., 1981—. Co-author: Using Microcomputers for Research, 1985. Contbr. articles to profl. jours. Mem. Am. Polit. Sci. Assn., Assn. for Computing Machinery, So. Polit. Sci. Assn., Midwestern Polit. Sci. Assn., Southwestern Polit. Sci. Assn. Office: North Texas State U Computing Ctr Denton TX 76203

BROOM, VERNON HERRIN, state justice; b. Marion County, Miss., Jan. 16, 1924; s. John Calvin and Bertha (Herrin) B.; student Pearl River Jr. Coll., Poplarville, Miss., 1941-43, Pratt Inst., Bklyn., 1943-44; B.B.A., U. Miss., 1948, LL.B., 1948; m. Clemetine Johnson; 2 children. Admitted to Miss. bar, 1948; practiced law, Columbia, Miss., 1948-70; dist. atty. 1st Jud. Dist. Miss., 1952-64; atty. Columbia Mcpl. Sch. Dist., 1967-69; judge Circuit Ct., 15th Jud. Dist., 1971-72; assoc. justice Miss. Supreme Ct., 1972-83, presiding justice, 1983—. Served with inf. U.S. Army, World War II; ETO. Decorated Bronze Star, Purple Heart. Mem. Miss. State Bar Assn. (commr. 1967-68), Marion County C. of C. (pres. 1969-70), Am. Legion, DAV, VFW. Democrat. Baptist. Clubs: Masons, Shriners. Office: Supreme Ct Bldg Jackson MS 39205

BROOME, O(SCAR) WHITFIELD, JR., educator, consultant; b. Monroe, N.C., Feb. 3, 1940; s. Oscar Whitfield and Irma (Hinson) B.; m. Julia Carol Renegar, June 14, 1964; children—Christine Irma, Michael Whitfield. A.B., Duke U., 1962; M.S., U. Ill., 1964, Ph.D., 1971. Instr. U. Ill., Urbana, 1965-67; prof. U. Va., Charlottesville, 1967—; exec. dir. Inst. Chartered Fin. Analysts, Charlottesville, 1978-84; vis. prof. U. Tex.-Austin, 1975, Duke U., Durham, N.C., 1977-78. Contbr. articles to profl. jours. Fellow Fin. Analysts Fedn.; mem. Am. Inst. C.P.A.s (bd. examiners 1980-82), Va. Soc. C.P.A.s, Fin. Mgmt. Assn., Phi Beta Kappa, Phi Kappa Phi, Beta Gamma Sigma. Home: 1460 Old Ballard Rd Charlottesville VA 22901 Office: U Va McIntire Sch Commerce Charlottesville VA 22903

BROPHY, GILBERT THOMAS, lawyer; b. Southampton, N.Y., July 15, 1926; s. Joseph Lester and Helen Veronica (Scholtz) B.; m. Canora Woodham Brophy, 1957 (div. 1983); 1 dau., Erin Woodham Brophy; m. Isabel Blair Porter; 1 stepdau., Laure Porter Thompson. B.S.B.A. with high honors in Acctg., U. Fla., 1949; LL.B., George Washington U., 1960; postgrad. Law Sch., U. Miami, 1970-73. Bar: Fla. 1960, U.S. Dist. Ct. D.C., 1970. Title examiner Jesse Phillips Klinge & Kendrick, Arlington, Va., 1959-60; ptnr. Beall, Beall & Brophy, Palm Beach, Fla., 1962-65; asst. city atty. West Palm Beach (Fla.), 1965-67; ptnr. Brophy & Skrandel, Palm Beach, 1968-70, Brophy & Aksomitas, Tequesta, Fla., 1974-75, Brophy, Genovese & Sayler, Jupiter, Fla., 1977-78, Brophy & Genovese, 1978-83; town atty. Lantana (Fla.), 1967-70; judge ad litem Village of Tequesta, 1970-72; town atty. Jupiter, 1974-75. Bd. dirs., disaster chmn. ARC, Palm Beach; past corr. sec. Palm Beach County Hist. Soc. Served with Inf., U.S. Army, 1944-46, World War II, 1951-54; Korea. Recipient Dedicated Service plaque Town of Jupiter, 1975. Mem. Attys. Title Guaranty Fund, Assn. Trial Lawyers Am., Palm Beach County Bar Assn., Nat. Mil. Intelligence Assn., Nat. CIC Assn., Assn. Former Intelligence Officers, NRA (life), Kappa Sigma, Phi Eta Sigma, Beta Gamma Sigma, Beta Alpha Psi, Phi Kappa Phi. Mem. exec. com. Republican Com. Martin County. Clubs: Rotary (pres. 1977-78), University (Washington); Elks, River Edge, Everglades Rifle and Pistol (hon. life). Home: Augusta D Riverbend Tequesta FL 33469 Office: 810 Saturn St Parkway Plaza Suite 15 Jupiter FL 33477

BROPHY, PATRICK JOSEPH, public relations agency executive, consultant; b. Oakland, Calif., Mar. 19, 1924; s. John Wilbur and Anna May B.; m. Norine Guillet, June 24, 1950; children—Julaine Brophy Brent, Moira Brophy Bakewell, Sean Patrick. B.S. in Bus. Adminstrn., Holy Cross Coll., Worcester, Mass., 1950; postgrad. Wayne State U., 1965-69. Publ. relations/sales promotion specialist, editor Oldsmobile Rocket News, Oldsmobile div. Gen. Motors Corp., Lansing, Mich., 1950-53, dist. sales rep., 1953-60, city mgr., Washington, 1960-63; planner, writer, account exec. Jam Handy Orgn., Detroit, 1963-69; regional publ. relations dir. Eaton Corp., Southfield, Mich., 1969-75; sales rep. State of Mich., mktg. services mgr. N.Y., Abitibi-Price, 1975-78; publicity dir. Saddlebrook Golf and Tennis Resort, Wesley Chapel, Fla., 1978-81; v.p. Sound Communications, Dunedin, Fla., 1981-83; pres. Brophy & Assocs., 1983—; pres., et al, inc., 1985—. Mem. Pub. Relations Soc. Am. (Silver Anvil award 1974), Roman Catholic. Lodge: K.C. Home: 53 Gulfwinds Dr W Palm Harbor FL 33563 Office: 53 Gulfwinds Dr Palm Habor FL 33563

BROSCHART, KAY RICHARDS, sociologist, educator; b. Youngstown, Ohio, Jan. 19, 1933; d. Lawrence Kay and Clara (Truesdale) Richards; m. James R. Broschart, Apr. 2, 1967; children—Christopher Lawrence, Jennifer Katherine. B.S. cum laude, Kent State U., 1958; M.P.H., Yale U., 1959, M.A., 1961, Ph.D., 1968. Instr., lectr., asst. prof. sociology Boston Coll., 1965-75, co-dir. Office Women and Career Options, 1974-75; asst. prof. Hollins Coll. (Va.), 1975-84, assoc. prof., 1984—, asst. to pres., 1977-81; cons. U.S. Office

Edn., 1980-86. Del., Va. 6th Dist. Dem. Conv., Va. State Dem. Conv., 1984-85. Recipient Emory Borgardus award, 1977; USPHS trainee, 1958-59; USPHS fellow Commonwealth Found., 1961-65; Carnegie Gilman faculty fellow, 1974-75; Mednick Meml. fellow, 1984. Mem. Am. Sociol. Assn., Eastern Sociol. Assn., AAUP, AAUW (Hollins Coll. corp. rep. 1977-81), Delta Psi Kappa, Kappa Delta Pi. Contbr. articles and revs. to profl. jours. Home: 2716 Crystal Spring Ave Roanoke VA 24014 Office: Dept Sociology Hollins College VA 24020

BROSKY, SANDRA CAREN, hospital administrator; b. Richmond, Va., June 1, 1955; d. Sherlee (Michael) Ginsberg. Student Sophie Newcomb Coll., 1973-75, U. South Fla., 1976; B.S. Nursing with honors, Emory U., 1978; M.H.A., Ga. State U., 1982. R.N. Staff nurse Crawford Long Hosp., Atlanta, 1978-82; adminstrv. resident Emory U. Hosp., Atlanta, 1982; dir. emergency services Kennestone Hosp., Marietta, Ga., 1982-84, asst. adminstr. clin. services div., 1984—. Mem. steering com. Women's Resource Ctr., Cobb County YWCA, Marietta, 1982-84. Recipient Outstanding Merit award Ga. State U., 1982. Mem. Ga. Hosp. Assn. (mem. profl. services council vol. cons. council on nursing 1982-83), Young Adminstrs. of Ga., Ga. Women's Health Adminstrn. Network, Sigma Theta Tau. Avocations: tennis; rafting; aerobics; photography. Office: Kennestone Hosp 677 Church St Marietta GA 30060

BROSMAN, PAUL WILLIAM, JR., retired linguistics educator; b. Macon, Ga., Sept. 16, 1927; s. Paul William and Katherine Elizabeth (Lewis) B.; m. Catharine Hill, Aug. 21, 1970; 1 child, Katherine Elliott. B.A., Tulane U., 1949, M.A., 1950; Ph.D., U. N.C., 1956. Asst. to assoc. prof. North Tex. State U., Denton, 1956-58; asst. to assoc. prof. U. New Orleans, 1958-65; assoc. prof. to prof. Tulane U., New Orleans, 1965-79. Contbr. articles to profl. jours. Served to 1st lt. USMC, 1950-52; Korea. Mem. Linguistic Soc. Am., Societas Lingusitica Europaea, South-Central MLA. Republican. Episcopalian. Club: Boston (New Orleans). Home: 7834 Willow St New Orleans LA 70118

BROTCHNER, RICHARD RAYMOND, industrial/mechanical engineer, consultant; b. Mpls., Feb. 25, 1944; s. Robert J. and Dorothy I. (Goldblum) B. B.S., Calif. State U.-Northridge, 1967; M.P.A., U. So. Calif., 1975. Ops./shift supr. The Flying Tiger Line, San Francisco, 1971-73; manpower controller Am. Airlines' Sky Chief Subs., 1973; dir. Manpower Devel. and Tng. Co., Merced, Calif., 1974; cons., group mgr. United Research Corp., Wofac, Inc., 1973-77; manpower cons. Orange County-Long Beach Health Consortium, Calif., 1974-75; mgr. hub and ramp operating systems, mgr. plans and programs Fed. Express Corp., Memphis, 1977-79, mgr. advanced tech. and research, 1979—. Spl. and res. dep. Shelby County Sheriff's Dept., Shelby County, Tenn. NASA postgrad. fellow, 1968-75; grad. teaching asst. Calif. State U., Northridge, 1966-68. Mem. Soc. Automotive Engrs., Air Cargo Handling Com., Blue Key, Pi Sigma Alpha. Lodge: Grand Krewe of Osiris. Home: 2321 Windy Oaks Dr Germantown TN 38138 Office: Fed Express Corp PO Box 727 Memphis TN 38104

BROTHERS, M(URIEL) ELIZABETH, college official; b. Bklyn.; d. Sydney Inman and Marguerite Olley (Taylor-Lindsay) B.; A.B. with distinction in Spanish, Vassar Coll., 1950; postgrad. Latin Am. Inst., N.Y. Sch. Employing Printers, Philanthrophy Tax Inst. Various editorial positions McCall Corp., 1951-62; devel. officer Mt. Holyoke Coll., South Hadley, Mass., 1962-67, 71-73; dir. publs. and dir. public info., 1967-71, dir. devel., 1973-80; asso. v.p. devel Rollins Coll., Winter Park, Fla., 1980—; dir. Mass. Congl. Fund, 1979-80; lectr., cons. fin. planning for women. Bd. dirs. Holyoke YWCA, 1976-79; trustee 1st Congl. Ch., Winter Park, 1981—; v.p. Christopher D. Smithers Found., N.Y.C.; bd. dirs. Crosby Found., Winter Park. Recipient Disting. Fund Raising award, 1969. Mem. Nat. Soc. Fund Raising Execs. (Outstanding Profl. Fund Raiser award 1985), Mt. Holyoke Alumni Assn. (hon.). Republican. Clubs: Cosmopolitan (N.Y.C.); University (Winter Park); Fla. Exec. Women (dir.) (Orlando); Mt. Holyoke of Del. (hon.). Author handbooks in field; contbr. articles to profl. publs. Home: 640 Park Ave N Winter Park FL 32789 Office: Rollins College Winter Park FL 32789

BROTHERS, WILLIAM JOHN, JR., agrl. warehousing firm exec.; b. Shelby, Miss., Mar. 11, 1920; s. William John and Anne (Kingston) B.; student Christian Bros. Coll., 1938-40, Memphis State U., 1940-41; m. Cassie Marie Campbell, Apr. 23, 1950; children—William John III, Brooke Ann Brothers Tappan. Plant mgr. Helena Chem. Co. (Ark.), 1957-69, v.p. mfg., 1969-72; pres. Blackhawk Warehouse & Leasing Co., Helena, 1970—. Commr. Ark. State Police, 1971-80; mem. CSC, 1966—, Helena Welfare Bd., 1968-70; past pres. Phillips County Indsl. Devel. Corp.; bd. dirs. Phillips County Community Coll., Helena; mem. adv. bd. to dean Bus. Sch., U. Ark. Served with USAAF, 1941-45; ETO, PTO. Recipient award for exceptional accomplishment Ark. Community Devel. Program, 1975. Mem. Ark. (dir., treas.), Helena chambers commerce. Democrat. Roman Catholic (ch. council). KC. Home: 123 Summit Dr Helena AR 72342 Office: PO Box 809 Helena AR 72342

BROTHERTON, THOMAS KEMPER, JR., company administrator; b. Charleston, W. Va., July 28, 1950; s. Thomas Kemper and Ethel Louise (Neff) B.; m. Dorothy Harrison Reynolds, June 19, 1971; children—Dorothy Allison, Hardin Thomas. B.A., U. N.C., 1972; M.B.A., U. Va., 1977, J.D., 1977. Industry dir. solar energy Reynolds Metals Co., Richmond, Va., 1977-79, nat. mgr. solar energy, 1979-80, gen. mgr. energy products, 1980—, market mgr. mill products, 1985—. Past deacon River Rd. Presbyn. Ch.; bd. dirs. Richmond Children's Mus. Mem. Solar Energy Industries Assn. (exec. com.). Clubs: Country of Va., Deep Run Hunt (Richmond).

BROUCEK, WILLIAM SAMUEL, printing plant manager; b. Statesboro, Ga., July 27, 1950; s. Jack Wolf and Emily Louise (Kupferschmid) B.; m. Sara Carolyn Bennett, May 10, 1975; children—Samuel Josiah, William Bennett. B.B.A., Ga. So. Coll., 1972. Adminstr. Willingway Hosp., Statesboro, Ga., 1972-73; dept. mgr. Deluxe Check Printers, Inc., Jacksonville, Fla., 1975-78, asst. prodn. mgr., 1978-82, asst. plant mgr., 1982-83, plant mgr., 1984—. Bd. dirs. Ga. So. Coll. Alumni Assn., Statesboro, 1980-81; vol. Am. Cancer Soc., Jacksonville, 1981-83. Mem. Stone Mountain Indsl. Park Assn., DeKalb County C. of C., Republican. Presbyterian. Clubs: Smokerise Swim (Stone Mountain, Ga.), YMCA, Aircraft Owners and Pilots Assn. Avocations: aviation; old cars. Office: Deluxe Check Printers Inc 2037 Mountain Ind Blvd Tucker GA 30084

BROUILLETTE, LYNN JOSEPH, physician; b. Marksville, La., Mar. 25, 1945; s. Amabe Joseph and Florence Rose (Borell) B.; B.S. in Zoology, Northwestern State Coll., Natchitoches, La., 1966; M.D., La. State U., 1970; m. Karen Bearden, Aug. 6, 1966; children—David, John, Paul. Intern, Confederate Meml. Med. Center, 1970-71, resident in ob-gyn, 1973-76; practice medicine specializing in ob-gyn, Natchitoches, 1976—; chief of staff Natchitoches Parish Hosp., 1980-82. Served with M.C., USN, 1971-73. Fellow Am. Coll. Ob-Gyn; mem. La. State Med. Soc., Am. Fertility Soc., Royal Soc. Medicine (affiliate), AAAS, Natchitoches Parish Med. Soc. Republican. Roman Catholic. Office: 114 E 5th St Natchitoches LA 71457

BROUN, E. C., JR., drilling equipment company executive; b. 1923; married. B.S., Tex. A&M U., 1947. Petroleum engr. Humble Oil & Refining Co., 1947-52; chief petroleum engr. Highland Oil Co., 1952-55; drilling supt. Henderson Drilling Co., 1955-57; v.p., gen. mgr. Southwest Industries, 1957-72; with Dresser Industries Inc., 1972-79, pres. Petroleum Services Group, 1975-78, pres. Oil Field Equipment Group, 1978-79; v.p. market devel. Hughes Tool Co., Houston, 1979-80, exec. v.p., pres. Product Tool Services, 1980—, also dir.; dir. Tex. Commerce Bank-Richmond/Sage N.A., Oceaneering Internat. Inc., Oil Corp. Served with U.S. Army, 1943-46. Office: Hughes Tool Co 6500 Tex Commerce Tower Houston TX 77002*

BROUSSARD, DONALD GLEN, safety engineer, consultant; b. West Memphis, Ark., May 19, 1954; s. Widley Jacob and Leola Marie (Harrington) B.; 1 child, Holly Ann. A.S. in Occupational Safety and Health, Delgado Coll., 1976; student in petroleum safety tech. Nicholls State U., 1980-84. Safety engr., loss prevention mgr. Gray & Co., Inc. Underwriters Mgrs., New Orleans, 1976-79; safety dir. Livingston/Pool Offshore, Houma, La., 1979-81, Bay Drilling Corp./Texaco Inc., New Orleans, 1981-84; safety engr., expert witness Occupational Safety & Health Cons., Schriever, La., 1984—; safety adminstr. Boeing Petroleum Services, New Orleans, 1985—; dir. South Central La. Safety Council, Houma, 1977-85, pres. Houma sect., 1985-86. Mem. Am. Soc. Safety Engrs. (cons. 1980), World Safety Orgn., Schriever Jaycees. Republican. Roman Catholic. Club: Endymion Carnival (New Orleans). Avocations: scuba diving, racquet ball, boxing, karate, dancing. Home: 131 Isle of Cuba Rd Schriever LA 70395

BROUSSARD, HUBY JOSEPH, industrial-marine supply company executive; b. Abbeville, La., Dec. 24, 1927; s. Clovis and Elva (Touchet) B.; m. Mary Ellen Melancon, July 12, 1947; children—Barry, Jerry, Jackie, Richard. Field hand rice farm, Gibson, La., 1948; parts mgr. Guarisco Motor Co., Morgan City, La., 1948-50; sales rep. Morgan City Supply, 1950-54, sales mgr., 1954-58, v.p. sales, 1958-71; pres. Am. Supply Co., Morgan City, 1971—, Two-Way Enterprises, Morgan City, 1969—; mem. adv. council ITT Jabsco Products, Costa Mesa, Calif., 1980-84. Inboard commr. Am. Power Boat Assn., East Detroit, Mich., 1964—, council mem., 1982-84. Mem. Nat. Assn. Wholesalers, So. Indsl. Distbr. Assn., La. Assn. Bus. and Industry, C. of C. (dir. 1979-81), St. Mary Indsl. Group (dir. 1980—). Democrat. Roman Catholic. Clubs: La. Dist. South Civitan (chpt. founder; lt. gov. 1961-64, gov. 1965-66), St. Mary Golf and Country pres. (pres. 1971, 74, 78) (Morgan City). Lodge: K.C. Office: Am Supply Co of Morgan City Inc PO Box 2602 Morgan City LA 70381

BROUSSARD, JOHN EDWARD, pharmacist; b. Abbeville, La., June 3, 1957; s. Edward John and Rose Marie (Guidry) B.; m. Margaret Marie Dugas, June 20, 1981; 1 dau., Constance Marie. B.S. in Pharmacy, N.E. La. U., 1982. Registered pharmacist, La. Staff pharmacist K-B Drugs, Lake Charles and Sulphur, La., 1982-83; pharmacist, owner, mgr. Thrifty-Way Pharmacy Lake Arthur, 1983—; v.p., dir. Thrifty Way Pharmacies of La., 1985—. Chmn. Leukemia Soc. Am., Lake Arthur, 1985; tchr. Roman Catholic Religious Study, Lake Arthur, 1984—; alderman Town of Lake Arthur, 1985—. Named Pharmacy Doctor, Nat. Assn. Retail Druggists, 1984. Mem. La. Pharmacist Assn. Democrat. Lodges: Kiwanis (bd. dirs. 1985-86), KC (3d degree, treas. 1985). Avocations: sports; games; youth work. Home: 1210 1/2 3d St PO Box AN Lake Arthur LA 70549 Office: Thriftyway Pharmacy Lake Arthur 110 Arthur PO Box AN Lake Arthur LA 70549

BROUSSARD, NORMAJ, artist, journalist; b. Lake Providence, La., Aug. 28, 1931; d. C. Thomas and Hazel Valli (Ainsworth) Edwards; student Stephen F. Austin State Coll., 1951-52, U. Tex., 1973—; mem. Internat. Workshop Danish Sch. Design, Copenhagen, 1973; m. Lee R. Broussard, Dec. 31, 1958; 1 dau., Cherie Antoinette; children from previous marriage—Bonnie Greening (Mrs. Allen P. Bennett), Billy E. Greening. Owner, The Chateau, Port Arthur, Tex., 1968—, Broussard's Mobile Villages, Port Arthur, 1960—, Studio Normaj, 1972—; pres. Travel Magic Corp., Broussard Enterprises; organizer, sponsor Gulf Coast Arts and Crafts Festival, 1970, Jefferson County (Tex.) Arts and Crafts Festival, 1972, Diamond Jubilee Fine Arts Show, 1973; tchr., lectr. in field; art dir. City of Port Arthur. Founder, Tex. Artists Mus. Soc., 1972, pres., 1973-74; mem. com. Tex. Constl. Rev. Commn., 1973—; pres. Am. Cancer Soc.; mem. Port Arthur Bicentennial Commn. Recipient numerous awards local and state art competitions including La. Art and Folk Festival, 1970-73, Sabine Area Art Show, 1972. Mem. Port Arthur Art Assn. Fine Arts Guild (pres. 1971), Diocesan Council Cath. Women (pres. 1965), Noon Bus. and Profl. Women's Club, Internat. Platform Assn., Tex. Fedn. Women's Clubs, Tex. Poetry South and Major Poets Club, S.E. Tex. Arts Council, Port Arthur C. of C., Zeta Phi Delphians (pres. 1967), Beta Sigma Phi, Roman Catholic (pres. altar soc. 1965, 66). Club: Heritage Antique Study (pres. 1973-74). Address: 4801 7th St Port Arthur TX 77642

BROWDER, JOHNIE MAE GOMILLION, retired educational administrator; b. McKenzie, Ala., Oct. 2, 1919; d. Thad Jackson and Irene (Lee) Gomillion; B.S., Troy State U., 1949; M.Ed., Auburn U., 1956; m. Ralph J. Browder, Dec. 15, 1939; children—Ralph Thaddeus, Tempie Leah Browder Mutschler. Tchr. public schs., 1943-46; tchr., guidance counselor McKenzie High Sch., 1946-65; supr. guidance and evaluation Butler County Public Schs., 1965-71; prin. W. O. Parmer Elem. Sch., Greenville, Ala., 1971-81, ret., 1982. Treas., adult Sunday sch. tchr. New Home Baptist Ch. Mem. Ala. Edn. Assn., NEA, Ala. Dept. Elem. Prins. Assn., Butler County Edn. Assn. (pres. 1973-74), Internat. Platform Assn., Delta Kappa Gamma, Kappa Delta Pi. Home: Route 1 McKenzie AL 36456

BROWDER, MICHAEL HEATH, clergyman, educator; b. Richmond, Va., Dec. 4, 1951; s. Arville Heath and Anna Marie (Ficke) B.; m. Susan Beers, July 8, 1978; children—Michael Heath, Marjorie Elizabeth. B.A., Duke U., 1973, Th.M., 1977, Ph.D., 1982; M.Div., Harvard U., 1976. Ordained to ministry United Methodist Ch., 1977. Minister, Prospect United Meth. Ch., 1976-78, King George United Meth. Ch., 1978-80, Highland Park United Meth. Ch., 1980-82; pastor Strasburg and Mt. Zion (Va.) United Meth. Chs., 1982—; instr. religion Shenandoah Coll. and Conservatory Music, 1983—; adj. faculty Wesley Theol. Sem. Mem. Shenandoah Democratic Com., Shenandoah Bd. Human Services; active Richmond Urban Inst. Recipient grants for lang. research. Mem. Assn. Bibl. Archeologists. Lodge: Masons. Author: Al-Biruni as a Source for Mani and Manichaeism, 1982; English Translation of the Coptic Manichaen Homilies, 1983; corr. Va. Advocate.

BROWER, DAVID JOHN, lawyer, urban planner, educator, administrator; b. Holland, Mich., Sept. 11, 1930; s. John J. and Helen (Olson) B.; m. Lou Ann Brown, Nov. 26, 1960; children—Timothy Seth, David John, II, Ann Lacey. B.A., U. Mich., 1956, J.D., 1960. Bar: Ill. 1960, Mich. 1961, Ind. 1961, U.S. Supreme Ct. 1971. Asst. dir. div. community planning Ind. U., Bloomington, 1960-70; assoc. dir. Ctr. for Urban and Regional Studies, U. N.C., Chapel Hill, 1970—; pres. Coastal Resources Collaborative, Ltd., Chapel Hill, 1980—. Author: (with others) Contitutional Issues of Growth Management, 1978; Growth Management, 1984, Special Area Management, 1985. Bd. dirs. Chapel Hill Day Care Ctr., 1978, N.C. Estuarine Sanctuary System, Raleigh. NSF grantee, 1977, 83—, NOAA sea grantee, 1978—. Mem. ABA, Am. Planning Assn. bd. dirs. 1982—, chmn.-founder planning and law div. 1978), Am. Soc. Pub. Adminstrn., Am. Inst. Cert. Planners. Democrat. Episcopalian. Home: 612 Shady Lawn Chapel Hill NC 27514 Office: Univ NC 108 Battle Ln Chapel Hill NC 27514

BROWER, WALTER JORDAN, physician; b. Birmingham, Ala., Feb. 5, 1921; s. Walter Scott and Elizabeth (Jordan) B.; B.A., U. Ala., 1942; M.D., Duke U., 1947; m. Miriam Timmons, Jan. 20, 1949; children—William Jordan, Carl Timmons, Caroline Elizabeth, Franklin Perry. Rotating intern Jefferson-Hillman Hosp., 1947-48, resident in radiology, 1948-51; instr. radiology Med. Coll. Ala., 1948-51; practice medicine specializing in radiology, Birmingham, 1955—; dir. dept. radiology VA Hosp., 1956-57; radiologist Doctors Hosp., Cullman, Ala.; cons. radiologist Cullman Hosp.; clin. asst. prof. Med. Coll. Ala., 1957—. Pres. Bangor Community Council, Ala., 1986-87. Served with Med. Dept., AUS, 1944-46; from lt. to capt. M.C., USAF, 1951-55. Fellow Am. Coll. Radiology (chpt. pres. 1969-70; councillor 1971-77), Am. Coll. Nuclear Medicine (pres. 1982-83); mem. Radiol. Soc. N.Am., So. Radiol. Conf. (charter, founder; chmn. 1974-75), Am., So. med. assns., Ala., Cullman County (chmn. bd. censors 1977, chmn. bd. health 1977) med. socs., Ala. Cattleman's Assn., Internat. Arabian Horse Assn., Nat. Skeet Shooting Assn. (life), Arlington Hist. Assn., So. Commemorative Soc., SCV, Soc. War 1812, Nat. Rifle Assn. (life), Delta Kappa Epsilon, Alpha Kappa Kappa. Episcopalian. Clubs: Masons, Shrine. Address: PO Box 1053 Cullman AL 35055

BROWN, ADRIAN WORLEY, manufacturing company executive; b. Orlando, Fla., Feb. 4, 1928; s. James Adrian and Madoline (Worley) B.; m. Mary Lou Morris; children—Adrian W., Nancy, Betsy. A.B., U. Fla., 1950, LL.B., 1955. Bar: Fla. 1955. V.p. Brown & Brown, Inc., Daytona Beach, Fla., 1955-61; chmn. Fla. Indsl. Commn., 1961-64; with Rock-Tenn Co., Norcross, Ga., 1964—, pres., chief exec. officer, 1967—, chmn., chief exec. officer, 1978—. Mem. Fla. Bar Assn., Ga. Bus. and Industry Assn. (chmn., mem. exec. com.), U.S. Indsl. Council (v.p., mem. exec. com.), Paperboard Packaging Council (dir., mem. exec. com., mem. sr. adv. council), Order of Coif, Phi Delta Phi, Phi Delta Theta. Methodist. Office: Rock Tenn Co 504 Thrasher St Norcross GA 30071

BROWN, ALEX SMITH, JR., industrial engineer; b. Tennille, Ga., Nov. 23, 1922; s. Alex Smith and Lillian (Daley) B.; B.S., The Citadel, 1947; grad. exec. program U. N.C. Sch. Bus. Adminstrn., 1971; m. Nancy Cockman, Dec. 4, 1965; 1 dau., Ellen Daley. Indsl. engr. Dan River Mills, Danville, Va., 1947-49; field engr. Am. Asso. Cons., 1949-56, chief engr., 1956-58, v.p., chief engr., dir., 1958-60; chief indsl. engr. Burlington Industries, Inc. Greensboro, N.C., 1960-77; corp. dir. indsl. engring. Dan River Inc., Danville, 1977—, v.p. indsl. engring., 1982—. Pres., Am. Soc. of Colombia, Medellin, 1957-58; trustee Davison Sch., Atlanta. Served to capt. AUS, 1943-46. Mem. Soc. for Advancement of Mgmt. (past pres., v.p.), Am. Inst. Indsl. Engrs., Assn. Citadel Men (dir. 1969-70). Republican. Baptist. Club: Greensboro Country. Home: 2307 Danbury Rd Greensboro NC 27408 Office: Dan River Exec Office 2291 Memorial Dr Danville VA 24541

BROWN, ALFRED WILLIAM, educator; b. Muse, Okla., June 19, 1932; s. Arthur Willie and Lela Mae B.; B.S. in Edn., E. Central State Coll., Ada, Okla., 1968; postgrad. in Corrections, Okla. State U., 1979; LL.B., LaSalle Extension U., 1979; m. Margie Nell Bohanan, July 22, 1961; 1 dau., Winifred Nell. Counselor, tchr., Tununak, Alaska, 1964-65; with Head Start program, Tununak, 1968-69; counselor, Shonto, Ariz., 1970-71; counselor, tchr. spl. learning problems, Kayenta, Ariz., 1971-72; prin., Barter Island, Alaska, 1971-72; dir. community health reps. Choctaw Nation, Talihina, Okla., 1972; prin. Paden (Okla.) Elem. Sch., 1973-74, Panama (Okla.) Public Schs., 1975; tchr. spl. reading problems Okla. State Reformatory, Granite, 1975—; adj. prof. Langston Urban Center, Tulsa; tchr. adult basic edn. Conners Correctional Center, Hominy, Okla. Bd. dirs. Osage Park Housing Authority. Served with AUS, 1951-55; Korea. Recipient spl. recognition award Center Internat. Security Studies, 1979. Mem. Okla. Edn. Assn. (del. 1981-83), Okla. Reading Council, NEA. Democrat. Club: Masons. Research on vocat. rehab. counseling. Home: Box 505 Talihina OK 74571

BROWN, ALVIN LLOYD, accountant; b. N.Y.C., Nov. 5, 1934; s. Andrew and Ruth (Levine) B.; m. Evelyn Bernice Epstein, July 31, 1955; children—Elliott Jeffery, Ruth Naomi, Sheri Marlene. B.B.A., U. Miami, 1957. C.P.A., Fla. Accountant Arthur Singer & Co., Miami Beach, Fla., 1957-66; ptnr. Brown & Brown, Hialeah, Fla., 1966-67, Caplan, Brown & Co., Miami, 1967-69 (name changed to Caplan, Morrison, Brown & Co.), 1969—; Bd. dirs. S. Dade Jewish Community Ctr., Greater Miami Jewish Fedn.; trustee Israel Bonds New Leadership Div. Served with USCG, 1952-55. Mem. Am. Inst. C.P.A.s, Fla. Inst. C.P.A.s, Greater Miami Tax Inst., Miss. Soc. C.P.A.s (speaker 1975), Acctg. Firms Assoc., inc. (dir.), Omicron Delta Kappa. Jewish. Lodges: Optimists (life mem.), B'nai B'rith. Home: 13322 SW 103 Pl Miami FL 33176 Office: 9795 S Dixie Hwy Miami FL 33156

BROWN, ARTHUR WAYNE, educator; b. Sheshequin, Pa., Apr. 20, 1917; s. Arthur L. and Helen E. (Laclair) B.; A.B., U. Scranton, 1937; M.A., Cornell U., 1938; Ph.D., Syracuse U., 1950; m. Dorothy C. Johnston, Sept. 17, 1938; children—Anne (Mrs. Allan Root), Margaret (Mrs. Frank O'Neill), Michael, Patricia (Mrs. Eugene Crabbe), Thomas, Arthur, Mary, Deborah. Prof. English, Utica Coll. of Syracuse U., 1955-63; prof. English, chmn. dept., dir. Inst. Humanities, Adelphi U., 1963-65, pres., 1965-67; dean faculties, dean Grad. Sch., Fordham U., 1967-68, v.p. for acad. affairs, 1968-69; pres. Marygrove Coll., Detroit, 1969-72; dean Sch. Liberal Arts and Scis., Baruch Coll., City U. N.Y., 1972-77; dean Coll. Arts and Scis. U. Miami, Coral Gables, Fla., 1977-85, prof. English, 1985—; Westchester dir. 1st Nat. City Bank. Sec., Catholic Commn. on Intellectual and Cultural Affairs, from 1970; exec. com. Mich. Colls. Found.; bd. dirs. Catholic Charities, Utica, 1960-62, United Fund, L.I., Fla. Endowment for Humanities; chmn. bd. dirs. St. Elizabeth Sch. Nursing, Utica, 1961-62; trustee Molloy Coll., L.I., 1969-73; bd. govs. St. Paul's Sch., Garden City, 1968-69, 73-74; v.p. Council on Edn. for Public Health, from 1979. Am. Council Learned Socs. grantee, 1961-62. Mem. AAUP, MLA, Newcomen Soc. N.Am. Author: Always Young for Liberty, 1956; William Ellery Channing, 1960; Margaret Fuller, 1964. Co-editor: (series) Great American Thinkers, 1964-73, World Leaders, from 1973. Office: U Miami Coll Arts and Scis Coral Gables FL 33124

BROWN, BAILEY, U.S. judge; b. Memphis, 1917; s. Joshua Goodlett and Lillian (Pearcy) B.; m. Doris Frances Lawhorn, Dec. 24, 1964; 1 son, Bailey. A.B., U. Mich., 1939; LL.B., Harvard, 1942. Bar: Tenn. bar. Partner firm Burch, Porter, Johnson & Brown, Memphis; judge U.S. Dist. Ct. for Western Tenn., Memphis; chief judge; judge U.S. Ct. Appeals for 6th Circuit, 1979—; mem. Jud. Conf. Com. on Ct. Adminstrn.; guest lectr. Southwestern U., Memphis. Pres. Memphis Symphony, 1958-60, Memphis Pub. Affairs Forum, 1955. Served to lt. USNR, 1942-46. Episcopalian (vestryman). Office: 2670 Union Extended Memphis TN 38112

BROWN, BARBARA LYNN, publishing executive; b. Cleve., Sept. 16, 1951; d. Lennart Uno and Louise Ulla (Borenius) Gunnerfeldt; B.Mus., Mich. State U., 1975; M.Ed., Fla. Atlantic U., 1976, Ed.S., 1980, Ed.D., 1982; m. Bronnie D. Brown, July 16, 1983; stepchildren—Joseph Paul, Sharon Sue. Editor's asst. Mich. State U., 1969-70; instr. flute Lansing Conservatory of Mus., 1970-73; instrumental tchr. Music for Am., Inc., 1974; research asst., editor monthly newsletter Center for Econ. Edn., Fla. Atlantic U., 1976-77; founder, pres. Lynnco Publs., Boca Raton, Fla., 1978—. Mem. Nat. Assn. Female Execs., Mensa, Phi Delta Kappa. Democrat. Lutheran. Author: Guidebook to Happiness, Multiple Sclerosis (The Guide to Successful Coping) 1980; The Art of Talking: A Handbook of Marital Communication, 1979. Home: 255 SW 7th St #2 Boca Raton FL 33432 Office: PO Box 734 Boca Raton FL 33429

BROWN, BARBARA STEIN, environ. scientist; b. Newark, Aug. 5, 1951; d. Louis and Louise (Mumper) Stein; student Am. U., 1969-71; B.S. in Biology, U. Miami, 1976, postgrad.; m. Ralph David Brown, Sept. 9, 1978; 1 child, Kristin Leigh. Sr. asso. scientist Environ. Sci. and Engring., Inc., Miami, 1978-83, staff scientist, mgr. water regulations dept., 1983—. Mem. Ecol. Soc. Am., Am. Inst. Biol. Scis., Assn. Women in Environ. Professions. Office: 2822 NW 79th Ave Miami FL 33122

BROWN, BENNETT ALEXANDER, banker; b. Kingsrgee S.C.; m. Mary Alice Rustin, Nov. 30, 1957; children—Charlotte, Bennett, Leila, Katherine. B.S., Presbyn. Coll., Clinton, S.C., 1950, La. State U. Sch. Banking, 1960; grad., Advanced Mgmt. Program, Harvard U., 1965. With Chem. Bank, N.Y.C., 1950; Fed. Res. Bank Atlanta, 1953-55; with Citizens & So. Bank, Atlanta, 1955—, chmn., chief exec. officer, 1979—, also dir.; dir. Citizens & So. Ga. Corp., Piggly Wiggly So., Inc., Vidalia, Ga., Graniteville Co., S.C.; adv. bd. Ga. So. and Fla. R.R. Co. Served with U.S. Army, 1951-53. Mem. Internat. Monetary Conf., Assn. Bank Holding Cos., Assn. Res. City Bankers, Atlanta C. of C. Presbyterian. Clubs: Capital City, Commerce (dir.). Address: Citizens and So Nat Bank 35 Broad St Atlanta GA 30399

BROWN, BILLIE AUGUSTINE, educator; b. Pangburn, Ark., Aug. 1, 1924; d. Prince Colombus and Icy May Wood; B.S. in Edn., Harding Coll., Searcy, Ark., 1962, M.S., 1966; M.A. in Guidance and Counseling, U. Central Ark., 1974; m. James A. Brown, Nov. 26, 1969; children by previous marriage—Terry Wood, Dawn Elizabeth, Benjamin McLove, Laura Delphine. Librarian, White County, Ark. 1947-52; U.S. postal clk., 1954; pub. sch. tchr., 1959—; art specialist Pulaski County (Ark.) Spl. Sch. Dist., 1978-79, instructional coordinator art, 1979—; co-founder, bd. advisers Ark. Young Artists Assn. Democratic committeewoman, 1978-82, 84—. Recipient 1st pl. award in pastel White County Art Show, 1957, 1st pl. in illus. poetry Ark. Festival Arts, 1973; Art Patron of Yr. award Ark. Young Artists Assn., 1985; Fair Housing Spl. Achievement award, 1985. Mem. Nat. Art Edn. Assn., Ark. Art Educators, Mid-So. Watercolorists, Ark. for Arts, Pulaski County Adminstrs. Assn., Am. Council for Arts, Ark. Curriculum Devel. Assn., AAUW, Delta Kappa Gamma. Democrat. Baptist. Home: 5302 Dreher Ln Little Rock AR 72209 Office: 1500 Dixon Rd Little Rock AR 72216

BROWN, BRENDA MAE, lawyer, educator; b. New Orleans, June 18, 1946; d. Thomas Oscar and Lucille (Holloway) B. B.A. in Spanish, Xavier U., 1969; M.A. in Spanish, So. Ill. U., 1971; cert., U. Costa Rica, 1967; J.D., Loyola Sch. Law, New Orleans, 1978. Bar: La. 1978, U.S. Dist. Ct. La. 1984. English tchr. Loyola City Coll., New Orleans, 1975-76; chief counselor Milne Boys Home, New Orleans, 1973-76; rehab. counselor Orleans Parish Prison, New Orleans, 1976-79; asst. dist. atty. Dist. Atty's. Office, New Orleans, 1979-84; assoc. Harris & Stampley, New Orleans, 1984—. Xavier U. scholar 1968; So. Ill. U. teaching assistant, 1969; Equal Opportunity fellow U. Ill. 1973. Mem. Louis A. Martinett Soc., Black Women Attys. Assn. Democrat. Roman Catholic. Home: 5114 Lakeview Ct New Orleans LA 70126 Office: Advocacy Ctr for the Elderly and Disabled 1001 Howard Ave Suite 300A New Orleans LA 70112

BROWN, CHARLES G. (CHARLIE), state attorney general; b. June 6, 1950; s. Charles G. and Emily Campbell B.; 1 child, Tara. Student Denison U.; J.D., Yale U. Staff atty. FTC, Washington; dir. W. Va. Atty. Gen.'s Antiturst Div.; dep. atty. gen. W.Va., 1979-82; sole practice law, W.Va., 1982-84; atty. gen. State of W. Va., Charleston, 1985—; gen. counsel W.Va. Consumer Fedn.; vice chmn. antitrust com. Nat. Assn. Attys. Gen. Mem. Phi Beta Kappa. Address: Attorney General's Office State Capitol 26 East Charleston WV 25305*

BROWN, CHARLES HENRY, psychologist, family therapist, consultant; b. Winston-Salem, N.C., July 30, 1949; s. Charles Henry and Marguerite Francis (Clark) B.; m. Janet Elaine Blanchard. B.A., Davidson Coll., 1971; M.A., Appalachian State U., 1975; Ph.D., U. So. Miss., 1979. Registered health service provider; lic. psychologist; cert. marital and family therapist, N.C. Psychologist Tri-County Mental Health Complex, Salisbury, N.C., 1978-79, Charlotte-Mecklenburg Mental Health Ctr., Charlotte, N.C., 1979-81; psychologist-ptnr. Charlotte Assocs. Family and Psychol. Services, 1980—. Mem. Acad. Psychologists in Marital, Sex and Family Therapy, Am. Assn. Marriage and Family Therapy, Am. Family Therapy Assn., Am. Psychol. Assn., Mecklenburg Psychol. Assn., N.C. Assn. Advancement Psychology, N.C. Psychol. Assn., N.C. Assn. Marriage and Family Therapy. Author tech. papers. Office: 515 Fenton Pl Charlotte NC 28207

BROWN, CHERYL KAY TYE, nurse, medical service executive; b. San Antonio, Feb. 28, 1956; d. Glenn Walter and Della I. (Felts) Tye; m. Kenneth E. Brown, Jr., Oct. 6, 1979. Emergency Med. Technician, Ind. Vocat. Tech. Coll., 1976; Nursing, A.D., U. Louisville, 1983. R.N.; cert. emergency med. technician, Ky. Emergency med. technician Louisville Emergency Med. Service, 1976-79, emergency med. technician paramedic, 1979-81, ops. supr., 1981—; nurse Humana Hosp. Southwest, Louisville, 1983—; instr. CPR, Am. Heart Assn., Louisville, 1978—, instr. advanced cardiac life support, 1979—, instr. trainer, 1983—, CPR instr. ARC, 1976—. Vol. Winterhelp Program, 1983—. Mem. Ky. Emergency Med. Technician Instrs. Assn. Democrat. Episcopalian. Office: Louisville Emergency Med Service 1805 S Brook St Louisville KY 40208

BROWN, CLAUDE LAMAR, JR., psychiatrist, educator; b. Mobile, Ala., Mar. 12, 1923; s. Claude Lamar and Pauline Johanna (Phifer) B.; m. Catherine McRaney, May 2, 1979; children by previous marriage—Claude Lamar, Paul William, Christianna Lori. B.S., Tulane U., 1943, M.D., 1945. Diplomate Am. Bd. Psychiatry and Neurology. Intern, City Hosp. Mobile, 1945-46; resident in psychiatry Menninger Found. Sch. Psychiatry, Topeka, 1948-51; practice medicine specializing in psychiatry, Mobile, 1951—; mem. staff Mobile Infirmary, Providence Hosp., Doctors Hosp., U. Med. Center Hosp., Southland Hosp., Mobile; clin. prof. psychiatry U. South Ala. Sch. Medicine, 1973—; mem. Ala. Mental Health Bd., 1959-71, chmn., 1967-69. Served to lt. USNR, 1946-48. Fellow Am. Psychiat. Assn.; mem. AMA, Ala. State Med. Assn., Ala. Dist. Br. Am. Psychiat. Assn. (pres. 1981), Mobile County Med. Soc. (pres. 1962). Methodist. Club: Mobile Yacht. Contbr. articles to profl. and popular publs. Office: 176 Louiselle St Mobile AL 36607

BROWN, CLAUDE P., transport company executive; b. Lithia Springs, Ga., July 12, 1917; s. James A. and Lula M. B.; m. Mary L. Stroud, Dec., 1941 (dec. Feb. 1981); children—Bruce, Jim (dec.), Sue, Bill; m. Grace Holman, Nov. 1982. Student, pubs. schs., Ga. Chmn. bd. Brown Transport Corp., Atlanta, 1946—, Tri Tractor, Cumming, Ga., 1980—. Bd. dirs. Old Time Gospel Hour, Lynchburg, Va., 1980—, Campus Crusade for Christ, San Bernardino, Calif., 1980—. Republican. Clubs: Capital City; Commerce (Atlanta); Lost Tree (North Palm Beach, Fla.). Office: Brown Transport Corp 352 University Ave SW Atlanta GA 30310

BROWN, CONNIE YATES, businesswoman; b. Carthage, Mo., Apr. 29, 1947; d. Charles Lee and Eunice Jane (Farmer) Yates; m. Larry Edward Brown, June 19, 1982; 1 step-dau., Tammy Lynn Brown. B.S., Pittsburg State U., 1969. With White Shield Oil and Gas/Petro-Lewis, Tulsa, 1969-74, dept. supt., 1971-74; with Southwestern Bell Telephone Co., 1975-79; owner, mgr. Abbyco, Inc., rental, sales carpet cleaning equipment, Tulsa, 1978—; lectr. in field. Named Rookie of Yr., Tulsa div. Southwestern Bell Yellow Pages, 1976; sales award winner Rug Doctor Licensee of Yr., 1981, 85. Mem. Home Economists in Bus. (treas. Okla. chpt.), Am. Home Econs. Assn., Met. Tulsa C. of C., Equipment Rental Dealers Assn. Eastern Okla., Tulsa Alumnae Panhellenic (dir. scholarships), Phi Upsilon Omicron, Alpha Gamma Delta (nat. dir. alumnae devel. 1984—). Lodge: Order of Rainbow for Girls. Home: 7806 S Evanston Ave Tulsa OK 74136 Office: 8600 S Lewis Ave Tulsa OK 74137

BROWN, CRAIG JAY, ophthalmologist; b. Fayetteville, Ark., Feb. 11, 1951; s. Connell Jean and Erma Dexter (Taylor) B.; m. Patricia Ruth Davis, Aug. 31, 1974. B.S. in Zoology, U. Ark., 1973, M.D., 1977. Diplomate Am. Bd. Ophthalmology. Intern Bapt. Med. Ctr., Naleriga, Ghana, 1977-78; resident in ophthalmology U. Mo., Columbia, 1978-81; practice medicine specializing in ophthalmology, Fayetteville, 1981—; attending physician Washington Regional Hosp., Fayetteville, 1984—. Contbr. articles to profl. jours. Justice of Peace for Washington County, Ark., 1972. Fellow Am. Acad. Ophthalmology, ACS; mem. AMA, Ark. Med. Soc. Methodist. Lodge: Lions. Avocations: invertebrate paleontology, medieval studies. Home: 10 Ranch Dr Fayetteville AR 72701 Office: 203 N College Ave Fayetteville AR 72701

BROWN, DALE, physician; b. Mosheim, Tenn., Jan. 26, 1915; s. Walter C. and Matilda (Hartman) B.; B.A., B.S., Carson-Newman Coll., 1937; M.D., U. Tenn., 1941; m. Kathryn Jones, June 14, 1942; children—Gale Ann (Mrs. Lynn Baumgartner), Dale. Intern, Nashville Gen. Hosp., 1942; practice medicine, Mosheim, 1943—; mem. staff Laughlin, Takoma hosps.; also lectr., geographer, photographer, explorer. Mem. Am. Acad. Family Physicians, AMA, World, So., Tenn., Greene County (pres. 1944-52) med. assns. Republican. Mason (32 deg., Shriner). Address: Box 38 Mosheim TN 37818

BROWN, DALE PATRICK, advertising executive; b. Richmond, Va., Aug. 11, 1947; d. Thomas Windom and Helen Mae (Curtis) P.; B.A. in Journalism, U. Richmond, 1968, M.A. in English, 1978. City news reporter Richmond Times-Dispatch, 1968-71; free-lance writer, 1971-73; public relations account exec. Martin Agy., Richmond, 1973-76, v.p. public relations, 1976-78, v.p., advt. account supr., 1978-79; mgr. communications services Mobil Chem. Co., Richmond, 1979-81; mgr. communications Whittaker Gen. Med. Corp., Richmond, 1981-83; v.p. advt., account supr. Martin Agy., Richmond, 1983-84, group v.p., 1984—. Publicity chmn. Richmond Friendship Force, 1977-78; public relations chmn. Richmond-First Club, 1978-79. Recipient Nat. award for outstanding collegiate journalism Pi Delta Epsilon, 1968, various awards for advt. and public relations campaigns, including Addy award Advt. Club of Richmond, 1975, Effie award Am. Mktg. Assn., 1979, Clio award, 1980, 81. Mem. Richmond Public Relations Assn., Advt. Club Richmond (bd. dirs. 1983—), Am. Mktg. Assn. (publicity chmn. Richmond chpt. 1983-84), Public Relations Soc. Am., Nat. Agri-Mktg. Assn. (dir. chpt. 1980-82). Baptist. Editor-in-chief The Messenger, 1966-67, The Collegian newspaper, 1967-68. Home: 419 N Davis Ave Richmond VA 23220 Office: 500 N Allen Ave Richmond VA 23320

BROWN, DANNY LEE, nurse; b. Salem, Ind., Feb. 14, 1957; d. Donald Lee and Bonnie Mae (Mitchell) B. B.S., Berea Coll., 1984. R.N., Ky., Fla. Nurse, supr. shift Cardinal Hill Hosp., Lexington, Ky., 1984-85; nurse Ft. Lauderdale Hosp., Fla., 1985—. Editor (phamphlet) Welcome to Danforth Residence Hall, 1982. Mem. Assn. Rehab. Nurses, Am. Nurses Assn., Am. Assn. Counseling and Devel., Am. Coll. Personnel Assn., Ky. Nurses Assn. Democrat. Avocation: reading. Home: 11033 NW 40th St Sunrise FL 33321 Office: Ft Lauderdale Hosp 1601 E Las Olas Blvd Fort Lauderdale FL 33301

BROWN, DAVID GRANT, university administrator, economist; b. Oak Park, Ill., Feb. 19, 1936; s. Wendell Jacob and Margaret (James) B.; m. Eleanor Lin Rosene, Aug. 16, 1958; children—Alison, Dirk. A.B., Denison U., 1958; M.A., Princeton U., 1960, Ph.D., 1961. Prof. econs. U. N.C., Chapel Hill, 1961-67; provost Drake U., Des Moines, 1967-70; provost Miami U., Oxford, Ohio, 1970-82; pres. Transylvania U., Lexington, Ky., 1982-83; spl. cons. Assn. Governing Bds., Washington, 1983-84; chancellor U. N.C., Asheville, 1984—. Author: The Market for College Teachers, 1965, The Mobile Professors, 1967, Leadership Vitality, 1979; editor: Leadership Roles of Chief Academic Officers, 1984. Fellow Am. Council Edn., 1966-67; vice-chmn. Lexington United, 1982-83; cons. Commn. Future of SUNY, 1983-85, Miss. Bd. Regents, 1984; bd. dirs. Western N.C. Tomorrow, 1984—; active Leadership Asheville, 1984-85. NSF grantee; U.S. Office Edn. grantee; U.S. Dept. Labor grantee; grantee Carnegie Corp., 1979; recipient Tanner-Fox award U. N.C., 1966; 100 Young Leaders Higher award Change Mag., 1978. Mem. Am. Assn. Higher Edn. (chmn. 1981-82), Higher Edn. Colloquium (chmn. 1984—), Am. Councilor Edn. Council (chief acad. officer 1979-80), Nat. Leadership Roundtable (bd. dirs. 1978-80), Nat. Council Acad. Affairs (chmn. 1975-76). Avocations: tennis; bicycling. Office: U NC Chancellors Office 1 University Heights Asheville NC 28804

BROWN, DEBBY LYNN, real estate broker; b. Richmond, Va., Jan. 6, 1953; d. Lennon Thomas Brown and Marie (Lloyd) Smith; m. Jeffrey Anton Stark, July 22, 1972 (div. Jan. 1976). Tel sel coordinator Allegheny Pepsi, Richmond, 1975-76; mktg. rep. Dr. Pepper, Washington, 1976-78; broker assoc. Merrill Lynch Realty, Miami, Fla., 1979; broker assoc. Bowers, Nelms & Fonville, Richmond, 1983—; vice chmn. Richmond Comml. Multiple Listing. Mem. women's council Big Bros. Big Sisters Miami, 1982-83. Named to Leading Edge Soc., Merrill Lynch Realty, 1981. Mem. Women's Council Realtors, Va. Assn. Realtors, Nat. Assn. Realtors. Republican. Mem. Disciples of Christ. Office: Bowers Nelms & Fonville Inc 8401 Patterson Ave Richmond VA 23229

BROWN, DENNIS CURRIE, school administrator; b. Niagara Falls, N.Y., June 18, 1941; B.A., Baldwin-Wallace Coll., 1963; M.Edn., SUNY-Buffalo, 1969; postgrad. U. Mass., 1974. Mem. math. dept., dean of students The Nichols Sch., Buffalo, 1964-71, The Randolph Sch., Huntsville, Ala., 1971—. Mem. Madison County United Way Com., Ala., 1974—, U. Ala.-Huntsville Study Task Force, 1984—, U. of Ala.-Huntsville Ann. Giving Campaign Com., 1982-84; mem. adminstrv. bd. Valley United Methodist Ch., Huntsville, 1975-76; bd. dirs. internat. div. Huntsville Little League, 1979, 80; bd. dirs. Huntsville-Madison County Newspaper-in-the-Classroom Program, 1978, chmn., 1982-84; bd. dirs. Huntsville-Madison County Clean Community System, 1977-83, chmn., 1979-81, bd. advisors, 1983—; bd. dirs. Huntsville Mental Health Assn., 1983—. Mem. Nat. Assn. Coll. Admissions Counselors, Ala. Assn. Ind. Schs. (v.p. 1979-81, pres. 1981-83, bd. dirs. 1983—), State Dept. of Edn. Adv. Com., Mid-South Assn. Ind. Schs. (bd. dirs. 1983—, sec. 1984—), Huntsville-Madison County C. of C., Alpha Sigma Phi, Phi Delta Kappa. Lodge: Rotary. Home: 1003 Drake Ave SE Huntsville AL 35802 Office: 1005 Drake Ave SE Huntsville AL 35802

BROWN, DENNISON ROBERT, mathematician, educator; b. New Orleans, May 17, 1934; s. Elihu Thomson and Floy Clements (Edwards) B.; m. Janet Madden, June 9, 1956; children—Robert, Alan. B.S., Duke U., 1955; M.S., La. State U., 1960, Ph.D., 1963. Instr. U. New Orleans, 1958-61; grad. asst. La. State U., Baton Rouge, 1961-63; asst. prof., assoc. prof. U. Tenn., Knoxville, 1963-67; assoc. prof. U. Houston, 1967-70, prof. dept. math., 1970—. Editor Semigroup Forum, 1970—; contbr. articles to profl. math. jours. Baseball coach Strake Jesuit Coll. Prep. Sch., Houston, 1981—. Served to lt. USN, 1955-58, Mediterranean. Mem. Am. Math. Soc., Math. Assn. Am. (lectr., cons. 1965—), Sigma Xi, Kappa Sigma. Methodist. Office: Dept Math U Houston University Park Houston TX 77004

BROWN, EARL STANLEY, optometrist; b. Houston, Jan. 9, 1950; s. Earl Dewey and Helen Marie (Nail) B.; m. Maria Louise De la Garza, May 14, 1977; 1 son, Gregory Earl. B.A. in Psychology, B.S. in Econs., Rice U., 1972; M.B.A., St. Mary's U., San Antonio, 1974; D.Optometric, U. Houston, 1978. Practice optometry ESB Corp., Bay City, Tex., 1979—, pres., 1983-85; pres. Earl S. Brown P.C., Bay City, 1982-85; tennis instr. Mem. Bay City Republican Steering Com., 1980-84. Mem. Tex. Assn. Optometrists. Baptist. Lodge: Lions. Avocation: farming. Home: Route 3 Box 242 Bay City TX 77414 Office: ESB Corp 3612 Ave F Bay City TX 77414

BROWN, ELLEN RUTH, theoretical physicist; b. N.Y.C., June 15, 1947; d. Aaron Joseph and Grace (Presser) Brown; B.S., Mary Washington Coll., 1969; M.S., Pa. State U., 1971; Ph.D. (Govs. fellow), U. Va., 1981. Physicist, Naval Weapons Lab., Dahlgren, Va., 1969; instr. physics Lord Fairfax Community Coll., Middletown, Va., 1971-74; engr. EG&G Washington Analytical Services Center, Dahlgren, Va., 1979—, head analysis and evaluation dept., 1982—; v.p. Windy Knoll Enterprises, Inc., Magnolia, Tex., 1981—. First violinist Coll. and Community Orch., Fredericksburg, Va., 1981—; mem. North Ferry Farms Civic Assn., 1979—. NSF Summer Sci. Faculty fellow, 1973; IEEE Summer Sci. Faculty fellow NASA, Langley, Va., 1974-75. Mem. Am. Phys. Soc., Sigma Xi. Club: Barry Lee Bressler Science (pres.). Home: PO Box 1397 Fredericksburg VA 22402 Office: EG&G PO Box 552 Dahlgren VA 22448

BROWN, FAYE POTTER, nurse, educator; b. Rockwood, Tenn., Feb. 6, 1937; d. James Abb and Evedna Marie (Paradise) Potter; m. Larry Gene Brown, May 23, 1977; children—Belinda, Donna Fraley, W. Robert. Diploma Sparks Meml. Hosp., Fort Smith, 1971; student So. State U., 1960-61, La. State U., 1975-76. County visitor Union County Welfare Dept., El Dorado, Ark., 1963-64; charge nurse Longleaf Nursing Home, Ruston, La., 1967-70; head nurse Lincoln Gen. Hosp., Ruston, 1971-72; instn. counselor Ruston State Sch., 1972-74; dept. head practical nursing N. Central Area Vo-tech, Farmerville, La., 1974-77; dept. head health occupations Ruston Vo-Tech, 1977—. Active March of Dimes Walkathon, Ruston, 1973; vol. nurse Spl. Olympics, 1973; rep. career day Bienville High Sch. (La.), 1973; mem. infection control com. Lincoln Gen. Hosp., 1976. Mem. Am. Nurses Assn., La. State Nurses Assn., Ruston Dist. Nurses Assn. (v.p. 1972-74, treas. 1974-76), La. Assn. Health Occupations Educators (cert. of appreciation 1984), Am. Heart Assn. (plaque of appreciation 1983), La. Vocat. Assn. Episcopalian. Avocations: reading; needlework; antiques; genealogy; travel. Home: Route 1 Box 256 Choudrant LA 71227 Office: Ruston Vo-Tech 1010 James St PO Box 1070 Ruston LA 71273

BROWN, FREDERICK RAYMOND, retired civil engineer; b. Peoria, Ill., Feb. 15, 1912; s. Lyman Harrison and Mary Ann (Weber) B.; m. Louise Grace Ferry, June 10, 1936; children—Sandra, Frederick Raymond, Roger. B.S. in Civil Engring., U. Ill., 1934. Registered profl. engr., Miss. With Waterways Experiment Sta., Vicksburg, Miss., 1934-85, Hydraulics Lab., 1934-60, Nuclear Weapons Effects Lab., 1960-69, tech. dir., Waterways Experiment Sta., 1969-85. Mem. Nat. Soc. Profl. Engrs., Soc. Am. Mil. Engrs., ASCE (hon.), Internat. Assn. Hydraulic Research. Methodist. Lodge: Rotary. Home: 105 Stonewall Rd Vicksburg MS 39180

BROWN, GEORGE ANTHONY, marketing representative; b. Atlanta, Dec. 13, 1960; s. George Odus and Barbara Ann (Kennedy) B. B.B.A. in Fin., U. Ga., 1983. System analyst Ga. Power Co., Atlanta, 1980-83; mktg. rep. IBM, West Palm Beach, Fla., 1983—. Mem. Boca Raton C. of C. (various coms.). Republican. Baptist. Avocations: snow skiing; travel; scuba diving. Home: 1117 C-1 Green Pine Blvd West Palm Beach FL 33409 Office: IBM 1665 Palm Beach Lakes Blvd West Plam Beach FL 33401

BROWN, GEORGE HAY, investment consultant; b. Denver, Feb. 4, 1910; s. Orville Graham and Clara Amsden (Topping) B.; m. Catherine Dorotha Smith, June 11, 1932 (dec. 1960); 1 child, Ann Catherine. A.B., Oberlin Coll., 1929; M.B.A., Harvard U., 1931; Ph.D., U. Chgo., 1945. Indsl. sales mgr. Mallinckrodt and Chem. Works, St. Louis, 1931-37; from instr. to prof. U. Chgo., 1937-54; dir. mktg. research Ford Motor Co., Dearborn, Mich., 1954-69; dir. U.S. Bur. Census, Washington, 1969-73; sec. to bd. The Conf. Bd., Inc., N.Y.C., 1973-83; vis. prof. U. N. Fla., Jacksonville, 1983-85; prs. A.C. Brown & Assocs., Inc., Sea Islands, Ga., 1984—. Author: International Economic Position of New Zealand, 1946. Contbr. articles to profl. jours. Campaign chmn. ARC of N.Y.C., 1974-79; trustee Fifth Ave Presbyn. Ch., 1980-83; mem. fair share com. Nat. ARC, Washington, 1980-83. Fellow Am. Statis. Assn. (nat. dir. 1972-75), Am. Mktg. Assn. (nat. pres. 1951-52); mem. Am. Econs. Assn., Market Research Council of N.Y., Assn. U. Bus. and Econ. Research (hon. life), Internat. Statis. Inst. Voorlaerg, Beta Gamma Sigma. Club: Harvard (N.Y.). Home: PO Box 98 Sea Island GA 31561 Office: AC Brown & Assocs PO Box 68 Sea Island GA 31501

BROWN, GERALD LEONARD, systems analyst, mathematician; b. N.Y.C., May 17, 1936; s. Murray and Ruth Florence (Lipman) B.; m. Joy Roseanne Skaller, July 16, 1967; 1 child, Amy M. B.S., U. Miami, 1958; M.S., MIT, 1960; Ph.D., U. Wis., 1965. Research staff mem. Sandia Labs., Albuquerque, 1965-70; Inst. Def. Analyses, Alexandria, Va., 1971—. Fellow Math. Research Ctr., U. Wis., 1963-65. Mem. Am. Math. Soc., Ops. Research Soc. Am. Jewish. Avocations: sports; photography. Home: 10265 Braddock Rd Fairfax VA 22032 Office: Inst Defense Analyses 1801 N Beauregard Alexandria VA 22311

BROWN, GLEN FRANCIS, geologist; b. Graysville, Ind., Dec. 14, 1911; s. Isaac El Nathan and Lois (Badger) B.; m. Laura Winifred Cameron, Feb. 9, 1941 (dec. 1974); 1 dau., Elizabeth H.; m. 2d, Helen Louise Royall White, Oct. 5, 1975. B.S., N.Mex. Sch. Mines, 1935; M.S., Northwestern U., 1940, Ph.D., 1949. Geologist, Philippine Bur. Mines, 1936-38; jr. geologist U.S. Geol. Survey, 1938-41, sr. geologist, 1941-44, sr. geologist Fgn. Econ. Administrn., 1944-46, geologist, 1946-48, acting chief mission to Thailand, 1949, chief field party, Saudi Arabia, 1950-54, chief Saudi Arabian project, Washington, 1955-56, geol. advisor Govt. of Saudi Arabia, 1956-57, sr. geologist U.S. Geol. Survey, 1957-60, geol. advisor World Bank mission to Saudi Arabia, 1960, to Kuwait, 1961, chief Saudi Arabian mission, 1963-69, staff geologist for Middle East, 1969-72, sr. staff geologist Nat. Ctr., Reston, Va., 1972—; cons. in field. Catherine White scholar; Disting. Service medal Dept. Interior, 1964. Fellow Geol. Soc. Am., Explorers Club, AAAS, Washington Geol. Soc.; mem. Soc. Econ. Geologists, Am. Geophys. Union, Am. Assn. Petroleum Geologists, Geol. Vereinigung, Soc. Geol. Applications Mineral Deposits, mem. N.Y. Acad. Sci., Am. Soc. Photogrammetry, Sigma Xi. Methodist. Club: Cosmos. Contbr. articles to profl. jours. Address: 2031 Royal Fern Ct Apt 21C Reston VA 22091

BROWN, GLENDA ANN WALTERS, dancing educator, administrator; b. Buna, Tex., July 22, 1937; d. Jesse Olaf and Kathryn Jeanette (Rogers) W.; m. David Dann Brown, Dec. 13, 1958; children—Kathryn Jean, Vanessa Lea. Grad. high sch., Beaumont, Tex. Asst. tchr. Widman Sch., Beaumont, Tex., 1952-55; owner Walters Sch. of Dance, Jasper, Tex., 1955-59, Allegro Acad. of Dance, Houston, 1981—; assoc. tchr. Emmamae Horn Sch., Houston, 1964-81; assoc. dir. Allegro Ballet Co., Houston, 1974-81, artistic dir., 1981—; mem. dance panel Cultural Arts Council, Houston, 1979—. Sec. Riedel Estates Civic Club, Houston, 1975-78; poll worker Rep. Party, Houston, 1970-81; mem. Cultural Arts Council of Houston, 1975—. Mem. Dance Masters of Am. (exam. chmn. chpt. 3 1980—), Southwestern Regional Ballet Assn. (exec. v.p. 1981—), Nat. Assn. Regional Ballet (bd. dirs. 1983—), Cultural Arts Council of Houston. Methodist. Avocations: camping; singing; golf; travelling. Office: Allegro Acad of Dance 1801 Dairy Ashford Suite 130 Houston TX 77077

BROWN, HARLAN JAMES, acquisition search, acquisition study executive; b. Altoona, Pa., Dec. 16, 1933; s. Lindsey Andrew and Emma Grace (Ackerman) B.; M.Engring. (Sch. grantee-in-aid), Colo. Sch. Mines, 1957; M.B.A., George Washington U., 1969; m. Judith Lynn Wix, Oct. 17, 1964 (div.); 1 son, Harlan James II. Field engr. Beckman Instruments Co., Arlington, Va., 1957-59; partner Shaheen, Brown & Day, Denver, Colo., 1959-60; v.p. Nat. Engring. Service subs. NESINC, Washington, 1960-63; pres. NSC Internat. Inc., engring. recruitment, pub., Washington, 1963-67; pres. Harlan Brown & Co., Inc., acquistion search, acquisition study, McLean, Va., 1967—; cons. in field; guest lectr. George Washington U., Washington, 1969, 70, 71, 75, FRS, 1975; lectr. sem. U. Toronto (Ont., Can.), 1970; cons., lectr. Nat. Congress Community Devel., Washington, 1975. Mem. IEEE, Am. Soc. Metall. Engrs., Am. Chem. Soc., Am. Mgmt. Assn., M-Club, Blue Key, Theta Tau, Sigma Delta Psi (pres. 1956-57), Alpha Tau Omega. Clubs: Washington Athletic, Regency Racquet. Author: (with Shuckett, Mock) Financing For Growth, 1971. Produced nation's first merger center expt., Cherry Hill, N.J., 1969. Home: 1800 Old Meadow Rd McLean VA 22102 Office: 6861 Elm St McLean VA 22101

BROWN, HAROLD EUGENE, district magistrate; b. Damascus, Ark., Jan. 6, 1935; s. Amos Eugene and Hazel Gladys (Thomas) B.; m. Carolyn Marie Sanders, Aug. 26, 1972; children—James Daryl, Deena Leigh, Cynthia Marie. Student U. Md. Overseas div. Verdun, France, 1962-64, Germanna Community Coll., 1978-84. Enlisted U.S. Army, 1954, advanced through grades to sgt. maj., 1977; White House liaison Chief of Staff Army, Washington, 1969-73; dep. dir. Def. Coop. Agy., New Delhi, India, 1973-77; post sgt. maj., co. comdr. Fort A.P. Hill, Bowling Green, Va., 1977-81; magistrate 15th dist. Supreme Ct. Va., Fredericksburg, 1982—; Decorated Cross Gallantry Rep. Vietnam, 1969; Commendation medal, Meritorious Service medal. Mem. Va. Magistrates Assn., Ret. Sgts. Maj. Assn. Republican. Baptist. Avocations: golf; photography; woodworking. Home: 6 Allen Ct Fredericksburg VA 22405 Office: 2127 Jefferson Davis Hwy Suite 101 Stafford VA 22554

BROWN, HARVEY CLAUDE, aerospace education specialist; b. Harlan County, Ky., Nov. 22, 1937; s. Harvey Lee and Gladys Edith (Sargent) B.; m. Janet Anne Hall, May 7, 1960; 1 child, Donna Lynette Brown Temple. Assoc. Applied Aerospace Sci., Community Coll. of Air Force, Montgomery, Ala., 1978, 79; B.S., Auburn U., 1982; M.S., Troy State U., 1985. Master air traffic controller, instr. Served as enlisted man U.S. Air Force, 1956-82, supt., seminar leader Air Traffic Control Sch., Biloxi, Miss., 1973-77, faculty advisor Air Force Sr. Non-Commd. Officers Acad., Montgomery, 1977-79, chief assoc. programs, 1979-80, dir. plans and evaluation, 1980-82, ret., 1982; dir. student testing program Dept. Def., Montgomery, 1982-84; aerospace edn. curriculum developer CAP, Montgomery, 1984—. Author: Applied Management Techniques, 1979; also learning packets. Neighbor leader Republican Party, Montgomery, 1982—. Recipient Meritorious Service medal Dept. Def., 1982. Mem. Am. Assn. for Counseling and Devel., Air Force Assn., Air Force Sgts. Assn. (v.p. 1978-79), Auburn U. Alumni Assn., Nat. Rifle Assn., Omicron Delta Epsilon, Phi Delta Kappa, Gamma Beta Phi. Episcopalian. Lodges: Masons (32 deg.), Shriners. Avocations: reading; walking. Home: 461 Planter's Rd Montgomery AL 36109 Office: Nat Hdqrs CAP Aerospace Edn (USAF) Maxwell AFB Montgomery AL 36112-5572

BROWN, HENRY ALAN, health care executive; b. N.Y.C., Nov. 9, 1948; s. Samuel and Caroline (Esformes) B.; m. Ellen Molomut, May 6, 1969; children—Jennifer Kaye, Rebecca Marci, Noah Adam. B.A., SUNY-Binghamton, 1970; M.B.A., Hofstra U., 1975. C.P.A., N.Y., Fla., Credit analyst Chase Manhattan Bank, N.Y.C., 1970-73; auditor Wolf & Co., 1973-75; regional fin. mgr., Humana, Inc., Louisville, 1975-80; mgmt. cons. Ernst & Whinney, Tampa, Fla., 1980-81; v.p. St. Mary's Hosp., West Palm Beach, Fla., 1981-85; pres. Network Healthcare Inc., Ft. Lauderdale, Fla., 1985—. Bd. dirs. Temple Beth Zion, 1983—. Fellow Healthcare Fin. Mgmt. Assn.; mem. Am. Inst. C.P.A.s, Fla. Inst. C.P.A.s. Office: Network Healthcare Inc 1895 W Commerical Blvd Fort Lauderdale FL 33309

BROWN, HORACE JACK, surgeon; b. Oxford, Miss., Dec. 19, 1934; s. Horace Brightberry and Dorothy Pittman (Seale) B.; m. Suzanne Neill, Sept. 6, 1957; children—Camille Suzanne, Brandon Neill, Shannon, Allison Elaine. B.S., U. Okla., 1956, M.D., 1959. Diplomate Am. Bd. Surgery. Intern Walter Reed Gen. Hosp., Washington, 1959-60; surgery resident Wilford Hall USAF Hosp., 1960-64; staff surgeon Mercy Hosp., Oklahoma City, 1969—, Edmond (Okla.) Meml. Hosp., 1974—; staff surgeon Presbyn. Hosp., Oklahoma City, 1969—, vice chmn. dept., 1975—; clin. instr. surgery U. Okla., 1969—; cons. Oklahoma City, Muskogee VA hosps., 1970—. Served to lt. col. USAF, 1958-69. Mem. ACS (sec.-treas. Okla. chpt. 1972), AMA, John Hunter Surg. Soc., Soc. Non-Invasive Vascular Technologists, Southwestern Surg. Congress, Okla. Med. Assn., Okla. Surg. Assn., Oklahoma City Surg. Soc., Phi Sigma, Alpha Epsilon Delta, Alpha Omega Alpha, Phi Beta Pi, Beta Theta Pi. Republican. Methodist. Contbr. articles to profl. jours. Home: 3305 Sorghum Mill Rd Edmond OK 73034 Office: 13439 N Broadway Suite 210 Oklahoma City OK 73114

BROWN, J.E. (BUSTER), state senator, lawyer; b. Dec. 10, 1940. B.S., Tex. A&I U.; J.D., U. Tex. Mem. Tex. Senate, mem. natural resources com., vice chmn. jurisprudence and adminstrn. coms. Republican. Office: Tex Senate PO Box 12068 Austin TX 78711*

BROWN, JAMES BARROW, bishop; b. El Dorado, Ark., Sept. 26, 1932; s. John Alexander and Ella May (Langham) B.; B.S., La. State U., 1954; B.D., Austin Presbyn. Sem., Austin, Tex., 1957; D.D., U. of South, Sewanee, Tenn., 1976; m. Mary Joanna Strausser, Oct. 23, 1942; 1 dau., Clare Elizabeth. Ordained priest Episcopal Ch., 1965; teaching fellow Princeton Theol. Sem., 1962-64; curate chs. in La., 1965-70; archdeacon of La., 1971-76; bishop of La., 1976—. Served as chaplain AUS, 1957-59. Alumni fellow Austin Presbyn. Sem., 1957, recipient Sam Bailey Hicks prize, 1957. Mem. La. Clergy Assn., Phi Delta Theta. Club: Rotary. Address: Box 15719 New Orleans LA 70175*

BROWN, JAMES DALTON, fish and wildlife biologist; b. Robersonville, N.C., Jan. 5, 1943; s. Dalton Archibald and Selma (James) B.; m. Patsy Stevenson, Bowling, June 20, 1965; children—Alisa Diane, Jarrett Tarkington. B.S., N.C. State U., 1965; M.S., U. Ark., 1967; Ph.D., U. Fla., 1972. Asst. prof. biology Indian River Community Coll., Ft. Pierce, Fla., 1970-72; fishery biologist U.S. Fish and Wildlife Service, Raleigh, N.C., 1973-76, fish and wildlife biologist, Washington, 1976-81; mgr. devel. program Dept. Interior; chief div. tech. services U.S. Fish and Wildlife Service, Atlanta, 1981—. Contbr. articles on southeastern wetlands to profl. jours. Recipient Spl. Achievement award U.S. Fish and Wildlife Service, 1974, 85. Mem. Am. Fisheries Soc., Soc. Wetland Scientists, Sigma Xi, Phi Kappa Phi, Phi Sigma, Gamma Sigma Delta. Home: 5039 Golf Link Ct Stone Mountain GA 30088 Office: US Fish and Wildlife Service 75 Spring St SW Suite 1276 Atlanta GA 30303

BROWN, JAMES EDWARD, horticultural specialist, educator; b. Quitman, Ga., Nov. 12, 1948; s. Prince W. and Willie Mae (Christian) B.; m. Mazie Louise Roper, Jan. 30, 1971; children—Wysteria Yolanda, Candace Ladawn. B.S., Ft. Valley State Coll., 1970; M.S., Tuskegee Inst., 1975; Ph.D., U. Ill., 1983. Lic. ins. agt., real estate agt., Tenn. Soil conservation trainee USDA, Marietta, Ohio, New Madrid, Mo. and Poplar Bluff, Mo., 1968-70; lab. asst. agr. dept. Ft. Valley (Ga.) State Coll., 1969-70; research asst. agr. dept. Tuskegee (Ala.) Inst., 1974-75; botanist, land and forest resources TVA, Norris, 1975-81; asst. prof., hort. specialist Tuskegee Inst., 1983—. Served to capt. U.S. Army, 1971-83. Decorated Army Commendation medal. Mem. Am. Soc. Plant Physiologists, Am. Soc. Hort. Sci., Tuskegee Inst. Alumni Assn., Sigma Xi, Phi Beta Sigma, Gamma Sigma Delta, Chi Gamma Iota, Alpha Zeta. Baptist. Club: Optimist. Lodge: Masons. Contbr. articles profl. jours.

BROWN, JAMES H., JR., state official; b. May 6, 1940; B.A., U. N.C.; J.D., Tulane U. Bar: La. 1966. Practice law, La.; mem. La. State Senate, 1972-80; sec. of state State of La., 1980—. Del., La. Constl. Conv., 1973. Democrat. Presbyterian. Office: Office Sec of State PO Box 94125 Baton Rouge LA 70804-9125

BROWN, JAMES MONROE, III, museum director; b. Bklyn., Oct. 7, 1917; s. James Monroe and Helen (Adriance) B.; B.A., Amherst Coll., 1939, M.A. (hon.), 1954; M.A., Harvard, 1946; m. Alice De Wolf Doggett, Nov. 16, 1946; children—Barbara Allison, Amy, Elizabeth. Asst. to dir. Inst. Contemporary Art, Boston, 1941, asst. dir., 1946-48; asst. to dir. Dumbarton Oaks Research Library and Collection, Washington, 1946; dir. William A. Farnsworth Art Mus., Rockland, Maine, 1948-51; dir. Corning Glass Center (N.Y.), 1951-63; dir. div. pub. affairs Corning Glass Works, 1956-59, dir. mgmt. devel., 1959-61; pres. Corning Glass Works Found., 1961-63; dir. Oakland (Calif.) Mus., 1963-68, Norton Simon, Inc. Mus. Art, Fullerton, Calif., 1968-69, Va. Mus. Fine Arts, Richmond, 1969-76, Soc. of Four Arts, Palm Beach, Fla., 1978—. Bd. dirs. Internat. Exhbns. Found.; adv. trustee Peabody Mus., Salem, Mass. Served with USNR, 1942-45. Mem. Am. Assn. Museums (pres. 1970-72, exec. com.), Assn. Art Mus. Dirs. Clubs: Harvard, Grolier, Explorers (N.Y.C.). Address: Soc of Four Arts Palm Beach FL 33480

BROWN, JAY CLARK, microbiology educator; b. Jersey City, June 23, 1942; s. John Robert and Vonna Lamme B.; m. Sallie Shepard Dietrich, June 26, 1965; children—Jeffrey F., Norman J., Michael E. B.A., Johns Hopkins U., 1964; Ph.D., Harvard U., 1969. Postdoctoral fellow MRC Lab. Molecular Biology, Cambridge, Eng., 1969-71; asst. prof. microbiology U. Va. Med. Sch., Charlottesville, 1971-76, assoc. prof., 1976—; mem. adv. com. personnel for research Am. Cancer Soc., 1979—; instr. physiology Marine Biol. Lab., Woods Hole, Mass., 1977-80. NATO fellow, 1969-70. Mem. Am. Soc. Microbiology, Am. Soc. Biol. Chemists. Democrat. Author: (with Flickinger) Medical Cell Biology, 1979. Office: Dept Microbiology U Va Med Center Charlottesville VA 22908

BROWN, JAY HOWARD JOEL, physician, consultant; b. Boston, May 10, 1941; s. Herman and Sylvia B.; children—Laura, Margaret. B.A., Harvard Coll., 1963; M.D., Boston U., 1967. Intern, St. Joseph Hosp., Syracuse, N.Y., 1967-68; resident Nat. Naval Med. Center, Bethesda, Md., 1968-70, 71-72; asst. prof. dept. anesthesiology Duke U., 1974-77; chief anesthesia service Moses Cune Hosp., Greensboro, N.C., 1977—; pres. Community Anesthesia Corp., Greensboro, 1983—. Pres., Devonshire Civic Assn., Durham, N.C., 1976-77. Served to lt. comdr. USN, 1968-74. Mem. Internat. Anesthesia Research Soc., Am. Soc. Anesthesiologists, Soc. Cardiovascular Anesthesiologists, N.C. Soc. Anesthesiologists, N.C. Med. Soc. Republican. Unitarian. Office: PO Box 10373 Greensboro NC 27404

BROWN, JOHN LOTT, university president; b. Phila., Dec. 3, 1924; s. John L. and Carolyn E. (Francis) B.; B.S., Worcester Poly. Inst., 1945; M.A., Temple U., 1949; Ph.D., Columbia U., 1952; m. Catharine Hertfelder, June 11, 1948; children—Patricia Carolyn, Judith Elliott, Anderson Graham, Barbara Smith. Mgr. personnel Olney foundry Link-Belt Co., Phila., 1948-50; tech. dir. Air Force contract dept. psychology Columbia U., N.Y.C., 1952-54; head psychology div. Aviation Med. Lab., Naval Air Devel. Center, Johnsville, Pa., 1954-59; dir. grad. tng. program physiology Sch. Medicine, U. Pa., Phila., 1962-65, asst., then asso. prof. physiology, 1955-65; dean Grad. Sch., Kans. State U., 1965-66, v.p. acad. affairs, 1966-69, prof. physiology and psychology, 1965-69; prof. optics and psychology U. Rochester (N.Y.), 1969-78, dir. Center for Visual Sci., 1971-78; prof. physiology, psychology and ophthalmology U. South Fla., Tampa, 1978—, pres., 1978—; mem. adv. com. on biotech. and human research NASA, 1965-69; chmn. com. on vision Nat. Acad. Scis.-NRC, 1965-70; mem. visual scis. study sect. NIH, 1967-71; chmn. vision research program com. Nat. Eye Inst., 1975-78; chmn. Tampa Bay area Research and Devel. Authority, 1979—; dir. Pioneer Savs. Bank. Vice chmn. Monroe County (N.Y.) Human Resources Health Task Force, 1970-71; bd. dirs. Fla. Gulf Coast Symphony, 1979-81, Tampa Gen. Hosp. Found., 1980-81; trustee Worcester Poly. Inst., 1970-83. Served with USN, 1943-46. Recipient Robert Goddard award Worcester Poly. Inst., 1969, Kans. Optometric award, 1968; NASA research grantee, 1975-77, Nat. Eye Inst. research grantee, 1972-79; USPHS research fellow 1959-61. Fellow Am. Psychol. Assn., Optical Soc. Am. (asso. editor Jour. 1972-77, mem. exec. com. Rochester chpt. 1975-76), AAAS; mem. Am. Physiol. Soc., Assn. for Research in Vision and Ophthalmology (pres. 1978, trustee 1974-78), Soc. for Neurosci., Psychonomic Soc., Greater Tampa C. of C. (governing bd. 1978—), Fla. Council of 100, Sigma Xi, Phi Gamma Delta, Phi Eta Sigma, Psi Chi, Phi Kappa Phi, Omicron Delta Kappa. Mem. Religious Soc. of Friends. Mem. editorial bd. Vision Research, 1971-77; contbr. numerous articles on psychology and physiology of vision to profl. jours. Office: 4202 Fowler Ave Tampa FL 33620

BROWN, JOHN ROBERT, federal judge; b. Funk, Nebr., Dec. 10, 1909; s. E.E. and Elvira (Carney) B.; A.B., U. Nebr., 1930, LL.D., 1965; J.D., U. Mich., 1932, LL.D., 1959; m. Mary Lou Murray, May 30, 1936 (dec.); 1 son, John R.; m. 2d, Vera Riley, Sept. 1979. Bar: Tex. 1932. Mem. firm Royston & Rayzor, 1932-55; judge U.S. Ct. Appeals, 5th circuit, 1955—, chief judge, 1967-79. Chmn., Harris County (Tex.) Republican Party, 1953-55. Served to maj. Transp. Corps, USAAF, 1942-46. Mem. Am., Tex., Houston bar assns., Am. Judicature Soc., Am. Law Inst., Maritime Law Assn. U.S., Assn. ICC Practitioners, Order of Coif, Phi Delta Phi, Sigma Chi. Presbyterian (elder). Clubs: Houston, Houston Country. Office: 11501 US Court House 515 Rusk St Houston TX 77002

BROWN, JOYCE ELISSA TAYLOR, educational administrator; b. Knoxville, Tenn., Jan. 20, 1947; d. Walter James and Hazel (Hartfield) Taylor; m. Garnett W. Brown, Aug. 8, 1970 (div. 1978); 1 child, Leigh Danielle. B.A., Knoxville Coll., 1969; M.Ed., Ga. State U., 1974, Ph.D., 1982. Cert. psychometrist, Ga., cert. tchr., Ga. Social worker Knoxville Community Devel. Corp., 1975; dir. fin. aid Knoxville Coll., 1975-77; mem. adminstrv. staff, instr. Ga. State U., Atlanta, 1978-83; dir. counseling and testing Johnson C. Smith U., Charlotte, N.C., 1983—; project counselor Atlanta Bd. Edn. Mem. Johnson C. Smith Community and Sch. Com., Charlotte, 1982; mem. Billingsville Sch.-Home Sch. Com., Charlotte, 1984-85; mem. seat belt com. Charlotte Sch. Bd., 1985. U.S. Dept. Edn. grantee, 1980. Mem. Am. Assn. Counseling and Devel., Nat. Assn. Personnel Workers, Am. Coll. Student Personnel Assn., Assn. for Non-White Concerns So. Assn. Coll. Students Affairs, Delta Sigma Theta. Democrat. Methodist. Avocations: reading, dancing, bowling, theatrical arts productions and singing.

BROWN, KENNETH ASHLEY, JR., mathematics and computer educator; b. Madisonville, Ky., Apr. 2, 1946; s. Kenneth Ashley and Violet Marie (Bond) B.; m. Betty Ann Orr, July 15, 1972; 1 child, James Jarrett. A.S. with high honors, Jr. Coll. Broward County, 1967; B.S. cum laude, Fla. Atlantic U., 1969, M.Ed., 1976. Cert. jr. coll. math. tchr., computer programming and math. tchr. Tchr. Nova High Sch., Ft. Lauderdale, Fla., 1970—; adj. faculty Broward Community Coll., Nova U., Ft. Lauderdale; panel mem. Com. on Am. Math. Competition, Alfred P. Sloane Found., 1984-85, mem. subcom. on Am. high sch. math. exam., 1986—. Contbr. articles to profl. publs. Recipient 2 D.X. Century Club awards Am. Radio Relay League. Mem. Math. Assn. Am. Baptist. Avocations: computer programming and electronics; amateur radio; pocket billiards. Home: 5711 SW 54th Ave Fort Lauderdale FL 33314 Office: Nova High Sch 3600 College Ave Fort Lauderdale FL 33314

BROWN, KENNETH RAY, banker, financial analyst; b. Cherokee, Okla., July 6, 1936; s. Tom Melton and Mary Elizabeth (Foster) B.; m. Marietta Verlene Nusz, Jan. 30, 1958 (dec. 1963); children—Kathryn Sue, Elizabeth Ann; m. Elizabeth Kay Callahan, Oct. 17, 1964; 1 child, Angela Kay. B.B.A., U. Okla., 1957. Chartered fin. analyst. Trainee, Liberty Nat. Bank and Trust Co. of Oklahoma City, 1957-59, trust investment officer, 1959-65, v.p., 1965-72, sr. v.p., 1972-80, exec. v.p., 1980—. Served with USAR, 1958-64. Mem. Okla. Soc. Fin. Analysts (pres. 1971-72), Econ. Club Okla. Democrat. Presbyterian. Avocation: photography. Office: Liberty Nat Bank & Trust Co PO Box 25848 Oklahoma City OK 73125

BROWN, LARRY DALE, Realtor; b. Ann Arbor, Mich., Sept. 23, 1936; s. Edward Nathaniel and Helen Marietta (Holl) B.; children—Cheryl, Brian, Christopher. Regional mgr. Am. Fin., Atlanta, 1957-73; v.p. Universal Guardian, Atlanta, 1973-77; Realtor Barton-Ludwig, Atlanta, 1977-79; Realtor, mgr. Remax, Northeast, Atlanta, 1979—. Vol. worker Republican Party, Dekalb County, Ga., 1968—. Served with U.S. Army, 1955-57. Named Mgr. of Yr. Remax Internat., 1982, Remax of Ga., 1982. Mem. Dekalb Bd. Realtors, Ga. Bd. Realtors, Nat. Bd. Realtors, Million Dollar Club (life). Lutheran. Lodge: Lions. Home: 3416 Ivy's Walk Atlanta GA 30340 Office: Remax Northeast 2200 Northlake Pkwy Suite 205 Tucker GA 30340

BROWN, L(ARRY) EDDIE, tax practitioner, real estate broker; b. Crawford, Tenn., Aug. 31, 1941; s. Earl and Lois Ovoca (Norrod) B.; m. Lillian Virginia Edwards, Feb. 9, 1965; children—Clifford Bruce, Michael Dwayne, Jennifer Noelle. B.B.A., Ga. State U., 1974, M.B.A., 1976. Cert. tax practitioner. Mgmt. trainee Citizens Bank, Cookeville, Tenn., 1963-65; office mgr. Redisco, Tampa, Fla., 1965-67; methods analyst Delta Air Lines, Atlanta, 1967-83; owner Brown Enterprises, College Park, Ga., 1971—; pres. So. Heritage Properties, Inc., 1984—. Served with USAF, 1959-63. Bd. dirs. Ga. Spl. Olympics, Atlanta, 1983-86. Mem. Nat. Assn. Income Tax Practitioners, Nat. Soc. Pub. Accts., Ga. Assn. Pub. Accts., Nat. Assn. Securities Dealers, Atlanta Bd. Realtors. Baptist. Clubs: Civitan (pres. Airport-Southside, Atlanta 1982-83, treas. Airport Area, Atlanta 1979-81, Civitan of Yr. chpt. 1982, bd. dirs. Ga. dist. north 1984-86, trustee Ga. dist. north Found. 1985-87), Masons. Office: Brown Enterprises 2479 Paul D West Dr College Park GA 30337

BROWN, LEROY RONALD, college administrator, counselor; b. Wadmalaw Island, S.C., Dec. 18, 1949; s. Willie Henry and Dorothy (Johnson) B.; m. Eva Elizabeth Choice, June 3, 1972; children—Tamyka M., Stephan L., Kristina V. B.S., Benedict Coll., 1971; Ed.M., U. Okla., 1973; Ed.D., NYU, 1980. Cert. counselor. Counselor, Medgar Evers Coll., Bklyn., 1974-80; dir. planning and research Denmark Tech. Coll., S.C., 1980-81, dean continuing edn., 1981-82; exec. v.p., dean of coll. Morristown Coll., Tenn., 1982-83; v.p. student services Midlands Tech. Coll., Columbia, S.C., 1983—; cons. So. Assn. Colls., Atlanta, 1983—; judge S.C. High Sch. Sci. Fair, 1983—. Treas. Dutch Fork Elem. Sch., Columbia, 1984-85; trustee Haskell Height First Baptist Ch., Columbia, 1984-85; bd. mem. United Black Fund, Columbia, 1985—; vol. S.C. Correctional Instn., Columbia, 1984—. Recipient Presdl. award NAFEO, 1985. Mem. Assn. for Counseling and Devel., Nat. Assn. Student Personnel Adminstrn., S.C. Tech. Edn. Assn. (Outstanding Tech. Educator award 1985), S.C. Coll. Personnel Assn. (chmn. awards com. 1984), Phi Delta Kappa, Omega Psi Phi. Democrat. Avocations: Gardening; antique furniture stripping and repair. Home: 225 Meadowlakes Dr Columbia SC 29203 Office: PO Box 2408 Columbia SC 29202

BROWN, LOUIS NOEL, JR., dentist; b. Atlanta, Apr. 9, 1955; s. Louis Noel and Edith Elizabeth (Ivie) B.; m. Elizabeth Anne Colmery, Aug. 4, 1984. Student Auburn U., 1973-74, U. Fla., 1974-76; D.D.S., Emory U., 1980. Practice dentistry, Tampa, Fla., 1980—. Dir. adv. bd. Fellowship Christian Athletes, Tampa, 1984. Mem. Hillsborough County Dental Soc., Fla. Dental Assn., ADA, Acad. Gen. Dentistry, S.E. Acad. Prosthedontics, Prosthetic Study Group, Hillsborough County Dental Emergency Service. Republican. Baptist. Lodge: Rotary. Avocations: water skiing; snow skiing; golf; tennis; basketball. Home: 4210 Glenhaven Ln Tampa FL 33624 Office: 1335 W Linebaugh Ave Tampa FL 33612

BROWN, MARCUS GORDON, educator; b. Miami, Fla., Mar. 14, 1908; s. David Chappel and Lula (Bell) B.; A.B., Columbia Union Coll., 1927; M.A., Emory U., 1936; Docteur ès Lettres, U. Dijon (France), 1939; Doctor en Filosofía y Letras, U. Madrid (Spain), 1940. Tchr. fgn. langs. high sch., Jacksonville, Fla., 1927-30, Boys' High Sch., Atlanta, 1930-36; instr. English and French, U. Fla., 1936-38; asst. prof. fgn. langs. Ga. Inst. Tech., Atlanta, 1940-42, asso. prof., 1942-43, prof., 1943-50; specialist U.S. Office Edn., 1944-46; cultural attache Am. embassy, Bogota, Colombia, 1950-52, Rio de Janeiro, Brazil, 1952-54; asst. chancellor Univ. System Ga., Atlanta, 1954-57; fgn. lang. coordinator Ga. State Dept. Edn., Atlanta, 1957-62; asso. prof. Romance langs. Memphis State U., 1963-67, prof., 1967-71, prof. modern langs., 1971-73; summer vis. prof. Duke U., 1941-44, U. Havana, 1943, U. Ga., 1947, U. Mont., 1948; vis. prof. Ft. Lewis Coll., 1975, Henderson State U., 1976-77, N.W. Miss. Jr. Coll., 1983; lectr. U.S. Dept. State, Latin Am., 1948-49, Spain and Portugal, 1957-58; lectr. numerous instns. and orgns. U.S. and abroad. Recipient Anchieta medal Municipality of Rio de Janeiro, Brazil, 1954; medals for excellence in French lang. and lit. French Govt., 1936. Mem. Sociedad Bolivariana de Colombia, Am. Assn. Tchrs. Spanish and Portuguese, Am. Assn. Tchrs. French, Am. Assn. Tchrs. Italian, Am. Assn. Tchrs. German, AAUP, MLA, S. Central MLA, Phi Sigma Iota, Sigma Delta Pi, Pi Delta Phi, Delta Phi Alpha. Author: Les Idées Politiques et Religieuses de Stendhal, 1939; La Vida y Las Novelas de Emilia Pardo Bazán, 1940; (with J. Russell) Bibliography for the Teaching of English to Foreigners, 1947; also translations, articles, condensations of Brazilian novels. Address: 2765 Ketchum Pl Apt 8 Memphis TN 38114

BROWN, MARTIN PARKS, state senator; b. Hart, Ga., Nov. 29, 1914; s. Heber C. and Hattie (Parks) B.; m. Joyce Winn, 1938; children—Jerry Parks, Sandra Joyce, Martin Boyce. Mcht.; cotton farmer; fertilizer dealer; mem. Ga. Ho. of Reps., 1961-66, Ga. Senate, 1968—. Served with U.S. Army, 1943-46, ETO. Decorated Battle Star. Democrat. Baptist. Office: Ga Senate State Capitol Atlanta GA 30334*

BROWN, MAUDE OPAL NORRIS, pharmaceutical company official; b. Benson, N.C., June 17, 1927; d. Ernest Hubert and Alma (Moore) Norris; student King's Bus. Coll., Raleigh, N.C., 1944-45; m. Robert William Brown, Sept. 26, 1948; children—Donna Rose, Robert William. Sec. to pres. Raleigh Bonded Warehouse, Inc., 1946-58; acting office mgr. Fed. Crop. Ins., Raleigh, 1958-61; dist. office mgr. Allied Chem. Corp., Raleigh, 1961-69; with Burroughs Wellcome Co., 1970—, adminstrv. secretarial mgr., Research Triangle Park, N.C., 1973-77, grants and projects costs adminstr., 1977—; sec., bd. dirs. Employees Credit Union, 1975-78. Mem. Am. Mgmt. Assn. Home: 310 Tiffany Circle Garner NC 27529 Office: Burroughs Wellcome Co 3030 Cornwallis Rd Research Triangle Park NC 27709

BROWN, MCTEER, banker; b. Sardinia, S.C., Oct. 31, 1927; s. Robert Roy and Bessie Elizabeth (McTeer) B.; m. Peggy Elizabeth Reed, June 19, 1957; 1 dau., Donna Elizabeth. B.S. in Bus. Adminstrn., U. S.C., 1950; postgrad. S.C. Bankers Sch., Columbia, S.C., 1964-66, Sch. of Banking of the South, La. State U., 1970-72. Asst. mgr. Comml. Credit Corp., Orangeburg, S.C., 1950-59; with First Nat. Bank in Orangeburg, 1960—, v.p., gen. auditor, 1977—. Served with USN, 1945-46. Mem. Am. Inst. Banking, Inst. Internal Auditors (cert. internal auditor), Am. Legion. Methodist. Club: Country Club of Orangeburg. Home: 1167 Austin St NE Orangeburg SC 29115 Office: 345 John C Calhoun Dr SE Orangeburg SC 29115

BROWN, MICHAEL NELSON, ins. broker; b. New Orleans, Feb. 12, 1946; s. Nelson Ernest and Mary Elaine (Brugier) B.; student Southeastern La. U., 1964-69, U. Ala., 1969, U. New Orleans, 1970-72; m. Karen Frances Sweitzer, Oct. 24, 1980; children—Keith Michael, Eric Neal. Marine underwriter Home Ins. Co., New Orleans, 1970-72, supr. marine dept., St. Louis, 1972-74; account exec. Corroon & Black, New Orleans, 1974-76, v.p., 1976-79, marine mgr., 1979-81, sr. v.p., 1980-81; v.p. Sherar, Cook, and Gardner, Inc., Metairie, La., 1981—; ptnr. Severn Assocs.; dir. Nat. River Acad. U.S., Wizard Ventures, Ltd.; speaker in field. Recipient cert. of merit City of New Orleans. Mem. Mariners Club New Orleans, Propeller Club U.S., La. DeMolay Assn. (pres. 1965-66, Legion of Honor award). Democrat. Clubs: Maritime Sq., Celtic. Home: 4311 Laurel St New Orleans LA 70115 Office: 2325 Severn Ave Metairie LA 70001

BROWN, MICHAEL STUART, geneticist; b. N.Y.C., Apr. 13, 1941; s. Harvey and Evelyn (Katz) B.; m. Alice Lapin, June 21, 1964; children—Elizabeth Jane, Sara Ellen. B.A., U. Pa., 1962, M.D., 1966. Intern, then resident in medicine Mass. Gen. Hosp., Boston, 1966-68; served with USPHS, 1968-70; clin. assoc. NIH, 1968-71; asst. prof. U. Tex. Southwestern Med. Sch., Dallas, 1971-74; Paul J. Thomas prof. genetics, dir. Center Genetic Diseases, 1977—. Recipient Pfizer award Am. Chem. Soc., 1976, Passano award Passano Found., 1978, Lounsbery award U.S. Nat. Acad. Scis., 1979; Lita Annenberg Hazen award, 1982. Mem. Nat. Acad. Scis., Am. Soc. Clin. Investigation, Assn. Am. Physicians, Harvey Soc. Home: 5719 Redwood Ln Dallas TX 75209 Office: 5323 Harry Hines Blvd Dallas TX 75235

BROWN, MILTON HENRY, horticulture society executive; b. Troy, N.Y., Jan. 9, 1916; s. Henry Arneche and Charlotte Hanneh (Bussa) B.; m. Elizabeth Ann Blair, June 15, 1946; 1 child, Bonnie Blair. A.B., U. Pitts., 1937; postgrad. George Washington U., 1946-50; grad. U.S. Nat. War Coll., 1958. Commd. 2nd lt. U.S. Army, 1937, advanced through grades to col., 1948; sr. exec. CIA, Washington DC, 1948-73; exec. dir. Am. Camellia Soc., Fort Valley, Ga., 1973—; dir. Internat. Camelia Soc., 1976-78, v.p., 1978-83. Author: The Camellia, 1978. Editor: Am. Camillian Yearbook, 1973—; The Camellia Jour., 1973—. Pres. PTA, Arlington, Va., 1952; founding chmn. Peach County Fine Arts Com., Fort Valley, 1980. Recipient cert. merit Garden Club Ga., Inc., 1984. Mem. Am. Assn. Bot. Gardens & Aboreta (assoc.), Am Assn. Mus. (assoc.), Garden Writers Assn. Am., Am. Camellia Soc. (editor 1973—, life). Republican. Presbyterian. Lodge: Kiwanis. Avocation: travel. Home: 409 W Church St Fort Valley GA 31030 Office: Am Camellia Soc PO Box 1217 Fort Valley GA 31030

BROWN, MILTON MCINTYRE, III, financial executive; b. Selma, Ala., June 11, 1945; s. Milton M. and Anne (Wells) B.; m. E. Casmira Eugene, Jan. 11, 1969; children—Milton McIntyre, Casmira-Anne Elizabeth. B.A. in Polit. Sci., Princeton U., 1973; M.B.A., Colgate Darden Grad. Sch. Bus. Adminstrn., 1975. Fin. and contract adminstr. Internat. Tech. Products, Washington, 1975-79; cons. Cresap, McCormick & Paget, Washington, 1980-83; fin. analyst CACI Inc., Arlington, Va., 1983-84; v.p. fin. and adminstrn. Cooper Wharton Wagoner, Inc., Arlington, Va., 1983—. Gen. mgr., coach N.W. Arlington Lions Soccer Assn., 1984—. Served with USAF, 1966-70. Republican. Club: Ivy. Address: 2450 N Jefferson St Arlington VA 22207

BROWN, MURIEL WINDHAM, librarian; b. Dallas, Nov. 19, 1926; d. Charles Wyatt and Gladys Mae (Patman) Windham; m. George W. Brown, II, Jan. 28, 1951; children—Laurence Windham, David Mitchum, Leslie Ann. B.A., So. Meth. U., 1949, M.A., 1950; M.L.S., North Tex. State U., 1974, postgrad., 1974—. Library assoc. Dallas Pub. Library, 1964-66, librarian lit. and history, 1966, children's librarian, 1966-72, head children's dept., 1967-69, children's selection new brs., 1972-77, children's lit. specialist, 1977—; cons. in field. Author: Books for You, 1981; compiler bibliographies for Behind the Covers, 1984. Mem. presch. edn. com. Am. Heart Assn., Dallas, 1982-83. Jesse Jones fellow, 1949. Mem. ALA (children's Notable books reevaluation com. 1983-86, Newbery award Com. 1984-85), Tex. Library Assn. (chmn. children's round table), So. Meth. U. Alumni Assn. (sec. 1972-73), Alpha Theta Phi, Beta Phi Mu, Alpha Lambda Sigma. Democrat. Unitarian. Home: 10415 Church Rd Dallas TX 75238 Office: Dallas Pub Library 1515 Young St Dallas TX 75201

BROWN, PATRICIA ANN, artistic director; b. Eastland, Tex., Sept. 10, 1929; d. Clifton Andrew and Alice Lucille (Adams) Horn; m. Gerald Leonard Brown, Sept. 16, 1951; children—James, Anthony, Sarah. Student pub. schs., Houston. Actress, Alley Theatre and East Coast, Houston, N.Y.C., 1947-51; producing dir. Magnolia Theatre, Long Beach, Calif., 1954-68; 1st dir. Theatre Communications Group, N.Y.C., 1960-61; theatre cons. Pat Brown & Assocs., Los Angeles, 1971-79; free lance dir., 1979-81; artistic dir. Alley Theatre, Houston, 1981—; mem. theatre panel Tex. Commn. on Arts, Austin, 1982—; mem. theatre arts adv. council Brown U., Providence, 1984—; panel mem. WGBH Ednl. Found., Boston, 1981, Corp. for Pub. Broadcasting, Washington, 1981. Margo Jones scholar, 1948-49; Anne Baxter scholar, 1949-50. Mem. Actors Equity Assn., Soc. Stage Dirs. and Choreographers. Office: Alley Theatre 615 Texas Ave Houston TX 77002

BROWN, PAUL RICHARD, ophthalmologist; b. Winston-Salem, N.C., May 7, 1930; m. Patricia Ann Barger, June 9, 1956; children—Deborah Gayle, Paul Richard. B.A., Catawba Coll., 1956; M.D., Wake Forest U., 1960. Diplomate Am. Bd. Ophthalmology. Intern, N.C. Bapt. Hosp., Winston-Salem, 1960-61; resident Eugene Talmadge Meml. Hosp., Med. Coll. Ga., Augusta, 1961-64; practice medicine specializing in ophthalmology, Ft. Myers, Fla.; mem. staffs Lee Meml. Hosp., Ft. Myers Community hosps. Mem. Fla. Ethics Commn., 1975-79; mem. grievance com. 20th Judicial Cir., Fla. Bar, 1980-82. Mem. Am. Acad. Ophthalmology. Republican. Baptist. Office: 1688 Medical Ln Fort Myers FL 33907

BROWN, RICHARD HARRIS, telephone company executive; b. New Brunswick, N.J., June 3, 1947; s. Harris Ransford and Winifred Veronica (Clelland) B.; m. Christine C. Demler, Sept. 27, 1969; children—Ryan, Allison. B.S., Ohio U., 1969. Mgr., Ohio Bell Tel. Co., Columbus and Toledo, 1969-74, dist. mgr., Toledo, 1974-79, div. mgr., Cleve., 1979-81; v.p. engring. United Telephone System, Inc., Westwood, Kans., 1981-82, v.p. ops. United Telephone Co. of Midwest, Overland Park, Kans., 1982-83, v.p. ops., chief operating officer United Telephone Co. of Fla., Altamonte Springs, Fla., 1983—, also dir.; bd. mgrs. Vista-United Inc., Kissimmee, Fla., 1983—. Bd. dirs. Northwest Ohio Cystic Fibrosis Found., Toledo, 1976-78; East Cleveland YMCA, 1978-80. Served with Army N.G., 1969-74. Mem. Orlando C. of C., Fla. State C. of C. (chmn. utilities communications com.). Republican. Clubs: Sertoma (past pres.), Rotary, Citrus, Sweetwater Country. Home: 1746 Alvarado Ct Longwood FL 32779 Office United Telephone Co of Fla PO Box 5000 Altamonte Springs FL 32715

BROWN, ROBERT CHARLES, college administrator; b. Coushatta, La., Feb. 9, 1945; s. John Theodore Brown and Bobby (Best) Campbell; m. Jill Lestage, June 8, 1968; children—Charles Hugh, Martha Ruth, John Lestage. B.A., Northwestern State U., 1967; M.A., La. State U., 1969, Ph.D., 1976. Instr. econs. Northwestern State U., Natchoches, La., 1969-71; Lang prof. Wingate Coll., N.C., 1976-80; prof. econs. McMurray Coll., Abilene, Tex., 1980—, asst. to pres., 1982-84, v.p., 1984—. Mem. Taylor County Red Cross Bd., Abilene, 1983-84. U.S. Dept. Labor fellow, 1975-76. Mem. Am. Econ. Assn., So. Econ. Assn., Blue Key, Phi Kappa Phi. Democrat. United Methodist. Avocations: Model railroads. Home: 3301 S 21st St Abilene TX 79605 Office: McMurray Coll PO Box 297 Abilene TX 79697

BROWN, ROBERT TINDALL, psychology educator; b. Greenwich, Conn., Jan. 3, 1940; s. Emerson Lee and Marguerite (Bangs) B.; m. Donna F. Ferris, June 25, 1964 (div. 1973); children—Ana Katherine, Julia Marguerite; m. 2d, Caryl Sue Lamb, Aug. 5, 1978. B.A., Hamilton Coll., 1961; Ph.D., Yale U., 1966; postgrad. U. Sussex, 1965-67. USPHS postdoctoral fellow U. Sussex, Brighton, Eng., 1965-67; vis. asst. prof. Coll. William and Mary, Williamsburg, Va., 1967-68; asst. prof. U. N.C., Chapel Hill, 1968-74, assoc. prof., Wilmington, 1974-79, prof. psychology, 1980—; mem. bd. cons. editors Ency. of Spl. Edn., 1985—. Co-editor: Perspectives on Bias in Mental Testing, 1984; Psychological Perspectives on Childhood Exceptionality: A Handbook, 1986. USPHS grantee, 1974-77. Mem. Am. Psychol. Assn., AAAS, Animal Behavior Soc., Psychonomic Soc., N.Y. Acad. Sci., Internat. Soc. Devel. Psychobiology, Sigma Xi. Home: 114 Buckeye Dr Route 4 Wilmington NC 28405 Office: Psychology Dept Univ NC Wilmington NC 28403

BROWN, SHIRLEY (PEGGY) KERN, interior designer; b. Ellensburg, Wash., Mar. 30, 1948; d. Philip Brooke and Shirley (Dickson) Kern; m. Ellery Kliess Brown, Jr., Aug. 7, 1970; children—Heather Nicole Coco, Rebecca Cherise, Andrea Shirley Serene, Ellery Philip. B.A. in Interior Design, Wash. State U., 1973. Apprentice, then interior designer L.S. Higgins & Assocs., Bellevue, Wash., 1969-72; interior designer ColorsPlus Interiors, Inc., Bellevue, 1972, Strawns Office Furniture & Interiors, Inc., Boise, Idaho, 1973-75, Empire Furniture Inc., Tulsa; owner Inside-Out Design Co. Ltd., Boise, 1973-82; interior designer Architekton, Inc., Tulsa, 1984—; lectr. schs., Meridian, Idaho, 1976, 78, Boise, 1980-81, Oral Roberts U., Tulsa. Mem. Am. Soc. Interior Designers (presdl. citation Oreg. chpt. 1977, dir. chpt. 1976-77, chmn. Boise subchpt. 1977-79, sec. 1980-81), Nat. Soc. Interior Designers, Idaho Hist. Co., AAUW, Wash. State U. Alumni Assn., Alpha Gamma Delta. Republican. Presbyterian. Club: Zonta. Author articles in field. Address: 9334 S 89th E Ave Tulsa OK 74133

BROWN, STEPHAN MARK, resource development consultant; b. Glendale, Calif., Mar. 7, 1943; s. Mackey E. and Grace (Ferguson) B.; m. Janet Eyre

Brookhart, Feb. 11, 1968; children—Theodore Mark, Stephan Thomas. Student Wash. State U., 1961-64, Eastern Wash. State U., 1964-67; B.A. in Ministry, Melodyland Sch. of Theology, 1978. In sales/personnel mgmt. Bon Marche, Seattle, 1966-68; personnel mgr. Squire Shops, Seattle, 1974; devel. services coordinator Melodyland Sch. of Theology, Anaheim, Calif., 1974-78, ordained to ministry Full Gospel Ch., 1978; founder, pres. Ctr. for Christian Services, Threshold Ministries and Helpline of South King County, Seattle, adminstr. First Bapt. Ch., Renton, Wash., 1978-80; resource devel. officer The Christian Broadcasting Network, Virginia Beach, Va., 1980-83; sr. cons. McConkey-Johnston, Inc., Dallas, 1983—; exec. dir. D.A.C.I., Dallas, 1983—; cons., lectr. in field. Lt., CAP. Served to sgt. Army N.G., 1966-72. Mem. Airplane Owners and Pilots Assn. Office: McConkey Johnston Inc 2995 LBJ Freeway 206W Dallas TX 75234

BROWN, STEPHEN MICHAEL, air force officer; b. Jackson, Mich., June 25, 1952; s. Harvey William and Ellen Ann (Norman) B.; A.A., Jackson County Community Coll., 1975; B.A. in Psychology, Siena Heights Coll., 1976; M.A. in Counseling, Central Mich. U. 1981; m. Kathleen Sue Felan, May 14, 1977; 1 son, Raymond Joseph. Joined U.S. Air Force, 1971, advanced through grades to capt., 1982; personnel specialist McConnell AFB, Kans., 1971-72, psychiat. technician USAF Hosp., 1972-74; youth specialist Adrian (Mich.) Tng. Sch., 1976-77; computer systems devel. officer/systems analyst Wright-Patterson AFB, Ohio, 1979-81, air force logistics command spl. projects mgr., 1981; test psychologist Randolph AFB, Tex., 1981—; drug and alcohol counselor; grad. teaching asst. Central Mich. U., 1977. Methodist. Club: Randolph AFB Officers. Home: 2406 French Sea San Antonio TX 78219 Office: USAF Occupational Measurement Center Randolph AFB TX 78150

BROWN, STEPHEN NEAL, electrical and mechanical engineer; b. Austin, Tex., July 30, 1952; s. Edward James and Alice Marie (Stewart) B.; m. Lisa Anne Runyon, Jan. 8, 1983. B.S. in Mech. Engring., U. Tex., 1975, M.S. in Mech. Engring., 1978, M.S. in Elec. Engring., 1984, postgrad. in elec. and computer engring., 1984—. Registered profl. engr., Tex. Jr. engr. IBM, Austin, 1975-76, assoc. engr., scientist, 1976-79, sr. assoc. engr., scientist, 1979—; grad. research asst. II, U. Tex.-Austin, 1984-85. Team leader CD, San Antonio, 1969; aquatic dir. summer camp Boy Scouts Am., Kerrville, Tex., 1973. Recipient Eagle Scout award Boy Scouts Am., 1969. Mem. IEEE Computer Soc., Assn. Computing Machinery, ASME (1st Place award for paper 1975), Eta Kappa Nu. Republican. Avocations: soccer; snow skiing. Home: 2000 Cedar Bend Dr Apt 126 Austin TX 78758 Office: IBM 62 T/008 11400 Burnet Rd Austin TX 78758

BROWN, STEVEN MARTIN, convenience store chain executive, oil company marketer, executive; b. Oklahoma City, Aug. 2, 1946; s. Barney U. and Virginia (Martin) B.; m. Ranell Bules, May 24, 1969; children—Matthew, Meredith Ranell. B.S. in Personnel Mgmt., Okla. State U., 1969. Pres. SAVE-A-STOP, Inc., Oklahoma City, 1973—; oil marketer, pres. Red Rock Petroleum Co., Inc., Oklahoma City, since 1984—. Chmn. family life com. Nichols Hills United Methodist Ch., 1976, mem. adminstrv. bd., sec. to adminstrv. bd., 1982-84, mem. fin. com., 1983, mem. bldg. and grounds com., 1984, chmn. council of ministries, 1985. Mem. Okla. Oil Marketers Assn. (dir., past pres., v.p., treas., nat. dir. to Nat. Oil Jobbers Council), Petroleum Marketers Assn. Am. (formerly Nat. Oil Jobbers Council) (Texaco brand com. 1977-79, motor fuel steering com. 1979-80, ops. and engring. com. 1978-79), Okla. Retail Grocers Assn. (dir. 1984), Travelers Aid Soc. Okla. (dir. 1980, chmn. nominations com. 1983, fin. com. 1984), Sigma Nu (corp. bd. 1984). Lodge: Lions (dir. 1972-73). Avocations: tennis; snow skiing; baking. Office: PO Box 82336 1801 SE Skyline Dr Oklahoma City OK 73148

BROWN, SUZANNE, physical education educator; b. Springfield, Mo., May 1, 1952; d. Ransome Lewis and Lois Wilba (House) B. Student S.W. Bapt. Coll., Bolivar, Mo., 1970-72; B.S. in Phys. Edn., S.W. Mo. State U., 1975; M.S. in Athletic Tng., Central Mo. State U., 1976. Women's athletic trainer S.W. Mo. State U., Springfield, 1976; instr. phys. edn., supr. horsemanship Berry Coll., Mount Berry, Ga., 1977—. Dir. Ga. High Sch. Rodeo Assn., 1982-83. Mem. AAHPER, Nat. Athletic Trainers Assn. (cert.), United Profl. Horseman's Assn., N.Am. Trial Ride Conf. Home: Hwy 27 N PO Box 357 Mount Berry GA 30149 Office: Berry Coll PO Box 357 Mount Berry GA 30149

BROWN, TRAVIS WALTER, oil drilling equipment company executive; b. Oklahoma City, June 18, 1934; s. H. Travis and Una Irene (Robison) B.; B.B.A., Okla. U., 1956; J.D., Oklahoma City U., 1962; m. Marilynn Davis, June 1, 1957; children—Deborah Sue, Travis Carson, Thomas Walter, Darla Lynn. Bar: Okla. 1962. With Geolograph Co., Oklahoma City, 1948-79, dir., 1960-79, pres., 1963-79; pres., gen. mgr. drilling equipment and services div. parent co. Geosource Inc., 1979-84; pres., dir. Geolograph Pioneer Inc., Geolograph Service Ltd. (Can.) Geolograph Pioneer (U.K.) Ltd., Chinese Am. Tech. Corp., 1984—; practiced in Oklahoma City, 1962—; pres., dir. Medearis Oil Well Supply Corp.; chmn. bd. Bowman Printing Co., 1977-79; v.p., dir. Geolograph Service Ltd. (Can.); sec., dir. Robinwood Farms Ltd.; officer, dir. Robinwood's Poor Boy Feed Co., Edmond, Okla., 1980—; pres. XIT Robinwood Pub. Co., pubs. Horse Digest, Leesburg, Va.; dir. Okla. Beef Inc.; former chmn. bd. Geolograph Medearis Service (U.K.) Ltd., London, Aberdeen and Singapore. Bd. dirs. Oklahoma County Fair. Served to lt. (j.g.) USNR, 1956-58. Named to Am. Cattleman's Hall of Fame, 1979. Mem. Okla. County Cattleman's Assn. (pres. 1975), Palomino Horse Breeders Am. (nat. pres. 1981—, nat. youth dir. 1973-78), Okla. Palomino Exhibitors Assn. (state youth dir., v.p. 1972-79, pres. 1979—), Internat. Brangus Breeders Assn. (chmn. promotions com.), Okla. Brangus Breeders Assn. (pres. 1982-83), Southwestern Okla. Brangus Breeders, N.W. Okla. Brangus Breeders, Indian Nations Brangus Breeders Assn., Okla. Horse Council (dir. 1981—, pres. 1983-85), Am. Quarter Horse Assn., Okla. Quarter Horse Assn., Am. Horse Show Assn. (palomino com. 1980—), Palomino Horse Breeders Owners Council (dir. 1985), Am. Petroleum Inst., Internat. Assn. Drilling Contractors (new equipment showcase com.), Ind. Oil Producers Assn., Okla. Oil Producers Assn., Calif. Ind. Oil Producers Assn., AIME, Soc. Petroleum Engrs., Canadian Diamond Drilling Assn., Am. Congress, Canadian Inst. Mining, Nat. Water Well Assn., Ind. Petroleum Assn. Am., ABA, Okla. Bar Assn., Okla. Poultry Fedn., World Cochin Family, Internat. Graphoanalysis Soc., Okla. Graphoanalysis Soc. Clubs: Cosmopolitan Internat. Civic (internat. pres. 1972-73, Disting. Service awards 1963-64, 66-67), Oklahoma City U. Alumni (dir.). Author: Freeze Branding of Horses, Cattle and Mules, 1982; co-author: Subsurface Geology, 1976. Contbr. articles to profl. jours. Home: Route 1 Box 154 Oklahoma City OK 73131 Office: PO Box 25246 Oklahoma City OK 73125

BROWN, WALDORF THOMAS, petroleum geologist; b. Richmond, Va., Feb. 28, 1957; s. Thomas Holt and Gertrude (Cheatham) B.; m. Beverly Kaye Carmichael, Sept. 4, 1982. B.S. in Geology, Va. State U., 1980. Geologist prodn. and devel. Prodn. div. Sun Exploration & Prodn. Co., Abilene, Tex., 1981—. Mem. Am. Assn. Petroleum Geologists, Soc. Profl. Well Log Analysts, Geol. Soc. Am., Nat. Assn. Black Geologists and Geophysicists. Democrat. Roman Catholic. Avocations: tennis; weight training; aerobics; travel. Home 3002 Rex Allen Dr Abilene TX 79606 Office: Prodn Div Sun Exploration & Prodn Co PO Box 2817 1 Century Plaza 1 Village Dr Abilene TX 79604

BROWN, WALTER STEVEN, training company executive; b. Birmingham, Ala., Feb. 12, 1938; s. William Samuel and Ethel (Whitley) B.; m. Toby Ann Tidwell, Mar. 21, 1953 (div. Sept. 1970); children—Beverly Ann, Cynthia L. Leigh; m. Marsha Lynn Dimsdale, Sept. 20, 1971; children—Stephanie Diane, William Steven. Exec. v.p. Sales Unltd., Inc., Birmingham, 1965-70; pres. Fortune Prodns., Inc., Atlanta, 1970-78; chmn. The Fortune Group, Atlanta, 1978—; v.p. Sales Mktg. Exec., Atlanta, 1985—. Author: 13 Fatal Errors Managers Make, 1985; (video system) Practical Sales Management; 1981; Creative Selling Skills, 1981. Bd. dirs. Jr. Achievement Greater Atlanta, 1983—. Mem. Nat. Speakers Assn. Republican. Avocation: golf. Office: The Fortune Group 4675 N Shallow Ford Rd Suite 200 Atlanta GA 30338

BROWN, WARREN JOSEPH, physician; b. Bklyn., July 17, 1924; s. Benjamin Oscar and Angela Marie (Cahill) B.; student Ursinus Coll., 1942-43; B.S., Bethany Coll., 1945; M.D., Ohio State U., 1949; m. Greet Roos, July 3, 1970; children—Warren James, Robert E., Suzanne J., Annemarie, Eric Jan. Reporter, Pottstown (Pa.) Mercury, 1942-43; intern U.S. Naval Hosp., Long Beach, Calif., Oceanside, Calif.; resident Pottstown Hosp., 1950-51; asso. Roos Loos Med. Group, Alhambra, Calif., 1951; pvt. family practice, Largo, Fla., 1953—; sr. civilian flight surgeon FAA, 1964—; pres. Aero-Med. Consultants, Inc., Largo, 1969—. Historian, Fla. Aviation Hist. Soc., 1978—, St. Petersburg-Clearwater-Tampa Hangar, Order of Quiet Birdmen, 1969-81. Served with USN, 1943-45, 49-50, 51-53. Diplomate Am. Bd. Family Practice. Fellow Am. Acad. Family Physicians; mem. Pinellas County Med. Assn., Fla. Med. Assn., Fla. Pilots Assn., Aircraft Owners and Pilots Assn. Christian. Author: Florida's Aviation History, 1980; Child Yank Over the Rainbow, 1977; Patients' Guide to Medicine, 9th edit., 1981; The World's First Airline: The St. Petersburg-Tampa Airboat Line, 1914, 1981 2d edit., 1984. Home: 14607 Brewster Dr Largo FL 33544 Office: 10912 Hamlin Blvd Largo FL 33544

BROWN, WILLIAM ALBERT, newspaper editor; b. Huntsville, Tex., Apr. 24, 1935; s. Clarence and Ora Etta (Wedgeworth) B.; m. Madeline Jo Ward, Dec. 21, 1966; children—Joe Frank, Keith Lee, Thomas Kirk. B.A., North Tex. State U., 1957. Sports editor San Angelo Standard-Times (Tex.), 1958-62; sports slotman Ft. Worth Star-Telegram, 1962-64; sports info. dir. U. Tex.-Arlington, 1964-72; mng. editor Tyler Courier-Times (Tex.), 1972-77, Waco Tribune-Herald (Tex.), 1977-85; editor Port Arthur News (Tex.), 1985—; nat. dir. Coll. Sports Info. Dirs., Chgo., 1970-72. Den leader Webelos, Boy Scouts Am., Waco, 1979; v.p. Lake Air Pee Wee Football, Waco., 1979-80; pres. Lake Air Little League, 1979-80. Mem. AP Mng. Editors Assn. (dir., Tex. 1983—, v.p. 1985, 1st place awards 1964-66), Tex. UPI Editors (pres. 1979-80), North and East Tex. Press Assn. (pres. 1978-79), Sigma Delta Chi. Democrat. Methodist. Club: Fish Pond Country. Home: 3727 Platt Ave Port Arthur TX 77640 Office: Port Arthur News 549 4th St Port Arthur TX 77641

BROWN, WILLIAM ALLEY, lawyer, educator; b. LaGrange, Tex., Sept. 5, 1921; s. Leon Dancy and Mary (Alley) B.; m. Ann Shafer, June 27, 1953; children—Ann Lenora, William A. Jr. B.B.A., U. Tex., 1942; I.A., Harvard U., 1943; J.D., U. Tex., 1948. Bar: Tex. 1948. Instr., U. Tex., Austin, 1946-50; ptnr. Powell, Wirtz, Rauhut, Reavley & Brown, Austin, 1950-61; v.p. and gen. atty. Brown & Root, Inc., Houston, 1961-83; prof. Tex. A&M U., College Station, 1983—. Served to 1st lt. U.S. Army, 1943-46. Mem. Sons Republic of Tex. Republican. Episcopalian. Clubs: Plaza (Bryan, Tex.); Frisch Auf Valley Country (LaGrange). Home: 2710 Pinehurst Bryan TX 77802

BROWN, WILLIAM LEE LYONS, JR., consumer products executive; b. Louisville, Aug. 22, 1936; s. William Lee Lyons and Sara (Shallenberger) B.; B.A., U. Va., 1958; B.S., Am. Grad. Sch. Internat. Mgmt., 1960; m. Alice Cary Farmer, June 13, 1959; children—William Lee Lyons III, Alice Cary, Stuart Randolph. Sales rep. Ariz., Brown-Forman Corp., Phoenix, 1960-61, v.p., Louisville, 1965-68, sr. v.p., 1968-72, exec. v.p., 1972-76, pres., chief exec. officer, 1976—; asst. v.p. Jos. Garneau Co. import div. Brown-Forman, N.Y.C., 1961-62, v.p., Paris, France, 1962-65; dir. Brown-Forman Distillers Corp., First Ky. Nat. Corp. Louisville, 1st Nat. Bank, Louisville. Diamond Shamrock Corp., Dallas. Bd. dirs. Ky. Center for Arts Endowment Fund, Louisville, Shakertown, Inc., Pleasant Hill, Ky.; pres., bd. govs. J.B. Speed Art Mus., Louisville mem. U. Va. Alumni Bd. Served to 1st lt. U.S. Army, 1958-59. Decorated chevalier de L'Ordre du Merite Agricole (France); hon. consul France. Mem. Soc. Sons Colonial Wars. Republican. Episcopalian. Clubs: Travellers (Paris); Fishers Island (N.Y.) Country; River Valley, Wynn Stay, Pendennis, Louisville Country (Louisville); University (N.Y.C.). Home: Fincastle Prospect KY 40059 also Fishers Island NY 06390 Office: 850 Dixie Hwy Louisville KY 40210

BROWN, WILSON GORDON, physician, educator; b. Bosworth, Mo., Jan. 18, 1914; s. Arthur Grannison and Clemma (Frock) B.; A.B., William Jewell Coll., 1935; M.D., Washington U., St. Louis, 1939; m. Anne Buckalew, Oct. 25, 1940; 1 son, Gordon Alan. Intern pathology Barnes Hosp., St. Louis, Mo., 1939-40; resident pathology St. Louis City Hosp., 1940-41; instr. pathology Washington U., 1945-51; clin. asso. prof. Baylor U. Coll. Medicine, Houston, 1951—; clin. prof. U. Tex. Med. Sch. at Houston, 1972—; pathologist, dir. labs. Hermann Hosp., Houston, 1951-71; dir. labs. Twelve Oaks Hosp., Houston, 1965—, Polly Ryon Hosp., Richmond, Tex., 1954—, Park Plaza Hosp., Houston, 1975—; partner Brown & Assos. Med. Labs., Houston, 1954—. Mem. adv. bd. Living Bank, Houston, 1968—; founding mem. Mus. Med. Sci., Houston, 1969—, trustee, 1969—, pres. bd. trustees, 1974-75. Bd. dirs. Ewing Center Inc., 1975-81, Am. Cancer Soc. Harris County (Tex.) Br., 1952, pres., 1967-68. Served to maj., M.C., AUS, 1942-46. ETO, MTO. Decorated Bronze Star medal. Diplomate Am. Bd. Clin. Pathology, Am. Bd. Anat. Pathology. Mem. Am., Tex. med. assns., Harris County Med. Soc., Coll. Am. Pathologists, Am. Soc. Clin. Pathology, Houston, Tex. socs. pathologists, Sigma Xi, Beta Beta Beta, Theta Chi Delta, Aeons, Phi Gamma Delta. Clubs: Forum of Houston, Warwick (Houston). Contbr. articles to various med. publs. Home: 3518 Westridge St Houston TX 77025 Office: 1213 Hermann Dr 252 Park Plaza Profl Bldg Houston TX 77004

BROWNE, RICHARD HAROLD, statistician, consultant; b. St. Louis, Sept. 24, 1946; s. Basil Campbell and Evelyn Beatrice (Biver) B.; m. Dennise Marie Richardson, Aug. 10, 1970. B.S., U. Mo.-Rolla, 1968; M.S., Okla. State U., 1970, Ph.D., 1973. Statistician M.D. Anderson Hosp., Houston, 1971-72; asst. prof. U. Tex. Health Sci. Ctr., Dallas, 1973-79; statistician Criterion Inc., Dallas, 1979-81; sr. mgmt. analyst Sun Co., Dallas, 1981-83; sr. biostatistician Teams, Inc., Dallas, 1983-85; sr. cons. RHB Cons. Services, Dallas, 1979—; adj. asst. prof. So. Meth. U., Dallas, 1974-77, Health Sci. Ctr., U. Tex.-Dallas, 1979-82; adj. assoc. prof. Tex. Women's U., Dallas, 1984—. Contbr. articles to profl. jours. Mem. Am. Statis. Assn., Biometric Soc. Republican. Club: Dallas Camera. Avocation: photography. Home: 2516 New Orleans St Apt 136 Dallas TX 75235

BROWNE, STEPHEN JAMES, management development specialist, consultant; b. N.Y.C., Sept. 25, 1953; s. Herbert William and Ardis Katherine (James) B.; m. Cleo Marie Vuolle, July 11, 1981. B.A., Rutgers U., 1975. Youth ctr. coordinator Piscataway Youth Resources Ctr., N.J., 1975-77; counselor Puerto Rican Assn. for Human Devel., Perth Amboy, N.J., 1978-79; project dir. Middlesex County Coll., Edison, N.J., 1979-82; div. personnel rep. Revco D.S., Inc., Twinsburg, Ohio, 1982-85, div. personnel mgr., 1985—; tng. cons. Cullinane Assocs., Edison, 1978-82. Chmn. Park Ave. Community Adv. Bd., Piscataway, N.J., 1976-77. Mem. Am. Soc. for Tng. and Devel., Livingston Coll. Assn. Grads. (sec. 1980-81). Avocations: hiking; camping; cross country skiing; photography. Office: Revco DS Inc 1925 Enterprise Pkwy Twinsburg OH 44087

BROWNING, GRAYSON DOUGLAS, philosophy educator; b. Seminole, Okla., Mar. 7, 1929; s. Grayson Douglas and Dorothea (Cook) B.; m. Susan Gilman, June 2, 1953 (div.); children—Tony, Luke, Lauren; m. 2d, Becky Jo Beck, July 15, 1972. B.A., U. Tex., Austin, 1954, M.A., 1955, Ph.D., 1958. From instr. to prof. U. Miami, Fla., 1958-69; vis. prof. U. Tex., Austin, 1969-71, prof., 1971—, chmn. dept. philosophy, 1972-76. Served with USAF, 1948-52. Mem. Am. Philos. Assn., Southwestern Philos. Soc. (pres. 1977), Fla. Philos. Soc. (pres. 1967), So. Soc. Philosophy and Psychology (pres. 1973), Soc. Advancement Am. Philosophy. Author: Act and Agent, 1964; Poems and Visions, 1965; editor Philosophers of Process, 1965; contbr. articles to profl. jours. Home: 185 Faubion Dr Georgetown TX 78628 Office: Dept Philosophy U Tex Austin TX 78712

BROWNING, JOE LEON, physical scientist; b. Huntington, W.Va., June 14, 1925; s. Jasper Kenna and Ethel Catherine (Woodall) B.; student U. Va., 1943-44; B.S. in Chemistry, Marshall U., 1947; postgrad. George Washington U., 1954-56; 1 dau., Jane Browning Brooks. Chemist, Chesapeake & Ohio Ry., Huntington, 1947-49, Allied Chem. & Dye Corp., South Point, Ohio, 1950-51, Internat. Nickel Co., Huntington, 1951; head, rocket motor combustion studies Naval Powder Factory, Indian Head, Md., 1951-53, head prodn. dept. lab., 1953-56, devel. engr. Polaris rocket motor U.S. Dept. Navy, Washington, 1956-58, dir. research and devel. Naval Propellant Plant, Indian Head, 1958-62, tech. dir. Naval Ordnance Sta., Indian Head, 1962-75; pres. Waldorf Investment & Land Corp., Indian Head, 1962-68, Waldorf Equity, Inc., Indian Head, 1971—; chmn. GEC Tech. Corp., Garland, Tex., 1980-82; dir. Video Scis. Inc., Dallas; pres. Pacific Flex, Inc., Los Angeles, 1982—; adj. prof. World Bus. Thunderbird Grad. Sch. Internat. Mgmt., Phoenix, 1971-72. Mem. Md. Gov's. Sci. Adv. Council, 1970-75. Navy Sr. Sci. Council, 1965-70. Served with USNR, 1943-46. Mem. AIAA, Am. Def. Preparedness Assn., Chi Beta Phi. Patentee in field.

BROWNING, LISA RITONDO, lawyer; b. Anniston, Ala., July 16, 1957; d. John Thomas and Rose Marie (Elwell) Ritondo; m. James Patrick Browning, Jr., Aug. 8, 1981. B.S., U. Ala., 1979, M.A., 1982, J.D., 1982. Bar: La. 1982. Acting treas.; dir. compliance, asst. corp. sec. New Orleans Commodity Exchange, 1982-83; v.p. and gen. counsel Howard, Weil, Labouisse, Friedrichs, Inc., New Orleans, 1983—. Mem. New Orleans Mus. Art, Friends of Audubon Zoo. Mem. ABA, La. Bar Assn., Futures Industry Assn., Omicron Delta Epsilon, Dobro Slovo. Home: 1429 Fern St New Orleans LA 70118 Office: Howard Weil Labouisse Friedrichs Inc Energy Centre 1100 Poydras St Suite 900 New Orleans LA 70163

BROWNLEE, PAULA PIMLOTT, college president, chemistry educator; b. London, June 23, 1934; d. John Richard and Alice A. (Ajamian) Pimlott; m. Thomas H. Brownlee, Feb. 10, 1961; children—Kenneth Gainsford, Elizabeth Ann, Clare Louise. B.A. with honors, Oxford U., 1957, M.A., 1959, D.Phil. in Chemistry, 1959. Research chemist Am. Cyanamid Co., Stamford, Conn., 1961-62; lectr. U. Bridgeport (Conn.), 1968-70; asst. prof. Rutgers Coll., Rutgers U., New Brunswick, N.J., 1970-73, assoc. prof. chemistry, assoc. dean, then acting dean Douglass Coll., 1973-76; dean faculty, prof. chemistry Union Coll., Schenectady, 1976-81; prof. chemistry, pres. Hollins Coll. (Va.), 1981—; dir. Colonial Am. Bank. Trustee Sci. Mus. Va., 1983—; bd. dirs. Roanoke Valley Sci. Mus., Roanoke Symphony. Fellow Chem. Soc. London; mem. Am. Chem. Soc., Am. Women in Sci., Assn. Va. Colls. (pres. 1985-86), Am. Assn. Higher Edn. (bd. dirs., chair 1983-84), Sigma Xi. Contbr. articles to profl. publs. Episcopalian. Home and Office: Hollins College VA 24020

BROWN-OLMSTEAD, AMANDA, public relations agency executive; b. Jackson, Miss., Oct. 7, 1943; d. J.A. and Iris (Williams) Brown; m. George T. Olmstead; children—Vanessa, Blake. Student in Liberal Arts, U. Miss., 1965. In pub. relations, fashion direction and coordination Rich's, J.P. Allen, and Saks Fifth Ave., 1965-71; founder, pres., owner A. Brown-Olmstead Assocs., Atlanta, 1972—; v.p. Pinnacle Group; instr. courses Emory U. and SBA. Bd. dirs. Atlanta chpt. Muscular Dystrophy, 1968-73, pres., 1972-73; adv. bd. YMCA Women of Achievement, 1983; founder Young Careers div. High Mus. Art, 1970; mem. annual ball com. Bot. Gardens, 1981-82, Piedmont Ball Com., 1975, 78; mem. Atlanta Clean City Commn., 1978-81, Leadership Atlanta, 1978, Central Atlanta Progress, 1983; active Atlanta Ballet, 1969-76. Recipient Gold Medal N.Y. Film and TV Festival, 1968; named one of Ten Outstanding Young People of Atlanta, 1976; featured as one of six young tycoons in fashion in U.S., Mademoiselle mag., 1970. Mem. Pub. Relations Soc. Am., Fashion Group, Atlanta C. of C. (Phoenix House award adv. bd. 1983). Democrat. Episcopalian. Clubs: Atlanta City, World Trade. Writer, dir. TV spl.: The Land of Cotton, 1968. Home: 36 Wakefield Dr Atlanta GA 30309 Office: 100 Peachtree St NE Suite 610 Atlanta GA 30303

BROYHILL, JAMES THOMAS, congressman; b. Lenoir, N.C., Aug. 19, 1927; B.S. in Bus. Adminstrn., U. N.C., 1950; LL.D. (hon.), Catawba Coll., Salisbury, N.C., 1966; m. Louise Robbins; children—Marilyn Broyhill Beach, Ed, Philip. Formerly exec. Broyhill Furniture Industries, Lenoir; mem. 88th-99th Congresses from 9th and 10th Dists. N.C., vice chmn. Congl. Textile Caucus, dean N.C. Congl. Del., ranking minority mem. House Energy and Commerce Com. Trustee, Wake Forest U., 1970-74; formerly vice chmn. bd. advs. Lees-McRae Coll., Banner Elk, N.C.; formerly mem. devel. bd. Lenoir-Rhyne Coll., Hickory, N.C. Baptist. Republican. Clubs: Masons, Shriners. Office: 2340 Rayburn House Office Bldg Washington DC 20515

BROYHILL, PAUL H., furniture manufacturing company executive; b. 1924; married. B.A., U. N.C., 1947. With Broyhill Furniture Industries Inc., Lenoir, N.C., 1947-86, salesman, 1947-50, v.p. sales and merchandising, 1950-60, pres., 1960-76, chmn. bd., 1976-86; chmn. Broyhill Furniture Rentals and Sales. Chmn. B.M.C. Investment Fund, Broyhill Found. Mem. Phi Beta Kappa. Address: Golfview Dr Box 500 Lenoir NC 28645

BRUCE, CHARLES JOY, insurance company executive; b. Columbia, S.C., Jan. 22, 1953; s. William Rankin and Jane Parsley (Emerson) B.; m. Diane Louise Smith, Oct. 27, 1955; 1 child, Merideth Louise. Student, Midlands Tech. Coll., 1973-75. With Seibels, Bruce & Co., Columbia, S.C., 1972—, loss control and safety rep., 1975-77, reins. rep., 1977, asst. v.p. adminstrv. dept., 1977-85, v.p., 1985—. Mem. Nat. Assn. Fleet Adminstrs. (dir.). Clubs: Columbia Sailing; Met. Bus., Tarantella; Forest Lake; Palmetto (Columbia).

BRUCE, JACKSON MILLER, lawyer; b. Charlottesville, Va., Sept. 22, 1942; s. Robert Jackson and Lena (Miller) B.; m. Sally Law, June 14, 1968; children—Shane Law, Robert Jackson II. B.A., U. Richmond, 1964; J.D., T.C. Williams Sch., 1978. Bar: Va. 1978, U.S. Ct. Appeals (4th cir.) 1978, U.S. Dist. Ct. (we. dist.) Va. 1979. Ins. adjuster Crawford & Co., Huntington, W.Va., 1965-66, br. mgr., Charlottesville, 1969-74, asst. claims mgr., Richmond, Va., 1974-76; claims adjuster USF&G Co., Richmond, 1967-69; ptnr. Gilmer, Sadler, Ingram, Sutherland & Hutton, Pulaski, Va., 1978—; pres. Charlottesville Claims Assn., Va., 1972. Bd. dirs. YMCA, Pulaski, 1984—. Mem. Pulaski C. of C. (bd. dirs. 1980), Huntington Jr. C. of C., ABA, Va. Bar Assn., Va. Trial Lawyers Assn., Assn. Trial Lawyers Am., Def. Research Inst., Pulaski Bar Assn., Twenty-seventh Jud. Cir. Bar Assn. (sec. 1986), Sigma Chi, Phi Alpha Delta. Presbyterian. Club: Thorn Spring Golf (Pulsaki). Lodges: Elks (past exalted ruler), Rotary (pres. 1986). Home: Route 2 Box 39 Pulaski VA 24301 Office: Gilmer Sadler Ingram Sutherland & Hutton PO Box 878 Pulaski VA 24301

BRUCE, JAMES W., JR., banking executive. Exec. v.p. Liberty Nat. Bank & Trust Co. of Oklahoma City. Office: Liberty Nat Bank & Trust Co 100 Broadway Oklahoma City OK 73102*

BRUCE, JOE, architectural/interior designer; b. Tulsa, Sept. 21, 1942; s. Melvin Ray and Helen F. (Smith) B.; m. Pamela Jan Badgwell, Dec. 11, 1961; children—Michael Joe, Jana Lynne. Student, U. Okla.; B.Arch., Ga. Tech. Inst., 1970, M.A. in Architecture/City Planning, 1972; B.A. in Bus. Adminstrn., Memphis State U., 1976. Pres. Archtl./Interior Design Cons., Atlanta; pres. Design Cons., Charlotte, N.C.; dir. interior design HTB, Inc., Tulsa, 1981-83; pres. Corporate Design, Inc., Tulsa, 1983—. Trustee, Tulsa Community Youth Home; mem. Nat. Hist. Rev. Bd. Served with USN, 1961-63. Mem. AIA (assoc.) Am. Soc. Interior Designers, Constructions Specifications Inst. Republican. Episcopalian. Home: 1117 S Norfolk Ave Tulsa OK 74120 Office: Corporate Pl PO Box 3627 Tulsa OK 74101

BRUCE, JOHN LARRABEE, dentist; b. Florence, S.C., Aug. 22, 1951; s. John Larrabee and Janie (Fields) B.; m. Emma Dennis Walters, Mar. 20, 1976; children—Elizabeth Dolan, Janie Catherine. B.S., Wofford Coll., 1973; B.S. in Pharmacy, Med. U. S.C., 1976, D.M.D., 1982. Staff pharmacist Med. U. S.C., Charleston, 1976-78; gen. practice dentistry, Florence, 1982—; clin. instr. Florence/Darl. Inst. Tech., 1984—; mem. staff Bruce Hosp., Florence, 1983—. Mem. ADA, Florence county Dental Soc., Delta Sigma Delta (life). Republican. Baptist. Lodge: Lions. Avocations: photography; tennis. Home: 1201 Madison Ave Florence SC 29501 Office: 521 S Dargan St Florence SC 29501

BRUCE, KATHLEEN THIRKELL, psychologist; b. Hull, Eng.; Am. citizen; d. Walter Bevan and Catherine (Graham) Thirkell. Litt.B., Douglass Coll., 1930; M.A., Columbia U., 1932. Lic. psychologist, N.J. Algebra tchr. North Bergen pub. schs., 1932-47, psychologist, 1947-61; psychologist Cliffside Park pub. schs., N.J., 1961-67, Weehawken, Secaucus and Guttenberg pub. schs., 1967-69, Ft. Lee pub. schs., N.J., 1968; gen. practice psychology, Ft. Lee, 1932—; cons. in field. Contbr. articles to profl. jours. Actice profl. and civic orgns. Zonta scholar, 1925. Mem. Brit. War Relief Soc. (chmn. mobile kitchen dr.), Am. Psychol. Assn. Republican. Espicopalian. Club: N.J. State Fedn. Women's (9th dist. v.p.). Avocations: traveling; arts; antiques; swimming.

BRUCH, VIRGINIA IRENE, librarian, author; b. Hickman, Ky., May 26, 1921; d. Thomas Terrell and Virginia Irene (Helm) Sullivan; m. Truman Elwood Bruch, Feb. 18, 1944; 1 child, Susan Irene Bruch Rose. B.S., Murray State U., 1943. Librarian, tchr. Union City High Sch., Tenn., 1943-44; librarian, cataloger FTC, Washington, 1949-55, Army Library, Washington, 1955-65; librarian, chief tech. services, 1965-80; researcher Boyhood Home of Robert E. Lee, Alexandria, Va., 1980—; librarian, tchr. First Christian Ch., Alexandria, 1960-72; owner, mgr. Jennie's Book Nook, Alexandria, Va., 1982—. Author: Beneath the Oaks of Ivy Hill, 1982; Proud Wanderers; My Mother's Family, 1984. Recipient Poetry prize Fed. Poet, Washington, 1956, Essay prize Va. Highlands Festival, Abingdon, Va., 1976, Outstanding Performance award Army Library, Washington, 1979, Commitment to Excellence award Dr. Elisha Dick chpt. DAR, Alexandria, 1980. Mem. ALA, DAR (librarian, chmn. lineage research 1980-83), Colonial Dames XVII Century (sec. 1984-85), Va. Hist. Soc., Ky. Hist. Soc., Tenn. Hist. Soc. Republican. Home: 15 W Howell Ave Alexandria VA 22301 Office: Boyhood Home of Robert E Lee 607 Oronoco St Alexandria VA 22314

BRUECHERT, CARL JOHN, engineering, construction executive; b. Parkersburg, Iowa, Aug. 14, 1914; s. Henry Nicholas and Jenetta (Plesscher) B.; m. Anna Bahlman Roper, Sept. 18, 1943; children—Louise Tucker, Elizabeth Rogers. B.S.E.E., Iowa State Coll., 1937. Engr., project mgr. Natkin & Co., Omaha, 1937-42, br. mgr., Lincoln, Nebr., 1946-49, div. mgr., dir., St. Louis, 1950-60; dir., chmn., treas., prin. stockholder Player & Co., Atlanta, 1961—. Pres. Little Cumberland Island Assn.; jr. warden St. Anne's Episcopal Ch. Served to lt. USNR, 1943-45. Decorated Norway Freedom medal, Commendation medal; named Metro Atlanta Engr. of Year, 1977. Fellow ASHRAE; mem. Nat. Soc. Profl. Engrs. (v.p. 1978-79), Mech. Contractors Assn. Am. Clubs: Cherokee Town and Country, Rotary. Home: 4810 Jett Rd NW Atlanta GA 30327 Office: 531 Bishop St NW Atlanta GA 30381

BRUHN, JOHN GLYNDON, university dean, medical sociologist; b. Norfolk, Nebr., Apr. 27, 1934; s. John Franz and Margaret Constance (Treiber) B. B.A., U. Nebr., 1956, M.A., 1958; Ph.D. in Med. Sociology, Yale U., 1961. Fulbright fellow in sociology dept. psychol. medicine U. Edinburgh, Scotland, 1961-62; instr. med. sociology U. Okla. Med. Ctr., Oklahoma City, 1962-63, asst. prof. dept. psychiatry and behavioral scis., 1963-64, asst. prof. preventive medicine and pub. health, 1964-67, assoc. prof. sociology in medicine dept. medicine, 1967-72, assoc. prof. human ecology, Sch. of Health, 1967-69, assoc. prof. preventive medicine and pub. health, 1967-70, prof., chmn. dept. human ecology Sch. of Health, 1969-72; assoc. prof. sociology U. Okla., Norman, 1967-72; instr. sociology Oklahoma City U., 1963; clin. investigator Okla. Med. Research Found., Oklahoma City, 1965-67; assoc. dean for community affairs U. Tex. Med. Br., Galveston, 1972-81, prof. preventive medicine and community health, 1972—, acting dean Sch. Allied Health Scis., 1979, 80-81, dean, spl. asst. pres. for community affairs, 1981—; prof. human ecology U. Tex. Sch. Pub. Health, Houston, 1975—; adviser, cons. numerous orgns.; lectr. in field; presenter at numerous confs. and workshops. Trustee United Way of Galveston, 1975-76, 85-86, exec. com., 1977-78, v.p. for agy. ops., 1978; chmn. health and human resources task force Goals for Galveston, 1974-75; chmn. tech. adv. com. on health promotion Health Systems Agy., Houston, 1978; mem. Health Promotion Adv. Council, 1979-80; bd. dirs. St. Vincent's House, 1974-75, William Temple Community House, 1974-78, Galveston County Cultural Arts Council, 1974-75, Galveston Alt. Sch. Program, 1976-77, Galveston County Coordinated Community Clinics, 1977-80, Galveston County Cancer Soc., 1979-80, Galveston County Heart Assn., 1980, Friends of Rosenberg Library, 1980-81, Galveston County Community Orch., 1979-85, Met. Houston chpt. March of Dimes, 1983—; mem. profl. adv. com. Galveston Mental Health Assn., 1984; mem. health professions adv. com. Coordinating Bd. Tex. Coll. and Univ. System, 1984—. Served with USAR, 1957-63. Recipient Career Development award Nat. Heart Inst., 1968-69; Outstanding Adminstrn. award Faculty Sch. Allied Health Scis., U. Tex. Med. Br.-Galveston, 1981, Nicholas and Catherine Leone award for adminstrv. excellence, 1983; grantee Nat. Heart Inst., NIH, 1968-69, Nat. Fund for Med. Edn., 1973-75, Tex. Regional Med. Program, 1974, Danforth Found., 1975, 76, 82, The Robert Wood Johnson Found., 1976-79, Charles Stewart Mott Found., 1979, Nat. Inst. Child Health and Human Devel., HEW, 1979-83, Moody Found., 1981, 83, HHS, 1981-84, Kempner Fund, 1982-84. Fellow Am. Pub. Health Assn. (task force on funding, so. br. 1973-74, standing com. pub. policy and resolutions, 1974), Am. Heart Assn., Royal Soc. Health; mem. Am. Sociol. Assn., AAAS, Assn. Am. Med. Colls., Am. Psychosomatic Soc., AAUP, Am. Soc. Allied Health Professions, Assn. Tchrs. Preventive Medicine, N.Y. Acad. Sci., Tex. Soc. Allied Health Professions, Alpha Kappa Delta, Sigma Xi. Author: (with Nader, Bryan, Parcel and Williams) Options for School Health, 1978; (with Wolf and Goodell) Occupational Health as Human Ecology, 1978; (with S. Wolf) The Roseto Story: An Anatomy of Health, 1979; (with Caballero, Hinkley and Purvis) A Doctor in the House?: Information for Parents and Spouses of Premedical and Medical Students, 3d edit., 1982; (with Philips and Levine) Medical Sociology: An Annotated Bibliography 1972-1982, 1985; also chpts. in books; contbr. numerous articles and book revs. to profl. jours.; mem. editorial bd. Health Values; Achieving High Level Wellness, 1979—, assoc. editor, 1980—; editorial bd. Jour. Allied Health, 1982—, Paedovita, 1983—, Family and Community Health, 1985—. Home: 7521 Beluche Galveston TX 77551 Office: Sch Allied Health Scis U TX Med Br Galveston TX 77550

BRUISTER, CARROLL LAFAYETTE, III, pharmacist; b. Clarksdale, Miss., Nov. 9, 1957; s. Carroll Lafayette and Janie Katherine (Crow) B.; m. Mary Louise Massey, Oct. 21, 1975; children—Shelley Nicole, Lindley Keryn, Lauren Denise. B.S. in Pharmacy, U. Miss., 1980. Dir. pharmacy HPI Health Care Services, Senatobia, Miss., 1980-82, Plymouth, N.C., 1982-84, DeWitt, Ark., 1984—. Mem. Tidewater Mental Health Bd., Washington, N.C., 1982-84; mem. Plymouth Vol. Fire Dept., N.C., 1982-84; speaker Washington County Pub. Schs., Plymouth, 1983. Delta Cotton Wives scholar, 1975. Mem. Am. Soc. Hosp. Pharmacists, Ark. Soc. Hosp. Pharmacists, Am. Pharm. Assn. Methodist. Lodges: Lions, Rotary. Avocations: fishing; hunting; flying; photography; skiing. Home: 502 W 2d St DeWitt AR 72042 Office: DeWitt City Hosp Pharmacy Hwy 1 and Madison St DeWitt AR 72042

BRUMFIELD, BRUCE CARLTON, university administrator, educator; b. New Rochelle, N.Y., Mar. 1, 1947; s. Perry Carlysle and Margaret Dorothy (Stagina) B.; m. Mary Jane Bloodworth, May 1, 1970; children—Robert Logan, Laura Lafe. B.B.A., Ga. So. Coll., 1969, M.B.A., 1970; D.B.A., Miss. State U., 1974. Head dept. bus. adminstrn. Jackson State U., Miss., 1974-78; coordinator M.B.A. program Ga. Coll., Milledgeville, 1978-83, dean Grad. Sch., 1980-83, dir. ctrs., assoc. prof. mgmt., 1983—; adj. prof. U. S.D., 1983—. Active staff Gov. Cliff Finch, Miss., 1976-80. Mem. Soc. Advancement Mgmt., Delta Sigma Pi, Beta Gamma Sigma. Republican. Methodist. Club: Computer (Macon, Ga.). Lodge: Rotary (Milledgeville). Avocations: collector of Disneyana, rare books, stamps, antiques, military weapons World War II and earlier, coins, ivory. Office: Ga Coll Milledgeville GA 31060

BRUMFIELD, SHANNON MAUREEN, speech and language pathologist; b. New Orleans, Sept. 14, 1946; d. Dr. Fred Orlan and Mary Kathleen (Maloney) B.; B.A., La. State U., 1968; M.A., Temple U., 1970; Ph.D., U. Fla., 1978. Speech therapist Sch. Dist. Upper Darby (Pa.), 1970-71; tchr. of deaf, rank tchr. Jefferson Parish Sch. Bd., La., 1971-74; instr. Holy Cross Coll., summer 1974; grad. asst. U. Fla., 1977; pvt. practice speech and lang. pathology, New Orleans, 1979—; lectr. La. Med. Sch. Sec., Les Amies Ensembles, 1979. Mem. jr. com. New Orleans Symphony, Opera, Friends of Zoo, Friends of Cabildo; active La. Council Performing Arts. Lic. speech pathologist, La.; cert. Council on Edn. of Deaf; cert. tchr. of speech and hearing handicapped (cert.), La. Mem. Am. Speech and Hearing Assn. (cert.), La. Speech and Hearing Assn., Am. Soc. Clin. Hypnosis, Am. Educators of Deaf, Internat. Assn. Logopedics and Phoniatrics, Alliance for Good Govt., Kappa Kappa Gamma. Clubs: Orleans, Jeunesse d'Orleans. Home: 2314 Calhoun St New Orleans LA 70118 Office: 4333 Loveland Metairie LA 70002

BRUMGARDT, JOHN RAYMOND, museum administrator; b. Riverside, Calif., Feb. 3, 1946; s. Reuben R. and Grace (Taylor) B.; m. Doris Ann Tarasko, Dec. 20, 1969; children—Jennifer, Thomas. B.A. in History, U. Calif.-Riverside, 1967, M.A., 1968, Ph.D., 1974; Mgmt. Devel. Cert., U. Colo., 1981. Riverside County historian Riverside Mus., Calif., 1974-76; head history div. Riverside County Parks, 1976-78; dir. Mus. of Western Colo., Grand Junction, 1978-84, Charleston Mus., S.C., 1984—; map surveyor Am. Assn. Mus., Washington, 1980—, mem. accreditation roster, 1982—; grants reviewer Inst. Mus. Services, 1981—. Editor: Civil War Nurse, 1980. Author: People of the Magic Waters, 1981. Contbr. articles to profl. jours. Mem. Colo. Humanities Com., Denver, 1981-84; chmn. Riverside County Bicentennial Com., Calif., 1975-76. Served to capt. U.S. Army, 1970-72. Haynes Found. fellow, 1968. Mem. Am. Assn. Mus., Mountain Plains Mus. Assn. (pres. 1983-84), S.E. Mus. Conf., S.C. Fedn. of Mus. Lutheran. Lodge: Rotary. Office: Charleston Mus 360 Meeting St Charleston SC 29403

BRUMLEY, IRA JON, oil and gas company executive; b. Pampa, Tex., 1939. B.B.A., U. Tex., 1961; M.B.A. Wharton Sch. Fin. U. Pa., 1963. Cons., Towers Perrin Forster & Crosby, Mgmt. Cons., 1964-67; with Southland Royalty Co., Fort Worth, 1967—, adminstrv. asst., 1967-69, asst. to pres., 1969-70, v.p., 1970-71, exec. v.p., 1971-73, pres., 1973-74, pres., chief exec. officer, 1974—, also dir. Office: Southland Royalty Co 200 InterFirst Tower Fort Worth TX 76102*

BRUNE, DAVID H., business executive; b. 1930. B.A., U. Tex., 1953, J.D., 1958. Sole practice, San Antonio, 1958-62; asst. mgr., mgr. San Antonio River Authority, 1962-68; mgr. Trinity River Authority, 1968-79; sr. exec. v.p. adminstrn. Southland Fin. Corp., 1979—; exec. v.p., chief operating officer Southland Land and Cattle Co.; pres., chief exec. officer Dallas County Utility and Reclamation Dist., 1982—.

BRUNE, KENNETH LEONARD, lawyer; b. Fort Madison, Iowa, Aug. 23, 1945; s. Bernard John and Colette Mary (Steffensmeier) B.; m. Judith Ann Sears, Oct. 17, 1970; children—James Bernard, Adrian Margaret, Sarah Anne. B.A., St. Ambrose Coll., 1967; M.A., U. Iowa, 1972; J.D., U. Tulsa, 1974. Bar: Iowa 1975, Okla. 1975, U.S. Dist. Ct. (we. and no. dist.) Okla. 1976, U.S. Ct. Appeals (10th cir.) 1976, U.S. Supreme Ct. 1980. Law clk. U.S. Dist. Ct. (no. dist.) Okla., Tulsa, 1975-77; asst. dist. atty., Tulsa County, Okla., 1977-78; judge dist. ct., Tulsa County, 1978-79; assoc. Holliman, Langholz, Runnels & Dorwart, Tulsa, 1980-81, ptnr., 1981-85; ptnr. Brune & Pezold, 1985—; gen. counsel Make Today Count, Tulsa, 1979-83, Okla. Oncology Nursing Soc., Tulsa, 1980-83; chmn. bd. Legal Services Eastern Okla., Tulsa, 1981, bd. mem., 1980—; judge temp. ct. appeals Okla. Supreme Ct., Tulsa, 1981; asst. prof. U. Tulsa Law Sch., 1984. Div. chmn. United Way, Tulsa, 1980-83. Served to 1st lt. U.S. Army, 1969-71, Vietnam. Decorated Bronze Star; St. Ambrose Coll. presdl. scholar, 1965-67. Mem. Okla. Bar Assn., Tulsa County Bar Assn. (speakers com. 1980-83), Delta Epsilon Sigma. Democrat. Roman Catholic. Home: 3519 S Florence Ave Tulsa OK 74105 Office: Brune & Pezold 6 E 5th St Suite 500 Sinclair Bldg Tulsa OK 74103

BRUNER, WILLIAM WALLACE, banker; b. Orangeburg, S.C., Nov. 6, 1920; s. Robert Raysor and Bessie (Livingston) R.; children—William W., Thomas W., James L. Acct. J.W. Hunt & Co., C.P.A.s, Columbia, S.C., 1945-48; with First Nat. Bank S.C., Columbia, 1948-84, sr. v.p., 1961-64, pres., 1964-84, also chmn. bd., dir.; pres., dir. First Bankshares Corp. S.C., 1972-84; chmn. S.C. Nat. Corp., 1984-85; dir. Spartan Mills, Spartanburg, S.C., Columbia Coca-Cola Bottling Co. S.C. Treas., United Fund Columbia, 1958-59, bd. dirs., 1956-58, chmn. large firms div., 1965, bd. dirs. treas., 1956-57; chmn. chpt. ARC, 1958-60, nat. fund vice chmn., 1960-61; trustee Providence Hosp., Columbia, chmn. fin. com., 1978-79, chmn. bd. trustees, 1980-82, mem. fin. com., treas., 1982—; trustee Bus. Partnership Found. U. S.C., Columbia, sec.-treas., 1972-73, chmn., 1985-86; treas. S.C. Soc. Crippled Children and Adults, 1967-70, v.p., 1970-71, pres., 1971-72; trustee Columbia Mus. Art and Sci., 1981—. Served to lt. comdr. USNR, 1941-45. C.P.A., S.C. Mem. Am. Inst. C.P.A.s, S.C. Assn. C.P.A.s, Columbia C. of C. (treas. 1961, v.p. 1962), Urban League Columbia (dir.), Am. (adv. com. on fed. legislation 1966-71, governing council 1972-74; dir. 1972-73, trustee fund for edn. in econs. 1976-77, chmn. 1977); S.C. (v.p. 1967-68, pres. 1970-71) bankers assns., U.S. C. of C. (banking, monetary and fiscal affairs com. 1977-79), Phi Beta Kappa, Beta Gamma Sigma, Sigma Nu. Methodist. Office: 1401 Main St Room 303B Columbia SC 29226

BRUNNER, THOMAS RUDOLPH, JR., telephone company public relations executive; b. Wichita, Kans., Sept. 20, 1946; s. Thomas R. and Mary Helen (Fitzgerald) B.; m. Lyndy Grant, Sept. 3, 1967; children—Sharon, Kylee. B.S. in Advt. and Pub. Relations, U. Kans., 1968. Accredited pub. relations. With Southwestern Bell, Topeka, 1968—, pub. relations mgr. Gulf Coast Region, Houston, 1980—. Pres. Greater Houston council Camp Fire; chmn. Midtown Assn. Winner Best Writing award, internat. competition Internat. Assn. Bus. Communicators, 1971. Mem. Soc. Consumer Affairs Profls. (pres. Houston chpt.), Pub. Relations Soc. Am., Corp., Relations Roundtable, Houston C. of C., Sigma Chi Alumni Assn. Home: 11007 Holly Springs Houston TX 77042 Office: 3100 Main Suite 1216 Houston TX 77001

BRUNO, ANGELO J., supermarket executive; b. 1922. With Bruno's Inc., Birmingham, Ala., 1946—, now pres., chief operating officer, also dir. Served with AUS, 1943-46. Office: Brunos Inc 2620 W 13th St Birmingham AL 35218*

BRUNO, JOSEPH, meat products company executive; b. 1914. With Bruno Bros., Birmingham, Ala., 1933-35; ptnr. Bruno's, Birmingham, 1935-46; owner Bruno's Inc., Birmingham, 1946—, chmn. bd., chief exec. officer. Address: Brunos Inc 2620 W 13th St W Birmingham AL 35218*

BRUNOW, CHARLES LLOYD, management consulting executive; b. New Orleans, Nov. 5, 1925; s. Henry F. and Eula M. Brunow; m. Gloria Yvonne Chandler, Nov. 2, 1945; children—Charles Lloyd, Susan, Sandra. B.S., Tex. A&M U., 1947. Registered profl. engr., Tex. Aerodynamic engr. McDonnell Aircraft Corp., St. Louis, 1947-51; lead engr. devel. Chance Vought, Dallas, 1951-55; chief aerodynamics, configuration mgr. Temco, Dallas, 1955-61; mgr. advanced system engring. Ling-Temco-Vought, Dallas, 1961-63, lance program dir., Warren, Mich., 1963-65; v.p. Ling-Temco-Vought Aerospace Corp., Warren, 1965-67, v.p. advanced programs Missiles and Space div., Dallas, 1967-69; v.p., gen. mgr. Kinetics Internat. div. LTV, 1969-71; pres., chmn. bd., founder Innocept, Inc., Dallas, 1971—. Served with USAAF, 1944-45. NSF grantee. Mem. Tau Beta Pi. Episcopalian. Club: Las Colinas Country. Home: 4009 Villa Grove Dallas TX 75252 Office: 1622A Beltline Rd Carrollton TX 75006

BRUNSON, GARION DENNIS, accountant; b. Dallas, Mar. 24, 1949; s. Roland Bryant and Cornia Helen (Crow) B.; B.B.A. in Acctg., Tex. Tech. U., 1971; m. Glenda Joy Slocumb, June 12, 1971; children—Jeffrey Glen, Joylynn. Instr., Tex. Bapt. Inst. and Sem., Henderson, 1971-74; instr. acctg. Commercial Coll., Odessa, Tex., 1975; acct. Howard Reed, Inc., Odessa, 1976-78; owner Garion Brunson, C.P.A., Odessa, 1978—. Mem. Odessa C. of C., Am. Inst. C.P.A.s, Tex. Soc. C.P.A.s, Tex. Restaurant Assn., Internat. Platform Assn. Republican. Baptist (fin. cons.; mem. bldg. com.). Clubs: Grandview Lions; Odessa Red Raider, Rotary. Home: 9017 Holiday St Odessa TX 79762 Office: 1207 W University St Odessa TX 79763

BRUNSON, LEON A., college administrator; b. Barnwell, S.C., Sept. 22, 1949; s. Ruebin and Mary Brunson; m. Carolyn Mackey, Sept. 2, 1972; children—Denise Darselle, Leon A. Jr. B.S., S.C. State Coll., 1973, M.Ed., 1981. Chief acct. Denmark Tech. Coll., S.C., 1973-78, bus. mgr., 1978—. Bd. dirs. Bamberg County Adult Devel. Ctr., Denmark, 1977-79. Recipient Presdl. award Denmark Tech. Coll., 1984. Mem. Nat. Assn. Accts., Nat. Assn. Coll. and Univ. Bus. Officers, So. Assn. Coll. and Univ. Bus. Officers, Bamberg C. of C. (bd. dirs. 1984-85). Club: Athletic Booster Denmark-Olar High Sch. (pres. 1984-85). Home: PO Box 459 Denmark SC 29042 Office: Denmark Tech Coll PO Box 327 Denmark SC 29042

BRUNSTETTER, MAUDE PHILLIPS, political science educator; b. Fayetteville, W.V., Mar. 12, 1931; d. George Erskine and Frances Virginia (Haptonstall) Phillips; m. George Worstall Brunstetter, Apr. 15, 1949 (div. 1976); 1 child, Mark Phillips. B.S. in Pub. Law, Columbia U., 1963, M.A. in Polit. Sci. and Govt., 1965, M. of Philosophy, 1976, Ph.D., 1981. Lectr., Fairleigh Dickinson U., Rutherford, N.J., 1966-68; Caldwell Coll., N.J., 1966-68, asst. prof., 1968-71; asst. prof. Salem Coll., W.Va., 1981, W. Va. State Coll., 1982—. Author: The Impact of the Reagan Administration on Higher Education, 1985; The Altomont Story, 1986. Contbr. articles to profl. jours. Mem. Fayette County Hist. Assn., W.Va., 1975—, Fayetteville Friends of the Library, W.Va., 1977—. Mem. Am. Polit. Sci. Assn., W.Va. Polit. Sci. Assn., Am. Acad. Polit. Sci., AAUW (div. rep. community affairs 1984-86, div. rep. cultural affairs 1982-84, task force chmn. Women's Worth, 1985), Phi Beta Kappa, Pi Sigma Alpha, Omicron Kappa. Democrat. Methodist. Home: 110 Fayette Ave Fayetteville WV 25840 Office: WVa State Coll Campus Box 115 Dept Polit Sci Institute WV 25112

BRUNTON, GEORGE DELBERT, educator, geologist; b. McGill, Nev., Dec. 20, 1924; s. Delbert W. and Mary Hilpa (Howey) B.; m. Gladys Ruth Wienke, Apr. 6, 1958; children—Stephen John, Kurt Michael. B.S., U. Nev., 1950; M.S., U. N.Mex., 1952; postgrad. Pa. State U., 1952-53; Ph.D., Ind. U., 1957. Research geologist Shell Devel. Co., 1953-55, Pure Oil Co., 1957-63, U.S. Gypsum Co., 1963-64, Oak Ridge Nat. Lab., 1964-80, Battelle Meml. Inst., 1980-82; chmn. dept. geology and geol. engring. U. Miss., University, 1983—. Served with U.S. Army, 1943-46. Fellow Am. Mineral. Soc. Contbr. articles to profl. jours. Office: Dept Geology and Geol Engring U Miss University MS 38677

BRUTON, JAY WARREN, JR., petroleum engineer; b. Perrin AFB, Grayson County, Tex., June 7, 1953; s. Jay Warren and Dorothy Jean (Braswell) B.; m. Jane Anne Earl, May 22, 1982 (div. July 1984). B.S. in Petroleum Engring., U. Tulsa, 1975; M.B.A., Houston Bapt. U., 1981. Drilling engr. Gulf Oil Corp., New Orleans, 1975-77, project engr., Houston, 1977-82; sr. drilling engr. AGIP Petroleum Co., Houston, 1982—. Deacon Woodhaven Baptist Ch., Houston, 1981. Mem. Soc. Petroleum Engrs. (jr.), Internat. Assn. Drilling Contractors (coordinating assoc. mem.). Republican. Baptist. Avocations: organist; raquetball; watersports. Home: 10515 Londonderry Dr Houston TX 77043 Office: AGIP Petroleum Co Inc 2950 N Loop W Suite 300 Houston TX 77092

BRYAN, CLARICE ADINA, lawyer; b. St. Thomas, V.I., Apr. 30, 1923; d. C. Arthur and Iza Anita (Lanclos) B.; A.B., Howard U., 1943; LL.B., Columbia U. and Howard U., 1949; 1 dau., Charlene Smith. Admitted to V.I. bar, 1950; tax assessor Govt. of V.I., 1950-60, asst. atty. gen., 1961-65, asst. commr. of labor, 1965-68, dir. consumer affairs, 1968-73; individual practice law, St. Thomas, 1950—; dir. People's Bank, 1971-75; trustee V.I. Retirement System. Vice pres. V.I. Constl. Conv., 1977, del., 1964, 81; mem. UN Status of Women Commn. Mem. ABA, Internat. Women Lawyers Assn., V.I. Bus. and Profl. Women (state pres. 1964-65). Roman Catholic. Home: 245A Bourne Field Saint Thomas VI 00801 Office: Room B2 Professional Bldg Saint Thomas VI 00801

BRYAN, CURTIS EUGENE, SR., educational administrator, consultant; b. Vanceboro, N.C., Sept. 6, 1938; s. Alfred Hilton and Betty Louise (Green) B.; m. Bethel Ellen Cherry, Oct. 9, 1959; children—Shuronia, Curtis, Jr., Daphne, Jennifer. B.S., Elizabeth City State U., 1960; student Va. State Coll., 1962-63, Coll. William and Mary, 1965-66, Old Dominion U., 1967-68; M.Ed., Temple U., 1968; Ph.D., NYU, 1977. Asst. prin. Portsmouth (Va.) Pub. Schs., 1966-68; dir. admissions Elizabeth City (N.C.) State U., 1968-70; asst. acad. dean, dir. continuing edn. and summer programs Del. State Coll., Dover, 1970-78; head div. edn. and human devel., dir. tchr. edn. Fayetteville (N.C.) State U., 1978-80; exec. v.p. Va. State U., Petersburg, 1980-82, interim pres., 1982-83, exec. v.p., 1983, v.p. adminstrn., 1983—. Author: Historically Black Colleges, 1977. Voter registration leader Petersburg NAACP, 1982-83. Recipient Dist. Service award City of Petersburg, 1982, Alpha Phi Alpha, 1967; named Most Outstanding Grad., Elizabeth City State U., 1960. Mem. NEA, Am. Assn. Higher Edn., Kappa Delta Pi, Phi Delta Kappa, Sigma Rho Sigma. Baptist. Home: 3360 Oakwood Circle Petersburg VA 23805 Office: Va State Univ Petersburg VA 23803

BRYAN, FRANK LEON, microbiologist, consultant, researcher; b. Indpls., Aug. 29, 1930; s. Frank Leslie and Marie Georgia (Vogt) B.; m. Ruth Ann McDonald, Aug. 30, 1952; children—Steven Harris, Sharryl Ann. B.S., Ind. U., 1953; M.P.H., U. Mich., 1956; Ph.D., Iowa State U., 1965. Instr. U. Mass., Amherst, 1956-58, also tng. officer New Eng. Field Tng. Sta.; tng. officer in environ. health Communicable Disease Ctr., Atlanta, 1958-63, research in salmonella, Ames, 1963-65; chief foodborne disease activity and scientist dir. Ctrs. for Disease Control, Atlanta, 1965-85; cons. in food safety and tng., Tucker, Ga., adj. prof. Emory U., Atlanta; sec. Internat. Commn. on Microbiol. Specifications for Foods, mem. com. Nat. Research Council, Nat. Acad. Scis.; lectr. foodborne disease epidemiology and control. Served to 1st lt. U.S. Army, 1953-55, to capt. USPHS, 1956-85. Recipient Norbert Sherman award, 1979, 82; Meritous Service medal USPHS, 1981. Mem. Am. Soc. Microbiology, Inst. Food Technologists, Internat. Assn. Milk, Food and Environ. Sanitarians, World Assn. Veterinary Food Hygienists (v.p.), Am. Pub. Health Assn., Nat. Assn. Sanitarians, Sigma Xi, Phi Tau Sigma, Gamma Sigma Delta. Author: (with Riemann) Foodborne Infections and Intoxications, 2d edit., 1979; (with others) Microorganisms in Foods 1, 1978, Microbiological Ecology for Foods, Vol. 1 and 2, 1980; Diseases Transmitted by Foods, 1982; contbr. articles to profl. jours.

BRYAN, HOB, lawyer, state senator; b. Amory, Miss., Dec. 5, 1952; s. Wendell Hobdy and Nadine (Morgan) B. B.A., Miss. State U., 1974; J.D., U. Va., 1977. Bar: Miss. 1977. Sole practice, Amory, 1977—; mem. Miss. Senate, 1984—. Democrat. Baptist. Office: Box 75 Amory MS 38821

BRYAN, JIM HUGH, insurance and investment company executive; b. Oklahoma City, Aug. 10, 1944; s. Everett P. and Lemma E. (Moore) B.; m. Pamela S. Jones, Dec. 19, 1964; children—Sharla, Vanessa. B.S. in Psychology, Bethany Nazarene Coll., 1968; M.S. in Psychology, Okla. State U., 1970. C.L.U.; chartered fin. cons. Pvt. practice psychology, Northeastern Iowa, 1970-77; owner, mgr. Bryan Farms, Edmond, Okla., 1977-79; owner, pres. Bryan Ins. and Investment Co., Edmond, 1979—. Chmn. Econ. Devel. Council, Edmond, 1981-82; bd. dirs. Edmond Indsl. Trust Authority; mem. commn. for city ordinance devel. City of Edmond, 1982. Recipient Property Co. award Shelter Ins. Munich (W.Ger.), 1982. Democrat. Lutheran. Clubs: Am. Businessmen's, Edmond Exchange. Lodge: Masons. Home: 427 Ramblewood Terr Edmond OK 73034 Office: Bryan Ins & Investment Co 111 N Broadway Suite B Edmond OK 73034

BRYAN, VIRGINIA SCHMITT, educational administrator; b. Ironwood, Mich., Jan. 25, 1922; d. John Arvid and Emily Virginia (Norvell) Schmitt; m. Paul Robey Bryan, Jr., Aug. 27, 1941; children—Paul John, Elizabeth Virginia Bryan Dover. B.S., U. Mich., 1948, M.S., 1950; Ph.D., Duke U., 1955. Research assoc. in botany Duke U., Durham, N.C., 1953-65, asst. dean, sr. research assoc. in botany, 1965—, coordinator for curriculum, 1975—. NSF grantee, 1973-75. Mem. AAAS, Am. Bryol. Soc. (sec. 1957-59), Sigma Xi (sec. chpt. 1979-83). Researcher cytobryology, 1953-75. Home: 1108 Watts St Durham NC 27701 Office: 113 Allen Bldg Duke Univ Durham NC 27706

BRYANT, CHARLES EDWARD, SR., computer scientist, aerospace executive; b. Atlanta, July 15, 1924; s. John Thomas and Mary (Driskell) B.; m. Elizabeth Roberson, Dec. 24, 1950; children—Charles Edward, Jr., Michelle P. A.B., Morehouse Coll., 1949; B.Arch., Howard U., 1955; cert. Emory U., 1969. Engring. technician Lockheed Ga., Co., Marietta, Ga., 1956; programmer, 1956-58, supr., programmer, 1958-67, dept. mgr., 1967-82, div. mgr., 1982—; cons. AID, Washington, 1964. Mem. Nat. Security Seminar, Carlisle Barracks, Pa., 1976; bd. dirs. Goodwill Industries, Atlanta, 1968—, Marist Coll., Atlanta, 1969. Recipient Equal Opportunity award Atlanta Urban League, 1960; named Man of Yr., Lockheed Mgmt. Club, 1974, Man of Yr. Omega Psi Phi, 1962. Mem. Nat. Mgmt. Assn. (bd. commrs., Man of Yr. 1974), Assn. Computing Machinery, Atlanta C. of C., NAACP (bd. dirs. 1974), Atlanta Gardsman (pres. 1968-69), Omega Psi Phi. Methodist. Avocations: architecture; art; tennis; swimming. Home: 648 Waterford Rd NW Atlanta GA 30318 Office: Lockheed Ga Co 86 S Cobb Dr Marietta GA 30063

BRYANT, DEBORAH REID, university official, counselor, student affairs; b. Elmira, N.Y., Dec. 31, 1950; d. Wilbur James and Beatrice (Bonner) Reid; m. Cleveland Walker Bryant, Jr., July 3, 1976; 1 child, Jason Reid. B.S. in Phys. Edn., Health, Recreation, Boston U., 1972; M.Ed. in Counseling, SUNY-Brockport, 1975. Cert. counselor. Asst. dir. ednl. opportunity program Corning Community Coll., N.Y., 1972-73; child devel. practitioner, cons. Comprehensive Interdisciplinary Devel., Elmira, N.Y., 1973-74; asst. dir. student activities Monroe Community Coll., Rochester, N.Y., 1975-77; asst. dean student devel. U. New Orleans, 1978-81; dir. ctr. commuter services Loyola U., New Orleans, 1981—. Bd. dirs., family life task force S. Central Conf. United Ch. of Christ. Afro-Am. scholar Boston U., 1972. Mem. So. Assn. Coll. Student Affairs, La. Assn. Women Deans, Adminstrs. and Counselors, Assn. Coll. Unions Internat., Nat. Entertainment and Campus Activities Assn., Am. Assn. Counseling and Devel., Am. Coll. Personnel Assn. (mem. various coms.), La. Coll. Personnel Assn. (mem. exec. bd.), Delta Sigma Theta. Democrat. Avocations: walking; exercising; reading. Office: Loyola U 6363 St Charles Ave New Orleans LA 70118

BRYANT, GEORGE MACON, chemist; b. Anniston, Ala., Aug. 3, 1926; s. Fred Boyd and Jessie Elizabeth (Macon) B.; m. Mary Lee Miles, Sept. 9, 1950; children—Fred Boyd II, George Macon. B.S. in Physics, Auburn U., 1948; M.S., Inst. Textile Tech., 1950; Ph.D., Princeton U., 1954. Research chemist research and devel. ctr. Union Carbide Corp., South Charleston, W.Va., 1954-58, group leader, 1958-66, assoc. dir., 1966-75, corp. research fellow, 1975—. Served with USN, 1944-46. Fellow Textile Inst.; mem. Am. Chem. Soc. (award for sci. achievement 1979), Am. Assn. Textile Chemists (Milson award 1982), Fiber Soc. (award for disting. early achievement 1964), Sigma Xi, Phi Kappa Phi. Democrat. Presbyterian. Contbr. articles to profl. jours.; patentee in field. Home: 1204 Williamsburg Way Charleston WV 25314

BRYANT, HENRY HERBERT, surgeon; b. Welaka, Fla., Feb. 1, 1921; s. Henry Herbert and Sara (Harris) B.; B.S., Emory U., 1942, M.D., 1944; m. Jean Quick, June 23, 1945; children—Carol Anne, Elizabeth Gail, Lauren Jean. Intern, 1944-45; practice medicine specializing in surgery, Coral Gables, Fla., 1952—; clin. prof. surgery U. Miami Med. Sch., 1983—; mem. staff South

Miami Hosp. (Fla.), Doctors Hosp., Coral Gables, Fla. Served to capt. M.C., AUS, 1945-47. Mem. AMA, Fla. Med. Assn., Dade County Med. Assn., Southeastern Surg. Assn., ACS. Republican. Methodist. Diplomate Am. Bd. Surgery. Home: 7340 SW 77th Ct Miami FL 33143 Office: 1544 Venera Ave Coral Gables FL 33146

BRYANT, HOWARD LOUIS, real estate appraiser and broker, cons., farmer; b. Drewryville, Va., Dec. 7, 1921; s. Lewis Harum and Bessie Elizabeth (Vick) B.; student U. Va., Va. Commonwealth U.; m. Maude Gertrude Bryant, June 5, 1942; children—Stephen L., Robyn Denise. Owner, operator Merrydale Farm, Boykins, Va., 1941—, Boykins Hardware Co., also Boykins Tractor & Implement Co., 1947-50; contractor, real estate developer, 1950-62; sr. appraiser Va. Dept. Hwys., 1963—; pres. Howard L. Bryant and Assocs., Ltd., 1986—; guest lectr. Mem. Colonial Heights (Va.) Bd. Zoning Appeals. Mem. Am. Soc. Appraisers (sr. mem.), Assn. Fed. Appraisers, Am. Right of Way Assn., Nat. Assn. Review Appraisers. Baptist. Clubs: Engineers, 2001. Lodges: Lions (dir.), Masons, Shriners, Order Eastern Star. Home: 300 Nottingham Dr Colonial Heights VA 23834 Office: Howard L Bryant & Assocs 300 Nottingham Dr PO Box 415 Colonial Heights VA 23834 also Hwy 670 PO Box 381 Boykins VA 23827

BRYANT, IRA HOUSTON, III, lawyer; b. San Antonio, Aug. 30, 1942; s. Ira Houston and Florence (Kimberlin) B.; m. Judith Ann Bryant, Mar. 13, 1971; children—Ira Houston IV, Andrew Nelson, Jennifer Ann. B.A., Oklahoma City U., 1965, J.D., 1973. Bar: Okla., 1973. Physicist, White Sands Missile Range, N.Mex., 1965-70; ins. adjuster U.S. Fidelity & Guaranty Co., Oklahoma City, 1971-72; assoc. Robert Leyton Wheeler, Inc., Oklahoma City, 1973-77, Kerr, Davis, Irvine, Krasnow, Rhodes & Semtner, Oklahoma City, 1977-79; ptnr. Bryant & Scribner, Oklahoma City, 1979-83, Claunch, Bryant & Scribner, 1983—. Mem. Oklahoma City Mineral Lawyers Soc., Oklahoma City Title Attys. Assn., Rocky Mountain Mineral Law Found., Phi Delta Phi. Republican. Methodist. Club: Sportsman's Country (Oklahoma City). Home: 6001 N State Oklahoma City OK 73122 Office: 710 Union Plaza 3030 Northwest Expressway Oklahoma City OK 73112

BRYANT, JOHN BRADBURY, economics educator, consultant; b. Washington, July 7, 1947; s. Royal Calvin and Martha Preble (Jones) B.; m. Evelyn Sandra Seltzer, June 24, 1973; 1 child, Aryn Royale. B.A., Oberlin Coll., 1969; M.S., Carnegie-Mellon U., 1973, Ph.D., 1975. Economist, Bd. Govs. FRS, Washington, 1974-77; sr. economist Fed. Reserve Bank, Mpls., 1977-81; assoc. prof. U. Fla., Gainesville, 1980-81; cons. Fed. Reserve Bank, Dallas, 1983—; Fox assoc. prof. Rice U., Houston, 1981-84, Fox prof. econs., 1984—. Contbr. articles to profl. jours. Office: Dept Econs Rice U PO Box 1892 Houston TX 77251

BRYANT, JOHN WILEY, congressman; b. Lake Jackson, Tex., Feb. 22, 1947; s. Robert Link and Billie Rae (Willey) B.; m. Janet Elizabeth Watts, Dec. 28, 1968; children—Amy, John Wiley, Jordan. B.A., So. Meth. U., 1969; J.D., So. Meth. U., 1972. Bar: Tex. 1972. Atty. at law Stanford and Bryant, Dallas, 1972—; chief counsel Tex. senate Subcom. on Consumer Protection, Austin, 1973; adminstrv. asst. Tex. Senate, Austin, Dallas, 1972-73; mem. Tex. Ho. of Reps., 1973-82, 98th Congress from 5th dist. Tex.; mem. exec. com. U.S. Ho. dem. Study Group, 1983. Named Hardest Working Mem. Tex. Capital Press Corps., 1977, Outstanding Legislator Tex. Monthly Mag., 1977, 79, One of Five Outstanding Young Texans Tex. Jaycees, 1979. Mem. Old Scyene Hist. Soc., Hist. Preservation Soc., Deaf Action Center Dallas (bd. dirs.), Lion's Eye Bank (Dallas) (life). Democrat. Methodist. Lodge: Rotary. Home: 8035 E R L Thornton St Dallas TX 75228 Office: US Ho of Reps 506 Cannon House Office Bldg Washington DC 20515

BRYANT, JUDSON STURGIS, architect; b. Charlotte, N.C., Oct. 4, 1950; s. Judson Sturgis and Cecelia Francis (Ferrari) B. B.Arch., Pratt Inst., 1974; postgrad. Clayton Coll., 1975-76. Registered architect, Ga. Designer, Dorothy Draper, Inc., N.Y.C., 1972-73; v.p. Space Mgmt. Cons., N.Y.C., 1973-76; jud. facility cons. State of Ga., Atlanta, 1976-80; chief exec. officer Byrant Architect, Ltd., Avondale Estates, Ga., 1980—; tech. asst. Am. U., Washington, 1973-84; mem. faculty Nat. Coll. State Judiciary, Reno, Nev., 1975-76; adv. Nat. Rural Ctr., Washington, 1979-80. Mem. com. for hist. preservation State Bar of Ga., Atlanta, 1982; com. mem. Goals for DeKalb, Decatur, Ga., 1984; mem. Devel. Authority, Avondale Estates, 1985. Mem. AIA, Constrn. Specifications Inst. Atlanta, Am. Judicature Soc., Avondale Estates C. of C. Roman Catholic. Avocations: trap, skeet shooting; fly fishing; canoeing. Office: Bryant Architect Ltd PO Box 99 120 Avondale Rd B-2 Avondale Estates GA 30002

BRYANT, LELAND MARSHAL, advertising executive; b. Gainesville, Ga., Apr. 28, 1950; s. William Marcus and Perrie Lou (Milner) B.; student (Alfred P. Sloan fellow) Vanderbilt U., 1968-70; B.B.A. with honors, U. Tex., Austin, 1972; M.B.A. (William E. Newcomb fellow), U. Pa., 1978; m. Rebecca Lea Biegert, Sept. 2, 1973; children—Shauna Rebecca, Natalie Anne, Marcus Bradley, Preston Jacob. Staff asst. Southwestern Life Ins. Co., Dallas, 1973; comml. real estate salesman, Dallas, 1974; mgr. Southwestern Life Ins. Co., Dallas, 1975-76; accountant Arthur Andersen & Co., Dallas, 1978-81; v.p. fin. Walter Bennett Co., Dallas, 1981—. Mem. Am. Inst. C.P.A.s, Tex. Soc. C.P.A.s. Home: 9205 Club Glen Dr Dallas TX 75243 Office: Suite 600 16479 Dallas Pkwy Dallas TX 75248

BRYANT, MICHAEL DAVID, engineering educator, researcher; b. Danville, Ill., Feb. 8, 1951; s. David Kinley and Helen (Jacob) B.; m. Eugenia Sturino, Sept. 9, 1978; children—David, Daniella, Christina. B.S., U. Ill.-Chgo., 1972; M.S., Northwestern U., 1980, Ph.D., 1981. Asst. prof. engring. N.C. State U., Raleigh, 1981-85, assoc. prof., 1985—. Contbr. articles to profl. jours. Recipient Presdl. Young Investigator award NSF, 1985. Mem. ASME, IEEE, Soc. Mfg. Engrs., Soc. Indsl. and Applied Math. Avocations: weightlifting; music. Office: NC State U Raleigh NC 27695

BRYANT, RICHARD MILES, clinical psychologist; b. Princeton, Ill., June 6, 1932; s. Miles William and Amanda (Kaar) B.; m. Patricia Ruth Patton, Aug. 20, 1955; children—Richard Miles, Jr., William Patton, Melissa Ruth. B.A., Washington U., St. Louis, 1954; student U. Iowa, 1954-55; Ph.D., U. Tex., 1958. Diplomate Am. Bd. Profl. Psychology. Chief clin. psychology sect. Mental Hygiene Consultation Service, Ft. Leonard Wood, Mo., 1958-60; supr. psychol. services Juvenile Residential Treatment Program, State Hosp., Fulton, Mo., 1960-63; part-time asst. prof. psychology Lincoln U., Jefferson City, Mo., 1960-63; spl. lectr. William Woods Coll., Fulton, Mo., 1960-63; sr. clin. psychologist Children's Med. Ctr., Tulsa, 1963-64, dir. psychol. services, 1964-75; pvt. practice clin. psychology, Tulsa, 1975—; past chmn. Okla. Bd. Examiners Psychologists. Mem. Am. Psychol. Assn., Midwestern Psychol. Assn., Southwestern Psychol. Assn., Okla. Psychol. Assn. (sec.-treas. 1969-71, pres. 1972-73), Am. Soc. Clin. Hypnosis, Tulsa Psychol. Assn. (past pres.), Sigma Xi, Kappa Alpha. Home: 5353 S Joplin Ave Tulsa OK 74135 Office: Springer Clinic 6160 S Yale Ave Tulsa OK 74136

BRYANT, ROBERT PARKER, restaurant company executive; b. S.I., N.Y., May 12, 1922; s. Thomas Vincent and Rosanna (McRoberts) B.; m. Barbara Carlson, Nov. 13, 1953; children—Elizabeth, Robert, Christine, Cahterine, Martha. B.S., Cornell U., 1947. Food mgr. Pa. R.R. Dining Car System, 1952-56; cons. Booz Allen & Hamilton, N.Y.C., 1956-58; v.p. Frank G. Shattuck Co., N.Y.C., 1958-66; group v.p. Marriott Corp., Washington, 1966-74; v.p. Marc's Big Boy Corp. (Marriott franchise), Milw., 1974-75; group v.p. Burger King Corp., Miami, Fla., 1975-76; pres. Dobbs Houses, Inc. subs. Squibb Corp., 1976—; vice chmn., dir. Carson Pirie Scott & Co., 1980—, West Electric Co., Toronto, Ont., Can.; dir. Commerce Union Bank, Memphis. Bd. dirs. Goodwill of Memphis, Goodwill of Am., Boy Scouts Am.; mem. curriculum council Memphis Bd. Edn. Mem. Nat. Restaurant Assn., Phi Delta Theta. Clubs: N.Y. Athletic, Touchdown of N.Y., Econ., Univ. (Memphis); Union League (Chgo.). Lodge: Rotary. Home: 1217 Brookfield Rd Memphis TN 38117 Office: Dobbs Houses Inc 5100 Poplar Ave Memphis TN 38137*

BRYANT, TERRY COLON, printing company executive; b. Oakland, Calif., Oct. 15, 1944; s. James Terrell and Billye Bess (Hunt) B.; m. Judith Carol Ferguson, Dec. 17, 1965 (div. 1980); children—Kristi Lynn, Jason Kyle, Cody Blake, James Anthony; m. Janet Garrison, Feb. 8, 1954. B.S., U. Tex.-Arlington, 1967. Basic line engr. Gen. Dynamics, Fort Worth, 1967-69; design engr. dist. 2, Tex. Hwy. Dept., Fort Worth, 1969-71; gen. mgr. East Side Printing, 1971-72; sales Colorcraft, 1972-74; sales mgr. Sprint Press, 1974-78; v.p. TM Graphics, 1978—. Recipient Disting. Salesman award Sales and Mktg. Execs. Ft. Worth. Mem. Printing Industries Am., Master Printers Am., Ft. Worth C. of C., West Tex. C. of C., Tex. Assn. Businesses, Ad Club of Ft. Worth. Republican. Baptist. Club: Sertoma. Office: TM Graphics 2924 Bledsoe Fort Worth TX 76114

BRYANT, THOMAS MONROE, newspaper publisher; b. Florence, S.C., Oct. 7, 1941; s. Monroe Lucas and Evelyn (Fore) B.; m. Linda Kay Stutts, Aug. 14, 1965; 1 child, Thomas Monroe, Jr. A.A., Brevard Coll., 1962; B.A., Elon Coll., 1965. With circulation dept. Daily Times News, Burlington, N.C., 1965-66, advt. rep., 1966-70, asst. advt. mgr., 1970-72, advt. mgr., 1972-76; pub. City County News & Outlook, Burlington, 1976—; dir. 4th Estate Inc., Burlington. Editor (mag.) Co. Shops Mall (award), 1977, Outlet Outlook (award), 1981. Pres. Alamance dist. Boy Scouts Am., Burlington, 1984. Served with USMCR, 1961-67. Mem. N.C. Press Inst., Nat. Advt. Execs. Assn. (v.p. 1975-76), Mid Atlantic Advt. Assn., Alamance Wildlife Club, Alamance County Conservation Club. Avocations: duck hunting; raising labrador retrievers; canoeing; camping. Home: 506 N Gurney St Burlington NC 27215 Office: City County News & Outlook 223 E Davis St Burlington NC 27215

BRYANT, TIMOTHY KENT, industrial engineer, automotive company executive; b. Goshen, Ind., June 4, 1946; s. Kenneth M. and Ruby E. (Deafenbaugh) B.; m. Barbara J. Baldwin, June 14, 1970; children—Kevin Scott, Jonathan Edward, Ted Allan. B.S. in Indsl. Engring., Purdue U., 1968; M.S. in Engring. Adminstrn., U. Tenn., 1980. Indsl. engr. Bendix Energy Controls div. Bendix Corp., South Bend, Ind., 1968-70, Bendix Automotive Service, South Bend, 1970-73, sr. indsl. engr. Bendix Automotive Aftermarket, Jackson, Tenn., 1973-81, supr. indsl. engring., 1981—; div. EPA coordinator, 1980—. Pres. Beech Bluff PTA, 1980-83; pres. council Madison County PTA, 1983—; pres. Families in Action, 1985—; supt. Beech Bluff United Methodist Ch. Mem. Am. Inst. Indsl. Engrs., Am. Soc. Safety Engrs. Republican. Home: RD 2 Box 5 Beech Bluff TN 38313 Office: Bendix-Automotive 1094 Bendix Dr Jackson TN 38301

BRYANT, WINSTON, lieutenant governor of Arkansas; b. Donaldson, Ark., Oct. 3, 1938. B.A., Ouachita Bapt. U., 1960; LL.B., U. Ark., 1963; LL.M. in Adminstrv. Law, George Washington U., 1970. Bar: Ark. bar 1963. Individual practice law, Malvern, Ark., 1964-66, 71-75; atty. Ark. Ins. Commn., 1966; asst. U.S. atty. for Eastern Dist. Ark., 1967; legis. asst. to Senator from Ark., 1968-71; dep. pros. atty. Hot Spring County, Ark., 1971-75; mem. Ark. Ho. of Reps., 1973-76; sec. of state State of Ark., Little Rock, 1976-80, lt. gov., 1981—; instr. polit. sci. Ouachita Bapt. U., 1971-73, Henderson (Ark.) State U., 1973—. Mem. Ark. Youth Services Planning Adv. Council, 1974, Ark. Gov.'s Ad Hoc Com. on Workmen's Compensation, 1975. Served to capt., inf. U.S. Army, 1963-64. Mem. ABA, Ark. Bar Assn. (ho. of dels.), Malvern C. of C. (pres. 1972), Am. Legion, Ark. Farm Bur. Baptist. Office: Office of Lt Gov State Capitol Little Rock AR 72201*

BRYSON, ALAN DOUGLAS, pharmacist; b. Anderson, S.C., Aug. 31, 1955; s. Melvin Talmage and Romola C. (Collins) B.; m. Charlene Margaret Work, Dec. 20, 1975; 1 child, Lori Ann. B.S. in Chemistry, Cumberland Coll., 1977; B.S. in Pharmacy, Samford U., 1980. Registered pharmacist, Ala. Analytical chemist So. Testing Labs., Birmingham, Ala., 1977-78; intern pharmacist Big B Drugs, Birmingham, 1980-81; registered pharmacist Big B Drugs, Dothan, Ala. 1981—. Recipient Eagle Scout award Boy Scouts of Am., 1970. Mem. Wireglass Pharm. Assn., Ala. Pharm. Assn., Dothan Jaycees, Kappa Psi. Republican. Baptist. Avocations: guitar; tennis. Home: 23 Chadwick Circle Dothan AL 36301 Office: Big B Discount Drugs Inc 833 S Oates St Dothan AL 36301

BRYSON, FRED WYLIE, psychologist, educator; b. Midlothian, Tex., July 2, 1922; s. Charles Wilburn and Mollie Lee (Wylie) B.; m. Vivian E. Hintze, Sept. 8, 1950; 1 son, Mark H. B.A., Bethel Coll., 1943; D.Div., 1981; M.A., Scarrit Coll., 1945; Ph.D., N.Tex. State U., 1963; L.H.D. (hon.), Baker U., 1978; postgrad. Vanderbilt U., So. Methodist U., UCLA. Lic. psychologist, Tex. Tchr., Calico Rork High Sch. (Ark.), 1943-44; mem. faculty Colegio Americana, U. Columbia, Cali, 1945-47; mem. faculty So. Methodist U., Dallas, 1947—, prof. counseling, dir. liberal arts degree program, 1968—; dean students, internat. programs, Fulbright lectr U. San Marios, Lima, Peru, 1967; interim pres. Bethel Coll., McKenzie, Tenn., 1975, chmn. bd., 1975—; dir. Presbyterian Village North and Health Care Ctr.; sole practice psychologist, Dallas, 1971—; cons. Coca Cola Bottling Co., Dallas, Baton Rouge, Flynn Co. Trustee, Presbyterian Hosp., Dallas; pres. Dallas UN Assn.; sponsor Blue Key Nat. Honor Fraternity. Recipient Disting. service award Bethel Coll.; Fulbright lectr. Lima, Peru. Mem. Am. Psychol. Assn., Tex. Psychol. Assn., Dallas Psychol. Assn., Am. Personnel Assn., Tex. Personnel Assn., Presbyterian. Lodge: Masons. Spl. aide to Bob Hope, 1972 Christmas Tour; bldg. named Bryson Hall, Shiloh Presbyterian Ch., Midlothian, Tex. Home: 3504 Villanova Dallas TX 75225 Office: So Methodist U Dallas TX 75275

BRYSON, LEE, groceries company executive. Exec. v.p. Piggly Wiggly Corp., Jacksonville, Fla. Office: Piggly Wiggly Corp PO Box 149 Jacksonville FL 32201*

BUBRIG, ROSS VINCENT, industrial company executive; b. New Orleans, Oct. 27, 1950; s. Steve Gerald and Maude Anabelle (Buras) B.; m. Susan Julia Bonneval, July 14, 1973; children—Michael Ross, Adrianne S. B.S. in Elec. Engring., La. State U., 1973. Registered prof. engr., La. Field engr. SECO Industries, Inc., Harvey, La., 1973-74, asst. mgr. Harvey dist., 1974-75, fabrication mgr., 1975-76, Houston dist. mgr., 1976-77, project mgr., Baton Rouge, La., 1977-78, internat. sales engr., Harvey, 1978-80, mgr. internat. ops., 1980-83, v.p. internat. ops., 1983—. Bd. dirs. OLPH Sch. Mem. La. Engring. Soc. Roman Catholic.

BUCELO, ARMANDO J., JR., lawyer; b. Havana, Cuba, Sept. 18, 1952; came to U.S., 1962; s. Armando De Jesus and Maria Del Carmen (Menendez) B.; m. Beatriz del Calvo, Nov. 20, 1981. A.A., Miami U., 1973; B.S., U. Miami (Fla.), 1976, J.D., 1979. Bar: Fla. 1979. Assoc. Snyder Stern & Young, Miami, 1977-78, Fuller & Feingold, Miami, 1978-79; sr. ptnr. Castrillo & Bucelo, Miami, 1979-81; sr. ptnr. Law Offices of Armando J. Bucelo, Jr., Miami, 1981—; atty. City of Miami Youth Baseball Acad.; legal advisor assns. Contbg. author: Condominium & Cluster Housing, 1979; newspaper columnist. Atty., bd. dirs. Dade County Republican party; bd. dirs. YMCA Internat. Club, ARC, Latin br.; bd. dirs. Crime Prevention, Miami; mem. Dade County Rental Housing Authority Bd.; v.p., dir. Downtown Miami Bus. Assn. Recipient Optimist Honor award, 1971; Sertoma Honor award, 1971; YMCA Honor Man award, 1972, 77, 83; Deportes Mag. award, 1972; Lincoln-Marti award, 1971; City of Miami Appreciation award, 1979; Dade County Appreciation award, 1979; Fla. Lions Athletic Assn. Honor award, 1982; Liceo Martiano Man of Yr. award, 1983; One of 100 Most Influential Hispanics in U.S., Hispanic Bus. Mag. Mem. Fla. Bar, Dade County Bar Assn., ABA, Assn. Trial Lawyers Am., Acad. Fla. Trial Lawyers, Assn. Immigration and Naturalization Lawyers, Inter-Am. Bar, Cuban Am. Bar Assn. (v.p., dir.). Republican. Roman Catholic. Clubs: Cuban Sertoma (dir.), Optimists (pres.), Am. Office: 1950 SW 27th Ave Miami FL 33145

BUCHAN, DOUGLAS CHARLES, petroleum co. exec.; b. Bklyn., Aug. 4, 1936; s. Charles J. and Amelia P. (Petraca) B.; student U. Fla., 1954-56; m. Beverly Ann Wilcox, Mar. 7, 1970; 1 son, Paul Douglas. Pres., Buchan Gas Co., St. Petersburg, Fla., 1955—, Buchan Oil Co., St. Petersburg, 1966—, Site Mgmt. Inc., St. Petersburg, 1975—, Grill Parts Distbrs. Pres., Pinellas County Republican Ivory Club; chmn. Pinellas campaign George Bush for Pres., also chmn. various polit. campaigns; mem. White House Advance Team for Fla., U.S. Senate Small Bus. Adv. Com., 1984-86. Served to 1st lt. U.S. Army, 1958-65. Mem. Nat. Oil Jobbers Council, Nat. Liquified Petroleum Gas Assn., Fla. Petroleum Marketers Assn. (v.p.), Oil Fuel Inst. Fla. (pres., chmn. bd.). Episcopalian. Club: St. Petersburg Yacht. Home: 1067 42d Ave NE Saint Petersburg FL 33703 Office: Buchan Oil Co 4555 38th St N Saint Petersburg FL 33714

BUCHAN, RUSSELL PAUL, gas company executive, publisher; b. St. Petersburg, Fla., May 24, 1947; s. Charles Joseph and Amelia (Petraca) B.; B.S. in Econs. magna cum laude, Stetson U., 1969; M.A., Vanderbilt U., 1975. Asst. to pub. Trend Publs., Tampa, Fla., 1971-74; book editor South Mag., Tampa, 1973-74; owner, v.p. Buchan Gas Co., St. Petersburg, 1968—, v.p., gen. mgr., 1975—; pub. Buchan Publs., St. Petersburg, 1980—; host radio talk show Sta. WTAN, Clearwater, Fla. Mem. Pinellas County Gas Adv. Bd., 1979—, vice chmn., 1982-83; bd. dirs. Eckerd Coll. Library Friends, 1971—, chmn., 1982. Recipient Outstanding Sr. award Stetson U., 1969; Woodrow Wilson fellow, 1969. Mem. St. Petersburg Mus. Fine Arts, Pinellas County Gas Assn. (sec.-treas. 1977-78, pres. 1979-80), Fla. Young Gassers (dist. dir. 1979-81), Nat. LP Gas Assn., Fla. LP Gas Assn. (dir. 1979-81), Fla. Mag. Assn. (treas. 1974-75), Internat. Wine and Food Soc. (br. chmn. St. Petersburg 1979-80), Confrerie de la Chaine des Rotisseurs, Brotherhood Knights of Vine, Order of Dali. Republican. Roman Catholic. Contbr. book revs. and articles on wine to various publs. Office: Buchan Gas Co 6150 49th St N St Petersburg FL 33709

BUCHANAN, BRUCE, II, political science educator; b. Shelby, Mont., July 28, 1945; s. Neil and Dorothy Jean (Gallup) B.; m. Susan Safford Bright, June 10, 1964 (div. June 1976); m. Stephanie Ann Sokolewicz, Jan. 3, 1981; children—Kathryn Elaine, Douglas Neil. A.B., Stanford U., 1967; M.A., Yale U., 1969, M.Philosophy, 1970, Ph.D., 1972. Prof., U. Ga., Athens, 1973-74, U. Tex., Austin, 1974—; cons. U.S. Dept. HHS, Washington, 1979-80. Author: The Presidential Experience, 1978; The Citizens Presidency, 1986. Mem. Am. Polit. Sci. Assn., Presidency Research Group, Am. Soc. Pub. Adminstrn., Ctr. Study Presidency. Avocations: sports, gardening. Home: 1304 Wilshire Blvd Austin TX 78722 Office: U Tex Dept Govt Austin TX 78712

BUCHANAN, EMMETT LASCAR, JR., sales executive; b. Detroit, Feb. 1, 1920; s. Emmett Lascar and Lillian (Kreekun) B.; m. Betty Jean Pounders, June 30, 1951 (dec. 1977); children—Shirley Jean, Nancy Joyce; m. 2d, Elsie Gaynell Hunter, July 3, 1978. Student U. Mo., 1938-39. Salesman Bankers Life Ins. Co., John Hancock Ins. Co., Proctor & Gamble, 1940-42, Health-Mor, Chgo., 1942-45; regional mgr. Animal Health div. Burroughs Wellcome Co., 1946-79; mgr. South Central region Starbar div. Zoecon Industries, Dallas, 1979—, product and sales tng. mgr., 1982—, sales mgr. Temple Tag div., 1984—. Served with AUS, 1942-45; PTO. Mem. Entomology Soc. Am., Tex. Producers Vet. Supplies (v.p. 1960). Methodist. Club: San Antonio Golf Assn. Home: PO Box 29424 San Antonio TX 78229 Office: 12005 Ford Rd Suite 800 Dallas TX 75234

BUCHANAN, ERNEST TREZEVANT, college dean, lawyer; b. Sanford, N.C., May 31, 1940; s. Ernest T. and Curry (Golden) B.; m. Susan Henry, Sept. 13, 1969; children—Mary Pegram, Ernest T. IV, Molly Golden. B.A., Duke U., 1962; J.D., U. Fla., 1966; Ph.D., Fla. State U., 1972. Bar: Fla. 1967, Va. 1975. Assoc. Bell, King & Brown, Ft. Lauderdale, Fla., 1966-68; atty. Mcpl. Code Corp., Tallahassee, Fla., 1968-70, Fla. State U., Tallahassee, 1970-73; dean Tidewater Coll., Virginia Beach, Va., 1973—. Contbr. monographs to profl. publs. Mem. City Council, Virginia Beach, 1982-83; chmn. Virginia Beach Tomorrow, 1984. Named Ambassador Extraordinaire, City of Virginia Beach, 1985. Mem. Nat. Assn. Student Personnel Adminstrs. (pres. 1982, Outstanding Leadership award 1985), Va. Assn. Student Personnel Adminstrs. (Outstanding Membership award 1985). Episcopalian. Office: Tidewater Community Coll 1700 College Crescent Virginia Beach VA 23456

BUCHANAN, JOHN CHALKLEY, physician, state senator; b. Darwin, Va., Jan. 20, 1911; s. Noah Jackson and Minnie (Willis) B.; B.S., U. Va., 1933, M.D., 1951; m. Carol King Phipps, July 17, 1945. Intern, Jefferson-Hillman Hosp., Birmingham, Ala., 1951-52; resident in internal medicine U. Va. Hosp., Charlottesville, 1952-55; practice medicine specializing in internal medicine, Wise, Va., 1956—; mem. Va. Senate, 1972—. Mem. adv. bd. Clinch Valley Coll., 1971—; mem. Wise County Housing and Devel. Authority, 1971—. Served in USN, 1942-46. Diplomate Am. Bd. Internal Medicine. Mem. Nat. Conf. State Legislatures. Democrat. Home: PO Box 1006 Wise VA 24293 Office: Wise Clinic Wise VA 24293

BUCHANAN, WILLIAM CHARLES, university library director; b. Cuba Landing, Tenn., June 25, 1940; s. Charles Dee and Annie Verina (Chance) B.; m. Madeline Lieber, Aug. 28, 1971; 1 son, Charles Philip. B.A., Belmont Coll., 1964; M.Ed., Middle Tenn. State U., 1967; M.S. in L.S., La. State U., 1971, Ed.D., 1978. Library dir. George C. Wallace Community Coll., Selma, Ala., 1971-77; asst. prof. edn. U. Central Ark., Conway, 1977-78; asst. prof. library sci. East Carolina U., Greenville, N.C., 1978-80; prof. edn. Northwestern State U., Natchitoches, La., 1980-81, library dir., 1981—; tchr. English Ga. Pub. Schs., Cartersville, 1964-66, Tenn. Pub. Schs., Waverly, 1966-67, Ga. Pub. Schs., Rossville, 1968-69. Mem. La. Library Assn. (chmn. com.), ALA, Phi Kappa Phi, Phi Delta Kappa (sec. 1983-84), Beta Phi Mu. Democrat. Mem. Church of Christ. Lodge: Kiwanis. Home: PO Box 797 Natchitoches LA 71457

BUCHMANN, MOLLY O'BANION, choreographer, dance teacher; b. Baton Rouge, Nov. 22, 1949; d. James Dennis and Annie Laurie (Joffrion) O'B.; m. Fred J. Buchmann, Aug. 23, 1969; children—F. Jason, Dennis Andrew. B.S. in Secondary Edn., La. State U., 1971, M.S. in Dance, 1973. Owner, mgr. Dancer's Workshop, Baton Rouge, 1973—; artistic dir. Baton Rouge Ballet Theatre, 1976—; dance tchr. Baton Rouge Magnet High Sch., 1979-85; choreographer Baton Rouge Little Theatre, 1983—, Aubin Ln. Dinner Theatre, Baton Rouge, 1980-82; vis. artist Arts and Humanities Council of Greater Baton Rouge, 1976. Choreographer numerous works. Editor: (newsletter) La. Dance News, 1976-77. State of La. Div. of Arts choreographic grantee, 1982; La. State U. Alumni Fedn. scholar, 1967. Mem. Southwest Regional Ballet Assn. (bd. dirs., sec. 1984-86). Democrat. Roman Catholic. Office: Dancers' Workshop 3875 Government St Baton Rouge LA 70806

BUCHMEYER, JERRY, U.S. dist. ct. judge; b. Overton, Tex., Sept. 5, 1933; student Kilgore Jr. Coll., 1953; B.A., U. Tex., 1955, LL.B., 1957. Admitted to Tex. bar, 1957; asso. firm Thompson, Knight, Simmons & Bullion, Dallas, 1958-63; partner, 1963-68, sr. partner, 1968-79; now judge U.S. Dist. Ct., No. Dist. Tex., Dallas. Mem. Am. Bar Assn., Dallas Bar Assn. (pres. 1979), State Bar Tex. (chmn. com. 1978-79). Office: US Courthouse Room 15A3C 1100 Commerce St Dallas TX 75242

BUCHOLTZ, NANCY MARIE, insurance executive; b. St. Paul, Oct. 8, 1953; d. Carroll Edward and Dorothy Beatrice (Jacobson) Hansen; m. Jack Edward Bucholtz, June 16, 1978 (div.). Student Concordia Coll., 1972-74. Ratercoder Milw. Ins. Co., 1976-77; rater NN Risk Mgmt. Services, Inc., Milw., 1977-80, asst. underwriter, 1980, account supr., 1980-81, sr. account supr., 1981-82, staff asst., 1982-84; with Houston Casualty Co., aviation underwriter, 1984-85; account asst. Frank B. Hall, 1984—; dir. Wis. Found. Ins. Edn., Inc., Madison, 1983, sec./treas., 1984, pub. relations chmn., 1984. Mem. Nat. Assn. Ins. Women, Ins. Women Milw. (edn. chmn. 1980-82, state orgn. chmn. 1983, membership dir. 1983, 84, sec. 1984, nominated Ins. Woman of Yr. 1983-84). Lutheran. Club: NN Women's (v.p. 1978-79, pres. 1980) Home: 7942 Grow Ln Houston TX 77040 Office: Frank B Hall 1000 Cashco Tower Eight Greenway Plaza Houston TX 77046

BUCK, CLEO EUGENE, JR., oil company executive; b. Houston, Mar. 4, 1931; s. Cleo Eugene Sr. and Lillian Mary (Monismith) B.; m. Gracie Darlene Seim, Aug. 18, 1954 (div. May 1977); children—Kathleen Marie, Dean Winton. B.S. in Geology, U. Tex., 1954. Exploration geologist Humble Oil Co., Midland, Tex., 1954-64; sr. geol. engr. Tenneco, 1964-72; div. geologist Apexco, Tulsa, Okla., 1972-74; div. mgr. Herndon O&G, 1974-81; v.p. Universal Energy, 1981-84; pres. Silver Eagle Co., Tulsa, 1984—. Mem. Am. Assn. Petroleum Geologists, Am. Inst. Profl. Geologists (cert.), Western Tex. Geol. Soc., Tex. Geol. Soc. Avocations: cameras; motorcycling; swimming; archeology. Home: Box 233 Tulsa OK 74101

BUCK, HARVEY SHARPE, judge; b. Tchula, Miss., July 19, 1921; s. George Thad and Florence (Baine) B.; B.S., Miss. State U., 1942; LL.B., U. Miss., 1956, J.D., 1968; m. Helen Eugenia Poirier, July 20, 1946; children—Brenda Poirier Buck Moore, George Thad II, Janis Parrish Buck Smith. Bar: Miss. 1955. Practiced in West Point, 1956—; city judge, West Point, 1958-60; dist. atty. 16th Jud. Dist. Miss., West Point, 1960-76, circuit judge, 1976—; preceptor clin. legal edn. program U. Miss. Law Sch., 1971—. Mem. Gov.'s Commn. Criminal Justice Standards, 1974-75, Miss. Commn. Jud. Performance, 1982—. Served to maj. AUS, 1955. Mem. Am., Miss., Clay County (pres. 1966-68) bar assns., Nat. Dist. Attys. Assn. (dir.), Miss. Prosecutors Assn. (pres. 1971-72), Miss. Circuit Judges Assn. (v.p. 1980, pres.-elect 1980, chmn. 1981), Clay County C. of C. (pres. 1968). Presbyn. (elder). Clubs: Masons, Shriners (Meridian). Home: Old Waverly Rd West Point MS 39773 Office: 203 Jordan S West Point MS 39773

BUCK, JACK BRUCE, dentist, consultant, administrator; b. San Angelo, Tex., Feb. 28, 1927; s. Henry E. and Eleanor (Clayton) B.; m. Bobbie Davis. B.A., Tex. A&I Coll., 1954; B.S., 1956; D.D.S., U. Tex.-Houston, 1960; M.P.H., U. N.C., 1974. Asst. chief Dental Bur., Tex. State Dept. Health,

Austin, 1973-74; asst. dir. Dallas City Dental Health Dept., 1974-78, dir., 1978-81; exec. dir. Dental Health Programs, Inc., Dallas, 1981-85, dental cons. Region VI, USPHS, Dallas, 1976—; assoc. prof. Baylor Coll. Dentistry, Dallas, 1978—. Editor, gen. mgr. Eleventh Hour Jour., 1972-73. Contbr. articles to profl. jour. Bd. dirs. The Sci. Place, Health and Science Mus., Dallas, 1981—, Health Sci. Mus., Dallas, 1981—. Served with USMC, 1944-49. Fellow Am. Coll. Dentists, Internat. Coll. Dentists, Acad. Internat. Dentists, Am. Acad. Gen. Dentistry, Tex. Pub. Health Assn. (chmn. 1974-75). Lodges: Rotary, Masons. Home: 3520 Timberview Rd Dallas TX 75229 Office: Dental Health Programs Inc 8700 Stemmond Freeway Suite 328 Dallas TX 75247

BUCK, JAMES ARNOLD, utility official, consultant; b. Evanston, Ill., Dec. 7, 1948; s. Arnold Queese and Carol Jean (Tait) B.; children—Marguerite Josephine, Lea Christine. B.S. in Journalism, So. Ill. U., 1972. Site rep. N. Anna Nuclear Power Sta., 1976-77, sr. pub. relations rep. corp. hdqrs., Richmond, Va., 1977-78, supr. community relations Bath County pumped storage project, Mountain Grove, Va., 1978-80, dir. media/community relations, No. Va. region, 1980—; pres., chief exec. officer McQuistan Assoc.; guest lectr. energy, pub. relations, legis. affairs. Chmn. legis. affairs com., lobbyist Fairfax County C. of C., 1982-84; mem. legis. affairs com. Greater Washington Bd. Trade, 1984-86; dir., treas. Springfield Breakfast Rotary Club, 1981-84; past mem. Fairfax Com. of 100; pres. Highland County Jaycees, 1978-80; active Richmond Jaycees, 1978; sec. Monterey Lions Club, 1979-80. Served with USN, 1972-76. Mem. No. Va. Press Club (sec. 1982-84, v.p. 1984-86), Pub. Relations Soc. Am. (asst. sec. chpt. 1981-83), Soc. Consumer Affairs Profls., Relations Soc. Am. (regional dir. Va. chpt. 1979-80). Roman Catholic. Home: 6001 Queenston St Springfield VA 22152 Office Va Power 12316 Lee-Jackson Meml Hwy Fairfax VA 22033

BUCK, JANIECE TERRELL, educational consultant; b. Arkadelphia, Ark., Aug. 6, 1934; d. Sadie Bledsoe Terrell; m. E.W. Buck, Aug. 15, 1951 (div. 1983); children—Jana L. Buck Hedrick, Larry W., Gary L. Assoc. Bus. Adminstrn., Kilgore Jr. Coll., 1965; B.S. cum laude, Stephen F. Austin U., 1967, M.A. in Edn., 1973. Lic. profl. counselor, Tex. Tchr. bus. edn. Kilgore Ind. Sch. Dist., Tex., 1967-73; high sch. counselor, 1974-79; cons. region VII Ednl. Service Ctr., Kilgore, 1979-84; counselor Kilgore Jr. Coll., 1982; curriculum dir. Palestine Ind. Sch. Dist., Tex., 1984-85; cons. Tex. Edn. Agy., Austin, Tex., 1985—. Mem. Am. Assn. Counseling and Devel., Tex. Assn. Counseling and Devel. (dir. 1981-85), Pinewoods Assn. for Counseling and Devel. (pres. 1984-85), Am. Sch. Counselors' Assn., Nat. Vocat. Counselor's Assn., Tex. Assn. Sch. Counselors, Tex. Career Counselor Assn. (dir. 1981-85), Am. Assn. Supervision and Curriculum Devel., Tex. Assn. Supervision and Curriculum Devel., Tex. Council for Women Sch. Execs. (treas. 1984-86), Tex. Assn. Sch. Adminstrs. (supt.'s workshop com. 1983-84). Alpha Delta Kappa. Avocations: cooking; sewing. Home: 12213 B Running Bird Austin TX 78758 Office: Tex Edn Agy 1701 W Congress Austin TX 78701

BUCKHAM, JAMES ANDREW, consultant, retired chemical corporation executive; b. Mpls., Sept. 15, 1925; s. Clifford James and Irene Eleanor (Ackerson) B.; m. Margaret van Leeuwen, Feb. 20, 1954; children—Judy, Craig, Peggy. B.S., U. Wash., 1945, M.S., 1948, Ph.D., 1953. Engr., Standard Oil Co. of Calif., 1948-50; research engr. Calif. Research & Devel. Corp., 1950, 53-54; instr. chem. engring. U. Wash., Seattle, 1951-53; research engr. Phillips Petroleum Co., 1954-63, research supr., 1963-66; research mgr. Allied Chem. Corp., Idaho Falls, Idaho, 1966-71, asst. gen. mgr., 1971-76, pres. Allied Gen. Nuclear Services, Barnwell, S.C., 1976-84; cons., 1984—; resident head chem. engring. U. Idaho, Idaho Falls, 1954-70. Served to lt. U.S. Navy Res., 1943-46. Mem. Am. Inst. Chem. Engrs. (chmn. Idaho sect. 1956, chmn. nuclear engring. div. 1970, Robert E. Wilson award 1974, chmn. nat. program com. 1977, bd. dirs. 1980-83), Am. Nuclear Soc. (chmn. eastern Idaho sect. 1974), Am. Chem. Soc., Atomic Indsl. Forum (chmn. subcom. on reprocessing 1981-83). Contbr. chpts. to books, articles in field to profl. jours. Patentee continuous dissolver-extractor for processing metal. Home and Office: Route 1 Box 196 Aiken SC 29801

BUCKLER, ELEANORE SMALL, science consultant; b. Balt., May 26, 1943; d. Joseph Warder III and Eleanore Catherine (Jordan) Small; m. Edward St. Clair Buckler III, Nov. 26, 1965; children—Edward IV, Joseph. B.S., Purdue U., 1965. Bacteriologist, Prince Georges Gen. Hosp., Cheverly, Md., 1965-66, George Washington Hosp., Washington, 1966-67; med. technologist, Arlington, Va., 1967-70; sci. cons. Jamestown Elem. Sch., Arlington, 1981—; mem. sci. adv. com. Arlington County pub. schs., 1981—. Treas. Arlington PTA Elem. Sch., 1977-78, Arlington PTA Jr. High Sch., 1984—; v.p. Coop. Pre-Sch., Arlington, 1974-77; den mother Boy Scouts Am., Arlington, 1978-81; pres. Arlington Outdoor Edn. Assn., 1984—. Mem. Nat. Sci. Tchrs. Assn. Democrat. Avocations: birdwatching; flower identifying; canoeing; hiking; camping; gardening. Home: 4913 N 33d Rd Arlington VA 22207

BUCKLEY, JACK BOYD, mechanical/electrical engineer; b. Fort Wayne, Ind., Feb. 6, 1926; s. Chauncey Jason and Ruth W. (Boyd) B.; student Ind. State U., 1944, Kans. State U., 1944-45, Purdue, 1947; B.S. in C.E., Rice Inst., 1948; postgrad. U. Houston, 1948-49; m. Helen C. Sartwelle, Jan. 18, 1952; children—Elizabeth Ann (Mrs. Christopher Till), James S., Steven B., William H. Vice chmn. bd., dir. I.A. Naman & Assos. and I.A. Naman & Assos. West, Inc., Houston, 1949—, also dir.; pres. Internat. Engrs., Inc., Houston; dir. Port City Stockyard, Tex. Agribus. Co., Inc. Mem. Houston Air Conditioning Bd., 1974-78, Houston Gen. Appeals Bd., 1978—. Mem. Aldine (Ind.) Sch. Bd., 1954-55; adv. council Am. Arbitration Assn. Served with USNR, 1944-46. Registered profl. engr., Tex. Fellow ASHRAE (chpt. pres. 1961); mem. Constrn. Specifications Inst. (chpt. pres. 1973-74), Nat., Tex. socs. profl. engrs., Am. Hosp. Assn., Internat. Conf. Bldg. Ofcls., Nat. Fire Protection Assn., Illuminating Engring. Soc., Smoke Control Assos., Am. Cons. Engr. Council, Houston Livestock Show and Rodeo (life), Nat. Rifle Assn. (life), Am. Forestry Assn., Am. Mgmt. Assn., Soc. Fire Protection Engrs., Constrn. Industry Council Houston, Houston Zool. Soc. (dir. 1969-73). Rotarian. Club: 100 (life, dir. 1975) (Houston). Cons. editor Specifying Engr. Mag., 1974—. Contbr. articles to profl. jours. Home: 10047 Del Monte Dr Houston TX 77042 Office: 2 Greenway Plaza E No 520 Houston TX 77046

BUCKLEY, JANET LOUISE, insurance company executive; b. Charleston, W. Va., Sept. 11, 1934; d. Opha Vincent Simmons and Stellena (Ramsey) Legge; m. Charles Walton Buckley, Aug. 15, 1952; (div. 1971); children—Crystal Renee, Gregory Charles. Student Charleston Sch. Commerce, 1951-52. Cert. profl. ins. woman. Account supr. McNeer Ins. Agy, Charleston, 1952-56; acct. supr. Wehrle-Goff Ins. Agy., Charleston, 1956-64, Comml. Ins. Service, Charleston, 1964-71; account exec., v.p. McDonough Caperton Charleston Inc., 1971—. Recipient Spirt of McDonough Award, 1982. Mem. Charleston Assn. Inc. Women (pres. 1976-77, edn. chmn. 1979—, Blanche Barry Edn. award 1976-81), Nat. Assn. Ins. Women, Ind. Ins. Agts. W.Va. (vice chmn. edn.), Ins. Inst. Am. (accredited adv.). Republican. Baptist. Home: PO Box 784 Big Chimney WV 25302 Office: McDonough Caperton Charleston Inc One Hillcrest E Charleston WV 25326

BUCKNER, GERALD LELAND, USAF officer, science and mathematics educator; b. Shelby, N.C., Jan. 10, 1953; s. Floyd Leland and Nancy Lee (Hill) B.; m. Linda Marie Johnan, June 7, 1975; children—Kara, Andrew, Matthew. B.S. in Phys. Sci., U.S. Mil. Acad., 1975; M.A. in Mgmt., Webster U., 1981; grad. Squadron Officer Sch., 1983; M.S. in Space Tech., Fla. Inst. Tech., 1985. Commd. 2d. lt., U.S. Army, 1975, advanced through grades to capt., 1979; 2d. lt., Vulcan platoon leader U.S. Army, Ft. Bragg, N.C., 1975-76; redeye sect. leader, Ft. Bragg, 1977, battery exec. officer, 1978; battery comdr. Camp Stanley, Korea, 1979-80; capt., br. chief, Ft. Bliss, Tex., 1980-81; capt. USAF Savannah River Lab., Aiken, S.C., 1981-82; capt., nuclear research officer Air Force Tech. Applications Center, Patrick AFB, Fla., 1982-85; instr. algebra, phys. sci. Brevard Community Coll., 1983-85. Mem. Citrus Council Girl Scouts Am., 1982-85. Decorated Army Commendation medal with 2 oak leaf clusters, Nat. Def. Service medal, Air Force Commendation medal, Air Force Tech. Applications Center Outstanding Unit award. Mem. Air Force Assn., Assn. Graduates, Nat. Space Inst. Home: 336 Apricot Ln Wright Patterson AFB OH 45433

BUCKNER, KATHRYN TRIMBLE CURRENT, accountant, educator, administrator; b. Chariton, Iowa, June 18, 1926; d. Charles Ralston and Blanche Bernice (Cloe) Trimble; m. James Philip Current, Feb. 14, 1945 (dec. Feb. 1968); 1 son, James Philip; m. 2d, Newt M. Buckner, May 29, 1971. Student, Ball State Tchrs. Coll., 1948-49, Ind. U., 1958-59; B.B.A., Ga. State U., 1961, M.B.A., 1965, D.B.A., 1971. C.P.A., Ga. Sec. various firms, Pensacola, Fla., 1943-45, Santa Ana, Calif., 1945-46; acct., office mgr. Thomas J. Marimon Auto Sales & Service, Valparaiso, Ind., 1950-55, Boney & Mellette Dodge Auto Sales & Service, Anaheim, Calif., 1955-56; acctg. jr. Woodrow Hulme, C.P.A., Ardmore, Okla., 1957-58, Ralph M. Braswell, C.P.A., Atlanta, 1956-57, 59-61; acct., auditor, assoc. William T. Hankins, C.P.A., Atlanta, 1961, 62-66; asst. prof. acctg. Ga. State U., Atlanta, 1966-74, assoc. prof., 1974-86, prof., 1986—; dir. Master of Taxation program Sch. Accountancy, 1979—; lectr. in field; commr. Internal Revenue Roscoe Egger's Group, 1982. Recipient Dean's key Ga. State U., 1960, W.S. Kell Scholarship award, 1961, Faculty Appreciation award, 1975, 76. Mem. Am. Acad. Acctg. Historians, Am. Acctg. Assn., Am. Inst. C.P.A.s, Am. Soc. Women Accts. (scholarship, 1959, pres. Atlanta chpt. 1964-65), Am. Woman's Soc. C.P.A.s (nat. pres. 1983-84), Ga. Soc. C.P.A.s (Silver Key award 1960), Nat. Assn. Accts. (pres. Atlanta chpt. 1975-76, most valuable mem., 1975-76, pres. Dixie Council 1980-81), Am. Woman's Soc. C.P.A.s Ga., Inc. (charter), Crimson Key Honor Soc., Phi Chi Theta (scholarship key award 1961), Beta Alpha Psi (appreciation award 1973). Author: Littleton's Contribution to the Theory of Accountancy, 1975; contbr. articles to profl. jours. Home: Route 1 Box 60 Ono Rd Palmetto GA 30268 Office: Sch Accountancy Ga State U University Plaza Atlanta GA 30303

BUCKNER, MARILYN, beverage company executive, management development administrator; b. Oneonta, Ala.; d. Remus Wilson and Annie Ruth (Whited) B.; m. Richard E. Phillips, Jr., Sept. 2, 1976. B.A., Ga. State U., 1973, Ed.M., 1974, Ed.S., 1981, Ph.D., 1984. Cert. rehab. counselor. Instr., Ga. State U., Atlanta, 1979-80; rehab. cons. Crawford & Co., Atlanta, 1980; dir. human resources tng. Floyd Jr. Coll., Rome, Ga., 1980-81; mgmt. devel. specialist, Coca-Cola Co., Atlanta, 1981-83, mgr. mgmt. devel., 1983—. Co-author: Tools of the Trade, 1981. Mem. Human Resource Planning Soc., Am. Soc. for Tng. and Devel. Office: The Coca-Cola Co PO Drawer 1734 Atlanta GA 30301

BUCUR, JOHN CHARLES, neurological surgeon; b. Youngstown, Ohio, Mar. 5, 1925; s. John and Victoria (Marginean) B.; B.S., Ohio U., 1947; postgrad. U. Biarritz (France), 1946; M.D., U. Pitts., 1951, M.Surgery, 1952; m. Emily Leanne Elmore; children—John Ellsworth, Dean Charles, Victoria Ann, Michael Paul, Teri Leanne. Intern, Western Pa. Hosp., Pitts., 1951-52; resident in neurosurgery Long Beach (Calif.) VA Hosp., 1953-56, staff neurosurgeon, 1956-57; neurosurg. cons. Harbor Gen. Hosp., Torrance, Calif., 1956-57; practice medicine specializing in neurol. surgery, Falls Church, Va., 1957—; chief staff Nat. Orthopedic and Rehab. Hosp., Arlington, Va., 1973; chief neurol. surgery Fairfax Hosp., Falls Church, 1961-75, Nat. Orthopedic and Rehab. Hosp., Arlington, 1957-79, No. Va. Drs. Hosp., Arlington, 1963—, Arlington Hosp., 1977—; sr. attending neurosurgeon Alexandria Hosp., 1959—, Circle Terrace Hosp., Alexandria, Va., 1962—; sec., dir. 7 Corners Med. Bldgs., Inc., Falls Church, 1958—; partner Edward R. Lang, M.D., Falls Church, 1969—. Mem. Va. Gov.'s Com. for Regional Med. Program, dir. regional med. program, 1969-77; bd. dirs. Nat. Hosp. for Orthopedics and Rehab. Served with U.S. Army, 1943-45; ETO. Diplomate Am. Bd. Neurol. Surgery. Fellow ACS; mem. Am. Assn. Neurol. Surgeons, Mid-Atlantic Neurosurgery Soc., Washington Acad. Neurosurgery, Neurosurg. Soc. Vas., No. Va. Acad. Surgery, Congress Neurol. Surgeons, Pan Am. Med. Assn., So. Med. Assn., Arlington County Med. Soc., Va. Health Assn. (pres.), Fairfax County Med. Soc., Am. Legion. Methodist. Club: Masons. Office: 6305 Castle Pl Falls Church VA 22044

BUCY, GERALD GLENN, contractor, engineer; b. Murray, Ky., Oct. 22, 1950; s. William Edwin and R. Alene (Chilcutt) B.; m. Carol Sue Hawthorne, Aug. 22, 1970 (div. 1981). Student David Lipscomb Coll., 1968-71; B.S. in Civil Engring., U. Tenn., 1973. Lic. profl. engr., contractor, Tenn. Field engr. Hardaway Constrn. Co., 1972-73; area engr. constrn. div. E.I. DuPont Co., 1973-75; project mgr. McCullough Assocs., Inc., Murfreesboro, Tenn., 1975-77, Century Constrn. Co., Franklin, Tenn., 1977-81; owner, pres. Harpeth Constrn. Co. & Gerald G. Bucy, Cons. Engr., Brentwood, Tenn., 1981—. Mem. Tenn. Soc. Profl. Engrs., Nat. Soc. Profl. Engrs., ASCE, Nat. Homebuilders Assn. Mem. Ch. of Christ. Club: Maryland Farms Racquet & Country (Brentwood). Home: 400 Watercress Dr Franklin TN 37064 Office: Harpeth Constrn Co 9000 E Church St Brentwood TN 37027

BUCY, PAUL C., neurosurgeon, editor; b. Hubbard, Iowa, Nov. 13, 1904; s. Isaac and Lillian (Clancy) B.; m. Evelyn Richards, June 12, 1927; children—Paul Craig, James Gordon. B.S., U. Iowa, 1925, M.S., 1927, M.D., 1927. Instr., then asst. prof., assoc. prof. then head div. neurology and neurosurgery, U. Chgo., 1927-41; prof. neurology and neurosurgery U. Ill., Chgo., 1941-54, Northwestern U., Chgo., 1954-72, Bowman Gray Sch. Medicine, Winston-Salem, N.C., 1973—; cons. to Nat. Inst. Neurol. and Communicative Disorders and Stroke, NIH; pres. 2d Internat. Congress Neurol. Surgeons. Recipient cert. of accomplishment U. Iowa; Disting. Service award U. Chgo.; named hon. prof. neurology and neurosurgery, U. Minas Gerais (Brazil). Mem. Soc. Neurochir. de lang. Francaise (hon.), Soc. Francaise de Neurol. (hon.), Soc. Ital. di Neurochir. (hon.), Am. Assn. Neurosurgeons (pres.), Soc. Neurol. Surgeons (pres.), Am. Neurol. Assn. (hon. mem., pres.), World Fedn. Neurosurgery Socs. (pres.), Am. Physiol. Soc., AMA, ACS, Am. Surg. Assn. Clubs: Chgo. Literary, University (Chgo.). Editor Surg. Neurology, 1972-85. Contbr. numerous articles to profl. jours. Home: PO Box 1441 Tryon NC 28782 Office: PO Box 1457 Tryon NC 28782

BUDALUR, THYAGARAJAN SUBBANARAYAN, chemistry educator; b. Tiuvarur, India, July 14, 1929; s. Subbanarayan Subbuswamy and Parvatham (Copalakrishnan) B.; came to U.S., 1969, naturalized, 1977; M.A., U. Madras, 1951, M.Sc., 1954, Ph.D., 1956; children—Chitra, Poorna, Kartik. Reader organic chemistry U. Madras, 1960-68; prof. chemistry U. Idaho, Mosow, 1968-74; prof. chemistry, dir. div. earth phys. sci. U. Tex., San Antonio, 1974—; lectr. in field. Recipient Intra Sci. Research award, 1966. Fellow Am. Chem. Soc., Am. Inst. Chemists; mem. Chem. Soc. London, N.Y. Acad. Sci., Nat. Commn. Cert. Chemists, Sigma Xi. Club: Lions. Author: Mechanisms of Molecular Migrations; Selective Organic Transfomations. Editorial bd. chem. jours.; contbr. articles to profl. jours. Home: 12711 Interstate 10 W #1914 San Antonio TX 78230 Office: San Antonio TX 78285

BUDZINSKY, ARMIN ALEXANDER, investment banker; b. Steyr, Austria, Nov. 25, 1942; came to U.S., 1951, naturalized, 1957; s. Alexander Wladimir and Maria Gisella B.; A.B., John Carroll U., 1964; M.A. (NDEA fellow, Fulbright fellow), Rutgers U., 1969; M.B.A., U. Chgo., 1974; m. Pamela Plimmer, Oct. 29, 1978; 1 dau., Andrea. Instr. in English, Cleve. State U., 1969-72; corp. fin. cons. Citibank NA., N.Y.C., 1974-76; project fin. Dean Witter & Co., N.Y.C., 1976-77; v.p. oil and gas financing Merrill Lynch Pierce Fenner & Smith, N.Y.C., 1977-83; v.p. corp. fin. Dunoco Corp., Houston, 1983; pres. Porcari Fearnow Capital Markets, Inc., Houston, 1983—; mem. industry adv. com. N.Am. Assn. Security Adminstrs. Mem. Oil Investment Inst., U. Chgo. Grad. Sch. Bus. Alumni Assn. (trustee 1982-83). Home: 4510 Shetland Ln Houston TX 77027 Office: 1800 Bering Suite 800 Houston TX 77057

BUE, CARL OLAF, JR., judge; b. Chgo., Mar. 27, 1922; s. Carl Olaf and Mabel Port (Shollar) B.; m. Mary Kathryn Waring, Dec. 27, 1948; children—Kathryn Anne, Richard Charles. A.A., U. Chgo., 1942; student, U. Rome, Italy, 1945; Ph.B., Northwestern U., 1951; LL.B., U. Tex., 1954. Bar: Tex. bar 1954. Asso. firm Royston, Rayzor & Cook, Houston, 1954-58, mem. firm, 1958-70; U.S. dist. judge So. Dist. Tex. (Houston div.), 1970—; lectr. various law schs. and admiralty seminars in Tex. and other states. Contbr. articles to profl. jours. Served to capt., Adj. Gen. Dept. AUS, 1942-46; MTO. Recipient Good Citizenship medal Houston chpt. SAR, 1975, Joe R. Greenhill award Tex. Municipal Cts. Assn., 1976-77. Mem. Am., Fedn., Tex., Houston bar assns., Maritime Law Assn. of U.S., Am. Judicature Soc., English Speaking Union, Houston Philos. Soc. at Rice U., Alpha Delta Phi, Phi Alpha Delta. Republican. Lutheran. Home: 338 Knipp Rd Houston TX 77024 Office: US Courthouse 515 Rusk Ave Houston TX 77002

BUEHRING, NORMIE WILLIE, agronomist, researcher; b. Karnes City, Tex., June 5, 1939; s. Louis H. and Elsie (Rosenbrock) B.; m. Carol Lynn Schulze, July 20, 1968; children—Jason Paul, Nathan Wade. B.S., Tex. A&I U., 1967; M.S., Okla. State U.-Stillwater, 1969, Ph.D., 1972. Soil fertility technician ARS, U.S. Dept. Agriculture, Weslaco, Tex., 1967; research asst. Okla. State U.-Stillwater, 1967-71, lab. instr., 1971-72; asst. agronomist Miss. State U.-Verona, 1972-79, assoc. agronomist, 1979-83, asst. supt. and agronomist, 1984—. Water Resources Inst. Research grantee, 1977-79; Miss. Soybean Promotion Bd. research grantee, 1979-85; Deere & Co. research grantee, 1982-86; BASF Wyandotte Corp. research grantee, 1983-85. Mem. So. Weed Sci. Soc., Weed Sci. Soc. Am., Am. Soc. Agronomy, Sigma Xi, Gamma Sigma Delta. Lutheran. Contbr. numerous articles to profl. jours. Office: PO Box 456 Verona MS 38879

BUENO, JUAN ANTONIO, landscape architect, engr.; b. Havana, Cuba, Aug. 3, 1947; came to U.S., 1960, naturalized, 1972; s. Juan Rafael and Zaida Antonieta (Bueno) Rodriguez; student Catholic U. Am., 1965-67; B.S. in E.E., U. Miami, 1969; m. Teresita Falcon, July 29, 1972. Engr., Eastman Kodak Co., Rochester, N.Y., 1969-72; engr. Smith Korach Hayet Haynie, Miami, Fla., 1972-73; engr. H.J. Ross, Miami, 1973-74; pres. Planners & Designers, Inc., Coconut Grove, 1974-77; partner Falcón & Bueno, Coconut Grove, Fla., 1978—. Registered landscape architect, Fla.; registered profl. engr., Fla. Mem. Am. Soc. Landscape Architects (recipient design awards), Archtl. Club Miami. Democrat. Roman Catholic. Club: Friends of Photography. Contbr. articles to profl. jours. Home and office: 4061 Battersea Rd Coconut Grove FL 33133

BUERKLE, RICHARD LOUIS, commercial real estate executive; b. Jonesboro, Ark., Jan. 11, 1947; s. Bill and Marvine (Matthews) B.; B.B.A., Ark. State U., 1971; M.B.A. with honors, So. Meth. U., 1972; m. Lena Ann Weston, Aug. 14, 1971; children—Richard Louis II, Ryan Lee. Comml. loan officer Glenn Justice Mortgage Co., Dallas, 1971-72, Equitable Life Assurance Soc. U.S., Dallas, 1972-73; v.p. s.w. div. Alpert Investment Corp., Dallas, 1973-76; chmn. bd., pres. Buerkle Investment Corp., Arlington, Tex., 1976—; guest lectr. numerous real estate seminars, univ. classes, banquets; dir. Real Estate Today TV series; expert witness before cts. and city govts. Exec. com. bus. adv. council U. Tex., Arlington, 1978-82; dir. Women's Haven of Arlington; bd. deacons 1st Bapt. Ch. of Arlington; Ark. state chief Order of Arrow, Boy Scouts Am., 1966, mem. Eagle Scout, Vigil. Served with USMC, 1966-68; Vietnam. Lic. real estate broker, Tex. Mem. Internat. Council Shopping Centers, Dallas and Ft. Worth Apt. Assn., Beta Gamma Sigma. Republican. Office: 3031 Suite B Harwood Blvd Bedford TX 76021

BUESCHER, MARGARET MCCULLOUGH, investment banker; b. Kerrville, Tex., May 29, 1954; d. David and Mary Holman (Myers) McCullough; m. James Elmer Buescher Jr., Nov. 24, 1979. B.A., Vanderbilt U., 1976. Chartered fin. analyst. Asst. v.p. investment dept. City Nat. Bank, Austin, Tex., 1976-79; v.p. to trust investment group Tex. Commerce Bank, Houston, 1980—. Mem. Houston Soc. Fin. Analysts (asst. treas. 1983-84), Inst. Chartered Fin. Analysts, Kappa Alpha Theta Alumni. Republican. Presbyterian. Avocations: golf; travel; gardening. Office: Texas Commerce Bank 600 Travis Houston TX 77002

BUESS, LARRY DUANE, mathematics educator; b. Wharton, Ohio, Feb. 22, 1941; s. Lawrence Avery Buess and Lillie Marie (Jones) Mason; m. Sharon Kay Weeks, June 8, 1963; children—Kent Duane, Michelle Eloie, Brent James, A.B., Olivet Nazarene Coll., 1963; M.A.T., Purdue U., 1968; M.S., George Peabody Coll., 1976. Tchr. math. Prairie Heights Schs., LaGrange, Ind., 1963-64, Fremont Schs., Ind., 1964-68; prof. math. Mt. Vernon Nazarene Coll., Ohio, 1968-69, Trevecca Nazarene Coll., Nashville, 1978—; dir. schs. Nazarene Evang. Schs., Lebanon, 1969-77, Syria, Jordan, 1977-78. Mem. Nat. Council Tchrs. Math., Math. Assn. Am. Avocations: computer programming, automotive mechanics. Home: 222 Worley Dr Nashville TN 37217 Office: Trevecca Nazarene Coll Nashville TN 37217

BUFKIN, ISAAC DAVID, energy diversified company executive; b. Haynesville, La., May 16, 1922; s. Floran E. and Pauline E. B.; B.S., La. Tech. U., 1948; m. Lee Elmo Renfrow, Apr. 23, 1944; children—Peggy Bufkin Gerst, David Michael. Mech. engr. NACA, Langley Field Va., 1948-49; with Tex. Eastern Transmission Corp., Houston, 1949-79, v.p. gas mktg. and rates, 1968-71, v.p. gas ops., 1971-79; exec. v.p. Tex. Eastern Corp., Houston, 1979, pres., chief operating officer, 1979-80, pres., chief exec. officer, 1980-84, chmn. bd., 1980-84, chmn. bd., chief exec. officer, 1984—; dir. First City Nat. Bank Houston. Transwestern Pipline. Bd. dirs. Conf. Bd. Gas Research Inst., Am. Petroleum Inst.; mem. Nat. Petroleum Council, 1980-81. Served with USAAF, 1943-46. Mem. La. Engring. Soc., Nat. Soc. Profl. Engrs., Am. Gas Assn., Pacific Coast Gas Assn., New Eng. Gas Assn., Soc. Gas Lighting, Gas Men's Roundtable Washington. So. Gas Assn., Interstate Natural Gas Assn. Am. (dir.). Newcomer Soc N. Am., Houston C. of C. (bd. dirs.). Baptist. Office: PO Box 2521 Houston TX 77001

BUFLER, CAROLE ORME, distbn. co. exec.; d. James Erskine and Elisabeth Margaret (Bishop) Orme; B.A., Trinity U., 1961; M.A., Incarnate Word Coll., 1980; m. Raymond Bufler; 1 son, Michael. Tchr. English, Macarthur High Sch., San Antonio, 1961-64; mem. faculty continuing edn. div. San Antonio Coll., 1972-77; program devel. coordinator U. Tex., San Antonio, 1978-79; comml. and investment broker Owens & Assos., San Antonio, 1979-81; mng. partner Southtex Distbrs., San Antonio, 1981—; mem. faculty bus. adminstrn. San Antonio Community Coll. Dist.; faculty continuing edn. div. St. Mary's U. Mem. adv. council on women's programs Incarnate Word Coll., San Antonio; mem. Arts Council of San Antonio; program dir. San Antonio Literacy Council, 1976-78; program dir. Covenant Presbyn. Ch., 1974-76. Mem. Women in Communications, Adult Edn. Assn., San Antonio Mus. Assn., North San Antonio C. of C., AAUW (steering com. conf. 1980, named Outstanding Woman in Bus. San Antonio chpt. 1980), AAUW. Home: 614 Golfcrest San Antonio TX 78239 Office: 10205 Oasis St Suite 120 San Antonio TX 78216

BUFORD, DELORES PHIFE, researcher, educator; b. Dallas, Dec. 18, 1933; d. George Jefferson and Louisa May (Daniel) Phife; m. Thomas Oliver Buford, Dec. 27, 1954; children—Russell Warren, Robert Carl, Anna Louise. B.A., North Tex. State U., 1954; postgrad. Boston U., 1958-60; M.A., Furman U., 1974; Ed.D., Nova U., 1982. Tchr. Dallas Pub. Sch. Dist., 1954-55; tchr. high sch. Ft. Worth Pub. Sch. Dist., 1955-58; mem. steering com. Jr. Great Books Program, Greenville County (S.C.) Pub. Schs., 1968-72; research assoc. Office Instnl. Planning and Research, Furman U., Greenville, S.C., 1974—, instr. ednl. research and learning process grad. div., 1977—. Mem. Greenville Fine Arts Festival Com., 1975; pres. Eastside High Sch. PTA, 1976. Mem. Assn. Instnl. Research, So. Assn. Instl. Research, S.C. Assn. Instl. Research, N.C. Assn. Instnl. Research, PEO (state exec. bd. 1980—, pres. 1985—). Democrat. Baptist. Scholarship to Edn. Fund Program named in her honor by Greenville br. AAUW, 1979. Home: Route 7 Regent Dr Greenville SC 29609 Office: Office Instnl Planning Furman U Greenville SC 29613

BUFORD, EVELYN CLAUDENE SHILLING, printing company executive; b. Fort Worth, Sept. 21, 1940; d. Claude and Winnie Evelyn (Mote) Hodges; student Hill Jr. Coll., 1975-76; m. Mar., 1982; children by previous marriage—Vincent Shilling, Kathryn Lynn Shilling Vassar. With Imperial Printing Co., Inc., Fort Worth, 1964-70, 77—, gen. sales mgr. comml. div., 1982—, corp. sec., 1977—; with Tarrant County Hosp. Dist., Fort Worth, 1973-77, asst. to asst. adminstr., 1981-82. Mem. Am. Mgmt. Assn., Exec. Women Internat. (dir., publs. chmn., v.p. 1984, pres. 1985); Nat. Assn. Female Execs., Presidents Club Tex. Republican. Methodist. Home: 100 Kenneth Ln Burleson TX 76028 Office: 1429 Hemphill Fort Worth TX 76104

BUFORD, MARK WAYNE, communications company executive; b. Pittsburg, Kans., Apr. 14, 1954; s. William Edward and Mary Eudella (Long) B.; student Pittsburg State U., 1972-75; m. Marcelyn Dendy, July 1, 1983; 1 child, Kasie Leigh McCanless. Asst. sports editor Pittsburg Pub. Co., 1972-76; sports writer/copy editor Okla. Pub. Co., Oklahoma City, 1976; sales/mktg. adminstr. Computype, Inc., Ann Arbor, Mich., 1976-78; product mktg. mgr. Harris Composition Systems, Melbourne, Fla., 1978-79, product mktg. mgr. Harris Distributed Office Systems div., 1979-84; product mgr. Harris Lanier Electronic Office Systems, 1984; product mktg. mgr. Harris Nat. Accounts div., 1984; product mktg. mgr. Harris Nat. Accounts div., Dallas, 1984—. Youth fellowship counselor United Meth. Ch., chmn. communications Custer Rd. United Meth. Ch., Plano, Tex. Recipient cert. of achievement Am. Legion Boys State of Kans., 1971; cert. of merit State of Kans. Scholarship Program Competition, 1971-72. Mem. Quill and Scroll, Sigma Tau Delta. Home: 2813 Ivanridge Ln Garland TX 75042 Office: 16001 Dallas Pkwy Dallas TX 75248

BUFORD, ROBERT PEGRAM, IV, chemical company executive; b. Richmond, Va., Sept. 14, 1949; s. Robert Pegram and Anne (Whitehead) B. B.A. in English, U. Va., 1972. Entertainment editor The Richmond Mercury, Va., 1972-73; writer corp. pub. relations Ethyl Corp., Richmond, 1974-78, editorial rep., 1978-80, coordinator corp. communications, 1980-82, mgr. corp. communications, 1982—; v.p., dir. The Company Corp., Richmond, 1982—; dir. Nepenthe Land Corp., 1984—. Exec. editor Clue Mag., 1984. Editor: May

Days: Crisis in Confrontation, 1970. Trustee, Friends Assn. for Children, Richmond, 1976-82; mem. Friends of the Anderson Gallery, 1982—. Recipient Henry Noble Taylor award, Seven Soc., U. Va., 1972. Democrat. Episcopalian. Club: Bull and Bear. Home: 6 N Plum St Richmond VA 23220 Office: Ethyl Corp 330 S 4th St PO Box 2189 Richmond VA 23217

BUICE, PATTERSON NALL, counselor; b. Atlanta, Mar. 2, 1934; d. Andrew Walton and Elizabeth (Merritt) Nall; m. Bonnie Carl, Dec. 14, 1957 (div.); children—Merrianne Dyer, Shannon, Sam, Bill (dec.), Chris. B.A., Peabody Coll., Oglethorpe U., 1956; M.Ed., Ga. State U., 1975, Ed.S., 1981; postgrad. U. Notre Dame, 1974-75; Advanced Standing, Emory U., 1982. Tchr., Atlanta Public Schs., 1956-58, Brenau Coll., Gainesville, Ga., 1972; instr. Tom Gordon's Parent Effectiveness Tng., 1972-73; counselor Holy Trinity Counseling Center, Decatur, Ga., 1976-78; pvt. practice counseling, Tucker, Ga., 1978-79, Macon, Ga., 1979-81; therapist Middle Ga. Mental Health, Macon and dir. therapeutic services Anneewakee Treatment Center, Rockmart, Ga., 1981—; asst. prof. behavioral scis. Brenau Coll., Gainesville, Ga., 1984-85, counsellor, 1984-85; dir. Peninsula Village, Peninsula Hosp., Knoxville, 1985—; vis. instr. Mercer U., Macon. Pres., Episcopal Churchwomen, Grace Ch., Gainesville, 1964-65, sr. warden, 1970-71; pres. Churchwomen United, Gainesville, 1965-67; bd. dirs. Yonah council Girl Scouts U.S.A., 1962-65, Gainesville Girls Club, 1968-73, pres. bd., 1971-73; bd. dirs. Gainesville Christian Study Center, 1970-72. Recipient Sidney-Sullivan award Peabody Coll., 1955; named Young Woman of Year, Gainesville, 1970. Mem. Am. Assn. Marriage and Family Therapists, Ga. Assn. Marriage and Family Therapists. Democrat. Home: Route 4 Box 400 Hillvale Dr Louisville TN 37777 Office: Peninsula Village Jones Bend Rd Louisville TN 37777

BUIGAS, OCTAVIO D., real estate development company executive; b. Havana, Cuba, Dec. 15, 1935; came to U.S., 1960; s. Ramon and Esther B.; m. Elena R. Buigas, children—Elean M., Octavio J., Ana M., Rosa, John Paul. B.A. in Architecture, Villanova U., Havana, Cuba, 1959. Registered architect, Fla., P.R. Pres., Ryerson & Haynes Realty, Inc., Miami, Fla., 1972-77; chmn. bd., chief exec. officer Southeast Enterprises, Inc., Miami, 1977—; sr. v.p. Buigas, Dorta-Duque & Assocs., Architects, Inc., Miami, 1972—; mem. Fla. East Coast adv. bd. Glendale Fed. Trustee, bd. dirs. Barry U., Miami, 1981—; mem. State of Fla. Adv. Com. on Regional Interstate Banking, 1983; mem. Fla. High Tech. and Industry Council. Mem. Miami Bd. Realtors, Soc. Am. Registered Architects, Greater Miami C. of C. (trustee). Home: 10361 SW 13th St Miami FL 33174 Office: Southeast Enterprises Inc 500 NW 165th St Rd 102 Miami FL 33169

BUKOWSKI, BARBARA ANN, researcher, merchant; b. Washington, Pa., Aug. 30, 1947; d. Anthony and Helen (Sovick) B.; R.N., Washington Hosp., 1968; B.S.N. cum laude, Duquesne U., 1970; M.P.H. cum laude, U. Pitts., 1975; A.B.D., U. Tex., 1979—. Nurse, mem. faculty Washington (Pa.) Hosp., 1968-74; profl. reviewer Appleton-Century-Crofts, N.Y.C., 1975-79; asst. prof. Erie Inst. Nursing, Villa Maria Coll., Pa., 1975-79; nurse, pub. health cons. The Meadows, Pa., 1971-75; pub. health cons., dir. Mack's Motor Co., Inc., Pa., 1976—; profl. adv. cons. Home Health-Home Care, Inc., Pasadena, Tex., 1980-85; ops. cons. HL&C Sales Contracting, Inc., 1982-85, Health Tech. Research, 1982—; adj. faculty Pa. Nurses Assn., 1980—; propr. Barbara's Antiques, 1980—; mem. com. protection of human subjects U. Tex., 1980-82; pres. bd. trustees Erie County Sr. Citizens Health Care Council, 1978-79; chmn. long range planning com. Erie County Health Edn. Council, 1978-79; dir., chmn. county sub-area council Health Systems, Inc., of Northwestern Pa., 1976-79. Hon. county exec., Erie, Pa., 1979; recipient awards USPHS, 1974, 75, 79-85. Mem. Am. Nurses Assn., Houston Health Policy Study Group, Tex. Nurses Assn., Am. Pub. Health Assn., Tex. Pub. Health Assn., Assn. Tchrs. in Grad. Programs in Community Health and Pub. Health Nursing, Nurses Coalition for Action in Politics, Sigma Theta Tau. Home and Office: 10103 Prospect Hill Houston TX 77064

BULCKEN, GEORGE WILLIAM, quality control engineer; b. Balt., July 26, 1929; s. George William and Mary S. (Ingham) B.; m. Carolyn Anne Brooks, Nov. 23, 1952; children—Cheryl, Cynthia, George William III, Richard. Student, Md. State Tchrs. Coll., 1948-51, Johns Hopkins U., 1957-59; A.B., Coll. of Mainland, Texas City, Tex., 1975; postgrad. U. Houston-Clear Lake, 1976-78. Registered profl. engr., Calif. Quality engr. Gen. Electric Co., 1962-72; supr. quality engring. Gray Tool Co., 1972-74; quality control mgr. Hydril; quality audit sect. mgr. Brown & Root; quality assurance mgr. Schlumberger; sr. quality engr. Bechtel Energy Corp., Houston, 1982—. Served with USNG, 1947-56. Recipient several aerospace awards Gen. Electric Corp., NASA commendations, 1967-70; Silver Snoopy award Apollo Astronauts, NASA, 1969. Mem. Am. Soc. for Quality Control (sr. mem., cert. quality engr.), Am. Soc. for Metals, Nat. Rifle Assn., Mensa, Intertel. Republican. Lodges: Masons, Shriners. Home: 5009 Casa Grande Dr Dickinson TX 77539 Office: Bechtel Energy Corp 5400 Westheimer Ct Houston TX 77252

BULGER, ROGER JAMES, university president, physician; b. Bklyn., May 18, 1933; s. William Joseph and Florence Dorothy (Poggi) B.; m. Ruth Ellen Grouse, June 8, 1960; children—Faith Anne, Grace Ellen. A.B., Harvard U., 1955, M.D., 1960; postgrad., Emmanuel Coll., Cambridge (Eng.) U., 1955-56. Intern, resident internal medicine U. Wash. Hosps., 1960-62, 64-65; postgrad. trainee infectious disease and microbiology U. Wash., 1962-63, 65-66; renal and metabolic diseases Boston U., 1963-64; asst. prof., then assoc. prof. medicine U. Wash. Med. Sch., Seattle, 1966-70; mem. dir. Univ. Hosp., Seattle, 1967-70; prof. community health scis., assoc. dean allied health Duke U. Med. Center, 1970-72; exec. officer Inst. Medicine, Nat. Acad. Scis., 1972-76; prof. internal medicine George Washington U. Sch. Medicine, 1972-76; prof. internal medicine, family and community medicine, dean Med. Sch. chancellor Worcester campus U. Mass., 1976-78; pres. U. Tex. Health Sci. Center, Houston, 1978—; mem. report rev. com. Nat. Acad. Scis.; adv. panel nat. health ins. com., ways and means com. U.S. Ho. Reps., 1975-76. Author: Hippocrates Revisited, 1973, also articles, chpts. in books; Mem. editorial bds. various jours. Bd. dirs. Georgetown U. Lionel de Jersey Harvard fellow, 1955-56. Fellow A.C.P.; mem. Inst. Medicine, Am. Soc. Microbiology, Infectious Disease Soc. Am., Am. Fedn. Clin. Research, Soc. Tchrs. Preventive Medicine, Am. Soc. Nephrology, Soc. Health and Human Values. Office: Office of Pres U Tex Health Sci Center at Houston PO Box 20036 Houston TX 77225

BULL, GEORGE ALBERT, banker; b. Red Lion, Pa., May 28, 1927; s. Mervin E. and Edna May (Gohn) B.; m. Grace Kathryn Rudolph, Nov. 13, 1949; children—Donna Carol, Diana Sue, David Alan. Student Grad. Sch. Banking, Rutgers U., 1961. From teller to cashier Citizens Nat. Bank, Front Royal, Va., 1947-64; asst. v.p., cashier Monticello Nat. Bank, Charlottesville, Va., 1964; asst. cashier Nat. Bank & Trust Co., Charlottesville, 1964-80, asst. to pres., 1980—; sr. v.p., treas. Jefferson Bankshares, Inc., Charlottesville, 1979—; pres., dir. Jefferson Data Service Inc., Charlottesville, Jefferson Properties, Inc., Charlottesville; dir. Jefferson Nat. Bank, Winchester, Va., Nat. Bank & Trust Co., Charlottesville, Va., Jefferson Mgmt. Inc., Charlottesville. Served with U.S. Army, 1945-46. Lodge: Masons. Home: 2315 Wakefield Rd Charlottesville VA 22901 Office: 123 E Main St Charlottesville VA 22901

BULLARD, EDGAR JOHN, III, museum dir.; b. Los Angeles, Sept. 15, 1942; s. Edgar John and Katherine Elizabeth (Dreisbach) B.; B.A., U. Calif. at Los Angeles, 1965, M.A., 1968. Asst. to dir., curator spl. projects Nat. Gallery Art, Washington, 1968-73; dir. New Orleans Mus. Art, 1973—; alt. mem. Citizens Stamp Adv. Com., 1969-71; mem. mus. adv. panel Nat. Endowment for Arts, 1974-77. Trustee, Ga. Mus. Art, U. Ga., Athens, 1975-80. Decorated Order of Republic (Egypt); Samuel H. Kress Found. fellow, 1967-68. Mem. Assn. Art Mus. Dirs. Internat. Council Museums, Am. Assn. Museums, Coll. Art Assn. Democrat. Episcopalian. Club: Nat. Arts (N.Y.C.). Author: Edgar Degas, 1971; John Sloan 1871-1951, 1971; Mary Cassatti: Oils and Pastels, 1972; A Panorama of American Painting, 1975. Home: 1805 Milan St New Orleans LA 70115 also Greenlea Deer Island ME 04627 Office: New Orleans Mus Art PO Box 19123 New Orleans LA 70179

BULLARD, JOHN MOORE, religion educator, church musician; b. Winston-Salem, N.C., May 6, 1932; s. Hoke Vogler and May Evangeline (Moore) B. A.B., U. N.C., 1953, A.M., 1955; M.Div., Yale U., 1957, Ph.D., 1962. Ordained to ministry United Meth. Ch., 1955. Asst. in instrn. Yale U., New Haven, 1957-61; asst. prof. religion Wofford Coll., Spartanburg, S.C., 1961-65, assoc. prof., 1965-70, Albert C. Outler prof. religion, 1970—, chmn. dept., 1962—; minister music (organist-choirmaster) Central United Meth. Ch., Spartanburg, 1961-72, Bethel United Meth. Ch., Spartanburg, 1972—; vis. prof. Biblical Lit. U. N.C., Chapel Hill, summers 1966, 67, U. N.C. at Charlotte, summer 1974; vis. prof. comparative religion Converse Coll., Spartanburg, S.C., 1984. Contbr. articles to profl. jours. Served with Naval ROTC, 1950-52. Grantee NEH summer seminar Harvard U. 1982; Fulbright-NEH grantee, Pakistan 1973, Fund for the Study of Gt. Religions in Asia, 1970-71; named Ky. Col. Mem. Soc. Biblical Lit. (pres. so. sect. 1968-69), Am. Acad. Religion, Am. Guild Organists (dean chpt. 1965-67), S.C. Acad. Religion (pres. 1974-75), New Bach Soc. (Leipzig), Phi Mu Alpha Sinfonia. Avocation: early keyboard music. Home: 1514 Fernwood-Glendale Rd Spartanburg SC 29302 Office: Dept Religion Wofford Coll N Church St Spartanburg SC 29301

BULLARD, RAYMOND LEE, railroad executive; b. Mayo, Fla., May 12, 1927; s. Fred Bascomb and Rosaline (Smith) B.; B.S. in Bus. Adminstrn., U. Fla., 1950; m. Clelia Boushee, Oct. 24, 1954; children—Clelia Bullard Davis, Jane Britt, Molly Bullard McRae, Roslyn Bullard Henderson. Asst. v.p. corp. communications CSX Transp., Jacksonville, Fla., 1973—. Bd. dirs. Jacksonville Symphony Assn.; bd. dirs. Goodwill Industries, pres., 1975; active North Fla. council Boy Scouts Am., Duval County unit Am. Cancer Soc.; mem. Jacksonville U. Council; past mem. public relations adv. council U. Fla. Served with USN, 1945-46, 50-51. Mem. R.R. Public Relations Assn. (v.p. 1965-66, 76-77), Public Relations Soc. Am. (pres. North Fla. chpt. 1975, 80), Ga. Press Assn., Fla. Press Assn. Republican. Baptist. Clubs: Timuquana Country, River. Home: 4705 Wadham Ln Jacksonville FL 32210 Office: 500 Water St Jacksonville FL 32202

BULLEIT, LOUIS AMIEL, engineering company executive; b. Corydon, Ind., Apr. 18, 1931; s. Charles Leo and Lorraine Eva (Albin) B.; m. Barbara Ann Limbach, Oct. 6, 1948; children—Douglas, Deborah, Jacqueline, Jeannie, Randall, Daniel, Teresa, Marie-Angela, James, Joseph, Mark. Draftsman, designer, assoc. ptnr. E. R. Ronald & Assocs., Louisville, 1951—. Active Cath. Youth Orgn., Confrat. of Christian Doctrine. Named Hon. Ky. Col. Mem. Elec. Clearing House Louisville, Internat. Assn. Elec. Insps., Illuminating Engring. Soc. (charter pres. Louisville chpt.). Roman Catholic. Lodge: KC. Home: Route 2 Old Vincennes Rd New Albany IN 47150 Office: ER Ronald & Assocs 1252 Starks Bldg Louisville KY 40202

BULLEN, ADELAIDE KENDALL (MRS. KENNETH SUTHERLAND BULLEN), anthropologist; b. Worcester, Mass., Jan. 12, 1908; d. Oliver Sawyer and Grace (Marble) Kendall, III; A.B. cum laude, Radcliffe Coll., 1943; grad. study Harvard, 1943-48, 50; m. Ripley Pierce Bullen, July 25, 1929 (dec.); children—Dana Ripley II, Pierce Kendall; m. 2d, Kenneth Sutherland Bullen, Mar. 22, 1980. Research anthropologist Health Center, Radcliffe Coll., 1943-44, Fatigue Lab., Harvard Grad. Sch. Bus. Adminstrn., 1944-46; civilian cons. in anthropology U.S. War Dept., 1946; anthropologist dept. anthropology, Peabody Mus., Harvard U., 1946-48, Fla. State Mus., 1949—. Fellow Am. Anthrop. Assn., AAAS, Royal Anthrop. Inst., London, Soc. Applied Anthropology; mem. Am. Assn. Phys. Anthropologists, Am. Psychosomatic Soc., Soc. Research in Child Devel., World Fedn. for Mental Health, N.Y. Acad. Sci., Authors League Am., Authors Guild, Sigma Xi. Clubs: Gainesville Garden, Gainesville Golf and Country, University Women's, Gainesville Woman's. Author: New Answers to the Fatigue Problem, 1956, paperback edit., 1980; also articles in field. Contbg. editor anthropology Handbook of Latin Am. Studies, Library of Congress, 1969-71. Home: 2720 SW 8th Dr Gainesville FL 32601 Office: Fla State Mus Univ Fla Gainesville FL 32611

BULLOCK, BOB, state government official; b. Hillsboro, Tex., July 10, 1929; s. Thomas A. and Ruth M. Bullock; B.A., Tex. Technol. U., 1955; LL.B., Baylor U., 1958; children by previous marriage—Lindy, Robert D. Admitted to Tex. bar, 1957; individual practice law, Hillsboro, 1957-59, Tyler, Tex., 1960-61, Austin, Tex., 1961-67; mem. Tex. Ho. of Reps., 1956-59; asst. atty. gen., Tex., 1967-68; legal counsel Office of Gov., State of Tex., 1969-71; sec. of state, Tex., 1971-73; comptroller of public accounts, Tex., 1975—. Alt. del. Dem. Nat. Conv., 1976. Served with USAF, 1951-54; Korea. Recipient Louisville Gold Medal award Mcpl. Fin. Officers Assn., 1978. Mem. Nat. Assn. State Auditors, Nat. Tax Assn., Nat. Assn. Tax Adminstrs., Fedn. Tax Adminstrs., N. Am. Gasoline Assn. Democrat. Home: PO Box 2243 Austin TX 78768 Office: LBJ Bldg 111 E 17th St Austin TX 78774

BULLOCK, ELBERT POPE, architect; b. Pensacola, Fla., Oct. 29, 1954; s. Ellis Way and Ann (Pope) B.; m. Jane McCauley Watson, May 24, 1980. Student Wofford Coll., Spartanburg, S.C., 1973-75; B.S., Auburn U. (Ala.), 1978, B.Arch., 1979. Registered architect, Ga. Intern architect Surber Barber, Atlanta, 1979-80, Jova/Daniels/Busby, Atlanta, 1980-81; project architect Cooper Carry & Assocs., Atlanta, 1981—; prin. E.P. Bullock Architect, Atlanta, 1983—. Archtl. works include: West Church St. Housing (recipient 1st Place award 1981). Mem. Pub. Adv. Council of Human Services Commn. ARC, Atlanta, 1983, mem. housing com., 1983; mem. Candler Park Neighborhood Assn., Atlanta, 1983. Mem. AIA. Republican. Episcopalian. Home: 1512 Emory Pl Atlanta GA 30307 Office: Cooper Carry Rd Atlanta GA 30306

BULLOCK, ELLIS WAY, JR., architect; b. Birmingham, Ala., Sept. 11, 1928; s. Ellis Way and Martha (Alexander) B.; m. Ann Pope, Nov. 28, 1950; children—Ellis Way III, Pope, Keith, Frank. B.Arch., Auburn U., 1954. Registered architect, Fla., Ala., Ga., Miss., S.C., N.C. Apprentice architect Yonge, Look & Morrison, Pensacola, Fla., 1954-58; owner Ellis Bullock Architect, Pensacola, 1958-73; pres. The Bullock Assocs., Pensacola, 1973—; treas. AIA Research Corp., Washington, 1980-81; chmn. Energy in Arch., Washington, 1980-82; mem. faculty adv. com. Auburn U. Sch. Architecture, 1980—; mem. Nat. Architecture Accrediting Bd., Washington, 1982—. Chmn. Pensacola Hist. Commn., 1967, City of Pensacola Archtl. Review Bd., 1968, Pensacola Bldg. Bd. of Appeals, 1970; 1st lt. U.S. Army, 1950-53. Recipient 1st Honor AIA-Navy, 1977, Award of Merit AIA-Navy, 1976, Outstanding Design USAF, 1980; named Profl. of Yr. Pensacola News Jour., 1977. Fellow AIA (dir. 1979-82, v.p. 1981-82); mem. Fla. Assn. AIA (pres. 1977), Clubs: Rotary, St. Andrews Soc. (Pensacola). Home: 2 Hyde Park Rd Pensacola FL 32503 Office: The Bullock Assocs Architects and Planners Inc 1823 N 9th Ave Pensacola FL 32503

BULLOCK, FRANK W., JR., federal judge; b. Oxford, N.C., Nov. 3, 1938; s. Frank William and Wilma Jackson (Long) B.; m. Frances Dockery Haywood, May 5, 1984. 1 child, Frank William III. B.S. in Bus. Adminstrn., U. N.C., 1961. LL.B., 1963. Bar: N.C., 1963. Assoc. Maupin, Taylor & Ellis, Raleigh, N.C., 1964-68; asst. dir. Adminstrv. Office of Cts. of N.C., Raleigh, 1968-73; ptnr. Douglas, Ravenel, Hardy, Crihfield & Bullock, Greensboro, N.C., 1973-82; judge U.S. Dist. Ct. N.C., Durham, 1982—. Mem. bd. editors N.C. Law Rev., 1962-63; contbr. articles to profl. jours. Mem. ABA, N.C. Bar Assn., Greensboro Bar Assn., N.C. Soc. of Cincinnati. Republican. Presbyterian. Clubs: Greensboro Country. Avocations: golf; tennis; running; history. Office: US Dist Ct PO Box 3807 Durham NC 27702*

BULS, BRUCE BURNETTE, financial executive; b. Rosenberg, Tex., Sept. 14, 1930; s. Edwin Richard and Lillie Mary (Koym) B.; student public schs., Rosenberg; m. Nelda Lea (Kitty) McDaniel, Mar. 6, 1953; children—Richard Lloyd, Michael Bruce. Asst. cashier/comptroller Rosenberg State Bank, 1948-55; br. mgr. Universal CIT Corp., N.Y.C., 1955-63; v.p. North Austin State Bank (Tex.), 1963-66; pres., chief exec. officer Mainland Bank & Trust, Texas City, Tex., 1966-68; pres., chmn. exec. com., chmn. bd., chief exec. officer Pioneer Casualty Ins. Co., San Antonio, 1968-70; v.p. sales and mktg. Royal Crest Homes, San Antonio, 1970-75; mng. broker South Tex. Real Estate, Seguin, 1975-76; comptroller, bus. mgr. Finkel Enterprises, San Antonio, 1976-77; exec. v.p. Gill Savs./Gill Cos., San Antonio, 1977-86; owner Assocs. in Mgmt. Services, 1986—; dir. S.W. Ins. Services, Gill Life Ins. Co., Gill Estate Planning and Bus. Ins., Inc., Gill Mng. Gen. Agy., Inc.; instr. Inst. Fin. Edn. Mem. econ. devel. steering com. Greater San Antonio C. of C., 1980—, mem. agri-bus. devel. steering com., 1980—, chmn. area relations task force, 1981—; mem. Bexar County (Tex.) Democratic Exec. Com., 1972; active San Antonio Live Stock Show. Served with USMC, 1950-52. Fellow Soc. Consumer Credit Execs., Am. Mgmt. Assn.; mem. Internat. Consumer Credit Assn., Tex. Consumer Fin. Assn. (dir., exec. com.), Tex. Bankers Assn. (officer, guest lectr.), Nat. Assn. Master Appraisers (master sr. appraiser), Nat. Assn. Realtors (CRB). Democrat. Clubs: Rotary (San Antonio); Toastmasters (hon.). Home: 196 Townsend Rd Seguin TX 78155 Office: 196-A Townsend Rd Seguin TX 78155 also 6025 Tezel Rd San Antonio TX 78250

BUMGARDNER, KATHRYN H., retired librarian; b. Nashville, Nov. 10, 1922; d. Max and Aline (Farrar) Hamrick; m. Walter Gaynor Bumgardner, July 21, 1948; children—Linda Browning, Donna Carol, Larry Gaynor; B.A., George Peabody Coll., Nashville, 1943; B.S. in Library Sci., Peabody Library Sch., 1944. Cert. librarian, Va., Ga. Librarian, White County High Sch., Sparta, Tenn., 1944-45; asst. librarian Abilene (Tex.) Christian Coll., 1946-48; catalog librarian Va. Commonwealth U., Richmond, 1966-69; assoc. librarian U. West Fla., Pensacola, 1970-74; asst. dir. Watauga Regional Library, Johnson City, Tenn., 1975-83; asst. dir. Lake Blackshear Regional Library, Americus, Ga., 1983-84. Mary Mildred Sullivan scholar, 1943. Mem. Southeastern Library Assn., AAUW. Republican. Mem. Ch. of Christ. Home: 4232 Bonway Dr Pensacola FL 32504

BUMGARNER, JOHN WESLEY, JR., maintenance and construction engineer; b. Newport, Tenn., Mar. 24, 1942; s. John Wesley and Maudie Lee B.; Asso. Sci. in Archtl. Tech., Walters State Community Coll., 1973; B.S., U. Tenn., Knoxville, 1978; m. Nancy Lee Harris, Jan. 24, 1962; children—Kimberly Faye, Donna Elaine; m. Faye B. Candela, May 11, 1984. Quality control lab. technician Chemetron Corp., Newport, 1962-71, environ. control technician, 1971-73; engring. designer Arapahoe Chems., Newport, 1973-78, maintenance planner, estimator, scheduler, 1978-79, asso. engr., 1979—; adj. faculty, mem. adv. com. archtl. tech. dept. Walters State Community Coll. Served with U.S. Army, 1966-68. Mem. Am. Mgmt. Assn. Democrat. Home: 704 Walnut St Newport TN 37821 Office: PO Box 480 Newport TN 37821

BUMPAS, GILES ANTHONY, purchasing exec.; b. Los Angeles, Oct. 28, 1941; s. Carl Leonard and Virginia Elizabeth (Waldo) B.; B.A. in Econs., Rice U., 1963; J.D., U. Tex., Austin, 1967. Buyer, Tex. Instruments, Dallas, 1969-74; dir. purchasing Seaco Computer Display, Garland, Tex., 1974-75; purchasing agt. Atlas Powder Co., Dallas, 1975-84; purchasing mgr. Veeco Integrated Automation, Dallas, 1984—. Bd. dirs. Dallas Met. Ballet, 1975-78; sponsor 500, Inc., Dallas, 1978, 84, 85, 86; bd. dirs. Dallas Dance Council. Served with C.E., U.S. Army, 1967-69. Republican. Methodist. Home: 4517 W Amherst St Dallas TX 75209 Office: 10480 Markison Rd Dallas TX 75238

BUMPERS, DALE L., U.S. senator; b. Charleston, Ark., Aug. 12, 1925; ed. U. Ark.; LL.B., Northwestern U., 1951; m. Betty Flanagan; children—Brent, Bill, Brooke. Owner Charleston Hardware and Furniture Co., 1951-66; admitted to Ark. bar, practiced in Charleston, 1951-70; owner cattle breeding farm, 1966-70; gov. Ark., 1971-75; U.S. senator from Ark., 1975—. Past chmn. United Fund, Boy Scouts Am. Fund, Cancer Fund. Former city atty., Charleston; past pres. Charleston Sch. Bd. Served with USMC, World War II. Recipient C. of C. Citizen's award. Democrat. United Methodist. Office: 229 Dirken Senate Office Bldg Washington DC 20510

BUNDY, WALTER EDWARD, III, eye surgeon, educator; b. Oak Hill, W.Va., Jan. 26, 1947; s. Walter Edward and Jane Cameron (Callison) B.; children—Walter Edward, IV., Graham Matthew, Peyton Carter. B.A., U. Va., 1969; M.D., Med. Coll. of Va., 1973. Diplomate Am. Bd. Ophthalmology. Intern Med. Coll-Va., 1973; resident Bascom Palmer Eye Inst., Miami, 1973-77; chief ophthalmology Naval Submarine Med. Ctr., 1977-79; fellow in glaucoma U. Wis., Madison, 1979-80, instr., ophthalmology, 1980; ptnr. Eye Surgeons of Richmond, Inc., Va., 1980—; instr. Med. Coll. Va., Richmond, 1981—. Richmond Area Heart Assn. fellow, 1964, Fight-for-Sight fellow, 1971, A.D. Williams scholar, 1971-72. Mem. New England Ophthal. Soc., Assn. Naval Aviators, Assn. Mil. Surgeons, Va. Otolaryngology and Ophthalmology Soc., Sigma Zeta. Clubs: St. Anthony (N.Y.C.); Commonwealth (Richmond); Country Club of Va. Office: Eye Surgeons of Richmond Inc 5855 Bremo Rd Suite 307 Richmond VA 23226

BUNN, SPRUILL G., restaurant chain executive. Pres., chief operating officer Hardee's Food Systems Inc., Rocky Mount, N.C. Office: Hardee's Food Systems Inc 1233 N Church St Rocky Mount NC 27801*

BUNTING, GARY GLENN, operations research analyst, educator; b. Toledo, Ohio, Mar. 19, 1947; s. Glenn Rose and Maxine (Hunt) B.; m. Glenda Marlene Mechum, Aug. 23, 1974; children—Wendy Daniele, Bradley Glenn. B.S., Auburn U., 1969; M.S., Troy State U., 1977. Research analyst City of Jacksonville, Fla., 1972-76; ops. research analyst U.S. Army Aviation Ctr., Ft. Rucker, Ala., 1976-78, U.S. Army Tng. Support Ctr., Ft. Eustis, Va., 1978-80, USAF Tactical Air Warfare Ctr., Eglin AFB, Fla., 1980-85, Office Sec. Def. Tng. Data and Analysis Ctr., Orlando, Fla., 1985—; adj. assoc. prof. U. West Fla., Ft. Walton Beach, 1982, Troy State U., Ft. Walton Beach, 1983—. Contbr. articles to profl. jours. Served with U.S. Army, 1969-71. Recipient Civilian Excellence award, USAF Tactical Air Warfare Ctr. and Air Force Assn., 1983. Mem. Air Force Assn. Republican. Lodge: Elks. Avocations: reading; photography. Home: 52 Sweetwater Creek Circle Oviedo FL 32765 Office: 3280 Progress Dr Orlando FL

BUNTON, LUCIUS DESHA, federal judge; b. Del Rio, Tex., Dec. 1, 1924; s. Lucius Desha and Avis Maurine (Fisher) B.; student U. Chgo., 1943-44; B.A., U. Tex., Austin, 1947, J.D., 1950; m. Mary Jane Carsey, June 18, 1947; children—Cathryne Avis Bunton Warner, Lucius Desha. Admitted to Tex. bar, 1949; individual practice law, Uvalde, Tex., 1950; asso. firm H.O. Metcalfe, Marfa, Tex., 1951-54; dist. atty. 83d Jud. Dist. Tex., 1954-59; mem. firm Shafer, Gilliland, Davis, Bunton & McCollum, Odessa, Tex., 1959-79; judge U.S. Dist. Ct. for Western Dist. Tex., Midland, 1979—; Trustee, Ector County (Tex.) Ind. Sch. Dist., 1967-76. Served with inf. U.S. Army, 1943-46. Mem. Tex. Bar Found. (charter), Am. Bar Assn., Am. Bar Found., Am. Coll. Probate Counsel, Am. Acad. Matrimonial Lawyers, State Bar Tex. (chmn. 1971-72, v.p. 1973-74, pres.-elect 1979). Baptist. Lodge: Masons (Marfa). Office: PO Box 1774 Midland TX 79701

BUNZL, RUDOLPH HANS, diversified manufacturing executive; b. Vienna, Austria, July 20, 1922; came to U.S., 1940, naturalized, 1944; s. Robert Max and Nellie Margaret (Burian) B.; B.S. in Chem. Engring., Ga. Inst. Tech., 1943; m. Rema R. Templeton, Apr. 6, 1947; children—Ann Mary Bunzl Kamoe, Carol Elizabeth Bunzl Showker; m. 2d, Esther R. Mendelsohn, Nov. 14, 1970. With Shell Chem. Co., Calif., 1943-54; v.p. Am. Filtrona Corp., Richmond, Va., 1954-59, pres., 1959-83, chmn., 1983—; dir. Sovran Bank, N.A., Richmond. Served with U.S. Army, 1944-46. Mem. Am. Inst. Chem. Engrs. Office: Am Filtrona Corp 8401 Jefferson Davis Hwy Richmond VA 23234

BURAS, BRENDA ALLYNN, public and government affairs executive; b. New Orleans, May 1, 1954; d. Allen Anthony and Gloria Short Buras. B.A.C. in Mgmt., Loyola U., New Orleans, 1976, M.B.A., 1984. Engr.'s asst. Texaco U.S.A., New Orleans, 1976-78, natural gas contracts analyst, 1978-80, pub. affairs asst., 1980-83, pub. affairs coordinator, 1983-85, pub. and govt. affairs coordinator, 1985—; owner Achievements Unlimited, motivational and communications counseling; lectr. Silva Mind Devel. and Stress Control. Loaned exec. United Way Greater New Orleans, 1978. Mem. Pub. Relations Soc. Am., Cross Keys Nat. Honor-Service Frat., Women in Communications, U.S. Figure Skating Assn., Silva Internat. Grad. Assn. Republican. Christian. Clubs: Dixieland Figure Skating, Press (New Orleans), YMCA (Lee Circle). Home: 1322 Tennobrahc St Arabi LA 70032 Office: PO Box 60252 400 Poydras St New Orleans LA 70160

BURCH, JOHN CHRISTOPHER, JR., investment banker; b. Nashville, Jan. 18, 1940; s. John Christopher and Frances Vivian (Harris) B.; m. Susan Marie Klein, Sept. 13, 1969; children—Frances Marie, Christina Polk, John Christopher III. B.A., Vanderbilt U., 1966. Credit analyst Bank N.Y., N.Y.C., 1966-70; v.p. instl. sales Loeb Rhoades & Co., N.Y.C., 1970-75, J.C. Bradford & Co., Nashville, 1976-82, Equitable Securities Corp., Nashville, 1982—. Active Com. Fgn. Relations, Nashville, 1976, N.C. Soc. Cin., Raleigh, 1979. Served with U.S. Army, 1962-65. Mem. Fedn. Fin. Analysts. Episcopalian. Clubs: Belle Meade Country, Cumberland (Nashville). Home: 705 Hillwood Blvd Nashville TN 37205 Office: Equitable Securities Corp First American Ctr Nashville TN 37238

BURCH, MARY RUTH, special education consultant; b. Altoona, Pa., Sept. 27, 1952; d. Stanley G. and Martina K. Burch; m. Jon S. Bailey, June 9, 1979. B.S., Fla. State U., 1974, M.S., 1976, Ph.D., 1982. Behavior program specialist Sunland Tng. Ctr., Tallahassee, 1977-78, qualified mental retardation profl., unit dir., 1978-80; exec. dir., spl. edn. dir. Behavior Mgmt. Consultants, Inc., Tallahassee, 1980—; invited cons. to retardation facilities in Eng., Belgium and Wales, 1981; mem. Van Dijk Inst. for Leaders in Deaf-Blind Edn., 1978; supr. Right-to-Read Program, 1972-74; mem. Nat. Com. Mentally Retarded Persons Leisure Service Needs, 1982—. Editor Autism Alert Newsletter, 1980-82; contbr. articles to various publs. Chairperson Human Rights Com. for

Retarded, Tallahassee, 1980-83; vol. worker St. Luke's Hosp., Jacksonville, 1967-70. Mem. Fla. Assn. for Behavior Analysis (co-editor quar. 1982), Internat. Soc. for Research and Rehab., Am. Assn. on Mental Deficiency, Assn. for Behavior Analysis, Council for Exceptional Children, Phi Kappa Phi. Avocations: ballet, Highland dancing, tennis. Home: 1708 Kathryn Dr Tallahassee FL 32308 Office: Behavior Mgmt Consultants Inc 1708 Kathryn Dr Tallahassee FL 32308

BURCHAM, ZELDA DEANE, nurse, nursing administrator; b. Wilmington, N.C., Jan. ', 1935; d. John James and Eunice Mae (Corbett) Pererson; m. Billy Brian Burcham Sr., June 15, 1957; children—Daphne, Brian, Mary Catherine. Diploma in nursing James Walker Meml. Hosp. of Nursing, 1956. Head nurse U.T. Med. Branch Galveston, Tex., 1961-62; operating room supr. Hardin Meml. Hosp., Kountze, Tex., 1963-69; home health nurse Home Health Agy., Kirbyville, Tex., 1969-70; pub. health nurse Hardin County Health Dept., Kountze, Tex., 1970-73; dir. nursing Hardin Meml. Hosp., 1973-76, Silsbee Doctors Hosp., Tex., 1976—. Service chmn. Am. Cancer Soc., Kountze, 1970-77. Mem. THA Soc. Hosp. Nursing Service Adminstra. Democrat. Presbyterian. Club: Silsbee Country. Avocations: golf; collecting Rockwell plates. Home: PO Box 1404 Silsbee TX 77656 Office: Silsbee Doctors Hosp Hwy 418 PO Box 1208 Silsbee TX 77656

BURDEN, DAVID LYNN, mining engineer; b. Owensboro, Ky., Apr. 9, 1952; s. Billy Phillip and Elizabeth Ann (Barnard) B.; m. Rosemary Lynn Reese, May 17, 1973; children—David Ross, Sarah Danielle. B.S. in Civil Engring., U. Ky.-Lexington, 1974. Registered land surveyor, Ky.; registered profl. engr., Ky., Ohio, Ind., Colo., Utah, Ill. Mgmt. trainee Peabody Coal Co., Star Mine, 1974-75, resident engr., 1975-77, project engr. eastern div., 1977-79, sr. project engr., 1979-83, sr. mine engr., Graham, Ky., 1983-84; asst. supr. Star South Mine, 1985—; instr. Community Coll., Madisonville, Ky., 1976-77. Recipient Tech. Achievement award Tri-State Council for Sci. and Engring., 1982. Mem. Ky. Soc. Profl. Engrs. (Outstanding Achievement in Mining award 1983, Young Engr. of Yr. 1984, pres. chpt. 1984), Nat. Soc. Profl. Engrs., Soc. Mining Engrs. of AIME, Western Ky. Mine Inst. (pres. 1983), Ky. Mine Inst. (pres. 1985). Democrat. Baptist. Lodge: Order Ky. Cols. Office: PO Box 66 Graham KY 42344

BURDETT, THOMAS STUART, JR., mechanical engineer; b. Point Pleasant, W.Va., Feb. 8, 1922; s. Thomas Stuart Burdett and Inez (Dess) Parker; m. Margaret Lee Thomas, Dec. 1, 1945; 1 child, Pamela. B.S. in Engring., U. Ky., 1950. Registered profl. engr., Calif. Engr., Sylvania, Emporium, Pa., 1950-63; mgr. engring. Raytheon Co., Newport, R.I., 1964-74; staff engr. E-Systems Inc., St. Petersburg, Fla., 1974—. Pres., Pinellas County Jr. Achievement, St. Petersburg, 1984—. Served to capt. USAF, 1941-45. Mem. Am. Inst. Indsl. Engrs., Am. Inst. Plant Engrs. Republican. Avocations: tennis; sailing. Home: 297 Monte Cristo Blvd Tierra Verde FL 33715 Office: E-Systems Inc 1501 72d St N St Petersburg FL 33733

BURDETTE, KEITH, state senator, business executive; b. Apr. 27, 1955. Student Parkersburg Community Coll. and Glenville State Coll. Pres., Keith Burdette Enterprises, Inc.; owner, mgr. Ford's Jewelers, Athens, Ohio; mem. W.Va. Senate, currently, vice chmn. govt. orgn. com., co-chmn. spl. joint com. on small bus.; bd. dirs. Western Dist. Guidance Ctr. Mem. Wood County Community Action. Recipient Outstanding Legislator award W.Va. Pub. Employees Assn.; Outstanding Citizen award Fraternal Order of Police. Mem. Jaycees. Democrat. Baptist. Office: W VA Senate State Capitol Charleston WV 25305

BURDETTE, WALTER JAMES, surgeon, educator; b. Hillsboro, Tex., Feb. 5, 1915; s. James S. and Ovazene (Weatherred) B.; m. Kathryn Lynch, Apr. 9, 1947; children—Susan, William J. A.B., Baylor U., 1935; A.M., U. Tex., 1936, Ph.D., 1938; M.D., Yale U., 1942. Diplomate Am. Bd. Surgery, Am. Bd. Thoracic Surgery. Intern Johns Hopkins Hosp., 1942-43; Harvey Cushing fellow surgery Yale U., 1943-44; resident in surgery New Haven Hosp., 1944-46; inst., asst., assoc. prof. surgery La. State U., 1946-55; vis. surgeon Charity Hosp. of La., 1946-55; cons. Touro Infirmary and So. Baptist Hosp., 1952-55, Oak Ridge Inst. Nuclear Studies Hosp., 1953-59; vis. investigator Chester Beatty Inst. Cancer Research, Brompton and Royal Cancer Hosp., London, 1953, Max Planck Institut Fuer Biochemie, Tuebingen, Germany, summer 1955; prof. clin. surgery St. Louis U. Sch. Medicine, 1956-57; prof., head dept. surgery U. Utah, 1957-65; dir. lab. clin. biology, surgeon-in-chief-Salt Lake Gen. Hosp., 1957-65; chief surgeon cons. VA Hosps., Salt Lake City, 1957-65; prof. surgery, assoc. dir. U. Tex.-M.D. Anderson Hosp. and Tumor Inst., Houston, 1965-72; prof. surgery, U. Tex., Houston, 1971—; adj. prof. pharmacology U. Houston, 1975—; pres. Nat. Biomed. Found., 1972—; cons. Hermann Hosp., Ctr. Pavilion Hosp., 1970—, St. Luke's Hosp., 1975—; Gibson Lectr. advanced surgery Oxford U., 1966; vis. prof. U. Oxford, spring 1965; ofcl. U. Congo, summer 1968. Chmn. Genetics study sect. NIH; cons. Nat. Cancer Inst.; mem. Nat. Adv. Cancer Council, Nat. Adv. Heart Council, Surgeons General's Com. on Smoking and Health; chmn. U.S.A. nat. com. Internat. Union Against Cancer; mem. Transplantation com. Nat. Acad. Scis.; chmn. working Cadre on cancer large intestine Nat. Cancer Soc.; elder, deacon Christian Ch. Recipient Baylor U. A.E.D. Disting. Alumnus award, 1983; Rockefeller travel fellow, summer 1957. Fellow ACS; mem. Soc. Surgery Alimentary Tract, Am. Assn. Cancer Research (dir.), Am. Cancer Soc. (chmn. research adv. council, mem. council on analysis and projection), Am. Surg. Assn., Soc. Clin. Surgery (treas.), Soc. U. Surgeons, AMA, Soc. Exptl. Biology and Medicine, Genetics Soc. Am., AAAS, Western Soc. Clin. Research, Am. Assn. Thoracic Surgery, Transplantation Soc., N.Y. Acad. Sci., Soc. Am. Naturalists, New Orleans Surg. Soc., Salt Lake City Surg. Soc., St. Louis Surg. Soc., Houston Surg. Soc., Tex. Med. Soc., Harris County Med. Soc., So., Western Surg. Assns., So. Thoracic Surg. Soc., Peruvian Cancer Soc. (hon.), Am. Assn. for Cancer Research, Soc. for Surgery Alimentary Tract, Am. Soc. Clin. Oncology, Am. Soc. for Cancer Edn., Tex. Surg. Soc., Assn. Yale Alumni in Medicine (exec. com. 1977), Soc. Internat. de Chirung, Phi Beta Kappa, Sigma Xi, Alpha Omega Alpha, Nu Sigma Nu. Editor, author: Etiology, Treatment of Leukemia, 1958; Methodology in Human Genetics, 1962; Methodology in Mammalism Genetics, 1962; Methodology in Basic Genetics, 1963; Primary Hepatoma, 1965; Carcinoma of The Alimentary Tract, 1965; Viruses Inducing Cancer, 1966; Carcinoma of the Colon and Antecedent Epithelium, 1970; Planning and Analysis of Clinical Studies, 1970; Invertebrate Endocrinology and Hormonal Heterophylly, 1974; mem. editorial bd.: Surg. Rounds; contbr. articles to med. and sci. jours. Home: 239 Chimney Rock Rd Houston TX 77024 Office: Plaza Med Ctr 1200 Binz St Suite 740 Houston TX 77004

BURDICK, GLENN ARTHUR, college dean; b. Pavillion, Wyo., Sept. 9, 1932; s. Stephen Arthur and Elizabeth (McClerg) B.; m. Joyce Mae Huggett, July 14, 1951; children—Stephen, Randy Glenn. B.S., Ga. Inst. Tech., 1958, M.S., 1959; Ph.D., MIT, 1961. Instr. physics Ga. Inst. Tech., 1958-59; mem. div. sponsored research MIT, 1961; sr. mem. research staff Sperry, 1961-65; mem. grad. faculty U. Fla., Tampa, 1963-65; assoc. prof. physics and math. U. South Fla., 1965-68, prof., 1968—, dean Coll. Engring., 1979—; pres. Internat. Soc. for Hybrid Microelectronics, 1973-47; dir. ABA Industries; cons. in field. Mem. Tampa Bay Region Fgn. Affairs Com., 1981—; mem. Mayor's Fgn. Trades Fair Com., 1982—. Served with USAF, 1950-54. Mem. IEEE (named Fla. West Coast Engr. of Yr. 1980), Am. Soc. Engring. Edn., N.Y. Acad. Sci., Am. R.R. Engrs. Assn., Nat. Fire Protection Agy., Phi Kappa Phi, Sigma Xi, Omicron Delta Kappa. Lodge: Rotary. Contbr. articles to profl. jours. Patentee in field. Home: 1005 Curlew Pl Tarpon Springs FL 33589 Office: Dean's Office College of Engineering University of South Florida Tampa FL 33620

BURES, PAUL LESLIE, JR., TV exec.; b. Cleve., Apr. 19, 1933; s. Paul Leslie and Margaret Elizabeth (Tompkins) B.; B.S., Miami U., Oxford, Ohio; m. Felicia M. Visconti, Sept. 26, 1966; children—Kristen Lee, Heather Elizabeth. Media supr. oil account J. Walter Thompson, Inc., N.Y.C., 1957-60; account, mktg. exec. Ogilvy & Mather, Inc., N.Y.C., 1960-66; sales exec. ABC-TV, N.Y.C., 1966-71; gen. sales mgr. KTRK-TV (Capital Cities Communications), Houston, 1971—; exec. com. TvB Sales Adv. Com., 1977—, co-chmn., 1980, chmn., 1981. Served with USCG, 1952-55. Mem. Nat. Acad. TV Arts and Scis., Am. Mgmt. Assn., Houston C. of C. Republican. Episcopalian. Script editor/adv.: Your Competitive Medium, 1979, The Sum of the Alternatives, 1978, Television: The Persuasive Medium, 1980, A New Perspective on the Changing 80's, 1981. Office: KTRK-TV 3310 Bissonnet St Houston TX 77005

BURFORD, ALEXANDER MITCHELL, JR., physician; b. Memphis, Mar. 21, 1929; s. Alexander Mitchell and Mary Young (Tittle) B.; B.S., Florence (Ala.) State Coll., 1951; M.D., U. Tenn., Memphis, 1957. Intern, U. Tenn., Knoxville, 1957-58, resident in pathology, Memphis, 1958-62; asso. pathologist Eliza Coffee Meml. Hosp., Florence, Ala., 1962-73, dir. lab., chief pathology, 1973—; practice medicine specializing in pathology, 1958—, Florence Pathologists P.C., 1977-83. Mem. Ala. Assn. Pathologists (pres. 1974-75), Coll. Am. Pathologists (del. 1972—), Birmingham Area Pathologists Assn., Am. Soc. Clin. Pathologists, Am. Assn. Blood Banks, Am. Forestry Assn., Am. Rifleman Assn., Nat. Wildlife Fedn., Florence C. of C., Friends of Florence-Lauderdale Pub. Library, Alpha Kappa Kappa, Kappa Mu Epsilon, Alpha Psi Omega. Home: 652 Howell St Florence AL 35630 Office: Eliza Coffee Meml Hosp PO Box 818 Florence AL 35631

BURGE, WILLIAM LEE, business information exec.; b. Atlanta, June 27, 1918; s. William Frederick and Leona (Payne) B.; ed. Ga. State Coll. Bus. Adminstrn., 1937-42; LL.D. (hon.), Mercer U., 1978; m. Willette Richey, Feb. 27, 1937; children—Judith Phillips, William Roger. With Equifax Inc. (formerly Retail Credit Co.), 1936—, br. mgr., Greensboro, N.C., 1949-51, div. mgr., Pitts., 1951-58, v.p., Atlanta, 1959-65, exec. v.p., 1964-65, pres., 1965-81, chief exec. officer, 1967-83, chmn. bd., 1976—, chmn. Equifax Inc. affiliates, Equifax Services Ltd. Can.; hon. dir. First Atlanta Corp. Nat. Service Industries; dir. Informes de Centrales of Mex. Gen. chmn. United Way, Atlanta, 1961; chmn. United Negro Coll. Fund., 1974-75; regional chmn. Nat. Alliance of Businessmen, 1969-70, 1981—; chmn. bd. regents Univ. System Ga., 1972-73; mem. coll. accreditation commn. So. Assn. Colls. and Sch.; bd. dirs. Council on Post Secondary Edn.; trustee Atlanta Arts Alliance, YMCA; mem. bd. Central Atlanta Progress; bd. dirs. Atlanta chpt. ARC. Served with AUS, World War II. Named Atlanta's Young Man of Year, 1948, one of Atlanta's Leaders of Tomorrow, Time mag., 1952, Alumnus of Yr., Ga. State U., 1968. Mem. Conf. Bd., Atlanta C. of C. (pres. 1966), Nat. C. of C. (panel on privacy), Jr. C. of C. (pres. 1947-48). Club: Kiwanis (pres. 1965). Home: 3659 Northside Dr NW Atlanta GA 30305 Office: 1600 Peachtree St NW Atlanta GA 30309

BURGEN, FRANK STANLEY, JR., building materials company executive; b. Ferriday, La., June 20, 1926; s. Frank Stanley and Louise (Randolph) B.; m. J. Ann Conway, Oct. 5, 1946; children—Constance Ann, Robert Stanley. B.C.S., U. Ga., 1954. Vice pres. mktg. Celotex Corp., Tampa, Fla., 1970-73, pres. Briggs div., Tampa, 1973-74, sr. v.p. parent co., Tampa, 1974-77, pres. bldg. products div., 1977-82, exec. v.p. parent co., 1982, pres., chief exec. officer, 1982—, also dir.; dir. Celotex-Marley, Inc., San Bernardino, Calif. Served with U.S. Army, 1944-46. Baptist. Avocations: tennis; golf. Office: The Celotex Corp 1500 N Dale Mabry Hwy Box 22602 Tampa FL 33622

BURGERT, JUDITH O'NEILL, ladies apparel executive; b. Boston, May 12, 1941; d. Forrest A. and Florence J. (Van Eck) O'Neill; m. Woodward Burgert, Jr., Mar. 6, 1965; children—Woodward III, Aimee Elizabeth. Student Chandler Sch. for Women, 1960, N.Y. Sch. Interior Design, 1967-69. Sec. to v.p. United Fruit Co., Boston, 1959; airline hostess internat. div. TWA, N.Y.C., 1961-65; owner Judy's Design Studio, Inc., Tallahassee, 1977—. Vice-pres. Civic Ballet Bd., 1976; active Jr. League Tallahassee, Med. Wives Aux., Tallahassee Symphony. Republican. Episcopalian. Club: Killearn Country (Tallahassee). Office: 3425 Thomasville Rd Tallahassee FL 32308

BURGESS, ELWOOD JOHNSON, JR., psychologist, mental health administrator; b. Warrenton, N.C., Apr. 9, 1956; s. Elwood Johnson and Belle (Limer) B.; m. Wendy Sharon Lopp, Sept. 7, 1985. B.S., Campbell Coll., 1979; M.A. in Clin. Psychology summa cum laude, Middle Tenn. State U., 1983. Psychol. asst. N.C. Dept. Corrections, Lillington, 1978-81, staff psychologist, Troy, 1983-84, cons. psychol. assoc., 1985—; staff psychologist Tenn. Dept. Vocat. Rehab., Smyrna, 1982-83; research assoc. Middle Tenn. State U., 1982; adult services dir. Lee-Harnett Mental Health Authority, Sanford, N.C., 1984—; cons. Rape and Family Violence Ctr., Sanford, 1984—, Central Carolina Tech. Coll., Sanford, 1984—. Mem. Coalition for Reducing Stress, Sanford; Assn. For Retarded Citizens, 1985. Mem. Am. Psychol. Assn., Tenn. Psychol. Assn., Middle Tenn. State Psychol. Assn., N.C. Psychol. Assn., Sigma Honor Fraternity (Hogan award 1983), Psi Chi Honor Fraternity. Democrat. Baptist. Clubs: Sanford Racquet, Sandhills Yacht, Lee County Tennis Assn. Office: Lee-Harnett Mental Health Authority 130 Carbonton Rd Sanford NC 27330

BURGESS, EUNICE LESTER, counselor; b. Madison, Fla., Dec. 17, 1935; d. Thomas and Rebecca (Royal) Lester; B.S. in Elem. Edn., Tuskegee Inst., 1958, M.Ed., in Psychology and Guidance, 1963; postgrad. U. N.C., 1967-68, U. South Fla., 1982—; m. Miller Burgess, Jr., Aug. 18, 1958; children—Brenda Joyce, Wanda Renee, Kenneth Bernard. Coordinator student affairs Tuskegee Inst., Ala., 1960-64; vocat. counselor Job Corps Center for Women, St. Petersburg, Fla., 1964-66; vocat. rehab. counselor State Dept. Edn., St. Petersburg, 1966-68; elem. counselor Pinellas County Sch. System, Clearwater, Fla., 1968-77; guidance coordinator St. Petersburg Vocat.-Tech. Inst., 1977-80, coordinator outreach recruitment, 1980—; cons. in career edn.; staff devel. tchr. in humanistic edn. Bd. dirs. NAACP, 1975—; v.p. Pinellas County (Fla.) Black Polit. Caucus, 1976-77; co-chmn. St. Petersburg Community Alliance, 1974-75; mem. Guidance Adv. Bd. Pinellas County, 1975-76; sec., treas. St. Petersburg Fair Housing Bd., 1976-78; mem. Pinellas Profl. Democratic Women's Club, 1976—; v.p. Pinellas County Biracial Adv. Com., 1980-82, pres., 1982-84. Recipient service award Elementary Div. of Fla. Sch. Counselor Assn., 1975, 1975; and leadership award St. Petersburg C. of C., 1975; outstanding performance award City of St. Petersburg, 1973; community service awards Bethune Cookman Alumni Assn., 1976, St. Petersburg C. of C., 1977; Outstanding Educator of Yr. award Suncoast C. of C. and Pinellas County Sch. Bd., 1983; Disting. Educator award Fla. Masons, 1983; Nat. Parent of Yr. award Tuskegee Inst., 1983; numerous others. Mem. Am., Fla., Suncoast (sec. 1981-82) personnel and guidance assns., Am. (human rights coordinator 1977-82), Fla. (v.p. post-secondary 1980-82, Eunice Burgess human rights award 1984), Suncoast sch. counselor assns., NEA, Am. Vocat. Guidance Assn., Fla. Vocat. Assn., Assn. Non White Concerns, Sickle Cell Found. Pinellas County, Zeta Phi Beta (Woman of Yr. 1976, treas. 1980-82). Democrat. Baptist. Home: 3012 DeSoto Way S Saint Petersburg FL 33712 Office: 901 34th St S Saint Petersburg FL 33712

BURGESS, GLEN DONAVON, coal company executive, private consultant; b. Charleston, W. Va., Aug. 26, 1951; s. Dave and Rethel Virginia (Carr) B.; m. Tonie Ann Simmons, Mar. 5, 1982; 1 child, Ashlee Donavon-Jean; children by previous marriage—D. Scott, Kirston Leigh, Ashlee Donavon, Jean. Assoc. in math. Hampton-Sidney Coll. (Va.), 1971; B.S. in Mining Engring., Va. Poly. Inst., 1973, B.S. in Mining Tech., 1974. Mng. ptnr. BurCarte Industries, Ltd., Charleston, 1974-76; v.p., gen. mgr. Investment Resources Australia, Charleston and N.Y.C., 1976-77; v.p. in charge prodn. Upper Elkhorn Coal Co., Harlen and Lexington, Ky., 1977-83; gen. mgr. prodn. Ashland Energies, Ltd., Lexington and N.Y.C., 1979—; dir. Upper Elkhorn Coal Co., Ashland Energies, Ltd. Mem. European Community-U.S.A. Businessman's Council, 1980, Lexington Citizens Council, 1980. Served to 1st lt. Army N.G., 1970-77. Mem. Soc. Mining Engrs. Lodge: Lions. Home: 144 Oakwood Rd Charleston WV 25314 Office: Ashland Energies Ltd Corporate Plaza Lexington KY 40575

BURGESS, OLIVER TAYLOR, hairstylist, cosmetologist; b. Dendron, Va., Aug. 29, 1918; s. Herman Oliver and Virginia (Trueheart) B.; student Kirby's Beauty Sch., Norfolk, Va., 1948, Robert France Hair Design Inst., N.Y.C., 1949;; m. Ida Majestic Chester, Dec. 17, 1941; 1 son, Oliver Taylor. Owner beauty salon, Wakefield, Va., 1948-50; owner beauty salons, Norfolk, 1950—, Taylor Burgess Hairstyling Salons, Inc., 1962—; guest stylist John H. Breck Co., in U.S. and Europe, 1957—. Served as cpl. 116th Inf., AUS, 1941-45; ETO. Decorated Purple Heart, Bronze Star. Mem. Nat. Hairdressers and Cosmetologists Assn., Norfolk Hairdressers Assn., Internat. Platform Assn., Intercoiffure Am. (parliamentarian 1977-83), Va. Hairdressers and Cosmetologists Assn. (pres. 1965-66), Norfolk C. of C., Wards Corner Bus. Men's Assn. Baptist (deacon). Clubs: Masons, Shriners, Lions. Home: 6435 Newport Ave Norfolk VA 23505 Office: 7500 Granby St Wards Corner Norfolk VA 23505

BURGIN, E. J., natural gas pipeline company executive; b. White Pine, Tenn., Sept. 27, 1927; s. Martin Lee and Virginia (Bailey) B.; m. Barbara Jean Inman, Dec. 28, 1971; 1 dau., Stacey Jean. B.S.M.E., U. Tenn., 1955; postrad., Stanford U., 1981. Vice pres. So. Ga. Natural Gas Co., Thomasville, 1955-58; gen. supt. ops. Fla. Gas Transmission Co., Winter Park, 1959-73, v.p. ops., 1974-77, v.p. mktg., 1978-81, exec. v.p., 1981—, dir., 1979—. Served to capt. U.S. Army, 1951-59. Mem. Am. Gas. Assn. (award of merit 1975), So. Gas. Assn., Fla. Natural Gas Assn. (dir.). Republican. Club: Rolling Hills Country (pres. 1979-81). Lodge: Masons. Home: 312 Pressview Ave Longwood FL 32750 Office: PO Box 44 Winter Park FL 32789

BURGIN, ROBERT F., medical center administrator; b. Orlando, Fla., Oct. 18, 1940; s. Robert H. and Helen Elizabeth (Fowler) B.; m. Glenda Sutton, Apr. 8, 1967; children—Carrie, Andrew. A.B. in History and Econs., Miami U., Oxford, Ohio, 1962; M.H.A., U. Mich., 1964. Resident, Bklyn. Hosp., 1963-64; dir. patient care adminstrn. Evanston Hosp., Ill., 1967-70; chief ops. Eugene Talmadge Meml. Hosp., Augusta, Ga., 1970-75; chief operating officer N.C. Meml. Hosp., Chapel Hill, 1975-81; pres. Meml. Mission Med. Ctr., Asheville, N.C., 1981—. Vice-chmn. Asheville Area Red Cross, 1984; trustee N.C. Hosp. Assn., 1985, Sun Alliance, 1985; mem. United Way Asheville, 1985. Mem. Am. Coll. Hosp. Adminstrs. Democrat. Methodist. Home: 599 Old Toll Rd Asheville NC 28804 Office: Meml Mission Med Ctr 509 Biltmore Ave Asheville NC 28801

BURGUIERES, PHILIP JOSEPH, metal products co. exec.; b. Franklin, La., Sept. 3, 1943; s. Denis P.J. and Emma L. (LeBlanc) B.; B.S. in Mech. Engring., U. Southwestern La., 1965; M.B.A., U. Pa., 1970; m. Cheryl A. Courrege, Aug. 21, 1965; children—Emily Louise, Philip Martial. Adminstrv. asst. Cameron Iron Works, Inc., Houston, 1971, controller European ops., 1972-75, v.p. corp. services, 1975-77, v.p. forged products div., 1977-79, exec. v.p. ops., 1979-81; pres. and chief operating officer, Cameron Iron Works, Inc., 1981—; dir. J.M. Burguieres Co., Ltd., New Orleans, 1st City Nat. Bank, Houston. Served with USN, 1966-69. Mem. ASME, Forging Industry Assn., Nat. Ocean Industries Assn., Petroleum Equipment Suppliers Assn., Tau Beta Pi, Pi Tau Sigma. Republican. Roman Catholic. Office: Cameron Iron Works Inc PO Box 1212 Houston TX 77251

BURK, RAYMOND FRANKLIN, JR., physician, medical educator, researcher; b. Kosciusko, Miss., Dec. 9, 1942; s. Raymond Franklin and Florence Annie (Davis) B.; m. Enikoe Vikor, June 17, 1967; children—Teresa Marie, Stephen Morrison. B.A., U. Miss., 1963; M.D., Vanderbilt U., 1968. Diplomate Am. Bd. Internal Medicine. Intern, Vanderbilt Hosp., Nashville, 1968-69, resident in medicine, 1969-70; asst. prof. medicine and biochemistry U. Tex. S.W. Med. Sch., Dallas, 1975-78; assoc. prof. medicine and biochemistry La. State U. Sch. Medicine, Shreveport, 1978-80; assoc. prof. medicine U. Tex. Health Sci. Ctr., San Antonio, 1980-82, prof., 1982—; researcher in field; mem. staff Med. Ctr. Hosp., Audie Murphy VA Hosp. Served to maj. U.S. Army, 1970-73. NIH grantee, 1974—. Mem. Am. Soc. Biol. Chemists, Am. Soc. Clin. Investigation, Am. Inst. Nutrition. Contbr. articles to profl. jours. Office: 7703 Floyd Curl Dr San Antonio TX 78284

BURK, SYLVIA JOAN, petroleum landman, author; b. Dallas, Oct. 16, 1928; d. Guy Thomas and Sylvia (Herrin) Ricketts; m. R. B. Murray, Jr., Sept. 7, 1951 (div. Jan. 1961); children—Jeffery Randolph, Brian BeVaughn; m. 2d, Bryan Burk, Apr. 26, 1973. B.A., So. Meth. U., Dallas, 1950, M.L.A., 1974; postgrad. U. So. Calif., 1973-74. Landman, E. B. Germany & Sons, Dallas, 1970-73; asst. mgr. real estate Atlantic Richfield Co., Los Angeles, 1973-74; landman Gold King Prodn. Co., Houston, 1974-76; co-owner Burk Properties, Houston, 1976—. Author: Petroleum Lands and Leasing, 1983, 2d edit., 1987. Mem. Am. Assn. Petroleum Landmen (dir. 1980-82, 2d v.p. 1982-83), Houston Assn. Petroleum Landmen (dir. 1978-79). Republican. Presbyterian. Clubs: Dallas Woman's, Sugar Creek Country. Office: Burk Properties Southwestern Bank Plaza Suite 555 12603 Southwest Freeway Stafford TX 77477

BURKE, JOHN ANDREW, JR., chemistry educator, administrator; b. Eastland, Tex., Dec. 14, 1936; s. John Andrew and Tom (Crowder) B.; m. Gwendolyn Mary Wright, July 7, 1962; children—Andrew, Christopher, Elizabeth. A.A., Paris Jr. Coll., 1957; B.S., Tex. Tech. Coll., 1959; M.S., Ohio State U., 1961, Ph.D., 1963. Asst. prof. Trinity U., San Antonio, 1963-66, assoc. prof., 1966-74, chmn. chemistry dept., 1969-76, prof., 1974, dean of scis., math. and engring., 1976—; trustee S.W. Research Inst., San Antonio, 1976-85. Contbr. articles to profl. pubs. in field. Active Leadership San Antonio, 1976-78. Research grantee Welch Found., 1965-70, NSF, 1971; equipment grantee NSF, 1968, 75. Fellow Am. Inst. Chemists; mem. Am. Chem. Soc. (chmn. San Antonio 1976-77, program chmn. regional meeting 1981), N.Y. Acad. Scis., AAAS, C. of C., Sigma Xi. Democrat. Presbyterian. Avocations: music; sports. Home: 125 Trillium San Antonio TX 78213 Office: Trinity U 715 Stadium Dr San Antonio TX 78284

BURKE, KAYE SLOAN, educator; B.S., U. Ill., 1969; M.S., 1978. Sec., McLean Community Ctr., Va., 1974-75, personnel com., 1974-76, rules procedures and fees com. chairperson, 1978-79, election chairperson, 1979-80, chmn. long-range planning, 1979-80, treas., 1979-80, vice chmn., county bd. liason, co-chmn. fin. com., 1980; bd. dirs. McLean Citizens Assn., 1977-82, chmn. planning and zoning com., 1978-80, 1st v.p., 1979-80, pres., 1980-82; customer adv. bd. VEPCO No. Va., 1981—; v.p. faculty senate Va., 1981—; instrnl. asst. math. No. Va. Community Coll., Annandalem 1976-78, chmn. math. search com., 1978-79, legis. liason, 1977—, master tchr. computer-assisted instrn., 1979-81, math. faculty mem., 1978-82, coordinator bus. and community relations, 1982—. Dist. rep. Fairfax County Park Authority, Va., 1983—; v.p. long range planning Friends of Turkey Run Farm Inc., 1981—; bd. suprs. County-wide Metro Task Force, 1980-84; Dranesville dist. supr. Falls Ch. Metro Task Force, 1980-84; co-chmn. transp. com. Fairfax County C. of C., 1982—; co chmn. airport access com. Washington-Dulles Task Forces, 1981—; hon. bd. dirs. Fairfax County Vol. Action, 1981—; advisor Tysons Transp. Assn. Inc., 1982—; program com. mem. Fairfax County Com. of 100, 1978—; McLean rep. Fairfax County Fedn. Citizens Assn., 1979—. Home: 7207 Churchill Rd McLean VA 22101 Office: No Va Community Coll 8333 Little River Turnpike Annandale VA 22003

BURKE, MARCUS B., museum curator, art educator; b. Apr. 10, 1947; m. Lenka Pichlikova. A.B. in English magna cum laude, Princeton U., 1969; M.T.S. in Ch. History, Harvard U., 1971; M.A. in Art History, Inst. Fine Arts NYU, 1973, Ph.D. in Art History, 1984. Ordained Am. Baptist Ch., 1973. Part time positions New Sch., and N.Y. Sch. Interior Design, N.Y.C., 1974-77; co-curator Art Mus. South Tex., Corpus Christi, 1976-79, Art Mus. South Tex./Instituto de Cultura Hispanica, Corpus Christi, 1979; instr. in art history Stephen F. Austin State U., Nacogdoches, Tex., 1979-83, curator Univ. Gallery, 1980-81, exec. com. dept. of art, dir. art dept. slide library; vis. asst. prof. art history SUNY-Purchase, 1983-85, mem. faculty in residence program, 1983-85; chief curator Meadows Mus. and Gallery, Dallas, 1985—; art dept. coordinator Tex. May Arts Festival, Nacogdoches, 1980, 81; Protestant chaplain Univ. Christian Found., NYU, 1971-74. Author exhbn. catalogues; contbr. articles in field; writer, interviewer videotape series in field, 1984-85. Vis. scholar J. Paul Getty Mus., 1984; research fellow Gladys Krieble Delmas Found., Venice, Italy, 1980; J. Clawson Mills research fellow Met. Mus. Art, N.Y.C., 1974-76; NYU scholar, 1972-74, fellow, 1977-78, Kress fellow, 1976-77. Mem. Phi Beta Kappa. Office: Meadows Mus and Gallery So Methodist Univ Dallas TX 75275

BURKE, ROBERT GENE, magazine editor, publisher; b. Waco, Tex., Oct. 7, 1928; s. Harry B. and Lillian Elizabeth (Wright) B.; m. Jane Hascall, Apr. 23, 1954; children—Melissa Jan Burke Steger, Tim R. B.A., Baylor U., 1950. Reporter Texarkana Gazette, Tex., 1950, Houston Chronicle, 1952-57; writer El Paso Natural, 1957-62; regional editor Oil and Gas Jour., Tulsa, 1962-69; editor in chief, assoc. publisher Offshore Mag., Houston, 1969—. Served with U.S. Army, 1950-52. Mem. Assn. Petroleum Writers (pres. 1967—), Nat. Ocean Industries Assn. (bd. dirs., sec. 1975—). Home: 710 N Wilcrest Dr Houston TX 77079 Office: Offshore Mag 1200 Post Oak Suite 106 Houston TX 77079

BURKES, WAYNE OLIVER, state senator; b. Philadelphia, Miss., Dec. 6, 1929; grad. Miss. Coll.; M.Div., New Orleans Bapt. Theol. Sem.; m. Ruthine Ferguson. Mem. Miss. Senate; ordained to ministry Bapt. Ch.; minister, educator, businessman. Mem. Hinds Jr. Coll. Edn. Assn., Miss. N.G. Assn. (past v.p.), Farm Bur., Clinton C. of C. (past pres.), Phi Delta Kappa, Kappa Delta Pi. Democrat. Club: Mason. Office: Miss State Senate Jackson MS 39205*

BURKHART, EDSEL JAY, civil engineer; b. Forest Hills, Pa., Feb. 4, 1920; s. Samuel Earl and Rose Ethel (Timmeney) B.; m. Florence Anne Seale, June 28, 1947; 1 child, Anne Burkhart Yoder. B.S. in Mech. Engring., Pa. State U., 1942; M.S. in Civil Engring., Tex. A&M U., 1947, postgrad., 1948-52. Registered profl. engr., Tex., La., Okla.; registered profl. surveyor, Tex., La. Civil engr. Tex. A&M Research Found. and Tex. A&M Engring. Expt. Sta.,

College Station, 1948-51; sec.-treas., co-owner, prin. engr. Spencer J. Buchanan and Assocs., Inc., cons. engrs., Bryan, Tex., 1951-82, also Soil Mechanics Inc., Bryan, 1956-82; pres., owner Buchanan/Soil Mechanics, Inc., Bryan, 1982—. Writer tech. research reports and USAF tech. manuals. Pres. Bryan Indsl. Found., 1960-62; pres. bd. trustees Bryan Pub. Library, 1971-75; pres. Arts Council Brazos Valley, Tex., 1972-73, 1st Presbyterian Ch. of Bryan Found., 1984—. Served to maj. C.E., U.S. Army, 1943-48, Res., 1948-57. Named Engr. of Yr., Tex. Soc. Profl. Engrs., 1974; recipient cert. of appreciation Coll. Engring., Tex. A&M U., 1978. Fellow ASCE; mem. ASTM, Am. Concrete Inst., Tex. and Southwest Cattle Raisers Assn., Tau Beta Pi, Pi Tau Sigma. Republican. Clubs; Briarcrest Country, Plaza, Century of Tex. A&M U. (Bryan). Lodges: Rotary (past pres. Bryan chpt.), Masons. Avocations: travel, golf, cattle raising, hunting. Home: 1626 Oakview Dr Bryan TX 77802 Office: Buchanan/Soil Mechanics Inc 206 N Sims St Bryan TX 77803

BURKHART, KAREN MOONEY, computer analyst; b. Gainesville, Ga., Sept. 10, 1958; d. Melvin Hoyt and Betty Modena (Vickers) Mooney; m. Charles Brad Burkhart, Mar. 22, 1980. B.S., Furman U., 1980. Application programmer Honeywell, Phoenix, 1980-81; lead analyst So. Co. Services, Atlanta, 1981—. Mem. So. Co. Services Profl. Devel. Assn. Republican. Baptist. Home: 3900 Camrose Ct Marietta GA 30062 Office: 64 Perimeter Center Atlanta GA 30346

BURKHOLDER, GEORGE VEEDER, urologist; b. Detroit, Jan. 31, 1934; s. Theodore McCoy and Margaret (Veeder) B.; m. Gretchen Bell Schneider, Apr. 20, 1963; children—Heidi, Matthew. B.A., Princeton U., 1956; M.D., Cornell U., 1960. Intern, N.Y. Hosp./Cornell Med. Ctr., N.Y.C., 1960, resident in surgery, 1961-63; resident in urology UCLA Sch. Medicine, 1963-67; staff urology Cleve. Clinic, 1969-70; practice medicine, specializing in urology, San Antonio, 1970—; asst. clin. prof. urologoic surgery U. Tex. Health Sci. Ctr., San Antonio, 1970-74, clin. assoc. prof., 1974-78, clin. prof., 1978—. Served to maj. M.C., U.S. Army, 1967-69. Mem. Soc. Pediatric Urology, AMA, Am. Urol. Assn., Bexar County Med. Soc., Tex. Med. Assn., San Antonio Urol. Soc. (pres. 1976-77), Am. Acad. Pediatrics, Tex. Med. Assn. (chmn. sect. urology 1976), ACS. Republican. Presbyterian. Club: Oak Hills Country. Contbr. articles to profl. jours. Office: 7950 Floyd Curl San Antonio TX 78229

BURLESON, CLAY ORVAL, real estate/insurance executive; b. Albemarle, N.C., Feb. 4, 1944; s. Cecil Clay and Mary Virginia (Cox) B.; m. Jacqueline Dell Ruth, Dec. 27, 1968; 1 son, Clay Baker. B.S. in Mktg., B.S. in Psychology, Western Carolina U., 1962. Cert. appraiser Am. Assn. Cert. Appraisers. With Sandoz Pharmaceuticals, Hanover, N.J., 1968-72, Carolina Color Corp., Salisbury, N.C., 1972-73; fin. planner, 1973-75; pres. Pilot Ins. & Realty Co., Salisbury, 1975—; cons. in field. Served with U.S. Army, 1966-68. Mem. Delta Sigma Phi. Republican. Presbyterian. Lodge: Rotary. Home: 625 N Craige St Salisbury NC 28144 Office: 516 W Innes St Salisbury NC 28144

BURLESON, KAREN TRIPP, lawyer; b. Rocky Mount, N.C., Sept. 2, 1955; d. Bryant and Katherine Rebecca (Watkins) Tripp; m. Robert Mark Burleson, June 25, 1977. B.A., U. N.C., 1976; J.D., U. Ala., 1981. Bar: Tex. 1981, U.S. Dist. Ct. (so. dist.) Tex. 1982, U.S. Ct. Appeals (fed. cir.) 1983. Law clerk Tucker, Gray & Espy, Tuscaloosa, Ala., 1978-81, to presiding justice Ala. Supreme Ct., Montgomery, summer 1980; atty. Exxon Prodn. Research Co., Houston, 1981—. Contbr. articles to profl. jours. Recipient Am. Jurisprudence award U. Ala., 1980, Dean's award, 1981. Mem. Houston Bar Assn. (internat. transfer tech. com. 1983-84), Houston Intellectual Property Lawyers Assn. (outstanding inventor com. 1982-84, student edn. com. 1985), Tex. Bar Assn. (antitrust law com. 1984-85), ABA, Am. Intellectual Property Lawyers Assn., Phi Alpha Delta (clerk 1980). Republican. Methodist. Office: Exxon Prodn Research Co PO Box 2189 Houston TX 77252

BURLESON, ROBERT JOE, orthopaedic surgeon; b. Birmingham, Ala., Oct. 20, 1918; s. Daniel Downs and Stella Lee (Collins) B.; A.B., U. Ala., Tuscaloosa, 1939; M.D., U. Louisville, 1943; M.S. in Orthopaedic Surgery, U. Minn., 1954; m. Mary Beth Hall, Mar. 29, 1943; children—Carol Jo, Genabeth, Robert Mark. Intern, USPHS-U.S. Marine Hosp., Stapleton, N.Y., 1943-44; surg. service U.S. Marine Hosp., Buffalo, 1944-46; fellow in orthopaedic surgery Mayo Clinic, 1951-54; gen. practice medicine and surgery, Decatur, Ala., 1946-51, specializing in orthopaedic surgery, Asheville, N.C., 1954-74; orthopaedics sports medicine Univ. Health Service, U. Ala., University, 1974-76, asso. prof. surgery, dir. surg. edn. Coll. Community Health Scis., 1977-85; mem. staff Tuscaloosa Orthopaedic Clinic, 1976-77, Ala. Crippled Children Program, Student Health Center, U. Ala.; past pres. N.C. Orthopaedic Assn. Deacon, elder, trustee, chmn. congregation First Christian Ch., Asheville, 1954-74; bd. dirs. Asheville Orthopaedic Hosp., Asheville Lions Club Workshop for Blind. Diplomate Am. Bd. Orthopaedic Surgery. Fellow Am. Acad. Orthopaedic Surgery; mem. Am. Orthopaedic Soc. for Sports Medicine, So. Med. Assn., Ala. med. assns., Tuscaloosa County Med. Soc., Eastern Orthopaedic Assn. (past pres.), Ala. Orthopaedic Soc. (past pres.), Mayo Clinic Alumni Assn., Mayo Orthopaedic Alumni Club, N.C. Commn. for Blind (life), Phi Chi, Phi Delta Theta. Republican. Presbyterian (elder). Clubs: Lions (pres. 1966, zone chmn. Internat. Dist. 31-A 1967); University. Contbr. articles to med. jours. Home: 3110 Firethorn Dr Tuscaloosa AL 35404

BURLINGAME, JAMES MONTGOMERY, lawyer; b. Great Falls, Mont., Dec. 25, 1926; s. James Montgomery and Eloise (Corbin) B.; B.A., Tulane U., 1949, J.D., 1950; m. Joella Claire Blache, June 15, 1950; children—James Montgomery IV, Ann Blache, John Marshall. Bar: La. 1950, U.S. Supreme Ct. 1961. Practiced in Washington, 1950; sr. ptnr. Jones, Walker, Waechter, Poitevent, Carrere and Denegre, New Orleans, 1953—. Served to ensign U.S. Maritime Service, 1944-46; to capt. AUS, 1950-52. Bd. trustees St. Martin's Protestant Episcopal Sch., 1968-81, 82—, pres., 1976-79; bd. dirs. Internat. Trade Mart, New Orleans, 1981—, chmn. pub. relations com., 1981-83, chmn. membership com., 1983-85. Bullard fellow Tulane U., 1980. Mem. La. (chmn. mineral sect. 1971-72), New Orleans (exec. com. 1980) bar assns., ABA, Internat. Bar Assn., Inter-Am. Bar Assn., Fed. Bar Assn., Am. Judicature Soc., Beta Theta Pi. Episcopalian. Clubs: Petroleum, New Orleans Country, Pickwick, Stratford, Plimsoll, Internat. House (New Orleans), Chaine des Rotisseurs, Commanderie de Bordeaux. Home: 433 Iona St Metairie LA 70005 Office: Pl St Charles 201 St Charles St New Orleans LA 70170

BURNET, THORNTON WEST, marketing executive; b. Cin., Aug. 27, 1917; s. David and Agnes McClung (West) B.; B.S. in Commerce, U. Va., 1940; m. Mary Elizabeth Charlton, Aug. 14, 1948; 1 son, Thornton West. Asst. treas. Lincoln Service Corp., Washington, 1941-50, v.p., sec., 1950-59; v.p. mktg. Am. Fin. Mgmt. Corp., Silver Spring, Md., 1959-77; v.p. mktg. ADS Agy., 1977-83; v.p., treas., dir. Monet Constrn. Co., Fairfax, Va., 1962-85; v.p., sec., dir. Worldwide Yellow Pages Service Co., 1979—. Committeeman, Boy Scouts Am., 1945—; pres. bd. trustees Fletcher Meml. Library, 1962—; trustee Children's Mission, Pitts., 1980-82; treas., trustee William C. Westlake Meml. Found., 1981—. Served with AUS, 1940-43. Mem. Alpha Kappa Psi. Republican. Episcopalian (vestryman, past sr. warden). Home: 10800 Hunters Valley Rd Vienna VA 22180

BURNETT, (CHARLES) DAVID, circuit court judge; b. Blytheville, Ark., Aug. 18, 1941; s. John David and Marjorie Flo (Wood) B.; m. Sonja Doris Harvey, Oct. 10, 1969; children—Jonathan David, Amanda Karen. B.A., U. Ark., 1963, J.D., 1966. Bar: Ark. 1966, U.S. Dist. Ct. (ea. dist.) Ark. 1966, U.S. Supreme Ct. 1970. Ptnr. Swift, Alexander & Burnett, Osceola, Ark., 1969-74; pros. atty. 2d Cir., State of Ark., Osceola, 1974-82, cir. ct. judge, 1982—; adj. prof. real estate and law Miss. County Community Coll., 1981—. Active Osceola Boys Club, Northeast Ark. Area council Boy Scouts Am.; sec., atty. Osceola Riverport Authority; mem. Miss. River Pkwy. Commn., 1972-77; mem. Dem. Central Com., Ark.; bd. dirs. 1st Christian Ch.; bd. dirs., bd. govs. Presbyn. Christian Day Sch.; mem. Criminal Detention Facilities Study Commn., Gov.'s Task Force on DWI, Gov.'s Task Force on Child Abuse. Served to capt. U.S. Army; Vietnam. Decorated Bronze Star, Army Commendation award, Vietnam Campaign Ribbon with 4 stars, Vietnamese Govt. Medal of Honor 1st class. Mem. ABA, Ark. Bar Assn., Northeast Ark. Bar Assn., Osceola Bar Assn. (past pres., sec.-treas.), Assn. Trial Lawyers Am., Ark. Pros. Attys. Assn. (sec. 1975, bd. dirs. 1976—, v.p. 1980-81, pres. 1981-82), Nat. Dist. Attys. Assn., Christian Legal Soc., Am. Legion, Osceola C. of C., Jr. C. of C., VFW, Phi Alpha Delta. Home: 618 Semmes St Osceola AR 72370 Office: PO Box 704 Suite 4 Professional Bldg Osceola AR 72370

BURNETT, EDMUND CODY, JR, psychologist, consultant; b. Arlington, Va., Apr. 7, 1952; s. Edmund Cody and Martha Grace (McCoy) B.; m. Ruth Ellen Reed, Aug. 7, 1976. B.A. cum laude, Wake Forest U., 1974; M.A., East Carolina U., 1976; Ph.D., U. So. Miss., 1982. Lic. psychologist, N.C. Div. E staff psychologist Caswell Mental Retardation Ctr., Kinston, N.C., 1976-77; staff psychologist I, Halifax County Mental Health Ctr., Roanoke Rapids, N.C., 1977-79, coordinator adult services, chief psychologist, 1982—; adj. prof. Wesleyan Coll., Rocky Mount, N.C., 1978; psychology intern VA Hosp., Durham, N.C., 1981-82; chmn. Domicilliary Adv. Com., Halifax, N.C., 1983—; cons. to. schs., industry; ancilliary staff psychologist Halifax Meml. Hosp., 1984—; pvt practice clin. psychology, 1985—. Author articles, papers in field. East Carolina U. fellow, 1974-76; U. So. Miss. fellow, 1979-81. Mem. Am. Psychol. Assn., N.C. Psychol. Assn., Southeastern Psychol. Assn., Psi Chi, Alpha Phi Omega (v.p. Winston-Salem 1970-74). Democrat. Presbyterian. Lodge: Kiwanis (treas. Roanoke Rapids 1983—). Avocations: tennis; running; hiking; camping; collecting antiques; cycling. Home: 427 Rightmyer Dr Roanoke Rapids NC 27870 Office: Halifax County Mental Health Ctr 210 Smith Church Rd Roanoke Rapids NC 27870 also Thanos Bldg 730 Roanoke Ave Roanoke Rapids NC 27870

BURNETTE, ADA M. PURYEAR, educational administrator; b. Darlington, S.C., Oct. 24; d. Theodore Lester and Floia (King) Peoples; B.A., Talladega Coll., 1953; postgrad. Chgo. State U., 1954-56; M.A., U. Chgo., 1958; postgrad. Fla. State U., 1977—, Fla. A&M U., 1980; children—Paul Puryear, Paula Lynn Puryear. High sch. math. tchr. Winston-Salem, N.C., 1953-54; elem. tchr. Chgo. Public Schs., 1954-58; reading clinician U. Chgo., 1958; dir. reading clinic, asst. prof. Norfolk State U., 1958-61, Tuskegee Inst., 1961-66; coordinator freshman math., asst. prof. math., Fisk U., 1966-70; adminstr. early childhood and elem. edn. State of Fla. Dept. Edn., Tallahassee, 1973—; hostess radio talk show, 1977-79; sec.-treas. Afro-Am. Research Assos., 1968-74; tutor, diagnostician, lectr., cons., planner, 1958—; cons. Job Corps, Alpha Kappa Alpha, Advancement Sch., pub. co.; lectr. univ. classes. Pres., PTA, 1975-76, v.p., 1983-84; del. state Democratic women's meeting, Fla., 1978, 79; mem. Dem. Exec. Com. Leon County, 1981—; mem. NAACP, United Fund com., Leon County 4C Bd.; pres. Norfolk Women's Interracial Council, 1960; mem. Urban League. Mem. Fla. Assn. Suprs. and Adminstrs., Fla. Council on Elem. Edn., Internat. Reading Assn., Fla. State Reading Assn., Assn. State Cons. on Early Childhood Edn., Alliance of Black Sch. Educators, Assn. for Supervision and Curriculum Devel., Fla. Assn. Supervision and Curriculum Devel., Internat. Reading Assn. (nat. early childhood com., nat. textbook com. nat. awards com., pres. 1983—), Nat. Assn. Elem. Sch. Prins., Fla. Assn. Elem. Sch. Prins., Nat. Assn. Edn. Young Children, Fla. Assn. Children Under Six, So. Assn. Children Under Six, Leon Assn. Children Under Six (pres. 1977), Assn. Childhood Edn. Internat., So. Assn. Colls. and Schs. (mem. elem. commn.), Phi Delta Kappa, Phi Kappa Phi (pres. 1985-86), Pi Lambda Theta, Alpha Kappa Alpha (treas., summer sch. dir., undergrad. adv.). Presbyterian (deacon). Clubs: Jack and Jill (pres., teen co-sponsor, chmn. pub. relations), Drifters (pres., nat. membership chmn. 1977-79, historian), Bridge, Fla. State U. Women's. Regular columnist profl. jours., 1974—; writer grants proposals; contbr. articles to profl. publs. Home: 3228 Constellation Ct Tallahassee FL 32312 Office: Dept Edn Knott Bldg Tallahassee FL 32301

BURNHAM, J.V., printing company executive; b. Pasagoula, Miss., May 23, 1923; s. George Luther and Eli Vashti (Hough) B.; A.A., Jones Jr. Coll., Ellisville, Miss., 1946; A.S., Rochester Inst. Tech., 1948; B.S., U. Houston, 1951. M.Ed., 1953; m. Patti Lauri Latham, May 18, 1946; children—James Steven, Jon Douglas, Richard Scott, Bruce Edward, Vernon Alan. Mgr., Progress-Item, Ellisville, 1948-51; asst. prof. graphic arts and journalism and asst. dir. printing dept. U. Houston, 1951-57; with Chas. P. Young; Houston, 1957—, estimator, prodn. supt. purchasing dir., 1957-67, asst. sec.-treas., 1967-69, v.p., 1969—; pres. Printing Industries of Gulf Coast, 1971-73, chmn. edn. com., 1960-70. Bd. dirs. Mus. Printing History, Tex. Printing Edn. Found.; mem. Republican Presdl. Task Force. Served to lt. (j.g.) USN, 1943-46, Named Houston Graphics Man of Year, 1968; named Man of Year, Printing Industries of Gulf Coast, 1970; recipient Scouter award Boy Scouts Am., 1966, Scoutmaster award, 1968; Benjamin Franklin award Houston Craftsmen's Club, 1971. Mem. Houston Advt. Fedn. Bus. and Profl. Advt. Assn., Nat. Eagle Scout Assn., Houston Litho Club, Houston Club of Printing House Craftsmen, Houston C. of C. (edn. com. 1970-81), Nat. Rifle Assn., U.S. Golf Assn. (assoc.), Franklin Mint Collectors Soc., Second Amendment Found., Gun Owners Am., Phi Delta Kappa. Methodist. Clubs: Braeburn Country, Newport Country, Westwood Shores Country, Landing at Seven Coves. Assoc. editor Am. Oceanography, 1968-71; S.W. corr. Inland Printer, 1952-60. Home: 6710 Tam O'Shanter Houston TX 77036 Office: 1616 McGowen Houston TX 77004

BURNLEY, DOROTHY ROCKWELL, state legislator; b. High Point, N.C., Feb. 27, 1927; d. Hubert J. and Ella N. Rockwell; student Hollins Coll., 1944-46; m. James H. Burnley III, Oct. 4, 1947; children—James H., Mary H., Ellen B., Judith L. Sec.-treas. Craftwood, Inc., High Point, N.C.; mem. N.C. Ho. of Reps., 1981—. Trustee, High Point Pub. Library; bd. dirs., past pres. High Point Women's Shelter; bd. dirs. High Point Mental Health Assn. Mem. Furniture City Woman's Club, High Point C. of C., U.S. C. of C., N.C. Library Assn. (pres. trustees sect.). Baptist. Office: NC Ho of Reps State Legis Bldg Raleigh NC 27611

BURNS, GROVER PRESTON, physicist, mathematician; b. nr. Hurricane, W.Va., Apr. 25, 1918; s. Joshua Alexander and Virgie (Meadows) B.; A.B., Marshall U., 1937; M.S., W.Va. U., 1941; student Duke U., 1939-40, U. Md., 1946; D.Sc., Colo. State Christian Coll., 1973; m. Julia Belle Foster, Nov. 4, 1941; children—Julia Corinne, Grover Preston. Tchr. high sch., W.Va., 1937-40; fellow W.Va., U., 1940-41; instr. physics U. Conn., 1941-42; asst. prof. Miss State Coll., 1942-44, acting head physics dept., 1944-45; asst. prof. physics Tex. Tech. Coll., 1946; assoc. prof. math. Marshall U., 1946-47; research physicist Naval Research Lab., Washington, 1947-48; asst. prof., chmn. physics dept. Mary Washington Coll., 1948-68, assoc. prof., chmn., 1968-69; quality control supr. Am. Viscose div. FMC Corp., 1950-67; pres. Burns Enterprises, Inc., Fredericksburg, Va., 1958—; mathematician Naval Surface Weapons Center, 1967-81; staff mathematician Sperry Univac, 1982—; cons. FMC Corp., 1984—. Served with AUS, 1945-46. Mem. Am. Phys. Soc., Am. Assn. Physics Tchrs., Fed. Profl. Assn., AAUP, Am. Def. Preparedness Assn., Reviewer, Am. Jour. Physics; contbr. articles to profl. jours., also CRC Handbook Chemistry and Physics. Patentee in field of thermometers, conductivity testers, star finders; research in fields of superconductivity, synthetic div., thermoelectricity, numerical integration, exterior ballistics, gunfire control models. Home: 600 Virginia Ave Fredericksburg VA 22401

BURNS, HAROLD DEWEY, engineering executive; b. Birmingham, Jan. 3, 1926; s. Dewey Gurley and Lucy (Polk) B.; m. Jeanne Bernice Tuley, Mar. 7, 1951; children—Dave Allen, Joann Lynn, Terry Lee. B.S. in Elec. Engring., Am. Inst. Engring., 1952; postgrad. Exec. Devel. program U. Ga., 1965, Bus. Adminstrn., Columbia U., 1968; M.B.A., U. West Fla., 1973. Engr., Daystrom Instrument, Archbald, Pa., 1952-53; maintenance foreman Lone Star Steel Co., Daingerfield, Tex., 1953-55; engr. Vitro Corp., Eglin AFB, Fla., 1955-60, dept. head, 1960-65, asst. mgr., 1965-68; mgr. Systems Engring. div. Automation Industries, Ft. Walton Beach, Fla., 1968-70, asst. mgr., Eglin AFB, 1970-76, dir. mktg. Ft. Walton Beach, 1976-83, v.p. strategic planning, 1983-85; v.p. Vitro Services Corp., Ft. Walton Beach, Fla., 1985—. Chmn. adv. com. Okaloosa-Walton Jr. Coll., 1965-70; charter mem. U. West Fla. Found., 1970—. Served with USN, 1943-48, 50-52. Recipient Student Achievement award Wall Street Jour., 1965. Mem. IEEE (sect. chmn. 1967), Am. Def. Preparedness Assn. (sect. dir. 1968), Assn. Old Crows (sect. dir. 1974-75). Methodist. Lodge: Lions. Contbr. articles to trade jours. Home: 921 N Whisperwood Ln Fort Walton Beach FL 32548 Office: Vitro Services Corp IRSP Div 715 Hollywood Blvd NW Industrial Park Fort Walton Beach FL 32548

BURNS, HENRY LEON, oil company executive; b. Shreveport, La., Aug. 13, 1948; s. Ellis Leon and Nonie Lee (Wyatt) B.; m. Sondra Rabon, Aug. 31, 1969; children—Tara Elizabeth, Henry Leon. B.S., Northwestern State U., 1970. C.P.A., La. Acct. Tex. Eastern Transmissions Corp., Shreveport, 1969, system analyst, 1970-71, auditor, controller, 1971-72; auditor Peat, Marwick, Mitchell, C.P.A.s, Shreveport, 1972-73; controller CBS Toys-Gym Dandy, Bossier City, La., 1973; fin. v.p. Splty. Oil Co., Shreveport, 1980-81; pres., owner, operator Burns Oil & Gas Exploration, Benton, La., 1981—. T.H. Harris Meml. scholar, 1966-67; Coll. Presdl. scholar, 1967-69. Mem. Am. Inst. C.P.A.s, La. Soc. C.P.A.s, Am. Acctg. Assn., Bossier City C. of C., Shreveport C. of C., U.S. C. of C., Nat. Riflemans Assn., Nat. Wildlife Fedn. Democrat. Baptist. Lodge: Rotary (pres. 1982-83) (Bossier City). Home: Hwy 18 3N Benton LA 71006 Office: PO Box 249 Benton LA 71006

BURNS, JOHNNY LEE, hospital administrator; b. Fayetteville, N.C., June 23, 1949; s. Johnnie Julius and Gwendelene V. (Naylor) B.; m. Cheryl Ann Greenberg, May 26, 1973; children—Adam Michael, Emily Elizabeth. B.A., Tulane U., 1971, M. Hosp. Administrn., 1979. Surg. sales rep. Am. Hosp. Supply Corp., New Orleans, 1976-78; asst. administr. Lakeside Hosp., Metairie, La., 1978-80; administr. Women and Children's Hosp., Odessa, Texas, 1981-82, Lee Meml. Hosp., Giddings, Texas, 1981-83; pres., chmn. bd. dirs. Inter Health Corp., Giddings, 1983—; mem. adv. council Capitol Area Planning Council, Austin, Tex., 1983-84; guest lectr. Tulane U., New Orleans, 1981—. Bd. dirs. State Home and School Texas Youth Commn., Giddings, 1982-85; Served to capt. U.S. Army, 1971-76. Named Outstanding Jr. Officer U.S. Army, Ft. Bragg, N.C., 1974; recipient Comendation medals U.S. Army, 1974. Mem. Am. Coll. Hosp. Adminstrs., Am. Acad. Med. Adminstrs., Am. Hosp. Assn., Texas Hosp. Assn., Am. Cancer Soc. (v.p. local chpt. 1982), Giddings C. of C. (dir. 1984-85). Lodge: Lions (v.p. local chpt. 1983-84, pres. 1984-85). Avocations: reading; tennis; golf; fishing. Office: Inter Health Corp PO Box 819 228 Petro Ctr Giddings TX 78942

BURNS, LAWRENCE ANTHONY, ecologist; b. Washington, Aug. 12, 1940; s. James William and Evelyn Elaine (Riddle) B.; m. Lea Liisa Salminen, Jan. 17, 1963 (div. 1972); 1 dau., Liisa Jacqueline; m. Karen Jean Ramey, July 4, 1975; children—Lara Ramey, Alexander Ramey. B.A., NYU, 1968; Ph.D., U. N.C., 1978. Research asst. U. N.C., Chapel Hill, 1968-71, U. Fla., Gainesville, 1973-76; research aquatic biologist, region 4, EPA, Naples, Fla., 1971-73, ecologist, Environ. Research Lab., EPA, Athens, Ga., 1977—. N.Y. State Regents fellow, 1968-71; recipient Civil Service Silver medal EPA, 1973. Mem. AAAS, Am. Inst. Biol. Scis., Am. Soc. Limnology and Oceanography, ASTM, Ecol. Soc. Am., Internat. Soc. Ecol. Modelling, N.Y. Acad. Scis., Soc. Environ. Toxicology and Chemistry, Amnesty Internat. (group coordinator 1981-84). Presbyterian. Contbr. articles to profl. jours. Office: Environmental Research Laboratory EPA College Station Rd Athens GA 30613

BURNS, MITCHEL ANTHONY, transportation services company executive; b. Las Vegas, Nev., Nov. 1, 1942; s. Mitchel and Zella (Pulsipher) B.; B.S. in Bus. Mgmt., Brigham Young U., 1964; M.B.A. in Finance, U. Calif., Berkeley, 1965; m. Joyce Jordan, Nov. 14, 1962; children—Jill, Mike, Shauna. With Mobil Oil Corp., N.Y.C., 1965-74, controller, 1970-72, cost-of-living coordinator, 1973, fin. analysis mgr., 1973-74; chief operating officer, exec. v.p., group v.p., treas., dir. corp. planning Ryder System, Inc., Miami, Fla., 1974-79, pres., dir., 1979—, chief exec. officer, 1983—, chmn. bd., 1985—, also dir.; pres., exec. v.p., chief fin. officer subs. Ryder Truck Rental, Inc., Miami, 1975-79. Office: 3600 NW 82d Ave Miami FL 33166

BURNS, NORMA DECAMP, architect; b. N.Y.C., Dec. 14, 1940; d. Cyrus and Stella (Werner) DeCamp; m. Robert Paschal Burns, Dec. 4, 1973; 1 child, Linda Paige, B.S., Fla. State U., 1962; M.Arch., N.C. State U., 1976. Registered architect, N.C. Tchr. high schs., Fla., Md., 1962-73; pres., owner Burnstudio Architects P.A., Raleigh, N.C., 1977—, WorkSpace, Inc., Raleigh, 1981—. Past chmn. City of Raleigh Appearance Commn.; mem. land use com Triangle J Council Govts.; mem. Downtown Adv. Com., Raleigh; bd. advisers Preservation Found. N.C., Raleigh, 1985—; mem. bus. adv. council Peace Coll., Raleigh, 1985—; councilman-at-large Raleigh City Council, 1985-87, mem. law and fin. com., comprehensive planning com., univ. liaison. Recipient numerous awards including Owens-Corning Energy award, 1984; Adaptive Reuse award Durham Preservation Soc., 1983, 84; cited in Ten Best Designs of 1984, Time Mag. Mem. AIA (nat. interiors com. 1981-84, nat. design com. 1985), chmn. N.C. nat. historic resources com. 1983-85), Nat. Trust Historic Preservation, Preservation Found. N.C. Office: Burnstudio Architects PA PO Box 25688 Raleigh NC 27611

BURNS, SANDRA K., lawyer, educator; b. Bryan, Tex., Aug. 9, 1949; d. Clyde W. and Bert (Rychlik) B.; 1 child, Scott. B.S., U. Houston, 1970; M.A., U. Tex.-Austin, 1972, Ph.D., 1975; J.D., St. Mary's U., 1978. Bar: Tex. 1978; cert. tchr., adminstr., supr. instrn., Tex. Tchr. Austin (Tex.) Ind. Sch. Dist., 1970-71; field coordinator depts. child devel./family life and home econs. tchr. edn. Coll. Nutrition, Textiles and Human Devel. Tex. Woman's U., Denton, 1974-75; instrnl. devel. asst. Office of Ednl. Resources div. instrnl. devel. U. Tex. Health Sci. San Antonio, 1976-77; legis. aide William T. Moore, Tex. Senate, Austin, fall, 1978, com. clk.-counsel, spring, 1979; legal cons. Colombotti & Assocs., Aberdeen, Scotland, 1980; contract atty. Republic Energy, Inc., Bryan, Tex., 1981-82; corporate counsel First Internat. Oil and Gas, Inc., 1983; contract atty. Humble Exploration Co., Inc., Dallas, 1984, ARCo, Dallas 1985; vis. lectr. Tex. A&M U., fall 1981, summer, 1981; lectr. home econ. Our Lady of the Lake Coll., San Antonio, fall, 1975. Mem. State Bar of Tex., ABA, Phi Delta Kappa. Democrat. Methodist. Contbr. articles on law and edn. to profl. jours. Address: 12126 Forestwood Circle Dallas TX 75244

BURNS, WILLIAM GOODYKOONTZ, marketing communications company executive; b. Vandalia, Ill., Aug. 23, 1935; s. Farrell Francis and Sarah J. (Goodykoontz) B.; B.A., Washington and Lee U., 1957; postgrad. U. Colo., U. Chgo.; children—Janean Mary, Pamela Ann. Grocery products promotion mgr. Wilson & Co., Inc., Chgo., 1957-67; dir. merchandising and sales tng. Blue-Cross-Blue Shield, 1967-71; v.p. mktg. Sammons Enterprises Inc., Dallas, 1971-74; owner William G. Burns Mktg. Communications Co., Bus. Express Press, Pigments of the Imagination, and Aqua Mart, Dallas, Burns Cattle Co., Klondike, Tex. Mem. Sales and Mktg. Execs. (past dir.), Sales Promotion Execs. (past pres.), Dallas Advt. League, Assn. Broadcasting Execs., Tex. Cattle Raisers Assn., Am. Quarter Horse Assn., Tex. Longhorn Breeders Assn. Am., Mktg. Communications Execs. Internat. Assn. (past dir.), Am. Simmental Assn., Dallas 40. Republican. Episcopalian. Club: Masons. Home: 4115 Lawngate Dr Dallas TX 75252 Office: 13601 Preston Rd Dallas TX 75240

BURNS, ZED HOUSTON, emeritus history educator; b. St. Paul, Nov. 3, 1903; s. John Ganble and Lois (Barncard) B.; m. Rubye McBride, Jan. 26, 1935; 1 dau., Cassandra Joyce. B.S., Auburn U., 1927, M.S., 1929; Ed.D., U. Cin., 1937; M.A., U. So. Miss., 1970, Ph.M., 1982. Counselor Guidance Ctr. Auburn U., 1946-48; prof. edn. Miss. U. for Women, Columbus, 1948-49; acad. dean Shorter Coll., Rome, Ga., 1949-50; chmn. psychology dept. U. So. Miss., Hattiesburg, 1950-56, chmn. dept. indsl. arts, 1956-68, prof. ednl. psychology, 1968-73; prof. psychology emeritus, 1973—; head dept. edn. and psychology Whitworth Coll., Brookhaven, Miss., 1974-76; prof. history Patrick Henry Jr. Coll., Gilbertown, Ala., 1982-84; cons. Bur. Hearings and Appeals, HEW, 1962-70. Served to maj. AUS, 1943-45. U. Cin. fellow, 1929-30, scholar, 1932-33. Fellow Am. Psychol. Assn.; mem. Southeastern Psychol. Assn., So. History Assn., Miss. Hist. Soc., So. Soc. Philosophy and Psychology, SAR, Sons Confederate Vets., Pi Kappa Alpha, Phi Alpha Theta, Phi Delta Kappa. Author: Ship Island in the Confederacy, 1971; Confederate Forts, 1977; contbr. articles to profl. jours. Home and Office: 1208 Marie St Hattiesburg MS 39401

BURNSIDE, MARY ARDIS, clinical psychologist; b. Milw., May 14, 1950; d. Glenn Grover and Chrystine (Mueller) B.; m. Bruce Edward Anderson, July 17, 1973; children—Aaron Hunter, Andrew Chase. B.A., Rice U., 1972; M.A., U. Houston, 1976, Ph.D., 1980. Lic. psychologist, Tex. Asst. prof. psychology Baylor Coll. Medicine, Houston, 1980—; pvt. practice clin. psychology, Houston, 1985—. Contbr. articles to profl. jours. Mem. Am. Psychol. Assn., Tex. Psychol. Assn., Houston Psychol. Assn. (pub. info. officer 1982-84). Office: 4710 Bellaire Blvd Bellaire TX 77401

BURR, DAVID ANTHONY, university administrator; b. Columbus, Kans., Apr. 19, 1925; s. Hugh Henry and Grace Elizabeth (Mitchell) B.; A.A., Northeastern Agrl. and Mech. Coll., Miami, Okla., 1948; B.A., U. Okla., 1952; LL.D. (hon.), Pepperdine U., 1981; m. Carol Jean Robinson, Nov. 18, 1962; children—Michael James, Kathleen Elizabeth, Thaddeus Mitchell. Editor, Sooner Mag., U. Okla., Norman, 1950-57; asst. to pres. U. Okla., 1957-59, asst. to pres. and dir. univ. relations and devel., 1959-68, v.p., dir. univ. community, 1968-71, v.p. devel., 1971-77, v.p. univ. relations and devel., 1977-79, v.p. univ. affairs, 1979—; coordinator, dir. U. Okla. leadership program, 1961; dir. Editorial Projects for Edn., Inc. Dir., Okla. Gov.'s Opportunity Program, 1964; mem. Civic Improvement Council, Norman, 1965; deacon 1st Presbyn. Ch., Norman, 1968-69, now elder. Served to lt. U.S. Army, 1944-46. Recipient Sibley award, 1956, disting. service citation U. Okla., 1983; named Outstanding Alumnus Northeastern Agrl. and Mech. U., 1971. Mem. Council Advancement and Support of Edn., Okla. Higher Edn. Alumni Council, U. Okla. Assn.,

Norman C. of C. (dir. 1968-70, 81—), Lambda Chi Alpha. Democrat. Home: 1409 Brookdale St Norman OK 73072 Office: 900 Asp Ave Norman OK 73019

BURR, TIMOTHY FULLER, lawyer; b. New Bedford, Mass., Oct. 18, 1952; s. John Thayer and Joan (Ames) B.; A.B., Harvard U., 1975; J.D., U. Miami, 1979; m. Marguerite Conti, Feb. 28, 1981; children—Emily Ames, Lisa Conti, David Thayer. Admitted to La. bar, 1979, also Supreme Ct., Circuit Ct. and Dist. Ct. bars; dir. firm McGlinchey, Stafford, Mintz, Cellini & Lang, New Orleans, 1979—, admiralty atty., 1979—. Mem. ABA, La. Bar Assn., Maritime Law Assn. U.S. Republican. Club: Harvard of La. Home: 8 Sleepy Hollow Ln Slidell LA 70458 Office: McGlinchey Stafford Mintz Cellini & Lang 643 Magazine St New Orleans LA 70130

BURRIS, CHARLES N., architect; b. Bay City, Tex., Oct. 30, 1950; s. Norwood H. and Barbara (Oliver) B.; m. Bonnie Schroeder, Feb. 7, 1970 (div. 1975); 1 child, Charles Michael. B. Environ. Design cum laude, Tex. A&M U., 1973. Registered architect, Tex. Designer M.O. Lawrence, Jr., Inc., Bryan, Tex., 1973-75, project architect, 1976; designer, project mgr. Jan Grierson, Inc., Austin, Tex., 1976-76; designer, mgmt. Burris Constrn. Co., Wharton, Tex., 1976-83; prin. Charlie Burris, Bryan, 1983-84; prin. Burris-Patterson, Architects, 1984—. Mem. AIA (pres.-elect Brazos chpt. 1986), Tex. Soc. Architects, Tau Sigma Delta. Democrat. Avocations: art; music; sailing; writing; outdoor activities. Home: Rt 3 Box 347 B College Station TX 77840 Office: 1707 Broadmoor Suite 200 Bryan TX 77805

BURROUGHS, JACK EUGENE, dentist, management consultant; b. Harlingen, Tex., Nov. 24, 1946; s. Jack Eugene and Virginia (Ayoub) B.; children by previous marriage—Brian A., Brad A. B.S., U. Tex. Arlington, 1969, D.D.S., U. Tex. Dental Br. Houston, 1973. Practice dentistry, Houston, 1973—; seminar leader, cons. Quest, Dallas, 1983—. Contbr. articles to profl. jours. Recipient Speaker awards Aspen Med.-Dental Conf., 1982, 83, 84, N.Am. Med.-Dental Assn., 1984, Am. Internat. Seminars, 1984. Fellow Acad. Gen. Dentistry; mem. ADA, Tex. Dental Assn., Houston Dist. Dental Soc., Houston Northwest C. of C. (bd. dirs.). Republican. Mem. Christian Ch. Clubs: Exchange (bd. dirs.), Toastmasters (officer). Avocations: body builder; runner. Office: Jack E Burroughs 17200 Red Oak Dr Houston TX 77090

BURROUGHS, JACK EUGENE, ceramic engineering executive; b. Marion, Ohio, Jan. 28, 1926; s. George Bay and Sada Marie (O'Connor) B.; m. Virginia Belle Ayoub, Feb. 24, 1946; children—Jack Eugene Jr., Teresa Ann Farr, Timothy Paul. B.S. in Ceramic Engring., U. Tex., 1957; M.S. in Nuclear Engring., So. Meth. U., 1963; postgrad. Ohio State U., 1971, Alfred U., Tex. Christian U. Chief engr. Miller Equipment, 1955-57; sr. research materials engr. Gen. Dynamics Corp., Ft. Worth, 1957-71, Dresser Industries, Houston, 1971-73, S & B Biomedics and Internat. Biomed., 1974-81; pres. Seecor Inc., Ft. Worth, 1981—; lectr. U. Tex.-Arlington. Served with USAF, 1944-46. Decorated Air medal and cluster, Air Force Commendation medal and cluster; Ohio State U. fellow, 1969-71. Fellow Am. Ceramic Soc., Soc. Advanced Materials and Process Engrs. (past pres.), Soc. Biomaterials (charter mem.); mem. Tex. Soc. Profl. Engrs., Sigma Xi. Contbr. numerous articles to profl. jours. Patentee in field. Home: 2005 Milam Ft Worth TX 76112 Office: 7731 Sand Dr Ft Worth TX 76118

BURRUS, JOHN NEWELL, sociology educator; b. Gilmer, Tex., Jan. 23, 1920; s. Herman Clifford and Beulah (Blalack) B.; m. Sarah Gray Emerson, 1983; A.B., U. Miss., 1942; M.A., La. State U., 1944, Ph.D., 1950; postgrad. U. Minn., 1945-47, Vanderbilt U., 1948. Grad. fellow La. State U. 1942-44, 48-49, research assoc., 1949-50; teaching fellow U. Minn., 1945-47; mem. faculty U. Miss., 1943-45, Vanderbilt U., 1947-48, U. Fla., 1950-51; faculty, chmn. dept. sociology U. So. Miss., Hattiesburg, 1951-70, 78-80, prof., 1957-70, disting. univ. prof., 1970—, mem. council univ. honors program, 1959-67. Past bd. dirs. ARC. Mem. So. Sociol. Soc. (nomination com. 1966-68, sect. chmn., mem. exec. com. 1955-58, awards 1976-78), Rural Sociol. Soc., Sigma Chi, Alpha Kappa Delta, Pi Gamma Mu, Phi Kappa Phi, Omicron Delta Kappa. Club: Kiwanis (dir. 1975—). Author: Life Opportunities: Differential Mortality in Mississippi, 1951; (with C.A. McMahan, R.H. Bradford) Manual to Accompany the Sociology of Urban Life, 1952; (with H.A. Pedersen, M.B. King) Mississippi Life Tables, 1954; Mississippi's People, 1950; (with others) Social Problems, 1955; mem. editorial bd. So. Quar., 1962-70, 76—, chmn., 1967-68; contbr. chpt. to A History of Mississippi, 1973; contbr. to Ency. Brit., also articles, book revs. to profl. publs. Home: 1305 Windsor Dr Hattiesburg MS 39401

BURRUS, ROBERT LEWIS, JR., lawyer; b. Richmond, Va., Sept. 16, 1934; s. Robert Lewis and Bessie (Hart) B.; m. Ann Williams, Aug. 1, 1964; children—David C., Peter T., Lewis G. B.A., U. Richmond, 1955; LL.B., Duke U., 1958. Bar: Va. 1958. Assoc., mem., now sr. ptnr. McGuire, Woods & Battle, Richmond, Va., 1958—; dir. Best Products Co., Inc., Heilig-Meyers Co., S&K Famous Brands, Inc., Wiland Services, Inc., Riverton Corp. mem. Council Higher Edn. Va.; chmn. Richmond Renaissance, chmn. exec. com.; chmn., Federated Arts Council of Richmond, 1981-84; dir., v.p. Hist. Richmond Found.; chmn. bd. assocs. U. Richmond, 1984—; mem. bldg. com. Va. Mus. Fine Arts, 1980—; bd. govs. St. Christopher's Sch., 1975-77, pres. Found.; mem. Nat. Council for the Law Sch., Duke U. Served to capt. USAR, 1963. Fellow ABA Found.; mem. Va. Bar Assn. (bd. govs., chmn. bus. sect. 1976-78), Richmond Bar Assn., Omicron Delta Kappa, Democrat. Episcopalian. Clubs: Commonwealth, Country of Va., Bull and Bear, Forum. Office: McGuire Woods & Battle One James Ctr Richmond VA 23219

BURRUSS, TERRY GENE, architect; b. Little Rock, Dec. 30, 1950; s. Alvin Eugene and Fern (Pelton) B.; B. Arch., B.A., U. Ark., 1973; m. Merilyn Kloss, Dec. 20, 1981; 1 child, Mamie Christine. Intern architect firm Robinson and Wassell, Inc., Little Rock, 1973-75; practice architecture Evo-Tech Prodn., Little Rock, and I.D.E.A., Eureka Springs, Ark., 1976-78; architect Store Planning Assos., San Francisco, 1978; asso. Design 3, Architects, Little Rock, Ark., 1979; v.p., div. mgr. Mehlburger, Tanner, Renshaw and Assocs., Little Rock, 1980-84; v.p. Mehlburger, Tanner & Assocs., 1984—; instr. Hatha Yoga, St. Francis House, Little Rock, 1978, Parapsychology Center, 1978-79. Mem. Ark. Environ. Barriers Council. Registered architect, Ark. Mem. AIA (state chmn. 1981), Nat. Trust Historic Preservation, Ark. Solar Coalition, U. Ark. Alumni Assn., Little Rock Jaycees (dir. 1981-83, sec. 1982-83), chmn. TV auction 1982). Alpha Phi Omega, Pi Kappa Alpha. Author: Flow Gently Sweet Alpha, 1972; Inflatables, An Alternative to the Deflated Classroom, 1973. Home: 1617 Battery St Little Rock AR 72202 Office: 201 S Izard St Little Rock AR 72201

BURSE, RAYMOND MALCOLM, university president; b. Hopkinsville, Ky., June 8, 1951; s. Joe Burse; m. Kim Maria Hatch; 1 son, Raymond Malcolm Jr. B.A. in Chemistry and Math., Centre Coll., 1973; postgrad. Oxford U., 1975; J.D., Harvard U., 1978. Assoc. Wyatt, Grafton & Sloss, now Wyatt, Tarrant & Sloss, Louisville, 1978-82; pres. Ky. State U., Frankfort, 1982—. Mem. council Nat. Collegiate Athletic Assn.; bd. dirs. Salvation Army, Frankfort, Frankfort YMCA, Thomas More Coll. Mem. ABA, Ky. Bar Assn., Frankfort and Franklin County C. of C. (bd. dirs.). Office: Office of Pres East Main St Ky State U Frankfort KY 40601

BURT, ARTHUR FARLOW, dentist; b. South Bend, Ind., Jan. 10, 1946; s. Farlow Berglund and Irene (Gradone) B.; m. Gail Ann Reynolds, Aug. 26, 1972; children—Kimberly Ann, Ashley Farlow. B.S., U. Fla., 1968; D.D.S., Med. Coll. Va., 1972. Gen. practice dentistry Albermarle Health Dept., Charlottesville, Va., 1972-73; assoc. dentist, Dunedin, Fla., 1973-76; pvt. practice dentistry, Clearwater, Fla., 1976—. Bd. dirs. Upper Pinellas Assn. for Retarded Citizens, Clearwater, 1980. Recipient Brotherhood award Fla. Assn. for Retarded Citizens, 1981; Boss of Yr. award Pinellas County Hygiene Soc., 1984. Mem. ADA, Upper Pinellas Dental Assn. (pres. 1984-85, ethics chmn. 1985; Cournoyer award 1981), West Coast Dental Assn. (chmn. council on assn. affairs, 1980-85), Fla. Dental Assn. (del. 1981-82). Republican. Presbyterian. Lodge: Rotary, (bd. dirs. 1986). Avocations: camping; boating. Office: 2708 Park Dr Clearwater FL 33575

BURT, MARLOW GERMAINE, arts administrator. B.A. in Edn., Oswego State U., 1960; postgrad. in econs. Syracuse U., 1962. Program adminstr. Syracuse U. Theatre; devel. dir. Sta. WCYN-TV, Syracuse; dir. N.H. Commn. on the Arts; exec. dir. St. Paul-Ramsey Arts and Sci. Council, until 1978; exec. dir. Ky. Ctr. for Arts, Louisville, 1978—; chmn. Nat. Endowment Arts City Spirit Panel, St. Paul, mem. nat. spl. projects panel; former chmn. bd. Minn. Pub. Radio. Past pres. St. Paul YMCA; mem. St. Paul Downtown Community Devel. Com. Mem. Nat. Assn. Community Arts Councils (exec. com.). Home: 14220 Harbour Pl Prospect KY 40059 Office: Ky Ctr Arts 5 Riverfront Plaza Louisville KY 40202

BURT, PHILIP BARNES, physicist, educator, consultant; b. Memphis, July 1, 1934; s. Louie Einsinger and Bess Maud (Bolton) B.; m. Harriet Grace Clack, June 24, 1954; children—Elizabeth Lynn, Constance Nicole, Sydney Faith, Timothy Clack. A.B., U. Tenn., 1956, M.S., 1958, Ph.D., 1961. Assoc. physicist Oak Ridge Nat. Lab., 1960, indsl. cons., 1965-71; sr. scientist Jet Propulsion Lab., Calif. Inst. Tech., Pasadena, 1961-65; vis. asst. prof. U. So. Calif., Los Angeles, 1963; from asst. prof. to prof. Clemson U., S.C., 1965—, head physics dept., 1982—. Author: Quantum Mechanics and Nonlinear Waves, 1981. Contbr. chpts. to books, articles to publs. NSF predoctoral fellow, 1960-61; NATO research grantee, Brussels, 1983—. Mem. Am. Phys. Soc., Am. Math. Soc., AAAS, Sigma Xi (Disting. Research Scientist 1985), Omicron Delta Kappa, Kappa Sigma. Baptist. Avocations: Swimming, flying. Home: 210 Wyatt Ave Clemson SC 29631 Office: Dept Physics Clemson U Clemson SC 29631

BURTON, BRONDA PARKER, nurse; b. Durham, N.C., Mar. 22, 1955; d. Charlie Raymond and Mildred Frances (Brown) Parker; m. William Harold Burton, Feb. 15, 1976; children—Cory Michael, Amy Hope, Toby Parker. Diploma, Watts Sch. Nursing, Durham, 1976. Lic. R.N., N.C., Va. Occupational therapy aide Durham Rehab. Ctr., 1971-73; assoc. nurse, area programmer Murdoch Ctr., Butner, N.C., 1976; staff nurse Meth. Retirement Home, Durham, 1978-79; activity dir. Melody Manor Rest Home, Boydton, Va., 1980-82; nursing supr. Burnette's Retirement Village, Louisburg, N.C., 1982-84; head nurse, R.N. supr., patient coordinator Hillhaven Convalesence Ctr., Raleigh, N.C., 1985—. Ch. pianist, asst. organist Centerville Bapt. Ch. (N.C.), 1982—, youth choir dir., 1982-84, program dir. Bapt. Young Women, 1982-84, dir. Women's Missionary Union, 1983-84, Young Women's dir., 1985—; assoc. mem. N.C. chpt. Arthritis Found., 1983—. Mem. Am. Nurses Assn. (cert. gerontol. nurse), N.C. Nurses Assn., Century Club Am. Nurses Found., N.C. Long Term Facilities Assn., N.C. Bapt. Nursing Fellowship. Office: Hillhaven Convalescent Ctr 616 Wade Ave Raleigh NC

BURTON, G(ENE) CRAIG, real estate financial executive; b. Louisville, Apr. 29, 1954; s. Gene Darrel and Jamie F. (Hefley) B.; student Southwestern U., Memphis, 1971-72; B.S. in Acctg. with honors, U. Ky., 1975; m. Gilda K. Knollenberg, Aug. 2, 1980. Auditor Arthur Andersen & Co., 1975-76, staff auditor, Dallas, 1976-77; staff acct., internal auditor Dixico, Inc., Dallas, 1977-78, mgr. external reporting, 1978-79, asst. controller, 1979-81, asst. treas., controller, 1981-83, treas., chief fin. officer, 1983-84; chief fin. officer, ptnr. Hill Zimmer & Assocs., 1984—; v.p., dir. Collins Exploration Co. C.P.A., Tex.; cert. mgmt. acct. Mem. Tex. Soc. CPAs, Nat. Assn. Accts., Am. Inst. CPAs. Republican. Mem. Ch. of Scientology.

BURTON, JACQUELINE JOYCE, college dean; b. Tupelo, Ark., Dec. 11, 1939; d. Henry Lester and Amanda Elizabeth (Rice) B. B.S. in Edn., Ouachita Bapt. U., 1961; M.R.E., Southwestern Theol. Sem., 1965; postgrad. U. Miss., summers. 1966, 68. Library and residence hall staff Ouachita Bapt. U., Arkadelphia, Ark., 1957-61; tchr. Newport Pub. Schs., Ark., 1961-63; girls' camp dir. Ark. Women's Missionary Union, Little Rock, 1965; counselor women So. Bapt. Coll., Walnut Ridge, Ark., 1965-80, Bapt. student union dir., 1975—, dean women, 1980—. Recipient Danforth Found. Leadership award, 1957. Mem. Ark. Bapt. Student Dir.'s Assn. (sec. 1979-80), Assn. Student Devel. of So. Bapt. Colls. and Univs. Democrat. Avocations: piano; tennis. Home: Box 48 SBC Walnut Ridge AR 72476 Office: So Bapt Coll Box 48 Walnut Ridge AR 72476

BURTON, JOHN LEE, banker; b. Blaine, Ky., Mar. 30, 1927; s. H.G. and Gladys Marie (Gambill) B.; student Morehead State U., 1943-44; m. Betty Jane Sherman, May 21, 1980; children—John Lee, Joseph Edward. Mcht., farmer, 1944-46; banker, 1946—. With Peoples Security Bank, Louisa, Ky., 1946—, pres., 1964—; v.p., dir. Grayson Rural Electric Coop. (Ky.), 1950—; pres., dir. Foothills Rural Telephone Coop., Staffordsville, Ky., 1966—; dir. East Ky. Power Corp., Winchester. Advisor, Ky. Gov.'s Econ. Devel. Commn., 1976; past agrl. chmn. Lawrence County; past mem. jury com. and election com. of Lawrence Co. Named hon. clk. Ct. Appeals Ky., 1976; hon. treas. State of Ky., 1978, hon. sec. state, 1980. Mem. Ky. Bankers Assn. (past sec., v.p., pres. group 9), Ind. Community Bankers Ky., Ky. Hist. Soc. Mem. Christian Ch. Home: Route 3 Box 258-D Catlettsburg KY 41129 Office: PO Box 60 Louisa KY 41230

BURTON, JOSEPH ALFRED, manufacturer's representative, state senator; b. Atlanta, Aug. 30, 1923; s. Louis Albert and Lillian Catherine (Stroupe) B.; m. Bessie Lucille Walraven, Apr. 15, 1950; children—Virginia Louise, Patricia Anne, Carolyn Jean, Lewis George. B.S. in Indsl. Mgmt., Ga. Tech. Inst., 1949. Pres. Joe Burton, Tucker, Ga., 1963—; mem. Ga. Gen. Assembly, 1973-83. Served with USAAF, 1942-45, USAF, 1951-52; Korea. Republican. Methodist. Home: 2598 Woodwardia Rd NE Atlanta GA 30345

BURTON, MILTON WALLING, carpet company executive; b. Travelers Rest, S.C., Feb. 22, 1940; s. Willie E. and Leona Martha (Buchanan) G.; m. Shirley D. Jahns, Nov. 8, 1975; children—Randy, Michele, Steven Young. Student U. Calif., 1964. Owner, pres. Carpets Unltd. & Circus Burgers, Iuka, Miss. Served with USMC, 1957-60. Recipient Edn. Friendship award Iuka PTA, 1985, Ann. Vol. award Tishomingo County Devel. Found., 1984. Mem. Tishomingo County Devel. Found., NE Miss. Local Planning Counsel (chmn. 1984—), Iuka C. of C. (past. dir.). Methodist. (mem. adminstrv. bd.). Lodges: Lions (dir., deputy dist. gov.), Rotary, Masons. Home: 502 Hwy 25 S Iuka MS 38852

BURTON, RALPH ASHBY, mechanical engineer; b. Shreveport, La., Oct. 31, 1925; s. Cleveland Cunningham and Sadie (King) B.; B.S., U. Ark., 1947; M.S., U. Tex., 1951, Ph.D., 1952; m. Nancy Gaines, Aug. 4, 1948 (dec.); 1 son, Ralph G. Research instr., U. Ark., Fayetteville, 1947-49; teaching fellow U. Tex., Austin, 1949-52; asst. prof. M.I.T., Cambridge, 1952-54; asso. prof. U. Mo., Columbia, 1954-58; staff scientist, sect. mgr. S.W. Research Inst., San Antonio, 1958-67; liaison scientist U.S. Office Naval Research, London, 1967-69; prof. mech. engring. Northwestern U., Evanston, Ill., 1969-80; head dept. mech. and aerospace engring. N.C. State U., Raleigh, 1980-85; pres. Burton Technologies, 1985—; spl. assignment Office of Naval Research, Arlington, Va., 1978-79. Recipient Small Bus. Innovation Research Phase I awards (2), 1985. Fellow ASME (centennial medallion Chgo. sect. 1980), Am. Soc. Engring. Edn., AAAS, AAUP, Sigma Xi. Republican. Presbyterian. Author: Vibration and Impact, 1958; editor: Thermal Deformation in Frictionally Heated Systems, 1980; patentee engine ignition enhancement. Home: 1825 Ridge Rd Raleigh NC 27607 Office: Mechanical and Aerospace Engineering NC State U Raleigh NC 27650

BURTON, RON D., educational foundation executive; b. Duncan, Okla., Sept. 22, 1946; s. Alton Head, Jr. and Nola Marie (Duvall) B.; B.B.A. in Acctg., U. Okla., 1969, J.D., 1974; m. Jetta Ellen Stewart, Sept. 1, 1967; children—Ronna Ellen, Josh Andrew. Bar: Okla. 1974. Acct. III, then dir. deferred giving U. Okla., Norman, 1969-78, trust officer, 1978—; treas., then assoc. exec. dir. U. Okla. Found., 1970-78, exec. dir., sec., 1978—. Ward 1 rep. Norman City Charter Revision Com., 1979-80; chmn. Sooner dist. Last Frontier council Boy Scouts Am.; bd. dirs., treas. Norman Pub. Sch. Found.; bd. dirs. U. Okla. Fed. Credit Union, 1975—, pres., 1978—; bd. dirs. Norman United Way Found. Served with USAR, 1971-72. Mem. Am. Bar Assn., Okla. Bar Assn., Cleveland County Bar Assn. Democrat. Christian Scientist. Lodge: Norman Rotary (bd. dirs. 1982—, pres. 1983-84). Home: 4001 Breckenridge Ct PO Box 5239 Norman OK 73070 Office: 100 Timberdell Rd Norman OK 73019

BURWELL, DUDLEY SALE, food distribution company executive; b. Ebenezer, Miss., Nov. 21, 1931; s. Clement Lucas and Winfree Henry B.; m. Joan Fay Berman, July 26, 1952; children—Lana, Dudley S., Joel B., Gregory Todd, Troy E. Student, Holmes Jr. Coll., 1950, Draughons Bus. Coll., 1951; grad. LaSalle Extension U., 1965. With Lewis Grocer Co., Indianola, Miss., 1954—, v.p., sec., 1972-79, pres., chief exec. officer, 1979—; pres., chief exec. officer Sunflower Stores, Inc., Indianola, 1979—, also dir.; dir. Planters Bank & Trust Co., Indianola. Bd. dirs. Miss. Econ. Council; v.p. Delta Council. Served with USMC, 1952-54. Mem. Am. Inst. C.P.A.s, Miss. Soc. C.P.A.s, Indianola C. of C. (pres. 1976-77). Methodist. Club: Rotary (pres. 1977-78). Home: 4 Morningside Dr Indianola MS 38751 Office: Hwy 49 S Indianola MS 38751

BURWELL, LEAH, pharmacist; b. Clarinda, Iowa, May 12, 1956; d. Matthew David and Judith Bonnel (Burwell) Mermelstein; B.S. in Pharmacy, U. Ky., 1978. Registered pharmacist, Ky. Pharmacy intern Cassell's Pharmacy, Lexington, 1977-78; pharmacy grad., pharmacist Pattie A. Clay Hosp., Richmond, Ky., 1979; pharmacist U. Ky. Med. Ctr., Lexington, 1979-81, VA Med. Ctr., Lexington, 1981-82, Humana Hosp., Lexington, 1982—, mem. diabetes teaching team, speaker, cons. Ctr. of Excellence in Diabetes, 1983—. Mem. Am. Soc. Hosp. Pharmacists, Bluegrass Pharm. Assn., Ky. Soc. Hosp. Pharmacists, Ky. Assn. Diabetes Educators. Avocations: piano; sewing; racquetball; golf; swimming; aerobic exercise. Home: 301 I Bainbridge Dr Lexington KY 40509 Office: Humana Hosp Lexington 150 N Eagle Creek Dr Lexington KY 40509

BURZYNSKI, STANISLAW RAJMUND, internist; b. Lublin, Poland, Jan. 23, 1943; s. Grzegorz and Zofia Miroslawa (Radzikowski) B.; came to U.S., 1970; M.D. with distinction, Med. Acad., Lublin, 1967, Ph.D., 1968. Teaching asst. Med. Acad. Lublin, 1962-67; intern, resident in internal medicine, Med. Acad., 1967-70; research asso. Baylor U., 1970-72, asst. prof., 1972-77; pvt. practice specializing in internal medicine, Houston, 1977—; dir. Burzynski Research Lab., 1977-83; pres. Burzynski Research Inst., Inc., 1983—. Nat. Cancer Inst. grantee, 1974 West Found. grantee, 1975. Mem. AAAS, Am. Assn. Cancer Research, AMA, Fedn. Am. Scientists, Harris County Med. Soc., Polish Nat. Alliance (pres. Houston chpt. 1974-75), Soc. Neurosci., Tex. Med. Assn., Sigma Xi. Roman Catholic. Contbr. articles profl. jours. Discoverer of antineoplastons components of biochem. def. system against cancer; described structure of Ameletin, 1st substance known to be responsible for remembering sound in animal's brain. Home: 5 Concord Cr Houston TX 77024 Office: 6221 Corporate Dr Houston TX 77036

BUSARD, THOMAS RICHARD, anesthesiologist; b. Muskegon, Mich., Dec. 11, 1923; s. Robert Ira and Florence Gertrude (Morrill) B.; m. Dolores M. Fisher, Nov. 28, 1946; children—Lucinda Jane, Thomas Alan, Roberta Ann, Patti Ellen, Gillian Sue. B.S. in Bus. Adminstrn., Northwestern U., 1948; M.D., U. Mich., 1959. Diplomate Am. Bd. Anesthesiology. Owner, mgr. Ford Co. Agy., Dowagiac, Mich.; intern Oakwood Hosp., Dearborn, Mich., 1959-60; resident U. Mich. Med. Ctr., Ann Arbor, Mich., 1960-62; practice medicine specializing in anesthesiology, Muskegon, Mich., 1962-73, Bradenton, Fla., 1973—; mem. staffs Manatee Meml. Hosp., Blake Meml. Hosp., Bradenton, Fla. Vice chmn. Sarasota Manatee Airport Authority, 1976-84. Served with AUS, 1943-45. Mem. AMA, Fla. Med. Assn., Manatee County Med. Soc., Am. Soc. Anesthesiologists, Fla. Soc. Anesthesiologists, Internat. Anesthesia Research Soc. Republican. Presbyterian. Clubs: Country, Elks (Bradenton). Home: 5050 18th Ave West Bradenton FL 33529 Office: 4700 Manatee Ave West Bradenton FL 33529

BUSCH, DAVID CARL, wholesaling and specialty retailing organization executive; b. Champaign, Ill., May 12, 1948; s. Harold Carl and Mary Jane (Shafer) B.; m. Rebecca Lynne Brown, June 13, 1970; children—Damian Matthew, Emily Lynne. B.S. in Mktg., U. Ill., 1970. Mgr. tng. Eisner div. Jewel Co., Inc., Champaign, 1970-77; dir. retail tng. Creative Mgmt. Inst., Hazelwood, Mo., 1977-80; dir. tng. and ops. Mayfair Foodtown Supermarkets, Elizabeth, N.J., 1980-81; dir. manpower tng. Malone & Hyde, Inc., Memphis, 1981-83, dir. human resources, 1983—. Author: (tng. manual) Supermarket Checker Certification Program, 1978, Managing Bottom Line Results, 1979. Bd. dirs. Jr. Achievement Greater Memphis, 1984—; pres. Dogwood Creek Homeowners Assn., Germantown, Tenn., 1984; personnel policy advisor Boys Clubs Memphis, 1984; bd. dirs., dir. mktg. Memphis Bus. Group of Health, 1985—. Mem. Am. Soc. Personnel Adminstrn., Am. Soc. Tng. and Devel., Food Mktg. Inst. (chmn. tng. and devel. forum 1985), Beta Theta Pi. Republican. Avocations: reading; swimming; tennis; golf. Home: 2596 Holly Springs Dr Germantown TN 38138 Office: Malone & Hyde Inc 3030 Poplar Ave Memphis TN 38111

BUSFIELD, ROGER MELVIL, JR., trade association executive; b. Ft. Worth, Feb. 4, 1926; s. Roger Melvil and Julia Mabel (Clark) B.; student U. Tex., spring 1943, summer 1946; B.A., Southwestern U., 1947, M.A., 1948; Ph.D., Fla. State U., 1954; m. Jean Wilson, Mar. 26, 1948 (div. Oct. 1960); children—Terry Jean, Roger Melvil III, Timothy Clark; m. Virginia Bailey, Dec. 1, 1962; 1 child, Julia Lucille. Asst. prof. Southwestern U., 1947-49; instr. U. Ala., 1949-50, Fla. State U., 1950-54; asst. prof. speech Mich. State U., 1954-60; editorial services specialist Oldsmobile div. Gen. Motors Corp., Lansing, Mich., 1960; gen. publs. supr. Consumers Power Co., Jackson, Mich., 1960-61; asso. dir. Mich. Hosp. Assn., Lansing, 1961-73; exec. dir. Ark. Hosp. Assn., Little Rock, 1973-81, pres., 1981—. Trustee, Central Mich. U., 1967-73, chmn., 1970; mem. Mich. Gov.'s Commn. on Higher Edn., 1972-74; mem. Ark. Gov.'s Emergency Med. Services Adv. Council, 1975—, chmn., 1978-84. Served with USMC, 1943-46. Named Tex. Outstanding Author, Theta Sigma Phi, 1958; recipient Disting. Alumnus award Southwestern U., 1971; Senate-House Concurrent Resolution of Tribute, Mich. Legis., 1973. Mem. Am. Soc. Assn. Execs., Ark. Soc. Assn. Execs. (pres. 1981-82), Public Relations Assn. Mich. (pres. 1966), Speech Communication Assn., Am. Coll. Hosp. Adminstrs., State Hosp. Assn. Exec. Forum, Am. Hosp. Assn. (council on legislation 1975-77; council allieds and govt. relations 1984-86), Am. Theatre Assn. Methodist. Club: Rotary (Little Rock). Author: The Playwright's Art, 1958, Arabic transl., 1964; (with others) The Children's Theatre, 1960; editor Theatre Arts Bibliography, 1964; contbr. articles to profl. jours.; author profl. motion picture scenarios. Home: 23 Covewood Conway AR 72032 Office: 1501 N University Suite 400 Little Rock AR 72207

BUSH, ARTHUR JOE, mining engr., educator; b. Washington, Mar. 27, 1922; s. Arthur Edward and Cassie (Rice) B.; m. Margaret Elizabeth Strausser, Dec. 25, 1956; children—Beryl Candice, Diane Denise. B.S., Mining Engring., Mo. Sch. Mines, 1947; M.S., 1963; M.S. Urban Planning, Transp., Purdue U., 1970. Registered profl. engr., Mo., Ind., Ky. Asst. mining engr. Fredericktown Lead Co., Mo., 1947-49; mining engr. Solvay Process Div., Allied Chem. & Dye Corp., Prairie du Rocher, Ill., 1949-53; acting asst. quarry supt., 1950-53; mining engr. Internat. Salt Co., Retsof, N.Y., 1953-55; engr. Frazier-Davis Constrn. Co., Morgantown, Pa., Marion, Ill., 1955-56; chief engr. Baroid Div., Nat. Lead Co., Malvern, Ark., 1956-60, instr., engring. graphics, U. Mo., Rolla., 1962-65; asst. prof. civil engring. Tri-State U., Angola, Ind., 1965-72; city coordinator, city engr. Kendallville, Ind., 1972-73; asso. prof. engring. tech. Western Ky. U., Bowling Green, 1974—; cons. on mining engring. Served to 1st lt., U.S. Army, 1943-46. Decorated Silver Star with oak leaf cluster. Mem. AIME, ASCE, Soc. Engring. Edn., Am. Rd. Builders Assn., Ky. Soc. Profl. Engrs., Nat. Soc. Profl. Engrs., Mammoth Cave chpt. Profl. Engrs., Am. Fencers Assn., Hobson House Assn., Am. Soc. Explosives Engrs., Steuben County Hist. Soc. Sertoma (Lewis B. Hershey chpt.), Sigma Xi, Pi Kappa Alpha, Sigma Gamma Epsilon, Tau Beta Pi. Clubs: Sertoma, Rolla Arts Group, Arts Alliance Bowling Green. Contbr. articles to profl. jours. Research in fields of explosives and dynamic creep. Home: 1927 Price St Bowling Green KY 41201 Office: Western Ky Univ Bowling Green KY 42101

BUSH, IDA FLORENCE, school counselor, educator; b. Vada, Ga., June 1, 1928; d. Walter and Pearl Florence (Johnson) Florence; m. Melvin Bush, May 20, 1946; children—Walter, Clarence, Benjamin, Portia, Reginald. B.S., Ft. Valley State Coll., 1957, M.S., 1958; student Savannah State Coll., 1948-49, 50, 51, 53, 54, 57; postgrad. Fla. A&M U., 1961-63, 69-70, 72, Atlanta U., 1960, 64, 69, Clark Coll., 1966. Tchr., Kestler Elem. Sch., Damascus, Ga., 1952-56, 58-61, 62-69; counsel or Washington High Sch., Blakely, Ga., 1961-62, Kestler Elem. Sch., 1969-71, Early County Elem. Sch., Blakely, 1971-82; counselor Early County High Sch., 1982-84, sch. test coordinator, sch. spl. edn. coordinator. Mem. Lonnie Chester Scholarship Found., 1982-83; mem. steering com. Early County Gov.'s Competition Project, 1981; mem. steering com. Early County Drug Awareness; mem. Early County Mental Health Adv. Council. Named Early County Tchr. of Year, 1959-60. Mem. NEA, Ga. Assn. Educators, Ga. Sch. Counselors Assn., Early County Assn. Educators. Democrat. Baptist. Club: Order Eastern Star.

BUSH, JOSEPH PAUL, psychologist, educator; b. San Diego, May 24, 1954; s. Bartholomew Michael and Lorraine (Touzet) B. B.A., U. Calif.-Santa Cruz, 1976; M.A., U. Va., 1980, Ph.D., 1983. Lic. clin. psychologist, Va. Psychology asst. Pineland Ctr., New Gloucester, Maine, 1977-78; chief psychology intern Augusta County Schs., Fishersville, Va., 1978-80; asst. dir. Ctr. for Youth and Family Studies, Charlottesville, Va., 1980-81; research coordinator Behavioral Medicine Lab., U. Fla., Gainesville, 1981-82; clin. psychology intern J. Hillis Miller Health Ctr., Gainesville, 1982-83; asst. prof. Va. Commonwealth U., Richmond, 1983—; practicum coordinator Clin. Psychology Program, Va.

Commonwealth U., Richmond, 1984—; psychol. cons. Med. Coll. Va., Richmond, 1983—. Contbr. articles to jours., chpts. to books. Va. Commonwealth U. biomed. grantee, 1985, 86, faculty grant-in-aid, 1984. Mem. Am. Psychol. Assn., Va. Psychol. Assn. (treas.), Soc. for Behavioral Medicine, Southeastern Psychol. Assn., Assn. for Advancement Behavior Therapy. Avocations: backpacking; map collecting. Office: Dept Psychology Va Commonwealth Univ 806 W Franklin St Box 2018 Richmond VA 23284-0001

BUSH, TED J., JR., state construction plans examiner; b. Portland, Oreg., Oct. 15, 1949; s. Ted J. and Anne Lee (Acton) B. Student Va. Poly. Inst. and State U., 1968-72. Designer, Fairfax Hosp., Falls Church, Va., 1977-85; constrn. plans examiner div. inspection services State of Va., Arlington, 1985—; owner Homeowners Design Service, Annandale, Va.; engring. technician County of Fairfax, 1973-77. Mem. vocat. edn. task force for drafting Fairfax County Pub. Schs., 1975-77. Mem. Nat. Wildlife Fedn., Fedn. Fly Fishers, Trout Unltd. (life; Va. council). Home: 1604 Woodmoor Ln McLean VA 22101 Office: Courthouse Rm 227 Arlington VA 22201

BUSH, WENDELL EARL, lawyer, govt. ofcl.; b. Little Rock, Dec. 10, 1943; s. David J. and Annie O. (Hamilton) B.; A.B., Philander Smith Coll., Little Rock; postgrad. Atlanta U.; J.D., Emory U.; postgrad. (Reginald Heber Smith fellow) U. Pa. Law Sch. Admitted to bar; staff Emory U. Community Law Clinic, Indpls. Legal Services Orgn.; dist. counsel Memphis dist. office EEO Commn., now sr. trial atty. H. Sol Clark fellow. Mem. Am., Nat. bar assns. Home: 3685 Winchester Park Circle Memphis TN 38118 Office: 1407 Union Ave Suite 502 Memphis TN 38103

BUSH, WILLIAM GEORGE, manufacturing company executive; b. Independence, Kans., Sept. 14, 1923; s. William Edward and Flava Inez (Griggs) B.; m. Miriam Ditto, Oct. 2, 1948 (div. 1973); children—William, Robert, Benton; m. 2d Margaret Pauline Ellis, June 14, 1974. B.B.A., N.Tex. State U., 1950. Dir., Williamson-Dickie Mfg. Co., Ft. Worth, 1960—, Dickies Indsl. Service, Inc., Ft. Worth, 1960—, Blessings Corp., Piscataway, N.J., 1979—; adv. dir. Liberty Mut. Ins. Co., Boston, 1980—. Served with U.S. Army, 1942-45. Republican. Methodist. Clubs: Petroleum (Ft. Worth), Emerald Bay (Tyler, Tex.). Office: Williamson-Dickie Mfg Co PO Box 1779 Fort Worth TX 76101

BUSING, WILLIAM RICHARD, research chemist, crystallographer; b. Bklyn., June 21, 1923; s. Waldemar Henry and Alice Wilmarth (Thompson) B.; m. June Thorndike, Aug. 25, 1951; children—Barbara Wilmarth Busing Wachs, Lesley Hazlewood, Richard Thorndike. B.A., Swarthmore Coll., 1943; M.A., Princeton U., 1948, Ph.D., 1949. Research assoc. chemistry dept. Brown U., 1949-51; instr. chemistry dept. Yale U., 1951-54; sr. research staff chemistry div. Oak Ridge Nat. Lab., 1954—; instr. chemistry Knoxville Coll., 1960-61, Oak Ridge Inst. Nuclear Studies, 1964-65; hon. research fellow U. Manchester (Eng.), 1962-63; instr. chemistry U. Tenn., Knoxville, 1968-69. Served to lt. j.g. USNR, 1944-46. Mem. Am. Crystallographic Assn. (pres. 1971, U.S. del. Internat. Congress Crystallography, Kyoto, Japan 1972, Amsterdam, The Netherlands, 1975, Martin J. Buerger award 1985), Phi Beta Kappa, Sigma Xi. Unitarian. Club: Smoky Mountains Hiking (pres. Knoxville 1984-85). Contbr. articles to profl. jours. Home: 317 Louisiana Ave Oak Ridge TN 37830 Office: Chemistry Div Oak Ridge Nat Lab PO Box X Oak Ridge TN 37830

BUSTAMENTE, ALBERT GARZA, U.S. congressman; b. Asherton, Tex., Apr. 8, 1935; m. Rebecca Pounders; children—Albert Anthony, John Marcus, Celina Elizabeth. Student San Antonio Coll., 1956-58; B.A., Sul Ross State Coll., 1961. Tchr., coach, 1961-68; congl. asst., 1968-71; Bexar County commr., 1973-78; Bexar County judge, 1979-84; mem. 99th Congress from Tex., 1985—. Mem. Nat. Council Mental Health Ctrs., Tex. Jail Commn. Address: Ho of Reps Office Office of House Members Washington DC 20515*

BUSTER, WILLIAM ROBARDS, SR., museum director; b. Harrodsburg, Ky., Oct. 10, 1916; s. John Shelby and Martha Lillard (Nooe) B.; student Centre Coll., 1934-35; B.S., U.S. Mil. Acad., 1939; grad. Command and Gen. Staff Sch., 1951, Army War Coll., 1964; m. Mildred Pine Martin, June 24, 1942; children—William Robards, Kathryn Martin, Martha Lillard. Commd. 2d lt., U.S. Army, 1939, advanced through grades to brig. gen., 1960; arty. comdr. 2d Armored Div., African Middle East and European Theatres, 1940-45; mem. plans and ops. div. War Dept. Gen. Staff European Sect., 1945-47; ret., 1947; mem. Res., 1947-53, Ky. N.G., 1953-69, corps arty. comdr., dep. adj. gen. of Ky., 1960-69; ret., 1969; dir. Ky. Hist. Soc., Frankfort, 1973-83, dir. emeritus, exec. advisor, 1983—; sr. advisor Ky. Oral History Commn. farmer, 1947—; dir. Home Fed. Savs. & Loan Assn., United Bank & Trust Co., Versailles, Ky. Pres. Woodford County Farm Bur., 1957-59; chmn. ARC Louisville Regional Blood Center, 1954-59, Central Ky. Council Camps and Hosps., 1955-58; chmn. bd. trustees Midway Coll. Decorated Legion of Merit, Bronze Star, Air medal, Silver Star with oak leaf cluster; Croix de Guerre avec palme. Mem. Ky. Archives and Records Commn., Ky. Adv. Commn. Public Documents. Ky. Hist. Records Adv. Bd. (coordinator), Ky. Civil War Round Table. Democrat Mem. Christian Ch. Clubs: Idle Hour Country, Lexington. Lodge: Midway Lions (pres. 1948-49). Editorial bd. Univ. Press of Ky., 1976—. Home: Audubon Farm Midway KY 40347 Office: Kentucky Historical Society Box H Frankfort KY 40601

BUTLER, BRUCE BAIRD, public health dentist; b. Schenectady, Dec. 17, 1930; s. Stannard McLean and Dorothy Faye (Baird) B.; m. Ann Giles, May 7, 1958; children—Charlotte, Priscilla, Martha, Elizabeth. B.Mus., Eastman Sch. of Music, 1953; D.D.S., Loyola U.-New Orleans, 1963; M.P.H., Tulane U., 1964. Diplomate Am. Bd. Dental Public Health. Resident in dental pub. health, Ga. Dept. Health, Atlanta, 1968-69; gen. practice dentistry, Metairie, La., 1969-71; chief of dental health New Orleans Health Dept., 1971-75; specialist in dental pub. health La. Dept. of Health and Human Resources, New Orleans, 1975—. Bd. dirs. Bastille Day Celebration. Served with U.S. Army, 1953-56, col. Dental Corps, Res. Mem. Res. Officers Assn. (state dental Surgeon La. dept.), Soc. Mayflower Desc. (dep. gov. gen. La. chpt.), Brewster Soc. (pres.), Am. Bd. Dental Pub. Health, ADA, La. Dental Assn., New Orleans Dental Assn., La. Pub. Health Assn., Am. Assn. Pub. Health Dentistry, SAR (pres. 1984-85), La. Pub. Health Assn. (pres. 1984-85), Assn. Mil. Surgeons of U.S., Round Table, Delta Omega Soc. Episcopalian. Clubs: Rotary (New Orleans), Pendennis. Home: 3206 Napoleon Ave New Orleans LA 70125 Office: PO Box 60630 New Orleans LA 70160

BUTLER, BURTRAM B., educational administrator; b. Chgo., Mar. 17, 1933; s. Julius Wales and Marion Stiger (Wright) B.; A.B., U. Miami (Fla.), 1952; A.M., U. N.Mex., 1953; M.A., Columbia U., 1954, Ed.D., 1955, Profl. Diploma, 1956. Adminstr., dir. Psychol. Service Ctr., Teaneck, N.J., 1955-62; headmaster, pres. trustees Graham-Eckes Sch., Palm Beach, Fla., 1963-68; cons. edn. and guidance, 1968—; headmaster William B. Travis Acad., Galveston, Tex., 1979—. Mem. Am. Assn. Sch. Adminstrs., Nat. Assn. Secondary Sch. Prins., Nat. Assn. Elem. Edn., Nat. Assn. Elem. Sch. Prins., AAUP, Am. Personnel and Guidance Assn., Nat. Vocat. Guidance Assn., Assn. Supervision and Curriculum Devel., Am. Psychol. Assn., N.Y. State Psychol. Assn., N.J. Psychol. Assn., Tex. Psychol. Assn., Acad. Psychologists in Marital and Family Therapy, Nat. Assn. Sch. Psychologists, Am. Sch. Counselor Assn., Tex. Assn. Profl. Educators, Tex. Assn. Sch. Adminstrs., Tex. Assn. Secondary Sch. Prins., Tex. Elem. Prins. and Suprs. Assn., Galveston Mental Health Assn., Palm Beach Civic Assn., Palm Beach Soc. Four Arts, Palm Beach Round Table, Soc. Colonial Wars, Cum Laude Honor Soc., Phi Delta Kappa, Kappa Delta Pi. Episcopalian. Office: Drawer 989 Main Post Office Bldg Galveston TX 77553

BUTLER, CHARLES ROBERT, health care official; b. Austin, Tex., Oct. 12, 1949; s. Raymond and Helen Marguerite (Evans) B.; B.S. in English and Journalism, Fla. State U., 1973; m. Pamela Ann Neal, Apr. 15, 1977; 1 child, Robert M. Tchr. English and journalism, Duval-St. Johns Counties, Fla., 1973-75; mng. editor Fla. Tennis & Golf Mag., 1976; account exec. Joe Luter & Assos., Advt. and Public Relations, 1977; dir. public relations Meml. Med. Ctr. Jacksonville (Fla.), 1978-82, dir. pub. affairs, 1983-84; dir. news, media relations Blue Cross and Blue Shield Fla., 1984—; v.p. mktg. Tampa Gen. Hosp., Fla., 1984—; pub. relations and advt. cons. Mem. Fla. Hosp. Assn. Public Relations Council (1st place award for external publs. 1980), Pub. Relations Soc. Am., Greater Jacksonville Hosp. Pub. Relations Council, Am. Soc. Hosp. Pub. Relations, Jacksonville Hosp. Pub. Relations Council (pres. 1979-80). Republican. Episcopalian. Club: University (Jacksonville). Home: 13143 Village Chase Circle Tampa FL 33624 Office: Tampa Gen Hosp Davis Island FL 33606

BUTLER, CONNIE MACK, chemical company executive; b. Greensboro, N.C., June 8, 1933; s. James Thomas and Pauline (West) B.; m. Rachel Marie Sizemore, Oct. 28, 1932. B.S. in Bus. Adminstrn., Rollins Coll., 1955; S.B.A., U. N.C., 1973. Chemist, sales rep., gen. mgr. Naugatuck Chem. Co. (Conn.), 1958-62; dir. mktg., v.p. mktg. Copdymer Rubber and Chem. Co., Baton Rouge, 1962-69; gen. mgr. chem. div. Milliken & Co., Spartanburg, S.C., 1970-78; dir. Petroleum Fermentations N.V., Amelia Island, Fla., 1978—; pres., chief exec. officer, dir. Petroferm USA, Amelia Island, 1978—; chmn. bd. Tamny Corp., Amelia Island, 1978—. Served with U.S. Army, 1956-58. Mem. Am. Chem. Soc., Soc. Chem. Industry. Clubs: Chemists (N.Y.C.); University (Jacksonville, Fla.). Office: Rt 2 Box 280 Amelia Island FL 32034

BUTLER, DONOVAN W., banker. Exec. v.p. Sun Bank Inc., Orlando, Fla. Office: Sun Banks Inc Sun Bank NA Bldg Orlando FL 32802*

BUTLER, ELIZABETH ANN, geologist; b. Meridian, Miss., Sept. 10, 1932; d. Franklin Walter and Serena (Hopper) McGee. B.S. in Geology, Millsaps Coll., 1955; M.S. in Geology, La. State U., 1957. Research geologist La. Geol. Survey, Baton Rouge, 1957-63; research geologist Sinclair Oil Corp., Tulsa, 1963-68; dir. paleontology Atlantic Richfield Co., Dallas, 1969-75, sr. geol. adviser, Los Angeles, 1975-80, asst. to exec. v.p. natural resources, 1977-80, sr. planning cons., 1980-81, mgr. stratigraphy and paleontology, Dallas, 1981—. Mem. Soc. Econ. Paleontologists and Mineralogists (sec.-treas. Gulf Coast sect. 1959-60, v.p. 1961-62), Am. Assn. Petroleum Geologists, Sigma Xi. Republican. Clubs: Brookhaven Country, Lancers. Contbr. articles on geology to profl. jours. Office: ARCO Exploration Co PO Box 2819 1601 Bryan St Dallas TX 75221

BUTLER, JOHN DANIEL, hospital administrator; b. Wichita, Kans., June 10, 1944; s. Arthur Hill and Frances Ann (Thorpe) B.; m. Martha Eugene Duty-Carstens, Nov. 26, 1965; children—Andrew, Eric. B.A., U. Houston, 1966; M.B.A., U. Utah, 1971. Asst. adminstr. St. Lukes Episc. Hosp., Houston, 1971-76; asst. adminstr. High Point Meml. Hosp., N.C., 1977-80, pres., 1980—. Bd. dirs. High Point United Way, 1980-84, Guilford County Mental Health Authority, 1983-86, Uwharrie Council Boy Scouts Am., 1980. Served to capt. USAF, 1967-71. Mem. High Point Mental Health Assn. (pres. 1980-81), Am. Coll. Hosp. Adminstrs., N.C. Hosp. Assn. (chmn.-elect bd. dirs.; chmn. dist. 1983). Democrat. Lutheran. Lodge: Kiwanis. Avocations: sailing; carpentry; hiking. Office: PO Box HP-5 601 N Elm St High Point NC 27261

BUTLER, JOHN PAUL, management consultant; b. Lexington, S.C., Sept. 6, 1935; s. Albert G. and Alma J. (Braswell) B.; m. Clare Vestal, Nov. 8, 1958 (div. 1978); children—Catherine, Thomas, Frank. B.S.M.E. (NROTC scholar), U. S.C., 1957; M.B.A., U. Conn., 1965. Sr. engr. Pratt & Whitney Aircraft, East Hartford, Conn., 1960-65; engring. supr. Westinghouse Electric Corp., Pitts., 1966-70, mktg. supr., 1971-76; dir. sales and mktg. Morgan div. Amca, Alliance, Ohio, 1977-78; sales dir. Mid-East, Westinghouse Electric Corp., Orlando, Fla., 1979-83; pres. Butler-Trappen Assocs., Orlando, 1984—. Republican committeeman. Served to lt., USN, 1957-60. Mem. ASME. Methodist. Contbr. articles to profl. jours.; patentee in field. Home: 215 Albrighton Ct Longwood FL 32779 Office: 6655 E Colonial Dr Orlando FL 32807

BUTLER, JOHN SCOTT, economist, educator; b. Waco, Tex., Mar. 28, 1950; s. Roy Francis and Barbara Goehring (Scott) B. B.A., Rice U., 1973; M.A., Cornell U., 1980, Ph.D., 1982. Acctg. clerk Hermann Hosp., Houston, 1973-75; teaching asst. U. Houston, 1975-76; teaching asst., fellow Cornell U., Ithaca, N.Y., 1976-79; research assoc. Mathematica Policy Research, Princeton, N.J., 1979-82, research economist, 1982; asst. prof. econs. Vanderbilt U., Nashville, 1982—. Grantee Inst. for Research Poverty, 1983, Dept Health and Human Services, 1983. Mem. Am. Econ. Assn., Econometric Soc., Am. Statis. Assn. Home: 1015 17th Ave S Apt 2 Nashville TN 37212 Office: Vanderbilt U Box 34-B Nashville TN 37235

BUTLER, MARILYN ANN, hospital nursing administrator; b. Crosby, Tex., Sept. 23, 1937; d. Frank Marin and Myrtle Lee (Becker) Smith; m. Richard Joe Butler, Dec. 2, 1960; children—Kimberly Lynn, Richard Scott. Diploma in nursing Lillie Jolly Sch. Nursing, Houston, 1958; postgrad. in health admstrn. U. Tex. Med. Br., Galveston, 1983-86. R.N., Tex. Surg. asst. C. M. Ashmore, M.D., Houston, 1958-61; head nurse, nursing supr. Meml. Hosp. System, Houston, 1962-77; nursing adminstr. Navarro Regional Hosp., Hosp. Corp. Am., Corsicana, Tex., 1981—. Mem. Am. Coll. Hosp. Adminstrs., Am. Soc. Nursing Service Adminstrs., Tex. Soc. Hosp. Nursing Service Adminstrs. (bd. dirs. 1983-85, pres.-elect 1985-86). Republican. Baptist. Home: 622 W 3d #2 Corsicana TX 75110 Office: Navarro Regional Hosp 3201 W Hwy 22 Corsicana TX 75110

BUTLER, MICHAEL LEE, public relations exec.; b. Sanford, Fla., May 3, 1947; s. Arthur L. and Christine (Stewart) B.; m. Jane Elizabeth Parks, Dec. 27, 1967; children—Lauren, Jenny. B.S. in Polit. Sci., U. Tenn., 1968. Public info. officer AEC, Oak Ridge, Tenn. and Washington, 1971-75, Clinch River Breeder Reactor, Oak Ridge, 1975-76; mgr. media relations TVA, Knoxville, 1976-80; chief speech writer Phillips Petroleum Co., Bartlesville, Okla., 1980-81; pres. Butler Communications, Knoxville, 1981—. Served with U.S. Army, 1968-71. Decorated Bronze Star. Recipient Knoxville Pub. Relations Practitioner of the Year award, 1983. Mem. Public Relations Soc. Am. Home: 18 Clark Pl Oak Ridge TN 37830 Office: Butler Communications 9041 Executive Park Dr Knoxville TN 37923

BUTLER, ROY, oil and gas exploration company executive; b. Rising Star, Tex., 1926. B.S., Tex. Tech. U., 1949, M.S., 1950. With Continental Oil Co., 1950-55, with subs. Samedan Oil Corp., 1955-74; with Noble Affiliates Inc., Ardmore, Okla., 1974—, pres., chief exec. officer, 1974—, also dir. Office: Noble Affiliates Inc 333 W Main St Ardmore OK 73401*

BUTLER, ROY FRANCIS, emeritus classics educator; b. Atlanta, May 4, 1914; s. Roy Edward and Mae Ellison (Kenner) B.; A.B. (Chattanooga Times scholar), U. Chattanooga, 1935; M.A., U. Tenn., 1938; PH.D. (Univ. scholar), Ohio State U., 1942; m. Barbara Goehring Scott, Nov. 17, 1943; children—Roy Francis, John Scott. Instr., U. Tenn., 1946, asst. prof. classics, 1947-48; instr. Ohio State U., 1946-47; asst. prof. classics Baylor U., 1947-49, assoc. prof., 1949-52, prof., 1952-84, chmn. dept. classics, 1958-84, prof. and chmn. emeritus classics, 1984—. Served with USAAF, 1942-45. Mem. Am. Philol. Assn., Oriental Soc. Am., Linguistic Soc. Am., Classical Assn. Middle West and South, Classical Assn. Southwestern U.S., AAAS. Author: Handbook of Medical Terminology, 1958, rev. 2d edit., 1972; The Meaning of Agapao and Phileo in the Greek New Testament, 1977; The Roman Numina, 1979; Sources of the Medical Vocabulary, 1980. Home: 2613 Starr Dr Waco TX 76710

BUTTION, THOMAS ROBERT, airline executive; b. Balt., Jan. 15, 1925; s. August Charles and Josephine M. (Stolba) B.; student public schs.; m. Dolores Rose Hengemihle, May 10, 1947; children—Robert Tod, Thomas Mark, Charles Randall. Exec. pilot L.C. Russell Co., 1947; pilot TWA, 1948; with Eastern Airlines Inc., 1949—, v.p. flight standards and tng., 1974-75, sr. v.p. flight ops., 1975—. Served with USAAF, 1943-45. Office: Eastern Airlines Inc Miami FL 33148

BUTTRAM, PRESTON LEE, oil and gas exploration company executive; b. Oklahoma City, Feb. 24, 1954; s. Dorsey Randal and Phyllis Green (Barnes) B.; m. Lianne Nelson, Aug. 18, 1979. Student Okla. U., 1972-74, Okla. City U., 1976. Gen. ptnr. PLB Ltd., Oklahoma City, 1977-79; propietor The Buttram Co., Edmond, Okla., 1980-85; pres., dir. Buttram Oil Properties Inc., Edmond, 1985—. Vol. Oklahoma City Festival of Arts, 1976-83, YMCA and YWCA, Oklahoma City, 1979, Oklahoma City Symphony, 1979-84, assoc. bd., 1980; sponsor Liberty Coll., Lynchburg, Va., 1983; vol. Chamber Music Orchestra, Oklahoma City, 1984; provider, counselor Metrochurch Ctr. Family Ministries, Edmond, 1985; precinct chmn. Republican Party, Edmond, 1985; county del. Rep. County Conv., Oklahoma City, 1985; del. Rep. State Conv., Oklahoma City, 1985. Mem. Oklahoma City Assn. Petroleum Landmen, Sigma Nu. Fundamentalist. Club: Bachelors (Oklahoma City) (pres. 1978-79). Office: Buttram Oil Properties Inc PO Box 2893 Edmond OK 73083

BUTTS, GLENN ALLEN, emergency medical technician; b. Boone, Iowa, May 13, 1951; m. Sheila Dianne Marshburn, June 22, 1974; children—Nathan, Alisha, Linnea. Assoc. Sci. in Aviation Tech., 1974; B.S. in Bus. Adminstrn., LeTourneau Coll., 1982; postgrad. No. Mich. U. Police Acad., 1976. Airport mgr., dir. airport pub. safety Delta County Airport, Escanaba, Mich., 1975-79; dir. emergency med. service City of Longview, Tex., 1980—. Bd. dirs. East Tex. Council of Govts., 1980-83, Am. Heart Assn., 1980—. Club: Kiwanis.

BUTZNER, JOHN DECKER, JR., federal judge; b. Scranton, Pa., Oct. 2, 1917; s. John Decker and Bess Mary (Robison) B.; B.A., U. Scranton, 1939; LL.B., U. Va., 1941; m. Viola Eleanor Peterson, May 25, 1946; 1 son, John Decker III. Admitted to Va. bar, 1941; practice in Fredericksburg, 1941-58; judge 15th and 39th Jud. Circuit of Va., 1958-62; U.S. judge Eastern Dist. Va., 1962-67; U.S. circuit judge 4th circuit Ct. Appeals, Richmond, Va., 1967-82, sr. circuit judge, 1982—. Served with USAAF, 1942-45. Home: 5507 Dorchester Rd Richmond VA 23225 Office: PO Box 2188 Richmond VA 23217

BUZARD, ROBERT SPURGIN, manufacturing company executive, electrical engineer; b. St. Joseph, Mo., Apr. 17, 1924; s. B. Frank and Catherine Mary (Spurgin) B.; m. Patricia Frances Ball, Aug. 28, 1948; children—Denise, Jeannie. B.S.E.E., Purdue U., 1949, M.S.E.E., 1956. Registered profl. engr., Tex. Sr. v.p. Vought Corp, LTV, Dallas, 1950-80, v.p. mktg., 1980-82, v.p. and gen. mgr. comml. div. E Systems, 1982-83; pres., chief exec. officer Electro Com Automation Inc., 1983—. Bd. dirs. Irving Community Hosp. Found.; mem. engring. vis. com. Purdue U. Served to capt. arty. U.S. Army, 1943-46. Recipient Disting. Engring. Alumni award Purdue U., 1980. Mem. Am. Def. Preparedness Assn., Am. Astronautical Soc. (dir. 1977-80), AIAA, IEEE, Irving (Tex.) C. of C., Eta Kappa Nu, Tau Beta Pi, Sigma Alpha Epsilon. Club: KC. Patentee servo-mechanism device. Office: PO Box 95080 Arlington TX 76005

BYERS, HAROLD HILL, religious organization executive; b. Bellwood, Pa., Nov. 26, 1928; s. Harold Hill and Ruth (Conley) B.; m. Phyllis E. Stahl, June 11, 1949 (div. Feb. 1975); children—Anne L., Stephen P., Cynthia R.; m. Jeanne McBeath Byers, Nov. 5, 1977. B.A., Ashland Coll. (Ohio), 1951; M.Div., Pitts. Theol. Sem., 1954; D.D. (hon.), Tusculum Coll., Greenville, Tenn., 1983. Ordained to ministry Presbyterian Ch. U.S.A., 1954; pastor Upper Buffalo Presbyn. Ch., Buffalo, Pa., 1951-55; assoc. pastor 1st Presbyn. Ch., Lansdowne, Pa., 1955-57; pastor 1st Presbyn. Ch., DuBois, Pa., 1957-64, Presbyn. Ch. of Apostles, Burnsville, Minn., 1964-73; program dir. Program Agy. Upcusa, N.Y.C., 1973-81; exec. Synod of South, Atlanta, 1981—. Mem. Acad. Parish Clergy. Office: Synod of the South 1001 Virginia Ave Room 217-C Atlanta GA 30083

BYERS, JERRY ALAN, engineer, consultant; b. Dallas, Nov. 6, 1952; s. Bernard and Phyliss (Wolens) B. B.S. in Indsl. Engring., U. Tex.-Arlington, 1976. Registered profl. engr., Tex. Engr., Gen. Dynamics, Fort Worth, 1976-78, Employers Ins. of Tex., Dallas, 1978—; owner, cons. Metroplex Engring. & Inspection, Dallas, 1983—. Coach Spl. Olympics, Dallas, 1985. Recipient Pres.'s award Employers Ins. Tex., 1980, 82. Mem. Tex. Soc. Profl. Engrs., Am. Soc. Safety Engrs. Republican. Jewish. Club: North Tex. Vintage Thunderbird (Dallas). Avocations: antique cars; golf; baseball; basketball; weight lifting. Home: 7510 Holly Hill #131 Dallas TX 75231 Office: Employers Ins of Texas PO Box 152009 Irving TX 75015-2009

BYERS, WILLIAM SEWELL, electrical engineer, educator; b. Ironton, Ohio, Oct. 3, 1925; s. William T. and Anna M. (Sewell) B.; B.E.E., Ohio State U., 1951; M.B.A., Rollins Coll., 1966; M.Eng., Pa. State U., 1969, M.Ed., 1972; Ed.D., Nova U., 1976; LL.D., Frank Ross Stewart U., 1981; m. Marjorie E. Reidel, Dec. 28, 1946; children—Thomas William, Robert M., Catherine G. Broadcast engr. Crosley Broadcasting Corp., Columbus, Ohio, 1949-51; dist. engr. Gen. Elec. Co., Syracuse, N.Y., 1951-55; staff engr., engring. mgr. Martin Marietta Aerospace Corp., Orlando, Fla., 1955-75; asso. prof. elec. engring. tech. U. Ala., Tuscaloosa, 1975-81, prof. and coordinator elec. engring. tech., 1981-83; prof., chmn. engring. tech. Murray State U. (Ky.), 1983-84, U. Central Fla., Cocoa, 1984—; academic advisor tech. Institut National d'Electricitie et d'Electronique at Boumerdes, Algeria, 1977-78; former adj. faculty Seminole Jr. Coll., Fla. So. Coll., Valencia Community Coll. Amateur radio operator. Nat. Sci. Found. grantee, 1968-69. Registered profl. engr., Fla., Ala., Mem. Soc. Wireless Pioneers (life), AAUP, Am. Soc. for Engring. Edn. (vice chmn. engring. tech. div.), Nat. Soc. Profl. Engrs., Mensa, IEEE (sr.), Capstone Engring. Soc., Pa. State Amateur Radio Club (hon. life), Tau Alpha Pi, Eta Kappa Nu. Home: 301 Westchester Dr Cocoa FL 32926 Office: 1519 Clearlake Rd Cocoa FL 32922

BYLSMA, GERALD L(EE), insurance agent; b. Albany, N.Y., Oct. 11, 1943; s. Donald and Marie Francis (Kneiper) B.; m. Sara Ellen Lampley, Dec. 16, 1967; children—Deborah Ann, Christine Marie. B.S. in Math., SUNY-Albany, 1970, M.S. in Math. Edn., 1971. Cert. math. tchr., N.Y., Ga. High sch. math. tchr. Warrensburg, N.Y., 1972-74, Columbus, Ga., 1974-78; life ins. agt., Albin/Bylsma Assocs., Columbus, 1978—. Served with U.S. Army, 1965-67. Recipient Silver Key, Ga. Internat. Life Ins. Co., 1981, 82, nat. quality and achievement awards, Nat. Assn. Life. Underwriters, 1981, 82, 83. Mem. Jehovah's Witnesses. Home: 1321 Melford Dr Columbus GA 31907 Office: Albin/Bylsma Assocs 701 4th St Phenix City AL 36867

BYRD, BETTE JEAN, artist, author; b. Columbia, Miss. Aug. 24, 1928; d. Rossie Dempsey and Edgie Irene (Cooper) McNeese; m. Jmes Peter Byrd, Dec. 26, 1953; (dec. Jan. 1982); children—William Patrick, Mark Andrew, Cynthi Denise. Student Holmes Jr. Coll., 1945-47; B.A., Millsaps Coll., 1949. Tchr., Satartia Jr. High Sch., Miss., 1949-50; exec. sec. Southland Co., Yazoo City, Miss., 1951-53; owner, mgr. Corner Cupboard Crafts, Atlanta, 1968-81; owner, sec. Bemby Co., Atlanta, 1978-82, owner, pres., 1982—. Artist, author: Rosemaling, A Celebration of Norwegian Folk Art, 1976; Tole and Decorative Painting Workbook, Vol. I, 1976, Vol. II, 1979; Paint Brush and Palette, 1981, Decorative Baskets, 1982; Decorative Stenciling, vol. 1, 2, 3, 1983, Cut, Pierced and Painted Lampshades, 1984; Folk Art Painting Plain and Fancy, 1985; Lampshades to Paint and Pierce, 1985; Old World Golden Treasures, 1986; contbg. author: Treasury of Decorative Painting, 1986; artist: Folk Art Designs vol 1, 1985, others; contbr. articles to craft mags. Mem. Nat. Soc. Tole and Decorative Painters (master decorative artist; pres. nat. 1978-79), Stencil Artisans League (pres., editor Newsletter 1986). Republican. Club: Sherbrooke Garden (pres.). Home: 2304 Sherbrooke Dr NE Atlanta GA 30345

BYRD, EDWARD TRAVIS, mortgage banker; b. Enterprise, Ala., Sept. 21, 1946; s. George Travis and Inez Elizabeth (Turner) B.; m. Barbara Betz, May 14, 1983. B.S., Livingston U. (Ala.), 1973. Vice-pres., Bowest Corp., Orlando, Fla., 1977-82; pres. Phoenix Comml. Fin., Orlando, 1982-83; pres. Fla. Comml. Mortgage Corp., Orlando, 1983—; dir. So. Consol. Inc., Orlando. Chmn. Orange County Democratic party (Fla.), 1983; bd. dirs. Orlando Opera Co., 1983. Served to capt. USAR. Mem. Fla. Mortgage Bankers Assn. (chmn. comml. loan com. 1981-82), Orlando Jaycees (v.p. 1977). Methodist. Lodge: Kiwanis. Home: 760 Thistle Ln Maitland FL 32751 Office: Fla Comml Mortgage Corp CNA Tower Suite 1540 255 S Orange Ave Orlando FL 32802

BYRD, JACK LYNN, petroleum engineer, executive; b. Miles, Tex., Nov. 12, 1934; s. Carl Lynn and Esther Mae (Morrow) B.; m. C. Marline Perkins, Aug. 26, 1955; children—Jeffrey Lynn, Gregory Owen, Shari Janice. B.S. in Petroleum Engring., Tex. Tech. U., Lubbock, 1956. Registered profl. engr., Tex. Jr. engr. Kewanee Oil Co., Okla., 1956-60, dist. supt., Borger, Tex., 1965, div. engr., Pampa, Tex., 1965-68, chief evaluation engr., Tulsa, 1968-72; v.p. and ops. mgr. Sound Refining, Tacoma, Wash., 1972-75; v.p. ops., exec. v.p. Hytech Energy Corp. (now Moran Exploration), Midland, Tex., 1975-79; v.p. and pres. Lacy & Byrd, Inc., Midland, 1979—; sr. and dist. engr. Walters & Shidler, Okla., 1960-65; Mem. Soc. Petroleum Engrs., Am. Petroleum Inst., Nat. Soc. Profl. Engrs., Ind. Petroleum Assn. Am., Permian Basin Petroleum Assn. Republican. Baptist. Club: Midland Country, Plaza. Home: 3100 Auburn Dr Midland TX 79705 Office: Lacy & Byrd Inc Sun Tower Suite 130 Midland TX 79702

BYRD, JAMES VERNON, law enforcement official; b. Columbia, La., May 11, 1934; s. William Graham and Rosa Florence (Kemp) B.; m. Norma Jeannette May, July 28, 1955; children—Cindy, Janet, Billy. Diploma in Traffic Police Adminstrn., Northwestern U., 1974. Trooper, La. State Police, Monroe, 1963-67, sgt., 1967-76, lt., 1975-84, capt., 1984—. Mem. La. State Troopers Assn., La. Police Officers Assn., Traffic Inst. Alumni Assn. Democrat. Baptist. Lodge: Masons. Home: PO Box 81 Old Bonita Rd Bastrop LA 71220 Office: Troop F La State Police 431 N Millhaven St Monroe LA 71203

BYRD, MICHAEL F., dancer, artistic director; b. Jacksonville, Fla., Nov. 30, 1950; s. Wilbur P. and Miriam (Rhodes) B.; m. Laurie Picinich, May 21, 1978; 1 child, Christopher Lawrance. B.A., U. Fla., 1972. Dancer, Met. Opera, N.Y.C., 1974, Classic Ballet, Closter, N.J., 1974-78; artistic dir. Fla. Ballet, Jacksonville, 1978—; cons. Duval Sch. of Fine Arts, Jacksonville, 1985; mem. adv. bd. Nat. Ballet Achievement Fund, Rutherford, N.J., 1984-85; active dancer Am. Guild Musical Artists, 1974—. Mem. State Dance Assn. Fla., Royal Acad. Dancing (student mem. 1975-79). Democrat. Methodist. Avocations: audio electronics; swimming; classical music. Office: Florida Ballet at Jacksonville 123 E Forsyth St Jacksonville FL 32202

BYRD, ROBERT CARLYLE, U.S. senator; b. North Wilkesboro, N.C., Nov. 20, 1917; s. Cornelius Sale and Ada (Kirby) B.; m. Erma Ora James, May 29, 1937; children—Mona Carole (Mrs. Mohammad Fatemi), Marjorie Ellen (Mrs. John Moore). Student, Beckley Coll., Concord Coll., Morris Harvey Coll., 1950-51, Marshall U., 1951-52; J.D., Am. U., 1963. Elected mem. W.Va. Ho. of Dels., 1946-50, W.Va. Senate, 1950-52; mem. 83d-85th Congresses, 6th Dist., W.Va.; U.S. senator from, W. Va., 1959—, Senate majority leader, 1977-79, Senate minority leader, 1980—. Named Most Influential Mem. U.S. Senate U.S. News & World Report Poll, 1979. Mem. Country Music Assn. (hon.). Democrat. Baptist. Lodge: Masons (33 deg.). Office: 311 Hart Senate Office Bldg Washington DC 20510*

BYRNES, VICTOR ALLEN, ophthalmologist; b. Tipton, Iowa, June 4, 1906; s. Victor Warren and Wilhelmina (Brauch) B.; m. Ethel M. Ahlberg-Seebach, June 6, 1929 (div. Aug. 1949); children—Donn A., Diane E. Byrnes Rury; m. Jean Beryl Crowly, Aug. 13, 1949. B.S., U. Iowa, 1927, M.D., 1929. Diplomate Am. Bd. Ophthalmology, Am. Bd. Preventive Medicine. Commd. 1st lt. U.S. Air Force, 1929, advanced through grades to brig. gen., 1956; asst. commandant USAF Sch. Aviation Medicine, 1943-44; comdr. Air Base and Convalescent Hosp., Nashville, Plattsburg Barracks, N.Y., 1944-45; staff surgeon Fifth Air Force, Okinawa, Japan, 1945-46; dir. edn. and clin. medicine div. USAF Sch. Aviation Medicine, 1946-53; dep. surgeon U.S. Air Forces in Europe, 1953-55; dir. profl. services Office Surgeon Gen., USAF, Washington, 1955-59; dir. med. edn. Mound Park Hosp., St. Petersburg, Fla., 1959-61; practice medicine specializing in ophthalmology, St. Petersburg, 1961-74; med. adjudicator VA, St. Petersburg, 1979—. Mem. editorial adv. bd. Jour. Aerospace Medicine, 1955-68; sect. editor Survey of Ophthalmology, 1959-68; mem. editorial adv. bd. Armed Forces Med. Jour., 1954-60; bd. editors Sight Saving Rev., 1961-70. Contbr. articles on ophthalmology to profl. jours. Decorated Legion of Merit with oak leaf cluster; recipient Gorgas medal Assn. Mil. Surgeons, 1955, Liljencrantz award Aerospace Med. Assn., 1958. Fellow Aerospace Med. Assn. (exec. council 1956-59), ACS (bd. govs. 1957-59), AMA (com. on aviation medicine 1957-59); mem. Am. Acad. Ophthalmology and Otolaryngology (exec. council 1957-61, honor award 1959), Am. Ophthal. Soc., Am. Assn. Ophthalmology, Soc. Mil. Ophthalmologists, Assn. for Research in Ophthalmology and Vision, Assn. Mil. Surgeons, Pan Am. Ophthal. Soc. (com. on space ophthalmology 1957), Mexican Ophthal. Soc. (hon.), Cuban Ophthal. Soc. (hon.), Pinellas County Med. Soc., Fla. Med. Assn., Alpha Omega Alpha. Republican. Lodge: Rotary. Home: 6110 Bahama Shores S Saint Petersburg FL 33705

CABANISS, WILLIAM JELKS, JR., machining company executive, state legislator; b. Birmingham, Ala., July 11, 1938; s. William Jelks and Florence Pierson (Sanson) C.; m. Catherine Hood Caldwell, July 20, 1962; children—Mary C., Frances C. B.A., Vanderbilt U., 1960. Dir. mktg. So. Cement div. Martin Marietta Corp., Birmingham, Ala., 1964-71; pres. Precision Grinding Inc., Birmingham, Ala., 1971—; mem. Ala. Ho. of Reps., 1978-82, Ala. State Senate, 1982—. dir. Am. South Bank, Protective Corp. Past pres., bd. dirs. Jr. Achievement Jefferson County. Served with U.S. Army, 1960-64. Home: 3812 Forest Glen Dr Birmingham AL 35213

CABLE, DWAYNE PAUL, management consultant; b. Hampton, Va., July 13, 1954; s. Paul Lyle Cable and Catherine (Hughes) Gaydos; Assoc. Degree in Acct., Assoc. Degree in Bus. Adminstrn., Wayne Community Coll., 1980; B.B.A., Western Carolina U., 1981, M.B.A., 1983; m. Deborah Ellen Sheffey, Nov. 10, 1973; children—Cheri N., J. Brett. Cons. project mgmt. and computer systems specialist, Goldsboro, N.C., 1978-80, Sylva, N.C., 1981—; dir. computer ops. Southwestern Tech. Coll.; ptnr. Cable and Assocs., Cullowhee, N.C., 1978—; pres. Concept Mgmt. Services, Sylva, N.C., 1983—; instr. Western Carolina U., 1980-83. Served with USAF, 1973-77. Mem. Western Carolina U. Data Processing Mgmt. Assn. (past pres.), Wayne Community Coll. Student Govt. Assn. (past pres.), Inst. Mgmt. Acctg., Am. Prodn. and Inventory Control Soc., Project Mgmt. Inst., Nat. Assn. Accts., Data Processing Mgmt. Assn., Phi Beta Lambda. Contbg. author: Microcomputers for Project Managers, 1982; author monograph: Organizing for Project Management; contbg. author: Accounting for Non-Business Majors. Home: Route 3 Box 283A Sylva NC 28779 Office: Southwestern Tech Coll 275 Webster Rd Sylva NC 28779

CABLE, JOHN LAURENCE, mathematics educator; b. Lancaster, N.Y., May 22, 1934; s. Laurence Nelson and Edith May (Wilson) C.; B.A., U. Buffalo, 1956, M.S., 1962. Tchr. Wilson Central Sch., N.Y., 1956-67; prof. math. Miami-Dade Community Coll., Miami, Fla., 1967-83; math. author Allyn & Bacon, Boston, 1974—, Macmillan, 1971—, Educulture, 1974—. Author: Patterns in the Sand, 1971, 75; Algebra Modules, 1974; Developing Skills in Algebra, 1974, 76, 79, 83; College Algebra, 1980; Algebra and Trigonometry, 1980; Elementary Algebra, 1984. Mem. Math. Assn. Am., Am. Math. Assn. Two Yr. Colls., Nat. council Tchrs. Math. Avocation: owner of standard bred horses. Office: 3446 SW 19th St Ocala FL 32674

CABRERA, JIMMY, professional speaker, seminar leader; b. Amherst, Tex., Sept. 26, 1944; s. George and Marie (Rodriguez) C.; m. Laural Anette Snelson, Aug. 23, 1975; children—Marcus John, Ale'tta Yvette, Chambray Lee. Assoc., Forest E. Olson Realtors, San Diego, 1973-76, br. mgr., 1976-77; regional dir. Champion Ltd., Scottsdale, Ariz., 1978-82; pres., profl. speaker Success Through Excellence, Inc., Houston, 1982—. Author: (audio cassette) Mastering the Art of Persuasion, 1983. Mem. Nat. Speakers Assn. (pres. Greater Houston chpt. 1984). Methodist. Home: 1827 Roanwood St Houston TX 77090 Office: Success Through Excellence Inc 1827 Roanwood St Houston TX 77090

CABRERA, RAUL D., accountant, health care company executive, consultant; b. Cienfuegos, Cuba, Apr. 10, 1951; came to U.S., 1961; s. Rigoberto and Hilda (Vazquez) C.; m. Lizette Martino, Sept. 28, 1978 (div.). B.B.A., Fla. Internat. U., 1984. Audit mgr. Deloitte Haskins & Sells, C.P.A.s, Miami, Fla., 1974-83; v.p., chief fin. officer CAC Health Plan, Inc., Miami, 1983—; dir. Nemesis Enterprises, Inc., Miami. Served with U.S. Army, 1970-71. Hon. Acctg. scholar Fla. Internat. U., 1973. Mem. Am. Inst. C.P.A.s, Fla. Inst. C.P.A.s, Health Care Mgmt. Assn. Republican. Roman Catholic. Office: CAC Health Care Plan Inc 1200 SW 1st St Miami FL 33101

CACCAMISE, GENEVRA LOUISE BALL, librarian; b. Mayville, N.Y., July 22, 1934; d. Herbert Oscar and Genevra (Green) Ball; B.A., Stetson U., DeLand, Fla., 1956; M.L.S., Syracuse U., 1967; m. Alfred Edward Caccamise, July 7, 1974. Tchr. elem. sch., Sanford, Fla., 1956-57, Longwood, Fla., 1957-58; tchr., librarian Enterprise (Fla.) Sch., 1958-63; librarian, media specialist Boston Ave. Sch., DeLand, Fla., 1963-82; head media specialist Blue Lake Elem. Sch., DeLand, 1982—; area dir. for Volusia County (Fla.) Edn. Assn., 1963-65. Charter mem. West Volusia Meml. Hosp. Aux., DeLand, 1962—; Girl Scout leader, 1955-56; bd. dirs. Alhambra Villas Home Owners Assn., 1972-76; trustee DeLand Public Library, 1977—, also sec., v.p.; pres. Violet Garden Circle, 1975-77. Mem. AAUW (2d v.p. chpt. 1965-67, rec. sec. 1961-65, 78-80, pres. 1980-82, parliamentarian 1982-84), Assn. Childhood Edn. (1st v.p. 1965-66, corr. sec. 1963-65), DAR (chpt. registrar 1969-80; asst. chief page Continental Congress, Washington 1962-65), Bus. and Profl. Women's Club (corr. sec. DeLand 1968-71, 2d v.p. 1969-70), Stetson U. Alumni Assn. (class chmn. for ann. fund drive 1968), Magna Charta Dames, Soc. Mayflower Desc., Colonial Dames XVII Century, Delta Kappa Gamma (chpt. pres. 1982-84). Democrat. Episcopalian. An author Volusia County manual Instructing the Library Assistant, 1965. Home: PO Box 241 DeLand FL 32721

CACHERIS, JAMES C., judge; b. Pitts., Mar. 30, 1933. B.S. in Econs., U. Pa., 1955; J.D. cum laude, George Washington U., 1960. Bar: D.C. 1960, Va. 1962. Asst. corp. counsel, Washington, 1960-62, pvt. practice, Washington and Alexandria, Va., 1962-71; judge 19th Jud. Circuit Ct. Va., Fairfax, 1971-83, U.S. Dist. Ct., Alexandria, 1983—. Mem. ABA, Va. Bar Assn., Fairfax County Bar Assn., Am. Judicature Soc. Office: US Dist Ct 200 S Washington St Alexandria VA 22314

CACUCI, DAN GABRIEL, nuclear physicist, engineer, educator; b. Romania, May 16, 1948; s. Gabriel D. and Malvina (Dan) C. M.S., Columbia U., 1973, M.Phil., 1977, Ph.D., 1978. Nuclear engring. assoc. III, Brookhaven Nat. Lab., 1975-76; lead engr. Ebasco Services Inc., N.Y.C., 1976-77; project leader Oak Ridge Nat. Lab., 1977-80, group leader, 1980—; assoc. prof. U. Tenn., Knoxville, 1983—. Columbia U. Merit fellow, 1972; Youth Found. Merit scholar, 1972-75; recipient Columbia U. Outstanding Achievements in Grad. Work citation, 1973, James D. Merriman Jr. Meml. award, 1977; recipient Oak Ridge Nat. Lab. Spl. Recognition award, 1983. Mem. Am. Nuclear Soc. (sec., nat. planning com. 1983—), N.Y. Acad. Scis., AAAS, Sigma Xi. Assoc. editor Nuclear Sci. and Engring., 1984—. Contbr. numerous articles to profl. publs. Office: Oak Ridge Nat Lab Engineering Physics Div PO Box X Oak Ridge TN 37831

CADDEL, BEVERLEY JOAN, safety consultant; b. Dallas, Sept. 12, 1943; d. Jesse C. and Delma Fay (Anderson) C. B.S., Tarleton State U., 1967; M.Ed., Stephen F. Austin State U., 1978. Tchr. Slaton Ind. Sch. Dist., Tex., 1978-79, Garland Ind. Sch. Dist., Tex., 1976-79; tech. rep. Hartford Ins. Group, Dallas, 1979-85, div. cons. in health care, 1985—. Chmn. campaign Am. Cancer Soc., 1976. Mem. Am. Soc. Safety Engrs., Am. Soc. Fire Protection Engrs., Internat. Health Care Safety Soc., Womens C. of C. (v.p. 1974-75), Friends Library (v.p. 1975-76). Mem. First Christian Ch. Avocations: scuba diving; travel study; Mayan culture; jewelry design. Home: 10103 Deermont Trail Dallas TX 75243 Office: Hartford Ins Group 5001 LBJ Freeway PO Box 927 Dallas TX 75221

CADDY, MICHAEL DOUGLAS, lawyer; b. Long Beach, Calif., Mar. 23, 1938; s. Frank Edward and Tabitha (Miles) C.; B.S. in Fgn. Service, Georgetown U., 1960; J.D., NYU, 1966. Bar: D.C. 1970, Tex. 1979. Practice in Washington and Tex.; exec. dir. Com. on Public Affairs, McGraw-Edison Co., N.Y.C., 1960-61; asst. to lt. gov. N.Y., 1962-65; asst. to exec. v.p. NAM, N.Y.C., 1966-67; Washington liaison Gen. Foods Corp., 1968-70; asso. Gall, Lane, Powell & Kilcullen, 1970-74; legis. counsel Nat. Assn. Realtors, Washington, 1975-76; atty. Office Tex. Sec. of State, 1980-81. Mem. Republican County Com., N.Y.C., 1965-66. Scholar, Intercollegiate Studies Inst., 1957-59. Mem. Am., D.C., Fed., Tex. bar assns., Am. Judicature Soc., Am. Econ. Assn., Am. Acad. Polit. and Social Sci., Internat. Platform Assn., Nat. Council Crime and Delinquency, Supreme Ct. Hist. Soc. Clubs: Houstonian (Houston); Union League (N.Y.C.); Nat. Economists (Washington). Author: The Hundred Million Dollar Payoff, 1974; How They Rig Our Elections, 1975; Understanding Insurance, 1984; Legislative Trends in Insurance Regulation, 1985. Home: 745 W Creekside Dr Houston TX 77024

CADE, RITA CORDE, infection control coordinator, utilization review coordinator; b. Dallas, Oct. 30, 1946; d. Oscar Laine and Lillian Lorraine (Kelley) Corde; m. Jerry Gene Cade, May 27, 1967; children—Sarah Lynn, Matthew Sean. B.A. in Biology, So. Meth. U., 1968; Assoc. Degree in Nursing, Nicholls State U., 1976. R.N., La. Water treatment bacteriologist City of Dallas, 1969; staff nurse Assumption Gen. Hosp., Napoleonville, La., 1976; staff nurse Thibodaux Gen. Hosp., La., 1977, infection control nurse, 1977—, utilization rev. coordinator, 1984—. Mem. Assn. for Practitioners Infection Control. Democrat. Roman Catholic. Avocations: raising horses; rabbits; gardening; needlework. Office: Thibodaux Gen Hosp PO Box 1118 Thibodaux LA 70302

CADWALLADER, DONALD ELTON, pharmacy educator; b. Buffalo, June 14, 1931; s. Donald E. and Catherine E. (Russell) C.; m. Cecelia Vidis, Feb. 13, 1961; children—Susan, Keith, Lynn. B.S. in Pharmacy, U. Buffalo, 1953; M.S. in Medicinal Chemistry, U. Ga., 1955; Ph.D. in Pharmaceutics, U. Fla., 1957. Research assoc. pharmacy dept. Sterling Winthrop Research Inst., Rensselaer, N.Y., 1958-60; sect. head pharmacy dept. White Labs., Kenilworth, N.J., 1960-61; asst. prof. Sch. Pharmacy U. Ga., 1961-64, assoc. prof., 1964-68, prof., 1968-77, prof., head dept. pharmacy, 1977-80, prof., head dept. pharmaceutics, 1980—. Author: Biopharmaceutics and Drug Interactions, 3d edit., 1983. Mem. Am. Pharm. Assn., Acad. Pharm. Scis., Am. Assn. Coll. of Pharmacy, Sigma Xi. Home: 470 Brookwood Dr Athens GA 30605 Office: Coll Pharmacy U Ga Athens GA 30602

CADY, DAVID CHRISTIAN, structural engineer; b. Birmingham, Mich., May 7, 1931; s. Leonard A. and Alma C. Cady; B.S., Mich. Technol. U., 1957; m. Barbara Lee Brown, Nov. 20, 1950; children—Charlene, David Christian, Rosanna Lyn, Phillip Lee, Brenda Jean. Sr. design engr. Gen. Dynamics, San Diego, 1961-68; design engr. LTV Aerospace Corp., Dallas, 1968-70; systems engr. McDonnel Aircraft Co., St. Louis, 1971-73; machine operator, product engr. Gardner Denver, Reed City, Mich., 1973-75; mine supt., chief engr. Gold Bond Bldg. Products (Va.), 1976-78; structural design contract engr., Brunswick, Marion, Va., 1978-79, Nordam, Tulsa, Okla., 1979; aircraft structural design contract engr. Swearingen Aircraft Co., San Antonio, 1979-80, Mooney Aircraft Co., Kerrville, Tex., 1980-82, Fairchild Aircraft Co., San Antonio, 1982-83, Gulfstream Aerospace Co., Bethany, Okla., 1983-85, E-Systems, Greenville, Tex., 1985, LTV, Grand Prairie, Tex., 1985—. Vol. docent Oklahoma City Zoo, 1983—; mem. CAP. Served with USAF, 1951-52. Club: Toastmasters Internat. (past pres. chpt., now ednl. v.p. chpt.).

CAESAR, THELMA FLORICE, child care administrator, bookkeeper, consultant; b. Lockhart, Tex., Jan. 17, 1935; d. Farom Maynard Spencer and Aslee (Miller) S.; m. Emmitt Bernell Stewart, June 21, 1962 (div.); 1 dau., Meta-Beryl Suzette Stewart; m. Joe Bill Caesar, Dec. 19, 1972. Student Del Mar Coll., 1953-55, Internat. Bus. Coll., 1960, Tex. A&I U., 1976. Med. sec., Corpus Christi, 1953-58; ednl. sec., Galveston, Tex., 1960-62; early caregiver, Corpus Christi, 1964-69; missionary and child care administrator So. Bapt. Home, Corpus Christi, 1969-79; asst. child care adminstr. Mary McLeod Bethune Day Nursery, Inc., Corpus Christi, 1979-83; adminstrv. asst. St. John Bapt. Ch., 1983—. Mem. adv. com. Mental Health-Mental Retardation; active YWCA, NAACP, Coastal Bend Migrant Council, Am. Cancer Soc., 1969-74; mem. consumer rev. bd. Planned Parenthood. Recipient NAACP award, 1973. Mem. Bay Area Assn. Edn. Young Children, Tex. Assn. Edn. Young Children, So. Assn. Edn. Young Children, Nat. Assn. Edn. Young Children, Nat. Assn. Female Execs., Tex. Assn. Child Devel. Assn., Tex. Child Care Adminstrs., Nat. Child Care Adminstrs. Baptist. Club: League and Loyal Ladies. Home: 6017 Orms Dr Corpus Christi TX 78412 Office: 5445 Greenwood Dr Corpus Christi TX 78417

CAFFEY, WILLIAM GARRETT, JR., retired bankruptcy judge, lawyer; b. Mobile, Ala., Jan. 13, 1919; s. William Garrett and Susan (Planck) C.; m. Marie Tonsmeire, Apr. 14, 1948; children—Susan Louise, Mary Garrett, Nancy Lee. A.B., U. Ala., 1940, J.D., 1947. Bar: Ala. 1947. Ptnr., Caffey, Gallalee & Caffey, Mobile, 1947-64; asst. U.S. atty. (part-time) U.S. Atty.'s Office so. dist. Ala., Mobile, 1948-54; judge 13th Jud. Cir. of Ala., Mobile, 1965-70; judge U.S. Bankruptcy Ct. So. Dist. Ala., Mobile, 1970-85; of councel Lyons, Pipes and Cook, Mobile. Mem. Ala. State Senate, 1958-62. Served to maj. AUS, 1941-46, 50-52; PTO. Mem. Mobile County Bar Assn. (hon. mem.), Ala. State Bar Assn. (spl. mem.), Phi Delta Phi. Democrat. Episcopalian. Home: 1915 Old County Rd Daphne AL 36526 Office: Lyons Pipes & Cook 2 N Royal St PO Box 2727 Mobile AL 36652

CAHOON, JACK, JR., mechanical engineer; b. Quincy, Fla., July 11, 1925; s. Jack and Mattie Lee (Cox) C.; B.S.M.E., Auburn U., 1948; M.S.M.E., U. Okla., 1958; m. Patty Sue Moore, Mar. 2, 1952; children—Douglas Mark, Jamie Carol. Combustion engr. Republic Steel, Gadsden, Ala., 1948-50; commd. 2d lt. USAF, 1950, advanced through grades to lt. col., 1968; various positions research and devel., to 1972; ret., 1972; sr. systems engr. Teledyne Brown, Huntsville, Ala., 1972-74, cons. engr., pres. sub. co., 1974-76; tech. dir. and quality mgr. ITT Henze Service div. ITT Grinnell Valve Co., Inc., Mobile, Ala., 1977—. Served with U.S. Army, 1946-47. Decorated Meritorious Service medal, various others. Mem. Am. Soc. Non-Destructive Testing (level III examiner penetrant testing 1978—), Am. Welding Soc., ASME (boiler and pressure vessel code subcom. on safety valve requirements, nat. bd. com. repair of safety and safety relief valves), Nat. Assn. Valve Rebuilders (sec.-treas. 1982-83), Ret. Officers Assn. Home: 6055 Highland Circle S Mobile AL 36608 Office: 2970 Cottage Hill Rd Suite 283 Mobile AL 36606

CAIN, GEORGE LEE, educator; b. Wilmington, N.C., Jan. 13, 1934; s. George Lee and Etta Maie (Jenkins) C.; m. Marilyn Amelia Alexander, Aug. 11, 1956; 1 child, Carolyn. B.S., MIT, 1956; M.S., Ga. Inst. Tech., 1962, Ph.D., 1965. Mathematician Lockheed Aircraft Co., Marietta, Ga., 1956-64; asst. dir. Sch. Math., Ga. Inst. Tech., Atlanta, 1973-78, from asst. prof. to assoc. prof., 1965-80, prof. math., 1980—. Contbr. articles to profl. jours. Served with U.S. Army, 1958. NSF fellow, 1964-65; Sigma Xi research awardee, 1963. Mem. Am. Math. Soc. Home: 402 Huntsman Way Marietta GA 30067 Office: Ga Inst Tech Sch Math Atlanta GA 30332

CAIN, JAMES M(ARSHALL), utility company executive; b. 1933; married. B.B.A., Tulane U., 1955, M.B.A., 1959. With New Orleans Pub. Service Inc., 1960-75, 78-83, v.p. adminstrn., to 1978, pres., chief exec. officer, dir., 1978-83; pres., chief exec. officer, dir. Middle South Services Inc., 1975-78; pres., chief exec. officer, dir. La. Power & Light Co., a Middle South Utilities Inc. Co., New Orleans, 1983—, also dir. Served to 1st lt. U.S. Army, 1955-57. Office: La Power & Light Co New Orleans Pub Service Inc PO Box 60340 New Orleans LA 70160

CAIN, LAURENCE SUTHERLAND, physics educator, consultant; b. Washington, Feb. 4, 1946; s. Leighton Aubrey and Beatrice (Sutherland) C.; m. Mary Jane Dimmock, Aug. 21, 1971; children—Rebecca Anne, Peter Laurence. B.S., Wake Forest U., 1968; M.S. in Physics, U. Va., 1970, Ph.D. in Physics, 1973. Research assoc. U. N.C., Chapel Hill, 1973-76, lectr., 1976-78; asst. prof. physics Davidson Coll. (N.C.), 1978-85, assoc. prof., 1985—; vis. prof. Wake Forest U., Winston-Salem, N.C., summer 1979; cons. in field. Bd. dirs. North Mecklenburg Child Devel. Assn., 1979—, treas., 1982—. NSF Research Equipment grantee, 1981; grantee Research Corp., 1981, 83, 85, 86. Mem. Am. Phys. Soc., Am. Assn. Physics Tchrs., AAAS, AAUP, Sigma Xi, Phi Beta Kappa, Kappa Mu Epsilon. Democrat. Presbyterian. Contbr. articles to profl. jours. Office: Dept Physics Davidson Coll Davidson NC 28036

CAIN, MARLA DEAN CHESTNUT, nurse; b. Marlinton, W.Va., Aug. 10, 1957; d. Murl Edward Chestnut and Eva Jane (Sharp) Madron m. David Russell Cain, June 28, 1980; children—Corey Russell, Brandon David. Diploma, Riverside Profl. Nursing Sch., 1980. Nurse/supr. Denmar Hosp., Hillsboro, W.Va., 1980-83; nurse, office nurse Dr. John Sharp, Marlinton, W.Va., 1983—; chmn. patient care conf. Denmar Hosp., 1982-83, patient care plan coordinator, 1982-83, mem. audit com., 1980-83. Co-dir. Little Miss Pocahontas Pageant, Marlinton, 1982, Miss Pocahontas Pageant, 1982-83; pageant judge Cherry River Festival, Richwood, W.Va., 1983. Mem. Bus. and Profl. Women's Club (v.p. 1982-84, pres.-elect 1985—, Young Careerist award 1982). Democrat. Methodist. Address: Route 1 PO Box 350 Marlinton WV 24954

CAIN, RUSSELL LYNN, real estate company executive; b. Belleville, Ill., Oct. 13, 1947; s. Roland and Virginia Cain; m. Doris B. Beel, Mar. 8, 1976. B.B.A., Tex. A&I U., 1969. Owner, operator Russell Cain Real Estate, Port Lavaco, Tex., 1974—. Dir. United Fund, Port Lavaco, 1975. Named one of Outstanding Young Men in Am., 1975. Mem. Bd. Realtors Calhoun County (bd. dirs. 1979—), Port Lavaca C. of C. Episcopalian. Club: Hatch Bend Country (Port Lavaca) (bd. dirs. 1983—). Lodges: Rotary, Masons. Home: 1640 Villa Dr Box 565 Port Lavaca TX 77979

CAIN, WILLIAM ALLEN, lawyer; b. Chgo., Nov. 9, 1924; s. Albert Paul and May (Gainer) C.; LL.B., DePaul U., 1946, J.D., 1971; m. Audrey Helene Rosin, Nov. 28, 1953; children—May Lydia, Jordan Scott. Admitted to Ill. bar, 1947, Fla. bar, 1978; former partner law firm Cain & Cernek, Chgo.; adj. prof. law U. Miami Sch. Law, 1979-81, adj. prof. trial advocacy, 1982—; mem. firm Cain and Cain, North Miami Beach, Fla. Past mem. caucus com. Sch. Dist. 108, Highland Park, Ill.; counsel Skokie Police Patrolmen's Assn., North Suburban Police Patrolmen's Assn. Commr. Sheriff Lake County Commn. Narcotics and Drug Abuse, 1972-73. Past pres. S.E. Clavey Homeowners Assn., Highland Park, Ill.; flotilla staff officer USCG Aux., 1974-82, North Miami, Fla., 1981—. Mem. bd. assocs. DePaul U., 1972-73. Mem. Am. Bar Assn. (com. criminal law, mem. speakers bur.), Ill. Bar Assn. (Am. citizenship com., com. on fair trial-free press 1977—), Fla. Bar Assn. (pvt. practitioner, entertainer and arts law coms., chmn. com. on representation indigents, liaison matrimonial law sect. for law colls., gen. practice sect. for continuing legal edn., mem. criminal law sect. ethics com. 1983-84), Fla. Bar (grievance com.), Dade County Bar Assn., (com. on criminal law and ethics, dir. 1983-84, mem. jud. poll com. 1983-84, lawyer referral service 1983-84), Chgo. Bar Assn., (past chmn. def. of prisoners com.; chmn. com. narcotics and drug abuse 1972), North Dade County Bar Assn., Acad. Fla. Trial Lawyers, Chgo. Trial Lawyers Club, Assn. Def. Lawyers, Fla. Assn. for Women Lawyers, Internat. Platform Assn., Am. Guild Variety Artists (mem. Chgo. br. exec. com., chmn. 1968), Nat. Assn. Def. Lawyers in Criminal Cases (Ill. chmn. strike force 1976-77), Am. Judicature Soc., Assn. Trial Lawyers Am., Nat. Geog. Soc., Vol. Talent Pool Highland Park, Ill. Mem. B'nai B'rith (dir. Lincolnwood 1974-75). Club: Belmont Yacht (dir. 1977-78). Profl. hypnotist, lectr. Starred on Pantomine Party, WBKB-TV, Chgo., 1953. Home: 1940 NE 119th Rd North Miami FL 33181 Office: 11755 Biscayne Blvd Suite 401 North Miami FL 33181

CAINE, NORA COOK, public relations specialist; b. Savannah, Ga., Mar. 17, 1949; d. Ellison Richards and Helen Brown Cook; B.A. in Journalism, U. Ga.; m. Martin Squier Caine, Nov. 27, 1976. Girl Friday, receptionist Sta. WSGA, Savannah, 1971; feature writer Savannah Morning News and Evening Press, 1971-73; asst. dir. community relations Candler Gen. Hosp., Savannah, 1973-74; communications dir. S.C. Hosp. Assn., Columbia, 1974-76; asst. public relations dir. Providence Hosp., Washington, 1976-77; asst. public relations dir. Suburban Hosp., Bethesda, Md., 1977-78; dir. public relations St. Joseph Hosp., Memphis, 1978-80; advt. and public relations cons., 1980-83; dir. mktg. and pub. relations St. Francis Hosp., Memphis, 1983—.

CAINE, ROBERT LLOYD, sociology educator; b. Fort Jackson, S.C., May 9, 1945; s. Edmund Arthur and Beatrice (Rothschild) C. B.A., Franklin and Marshall Coll., 1967; M.A., U. Ga., 1974, Ph.D., 1979. Asst. coordinator planning and evaluation Fulton County Health Dept., Atlanta, 1974-76; asst. prof. sociology Columbus Coll., Ga., 1976-83, assoc. prof., 1984—; ednl. cons. EduDisc Corp., Nashville, 1984—; lead programmer CBT, Inc., 1984—. Bd. dirs. Campaign for a Prosperous Ga., 1985; mem. adv. com. Public Interest Computer Assn., Washington, 1985. Mem. Am. Sociol. Assn., So. Sociol. Soc., Mid South Sociol. Soc., AAUP (v.p. 1980-81), Phi Kappa Phi. Avocation: Backpacking. Home: 2147 Palifox Dr Atlanta GA 30307 Office: Dept Psychology Sociology Columbus Coll Columbus GA 31993

CAIOLA, STEPHEN MICHAEL, pharmacist, educator; b. Akron, Ohio, Aug. 30, 1943; s. Stephen R. and Elizabeth R. (Alexander) C.; m. Judith Ann Siracusa, Mar. 18, 1967; children—Karen, Jeffrey, Gregory. B.S. in Pharmacy, Duquesne U., 1966; M.S., Ohio State U., 1969. Resident in pharmacy Ohio State U. Hosps., Columbus, 1968; instr., U. N.C., 1969-71, asst. prof., 1971-77, assoc. prof., 1977—, assoc. chmn. div. pharmacy practice, 1985—; asst. dir. pharmacy N.C. Meml. Hosp., Chapel Hill, 1969-71; dir. Pharmacy Services Orange-Chatham Comprehensive Health Services, Inc., Chapel Hill, 1974-82; cons. to Winston-Salem Health Care Plan, Inc.; program dir. N.C. Pharmacy Area Health Edn. Ctrs., 1985—. Active St. Thomas More Roman Cath. Ch. activities. Grantee Smith-Kline Corp., 1981. Mem. Am. Soc. Hosp. Pharmacists, Am. Pharm. Assn., Am. Assn. Colls. Pharmacy, N.C. Soc. Hosp. Pharmacists (Acheivement award 1979), N.C. Pharm. Assn., Rho Chi. Contbr. articles to profl. jours. Office: Sch of Pharmacy Beard Hall 200H U N C Chapel Hill NC 27514

CAIRNS, JOHN, JR., environmental science educator, researcher; b. Conshohocken, Pa., May 8, 1923; s. John and Eunice S. (Fesmire) C.; m. Jean Ogden, Aug. 5, 1944; children—Karen Jean, Stefan Hugh, Duncan Jay, Heather. A.B., Swathmore Coll., 1947; M.S., U. Pa., 1949, Ph.D., 1953. Curator limnology Acad. Natural Scis., Phila., 1948-66; prof. zoology U. Kans., Lawrence, 1966-68; univ. disting. prof. Va. Poly. Inst. and State U., Blacksburg, 1968—, dir. Univ. Ctr. Environ. Studies. Served with USN, 1942-46. Recipient Presdl. Commendation, 1971; Dudley award for outstanding publ. ASTM, 1978; superior achievement award; EPA, 1980; Founders award Soc. Environ. Toxicology and Chemistry, 1981; Morrison medal for outstanding accomplishments in environ. scis. U.S. Dept. Agr. Agrl. Research Service, 1984. Fellow AAAS; mem. Am. Microscopical Soc. (pres. 1980), Am. Water Resources Assn. (editorial bd. 1975-81, Icko Iben award for interdisciplinary research 1984), Inst. Ecology (founder), Acad. Natural Scis. (research assoc.). Unitarian. Author: Testing for Effects of Chemicals on Ecosystems, 1981; Artificial Substrates, 1982; Biological Monitoring, 1982; Modeling the Fate of Chemicals in the Aquatic Environment, 1982; contbr. chpts. to books, articles to profl. jours. Office: Ctr Environ Studies Va Poly Inst and State U Blacksburg VA 24061

CALARCO, ALLAN JOSEPH, university administrator; b. Hazelton, Pa., Aug. 17, 1955; s. Theodora (Calarco) Charnigo. B.A., East Strondsburg U., 1978; M.S., Shippensburg U., 1980. Area dir. U. N.C., Chapel Hill, 1980-83, asst. dir. housing, 1983-85, assoc. dir. housing, 1985—. Mem. N.C. Housing Officers (program chmn. 1984—), Am. Assn. Counseling and Devel., Assn. Coll. and Univ. Housing Officers, Am. Coll. Personnel Assn. Lodges: Order of Grail, Soc. Janus (adviser). Avocations: tennis; golf; going to beach. Office: 103A Carr Bldg Chapel Hill NC 27514

CALDERONE, JOSEPH DANIEL, campus ministry director, educator; b. Bryn Mawr, Pa., Feb. 26, 1948; s. Joseph Albert and Sara Jane (Giangiulio) C. B.A. in Social Scis. Villanova U., 1970, M.A. in Counseling, 1973. M.A. in Theology, Washington Theol. Union, 1975; Cert. Advanced Grad. Study in Higher Edn. Adminstrn., Northeastern U., 1976, Ed.D. in Higher Edn. Adminstrn., 1982. Ordained priest Roman Catholic Ch., 1973. Campus minister Villanova U., Pa., 1973-74; assoc. dir. campus ministry Merrimack Coll., North Andover, Mass., 1974-76, dir. campus ministry, 1976-78; diocesan dir. campus ministry, Orlando and Winter Park, Fla., 1978—; prof. mgmt. and counseling theory St. Leo Coll., St. Leo, Fla., 1984—; prof. bus. ethics Rollins Coll., Winter Park, Fla., 1983—. Mem. Nat. Assn. Diocesan Dirs. Campus Ministry (sec., treas. 1984—), Nat. Assn. Coll. and Univ. Chaplains (mem. at large 1985—). Democrat. Home and Office: 430 E Lyman Ave Winter Park FL 32789

CALDWELL, BILLY RAY, geologist; b. Newellton, La., Apr. 20, 1932; s. Leslie Richardson and Helen Merle (Clark) C.; m. Carolyn Marie Heath, May 9, 1979; children—Caryn, Jeana, Craig. Cert. petroleum geologist, Tex. Geologist, Geol. Engring. Service Co., Fort Worth, Tex., 1954-60; sci. tchr. Fort Worth and Lake Worth Sch. Dists., 1960-63; mgr. Outdoor Living, 1963-71; instr. geology Tarrant County Jr. Coll., Fort Worth, 1970—; petroleum geologist cons., Fort Worth, 1971—. Bd. dirs. Fort Worth and Tarrant County Homebuilders Assn., 1973. Named Dir. of Yr., Fort Worth Jaycees, 1966-67. Mem. Fort Worth Geol. Soc., Am. Assn. Petroleum Geologists, Soc. Profl. Well Log Analysts Geol. Soc. Am. Republican. Baptist. Avocations: traveling; gardening; church work. Home: 305 Bodart Ln Fort Worth TX 76108 Office: 101 Jim Wright Freeway Suite 402 Fort Worth TX 76108

CALDWELL, CHARLES ANDERSON, banker; b. Amory, Miss., Sept. 4, 1942; s. William Stanley and Martha Frances (Wade) C.; m. Sandra Delores Leech, Dec. 17, 1961; children—Diana Leigh, Kimberly Frances, Charles Anderson II. B.B.A., U. Miss., 1965, postgrad., 1972-73; postgrad. in bank ops. U. Wis.-Madison, 1977. Asst. mgr. Retail furniture Store, Amory, Miss., 1965-68; prodn. forecaster Rockwell Internat., Tupelo, Miss., 1968-70; ops. officer Bank of Miss., Tupelo, 1970-80, asst. v.p., loan officer, 1980—. Chmn. Monroe County Charmichael for gov. campaign, 1976; vol. Heart Fund, Tupelo, 1975, Lee County United Neighbors, Tupelo, 1970-80. Republican. Presbyterian. Lodge: Lions (pres. 1982-83, treas. 1983— Nettleton, Miss.). Avocations: golf; fishing; cooking. Home: 1221 Williamsburg Dr Amory MS 38821 Office: Bank of Miss PO Drawer B Nettleton MS 38858

CALDWELL, CLAUD REID, lawyer; b. Augusta, Ga., Sept. 18, 1909; s. John Mars and Ethel (Bennett) C.; student Acad. Richmond County, 1922-26; m. Josephine F. Clarke, June 30, 1940; children—Claud R., Kathryn C., James W. Admitted to Ga. bar, 1932, practiced in Augusta, 1934—; judge Municipal Ct., City of Augusta, 1948-49. Pres., Richmond County Independent Party, 1950-51; bd. dirs. Augusta chpt. ARC, YMCA; chmn. Augusta council Boy Scouts Am., 1949-50. Served with AUS, 1941-45; ETO; col. USAR (ret.). Recipient Distinguished Pistol Marksman award U.S. Army, 1965. Mem. Am., Ga., Augusta bar assns., Ga. Sport Shooting Assn. (dir., past pres.), Richmond County Hist. Soc., Mil. Order World Wars, Nat. Sojourners, Heroes of '96 (Gen. Oglethorpe chpt.), U.S. Power Squadron, Augusta Amateur Radio Club, Ret. Officers Assn. (Augusta chpt.), Am. Legion, Sons of Confederacy, Assn. U.S. Army, Am. Radio Relay League, Hephzibah Agrl. Club. Presbyn. (deacon). Mason (32 deg., Shriner). Clubs: Augusta Country, Augusta Sailing, Sudlow-Silver Bluff Rifle and Skeet. Home: 343 Hemlock Hill Rd Augusta GA 30909 Office: Southern Finance Bldg Augusta GA 30901

CALDWELL, GLYN GORDON, epidemiologist, physician; b. St. Louis, Jan. 14, 1934; s. Cecil Gordon and Zelma Mae (Peeler) C.; m. Mary Jean Pandolfo, Aug. 13, 1960; children—Michael Gordon, Elizabeth Ann, Thomas Gordon. B.S., St. Louis U., 1960; M.S., Mo. U., 1962, M.D., 1966. Diplomate Nat. Bd. Med. Examiners. Intern, USPHS Hosp., Brighton, Mass., 1966-67; resident in internal medicine Cleve. Met. Gen. Hosp., 1969-71; grad. instr. microbiology U. Mo., 1960-62; with USPHS, 1966-85, med. virologist-epidemiologist Ecol. Investigations Program, Ctr. Disease Control, Kansas City, Kans., 1967-69, chief leukemia and oncogenic virus activities, 1968-69, acting chief virus disease sect., 1968-69, chief oncology and teratology activities, 1971-73, biohazards cons., 1972-73, asst. to chief leukemia sect. cancer and birth defects br. Bur. Epidemiology, Atlanta, 1973-74, dep. chief, 1974-77, chief cancer br. chronic diseases div., 1977-81, chief cancer br. chronic diseases div. Ctr. Environ. Health, 1981-82, dep. dir. chronic diseases div., 1982-85; asst. prof. microbiology U. Kans., 1968-70; docent Kansas City Gen. Hosp., 1972-73; clin. asst. prof. medicine U. Mo., Kansas City, 1972-73; clin. asst. prof. preventive medicine and community health Emory U., Atlanta, 1975-85, dir. Atlanta Cancer Surveillance Ctr., 1976-77; mem. adv. bd. Ctr. for Disease Control, 1979-84; mem. subcom. on Three Mile Island, Interagy. Radiation Research Com., 1980-84; mem. com. on health research initiatives on radiation research HHS, 1980-85; mem. fed. interagy. central coordinating com. for radiation planning and preparedness Fed. Emergency Mgmt. Agy., 1980-85, mem. subcom. on fed. response, 1982—; mem. dosimetry assessment adv. com. Dept. Energy, 1980-85; asst. dir. Ariz. Dept. Health Services, state epidemiologist, 1985—. Served with Signal Corps, U.S. Army, 1954-60. St. Louis U. scholar, 1952-53; recipient McComas History of Medicine prize U. Mo., 1966, Commendation medal USPHS, 1980. Fellow Am. Coll. Epidemiology; mem. Internat. Assn. Comparative Research on Leukemia and Related Diseases, Am. Soc. Preventive Oncology, Am. Soc. Microbiology, Commd. Officers Assn. USPHS (pres. Atlanta br. 1976), Soc. Epidemiologic Research, N.Y. Acad. Scis., Sigma Xi. Roman Catholic. Lodge: K.C. Contbg. editor Internat. Jour. Cancer Control and Prevention, 1979—. Contbr. articles to profl. jours.

CALDWELL, HAROLD LEROY, petroleum engineer; b. Pawnee, Okla., Aug. 14, 1925; s. Harold Ralph and Eula P. (Buckner) C.; B.S. in Petroleum Engring., U. Tulsa, 1951; m. Patricia T. Poorman, Dec. 24, 1948; children—Michael Alan, Douglas Owen. Exploitation engr. Sunray Oil Co., 1951-55; chief engr. Keener Oil Co., Tulsa, 1955-59, gen. supt. prodn., 1959-62; cons. engr., 1962-63; drilling engr. Fenix & Scisson, Inc., Tulsa, 1963-65; gen. prodn. supt. K.W.B. Oil Property Mgmt., Inc., 1965—; engr. Williams Bros. Engring. Co., 1967-74; mgr. Perrault-Caldwell, Inc., Tulsa, 1974-75; petroleum cons. Caldwell and Assos., Inc., 1975—. Served with AUS, 1943-46. Registered profl. engr., Okla. Mem. Am. Inst. Mining Engrs., Am. Petroleum Inst., Okla. State Profl. Engrs. Republican. Mem. Reorganized Ch. of Jesus Christ of Latter-day Saints. Home: 5129 S Richmond Tulsa OK 74135 Office: Suite 1118 320 S Boston Bldg Tulsa OK 74103

CALDWELL, JESSE BURGOYNE, JR., physician; b. Cherryville, N.C., Sept. 25, 1917; s. Jesse B. and Virginia (Harrill) C.; B.S., U. N.C., 1938; M.D., C.M., McGill U., Montreal, Que., Can., 1941; m. Martha McDowell Gunter, Mar. 27, 1948; children—Jesse Burgoyne III, Charles Gunter, Lawson Harrill and Martha Clyburn (twins). Intern, Kings County (N.Y.) Hosp., Bklyn., 1941-42, 45-46; asst. resident in pathology Bowman Gray Sch. Medicine, Winston-Salem, N.C., 1947, instr. ob-gyn, 1949-50; asst. resident in ob-gyn N.C. Baptist Hosp., Winston-Salem, 1947-49, resident in ob-gyn, 1949-50; practice medicine specializing in ob-gyn, Gastonia, N.C., 1950-78; ret., 1978; mem. staff Gaston Meml. Hosp., 1950-78, chief of staff, 1960—; cons. staff Kings Mountain (N.C.) Hosp., 1960-73; ob-gyn mem. faculty obstetric sect. So. Pediatric seminar, Saluda, N.C., 1956, 57; dir. Gastonia office First-Citizens Bank & Trust Co., Med. Mut. Ins. Co. N.C. Bd. dirs. Med. Found. N.C., 1963-66, 1970—; bd. dirs. N.C. Med. Peer Rev. Found., Inc., treas., 1973-80; bd. dirs. N.C. div. Am. Cancer Soc., 1976—; trustee U. N.C., 1957-65, Gaston County Library, 1960-79, chmn., 1968-79; trustee Gaston-Lincoln Regional Library, treas., 1967-79; trustee Charlotte (N.C.) Coll., 1963-65, Gaston County Hosp., 1967-70, Gaston Meml. Hosp., 1970-73, Schiele Mus. Natural History, 1975-78. Served to capt. M.C., U.S. Army, 1942-45; ETO. Decorated Bronze Star; recipient Disting. Service award U. N.C. Sch. Medicine, 1983. Diplomate Am. Bd. Ob-Gyn. Fellow ACS, Internat. Coll. Surgeons (N.C. credentials com. 1965-78); mem. AMA (del. from N.C. 1980—), N.C. Med. Soc., N.C. (councilor 7th dist. 1972-75, pres. 1976-77, mem. maternal welfare com. 1955-75, legis. com. 1958-59, 62-63, 65-66), N.C. Obstet. and Gynecol. Soc., South Atlantic Assn. Obstetricians and Gynecologists (mem. exec. com. 1961-64), Phi Chi. Democrat. Methodist (mem. ofcl. bd. 1963-66). Rotarian (pres. 1961-62). Club: Gaston Country (dir. 1965-67). Contbr. articles on gynecology to med. jours. Home: 1307 Park Ln Gastonia NC 28052

CALDWELL, JOHNNIE L., state comptroller Georgia; b. Taylor County, Ga., Aug. 10, 1922. Student, Woodrow Wilson Law Coll.; m. Martha Smisson, 1942; children—Patricia Ann, Barbara Sue, Johnnie L. Ga. State Rep., 1955-71; comptroller gen. State of Ga., Atlanta, 1971—; also atty. with law firm Thomaston & Zebulon. Address: Comptroller General 200 Piedmont Ave 7th Floor West Tower Atlanta GA 30334*

CALDWELL, PHILLIP MACK, architect, solar design and research consultant; b. Springfield, Mo., Nov. 6, 1942; s. Edwin Miller and Laveeda Ethel (Wood) C.; m. Renate Frieda Hans, Dec. 15, 1975; children—Sabine, Rebecca, Howard. B.A., U. Tex., 1964; M.A. in Architecture, Yale U., 1971; postgrad., diploma, Arch. Assoc. Sch., London, 1971; diploma (Hon.), La. Universidad Autonoma de Cd. Juarez, 1981. Registered architect, Tex., N.Mex., Colo. Architect-in-tng. various firms, 1967-74; pres. Architects Design Group, El Paso, Tex., 1974-75; owner, pres. Adobe Builders, El Paso, 1982—; owner, architect Mack Caldwell Architect, El Paso, 1976—; lectr. in field. Contbr. articles to profl. jours. Com. mem. to Amend Adobe Bldg. Code, El Paso, 1980. Recipient Solar Design award Solar Energy Research Inst., HUD, 1978, Outstanding Architecture Design award Tex. Soc. Architects, 1983. Mem. El Paso Solar Energy Assn. (bd. dirs. 1978-79), AIA, Tex. Soc. Architects. Democrat. Methodist. Club: Yale (El Paso). Avocations: documentary film making; journalism. Office: Mack Caldwell Architect 1429 E Yandell Dr El Paso TX 79902

CALDWELL, ROSSIE JUANITA BROWER, library service educator; b. Columbia, S.C., Nov. 4, 1917; d. Rossie Lee and Henrietta Olivia (Irby) Brower; m. Harlowe Evans Caldwell, Aug. 6, 1943 (dec. 1983); 1 adopted dau., Rossie Laverne Caldwell Jenkins. B.A., Claflin Coll., 1937; M.S., S.C. State Coll., 1952; M.S. in L.S., U. Ill., 1959. Tchr., librarian Reed St. High Sch., Anderson, S.C., 1937-39, Emmett Scott High Sch., Rock Hill, S.C., 1939-42, Wilkinson High Sch., Orangeburg, S.C., 1942-43, librarian, 1945-57; with War Dept., 1943-45; asst. prof. then assoc. prof. library service dept. S.C. State Coll., Orangeburg, 1957-83. Contbr. to book in field; author articles. Life mem. NAACP; trustee Christian Advocate: The United Methodist Ch. in S.C.; assoc. mem. Orangeburg Regional Hosp. Aux. Mem. ALA, S.C. Library Assn. (hon.), Southeastern Library Assn., AAUP (sec., historian), Friends of the Library, Phi Delta Kappa, Beta Phi Mu (hon.), Alpha Beta Alpha (hon.). Alpha Kappa Alpha. Methodist. Clubs: Links, As You Like It Bridge. Daus. of Isis. Home: 1320 Ward Ln Orangeburg SC 29115

CALDWELL, STEPHEN ADDISON, university dean; b. Humboldt, Tenn., Oct. 8, 1947; s. Thomas Weldon and Martha Irene (Richardson) C.; m. Lindy Carol Gardner, Aug. 11, 1972; children—Scarlett Richardson, Thomas William Atticus. B.A., Southwestern U., Memphis, 1968; postgrad. Memphis Theol. Sem., 1968-69; M.Div., Vanderbilt U., 1971. Ordained elder United Methodist Ch., 1972. Coordinator for housing Vanderbilt U., Nashville, 1971-72, asst. dean, 1972-77, dep. dean, 1977-78, assoc. dean, 1978—; referee Tenn. Secondary Sch. Assn., 1974—. Mem. Nat. Assn. Student Personnel Adminstrs., Tenn. Farm Bur., Tenn. Livestock Assn., Dickson County Livestock Assn. Home: Route 1 Box 191 Dickson TN 37055 Office: Box 1677 Station B Vanderbilt Nashville TN 37235

CALDWELL, WILLIE MITCHELL, II, school administrator; b. Dadeville, Ala., Sept. 20, 1942; s. Willie Mitchell and Carrie Lou (McHargue) C.; m. Lynne Pearson, Oct. 20, 1973; children—W. Mitchell (Trey) III, Ingrid Lynne. B.S., Jacksonville State U., 1964; M.Ed., Livingston U., 1968; A.A., Jacksonville State U., 1975. Tchr., coach high sch., Dadeville and Alexander City, 1964-70; coach basketball Jacksonville State U., 1971-74; prin. Dadeville Jr. Sr. High Sch., Dadeville, 1974—. Recipient Top 100 Athletes in 100 Yr. History award Jacksonville State U., 1984. Mem. Nat. Assn. Secondary Prins., NEA. Avocation: tennis. Home: Route 3 11 Bent Hickory Dadeville AL 36853 Office: Dadeville Jr Sr High Sch PO Box 28 Dadeville AL 36853

CALE, WILLIAM GRAHAM, JR., environmental sciences educator, researcher; b. Phila., Dec. 10, 1947; s. William Graham and Kathryn (Rowland) C.; m. Betty Jean Bryd, June 8, 1974. B.S., Pa. State U., 1969; Ph.D., U. Ga., 1975. Asst. prof. U. Tex.-Dallas, Richardson, 1975-80, assoc. prof. environ. scis., 1980—, assoc. dean, 1983-85, chmn. dept. environ. scis., 1985—; vis. scientist Oak Ridge Nat. Lab., 1981, 84, 85. Contbr. articles to profl. jours. NSF grantee, 1978, 81, 83, 85. Mem. Ecol. Soc. Am., Am. Inst. Biol. Scis., Internat. Assn. for Ecology, Internat. Soc. for Ecol. Modelling. Democrat. Avocations: tournament bridge; jogging. Home: 1617 Clemson Ct Plano TX 75075 Office: U Tex Dallas Box 830688 Richardson TX 75080

CALGAARD, RONALD KEITH, university president; b. Joice, Iowa, July 29, 1937; s. Palmer O. and Orrie Beatrice (Nessa) C.; B.A. summa cum laude, Luther Coll., 1959; M.A. (Woodrow Wilson fellow), U. Iowa, 1961, Ph.D. in Econs., 1963; m. Gene Rae Flom, June 14, 1959; children—Lisa Rae, Kent David. Instr. econs. U. Iowa, Iowa City, 1961-63; asst. prof. U. Kans., Lawrence, 1963-65, assoc. prof., 1967-72, prof. econs., 1972-79, assoc. vice chancellor, 1974-75, vice chancellor, 1975-79; pres. Trinity U., San Antonio, 1979—; dir. Alamo Savs. & Loan Assn.; cons. to govt. and industry. Bd. dirs. S.W. Research Inst., United Way ofSan Antonio; bd. govs. Inst. European Studies; adv. trustee San Antonio Art Inst.; bd. dirs. ARC Council Learned Socs. fellow, Santiago, Chile, 1965-67. Mem. Am. Econ. Assn., Midwest Econ. Assn., Western Econ. Assn., Midwest Assn. Latin Am. Studies, AAUP. Club: Rotary. Author: Economic Planning in Underdeveloped Countries, 1963. Office: Trinity U 715 Stadium Dr San Antonio TX 78284

CALHOON, STEPHEN WALLACE, JR., college administrator; b. Mt. Gilead, Ohio, Oct. 21, 1930; s. Stephen W. and Helen Rebecca (Jackson) C.; m. Louretta Ann Houser, Aug. 29, 1952; children—Melinda, Denise, Kevin. A.A., Central Wesleyan Coll., 1950; B.S., Houghton Coll., 1953; M.S., Ohio State U., 1958; Ph.D., 1963. Instr., Ohio State U., Columbus, 1960-63; asst. prof. chemistry Houghton Coll., N.Y., 1956-63, assoc. prof., 1963-70, prof., 1970-78, head dept. chemistry, 1971-78; dean Central Wesleyan Coll., Central, S.C., 1978—. Contbr. chpts. to books, articles to profl. jours. Mem. sci. adv. com. Congressman Lundine, N.Y., 1976-78; ednl. adv. com. S.C. Appalachian Council Govts., 1981—; dir. Wesleyan Evangelistic Ministeries, S.C., 1981—; bd. dirs. Clayton Geneol. Collection, S.C., 1983—. Served with U.S. Army, 1953-55. DuPont teaching fellow Ohio State U., 1959-63; NSF faculty teaching fellow Boston U., 1966; recipient Centennial Alumnus award Houghton Coll., 1983. Mem. Council Deans Ind. Colls. S.C. (pres. 1984-85), Acad. Deans So. States, Republican. Lodge: Rotary (dir. 1983-84). Avocations: backpacking; photography; reading; travel. Home: Box 436 CWC Central SC 29630 Office: Central Wesleyan Coll Central SC 29630

CALHOUN, ALICE ANN, communications specialist; b. Jacksonville, Fla., Oct. 11, 1947; s. Ashley Barnes and Virginia (Page) Calhoun. B.A., Columbia U., 1969; M.A., U. S.C., 1974, Ph.D., 1979. Teaching asst. U. S.C., 1969-74; asst. prof. English, coordinator humanities Morris Coll., Sumter, S.C., 1975-77, dir. honors program, 1979-83; instr. Greenville Tech. Coll. (S.C.), 1978-79; tech. writer/editor Savannah Bank & Trust (Ga.), 1983-84, asst. cashier, scheduling coordinator, 1984-85, asst. v.p., productivity officer, 1985—. Am. Shakespeare Inst. scholar, 1969; Lilly scholar Duke U., 1977-78, Nat. Endowment for Humanities grantee, 1981. Mem. Am. Film Inst., MLA, South Atlantic Modern Lang. Assn., Am. Inst. Banking, Soc. Tech. Communication. Democrat. Methodist. Author: (with James Boblenz) Style Manual for Technical Report Writing, 1983. Home: 19 W Gordon St Savannah GA 31401 Office: Savannah Bank & Trust 2 E Bryan Savannah GA 31401

CALHOUN, CRAIG JACKSON, sociologist, educator, consultant; b. Watseka, Ill., June 16, 1952; s. Jay Robert and Audrey Thelma (Jackson) C.; m. Pamela Frances DeLargy, Aug. 2, 1980. B.A., U. So. Calif., 1972; M.A., Columbia U., 1974; M.A. in Econs., U. Manchester (Eng.), 1975; D. Phil., Oxford U. (Eng.), 1980. Research assoc. Columbia U., N.Y.C., 1972-74; instr. U. N.C., Chapel Hill, 1977-80, asst. prof. sociology 1980-85, assoc. prof., 1985—; cons. N.Y. Office Econ. Devel., 1981-82; tech. advisor U.S. AID, Govt. of Sudan, 1984—. Editor: The Anthropological Study of Education, 1976; author: The Question of Class Struggle, 1982; also articles. Officer, del. Democratic Party, Orange County, N.C., 1980—. Recipient Kellogg Found. fellow, 1982-85; R.J. Reynolds Fund award U. N.C., 1985. Fellow Royal Anthrop. Inst.; mem. Am. Sociol. Assn. (chair sect. comparative hist. sociology 1984-85). Home: 101 Sidney Green St Chapel Hill NC 27514 Office: U NC Dept Sociology Chapel Hill NC 27514

CALHOUN, EVELYN WILLIAMS, social worker; b. Tyler, Tex., Sept. 12, 1921; d. James Stanley and Norma (Skelton) Williams; B.A., Baylor U., 1941; M.S.W., Worden Sch. Social Work, 1960; postgrad. U. Chgo., 1955-56; m. William Benjamin Calhoun, Jr., Mar. 15, 1942 (div. Mar. 1949); children—William Benjamin III, Anne Stanley (Mrs. Donald Elliot Loyd). Field worker Tex. Dept. Pub. Welfare, Tyler, 1953-55; field placement Salvation Army Family Service, Chgo., 1955-56; child welfare worker Tyler-Smith County Child Welfare Unit, 1957-59; field placement Tex. Inst. Rehab. and Research, Baylor U., Houston, 1959-60, med. social worker, 1960-64; research social worker pre-natal research project dept. obstetrics and gynecology U. Tex. Med. Br. at Galveston, 1964-66, supr. social service dept. obstetrics and gynecology, 1966-74, cons. satellite clinics, 1967-74, cons. family planning project, 1969-74, cons., supr. head and neck cancer service, ear, nose and throat, chest surgery and neurosurgery, 1974-78, cons., supr. plastic surgery and oral surgery service, 1975-78, supr. internal medicine services, otolaryngology, ophthalmology and dermatology, 1978-81; field instr. U. Houston Grad. Sch. Social Work, 1968-81. Bd. dirs. Galveston County Community Action Council, 1966-68, Galveston chpt. Am. Cancer Soc., 1974-81; trustee Houston Intergroup Assn., 1974-76. Lic. social psychotherapist, Tex.; cert. social worker, advanced clin. practitioner, Tex. Mem. Nat. Assn. Social Workers (chmn. research council San Jacinto chpt. 1963-64, dir. chpt. 1964-67, chmn. Galveston br. 1964-67, sec. 1967-68; group leader so. regional inst. 1966, alt. Tex. del. 1969-71, Tex. del. 1971-73, dir. 1969-73; alt. del. Tex. state council 1967), Acad. Cert. Social Workers, Galveston County Soc. Social Service Dirs. (sec. 1979-80), AAUW, Baylor Alumnae Assn., Daus. King (pres. 1976-78), Order De Moley, Delta Alpha Pi. Episcopalian. Toastmistress. Home: 2408 Ave O Galveston TX 77550

CALHOUN, FRANK WAYNE, lawyer, former state legislator; b. Houston, Apr. 15, 1933; s. Wilmer Cecil and Ruby Edith (Willis) C.; m. Suzanne Paden Davis, Dec. 14, 1985; children by previous marriage: Michael, David; m. Suzanne Paden Davis, Dec. 14, 1985. B.A., Tex. Tech U., 1956; J.D. U. Tex., 1959. Bar: Tex. 1959, U.S. Supreme Ct. 1965. Ptnr. Byrd, Shaw, Weeks & Calhoun, Abilene, Tex., 1959-73, Liddell, Sapp, Zivley & LaBoon, Houston, 1974—; mem. Tex. Ho. of Reps., 1966-75. Del., Tex. Constl. Conv., 1974; mem. exec. bd. Chisholm Trail council Boy Scouts Am.; mem. exec. com. Tex. Film Commn., 1979-83; chmn. San Jacinto Hist. Adv. Bd.; bd. dirs. Abilene YMCA; trustee Tex. Tech Law Sch. Found., Colo. Outward Bound Sch.; bd. govs. Southwest Outward Bound Sch. Served with USNR, 1951-53. Named Abilene's Outstanding Young Man, Jaycees, 1968; Disting. Service award State Bar Tex., 1969, 71, 73. Mem. ABA, Tex. Bar Assn. (past com. chmn.), Tex. Assn. Bank Counsel, Am. Judicature Soc., Abilene C. of C. (past dir.), Tex. Tech U. Ex-Students Assn. (past pres.), Nat. Soc. State Legislators (bd. govs., past program chmn., exec. com.), Tex. Archeol. Soc., Tex. State Hist. Assn., Sierra Club, Nat. Audubon Soc., Nat. Trust for Hist. Preservation, Houston Fine Arts Mus., SCV, St. Andrews Soc. Tex., Sons. Confederate Vets., Sigma Alpha Epsilon, Alpha Kappa Psi. Democrat. Methodist. Clubs: Rotary, Houston, Plaza, Austin. Contbg. editor Tex. Lawyers Weekly Letter, 1964. Home: 3040 Locke Ln Houston TX 77019 Office: 3040 Locke Ln Houston TX 77019

CALIFF, MARILYN ISKIWITZ, painter, quilt designer, photographer; b. Memphis, Apr. 27, 1932; d. Leonard and Esther (Walberg) Iskiwitz; m. Leon Herman Califf, Mar. 8, 1953; children—Randall Todd, Regina Ann. Student U. Miami, 1950-51, Memphis State U., 1951-52, Internat. U. of Saltillo, Mex., 1968; B.F.A. in Painting, Memphis Acad. Art, 1970. Tchr. painting Peabody Ctr. for Sr. Citizens, 1970; tchr. quilting and patchwork Tenn. Vocat. Rehab., Memphis State U. Continuing Edn., Shelby State Community Coll. Continuing Edn., 1973-76; owner, operator book and quilt design mail order bus., 1971—; owner, operator retail quilt and patchwork shop, 1975-82; lectr., cons. in field. Author: Your First Quilt, 1975; The Pillow Book, 1977. One-woman shows of paintings Seabrooks Gallery, Memphis, 1965, Memphis Athletic Club, 1965, Carnegie Pub. Library, Clarksdale, Miss., 1966, The Gallery Upstairs, Nashville, 1970, Mid-South Fair, Memphis, 1970; one-woman shows of quilts and paintings Theatre Memphis, 1980, Meridian Mus. Art, Miss., 1981; also group shows; represented in permanent collections: Brooks Meml. Art Gallery, Memphis; Baron Hirsch Synagogue, Memphis Jewish Community Ctr., Memphis Hebrew Acad. Day Sch. Recipient First prize in oils Mid-South Exhbn., Brooks Art Gallery, 1968, three Purchae prizes for quilts Tenn. Artist-Craftsman's Assn., 1972, Outstanding Women Who Work award Memphis C. of C., 1975. Home and Studio: 5305 Denwood Ave Memphis TN 38119

CALKINS, CARROL OTTO, research entomologist, educator; b. Sioux Falls, S.D., June 4, 1937; s. Glenn Keeler and Nell (Olson) C.; m. Janice Marie McGuire, Oct. 3, 1959; children—Debra Diane, Lori Lynn. B.S., S.D. State Coll., 1959, Ph.D., 1974; M.S., U. Nebr.-Lincoln, 1964. Cert. in ecology, behavior, agrl. entomology Am. Registry Profl. Entomologists. Entomologist, Agrl. Research Service, U.S. Dept. Agr., Lincoln, Nebr., 1960-64; research entomologist Agrl. Research Service, U.S. Dept. Agr., Brookings, S.D., 1964-72, Gainesville, Fla., 1972-77, 80—; head entomology sect. Seibersdorf Lab., IAEA, Vienna, Austria, 1977-80; instr. U. Nebr., 1961-64, S.D. State U., 1964-72; with U.S. Dept. Agr., Gainesville, Fla., 1980—; assoc. prof. U. Fla., Gainesville, 1981—. Served with Air N.G., 1960-66. Mem. Entomol. Soc. Am., Ecol. Soc. Am., AAAS, Fla. Entomol. Soc., Sigma Xi, Alpha Zeta, Gamma Sigma Delta. Roman Catholic. Lodge: Elks (Brookings, Elk of Year 1971). Contbr. articles in field to profl. publs. Office: Insect Attractants Behavior Basic Biology Research Lab PO Box 14565 Gainesville FL 32604

CALKINS, PATRICIA CALE, registrar; b. Congress Heights, Md., Nov., 18, 1937; d. Elbert James and Jane Dolores (Gessler) Cale; m. Sidney Donald Calkins, June 7, 1959; children—David Warren, James Edward. M.A. in Math., Winthrop Coll., 1969; B.A., Fla. State U., 1959. Teaching asst. Winthrop Coll., Rock Hill, S.C., 1969-71; instr. in developmental edn. York Tech. Coll., Rock Hill, 1971-72, instr. math., 1972-74, head acad. div., 1974-83, dean acad. div., 1983-85, registrar, 1985—. Sec. Charlotte Area Ednl. Consortium, N.C., 1983—. Mem. Nat. Council Tchrs. Math., Am. Assn. Women in Community and Jr. Colls., Assn. Women Deans, Assn. Ednl. Communications and Tech. Democrat. Office: York Tech Coll Hwy 21 By-pass Rock Hill SC 29730

CALLAHAM, BETTY ELGIN, librarian; b. Honea Path, S.C., Oct. 8, 1929; d. John Winfred and Alice (Dodson) C.; B.A. in History, Duke U., 1950; M.A. in History, Emory U., 1954, M.Librarianship, 1961. Tchr. public schs., N.C., Ga., S.C., 1950-60; field service librarian S.C. State Library, Columbia, 1961-65, dir. field services, 1965-74, dep. librarian, 1974-79, librarian, 1979—; coordinator S.C. Gov. Conf. on Public Libraries, 1965; coordinator S.C. Gov. Conf. on Library and Info. Services, 1979; S.C. rep. White House Conf. Library and Info. Sci., 1979. Mem. ALA (mem. council 1977-80), S.C. Library Assn. (chmn. public library sect. 1965, fed. relations coordinator 1976-80, various cons.), Southeastern Library Assn., Chief Officers of State Library Agys. (chmn. Southeastern del. 1983-84), Southeastern Library Network (trustee 1984—, vice chmn. bd. 1985-86), S.C. Women in Govt., South Carolinana Soc., Historic Columbia Found., Friends of S.C. State Mus., S.C. Assn. Pub. Library Administrs. Baptist. Home: 1830 St Michaels Rd Columbia SC 29210 Office: PO Box 11469 Columbia SC 29211

CALLAHAN, CHERYL MANN, educational administrator; b. Greenville, S.C., Mar. 9, 1949; d. Joseph Griffin and Alice Elizabeth (Capell) M.; m. Thomas Michael Callahan, July 15, 1972; children—Megan Elizabeth, Kathleen Michelle. B.A. in Sociology, U. N.C.-Greensboro, 1971; M.Ed. in Counseling, U. N.C.-Chapel Hill, 1972. Counselor, dir. orientation Del. State Coll., Dover, 1972-76; guidance counselor Guilford County Schs., Greensboro, N.C., 1977-79, internat. student advisor U. N.C., Greensboro, 1979-81, asst. to vice chancellor student affairs, 1979-83, asst. vice chancellor for student affairs, 1984—. Project coordinator Jr. League, Greensboro, 1982-83; instr. Family Life Council, 1981-83; external appraiser Jr. League, 1984—; mem. project independence bd. Greensboro Urban Ministry, 1985—. Mem. Nat.

Assn. Student Personnel Adminstrs. (N.C. coordinator 1984-85), Nat. Assn. Women Deans, Adminstrs., Counselors, So. Assn. Coll. Student Affairs (mem. conf. program com. 1984), Nat. Council Family Relations, Am. Coll. Personnel Assn., Am. Assn. Counseling and Devel. Democrat. Presbyterian. Office: Office Student Affairs Univ NC 147 Mossman St Greensboro NC 27412

CALLAHAN, DENNIS HILLIARD, produce broker; b. Columbia, S.C., Jan. 14, 1944; s. John Minch and Sevena Clarissa (Greene) Baum; m. Nancy Jean Hiers, Jan. 30, 1965; 1 dau., Rebecca Anne. Student St. Petersburg Jr. Coll., 1962-63; produce merchandizer Haber Produce & Tomato Co., Pensacola, Fla., 1966-69; Fla. field rep. Wash. State Apple Commn., 1969-71; banana sales mgr. Bud Antle, Inc., Salinas, Calif., 1971-72; produce broker Farmers Potato Distbrs., Inc., Jacksonville Beach, Fla., 1972-73; co-owner Atlantic Brokers, Inc., Neptune Beach, Fla., 1973—. Served with USAF, 1965-73. Republican. Lutheran. Clubs: Rotary (Jacksonville Beach); Rolls Royce Owners (dir.); Bentley Drivers; Valiant Air Command (recruiting officer); Exptl. Aircraft Assn. Office: 1556 Atlantic Blvd Neptune Beach FL 32233

CALLAHAN, H. L., congressman; b. Mobile, Ala., Sept. 11, 1932; m. Karen Reed; children—Scott, Patrick, Shawn, Chris, Cameron, Kelly. Grad. McGill Inst. Pres., chmn. bd., chief exec. officer Finch Cos., Mobile and Montgomery, Ala., 1964-84; former mem. Ala. Ho. of Reps., Ala. Senate, from 1978, chmn. joint house and senate com. on oil and gas lease monies; mem. 99th Congress from 1st Ala. Dist., mem. com. on pub. works and transp., com. on mcht. marine and fisheries. Active Boy Scouts Am., Ala. Safety Council. Served with USN, 1952-54. Mem. Ala. Movers Assn., Ala. Trucking Assn., Mobile Area C. of C. Club: Pleasant Valley Optimist. Lodge: Kiwanis. Office: 1631 Longworth House Office Bldg Washington DC 20515

CALLAHAN, JAMES FREDERICK, manufacturing company executive; b. Rochester, N.Y., Sept. 15, 1919; s. Maurice James and Mary M. (Pigage) C.; m. Berenice R. Norman, Mar. 12, 1945; 1 dau., Margaret Callahan Schofield. Grad. Rochester Bus. Inst., 1939; postgrad. Niagara U., 1940-41, NYU, 1977. With Fasco Industries Inc., Boca Raton, Fla., 1939—, v.p., 1972-80, exec. v.p., 1980, pres., vice chmn., 1980-84, chmn. bd., 1984—; pres. Elmwood Sensors Inc., Pawtucket, R.I. 1981-82, chmn., 1981—, chief exec. officer, 1981-85, also Elmwood Sensors Inc., Newcastle, Eng.; chmn. Torin Ltd., Swindon, Eng., 1985—; dir. Basic Systems, Inc., Houston, Westcode Inc., Frazer, Pa., Onan Corp., Mpls. Mem. Nat. Assn. Accts. (pres. Rochester chpt. 1956-57, nat. dir. 1957-58), Inst. Internal Auditors. Clubs: Royal Palm Yacht and Country, Boca Raton Hotel and Club. Office: 601 N Federal Hwy Boca Raton FL 33432

CALLAHAN, LLOYD MILTON, agronomist, educator; b. Hobart, Okla., Mar. 28, 1934; s. Clyde C. and Sadie J. (Thrower) C.; divorced; children—Rebecca, Wayne, Kevin, Robert. B.S., Okla. State U., 1959, M.S., 1961; Ph.D., Rutgers U., 1964. Cert. profl. agronomist. Research asst. and technologist-turf Okla. State U., 1959-61; research asst.-turf Rutgers U., 1961-64; asst. prof. U. Tenn., Knoxville, 1964-69, assoc. prof., 1969-78, prof. turfgrass mgmt., 1978—; mem. green sect. com. U.S. Golf Assn., 1966—. Author: Diseases of Turfgrass, 1978; also sci. papers and popular articles. Served with USMC, 1952-55, Korea. Ednl. grantee U.S. Golf Assn., 1961; recipient Outstanding Tchr. award U. Tenn. Coll. Agr., 1982. Mem. Tenn. Turf Assn. (exec. sec. 1966-72, Plaque 1972), Am. Soc. Agronomy (chmn. div. C-5, 1973, bd. dirs. 1972-74), Weed Sci. Soc. Am., Sigma Xi, Gamma Sigma Delta. Democrat. Methodist. Club: Knox Science (pres. 1969). Avocations: karate; hunting; fishing; camping. Home: 8500-8 Olde Colony Trail Knoxville TN 37923 Office: Dept Ornamental Horticulture U Tenn Plant Sci Bldg 259 Knoxville TN 37901

CALLAHAN, MARGUERITE POYNOR, academic adviser; b. Waco, Tex., July 6, 1947; d. Phelps and Norma Louise (Luther) Smith; divorced; children—David A., Alan, Pamela; m. 2nd Michael Thomas Callahan; stepchildren—Aaron, Mary, Nathan. B.A., So. Methodist U., 1969; M.Ed., N. Tex. State U., 1984, postgrad., 1985. Tchr. Park Cities Acad., Dallas, 1981-84; acad. adviser So. Meth. U., Dallas, 1985—, med. bd. reviewer, 1985; cons. testing CETA, Dallas, 1982, N. Dallas High Sch., 1983. PTA room mother McCulloch Middle Sch., Dallas, 1982-84; den mother Council 10, Boy Scouts Am., Dallas, 1979-80; group coordinator Dallas Charity Dog Show, 1975-77. Mem. Am. Assn. Counseling and Devel., Tex. Assn. Counseling and Devel., Tex. Sch. Counselors Assn., Kappa Delta Pi, Psi Chi, Phi Delta Kappa, Beta Beta Beta. Republican. Presbyterian. Clubs: Skye Terrier of Am.; Caledonian Dancers, Scottish Soc. (Dallas). Avocations: Scottish dancing and history, gardening, traveling. Home: 2921 Westminster St Dallas TX 75205 Office: Dedman Coll So Methodist Univ Dallas TX 75275

CALLAHAN, VINCENT FRANCIS, JR., publisher, state legislator; b. Washington, Oct. 30, 1931; s. Vincent Francis and Anita (Hawkins) C.; B.S. in Fgn. Service, Georgetown U., 1957; m. Dorothy Helen Budge, Aug. 27, 1960; children—Vincent Francis III, Elizabeth Lauren, Anita Marie, Cynthia Helen, Robert Bruce. Became partner Callahan Publs., 1957, pres., editor numerous publs., 1957—; dir. McLean Savs. and Loan Assn.; past pres. Ind. Newsletters Assn., Washington; mem. Va. Ho. of Dels., 1968—, minority leader, 1982-85. Candidate for lt. gov. Va., 1965; state fin. chmn. Rep. Party of Va., 1966-68; candidate for U.S. Congress, 1976; past dir. Washington Met. Council Govts. Served with USMC, 1950-53; as lt. USCGR, 1959-63; chmn. No. Va. Community Found. Mem. U.S. Naval Inst., Marine Tech. Soc., Am. Def. Preparedness Assn. Republican. Roman Catholic. Clubs: Nat. Press; Kiwanis (past pres.) (McLean, Va.); Bull and Bear (Richmond, Va.). Author eight books including; Missile Contracts Guide, 1958; Space Guide, 1959; Underwater Defense Handbook, 1963; Military Research Handbook, 1963. Home: 6220 Nelway Dr McLean VA 22101 Office: PO Drawer 1173 McLean VA 22101

CALLAN, KAY KILPATRIC, educational administrator; b. Cullman County, Ala., May 10, 1945; d. Floyd Gaines and Honor Jewel (Lankford) Kilpatric; B.A. in Music Edn. magna cum laude, St. Bernard Coll., Cullman, Ala., 1969; M.A. in Elem. Edn., U. Ala., Birmingham, 1975; m. Herlin Cranford Callan, May 25, 1968; children—James David, Paul Gaines. Tchr. music Cullman County Schs., 1969-71; elem. sch. tchr. Sacred Heart Sch., Cullman, 1971-75; remedial reading instr. Cullman County Schs., 1975-77, reading resource tchr., 1977-79; related subjects instr. Cullman Area Vocat. High Sch., 1979-82, chpt. II/basic skills coordinator, 1982-84, assoc. supt., 1984—, pvt. instr. piano, 1960-72. Organist, St. Andrew's United Methodist Ch., Cullman, 1964-79, mem. adminstrv. bd., mem. council ministries, children's coordinator, 1981. Mem. Internat. Reading Assn., NEA, Ala. Reading Assn., Ala. Edn. Assn., North Central Ala. Reading Assn. (charter), Cullman County Edn. Assn., Ala. Vocat. Assn., Cullman Vocat. Assn., Delta Kappa Gamma. Home: 1626 2d Ave NW Cullman AL 35055 Office: Cullman County Bd Edn 310 3d Ave SE Cullman AL 35055

CALLAWAY, CATHERINE LEWIS, accountant; b. Urbana, Ill., Dec. 17, 1934; d. Horace Lockwood and Mildred (Wilcox) Lewis; B.A., Agnes Scott Coll., 1955; postgrad. La. State U., 1956; M.P.A., Ga. State U., 1981; m. Mayson Augustus Callaway, Jr., June 8, 1957; children—Mayson Augustus III, Louise Ann, Eugene Lewis. Social worker Fulton County Dept. Public Welfare, Atlanta, 1956-58; personnel interviewer, cashier Sears, Roebuck & Co., Atlanta, 1970-75; field agt. team leader Ga. Dept. Revenue, 1975-77; accounts payable supr. Dept. Adminstrv. Services, State of Ga., Atlanta, 1977-78, accounts receivable supr., 1978-79, project cons., 1979—; treas. Namano Inc.; dir. Calack, Inc. Mem. Ga. Assn. C.P.A.s, Am. Soc. Women Accts. (1st v.p. Atlanta chpt.), Am. Women Soc. C.P.A.s, Assn. Women Accts., Assn. Govt. Accts. (dir. Atlanta chpt.), Ga. Property Mgmt. Council (pres.), Fiscal Officers State Ga., High Mus. Art, Methodist. Home: 1135 Stillwood Dr NE Atlanta GA 30306 Office: 1512 West Tower 200 Piedmont Ave Atlanta GA 30334

CALLAWAY, MARK CLAYTON, investment company executive; b. Dayton, Ohio, June 16, 1956; s. Fuller Earle Callaway, 3d and Wanda (Vogt) Warren; m. Debra Cerniglia, Jan. 16, 1982; 1 child, Fuller Earle. B.A., LaGrange Coll. (Ga.), 1981; postgrad. NYU, 1981-82. Adminstrv. asst. Hills & Dales, LaGrange, Ga., 1982; investment broker Johnson, Lane, Space Smith & Co., LaGrange, 1983; v.p. Lamon-Callaway, Inc., Atlanta, 1983—; mng. prin. Lamon-Callaway Group; pres. Lamon-Callaway Fin. Services, Inc., 1984—; Founding dir. Bank of Troup County, LaGrange. Trustee, Callaway Found., Inc., 1981—, Fuller E. Callaway Found., Inc., 1982—; bd. dirs. Alliance Theatre Co., Atlanta, 1983-86, U. Ga. Bot. Gardens, Athens, 1983-85; chmn. bd. advisors State Bot. Gardens Ga., 1984—; trustee Ga. Found. Ind. Colls., 1985—. Mem. Internat. Assn. Fin. Planners, Am. Assn. Individual Investors, LaGrange C. of C. (dir. 1984—). Republican. Baptist. Clubs: Piedmont Driving, Highland Country, Rotary (LaGrange). Home: 403 College Ave LaGrange GA 30240 Office: Lamon-Callaway Group 205 N Lewis St LaGrange GA 30240

CALLEN, JEFFREY P., dermatologist; b. Chgo., May 30, 1947; s. Irwin R. and Rose P. (Cohen) C.; B.S., U. Wis., 1969; M.D., U. Mich., 1972; m. Susan Beth Manis, Dec. 21, 1968; children—Amy, David. Intern. U. Mich. Affiliated Hosps., Ann Arbor, 1972-73, resident in internal medicine, 1972-75, resident in dermatology, 1975-77; practice medicine specializing in dermatology and internal medicine, Louisville, 1977—; asso. prof. dept. medicine, U. Louisville, 1977—; chief dermatology Louisville VA Hosp., 1983—. Bd. dirs. Actors Theatre Louisville. Recipient Award of Excellence for Sci. Exhibit, Ky. Med. Assn., 1978; diplomate Am. Bd. Internal Medicine, Am. Bd. Dermatology. Fellow ACP, Am. Acad. Dermatology (chmn. com. on audiovisual edn., chmn. task force on therapeutic agts., cons. editor Dialogues in Dermatology, editor-in-chief Dermavision 1984); mem. Ky. Med. Assn., AMA, Soc. Investigative Dermatology, Dermatology Found., Galens Hon. Med. Soc., Ky. Dermatol. Soc. (pres. 1986-87). Author: Dermatology: A Teaching Manual, 1977, 78; Manual of Dermatology, 1980 Yearbook; editor: Cutaneous Aspects of Internal Disease, 1980; editor spl. issue of Cutis, 1978, 79, 81, 83; contbg. editor Internat. Jour. Dermatology, 1979—; editor Cutis, 1980—; editor issues of Med. Clinics N. Am., 1980, 82, Primary Care, 1983, Clinics Rheumatic Diseases, 1982, Dermatology Clinics, 1983; Seminars in Dermatology, 1984; contbr. articles to profl. jours. Office: 310 E Broadway Louisville KY 40202

CALLENDER, CHRISTIE ANN, geologist; b. Portland, Oreg., Apr. 9, 1952; d. Joseph Anthony and Helen (Lash) Mayer; m. Arden Daniel Callender, Jr., Dec. 3, 1977. B.S. in Geology, Portland State U., 1976. Geol. asst. Texaco Inc., Houston, 1978, assoc. geologist, 1978-82, geologist, 1982-84, sr. geologist, 1984—. Vice pres. West Airport Homeowners Assn., Houston, 1984. Mem. Am. Assn. Petroleum Geologists, Houston Area Microbeam Analysis Soc. (vice chmn. 1981-85, chmn. 1985—) Microbeam Analysis Soc., Transmission/-Scanning Electron Microscopy. Roman Catholic. Avocation: aerobics instruction. Home: 12019 Ripple Glen Dr Houston TX 77071 Office: Texaco Inc PO Box 770070 Houston TX 77215

CALLOWAY, FRANCES AMANDA, hotel executive; b. Birmingham, Ala., July 6, 1950; d. John Clyde and Nettye M. (Phillips) C.; student U. Ala., 1969-73, Hotel Sch., U. Houston, 1978. Mem. mgmt. staff Jolly Inns, Inc., Birmingham, 1971-72; gen. mgr. Airways Inn, Jackson, Miss., 1972-80; sec.-treas. Intergulf Motels Inc., Jackson, 1975-80, exec. ops. officer, 1980—; exec. officer, mng. ptnr. Inn Host Ltd. Hospitality Property Group, 1980—; exec. v.p. Motor Hotel Investors Inc., Jackson, 1979-80, exec. ops. officer, 1980—. Chmn., Miss. Tourist Promotion Com., 1978-79; mem. adv. bd. Travel South, 1979-80. Mem. Miss. Hotel/Motel Assn. (dir. 1978-79, v.p. 1979-80, pres. 1980-81), Jackson Hotel/Motel Assn. (pres. 1979), Jackson C. of C. Democrat. Presbyterian. Club: The Club (Birmingham). Office: 1 Flowood Pl Jackson MS 39208

CALLUAUD, GUY, chef; b. Rabat, Morocco, July 26, 1948; s. Pierre Arsene and Marie (Bourdin) C.; m. Martine Edith Lazaro, Apr. 24, 1971; children—Frederique, Stephanie. Cert. Ecole Hotliere de Nice (France), 1967. Pvt. chef, N.Y.C., 1972; chef Pyramid Room, Fairmont Hotel, Dallas, 1974; chef, owner Calluaud French Restaurant, Dallas, 1974—, Calluaud Traiteur, Dallas, 1982—. Recipient Cartier award, 1982, Lords Locator Fine Dining award, 1981, Bus. Execs. Dining award, 1981. Mem. Tex. Restaurant Assn., Tex. Chef Assn. Roman Catholic. Office: 2619 McKinney St Dallas TX 75224

CALLUENG, ZINNIA GOLEZ, physician; b. Cadiz, Negros Occidental, Philippines, May 6, 1946; came to U.S., 1972; d. Arturo Tad-y and Aurora Yulo (Tionko) Golez; m. Jose Aurelio D. Callueng, June 23, 1974; children—David Alexander, Eric Anthony. M.D., U. of East, Ramon Magsaysay Meml. Med. Ctr., Philippines, 1971. Asst. instr. anatomy U. of East, Philippines, 1971, instr. biochemistry, 1974-76; resident in gen. practice Kirwood Gen. Hosp., Detroit, 1972-73; resident in pediatrics Mt. Carmel Mercy Hosp., Detroit, 1973-74; gen. practice medicine and acupuncture, Crystal River, Fla., 1979— Recipient Appreciation cert. Gifted Edn. Community Internship Program Citrus County, 1980, Crystal River Christian Acad., 1982. Fellow Am. Bd. Acupuncture Medicine; mem. AMA, Fla. Med. Assn., Citrus-Hernando County Med. Soc., Am. Soc. Contemporary Medicine and Surgery, Catholic Family Orgn. Crystal River. Club: Altrusa.

CALOGERO, PASCAL FRANK, JR., state supreme court justice; b. New Orleans, Nov. 9, 1931; s. Pascal Frank and Louise (Moore) C.; student Loyola U. La., 1949-51, J.D., 1954; children—Deborah Ann Calogero Applebaum, David, Pascal Frank III, Elizabeth, Thomas, Michael, Stephen, Gerald, Katherine. Bar: La. Partner firm Landrieu, Calogero & Kronlage, 1958-69, Calogero & Kronlage, 1969-73; gen. counsel La. Stadium and Exposition Dist., 1970-73; assoc. justice La. Supreme Ct., New Orleans, 1973—. Del. Dem. Nat. Conv., 1968. Served to capt. U.S. Army, 1954-57. Mem. ABA, La. Bar Assn., New Orleans Bar Assn., Greater New Orleans Trial Lawyers Assn. (v.p. 1967-69).

CALTON, JUDGE TERRY, JR., hospital system executive; b. Imboden, Va., June 3, 1931; s. Judge Terry and Flora Etta (Southard) C.; B.A., Berea (Ky.) Coll., 1953; M.S. in Adminstrv. Medicine, Columbia U., 1959; children—Michael, Anthony. Adminstrv. asst., asst. adminstr. Miners Meml. Hosp. Assn., Washington, 1955-57, adminstr., 1959-63; research asst. Columbia U., 1963-64; asst. to assoc. hosp. dir. Univ. Hosp., Lexington, Ky., 1965-71, hosp. dir., 1971-77; exec. v.p. Meth. Hosps. of Memphis, 1978-80, pres., 1981—; dir. Blue Cross/Blue Shield; dir. U.S. Security Ins.; precepter U. Mich. Program and Bur. Hosp. Adminstrn., Ga. State U. Inst. Health Adminstrs. Mem. membership assembly United Way Greater Memphis; bd. dirs. United Way; bd. dirs. Mid-South Found. Med. Care; mem. Gov.'s Select Com. Health Care Cost Containment.Served with M.S.C., U.S. Army, 1953-55. Fellow Am. Coll. Hosp. Adminstrs. (regent adviser to Tenn. regent); mem. Ky. Hosp. Assn. (life), Am. Hosp. Assn., Tenn. Hosp. Assn. (exec. com., chmn. bd., Blue Cross liaison com.; award for meritorious service 1983, leadership award 1984), Hosp. Alliance Tenn. (past pres.), Memphis Hosp. Council (past pres.), Mid-South Med. Ctr. Council (dir.), Health Care Coalition Memphis, Ky. Public Health Assn., Memphis Hosp. Dist., Am. Assn. Med. Colls. Hosp. Alliance Tenn. (pres., dir.). Methodist. Office: 1265 Union Ave Memphis TN 38104

CALVER, RICHARD ALLEN, college dean; b. Chillicothe, Ohio, Feb. 16, 1939; s. Richard L. and Katherine Mae (Roush) Bryan; student U. Hawaii, 1959-61; B.S. in Bus. Adminstrn., W.Va. U., 1963; M.S. in Bus., Va. Commonwealth U., 1970; C.A.G.S.E., Va. Tech. U., 1983, Ed.D., 1984; m. Glenda Leigh Davidson, Mar. 13, 1965. Mgmt. trainee Sears Roebuck & Co., 1963; mgmt. trainee Reuben H. Donnelley Corp., 1963-64, state publs. and customer relations mgr., 1964-68; state job analyst Va. Div. Personnel, Richmond, 1968-70; dean adminstrv. services S.W. Va. Community Coll., Richlands, 1970—; mem. accreditation team So. Assn. Colls. and Schs. Mem. Lebanon (Va.) Town Council, 1978-82. Served with USAF, 1957-61. Mem. Nat. Assn. Coll. and Univ. Bus. Officers, Nat. Council Community Coll. Bus. Officers (nat. bd. dirs.), So. Assn. Coll. and Univ. Bus. Officers, Assn. Sch. Bus. Officers of U.S. and Can., Am. Mgmt. Assn., Russell County (Va.) C. of C. (pres. 1975-76), Delta Tau Delta, Phi Kappa Phi, Phi Theta Kappa (hon.). Methodist. Lodges: Lions (pres. Lebanon club 1976-77), Shriners (pres. club 1974-75), Scottish Rite (32 deg.), Masons. Home: Lebanon Manor Lebanon VA 24266 Office: PO Box SVCC Richlands VA 24641

CALVERT, DELBERT WILLIAM, business executive; b. Bosworth, Mo., Jan. 29, 1927; s. William McKinley and Ruby Leona (Berrier) C.; B.S. in Civil Engring., U. Mo., 1952; m. Mary Lee Brown, Feb. 10, 1947 (div. Mar. 1971), children—Gary D., Danial L.; m. 2d, Melva Allen Hurst, Sept. 4. 1971; stepchildren—Holly Hurst, Allen Hurst. Asst. mgr. supply and transp. div. Phillips Petroleum Co., Bartlesville, Okla., 1952-63, asst. to v.p. Tex. Eastern Transmission Corp., Houston, 1963-65; mgr. diversification dept. No. Natural Gas Co., Omaha, 1965-68; pres. Williams Bros. Pipe Line Co., Tulsa, 1968-71; exec. v.p. The Williams Cos., Tulsa, 1971—, also dir.; chmn. bd. Williams Energy Co., 1975-79, also dir.; chmn., chief exec. officer Agrico Chem. Co., Tulsa, 1977—, also dir.; dir. Williams Exploration Co., Edgecomb Steel Co., Tulsa; fertilizer industry adv. com. FAO. Mem. exec. bd. Indian Nations council Boy Scouts Am., 1969—, pres., 1974-76; bd. dirs. Goodwill Industries Tulsa; mem. U. Mo. Devel. Fund, 1969—, chmn., 1972-73. Served with AUS, 1945-47. Mem. Okla. Petroleum Council (dir. 1968—, pres. 1977-78), Am. Petroleum Inst. (gen. com. div. transp. 1971). Phosphate Chems. Export Assn., Inc. (chmn. bd.), Internat. Superphosphate Mfrs. Assn. (v.p. N.Am. Region), Tulsa C. of C., Tau Beta Pi, Chi Epsilon, Pi Mu Epsilon. Republican. Clubs: Southern Hills Country, Tulsa, Summit Shangri-La (Afton, Okla.); Garden of the Gods (Colorado Springs, Colo.); Sky (N.Y.C.). Home: 2739 E 69th Pl Tulsa OK 74136 Office: One Williams Center Tulsa OK 74172*

CALVERT, WILLIAM PRESTON, radiologist; b. Warrensburg, Mo., July 2, 1934; s. William Geery and Elizabeth (Spaulding) C.; B.S., Mass. Inst. Tech., 1956; M.D., U. Pa., 1960; m. Mary Kay Kersh, Apr. 4, 1976. Intern. Pa. Hosp., Phila., 1960-61, resident in medicine, 1961-62, 64-66, chief med. resident, chief resident physician, 1965-66; resident in gastroenterology Jackson Meml. Hosp., U. Miami (Fla.), 1966-67, NIH fellow in gastroenterology, 1967-68, resident in radiology, 1968-71; radiologist Meml. Hosp., Hollywood, Fla., 1971-72; chief dept. radiology Larkin Gen. Hosp., South Miami, Fla., 1972-80, radiologist, 1980—; clin. instr. radiology U. Miami Sch. Medicine, 1971-76, now asst. clin. prof. dept. family practice, clin. asst. prof. radiology, 1984—. Bd. dirs. Wediko Farms Children's Services, Carbondale, Ill. Served with M.C., USAF, 1962-64. Diplomate Am. Bd. Nuclear Medicine, Am. Bd. Radiology. Mem. AMA, Fla. Med. Assn., Fla., Greater Miami radiol. socs., Soc. Nuclear Medicine, Radiol. Soc. N.Am., Explorers Club. Home: 6851 SW 106th St Miami FL 33156 Office: 7031 SW 62d Ave South Miami FL 33143

CAMERON, CAROL ANN, occupational therapist; b. Calypso, N.C., Mar. 8, 1954; d. Paul Carroll and Kathryn Jeanette (Gorham) C. Student U. Fla., 1972-73; A.A., Miami Dade Community Coll., 1976; B.S., Fla. Internat. U., 1978. Lic. occupational therapist, Fla. Legal sec. Blackwell, Walker, Gray, Powers, Flick and Hoehl, Attys. at Law, Miami, Fla., 1973-74, computer operator, clk., 1975-76; computer operator, legal sec., clk. Kelly Girl, Hialeah, Fla., 1977; staff occupational therapist Greynolds Park Rehab. Ctr., North Miami Beach, Fla., 1979, Easter Seal Soc. Dade County, Inc., Miami, 1979-80; dir. occupational therapy Hialeah Hosp., 1981—; speaker, adv. Telethon vol. Easter Seal Soc. Dade County, 1980. Mem. World Fedn. Occupational Therapists, Am. Occupational Therapy Assn., Fla. Occupational Therapy Assn., Ctr. Study of Sensory Integrative Dysfunction, Nat. Geog. Soc., Nat. Audubon Soc., Fla. Audubon Soc., Smithsonian Instn., Nat. Rifle Assn. Democrat. Baptist. Office: Hialeah Hosp 651 E 25th St Hialeah FL 33013

CAMERON, CHARLES CLIFFORD, banker; b. Meridian, Miss., Jan. 4, 1920; s. Daniel Baker and Bertha (Morris) C.; B.S., La. State U., 1941; m. Sara Anderson, Nov. 22, 1978; children—Sheryl, Randolph Morris, Cynthia and Cathy (twins). Engr. Standard Oil Co. N.J., 1945-49; with Cameron-Brown Co., Raleigh, N.C., 1949—, pres., 1951-66, chmn. bd., 1966—; vice chmn. exec. com., chmn. bd., chief exec. officer First Union Nat. Bank of N.C., from 1966, now exec. v.p., also dir.; chmn. bd., pres. 1st Union Corp., 1968-83, chmn., chief exec. officer, 1984—; dir. Charlotte br. Fed. Res. Bank of Richmond, So. Bell Tel. & Tel. Mem. Gov's Council for Econ. Devel.; treas. Bus. Devel. Corp. N.C.; mem. Army Adv. Com. N.C. Pres. United Fund Raleigh. Bd. dirs. Raleigh YMCA. Carolinas United Community Service; chmn. bd. trustees U. N.C. at Charlotte, v.p. Chapel Hill, chmn. bd. Dimensions for Charlotte-Mecklenburg; bd. dirs., exec. com. N.C. Citizens Assn. Served to col. AUS, 1941-45; ETO. Decorated Bronze Star. Named Boss of Year, Raleigh Jr. C. of C., 1964. Mem. Assn. Res. City Bankers, Newcomen Soc. N.Am., Nat. Assn. Real Estate Bds. (v.p. 1961), Raleigh Bd. Realtors (past pres.), N.C. Assn. Realtors (past pres., Realtor of year award 1959), Am. (pres. 1964; Distinguished Service award 1961), Carolinas (pres. 1955) mortgage bankers assns., Am. Inst. Real Estate Appraisers, U.S. C. of C., Am. Bankers Assn. (exec. com. mktg. div.), Charlotte C. of C. (pres. 1973), Assn. Registered Bank Holding Cos. (dir.), Scabbard and Blade, Alpha Chi Sigma, Phi Lambda Upsilon, Theta Xi (pres. 1941). Baptist (deacon). Clubs: Capital City (Raleigh); Country of N.C. (Pinehurst); Charlotte (N.C.) City, Charlotte Country, Quail Hollow Country. Home: 2633 Richardson Dr Charlotte NC 28211 Office: First Union Corp Charlotte NC 28288

CAMERON, CHARLES METZ, JR., medical educator; b. Morristown, Tenn., Dec. 20, 1923; s. Charles Metz and Mildred (Brown) C.; m. Vera L. Cheek, Nov. 25, 1948; children—Charles Metz III, Cheryl Lynn, David Alan. Student U. Tenn., 1942, N.C. State Coll., 1943, U. Ky., 1944, U. Miss., 1945; M.D., Vanderbilt U., 1948; M.P.H., U. N.C., 1955. Rotating intern U.S. Marine Hosp. System, 1949; dist. health officer Tenn. Dept. Pub. Health, 1949-52; physician USPHS, 1951-53; chief communicable disease control sect., accident prevention sect. N.C. Bd. Health, 1953-55; assoc. prof., prof. U. N.C. Sch. Pub. Health, 1955-68, acting chmn. dept., 1960-61; dir. N.C. Office Comprehensive Health Planning, 1967-68; prof. dept. health adminstrn. U. Okla. Health Scis. Ctr., Oklahoma City, 1968-80, 83—, chmn. dept., 1968-75, 83-84, dean Coll. Pub. Health, 1984—, also dir. Mid-Continent Comprehensive Health Plannning Ednl. Ctr. and Health Resources Info. Ctr.; dep. commr. Okla. State Dept. Health, 1980-82, chief Preventive Med. Service, 1982-83; med. dir. USPHS. Served with AUS, 1943-45. Mem. Delta Omega (nat. pres. 1962). Contbr. articles to profl. jours. Home: 3132 Goshen Dr Oklahoma City OK 73120

CAMERON, DEBORAH JANE, medical educator, microbiologist, immunologist; b. Hackensack, N.J., Aug. 14, 1949; d. Alan Duncan and Jane Katherine (Bocket) Cameron; m. Patrick Van David, June 22, 1985. B.S. in Biology, Tufts U., 1971; Ph.D. in Microbiology, Columbia Coll. Physicians and Surgeons, 1977. Research assoc. in microbiology Columbia U., N.Y.C., 1977; postdoctoral fellow, dept. medicine Harvard Med. Sch., 1977-79; instr. surgery Med. U. S.C., 1979-80, asst. prof., 1980—. Montgomery Maze fellow, 1972-77; NIH postdoctoral fellow, 1978-79; NIH grantee, 1981—. Mem. Am. Assn. Immunologists, Reticuloendothelial Soc., Sigma Xi. Republican. Presbyterian. Office: Department of Surgery 171 Ashley Ave Charleston SC 29425

CAMP, EHNEY ADDISON, III, mortgage banker; b. Birmingham, Ala., June 28, 1942; s. Ehney Addison and Mildred Fletcher (Tillman) C.; B.A., Dartmouth Coll., 1964; m. Patricia Jane Hough, Sept. 17, 1966; children—Ehney Addison IV, Margaret Strader. Sr. v.p. Cobbs, Allen & Hall Mortgage Co., Inc., Birmingham, 1965-72; v.p., gen. mgr. The Rime Cos., Birmingham, 1972-75; pres. Camp & Co., Birmingham, 1975—; dir. AmSouth Bancorp. Bd. dirs. Community Chest/United Way Jefferson, Walker and Shelby Counties. Served with USAF, 1965, Ala. Air N.G., 1966. Mem. Am. Mortgage Bankers Assn., Ala. Mortgage Bankers Assn. (treas. 1984-85, sec. 1985-86), Birmingham Real Estate Bd. Methodist. Clubs: Mountain Brook (bd. govs. 1976-77), Birmingham Country, The Club, Downtown, Jefferson, Shoal Creek (bd. dirs.). Lodge: Kiwanis (dir. 1977-78, 82-83, sec. 1983-84, v.p. 1985-86). Home: 3510 Victoria Rd Birmingham AL 35223 Office: 15 Office Park Circle Suite 100 Birmingham AL 35223

CAMP, MAX WAYNE, music educator; b. Arab, Ala., July 4, 1935; s. Roy Hubert and Alice Mellie (Cox) C. Mus.B., U. Ala., 1957; Mus.M., Peabody Coll., Vanderbilt U., 1965; D.M.E., Okla. U., 1977. Teaching assoc. Snead Coll., Boaz, Ala., 1965-67, Athens (Ala.) Coll., 1967-68; prof. music U. S.C., Columbia, 1970—; dir. Camp Sch. of Music, Huntsville, Ala., 1957-70; tchr. master classes at piano workshops. Mem. Music Tchrs. Nat. Assn., S.C. Music Tchrs. Assn., Pi Kappa Lambda, Phi Mu Alpha. Author: Developing Piano Performance: A Teaching Philosophy, 1981; Guidelines for Developing Piano Performance, Books I and II, 1985; contbr. articles to profl. jours. Home: 21 Sims Alley Columbia SC 29205 Office: Sch of Music University of South Carolina Columbia SC 29208

CAMP, N. HARRY, JR., clin. psychologist; b. Des Moines, Mar. 28, 1918; s. N. Harry and Hazel Grace (Hohl) C.; B.A., U. Chgo., 1940, M.A., 1941; D.Ed., U. Calif., Los Angeles, 1948; postgrad. Johns Hopkins U., 1963-65. Sch. prin., Sigourney, Iowa, 1941-42; teaching asst. U. Calif., Los Angeles, 1946-48; prof. edn. Bklyn. Coll., 1948-49; prof. edn. and guidance Bucknell U., 1949-53; dir. guidance and clin. services Balt. County Schs., 1953-56; dir. psychiat. clinic Sch. for Boys, Marianna, Fla., 1956-58; dir. guidance and clin. services Brevard County, Fla., 1958-60; vis. prof. U. Miami, Fla., 1957-60, Pa. State U., 1960-65, Hunter Coll., N.Y., 1974-76; pvt. practice clin. psychology, 1961—; speaker on learning disabilities. Served to ensign, USNR, 1942-45. Editor Edn. Mag., 1949-53, The School Counselor, 1953-58. Address: 7520 SW 105th Terr Kendall FL 33156

CAMP, THOMAS EDWARD, librarian; b. Haynesville, La., July 12, 1929; s. Charles Walter and Annie Laura (Brazzel) C.; m. Elizabeth Anne Sowar, Sept. 4, 1952; children—Anne Winifred, Thomas David. B.A., Centenary Coll. Shreveport, 1950; M.L.S., La. State U., 1953. Binding asst. La. State U. Library, Baton Rouge, 1951-53; circulation librarian Perkins Sch. Theology

Bridwell Library, So. Meth. U., Dallas, 1955-57; librarian Sch. Theology, U. of South, Sewanee, Tenn., 1957—, assoc. univ. librarian, 1976—, acting univ. librarian, 1981-82. Co-author: Using Theological Libraries and Books, 1963; contbr. articles to profl. jours. Pres. Franklin County Assn. for Retarded, 1971-72. Served with AUS, 1953-55. Mem. Am. Theol. Library Assn. (exec. sec. 1965-67), ALA, Tenn. Library Assn. Democrat. Episcopalian. Home: Carruthers Rd Sewanee TN 37375 Office: U of South Library Sewanee TN 37375

CAMPBELL, ANTHONY, director counseling and career planning center; b. Bklyn., Aug. 8, 1955; s. Albert Henry and Francis Campbell; m. Melissa Lee Scott, May 21, 1977; children—Thomas Albert, Mary Elizabeth. B.S., James Madison U., 1977; M.Ed., U. Ga., 1979. Counselor, counseling and testing U. Ga., Athens, 1979; asst. dir. counseling and career devel. St. Mary's Coll., Notre Dame, Ind., 1979-81; dir. ctr. counseling and career planning Hampden-Sydney Coll., Va., 1981—; dir. Va. Coll. Placement Assn., Richmond, 1983—. Contbr. articles to profl. jours. Mem. steering com. Widowed Persons Service, Farmville, Va. 1984. Recipient Merit award Va. Vocat. Guidance Assn., 1984, cert. of merit N.Y. State Legislature, 1985; named Outstanding Alumni Newfield High Sch., Selden, N.Y, 1985. Mem. Va. Coll. Placement Assn. (dir. 1982—), Am. Coll. Personnel Assn. (directorate commn. VI 1980-84), So. Coll. Placement Assn. (mem. research com. 1980—), Farmville Jaycees, Phi Kappa Phi. Democrat. Roman Catholic. Avocations: tall ship collection, racquetball, historical biography. Home: PO Box 726 Hampden-Sydney VA 23943 Office: Ctr Counseling and Career Hampden-Sydney Coll Hampden-Sydney VA 23943

CAMPBELL, BRUCE GILMAN, chief of police; b. Manistee, Mich., Aug. 26, 1948; s. Roger Lee and Annabelle (Peterson) C.; m. Sandra Thomas, Dec. 10, 1975; children—Alexander Thomas, Megan Lee. B.A., Coll. of V.I., 1973; postgrad. FBI Nat. Acad., 1975, John Jay Coll., 1978-79, U. Va.-Quantico, 1973, 75, Sr. Mgmt. Inst. for Police, 1983; M.B.A., Fla. Inst. Tech., 1985. Police officer Dept. Pub. Safety, St. Thomas, V.I., 1970-73, police sgt., 1973-75, dir. prosecutor's investigation unit, 1975-77, supr. detectives, 1977-78, dep. commr., 1979-80; chief of police City of Melbourne, Fla., 1980—; assoc. Long and Assocs., Fort Lauderdale, Fla., 1984-85; Named Outstanding Young Man, U.S. Jaycees, 1982. Mem. Brevard County Assn. Chiefs of Police (pres. 1984—), Internat. Assn. Chiefs of Police, Internat. City Mgmt. Assn., Fla. Police Chiefs Assn. Lodges: Fraternal Order of Police (trustee 1982-85). Home: 28 Spruce St Brattleboro VT 05301 Office: Melbourne Police Dept 650 N Apollo Blvd Melbourne FL 32935

CAMPBELL, CARROLL ASHMORE, JR., congressman; b. Greenville, S.C., July 24, 1940; s. Carroll Ashmore and Anne (Williams) C.; m. Iris Rhodes, Sept. 5, 1959; children—Carroll Ashmore, III, Richard Michael. Ed., McCallie Sch., U. S.C., Am. U. Pres. Handy Park Co., 1960-78; mem. S.C. Ho. of Reps., 1970-74, S.C. Senate, 1976; exec. asst. to Gov. S.C., 1975; mem. 96th-99th Congresses from S.C. 4th Dist.; mem. banking, fin. and urban affairs com., com. on House adminstrn., appropriations com., ways and means com., asst. regional whip, Tenn. and Carolinas; farmer, Fountain Inn, S.C. Del. Republican. Conv., 1976, 80, 84; mem. Nat. Republican Congl. Com., Textile Caucus, S.C. Gov.'s Com. on Employment of Handicapped; mem. adv. council White House Conf. on Handicapped Individuals; chmn. March of Dimes; hon. chmn. Arthritis Found. Dr. Recipient Disting. Service award Jaycees; Citizenship award Woodmen of World; K.C. award; Rehab. Assn. Citizenship award; Guardian of Small Bus. award Nat. Fedn. Inst. Bus.; Disting. Service award Ams. for Constl. Action; Watchdog of Treasury award Nat. Associated Businessmen. Episcopalian. Clubs: Sertoma (Citizenship award), Masons, Chowder and Marching. Office: 106 Cannon House Office Bldg Washington DC 20515

CAMPBELL, CHARLES EDWARD, oil company executive; b. Washington, Apr. 16, 1946; s. Charles Edward and Helen Campbell; m. Judy Lodewyk, Aug. 22, 1971; children—Mandy Darnell, Nicholas William. B.A., Calif. State. U.-Sacramento, 1981, M.A., 1983; postgrad. Columbia Pacific U., 1983—. Sr. product engr. Baker Prodn. Service Inc., Houston. Served with USAF, 1964-67. Mem. Am. Mgmt. Assn., Am. Inst. Mech. Engrs., Instrument Soc. Am. (sr.), IEEE, Soc. Petroleum Engrs. Home: 7723 Creekfield Dr Spring TX 77379 Office: Baker Prodn Service Inc 350 N Belt St Houston TX 77060

CAMPBELL, CHARLES HARVEY, physician; b. Nixon, Tex., June 21, 1941; children—Charles, Colin, Clayton, Courtney. B.A., U. Tex., 1963; M.D., Tulane U., 1967. Intern, Charity Hosp., New Orleans, 1967-68; resident Alton Ochsner Found. Hosp., New Orleans, 1970-73, Baylor Coll. Medicine, Houston, 1973-74; practice medicine specializing in retina surgery, Corpus Christi, Tex., 1975—; mem. staff Meml. Med. Ctr., Driscoll Found. Children's Hosp., Spohn Hosp., all Corpus Christi. Diplomate Am. Bd. Ophthalmology. Fellow ACS; mem. Tex. Med. Polit. Action Com. (vice chmn.), Tex. Med. Assn., AMA, Nueces County Med. Soc., I.C.S., Am. Acad. Ophthalmology, Tex. Ophthalmology Assn., Tex. Soc. Ophthalmology and Otolaryngology, Pan Am. Assn. Opthalmology, Internat. Soc. Eye Surgeons. Home: 5540 Saratoga Corpus Christi TX 78413 Office: 1712 Sante Fe St Corpus Christi TX 78404

CAMPBELL, DAVID GWYNNE, petroleum company executive, geologist; b. Oklahoma City, May 2, 1930; s. Lois Raymond Henager and LaVada (Ray) Henager Campbell; B.S. in Geology, U. Tulsa, 1953; M.S. in Geology, U. Okla., 1957; m. Janet Gay Newland, Mar. 1, 1958; 1 son, Carl David. Petroleum geologist Lone Star Producing Co., Oklahoma City, 1957-65; exploration project geologist Tenneco Oil Co., Denver, Oklahoma City, 1965-71, dist. exploration geologist, Oklahoma City, 1971-73, div. geol. cons. Mid-Continent div., 1973-77; exploration mgr. Mid-Continent div. Leede Exploration, Oklahoma City, 1977-80; pres. Earth Hawk Exploration, Oklahoma City, 1980—; div. mgr. Mid-Continent div. Petro Corp, Oklahoma-City, 1983—. Active Last Frontier council Boy Scouts Am., 1960-73, edn. chmn. Eagle dist., 1963-67, asst. scoutmaster Wiley Post dist., 1971-73; Oklahoma County rep. to Cherokee Nation, 1976-78; mem. search com. U. Okla. Coll. Geoscis., 1985—. Served with USNR, 1949-53; with U.S. Army, 1953-55. Recipient cert. of recognition Okla.-Kans. Oil and Gas Assn., 1982. Mem. Am. Petroleum Inst., Am. Assn. Petroleum Geologists (info. com. nat. conv. 1968, field trips chmn. nat. conv. 1978, mem. ho. of dels. 1980—, nat. chmn. ho. of dels. 1981-82, mem. exec. com. 1981-82, trustee found. 1983—, chmn. nominating com. 1984-85, adv. council 1984—, councillor Mid-Continent sect. 1984—, chmn. liaison subcom. of astrogeology com. 1984-85, awards com. 1985-86), Oklahoma City Geol. Soc. (public relations chmn. Speakers Bur. 1963-64, chmn. stratigraphic code com. 1967-68, mem. exec. bd. 1968-69, advt. mgr. Shale Shaker 1969-71, rep. to Am. Assn. Petroleum Geologists ho. of dels. 1980-83, 80-83, 83-86, by-laws and articles of incorporation com. 1986—, Outstanding Service cert. 1984), Okla. Ind. Petroleum Assn., Tulsa Geol. Soc., Ind. Petroleum Assn. Am, AAAS, N.Y. Acad. Scis., U.S. C. of C., Oklahoma City C. of C., Okla. Hist. Soc., Cherokee Nat. Hist. Soc. (dir., chmn. solicitation com. Heritage Council 1983), Mus. Cherokee Indian Assn., Thomas Gilcrease Mus. Assn. Oklahoma City Geol. Discussion Group (pres. 1975-76), Sigma Xi. Club: Oklahoma City Petroleum. Contbr. articles to Jour. Cherokee Studies. Home: 6109 Woodbridge Rd Oklahoma City OK 73132 Office: 210 W Park Ave Suite 3131 Oklahoma City OK 73102

CAMPBELL, GEORGE EMERSON, lawyer; b. Piggott, Ark., Sept. 23, 1932; s. Sid A. and Mae (Harris) C.; J.D., U. Ark., 1955; m. Joan Stafford Rule, Apr. 9, 1973; children—Dianne, Carole. Admitted to Ark. bar, 1955, U.S. Supreme Ct. bar, 1971; asso. firm Kirsch, Cathey & Brown. Paragould, Ark., 1955; law clk. Asso. Justice Ark. Supreme Ct., 1959-60; mem. Rose Law Firm and predecessors, Little Rock, 1960—; spl. chief justice Ark. Supreme Ct., 1977. Mem. Ark. Ednl. TV Commn., 1976—, vice chmn., 1978-80, chmn., 1980-82; exec. sec. Ark. Constl. Revision Study Commn., 1967-68; chmn. Ark. Constl. Conv. Prep. Commn., 1968-69; del. Seventh Ark. Constl. Conv., 1969-70; bd. dirs. Ark. Orch. Soc., 1981—. Served with USNR, 1955-59. Recipient Disting. Citizen award, Nat. Mcpl. League, 1973. Fellow Ark. Bar Found.; mem. Am. Bar Assn., Ark. Bar Assn., Pulaski County Bar Assn., Am. Law Inst., Nat. Mcpl. League. Presbyterian. Club: Country Club of Little Rock. Home: 4 Kingston Dr Little Rock AR 72207

CAMPBELL, HUGH GREGORY, mathematics educator, author; b. Orlando, Fla., Mar. 10, 1932; s. Wendell Whitcomb and Margaret Caroline (Gregory) C.; m. Virginia Allen Loy, May 26, 1951; children—Hugh Gregory, Jr., Virginia Loy Campbell Bollinger, Allen Webb. B.S., Fla. State U., 1954, M.S., 1955. Asst. prof. Va. Poly. Inst. and State U., Blacksburg, 1955-58, assoc. prof., 1958-72, prof. math., 1972—, v.p. Arts and Scis. Faculty Assn., 1969-71, mem. univ. council, 1969-71, mem. faculty senate, 1969-72. Author: (math. textbooks) Linear Algebra with Applications, 1971, 2d edit., 1980; An Introduction to Matrices, Vectors, and Linear Programming, 1965, 2d edit., 1977; Linear Algebra with Applications Including Linear Programming, 1971; Matrices with Applications, 1968; (with Robert E. Spencer) Finite Mathematics and Calculus, 1977; A Short Course in Calculus with Applications, 1975; Finite Mathematics, 1974. Chmn. adv. bd. Blacksburg Parks and Recreation Dept., 1983—. Mem. Am. Math. Soc., Math. Assn. Am. Episcopalian. Office: Va Poly Inst and State U Dept Math Blacksburg VA 24061

CAMPBELL, HUGH THOMAS, football coach; b. San Jose, Calif., May 21, 1941. B.S., Wash. State U., 1963. Football player Can. Football League, Sask. Roughriders, 1963-69; football coach Whitworth Coll., 1970-76, Edmonton Eskimos, 1977-82; head coach Los Angeles Express, 1983, Houston Oilers, 1984—. Address: Houston Oilers PO Box 1516 Houston TX 77001*

CAMPBELL, J. JEFFREY, restaurants and holding company executive. Chmn., chief exec. officer Burger King Corp.; v.p. Pillsbury Co. Office: 7360 N Kendall Dr Miami FL 33156

CAMPBELL, JAMES EDWARD, political science educator; b. Portland, Maine, July 31, 1952; s. Wallace Joseph Jr. and Mary Elizabeth (Murphy) C. A.B., Bowdoin Coll., 1974; M.A., Syracuse U., 1980, Ph.D., 1980. Assoc. prof U. Ga., Athens, 1980—; congl. fellow Am. Polit. Sci. Assn., Washington, 1979-80; cons. Republican Nat. Com., Washington, 1981. Contbr. articles to profl. jours. Legis. asst. to congressman, 1979, to U.S. senator, 1980; state chmn. Nat. Com. Scholars Reagan-Bush, Athens, 1984. U. Ga. grantee 1981, 83, 85. Fellow Inst. Behavioral Research; mem. Am. Polit. Sci. Assn., So. Polit. Sci. Assn., Midwest Polit. Sci. Assn., Phi Beta Kappa. Avocation: Softball. Home: 364 Parkway Dr Athens GA 30606 Office: U Ga Dept Polit Sci Baldwin Hall Athens GA 30602

CAMPBELL, JOHN CLYDE, III, accountant, association executive; b. Buffalo, Dec. 3, 1944; s. John C. and Dorothy G. (McKenna) C.; B.A., SUNY, Buffalo, 1967, M.B.A., 1969; postgrad. Va. Commonwealth U., 1980; M.A., Central Mich. U., 1984; m. Maureen Theresa Butler, Oct. 31, 1970; children—John Clyde IV, Justin Wallace. Va. rep. at large Am. Cancer Soc., Richmond, 1972-73; Va. sales rep. Met. Life Ins. Co., Richmond, 1973-78; Va. adminstr. long range devel. Am. Heart Assn., Richmond, 1978—. Founding chmn. Richmond Area Alliance, 1975; pres. Duntreath Assn., 1980; chmn. scouting com., cubmaster Boy Scouts Am., 1981-83; chmn. Richmond Area Inter-Club Council, 1981-82, dir. 1982—. Served with AUS, 1969-72. Mem. U.S. Jaycees (Spoke award 1974), Richmond West End Jaycees (dir. 1974), Life Underwriters Assn., Soc. Heart Assn. Profl. Staff (fellow 1982-83), Res. Officer Assn. U.S., Internat. Platform Soc., Nat. Soc. Fund Raising Execs., Assn. Retarded Citizens. Republican. Club: Civitan (dir.). Home: 6809 Edmonstone Ave Richmond VA 23226 Office: 316 E Clay St Richmond VA 23219

CAMPBELL, JOHN THOMAS, counselor, university official; b. Gallipolis, Ohio, June 29, 1958; s. John Ivor and Kathryn Helena (Edwards) C. B.S., Rio Grande Coll., 1981; Ed.M., Miami U., 1983. Asst. freshman adv. Miami U., Oxford, Ohio, 1981-82, head resident adv., 1982-83; counselor to students U. South Fla., Tampa, 1983-85, instr., 1984-85, asst. to assoc. dean of students, 1984-85; area coordinator Office Residence Life, So. Methodist U., Dallas, 1985—. Vol. Health Rehab. Services, Tampa, 1983-84. Mem. Am. Coll. Personnel Assn., Nat. Assn. Student Personnel Assn., So. Assn. Coll. Student Affairs, Assn. Coll. Univ. Housing Officers, Civitan Internat. (bd. dirs. 1983-84, sgt. 1983-84, v.p. elect. 1984-85). Republican. Presbyterian. Avocations: golf; tennis; jogging; basketball. Office: Residence Life So Methodist U Box 452 Dallas TX 75275

CAMPBELL, JOHN TUCKER, South Carolina secretary of state; b. Calhoun Falls, S.C., Dec. 12, 1912; s. John Brown Gordon and Mary (Tucker) C.; student U. S.C., 1941-42; m. Gertrude Davis, Jan. 4, 1936; children—James Gordon. Pres. Campbell Drug Stores, Columbia, S.C., 1938—; mem. Columbia City Council, 1954-58, 66-70, mayor, 1970-78; sec. state State of S.C., 1979—. Served with USAAF, 1943-46. Mem. S.C. Pharm. Assn. (dir. 1971-73), Nat. League Cities, S.C. Municipal Assn. (pres. 1972-73). Methodist. Mason (Shriner). Clubs: Optimist Internat. (state gov. 1964-65); Palmetto. Office: PO Box 11350 Columbia SC 29214

CAMPBELL, JONATHAN WESLEY, physicist, aerospace engineer; b. Alexander City, Ala., Sept. 1, 1950; s. Harry Underwood and Sarah Ruth Campbell; m. Mary Magdalene Sanders, Dec. 11, 1974; 1 son, Jason Jonathan. B.S., Auburn U., 1972, M.S., 1974; M.S., U. Ala., 1980. Coop. engr. Pratt & Whitney Aircraft, West Palm Beach, Fla., 1968-70; instr. physics Auburn U., 1972-74; physicist, aerospace engr. Missile Intelligence Agy., Huntsville, Ala., 1978-80; physicist, aerospace engr., exec. asst. to dir., lead engr. space telescope fine guidance sensor NASA/Marshall Space Flight Ctr., Huntsville, Ala., 1980—; cons. Starflight Assocs. Served to capt. AUS, 1975-78. Recipient Eagle Scout award. Mem. AIAA, Air Force Assn., Res. Officer Assn., Aircraft Owners and Pilots Assn., Tau Beta Pi, Sigma Gamma Tau. Methodist. Home: 3713 Old Railroad Bed Rd Harvest AL 35749 Office: DX01 NASA Marshall Space Flight Ctr Huntsville AL 35812

CAMPBELL, JUDITH KURTZ, university administrator; b. Phila., Dec. 27, 1945; d. Jules and Esther D. (Woloshin) Kurtz; m. Robert Craig Campbell III, Dec. 26, 1967 (div. Nov. 1977); children—David Philip Lee, Brett William. B.S. in Edn., U. Pa., 1967; M.S. in Counseling, U. South Ala., 1984. Caseworker Mobile County Dept. Pensions and Security, Mobile, Ala., 1970-73; dir. social work Wilmer Hall Episcopal Home, Mobile, 1973-77; owner, pres. Profiles, Inc., Mobile, 1977-81; dir. tech. programs and human services U. South Ala., Mobile, 1981—; cons. Morrison, Inc., Mobile, 1978—. Editor Art Patron's League Newsletter, Mobile, 1976-77. Pres. Vol. Coordinators, Mobile, 1976; v.p. Austin PTA, Mobile, 1977-78; mem. adv. com. Mobile County Pub. Schs., 1977; bd. dirs. Chandler br. YMCA, Mobile, 1977-80; mem. adv. bd. Wilmer Hall Children's Home, Mobile, 1978-80. Mem. Am. Soc. for Tng. and Devel., Am. Mgmt. Assn., Am. Personnel and Guidance Assn., Nat. U. Continuing Edn. Assn., Ala. Assn. of Continuing Edn. and Services, Am. Soc. Engring. Edn. Avocations: swimming; tennis; scuba diving; white water rafting; creative writing. Office: U South Ala 2002 Old Bay Front Rd Mobile AL 36615

CAMPBELL, JUDY GAYLE, management development consultant; b. Port Arthur, Tex., Jan. 23, 1948; d. Lawrence Joseph and Josephine V. Bouillion; B.A., Lamar U., 1970; m. Raymond Campbell, Mar. 21, 1970. Govt. tchr. Thomas Jefferson High Sch., Port Arthur, 1970-72; corp. tng. mgr. Foley's, Houston, 1972-81; sr. cons. Mohr Devel. Inc., Houston, 1981-82; mgr. tng. devel. Goldking Prodn. Co., Houston, 1982—; pub. speaker for profl. and bus. groups; internal and external cons. for human resources. instr. Houston Community Coll., Houston Bapt. U., U. Houston, 1976-82. Chmn. for Houston region U. Tex. Adv. Council. Mem. Am. Soc. Tng. and Devel. (sec. 1980, 81, pres. 1982, asst. regional dir. 1983-85). Roman Catholic. Home: 222Q7 Wetherburn St Katy TX 77449

CAMPBELL, KATHERINE WILSON, nursing administrator; b. Knoxville, Tenn., Apr. 23, 1940; d. William Caldwell and Katherine Lucille (Bolt) Wilson; m. John Morton Gardner, June 12, 1959 (div. 1971); children—Mary Ellen Bolinger, Katherine Paige Mounce, Julia Gale, John Morton, Jr.; m. George William Campbell, Aug. 5, 1980. B.S., U. Tenn., 1961; nursing diploma St. Mary's Sch. Nursing, Knoxville, 1973. Cert. emergency nurse. Staff nurse Fort Sanders Hosp., Knoxville, 1973-74, 76-78, clin. nursing coordinator emergency dept., 1978—; staff nurse Canal Zone Co., Gorgas Hosp., C.Z., 1974-76. Bd. dirs. Rape Crisis Ctr., Knoxville, 1978. Mem. Am. Acad. Med. Adminstrs. (affiliate), Emergency Nurses Assn. (pres. chpt. 1980, 83), East Tenn. Emergency Med. Symposium (program chmn. 1980, 85). Baptist. Home: 7020 Stagecoach Trail Knoxville TN 37909 Office: Fort Sanders Hosp 1901 Clinch Ave Knoxville TN 37916

CAMPBELL, LEONARD GENE, university president; b. Krebs, Okla., Oct. 15, 1933; s. Thomas Allen and Tempie (Woodall) C.; m. Linda Lou Bailey, May 22, 1958; 1 dau., Kristi Lynn. B.S., Southeastern Okla. State Coll., 1958; M.A., U. Okla., 1964, Ed.D., 1970. Tchr., coach Amarillo (Tex.) pub. schs., 1960-61, Moore (Okla.) High Sch., 1961-63; prin. Moore (Okla.) Jr. High Sch. and Moore High Sch., 1963-65; asst. supt. Moore (Okla.) pub. schs., 1965-70; supt. Western Heights Pub. Schs., Oklahoma City, 1970-75; pres. Southwestern Okla. State U., Weatherford, 1975—. Served with USN, 1952-54. Mem. NEA, Okla. Edn. Assn., Am. Assn. Sch. Adminstrs., Okla. Assn. Sch. Adminstrs., Central Dist. Okla. Edn. Assn. (pres. 1973-74), Okla. Textbook Commn. (chmn. 1972-74). Democrat. Baptist. Lodges: Lions; Kiwanis; Rotary. Office: Southwestern Okla State U Office of Pres Weatherford OK 73096*

CAMPBELL, LUCY BARNES, librarian; b. Windsor, N.C., Oct. 30; d. Eley and Frankie Elizabeth (Carter) Barnes; B.A., N.C. Central U., 1941, B.L.S., 1942, M.L.S., 1960; m. Alfonso L. Campbell, Sr., May 4, 1946; children—Alfonso L., Sharon I. Librarian, Darden High Sch., Wilson, N.C., 1942-45; asst. librarian Ala. State U., Montgomery, 1945-63; circulation librarian Hampton Inst., Huntington Library, Hampton, Va., 1963, acting dir., coordinator student activities, 1964, asst. reference librarian, 1964-65, asst. prof./head periodicals dept., 1966-84, coordinator residence hall reading rooms, 1967-73; participant Inst. Black Studies Librarianship, Fisk U., summer 1970. Solicitor, United Negro Coll. Fund, 1964-70, Hampton Inst. Peninsula Ann. Fund Campaign, 1972-78. Recipient citation for service and leadership Ala. State U., 1962; cert. of merit Women's Senate, 1965, named Mother of Yr., 1965, Mother of Men of Hampton, 1968 (all Hampton Inst.). Mem. ALA, Assn. Coll. and Research Libraries, Southeastern, Va. library assns., Assn. Study of Afro-Am. Life and History, YWCA, Black Caucus, NAACP (life), Alpha Kappa Alpha (life). Baptist. Club: Women's Service League. Lodge: Order Eastern Star. Author: Black Librarians in Virginia, 1976; The Story of the Hampton Institute Library School, 1925-39, 1976.

CAMPBELL, MICHAEL EUGENE, state agency official, psychologist; b. Sentinel, Okla., Mar. 1, 1950; s. Leland Eugene and Betty Louise (Tierce) C.; m. Teresa Louise Hankins, Jan. 2, 1971; children—Tamara, Shana, Maia. B.A., Baylor U., 1972, M.A., 1974, Ph.D., 1976. Lic. psychologist, Tex. Asst. prof. Our Lady of the Lake U., San Antonio, 1975-79; research scientist Systems Research, San Antonio, 1980-83; tng. dir. Office State Comptroller, Austin, Tex., 1984—. Contbr. articles to profl. jours. Vice pres. U. Roundtable, San Antonio, 1984. Danforth Found. assoc., 1979-85. Mem. Am. Psychol. Assn., Southwestern Psychol. Assn., AAAS, N.Y. Acad. Sci., Soc. Neurosci. Home: 501 Noton St Pflugerville TX 78660 Office: Comptroller Public Accounts 111 W 17th St Austin TX 78711

CAMPBELL, MICHAEL WEYMOUTH, oil co. exec.; b. Amarillo, Tex., Oct. 31, 1948; s. Thomas Henry and Mary Ann (Weymouth) C.; student Tex. Tech. U., 1965; B.B.A., El Centro Coll., 1967; Ph.D. (hon.), Acad. Life Studies, 1974; m. Mary Margret Larson, Dec. 7, 1968; children—Michael Weymouth, Sarah Elizabeth. Data processor Blue Cross Med., Dallas, 1968-70; with Weymouth Corp., Amarillo, 1970—, pres., chmn. bd., 1976—. Bd. dirs. Amarillo Art Center, 1981, Amarillo Kidney Found., 1981, Tex. Tech. U., 1981; founding pres. Amarillo Hist. Preservation Soc., 1978. Mem. Tex. Cattle Raisers Assn., Southwestern Cattle Raisers Assn., Ind. Producers Assn. Am., Tex. Cattle Feeders. Republican. Episcopalian. Clubs: Rotary, Amarillo, Amarillo Country. Home: 3204 Ong St Amarillo TX 79109 Office: 600 Plaza I Amarillo TX 79101

CAMPBELL, OLGA MARGARET, psychologist; b. Altrincham, Cheshire, Eng., June 20, 1943; came to U.S., 1968, naturalized, 1981; d. John Wilkinson and Margaret (Warmisham) Talbot; m. Phalguni Sekhar Roy, Sept. 5, 1964 (div. 1973); m. James Donald Campbell, Nov. 1, 1974 (div. 1980). B.S., Marywood Coll., 1972; M.A., Abilene Christian U., 1975; Ph.D., U. Tex., 1983. Lic. psychologist, Tex. Psychologist, Big Spring State Hosp., Tex., 1973-74, 80-84, Vernon State Hosp., Tex., 1974-76, Rusk State Hosp., Tex., 1976-77; pvt. practice psychology, Midland, Tex., 1985—. Bd. dirs. Permian Basin Ctr. for Battered Women and Their Children, Midland, 1985. Mem. Am. Psychol. Assn., Tex. Psychol. Assn., Soc. Personality Assessment, Mensa, Intertel. Office: 3325 W Wadley Suite 231 Midland TX 79707

CAMPBELL, PATRICIA, librarian; b. Austin, Tex., Dec. 9, 1941; d. Lloyd Walton and June (Rousseau) C.; m. Lamar Allen III, May 31, 1969 (div. 1978). B.S., U. Tex., 1963; M.L.S., N. Tex. State U., 1970. Provisional teaching cert., Tex. Librarian, Leslie A. Stemmons Elem. Sch., Dallas Ind. Sch. Dist., 1963-69, Forestridge Elem. Sch., Richardson Ind. Sch. Dist., Dallas, 1969—. Mem. Tex. Library Assn., Dallas County Library Assn., Richardson Edn. Assn., Dallas Hist. Preservation Soc., The 500 Inc. Democrat. Methodist. Home: 6423 Danbury St Dallas TX 75214 Office: 10330 Bunchberry St Dallas TX 75243

CAMPBELL, RALPH PURCELL, JR., mental health/substance abuse administrator; b. Alexandria, La., Feb. 8, 1933; s. Ralph Purcell and Oma Vesta (Arrington) C.; m. Betty Lucille Stacey, Aug. 18, 1962; children—Robert Keith, David Brian, Julie Ann. B.A., La. Coll., 1956; C.S.W., La. State U., 1961, M.S.W., 1962. Clin. Social worker Lake Charles Mental Health Center, Lake Charles, La., 1962-64; chief social worker East La. State Hosp., Jackson, 1964-67; chief social worker Mental Health Center, Buncombe County (N.C.), Asheville, 1967-68; adminstr. Blue Ridge Mental Health Center, Asheville, N.C., 1968-72; dep. adminstr. Div. Substance Abuse, Office of Mental Health and Substance Abuse, Dept. Health and Human Resources, Baton Rouge, La., 1972-81, dir. Div. Adminstrv. Services, 1981-84, div. dir. Office of Prevention and Recovery from Alcohol and Drug Abuse, 1984—. Served with U.S. Army, 1957-58. Mem. Nat. Assn. Social Workers, Mental Health Assn. Baton Rouge, Acad. Cert. Social Workers La. Democrat. So. Baptist. Club: Pelican Woodcarvers Guild (sec., treas.), Jr. C. of C. (past office holder), (Lake Charles and Jackson). Office: 2744-B Wooddale Blvd Baton Rouge LA 70892

CAMPBELL, REGINALD LAWRENCE, industrial hygienist, educator; b. Hartford, Conn., Apr. 8, 1943; s. Reginald L. and Etta M. (Ashton) C.; student Amherst Coll., 1961, Yale U. Sch. Medicine, 1965-67; Asso. Sci., Hahnemann Med. Coll., 1975; B.A., Fairmont State Coll., 1977; M.S., Marshall U., 1980. Propr., dir. Campbell Clin. Lab., Amherst, Mass., 1963-65; staff therapist St. Joseph's Hosp., Stamford, Conn., 1966-67; staff therapist Yale-New Haven Hosp., 1967-70; asst. research cardiothoracic surgery Yale U. Sch. Medicine, 1967-70; guest lectr. Royal Melbourne (Australia) Hosp., Monash U., 1968, Royal North Shore Hosp., U. Sydney (Australia), 1968; chief anesthetic technologist Montreal (Que.) Gen. Hosp., McGill U. Sch. Medicine, 1970; tech. dir. sect. respiratory disease services Danbury (Conn.) Hosp., 1970-72; dir. respiratory program adj. faculty Western Conn. State Coll., Danbury, 1970-72; sr. instr. medicine Sch. Respiratory Therapy, Hahnemann Med. Coll., Phila., 1972-75, asst. prof. dept. medicine Coll. Allied Health Professions, 1974-75; adminstr. So. W.Va. Lung Center, Inc., Beckley, 1975-77; cons. respiratory therapy program Fairmont (W.Va.) State Coll., 1975-76, Bluefield (W.Va.) State Coll., 1975-76; tech. cons. W.Va. Gov.'s Coal Worker's Respiratory Disease Control Program, 1975-78; indsl. hygienist Nat. Mine Health and Safety Acad., U.S. Dept. Interior, Beckley, W.Va., 1978-79; instr. occupational lung diseases and occupational health Nat. Mine Health and Safety Acad., U.S. Dept. Labor, Beckley, 1979-83, Inst. Occupational Health, 1983—; guest lectr. mil. history and firearms various mil. instns., 1965-69. Squadron comdr. CAP, Beckley, 1978-80, Lewisburg, 1980-83; wing safety officer, 1983—; mem. Pa. Gov.'s Task Force on Black Lung, 1974-75. Mem. Am. Public Health Assn., Am. Assn. Indsl. Hygiene, Am. Assn. Safety Engrs., Am. Assn. for Respiratory Therapy, Can. Soc. Respiratory Technologists, Am. Thoracic Soc. (asso. mem.), W.Va. Soc. Respiratory Therapy, Mil. Hist. Soc. S. Africa, Mil. Hist. Soc. Australia, Wheelchair Pilots Assn., Kappa Delta Pi, Yale Sch. Respiratory Therapy Alumni Assn. (pres. 1966-71). Democrat. Presbyterian. Clubs: Lions, Masons, Ruritan. Contbr. articles to profl. publs. Home: Route 1 Box 51-A Alderson WV 24910 Office: PO Box 1166 Beckley WV 25802

CAMPBELL, ROBERT GORDON, music educator; b. Camden, Ark., May 24, 1922; s. Charles Milton and Edith Harriet (Newman) C.; m. Nancy Brough Patterson, May 27, 1949; children—Shirley, Catherine, Gordon, Betty. B.A., Hendrix Coll., 1943; B. Mus., U. Tex., 1948, M. Mus., 1950; Ph.D., Ind. U., 1966. Mus. instr. U. Tex.-Austin, 1950-52; mus. instr. So. Ark. U., Magnolia, 1952-55, asst. prof., 1955-57, assoc. prof., 1957-64, prof. mus., 1964—, chmn. div. of fine arts, 1964-80. Pres. of bd. So. Ark. Symphony, El Dorado, 1967-68. Served with USAAF, 1943-46, ETO. Mem. Mus. Tchrs. Nat. Assn. (exec. bd. mem. 1968-72), Ark. State Mus. Tchrs. Assn. (pres. 1967-68), Am. Musicological Soc., Coll. Mus. Soc., Mus. Library Assn., Pi Kappa Lambda, Phi Mu Alpha Sinfonia. Democrat. Presbyterian. Avocations: swimming; bird watching. Home: 508 Margaret St Magnolia AR 71753 Office: So Ark U Box 1398 So Ark U Magnolia AR 71753

CAMPBELL, ROBERT M., state supreme court justice; b. Mar. 1, 1935; B.A., Tex. Wesleyan Coll.; J.D., Baylor U. Admitted to Tex. bar, 1964; practiced in Waco, Tex.; justice Tex. Supreme Ct., Austin, 1978—. Mem. ABA,

Waco-McClennan County Bar Assn., State Bar Tex., Tex. Trial Lawyers Assn., Delta Theta Phi. Office: Supreme Ct Bldg Austin TX 78711

CAMPBELL, ROBERTA JUNE, auditor; b. Atlanta, Oct. 17, 1947; d. Robert Miles and Eunice (O'Neal) Saul; B.B.A. (Ga. Educators Assn. fellow), Ga. State U., 1970, M.Profl. Acctg. and Bus. Info. Sci. (Univ. fellow), 1978; m. Lloyd Ray Campbell; children—Michael, Sara, Brian. Sr. acct. textile ops. Oxford Industries, Inc., Atlanta, 1969-71; corp. auditor U.S. Dept. Treasury, Atlanta, 1971-76; fin. systems dir. Indsl. Devel. Research Council, Atlanta, 1976-81; sr. EDP/fin. specialist Met. Atlanta Rapid Transit Authority, EDP auditor/specialist, 1981—; mem. adult edn. acctg. faculty Ga. U. System, 1972-76; cons., lectr. in field. Mem. Assoc. Info. Mgrs., Info. Industry Assn., Inst. Internal Auditors (EDP seminar chmn. 1985), Women's Transp. Seminar, Ga. State U. Alumni Assn. Co-author: Industrial Park Growth, 1979; New Industries of the Seventies, 1978, 2d edit. 1980; Composite Case History of New Facility Location-Utility Services, 1978; 5000 Growth Firms, 1981; Effective Auditing of Personnel, Payroll and Risk Management, 1983. Home: 2848 N Deshong Rd Stone Mountain GA 30087 Office: 401 W Peachtree St Suite 2000 Atlanta GA 30305

CAMPBELL, SALLY WORTHINGTON, freelance writer, editor, public relations consultant; b. Pitts., Jan. 3, 1947; d. Aubrey Walter and Marie Ruth (Henningsen) Worthington; B.A. in Journalism, Auburn U., 1968; m. John Jette Campbell, Aug. 31, 1968; children—Ashley, Heather, John Jette, Jr. Reporter-intern Montgomery, Ala. Jour., 1968; asst. editor Auburn (Ala.) Extension Service, 1968-69; tchr. lang. arts Nichols Jr. High Sch., Tuskegee, Ala., 1969-70; editor Where Mag., Houston, 1971-79, Southwestern editorial supr., 1979; dir. public relations Austin (Tex.) Civic Ballet, 1980-82, v.p. performance, 1983-84, v.p. spl. events, 1984-85, also bd. dirs.; cons. public relations Retinitis Pigmentosa Found., Houston, 1979. Vice pres. Austin Jr. Forum, 1981-82; loaned exec. Capital Area United Way, 1983; mem. Laguna Gloria Mus. Women's Art Guild, 1980—; writer for KTBC-TV 1st place award Region II public service announcement competition, Tex. Broadcasters Assn., 1981. Mem. Women in Communications, Leadership Austin, Alpha Omicron Pi. Republican. Presbyterian. Home and Office: 7705 Bramblewood Circle Austin TX 78731

CAMPBELL, SEAN STEPHEN, yacht company executive; b. Paris, Sept. 18, 1947; came to U.S., 1952; s. Stephen James and Elizabeth (Barbier) C.; m. Kathleen Sakala, Oct. 12, 1974 (div. 1980); m. Mary A. Reischmann, 1984. B.A., Hobart Coll., 1970; student Hebrew U., 1969. Counselor, asst. to pres. Kingsborough Coll., N.Y.C., 1970-72; pres. Lutetia Prodns., 1972-75; dir. ships and piers South Street Seaport, 1975-76; sales and purchasing mgr. Ross Yacht, Clearwater, Fla., 1976; mgr. R.B. Grove, 1977—; pres. Illusion Yachts, 1984—. Home: 835A E Gulf Blvd Indian Rocks Beach FL 33535 Office: 3862 E Bay Dr 244 Largo FL 33541

CAMPBELL, STEPHEN LAVERN, mathematics educator, researcher; b. Belle Plaine, Iowa, Dec. 8, 1945; B.A., Dartmouth Coll., 1967; M.S., Northwestern U., 1968, Ph.D., 1972. Asst. prof. N.C. State U., Raleigh, 1972-76, assoc. prof., 1976-81, prof. math., 1981—. Author: Singular Systems of Differential Equations, 1980, Singular Systems of Differential Equations II, 1982; Generalized Inverses of Linear Transformations, 1979; author research papers. Editor: Recent Applications of Generalized Inverses, 1982; editorial bd. Linear Algebra and Its Applications, 1982-83. Research grantee NSF, Air Force Office Sci. Research. Mem. Soc. Indsl. and Applied Math. (editorial bd. Jour. of Algebraic and Discrete Methods 1983—). Office: Dept Math Box 8205 NC State Univ Raleigh NC 27695-8205

CAMPBELL, THOMAS CORWITH, economics educator, researcher, administrator; b. Manquin, Va., Mar. 19, 1920; s. Thomas Corwith and Pearl (Gravatt) C.; m. Martha Burdine Gordon, Apr. 17, 1943; children—Thomas III, Gordon. A.B., Lynchburg Coll., 1942; M.A., U. Pitts., 1947, Ph.D., 1948. Prof. W.Va. U., Morgantown, 1948-80, dean coll. bus. and econs., 1964-68; prof. Va. Commonwealth U., 1980—; econ. adviser Govt. of Kenya, Nairobi, 1966-70; economist part-time U.S. Bur. Mines, 1947-77, U.S. Dept. Energy, 1978-80. Chmn. Gov.'s Council Econ. Advisers, Charleston, W.Va., 1968-70; mem. Morgantown Planning Commn., 1978-80, Charleston Regional Export Expansion Council, 1966-80. Served to capt. USNR, 1942-46. Recipient U.S. Dept. Transp. research contract, 1978-80. Mem. Am. Econ. Assn., AAUP. Mem. Christian Ch. Contbr. articles to profl. jours. Home: 4014 Fauquier Ave Richmond VA 23227 Office: Dept Econs Va Commonwealth U 1015 Floyd Ave Richmond VA 23284

CAMPBELL, THOMAS DOUGLAS, lawyer, consultant, real estate developer; b. N.Y.C., Jan. 5, 1951; s. Edward Thomas and Dorothy Alice (Moore) C.; m. Mary Anne Campbell, Dec. 22, 1978; 1 dau., Kristen Anne. B.A., U. Del., 1972; J.D., U. Pa., 1976. Bar: Del. 1977. Law clk. Law Offices Bayard Brill & Handleman, Wilmington, Del., 1974-77; Washington rep. Standard Oil Co. (Ind.), 1978-85; pres. Thomas D. Campbell & Assocs., Inc., 1985—; govt. affairs rep. Northeastern U.S., Standard Oil Co. Ind., 1977-78; campaign cons. campaign steering coms. for congressional and senatorial campaigns. Served with U.S. Army, 1968-69, USAF, 1969-77. Mem. ABA, Del. Bar Assn., World Affairs Council, Nat. Trust for Historic Preservation, Phi Beta Kappa, Phi Kappa Phi, Omicron Delta Epsilon, Omicron Delta Kappa. Republican. Episcopalian. Home and office: 517 Queen St Alexandria VA 22314

CAMPBELL, THOMAS MARK, oil company executive, energy consultant; b. Lansdown, Pa., Mar. 14, 1942; s. Thomas J.J. and Mary (Johnson) C.; m. Melva F. Espana, Aug. 2, 1977; children—Marisol, Vanessa, Thomas Moises, Penelope. B.S. in Geology, Villanova U., 1964; Ph.D., U. N.C., 1967. Geophysicist, Aero Service Corp., Phila., 1967-71; mgr. McPhar Geophysics, Toronto, Ont., Can., 1971-73; owner, cons. Consulgesa, Guatemala, 1973-80; sr. scientist S.W. Research Inst., San Antonio, 1980-82; pres. Poza Rico Co., Inc., San Antonio, 1982—; cons. Geosurvey Internat., Nairobi, Kenya, 1976-77; acting gen. mgr. Minas San Cristobal, El Salvador, 1979; cons. Norsk Hydro, Oslo, Norway, 1982, Petro Fina, Brussels, Belgium, 1983. Designer in field. Inventor in field. Adv., Consejo Mcpl., PTO, Ayacucho, Venezuela, 1971, Cook Inlet Native Peoples' Assn., Anchorage, 1975, West Lake Master Water Plan, D'Doma, Tanzania, 1977; mediator Nat. Fedn. Mine Workers, El Salvador, 1979. Mem. Am. Assn. Petroleum Geologists, South Tex. Geol. Soc., Soc. Exploration Geophysicists, European Assn. Exploration Geophysicists, San Antonio Geophys. Soc. Roman Catholic. Avocations: hiking; physical fitness: family travel; economics. Home: 5606 Ridge Run San Antonio TX 78250 Office: Pozo Rico Co Inc 5606 Ridge Run San Antonio TX 78250

CAMPBELL, VERNON DEENE, wire products company executive; b. Ft. Smith, Ark., June 24, 1944; s. Johnnie Vernon and Effie Tabitha (Dean) C.; m. Susan Kay Griffin, June 14, 1964; children—Eric Dean, Aaron David, Sean Allen. Student U. Ark., 1962-63; degree in advanced electricity O.T. Autry Vocat.-Tech. Sch., Enid, Okla., 1966; degree in emergency med. tech. Ark. Valley Vocat.-Tech. Sch., Ozark, Ark., 1982. Ordained to ministry Assemblies of God Ch., 1971. Technician, Okla. Gas & Electric Co., Enid, 1963-68, Serv-Air Inc., Vance AFB, Enid, 1968-69; mgr. die cast div. Gen. Electric Co., Ft. Smith, Ark., 1969; plant engr. Spalding Inc., Ft. Smith, 1970-75; plant engr. So. Steel & Wire Co., Ft. Smith, 1975-82, plant mgr., 1982—; pastor Assembly of God Ch., Van Buren, Ark., 1977—. Mem. pretreatment com. City of Ft. Smith; mem. adv. trustee bd. Sparks Regional Med. Ctr.; chmn. bd. dirs. Sebastian County chpt. ARC, 1979—, dist. chmn., 1976—; instr. first aid and instr. trainer CPR, ARC, 1972—. Recipient gold medal award Nat. Sports Found., 1974; Outstanding Service award Polk County chpt. ARC, 1980, Sebastian County chpt., 1980; Clara Barton award ARC, 1984. Mem. Ark. Fedn. Water and Air Users (bd. dirs., mem. hazardous waste mgmt. task force), West Ark. Pilots Assn. Republican. Home: PO Box 384 1108 22d St Barling AR 72923 Office: PO Box 6537 3501 S Tulsa St Fort Smith AR 72906

CAMPBELL, WALTER MALCOLM, investment counselor, economic consultant; b. Toledo, Ohio, Nov. 25, 1931; s. Walter Miner and Ethel Cora (Schmide) C.; m. Jacqueline Adel Hoover, June 11, 1960; children—Douglas Malcolm, Cameron Elizabeth, Charles Walter. B.S., Bowling Green U., 1957; M.Bus., U. Ky., 1959. Chartered fin. analyst; chartered investment counselor. Investment officer Brown Bros. Harriman, Chgo., 1960-67; mng. prin. Drexel, Harriman, Ripley, Chgo., 1967-70; sr. v.p. Jefferson Nat. Life, Indpls., 1970-72; v.p. Montag & Caldwell, Atlanta, 1973-79; pres. Piedmont Capital Mgmt., Atlanta, 1979 ; cons. Nat. Assoc. Life Co., Atlanta, 1979 ; mem. investment adv. com. Life Office Mgmt., Atlanta, 1983—. Contbr. articles to profl. jours. Served with USN, 1951-55. Fellow Fin. Analysts Fedn.; mem. Atlanta Fin. Analysts, Inst. Chartered Fin. Analysts, Nat. Assn. Life Cos., Investment Counsel Assn. Am. (assoc.). Republican. Avocations: reading; golf; swimming. Office: Piedmont Capital Mgmt Assn 3312 Piedmont Rd Suite 320 Atlanta GA 30305

CAMPBELL, WANDA EVANELL, accountant; b. Santa Anna, Tex., Mar. 21, 1931; d. William C. and Golda A. (Griffith) Price; ed. Santa Anna public schs., LaSalle Bus. Coll., corr. courses Tex. Tech U.; m. Billy John Campbell, Aug. 14, 1948; 1 son, Donnie Lynn. Acct., N.W. Purcell Public Acct., Coleman, Tex., 1964-68; acct. A.T. Kramer, Wichita Falls, Tex., 1968; acct., tax acct., office mgr. Jordan & Scherer C.P.A.s, 1968-80; acct., tax acct., controller, supr. acctg. dept. Inter Systems Corp., Dallas, also pvt. practice tax acctg., 1980—; treas. InterSystems Corp. Enrolled agt., IRS. Mem. Nat. Soc. Public Accts., Nat. Soc. Notaries. Home: 1829 Clark Trail Grand Prairie TX 75052 Office: 9900 N Central St Dallas TX 75231

CAMPBELL, WILLIAM EDWARD, valuation consultant; economist; b. Elgin, Tex., Sept. 16, 1946; s. William Edward and Edyth Pauline (Johnson) C.; m. Pamela S. Moody, Sept. 2, 1967 (div. Mar. 1973); 1 son, Colin Scott; m. Julie Elizabeth Bunge, Apr. 3, 1982. B.A. in Econs., Tex. A&M U., 1970, M.B.A. in Mgmt., 1971. Grad. asst. Tex. A&M U., College Station, 1970; instr. in econs. Galveston Coll. (Tex.), 1971-73; mgr., regional economist First City Bancorp., Houston, 1974-78; economist RPC, Inc., Austin, Tex., 1978-79; account rep. ADP Network Services, Houston, 1979-80; mgr. Profit Techs. Corp., Houston, 1980-81; investment broker Prudential-Bache Securities, Houston, 1981-85; valuation cons. Marshall and Stevens, Houston, 1985—; cons. economist to pvt. investors, Galveston, 1972-74. Author: Geopressured-Geothermal Economic and Financial Evaluation, 1979; author, originator ann. booklet: Inside Texas, An Economic Prospective, 1974-78; co-author Financial Facts newsletter, 1974-78; contbr. numerous articles to profl. jours. Bd. dirs. Loft-On-Strand Art Gallery, Galveston, 1974-76. Mem. Nat. Assn. Bus. Economists, Houston Mus. Fine Arts. Club: Galveston Yacht. Home: 1849 Marshall Apt 28 Houston TX 77098 Office: Marshall and Stevens 1300 Hercules Suite 110 Houston TX 77058

CAMPBELL, WILLIAM J., judge; b. Chgo., Mar. 19, 1905; s. John and Christina (Larsen) C.; grad. St. Rita Coll. Prep. Sch., 1922; J.D., Loyola U., 1926, LL.M., 1928, LL.D., 1955, Litt.D., 1965, J.C.D., 1967; m. Marie Agnes Cloherty, 1937; children—Marie Agnes (Mrs. Walter J. Cummings), Karen (Mrs. James T. Reid), Roxane (Mrs. Wesley Sedlacek), William J., Christian, Thomas. Admitted to Ill. bar, 1927; Ill. adminstr. Nat. Youth Adminstrn., 1935-38; U.S. dist. atty. No. Dist. of Ill., 1938-40; judge U.S. Dist. Ct., 1940—, chief judge, 1959-70; asst. dir. Fed. Jud. Center, Washington, 1974—. Mem. citizens bd. U. Chgo., Loyola U., Barat Coll. of Sacred Heart; bd. dirs. Catholic Charities Chgo.; co-founder Cath. Youth Orgn. Chgo., 1930; mem. exec. bd. Chgo. council, also nat. exec. bd. Boy Scouts Am. Mem. Am. Bar Assn., Ill. Bar Assn., Chgo. Bar Assn., Fed. Bar Assn., Jud. Conf. U.S. (chmn. com. on budget 1955-69). Clubs: Law, Ill. Athletic, Union League, Standard (Chgo.); La Coquille (Manalapan, Fla.). Home: 400 S Ocean Blvd Villa 305-A Manalapan FL 33462 Office: 401 Fed Bldg 701 Clematis St West Palm Beach FL 33401

CAMPER, NYAL DWIGHT, plant physiology educator; b. Lynchburg, Va., May 12, 1939; s. Herbert Nyal and Grace Irene (Leedy) C.; m. Margaret Jane Bratton, Feb. 23, 1946; children—Shea Lynn, Britney Dawn. B.S., N.C. State U., 1962, Ph.D., 1967. Asst. prof. dept. plant pathology and physiology Clemson U. (S.C.), 1966-71, assoc. prof., 1971-77, prof., 1977—. NSF grantee, 1968-70; U.S. Dept. Agr. grantee, 1976-79, 83-85; Water Resources Inst. grantee, 1976-79; Cotton Ins. grantee, 1972-75. Mem. Am. Soc. Plant Physiologists, Am. Chem. Soc., Weed Sci. Soc. Am., Internat. Assn. for Plant Tissue Culture, Sigma Xi. Contbr. articles to profl. jours. Office: Dept of Plant Pathology & Physiol Clemson U Clemson SC 29631

CANARINA, OPAL JEAN, nurse, administrator, educator, consultant, lecturer; b. Geneva County, Ala., Mar. 21, 1936; d. O. Lee and L. Ellen (Box) Peacock; m. Miles Steven Bajcar, June 27, 1953 (div.); children—Debra Lynn-Wilson; Wayne Steven; m. Arnold R. Canarina, June 19, 1965; children—Catherine Mary, Christopher John, Charles Benjamin. B.S.N. summa cum laude, George Mason U., Fairfax, Va., 1976, M.S.N., Vanderbilt U., 1981. R.N., Va., Tenn., Okla., Utah, Ky. Staff and charge nurse Georgetown U. Hosp., Washington, 1976; charge nurse ob-gyn Vanderbilt U. Hosp., Nashville, 1976-77; charge nurse labor and delivery service Baptist Hosp., Nashville, 1977-80; asst. prof. dept. baccalaureate nursing Austin Peay State U., Clarksville, Tenn., 1981-83; dir. nursing services Meml. Hosp., Guymon, Okla., 1983-85; dir. women's ctr./maternal-child nursing McKay-Dee Hosp. Ctr., Ogden, Utah, 1985—; cons. to middle Tenn. area health and nursing issues. Recipient cert. of excellence R.N.s on campus George Mason U., 1976. Mem. Tenn. Nurses Assn. (legis. chmn. dist. 13, 1982—, pres. 1982), Va. Nurses Assn. (Student Nurse of Yr. award 1975), Am. Nurses Assn., Am. Nurses Found., Nurses Assn. Coll. Ob-Gyn, Sigma Theta Tau, Alpha Chi.

CANCHOLA, DENISE ANN, nurse; b. San Antonio, Apr. 7, 1955; d. Oscar S. and Gabriela (Garza) C. B.A. in Biology, Trinity U., 1977; M.S.N. in Adult Psychiatry, Yale U., 1981. Lab. technician San Antonio State Hosp., 1978; clinician Conn. Community Mental Health, New Haven, 1981; charge nurse Med. Pool, San Antonio, 1981-82, Villa Rosa Hosp., San Antonio, 1982; head nurse Highland Park Hosp., Miami, Fla., 1982-83; aftercare coordinator North Miami Community Mental Health Ctr. Mem. Nat. Hispanic Nurse's Assn. (lectr. 1981—), Am. Nurses Assn. Democrat. Roman Catholic. Office: North Miami Community Mental Health Ctr 9400 NW 12th Ave Miami FL 33150

CANDLER, DAVID EDWARD, aircraft leasing company executive, accountant; b. Takoma Park, Md., Sept. 8, 1943; s. Coye Snivery and Frances Odelle (Hudson) C.; m. Connie Rae Campbell, May 12, 1969; children—Michelle Anne, Christina Marie. B.C.S. with honors, Benjamin Franklin U., 1967; M.B.A. with honors, Loyola Coll., Balt., 1980. C.P.A., Md. Acct. various firms, Washington and Md., 1965-71; dir., chief fin. officer Onmi Investment Corp., Washington, 1971-74; dir., exec. v.p. Advanced Air Concepts, Inc., Balt., 1974-75; with Fairchild Industries, Inc., Germantown, Md., 1975-81; v.p. contracts and fin. services Fairchild Aircraft Corp., San Antonio, 1981-84; v.p. Fairchild Credit Corp., Germantown, Md., 1981-84, Metro Credit Corp., Germantown, 1982-84; v.p. air transp. PLM Transp. Equipment Corp., San Francisco and San Antonio, 1984—. Mem. Am. Inst. C.P.A.s, Md. Assn. C.P.A.s, Benjamin Franklin U. Alumni Assn. Republican. Baptist. Office: PLM Transportation Equipment Corp 45 NE Loop 410 Suite 840 San Antonio TX 78216

CANDLER, JOHN SLAUGHTER, II, lawyer; b. Atlanta, Nov. 30, 1908; s. Asa Warren and Harriet Lee (West) C.; m. Dorothy Bruce Warthen, June 13, 1933; children—Dorothy Warthen (Mrs. Joseph W. Hamilton, Jr.), John Slaughter. A.B. magna cum laude, U. Ga., 1929; J.D., Emory U., 1931. Bar: Ga. 1931. Partner Candler, Cox & Andrews and other firms, 1931—; dir. Leon Propane, Inc., Weatherly Corp., The D.M. Weatherly Co., Sungas, Inc., others; dep. asst. atty. gen. State of Ga., 1951-68. Mem. Greater Atlanta Council USO, 1969—, exec. com., 1970-79, pres., 1974-75; trustee Ga. Student Ednl. Fund; trustee Kappa Alpha Scholarship Fund, pres., 1970-72. Served from capt. to col. USAR, 1941-46. Decorated Commendation Ribbon. Fellow Am. Coll. Probate Counsel (regent 1968-74), Internat. Acad. Law and Sci., Ga. Bar Found.; mem. Nat. Tax Assn.-Tax Inst. Am. (Tax Inst. Am. adv. council 1969-72), Newcomen Soc., Am. Judicature Soc., State Bar Ga. (chmn. sect. fiduciary law 1964-65), ABA, Atlanta Bar Assn., Internat. Platform Assn., Atlanta Estate Planning Council (pres. 1963-64), Lawyers Club of Atlanta, Am. Legion (post comdr. 1949-50), Res. Officers Assn. U.S. (state pres. 1946, nat. exec. com. 1947), Mil. Order World Wars, English-Speaking Union, U.S. Power Squadrons, Phi Beta Kappa, Phi Kappa Phi, Phi Delta Phi, Kappa Alpha Order, Sigma Delta Chi. Episcopalian (vestryman 1953-56, sr. warden, 1955, cathedral trustee 1957-67, Lay reader 1971—). Clubs: Masons, Kiwanis, Atlanta Touchdown, Piedmont Driving, Capital City, Commerce, Peachtree Racket, Ft. McPherson Officers; Oglethorpe (Savannah); Army-Navy (Washington). Home: 413 Manor Ridge Dr NW Atlanta GA 30305 Office: 610 Eight Piedmont Center 3525 Piedmont Rd NE Atlanta GA 30305

CANDOLL, I. CARL, educational administrator. Supt. of schs. Ft. Worth. Office: 3210 W Lancaster Fort Worth TX 76107*

CANFIELD, CHARLES ROBERT, bookstore director; b. Elkins, W.Va., Jan. 29, 1933; s. Ceriel Leon and Margaret Susan (Wickwire) C.; m. Juanita Mae Long, Feb. 22, 1953; children—Melody Ann, Phyllis Rae, Charlene Roberta, Margaret LaVonne. B.S. in Mktg., Am. U., 1966. Bookstore mgr. George Washington U., Washington, 1963-66, U. Alta., Edmonton, Can., 1966-68; mdse. mgr. U. R.I., Kingstown, 1969-73; student union dir. Rensselaer Poly. Inst., Troy, N.Y., 1973-79; dir. bookstores U. Miami, Coral Gables, Fla., 1979—. Pres. Cosmopolitan Internat., Edmonton, 1968. Mem. Nat. Assn. Coll Stores (officer, trustee, 1984—, mgmt. seminar faculty, 1981-84, regional speaker, 1983, chmn. fin. survey com. 1983-84), Fla. Assn. Coll. Stores (pres. 1983). Served with USN, 1952-56. Democrat. Lodge: Lions. Avocations: golf; bowling; sailing; swimming. Home: 6706 SW 113th Ct Miami FL 33173 Office: U Miami Bookstore PO Box 8086 Coral Gables FL 33124

CANGEMI, JOSEPH PETER, psychology educator, consultant; b. Syracuse, N.Y., June 26, 1936; s. Samuel and Marion Cangemi; m. Amelia Santalo, Oct. 6, 1962; children—Michelle M., Lisa Anne. B.S., SUNY-Oswego, 1959; M.S., Syracuse U., 1964; Ed.D., Ind. U., 1974. Instr., adminstr. Syracuse Pub. Schs., 1959-60, 61-64, Carol Morgan Sch., Santo Domingo, Dominican Republic, 1960-61; staff indsl. relations Orinoco Mining div. U.S. Steel Corp., Puerto Ordaz, Venezuela, 1965-68; from asst. prof. to assoc. prof. psychology Western Ky. U., Bowling Green, 1968-78, prof., 1979—; cons. various U.S. and fgn. corps. Decorated by Govt. State of Santander (Colombia); recipient Excellence in Teaching award Coll. Edn. Western Ky. U., 1979, award Firestone Tire & Rubber Co., 1981, Dayton Tire & Rubber Co., 1982, Disting. Pub. Service award Western Ky. U., 1983, Disting. Alumnus award SUNY-Oswego, 1983. Mem. Am. Personnel and Guidance Assn., Nat. Vocat. Guidance Assn., Acad. Mgmt., Interam. Soc. Psychology, Internat. Council Psychologists. Club: Bowling Green Country. Author: Higher Education and the Development of Self-Actualizing Personalities, 1977; Effective Management-A Humanistic Perspective, 1980; Higher Education in the United State and Latin America, 1982; La Generencia Participativa (Colombia), 1983; Perspectives in Higher Education, 1983; Participative Management, 1984. Editor: Psychology: A Quar. Jour. of Human Behavior, 1977—; Jour. Human Behavior and Learning, 1983—; Orgn. Devel. Jour., 1983—. Home: 1305 Woodhurst Dr Bowling Green KY 42101 Office: Psychology Dept Western Ky U Bowling Green KY 42101

CANIPE, STEPHEN LEE, educational administrator; b. Lincolnton, N.C., Jan. 9, 1946; s. Clayton Lee and Edna Jeanette (Farmer) C.; B.S. in Biology cum laude, Appalachian State U., 1968; M.S. in Biology (NSF fellow), Mich. State U., 1973; Ed.D. in Ednl. Adminstrn., Duke U., 1982; m. Sharon Wilbourne, Apr. 1, 1972; children—Martha Murray, David Jacob. Lab. asst. USPHS, Savannah, Ga., 1968-69; tchr. high sch. biology Charlotte, N.C., 1969-76, asst. prin., 1976-77; N.C. sci. cons., Raleigh, 1977-78; supr. ednl. services Duke Power Co., Charlotte, N.C., 1978-79, dir. employee communications, 1979-81, dir. adminstrn. and devel., 1981-83; prin. West Lincoln Sr. High Sch., Lincolnton, N.C., 1983—; instr. Central Piedmont Community Coll., 1976-78; adj. prof. Gaston Coll., 1984—; cons. Project ALIVE, 1979-81. Charter mem. Metrolina Environ. Concern Assn., 1970-77; mem. mayor's energy adv. com., 1979. Mem. Internat. Assn. Bus. Communicators, Carolinas Assn. Bus. Communicators, Assn. for Supervision and Curriculum Devel., Public Relations Soc. Am., Phi Delta Kappa, Kappa Delta Pi, Beta Beta Beta. Episcopalian. Club: Rotary. Author: Valuing the Environment, 1975: High School Animal Behavior, 1977. Home: 115 Fox Run Denver NC 28037 Office: Route 1 Box 363 Lincolnton NC 28092

CANN, SHARON LEE, health science librarian; b. Ft. Riley, Kans., Aug. 14, 1935; d. Roman S. and Cora Elon (George) Foote; m. Donald Clair Cann, May 16, 1964. Student Sophia U., Tokyo, 1955-57; B.A. Sacramento (Calif.) State U., 1959; M.S.L.S., Atlanta U., 1977. cert. health scis. librarian. Recreation worker ARC, Korea, Morocco, France, 1960-64; shelflister Library Congress Washington, 1967-69; tchr. lang. Ctr., Taipei, Taiwan, 1971-73; library tech. asst. Emory U., Atlanta, 1974-76; health sci. librarian Northside Hosp., Atlanta, 1977-85; librarian Area Health Edn. Ctr.'s Learning Resources Ctr., Morehouse Sch. Medicine Multi-Media Ctr., Atlanta, 1985—; library cons., 1985—. Editor Update, publ. Ga. Health Sis. Library Assn., 1981; contbr. articles to publs. Chmn. Calif. Christian Youth in Govt Seminar, 1958. Named Alumni Top Twenty, Sacramento State U., 1959. Mem. ALA, Med. Library Assn., Spl. Library Assn. (dir. South Atlantic chpt. 1985), Ga. Library Assn. (spl. library div. chmn. 1983-85), Ga. Health Scis. Library Assn. (chmn. 1981-82), Atlanta Health Sci. Library (chmn. 1979), Am. Numis. Assn. Club: Toastmasters (Atlanta) sec.-treas. 1983-84). Home: 5520 Morning Creek Circle College Park GA 30349 Office: 720 Westview Dr SW Atlanta GA 30314

CANNADY, WILLIAM TILLMAN, architect, educator; b. Houston, Oct. 12, 1937; s. Henry Hillard and Mary Elizabeth (Cummins) C.; m. Mollie Rehmet, Sept. 10, 1966; children—Sarah Katherine, Lucinda O'Neill. B.Arch., U. Calif.-Berkeley, 1961; M.Arch., Harvard U., 1962; postgrad. U. London, 1970. Mem. team Progressive Design Assocs., Cambridge, Mass., 1961-62; project designer Mario Ciampi, FAIA, San Francisco, 1962-63; planner Lawrence Lacke, AIA, Knorr & Elliot, AIA Associated Architects, San Francisco, 1963; project designer Airport Architects, Goleman & Rolfe, Pierce & Pierce, Houston, 1963-64; mem. faculty Rice U. Sch. Architecture, Houston, from 1964, then prof.; sole practice William Cannady, AIA, Architects and Planners, Houston, 1965-68; design group leader Caudill Rowlett Scott, Houston, 1968-69; design cons. Llewelyn-Davies, Weeks, Forestier-Walker, and Bor, London, 1970; v.p. Omniplan Inc., Houston, Dallas, 1970-72; pres. William T. Cannady & Assocs. Inc., Houston, 1972—; vis. lectr., critic in architecture to numerous univs. Served with USMC Res., 1955-62. Recipient of numerous awards for excellence in architecture. Fellow AIA (juror); mem. Houston Philos. Soc. (treas. 1981-82, v.p., 1982-83). Republican. Episcopalian. Club: Faculty (Rice U.); Round Top Rifle Assn.; Houston City. Contbr. articles to profl. jours. and lectr. to profl. confs. Home: 2246 Quenby Houston TX 77005 Office: 2403 Sunset Houston TX 77005

CANNON, HUGH, lawyer; b. Albemarle, N.C., Oct. 11, 1931; s. Hubert Napoleon and Nettie (Harris) C.; A.B., Davidson Coll., 1953; B.A. (Rhodes scholar) Oxford U., 1955, M.A., 1960; LL.B., Harvard U., 1958; m. Lorrie Clark, July 17, 1979; children by previous marriage—John Stuart, Marshall, Martha Janet. Admitted to N.C. bar, 1958, D.C. bar, 1978, S.C. bar, 1979; mem. staff U. N.C. Inst. Govt., Chapel Hill, 1959; mem. firm Sanford, Phillips, McCoy & Weaver, Fayetteville, 1960; asst. to Gov. of N.C., Raleigh, 1961; dir. adminstrn. State of N.C., 1962-65, state budget officer, 1963; mem. firm Sanford, Cannon, Adams & McCullough, Raleigh, 1965-79; individual practice law, Charleston, S.C., 1979—. Parliamentarian NEA, 1965—; lectr. N.C. State U., Raleigh, part-time, 1965, 66. State dir. N.C. Emergency Resources Planning Com., 1962-65; pres. Friends of Coll., Raleigh, 1963; alt. del. Democratic Nat. Conv., 1964; chief parliamentarian, 1976, 80, 84; bd. govs. U. N.C., 1972-81; trustee Davidson Coll., 1966-74. Mem. Phi Beta Kappa, Omicron Delta Kappa, Phi Gamma Delta. Democrat. Episcopalian. Home: 32 Murray Blvd Charleston SC 29401 Office: 1625 Savannah Hwy Charleston SC 29407

CANNON, JAMES RUSSELL, educator; b. Trenton, Tenn., Apr. 10, 1927; s. Ree Clinton and Opal Mai (Hassell) C.; m. Betty Jean Bowen, July 24, 1949; children—Sherry Lynn, Patricia Ann, Cathy Jean. B.S., Bethel Coll., 1953; M.A., Memphis State Coll., 1956; postgrad. Purdue U., 1957, Vanderbilt U., 1959, Middle Tenn. State U., 1970-71. Tchr., asst. prin. Dyersberg High Sch., Tenn., 1953-56; math. specialist Tenn. Dept. Edn., Nashville, 1959-67, adminstr., 1967-73, asst. commr., 1973-75, dir., 1975-82, asst. to commr., 1982—; v.p. State Suprs. Math. Exec. com. Davidson County Republican Party, Nashville, 1982—. Served with USN, 1945-46. Baptist. Club: Rotary (bd. dirs.). Lodge: Masons. Avocations: hunting; aviation. Home: 3001 Melody Ln Nashville TN 37214 Office: State Dept Edn 1150 Menzler Rd Nashville TN 37210

CANNON, JESSE DEES, JR., architect, urban designer; b. Portsmouth, Va., Oct. 11, 1947; s. Jesse Dees and Constance (Paradiso) C. B.Arch., La. State U., 1972. Registered architect. Archtl. draftsman Mathes, Bergman, New Orleans, 1976-77; architect Audubon Constrn. Corp., New Orleans, 1977-79; architect Archtl. Planning & Design, New Orleans, 1979-80; dir. planning GGS Cons., Ltd., Metairie, La., 1980-82; owner, prin. Jesse Cannon Assocs., Metairie, La., 1982—. Mem. Vieux Carré Commn., New Orleans, 1985-86; bd. dirs. Pharm. Mus. Served with USN, 1968-69: Vietnam. Mem. AIA (Outstanding Service award New Orleans 1982, honor award for design 1986, chpt. pres.-elect 1986, chpt. pres. 1987), La. Architects Assn., New Orleans C. of C., Preservation Resource Ctr., New Orleans, Nat. Trust Hist. Preservation, Soc. Am. Mil. Engrs., Res. Officers Assn., Naval Res. Assn., U.S. Naval C.E. Corps.

Democrat. Roman Catholic. Office: 1540 Chickasaw Ave #102 Metairie LA 70005

CANNON, LUCINDA SAMFORD, civic worker; b. Opelika, Ala., Apr. 7, 1947; d. William James and Evlyn (Barnett) Samford; student Wesleyan Coll., Macon, Ga., 1965-68; B.S., Auburn U., 1969, M.Ed., 1971; 1 son, Edmund Rasha. Tchr., Brookwood Forest Elem. Sch., Mountain Brook, Ala., 1971-73, Julius T. Wright Sch. for Girls, Mobile, Ala., 1973-74; sales agt. Metcalf Realty Co., Inc., Birmingham, Ala., 1978—; vol. U. Ala. at Birmingham Hosp., 1971-73; circle chmn. Dauphin Way United Methodist Ch., Mobile, 1975-77; jr. bd. dirs. Florence Crittendon Home for Unwed Mothers, Mobile, 1975-77; bd. dirs. Art Patrons League, Mobile, 1975-77, Christian Women's Club, Mobile, 1975-77; circle chmn. Canterbury United Meth. Ch., Birmingham, 1979-80, mem. Family Life Council, 1981—, sec. adminstrv. bd., 1984-85; mem. arrangement com. North Ala. United Meth. Conf.; mem. exec. bd. Jefferson County (Ala.) Auburn Club, 1980—, publicity chmn., 1983, treas., 1984, sec., 1985; treas. Salvation Army Aux., Birmingham, 1981—; mem. ladies' com. Hall of Fame Bowl, Birmingham, 1981—; mem. Ala. Space Sci. Exhibit Commn., 1981—; chmn. U.S. Space Camp Com., 1982—. Mem. Birmingham Bd. Realtors, Service Guild Birmingham, Friends of Emmet-O'Neal Library, Kappa Kappa Gamma (sec. alumnae 1979—). Clubs: Bordeaux Dance, Birmingham Stallions Booster. Home: 3920 Forest Ave Birmingham AL 35213

CANNON, MARY EVELYN, school nurse; b. Meridian, Miss., Sept. 2, 1949; d. Hassel Dearing and Evelyn Ruth (Taylor) Wade; m. William Auston Cannon, July 5, 1968; 1 son, William Christopher. A.A.S., Hinds Jr. Coll., 1977. Registered nurse, Miss., La. Staff nurse St. Charles Hosp., Newellton, La., 1968-79; gen. migrant sch. nurse Tensas Parish Sch. Bd., St. Joseph, La., 1979—; spl. edn. adv. council mem., St. Joseph, La., 1983-85, assessment team mem., 1979—. Pres. Parent Adv. Council, Newellton, 1981-82; pres. Newellton High Sch. Band Boosters; v.p. Dist. Adv. Council, St. Joseph, 1982-83. Mem. La. Sch. Nurse Orgn., Nat. Assn. Sch. Nurses. Democrat. Home: PO Box 206 Newellton LA 71357

CANNON, RONALD EDGAR, association executive; b. Beaumont, Tex., Feb. 12, 1926; s. Adron D. and Nora (Hairston) C.; m. Ruth Womack, Nov. 15, 1945; children—Scott, Kathleen. B.S. in Mech. Engring., La. Tech. U., 1948. Registered profl. engr., Tex. Engr. Gulf Oil Corp., Port Arthur, Tex., 1948-56; tech. editor McGraw Hill Pub. Co., Houston, 1956-57; exec. dir. Gas Processors Assn., Tulsa, 1957—, recipient Hanlon award, 1982. Editor: Engineering Data Book, 1972. Served to lt. USNR, 1943-46. PTO. Mem. ASTM (sub-com. officer), Internat. Standards Orgn. (work group chmn.). Republican. Office: Gas Processors Association 1812 First Pl Tulsa OK 74103

CANONICO, DOMENIC ANDREW, engineering company executive; b. Chgo., Jan. 18, 1930; s. Angelo Anthony and Anna (Contratto) C.; m. Colleen Margaret Jennings, Aug. 27, 1955; children—Judith Canonico Asreen, Mary Carol, Angelo Edward, Domenic Michael, Catherine Ann. B.S. in Metall. Engring., Mich. Tech. U., 1951; M.S. in Metall. Engring., Lehigh U., 1961, Ph.D. in Metall. Engring., 1963. Group leader Pressure Vessel Tech. Lab., Metals and Ceramics Div., Oak Ridge Nat. Lab. (Union Carbide Corp.), Oak Ridge, 1965-81; dir. Metall. & Materials Lab. Combustion Engring., Inc., Chattanooga, 1981—; lectr., cons., researcher in field. Served with the USAF, 1952-53; Korea. Fellow Am. Soc. Metals; mem. ASME (mem. main com. boiler and pressure vessel code), Am. Welding Soc. (Lincoln Gold Medal 1980, Disting. Service award NE sect. 1978, Rene D. Wasserman award 1977, Adams lectr. 1983), Sigma Xi. Roman Catholic. Club: Walden (Chattanooga). Home: 3 Big Rock Rd Signal Mountain TN 37377 Office: 911 West Main St Chattanooga TN 37402

CANOPARI, GERALD EUGENE, banker; b. Hartford, Conn., Mar. 13, 1944; s. Mario Louis and Mary (Filmore) C.; m. Donna Ann Skiba, Sept. 20, 1965 (div. June 1981); children—Gina Lynn, Lisa Lynn. B.S.B.A., U. Hartford, 1966; M.B.A., U. Tampa, 1979. Security analyst Hartford Nat. Bank & Trust, 1966-68; br. mgr. New Britain Bank & Trust, Conn., 1968-69; registered rep. Shearson Lehmen Bros., Hartford, 1969-71; investment mgr. First Nat. Bank, Clearwater, Fla., 1971—; instr. Fla. Trust Sch., Gainsville, 1976—, sch. dir., 1984-85; instr. St. Petersburg Jr. Coll., Clearwater, 1973-83. Chmn. Suncoast YMCA Investment Com., Clearwater, 1985—. Mem. Central Fla. Soc. Fin. Analysts (charter). Republican. Roman Catholic. Avocations: woodworking; deep sea fishing. Home: 1429 Forest Rd Clearwater FL 33515 Office: First Nat Bank Clearwater 400 Cleveland St Clearwater FL 33515

CANTOR, IRVIN VICTOR, lawyer; b. Richmond, Va., June 9, 1953; s. Leo Joseph and Mary Frances (Cohen) C. B.S., U. Va., 1975, J.D., 1978. Bar: Va. 1978. Law clk. Va. Supreme Ct., Richmond, 1978-79; ptnr. firm Rilee, Cantor, Arkema, Edmonds, Richmond, 1979—; ptnr. World Class, Inc., Richmond, 1983—. Bd. dirs. Richmond Tennis Patrons, Tennis Found. Richmond, Historic Richmond Found. Zeta Beta Tau Nat. Found. scholar, 1973. Mem. Va. Bar Assn., Richmond Bar Assn., Va. Trial Lawyers, Richmond Trial Lawyers, U.S. Tennis Assn., U. Va. Alumni Assn. Clubs: Bull and Bear, Westwood Racquet. Office: 1011 E Main St Richmond VA 23219

CANTRELL, WESLEY E., SR., office equipment company executive; b. 1935. Student, So. Inst. Tech. With Lanier Business Products, Inc., 1955—, v.p., 1966-72, exec. v.p., 1972-77, pres., dir. 1977—. Address: Lanier Business Products Inc 1700 Chantilly Dr Atlanta GA 30324*

CANTY, HOLLY MERRILL, police polygraph examiner; b. Alexandria, Va., Nov. 17, 1952; d. Vernon Elbert and Mary (Chapura) Hicks; m. Henry Canty; children—Mary Stefana, Edna Kristin. A.A., No. Va. Community Coll., 1976; Police polygraphist Alexandria Police Dept., 1981-85; self-employed polygraph examiner, 1981—. Recipient Profl. Excellence award Richard O. Arther, 1984; Outstanding Service award Am. Assn. Police Polygraphers, 1984, 85. Mem. Am. Assn. Police Polygraphers (sec. 1982-83, sec./treas. 1983—), Am. Polygraph Assn., Va. Polygraph Assn., Md. Polygraph Assn., Tex. Assn. Polygraph Examiners. Republican. Roman Catholic. Avocations: swimming; beaching; astrology; traveling.

CAPEHART, ORVEL HOLLIS, county official; b. Vera, Tex., Apr. 18, 1909; s. John Ode and Nancy Jerusha (Kendrick) C.; m. Ruth J. Burchard, Mar. 25, 1953. Student, Altus Bus. Coll., 1929-30, Tex. Hwy. Patrol Sch., 1941. Constable Knox County, Tex., 1932-35; dep. sheriff, Knox County, 1935-41; patrolman Tex. Hwy. Patrol, Midland, Van Horn, Alpine, El Paso, 1941-46; sheriff, tax assessor Culberson County, Van Horn, 1947-73. Precinct chmn. Democratic Com., Van Horn, 1972-80. Recipient Plaque award Citizens of Culberson County, 1972, Hon. Resolution award State House of Reps., numerous commendations from Pres., govs., FBI offls. Mem. Tex. Tax Assessor Collectors Assn., Sheriffs Assn. Tex., Am. Fedn. Police (award 1972). Methodist. Lodge: Rotary (pres. local chpt. 1975-76). Avocation: flying. Home: Box 336 Van Horn TX 79855

CAPEL, RANDOLPH ALLAN, home builder; b. Richmond, Va., June 17, 1955; s. James Dempsey and Doris Ann (Prentice) C.; m. Judy Carol Arrington, Feb. 19, 1977; children—Julie Elizabeth, Grady Allan. B.A., Hampden-Sydney Coll., 1977. Salesman, So. Insulators, Richmond, Va., 1977; owner, pres. G & R Builders, Inc., Richmond, 1978—; dir. H.O.W. Corp., Richmond. Bd. dirs. YMCA South Richmond, 1981—. Recipient Cert. of Merit as chmn. of Young Builder, Home Builders and Assoc. Council, 1981-82; Life Spike, Nat. Assn. Home Builders, 1985. Mem. Nat. Assn. Home Builders, Home Builders Assn. Richmond (dir.). Republican. Baptist. Avocations: hunting; fishing; camping; gardening. Home: 2205 Oakwater Ct Richmond VA 23235 Office: G & R Builders Inc 7635 Hull St Richmond VA 23235

CAPELLE, KENNETH EARL, real estate executive; b. Fonddulac, Wis., May 25, 1938; s. Ira Richard and Aimee Cecelia (Dignin) C. B.A., U. So. Fla., 1964; postgrad. Stetson U. Coll. Law, 1965-66. Exec. trainee 1st Nat. Bank of Atlanta, 1966-68; mktg. rep. IBM, Atlanta, 1968-71; mgr. S.E. div. Centurion Devel., Atlanta, 1973-77; v.p. Gallery of Homes, Inc., Atlanta, 1978-83; pres. Transfer Location Corp., Dallas, 1983—; mem. editorial com. Employee Relocation Council, Washington, 1982-83. Served with USMC, 1957-60. Republican. Episcopalian. Contbr. articles to profl. jours. Home: Route 2 Box 256 Argyle TX 76226

CAPEN, RICHARD GOODWIN, JR., publisher; b. Hartford, Conn., July 16, 1934; s. Richard and Virginia (Hufbauer) C.; m. Joan Lees Lambert; children—Christopher G., Kelly L., Catherine K. A.B., Columbia U., 1956. Dir. pub. affairs Copley Newspapers, LaJolla, Calif., 1961-69, v.p., 1971-76, sr. v.p., 1976-79; sr. v.p. ops. Knight-Ridder Newspapers, Inc., Miami, 1979-83, mem. exec. com., 1981—; chmn., pub. Miami Herald Pub. Co., Miami, 1983—; dep. asst. sec. pub. affairs Dept. Def., Washington, 1968, then asst. for legis. affairs; corp. dir., chmn. newspaper adv. bd. UPI, 1977-79; dir. Newspaper Advt. Bur., 1984. Vice chmn. San Diego Econ. Devel. Corp., 1978-79; mem. Orange Bowl Com., 1982—; mem. Fla. Council of 100, 1984—; mem. nat. com. on innovations in state and local govt. Ford Found., 1985—; mem. adv. council Stanford U. Grad. Sch. Bus., 1985—. Served to lt. (j.g.) USN, 1956-59. Recipient Disting. Service medal Dept. Def., 1971; Freedoms Found. awards (8); named San Diego's Outstanding Young Man, San Diego Jaycees, 1967, one of five Outstanding Young Men, Calif. Jaycees, 1969. Mem. Interam. Press Assn. (bd. dirs. 1983—), San Diego C. of C. (pres. 1977-79). Republican. Presbyterian. Office: One Herald Plaza Miami FL 33101

CAPERTON, KENT A., state senator, lawyer; b. Aug. 2, 1949. Grad. Tex. A&M U.; J.D., U. Tex. Mem. Tex. Senate, mem. fin., jurisprudence, and state affairs coms. Democrat. Office: Tex Senate PO Box 12068 Austin TX 78711*

CAPERTON, TROY ROSS, architect; b. Seguin, Tex., May 31, 1955; s. Charles Gillam and Laverne (Howell) C.; B.Arch. with honors, U. Tex., Austin, 1978; grad. diploma Archtl. Assn. Sch. Architecture, London, 1980. Archtl. designer firms in Tex. and Alaska, 1977-79; archtl. designer Albert C. Martin & Assocs., Houston, 1980-81, Ferrenz, Taylor, Clark & Assocs., N.Y.C., 1982-84, Richard H. Mycue Architects, San Antonio, 1984-85; ptnr. firm Ar.co.tects, San Antonio, 1986; prin. works include Guadalupe County Mental Health/Mental Retardation Clinic, Seguin, 1977, Plaza Hotel restoration, New Braunfels, Tex., 1977, Point Hope (Alaska) Sch., 1978, Exxon Chem. Plant Adminstrv. Bldg., Baytown, Tex., 1980. Vol. worker San Antonio Met. Ministry, shelter for homeless. Minnie Stevens Piper scholar, 1973; Houston Endowment scholar, 1973. Mem. AIA (asso.), Soc. Archtl. Historians, Archtl. Assn. U.K., Tex. Soc. Architects, Exec. and Profl. Assn., Internat. Platform Assn. Houston, Mensa, Lambda Chi Alpha. Episcopalian. Home: PO Box 294 Stockdale TX 78160

CAPITO, MARY ANN MCNEIL, pharmacist; b. Wheeling, W.Va., Jan. 6, 1954; d. John Eugene and Anna Theresa (Kuca) McNeil; m. Richard Anthony Capito, June 10, 1978; 1 child, Eric Anthony. B.S. in Pharmacy, W.Va. U., 1977. Pharmacy asst. mgr. People's Drug Store, Annandale, Va., 1977-78; pharmacy mgr. Rite Aid, South Charleston, W.Va., 1978-80; supr. ops. W.Va. Poison Ctr., Charleston, 1980-82; dir. pharmacy Eye and Ear Clinic, Charleston, 1982-83; pharmacist Trivillians Pharmacy, Charleston, 1981—; cons. Kanawha Hospice, Charleston, 1981-82. Editor: Toxic News Today, 1981. Active Young Democrats Rockefeller, Charleston, 1980, Blessed Sacrament Community Service, South Charleston, 1983—, Kanawha Med. Aux., Charleston, 1984—. Mem. Kanawha Pharmacy Assn. Democrat. Roman Catholic. Club: Culture (charter mem. 1984—). Home: 201 Autumn Dr Dunbar WV 25064 Office: Trivillians Pharmacy 215 35th St Charleston WV 25304

CAPLAN, ALAN MARK, communications executive; b. Newton, Mass., Mar. 23, 1948; s. Samuel David and Sara Edith (Leib) C.; m. Wendy Ellen Bogen, Nov. 30, 1974; children—Andrew Bogen, Benjamin Bogen. B.A., U. Miami, 1970. Product sales mgr. The Merit Corp., Cambridge, Mass., 1970-76; account exec. WEZE Radio, Boston, 1977; sales mgr. WITS Radio, Boston, 1977-81; account exec. WHDH Radio, Boston, 1981; sales mgr. CBS Radio Reps., Atlanta, 1981—. Mem. Atlanta Broadcasting and Advt. Club, Atlanta Radio Reps. Assn. (pres.), Am. Mgmt. Assn. Home: 7575 Hunters Woods Dr Dunwoody GA 30338 Office: 11 Piedmont Center Suite 608 Atlanta GA 30305

CAPLAN, LESTER, educator, optometrist; b. Balt., Mar. 27, 1924; s. Hyman and Jeannette (Frank) C.; student Wheaton Coll., 1943-44, U. Md., 1946-47; B.S. in Visual Optics, No. Ill. Coll. of Optometry, 1949, O.D. summa cum laude, 1949; M.Ed., Loyola Coll., Balt., 1967; m. Florence Shenker, Sept. 8, 1946 (dec. Jan. 1979); children—Bruce E., Eric Scott; m. Arlene Cohen, Jan. 10, 1981; Harriet Wilder, Cohen Lori Wilder. Practice optometry, Balt., 1950-79; chief of staff Contact Lens Clinic, Optometric Center of Md., 1975-77; vision cons. Prince George's County (Md.) public schs., 1968-70; optometric cons. and clinician Sinai-Druid Comprehensive Child Care Clinic, 1967-68; cons. and instr. Optometric Technician's program, Howard Community Coll., 1976-79; cons. to Indian Health Service, USPHS, 1969—, FDA, 1975—; adv. to dir. profl. service Fed. Health Programs Services, 1972-76; prof. Sch. of Optometry, U. Ala., Birmingham, 1979—, chief div. contact lens services, assoc. prof. Sch. of Community and Allied Health, 1979-81, dir. optometric technician program, 1979-81, assoc. prof. dept. psychology Grad. Sch., 1975—; guest lectr. various colls. and univs., 1970—; mem. adv. council Md. Comprehensive Health Planning Agy., 1971-77; alt. mem. adv. group to Md. Statewide Profl. Standards Rev. Council, 1978-79; mem. Md. Bd. Examiners in Optometry, 1975-79. Pres., Beth Israel Congregation, Randallstown, Md., 1966-67; prof. adv. com. Optometric Center of Md., 1973-75, v.p., 1975. Served with Signal Corps, U.S. Army, World War II; PTO. Named Md. Optometrist of Year, 1974; Disting. Practitioner in Optometry, Nat. Acads. Practice. Fellow Am. Acad. Optometry; hon. mem. Md. Optometric Assn.; mem. Am. Optometric Assn. (Named Nat. Optometrist of the Year 1975), Ala. Optometric Assn., Am. Public Health Assn. (gov. council 1981—), Optometric Hist. Soc. Contbr. author, Public Health and Community Optometry; contbr. articles to jours. in optometry. Home: 3020 Sharpsburg Circle Birmingham AL 35213 Office: Univ Alabama at Birmingham Sch of Optometry University Station Birmingham AL 35294

CAPLES, BARBARA BARRETT, artist; b. Providence, Oct. 28, 1914; d. Colin Douglas and Edna Amelia (Fraser) B.; m. James Stephen Caples, June 29, 1940; children—Cynthia Barrett, Sara Elizabeth Caples Jefferson. B.A. magna cum laude, Smith Coll., 1936; postgrad. in art and design Yale U., 1936-38. One-woman shows 1st Nat. Bank, Washington, 1968, 69, Alexandria Community Y, Va., 1968, Art League, Alexandria, 1970, Smith Coll., Northampton, Mass., 1970, Carlsbad Mus., N.Mex., 1980; group shows N.Y. Watercolor Club, N.Y.C., 1938, Am. Watercolor Soc., N.Y.C., 1938, Soc. Washington Printmakers, 1965-78, Boston Printmakers Soc., Lincoln, Mass., 1969, Disting. Mid-Atlantic Artists, U. Del., Newark, 1980; represented in permanent collections Smith Coll., U. Va., Carlsbad Mus., N.Mex. Mem. Alexandria Tourist Council, 1983—, treas., 1984. Recipient First award Canal Zone Art Assn., 1949, First award St. Andrew's Religious Art Exhbn., 1965. Mem. Art League (bd. dirs. 1969, various awards), No. Va. Fine Arts Assn. (various awards), Alexandria Assn., Alexandria Hist. Soc. (sec. 1978), Alexandria Hist. Found., Phi Beta Kappa. Democrat. Episcopalian. Club: Smith Coll. (Washington). Avocations: piano; bird watching; travel. Home: 1111 Roan Ln Alexandria VA 22302

CAPPETO, MICHAEL ARNOLD, educator; b. Union, N.J., Dec. 17, 1947; s. James J. and Constance (Conza) C.; m. Beverlee A. Johnson, Dec. 19, 1970; children—Christine, Jennifer. B.A., James Madison U., 1970, M.S., 1971; Ed.D., Va. Poly. Inst., 1977. Asst. dir. student affairs Va. Mil. Inst., Lexington, 1971-74; asst. dean students Washington and Lee U., Lexington, 1975-78, assoc. dean students, 1978—; evaluator career planning program, counselor edn. dept. Coll. Edn. U. Va., 1980-81; chmn. on-campus eval. com. Coll. Placement Council, 1984—. Chmn., Rockbridge County Community Services Bd., Lexington, 1984-85. Mem. Va. Assn. Student Personnel Adminstrs. (pres. 1983-84; Outstanding Student Personnel Profl. award 1985), Nat. Assn. Student Personnel Adminstrs. (dir. membership recruitment and orientation for Va. 1978-80), Nat. Assn. Campus Activities (southeastern unit chmn. 1973-74), Am. Coll. Personnel Assn., So. Assn. Coll. Student Affairs. Roman Catholic. Office: Washington and Lee U Lexington VA 24450

CAPPS, JAMES BARRI, mortgage banker; b. Paterson, N.J., Jan. 31, 1946; s. Aaron and Mae (Joel) C.; B.A. in Sociology, N.C. State U., 1971; m. Katherine Lawing, Oct. 10, 1970; 1 dau., Holly Elizabeth. Mgr., asst. v.p. Cameron Brown Co., Arlington, Va., 1971-74; loan officer, asst. v.p., Colonial Mortgage Service Co., Annandale, Va., 1974-76; mgr., v.p., 1977-81; v.p., mgr. Kissell Mortgage Co., 1981—; mgr., partner, asst. v.p. Baker Mortgage Co., Fairfax, 1976-77. Mem. No. Va. Bd. Realtors, Mortgage Bankers Assn., No. Va. Builders Assn., Kappa Alpha. Clubs: Country (Fairfax), River Bend Country. Home: 1310 Timberly Ln McLean VA 22102 Office: 7700 Little River Turnpike Annandale VA 22003

CAPPS, JAMES HARLAN, life underwriter, missionary; b. Decatur, Tex., Feb. 10, 1943; s. James Ambers and Una (Fox) C.; children—Marthel L., Easter A. B.D., Mexican Bapt. Theol. Sem., 1972; B.Theology in Div., Cascades of Glory Bapt. Sem., 1973, Dr. Fgn. Missions and Relations (hon.), 1973. Bus. and personal agt. Am. Gen./Life and Casualty, Houston, 1982-84; assoc. sales mgr. Am. Gen. Life & Accident Ins. Co., Angleton, Tex., 1984-86, assoc. sales mgr., Dallas, 1986—; mgr. Automobile Club Mo., St. Louis, 1964-67; fgn. missionary Faith Bapt. Missions, Houston, 1968-74; regional lang. missionary So. Bapt. Conv., Atlanta, 1974-77; pres. Capps Aluminum, Inc., Houston, 1977-82; pastor Iglesia Bapt. Meml. Ch., Houston, 1981-83. Bd. dirs. Houston Home Improvement Council, 1981; pres., bd. dirs. Faith Bapt. Missions, Houston, 1968-83. Recipient Plaque of Appreciation, Houston Home Improvement Council, 1981, also numerous sales awards in insurance. Lic. in fire and casulty ins. Mem. Nat. Assn. Life Underwriters, Two Million Dollar Club. Republican. Home: 11511 Ferguson Rd Box 1634 Dallas TX 75228 Office: 10675 E Northwest Hwy Dallas TX 75238

CAPPS, THOMAS CULLEN, international training and evaluation consultant; b. Mobile, Ala., July 15, 1942; s. John Mills and Ethel Reberta (Draper Turner) C.; m. Jessica Fried, Aug. 15, 1974. B.B.A., Tulane U., 1965. Internal cons. Ruberoid Co., N.Y.C., 1965-68; audit supr. G.A.F. Corp., N.Y.C., 1968-72, Amtrak, Washington, 1972-73; exec. counselor M&M Internat., Washington, 1973-74; dir. audits Drug Fair, Inc., Washington, 1974-75; dir. seminars Ins. Internal Auditors, Altamonte Springs, Fla., 1976-79; pres. TC & Assocs., North Palm Beach, Fla., 1979—. Author: An Anthology of Auditing, 1984. Home: 11333 Knights-Griffin Rd Thonotosassa FL 33592 Office: TC & Assocs 961 Ocean Dr North Palm Beach FL 33408

CAPRITTO, ANTHONY JOSEPH, lawyer; b. New Orleans, July 11, 1931; s. Philip Joseph and Marie Virginia (Longo) C.; m. Eileen Mary Frisbee, June 6, 1964; children—Ann, Jane, Michael, Margaret, Elizabeth, Alice, Judith, David, Mary. B.B.A., Loyola U., New Orleans, 1953, J.D., 1959. Bar: La. 1959, U.S. Dist. Ct. (ea. dist.) La. 1959, U.S. Ct. Appeals (5th cir.) 1965, U.S. Supreme Ct. 1971. Sole practice law, New Orleans, 1959—; gen. counsel Bank of La., New Orleans, 1979—. Mem. legal com., bd. dirs. New Orleans Opera Assn., 1975—; commr. La. Civil Service Commn., Baton Rouge, 1979—; pres. Cath. Charities, New Orleans, 1980, La. Cystic Fibrosis Found., 1976-78; pres. Christian Bros. Found., New Orleans, 1985. Served to capt. U.S. Army, 1953-55. Mem. La. Bar Assn., Assn. Trial Lawyers Am., Am. Arbitration Assn. (arbitrator), Am. Judicature Soc., La. Trial Lawyers Assn., St. Thomas More Cath. Law Assn. (pres. 1980-85). Democrat. Roman Catholic. Club: Semreh. Home: 500 Turquoise St New Orleans LA 70124 Office: Suite 811 234 Loyola Bldg 234 Loyola Ave New Orleans LA 70112

CAPUTO, ANNE SPENCER, information science educator; b. Eugene, Oreg., Jan. 14, 1947; d. Richard J. and Adelaide Bernice (Marsh) Spencer; m. Richard Philip Caputo, July 15, 1977; 1 child, Christopher Spencer Caputo. B.A. in History, Lewis and Clark Coll., Portland, Oreg., 1969; M.A., U. Oreg., 1971; M.A.L.S., San Jose State U., 1976. Librarian San Jose State U., Calif., 1972-76; online instr. DIALOG Info. Services, Palo Alto, Calif., 1976-77, chief info. scientist, Washington, 1977—; asst. prof. info. sci. Catholic U. Am., Washington, 1978—; online cons. Nat. Com. Library-Info. Sci., Washington, 1980-82; bd. dirs. ASK!, Washington, 1981—. Author: Brief Guide to DIALOG Searching, 1979. Contbr. articles to profl. jours. Named Info. Sci. Tchr. of Yr., Catholic U. Am., 1983. Mem. Am. Soc. for Info. Sci. (officer, chair Potomac Valley chpt. 1985-86), ALA, Spl. Library Assn., D.C. Library Assn. Republican. Episcopalian. Avocation: photographing architectural details on National Trust buildings. Home: 5314 26th Rd N Arlington VA 22207 Office: DIALOG Info Services 1901 N Moore St Suite 809 Arlington VA 22209

CARAWAN, ROY EUGENE, food scientist, educator, consultant; b. Southport, N.C., June 9, 1943; s. Cleveland Eugene and Mildred Ruth (Lorang) C.; m. Deborah Windsor Stallings, Dec. 20, 1964; children—Russell Eugene, Ashley Windsor. B.S., N.C. State U., 1966, M.S., 1970; Ph.D., Ohio State U., 1977. Grad. research asst. dept. food sci. N.C. State U., Raleigh, 1966-68, extension specialist in food engring., 1968—, asst. prof. food sci., 1978-81, assoc. prof., 1981—; prin. Roy E. Carawan, Cons., Cary, N.C., 1969-76, Roy E. Carawan and Assocs., Cons., Cary, 1976—. Chmn. Cary area Ducks Unltd., 1980-82; mem. Wake County (N.C.) Bd. Edn., 1981-85; vice chmn. N.C. Alliance Pub. Edn., 1981-82; bd. dirs. Wake Opportunities, Inc., 1981-82. Named Citizen of Yr., Cary C. of C., 1983. Mem. Inst. Food Technologists (profl.), Carolina-Va. IFT, Water Pollution Control Fedn., N.C. Water Pollution Control Assn., N.C. Assn. Coop. Extension Specialists, Am. Dairy Sci. Assn., N.C. State Employees Assn., N.C. Congress Parents and Tchrs. (life; bd. mgrs. 1980-82), N.C. Jaycees (Top Ten Spokes award 1972, One of Five Outstanding Young Men in N.C. 1979, presdl. aide 1977-78, regional chmn. 1977, state project chmn. 1978), Cary Jaycees (life; treas. 1971-72, v.p. 1972-73, pres. 1973-74, state bd. dirs. 1977-78, Outstanding Young Man 1979), Cary C. of C. Pres.'s Club 1982, edn. com. 1983-84), N.C. State U. Alumni Assn., N.C. State U. Wolfpack Club, Sigma Xi, Gamma Sigma Delta, Epsilon Sigma Phi, Phi Tau Sigma, Sigma Pi. Republican. Methodist. Clubs: Kildare Farms Racquet and Swim, Civitan (charter mem., pres.-elect Cary 1980-81); N.C. State U. Faculty (Raleigh); Pollocks Ferry (Tillery, N.C.). Author numerous extension publs.; author profl. reports; contbr. articles to profl. publs. Home: 135 Castlewood Dr Cary NC 27511 Office: 129 Schaub Hall NC State U Raleigh NC 27650

CARDEN, ZACHARY FRANK, JR, dentist; b. Chattanooga, June 19, 1941; s. Zachary Frank and Mable (Torbett) C.; m. Anne Fowler, Jan. 28, 1967; children—Heather Anne, Zachary Frank III. B.S., Carson-Newman Coll., 1963; Med. Technologist, Erlanger Hosp., Chattanooga, 1964; D.D.S., U. Tenn., 1974. Med. technologist Erlanger Hosp., Chattanooga, 1964-65, 68-70; pvt. practice dentistry, Chattanooga, 1974—. Pres. Civic Art League, Chattanooga, 1980. Served to capt. U.S. Army, 1965-68. Decorated Army Commendation medal. Mem. ADA, Am. Acad. Oral Medicine (oral medicine award 1974), Tenn. Dental Assn. (del. 1983-85), Lookout Dental Study Group (pres. 1975), 3d Dist. Dental Soc. (chmn. peer rev. 1983-85), Chattanooga Craniomandibular Study Group (pres. 1985-86). Republican. Baptist. Clubs: Tenn. Watercolor Soc., Ga. Watercolor Soc., Ky. Watercolor Soc. Avocations: watercolor painting; golf. Office: Lake Hills Profl Bldg 4216 Cross St Chattanooga TN 37416

CARDENAL-VIVAS, JOSE, machinery company executive; b. Granada, Nicaragua; came to U.S., 1959; s. Jose Cardenal-Arguello and Violeta Vivas-Chamorro; m. Martha Hueck, Jan. 24, 1965; children—Jose Ignacio, Juan Carlos, Mauricio. B.C.E., Ga. Inst. Tech., 1964; M.B.A. cum laude, Instituto Centroamericano de Administracion de Empresas, Managua, Nicaragua, 1970. Profl. civil engr., Nicaragua. Engr., planning div. Harza Engring. Co., Chgo., 1965-66; engr., irrigation dept. Instituto de Fomento Nacional, Managua, 1967-68; internat. adviser First Nat. Bank of Chgo., Chgo., 1970; gen. mgr. Nicaragua Machinery Co., Managua, 1971-79; pres. Richards Tractors & Emplements, Inc., Homestead, Fla., 1981—, Sandland Equipment Corp., Fort Myers, Fla., 1982—; dir. Central Bank of Nicaragua, 1973-78. Mem. ASCE, Homestead C. of C. Republican. Roman Catholic. Clubs: Nejapa Country (Managua); Cocibolca Jockey (Granada, Nicaragua). Office: 550 N Flagler Ave Homestead FL 33030

CARDOSO, ÁLVARO EDMUNDO, civil engineer; b. Bogotá, Colombia, Mar. 8, 1936; s. Joaquín Emilio and Lola (Vargas) C.; m. Shelby Jean Rayder, Sept. 8, 1956; children—Carmen Marcela, Yolanda Roxanna. B.S.C.E., Ga. Inst. Tech., 1958, M.S.C.E., 1970. Registered profl. engr., Ga., Fla., Colombia. With Colombian Govt., 1958-65; civil engr. Law Engring. Testing Co., 1966-70, Ga. Power Co., Atlanta, 1970-75; internat. mgr. Brainard Kilman Drill Co., Atlanta, 1975-80, Latin Am. sales law engr. Latin Am. div., Atlanta, 1980—. Consul of Colombia, Atlanta, 1967—; vice chmn. Atlanta Council for Internat. Visitors, 1970-72. Recipient Non-Mem. Appreciation award Hispanoam. Club, 1981. Mem. ASCE. Club: Gun (Bogotá).

CARDOSO, ANTHONY ANTONIO, artist, educator; b. Tampa, Fla., Sept. 13, 1930; s. Frank T. and Nancy (Messina) C.; B.S. in Art Edn., U. Tampa, 1954; B.F.A., Minn. Art Inst., 1965; M.A., U. So. Fla., 1975; Ph.D., Elysion Coll.; m. Martha Rodriguez, July 27, 1954; children—Michele Denise, Toni Lynn. Art instr., head fine arts dept. Jefferson High Sch., Tampa, 1952-67, Leto High Sch., Tampa, 1967—, instr. adult art edn., 1965—; supr. art and humanities program, dir. Hillsboro County Schs., Tampa; rep. Tampa Art Council; painter, 1952—; one-man shows include Warren's Gallery, Tampa, 1974, 75, 76, Tampa Realist Gallery, Tampa, 1975; group shows include

Rotunda Gallery, London, Eng., 1973, Raymon Duncan Galleries, Paris, France, 1973, Brussells (Belgium) Internat., 1973; represented in permanent collections Minn. Museum, St. Paul, Tampa Sports Authority Rep. Tchrs.' Art Council, Tampa, 1971—, Tampa Arts' Council, 1978—; mem. Latin Quarter Art Gallery, Tampa, 1970—. Recipient Prix de Paris Art award Raymon Duncan Galleries, 1970, Salon of 50 States award Ligoa Duncan Gallery, N.Y.C., 1970, Latham Found. Internat. Art award, 1964, XXII Bienniel Traveling award Smithsonian Instn., 1968-69, Purchase award Minn. Mus., 1971, First award Fla. State Fair, 1967, accademia Italia Gold Medal, 1981-82; Merit award Palazzo della manifestazioni, Italy, 1984; Centrod Studi-Nazioni, Premio-Statua della Vittoria, 1985. Democrat. Roman Catholic. Executed murals at Suncoast Credit Union Bldg., Tampa, 1975, Tampa Sports Authority Stadium, 1972. Home: 3208 Nassau St Tampa FL 33607 Office: 901 E Kennedy Blvd Tampa FL 33601

CARDWELL, SUE POOLE, reclamation services company executive; b. Clearfield, Pa., Oct. 31, 1952; d. Robert Thomas Poole and Mary B. (Edwards) (stepmother) and Patricia Alice (Coleman) (stepmother) P.; m. Charles Howard Cardwell, Nov. 24, 1979; children—Jonathon Aaron, Jacqueline Leigh. Clk.-typist Ky. Dept. Mines and Minerals, 1974; sr. reclamation insp. div. reclamation Ky. Dept. Natural Resources, Madisonville, 1974-77; pres. Reclamation Services Unltd., Inc., Madisonville, 1977—; chmn. West Ky. adv. group Office Surface Mining, Dept. Interior, 1979—; adv. bd. U. Ky. Symposium on Surface Mining Reclamation and Hydrology, also mem. exec. adv. com.; mem. Ky. Adv. Com. on Strip Mine Regulation, 1979—; mem. exec. bd. Ky. Task Force on Exploited and Missing Children; bd. dirs., sec. Ky. Alliance for Missing and Exploited Children; mem. Rep. Senatorial Inner Circle, 1984—. Served with WAC, 1972-73. Named hon. Ky. col.; named to W.Va. Ship of State. Mem. West Ky. Coal Operators Assn. (dir.), Hazardous Materials Control Research Inst., Mining and Reclamation Council Am. (chmn. reclamation subcom.), Profl. Reclamation Assn. Am. (bd. dirs., charter), W.Va. Surface Mine Assn., Nat. Reclamation Assn. West Ky. contbg. editor Ky. Coal Jour. Office: 12 Hartland Ave Madisonville KY 42431

CAREK, DONALD J(OHN), child psychiatry educator; b. Sheboygan, Wis., Aug. 10, 1931; s. Peter and Rose (Gergisch) C.; m. Frances M. Schaefer, Jan. 28, 1956; children—Carla, Thomas, Therese, Peter, Mary Beth, Christopher. M.D., Marquette U., 1956. Diplomate Am. Bd. Psychiatry and Neurology, examiner in child psychiatry, examiner in psychiatry. Intern, Walter Reed Army Hosp., 1956-57; resident U. Mich. Hosps., 1959-63; pediatrician Ft. Meyers Dispensary, Arlington, Va., 1958-59; instr. psychiatry U. Mich. Sch. Medicine, Ann Arbor, 1962-65, asst. prof., 1965-66; dir. day care Children's Psychiat. Hosp., Ann Arbor, 1965-66; assoc. prof. psychiatry and pediatrics Med. Coll. Wis., Milw., 1966-74; acting chmn. div. human behavior Med. Coll. Wis., Milw., 1970-73, prof. psychiatry, 1974-76; pres. med. staff Milw. Psychiat. Hosp., 1971-73; prof. psychiatry and pediatrics, chief Youth Div. Med. U. S.C., Charleston, 1976—. Bd. dirs. Cedarcrest Girls Residential Treatment Center, 1969-71. Served to capt. USAR, 1957-59. NIMH child psychiatry tng. grantee, 1979-81, 84-87. Fellow Acad. Child Psychiatry (com. on adolescent psychiatry 1979-85), Am. Psychiat. Assn., Am. Coll. Psychiatrists; mem. AMA, Am. Orthopsychiatry Assn., AAAS, Am. Assn. Med. Colls., Am. Psychosomatic Soc., Soc. Profs. Child Psychiatry, S.C. Med. Assn., S.C. Dist. Br. Am. Psychiat. Assn., So. Psychiat. Assn., Charleston County Med. Soc., Alpha Omega Alpha, Alpha Sigma Nu. Roman Catholic. Co-author: Guide to Psychotherapy, 1966; author: Principles of Child Psychotherapy, 1972; contbr. articles to profl. publs. Home: 723 Kirk Ct Mount Pleasant SC 29464 Office: Med Univ of SC 171 Ashley Ave Charleston SC 29425

CAREW, JAMES LESLIE, geology educator, geologist, researcher; b. Lydney, Eng., May 2, 1945; came to U.S., 1946; s. Ernest W. and Joyce M. (Andrews) C. A.B. in Geology and Biology, Brown U., 1966; M.A. in Geology, U. Tex.-Austin, 1969, Ph.D. in Geology, 1978. With dept. geology Williams Coll., Williamstown, Mass., 1972-75, marine scientist Williams Coll./Mystic Seaport Program, 1977-80; with dept. geology Rensselaer Poly. Inst., Troy, N.Y., 1975-77; U. South Fla., Tampa, 1981; assoc. prof. geology Coll. Charleston (S.C.), 1981—. Pres. Forest Lakes Civic Club, 1982-84. Chevron Oil Co. fellow, 1969; Cuyler Meml. scholar, 1970; So. Regional Edn. Bd. grantee, 1983, 85; Alfred P. Sloan Found. research grantee, 1973; Harbor Br. Found. grantee, 1983, 84; Coll. of Charleston grantee, 1985, other grants. Mem. Geol. Soc. Am., Soc. Econ. Paleontologists and Mineralogists, Paleontol. Soc., Carolina Geol. Soc., Bahamas Nat. Trust, AAAS, Sigma Xi, Sigma Gamma Epsilon, Phi Kappa Phi. Contbr. articles and abstracts to profl. lit.

CAREY, MALCOM TIMOTHY, automatic welding equipment manufacturing company executive; b. Wilmington, Del., Jan. 28, 1944; s. Lewis Ziegler and Sarah Katherine (Malcom) C.; B.E., Vanderbilt U., 1966; M.B.A., Stanford U., 1968; m. Bobbie N. Robinson, Mar. 9, 1979; children—Keith Timothy, Kevin Uno, Timothy John. Asst. to v.p. corp. devel. Crutcher Resources Corp., Houston, 1972-73; v.p. fin. Cerro Negro S.A., Venezuelan subs. Crutcher Resources Oil Well Drilling and Workover, 1973-75; v.p. Gulf Consol. Internat., Latin Am., 1975-77; asst. to pres. Crutcher Resources Corp., Houston, 1977-78; asst. to pres. Crutcher Resources Corp. Automatic Welding div. Crutcher Resources Corp., Houston, 1978-79, pres., 1979—; pres. CRC Welding Systems, Inc., subs. Crutcher Resources Corp., Houston, 1981-84, CRC-Evans Automatic Welding div. CRC-Evans Pipeline Internat. Inc., 1985—. Served to lt. C.E., USN, 1968-72. Mem. Am. Welding Soc., Young Pres.' Orgn. Clubs: Champions Golf, Reveneaux Country, University (Houston). Home: 16210 Chipstead St Spring TX 77373 Office: 50 Briar Hollow Ln Houston TX 77027

CARGILL, OTTO ARTHUR, JR., lawyer; b. Oklahoma City, May 30, 1914; s. Otto Arthur and Delia Ann (Arnold) C.; LL.B., Cumberland U., 1934; m. Rebecca Kay; children—Otto Arthur III, Carole Sue Cargill Lash, Henson, Christina Cargill Best, John Russell, Angela Beth, Kima Leigh, Jennifer Ann. Admitted to Okla. bar, 1935; U.S. Dist. Cts., Western, No., Eastern dists. Okla., U.S. Ct. of Appeals, 10th Circuit, U.S. Supreme Ct.; practiced in Oklahoma City, 1935—. Pres., Buffalo Breeders of Am., Inc. Served with U.S. Army, 1943. Fellow Internat. Acad. Trial Lawyers; mem. Oklahoma City C. of C., Am., Okla., Oklahoma County bar assns., Assn. Trial Lawyers Am., Okla. Trial Lawyers Assn. (pres. 1947, 63), Nat. Assn. Criminal Def. Lawyers (co-chmn. membership com. 1971), Am. Judicature Soc., Law-Sci. Acad. Am. (founding mem., Gold Medal award 1969), Am. Bd. Trial Advocates. Democrat. Baptist. Club: Petroleum. Home: 6401 NW 164th St Edmond OK 73034 Office: 408 Park-Harvey Center 200 N Harvey Oklahoma City OK 73102

CARITHERS, CORNELIA MORSE, physician; b. Winsted, Conn., Mar. 15, 1913; d. Charles Milton and Susanna (Davis) Morse; m. Hugh Alfred Carithers, July 27, 1942; children—Susan C. Callender, Hugh A., Starr C. Waddell. A.B., Cornell U., 1934, M.D., 1938. Diplomate Am. Bd. Pediatrics, 1944. Intern in medicine Bellevue Hosp., N.Y.C., 1938-39, intern in chest medicine, 1939, intern, asst. resident, resident in pediatrics, 1939-42; practice medicine specializing in pediatrics, Jacksonville, Fla., 1942—; clin. asst. prof. U. Fla., Gainesville, 1960-. Bd. dirs. Family Resource. Recipient Beal award Duval County Med. Soc., 1969; Outstanding Achievement plaque Children's Service Child Abuse, 1979. Mem. Am. Med. Women's Assn., Pan-Am. Med. Women's Assn. (program chmn. 1974-76), Am. Acad. Pediatrics (mem. nat. opportunities for women in medicine com. 1983—), AMA, Fla. Pediatric Soc., N.E. Fla. Pediatric Soc. (pres. 1981-84), DAR, Mortar Board, Phi Beta Kappa, Alpha Omega Alpha. Episcopalian. Club: Jacksonville Pan-Hellenic. Home: 3010 St Johns Ave Jacksonville FL 32205 Office: 1661 Riverside Ave Suite I Jacksonville FL 32204

CARLEY, JOHN WESLEY, III, health care industry consultant; b. Dallas, Dec. 15, 1942; s. John Wesley and Velma Ruth (Miller) C. B.S. in Psychology, North Tex. State U., Denton, 1964, M.S. in Psychology, 1965, Ph.D. in Psychology and Human Resource Mgmt., 1970; postgrad. Harvard Grad. Sch. Bus. Adminstrn., 1980. Lic. psychologist, Tex. Dir. spl. projects Austin State Sch., 1971-75; asst. dep. commr. Tex. Dept. Mental Health-Mental Retardation, 1976-78, dep. commr., 1978-83; sr. cons. Tex. Devel. Group, Austin, 1982—. Author: Your Town and You, 1975; also articles; co-author: (film) Series on Mentally Retarded, 1975 (Best in Humanities award Internat. Film Festival 1975). Com. mem. Gov.'s Com. on Handicapped, Austin, 1981; mem. task force on productivity Tex. Legislature, 1982; fund raiser United Way, 1982. Mem. Am. Psychol. Assn., Soc. Indsl. Psychology; fellow Am. Assn. Mental Deficiency. Republican. Methodist. Avocations: reading; computers. Home: 2505 Woodmere St Dallas TX 75233 Office: 817 W Davis St Dallas TX 75208

CARLEY, THOMAS GERALD, engineering science and mechanics educator; b. Greenville, Miss., July 3, 1935; s. Charles Team and Ruby Alice (McClendon) C.; m. Carol Glee Lorette, June 5, 1967; children—Laura Richey, Jack McClendon. B.S. in Mech. Engring., La. State U., 1958, M.S. in Engring. Mech., 1961; Ph.D. in Theoretical and Applied Mechs., U. Ill., 1965. Registered profl. engr., Tenn. Asst. prof. U. Ky., Lexington, 1961-62; research engr. The Boeing Co., Huntsville, Ala., 1965-66; asst. prof. mech. engring. So. Meth. U., Dallas, 1966-68; asst. prof. engring. sci. and mechs. U. Tenn., Knoxville, 1968-69, assoc. prof., 1969-77, prof., 1977—; cons. in structural mechanics, vibration and noise. Pres. So. Appalachian Sci. & Engring. Fair, 1981, 82. Mem. ASME, ASEE, Am. Acad. Mechanics, Am. Soc. for Engring. Edn. Home: 7113 Merrick Dr Knoxville TN 37919 Office: Dept Engring Sci & Mech Univ TN Knoxville TN 37916

CARLIN, WILLIAM BERNARD, II, advertising executive; b. Jackson, Miss., July 14, 1950; s. William Bernard and Betty Courtney (Bankston) C.; m. Pamela Ann McFarland, Nov. 8, 1975; 1 dau., Emily Katherine. B.S., U. So. Miss., 1972. Info. specialist Instns. Higher Learning State of Miss., Jackson, 1973-76; dir. membership services Nat. Assn. Corrosion Engrs., Houston, 1976-81, bus. mgr. publs., 1981-82; tech. publs. mgr. Camco, Inc., Houston, 1982-83; chief exec. officer Carlin & Co., Natchez, Miss., 1983—. Mem. Internat. Assn. Bus. Communicators, Nat. Assn. Corrosion Engrs. Episcopalian. Office: PO Box 2233 Natchez MS 39120

CARLISLE, DWIGHT L., JR., company executive; b. Alexander City, Ala., Nov. 7, 1935; s. Dwight L. Carlisle; m. Sarah Wilbanks; children—Danice, Rebecca, Meredith. B.S. in Textile Engring., Auburn U., 1958. Asst. gen. supt. Russell Corp., Alexander City, Ala., 1968-70, gen. supt., 1970-71, v.p. mfg., 1971-80, exec. v.p., 1980-82, pres., chief operating officer, 1982—, also dir.; dir. First Nat. Bank, Alexander City. Bd. dirs. Russell Hosp., Alexander City, 1984—. Mem. Ala. C. of C. (bd. dirs.). Office: Russell Corp Lee St Alexander City AL 35010

CARLISLE, JOHNNIE, educator; b. Wedowee, Ala., Sept. 14, 1921; d. John William and Hattie (Burrow) Carlisle; B.S., Ala. Coll., 1942; M.S., Columbis U., 1949; Ph.D., U. Tenn., 1975; m. Gordon Lee Carlisle, Oct. 15, 1950. Vocat. home econs. tchr. Gordo (Ala.) High Sch., 1942-43; supervisory tchr. vocat. home econs. Montevallo (Ala.) High Sch., 1943-45; supervisory tchr. home econs. and sci. Memphis State Tng. Sch., 1945-46; tchr. home econs. Miami Beach (Fla.) High Sch., 1946-50; asst. prof. home econs. Ala. Coll., Montevallo, 1950-57; tchr. Larrymore Elem. Sch., Norfolk, Va., 1958-59; substitute tchr. Oceanside (Calif.) Jr.-Sr. High Sch., 1960-61; tchr. biology, physics and gen. sci. Randolph County High Sch., Wedowee, Ala., 1961-62; asst. prof. home econs. U. Montevallo (Ala.), 1965—, assoc. prof., 1973-83, prof., 1983—; state advisor Coll. Home Econs. Clubs, 1954-55; mem. Ala. Nutrition Council, 1971-74, Birmingham Regional Nutrition Com., Inc., 1977-83; area worker March of Dimes, 1964-65. Recipient Disting. Service award for Grey Lady activities Kennedy Gen. Hosp., 1946; Nat. Teaching Fellowship grantee, 1967-68. Mem. Ala. Home Econs. Assn. (panel participant), Am. Home Econs. Assn., Nutrition Today Soc., Soc. for Nutrition Edn., Joint Legis. Council of Ala., Omicron Nu (nat. scholarship com.). Democrat. Baptist. Contbr. articles to profl. jours. Home: 365 Nabors St N Montevallo AL 35115 Office: 102 Bloch Hall Sta 101 Univ of Montevallo Montevallo AL 35115

CARLOS, MICHAEL C., wine, spirits and linen service wholesale company executive; b. Atlanta, Jan. 14, 1927; s. Chris and Helen (Spanos) C.; m. Thalia Noras, Dec. 25, 1963; 1 son, Chris Michael. Student, Ga. State U. Pres., chief operating officer Nat. Distbg. Co., Inc., Atlanta. Trustee Ga. State U. Found.; bd. visitors Emory U. Woodward Acad.; bd. dirs. Atlanta Arts Alliance/High Mus. Art. Home: 3695 Randall Mill Rd NW Atlanta GA 30327 Office: One National Dr SW Atlanta GA 30336

CARLSEN, CHRISTIAN EDWARD, oil company executive, real estate consultant; b. Indpls., Mar. 9, 1951; s. Christian Elmer and Roberta Ann (Cramer) C.; m. Susan Taylor Rogers, June 26, 1971; children—Heather Leigh, Brian Christian. B.A., B.S., U. Fla., 1973. Lic. real estate broker, mortgage broker, Fla. Founder, operator, C.E. Carlsen & Assocs., Ft. Lauderdale, Fla., 1974—; v.p. Multicon Devels., Inc., Ft. Lauderdale, 1975-77; real estate officer Equibank, N.A., Pitts., 1977-79; exec. v.p. Cem-A-Care Fin., Inc., Ft. Lauderdale, 1979-81; founder, chmn. bd., pres. Fla.-Penn Oil & Gas, Inc., Ft. Lauderdale, 1981—. Contbg. mem. Children's Home Soc. Broward County. Mem. Pine Crest Sch. Alumni Assn. (dir.). Republican. Club: Coral Ridge Country (Ft. Lauderdale). Office: 600 Corporate Center Dr Suite 502 Fort Lauderdale FL 33334

CARLSON, BRUCE ALTON, lawyer, lobbyist; b. Akron, Ohio, Oct. 22, 1954; s. Clarence F. and Juanita E. (Day) C.; m. Lisa Anne Freeman, Jan. 13, 1978; 1 child, John Freeman. B.S.B.A., U. Akron, 1977, M.B.A., 1983; J.D., Am. U., 1981. Bar: Va. 1982, Ohio 1983. Pres., Apt. Services, Akron, 1970-74; field rep. N.C. Republican Party, Raleigh, 1974; adminstr. Am. U., Washington, 1978-82; pres. B.A. Carlson & Assocs., Reston, Va., 1982—; ptnr. Carlson & Fay, McLean, Va., 1982-84; prin. Bruce Alton Carlson, P.C., McLean, Va., 1984—; lobbyist No. Va. Apt. Assn., 1984—. Author articles in field. Chmn., Akron Rep. Youth Com., 1971-73; del. Ohio Rep. Conv., 1972. Charles Edison scholar, 1974. Mem. McLean Bar Assn., Akron Bar Assn., No. Va. Apt. Assn. (counsel). Congregationalist. Home: 13607 Copper Ridge Dr Herndon VA 22071 Office: Bruce Alton Carlson PC 1319 Vincent Pl McLean VA 22101

CARLSON, GERALD PAUL, physical education educator; b. Two Harbors, Minn., Sept. 20, 1941; s. Paul H. and Vivian L. Carlson; B.S., Northland Coll., 1963; M.S., U. Colo., 1964; Ph.D., U. Utah, 1973; m. Beth Hulsey, Jan. 12, 1980; children by previous marriage—Deborah Ann, Mark Allen. Teaching asst. dept. phys. edn. U. Colo., Boulder, 1963-64; instr. health and phys. edn. Northland Coll., Ashland, Wis., 1964-68, asst. football coach, 1964-68, head wrestling and tennis coach, 1964-68, dir. student housing and student union, 1964-65; assoc. prof., chmn. health, phys. edn. and recreation U. Colo., Denver, 1968-80, adminstrv. intern, Office of the Chancellor, 1974-77; nat. coordinator for Phys. Edn. Public Info. Project, 1977-79; head dept. phys. edn. and recreation U. Southwestern La., Lafayette, 1980—. Recipient Honor award Colo. Assn. Health, Phys. Edn., Recreation, and Dance, 1980. Mem. AAHPERD (award 1973), Nat. Assn. for Phys. Edn. in Higher Edn., So. Dist. Assn. for Health, Phys. Edn., Recreation, and Dance, La. Assn. for Health, Phys. Edn., Recreation, and Dance, Phi Delta Kappa, Delta Psi Kappa. Co-author: Bowling Basics; contbr. 25 articles on phys. edn. to profl. jours. Office: Dept of Health Phys Edn and Recreation U Southwestern LA PO Box 196 Lafayette LA 70504

CARLSON, GREGORY CLAYTON, pharmacist; b. Rockford, Ill., Oct. 6, 1947; s. Richard Clayton, and Ella Kathryn (Cooney) C.; m. Jane Rhoda, Aug. 3, 1974; children—Christine Rhoda, Richard Clayton, Stephen Gregory. B.S. in Pharmacy, Mercer U. Sch. Pharmacy, 1975, D.Pharmacy, 1976. Lic. pharmacist, Ga., Va. Asst. prof. clin. pharmacy Mercer U., Atlanta, 1976-78; dir. pharmacy R.J. Reynolds-Patrick County Meml. Hosp., Stuart, Va., 1978—; preceptor Va. Commonwealth U. Med. Coll., Sch. Pharmacy, 1979—; cons. Health Systems Assn., Stockton, Calif., 1983—, nursing homes, 1985-85. Served with U.S. Army, 1969-72, Vietnam. Named to Outstanding Young Men of Am., 1982. Mem. Am. Soc. Hosp. Pharmacists, Am. Pharm. Assn., Va. Soc. Hosp. Pharmacists. Republican. Baptist. Lodge: Rotary (pres.). Avocations: running; family recreation. Home: Route 2 Box 14Aa Stuart VA 24171

CARLSON, M(ASON) RANDOLPH, II, lawyer; b. Norfolk, Va., Apr. 26, 1956; s. Mason Randolph and Doris Jean (Owens) C. B.B.A., Old Dominion U., 1978; J.D., Coll. William and Mary, 1981. Bar: Va. Asst. commonwealth atty. (prosecutor), Office of Commonwealth Atty., Norfolk, 1981-83; gen. ptnr. firm Jones and Carlson, Norfolk, 1983—. Bd. dirs. Parents United, Norfolk, Com. for Prevention of Child Abuse, 1985. Recipient Wall St. Jour. award Old Dominion U., 1978. Mem. Norfolk/Portsmouth Bar Assn., Assn. Trial Lawyers of Am. Office: Jones and Carlson 800 Plaza One Norfolk VA 23510

CARLSON, MAURICE IRWIN, English language, educator, editor; b. Fulton, Ky., July 26, 1914; s. Peter Arvid and Della Elizabeth (Irwin) C.; B.A. with honors, Southwestern Coll., Memphis, 1936; M.A., Vanderbilt U., 1937; postgrad. Brown U., La. State U., 1938-39; m. Martha Elizabeth Deniger, Jan. 13, 1939; children—Martha Ann, Martha Elizabeth Carlson Crain. Agt., br. mgr. Acacia Mut. Life Ins. Co., Memphis, New Orleans, field supr., Washington, 1941-47; mgr. N.Tex. dept. Reliance Life Ins. Co. Pitts., Dallas, then supt. agys., Pitts., 1947-51; v.p. Universal Life and Accident Ins. Co., Dallas, 1951-59; with Life Ins. Co. N.Am., Tex., 1959; pres., dir. Reliance Life and Accident Ins. Co. Am., Dallas, 1959-65; mem. English and Greek faculties U. Tex., Arlington, 1966—, editor Arlington Quar., 1967—; guest lectr. So. Meth. U., U. Tex., Arlington; a founder weekly newspaper Hudkins Jour. (now Dallas County Jour.), 1962. Gen. chmn. Dallas County Cancer Crusade, 1954, Dallas County chpt. Nat. Kidney Disease Found., 1960; organizer Greater Dallas Citizens Com. for Old-Time Celebration Am. Ind. Day, 1961, chmn. adv. bd., 1961-67; pres. Bible class Park Cities Baptist Ch., Dallas, 1977; chmn. adv. bd. Operation LIFT, 1962-65; pres. Dads' Club So. Meth. U., 1963-64; exec. v.p. Dallas Am. Revolution Bicentennial Corp., 1975-76; chmn. Dallas County Republican Exec. Com., 1958-60; co-founder Dallas Charter League, 1961, exec. com., 1961-65, pres., 1965; bd. dirs. Dallas Council on World Affairs, also 1st v.p., chmn. exec. com., 1977; bd. dirs. Dallas UN Assn. U.S. C.L.U. Mem. Dallas Forum, Tex. Bur. Econ. Understanding (pres. 1971). Author: Aubrey Beardsley: A Study in Decadence, 1937; book reviewer Dallas Times-Herald, 1950—. Home: 6016 Chalet Ct Apt 5221 Dallas TX 75205 Office: English Dept Room 19035 U Tex at Arlington Arlington TX 76019

CARLTON, ALWIN HORATIO, mech. engr.; b. Birmingham, Ala., Feb. 24, 1933; s. Basil Brown and Nannie Hope (Lee) C.; B.S., Auburn U., 1960; postgrad. U. Tenn., 1965-67; m. Dorothy Emma Bowles, Sept. 16, 1952; children—Patricia Ann, Linda Jane, James Alwin, Robert Duane. Mech. engr. Holston Def. Corp., Kingsport, Tenn., 1960-72, chief engr., 1972-79, supt. utilities, 1979-83, supt. mfg. services, 1983—. Bd. dirs. Community Chest Kingsport, 1974—. Registered profl. engr., Tenn. Mem. ASME, Tenn. Soc. Profl. Engrs. (dir. Upper East Tenn. chpt. 1978-79, pres. Upper East Tenn. chpt. 1983—). Baptist (deacon). Clubs: Bays Mountain Flying, Elks. Home: 1308 Dupont Dr Kingsport TN 37664 Office: Holston Def Corp Kingsport TN 37660

CARLTON, CATHERINE KENNEY, physician, osteopathic surgeon; b. Laredo, Tex., Oct. 20, 1915; d. Charles Francis and Helene (Larmoyeux) K.; m. Elbert P. Carlton, June 11, 1941 (dec. 1972); children—Cathy Carlton Landon, Helen McFall, Jane Carlton Toone; m. Eugene Hightower, May 23, 1974. Student, Incarnate Word Coll., San Antonio, 1933, U. Tex.-Arlington, 1934; D.O., Kirksville Coll. Osteo. Medicine, Mo., 1938. Cert. Am. Acad. Osteopathy; cert. in gen. practice; lic. physician, Tex. Mem. staff Fort Worth Osteo. Hosp., 1946—; practice in osteopathy, 1939—; clin. prof. Tex. Coll. Osteo. Medicine, 1970—; cons. and lectr. in field. Contbr. articles to profl. jours. Mem., NCCJ, Fort Worth, 1984—. Named Outstanding Alumnus, Kirksville Coll. Osteo. Medicine, 1965; recipient Meritorious Service award Tex. Coll. Osteo. Medicine, 1975; Outstanding Profl. Accomplishments award Zonta Club, Fort Worth, 1976, Edna Gladney Aux. Service award, Fort Worth, 1978, Founders medal Tex. Coll. Osteo. Medicine, 1983. Mem. Am. Acad. Osteopathy (pres. 1976-77), Kirksville Alumni Osteo. Assn. (pres. 1979-80), Tex. Acad. Osteopathy (pres. 1969-71). Republican. Roman Catholic. Clubs: Nat. Council Cath. Women (pres. 1952-53), Zonta; Women of Rotary; St. Mary's Parish Council; Fort Worth Diocese. Avocations: swimming; walking; reading. Home: 2505 Ryan Place Dr Fort Worth TX 76110 Office: 815 W Magnolia Ave Fort Worth TX 76104

CARMACK, COMER ASTON, JR., steel company executive; b. Phenix City, Ala., June 26, 1932; s. Comer Aston and Mary Kate (Mills) C.; A.S., Marion Mil. Inst., 1951; B.S., Ala. Poly. Inst., 1954; m. Blanche Yarbrough, Nov. 30, 1957; children—Comer Aston, Mary Kate. Project mgr. Muscogee Iron Works, Columbus, Ga., 1956-58, v.p. engring., 1958-73, pres., 1973—; exec. v.p. Universal Drives & Services. Past bd. dirs. Better Bus. Bur. Served with USAF, 1954-56. Registered profl. engr., Calif. Mem. ASTM, Nat. Soc. Profl. Engrs., Ga. Soc. Profl. Engrs., Ga. Archtl. and Engring. Soc. (past pres., dir. Columbus chpt.), Order of Engr., Chattahooche Valley Safety Soc., Columbus Engring. Soc. Methodist. Club: Columbus Country. Office: 1324 11th Ave Columbus GA 31994

CARMAN, JOHN ELWIN, journalist; b. Des Moines, Nov. 25, 1946; s. Paul Herbert and Trace Emma (Becker) C.; m. Leslie Debbs Hill, Feb. 15, 1975 (div. 1982); m. Janice Faller, Sept. 21, 1985. B.A., Kenyon Coll., 1968; M.S. in Journalism, Northwestern U., 1970. Reporter, Des Moines Register, 1967, Duluth News-Tribune (Minn.), 1968-69, Milw. Jour., 1970-72; reporter, columnist Mpls. Star, 1972-82; columnist Atlanta Jour. and Constitution, 1982—. Recipient Page One award Twin Cities Newspaper Guild, 1975; AP Ann. award Minn. AP, 1977; Green Eyeshade award Sigma Delta Chi, 1985. Mem. TV Critics Assn. (bd. dirs.). Home: 42 W Ferry Dr Atlanta GA 30319 Office: Atlanta Jour and Constitution 72 Marietta St NW Atlanta GA 30303

CARMICHAEL, JOHN LESLIE, JR., political science educator; b. Birmingham, Ala., Apr. 5, 1930; s. John Leslie and Grace (Donald) C.; m. Neva Kyser, Aug. 3, 1968; 1 child, Lesley Erwin. B.A., Vanderbilt U., 1951; M.A., Columbia U., 1956; J.D., George Washington U., 1958; Ph.D., U. Ala., 1972. With land dept. Shell Oil Co., New Orleans, 1960-66; grad. fellow U. Ala., University, 1966-69, lectr., Birmingham, 1969-72, asst. prof., 1972-76, assoc. prof. polit. sci., 1976—. Co-editor: Employment and Labor Relations Policy, 1980. Contbr. articles to profl. jours. Bd. dirs. Campus Counseling Ctr., Birmingham, 1972-80; mem. Birmingham Com. on Fgn. Relations, 1970; elder South Highland Presbyterian Ch., Birmingham, 1977-80, 83—, clk. of session, 1985. Served with U.S. Army, 1952-54. Mem. Am. Polit. Sci. Assn., So. Polit. Sci. Assn., Policy Studies Orgn. (bd. editors 1978-80), Kappa Sigma. Club: Mountain Brook Swim and Tennis. Avocation: tennis. Home: 2916 Thornhill Rd Birmingham AL 35213 Office: Dept Polit Sci U Ala Birmingham AL 35294

CARMICHAEL, WILLIE FRANKLIN, JR., science educator; b. Atlanta, Mar. 18, 1939; s. Willie Franklin and Inez Yvonne (White) C. B.A., Morris Brown Coll., 1961; M.A., Atlanta U., 1965, Ed.S., 1967. Cert. tchr., Ga. Tchr. sci. Winder City Bd. Edn., Ga., 1961-63, Atlanta Bd. Edn., 1963—, Washington Evening Sch., Atlanta, 1971—; mem. staff biomed. Scis. program Emory U., Atlanta, 1980-83; cons. on central cities Atlanta Bd. Edn., summer 1968; tchr. Price Community Sch., Atlanta, 1967-68. Author (with others) Atlanta Pub. Schs. Rev. Biology Curriculum Guide, 1978. Founder Assn. to Revive Grant Park, Atlanta, 1973; co-founder Dogwood City Landmarks, Atlanta, 1981; mem. No In-Town Piggyback Coalition, Atlanta, 1984; trustee Historic Oakland Cemetery, Inc., Atlanta, 1984. Named Tchr.-of-Yr., Fulton High Sch., Atlanta, 1974, Outstanding Secondary Educator of Am., 1974; recipient Tchr. Spotlight award Washington High Evening Sch. newspaper, 1974, Sci. Project Sponsor award Am. Soc. Microbiology, 1976, Student Tchr. Achievement Recognition award Kiwanis Club Atlanta, 1981, 82, 83, Fire Prevention award Atlanta Fire Bur., 1982, 83, 84, 85, Disting. Service Citation Atlanta-Fulton County Emergency Mgmt. Agy., 1985 subject of yearbook dedication Fulton High Sch., 1978. Mem. Nat. Sci. Tchrs. Assn., Ga. Sci. Tchrs. Assn., Nat. Sci. Suprs. Assn., Ga. Edn. Assn., NEA, Assn. Supervision and Curriculum Devel., Atlanta Preservation Ctr., Nat. Trust Historic Preservation, Victorian Soc. Am. (Atlanta chpt.), Ga. Conservancy, Atlanta Bot. Garden, Ga. Bot. Soc., Ga. Ornithology Soc., Am. Meteorol. Soc., Nat. Audubon Soc., Ga. Trust Historic Preservation, Omega Psi Phi. Mem. African Methodist Episcopal Ch. Home: 1225 Boulevard Dr SE Atlanta GA 30317

CARMODY, BASIL TERENCE, construction company executive; b. New Haven, Mar. 23, 1937; s. Edward T. and Dorothy C. C.; m. Ann Pendleton Powell, Aug. 24, 1963; children—Lycia McRae, Nathaniel Chase. B.A., Yale U., 1958; M.A., Harvard U., 1963, postgrad. Mem. staff Arthur D. Little, Inc., Cambridge, Mass., London, Brussels, Belgium, 1963-72; sr. v.p. United Va. Bankshares, Richmond, 1972-79; pres. Eastern Homes Corp., Richmond, 1980—. Vice chmn. Va. State Water Control Bd., 1973-75. Mem. Am. Bankers Assn. (exec. com. real estate 1978-79). Home: 9 Roslyn Rd Richmond VA 23226 Office: 8900 Three Chopt Rd Richmond VA 23229

CARMONA-AGOSTO, VIVIAN, technical writer, editor; b. San Juan, P.R., June 8, 1952; d. Jose Ramon and Maria Altagracia (Agosto) Carmona; B.A. cum laude, U. P.R., 1974; postgrad. Inter-Am. U., 1975-77, U. Tex., Austin, 1981—. Translator, Cariduro Express, Fajardo, P.R., 1974; asst. editor Noreste News, Fajardo, 1974; housing and media coordinator Palmas del Mar Resort, Sea Pines Corp., P.R., 1974; employment interviewer Dept. Labor, Fajardo, 1975-76; spl. agt. FBI, Washington, 1976; tng. specialist Petroleum Extension Service, U. Tex., Austin, 1978-79, tech. writer/editor III, 1980—. Active Whitestone Retirement Home, Austin. Roman Catholic. Clubs: Koinonia, U.

Tex. Bellydance. Translator: Conceptos Basicos de Perforaction, 1979; rewrote, updated: The Rotary Rig and Its Components, 1979; The Bit, 1980; Safety on the Rig, 1980. Home: Apt 104 3121 Speedway Austin TX 78705 Office: Balcones Research Center 33,10100 Burnet Rd Austin TX 78758

CARNAHAN, RICHARD HENRY, JR., dentist; b. San Antonio, Aug. 12, 1942; s. Richard Henry and Adele (Cherry) C.; m. Blaire Busby, Aug. 4, 1967; children—Carey Busby, Colleen Douglas, Richard H. Student U. Tex., 1960-64, Trinity U., 1965-66, 73; D.D.S., Baylor U., 1970. Gen. practice dentistry, San Antonio, 1970—; asst. clin. prof. U. Tex. Health Sci. Ctr., San Antonio, 1979-82, assoc. clin. prof. dentistry, 1982—; lectr. infield; mem. State Bd. of Health Dental Adv. Com., 1980—, chmn., 1983-85. Vestryman, St. Lukes Episcopalian. Ch., 1971-72; spl. divs. judge Alamo Regional Sci. Fair, 1971-72, 74-77; bd. dirs. Good Samaritan Community Ctr., 1973—; pres. U. Tex. Ex-Students Assn., 1984—; campaign mgr. Cecil Bain San Antonio River Authority Campaign, 1978-79; tri-chmn. fin. com. County Commr. Jeff Wentworth's Re-election Campaign, 1980. Recipient Bernhard Gottlieb Meml. award Baylor U., 1970. Mem. ADA, Tex. Dental Assn. (council chmn. 1982-83), San Antonio Dist. Dental Soc. (del. state ho. 1981-83), Tex. State Bd. Dental Examiners (select com. on advt. 1977-79), S.W. Soc. Oral Medicine (pres. 1978-80), Am. Acad. Gold Foil Operators, Greater San Antonio C. of C. (bd. dirs. 1980-83), Acad. Operative Dentistry, S.W. Soc. Denture Prosthesis (sec.-treas. 1978-80), Internat. Coll. Dentists, S.W. Acad. Restorative Dentistry, Tex. Gnathological Soc., Am. Coll. Dentists, Am. Acad. Restorative Dentistry, Baylor Dental Alumni Assn. (trustee 1974-82, pres. 1979-80), Psi Omega. Republican. Episcopalian. Clubs: Houston Gold Foil Study (dir. 1975-77), San Antonio German, Tex. Cavaliers, Baylor Century (dir. 1979-81, chmn. 1977-79). Home: 115 Camellia Way San Antonio TX 78209 Office: 105 El Prado Dr W San Antonio TX 78212

CARNALL, GEORGE HURSEY, II, lawyer, business executive; b. Ft. Smith, Ark., Feb. 19, 1947; s. George and Kathleen (Browne) C.; m. Janet Spaulding, Aug. 28, 1971; children—Clayton Wilson, Abigail Browne, Kevin Joseph. B.S. in Econs., Bus. Adminstrn., Millikin U., Decatur, Ill., 1969; J.D., Vanderbilt U., 1974. Bar: Tenn. 1974, U.S. Dist. Ct. (we. dist.) Tenn. 1974. Assoc., Arnoult & May, Memphis, 1974-76, Watson Cox & Arnoult, Memphis, 1976-79; pres. Fantastic Sam's the Original Family Haircutters Franchise; gen. counsel S.M.R. Enterprises, Inc., Memphis, 1980—. Contbr. articles to legal jours. Bd. dirs. Teen Challenge, Memphis, 1983, First Assembly Christian Sch., Memphis, 1982. Served with U.S. Army, 1969-71. Mem. ABA, Tenn. Bar Assn., Memphis and Shelby County Bar Assn., Phi Kappa Phi. Mem. Assembly of God Ch. Home: 6870 Wytham St Memphis TN 38119 Office: SMR Enterprises Inc 3180 Old Getwell Rd Memphis TN 38181-0845

CARNESOLTAS, ANA-MARIA, lawyer; b. Havana, Feb. 9, 1948; came to U.S., 1962, naturalized, 1969; d. Manuel Ramon and Zenaida de las Mercedes (Enriquez) C.; B.A., U. Calif.-Santa Barbara, 1970; J.D., Loyola U., Los Angeles, 1978. Bar: Calif. 1978, Fla. 1979. Dep. probation officer Santa Barbara County, Calif., 1970-73; personnel analyst Los Angeles County, Calif., 1973-77; dep. dist. atty. Los Angeles County, 1978-80; asst. U.S. atty. So. Dist. Fla., Miami, 1980-82; sole practice, Miami, 1982-83; asst. city atty. Miami, 1983—; hostess The Local Perspective, Radio WNWS, Miami, 1984. Bd. dirs. Greater Miami chpt. Am. Heart Assn., 1983-85 Mem. Calif. Probation, Parole and Corrections Assn. (v.p. Santa Barbara chpt. 1972-73), Cuban-Am. Attys. Council Los Angeles (sec. 1980), Cuban Am. Bar Assn. (dir. 1983, sec. 1984), Fla. Assn. Women Lawyers, ABA, Fed. Bar Assn., Dade County Bar Assn. (criminal cts. com. 1983-84), Fla. Bar (civil procedure rules com. 1984-87, voluntary bar liaison com. 1984-86), Calif. Dist. Attys. Assn., Assn. Trial Lawyers Am., Latin Bus. and Profl. Women (rec. sec. 1982-83, 1st v.p. 1983-84), Coalition Hispanic Am. Women; YWCA Networking Club. Office: 169 E Flagler St Suite 1101 Miami FL 33131

CARNEY, ALMA JEAN, health center director; b. Brownsville, Tenn., Sept. 1, 1943; d. Augusta and Ora (Mathis) Thomas; m. Willie Edward Carney, Oct. 22, 1979; B.S., U. Tenn., Knoxville, 1973; postgrad. publ. adminstrn. U. Tenn.-Knoxville and Memphis State U., 1974-75, 82—. County agt. for children Peabody Coll., Nashville, Brownsville, 1975; eligibility counselor Tenn. Dept. Human Services, Brownsville, 1976; health planner Douglas Community Health Recreation Council, Stanton, Tenn., 1977-79, project dir., 1979—. Chmn. housing affairs NAACP, 1988-83, sec., 1978-79. U. Tenn. Minority scholar, 1973; recipient Outstanding Services award Tenn. Assn. Retarded Citizens, 1978. Mem. Tenn. Voters Council, Tenn. Public Health Assn., Assn. Primary Health Care Centers (treas.), Tenn. Primary Care Adv. Bd., Am. Publ. Health Assn., Nat. Assn. Community Health Centers. Democrat. Baptist.

CARNEY, BRUCE HAY, physician; b. Garrett, Pa., Mar. 13, 1916; s. W.H. Bruce and Lydia (Hay) C.; m. Dorothy Lee Morrison, Sept. 4, 1949; children—Bruce M., Suzanne F., Kenneth B., Martha F. B.S., Wagner Coll., 1937; M.A., Columbia U., 1939; Ph.D., NYU, 1944, M.D., 1948. Intern, Bellevue Hosp., N.Y.C., 1948-49, resident, 1950-52; resident Woman's Hosp., Detroit, 1949-50; practice obstetrics and gynecology, Norristown, Pa., 1953-77, Franklin, N.C., 1977—; chief staff Angel Hosp., Franklin, 1980-81, 82-83. Mem. Norristown Area (Pa.) Sch. Bd., 1965-72. Served with U.S. Army, 1942-44. Fellow Am. Coll. Obstetricians and Gynecologists; mem. Montgomery County Med. Soc. (editor bull. 1954-75). Democrat. Lutheran. Club: Masons. Home and Office: 740 Bryson City Rd Franklin NC 28734

CARNEY, BRUCE WILLIAM, astronomer, educator; b. Guam, Mariana Islands, Nov. 30, 1946; s. William Robert and Anne Elizabeth (Skow) C.; m. Lynn Christopher, Dec. 18, 1971. B.A., U. Calif.-Berkeley, 1969; A.M., Harvard U., 1971, Ph.D., 1978. Carnegie fellow dept. terrestrial magnetism Carnegie Inst. Washington, 1978-80; asst. prof. astronomy U. N.C., Chapel Hill, 1980-85, assoc. prof., 1985—; chmn. users com. Kitt Peak Nat. Obs., Tucson, 1983—; mem. astronomy adv. com. NSF, Washington, 1984—; mem. dirs. adv. com. Nat. Optical Astronomy Obs., Tucson, 1984—. Contbr. articles to profl. publs. Served with U.S. Army, 1971-74. NSF grantee, 1981, 83. Mem. Internat. Astron. Union, Am. Astron. Soc., Astron. Soc. Pacific. Democrat. Avocations: Egyptology, hiking. Office: U NC Dept Physics and Astronomy Phillips Hall 039A Chapel Hill NC 27514

CARNEY, KAREN, dentist, educator; b. Kansas City, Mo., Nov. 24, 1950; d. Thomas Martin and Pauline (Ernst) C.; m. Michael R. Amonett, Nov. 3, 1979. B.S. in Chemistry, Loyola U., 1972; D.D.S., La. State U., 1978. Gen. practice dentistry, Jackson, Miss., 1978—; clin. asst. prof. restorative dentistry U. Miss. Med. Ctr., 1979—. Mem. ADA, Miss. Dental Assn., Jackson Dental Soc., Omicron Kappa Upsilon. Office: 2419 McFadden Rd Jackson MS 39204

CARO, CHARLES CRAWFORD, microcomputer company executive, international consultant; b. Champaign, Ill., Feb. 15, 1946; s. William Crawford and Marian Dell (Heischmidt) C.; m. Sallye Simons, Dec. 18, 1977; 1 child, Mark Christopher. B.A., U. South Fla., 1973, M.A., 1976. Program support specialist Bendix/SIYANCO, Riyadh, Saudi Arabia, 1973-74; chmn., chief exec. officer Caro Internat. Trade and Relations Corp. (CITAR), Tampa, Fla. and Jeddah, 1976-79, dir., 1976-79; mng. dir. Architect Lee Scarfone Assocs. (ALSA), Al-Khobar, Saudi Arabia, 1979-80; exec. dir. Caro Research Assocs., Tampa and New Orleans, 1980—; pres., chief exec. officer MICROFINE, Inc., Tampa, 1983—, also dir.; bd. dirs. Action Conc. Servives Inc., 1986—. Contbr. articles to publs. in field. Parliamentarian, Hillsborough Democratic Exec. Com., Tampa, 1982—. Served with U.S. Army Security Agy., 1967-71. Mem. UNIR Project, Am. Microcomputer Dealers Assn. (life), Assn. Computing Machinery (Computer & Soc. special interest group), Internat. Platform Assn., Phi Kappa Phi, Pi Sigma Alpha. Episcopalian. Club: Tiger Bay (Tampa). Home: 1607 Deleon Tampa FL 33606 Office: Caro Research Assocs 202 S 22nd StTampa FL 33606

CAROTHERS, DAVID EUGENE, steel company executive; b. Ashland, Ohio, Aug. 15, 1951; s. Ivan Grant and Virginia Loris (Hibbs) C.; m. Karen Renee Bevan, July 1, 1972; children—David Ross, Kristin Renee, Jonathan Charles. B.A., Baldwin-Wallace Coll., 1981. Trooper Ohio State Hwy. Patrol, Columbus, 1972-78; interviewer U.S. Steel Corp., Lorain, Ohio, 1978-79, safety engr., 1979-81, prodn. supr., 1981-82, gen. supr. safety, McKeesport, Pa., 1982-83, dept. mgr. safety indsl. hygiene and security, Fairfield, Ala., 1983—. Mem. Am. Soc. Safety Engrs. (v.p. Ala. chpt. 1984—, pres. chpt. 1985), Bus. Council Ala. (safety com. 1984—), Greater Birmingham Safety League (bd. dirs. 1985), Alpha Sigma Lambda. Avocations: running; reading; computers; classical music. Office: United States Steel Corp Fairfield Works PO Box 599 Fairfield AL 35064

CAROW, RAYMOND EDWARD, communications company executive; b. Bklyn., Dec. 13, 1922; s. Edward and Jennie (Altenburg) C.; m. Elise Frost, Aug. 16, 1969; stepsons, Jameson, Jasen; children by previous marriage—Kathleen, Karen, Kurt, Cassandra. B.A., Hofstra U., 1950, postgrad., 1950-51. Prodn. mgr. WEAR-TV, Pensacola, Fla., 1953-55; mgr. WCTV, Tallahassee, 1955-57; gen. mgr. WALB-TV, Albany, Ga., 1957—; v.p. Gray Communications Systems, Inc., Albany, 1967—. Bd. dirs. Salvation Army. Served to lt. comdr. USNR, 1942-46, 50-53. Named Broadcaster of Yr., Ga. Assn. Broadcasters, 1965. Mem. Albany C. of C., U.S. Navy League, Ga. Assn. Broadcasters (pres. 1964-65). Republican. Methodist. Club: Doublegate Country. Home: 2218-A Old Dominion Rd Albany GA 31707 Office: Gray Communications Systems Inc PO Box 3130 Albany GA 31708

CARPENING, WAYNE, city official. Mayor, City of Winston-Salem, N.C. Office: PO Box 2511 Winston-Salem NC 27102*

CARPENTER, ADDIE FLOWERS, nurse; b. Bellville, Tex., Aug. 27, 1949; d. Addison Johnson and Sue Elizabeth (Powers) Flowers; m. Robert James Carpenter, Jr., Aug. 21, 1970; 1 child, Craig Barrett. B.S., Tex. Woman's U., 1971. Surg. nurse M.D. Anderson Hosp., Houston, 1971-72; head nurse nursery St. Lukes Episcopal Hosp., Houston, 1972-74; research nurse Baylor Coll. Medicine, Houston, 1980-81; genetics research assoc. Emergency Aid Coalition, Houston, 1984—, bd. dirs., 1985. Fellow Am. Soc. Tng. and Devel. Democrat. Baptist. Club: Aeros Soccer (Houston) (statistician 1983). Avocations: aerobic dancing; literature. Home: 9223 Ilona Ln Houston TX 77025

CARPENTER, BENJAMIN HARRISON, JR., chemical engineer; b. Buckhannon, W.Va., Apr. 5, 1921; s. Benjamin and Mary Maurine (Westfall) C.; m. Marilynn J. May, June 8, 1941; children—Martha Jo Azzone, Marilynn Jane Hoch, May Sue; m. 2d Alma Beatrice Grindstaff, Feb. 27, 1981. B.S., W.Va. Wesleyan U., 1941; M.S. in Ch.E., W.Va. U., 1961. Registered profl. engr., W.Va., N.C. Analytical chemist Union Carbide Corp., 1941-43, in specifications devel., 1944-47, research chemist analytical methods, 1948, mgr. quality control systems, 1949-53, group leader research, 1954-63, staff sr. research cons. unit processes, 1964-69; sr. research engr. Research Triangle Inst., Research Triangle Park, N.C., 1970-79, mgr. indsl. studies dept., 1980-81, sr. program devel. engr., 1982—. Mem. Am. Chem. Soc., AIME, Assn. Iron and Steel Engrs., Am. Statis. Assn., Sigma Xi. Republican. Baptist. Clubs: Century, Copa, Lords and Ladies, Toppers, Elks. Office: 1220 Huntsman Dr Durham NC 27713

CARPENTER, GENE CHARLES, engineering geologist; b. Columbus, Ohio, Nov. 2, 1935; s. John Patrick and Louise May (Adkins) C.; m. Karen Kemmish, Aug. 15, 1974; children—Brent, Christine, Michelle. B.Sc., Ohio State U., 1958; M.Sc., U. Cin., 1960, Ph.D., 1975. Cert. geologist. Ptnr., mgr. Earth Sci. Labs., Cin., 1960-63; owner, cons. Carpenter & Assocs., Cin., 1963-65; pres. Shield Petroleum, Cin., 1965-67, Carpenter Devel., Phoenix, 1967-76, Carpenter & Assocs., Tulsa, 1976—; dir. Western Resources, Tulsa, 1976-79. Contbr. articles to profl. jours. Mem. Am. Assn. Petroleum Geologists, Am. Inst. Profl. Geologists. Republican. Lodge: Rotary. Avocations: photography; flying; writing; swimming. Office: Carpenter & Assocs Ltd Box 52250 Tulsa OK 74152

CARPENTER, JOHN W., corporate executive; b. 1952. B.B.A., Tex. Tech. U., 1974; M.B.A., U. Tex., 1977. Distbr., 1st Southwest Co., 1971; with Las Colinas Corp., 1975; mgmt. trainee Southland Life Ins. Co., Dallas, 1976-77; project coordinator Las Colinas Corp., 1977-78; pres. Southland Investment Properties Co., 1978, exec. v.p. Southland Fin. Corp., Dallas, 1979—, also dir. Office: Southland Life Ins Corp 409 N Olive St Dallas TX 75201*

CARPENTER, RICHARD GLYNN, college president; staff development consultant; b. Bogalusa, La., Aug. 7, 1953; s. Dallas William and Ruth (Boone) C.; m. Marjorie Stogner, Feb. 19, 1953. A.A., Southwest Miss. Jr. Coll., 1972; B.A., Northwestern U., 1974, M.Ed., 1976; Ph.D., N.C. State U., 1980. Lic. pvt. pilot. FAA. Tchr., dir. high sch. band La. Pub. Sch. System, 1974-78; instr. Grad. Sch. N.C. State U., 1979-80, staff devel. cons., 1979—; acad. v.p. Somerset Community Coll., U. Ky., 1980-84, pres., 1984—. Active Southcentral Ky. United Way Found.; bd. dirs. Southcentral Ky. Performing Arts Council, Indsl. Found. Pulaski County. Grantee in field. Mem. Am. Assn. Acad. Affairs Adminstrs., Nat. Soc. for Performance and Instrn., Am. Assn. Adult and Continuing Edn., Somerset/Pulaski County C. of C. Republican. Methodist. Lodge: Somerset Rotary. Author: The Programming Process in Non Formal Adult Education, 1981; Needs Assessment in Continuing Education, 1980; Community Development and Leadership, 1982, others. Home: 3713 Heather Way Somerset KY 42501 Office: 808 Monticello Rd Somerset KY 42501

CARPENTER, ROBERT DURWARD, mortician; b. Huntington, W.Va., Sept. 8, 1932; s. Veri S. and Zelma (Wagstaff) C.; A.B.S., Marshall U., 1952; grad. Cin. Coll. Mortuary Sci., 1953; Ph.D. (hon.), Marlow U., 1956; grad. Nat. Emergency Tng. Ctr., Emmitsburg, Md.; m. Grace Evelyn Edwards, May 28, 1954; children—Robert David, Timothy Durward. Pres., Klingel-Carpenter Mortuary, Inc., Huntington, W.Va., 1964—; mem. staff Marshall U. Med. Sch., Huntington, 1977—, dir. mortuary services, 1978-79; dir. Chesapeake (Ohio) area Bd. Trade, 1970-75. Mem. Civic Center Adv. Bd., City of Huntington, 1975-76, pres. Huntington Econ. Devel. Bd., 1972-73; chmn. Huntington Fire Dept. Adv. Bd., 1962-65; campaign chmn. United Fund and Red Cross Drive, 1968-69; mem. bd. deacons Presbyn. Ch., 1956-65, 69-75, co-chmn. World Wide Missions, 1958, chmn. property com., 1958-60; bd. dirs. Nat. council Boy Scouts Am., 1976-77; bd. dirs. Civil Emergency Def., 1954-79, chmn., 1959-60, mem. adv. com. for County and City, 1973-76; bd. dirs. Tri-State Fire Sch., 1958-79, chmn., 1962-76; bd. dirs. ARC, 1956-58; bd. dirs. March of Dimes, 1964-77, v.p., 1969; bd. dirs. Stella Fuller Settlement, 1959-77, pres., 1962-64; bd. dirs. Cin. Found. Mortuary Sci., 1977-81, W.Va. Heart Assn., 1972-73, Cabell Area Heart Assn., 1969-77, United Comml. Travelers Tri State Council, 1967-68. Recipient March of Dimes Service award, 1976, Mayor's award, Huntington, W.Va., 1972, Outstanding Service award Tri State Execs. Club, 1969; named Hon. W.Va. Fire Marshall, 1968, Ky. Col., 1970. Fellow Royal Soc. Health of London; mem. Huntington C. of C. (dir. 1969-71, chmn. crime prevention com. 1974-75), Navy League (pres. Tri-State area 1975), Jr. C. of C., U.S. C. of C., Presidents Assn., Fla. Land Owners League, Internat. Platform Assn., Internat. Assn. of Fire Fighters (hon. mem.), Tri-State Audubon Soc., SAR, Central Ohio Valley Indsl. Council, Marshall U. Alumni Assn., Associated Funeral Dirs. Service Internat. (pres. 1979-80), Nat. Funeral Dirs. Assn. (chmn. disaster com. for U.S.), W.Va. Funeral Dirs. Assn. (pres. 1962-63), So. W.Va. Funeral Dirs. Assn. (pres. 1955-58), Internat. Thanatopractic Assn., Ohio Funeral Dirs. Assn., W.Va. Hist. Soc., Nat. Hist. Soc., U.S. Naval Inst., Pi Sigma Eta. Clubs: Elks, Big Green, Rotary (pres. Huntington 1977, dist. gov. 1980-81, Paul Harris fellow 1982). Address: PO Box 2125 328 6th Ave Huntington WV 25721

CARPENTER, STANLEY HAMMACK, retired engineering research and development company executive; b. Hattiesburg, Miss., Jan. 21, 1926; s. Henry Herbert and Esther Mae (Cooper) C.; m. Catherine Jane Sadler, Nov. 29, 1946; children:13 Stanley Hammack, Louise N., Catherine D., Mary C. B.S., Tulane U., 1946; U.S. Naval Postgrad. Sch., 1956; Aero. Engr., Calif. Inst. Tech., 1957; M.S., U. So. Calif., 1982; cert. safety profl.; Enlisted U.S. Navy, 1944, commd. 2d lt. U.S. Marine Corps, 1946, advanced through grades to col., 1968; liaison officer Naval Weapons Center, China Lake, Calif., 1959-62; comdg. officer 1st Marine Corps A4E Squadron, 1963-65; aide to asst. sec. navy for research devel., 1965-68; Viet Nam combat tour officer in charge Chu-Lai Air Base, commdg. officer Marine Wing Support Group, 1968-69; staff officer, dir. def. research engring., asst. chief of staff and div. chief Marine Corps Devel. Center, Quantico, Va., 1971-74; ret., 1974; aero. engr., sr. program mgr. Unified Industries, Inc., Springfield, Va., 1975-86, now ret. Decorated Legion of Merit, Air medal. Mem. Marine Corps Aviation Assn., First Marine Div. Assn., Marine Corps Assn., Assn. Naval Aviation, Tailhook Assn., Marine Corps Res. Officers Assn., Ret. Officers Assn., Marine Corps League, Navy League, Marine Corps Hist. Found., Naval Aviation Mus., Exptl. Aircraft Assn., Aircraft Owners and Pilots Assn., Nat. Aero Club, System Safety Soc., Am. Soc. Safety Engrs., Nat. Safety Mgmt. Soc., Human Factors Soc., Tulane U. Alumni Assn., Calif. Inst. Tech. Alumni Assn., Phi Beta Kappa, Omicron Delta Kappa, Kappa Sigma, Kappa Delta Phi. Roman Catholic. Home: 8404 Bound Brook Ln Alexandria VA 22309

CARPENTER, THOMAS GLENN, university president; b. Atlanta, Ga., Feb. 27, 1926; s. Walker G. and Loreta (Jackson) C.; B.S. in Bus. Adminstrn., Memphis State U., 1949; M.A. in Econs., Baylor U., 1950; Ph.D. in Econs., U. Fla., 1963; m. Oneida Claire Pruette, Oct. 30, 1948; children—Debra Claire, Thomas Glenn. Asst. dir. housing U. Fla., Gainesville, 1957-64, instr. econs., 1956-57; dir. auxs. Fla. Atlantic U., Boca Raton, 1964; bus. mgr., v.p. U. W.Fla., Pensacola, 1965-69; pres. U. N.Fla., Jacksonville, 1969-80; pres. Memphis State U., 1980—; dir. Delta Life and Annuity, Memphis; trustee First Am. Bank Memphis. Bd. dirs. Chickasaw council Boy Scouts Am.; mem. Lenoir-Rhyne Coll. Devel. Bd. Served with USN, 1944-46. Mem. So. Assn. Colls. and Schs. (chmn. exec. council from 1981), Memphis C. of C. (bd. dirs.), Phi Delta Theta, Phi Kappa Phi, Beta Gamma Sigma, Omicron Delta Kappa. Presbyterian. Office: Memphis State Univ Southern Ave Memphis TN 38152

CARPENTER, WILLIAM LEVY, architect, engineer, planner; b. Columbia, S.C., May 26, 1926; s. Levy Leonidas and Lucille (O'Brien) C.; student N.C. State U., 1943-44; B.S., U.S. Naval Acad., 1947; m. Blanche Augusta Owen, Apr. 10, 1948; children—Becky Carpenter Bouton, William Owen, Robert Meadors. Staff engr. Celanese Corp., Charlotte, N.C., 1954-56; power plant design engr. J.E. Sirrine Co., Greenville, S.C., 1956-62, v.p. dept. mech. engring., 1962-69; v.p. bus. devel., 1969-74, exec. v.p., 1974-75, pres., chief exec. officer, 1976-83; vice chmn. CRS Sirrine, Inc., Greenville, 1983—; chmn. Non-Woven Industries, Inc., 1972-77; dir. S.C. Nat. Bank. Bd. dirs. St. Francis Community Hosp., Greenville, 1980, chmn., 1985—. chmn. United Way Campaign, Greenville County, S.C., 1980, pres., 1983. Served to lt. comdr. USNR, 1947-53. Registered profl. engr., S.C. Mem. S.C. Assn. Cons. Engrs., Cons. Engrs. Council (nat. dir. 1966-69), Greater Greenville C. of C. (pres. 1978). Baptist (chmn. bd. deacons 1973-74). Club: Greenville Country. Home: 227 Seven Oaks Dr Greenville SC 29605 Office: CRS Sirrine Inc PO Box 5456 Greenville SC 29606

CARR, ADAM FYFE, psychologist; b. Urbana, Ill., Dec. 27, 1948; s. Arthur Japeth and Marion Elizabeth (Grudier) C. B.A., Kalamazoo Coll., 1971; M.A., Dalhousie U., 1973, Ph.D., 1976. Lic. psychologist, Tenn. Asst. prof. psychology Trent U., Peterborough, Ont., Can., 1976-77; research assoc. U. Kans., Lawrence, 1977-79; asst. prof. criminal justice Ill. State U., Normal, 1979-80; indsl. psychologist S.D. Govt., Pierre, 1980-82; psychologist City of Memphis, 1983—. Contbr. articles to profl. jours. Killam fellow Dalhousie U., 1971-76. Mem. Am. Psychol. Assn., Tenn. Psychol. Assn., Memphis Area Psychol. Assn., Phi Beta Kappa. Avocations: running; cycling; photography, birding. Home: 65 S Fenwick Rd Memphis TN 38111 Office: City of Memphis Employment Bur 125 N Mid America Mall Memphis TN 38103

CARR, ANNA WEAVER, cytogenetic technologist; b. Hickory, N.C., Dec. 8, 1930; d. Robert and Mary Beatrice (Simms) Weaver; B.S. cum laude, Va. Union U., 1957; divorced; children—Inga Maria, Troi Lovette. Lab. technician child devel. study project NIH, 1958-64; with Va. Health Dept., Med-Coll. Va.-Va. Commonwealth U., Richmond, 1964—, cytogenetic lab. specialist, 1976—, supr. cytogenetic lab., 1980—. Bd. dirs. Richmond Community Hosp., 1971—; rec. sect. Va. Crusade for Voters Meetings, 1974-75, 83; pres. Richmond chpt. Tots and Teens Inc., 1972-74. Named Miss Va. Union U., 1956-57. Mem. Assn. Cytogenetic Technologists (dir.), Continental Socs. (chpt. fin. sec. 1978-80), NAACP, Delta Sigma Theta (chpt. pres. 1956-57). Baptist. Home: 1502 Sharpsburg Ct Richmond VA 23228 Office: Sanger Hall 11th and Marshall Sts Richmond VA 23298

CARR, GEORGE C., judge; b. 1929. B.S., B.A., J.D., U. Fla., Gainesville. Bar: Fla. bar 1954. Presently U.S. dist. judge Dist. of Middle Fla., Tampa. Mem. Am. Bar Assn. Office: US Dist Ct PO Box 3309 Tampa FL 33601

CARR, GORDON LEE, psychologist, educator; b. Belleville, Ill., Dec. 4, 1942; s. Elbert Hamilton and Hilda Katherine (Scheid) C.; m. Carolyn F. Pounders, June 13, 1974; children—Jon, Shannon, Patrick. B.A., So. Ill. U., 1965; M.S., Syracuse U., 1967, Ph.D., 1969. Lic. clin. psychologist, Miss. Staff psychologist Norristown State Hosp., Pa., 1969-72; staff psychologist St. Louis VA Med. Ctr., 1972-74; dir. internship VA Med. Ctr., Biloxi, Miss., 1974-84, chief psychologist, 1984—. USPHS fellow, 1965-66, 66-67. Mem. Am. Psychol. Assn. Republican. Club: Pass Christian Yacht (Miss.). Lodge: Elks. Home: PO Box 4274 Gulfport MS 39502 Office: Psychology Service 116B-1 VA Med Ctr Biloxi MS 39531

CARR, HAROLD NOFLET, airlines executive; b. Kansas City, Kans., Mar. 14, 1921; s. Noflet B. and Mildred (Addison) C.; B.S., Tex. A&M U., 1943; postgrad. Am. U., 1944-45; m. Mary Elizabeth Smith, Aug. 5, 1944; children—Steven Addison, Hal Douglas, James Taylor, Scott Noflet. Asst. dir. route devel. Trans World Airlines, Inc., 1943-47; exec. v.p. Wis. Central Airlines, Inc., 1947-52; mem. firm McKinsey & Co., 1952-54; dir. Republic Airlines, Inc., 1952—, chmn. bd., 1979-84, chmn. exec. com., 1984—; pres. N. Central Airlines, Inc., 1954-69, chmn. bd., 1965-79; professorial lectr. mgmt. engring. Am. U., 1952-62; dir. Dahlberg Inc., Ross Industries, Inc., Republic Energy, Inc., Cayman Water Co., Governor's Sound, Ltd., First Nat. Bank Bryan, Cayman Mile Ltd., OMI, Inc.; mem. devel. council Coll. Bus. Adminstrn., Tex. A&M U., adv. com. Tex. Transp. Inst., Tex. A&M U. System. Trustee, Tex. A&M Research Found.; bd. nominations Nat. Aviation Hall Fame. Served with AUS, 1942-43. Mem. World Bus. Council, Smithsonian Assos., Am. Mgmt. Assn., Air Transport Assn., Minn. Execs. Orgn., Tex. A&M Century Club and Former Students Assn., Nat. Aero. Assn. (Washington), Am. Assn. Airport Execs., Nat. Def. Transp. Assn., Am. Econ. Assn., Stearman Alumnus Club, Pine Beach Peninsula Assn., Beta Gamma Sigma. Episcopalian. Clubs: Nat. Aviation, Aero (Washington); Wings (N.Y.C.); Aggie (dir.), Briarcrest Country (Bryan, Tex.); Racquet (Miami); Gull Lake Yacht (Brainerd, Minn.); Minneapolis. Office: PO Box H Bryan TX 77805

CARR, HOWARD ERNEST, ret. ins. agy. exec.; b. Johnson City, Tenn., Oct. 4, 1908; s. William Alexander and Gertrude (Feathers) C.; B.S., E. Tenn. State U., 1929; M.Ed., Duke, 1935; postgrad. U. N.C., 1938-39; m. Thelma Northcutt, June 11, 1937 (dec. Oct., 1972); 1 son, Howard Ernest. Supt., Washington Coll. (Tenn.), 1929-35; ednl. advisor U.S. Office Edn., Ft. Oglethorpe, Ga., 1935-37; prin. Greensboro (N.C.) city schs., 1937-42; dir. activities First Presbyn. Ch., Greensboro, 1946-47; with Jefferson Standard Life Ins. Co., Greensboro, 1947—, spl. rep., 1947-54, supr. agy. Greensboro, 1964, mgr., 1964-67; pres. Everett's Lake Corp. Chmn. Guilford County Bd. Edn., 1950-77; vice chmn. N.C. Gov's Com. Edn., 1956-60; N.C. rep. White House Conf. Edn., 1955. Mem. adv. com. Greensboro div. Guilford Coll., 1958—; head Guilford County Cancer Drive, 1956, bd. dirs. Cancer Soc., 1956—; v.p. N.C. State Sch. Bds. Assn., 1959-61; bd. dirs. Greensboro Jr. Mus., 1956-62, Sternberger Found. Served to lt. with USNR, 1942-46, asst. head motion picture dept., Washington; to capt., 1951-54, as head motion picture dept; ret. as capt., 1968. Recipient Nat. Quality award, Nat. Assn. Life Underwriters, 1948—; named Boss of the Year, Lou-Celin chpt. Am. Bus. Woman's Assn., 1967; W.H. Andrews, Jr. award, 1985. Mem. Nat. C. (pres. 1964-65; Man of Year award 1969), Greensboro (pres. 1956-57) assns. life underwriters, N.C. Leaders Club, Greensboro C. of C. (chmn. edn. com. 1960-62). Presbyn. (elder). Mason (32 deg.), Kiwanian (pres. Greensboro 1951). Author: History of Higher Education in East Tennessee, 1935. Home: 3927 Madison Ave Greensboro NC 27410 Office: Jefferson Sq Greensboro NC 27401

CARR, JAMES GILES, psychologist; b. DeLand, Fla., Oct. 10, 1925; s. James Clark and Freta Claire (Tompkins) C.; m. Sara Ann Creech, July 15, 1949; children—Gavin Patrick, Michael Scott. B.A., Duke U., 1949; M.Ed., U. Fla., 1957, Ed.D., 1962. Lic. psychologist, N.C., Va. Math. instr., counselor Gainesville High Sch., Fla., 1957-59; instr., counselor U. Fla.-Gainesville, 1959-63; asst. prof. psychology U. Ga., Athens, 1963-65; staff psychologist Rohrer, Hibler & Replogle, Charlotte, N.C., 1965-67; sole practice mgmt. psychology, Charlotte, 1967—. Contbr. articles to mags. Served to lt. comdr. USN, 1952-53. Mem. Am. Psychol. Assn., N.C. Psychol. Assn., Sales and Mktg. Execs. Internat. Democrat. Baptist. Avocation: music. Home and Office: 2916 Goneaway Rd Charlotte NC 28210

CARR, KENNETH WILSON, JR., safety engineer; b. Richmond, Va., July 12, 1934; s. Kenneth Wilson and Enna (Branch) C.; student in Civil Engring., Va. Poly. Inst., 1953-56, Bituminous Mixture Sch., U. Va., 1957, various tng. schs.; m. Mary Annette Hachett, Mar. 12, 1960; children—James Douglas, Richard Stuart, Kenneth William. Hwy. engr. Va. Dept. Hwys., 1956-60; safety engring. rep. Aetna Casualty & Surety Co., Richmond, 1960-65, supt. engring. dept., Norfolk, Va., 1965-70, mgr. engring. dept., 1970-78, mgr. engring. dept., Nashville, 1978-84, Washington, 1984—; designer, instr. indsl. and constrn.

safety courses Old Dominion U., Tidewater Community Coll., 1970-77; lectr. on mgmt. Middle Tenn. State U., 1979-80. Little League baseball coach, 1971-77, football coach, 1974-78; chmn. adminstrv. bd., Sunday Sch. supt., adult tchr. United Ch. of Christ, Chesapeake, Va., 1965-77; lay leader, adult tchr. Mechanicsville Meth. Ch., 1960-65; mem. adminstrv. bd. Bethlehem Meth. Ch., Franklin, Tenn., 1979-81. Recipient Outstanding Vol. award ARC, 1977; registered profl. engr.; internat. cert. hazard control mgr. Mem. Am. Soc. Safety Engrs. (profl.; regional v.p., 1976-79, chpt. pres., 1968-69), Vets. of Safety, Fed. Safety Council, Asso. Builders and Contractors (safety com.). Republican. Lodge: Masons. Home: 4217 High Ridge Rd Haymarket VA 22069 Office: 7926 Jones Branch Dr Mc Lean VA 22102

CARR, MARJORIE BARNWELL, pediatrician; b. Kinston, N.C., Sept. 29, 1949; d. Robert Franklin and Marjorie (Rhodes) Barnwell; m. Robert Winston Carr, Jr., June 7, 1975. B.S. in Zoology, U. N.C., 1971, M.D., 1976. Intern N.C. Meml. Hosp., Chapel Hill, 1976-77, resident, 1977-79, fellow, 1979-80; pediatrician Fleming, Edwards, Goldman, Carr, Raleigh, N.C., 1980—; bd. dirs. Frankie Lemmon Developmental Presch., 1981—, v.p., 1982-83, sec., 1983-86; bd. dirs. Wake-Up for Children, Raleigh, 1981-83; mem. Wake County Task Force for Handicapped Children, 1982—, chmn., 1985-86; mem. Project O-3. Mem. Big Sister Program, Durham, 1976-78, Education for Ministry, 1985—; mem. Christ Ch. Young Adults, Raleigh, 1982—; pres. Raleigh Area Masters Swim Team, 1980-82. Fellow Am. Acad. Pediatrics; mem. AMA, N.C. Pediatric Soc. (mem. liason com., com. for care of handicapped children), Wake County Med. Soc., Kappa Delta. Democrat. Episcopalian.

CARR, PATRICK E., U.S. dist. ct. judge; b. Jasper County, Miss., Oct. 2, 1922; s. Eugene A. and Sarah (Finnegan) C.; grad. St. Bernard Jr. Coll.; LL.B., Loyola U.; m. Jean Massey, Dec. 20, 1947; children—Karen, Stanley, Judy, Janice, Pat, Mary, Brian. Admitted to La. bar, 1950; pvt. practice, Metaire, La., 1950-75; judge La. Dist. Ct., 24th Jud. Dist., 1975-79; now U.S. Dist. Ct. judge, Eastern Dist. La., New Orleans. Served with U.S. Army, 1942-45. Mem. Am. Bar Assn., Jefferson Parish Bar Assn., La. State Bar Assn., VFW (nat. comdr.). Democrat. Office: US Courthouse 500 Camp St Chambers C-376 New Orleans LA 70130

CARR, THOMAS ELDRIDGE, lawyer; b. Austin, Tex., Aug. 16, 1953; s. Peter Gordon and Margaret (Johnson) C.; m. Cathy Diane Franson, Dec. 18, 1977; 1 child, Christopher Allen. B.A., Tex. Tech U., 1975, J.D., 1977. Bar: Tex. 1978, U.S. Dist. Ct. (no. dist.) Tex. 1978, U.S. Ct. Appeals (5th cir.) 1981, U.S. Supreme Ct. 1982. Assoc. Morgan, Gambill & Owen, Fort Worth, 1978-81; ptnr. Morgan, Owen, & Carr, Fort Worth, 1981-85, Quillin, Owen & Thompson, Fort Worth, 1985—. Co-author: Of Counsel to Classrooms: A Resource Guide to Assist Attorneys and Teachers in Law Focused Education. Active Benbrook City Council, Tex., 1984—, Park and Recreation Bd., Benbrook, 1981-84; mem. exec. bd. Longhorn council Boy Scouts Am., 1983—; mem. devel. bd. Western Nat. Bank Tex., Fort Worth, 1983—; mem. Home Rule Charter Commn., Benbrook, 1983. Named one of Outstanding Young Men of Am. Mem. ABA, Fort Worth Tarrant County Young Lawyers Assn. (pres. 1983), Tex. Young Lawyers Assn. (bd. dirs. 1984—). Clubs: Petroleum, Lost Creek Country (Fort Worth). Office: Quillin Owen & Thompson 550 Bailey Ave Suite 530 Fort Worth TX 76107

CARRABBA, MICHAEL PAUL, aircraft components manufacturing company executive; b. Dayton, Ohio, Jan. 31, 1945; s. Paul G. and Margie (Nichols) C.; student Miami Dade Jr. Coll., 1964—. Gen. mgr. D&C—Airparts Corp., Hialeah, Fla., 1969-70, pres., owner, 1970—, also chmn. bd.; pres. D.C. A/P Battery Co., 1974—, D.C. A/P Battery of Europe, D.C. Battery Exide div. M.P.C. & Assos., 1969—. Served with USMCR, 1962-66. Mem. Nat. Pilots Assn., Profl. Aviation Maintenance Assn., Nat. Air Transp. Conf., Nat. Bus. Aircraft Assn., Am. Helicopter Soc., Aviation Maintenance Found. Home: 10305 SW 53d St Cooper City FL 33055 Office: 485 W 27th St Hialeah FL 33010 also PO Box 700 Hialeah FL 33011

CARRENO, OCTAVIO B., ophthalmologist; b. Havana, Cuba, May 14, 1936; came to U.S., 1961, naturalized, 1967; s. Bienvenido and Graciela (Otero) C.; m. Cenaida Canales, Apr. 23, 1960; children—Teresa, Octavio. B.S., Inst. Secondary Edn., Havana, 1953; med. degree U. Madrid Sch. Medicine, 1960. Diplomate Am. Bd. Ophthalmology. Intern, Mt. Sinai Hosp., Miami Beach, Fla., 1962-63; ophthalmology resident U. Tex.-Galveston, 1965-68; fellow ophthalmology Mount Sinai Hosp., Miami, Fla., 1970-71; prof. opthalmology U. Tex. Med. Sch., Galveston, 1975-76; practice medicine specializing in ophthalmology, Miami, 1976—; pres. staff Bascom Palmer Eye Inst., Miami, 1982-84; chief ophthalmology Mercy Hosp., Miami, 1983-85. Served with armed forces, 1968-70. Mem. Dade County Med. Assn., Fla. Med. Assn., Fla. Soc. Ophthalmology, Am. Acad. Ophthalmology, World Med. Assn. Republican. Roman Catholic. Clubs: Jockey, Big Five. Home: 1221 Obispo Ave Coral Gables FL 33134

CARRENO, PABLO A., food manufacturing company executive, engineering company executive; b. Havana, Cuba, Apr. 11, 1925; s. Pable F. and Maria C. (Camps) C.; m. Josefina Lopez-Ona; children—Pablo, Alberto, Josefina. B.S. in Chem. Engring., Havana U., 1946, B.S. in Agrl. Engring., 1947; postgrad. La. State U., 1947, Alexander Hamilton Inst., 1972. Research engr. Am. Cyanamid Co., Stamford, Conn., 1947-48; mgr. Transportes and Almacenes Covadonga, S.A., L.V., Cuba, 1948-50; shift supr. Cia Rayonera Cubana, Matanzas, Cuba, 1950-53; gen. supt. Central Sta. Lutgarda, S.A., L.V., Cuba, 1953-60; v.p. prodn. Gulf and Western Food Products, Miami, Fla., 1961—; sec./treas. C&A Engring. Co., Miami, 1979—. Active charity drives. Mem. Am. Soc. Sugar Cane Technologists (1st v.p.), Am. Soc. Chem. Engrs., Sugar Industry Tech. (dir.), Agrl. Engrs. Soc. Republican. Roman Catholic. Club: Big — 5 — (Miami). Author tech. papers. Home: 9321 SW 69th St Miami FL 33173 Office: PO Box 86 South Bay FL 33493

CARRERE, CHARLES SCOTT, judge; b. Dublin, Ga., Sept. 26, 1937; B.A., U. Ga., 1959; LL.B., Stetson U., 1961. Admitted to Fla. bar, 1961, Ga. bar, 1960; law clk. to U.S. Dist. judge, Orlando, 1962-63; asst. U.S. atty. Middle Dist. Fla., 1963-66, chief trial atty., 1965-66, spl. asst. to U.S. atty., 1966-67; partner firm Harrison, Greene, Mann, Rowe & Stanton, St. Petersburg, 1970-80; county judge Pinellas County (Fla.), 1980—. Served with inf. AUS. Mem. Am., Fla., St. Petersburg bar assns., Stetson Lawyers Assn. (dir. 1968), Phi Beta Kappa, Phi Delta Phi. Home: PO Box 41707 Saint Petersburg FL 33743

CARRICO, HARRY LEE, state justice; b. Washington, Sept. 4, 1916; s. William Temple and Nellie Nadalia (Willett) C.; jr. certificate George Washington U., 1938, J.D., 1942; LL.D. (hon.), U. Richmond (Va.), 1973; m. Betty Lou Peck, May 18, 1940; 1 dau., Lucretia Ann. Admitted to Va. bar, 1941; with firm Rust & Rust, Fairfax, 1941-43; trial justice Fairfax County, Va., 1943-51; pvt. practice, Fairfax, 1951-56; judge 16th Jud. Circuit Va., 1956-61; justice Supreme Ct. Va., 1961—, chief justice, 1981—. Bd. dirs. Conf. of Chief Justices, 1985—. Served to ensign USNR, 1945-46. Recipient Alumni Achievement award George Washington U., 1972. Mem. McNeill Law Soc., Order of Coif, Phi Delta Phi. Episcopalian. Home: 9303 Cragmont Dr Richmond VA 23229 Office: Supreme Ct Bldg Richmond VA 23210

CARRINGTON, JOY HARRELL, artist, art teacher; b. Jacksonville, Tex.; d. Benjamin German and Mollie Elizabeth (Anderson) Harrell; m. William Lorrin Carrington, Sept. 20, 1934. Student Kansas City Art Inst., 1924-26, Am. Acad. Art, Chgo., 1927, Nat. Acad. Art, Chgo., 1928, Art Inst. Chgo., 1946, Art Students League, N.Y.C., 1948-51. Comml. artist Montgomery Ward Co., Kansas City, Ft. Worth, Chgo., 1925-28; staff artist Hartman Furniture Co., Chgo., 1928-29; free-lance artist, N.Y.C., 1930, San Antonio, 1931-34; staff artist Handelan & Staff, Chgo., 1935-36; art tchr. Joy Carrington Studio, Medina, Tex., 1965—, Dietert Sr Citizen Claim, Kerrville, Tex., 1975. One-woman exhbns. include: Witte Meml. Mus., San Antonio, 1963, Meinhard Gallery, Houston, 1973, Rotunda Art Gallery, Houston, 1984; group exhbns. include: McNamara O'Connor Hist. and Fine Arts Mus., Victoria, Tex., 1968, Panhandle Plains Mus., Canyon, Tex., 1969-80, Am. Artists Profl. League, N.Y.C., 1976-83, Coppini Acad. Fine Arts, San Antonio, 1955-85, Springville Mus. Art, Utah, 1985; represented in permanent collections including: Long Barrack Mus., Alamo, San Antonio, Coppini Acad. Fine Arts, San Antonio; illustrator: Illuminated Memorial Book, 1962; illuminated manuscript Daughters of the Republic of Texas, 1963; bicentennial illumination Daughters of the American Revolution, 1976. Recipient Best of Show award Coppini Acad. Fine Arts, 1983, 3d place, 1984, honorable mention, 1985. Mem. Am. Artists Profl. League (Grumbacher award 1969), Nat. Soc. Arts and Letters, San Antonio Watercolor Group. Club: Kerrville Art. Avocations: flower gardening; traveling. Home: T-Anchor Ranch Route 16 Box 30 Medina TX 78055

CARRINGTON, LOWRY LEWIS, mathematics educator, real estate consultant; b. Paris, Tex., July 15, 1937; s. Lewis A. and LeOla (Rhodes) C.; m. Glenna Oglesby, Sept. 7, 1957; 1 child, LaDonna Joye. A.A., Paris Jr. Coll., 1957; B.A., E. Tex. State U., 1960, M.A., 1967; postgrad. U. Tex.-Austin, 1966-67, U. Kans.-Lawrence, 1966, U. Mo.-Rolla, 1969, Columbia U., 1971. Tchr. Paris Pub. Schs., 1961-66; instr. math. Paris Jr. Coll., 1967—; real estate cons. Carrington Properties, Paris, 1970—. Mem. Tex. Jr. Coll. Tchrs. Assn., Math. Assn. Am., Nat. Assn. Realtors, Tex. Assn. Realtors, Nat. Assn. Homebuilders. Republican. Methodist. Club: Paris Rotary (dir. 1978). Avocations: sports; collecting; gardening. Home: 1040 Johnson Woods Dr Paris TX 75460 Office: Carrington Realtors 1954 Clarksville St Paris TX 75460

CARRINGTON, PAUL BUTLER, periodontist, educator; b. Eldorado, Ark., Oct. 5, 1927; s. Hamilton Kelso and Hazel (Butler) C.; m. Vivienne Lemley Manning, Apr. 14, 1984; children from previous marriage—Stephen, David, Angela. A.A., Magnolia A&M Coll., 1949; D.D.S., Baylor U., 1954, B.S.D. in Dentistry, 1960; B.A., So. State Coll., 1959. Practice dentistry specializing in periodontics and endodontics, Dallas, 1960—; pres. Paul B. Carrington, D.D.S., Inc., Dallas, 1970—; tchr. Baylor Coll. Dentistry, Dallas, 1960-63, 76-82. Editor Dallas County Dental Jour. Contbr. articles to dental publs. Dental missionary Wycliffe Bible Translators, Peru, 1966; area dir. Inst. in Basic Youth Conflicts, Dallas, 1970s. Served to 1st lt. U.S. Army, 1945-48, capt. USN, 1953-59. Fellow Acad. Gen. Dentistry (award 1965); mem. Tex. Dental Assn., ADA, Am. Acad. Periodontology, Am. Assn. Endodontists, Res. Officers Assn (life). Republican. Baptist. Avocations: philately; travel. Office: 10405 E Northwest Hwy Dallas TX 75238

CARRITHERS, ROBERT WILSON, pharmacist, realtor, insurance agent; b. Shelbyville, Ky., July 2, 1950; s. Robert Clay and Norma Janet (Spears) C.; m. Betty Jane Pike, June 13, 1981; 1 child, Cassandra Aine. B.S. in Pharmacy, U. Ky., 1974. Registered pharmacist, Ky. Pharmacist, mgr. W.T. Froman Drug, Inc., Taylorsville, Ky., 1974—; life and health agt. Mass. Indemnity and Life Ins. Co., Mt. Washington, Ky., 1984—. Chmn. Spencer County br. Ky. Retail Fedn., Taylorsville, 1984—. Mem. Nat. Assn. Retail Druggists, Ky. Assn. Retail Druggists, Nat. Fedn. Ind. Bus., Nat. Bd. Realtors, Ky. Bd. Realtors. Democrat. Baptist. Avocations: golf; music. Home: 104 Hilltop Dr Mount Washington KY 40047 Office: W T Froman Drug Inc Main St Box 217 Taylorsville KY 40071

CARROLL, CHARLES LEMUEL, JR., mathematician; b. Whitsett, N.C., Sept. 16, 1916; s. Charles Lemuel and Erma Ruth (Greason) C.; m. Geraldine Budd, June 8, 1938; children—Geraldine Heitman, Charlda Sizemore, Charles Lemuel III. B.S., Guilford Coll., 1936; A.M., U. N.C., 1937, Ph.D., 1945. Instr. math. Ga. Inst. Tech., Atlanta, 1939-42; assoc. prof. math. N.C. State U., Raleigh, 1946-55; research adminstr. Air Force Office Sci. Research, Balt., 1955-56; mgr. systems analysis RCA Service Co., Patrick AFB, Fla., 1956-61; asst. dir. Aerospace Corp., Atlantic Missile Range, Fla., 1961-62; mgr. tech. staff Pan Am World Airways, Patrick AFB, 1962-72; mgr. info. systems Pan Am World Services, Cocoa Beach, Fla., 1972—. Elder, Eastminster Presbyn. Ch., Indialantic, Fla., 1962—; bd. dirs. South Brevard YMCA, Melbourne, Fla., 1959-65, v.p., 1962-63. Served to lt. comdr. USNR, 1943-57. Assoc. fellow AIAA; mem. Am. Math. Soc., Inst. Math. Stats. Sigma Xi. Democrat. Home: 109 Michigan Ave Indialantic FL 32903 Office: Pan Am World Services Inc 1325 N Atlantic Ave Cocoa Beach FL 32931

CARROLL, CHARLES MICHAEL, educator; b. Otterbein, Ind., Mar. 5, 1921; s. James William and Catherine Doretta (Bohan) C.; B.M., Ind. U. at Bloomington, 1949; M.M., Fla. State U., Tallahassee, 1951, Ph.D., 1960; m. Mary Lipford Rosenbush, Sept. 4, 1951; children—Charles Michael, Mary Catherine, Theresa Jane, William Rosenbush. Asst. coordinator music services Ind. U., 1949-50; instr. music Fla. State U., 1950-53; concert mgr. symphony orchs. Toledo, Washington, Savannah, Ga., 1953-58; prof. music Pensacola (Fla.) Jr. Coll., 1960-64; prof. St. Petersburg (Fla.) Jr. Coll., 1964— music critic Tallahassee Democrat, 1950-53, St. Petersburg Evening Independent, 1976—. Served to capt., AUS, 1942-46; ETO. Mem. Am. Symphony Orch. League (v.p. 1955-56), Am. Musicol. Soc. (nat. council 1974-77, chmn. chpt. 1974-76), Am. Soc. Eighteenth-Century Studies (exec. bd. region 1974-82, regional pres. 1979-80), Coll. Music Soc. (editor 1979-83, nat. council 1978-81, chmn. chpt. 1979-80). Author: The Great Chess Automaton, 1975; contbr. articles to profl. jours. Home: 1701 80th St N Saint Petersburg FL 33710

CARROLL, CHARLOTTE ANNE, nurse; b. Sweeden, Ky., Oct. 26, 1944; d. Loren Dee and Annie Pauline (DeWeese) Pruitt; m. Chester Dwight Carroll, June 10, 1967. Diploma, Glasgow Sch. Practical Nursing (Ky.), 1982; student Western Ky. U., 1977—. Sitter in home, Rhoda, Ky., 1972-73, Sweeden, part-time 1973-81; dairy hand Webb & Son Dairy Farm, Sweeden, 1979-80; clk. Lane's Furniture Store, Sweeden, part-time 1981-82; charge nurse Medco Nursing Home, Bowling Green, Ky., 1982-83; nurse Med. Ctr., Bowling Green, 1983—. Mem. Glasgow Sch. Practical Nursing Alumni Assn. (v.p. 1982-84). Democrat. Baptist. Home: PO Box 203 Sweeden KY 42285 Office: Med Ctr 250 Park St Bowling Green KY 42210

CARROLL, EDWARD ELMER, JR., nuclear engineering educator, consultant; b. North Bergen, N.J., Feb. 13, 1930; s. Edward Elmer and May Rita (Sullivan) C.; m. Joann Marie Harrington, Dec. 27, 1959 (dec. 1971); children—Cynthia, Megan, Edward, III; m. 2d, Thuy Thanh Tong, Dec. 12, 1975; children—Thanh-Mai, Giang Thanh. B.A., Harvard U., 1950; M.S., U. Pa., 1952, Ph.D., 1959. Sr. scientist Westinghouse Bettis Lab., West Mifflin, Pa., 1959-64; fellow scientist Westinghouse Electric Corp., Pitts., 1964-66; assoc. prof. nuclear engring. U. Fla., Gainesville, 1966-70, asst. dean Coll. Engring., 1971-74, acting chmn. nuclear engring., 1976-79, prof. nuclear engring. scis., 1972—. vis. staff mem. Los Alamos Nat. Lab., 1970-71. Bd. dirs. Cath. Charities, Inc., North Fla., 1980—. Served to lt. (j.g.) U.S. Navy, 1952-55. Mem. Am. Phys. Soc., Am. Nuclear Soc., Soc. Photo Optical Instrumentation Engrs., Sigma Tau, Tau Beta Pi. Contbr. articles to profl. publs.; patentee in field.

CARROLL, FELIX ALVIN, JR., chemistry educator; b. High Point, N.C., Aug. 17, 1947; s. Felix Alvin and Addie (Doss) C.; m. Linda Carol Crutchfield, July 15, 1972; children—Heather Elaine, Brandon Russell. B.S. with highest honors in Chemistry, U. N.C., 1969; Ph.D. in Organic Chemistry, Calif. Inst. Tech., 1972. Asst. prof. Davidson Coll., N.C., 1972-80, assoc. prof., 1980—. Author numerous research articles. Patentee in field. Research grantee NSF, Research Corp., Petroleum Research Fund, Camille and Henry Dreyfus Found., Pitts. Conf. Grants Program, N.C. Bd. Sci. and Tech. Mem. Am. Chem. Soc. (program chmn. 35th Southeast regional Meeting 1983), AAAS, Inter-Am. Photochem. Soc. Quaker. Club: Wildcat Investment (pres. 1978-79, sec. 1976-77) (Davidson, N.C.). Avocations: gardening; photography. Home: PO Box 1647 Davidson NC 28036 Office: Dept Chemistry Davidson Coll Davidson NC 28036

CARROLL, FRANK IVY, organic chemist; b. Norcross, Ga., Mar. 28, 1935; s. Frank Edwin and Jewel (Ivy) C.; m. Sara Mildred Castleman, June 8, 1957; children—Wayne, Connie. B.S., Auburn U., 1957; Ph.D., U. N.C., 1961. Chemist, Research Triangle Inst., Research Triangle Park, N.C., 1960-64, sr. chemist, 1964-68, group leader, 1968-71, asst. dir., 1971-75, dir., 1975—; adj. prof. textile chemistry N.C. State U., Raleigh, 1982—. Patentee in field (2); contbr. articles to profl. jours. Fellow Am. Chem. Soc.; mem. Am. Chem. Soc., AAAS, Sigma Xi, Phi Lambda Upsilon. Avocations: fishing; hunting; tennis. Home: 5124 N Willowhaven Dr Durham NC 27712 Office: Research Triangle Inst PO Box 12194 Research Triangle Park NC 27709

CARROLL, FRANK MORRIS, college dean, conductor; b. Norfolk, Va., Mar. 19, 1928; s. Richard Norman and Annie Laurie (Morris) C.; m. Constance Knox, Aug. 17, 1963; children—Frank Knox, Arthur Richard. B. Music, Shenandoah Conservatory, 1950; M. Music Coll. Music Cin., 1952; Ph.D., Eastman Sch. Music, 1960. Asst. prof. Md. State Coll., Princess Anne, 1961-63; assoc. prof. Salisbury State Coll., Md., 1963-66; prof. U. Wis., Superior, 1966-69; dean, sch. music Centenary Coll., Shreveport, La., 1969-74, 79—; dept. chmn. Appalachian State U., Boone, N.C., 1974-79; condr. Marshall Symphony, Tex., 1966-68, Longview Symphony, Tex., 1968-69, 79—; bd. dirs. Shreveport Symphony, 1984—, Shreveport Opera, 1979-82. Composer: Old Woman and the Pig, 1966; Concerto for Piano, 1969 (1st prize concerto category Wis.); Suite for Violin and Piano, 1968. Mem. Nat. Fed. Music Clubs (nat. chmn. orchs. 1983—), La. Music Tchrs. Assn. (chmn. for theory, composition 1984—). Roman Catholic. Avocations: horticulture; Spanish language and culture. Home: 518 Sophia Ln Shreveport LA 71115 Office: Dean Music Centenary Coll 2911 Centenary Blvd Shreveport LA 71104

CARROLL, GEORGE JOSEPH, physician; b. Gardner, Mass., Oct. 14, 1917; s. George J. and Kathryn (O'Hearn) C.; A.B., Clark U., 1939; M.D., George Washington U., 1944. Intern, Worcester (Mass.) City Hosp., 1944-45; resident Doctors Hosp., 1945-46, Sibley Hosp., 1948-49, VA Hosp., 1949-50, all Washington; asst. pathologist D.C. Gen. Hosp., 1950-51, pathologist, 1951-52; practice medicine, specializing in pathology, Suffolk and Franklin, Va., 1952—; pathologist Louise Obili Meml. Hosp., Suffolk, Southampton Meml. Hosp., Franklin, Greensville Meml. Hosp., Emporia, Va., all 1952—; instr. pathology Med. Sch., Georgetown U., Washington, 1950-52; instr. clin. micrology Am. U., Washington, 1950-51; asso. clin. prof. pathology Med. Coll. Va., Richmond, 1968—; clin. prof. pathology Health Sci. Center, Va. Commonwealth U., Richmond, 1970—. Mem. Va. Bd. Med. Examiners, 1967—, sec., treas., 1970—. Bd. dirs. Va. div. Am. Cancer Soc., 1955-62, Va. Med. Service Assn., 1960-71. Diplomate Am. Bd. Pathology. Fellow Am. Soc. Clin. Pathologists (dir. 1969-75, 1st v.p. 1974-75, pres. 1976-77), Coll. Am. Pathologists, A.C.P.; mem. Am. Assn. Blood Banks, Va. Soc. Pathology (sec., treas. 1954-68, pres. 1973-74, mem. council), Va. Med. Soc. (mem. ho. of dels. 1960-80), Med. Soc. Va., So. Med. Assn. (councillor from Va. 1965-70, chmn. council 1969-70, 1st v.p. 1971-72, pres. 1973-74), 4th Dist. Med. Soc. Va. (pres. 1968), Internat. Acad. Pathology, AMA, George Washington, D.C. (asso.), Seaboard (past pres.) med. socs., Am. Soc. Clin. Pharmacy and Therapeutics, Soc. Nuclear Medicine. Rotarian. Home: 219 Northbrooke Ave Suffolk VA 23434 Office: Louise Obici Meml Hosp Suffolk VA 23434

CARROLL, MARY ANN, philosophy educator; b. Baton Rouge, May 31, 1947; d. Frank Theodore Jr. and Patricia Ann (Farr) C.; m. Bruce Nicholas Richter, Sept. 1, 1967 (div. Dec. 1980). B.A., U. New Orleans, 1969; M.A., U. N.C., 1971, Ph.D., 1973. Lectr. U. N.C., Chapel Hill, summer 1973; asst. prof. Appalachian State U., Boone, N.C., 1973-77, assoc. prof., 1977-83, prof. philosophy, 1983—; applied ethics cons. Mem. Am. Philos. Assn., So. Soc. for Philosophy and Psychology, N.C. Philos. Soc., Am. Assn. Philosophy Tchrs. Author: The Right to Treatment and Involuntary Commitment; also book revs. Co-author: Moral Problems in Nursing: Case Studies, 1979; Ethics in the Practice of Psychology, 1984; author: The Right to Treatment and Involuntary Commitment. Office: Philosophy-Religion Department Appalachian State Univ Boone NC 28608

CARROLL, RICHARD FRANK, exploration geologist; b. Abilene. Tex., Oct. 10, 1956; s. Arthur Lee and Margaret Ramona (Wilkinson) C. B.S. in Geol. Scis., U. Tex., 1980. Geologist exploration AGIP Petroleum Co., Inc., Houston, 1981-84, Ultramar Oil & Gas, Ltd., Houston, 1985—. Mem., Houston Mus. of Fine Arts, 1984—. Mem. Am. Assn. Petroleum Geologists, Houston Geol. Soc., Soc. of Econ. Palentologists and Mineralogists of AIME. Democrat. Presbyterian. Avocations: painting; sculpting; raquetball. Home: 1133 Merrill Houston TX 77009 Office: Ultramar Oil & Gas Ltd 16825 Northchase Suite 1200 Houston TX 77060

CARROLL, ROBERT ALLEN, educational administrator; b. El Dorado, Ark., Jan. 31, 1944; s. Robert L. and Vivian (Allen) C.; m. Hope McCutchen, Nov. 22, 1966; children—Jenni, Brad. B.A. in Journalism, Northeast La. U., Monroe, 1968; M.A. in Journalism, East Tex. State U., 1975. News reporter News-Times, El Dorado, Ark., 1962-64, Morning World, Monroe, La., 1964-66; asst. city editor News-Star-World, Monroe, 1966-70; asst. dir. pub. relations Northeast La. U., Monroe, 1970-73, dir. pub. relations, 1973—. Dir. communications United Way of Ouachita, Monroe, 1984, 85. Recipient Feature Writing award UPI, 1966, Pacesetter award City of Monroe, 1970, Achievement award Council Advancement and Support of Edn., 1979. Mem. Pub. Relations Assn. La. (pres. 1985, Practitioner of Yr. 1983), La. Higher Edn. Pub. Relations Assn., So. Pub. Relations Assn., West Monroe C. of C. (bd. dirs. 1985), Sigma Delta Chi. Democrat. Baptist. Lodge: Rotary. Avocations: fishing; hunting; coin collecting. Home: 100 Teakwood Dr West Monroe LA 71291 Office: Northeast La U 700 University Dr Monroe LA 71209

CARROLL, SEAVY ALEXANDER, lawyer, former judge; b. Lumberton, N.C., Feb. 4, 1918; s. Samuel Willard and Berta (Butler) C.; m. Virginia Brooks Corbett, Nov. 16, 1956; children—Carrie, Catherine, Wesley, Martha, Ernest. B.A., Wake Forest U., 1940, LL.B., 1946, J.D., 1970; postgrad. St. Andrews Coll., Eng., 1959, Ind. U., 1965, Nat. Coll. State Judiciary, 1973. Bar: N.C. 1947, U.S. Dist. Ct. (ea. dist.) N.C. 1948. Adviser Duke Legal Aid Clinic, 1946-47; sole practice, Fayetteville, N.C., 1947-58; ptnr. Carroll & Herring, Fayetteville, 1958-59; missionary United Methodist Ch., Rhodesia, 1959-70; supt. schs. Nyadiri, Rhodesia, 1960; dir. publicity and promotion, Salisbury, Rhodesia, 1961-69; judge Cumberland County Recorders Ct., 1952-56, 12th Jud. Dist., 1970-74; sole practice, Fayetteville, 1974—; atty. Town of Spring Lake, N.C., 1974-78; adviser Duke Legal Aid Clinic. Chmn., United Fund, 1949; mem. N.C. Senate, 1957-59. Mem. ABA, N.C. Bar Assn., 12th Jud. Dist. Bar Assn., Cumberland County Bar Assn. Democrat. Contbr. articles to religious jours. Home: 2404 Morganton Rd Fayetteville NC 28303 Office: 115 S Cool Spring St Fayetteville NC 28301

CARROLL, STAN J., insurance broker; b. Avon, S.D., Aug. 6, 1925; s. Raymond James and Genevieve Delores (Waggoner) C.; m. LaVoin B. Payne, Apr. 19, 1958; children—Christiana Moreno, Jay Bradford. B.A., Cornell Coll., 1949; postgrad. in secondary edn. Colo. State U. Spl. agt. Am. Surety Co., San Francisco, 1950-52; sales rep. Levi Strauss & Co., San Francisco, San Jose, Calif., Phoenix, Shreveport, La., Little Rock, Denver, Corpus Christi, Tex., 1952-69; franchise owner Mr. Swiss stores, Tex., 1969-72; ins. broker and agt. Mony and Mony Securities Corp. Houston, 1972—. Bd. dirs. Harris County Water Dist. (Tex.), 1970-79. Served with USNR, 1943-64; PTO. Mem. Nat. Assn. Life Underwriters (Nat. Sales Achievement award 1976, 80, Nat. Quality award, 1976, 80), Health Underwriters Assn. Am. (Health Quality award 1976, 79), Million Dollar Round Table, Tex. Life Underwriter (Tex. leader 1979), Cornell Coll. Alumni Assn. (class agt.), Houston C. of C. Republican. Methodist. Club: Kiwanis (Houston) (v.p. 1979). Home: 1610 Mossy Stone Houston TX 77077 Office: 5847 San Felipe St Suite 1400 Houston TX 77057

CARROW, DONALD JAMES, physician; b. Miami, Fla., May 1, 1934; s. James and Dorothy (Tuck) C.; B.S., U. Miami, Coral Gables, Fla., 1962; postgrad. Roosevelt U., Chgo., 1963-64; M.D., U. Louisville, 1969; m. Deborah Ann Ray, June 8, 1979. Intern, U. Louisville Affiliated Hosps., 1969-70, resident in anesthesiology, 1970-72; staff Clark County Meml. Hosp., 1971, Norton Meml. Infirmary, Louisville, 1972, Suburban Hosp., Louisville, 1972; asst. to dir. anesthesiology Norton Children's Hosp., Louisville, 1974-77; dir. anesthesiology Med. Center Hosp., Largo, Fla., 1978-79; founder, head Largo Ctr. for Preventive and Gen. Medicine, 1980—; staff Univ. Gen. Hosp., Seminole, Fla., 1981—; clin. instr. Louisville Sch. Medicine, 1970-72, instr., 1972-74, asst. prof., 1974-77. Served with U.S. Army, 1952-55. Mem. AMA, Ky. Med. Assn., Am. Soc. Anesthesiologists, Ky. Soc. Anesthesiologists, La. Soc. Anesthesiologists, So. Med. Assn., Pinellas County Med. Soc., Am. Acad. Med. Preventics, Internat. Acad. Preventive Medicine, Largo C. of C. Republican. Club: Kiwanis. Contbr. articles to profl. jours. Office: 147 N Belcher Rd Suite 4 Largo FL 33541

CARRUTH, ALLEN HIGGINS, insurance company executive; b. Houston, Sept. 7, 1919; s. B.F. and Frances (Headly) C.; m. Ethel Mae Greasley, Feb. 28, 1943; children—Carolyn Carruth Rizza, J. Allen, Brady F. Student U. Tex., 1937-38; B.S. in Econs., U. Pa., 1942. With firm John L. Wortham & Son, Houston, 1946—, ptnr., 1950—, mng. ptnr., 1965—, chmn. exec. com., 1978—; dir., mem. exec. com., chmn. audit com. Am. Gen. Corp.; dir., mem. exec. com., chmn. audit com. Entex; dir. Allied Bank of Tex. Pres. bd. dirs. Wortham Found.; bd. dirs. Houston Grand Opera; mem. exec. com., bd. dirs. Houston Soc. for Prevention Cruelty to Animals, 1950—; chmn. bd., past pres. Houston Livestock Show and Rodeo, 1979-81. Served to maj. USAAF, 1941-46. Named Westerner of Yr., Houston Farm and Ranch Club, 1982; Humanitarian of Yr., Houston Soc. for Prevention Cruelty to Animals, 1980. Mem. Nat. Assn. Casualty and Surety Agts. (dir., pres., mem. exec. com.), Houston C. of C. (past dir.), Santa Gertrudis Breeders Internat. (past officer and dir.). Presbyterian. Home: 5545 Candlewood Dr Houston TX 77056 Office: PO Box 1388 Houston TX 77251

CARRUTHERS, ROBERT LYNN, building materials company executive, insurance and real estate executive; b. Memphis, Mar. 9, 1943; s. Stanley and Doris Carruthers; m. Sally Kosloski, July 19, 1961; 1 child, Mary Catharine. Student Memphis State U., 1965-68. Prodn. mgr. Alpha Chem. Corp., Collierville, Tenn., 1966-66, 68-70; developer Residential Subdivs., Collierville, 1973—; pres., v.p. Carruthers Harris Ins. Co., Collierville, 1975—; pres. Carruthers Ready Mix Co., Collierville, 1974—. Named to Circle Agt. Council Continental Ins., 1984-85. Mem. Associated Builders and Contractors (treas. 1983-84, v.p. 1984-85), Tenn. Bldg. Materials Assn., Memphis Ready Mix Assn. (v.p. 1983-84), Tenn. Constrn. Coalition (bd. dirs. 1986—). Episcopalian. Avocations: hunting; tennis. Lodge: Rotary (pres. 1977). Home: 11944 E Holmes Collierville TN 38017 Office: Carruthers Ready Mix Inc PO Box 368 Collierville TN 38017

CARRY, L. RAY, mathematics educator, researcher; b. Ector, Tex., Aug. 27, 1932; s. O.R. and Oleta (Ramey) C.; m. Mary Joyce Cobern, May 6, 1951; children—Rodney Lynn, Lisa Carry Barbour, Susan Carry Craig. B.A., North Tex. State U., 1952, M.S., 1960; M.S., Stanford U., 1964, Ph.D., 1968. Elec. engr. S.W. Bell Telephone Co., Dallas, 1952-58; math. instr. North Tex. State U., Denton, 1958-61; instrumentation engr. Lockheed, Sunnyvale, Calif., 1961-62; math. instr. Foothill Coll., Los Altos Hills, Calif., 1964-65; research assoc. Sch. Math. Study Group, Stanford, Calif., 1965-68, cons., 1968-72; prof. U. Tex., Austin, 1968—; cons. Project Math. Devel. Children, Tallahassee, Fla., 1974-76. Co-author: Field Mathematics Program, 1973; contbr. articles to profl. jours. NSF grantee, 1978-80. Mem. Math. Assn. Am., Nat. Council Tchrs. Math (chmn. research jour., editorial bd. 1976-77), Am. Ednl. Research Assn. (steering com. 1970, 80). Republican. Avocation: house restoration. Office: Dept Math U Tex-Austin Austin TX 78712

CARSON, CULLEY CLYDE, III, urologist; b. Westerly, R.I., Feb. 25, 1945; s. Culley Clyde, Jr., and Dorothy (Scarborough) C.; B.S., Trinity Coll., 1967; M.D., George Washington U., 1971; m. Mary Jo McDonald, Aug. 10, 1970; children—Culley Clyde IV, Hilary. Intern, Dartmouth Med. Center, 1971-72, resident in surgery, 1971-73; fellow in urology Mayo Clinic, 1975-78; instr. urology U. Minn. Mayo Med. Sch., 1978; asst. prof. urology Duke U. Med. Center, Durham, N.C., 1978-84, assoc. prof., 1984—; chief urology Durham VA Hosp. Served to maj. M.C., USAF, 1973-75. Am. Heart Assn. research fellow, 1969; O'Dea travel fellow, 1978; recipient Calvin Klopp research award, 1971, Friedman research prize, 1971; named Command Flight Surgeon of Yr., USAF, 1974. Diplomate Am. Bd. Urology. Fellow ACS; mem. AMA, Am. Urol. Assn., Internat. Société d'Urologie, Am. Fertility Soc., Univ. Urol. Forum, AAAS, N.Y. Acad. Scis., Sigma Xi, Psi Chi, Alpha Omega Alpha. Clubs: Durham Sports, Duke U. Faculty, Mayo Alumni Assn. Club: Trinity (Hartford). Author: Endourology, 1985; Atlas of Urologic Endoscopy, 1986; contbr. chpts. in urol. texts. Home: 2719 Spencer St Durham NC 27705 Office: Duke University Medical Center Durham NC 27710

CARSON, DALE GEORGE, sheriff; b. Amsterdam, Ohio, Jan. 16, 1922; s. Dale C. and Lillian A. (George) C.; m. Doris Newell, Sept. 1, 1946; children—Dale, Chris, Cindy. B.A., Ohio State U., 1949; grad., Nat. Execs. Inst., FBI Acad., 1976. Spl. agt. FBI, 1951-58; sheriff, Duval County, 1958-68, Jacksonville and Duval County, 1968—; Vice chmn. Nat. Commn. on Police Standards and Goals, 1971—. Contbr. numerous articles to law enforcement jours. Served with AUS, 1942-46. Mem. Am. Soc. Criminologists, Fla. Sheriffs Assn. (pres. 1970-71), Nat. Sheriffs Assn. (dir.). Clubs: Masons (Shriner), Civitan. Home: 1671 Woodmere Dr Jacksonville FL 32210 Office: PO Box 2070 Jacksonville FL 32202

CARSON, DAVID COSTLEY, psychologist, health care administrator; b. Dallas, Oct. 18, 1921; s. William Henry and Eula Lee (Costley) C.; B.A., So. Meth. U., 1943; postgrad. U. Chgo., 1943-46; M.A., U. Tex., 1950, postgrad., 1950-52; m. Barbara Dame, Aug. 22, 1946; children—Jonathan David, Laurel, Bruce Alan. Psychologist, Tex. State Youth Devel. Council, Austin, 1952-53; counselor, planner Tex. Edn. Agy., Austin, 1953-67; project dir. Planning Comm. for Vocat. Rehab., Olympia, Wash., 1967-70; exec. dir. Group Health Coop. S. Central Wis., Madison, 1972-76; pres. Austin Health Maintenance Orgn., Inc., 1978-84; cons. health care adminstrn., 1969—; pres. WindWatts, Inc., 1974—. Sec. Dane County Arts Commn., 1975-78; pres., bd. dirs. Austin Ballet Soc., 1955-67; pres. bd. trustees McDade Ind. Sch. Dist., 1986—. Served with M.C., U.S. Army, 1946-48. VA fellow, 1948-49. Mem. AAAS, Bastrop County Audubon Soc. (pres. 1986—), Phi Delta Kappa, Psi Chi. Author: Satellite HMO, 1972; Rehabilitation Advance, 1969; co-author: Rehabilitation in Washington State, 1968. Home and Office: PO Box 4856 McDade TX 78650

CARSON, GAYLE NORMA, management consultant; b. Albany, N.Y., Feb. 19, 1938; d. Bernard and Sylvia (Smith) Cohn; m. Norman Dale DeVecht, Nov. 27, 1963; children—Steven, Tracy, Scott. B.A., Emerson Coll., 1959; Ed.D., Nova U., 1982. Pres., Fla. Casting Agy., 1959-80; dir. Gayle Carson Cosmetics, Miami, Fla., 1959-80; pres. Gayle Carson Career Schs., various locations, 1959-80; pres. Gayle Carson Presents, Miami, 1972—, Gayle Carson Acad., 1981—, Gayle Carson & Assocs., 1983—; prof. dept. devel. U. Miami, 1982-84. Chmn. bd. dirs. Dade div. Better Bus. Bur. of South Fla., 1983-85; bd. dirs. Gold coast Hotel Sales Mgmt. Assn., 1977-84, Meeting Planners, Internat., 1980-83. Named Dade County's Outstanding Bus. Woman of 1980, Am. Bus. Women's Assn.; Mem. of Year, Fla. Speakers Assn., 1982-84. Mem. Modeling Assn. Am. Internat. (pres. 1973-75), Gold Coast Am. Women in Radio and TV (pres. 1980-82), South Fla. Meeting Planners (pres. 1982-83), Fla. Speakers Assn. (pres. 1982-84), Fashion Group of Miami (dir.), Fla. Assn. Pvt. Schs. (dir. 1976-78), Fla. Real Estate Educators Assn. (sec. 1976-77), Miami Beach C. of C., Am. Soc. Tng. and Devel. (dir. Miami 1984—, v.p. communications 1985, v.p. programming 1986). Co-author: Star Spangled Speakers, 1982; contbr. articles to profl. jours. Address: 2957 Flamingo Dr Miami Beach FL 33140

CARSON, PAUL JOHN, executive; b. San Antonio, Nov. 26, 1938; s. John Chris and Sophia Georgia C.; m. Diana Candace Milam, July 3, 1963; 1 son, John Murrah. B.B.A., U. Tex., 1960. With Dun & Bradstreet, Houston, 1960-61; account exec. L.R. Sheffer Advt., 1962-63; ptnr. Criezis & Carson, Houston, 1963-65; founding ptnr. Media Assocs. Publ. Co., Houston, 1966—; pres. Southland Communications Corp., Houston, 1969—; dir. Walden Enterprises, Prince Food Systems. Mem. Am. Assn. Advt. Agys., Houston Advt. Assn. Republican. Greek Orthodox. Office: 1708 Hwy Six S Houston TX 77077

CARSON, ROBERT CHARLES, psychology educator, administrator, author; b. Providence, Jan. 6, 1930; s. Robert E. Carson and May (O'Bourne) Hamill; m. Mary Anne Mako, June 25, 1955 (div. 1977); children—David, Carolyn; m. Tracey Leigh Potts, Sept. 2, 1977; 1 child, Kelly. A.B., Brown U., 1953; M.A., Northwestern U., 1955; Ph.D., 1957. Diplomate Am. Bd. Profl. Psychology. Asst. prof. U. Chgo., 1957-60; from asst. prof. to prof. Duke U., Durham, N.C., 1960—, chmn. dept. psychology, 1981-85. Author: Interaction Concepts of Personality, 1969. Co-author: Abnormal Psychology and Modern Life, 1980. Served with USN, 1948-49. NIMH fellow, 1967-68. Fellow Am. Psychol. Assn.; mem. N.C. Psychol. Assn. (pres. 1967-68), Phi Beta Kappa. Avocations: woodworking; tennis. Home: 1734 Tisdale St Durham NC 27705 Office: Dept Psychology Duke U Durham NC 27706

CARSON, THOMAS MOORE, librarian; b. Pecos, Tex., June 5, 1917; s. Robert Kimbrough and Ruby Alice (Moore) C.; B.S. in Edn. with honors, U. Tex., El Paso, 1971; M.L.S., U. Tex., Austin, 1971; m. Lois Violet Luce, July 24, 1937; children—Patricia Kay, Pamela Lee, Thomas Moore. Toolmaker, Corona Clipper Co. (Calif.), 1937-41, plant insp., 1946; edn. counselor, Ft. Bliss, Tex., 1972-74; dir. El Paso County Library, Fabens, Tex., 1975-81; mil. occupational splty. librarian William Beaumont Army Med. Center, El Paso, 1981—; cons. Am. Research Corp. (El Paso). Bd. dirs. Allied Mil. Host Family Program, 1972—. Served with U.S. Army, 1934-36, 41-45, 46-68. Decorated Army Commendation medal. Mem. ALA, Tex. Library Assn., S.W. Library Assn., Border Regional Library Assn., El Paso Public Library Assn., Ret. Officers Assn., Mil. Order World Wars, Council Abandoned Mil. Posts Dept. of the Rio Grande (past pres.). Baptist. Clubs: Masons, Nat. Sojourners. Home: 8719 Marble Dr El Paso TX 79904 Office: Army Edn Center William Beaumont Army Med Center El Paso TX 79920

CARSON, WAYNE GARY, consulting firm executive; b. Arlington, Va., Mar. 24, 1946; s. Roy and Olivia (Weir) C. B.S., U. Md., 1969. Dep. chief Burke (Va.) Vol. Fire Dept., 1962-70; fire protection engr. Chesapeake div. Naval Facilities Engring. Command, Washington, 1969-71; fire protection engr. Trans World Airlines, Kennedy Space Center, Fla., 1970-71; loss prevention engr. Potomac Electric Power Co., Washington, 1971-73; instr. No. Va. Community Coll., Annandale, 1972-78; owner, pres. Carson Assocs., Inc., Warrenton, Va., 1973—; tech. cons. Fire Safety in Correctional Facilities, Nat. Inst. Corrections, 1981—. Chmn. pastor parish com. Warrenton Methodist Ch. Registered profl. engr., Pa., Va., D.C., N.C., Ohio. Mem. Soc. Fire Protection Engrs., Nat. Fire Protection Assn. (mem. Life Safety Code subcom. on detention and correctional occupancies), Am. Soc. Safety Engrs., Internat. Assn. Arson Investigators, Bldg. Ofcls. Conf. Am., Internat. Conf. Bldg. Ofcls., So. Bldg. Code Congress Internat. Office: Route 3 Box 286-B Warrenton VA 22186

CARSWELL, KIMBERLY ELISE, statistician; b. Augusta, Ga., Feb. 19, 1957; d. Manley Wallace and Frances Etoila (Herd) C.; m. David Michael Smith, Dec. 22, 1984. B.S., U. N.C.-Greensboro, 1979, M.A., 1984. Sr. tech. info. services specialist CIBA-GEIGY Corp., Greensboro, 1982—. Mem. campaign com. United Way, Greensboro, 1983. Mem. Am. Statis. Assn. Avocations: sewing; crafts; cycling; walking. Home: 801 W Bessemer Greensboro NC 27408 Office: CIBA-GEIGY Corp 410 Swing Rd Greensboro NC 27409

CARTER, ANNE DYKES, pharmacist; b. Troy, Ala., Mar. 20, 1954; d. James Frank and Annie Lois (Shipman) Dykes; m. Elkin Bragg Carter, Nov. 19, 1977; 1 child, Laurel. B.S. in Pharmacy, Auburn U., 1976. Chief pharmacist Barbour County Hosp., Eufaula, Ala., 1977; relief pharmacist Dykes Drugs and Louisville Drugs, Ala., 1977-80; asst. mgr. Harco Drugs, Eufaula, 1980, Central Drug Co., Abbeville, Ala., 1980-84; relief pharmacist Price Drug Co., Eufaula, 1984—; pharmacy cons. Barbour County Nursing Home, Eufaula, 1977, Eufaula Geriatric Ctr., 1982-84. Mem. Ala. Pharm. Assn., Barbour County Pharm. Assn. (program chmn. 1984-85), Auburn Pharmacy Alumni Assn. Baptist. Club: Camerata (Eufaula) (historian 1980-81). Avocations: reading; cooking; hand sewing; swimming; skeet shooting. Home: 411 Inlet Rd Eufaula AL 36027 Office: Price Drug Co 106 S Broad St Eufaula AL 36027

CARTER, ARTHUR D., JR., oil and gas company executive; b. Houston, 1937; married. B.S., U. Tex., 1960. Field engr. N.D. Geol. Survey, 1960-62; dist. area engr. Tex. Pacific Oil Co., 1962-68; dist. petroleum engr. Tex. Oil & Gas Corp., 1968-70, staff reservoir engr., 1970-73, asst. chief engr., then chief engr., 1973-75, v.p., mgr. mid-continent dist., 1975-78, sr. v.p., mgr. prodn. and exploration no. region, 1978-81, exec. v.p., mgr. prodn. and exploration, then exec. v.p. prodn. and exploration, Dallas, 1981—. Served to 1st lt. USNG, 1955-65. Office: Tex Oil & Gas Corp 1507 Pacific Dallas TX 75201*

CARTER, ARTHUR LINWOOD, JR., savings and loan executive; b. Washington, June 27, 1948; s. Arthur Linwood and Doris (Fullerton) C.; m. Leah Kidd, Jan. 13, 1973; children—Michelle Lynn, Rebecca Anne. B.A., George Mason U., 1970. Asst. controller Piedmont Fed. Savs. & Loan Assn., Manassas, Va., 1970-80, savs. officer, 1980—, v.p., 1981—. Sec.-treas. Prince William Multiple Sclerosis Soc., Manassas, 1980. Mem. Fin. Mgrs. Soc., Prince William-Greater Manassas C. of C. (pres. 1983-84, Mem. of Yr. 1978-79). Club: Kiwanis. Home: 9252 Longstreet Ct Manassas VA 22110 Office: Piedmont Fed Savs Bank 9324 West St Manassas VA 22110

CARTER, DAVID EDWARD, communications executive; b. Ashland, Ky., Nov. 24, 1942; s. Victor Byron and Lillie Elzena (Clarke) C.; A.B., U. Ky., 1965; M.S., Ohio U., 1967; m. Linda Louise Gibson, May 31, 1969; children—Christa Ann, Lauren Louise. Dir. advt. Wheeler & Williams Co., Ashland, 1965-66; instr. U. Ky., 1967-70; dir. communications Ky. Electric Steel Co., Ashland, 1970-77; pres. David E. Carter Corporate Communications, Inc., Ashland, 1977—; dir. Home Fed. Savs. & Loan Assn., Ashland, Decathlon Corp., Hanover Pub. Co. Scoutmaster, Tri-State Area Council Boy Scouts Am., 1970-77, dist. commr., 1977-78, recipient dist. award of merit, 1975. Mem. Nat. Acad. TV Arts and Scis., N.Y. Art Dirs. Club, Am. Inst. Graphic Arts. Republican. Methodist. Author: It's Not the Money—It's The Principle, 1975; Book of American Trade Marks, 10 vols., 1972-86; Designing Corporate Symbols, 1975; Corporate Identity Manuals, 1976; Letterheads/1, 1977; Ideas for Editors, 1977; Letterheads/2, 1979; Best Financial Advertising, 1979; Letterheads/3, 1981; Best Financial Advertising/2, 1981; Letterheads/4, 1983; Designing Corporate Identity for Small Companies, 1985; How to Improve Your Corporate Identity, 1986. Home: 4727 Southern Hills Dr Ashland KY 41101 Office: 1505 Carter Ave Ashland KY 41101

CARTER, DONALD, professional basketball team executive. Pres., Dallas Mavericks, Nat. Basketball Assn. Office: care Dallas Mavericks Reunion Arena 777 Sports St Dallas TX 75207

CARTER, DONNA DEAN, architect, planner; b. Dayton, Ohio, June 18, 1952; d. Daniel Dean and Dorothy Rosetta (Reeves) Carter; m. Michael Gagarin, May 27, 1974; children—Daniel Porter, Alexandra Carter. B.A., Yale U., 1974; postgrad. Am. U., Cairo, 1972-73, U. Tex.-Austin, 1975; M.Arch., U. Calif.-Berkeley, 1977. Registered architect, Tex. Designer 3D/Internat., Austin, Tex., 1977-78, Graeber Simmons & Cowan, Inc., Austin, 1978-81; prin. Carter Design Concepts, Austin, 1981; ptnr. Carter & Parshall Assocs., Austin, 1981-85; prin. Carter Design Assocs., Austin, 1985—; guest lectr. U. Tex. Continuing Edn, U. Tex. Dept. Architecture summer acad. Mem. Downtown Revitalization Task Force, City of Austin, Congress Ave. Task Force, City of Austin; bd. dirs. Ecology Action, Inc., 1980-86, Heritage Soc. Austin, Women and Their Work; mem. adv. panel Art in Pub. Places; mem. planning council Holy Cross Hosp. Ford Found. fellow Am. U., 1972-73. Mem. Tex. Soc. Architects, AIA (dir. Austin chpt. 1981-82), Soc. Am. Registered Architects, Am. Planning Assn., Tex. Solar Energy Soc., Soc. Archtl. Historians, Nat. Trust for Hist. Preservation, Tex. Hist. Found., Heritage Soc. Austin (mem. preservation com.). Office: 817 W 11th St Austin TX 78701

CARTER, FAIRIE LYN, chemist; b. Biloxi, Miss., Oct. 1, 1926; d. William Raymond and Velma Carter. B.S., Miss. U. Women, 1948; M.A., U. N.C., 1950. Chemist, asst. curator Acad. Natural Scis., Phila., 1950-54; chemist Eastern Regional Research Ctr., U.S. Dept. Agr., Phila., 1955-57, So. Regional Research Ctr., New Orleans, 1957-65; prin. chemist Forest Service, U.S. Dept. Agr., Gulfport, Miss., 1965-84. Mem. Am. Chem. Soc., Am. Oil. Chemists Soc., Entomol. Soc. Am., Sigma Xi. Baptist. Club: Order Eastern Star. Contbr. articles to profl. jours. Home: 525 E Water St Biloxi MS 39530

CARTER, H. KENNON, physicist; b. Athens, Ga., Apr. 23, 1941; s. Hubert H. and Mildred (Kennon) C.; m. Barbara W., Aug. 11, 1962; children—Barbara Leigh, Joanna Ruth, Daniel Kennon. B.S. in Physics, U. Ga., 1963; M.S., La. State U., 1965; Ph.D., Vanderbilt U., 1969. Asst. prof. physics Furman U., Greenville, S.C., 1968-74; scientist in physics univ. isotope separator Oak Ridge Assoc. Univs., 1974-85, dir., Tenn., 1985—. Mem. Am. Phys. Soc. Methodist. Avocations: boating; hiking. Home: 110 Newcrest Ln Oak Ridge TN 37830 Office: Oak Ridge Associated Univs Oak Ridge Nat Lab Bldg 6008 PO Box X Oak Ridge TN 37831

CARTER, JAMES BYARS, allergist; b. Dallas, July 15, 1934; s. Algie Billie and Naomi (Byars) C.; B.A., U. Tex., Austin, 1956; M.D., U. Tex.-Galveston, 1959; M.S., U. Minn., 1966; m. Jean Foxhall Clement, Apr. 4, 1970; children—Gregory James, Kathleen Jo, William Adam, John Gregory. Intern, Letterman Gen. Hosp., San Francisco, 1959-60; resident internal medicine Mayo Grad. Med. Sch., Rochester, Minn., 1963-66; practice medicine, specializing in internal medicine, partner Capital Med. Clinic, Austin, 1967-71; resident allergy and immunology Kaiser Found. Hosp., San Francisco, 1971-73; asso. Allergy Assos., Austin, 1973—; pres. staff Seton, St. David's, Shoal Creek, Brackenridge hosps., Austin, 1973—. Cub scout den leader Boy Scouts Am., Austin, 1974-75, asst. scoutmaster, 1974-75, scoutmaster, 1976-82. Served with USAF, 1959-63. Mead Johnson scholar, 1965-66; Am. Coll. Allergists and Am. Acad. Allergy grantee, 1971-72. Diplomate Am. Bd. Internal Medicine, Am. Bd. Allergy and Immunology. Fellow Am. Coll. Allergists, A.C.P., Am. Acad. Allergy (sports medicine com.), Am. Coll. Chest Physicians; mem. Travis County Med. Soc., Tex. Med. Assn. (careers com. 1982—), Am. Assn. Certified Allergists, AMA, Am. Tb Soc. (dir. 1967-70), S.W. Allergy Forum, SAR (v.p., chaplain Patrick Henry chpt.), Austin Geneal. Soc., 1st v.p., bd. dirs. 1982-84). Episcopalian (asst. Sunday sch. supt. 1973-74, lay reader 1977, vestryman 1981-84, lay chalice bearer). Contbr. articles to profl. jours. Office: Suite 100 1510 W 34th St Austin TX 78703

CARTER, JAMES CLARENCE, university president, educator; b. N.Y.C., Aug. 1, 1927; s. Clarence S. and Elizabeth (Dillon) C. B.S. in Physics, Spring Hill Coll., 1952; M.S., Fordham U., 1953; Ph.D., Cath. U. Am., 1956; S.T.L., Woodstock Coll., 1959. Joined S.J., 1947; instr. Loyola U., New Orleans, 1960, asst. prof., 1960-67, assoc. prof., 1967—, v.p. 1970-74, pres., 1974—; dir. edn. New Orleans Province, S.J., 1968-70; dir. Internat. Trade Mart, 1975—. Mem. high edn. facilities com. State of La., 1971-73; chmn. Mayor's Com. Ednl. Uses CATV, 1972; mem. Council for Better La., 1974—, La. Ednl. TV Authority, 1977-83; bd. dirs. Internat. House, 1975, Boys' Clubs Greater New Orleans, 1974-79, Met. Area Com., 1974—; mem. adv. bd. Inst. Politics New Orleans, 1970—; chmn. La. selection com. Rhodes Scholarship, 1978; trustee Regis Coll., Xavier U., Cin., Loyola U. Chgo.; dir. New Orleans Pub. Service, Inc. Named to Hall of Fame, St. Stanislaus High Sch., 1974. Mem. Palmes Academiques, Am. Assn. Higher Edn., AAUP, Assn. Governing Bds. Univs. and Colls., Fgn. Relations Assn. New Orleans, Am. Phys. Soc., Am. Assn. Physics Tchrs., Nat. Cath. Ednl. Assn., Albertus Magnus Guild, Assn. Jesuit Colls. and Univs. (chmn. acad. v.p. conf. 1971-74), Nat. Assn. Ind. Colls. and Univs. (dir. 1977-81), Am. Council Edn., Assn. Am. Colls., Sigma Xi, Beta Gamma Sigma. Club: Plimsol, City. Home: 6363 St Charles Ave New Orleans LA 70118

CARTER, JAMES EARL, JR. (JIMMY), former President of U.S.; b. Plains, Ga., Oct. 1, 1924; s. James Earl and Lillian (Gordy) C.; student Ga. Southwestern Coll., 1941-42, LL.D., 1981; student Ga. Inst. Tech., 1942-43, D.E. (hon.), 1979; B.S., U.S. Naval Acad., 1946; postgrad. Union Coll., 1952-53; LL.D., Morehouse Coll., 1972, Morris Brown Coll., 1972, U. Notre Dame, 1977, Emory U., 1979, Kwansei Gakuin U., 1981; Ph.D. (hon.), Weizmann Inst. Sci., 1980, Tel Aviv U., 1983; D.H.L. (hon.), Central Conn. State U., 1985; m. Rosalynn Smith, July 7, 1946; children—John William, James Earl III, Donnel Jeffrey, Amy Lynn. Farmer, warehouseman, Plains, Ga., 1953-77; mem. Ga. Senate, 1963-67; gov. Ga., Atlanta, 1971-75; Pres. U.S., 1977-81; Univ. Disting. prof. Emory U., Atlanta, 1982—, founder sr. fellow Carter Ctr., 1982. Chmn. congressional campaign com. Democratic Nat. Com., 1974; candidate Dem. nomination Pres. U.S., 1976; mem. Sumter County (Ga.) Sch. Bd., 1955-62, chmn., 1960-62; mem. Americus and Sumter County Hosp. Authority, 1956-70; bd. dirs. Ga. Crop Improvement Assn., 1957-63, pres., 1961; mem. Sumter County Library Bd., 1961; pres. Plains Devel. Corp., 1963; chmn. West Central Ga. Area Planning and Devel. Commn., 1964; pres. Ga. Planning Assn., 1968; state chmn. March of Dimes, 1968-70. Served with U.S. Navy, 1946-53. Recipient Gold medal Internat. Inst. Human Rights, 1979; Internat. Mediation medal Am. Arbitration Assn., 1979, Martin Luther King, Jr. Nonviolence Peace prize, 1979, Internat. Human Rights award Synagogue Council Am., 1979, Conservationist of Yr. award, 1979, Harry S. Truman Pub. Service award, 1981, Ansel Adams Conservation award Wilderness Soc., 1982, Disting. Service award So. Bapt. Conv., 1982, Human Rights award Internat. League Human Rights, 1983, World Meth. Peace award, 1985. Club: Lions (dist. gov. 1968-69). Author: Why Not the Best?, 1975; A Government as Good as Its People, 1977; Keeping Faith: Memoirs of a President, 1982; Negotiation: The Alternative to Hostility, 1984; The Blood of Abraham, 1985. Home: 1 Woodland Dr Plains GA 31780 Office: 75 Spring St SW Atlanta GA 30303

CARTER, JAMES EDWARD, JR., retired dentist, association official; b. Augusta, Ga., July 1, 1906; s. James Edward and Emma (Barnett) C.; D.D.S., Howard U., 1930; postgrad. Haines Normal and Indsl. Inst., 1920-24; m. Marjorie Butler, Jan. 7, 1928; 1 son, James Edward III. Pvt. practice dentistry, Augusta, 1930-81. Mem. Nat. Council YMCA, 1958-64, 67-69; chmn. 9th St. YMCA, Augusta, 1950-57; active United Coll. Fund, Cancer Dr., United Chest Fund, Boy Scouts Am. Del. Republican Nat., Conv., 1960. Bd. dirs. Augusta-Richmond County Library. Recipient Achievement award in pub. service Upsilon Sigma chpt. Omega Psi Phi, 1949; award of merit Georgia Dental Soc., 1961; 55 Year award Thankful Bapt. Ch., 1973; Howard U. Alumni Dental Achievement award, 1982; Spl. award Stoney Med., Dental and Pharm. Soc., 1983. Fellow Internat. Coll. Dentists, Am. Coll. Dentists, Royal Soc. Health, Acad. Gen. Dentistry, World Wide Acad. Scholars, Acad. Dentistry Internat.; mem. Nat. (life; past pres.; mem. exec. bd. 1940-52), Am. (life), Ga. (life, pres. 1940-41, 35-year service plaque) dental assns., Stoney-Med. and Dental Soc. (pres. 1961-63), Acad. Gen. Dentistry, John A. Andrew Clin, Soc. (pres. dental sect. 1947), Fedn. Dentaire Internationale, Pierre Fauchard Acad., Omega Psi Phi (past basilius Psi Omega chpt. 1936-37, treas. 7th dist. 1943-75; recipient achievement award human relations Psi Omega chpt. 1963, 50 Year Pin), Sigma Pi Phi, Omicron Kappa Upsilon. Republican. Baptist (chmn. bd. trustees 1937-77, chmn. emeritus, deacon 1961—). Clubs: Frontiers (Augusta, Ga.); Optimist Internat. Home: 2347 Fitten St Augusta GA 30904

CARTER, JANET LYNN, design and color consultant; b. McKeesport, Pa., Oct. 14, 1948; d. Herbert Sample and Mildred (Obradovich) C. Student, Art Inst. Pitts., 1967-69, LaRoche Coll, Pitts., 1980-81. Designer, Kitchen Trends, Pitts., 1970, L.S. Ayers Dept. Store, Ft. Wayne, Ind., 1970, Empire Furniture Co., Pitts., 1971-74, Begandy Furniture Store, Pitts., 1974-76; instr. Art Inst. Pitts., 1976-77; design, color cons. Eljer Plumbing Ware, Pitts., 1977-81; merchandising mgr. Mid-State Tile Co., Lexington, N.C., 1981—; instr. continuing edn. dept. Community Coll. Allegheny County, Pitts., 1974-76; speaker, cons. design and color coordination, 1975—. Mem. citizens com. West Mifflin (Pa.) Sch. Dist., 1981; mem. exec. com. Uwharrie council Boy Scouts Am., 1983. Mem. Am. Soc. Interior Designers (pres. 1981), Color Mktg. Group (chair holder 1982, dir. 1984), Internat. Mgmt. Council. Democrat. Presbyterian. Club: Toastmasters. Office: Mid-State Tile Co PO Box 1777 Lexington NC 27292

CARTER, JOHN H(ENRY), telecommunications company executive; b. Thomaston, Ga., Sept. 26, 1948; s. Gus and Rosa (Matthews) C.; m. Susan Gibson, Aug. 20, 1970; children—Gregory L., Candace M. B.A., Morris Brown Coll., Atlanta, 1970; M.S., U. Utah, 1977. Tchr. Cambridge Sch. System (Mass.), 1970; with So. Bell Telephone Co., Atlanta, 1972-77, 80-84, bus. office mgr., 1976-77, dist. mgr.-personnel, 1980-82, dist. mgr.-corp. planning, 1982-84; dist. mgr.-EEO/goals analysis AT&T, Basking Ridge, N.J., 1977-80; ops. mgr.-purchasing adminstrn. BellSouth Services Corp., Atlanta, 1984—; vis. prof. Pholander-Smith Coll., Little Rock, 1982; bd. dirs. Atlanta Met. Fair Housing, 1983. Loaned exec. Fulton County Commn. (Ga.), 1981, vice chmn. zoning ordinance rev. com., 1983; pres. Huntington Community Assn., Atlanta, 1981-82; chmn. adv. bd. Douglas High Sch., Atlanta, 1983-84; v.p. Seaborn Lee Sch. PTA, Atlanta, 1983-84; mem. Clark Coll. Allied Health Com., Atlanta. Served with U.S. Army, 1970-72. Named Jaycee of Yr., Mt. Olive Jaycees (N.J.), 1979; Outstanding Businessman of Yr. award, Douglass High Sch., 1984. Methodist. Home: 3465 Somerset Trail Atlanta GA 30331 Office: BellSouth Services 675 W Peachtree St NE Atlanta GA 30375

CARTER, JOHN THOMAS, educational administrator, writer; b. Mantee, Miss., Dec. 16, 1921; s. John Franklin and Mattie (George) C.; m. Frances Tunnell, Mar. 16, 1946; children—John W., Nell Carter Branum. Student Clarke Coll., 1940-42; student Miss. State U., 1942-43, B.S., 1947; M.S., U. Tenn., 1948; Ed.D., U. Ill., 1954. Cert. tchr. Tchr., prin. Maben Consol. Sch., Miss., 1946-47; faculty Wood Jr. Coll., Mathiston, Miss., 1947-48; faculty, farm supt. Clarke Coll., Newton, Miss., 1948-56; faculty, dean. Sch. Edn., Samford U., Birmingham, Ala., 1956—. Author 6 books for children and youth, 1958-75, including: East is West, 1965; Witness in Israel, 1969; Sharing Times Seven, 1971. Regional dir. Aerospace Edn. CAP, 1970-84. Served with U.S. Army, 1942-45, NATOUSA, ETO. Recipient Brewer award CAP, 1977, Crown Circle award Nat. Congress Aerospace Edn., 1983. Mem. Assn. Tchr. Educators (pres. 1970-71), Assn. Colls. for Tchr. Edn. (exec. bd. 1983—), Assn. for Supervision and Curriculum Devel., Kappa Delta Pi (treas. 1980—), Phi Delta Kappa (v.p. 1982-83). Republican. Baptist. Club: Kiwanis. Avocations: flying; travel. Home: 2561 Rocky Ridge Rd Birmingham AL 35243 Office: Sch Edn Samford U Birmingham AL 35229

CARTER, KAREN ELAINE, geophysicist, photographer, writer; b. Houston, Oct. 8, 1957; d. Donald Walker and Florence Augusta (Barron) Lanning; m. Kent Ellsworth Carter, Aug. 14, 1982. B.S. in Physics, Stephen F. Austin U., 1979; postgrad. toward M.B.A., U. Houston, 1983—. Geophysicist Texaco, Inc., Houston, 1980-83; sr. geophysicist Amerada Hess Corp., Houston, 1983—. Recipient Freshman Fellowship award in Physics, Stephen F. Austin State U., 1976. Mem. Am. Assn. Petroleum Geologists (assoc.), Soc. Exploration Geophysicists, NOW, Sigma Pi Sigma. Avocations: horse training; riding; triathalons; racquetball.

CARTER, KENNETH WAYNE, advertising agency executive; b. Muskogee, Okla., Sept. 8, 1954; s. Ira Carter and Doris Marie (Hickerson) McCoy. B.A. in Journalism, So. U., 1976. Sports dir. Sta. KALO, Little Rock, 1976; dir. pub.

relations Dallas chpt. Am. Heart Assn., 1977-81; exec. v.p. Focus Communications Group, pub. relations and advt., Dallas, 1981—. Mem. steering com. City of Dallas Public Info. Task Force; chmn. community relations United Way; bd. dirs., chmn. pub. relations com. Dallas Regional Minority Purchasing Council. So. U. Alumni Fedn. scholar, 1973; recipient Target Impact award Tex. affiliate Am. Heart Assn., 1980. Mem. Pub. Relations Soc. Am. (sec. 1981-82, dir., nat. minority affairs com.), Dallas/Ft. Worth Assn. Black Communicators, Tex. Pub. Relations Assn., Internat. Assn. Bus. Communicators, Dallas Advt. League. Baptist. Office: 711 Elm St Suite 2 Dallas TX 75202

CARTER, LARRY DEAN, optometrist; b. Birmingham, Ala., Mar. 25, 1950; s. Samuel and Moveline O. (Shotts) C.; m. Sonia Kaye Ingle, May 27, 1977; children—Hollie Nell, Daniel Larry. B.S. in Physiol. Optics, U. Ala., 1975, O.D., 1975. Gen. practice optometry, Hamilton Ala., 1975—. Councilman City of Hamilton, 1980-84; pub. adv. com. Northwest Ala. Council Local Govt., Florence, 1981-84; trustee So. Council Optometry, Atlanta, 1981-84. Mem. Am. Optometric Assn., Ala. Optometric Assn. (pres. 1982-83). Lodge: Kiwanis (pres. 1978-80). Avocations: fishing; family. Home: PO Box 7 Hamilton AL 35570 Office: 2006 Military St Hamilton AL 35570

CARTER, LIEF HASTINGS, law and politics educator; b. N.Y.C., Oct. 9, 1940; s. Robert Spencer and Cynthia (Root) C.; m. Nancy Saunders Batson, Dec. 22, 1963; children—Stephen Hastings, Robert Benjamin, Laura Elizabeth. A.B., Harvard U., 1962, LL.B., 1965; Ph.D., U. Calif.-Berkeley, 1972. Bar: D.C. 1966. Assoc. Kirkland, Ellis, Washington, 1965-66; vol. Peace Corps, La Paz, Bolivia, 1966-67; lectr. U. Calif.-Berkeley, 1967-68; prof. U. Tenn., Chattanooga, 1971-73; prof. law and politics U. Ga., Athens, 1973—; program reviewer NEH, Nat. Inst. Edn. Author: The Limits of Order, 1974; Reason in Law, 1979, 2d edit., 1984; Administrative Law and Politics, 1983; Contemporary Constitutional Lawmaking, 1985. Choral dir. St. Gregory the Great Episcopal Ch., Athens, 1982—. Recipient Beaver Spl. Teaching award U. Ga., 1984, Josiah Meigs Teaching award U. Ga., 1984. Mem. Am. Polit. Sci. Assn. (bd. dirs. law sect. 1984-85, Edward Corwin award 1973), Am. Soc. for Pub. Adminstrn. (edn. coordinator 1984-86), So. Polit. Sci Assn., Law and Soc. Assn. Democrat. Avocations: Harpsichord performing; choral conducting; squash. Home: 475 Forest Rd Athens GA 30605 Office: U Ga Dept Polit Sci Baldwin Hall Athens GA 30602

CARTER, LUTHER FREDERICK, public administration educator; b. Kenova, W.Va., May 30, 1950; s. Luther and Elaine (Jones) C.; m. Theresa Gayle Siskind, Dec. 18, 1975; 1 child, Bryan. B.A., U. Central Fla., 1972; M.Pub. Adminstrn., U. S.C., 1976, Ph.D., 1979. Asst. prof. govt. Western Ky. U., Bowling Green, 1979-80; asst. prof. pub. adminstrn. U. Central Fla., Orlando, 1980-81; assoc. prof. polit. sci. Coll. Charleston, S.C., 1981—; dir. inst. for pub. affairs, 1984—. Author: Electoral Perference and Reform Choice, 1980; (with others) Personnel: Managing Human Resources, 1985. Editor: (with others) Mobilization and the National Defense, 1985; Government in the Palmetto State, 1983. Contbr. articles to profl. jours. Served to 1st lt. USMC, 1972-75, comdg. officer Res. Grantee Dept. Def. 1983—, Dept. Edn. 1983—, Fed. Emergency Mgmt. Agy., 1984. Mem. Am. Soc. Pub. Adminstrn. (chapt. pres. 1983-84), Southeastern Conf. Pub. Adminstrn. (chmn. 1984—), Am. Polit. Sci. Assn. Democrat. Roman Catholic. Home: 855 Longbranch Dr Charleston SC 29407 Office: Inst Pub Affairs Coll Charleston 114 Wentworth Charleston SC 29424

CARTER, MARILYN RAY, nurse; b. Galveston, Tex., May 25, 1931; d. Raymond J. and Elizabeth E. (Weyer) Hansen; m. Wade V. Carter, Jr., Feb. 21, 1957; children—Renee, Wade, Kim, Vanette. R.N., St. Mary's Sch. Nursing, 1951. Head nurse VA Hosp., Houston, 1953-56; psychiat. nurse Panama Canal Co., Balboa, C.Z., 1956-79; charge nurse Starlight Hosp., Center Point, Tex., 1982—; reporter Canal Record, 1981-82. Founder, chmn. Hill Country Zonian's Assn., Kerrville, 1979-82; chmn. Hill Country Youth Ranch Charity Ball, 1977; poll clk. local, fed. elections, 1981-83. Vol. Salvation Army, 1979-82, Cowboy Artists Am. Mus. Named Nurse of Yr., VA Hosp., Houston, 1954; recipient Outstanding Job Performance award U.S. Civil Service, 1968. Mem. Tex. Nurses Assn., Panama Canal Soc. Fla., Am. Assn. Ret. Persons. Lutheran. Club: Hill Country Zonians.

CARTER, MEDORA ABBOTT, financial analyst; b. Washington, July 18, 1953; d. Jackson Miles and Frances Elizabeth (Dowdle) A.; m. Donald Lynwood Carter, May 14, 1983. Student Chowan Jr. Coll., 1971-72, J. Sargeant Reynolds and Va. Commonwealth U., 1973-76; grad. with honors Am. Inst. Banking, 1981. Asst. cashier, br. mgr. Dominion Nat. Bank, Vienna, Va., 1977-82; fin. analyst TYMNET, Inc., Vienna, 1984—. Mem. Colonial chpt. Republican Women's Club, Alexandria, Va., 1985—; mem. membership drive com. Fairfax County C. of C., 1981, 82; treas. Kings Park Shopping Ctr. Mcht.'s Assn., Springfield, Va., 1981; page DAR 1976 Va. State Conv., also active mem. Recipient Outstanding Achievement award Nat. Assn. Banking Women No. Va., 1981. Episcopalian. Office: TYMNET Inc 2070 Chain Bridge Rd Vienna VA 22180

CARTER, PURVIS MELVIN, history educator; b. Columbus, Tex., Nov. 22, 1925; s. Earnest and Daisy Sammie (Jones) C.; A.B., Tillotson Coll., 1948; M.A., Howard U., 1950; postgrad. U. Denver, 1954, 55; Ph.D., U. Colo., 1970; m. Gwendolyn M. Burns, June 1, 1956; children—Purvis Melvin, Frederick Earl, Burnest Denise. Tchr.-coach Harlingen (Tex.) Ind. Sch. Dist., 1950-55; instr. dept. history Prairie View A & M U., 1956-60, asst. prof., 1960-66, assoc. prof., 1966—, exchange prof. Prairie View A&M-Tex. A&M U., 1981; cons., lectr. Tex. observance Black History Month; cons. race relation activities; cons. Fgn. Relations series U.S., Office Historian, U.S. Dept. State; tchr. Bethlehem Study course Bethlehem Meth. Women Soc. Christian Service; cons. World Without War Council, U. Chgo., 1981; Mem. Tex. Hist. Commn.; active Waller High Sch. Tex. Booster Club, Sam Houston Area council Boy Scouts Am. Served with USMCR, 1944-46. Recipient Social Sci. Found. scholarship, 1954; U. Colo. fellowships, 1968-70; Tchr. of Yr. award Prairie View A. and M. U. Mem. So., Tex., Waller County hist. socs., Orgn. Am. Historians, Western History Assn., Assn. Study Negro Life and History, AAUP, Soc. Historians Am. Fgn. Relations, Phi Epsilon chpt. Phi Alpha Theta. Methodist (lay leader 1970-72). Author: Congressional and Public Reaction to Wilson's Caribbean Policy 1913-1917, 1977; The Black Press and Its Counterparts: Reaction to the Application to Wilson's Caribbean Policy in Haiti; compiler index Jour. Negro History, Vols. 1-54; compiler The Negro in Periodical Literature 1970-74, Jour. Negro History. Contbr. articles to profl. publs. Home: PO Box 2243 Prairie View TX 77445 Office: Dept History Prairie View A&M U Prairie View TX 77445

CARTER, RALPH GORDON, political science educator; b. Belton, Tex., Feb. 7, 1952; s. Ralph Gordon Jr. and Gwendolyn Lorene (Birkes) C.; m. Nita Fern Mullen, Dec. 28, 1973. B.A. summa cum laude, Midwestern State U., 1974; M.A., Ohio State U., 1977, Ph.D., 1980. Asst. prof. Wichita State U., Kans., 1978-82; asst. prof. polit. sci. Tex. Christian U., Ft. Worth, 1982—, interim dept. chmn., summers 1983, 84, dorm adviser, 1983-84, 84—; adj. asst. prof. Tabor Coll., Hillsboro, Kans., 1982; cons. Ft. Worth Star-Telegram, 1984. Program planner U.S. Com. for UNICEF, Dallas, Ft. Worth, 1984—; speaker Jewish Ctr., Ft. Worth, 1985. Mem. Am. Polit. Sci. Assn., Internat. Studies Assn., Kappa Sigma. Democrat. Methodist. Avocations: running; gardening. Home: 8017 Hunnicut St Dallas TX 75228 Office: Tex Christian U Box 32873 Fort Worth TX 76129

CARTER, RICHARD BRENTS, counselor; b. Trinidad, Colo., Sept. 23, 1948; s. Brents and Catherine Ann (Ferris) C.; m. Laveda Faye DePriest, Oct. 3, 1969; 1 child, Phillip Brents. B.S.Ed., U. Central Ark., 1969, M.S.Ed., 1971; M.S.Ed., Ark. State U., 1975, Edn.S., 1982. Tchr. mentally retarded Yerger Jr. High Sch., Hope, Ark., 1969-70; tchr. mentally retarded Sante Fe Pub. Schs., 1970-71; tchr. Elaine Pub. Schs., Ark., 1971-74; counselor Harrisburg Elem. Sch., Ark., 1974-79; guidance specialist Ark. Dept. Edn., Little Rock, 1979-84; counselor Great Falls Elem. Sch., S.C., 1985—. Assoc. editor Jour. Peer Facilitator Quar., 1984-85. Mem. Am. Assn. Counseling and Devel., Am. Sch. Counselor Assn., Am. Assn. Counselor Edn. and Supervision, S.C. Assn. Counseling and Devel., Phi Delta Kappa. Avocations: camping. Home: 1548 Arlene Dr Columbia SC 29204 Office: Great Falls Elem Sch 301 Dearborn St Great Falls SC 29055

CARTER, ROSALYNN SMITH, wife of former President of United States; b. Plains, Ga., Aug. 18, 1927; d. Edgar and Allie (Murray) Smith; m. James Earl Carter, Jr., July 7, 1946; children—John William, James Earl III, Donnell Jeffrey, Amy Lynn. Grad., Ga. Southwestern Coll.; D.H.L. (hon.), Morehouse Coll., 1980. Author: First Lady from Plains, 1984. Mem. Ga. Gov.'s Commn. to Improve Service for the Mentally and Emotionally Handicapped, 1971-74; vol. Ga. Regional Hosp., Atlanta; hon. chmn. Ga. Spl. Olympics for Retarded Children, Pres.'s Commn. on Mental Health; hon. chmn. bd. trustees John F. Kennedy Center Performing Arts; bd. dirs. Nat. Assn. Mental Health; campaigned independently during 1976 and 1980 Presdl. Campaigns. Recipient Vol. of Yr. award Southwestern Assn. Vol. Services. Address: Plains GA 31780

CARTER, TERESA RHODES, nurse; b. Morganton, N.C., Oct. 8, 1956; d. Daniel Edward and Bernice (Grigg) Rhodes; m. Mark Clinton Carter, Dec. 18, 1977. A.B. in Early Childhood Edn., Lenoir-Rhyne Coll., 1978, B.S.Nursing, 1983. Lic. R.N., tchr., N.C. Tchr., Hallsboro (N.C.) High Sch., 1978-79, Statesville (N.C.) High Sch., 1979-80; nursing asst. Catawba Meml. Hosp., Hickory, N.C., 1980-83; nurse Glenn R. Frye Hosp., Hickory, 1983; nurse Charlotte (N.C.) Meml. Hosp., 1984—. Mem. Am. Nurses Assn., Santa Filomena, Chi Beta Phi, Delta Zeta. Methodist. Home: 311 Beacon Hills Rd Indian Trail NC 28079 Office: Charlotte Memorial Hosp 1000 Blythe Blvd Charlotte NC 28232

CARTER, THOMAS ELMER, engineering official, speaker; b. Hominy, Okla., Aug. 2, 1942; s. George Arthur and Zettie (Palmer) C.; m. Sandra Dell Veach, June 2, 1963. B.S., Okla. State U., 1965, M.S., 1971; M.B.A., U. Houston, 1981. Sr. indsl. engr. Champion Papers, Pasadena, Tex., 1977-81; mgr. maintenance services Houston Chronicle, 1981—; lectr. grad. level mgmt. U. Houston-Clear Lake, 1982—. Served to capt. USAF, 1962-77; lt. USNR, 1979—. Decorated Air Force Commendation medal (3). Mem. Inst. Indsl. Engrs. (sr.), Nat. Speakers Assn., Alpha Pi Mu. Republican. Baptist. Club: Toastmasters (lt. gov. Gulf Coast div.). Office: 801 Texas Ave Suite 628 Houston TX 77002

CARTER, W(ILBUR) LEE, III, insurance company executive; b. Greensboro, N.C., June 17, 1952; s. Wilbur Lee, Jr. and Martha (Sauvain) C. B.Sc., U. N.C., 1975. Mktg. asst. So. Life Ins. Co., Greensboro, 1976-77, agt., Atlanta, 1977-78, exec. asst., Greensboro, 1979-80, investment analyst, 1980-81, asst. v.p., 1981-83, v.p. investments, 1983—. Loan exec. United Way Greensboro, 1981-82; active United Negro Coll. Fund, 1980—, Leadership Greensboro, 1982-83; bd. dirs. United Arts Council Greensboro, 1980-84, Greensboro Jr. Achievement, 1980—, Woodberry Forest Sch., 1967-70. English Speaking Union scholar Wrekin Coll., Shropshire, Eng., 1970-71. Fellow Life Membership Assn.; mem. Life Underwriters Polit. Action Com., N.C. Soc. Fin. Analysts, Greensboro Assn. Life Underwriters, Nat. Assn. Life Underwriters, Mortgage Bankers Assn. N.C. (income property com.), Greensboro Jaycees (dir. 1980-82). Democrat. Presbyterian. Club: Greensboro Country. Home: Route 1 Box 134 Hudson Rd Summerfield NC 27358 Office: One Southern Life Ctr PO Box 21887 Greensboro NC 27420

CARTER, WILLIAM CLARENCE, insurance agent; b. Mayodan, N.C., Mar. 29, 1928; s. William Comer and Lucy Pearl (Barrow) C.; B.A., Randolph-Macon Coll., 1950; m. Phyllis Jane Stephenson, Apr. 28, 1951; children—Anne Carter Marrin, Mary Claire. With Fidelity Mut. Life Ins. Co., Richmond, Va., 1953-56; gen. agt. Fidelity Bankers Life Ins. Co., Richmond, 1956—. Served as capt. USMC, 1951-53. C.L.U. Mem. Am. Soc. C.L.U., Estate Planning Council, Million Dollar Roundtable. Episcopalian. Clubs: Bull and Bear, Hermitage Country (Richmond). Home: 103 Rose Hill Rd Richmond VA 23229 Office: Monroe Park Towers Suite 24 520 W Franklin St Richmond VA 23220

CARTMILL, MATT, anatomy educator; b. Los Angeles, Jan. 4, 1943; m. Mary Kaye Brown, May 29, 1971; 1 dau., Erica A. B.A. summa cum laude in Anthropology, Pomona Coll., 1964; M.A., U. Chgo., 1966, Ph.D. in Anthropology, 1970. Assoc. in anatomy Duke U., Durham, N.C., 1969-70, asst. prof. dept. anatomy, 1970-72, asst. prof. depts. anatomy and anthropology, 1972-74, assoc. prof., 1974-81, prof. dept. anatomy, 1981—, assoc. prof. dept. anthropology, 1981-83, prof., 1983—, dir. Primate Facility, spring 1977. Hon. Woodrow Wilson fellow, 1964; NSF fellow, 1964-69; Am. Council Learned Soc. summer scholar, 1962; Wenner-Gren Found. grantee, 1966, 67; NIH grantee, 1970; recipient Student AMA Med. Teaching award, 1971; NIH Research Career Devel. award, 1975-79; NSF grantee, 1982-85; Guggenheim fellow, 1985-86. Fellow AAAS; mem. Am. Anthrop. Assn., Am. Assn. Phys. Anthropologists, Am. Soc. Mammalogists, Am. Soc. Vertebrate Paleontologists, Internat. Primatol. Soc., Sigma Xi (grantee 1968). Mng. editor Internat. Jour. Primatology, 1980—. Contbr. numerous articles to profl. jours. Office: Dept Anatomy Duke U Durham NC 27710

CARTNER, JOHN A., consulting engineer; b. Jacksonville, N.C., Nov. 6, 1947; s. John Alexander and Anna Gertrude (Hardison) C.; m. Tanya Lynn Morris, Feb. 18, 1978; children—Christian W.J., Natalie V.O. B.S.c., U.S. Merchant Marine Acad., 1969; M.Sc., U. Ga., 1974; M.B.A., Ga. State U., 1978; Ph.D., U. Ga., 1975. Cadet to master U.S. Mcht. Marine, 1969—; postdoctoral trainee U.S. Army Research Inst., 1975-78; dir. marine transp. systems Grumman Data Systems Corp., Bethpage, N.Y., 1980-81; v.p. IMA Resources, Inc., Washington, 1981; pres., chief operating officer Phillips Cartner & Co., Inc., Alexandria, Va., 1981-84, chmn., chief exec. officer, 1985—; dir. Alexandria Seaport Found., USMMA Found., Kings Point, N.Y. Chesapeake Crane Co., Inc., Alexandria, Va., 1985—; chmn. Simat Internat., Ltd., Washington, 1985—. Contbr. articles to profl. jours. Served to lt. USNR, 1969-73. Recipient Outstanding Profl. Achievement, U.S. Mcht. Marine Acad., 1984. Mem. Soc. Naval Architects and Marine Engrs., N.Y. Acad. Scis., Inst. Navigation U.S. Republican. Episcopalian. Club: Downtown Athletic. Address: 203 S Union St Alexandria VA 22314

CARTWRIGHT, AUBREY LEE, JR., research physiologist, nutritionist; b. Elizabeth City, N.C., Jan. 13, 1952; s. Aubrey Lee and Eva Marie (Copeland) C.; m. Elaine Cayton Twiddy, Aug. 18, 1973; children—Ian Lee, Lauren Elaine, Morgan Blair. B.S. in Animal Sci., N.C. State U., 1975, M.S. in Nutrition, 1979, Ph.D. in Nutrition, 1982. Research physiologist U.S. Dept. Agriculture, Agrl. Research Service, Richard B. Russell Research Center, Athens, Ga., 1982-84, U.S. Dept. Agriculture, Agrl. Research Service, Poultry Research Lab., Georgetown, Del., 1984—. Mem. Council for Agrl. Sci. and Tech., N.Y. Acad. Scis., Am. Soc. Animal Sci., Poultry Sci. Assn., Am. Inst. Nutrition, Fedn. Am. Socs. for Exptl. Biology, Sigma Xi. Mem. Christian Ch. (Disciples of Christ). Lodge: Mason. Contbr. articles to various publs.

CARTWRIGHT, CHARLES NELSON, lawyer; b. Ft. Worth, July 22, 1933; s. Charles L. and Mildred (Epperson) C.; student U. Houston, 1952; B.A., U. Tex., 1956, J.D., 1960; m. Suzanne Oberwetter, Sept. 5, 1956; 1 son, Charles Rea. Admitted to Tex. bar, 1960; asst. city atty. Corpus Christi (Tex.), 1960-63; assoc. Utter & Chase, Corpus Christi, 1964-67, ptnr., 1967-73; mem. firm Howard, McDowell & Cartwright, Corpus Christi, 1973-76, Prichard, Peeler, Cartwright & Hall, Corpus Christi, 1976—; instr. real estate law Del Mar Coll., Corpus Christi, 1965-68, guest lectr., 1968-70. Mem. City Zoning and Planning Commn. Corpus Christi, 1970-76, chmn., 1973-76; chmn. adv. bd. Mcpl. Legal Studies Center, 1982-84; research fellow Southwestern Legal Found., Dallas, 1978—, mem., 1973—. Co-author: Texas Civil Trial Handbook, 1984. Served to 2d lt. AUS, 1957. Fellow Tex. Bar Found. (life); mem. Am., Nueces County (pres. 1975-76) bar assns., State Bar Tex. (past chmn. continuing legal edn., dir. State Bar Coll. 1984—), Nueces County Trial Lawyers Assn. (dir. 1970-71), Am. Soc. Hosp. Attys., Corpus Christi C. of C., Leadership Corpus Christi, Aircraft Owners and Pilots Assn., Nat. Rifle Assn. Lodges: Masons, Kiwanis. Home: 334 Cape Hatteras Corpus Christi TX 78412 Office: Guaranty Bank Plaza Corpus Christi TX 78475

CARTWRIGHT, PHILLIP AUGUST, economics educator, economic forecasting project administrator, consultant; b. Springfield, Ill., Dec. 29, 1953; s. Thomas Hume and Miriam (Beyer) C.; m. Blanche Victoria Baumann, July 30, 1977. B.A. with honors, Tex. Christian U., 1975, M.A., 1976; M.S., U. Ill., 1980, Ph.D., 1982. Grad. asst. Tex. Christian U., Ft. Worth, 1975-76; econ. analyst Tex. Am. Bancshares, Ft. Worth, 1976-78; teaching asst. U. Ill., Urbana-Champaign, 1978-80; research asst. Bur. Econs. Bus. Research, 1980-82; asst. prof. econs., dir. Ga. Econ. Forecasting Project, Athens, 1982—; econ. commentator Atlanta Jour.-Constn., 1984—. Contbr. articles to profl. jours. U. Ill. fellow, 1982; U. Ga. grantee, 1985—. Mem. Am. Econ. Assn., Am. Statis. Assn., Econometric Soc., Assn. for Univ. Bus. Econ. Research (chmn. fed. stats. commn. 1983—), Internat. Inst. Forecasters, So. Econ. Assn. Avocations: collector of fine prints; tennis. Office: U Ga Div Research Coll Bus Adminstrn Brooks Hall Athens GA 30602

CARTWRIGHT, WALTER JOSEPH, sociology educator; b. Carona, Kans., Apr. 26, 1922; s. James William and Agnes (Whitehead) C.; m. Bettye D. Atkins, June 6, 1948; children—Joseph Daniel, Deborah. Student Texarkana Coll., 1939-41; A.B., So. Methodist U., 1943; Th.M., 1946; M.A., U. Tex., 1960, Ph.D., 1964. Pastor, United Meth. Ch., Tex., 1944-62; asst. prof. Tex. Tech. Coll., Lubbock, 1962-65, assoc. prof., 1965-68; chmn. dept. Tex. Tech. U., Lubbock, 1968-74, prof. sociology, 1969—; adv. vice chmn. Com. Aging, South Plains Govt. Assn., 1973-82; mem. community service adv. com., coordinator Bd. Tex. Coll. Univs. System, 1968-70; cons. Tex. Commn. Alcoholism, Austin, 1965-67. Co-editor, co-author: Sociological Perspectives, 1968. Bd. dirs. Vis. Nurses Assn., Lubbock, 1980—; bd. dirs. Golden Age Home, Lockhart, Tex., 1958-62; mem. projects bd. Internat. Ctr. Arid Semi-arid Lands, Lubbock, 1968-68. Fellow Am. Sociol. Assn.; mem. Southwest Social Sci. Assn., Rocky Mountain Social Sci. Assn., So. Sociol. Soc., Law Soc. Assn., Phi Beta Kappa. Democrat. Methodist. Lodges: Masons, Lions, Rotary. Avocations: gardening; showing prize iris. Home: 7904 Joliet Ave Lubbock TX 79423 Office: Tex Tech U PO Box 4590 Lubbock TX 79409

CARULLA, RAMON, painter; b. Havana, Cuba, Dec. 7, 1938; s. David and Lydia (Trujillo) C.; m. Teresa Chacon, Mar. 14, 1964; children—Carlos A., Janik. Student U. Havana Sch. Law, 1960-62. Asst. to pres. Virginia Miller Galleries, Coconut Grove, Fla., 1976-79; artist, Miami, Fla., 1979—; lectr. in field. Represented in permanent collections at Detroit Inst. Art., Cin. Art Mus., Société D'Artistes Internat., Paris, Mus. Tamayo, Mexico City, Mus. Fine Art, Montreal Que., Can., Mus. Modern Art of Latin Am., Washington, New Sch. Social Research, N.Y. Cintas fellow, Internat. Inst. Edn., N.Y., 1974, 80. Recipient Sylvia Davidowics award for painting Met. Mus. and Art Ctr., 1981; 1st prize VI Biennial Graphic Art, San Juan, 1983. Republican. Roman Catholic. Home and office: 4735 NW 184th Terr Miami FL 33055

CARUSO, SALVATORE ANTHONY, social worker, city official; b. New Orleans, Aug. 25, 1941; s. Frank Salvatore and Josephine Delores (Vitale) C.; B.A., La. State U., 1965; M.S.W. (Public Health scholar), Tulane U., 1971; m. Mary Martha Joachim, Jan. 21, 1967; children—Salvatore Anthony, Mary Martha. Employment interviewer La. Employment Service, New Orleans, 1965-67, employment technician, 1967-69; dist. exec. Boy Scouts Am., New Orleans, 1967; employment counselor Holman Vocat. Center, New Orleans, 1969-70; chief social worker, behavioral sci. coor. children and youth project Driscoll Children's Hosp., Corpus Christi, Tex., 1972-73; exec. dir. Big Bros. of Greater New Orleans, 1973-75; asst. prof. La. State U. Med. Center, New Orleans, 1975—, also assoc. dir. Human Devel. Ctr., 1984-85; pvt. practice social work, New Orleans and Slidell, La., 1973—. Bd. dirs. Youth Services, New Orleans, 1976-78; mem. Slidell City Council, 1978-82, v.p., 1979-80, pres., 1980; chmn. bd. St. Tammany Parish Hosp. Service Dist., 1982-85; mayor, Slidell, 1985—. Named hon. dep. atty. gen. State of La., hon. dep. civil sheriff Orleans Parish; recipient Outstanding Service award Big Bros. Greater New Orleans, 1975; hon. goodwill ambassador State of La.; award for service Slidell Meml. Hosp., 1985; Outstanding Service award La. State U., 1986. Mem. Nat. Assn. Social Workers, Acad. Cert. Social Workers, Slidell C. of C., Order Sons of Italy in Am. Democrat. Roman Catholic. Lodges: K.C., Rotary. Home: 3842 Brookwood Dr Slidell LA 70458 Office: Mayor's Office City Hall 2056 2d St Slidell LA 70458

CARVEL, MARY JANE, real estate broker; b. St. Louis, Aug. 23, 1920; d. Conrad Arthur and Otillia Mary (Brefeld) Wellings; student selected courses U. Houston, 1938-39, Houston Conservatory Music, 1949-54; m. Vincent Carvel, Apr. 25, 1942 (dec. 1943). Various secretarial positions in oil industry, 1937-39; appraiser Nat. Bank Commerce (now Tex. Commerce Bank), Houston, 1949-55; asst. to pres. Weaver Drilling Co., Houston, 1955-59; co-owner, builder 1st garden apts. in Houston, 1959-60; founder, propr. Mary Jane Carvel, Interiors, Houston, 1960—; owner, founder Mary Jane Carvel Realtors, Houston, 1974—; co-owner Bayou on the Bend Apts., Timberline Office Bldg. and owner 17 miscellaneous propoerties. Founder, chmn. bd., bd. dirs. Sanctuary for Unwanted Animals, Houston, 1981—; bd. dirs. Carvel Animal Relief Endowment; charter mem. Republican Presdl. Task Force. Mem. Nat. Realtors, Tex. Bd. Realtors, Houston Bd. Realtors, Houston Apt. Assn. Roman Catholic. Office: 5213 Memorial Dr Houston TX 77077

CARVER, JAMES LEWIS, building contractor; b. King George County, Va., Mar. 6, 1925; s. George Thomas and Fannie Mae (Shelton) C.; m. Myrtis Virginia Henderson, Oct. 20, 1955. Exec., Carver's Floor Service, Fredericksburg, Va., 1949-70; pres. Fredericksburg Real Estate Sales, Inc., Clearview Hts., Ltd., Fredericksburg Devel. Corp., Spotslee Investors, Spring Valley Devel. and Rentals; adv. bd. Central Fidelity Bank. Served with USAF, 1943-46. Mem. Am. Contract Bridge League (life master), Am. Legion, D.A.V. Clubs: Elks, Fredericksburg Country. Home: 1102 Westwood Dr Fredericksburg VA 22401 Office: 1002 Prince Edward Fredericksburg VA 22401

CARWILE, WALTER DEWITT, JR., accountant, adult home administrator; b. Campbell County, Va., Mar. 13, 1922; s. Walter DeWitt and Hessie Mae (Finch) C.; A.B., Lynchburg Coll., 1950; m. Kathryn Mae Wingfield, Dec. 18, 1948; children—Kathie Mae, Cynthia Ann, Gwynne Annette. With Pilot Life Ins. Co., Lynchburg, Va., 1950-52, N&W Mfg. Co., 1952-53; mem. acctg. staff Gt. Am. Industries, Bedford, Va., 1954-55; asst. mgr., asst. dir. Elks Nat. Home and Hosp., Bedford, 1955—. Dist. dir. Cancer Soc., 1980-81. Served with AUS, 1942-45; ETO. Decorated Purple Heart. Cert. adminstr. Homes for Adults. Mem. Bedford County C. of C., Va. Assn. Homes for Adults. Republican. Wesleyan. Clubs: Ruritan, Gideons Internat., Elks (trustee Lynchburg lodge). Home: Hwy 460 Box 26 Thaxton VA 24174 Office: Elks Nat Home Bedford

CARY, JOHN BARRY, JR., marketing company executive, lawyer; b. Richmond, Va., Sept. 10, 1938; s. John Barry and Katherine Roy (Gordon) C.; m. Janet Marie Landes, June 22, 1974 (div. June 1976). A.B. in English, Va. Mil. Inst., 1960; J.D., U. Va., 1971; diploma U.S. Army War Coll., 1983. Bar: Va. 1971, D.C. 1972, U.S. Supreme Ct. 1975. Commd. 2d lt. U.S. Army, 1960, advanced through grades to col. Res., 1984—; law clk. Superior Ct. D.C., 1971-72; atty.-adviser FCC, Washington, 1972-76; sr. atty.-adviser, 1976-82; pres. Cary Enterprises, Arlington, Va., 1982—. Author text exam, 1976. Fundraiser Va. Mil. Inst., Lexington, 1960-70, 76, 85, alumni class pres., 1970—; fundraiser Durette for Gov., Richmond, Va., 1985; trustee, ptnr. The Old Mansion, Bowling Green, VA., 1970—; bd. govs. Preston Library, Va. Mil. Inst., 1984—. Mem. Fed. Bar Assn., Res. Officers Assn. (officer 1972-73, 85, exec. com. Am. Vets. com. 1986—, chmn. adviser U.S. Congl. Adv. Bd. 1982-83), U.S. Army War Coll. Alumni Assn., Soc. Cin., Am. Legion, Spl. Forces Assn., Kappa Alpha, Phi Delta Phi. Clubs: Torch Internat., Country of Va. Republican. Presbyterian. Avocations: weight lifting; running; reading. Home and Office: 6835-B N Washington Blvd Arlington VA 22213

CASARIEGO, JORGE ISAAC, psychiatrist; b. Havana, Cuba, Apr. 25, 1945; came to U.S., 1960, naturalized, 1970; s. Isaac Alberto Casariego and Elena Mercedes Portela de Casariego; B.S., U. New Orleans, 1967; M.D., La. State U., 1969. Med. intern Jewish Hosp. Bklyn., N.Y.C., 1969-70; psychiat. resident N.Y. Med. Coll., N.Y.C., 1970-71, Walter Reed Army Hosp., Washington, 1971-73; chief psychiatry clinic U.S. Army Hosp., Heidelberg, W.Ger., 1973-75; clin. instr. dept. psychiatry Sch. Medicine U. Miami (Fla.), 1976-78, asst. prof. psychiatry, 1978—; practice medicine specializing in psychiatry, Miami, 1976—; med. dir. drug dependence outpatient unit VA Med. Center, Miami, 1976, dir. crisis intervention program, 1976—, attending psychiatrist, 1976—; attending psychiatrist Jackson Meml. Hosp. and U. Miami Hosps., 1976—; chmn. continuing psychiat. edn. com. U. Miami, 1980-83; invited examiner Am. Bd. Psychiatry. Served with M.C., U.S. Army, 1971-75. Diplomate Am. Bd. Psychiatry and Neurology. NIH Tropical Medicine fellow, U. Recife (Brazil), 1968; recipient Physician's award AMA, 1977, 81. Mem. Am. Psychiat. Assn. (observer-cons. Council on Internal Orgn. 1979-81), South Fla. Psychiat. Soc. (chmn. membership com., 1978-80, mem. continuing edn. com. 1980-81, chmn. Spanish speaking com. 1981-82, chmn. continuing med. edn. com. 1982-84), Cuban Med. Assn. in Exile, Fla. Psychoanalytic Soc., Com. of 1000 (Washington), Aesculapians. Editor-in-chief The Tiger Rag, La. State U., 1968-69; reviewer, contbr. articles Am. Jour. Psychiatry; contbr. articles to profl. publs. Office: 1900 Coral Way Suite 202 Miami FL 33145

CASE, GERALD CLARENCE, ins. co. exec.; b. Peoria, Ill., Aug. 10, 1937; s. Clarence A. and Edna B. Case; B.S. in Polit. Sci. and Mktg., U. Mo., 1959; m. Janet Marie Dunagan, Nov. 28, 1959; children—Kimberly Marie, Gregory

Gerald, Bradley Gerald. Area sales rep. Proctor & Gamble Distbg. Co., Dade and Monroe counties, Fla., 1959-62, office head salesman, 1962-64, unit mgr. for Pitts. and Charleston, W.Va., 1964-65; exec. v.p. Scope Co., Miami, Fla., 1965-68; spl. agt. Mass. Mut., Fla., 1968-71, asst. to gen. agt. Miami area, 1971-72; asso. Hale & Jones, Inc., Miami, 1970-72; agy. mgr. Bankers Life Co. of Des Moines, Miami, 1972—; dir. Community Bank of Homestead, chmn. exec. com., 1975-78. Mem. Dade County (Fla.) Transp. Adv. Com., 1974-75; chmn. com. fin. Silver Palm Meth. Ch., 1974-78. Served with U.S. Army, 1956-58. Mem. Miami Assn. Life Underwriters (v.p. 1973-78), Gen. Agts. and Mgrs. Miami (dir. 1973—, pres. 1979), Fla. Gen. Agts. and Mgrs. Assn. (pres. 1983-84), Greater Homestead Motel Assn. (pres. 1970-72), Redlands Citizen Assn., Homestead South Dade C. of C. (dir. 1974-78), Phi Delta Theta. Democrat. Clubs: Elks, Rotary (pres. 1976-78) (Homestead); Miami Dolphin Booster; Redlands Golf and Country. Home: 14925 SW 232d St Goulds FL 33170 Office: 10621 SW 88th St Miami FL 33176

CASE, STEVEN THOMAS, biochemistry educator, molecular/cellular biologist; b. N.Y.C., Jan. 18, 1949; s. Truman Gordon and Peggy (Pappas) C.; m. Gay Lynn Moore, June 12, 1971; children—Chad Erik, Jill Lynn. B.S., Widner Coll., 1969; M.S., Wilkes Coll., 1971; Ph.D. in Cellular and Molecular Bioloy, U. So. Calif., 1974. Postdoctoral fellow Karolinska Inst., Stockholm, 1975-77; postdoctoral assoc. Yale U., New Haven, 1977-78; asst. prof. biochemistry U. Miss. Med. Ctr., Jackson, 1979-83, assoc. prof., 1983—; mem. research adv. and policy com. Miss. affiliate Am. Heart Assn., 1981-84. Served to capt. U.S. Army, 1974-75. Recipient Nat. Research Service award NIH, 1975-78; grantee NIH, 1979-84, Am. Heart Assn., 1982-84, NSF, 1985—; recipient U.S. Congl. Antarctic Services medal, 1985. Mem. Am. Soc. Biol. Chemists, Am. Soc. for Cell Biology, Sigma Xi. Editor Gene, 1983—; contbr. articles to sci. research jours. Home: 133 Dogwood Circle Brandon MS 39042 Office: Dept Biochemistry U Miss Med Ctr 2500 N State St Jackson MS 39216

CASEMAN, AUSTIN BERT, civil engineering educator; b. Phoenix, Feb. 13, 1922; s. Artie B. and Winnie (Yergensen) C.; m. Susan Louise Burleson, Nov. 9, 1946; 1 child, Cathy Anne. B.S. in Civil Engring., Utah State U., 1947, M.S. in Civil Engring., 1948; Sc.D. in Civil Engring., MIT, 1961. Registered profl. engr., Ga. Instr., then asst. prof. civil engring. Wash. State U., 1948-56; assoc. prof. civil engring. Ga. Inst. Tech., Atlanta, 1956-62, prof., 1962—; with City Planning Commn., Logan, Utah, summer 1948; structural engr. Boeing Aircraft, Seattle, summer 1951, U.S. Army C.E., Walla Walla, Wash., summer 1952, Douglas Aircraft, Long Beach, Calif., summer 1953, Lockheed Aircraft, Marietta, Ga., summer 1956. Served to 1st lt. U.S. Army, 1943-46. Decorated Bronze Star. Faculty fellow NSF, 1957-59. Mem. Am. Concrete Inst. (past pres. Atlanta chpt.), ASCE (faculty award student chpt. Ga. Inst. Tech. 1968), Blue Key, Sigma Xi, Chi Epsilon, Sigma Tau, Phi Kappa Phi, Pi Kappa Alpha. Mormon. Home: 2136 Kodiak Dr NE Atlanta GA 30345 Office: Sch Civil Engring Ga Inst Tech Atlanta GA 30332

CASEY, ALBERT VINCENT, retired airline executive; b. Boston, Feb. 28, 1920; s. John Joseph and Norine (Doyle) C.; A.B., Harvard, 1943, M.B.A., 1948; m. Eleanor Anne Welch, Aug. 25, 1945; children—Peter Andrew, Judith Anne. With S.P. Ry., 1948-61, asst. v.p., asst. treas., San Francisco, 1953-61; v.p., treas. Ry. Express Agy., N.Y.C., 1961-63; v.p. finance Times-Mirror Co., Los Angeles, 1963-64, exec. v.p., dir., 1964-66, pres., mem. exec. com., 1966-74; chmn. bd., pres. Am. Airlines, 1974-80, chmn. bd., chief exec. officer, 1980-85; dir. Times Mirror Co., Sears, Roebuck and Co., LTV Corp., Colgate-Palmolive Co., Am Internat., AMR Corp., Am. Airlines, Inc. Mem. Exec. Council on Fgn. Diplomats; bd. govs. Dallas Symphony Assn.; Served to 1st lt. AUS, 1942-46. Clubs: Dallas Petroleum, Dallas, Dallas Country (Dallas); Eldorado Country (Indian Wells, Calif.). Office: 2626 Republic Bank Tower Dallas TX 75201

CASEY, CATHERINE SUE, pediatrician, educator; b. Washington, Feb. 23, 1948; d. John Roland and Edna Hope (Batcheller) C. B.S., Coll. William and Mary, 1970; M.D., Med. Coll. Va., 1974. Diplomate Am. Bd. Pediatrics. Intern, Children's Hosp. Phila., 1974-75, resident, 1975-77; practice medicine specializing in pediatrics, Arlington, Va., 1977—; asst. clin. prof. pediatrics Georgetown U. Sch. Medicine, 1980—. Chmn. Project Santa Ana, humanitarian relief project, 1984—. Fellow Am. Acad. Pediatrics; mem. Am. Med. Women's Assn. (br. pres. 1983-84), Med. Soc. Va., No. Va. Pediatric Soc. (v.p. 1983-84, pres. 1984-85), Arlington County Med. Soc. (treas. 1984-85, sec. 1985, v.p. 1986). Democrat. Episcopalian. Office: 1715 N George Mason Dr Suite 205 Arlington VA 22205

CASEY, JOE, law enforcement official. Chief of police, Nashville. Office: City Hall 107 Metropolitan Courthouse Nashville TN 37201*

CASEY, MICHAEL KIRKLAND, business executive, lawyer; b. Wheeling, W.Va., Jan. 24, 1940; s. Clyde Thomas and Joan Ferrell (McLure) C.; m. Mary Ann McCarten, Jan. 29, 1969; children—Michael Kirkland II, Mary Larkin, Colin McCarten. Student U. Notre Dame, 1957-58; B.S., W.Va. U., 1964; J.D., George Washington U., 1967. Bar: D.C. 1974, U.S. Dist. Ct. D.C., U.S. Ct. Appeals (D.C. cir.). Cons. to White House, Washington, 1977-81, handled overseas Presdl. missions in India, Western Europe, Brazil and Middle East; dir. White House Conf. on Small Bus., Washington, 1979-80; assoc. adminstr. for investment SBA, Washington, 1980-81; chmn. bd. MCW Internat. Ltd., Alexandria, Va., 1981—; cons. Churchill Internat., San Francisco, 1981—. Advance man Kennedy for Pres. Com., 1968, spl. asst. Muskie for Pres. Com., 1972, asst. campaign mgr. Jackson for Pres. Com., 1976, campaign mgr. Carter-Mondale Reelection Com. in Mo. and Ill., 1980. Served with USMC, 1958-61, Mediterranean. Recipient Presdl. Cert., Pres. of U.S., 1977, 78, 79, plaque White House Commn. on Small Bus., 1980, Disting. Service award SBA, 1980. Mem. ABA, D.C. Bar Assn., Nat. Democratic Club. Roman Catholic. Club: Belle Haven Country (Alexandria). Avocations: reading; tennis; skiing. Home: 6115 Vernon Terr Alexandria VA 22307 Office: MCW Internat Ltd 301 N Fairfax St Suite 110 Alexandria VA 22320

CASHIN, JOHN GREGORY, restaurant executive; b. Bklyn., Nov. 24, 1925; s. Leo Ignatious and Mildred (Hess) C.; m. Helen Heath, Dec. 19, 1948; children—Heath, Bridgett, Jason, Cara, Adam, Erin. Student U. De San Marcos, Lima, Peru, 1948, Mexico City Coll., 1948; B.A., Colgate U., 1949. With Charles W. Hoyt Advt. Agy., 1950; dist. mgr. McGraw-Hill Publishing Co., Cleve., 1951-63; pres., editor, publisher Cashin Publishing Co., Cleve., 1963-69; pub., editor Dare Mag., 1963-68; pres. Cashin's Restaurant Group, Atlanta, 1974—. Bd. dirs. USO; trustee Ga. Horse Found.; active Atlanta Zool. Soc.; pres. 2000 Neighbors Assn. Served with USAAF, 1943-45. Named Ga. Restaurateur of Yr., 1982. Mem. Assn. for U.S. Army (exec. com.), Ga. Hospitality and Travel Assn. (bd. dirs., pres. restaurant div. 1985, trustee health benefit trust). Club: Atlanta Polo. Editor, pub. Dare Mag., 1963-68. Home and Office: 5905 Long Island Dr Atlanta GA 30328

CASHION, JERRY CLYDE, historian; b. Statesville, N.C., Nov. 18, 1940; s. Benjamin Harrison and Alma (Spears) C.; A.B., U. N.C., 1963, Ph.D., 1979. Teaching asst. U. N.C., Chapel Hill, 1964-70, instr., 1971-74; contract researcher N.C. div. Archives and History, Raleigh, 1965-69, research supr., 1975—; vis. prof. N.C. State U., Raleigh, 1978, 81. Mem. Hist. Soc. N.C. (sec. 1981—), So. Hist. Assn. (life), N.C. Lit. and Hist. Assn., Hist. Preservation Soc. N.C., Phi Gamma Delta (advisor 1965—, Durance award 1980). Author: Fort Butler and Cherokee Removal from N.C., 1970; co-author: Fort Dobbs, 1976; editor: Guide to N.C. Highway Historical Markers, 1979. Home: 1104 Mordecai Dr Raleigh NC 27604 Office: 109 E Jones St Raleigh NC 27611

CASKEY, OWEN LAVERNE, psychology educator; b. Corsicana, Tex., Mar. 10, 1925; s. Price Hamilton and Esma Eulysses (Lisman) C.; m. Shirley Jean Larned, Apr. 10, 1981; children—Leigh Ann, Deborah Jane. B.S., Tex. Tech U., 1947, M.Ed., 1948; Ed.D., U. Colo., 1952. Lic. psychologist, Tex.; lic. profl. counselor, Tex. Tchr. Lubbock (Tex.) Pub. Schs., 1941-43; instr. Tex. Tech U., Lubbock, 1947-50, prof. ednl. psychology, 1964-83, prof. emeritus, 1983—, v.p. student affairs, 1968-70, assoc. v.p. acad. affairs, 1970-73, dir. instructional research, 1974-81, assoc. dean. Coll. Edn., 1976-78; asst. prof. Colo. State U., 1950-53, assoc. prof., 1954-58; counseling psychologist VA, Denver, 1954; cons. psychologist Rohrer, Hibler & Riplogle, Dallas, 1958-63; assoc. prof. Okla. State U., 1963-64; psychologist El Paso (Tex.) Pub. Schs., 1981—; cons. to state and govt. agys. Chmn. Community Planning Council, 1973-75; Bd. dirs. United Way, 1973-75, mem. budget com., 1973-79, mem. long-range planning com., 1978-80; bd. dirs. South Plains Health System, 1976-81, mem. exec. com., 1978-81. Served to lt. (j.g.) USN, 1943-46; ETO. Fellow VA, 1954, U. Colo., 1954; recipient numerous research grants, 1966—. Mem. Am. Psychol. Assn., Am. Personnel and Guidance Assn., Am. Coll. Personnel Assn., Nat. Vocat. Guidance Assn., Am. Counselor Educators and Suprs., Soc. for Accelerated Learning and Teaching, Tex. Personnel and Guidance Assn., Tex. Psychol. Assn. Methodist. Contbr. numerous articles to profl. jours. Home: 8201 Edgemere St El Paso TX 79925 Office: 4931 Hercules Ave El Paso TX 79904

CASKEY, WILLIAM EDWARD, JR., psychologist, educator; b. Springfield, Ohio, Feb. 6, 1925; s. William Edward and Bernice Florence (Allen) C.; m. Marylou Ferrante, June 15, 1951 (div. Oct. 1970); children—J. Edward, Karen Lorraine, Wesley Craig; m. Judith Mast, Apr. 15, 1971. B.S. in Edn., Kent State U., 1949, M.A., 1965, Ph.D., 1973; M.Div., Drew U., 1954. Dir. pupil personnel Orrville City Schs., Ohio, 1966-68, Portage County Sch., 1969-70, West Holmes Local Schs., Millersburg, Ohio, 1971-75; sch. psychologist Tuscarawas County Sch., New Philadelphia, Ohio, 1970-71; faculty East Tenn. State U., Johnson City, 1975—; psychol. cons. Appalachian Regional Child Devel., Johnson City, 1979—; psychologist, cons. Unicoi County Sch., Erwin, Tenn., 1980-84; spl. edn. cons. Appalachian Psychol. Cons., Johnson City, 1981—. Contbr. articles to profl. jours. Served as pfc. USAF, 1943-45. Research Council East Tenn. State U. grantee, 1983; honored for services Tenn. Dept. Health, 1979-85. Mem. Am. Psychol. Assn., Nat. Assn. Sch. Psychologists (cert.), Council Exceptional Children, Am. Assn. Mental Deficiency, Assn. Retarded Citizens (pres. 1979-81), Internat. Assn. Sch. Psychologists, NEA, Assn. Brain Research. Methodist. Lodge: Masons (master 1967-68). Avocations: fishing, reading, weightlifting, running, swimming. Home: 1004 Southwest Ave Johnson City TN 37601 Office: E Tenn State Univ Box 18940 A East Tenn State U Johnson City TN 37614

CASLER, DENNIS JOSEPH, accountant; b. Hoboken, N.J., Feb. 3, 1945; s. Walter Francis and Elizabeth Ann (McGovern) C.; m. Carolyn Joyce Woerner, May 22, 1971 (div. 1981). B.S., Fairleigh Dickinson U., 1971. C.P.A., Fla. Acct., UPS, 1965-67; internal auditor Gentry Internat., 1967-69; controller Hoboken Model Cities Program, N.J., 1969-73; sr. acct. Tanner & Assocs., New Port Richey, Fla., 1973-75; controller Uitewyk Corp., Tampa, Fla., 1975-81; pres. Dennis J. Casler, C.P.A., Clearwater, Fla., 1981—; seminar instr., cons. small bus. Resource Mgmt. Inc. Mem. Citizen adv. council Pasco County Comprehensive Health Agy., 1976-77. Mem. Am. Inst. C.P.A.s, Fla. Soc. C.P.A.s. Club: Kiwanis. Office: 2566 McMullen Booth Rd Suite G Clearwater FL 33519

CASLER, WILLIAM FRANKLIN, veterinarian, lawyer; b. St. Petersburg, Fla., Aug. 5, 1924; s. George Franklin and Virginia Dawn (Parsons) C.; children—William F., Paul D., Gregory D., Christopher E., Mark D., Brent B., Jonathan W., Joseph C., Steven W. B.S., Mich. State U., 1952, D.V.M., 1955; J.D., Stetson U., 1965. Bar: Fla. 1965, U.S. Dist. Ct. (mid. dist.) Fla. 1966, U.S. Ct. Ct. Appeals (5th cir.) 1969, U.S. Ct. Appeals (D.C.) 1976, U.S. Supreme Ct. 1970. Coach, Fla. Mil. Acad., St. Petersburg, 1946-49; owner, veterinarian Animal Med. Ctr., St. Petersburg, 1956-76; ptnr. Piper & Casler, St. Petersburg, 1971-76; prin. William F. Casler, Sr., Atty. at Law, St. Petersburg Beach, Fla., 1976—; veterinarian Suncoast Animal Clinic, St. Petersburg Beach, 1976—; vis. prof. Coll. Vet. Medicine, U. Fla., Gainesville, 1972—. Pres., St. Petersburg Soc. Prevention Cruelty to Animals; pres. St. Petersburg Boys Choir. Served to capt. inf. U.S. Army, 1943-46. Decorated Bronze Star with oak leaf cluster, Purple Heart, Combat Infantryman Badge. Named Fla. Veterinarian of Yr., Fla. Vet. Med. Assn., 1972. Mem. Fla. Vet. Med. Assn. (pres. 1970), Pinellas County Vet. Med. Soc (pres.), AVMA (jud. counsel 1975—), AVMA, Pinellas County Lawyers Assn., Fla. Bar Assn., ABA. St. Petersburg C. of C. Democrat. Episcopalian. Club: Sertoma. Home: 11778 88th Terrace N Seminole FL 33542 Office: 7217 Gulf Blvd Saint Petersburg Beach FL 33706

CASON, DICK KENDALL, physician; b. Beaumont, Tex., June 27, 1922; s. Dick Kendall and Maurine (Mills) C.; B.A., Rice U., 1945; M.D., U. Tex., 1945; m. Maxine Skocdopole, Apr. 4, 1946; children—Dick Mills, Alma Christine. Intern, Kings County Hosp. Bklyn., 1945-46; med. resident Meth. Hosp., Dallas, 1948-49; gen. practice medicine, Hillsboro, Tex., 1949—; staff mem. Grant-Buie Hosp.; charter mem. Am. Bd. Family Practice. Pres. Hillsboro Indsl. Devel. Found., 1955-60; pres. Indsl. Found., 1979—. Served from 1st lt. to capt., AUS, 1946-48. Fellow Royal Soc. Health (Eng.); mem. Hill County Med. Soc. (pres. 1951), Tex. Med. Assn. (alt. del. to AMA 1980-84, del. to AMA 1984—), Am. Acad. Gen. Practice, N.Y. Acad. Sci., Internat. Horn Soc., C. of C., Hill County Soc. Crippled Children, Royal Soc. Medicine (affiliate). Presbyterian (elder). Clubs: Hillsboro Country, Rotary (pres. Hillsboro 1955). Contbr. articles to profl. jours. Home: 1303 Park Dr Hillsboro TX 76645 Office: 150 Circle Dr Hillsboro TX 76645

CASON, LOUIE LANDER, JR., insurance company executive; b. Atlanta, Sept. 2, 1948; s. Louie Lander and Mary (Martin) C.; m. Dorothy Walker, June 25, 1977; children—Louie Lander, William Hammond, Frank Walker. Student, Clemson U., 1966-68; B.B.A. in Fin., U. Ga., 1970; postgrad., Ga. State U., 1972-82, Am. Coll., 1974—. Credit mgr. Trust Co. Bank, Atlanta, 1972-74; sales rep. Met. Life Ins. Co., Atlanta, 1974-79; pres. Cason and Cason, Atlanta, 1979-81; sales mgr. dist. Guardian Life Ins. Co., Columbia, S.C., 1981—. Chmn. registration Atlanta March of Dimes, 1976-78; chmn. com. Atlanta Heart Assn., 1979-81; team leader Joint Tech. Ga. Devel. Fund, 1979—. Mem. Nat. Assn. Life Underwriters (bd. dirs. 1983-85), Am. Soc. Chartered Life Underwriters (chmn. com. 1979), Atlanta C. of C. (bd. dirs. 1982), Sigma Pi. Clubs: Atlanta City; Palmetto (Columbia). Office: Guardian Life Ins Co Am 1401 Main St Suite 825 Columbia SC 29201

CASOTTI, STEVEN L., financial and tax consultant; b. Estherville, Iowa, Dec. 17, 1948; s. Alfred B. and Doris M. (Raisbeck) C.; m. Elizabeth Jean McNealey, Dec. 27, 1968. B.G.S., U. Nebr.-Omaha, 1973; P.M.D., Harvard Grad. Sch. Bus. Adminstrn., 1984. C.P.A. Tax mgr. Arthur Andersen & Co., Omaha, 1973-77; controller Tradco-Vulcan, Ltd., Dhahran, Saudi Arabia, 1978-80, Vulcan Materials Co., Winston-Salem, N.C., 1980-83, dir. bus. planning, 1984-85; acct. Touche Ross & Co., Winston-Salem, 1985—. Fund raiser Friendship Force, Winston-Salem; ambassador to USSR, Friendship Force of N.C., 1982. Irwin scholar, 1972. Mem. Am. Inst. C.P.A.s, Nebr. Soc. C.P.A.s (Gold Cert. award 1973), N.C. Assn. C.P.A.s, Harvard Club of the Carolinas, Beta Alpha Psi. Republican. Lutheran. Avocations: tennis; travel; photography; personal computer programming. Home: 887 Moyers Rd Winston-Salem NC 27104 Office: Casotti & Assocs Inc 887 Moyers Rd Winston-Salem NC 27104

CASPERSEN, FINN MICHAEL WESTBY, financial company executive; b. N.Y.C., Oct. 27, 1941; s. Olaus Westby and Freda C.; m. Barbara Caspersen, June 17, 1967. B.A. With honors in Econs., Brown U., 1963; LL.B. cum laude, Harvard U., 1966; LL.D., Hood Coll.; H.H.D., Washington Coll., Chestertown, Md. Bar: Fla. 1966, N.Y. 1967. Assoc. Dewey, Ballantine, Bushby, Palmer & Wood, N.Y.C., 1969-72; assoc. counsel Beneficial Mgmt. Corp., Wilmington, Del., 1972-75; chmn. bd., chief exec. officer, mem. exec. com. Beneficial Corp., 1976—; dir., mem. exec. com. Beneficial Nat. Bank; dir. Beneficial Nat. Bank, U.S.A. Wilmington; chmn. bd., chief exec. officer Beneficial Fin. Internat. Corp.; dir. Beneficial Internat. Ins. Co. Ltd., Am. Centennial Ins. Co., Consol, Marine Ins., BFC Agy., Inc., BFC Ins. Agy. Am., BFC Ins. Agy. Nev., Guaranty Life Ins. Co. Am., Clark Hill Sugary; dir., pres. Tri-Farms Inc.; dir., Westby Corp., Westby Mgmt. Corp.; chmn. 35th Ann. N.J. Bus. Conf., Rutgers U. Grad. Sch. Mgmt. and Sales Execs. Club N.J., 1983; gen. counsel, dir. Central Nat. Life Ins. Co. of Omaha, 1974-76. Trustee Camp Nejeda Found. for Diabetic Children, Com. Econ. Devel.; mem. nominating com. Morristown Meml. Hosp.; former mem. N.J. Bd. Higher Edn.; bd. dirs., v.p. O.W. Caspersen Found.; chmn. bd. trustees, mem. exec. com. Peddie Sch., Hightstown, N.J.; chmn. Waterloo Found. for Arts, Inc.; trustee James S. Brady Presdl. Found., Savs. Forum; pres. Coalition of Service Industries, Inc., Washington; mem. adv. com. to exec. bd. Morris-Sussex Area Council Boy Scouts Am.; mem. corp. Cardigan Mountain Sch., bd. dirs. Shelter Harbor Fire Dist., Westerly, R.I., Harbor Island Inc., Tampa; adv. bd. Nat. Ctr. Fin. Services, Earl Warren Inst., U. Calif.; adv. bd. Inferential Focus, N.Y.C.; bd. govs. Winterthur Mus. Corp. Council, Wilmington, Del.; trustee emeritus Brown U. Served to lt. USCG, 1966-69. Recipient President's medal Johns Hopkins U.; named Civic Leader of Yr. YMCA, 1982. Mem. Am. Fin. Services Assn. (trustee, chmn. govt. affairs com.), Conf. Bd., Gladstone Equestrian Assn. (chmn. bd. trustees), Am. Horse Shows Inc. (driving com.), Partnership for N.J. (charter), N.J. State Police Library and Mus. Assn. (trustee), ABA, Fla. Bar Assn., N.Y. Bar Assn. Clubs: Harvard; Knickerbocker (N.Y.C.); University (Sarasota, Fla.); Wilmington.

CASSARA, ERNEST, historian; b. Everett, Mass., June 5, 1925; s. Gaetano and Amelia (St. George) C.; A.B., Tufts Coll., 1952, B.D., 1954; Ph.D., Boston U., 1957; postdoctoral student Cambridge U., 1962-63; m. Beverly Alfretta Benner, Feb. 7, 1949; children—Shirley, Catherine, Nicholas Ernest. Announcer, Sta. WORC-AM, Worcester, Mass., 1945-47; news editor Sta. WBET, Brockton, Mass., 1947-50; instr., asst. prof., asso. prof. Tufts U., Medford, Mass., 1955-66; interim dir. Albert Schweitzer Coll., Churwalden, Switzerland, 1963-64; prof., dean Goddard Coll., Plainfield, Vt., 1966-70; prof. George Mason U., Fairfax, Va., 1970—, chmn. dept. history, 1970-74. Trustee, Billerica (Mass.) Hist. Soc., 1953-58, Bennett Public Library, 1954-58; mem. Town Meeting Billerica, 1955-56; mem. Democratic Town Com. Plainfield (Vt.), 1967-70; mem. Am. Bicentennial Com., City of Fairfax, 1974-75; life mem. alumni council Tufts U., 1969—. Fulbright prof. U. Munich, 1975-76; George Mason U. Found. grantee, 1972-73. Mem. AAUP, Am. Hist. Assn., Orgn. Am. Historians, Am. Studies Assn., Deutsche Gesellschaft für Amerikastudien. Democrat. Unitarian Universalist. Author: History of the United States of America: a Guide to Information Sources, 1977; The Enlightenment in America, 1975; Universalism in America: a Documentary History, 1971, new edit., 1984; Hosea Ballou: the Challenge to Orthodoxy, 1961, 82. Office: 4400 University Dr Fairfax VA 22030

CASSEL, JOHN ELDEN, accountant; b. Verden, Okla., Apr. 24, 1934; s. Elbert Emry and Erma Ruth (McDowell) C.; m. Mary Lou Malcom, June 3, 1953; children—John Elden, James Edward, Jerald Eugene. Plant mgr., also asst. gen. mgr. Baker and Taylor Co., Oklahoma City, 1966-71; paymaster, office mgr. Robberson Steel Co., Oklahoma City, 1971-76; pvt. investor, 1976—. Democrat. Methodist. Home: 2332 NW 118th St Oklahoma City OK 73120

CASSEL, MARWIN SHEPARD, lawyer; b. N.Y.C., July 4, 1925; s. Irwin M. and Mana-Zucca Cassel; m. Leslie Stein, Nov. 24, 1983; 1 child, Michael Alan; children by previous marriage—Bradley William, James Scott, Thomas Drew.J.D., U. Fla., 1949. Bar: Fla. 1949, D.C. 1980. Sr. ptnr. Broad and Cassel, Miami, Fla., 1985—; chmn. bd., pres. Internat. Savs. and Loan Assn., Miami, 1980-83. Vice chmn. Miami Beach Redevel. Authority, 1978-82; bd. dirs., treas. Downtown Miami Bus. Assn., 1985-86; bd. dirs. Friends of Arts, Lowe Gallery, Coral Gables, Fla., 1985—; mem. nat. jud. council Democratic Nat. Com., 1976-80. Served with USAAF, 1943-45. Named Outstanding Alumni U. Fla., 1979. Mem. ABA, Fla. Bar Assn. Jewish. Clubs: Bankers, Jockey (Miami). Office: 2 S Biscayne Blvd Miami FL 33131

CASSENS, BARBARA ANN, mathematics and computer educator, consultant; b. Vienna, Mo., Dec. 11, 1943; d. Alex J. and Lucy G. (Volmert) Arunski; m. Simon Patrick Cassens, Dec. 29, 1962; children—Edward Gerard, Mary Alesia. B.S. in Math., St. Louis U., 1964, M.S., 1968; postgrad. SUNY-Oswego, 1970-75, Central State U., Edmond, Okla., 1980-83. Cert. tchr., N.Y., Okla. Tchr. math. Villa Duchesne Sch., St. Louis, 1964-65; lectr. math. SUNY-Oswego, 1968-70; tchr. math. City Sch. Dist. Oswego, 1970-77, Watervliet (N.Y.) City Sch. Dist., 1977-79; Chpt. I math specialist Edmond Sch. Dist., 1979—; ind computer programmer, 1982—; workshop presenter. Mary Clemens scholar, 1961-64. Mem. Nat. Council Tchrs. Math., Pi Mu Epsilon. Democrat. Roman Catholic. Home: 409 Partridge Ln Edmond OK 73034

CASSIBRY, FRED JAMES, federal judge; b. D'Lo, Miss., Sept. 26, 1918; s. Reginald E. and Lelia (Garner) C.; B.A., Tulane U., 1941, LL.B., 1943; m. Lorraine E. Patterson, Dec. 21, 1940; 1 dau., Elizabeth; m. Muriel D. Belsome, Feb. 13, 1974; 1 dau., Cathryn. Bar: La. 1944. Practice law, New Orleans, 1947-61; mem. firms Cassibry & Zengel, 1946-47, Dymond & Cassibry, 1950-55, Cassibry, Jackson & Hess, 1955-61; judge Civil Dist. Ct., Parish of Orleans, 1961-66; judge U.S. Dist. Ct. Eastern Dist. La., 1966—; mem. com. on jud. ethics La. Supreme Ct., 1965-66; instr. fed. procedure Tulane U. Mem. city council New Orleans, 1954-60; mem. bd. commrs. New Orleans City Park, 1962-68. Del. Democratic Nat. Conv., 1956. Served from ensign to lt. (j.g.), USNR, 1944-46. Mem. Fed., La., New Orleans bar assns., La. Dist. Judges (pres. 1963), 5th Circuit Dist. Judges Assn. (pres. 1974-75), Tulane U. Alumni Assn. (exec. com. 1962-65), Blue Key (hon.), Order of Coif (hon.). Home: 45 Hawk St New Orleans LA 70124 Office: US Dist Ct 500 Camp St New Orleans LA 70130

CASSIDY, MARY FRANCES, special educator; b. Anson County, N.C., May 6, 1934; d. William Bennett and Julia Grace Meachum; m. Samuel Lafayette Cassidy, June 5, 1955; children—Mary Glenda, Samuel Layfayette (dec. 1979). A.A. with honors, Brevard Jr. Coll., 1954; student U. N.C., 1954-55; A.B. in Elem. Edn., U. S.C., 1960, M.Ed., 1969; cert. Winthrop Coll., 1977. Tchr. English and math. Hillcrest Sch., Sumter County, S.C., 1956; tchr. Camden Primary Sch., Kershaw County, S.C., 1960-67, Lugoff Elem. Sch., Kershaw County, 1967-71, Jr. Vocat. Sch., Kershaw County, 1971-72, Richland County, 1972-73, Camden Elem. Sch., Kershaw County, 1973-74; itinerant tchr. orthopedically handicapped Kershaw County, 1979—; lic. pvt. pilot. Fed. grantee in spl. edn., 1965. Mem. Council Exceptional Children. Republican. Baptist. Club: Breakfast of S.C. Home: PO Box 2 Hwy 34 Lugoff SC 29078 Office: Clyde Walton Educational Bldg DuBose Ct Camden SC 29020

CASSILL, ERNEST CRAMER, resort owner; b. Bridgewater, Iowa, Aug. 21, 1909; s. Charles and Lida C. (Cramer) C.; m. Estelle S. Strohbeen, Dec. 31, 1939. B. Commerce, U. Iowa, 1931. Bar: Iowa 1935. Newspaper pub. Iowa Falls, Iowa, 1939-49; owner drug store Iowa Falls, 1941-49; investigator FBI, 1942-45; owner Sea Castle Resort, Pompano Beach, Fla., 1951—, Sun Castle Resort, Pompano Beach, 1958—, Traders Resort, Pompano Beach, 1964-81; mem. Presdl. Task Force, 1980—. Mem. Sigma Chi, Phi Delta Phi. Republican. Lutheran. Home and Office: 1380 S Ocean Blvd Pompano Beach FL 33062

CASSIN, WILLIAM BOURKE, lawyer; b. Mexico City, Sept. 11, 1931 (parents Am. citizens); s. William Michael and Elouise (Hall) C.; m. Kristi Shipnes, July 15, 1961; children—Clay Brian, Michael Bourke, Macy Armstrong. A.B., Princeton U., 1953; J.D., U. Tex., 1959. Bar: Tex. 1959. Clk. to Judge Warren L. Jones, 5th U.S. Circuit Ct., 1959-60; asso. firm Baker & Botts, Houston, 1960-70; v.p., gen. atty. United Gas Pipe Line Co., Houston, 1970-73, sr. v.p., gen. atty., 1973, exec. v.p., gen. counsel, dir., exec. com., 1974-84; exec. v.p., gen. counsel, mem. exec. com. United Energy Resources, Inc., Houston, 1976-84, dir., 1976—; of counsel Mayer, Brown & Platt, 1985—. Gen. counsel Harris County Republican Party, 1963-64, 67-68, Houston Grand Opera Assn., 1961-70; dir. or trustee Houston Grand Opera Assn., Houston Ballet Found., Harris County Heritage Soc., Armand Bayou Nature Center, Gulf and Gt. Plains Legal Found., Legal Found. Am., Tex. Mil. Inst., Atwill Meml. Chapel Assn., Associated Republicans of Tex. vestryman Christ Ch. Cathedral, Houston, 1971-73, 80-82. Served to lt., airborne arty., AUS, 1953-57, capt. USA ret. Fellow Tex. Bar Found.; mem. Am., Tex., Houston, Fed., Fed. Energy bar assns., Order of Coif, Phi Delta Phi. Republican. Clubs: Houston Country, Bayou, Ramada, Allegro, Texas, Houston Met. Racquet (Houston); Argyle (San Antonio); Army and Navy (Washington); Princeton (N.Y.C.); Princeton Terr. Home: 1 S Wynden Dr Houston TX 77056 Office: 3600 Republic Bank Ctr Houston TX 77002

CASTAGNA, WILLIAM JOHN, U.S. district judge; b. Phila., June 25, 1924; s. Charles and Ninetta Castagna; student U. Pa., 1941-43; LL.B., J.D., U. Fla., 1949; m. Carolyn Ann Spoto, Sept. 1, 1954; children—Charles N., William D., Lisa Ann, Catherine Alice. Admitted to Fla. bar, 1949; practice in Miami, 1949-50; Clearwater, 1951-79; partner firm MacKenzie, Castagna, Bennison & Gardner, 1970-79; U.S. dist. judge Middle Dist. Fla., 1979—. Served with USAAF, 1943-45. Mem. Am. Bar Assn., Fed. Bar Assn., Am. Trial Lawyers Assn., Am. Judicature Soc., Fla. State Bar (bd. govs., seminar lectr.), Acad. Fla. Trial Lawyers, Clearwater Bar Assn. (pres. 1965). Democrat. Club: Masons. Office: PO Box 3424 Tampa FL 33601

CASTIGLIONE, ROBERT FRANK, optometrist, air force officer; b. Hackensack, N.J., Apr. 1, 1942; s. Frank Robert and Eleanore Elizabeth (Piotrkowski) C.; m. Catherine Agnes Herrington, Nov. 22, 1965; children—Robert Frank, Victoria, Anthony Gregory, Dominic Houston. A.A., Miami-Dade Jr. Coll., 1963; B.S., So. Coll. Optometry, 1964, O.D., 1966; student Air Command and Staff Coll., 1982-83. Gen. practice optometry, Miami, Fla., 1968-72; commd. 1st lt. U.S. Army, 1966-68; advanced through grades to lt. col. U.S. Air Force, 1972—; staff optometrist Columbus (Miss.) Air Force Hosp., 1972-75; chief optometry Service Clark AFB Hosp., Philippines, 1975-78; asst. dir. optometry Randolph AFB Hosp., San Antonio, 1978-80, dir. optometric services, 1980-82; dir. optometric service Randolph AFB and Officers Tng. Sch., 1983—; cons. optometry Air Tng. Command Surgeon Gen.; mem. faculty Miami-Dade Jr. Coll. Optometric Technician Program, 1969-72. Contbr. articles to profl. jours. Mem. Catholic Sch. Bd., Columbus, 1972-75, trustee, 1974-75. Fellow Am. Acad. Optometry (chmn. admittance com. for fed. service optometrists 1986—); mem. Am. Optometric Assn., Nat. Eye Research Found., Am. Public Health Assn., Dade County Optometric Assn. (dir. 1968-72), Armed Force Optometric Soc. (liaison Pacific area 1975-78), Jr. Officers Council (treas. Columbus AFB 1974), Jr. Officers Clark AFB (v.p. 1977-78), Omega Delta (rush chmn. 1965). Republican. Roman Catholic. Clubs: Optimists (Nor-Isle), KC (Marian Council), Officers (adv. council Randolph AFB 1980—). Office: Optometry Clinic 12 SG USAF CI Randolph AFB TX 78148

CASTILLO, ERNESTO RICARDO, insurance company official, lawyer; b. Havana, Cuba, Nov. 12, 1926; came to U.S., 1961; s. Jose and D. Sara (Gomez) C.; m. Silvinia C. Cano, Aug. 6, 1950; children—Silvinia M., Sara M., Ernest F. J.D., Havana U., 1950. Bar: Havana 1950. Mem. firm Cardenas K. Salgado, Havana, 1950-61; regional mgr. Am. Internat. Underwriters Tex., Inc., Dallas, 1976-83, Global div. mgr. Am. Internat. Group, Dallas, 1983—. Republican. Roman Catholic. Clubs: Dallas Athletic, 2001, Country, Insurance (Dallas). Office: American Internat Cos 2001 Bryan Tower Dallas TX 75201

CASTILLO, LUCY NARVAEZ, real estate investor; b. Guayaquil, Ecuador, June 25, 1943; came to U.S., 1965, naturalized, 1972; d. Jose N. and Teresa (Sanchez) Narvaez; student St. Peters Coll., 1971, Emory Riddle U., 1977; Ph.D. in Psychology, Kensington U., 1981; m. Boris Castillo, Apr. 20, 1964 (div.); children—Sylvia, Boris M. Sales agt. Globe Travel Bur., Bklyn., 1967; asst. supr. files Franklin Nat. Bank, N.Y.C., 1968; corp. sec. Castillo Med. Assos., P.A., Panama City, Fla., 1972-74; mgr. Bell Med. Group Med. Clinic, Los Angeles, 1974-76; pres. Lunar Enterprises, Inc., import-export co., Daytona Beach, Fla., 1976-78; real estate broker Watson Realty, Inc., Ormond Beach, Fla., after 1978; now owner, dir. Today's Fashions; pres. Lucy Motors Cia. Lta. Recipient award of merit Challenge to Am., 1979. Mem. Daytona Beach Bd. Realtors. Republican. Author: (fiction) For Better or For Worse, 1979. Home: 6450 Milk Wagon Ln Miami Lakes FL 33014 Office: 6250 NW 35th Ave Miami FL 33147

CASTINEIRA, JUAN ANTONIO, electrical/mechanical engineer; b. Havana, Cuba, Nov. 17, 1931; came to U.S., 1962; s. Juan Antonio and Maria Aurora (Diaz) C.; m. Migdalia Alfonso, Dec. 4, 1955; children—Mayra, Barbara Marlene, Ana Marisela, John Anthony. M.E.E., Havana U., 1959. Registered profl. engr., Fla., Tex. Instruments engr. Hershey Sugar Corp., 1954-62; power plant engr. Sugar Mills S. Fla., 1962-68; project engr. MCN Inc., 1968-80; owner, pres. Columbia Engring., Miami, Fla., 1981—; v.p., owner Columbia Electric Inc., Miami, 1981—. Campaign coordinator Republican party, Coral Gables, Fla., 1980. Mem. Nat. Soc. Profl. Engrs., Fla. Engring. Soc., Cuban Engring. Soc. Roman Catholic. Home: 2114 SE 98 Ave Miami FL 33165 Office: Columbia Engring 2114 SW 98 Ave Miami FL 33165

CASTOR, ELIZABETH B., state senator; b. Glassboro, N.J., May 11, 1941; d. Joseph L. and Gladys (Wright) Bowe; m. Donald F. Castor, 1966; children—Katherine, Karen, Frank. B.A., Glassboro State Coll., 1963; M.A., U. Miami (Fla.), 1968. Mem. Hillsborough County Bd. Commrs. (Fla.), 1972-76, chmn., 1975-76; mem. Fla. Senate, 1976—; mem. Hillsborough County Environ. Protection Commn., 1972-76, chmn., 1973-74; mem. exec. bd. Tampa Bay Regional Planning Council, 1972-76. Bd. dirs. Hillsborough Hosp. and Welfare Bd., 1972-76, chmn., 1973-74. Mem. U. Fla. Ctr. for Govt. Responsibility (dir. 1977), U.S. Fla. Council Advisors, LWV (Hillsborough County pres. 1969-71, state bd. mem.), Athena Soc., Town 'N Country Jaycees (Good Govt. award 1975), Phi Gamma Mu. Recipient Outstanding Legislator of Yr. award FEA, 1977. Democrat. Lutheran. Office: Fla Senate Senate Office Bldg Tallahassee FL 32304*

CASTRO, ALBERT, scientist, educator; b. San Salvador, El Salvador, Nov. 15, 1933; s. Alberto Lemus and Maria Emma (de la Cotera) C.; B.S., U. Houston, 1958; postgrad. Baylor U., 1958; Ph.D., U. El Salvador, 1962; M.D., Dominican Republic, 1982; m. Jeris Adelle Goldsmith, Oct. 19, 1956; children—Stewart, Sandra, Alberto, Juan, Richard. Came to U.S., 1952. Asst. prof. microbiology and biochemistry U. El Salvador, San Salvador, 1958-60, asso. prof. dental and med. sch., 1960-63, prof., head dept. basic sci., 1965-68, dir. research in basic sci. dental sch., 1964-68, co-dir. grad. research, 1965-66, bd. dirs. dental sch., 1961-66, mem. research and scholarship com., 1964-65; asst. prof. pediatrics, co-dir. pediatrics metalobic lab. U. Oreg., Portland, 1969-73; dir. endocrinological dept. and research unit United Med. Lab., Portland, 1970-73; sr. scientist Papanicolaou Cancer Research Inst., Miami, Fla., 1973-75; asso. prof. pathology and medicine U. Miami, 1973-77, prof. pathology, medicine and microbiology, 1977—; coordinator Inter Am. Tech. Transfer and Tng. Program, 1976—. NIH postdoctoral fellow, 1966-70; U. Oreg. Med. Sch. grantee, 1966-69; Northwest Pediatric Research fellow, 1971. Fellow Am. Inst. Chemists, Royal Soc. Tropical Med. and Hygiene; mem. N.Y. Acad. Scis., Am. Chem. Assn. Am. Assn. Microbiology, AAAS, Tooth and Bone Research Soc., Acad. Sci. El Salvador. Roman Catholic. Contbr. over 200 publs. to nat. and internat. sci. jours.; basic research in diabetes, hypertension and immunochemistry. Home: 6275 SW 123d Terr Miami FL 33156 Office: Univ of Miami Sch Medicine Dept Pathology (R40) PO Box 016960 Miami FL 33101

CASTRO, ÁNGEL, accountant, author, educator; b. Bolondrón, Matanzas, Cuba, Aug. 7, 1930; came to U.S., 1961; s. Ángel and Dolores (Martínez) C.; m. Rula Lappas, Feb. 24, 1973; 1 son, Alexander. Bachellor, Havana State U., 1949; M.B.A., Havana U., 1955, J.D., 1960, LL.D., 1961; Doctorate in Spanish Law, Norte de Oriente U. (Cuba), 1958. C.P.A., Cuba. Prof., José Martí Nat. U., Havana, 1954-60, dean, 1957-60; head Spanish dept., tchr. Rolfe (Iowa) High Sch., 1965-66; asst. prof. Spanish lang. and lit. Carroll Coll., Waukesha, Wis., 1966-67; asst. prof. Spanish lang. and lit. Hampton (Va.) Inst., 1967-68; cons. Va. Community Colls., Thomas Nelson Community Coll., Hampton, 1968; dir. Summer Insts. to retrain high sch. tchrs. French, German and Spanish in fgn. lang. methodology, 1969-70; asst. prof. Spanish lang. and lit. Old Dominion U., Norfolk, Va., 1968-72; acct. Arthur Young & Co., N.Y.C., 1973—; pres. Angel Castro & Co., North Miami Beach, Fla., 1977-83; sr. acct. Angel Castro Accts., 1982—; instr. Fla. Career Coll., 1983—; instr. acctg. Bauder Coll. Author: José Martí: Páginas Literarias, 1969; Refugiados, 1970; Cuentos de New York, 1973; Poemas del Destierro, 1971. Republican. Home: 1271 NE 179th St North Miami Beach FL 33162

CASTROW, FRED(ERICK) F(RANCIS), II, dermatologist; b. Houston, Oct. 15, 1935; s. Frederick F., Sr. and Mattie Wells (Johnson) C.; m. Janet I. Schatzman, June 27, 1959; children—Fred F. III, James R., Sharon L. B.A., U. Tex., Austin, 1958; M.D., U. Tex.-Galveston, 1961. Diplomate Am. Bd. Dermatology. Intern, U.S. Naval Hosp., San Diego, 1961-62; resident in dermatology, U. Tex. Med. Br., Galveston, 1965-68; practice medicine specializing in dermatology, Houston, 1968—; mem. staff Meml. Hosp. System, chief dermatology sect., 1979-81, 86—; mem. staff Hermann Hosp. Meml. City Gen. Hosp., Rosewood Gen. Hosp., Sharpstown Gen. Hosp.; clin. asst. prof. dermatology Baylor Coll. Medicine, Houston; clin. assoc. prof. dermatology U. Tex. Med. Sch., Houston, U. Tex. Med. Br., Galveston. Contbr. numerous articles to med. jours. Served to lt. M.C., USN, 1960-65. McLaughlin fellow U. Tex. Med. Br., Galveston, 1959. Fellow Am. Soc. Dermatopathology, Am. Acad. Dermatology (bd. dirs. 1986—), Am. Dermatol. Assn., Houston Dermatol. Soc. (pres. 1978), Tex. Dermatol. Soc., Am. Soc. Dermatologic Surgery (pres. 1985), Dermatology Found., South Central Dermatologic Congress, Harris County Med. Soc. Tex. Med. Assn., AMA, Alpha Epsilon Delta (Order of Aesculapius 1957), Mu Delta, Alpha Kappa Kappa. Republican. Methodist. Office: 7777 Southwest Freeway Suite 1014 Houston TX 77074

CASWELL, JOHN BEVERIDGE, human resources consultant; b. Hartford, Conn., Dec. 28, 1938; s. Philip Jr. and Evelyn G. (Beveridge) Caswell Russell; m. Heather F. Livingstone, July, 1974; children—John Beveridge, Pamela T. Camard, Jeffrey F., Philip A.L., Elizabeth S. B.A., Brown U., 1960; M.B.A., Columbia U., 1961. Adminstrv. asst. R.I. Trust NB, Providence, 1961-64; pres., chief operating officer Stanhome, Inc., Westfield, Mass., 1964-84; pres., chief exec. officer Internat. Info. and Investments, Inc., Tampa, Fla., 1985—, Omnia Profile, Inc., Tampa, 1985—, Fiscal Check-Up, Inc., Tampa, 1985—; dir. Berkshire Life Ins. Co., Pittsfield, Mass. Mem. Nat. Assn. Corp. Dirs. Republican. Episcopalian. Clubs: Longmeadow Country (Mass.); Centre (Tampa, Fla.). Home: 4803 Culbreath Island Rd Tampa FL 33629 Office: Internat Info & Investments Inc 4830 W Kennedy Blvd Suite 330 Tampa FL 33609

CATANIA, SUSAN LOVELAND, medical device manufacturing company executive; b. Key Biscayne, Fla., May 21, 1953; d. Steven and Helen (McCollum) Loveland; m. Patrick Michael Catania, Jan. 28, 1976; 1 dau., Susan Meghan. B.S. in Nursing, U. Tenn., 1975. Registered nurse, Fla. Nurse ICU, Coral Gables Hosp., Fla., 1975-76; rotating charge nurse CCU, Jackson Meml. Hosp., Miami, 1976-79, nursing supr. central services, 1979-80, dir. patient relations, asst. adminstr. operating room, recovery room and anesthesiology, 1980-81; ednl. programs coordinator Cordis Corp., Miami, 1982-84, sr. ednl. program's coordinator, supr., 1984-85, prin. ednl. programs coordinator, supr., 1985—. Author audiovisual program Cordis Guide to Interpretation of DDD Pacer ECGs, 1984. Vol. United Way Campaign, Miami, 1982. Recipient letters of commendation Miami's chief dir. fire and Pub. Health Trust, Miami, 1981; named Outstanding Young Woman Am., U.S. Jaycees, 1984; Key Biscayne Women's Club scholar U. Tenn., Knoxville, 1971. Mem. Am. Assn. Critical Care Nurses, Council Continuing Edn. of Am. Nurses Assn., Am. Nurses Assn., Am. Heart Assn. Republican. Presbyterian. Club: Biscayne Bay Yacht Racing Assn. (Coconut Grove, Fla.). Office: Cordis Corp Dept Ednl Services PO Box 025700 Miami FL 33102

CATES, CONRAD WAYNE, food company sales executive; b. Greensboro, N.C., June 5, 1930; s. John Henry and Minnie Roxie (James) C.; m. Nancy Mae Moore, Jan. 20, 1951; children—Karen Moore Cates Cumbia, Nancy Beth Cates Hamilton. B.S.B.A., U. N.C., 1952. Boys work sec. YMCA, Greensboro, 1952-53, phys. dir., 1953-54; prodn. mgr. Cone Mills Corp., Greensboro, 1954-56; sales rep. RT French Co., Greensboro, 1956-58, dist. mgr., 1958-65, div. sales mgr., Falls Church, Va., 1965—. Founder Burke Centre Swim Assn., Burke, Va., 1977; com. chmn. Burke Centre Conservancy, 1977—; vol. Washington Spl. Olympics, 1979-83; campaign worker Nat. Republican Party, Va., 1978—; elder, choir mem. Grace Presbyn. Ch. Recipient Humanitarian award ARC, Greensboro, 1955; Toastmaster of Yr. award Toastmasters Internat., Greensboro, 1955; Sales Mgr. of Yr. award R. T. French Co., 1970, 76; Outstanding Service award Burke Centre Swim Assn., 1980. Mem. U. N.C. Alumni Assn. (life), Washington Grocery Wheels (bd. dirs. 1975—, pres. 1979-80). Clubs: Encore Cotillion (pres. 1963) (Greensboro); Occoquan Yacht (social chmn. 1985) (Va.). Lodges: Masons, Odd Fellows. Avocations: golf; sailing; swimming. Home: 9920 Natick Rd Burke VA 22015 Office: RT French Co 207 Park Ave Falls Church VA 22046

CATES, JOHN CARRINGTON, audio-visual production company executive, drug abuse consultant; b. Texas City, Tex., May 30, 1951; s. W. H. and Ernestine (Wood) C.; m. Mary Susan Perry, June 21, 1980. B.S. in Edn., U. Houston, 1972; cert. in drug abuse counseling, Palmer Drug Abuse Program, 1976. Cert. tchr., Tex. Tchr. elem. sch. Houston Ind. Sch. Dist., 1972-75; founder, dir. Palmer Drug Abuse Program Gen. Ednl. Devel. Program, Houston, 1976-80; founder, sr. counselor Palmer Drug Abuse Program, Fort Bend County, Tex., 1977-78; v.p., corp. sec. N.Am. Video Prodns., Inc., Richardson, Tex., 1980—. Mem. cable communications com. Dallas County Red Cross, 1981—. Mem. Dallas Communications Council (charter), Dallas Producers Assn., Internat. Assn. Bus. Communicators, Dallas C. of C. Co-creator album Off The Streets, 1981. Office: 725 S Central St Suite C3 Richardson TX 75080

CATHEY, CRAIG WAYNE, design firm executive; b. Fort Worth, July 22, 1947; s. James J. and Margie E. (Johnson) C.; m. Barbara Young, Mar. 2, 1985. B.B.A., North Tex. State U., Denton, 1972. Ops. mgr. Mr. Gatti's Restaurants, Inc., Austin, Tex., 1972-74; owner Fargo's Restaurants, Inc., San Antonio, 1974-77; v.p. Cathey, Marince & Bennett, Dallas, 1977—. Recipient Best of Tex. award Tex. Soc. Pub. Relations, 1983. Mem. Sales and Mktg. Execs. Dallas, Dallas Advt. League, Internat. Assn. Bus. Communicators, Dallas C. of C. Democrat. Club: Toastmasters. Contbr. photographs to various periodicals. Home: 5622 W Hanover Dallas TX 75209 Office: 8585 Stemmons Suite M-29 Dallas TX 75247

CATHEY, VANCE LEROY, textile company executive; b. Roanoke, Ala., May 4, 1921; s. Melvin Leroy and Frances Mae (Brannan) C.; m. Margaret Anderson Scott, Nov. 5, 1948; children—Elizabeth, Vance Leroy. B.S. in Textile Engring. Ga. Inst. Tech., 1943. With West Point Pepperell (Ga.), 1946—, indsl. engring. and plant mgmt., 1946-69, v.p. mfg. indsl. fabrics div., 1969-74, corp. v.p. personnel, 1974—. Served to lt. j.g. submarine service USNR, 1943-46. Mem. Am. Soc. of Personnel Execs., Ala. Textile Mfg. Assn. (bd. dirs.), So. Indsl. Relations Conf. (bd. dirs.), Unemployment Benefits Advisors (bd. dirs. Washington), Ala. Safety Assn. (bd. dirs.), West Point C. of C. Presbyterian. Club: Riverside Country (West Point). Lodges: Masons, Rotary (pres. 1982-83). Office: West Point Pepperell Box 71 Corp Hdqrs West Point GA 31833

CATHEY, WILLIAM BLAIR, geologist, oil and gas exploration consultant; b. Columbia, Tenn., Nov. 30, 1954; s. Cecil Blair and Mary Lou (Sawyer) C.; m. Victoria Ann Russell, Oct. 18, 1974. B.A. in Geology, U. Tenn., 1977, M.S. in Geology, 1980; postgrad. Tulane U., 1982-83. Coop geologist Union Carbide, Oak Ridge, Tenn., 1975-77; assoc. geologist Exxon Minerals, Denver, 1978; prodn. geologist Conoco, Inc., New Orleans, 1980-81; exploration geologist Shell Oil Co., New Orleans, 1981-83; supr. phosphate-auisition Occidental Petroleum, Columbia, Tenn., 1984—; pres. Tnread, Inc., Knoxville, Tenn., 1983-84; grad. asst. in geology U. Tenn., Knoxville, 1978; grad. research fellow Oak Ridge Assoc. Univs., Tenn., 1979. Recipient Tarr award U. Tenn., 1977. Mem. Am. Assn. Petroleum Geologists, Geol. Soc. Am., New Orleans Geol. Soc., Phi Kappa Phi, Sigma Gamma Epsilon (v.p. 1979-80). Methodist. Club: Maury County Gun (Columbia, Tenn.). Lodge: Kiwanis. Avocations: hiking; camping; hunting; fishing. Home: 1098 Rolling Fields Circle Columbia TN 38401 Office: Occidental Petroleum PO Box 591 Columbia TN 38402-0591

CATOE, JAMES RANDALL, banker; b. Houston, Sept. 29, 1952; s. James Arman and Annie Louise (Royall) C.; m. Kathy Frey, Mar. 28, 1981. A.A., San Jacinto Coll., 1973; B.B.A., U. Houston, 1975; M.B.A., 1976. Systems analyst Arthur Andersen & Co., Houston, 1977-78; mktg. research cons. Gelb Cons. Group, Houston, 1978-79; v.p., mgr. bus. devel services MBank Houston, 1979—; instr. mktg. principles U. Houston, evenings 1979-81. R.C. Baker Found. scholar, 1973-75; Heyne fellow U. Houston, 1975-76. Mem. Am. Mktg. Assn. (dir. 1980-81, treas. 1981-82, v.p. 1982-83), Research Roundtable, Am. Inst. Banking, Houston C. of C. (commerce research adv. com.), Phi Kappa Phi, Beta Gamma Sigma, Kappa Alpha, Delta Sigma Pi. Office: 910 Travis St Houston TX 77002

CATRON, MICHAEL STANLEY, printing company executive; b. Montgomery, Ala., Mar. 19, 1947; s. Evorit Leroy and Jacqueline Jean (Ingels) C.; B.S. in Metall. Engring., Auburn U., 1970; M.B.A. cum laude in fin., U. Louisville, 1975; m. Mary Ann Zoeller, Mar. 23, 1978; children—Jennifer Leigh, James Crawford. Prodn. supr., process engr. Union Carbide Co., Sheffield, Ala., 1970-71; field sales engr. Tex. Instruments, Louisville, 1972-75, field sales engr., Dallas, 1976-77, product mgr., 1977, purchasing supr., 1977-78; area mgr. Aero-Go, Louisville, 1975-76; regional mgr., U.S. direct mktg. mgr., export mgr. Tex. Instruments Supply, Inc., Dallas, 1978-80; product mgr. Harris Corp., Dallas, 1980; pres. Artesian Press, Inc., Dallas, 1980—; chmn., chief exec. officer M Press, Inc., Dallas, 1983—. Mem. Am. Mgmt. Assn. Republican. Episcopalian. Club: Brookhaven Country. Office: 8900 Premier Row Dallas TX 75249

CATTIE, EUGENE GERARD, loan authority executive; b. Phila., July 13, 1948; s. Joseph Pierre and Agnes Gail (Seidle) C.; m. Margaret Theresa Ezokas, Nov. 7, 1970; children—Sean, Eugene, Mark, Jason. B.S., LaSalle Coll., 1974. Asst. bursar LaSalle Coll., Phila., 1967-72, dir. fin. aid, 1972-77; pres. Va. Edn. Loan Authority, Richmond, 1977—. Served to sgt. USMC, 1966-72. Mem. Nat. Council Higher Edn. Loan Programs (treas. 1982-84, pres.-elect 1986), Nat. Assn. Fin. Aid Adminstrs., Eastern Assn. Fin. Aid Adminstrs., So. Assn. Fin. Aid Adminstrs., Vir. Assn. Fin. Aid Adminstrs., Pa. Assn. Fin. Aid Adminstrn. (trainer 1974-76), Bond Club N.Y. Roman Catholic. Avocations: jogging; fishing. Office: Va Edn Loan Authority 737 N Fifth St Richmond VA 23219

CAUBLE, HERMAN W., clergyman. Bishop, Lutheran Ch. S.C., Columbia. Office: 1003 Richland St PO Box 43 Columbia SC 29202*

CAUDELL, JOY LARAINE (LORI), hospital administrator; b. Toccoa, Ga., Aug. 14, 1948; d. Dwain and Nell Marie (Smith) C.; B.S. in Home Econs., U. Ga., 1970; M.B.A., U. South Ala., 1979. Tng. instr. Davis Bros., Inc., Atlanta, 1970-72; asst. to food service dir. West Paces Ferry Hosp., Atlanta, 1972-74; dir. food services Drs. Hosp., Mobile, Ala., 1974-79; adminstrv. asst. Indian Path Hosp., Kingsport, Tenn., 1979-80, asst. adminstr., 1980-82; adminstr. Johnson City (Tenn.) Eye & Ear Hosp., 1982—; food service cons., 1974-79. Faculty Center for Health Studies, Nashville, Tenn.; bd. dirs., mem. exec. com. East Tenn. Regional Organ Procurement Agy. Sunday sch. tchr. Colonial Heights Baptist Ch.; adv. Experience Based Career Edn. Program, Murphy High Sch., 1977-79; bd. dirs. United Way Washington County; v.p. Upper East Tenn. Hosp. Dist. Mem. Nutrition Today Soc., Assn. Bus. Grad. Students (dir. 1978-79), Assn. M.B.A. Execs., Johnson City C. of C. (health services council), U. Ga. Alumni Assn., U. South Ala. Alumni Assn. Home: Route 11 Box 335 Johnson City TN 37615 Office: Johnson City Eye and Ear Hosp 203 E Watauga Johnson City TN 37601

CAUDILL, DIANE SUE, business education educator; b. Louisville, Dec. 1, 1951; d. Paul Stewart and Sarah Elizabeth (Shelburne) Gritton; m. Donald Edward Caudill, Dec. 29, 1973; children—Jeffrey Carl, Briana Elizabeth. B.S., Morehead State U., 1973, M.Bus. Ed., 1985. Bus. edn. instr. Carter County Bd. Edn., Grayson, Ky., 1974-76, Ky. Christian Coll., Grayson, 1980—. Youth group leader Ch. Christ, Grayson, 1974-75, Sunday Sch. tchr., 1980—; den mother Boy Scouts Am., Grayson, 1984—; Republican. Avocations: Reading; swimming; tennis. Home: Route 4 Box 628 Grayson KY 41143

CAUDILL, DONALD W., marketing educator, consultant; b. Norton, Va., July 31, 1958; s. Alfred and Shirley (Wampler) C. B.S., Berea Coll., 1980; M.B.A., Morehead State U., 1981; postgrad. Va. Poly. Inst. and State U., 1981-83, Memphis State U., 1983—. Instr. mktg. Va. Poly. Inst. and State U., Blacksburg, 1981-83; asst. prof. mktg. U. Tenn.-Martin, 1984-85, U. North Ala., Florence, 1985—; cons. small businesses and corps. Contbr. articles to profl. jours. Fellow Acad. Mktg. Sci.; mem. Am. Mktg. Assn., Assn. Consumer Research, So. Mktg. Assn., Southwestern Mktg. Assn., Am. Psychol. Assn., Alpha Kappa Psi. Avocations: swimming; writing; traveling. Home: 723 E Powell River Dr Norton VA 24273

CAUTHEN, CHARLES EDWARD, JR., retail food and department store executive; b. Columbia, S.C., Oct. 26, 1931; s. Charles Edward and Rachel (Macaulay) C.; B.A., Wofford Coll., 1952; certificate Charlotte Meml. Hosp. Sch. Hosp. Adminstrn., 1956; M.S. in Bus. Adminstrn., Kennedy-Western U.; m. Hazel Electa Peery, June 13, 1959; children—Portia Cauthen White, Sara McMaster, Rachel Cauthen Rohrer, Sidney Peery. Asst. adminstr. Union Meml. Hosp., Monroe, N.C., 1956-58; adminstr. Lowrance Hosp., Inc., Mooresville, N.C., 1958-61; v.p., mgr. Va. Acme Market, Bluefield, W.Va., 1961-68; v.p. Acme Markets and A-Mart Stores, (name now Acme Markets of Tazewell, Va., Inc.), North Tazewell, Va., 1965—, exec. v.p., 1968-71, pres., 1971—, also dir.; dir. Bluefield Supply Co. (W.Va.); pres. Doran Devel. Corp., 1971—, Big A Market, Inc., 1981—. Deacon, elder, trustee Westminster Presbyn. Ch., Bluefield, W.Va. Served to 1st lt. AUS, 1952-54. Decorated Army Commendation medal, Combat Med. badge. Mem. W.Va. Assn. Retail Grocers (v.p., dir. 1968-82), Va. Food Dealers Assn. (dir. 1978), Bluefield Sales Exec. Club (dir. 1965-67). Republican. Rotarian (dir. 1966). Home: 810 Parkway Bluefield WV 24701 Office: Box 246 Railroad Ave North Tazewell VA 24630

CAVALLARO, JOSEPH JOHN, microbiologist; b. Lawrence, Mass., Mar. 18, 1932; s. John and Salvatrice (Zappala) C.; m. Kathleen Frances Kraus, Dec. 2, 1972; children—Theresa Margaret, Sandra Marie, Elizabeth Camille, Danielle Kay, Gina Kathleen. B.S., Tufts U., 1952; M.S., U. Mass., 1954; Ph.D., U. Mich., 1966. Pub. health sanitarian Hartford (Conn.) Health Dept., 1954-55, 57-61; teaching assoc. dept. microbiology U. Mass., Amherst, 1961-62; research virologist Med. Research Labs., Charles Pfizer & Co., Groton, Conn., 1966-67; research asso. dept. epidemiology Sch. Pub. Health, U. Mich., Ann Arbor, 1967-70; microbiologist, diagnostic immunology tng. br. Ctrs. for Disease Control, Atlanta, 1971—; lectr. resident pathologists Grady Meml. Hosp., Atlanta, 1975; asst. prof. pathology Morehouse Sch. Medicine, 1982-85, clin. assoc. prof., 1986—; adj. asst. prof. pathology and lab. medicine Emory U. Sch. of Medicine, 1985—. Served with M.C., AUS, 1955-57. Registered specialist microbiologist Nat. Registry Microbiologist, Am. Acad. Microbiology. Fellow Am. Acad. Microbiology; mem. Am. Soc. Microbiology, Am. Assn. Immunologists, N.Y. Acad. Sci., Sigma Xi. Democrat. Roman Catholic. K.C. Contbr. articles to profl. jours. Home: 1325 Balsam Dr Decatur GA 30033 Office: 1600 Clifton Rd Atlanta GA 30333

CAVALLO, JOSEPH CHARLES, JR., clergyman; b. Riverside, Calif., Jan. 12, 1944; s. Joseph Charles and Ruth Caroline (Elfner) C. A.A., St. Thomas Seminary, 1964; B.A. in Philosophy, St. Mary's U., 1966; M.Div., St. Meinard Seminary, 1970. Ordained priest Roman Catholic Ch., 1970; asst. pastor Immaculate Heart of Mary, Atlanta, 1970-71, Sacred Heart Ch., Atlanta, 1971-74, St. Jude Ch., Sandy Springs, Ga., 1974-75, St. Thomas Ch., Smyrna, Ga., 1975-77; chaplain Emory U., Atlanta, 1977-81, Atlanta U. Ctr., 1981-86; pastor Our Lady of Lourdes Ch., Atlanta, 1986—; chaplain Civil Air Patrol, DeKalb County, Ga., 1971-81; pres. Atlanta Senate of Priests, 1979-81; chaplain Dignity, Atlanta, 1979—. Chmn. bd. So. Center for Mil. and Vet. Rights, Atlanta, 1978; co-pres. Ecumenical Coalition of Ch. and Labor, Atlanta, 1979-83; mem. bd. Urban Tng. Orgn., Atlanta, 1981-83. Served to maj., Air Force CAP, 1971-81. Mem. Atlanta Bus. and Profl. Guild. Lodge: Rotary. Office: St Anthony Catholic Ch 928 Gordon St Atlanta Ga 30310

CAVANAUGH, CHARLES ARTHUR, pharmacist, typing service executive; b. Boston, Nov. 9, 1935; s. Bartholomew Cavanaugh and Sylvia Viola (Thomas) Cavanaugh Bagley; m. Gloria Ann Harden, Feb. 17, 1962; children—Charles Andrew, Angela Claire. B.S. in Pharmacy, Auburn U., 1961. Registered pharmacist, Ala., Ga., Pharmacist-mgr. Lee Drug Co., Columbus, Ga., 1961-64; pharmacist, owner, operator Banks' Pharmacy, Columbus, 1964-73; state narcotics officer Ala. Diversion Investigative Unit, Montgomery, 1973-74; pharmacist-mgr. Reed Drug Co., Atlanta, 1974—; adminstrv. chief exec. officer Trans-Tex Services, Phenix City, Ala., 1979—. Mem. Lakewood Bapt. Ch., Phenix City, Ala. Served with USAF, 1954-58. Named hon. lt. col. aide-de-camp Gov. Ala., 1974. Mem. Ala. Pharm. Assn. (vice chmn. acad. chain store practice 1981, ho. of dels. 1981), Columbus Track Club, Rho Chi, Delta Upsilon (charter mem. Auburn U. chpt.). Lodge: Gideons Internat. (treas. 1976). Home: PO Box 701 Route 5 Box 28 Phenix City AL 36867 Office: Reed Drug Co 515 Wharton Circle SW Atlanta GA 30336

CAVANAUGH, CHARLES WILLIAM, professional ice skater; b. Freeport, Ill., Oct. 7, 1919; s. Charles Lawrence and Laura Henrietta (Holsinger) C.; m. Lucille Jeannette Risch, Apr. 12, 1947; children—Dennis Alan, Martine Del. Student public schs., Rockford, Ill. Mem. acrobatic adagio ice skating team (with Lucille Jeannette Cavanaugh), 1947-77; appeared in various ice skating shows and at various hotels and theaters, 1947-77, with Barry Ashton's French Style Revuew, 1959-70, S.S. Leonardo Da Vinci, Italian ship and other ships, 1970-73, Americana Hotel, San Juan, P.R., 1974-75; on tour of Southwestern U.S. with plastic ice, 1976-77; cons. U.S. amateur and profl. skaters. Active campaign John B. Anderson for Pres., 1980, Ronald Reagan for Pres., 1984. Mem. AGVA. Lutheran. First ice skater to put on show aboard a ship. Office: 2817 S Ocean Dr Jacksonville Beach FL 32250

CAVANAUGH, LUCILLE JEANNETTE, professional ice skater; b. Hackensack, N.J., Oct. 25, 1927; d. Charles F. and Thelma Rosemond (King) Risch;m. Charles William Cavanaugh, Apr. 12, 1947; children—Dennis Alan, Martin Del. Grad. Tutoring Sch. N.Y., N.Y.C., 1944; Mem. acrobatic adagio ice skating team (with Charles William Cavanaugh), 1947-77; appeared in various ice skating shows and at various hotels and theaters, 1947-77, with Barry Ashton's French Style Revue, 1959-70, S.S. Leonardo Da Vinci, Italian ship, and other ships, 1970-73, Americana Hotel, San Juan, P.R., 1973-75; on tour of Southwestern U.S. with plastic ice, 1976-77; cons. U.S. amateur and profl. skaters. Active campaign John B. Anderson for Pres., 1980, Ronald Reagan for Pres., 1984. Mem. AGVA. Lutheran. First ice skater to put on a show aboard a ship. Office: 2817 S Ocean Dr Jacksonville Beach FL 32250

CAVAZOS, LAURO FRED, university president; b. King Ranch, Tex., Jan. 4, 1927; s. Lauro Fred and Tomasa (Quintanilla) C.; B.A., Tex. Tech. U., 1949, M.A., 1951; Ph.D., Iowa State U., 1954; m. Peggy Ann Murdock, Dec. 28, 1954; children—Lauro, Sarita, Ricardo, Alicia, Victoria, Roberto, Rachel, Veronica, Tomas, Daniel. Teaching asst. Tex. Tech U., Lubbock, 1949-51, prof.

biol. scis., pres., 1980—, prof. anatomy, pres. Univ. Health Scis. Center, 1980—; instr. in anatomy Med. Coll. Va., 1956-60, asst. prof. anatomy, 1956-60, asso. prof., 1960-64; prof., chmn. anatomy Tufts U. Sch. Medicine, Boston, 1964-72, prof. anatomy, asso. dean, 1972-73, prof. anatomy, acting dean, 1973-75, prof. anatomy, dean, 1975-80; spl. and sci. staff N.Eng. Med. Center Hosp., Boston, 1974-80; adv. com. fellows program Nat. Bd. Med. Examiners, 1978; project site vis. Nat. Library of Medicine, 1978; cons. Council Med. Edn., Tex. Med. Assn., 1980-85; active Pan Am. Health Orgn., bd. regents Uniformed Services Univ. of Health Scis., 1980—. Bd. dirs., chmn. Tex. Tech. U. United Way Campaign, 1980; mem. Tex. Gov.'s Task Force on Higher Edn., 1980-82; mem. Gov.'s Higher Edn. Mgmt. Effectiveness Council, 1980-82, chmn., 1981-82; mem. biomed. library rev. com. Nat. Library of Medicine, NIH, 1981-85; chmn. City of Lubbock Boy Scout Campaign, 1981; chmn. edn. com. Tex. Sci. and Tech. Council, 1984-85; trustee S.W. Research Inst., 1982—; mem. selection panel NASA Journalist-in-Space Project, 1986—. Served with U.S. Army, 1945-46. Elected Disting. Grad., Tex. Tech. U., 1977, hon. mem. Tufts Med. Alumni Assn., 1976, edn. and teaching awards from graduating med. class, five years. Recipient Alumni Achievement awards Iowa State U., 1979. Mem. Am. Assn. Anatomists, Endocrine Soc., Histochem. Soc., AAAS, Assn. Am. Med. Colls., WHO, Pan Am. Assn. Anatomy (founding, councilor from U.S., rep Am. Assn. Anatomy, 1974—), Philos. Soc. Tex., Lubbock C. of C. (bd. dirs.), Sigma Xi. Roman Catholic. Editorial bds. Anatomical Record, 1970-73, Med. Coll. of Virginia Quarterly, 1964— Tufts Health Sci. Rev., 1972—, Jour. Med. Edn., 1980-85; contbr. articles to textbooks, jours. Office: Office of the President Texas Tech Univ Box 4349 Lubbock TX 79409

CAVER, TROY VERNON, management educator, consultant; b. Bonnendale, Ark., Dec. 1, 1940; s. Clarence Vernon and Myrtle (Ketchum) C.; m. Lorraine Dawn Paul, Sept. 5, 1964; children—Troy Alan, Tonya Lorraine. B.S.E., Henderson U., 1962; M.S. in Elec. Engring., U. Tex.-El Paso, 1970; M.B.A., Marymount Coll.-Va., 1982. Registered profl. engr., Tex. Commd. 2d lt. U.S. Army, 1962, advanced through grades to lt. col., 1979; chief test policy br. Army Tng. and Doctrine Command Hdqrs., Ft. Monroe, Va., 1974-77; program coordinator office program mgr. Div. Air Def. Gun, Dover, N.J., 1978-80; dir. long range planning Army Staff, Pentagon, Arlington, Va., 1980-82, ret., 1982; dir. market devel. Singer Kearfott div. Singer Corp., Little Falls, N.J., 1982-83; prof. mgmt. Def. Systems Mgmt. Coll., Ft. Belvoir, Va., also pres. Profit and Performance Enhancement Group, 1983—; cons. aerospace cos., 1983—; mktg. cons. Westwell Computer Assocs., Upper Marlboro, Md., 1983. Contbr. articles to profl. jours. Bd. dirs. Springfield Ch. of Nazarene, Va., 1985. Decorated Legion of Merit, Meritorious Service medal, Bronze Star (3), Army Commendation medal (3), Air medal. Mem. Tex. Assn. Profl. Engrs., N. Am. Soc. Corp. Planners. Home: 7012 Flax St Springfield VA 22152 Office: Def Systems Mgmt Coll Fort Belvoir VA 22060

CAZALAS, MARY REBECCA WILLIAMS, lawyer; b. Atlanta, Nov. 11, 1927; d. George Edgar and Mary Annie (Slappey) Williams; R.N., St. Joseph's Infirmary Sch. Nursing, 1948; postgrad. Vanderbilt U., 1950-51, U. Ga., 1951-52; B.S., Ogelthorpe U., 1954; M.S. in Anatomy, Emory U., 1960; J.D., Loyola U., 1967; m. Albert Joseph Cazalas. Gen. duty nurse St. Joseph's Infirmary, Atlanta, 1948-50, Vanderbilt U. Hosp., Nashville, Tenn., 1950-51, Johns Hopkins Hosp., Balt., 1953; instr. maternity nursing St. Joseph's Infirmary Sch. Nursing, Atlanta, 1954-59; med. researcher urology Tulane U. Sch. Medicine, New Orleans, 1961-65; legal researcher Fourth Circuit Ct. Appeals, New Orleans, 1965-71; admitted to La. bar, 1967, practiced in New Orleans, 1967-71; asst. U.S. atty., New Orleans, 1971-79; supervising trial atty. Equal Employment Opportunity Commn., 1979—. Mem. New Orleans Mayor's Drug Abuse Adv. Com., 1976-79; mem. Task Force Area Agency on Aging, 1976-78; mem. Pres.'s Council Loyola U.-New Orleans. Recipient awards Am. Jurisprudence, 1963, Loyola Law Rev., 1967; 1st place for oil painting Fed. Bus. Assn., 1973; Superior Performance award U.S. Dept. Justice, 1974; cert. of appreciation Fed. Exec. Bd., 1975, 76, 77, 78; Outstanding Cardinal Key Rev. E. A. Doyle award, 1976. Mem. D.A.R., Fed. Bus. Assn. (dir. 1972-76, sec. 1976, v.p. 1976—, pres. 1976-78), Fed. (pres. New Orleans chpt. 1974-75, mem. nat. council 1974—, chmn. nat. drug abuse com. 1976-80), Am., La., New Orleans bar assns., Nat. Assn. Women Lawyers, Nat. Health Lawyers Assn., Am. Judicature Soc., New Orleans Art Assn., Federally Employed Women (chmn. fed. women's program 1976-78), New Orleans Bus. and Profl. Women's Club (dir. 1979—), New Orleans Mus. Art, City Park Mid-City Improvement Assn., Emory U., Ogelthorpe U., Loyola U. alumni assns., Loyola Law Alumni (v.p. 1975-76, bd. dirs. 1974-75, 77), Cardinal Key, Leconte, Phi Sigma, Alpha Epsilon Delta, Phi Delta Delta, Phi Alpha Delta (vice justice New Orleans 1974-76, justice 1976-78). Democrat. Roman Catholic. Author textbook; contbr. articles to profl. jours. Home: 1116 City Park Ave New Orleans LA 70119 Office: 600 South St New Orleans LA 70130

CEBALLOS, LEONARDO MIGUEL, engineering company executive; b. Havana, Cuba, June 4, 1953; s. Leonardo Antonio and Concepcion (Roldan) C.; B.S., B.A., Swarthmore Coll., 1975; m. Maria M., Nov. 21, 1975. Salesman Structural Steel System-Cupriocl, Inc., San Juan, P.R., 1972-75, mgr. constrn., 1975-77, v.p., 1977-82, pres., 1983—; pres. P.R. Steel Erectors, 1982—; asso. Morales & Ceballos, Engrs., 1977-80. Walter M. and Florence Schirra scholar, Soc. Am. Mil. Engrs., 1974-75. Mem. ASCE, Colegio de Ingenieros & Agrimensores de Puerto Rico, P.R. C. of C., Sigma Xi. Roman Catholic. Club: Casade España. Home: 61-63 Apt 501 Santiago Iglesias Santurce PR 00901 Office: G P O Box 1366 San Juan PR 00936

CELLUM, MARY ANNA, educator; b. Tishomingo, Okla., Feb. 26, 1919; d. Herbert and Pearl Leta (McCool) Johnson; A.S., Murray State Coll., Tishomingo, 1938; student Okla. U., Norman, 1939; B.S., Southeastern State U., Durant, Okla., 1941; m. James Myrl Cellum, May 27, 1944; children—Jonathan Myrl, James Steven, Rick Wayne, Thomas Russell; 1 stepdau., Barbara Kay. Tchr., Edcouch (Tex.)-Elsa Schs., 1941-42, 56—, now tchr. math. lab. jr. high sch.; tchr. Wapanucha (Okla.) High Sch., 1942-43, public schs., La Villa, Tex., 1943-45. Mem. NEA, Tex. Tchrs. Assn., Assn. Supervision and Curriculum Devel., Tex. Classroom Tchrs. Assn., Beta Sigma Phi (charter mem. Pi Upsilon chpt.). Democrat. Methodist. Club: Jr. Study. Address: PO Box 202 Edcouch TX 78538

CEMEN, IBRAHIM, geology educator; b. Bursa, Turkey, July 23, 1951; came to U.S., 1975; s. Rahmi and Hikmet (Bollu) C.; m. Pamala Byrd, Aug. 20, 1983. B.S. in Geology, Istanbul U., Turkey, 1974; M.S. in Geology, Ohio U., 1977; Ph.D. in Geology, Pa. State U., 1982. Geologist Mining Exploration and Research Inst., Ankara, Turkey, 1974-75; asst. prof. geology Ohio U., Athens, 1982-83, Okla. State U., Stillwater, 1984—. Author: (with others) Geology of Selected Areas in Southern Great Basin California, 1982. Contbr. articles to profl. jours. Recipient Disting. Alumni award Ohio U., 1983; dean's starter grantee Okla State U., 1984—. Mem. Am. Assn. Petroleum Geologists, Geol Soc. Am., Am. Geophys. Union. Home: 807 Dryden Circle Stillwater OK 74075 Office: Okla State U 148 Physical Sciences Stillwater OK 74078

CERNUDA, CHARLES EVELIO, physician; b. Tampa, Fla., June 19, 1941; s. Evelio Perez and Angelina (Leto) C.; B.A., Emory U., 1963, M.D., 1968; m. Mary Margaret McElory, Nov. 24, 1967; children—Mary Robin and Meredith Lynley (twins), Lindsey Elizabeth. Intern, Emory U. Affiliated Hosps., Atlanta, 1968-69, resident in internal medicine, 1969-70, fellow in pulmonary disease, 1970-72; practice medicine specializing in internal medicine and pulmonary disease, Tampa, 1974—; med. dir. ICU, pulmonary lab. and respiratory therapy depts. St. Joseph's Hosp., 1974—, sec. treas., 1977-81, pres.-elect med. staff, 1982, pres. med. staff, 1982-85; med. dir. pulmonary lab. and respiratory therapy depts. Centro Asturiano Hosp., 1974—, vice chief med. staff, 1975-78; dir. Commerce Bank Tampa. Trustee Berkeley Prep. Sch., Tampa, 1985—. Served with M.C., USAF, 1972-73. Diplomate Am. Bd. Internal Medicine, also Sub-Bd. Pulmonary Disease. Fellow Am. Coll. Chest Physicians, ACP; mem. Nat. Assn. Med. Dirs. Respiratory Care, So. Med. Assn., Fla. Med. Assn., AMA, Am., Fla. thoracic socs., Fla. Soc. Internal Medicine, Hillsborough County Med. Assn. (chmn. bd. censors 1981-82), West Coast Acad. Medicine (sec.-treas. 1981-83), Am. Soc. Internal Medicine. Democrat. Episcopalian. Clubs: Univ. Tampa Yacht and Country, Rotary of Ybor City (Tampa). Home: 4930 Andros Dr Tampa FL 33609 Office: 4900 N Habana Ave Tampa FL 33614

CERTUSI, JOHN ARTHUR, JR., spectrochemical instrumentation company executive, vocalist, recording consultant; b. Panama City, Fla., June 18, 1953; s. John Arthur and Mary Ann (Murdza) C.; m. Catherine Salovardos, Nov. 24, 1979 (dec. Feb. 1981). B.S., Boston State Coll., 1975. Analytical chemist Shipley Chem. Co., Newton, Mass., 1975-77; project mgr. Jarrell Ash Co., Waltham, Mass., 1978-83; regional mktg. rep. Allied Analytical Systems, Waltham, 1983—. Mem. Soc. Applied Spectroscopy, Am. Foundrymen's Soc. Avocations: composing and recording music; reading; golf; athletics. Home: 307 Park Colony Dr Norcross GA 30093

CERVENY, FRANK STANLEY, bishop; b. Springfield, Mass., June 4, 1933; s. Frank Charles and Julia Victoria (Kulig) C.; B.A., Trinity Coll., Hartford, Conn., 1955, M.Div. (hon.), 1977; M.Div., Gen. Theol. Sem., N.Y.C., 1958; M.Div. (hon.), U. of South, 1977; m. Emmy Pettway, Nov. 1, 1961; children—Frank Stanley, Emmy Pettway, William DeMoville. Asst. rector Ch. of Resurrection, Miami, Fla., 1958-60; asso. priest, dir. Christian edn. Trinity Ch., N.Y.C., 1960-63; rector St. Lukes Ch., Jackson, Tenn., 1963-68, St. Johns Ch., Knoxville, Tenn., 1968-72; dean Fla., rector St. John's Cathedral, Jacksonville, 1972-74; bishop Diocese of Fla., Jacksonville, 1974—; bd. mem. Com. of 200 of Nat. Ch.; chmn. Presiding Bishops Com. on Renewal; chmn. bd. Episcopal High Sch., Jacksonville; chmn. evangelism House of Bishops; chmn., adviser Center for Christian Spirituality, N.Y.C.; mem. nat. bd., adviser Brotherhood of St. Andrew. Commr., Bicentennial Com. of Jacksonville; mem. Mayor's Com. on Human Relations, Jackson; bd. dirs. Heart Fund, Mental Health Assn., YMCA, Cerebral Palsy Assn., Travelers Aid Soc., Community Planning Council, Jacksonville; trustee Gen. Theol. Sem., N.Y.C., U. of South, Sewanee, Tenn. Club: Rotary. Office: 325 Market St Jacksonville FL 32202

CESAR, THOMAS EUGENE, health services center executive; b. Riverside, Calif., Aug. 25, 1944; s. Edmund Broadman and Annette (Thomas) C.; A.A., Santa Monica City Coll., 1965; B.S., Calif. State U.-Los Angeles, 1969; M.A., Boston State Coll., 1976; m. Amber Henson, Aug. 24, 1968; children—Todd Alan, Eric Thomas. Tchr. Pilgrim Sch., Los Angeles, 1971-73; staff asst. Mass. Bd. Regional Community Colls., Boston, 1974-75; unit mgr. Mt. Auburn Hosp., Cambridge, Mass., 1976-78; exec. dir. Rehab. Services of Wake County, Raleigh, N.C., 1978—. Served with USAF, 1965-68. Mem. Assn. Retarded Citizens, Health Affairs Roundtable Wake County, Nat. Assn. Rehab. Agys. Office: Rehab Services Wake County 3004 New Bern Ave Raleigh NC 27610

CHABOT, PHILIP LOUIS, JR., lawyer; b. Coaldale, Pa., Mar. 23, 1951; s. Philip Louis and Dorothy Louise (Casselberry) C.; m. Karen Sue Pirko, June 6, 1970 (div. 1981); m. Lynne Marx, Nov. 23, 1985; 1 child, Alexander. B.A. with high honors, U. Va., 1973, J.D., 1976. Bar: Va. 1976, D.C. 1976, U.S. Ct. Claims 1978, U.S. Dist. Ct. D.C. 1976, U.S. Dist. Ct. (ea. dist.) Va. 1984, U.S. Ct. Appeals (1st, 2d, 4th, 5th, 8th, 9th and 10th cirs.), U.S. Ct. Appeals (D.C. cir.) 1976, U.S. Supreme Ct. 1979. Assoc. Northcutt Ely, Washington, 1976-77; prin. Duncan, Weinberg & Miller, P.C., Washington, 1978-84; pres. Philip Chabot, Chartered, Washington and Alexandria, Va., 1984—; aide U.S. Senator John V. Tunney, 1973, U.S. Senator William V. Roth, 1974-75; adj. prof. law Am. U., Washington, 1977-81; asst. to dir. com. on tech., transfer and utilization Nat. Acad. Engring., Washington, 1973-74. Editor: (newsletter) Stateline, 1983—. Democratic candidate Va. Ho. of Dels., 44th House Dist., Va., 1983; bd. dirs., sec. Mt. Vernon-Lee Cultural Ctr. Found., Inc., Fairfax, Va., 1984—; state coordinator Youth Coalition for Muskie, Va., 1972; mem. Fairfax Com. 100, 1983—; mem. Mt. Vernon Dem. Com., 1982—; mem. Fairfax County Dem. Com., 1982—; mem. citizens adv. bd. Mt. Vernon Nursing Ctr., Fairfax, 1982—; bd. dirs. Gum Springs Hist. Soc., Inc., 1985—; trustee Va. Outdoors Found., 1982—; trustee, vice chmn. Fairfax County Uniformed Retirement System Bd., 1982—; nat. vice chief Order of Arrow Boy Scouts Am., 1968-70. Recipient Eagle Scout award Boy Scouts Am., 1964. Mem. ABA, Va. State Bar Assn., Va. Trial Lawyers' Assn., D.C. Bar Assn., Mt. Vernon-Lee C. of C., Fairfax C. of C., Alexandria C. of C. Avocation: sailing. Home: 2201 Sherwood Hall Ln Alexandria VA 22306 Office: 600 Cameron St Alexandria VA 22314 also 1317 F St NW 311 Washington DC 20004

CHABROW, PENN BENJAMIN, lawyer; b. Phila., Feb. 16, 1939; s. Benjamin Penn and Annette (Shapiro) C.; m. Sheila Sue Steinberg, June 18, 1961; children—Michael Penn, Carolyn Debra, Frederick Penn. B.S., Muhlenberg Coll., Allentown, Pa., 1960; J.D., George Washington U., 1962, LL.M. in Taxation, 1968; postgrad. in econs. Harvard U. Bar: Va. 1963, D.C. 1964, Fla. 1973, U.S. Supreme Ct. 1972, U.S. Tax Ct. 1964, U.S. Ct. Claims 1974, U.S. Ct. Appeals (D.C. cir.) 1964; cert. tax atty., Fla. Tax law specialist IRS, Washington, 1961-67; tax counsel C. of C. U.S., Washington, 1967-74; sole practice, Miami, Fla., 1974—; pres. Chermere—Forum Imports, Inc., Coral Gables, Fla.; lectr. fed. taxation Barry U., 1977-81. Mem. ABA, Fla. Bar Assn., Fed. Bar Assn., Va. Bar Assn., D.C. Bar Assn., Greater Miami Estate Planning Council, Phi Alpha Delta, Phi Sigma Tau. Contbr. articles profl. jours. Office: 2222 Ponce De Leon Blvd 3d Floor Coral Gables FL 33134

CHACKO, RANJIT CHERIAN, psychiatrist, psychiatry educator; b. Sri Lanka, July 23, 1948; s. Koppara Chandy and Grace Sarah (Cheriyan) C.; came to the U.S., 1974; naturalized, 1982; m. Danuta Susan, Apr. 15, 1978; children—Kristina Rachel Cheriyan, Marissa Evelyn Natalie. M.B.B.S., 1971. Diplomate Am. Bd. Psychiatry and Neurology, Intern, Wellington Hosp. (N.Z.), 1972-73; resident in psychiatry Mt. Sinai Hosp., N.Y.C., 1974-77; clin. dir. Ripley Mental Health Clinic, Houston, 1977-78; clin. dir. Denver Harbor Mental Health Clinic, Houston, 1978-79; asst. prof. psychiatry Baylor Coll. of Medicine, Houston, 1977-85, assoc. prof., 1985—, assoc. dir. community and social psychiatry programs, 1980—; clin. dir. Mid-City Adult and Geriatric Psychiatry Clinic, Houston, 1980—. Mem. Am. Psychiat. Assn., AMA, Am. Pub. Health Assn., Gerontol. Soc. Am. Republican. Episcopalian. Contbr. articles to profl. jours. in field. Office: 1 Baylor Plaza Houston TX 77030

CHAFFIN, GAYLE PATRICK, bank executive; b. East Liverpool, Ohio, Feb. 5, 1950; s. Gayle Adrian and Helen Patricia (O'Driscoll) C.; m. Deborah June Flaherty, Aug. 14, 1971; children—Pamela Ann, Patrick. B.A., La. State U., 1972; M., U. Okla., 1980. Commd. 2d lt. U.S. Army, advanced through grades to capt. 1976; now maj. USAR; tng. specialist Hibernia Nat. Bank, New Orleans, 1981-83, mgr. recruiting, 1983—; tng. cons. Tulane U., 1981—. Author: (textbook) Sales Technology, 1982. Contbr. articles to profl. jours. Recipient La. Cross Merit award, 1982. Democrat. Roman Catholic. Avocations: sailing; racket sports. Home: 4913 Grand Terre Dr Marrero LA 70072 Office: Hibernia Nat Bank PO Box 61540 New Orleans LA 70161

CHAFFINS, ROBERT KAY, oil company executive, real estate specialist; b. Huntington, W.Va., Sept. 24, 1951; s. Miles Kay and Mary Josephine Chaffins; m. Teresa Kay Slover, July 15, 1970; children—Robert Michael, Kristi Michelle. B.A., Marshall U., 1978. Legal asst. firm Marshall & St. Clair, Attys. at Law, Huntington, 1973-78; legal asst. Ashland Oil, Inc., (Ky.), 1978-82, mgr. real estate services, 1982—; lectr. Marshall U. Chmn. bd. dirs. Ceredo-Kenova Community Ctr., Kenova, W.Va., Ceredo-Kenova War Meml. and Library Commn., Kenova; active Madison County Youth Soccer League, Richmond, Ky., Clark-Moores Intramural Basketball League, Richmond, Ceredo-Kenova Buddy Basketball League, Kenova, Ceredo-Kenova Little League, Wayne County Youth Soccer League, Ceredo, W.Va., Ceredo-Kenova Midget Football League, Kenova, Southeastern Jr. Pro Basketball League, Lexington, Ky. Mem. Marshall U. Alumni Assn., Eastern Ky. U. Alumni Assn., Zeta Beta Tau. Democrat. Baptist. Clubs: Arlington Assn., Foresters (Toronto, Can.). Home: 70 Boone Trail Richmond KY 40475 Office: Ashland Oil Inc 3499 Dabney Dr Lexington KY 40509

CHAFIN, ANDREW, planning adminstr.; b. Matewan, W.Va., Jan. 14, 1937; s. Tom C. and Hazel (Isaac) C.; M.A., U. No. Colo., 1972; B.A., U. Charleston, 1967; m. Vickie Griffith, Jan. 12, 1962; children—Andrew Kurt, Lorraine, Adrienne. Planning technician W.Va. State Road Commn., Charleston, 1963-67; planner W.Va. Dept. Commerce, Charleston, 1967-68; exec. dir. Tug Valley C. of C., Williamson, W.Va., 1968; exec. dir. Cumberland Plateau Regional Planning Commn., Lebanon, Va., 1968—; chmn. Cumberland Plateau Regional Housing Authority, Lebanon, 1978—. Served with AUS, 1959-61. Mem. Am. Soc. Public Adminstrn., Am. Planning Assn. So. Baptist (deacon). Office: Box 548 Lebanon VA 24266

CHAFIN, HARRY TRUMAN, state senator; b. July 10, 1947; s. Tom C. and Hazel Marie C.; B.B.A., Marshall U.; postgrad. Detroit Coll. Law, U. Mich.; J.D., Emory U. Atty.; judge City of Williamson, W.Va.; mem. W.Va. senate, 1982—, vice chmn. judiciary com.; mem. gov.'s judicial adv. com. W.Va. Mem. W.Va. State Democratic Exec. Com.; pres. Mingo County Commn., 1979-82. Mem. ABA, W.Va. Bar Assn., Mingo County Bar Assn. (past pres.), Trial Lawyers Am., W.Va. Trial Lawyers Assn., Pi Kappa Alpha. Lodge: Elks. Office: W Va Senate Charleston WV 25305*

CHAGUI, JULIO ALBERTO, export executive; b. Barranguilla, Colombia, May 31, 1945; s. Julio Chagui and Alicia de La Rosa; m. Martha Cecilia Orozco, July 22, 1967; children—Martha Patricia, Claudia, Andres Felipe. Student U. de Mexico, U. Javeriana, Bogota, Columbia. Sales mgr. Grasas y Aceites Chagui, Barranquilla, Colombia, 1966-68; pres., co-owner Centro Decorativo, Barranquilla, 1969-75; pres., owner Decor House, Barranquilla, 1976—; pres., owner Claumar Exports Inc. and Italbagno, Miami, Fla. Office: Italbagno 1 NE 40 St Miami FL 33137

CHAIN, BOBBY LEE, electrical contractor, former mayor; b. Hattiesburg, Miss., Sept. 19, 1929; s. Zollie Lee and Grace (Sellers) C.; B.S., U. So. Miss., Hattiesburg, 1974; D.B.A. (hon.), William Carey Coll., Hattiesburg; m. Betty Sue Green, June 30, 1967; children—Robin Ann, Laura Grace, Bobby Lee, John Webster. Chief electrician Miss. Power & Light Co., Natchez, 1950-53; asst. to gen. supt. atomic energy plant Allegany Electric Co., Oak Ridge, 1954-55; owner, chmn. bd. Chain Electric Co., Hattiesburg, 1957—, Chain Lighting & Appliance Co., Hattiesburg, 1957—; owner, pres. Chainco, Inc., oil properties, Hattiesburg, 1974—; dir. Deposit Guaranty Nat. Bank, Jackson, Deposit Guaranty Corp., Jackson; adv. dir. Deposit Guaranty Nat. Bank, Hattiesburg; mem. Interstate Oil Compact Commn., 1972—; nat. adv. council SBA, 1966-67; dir. Miss. Econ. Council, 1982-83; mayor City of Hattiesburg, 1980-85. Past mem., past pres. Miss. Trustees Instns. Higher Learning; alt. del. Democratic Nat. Conv., 1964; mayor of Hattiesburg, 1980-85; past mem. So. Regional Edn. Bd., Postsecondary Edn. Bd. Served with AUS, 1950. Recipient Albert Gallatin award Zurich Am. Ins. Co., 1975; Disting. Service award U. So. Miss., 1976; Compatriot in Edn. award Kappa Delta Pi, 1976; Recognition plaque City of Hattiesburg, 1961-68; Hub award, 1979; Continuous Outstanding Service award U. So. Miss., 1980; Liberty Bell award, 1980; Service to Edn. award Phi Delta Kappa, 1980; Bobby L. Chain Tech. Ctr. named in his honor; Bobby L. Chain Mcpl. Airport named in his honor. Mem. Newcomen Soc. N.Am., U. So. Miss. Alumni Assn. (Outstanding Service award 1972; Sales and Mktg. Man of Yr. award 1981), Hattiesburg C. of C. (past dir.), Omicron Delta Kappa, Beta Gamma Sigma. Baptist. Clubs: Kiwanis, Hattiesburg Country, U. So. Miss. Century, Shriners, Elks; Univ., Capitol City (Jackson, Miss.). Home: 312 6th Ave Hattiesburg MS 39401 Office: PO Box 2058 Hattiesburg MS 39401

CHALKER, DURWOOD, elec. utility holding co. exec.; b. Breckenridge, Tex., Aug. 22, 1923; s. Robert Nathaniel and Leona Blanche (Cook) C.; B.S. in E.E., Tex. A&M U., 1950; student Harvard U. Bus. Sch., 1978; m. Vada Ray McAdams, Dec. 22, 1953; children—Daniel Joseph, David James, Jason Paul. With West Tex. Utilities Co., Abilene, 1950-79, asst. chief engr., 1960-67, exec. asst., 1967-68, v.p., 1968-75, pres., 1975-76, pres., chief exec. officer, 1979-79; chmn., chief exec. officer Central Power and Light Co., 1979-80, S.W. Corp. and Central and S.W. Services, Inc., Dallas, 1980—; dir. Central Power & Light Co., Corpus Christi, Public Service Co. of Okla., Tulsa, Southwestern Electric Power Co., Shreveport, West Tex. Utilities Co., Abilene. Second v.p. Abilene Indsl. Found., 1979-80; bd. dirs. Hendrick Med. Center Found., 1975-79; bd. dirs. West Tex. Rehab. Center, 1976—, mem. exec. com., 1978-79; mem. Dallas County adv. bd. Salvation Army, 1981; mem. Circle 10 Sustaining Membership Enrollment, Boy Scouts Am., 1981; chmn. Big Gifts div. United Way of Met. Dallas, 1982. Served with USNR, 1943-46, 50-52. Mem. Abilene C. of C. (past dir., chmn. indsl. mfg. com.), West Tex. C. of C. (mem. exec. com. 1977-80), South Tex. C. of C. (past dir., mem. exec. com.), Dallas C. of C. (bd. dirs. 1981-82), Tex. Soc. Profl. Engrs., Edison Electric Inst., IEEE, Tex. A&M Exec. Program (dir.). Baptist. Clubs: City, Northwood. Home: 9035 Broken Arrow Ln Dallas TX 75209 Office: 2700 One Main Pl Dallas TX 75202

CHALMERS, DAVID BAY, SR., oil company executive; b. Denver, Nov. 17, 1924; s. David Twiggs and Dorritt (Bay) C.; 1 son, David Bay. Ed. Dartmouth Coll., 1947, Tuck Sch. Bus.; grad. advanced mgmt. Harvard U., 1966. With Bay Petroleum, Denver, 1951-55; v.p. Tenneco Oil Co., Houston, 1955-67, Occidental Petroleum Corp., Houston, 1967-68; pres. Can. Occidental Petroleum, Ltd., Calgary, Alta., Can., from 1968—; pres., chief exec. officer Petrogas Processing Ltd., Calgary, until 1973; chmn. bd., chief exec. officer Coral Petroleum, Inc., Houston, 1973—; dir. United Refining Inc., Leeward Petroleum Co., Coral Petroleum Can. Served to 1st lt. USMC, 1943-45, 49-50; Korea. Mem. Tex. Ind. Petroleum and Royalty Owners Assn., Nat. Petroleum Refiners Assn., Houston C. of C., 25 Yr. Club of Petroleum Industry. Republican. Episcopalian. Clubs: Lakeside Country, The Houston, Petroleum, Houstonian, The Heritage, Riverbend Country, Plaza (Houston); Denver Country, Petroleum (Denver); Plaza of Hololulu, Waialae Country (Honolulu); Metropolitan, Town of Jamestown. Office: PO Box 19666 Houston TX 77224

CHALMERS, PATRICK JOSEPH, fire protection systems company sales executive, photographer; b. Springfield, Ill., Jan. 15, 1941; s. Joseph William and Agnes Cecilia (McGill) C.; m. Susan Kay Mounts, Dec. 29, 1962; children—Michael E., Patrick S., Kevin D. Grad. in bus. adminstrn. Alexander Hamilton Inst., N.Y.C., 1969-71; cert. in acctg. La Salle Extension U., Chgo., 1965-69; student in econs. Millikin U., 1960-71. Pres., Chalmers, Inc., Decatur, Ill., 1959-78; br. mgr. VikingFire Protection Co., Peoria, Ill., 1978-80; br. mgr. Grinnell Fire Protection Co., Albuquerque, 1980-81, spl. hazards rep., Houston, 1982, sales rep., 1982-83; sales mgr. Grunau Co., Inc., Houston, 1983-84; pres., owner Mktg. Services, Houston, 1984—; v.p. Gamco Internat., Inc., Houston, 1984—; free-lance photographer, Crosby, Tex., 1982—; prin. Patrick Chalmers Photog., Crosby, 1983—; sports corr. Houston Community News, 1983. Founder, pres. East Lake Houston Soccer Club, 1982, dir. pub. relations, 1983—. Mem. Nat. Inst. Cert. Engring. Technicians (assoc. engring. tech.; Level II award 1983, Level III award 1984), Assoc. Photographers Internat., Soc. Mfg. Engrs. Republican. Mem. Christian Ch. (Disciples of Christ). Clubs: Millikin Vets. (v.p. 1970-71) (Decatur); Newport Country (Crosby). Lodge: Masons (3d deg.), York Rite. Office: Mktg Services 12620 North Freeway Suite 218 Houston TX 77060

CHAMBERS, ANNE COX, newspaper executive, former diplomat; b. Dayton, Ohio. Student Finch Coll., N.Y.C.; hon. degrees: D.Pub. Service, Wesleyan Coll., 1982; D.H.L., Spelman Coll., 1983; LL.D., Oglethorpe U., 1983. Chmn. bd. Atlanta Jour.-Constn.; Am. ambassador to Belgium, 1977-81; chmn. Lacoste/Sch. of the Arts in France, Inc. dir. Cox Enterprises, Inc., Cox Communications, Coca-Cola Co. Bd. dirs. Atlanta Arts Alliance, High Mus. Art, Cities in Schs., Am. Ditchley Found.; trustee So. Ctr. Internat. Studies, Mus. Modern Art; mem. internat. council Mus. Modern Art, nat. com. Whitney Mus. Am. Art. Mem. Council Fgn. Relations. Address: 426 W Paces Ferry Rd NW Atlanta GA 30305

CHAMBERS, CONSTANTINE PETER, physician; b. Mikrothive, Almyros, Greece, June 12, 1935; s. Petros Constantinos and Vasilicki (Mamalis) Tsambiras; m. Elaine Varney, July 22, 1962; children—Peter, George, Lisa. Grad. Am. Agrl. & Indsl. Inst., Greece, 1956; B.S., Wilmington Coll., 1960; D.O., Kirksville Coll. Osteopathy & Surgery, 1966. Intern, Doctors Hosp., Tucker, Ga., 1966-67; gen. practice osteo. medicine, Tucker, 1967-80; hair transplant practitioner, Clearwater, Fla., 1980—. Author: Baldness and the Reliable Alternative, 1980; Are Bald Men Sexier?, 1985. Mem. Am. Osteopathic Assn., Ga. Osteopathic Assn., Fla. Osteopathic Med. Assn., Am. Coll. Gen. Practitioners. Republican Greek Orthodox. Office: 1245 Rogers St Clearwater FL 33516

CHAMBERS, JAY LEE, clinical psychologist; b. Providence, Ky., Apr. 7, 1923; s. Jay Lee and Anna Royston (Griggs) C.; m. Willa Marie Browning, June 1, 1952; children—Ann Marie, Carol Louise. B.A., George Washington U., 1948; M.A., U. Ky., 1952, Ph.D., 1954. Chmn. psychology dept. Muskingum Coll., New Concord, Ohio, 1954-56; dir. psychol. services Eastern State Hosp., Williamsburg, Va., 1956-58; dir. Charles L. Mix Meml. Fund, Inc., Americus, Ga., 1958-64; dir. psychol. services Ky. State Hosp., Danville, 1964-66; clin. psychologist Student Health Services, Fla. State U., Tallahassee, 1966-70; dir. Ctr. for Psychol. Services, Coll. William and Mary, Williamsburg, 1970—. Served with USMCR, 1942-46. Mem. Am. Psychol. Assn., Southeastern Psychol. Assn., So. Soc. for Philosophy and Psychology. Democrat. Contbr. articles to profl. jours. Home: 116 Indian Springs Rd Williamsburg VA 23185 Office: Coll William and Mary Williamsburg VA 23185

CHAMBERS, JOHN LEE, optometrist; b. Rogersville, Tenn., May 29, 1951; s. Joe Alvie and Emily Ellen (Smith) C.; m. JoAnn M. White, Nov. 18, 1976; children—Nicole Lee, Charlotte Duke. O.D., So. Coll. Optometry, Memphis, 1976. Pvt. practice optometry, Rogersville, Tenn., 1977—. Mem. bd. Park and Recreation Com., Rogersville, 1979; pres. Assn. for Preservation of Tenn. Antiquities, Rogersville, 1981; coach Rogersville Flying Fish Swim Team, 1981-83. Mem. East Tenn. Optometry Assn. (pres. 1981-82, rep. 1983-84).

Republican. Presbyterian. Lodge: Rotary. Home: PO Box 250 Rogersville TN 37857

CHAMPAGNE, MARIAN GROSBERG, lawyer; b. Schenectady, Dec. 17, 1915; d. Joseph E. and Rae Grosberg; m. Herbert Champagne, Aug. 18, 1940 (dec. May 1966); children—Emily, Margot J. B.A., Smith Coll., 1936; LL.B., Albany Law Sch., 1955, J.D., 1968. Bar: N.Y. 1956. Practice with Herbert Champagne, 1956-66; assoc. Wood Morris Sanford & Hatt, 1966-71. Author: The Cauliflower Heart, 1944; Quimby and Son, 1962; Facing Life Alone, 1964. Mem. Fla. Mental Health Bd., 1975-78, Sarasota Mental Health Clinic, 1980-82. Mem. AAUW. Republican. Unitarian. Club: Smith Alumnae (Sarasota). Home and Office: 3276 Pinecrest St Sarasota FL 33579

CHAMPAÑA, JOSIE ANNE M. GAGNERON, beverage company executive; b. Port Au Prince, Haiti, Mar. 19, 1947; d. Raymond Champana and Germaine Gagneron (O'Henry) Martelly; divorced; 1 son, Joseph Patrick Michael Mottion Champaña. B.B.A., NYU, 1968. Exec. asst., project fin. mgr. William Sigal & Assocs., San Juan, P.R., 1969-72; exec. asst. to mktg. mgr. Latin Am. and Caribbean, Confed Life Ins. Co., San Juan, 1972-76; advt. and promotions mgr. Latin Am., Caribbean, Tobacco Exporters Internat., Alfred Dunhill Ltd., P.R. and Colombia, S.Am., 1976-80; mgr. external affairs and pub. relations Caribbean Refrescos Inc., subs. Coca-Cola Co., Cidra, P.R., 1980—; adminstrv. cons., sales promotions. Mem. Pub. Relations Soc. Am., P.R. C. of C., Mfrs. Assn. P.R., Conv. Bur. P.R., Sales and Mktg. Assn., Am. Assn. Pub. Relations, Am. Assn. P.R. and U.S.A. Republican. Roman Catholic. Clubs: Casa Espana, La Rotiserie, Juliana's, Caribe Hilton Hotel. Office: PO Box CC Cidra PR 00639

CHAMPION, PAUL HENRI, citrus grower, national trust examiner; b. Orlando, Fla., Dec. 24, 1945; s. Paul Henri and Marion Alice (Joyce) C.; B.S., U. West Fla., 1968; M.B.A., Stetson U., 1970. Asst. trust examiner Regional Adminstr. of Nat. Banks, Atlanta, 1971-74, nat. trust examiner, 1974-78, examiner-in-charge Atlanta Trust Subregion, 1976, nat. bank examiner, 1978—; chmn. bd. Tuscawilla Properties, Inc., Leesburg, Fla., 1974—; tech. edn. specialist Comptroller of Currency, Washington, 1976-78; instr. mgmt. techniques Fed. Fin. Instns. Council, 1977—. Recipient Spl. Achievement award Dept. Treasury, 1978; Comptroller of Currency Spl. Recognition award Comptroller of Currency, 1978, cert. of appreciation, 1982. Mem. Soc. for Advancement Mgmt. Republican. Roman Catholic. Club: Kingwood Country. Home: 1365 Kingwood Dr Box 5658 Kingwood TX 77339 Office: 1201 Elm St Suite 3800 Dallas TX 75270

CHAMPION, WILLIAM LANCASTER, exploration geologist; b. Sadieville, Ky., Mar. 20, 1925; s. Ebon and Laura (Lancaster) C.; m. Trudy Caywood, Aug. 27, 1946; children—William Lancaster, Jr., Katherine Carr, Laura, Carol. B.S., U. Ky., 1950; postgrad. U. Houston, 1962. Geologist U.S. Geol. Survey, N.Mex., La., 1950-54, Houston Oil Co. Tex., Shreveport, La., 1954-56, Atlantic Refining Co., Houston, 1956-63; pvt. practice as geologist, Houston, 1963—. Editor: Sipes Bull. 11, 1985; assoc. editor Sipes Bull. 10, 1984. Served to lt. (j.g.) USNR, 1943-46, ETO, PTO. Mem. Soc. Ind. Profl. Earth Scientists (cert., pres. 1982), Am. Assn. Petroleum Geologists (cert., del. 1984—), Houston Geol. Soc. (mem. exec. com. 1985—), Petroleum Club. Home: 3601 Allen Pkwy 715 Houston TX 77019 Office: 911 Walker 1143 Houston TX 77002

CHAMPION, WILLIAM RALPH, computer science educator; b. Jackson, Miss., Feb. 17, 1938; s. William R. Champion and S.L. (Bonner) Fleming. A.B., U. Ala., 1960. Programming instr. Acad. Computer Tech., Houston, 1969-70, Coastal Carolina Community Coll., Jacksonville, N.C., 1970-73; bus. programmer Belo Corp., Dallas, 1973-74; sr. instr. Tex. Inst. Dallas, 1974-80; assoc. prof. computer sci. DeVry Inst. Tech., Irving, Tex., 1980—; adj. tchr. Tarrant County Community Coll., Hurst, Tex., 1982-84; pascal tutoring, Dallas, 1980-81. Author: Pascal for Business, 1984. Recipient Teaching Excellence award Delta Chi, 1983. Mem. Data Processing Mgmt. Assn., Assn. Systems Mgmt. Democrat. Baptist. Avocation: correspondence chess. Office: DeVry Inc 4250 N Beltline Irving TX 75038

CHAMPNEY, RAYMOND JOSEPH, advertising agency executive; b. N.Y.C., Aug. 6, 1940; s. Raymond Joseph and Florence (McConnell) C.; m. Anne Kelly, Jan. 10, 1976. Student CCNY, 1961-63; B.S. in Mktg., NYU, 1965. With BBDO Advt., N.Y.C., 1964-66, McCann Erickson Advt., 1966-68, Clinton E. Frank Advt., 1968-71, Norman Craig & Kummel Advt., 1971-73, Doyle Dane Bernbach Advt., 1973-74, Guest Pub. Co., 1974-77, Bozell & Jacobs Advt., 1977-79; pres. Weekley & Champney Advt., Dallas, 1979—. Served with U.S. Army, 1959-61. Mem. Sales Mktg. Execs., Dallas Ad League. Home: 1212 Spargercrest Dr Bedford TX 76021 Office: Weekley & Champney Advt 1440 W Mockingbird Ln Suite 300 Dallas TX 75247

CHAN, CHIU YEUNG, mathematics educator; b. Hong Kong, Feb. 28, 1941; came to U.S., 1969; s. Hak Tan and Ching Yuen (Lam) C.; m. Mui Lai Tania Lee, May 6, 1970; children—Andy Sung-Kin, Gary Sung-Hong. B.Sc., U. Hong Kong, 1964, Spl. B.Sc., 1965; M.Sc., U. Ottawa, 1967; Ph.D., U. Toronto, 1969. Asst. prof. Fla. State U., Tallahassee, 1969-74, assoc. prof., 1974-81, prof., 1981-83; prof. math. U. Southwestern La., Lafayette, 1982—. Contbr. articles to math. jours. Mem. Am. Math. Soc., Soc. Indsl. and Applied Math., Am. Acad. Mechanics. Home: 102 Autumn Oak Bend Lafayette LA 70508 Office: Dept Math U Southwestern La Lafayette LA 70504

CHANCE, (MARI) SUE, psychiatrist; b. Paris, Tex., Apr. 27, 1942; d. John Bruce and Ella Winifred (McDaniel) Scott; m. Garland James Bankston, 1957 (div. Aug. 1961); children—Kenneth James, Bankston Scott; m. Thomas E. Chance, Jr., Jan. 1, 1976. B.A. in Psychology, Angelo State U., 1971; M.D., U. Tex. Med. Br., 1978. Social worker Tex. Dept. of Welfare, San Antonio and Ft. Worth, 1972-73; intern U. Okla., Oklahoma City, 1978-79; resident Menninger Found., Topeka, Kans., 1980-83; practice medicine specializing in psychiatry; staff Ctr. Psychiatrists, Norfolk, Va., 1981-82, Wetcher Clinic, Houston, 1983—; med. dir. Adult Therapeutic Community Mainland Ctr. Hosp., Texas City, Tex., 1984—; cons. to nursing homes in area. Contbr. articles to profl. jours. Bd. dirs. Bay Area Council on Drug and Alcohol Abuse, Houston, 1984. Mem. Am. Psychiat. Assn., Am. Assn. for Geriatric Psychiatry, Houston Geriatric Soc., Soc. for Clin. Exptl. Hypnosis, Am. Soc. For Clin. Hypnosis, Houston Assn. for Bus. and Profl. Women, Alpha Chi. Avocations: writing; genealogy. Office: Wetcher Clinic 16902 El Camino Real Suite 2C Houston TX 77058

CHANDLER, A. LEE, state judge, b. Orangeburg, S.C., Dec. 16, 1922; s. William E. and Ella Rowe (Dukes) C.; m. Martha Nell Wilkins, Dec. 30, 1945; 1 child, Jane. Student The Citadel, 1940-43, U. S.C. Law Sch., 1946-47; A.B., George Washington U., 1950. County atty. Darlington County, S.C., 1963-73; mem. S.C. Ho. of Reps., 1973-76; judge S.C. Cir. Ct., 4th Jud. Cir., 1976-84; judge S.C. Supreme Ct., 1984—. Address: PO Box 9 Darlington SC 29532*

CHANDLER, EDY J(OAN), collectable memorabilia sales executive, artist, photographer; b. New Rochelle, N.Y., July 26, 1951; d. Henry and Ceil (Sandler) C. Student, Mus. Fine Arts Sch., 1970-72. Freelance artist, Houston, 1968—; mgr. Bellaire Rare Books and Coins, Houston, 1969-70; buyer Foley's Record Dept., Houston, 1970-72; owner, appraiser Chandler's Nostalgia, Houston, 1972—; supr. graphic arts dept. Tex. Art Supply, Houston, 1985—. Photographer of books and articles. Contbr. articles to profl. jours. Avocations: collecting books; fantasy memorabilia; miniatures. Home: Box 20664 Houston TX 77225 Office: Chandler's Nostalgia 2821 Fondren Houston TX 77063

CHANDLER, JAMES WENDELL, public relations executive; b. Winnfield, La., Oct. 19, 1932; s. Wendell L. and Callie (Jones) C.; m. Jimmie Ruth Carter, Aug. 27, 1950; children—Steven Michael, Kay Lynne. Student Marietta Coll., 1956-57, W. Liberty State U., 1958-60. Reporter, Wheeling Intelligencer, 1957-59; editor Weirton Steel Co. div. Nat. Steel, 1959-64; mgr. communications Allegheny Ludlum Industries, Inc., 1964-71; dir. pub. relations Dayton Press, Inc., 1971-77; v.p. corp. communications NCNB Corp., Charlotte, N.C., 1977-83, v.p., dir. pub. relations, Tampa, Fla., 1984—. Contbr. articles to profl. jours. Served with USAF, 1951-55. Mem. Pub. Relations Soc. Am., Club: Tampa, Temple Terrace Golf and Country. Home: 1724 Magdalene Manor Dr Tampa FL 33613 Office: NCNB Corp PO Box 25900 Tampa FL 33630

CHANDLER, JOHN BRANDON, JR., lawyer; b. Boston, Sept. 25, 1939; s. John Brandon and Juliette (Blackburn) C.; diploma Ga. Mil. Acad., 1957; B.A., Vanderbilt U., 1961, J.D., 1964; student Instituto Technilogico y Estudios Superiores de Monterrey, 1959; 1 son, John Brandon III; m. Helen Elizabeh Demski, Mar. 22, 1986. Admitted to Tenn. bar, 1964, Fla. bar, 1967, U.S. Supreme Ct. bar, 1971; asso. firm Rogers, Towers, Bailey, Jones & Gay, Jacksonville, Fla., 1966-73, partner, 1973—. Panel mem. Am. Arbitration Assn. Pres. Jacksonville Beach Young Republican Club, 1967. Served to capt. AUS, 1964-66. Mem. ABA (regional chmn. discovery com. litigation sect.), Fla. (labor law com.), Tenn., Jacksonville (gov. 1975-80) bar assns., Phi Delta Phi (pres. Malone Inn 1964), Kappa Alpha Order. Clubs: Jacksonville Vanderbilt (pres. 1973-84), Fla. Yacht, Sawgrass, Seminole, Ponte Vedra, University, Friars, Ye Mystic Revelers. Contbr. articles to profl. jours. Home: 2025 Oceanfront Atlantic Beach FL 32233 Office: 1300 Gulf Life Dr Jacksonville FL 32207

CHANDLER, PHILIP P., educator. Dir. Okla. State U. Tech. Inst., Oklahoma City. Office: Dept Technology Okla State U Tech Inst 900 N Portland St Oklahoma City OK 73107*

CHANDLER, REUBEN CARL, business executive; b. Lawrenceville, Ga., Oct. 25, 1917; s. Reuben C. and Florine (Doster) C.; grad. Marist Coll., Atlanta, 1935; student Ga. Inst. Tech., 1935-37; A.B., Emory U., 1941; postgrad. Atlanta Law Sch., 1946-48; D.Sc. (hon.) in Bus. Adminstrn., Detroit Inst. Tech., 1960; m. Sarah Megee, Oct. 27, 1940; children—Carla Evalynee Chandler Gurkin, Robert Megee, David Pratt, Craig D. Sales rep. Gen. Motors Acceptance Corp., Atlanta, 1941-42; asst. dir. tng. Southeastern Shipbldg. Corp., Savannah, Ga., 1942-43; prodn. mgr. Mead-Atlanta Paper Co., 1946-49; salesman Union Camp Corp. (formerly Union Bag & Camp Paper Corp.), 1949-50, dist. sales mgr., Trenton, 1950-51, Eastern div. sales mgr., 1951-52, dir. corrugated container and bd. sales, N.Y.C., 1952, v.p. sales, 1952-55; chmn., chief exec. officer, chmn. exec., fin. coms. Standard Packaging Co., N.Y.C., 1955-66; chmn. bd. Crowell-Collier Pub. Co., N.Y.C., 1957; ltd. partner Elliott & Co., investment bankers, N.Y.C., 1960-62; chmn bd. J.D. Jewell, Inc., Gainesville, Ga., 1962-72, pres., 1969—, also chmn. exec. com., dir.; pres. Identiseal Systems, Atlanta, 1972—, Perkins-Goodwin Mgmt. Services Co., N.Y.C., 1973—, Am. Resources Corp., Berles Corp., Paterson, N.J., 1982-84, Nat. Packing Industries Corp., Paterson, 1982-84; chmn. bd. Lanier Mortgage Corp., Gainesville, Ga., 1973—; pres., chief exec. officer Duncan & Copeland, Inc., 1976-79, Va. Packaging Supply Co., McLean, 1979-84; dir. Am. Agy. Life Ins. Co., Atlanta, Berry Steel Corp., Edison, N.J. Trustee Detroit Inst. Tech., 1960—, Christ Ch. Sch., Short Hills, N.J., 1963—, Brenau Coll., 1968—, Emory U., Atlanta, 1972—, Ga. Found. for Ind. Colls., 1969—, Charter Sch., Gt. Falls, Va.; bd. dirs. Am. Soc. Indsl. Security Found. Served as lt. USNR, 1943-46. Lt. col. aide de camp Gov.'s staff Ga., 1951-52, 70-72. Recipient Man of Yr. award Am. Jewish Com., 1964; Horatio Alger award, 1965; Achievement award Delta Tau Delta, 1966; named Disting. Alumnus, Marist Sch., 1985. Mem. Savannah Jr. C. of C. (v.p. 1942-43), Gainesville C. of C., Navy League (life), Def. Orientation Conf. Assn., Am. Pulp and Paper Mill Supts. Assn. (life), Emory U. Alumni Assn. (pres. 1965, Honor award 1968), Ga. Tech. Nat. Alumni Assn. (nat. adv. bd. 1964 —), Ga. Poultry Fedn. (mem. round table 1970—), Tenn. Wesleyan Coll. Parents Assn., U.S. Navy Supply Corps Assn. (trustee 1972—), Delta Tau Delta (life), Alpha Delta Sigma, Omicron Delta Kappa. Baptist. Mason. Elk. Clubs: Atlanta Athletic, Commerce (Atlanta); N.Y. Area Emory (pres. 1964), Sky, University, Union League, Economic (N.Y.C.); Washington Golf and Country (Arlington, Va.); Chattahoochee Country (Gainesville); Sea Pines Plantation (Hilton Head Island, S.C.). Address: 4101 Dunwoody Club Dr Apt 25 Dunwoody GA 30338

CHANDLER, ROBERT CHARLES, hospital administrator; b. Birmingham, Ala., Apr. 15, 1945; s. Coleman Duke and Myrtle (Cleveland) C.; m. Cynthia Brightwell, June 15, 1968; children—Jason Charles, Jonathan Robert. B.S. in Pharmacy, Samford U., 1968; M.S. in Hosp. and Health Adminstrn., U. Ala.-Birmingham, 1972. Registered pharmacist. Pharmacy intern Carraway Methodist Hosp., Birmingham, 1968-69; chief pharmacist Holy Family Hosp., Birmingham, 1969-70; v.p. Ft. Sanders Med. Ctr., Knoxville, Tenn., 1971-78; sr. v.p. Bapt. Med. Ctrs., Birmingham, 1978-79, exec. v.p. Princeton, 1979-85; pres. E. Tenn. Bapt. Hosp., Knoxville, 1985—; bd. dirs. Ala. Quality Assurance Found., Birmingham, 1984-85, Ala. Med. Rev., Birmingham, 1980-84; adv. bd. Blue Cross/Blue Shield, Birmingham, 1983-85; liaison com. Jefferson County Med. Soc., Birmingham, 1984-85. Div. chmn. United Way, Birmingham, 1984; Sunday Sch. tchr. Dawson Bapt. Ch., Birmingham. Recipient Cert. Appreciation, Tenn. Gov. Ray Blanton, 1978, Disting. Service award Tenn. Com. on Employment of Handicapped, 1978, Award of Excellence Ala. Pub. Relations Council, 1979. Fellow Am. Coll. Hosp. Adminstrs.; mem. Birmingham Regional Hosp. Council (pres. elect 1985), Ala. Hosp. Assn. (trustee 1984-85), Birmingham C. of C. (chmn. health services com. 1980). Republican. Club: The Club (Birmingham). Lodge: Rotary (mem. group study exchange, 1977). Office: E Tenn Baptist Hosp PO Box 1788 Knoxville TN 37901

CHANDLER, SADIE ARNETTE, state educational administrator, consultant; b. Port St. Joe, Fla., July 5, 1933; d. David Crockett and Roxie Mae (Whitehead) Arnette; m. James William Herschel Chandler, Jr., Sept. 16, 1956; children—Richard Allan, Kathi Lynn Chandler Adams. B.A., Stetson U., 1956; M.Ed., Middle Tenn. State U., 1969, Ed. S.,1982. Tchr., choral dir. Franklin County High Sch., Winchester, Tenn., 1965-69, guidance counselor, 1969-77; instr. Motlow State Community Coll., Tullahoma, Tenn., 1971-74; dir. career edn. Tenn. Dept. Edn., Nashville, 1978-80, dir. staff devel., 1980—; cons. Univ. Counselor, Murfreesboro, Tenn., 1970, 74, 75; mem. nat. task force career edn. communication, Washington, 1979; bd. dirs. Nat. Council States Inservice Edn., Tenn., 1984-88. Task force dir. State Plan Career Edn., 1978, Tenn. Instructional Model, 1984. Recipient Outstanding Service award Franklin County Jaycees, 1976. Mem. Tenn. Assn. Suprs. and Curriculum, South Tenn. Personnel and Guidance Assn. (pres., counselor 1976), Middle Tenn. Edn. Assn. (chmn., Counselor of Yr. award 1966-67), Bus. and Profl. Women, Phi Delta Kappa, Delta Kappa Gamma (pres. 1980-82). Methodist. Clubs: LeConte, Capitol Hill. Avocations; pageant director; musical director; organist. Home: Route 1 Decherd TN 37324 Office: Tenn Dept Edn Room 202 1150 Menzler Rd Nashville TN 37210

CHANDLER, STEPHEN S., judge; b. Blount County, Tenn., Sept. 13, 1899; s. Stephen Sanders and Evelyn Amelia (Johnson) C.; student U. Tenn., 1917-18; J.D., U. Kans., 1922; m. Margaret Patterson, 1922 (dec.); children—Frances Patterson (Mrs. Sim K. Sims), Stephen Sanders III, Frank Patterson. Pvt. law practice in Oklahoma City, 1922-43; U.S. dist. judge for Western Okla., 1943—, chief judge, 1956-69. Mem. law faculty Oklahoma City U., 1957-60. Recipient Hatton Sumners award, 1961; named to Okla. Hall of Fame, 1960. Mem. various bar and other legal assns., Sigma Alpha Epsilon, Phi Delta Phi, Order of Coif. Democrat. Methodist. Mason (Shriner). Clubs: Oklahoma City Golf, Lotus, Petroleum, Rotary (pres. 1940-41); Nat. Press (Washington). Home: Oklahoma City OK 73101 Office: US Court House PO Box 895 Oklahoma City OK 73101

CHANDLER, WILLIAM HENRY, lawyer; b. Hemingway, S.C., May 5, 1948; s. William Jackson and Margaret Eloise (Nelson) C.; m. Ann Rodgers Tomlinson, July 31, 1982; children—Jared Witherspoon Nelson, Martha Elizabeth Hartman, Ann Paisley Snowden. A.B., U. S.C., 1970, J.D., 1973. Bar: S.C. 1973, U.S. Dist. Ct. (we. dist.) La. 1975, U.S. Dist. Ct. S.C. 1973, U.S. Ct. Mil. Appeals 1974. Ptnr., Chandler & Ruffin, Hemingway, 1978-84, Askins, Chandler, Ruffin and Askins, Hemingway, 1984—; town atty. Stuckey (S.C.), 1979—; atty. Lawyers Title Ins. Co., Fed. Land Bank, Title Ins. Co. Minn., 1978—; instr. bus. law Williamsburg Tech. Coll., Kingstree, S.C., 1978-79. Supt. ch. sch. First Presbyn. Ch., Bossier City, La., 1975-77; lay speaker Presbytery of the Pines, Presbyn. Ch. U.S., Bossier City, 1976-77; vice-chmn. Williamsburg County Bd. Trustees, 1979-84; ruling elder Indiantown Presbyn. Ch., Hemingway, 1980—. Served as capt. JAGC, USAF, 1974-78; to maj. Res. Mem. ABA, Am. Legion, SAR, French Huguenot Soc., S.C. Bar Assn., S.C. Geneal. Soc., South Caroliniana Library Soc., S.S. Hist. Soc., Williamsburg County Bar Assn., Williamsburg County Hist. Soc., Three Rivers Hist. Soc. (pres.), St. Andrews Soc., Charleston Preservation Soc., PTA, Phi Eta Sigma, Omicron Delta Kappa, Phi Delta Phi. Presbyterian. Lodge: Masons (Hemingway). Club: Hog Crawl Hunting. Home: Route 1 Box 189 Hemingway SC 29554 Office: PO Box 218 Hemingway SC 29554

CHANDWANI, ARJAN DHALUMAL, consulting engineer; b. Umarkot, Sind, Pakistan, June 15, 1936; s. Dhalumal and Gyanidevi Chandwani; came to U.S., 1966, naturalized, 1974; M.S. in Civil Engring., U. Cin., 1968; m. Meera M. Nebhrajani, July 21, 1969; children—Alpana, Sunita, Sanjay, Shalni, Manesh. Gazetted officer Central Designs Orgn., Ahemdabad, India, 1961-66; project mgr. Dade County Aviation Dept., Miami, Fla., 1972-80; project mgmt. specialist Rapid Transit System, Dade County Office of Transp., Miami, 1980-82; pvt. practice cons. engr.; founder, pres. Fla. State Constrn. Coll. Inc., Hollywood; adj. faculty mem. Broward Community Coll., Embry Riddle Aero. U. Mem. Am. Mgmt. Assn., India Assn. of U. Detroit, India Club. Met. Dayton, Am. Assn. Airport Execs., India Assn. Greater Miami (pres. 1978-79). Democrat. Hindu. Club: Kiwanis (pres. club 1979-80). Contbr. articles to profl. jours. Home: 2560 Azalea Ave Miramar FL 33025 Office: 7832 Davie Rd Extension FL 33024

CHANEY, FLOYD TONEY, mine maintenance executive; b. Orville, W.V., Feb. 8, 1937; s. James Toney and Pearl Virginia (Curry) C.; m. Martha Catherine Douglas, Aug. 20, 1960; children—Vanessa, James, Kathy. B.S.E.E., Fla. Inst. Tech., 1959; M.B.A., Southwestern U., Tucson, 1983. Chief electrician Amherst Coal Co., Lundale, W.Va., 1963-65; constrn. mgr. Lummus Constrn. Co. N.Y.C. 1965-72; asst. maintenance supt. Youngstown Sheet and Tube, Dehue, W.Va., 1972-74; chief electrician, asst. project engr., tng. instr. Wheeling-Pittsburgh Steel, Omar, W.Va., 1974-78; gen. elec. foreman Conners Steel Co., Huntington, W.Va., 1978-80; maintenance supt., Martiki Mine, Mapco Inc., Lovely, W.Va., 1980-83; maintenance supt. Morton Salt Co., Weeks Island, La., 1984—; karate instr. Amateur radio operator Navy Mil. Affiliate Radio Service W.Va., 1974—; instr. CPR W.Va. Heart Assn. Served to capt. USN, 1953-59; Korea. Mem. Aircraft Owners and Pilots Assn., Democrat. Methodist. Home: 124 Vera Cruz New Iberia LA 70560 Office: Morton Salt Co Box 1496 New Iberia LA 70560

CHANG, JOSEPH JAWSHIN, researcher, consultant; b. Taiwan, China, Nov. 21, 1944; s. Fusan and Dankun (Lin) C.; m. Susie S. Hwang, Aug. 20, 1973; children—Eugene, Victor. B.S. in Chem. Engring., Nat. Cheng-Kung U., Taiwan, 1966; M.S., U. Mo., 1970, Ph.D., 1973. Registered profl. engr., N.J., Fla. Postdoctoral fellow U. Mo. Materials Research Center, Rolla, 1973-74; research staff Western Electric Co., Engring. Research Center, Princeton, N.J., 1974-78; research engr. Jelco Labs., Johnson & Johnson, Tampa, Fla., 1978-80, project leader div. Critikon Inc., Tampa, 1980—. Served to 2d lt. Chinese Army, 1966-67. Mem. AAAS, Am. Inst. Chem. Engrs., Nat. Soc. Profl. Engrs., Am. Assn. Med. Instrumentation, AMA, Sigma Xi. Patentee Fabricating printed circuits, 1978; pretreatment electrochem. oxygen sensor, 1983. Home: 7013 W Linebaugh Ave Tampa FL 33625

CHANG, LIE-PING, osteopathic physician; b. Taipei, Taiwan, Republic of China; came to U.S., 1972, naturalized, 1980; s. Shu-Liang and Yi-Kun (Li) C.; m. Bernadette Yong, Mar. 23, 1979. B.A. in Biology, Cath. U. Am., 1976; D.O., Kirksville Coll., Mo., 1980. Diplomate Am. Bd. Family Practice, Am. Bd. Osteo. Physicians and Surgeons. Intern, then resident Meml. Gen. Hosp., Union, N.J., 1980-82; gen. practice osteo. medicine Osteo. Family Physicians Ltd., Alexandria, Va., 1982—; staff attending physician Alexandria Hosp., Va., 1982—, Circle Terr. Hosp., Alexandria, 1982—, Nat. Hosp. for Orthopedics and Rehab., Arlington, Va., 1983—; clin. instr. Kirksville Coll. of Osteo. Medicine, 1984—. Served to capt. USAR, 1981—. Mem. Am. Osteo. Assn., Am. Coll. Gen. Practitioners (pres. Va. chpt. 1984-86), Va. Osteo. Med. Assn. (program chmn. 1984, 85, sec., treas. 1985-87), Washington Osteo. Assn. (v.p. 1984-85), Assn. Mil. Surgeons U.S. (medals 1985). Republican. Roman Catholic. Club: Mil. Dist. of Washington Officers. Lodge: Rotary. Avocations: oil painting, traveling. Office: Osteo Family Physicians Ltd 1225 Martha Custis Dr Suite C-7 Alexandria VA 22302

CHANG, PHILIP TUN YAU, architect; b. Canton, China, Sept. 19, 1936; came to U.S., 1959; s. Ngai Pak and Shui King Chang; m. Lily Kwan, May 1964; 1 child, Audrey. B.Sc. in Civil Engring., Chu Hai Coll., Hong Kong, 1958; B.Arch., Rice U., 1962, M.Arch., 1963. Cert. Nat. Council Archtl. Registration Bds. Designer, Aeck Assocs., Atlanta, 1962-71; chief designer Koetter, Tharp & Cowell, Architects, Houston, 1971-73; project designer Neuhaus & Taylor, Architects Houston, 1973-75; prin. Philip Chang Assocs., Architect, Houston, 1975—. Mem. AIA. Tau Sigma Delta. Roman Catholic. Home: 9218 Ilona Houston TX 77025 Office: 4660 Beechnut Houston TX 77096

CHANG, YUNG-KWANG, physicist, researcher; b. Linlin, Hunan, China, June 6, 1941; came to U.S., 1965, naturalized, 1976; s. Pao-Liang and Mei-Chen (Tsao) C.; m. Susan S.S. King, Mar. 19, 1967; children—Joseph, Daniel. B.S. in Physics, Nat. Taiwan U., 1964; M.A. in Physics, U. Oreg., 1968, Ph.D. in Physics, 1974. Postdoctoral fellow Argonne Nat. Lab., Ill., 1974-76; mem. research staff Oak Ridge Nat. Lab., 1976—; vis. physicist Kernforschungsanlage Julich, Fed. Republic Germany, 1981-82, 83. Contbr. articles on physics, crystal growth and instrumentation to profl. jours. Prin., Chinese Lang. Sch., Knoxville, Tenn., 1977-80, 82—. Mem. Am. Phys. Soc., Am. Assn. for Crystal Growth. Baptist. Office: Oak Ridge Nat Lab Solid State Div Bldg 2000 Oak Ridge TN 37831

CHAPLIN, JAMES PAUL, broadcast executive, writer; b. Lockport, N.Y., July 6, 1940; s. Raymond Joseph and Bonita (Kessler) C.; m. Starr Macfarland, May 1, 1965 (div.); 1 son, David; m. 2d, Patricia Maureen Needham, Sept. 2, 1967; children—Jennifer, Jessica, Lauren. Student Fredonia (N.Y.) State Tchrs. Coll. Actor as Bozo the Clown, announcer Sta. WSPD-TV, Toledo, 1969-72; music dir., announcer Sta. WSPD Radio, Toledo, 1972-73; music announcer Sta. WDAE Radio, Tampa, Fla., 1973-75; sales mgr. Sta. WOVV Radio, Ft. Pierce, Fla., 1976-78; v.p., sales mgr., dir. Indian River Broadcast Internat., Ft. Pierce, 1978-81; v.p., gen. mgr., dir. Roth Broadcasting, Inc., Ft. Pierce, 1981—1981-84; pres. Southwind Broadcastng, Inc., 1985—. Author: Psychic in the Devil's Triangle, 1975; Encounters in the Devil's Triangle, 1977. Candidate for mayor of Ft. Pierce, 1983; mem. Ft. Pierce Planning and Zoning Bd., 1983; pres. Indian Riverland YMCA, 1980-81, dir., 1977—. Named Sertoman of Yr., Sertoma Club St. Lucie County, 1980. Mem. Fla. Assn. Broadcasters (dir., v.p. for radio 1985-86, pres. 1986-87), Treasure Coast Advt. Fedn. (pres. 1980-81). Republican. Club: Ft. Pierce Exchange. Lodge: Ft. Pierce Rotary. Office: Southwind Broadcasting Inc PO Box 3032 Fort Pierce FL 33448

CHAPMAN, ALVAH HERMAN, JR., newspaper executive; b. Columbus, Ga., Mar. 21, 1921; s. Alvah Hermann and Wyline (Page) C.; B.S., The Citadel, 1942; m. Betty Bateman, Mar. 22, 1943; children—Dale Page Chapman Webb, Chris Ann Chapman Hilton. Bus. mgr. Columbus Ledger, 1945-53; v.p., gen. mgr. St. Petersburg (Fla.) Times, 1953-57; pres., pub. Morning News and Evening Press, Savannah, Ga., 1957-60; pres. Savannah News-Press, Inc., 1957-60; exec. Knight-Ridder Newspapers, Inc., Miami, Fla., 1960—, exec. com., 1960—, exec. v.p., 1967-73, pres., 1973-82, chief exec. officer, 1976—, chmn., 1982—; v.p., gen. mgr. Miami Herald, 1962-70, pres., 1970-82; lectr. Am. Press Insts., Columbia U. Served from 2d lt. to maj. USAAF, World War II. Decorated D.F.C. with 2 oak leaf clusters, Air medal with 5 clusters (U.S.); Croix de Guerre; named Dade County's Outstanding Citizen of 1968-69; recipient Bus. Leader of Yr. award, 1980; Sand in My Shoes award Greater Miami C. of C., 1982; named Internat. Businessman of Year, Brigham Young U., 1984. Mem. Am., So. newspapers pubs. assns. Methodist. Home: 4255 Lake Rd Miami FL 33137 Office: Miami Herald 1 Herald Plaza Miami FL 33101

CHAPMAN, HOWARD REED, city and county transportation engineer, consultant; b. Dayton, Ohio, Aug. 3, 1946; s. Roy Howard and Elvira Evelyn (Riccio) C.; m. Rosemary O'Donohue, Dec. 7, 1968; children—Lara, Amy, Jennifer, Gregory. B.S.C.E., Va. Mil. Inst., 1968; M.E., U. S.C., 1970. Registered profl. engr. S.C., Fla. Engr. Va. Dept. Hwys., Richmond, 1968; project engr. Wilbur Smith & Assocs., Columbia, S.C., 1968-70; asst. dir. Charleston (S.C.) Dept. Traffic and Transp., 1970-71, dir., 1971-77; city engr. and chief transp. div. City of Boca Raton (Fla.), 1977; dir. Dept. Traffic and Transp., Charleston, 1978—; cons. Charleston County, Town of Mt. Pleasant, S.C.; guest lectr. U. S.C., Clemson, U., Coll. of Charleston. Mem. exec. com. Palmetto Safety Council, 1974-81, treas., 1982-83, v.p., 1984-85. Served to lt. USAFR, 1968-70. Mem. Nat. Soc. Profl. Engrs., Inst. Transp. Engrs. (M.J. Hensley Outstanding Individual Activity award, so. sect. 1982, Transp. Engr. of Yr. S.C. div. 1983; sec.-treas. so. sect. 1983-84, v.p. 1984-85, pres. 1985—), ASCE, Kappa Alpha. Roman Catholic. Home: 1254 Oldwanus Dr Mt Pleasant SC 29464 Office: 180 Lockwood Dr Ext Charleston SC 29403

CHAPMAN, HUGH MCMASTER, banker; b. Spartanburg, S.C., Sept. 11, 1932; s. James Alfred and Martha (Marshall) C.; B.S. in Bus. Adminstrn., U. N.C., 1955; m. Anne Allston Morrison, Dec. 27, 1958; children—Anne Allston, Rachel Buchanan, Mary Morrison. With Citizens & So. Nat. Bank S.C., 1958—, asst. pres., Columbia, 1968-71, pres., 1971-74, chmn. bd., 1974—, also dir.; chmn. bd. C & S Corp., 1974—. Mem. S.C. Commn. on Higher Edn.,

1971-75. Trustee, Benedict Coll., Columbia, S.C. Found. Ind. Colls., Com. for Econ. Devel., Duke Endowment; ruling elder Presbyn. Ch. Served to 1st lt. USAF, 1955-57. Named Distinguished Eagle Scout, Palmetto council Boy Scouts Am., 1972. Mem. S.C. Bankers Assn. (pres. 1976-77), Zeta Psi. Club: Augusta Nat. Golf. Home: 5033 Wittering Dr Columbia SC 29206 Office: PO Box 727 Columbia SC 29222

CHAPMAN, JAMES, congressman; b. Mar. 8, 1945. B.B.A., U. Tex.; J.D., So. Methodist U. Dist. atty. State of Tex., 1977-85; mem. 99th Congress from 1st Tex. Dist. Office: US Ho of Reps Washington DC 20515

CHAPMAN, JOHN ANDREW, organization executive; b. Evanston, Ill., Oct. 12, 1928; s. Roger Edington and Margaret Holloway (Morgan) C.; m. Betsy Ann Miller, June 23, 1951; children—Andrew Kern, Jean Goodwin Ostrand, Margaret Miller, Peter Stark. B.S., Northwestern U., 1950. Cert. chamber exec. Asst. dir. pub. recreation Northwestern U., Evanston, Ill., 1950-54; asst. mgr. C. of C., Joliet, Ill., 1954-57, exec. v.p., Benton Harbor, Mich., 1957-67, pres., Muskegon, Mich., 1967-74, Charleston, W.Va., 1974—. Com. chmn. Salvation Army, Charleston, 1980-82, Goodwill Industries, Charleston, 1982—. Served with USAF, 1951-52. Mem. Am. C. of C. Execs. (bd. dirs. 1981-84), So. C. of C. Execs. (bd. dirs. 1985—), W.Va. C. of C. Execs. (pres. 1977-78). Republican. Episcopalian. Clubs: Edgewood Country, Anvil (sec. 1977—) (Charleston). Avocations: Canadian coins; Canada. Office: Charleston Chamber of Commerce 818 Virginia St E Charleston WV 25301

CHAPMAN, JOSEPH, advt. mgr.; b. Saltville, Va., June 15, 1936; s. Lawrence Allen and Kansas Sarah Chapman; m. Wanda Faye Barnett, Dec. 20, 1957; 1 dau., Donna Jo. Artist, Newspaper Agy. Corp., Charleston, W.Va., 1959-60; pictorial artist, designer Stanford Signs Inc., Bluefield, W.Va., 1960-67; elec. sign designer Allen Displays, Inc., Greensboro, N.C., 1967-72; prodn. artist Allen Wendt & Assos., Charlotte, N.C., 1972-73; advt. dir. retail div. Salem Carpets, Winston-Salem, N.C., 1973-79; advt. coordinator N.Y. Carpet World, Winston-Salem, 1979-80; advt. mgr. Nat. of Lexington (N.C.), 1980—; adv. com. comml. art Guilford Tech. Inst., 1970-72. Served with U.S. Army, 1957-59. Mem. Piedmont Triad Advt. Fedn. (treas. 1977-78, dir. 1979). Home: 2424 Smithwick Rd Kernersville NC 27284 Office: 400 National Blvd Lexington NC 27292

CHAPMAN, MARY LOUISE SHIPPY SHARPNACK, school headmaster; b. Brownsville, Pa., Mar. 11, 1926; d. Clarence Bugher and Flora Messmore (McCune) Sharpnack; m. Donald E. Chapman, Sept. 16, 1950; children—Mary Beth Chapman McLeod, Laura McCune. B.A., Mt. Union Coll., 1948; M.A., Middle Tenn. State U., 1961; S.T.M., U. of South, 1978; D.Min., U. of South/Vanderbilt U., 1980. Office mgr. Brantzen & Kluge, N.Y.C., 1950-52; tchr. aeros. and sci. St. Andrew's Sch., Tenn., 1954-70; tchr. math. St. Mary's; head dept. sci. Augusta Prep. Sch., Ga., 1970-79, headmaster, 1979—. Lt. col. CAP, past dir. cadets Ga. Wing, past squadron comdr. Mem. Ga. Assn. Ind. Schs. (bd. dirs. 1983—; Disting. Teaching award 1979), Mid.-South Assn. Ind. Schs. (bd. dirs. 1983—), Alpha Chi Omega. Episcopalian. Contbr. articles to profl. jours. Home: 111 Aiken Rd Graniteville SC 29829 Office: Augusta Prep Sch PO Box 4690 Martinez Augusta GA 30907

CHAPMAN, NETTLES FORD, JR., oil well drilling contractor; b. Indianola, Miss., Nov. 6, 1909; s. Nettles Ford and Ara Montaque (Sutton) C.; m. Geraldine Athena Layton, Feb. 15, 1945; children—Martha, Scott. Student Schreiner Inst., 1925-28, Sun Flower Jr. Coll., 1928-29. Contractor in oil well drilling, ind. producer, Midland, Tex., 1945—. Chmn. County Republican Com., 1956-64; del. nat. convs., 1956; v.p. Permian Basin Petroleum Mus., 1974—. Served with U.S. Army, 1941-45. Named Disting. Alumnus, Schreiner Coll., 1980; inducted into permian Basin Petroleum Mus. Hall of Fame, 1981. Mem. Internat. Assn. Drilling Contractors, Mid-Continent Oil and Gas Assn., Permian Basin Petroleum Assn. (pres. 1969-70), Tex. Ind. Oil Products Assn. Republican. Presbyterian. Clubs: Midland Country, Midland Petroleum. Discoverer Chapman Field, 1948, Ken Regan Field, 1951, Ford Field, 1956 (all Reeves County, Tex.), Geraldine Field, Culbertson County, Tex., 1957. Home: 2004 Humble Ave Midland TX 79705 Office: 430 Claydesta St Midland TX 79705

CHAPMAN, RAYBURN KEITH, accountant; b. Carthage, Tex., Jan. 24, 1952; s. Grady Chapman and Jean (Smith) Brannon; m. Lacy Lane Thomas, June 1, 1974; children—Keric, Amanda. B.B.A., U. Tex., 1974. C.P.A., Tex. Staff acct. Touche Ross & Co., Dallas, 1974-77; asst. treas. So. Baptist Annuity Bd., Dallas, 1977-79; acct. Fox Byrd & Co., Dallas, 1979-81; ptnr. Chapman, Robinson & Co., Carthage, 1981—. Mem. Am. Inst. C.P.A.s, Tex. Soc. C.P.A.s, Panola County C. of C. (pres.), Panola County Indsl. Devel. Found., Carthage Downtown Devel. Found. Republican. Baptist. Lodge: Lions. Office: 309 W Sabine St Carthage TX 75633

CHAPMAN, RICHARD DRAKE, university administrator, psychology educator, consultant; b. Ogdensburg, N.Y., Feb. 8, 1947; s. Harold Frederick and Marion (Drake) C. B.A., Hamilton Coll., 1969; Ph.D., U. Va., 1975. Counselor SUNY, 1970-80; dir. univ. counseling service, lectr. psychology U. of South, Sewanee, Tenn., 1980—. Active various regional and local health planning activities and orgns. Mem. Assn. for Study Higher Edn., Am. Assn. for Counseling and Devel., Am. Psychol. Assn., Am. Coll. Health Assn., Nat. Assn. Student Personnel Adminstrs., Am. Assn. for Higher Edn., Mensa, Phi Delta Kappa, Alpha Delta Phi. Republican. Baptist. Clubs: Walden, Ecce Quam Bonum. Avocations: football officiating, parliamentary procedure. Home: Mississippi Ave Sewanee TN 37375 Office: U of South SPO 1238 Sewanee TN 37375

CHAPMAN, ROBERT FOSTER, federal judge; b. Inman, S.C., Apr. 24, 1926; s. James Alfred and Martha (Marshall) C.; B.S., U. S.C., 1945, LL.B., 1949; m. Mary Winston Gwathmey, Dec. 21, 1951; children—Edward, Foster, Winston. Admitted to S.C. bar, 1949; assoc. firm Butler & Moore, Spartanburg, 1949-51; partner firm Butler, Chapman & Morgan, Spartanburg, 1953-71; U.S. dist. judge for S.C., 1971-81; judge U.S. Ct. Appeals (4th cir.), 1981—. Chmn. S.C. Republican Party, 1961-63. Served to lt. USNR, 1943-46, 51-53. Fellow Am. Coll. Trial Lawyers. Presbyn. (ruling elder). Home: 1822 Fair St Camden SC 29020 Office: Federal Court House Columbia SC 29202

CHAPPELL, BARBARA KELLY, child welfare consultant; b. Columbia, S.C., Oct. 17, 1940; d. Arthur Lee and Katherine (Martin) Kelly; 1 child, Kelly Katherine. B.A. in English and Edn., U. S.C., 1962, M.S.W., 1974. Cert. secondary tchr., Hawaii, Tex.; cert. social worker, S.C. Tchr. English, Leilehua and Radford High Schs., Honolulu, 1962-65, Alamo Heights High Sch., San Antonio, 1965-67; caseworker Dept. Social Services, Columbia, 1969-70; supr. Juvenile Placement and Aftercare, Columbia, 1970-72; cons. child welfare Edna McConnell Clark Found., N.Y., 1974-75; dir. Children's Foster Care Rev. Bd. System, Columbia, 1975-85; pvt. child welfare cons., 1985—; founder first citizen foster care rev. bd. system in country, 1974; condr. numerous confs. and seminars throughout U.S. Author child welfare articles; coordinator A Child's Rights to Parents, Columbia, 1970-75. Episcopalian. Home and Office: 3215 Girardeau Ave Columbia SC 29204

CHAPPELL, MOSES ELLSWORTH, JR., diversified company executive; b. Texarkana, Tex., Jan. 3, 1911; s. Moses Ellsworth and Eugenia (Buchanan) C.; m. Mary Catherine Sloan, June 13, 1932; 1 dau., Gretchen Kay. B.S., Tex. Christian U., 1931, M.A., 1932. C.P.A., Tex. Chief acct. Marvin D. Evans Co., Ft. Worth, 1935-47; ptnr. R.A. Moore & Co., Ft. Worth, 1947-50; v.p. Bass Bros. Enterprises, Inc. and assoc. cos., Ft. Worth, 1950-76; v.p., dir. Sid W. Richardson Found., Ft. Worth, 1963—; dir. Mel Wheeler, Inc., Denton, Tex. Mem. Am. Soc. C.P.A.s, Tex. Soc. C.P.A.s. Presbyterian. Clubs: Ridglea Country; Petroleum (dir. 1953-58, pres. 1955) (Ft. Worth).

CHAPPELL, WILLIAM V., JR., congressman, lawyer; b. Kendrick, Fla., Feb. 3, 1922; s. William Venroe and Laura C.; children—Judy Chappell Gadd, Deborah Chappell Bond, William V. III, Christopher. B.A., U. Fla., 1974, LL.B., 1949, J.D., 1967, D.Aero. Law, Embry-Riddle Aero. U., 1977; LLD. (hon.), Flagler Coll., 1978. Bar: Fla. Sole practice; county pros. atty., 1950-54; mem. Fla. Ho. of Reps., 1954-65, 66-68, speaker, 1961-63; mem. congresses from 4th Fla. Dist.; mem. appropriations com., ranking majority mem. def. subcom., mem. energy and water and mil. constrn. subcoms. Past v.p. Marion County Young Democrats. Recipient Allen Morris awards Most Valuable Mem. of House and Most Effective in Debate, Disting. Service award Ams. for Constn. Action, Statesman citation Am. Conservative Union, Watch Dog of Treasury award Nat. Assoc. Small Bus. Men, Guardian of Small Bus. citation Nat. Fedn. Ind. Bus., Commendation award Fla. Wildlife Fedn. and Nat. Wildlife Fedn., 19—, Triple-E citation Nat. Environ. Devel. Assn. Mem. Am. Legion, Res. Officers Assn., VFW, Fraternal Order Police, Am. Assn. Ret. Persons, Nat. Assn. Retired Fed. Employees, SCV, ABA, Am. Trial Lawyers Assn., Fla. Bar, Blue Key. Lodges: Lions, Elks, Moose, Masons, Shriners. Methodist. Office: 2468 Rayburn House Office Bldg Washington DC 20515

CHAR, WASHINGTON TIENTSIN, structural engineer, consultant; b. Honolulu, Aug. 26, 1924; s. Yew and Helen Mow C.; m. Rose Lum, Aug. 1, 1948; children—Karen, Dexter, Jill, Orrin. B.S.C.E., Washington U., St. Louis, 1949; M.S.C.E., Ga. Inst. Tech., 1950; M.B.A., St. Louis U., 1961. Registered profl. engr., Hawaii. Chief structural engr. U.S. Army C.E., Honolulu, 1951-54, gen. engr., Liverno, Italy, 1954-59; project mgr. Lublin, McGaughy and Assocs., Honolulu, 1961-63; dep. Air Force regional engr. USAF, Taiwan, Thailand, 1963-70; chief structural engr. U.S. Army C.E., Huntsville, Ala., 1970-84; cons. State Farm Ins., 1983-85; lectr. U. Ala., 1983-85. Served to lt. USAF, 1950. Named Engr. of Yr., Nat. Soc. Profl. Engrs. and ASCE, 1978; Achievement award Soc. Am. Mil. Engrs., 1977. Mem. ASCE (past pres.), Am. Concrete Inst., Soc. Am. Mil. Engrs. (past pres.). Republican. Methodist. Club: Huntsville (Ala.) Athletic.

CHARDKOFF, RICHARD BRUCE, history educator; b. Chgo., Mar. 20, 1940; s. Moses Austin and Naomi Wexler C.; m. Joan Roslyn Corb, June 7, 1944; children—Deena Michelle, Leslie Nicole. Assoc. dir. C.Z. br. Fla. State U., Panama, 1967-69; assoc. prof. history Radford (Va.) Coll., 1969-71; prof. history, dir. gen. studies curricula, dir. developmental edn. N.E. La. U., Monroe, 1971—; mem. rev. panel for submission proposals NEH, 1982-83; mem. La. Exec. Com. for Humanities, 1975—. Trustee, Monroe Little Theater. Fla. State U. grad. research fellow, 1966; Exxon Faculty Forum fellow, 1975; NEH grantee, 1972, 73, 74. Mem. Conf. Latin Am. History, S.W. Social Sci. Assn., Southeastern Conf. of Latin Americanists, Pi Sigma Alpha, Phi Alpha Theta. Club: Lions (Monroe). Lodge: Masons. Contbr. articles to profl. jours.

CHARLES, BALLENGER EUGENE, power company executive; b. Sneads, Fla., July 5, 1923; s. Lee and Mattie Charles; m. Carolyn McDonald; children—Ballenger E., Jr., Terry L. A.A., Chipola Jr. Coll., 1953; student Internat. Corr. Sch., 1954-57. Metalsmith, J.S. Walters, 1947-49; yard clk. A.C.L. RR, 1951-53; with Gulf Power Co., 1953—, plant supr., 1965-76, supr. ops., 1976-81, generating plant safety and tng. supr., 1981—. Chmn. Ala. and West Fla. council Boy Scouts Am.; mem. Nat. Congress PTA, Fla. Sch. Bd. Assn., Apalachee Correctional Inst.; past city councilman Sneads; past bd. dirs. Chipola Jr. Coll.; mem. Jackson County Bd. Pub. Instrn.; mem. Fla. Regional Corrections Adv. Council. Ch. Served with USN, World War II. Mem. Sneads High Sch. Alumni Assn., Chipola Jr. Coll. Alumni Assn. Methodist. Lodge: Masons. Home: PO Box 216 Sneads FL 32460

CHARLES, BRONSON HIGH, artist; b. Ft. Worth, Sept. 16, 1923; d. Thomas Russell and Lettie J. (Milner) High; m. Henry Lee Charles, Oct. 18, 1973; children by previous marriage—Thomas Randall Black, Suzanne Douglas Black, Warren Mitchell Black, Nancy Leigh Black. B.F.A., Tex. Christian U., 1944; M.F.A., U. Tex.-Dallas, 1983. Advt. mgr. various dept. stores, Dallas, Tulsa, 1956-67; free lance artist/illustrator, Chgo., Dallas, 1967-69; account exec. Glass Hughes Advt., Dallas, 1969-70, W.W. Sherrill Advt., Dallas, 1970-71. One woman shows in oil portraits include Williams Center, Tulsa, Okla. Trails Gallery, San Antonio, Eagles Nest Gallery, Dallas, Dallas Communications Complex, Menasco Galleries, Shreveport, La., Barrington, Ill. Art Assn., Portraits South, Raleigh, N.C., Am. Soc. Portrait Artists; commissioned portraits include: V.P. George Bush, W. Herbert Hunt family, Dallas, Gary Adams and Buddy Parker families, Tulsa, Dr. Robert Plant Armstrong, Dallas, Dallas Cowboy football players. Active in fund-raising Am. Diabetes Assn., Dallas, 1984, Am. Cancer Soc., Dallas, 1980. Recipient 1st place art-oils, Am. Psychiatric Assn., 1985. Mem. Artists and Craftsmen Assoc., Am. Soc. Portrait Artists. Salagundi Club, Assemblage, Portrait Club of N.Y., D-Art, Am. Psychiatric Aux. Art Assn. (chpt. pres. 1983-84, nat. pres. 1983-84). Address: 3831 Turtle Creek 2C Dallas TX 75219

CHARLES, JEFFREY MARK, toxicologist; b. N.Y.C., Aug. 19, 1951; s. Lall and Bernice Selma (Goldstein) C.; m. Linda Ann Ryan, July 5, 1969; 1 son, Robert Andrew. B.A. in Biology and Chemistry, U. Va., 1973; Ph.D. in Physiology and Pharmacology, Duke U., 1976. Diplomate Am. Bd. Toxicology. NIH postdoctoral fellow in toxicology dept. pharmacology, Duke U., Durham, N.C., 1976-77; team leader Toxic Effects Br., EPA, Research Triangle Park, N.C., 1977-79; toxicologist agrl. div. CIBA-Geigy Corp., Greensboro, N.C., 1979-81, staff toxicologist, 1981-83; toxicologist Union Carbide Agrl. Products Co., Research Triangle Park, 1983—. NIH fellow, 1973-76. Mem. Soc. Toxicology, Am. Coll. Toxicology, Am. Indsl. Hygiene Assn., Am. Chem. Soc., Sigma Xi. Contbr. articles to profl. jours. Office: Union Carbide Agrl Products Co PO Box 12014 Research Triangle Park NC 27709

CHARLES, JOHN FRANKLYN, marriage and family therapist, clergyman; b. St. Paul's, Antigua, W.I., Sept. 10, 1937; came to U.S., 1978; s. Christopher Cornelius and Celestine Rebecca (James) C.; m. Delpha Louista Buntin, Dec. 19, 1982. B.Div., U. London, 1976; M.S.Ed., U. Miami, Fla., 1979, Ed.S., 1981; Ph.D., Calif. Coast Coll., 1985. Ordained to ministry United Methodist Ch., 1974. Tchr. Grammar Sch., St. John's, Antiqua, 1959-67; chaplain, tutor Wesley Coll., Belize City, Belize, 1971-72; minister religion Meth. Ch., W.I., Road Town, 1972-78; vocat. counselor CETA, U. Miami, Coral Gables, Fla., 1980-82; psychometrist, psychologist Consortium, Miami, 1981-85; marriage therapist Charles' Cons. Bur., Miami, 1983—; assessor Magistrate Ct., Brit. V.I., 1976-78; cons. Corrections Ctr., Miami, 1980-81. Mem. U.S. Presdl. Task Force, 1984; pres. Gideons Internat., Antigua, 1962-67. Meth. Conf. scholar, 1968; U. Miami grantee, 1980. Mem. Am. Assn. Counseling and Devel., Fla. Assn. Counseling and Devel. Avocations: travel; swimming; yoga; table tennis; international affairs. Office: PO Box 248631 Miami FL 33124

CHARLES, MICHAEL HARRISON, architectural interior designer; b. Fort Lauderdale, Fla., Feb. 8, 1952; s. Melvin Mowrer and Ann (Cookus) C. B.A., U. Fla., 1976; A.S., Fla. Jr. Coll., 1982. Cert. Nat. Council Interior Design. Ptnr., v.p. St. Johns Lighting Design, St. Augustine, Fla., 1978-81; archtl. interior designer KBJ Architects, Inc., Jacksonville, Fla., 1982—; owner Michael H. Charles Assocs., Cons., St. Augustine, 1984—. Mem. Inst. Bus. Designers (regional dir.), Am. Soc. Interior Designers, AIA (affiliate), SCW, SR, Colonial Soc. Pa., SAR (state v.p. 1982—). Republican. Episcopalian. Clubs: Ponte Vedra (Fla.); Seminole (Jacksonville). Avocation: genealogy. Home: 18 Carrera St Saint Augustine FL 32084 Office: KBJ Architects 510 Julia St Jacksonville FL 32202

CHARLES, RONALD ALLAN, businessman, educator; b. N.Y.C., Feb. 20, 1944; s. Norman B. and Louise (Roscoe) C. B.A., The Citadel, 1965, M.A., 1976, M.Ed., 1983; Ph.D., U. S.C., 1978. Cert. examiner Nat. Bd. Judo Examiners. Tchr. English, East-West Cultural Inst., Tokyo; tutor English dept. Chiba Inst. Tech. (Japan), 1968-69; tchr. world history, econ. and world geography North Charleston High Sch. (S.C.), 1975-76; instr. Coll. Edn. U. S.C., 1976-77, grad. asst., 1977-78; instr. Program for Afloat Coll. Edn., U. S.C., 1978-79; resident dir. Fla. State U. On-Shore Edn. Program, Charleston, S.C., 1979-80; founder, dir. Samurai Judo Assn., Goose Creek, 1980—; pres. S.C. Judo, Inc., Goose Creek, S.C., 1981—; coach The Citadel Judo Team, Charleston, 1979-80; instr. Brentwood Bushi Dojo Judo Club. Pres., Brentwood Middle Sch. Adv. council, 1981—. Served with U.S. Army, 1966-68. Recipient Best Poem award The Crucible, 1977; Best Judged Bicentennial Poem, Alumni News, 1976. Mem. Nat. Council Social Studies, Coll. and Univ. Faculty Assembly, NEA, Eastern Ednl. Research Assn. (affective edn. spl. interest group), S.C. Edn. Assn., S.C. Council for Social Studies, Charleston County Edn. Assn., Profl. Assn. Diving Instrs. (master), Mensa (chpt. pres. 1983—), Phi Delta Kappa. Author: In Our Own Way, 1965; editor The Shako, 1964-65; contbr. articles and numerous poems to lit. jours. Home and Office: 113 Camellia Rd Goose Creek SC 29445

CHARLSON, GEORGE WAYNE, aerospace company administrator; b. Camp Forrest, Tenn., Oct. 28, 1943; s. George Samuel and Virginia E. (Anderson) C. A.A., Cameron State U., 1964; B.S. in Fin., Okla. State U., 1966; cert. in Govt. Contract Mgmt., UCLA, 1973; M.S. in Mgmt., Troy State U., 1977. Commd. officer U.S. Army, 1966, advanced through ranks to maj., 1982, logistics engr. Martin Marietta Aerospace Co., Orlando, Fla., 1978-80, subcontract adminstr., 1980-82, program material rep. to critical procurement adminstr., 1982-83, sr. program rep., 1983—. Decorated Bronze Star medal, Army Commendation medal, Army Commendation medal with oak leaf. Mem. Delta Sigma Pi, Phi Theta Kappa. Republican. Lutheran. Avocation: scuba diving. Home: 4725 Chevy Pl Orlando FL 32811

CHARLTON, GORDON TALIAFERRO, JR., clergyman; b. San Antonio, Sept. 29, 1923; s. Gordon Taliaferro and Enid Lynn (Jones) C.; m. Landon Cutler Crump, Dec. 23, 1948; children—Virginia Ellen, David Holland, Frank Duncan. B.A., U. Tex., 1944; M. Div., Va. Theol. Seminary, 1949, D.D. (hon.), 1974. Ordained priest Episcopal Ch., 1949; rector St. Matthew's Ch., Fairbanks, Alaska, 1951-54, Christ Ch., Mexico City, 1958-63, St. Andrew's Ch., Wilmington, Del., 1963-67; personnel sec. overseas dept. Nat. Episcopal Ch., 1954-58; asst. dean Va. Theol. Seminary, 1967-73; dean Episc. Theol. Seminary Southwest, 1973-82; bishop suffragan Episc. Diocese Tex., Houston, 1982. Served with USN, 1943-46.

CHARLTON, MARGARET ELLEN JONSSON, civic worker; b. Dallas, Aug. 7, 1938; d. John Erik and Margaret Elizabeth (Fonde) Jonsson; student Skidmore Coll., 1956-57, So. Meth. U., 1957-60; children—Laura, Emily, Erik. Dir., Sta. KRLD, Dallas, 1970-74; 1st woman dir. First Nat. Bank Dallas (name now Interfirst Bank Dallas), 1976—, vice-chmn. dirs. trust com. First woman trustee Meth. Hosp., 1972-82, mem. exec. com., 1977-80; mem. corp. bd. Meth. Hosps. Dallas, 1980-82; pres. Jonsson Found.; bd. dirs., chmn. exec. com. Lamplighter Sch., 1967—; bd. dirs. Winston Sch., 1973-84; mem. adv. bd. Susan G. Komen Found. for Cancer Research, 1983—; bd. dirs., mem. exec. com. Episcopal Sch. Dallas, 1976-83; bd. dirs. Found. for Callier Center and Communication Disorders, 1967—, v.p., 1974—; mem. vis. com. dept. psychology MIT, 1978—; past chmn. Crystal Charity Ball; past bd. dirs. Children's Med. Center, Hope Cottage, Children's Bur., Baylor Dental Sch., Dallas Health and Sci. Mus., Dallas YWCA, Dallas Day Nursery Assn.; mem. vis. com. Stanford U. Libraries; hon. life trustee Dallas Mus. Art.; nat. adv. bd. Ctr. Strategic and Internat. Studies; pres. MIC Fund; mem. collectors' com. Nat. Gallery Art; mem. internat. council Mus. Modern Art. Margaret Jonsson Charlton Hosp. named in her honor, Dallas, 1973. Mem. Jr. League Dallas (sustaining). Republican. Clubs: Dallas Woman's, University (bd. govs.), Tower.

CHARLTON, NINA, petroleum landman; b. Hopkins County, Tex., Aug. 21, 1932; d. Dave E. and Lela May (Wofford) C.; ed. Sulphur Springs (Tex.) pub. schs. Cashier, bookkeeper Bealls Dept. Store, Sulphur Springs, 1949-52; clk. Lone Star Gas, Sulphur Springs, 1952-62; bookkeeper, teller City Nat. Bank, Sulphur Springs, 1962-70, receptionist, sec. to pres., 1965-70; credit clk. Portland Gen. Electric, Oregon City, Oreg., 1970; bookkeeper C.E. Wingo Feed Mill, Sulphur Springs, 1970-72; machine operator H.D. Lee Mfg. Co., Sulphur Springs, 1972; typist, clk., sec. M.C. Bailey Abstract Co., Sulphur Springs, 1972-74; abstracter Morris Abstract Co., Sulphur Springs, 1974-75; ind. landman for energy co., Sulphur Springs, 1975—. Mem. Am., E. Tex. assns. petroleum landmen. Baptist. Address: PO Box 8606 Tyler TX 75711

CHARSINSKY, KENNETH, geologist; b. Newark, Sept. 3, 1954; s. Isadore and Rae (Grossman) G. B.A., Kean Coll., 1975; M.S., Rensselaer Poly. Inst., 1976. Region ops. geologist Cities Service Oil & Gas Corp., Houston, 1977—. Mem. Am. Assn. Petroleum Geologists, Soc. Econ. Paleontologists and Mineralogists, Houston Geol. Soc. Avocations: fishing; basketball; music; theater; football. Home: 12326 Meadowdale Dr Meadows TX 77477 Office: Cities Service Oil & Gas Corp 1980 Post Oak Blvd (Poc II) Houston TX 77227

CHASE, GAYLORD RICHARD, JR., restaurant owner; b. Amarillo, Tex., Mar. 28, 1953; s. Frances (Schaer) C.; m. Lucia Caton Carter, July 17, 1976 (div. Jan. 1978); m. Margaret Anne Wallace, Oct. 6, 1979; 1 dau., Alexis Anne. B.A. in Polit. Sci., So. Meth. U., 1975. Account exec. KOLE Radio, Port Arthur, Tex., 1975-76; researcher, analyst Consumer Behavior Center, Dallas, 1976-79; sr. sales cons. TM Prodns., Dallas, 1979-81; dir. sta. relations Sunbelt Network, Dallas, 1981-82; account exec. KZZB Radio, Beaumont, Tex., 1982; co-owner Hoffbrau Steaks, Beaumont, Tex., 1982—, RK's Oyster Bar, Beamount, Tex. pres. ChaseM, Inc., Beaumont. Past pres. White Rock West Townhomes, Dallas. Mem. Gulf Coast Conservation Assn., Duncks Unlimited. Office: 2310 N 11th St Beaumont TX 77703

CHASE, HELEN CHRISTINA MATULIC, biostatistician, consultant; b. N.Y.C., Mar. 21, 1917; d. Jozef and Kristina (Gerwich) Matulic; m. Donald Frederick Chase, Jr., Nov. 5, 1942. A.B., Hunter Coll., 1938; M.S., Columbia U., 1951; D.P.H., U. Calif.-Berkeley, 1961. Unemployment ins. claims examiner N.Y. Labor Dept., Albany, 1939-48; biostatistician, then prin. biostatistician N.Y. Health Dept., Albany, 1948-63; health statistician, chief mortality stats. HEW, Washington, 1963-69, Medicare statistician, 1973-75, dep. chief epidemiologic studies Bur. Radiol. Health, Rockville, Md., 1975-80; cons., 1980—; lectr. Cath. U., Washington, 1966-76; dir. research Assn. Schs. Allied Health Professions, Washington, 1969-71; staff assoc. Nat. Acad. Scis., Washington, 1971-72. Columbia U. fellow, 1950-51; U. Calif.-Berkeley fellow, 1955-57. Fellow Am. Pub. Health Assn. (Lowell J. Reed award 1979), Am. Statis. Assn.; mem. Am. Epidemiol. Soc., Delta Omega. Presbyterian. Author: International Comparison of Infant, Perinatal and Early Childhood Mortality: United States and Six European Countries, 1967. Contbr. numerous articles to profl. jours. Home and Office: 3410 Stonehaven Ct E Palm Harbor FL 33563

CHASE, STEPHEN FOREST, periodontist; b. Chgo., Mar. 11, 1943; s. Edward George and Theresa (Zechman) C.; m. Donna Addison, Jan. 24, 1983; children—Debra Lauren, Emily Joy. Grad., U. Fla., 1964; D.D.S., Med. Coll. Va., 1968; Cert. in periodontology Boston U., 1970. Practice dentistry specializing in periodontics, Miami, Fla., 1972—; guest lectr. in field. Served to capt. U.S. Army, 1970-72. Mem. Am. Acad. Periodontics, ADA, Fla. Dental Assn. Avocations: jogging; snow skiing; sailing; fishing. Office: Abel and Chase DDS PA 7600 Red Rd Miami FL 33143

CHASKIN, MEL, research and development executive; b. N.Y.C., June 19, 1941; s. Albert B. and Annette C.; B.S., NYU, 1965; m. Mary G. Reifer, Aug. 29, 1965; children—Adam Scott, Marni Lyn. Software engr. Grumman Aircraft Enging. Corp., 1965-67; sr. system engr. ITT, 1967; system flight test pilot Lear Siegler, Inc., 1967-71; dep. dir., program mgr. USAF, 1971-73, dir. advanced space communications, 1973-77, acting dept. World-wide Mil. Command and Control System Enging., Office Sec. of Def., Washington, 1977-81; v.p., pres. Washington div. Horizons Tech., Inc., McLean, Va., 1981-84; pres. Vanguard Research, Inc., Fairfax, Va., 1984—. Mem. Pres.'s Mgmt. Improvement Council, 1980-81; pres. Gt. Falls PTA, 1980-82. Mem. Air Force Assn., Armed Forces Communications and Electronics Assn. Republican. Jewish. Club: Optimists (dir. Great Falls). Home: 10305 Brandenburg Ct Great Falls VA 22066 Office: 2810 Old Lee Hwy Suite 200 Fairfax VA 22031

CHASTAIN, DAVID LEE, JR., medical technologist; b. Tuscaloosa, Ala., Nov. 15, 1943; s. David Lee and Ozelle (Smith) C.; A.A., Polk Jr. Coll., Winter Haven, Fla., 1970; B.S., Fla. So. Coll., 1971; M.T., Orange Meml. Hosp. Sch. Med. Tech., 1972; m. Kiyoko Matsumoto, Dec. 7, 1965; 1 son, Stephen Herrick. Chief technologist Damon Med. Labs., Inc., North Miami Beach, Fla., 1972-73; asst. mgr. automated chemistry dept. Coulter Diagnostics, Inc., Hialeah, Fla., 1973-75; dir. research and devel. BioMed. Products Corp., Ft. Lauderdale, Fla., 1975-76; research assoc. Coulter Electronics, Inc., Hialeah, 1976-80; med. lab. technologists, evening supt. Cypress Community Hosp., Pompano Beach, Fla., 1980-83; sr. scientist Coulter Diagnostics, Hialeah, 1983—. Served with Med. Service Corps, U.S. Army, 1962-68; Korea, Japan, Vietnam. Lic. clin. lab. supr., Fla. Mem. Am. Med. Technologists, Am. Soc. for Med. Tech., Am. Soc. Clin. Pathologists, AAAS, Am. Chem. Soc., N.Y. Acad. Scis. Patentee in field. Home: 1137 NW 19th Ave Fort Lauderdale FL 33311 Office: Coulter Diagnostics Hialeah FL

CHASTAIN, MERRITT BANNING, JR., lawyer; b. Shreveport, La., Jan. 28, 1940; s. Merritt Banning and Lydia (Spock) C.; m. Virginia Anne Ferguson, July 21, 1962; children—Merritt Banning III, Grayson Anne. B.S., U. Okla., 1962; J.D., La. State U., 1967. Bar: La. 1967, U.S. Dist. Ct. (we. dist.) La. 1968, U.S. Dist. Ct. (ea. dist.) La. 1972, U.S. Ct. Appeals (5th cir.) 1972, U.S. Supreme Ct. 1979. Law clk. La. Ct. Appeals (2d cir.), Shreveport, 1967-68; assoc. Smitherman, Lunn, Chastain & Hill Shreveport, 1968-72, ptnr., 1972—; mng. dir. Nat. Assn. Pipe Coating Applicators, 1979—; spl. counsel La. Pub. Facilities Authority, 1985—. Dir., sec. United Mercantile Bank, Shreveport, 1981—. Chmn. United Way of Shreveport/Bossier City, 1975; pres. Vols. Am., 1976, Norwela council Boy Scouts Am., 1977-78, Ark.-La.-Tex. Tax Inst., 1977; exec. v.p. Shreveport Symphony Soc., 1981; bd. dirs. Shreveport Opera,

1981—, sec., 1981—; trustee Loyola Coll. Prep. Sch., 1984—, exec. com., 1985. Served to 1st lt. U.S. Army, 1962-64. Named Outstanding Young Man of La., La. Jaycees, 1975, Outstanding Young Man of Shreveport, Shreveport Jaycees, 1975. Mem. ABA (La. mem. chmn. 1976-82), La. State Bar Assn. (spl. com. 1974-75), Shreveport Bar Assn., (exec. council 1971-75, sec.-treas. 1972, bd. govs. young lawyer's sect. 1967-74, pres. young lawyer's sect. 1974). Democrat. Episcopalian. Clubs: Cambridge, University, Pierremont Oaks Tennis (Shreveport). Home: 330 Corinne Circle Shreveport LA 71106 Office: Smitherman Lunn Chastain & Hill 717 Comml Nat Bank Bldg Shreveport LA 71101

CHASTAIN, WAYNE HOLT, health care company executive; b. Jacksonville, Fla., Sept. 3, 1934; s. Eugene C. and Elinor (Bennett) C.; m. Kay Fenn, Dec. 27, 1956; children—Wendy, Dane, Brett. B.A., Stetson U., 1956; postgrad. Wake Forest U., 1958-59. Dir. Camp Ridgecrest for Boys, Ashville, N.C., 1959-64; bus. cons., 1965-67; dir. mgmt. services BSSB Corp., Nashville, 1967-81; pres., founder, chief exec. officer Medinc Co., Nashville, 1981—; also dir.; dir. Mgmt. Inc., Nashville, I corp., Nashville, 1984—, Horizon Films, Nashville; creator, tchr. of AretÉ seminars, 1981—. Served with USN, 1956-57. Mem. Am. Mgmt. Assn., Fin. Exec. Inst., Inst. Fin. Analysts (past pres.). Democrat. Baptist. Lodge: Rotary. Avocations: jogging, reading, scuba diving, snow skiing. Home: Five Coves Route 3 Gallatin TN 37066 Office: Medinc 230 Great Circle Dr Nashville TN 37228

CHASTEEN, RICHARD STEPHEN, contractor, former army officer; b. Louisville, Oct. 7, 1955; s. Doyle William and Serena Jan (Conn) C.; m. Shelley Renee Bettis, Apr. 5, 1980. B.S.Ed. cum laude, U. Ga., 1978. Commd. 2d lt. U.S. Army, 1978, advanced through grades to capt., 1978; exec. officer hdqrs. command, Ft. McPherson, Ga., 1978-80, platoon leader Blackhawk Helicopter Platoon, 101st Aviation Bn., Ft. Campbell, Ky., 1980-82, bn. adj., 1983-84; gen. contractor, Lafayette, Ga., 1984—. Decorated Army Commendation medal. Mem. Army Aviation Assn. Am., Assn. U.S. Army, Nat. Rifle Assn., Zeta Beta Tau. Baptist.

CHATMAN, VERA ANN STEVENS, psychologist, researcher; b. Wilson, N.C., Sept. 7, 1948; d. Paul Lee Stevens and Bernetha (Pettiford) Morgan; m. James Evans Chatman, Mar. 29, 1975; children—Joi Stevens, Jamie Evette. B.A., Fisk U., 1966, M.A., 1972; Ph.D., George Peabody Coll., Vanderbilt U., 1976. Cert. sch. psychologist, Tenn. Sch. psychology intern Sumner County Bd. Edn., Gallatin, Tenn., 1974-75; asst. project dir. Community Mental Health Ctr., Meharry Med. Coll., Nashville, 1975-78, dir. research and eval., 1978-82, assoc. dir., 1982-84, project coordinator RWJ Hosp. Initiative, 1984—. Author: (manual) Everything You Wanted to Know About the CMHC But Was Afraid to Ask, 1982. Bd. dirs. Alive Hospice, Inc., 1974—, Tenn. Mental Health, 1980-84, Sr. Services Network, 1984—; mem. Mayoral Task Force, Nashville, 1984—; v.p. programming YWCA, Nashville, 1978; room parent U. Sch. Nashville Parent Aux., 1984. Recipient Humanitarian award DAV, Nashville, 1980, Outstanding Young Women Am. award, 1975; NIMH fellow. Mem. Am. Psychol. Assn., Assn. Gerontology Higher Edn., Gerontol. Soc. Am., Nat. Council Aging, Inc. Democrat. Baptist. Avocations: reading; computers. Home: 3817 Augusta Dr Nashville TN 37207 Office: Meharry Med Coll 1005 D B Todd Blvd Nashville TN 37208

CHATMON, LAVERNE GUICE, nurse; b. Birmingham, Ala., May 17, 1919; d. Thomas Jefferson and Minnie (Waters) G.; m. Warren Pete Chatmon, Mar. 23, 1939 (dec. 1968); children—Warren Pete, Gwendolyn Clarita Chatmon Corrin. Student Carraway Meth. Sch. Nursing, Birmingham. R.N., Ala. Supr., Stillman Hosp., Tuscaloosa, Ala., 1940-41; staff nurse Jefferson County Dept. Health, Birmingham, 1947—, health info. referral nurse, 1976—. Mem. Health Workers Assn., Chi Eta Phi (sec. 1980—). Democrat. Baptist. Clubs: 900 6th St. Block, 36'ers. Home: 947 6th St W Birmingham AL 35204 Office: Jefferson County Dept Health 1400 6th Ave S Birmingham AL 35233

CHAUVIN, WILLIAM DONOHUE, shrimp market analyst, association administrator; b. Houma, La., Apr. 8, 1937; s. John A. and Bertha M. (Aldrete) C.; m. Karen Chapman, Nov. 7, 1959; children—Elizabeth, Eric, Deanna, Stephanie. B.A., San Francisco State U., 1962. Exec. v.p. John A. Chauvin, Inc., Gretna, La., 1962-78; pres. Seafood Purchasing Dirs., Inc., New Orleans, 1978-79; pres. Shrimp Notes Inc., New Orleans, 1979—; exec. dir. Am. Shrimp Processors Assn., New Orleans, 1981—; pres. Shrimp World Inc., New Orleans, 1984—; mem. Gulf of Mex. Fishery Mgmt. Council, 1984—; mem. adv. com. Gulf States Marine Fisheries Commn., Nat. Fisheries Inst., Washington, Nat. Food Processors Assn., Inc. Contbr. articles to profl. jours. Home and Office: Shrimp Notes Inc 417 Eliza St New Orleans LA 70114

CHAVERS, DEAN, management consultant; b. Pembroke, N.C., Feb. 4, 1941; s. Luther C. and Dorothy M. (Godwin) C.; B.A., U. Calif., Berkeley, 1970; M.A., Stanford U., 1973, Ph.D., 1976; m. Antonia Navarro, Apr. 26, 1970; children—Cynthia Christine, Monica Lynn, Celia Ricarda. Asst. prof. Calif. State U., Hayward, 1972-74; pres. Indian Edn. Assocs. Palo Alto, Calif., 1975-77, Native Am. Scholarship Fund, Palo Alto, 1970-78; pres. Bacone Coll., Muskogee, Okla., 1978-81; mgmt. cons., Albuquerque, 1985—. Mem. com. on equal edni. opportunity Calif. Postsecondary Edn. Commn., 1977-78. Served to capt. USAF, 1963-68. Decorated D.F.C., Air medal. Ford Found. fellow. Mem. Nat. Congress Am. Indians, Internat. Communication Assn. Democrat. Baptist. Club: Rotary Internat. Mng. editor Indian Voice, 1971-73; contbr. articles to profl. jours. Address: 6709 Esther Ave NE Albuquerque NM 87109

CHÁVEZ-GARCÍA, SYLVIA, psychotherapist; b. San Antonio, Jan. 27, 1946; d. Manuel Gonzales and Carolina (Pena Padilla) Chavez; children—Rafael Robert, Miguel Antonio. B.A., Incarnate Word Coll., 1968; M.A., St. Mary's U., 1978; M.T.S., Oblate Sch. Theology, 1984; postgrad. Tex. A&M, 1987. Lic. profl. counselor; cert. social worker; advanced clin. practitioner. Tchr. Central Catholic Sch., San Antonio, 1968-69, Am. Sch., Monterrey, Mex., 1969-71; research assoc. Cardiovascular Research Inst., San Francisco, 1971-73; program coordinator Drug Awareness Ctr., San Antonio, 1979-83; tng. coordinator San Antonio Council on Alcoholism, 1984-85, project dir., 1985—; pvt. practice psychotherapy, San Antonio, 1978—. Bd. dirs. Bexar County Women's Shelter, San Antonio, 1981-85; mem. adv. bd. Omega Retreat Ctr., Boerne, Tex., 1978—; chmn. Family Life Commn., Archdiocese San Antonio, 1983-84. Mem. Assn. Christian Therapists, Community Catholic Counselors, Mental Health Counselors Assn., Assn. for Counseling and Devel., Tex. Conf. Chs. (mem. substance abuse prevention task force), Women's Ordination Conf. Democrat. Home: 4711 Trailwood San Antonio TX 78228 Office: San Antonio Council on Alcoholism 1222 N Main St Suite 406 San Antonio TX 78212

CHEATHAM, EUGENE RALPH, real estate company executive, computer service company executive; b. Oklahoma City, July 12, 1932; s. Eugene Ralph and Madeline E. (Brown) C.; m. Sylvia E. Gentner, Aug. 22, 1956 (div. Feb. 1970); children—Richard E., Kent M., Brad J., Jeff R., Mary E.; m. Mary Lee Johnson, June 23, 1971. B.S. in Chem. Engring., U. Okla., 1960; postgrad. U. St. Louis, 1962. Registered profl. engr., Okla.; lic. real estate broker, lic. ins. agt., Tex. Design engr. J.F. Pritchard Engring. Co., Kansas City, Mo., 1960-62; sales engr. Rockwell Internat., Kansas City, 1962-64; sr. sales engr. Taylor Instruments, Lakeland, Fla., 1964-71; mgr. instrumentation C.T. Main Co., Boston, 1972; pres. Paneltech, Ltd., Lakeland, Fla. and Houston, 1973—, Tejas Computer Services, Ltd., Houston, 1982—; pres. Home At Last Realty, Houston, 1986—; instrumentation cons.; staff mem. Engring. Socs. Commn. on Energy Task Force project Dept. Energy. Mem. Instrument Soc. Am., Houston Bd. Realtors, Microcomputer Users of Houston. Computer sci. editor West Houstonian; pub. Realtors Money Machine Newsletter. Home: 7635 Club Lake Dr Houston TX 77095 Office: PO Box 218070 Houston TX 77218

CHEATHEAM, O. NEWELL, building designer; b. Wichita Falls, Tex., Nov. 16, 1946; s. Llannis Denton and Irene (Cubine) C.; m. Sharon Kay Wilcox, June 29, 1978; children—Shawn, Candice, Crystal, Shannon. Student in architecture and biology Midwestern U., 1965-67, U. Houston, 1968-71; student Ahrens SW Sch. Real Estate, 1977. Comml. designer, store planner, designer J. Weingarten Inc., Houston, 1969-71; bldg. designer Keeper Co., 1973, Joe Laverge & Assoc., 1974; ins. salesman, fin. planner Lincoln Nat. Life Ins. Co., 1974-75; sr. assoc., bldg. designer Charles Smith & Assoc., 1976-78; pres., owner Newell's Designs, Inc., Houston, 1972—; ins. salesman, fin. planner A.L. Williams rep. Mass. Indemnity & Life Ins. Co. Pres., Mason Rd. Improvement Assn., 1979-81. Mem. Katy C. of C., Katy Area Jaycees (v.p. 1978, numerous awards), West Houston C. of C. (govt. affairs com.), Nat. Assn. Homebuilders, Greater Houston Homebuilders Assn. (assoc. council), Tex. Inst. Bldg. Design (bd. dirs., Design award 1978-82), Am. Inst. Bldg. Design, AIA, Tex. Inst. Architects. Republican. Baptist. Avocations: Fishing; duck and goose hunting; camping; bow hunting. Office: Newells Designs Inc PO Box 55492 Houston TX 77055

CHEE, ANTHONY NGIK CHOONG, scientist, educator; b. Taiping, Malaysia, Feb. 9, 1942; came to U.S., 1962, naturalized, 1972; s. Fook On and Ah Yin (Lau) C.; B.S. (scholar), St. Edward's U., 1966; M.A., U. Mass., 1968; Ed.D., U. Houston, 1979; m. Ann Ping Sze, Dec. 27, 1969; children—Andy, Lawrence. Lab. asst. Coll. Physicians and Surgeons, Columbia U., N.Y.C., 1964; teaching fellow dept. zoology U. Mass., Amherst, 1966-68, NIH fellow, 1969; research asso. Baylor Coll. Medicine, Houston, 1972-75; chmn. biology faculty Houston Community Coll., 1975—; biomed. researcher Tex. Med. Center, Houston, 1971-78; adj. assoc. prof. U. Tex., 1980—; vis. prof. U. Nanjing, Peoples' Republic of China, 1985; sci. fair judge, guest lectr. schs. and colls.; vis. prof. U. Nanjing, Peoples Republic China, 1985. Recipient Outstanding Teaching award Houston Community Coll., 1980-81; John P. McGovern Outstanding Teaching award U. Tex., 1985; USPHS scholar U. Tex., 1970. Mem. AAAS, Nat. Sci. Tchrs. Assn., AAUP, Am. Assn. Clin. Chemists, Tex. Acad. Sci., Sigma Xi. Roman Catholic. Club: Chinese Profl. Author: (with others) Biology, A Laboratory Experience, 1978, 2d edit., 1982; Anatomy and Physiology—A Dynamic Approach, 1979, 3d edit., 1985; editor: Contemporary Biology—A Process Approach, 1980, 2d edit., 1982; contbr. articles to profl. jours. Home: 8914 Sterlingame St Houston TX 77031 Office: 22 Waugh Dr Houston TX 77007

CHEN, CHIA-MING, resin chemist, wood scientist, educator; b. Chia-Yi, Taiwan, July 20, 1935; came to U.S., 1967, naturalized, 1974; s. Pi-Ching and Jong (Huang) C.; m. Shu-Hsien Lai, Sept. 27, 1963; children—Edward Po-Chung, Frederick Yen-Ching. B.S., Chyng-Hsing U., Taichung, Taiwan, 1958; M.S., U. Tokyo, 1963, Ph.D., 1966. Research assoc. Yale U. Sch. Forestry, New Haven, 1967-68; products devel. engr. Champion Bldg Products, Seattle, 1968-69; wood scientist, resin chemist chem. div. Ga.-Pacific Corp., Decatur, Ga., 1969-71; sr. wood scientist, assoc. prof. U. Ga. Sch. of Forest Resources, Athens, 1971—, mem. grad. faculty; cons. in field to various cos. Mem. Athens Internat. Council. Registered forester, Ga.; U.S. Dept. Agr. grantee, 1982-85. Fellow Am. Inst. Chemists; mem. Am. Chem. Soc., Forest Products Research Soc., N.Am. Taiwanese Profs.' Assn., Adhesion Soc., Formosan Assn. Pub. Affairs (pres. chpt. 1986-88). Club: Formosan (pres. and faculty adviser Athens chpt.). Contbr. numerous articles on resin and adhesive chemistry, wood sci. and tech. to profl. jours.; patentee in field. Home: 205 Dove Valley Dr Athens GA 30606

CHEN, LINDA LI-YUEH HUANG, educator, consultant, researcher; b. Tokyo, Mar. 22, 1937; d. Chun Mu Huang and Chung Tien (Lin) H.; m. Boris Yuen-jien Chen, Dec. 23, 1961; children—Audrey Huey-wen, Lisa Min-yi. B.S. in Pharmacy, Nat. Taiwan U., 1959; Ph.D. in Biochemistry, U. Louisville, 1964. Research assoc. dept. biochemistry U. Louisville, 1964-66; from asst. prof. to assoc. prof. dept. nutrition and food sci. U. Ky., Lexington, 1967-79, prof., 1979—, chmn. dept., 1983—. Mem. Am. Inst. Nutrition, Am. Soc. Clin. Nutrition, Inst. Food Technologists, Gerontol. Soc. Am. Democrat. Presbyterian. Author: Laboratory Manual of Nutritional Biochemistry, 1974; Eating Right for Healthier Life-A Nutrition Handbook for Older Persons, 1982; Nutritional Aspects of Aging, Vols. I and II, 1986; contbr. articles to profl. jours. Home: 531 S Bend Dr Lexington KY 40503 Office: 212 Funkhouser Bldg U Ky Lexington KY 40506

CHEN, PING-FAN, geologist; b. Kiangyin, Kiangsu, China, May 13, 1917; s. Mou-Chu and Lan-yin (Men) C.; B.S., Nat. Central U. China, 1938; M.S., U. Cin. (fellow), 1956; Ph.D. (fellow), Va. Poly. Inst. and State U., 1959; m. Tsing-fang Tsao, Jan. 1, 1947 (dec.); children—Jane, June, Julia; m. 2d, Esther Fu-Mei Yang, Aug. 10, 1979; came to U.S., 1956, naturalized, 1969. Petroleum geologist Nat. Geol. Survey China, 1938-46; sr. petroleum geologist Chinese Petroleum Corp., Taiwan, 1946-55; stratigrapher W.Va. Geol. Survey, Morgantown, 1960—; adj. prof. W.Va. U., 1975—. Adviser W.Va. U. Chinese Student Assn., 1962-81. Mem. Geol. Soc. China, Chinese Engrs. Assn., Chinese Assn. Advancement Scis., Sigma Xi, Sigma Gamma Epsilon. Author: Mineral Resources of China, 1954; New Outlook for the Oil Fields of Taiwan, 1949; Tectonic Analogies and Antitheses between Taiwan and the Appalachians, 1976; Lower Paleozoic Stratigraphy in the Central Appalachians, 1978. Home: 1277 Dogwood Ave Morgantown WV 26505 Office: PO Box 879 Morgantown WV 26505

CHEN, TAR TIMOTHY, biostatistician; b. Fuching, China, June 23, 1945; came to U.S., 1967, naturalized, 1979; s. Lin-Tsang and Ai-Ging (Chang) C.; m. Meei-Ming Li, Aug. 9, 1969; children—Stephen, Daniel. B.S., Nat. Taiwan U., 1966; M.S., U. Chgo., 1969, Ph.D., 1972. Statistician, Ill. Bell Telephone, Chg., 1971-73; asst. prof. Calif. State U.-Hayward, 1973-74; vis. assoc. prof. Chung-Hsing U., Taichung Taiwan, 1974-75; biostatistician The Upjohn Co., Kalamazoo, 1975-79; asst. prof. biometrics U. Tex. System Cancer Ctr., Houston, 1979-84; sr. biostatistician Alcon Labs., Fort Worth, 1984—. Contbr. articles to profl. jours. Deacon, Houston Chinese Ch., 1981-83. Served to 2d lt. Republic of China Army, 1966-67. Mem. Am. Statis. Assn., Biometric Soc., Sigma Xi. Office: Alcon Labs 6201 S Freeway PO Box 1959 Fort Worth TX 76101

CHENAULT, MYRON MAURICE, university administrator; lawyer; b. Richmond, Ind., Mar. 3, 1949; m. Vivian Michele Chiles, June 28, 1975; 1 child Myron. B.A., Manchester Coll., 1971; J.D., Valparaiso U., 1974. Bar: Ohio, U.S. dist. ct. (no. dist.) Ohio. Asst. v.p. Bowling Green U., Ohio, 1978-80, assoc. v.p., legal staff cont. relations, 1980-82; vice chancellor for devel. affairs Winston-Salem State U., N.C., 1982—; exec. sec. Winston-Salem State U. Found., Inc., 1982—. Vol., bd. dirs. Nature Sci. Ctr., 1985—, Southeastern Ctr. Contemporary Art, 1985—, Winston-Salem Housing Found., 1984—; mem. Leadership Winston-Salem. Mem. Ohio Bar Assn., ABA, Council for Advancement and Support of Edn., Phi Alpha Delta, Omicron Delta Kappa, Phi Beta Sigma. Democrat. Presbyterian. Avocations: jogging; racquetball; reading. Home: 4271 Mill Creek Rd Winston-Salem NC 27106 Office: Winston-Salem State U PO Box 13325 Winston-Salem NC 27110

CHENAUSKY, ANTHONY, aircraft electronics company executive; b. El Paso, Tex., Nov. 26, 1960; s. Richard Donald and Margie (Perez) C.; m. Cheryl Lynn Farner, Dec. 26, 1983. Student U. Tex.-El Paso, 1978-79. Cert. aircraft radio repairman and pilot FAA. Part-time installer Avionics Assocs., El Paso, 1978, installation dept. co-foreman, 1979, installation dept. supr., 1981, v.p., 1981—; pres., owner Chenausky Investments, El Paso, 1983—. Mem. Credit Bur. El Paso, El Paso Apt. Assn., Aircraft Owners and Pilots Assn. Roman Catholic. Home: 1404 Sun Meadow Ln El Paso TX 79936 Office: 6825 Convair Rd El Paso TX 79925

CHENOWETH, PHILIP ANDREW, consulting geologist; b. Chgo., Aug. 21, 1919; s. Joseph Gayne and Helen Gilette (Burton) C.; m. Marilyn Myers, Apr. 11, 1952; children—Kathryn, Amelia. B.A., Columbia Coll., 1946; M.A., Columbia U., 1947, Ph.D., 1949. Asst. prof. geology Amherst Coll., 1949-51; asst. dist. geologist Sinclair Oil & Gas Co., Ardmore, Okla., 1951-54; assoc. prof. geology U. Okla., 1954-60; research assoc. Sinclair Research Labs., 1960-68; cons. geologist, Tulsa, 1968—; dir. Soaring Eagle Oil Co. Chmn. higher edn. subcom. Goals for Tulsa. Served with AUS, 1941-45. Fellow Geol. Soc. Am., Explorers Club; mem. Am. Assn. Petroleum Geologists, Am. Inst. Profl. Geologists, Tulsa Geol. Soc. (hon.), Oklahoma City Geol. Soc., Rocky Mountain Assn. Geologists, Democrat. Episcopalian. Contbr. numerous articles to profl. jours. Home: 5828 E 62d Pl Tulsa OK 74136 Office: 7010 S Yale Suite 216 Tulsa OK 74136

CHERAMIE, CARLTON JOSEPH, lawyer, business consultant; b. Raceland, La., Sept. 29, 1952; s. Antoine Joseph and Gladys Marie (Plaisance) C.; m. Myra Joan Diaz, July 15, 1973; 1 child, Andrea Ragan. B.A., Nicholls State U., Thibodaux, La., 1973; J.D., La. State U., 1976. Bar: La. 1976, U.S. Dist. Ct. (ea. dist.) La. 1977, U.S. Dist. Ct. (we. dist.) La. 1977, U.S. Ct. Appeals (5th cir.) 1982, U.S. Ct. Appeals (10th cir.) 1984, U.S. Supreme Ct. 1984. Law clk. Dist. Ct. 19th Jud. dist., Baton Rouge, 1975-76; assoc. Diaz & Herrin, Golden Meadow, La., 1976-77; assoc. Law Office of Ed Diaz, Golden Meadow, 1977-79; ptnr. Diaz & Cheramie, Golden Meadow, 1979-83, Cheramie & Smith, Cut Off, La., 1983—; pres., dir. Tradewinds Marine, Cut Off, 1982—; corp. cons. First Am. Investments, Dallas; atty. Town of Golden Meadow, 1980-83; dir. Westwind Capital, Cut Off. State advisor U.S. Congl. Adv. Bd., Cut Off, 1980. Mem. Fed. Bar Assn., Assn. Trial Lawyers Am., La. Trial Lawyers Assn., ABA, Phi Alpha Theta, Phi Delta Phi. Republican. Roman Catholic. Home: 134 W 47th St Cut Off LA 70345 Office: Cheramie & Smith 2024 W Main St Cut Off LA 70345

CHERIAN, SUNNY K., accountant; b. Kerala, India, July 11, 1936; s. Cherian and Anna C.; m. Gracy Verghese, Jan. 7, 1974; children—Sarah, Paul. Student, C.M.S. Coll., India, 1953-55, Indian Bus. Coll., 1953-54, Laxmi Coll., India, 1955-57; LL.B., Govt. Law Coll., India, 1961; M.C.L., George Washington U., 1973. C.P.A., Va. Acct. in tng. Marfatia and Co., C.P.A.s, India, 1956-61; mgmt. trainee Express Group Newspapers and News Services Ltd., Bombay, India, 1961; ptnr. Jaitly Cherian Luthra Assocs., C.P.A.s, New Delhi, India, 1962-75; audit mgr. internal audit Bennett, Coleman & Co., Ltd., No. India, 1963-65; commr. for stamp duties and legal consul Ministry of Land and Survey, No. Nigeria, 1965-68; controller Ministry Land and Survey, Ministry Town and Country planning, Fed. Ministry Mines and Power, No. Nigeria, 1965-68; fin. officer Ministry Natural Resources and Coops., Nigeria, 1968-69; sub contract acct. Robert Millard & Co., C.P.A.s, Md., 1970; sr. acct., auditor Burton K. Myers & Co., C.P.A.s, Va., 1971, John Henderson & Co., C.P.A.s, Washington, 1972; pvt. practice acctg., Va., 1973-78; mgmt. auditor Papua New Guinea, 1978; ombudsman/commr. Ombudsman Commn., 1978-79; profl. pub. fin. UN Econ. Commn. for Africa, 1979-81; pvt. practice internat. cons., Falls Church, Va., 1981—; v.p. fin. Sarah Cherian Internat., Inc., 1981—; asst. prof. Dundalk Community Coll., 1983—. Sec.-treas. Soc. Internat. Devel., Addis Ababa chpt., 1980-81; sec., staff council UN Econ. Commn. for Africa, 1980-81; mem. coordinating team UN Inter Agy. Staff Council, Ethiopia, 1981; mem. India-Papua New Guinea Cultural Com., 1978-79; mem. India-Papua New Guinea Trade and Tng. Com., 1978-79. Recipient Commendations, Permanent Secs. Ministries Land and Survey, 1966, 67, Commendation, Mil. Gov. Sultan Nigeria, 1968. Mem. Internat. Ombudsman Assn., Inst. Chartered Secs. and Adminstrs., Inst. Chartered Accts. India, Am. Bar Assn., Inst. C.P.A.s, George Washington U. Law Alumni. Democrat. Episcopalian. Home: 5519 N 24th St Arlington VA 22205 Office: 5827 Columbia Pike Suite 315 Falls Church VA 22041

CHERNENKO, JOHN G., state senator; b. Apr. 30, 1924; m. Kathryn Joyce Smith; children—Gary C., Marc B., Janet Ann. U.S. Marshal, 1961-69; mem. W.Va. senate, 1982—. Mem. Bethany Coll. Parents Council; treas. Brooke County Mus. Commn. (W.Va.); bd. dirs. Tri-State Council on Alcoholism; zoning office Wellsburg, W.Va., also bldg. inspector; chmn. Brooke County Democratic Exec. Com. Served with U.S. Army. Decorated Purple Heart with cluster, Bronze Star. Mem. U.S. Marshals Assn. (v.p. 4th jud. cir.). Methodist. Lodges: Elks, Am. Legion, VFW, Fraternal Order Police. Office: W Va Senate Charleston WV 25305*

CHERNOFF, ROY, hospital administrator; b. N.Y.C., Nov. 19, 1947; s. George and Sara (Leach) C.; m. Alice Helen Gortz, Sept. 12, 1969; 1 child, Greg M. B.S. in Acctg., Hunter Coll., 1970; M.B.A. in Hosp. Adminstrn., U. Miami, 1982. Mgr. syndicate ops. Bache and Co., N.Y.C., 1971-72; sr. acct. Siedman and Siedman, White Plains, N.Y., 1972-73; asst. bus. mgr. CUNY, 1973-75; fin. analyst Union Carbide, Tarrytown, N.Y., 1976-77; asst. adminstr. Grant Ctr. Hosp., Miami, Fla., 1977-82; adminstr. Fair Oaks Hosp., Delray Beach, Fla., 1982—. Bd. dirs. Concept House, Miami, 1982-84. Mem. Hosp. Fin. Mgmt. Assn., Palm Coast Hosp. Council, Greater Palm Beach Health Coalition, Nat. Assn. Pvt. Psychiat. Hosps. Avocation: golf. Office: Fair Oaks Hosp at Boca-Delray 5440 Linton Blvd Delray Beach FL 33445

CHERRY, CHARLES LEWIS, petroleum exploration company executive; b. Platteville, Colo., Mar. 5, 1926; s. Ernest Joseph and Mildred Helen (Hall) C.; m. Eleanor Marie Rasmussen, Dec. 22, 1946; children—Bryan Alan, Jilleen Marie Cherry Day. Student Colo. State Coll. Edn., 1946-47; B.S., U. Wyo., 1950. Regional geologist Royal Resources Corp., Denver, 1969-71; pvt. practice cons. geologist, Littleton, Colo., 1971-78; staff geologist Natural Resources Corp., Denver, 1972-73; pres. Charles L. Cherry and Assocs., Inc., Fayette, Ala., 1978—. Author: (with others) Geology of the Paradox Basin, 1953. Served with USMC, 1943-45, PTO. Decorated Bronze Star, Purple Heart. Mem. Am. Assn. Petroleum Geologists, Rocky Mountain Assn. Geologists, Am. Petroleum Inst. (Warrior Basin chpt. bd. dirs. 1984), Fayette C. of C. (bd. dirs. 1985), Ala. Sight Conservation Assn. (bd. dirs. 1985-86). Republican. Lodges: Lions (pres. 1981-82), Exchange Club. Avocations: fishing; hunting. Home: 521 11th St NW Fayette AL 35555 Office: Charles L Cherry and Assocs 1600 Temple Ave N Fayette AL 35555-0877

CHERRY, JEAN SMITH, university official; b. Rosenberg, Tex., Apr. 9, 1944; d. Omar and Elouise (Beard) Smith; m. Tom Beverly Cherry, Jr., Sept. 21, 1974; 1 child, Gala Diane. B.A., So. Meth. U., 1966. Tchr., Leysin Am. Sch. (Switzerland), 1966-67; substitute tchr. Bryan Ind. Sch. Dist. (Tex.), 1967; tchr. College Station Ind. Sch. Dist. (Tex.), 1967-68; salesperson Heffer's Paperback Shop, Cambridge, Eng., 1968-69; tchr. Garland Ind. Sch. Dist. (Tex.), 1969-72; agt. Titche's World Travel Bur., Dallas, 1972-75; asst. to dean Meadows Sch. Arts, So. Meth. U., Dallas, 1975—; v.p. Omar Smith Enterprises Inc.; ptnr. Smith Dairy Queens. Mem. Dallas Civic Chorus, 1969—; mem. bd. Campus Y, So. Meth. U., 1984—. Recipient M award So. Meth. U., 1983. Home: 3110 Milton St Dallas TX 75205 Office: Meadows Sch Arts So Meth U Dallas TX 75275

CHERRY, SANDRA WILSON, lawyer; b. Little Rock, Dec. 31, 1941; d. Berlin Alexander and Renna Glen (Barnes) Wilson; m. John Sandefur Cherry, Jr., Sept. 24, 1976; 1 dau., Jane Wilson. B.A., U. Ark., 1962; J.D., U. Ark. Sch. Law, 1975. Bar: Ark., 1975, U.S. Dist. Ct. (ea. dist.) Ark., 1979, U.S. Supreme Ct. 1979, U.S. Ct. Appeals (8th cir.) 1979. Tchr. social studies Little Rock Sch. Dist., 1966-70; chmn. social studies dept. Horace Mann Jr. High Sch., Little Rock, 1970-72; asst. U.S. atty. Dept. Justice, Little Rock, 1975-81, 83—; commr. Ark. Pub. Service Commn., Little Rock, 1981-83; adj. instr. U. Ark. at Little Rock Sch. Law, Little Rock, 1980. Contbr. case note to Ark. Law Rev., 1975. Bd. dirs. Gaines House, Inc.; pres. U. Ark. at Little Rock Law Sch. Assn., 1980-81, bd. dirs., 1982. Mem. ABA, Ark. Bar Assn. (Ho. of Del. 1984—), Pulaski County Bar Assn., Ark. Women Lawyers Assn., Jr. League Little Rock (bd. dirs. 1974), Pi Beta Phi. Democrat. Presbyterian. Home: 4100 S Lookout St Little Rock AR 72205 Office: US Attys Office PO Box 1229 Little Rock AR 72203

CHESHIER, RANDOLPH (RANDY) L(EE), investment consultant; b. Dallas, Sept. 20, 1956; s. Lee Banie, Jr., and Doris Louise (Weaver) C. B.A. in Anthropology, So. Meth. U., 1977; B.B.A. in Fin., U. Tex.-Austin, 1980. Credit analyst, Republic Bank Houston, 1980-81, Standard Chartered Bank Internat., Houston, 1981; sr. fin. analyst Barclays Bank Internat., Houston, 1981-83; research div. Southwest Securities, Dallas, 1983-84; pres., founder Investexas Fin. services Inc., Dallas, 1985—; arbiter Better Bus. Bur. Active Dallas Mus. Fine Arts, Smithsonian Instn., Mus. Natural History, N.Y.C. Mem. Fin. Analysts Fedn., Nat. Assn. Bus. Economists, Dallas Assn. Investment Analysts, So. Meth. U. Young Alumni Assn., Phi Beta Kappa, Phi Eta Sigma. Republican. Episcopalian. Club: Texas Exes. Author investment research reports, newsletters.

CHESHIRE, RICHARD DUNCAN, university president; b. Mineola, N.Y., Aug. 12, 1936; s. Leslie G. and Catherine C. Cheshire; A.B., Colgate U., 1958; M.Ed., U. N.H., 1961; Ph.D., N.Y. U., 1973; m. Roberta Ann Jeans, Sept. 6, 1958; children—Jennifer, Jonathan, Camilla. Tchr. Am. history Chatham (N.J.) High Sch., 1959-60; asst. to v.p., alumni fund sec. Colgate U., 1960-62; dir. devel. Dickinson Coll., 1963-65; asst. to pres., v.p. univ. relations Drew U., Madison, N.J., 1966-73; v.p. public affairs, lectr. edn. Colgate U., 1973-77; pres., prof. history U. Tampa (Fla.), 1977—; cons. Ford Found., 1968-69. Pres., N.J. Shakespeare Festival, 1972; bd. dirs. Fla. Gulf Coast Symphony, Tampa Museum Fedn., Tampa Bay Arts Center, Tampa Prep. Sch., Greater Tampa United Way; mem. Fla. Council 100, Tampa Bay Area Com. Fgn. Relations. Mem. Greater Tampa C. of C. (dir.). Clubs: Univ. (N.Y.C. and Tampa). Div. editor: Handbook of Institutional Achievement, 1976. Office: 401 W Kennedy Blvd Tampa FL 33606

CHESHIRE, WILLIAM POLK, newspaper editor; b. Durham, N.C., Feb. 2, 1931; s. James Webb and Anne Ludlow (McGehee) C.; A.B., U. N.C., 1958; m. Lucile Geoghegan, Aug. 1, 1959; children—William Polk, Helen Wood, James Webb. Reporter, Richmond (Va.) News Leader, 1958-61; asso. editor Charleston (S.C.) Evening Post, 1963-68, The State, Columbia, S.C., 1968-72; editorial dir. Capital Broadcasting Co., Raleigh, N.C., 1972-75; editorial page editor Greensboro (N.C.) Record, 1975-78; editor-in-chief Charleston (W.Va.) Daily Mail, 1978-84; editor, editorial pages Washington Times, 1984—; prof. journalism U. Charleston, 1979-83. Bd. dirs. Sunrise Mus.; Charleston (W.Va.)

United Way. Served with USCG, 1952-56. Recipient Council for the Def. Freedom award, 1980; Freedoms Found. George Washington Honor medal, 1975. Mem. N.C. Soc. of Cincinnati (v.p. 1982-85), Am. Soc. Newspaper Editors, Nat. Conf. Editorial Writers, Sigma Delta Chi (pres. Piedmont chpt. 1978). Home: 124 Cameron Mews Alexandria VA Office: 3600 New York Ave NE Washington DC 20002

CHESLEY, WILLIAM RORAH, advertising agency executive; b. Pitts., Dec. 24, 1928; s. John Osborne and Eugenia Rorah C.; B.A., U. Pitts., 1951; m. Shirley Ann Tanner, Sept. 10, 1955; children—John Osborne II, Janet Tanner, Mary Ellen. Account asst. Ketchum, McLeod & Grove, Pitts., 1951-53; advt. mgr. tar products div. Koppers Co., Pitts., 1955-57; account exec. Fuller & Smith & Ross, Pitts., 1957-60; mgr. advt. and sales promotion Corry Jamestown Corp., Corry, Pa., 1960-63; account exec. Jayme Orgn., Cleve., 1963-66; copy dir. Griswold-Eshleman, Pitts., 1966-68; prin. Creative Bus. Communications, Pitts., Miami Shores and Orlando, Fla., 1968—. Bus. adminstr. Miami Shores Presbyn. Ch., 1982-84. Served to 1st lt. arty. U.S. Army, 1953-55. Recipient 1st award, div. 1 TF Club of Cleve., 1961. Mem. Ch. Bus. Adminstrs. Assn. (pres.), Scottish-Am. Soc. Central Fla., Clan MacLean Soc. U.S.A. Republican. Presbyterian. Home and Office: 1716 Woodside Ct Kissimme FL 32743

CHESNUTT, CAROLYN CRAWFORD, association executive; b. Maryville, Tenn., Sept. 16, 1933; d. John Calvin, Jr. and America Arey (Moore) Crawford; B.A. (Presser Found. Music scholar), Agnes Scott Coll., 1955; M.Ed. (Ednl. Research fellow), U. S.C., 1972; M.S., Ga. Inst. Tech., 1979; children—John Calvin, Thomas Walter, Margaret America, Carolyn Christian. Asst. librarian, Hartsville, S.C., 1965-66; instr. math. and psychology secondary schs., Ga. and S.C., 1966-75; asst. to dean engring. Ga. Inst. Tech., Atlanta, 1975-77; exec. dir. Southeastern Consortium for Minorities in Engring., Atlanta, 1977—. Organist, choirmaster various churches, 1951—; campaign chmn. Community Concert Assn., 1968-70, pres., 1972-74; v.p. Hartsville Arts Council, 1968-72; com. to restructure bds. and agencies Presbyterian Ch. U.S., 1968-71; gen. exec. bd. Presbyn. Ch. U.S., 1971-72; pres. PTA, 1973. Alfred P. Sloan Found. grantee, 1977-81; NASA grantee, 1982-84. Mem. Nat. Assn. Pre-Coll. Dirs. (charter, chmn.), Soc. Women Engrs., Am. Soc. Engring. Edn., Am. Guild Organists, NEA, S.C. Edn. Assn. Office: Southeastern Consortium for Minorities in Engineering Georgia Institute of Technology Atlanta GA 30332

CHESNUTT, EDWIN LEE, JR., manufacturing executive; b. Atlanta, Mar. 4, 1940; s. Edwin Lee and Mary Ellen (Bell) C.; B.S. in Engring., Duke U., 1963; M.B.A., U. N.C., 1964; grad. advanced mgmt. program Harvard Bus. Sch., 1982; m. Ann Tanner, Nov. 17, 1977; 1 son, Edwin Lee III; 1 stepson, James Harold Mason III. With Cryovac div. W.R. Grace Co., Duncan, S.C., 1964—, dir. mktg., 1975-77, v.p. mktg., planning, and new bus. devel., 1977—. Mem. Greenville County (S.C.) Devel. Bd., 1971-74, chmn., 1974; trustee United Way of Greenville, 1969-76; pres. Jr. Achievement of Greenville, 1975-76, v.p., 1974-75, sec.-treas., 1973-74; mem. Greenville County Planning Commn., 1976-82, vice chmn., 1977, 81, 82; bd. dirs. Am. Cancer Soc., Greenville, 1975, Greenville Housing Found., 1971-73; v.p. Community Council of Social and Welfare Agys., 1973-74. Named Boss of Yr., Nat. Secs. Assn., Greenville, 1974, Young Man of Yr., Greenville Jaycees, 1973; S.C. Young Man of Yr., S.C. Jaycees, 1974. Mem. Soc. Plastics Engrs., Am. Mgmt. Assn., Soc. Profl. Planners, Greenville C. of C. (v.p. 1973-74). Republican. Episcopalian. Office: PO Box 464 Duncan SC 29334

CHEVALIER, ROGER ALAN, astronomy educator, consultant; b. Rome, Sept. 26, 1949; s. Frank Charles and Marion Helen (Janhke) C.; came to U.S., 1962; m. Margaret Mary With, July 27, 1974. B.S. in Astronomy, Calif. Inst. Tech., 1970; Ph.D. in Astronomy (Woodrow Wilson and NSF fellow), Princeton U., 1973. Asst. astronomer Kitt Peak Nat. Obs., Tucson, 1973-76, assoc. astronomer, 1976-79; assoc. prof. astronomy U. Va., Charlottesville, 1979-85, prof. astronomy, chmn. dept., 1985—; dir. Leander McCormick Obs., 1985—; cons. Lawrence Livermore Nat. Lab., Livermore, Calif., 1981—. Contbr. numerous research articles to Astrophys. Jour., other astronomy and physics jours. Mem. Am. Astron. Soc., Internat. Astron. Union, Ill. Sci. Lectr. Assn. (v.p. 1975—), Sigma Xi. Home: 1891 Westview Rd Charlottesville VA 22903 Office: Dept Astronomy U Va PO Box 3818 Charlottesville VA 22903

CHEVES, HARRY LANGDON, JR., physician; b. Birmingham, Ala., Oct. 17, 1924; s. Harry Langdon and Myrtle (Churchill) C.; A.B., Mercer U., 1949; M.D., Med. Coll. Ga., 1953; m. Lois Rebecca Corry, Dec. 25, 1949; children—Rebecca Churchill, Harry Langdon III; m. 2d, Mary Agnes Moon; 1 son, Harry Michael. Intern, Univ. Hosp., Augusta, Ga., 1953-54; practice medicine, East Point, Ga.; mem. staff S. Fulton Hosp., chief of staff, 1980-81. Served with USAAF, 1942-46. Fellow Internat., Am. colls. angiology; mem. Royal Soc. Health, AMA, So. Med. Assn., Med. Assn. Atlanta, Atlanta, So. Dist. (past pres.) med. socs., Am. Geriatric Soc., Med. Assn. Ga., Ga. Heart Assn., Phi Delta Theta. Clubs: Am. Antique Automobile, Classic Car Club Am., Packard Automobile Classics, Rolls-Royce Am., Rolls-Royce Owners, Model A, Chrysler Restorers. Home: 333 Plantation Circle Riverdale GA 30296 Office: 2726 Felton Dr East Point GA 30344

CHEWNING, WILLIAM JEFFRIES, III, broadcasting executive, publisher; b. Washington, May 14, 1931; s. William Jeffries Chewning Jr. and Margo (Couzens) Chewning Bryant; m. Mary Chapman, Sept. 1953 (div. 1956), Rachael Kay James, Nov. 28, 1958; children—Kimberly Kay, Stephanie Couzens. B.S. in Agronomy, Phelps Sch., Malvern, Pa., 1949, B.S. in Farm Mgmt., 1950. Cert. restricted radio, FCC. Photographer, Republican. Nat. Com., Washington, 1947; news photographer Times Herald, Washington, 1947-50; cons., editor Herbert Bryant, Inc., Alexandria, Va., 1955-64, Soil Adv. Assts., Alexandria, 1964-71; news dir. UPI, Sta. WAGE, Leesburg, Va., 1971-77; chief exec. officer William J. Chewning Communications Co., Waterford, Va., 1977—, CNI World News Service, Leesburg, Va., 1977—. Author: Outward Bound East Africa, 1975. Editor: JCH Bryant/Life and Times, 1984. Pres., Va. Knolls Civic Assn., Leesburg, 1966-69. Served to sgt. USAF, 1951-55. Recipient Outstanding Journalism East Africa award Am. Inst. Fgn. Service, 1974, Best News Operation award Va. Assn. Broadcasters, 1976, Outstanding Broadcast China award Lead Line Assn., 1978. Mem. Nat. Steeplechase Assn. Episcopalian. Clubs: Va. Soc. of Cin., Nat. Press, Washington Press. Lodge: Kiwanis (bd. dirs. 1982-84). Avocations: long distance walking; swimming; horse show jumping; polo. Office: CNI World News Service PO Box 621 Leesburg VA 22075

CHI, LOTTA C(HAI) J(UI) LI, research and development company executive; b. N.Y.C., Dec. 5, 1930; d. Chen Pien and Han Chih (Tang) Li; B.S., Heidelberg Coll., Tiffin, Ohio, 1953; M.S., Rutgers U., 1955; m. Michael Chi, June 15, 1957; children—Loretta, Maxwell. Virologist NIH, Bethesda, Md., 1956-63; sec., treas. Chi Assos., Inc., Arlington, Va., 1975-80, contract mgr., 1975-80, v.p., 1980—; pres. L Chi Assos., 1983—; cons. in field. Chmn. Li Chen-pien Meml. Found. Fellow Am. Soc. Microbiology, N.Y. Acad. Scis., Nat. Assn. Women Bus. Owners, Internat. Biog. Assn.; mem. Am. Biog. Inst. (research bd. advisers), Sigma Xi. Democrat. Home: 2721 N 24th St Arlington VA 22207 Office: 2045 N 15th St Arlington VA 22201

CHICHESTER, JOHN H., state senator; b. Fredericksburg, Va., Aug. 26, 1937; m. Sydney Collson. Grad. Va. Poly. Inst. Mem. Va. Senate, 1978—. Mem. Big Bros. Served with USAR, 1956-62. Mem. Fredericksburg Jaycees. Republican. Presbyterian. Lodges: Masons, Shriners, Rotary (past pres.). Office: Va Senate Gen Assembly Bldg 9th and Broad Sts Richmond VA 23219*

CHICKOWSKY, CAROLL EVE, designer, consultant, educator; b. Detroit, Apr. 30, 1935; s. John and Constance Helen (Jastremsky) C. Student U. Mich., 1953-54; B.Indsl. Design, Pratt Inst., 1958; postgrad. U. Mo., 1979. Designer various cos., Detroit, Chgo., Calif., 1962-75; project mgr. Hosp. Bldg. and Equipment, St. Louis, 1975-79; dir. interiors Geren & Assocs., Ft. Worth, 1979-82; prin. Ergonomics Co., Ft. Worth, 1981—; cons. Henmi & Assoc., St. Louis, 1982—; instr. Tex. Christian U., Ft. Worth, 1981-82, Washington U., St. Louis, 1982-83. Kate Maremont Found. grantee, 1964. Mem. Inst. Bus. Designers (assoc.), AIA (dir. interiors com.), Illuminating Engring. Soc. Creator permanent exhibit Mus. Sci. and Industry, Chgo., 1964, TV/documentation on low income living quarters. Office: Ergonomics 612 N Bailey Fort Worth TX 76107

CHICONE, JERRY, JR., citrus grower; b. Orlando, Fla., Nov. 19, 1934; s. Jerry J. and Maude Lee (Kirkland) C.; m. Sue Throckmorton, Sept. 12, 1959; children—Jay, Cary, Susan. B.S. in Bus. Adminstrn., U. Fla., 1956. Ptnr., Chicone Groves, Orlando, 1958—; dir. First Fed. Savs. & Loan Assn., Orlando, Fla. Citrus Mut., Lakeland. Author: History of Orlando Jaycees, 1977. Chmn. Downtown Devel. Bd. Orlando, 1979-80, Am. Heart Assn., 1978-80. Named Downtowner of Year, Downtown Orlando, 1981; Vol. of Year, Am. Heart Assn., 1981; Citizen of Year, Kiwanis, 1980; Spokesman of Year, Chem. Mag., 1978. Mem. Nat. Fedn. Ind. Bus. (dir.), Orlando C. of C. (dir.), Fla. Agribus. Inst., Sigma Chi. Republican. Clubs: Univ., Citrus. Office: Chicone Groves PO Box 7636 Orlando FL 32854

CHIDNESE, PATRICK N., lawyer; b. Neptune, N.J., May 26, 1940; s. Louis and Helen C.; m. Rene E. Chidnese, Aug. 19, 1968; 1 child, Krista; m. Kathy J. Chidnese, Feb. 16, 1985; 1 child, Patrick. B.A., U. Miami, 1964, J.D., 1968. Assoc. Sinclair, Louis & Huttoe, Miami, 1968-69; assoc. Stephens, Demos, Magil & Thornton, Miami, 1969-70; assoc. Howell, Kirby, Montgomery, D'Aiuto, Dean & Hallowes, Fort Lauderdale, Fla., 1970-71; sole practice, Fort Lauderdale, 1971—; county atty. Broward County Juvenile Ct., 1971-72. Mem. Fla. Bar Assn. (chmn. auto ins. com. 1977-78, chmn. 17th jud. circuit legis. com. 1977-80), Broward County Bar Assn., Acad. Fla. Trial Lawyers, Broward County Trial Lawyers Assn. (bd. dirs. 1974-80). Office: 201 SE 12th St Fort Lauderdale FL 33316

CHIERI, PERICLE ADRIANO C., educator, cons. mech. and aero. engr., naval architect; b. Mokanshan, Chekiang, China, Sept. 6, 1905; s. Virginio and Luisa (Fabbri) C.; Dr. Engring., U. Genoa, Italy, 1927; M.E., U. Naples, Italy, 1927; Dr. Aero. Engring., U. Rome, 1928; m. Helen Etheredge, Aug. 1, 1938. Came to U.S., 1938, naturalized, 1952. Naval architect, mech. engr. research and exptl. divs., submarines and internal combustion engines, Italian Navy, Spezia, 1929-31; naval architect, marine supt. Navigazione Libera Triestina Shipping Corp., Libera Lines, Trieste, Italy, 1931-32, Genoa, 1933-35; aero. engr., tech. adviser Chinese Govt. commn. aero. affairs, Nat. Govt. Republic of China, Nanchang and Loyang, 1935-37; engring. exec., dir. aircraft materials test lab., supt. factory's tech. vocat. instrn., SINAW Nat. Aircraft Works, Nanchang, Kiangsi, China, 1937-39; aero. engr. FIAT aircraft factory, Turin, Italy, 1939; aero. engr. and tech. sec. Office; Air Attache, Italian Embassy, Washington, 1939-41; prof. aero. engring. Tri-State Coll., Angola, Ind., 1942; aero. engr., helicopter design Aero. Products, Inc., Detroit, 1943-44; sr. aero. engr. ERCO Engring. & Research Corp., Riverdale, Md., 1944-46; asso. prof. mech. engring. U. Toledo, 1946-47; asso. prof. mech. engring., faculty grad. div. Newark (N.J.) Coll. Engring., 1947-52; prof., head dept. mech. engring. U. Southwestern La., Lafayette, La., 1952-72; cons. engr., Lafayette, 1972—; research engr., advanced devel. sect., aviation gas turbine div., Westinghouse Electric Corp., South Philadelphia, Pa., 1953; exec. dir. Council on Environment, Lafayette, 1975—. Instr. water safety ARC Nat. Aquatic Schs., summers 1958-67. Bd. dirs. Lafayette Parish chpt. ARC. Registered profl. engr., Italy, N.J., La., S.C.; chartered engr., U.K. Fellow Royal Instn. Naval Architects London (life); asso. fellow Am. Inst. Aeronautics and Astronautics; mem. Soc. Naval Architects and Marine Engrs., AAAS, AAUP (emeritus), Am. Soc. Engring. Edn. (life), ASME, Soc. Automotive Engrs., Instrument Soc. Am., Soc. Exptl. Stress Analysis, Nat. Soc. Profl. Engrs., N.Y. Acad. Scis., La. Engring. Soc., La. Tchrs. Assn., AAHPER, La. Acad. Scis., Commodore Longfellow Soc., Cons. Engrs. Council La., Phi Kappa Phi, Pi Tau Sigma (hon.). Home: 142 Oak Crest Dr Lafayette LA 70503 Office: PO Box 52923 OCS Lafayette LA 70505

CHILCOTE, THOMAS FRANKLIN, retired college president, clergyman; b. Dayton, Pa., May 25, 1918; s. Thomas Franklin and Emma Jane (Peters) C.; m. Margaret Virginia Mossor, Sept. 18, 1943; children—Wayne Leslie, Deborah Jean. Student, Taylor U., 1936-38; B.A., U. Pitts., 1940; postgrad. Western Theol. Sem., 1940-41; M.Div., Boston U., 1943; D.D. (hon.), U. Chattanooga, 1955; postgrad. Harvard Inst. Ednl. Mgmt., 1973. Ordained elder Methodist Ch., 1943. Pastor, McCandless Ave Meth. Ch., Pitts., 1939-41, Walnut Ave. Meth. Ch., Roxbury, Mass., 1942-43, Cresson (Pa.) Meth. Ch., 1943; news editor The Christian Advocate, Chgo., 1943-45; mng. editor New Life Mag., Nashville, 1945-48; pastor First Meth. Ch., Chattanooga, 1948-55; supt. Abingdon (Va.) dist. Meth. Ch., 1955-58; pastor First Meth. Ch., Maryville, Tenn., 1958-62; sr. minister Fountain City United Meth. Ch., Knoxville, Tenn., 1962-68, First United Meth. Ch., Oak Ridge, 1968-70, First Broad St. United Meth. Ch., Kingsport, Tenn., 1970-73; pres. Emory and Henry Coll., Emory, Va., 1973-84; del. World Meth. Conf., Oxford and Oslo, 1951-61, Pacific Rim Higher Edn. Seminar in Far East, 1980; mem. Theol. Study Commn. on Doctrine and Doctrinal Standards, United Meth. Ch., 1968-72, mem. uniting conf., 1970. Mem. Alpha Pi Omega. Republican. Methodist. Author: Quest for Meaning, God's Twenty-Two, 1982. Home: 1325 Highland Prk Dr Seymour TN 37865

CHILD, CHARLES JUDSON, JR., bishop of Atlanta, Episcopal Church; b. North Bergen, N.J., Apr. 25, 1923; s. Charles Judson and Alice Sylvia (Sparling) C. B.A., U. of the South, 1944, M.Div., 1947, D.D. (hon.), 1978; Lic. in Theology, St. Augustine Coll.-Eng., 1961. Ordained priest Episcopal Ch., 1948, bishop, 1978. Asst., St. Paul's Episc. Ch., Paterson, N.J., 1947-51; rector St. Bartholomew's Episc. Ch., Ho-Ho-Kus, N.J., 1951-67; canon pastor Cathedral of St. Philip, Atlanta, 1967-78; bishop suffragan Diocese of Atlanta, 1978-83, bishop, 1983—. Home: 3138 Peachtree Dr NE Atlanta GA 30305 Office: Episcopal Diocese of Atlanta 2744 Peachtree Rd NE Atlanta GA 30363*

CHILDERS, CHARLENE DINSMORE, systems analyst; b. Canton, Ga., Nov. 6, 1946; d. James Edwin and Hazel Willine (Fowler) Dinsmore; m. Terry Wayne Childers, Mar. 30, 1971; children—Christopher Donahue, David Wayne. B.S., U. Ga., 1968. Programmer, U. Ga., Athens, 1968; data processing coordinator Ga. Hosps. Computer Group, Atlanta, 1969-70; programmer Fulton County Data Processing, Atlanta, 1972-73, sr. programmer, 1973-74, programmer analyst, 1974-75, analyst, 1975-76, sr. analyst, 1976-79, project mgr., 1979-82; sr. systems analyst Georgia Pacific, Atlanta, 1982-85, Mass. Indemnity Life Ins. Co., Duluth, Ga., 1985—. Mem. Math. Assn. Am., Pi Mu Epsilon, Alpha Lambda Delta. Libertarian. Lutheran. Club: Peachstate Region Porsche of Am. Home: 2412 Pine Cove Dr Tucker GA 30084 Office: 3120 Breckenridge Blvd Duluth GA 30199

CHILDERS, PERRY ROBERT, government agency administrator; b. Monticello, Ky., July 17, 1932; s. Charles T. and Leva M. (Spradlin) C.; B.A., U. Ky., 1958; M.A. (Grad. fellow), U. Ga., 1961, Ed.D., 1963; m. Mary Aliece Carpenter, Jan. 2, 1983; children—William Charles, Richard Calvin, Linda Louise, Leva Catherine. Asst. prof. psychology U. Ky., 1963-65; mgmt. psychologist Rohrer, Hibler & Replogle, Atlanta, 1966-67; asso. prof. psychology U. Fla., 1967-68, U. Wis., 1968-73; dep. supt. edn. State of La., 1973; dir. evaluation and monitoring, social and rehab. service HEW, Atlanta, after 1974; dir. quality control Social Security Adminstrn., after 1977, state program officer, 1980—, dep. commr. Tenn. Dept. Human Services, 1979-80; psychol. cons. to bus. mgmt. Recipient Spl. Achievement award HEW, 1976; Outstanding Performance award, 1977, 81; lic. psychologist, Wis. Author publs. in field. Office: 101 Marietta St Atlanta GA 30323

CHILDERS, RAYMOND FAYNE, insurance agency executive; b. Emory, Tex., Oct. 25, 1931; s. Raymond Franklin and Mattie Gertrude (Latham) C.; m. Tommye Gene Fuller, Oct. 25, 1967; children—Tamela Gayle, Derek Fayne. B.S., Stephen F. Austin Coll., 1956. Owner, mgr. ins. agy., Bedford, Tex., 1967—; dir. Grand Bank, Bedford. Presbyterian. Lodge: Masons. Avocations: hunting; fishing. Home: 413 Westcliff Euless TX 76040 Office: 1100 Airport Freeway Suite 100 Bedford TX 76022

CHILDERS, WILLIAM EDWARD, petroleum company executive; b. Albany, Tex., Sept. 26, 1936; s. J. Glenn and Jewel Inez (Miller) C.; m. M. Jeanice Montgomery, June 11, 1959; children—Dan Hal, Stuart Chad. Registered profl. engr., Calif.; cert. safety profl. B.S. in Bus., U. Corpus Christi, 1961; M.S. in Occupational Safety and Health, Western States U., 1985. Asst. corp. safety dir. El Paso Products Co., Odessa, Tex., 1960-72; mgr. safety Hess Oil Virgin Islands Corp., St. Croix, V.I., 1972-74; res. safety engr. B.P. Alaska Inc., Anchorage, 1974-77; loss prevention mgr. P.T. Arun/Mobil Oil Exploration Co., Lhocksumawe, Indonesia, 1977-78; staff adviser safety, environ. Mobil Exploration Norway, Stavander, 1978-79; corp. mgr. safety Champlin Petroleum Co., Ft. Worth, 1979—. Mem. steering com. Gov.s Task Force on Safety and Health, Alaska, 1975. Named Safety Engr. of Yr., State of Alaska, 1976. Mem. Am. Soc. Safety Engrs. (pres. Permian Basin chpt. 1969), Nat. Fire Protection Assn., Internat. Assn. Safety Profls. (life), Vet. of Safety. Home: 1202 Cimmaron DCBE Granbury TX 76048 Office: Champlin Petroleum Co 801 Cherry St Fort Worth TX 76101

CHILDRESS, JAMES FRANKLIN, religious studies educator; b. Mt. Airy, N.C., Oct. 4, 1940; s. Roscoe Franklin and Zella (Wagoner) C.; m. Georgia Monroe Harrell, Dec. 21, 1958; children—Albert Franklin, James Frederic (twins). B.A., Guilford Coll., 1962; B.D. cum laude, Yale Divinity Sch., 1965; M.A., Yale U., 1967, Ph.D., 1968. Asst. prof. U. Va., Charlottesville, 1968-71, assoc. prof., 1971-75, prof. religious studies, 1975—, chmn. dept., 1972-75, prof. religious studies and med. edn., 1981-83, Commonwealth prof. religious studies and prof. med. edn., 1983—; Joseph P. Kennedy Sr. prof. Christian Ethics, Kennedy Inst. Ethics, Georgetown U., 1975-79; vis. prof. Union Theol. Sem., Va., 1969, U. Chgo. Divinity Sch., fall 1977, Princeton U., spring 1978. Fellow George Day, Yale U., 1965-66; Kent fellow, 1966-68; Rockefeller fellow, 1967-68; Am. Council Learned Socs. fellow, 1972-73; Harvard U. Law Sch. fellow, 1972-73; Guggenheim fellow, 1984-85; Wilson Ctr. fellow, 1984-85. Mem. Am. Acad. Religion, Soc. Christian Ethics, Am. Soc. for Social and Polit. Philosophy, Am. Theol. Soc., Duodecim, Soc. for Health and Human Values, Inst. Soc., Ethics and Life Scis. (fellow). Quaker. Author: Civil Disobedience and Political Obligation, 1971; (with Tom L. Beauchamp) Principles of Biomedical Ethics, 1979, 2d. edit., 1983; Priorities in Biomedical Ethics, 1981; Moral Responsibility in Conflicts, 1982; Who Should Decide? Paternalism in Health Care, 1982; contbr. articles on religious studies and med. ethics to profl. jours. Office: Dept Religious Studies Cocke Hall U Va Charlottesville VA 22903

CHILDRESS, LEONARD, communications analyst; b. Kermit, Tex., Sept. 24, 1953; s. Troy and Virginia Lorene C.; m. Beverly Ann Duhart, July 8, 1983. B.A., Tex. Tech. U., 1976; M.P.A., U. Tex., 1978. Account exec. AT&T, St. Louis, 1978-80, sales office mgr., Houston, Tex., 1980-82, market adminstr., 1982—. Active Tex. Coalition Black Democrats, Progressive Action League, NAACP, League of United Voters. Mem. Am. Mktg. Assn., Am. Mgmt. Assn. Baptist. Home: 11518 Brighton Stafford TX 77477

CHILDS, RAND HAMPTON, data processing executive; b. Charlotte, N.C., Oct. 20, 1949; s. Wade Hampton and Francis Marion (Rand) C.; m. Anne Elizabeth Turner, Jan. 4, 1986. B.S. in Chemistry, Ga. Inst. Tech., 1971, M.S. in Chemistry, 1977; postgrad. Eidgenossische Technische Hochschule, Zurich, Switzerland, 1971-72. Systems analyst Ga. Inst. Tech., Atlanta, 1974-80, mgr. data processing, 1980-83, assoc. dir. office of computing services, 1983—; cons. in field. World Student Fund Scholar Ga. Inst. Tech. and Swiss Govt., 1971-72. Mem. AAAS, Am. Chem. Soc., Assn. Computing Machinery, VIM (Control Data Corp. User Group), Sigma Xi, Alpha Iota Delta of Chi Psi, Atlanta. Contbr. articles to profl. jours. Home: 106 Rosaire Pl NW Atlanta GA 30327 Office: Office of Computing Services Ga Inst Tech Atlanta GA 30332

CHILES, EDDIE, professional sports team executive, company executive. B.S. in Petroleum Engring., U. Okla. Founder, chmn. bd. Western Co. N. Am., Seagraves, Tex.; chmn. bd., pres., chief exec. officer Tex. Rangers Baseball Team, Arlington, Tex., 1980—. Office: Tex Rangers Arlington Stadium PO Box 111 Arlington TX 76010*

CHILES, HARRELL E., oil company executive; b. 1910. Student U. Okla., 1934. With Reed Roller Cit Co., 1934-39; with Western Co. of N. Am., Ft. Worth, 1939—, chmn., dir. Address: Western Co of N Am 6000 Western Pl Fort Worth TX 76107*

CHILES, LAWTON MAINOR, U.S. senator; b. Lakeland, Fla., Apr. 3, 1930; s. Lawton Mainor and Margaret (Patterson) C.; m. Rhea May Grafton, Jan. 27, 1951; children—Tandy M., Lawton Mainor III, Edward G., Rhea Gay. B.S., U. Fla., 1952; LL.B., 1955; LL.B. hon. degrees, Fla. So. Coll., Lakeland, 1971, Jacksonville U., 1971. Bar: Fla. bar 1955. Practiced in, Lakeland, 1955-70, U.S. senator from, Fla., 1971—; Mem. Fla. Ho. of Reps., 1958-66, Fla. Senate, 1966-70. Trustee U. Fla. Law Center, 1968—, Fla. So. Coll., 1971—, Eckerd Coll., St. Petersburg, Fla., 1971—. Served as lt. AUS, 1952-54. Mem. Phi Delta Phi, Alpha Tau Omega. Presbyterian. Office: 250 Russell Senate Office Bldg Washington DC 20510*

CHILTON, CRAIG, marketing company executive; b. Jersey City, Aug. 5, 1941; s. Chester Calvert and Violette Frances (Mabbitt) C.; student Central Coll., Pella, Iowa, 1959-61, 63-65, B.A., 1965; postgrad. in anthropology U. of Ams., Mexico City, 1964; postgrad. in geology and geography U. No. Iowa, 1971-74; children—Craig A., Wendy Jo, Brian D. Tchr. schs. Casa Grande, Ariz., 1965-66, Lancaster, Calif., 1966-69; tech. writer for research and devel. div. Chamberlain Mfg. Corp., Waterloo, Iowa, 1972-74; tchr. East Greenbush, N.Y., 1974-77; pres. Xanadu Enterprises, Goochland, Va., 1977-84; chmn. bd., gen. coordinator Questron Corp., Richmond, Va., 1984—; lectr. in field. Served with USAF, 1961-63. NDEA grantee Rutgers U., 1966. Mem. Ref. Ch. in Am. Club: Kiwanis (Key Club program dir., 1958-59). Guest radio and TV shows; author: How to Get Paid $30,000 a Year to Travel Without Selling Anything, 1979; How To Get Paid $200 a Day to Travel Without Selling Anything, 1979. Home: 2012 Grove Ave Richmond VA 23220 Office: Questron Corp Suite 15 Byrd Bldg 1910 Byrd Ave Richmond VA 23230

CHILTON, HORACE THOMAS, pipeline company executive; b. San Antonio, June 18, 1923; s. Horace Thomas and Lear Isabel (Word) C.; B.S. in Mech. Engring., U. Tex., 1947, B.A. in Bus. Adminstrn., 1947; Advanced Mgmt. Program, Harvard U., 1958; m. Betty Jane Gray, Oct. 18, 1947; children—Thomas G., William D. Engr., Stanolind Pipe Line Co., Tulsa, 1947; div. chief engr. Service Pipe Line Co., Lubbock, 1950—, asst. gen. mgr., 1960; mgr. products pipelines, lake tankers and barges Amoco Oil Co., Chgo., from 1963; gen. mgr. transp., pres. Amoco Pipeline, 1971-74; pres., chief exec. officer Colonial Pipeline, Atlanta, 1975—. Mem. U. Tex. Engring. Advisory Found. Bd., 1977—. Served with USN, 1944-46. Mem. Nat. Petroleum Council, Assn. Oil Pipe Lines (chmn. 1983-84), Am. Petroleum Inst. (dir. 1975—), Beta Theta Pi. Presbyterian. Club: Cherokee Town and Country (Atlanta). Home: 8290 River Landing Way Atlanta GA 30338 Office: 3390 Peachtree Rd NE Atlanta GA 30326 also Box 18855 Atlanta GA 30326

CHILTON, JACK KING, medical equipment company executive; b. Adairsville, Ga., July 14, 1934; s. Stuart King and Julia Mae (Shaw) C.; m. Jeannine M. Maltby, Apr. 9, 1960; children—Jack King, Chris, Carol. Student West Ga. Coll., 1953-54; B.F.A., U. Ga., 1957, postgrad., 1957-58. Sales trainee U.S. Rubber Corp., Atlanta, 1960-61; sales mgr. Puritan-Bennett Corp., Atlanta, 1961-76; pres. Chilton's Anesthesia & Respiration Equipment, Atlanta, 1976—; mktg. cons. bd. Marathon Med. Mfg., Denver, 1982—; mktg. cons. Bio-Med Devices, Stamford, Conn., 1979—. Pres., Briarcliff Community Sports, Atlanta, 1975, Dugout Club, Atlanta, 1982. Served with USN, 1951-53. Named outstanding ofcl. Atlanta Football Ofcls. Assn., 1983; recipient Silver Circle award Alpha Tau Omega, 1981. Mem. Am. Assn. Respiratory Therapists, Ga. Soc. Respiratory Therapists. Republican. Methodist. Home: 2641 Mercedes Dr NE Atlanta GA 30345 Office: Chilton's Anesthesia & Respiration Equipment Inc 2641 Mercedes Dr NE Atlanta GA 30345

CHIN, HONG WOO, physician; b. Seoul, Korea, May 14, 1935; came to U.S., 1974; s. Jik Hyun and Woon Kap (Park) C.; m. Soo Ja Cheung, Dec. 27, 1965; children—Richard, Helen, Kisik. M.D., Seoul Nat. U., 1962, Ph.D., 1974. Diplomate Am. Bd. Radiology. House officer, chief resident dept. radiation oncology McGill U., Royal Victoria Hosp. and Montreal (Can.) Gen. Hosp., 1975-79; asst. prof. radiation, head, neuro-radiation oncology sect. U. Ky. Hosp., Lexington, 1979—. Served to lt. comdr. Korean Navy, 1967-70. Mem. AMA, Am. Coll. Radiology, AAAS, Am. Soc. Therapeutic Radiologists, N.Y. Acad. Scis., Radiation Research Soc., Radiol. Soc. N.Am., Can. Assn. Radiologists. Contbr. articles to profl. jours.; also invited author. Office: 800 Rose St Lexington KY 40536

CHIN, RICCARDO FAY, artist; b. Hong Kong, July 16, 1935; s. Lan Den and Mee Yee (Wong) C.; came to U.S., 1951, naturalized, 1966; B.A., SUNY, 1958; M.F.A., Normal U., Taiwan, 1982; m. Helen Leong, Sept. 21, 1959; children—Steven, Deborah. Staff artist Automation Lab., Inc., Mineola, N.Y., 1960-61; asst. art dir. Tech. Illustrators-Omnibus Tech. Industries, Inc., Hempstead, N.Y., 1961-62; free lance artist, 1962-64; pres. Bertrick Asso. Artists, Inc., Seaford, N.Y., 1964-74; lectr. Chinese culture L.I. U., 1971-73; lectr., demonstrator East West style watercolor on rice papers, 1968—; tchr. Chinese cooking with western ingredients, 1964—; exhbns. of watercolors in U.S. and Far East. Served with AUS, 1958-60. Recipient numerous art awards. Mem. Artists Fellowship, Am. Artists Profl. League, Nat. Art League, Art League Nassau County, Long Beach Art Assn. (v.p. 1972—), Sumi-E Soc. Am., Chinese Calligraphy Assn. N.Y., Virginia Beach Arts Ctr. Clubs: Salmagundi (N.Y.C.); K.C. Author: Chinese Cooking with an American Touch; Chinese

Hors d'Oeuvre with an American Touch, 1976; perfected method for hand making rice paper with watercolor control texture. Home: 902 W Market St Greensboro NC 27401

CHINKES, HY, management consultant, financial planner; b. Tighina, Roumania, Oct. 14, 1918; s. Max and Anna (Crausman) C.; m. Sophie Jacobs, July 1942 (div. 1955); children—Joel David, Barbara Rebecca; m. 2d, Charlotte Flora Maisel, Sept. 11, 1956. Mfrs. rep. to various photog. cos., 1956-58; pres., founder Crown Camera, Atlanta, 1958-76; fin. planner Consol. Planning, Atlanta, 1976—; spl. place ops. supr. U.S. Census Bur., Atlanta, 1980; pres., chief exec. officer Employment World, Atlanta, 1980-81; founder, chief exec. officer A.P.D. Fin. Services, Atlanta, 1976—; pres., founder Ind. Camera Stores, Atlanta, 1974-76; pres. Atlanta City Salesman's Club, 1975; treas. Service Corps Ret. Execs., Atlanta, 1976—; mem. White House Council Small Businesses, 1978. Founder, mem. bd. Jewish Vocat. Service, Atlanta, 1962—; house dist. chmn., mem. county exec. com. Democratic Party, Atlanta, 1970—; chmn. Devel. Authority Fulton County, Atlanta, 1976-82; mem. allocation panel mem. United Way, Atlanta, 1977—. Democrat. Lodge: Masons. Home: 5335 Chemin De Vie Atlanta GA 30342

CHIRKINIAN, GEORGE WILLIAM, chiropractic physician; b. Richmond, Va., Sept. 21, 1947; s. George William and Frances Carolyn (Box) C.; m. Sharon Juanita Mason, June 18, 1968; children—Tara Lynn, Amanda Kay, Melanie Ann, George William. A.A.S., John Tyler Community Coll., Richmond, 1972-74; student Va. Commonwealth U., 1974-75; B.S. in Biology, Logan Coll., 1976, D.Chiropractic, 1978, cert. applied acupuncture, 1980; D.Homeopathy, Brandon (Fla.) Med. Inst., 1981-82. Physician's asst. Commonwealth of Va., 1972-75; clinic dir., instr. Logan Coll. Chiropractic, St. Louis, 1978-80; gen. practice chiropractic medicine, Richmond, 1980—. Served in M.C., USAF, 1967-71. Recipient Instr. of Yr. award Logan Coll. Chiropractic, 1980. Mem. Am. Chiropractic Assn., Va. Chiropractic Assn., Chi Rho Sigma. Author: Kinesiology Memory Book, 1978; editor student newspaper, 1976-78, Sherwood Forest lit. mag., 1974; contbr. articles to news jour., 1981, 82. Office: 3509 Jefferson Davis Hwy Richmond VA 23234

CHISHOLM, MICHAEL PATRICK, therapist, publisher, author, fin. advisor; b. Cumberland, Md., Jan. 11, 1940; s. Robert V. and Lois C.; B.S. in Psychology cum laude, U. Md., 1961; postgrad. in counseling psychology Beacon Coll., Washington, 1981—; m. Judy Janice Burke, Sept. 13, 1963; children—Lisa, Christopher, Benjamin. Clin. psychologist Control Data Corp., Washington, 1962-64; salesman Blue Ridge Sales, Inc., Winchester, Va., 1964-66, regional mgr., 1966-68, sales mgr., 1968-70, v.p., 1970-75, pres., 1975-76, also dir. editor, pub. Taurus Newsletter, weekly commodity adv. service, 1976—. Registered commodity trading advisor and commodity pool operator Commodity Futures Trading Commn. Mem. Internat. Transactional Analysis Assn., Orthopsychiat. Assn., Assn. for Humanistic Psychology, Nat. Psychiat. Assn., Am. Group Psychotherapy Assn., Mensa. Author: Games Investors Play; The Master Keys to Riches in Commodity Trading. Home: One S Washington St Winchester VA 22601

CHISHOLM, TOMMY, lawyer, utilities exec.; b. Baldwyn, Miss., Apr. 14, 1941; s. Thomas Vaniver and Ruby (Duncan) C.; B.S. in Civil Engring., Tenn. Tech. U., 1963; J.D., Samford U., 1969; M.B.A., Ga. State U.; m. Janice McClanahan, June 20, 1964; children—Mark Alan (dec.), Andrea, Stephen Thomas, Patrick Ervin. Civil engr. TVA, Knoxville, Tenn., 1963-64; with So. Services, Inc., 1963-73, coordinator spl. projects, Atlanta, 1971-73; admitted to Ala. bar, 1969; asst. to pres. So. Co., Atlanta, 1973-75; mgr. adminstrv. services Gulf Power Co., Pensacola, Fla., 1975-77; sec., asst. treas. So. Co., Atlanta, 1977—; sec., house counsel So. Co. Services Inc., Atlanta, 1977-82, v.p., sec., house counsel, 1982—; v.p., corp. sec. So. Electric Internat., Inc., 1981—. Registered profl. engr., Ala., Fla., Ga., Miss., Del., Ky., La., N.C., P.R., S.C., Tenn., Va., W.Va. Mem. ABA, Ala. State Bar, ASCE, Am. Soc. Corp. Secs., Phi Alpha Delta. Lodge: Rotary. Home: 1611 Bryn Mawr Circle Marietta GA 30067 Office: 64 Perimeter Center E Atlanta GA 30346

CHISHOLM, WILLIAM DEWAYNE, contract manager; b. Everett, Wash., Mar. 1, 1924; s. James Adam and Evelyn May (Iles) C.; B.S. in Ch.E., U. Wash., 1949, B.S. in Indsl. Engring., 1949; M.B.A., Harvard U., 1955; m. Esther Troehler, Mar. 10, 1956; children—James Scott, Larry Alan, Brian Duane. Chemist, unit leader, tech. rep. The Coca-Cola Co., Atlanta and Los Angeles, 1949-59; contract adminstr. Honeywell Inc., Los Angeles, 1959-61, mktg. adminstr., 1961-64, contracts work dir., 1964-66, contracts mgr., Clearwater, Fla., 1966-73, contracts supr., 1973-75, sr. contract mgmt. rep., 1975-80, prin. contract mgmt. rep., work dir., 1980-82, contracts mgr. profl. devel. and mgmt. practices, 1982—; adj. faculty Fla. Inst. Tech. Contbr. articles to profl. jours. Trustee, John Calvin Found.; mem. budget adv. bd., City of Clearwater, 1983-85; commr. to 196th gen. assembly Presbyterian Ch. (U.S.A.), 1984. Served with USN, 1944-46. Cert. profl. contracts mgr. Fellow Nat. Contract Mgmt. Assn. (chmn. S.E. region fellows 1984-86, past nat. dir., pres., v.p. Suncoast chpt.). Republican. Presbyterian (elder). Club: Breakfast Optimist of Clearwater (dir. 1982—, disting. sec.-treas. 1983-84, disting. pres. 1984-85). Home: 1364 Hercules Ave S Clearwater FL 33546 Office: Honeywell Inc 13350 US Hwy 19 S Clearwater FL 33546

CHISHOM, ANDREW JAMES, criminal justice educator; b. Augusta, Ga., Oct. 17, 1942; s. Junious and Janie (Robinson) C.; m. Lottie A. Screen, Sept. 17, 1967; children—Mark, André, Wendi. B.Criminology, U. Md.-Balt., 1969; M.A., U. Ga., Atlanta, 1972, Ph.D., 1974; postgrad. Harvard U., 1981. Counselor and supr. Juvenile Placement, Greenville, S.C., 1969-70; U.S. Marshall, S.C., 1976; prof. dept. criminal justice U. S.C., Columbia, 1974—, asst. to pres. minority affairs 1979-81; pres. Palmetto Security, Columbia, 1982—. Chmn. bd. dirs. Midland Vocat. Rehab., Columbia, 1984—, Columbia Community Relations Council, 1984—; founding mem. Crime Stoppers of the Midlands, 1977—. Served to lt. comdr., USN, 1983—. Recipient Andy Chishom-Museum Key to Augusta, Ga., 1984. Mem. Am. Correctional Assn., Am. Police Found., Nat. Blacks in Law Enforcement Execs., C. of C. of Columbia (bd. dirs. 1984—); Omicron Phi. Clubs: 7:30 Breakfast, Luncheon (pres.). Lodge: Masons. Address: Palmetto Security Systems 2110 Wallace St Columbia SC 29201

CHISOLM, GRACE BUTLER, university administrator; b. New Orleans; d. Washington Roosevelt and Althea (Landry) Butler; 1 child, Olethia Elise. B.S. in Music Edn., Xavier U., La., 1958; Mus.M., Northwestern U., 1962; 6th yr. cert. ednl. adminstrn. and supervision Queens Coll., 1972; Ph.D., NYU, 1976. Tchr. music and English, Rivers Frederick Jr. High Sch., New Orleans, 1958-63; tchr. music Bd. Edn. N.Y.C. 1963-69, also acting chmn. music dept. Jr. High Sch. III, Bklyn., 1964-69; dir. coll. prep. and career program Title I, Community Sch. Dist. 16, Bklyn., 1969-73; adj. lectr. Queens Coll., 1974-75; assoc. dir. Univ. Council for Ednl. Adminstrn., Columbus, 1976-78; assoc. prof. ednl. adminstrn. N. Tex. State U., Denton, 1978-83; assoc. prof. ednl. adminstrn. and interdisciplinary edn. Tex. A&M U., College Station, 1983—, asst. to pres., 1985—. Contbr. articles to profl. jours. Eisman scholar, 1962; Edward R. Shaw scholar, 1974; fellow Nat. Fellowship Fund, 1975-76, NYU, 1973-75. Mem. AAUW, Am. Ednl. Research Assn., Assn. Supervision and Curriculum Devel., Brazos Valley Symphony Soc., Nat. Assn. Women Deans, Adminstrs. and Counselors, Nat. Conf. Profs. Ednl. Adminstrn., Tex. Assn. Supervision and Curriculum Devel. Tex. Profs. Ednl. Adminstrn., Delta Sigma Theta, Phi Delta Kappa. Office: Asst to Pres Tex A&M Univ College Station TX 77843

CHISOLM, JACK TAYLOR, physician; b. Birmingham, Ala., July 27, 1923; s. Joseph James and Lillie Tom (Thomasson) C.; student Samford U., 1941-43; Stanford U., 1944; M.D., Med. Coll. Ala., 1947; m. Martha Lee Hatcher, Feb. 7, 1953; children—James Edward, John Craig, Patrick Taylor. Intern, St. Louis City Hosp., 1947-48; resident in surgery Hackensack (N.J.) Hosp., 1948-49, Scott & White Clinic, Temple, Tex., 1949-50, 53-55; pvt. practice medicine, specializing in surgery, Dallas, 1955—; mem. med. staff St. Paul Hosp., Presbyn. Hosp., both Dallas; med. dir. Employers Nat. Life Ins. Co.; med. advisor Employers Casualty Co. Served with AUS, 1943-44, USNR, 1951-53. Diplomate Am. Bd. Surgery. Mem. Am., Tex., So. med. assns., Dallas County Med. Soc. (pres. 1972), A.C.S., Dallas Soc. Gen. Surgeons (pres. 1983-84). Baptist. Home: 6531 Prestonshire St Dallas TX 75225 Office: 8210 Walnut Hill Ln Dallas TX 75231

CHITTENDEN, MARK EUSTACE, JR., marine fisheries educator; b. Jersey City, N.J., July 30, 1939; s. Mark Eustace and Margaret Beaumont (Neil) C.; m. Susan Rae Morrison, Jan. 22, 1967; children—Laura Lynne, Julie Anne. B.A., Hobart Coll., 1960; M.S., Rutgers U., 1965, Ph.D., 1969. Fisheries biologist N.J. Div. Fish and Game, 1960-64; research fellow dept. environ. sci. Rutgers U., 1964-67, research asst., 1967-68, research assoc., 1968-69; asst. prof. marine fisheries Coll. William and Mary, 1969-72, U. Va., 1969-72; assoc. marine scientist Va. Inst. Marine Sci., Gloucester Point, 1969-72; asst. prof. dept. wildlife and fisheries sci. Tex. A&M U., College Station, 1973-77, assoc. prof., 1977-84, prof., 1984; prof. Va. Inst. Marine Sci., Coll. William and Mary, Gloucester Point, 1984—. Mem. Am. Fisheries Soc., Am. Soc. Ichthyologists and Herpetologists, AAAS, Gulf and Caribbean Fisheries Inst., Am. Inst. Fisheries Research Biologists, Nat. Geog. Soc., Nat. Wildlife Fedn. Contbr. numerous articles to profl. jours. Office: Va Inst Marine Sci Gloucester Point VA 23062

CHIVERS, LINDA RUTH, education administrator; b. Atlanta, Aug. 11, 1947; d. Forrest James and Mary Lou (Sills) C. B.S., Ga. Southern Coll., 1969, M.S.T., 1974; Edn. Specialist, Ga. State U., 1984. Tchr., Richmond County Bd. Edn., Augusta, Ga., 1969-75; tchr. DeKalb County Bd. Edn., Decatur, Ga., 1975-80, adminstr., 1980—, asst. prin. Gordon High Sch., 1980—. Mem. Assn. Supervision and Curriculum Devel., DeKalb Assn. Adminstrs., Ga. Edn. Assn., DeKalb Assn. Educators, Common Cause, LWV. Democrat. Presbyterian. Home: 2187 Cloverdale Dr Atlanta GA 30316

CHMIELEWSKI, WALTER BENEDICT, JR., electrical engineer; b. Sloan, N.Y., Mar. 27, 1937; s. Walter Benedict and Sophie Josephine (Dabrowski) C.; m. Ana Maria Medellin, Nov. 24, 1962; children—Carol Ann, Mark Christopher. B.S.E.E., U. Buffalo, 1962; M.B.A., U. Dallas, 1975. Registered profl. engr., Tex. Devel. engr. Home Metal Products, Plano, Tex., 1972-74; field engr. Employers Ins. Tex., Dallas, 1974-76; dist. engr. Employers Casualty Co., Birmingham, Ala., 1976-79; br. engring. mgr. Employers Ins. Tex., Houston, 1979-83, dist. engr. mgr., 1983—; engring. vice chmn. Home Ventilation Inst., Chgo., 1973-74. Contbr. articles to profl. jours. Rules/safety chmn. Houston Engring. Sci. Fair, 1983—. Served to capt. USAF, 1961-67. Mem. Am. Soc. Safety Engrs. Republican. Roman Catholic. Lodge: K.C. (youth dir.). Avocations: computer programming; tennis; swimming; hunting. Home: 17303 Broken Back Dr Crosby TX 77532 Office: Employers Ins Tex 2000 Bering Dr Houston TX 77057

CHO, JAI HANG, hematologist, oncologist, educator; b. Busan, Republic of Korea, May 1, 1942; came to U.S., 1972; s. Neung Whan and Heo Jai (Min) C.; m. Jawon Nam, Oct. 8, 1971; children—Karen, Austin. M.D., Catholic Med. Coll., Seoul, Republic of Korea, 1968. Diplomate Am. Coll. Internal Medicine. Intern, White Plains Hosp., N.Y., 1972-73; resident in internal medicine Nassau Hosp., Mineola, N.Y., 1973-76; fellow in hematology and oncology U. South Fla. Med. Coll., Tampa, 1976-79; practice medicine specializing in hematology and oncology, Tampa, 1979—; mem. staff Univ. Community Hosp., St. Joseph Hosp.; clin. asst. prof. medicine U. South Fla. Med. Coll., 1985—. Served to capt. Korean Army, 1968-71. Mem. AMA, ACP, Fla. Med. Assn., Hillsborough County Med. Assn. Lodge: Rotary. Avocations: cars; golf. Home: 4507 Sweetwater Lake Dr Tampa FL 33613 Office: Northside Med Ctr 13550 N 31st St Tampa FL 33613

CHOPPIN, S(AMUEL) WALKER, banker; b. Nashville, Jan. 31, 1948; s. Samuel Walker and Mildred Evelyn (Goad) C.; m. Marees Henry, Jan. 7, 1984; 1 son, William Henry; m. Jamie Parsley, Sept. 14, 1970 (div. 1980); children—Brian Walker, Laura Elizabeth. B.A., Vanderbilt U., 1970; M.B.A., U. N.C., 1974. Cert. mgmt. acct. Banking officer Commerce Union Bank, Nashville, 1974-77; v.p., treas. Tenn. Natural Gas Lines, Nashville, 1977-80; sr. v.p. Commerce Union Bank, 1980—. Chmn. trustees Samaritan Ctr. Inc., Nashville, 1984-85. Served to lt. (j.g.) USNR, 1970-72. Mem. Fin. Mgrs. Assn. (pres. 1982-83), Nashville Soc. Fin. Analysts. Republican. Presbyterian. Home: 621 Lynwood Blvd Nashville TN 37205 Office: Commerce Union Bank One Commerce Place Nashville TN 37219

CHORGHADE, MUKUND SHANKAR, organic chemist, researcher, educator; b. Jabalpore, India, Apr. 23, 1953; s. Shankar Laxman and Suhasini Vimal (Telang) C. B.S., U. Poona (India), 1971, M.S., 1973; Ph.D., Georgetown U., 1983. Research fellow Nat. Chem. Lab., Poona, 1973-74; officer Bank of Maharashtra (India), 1974-75; chief teaching and research fellow Georgetown U., Washington, 1979-81, chemistry instr., 1981-82; postdoctoral research assoc. U. Va., Charlottesville, 1982—; synthetic chemist Georgetown U. Med. Sch., 1979; NMR specialist, Preston Publs., 1979; tech. translator Drug Enforcement Adminstrn., 1978—. Elected exec. officer India Cultural Coordination Com., Washington. Open merit scholar Govt. Maharashtra, 1969-70; merit scholar Poona U., 1971-73; recipient High Explosive Factory Silver Jubilee Commemoration award, 1973; recipient Poona U. German Assn. award, 1974, Hercules Corp. award, 1976-77, grad. student research prize Sigma Xi, 1982; jr. research fellow Council Sci. and Indsl. Research, India, 1973-74. Contbr. writings to sci. publs. and profl. confs. Office: Room 248 Dept Chemistry Univ Va Charlottesville VA 22901

CHOUN, ROBERT JOSEPH, JR., educator; b. Bridgeport, Conn., Aug. 17, 1948; s. Robert Joseph and Mildred Fitz C.; A.A., Luther Coll., 1969; B.A., Gustavus Adolphus Coll., 1971; M.R.E., Trinity Evangelical Div. Sch., 1974; M.A., Wheaton Coll., 1975; D.Min., Faith Sem., 1980; postgrad. North Tex. State U., 1978—; m. Jane Willson, July 12, 1975. Media relations asst. Am. Bible Soc., N.Y.C., 1969-74; asst prof. Christian edn. Dallas Theol. Sem., 1977—, adj. prof. edn., 1978—; seminar leader early childhood Internat. Center Learning, Ventura, Calif., 1977—; minister edn. Pantego Bible Ch., Arlington, Tex., 1975—. Contbr. articles to profl. jours. and mags. Mem. bd. evaluation Pioneer Ministries, Wheaton, Ill. Mem. Nat. Assn. Dirs. Christian Edn., Christian Camping Internat., Booth Meml. Astronomical Soc., Kappa Delta Phi, Phi Delta Kappa. Home: 818 Clover Park Dr Arlington TX 76013 Office: 2203 W Park Row Arlington TX 76013

CHOW, DAVID KIMKWONG, ophthalmologist, entrepreneur, banker; b. Hong Kong, Jan. 13, 1947; came to U.S., 1972, naturalized, 1985; s. Kam Wai and Wai Chen (Wong) C.; m. Diane Lane, Oct. 10, 1981; 1 child, Lauren. Assoc. of Inst. Bankers, London, 1968; Assoc. Chartered Inst. Secs. and Adminstrs., London, 1971; B.A., La. State U., 1974; M.P.H., M.D., Emory U., 1978. Diplomate Am. Bd. Ophthalmology, Nat. Bd. Med. Examiners. Gen. surgery intern Washington Hosp. Ctr., D.C., 1978-79, ophthalmology resident, 1979-82; banker Hang Seng Bank Ltd., Hong Kong, 1964-71; chmn., chief exec. officer Man Lee Corp., Alexandria, Va., 1984—; practice medicine specializing in ophthalmology, Alexandria, 1982—; active real estate devel. and partnerships worldwide, 1964—. Mem. chmn.'s com. bus. adv. bd. U.S. Senatorial Com., Washington, 1981. Mem. Am. Acad. Ophthalmology, AMA, D.C. Med. Soc., Alexandria Med. Soc. Roman Catholic. Home: 5909 Dawes Ave Alexandria VA 22311 Office: 4900 Leesburg Pike Suite 212 Alexandria VA 22302

CHRISCOE, CHRISTINE FAUST, indsl. trainer; b. Atlanta, Oct. 29, 1950; d. Henry Charles and Shirley Faye (Birdwell) Faust; B.A., Spring Hill Coll., 1973; postgrad. Ga. State U., 1974—; m. Ralph D. Chriscoe, June 25, 1983. Trainer, Fed. Res. Bank, Atlanta, 1973-77; project mgr., tng. dept. Coca Cola U.S.A., Atlanta, 1977-79, sr. project mgr., 1979-81, mgr. tech. tng., 1981-83, mgr. sales, mgmt. and mktg. tng., 1983-85, mgr. bottler tng., 1985—. Trustee Ga. Shakespeare Festival, 1985. Mem. Internat. TV Assn., Am. Soc. Tng. and Devel. Roman Catholic. Office: PO Drawer 1734 Atlanta GA 30301

CHRIST, JOHN ERNEST, plastic surgeon, physiologist; b. Ipswich, Mass., Aug. 27, 1946; s. Christ John and Effie (Vasiliadis) C.; m. Gay Simons, Sept. 19, 1981; children—Alexandra, Nicholas. B.S. cum laude, U. Miami, Coral Gables, 1968; M.D., Baylor Coll. Medicine, 1973, Ph.D., 1974. Diplomate Am. Bd. Plastic Surgery. Instr. physiology Baylor Coll. Medicine, Houston, 1973-74; intern Nassau Hosp, Mineola, N.Y., 1974-75; resident in surgery SUNY, Stony Brook, 1975-78; resident in plastic surgery Baylor Coll. Medicine, 1978-80, inter. physiology, 1979—; practice medicine specializing in plastic surgery, Houston, 1980—. Contbr. articles to med. jours. Pres. Museum Area Mcpl. Assn., Houston, 1983-84. Mem. AMA, Tex. Med. Assn., Harris County Med Soc., Am. Soc. Plastic and Reconstructive Surgery, Am. Physiol. Soc. Mem. Greek Orthodox Ch. Lodge: Ahepa. Office: 6560 Fannin St Houston TX 77030

CHRISTEN, MONICA SUE, university administrator; b. Appleton, Wis., May 1, 1953; d. Wilbert Frank and Marjorie Louise (Wentzel) C. B.S., U. Wis.-Stevens Point, 1975; M.A., Ball State U., 1977. Residence hall dir. Northeast Mo. State U., Kirksville, 1977-79; asst. area coordinator Tex. A&M U., College Station, 1979-81, area coordinator, 1981—. Crisis helper Crisis Hotline, Bryan, Tex., 1983-84. Mem. Am. Coll. Personnel Assn., Am. Assn. Counseling and Devel. Assn. Coll. and Univ. Housing Officers, Nat. Assn. for Female Execs., Phi Delta Kappa. Avocations: reading; needlework; biking; traveling; Home: PO Box 749 College Station TX 77841 Office: Dept Student Affairs 103 YMCA Bldg Tex A&M U College Station TX 77843

CHRISTENSEN, JEAN, musicology educator, author; b. San Bernardino, Calif., Oct. 23, 1940; d. Harold Maxwell and Kathleen Mary (Hatcher) Barnes; m. Jesper Skov Christensen, Mar. 9, 1977; children—Isabella Marie, Nikolaj Mandrup. B.A., Pomona Coll., 1962; M.A., U. Calif.-Riverside, 1970, Ph.D., UCLA, 1979. Assoc. prof. musicology U. Louisville, Ky., 1979—. Author: Arnold Schoenberg's Oratorio Die Jakobsleiter, 1979; From the Schoenberg Literary Legacy: A Catalog of Neglected Items, 1984. Denmark-Amerika Found. grantee, Copenhagen, 1975-77; grantee Martha Baird Rockefeller Fund for Music, 1978-79, Amerika-Danmark Fondet, Copenhagen and Arhus, 1983. Fellow Arnold Schoenberg Inst., Louisville Jazz Soc. (bd. dirs., editor newsletter 1984—); mem. Soc. for Music Theory, Internat. Soc. for Contemporary Music, Am. Musicol. Soc. Office: Sch of Music U Louisville Louisville KY 40292

CHRISTENSEN, KURT KJELD, engineer, scientist; b. Oslo, Norway, Sept. 1, 1957; parents U.S. citizens, s. Wayne John and Arlene (Mitchell) C. B.S. in Physics, Va. Poly. Inst. and State U., 1981, B.S. in Math., 1983, M.S. in Elec. Engring., 1984. Lic. engr.-in-tng.; lic. FCC radio telephone operator. Broadcast engr. Blacksburg Town Council, Sta. WUVT-FM, 1979-82; elec. design engr. Tex. Instruments, McKinney, Tex., 1983—; researcher artificial intelligence Radar Systems Div., 1984—; elec. engr., cons. Animated Concepts, Richardson, Tex., 1984—. Patentee in field. Mem. zoning evaluation team McKinney Heights Homeowners Assn., 1985. Mem. IEEE, Soc. Physics Students, Laser Inst. Am., N.Y. Acad. Scis., Soc. Automotive Engrs., ASME, Math. Assn. Am., Am. Radio Relay League, Assn. Computing Machinery, Assn. Computational Linguistics, Sigma Pi Sigma, Mu Phi Epsilon. Avocations: woodworking, skydiving, amateur radio, computer programming, holography. Home: 1913 Wisteria Way McKinney TX 75096 Office: Tex Instruments PO Box 801 M/S 8025 McKinney TX 75069

CHRISTENSEN, MARGARET ANNA, human resource consultant, registered nurse; b. San Francisco, Nov. 10, 1938; d. John Bernard and Catherine (Scott) Thielen; m. Robert Edwin Christensen, June 24, 1961; children—Marthe Elizabeth, Katrina Marie, Andrea Susan. B.S., Wichita State U., 1978; Ed.M., Central State U., Okla., 1984; postgrad. Okla. State U., 1984—. Staff devel. supr. St. Joseph Med. Ctr., Wichita, Kans., 1972-79; head nurse Baptist Med. Ctr., Oklahoma City, 1970-80; clin. supr. Mercy Health Ctr., Oklahoma City, 1980-81, staff devel. coordinator, 1981-84; prin. Human Resource Cons., Inc., Edmond, Okla., 1985—; dir. planning and devel. Allied Nursing Care, Inc., Oklahoma City, 1984-85; mgmt. cons., 1982—. Author human resource devel. process, 1984; (booklet) Live-In Companion Guide, 1984. Mem. Parents for Child Safety Assn., Oklahoma City, 1983—. Mem. Am. Assn. Adult and Continuing Edn., Am. Soc. Tng. and Devel., Okla. Inservice Edn. Assn., Nat. League Nursing, Okla. Lifelong Learning Assn., Edmond C. of C., Alpha Chi, Kappa Delta Pi. Republican. Roman Catholic. Home: 2809 Summer Set Trail Edmond OK 73034 Office: Human Resource Cons Inc 2 E 11th St Suite 19 Edmond OK 73034

CHRISTIAN, FRANCES MARIE, social worker, educator; b. Richmond, Va., Dec. 7, 1948; d. Washington M. and Annie M. Mayo (Brown) Christian. Student, Davis and Elkins (W.Va.) Coll., 1967-70; B.A. cum laude, Howard U., 1972; M.S.W., U. Mich., 1974. Lic. clin. social worker, Va. Psychiat. social worker Meml. Guidance Clinic, Richmond, 1974-76; part-time instr. J. Sargent Reynolds Community Coll., Richmond, 1978-81; instr., dept. psychiatry Med. Coll. Va., Richmond, 1976—; part-time staff therapist, cons. Family and Children's Services, Richmond, 1982—; gov.'s appointee Social Work Licensing Bd., Va. Dept. Health Regulatory, 1980-85, chmn., 1983—. Chmn. East End Mental Health Clinic adv. bd., Richmond, 1977-82; bd. dirs. Richmond Area Assn. for Retarded Citizens, membership chmn., 1979-81. Recipient Outstanding Vol. Service award City of Richmond East End Mental Health Clinic Adv. Bd., 1982; mem. Richmond Citizens' Adv. Bd. Comprehensive Mental Health Clinics, 1982—, vice chmn., 1982-83. Mem. Nat. Assn. Black Social Workers, Inc. (membership chmn. Richmond chpt.), Va. Commonwealth U. Black Edn. Assn., Howard U. Alumni Assn., Richmond Jazz Soc., NAACP. Democrat. Contbr. articles to profl. jours. Home: 3302 Hazelhurst Ave Richmond VA 23222 Office: Med Coll Va Outpatient Psychiatry Clinic 307 College St Box 253 Richmond VA 23298

CHRISTIAN, HUGH, broadcasting executive; b. Athens, Ga., Mar. 10, 1943; s. L.H. and Sara (Bradbury) C.; m. Claudia Elaine Craft, June 25, 1967; children—Christelle, Cherylle, Cheri; m. Carolyn F. Bowen, May 1, 1982. B.B.A. in Acctg., U. Ga., 1966. Lic. broadcast engr., FCC. Mgr., Beechwood Cinema, Athens, 1961-66; asst. mgr., chief engr. Sta. WRFC, Athens, 1970-72, pres., dir. Radio Athens, Inc., (WRFC, Athens and WFOX, Gainesville, Ga.), 1976-83; account exec. Merrill Lynch Co., Athens, 1972-74; owner, mgr. Padgett Bus. Services of Augusta (Ga.), 1974-76; co-owner, co-pres., co-chmn. AM 96, Inc. (Sta. WRFC), 1983—. Bd. dirs. Athens/Clarke County unit Am. Cancer Soc., 1976—, Athens Heart Assn., 1982—; exec. com. Clarke County Democratic party, 1979—. Served to capt. USAF, 1967-70. Ger. Mem. Ga. Assn. Pub. Accts., Athens Area C. of C. (chmn. mem. relations div. 1980-83, dir.), Athens Assn. Computer Users, Athens IBM PC User Group (pres. 1985), Tau Kappa Epsilon (chpt. adviser). Club: Athens Adclub (dir., membership chmn.). Home: 540 S Milledge Ave Athens GA 30605 Office: Sta WRFC 255 S Milledge Ave Athens GA 30605

CHRISTIAN, JOHN CATLETT, JR., lawyer; b. Springfield, Mo., Sept. 12, 1929; s. John Catlett and Alice Odelle (Milling) C.; A.B., Drury Coll., 1951; LL.B., Tulane U., 1956; m. Peggy Jeanne Cain, Apr. 12, 1953; children—Cathleen Marie, John Catlett III, Alice Cain. Admitted to La. bar, 1956, Mo. bar, 1956, to practice before Supreme Ct. U.S., Fifth Circuit Ct. Appeals, Western and Eastern Dists. Fed. Cts. La.; assoc. firm Porter & Stewart, Lake Charles, La., 1956-58; assoc. firm, then ptnr. firm Wilkinson, Lewis, Wilkinson & Madison, Shreveport, La., 1958-64; ptnr. firm Milling, Benson, Woodward, Hillyer & Pierson, New Orleans, 1964—; pres. Sherburne Land Co., 1974-83; dir. Emerald Land Co. Pres. Kathleen Elizabeth O'Brien Found., 1963—. Served with USMC, 1951-53. Fellow Am. Coll. Trial Lawyers; mem. Am., Mo., Fed., La. bar assns., Am. Judicature Soc., La. Landowners Assn. (dir. 1983—), Omicron Delta Kappa, Phi Delta Phi, Kappa Alpha Order. Clubs: Boston, Essex, Plimsoll, Petroleum (New Orleans), Beau Chene Country. Home: 807 Tete L'ours Dr Mandeville LA 70448 Office: Whitney Bank Bldg New Orleans LA 70130

CHRISTIAN, LYLE MCCLELLAN, funeral home owner; b. Churchill Hill, Tenn., July 15, 1928; s. James Wiley and Lucy Ellen (Hutchinson) C.; m. Virginia Anne Denise, Dec. 17, 1950; children—Christopher McClellan, Kari Anne. Diploma, John A. Gupton Sch. Mortuary Sci., 1948; B.S. in Bus. Adminstrn., U. Tenn.-Knoxville, 1958. Lic. funeral dir., embalmer. Cons., Bluefield Casket Co., Va., 1958-60, Internat. Order of Golden Rule, Springfield, Ill., 1960-62, Am. Soc. Funeral Dirs., Jacksonville, Fla., 1962-65; pres., owner Bass Funeral Home, Rock Hill, S.C., 1965—; mem. S.C. State Bd. Funeral Service, 1976-79. Bd. dirs. Salvation Army Rock Hill, 1976, 83, YMCA Rock Hill, 1976-79, 83—. Served with USMC, 1946-48, 50-51. Recipient Leadership & Service award Rock Hill C. of C., 1970, 77. Mem. S.C. Funeral Dirs. Assn. (pres. 1974-75), Nat. Funeral Dirs. Assn., Nat. Selected Morticians, Internat. Order Golden Rule, Associated Funeral Dirs. Soc., Rock Hill C. of C. Clubs: Rotary. Home: 2531 Shiland Dr Rock Hill SC 29730 Office: Bass Funeral Home 331 E Main St Rock Hill SC 29731

CHRISTIAN, ROBERT RAYMOND, biology educator, researcher; b. Phila., Sept. 2, 1947; s. Raymond and Dorothy Weida (Seidel) C.; m. Carol Ann Rich, Sept. 5, 1970; children—David Joseph, Juliet. A.B., Rutgers U., 1969; M.S., U. Ga., 1972, Ph.D., 1976. Asst. instr. biology Rutgers U., Camden, N.J., 1970-72; asst. prof. Drexel U., Phila., 1976-81; research assoc. U. Ga., Athens and Sapelo Island, 1979-80; assoc. prof. biology East Carolina U., Greenville, N.C., 1981-85, prof., 1985—. Recipient Outstanding Dissertation award U. Ga., 1976; grantee EPA, N.C. Sea Grant Program and others. Mem. Atlantic Estuarine Research Soc. (pres. 1982-84), Am. Soc. Microbiology, AAAS, Ecol. Soc. Am., Sigma Xi. Democrat. Episcopalian. Contbr. articles to profl. jours., books and symposia volumes. Home: 3208 Ellsworth Dr Greenville NC 27834 Office: Biology Dept East Carolina U Greenville NC 27834

CHRISTIAN, THOMAS FRANKLIN, JR., aerospace engineer; b. Macon, Ga., Mar. 2, 1946; s. Thomas Franklin and Lucille Vanessa (Solomon) C.; B.A.E., Ga. Inst. Tech., 1968, M.S.A.E., 1970, Ph.D., 1974; M.S. in Engring. Adminstrn., U. Tenn., 1976; m. Jan McGarity, Apr. 30, 1983; 1 child, Ellen Caroline. Sr. design engr. nuclear analytical engring. Combustion Engring., Inc., Chattanooga, 1973-77; team mgr. IF-1 pilot plant Procter & Gamble, Macon, 1977-80; program mgr. durability and damage tolerance assessment, Warner Robins Air Logistics Center, Robins AFB, Ga., 1980-85, chief engr., 1985—; adj. prof. math. Cleveland State Community Coll., 1976-77; adj. prof. engring. Mercer U., 1986—. Bd. dirs. Warner Robbins Little Theatre. Registered profl. engr., Ga., Tenn.; cert. profl. logistician. Mem. N.Y. Acad. Scis., AIAA (assoc. fellow), ASME, Soc. for History Tech., Soc. for Exptl. Stress Analysis, AAAS, Soc. Logistics Engrs. (Ga. state bd. dirs., Schoenberg award 1985), ASTM, Air Force Assn., Middle Ga. Art Assn., Ga. Inst. Tech. Alumni Assn., Macon Little Theater, Order of Engr., Sigma Xi, Pi Tau Chi. Methodist. Home: 101 Chadwick Dr Warner Robins GA 31088 Office: WR ALC/MMSR Robins AFB GA 31098

CHRISTIAN, THOMAS WILLIAM, lawyer; b. Tuscaloosa, Ala., Aug. 23, 1938; s. George William and Grace (Mandeville) C.; m. Dorothy Rosamond, Jan. 23, 1965; children—George, Ed, Delia. A.B., U. Ala., 1960, LL.B., 1965. Bar: Ala. 1965, U.S. Dist. Ct. (no. dist.) Ala. 1965, U.S. Ct. Appeals (5th cir.) 1971, U.S. Supreme Ct. 1973. Ptnr. firm Balch & Bingham, Birmingham, Ala., 1965-81, firm Rives & Peterson, Birmingham, 1981—. Served to lt. U.S. Army, 1961-63. Fellow Am. Coll. Trial Lawyers; mem. ABA, Ala. State Bar, Birmingham Bar Assn. (pres. 1984), Ala. Defense Lawyers Assn. (pres. 1979), Internat. Assn. Ins. Counsel. Presbyterian. Clubs: Birmingham Country, Downtown, Redstone. Avocations: fishing; jogging; nautilis. Home: 3756 Dunbarton Dr Birmingham AL 35223 Office: Rives & Peterson 1700 Fin Center Birmingham AL 35203-2696

CHRISTIAN-GARY, COLLDEN OLLIE, social work educator; b. Ocala, Fla., Sept. 22, 1946; d. Homer Alfred and Ollie (Collden) Gary; m. Frederick Ade Christian, Dec. 11, 1971; children—Frederick Gary, Angella YeWande. B.S., Paine Coll., 1968, M.S.W., La. State U., 1971, M.A., 1980, Ph.D., 1986. Field supr. So. U., Baton Rouge, 1971-76, also social work instr; clin. social worker Dept. Corrections, Baton Rouge, 1971, coordinator symposium on institutionalized youth, 1974; social worker Sante Fe Jr. Coll., Gainesville, Fla., summer 1970; teaching asst. La State U., Baton Rouge, 1981-84, asst. prof. social work, 1984—. lectr., 1984, Active Mt. Zion Meth. Ch., Ocala, 1961-71; vol. nursing home, Baton Rouge, 1981-82; tchr. illiterate adults Augusta Community Ctr., Augusta, Ga., 1968; asst. tchr. Mt. Carmel Ch., Baton Rouge, 1982—. La State U. scholar, 1981-84; NIMH grantee, 1969-71. Mem. Am. Social. Assn., Sociol. Inquiry, Family Relations Council La., Alpha Kappa Delta, Phi Lambda Pi. Democrat. Avocations: piano; violin; horse-riding; poetry; exercise.

CHRISTIANSEN, MARJORIE MINER, nutrition educator; b. Canton, Ill., Feb. 28, 1922; d. John Ernest and Margaret Ellen (Wilson) Miner; m. Theodore Leo Christiansen, Aug. 10, 1951; 1 dau., Karen Lee. Student Joliet Jr. Coll., 1939-41, Iowa State U., 1941-42; B.S., U. N.Mex., 1949, M.A., 1955; Ph.D., Utah State U., 1967. Registered dietitian, N.Mex., Va. Instr. sci. and nutrition Regina Sch. Nursing, Albuquerque, 1950-64, project dir., 1966-69; project dir., adj. prof. U. Albuquerque, 1969; prof. home econs. James Madison U., Harrisonburg, Va., 1969-84, prof. emeritus, 1984—; nutrition cons. Mental Devel. Ctr., Albuquerque, 1968-69; project dir. Dietary Mgmt. Seminars, VA Regional Med. Program, 1973-76. Mem. adv. Com. on spl. edn. Harrisonburg (Va.) pub. schs., 1972-84. Utah State U. fellow, 1963-67; grantee Corn Products Co., 1965, Nurse Tng. Act Pub. Health Service, 1966-69. Mem. Am. Dietetic Assn., Va. Dietetic Assn. Methodist. Contbr. articles to profl. jours. Home: 94 Laurel St Harrisonburg VA 22801

CHRISTIE, LAURENCE GLENN, JR., surgeon; b. Houston, May 13, 1930; s. Laurence Glenn and Tommie Katherine (Myers) C.; B.S., Washington and Lee U., 1953; M.D., Med. Coll. Va., 1957; m. Constance Graham Kelsey, Sept. 15, 1973; 1 dau. Susan Elizabeth. Intern surgery Med. Coll. Va., 1957-58, resident surgery, 1957-62; practice medicine specializing in gen. and vascular surgery, Ft. Smith, Ark., 1962-63, Richmond, Va., 1963—; clin. instr. Med. Coll. Va., Richmond, 1963—; mem. active staff Henrico Doctors Hosp.; courtesy staff Stuart Circle Hosp., Grace Hosp., St. Mary's Hosp., Richmond Meml. Hosp., St. Luke's Hosp.; mem. courtesy staff Retreat Hosp.; chmn. dept. surgery chmn. med. exec. com., med. dir. Henrico Doctors Hosp., also vice chmn. bd. trustees, 1981—, chief staff, 1982—; courtesy staff Richmond Met. Hosp.; pres. Med. Planning Corp. Mem. sci. adv. bd. Richmond chpt. Nat. Found. for Ileitis and Colitis, Inc. Diplomate Am. Bd. Surgery. Fellow A.C.S.; mem. Southeastern Surg. Congress, So. Med. Assn., Richmond Acad. Medicine, Richmond Surg. and Gynecol. Soc., Med. Soc. Va., AMA, Humera Soc. Episcopalian. Clubs: Bull and Bear, Irish Setter of Greater Richmond, Irish Setter of Am. Contbr. articles to profl. jours. Home: Killagay Crozier VA 23039 Office: Suite 402 7605 Forest Ave Richmond VA 23229

CHRISTIE, MARY LOU BRANDON, educator; b. Waverly, Iowa, Nov. 7, 1917; d. William Lewis and Mary Wilson (Cooke) Brandon; A.B., John B. Stetson U., 1942; M.S., Fla. State U., 1969, doctoral studies, 1969-71; m. William Traugott Christie Jr., May 2, 1942 (div. Oct. 1970), remarried May 18, 1974; children—Mary Elizabeth, Lewis Traugott, Terris Jean. Tchr., Orange City (Fla.) Elementary Sch., 1939-43; tchr., dir. girls phys. edn. Leon High Sch., Tallahassee, 1943-45; owner, mgr. Christie's Kiddie Kottage-Juvenile Retail Store, Tallahassee, 1948-61; tchr. Fed. Correctional Instn., Tallahassee, 1966-67; counselor Leon County Juvenile Ct., Tallahassee, 1969-70, supr. tng., 1970-71; dir. tng., youth counselor supr. Bur. Field Services, Fla. Div. Youth Services, Tallahassee, 1971-75, dist. coordinator vol. programs, 1972-75, acting regional dir. Bur. Community Service, 1975—, vol. program specialist, 1975-76; instr. Lively Vocat. Tech. Center, 1976-83; tchr. piano, Tallahassee, 1934-48, 62-74; guest lectr. Fla. State U., also Fla. A. and M. U., 1967-71. Mem. Leon County Sch. Bd., 1965-69, chmn. bd., 1968; mem. Fla. Gov.'s Task Force on Standards. Chmn. adv. com. Sunland Hosp., Tallahassee, 1969-70; sec., dir. Leon Assn. for Retarded Children, 1969-70; mem. Leon County Assn. Community Services. Bd. dirs. Easter Seal Rehab. Center, 1953—, sec., 1955-65; bd. dirs. Vol. Action Center of Leon County; adv. bd. Supplementary Assistance Center Leon County, Fla. Assn. Health and Social Services, Inc. Mem. NEA, Fla. Teaching Profession Assn., Leon County Tchrs. Assn., Tallahassee Music Tchrs. Assn., D.A.R. (regent 1959-61), Fla. Council on Crime and Delinquency, Lambda Alpha Epsilon. Baptist. Club: Tallahassee Womans. Author: A Model for the Training of Interns in Juvenile Corrections, 1974; Informational Manual for Full-time Vocational Training, 1977. Home: 1437 Chowkeebin Nene Tallahassee FL 32301

CHRISTILLES, WILLIAM EDWARD, mathematics educator; b. San Antonio, June 16, 1931; s. Emil Sabastion and Mildren (Christian) C.; m. Joy Ann Alsbury, Apr. 17, 1950; children—Susan Joy, Robert Edward. B.S. in Math., Trinity U., 1956; M.S. in Math., 1960. Tchr., St. Mary's U., San Antonio, 1960-74; tchr. math., San Antonio, 1974—. Contbr. articles to profl. jours. Mem. Am. Math. Soc., Math. Am. Republican. Methodist. Avocation: table tennis. Home and Office: 3534 Rock Creek Run San Antonio TX 78230

CHRISTMAN, ARTHUR CASTNER, JR., government official, physicist; b. North Wales, Pa., May 11, 1922; s. Arthur Castner and Hazel Ivy (Schirmer) C.; m. Marina Ilia Diterichs, Apr. 17, 1945; children—Candace Lee Christman Cupps, Tatiana Marina Christman Harvey, Deborah Ann Christman Clark, Arthur Castner III, Keith Ilia, Cynthia Ellen. B.S. in Physics, Pa. State U., 1944, M.S. in Physics, 1950. Teaching asst. Pa. State U., State College, 1943-44, grad. asst., 1946-48; instr. George Washington U., Washington, 1948-51; physicist Ops. Research Office, Johns Hopkins U., Chevy Chase, Md., 1951-58; sr. physicist Stanford Research Inst., Menlo Park, Calif., 1958-62, head ops. research group, 1962-64, mgr. ops. research, 1965-67, dir. opns. research dept., 1968-71, dir. tactical weapons systems, 1971-75; sci. advisor to comdg. gen. and dep. chief of staff combat devels. U.S. Army Tng. and Doctrine Command, Ft. Monroe, Va., 1975—; cons. U.S. Navy, Washington, 1950-51. Contbr. numerous articles to profl. jours. and mil. publs. Umpire, Palo Alto (Calif.) Little League, 1962-72. Served to lt. USN, 1944-46, PTO. Decorated Meritorious Civilian Service award Dept. Army, 1983; recipient Meritorious Exec. award, 1985. Fellow AAAS; mem. Am. Phys. Soc., Ops. Research Soc. Am., Sci. Research Soc., Sigma Xi, Sigma Pi Sigma, Delta Chi. Republican. Baptist (deacon, trustee). Home: 102 Sherwood Dr Williamsburg VA 23185 Office: Hdqrs Tng and Doctrine Command Fort Monroe VA 23651

CHRISTOPHER, FLOYD HUDNALL, JR., tobacco company executive; b. Franklin, Va., Dec. 9, 1933; s. Floyd Hudnall and Dorothy Eberwine (Ames) C.; m. Claire Penn Cannon, Feb. 11, 1961; children—John H., Ashley Penn, David Ames. B.Chem.Engring., U. Va., 1955; S.M., MIT, 1959. With R.J. Reynolds Industries, Inc., 1959; v.p. R.J. Reynolds Tobacco Co., Winston-Salem, N.C., 1976-79, sr. v.p., 1981-83, exec. v.p., 1983—, dir., 1981—; pres., chief exec. officer RJR Archer, Inc., 1979-81, dir., 1979—; dir. Wachovia Bank & Trust Co. Bd. dirs. United Way Forsyth County, 1978—, Reynolda House Mus. Am. Art; bd. visitors Wake Forest U., Winston-Salem; bd. overseers Sweet Briar Coll. (Va.); mem. com. Winston-Salem Found.; chmn. bd. United Way Forsyth County, 1986. Served to lt. (j.g.) USN, 1955-57. Mem. Aluminum Assn. (dir. 1979-81), Winston-Salem C. of C. Republican. Episcopalian. Clubs: Old Town (bd. govs.), Twin City (Winston-Salem), Rotary. Home: 2837 Reynolds Dr Winston-Salem NC 27104 Office: 401 N Main St Winston-Salem NC 27102

CHRISTOPHER, JOYCE MAE, media resource specialist, librarian; b. Carthage, Tex., Aug. 13, 1933; d. Elmer and Cora L. (Willis) Guinn; m. Clyde Christopher, June 13, 1953 (div. July 1980); children—Gerald Allen, Mitchell Claude, Michael Clyde. B.S., Praire View A&M Coll., 1966, M.Ed., 1969, M.S., 1981. Cert. elem. tchr., librarian, learning resources specialist, Tex. Librarian, Cypress-Fairbanks Ind. Sch. Dist., Houston, 1966—. Youth dir. Bethlehem United Meth. Ch., Hempstead, Tex., 1970—; leader Boy Scouts Am., 1977-79; mem. Jack and Jill, Inc. of Am., Prairie View, 1970-79. Mem. ALA, Tex. Library Assn., Tex. Tchrs. Assn., NEA, Alpha Kappa Alpha, Delta Kappa Gamma. Democrat. Home: Hill and Smith Sts PO Box 2782 Prairie View TX 77446 Office: Cy-Fair High School 22602 Hempstead Hwy Houston TX 77040

CHRISTOPHER, TOM ALLEN, accountant; b. Richmond, Ky., Dec. 19, 1947; s. Clyde Tom and Mary Kaye (Howell) C.; m. Sally Lou Zartman, Dec. 21, 1968; children—Laura Beth, David Thomas, John Allen. B.S., Georgetown Coll. (Ky.). C.P.A., Ky. Staff acct. Arthur Young & Co., Cin., 1969-71; mgr. Robinson & Hughes, C.P.A.s, Danville, Ky., 1971-74; tnr. Robinson, Hughes & Christopher, Danville, 1974-77, mng. ptnr., 1977—. Bd. dirs. Christian Appalachian Project, Lancaster, Ky., Living Word Evangel. Assn., Lexington, Ky.; deacon 1st Baptist Ch., Danville. Mem. Ky. Soc. C.P.A.s (mgmt. adv. services com. 1978-79, mgmt. acctg. practice com. 1981-83), Am. Inst. C.P.A.s, Accts. Computer Users Tech. Exchange, Danville C. of C. (dir.). Office: Robinson Hughes & Christopher CPAs 459 W Green St Danville KY 40422

CHRISTY, AUDREY MEYER, public relations consultant; b. N.Y.C., Mar. 11, 1933; d. Mathias J. and Harriet Meyer; B.A., U. Buffalo, 1967; m. James R. Christy, Apr. 19, 1952; children—James R., III, Kathryn M., John T., Alysia A., William J. Public relations officer Turgeon Bros., Buffalo, 1968-69; mem. public relations staff Sch. Fine Arts, U. Nebr., Omaha, 1972; public relations exec. Mathews & Clark Advt., Sarasota, Fla., 1974-75; profiles editor Tampa Bay mag., Tampa, Fla., 1972; public relations cons. Bildex Corp., 1973-79; owner, operator Christy & Assos., Venice, Fla., 1976—. Vice chmn. Erie County March of Dimes, 1970; bd. dirs. Sarasota chpt. Am. Cancer Soc.; mem. S.W. Fla. Ambulance Adv. Com., 1981-86; pres. Community Health Edn. Council, 1983; mem. community adv. bd. Jr. League Sarasota. Recipient various advt. awards. Mem. Public Relations Soc. Am. (Community Service award 1985), Sarasota Manatee Press Club, Sarasota County C. of C. (bd. dirs. 1984-86, exec. com. 1984-85, vice chmn. membership 1984, vice chmn. mktg. 1985, chmn. speakers bus. 1986), Sarasota Manatee Press Club (dir.), LWV (editor Sarasota publ. 1978-79). Address: 216 Bayshore Circle Venice FL 33595

CHRISTY, TINA SUZANNE, banker; b. Sacramento, Nov. 11, 1955; d. Clayton R. and Mary Micki (O'Keefe) C. B.A. summa cum laude, Tex. Luth. Coll., 1979. Sec. Nat. Sharedata Corp., San Antonio, 1973-74; mil. banking rep. Broadway Nat. Bank, San Antonio, 1975-77; asst. auditor Broadway Nat. Bank, San Antonio, 1977-78; asst. to cashier Merc. Bank and Trust Co., San Antonio, 1979-80; auditor First City Bank-Central Park, San Antonio, 1980-82, asst. v.p. ops., 1982-83; v.p., cashier, sec. bd. dirs. First City Bank, Forum N.A., San Antonio, 1983—. Mem. regional exec. bd. Muscular Dystrophy Assn., chpt. sec., broadcasting coordinator ann. telethon; vol. Girl Scouts U.S.A.; vol. Distributive Edn. Clubs Am., KLRN Pub. TV Auction. Mem. Am. Inst. Banking (bd. dirs., treas. chpt.), Bank Adminstrn. Inst., Inst. Internal Auditors, San Antonio Security Assn., Alpha Chi. Republican. Roman Catholic. Office: PO Box 5935 San Antonio TX 78201

CHU, CHAUNCEY CHENG-HSI, language educator, linguistic researcher; b. Jiangsu, China, Nov. 21, 1930; came to U.S., 1963; s. He-Lin and Wan-Yue (Mao) C.; m. Cheng-Yung Yang, Feb. 28, 1966; children—Jerome, Gary. B.A., Taiwan Normal U., 1953, M.A., 1959; M.A., U. Tex., 1964, Ph.D., 1970. English instr. Tainan 2d High Sch., Taiwan, 1954-57; instr., asst. prof. Taiwan Normal U., Taipei, 1959-67; asst. to assoc. prof. U. Fla., Gainesville, 1970-84, prof. language, 1984—, dir. linguistic program, 1979-82; mem. acad. adv. bd. U. Central China, Wuhan, 1982—. Editorial bd. Student Book Co., Taipei, 1979—. Served to 2d lt. Air Force, 1955-57. Recipient Disting. Teaching award U. Fla. 1975. Mem. Linguistic Soc. Am., Chinese Lang. Tchrs. Assn., Southeastern Conf. Linguistics (pres. 1981-82), Linguistics Assn. Can., Linguistics Assn. U.S., Gulf Tchrs. English for Speakers of Other Languages Assn. Avocations: jogging, swimming, basketball, reading, classical music. Office: U Fla Linguistics Program Gainesville FL 32611

CHUBIN, DARYL EVAN, sociologist, educator; b. Chgo., Jan. 8, 1947; s. Alvin and Shirley S. (Poet) C.; m. Vicki Bluestone, Dec. 22, 1968; children—Rand, Jessica. Student U. Ill.-Chgo., 1965-66; A.B., Miami U., Oxford, Ohio, 1968; A.M., Loyola U., Chgo., 1971, Ph.D., 1973. Instr. So. Ill. U., Edwardsville, 1972-73; research assoc. Cornell U., 1973-76, acting asst. prof., 1974-76; vis. asst. prof. U. Pa., 1976-77; asst. prof. social scis. Ga. Inst. Tech., 1977-82, assoc. prof., 1982-85, prof., 1986—, dir. tech. and sci. policy program, 1982—; vis. assoc. prof. Program on Sci., Tech. and Society, Cornell U., 1983-84; cons. in field. Johnson Wax fellow, 1980. Mem. AAAS, Am. Sociol. Assn., Soc. Social Studies of Sci. (founding), Sigma Xi. Author: (with K.E. Studer) The Cancer Mission: Social Contexts of Biomedical Research, 1980; Sociology of Sciences, 1983; Interdisciplinary Research and Analysis, 1986. Contbr. articles to profl. jours. Office: Sch Social Scis Ga Inst Tech Atlanta GA 30332

CHUNG, JAE WAN, economics educator; b. On Yang, Korea, Apr. 26, 1937; came to U.S., 1965; s. Il Hee and Bo Boon (Kim) C.; m. Soojun Lee, May 23, 1967; children—Caroline, Edward. B.Commerce, Seoul Nat. U., Korea, 1962; Ph.D. in Econs., NYU, 1972. Mem. profl. research staff Bank of Korea, Seoul, 1962-65, adviser, 1981; vis. prof. Seoul Nat. U., 1981; asst. prof., then assoc. prof. econs. George Mason U., Fairfax, Va., 1972—; seminar cons. Inter-Am. Def. Coll., Washington, 1975-80. Area corr. So. Econ. Jour., Washington, 1983—. Contbr. articles to profl. publs. Mem. Am. Econ. Assn., So. Econ. Assn. Office: Dept Econs George Mason U 4400 University Dr Fairfax VA 22030

CHUPIK, EUGENE JERRY, business executive, financial consultant; b. Temple, Tex., Jan. 22, 1931; s. Jerry Joe and Annie E. C.; m. Betty Lou Fletcher, Feb. 2, 1957; children—Stephen, Donald. B.B.A., U. Tex., Austin, 1957. Auditor, Peat, Marwick, Mitchell & Co., Dallas, 1957-61; comptroller Vantex Enterprises, Inc., Dallas, 1961-64, v.p., 1964-66, exec. v.p., 1966—. Served with USN, 1949-54. Mem. Petroleum Accts. Soc., Dallas C. of C., Nat. Fedn. Ind. Bus., Real Estate Fin. Execs. Assn. Republican. Methodist. Club: Northwood Country (Dallas). Home: 4500 Stanhope Dallas TX 75205 Office: Vantex Enterprises Inc 1825 W Mockingbird Dallas TX 75235

CHURCHILL, FREDERICK CHARLES, research chemist; b. Pitts., Nov. 7, 1940; s. Frederick C. and Mary Alleen (Thomas) C.; B.S. summa cum laude, Lafayette Coll., 1962; M.A., Harvard U., 1964; student Georgetown U., 1968-69; Ph.D., U. Ga., 1980; m. Nancy Lee McMurran, Apr. 3, 1970; children—Celeste Marie, Christopher Frederick. With Tech. Devel. Labs., Centers for Disease Control, U.S. Dept. Health and Human Services, Savannah, Ga., 1964-73, Atlanta, 1973-82, scientist, dir. in Ctr. Infectious Diseases, Atlanta, 1981—. Nat. Presbyn. scholar, 1958-62; USPHS Commendation medal, 1983. Mem. Am. Chem. Soc., Commd. Officers Assn. of USPHS, Atlanta Chromatography Discussion Group, Mensa, Intertel, Phi Beta Kappa. Presbyn. Author publs. in field; lectr. sci. meetings. Home: Route 1 Box 5864 Auburn GA 30203 Office: Centers for Disease Control Center for Infectious Diseases Atlanta GA 30333

CHURCHILL, STANLEY WINSTON, college dean; b. Clinton, Okla., Sept. 24, 1931; s. Alton I. and Mildred (Green) C.; m. Martha Jo Vaughan, Dec. 5, 1958; children—Terre Renee, Kindra Kay. B.S., Southwest Tex. State U., 1958, M.Ed., 1962. Tchr. indsl. cooperative tng., New Braunfels, Tex., 1958-59, Grand Prairie, Tex., 1959-61, Seguin, Tex., 1965-67; dean vocat. and tech. edn. Temple Jr. Coll., Tex., 1967—. Mem. Emergency Med. Service, 1982—, Central Tex. Council of Govt., 1983-84; mem. exec. bd. Pvt. Industry council, 1984—. Served to 1st lt. USAF, 1951-55, Korea. Recipient Outstanding Law Enforcement award Temple Police Dept., 1978, Instr. award Tex. Safety Assn., 1981, 82. Mem. Post Secondary Deans and Dirs. Orgn. (bd. dirs.). Lodge: Optimist (Optimist of Yr. award 1969). Avocations: golf, leather craft, radio controlled models, boating. Office: Temple Jr Coll 2600 S 1st St Temple TX 76502

CHURNET, HABTE GIORGIS, geology educator, researcher; b. Shewa, Ethiopia, May 9, 1946; came to U.S., 1975; s. Churnet Argaw and Yeshewa Mebrat Tilahun; m. Enat Negussie, Jan. 17, 1983; children—Dargay H., Bethlehem Habte. B.Sc., Haile Selassie I U., Addis Ababa, Ethiopia, 1969; postgrad. Leeds U. (Eng.), 1972; Ph.D., U. Tenn., 1979. Lectr. dept. geology Haile Selassie I U., 1971-74, chmn. dept. geology, 1974-75; asst. prof. geoscis. dept. U. Tenn., Chattanooga, 1980-83, assoc. prof., 1983—. U.S. Geol. Survey grantee, 1983-84; U. Tenn.-Chattanooga faculty research grantee, 1980-82. Mem. Geol. Soc. Am., AAAS. Author: Titchet, 1974. Office: 615 McCallee Ave Breteske Hall U Tenn Geoscis Chattanooga TN 37402

CHUTKOW, LEE ROBINSON, physician; b. Denver, Feb. 10, 1927; s. Samuel and Yvette (Robinson) C.; m. Mary Lou Murdock, June 1957 (div.); 1 child, John; m. Betty Miller Hanish, June 3, 1973; children—Jennifer Hanish Chutkow Baldwin, Jonathon Hanish. Ph.B., U. Chgo., 1948; M.D., U. Colo., 1954; Diplomate Am. Bd. Psychiatry and Neurology. Intern, Strong Meml. Hosp., Rochester, N.Y., 1954-56; resident in psychiatry U. Colo. Med. Ctr., Denver, 1956-59; pvt. practice psychiatry, Newark, 1959-64, Los Alamos, N.Mex., 1964-68, Louisville, 1969—; clin. dir. Central State Hosp., Louisville, 1982—; clin. faculty dept. psychiatry U. Louisville. Active Am. Jewish Com. Served with USN, 1945-46. Mem. AMA, Am. Psychiat. Assn. Democrat. Jewish. Lodge: B'nai B'rith. Home: 3019 Colonial Hill Rd Louisville KY 40205

CICET, DONALD JAMES, lawyer; b. New Orleans, May 24, 1940; s. Arthur Alphonse and Myrtle (Ress) C. B.A., Nicholls State U., 1963; J.D., Loyola U., New Orleans, 1969. Bar: La. 1969, U.S. Dist. Ct. (ea. dist.) La. 1971, U.S. Ct. Appeals (5th cir.) 1971, U.S. Supreme Ct. 1972, U.S. Dist. Ct. (mid. dist.) La. 1978, U.S. Dist. Ct. (we. dist.) La. 1979. Sole practice, Reserve, La., 1969—; staff atty. La. Legis. Council, 1972-73; legal counsel Nicholls State U. Alumni Fedn., 1974-76, 78-80; spl. counsel Pontchartrain Levee Dist., 1976—; civil service referee La. Dept. Civil Service, 1981—. Served with AUS, 1964, USNG, 1964-70. Recipient Am. Jurisprudence award Loyola U., 1968. Mem. 40th Jud. Dist. Bar Assn., (pres. 1985—), La. Bar Assn. (ho. dels. 1973-77, 79-85), ABA, La. Trial Lawyers Assn., Assn. Trial Lawyers Am., Nicholls State U. Alumni Fedn. (exec. council 1972-76, 77-85, pres. 1982, James Lynn Powell award 1980), Am. Judicature Soc. Roman Catholic. Home: 124 W 1st St Reserve LA 70084 Office: Suite 100 2810 W Airline Hwy Reserve LA 70084

CICOLANI, ANGELO GEORGE, research company executive, operating engineer; b. Norwood, Mass., Mar. 4, 1933; s. Luigi and Maria (Fossa) C.; m. Marilyn Adell Griffith, June 4, 1955 (div. 1968); children—George, Susanne, Diana; m. Reda Jeanne McWhorter, July 9, 1969 (div. 1978); children—Julie Pingree, Jennifer. Student Northeastern U., 1950; B.S., U.S. Naval Acad., Annapolis, Md., 1955; Profl. Cert., Advanced Nuclear Powwer Sch., 1960; B.S., Naval Postgrad. Sch., 1969. Commd. ensign U.S. Navy, 1955, advanced through grades to lt. comdr., 1975, chief reactor operator, 1958-62, exec. officer, 1963-67, systems analyst, Arlington, Va., 1969-75; cons. Arlington, 1975-77; sr. reseacher R&D Assocs., Arlington, 1977—, program mgr., 1977—. Author: The Role of Systems Analysis, 1974. Author, editor Mineral Minutes Jour., 1972 (best newsletter 1974); designer Low Speed Ram-Jet, 1954 (Inst. Aeronautical Scis. 1st Place award). Pres. bd. dirs. Dumbarton Concert Series, Washington, 1982—. Mem. Ops. Research Soc. Am., Naval Inst., Mineral Soc. D.C. (pres. 1972-77), Ret. Officers Am., Nature Conservancy. Office: R & D Assocs 1401 Wilson Blvd Arlington VA 22209

CIKRA, ALDER A., restaurant owner and developer; b. Doylestown, Ohio, Apr. 18, 1946; b. Alder and Mary Wanda (Perity) C.; m. Susan Elizabeth Board, Dec. 6, 1974; 1 dau., Rebecca Suzanne. B.S., Ohio State U., 1969. Sales mgr. Keller Bldg. Products, Canton, Ohio, and Miami, Fla., 1972-74; asst. v.p. sales and mktg. Keller Industries, Miami, 1974-77, v.p. sales and mktg., 1977-79; owner Uncle Al's Restaurant and Lounge, Davie, Fla., 1979—. Served to capt. U.S. Army, 1969-71. Named to Million Dollar Club, Keller Industries, 1973. Mem. Fla. Restaurant Assn. Republican. Roman Catholic. Patentee design for wood slatted aluminum furniture. Office: 8200 Griffin Rd Davie FL 33328

CIMIJOTTI, LEW F., architect; b. Mason City, Iowa, May 18, 1931; s. Leo M. and Mary E. (Pedelty) C.; A.A., Mason City Jr. Coll., 1951; B.S., Iowa State U., 1958; m. Patricia J. Kennedy, Sept. 17, 1956 (div. Dec. 1982); children—Mark Trenton, Bruce Trenton, Laura Denise (dec.). Practice architecture, Chgo., 1960-65, Fairborn, Ohio, 1965-68; with HUD, 1968-78, dep. dir. ops., 1971-75, chief architect, Jacksonville, Fla., 1975-78; field cons., 1978—; prodn. mgr. Space Jour. mag., Huntsville, Ala., 1958. Served with AUS, 1956-58. Recipient Lincoln Arc Welding Found. award, 1958. Mem. Ill. Soc. Architects, Am. Registered Architects, AIA, Toastmasters Internat. Office: PO Box 8176 Jacksonville FL 32239

CINQUEMANI, LAWRENCE VINCENT, sales executive; b. Bklyn., July 22, 1940; s. Paolo G. and Frances (Tombrello) C.; children—Lauren, Jennifer. Student Queens Coll., 1958-59. Regional sales mgr. Field Enterprises Ednl. Corp., Chgo., 1973-77; div. sales mgr. Lexington Andrews Corp., N.Y.C., 1977-80; exec. v.p., gen. mgr. Housecraft Service Co., Houston, 1980—; sales cons. Portogallo Inc., N.Y.C., 1979. Co-chmn. United Way, Manhattan, 1971. Served to cpl. USMC, 1961-66. Roman Catholic. Clubs: Plaza (Houston); Governors. Avocations: photography; cooking; tennis. Home: 810 Fleetwood PL Dr Houston TX 77079 Office: Housecraft Service Co 1217 W Loop N Suite 160 Houston TX 77055

CINTRÓN, EMMA VARGAS, clinical psychologist, educational counselor; b. Yauco, P.R., Aug. 8, 1926; d. José Vargas Bocheciamppi and María Teresa Rivera de Vargas; B.A. in Sociology summa cum laude, Inter Am. U., San Germán, P.R., 1973, M.A. in Counseling and Guidance summa cum laude, 1974; postgrad. in psychology Centro Caribeño de Estudios Postgraduados; Ph.D. in Counseling Psychology, Columbia Pacific U., Calif., 1985; m. Jorge N. Cintrón, Feb. 14, 1948; children—Lisi Cintrón Vazquez, Ileana Cintrón Vazquez. Weekly columnist newspaper El Mundo, San Juan, P.R., 1979—; advisor for dormitories Inter-Am. U., San Germán, P.R., 1978-79, part-time prof. dept. edn., 1976-77, cons. orientation center, 1974-76; bus. mgr. U. P.R. Law Rev., Rio Piedras, 1963-71. Recipient Journalism award P.R. Inst. Lit., 1984; award for disting. service to community Hijos del Antiguo San Juan, 1985. Mem. P.R. Psychol. Assn., Nat. Hispanic Psychol. Assn. Am. Assn. Counseling and Devel., P.R. Assn. Counseling and Devel., China de Oro, Phi Delta Kappa (editor Phi-De-Ka; Disting. Kappan of Yr. 1981). Methodist. Clubs: Lions (Domadoras), Grandmothers (hon. grandmother 1983), San German. Contbr. articles to newspapers including El Mundo, P.R. Profl., Impacto, Colinas, Puerto Rico Evangélico. Home and Office: Box 2547 San Germán PR 00753

CIRE, GEORGE EDWARD, U.S. district judge; b. Houston, Sept. 29, 1922; s. Jorda Michael and Ida Marie (Melancon) C.; B.S. in Commerce, St. Edward's U., Austin, Tex., 1946; LL.B., U. Tex., Austin, 1948; m. Mary Margaret Scott, July 12, 1954; children—Scott Edward, George Edward, Mary Margaret Cire Hicks, Stephen Edward, Jennifer Elizabeth. Admitted to Tex. bar, 1948; partner firm Cire & Jamail, Houston, 1956-64; judge 165th Dist. Ct. Tex., 1964-76, 14th Ct. Civil Appeals Tex., 1976-79; U.S. dist. judge So. Dist. Tex., 1979—. Served to capt. USMCR, 1943-46, 50-52. Decorated Silver Star, Purple Heart. Mem. State Bar Tex. (chmn. dist. grievance com. 1958), Houston Bar Assn., Phi Delta Phi. Democrat. Roman Catholic. Address: 11126 US Courthouse 515 Rusk Ave Houston TX 77002

CISNE, MAXWELL GERARD, accountant; b. Champaign, Ill., Dec. 28, 1936; s. Richard Gerard and Margaret (Maxwell) C.; m. Mary Ann Inwood, Aug. 27, 1960; children—Katrin Neill, Mary Megan. B.S., U. Ill., 1958; M.S., U. Richmond, 1964. C.P.A., Va. Staff acct. Reynolds Metals Co., Richmond, Va., 1960-65; mgr. Peat, Marwick, Mitchell & Co., 1965-72, Arthur Young &

Co., 1972-73; ptnr. Kuehl & Cisne, 1973-79, Gary, Stosch, Walls & Co., 1979—; instr. acctg. U. Richmond, 1970-71, Richmond chpt. Am. Inst. Banking, 1971-72, Va. Commonwealth U., 1971-80. Treas., bd. dirs. Hope Housing Inc., Hope Village, Inc., 1969-76; account exec. United Givers Fund, 1972-74, group chmn., 1974-76, mem. agy. evaluation com., 1981—; pres. Richmond First Club, 1977-78; past mem. and vice-chmn. Richmond Mental Health Mental Retardation Services Bd., 1974-80; bd. dirs. Southampton Citizens Assn., 1972-74; deacon, treas., elder First Presbyterian Ch., 1972—, supt. ch. sch., 1977-78. Served to lt. USNR, 1958-60. Mem. Nat. Assn. Accts. (chpt. pres. 1980-81), Am. Inst. C.P.A.s, Va. Soc. C.P.A.s (chpt. pres. 1978-79), Phi Delta Theta. Home: 8 Partridge Hill Richmond VA 23233 Office: 700 E Main Bldg Richmond VA 23219

CISNEROS, HENRY G., mayor, educator; b. San Antonio, June 11, 1947; s. J. George and Elvira (Munguia) C.; m. Mary Alice Perez; children—Teresa Angelica, Mercedes Christina. B.A., Tex. A&M U., 1969, M. Urban and Regional Planning, 1970; M.P.A., Harvard U., 1973; D.Public Adminstrn., George Washington U., 1975. Adminstrv. asst. to city mgr., San Antonio, 1968, Bryan, Tex., 1968, asst. dir. dept. model cities, San Antonio, 1969-70; asst. to exec. v.p. Nat. League Cities, Washington, 1970-71; White House fellow asst. Sec. of HEW, Washington, 1971-72; teaching asst. dept. urban studies and planning M.I.T., 1972; mem. faculty div. environ. studies U. Tex., San Antonio, 1974—, asst. prof., 1974—; mem. City Council, San Antonio, 1975-81; mayor City of San Antonio, 1981—. Trustee City Pub. Service Bd., City Water Bd., San Antonio; chmn. Fire and Police Pension Fund, San Antonio; mem. strategy council Nat. Democratic Party; mem. Twentieth Century Fund Ednl. Task Force, Eisenhower Found., com. on visual arts Tex. A & M U., bus. adv. com. Trinity U.; tri-chmn. United San Antonio; bd. dirs. San Antonio Symphony Soc., 1974-75. Office: Office of the Mayor PO Box 9066 San Antonio TX 78285

CISSEL, NORMAN RALPH, retired accountant; b. Washington, Dec. 9, 1911; s. William and Emma (Pearson) C.; B.C.S., Benjamin Franklin U., 1935; m. Dorothy E. Fleming, Sept. 14, 1940 (div.); 1 son, William F. With V.I. Corp. (formerly V.I. Co.), Christiansted, 1936-51, comptroller, 1940-51; territorial acctg. exec. OPS, Charlotte Amalie, V.I., 1952-53; supervisory auditor, asst. comptroller Govt. Comptroller of V.I., Charlotte Amalie, 1957-61; pvt. practice as C.P.A., St. Croix, V.I. 1952-66; sr. partner Cissel & Ellis, C.P.A.s, 1966-71 (merged with Seidman & Seidman, C.P.A.s, 1971); cons. partner Seidman & Seidman, C.P.A.s, 1971-74. Mem. Food Commn. Municipality of St. Croix, 1946-49; mem. Banking Bd. V.I., 1949-72, 77-79, chmn., 1949-54; mem. Tax Exemption Bd. Municipality of St. Croix, 1951-55; pres. V.I. Bd. Public Accountancy, 1957-72; mem. investment bd. V.I. Unemployment Compensation, 1963—; mem. V.I. Bd. Tax Rev., 1977-84. C.P.A., V.I. Mem. Nat. Assn. State Bds. Accountancy, Am. Inst. C.P.A.s (council 1960-67), V.I. Soc. C.P.A.s (pres. 1952-72), Inst. Internal Auditors, Nat. Assn. Accts., Am. Acctg. Assn., Mcpl. Fin. Officers Assn. Home: Estate La Reine Box C Kingshill PO St Croix VI 00850

CISSIK, JOHN HENRY, air force officer, aerospace physiologist; b. Great Neck, N.Y., Aug. 18, 1943; s. John Peter and Gladys Lucille (Moore) C.; B.A., U. Tex., Austin, 1965, M.A., 1967; Ph.D. in Physiology, U. Ill., 1972; m. Dorothy Paulette Allen, Dec. 21, 1965; 1 son, John Mark. Commd. 2d lt. USAF, 1967, advanced through grades to lt. col., 1982; aerospace physiologist, physiol. tng. unit Wright-Patterson AFB, Ohio, 1967-69, Andrews AFB, Washington, 1969-70; aerospace physiologist, lab. officer USAF Med. Center, Scott AFB, Ill., 1972-80, Keesler AFB, Miss., 1980-84; instr. physician asst. course Sch. Health Care Scis., Sheppard AFB, Tex., 1984-85; research physiologist Clin. Research Facility, Wilford Hall Med. Ctr., Lackland AFB, Tex., 1985—; coordinator USAF Phase II Cardiopulmonary Lab. Specialist Tng. Course, 1972-84; cons. in field. USAF rep. to Fed. Interagy. Com., 1975-78, Am. Assn. Respiratory Therapists, 1974—, Bd. Schs., 1975-79, Nat. Soc. Cardiopulmonary Technologists, 1973—. Cert. instr. CPR; registered respiratory therapist, 1983. Asso. Fellow Aerospace Med. Assn.; mem. Nat. Soc. Cardiopulmonary Technologists (registered, editorial adv. com. 1975-79, chmn. editorial adv. com. 1977-79, 83—, editor Analyzer 1984—), Am. Coll. Sports Medicine, Am. Thoracic Soc., Am. Assn. Physicians Assts., Chi Gamma Iota, Phi Sigma. Editorial adv. bd. Jour. Cardiovascular and Pulmonary Tech., 1975-84, Jour. Allied Health, 1978-83, Applied Cardiology, 1984—. Respiratory therapy adv. bd. Belleville Area Coll., 1979-80. Research, publs. on respiratory nitrogen prodn. in man and pulmonary physiology. Office: Wilford Hall Med Ctr/SGS Lackland AFB TX 78236

CISSNA, KENNETH NORMAN, communication educator; b. San Francisco, July 10, 1948; s. Norman Clark and Jeanne Katherine (Miller) C.; m. Linda Ann Surbaugh, June 6, 1971 (div. 1975); m. Donna Roberta Leone, June 20, 1977 (div. 1982); m. Susan Farl Shackelton, Nov. 13, 1982. B.A. magna cum laude, Humboldt State Coll., 1970; M.S., So. Ill. U., 1971; Ph.D., U. Denver, 1975. Research asst. Internat. Services Div. and dept. speech, So. Ill. U., Carbondale, 1970-71; adj. instr. speech, Coll. of Redwoods, Eureka, Calif., 1972; grad. teaching asst. dept. speech communication U. Denver, 1973-75; asst. prof. communication, dir. grad. programs dept. communication, St. Louis U., 1975-79, assoc. prof., 1979; asst. prof. communication U. South Fla., Tampa, 1979-82, assoc. prof., 1982—, dir. grad. studies dept. communication, 1985—, grievance rep. United Faculty Fla., 1981—, grievance chmn., 1983-84; dir., instr. workshops, confs., colls., univs., ch. bus. and civic groups; invited participant seminars, U.S., Japan. Bd. govs. Speech and Theatre Assn. Mo., 1977-79. Recipient various grants; Dean's scholar U. Denver, 1973; recipient 1st Ann. Alumni Prof. award, U. South Fla., 1981; Mem. AAUP, Fla. Speech Communication Assn. (1st v.p. 1985-86), Internat. Communication Assn. (life), Soc. for Study of Symbolic Interaction, So. Speech Communication Assn. (life), Speech Communication Assn. (life, vice chmn. applied communication sect. 1985-86). Democrat. Club: Quail Hollow Golf and Country. Editor: Jour. Applied Communication Research, 1981-86, Tng. Manual for Community Leadership Development, 1975. Contbr. writings to books, monographs, periodicals. Home: Quail Cote 107 Quail Hollow Blvd Wesley Chapel FL 34249 Office: Dept Communication Univ S Fla Tampa FL 33620

CIVEY, GEORGE ARNOTT, III, art historian, critic; b. Des Moines, Jan. 20, 1944; s. George Arnott and Annette Newcomer (Foley) C.; B.A., Transylvania U., Lexington, Ky., with distinction, 1966; M.A., U. Iowa, Iowa City, 1971; postgrad. U. N.C., Chapel Hill, 1974—; m. Mary Janet Eberwein, Aug. 22, 1969; 1 dau., Jorgianne Irene. Research asst. art history U. Iowa, Iowa City, 1970-71; instr. art history and criticism Memphis State U., 1971-74; teaching asst. art history U. N.C., Chapel Hill, 1974-75; asst. prof. art Eastern Ky. U., Richmond, 1975—; cons. in field. Served with USAF, 1966-68. Recipient Excellence in Teaching award Coll. Arts and Scis., Eastern Ky. U., 1977-78; Transylvania U. acad. scholar, 1962-66; NDEA fellow U. Iowa, 1968-70. Mem. Coll. Art Assn. Am., S.E. Coll. Art Conf., Am. Soc. for Info. Sci., Assn. for Computing Machinery, AAUP (sec. chpt. 1978-80, chpt. v.p. 1981-82, pres. 1983-84), Arlington Assn., Delta Sigma Phi. Democrat. Presbyterian. Club: Lions (pres. 1983-84). Author: Selected Aspects of the History of French Painting During the Bourbon Restoration 1814-1830, 1975—. Contbr. to Metalsmith, Goldsmith's Jour. Home: 103 Cartier Dr Richmond KY 40475 Office: 425 Jane Campbell Fine Arts Complex Eastern Ky U Richmond KY 40475

CIZIK, ROBERT, manufacturing executive; b. Scranton, Pa., Apr. 4, 1931; s. John and Anna (Paraska) C.; m. Jane Morin, Oct. 3, 1953; children—Robert Morin, Jan Catherine, Paula Jane, Gregory Alan, Peter Nicholas. B.S., U. Conn., 1953; M.B.A., Harvard U., 1958; LL.D. (hon.), Kenyon Coll., 1983. Acct., Price Waterhouse & Co. (C.P.A.s), N.Y.C., 1953-54, 56; fin. analyst Exxon U.S.A., N.J., 1958-61; with Cooper Industries, Inc., Houston, 1961—, exec. asst. corp. devel., treas., controller, 1963-67, v.p. for planning, 1967-69, exec. v.p., 1969-72, pres., 1972—, chief exec. officer, 1975—, chmn. bd., 1983—, also dir.; dir. First City Bancorp. Tex., NBC, Inc., Temple Inland Inc., RCA Corp., N.Y.C.; v.p. Machinery and Allied Products Inst. Bd. dirs. Central Houston, Inc., Nat. Bus. Com. for Arts; co-chmn. Houston Lyric Theater Found.; mem. Houston Bus. Com. for Arts; trustee Center for Internat. Bus., Conf. Bd.; mem. exec. com. Houston Grand Opera; trustee Com. Econ. Devel.; mem. Soc. Founders, Am. Leadership Forum. Served to 1st lt. USAF, 1954-56. Clubs: Coronado, Houston Ctr., Houston Petroleum, River Oaks Country, Ramada, Forum of Houston (founding). Office: PO Box 4446 Houston TX 77210

CLACK, DOUGLAS MAE, training and management consultant; b. San Antonio, July 10, 1943; d. Douglas and Ida Mae (Norwood) Campbell; m. Floyd Broadnax, Jr., Oct. 2, 1962 (dec.); m. Charles Leonard Clack, Sr., Aug. 6, 1966 (div. Aug. 1973); 1 son, Charles Leonard. B.B.A., U. Tex.-San Antonio, 1977; M.S., St. Mary's U., San Antonio, 1982. Sec. and clerical positions Frost Nat. Bank, Southwestern Bell Telephone Co., United Services Automobile Assn., San Antonio, 1964-75; adminstrv. officer I food service personnel San Antonio Ind. Sch. Dist., 1977-83; v.p. Diverse Data Systems, Inc., San Antonio, 1983—; instr., cons. Tex. Edn. Agy. Vol. San Antonio voter registration, 1977—, Am. Cancer Soc., 1973—; mem. PTA, 1973—; mem. adv. council Ella Austin Community Clinic; coordinator New Mt. Pleasant Baptist Ch. Ann. Tea, 1983; mem. adv. com. Bexar County Women's Ctr.; mem. Bus. and Profl. Women; mem. Black Coalition San Antonio; charter mem., mem. adv. council Bexar County Women's Mentor Program. Recipient Black Achiever in Adminstrn. award Gamma Phi Lambda, 1982. Mem. San Antonio Adminstrn. and Suprs. Assn., Tex. State Tchrs. Assn., NEA, Tex. Sch. Food Service Assn., Iota Phi Lambda, U. Tex. Alumni Assn., San Antonio Bus. and Profl. Women's Orgn. Club: Rising Star Toastmistress (charter). Contbr. articles to profl. publs. Office: PO Box 33126 San Antonio TX 78233

CLAGETT, ARTHUR F(RANK), JR., sociology educator, social psychologist; b. Little Rock, Dec. 3, 1916; s. A.F. and Mary Gertrude (Bell) C.; m. Dorothy Ruth Pinckard, Dec. 23, 1954. B.A. in Chemistry, Baylor U., 1943; M.A. in Psychology, U. Ark., 1957; Ph.D. in Sociology, La. State U., 1968. Shift chemist Celanese Corp., Cumberland, Md., 1942-44; shift supr. penicillin prodn. Comml. Solvents Corp., Terre Haute, Ind., 1944-45; research supr. streptomycin pilot plant Schenley Labs., Lawrenceburg, Ind., 1945-48; asst. mgr. Clagett's Feed and Seed Store, Donna, Tex., 1948-50; med. service rep. Blue Line Chem. Co., St. Louis, 1952-56; prison classification officer La. State Penitentiary, 1956-59, classification supr. new admissions, 1959-60; counseling psychologist, Baker, La., 1960-64; asst. prof. sociology Lamar State Coll. Tech., Beaumont, Tex., 1964-66; assoc. prof. sociology Stephen F. Austin State U., Nacogdoches, Tex., 1968-83, prof., 1983—, mem. univ. research council, 1973-75, Sch. Liberal Arts council, 1970-71, 78-79. Mem. editorial bd. Quar. Jour. Ideology, 1982—. Contbr. articles to profl. jours. Mem. Am. Soc. Criminology, Am. Acad. Criminal Justice Scis., Am. Sociol. Assn., Inst. Criminal Justice Ethics, ACLU. Methodist. Avocations: reading; fishing. Home: 609 Egret Dr Nacogdoches TX 75961 Office: PO Box 6173 Stephen F Austin Sta Nacogdoches TX 75962

CLAIBORN, EDWARD LEE, economics educator; b. Kimberly, Idaho, Apr. 3, 1933; s. Jack Dewey and Emily M. (Wall) C.; m. Shirley Grace Mason, Aug. 31, 1952; children—Candis Sue, Kelley Ann. B.S., U. Idaho, 1955; M.A., Princeton U., 1961, Ph.D., 1964. Commd. 2d lt. U.S. Air Force, 1955, advanced through grades to col., 1976, ret., 1981; mem. econs. faculty U.S. Air Force Acad., 1961-77; prof. aerospace studies U. Calif.-Berkeley, 1977-81; prof. econs. Va. Mil. Inst., Lexington, 1981—. Decorated Legion of Merit with oak leaf cluster, D.F.C., Air medal with 7 oak leaf clusters. Mem. Am. Econs. Assn., Air Force Assn. (bd. advisors 1980-81), AAUP. Presbyterian. Club: Rotary (Lexington, Va.). Home: 4 Woodduck Rd Lexington VA 24450 Office: 239 Scott Shipp Hall Va Mil Inst Lexington VA 24450

CLAIBORNE, JERRY WAYNE, accountant; b. Little Rock, Oct. 25, 1943; s. William A. and Irma L. (Coleman) C.; B.B.A., Baylor U., 1965; m. Mildred Keller Phillips, July 13, 1968; children—Courtney, Adam, Amanda. With Peat, Marwick, Mitchell & Co., 1965—, Houston, 1965-70, N.Y.C., 1970-73, partner, Houston, 1973—. Mem. exec. com. of bd. Houston Grand Opera, 1979—, 1st v.p., 1981—. Served in U.S. Army, 1967. C.P.A., N.Y., Tex. Mem. Am. Inst. C.P.A.s, N.Y. State Soc. C.P.A.s, Tex. Soc. C.P.A.s. Roman Catholic. Clubs: Coronado, Houston Racquet. Home: 5661 Bayou Glen Houston TX 77056 Office: 3000 Republic Bank Ctr Houston TX 77210

CLAMANN, H. PETER, physiology educator; b. Berlin, Nov. 18, 1939; came to U.S., 1947, naturalized, 1957; s. Hans Georg and Maria (Mueller) C.; m. Eva Maria Schoffel, Apr. 15, 1967; children—Alexander, Michael. B.S. in Math., St. Mary's U., San Antonio, 1961; Ph.D. in Biomed. Engring., Johns Hopkins U., 1968. Research assoc. Harvard Med. Sch., Boston, 1970-72, instr., 1972-73; asst. prof. Med. Coll. Va., Richmond, 1973-78, assoc. prof. physiology, 1978—; guest docent U. Zürich, Switzerland, 1983-84. Contbr. articles to profl. jours. and chpts. to scholarly books. Served to capt. U.S. Army, 1968-70. Recipient NIH fellowships and research grants. Mem. Soc. Neurosci., Am. Physiol. Soc., IEEE, Biomed. Engring. Soc. (sr. mem.), Schweizerische Physiologische Gesellschaft, Richmond Area Bicycling Assn. (pres. 1981). Avocations: photography, bicycle touring. Home: 4001 Laurelwood Rd Richmond VA 23234 Office: Dept Physiology and Biophysics Med Coll Va Box 551 MCV Sta Richmond VA 23298

CLAMPITT, MARTHA REDDING, interior designer; b. North Wilkesboro, N.C., Jan. 11, 1947; d. Dewey Wayne and Pansy Lucille (Sale) Redding; m. Otis Clinton Clampitt, Jr., Apr. 3, 1971. B.S., U. N.C.-Greensboro, 1971; M.A. in Art summa cum laude, Miss. Coll., 1985. Advt. copywriter Jordan Marsh, Greensboro, N.C., 1971-73; interior designer Oldtown Drapery, Winston-Salem, N.C., 1973-76, interior design mgr. Shade Shop, Inc., Columbia, S.C., 1976-80; interior designer Warren Wright's, Jackson, Miss., 1981-83, Architects Plus, Jackson, 1985—. Sec. Treasure Cove Homeowners Assn., Madison, Miss., 1983-84; sect. leader, exec. com., mem. choir 1st Baptist Ch., Jackson, 1983—; active Miss. Mus. of Art Aux., Jackson Symphony League, Miss. Ballet League. Mem. Am. Soc. Interior Designers (assoc., chmn. self-testing exercises for pre-profls. 1984-86), Comml. Interior Design Guild, Miss. Artists Guild. Democrat. Avocations: sailing, skiing, painting, photography, antiques. Home: 3032 Tidewater Ln Madison MS 39110 Office: Architects Plus 3780 I-55 North Frontage Rd Jackson MS 39211

CLAPP, ALLEN LINVILLE, energy research company executive; b. Raleigh, N.C., Oct. 8, 1943; s. Byron Siler and Alene Linville (Hester) C.; m. Anne Stuart Calvert, Dec. 18, 1966. B.S. in Engring. Ops., N.C. State U., 1967, M. Econs., 1973. Registered profl. engr., N.C., N.J. Asst. engr. Booth-Jones and Assocs., Raleigh, 1965-67; assoc., 1969-71; chief ops. analysis N.C. Utilities Commn., Raleigh, 1971-77, engring. and econs. advisor to commrs., hearing examiner, 1977-82; dir. tech. assessment N.C. Alternative Energy Corp., Research Triangle Park, 1982-85; mng. dir. Clapp Research Assocs., 1985—; pvt. practice electric safety cons., Raleigh, 1971—; chmn. Nat. Elec. Safety Code Com., 1984—; lectr. in field. Author: National Electrical Safety Code Handbook, 1984; Assembly and Testing of Aerial Mines, 1968. Contbr. articles to profl. jours. Co-chmn. Brookhaven/Deblyn Park Action Com., Raleigh. Served with U.S. Army, 1967-69. Recipient Cert. of Recognition and Appreciation Aerial Mine Lab., 1969. Mem. Nat. Soc. Profl. Engrs., Profl. Engrs. N.C. (pres. 1980, Disting. Service award central Carolina chapt. 1978), N.C. Assn. Professions (pres. 1981), IEEE, Power Engring. Soc., Nat. Safety Council, Am. Soc. Safety Engrs., Am. Econs. Assn., Am. Statis. Assn., Assn. Energy Engrs., Indsl. Applications Soc., Am. Fin. Assn. Democrat. Baptist. Avocations: competitive target shooting; photography; raising orchids. Home: 3206 Queens Rd Raleigh NC 27612 Office: Clapp Research Assocs Suite 200 5124 Burr Oak Circle Raleigh NC 27612

CLAPP, JOHN GARLAND, JR., agronomist, manufacturing company executive; b. Greensboro, N.C., Oct. 27, 1936; s. John G. and Edna R. (Robinson) C.; m. Gladys L. Cobb, May 30, 1959; children—J. Randal, Lisa D., G. Keith. B.S., N.C. State U., 1955, M.S., 1959, Ph.D., 1961. Asst. prof. crop sci. N.C. State U., Raleigh, 1961-66, assoc. prof., 1966-75; agronomist Allied Chem. Corp., Greensboro, N.C., 1975-84; research agronomist Arcadian Corp., 1984—. Recipient citation for meritorious service Am. Soybean Assn., 1974; award of recognition Nat. Fertilizer Solutions Assn., 1977. Mem. Am. Soc. Agronomy (Geigy award 1972), Soil Sci. Soc. Am., Crop Sci. Soc. Am., Weed Sci. Soc. Am., Plant Growth Regulation Soc. Am. Patentee fertilizer innovation. Home: 310 Clapp Farms Rd Greensboro NC 27405 Office: Arcadian Corp 310 Clapp Farms Rd Greensboro NC 27405

CLAPP, ROGER HOWLAND, advertising executive; b. Scarsdale, N.Y., May 11, 1928; s. Kenneth J. and Louise (Allen) C.; m. Patricia Townshend, June 26, 1954; children—Roger Howland Jr., Georgia Louise, Sarah Townshend. B.A. cum laude, Amherst Coll., 1954. Vice pres., assoc. media dir. Benton & Bowles, Inc., N.Y.C., 1954-67; v.p., media dir. Rumrill-Hoyt Inc., N.Y.C., 1967-72; advt. dir. Richmond (Va.) Newspapers, Inc., 1972—. Active Central Richmond Assn. Served with USN, 1948-52. Recipient Silver medal Am. Advt. Fedn., 1980. Mem. Internat. Newspaper Advt. and Mktg. Execs. (2d v.p.), Mid-Atlantic Newspaper Advt. and Mktg. Execs., Advt. Club of Richmond, Sales and Mktg. Execs. of Richmond, Met. Richmond C. of C., Retail Mchts. Assn. Greater Richmond. Clubs: Bull and Bear, Brandermill Country.

CLAPPER, JAMES MICHAEL, management educator, consultant; b. Boston, July 25, 1946; s. John Clarence and Joan Ruth (McCarthy) C.; m. Deborah Musgrove, June 14, 1969; children—Sasha McCarthy, Evan Howes. B.S. in Mgmt., Rensselaer Poly. Inst., 1968, M.S., 1970; Ph.D. in Bus. Adminstrn., U. Mass.-Amherst, 1974. Instr. bus. adminstrn. U. Mass., 1969-73; asst. prof. mktg. U. S.C., Columbia, 1973-75; asst. prof. mgmt. Wake Forest U., Winston-Salem, 1975-79, assoc. prof. Babcock Grad. Sch., 1980—, dir. MBA exec. program, 1980-83, assoc. dean, 1982—; commodity industry specialist U.S. Dept. Commerce, Washington, 1979, assoc. dir. Office of Bus. Liaison, 1980; mem. White House Task Force on Energy Conservation Outreach, 1980. Bd. dirs., treas. Greenspring Food Coop., Winston-Salem, 1980-82; mem. mktg. adv. com. Winston-Salem/Forsyth County Arts Council, 1982-85; mem. United Way Communications Com., 1984—; bd. dirs. Salvation Army Boys Club, Winston-Salem, 1986—. Served with USAR, 1970-76. Am. Assembly Collegiate Schs. of Bus. fellow, 1979-80. Mem. Decision Scis. Inst. (book rev. editor for Decision Line 1976-79, v.p. 1982-84, pres.-elect 1986), Am. Mktg. Assn., So. Mktg. Assn., Acad. Mktg. Sci., Epsilon Delta Sigma, Alpha Iota Delta. Contbr. articles to profl. jours. Office: PO Box 7659 Winston Salem NC 27109

CLAPPER, THOMAS H., state official; b. Plainfield, N.J., Mar. 12, 1943; s. Thomas Wayne and Anna M. (Anderson) C. Student, Regis Coll., Denver, 1962-64; B.A., U. Calif.-Riverside, 1966; M.A., Calif. State U.-Fullerton, 1967; Ph.D., U. Okla., 1983. Teaching asst. U. Okla., Norman, 1972-74; adj. instr. South Okla. Community Coll., Oklahoma City, 1974-75; research asst. Okla. Legis. Council, Oklahoma City, 1974-75, research assoc., 1977-80; mem. com. staff Okla. Senate, Oklahoma City, 1980—. Co-author: Oklahoma Legislative Manual, 1980. Served with USAF, 1967-69, to 1st sgt. Res. Mem. Am. Soc. Pub. Adminstrn., Polit. Sci. Assn., Okla. Polit. Sci. Assn., Air Force Assn., Air Force Sgts. Assn., Assocs. Western History Collection (charter), Pi Sigma Alpha, Pi Alpha Alpha. Democrat. Roman Catholic. Avocation: Reading. Home: 12104 Camelot Pl Oklahoma City OK 73120 Office: Senate Com Staff State Capitol Oklahoma City OK 73105

CLARE, GEORGE, safety engineer; b. N.Y.C., Apr. 8, 1930; s. George Washington and Hildegard Marie (Sommer) C.; student U. So. Calif., 1961, U. Tex., Arlington, 1963-71, U. Wash., 1980; m. Catherine Saidee Hamel, Jan. 12, 1956; 1 son, George Christopher. Enlisted man U.S. Navy, 1948, advanced through grades to comdr., 1968; naval aviator, 1951-70; served in Korea; comdr. Res., 1963-70; ret., 1970; mgr. system safety Vought Missiles and Advanced Products div., Dallas, 1963—. Mem. Nat. Republican Com., Rep. Senatorial Com., Rep. Congl. Com., Tex. Rep. Com., Citizens for Republic. Decorated Air medal with gold star, others; cert. product safety mgr. Mem. AIAA, Am. Security Council, Internat. Soc. Air Safety Investigators, System Safety Soc., Am. Def. Preparedness Assn., Assn. Naval Aviation, Ret. Officers Assn. Roman Catholic. Home: 817 N Bowen Rd Arlington TX 76012 Office: Vought Missiles and Advanced Products Div PO Box 650003 Dallas TX 75265

CLARK, ALBERT EDWIN, retired journalist; b. Chatham County, N.C., May 12, 1915; s. Walter Budd and Mary Hughes (Burns) C.; m. Naomi Ruth Rouse, Aug. 22, 1942; children—Albert Edwin, George B., Carolyn (dec.). A.A., Campbell Coll., 1937; student U. N.C., 1939-40. Reporter Greensboro Daily News, N.C., 1940-45, Evening Sun, Balt., 1945; reporter Wall Street Jour., Washington, 1945-60, bur. chief, 1953-60; asst. mng. editor U.S. News and World Report, Washington, 1960-77; free-lance writer articles on local, state and nat. current events for local and state newspapers, 1980—. Active mem. Men of Ch., 1st Presbyterian Ch., New Bern, N.C., also Sr. Citizens Club. Recipient Disting. Alumnus award Campbell U., Buies Creek, N.C., 1968. Home: 2000 Williamson Dr New Bern NC 28560

CLARK, ALBERT HATCHER, finance educator, consulting economist; b. Americus, Ga., Feb. 9, 1931; s. George Amos and Maida Louise (Hatcher) C.; m. Edith Marion Lloyd, Sept. 1, 1957; children—Cynthia Anne, Kathryn Jean, Constance Lyn. B.B.A., U. Ga., 1952, M.B.A., 1956; Ph.D., U. Pa., 1961. Instr. econs. Clemson U., S.C., 1956; dir. exams Am. Coll., Bryn Mawr, Pa., 1959-61; prof. fin. Ga. State U., Atlanta, 1961—; cons. economist, 1961—. Fellow Ford Found., 1956-58, Heubner Found 1958-59. Mem. Am. Fin. Assn., So. Econ. Assn., Atlanta Soc. Fin. Analysts. Home: 2822 Foster Ridge Rd Atlanta GA 30345 Office: Ga State U University Plaza Atlanta GA 30303

CLARK, BECKY JO DAVIS, health administrator; b. Columbia, S.C., Sept. 3, 1938; d. Clifton Lee and Olive (Casey) Davis; m. James Edwin Clark, Sept. 8, 1956; children—Teresa, Dave, Melissa. B.S. with distinction, Miss. State U., 1970; M.Ed., Clemson U., 1975. Instr., Tri County Tech. Coll., Pendleton, S.C., 1970-73, adv. com., 1973-78; project dir. Clemson Child Devel. Ctr., 1973-78; project adminstr. Appalachia I Pub. Health Dist., Anderson, S.C., 1978-81, dist. planner, 1981-84; project dir. Coll. Nursing, Clemson U., 1984—. Bd. dirs. Pickens County Planning and Devel. Commn. (S.C.), 1977-85, chmn., 1981-84; bd. dirs. United Way, 1975-82, Easter Seals Assn., 1981-84. Mem. Am. Pub. Health Assn., S.C. Pub. Health Assn., S.C. Employee Assn. Baptist. Clubs: Keowee Key Sailing, Clemson Gourmands. Contbr. articles to profl. publs. Home: 114 E Brookwood Dr Clemson SC 29631 Office: Clemson U Coll Nursing Clemson SC 29631

CLARK, BERNARD F., natural gas company executive; b. 1921; B.S., Fordham U., 1942; M.B.A., Harvard U., 1949. Chemist, Pan-Am. Refining and Transport Co., 1947-49; asst. v.p. sales Baker J.T. Chem. Co., 1949-51; asst. exec. v.p. Pan-Am. So. Corp., 1951-56; with Mitchell Energy & Devel. Corp., 1956—, asst. to pres., 1956-57, v.p., gen. mgr., 1957-63, exec. v.p., 1963-79, vice chmn., dir., 1979—. Served to maj. U.S. Army Air Corp, 1942-46. Address: Mitchell Energy & Devel Corp 2001 Timberlock Pl The Woodlands TX 77380*

CLARK, BILLY PAT, physicist; b. Bartlesville, Okla., May 15, 1939; s. Lloyd A. and Ruby Laura (Holcomb) C.; B.S., Okla. State U., 1961, M.S., 1964, Ph.D., 1968. Grad. asst. dept. physics Okla. State U., 1961-68; postdoctoral research fellow dept. theoretical physics U. Warwick, Coventry, Eng., 1968-69; sr. mem. tech. staff Booz-Allen Applied Research, 1969-70; sr. mem. tech. staff field services div. Computer Scis. Corp., Leavenworth, Kans., 1970-73, sr. mem. tech. staff, field services div., Hampton, Va., 1973-76; head quality assurance engring. Landsat project applied tech. div. Computer Scis. Corp., 1976-77, mgr. data quality assurance sect., 1977-79, sr. system scientist on staff to engring. dept. mgr., 1979-80, sr. scientist on staff to dir. NASA image processing ops., 1980-82, sr. prin. engr./scientist on staff to dir. NASA sci. and applications operation Systems Scis. div., 1982-83, tech. advisor to dir. ops. NOAA Landsat Program, CSC, 1983—, rep. Landsat Tech. Working Group, 1982—. Undergrad. scholar Phillips Petroleum Co., 1957-61, Am. Legion, 1957-58, Okla. State U., 1957-58. Mem. Am. Acad. Polit. and Social Sci., Internat. Platform Assn., Am. Phys. Soc., AAAS, IEEE, Soc. for Photo-optical Instrumentation Engring., Internat. Soc. for Photogrammetry and Remote Sensing, N.Y. Acad. Scis., Pi Mu Epsilon, Sigma Pi Sigma. Club: Victory Hills Golf and Country (Kansas City, Kans.). Author or co-author tech. publs. Home: 502 S Hamilton St Dewey OK 74029

CLARK, CHARLES, judge; b. Memphis, Sept. 12, 1925; s. Charles and Anita (Massengill) C.; student Millsaps Coll., 1943-44, Tulane U., 1944; LL.B., U. Miss., 1948. Admitted to Miss. bar, 1948; mem. firm Wells, Thomas & Wells, Jackson, Miss., 1948-61, Cox, Dunn & Clark, Jackson, 1961-69; spl. asst. to atty. gen. State of Miss., 1961-66; judge U.S. Ct. Appeals, 5th Circuit, Jackson, 1969—, chief judge, 1981—. Served to lt. USNR, 1943-46, 51-52. Mem. Miss. Bar Assn., Am. Coll. Trial Lawyers, Jud. Conf. U.S. (chmn. com. budget). Episcopalian. Home: Jackson MS Office: US Courthouse Jackson MS 39205

CLARK, CHARLES DANIEL, automobile dealer; b. Peoria, Ill., May 28, 1917; s. Richard Fardon and Melba Iona (Kirkpatrick) C.; B.A., U. Mich., Ann Arbor, 1939; m. Dorothy Elizabeth Van Gelder, Jan. 3, 1942; children—Kirk Allen, Robin Anne. Apprentice purser S.S. Santa Lucia, Grace Lines, N.Y.C., 1939-40; sales mgr. Carpenter Chevrolet Co., McAllen, Tex., 1940-41, v.p., 1945-50; pres. Charles Clark Chevrolet Co., McAllen, 1951—; dir. McAllen State Bank; Charles and Dorothy Clark lectureship in fine arts U. Tex.-Austin, 1985. City commr. City of McAllen, 1950-52. Served to maj., USAAF, 1941-45. Decorated D.F.C., Air Medal with oak leaf clusters. Nat. com. Univ. Art Mus., U. Calif. at Berkeley, 1969-70; Council of Friends U. Mich. Mus. Art, 1972-78; mem. Coll. Fine Arts Found. adv. council U. Tex. at Austin, 1972—; mem mus adv panel Tex. Commn. Arts and Humanities, 1972-74. Mem. McAllen C. of C. (pres. 1957, outstanding citizen 1958), Tex. Automobile Dealer Assn. (award personnel relations 1963, v.p. 1965-66), Delta

Upsilon. Episcopalian. Home: 404 Lindberg Ave McAllen TX 78501 Office: PO Box 938 McAllen TX 78501

CLARK, CHARLES EDGAR, construction company executive; b. Royal Oak, Mich., Oct. 3, 1946; s. Wallace S. and Zelda Rose (Largent) C.; m. Wanda Jean Tebbe, Oct. 9, 1970; children—Lisa, Susan, Teresa. Student Brigham Young U., 1964-65, Calif. State Coll.-Long Beach, 1966-68. Cert. gen. contractor, Fla. Field clk., asst. supt., supt., asst. project supt. Levitt & Sons, Detroit, 1969-71; project supt. Multicon Corp., 1971-72, regional mgr., Cleve., 1972-73; project mgr. Tekton Corp., West Palm Beach, Fla., 1973-74; gen. supt. Ahrens & Son, Inc., West Palm Beach, 1974-76; pres. Clark Constrn. Service, Inc., West Palm Beach, 1976—, dir., 1978—; dir., v.p. Stephen A. Brock Architects, Inc.; mem. pres.'s adv. council for Republic Steel Bldg. Corp., 1982; mem. pres.'s adv. bd. Kirby Bldg. Systems, 1984-85. Mem. Republican Nat. Com. Recipient corp. awards Kirby Bldg. Systems, 1978, 79, 81, 82, 83, 84. Mem. Nat. Assn. Home Builders, Metal Bldg. Dealers Assn., West Palm Beach C. of C., Stuart C. of C., Palm Beach Gardens C. of C. Republican. Presbyterian. Lodge: Moose. Home: 16887 97th Way N Jupiter FL 33458 Office: 6667 42nd Terr N West Palm Beach FL 33407

CLARK, DAVID RANDOLPH, wholesale grocer; b. Columbia, S.C., Mar. 25, 1943; s. Joseph Wilbur and Josephine (Timberlake) C.; m. Carole Jane Cooper, Aug. 21, 1965; 1 dau., Catherine. B.A., Wofford Coll., 1965; M.B.A., U. S.C., 1966. Vice pres., gen. mgr. Thomas & Howard Co., Spartanburg, S.C., 1969-77; pres. Thomas & Howard Co., Columbia, S.C., 1977—; chmn. T & H Ins. Agy., Inc.; dir. Timberlake Grocery Co. Mem. campaign cabinet United Way, 1975; mem. nat. alumni bd. Wofford Coll.; bd. dirs. Indian Waters council Boy Scouts Am. Served to 1st lt. U.S. Army, 1967-68. Mem. Nat. Am. Wholesale Grocers Assn., S.C. Assn. Convenience Food Stores (dir.), Scabbard and Blade, Phi Beta Kappa, Pi Gamma Mu, Pi Kappa Alpha. Episcopalian. Clubs: Rotary (dir.) Forest Lake. Home: 6307 Goldbranch Rd Columbia SC 29206 Office: PO Box 947 Columbia SC 29202

CLARK, DAYLE MERITT, civil engineer; b. Lubbock, Tex., Sept. 5, 1933; s. Frank Meritt and Mamie Jewel (Huff) C.; B.S., Tex. Tech. U., 1955; M.S., So. Meth. U., 1967; m. Betty Ann Maples, Apr. 11, 1968; 1 dau., Alison. Field engr. Chgo. Bridge & Iron Co., 1955; mgr. L.K. Long Constrn. Co., 1958-64; faculty U. Tex., Arlington, 1964—; expert witness numerous ct. cases, 1969-86; cons. AID, 1966, NSF, 1967-68. Served to capt. USAF, 1955-57. Mem. ASCE (pres. Dallas br. 1986-87). Club: Rotary. Editor: Tex. Civil Engr., 1967-71. Contbr. papers, reports to profl. lit. Office: PO Box 185 Arlington TX 76004

CLARK, DONALD OTIS, lawyer; b. Charlotte, N.C., May 30, 1934; s. Erwin and Ruby Lee (Church) C.; A.B., U. S.C., 1956, J.D. cum laude, 1963; M.A., U. Ill., 1957; m. Jo Ann Hager, June 15, 1957 (div. Mar. 1980); children—Deborah Elise, Stephen Merritt. Admitted to S.C. bar, 1963, Ga. bar, 1964; clk. firm Cahill, Gordon, Reindel, Sonnett & Ohl, N.Y.C., summer, 1962; practiced in Atlanta, 1963—; mem. firm Candler, Cox, McClain & Andrews, Atlanta, 1968-70, McClain, Mellen, Bowling & Hickman, Atlanta, 1970-75; partner firm King & Spalding, Atlanta, 1975-78; sr. partner firm Hurt, Richardson, Garner, Todd & Cadenhead, Atlanta, 1978—; mem. dist. export council U.S. Dept. Commerce, 1974—; adj. prof. law Emory U., 1970—, U. S.C., 1974; lectr. Ga. State U., 1972—; lectr. numerous internat. trade seminars and workshops. Served to capt., USAF, 1957-60. Decorated knight Sovereign Order St. John of Jerusalem, Knights of Malta; knight and minister of justice Sovereign Order of New Aragon; Sungrye medal (Korea); recipient Nat. Leadership medal Air Force Assn., 1956, Coll. award Am. Legion, 1956, Outstanding Sr. award U. S.C., 1956; named hon. consul Republic of Korea, 1972—. Mem. Atlanta, Am., S.C. bar assns., state bars Ga., S.C., Lawyers' Club of Atlanta, Am. Judicature Soc., Am. Soc. Internat. Law, Atlanta C. of C., Ga. C. of C. (exec. coms. Internat. Councils), Inst. Internat. Edn. (chmn. Southeastern regional adv. bd. 1974—, nat. trustee), So. Consortium Internat. Edn. Inc. (dir.), Wig & Robe, Sigma Chi (pres. 1956, Province Balfour award 1956), Omicron Delta Kappa, Kappa Sigma Kappa, Phi Delta Phi (pres. 1963, Province Grad. of Yr. award 1963). Author German govt. study on doing bus. in Southeastern U.S., 1974. Editor-in Chief S.C. Law Rev., 1963. Contbr. articles to profl. jours. Home: 712 W Paces Ferry Rd NW Atlanta GA 30327 Office: 1100 Peachtree Center Harris Tower 233 Peachtree St NE Atlanta GA 30043

CLARK, EMORY EUGENE, financial planning executive; b. Opelika, Ala., Jan. 24, 1931; s. Bunk Henry and Dorothy (Bolt) C.; grad. pub. schs.; m. Jean F. Reed, Sept. 30, 1951; children—Steven E., Michael E. With Mgrs. Life Ins. Co., 1956-74, agt., supr., Los Angeles, 1956-60, mgr. Hawaii br., 1960-65, Pitts. br., 1965-68, Houston br., 1968-74; with Jefferson Standard Life Ins. Co., Fort Worth, 1974-82; fin. planner E.F. Hutton & Co., Inc., 1983—. Served with AUS, 1950-56. Mem. Fort Worth Life Underwriters Assn., Am. Soc. Life Underwriters, Fort Worth Soc. Life Underwriters, Ft. Worth Securities Dealers Assn. Home: 8109 Meadowbrook Dr Fort Worth TX 76112 Office: 3005 Tex Am Bank Bldg Fort Worth TX 76102

CLARK, FAYE LOUISE, drama and speech educator; b. La., Oct. 9, 1936; student Centenary Coll., 1954-55; B.A. with honor, U. Southwestern La., 1962; M.A., U. Ga., 1966; m. Warren James Clark, Aug. 8, 1969; children—Roy, Kay Natalie. Tchr., Nova Exptl. Schs., Fort Lauderdale, Fla., 1963-65; faculty dept. drama and speech DeKalb Community Coll., Atlanta, 1967—, chmn. dept., 1977-81. Pres., Hawthorne Sch. PTA, 1983-84. Mem. Ga. Theatre Conf. (sec. 1968-69, rep. to Southeastern Theatre Conf. 1969), Ga. Psychol. Assn., Ga. Speech Assn., Atlanta Ballet Guild, Southeastern Theatre Conf., Atlanta Artists Club (sec. 1981-83, dir. 1981—), Young Women of Arts, High Mus. Art, Phi Kappa Phi, Pi Kappa Delta, Sigma Delta Pi, Kappa Delta Pi, Thalian-Blackfriars. Presbyterian. Club: Lake Lanier Sailing. Home: 2521 Melinda Dr NE Atlanta GA 30345 Office: Humanities Div DeKalb Community Coll North Campus Dunwoody GA 30338

CLARK, FRANK RINKER, JR., ret. pipe line co. exec.; b. Washington, May 4, 1912; s. Frank Rinker and Theresa Louise (Burton) C.; student Northwestern U., 1930-33, U. Tulsa, 1933-35, Harvard Law Sch., 1935-36, U. Okla. Law Sch., 1936-38, U. Tulsa, 1939-42, 45-47; m. Evelyn Crews, June 27, 1943 (dec. July 1972); children—Theresa Lynn, Frank Robert; m. 2d, Annelle Macon Beaty, June 3, 1973. Claims adjuster Travelers Ins. Co., 1938; trainee Helmerich & Payne, Tulsa, 1938-39; law clk. Settle, Monnet & Clammer, Tulsa, 1939-42; prodn. planning Douglas Aircraft Co., 1942-45; tax accountant Exxon Pipeline Co. (formerly Interstate Oil Pipe Line, later Humble Pipe Line Co.), 1945-50, tax atty., 1950-63, sec., 1955-77, treas., 1958-61, 63-77; treas. Dixie Pipeline Co., 1966-76, sec., 1972-76; admitted to Okla. bar, 1938, also U.S. Supreme Ct. bar. Mem. Am., Okla. bar assns., Am. Soc. Corporate Secs., Houston Soc. Fin. Analysts, Sigma Chi. Republican. Presbyterian (elder). Club: East Ridge Country (Shreveport, La.). Home: 125 Harpeth Trace Dr Nashville TN 37221

CLARK, FRANKLIN TAYLOR, school principal; b. Cape Girardeau, Mo., Jan. 31, 1949; s. Bayard Stockton and Charlotte (Cheever) Cushwa C.; m. Susan Carol Cartwright, June 29, 1974; children—Sarah Hadley, Annalise Taylor. B.A., U. Rochester, 1971; M.Ed. Adminstrn., U. Va., 1978. Tchr., Kent Jr. High Sch., Prince George's County, Md., 1972-74, tutor coordinator Kenmoor Jr. High, 1974-75; tchr. English, Am. Sch. in Japan, Tokyo, 1975-77; asst. prin. Culpeper County High Sch. (Va.), 1978—. Bd. dirs. Mental Health Assn. Mem. Nat. Assn. Secondary Prins. Democrat. Episcopalian. Club: Culpeper Recreation. Home: Sheftan Oaks Route 1 Box 344 Culpeper VA 22701 Office: Culpeper County High Sch Culpeper VA 22701

CLARK, GEORGE BRYAN, geophysicist; b. Rogers, Ark., Aug. 5, 1925; s. George Washington and Grace Opal (Van Der Pol) C.; B.S., Ark. State U., 1943; Ph.D., Columbia Pacific U., 1981; m. Therese Glöbl, June 27, 1956 (dec. May 1968); children—Gracia, George, Johanna; m. Elsa M. Torres, Jan. 16, 1983. From trainee to sr. geophysicist Teledyne Co., 1945-65; sr. quality control geophysicist Petty Labs., 1965-67; cons., 1967-74; sr. profl. geophysicist Amerada Hess Co., 1974-80; chief geophysicist Imperial Chem. Industries, New Orleans, 1980-83; area geophysicist Atlantic Richfield, Lafayette, La., 1983-86; cons., 1986—; exec. reservist FEMA, 1986—. Mem. Soc. Exploration Geophysicists, European Assn. Exploration Geophysicists, Air Force Assn., Am. Ordnance Assn., Am. Def. Preparedness Assn., S.W. La. Geophys. Soc. (past officer; award for services 1972, 73, 74), U.S. Naval Inst. Home: Route 1 Box 620 Carencro LA 70520

CLARK, HAROLD STEVE, architect; b. Amarillo, Tex., Feb. 10, 1947; s. Harold John and Joyce Elmore (Fleming) C.; m. Billy June Martin, June 1, 1968 (div. 1974); m. Lonna Paulette Thomas, Aug. 1, 1977; children—Lori Denise Pruett, Jimmy Scott Stoddard, Lindsay Dawn. Student Amarillo Jr. Coll., 1965-66, 67-68; B.Arch., Tex. Tech. U., 1975. Registered architect, Tex. Asst. mgr. trainee S.H. Kress Co., Amarillo, 1963-66; asst. mgr. C.R. Anthony Co., Amarillo, 1966-68; chief draftsman City of Amarillo, Engr., 1968-71; job capt. Huckabee and Donham, Andrews, Tex., 1975-77; sr. assoc. Covington and Taylor, Odessa, Tex., 1977—. Archtl. works include: First Savs. and Loan, Odessa, Ector County Library, Tex., Ratliff Stadium, Temple Baptist Ch., Odessa. Charter contbr. Statue of Liberty Ellis Island Found., 1983—. Served with USMCR, 1966-72. Mem. AIA, Tex. Soc. Architects, Nat. Council Archtl. Registration Bds., Tex. Tech. U. Archtl. Alumni Assn., Odessa C. of C. Republican. Baptist. Avocations: golf; hunting. Home: 2522 Cambridge St Odessa TX 79761 Office: Covington and Taylor 2651 Parkway Suite B Odessa TX 79761

CLARK, HAROLD WHITE, securities company executive; b. Sparta, Tenn., Sept. 1, 1922; s. William Fred and Eula Pearl (Barlow) C.; B.A., Vanderbilt U., 1943; m. Gloria Gambill, July 20, 1946; children—Carol Clark Elam, Harold White, Gloria Clark Angell. With J.C. Bradford & Co., 1947-48; v.p. Clark, Landstreet & Kirkpatrick, Inc., 1949-62; pres. The Cherokee Securities Co., Nashville, 1962—. Trustee Montgomery Bell Acad., Harpeth Hall Sch., Tenn. Sch. for Blind; mem. Vanderbilt Intercollegiate Athletic Bd.; chmn. Justin Potter Med. Scholarship Com. Vanderbilt U. Sch. Medicine. Served to lt. USNR, 1943-46; ETO. Mem. Nat. Assn. Securities Dealers (past chmn. Dist. 7), Securities Industry Assn. (dir.), Pub. Securities Assn. (dir.), Vanderbilt U. Alumni Assn. (pres. 1968-69), Nashville C. of C. (chmn. sports com.). Presbyterian. Clubs: Belle Meade Country, Cumberland, Nashville City. Home: 1015 Lynwood Blvd Nashville TN 37215 Office: 3200 West End Ave Nashville TN 37202

CLARK, ISAAC EDGAR, publisher; b. Schulenburg, Tex., Dec. 9, 1919; s. Harvey Robert and Annie Ruby (Miekow) C.; B.A., U. Tex. at Austin, 1941, M.A., 1945; m. Lila Rhea Norwood, Sept. 1, 1945; children—Candace Ann, Robin Rhea. Rancher, 1945—; tchr., theatre dir., publs. dir., lang. arts coordinator Schulenburg Pub. Schs., 1945-77; founder, owner I.E. Clark, Inc., pub. plays and books for theatre, 1959—; tchr. Newspaper Fund seminars U. Tex. at Austin, summers 1961-66; regional observer for Nat. Observer, 1961; mem. Tex. Edn. Agy. Commn. for Lang. Arts Curriculum Revision, 1958-59, State Com. Devel. of Speech-Drama Publ. of Tex. Edn. Agy., 1960-61. Mem. Fayette County His. Survey Com., 1969—; founder, artistic dir., bd. dirs., officer Backstage, Inc., Fine Arts Council for South Central Tex., 1969—; adv. dir. 1st Nat. Bank of Schulenburg, 1974-80. Democratic precinct chmn., Fayette County Dem. Exec. Com., 1955-80; county campaign chmn., Lyndon B. Johnson, 1949, 55; area campaign chmn. Tex. Lt. Gov. Bill Hobby, 1972. Bd. dirs. Schulenburg Hist. Soc. Recipient Finest Journalism Tchr. in Tex. award U. Tex. Interscholastic League, 1967; Order Golden Quill, 1977; named Hon. State Farmer, Future Farmers Am., 1956; Newspaper Fund fellow, 1959. Mem. Am. Theatre Assn. (nat. chmn. play publishers panel 1977, edtior Secondary Sch. Theatre Jour. 1982-83), Am. Community Theatre Assn., Childrens Theatre Assn., Tex. Secondary Theatre Conf. (dir., Newsletter editor, 1966-69, mem. Interscholastic League adv. com.), Tex. Ednl. Theatre Assn., Modern Music Masters (hon. life), English Speaking Union, Farm Bur., Phi Beta Kappa, Delta Tau Delta, Sigma Delta Chi, Phi Eta Sigma. Methodist. Mason (Shriner). Author: (plays) Twelve Dancing Princesses, 1969; Hansel and Gretel, 1970; It's A Dungaree World, 1974; Once Upon a Texas, 1985; also several one-act plays including The Christmas Dream, transl. into Spanish, produced TV, Ecuador, 1973; (pageant) Fate of Fayette, 1986. Home: Bermuda Valley Farm Schulenburg TX 78956 Office: PO Box 246 Schulenburg TX 78956

CLARK, JAMES KERMIT, JR., real estate executive; b. Atlanta, Nov. 17, 1942; s. George W. and Jean (Scutaro) K. B.B.A., U. Ga., 1965; grad. Realtor Inst. Ga., 1973. Lic. real estate broker, Ga. Chief appraiser First Fed. Savs. & Loan Assn., Atlanta, 1965-67; comml. appraiser Draper-Owens Co., Atlanta, 1967-69; partner, pres. Tri-City Comml. Sales, Inc., College Park, Ga., 1969—; dir. Tri-City Realty & Mgmt., Inc. Mem. Nat. Assn. Realtors, Ga. Assn. Realtors, Atlanta Bd. Realtors (comml. adv. council), Million Dollar Club (active life), Atlanta C. of C. (Southside devel. task force), Phi Kappa Alpha. Republican. Baptist. Office: Tri-City Comml Sales Inc 5529 Old National Hwy College Park GA 30349

CLARK, JAMES ROBERT, fund raising company executive; b. Knoxville, Tenn., Jan. 28, 1948; s. Willis R. and Theresa M.C.; m. Linda Diane Hilburn, Sept. 11, 1971; children—Zachary, Preston, Rowland. B.B.A., Ga. So. Coll., 1972. Bus. devel. officer Park Nat. Bank, Knoxville, 1972-76; dir. devel. Harrison Chilhowee Acad., Seymour, Tenn., 1976-79; v.p. devel. Carson-Newman Coll., Jefferson City, Tenn., 1979-82; pres. J. Robert Clark & Assocs., Knoxville, 1982—. Mem. Nat. Soc. Fund Raising Execs., Bapt. Pub. Relations Assn., Knoxville C. of C. Republican. Baptist.

CLARK, JOHN MICHAEL, publisher, researcher; b. Tulsa, Okla., July 7, 1948; s. Don Emmett and Lois Anne (Fivash) C.; m. Jacqueline Marie Claire Bradford, Aug. 19, 1976 (div. Aug. 1977); m. Marjorie Louise Gilliam, Mar. 5, 1983 (div. Mar. 1986); stepchildren—Michael Wayne Carver, Keith Alan Carver. A.B.A., No. Okla. Coll., Tonkawa, 1969; B.A., NYU, 1973. Adminstr., copywriter McCann-Erickson, N.Y.C., 1970-73; advt. mgr. Schwarz/Mann div. Becton-Dickinson, Orangeburg, N.Y., 1973-75; dir. advt. Badger Meter, Inc., Tulsa, Okla., 1975-79; dir. corp. communications Hinderliter, Tulsa, 1979-82; publisher, founder, pres. Market Media, Broken Arrow, Okla., 1982—. Author: Clinical Use of RIA, 1974; author monthly newsletter, 1983, regional food trade and culinary assn. publs., 1983—. Mem. Phi Beta Lambda (founder No. Okla. Coll. chpt., pres. 1968-69). Republican. Baptist. Home: 2019 W Toledo St Broken Arrow OK 74012

CLARK, JOHN STEVEN, lawyer, attorney general of Arkansas; b. Leachville, Ark., Mar. 21, 1947; s. John Willis and Jean (Bearden) C.; children—Donna Marie, Anna Katherine. B.A., Ark. State U., 1968; J.D., U. Ark., 1971. Bar: Ark. 1971, U.S. Supreme Ct. 1978. Assoc. Sharp & Sharp, Brinkley, Ark., 1971-73; asst. prof., asst. dean U. Ark. Sch. Law, Fayetteville, 1973-76; exec. sec. Gov. David Pryor, Little Rock, 1976-78; assoc. Clark & Nichols, Little Rock, 1978-79; atty. gen. State of Ark., Little Rock, 1979—. Served to capt. USAR. Bd. dirs. Ark. chpt. Multiple Sclerosis Soc. Named Employer of Yr., Ark. Council for Blind, 1979; Ark. Outstanding Young Man, Ark. Jaycees, 1979; recipient Humanitarian Service award United Cerebral Palsy, 1981; Disting. Alumni award Ark. State U., 1985. Fellow Ark. Inst. Politics and Govt.; mem. Ark. Bar Assn. (trustee continuing legal edn. fund, mem. ho. of dels., chmn. young lawyers sect.), Ark. Inst. Continuing Legal Edn. (bd. dirs.). Democrat. Methodist. Avocation: jogging. Office: Office of Atty General 201 East Markham Heritage West Bldg Little Rock AR 72201

CLARK, JOHN WAYNE, communications executive; b. Muncie, Ind., Jan. 31, 1945; s. J. Owen and Doris Jean (Smith) C.; m. Carole Elaine Lauck, Sept. 2, 1972. B.A., Ind. U., 1968; postgrad. U. London, 1967, Am. U., 1970. Campaign staff William Ruckelshaus for U.S. Senator campaign, Ind., 1968; legis. aide Lt. Gov. of Ind., 1969; minority floor asst. U.S. Ho. of Reps., 1970; aide to Congressman, 1970; asst. dir. congressional affairs U.S. EPA, 1970-73; dir. communications Wheelabrator-Frye Signal Co., 1973-75; asst. dir. congressional affairs U.S. Dept. Energy, 1976-77; v.p. Am. Gas Assn., Arlington, Va., 1978—; adv. bd. Americans for Energy Independence, 1979; adv. com. on voluntary fgn. aid U.S. AID. Recipient EPA Bronze medal for disting. service, 1973. Mem. Pub. Relations Soc. Am. (exec. com. utilities sect.; accredited), Alpha Tau Omega. Office: 1515 Wilson Blvd Arlington VA 22209

CLARK, KEITH COLLAR, musician, educator; b. Grand Rapids, Mich., Nov. 21, 1927; s. Harry Holt and Bethyl June (Collar) C.; student of Pattee Evenson and Clifford Lillya, 1943-45, Lloyd Geisler, 1947-48, Armando Ghitalla, 1974; m. Marjorie Ruth Park, Dec. 8, 1951; children—Nancy Clark Mc Colley, Sandra Clark Masse, Karen, Beth Anne Clark Barnard. Trumpeter with Grand Rapids Symphony Orch., 1943-46; cornetist U.S. Army Band, Washington, 1946-66; ret., 1966; tchr. Montgomery (Md.) Coll., 1964-66; asso. prof. brass instruments Houghton (N.Y.) Coll., 1966-80, condr. Houghton Coll. Symphony Orch., 1966-78, Houghton Coll. Concert Band, 1975-80; cons., asst. project dir. Dictionary American Hymnology, 1980-81; prin. trumpet S.W. Fla. Symphony Orch., 1982—; tchr. Roberts Wesleyan Coll., Rochester, N.Y., 1969-70, Edison Community Coll., Ft. Myers, Fla., 1984—; music dir. Maryland Ave. Bapt. Ch., Washington, 1947-51, Cherrydale Bapt. Ch., Arlington, Va., 1953-60, Christ Meth. Ch., Arlington, 1961-65, Houghton Wesleyan Ch., 1967-68, Central United Meth. Ch., Ft. Myers, Fla., 1981-82; soloist Today program NBC-TV, 1956. Pastor, Sterling (Va.) Bapt. Ch., 1951-53. Mem. Nat. Sch. Orch. Assn. (v.p. 1974-76, Honor award 1976, 80), Am. Symphony Orch. League, Internat. Trumpet Guild, Hymn Soc. Am., Hymn Soc. Gt. Britain and Ireland, Ch. Music Soc., Nat. Ch. Music Fellowship (pres. 1967-69), S.W. Fla. Symphony and Chorus Assn. (exec. bd. 1982—), Sonneck Soc. Republican. Author: A Selective Bibliography for the Study of Hymns, 1980. Contbr. articles on music to profl. publs. Selected to sound Taps for funeral of President John F. Kennedy, 1963; participant ceremonies and concerts for Presidents Truman, Eisenhower and Johnson. Home: 1691 N Flossmoor Rd Fort Myers FL 33907

CLARK, KENNETH E., psychologist, educator; b. New Madison, Ohio, Dec. 18, 1914; s. Harry H. and Nellie B. (Trempo) C.; m. Helen T. Titelmaier (div. 1983); children—Patricia, Virginia, Joyce; m. Miriam B. Bittker, May 25, 1983. B.S. in Math., Ohio State U., 1935, M.A. in Psychology, 1937, Ph.D. in Psychology, 1940. Prof. psychology U. Minn., 1956-60, dept. chmn., 1957-60, assoc. dean grad. sch., 1960; prof. and dean Coll. Arts and Scis., U. Colo., Boulder, 1961-63, U. Rochester, N.Y., 1963-80; pres. Ctr. for Creative Leadership, Greensboro, N.C., 1981-85; cons. Office Sci. and Tech., 1961-69; mem. Army Sci. Bd., 1977-82, Pres.' Nat. Medal of Sci. Com., 1962-65; mem. bd. Overseers Ctr. for Naval Analysis, 1968-81, Smith Richardson sr. scientist, 1985—. Author: America's Psychologists, 1957; Vocational Interests of Non-professional Men, 1961 (Am. Personnel and Guidance Assn. citation for research excellence 1963); editor: Psychology (G.A. Miller), 1970; editor Jour. Applied Psychology, 1961-70. Trustee St. John Fisher Coll., Rochester; bd. mgrs. Meml. Art Gallery, U. Rochester, 1963-81; bd. dirs. Civic Music Assn., Rochester, 1968-71, Eastern Music Festival, Greensboro, 1983. Served to lt. (j.g.) USN, 1944-46. Recipient Edward K. Strong Gold medal, 1967, Centennial Achievement award Ohio State U., 1970, Alumni citation U. Rochester, 1973, Outstanding Teaching award Arts Coll. Student Bd., U. Minn. Fellow Am. Psychol. Assn. (v.p. 1966-68, trustee pres. 1968-70); mem. Psychology for Legis. Action Now (chmn. 1976-82, trustee), Assn. for Advancement of Psychology (chmn. bd. trustees 1974-75). Home: 10 St Augustine Sq Greensboro NC 27408 Office: Ctr for Creative Leadership PO Box P-1 Greensboro NC 27402

CLARK, KIRK ALLEN, automobile dealer, insurance agent; b. McAllen, Tex., May 2, 1946; s. Charles Daniel and Dorothy VanGelder) C.; m. Sharon Rees Waite, Aug. 13, 1969 (div. Aug. 1981); children—Charles Kenneth, Anne Karen; m. Jeri Clare La Masters, May 1, 1982. B.S., U. N.Mex., 1969. Dealer, Charles Clark Chevrolet Co., McAllen, Tex., 1969—; agt. Clark Ins. Agy., 1973—; ptnr. Tejas Life Ins. Co., 1981—; cons. automobile safety U.S. Congressman John Bryant, Washington. Fin. chmn. State Senator Hector Uribe, 1983; bd. dirs. Trinity Sch., Pharr, Tex., 1983—; area dir. Auto-Pac, Austin, Tex., 1983—. Mem. Chevrolet Dealers Advt. Assn. (pres., founder Lower Rio Grande Valley chpt. 1979—). Democrat. Episcopalian. Clubs: McAllen 100 (pres.), McAllen Swim (v.p. 1984). Lodge: Rotary (dir.). Home: 500 N Rose Ellen Circle McAllen TX 78501 Office: Charles Clark Chevrolet Co 909-915 Hwy Ave McAllen TX 78501

CLARK, MAGGIE MAGEE, advertising executive; b. Jackson, Miss., May 21, 1949; d. Ewell and Mary Louella (Bond) Magee; m. Charles Ernest Youens, Nov. 22, 1970 (dec. Oct. 15, 1971); m. Gene Estes Clark, Sept. 26, 1975; 1 son, Charles Kenneth Youens. B.S., U. So. Miss., 1971. Traffic dir. Sta. WHHY-AM-FM, Montgomery, Ala., 1971, stas. WJDX-WZZQ, Jackson, 1971-72; media dir. Gene Clark Advt., Inc., Jackson, 1973—, also agy. prin. Active Muscular Dystrophy Assn., 1979-81, Jackson Zoo, 1978-80. Recipient Gold award Greater Jackson Ad Club, 1977, 78, 80. Mem. Am. Advt. Fedn. (dist. officer 1981—; medal of Merit 1983, 1st place 1980; nat. pub. service com. 1980, chmn. 1981-83), Southwestern Assn. Advt. Agys., Miss. Assn. Advt. Agys. Club: Greater Jackson Advt. (pres. 1979-80). Office: 5265 Clinton Blvd Jackson MS 39209

CLARK, MAXINE LORRAINE, psychology educator; b. Cin., Oct. 27, 1949; d. Riley Ryan and Anna Juanita (Pickett) C.; children—Cheri Marie, Ramel Akil. B.A., U. Cin., 1972; A.M., U. Ill., 1975, Ph.D., 1979. Asst. prof. Va. State U., Petersburg, 1976-80; assoc. Wake Forest U., Winston-Salem, N.C., 1980—; cons. in field. Mem. editorial bd. Jour. Youth and Adolescence, 1985—; contbr. articles to profl. jours.; columnist Winston-Salem Chronicle, 1984-85. Counselor, Rape Response, Winston-Salem, 1983-85; bd. dirs. Family Violence Bd., 1985—. NEH fellow, 1979; Inst. Social Research fellow, 1979. Mem. Am. Psychol. Assn., Am. Ednl. Research Assn. (affirmative action co-chmn. 1985—), Southeastern Psychol. Assn. Democrat. Baptist. Avocations: weight lifting; racquetball. Office: Dept Psychology Box 7778 Wake Forest U Winston-Salem NC 27109

CLARK, OUIDA OUIJELLA, public relations executive, educator; b. Birmingham, Ala., Dec. 7, 1949; d. Fred and Johnnie (Norrington) C. B.A. in Spanish Edn., Dillard U., New Orleans, 1971; grad. cert. pub. relations Am. U., 1973, U. Valencia (Spain), 1974; cert. journalism NYU, 1972; postgrad. U. Chgo., 1980. Fgn. Service intern USIA, 1971; freelance pub. relations cons., 1972-76; tchr. English as 2d lang. Arlington (Va.) Pub. Schs., 1976-78; founder, pres. Clark Prodns., Ltd., Inc., Little Rock, 1981—; pres., founder Global Pub. Relations, Inc., Washington, 1976, and Little Rock, 1981—; multi lingual freelance pub. relations cons.; research assoc. Philander Smith Coll., 1980-81. Recipient Pub. Relations award Nat. Powderly Alumni Assn., 1977; Ark. Endowment Humanities grantee, 1982. Mem. Pub. Relations Soc. Am., Am. Film Inst., Nat. Press Club, Capital Press Club. Baptist. Contbr. articles to profl. jours.; patent Nat. Directory of Music and Dance Studios, 1978, rev., 1980. Office: PO Box 583 Little Rock AR 72203

CLARK, PAUL LAWRENCE, city official, safety engineer; b. New London, N.H., May 11, 1937; s. Erwin Willis and Blanche (Palmer) C.; m. Faustine Jane Stanhope, Nov. 9, 1957 (div. June 1974); m. Opal Mae Rutledge, Dec. 26, 1974; children—Steven, Larry, Richard, Sharon. Enlisted U.S. Air Force, 1955, advanced through grades to master sgt., 1971; safety supt. various locations U.S. and overseas, 1970-76, ret., 1976; safety officer City of Houston, 1977-83, adminstr. accident prevention and loss control, 1983—. Author: Municipal Safety Management, 1981. Merit badge counselor Boy Scouts Am., 1977—; pres. Hunters Glen Civic Assn., Missouri City, Tex., 1980-83. Mem. Am. Soc. Safety Engrs., Pub. Risk and Ins. Mgmt. Assn., Tex. Safety Assn. (bd. dirs. 1981-84, v.p. pub. employees 1982-84), Safety Council Greater Houston (exec. com. 1977—). Republican. Methodist. Avocations: woodworking; gardening. Home: 16303 Quailynn Ct Missouri City TX 77489 Office: City of Houston Accident Prevention and Loss Control 806 Main St Houston TX 77002

CLARK, RICHARD, cons.; b. Tampa, Fla., Aug. 20, 1927; s. Charles C. and Rhetta (Lang) C.; student Fla. Mil. Acad., St. Petersburg; grad. Royal Sch. Work Study, Portsmouth, Eng., 1960; grad. Indsl. Engring. Sch., Proctor & Gamble Co., 1960; m. Patricia Anne Gay, Sept. 23, 1966; 1 dau., Gayle Marguerite; children by previous marriage—Betty Jo, Sandra Jean, Beverly Ann. Served as enlisted man U.S. Navy, 1945-66; indsl. engr. Stanwick Corp., Norfolk, Va., 1966-67; photographer Meml. Hosp., Sarasota, Fla., 1967-68; office mgr. sales Esquire Pools, Sarasota, 1968-69; field engr. Ionics Inc., Boston, 1969-70; br. mgr. Nor-Cal Engring. Co., Sarasota, 1970-77; v.p. purchasing Outdoor World/Nor-Cal Distributing Co. Inc., Bradenton, Fla., 1977-81; swimming pool trade cons., Sarasota, 1981—. Recipient various mgmt. awards. Mem. Nat. Swimming Pool Inst., Am. Mgmt. Assn., C. of C., Fleet Res. Assn. Republican. Clubs: Masons, Grotto. Home and Office: 4409 S Lockwoodridge Rd Sarasota FL 33581

CLARK, RICHARD LEE, radiologist; b. Mt. Vernon, N.Y., June 1, 1940; s. Kenneth Fenton and Gertrude Lathrop (Dezendorf) C.; B.A. magna cum laude, Oberlin Coll., 1962; M.D., Johns Hopkins U., 1966; m. Linda Lenore Horne, Aug. 27, 1963; children—Jonathan Kenneth, Jennifer Lee. Intern, U. Ky. Med. Center, Lexington, 1966-67; resident in radiology Johns Hopkins Hosp., Balt., 1967-70, chief resident, instr., 1970-71; asso. prof. radiology U. N.C., Chapel Hill, 1973-83, prof., 1983—; dir. diagnostic radiol. research, 1973-79, adv. to med. class of 1981; cons. to Chief Med. Examiner, N.C., 1973—; dir. div. gen. radiology N.C. Meml. Hosp., 1979—. Bd. dirs. Chapel Hill Village Orch.; trustee Eno River Unitarian-Universalist Fellowship. Served with USPHS, 1971-73. Recipient Henry Strong Denison award Johns Hopkins U., 1965-66; faculty research grantee N.C., 1974-75; NIH research grantee, 1976-79, James Picker Found. scholar 1975-79. Diplomate Am. Bd. Radiology. Mem. Assn. Univ. Radiologists, Soc. Uroradiology, Am. Coll. Radiology, Radiol. Soc. N.Am., N.C. Med. Soc., Johns Hopkins Med. Assn., Johns Hopkins U. Alumni Assn., Durham Orange County Med. Soc., Sigma Xi. Unitarian-Universalist. Clubs: Oberlin Alumni of N.C. (co-pres. 1975-77).

Co-author: Renal Microvascular Disease, 1980. Contbr. numerous articles to profl. jours. Home: Rt 4 Box 529 Chapel Hill NC 27514 Office: Dept Radiology U NC Sch Med Chapel Hill NC 27514

CLARK, ROBERT LLOYD, JR., librarian; b. McAlester, Okla., Sept. 12, 1945; s. Robert Lloyd and Fairel Ruth (Nelson) C.; B.A., U. Okla., 1968, M.L.S., 1969; children—Roberta, Johnathan. Dir. div. archives and records Okla. Dept. Libraries, Oklahoma City, 1968-72, data processing coordinator, 1972-73, dir., 1976—; asst. dir. pub. services Jackson (Miss.) Met. Library System, 1973-74; dir. Mid-Miss. Regional Library, Kosciusko, 1974-76; sec. Okla. Archives and Records Commn., from 1976; ex officio sec. Okla. Arts and Humanities Council, from 1976; sec. adv. council Library Services and Constrn. Act., from 1976. Mem. ALA (chmn. pub. library assn. interlibrary coop. 1974-77, mem. standards com. from 1979), Okla. Library Assn., Southwestern Library Assn. (pres. from 1980), Amigos Bibliog. Council (exec. bd. 1977-80), Assn. State Libraries (bd. dirs. 1977-80), Assn. Chief Officers of State Library Agys. (chmn. legis. com. 1979-81). Author: Archive-Library Relations, 1976. Office: 200 NE 18th St Oklahoma City OK 73105

CLARK, ROY CLYDE, bishop; b. Mobile, Ala., July 24, 1920; s. Clyde Columbus and Lelia B. (Cochran) C.; m. Esther Maddox, June 7, 1945; children—Lynn B., Susan. B.A., Millsaps Coll., 1941, D.D., 1962; B.D., Yale U., 1944; H.H.D., Columbia Coll., S.C., 1981. Ordained deacon Meth. Ch., 1944, elder, 1946, bishop, 1980. Pastor various chs., Pasacagoula and Wesson, Miss., 1944-49, Centreville and Forest, Miss., 1949-53, Capital Street Meth. Ch., Jackson, Miss., 1953-63, St. John's Meth. Ch., Memphis, 1963-67, West End United Meth. Ch., Nashville, 1967-80; bishop United Meth. Ch., Columbia, 1980—; dir., pres. Assn. Christian Tng. and Service, Nashville, 1977-83; dir. gen. bd. global ministries United Meth., Ch., N.Y.C., 1980—; trustee Lake Junaluska Assembly, N.C., 1980—. Author: Expect a Miracle, 1976. Mem., chmn. Jackson Appeal Rev. Bd., 1957-61; pres. Family Service Assn., Jackson, 1963; dir. Council Community Services, Nashville, 1976-80; trustee Emory U., Atlanta, 1980—. Named Alumnus of Yr. Millsaps Coll., 1957. Mem. World Meth. Council. Office: United Methodist Ch Columbia Area 4908 Colonial Dr 08 Columbia SC 29203

CLARK, ROY THOMAS, JR., educator, administrator; b. Lockhart, Tex., Feb. 22, 1922; s. Roy Thomas and Ada Louise (Masur) C.; B.S. in Chemistry, S.W. Tex. State Coll., 1947, M.A. in Chemistry, 1950; m. Lavanie Anne Busby, Jan. 3, 1948; 1 son, Thomas David. Commd. 2d lt. USAAF, 1943; advanced through grades to lt. col. USAF, 1966; various assignments U.S., 1943-59; project officer propulsion br. Agena div. Directorate Space Systems, Air Force Ballistic Missile Div., Los Angeles, 1959-60; chief propulsion sect., astrovehicle br. Agena div. Office Dep. Comdr. Satellite Systems, Space Systems Div., Los Angeles, 1960-61; asst. prof. chemistry USAF Acad., Colo., 1961-63, asso. prof., 1963-64; student Air Force Inst. Tech., Edn.-with-Industry Program, Aerojet Gen. Corp., Sacramento, 1964-65; project officer 6595th Aerospace Test Wing, Vandenberg AFB, Calif., 1965-66; chief Titan Launched Satellite Systems Office, 1966-69; ret., 1969; adminstrv. officer dept. chemistry U. Tex. at Austin, 1969-84. Decorated Air medal, Air Force Commendation medal, Meritorious Service medal. Mem. Am. Chem. Soc. Episcopalian. Home: 7711 Shadyrock Dr Austin TX 78731

CLARK, RUDOLPH BLANSETT, insurance executive; b. Delton, Va., Oct. 31, 1923; s. Lloyd George and Clydie (Blansett) C. B.A., Lincoln Meml. U., Harrogate, Tenn., 1948; B.S. in Library Sci., Peabody Coll., 1948. Librarian, Union Coll., Barbourville, Ky., 1949-52, Lincoln Meml. U., 1952-72; pres. Clark Ins. Agy., Harrogate, 1954—; mem. trust com. Comml. Bank, Middlesboro, Ky., 1962—; real estate appraiser. Mem. Nat. Assn. Realtors, Insurors of Tenn. (cert.), Nat. Assn. Real Estate Appraisers (cert.), Profl. Ins. Agts. Home and Office: PO Box 96 Harrogate TN 37752

CLARK, SAM DAVID, real estate investor; b. Kingsport, Tenn., Dec. 12, 1948; s. Harless L. and Lucille Nellie (Bullion) C. Student East Tenn. State U., 1970-74. Personnel officer Holston Defense Corp., Kingsport, 1968-70; real estate broker C. P. Edwards III, Kingsport, 1971-76; pres. Cherokee News, Kingsport, 1978—. Democrat. Home: 210 W Wanola Ave Kingsport TN 37660 Office: Cherokee News 311 Cherokee St Kingsport TN 37660

CLARK, STAN, assn. exec.; b. Oakland, Calif., Aug. 27, 1927; s. Otto and Luella (Vestal) C.; A.B., San Jose (Calif.) State Coll., 1954, M.A., 1956; postgrad. Stanford U., 1959-60; m. Faye Juhls, Aug. 31, 1952 (div. May 1980); children—Valerie, Laury, Steven; m. 2d, Nancy Wood, June 1, 1980. Dir. aux. services San Jose City Coll., 1956-62, Calif. State U., Hayward, 1963-68, SUNY, Cortland, 1968-70, SUNY, New Paltz, 1970-72; exec. dir. Nat. Assn. Coll. Aux. Services, Cortland, 1972—; part-time tchr. acctg. San Jose City Coll., 1958-61, Foothill Coll., Los Altos, Calif., 1962-63, Chabot Coll., Hayward, 1964-67; cons.; pres. Calif. Assn. Coll. Stores, 1962. Bd. dirs. Higher Edn. Adminstrn. Referral Service, Washington, 1971—. Served with USAAF, 1945-47. Mem. Nat. Assn. Coll. Aux. Services (sec.-treas. 1969—), Eastern Assn. Coll. Aux. Services (sec.-treas. 1969—), Coll. Stores Assn. N.Y. State (sec.-treas. 1969-72), Tau Delta Phi.

CLARK, STEPHANIE LOUISE, educational administrator; b. Des Moines, Mar. 19, 1958; d. Reber Fields, Jr., and Elizabeth Louise (O'Master) C. B.S., Ark. Tech. U., 1980; M.A., Northwestern State U., Natchitoches, La., 1983, M.Ed., 1985. Cert. math. tchr., Ark., S.C. Math. tchr. Cabot Pub. Schs., Ark., 1980-81; Panhellenic adviser Northwestern State U., 1981-83, asst. to dir. student services, 1981-83; student devel. specialist Clemson U., S.C., 1983—, coordinator ednl. placement, 1983—. Named Outstanding mem. ATU Panhellenic Council, 1980. Mem. Am. Coll. Personnel Assn., Am. Assn. Counseling and Devel. (grad. liaison 1982-83), Cardinal Key (life), Kappa Delta Pi (life), Phi Mu (life). Home: Route 4 Box 119 Central SC 29630 Office: Office Ednl Services and Placement Clemson U 418 Tillman Hall Clemson SC 29634

CLARK, THOMAS ALONZO, judge; b. Atlanta, Dec. 20, 1920; s. Fred and Prudence (Sprayberry) C.; m. Betty Medlock, July 16, 1978; children—Thomas A., Christopher S., Julia M.; stepchildren—Allen L. Carter, Rosalyn Lackey Howell. B.S., Washington and Lee U., Lexington, Va., 1942; LL.B., U. Ga.-Athens, 1949. Sole practice, Bainbridge, Ga., 1949-55; ptnr. Dykes, Marshall & Clark, Americus, Ga., 1955-57; assoc. Fowler, White et al, Tampa, Fla., 1957-61; sr. ptnr., shareholder Carlton, Fields et al, Tampa, 1961-79; judge U.S. Ct. Apls. 5th cir., 1979-81, 11th cir., Atlanta, 1981—; mem. Fla. Supreme Ct. commn. to study structure of appellate courts in Fla., 1978-79. Rep., Ga. Legislature, 1951-52; pres. Fla. Assn. Retarded Citizens, 1974-75. Fellow Am. Coll. Trial Lawyers; mem. ABA, Ga. Bar Assn., Fla. Bar Assn. (chmn. trial lawyers sect. 1971-72), Am. Judicature Soc. Office: US Ct Appeals 11th Circuit 56 Forsyth St Atlanta GA 30303

CLARK, THOMAS GATES, consulting forester; b. Uniontown, Pa., May 10, 1920; s. Guy Moser and Nelle (Gates) C.; B.S., W.Va. U., 1942; M.F., U. Mich., 1946; postgrad. U. Miami, 1943—; m. Rhodo Mildred Shortridge, Jan. 19, 1944; children—Conrad W., Timothy Ritner, Guy Alan, Bruce Shortridge, Daniel Quentin. With U.S. Forest Service, W.Va., Pa., Vt., Va., 1946-52; self-employed cons. forester, Morgantown, W.Va., 1953—; partner Arkley Forest Lands, 1965—; sec.-treas. Krakrow Corp., oil and gas producers, 1974—; mem. W.Va. Ho. of Dels., 1979-81. Served with AC, USNR, 1942-45. Decorated D.F.C. Mem. Assn. Cons. Foresters (nat. pres. 1963-64), Soc. Am. Foresters, Forest Farmers Assn. (dir.), Wildlife Soc. Home: 436 Callen Ave Morgantown WV 26505 Office: 432 Callen Ave PO Box 1046 Morgantown WV 26505

CLARK, WILLIAM JOHN, JR., traffic management specialist; b. Pautexant, Md., Mar. 7, 1951; s. William John Clark and Dorothea Lee (Holcombe) Cotton; m. Charlene Jeanette Davis, Aug. 25, 1978; children—Joseph Shannon, Christine Diana. B.S., Wayland Baptist U., 1981; A.A., Vernon Regional Jr. Coll., 1981. Commd. E-1 USAF, 1970, advanced through grades to E-6 (tsgt.), 1982; aircraft weight and balance specialist U.S. Air Force, 1970-82, tech. instr., 1977-81; 2d lt. transp. officer U.S. Army Res., 348th Trans Bn (TML), Houston, 1983—; traffic mgr. NASA, Houston, 1983—. Decorated Air medal with three oak leaf clusters; recipient Master Instr. award USAF, 1980. Republican. Roman Catholic. Avocations: fishing; tennis. Home: 402 Charidges Dr Houston TX 77034 Office: NASA Johnson Space Ctr Houston TX 77058

CLARKE, CLIFFORD MONTREVILLE, health association executive; b. Ludowici, Ga., July 20, 1925; s. Clifford Montreville and Lella Bertrue (Hightower) C.; A.B. in Polit. Sci., Emory U., 1951. Radio engr., announcer WSAV, Savannah, 1941-43; pub. relations dir. Ga. dept. Am. Legion, 1945-47; instr. Armstrong Coll., Savannah, 1947-48; asst. supt. Savannah Park and Tree Commn., 1951; instr., supr. tng. dept. Lockheed Aircraft Corp., Marietta, Ga., 1951-52, mgr. employee services dept., 1952-53; exec. v.p. Asso. Industries, Ga, 1953-68; pres. Ga. Bus. and Industry Assn., Atlanta, 1968-73; exec. dir. Bicentennial Council Thirteen Original States, Atlanta, 1973-75; pres. Arthritis Found., 1975—; mem. Am. Soc. Assn. Execs., 1955—, bd. dirs., 1958-67, mem. exec. com., 1960-67, treas., 1962-64, sr. v.p., 1964-65, pres., 1965-66; pres. Ga. Soc. Assn. Execs., 1958-60; v.p., chmn. state assn. group Nat. Indsl. Council, 1970-72. Mem. Ga. Urban and Tech. Assistance Adv. Council, 1965-70, Ga. Intergovtl. Relations Commn., 1966; mem. Ga. Ednl. Improvement Council, 1964-69, chmn., 1967-69, vice chmn., 1970-71; mem. Forward Ga. Commn., 1969-72; vice chmn. Ga. Commn. for Nat. Bicentennial Celebration, 1969-72, chmn., 1973-74; chmn. Chartered Exec. Chartering Bd., 1969-71; mem. Cert. Assn. Exec. Bd., 1978-80; mem. policy com. U. Ga. Grad. Sch. Bus.; adv. bd. Ga. Vocat. Rehab.; mem. Nat. Arthritis Adv. Bd., 1977-80. Bd. dirs. Arthritis Found. Ga., 1965-71, Atlanta Community Services to Blind, Coop. Services for Blind, 1964-71, Atlanta Sch. Art, Atlanta Conv. Bur., 1968-71, Nat. Health Council, 1978-81, trustee Am. Soc. Assn. Execs. Found. Served with inf. AUS, World War II. Decorated Purple Heart with 2 oak leaf clusters. Office: 1314 Spring St NW Atlanta GA 30309

CLARKE, EDWINA TYNES, government official; b. Miami, Fla., Sept. 3, 1942; d. Ismor I. Tynes; m. Andrew C. Clarke, July 4, 1959; children—Andrew II, Candice, Dexter, Simone. A.A., Miami-Dade Jr. Coll.; B.B.A., Fla. Internat. U.; postgrad U. Miami. Clk., typist Jackson Byrons Dept. Store, Miami, 1960-64; clk. U.S. Postal Service, Miami, 1965-75, EEO counselor, 1975-78, EEO investigator, 1978—, supr., 1976. Vice pres. South Dade br. NAACP, 1983; pres. Miami Blacks in Govt., 1981; mem. nat. bd. dirs. Blacks in Govt.; mem. Miami Urban League, Children Home Soc. Coll. Entrance Exam Bd. scholar, 1974; John F. Kennedy/Martin Luther King scholar, 1974. Fellow Urban League Leadership Devel. Ctr.; mem. Nat. Alliance Postal Fed. Employees (chmn. edn. com.), Fla. Internat. U. Alumni Assn., Phi Lambda Pi, Phi Theta Kappa. Democrat. Baptist. Home: 13960 Harrison St Miami FL 33176 Office: PO Box 57087 Miami FL 33157

CLARKE, HAROLD G., justice Supreme Ct. Ga.; b. Forsyth, Ga., Sept. 28, 1927. J.D., U. Ga., 1950. Bar: Ga. 1950. Mem. Ga. State Legislature, 1961-71; chmn. Ga. Inst. for Continuing Legal Edn.; justice Ga. Supreme Ct., 1979—. Fellow Am. Coll. Trial Lawyers, Am. Bar Found.; mem. ABA, Flint Circuit Bar Assn. (pres. 1960-61), Am. Judicature Soc. (bd. dirs.), State Bar Ga. (gov. 1971—, exec. com. 1973—, pres. 1976-77), Omicron Delta Kappa. Office: Supreme Ct Judicial Bldg Atlanta GA 30334

CLARKE, J. CALVITT, JR., federal judge; b. Harrisburg, Pa., Aug. 9, 1920; s. Joseph Calvitt and Helen Caroline (Mattson) C.; B.S. in Commerce, U. Va., 1944, LL.B., 1944; m. Mary Jane Cromer, Feb. 1, 1943; children—Joseph Calvitt III, Martha Tiffany. Admitted to Va. bar, 1944, practiced in Richmond, Va., 1944-74; partner firm Bowles, Anderson, Boyd, Clarke & Herod, 1944-60, firm Sands Anderson, Marks and Clarke, 1960-74; judge U.S. Dist. Ct. Eastern dist. of Va., 1975—; mem. 4th Circuit Judicial Conf. 1963; hon. consul for Republic of Bolivia, 1959-75. Chmn. Citizen's Advisory Com. on Joint Water System for Henrico and Hanover counties, Va., 1968-69; mem. Mayor's Freedom Train Com., 1948-50; del. Young Republican Nat. Conv., Salt Lake City, 1949, Boston, 1951; chmn. Richmond (Va.) Republican Com., 1952-54; candidate for Congress, 1954; chmn. Va. 3d Dist. Rep. Com., 1955-58, 74—, Va. State Rep. Conv., 1958—; co-founder Young Rep. Fedn. of Va., 1950, nat. committeeman, 1950-54; chmn. Speakers Bur., Nixon-Lodge campaign, 1960, mem. fin. com., 1960-74; chmn. Henrico County Republican Com., 1956-58, fin. chmn., 1956—; pres. Couples Sunday Sch. class Second Presbyn. Ch., Richmond, Va., 1948-50, mem. bd. deacons, 1948-61, elder, 1964—; bd. dirs. Family Service Children's Aid Soc., 1948-61, Gambles Hill Community Center, 1950-60. Christian Children's Fund, Inc., 1960-67, Children, Inc., 1967-75, Norfolk Forum, 1978-83; mem. bd. of chancellors Internat. Consular Acad., 1965-75; trustee Henrico County Pub. Library, chmn., 1971-73. Mem. Va. State Bar (mem. 3rd dist. com. 1967-70, chmn. 1969-70), Am. Judicature Soc., Am. Va. (vice chmn. com. on cooperation with fgn. bars 1960-61) bar assns., Richmond Jr. C. of C. (dir. 1946-50), Delta Theta Phi. Clubs: Windmill Point Yacht, Westwood Racquet (pres. 1961-62), Commonwealth. Office: 325 US Courthouse Norfolk VA

CLARKE, MARY WHATLEY, writer; b. Palo Pinto, Tex., June 11, 1899; d. Cephas Vachel and Narcie Isabella (Abernathy) Whatley; student N.Mex. State Normal Sch., 1925; m. James Coltman Dunbar, Oct. 27, 1920 (dec. 1923); 1 dau., Mary Murray Dunbar Harper; m. 2d, Joe A. Clarke, Nov. 15, 1941 (dec. 1971). Owner, pub. Norwood (Man.) Press, 1924-26; advt. dept. Hudson's Bay Co., Winnipeg, Can., 1926-27; advt. mgr. Mineral Wells (Tex.) Daily Index, 1928-33, Breckenridge (Tex.) Am., 1939; pub. Palo Pinto (Tex.) County Star, 1933-44; writer; books include: The Palo Pinto Story, 1957; Life in the Saddle, 1963; David G. Burnet, First President of Texas Republic, 1969; Thomas J. Rusk; Soldier, Statesman, Patriot, 1971; Chief Bowles and the Texas Cherokees, 1971; The Swenson Saga and SMS Ranches, 1976; A Century of Cow Business, 1976; The Slaughter Ranches and Their Makers, 1979; John Simpson Chisum, 1984; contbr. numerous stories and articles to the Cattleman. Woman's bd. Ft. Worth Children's Hosp., pres., 1955-56. Mem. Tarrant County Hist. Soc. (past pres., award), W. Tex. Press Assn. Presbyterian. Club: Ft. Worth Woman's. Home: 3605 Bellaire Dr S Fort Worth TX 76109

CLARKE, RICHARD WALLACE, aviation consulting company executive; b. Jacksonville, Fla., Sept. 8, 1946; s. Gerald Mordaunt and Doris Mildred (Parker) C.; 1 child, William Bartley. B.A. with dept. honors in Polit. Sci., U. Gla., 1967; M.S. in Safety, U. So. Calif.-Arlington, Va., 1979. Cons. Quadel Corp., Rockville, Md., 1976-77; staff engr. Air Line Pilots Assn., Washington, 1977-81; mng. ptnr. SO-CAL Safety Assocs., Reston, Va., 1981-84; v.p. Events Analysis, Inc., Oakton, Va., 1984—. Editor newsletter Accident Prevention Bull., 1980-81; author paper, article. Campaign vol. John Glenn Presdl. Com., Washington, 1983-84. Served to pilot USN, 1968-75, comdr. USNR, 1968—, U.S., Southeast Asia. Recipient Navy Achievement medal, 1975. Mem. System Safety Soc. (chpt. sec. 1984—), Am. Soc. Safety Engrs., Soc. Automotive Engrs. (assoc.), Internat. Soc. Air Safety Investigators (assoc. editor jour. 1984—), Aero Club of Washington, Quiet Birdmen. Democrat. Episcopalian. Avocations: Sailing; flying; photography; writing. Office: Events Analysis Inc 12101 Toreador Ln Oakton VA 22124

CLARKE, ROBERT, financial and tax consultant; b. Rome, N.Y., Apr. 14, 1934; s. Wesley Ray and Patricia Ann (Dollard) C.; m. Arleen Ilona Barry, Nov. 2, 1984; children—Thomas, Stewart, Gregory. B.S., Syracuse U., 1961, M.B.A., 1962; Ph.D., U. Ill., 1967. Prof. taxation U. Mich., Ann Arbor, 1967-70, U. N.C., Chapel Hill, 1970-73, U. Houston, 1973-74, Rice U., Houston, 1974-79; pres. Clarke & Simmons, Inc., Houston, 1979—; dir. ZI Builders, Inc., San Antonio, Selective Coach, Inc., Houston; gen. ptnr. C&S/West Houston, Ltd., 1984—. Coauthor: Accountants' Handbook, 1970; Federal Taxation; Individual Taxes, 1977-83; Corporations, Partnerships, Trusts and Estates, 1977-83; also articles. Served with USAF, 1953-57. Fellow Haskins and Sells Found., 1961, Arthur Andersen & Co., 1966, Am. Acctg. Assn., 1964-65; scholar Bet Alpha Psi, 1961, Fin. Exec. Inst., 1961, N.Y. State Soc. C.P.A.s, 1961, Alpha Kappa Psi, 1961; Tchr. of Yr. award U. Ill., 1964. Mem. Am. Taxation Assn., Am. Acctg. Assn., Beta Gamma Sigma, Beta Alpha Psi, Phi Kappa Phi, Alpha Kappa Psi. Avocations: running; golf. Office: Clarke & Simmons Inc 10500 Richmond Ave Suite 148 Houston TX 77042

CLARK-HOLMES, WILLIAM DONALD, surgeon, otolaryngologist, educator; b. Abilene, Tex., June 28, 1940; s. Sidney Holmes and Mary L. Holmes (Davis) C.; children—Stephen, William Jr., David. D.D.S., U. Tex., 1965, M.D., 1970. Diplomate Am. Bd. Otolaryngology. Intern Brooke Gen. Hosp., 1970-71; resident Walter Reed Hosp., 1972-75; chief of surgery Lyster Army Hosp., Ft. Rucker, Ala., 1975-77; practice medicine specializing in otolaryngology, Key West, Fla., 1977-81; asst. prof. otolaryngology, U. Tex. Med. Br., Galveston, 1981-85. Served to lt. col., U.S. Army, 1965-77. Fellow ACS, Internat. Coll. Surgeons. Republican. Baptist. Contbr. articles to profl. jours., chpts. to texts. Home: 800 La Mancha El Paso TX 79922 Office: 2801 Missouri St Suite 30 Las Cruces NM 88001

CLARKSON, KENNETH WRIGHT, economics educator; b. Downey, Calif., June 30, 1942; s. William Wright and Constance (Patch) C.; A.B., Calif. State U., 1964; M.A., UCLA, 1966, Ph.D., 1971; m. Mary Jane Purdy, June 20, 1965; children—Steven Wright, Thomas David. Economist, Office Mgmt. and Budget, Washington, 1971-72; asst. prof. econs. U. Va., 1969-75; prof. econs. U. Miami, Coral Gables, Fla., 1975—, dir. Law & Econs. Center, 1981—; assoc. dir. office Mgmt. and Budget, Washington, 1982-83; cons. in field. Mem. adv. bd. Reagan/Bush Transition Team, Washington, 1980; mem. Pres.'s Task Force on Food Assistance, 1983; mem. governing bd. Credit Research Ctr., Purdue U., 1981—. NSF grantee, 1972-74. Mem. Am. Econ. Assn., Am. Bus. Law Assn., Western Econ. Assn., Sigma Xi. Author: Food Stamps and Nutrition, 1975; Intangible Capital and Rates of Return, 1977; co-author: Correcting Taxes for Inflation, 1975; Distortions in Official Unemployment Statistics, 1979; West's Business Law, 2d edit., 1983; The Federal Trade Commission Since 1970, 1981; Industrial Organization, 1982; Economics Sourcebook of Government Statistics, 1983; contbr. numerous articles in field. Home: 15925 SW 77th Ct Miami FL 33157 Office: 1541 Brescia Ave Coral Gables FL 33146

CLARY, KENNETH EUGENE, medical supply company executive; b. Gaffney, S.C., Dec. 9, 1941; s. Glenn Elmore and Margaret Macy (Cantrell) C.; m. Victoria Louise Barker, June 17, 1967; children—Kevin Alexander, Partick Stephen. B.S. in Biology, Clemson U., 1964. Textile chemist Lyman Printing & Finishing Co., Lyman, S.C., 1965-69; tech. sales rep. Picker Nuclear Co., Charlotte, N.C., 1969-73, New Eng. Nuclear Co., Raleigh, N.C., 1973-78; nat. dir. sales MCB Mfg. Chemists, Cin., 1978-80; owner, operator Am. Sci. & Chem. Co., Houston, 1980—; pres. Knightsbridge Med. Inc., Houston, 1980—. Mem. Am. Chem. Soc. Republican. Episcopalian. Club: Raveneaux Country (Spring, Tex.). Address: 8807 Chelmsford Ln Spring TX 77379

CLARY, RONALD GORDON, ins. agy. exec.; b. Moultrie, Ga., May 2, 1940; s. Ronald Ward and Hazel Collins C.; student Young Harris Coll., 1958-60; B.B.A. in Ins., U. Ga., 1962; LL.B., Woodrow Wilson Coll. Law, 1966. Field rep. Comml. Union Ins. Cos., 1962-67; ind. ins. agt., 1967—; ins. agt., sec. of agy. Day, Reynolds & Parks, Gainesville, Ga., 1970—. Mem. Ga. Assn. Ind. Ins. Agts., Gainesville Assn. Ind. Ins. Agts. (past pres.), Am. Legion. Republican. Baptist. Club: Elks. Home: 510 Bradford St Gainesville GA 30501 Office: Day Reynolds & Parks 611 Spring St Gainesville GA 30501

CLARY, WARREN THOMAS TIMMONS, manufacturing company executive; b. Midland, Tex., Jan. 23, 1952; s. Robert Artemus and Dorothy Jean (Timmons) C. B.A. with honors, N. Tex. State U., 1975. Consumer communications asst. Sony Corp., Dallas, 1977-79; radio communications rep. Motorola, Dallas, 1979-82, sales communications mgr., 1982—; pres. elect Bus. Exchange, Dallas. Democrat. Roman Catholic. Club: Fort Worth Boat. Office: 3320 Beltline Rd Dallas TX 75234

CLAUSEL, NANCY KAREN, clergywoman, pastoral counselor; b. Jackson, Tenn., Jan. 1, 1948; s. Clinton Prentice and Martha Juanita (Felker) C.; married; children—Richard D. Harwood Jr., Kara Denise Harwood. Student Lambuth Coll., 1966-67, George Peabody Coll. for Tchrs.; B.S. in Edn., Memphis State U., 1971; M.Div. summa cum laude, Memphis Theol. Sem., 1980. Ordained to ministry United Meth. Ch. Dir. Christian edn. Grimes United Meth. Ch., Memphis, 1977-79, Wesleyan Hills United Meth. Ch., Memphis, 1979-80; assoc. minister St. James United Meth. Ch., Memphis, 1981-82; dir. Wesley Pastoral Counseling Ctr., Memphis, 1982-85; co-dir. Connection: Holistic Counseling Ctr., Memphis, 19—; co-founder, co-minister The Connection Ch.; bd. dirs. Wesley Found.-Memphis State, 1979-80, 82-84; vice chmn. commn. on status and role of women Memphis Ann. Conf., 1980—; chmn. work area on worship McKendree Dist. Memphis Ann. Conf., 1980-84; mem. Bd. Pensions Memphis Ann. Conf., 1983-84; supervising pastor Candidacy for Minister program Memphis Ann. Conf., 1984—. Vol. Johnson Aux. City of Memphis Hosp., 1975; sec. Peacemakers Memphis, 1979; clergy rep. adv. bd. Memphis chpt. Parents Without Ptnrs., 1984-85; mem. Network, Memphis, 1984—. Mem. Internat. Transactional Analysis Assn. (clin. mem. 1981—, provisional teaching mem. 1982—), Am. Assn. for Counseling and Devel., Assn. for Specialists in Group Work, Memphis Ministers Assn. (treas. 1985—), Phi Kappa Phi. Avocations: aerobics; music. Home: 1775 B 6th Crompton Pl Memphis TN 38134

CLAXTON, LAWRENCE JACK, marketing executive, educator; b. Lebanon, Mo., Feb. 12, 1954; s. Jackie Ray and Freda May (Winfrey) C.; m. Patti Jean Spain, July 14, 1979; 1 son, Matthew Carl. B.S. in Mgmt., Southwestern Okla. State U., 1977, M.B.A., 1979. Supr. pub. health stats. Okla. Dept. Health, Oklahoma City, 1979-86; dir. research and mktg. A Chance to Change, Inc., The Chem. Dependency Inst. of Okla., 1986—; adj. faculty mktg. dept. Central State U. Sch. Bus., 1980—, bus. dept. Oklahoma City Community Coll., 1981-82. Mem. Southwestern Alumni Assn. (dir. 1981—), Southwestern Sch. Bus. Alumni Assn. (pres. 1980—), Assn. Vital Records and Health Stats. (assoc.). Republican. Baptist. Home: 1101 S Bouziden Dr Moore OK 73160 Office: A Chance to Change Inc 5015 N Penn St Suite 100 Penn Park Office Complex Oklahoma City OK 73112

CLAY, CATESBY WOODFORD, coal corporation executive; b. Paris, Ky., July 25, 1923; s. Brutus J. and Agnes (McEvoy) C.; m. Elizabeth Gerwin, Dec. 30, 1959. B.S. in Bus., Georgetown U., 1948. With Ky. River Coal Corp., Lexington, 1948—, sec., 1950-61, v.p., 1961-69, pres., 1969—, chmn. bd. dirs., 1976—; pres. Runnymede Farm, Inc., Paris, Ky., 1973, dir., 1973—; dir. Churchhill Downs, Inc., Louisville, 1944, pres., dir. KRCC Oil and Gas Co., 1981—. Bd. dirs. Triangle Found., Inc., Lexington, 1980. Mem. Lexington C. of C. Roman Catholic. Club: Lafayette. Home: 616 Cynthiana Rd Paris KY 40361

CLAY, HARRIS AUBREY, chem. engr.; b. Hartley, Tex., Dec. 28, 1911; s. John David and Alberta (Harris) C.; B.S., U. Tulsa, 1933; Ch.E., Columbia U., 1939; m. Violette Frances Mills, June 19, 1948 (dec. June 1972); m. 2d, Garvice Stuart Shotwell, Apr. 28, 1973. Pilot plant operator Phillips Petroleum Co., Burbank, Okla., 1939-42, resident supr. Burbank pilot plants, 1942-44, process design engr., Bartlesville, Okla., 1944-45, process engring. supr. Philtex Plant, Phillips, Tex., 1946-56, tech. adviser to pilot plant mgr., Bartlesville, 1957-61, chem. engring. assoc., 1961-74; cons. engr., 1974—; chmn. tech. com. Fractionation Research, Inc., 1966-71, mem. tech. com., 1972-73. Mem. dist. commn. Boy Scouts Am. Fellow Am. Inst. Chem. Engrs.; mem. Am. Chem. Soc., Electrochem. Soc. Presbyterian. Clubs: Elks, Lions. Contbr. articles to profl. jours. Patentee in field. Home: 1723 Church Ct Bartlesville OK 74006

CLAY, JAMES HARVEY, tool company executive; b. Ft. Monmouth, N.J., Mar. 10, 1950; s. James Watkins and Kathryn (Wegamen) C.; m. Delores Annalee Brander, Mar. 25, 1972; children—Anita Marie, James Eric, Neil Allen. B.S. in Bus. Adminstrn., Monmouth Coll., 1976, M.B.A., 1977; postgrad. U. Mich., 1981, Cornell U., 1982. With Gen. Cable Corp., Woodbridge, N.J., 1977-80, pricing analyst, 1977-78, product analyst, 1978-79, market analyst, 1979-80; market analyst Harding Bros., Inc., Elmira, N.Y., 1980-81, mgr. mktg. adminstrn., 1981-82; v.p. sales and mktg. Utica Tool Co., Orangeburg, S.C., 1982—. Pres., Monmouth County Rifle and Pistol Club, Freehold, N.J., 1980; treas. Landing Homeowners Assn., Orangeburg, 1983-85. Served with USAF, 1968-72. Mem. Am. Mktg. Assn., Assn. M.B.A. Execs. Methodist. Club: Orangeburg Country. Lodge: Masons. Office: PO Box 1807 Cameron Rd Orangeburg SC 29115

CLAY, LYELL BUFFINGTON, newspaper publisher, broadcasting executive; b. Balt., Dec. 15, 1923; s. Buckner and Juliet Lyell (Staunton) C.; B.A., Williams Coll., 1944; LL.B., U. Va., 1948; M.A., Marshall U., W.Va., 1956; M.B.A., W.Va. U., 1975; grad. Advanced Mgmt. Program, Harvard U., 1967; m. Patricia Kennedy, Dec. 3, 1949 (dec.); children—Whitney Kennedy, Ashton deLashmet, Leslie Staunton, Courtney Buffington. Chmn. bd. Clay Communications, Inc., Charleston, W.Va., 1970—; co. pubs. Charleston Daily Mail, Beckley (W.Va.) Register/Herald, Beckley, Shelby Daily Star, N.C., Enquirer Jour., Monroe, N.C.; operator TV stas. in N.C., Miss. and Tex., also WCHV-WWWV radio, Charlottesville, Va.; pres. Clay Realty Co., Charleston, 1957—; admitted to W.Va. bar, 1948. Trustee, U. Charleston, 1967-84; city solicitor, Charleston, 1951-56. Served in USMC, 1945; comdr. JAGC, USNR, ret. Mem. Am. Newspapers Pubs. Assn. (past dir.), W.Va. State Bar, Charleston Area C. of C. (past pres.), W.Va. Press Assn. (past pres.). Presbyterian. Clubs: Edgewood Country, Charleston Rotary (past pres.). Home: PO Box 2993 Charleston WV 25330 Office: 1001 Virginia St Charleston WV 25301

CLAY, ORSON C., insurance executive; b. 1930; B.S., Brigham Young U., 1955; M.B.A., Harvard, 1959; married. Dir. econ. div. Continental Oil Co. Ltd., London, 1964, gen. mgr. adminstrn. and ops., 1965, asst. mgr. marine transp., N.Y.C., 1966-68; exec. asst. fin. Pennzoil United Inc., Houston, 1968-70; exec. v.p. fin., treas. Am. Nat. Ins. Co., Galveston, Tex., 1970-73, sr. exec. v.p., treas., 1973-77, chief exec. officer, dir., 1978—; pres., chmn., dir. Am. Nat. Life Ins. Co. Tex. chmn., dir. Am. Nat. Property & Casualty Co., Am. Nat. Gen. Ins. Co.; Standard Life & Accident Ins. Co.; chmn., dir. Commonwealth Life & Accident Ins. Co.; vice chmn., dir. Tex. Life, Accident, Health, Hosp. Service Ins. Guaranty Assn.; v.p., dir. Am. Nat. Real Estate Mgmt. Corp.; dir. Am. Printing Co.; adv. dir., mem. exec. com. First City Nat. Bank, Houston; dir., mem. exec. com. Securities Mgmt. & Research, Inc. Trustee United Way Galveston; bd. dirs. Tex. Research League, Galveston Indsl. Devel. Corp. mem. investment adv. com. for permanent univ. fund U. Tex. System. Mem. Brigham Young U. Alumni Assn., Tex. Life Ins. Assn. (chmn.). Served to lt. USMCR, 1955-57. Office: 1 Moody Plaza Galveston TX 77550

CLAY, WILLIAM MCCAULEY, petroleum geologist, geophysicist; b. Richmond, Va., Nov. 10, 1954; s. James H.B. and Betty Wilda (Fahrbach) C.; m. Aurelia Ann Broussard, May 15, 1982; 1 child, Dana. B.S. in Geophysics, Va. Inst. Tech., 1978. Geophysicist, Tenneco Oil Co., Houston, 1977-80; geologist, geophysicist Dynamic Exploration, Lafayette, La., 1980—. Mem. Am. Assn. Petroleum Geologists, Soc. Exploration Geophysicists, Lafayette Geol. Soc., S.W. La. Geophys. Soc. Avocations: hunting; fishing; gardening. Home: 209 Bocage Circle Lafayette LA 70503 Office: Dynamic Exploration Ltd PO Box 52889 Lafayette LA 70505

CLAYBROOK, RICHARD ALLEN, JR., lawyer; b. Richmond, Va., May 13, 1952; s. Richard Allen Sr. and Elizabeth Lee (McNeal) C. B.A., Bridgewater Coll., 1974; J.D., U. Richmond, 1977. Bar: Va. 1978. Staff asst. Office of Gov. Va., Richmond, 1978-80, 1981-82; dep. dir. Va. Liaison Office, Washington, 1980-81; research dir. Coleman for Gov. Com., Richmond, 1981; ptnr. Kaylor & Claybrook, Harrisonburg, Va., 1982-84; asst. Commonwealth's atty. Harrisonburg and Rockingham County 1984—; lectr. bus. law Bridgewater Coll., Va., 1982-83. Chmn. City Republican com., Harrisonburg, 1984—, Named Outstanding Young Men Am. 1978-85. Mem. Harrisonburg-Rockingham Bar Assn., Va. Trial Lawyers Assn., Harrisonburg-Rockingham C. of C. (chmn. legis. affairs com. 1984-85), Bridgewater Coll. Alumni Assn. (pres. 1982-83), Alpha Chi Lambda. Methodist. Club: Bridgewater Ruritan. Office: Rockingham County Courthouse Harrisonburg VA 22801

CLAYTON, CARL A., university dean; b. Greensboro, N.C., Nov. 15; s. William A. and Mary (Moore) C.; m. Barbara F. Bennett; children—Michelle, Alan. B.S., Appalachian State Tchrs. Coll., 1967; M.A., Appalachian U., 1968; Ed.D., U. S.C., 1981. Instr. bus. and econs. U. S.C.-Florence, 1968, bus. mgr. and instr., 1969; dir. U. S.C.-Salkehatchie, Allendale, 1970—, asst. prof., 1976, now dean of univ.; mem. transfer com. S.C. Commn. of Higher Edn. Bd. dirs. Swallow Savannah Meth. Ch., Allendale; mem. alumni council U. S.C. Named Friend of Campus, U. S.C.-Salkehatchie, 1981. Mem. Walterboro-Colleton C. of C., Barnwell County C. of C., Nat. Univ. Continuing Edn. Assn., Allendale County Civic Assn., Bamberg County C. of C., So. Assn. Community and Jr. Colls., Nat. Conf. Regional Campus Adminstrs., Allendale Coll. Bus. Assn. Avocations: restoration of automobiles; hunting; fishing; tennis; swimming. Home: PO Box 27 Fairfax SC 29827 Office: U SC-Salkehatchie PO Box 617 Allendale SC 29810

CLAYTON, DONALD DOUGLAS, market researcher, management consultant; b. Pasadena, Calif., Jan. 14, 1960; s. Donald Delbert and Mary Lou (Keesee) C. B.A. in Bus., Rice U., 1983, B.A. in Geology, 1983. Cons. Winick & Assocs., Houston, 1983-84, Am. Metro/Study, Houston, 1984—; chmn. bd. dirs. Intertech Cons., Inc., Houston, 1984—. Mem. Am. Assn. Petroleum Geologists, Urban Land Inst., Mensa. Presbyterian. Avocations: entrepreneurism; music; racquet sports; automobile restoration. Home: 901 Bomar St Houston TX 77006

CLAYTON, EVELYN WILLIAMS, accountant, company executive; b. Durham, N.C., Feb. 11, 1951; d. Virge and Inez Florence (Jordan) Williams; m. Archie L. Clayton, Mar. 1, 1972 (div. May 1975); 1 child, Dorel. Student Durham Tech. Inst., 1969-71, Durham Bus. Coll., 1971-72, U. N.C.-Chapel Hill, 1977-81; A.B.A., Durham Tech. Inst., 1971. C.P.A. Fiscal officer Durham County Health Dept. (N.C.), 1974-82; dir. fin. MedVisit Inc., Butner, N.C., 1982—; exec. dir., pres. EC & Assocs., fin. mgmt. and cons. firm, Durham, 1982—. Mem. Durham Com. on Affairs of Black People; cubmaster, Pack 442, Boy Scouts Am.; active congl. campaign Kenneth B. Spaulding, 1985. Mem. N.C. Assn. Home Care (treas. 1980-83), N.C. Public Health Assn., NAACP. Democrat. Baptist. Home: 112 S Driver Ave Durham NC 27703 Office: EC & Assocs 2514 University Dr Durham NC 27707

CLAYTON, ROBERT LOUIS, educational consultant; clergyman; b. Pensacola, Fla., Feb. 25, 1934; A.B., Talladega Coll., 1955; B.D., Hood Sem., 1959; S.T.M., Interdenoml. Theol. Center, 1965; m. Minnie Harris, June 22, 1957; children—Robert Joel, III, Myrna Audenise. Ordained to ministry African Methodist Episcopal Zion Ch., 1955; coll. chaplain, chmn. dept. sociology Ala. A. and M. Coll., 1959-63; asso. minister Shaw Temple AME Zion Ch., Atlanta; instr., dir. publicity Interdenoml. Theol. Center, 1964-65; chmn. dept. sociology, placement dir. Livingstone Coll., 1965-68; coll. minister Spelman Coll., 1968-69; nat. dir. Black Coll. Placement Dirs., Atlanta, 1968-72; regional dir. Am. Coll. Testing Program, Atlanta, 1972-75, dir. spl. services, Atlanta, 1975-81, dir. minority programs, 1976-81; dir. mktg. and planning Talladega (Ala.) Coll., 1981-82; program dir. Robert R. Moton Inst., Gloucester, Va., 1982—. Danforth Found. Sem. Intern Dillard U., New Orleans, 1957-58; pres., exec. dir. C.E.S.H.E.P.; cons. Office Edn. Bd. dirs. W. J. Walls Found., N.Y.C.; 1st v.p. Concerned Citizens of S.W. Atlanta. Danforth Campus Ministers grantee, 1963-64. Mem. Am. Personnel, Guidance Assn., Am. Sch. Counselors Assn., Am. Coll. Pres. Assn., Assn. Measurement and Evaluation in Guidance, Assn. for Non-White Concerns in Personnel and Guidance (past pres.), Nat. Vocat. Guidance Assn., Nat. Assn. of Coll. and Univ. Chaplains, Nat. Acad. Advisors Assn., Nat. Assn. Coll. Adminstrn. Ofcls., Alpha Phi Alpha. Democrat. Author: Counseling Non-White Students; contbr. numerous articles to profl. jours. Home: 668 Waterford Rd NW Atlanta GA 30318 Office: Robert Russa Moton Meml Inst Box 1070 Gloucester VA 23061

CLAYTON, WILLIAM HOWARD, university administrator; b. Dallas, Aug. 16, 1927; s. William Howard and Blanche (Phillips) C.; m. Joy May; children—Jill, Greg. B.S. in Physics and Math., Bucknell U., 1949; Ph.D. in Phys. Oceanography, Tex. A&M U., 1956. Instr. Bucknell U., Lewisburg, Pa., 1948-49; assoc. in oceanography, instr. math. Tex. A&M U., Galveston, 1954-56, prof. oceanography and meteorology, 1965—, dean Coll. Marine Scis., 1971-74, provost Moody Coll. Marine Scis. and Maritime Resources, 1974-77, pres., 1977—, pres. University System, 1977—; dir. Bank of West Contbr. articles to profl. jours. Adv. bd. Tex. A&M U. Press; bd. dirs. Galveston United Way, 1978—; commr. Police and Fire Dept. Civil Service Bd., City of Galveston, 1976—; directorate com. UNESCO's Project 5b Man and the Bioshpere Program, 1975—; sec.-treas. Tex. Coastal Higher Edn. Authority, Inc., 1981—; chmn. Gulf Univs. Research Consortium, 1977-79. Mem. Am. Meteorol. Soc., Am. Geophys. Union, Sigma Xi, Pi Mu Epsilon, Sigma Pi Sigma, Phi Kappa Phi, Sigma Phi Epsilon. Home: 54 Adler Circle Galveston TX 77550 Office: TEX A&M U-Galveston PO Box 1675 Galveston TX 77553

CLAYTOR, ROBERT BUCKNER, railroad executive; b. Roanoke, Va., Feb. 27, 1922; s. William Graham and Gertrude Harris (Boatwright) C.; m. Frances Tice, Sept. 25, 1943; children—Jane Gordon (Mrs. Samuel J. Webster), Robert Harris, John Preston. A.B. cum laude, Princeton U., 1943; J.D., Harvard U., 1948; L.H.D. (hon.), Hollins Coll., 1982. Admitted to Mass. bar, 1948, N.Y. bar, 1949, Va. bar, 1952; atty. AT&T, 1948-51; solicitor Norfolk & Western R.R., Roanoke, 1951-54, asst. gen. solicitor, 1954-56, asst. gen. counsel, 1956-60, gen. solicitor, 1960-64, v.p. law, 1964-68, sr. v.p., 1968-70, exec. v.p., 1970-80, pres., 1980-81, chief exec. officer, pres., 1981-82, dir., 1970—; chmn., chief exec. officer, dir. Norfolk So. Corp., Norfolk, 1982—; dir. Piedmont Aviation, Inc., Sovran Fin. Corp., Ga.-Pacific Corp., Greater Norfolk Corp., Richardson-Wayland Elec. Corp., Assn. Am. R.R.s. Chancellor, Episcopal Diocese Southwestern Va., 1969-74, trustee diocese funds; bd. trustees Va. Found. Ind. Colls., Eastern Va. Med. Found., Lewis Gale Hosp., Protestant Episcopal Theol. Sem., Va., Hollins Coll.; bd. regents Mercersburg Acad., 1981—; bd. visitors Va. Poly. Inst. and State U.; bd. dirs. Va. Opera Assn. Served to 1st lt. AUS, 1943-46. Mem. Am., Va., Roanoke bar assns., The Bretton Woods Com., The Conf. Bd., Va. Bus. Council, Nat. Coal Council, Bus. Roundtable, Phi Beta Kappa. Episcopalian. Clubs: Princeton, Sky, Links (N.Y.C.); Metropolitan (Washington); Norfolk, Harbor (Norfolk); Yacht and Country; Shenandoah (Roanoke). Office: Norfolk Southern Corp One Commercial Pl Norfolk VA 23510-2191

CLELAND, JOSEPH MAXWELL, state official; b. Atlanta, Aug. 24, 1942; s. Joseph Hugh and Juanita (Kesler) C. B.A., Stetson U., 1964; M.A., Emory U., 1968. Adminstr. VA, Atlanta; state senator Ga. Gen. Assembly; now sec. of state, Ga. Served to capt. U.S. Army, 1965-68. Decorated Silver Star, Bronze Star, Soldier's medal. Recipient Jefferson award for pub. service, 1977; Neal Pike Rehab. award Boston U., 1978. Democrat. Methodist. Author: Strong at the Broken Places. Office: State Capitol Bldg Atlanta Ga 30334

CLEMENT, CHARLES DAVE, petroleum products wholesaler, farmer; b. Borger, Tex., Feb. 23, 1948; s. Everett Dave, Jr., and Willie Leona (Mackie) C.; m. Branda Timmons, Aug. 26, 1982 (div. 1976); 1 dau., Sally Rae; m. 2d, Jolene Marie Rempe, June 30, 1978; children—Patrick Dave, John Philip. Student Tex. Tech. U., 1966-68. Owner farm, Perryton, Tex., 1968—; asst. yard mgr. Carey Lumber Co., Norman, Okla., 1977-78; owner D & D Petroleum Inc., Perryton, 1978—. Vice pres. Parish Council of Immaculate Conception Roman Catholic Ch., Perryton, 1982—, spl. minister of the Eucharist, 1983—. Served with USN, 1968-69. Mem. Tex. Oil Marketers Assn., Nat. Assn. Texaco Wholesalers, Nat. Fedn. Ind. Bus., Ochiltree County C. of C. Home: 2005 Jackson Dr Perryton TX 79070

CLEMENT, RICHARD FERDINAND, JR., uranium mining company executive, geologist; b. Woburn, Mass., Sept. 22, 1943; s. Richard Ferdinand and Gladys Winsbay (Whittle) C.; m. Jeanne Ellen Colt, Nov. 11, 1967; 1 child, Richard F. III. B.S., Boston Coll., 1965; M.S., U. Vt., 1967. Exploration geologist Mobil Oil Corp., Oklahoma City, 1967-69, planning assoc., N.Y.C., 1976-78; sr. geologist Mobil Spl. Energy, Denver, 1969-74, ops. coordinator, 1974-76; v.p. Mobil Energy Minerals, Melbourne, Australia, 1978-83; v.p., Uranium Resources Inc., Richardson, Tex., 1983—, also dir. Mem. Am. Assn. Petroleum Geologists (assoc.). Avocations: Golf, game fishing. Office: Uranium Resources Inc 1600 Promenade Ctr Richardson TX 75080

CLEMENTS, BERNADETTE STONE, ballet director; b. Mobile, Ala., Aug. 25, 1943; d. J.W. Stone and Vera (Enger) Stone Faulkner; m. Vernon Gaylord Clements, June 6, 1964; children—Enger Bernadette, William Patrick, Vernon Scott. Student Ballet Arts Studio, N.Y.C., 1961-62. Founder, dir. Ft. Walton Beach Ballet Acad. (Fla.), 1966—; founder, artistic dir. Ft. Walton Beach Ballet Co., 1969—. Pres. Jr. Service League, 1974; mem. dance panel Fine Arts Council Fla. Alt. Miss Ala., 1964; named Outstanding Co. Mem., Mobile Civic Ballet, 1964, Outstanding Mem. Jr. Service League, 1973. Mem. Nat. Assn. Regional Ballet (regional coordinator 1977-79), Southeastern Regional Ballet Assn. (pres. 1980), State Dance Assn. Fla. (pres. 1981). Office: 101 Chicago Ave Fort Walton Beach FL 32548

CLEMENTS, CYNTHIA LEA, librarian; b. Dallas, May 23, 1950; d. Archie Bob and Dorothy Maye (Cofer) Clements. B.A. in Hist., U. Dallas, Irving, 1972; M.L.S., Tex. Woman's U., Denton, 1974; M.A. in Humanities, U. Tex.-Dallas, Richardson, 1980; postgrad. U. London, Paris Am. Acad. through Am. U. Librarian, evening mgr. Richland Coll., Dallas, 1974-82, acquisitions evening librarian, 1982—, collection devel. librarian, 1984—; cons. Belo. Corp., Dallas, 1981. Editor: U. Dallas Coll. Annual, 1971, 72, Tex. Library Jour., 1978-80; author, talent videotapes Library Instrn. series, 1983; on-line computer system manual for Dallas County Community Coll. Dist., 1983; contbr. articles to publs., designer brochures. Tex. Woman's U. scholar, 1974. Mem. ALA, Tex. Library Assn., Dallas County Library Assn., Alliance Française. Democrat. United Methodist. Home: 4116 Shackelford Dr Mesquite TX 75150 Office: Richland Coll LRC 12800 Abrams Rd Dallas TX 75243

CLEMENTS, MICHAEL ROBERT, banker; b. Jersey City, Oct. 26, 1943; s. Arthur and Jeanne (Rosier) C.; m. Karen Margaret Nevins, Oct. 9, 1965; children—Kim Michele, Michael Matthew. A.A.S., Pace U., 1972; student Sch. Banking of the South, 1976-78. CDP, Data Processing Mgmt. Assn. Systems analyst Bank of N.Y., 1961-68; systems research officer First Jersey Nat. Bank, Jersey City, 1968-72; sr. v.p. Flagship Services Corp., Tampa, 1972-80, acting chief operating officer, 1980, sr. v.p., 1980—; dir. Fla. EFTS Inc.; instr. Am. Inst. Banking, 1976-81. Area coordinator Connally for Pres. campaign, 1980; pres. Countryside High Sch. Dance/Drill Team Parents Assn., 1981-82. Served with USNR, 1965-67. Named Boss of Yr., Am. Bus. Woman's Assn., 1981-82. Mem. Am. Bankers Assn. (Bank Card adv. bd.), Fla. Bankers Assn. (past chmn. Bank Card com.), Data Processing Mgmt. Assn. (dir. 1969-71). Republican. Roman Catholic. Club: Countryside Country. Home: 5002 Whalers Way Orlando FL 32822 Office: Sunbank Service Corp 7632 Southland Blvd Orlando FL 32809

CLEMENTS, OMAR RANDOLPH, petrochem. co. exec.; b. Ida, La., Aug. 14, 1925; s. Quilla Z. and Vada (Slay) C.; B.S. in Chem. Engring., La. Tech. U., 1950; m. Lovenia Holder, Dec. 22, 1950; 1 son, Terrence Christopher. Plant engr. S.W. Gas Producing Co., Dubach, La., 1950-51; field service engr. Western Co., Midland, Tex., 1951-52, Henderson Engring. Co., Shreveport, La., 1952-53; sr. process engr. El Paso Natural Gas Co., El Paso, Tex., 1953-54, asst. chief process engr., 1954-56, chief process engr., 1956-60; ops. supr. El Paso Products Co., Odessa, Tex., 1960-64, ops. mgr., 1964-65, ops. and maintenance mgr., 1965-66, complex mgr., 1966-67, gen. mgr. mfg., 1967-69, asst. v.p., 1969-72, v.p., 1972-77, sr. v.p., 1979-83, pres., 1984—, also dir.; exec. v.p. El Paso LNG Service Co., Paris, 1977-79; dir. El Paso Products Service Co., Utah Natural Gas Co., El Paso Products Pipeline Co., El Paso Polyolefins Co. Pres. bd. trustees Odessa Coll. 1968-76. Served with U.S. Army, 1943-45. Registered profl. engr., Tex. Mem. Am. Inst. Chem. Engrs., Nat. Soc. Profl. Engrs., Tex. Soc. Profl. Engrs., Tex. Assn. Bus. (dir., regional chmn., 1974-76, exec. com., 1978-80), West Tex. C. of C. (v.p., dir., 1970-76), Odessa C. of C. (dir., 1970-76). Republican. Presbyterian. Clubs: Odessa Country, Mission Country; Santa Teresa Country (El Paso). Office: PO Box 3986 Odessa TX 79760

CLEMENTS, WOODROW WILSON, beverage company executive; b. Tuscaloosa, Ala., July 30, 1914; s. William Houston and Martha (Christian) C.; student Howard Coll., Birmingham, Ala., 1932-33; student U. Ala., 1933-35, L.H.D. (hon.), 1974; m. Eloise Davis, Mar. 20, 1937; 1 son, Wayne Wilson; m. Virginia Thomas, 1982. Began as route salesman advancing to sales mgr. Dr Pepper Bottling Co., Tusculoosa, 1935-42; with Dr Pepper Co., 1942—, successively dist. mgr., sales promotion mgr., asst. mgr. bottler service, gen. sales mgr., 1942-49, 49-51, v.p., gen. sales mgr., 1951-58, v.p. mktg., 1958-67, exec. v.p., dir., 1967-68, pres., 1969—, chief exec. officer, 1970—, chmn., 1974—; past dir. Inter First Bancshares, Fidelity Union Life. Past dir. Council Opportunities Selling; exec. council Internat. and Comparative Law Center; mem. Cotton Bowl Council; gen. chmn. Dallas Salute to Vietnam Vets., 1973; devel. council Tex. Sports Hall of Fame; adv. council Nat. Alliance Businessmen, Council Religious Heritage Am., Salvation Army; mem. alumni council Pres.'s Cabinet U. Ala. Bd. visitors U. Ala. Coll. Commerce and Bus. Adminstrn.; bd. dirs. North Tex. Commn., Internat. Trade Conf. S.W. So. Meth. U., Greater Dallas Crime Commn., Dallas Council World Affairs, Dallas Civic Opera, Dallas Citizens' Council, Citizens Traffic Safety Commn. Greater Dallas, Boy Scouts Am., Better Bus. Bur. Met. Dallas; trustee Baylor U. System; chmn. bd. govs. Jr. Achievement Dallas, others. Recipient Mktg. Man of Decade award Am. Mktg. Assn., 1970; Golden Plate award Am. Acad. Achievement, 1970; George Washington certificate Freedoms Found. at Valley Forge, 1975; Entrepreneur of Yr. award So. Meth. U. Sch. Bus., 1975; Beverage Industry Man of Yr. award Beverage Industry publ., 1976; Chief Exec. Officer of Yr. in Beverage Industry award Fin. World, 1977; Horatio Alger award, 1980; Disting. Am. award Nat. Football Hall of Fame, 1980; Beverage Hall of Fame award, 1982. Mem. Sales and Mktg. Execs. Internat. (regional v.p., pres. 1968-69, chmn. bd. 1969-70, Disting. Salesman award 1972), Dallas Personnel Assn. (dir.), S.W. Sales Execs. Council (pres.; named Disting. Sales Exec. 1969), Dallas Sales Exec. Club (pres. 1957), Dallas C. of C. (dir.). Clubs: Dallas Country, Chaparral, City, Tower. Lodge: Rotary. Office: PO Box 655086 Dallas TX 75265

CLEMMONS, FRANCES ANNE MANSELL (MRS. SLATON CLEMMONS), government official; b. Camden, Miss., Dec. 21, 1915; d. Otho Franklin and Pearl (Dunlap) Mansell; B.S., Belhaven Coll., 1937, Mus.B., 1937; m. Rowe Sanders Crowder, Dec. 17, 1938 (div. Mar. 1954); children—Rowe Sanders, Frances Elizabeth; m. 2d, Slaton Clemmons, Nov. 21, 1965. Owner, operator Crowder Art Gallery, Jackson, Miss., 1946-50; dept. mgr., buyer Valley Dry Goods Co., Vicksburg, 1954-56; with Social Security Adminstrn., 1956-83, asst. dist. mgr., Rome, Ga., 1962-83. Mem. Ga. Citizens Adv. Council on Energy (pres. Rome chpt.), Floyd County Merit Bd., Salvation Army Aux. Mem. Rome Community Concert Assn., Rome Little Theatre, Rome C. of C. Democrat. Presbyterian. Club: Quota Internat. (pres. Rome club 1974-75, 75-76; dist. lt. gov. 1979-80, dist. gov. 1980-81, 81-82, dir. South area 1984—) (Rome). Home: 412 E 3d Ave Rome GA 30161

CLEMMONS, JACK DEAN, educational administrator; b. Mount Pleasant, Tex., Nov. 12, 1948; s. Fred Madison and Una Mae (Bradley) C.; m. Candace Lynne Ragsdale, Nov. 17, 1967; children—Bryan Scott, Brandon Lee. B.S., East Tex. State U., 1972; M.Ed., North Tex. State U., 1979; Ed.D., Tex. A&M U., 1984. Tchr., coach Mesquite Ind. Sch. Dist., Tex., 1973-77, Keller Ind. Sch. Dist., Tex., 1977-79, Eagle-Mount-Saginaw Ind. Sch. Dist., Fort Worth, 1979-80; elem. prin. Waller Ind. Sch. Dist., Tex., 1980-84; high sch. prin. White Deer Ind. Sch. Dist., Tex., 1984-85; asst. supt. ednl. services Athens Ind. Sch. Dist., Tex., 1985—. Mem. Nat. Assn. Secondary Sch. Prins., Tex. Assn. Secondary Sch. Prins., Tex. Assn. Gifted and Talented, Assn. Suprs. and Curriculum Dirs., Tex. Assn. Community Schs., Tex. Assn. Sch. Adminstrs. Republican. Baptist. Lodge: Lions. Avocations: hunting; fishing; motorcycle riding; jogging. Home: Box 2236 Athens TX 75751 Office: Athens Ind Sch Dist Box 112 Athens TX 75751

CLEMMONS, SLATON, lawyer; b. Rome, Ga., July 19, 1909; s. Thomas Edmondson and Annie Ross (Slaton) C.; student Davidson Coll., 1926-27; J.D., U. Ga., 1929; postgrad. U. Pa., 1929-30; m. Starr Reynolds Quigg, 1939 (div. 1957); children—Diana Edmondson, Byard Quigg, Thomas Slaton; m. 2d, Frances Mansell Crowder, Nov. 1965. Admitted to Ga. bar, 1929, U.S. Supreme Ct. bar, 1937; practiced in Rome, 1930-35, 46-54; spl. atty. U.S. Dept. Justice, 1935-37, 42-46; spl. atty. gen. Ga., 1938-39; spl. asst. to atty. gen. U.S., 1940-41; asst. U.S. atty. No. dist. Ga., 1954-62; 1st asst. U.S. atty., 1962-70, ret., 1970. Served as lt. (j.g.) USNR, 1942. Mem. Ga., Rome (past pres.) bar assns., Am. Legion, Mil. Order World Wars, Phi Delta Phi, Sigma Alpha Epsilon. Democrat. Presbyn. Mason. Clubs: Coosa Country, Nine O'clock Cotillion (Rome, Ga.).

CLEMON, U. W., federal judge; b. Birmingham, Ala., Apr. 9, 1943; m. Barbara Lang; children—Herman Issac, Addine Michele. Admitted to Ala. bar; partner firm Adams and Clemon and predecessor, Birmingham, 1969-80; fed. judge U.S. Dist. Ct., No. Dist. Ala., Birmingham, 1980—; mem. Ala. Senate, 1974-80. Recipient Law and Justice award SCLC, 1980. Mem. Am. Bar Assn. (exec. council 1976-79), Alpha Phi Alpha. Office: 305 Fed Courthouse Birmingham AL 35203

CLEMONS, ROBERT RICKARD, exploration geologist, consultant medical image processing; s. Robert Oliver and Harriet Louise (Rickard) C. B.S. in Geology, U. Utah, 1967; M.S., Tex. Tech U., 1980, Ph.D., 1984. Commd. 2d lt. U.S. Air Force, 1967; advanced through grades to maj., 1981; adminstrv. mgmt. officer, Clark AFB, Philippines, 1973-74, intelligence applications officer, 1974-79; sr. geologist Amerada Hess Corp., Tulsa, 1980—; mem. sci. steering group Geopotential Research Mission, 1983—; cons. image processing ORU Med. Ctr., Tulsa, 1984—. Contbr. articles to profl. jours. Adviser CAP, Tulsa, 1980—. Mem. Geol. Soc. Am., Am. Geophys. Union, Am. Assn. Petroleum Geologists, Geosci. and Remote Sensing Soc., Am. Soc. Photogrammetry, Sigma Xi, Phi Kappa Phi, Sigma Gamma Epsilon. Republican. Club: Tex. Navy (adm. 1975—). Lodges: Masons (master 1967—), Order of Sword (grand chancellor 1978—). Avocations: scuba diving, sailing; being a journeyman curmudgeon. Home: PO Box 2931 Tulsa OK 74101 Office: Amerada Hess Corp PO Box 2040 Tulsa OK 74102

CLENDENIN, JOHN L., telecommunications company executive; b. El Paso, Tex., May 8, 1934; s. Thomas Pipes and Maybelle Baumann C.; m. Margaret Ann Matthews, Aug. 30, 1954; children—Elizabeth Ann, Linda Susan, Mary Kathryn, Thomas Edward. B.A., Northwestern U., 1955. With Ill. Bell Telephone Co., 1955-78, v.p., 1975-78; v.p. ops. Pacific N.W. Bell, Seattle, 1978-79; v.p. AT&T, 1979-81; pres. So. Bell Tel. & Tel. Co., Atlanta, 1981-82, chmn. bd., 1982-83; pres., chief exec. officer BellSouth Corp., Atlanta, 1984, chmn., chief exec. officer, 1984—, also dir.; dir. First Atlanta Corp., First Nat. Bank Atlanta, Equifax Inc., Atlanta, Nat. Service Industries, Inc., Atlanta, Capital Holding Corp., Louisville, R.J. Reynolds Industries, Inc., Winston-Salem, N.C. Pres. Atlanta area council Boy Scouts Am.; bd. dirs. Atlanta Arts Alliance, Atlanta Symphony Orch. League, Central Atlanta Progress Inc. Martin Luther King, Jr. Ctr. for Nonviolent Social Change, Morris Brown Coll., Atlanta, Oglethorpe U., Atlanta; southeast regional chmn. Nat. Alliance Bus., United Way Am.; v.p. Atlanta United Way; pres. Atlanta C. of C. Served with USAF, 1956-59. Presbyterian. Clubs: Commerce, Cherokee Town and Country, Piedmont Driving (Atlanta); Mid-Am. (Chgo.). Lodge: Rotary. Office: BellSouth Corp 675 W Peachtree St NE Atlanta GA 30375

CLENDENIN, MARTHA ANNE, anatomist, physical therapist; b. Salem, Ohio, Jan. 26, 1944; d. William E. and Ellen I. (Esterly) C. B.S., Med. Coll. Va.-Richmond, 1965, M.S., 1970, Ph.D., 1972. Lic. phys. therapy, N.C., Fla. Staff phys. therapist Duke U. Hosp., Durham, N.C., 1965-67; asst. prof. anatomy Eastern Va. Med. Sch., Norfolk, 1973-79, assoc. prof., 1979-83; prof., chmn. phys. therapy U. Fla., Gainesville, 1983—. NIH fellow, 1972-73; grantee Tidewater Heart Assn., 1976-77, Intramural Biomed. Research and Devel., 1978-82, Va. Heart Assn., 1979-80. Mem. Soc. Neurosci., So. Soc. Anatomists, Am. Phys. Therapy Assn., Va. Acad. Sci., AAAS, Am. Assn. Anatomists, Sigma Xi. Contbr. articles to profl. jours. Office: Sch Phys Therapy JHM Health Ctr Box J-154 Univ Fla Gainesville FL 32610

CLENDENING, JOHN ALBERT, geologist; b. Martinsburg, W.Va., Mar. 6, 1932; s. Charles and Florence M. (Remsburg) C.; m. Cleo Dorothy Bond, Sept. 26, 1954; children—Kyra, Rebecca, Shawna. B.S. in Geology, W.Va. U., 1958, M.S. in Geology, 1960, Ph.D., 1970. Coal geologist, palynologist W.Va. Geol. Survey, Morgantown, 1960-68; geologist Pan Am. Petroleum Corp., Fort Worth, 1968-71, Amoco Prodn. Co., Houston, 1971—. Contbr. articles to profl. jours. Bd. dirs. Westador Civic Assn., Houston, 1984-85. Fellow Geol. Soc. Am.; mem. Am. Assn. Stratigraphic Palynologists (councilor 1975-76, v.p. 1976-77, sec.-treas. 1978-82, pres.-elect 1982-83, pres. 1983-84), Am. Soc. for Organic Petrology (pres. 1983-84), Am. Assn. Petroleum Geologists, Houston Geol. Soc. Lodges: Knights of Malta, Masons, KT. Avocations: golf; bagpipes. Home: 1018 Tulip Tree Ln Houston TX 77090 Office: Amoco Prodn Co PO Box 3092 Houston TX 77253

CLESI, PHILIP JOHN, consulting actuary; b. New Orleans, Oct. 26, 1945; s. John Joseph and Ethel Ann (Battistella) C.; div.; 1 son, Cameron. B.S. in Math., U. New Orleans, 1968, M.S., 1969. Enrolled actuary. Actuarial asst. Bankers Life & Casualty Co., Chgo., 1970-73; asst. actuary Pan-Am. Life Ins. Co., New Orleans, 1973-76; cons. actuary Groves & Clesi Cons. Actuaries, New Orleans, 1976-81; pres., chmn. bd. Clesi Actuarial Assocs., Inc., 1981—. Mem. Am. Soc. Pension Actuaries, Am. Acad. Actuaries, Soc. Actuaries (assoc.), U. New Orleans Alumni Assn. (recipient Cert. Service in Legis. Relations). Republican. Roman Catholic. Home and office: 3342 Esplanade Ave New Orleans LA 70119

CLEVELAND, SIDNEY E(ARL), psychologist; b. Boston, Jan. 22, 1919; s. Herbert Carlos and Edith (Willey) C.; m. Marjorie Spacht, Nov. 27, 1942; children—John Alvin, Carol Tennant, Mark Eastman, Sarah Downing. A.B., Brown U., 1941; M.A., U. Nebr., 1942; Ph.D., U. Mich., 1950. Lic. psychologist, Tex. Staff psychologist VA Med. Ctr., Houston, 1950-57, asst. chief, 1957-62, chief psychology sevice, 1962—; prof. clin. psychology Baylor Coll. Medicine, Houston, 1957—; pvt. practice psychology, Houston, 1961—. Author: (with others) Body Image and Personality, 1968. Contbr. articles to profl. jours. Served to comdr. USN, 1942-46. Fellow Am. Psychol. Assn., (pres. div. 18 1980-81), Assn. VA Chief Psychologists (pres. 1980-81, Leadership award 1982). Home: 12021 Tall Oaks Houston TX 77024

CLEVELAND, VIRGINIA BESS, sociology educator, administrator; b. Lebanon, Ky., Feb. 16, 1948; s. Joseph Claybrooke and Virginia (Lankford) C.; B.A., Western Ky. U., 1970, M.A., 1974. Assoc. prof. sociology Jefferson Community Coll., Louisville, Ky., 1975—, chairperson behavioral and social scis. div., 1982—. Mem. So. Sociol. Soc., Anthropologists and Sociologists of Ky., Ky. Assn. Community Coll. Profs. (treas. 1983—). Home: 404 Wallace Ave Louisville KY 40207 Office: Jefferson Community Coll 109 E Broadway Louisville KY 40202

CLEVENGER, FRANKIE DENISE, pharmacist; b. Newport, Tenn., Sept. 4, 1957; d. James and Winnifred (Frazier) C. B.S. in Pharmacy, Mercer Coll. Pharmacy, 1983. Intern Jabo's Pharmacy, Newport, Tenn., 1975-83; pharmacist Clayton Gen. Hosp., Riverdale, Ga., 1983-84, Dekalb Gen. Hosp., Decatur, Ga., 1983-84, Revco Discount Drug, Johnson City, Tenn., 1984—. Mem. Am. Soc. Hosp. Pharmacists, Am. Pharm. Assn., Ga. Pharm. Assn., Am. Apothecary Assn., Kappa Epsilon, Kappa Psi. Avocations: jogging; basketball; softball; water skiing; traveling; macrame; sewing. Home: 1811 Lakeview Dr Apt E-7 Johnson City TN 37601

CLEVES, MARIO ALBERTO, biostatistician, systems analyst; b. Paris, Nov. 26, 1954; came to U.S., 1978; s. Alfonso and Beatriz (Saa) C.; m. Pattie Jane Adams, Aug. 14, 1982; 1 child, Phillip Alfonso. B.S. in Med. Tech., U. Okla., 1980, M.S. in Biostats., 1983. Registered med. technologist. Med. technologist Okla. Children's Hosp., Oklahoma City, 1979-84; health data analyst Okla. Found. for Peer Revs., Oklahoma City, 1984-85, sr. systems analyst, 1985—. USPHS grantee Okla. U. Scis. Ctr., Oklahoma City, 1983—. Mem. Am. Soc. Med. Technologists, Am. Soc. Clin. Pathologists, Am. Statis. Assn. Roman Catholic. Office: Okla Found for Peer Rev 601 NW Expressway Oklahoma City OK 73118

CLICK, MARGARET RIDDLE-LAWTON, guidance counselor, researcher; b. Pitts., May 20, 1942; d. Forest Leroy and Grace Elizabeth (Riddle) Lawton; m. Dewitt Ernest Click, Nov. 24, 1974. B.A., Knox Coll., 1964; M.Ed., E. Stroudsburg Coll., 1974; Ph.D., U.Fla., 1986. Cert. sci. tchr., sch. counselor, leader human potential seminars. Tchr. Gwynns Falls Jr. High Sch., 1964, Lombard Jr. High Sch., Galesburg, Ill., 1965, San Pablo Jr. High Sch., Calif., 1966-67, Sparta Jr. High Sch., N.J., 1968-71, Helen Morgan Elem. Sch., 1972, Stillwater Jr. High Sch., N.J., 1973, Umatilla High Sch., Fla., 1974-81; owner, operator, tch. Inst. for Advanced Edn., Totowa, N.J., 1972-73; spl. project writer and workshop leader, 1976; sponsor Brain Bowl Team Umatilla High Sch., 1977, human potential leader, 1979; sch. counselor Lake County Schs., Leesburg, Fla., 1983—. Author of gifted curriculum: Biochemistry, 1979. Vol. Youth Programs, Lake County, Fla., 1976-79; leader Human Potential Seminars, Lake County, 1979. Grantee NSF, 1963, NDEA Lake County, 1975. Mem. AAUP, Am. Assn. Counseling and Devel., Am. Sch. Counseling Assn., Alpha Delta Kappa (sec. 1980-81), Kappa Delta Pi, Phi Delta Kapp, Chi Sigma Iota, Pi Lambda Theta. Republican. Presbyterian. Club: Exptl. Aircraft Assn. Avocations: private pilot; scuba diving; piano; painting; tennis. Home: 235 Lakeview St Box 1039 Umatilla FL 32784

CLIFFORD, PAUL ARTHUR, former art museum curator, lecturer; b. Framingham, Mass., Dec. 3, 1915; m. Virginia Petty, June 28, 1939. B.A., Marietta Coll., 1937. Curator pre-Columbian collection Duke U. Mus. Art, Durham, N.C., 1973-81, emeritus, 1981—; lectr. dept. continuing edn. Duke U., 1974-81; lectr. Mint Mus. Art, Charlotte, N.C., Hollywood (Fla.) Art Ctr., Birmingham Art Mus., Huntsville Mus. Art, U. N.C.-Wilmington, U. Nev.-Las Vegas, others; cons. EPCOT Ctr., others. Recipient award of Spl. Recognition N.C. Mus. Council, 1981. Fellow Instituto Interamericano; mem. Am. Soc. Appraisers (sr. appraiser; chpt. pres. 1982-83), Textile Mus. Republican. Club: Torch. Author articles in field. Home and Office: 315 Geitner Ave Newton NC 28658

CLIFFORD, PAUL INGRAHAM, psychologist, assn. exec.; b. Martinsburg, W.Va., Jan. 22, 1914; s. J. Paul and Mabel (Douglass) C.; B.S., Shippensburg, State U., Pa., 1938; A.M., Atlanta U., 1948; Ph.D., U. Chgo., 1953; m. Elizabeth Edith Sterrs, Jan. 21, 1950 (dec.); m. 2d, Margaret Washington Cabiness, Nov. 26, 1975. Civilian administrv. asst. USAAF, 1941-46; prof. chemistry Paine Coll., Augusta, Ga., 1947-48; instr. in edn. Atlanta U., 1948-51, asst. prof., 1952-54, asso. prof., 1954-57, prof., 1957-68, registrar, 1954-66, dir. admissions, 1954-66, dir. summer sch., 1957-68; staff psychologist Am. Mgmt. Psychologists, Inc., 1966—, v.p., dir., 1969—, nat. dir. profl. services, 1969-71; prof., chmn. dept. psychology S.C. State Coll., 1971-76; psychologist Career Mgmt. Atlanta, Inc., 1976—; dir. Summer Sch. Atlanta U., 1982—, adj. prof., 1980-85; cons. U.S. Office Edn., 1961—; vis. prof. edn. U. Calif. at Berkeley, 1968-69; cons. psychologist various indsl. orgns. Bd. dirs. So. Fellowships Fund, Nat. Fellowships Fund; trustee Zale Found., Dallas. Lic. psychologist, Ga., Ill. Fellow AAAS, Ga., Pa. psychol. assns.; mem. Am., Southeastern, S.C., Ill. psychol. assns., Soc. for Psychol. Study Social Issues, Nat. Soc. Study Edn., AAUP, Assn. Higher Edn., NEA, Am. Ednl. Research Assn., Am. Assn. Counseling and Devel., Nat. Vocat. Guidance Assn., Nat. Assn. Guidance Suprs., Assn. Counselor Edn. and Supervision, Assn. Measurement Edn. and Guidance, Nat. Council on Measurement in Edn., Am. Acad. Polit. and Social Scis., N.Y. Acad. Scis., Internat. Platform Assn., Phi Delta Kappa, Omega Psi Phi. Episcopalian. Author monograph, articles for ednl. and psychol. jours. Home: 859 Woodmere Dr NW Atlanta GA 30318

CLIFT, ANNIE SUE, nursing educator; b. Newbern, Tenn., Nov. 29, 1931; d. James L. and Mollie Sue (Gelzer) C.; B.S.N., U. Tenn. Sch. Nursing, 1954; cert. Tokyo Sch. Japanese Lang., 1964; M.R.E., Southwestern Bapt. Theol. Sem., 1967; student Union U. Extension, 1955-56, Memphis State Coll., 1956; M.N. in Rehab., Emory U., 1969. Gen. duty staff nurse John Gaston Hosp., Memphis, 1954-55; staff nurse Memphis and Shelby County Public Health Dept., Memphis, 1955-56; supr., asst. dir. nurses Parkview Hosp., Dyersburg, Tenn., 1956-59, acting dir. nurses, 1958; charge nurse (part-time) Harris Hosp., Fort Worth, 1959-60, W.I. Cook Meml. Hosp. Center for Children, Fort Worth, 1960; missionary nurse, fgn. mission bd. So. Bapt. Conv., Richmond, Va., 1961-75; gen. duty nurse Japan Bapt. Hosp., Kyoto, 1964-66, ednl. dir., 1966-67; instr. (part-time) Japan Bapt. Sch. Nursing, Kyoto, 1966-67; charge nurse, in-service dir. Jibla (Yemen) Bapt. Hosp., 1969-71; clin. instr. ob-gyn. Japan Bapt. Sch. Nursing, Kyoto, 1971-72, exec. dir., 1971-72; asst. prof. nursing U. Tenn., Martin, 1973-81, asso. prof., 1981—. Missionary, Fujisawa (Japan) Bapt. Ch., 1962-64; youth dir. Kyohoku Bapt. Mission, Kyoto, 1964-67; ednl. dir. Kitayama Bapt. Ch., Kyoto, 1971-72; instr. English as second lang. various schs. and hosps. in Japan, 1962-66, 71-72; Children's Sunday sch. tchr. Emmaus Bapt. Ch., 1972-77; dir. Acteens Dyer Bapt. Assn., 1976-77. Mem. Am. Nurses Assn., Tenn. Nurses Assn., Assn. Rehab. Nurses, Am. Congress Rehab. Medicine. Baptist. Contbr. book revs. on rehab. and phys. medicine to profl. publs. Home: Route 2 Newbern TN 38059 Office: Dept Nursing U Tenn Martin TN 38238

CLIFTON, DAVID SAMUEL, JR., research executive, economist; b. Raleigh, N.C., Nov. 15, 1943; s. David Samuel and Ruth Centelle (Parker) C.; m. Karen Lisette Buhrer (div. 1980); children—Derek Scott, Mark David; m. Eileen Lois Cooley, July 30, 1983. B.I.E., Ga. Inst. Tech., 1966; M.B.A. in Econs., Ga. State U., 1970, Ph.D. in Econs., 1980. Customer facilities engr. Lockheed-Ga. Co., Marietta, 1966-70; prin. research sci. Ga. Tech Research Inst., Atlanta, 1970—, dir. econ. devel. lab., 1979—; dir. Sea Adventure Unltd., Inc., Atlanta, 1984—; cons. UN Indsl. Devel. Orgn., Vienna, 1982, Inst. de Adminstn. Cientifica de los Empresos, Mexico City, 1978. Author: (with others) Project Feasibility Analysis, 1977. Contbr. articles to profl. jours. Mem. Am. Econs. Assn., Sigma Xi. Club: Atlanta Power Squadron. Avocation: sailing. Office: GA Tech Research Inst Econ Devel Lab Atlanta GA 30332

CLIFTON, GLENN ALVIN, respiratory therapist; b. Lincoln, Nebr., Feb. 17, 1945; s. Glenn Alvin and Grace Adeline (Carey) C.; A.A., St. Petersburg Jr. Coll., 1975; m. Edna Brady, Dec. 17, 1973; 1 dau., Laura Marie. Chief respiratory therapist Apollo Med. Center, St. Petersburg, Fla., 1970-71; ednl. dir. respiratory therapy dept. Jackson Meml. Hosp., Miami, 1971-72; clin. coordinator respiratory therapy program St. Petersburg Jr. Coll., Clearwater, Fla., 1972-76; tech. dir. respiratory services Tampa (Fla.) Gen. Hosp., 1976—; dir. patient services Saron Home Breathing Care, Inc., 1983—; cons. St. Petersburg Vocat. Tech. Inst., 1976—, Appleton-Century-Crafts, Med. Pub. Div., 1978—; affiliate faculty mem. St. Petersburg Jr. Coll., Clearwater, Fla., 1976—, St. Petersburg Vocat. Tech. Inst., 1976—. Mem. Am. Assn. Respiratory Therapy (pres. Central Fla. chpt.), Nat. Bd. Respiratory Therapy, Am. Heart Assn., Fla. Heart Assn., Gulf Coast Lung Assn. Democrat. Home: 7000 52d Ln Pinellas Park FL 33565 Office: Tampa Gen Hosp Davis Islands Tampa FL 33606

CLIFTON, PHILIP KIRKER, lawyer, investor, consultant; b. Breckenridge, Tex., Aug. 2, 1920; s. Henry Brainard and Helena (Kirker) C.; m. Roberta Williamson, Mar. 22, 1945; children—Karen Clifton Flick, Lee Clifton O'Brien. B.A., Centenary Coll., 1942; LL.B., U. Houston. Bar: Tex. 1965, La. 1966. Vice-pres., dir. Williamson Sales Co., Shreveport, La., 1945-62; sole practice, Houston, 1965—. Mem. Nat. Republican Task Force, 1981-83. Served to lt. USNR, 1942-45. Mem. State Bar Tex., La. State Bar, Houston Bar Assn. Republican. Baptist (deacon). Clubs: Houston, University. Lodge: Masons.

CLIFTON, YERGER HUNT, English literature educator; b. Jackson, Miss., July 26, 1930; s. Yerger Hunt and Sudie Cocke (Wilson) C. B.A., Duke U., 1952; student law Washington and Lee U., 1952-53; M.A., U. Va., 1958; Ph.D., Trinity Coll., Dublin, Ireland, 1962; postgrad. Oxford U., U. Munich. Instr., Coll. William and Mary, Williamsburg, Va., 1958-59, U. Ky., Lexington, 1962-65; vis. lectr. Youngstown U. (Ohio), 1964-65; lectr. humanities Memphis Coll. Arts, 1966-69; asst. prof. English lit. Rhodes Coll., Memphis, 1965-70, assoc. prof., 1970-77, prof., 1977—; dean Brit. studies Univ. Coll. of Oxford U., 1970-79, St. John's Coll., 1980—, So. Coll. Univ. Union, pres. 26th So. Lit. Festival, 1967, trustee, 1967-70. Served to lt. USNR, 1953-56. Menkenmeller fellow, 1952-53. Mem. AAUP, MLA, Oxford Soc., Green Ribbon Soc., Phi Kappa Sigma. Republican. Episcopalian. Clubs: Athenaeum, Oxford and Cambridge Univs. (London); Monteagle (Tenn.) Assembly. Author: Angelic Knowledge in Paradise Lost, 1958; Milton and the Fall of Man, 1962. Home: 2907 Iroquois Rd Memphis TN 38111 Office: 2000 North Pkwy Memphis TN 38112

CLINE, ANN, artist, designer; b. Greensboro, N.C., Apr. 7, 1933; d. Grady Alton and Mae Josephine (Karsten) Merriman; scholar Cooper Union, N.Y.C., 1954, Fashion Inst. Tech., 1957, Arts Students League, 1961-62, Fine Arts Acad., 1962-63, Joachim Simon Atelier, Tel Aviv, 1962; A.B., N.E. La. U., Monroe, 1971; m. S.C. Johananoff, Mar. 9, 1959 (div. 1973); 1 child, Pamela; m. Francis X. Cline, Feb. 14, 1973. Asst. designer Adele Simpson Couture, 1959; pres. Johananoff Designs, 1967-70, Ann Cline Art Objects, Monroe, La., 1975—; pres. 165 North Properties; artist; works exhibited in group shows Haifa Mus., 1961, Am. Watercolor Soc., 1962; one person shows include: Barzansky Gallery, 1962, La. Polytech. U. Art Gallery, 1967, Mittel's Art Gallery, 1969, N.E. La. U., 1973, 71, Am. Consulate, Tel Aviv, 1962, Contemporary Gallery, Dallas, 1970, Brooks Gallery, Memphis, 1971, 14th Ann. Delta Art Exhbn. Nat. Found. Arts, 1971, Jackson Arts Ctr. Ann. Exhbn., Miss., (prize award 1971), 22d Ann. Delta Exhbn., Ark. Arts Center, 1972, 79, Mayor's Show, Monroe, 1979, Wesley Found. Award Show, 1979, 80, 81, others. Bd. dirs. La. Council Performing Arts, 1974; rep. Gov.'s Conf. Arts; bd. adjustments Monroe Zoning Commn.; trustee Masur Mus., 1974-75; bd. dirs. Little Theater of Monroe, 1975-76; bd. dirs. Women of the Ch., Episcopal Ch., 1977-78, mem. Daus. of the King, 1979-82, chmn. meml. com. Recipient Young Designer competition award Fontana of Rome, 1957, 1st prize Fashion Inst. Tech., 1957, Young Designer's award Women's Wear Daily, 1960, 1st prize, Arts Students League, 1961, 2d prize, 1963, 2d prize Fine Arts Acad., 1962, 1st prize, Woodstock Gallery, 1962, 1st prize, La. Folk Art Festival, 1966, 68, 72, prize awards Temple Emmanuel Ann., Dallas, 1969, 71, 74. Mem. Butler Soc. Clubs: Bayou Desiard Country, Lotus, Illustrator: Jessie Strikes Louisiana Gold, 1969. Home and Office: 503 Speed Ave Monroe LA 71201

CLINE, PAUL CHARLES, political science educator, state legislator; b. Clarksburg, W.Va., Dec. 26, 1933; s. Kemper P. and Irene (Neff) C.; m. Diane Chilcote, Aug. 10, 1958; children—Alice J., Camille N. A.B., W.Va. U., 1956, J.D., 1957, M.A. in Polit. Sci., 1961; Ph.D., Am. U., 1968. Bar: W.Va., 1957. With law firm, Huntington, W.Va., 1959-60; from instr. to prof. James Madison U., Harrisonburg, Va., 1961—; mem. Va. Ho. of Dels., 1986—. Active Shenandoah Valley Folklore Soc.; past councilman City of Harrisburg, 1972-76. Served with U.S. Army, 1957-59. Mem. Am. Polit. Sci. Assn., Internat. Polit. Sci. Assn. Democrat. Methodist. Lodge: Masons. Author: Practical Law, 1978; By the Good People of Virginia, 1983; contbr. articles to profl. jours. Home: 221 Dixie Ave Harrisonburg VA 22801 Office: Dept Political Science James Madison University Harrisonburg VA 22807

CLINGMAN, WILLIAM HERBERT, JR., mgmt. cons.; b. Grand Rapids, Mich., May 5, 1929; s. William Herbert and Elizabeth (Davis) C.; B.S. with distinction and honors in Chemistry, U. Mich., 1951; M.A., Princeton U., 1954, Ph.D., 1954; m. Mary Jane Wheeler, Feb. 6, 1951; children—Mary Constance, James Wheeler. Chemist, Am. Oil Co., Texas City, Tex., 1954-57, group leader, 1957-59; head thermoelectric sect. Tex. Instruments, Inc., Dallas, 1959-61, dir. energy research lab., 1961-62, mgr. corporate research and devel. mktg. dept., 1962-67; pres. W.H. Clingman Co., Inc., Dallas, 1967—; dir. Graham Magnetics Inc., 1974-77; speaker, cons. SBA, 1967-70; mem. adv. com. on sci., tech. and economy Nat. Planning Assn., 1966-67. Mem. Am. Chem. Soc., IEEE, Assn. Computing Machinery, Sigma Xi. Club: Brook Hollow Golf (Dallas). Mem. editorial adv. bd. Jour. Advanced Energy Conversion, 1961-66. Home: 4416 McFarlin St Dallas TX 75205 Office: 717 N Harwood St Suite 800 Dallas TX 75201

CLINTON, MARIAN MARIE, special education consultant, counselor; b. White Salmon, Wash., Nov. 16, 1946; d. Virgil C. and Cleo Marie (Young) Haddock; m. Robert J. Clinton, July 31, 1971. B.S., So. Ill. U., 1971; M.Ed., Tex. Woman's U., 1979, postgrad., 1984—. Lic. profl. counselor, Tex. Tchr. of emotionally disturbed Irving Ind. Sch. Dist., Tex., 1971-73; tchr. emotionally disturbed Hurst-Euless-Bedford Ind. Sch. Dist., Bedford, Tex., 1973-75, spl. edn. cons., 1975—; marriage and family counselor William Kennedy and Assocs., Bedford, 1980—. Recipient DAR award, 1965; Danforth Found. award, 1965. Mem. Council for Exceptional Children, Council for Children with Behavioral Disorders, Tex. Council for Adminstrs. and Suprs. in Spl. Edn., Am. Assn. Marriage and Family Therapists, Am. Personnel and Guidance Assn., Tex. Elem. Prins. and Suprs. Assn., Assn. Learning Disabilities, Assn. Tex. Profl. Educators, Tex. Assn. Supervision and Curriculum Devel., Delta Kappa Gamma. Republican. Methodist. Home: 3500 Blue Quail Ln Bedford TX 76021 Office: Hurst-Euless-Bedford Ind Sch Dist 1749 Central Dr Bedford TX 76002

CLINTON, MARTHA LINDA, nursing administrator; b. Dillon, Mont., June 12, 1949; A.S. in Nursing, Cleveland State Community Coll., 1971; B.S. in Pub. Health Edn., U. Tenn.-Knoxville, 1976, M.P.H., 1978. Staff nurse Fort Sanders Regional Med. Ctr., Knoxville, 1971-77; hosp. supr. St. Mary's Med. Ctr., Knoxville, 1977-78, asst. dir. nursing, 1978-80, dir. nursing, 1980—. Arbitrator Better Bus. Bur., Knoxville, 1985. Mem. Am. Nurses Assn., Tenn. Nurses Assn., Am. Heart Assn. (chmn. state nursing com., flying high award 1979), Internat. Orgn. Women Pilots (chpt. news reporter 1983-84). Avocations: flying; softball; running. Office: St Marys Med Ctr Oak Hill Ave Knoxville TN 37917

CLINTON, WILLIAM J., governor of Arkansas; b. Hope, Ark., Aug. 19, 1946; B.S. in Internat. Affairs, Georgetown U., 1968; postgrad. (Rhodes scholar), U. Coll., Oxford (Eng.) U., 1968-70; J.D., Yale U., 1973; married; 1 dau. Prof. law U. Ark. Sch. Law at Fayetteville and ltd. individual practice law, 1973-76; atty. gen. Ark., 1977-79, gov. Ark., 1979-81, 83—; of counsel firm Wright, Lindsey & Jennings, Little Rock, 1981-83. Chmn. bd. Ark. Housing Devel. Corp.; coordinator Ark. campaign Carter for Pres., 1976; chmn. state and local election div. Dem. Nat. Com. Mem. Am., Ark. bar assns., Nat. Assn. Attys. Gen. Democrat. Office: Office of Governor State Capitol Room 250 Little Rock AR 72201

CLIZER, HERALD KENNETH, meat processing company executive; b. Savannah, Mo., Oct. 31, 1932; s. Kenneth Herman and Iva May (Sheppard) C.; m. Martha Francis, Jan. 10, 1963. B.S. in Agr., U. Mo., 1954. Vice pres. Wilson Foods, Oklahoma City, 1970-81; chmn. Buring Foods, Memphis, 1981—; dir. Nat. Agr. Hall of Fame, Kansas City, Kans., 1971-76, v.p. Kansas City C. of C., 1967-70. Served to capt. U.S. Army, 1954-56. Methodist. Clubs: Economic, Chickasaw Country (Memphis). Lodge: Rotary. Avocation: golf. Office: Buring Foods 1837 Harbor Ave Memphis TN 38113

CLOER, CARROLL MARTIN, textile company official; b. Patterson, N.C., Jan. 29, 1926; s. Carl Elisha and Nancy Lois (Holder) C.; B.S. in Textile Engring., N.C. State U., 1950; grad. Air War Coll.; m. Rachel Tuttle, Oct. 2, 1954. Supr., Hudson Mills Co. (N.C.), 1950-52; foreman Pacific Mills Co., Rhodhiss, N.C., 1953-58; quality control supr. Burlington Industries, Rhodhiss, 1959-61; quality control supt. Beaunit Fibers, Elizabethton, Tenn., 1961-68; assoc. prof. textiles Danville (Va.) Community Coll., 1969-70; mfg. mgr. Virginia Mills Co., Swepsonville, N.C., 1970-71; quality control mgr. Firestone Fibers & Textiles Co., Gastonia, N.C., 1971-83, sr. process engr., 1983—. Served with USAAF, 1944-45; maj. Res. ret. Decorated Air medal with 3 oak leaf clusters. Mem. Am. Soc. Quality Control (cert. quality engr.), Am. Inventory and Prodn. Mgmt. Soc., ASTM, Mensa. Office: PO Box 1278 Gastonia NC 28052

CLOGAN, PAUL MAURICE, educator; b. Boston, July 9, 1934; s. Michael J. and Agnes J. (Murphy) C.; B.A., Boston Coll., 1956, M.A., 1957; Ph.D., U. Ill., 1961; F.A.A.R., Am. Acad. in Rome, 1966; m. Julie Sydney Davis, June 27, 1972; children—Michael Rodger, Patrick Terence, Margaret Murphy. Asst. prof. Duke U., 1961-65; asso. prof. Case Western Res. U., Cleve., 1965-72; prof. English, N. Tex. State U., Denton, 1972—; vis. prof. U. Keele (Eng.), 1965, U. Pisa (Italy), 1966, U. Tours (France), 1978; vis. mem. Inst. Advanced Study, Princeton, N.J., 1970, 77; cons. Library of Congress, Ednl. Testing Service, Nat. Endowment Humanities, Nat. Acad. Scis., NRC Commn. Human Resources, Am. Council Learned Socs., Nat. Enquiry into Scholarly Communication, Chilton Research Services, Am. Arts Assn. Mem. nat. screening com. Inst. Internat. Edn., 1984—. Duke Endowment grantee, 1961-62; Am. Council Learned Socs. grantee, 1963-64, 70-71; Am. Philos. Soc. grantee, 1964-69; sr. Fulbright-Hays postdoctoral research fellow, Italy, 1965-66, research grantee, France, 1978; Prix de Rome fellow, 1966-67; Bollingen Found. fellow, 1966; Nat. Endowment Humanities fellow, 1969-70, grantee, 1986; N. Tex. State U. Faculty grantee, 1972-75, 80-81. Mem. Internat. Assn. Univ. Profs. English, MLA (exec. com. 1980-84, del. assembly 1981-84, 86—), Mediaeval Acad. Am. (nominating com. 1975-76, John Nicholas Brown Prize com. 1980-83), Internat. Comparative Lit. Assn., Internat. Arthurian Soc., Modern Humanities Research Assn. Democrat. Roman Catholic. Author: The Medieval Achilleid of Statius, 1968; Social Dimensions in Medieval and Renaissance Studies, 1972; In Honor of S. Harrison Thomson, 1970; Medieval and Renaissance Studies in Review, 1971; Medieval and Renaissance Spirituality, 1973; Medieval Historiography, 1974; Medieval Hagiography and Romance, 1975; Medieval Poetics, 1976; Transformation and Continuity, 1977; Innovation and Tradition, 1978; Byzantine and Western Studies, 1983; Fourteenth and Fifteenth Centuries, 1986; editor Medievalia et Humanistica: Studies in Medieval and Renaissance Culture, 1970—; contbr. articles to profl. jours. Office: PO Box 13348 North Texas Station Denton TX 76203

CLOKE, WILMA JEAN NEWSOM, business executive, educator; b. Breckenridge, Tex., Dec. 1, 1928; s. Clarence William and Mary Anita (Taylor) Newsom; m. Arthur L. Cloke, June 5, 1948 (dec.); children—Linda Cheryl Cloke Hettick, Victoria Lynn Cloke Mallory. B.S., Tex. Christian U., 1950; M.A., U. Redlands, 1964; postgrad. U. Tex. 1950, U. Dayton, 1960-61, Pepperdine Coll., 1961-62, Los Angeles State Coll., 1961, LaSalle Sch. Law, 1962-64, Claremont Coll., 1970—; Ph.D. (hon.), Colo. State Christian Coll., 1973. Tchr. various schs., Tex., 1949-53, 57-59, Ohio, 1959-61, Inglewood (Calif.) pub. schs., 1961-62, Highland (Calif.) Jr. High Sch., 1962-67, Serrano Jr. High Sch., Highland, 1967-82, Mansfield Ind. Sch. Dist., Fort Worth, 1982-83; gen. ptnr. Am. Heritage Mortgage Co., 1983—; owner, dir. Camp Sugar Cone, 1967-71; pres., past chmn. bd. Desert Rent-A-Car, Inc., San Bernardino, Calif.; assoc. broker Desert Adminstrv. Service; mem. White House Conf. Edn., 1960; mem. Smithsonian Inst.; mem. adv. bd. San Bernardino assmebly 78 Order Rainbow for Girls, 1965-70, mother adviser Mt. Shadow assembly. Mem. AAUW, NEA, Internat. Platform Assn., World Affairs Council, Mortgage Bankers Assn., Nat. Assn. Home Builders, Greater Ft. Worth Bd. Realtors, Ft. Worth City C. of C., Marquis Biog. Library Soc. (dir.), Smithsonian Assocs., Tex. Christian U. Women's Execs., Calif. Tchrs. Assn., San Bernardino Tchrs. Assn. (mem. personnel policy com. 1965—), Alpha Delta Kappa. Mem. Disciples of Christ. Club: Century II. Lodge: Order Eastern Star, Officers' Wives. Home: 1800 Wisteria Ct Fort Worth TX 76111

CLONTZ, ROBERT SHIRLEY, wildlife artist; b. Wilmington, N.C., Dec. 21, 1941; s. Robert Luther and Maxine (Baysden) C.; m. Carol McCoy Price, Feb. 22, 1964; children—Robert Baysden, John Bradley. Student Emory and Henry Coll. With engring. dept. Newport News Shipbuilding Co. (Va.), 1964-80; v.p. Chesapeake Dimensions, Smithfield, Va., 1983—; one man shows: Twentieth Century Gallery, Williamsburg, Va., 1980, Windmill Point Yacht Club, Whitestone, Va., 1983, Village Gallery, Virginia Beach, Va., 1983; group shows include: Yesterday and Today Gallery, Hillsborough, N.C., 1981, 82, 83, 84, 85, 86; Philip Morris Research Ctr., Richmond, Va., 1984; represented in permanent collections: Perdue Farms, Salisbury, Md., Biomed. Reference Labs., Burlington, N.C., others. Recipient numerous printing industry awards. Mem. Back Bay Wildfowl Guild, Ducks Unltd. (Artist of Year 1984), Ward Found., Va. Wildlife Fedn. Baptist. Home and office: RFD 2 Box 207 Smithfield VA 23430

CLOSSER, PATRICK DENTON, artist, radio evangelist; b. San Diego, Apr. 27, 1945; s. Edward and Helen Thompson. Diploma Am. Schs. of Cinema, 1970; D.Cinema Arts (hon.), World U., Ariz. Artist, Sta. KBFI-TV, Dallas, 1972-73; with Stas. KVTT and KDTX, Dallas, 1976-81; worked on TV commls. for Dr. Pepper, Am. Chiropractic Assn., feature movies Operation Red Star, Mars Needs Women, show Comment on Our Times, Bible's Forecast; evangelist Stas. KDTX-FM, KVTT-FM; worked on theatre trailers, network TV shows, Nelson Golf Classic, Operation Entertainment; radio evangelist Sta. KXVI, NTRB (North Tex. Radio for the Blind); religious broadcaster Sta. KTXO, Sherman, Tex., Sta. WINB/World Internat. Broadcasters (shortwave) Red Lion, Pa., Radio Africa. Mem. nat. adv. bd., bd. researchers. Am. Biog. Inst. Named to Life History Center, Conroe, Tex.; recipient medals Am. Biog. Inst. Fellow Internat. Biog. Assn. (life); mem. Anglo-Am. Acad., Internat. Christian Broadcasters Assn., Soc. Motion Picture and TV Engrs., Internat. Platform Assn. Home: PO Box 20881 Dallas TX 75220

CLOUD, BRUCE BENJAMIN, construction company executive; b. Thomas, Okla., Feb. 15, 1920; s. Dudley R. and Lillian (Sanders) C.; B.C.E., Tex. A. and M. U., 1940; m. Virginia Dugan, June 5, 1944; children—Sheila Marie Cloud Kiselis, Karen Susan, Bruce Benjamin, Deborah Ann Cloud Mixon, Virginia Ann. With H.B. Zachry Co., San Antonio, 1940-42, 55—, exec. v.p., 1963—, also dir.; partner Dudley R. Cloud & Son, constrn., San Antonio 1946-55. Mem. adv. council Boysville Inc., 1978-79; mem. adv. bd. Tex. Transp. Inst., 1981—; bd. dirs. Tex. State Tech. Found., 1984—. Served to lt. col. C.E., AUS, 1942-46, ETO. Recipient Pro Deo Et Juventute award Nat. Council Catholic Youth; registered profl. engr., Tex. Mem. Tex. Assn. Gen. Contractors (dir. hwy. and heavy br. 1947-48, 72-76, pres. 1974), Am. Concrete Paving Assn. (v.p. 1970-74, dir. 1970—, 1st v.p. 1975-75, pres. 1976), Nat. Asphalt Paving Assn., Tex. Hotmix Paving Assn. (dir. 1972). Nat. Assn. Gen. Contractors (dir. 1976—, mem. exec. com. 1978-79, chmn. heavy div. 1979), San Antonio Livestock Assn. (life), Nat., Tex. socs. profl. engrs., Tex. Good Rds.-Transp. Assn. (dir. 1974-79, exec. com. 1975-85). AIM, Am. Mgmt. Assn., San Antonio C. of C. (chmn. better roads task force 1978-79, 85-86), Cons. Contractors Council Am., Holy Name Soc. (v.p. 1962-63), Noctural Adoration Soc. Club: K.C. (3 deg.). Home: 127 Cave Ln San Antonio TX 78209 Office: PO Box 21130 San Antonio TX 78285

CLOUSE, JAMES PAUL, agricultural education educator; b. Hope, Ind., Aug. 23, 1922; s. Miller M. and Mary N. (Marlin) C.; m. Barbara L. Southard, Mar. 26, 1949; children—Ellen, James, Susan, Peter. B.S., Purdue U., 1947, M.S., 1951, Ph.D., 1959. Cert. tchr. Ind., Va. Prof. agrl. edn. Purdue U., West Lafayette, Ind., 1958-73; prof. agrl. edn. Va. Poly. Inst. and State U., Blacksburg, 1973—; trustee Future Farmers of Am. Found.; cons. in Sudan, Kenya, Brazil and Panama. Served with USAAF, 1942-46. Mem. Am. Vocat. Assn., Future Farmers of Am. Alumni, AAUP, Nat. Vocat. Agrl. Tchrs. Assn., Am. Assn. Tchr. Educators in Agr., Toastmasters Internat., Omicron Tau Theta, Phi Delta Kappa, Sigma Delta Xi, Gamma Sigma Delta. Presbyterian. Home: RD 4 Box 136 Blacksburg VA 24060 Office: 122 Lane Hall Va Poly Inst and State U Blacksburg VA 24060

CLOWER, DONNA DARLENE, communications corporation executive; b. Loudon, Tenn., Jan. 23, 1956; s. Raymond Edward and Charlene Josephine (Pesterfield) C. B.B.A., Middle Tenn. State U., 1977. Cons., ACDS, Inc., Nashville, 1976; computer operator Rutherford Hosp., Murfreesboro, Tenn., 1976-78; cons. Earl Swensson Assocs., Nashville, 1978; personnel cons. Sanford Rose Assocs., Nashville, 1978-79; systems programmer South Central Bell Co., Nashville, 1979-84, staff mgr., 1984—. Vol., Telephone Pioneers Am., Nashville, 1979—, Spl. Olympics, Nashville, 1983—. Baptist. Office: South Central Bell Co PO Box 39 Nashville TN 37202

CLOYD, HELEN MARY, educator, accountant; b. Austria-Hungary, 1918; d. Valentine and Elizabeth (Kretschmar von Kienbusch) Yuhasz; came to U.S. 1922, naturalized, 1928; B.S., Eastern Mich. U., 1953; M.A., Wayne State U., 1956; Ph.D., Mich. State U., 1963; m. George S. Smith, Mar. 4, 1939 (dec.); children—George, Nora; m. Chester L. Cloyd, Apr. 16, 1960 (dec.). Pub. accounting Haskins & Sells, Detroit, 1945-53; tchr. Marine City (Mich.) High Sch., 1954-59; instr. acctg. Central Mich. U., Mt. Pleasant, 1959-60; asst. prof. Wayne State U., Detroit, 1960-61; tchr. Grosse Pointe (Mich.) High Sch.,

1961-64; asso. prof. acctg. Ball State U., Muncie, Ind., 1964-71; prof. Shepherd Coll., Shepherdstown, W.Va., 1971-76; now asso. prof. George Mason U., Fairfax, Va. Recipient McClintock Writing award C.P.A., Mich., Ind., W.Va. Mem. Am. Inst. C.P.A.'s, Am. Acctg. Assn., Am. Econs. Assn., AAAS, Assn. Sch. Bus. Ofcls., Delta Pi Epsilon, Pi Omega Pi, Pi Gamma Mu. Clubs: Order Eastern Star, White Shrine. Contbr. numerous articles to publs. Home: PO Box 186 Inwood WV 25428 Office: George Mason U Fairfax VA 22030

CLOYD, LEILAH FRANCES SPEARS, real estate consultant; b. Dallas; d. William Thomas and Leilah (Pelt) Spears; m. Marshall Sadler Cloyd, Feb. 14, 1942; children—Marshall P., Malcolm E. B.A., So. Meth. U., 1930, LL.B., 1932, LL.M., 1959. Guest lectr. So. Meth. U. Law Sch., 1960-61; assoc. Ebby Halliday Comml. Real Estate; v.p. Day Realty Tex., Dallas, 1979-81; real estate cons., Dallas, 1981—. Bd. dirs. Dallas Grand Opera Assn.; adv. chmn. Southwestern Hospitality Bd. Met. Opera; mem. women's com. Dallas Theater Ctr., 1960—; mem. women's com. Dallas Civic Ballet; mem. women's guild Dallas Civic Opera Soc., Dallas Art Mus. League, Dallas Mus. Fine Arts. Mem. ABA, Nat. Assn. Realtors, Internat. Real Estate Fedn., Nat. Arbitration Assn. (mem. panels), Tex. Bar Assn., Tex. Bd. Realtors, Dallas Bar Assn., Dallas Bd. Realtors, Daus. Republic of Tex. Pi Beta Phi. Clubs: Dallas Country, Dallas Woman's, Dallas Dinner Dance, Dallas Garden; Thalia; Carrousel; Cadence.

CLUFF, SUSAN KAYE, nurse; b. Ottumwa, Iowa, July 12, 1952; d. Donald Byron and Elsbeth Gwendolyn (Nutt) Abbey; m. Gary Eugene Fetters, Aug. 29, 1970 (div.); children—Shanon Kristi, Jaime Dion; m. John Max Cluff, Dec. 13, 1980. R.N., Okla. A.A. in Applied Sci. and Nursing, Tulsa Jr. Coll., 1980. Staff nurse Hillcrest Med. Ctr., Tulsa, 1980-81, asst. head nurse, 1981-82, head nurse urology-nephrology-neurology, 1982—. Recipient Outstanding Scholastic Achievement award Rotary-Anns, Tulsa, 1980. Democrat. Home: 4206 W Urbana Ct Broken Arrow OK 74012 Office: Hillcrest Med Ctr 1120 S Utica St Tulsa OK 74104

CLUM, DENNIS PATRICK, banker; b. Poughkeepsie, N.Y., May 1, 1925; s. Frederick J. and Margaret M. (Murphy) C.; B.A., Union Coll., Schenectady, 1947; LL.D., Fordham U., 1951; m. Dorothy M. Diederichs, Oct. 14, 1953 (div. Oct. 1973); children—Dennis Patrick, Robert, Laura; m. 2d, Lucille Michaud, Sept. 5, 1975. Sr. v.p., trust officer, dir. Miami Beach, First Nat. Bank (Fla.), 1954-71; sr. v.p., dir. United Bancshares of Fla., Inc., 1965-71; exec. v.p., trust officer First State Bank of Miami (Fla.), 1972, also dir.; v.p. Barnett Banks Trust Co., N.A. Past pres. Estate Planning Council Dade County; bd. dirs. Miami Heart Inst., Miami Opera Guild, Com. of 100 Miami Beach; past chmn. Dade Found.; chmn. endowment fund com. U. Miami. Served to lt. USNR, 1943-46, 51-54. Mem. Corporate Fiduciaries Assn. Clubs: Surf, La Gorce, Miami Shores Country, Standard, Beach Colony (past pres.), Miami, Army and Navy, Palm Bay, Jockey. Home: 1430 NE 102d St Miami Shores FL 33138 Office: 7900 NE 2d Ave Miami FL 33138

COAKER, JAMES WHITFIELD, mechanical engineer; b. Boston, Nov. 12, 1946; s. George W. and Margaret N. Coaker; m. Ruth Johnson, May 17, 1969; children—James W., John A. B.S.M.E., Lafayette Coll., 1968; M.S.B., Va. Commonwealth U., 1976. Registered profl. engr., Va. Application engr., pump and condenser div. Ingersoll-Rand Co., Richmond, Va., 1972-76; project mgr. Reco Industries, Inc., Richmond, 1976-77, asst. mgr. engring., 1977-79, mgr. engring., 1979-83; systems engr., program mgr. Advanced Tech., Inc., Arlington, Va., 1983—. Served with USN, 1969-72; to comdr. USNR. Mem. ASME (dir. Central Va. sect.), Nat. Soc. Profl. Engrs., Nat. Council Engring. Examiners (affiliate), Assn. Computers in Mfg., Nat. Computer Graphics Assn. Contbr. tech mgmt articles to profl. jours. Home: 11675 Captain Rhett Ln Fairfax Station VA 22039 Office: Advanced Tech Inc Suite 300 1725 S Jefferson Davis Hwy Arlington VA 22202

COATS, ANDREW MONTGOMERY, lawyer, mayor; b. Oklahoma City, Jan. 19, 1935; s. Sanford Clarence and Mary Ola (Young) C.; m. Linda M. Zimmerman; children—Michael, Sanford. B.A., U. Okla., 1957, J.D., 1963. Assoc. Crowe and Dunlevy, Oklahoma City, 1963-67, ptnr., 1967-76, sr. trial ptnr., 1980—; dist. atty. Oklahoma County, Oklahoma City, 1976-80; mayor Oklahoma City, 1983—; vis. prof. law U. Okla., 1968-71; pres. Oklahoma County Legal Aid Soc., 1972-73, Okla. Young Lawyers Conf., 1968-69; dir. Meml. Bank, N.A., Oklahoma City. Democratic nominee U.S. Senate, 1980. Served to lt. USN, 1960-63, Taiwan. Named Outstanding Lawyer in Okla., Oklahoma City U., 1977. Fellow Am. Coll. Trial Lawyers; mem. ABA, Okla. Bar Assn., Oklahoma County Bar Assn. (pres. 1976-77), Phi Beta Kappa (pres. 1975), Pi Kappa Alpha (pres. 1956), Phi Delta Phi (pres. 1962), Order of Coif. Episcopalian. Clubs: Oklahoma City Golf and Country (bd. dirs. 1977-80), Beacon, Petroleum, White Hall. Office: Crowe and Dunlevy Mid-America Tower 20 N Broadway Oklahoma City OK 73102

COBB, ALTON BERNARD, state official; b. Madison County, Miss., Oct. 19, 1928; s. Joseph Harrison and Winnie Ora (Mabry) C.; B.A., U. Miss., 1950; M.D., Johns Hopkins U., 1954; M.P.H., Tulane U., 1960; m. Mary O'Connor, Sept. 26, 1954; children—Mary Alene, Tommy, Susan. Intern, Charity Hosp., New Orleans, 1954-55; resident in pub. health Miss. State Bd. Health, Jackson, 1960-62, dir. chronic illness services, Jackson, 1962-68, state health officer, 1973—; county health officer Sunflower County, Miss., 1957-59; dir. comprehensive health planning, Exec. Dept. State of Miss., Jackson, 1968-69; dir. Miss. Medicaid Commn., 1969-73; vis. asst. prof. pub. health adminstrn. Tulane U., 1969—; clin. prof. preventive medicine U. Miss., Jackson, 1973—, mem. numerous state med. bds. Served with M.C., U.S. Army, 1955-57. Diplomate Am. Bd. Preventive Medicine Pub. Health. Mem. Central Med. Soc., Am. Coll. Preventive Medicine, Am. Pub. Health Assn., Miss. State Med. Assn. Presbyterian. Club: Rotary. Contbr. articles to med. jours. Office: 2423 N State St PO Box 1700 Jackson MS 39215

COBB, CHARLES KENCHE, JR., real estate executive, lawyer; b. Canton, Ga., Aug. 23, 1934; s. Charlie Kench and Alice (Enloe) C.; m. Carolyn Webb, Aug. 31, 1963; children—Charlie Kenche, Catherine Elizabeth. B.S., Ga. Inst. Tech., 1956; M.B.A., Harvard U., 1962; LL.D., Woodrow Wilson Sch. Law, 1968. Pres. Am. Printing and Finishing Co., 1964; real estate exec. Sharp-Boylston Co., 1965-69, Charles Cobb Properties, Atlanta, 1969—; admitted to Ga. bar, 1969; sole practice, Atlanta, 1969—; pres. Sterling Land Co., 1972—, Bridgewood Properties, Inc., 1982—; cons. real estate investments. Fin. chmn. Gadrix for Congress campaign, 1976; exec. com. Ga. Tech. Wesley Found.; bd. dirs. Ga. Tech. YMCA, Atlanta Area Council Boy Scouts Am.; trustee Reinhardt Coll., also chmn. fin. com., treas.; ofcl. bd. Northside Methodist Ch., former lay leader. Served to lt. USAF, 1956-59. Named Ga. Exchangor of Yr. 1971, 85. Mem. Ga. Bar Assn., Atlanta Bd. Realtors (Million Dollar Club, parliamentarian), Ga. Assn. Realtors, Nat. Assn. Realtors, Realtors Comml. Council (vice chmn.), Cherokee Bd. Realtors, Ga. Assn. Real Estate Exchangors (dir., past pres.), Ga. Tech. Alumni Assn. (trustee), Omicron Delta Kappa. Club: Fairington Golf and Tennis, Buckhead 50, Ga. Tech. ANAK Soc., Masons. Home: 2851 Howell Mill Rd NW Atlanta GA 30327 Office: One Northside 75 Suite 102 Atlanta GA 30318

COBB, DAVID KEITH, accountant; b. Calhoun City, Miss., Mar. 2, 1941; s. Bayne and Frances C.; m. Dorothy Hill, June 15, 1963; children—Paul, John, Mark. B.S., U. So. Miss., 1963. C.P.A., Miss., Fla. With Peat, Marwick, Mitchell & Co., Jackson, Miss., 1963-75, mng. ptnr., Orlando, Fla., 1971-75, Fort Lauderdale, Fla., 1975—. Chmn. local chpt. Nat. Multiple Sclerosis Soc., 1983; treas. South Fla. Coordinating Council, 1983-85; chmn. Broward Pub. Library Found., 1983-86; pres. Central Fla. Kidney Found., 1975; bd. dirs. Broward Workshop, Project Horizon, Crimestoppers, Leadership Broward. Mem. Am. Inst. C.P.A.s, Govt. Fin. Officers Assn., Fla. Inst. C.P.A.s, Broward Workshop, Fort Lauderdale Area C. of C. Republican. Presbyterian. Clubs: Lauderdale Yacht, Tower (Fort Lauderdale).

COBB, JEAN GROSS, advertising executive; b. Omaha, Mar. 13, 1952; d. Lawrence Emmett and Marie Christine (Groover) Gross; m. Randolph Hunt Cobb, June 28, 1974 (div. June 1985); 1 child, Ryan Hunt. Student Vanderbilt U., 1970-71; A.B. in Journalism cum laude, U. Ga., 1974; postgrad. Sch. of Bank Mktg., U. Colo., 1980-81. Media buyer, asst. prodn. mgr., traffic mgr. Metzdorf Advt. Agy., Houston, 1976-78; communications mgr. RepublicBank Houston, 1978-82; communications mgr., gen. banking group RepublicBank Corp., Houston, 1982-83, corp. advt. mgr., 1983; account supr. Erickson & Co. Advt., 1983-84; advt. dir. Computer Craft, Houston, 1984—. Recipient Clio Advt. award, 1982. Mem. Am. Women in Radio and TV, Houston Advt. Fedn., Bank Mktg. Assn. (Best of TV, Best of Radio, Best of Print awards 1982, Mktg. Excellence award Gulf Coast chpt. 1981, 82). Home: 14115 Greenway Dr Sugar Land TX 77478 Office: 1616 S Voss Suite 900 Houston TX 77057

COBB, LOREN, mathematician; b. Boston, May 8, 1948; s. John C. and Helen (Imlay) C.; m. Barbara Fitch, May 24, 1975. B.A., Cornell U., 1970, M.A., 1971, Ph.D., 1973. Asst. prof. sociology U.N.H., Durham, 1972-77; post-doctoral fellow in psychiatry, U. South Fla., Tampa, 1977-79; asst. prof. biometry Med. Sch. U.S.C., Charleston, 1979-81, asso. prof., 1981—. Past treas., N.H. ACLU, Woodrow Wilson Fellow (hon.), 1969-70. Mem. Soc. Indsl. and Applied Math., Am. Statis. Assn., Am. Sociol. Assn., Inst. Mathematical Stas., AAAS. Author: Mathematical Frontiers of the Social and Policy Sciences, 1981; contbr. articles to profl. jours. Home: 317 Molasses Lane Mt Pleasant SC 29464 Office: Dept Biometry Med U of SC Charleston SC 29425

COBB, MARNEE (ALLISON) CORYELL, mathematics educator, coach; b. Clearwater, Fla., June 7, 1952; d. Richard Woodley and Tetula May (McMullen) Coryell; m. Michael Eugene Cobb, July 5, 1975; 1 dau., Cara Elizabeth. B.S., Fla. So. Coll., 1974. Cert. tchr. math. and phys. edn., Fla. Math. tchr. Bartow (Fla.) Jr. High Sch., 1974—, basketball coach, 1975-77, varsity cheerleader sponsor, 1978-83; volleyball official Fla. High Sch. Activities Assn., 1975-78. Columnist weekly column on women's sports, 1975-77. State chmn. pages Fla. State Soc. DAR, 1980-82, state chmn. jr. membership, 1978-80; chpt. regent Cary Cox chpt. Nat. Soc. DAR, 1980-82. Named Volleyball Coach of Yr. Polk County, Ledger Pub. Co., 1983, Outstanding Jr. Mem. Fla. State Soc. DAR, 1980. Mem. Fla. Athletic Coaches Assn. (dist. 9 coach of yr. volleyball 1983), Fla. Council Tchrs. of Math, Polk County Council Tchrs. of Math., Bartow Jr. High Parent-Tchr.-Student Assn. (adv. com. 1979-80), NEA, Polk Edn. Assn., Kappa Delta Pi, Zeta Tau Alpha (chpt. gen. advisor Fla. So. Coll. 1977-83, treas. 1972-73), Polk County Alumnae Assn. Polk County (pres. 1979-81). Office: Bartow Jr High Sch 550 E Clower St Bartow FL 33830

COBB, WILLIAM DANIEL, III, educational administrator; b. Conway, Ark., June 30, 1937; s. William Daniel, Jr. and Edna Earle (Speed) C.; m. Rosemary Jeanne Walker, Oct. 26, 1963; children—David Elliott, Enid Karisa, Jamie Elisa, Sarah Jeanne. A.B with distinction and honors, Transylvania U., 1958; B.D., Yale U., 1961, S.T.M.; 1962; A.M., U. Chgo., 1964, Ph.D., 1966. Ordained to ministry Christian Ch. (Disciples of Christ), 1961. Instr., YMCA Jr. Coll., Chgo., 1963-65; chaplain Eureka Coll., Ill., 1965-67, prof. philosophy and religion, 1965-77, chair humanities div., 1967-71, dir. gen. studies, 1971-77; v.p., dean faculty Bethany Coll., W.Va., 1977—; trustee Lexington Theol. Sem., Ky., 1983—; mem., pres.-elect alumni council Disciples Div. Ho., U. Chgo., 1983—; evaluator-cons. North Central Assn., Chgo., 1983—; mem. adv. council W.Va. Dept. Edn., Charleston, 1978-84; evaluator NEH, Washington, 1984—. Contbr. articles and revs. to religious and edn. jours. Elder, choir dir. Eureka Christian Ch., 1968-77; elder Bethany Meml. Ch., 1977—. Mem. Am. Acad. Religion, Soc. Christian Ethics, Assn. Disciples for Theol. Discussion, Am. Acad. Academic Deans, W.Va. Assn. Acad. Deans (pres. 1983-84), Phi Kappa Tau. Democrat. Avocations: tennis, basketball, mystery novels. Home: 113 Logan Ct Box 449 Bethany WV 26032 Office: Bethany Coll Cramblet Hall Bethany WV 26032

COBB, WILLIAM NEAL, dentist; b. Atlanta, May 9, 1939; s. Billy Sunday and Frances Virginia (Leach) C.; m. Betty Jane Hefner, June 28, 1959; children—William Mark, Kimberly Leigh, Sheri Elizabeth. Student North Ga. Coll., 1957-58, Ga. State Coll., 1962-64; D.D.S., Emory U., 1968. Pvt. practice gen. dentistry, Cleveland, Ga., 1970—. Bd. dirs. Lanier Orch. League, Gainesville, Ga., 1984—; adv. bd. Village Health Clinic, Helen, Ga.; elder Helen Presbyn. Ch. Served to capt. Dental Corps, U.S. Army, 1968-70. Recipient 1st Boss of Yr. award Hall County Dental Assts. Assn., 1973, Service award White County Recreation and Parks Bd., 1975-76, Service award Appalachian Ga. Health Systems Agy., 1979-81. Mem. ADA, Acad. Gen. Dentistry, Ga. Dental Assn., No. Dist. Dental Soc. of Ga., White County C. of C. (bd. dirs. 1984), Xi Psi Phi. Club: Rotary (pres.-elect White County 1985—). Home: Route 1 Sautee-Nacoochee GA 30571 Office: PO Box 496 Cleveland GA 30528

COBBE, JAMES HAMILTON, economics educator; b. London, July 24, 1946; came to U.S., 1968, naturalized, 1985; s. Clifford James and Beatrice Aileen (Blake) C.; m. Louise Grant Barrett, June 14, 1969; 1 child, Andrew van Leer. B.A., U. Cambridge, 1968; M.Philosophy, Yale U., 1970, Ph.D., 1977. Fellow Yale U., New Haven, 1968-72; research economist Carnegie Endowment for Internat. Peace, N.Y.C., 1971; lectr. in econs. London Sch. Econs. and Polit. Sci., 1972-73, U. Botswana, Lesotho and Swaziland, Roma, Lesotho, 1973-76; asst. prof. econs. Fla. State U., Tallahassee, 1976-81, assoc. prof., 1981-86, prof., 1986—, assoc. dean Coll. Social Scis., dir. interdisciplinary program social sci., 1985—; sr. research fellow Inst. So. African Studies, Nat. U. Lesotho, 1981-82; cons. in field. Author: Governments and Mining Companies in Developing Countries, 1977; Lesotho: Dilemmas of Dependence in Southern Africa, 1985. Contbr. articles to profl. publs., chpts. to books. Mem. Am. Econ. Assn., So. Econ. Assn., Eastern Econ. Assn., African Studies Assn., Soc. Internat. Devel. Clubs: Hawks (Cambridge, Eng.); Leander (Henley, Eng.). Home: 2012 E Randolph Circle Tallahassee FL 32312 Office: Fla State U Dept Econs Tallahassee FL 32306

COBBS, JAMES HAROLD, petroleum engineer; b. Bristow, Okla., Aug. 25, 1928; s. Harold M. and Ella (Rouintree) C.; B.S., U. Okla., 1949, postgrad., 1949-51; postgrad. U. Tulsa, 1955-67; m. Charlotte Marie Fisher, Aug. 16, 1953; children—James Harold, David C., Gregory L., Matthew L. Grad. asst. U. Okla., 1949-51; asso. engr. Tidewater Oil Co., Midland, Tex., 1951-52, reservoir engr., Houston, 1952-55, div. reservoir engr., Tulsa, 1955-59; pvt. practice engring., Tulsa, 1959-63, 69—; pres. Cobbs Engring. Inc.; sr. engr. Fenix & Scisson, Inc., Tulsa, 1963-69. Com. chmn., scoutmaster Indian Nations council Boy Scouts Am., 1962—; instr. first aid A.R.C., 1969—. Precinct chmn. Republican party, 1961-62. Fellow AAAS; mem. Soc. Petroleum Engrs., Nat., Okla. socs. profl. engrs., Inst. Shaft Drilling Tech., Vols. in Tech. Assistance, Nat. Oil Mfrs. and Dels. Soc., Sigma Phi Epsilon. Mem. Christian Ch. (elder, chmn. bd. 1971-72, 79). Contbr. articles to profl. jours. Patentee in field. Home: 5144 S New Haven St Tulsa OK 74135 Office: 5350 E 46th St Tulsa OK 74135

COBEY, WILLIAM WILFRED, JR., congressman, management consultant; b. Washington, May 13, 1939; m. Nancy Sullivan, Feb. 20, 1965; children—Billy, Cathy. B.S. in Chemistry, Emory U., 1962; M.S. in Mktg., U. Pa., 1964; M.Ed. in Health and Phys. Edn., U. Pitts., 1968. Dir. athletics U. N.C., Chapel Hill, 1976-80; prin. Cobey and Assocs. mgmt. cons., Chapel Hill, N.C., 1982-85; mem. 99th Congress from 4th N.C. Dist., mem. com. on sci. and tech. com. on small bus. Past pres. Chapel Hill-Carrboro YMCA; active Am. Field Service, Fellowship Christian Athletes, Boy Scouts Am. Republican candidate for lt. gov. N.C., 1980, for U.S. Congress, 1982. Office: 510 Cannon House Office Bldg Washington DC 20515

COBLE, HOWARD, congressman; b. Greensboro, N.C., Mar. 18, 1931. Student Appalachian State U., 1949-50; A.B. in History, Guilford Coll., 1958; J.D., U. N.C., 1962. Bar: N.C. 1962. Mem. N.C. Ho. of Reps., from 1969; asst. U.S. atty. middle dist. N.C., 1969-73; commr., sec. N.C. Dept. Revenue, 1973-77; mem. N.C. Ho. of Reps., 1979-83; assoc. Turner, Enochs & Sparrow, Greensboro, 1979-83; mem. 99th Congress from N.C. 6th dist.; mem. judiciary and small bus. coms. Served with USCG, 1952-56. Mem. Am. Legion, VFW, N.C. Bar Assn., N.C. State Bar, Greensboro Bar Assn. Presbyterian. Lodge: Lions. Office: 513 Cannon House Office Bldg Washington DC 20515

COCHRAN, CAROLYN, librarian; b. Tyler, Tex., July 13, 1934; d. Sidney Allen and Eudelle (Frazier) C.; m. Guy Milford Eley, June 1, 1963 (div.). B.A., Beaver Coll., 1956; M.A., U. Tex., 1960; M.L.S., Tex. Woman's U., 1970. Librarian, Canadian (Tex.) High Sch., 1970-71; rep. United Food Co., Amarillo, Tex., 1971-72; librarian Bishop Coll., Dallas, 1972-74; interviewer Tex. Employment Commn., Dallas, 1975-76; librarian St. Mary's Dominican, New Orleans, La., 1976-77; librarian DeVry Inst. Tech., Irving, Tex., 1978—; with Database Searching Handicapped Individuals, Irving, Tex., 1983—; vol. bibliographer Assn. Individuals with Disabilities, Dallas, 1983—. Mem. Am. Coalition of Citizens with Disabilities, 1982—, Assn. Individuals with Disabilities, 1982—, Vols. in Tech. Assistance, 1985—, Radio Amateur Satellite Corp., 1985—. HEW fellow, 1967; honored Black History Collection, Dallas Morning News, Bishop Coll., Dallas, 1973. Mem. ALA, Spl. Library Assn. Club: Toastmistress (pres. 1982-83) (Irving). Reviewer Library Jour., 1974, Dallas Morning News, 1972-74, Amarillo Globe-News, 1970-71.

COCHRAN, GEORGE CALLOWAY, III, banker; b. Dallas, Aug. 29, 1932; s. George Calloway and Miriam (Welty) C.; m. Jerry Bywaters, Dec. 9, 1961; children—Mary, Robert. B.A., So. Meth. U., 1954; J.D., Harvard U., 1957. Bar: Tex. 1957. Assoc. Leachman, Gardere, Akin & Porter, Dallas, 1961-62; with Fed. Res. Bank Dallas, 1962—, v.p., 1973-76, sr. v.p., 1976—; mem. part time faculty So. Meth. U. Law Sch., 1973. Mem. Hist. Landmark Task Force City Dallas, 1974-77. Served to capt. USAF, 1958-60. Mem. ABA, Tex. Bar Assn., Dallas Bar Assn., Phi Beta Kappa. Methodist. Home: 3541 Villanova St Dallas TX 75225 Office: 400 S Akard St Dallas TX 75222

COCHRAN, GEORGE MOFFETT, judge; b. Staunton, Va., Apr. 20, 1912; s. Peyton and Susie (Robertson) C.; B.A., U. Va., 1934, LL.B., 1936; m. Marion Lee Stuart, May 1, 1948; children—George Moffett, Harry Carter Stuart. Bar: Md. 1936, Va. 1935. Assoc. firm, Balt., 1936-38; ptnr. firm Peyton Cochran and George M. Cochran, Staunton, 1938-64, Cochran, Lotz & Black, Staunton, 1964-69; justice Supreme Ct. Va., Richmond, 1969—; pres. Planters Bank & Trust Co., Staunton, 1963-69. Chmn. Woodrow Wilson Centennial Commn. of Va., 1952-58, Va. Cultural Devel. Study Commn., 1966-68; mem. Va. Commn. on Constl. Revision, 1968-69, Jud. Council of Va., 1963-69. Mem. Va. Ho. of Dels., 1948-66, Va. Senate, 1966-68. Chmn. bd. dirs. Stuart Hall; bd. visitors Va. Poly. Inst., 1960-68; trustee Mary Baldwin Coll., 1967-81. Served to lt. comdr. USNR, 1942-46. Mem. Am. Bar Assn., Va. Bar Assn. (pres. 1965-66), Soc. of Cincinnati, Raven Soc., Phi Beta Kappa, Phi Delta Phi, Beta Theta Pi. Episcopalian. Office: Masonic Temple Bldg Staunton VA 24401 also Supreme Ct Bldg Richmond VA 23210

COCHRAN, OLIVE LEIGH MYATT, former educational administrator; b. Monroe, La., Sept. 8, 1907; d. Webster Andrew and Martha Fidelia (Morton) Myatt; student La. State Normal Coll., 1923-25; kindergarten cert. Harris Tchrs. Coll., 1926; B.S. cum laude, La. State U., 1942; M.Ed., N.E. La. U., 1962; m. Raymond Nevitt Cochran, June 4, 1940 (dec. 1985); children—Kathleen N., Susan Cochran Mingledorff. Tchr. rural schs., Ouachita Parish, La., 1925-27, Georgia Tucker Elem. Sch., Monroe, 1927-43, 55-62; tchr., owner Cochran Nursery Sch., 1949-51; supr. elem. edn. Monroe Sch. System, 1962-67, dir. elem. curriculum, 1967-73; organizer first spl. edn. classes Monroe schs., 1964; supr. spl. edn. Monroe City schs., 1964-73; ret., 1973. Active CD. during World War II. Mem. Internat. Reading Assn. (dir. local unit 1970-73), Assn. Childhood Edn. Internat. (br. pres. 1967-71, treas. 1971-83), La. Assn. Childhood Edn. Internat., AAUW, Delta Kappa Gamma, Sigma Tau Delta. Republican. Baptist. Home: 1105 N 7th St Monroe LA 71201

COCHRAN, TED ALAN, communications company executive; b. Atlanta, Aug. 4, 1946; s. William Allen and Dorothy Marcelle (Hall) C.; m. Ann Foster Girtman, Aug. 14, 1970; children—Franklin, Marie. B.B.A. in Mgmt., Ga. State U., 1979. Computer operator Decatur Fed. Savs. & Loan, Ga., 1967-69, lead operator, 1971-74, programmer/analyst, 1974-77; systems analyst So. Bell Telephone Co., Atlanta, 1978—; pres., owner Cochran Computer Consulting, Stone Mountain, Ga., 1984—. Served to Sgt. U.S. Army, 1969-71. Mem. Dekalb Hist. Soc., Mountain Shadow Civic Club, Golden Key, Mortar Bd. Republican. Methodist. Club: Apple Computer. Avocations: woodworking; photography; computers. Home: 4870 Forestglade Ct Stone Mountain GA 30087 Office: Cochran Computer Consulting 4870 Forestglade Ct Stone Mountain GA 30087

COCHRAN, THAD, U.S. Senator; b. Pontotoc, Miss., Dec. 7, 1937; s. William Holmes and Emma Grace (Berry) C.; B.A., U. Miss., 1959, J.D. cum laude, 1965; postgrad. (Rotary Found. fellow), U. Dublin (Ireland), 1963-64; m. Rose Clayton, June 6, 1964; children—Thaddeus Clayton, Katherine Holmes. Admitted to Miss. bar, 1965, practiced in Jackson, 1965-72; asso. firm Watkins & Eager, 1965-72; mem. 93d-95th congresses from Miss.; mem. U.S. Senate from Miss., 1979—. Mem. exec. bd. Andrew Jackson council Boy Scouts Am., 1973—. Served to lt. USNR, 1959-61. Named Outstanding Young Man of Jackson, 1971, One of Three Outstanding Young Men of Miss., 1971. Mem. Am., Miss. (pres. young lawyers sect.) bar assns., Omicron Delta Kappa, Phi Kappa Phi, Pi Kappa Alpha. Republican. Baptist. Club: Rotary. Office: US Senate Washington DC 20510

COCHRANE, JAMES HARWOOD, JR., transportation company executive, architect; b. Richmond, Va., Aug. 25, 1953; s. James Harwood and Louise Carr (Blanks) C.; m. Judy Gail Alspaugh, Aug. 29, 1981. B.Arch., Va. Poly. Inst. and State U., 1984; Transp. Mgmt. cert. U. Richmond, 1981, M.B.A., 1986. Cert. freight claims profl. Architect intern Overnite Transp. Co., Richmond, 1978-79, asst. ops. mgr., 1983—; architect intern Jack Kincaid, ALA, Newton-Conover, N.C., 1979, Ballou & Justice, Architects & Engrs., Richmond, 1979-80, Ben R. Johns, Jr., AIA, Richmond, 1980-81, Leadbetter Bldgs. Inc., Ashland, Va., 1981-82, Wright, Cox & Smith, Richmond, 1982-83. Mem. Rockville Jr. C. of C. (charter). So. Baptist. Kappa Alpha Order. Home: 1 Loblolly Ln Rockville VA 23146 Office: Overnite Transp Co 1000 Semmes Ave Richmond VA 23224

COCKE, JAMES GILBERT, SR., electronics company executive; b. Chgo., Sept. 15, 1947; s. Charles Gilbert and Mary Belle (LeMaster) C.; m. Nancy Jane Albert, Jan. 13, 1967; children—Kristin Mary, James Gilbert, Timothy James. B.S. in Bus. Adminstrn., Roosevelt U., Chgo., 1973, M.S. in Acctg., 1976. Acctg. mgr. Teledyne Brown, Huntsville, Ala., 1976-78; controller Teledyne MEC, Palo Alto, Calif., 1978-80; dir. fin. E-Systems, Inc., Memcor, Tampa, Fla., 1980-82, div. controller, 1982-83, v.p. fin. and adminstrn., 1983—; guest lectr. Def. Systems Mgmt. Coll., Ft. Belvoir, Va., 1980—. Mem. Polit. Action Com., Dallas, 1983—. Served with USMC, 1965-68. Decorated Bronze Star. Mem. Nat. Contract So. Mgmt. Assn. Republican. Avocations: stamp collecting; woodworking. Home: 4223 Water Oaks Ln Tampa FL 33674 Office: E-Systems Inc Memcor Div PO Box 23500 Tampa FL 33630

COCKE, WILLIAM MARVIN, JR., plastic surgeon; b. Balt., Aug. 2, 1934; s. William M. and Clara E. (Bosley) C.; B.S., Tex. A&M Coll., 1956; M.D., Baylor U., 1960; children—William Marvin III, Catherine Lynn, Deborah Kay, Brian Thomas, Gregory William. Intern, Vanderbilt U. Hosp., Nashville, 1960-61; fellow gen. surgery Ochsner Clinic and Found. Hosp., New Orleans, 1961-64; Am. Cancer Soc. clin. research fellow surgery Ochsner Clinic, 1962-63; chief resident surgery, clin. dir. Monroe (La.) Charity Hosp., 1963-64; resident head and neck surgery Roswell Park Inst., Buffalo, 1965; resident in plastic surgery N.Y. Hosp.-Cornell Med. Center, 1964-66; practice medicine specializing in plastic surgery; clin. instr. plastic surgery U. Tex. Med. Sch., San Antonio, 1968; asst. prof. surgery Vanderbilt U. Sch. Medicine, Nashville, 1968-69, developer div. plastic surgery, 1969, asst. clin. prof. plastic surgery, 1969-75; assoc. prof. surgery Ind. U. Sch. Medicine, Indpls., 1975-76; chief plastic surgery Wishard Meml. Hosp., Ind. U. Med. Center, Indpls., 1975-76; asso. prof. surgery U. Calif., Davis, 1976-79, chmn. dept. plastic surgery, 1976-79; mem. staff Kaiser Found. Hosp., Sacramento, 1976-79; cons. plastic surgery VA Hosp., Martinez, Calif., 1976-79; prof. surgery, chief div. plastic surgery Tex. Tech U. Sch. Medicine, 1979-80; pvt. practice plastic surgery, Bryan, Tex., 1979—; clin. prof. surgery, researcher Tex. A&M U. Sch. Medicine, 1980—. Scis. Ctr. Served with USAF, 1966-68. Diplomate Am. Bd. Plastic Surgery. Fellow A.C.S.; mem. Am. Assn. Plastic Surgeons, Am. Soc. Plastic and Reconstructive Surgery, Tex. Soc. Plastic Surgeons, Southeastern Soc. Plastic Surgeons, Pan Am. Med. Soc., Assn. Acad. Surgery, Soc. Head and Neck Surgeons, Internat. Soc. Aesthetic Plastic Surgeons, Alton Oshsner Surg. Soc., Tex. Med. Assn., AMA, Brazos-Robertson County (Tex.) Med. Soc., Herbert Conway Soc. Author: Breast Reconstruction Following Mastectomy for Carcinoma, 1977; (with John S. Silverton and R.McShane) Basic Plastic Surgery, 1979; (with White, Lynch and Vermeyden) Wound Care; contbr. articles on reconstructive surgery to jours. in medicine. Office: 1737 Briarcrest Dr Suite 18 Bryan TX 77801

COCKERHAM, COLUMBUS CLARK, population and quantitative geneticist, educator, consultant; b. Mountain Park, N.C., Dec. 12, 1921; s. Corbett C. and Nellie Bruce (McCann) C.; m. Joyce Evelyn Allen, Feb. 26, 1944; children—C. Clark, Jr., Jean Allen, Bruce Allen. B.S., N.C. State Coll.-Raleigh, 1943, M.S., 1949; Ph.D., Iowa State U., 1952. Asst. prof. dept. biostats. U. N.C., Chapel Hill, 1952-53; assoc. prof. dept. exptl. stats. N.C. State U., 1953-59, prof. dept. stats., 1959-72, William Neal Reynolds prof. stats. and genetics, 1972—; mem. genetics study sect. NIH, 1965-69; cons. Adv. Com. on Protocols for Safety Evaluation FDA, 1967-69. Served to lt. USMC, 1943-46. Recipient N.C. award in field of sci., 1976; O. Max Gardner award, 1980; D.D. Mason faculty award, 1983; Nat. Inst. Gen. Med. Scis. grantee, 1960—. Fellow Am. Soc. Agronomy; mem. Nat. Acad. Scis., AAAS, Am. Soc. Animal Sci., Am. Soc. Human Genetics, Am. Soc. Naturalists, Biometric Soc., Genetics Soc.

Am., Genetics Soc. Japan (fgn. hon. mem.). Mem. editorial bd. Genetics, 1969-72, Genetic Epidemiology, 1984—; editor: Theoretical Population Biology, 1975-81, assoc. editor, 1982—; assoc. editor: Am. Jour. Human Genetics, 1978-80; contbr. articles to profl. jours. Office: Dept Statistics NC State Univ Box 8203 Raleigh NC 27695

CODD, RICHARD TRENT, JR., educator, computer scientist; b. Norfolk, Va., June 1, 1945; s. Richard Trent and Mildred Joyce C.; m. Celine Marie Morisset, Aug. 10, 1968; children—Richard Trent, III, Patrick Timothy, Matthew Paul. A.A., Miami-Dade Community Coll., 1967; B.S., U. Miami, 1970, M.A., 1974; B.S., Fla. Internat. U., 1985. Lic. tchr., ednl. adminstr. Fla. Audio technician U. Miami, Coral Gables, Fla., 1968-71; tchr. Archbishop Curley High Sch., Miami, Fla., 1972-74; tchr. St. Brendan High Sch., Miami, 1974-80, adminstr., 1980—, asst. prin., 1981—, dir. computer services, 1981—; instr. St. Thomas U., Opa Locka, Fla., 1980—, St. John Vianney Coll. Sem., Miami, 1985—; software systems developer Archdiocese of Miami, 1984—; bd. dirs. Archdiocese of Miami Credit Union, 1979-80. Developer Master Acad. Record/Scheduling ADP System. Mem. Math. Assn. Am. Democrat. Roman Catholic. Avocations: Music; hiking; boating. Office: St Brendan High Sch 2950 SW 87th Ave Miami FL 33165

CODDING, FREDERICK HAYDEN, lawyer; b. Hopewell, Va., Dec. 13, 1938; s. Francis Chadwick and Ruthcille Sharon (Craven) C.; A.B., Coll. William and Mary, 1962; J.D., Georgetown U., 1966; m. Judith Willis Hawkins, Apr. 30, 1966; children—Forrest Hayden, Judith Chadwick, Cally Willis, Clare Catharine. Legal asst. VA, Washington, 1963-65; Capitol Hill reporter, editor Congl. Monitor, Washington, 1966; admitted to Va. bar, 1966, D.C. bar, 1968; law clk. to chief judge D.C. Ct. Appeals, 1966-68; individual practice law, Va. and Washington; v.p., counsel Nat. Assn. Miscellaneous, Ornamental and Archtl. Products Contractors, Fairfax, 1970—; counsel, dir. Nat. Assn. Reinforcing Steel Contractors, Fairfax, 1970—. Mem. federally established rev. bds. for constrn. industry, N.Y.C. Bldg. Standards Com. Counsel, Fairfax County Youth Club; pres., counsel Fairfax Police Youth Club; mem. Fairfax City Sch. Bd. Mem. Am., D.C., Va., Fairfax bar assns., Nat. Council Erectors, Fabricators and Riggers, Sigma Nu. Editor, pub. legislative, adminstrv., bldg. and constrn. industry newsletters, reports. Office: 10382 Main St Fairfax VA 22030

CODINGTON, LEWIS LANCASTER, bookstore executive; b. Kwangju, South Korea, July 9, 1956 (parents Am. citizens); s. Herbert Augustus and Mary Littlepage (Lancaster) C.; m. Elisabeth Caroline Schaffers, Dec. 16, 1978; children—Wilhelmus, Julia. B.A. cum laude, Covenant Coll., 1978; M.B.A., U. Del., 1980. Asst. to registrar Covenant Coll., Lookout Mountain, Ga., 1977-78, personnel dir., 1980-82; owner, mgr. Christian Book Nook, Alcoa, Tenn., 1982—; research asst. U. Del., Newark, 1978-79. Youth leader Cedar Springs Presbyn. Ch., Knoxville, Tenn., 1984—. Mem. Christian Booksellers Assn. Midland Mchts. Assn. (fin. com. 1985—). Republican. Avocations: tennis; walking; reading; travelling. Home: Route 3 Box 535 Louisville TN 37777 Office: Christian Book Nook Midland Ctr Alcoa TN 37701

CODY, JACQUELINE JO, training and development specialist, artist; b. Blackwell, Okla., Dec. 11, 1927; d. Howard Spencer and Alberta Hope (Keeley) Brown; m. Harvey Hobson Cody, Jr., July 17, 1948; children—Candace Ann, Harvey Hobson III, Christopher Miles. A.A., UCLA, 1947; B.S., U. Okla., 1965, M.S. in Polit. Sci., 1972. Artist, illustrator U.S. Air Force, Tinker AFB, Oklahoma City, 1952-54, communications instr., 1955-60, employee devel. specialist, 1960-73, chief tech. tng., 1974-81, chief employee devel. and tng., 1982—; art and drama coach YMCA, Oklahoma City, 1955-57; mem. accrediting com. Rose State Coll., Midwest City, Okla., 1975; adv. bd. elec. engring. tech. Okla. State Tech. Inst., 1980—; adv. bd. prodn. engring. So. Oklahoma City Jr. Coll., 1979; Okla. Adv. Bd. for Postsecondary Edn., 1986—. Author: Count Me In, 1968; Something Else, 1970; Where Its At, 1971; Are You Ready For This?, 1972. Coordinator Community Edn. and Tng. Act, Tinker AFB, Okla., 1970's, Combined Fed. Campaign for Directorate of Personnel, Tinker AFB, 1983, 84; lectr. in art various women's groups, Shawnee and Oklahoma City, 1950—. Recipient Sustained Superior award Tinker AFB, 1956, 60, Quality Step Increase, Tinker AFB, 1968, Meritorious Civilian Service award U.S. Air Force, 1969, Excellent Ratings award Tinker AFB, 1982, 84. Mem. Tinker Mgmt. Assn., Am. Soc. Tng. and Devel. Democrat. Methodist. Avocations: flying, drawing, painting.

CODY, WALTER JAMES MICHAEL, state attorney general; b. Mar. 13, 1936; m. Suzanna Marten; children—Jane, Michael. B.A. with distinction, Southwestern U., 1958; LL.B., U. Va., 1961. Bar: Tenn. 1961. Lectr. Memphis State U. Sch. Law; instr. polit. sci. Southwestern U., Memphis; U.S. atty. Western Dist. Tenn., 1977-81; staff atty. City of Memphis, 1981-83; ptnr. Burch, Porter & Johnson, Memphis, 1961-77, 81-84; atty. gen., reporter State of Tenn., 1984—. Active Memphis Acad. Arts; co-founder Memphis and Shelby County Bar Assn. Neighborhood Legal Service Project; participant Boston Marathon; bd. dirs. Memphis March of Dimes, Multiple Sclerosis Soc.; Orpheum; chmn. 1984 Crusade Cancer Drive. Mem. Memphis Bar Assn., Shelby County Bar Assn., ABA, Fed. Bar Assn., Tenn. Bar Assn., Nat. Assn. Former U.S. Attys. Address: 450 James Robertson Pkwy Nashville TN 37219

COE, JACK MARTIN, lawyer; b. Orange, N.J., Mar. 25, 1945; s. Irving and Evelyn (Phillips) C.; m. Diana Jean Martino, Oct. 24, 1981. B.A., U. Va., 1967; A.M., Brown U., 1969; J.D., U. Fla., 1975. Bar: Fla. 1975, U.S. Ct. Appeals (5th cir.) 1976, U.S. Dist. Ct. (so. dist.) Fla. 1976, D.C. 1978, U.S. Supreme Ct. 1978, U.S. Ct. Appeals (11th cir.) 1981. Assoc. Adams, George, Lee & Schulte, Miami, Fla., 1975-77, Thomas E. Lee Jr., P.A., Miami, 1977-78; ptnr. Lee, Schulte, Murphy & Coe, P.A., Miami, 1978—; alumni dir. Sta. WUVA, U. Va., Charlottesville, 1977—. Active in Tiger Bay Polit. Club, Miami, 1978—. Served to 1st lt. USAF, 1969-72. Mem. ABA, Assn. Trial Lawyers Am., Acad. Fla. Trial Lawyers, Dade County Bar Assn., Palm Beach County Bar Assn. Democrat. Home: 1546 Catalonia Ave Coral Gables FL 33134 Office: Lee Schulte Murphy & Coe PA Suite 800 200 SE First St Miami FL 33131

COFFEY, GLENN HARRIS, petroleum geologist; b. Lafayette, La., Oct. 18, 1953; s. Andy Murray and Katherine (Harris) C. B.S. in Geology, U. Southwest La., 1974. Grad. asst. La. State U., 1975; production geologist Gulf Oil Co., Lafayette, La., 1975-77; dist. geol. mgr. Marion, Corp., Lafayette, 1977-79; dir. Frontier Energy Corp., Houston, 1981-85; geologist, owner Coffey Oil Co., Lafayette, 1979—. Bd. dirs. Holy Family Ctr. Orphanage, Abbeville, La. Recipient 300 Game award Am. Bowling Congress, 1974. Mem. Soc. Independent Earth Scientists (cert.). Lafayette Geol. Soc., Am. Assn. Petroleum Geologists (cert.), Nat. Rifle Assn. (life), U.S. C. of C., Sigma Gamma Epsilon. Avocations: hunting; tennis; bowling; geology student assistance programs. Office: Coffey Oil Co 510 E University PO Box 53606 Lafayette LA 70505

COFFEY, KITTY ROBERTS, home economics educator; b. Jefferson City, Tenn., Nov. 19, 1942; d. William Oliver and Verdie Irene (Cluck) Roberts; m. Benjamin Bruce Coffey, Sept. 27, 1969; B.S., U. Tenn.-Knoxville, 1965, M.S., 1966, Ph.D., 1977; student Merrill-Palmer Inst., Detroit, 1965, U. Iowa, 1969. Registered dietitian. Instr., Coll. Home Econs. U. Ala.-Tucscaloosa, 1966-69; asst. prof. Child Devel. Center, U. Tenn. Center for Health Scis., 1969-74; instr. dept. nutrition and food scis. Coll. Home Econs., U. Tenn.-Knoxville, 1974-77; assoc. prof., coordinator home econs. dept., chmn. div. social scis. Carson-Newman Coll., 1977—; cons. Mem. Am. Dietetic Assn., Tenn. Dietetic Assn., Am. Home Econs. Assn., Tenn. Home Econs. Assn., Soc. Nutrition Edn., Inst. Food Technologists, Nat. Council Adminstrs. Home Econs., Sigma Xi, Omicron Nu, Kappa Omicron Phi, Phi Kappa Phi, Alpha Lambda Delta. Methodist. Club: Soma Sala Federated Women's. Contbr. articles in nutrition jours.

COFFEY, SMITH DWIGHT, psychologist, human resource consultant; b. Greensboro, N.C., Nov. 24, 1946; s. Paul Pershing and Helen Corine (Pitts) C.; m. Carolyn Bruce Little, Aug. 31, 1969 (div. Oct. 1979); 1 child, Catherine Smith. A.A., Wingate Coll., 1967; B.A., U. N.C., 1969; M.A. in Clin. Psychology, Appalachian State U., 1974; M.B.A., U. N. Fla., 1983. Lic. psychol. assoc., N.C. Rehab. therapist John Umstead Hosp., Butner, N.C., 1969-72; dir. child services Mecklenburg Mental Health, Charlotte, N.C., 1973-79; clin. services coordinator Child Guidance Clinic, Jacksonville, Fla., 1979-82; corp. assessment adminstrs. Blue Cross and Blue Shield of Fla., Jacksonville, 1984—; psychol. examiner, Charlotte, 1977-79; child abuse cons. Children's Haven of Clay County, Orange Park, Fla., 1982-83. Creator TV series, 1978. Bd. dirs. Mecklenburg Child Abuse & Neglect Council Charlotte, 1976-77; mem. human resource bd. Central Piedment Community Coll., Charlotte, 1977; mem. Mecklenurg Comm. on Status of Women, Charlotte, 1977-78; bd. dirs. Clay County Mental Health Adv. Bd., Orange Park, Fla., 1980-82. Recipient award Gov. Council on Child Services Office of Gov. N.C., 1979. Mem. Am. Psychol. Assn. (assoc.), Am. Soc. Personnel Adminstrs., Sigma Chi. Democrat. Presbyterian. Avocations: sailing, tennis, travel. Home: 512 Lancaster St Jacksonville FL 32204 Office: Blue Cross & Blue Shield of Fla 532 Riverside Ave Jacksonville FL 32231

COFFIELD, CONRAD EUGENE, lawyer; b. Hot Springs, S.D., Nov. 26, 1930; s. Eugene M. and Alice (Hotvet) C.; m. Maggie Lee Murphey, Aug. 1, 1953; children—Conrad Eugene, Michael, Megan, Edward, Philip. Student S.D. Sch. Mines and Tech., 1948-49; B.B.A., Washington U., St. Louis, 1952; LL.B., U. Tex., 1959. Bar: Tex. 1959, N.Mex. 1959. Practiced in Roswell, N.Mex., 1959-66, Midland, Tex., 1966—; mem. firm Hervey, Dow & Hinkle, 1959-64; gen. ptnr. Hinkle, Cox, Eaton, Coffield & Hensley, Roswell, 1964-66, resident ptnr., Midland, 1966—; dir. Republic Bank, Midland. Trustee Petroleum Mus., Library and Hall of Fame; bd. govs. Midland Community Theatre. Served with USCGR, 1952-56. Fellow Tex. Bar Found.; mem. Am., Tex., N.Mex., Midland County bar assns., N.Mex. Oil and Gas Assn. Episcopalian (vestryman). Clubs: Midland Petroleum, Midland Country. Home: 2813 W Dengar St Midland TX 79701 Office: Blanks Bldg Midland TX 79701

COFFMAN, CHARLIE QUINN, education educator; b. Lula, Miss., Feb. 20, 1923; s. Tulus Jackson and Addie (Mick) C.; m. J'Nell Posey, Aug. 23, 1947; children—Deborah, Marilyn. B.S. in Edn., Delta State Coll., 1948; M.A. in Sch. Adminstrn., U. So. Miss., 1953; Ed.D., U. Miss., 1964; postdoctoral U. Pitts., 1969-70. Cert. tchr., adminstr., Miss., N.C. Supt. of schs., Arcola, Miss., 1953-56, Cleveland, Miss., 1957-61; asst. supt. schs., Hinds County, Miss., 1961-68, assoc. dir. higher edn., 1969-79; dir. lay renewal United Meth. Ch., 1968-69; prof. edn. Fayetteville (N.C.) State U., 1979, asst. dir. grad. studies program, 1985—; dir. fed. programs and planning in higher edn. State of Miss. Active ARC. Served with USMC, 1941-45. Decorated Purple Heart; grad. fellow U. Miss., 1963. Mem. Am. Assn. Sch. Adminstrs., Nat. Assn. Secondary Sch. Prins., Assn. Supervision and Curriculum Devel., Phi Delta Kappa. Democrat. Methodist. Lodges: Masons, Rotary (pres. 1985-86), Lions. Contbr. articles to profl. jours.

COFFMAN, JAMES BARRY, real estate development company executive; b. Dallas, Nov. 19, 1942; s. Thomas Ray and Emma Helen (Lewis) C.; m. Cynthia Dianne Goerner, June 22, 1968; 1 son, Kevin Todd. B.B.A., Sam Houston State U., 1965. Chartered fin. analyst. Trust investment officer Tex. Commerce Bank, Austin, 1965-72; v.p., dir. West Georgetown Devel. Co. (Tex.), 1981—, S.C.B. Devel. Co., Georgetown, 1976—, Serenada Tennis, Inc., Georgetown, 1972—; pres., dir. Sierra Lima Jet Service, Inc., Georgetown, 1976—. Served with USAF, 1965-71. Mem. Inst. Chartered Fin. Analysts, Austin-San Antonio Soc. Fin. Analysts, Georgetown C. of C. Republican. Clubs: Serenada Racquet, Georgetown Country. Office: West Georgetown Devel Co 301 Toledo Terr Georgetown TX 78626

COFFMAN, JOHN EDWIN, geographer, educator; b. Robstown, Tex., Feb. 17, 1942; s. Carl Simeon and Zada Lee (White) C.; A.A., Del Mar Coll., 1960; B.A., UCLA, 1967, M.A., 1968, C.Phil., 1970, Ph.D., 1972. Tech. pubs. and media display cons., N.Y. and Calif., 1960-65; instr. geography Calif. State U., Fullerton, 1970, Calif. State Coll., Dominguez Hills, 1970; from instr. to assoc. prof. U. Houston, 1970—; mem. regional selection com. Office of Edn., 1970—. Lectr. Rice U., U. St. Thomas, Women's Inst. of Houston. Mem. Nat. Council Geog. Edn. (life), Assn. Am. Geographers, Am. Geog. Soc., Assn. Pacific Coast Geographers, Southwestern Social Sci. Assn., Southwest Conf. Asian Studies, Nat., Tex. councils social studies, Calif. Council Geography Tchrs., Assn. Asian Studies, Western Social Sci. Assn., Conf. Latin Am. Geographers, Geog. Educators Tex. (founder), AAUP (past pres. U. Houston chpt.), AAAS, Soc. Econ. Botany, Alaska Geog. Soc., Sigma Xi, Phi Theta Kappa, Gamma Theta Upsilon; fellow Royal Geog. Soc. (London), Explorers Club, U.S. Naval Inst., Omicron Delta Kappa. Author coll. and elem. level social studies textbooks; contbr. articles to profl. jours., Funk & Wagnalls, World Book Ency. Home: Route 5 Box 692 Porter TX 77365 Office: Dept Econs U Houston University Park Campus Houston TX 77004

COFRAN, GEORGE LEE, mgmt. cons.; b. Buffalo, Sept. 30, 1945; s. Louis Lee and Virginia Carolyn (Breneman) C.; B.S.E.E., Purdue U., 1967; M.B.A., Dartmouth Coll., 1969; m. Jane Ann Kimsey, Apr. 24, 1969; children—Jeffrey Todd, Jennifer Renee. Systems analyst Burlington Mgmt. Services, Greensboro, N.C., 1969-70; mgmt. cons. Arthur Young & Co., Houston, 1971-77; pres. Cofran & Assos., Inc., Houston, 1977—; comml. arbitrator Am. Arbitration Assn.; speaker, lectr. in field. Bd. dirs., pres. Huntwick Civic Assn., Houston; charter v.p. Active Corps of Execs., SBA, 1974, 75. Served to 1st lt., AUS, 1970-71. Decorated Army Commendation medal; C.P.A., Tex.; cert. data processing Data Processing Mgmt. Assn. Mem. Am. Inst. C.P.A.s, IEEE, Assn. Systems Mgmt. (past pres., dir. Houston chpt., Outstanding Service award Houston chpt. 1978-79), Tau Beta Pi. Clubs: Raveneaux Country; Olde Oaks Racquet, Huntwick Racquet (Houston). Home: 5610 Ascalon Circle Houston TX 77069 Office: 14611 Benfer Rd Houston TX 77069

COGGESHALL, NORMAN DAVID, oil company executive; b. Ridgefarm, Ill., May 15, 1916; s. Lester B. and Grace (Blaisdell) C.; m. Margaret Josephine Danner, Aug. 22, 1940; children—Nancy Ellen Von de Ohe, David M., M. Gwen Calabretta, Philip A. B.A., U. Ill., 1937, M.S., 1938, Ph.D., 1942. Tcrh. physics U. Ill., 1942-43; scientist Gulf Oil Research, Pitts., 1943-50, asst. dir. physics div., 1950-55, dir. analytical sci. div., 1955-61, dir. phys. scis. div., 1961-67, v.p. process scis., 1967-70, v.p. exploration and prodn., 1970-76, v.p. tech. govt. coordination, 1976-81; pvt. investor and pvt. cons., Lynn Haven, Fla., 1981—. Recipient Resolution of Appreciation, Am. Petroleum Inst., 1970. Fellow Am. Phys. Soc.; mem. Am. Chem. Soc. (award in chem. instrumentation 1970), Spectroscopy Soc. Pitts., Bay County C. of C. (mil. affairs com.). Republican. Clubs: St. Andrews Bay, Yacht (Panama City, Fla.). Lodge: Rotary. Contbg. author: Colloid Chemistry, 1946; Physical Chemistry of Hydrocarbons, 1950; Organic Analysis, 1953; Advances in Mass Spectrometry, 1963; contbr. articles to tech. jours.; patentee in field. Home and Office: 701 Driftwood Dr Lynn Haven FL 32444

COGGESHALL, PETER COLLIN, paper products manufacturing company executive; b. Darlington, S.C., Sept. 22, 1915; s. Robert Werner and Mary Beulah (Walden) C.; m. Rosanne Howard, Jan. 24, 1942; children—Peter Collin, Rosanne Howard. A.B., U. S.C., 1936; M.B.A., Harvard U., 1938. Research staff Harvard U., 1938-39; with Sonoco Products Co., Hartsville, S.C., 1939—, v.p., 1961-76, exec. v.p., 1976—, also dir.; dir. Sonoco Internat. Co. Trustee McLeod Regional Med. Center, Florence, S.C., Coker Coll., Hartsville, S.C. Served as officer AUS, 1943-45. Mem. Phi Beta Kappa, Omicron Delta Kappa, Alpha Tau Omega. Presbyterian. Clubs: Damon Gun, Rotary. Home: 547 Lakeshore Dr Hartville SC 29550 Office: Sonoco Products Co 2d St Hartsville SC 29550

COGGESHALL, ROBERT WALDEN, ret. govt. ofcl.; b. Darlington, S.C., Sept. 11, 1912; s. Robert Werner and Beulah (Walden) C.; B.S., U. S.C., 1932; M.A., George Washington U., 1964; postgrad. Am. U., 1964-69; m. Ellie Mason Thomas, Sept. 3, 1934; children—Peter Collin V., John Pennington. Adminstrv. analyst Home Owners Loan Corp., Washington, 1934-41; budget analyst Fed. Works Agy., 1941-43; asst. dep. adminstr. for rent control OPA, 1943-46; chief systems and procedures Bur. Reclamation, 1946-53; editor Postal Manual, Office Postmaster Gen., 1954; chief mgmt. analysis Bur. Indian Affairs, 1954-57; chief div. mgmt. sci. Office of Sec., Dept. Interior, 1957-68; fellow Brookings Instn., 1968-69; mem. faculty U.S. Dept. Agr. Grad. Sch., 1959-65. S.C. chmn. Common Cause, 1974-75. Mem. Alpha Tau Omega. Episcopalian. Author: Administrative Functions of the Fish and Wildlife Service, 1958; Coordination of Federal Oceanography, 1963. Home: Shaggy Acres Ballentine SC 29002

COGGINS, DELBERT RONALD, school administrator; b. Tallapoosa, Ga., Apr. 10, 1941; s. Herman and Bernice Missouri (Bentley) C.; m. Anne Clark, Jan. 26, 1963; children—Jon Clark, David Christian. B.A., Union U., Jackson, Tenn., 1963; M.Ed., Memphis State U., 1975. Cert., tchr., adminstr., Tenn., Ga. Tchr., Ensworth Sch., Nashville, 1965-69; headmaster Tunica Inst. (Miss.), 1969-73; headmaster Grace-St. Luke's Episcopal Sch., Memphis, 1973-75; headmaster Holy Innocents' Episc. Sch., Atlanta, 1975-83; asst. headmaster Webb Sch., Bell Buckle, Tenn., 1983—; dir. Ga. Episc. Fed. Credit Union, Atlanta, 1977-80; chairperson vis. coms. So. Assn. Colls. and Schs., Atlanta, 1978-83. Lay reader Episc. chs., Atlanta and Memphis, 1974-83; bd. dirs. North Springs High Sch. Parent, Tchr. and Student Assn., Atlanta, 1979-81. Honored for Contbns. to Edn., Roundtable Vanderbilt U., 1983. Mem. Atlanta Area Assn. Ind. Schs. (sec. 1978-79, v.p. 1979-80, pres. 1980-81), Ga. Assn. Ind. Schs. (v.p. 1980-81, pres. 1981-82, exec. com. 1982-83), Jaycees. Home: Route 2 Box 108A Bell Buckle TN 37020 Office: Webb Sch Hwy 82 Bell Buckle TN 37020

COGGINS, SONJA IRENE, insurance company executive; b. Pensacola, Fla., Oct. 9, 1944; d. John R. Meadows and Louise (Wallace) Christensen; m. James Albert Coggins, Nov. 20, 1962; children—Daniel E., John L. A.A., Pensacola Jr. Coll., 1964. With Mitchell Realty Co., Biloxi, Miss., 1965-66, Baronich Ins. Co., Biloxi, 1966-74, Assoc. Ins. Co., Pensacola, 1974-83; agt. Lee Ins. Agy., Pensacola, 1983—. Mem. Escambia County Assn. for Retarded Citizens, Pensacola, 1980—. Mem. Nat. Assn. Ins. Women Internat., Ins. Women of Pensacola (pres. 1977-78, 80-81, Ins. Woman of Year 1978), Pensacola Life Underwriters (bd. dirs. 1980—). Republican. Baptist. Lodge: Warrington Elkettes. Home: 4220 Langley Ave Pensacola FL 32504 Office: James Lee & Assocs Inc PO Box 16070 7 S Warrington Rd Pensacola FL 32507

COGHILL, MARVIN W., tobacco company executive. Pres. Standard Comml. Tobacco Co., Wilson, N.C. Address: Standard Commercial Tobacco Co PO Box 450 Wilson NC 27893*

COGSWELL, PATRICK FINIS, chemist; b. Sherman, Tex., Mar. 17, 1929; s. Howard Winwood and Jhonnie Catherine (Page) C.; m. Claudette Frances Speaker, Apr. 8, 1955; children—Patricia, Janis, Thomas, Scott. B.S., Austin Coll., 1951. Analytical chemist Core Labs., Inc., Dallas, 1954-58, Kerr-McGee Oil Industries, Cushing, Okla., 1958-62; analytical research group supr. Goodrich-Gulf Chem., Port Neches, Tex., 1962-65; quality control supr. Ethyl Corp., Houston, 1965-68; quality assurance group leader Alcon Labs., Inc., Ft. Worth, 1969—. Mem. adv. bd. Pastoral Care Center, Brite Div. Sch., 1980—. Mem. Am. Chem. Soc., Dallas Soc. Analaytical Chemists, Am. Soc. Quality Control. Republican. Christian Ch. Contbr. articles to profl. jours. Home: 3436 Winifred St Fort Worth TX 76133 Office: 6201 S Freeway Fort Worth TX 76134

COHEN, BARBARA HELEN, medical center executive, nurse; b. Lincoln, Kans., Feb. 6, 1931; d. Alfred Edison and Helen Lucinda (Bird) Strange; m. David Arnold Cohen; 1 child, Benjamin C. Diploma in Nursing, Research Hosp., 1952; B.S. in Nursing, Mo. U., 1955; M.S. with honors in Nursing, Washington U., 1959; postgrad., U. Houston, 1964-65. R.N. Asst. prof. nursing Tex. Women's U., Houston, 1960-63; hemodialysis nurse, technician St. Luke's Hosp., Houston, 1963-66; asst. prof. nursing Washington U., St. Louis, 1966-67, U. Ill., Chgo., 1967-68; quality assurance coordinator Kaiser Permanente Med. Ctr., Santa Clara, Calif., 1974-80; infection control coordinator Seton and St. David's Hosps., Austin, Tex., 1981—; research asst. Washington U., St. Louis, 1958-60. Active in Eanes Community Edn. Com., Austin, 1984. Pub. Health Service grant 1958. Mem. Assn. Practitioners in Infection Control, Tex. Soc. Infection Control Practitioners, Austin Area Infection Control Com. Home: 3605 Ripple Creek Dr Austin TX 78746 Office: St David's Hosp 919 E 32d St Austin TX 78765

COHEN, BARRY MENDEL, historian; b. Dallas, Feb. 1, 1939; s. Ben and Marjorie Joyce (Novich) C.; B.A., Rice U., 1960; M.A., U. Tex., 1964, Ph.D., 1980; postgrad. (fellow) U. Ill., summer 1974; m. Rosalee Valent-Torres, July 30, 1967. Instr. history Tex. Arts and Industries U., Kingsville, 1965-67; prof. social sci. Chowan Coll., Murfreesboro, N.C., 1969-73; exec. Cohen Candy Co., Dallas, 1973-83; asso. sales mgr. McCraw Candy, 1981-83; owner BMC Brokerage, 1983—; lectr. Richland Coll., Dallas, 1976-77, Mountain View Coll., Dallas, 1977-84, U. Tex. at Dallas, summer 1977; symposium speaker 14th Internat. Genetics Congress, Moscow, 1978; invited speaker John Innes Inst., Norwich, Eng., 1984. Mem. nat. bd. advisers Ad Hoc Com. for Intellectual Freedom. Bd. dirs. Kleberg County Community Action, 1966-67, Chowanoke Area Devel. Assn., 1971. Mem. Am. Hist. Assn., Am. Assn. for Advancement Slavic Studies, AAUP. Democrat. Jewish. Contbr. articles to profl. jours. and newspapers. Home and Office: 3527 Granada St Dallas TX 75205

COHEN, EDWIN SAMUEL, lawyer, educator; b. Richmond, Va., Sept. 27, 1914; s. LeRoy S. and Miriam (Rosenheim) C.; m. Helen Herz, Aug. 31, 1944; children—Edwin C., Roger, Wendy, B.A., U. Richmond, 1933; J.D., U. Va., 1936. Bar: Va. 1935, N.Y. 1937. Assoc. Sullivan Cromwell, N.Y.C., 1936-49; ptnr. Root, Barrett, Cohen Knapp & Smith and predecessor, N.Y.C., 1949-65, counsel, 1965-69; prof. law U. Va., Charlottesville, 1965-68, Joseph M. Hartfield prof., 1968-69, 73-85, prof. law emeritus, 1985—; faculty Ctr. Advanced Studies, 1973-74; asst. sec. treasury for tax policy, 1969-72, under sec. treasury, 1972-73; counsel Covington & Burling, Washington, 1973-77, ptnr., 1977—; mem. and counsel adv. group on corp. taxes Ways and Means Com. Ho. of Reps., 1956-58, mem. adv. cons. on corps. Am. Law Inst. Fed. Income Tax Project, 1949-54, mem. adv. group Fed. Estate and Gift Tax Project, 1964-68; mem. Va. Income Tax Conformity Study Commn., 1970-71; cons. Va. Income Tax Study Commn., 1966-68; mem. adv. group commr. internal revenue, 1967-68. Recipient Alexander Hamilton award Treasury Dept. Mem. Am. Judicature Soc., ABA (chmn. com. on corp. stockholder relationships 1956-58, mem. council 1958-61, chmn. spl. com. on substantive tax reform 1962-63, chmn. spl. con. on formation tax policy 1977—), Va. Bar Assn., D.C. Bar Assn., N.Y. State Bar Assn., Va. Tax. Conf. (planning com. 1965-68, 85—), Assn. Bar City N.Y., N.Y. County Lawyers Assn., Am. Law Inst., Am. Coll. Tax Counsel, U.S. C. of C. (dir., chmn. taxation com. 1979-84), Order of the Coif, Raven Soc., U. Va., Phi Beta Kappa, Omicron Delta Kappa, Pi Delta Epsilon, Phi Epsilon Pi (Nat. Achievement award). Clubs: Broad Street, Farmington, Colonnade, Boar's Head, International (Washington); Capitol Hill, Nat. Lawyers. Home: 104 Stuart Pl Ednam Forest Charlottesville VA 22901

COHEN, EUGENE ERWIN, university and health institute administrator; b. Johnstown, Pa., Nov. 1, 1917; s. Leroy Samuel and Ann (Aronson) C.; B.B.A., U. Miami (Fla.), 1941, M.B.A., 1951; postgrad. Wayne State U., 1944-45, U. N.C., 1951-52; m. Lee Woodard Edmundson, Dec. 31, 1944; children—William Palmer, Margaret Gene, Ann Woodard. Mem. faculty U. Miami, 1945—, assoc. prof. acctg., 1954-67, prof. acctg., 1967-79, prof. emeritus, 1979—, treas., 1957-79, v.p., 1958-79, v.p. emeritus, 1979—; treas. Howard Hughes Med. Inst., 1979—, also treas. univ. Research Found.; v.p., dir. Dormitory Housing Assn., Inc.; chmn., pres. Laurel Corp., 1971-73; dir. chmn. Miami br. Fed. Res. Bank, 1983, 85—, dir., 1983—; dir. Am. Bankers Ins. Co. Fla., Am. Laser Corp., Garrett & Co., Garrett Trust; stockholder's agt. Fla. Fed. Savs. and Loan Assn.; cons. Greyhound Corp., Plastetics, Inc., Reynolds & Co., NSF, NIH, U.S. Office Edn., So. Assn. Colls. and Schs., J.L. Mailman Found., A.L. Mailman Family Found.; rep. Univ. Corp. for Atmospheric Research, 1969-73; mem. com. taxation Am. Council Edn. Pres., Orange Bowl Com., mem., 1950—; asso. mem. Internat. Center Coral Gables, 1973—, also New World Center at Miami Com.; mem. Miami Mayor's Spl. Adv. Com. on Interama, 1969-72; bd. dirs. Miami Goodwill Industries, Dade County Citizens Safety Council, Greater Miami Indsl. Commn.; chmn. Dade County Higher Edn. Facilities Authority, 1969-81, Jackson Found., 1972—; vice chmn. bd. Nat. Children's Cardiac Hosp.; mem. Health Systems Agency of S. Fla.; bd. dirs. Family Services, Miami, 1968-74, Heart Learning Resources Center; trustee United Way Dade County, White Belt Found. Served to maj. U.S. Army, 1941-45. Recipient Disting. Alumni award U. Miami, 1961, Disting. Grad. Alumnus award, 1963. Mem. Dade County C. of C., Am. Mgmt. Assn., Nat. Assn. Coll. and Univ. Bus. Officers (dir.), So. Assn. Coll. and Univ. Bus. Officers (pres. 1963), Coll. and Univ. Personnel Assn., Coll. and Univ. Housing Officers Assn., Nat. Assn. Cost Accts., Fin. Execs. Inst. (founder mem. Fla. chpt., chpt. pres. 1963), Fin. Analysts Soc. Miami, Econ. Soc. S. Fla., Miami Beach Com. of 100, Hist. Assn. So. Fla. (dir.), The Miamians, Coral Gables Com. of 21, Friends of Univ. Library, Newcomen Soc., Iron Arrow, Omicron Delta Kappa, Alpha Phi Omega, Phi Mu Alpha, Alpha Kappa Psi, Beta Gamma Sigma. Clubs: Univ. Yacht, Miami; Ocean Reef Yacht and Country (Key Largo, Fla.). Cons. editor Coll. and Univ. Bus. Mag., 1963-68. Author articles in field. Home: 6700 SW 117th St Miami FL 33156 Office: Howard Hughes Med Inst PO Box 330837 Coconut Grove FL 33133

COHEN, GETTYS, JR., dentist; b. Spartanburg, S.C., Feb. 14, 1944; s. Gettys and Lula Mae (Foster) C.; m. Shirley O'Neal, June 15, 1968; children—Johnathan Ashley, Christopher Brian. B.S., Benedict Coll., 1966; postgrad., S.C. State Coll., 1966-67, Wofford Coll., 1968-69; D.D.S., Howard U., 1974. Tchr. Spartanburg City Schs., 1966-70; instr. Coll. Dentistry, Howard U., Washington, 1974-76; pvt. practice dentistry, Washington, 1974-76, Smithfield, N.C., 1976—; assoc. dir. dentistry Cherry Hosp., Goldsboro, N.C., 1976-84; dir. dentistry Eastern Regional Dept. Corrections, Maury, N.C., 1984—, N.C. Dept. Corrections, Maury, 1984—; career cons. Johnston County Schs., Smithfield, 1978—. Mem. Johnston County Citizens Assn., Smithfield, 1978—; chmn. bd. trustees St. John Ch., Selma, N.C., 1981—. Served with USN, 1963-71. Howard U. scholar, 1972. Mem. ADA, Nat. Dental Assn., N.C. Dental Assn., Oral Cancer Soc., Old North State Dental Soc. (com. chmn. 1985), Omega Psi Phi (sec. 1983-85), Chi Delta Mu. Democrat. Methodist. Club: Progressive Men's (Smithfield). Lodge: Masons. Avocations: biking; fishing; tennis; gardening. Home: 3 Aspen Dr Smithfield NC 27577 Office: Hwy 301 N Smithfield NC 27577

COHEN, HARVEY STUART, architect; b. Florence, S.C., Dec. 17, 1951; s. Leonard Barry and Mildred (Friedman) C.; m. Sara Jane Lundin, Sept. 21, 1975; 1 child, Lauren Elizabeth. B.A., Washington U., St. Louis, 1974; M.Arch., Ga. Inst. Tech., 1980. Registered architect, Ga., Nat. Council Archtl. Registration Bds. Planner, Space Mgmt. Cons., Seattle, 1975-80; architect Heery Internat., Atlanta, 1980-83; project mgr. Odell Assocs., Charlotte, N.C., 1983-85; project mgr. Wilkerson Assocs., Inc., Charlotte, N.C., 1985—; com. mem. Architect for Health, Washington, 1983—. Mem. AIA, Am. Assn. Hosp. Planners, Environ. Design/Research in Architect. Democrat. Avocations: running; camping; traveling. Office: Wilkerson Assocs Inc Suite 160 2 Parkway Plaza Charlotte NC 28210

COHEN, KATTY WEINER, gerontologist, consultant, counselor; b. Santiago, Chile, July 16, 1949; came to U.S., 1969, naturalized, 1975; d. Bernat K. and Lidia Weiner; children—Emily Beth, Gail Marie. B.A., Ohio Dominican Coll., 1971; M.S., Nova U., 1981. Lic. mental health counselor, Fla. Counselor V State of Ohio Manpower Tng. Ctr., Columbus, 1972-73; dir. vols. Heritage House, Jewish Nursing Home, Columbus, 1975-76; asst. activities dir. Boca Raton Convalescent Ctr., Fla., 1977-78; social services dir., activities coordinator St. Andrews Estates Nursing Home, Boca Raton, 1979-81; counselor The South Florida Geriatric Ctr., Boca Raton, 1981-82; exec. dir., v.p. Nat. Adult Enrichment Ctr., Boca Raton, 1982-84; gerontologist Adult Care Cons., Boca Raton, 1984—; adj. prof. Coll. of Boca Raton, 1985—; cons. to Alzeihmers groups and children of aging parents support groups, nursing homes and retirement communities. Mem. Gerontol. Soc. Am., Fla. Geriatric Assn., Am. Assn. Counseling Devel., Nat. Council on Aging. Nat. Inst. Adult Day Care, Fla. Assn. Adult Day Care, Fla. Council on Aging, Fla. Health Care Assn. Jewish. Office: Adult Care Cons Services 6372 La Costa Dr #302 Boca Raton FL 33434

COHEN, LOUIS RALPH, paper company executive; b. Houston, Mar. 30, 1917; s. Leo Moses and Sadie (Kaufmann) C.; m. Reva Dorothy Blinderman, Dec. 21, 1941; children—Diana Louise Cohen Gordon, Lawry Martin. Student pub. schs., Houston. Office boy to v.p. Magnolia Paper Co., Houston, Dallas and Corpus Christi, Tex., 1934-59; asst. mgr. Pollock Paper Co., Houston, 1959-63; mgr. Century Papers, Inc., Dallas, 1963-72; v.p. Kaymac Paper Co., Dallas, 1971-80; corp. mdse. mgr. Pollock Paper Distributors, Dallas, 1980—. Chmn., Dallas Jewish Com. on Scouting; active North Trails Dist., Circle 10 council Boy Scouts Am.; pres. Willow Meadows Civic Club, Houston, 1957; past pres. Temple Shalom, Dallas. Served to capt. M.S.C., U.S. Army, 1942-46. Mem. Southwestern Paper Merchants Assn. (pres.). Club: Rotary (past pres.). Home: 3711 Truesdell Pl Dallas TX 75244 Office: PO Box 660005 Dallas TX 75266

COHEN, MARTIN DAVID, psychologist, educator; b. Bklyn., Jan. 24, 1947; s. Norman D. and Millicent (Rome) C.; m. Sara Jane Reisman, Aug. 18, 1968; children—Daniel Adam, Gillian Elizabeth. B.A., Lehigh U., 1968; Ph.D., Temple U., 1976. Mem. psychol. staff Hillsborough Community Mental Health Ctr., Tampa, Fla., 1973-77, dir. community oriented services, 1977-80, chief psychologist, 1979-80; gen. practice in psychology, Tampa, 1977—; co-founder, dir. Suncoast Ctr. Consultation, Edn. and Growth, Tampa, 1980—; clin. dir. The LIFE Center, Tampa, 1981—; co-founder, dir. Suncoast Ctr. for Attitudinal Healing, Tampa, 1981-84; mem. clin. faculty dept. psychiatry U. South Fla. Coll. Medicine, Tampa, 1977-79, mem. adj. faculty dept. psychology, 1980-85; mem. adj. faculty Hillsborough Community Coll. Human Services Program, Tampa, 1980-85; mem. adj. faculty Goddard Grad. program Vt. Coll., Montpelier, 1982—; cons. in field. Mem. health adv. com. Head Start Program, Hillsborough County (Fla.) Policy Council, 1977-82; bd. dirs. Community Council on Child Abuse and Neglect, 1978-83, v.p., 1981-82; mem. adv. bd., tng. cons. Rape Crisis Ctr., 1979—; mem. Hillsborough-Manatee (Fla.) Dist. Human Rights Advocacy Com., 1982-84. Recipient Outstanding Service award Hillsborough County Head Start Program, 1980; NIMH fellow Temple U., 1972. Mem. Am. Psychol. Assn., Fla. Psychol. Assn. (exec. council 1978-84, pres. pub. service div. 1980-84). Lectr. to profl. confs., seminars and workshops; developer: model program in mental health prevention, 1979; prepared parenthood course, Tampa, 1981; co-producer Options for Living, TV programs, Tampa, 1981-82. Home: 510 Crestover Dr Temple Terrace FL 33617 Office: 5035 E Busch Blvd #6 Tampa FL 33617

COHEN, MEREDITH JOSEPH, lawyer; b. Orlando, Fla., Aug. 3, 1929; s. Barney J. and Dorothy (Collman) C.; m. Audrey E. Mayer, Mar. 11, 1956; children—Robert, Wendy, Jennifer, Arthur. B.S. with honors, U. Fla., 1950, J.D., 1952. Bar: Fla. 1952, U.S. Supreme Ct. 1964; cert. marital and family law Fla. Bar. Asst. pros. atty. State of Fla., 1955-59, 65-69; sole practice, Orlando, Fla., 1960-65, 69—; adj. prof. law office mgmt. Valenicia Community Coll., 1978-81. Served as 1st lt. JAGC, AUS, 1952-55. Decorated Bronze Star. Fellow Am. Acad. Matrimonial Lawyers; mem. ABA, Fla. Bar Assn. (chmn. criminal law sect. 1981-82, exec. council family law sect.), Assn. Trial Lawyers Am., Acad. Fla. Trial Lawyers, Nat. Assn. Criminal Def. Lawyers, Orange County Bar Assn. (chmn. family law sect. 1982-83). Jewish. Clubs: Toastmasters Internat., Shriners. Office: Suite 516 Bradshaw Bldg 14 E Washington St Orlando FL 32801

COHEN, PINYA, microbiologist; b. Burlington, Vt., Dec. 23, 1935; married; 1 child. B.S., Delaware Valley Coll., 1953; M.S., U. Ga., 1959; Ph.D., Purdue U., 1964. Research microbiologist NIH, Bethesda, Md., 1964-68, chief blood and blood derivatives sect., 1968-72; dir. plasma derivatives br. FDA, Bethesda, Md., 1972-76; dir. quality control and regulatory affairs Merieux Inst., Inc., Miami, Fla., 1976-79, v.p. quality control and regulatory affairs, 1979—, asst. sec., 1977—, asst. treas., 1978—, adv. Univ. without Walls Morgan State Coll., Balt., 1972-74; mem. adv. panel to com. on public-pvt. sector relations in vaccine innovation Nat. Acad. Scis., 1983-84. U. Ga. scholar, 1957; NIH fellow, 1961-64. Mem. AAAS, Am. Soc. Microbiology, Internat. Assn. Biol. Standardization, Internat. Soc. Blood Transfusion, N.Y. Acad. Scis., Sigma. Xi. Contbr. article to profl. jours. Office: Merieux Inst 7855 NW 12th St Suite 114 Miami FL 33126

COHEN, ROBERT STRIB, animal science educator, swine nutritionist, consultant, computer programmer; b. Austin, Tex., Sept. 13, 1943; s. Robert Quincy and Opal (Stribling) C.; m. Jane Elizabeth Watkins, Dec. 2, 1967. B.S., Tex. A&M U., 1965, M.S., 1972, Ph.D., 1975. Cert. animal scientist. Jr. asst. extension agt. Tex. A&M U. System, Tex. Agrl. Extension Service, Georgetown, 1965-66, asst. county agrl. agt., Eastland, 1966-69; grad. asst. dept. animal sci. Tex. A&M U., 1970-74, asst. prof. continuing edn. depts. animal sci. and agrl. edn., 1974-78, extension swine specialist Tex. Agrl. Extension Service, Lubbock, 1979—. Served with USAFR, 1965-71. Recipient Disting. Service award Vocat. Agrl. Tchrs. Assn. Tex., 1978; Nat. 4-H Club Congress scholar, 1961. Mem. Am. Soc. Animal Sci., Tex. Agrl. Extension Service Specialists Assn. (chpt. dir. 1981-82, sec. 1983), Am. Farm Bur. Fedn., Tex. Farm Bur. Fedn., Lubbock County Farm Bur. Fedn., Lubbock C. of C. (chmn. livestock industry com. 1983, chmn. agrl. ambassadors 1984), 4-H Club (10 yr. award 1963), Aircraft Owners and Pilots Assn., Lubbock Agr. Club, Lubbock Computer Club; assoc. mem. Nat. Pork Producers Assn., Tex. Pork Producers Assn., West Tex. Pork Producers Assn. Lodge: Masons. Columnist, S.W. Farm Press; contbr. articles to profl. jours. Home: 5609 70th St Lubbock TX 79424 Office: Tex Agrl Extension Service Tex A&M U Route 3 Box 213AA Lubbock TX 79401

COHEN, STEPHEN IRA, lawyer, state senator; b. Memphis, May 24, 1949; s. Morris David and Genevieve (Goldsand) C. B.A., Vanderbilt U., 1971; J.D., Memphis State U., 1973. Bar: Tenn. 1974. Sole practice, 1974-75; legal advisor Memphis Police Dept., 1975-78; mem. Shelby County Commn., 1978-80; sole practice, Memphis, 1978—; mem. Tenn. Senate, 1982—; interim judge Gen. Sessions Ct., 1980; v.p. Tenn. Constnl. Conv., 1977; del. Democratic Nat. Conv., 1980. Mem. Memphis-Shelby County Bar Assn., Memphis-Shelby County Trial Lawyers Assn., Wolf River Soc. Home and office: 178 S McLean St Apt 1 Memphis TN 38104

COHN, DAVID MARK, physician; b. N.Y.C., Apr. 8, 1953; s. Gerald and Irene (Koplin) C. B.A., SUNY-Albany, 1975; M.D., U. Miami, 1982. Intern in ob/gyn Jackson Meml. Hosp., Miami, Fla., 1982-83, intern in internal medicine, 1983-84, resident in internal medicine, 1984-86; practice. internal medicine, Miami, Fla., 1982—. Mem. ACP, Dade County Med. Assn. Democrat. Jewish. Avocations: sports; dogs; reading; travel. Home: 7515 SW 54th Ave Miami FL 33143 Office: Jackson Meml Hosp Dept Medicine Miami FL 33136

COHN, ROBIN JEAN, public relations executive, consultant; b. Portsmith, Va., Oct. 18, 1952; d. Murry and Mildred (Shachtman) Cohn. B.A. magna cum laude (Pres.'s scholar), Temple U., 1974. Dir., David Gary Ltd., Ft. Lauderdale, Fla., 1974-75; advt. mgr. Tamarac Topic (Fla.), 1975-76; dir. pub. relations Biscayne Med. Ctr., Miami, Fla., 1976-78; staff v.p. Air Fla., Miami, 1978-84, Alamo Rent A Car, 1984—; guest lectr. U. Miami. Mem. pub. relations com. Miami's For Me, 1982, 83, host com., 1983; active Leadership Miami, 1982-85, Miami Forum, 1981—, Fla. Tourism Adv. Council, 1983—; bd. dirs. Miami City Ballet, 1985—, Project Horizon, 1986—; mem. pub. relations com. Broward County Arts Council, 1984—. Mem. Aviation and Space Writers Assn., Soc. Am. Travel Writers. Office: Alamo Rent A Car PO Box 22776 Fort Lauderdale FL 33335

COIT, ROBERT DANIEL, lawyer; b. Enterprise, Miss., Mar. 31, 1930; s. Robert Edwin and Faye (Armstrong) C.; student Meridian Jr. Coll., 1947-49; B.S., Miss. State Coll., 1952; LL.B., U. Miss., 1956; m. Elna Faye Haden, Aug. 2, 1959; children—Lauren Faye, Linda Ann, Nancy Margaret, Edwin Daniel. Admitted to Miss. bar. 1956; since practiced in Meridian, mem. firm Huff & Williams, 1956-62, gen. practice, 1962—. Mem. Selective Service Bd., 1965-75; incorporator, pres. Lamar Sch. Found., 1964-72; trustee Beauvoir, 1976-78, bd. dirs., 1979—, pres., 1979-80; bd. dirs. Beauvoir Devel. Found. Served to lt. AUS, 1952-54; capt. Res. Col. on Gov.'s Staff, 1972-76. Mem. Miss. State, Lauderdale County bar assns., Miss. Forestry Assn., Phi Alpha Delta, SCV (comdr. Miss. div. 1976-78, Tenn. dept. 1980-81), Miss. Pvt. Sch. Assn. (dir. 1965-77), Miss. Hist. Soc., Am. Legion. Presbyterian. Masons (treas.). Home: 2305 36th Ave Meridian MS 39305 Office: Lamar Bldg Meridian MS 39302

COKE, C(HAUNCEY) EUGENE, consulting company executive, scientist, educator, author; b. Toronto, Ont., Can.; s. Chauncey Eugene and Edith May (Redman) C.; B.Sc. cum laude in Chemistry, U. Man., also M.Sc. magna cum laude; M.A., U. Toronto; postgrad. Yale U.; Ph.D., U. Leeds, Eng., 1938; m. Sally B. Tolmie, June 12, 1941. Dir. research Courtaulds (Can.) Ltd., 1939-42; dir. research and devel. Guaranty Dyeing & Finishing Co., 1946-48; various exec. research and devel. positions Courtaulds (Can.) Ltd., Montreal, 1948-59; dir. research and devel., mem. exec. com. Hart-Fibres Co., 1959-62; tech. dir. textile chem. Drew Chem. Corp., 1962-63; dir. new products fibers div. Am. Cyanamid Co., 1963-68, dir. application devel., 1968-70; pres. Coke & Assos. Consultants, 1970-78, chmn., 1978—; pres. Aqua Vista Corp. Inc., 1971-74; vis. research prof. Stetson U., 1979—. Vice chmn. North Peninsula adv. bd. Volusia County Council, 1975-78; bd. dirs. Council of Assns. of N. Peninsula, 1972-74, 76-77; mem. Halifax Area Study Commn., 1972-75. Served from 2d lt. to maj. RCAF, 1942-46. Recipient bronze medal Can. Assn. Textile Colourists and Chemists, 1963. Fellow Royal Soc. Chemistry (life) (Gt. Britain), Textile Inst. (Gt. Britain), Soc. Dyers and Colourists (Gt. Britain), Inst. Textile Sci. (co-founder, 3d pres.), Chem. Inst. Can. (life), AAAS, N.J. Acad. Sci., Am. Inst. Chemists; mem. Am. Assn. Textile Technology (life, past pres., recipient Bronze medal 1971), Can. Assn. Textile Colourists and Chemists (past pres., hon. life), N.Y. Acad. Scis. (life), Fla. Acad. Scis. Clubs: Greater Daytona Beach Republican Men's (pres. 1972-75), Rep. Pres.'s Forum (pres. 1976-78, v.p. 1978—), The Chemist's. Author articles in field. Home: 26 Aqua Vista Dr Ormond Beach FL 32074 Office: Ormond by the Sea FL 32074

COKER, CHARLES W., JR., oil company executive; b. 1933. B.A., Princeton U., 1955; M.B.A., Harvard U., 1957. With Sonoco Products Co., 1958—, v.p. adminstrn., 1961-66, exec. v.p., 1966-70, pres., chief exec. officer, 1970—; dir. NCNB Corp., First Fed. Savs. & Loan Assn., N.C. Nat. Bank. Served with USAR, 1957-63. Address: Sonoco Products Co Inc N Second St Hartsville SC 29550*

COKER, CYNTHIA CAROLE, dance educator, artistic director; b. Hugoton, Kan., Dec. 18, 1952; d. Kenneth and Mildred (Gaskill) Greenwood; m. Chester Cross Coker, Aug. 2, 1980; children—Chester Ehren, Kenneth Clifton. B.F.A., So. Meth. U., 1973, M.F.A., 1975. Faculty communications dept. Pan Am. U., Edinburg, Tex., 1976—, choreographer summer stock theatre, 1976—; owner, dir., tchr. Edinburg Dance Acad., 1977—; owner, dir. Cynthia Coker & Co., Dance Acad., 1982—; artistic dir., founder Edinburg Dance Theatre, 1978—; choreographer Pan Am. U. Opera and Musical Theatre prodns. Mem. Nat. Assn. for Regional Ballet. Republican. Presbyterian. Office: 225 S Closner St Edinburg TX 78539

COKER, THOMAS M., JR., judge; b. Hialeah, Fla., Feb. 25, 1926; s. Thomas M. and Mary Thelma (Lansford) C.; m. Norma L. Albrektsen, July 2, 1949; children—Terry Ann Monroe, Cynthia Lee, Thomas Nielsen. B.B.A., J.D., U. Miami. Practice law, Broward County, Fla., 1955-76; county solicitor, 1955-66; pub. defender Broward County, 1966-67; judge Circuit Ct., Ft. Lauderdale, 1977—. Served with USN, 1943-46. Mem. Fla. Bar Assn. Lodge: Elks (pres. Fla. assn. 1984-85). Office: Broward County Courthouse 201 SE 6th St Suite 910 Fort Lauderdale FL 33301

COLBERG, EDWIN J., financial analyst, communications company executive; b. San Juan, P.R., Jan. 14, 1950; s. Edwin J. Colberg-Ramírez and Carmen García; B.B.A., U. P.R., 1971; M.B.A., Interam. U., 1972; m. Mildred Amador, July 22, 1972; children—Andrew F., Eugene J. Asst. to credit mgr. Puerto Rican Cement, San Juan, 1972-73; fin. planning mgr. ITT Caribbean Mfg. Co., San Juan, 1973-75; asst. comptroller ITT Bus. Communications Corp., Río Piedras, 1976-79, comptroller, 1979—. Mem. Nat. Assn. Accts., Assn. M.B.A. Execs., P.R. Fin. Analysts Assn. Home: E-7 4th St Montebello Estates Trujillo Alto PR 00760 Office: Rd 1 Km 14.1 Río Piedras PR 00926

COLBERT, ROBERT B., JR., apparel company executive; b. Columbus, Ga., Sept. 24, 1921; s. Robert B. and Mae (Hindsman) C.; student Emory U., U. Ga.; m. Margaret Moore, Mar. 22, 1942; children—Margaret, Bert, John. Chmn. bd., dir. Wayne-Gossard Corp., Chattanooga; chmn. bd., dir. Signal Knitting Mills, Chattanooga, H. W. Gossard Co., Chgo.; dir. Union Planters Nat. Bank Memphis, Union Planters Corp., Memphis. Served with USNR, World War II. Office: 701 Market St Suite 922 Chattanooga TN 37401

COLBOURN, TREVOR, university president, historian; b. Armidale, New South Wales, Australia, Feb. 24, 1927; came to U.S., 1948; s. Harold Arthur and Ella Mary (Henderson) C.; m. Beryl Richards Evans, Jan. 10. 1949; children—Katherine Elizabeth, Lisa Sian Elinor. B.A. with honors, U. London, 1948; M.A., Coll. William and Mary, 1949, Johns Hopkins, 1951, Ph.D., 1953. From instr. to asst. prof. Pa. State U., 1952-59; from asst. prof. to prof. Am. history Ind. U., 1959-67; dean Grad. Sch., prof. history U. N.H., 1967-73; v.p. for acad. affairs San Diego State U., 1973-77, acting pres., 1977-78; pres. U. Central Fla., Orlando, 1978—; state rep. Am. Assn. State Colls. and Univs. Author: The Lamp of Experience, 1965, The Colonial Experience, 1966, (with others) The Americans: A Brief History, 1972, 4th edit., 1985; Co-editor: The American Past in Perspective, 1970; editor: Fame and the Founding Fathers, 1974. Mem. Am. Hist. Assn., Orgn. Am. Historians. Home: 207 Ranch Rd Winter Park FL 32792 Office: U Central Fla PO Box 25000 Orlando FL 32816

COLBURN, JAMES ALLAN, lawyer; b. Huntington, W.Va., July 5, 1942; s. Ray S. and Edith Abigail (Blood) C.; m. Virginia Ann Carter, June 19, 1965; children—Heather Lara, Sarah Carter. A.B., Davidson (N.C.) Coll., 1964; J.D., Rutgers U., 1967; postgrad. Marshall U., Austin Peay State U. Bar: W.Va. 1970, U.S. Dist. Ct. (no. and so. dists.) W.Va. 1970, U.S. Ct. Appeals (4th cir.) 1973, U.S. Tax Ct. 1982, U.S. Supreme Ct. 1983. Assoc., Levy & Patton, 1970-72; sole practice, Huntington, W.Va., 1973-75; ptnr. Baer, Napier & Colburn, Huntington, 1975-81; ptnr., pres. Baer, Colburn & Morris, L.C., Huntington, 1981—; instr. legal asst. program Marshall U., 1978-82; lectr. in field. Asst. pros. atty. Cabell County, 1977-79, spl. pros. atty., 1985-86; spl. pros. atty. Nicholas County, W.Va., 1985-86. Served with U.S. Army, 1968-70. Mem. W.Va. Bar Assn., ABA, Assn. Trial Lawyers Am., Union Internat. des-Advocats, Cabell County Bar Assn. (pres. 1960), Nat. Assn. Dist. Attys. Democrat. Presbyterian. Office: 731 5th Ave Huntington WV 25701

COLE, BARBARA ANNE, nurse, crisis counselor; b. Waltham, Mass., July 29, 1949; d. George Joseph Sargent and Doris Anne (Holloway) Sargent Sullivan; m. Walter Brayton, Dec. 31, 1972. A.S., Coll. St. Mary, Omaha, 1975; M.S., U. No. Colo., 1982; A.A., Miss. Gulf Coast Jr. Coll., 1983; B.S., U. So. Miss., 1984. Psychiat. nurse Richard Young Meml. Hosp., Omaha, 1975-76; operating room nurse Moore Meml. Hosp., Pinehurst, N.C., 1976-77; research nurse Urological Assocs. So. Ariz., Tucson, 1977-79, nursing adminstrn., 1979-81; ICU/CCU nurse Gulf Coast Community Hosp., Biloxi, Miss., 1981-82; med./surg. nurse Garden Park Community Hosp., Gulfport, Miss., 1982—. Sr. assembly rep. U. So. Miss., Hattiesburg, 1983—. Served with USAF, 1968-72; capt. Res., 1972—. Decorated Air Res. Forces Meritorious Service medal, Armed Forces Res. medal, Air Force Commendation. Mem. Am. Nurses Assn., Nat. Students Nurses Assn., Miss. Nurses Assn., Res. Officers Assn. U.S., U.S. Olympic Soc., Nat. League POW-MIA Families, Ctr. Environ. Edn., Animal Protection Inst., Ariz. Sonora Desert Museum, Sigma Theta Tau. Republican. Baptist. Office: Garden Park Community Hosp 1501 45th Ave Gulfport MS 39501

COLE, CAROLYN LEE, oil company executive; b. Mpls., Sept. 25, 1943; d. Robert Stanford and Audrey Jean (Gabrielson) Coe; m. Kynn Monroe Cole, Aug. 15, 1964; 1 son, Christopher Kynn. B.A., U. Tex., 1966. Owner, pub. Ridgewood News, Garland, Tex., 1970-73; asst. corp. sec. Xenerex Corp., Dallas, 1979—. Bd. dirs. Dallas County Heritage Soc., 1978-82; mem. parks and recreation com. Goals for Dallas, 1976—; mem. women's com. Dallas Ballet, 1982—, Dallas Theater Ctr., 1981—; mem. Dallas Civic Opera, 1982—. Mem. Gamma Phi Beta, Republican. Lutheran. Club: Willow Bend. Office: Xenerex Corp 3400 Southland Ctr 400 N Olive Dallas TX 75201

COLE, CLYDE CURTIS, JR., association executive; b. Ft. Smith, Ark., May 4, 1932; s. Clyde Curtis and Alta Mae (Lasater) C.; m. Marcia Anne Johnson, Nov. 25, 1953 (div. 1973); children—Clyde Curtis, Deborah Dianne, Douglas Scott, Mark Johnson; m. Joyce L. Ruis, July, 1974. Asso. in Arts and Scis., Northeastern A. and M. Coll., Miami, Okla., 1952; B.A. in History, Econs. and Polit. Sci., Eastern N.Mex. U., Portales, 1954; postgrad., U. N.Mex. Coll. Law, 1954-55; grad., Inst. Organizational Mgmt., U. Colo., 1965. Mgr. Guymon (Okla.) C. of C., 1955-57; asst. dir., exec. dir. Okla. Devel. Council, Oklahoma City, 1957-59; dir. Indsl. Devel. Commn., Columbia, S.C.; and mgr. indsl. dept. Columbia C. of C., 1959-61; exec. dir. Greater Enid (Okla.) C. of C., 1961-65, South Bend-Mishawaka Area C. of C., Ind., 1965-67; exec. v.p. Met. Tulsa C. of C., 1967—; pres. Industries for Tulsa, Inc.; faculty Insts. Orgn. Mgmt., U. Colo., 1964, 65, 69-72, U. Ga., 1971, 75, Tex. Christian U., 1971-72, Santa Clara U., 1971-72, Mich. State U., 1972, So. Meth. U., 1975-76; Mem. Gov's Econ. Adv. Council, 1963-65. 1st v.p., bd. dirs. Okla. Good Rds. and Sts. Assn., 1962-65; sec.-treas. So. Indsl. Devel. Council, 1963-64, Econ. Devel. Commn., Tulsa, 1969—; mem. Tulsa Indsl. Authority, 1969—; mem. dean's adv. council Tulsa U., 1972-76; mem. Okla. Citizen's Adv. Council on Goals for Higher Edn.; bd. dirs. Ark. Basin Devel. Assn., Jr. Achievement of Greater Tulsa, Indian Nations Council of Govts.; bd. regents Insts. Orgn. Mgmt. Mem. Am. C. of C. Execs. Assn. (past chmn., mem. bd., sr. counselor), So. Assn. C. of C. Execs. (past pres.), Okla. C. of C. Execs. (past pres.). Home: 4305 S Birmingham Ave Tulsa OK 74105 Office: 616 S Boston Ave Tulsa OK 74119

COLE, JOHN L., JR., city official; b. Johnstown, Pa., Nov. 8, 1928; s. John L. and Susie L. (Stamper) C.; divorced; 1 dau., Keia D. Student U. Buffalo, 1956-58; diploma Bryant & Stratton Bus. Inst., Buffalo, 1960. Exec. asst. City of Cleve., 1966-69, compliance officer, 1969-72; asst. to gen. mgr. for equal employment opportunity Met. Atlanta Rapid Transit Authority, 1972—. Bd. dirs. Cleve. Urban League, 1971 (Outstanding Service award 1971). Served with U.S. Army, 1951-53; Korea. Recipient Meritorious Pub. Service award NAACP, 1971; Cleve. City Council resolution, 1973, Berkeley G. Burrell Pvt. Sector award Nat. Bus. League. rMem. Am. Pub. Transit Assn. (chmn. minority affairs com. 1975-80), Com. To Increase Minority Profls. Engring. and Architecture, Greater Cleve. Growth Assn. (dir.), Conf. Minority Transp. Ofcls. (Ann. Sibling award 1980). Home: 2691 Laurens Circle Atlanta GA 30311

COLE, MARK JULIAN, psychologist; b. Alexandria, La., Nov. 1, 1955; s. Henry Buford Jr. and Bernice Pauline (Beavers) C.; m. Janice Lynn Haynes, June 16, 1979. B.A. in Psychology, Northeast La. U., Monroe, 1978, M.S. in Clin. Psychology, 1982. Intern, Delhi Guest Home, La., 1982; dir sch. psychology Union Parish Sch. Bd., Farmerville, La., 1982-83; program dir. Westside Habilitation Ctr., Cheneyville, La., 1983—. Mem. Am. Psychol. Assn., La. State U. Alumni Fedn. Republican. Methodist. Avocations: music; photography; fishing. Home: PO Box 427 Ball LA 71405 Office: Westside Habilitation Ctr Boyd at Klock St Cheneyville LA 71325

COLE, MICHAEL HENRY, rental car executive; b. Atlanta, Oct. 5, 1943; s. Todd Godwin and Inez (Hamilton) C.; m. Linda Carol Hanson, Feb. 3, 1968; 1 son, Todd Godwin. B.E.E., U. Fla., 1965; M.B.A., Fla. Atlantic U., 1970. Registered profl. engr., Fla.; C.P.A., Fla. Systems analysis engr. Systems Engr. Labs., Ft. Lauderdale, 1965-69; v.p. fin. Data Research, Ft. Lauderdale, 1970-71; mgr. cargo acctg. Eastern Airlines, Miami, Fla., 1972-80; v.p. fin. and treas. Alamo Rental Car, Inc., Ft. Lauderdale, 1980—. Mem. Am. Inst. C.P.A.s, Fla. Soc. C.P.A.s. Republican. Lutheran. Club: Ft. Lauderdale Country. Office: Alamo Rent A Car Inc 1401 S Federal Hwy Fort Lauderdale FL 33335

COLE, NANCY BERKEY, theater educator and director; b. Bklyn., July 9, 1936; d. Gerald Kirk and Jessie McMurray (Mincher) Berkey; m. Stephen R. Cole, May 17, 1958 (div.); children—Paula Murray and Leslie Jordan (twins). A.B. magna cum laude, Ind. U., 1959; M.F.A. in Acting, U. Iowa, 1964. Instr. English dept. U. Nebr., 1964-66; instr. theatre dept. Cornell U., Ithaca, N.Y., lectr./specialist music dept. Ithaca Coll., 1970-74; actress, dir. Ithaca Summer Repertory, Dartmouth Coll. Summer Repertory, Hanover, N.H., Front St. Theatre, Memphis, Ledges Playhouse, Grand Ledge, Mich. and Lincoln, Nebr., 1970-75; asst. prof. theatre Washington U., St. Louis, 1974-76; assoc. prof., chmn. dept. theatre U. South Fla., Tampa, 1976—, prof., 1982—, producer theatre, related programs, dance concerts Coll. Fine Arts TV Series (on adminstrv. leave, N.Y.C., 1984-85); dir. Hangar Theatre, Ithaca, N.Y., Cornell Savoyards, Ithaca, Palisades Theatre, St. Petersburg, Fla. Chief researcher Introduction to the Theatre (Oscar Brockett), 1962-63. Woodrow Wilson fellow, 1958-59; recipient nat., regional awards Am. Coll. Theatre Festival, 1979-80, 81-82; Washington U. research grantee, summer 1975. Mem. Am. Theatre Assn. (chmn. N.Y. conv. Women in Theatre 1982), Dramatists Guild (assoc.), Tampa Athena Soc., Phi Beta Kappa. Democrat. Episcopalian. Office: Dept Theatre U So Fla Tampa FL 33620

COLE, PATRICIA NEAL, medical librarian, consultant; b. Bear, Del., May 30, 1941; d. Taylor McKinney and Lillian Marie (Kohler) Neal; m. William Lee Cole, June 13, 1964; 1 dau., Lynn Marie. Circulation asst. E.I. Dupont DeNemours & Co., Newark, Del., 1960-64, U. Tenn., Knoxville, 1964-65; med. librarian Fla. Hosp., Orlando, 1972-82, Winter Park (Fla.) Meml. Hosp., 1982—; lectr. U. Central Fla., 1975-83; cons. Orlando Regional Med. Ctr. Library, S. Lake Meml. Hosp. Library, S. Seminole Hosp. Library, Longwood, Fla., 1984, Lake Wales Hosp. Assn., Inc., 1985, 86. Fund raiser Fla. Symphony Youth Orch., Orlando, 1982. Mem. Med. Library Assn., So. Regional Med. Library Assn., Central Fla. Library Assn., Southeastern Conf. Hosp. Librarians, Fla. Health Scis. Library Assn. (treas. 1976, program coordinator 1977, membership chmn. 1978), Winter Park Med. History Soc. (bd. dirs. 1986). Home: 2415 Sherbrooke Rd Winter Park FL 32792 Office: Med Staff Library Winter Park Meml Hosp 200 N Lakemont Winter Park FL 32792

COLE, RICHARD LOUIS, university dean, educator; b. Dallas, Jan. 25, 1946; s. Louis Ray and Mary Francis (Steely) C.; m. Pamela June Jacobs, Nov. 21, 1968; children—Jonathan, Ashley. B.A., North Tex. State U., 1967, M.A., 1968; Ph.D., Purdue U., 1973. Asst. prof. George Washington U., Washington, 1973-78, assoc. prof., 1978-79; research scholar Yale U., New Haven, 1979-80; prof. polit. sci. U. Tex.-Arlington, 1980—, dean Inst. Urban Studies, 1980—; cons. in field. Author: Citizen Participation, 1974; Introduction to Political Inquiry, 1980; Politics and Policy Making in Texas, 1986; Urban Life in Texas,

1986; also articles. Active Leadership Arlington, 1980, Accent Arlington, 1981—; council mem. Boy Scouts Am., Arlington, 1985. Mem. S.W. Polit. Sci. Assn. (v.p. 1983-84), Am. Polit. Sci. Assn., Southwestern Social Sci. Assn. Democrat. Methodist. Home: 704 Tanglewood St Arlington TX 76012 Office: Inst Urban Studies U Tex-Arlington PO Box 19588 Arlington TX 76019

COLE, ROBERT BATES, lawyer; b. Scarborough, Eng., Feb. 9, 1911; s. William and Mary Elizabeth (Bates) C.; brought to U.S., 1911, naturalized, 1914; A.B., U. Fla., 1932, J.D., 1935; m. Frances Lee Arnold, June 23, 1937; children—Charles Robert, George Thomas, Richard Phillip. Admitted to Fla. bar, 1935, since practiced in Miami; mem. firm Mershon, Sawyer, Johnston, Dunwody & Cole, Miami, Fla., from 1946, now of counsel; sec., dir. Major Appliances, Inc., Miami, 1953—, Lennar Corp., Miami, 1969—, chmn. exec. com., gen. counsel, 1984—; sec., treas., dir. Fla. Dairy Producers Coop., Orlando, 1962—. Pres. 200 Club Greater Miami, 1986. Trustee Bapt. Hosp. Miami, Inc. Mem. Nat. Assn. Coll. and Univ. Attys., Am., Dade County bar assns., Fla. Bar, Phi Delta Phi, Sigma Chi. Baptist. Clubs: Miami; Riviera Country (past pres.) (Coral Gables, Fla.). Home: 2301 Alhambra Circle Coral Gables FL 33134 Office: Southeast Financial Ctr 4500 Miami FL 33131

COLEMAN, ALAN BROUSE, financial management educator; b. San Francisco, Jan. 11, 1929; s. Alan Brouse and Hazel Virginia (Deane) C.; m. Janet M. Saville, July 4, 1953; children—Kathleen, Frances Jennifer. B.A., U. San Francisco, 1952; M.B.A., Stanford U., 1956, Ph.D., 1960. Mem. faculty Grad. Sch. Bus., Harvard U., 1958-62, Stanford U. Grad. Sch. Bus., 1962-70; dean ESAN, Lima, Peru, 1963-66; v.p., treas. U.S. Natural Resources, Inc., 1970-71; pres., chief exec. officer Yosemite Park and Curry Co., Calif., 1971-73; pres., chief adminstrv. officer Sun Valley Co., Idaho, 1973-74; Caruth Prof. fin. mgmt. So. Meth. U., Dallas, 1974—, dean Edwin L. Cox Sch. Bus., 1975-81, pres. Southwestern Grad. Sch. of Banking Found., 1980—; cons. Treas., trustee Family Service Assn. Mis-Peninsula; mem. adv. bd. East Palo Alto br. Bank Am.; bd. dirs. Stanford Credit Union; mem. adv. bd. Amigos de las Americas, Houston; treas. Dallas United Nations Assn.; active Salvation Army, Dallas; mem. adv. council Dallas Community Chest Trust Fund; adv. dir. Army and Air Force Exchange Service World Hdqrs., Dallas. Served to 1st lt. U.S. Army, 1952-54. Recipient Palmas Magisteriales, Orden de Commendador (Peru); Ford Found. fellow, 1956-57; Am. Numis. Soc. fellow, 1980—. Mem. Fin. Mgmt. Assn., Fin. Execs. Inst., Am. Fin. Assn., Beta Gamma Sigma. Author: (with Hempel and Simonson) Bank Management: Text and Cases, 1983; (with Robichek) Management of Financial Institutions, 1967, 77; (with Vandell) Case Problems in Finance, 1962; (with Marks) Cases in Commerical Bank Management, 1962. Home: 4253 Rickover Circle Dallas TX 75234 Office: 6211 W Northwest Hwy Suite 2906 Dallas TX 75225

COLEMAN, BEN LEWIS, funeral director; b. Metter, Ga., July 20, 1936; s. Bascom Anthony and Gladys (Mercer) C.; A.A., Allan Hancock Jr. Coll., 1960; grad. Dallas Coll. Mortuary Sci., 1964; m. Shirley Diann Hardee, Nov. 24, 1955; 1 son, Mark Andrew. With Ed C. Smith & Bro. Funeral Home, Dallas, 1964-66; intern, funeral dir. East Funeral Home, Texarkana, Tex., 1966-68; gen. mgr. Ed C. Smith Funeral Home, 1973-82; gen. mgr., dir. ops. Ware-Crest, Inc., Ft. Worth, 1982-84, v.p., 1984—; lectr. in field. Served with USAF, 1955-63. Mem. Nat. Funeral Dirs. Assn., Tex. Funeral Dirs. Assn., Dallas County Funeral Dirs. Assn., East Dallas C. of C. (dir. 1982-83), Internat. Order Golden Rule, Mu Sigma Alpha. Club: Rotary. Home: 9136 Bretshire Dallas TX 75228 Office: 4419 Samuel Blvd Dallas TX 75228

COLEMAN, BRYAN DOUGLAS, lawyer, corporate executive, educator; b. Texarkana, Tex., Aug. 16, 1948; s. William Bryan and Armeda (Crawford) C.; m. Tommye Lou Bettis, Jan. 31, 1984. A.S., Texarkana Coll., 1968; B.S. in B.A., Stephen F. Austin U., 1970; postgrad. Rice U., 1971-73; J.D. (E.E. Townes award, Am. Jurisprudence award), South Tex. Coll. Law, 1973; grad. JAG Sch., U.S. Army, 1978. Bar: Tex. 1973, U.S. Dist. Ct. (so. dist.) Tex. 1974, U.S. Ct. Appeals (11th cir.) 1982, U.S. Ct. Appeals (5th cir.) 1975. Quality control insp. Lone Star Ammunition Plant, Texarkana, 1966-68; law clk. Fulbright & Jaworski, Houston, 1970-71, Boswell, O'Toole, Davis & Pickering, Houston, 1971-72, Helm, Pletcher & Hogan, Houston, 1972-73; assoc. Law Office Gus Zgourides, Houston, 1973-76, Ray & Coleman, P.C., Houston, 1976—; dir. Med. Assurance Group, Houston, 1978—; counsel Gt. SW Life Ins. Co., Houston, 1983—; instr. U. Houston, 1979-81. Mem. Republican Nat. Com., 1983—. Served to comdr. Army ROTC, 1972-73, to 1st lt. U.S. Army, 1973-79. Mem. ABA, State Bar Tex. (founder law student div. 1973, chmn. grievance com. 1979-81), Assn. Trial Lawyers Am., Tex. Trial Lawyers Assn., Am. Judicature Soc., Houston Bar Found., Houston Bar Assn., Alpha Kappa Psi (sec. 1969-70), Alpha Phi Omega (pledge trainer 1970) Delta Theta Phi. Home: 3510 Saratoga Houston TX 77088 Office: 500 Great Southwest Bldg Houston TX 77002

COLEMAN, DON ELDRIDGE, SR., nursing home company and radio executive; b. Fayetteville, W.Va., Apr. 26, 1937; s. Fred Richard and Jessie Wallace (Donnally) C.; m. Naomi E. Deal, May 4, 1957 (div. 1981); children—Pamela Lynn, Denise Crystal, Donald Eldridge. Student Beckley Coll., 1965-68. Sales mgr. Sta. WLOG, Logan, W.Va., 1956-61, Sta. WMON, Montgomery, W.Va., 1965-68; gen. mgr. Wyo. Broadcasting Co., Pineville, W.Va., 1968-76; nat. sales rep. Aken Sign Co., Bluefield, W.Va., 1976-80; adminstr. Mountain Sunset, Inc., Beckley, W.Va., 1980—; controlling stockholder Radio Sta. WLOG, Logan, The DonCo Corp.; dep. commr. W.Va. State Athletic Commn., Charleston, 1968-73; advisor W.Va. Dept. Health, Charleston, 1980-82. Chmn. Wyo. Children's Toy Fund, W.Va., 1969-71. Served with USAF, 1961-65, Korea. Recipient Helping Hand award Wyo. Crippled Children's, 1970, Disting. West Virginian award Gov. of W.Va., 1972. Mem. Assoc. Photographers Internat., Pineville Jaycees (pres. 1969-71). Democrat. Baptist. Club: International. Lodge: Lions. Home: PO Box 1800 Logan WV 25601 Office: Mountain Sunset Inc 118-20 Antonio Ave Beckley WV 25801 also Chestnut and Kanada Sts Logan WV 25601

COLEMAN, FRANK CARTER, physician, educator, pathology and laboratory management consultant; b. Jackson, Miss., May 14, 1915; s. Francis Marion and Emma (Carter) C.; B.A., Miss. Coll., 1935; M.D., Tulane U., 1941; m. Ruth Yvonne Ellzey, Sept. 2, 1937; children—Nancy Ruth (Mrs. James Lujan), Stephen Carter, John Timothy, Jeanne Laurie. Intern Touro Infirmary, New Orleans, 1941-42, resident in pathology, 1942-45, asst. dir. pathology, 1945; practice medicine specializing in pathology, Des Moines, 1945-64, Tampa, Fla., 1964—; dir. labs. Mercy Hosp., Des Moines, 1945-64, Patterson Coleman Labs., Tampa, 1964-77; dir. dept. pathology Centro Asturiano Hosp., Tampa, 1964—, Citrus Meml. Hosp., Inverness, Fla., 1964-76, Hillsborough County Hosp., Tampa, 1964-76, Jackson Meml. Hosp., Dade City, 1965-77, Hardee Meml. Hosp., Wauchula, Fla., 1970-74, Centro Espanol Hosp., Tampa, 1967-77, DeSoto Meml. Hosp., Arcadia, Fla., 1969-77, Community Hosp., New Port Richey, 1971-77, Tarpon Springs (Fla.) Gen. Hosp., 1967-77, West Pasco Hosp., New Port Richey, 1966-77, G. Pierce Wood Meml. Hosp., Arcadia, 1971-77; resident asst. in pathology Sch. Medicine Tulane U., 1942-44, instr. pathology, 1944-45; asst. clin. prof. dept. pathology Coll. Medicine U. Nebr., 1951—; clin. prof. pathology U. South Fla., Tampa, 1972—; med. dir. Southwest Fla. Blood Bank, 1971-75. Mem. Pres.'s Com. Health Services Industry, 1972-73, Gov.'s Community Hosp. Edn. Council, 1971—; mem. subcom. profl., sci. and tech. manpower Nat. Manpower Adv. Com. Dept. Labor, 1973-74; mem. spl. com. nation's health care needs C. of C. U.S., 1977-79. Pres. Gulf Coast Symphony, 1975-76, chmn. Master Bd., 1978-79; bd. dirs. Blue Shield of Fla., 1967-70; bd. dirs. Am. Med. Polit. Action Com., 1960-69, chmn., 1965-67; pres. Fla. Med. Polit. Action Com., 1980—; bd. regents Uniformed Services U. of Health Scis., 1982—, life mem. Pres.'s Council U. South Fla.; bd. fellows U. Tampa, 1980—. Recipient award of merit Iowa Med. Soc., 1957; Sci. Products Found. award for outstanding service to pathology and medicine, 1965; Disting. Service award Am. Soc. Clin. Pathologists and Coll. Am. Pathologists, 1978; spl. award for contbns. and activities in fostering pvt. practice pathology Am. Pathology Found., 1979; diplomate Am. Bd. Pathology (life trustee). Fellow Am. Soc. Clin. Pathologists, Coll. Am. Pathologists (life; govs. 1953-58, pres. 1960-69, mem. nat. legis. com. 1966-69 chmn. council on govt. affairs 1971-78, archivist, historian 1979—, adviser commn. profl. relations 1984—), A.C.P., Am. Coll. Chest Physicians; mem. AMA (chmn. council legislative activities 1963-64, chmn. council health manpower 1972-74, pres. 1984-85, profl. standards rev. orgns. adv. com. 1973-74, awards 1974), Fla. Med. Assn. (chmn. council on legislation 1979-80, exec. com., bd. govs. 1981-82, pres. 1984-85), pres. 1984-85, liaison with Blue Cross/Blue Shield of Fla. 1983—), Hillsborough County Med. Soc. (pres. 1979-80, chmn. membership com. 1966-70, mem. exec. council 1967-70, chmn. pub. service com. 1970-72, del. to Fla. Med. Assn.), Am. Assn. Pathologists and Bacteriologists, Am. Assn. Blood Banks (pres. 1968-69, dir.), Fla. Soc. Pathologists (chmn. ins. com. 1966-68, chmn. com. contractual and profl. ethics 1968-69), Soc. Nuclear Medicine, Am. Soc. Cytology, Fla. Assn. Blood Banks (pres. 1970-71), Internat. Acad. Pathologists, Tampa C. of C. (chmn. air pollution task force 1971-72, chmn. med. sch. com. 1966-67, chmn. health care com. 1969-74, gov. 1974-77), Theta Kappa Psi, Alpha Omega Alpha. Presbyterian. Clubs: Krewe of Venus, University, Carrollwood Village Golf and Tennis, Avila Golf and Country, Rotary. Contbr. articles to profl. jours. Contbg. editor Recent Advances in Clinical Pathology, 1971. Home: 16407 Zurraquin Ct Tampa FL 33612 Office: 4710 N Habana Ave Suite 405 Tampa FL 33614

COLEMAN, GEORGE WILLARD, financial consultant; b. June 11, 1912; married. B.A., U. Ariz., 1934; M.A., Washington U., St. Louis, 1935, Ph.D., 1939. Asst. in econs. Washington U., St. Louis, 1935-39; lectr. econs. Grad. Sch., 1955-59; economist Merc. Trust Co., St. Louis, 1939-66; econ. adviser Am. Bankers Assn., 1966-67, dep. dir., 1967-74; cons. bd. govs. Fed. Res. System, 1974-76; adviser IMF, 1975-80; internat. fin. cons. to various cos. and banks, 1980—. Mem. long-term planning com. Greater St. Louis council Girl Scouts U.S.A., 1962-66. Contbr. articles to publs. in fields of econs. and banking. Mem. Artus, Phi Beta Kappa, Pi Sigma Alpha. Home: 607 Sunset Towers 11 Sunset Dr Sarasota FL 33577

COLEMAN, HOWARD S., government official; b. Everett, Pa., Jan. 10, 1917; s. Howard Soloman and Amy Elizabeth (Ritchey) C.; B.S., Pa. State U., 1938, M.S., 1939, Ph.D. (Grad. fellow), 1942; m. Jeannette Eve, Dec. 29, 1968; children—Michael, Madeline, Tom, Carl. Asst. prof. Pa. State U., State College, 1941-47, dir. optical inspection lab., 1941-47; asso. prof., dir. optical research lab. U. Tex.-Austin, 1947-51; dir. sci. research Bausch & Lomb, Inc., Rochester, N.Y., 1951-54, mgr., v.p. research and engring. 1954-62; head physics research dept., tech. asst. to v.p. Melpar, Inc., Falls Church, Va., part-time, 1964-68; prof. elec. engring., dean Coll. Engring., U. Ariz., Tucson, 1964-68; asst. to pres. Kollsman Instrument Corp., N.Y.C., part-time 1966-68; research engring. scientist Schellenger Research Labs., U. Tex.-El Paso, 1968-69, dir. Spl. Projects Center, 1969-75; dir. Howard S. Coleman & Assos., El Paso, 1968—; spl. asst., program mgr., dep. dir. solar energy div., Energy R&D Adminstrn., Washington, 1976-77; with U.S. Dept. Energy, Washington, 1977—, prin. dep. asst. sec. conservation and renewable energy, 1981-83, dir. solar thermal tech. div., 1983—; cons. to various orgns., 1942-75. Registered profl. engr., Tex., Ariz., Va. Fellow Optical Soc. Am., Rochester Mus. and Sci. Center; mem. Am. Assn. Physics Tchrs., AIAA, Am. Inst. Physics, Am. Geophysics Union, Am. Meteorol. Soc., Am. Phys. Soc., Am. Soc. Engring. Edn., Am. Soc. Metals, Inst. Aero. Scis., Tex. Soc. Profl. Engrs., Nat. Soc. Profl. Engrs., N.Y. Acad. Scis., Soc. Photo-Optical Instrumentation Engrs., Illuminating Engring. Soc., Sigma Xi, Alpha Nu, Pi Mu Epsilon, Sigma Pi Sigma, Delta Sigma Phi. Contbr. numerous articles to publs. Home: 4800 Stanton St El Paso TX 79902 Office: PO Box 26368 El Paso TX 79926 also 1000 Independence Ave Washington DC 20585

COLEMAN, HOYTE ALONZA, educational administrator; b. Inverness, Ala., Feb. 9, 1931; s. Claude and Annie (Pitts) C.; m. Juanita Lampley, May 17, 1953; 1 son, Mark Krishna. B.A., Fla. So. Coll., 1966; M.S., U. So. Calif., 1969. Cert. counselor. Commd. sgt. U.S. Air Force, 1948, advanced through grades to chief master sergeant, 1969, ret., 1973; dir. spl. services program Valencia Community Coll., Orlando, Fla., 1973—. State Democratic committeeman for Seminole County (Fla.), 1975—. Decorated Air Force Commendation medal with 2 oak leaf clusters. Sears Roebuck Found. fellow, 1983. Mem. Am. Mgmt. Assn., Am. Personnel and Guidance Assn., Southeastern Assn. Ednl. Opportunity Program Personnel, Fla. Assn. Ednl. Opportunity Program Personnel. Moravian. Guest editorialist Orlando Times, 1980—. Home: 325 Ravenrock Ln Longwood FL 32750 Office: Valencia Community Coll PO Box 3028 Orlando FL 32802

COLEMAN, JEAN BLACK, nurse; b. Sharon, Pa., Jan. 11, 1925; d. Charles B. and Sue E. (Dougherty) Black; m. Donald A. Coleman, July 9, 1946; children—Sue Ann Coleman Lynn, Donald Ashley. R.N., Spencer Hosp. Sch. Nursing, Meadville, Pa., 1945; student Vanderbilt U., 1952-54. Nurse, dir. nursing Bulloch Meml. Hosp., Statesboro, Ga., 1948-51, nurse supr. surgery, 1954-67, dir. nursing, 1967-71; physician's asst., 1951-52; physician's asst., nurse anesthetist to Robert H. Swint, Statesboro, 1971—. Named Woman of Year in Med. Field, Bus. and Profl. Women, 1980. Mem. Am. Nurses Assn., Ga. Nurses Assn., Am. Acad. Physicians Assts., Ga. Assn. Physicians Assts. (dir. 1975-79, v.p. 1979-80, pres. 1980-81). Democrat. Roman Catholic.

COLEMAN, JOHN HARROD, municipal bond specialist; b. Jacksonville, Fla., May 2, 1926; s. John H. and Mary Ellen (Joseph) C.; student The Citadel, 1943; B.A. with honors, U. Fla., 1949; postgrad. Goethe U. (Germany), 1956; cert. Sorbonne, Paris, 1957, others. With Marine Midland Trust Co., N.Y.C., 1960-66; fin. advisor Roosevelt & Son, N.Y.C., 1966-72; v.p. First Equity Corp. Fla., Tampa, 1972-75, Shearson Loeb Rhoades, Miami, Fla., 1975-79, NCNB Nat. Bank of Fla., Boca Raton, Fla., 1979-86, First Nat. Bank in Palm Beach, Boca Raton, 1985—. Served with USNR, 1944-46, 51-52. Mem. Soc. Colonial Wars, St. Nicholas Soc., English Speaking Union, SR, Order of Crown of Charlemagne, Baronial Order of Magna Charta. Democrat. Presbyterian. Clubs: Municipal Bond N.Y., Municipal Forum N.Y., Union, Selva Marina Country, St. Andrews Soc. Home: 333 N Ocean Blvd 1008 Deerfield Beach FL 33441 Office: 150 E Palmetto Park Rd Boca Raton FL 33432

COLEMAN, LINDA HOOKER, microprocessor design consultant; b. Frankfurt, Germany, Sept. 26, 1955; came to U.S., 1957, naturalized, 1960; d. Winford Macon and Kathryn (Holt) Hooker; m. Gregory E. Coleman, July 1984. B.S. in Electronics Tech., summa cum laude, U. Houston, 1984. Cert. Reiki therapist; lic. real estate salesman, Tex. Sec. to v.p. IWECO, Inc., Houston, 1974-75; exec. sec. to v.p. Fisk Electric Co., Houston, 1975-77; exec. sec. U. Houston, 1977-79, lab. asst., 1979, electronics technician, 1979-81; microprocessor designer Stewart & Stevenson, Houston, 1981-84; field engr. Hewlett Packard Co., 1984—. Bd. dirs. Esoteric Philosophy Ctr., sec., 1986. Nat. Merit scholar, 1973, Jesse H. Jones scholar U. Houston, 1979. Mem. IEEE, Nat. Assn. Female Execs., Am. Internat. Reiki Assn., Tau Alpha Pi (sec. 1983—), Phi Kappa Pi. Republican. Home: 947 Oak Meadow Houston TX 77017

COLEMAN, MARK ELLIOTT, land development company executive; b. Cleve., Feb. 26, 1949; s. Robert Franks and Mary Veronica (Churchill) C. Grad. archtl. engrig. U. Notre Dame, 1972. Project engr. Merit Devel., Atlanta, 1972-75; project mgr. Abrams Industries, Atlanta, 1975-78; pres. RMC Constrn., Atlanta, 1978-82, Benmark Industries, Atlanta, 1982—; cons., 1982—. Republican. Roman Catholic. Club: Atlanta Country (Marietta). Office: Benmark Industries 90 W Wievca Rd Suite 210 Atlanta GA 30342

COLEMAN, MARY DELORSE, political science educator, consultant, researcher; b. Forest, Miss., June 5, 1954; d. John Henry and Catherine (Payton) C.; m. Joe Willie Laymon, Mar. 30, 1974 (div. 1980); 1 son, Kiese. B.A., Jackson State U., 1975; M.A., U. Wis., 1977, Ph.D., 1984. Research asst. Inst. for Policy Studies, Washington, 1975; research asst. Center for Eval. and Research, Madison, Wis., 1978; teaching asst. U. Wis.-Madison, 1979; asst. prof. polit. Sci. Jackson (Miss.) State U., 1979—; cons. Ford Found.; computer assisted instruction module developer, Jackson State U.; adj. fellow So. Edn. Found.; co-project dir. So. Legis. Behavior. Vol. coordinator congressional campaign of Leslie McHlemone, 1980; v.p. Miss. ACLU, 1983. Recipient Black Politics award Jackson State U., 1975; U. Wis. fellow, 1976-79; Ford Found. fellow, 1980-84; NSF grantee, 1982-85. Mem. Am. Polit. Sci. Assn., Nat. Conf. Black Polit. Scientists, AAUW. Baptist. Author: Gender and Civic Orientations as Correlates of Efficacy, 1982. Home: 527 Morton Rd Forest MS 39074 Office: Jackson State U 1365 Lynch St Jackson MS 39217

COLEMAN, MICHAEL DORTCH, physician; b. Jackson, Tenn., June 19, 1944; s. Ivery R. and Kathleen (Campbell) C.; B.A. in Chemistry, U. Ark., 1966; M.D., Duke U., 1970; m. Judi Gail Sabin; children by previous marriage—Michael Dortch, Christopher Mathew. Intern, Duke U. Med. Sch., Durham, N.C., 1970-71, resident internal medicine, 1971-72, nephrology fellow, 1972-74; practice medicine specializing in nephrology, Durham, 1972-74, Kannapolis, N.C., 1973-74, Ft. Smith, Ark., 1974—; nephrology cons. Cabarras County Hosp., Kannapolis, 1973; chief dept. nephrology Holt Krock Clinic, Ft. Smith, 1974—, dir. dialysis Holt Krock Dialysis Center, 1974—, Sparks Regional Med. Center, Ft. Smith, 1974—, St. Edward's Mercy Med. Center, Ft. Smith, 1980—; asso. prof. medicine U. Ark., Ft. Smith, 1976—; mem. med. rev. bd. Ark. Kidney Disease Commn., 1974—; nephrology cons., 1974—; mem. exec. com. and med. rev. bd. Ark.-Okla. Endstage Renal Disease Council, 1977—. Bd. dirs. Ark. Tennis Assn., Jr. Tennis Council. Diplomate Am. Bd. Internal Medicine. Mem. Internat. Soc. Nephrology, Renal Physician Assn., Am. Soc. Nephrology, Am. Heart Assn., AMA, Ark. Med. Assn., Sebastian County Med. Assn., Alpha Omega Alpha. Clubs: Ft. Smith Racquet, Hardscrabble Country. Contbr. articles to med. jours. Office: 1500 Dodson St Fort Smith AR 72901

COLEMAN, ROBERT E., textile company executive; b. Greenville, S.C., 1925; B.S., N.C. State U., 1950. Supr., Graniteville Co. (S.C.), 1950-52; asst. supt. Anchor Rome Mills, Inc., Rome, Ga., 1952-55; with Riegel Textile Corp., 1955—, exec. v.p., 1969-73, pres. from 1973, chief operating officer, 1973-74, chief exec. officer, 1974—, chmn. bd., 1975—, also dir. Address: Suite 800 Green Gate Park 25 Woods Lake Rd Greenville SC 29607

COLEMAN, RON, congressman; b. El Paso, Tex., Nov. 29, 1941; m. Tammy Biel; 1 dau., Kimberly Michelle. B.A., U. Tex.-El Paso, 1963, J.D., 1969; postgrad. in law, Kent U., Canterbury, Eng., 1981. Bar: Tex. 1969. Tchr. El Paso Pub. Schs., 1967; practice law El Paso, 1969; asst. county atty., Tex., 1969-71, 1st asst. county atty., from 1971; mem. Tex. Ho. of Reps., 1973-82, 98th Congress from 16th dist. Tex.; majority whip at-large, rep. Democratic Congl. Campaign Com., mem. subcoms. research and devel. and mil. personnel and compensation of armed services com., subcom. commerce, consumer and monetary affairs of govt. ops. com., govt. info., justice and agr. com., govt. activities and transp. com. 98th Congress from 16th dist. Tex.; founder, organizer Border Caucus; mem. Vietnam Vets. Caucus, Congl. Hispanic Caucus, Sunbelt Caucus, Environ. and Energy Study Conf., Arms Control and Fgn. Policy Caucus. Author: Pub. Sch. Fin. Act. Tex. Del. Tex. Constl. Conv., 1974. Named One of 10 Best Legislators Tex. Monthly mag.; recipient Adminstrn. Justice award State Bar Tex., 1973, Legis. award State Bar Tex., 1979, Environ. award, 1977, award for edn. Tex. Assn. Sch. Adminstrs. and Sch. Bds., 1977, cert. Tex. Compensatory Edn. Assn., 1979. Office: US House of Reps Washington DC 20515

COLEMAN, SYLVIA ETHEL, research biologist; b. Gainesville, Fla., Mar. 23, 1933; d. John Melton and Jessie Lee C.; m. Henry Carl Aldrich, Jan. 1, 1978. B.S., U. Fla., 1955, M.S., 1956, Ph.D., 1972. Grad. teaching asst. U. Fla., Gainesville, 1955-56; med. bacteriologist Mound Park Hosp., St. Petersburg, Fla., 1959-60; research microbiologist Bay Pines VA Med. Center, St. Petersburg, 1960-67; grad. teaching asst. dept. microbiology U. Fla., Gainesville, 1967-71; electron microscopy technician U. Fla., 1972; research biologist VA Med. Center, Gainesville, 1972—; adj. asst. prof. microbiology U. Fla., Gainesville, 1976—, adj. postdoctoral fellow dept. botany, 1979. Pres. univ. br. N. Fla. chpt. Nat. Multiple Sclerosis Soc., 1980-82. Mem. Am. Soc. Cell Biology, Am. Soc. Microbiology (Pres. award 1961), Am. Assn. Pathologists, Electron Microscopy Soc. Am., Histochem. Soc., S.E. Electron Microscopy Soc., Fla. Acad. Scis., N.Y. Acad. Scis., Sigma Xi (Annual award 1972), Alpha Lambda Delta. Democrat. Mem. United Ch. of Christ. Contbr. articles in field to profl. jours. Home: 122 NW 28th Terrace Gainesville FL 32607 Office: Research Service 151 VA Med Center Gainesville FL 32602

COLEMAN, VIRALENE J., English educator; b. Waterloo, Ark., Feb. 5, 1928; d. James Johnson and Estella (Ellis) Ingram; m. Elijah Coleman; children—Ronald, Sandra. B.A. in English, Ark. M&N Coll., 1950; M.A. in English, 1959, Ph.D., 1969. Prof. English, U. Ark., Pine Bluff, 1973-79, chmn. dept. English, 1974—; cons. NEH, Washington, Ark. Endowment for Humanities, Little Rock, 1978—; reader Ednl. Testing Service, N.J., 1983—. Recipient Disting. Tchr. in Div. Arts and Scis. award U. Ark.-Pine Bluff, 1984, Ark. Humanist of Yr. award Ark. Endowment for Humanities, 1984. Mem. Nat. Council Tchrs. English (past regional dir.), Coll. Composition Communication (past mem. exec. com.), Ark. Philol. Assn. (past pres.), Delta Sigma Theta. Republican. Presbyterian. Avocations: reading; sewing; playing piano; jogging. Home: Route 4 Box 208A Pine Bluff AR 71601 Office: U Ark Pine Bluff AR 71601

COLEY, MARY LOVE, librarian; b. Erwin, Tenn., Sept. 24, 1940; d. Byrd Thomas and Pauline (Love) Garland; m. George Clinton Coley, Mar. 29, 1959; children—Stephen Lee, Martha Love, George Michael. B.S., E. Tenn. State U., 1981. Cert. English tchr., library media. Librarian, Unicoi County (Tenn.) Bd. Edn., Erwin, 1981—. Pres. Tenn. Fedn. Women's Clubs Dist. 1, 1982-84; mem. Gen. Fedn. Women's Clubs, Erwin Woman's Club; founder, edn. chmn. Erwin Monday Club, 1982-84. Recipient 3 Star award Gen. Fedn. Women's Clubs, 1982; Outstanding Vol. Tenn. award Tenn. Fedn. Women's Clubs, 1982; Library Media award E. Tenn. State U., 1981. Mem. Unicoi County Edn. Assn., Tenn. Edn. Assn., NEA, ALA, Nat. Council Tchrs. English. Republican. Mem. Christian Ch. Office: Evans Elem Sch Erwin TN 37650

COLI, GUIDO JOHN, JR., chemical company executive; b. Richmond, Va., Sept. 12, 1921; s. Guido and Rena (Pacini) C.; B.S., Va. Poly. Inst., 1941, M.S., 1942, Ph.D., 1949; m. 2d, Gertrude Maria Karl, Nov. 4, 1972; children by previous marriage—Pamela, Patricia, Deborah, Richard. Asst. engr. Va. Health Dept. bur. indsl. hygiene, 1941; asso. chemist Naval Research Lab., 1942-43; instr. chem. engring. Va. Poly. Inst., 1947-48; chem. engr. Mobil Oil Co., Paulsboro, N.J., 1949-50; with Allied Chem. Corp., N.Y.C., 1950-72, group v.p. corp., 1968-72, dir., 1970-72, pres. Am. Enka Co., Enka, N.C., 1972—; dir. Akzona, Inc. Mem. Gov. Va. Commn. to Establish Urban Univ. in Richmond Area, 1966-67; mem. adv. council Coll. of Engring., Va. Poly. Inst.; trustee St. Joseph's Hosp., Asheville, N.C.; pres. Mountain Health Services, Asheville. Served to lt. USNR, 1943-46. Registered profl. engr., N.Y., Va. Fellow Am. Inst. Chemists; mem. Am. Chem. Soc. (chmn. Va. 1957). Am. Inst. Chem. Engrs., Sigma Xi, Phi Lambda Upsilon, Tau Beta Pi, Phi Kappa Phi, Alpha Kappa Psi. Club: University (N.Y.C.). Office: Enka NC 28728

COLLETT, ROBERT WAYNE, rental equipment executive; b. Connellsville, Pa., Feb. 22, 1922; s. Okey Wayne and Nona (Cross) C.; m. Hilda Ashworth, Jan. 29, 1944; children—Connie Collett Gatz, John W., Gregory Cross. Student Chgo. Acad. Fine Arts, 1947; grad. Squadron Officers Sch., Air U., 1951; cert. rental mgr. Appalachian State U., 1983. Pres. and chief exec. officer Arrow-Rents, Inc., Montgomery, Ala., 1954—; dir. Am. Rentall Inc., New Orleans, 1964—. Candidate City Commn., Montgomery, 1966, Ho. of Reps., State of Ala., 1970. Served to capt. USAAF, 1942-52; ETO. Mem. Am. Rental Assn. (dir. 1958-61, pres. 1963-64; Rental Man of Yr. southeast region 1980; Disting. Service award 1967). Republican. Presbyterian. Lodge: Kiwanis of Capital City (bd. dirs. 1956-59, pres. 1967). Home: 1238 Vaughn Rd Pike Rd Montgomery AL 36064 Office: Arrow-Rents Inc 5600 Calmar Dr Montgomery AL 36116

COLLEVECCHIO, EMIDIO JOSEPH, dentist, naval officer; b. Camden, N.J., Aug. 15, 1929; s. Domenico and Mary (Dinino) C.; m. Pauline Chabon, May 26, 1956; children—Donna, Edward, Ann, Vincent, Carolyn. B.S. in Biology, St. Joseph's U., 1951; D.D.S., Temple U., 1955. Commd. lt. (j.g.) U.S. Navy, 1955, advanced through grades to vice capt., 1972; gen. practice dentistry, Audubon, N.J., 1958-61; dir. clin. services U.S. Navy, Camp Lejeune, N.C., 1980-83, exec. officer of dental command, 1983-84. Mem. ADA, Assn. Mil. Surgeons of U.S., Ret. Officers Assn. Home: 9010 Stockton Ct Orlando FL 32817 Office: Naval Officer Dental Clinic Naval Tng Ctr Orlando FL

COLLEY, JOHN GEIST, real estate broker, consultant; b. Nashville, Jan. 17, 1921; s. William Hubert and Mary Agnes (Geist) C.; m. Nannie Mildred Smith, Nov. 26, 1941; children—Susan Hope, John, II (dec.), William Lee, Josephine Lynn. B.S., Middle Tenn. State U., 1947; M.S., George Peabody Coll. Tchrs., 1950. Real estate broker, appraiser, 1957. Metallurgist Avco, Smyrna, Tenn., 1939-43; tchr. Tenn. City Schs., 1947-57; supt. Tenn. State Park, Lebanon, 1950-53; supr. Ford Motors Co., Nashville, 1957-82; real estate broker, Nashville, 1957—; cons. Colley Real Estate, Nashville, 1957—; tchr. adult program real estate Met. Nashville Bd. Edn., 1984. Served with USMC, 1943-46. Decorated Purple Heart; recipient Improvement grant Ford Motor Co., 1961; Prodn. award, Safety award, 1978. Mem. Internat. Orgn. Real Estate Appraisers. Democrat. Lodges: K.C., Elks. Office: 785 Old Hickory Blvd Nashville TN 37027

COLLIER, CONSTANCE HEINS, financial executive; b. Raleigh, N.C., Sept. 6, 1940; d. William Edward and Dorothy (Kimball) Clenney; m. John Alan Brocksmith, Mar. 10, 1959 (div. 1981); children—John Alan, Leslie Kathryn, Amy Ann. Student anthropology Ga. State U., 1981—. Treas. Tennis Sales South, Inc., Tucker, Ga., 1971—; v.p. Diversified Sports Distbg., Inc.,

Tucker, 1980-81, treas., 1981—. Editor newsletter Exec. Bd. Westminster Schs., Atlanta, 1981—. Mem. Soc. Am. Archaeology, Southeastern Archaeol. Soc., Am. Anthrop. Assn., Blue Key, Mortar Bd., Golden Key. Democrat. Methodist. Club: Ga. State Anthropology (pres.). Home: 2232 DeFoors Ferry Rd Atlanta GA 30318

COLLIER, DAVID FRANKLIN, automobile dealer; b. Louisburg, N.C., June 14, 1919; s. William Edward and Maggie (Taylor) C.; m. Mary S. Smedley, Feb. 29, 1944; children—Michael Allan, Lynn Louise, Susan Taylor, David Scott. Student Louisburg Coll., 1936-37. Owner auto dealership Tacoma, Wash., 1946-54; owner, pres. Collier Auto Sales, Orlando, Fla., 1954—. Served to chief warrant officer, USN, 1939-46. Recipient commendations capt., U.S.S. Lexington, 1941, comdr. escort carrier Pacific Fleet, 1944, condr. Pacific Fleet, 1945, award Time Mag., 1980. Mem. Nat. Automobile Dealers Assn. (Quality Dealer award 1980), Fla. Automobile Dealers Assn. (past dir.), Central Fla. Automobile and Truck Dealers Assn. (dir. 1962—), Central Fla. Ind. Auto Dealers (hon. life, past pres.), Central Fla. Sales and Mktg. (hon. life, dir., past pres. Orlando), VFW, Orlando Area C. of C. (dir., v.p.). Democrat. Presbyterian. Clubs: Orlando Country, Citrus, University, Elks. Office: 2150 W Colonial Dr Orlando FL 32804

COLLIER, JERRY WAYNE, nuclear engineer; b. Charlottesville, Va., Apr. 14, 1956; s. James Irving, Jr. and Eura Gay (Strickler) C.; B.S. in Nuclear Engring., U. Va., 1978; m. Tandy Lee Tucker, June 2, 1979; children—John Vernon, Steven Wayne. Nuclear research reactor operator U. Va. Reactor Facility, 1977-78; jr., then asst. test engr. Oconee Nuclear Sta., Duke Power Co., 1978-81, asst. reactor engr., 1981-83, assoc. reactor engr., 1983-84, reactor engr., 1984—. Mem. Am. Nuclear Soc., ASME, U. Va. Alumni Assn. Republican. Baptist. Home: Furman L Smith Memorial Hwy Six Mile SC Office: Oconee Nuclear Station PO Box 1439 Seneca SC 29679

COLLIER, LOUIS MALCOLM, physicist, community service worker, educator; b. Little Rock, May 19, 1919; s. Albert and Ludia (Lewis) C.; B.S. (La. Legis. scholar), Grambling State U., 1954; M.S., Okla. State U., 1960, postgrad., 1962-64; postgrad. Cornell U., 1961; m. Pearlie B. May, June 6, 1947; children—James Bernard, Irving Orlando, Albert Jerome, Phillip Louis, Eric Wayne. Tchr., chmn. sci. and math. dept. Central High Sch., Calhoun, La., 1955-62; instr. physics and math. So. U., New Orleans, 1962-64, asst. prof., 1964-66, asso. prof. physics, Shreveport, La., 1967-75, chmn. dept. physics, 1975-77; formerly chmn. sci. and math. dept. Hopewell High Sch., Dubach, La.; mem. Caddo-Bossier Community Council, Shreveport, 1972—, mem. exec. com., 1975-77; v.p. Newton Smith PTA, 1973-74, pres., 1975-77; pres. Cooper Road Area PTA, 1975-77; v.p. 7th Dist. Bicentennial Com.; mem. Caddo Parish (La.) Bicentennial Commn, 1973-76, also Shreveport Regional Bicentennial Commn., serving on Art and Cultural Task Force and on Black Cultural Com., 1975-76; bd. dirs. Shreveport Performing Arts Council, 1975-77, treas., 1976-77; mem. Shreveport's Mayor's Com. on Youth Services, 1974; bd. dirs. Caddo chpt. ARC; bd. dirs. George Washington Carver br. YWCA, 1972, sec. bd., 1972-76, dir. publicity, 1976—, chmn. bd. mgmt., 1978-79; program dir. Sunday Morning radio program Youth Wants to Know, 1972-77, bus. mgr., Shreveport, 1972-77; v.p. Shreveport chpt. Nat. Pan Hellenic Council, Inc., 1972-74, pres., 1974-79; v.p. Caddo Community Action Agy., 1972-77, chmn. fin. com., 1972-77; pres. Cooper Road Health Club, 1973-77, Cooper Rd. Med. Bd., 1975-77; chmn. edn. com. Cooper Road Adv. Council, 1974-77; mem. Cooper Road Vol. Fireman's Assn., 1971-77, sec., 1972-73; sec. Cooper Road Adv. Council, 1976-77; vol. counselor Caddo Parish Juvenile Ct., 1972-77; adv. Caddo Parish 4-H Club, 1975-77. Served to sgt. U.S. Army, world War II. Recipient Ednl. Leadership award Ouachita Parish (La.), 1959, NSF award, 1970, Urban League award Dept. Commerce, 1975, Community Leadership and Service award George Washington Carver br. YMCA Bd., 1975, Bicentennial Commn. award City of Shreveport, 1976, Leadership and Service award Nat. Pan Hellenic Council, 1976, Top Citizens award Caddo Edn. Assn. and Caddo Tchrs. Assn., 1977, Found. for Econ. edn. award, 1978, Citizenship award Shreveport chpt. NAACP., 1978; award for dedicated service to community Cooper Road Adv. Council of Caddo Community Action Agy., 1978, Disting. and Outstanding Community Service award Caddo Community Action Agy., Inc., 1979; named Tchr. of Yr., Freedom Found., 1962, recipient Freedom Found. award, 1977; Shell Merit fellow, 1962. Mem. AAAS (research participation award 1961, Fellowship award 1962-64), Nat. Assn. Mathematicians, AAUP, Nat. Council Tchrs. Math., Nat. Sci. Tchrs. Assn., La. Acad. Sci., La. Edn. Assn. (Ednl. Leadership award 1973, Sci. Edn. award 1976, program coordinator 1976-77), NEA, La. Assn. Educators, Am. Legion (post child welfare officer 1975-77, adv. Sons of Am. Legion 1976-77, Leadership, Scholarship and Service award, post Meritorious Service award 1978, Area Meritorious Service award 1979), Sigma Phi Sigma (hon. award 1975), Phi Beta Sigma (Community Service award 1976, Meritorious Service award Gulf Coast region 1977, Appreciation award Epsilon Eta chpt. 1977, Disting. Service award Gulf Coast Region 1978, Appreciation award Epsilon Eta chpt. 1978, regional dir. 1979—), Alpha Xi Sigma. Club: Kiwanis (pres. club 1974-75, Outstanding Club Leadership award 1975). Home: 3031 Oak Forest St Shreveport LA 71107 Office: So U 3050 Cooper Rd Shreveport LA 71107

COLLINS, CHARLES DANIEL, oil company executive, geologist; b. Dallas, Nov. 11, 1955; s. John Daniel and Juanita Francis (Johnson) C.; m. Ellen Marie Real, Aug. 22, 1975; children—Sean Daniel, Kasey Shea. B.S. in Geology, Stephen F. Austin State U., Nacogdoches, Tex., 1979. Unit mgr. Splty. Logging Co., Gonzales, Tex., 1979-80; geologist Champlin Petroleum Co., Corpus Christi, Tex., 1980-81; exploration geologist Sulpetro Resources, Dallas, 1981-82; sr. Geologist Big Chief Exploration Co., Gillette, Wyo., 1982-83; dir. geol. services Spectrum Engergy, Inc., Dallas, 1983-85, v.p., 1985—; cons. geologist, Dallas, 1984—. Mem. Am. Assn. Petroleum Geologists, Corpus Christi Geol. Soc. Baptist. Avocations: golf, guitar, writing, painting. Home: 917 Charles Dr Ada OK 74820 Office: Spectrum Energy Inc Route 3 Box 297 Ada OK 74820

COLLINS, CLAUDE CHARLES, fin. services co. exec.; b. West Palm Beach, Fla., Sept. 14, 1946; s. Claude Charles and Winifred (Farr) C.; student U. Fla., 1964-67; children—Christian, Cara. Ins. mktg. rep. State of Fla., 1967-68; fin. and mktg. cons. to several ins. cos., 1969-71; pvt. cons. investments, ins. and tax strategies; v.p. IMC Am., Tampa, Fla., 1973-75; propr. MDA Fin., DeLand, Fla., 1976-79; founder, pres. Seos Found., Inc., DeLand, 1977—, Sterling-Forbes Holdings, Inc., DeLand, 1979—; agt. and exclusive U.S. rep. Finlay Trust Group; internat. fin. cons. Served with U.S. Army, 1968. Mem. Nat. Assn. Fin. Cons., Real Estate Securities and Syndication Inst., Internat. Soc. Financiers, Mcht. Brokers Exchange. Republican. Club: Internat. Order Flangers. Home: Beresford Rd DeLand FL 32720 Office: PO Box 622 DeLand FL 32720

COLLINS, CORNELIA DEMING, educator; b. Hartford, Conn., Aug. 18, 1921; d. Edward Adams and Evelyn Mary (Staley) Deming; m. James Foster Collins, Dec. 30, 1944; children—Lauren F. Collins Mitchell, Kenneth D., C. Staley. B.A., Smith Coll., 1943; M.A. in Social Work, Columbia U., 1945. Field advisor, nat. del., nat. com. mem. Girl Scouts U.S.A., 1944—; trustee Laubach Literacy Internat., Syracuse, N.Y., 1966—; bd. dirs. Literacy Council No. Va., 1969—, Va. Literacy Coalition, 1984—. Home: 6804 Sorrell St McLean VA 22101

COLLINS, DANIEL LYNN, air force officer, psychologist; b. Sioux Falls, S.D., Sept. 27, 1951; s. William Hoffman and Theresa Carolina (Gedstead) C.; m. Cynthia Rebecca Gerlich. July 21, 1979; 1 child, Jason Daniel. B.S., S.D. State U., 1974; Ph.D. magna cum laude, Uniformed Services U. Health Scis., 1984. Commd. 2nd lt. U.S. Air Force, 1974, advanced through grades to maj., 1985; aviator, exec. officer Hill Air Force Base, Utah, 1976-79; chief drug and alcohol rehab. program, 1978-79; liason officer U.S. Force Inst. Tech., Wright Patterson AFB, Ohio, 1980-84; chief testing function U.S. Air Force Human Resources Lab., Lackland AFB, Tex., 1984—. Contbr. articles to profl. jours. Adv. Explorer Scouts, Lackland AFB, 1984-85; organizer Neighborhood Watch, San Antonio, 1984. Recipient Nat. Safety Council award, 1977; Air Force Inst. Tech. scholar, 1980-84. Mem. Am. Psychol. Assn., Air Force Human Resources Lab., Air Force Assn., Nat. Acad. Scis. (com. 1980-84), AAAS. Lutheran. Clubs: Brooks Air Force Base Officers, Company Grade Officers (liason officer 1984-85), Nat. KayPro Users Group. Home: 1734 Copperfield San Antonio TX 78251 Office: US Air Force Human Resources Lab Bldg 578 Brooks Air Force Base TX 78235-5601

COLLINS, GLENDA BARDWELL, educator, civic worker; b. Grenada, Miss., Sept. 21, 1941; d. Robert Lee and Irene (James) Bardwell; B.F.A., Miss. State Coll. for Women, 1963; M.Ed., U. New Orleans, 1975; m. M. B. Collins, June 30, 1963 (div.); 1 dau., Cathleen Kelly. Tchr. art Memphis City Sch. System, 1964-68, Met. Nashville-Davidson County Schs., 1969-72, St. Bernard Parish Schs., 1973-76, St. Tammany Parish, Salmen High Sch., Slidell, La., 1976—; co-chmn. Bicentennial Festival of Arts for Children, New Orleans, 1976; exhibitor Internat. Trade Mart, New Orleans, 1976; tchr., cons. State-wide Inservice Program. Co-founder, pres. Council for Victims of Family Violence in St. Tammany Parish, 1979-80; founder, pres. St. Tammany Parish Pres.' Commn. on Needs of Women; active ERA, United, ERAmerica, Speakers Bur. Slidell, Talent Bank of Women; active polit. campaigns; photographer La. Women's Conf., Baton Rouge; works include La. Internat. Women's Year banner cover photograph. Mem. NEA, La. Assn. Educators, St. Tammany Parish Assn. Educators (v.p.), Nat. Assn. Art Educators, La. Art Educators Assn., St. Tammany Parish Assn. Art Educators (pres.), Slidell Art League. Methodist. Club: Bus. and Profl. Women's (Woman of Year 1978-79). Home: PO Box 916 Slidell LA 70459 Office: Salmen High School PO Box 787 Slidell LA 70459

COLLINS, HARRY DAVID, construction claims consultant; retired army officer; b. Brownsville, Pa., Nov. 18, 1931; s. Harry Alonzo and Cecelia Victoria (Morris) C.; B.S. in Mech. Engring., Carnegie Mellon U., 1954; M.S., U.S. Naval Postgrad. Sch., 1961; m. Suzanne Dylong, May 11, 1956; children—Cynthia L., Gerard P. Commd. 2d lt. C.E., U.S. Army, 1954, advanced through grades to lt. col. 1969; comdr. 802d Heavy Engr. Constrn. Bn., Korea, 1972-73; dep. dist. engr. Army Engr. Dist., New Orleans, 1973-75; ret., 1975; v.p. deLaureal Engrs., Inc., New Orleans, 1975-78; v.p. Near East mktg. Kidde Cons., Inc., 1978-82; dir. new bus. devel. for Middle East, Am. Middle East Co., Inc., 1982-84; sr. cons. Wagner, Hohns, Inglis, Inc., 1984—. Decorated Legion of Merit, Bronze Star, Meritorious Service medal; registered profl. engr., Miss., La. Mem. ASME, Am. Soc. Mil. Engrs., La. Engring. Soc., Sigma Xi. Home: 2024 Audubon St New Orleans LA 70118

COLLINS, JAMES CHALLACOMBE, accountant; b. Oklahoma City, Sept. 8, 1950; s. William F. Jr. and Jeanne (Hill) C.; m. Rebecca McGough, Apr. 8, 1978; 1 child, Robert Wilson. B.B.A., U. Okla., 1972. C.P.A., Okla.; chartered bank auditor. Sr. acct. Touche Ross & Co., Oklahoma City, 1972-76; sr. mgr. Ernst & Whinney, Oklahoma City, 1976—. Fellow Life Mem. Inst.; mem. Okla. Mus. Art, Okla. Zool. Soc., Young Men's Dinner Club, Am. Inst. C.P.A.'s, Okla. Soc. C.P.A.'s, Nat. Assn. Accts. Lodge: Lions. Avocations: golf; gardening. Home: 2334 NW 58th St Oklahoma City OK 73112 Office: Ernst & Whinney 2600 Liberty Tower Oklahoma City OK 73102

COLLINS, JAMES DEAKIN, III, real estate company executive; b. Washington, Dec. 22, 1943; s. James Deakin and Clare (Grovenstein) C.; m. Elizabeth Joy Willen, Feb. 18, 1967; children—James Deakin, IV. B.S. in Indsl. Mgmt., Ga. Inst. Tech., 1966. Asst. v.p. Cobbs Allen & Hall Mortgage Co., Birmingham, 1972-76; v.p. Jackson Co., Birmingham, 1976-82; asst. v.p. Camp & Co., Birmingham, 1982-85; v.p. Am. Storage Properties, Inc., Birmingham, 1985—. Served to capt. USMC, 1966-71. Decorated D.F.C., 33 Air medals, Vietnamese Cross of Gallantry with Silver star. Methodist. Office: 300 Cahaba Park S Suite 114 Birmingham AL 35243

COLLINS, JODEAN THORNTON, banker; b. Corsicana, Tex., July 9, 1930; s. Walter Thornton and Olivia Christine (Martin) C.; B.B.A. in Banking and Fin., U. Tex., Austin, 1952; m. Annella Wray Hunter, Dec. 14, 1956; children—Cindi Karen Collins Koder, Cari Lynda. Credit analyst 1st Nat. Bank of Ft. Worth, 1952; asst. v.p. T.J. Bettes Co., 1954-59; co-owner Autrey & Collins Constrn. Co., 1959-65; chmn. bd. Providence Park, Inc., Dallas, 1965—, Excel Corp., Dallas, 1965—, Majestic Savs. Assn., McKinney, Tex., 1976—, Lawyers Title Co. Central Colo., 1976—, Sofco, Inc., 1976—, Glenwood Life Ins. Co., Heritage Subaru, Interstate Capital Corp., Dallas, 1983—, Heritage Oldsmobile, Plano, 1984—; dir. Interfirst Bank, Carrollton, Fiduciary Trust Co. S.W., Interstate Services Corp., Blue Bell, Pa. Served to 1st lt. USAF, 1952-54. Mem. Nat. Savs. and Loan League, U.S. League Savs. Assn., Tex. Savs. and Loan League. Republican. Methodist. Clubs: Bent Tree Country, Arrowhead Country (Dallas); Vail, Country of the Rockies (Colo.). Home: 6934 Leameadow Dr Dallas TX 75248 Office: 5314 Arapaho Rd Dallas TX 75248

COLLINS, LEROY, JR., realtor, data processing company executive; b. Tallahassee, Sept. 3, 1934; s. LeRoy and Mary Call (Darby) C.; m. Jane Sisson, 1959; 4 children. B.S., U.S. Naval Acad., 1956. Commd. ensign U.S. Navy, 1956, advanced through grades to lt. comdr., 1966, res., 1966; asst. to pres. Fla. Power and Light Co., Miami, 1966-68; salesman IBM Corp., Tampa, Fla., 1968-69; pres., dir. Fla. Credit Service Center, Inc. (name changed to Fin. Transaction Systems, Inc. 1981), Tampa, 1969—; pres., dir. Fla. Service Center, Inc. (name changed to Telecredit Service Center, Inc. 1977), Tampa, 1977-80; exec. v.p., dir. Telecredit, Inc., Los Angeles, 1978-80; pres., broker Dynamic Realty of Tampa, Inc., 1980—; dir. Payment Systems Inc. Tampa; mem. Tampa adv. bd. Atlantic Nat. Bank of Fla. Vestryman St. Andrew's Episcopal Ch., Tampa, 1972-75, 77-80, 81-84; adv. bd. Hillsborough Community Coll., Tampa, 83-85. Served to rear adm. USNR, 1966—. Mem. Golden Triangle Civic Assn., Lodges: Ye Mystic Krewe Gasparilla, Kiwanis of Tampa (past pres.). Democrat. Home: 418 Blanca Ave Tampa FL 33606 Office: PO Box 22377 Tampa FL 33622

COLLINS, MARILEE FASSERO, music educator; b. Litchfield, Ill., Sept. 2, 1945; d. Arthur and Emma Louise (Bowen) Fassero; m. Michael Davisson Collins, Nov. 24, 1978; 1 child, Benjamin Judson. B.S., Memphis State U., 1968; M.S., No. Ill. U., 1971. Tchr. Sycamore Pub. Schs., Ill., 1968-74, Tulsa Pub. Schs., 1975—; dir. children's choir Boston Ave. Methodist Ch., Tulsa, 1978-81; pianist Theatre Tulsa, 1975-77; owner Lorenzo's Hickory Kitchen restaurant. Editor: Loaves and Fishes and Other Dishes, 1979. Nd. dirs. Tulsa Educators Polit. Action Com., 1979. Mem. NEA, Okla. Edn. Assn., Tulsa Classroom Assn., Sigma Alpha Iota. Republican. Home: 1728 E 56th St Tulsa OK 74105 Office: Tulsa Pub Schs 3111 E 56th St Tulsa OK 74105

COLLINS, MARTHA LAYNE, governor of Kentucky; b. Shelby County, Ky., Dec. 7, 1936; d. Everett Larkin and Mary Lorena (Taylor) Hall; student Lindenwood Coll., St. Charles, Mo., 1955-56; B.S., U. Ky., 1959; m. Bill Collins, July 3, 1959; children—Stephen Louis, Marla Ann. Tchr. public schs., Ky., 1959-63; lt. gov. State of Ky., 1979-83, gov., 1983—; vice-chmn. Nat. Conf. Lt. Govs., 1982, chmn., 1983. Mem. Woodford County (Ky.) Democratic Exec. Com., 1963; mem. Dem. Nat. Com., 1972-76; del. Dem. Nat. Conv., 1972, chmn., San Francisco, 1984; chairwoman Ky. Com. for Carter, 1976; mem. Ky. State Dem. Central Exec. Com., 1972-79, sec., 1974-79; clk. Ct. of Appeals, 1975; clk. Supreme Ct. of Ky., 1975-79; mem. Ky. Commn. on Women; exec. dir. The Friendship Force, Ky., 1977; trustee So. Bapt. Theol. Sem. Mem. U. Ky. Alumni Assn. Baptist. Clubs: Jaycee-ettes (past pres. Woodford County), Bus. and Profl. Women's, Order of Eastern Star. Office: Gov's Office State Capitol Frankfort KY 40601

COLLINS, MARY ANN, nurse; b. Grundy, Va., Jan. 23, 1950; d. Larry and Ruby Evelyn (Laws) Skeens; m. Robert Austin Smith, June 28, 1969 (div. 1976); 1 son, Darrell Austin; m. 2d. Gary Wayne Collins, Oct. 23, 1976; 1 son, Nicholas Wayne. Student Pikeville Coll., 1968, East Tenn. State U., 1968-69, Old Dominion U., 1969-70, 73-76; A.S., Southwest Va. Community Coll., 1973, A.A.S., 1979. Nursing coordinator Buchanan Gen. Hosp., Grundy, Va., 1979-81, inservice dir., 1983-84; infant care instr. Buchanan-Dickenson Health, Grundy, Va., 1981-82. Baptist. Office: Buchanan Gen Hosp Route 4 Box 335 Grundy VA 24614

COLLINS, MICHAEL JAMES, investment company executive; b. Orange, N.J., July 30, 1944; s. James Mitchell and Dorothy Colville (Dann) C.; m. Wynell Madison Roach, Nov. 14, 1982; 1 dau., Catherine Elise. B.A., Stanford U., 1967; grad. Am. Inst. Fgn. Trade, 1968; M.B.A., Harvard U., 1970. Vice pres. acquisition product devel. APC Industries, Inc., Austin, Tex., 1969-70; asst. to pres. Fidelity Union Life Ins. Co., Dallas, 1970-71, v.p. spl. ops, 1971-72, chmn. bd., pres., chief exec. officer, 1972-82; pres., dir. Allianz Investment Corp., 1980-82; pres., chief exec. officer Collins Capital Co., Dallas, 1982—, Expertel, Inc., 1984—; chmn. investment adv. com. Taylor & Turner; pres., dir. Collins Diversified, Inc. Vice pres., bd. dirs. Carr P. Collins Found.; bd. dirs. Dallas County Community Coll. Dist. Found., Colo. Outward Bound Sch., Sta. KERA-TV; trustee, Dallas Mus. Art. Recipient Douglas MacArthur Freedom medal; Pub. Service Commendation USCG, 1975; named Outstanding Young Man of Am., U.S. Jaycees, 1978. Mem. Young Pres.'s Orgn. Clubs: City, Petroleum, Preston Trail Golf, Willow Bend Polo Hunt. Office: Collins Capitol Co 2670 One Dallas Centre Dallas TX 75201

COLLINS, NEAL WESLEY, nurse anesthetist, educator; b. Amarillo, Tex., June 15, 1935; s. Charles F. and Helen L. (Krilling) C.; m. Marjorie Dolores Dawson, Dec. 21, 1958; children—Michelle R., Greggory N., Melanie K. B.S. in Nursing, Baylor U., 1960; M.S. in Nursing, U. Tex., 1969; grad. U.S. Army Sch. Anesthesia, Brooke Gen. Hosp., 1962. Cert. registered nurse anesthetist, 1962. Dir. Sch. Anesthesia for Nurses, Tripler Army Med. Center, Honolulu, 1970-73, Erlanger Med. Ctr., Chattanooga, 1973-80, Wichita Falls (Tex.) Gen. Hosp., 1981—. Vice-pres. Hawaii Assn. Nurse Anesthetists, 1972; pres. Tenn. Assn. Nurse Anesthetists, 1979; mem. Nat. Council Accreditation Nurse Anesthesia Schs./Programs, 1977-83. Served to col. U.S. Army Nurse Corps, 1960-83. Decorated Army Commendation medal. Mem. Am. Assn. Nurse Anesthetists, Tex. Assn. Nurse Anesthetists, Anesthesia Research Soc., Res. Offices Assn. Republican. Baptist. Home: 4414 Nassau St Wichita Falls TX 76308 Office: PO Box 5184 Wichita Falls TX 76307

COLLINS, RALPH EARL, III, fire protection engineering consultant, educator; b. Washington, Dec. 27, 1939; s. Ralph Earl and Marguerite Mary (Scruggs) C.; m. Joan M. Bielaski, Sept. 3, 1960. B.S., in Engring Fire Protection, U. Md., 1964. Sr. field engr. Factory Ins. Assn., Phila., 1964-67; asst. mgr., sr. engr. fire protection TWA, Kennedy Space Ctr., Fla., 1967-71; v.p. property loss control Johnson & Higgins, Richmond, Va., 1971—; adj. faculty fire sci. Valentin Jr. Coll., Orlando, Fla., Brevard Jr. Coll., Cocoa, Fla., John Tyler Community Coll., Chester, Va., J. Sargeant Reynolds Community Coll., Henrico, Va. Sec. Landover Hills, Md. vol. fire dept., Brentwood, Md. vol. fire dept.; pres. Crestwood PTA, 1973; v.p. Chesterfield County Council PTA's; pres. Southham Civic Assn., 1974. Mem. Soc. Fire Protection Engrs. (pres. elect), Am. Soc. Safety Engrs., System Safety Soc., Bldg. Officials and Code Adminstrs., Nat. Fire Protection Assn., Richmond Joint Engrs. Council, Am. Assn. Engring Soc., Va. Fire Prevention Assn. Roman Catholic. Club: Engrs. of Richmond. Home: 1123 Joliette Rd Bon Air VA 23235

COLLINS, ROBERT FREDERICK, federal judge; b. New Orleans, Jan. 27, 1931; s. Frederick and Irma V. (Anderson) C.; B.A. cum laude, Dillard U., 1951, LL.D., 1979; J.D., La. State U., 1954; grad. spl. summer course Nat. Jud. Coll., U. Nev., 1973; m. Aloha Collins, Dec. 28, 1957; children—Francesca Collins McManus, Lisa Ann, Nanette C., Robert A. Bar La. 1954. Mem. firm Augustine, Collins, Smith & Warren, New Orleans, 1956-59; instr. law So. U., 1959-61; sr. partner firm Collins, Douglas & Elie, New Orleans, 1960-72; asst. city atty.-legal adv. New Orleans Police Dept., 1967-69; judge ad hoc Traffic Ct., New Orleans, 1969-72; atty. Housing Authority New Orleans, 1971-72; judge magistrate sect. Criminal Dist. Ct., Orleans Parish, La., 1971-78; judge U.S. Dist. Ct., Eastern Dist. La., 1978—; asst. bar examiner State of La., 1970-78. Bd. dirs. New Orleans Housing Council, 1962-64, Social Welfare Planning Council, New Orleans, 1965-67, Dryades St. YMCA, New Orleans, 1963-65, New Orleans Urban League, 1970-72, 75; mem. La. State Welfare Bd., 1970-72; trustee Loyola U., New Orleans, 1977-83. Served with U.S. Army, 1954-56. Mem. La. State Bar Assn., Nat. Bar Assn. (regional dir. 1964-65), Am. Bar Assn., Louis A. Martinet Legal Soc. (pres. 1959-60), Am. Judicature Soc., Fifth Circuit Dist. Judges Assn. Democrat. Roman Catholic. Office: 500 Camp St Suite 465 New Orleans LA 70130

COLLINS, SALLY ANN, computer programmer; b. Balt., Oct. 26, 1939; d. Oliver Guth Matthews and Betty Jane (Mamaux) M.; m. Fredric Pittman Harris, Oct. 26, 1957 (div.); 1 son, Kristopher David; m. 2d, James Eugene Collins, Mar. 18, 1963 (div.); 1 son, Robert James. Cert. Elec. Computer Programming Inst., 1970; student Broward Community Coll., 1981—. With Shadeland Plant, Western Electric Co., Indpls., 1964-70; programmer L.S. Ayres and Co., Indpls., 1970-73; programmer/operator Data Develco, Oakland Park, Fla., 1973; programmer I through programmer/analyst II Broward County Bd. County Commrs., Ft. Lauderdale, Fla., 1973—. Active Republicans for Reagan, Ft. Lauderdale, 1976, Broward Hist. Commn., Ft. Lauderdale, 1976, Broward Community Blood Ctr., 1974—, Broward Community Bond Drive, 1978. Recipient departmental award in police sci. Broward Community Coll., 1983; photography award Broward Hist. Commn., 1980. Mem. Psi Iota Xi (conductress Theta Alpha chpt. 1971-72). Club: Gold Coast Toastmistress sec., v.p. 1974-76, award 1976). Contbr. articles to profl. jours. Home: 601 N Rio Vista Blvd Apt 108 Fort Lauderdale FL 33301 Office: Broward County Courthouse 201 SE 6th St Room 1002 Fort Lauderdale FL 33301

COLLINS, THOMAS ASA, clergyman, educational consultant; b. Rome, Ga., Aug. 31, 1921; s. Earle Strathmore and Hazel (Alverson) C.; m. Anna E. Galloway, Aug. 17, 1944; children—Faye Anne Collins Rivers, Thomas Asa, Robert Earle, William Ray. B.A., Asbury Coll., 1941, B.D., 1944; M.Div., Emory U., 1944; D.D. (hon.), High Point Coll. Ordained to ministry Methodist Ch., 1944. Pastor, Atlanta, 1942-43, Talbot, Ga., 1943-44, Gatesville, N.C., 1944-49, Raleigh, N.C., 1949-53; exec. dir. Meth. Conf. Bd. Missions, 1953-59; 1st pres. N.C. Wesleyan Coll., Rocky Mount, 1959-75; sr. pastor St. Mark's United Meth. Ch., Raleigh, 1980—; prin. tchr. high sch. Gates County, 1944-46; dir. People's Bank and Trust Co., Rocky Mount, N.C., 1966-69. Del. gen. conf. and jurisdictional confs. Meth. Ch., 1960, 64, 68; pres. N.C. Council Chs., 1967-70; mem. bd. commn. Christian edn. Nat. Council Chs., 1959-68. Named N.C. Tar Heel of Week, 1959. Mem. Am. Acad. Religion, Am. Assn. Colls. Democrat. Clubs: Ruritan (pres. 1947-49), Kiwanis (pres. 1959, lt. gov. 1974-75) (Rocky Mount). Sermon editor Carolina Cooperator, 1949—; contbr. articles to religious jours. Home: 208 Ellwood Dr Raleigh NC 27609

COLLINS-EILAND, KAREN WISLER, psychologist; b. Oklahoma City, Mar. 25, 1949; d. Charles C. and Frances Joan (Higgins) Wisler; B.A. with honors, Stephen F. Austin State U., Nacogdoches, Tex., 1973; M.A., Tex. Christian U., 1978, Ph.D., 1979; m. David C. Eiland. Asst. prof. Dickinson (N.D.) State Coll., 1979-80; research asst. prof. psychiatry U. Tex. Med. Br., Galveston, 1980-81, asst. prof. dept. ob-gyn and sr. asso. Office Ednl. Devel., 1981—. Mem. Am. Psychol. Assn., Am. Ednl. Research Assn., Sigma Xi, Psi Chi, Alpha Kappa Delta, Alpha Chi, Delta Zeta. Methodist. Contbr. articles to profl. jours. Office: Dept Ob-Gyn U Tex Med Br Room 313 MW E-87 Galveston TX 77550

COLLMER, ROBERT GEORGE, university administrator, English educator; b. Guatemala, Central Am., Nov. 28, 1926 (parents Am. citizens); s. G. Russell and Constance Ethel (Cravener) C.; m. Linnie Maffett Burney, Jan. 5, 1948 (dec. 1979); children—Carol Linda Collmer McLaren, Mark Wesley; m. Alys Edney, July 4, 1981. B.A., Baylor U., 1948, M.A., 1949; Ph.D., U. Pa., 1953. Asst. instr. U. Pa., Phila., 1949-52; instr. Phila. Coll. of Bible, Phila., 1952-54; from assoc. prof. to prof., chmn. dept. English, Hardin-Simmons U., Abilene, Tex., 1954-58, 61; Smith-Mundt vis. prof. Inst. Tecnologico, Monterrey, Mex., 1958-60; independent researcher U. Leiden, Netherlands, 1960; academic dean, prof. Wayland Baptist U., Plainview, Tex., 1961-66; Fulbright vis. prof. Universidad Nacional, Asuncion, Paraguay, 1966-67; prof. English, Tex. Tech U., Lubbock, 1967-73; prof., chmn. dept. English, Baylor U., Waco, 1973-80, dean grad. studies and research, 1979—. Editor: (with others) American Bypaths, 1980; The English Journals of Lodewijck Huygens, 1982. Contbr. articles to profl. jours. Served to cpl. U.S. Army, 1945-46. Fellow Rockefeller Found. 1958, Smith-Mundt, 1958-60, Fulbright-Hays, 1966-76; grantee Dutch Ministry Edn. Scis., 1981, Fulbright-Hays sr. research grantee 1982. Mem. Deans Conf. So. Assn. Bapt. Schs. (pres. 1963-64), S. Central Renaissance Conf. (pres. 1970-71), Assn. Tex. Grad. Schs. (pres. 1982-83), Conf. Christianity and Lit. (pres. 1982-85), Conf. Coll. Tchrs. of English (pres. 1983-84). Democrat. Avocations: traveling to Latin Am. and Europe. Home: 2801 Wooded Acres Dr Waco TX 76710 Office: Grad Sch Baylor U Waco TX 76798

COLLURA, JAMES GERARD, quality control administrator; b. Rockville Center, L.I., N.Y., Feb. 18, 1947; s. Frank Leonard and Florence Marie (Seaman) C.; diploma Burlington County Vocat. Tech. Sch., 1966; student U.S. Govt. Pkg. Sch., Aberdeen, Md., 1974; student Rider Coll., 1975—; numerous specialized courses; m. Frances Elaine Heydorn, Oct. 7, 1967; children—James Gerard, Michele Lynn, Melanie Ann. Chuck turret operator De-Laval Turbine Inc., Trenton, N.J., 1968-69, insp. quality control, 1969-74, quality control supr., 1974-83, sr. mfg. engr., 1983-84, div. quality circle coordinator, 1984—; staff writer DeLaval Digest. Served with Seabees, USN, 1966-68. Mem. Atco Dragracing Assn., Drag Bike Racing Assn., Internat. Assn. Quality Circles. Roman Catholic Lodge: Moose. Home: Oakdale Subdiv 3012 Oakdale Dr

Monroe NC 28110 Office: Transam Delaval Inc Pyramid Pump Div PO Box 447 Monroe NC 28110

COLMER, WILLIAM MEYERS, JR., obstetrician-gynecologist, medical administrator; b. Meridian, Miss., Nov. 22, 1919; s. William Meyers and Ruth (Miner) C.; m. Kathryn Mai Hoffman, Sept. 21, 1951; children—Meyers Hoffman, William Galloway. B.A., Vanderbilt U., 1941, M.D., 1944. Diplomate Am. Bd. Ob-Gyn. Rotating intern U.S. Naval Hosp., Bethesda, Md., 1944-45; intern in ob-gyn, asst. resident Vanderbilt U. Hosp., 1946-48; resident in ob-gyn Nashville Gen. Hosp., 1948-49; chief resident in ob-gyn U. Ark. Hosp., 1949-50; pvt. practice ob-gyn, Pensacola, Fla., 1954-80; med. dir. Med. Ctr. Clinic and West Fla. Hosp., Pensacola, 1980—. Participant Health Systems Agy. N.W. Fla., 1976-81, chmn., 1976-77; former mem. N.W. Fla. Comprehensive Health Planning Council; mem. Statewide Health Coordinating Council Cert. Need Task Force, 1981. Fellow ACS; mem. Am. Coll. Obstetricians and Gynecologists, Am. Acad. Med. Dirs., Am. Coll. Physician Execs., Fla. Med. Assn. (com. health systems agys. 1978-80, com. health planning 1981, com. bus. and industry 1982, com. health care fin. 1983). Democrat. Episcopalian. Contbr. articles to med. jours. Home: 555 El Cerrito Pl Pensacola FL 32503 Office: PO Box 151 Medical Center Clinic Pensacola FL 32591

COLON, GUSTAVO ALBERTO, plastic surgeon; b. Ponce, P.R., June 14, 1938; s. Gustavo Enrique and Araceli (de Ramery) C.; B.A., Johns Hopkins U., 1960; M.D., U. Md., 1964; m. Nairda Muniz, June 23, 1962; children—Gene, Albert, Lisa, Nairda. Intern, USPHS Hosp., Balt., 1964-65; resident in surgery USPHS Hosp., New Orleans, 1965-69; resident in plastic surgery Tulane U., New Orleans, 1969-71, assoc. prof. plastic surgery, 1972—; chief plastic surgery USPHS Hosp., New Orleans, 1971-72; pvt. practice plastic surgery, Metairie, La., 1972—; mem. staff East Jefferson Gen. Hosp., Touro Infirmary, Lakeside Hosp.; staff Drs. Hosp. of Jefferson, chmn. bd.; 1982-85. Served with USPHS, 1964-71. Diplomate Am. Bd. Plastic Surgery. Decorated U.S. Coast Guard Commendation Ribbon. Fellow A.C.S.; mem. Am. Soc. Plastic and Reconstructive Surgery, AMA, A.C.S., Am. Burn Assn., Am. Soc. Aesthetic Surgery, Am. Cleft Palate Assn., New Orleans Surg. Soc. Roman Catholic. Home: 4801 Hessmer Ave Metairie LA 70002 Office: 4204 Tueton St Metairie LA 70002

COLONEY, WAYNE HERNDON, civil engineer; b. Bradenton, Fla., Mar. 15, 1925; s. Herndon Percival and Mary Adore (Cramer) C.; B.C.E. summa cum laude, Ga. Inst. Tech., 1950; m. Anne Elizabeth Benedict, June 21, 1950; 1 dau., Mary Adore. Project engr. Constructora Gen., S.A., Venezuela, 1948-49, Fla. Rd. Dept., 1950-55; hwy. engr. Gibbs & Hill, Inc., Guatemala, 1955-57, project mgr., Tampa, Fla., 1957-59; project engr., then asso. J.E. Greiner Co., Tampa, 1959-63; partner Barrett, Daffin & Coloney, Tallahassee, 1963-70; pres. Wayne H. Coloney Co., Inc., Tallahassee, 1970-77, chmn. bd. chief exec. officer, 1977-83; pres., sec. Tesseract Corp., 1975-83; chmn. bd., chief exec. officer Coloney Co. Cons. Engrs., Inc., 1978—; chmn. adv. com. Area Vocat. Tech. Sch., 1965-78. Pres. United Fund Leon County, 1971-72; bd. dirs. Springtime Tallahassee, 1970-72, pres., 1981-82; bd. dirs. Heritage Found., 1965-71, pres., 1967; mem. Pres.'s Adv. Council on Indsl. Innovation, 1978-79; bd. dirs. LeMoyne Art Found., 1973, v.p., 1974-75; bd. dirs. Goodwill Industries, 1972-73, Tallahassee-Popoyan Friendship Commn., 1968-73; mem. Adv. Com. for Hist. and Cultural Preservation, 1969-71. Served with AUS, 1943-46. Named Fla. Small Bus. Person of Year, 1981. Registered profl. engr. and surveyor, Fla., Ga., Ala., N.C., also Nat. Council Engring. Examiners. Fellow ASCE; mem. Nat. Soc. Profl. Engrs., Fla. Engring. Soc. (sr.), Am. Water Works Assn., Fla. Inst. Cons. Engrs., Fla. Soc. Profl. Land Surveyors, Tallahassee C. of C., Anak, Koseme Soc., Phi Kappa Phi, Omicron Delta Kappa, Sigma Alpha Epsilon, Tau Beta Pi. Episcopalian. Clubs: Killearn Golf and Country; Governors. Contbr. profl. jours. Patentee roof framing system, tile mounting structure, curler rotating device, bracket system for roof framing. Home: 3219 Thomasville Rd #1-D Tallahassee FL 32312 Office: PO Box 668 Tallahassee FL 32302

COLORADO, ANTONIO J., lawyer; b. N.Y.C., Sept. 8, 1939; s. Antonio J. and Isabel (Laguna) C.; B.S. in Engring. Mgmt., Boston U., 1962; LL.B. cum laude, U. P.R., 1965; LL.M., Harvard U., 1966; m. Delia Castillo, Jan. 9, 1965; children—Delia Isabel, Ana Maria, Antonio Jose. Admitted to P.R. bar, 1966, U.S. Ct. Appeals bar, 1966; legal tax adv. Econ. Devel. Adminstrn. of P.R., 1966-68; exec. asst. to adminstr., 1968-69; mem. firm Baker & Woods, San Juan, P.R., 1969-72; partner firm Trias, Francis, Doval, Colorado and Carlo, San Juan, 1972-76; partner firm Antonio J. Colorado, San Juan, 1976-79; partner firm Colorado Martinez & Odell, San Juan, 1979—; lectr. taxes U. P.R. Law Sch., 1978-79, Inter-Am. U., 1979. Mem. P.R. Tax Reform Commn., 1975; mem. P.R. Bd. Bar Examiners, 1974-77. Mem. P.R. Bar Assn. (pres. constl. law commn. 1977, dir. 1978-79), P.R. Mfrs. Assn. (dir.), Am. Bar Assn., InterAm. Bar Assn. Club: Casino de Puerto Rico. Home: 780 Diana St San Juan PR 00923 Office: PH Suite Popular Center Bldg Hato Rey San Juan PR 00918

COLSON, BILL, lawyer; b. Miami, Nov. 25, 1924; s. W.W. Colson and Catherine A. (Frieden) Colson Tate; m. Martha Frances Wynns, June 11, 1948; children—William R., Dean Churchill, Catherine Wynns Colson Arbuckle. J.D., U. Miami, 1948. Bar admittee: Fla. 1948, D.C. 1978. Assoc., Worley's Gautier, 1948-51; ptnr. Nichols, Gaither, Beckham, Colson, Spence & Hicks, Miami, 1951-67; ptnr. Colson, Hicks & Eidson and predecessors, Miami, 1967—. Co-chmn. Com. for a Better Miami, 1970, pres. Community Mental Health Services Found., Miami, 1972-74; pres. Miami's 1976 Bicentennial Pageant; pres., trustee Center for Fine Arts, 1984—; mem. Orange Bowl Com.; vice chmn. Miami Citizens Against Crime, 1981; trustee U. Miami, 1971-77; chmn. Leadership Miami, 1978—. Recipient Miami-Dade C. of C. Achievement award, 1976; Big Orange award, 1977, NCCJ Silver medallion, 1977; Urban League Greater Miami The Reuben Askew award for outstanding service, 1981. Fellow Internat. Acad. Trial Lawyers, Acad. Fla. Trial Lawyers; mem. Assn. Trial Lawyers Am. (nat. pres. 1964-65), ABA, Am. Coll. Trial Lawyers, Inner Circle Advs., Trial Lawyers Pub. Justice (v.p.), Greater Miami C. of C. (pres. 1976-77). Democrat. Presbyterian. Office: Southeast Fin Center 200 S Biscayne Blvd 54th Floor Miami FL 33131

COLSON, LUCY WIGGINS, pharmacist; b. Monroeville, Ala., Dec. 11, 1951; d. James Morgan and Mabel Maxine (Stucey) W.; m. Robert Ellis Colson, Mar. 8, 1975. B.S., Auburn U., 1975; D.Pharmacy, U. Tenn., 1982. Registered pharmacist, Ala., Tenn. Staff pharmacist Meharry Med. Sch., Nashville, 1975; chief pharmacist K Mart Pharmacy, Nashville, 1975-82; pharmacist Albertson's, Huntsville, Ala., 1982-85, Bruno's Food & Pharmacy, Huntsville, 1985—; drug related cons., Nashville, 1975-76. Author: Monroe and Conecuh County Marriages, 1983; contbr. articles to various publs. Com. chmn. Madison County Young Republicans, Huntsville, 1980; active Rep. Women, Huntsville; del. Rep. Nat. Conv., 1984. Mem. Madison County Pharm. Assn., Ala. Pharm. Assn., Nat. Assn. Retail Druggists, Huntsville Friends of Library (bd. dirs. 1981-85), Hunts Spring DAR (historian 1984—), Christian Women's Fellowship, UDC. Lodge: Woodmen of World (sec.-treas. 1982-84, trustee 1980-82). Home: 9403 Danese Ln SE Huntsville AL 35803 Office: Bruno's Food & Pharmacy Bailey Cove Rd Huntsville AL 35802

COLSON, WENDELL H., banker. Exec. v.p. Sun Banks Inc., Orlando, Fla. Address: Sun Banks Inc Sun Bank NA Bldg Orlando FL 32802*

COLSTON, STEPHENIE WEBBER, mental health administrator; b. Odessa, Tex., Aug. 6, 1950; d. Selwyn Sanford and Rosamond Jack (Stephenson) Webber; 1 son, Todd. B.A., U. Okla., 1972, M.A., 1974, postgrad., 1982—. Grad. research asst. pub. adminstrn., grad. teaching asst., adj. prof. polit. sci. U. Okla., S. Oklahoma City Jr. Coll., 1973-75; research asst. Okla. State Legis. Council, 1975-76, sr. research assoc., 1977-78, research analyst, 1978-79, coordinator research and reference services div., 1979-80; dir. fiscal services, dir. bill drafting Okla. State Senate, 1980-82; chief ops. Okla. State Dept. Mental Health, Oklahoma City, 1982-85; acting asst. supt. adminstrn. Western State Hosp., Ft. Supply, Okla., 1983; exec. dir. Taliaferro Mental Health Ctr., Lawton, Okla., 1985—. Mem. ACLU, Assn. Am. Mgmt. Assn., Mental Health Adminstrs., Am. Pub. Health Assn., Am. Soc. Pub. Adminstrn., Pi Sigma Alpha. Author: (with T. R. Carr) State and Urban Policy: An Annotated Bibliography, 1975. Home: 7101 Woodland Dr Lawton OK 73505 Office: 602 SW 38th St Lawton OK 73505

COLVIN, EUTA MILLER, surgeon; b. Chester, S.C., Nov. 13, 1918; s. D. Euta and Havilene (O'Donnell) C.; m. Dorothy Eugenia Horner, Dec. 22, 1942; children—William Euta, Donald Horner Colvin. B.S., Furman U., 1936-40; M.D., Med. U. S.C., 1943. Diplomate Am. Bd. Surgery. Intern Roper Hosp., Charleston, S.C., 1944, Greenville (S.C.) Gen. Hosp., 1946; surg. preceptorship with pvt. physician, Spartanburg, S.C., 1946-50; resident Lawson VA Hosp, Emory U. group, Atlanta, 1950-52; practice surgery, Spartanburg, 1952—; established Surg. Assoc. of Spartanburg, P.A. 1957; attending surgeon Spartanburg Gen. Hosp., 1952—, former chief staff, chief surgery; attending surgeon Mary Black Meml. Hosp., 1953—; courtesy surg. staff. Drs. Meml. Hosp., 1975—; clin. prof. surgery Med. U. S.C., 1976—. Bd. dirs., treas. S.C. Polit. Action Com., 1974—; mem. session 1st Presbyn Ch., Spartanburg, pres. 1982; bd. dirs. S.C. Dept. Health and Environ. Control. Fellow ACS (S.C. gov.-at-large 1978—, chmn. state adv. com. 1976-78); mem. S.C. Med. Assn. (chmn. council 1979-81, pres. 1982-83) AMA, Spartanburg County Med. Assn. (pres. 1955), So. Med. Assn., Southeastern Surg. Congress, S.C. Surg. Soc. (pres. 1978-79), Am. Trauma Soc., S.C. Inst. Med. Edn., Research (bd. dirs., pres.), Alpha Omega Alpha. Contbr. articles to profl. publs. Home: 102 Rosewood Ln Spartanburg SC 29302 Office: 711 N Church St Spartanburg SC 29303

COLVIN, GERALD FRANKLIN, psychology educator, administrator, consultant; b. Jefferson, Tex., June 9, 1939; s. Jackson William and Rowena Berneice (Self) C.; m. Gayle Frances De Groat, July 26, 1959; children—Guy, Gaye. B.A., Union Coll., 1961; M.Ed., U. Ark., 1967, Ed.D., 1968; Ph.D., U. Ga., 1980. Cert. counselor, adminstr. Tenn. Grad. tchr. Loma Linda U., Loma Linda, Calif., 1970-72; dept. chmn. So. Coll., Collegedale, Tenn., 1972-79, 84-86, div. chmn., 1979-82; acad. dean. SAC, Keene, Tex., 1982-84; motivation speaker Andrews U. Inst., Berrien Springs, Mich., 1985. Author: Days of Lilac, 1971; Now Will I Sing, 1982; Homespun, 1985; Issues in Psychology and Religion, 1985. Ch. elder, Collegedale, 1985. Mem. Am. Psychol. Assn., Phi Delta Kappa. Avocations: walking; micro-computers; gardening. Office: Southern Coll Box 370 Collegedale TN 37315-370

COLWELL, CHARLES CARTER, English educator; b. Chgo., Aug. 19, 1932; s. Ernest Cadmen and Annette (Carter) C.; m. Ann Knox, 1952; children—Christopher James, Knox Cadmen, Joshua Edwards. B.A., U. Chgo., 1949; M.A., Cambridge U., 1957; Ph.D., Emory U., 1958. Instr. English, Emory-at-Oxford, 1952, 55; asst. prof. English, Stetson U., DeLand, Fla., 1958-64, assoc. prof., 1964-70, prof. English and humanities, 1970—, Nell Carlton prof. English, 1982-83. Served to sgt. AUS, 1953-55. Danforth fellow, 1955-58, assoc., 1968—; Emory U. fellow, 1957; recipient William Hugh McEniry award, 1980. Democrat. Methodist. Author: A Student's Guide to Literature, 1968; The Tradition of British Literature, 1971; (with James Knox) What's the Usage? A Writer's Guide to English Grammar and Rhetoric, 1973, The Complete Term Paper, 1974; contbr. articles and revs. to profl. publs.; movie reviewer Daytona Beach News-Jour. Home: 818 E Church St DeLand FL 32724 Office: Stetson U English Dept DeLand FL 32720

COLWELL, JAMES LEE, educator; b. Brush, Colo., Aug. 31, 1926; s. Francis Joseph and Alice (Bleasdale) C.; m. Claudia Alsleben, Dec. 27, 1957; children—John Francis, Alice Anne. B.A., U. Denver, 1949; M.A., U. No. Colo., 1951; cert. Sorbonne, Paris, 1956; diploma U. Heidelberg (Ger.), 1957; A.M. (Univ. fellow), Yale U., 1959, Ph.D. (Hale-Kilborn fellow), 1961. Tchr. high sch., Snyder and Sterling, Colo., 1948-52; civilian edn. adviser U.S. Air Force, Japan, 1952-56; asso. dir. Yale Fgn. Student Inst., summers 1959-60; asst. dir. European div. U. Md., Heidelberg, 1961-65; dir. Office Internat. Edn., asso. prof. Am. lit. U. Colo., Boulder, 1965-72; prof. Am. studies, chmn. lit. U. Tex. Permian Basin, Odessa, 1977-82, K.C. Dunagen prof. humanities, 1984—, dean Coll. Arts and Edn., 1972-77, 1982-84.Mem. nat. adv. council Inst. Internat. Edn., 1969-75. Vice pres. Ector County chpt. ARC, 1974-76; mem. Ector County Hist. Commn., 1973-75. Served with USAAF, 1945; brig. gen. USAF Res. (ret.). Mem. AAUP, Am. Studies Assn., Western Social Sci. Assn. (life; pres. 1974-75), MLA, NEA (life), Orgn. Am. Historians (life), South Central MLA, Permian Basin Hist. Soc. (life; pres. 1980-81), Air Force Assn. (life), Air Force Hist. Found. (life), Res. Officers Assn. (life), Ret. Officers Assn. (life), Phi Beta Kappa. Unitarian-Universalist. Contbr. articles to learned jours. Home: 1501 Westbrook Ave Odessa TX 79761

COMBEST, LARRY ED, congressman; b. Memphis, Tex., Mar. 20, 1945; s. Nelson and Callie (Gunter) C.; m. Sharon McCurry, Sept. 10, 1981. B.B.A., W. Tex. State U., 1969. Asst. to U.S. Senator John Tower, Washington, 1971-78; prin. Combest Distbg. Co., Lubbock, Tex., 1978-84; mem. 99th Congress from 19th Tex. Dist. Republican. Methodist. Lodges: Lions, Rotary. Office: Office of House Mems House of Representatives Office Washington DC 20515

COMBS, JERALD FORESTER, optometrist; b. Harlan, Ky., Apr. 25, 1949; s. Judge Forester and Madge (Harrison) C.; m. Judith Ann Breedlove, Nov. 24, 1979; 1 dau., Elizabeth LeAnn. B.S., Eastern Ky. U., 1972; B.S., U. Ala., 1974, O.D., 1976. Optometrist, Whitesburg, Ky., 1976-77, Paintsville, Ky., 1977-82, Martin and Inez, Ky., 1982—. Mem. Am. Optometric Assn., Ky. Optometric Assn. (2d v.p. 1984-85; 1st v.p. 1985-86, pres. elect 1986-87), Eastern Ky. Optometric Soc. Democrat. Methodist. Lodges: Lions, Kiwanis, (pres. 1985-86), Masons, Shriners. Home: Box 306 Paintsville KY 41240 Office: 127 Main St Box 1307 Inez KY 41224

COMBS, KINCHEON V., air national guard officer, civil engineer; b. Fairfax, Ala., Apr. 22, 1929; s. Robert James and Mary Katherine (Adams) C.; m. Juanita Black, Nov. 11, 1950; children—Cathryn J., Robert V. II, J. Carol, Ken V., Jr., Frances D. Assoc. in Sci., Jones Jr. Coll., 1954; B.S.C.E., Miss. State U., 1956. Staff engr. Miss. Nat. Guard, Jackson, 1956-65; commd. capt. Air Nat. Guard, U.S. Air Force, 1965; advanced through grades to col., 1977; base engr. Air N.G., Gulfport, Miss., 1965-77, comdr., 1977—; advisor Regional Airport Authority, Gulfport, 1977—; mem. U.S. Atty.'s Coordination Commn. So. Miss., 1983—. Contbr. articles on mil. engring. to profl. jours. Pres. bd. trustees Gulfport Sch. Dist., Miss., 1984—; sec. Gulfport Civil Service Commn., 1970-75; pres. Miss. Coast Crime Commn., Gulfport, 1978-80. Recipient Silver Beaver award Boy Scouts Am., 1971; Thanks Badge Girl Scouts Am., 1982; citation FAA, Atlanta, 1980. Mem. Miss. Nat. Guard Assn. (pres. 1980-81, bd. dirs. 1976-79, Commendation 1981). Methodist. Lodges: Rotary (Gulfport), Kiwanis (Pres. Gulfport 1977-78), Mason (32 degree), Shriners (pres. Miss. Coast club 1972-73). Home: 31-55th St Gulfport MS 39501 Office: Air Nat Guard Regional Airport Gulfport MS 39501

COMBS, LEON LAMAR, chemistry educator; b. Meridian, Miss., Sept. 19, 1938; s. Leon Lamar and Roberta Weems (Bunch) C.; m. M. Carol Hardee, Feb. 17, 1962; 1 child, Jeffrey L. B.S., Miss. State U., 1961; postgrad. U. Louisville, 1962-64; Ph.D., La. State U., 1968. Polymer chemist Devoe & Reynolds Co., Louisville, 1961-64; teaching and research asst. La. State U., Baton Rouge, 1964-67; from asst. prof. to prof. chemistry and physics, head dept. chemistry Miss. State (Miss). U., 1967—; vis. prof. quantum chemistry U. Uppsala (Sweden), 1977-78. Sunday Sch. tchr. Faith Baptist Ch. Exxon Research fellow, 1965; recipient research award Swedish Research Council, 1977, 79. Mem. Am. Chem. Soc. (Outstanding Chemist award), Am. Phys. Soc., Sigma Xi, Phi Lambda Upsilon, Phi Kappa Phi (pres. 1985-86). Contbr. articles to profl. jours. Office: Drawer CH Mississippi State University Mississippi State MS 39762

COMBS, PETER ARTHUR, architect, contractor; b. Columbus, Ohio, Jan. 11, 1942; s. Arthur Wright and Mildred (Mitchell) C.; m. Pam Heckman, 1966 (div. 1970); m. Nancy Buford, Feb. 14, 1973; 1 child, Jonathan Buford. B.A. in Architecture, U. Fla., 1960. Architect John Portman & Assocs., Atlanta, 1970-73, Peter A. Combs & Assocs., Atlanta, 1973—; specialist bldg. allergy free constrn. Served with U.S. Army, 1962-64. Mem. AIA, Nat. Assn. Home Builders. Home: 778 Brookridge Dr NE Atlanta GA 30306 Office: Peter A Combs & Assocs 2160 Briarcliff Rd NE Atlanta GA 30329

COMEGYS, JOHN STAFFORD, geologist, investor; b. Shreveport, La., Dec. 15, 1955; s. William McLoyd and Emily Anne (Glassell) C.; m. Pamela Jeter, Oct. 22, 1983; 1 child, Emily Anne. B.A., La. Tech. U., 1981; B.S. in Geology, Centenary Coll., 1982. Mud-logger So. Mud-Logging, Monroe, La., 1978-79; geologist Comegys Operating, Shreveport, La., 1982-84, 85—, Sugar Creek Prodn., Shreveport, 1984-85, Mem. Young Energy Forum, Shreveport, 1985. Mem. Am. Assn. Petroleum Geologist, Geol. Soc. Am., Shreveport Geol. Socs., Sigma Gamma Epsilon. Democrat. Epscopalian. Clubs: Petroleum (Shreveport), Like-Four Ltd. (Shreveport). Avocations: hunting, golf, racketball, swimming. Office: Comegys Operating Co 625 American Tower Shreveport LA 71101

COMISSIONA, SERGIU, conductor; b. Bucharest, Rumania, June 16, 1928; s. Isaac and Jean L. (Haufrecht) C.; ed. music conservatoire, Bucharest; Mus.D., Peabody Conservatory Music, 1972; L.H.D. (hon.), Towson State U., 1980; D.F.A. (hon.), Washington Coll., Chestertown, Md., 1980, Western Md. Coll.; hon. doctorate Johns Hopkins U.; m. Robinne Florin, July 16, 1949. Mus. dir. Rumanian State Ensemble Orch., 1950-55; prin. condr. Rumanian State Opera, 1955-59; musical dir. Haifa (Israel) Symphony, 1959, Israel Chamber Orch., 1960-65, Goteburg (Sweden) Symphony Orch., 1966-69; mus. adviser, condr. Ulster Orch., Belfast, Ireland, 1967-69; mus. dir. Balt. Symphony Orch., 1969-84; musical adviser Temple U. Music Festival, 1975-76, artistic dir., 1976-80; music adviser Am. Symphony Orch., 1978-82; artistic adviser Houston Symphony Orch., 1980-83, music dir., 1983— permanent guest condr. Radio Philharm. Orch. of Netherlands, 1982-84, chief condr., 1984—. Decorated Order Merit 2d Class (Rumania); winner internat. competition for young condrs., Besancon, France, 1956; recipient Gold medal award City of Goteborg, 1973; Ditson Condr.'s award Columbia U., 1979. Mem. Royal Swedish Acad. Music (hon.). Office: 615 Louisiana Houston TX 77002

COMOLA, JAMES PAUL, government official; b. Leland, Miss., Nov. 16, 1931; s. Wilson and Freda (Saba) C.; student Hinds Jr. Coll., 1950; B.A., Millsaps Coll., 1957; profl. social worker Fla. State U., 1958; postgrad. U. Miss., 1959-62; M.A. in Urban Planning, U. Tex. at Arlington, 1975; m. Beverly L'Hote Hoffman; children—James Paul, Jon Ronald. Asst. buyer Kennington's, 1954-57; dir. Miss. Dept. Pub. Welfare, Yazoo County, 1957-59; tech. Liaison Commn. Small Watersheds, U.S. Ho. of Reps., 1959-60; exec. v.p. Miss. Rivers and Harbors Assn., 1960-62; asst. gen. mgr. Trinity Improvement Assn., Arlington, Tex., 1962-66, gen. mgr., 1967-70; asst. regional adminstr. EPA, Dallas, 1970-77; EPA liaison to SW Fed. Regional Council, 1977-82, program analyst, EPA, Dallas, 1982—; clin. instr. community medicine U. Tex. Southwestern Med. Sch., Dallas; cons., 1970—. Mem. Bedford City Council, Tex., 1963-65, chmn. mid-cities adv. council, 1963-66. Served with USN, 1950-54. Recipient award Rivers and Harbors Assn. Miss., 1962; Appreciation award Bedford Council Good Govt., Bedford, 1966. Mem. Am. Inst. Planners (asso.), Urban Land Inst., Assn. Tchrs. Preventive Medicine, Soil Conservation Soc. Am., Audubon Soc., Ducks Unltd., Okla. Coalition for Clean Air. Club: Lions (dir. Bedford). Editor Trinity Valley Progress, 1963-67. Contbr. articles to profl. jours. Home: 12731 Burning Log Ln Dallas TX 75243 Office: 1201 Elm St Dallas TX 75270

COMPAGNO, RALPH EDWARD, contractor; b. New Orleans, Feb. 8, 1925; s. Emil A. and Leona (Schmidt) C.; m. Patricia Koenenn, Sept. 18, 1953; children—Ralph Edward, Daniel R. B.E. in Civil Engring., Tulane U., 1945. Registered profl. engr., Ala., Miss., La. Engr., Freeport Sulphur Co., New Orleans, 1946-48, Avondale Marine Ways, New Orleans, 1948-49, Delta Drainage & Constrn. Co., Greenville, Miss., 1949-51, William E. Mallett & Assocs., Greenville, 1951-52; engr., estimator Farmer Constrn. Co., Mobile, Ala., 1954-58; sec.-treas., mgr. Flaco Corp., Whistler, Ala., 1958-78; v.p., mgr. road materials div. Radcliff Materials, Inc., Mobile, 1978—; mem., sec.-treas. Ala. Licensing Bd. for Gen. Contractors, Montgomery, 1983—. Sr. warden St. Paul's Episcopal Ch., 1969-70; treas., chmn. fin. com. Episc. Diocese of Central Gulf Coast; bd. dirs. Met. YMCA, 1976-83; chmn. rds. and sts. com. Mobile Area C. of C., 1977-79, 83—, chmn. spl. task force Cochrane Bridge, 1978—. Served to lt. C.E., USNR, 1943-46, 52-54. Fellow ASCE; mem. Soc. Am. Mil. Engrs., Ala. Rd. Builders Assn., Am. Rd. and Transp. Builders Assn., Mobile County Rd. Builders Assn. Lodge: Rotary. Home: 4550 Knigh Way Dr Mobile AL 36608 Office: Radcliff Materials Inc Mobile AL 36652

COMPTON, ASBURY CHRISTIAN, justice Supreme Ct. Va.; b. Portsmouth, Va., Oct. 24, 1929; s. George Pierce and Edyth Gordon (Christian) C.; B.A., Washington and Lee U., Lexington, Va., 1950, LL.B., 1953, LL.D. (hon.), 1975; m. Betty Stephenson, Nov. 17, 1953; children—Leigh Christian, Mary Bryan, Melissa Anne. Admitted to Va. bar, 1957; partner firm May, Garrett, Miller, Newman & Compton, Richmond, 1957-66; judge Richmond City Law and Equity Ct., 1966-74; justice Supreme Ct. Va., 1974—. Trustee, Collegiate Schs., Richmond, 1972—, chmn., 1978-80; mem. adminstrv. bd. Trinity United Methodist Ch., Richmond, 1974-78; trustee Washington and Lee U., 1978—. Served as officer USNR, 1953-56. Recipient Letter of Commendation. Mem. Va. Bar Assn., Va. State Bar, Bar Assn. Richmond, Washington and Lee U. Alumni Assn. (past pres., dir.), Omicron Delta Kappa, Phi Kappa Sigma, Phi Alpha Delta. Club: Country of Va. Home: 5508 Queensbury Rd Richmond VA 23226 Office: PO Box 1315 Richmond VA 23210

COMPTON, ESTHER A., mathematics educator; b. Wabash, Ind., Mar. 28, 1908; d. Joseph John and Ida May (Kanower) Compton. A.B., Ind. U., 1930, A.M., 1933; M. Art Teaching, Mich. State U., 1962. Tchr. Butler Twp. High Sch., Peru, Ind., 1931-32; instr. Wood Jr. Coll., Mathison, Miss., 1935-41; tchr. Williamsport Jr. High Sch., Ind., 1943-45, Banquo High Sch., Marion, Ind., 1941-43; insp. Gen. Tire, Wabash, Ind., 1945-47; instr. math. and social sci. Cumberland Coll., Williamsburg, Ky., 1947—; faculty adviser Bapt. Student Union, 1948-60. Mem. Math. Assn. Am., Soc. Am. Math., Nat. Council Tchrs. Math. Clubs: Williamsburg Women's (pres. 1972-75), Cumberland County Women's (pres. 1977-78). Avocation: gardening. Home: Box 153 Williamsburg KY 40769

COMPTON, LARRY CURTIS, consultant; b. Greenville, S.C., July 17, 1942; s. Homer Stanley and Margie Ruth (Smith) C.; m. Iris Latimore, Apr. 2, 1965; children—Larry Curtis, Kelly Cathrine. Student U. S.C., 1960-61. Comml. artist Compton-Campbell Co. 1961-66; agt. trainee Hartford Ins. Co., 1966-67, Aetna Ins. Co., 1967-68; salesman Edens-Turbeville Agy., 1966-69; v.p. Curtis Brooks & Co., 1969; So. regional bd. Consumer Protection Agy., 1976-81; dist. mgr. County Yellow Pages, Greenville, S.C., 1983; gen. mgr. McCorkle Oil Co. Inc., Greenville, 1983; pres. Southern Yellow Pages Inc., Asheville, N.C., 1985—; advt., Greenville, 1984—. Chpt. sec. Batesburg Leesville Jaycees, 1966-71, v.p., 1966—; sec., chmn. United Fund, 1967-68. Recipient Rookie of Yr. award Batesburg Leesville Jaycees, 1966, Spark Plug award, 1967, Pres.' Cap, Palmetto State Lite, 1972; named Boss of the Yr., WMMU Radio, 1971. Republican. Methodist. Home: 202 Tindall Rd Greenville SC 29609 Office: 2552 N Pleasantburg Dr Greenville SC 29609

COMPTON, SUSAN LANELL, retired librarian; b. Batesville, Ark., Aug. 20, 1917; d. Thomas Smith and Susan (Whitlow) Compton; B.S. in Edn., Ark. State Tchrs. Coll., 1939; B.S. in L.S., Peabody Coll. Tchrs., 1948. Asst. cataloger U. Ark. Gen. Library, Fayetteville, 1948-49; head catalog dept. Ark. Library Commn., Little Rock, 1949-77, chief cataloger, bibliographer, indexer, 1977-79; free-lance writer. Mem. Nat. League Am. Pen Women (v.p., program chmn. Ark. Pioneer br. 1972-74, pres. 1974-76), AAUW, Ark. Hist. Assn., Ark. Fedn. Women's Clubs. Christadelphian. Author: Beauty Transient & Other Poems, 1969; Looking Forward to a New Day, 1984. Contbr. to Collier's Ency., 1970-76; editor quar. library bull. Ark. Libraries, 1949-74. Home: 620 N Oak St Little Rock AR 72205

COMRAS, REMA, librarian; b. N.Y.C., Oct. 26, 1936; d. Manuel and Zita (Kessel) C.; m. Jose Simonet, June 22, 1981. B.A., U. Fla., 1958; M.L.S., Syracuse U., 1960. Librarian, Queensborough Pub. Library, N.Y.C., 1960-61, Spl. Services, U.S. Army, Federal Republic Ger. and France, 1962-64; asst. head librarian City of Hialeah Library, Fla., 1964-73, library dir., 1973—. Mem. ALA, Fla. Library Assn., Dade County Library Assn., Beta Phi Mu. Office: City of Hialeah Library 190 W 49th St Hialeah FL 33012

CONARKO, JEANNE MARIE, music educator, singer; b. Kankakee, Ill., Aug. 21, 1946; d. Kenneth Louis and Rita Lorene (Blanchette) Beaupre; m. John Robert Conarko, July 13, 1968; children—Joseph John, Jeffrey James, Jennifer Elizabeth. B.A. in Voice, Coll. of St. Francis, 1968. Cert. music tchr. K-12, Ill., Iowa, Tex. Tchr. music Riverdale (Iowa) Jr. High Sch., 1968-71, St. Pius X Sch., San Antonio, 1979-82, 83-85, Bowden Elem. Sch., San Antonio Ind. Sch. Dist., 1985—; choir dir. Patrick Henry Village Army Chapel, Heidelberg, W. Ger., 1975-78, St. Helena Cath. Ch., San Antonio, 1980—; appearances include The Sound of Music, San Antonio, Showboat, San Antonio, 1982, The King and I, San Antonio, 1981, South Pacific, San Antonio, 1979. Active Bettendorf (Iowa) Community Theatre, Kelley Players, Stuttgart, W. Ger., Roadside Theatre, Heidelberg, San Antonio Little Theatre. Mem. Nat. Childbirth Edn. Assn. (pres. Bettendorf 1970), Nat. Pastoral Musicians, Tex. Choral Dirs. Assn., Tex. State Tchrs. Assn., Alpha Psi Omega. Clubs: World-Wide Marriage Encounter, Heidelberg Internat. Ski, Volksmarching.

CONAWAY, DANIEL EDWIN, advertising executive; b. Memphis, Oct. 10, 1949; s. Frank Elmer and Jessica Kathryn (Alley) C.; m. Nora Gorman Ballenger, Dec. 19, 1970; children—Hallie Elizabeth, Gaines Alley. B.S. in Communications, U. Tenn.-Knoxville, 1971. Copywriter, Brick Muller, Swearingen & Dorrity Advt., Memphis, 1971-74; v.p., creative dir. Brick Muller & Swearingen Advt., Memphis, 1974-77; exec. v.p. creative dir. Swearingen & Conaway Communications, Memphis, 1977-83, pres., 1984—; guest lectr. U. Tenn., Memphis State U. Mem. communications com. Episcopal Diocese of Tenn., 1981-83; pres. Memphis and Shelby County unit Am. Cancer Soc., 1983-84; bd. dirs. Boys Clubs of Memphis, 1979—, Youth Concert Ballet, 1979-84, Lakeside Hosp., Mental Health Soc. Memphis, 1982-83, Concerts Internat., 1982—, Muscular Dystrophy Assn. Memphis, 1973-74; bd. dirs. The Phoenix Inc., 1977-83, pres., 1981-82; participant Leadership Memphis, 1982, pres. alumni, 1982-83, trustee, 1984—. Recipient Edith S. Joel award as outstanding advt. alumnus U. Tenn., 1983; J.H. Mednikow award as outstanding mem. of The Phoenix, 1983. Mem. Am. Advt. Fedn., Memphis Advt. Fedn. Episcopalian. Club: Chickasaw Country. Office: 3259 Whitebrook Plaza Memphis TN 38118

CONCANNON, JAMES THOMAS, pharmacology educator; b. Shamokin, Pa., Apr. 18, 1951; s. Mary Dolores (Sokalaskie) C. B.S. in Psychology, St. Joseph's Coll., 1973; M.A. in Psychology, SUNY-Binghamton, 1975, Ph.D. in Psychology, 1977. Postdoctoral research assoc. Kent State U., Ohio, 1977-79; asst. prof. psychology U. R.I., Kingston, 1979-80; research instr. pharmacology Northeastern Ohio Univ. Coll. Medicine, Rootstown, 1980-82, research asst. prof., 1982-84; asst. prof. pharmacology Southeastern Coll. Osteo. Medicine, 1984—; teaching asst. SUNY-Binghamton, 1974-76, instr., 1977. Contbr. articles to profl. jours. and papers to profl. meetings. Fellow Nat. Inst. Alcohol Abuse and Alcoholism, 1976-77, NIH, 1977-79; grantee NIH, 1980-81, Northeastern Ohio Coll. Medicine, 1982, Occupational Health, 1982-84, Northeastern Ohio Univs. Coll. Medicine, 1983-84. Mem. Soc. Neuroscis., Am. Psychol. Assn. (mem. psychopharmacology, exptl. and gen. divs.), Internat. Soc. Devel. Psychobiology Soc. Stimulus Properties of Drugs, AAAS, Eastern Psychol. Assn., MIdwestern Psychol. Assn., N.Y. Acad. Sci., Sigma Xi. Office: Southeastern Coll Osteopathic Medicine 1750 NE 168th St North Miami Beach FL 33162

CONCODORA, PATRICIA JANE, interior designer; b. Jersey City, Aug. 3, 1948; d. Patrick Joseph and Susan Mildred (Capone) Woods; m. Joseph Anthony Concodora, June 15, 1969; children—Stephanie Lynn, Jacqueline Leigh. B.A., in Biology and Chemistry, Caldwell Coll., 1970; B.F.A. in Interior Design, Va. Commonwealth U., 1981, M.F.A. in Interior Design, 1985. Asst. scientist Philip Morris U.S.A., Richmond, Va., 1969-73; designer Creative Interiors, Midlothian, Va., 1980-84; head interior design Interplan/Interiors, Richmond, 1984-85; designer Deep Run Design Group, Richmond, 1985—. Mem. Interior Bus. Designers (affiliate), Va. Orchid Soc. (bd. dirs. 1983-84). Roman Catholic. Avocation: raising orchids. Home: 14011 Chepstow Rd Midlothian VA 23113 Office: Deep Run Design Group Deep Run Bus Ctr Richmond VA 23219

CONCORDIA, CHARLES, consulting engineer; b. Schenectady, June 20, 1908; s. Francis G. and Susie Elizabeth (Decker) C.; m. Frances Butler, Dec. 18, 1948; Sc.D., Union Coll., 1971. With Gen. Electric Co., 1926-73, with engring. lab., 1926-31, with advanced engring. program, 1932-35, electric utility systems application engr., Schenectady, 1936-49, cons. engr., 1949-73; cons. engr., Venice, Fla., 1973—. Recipient Coffin award, 1942, Steinmetz award, 1973; Lamme medal Am. Inst. Elec. Engrs., 1961; named Engr. of Yr., Schenectady Profl. Engrs. Soc., 1963. Fellow IEEE, ASME, AAAS; mem. Nat. Soc. Profl. Engrs., Nat. Acad. Engring., Conf. Internationale de Grands Reseaux Electriques. Republican. Presbyterian. Club: Venice Yacht. Author: Synchronous Machines, 1951; contbr. over 120 articles to profl. jours.; patentee in field. Home and Office: 702 Bird Bay Dr W Venice FL 33595

CONDE, CESAR AUGUSTO, physician; b. Lima, Peru, Oct. 31, 1942; s. Aurelio Vicente and Mercedes (Portocarrearo) C.; M.D., San Marcos U. (Lima, Peru), 1967; m. Maria C. Perez-Teran, Sept. 8, 1972; children—Cesar R., Jorge C., Enrique A. Intern, Phila. Gen. Hosp., U. Pa., 1968-69; resident Henry Ford Hosp., Detroit, 1969-71; resident cardiology Mt. Sinai Hosp. and Mt. Sinai Sch. Medicine, 1971-73, asst. prof. medicine and cardiology, 1973-74; asst. clin. prof. medicine and cardiology U. Miami, 1974-78, asso. clin. prof., 1978-84, clin. prof., 1984—, chief div. cardiology Parkway Gen. Hosp., Miami, Fla., 1977-84; chief staff Parkway Regional Med. Ctr., Miami, 1984—. . Fellow Am. Coll. Cardiology, A.C.P., Nat. Council Clin. Cardiology; mem. Am. Heart Assn. (pres.-elect Greater Miami), Miami Heart Assn. (dir.). Roman Catholic. Club: Big Five (Miami). Home: 8100 Los Pinos Blvd Miami FL 33143 Office: 16800 NW 2d Ave North Miami Beach FL 33169 also 1295 NW 14th St Miami FL 33125

CONDE, JUDITH SHERROW, Spanish language educator; b. Danville, Ky., Oct. 27, 1948; d. Mary (Hamm) Hollon; m. Clemente Conde, Feb. 7, 1970; children—Maria Dolores, Elisa Renee. Diploma U. de Guadalajara, Mex., 1969; B.A., Berea Coll., 1970; M.A., U. Ky., 1974, Ph.D., 1977. Spanish tchr. St. Michael's High Sch., Los Angeles, 1970-71; grad. teaching asst. U. Ky., Lexington, 1972-77; assoc. prof. Spanish, head modern lang. dept. Asbury Coll., Wilmore, Ky., 1977—, sponsor Spanish Club, 1977-79, Fgn. Lang. Club, 1985—. Author: (etymological vocabulary) Vocabulario Etimologico de Poridat de las Poridades, 1981. Contbr. articles to profl. jours. Grantee U. Ky., 1976, Asbury Coll., 1977, 80, 85. Mem. Am. Assn. Tchrs. of Spanish and Portuguese, MLA, Ky. Council on Teaching Fgn. Langs., South Atlantic MLA. Democrat. Baptist. Avocations: reading; sewing; crafts, computer programs for foreign languages. Office: Asbury Coll Wilmore KY 40390

CONDIT, PAUL ARTHUR, JR., manufacturing company executive; b. Paul Arthur and Dorothy Ann (Murphy) C.; student Allen Mil. Acad., Bryan, Tex., 1953-58, U. Houston, 1958-66; m. Lois Jobe Condit, Jan. 7, 1967; children—Garth, Paul, Laura. With Paul-Condit Co., Inc., Houston, 1958-72; pres., chmn. bd. Environ. Products, Inc., Houston, 1969—; v.p. Wesco Equipment Inc., Houston, 1972-82; pres. Centriflow Inc., 1982—. Mem. Houston Engring. Sci. Soc., Instrument Soc. Am. Republican. Presbyterian. Clubs: Planetary Soc., Woodlands Country. Patentee in field. Home: 1 Sandlily Ct Woodlands TX 77380 Office: Woodlands TX 77380

CONDOM, JAIME ERNESTO, hospital administrator, physician; b. Mariel, Cuba, Feb. 27, 1932; s. Jaime Simeon and Maria Matilde (Valera) C.; B.S., U. Havana, 1957; M.D., U. Madrid, 1962; m. Kathryn Du Cloux, Dec. 5, 1974; children—Marie Elizabeth, Kathryn Leigh, Valerie DuCloux. Came to U.S., 1960, naturalized, 1966. Intern, Mobile (Ala.) Gen. Hosp., 1962-63; staff physician Searcy State Hosp., Mt. Vernon, Ala., 1963-68, acting clin. dir., 1968-69, clin. dir., 1969-70, acting supt., clin. dir., 1970, supt., 1970-83; supt. Thomasville, Andalusia and Eufaula Adjustment Centers, 1975-83; asso. prof. psychiatry U. South Ala. Sch. Medicine, 1977—; supt. Bryce Hosp., Tuscaloosa, Ala., 1979; asso. commr. mental health State of Ala., 1981-83; supt. S.C. State Hosp., 1984—. Bd. dirs. Mobile Mental Health Assn. Recipient Physician's Recognition award AMA, 1970. Mem. Assn. Med. Supts. Mental Hosps., Med. Assn. State Ala., Mobile County Med. Soc., Gulf Coast Soc. Neurology, Psychiatry, Neurosurgery and Psychology. Address: Searcy Hosp PO Box 545 Mount Vernon AL 36560

CONDON, DONALD STEPHEN, real estate investment adviser and broker; b. Bklyn., Dec. 26, 1930; s. Joseph Francis and Helen (Carboy) C.; m. Cristina Maria Basarrate, Sept. 27, 1969; children—Gregg, Mark, Brian, Alexander, Kevin. Student (scholar) Oberlin Coll., 1949-50; B.A. (scholar), Northwestern U., 1953; postgrad. U. Detroit, 1956. Mem. sales and mktg. dept. Owens-Corning Fiberglas, 1955-63; v.p., gen. mgr. Howard T. Keating Co., Birmingham, Mich., 1963-65; chief exec. officer Condon Investment & Devel. Corp., Bloomfield Hills, Mich., 1965-69; pres. Condyne, Inc., N.Y.C., 1969-74; chmn., dir. Parr, O'Mara, Condon & Assos., Inc., N.Y.C. and Palm Beach, Fla., 1974-81; pres. The Condon Corp., Palm Beach, Fla., 1981—; lectr. Practising Law Inst., 1970-71. Served with Signal Corps, U.S. Army, 1953-55. Recipient Sales Builder award Owens-Corning Fiberglas, 1959, Am. Home Builders award for design, 1964, Practical Builders Top Merchandising award, 1966, Mktg. Mgr. of Yr. award Nat. Assn. Home Builders, 1967, Product of Year award Mich. C. of C., 1968, Assn. Indsl. Mgmt. award, 1972. Mem. Internat. Platform Assn., Phi Gamma Delta. Contbr. articles to House and Home, Profl. Builder mag., Bus. Week, Instn. Investor, others. Clubs: N.Y. Athletic; Birmingham Athletic; Beach (Palm Beach); PGA Nat. Golf. Home: 255 Bahama Ln Palm Beach FL 33480 Office: 101 Bradley Pl Suite 205 Palm Beach FL 33480

CONDON, WILLIAM JAMES, librarian; b. Portsmouth, N.H., Nov. 13, 1928; s. James Joseph and Helen Marjorie (Burton) C.; m. Jane Elizabeth Sharp, Feb. 24, 1973; children—James, Mary Elizabeth, Tracy. A.B., Union Coll., 1952; M.S.L.S., Western Res. U., 1954. Librarian, Enoch Pratt Free Library, Balt., 1954-58; mgr. tech. library aircraft nuclear propulsion dept. Gen. Electric Co., Cin., 1958-62; corp. librarian System Devel. Corp., Santa Monica, Calif., 1962-65; mgr. reference dept. NASA Info. Facility, College Park, Md., 1965-67; systems analyst System Devel. Corp., Falls Church, Va., 1967-69; chief library br. Def. Atomic Support Agy., Washington, 1969-71; dir. Swisher Library, Bolles Prep. Sch., Jacksonville, Fla., 1971-76; dir. Clay County Pub. Library, Green Cove Springs, Fla., 1976-81; corp. librarian Blue Cross & Blue Shield Fla., Jacksonville, 1981—. Del., Gov.'s Conf. on Libraries and Info. Sci., Tallahassee, 1979, White House Conf. Libraries and Info. Sci., Washington, 1980. Served with USN, 1946-48. Mem. Am. Soc. Info. Scientists, Spl. Libraries Assn., Nat. Soc. Arts and Letters. Clubs: Rotary, Sertoma. Home: 1560 Lancaster Terr Apt 1106 Jacksonville FL 32204 Office: 532 Riverside Ave Jacksonville FL

CONDRILL, JO ELLARESA, logistician, speaker; b. Hull, Tex., Oct. 25, 1935; d. Freddie and Ida (Donatto) Founteno; m. Edwin Leon Ellis, Jan. 9, 1955 (div. 1979); children—Michael Edwin, James Alcia, Resa Ann, Thomas Matthew; m. Donald Richard Condrill, Sept. 21, 1980 (div. 1985). B.S. in Bus. Adminstrn., Our Lady of the Lake U. San Antonio, 1982; grad. Logistics Exec. Devel. Course, Army Logistics Mgmt. Ctr., 1985. cert. seminar coordinator. Sec. U.S. Air Forces, Wiesbaden, Germany, 1968-73, Air Force Mil. Tng. Ctr., San Antonio, 1973-77; editorial asst. Airman Mag., San Antonio, 1978; mgmt. analyst San Antonio Air Logistics Ctr., 1979-81, inventory mgr. ground fuels Detachment 29, Alexandria, Va., 1981-83; owner Seminars by Jo, Alexandria, 1984—; logistics plans officer, Mil. Dist. Washington, 1983-85, chief logistics plans ops. and mgmt., 1985—; field instr. Golden State U., Los Angeles, 1985—. Instr. Fairfax County Adult Edn., Springfield, Va., 1984; vol. aide ARC Wilford Hall Hosp., San Antonio, 1978; constn. drafter KC Women's Aux., San Antonio, 1977; den mother Boy Scouts Am., San Antonio, 1967. Recipient Cert. of Achievement, Dept. Army, 1984; Best Speaker award Def. Logistics Agy. Toastmasters, Alexandria, 1984. Mem. Soc. Logistics Engrs., Federally Employed Women, Assn. U.S. Army, Nat. Assn. Female Execs. Republican. Roman Catholic. Club: Toastmasters (pres. Def. Logistics Agy. 1984, instr. Washington 1985, speaker dist. 36 1984—). Avocations: Travel; dancing; reading; listening. Home: PO Box 11812 Alexandria VA 22312

CONE, CARL BRUCE, historian; b. Davenport, Iowa, Feb. 22, 1916; s. Carl S. and Lena (Petersen) C.; B.A., U. Iowa, 1936, M.A., 1937, Ph.D., 1940; D.Litt., U. Ky., 1984; m. Mary Louise Regan, Dec. 20, 1942; 1 son, Carl Timothy. Instr. history Allegheny Coll., Meadville, Pa., 1940-41; asst. prof. history La. State U., Baton Rouge, 1942-47; asst. prof. U. Ky., Lexington, 1947-49, asso. prof., 1949-56, prof., 1956-81, prof. emeritus, 1981—, chmn. dept., 1965-70. Mem. Lexington Civil Service Commn., 1958-68; mem. Lexington Library Bd., 1978-83. Guggenheim Found. fellow, 1963-64; recipient Disting. Citizen award Lexington-Fayette Urban County Govt., 1981. Mem. So. Hist. Assn. (mem. exec. council), Am. Cath. Hist. Assn. (pres. 1967), So. Conf. Brit. Studies (chmn. 1972). Republican. Roman Catholic. Author: Torchbearer of Freedom, 1952; Burke and the Nature of Politics, Vol. I, 1957, Vol. 2, 1964; The English Jacobins, 1968; Hounds in the Morning, 1981; also articles. Home: 203 Sycamore Rd Lexington KY 40502 Office: Dept History U Ky Lexington KY 40506

CONE, GEORGE WALLIS, lawyer; b. Augusta, Ga., July 20, 1945; s. William Harry and Agnes M. (Hill) C.; student Clemson Coll., 1963-64; B.S. in Pharmacy, U. Ga., 1967, J.D., 1973; m. Patricia Ann Stabenow, Dec. 28, 1967; children—Jennifer Lee, Laura Katherine, David Wallis. Pharmacist-in-charge Walterboro Drug, Inc. (S.C.), 1967-76; admitted to Ga. bar, 1973, S.C. bar, 1974; atty. firm McLeod, Fraser & Unger, Walterboro, 1976—. Mem. S.C. Bd. Pharmacy, 1981—; bd. dirs. S.C. Humane Assn., 1978—, treas., 1979—; bd. dirs. Colleton County chpt. SPCA, 1975—, pres., 1975-77; mem. Colleton County Alcohol and Drug Abuse Com., 1979-81, chmn., 1980-81; bd. dirs. Public Defender Corp. Colleton County, 1978—, sec., 1979—; mem. Colleton County Bd. Voter Registration, 1982—; bd. dirs. Lowcountry Community Action Agy., 1980—, sec., 1983—. Served with S.C. Army N.G., 1970-76. Mem. Nat. Assn. Bds. Pharmacy (adv. com. bur. voluntary compliance 1983—), Am. Pharm. Assn., Nat. Assn. Retail Druggists, Am. Soc. Pharm. Law, ABA, State Bar Ga., S.C. Bar Assn., S.C. Trial Lawyers Assn., S.C. Pharm. Assn. (ho. of dels. 1975-76, 77-78, 79—), Colleton County Bar Assn., 14th Dist. Pharm. Assn. (pres. 1980-82), Delta Chi, Phi Alpha Delta. Democrat. Baptist. Club: Sertoma (pres. 1977-78) (Walterboro). Notes editor Ga. Jour. Internat. and Comparative Law, 1971-72, revs. and comments editor, 1972-73. Home: PO Box 233 Walterboro SC 29488 Office: PO Box 230 Walterboro SC 29488

CONERLY, EVELYN NETTLES, educational consultant, counselor; b. Baton Rouge, Aug. 25, 1940; d. Noel Douglas and Evelyn Elsie (Pratt) Nettles; children from previous marriage—Douglas Wayne, Kelee Lynne. B.S., La. State U., 1962, M.Ed., 1965, Ph.D., 1973. Tchr., East Baton Rouge Parish Pub. Schs., La., 1962-67, elem. librarian, 1967-73, prin., 1973-81, elem. library supr., 1981-83, prin., 1983-84; ednl. cons., counselor, Baton Rouge, 1984—. Co-author: Principals' Pointers for Parents, 1985. Mem. Assn. Tchr. Educators (pres. La. 1981-82), Internat. Reading Assn., La. Reading Assn., Am. Assn. Counseling and Devel., Am. Mental Health Counselors Assn., La. Ret. Tchrs. Assn., Phi Kappa Phi, Phi Delta Kappa, Delta Kappa Gamma. Presbyterian. Club: Zonta. home: 4965 Abelia Ct Baton Rouge LA 70808

CONESA, MIGUEL A. OSUNA, artist; b. Ponce, P.R., Sept. 29, 1952; s. Antulio Conesa Maldonado and Irma Osuna Yordan; m. Reina Inés Conesa, Aug. 29, 1980; 1 dau., Karina Inés. Student, Cath. U., Ponce, 1971-72, Escuela Artes Plásticas, San Juan, P.R., 1972. One-man shows: Gertrude Herbert Art Inst., Augusta, Ga., 1976, Ponce Art Mus., 1980, U. P.R. Library, 1980; group shows: Am. Painters In Paris, 1975-76, High Mus., Atlanta, 1976, Instituto de Cultura, San Juan, 1980, U. Aiken (S.C.), 1981, Gallery II, Charlottesville, Va., 1983, others. Served with U.S. Army, 1972-74. Mem. Internat. Platform Assn. Home: Ext Rambla Calle D-648 Ponce PR 00731

CONESCU, PAUL VICTOR, orthopedic surgeon; b. Bklyn., Sept. 3, 1943; s. Sidney and Diana (Kass) C.; m. Lizabeth Green, July 3, 1967; children—Ronald, Jeremy. B.M.E., Rensselaer Poly. Inst., 1965; M.D., N.Y. Med. Coll., 1969. Diplomate Am. Bd. Orthopedic Surgery. Intern, Beth Israel Med. Center, N.Y.C., 1969-70, resident in gen. surgery, 1970-71; research assoc. USPHS, Balt., 1971-73; clin. assoc. Surgery Br. Nat. Cancer Inst., Bethesda, Md., 1973-74; resident in orthopedic surgery, U. Conn. Health Center, Hartford, 1974-77; practice medicine specializing in orthopedic surgery, Atlanta, 1977—; attending physician DeKalb Gen. Hosp., Decatur, Ga., 1977—, Humana Hosp.-Gwinett, Snellville, Ga., 1981—. Fellow ACS, Am. Acad. Orthopedic Surgeons; mem. So. Med. Assn., Med. Assn. Ga., DeKalb Med. Soc., Atlanta Orthopedic Soc. Office: 487 Winn Way Suite 101 Decatur GA 30030

CONEWAY, CHARLES RICHARD, JR., civil engineer, consultant; b. Houston, July 31, 1946; s. Charles Richard and Wayne Estelle (Sandifer) C.; m. Mary Eleanor Hotchkiss, June 19, 1971; 1 son, Casey Wayne. B.S., Tulane U., 1968; B.S.C.E., U. Houston, 1973, M.S.C.E., 1976. Registered profl. engr., Tex. Project engr. Lockwood, Andrews & Newman, Inc., Houston, 1973-80, mgr. Austin office, 1981-83; pres. Coneway and Assocs., Inc., 1983—; lectr. U. Houston. Vice pres. Southwest Civic Club, Houston, 1979-80; v.p. Lost Creek Neighborhood Assn., Austin, 1983; bd. dirs. Wild Basin Wilderness Reserve. Served with USN Air Res., 1969-79, Tex. Air N.G., 1979-81, USAFR, 1981—. Recipient Outstanding Young Engr. of Yr. award, Tex. Soc. Profl. Engrs., 1978. Mem. Tex. Soc. Profl. Engrs. (pres. elect chpt.), Nat. Soc. Profl. Engrs., Res. Officers Assn., ASCE, Am. Acad. Environ. Engrs., Am. Waterworks Assn., Young Men's Bus. League, Water Pollution Control Fedn., Austin C. of C. Presbyterian. Club: Headliners. Home: 1509 Wilson Heights Dr Austin TX 78746 Office: 3316 Bee Cave Rd Suite 3 Austin TX 78746

CONGER, AMY, art educator. B.A. in Art History, Skidmore Coll., 1964; M.A. in Art History, U. Iowa, 1966; postgrad. Washington U., St. Louis, 1966-67, Lake Forest Coll., 1977; Ph.D. in Art History, U. N.M., 1982. Instr. art history So. Ill. U., Edwardsville, 1966-67; asst. prof. architecture and fine arts U. Chile, Santiago, 1972-74; researcher, interpreter dept. collections and exhbns., Art Inst. Chgo., 1975-76; part-time lectr. Extension Coll., Coll. DuPage, Glen Ellyn, Ill., 1976; asst. prof. art history and photography, So. Ill. U., Edwardsville, 1976-77; asst. U. N.M., 1978-79, tchg. assoc. dept. art, part-time lectr. Honors Coll. and dept. continuing edn., 1979; vis. prof. postgrad. faculty dept. philosophy U. Mex., Mexico City, 1982; guest curator San Francisco Mus. Modern Art, 1982-83; asst. prof. dept. art Coll. Arts and Humanities, Corpus Christi State U., 1983—. Contbr. articles to profl. jours.; participator in several nat. and internat. photographic shows. Grantee Latin Am. Inst. U. N.M., Tinker Found., Grad. Student Assn., Fulbright-Hays; fellow Beaumont Newhall, 1981-82, AAUW, 1971-72, Woodrow Wilson, 1968.

CONGER, CLINTON BEACH (PAT), retired editor; b. Copenhagen, Mar. 17, 1917 (parents Am. citizens); s. Seymour Beach II and Lucile (Bailey) C.; m. Barbara Heath, Sept. 14, 1943 (div. 1945); m. Charlotte Doretta Dahl, Feb. 15, 1947; children—Dahlia Jean, Lucile Bailey, Patricia Jean. B.A. in Polit. Sci., U. Mich., 1938; postgrad. Nat. War Coll., 1961; M.A. in Internat. Affairs, George Washington U., 1967. String corr. various orgns., 1930-39; staff corr. United Press, Detroit, 1939, fgn. corr., Oslo, Copenhagen, Zurich, Berlin, 1940-41, Bad Nauheim, Germany, 1941-42, war corr., 1942-45, mgr. for Germany, 1945-48; sports editor, asst. to pub. Los Angeles Mirror, 1948-51; intelligence officer, sr. editor current intelligence CIA, 1951-79, ret. Author: (with others) This Is The Enemy, 1942. Recipient Disting. Intelligence medal CIA, 1979. Mem. Nat. Press Club, Central Intelligence Retirees Assn., Assn. Former Intelligence Officers, Sigma Delta Chi (life), Sigma Phi. Republican. Episcopalian. Avocations: traveling; football. Home and Office: 8380 Greensboro Dr 312 McLean VA 22102

CONGER, STEPHEN HALSEY, lumber company executive; b. Asheville, N.C., July 14, 1927; s. Allen Ford and Margery (Evans) C.; m. Marian Lansdell Meiere, June 29, 1951; children—Susan de Camp, Stephen Halsey, Robert Cody Lansdell, Marian Lansdell Meiere. B.S.F., U. Ga., 1949. With Forester Coastal Lumber Co., Lake City, S.C., 1949-52; asst. sales mgr. Commonwealth Lumber Corp., Murphy, N.C., 1952-53; salesman Ga. Pacific Corp., Augusta, 1953-54; sales mgr. Coastal Sales Co., Weldon, N.C., 1953-59, pres., 1960-69; pres. Pioneer Lumber Corp., Dailey, W.Va., 1961-70; exec. v.p., sec., dir. Coastal Lumber Co., Weldon, 1969—; v.p., sec., dir. Dubarco Lumber Co., Havana, Fla., 1970-73, Frazee Lumber Co., Hopwood, Pa., 1978-80, Summit Lumber Co., Hopwood, 1978-80; pres. Coastal Lumber Internat., 1972—; exec. v.p., dir. Coastal Lumber Co. of Va., 1980—; v.p., dir. Sheffield Lumber Co., Suffolk, Va., 1980-84; v.p., dir. Coastal Lumber Co. of Miss., Meridian, 1985—. Treas., N.C. Pvt. Sch. Assn., 1973-77; county chmn. Halofax County Republican Com., 1960-65, 68-69; del. Rep. Nat. Conv., 1964, 68; treas. Am. Party N.C., 1969-71. Served with C.E., AUS, 1946-48. Mem. So. Cypress Mfg. Assn. (pres. 1974—), Nat. Forest Products Assn. (dir. 1969—), Soc. Am. Foresters, Nat. Lumber Exporters Assn. (dir. 1976-78), So. Hardwood Lumber Mfg. Assn. (dir. 1976-80), Appalachian Hardwood Mfrs. Assn. (dir. 1978-84), Nat. Hardwood Lumber Assn. (dir. 1982—), SAR, Newcomen Soc., Holland Soc. N.Y., Sigma Alpha Epsilon. Baptist. Clubs: Wintergreen Country, Chockoyotte Country, Capital City. Home: 509 Sycamore St Weldon NC 27890 also 11 Roanoke Shores Littleton NC 27850 Office: Box 829 Weldon NC 27890

CONINE, DEBORAH ANN, automobile distributorship official; b. Hot Springs, Ark., Dec. 10, 1948; s. Thurman Reeves and Nicoletta Louise (Rose) Hollingshead; 1 dau., Rebecca Shayne. B.S., Phillips County Community Coll., 1973; postgrad. U. Ark. Co-mgr. Holiday Inn, Helena, Ark., 1975-78; gen. mgr. Tramps Restaurant, Little Rock, 1978-80; advt. and communications mgr. Subaru South, Inc., Little Rock, 1980—. Recipient Disting. Pub. Service award Ark. Arthritis Found., 1982; award for excellence in advt., 10th dist. Am. Advt. Fedn., 1983; Am. Advt. Fedn. 10th Dist. scholar, 1982. Mem. Internat. Assn. Bus. Communicators (treas. 1983), Ark. Advt. Fedn., Pub. Relations Soc. Am., Pulaski County Automobile Dealers Assn., Alpha Delta Sigma. Republican. Methodist. Editor Internat. Assn. Bus. Communicators Newsletter, 1982. Home: 7 Myrtle Ln Little Rock AR 72207 Office: Subaru South Inc 8923 Fourche Dam Pike Little Rock AR 72206

CONKEL, ROBERT DALE, pension consultant, lawyer; b. Martins Ferry, Ohio, Oct. 13, 1936; s. Chester William and Marian Matilda (Ashton) C.; m. Elizabeth A. Cargill, June 15, 1958; children—Debra Lynn Conkel McGlone, Dale William, Douglas Alan; m. 2d, Brenda Jo Myers, Aug. 2, 1980. B.A., Mt. Union Coll., 1958; J.D. cum laude, Cleve. Marshall Law Sch., 1965; LL.M., Case Western Res. U., 1972. Bar: Ohio 1965, U.S. Tax Ct. 1974, U.S. Supreme Ct. 1974, Tex. 1978, U.S. Ct. Appeals (5th cir.) 1979. Supr., Social Security Adminstrn., Cleve., 1958-65; trust officer Harter Bank & Trust Co., Canton, Ohio, 1965-70; exec. v.p. Am. Actuaries, Inc., Grand Rapids, Mich., 1970-73, pension cons., S.W. regional dir., Dallas, 1974—; mgr. plans and research A.S. Hansen, Inc., Dallas, 1973-74; sole practice, Dallas, 1973—; mem. devel. bd. Met. Nat. Bank, Richardson, Tex.; instr. Am. Mgmt. Assn., 1975, Am. Coll. Advanced Pension Planning, 1975-76. Sustaining mem. Republican Nat. Com., 1980—. Enrolled actuary, Joint Bd. Enrollment U.S. Depts. Labor and Treasury. Mem. ABA (employee benefit com. sect. taxation), Ohio State Bar Assn., Tex. Bar Assn., Dallas Bar Assn., Am. Soc. Pension Actuaries (dir. 1973-81), Am. Acad. Actuaries. Contbr. articles to legal publs.; editorial adv. bd. Jour. Pension Planning and Compliance, 1974—. Office: PO Box 31481 Dallas TX 75231

CONKLIN, DORMAN STAHL, JR., training and development executive; b. Ancon, C.Z., Panama, Dec. 22, 1945; s. Dorman Stahl and Olivia (Fowler) C.; m. Judy Culpepper, Mar. 3, 1967 (div. 1976); 1 dau., Jennifer Dawn; m. Lynette Ingram, Nov. 17, 1977. B.S., U. So. Miss., 1967; M.S. in Environ. Health, East Tenn. State U., 1971. Registered sanitarian; cert. CPR instr.; cert. trainer employee performance appraisal system. With Miss. Dept. Health, 1967—, county sanitarian, Meridian, 1967-70, chief sanitarian, Laurel, 1971-73, adv. sanitarian, Jackson, 1973-74, supr. tng. environ. health, 1974-79, adminstrv. asst., 1979-81, tng. dir., 1981-85; mgr. corp. tng. So. Vital Dataplex, Flora, Miss., 1985—; vice chmn. Miss. Tng. and Devel. Consortium, Jackson, 1981—; conv. coordinator Nat. Rural Primary Care Assn., Waterville, Maine, 1981-82; cons. audiovisual coordinator, Nat. Assn. Emergency Med. Technicians, Newton Highlands, Mass., 1982-83, SE Region High Blood Pressure Found., Atlanta, 1983. Mem. Am. Soc. Tng. and Devel. (pres.-elect Miss. chpt. 1984—), Miss. Pub. Health Assn. (pres. 1979-80), Miss. Environ. Health Assn. (pres. 1980-81), Miss. Conservation Edn. Commn., Miss. Bd. Registration for Sanitarians (sec. 1979-82), State Employees Assn. Miss., Am. Record Mgmt. Assn. (publicity chmn. 1985—). Republican. Methodist. Club: Lions. Home: 271 Glenside Dr Jackson MS 39211 Office: So Vital Dataplex Box 236 Flora MS 39071

CONKWRIGHT, CHARLES TERRY, pharmacist; b. Hartford, Ky., May 31, 1951; s. Charles William and Charlotte Fern (Phelps) C.; m. Patricia Joan Boswell, May 21, 1977; 1 child, Sarah Ellen. B.S. in Pharmacy, U. Ky., 1975. Pharmacist Begley Drug Co., Richmond, Ky., 1975-76, Our Lady of Mercy Hosp., Owensboro, Ky., 1976-79; chief pharmacist Ohio County Hosp., Hartford, Ky., 1979-83; staff pharmacist Ireland Army Hosp., Fort Knox, Ky., 1983—. Chmn. of adminstrv. bd. Dundee United Meth. Ch., Ky., 1984—. Mem. Ky. Pharmacists Assn. Republican. Lodge: Masons (master 1980, 81, 84, sec. 1985—). Home: Route 1 Box 62 Boswell Rd Dundee KY 42338 Office: Ireland Army Community Hosp Bldg 851 Fort Knox KY 40121

CONLEY, GLEN TAYLOR, corporation executive; b. Wanette, Okla., Dec. 28, 1923; s. Taylor and Pearl (Waddle) C.; m. Hazel Carla Sandrini, Oct. 3, 1956; 1 son, Kelly Ugo. Student, Bakersfield Jr. Coll., (Calif.). Foreman Bechtel Corp., San Francisco, 1952-53; supt. Fluor Corp., Los Angeles, 1953-56; v.p. Paul Hardeman, Inc., Los Angeles, 1956-64; pres. Conley Contractors, Montebello, Calif., 1964-66, Fischbach & Moore, Internat., Dallas, 1966-80, Fischbach & Moore, Inc., 1980—. Served to tech. sgt. U.S. Army, 1943-46; Japan. Decorated Presdl. Citation Combat Infantryman's Badge with 6 gold stars. Roman Catholic. Lodges: Beavers; Elks. Office: Fischbach & Moore Inc 11030 Ables Ln Dallas TX 75229

CONLEY, JAMES FRANKLIN, geologist; b. Logan, N.C., Dec. 28, 1931; s. Thaddeus Lafayette and Mallie Marie (Morehead) C.; m. Ellen Marie Reedy, Dec. 23, 1954; children—James Franklin, John Horace, David Lauren. B.A., Berea Coll., 1954; M.S., Ohio State U., 1956; Ph.D., U.S.C., 1981. Geologist, N.C. Div. Mineral Resources, Raleigh, 1957-65; geologist Va. Div. Mineral Resources, Charlottesville, 1965—; adj. prof. dept. environ. scis. U. Va., 1982—. Mem. Carolina Geol. Soc., AIME, Am. Assn. Petroleum Geologists, Potomac Geophys. Soc., Am. Inst. Profl. Geologists, Va. Acad. Sci., Geol. Soc.

Am. Contbr. articles to sci. jours. Home: 1614 Trailridge Rd Charlottesville VA 22903 Office: PO Box 3667 Charlottesville VA 22903

CONN, JAMES STEPHEN, clergyman; b. Leadwood, Mo., Jan. 26, 1945; s. Charles W. and Edna Louise (Minor) C.; m. Patricia Elizabeth Miller, Oct. 24, 1965; children—Gregory, Christopher, Jeremy. Grad. Lee Coll., Cleveland, Tenn., 1966. Ordained to ministry Church of God, 1966. Pastor Ch. of God, Casper, Wyo., 1966-67, state youth dir., Albuquerque, 1967-68, pastor, Cleveland, Tenn., 1968-72, new field evangelist, Pineville, W.Va., 1972-73, dist. overseer, Harrisburg, Pa., 1973-77; pastor, founder Maranatha Fellowship, Augusta, Ga., 1977—. Mem. nat. bd. govs. Am. Coalition for Traditional Values, Washington, 1984—. Author: Damascus Appointment, 1976; Run With the Vision, 1977; Miracles Don't Just Happen, 1979. Contbr. articles to profl. jours. Editorial columnist Augusta Chronicle Herald, 1982—. Republican. Avocations: mountain climber; farmer. Home: 1036 Conn Rd Evans GA 30809 Office: Maranatha Fellowship PO Box 4597 Augusta GA 30907

CONNALLY, HERSCHEL JOSEPH, judge; b. San Angelo, Tex., July 15, 1935; s. Herschel Christian and Hazel Corinne (Faris) C.; student Southwestern U., 1953-54, 1957, San Angelo Coll., 1955-56; student U. Tex., 1960-61, J.D., 1964; m. Lanita Connally; children—Vella Katherine, Jennifer Robin, Matthew Caleb. Admitted to Tex. bar, 1964; practiced in Abilene, Tex., 1964, Odessa, 1964—; mem. firm Jackson & Jackson, Abilene, 1964; mem. firm Turpin, Smith, Dyer, Harman & Dawson, Odessa, 1964-74, partner, 1967-74; individual practice law, 1974-77; county judge Ector County, Tex., 1975-77; judge 244th Dist. Ct., 1977—. Chmn. zoning bd. adjustment City of Odessa, 1972-74; mem. Tex. Bd. Pvt. Investigators and Pvt. Security Agys., 1973-77, chmn., 1975-77; v.p. Presidential Mus. Odessa, 1971-75, trustee, 1969-75; mem. Tex. Dem. Exec. Com., 1972-76; campaign mgr. U.S. Senator Lloyd Bentsen, 1970, Gov. Dolph Briscoe, 1972. Served with AUS, 1958-60. Mem. State Bar Tex., Ector County Bar Assn. (chmn. grievance com. 1972, v.p. 1976), Kappa Sigma, Phi Alpha Delta. Democrat. Methodist. Club: Exchange (Odessa). Office: Room 300 Ector County Ct House Odessa TX 79761

CONNAWAY, ROBERT WALLACE, artist, computer programmer; b. Dothan, Ala., Nov. 5, 1956; s. Charles Earl and Ina Lee (Wallace) C.; m. Catherine Coyne. B.Info. Systems Tech., U. No. Fla., 1981; B.A. cum laude, Flagler Coll., 1978. Computer programmer Mgmt. Info. Systems Group, 1981-83; computer analyst/programmer Grumman St. Augustine Corp., 1985—; flight line attendant, free-lance artist Aero Sport Inc., St. Augustine, Fla., 1978-83; founder, prin. Aviation Art Works, St. Augustine, 1978—; Recipient Art awards Sr. Honors Project, 1978; Honorable Mention award Audubon Soc. Art Show, St. Augustine, 1978. Mem. St. Augustine Art Assn., Aircraft Owners and Pilots Assn., Exptl. Aircraft Assn. Episcopalian. Commn.: mural St. Augustine Mcpl. Airport, 1982; exhibited Fly-In art show Exptl. Aircraft Assn., 1980. Home: 416 Arredondo Ave Saint Augustine FL 32084 Office: Grumman Corp St Augustine Hwy 1 N Saint Augustine FL 32084

CONNELL, GEORGE HERMAN, JR., lawyer; b. Atlanta, June 11, 1944; s. George Herman and Frances Lamar (Lowe) C.; children—Sarah Lamar, George Herman, III. B.A., Brown U., 1966; J.D., U. Ga., 1969. Bar: Ga. 1970, U.S. Supreme Ct. 1978, U.S. Ct. Appeals (11th cir.) 1982. Asst. U.S. atty. No. Dist. Ga., Atlanta, 1971-72; ptnr. Long, Weinberg, Ansley & Wheeler, Atlanta, 1972-78; sole practice, Atlanta, 1978—. Pres. North X Northwest Civic Assn., 1979-81. Mem. ABA, Atlanta Bar Assn., State Bar Ga. Assn., Ga. Def. Lawyers Assn., Brown U. Club Atlanta (pres. 1978—). Methodist. Clubs: Capital City Lawyers (Atlanta). Office: Suite 1770 Galleria Tower One Hundred 100 Galleria Pkwy NW Atlanta GA 30339

CONNELL, MATTHEW JOSEPH, educational administrator; b. Phila., Oct. 20, 1954; s. Gerald Francis and Claire Veronica (Wilson) C.; m. Evelyn Baxevane, Nov. 13, 1982. B.A., Bloomsburg State Coll., 1977; M.A., Indiana U. of Pa., 1979. Asst. dir. of campus activities Ithaca Coll., N.Y., 1979-82; dir. student activities ctr. North Tex. State U., Denton,, 1982—; cons. student activities office SUNY Upstate Med. Ctr., Syracuse, N.Y., 1981. Softball coach Spl. Olympics, Denton, 1984; mem. Assn. for Retarded Citizens, Denton, 1982—. Recipient Service Key award Bloomsburg State Coll., 1977; named One of Outstanding Young Men in Am., U.S. Jaycees, 1983. Mem. Assn. Coll. Unions Internat., Am. Assn. Counseling and Devel., Assn. Coll. Personnel Adminstrs., Assn. Coll Unions Internat. Avocations: jogging, reading, writing, baking, camping. Home: 1906 Azalea St Denton TX 76205 Office: North Tex State U Box 13705 Denton TX 76203

CONNELL, SUZANNE (SPARKS) MCLAURIN, retired librarian; b. Bennettsville, S.C., Sept. 12, 1917; d. John Bethea and Aleine (McLeod) McLaurin; A.B., Woman's Coll. of U. N.C., 1938; A.B in L.S., U. N.C., 1940; 1 child, John Alexander (dec.). Library asst. Mt. Pleasant br. D.C. Public Library, Washington, 1940-41; post librarian Camp Sutton, N.C., 1943-44; post librarian McGuire Gen. Hosp., Richmond, Va., 1945-46, chief librarian McGuire VA Hosp., 1946-52, 59-62; chief librarian VA Hosp., Lake City, Fla., 1952-56; cataloger, chief books acquisitions, chief books circulation, asst. chief documents acquisitions Air U. Library, Maxwell AFB, Ala., 1956-59; head extension, head circulation Greensboro (N.C.) Public Library, 1962-63; reference librarian, asst. and acting base librarian Marine Corps Base, Camp Lejeune, N.C., 1963-66; part time cataloger Wilmington (N.C.) Public Library, 1967-75. Past vol., ARC, U.S. Naval Hosp., Marine Corps Base, Camp Lejeune, N.C., also local hosp. and nursing home. Mem. ALA (pres. assn. hosp. and instn. libraries 1955-56), Phi Beta Kappa. Methodist. Contbr. articles to Brit. and Am. periodicals. Home: 249 E 11th St Apt 253-B Southport NC 28461

CONNELL, WESSIE GERTRUDE, library administrator; b. Cairo, Ga., Nov. 21, 1915; d. John H. and Gertrude (Pearce) C. Grad. high sch. Dir., Cairo Pub. Library (name changed to Roddenbery Meml. Library 1964), 1939—; cons., speaker to library and ednl. orgns. Contbg. author: Wonderful World of Books, 1952; Public Relations for Libraries, 1972; library columnist Cairo Messenger. Advisor Grady County Courthouse Bldg. Com., 1983; pres. Wesleyan Service Guild, Methodist Ch., 1960-61. Recipient John Cotton Dana publicity awards, 1948, 49, 58, 59; Library Pub. Relations Council award, 1950; Garden Club Ga. Merit award, 1961; named Cairo Kiwanis Citizen of Yr., 1948; Woman of Yr., Rotary, Kiwanis and Lions clubs, 1959; plaque exemplary service Ga. Adult Edn. Assn., 1985. Mem. Ga. Library Assn., Southeastern Ga. Library Assn., ALA, Library Pub. Relations Council, Ga. Adult Edn. Council, Ga. Hist. Soc., Ga. Council Pub. Libraries (adv. council), Ga. Writers Assn., Oral History Council, Delta Kappa Gamma. Clubs: Cairo Women, Cairo Book (hon.), Camellia Garden (hon.). Home: 410 N Broad St Cairo GA 31728 Office: Roddenbery Memorial Library 320 N Broad St Cairo GA 31728

CONNELLY, JOHN LAWRENCE, college dean; b. Dickson, Tenn., July 19, 1929; s. John Neely and Thelma (Hammon) C.; m. Edythe Dickens, Aug. 19, 1953. B.S., Middle Tenn. U., 1950; M.A., Peabody Coll. Vanderbilt U., 1951. Chmn. English dept. East High Sch., Nashville, 1952-55; staff Peabody Coll., Nashville, 1955-60; instr. English, U. Tenn., Nashville, 1958-60; co-owner Advanced Equipment Co., Nashville, 1960-80; dean students Aquinas Jr. Coll., Nashville, 1980—; antique furniture cons. Furniture Corner, Nashville, 1984—. Author books and articles on local history. Contbr. to Tenn. Hist. Quar. Chmn. Met. Hist. Commn., Nashville, 1985—; chmn., founder Nashville Oktoberfest, 1980; mem. Tenn. Homecoming Commn. Named hon. Ky. col., 1963, hon. Tenn. squire, 1980. Mem. Tenn. Hist. Soc., Met. Opera Guild, So. Hist. Soc., Checkwood Bot. Assocs. Methodist. Avocations: boating; history; antique American furniture collecting. Home: 4204 Hood Ave Nashville TN 37215

CONNELLY, LEWIS BRANCH SUTTON, lawyer; b. St. Louis, Sept. 17, 1950; s. Lewis Branch and Mary Ellen (Henneberger) C.; m. Anna Kristina Cook, Oct. 15, 1977; children—Christopher Sutton, Jeffrey Scott. B.A., Vanderbilt U., 1972; J.D., U. Tenn., 1977. Mem. Smith, Cohen, Ringel, Kohler & Martin, Atlanta, 1977-79, Cook & Palmour, Summerville, Ga., 1979—. Staff mem. Tenn. Law Rev., 1975-77. Mem. ABA (complex crime com. litigation sect. 1982—, consumer affairs com. corp. banking sect. 1982—), Assn. Trial Lawyers Am., Nat. Assn. Criminal Def. Lawyers, Ga. Assn. Criminal Def. Lawyers. Democrat. Presbyterian. Office: Cook & Palmour 128 S Commerce St Summerville GA 30747

CONNELLY, THOMAS FRANCIS, JR., educational administrator; b. Durham, N.C., Nov. 27, 1942; s. Thomas Francis and Mary Katherine (Kinton) C.; m. Mary Lou Masten, Nov. 25, 1967; children—Kinton Reid, Perry Elizabeth, Allison Morning. B.A., Hampden-Sydney Coll., 1965; M.H.A., Duke U., 1967; Ed.D., U. Ky., 1976. Asst. to exec. v.p. Ky. Hosp. Assn., Louisville, 1967-70; coordinator allied health Eastern Ky. U., Richmond, 1970-72; dir. office spl. programs U. Ky., Lexington, 1972-79; dean Sch. Nursing and Health Scis., Western Carolina U., Cullowhee, N.C., 1979—; dir. Appalachian Regional Hosp., Inc., Lexington, Ky., 1984—; vis. fellow Western Australian Inst. Tech., Perth, 1982. Contbr. articles to profl. pubis. Recipient Community Service award Ky. Hosp. Assn., 1970; Outstanding Young Men of Ky. award Ky. Jaycees, 1972; Better Life award Ky. Nursing Home Assn., 1972; Meritorious Service award Ky. League Nursing, 1975. Fellow Am. Soc. Allied Health Profls. (bd dirs. 1977-79, sec. 1979-81); mem. Nat. League for Nursing (bd. dirs. 1977-79). Avocations: skiing, model ship building, record collecting. Home: Route 3 Box 493-F Sylva NC 28779 Office: Sch Nursing and Health Scis Western Carolina U Cullowhee NC 28723

CONNER, LABAN CALVIN, librarian; b. Ocala, Fla., Feb. 18, 1936; s. Laban Calvin and Dorothy Helen (Todd) C. B.Gen.Edn., U. Nebr., 1959; M.S. in Library Edn., Emporia State U., 1964; Ed.S., Nova U., 1979; Ph.D., Pacific Western U., 1980. Tchr., Liberty City Elem. Sch., Dade County, Fla., 1959-63; library/media specialist Dade County Pub. Schs., 1963-68, coordinator library services, 1968-70; asst. prof. library Miami-Dade Community Coll., 1970-73; library/media specialist Dade County Pub. Schs., 1973-81; dir. libraries Fla. Meml. Coll., Miami, 1981—. Mem. United Tchrs. Dade, Dade County Media/Specialists Assn., ALA, Fla. Library Assn., Am. Fedn. Tchrs. Served with USAF, 1956-59. Democrat. African Methodist Episcopal. Home: 18601 NW 39th Ave Opa Locka FL 33055 Office: Fla Meml Coll 15800 NW 42nd Ave Miami FL 33054

CONNER, VALERIE JEAN, history educator; b. Jennings, La., Oct. 23, 1945; d. John Louis and Mary Valerie (Wartelle) C. B.A., Loyola U. of South, New Orleans, 1967; M.A., U. Va., 1969, Ph.D., 1974. Mem. staff Com. on Style and Drafting, La. Constl. Conv., 1973; asst. prof. history Fla. State U., Tallahassee, 1974-81, assoc. prof., 1982—, mem. adv. bd. Univ. Press. Author: The National War Labor Board, 1983. Woodrow Wilson fellow, 1967-68; Virginia Wilson fellow, 1968-72; Fla. State U. faculty devel. grantee, 1978. Mem. Orgn. Am. Historians. Democrat. Roman Catholic. Home: 534 E Oakland Ave Tallahassee FL 32301 Office: Dept History Fla State U Tallahassee FL 32306

CONNER, WARREN WESLEY, lawyer, title company executive; b. Cat Spring, Tex., Aug. 14, 1932; s. George William and Freida Johanna (Kollatschny) C.; m. Suzanne Rosser, Oct. 29, 1955; children—Connie Suzanne, Cathy Lorrane; m. Sharon Ann Welch, July 28, 1978. B.B.A., So. Meth. U., 1959; J.D., 1963. Bar: Tex. 1963, U.S. Dist. Ct. (so. dist.) Tex. 1971. Ptnr., Sheehan & Conner, Friona, Tex., 1963-65; founder, ptnr. Conner, Odom and Clover, P.C., Sealy, Tex., 1965—; pres. Sealy Title Co.; dir. Citizens State Bank, Sealy, Industry Telephone Co. Served with U.S. Army, 1953-55. Mem. State Bar Tex., Austin County Bar Assn. (past pres.), Am. Legion. Presbyterian. Club: Safari. Lodges: Mason, Shriners, Rotary (past pres.). Home: 403 Fowlkes Sealy TX 77474 Office: PO Box 570 Sealy TX 77474

CONNOLLY, JOHN W., JR., oil company executive; b. 1929. Salesman Carter Oil Co., 1951-58; pres., dir. Eastern Seaboard Petroleum Co., Inc., 1958—. Address: Eastern Seaboard Petroleum Co Inc 6531 Evergreen Ave Jacksonville FL 32206*

CONNOR, JOSEPH MICHAEL, restaurant owner; b. Knoxville, Tenn., Mar. 3, 1951; s. Joseph Michael and Helen Marie (Mabry) C.; m. Carol Anne Gray, June 10, 1975; children—Amanda, Ryan. B.A., U. Tenn., 1974. Gen. mgr. Steak & Ale Restaurant, Dallas, 1973-82; pres. Grady's Inc., Knoxville, Tenn., 1982—. Annual gala ofcl. March of Dimes, Knoxville, 1983; Recipient Achievement award Steak & Ale Restaurants, Orlando, Fla., 1981. Mem. Nat. Restaurant Assn., Tenn. Restaurant Assn., Knoxville C. of C. (com. mem. 1983), D'Lite of N.C. (bd. dirs.). Republican. Roman Catholic. Home: 12103 Valley Trail Knoxville TN 37922 Office: Grady's Inc 318 Gay St NW Suite 201 Knoxville TN 37917

CONNORS, ROBERT MICHAEL, corporation financial executive; b. Camden, N.J., Dec. 5, 1933; s. William Brendon and Mary (McGrath) C.; m. June D. Terrel, Oct. 6, 1956; children—Debra Lynn, Patricia Anne, Robert Michael, Carol June. Acctg. cert. Rutgers U.-South Jersey Div., 1953; B.S. in Bus. Adminstrn. in Acctg., U. Fla., 1960. With Ernst & Whinney, Atlanta and Miami, Fla., 1960-68; asst. to pres. Keller Industries, Inc., Miami, 1968-69, treas., 1969-74, corp. sec. and treas., 1974-75, v.p. and treas., 1975-77, sr. v.p., 1977-80, sr. v.p. and corp. treas., 1980—, also dir. Advisor, Miami Jr. Achievement, 1967. Served with U.S. Army, 1954-56. C.P.A., Fla. Mem. Am. Inst. C.P.A.s, Fla. Inst. C.P.A.s, Nat. Assn. Accts., Risk Ins. Mgmt. Soc. Democrat. Roman Catholic. Office: 18000 State Rd Nine Miami FL 33162

CONOLE, RICHARD CLEMENT, management executive; b. Binghamton, N.Y., Dec. 7, 1936; s. Clement V. and Marjorie E. (Anable) C.; student Wharton Sch., Moore Sch. Engring., U. Pa., 1955-60, Clarkson Coll., 1956-57; children—Margaret Ann, Linda Elizabeth; m. Sharyn Stafford, Apr. 18, 1969; 1 dau., Samantha Erin. Data processing dept. Campbell Soup Co., Inc., Camden, N.J., 1954; draftsman Gannett, Fleming, Corddry & Carpenter, Inc., Ardmore, Pa., 1955-56; plant mgr., office mgr. Tabulating Card Co., Inc., Princeton, N.J., 1957-59, asst. to pres., asst. sec.-treas., sec. 1959; pres., dir. Data Processing Supplies Co., Inc., Princeton, 1959; sec., dir. Whiting Paper Co., Inc., Princeton, 1959, pres., 1961-62; pres., dir. Mercer-Princeton Realty Co., Inc., Princeton, 1959-61; pres. Am. Bus. Investment Co., Inc., Princeton, 1960; pres., dir. Business Supplies Corp. Am., Skytop, Pa., 1962-65, Gen. Bus. Supplies Corp., Ardmore, 1965-71; chmn. bd. Nat. Productive Machines, Inc., Elkridge, Md., 1965-71; v.p., chmn. finance com., dir. Pocono Internat. Raceway Inc., 1964-74; pres. Gen. Automotive Supplies Co., 1971-72; pres., dir. Autoberfest, Inc., 1973—, Promotional Printing Ltd., 1973; pres. The World Series of Auto Racing Corp., 1973-78, Tex. World Speedway Inc., 1976—, Speedway Mgmt. Corp., 1978—, Mobile Home Value Ctr., Inc., 1983—, Tex. World Affordable Homes Inc., 1983—, Gt. Tex. Truck Stop, Inc., 1983; sales cons. Hess & Barker, 1972-76; mem. competition com. U.S. Auto Club, 1976—; founder Tex. 500, Tex. Grand Prix, Tex. Race of Champions. Treas., chmn. fin. com. Allen Acad. and Tex. Pvt. Sch. Found., Inc., 1986—. Mem. U.S. Squash Racquets Assn. (life), Phila. Squash Racquets Assn. (life), Tex. Manufactured Housing Assn., Nat. Greyhound Assn., Tex. Greyhound Assn. Clubs: Skytop (Pa.); Phila. Country, Merion Cricket (Haverford, Pa.); Manor (Pocono Manor, Pa.). Patentee magnetic printer cylinder, 1970. Home: Box 9191 College Station TX 77840 also Camp Creek Lake New Baden TX Office: Box AJ College Station TX 77840

CONOVER, PATRICIA KATHRYN, educational coordinator; b. Mt. Holly, N.J., Jan. 2, 1944; d. Joseph Anthony and Kathryn (Gidzinski) Lajkowicz; m. Lyman Harris Conover, June 6, 1964; children—Christine Frances, Susan Cathleen, Matthew Lyman. A.Gen. Studies, C.P.S., Miami-Dade Community Coll., 1980, A.S., 1981; .B.S., Barry U., Miami, Fla., 1983. Sec. Levitt & Sons, Inc., Levittown, N.J., 1961-65; sec. to pres. Lawn Craft, Inc., Fords, N.J., 1965-66; purchasing sec. Johnson & Johnson, New Brunswick, N.J., 1966-67; contracts sec. Curtiss-Wright Corp., Buffalo, 1967-69; sales sec. Allstate Ins. Co., Succasunna, N.J., 1969-70; spl. projects coordinator-ednl. programs Miami Children's Hosp., 1977—; corp. sec. Counterpoint Info. Systems, Inc., Miami, 1978—; cons. in field; instr. Miami-Dade Community Coll., Dade County Pub. Schs. Active Colonial Dr. Citizens Assn., Miami, 1977—; block capt. Neighborhood Crimewatch Network, Miami, 1979-82. Mem. Amaneunsis Soc. (founding; sec. 1982-83, v.p. 1980-81, pres. 1981-82), Nat. Secs. Assn. (cert. profl. sec. 1980, chaplain 1981-82), CPS Soc. Fla., Internat. Word/Info. Processing Assn., Assn. M.B.A. Execs., Phi Theta Kappa. Democrat. Roman Catholic. Home: 10431 SW 162 Terr Miami FL 33157 Office: Miami Children's Hosp 6125 SW 31 St Miami FL 33155

CONRAD, HAROLD THEODORE, psychiatrist; b. Milw., Jan. 25, 1934; s. Theodore Herman and Alyce Barbara (Kolb) C.; A.B., U. Chgo., 1954, S.B., 1955, M.D., 1958; m. Elaine Marie Blaine, Sept. 1, 1962; children—Blaine, Carl, David, Erich, Rachel. Intern USPHS Hosp., San Francisco, 1958-59; commd. sr. asst. surgeon USHPS, 1958, advanced through grades to med. dir., 1967; resident in psychiatry USPHS Hosp., Lexington, Ky., 1959-61, Charity Hosp., New Orleans, 1961-62; chief psychiatry USPHS Hosp., New Orleans, 1962-67, clin. dir., 1967; dep. dir. div. field investigations NIMH, Chevy Chase, Md., 1968; chief NIMH Clin. Research Ctr., Lexington, 1969-73; cons. psychiatry, region IX, USPHS, HEW, San Francisco, 1973-79; dir. adolescent unit Alaska Psychiat. Inst., Anchorage, 1979-81, supt., 1981-85; assoc. prof. psychiatry U. Wash. Med. Sch., 1981-86; med. dir. Bayou Oaks Hosp., Houma, La., 1986—. Decorated Commendation medal; recipient various community awards for contbns. in field of drug abuse and equal employment opportunity for minorities. Diplomate Am. Bd. Psychiatry. Fellow Royal Soc. Health, Am. Psychiat. Assn.; mem. AMA, Alpha Omega Alpha, Alpha Delta Phi. Contbr. articles to profl. jours. Home: 855 Belanger St Houma LA 70360

CONRAD, JOSEPH HENRY, animal nutrition educator; b. Cass County, Ind., Dec. 7, 1926; s. Ferdinand M. and Marie E. (Hubenthal) C.; m. Frances Ash, June 18, 1950; children—Kenneth A., Leonard J., Carol Ann, Joseph C. B.S., Purdue U., 1950, M.S., 1954, Ph.D., 1958; prof. honoris causa, Fed. U. Viçosa, Brazil, 1965. Asst. prof. Purdue U., West Lafayette, Ind., 1958-63, assoc. prof., 1963-68, prof., 1968-71; animal scientist Fed. U. Viçosa, 1961-65; prof. and coordinator tropical animal sci. programs, U. Fla., Gainesville, 1971—. Co-author: Swine Production, 1982; contbr. monographs and numerous articles on animal nutrition and tropical animal prodn. to profl. jours. Served with USN, 1944-46. Recipient Disting. Nutritional award Distillers Feed Research Council, 1964. Mem. Am. Soc. Animal Sci., Sociedade Brasileria de Zootecnia, Latin Am. Soc. Animal Prodn., World Assn. Animals Prodn. (v.p.), Sigma Xi, Gamma Sigma Delta, Purdue U. Alumni Assn. (life; pres.'s council). Republican. Baptist. Home: 1824 NW 10th Ave Gainesville FL 32605 Office: Animal Sci Bldg 125B U Fla Gainesville FL 32611

CONSTANGY, HERBERT WILLIAM (BILL), JR., lawyer, author; b. Atlanta, Aug. 26, 1942; s. Herbert William and Janet Udell (Kassel) C.; m. Deborah Newsome, Apr. 4, 1970; 1 son, Herbert William III. B.A., Wake Forest U., 1964; J.D., Duke U., 1967. Bar: N.C. 1968, U.S. Dist. Ct. (we. dist.) N.C. 1971, U.S. Ct. Appeals (5th cir.) 1971, U.S. Ct. Appeals (4th cir.) 1975, U.S. Supreme Ct. 1975. Sole practice, Charlotte, N.C., 1973-78, 81—; assoc. Palmer, Jonas & Mullins, Charlotte, 1971-73; ptnr. Constangy, Goines, Buckley & Boyd, Charlotte, 1978-81. U.S. Congl. intern, 1966; pres. State Student Legislature of N.C., 1963-64; student body pres. Wake Forest U., 1964. Hankins scholar Wake Forest U., 1960-64. Mem. Assn. Trial Lawyers Am., Authors Guild, Inc., Author's League Am., N.C. Bar Assn., N.C. Acad. Trial Lawyers, Mecklenburg County Bar Assn. (sec.-treas. 1979-80), Charlotte/-Mecklenburg Wake Forest Alumni Assn. (pres. 1981-83), Omicron Delta Kappa. Author: North Carolina Employer-Employee Handbook, 1976; Concerted Activity by Non-Union Employees, 1983; Employment Contract Covenants Not to Compete, 1974. Home: 3931 Sulkirk Rd Charlotte NC 28210 Office: 122 N McDowell St Charlotte NC 28204

CONSTANTIN, JAMES ALFORD, business administration educator; b. Tulsa, Okla., June 15, 1922; s. Jules Joseph and Nelle Goff (Alford) C.; m. Wanda Anita Moyer, May 18, 1941; children—Katherine Constantin Beaird, James Alford, Anne Constantin Calinsky, Jules Joseph. B.B.A., U. Tex.-Austin, 1943, M.B.A., 1944, Ph.D., 1950. Instr., U. Tex., 1946-47; asst. prof., assoc. prof. U. Ala., 1947-52, asst. dir. Bur. of Bus. Research, 1947-52; assoc. prof. U. Wash., 1952-53; assoc. prof., then prof. bus. adminstrn. U. Okla., Norman, 1953—, David Ross Boyd prof., 1969—; cons. in field; dir. several cos. Served with AC, U.S. Army, 1942-43. Recipient Teaching award Merrick Found., 1980; teaching award Soc. Mfg. Engrs., 1984, Freedoms Found. at Valley Forge, 1985. Mem. Transp. Research Forum, Am. Soc. Traffic and Transp., Nat. Council Phys. Distbn. Mgmt. Author: (with W.J. Hudson) Motor Transportation 1958, Principles of Logistics Management, 1966; (with W.N. Peach) Zimmermann's World Resources and Industries, 3d edit., 1972; (with R.E. Evans, M.L. Morris) Marketing Strategy and Management, 1976; contbr. in field. Home: 520 Merrywood Ln Norman OK 73069 Office: 307 W Brooks #10 Norman OK 73019

CONWAY, FRENCH HOGE, lawyer; b. Danville, Va., June 11, 1918; s. Lysander Broadus and Mildred (Hoge) C.; B.S., U. Va., 1942, J.D., 1946; m. Louise Throckmorton, Feb. 3, 1961; children—French Hoge, William Chenery, Helen (Mrs. Carlton Bedsole), Donna L. Starnes. Admitted to Va. bar, 1942, since practiced in Danville; mem. firm Clement, Conway & Winston, 1950-60. Sec., Danville City Bd. Rev., 1985—; v.p. Va. Election Bd. Assn., 1974. Served with USNR, 1942-46. Mem. Am., Va., Danville (pres. 1985-86) bar assns., Am. Trial Lawyers Assn., Va. Trial Lawyers Assn., Soc. Cincinnati in State of Va., Ret. Officers Assn., Boat Owners Assn. U.S. Club: Danville Execs. Kiwanian, Mason. Home: 912 Main St Danville VA 24541 Office: 105 S Union St Danville VA 24541

CONWAY, JAMES DONALD, physician; b. Newark, May 2, 1946; s. James M. and Dorothy (Kelly) C.; B.A., St. Olaf Coll., 1968; M.D., U. Ill., 1972, M.S., 1972. Intern, Cornell Coop. Hosp., N.Y.C., 1972, resident, 1973-74; fellow infectious disease U. Mich., Ann Arbor, 1974-76; sr. resident medicine La. State U., New Orleans, 1978-79; co-dir. critical care medicine So. Md. Hosp., Clinton, 1979; assoc. prof. internal medicine, emergency medicine La. State U., 1980—; pvt. practice medicine specializing in infectious diseases, New Orleans, 1980—. Recipient Research award U. Ill., 1973; Mich. Heart Assn. fellow research award, 1974. Mem. Am. Soc. Microbiology, Soc. Critical Care Medicine, ACP, Underwater Med. Soc. Contbr. articles to profl. jours. Home: 1528 7th St New Orleans LA 70115 Office: 5720 Magazine St New Orleans LA 70115

CONWAY, KATHRYN LOUISE, university media specialist; b. Henry County, Va., Jan. 30, 1950; d. Richard Earl and Josephine Hope (Leftwich) C.; B.F.A., U. N.C., Chapel Hill, 1975, postgrad. in communication, 1980—, cert. univ. mgmt. devel. program, 1981; cert. Young Execs. Inst., 1983. Advt. writer Sta. WTOB, Winston Salem, N.C., 1969; research asst. U. N.C., Chapel Hill, 1971, 73, photographer Photo Lab., 1974-75, assoc. dir. Media and Instructional Support Center, 1976—, dir. telecommunications devel., 1982—; mem. functional working group video Microelectronics Ctr. of N.C. Tech. Working Group-Communications; chairperson bd. Sta. WXYC-FM; mem. steering com., interim bd. dirs. N.C. Public Radio Assn.; lead actress Desperadoes, Pocket Theatre, off-off-Broadway, 1978, The Fate of my Joy teleplay Sta. WUNC-TV, Chapel Hill, 1978; mem. Chapel Hill Adv. Com. on Cable TV, 1979; mem. U. N.C.-Chapel Hill Adv. Com. Planning Process, 1984. Mem. Am. Mgmt. Assn. (cert. Fundamentals Data Communication), Am. Assn. Higher Edn., N.C. Ind. Film and Video Assn., U. N.C.-Chapel Hill Mgrs. Assn. (pres. 1983), Assn. Ednl. Communications and Techs. Democrat. Home: Route 7 Box 2 Chapel Hill NC 27514 Office: PARS Bldg 312 208 N Columbia St Chapel Hill NC 27514

CONWAY, SUZANNE, hospital administrator; b. Waco, Texas, Sept. 22, 1951; d. William Thomas Olsen; m. Allen David Pittman, Jan. 14, 1974 (dec. 1979); 1 child., Allison; m. Lucian Gideon Conway, Jr., Apr. 10, 1981; children—Luke, Elizabeth. B.A., Baylor U., 1973, M.B.A., 1985. Bank teller Republic Bank Waco, Texas, 1973-74; tchr. Am. Prepatory Inst., Ft. Hood, Texas, 1974, Killeen Independent Sch. Dist., Tex., 1974-79; hosp. administr. Methodist Home Children's Guidance Ctr., Waco, 1982—. Tchr. pastor's class First Baptist Ch. Woodway, Waco, 1982-84; mem. Midway Schs. P.T.A., Waco, 1983-85, Waco Hist. Found., 1985. Named Outstanding Tchr., Killeen High Sch., 1977. Mem. Health Care Fin. Mgmt. Assn., Nat. Assn. Female Execs., Sigma Iota Epsilon. Club: Roundtable. Office: Methodist Home Children's Guidance Ctr Waco TX 76708

CONWELL, HALFORD ROGER, physician; b. Cin., Jan. 28, 1924; s. Halford Fredrick and Erma Pearl (Cornelius) C.; B.A., U. Wooster, 1948; M.A., U. Louisville, 1950; M.D., U. Cin., 1955; m. Margaret Ann King, Dec. 15, 1965; children—Mark A., Sherri L. Intern, Christ Hosp., Cin., 1955-56; resident Maumee Valley Hosp., Toledo, 1956-57, Baylor U. Hosp., Houston, 1957-58; gen. practice medicine and aviation medicine, Huntsville, Tex., 1959—; mem. staff Huntsville (Tex.) Meml. Hosp., chief of staff, 1974-75, chief medicine, 1976-80; cons. Tex. Dept. Corrections, 1970-80; sr. U.S. med. officer Brit. Caledonian Airways; cons. Aeromexico; mem. Walker County Hosp. Dist., 1975—, chmn., 1976-79; med. dir. Planned Parenthood Assn., Huntsville, 1975-77; asst. dean of men, instr. psychology Heidelberg U., Tiffin, Ohio, 1950-51; instr. psychology Cin. Coll.; sr. med. examiner FAA; examiner C.A.A. (U.K.). Trustee Biol. Analysis and Research Found.; mem. adv. council liberal arts Sam Houston State U. capt. (hon.) Tex. Internat. Airline. Served to lt. USNR, 1942-46. Recipient safe pilot award Nat. Pilots Assn. Fellow Am. Soc. Abdominal Surgeons, Airline Med. Dirs. Assn.; asso. fellow Aerospace Med. Assn., Brit. Assn. Aerospace Medicine, Latin Am. Aviation Med. Assn.; mem. AMA, Tex. Med. Assn., Walker-Madison-Trinity Med. Soc. (pres. 1974-75), Civil Aviation Med. Assn. (v.p. 1968-80, dir. 1968—, pres. 1980-81), Mitchell Pediatric Soc., Academie Internationale de Medicine Aeronatque et Spatiale,

Confederate Air Force, Friends of RAF Mus., Order Ky. Cols., Psi Chi. Club: Drs. Lodge: Masons. Home: 825 Cherry Hills Elkins Lake TX 77340 Office: 2800 Lake Rd Huntsville TX 77340

CONWELL, JOSEPH THOMAS, lawyer; b. Oakman, Ala., Nov. 9, 1914; s. Joe D. and Elma Pettus (Wells) C.; student Transylvania Coll., 1934-35; B.A., U. Ala., 1937, LL.B., 1940; m. Winifred Maxwell, June 25, 1946; 1 son, Joseph Thomas. Admitted to Ala. bar, 1940; pvt. practice law, Jasper, Ala., 1940-42, Birmingham, Ala., 1946-48, Huntsville, Ala., 1955—; atty. ICC, Atlanta, 1948-49; claim and ins. investigator, San Francisco, 1949-54. Mem. nat. honor sec. Walker County High Sch.; mem. Madison County Democratic exec. com. Served with AUS, World War II. Mem. Am., Ala., Huntsville-Madison County (meml. com.) bar assns., Am. Judicature Soc., Ala. Trial Lawyers Assn. (gov.), Farrah Law Soc., Civitan Club, Am. Legion. Episcopalian. Lodge: Woodmen of World. Club: Century of U. Ala. Contbr. articles to profl. publs. Home: 7118 Chadwell Rd SW Huntsville AL 35802 Office: Conwell Legal Bldg 607 Madison St Huntsville AL 35801 Office: Conwell Legal Bldg 607 Madison St Huntsville AL 35801

CONYERS, J. C., drilling engineer; b. Saint Jo, Tex., Oct. 31, 1937; s. Joe Crump and Ellie Evelyn (Ray) C.; student (Alfred P. Sloan scholar), Dartmouth Coll., 1956-58; B.S. in Geology (Am. Petroleum Inst. scholar), Tex. Technol. U., 1962; m. Dinah Gunter, Sept. 3, 1960. Cons. geologist, Dallas, 1962-63; logging supr. Monarch Logging Co., Aransas Pass, Tex., 1963-68; data engr. Dresser-Magcobar, Houston, 1969-70, data supr. Dresser Internat., Singapore, 1971-73, devel. engr., tech. services engr., tng. coordinator, tng. mgr., div. tech. services mgr., div. products applications mgr. Dresser-Swaco, Houston, 1973-81; tech. service mgr. oil tools div. Servco div. Smith Internat., Houston, 1981-82, bus. devel. mgr. Drilco div., 1982—; guest lectr. various univs. Mem. Soc. Petroleum Engrs., Am. Assn. Petroleum Geologists, ASME, Houston Geol. Soc. Baptist. Home: 6622 Montauk Houston TX 77084 Office: 16740 Hardy St Houston TX 77205

COODY, RICHARD HOWARD, general contractor; b. Dodge County, Ga., Jan. 27, 1931; s. Robert W. and Audrey S. (Shepard) C.; m. Joyce M. Moore, June 15, 1951; children—Richard H., Robin C. Student Dodge County pub. schs. Job supt. home constrn. Eastman, Ga., 1948-55; job. supr. A.C. Samford, Inc. also A.C. Samford Overseas, Inc., Albany, Ga., 1954-62; owner R.H. Coody and Assoc., Albany, 1972-76, Brookstone, Inc., Albany, 1976—. Bd. dirs. Sowega Youth Home, Albany, 1960-70. Mem. Gen. Contractors Am. (Ga. br.). Methodist. Club: Radium Country. Lodges: Masons, Shriners, Elks. Home: 5002 Holly Hill Rd Albany GA 31707 Office: 233 Flint Ave Albany GA 31707

COOIL, BRUCE KIMO, mathematical statistician, statistics educator; b. Honolulu, Mar. 26, 1953; s. Bruce James and Drea Georgia (O'Connell) C.; m. Julia Ellen Buzzell, June 26, 1976. B.S., Stanford U., 1975, M.S., 1976; Ph.D., Wharton Sch., U. Pa., 1982. Biostatistician Inst. Health Research, San Francisco, 1976-78; research and teaching fellow Wharton Sch., Phila., 1978-82; asst. prof. stats. Owen Grad Sch., Vanderbilt, U., Nashville, 1982—. Contbr. articles to profl. jours. Dean's fellow Wharton Sch., 1978-79; Vanderbilt U. grantee, 1984—. Mem. Am. Statis. Assn., Inst. Math. Stats., Inst. Mgmt. Sci., Phi Beta Kappa. Unitarian. Office: Vanderbilt U Owen Grad Sch 401 21st Ave S Nashville TN 37203

COOK, ANNABELLE LEMON, ednl. adminstr.; b. Jane Lew, W.Va., Aug. 22, 1930; d. Clyde and Della (Cooper) Lemon; student Freed Hardeman Coll., 1949-50, U. So. Miss., 1960-61; B.S., La. State U., 1970; M.S., Fla. Internat. U., 1979; m. Lynn Odell Cook, Apr. 6, 1950; children—Beverly Cook Watkins, Russell, Melanie Cook Mitchell, Paul. Tchr. elem. sch., Baton Rouge, La., 1970-71, Miami, Fla., 1972-77; asst. prin. Atlantic Christian Sch., Miami, 1977, prin., 1978-79, supt. elem. brs., 1980—. Mem. Assn. Supervision and Curriculum Devel. Mem. Ch. of Christ. Home: 7105 SW 84th Ave Miami FL 33143 Office: Atlantic Christian School 8445 Sunset Dr Miami FL 33143

COOK, CLAYTON HENRY, rancher; b. Moundridge, Kans., Apr. 21, 1912; s. Herbert and Bertha (Wilkening) C.; student public schs., Moundridge; m. Margery Maxine Manning, Apr. 13, 1941; children—Larry Clayton, Ronald Leigh, Michael Craig, Melanie Beth. Engaged in ranching, Vega, Tex. Mem. Tex. Econ. Commn., 1950-57-59, 62—; mem. Gov.'s Com. on Aging, Tex. Constn. Revision Com.; profl. actor; play critic, judge Tex. U. Interscholastic League; past mem. governing bd. Amarillo Little Theatre; mem. governing bd. High Plains Center Performing Arts; bd. dirs. Friends of Fine Arts West Tex. State U., Amarillo Symphony; chmn. Oldham County Democratic Exec. Com. Mem. Internat. Platform Assn. (chmn.). Methodist. Clubs: Masons, Kiwanis (lt. gov. Tex.-Okla. dist. 1959, chmn. new club bldg. 1960, chmn. past lt. govs. 1967); Amarillo Knife and Fork (dir.). Home: Box 57 Vega TX 79092

COOK, DAVID HALL, training specialist; b. Prattville, Ala., Oct. 4, 1930; s. Klink Woodworth and Jennie Lucille (Hall) C.; B.B.A., George Washington U., 1974, M.A.Ed., 1977; m. Joyce Jannell Fralic, Dec. 20, 1972; children—David Hall, John. With Computer Scis. Corp., Springfield, Va., 1967—, sr. engr., 1971-74, sect. mgr., 1977-79, tng. mgr., 1980—, tchr. naval sci. Navy High Sch. ROTC Program, 1974-77. Neighborhood commr. Boy Scouts Am., 1966-73. Served with U.S. Navy, 1947-67. Mem. AAAS, Soc. Interdisciplinary Studies, U.S. Naval Inst., Am. Soc. Tng. and Devel., N.Y. Acad. Sci., Fleet Res. Assn., Phi Delta Kappa (pres. George Washington U. chpt. 1982-83). Club: George Washington U. Lodges: Masons, Shriners. Home: 6217 Dana Ave Springfield VA 22150 Office: 6565 Arlington Blvd Falls Church VA 22046

COOK, DORIS MARIE, accountant, educator; b. Fayetteville, Ark., June 11, 1924; d. Ira and Mettie Jewell (Dorman) C.; B.B.A., U. Ark., 1946, M.S., 1949; Ph.D., U. Tex., 1968. Staff acct. Haskins & Sells, Tulsa, 1946-47; instr. acctg. U. Ark., Fayetteville, 1947-52, asst. prof., 1952-62, assoc. prof., 1962-69, prof., 1969—. C.P.A., Okla., Ark. Mem. Fayetteville Bus. and Profl. Women's Club (pres. 1973-74, 75-76), Ark. Fedn. Bus. and Profl. Women's Clubs (chmn. found. com. 1975-77, treas. 1979-80), Ark. Soc. C.P.A.s (v.p. 1975-76, pres. N.W. Ark. chpt. 1980-81), sec. Student Loan Fund Found. 1981-85, chmn. pub. relations com. 1984-87, treas. 1985—), Am. Acctg. Assn. (chmn. membership for Ark. 1981-82, chmn. nat. membership com. 1982-83, chmn. Arthur Carter scholarship com. 1984-85, chmn. membership for arts 1985-86), Am. Inst. C.P.A.s, Acad. Acctg. Historians (trustee 1985—), Am. Woman's Soc. C.P.A.s, Ozarks Econ. Assn. (editor Newsletter 1982-85), Mortar Bd., Beta Gamma Sigma, Beta Alpha Psi (pres. nat. council 1977-78, editor newsletter 1973-77, dir. regional meetings 1978-79), Phi Gamma Nu, Alpha Lambda Delta, Delta Kappa Gamma (sec. 1976-78, pres. 1978-80), Phi Kappa Phi. Contbr. to profl. jours. Home: 1115 Leverett St Fayetteville AR 72701 Office: Dept Accounting U Ark Fayetteville AR 72701

COOK, EDWARD H., association executive. Pres., Oklahoma City C. of C. Office: Oklahoma City C of C One Santa Fe Plaza Oklahoma City OK 73102*

COOK, EDWARD WILLINGHAM, diversified industry executive; b. Memphis, June 19, 1922; s. Everett Richard and Phoebe (Willingham) C.; m. Patricia Long, Mar. 17, 1973; children—Edward Willingham Jr., Everett Richard II, Barbera Cook Brooks, Mark W., Patricia Kendall. A.B., Yale U., 1944. With Cook & Co., Memphis, 1946-68, pres., 1956-68; pres. Cook Industries, Inc., Memphis 1968-74, chmn., chief exec. officer, 1974-81; pres., chmn., chief exec. officer Cook Internat., Inc., Palm Beach, Fla., 1981—; mem. Cotton Adv. Com., 1964-68. Mem. Shelby County Quar. Ct., Memphis, 1948-66; chmn. Memphis-Shelby County Airport Authority, 1968-81; mem. exec. com. Nat. Council U.S.-China Trade, Washington, 1973-78; mem. Pres.' Export Council, Washington, 1973-79; bd. dirs. Chgo. Bd. Trade, 1974-76, First Tenn. Nat. Corp., Memphis, Tenn. Taxpayers Assn., Nashville, Planned Parenthood Palm Beach Area, 1984—, Palm Beach Civic Assn., Inc., 1984—. Served to maj. USAAF, 1943-45. Decorated DFC, Bronze Star, Air medal with six oak leaf clusters. Mem. So. Cotton Assn. (past pres.), Cotton Council Internat. (bd. dirs. 1964-65), Am. Cotton Shippers Assn. (past pres.), Cotton Council Adminstrs. (bd. dirs. 1962-65). Episcopalian. Clubs: Memphis Country, Memphis Hunt & Polo; Links (N.Y.C.); Everglades, Bath & Tennis, Palm Beach Polo and Country. (Palm Beach). Office: 322 Royal Poinciana Plaza Palm Beach FL 33480

COOK, ERNEST EWART, oil exploration company executive; b. Wiltshire, Eng., Mar. 23, 1926; s. Edgar John and Dorothy May (Wiltshire) C.; B.A. in Natural Scis., Cambridge (Eng.) U., 1946, M.A., 1950; 1 dau., Julia Ann; came to U.S., 1946. Geophysicist, Cia Shell de Venezuela, Maracaibo, 1947-56; chief geophysicist Pakistan Shell Oil Co., Karachi, 1956-57; with Signal Oil & Gas Co., 1957-67, internat. exploration mgr., Los Angeles, 1966-67; v.p. Seismic Computing Corp., Houston, 1968-70; chmn. Invent Inc., Houston, 1971-78; pres. Zenith Exploration Co. Inc., Houston, 1978-83; chmn. Barnsdall Geo-Technologies Inc., 1983-84; dir. Triton Energy Corp., Dallas, Triton Europe, Plc., London. Fellow Geol. Soc. London; mem. Soc. Exploration Geophysicists, Soc. Petroleum Engrs., Marine Tech. Soc., Am. Geophys. Union, Am. Assn. Petroleum Geologists. Office: Suite 202 9225 Katy Freeway Houston TX 77024

COOK, FREDERICK LEE, mathematics educator; b. Balt., Mar. 15, 1940; m. Barbara Lee Blackburn, Aug. 17, 1962; children—Merren Elizabeth, Mary Catherine. B.S. in Applied Math., Ga. Inst. Tech., 1961, M.S. in Applied Math., 1964, Ph.D., 1967. Reservoir analyst Exxon Corp., Houston, 1967; research mathematician NASA, Huntsville, Ala., 1967-69; mem. faculty U. Ala., Huntsville, 1969—, chmn. dept. math., 1977-85. Bd. dirs. Mental Health Assn., Madison County, 1977—, v.p., 1979-81, pres., 1981-82. Served to capt. U.S. Army, 1967-69. Mem. Am. Math. Soc., Ala. Assn. Coll. Tchrs. Math. (pres. 1976-77), Math. Assn. Am. (chmn. southeastern sect. 1984-85), Soc. Indsl. and Applied Math., Sigma Xi. Contbr. articles to profl. jours. Home: 804 Cleermont Dr Huntsville AL 35801 Office: Dept Math Univ Alabama in Huntsville Huntsville AL 35899

COOK, GERALD, electrical engineering educator; b. Hazard, Ky., Oct. 31, 1937; s. Rudolph H. and Rose I. (Boyer) C.; m. Nancy Anne Gillispie, June 9, 1962; children—Gerald Boyer, Allan Binford. B.S., Va. Poly. Inst., 1961; M.S., MIT, 1962, Sc.D., 1965. Lectr. U. Colo., Colorado Springs, 1966-68; asst. prof. U.S. Air Force Acad., Colorado Springs, 1966-68; assoc. prof. U. Va., Charlottesville, 1968-73, prof., 1973-80; prof., dept. chmn., Vanderbilt U., Nashville, 1981-85; Earle Co. Williams prof. elec. engring. George Mason U., Fairfax, Va., 1985—; vis. prof., Tech. U. Denmark, 1979-80. Editor IEEE Trans. on Indsl. Electronics, 1984— Recipient Cert. of Achievement, U.S. Army, 1981; NSF fellow, 1961-64. Fellow IEEE (pres. Indsl. Electronics Soc. 1982-84, Centennial medal 1984), Am. Soc. Engring. Edn. (Outstanding Research award, Southeast sect. 1971), Sigma Xi, Eta Kappa Nu, Phi Kappa Phi, Tau Beta Phi. Home: 10855 Weisiger Ln Oakton VA 22124 Office: Dept Electrical and Computer Engineering George Mason Univ Fairfax VA 22030

COOK, HAROLD DALE, federal judge; b. Guthrie, Okla., Apr. 14, 1924; s. Harold Payton and Mildred Arvesta (Swanson) C.; (div.) children—Harold Dale II, Caren Irene, Randall Swanson. B.S. in Bus., U. Okla., 1950, LL.B., 1950, J.D., 1970. Bar: Okla. bar 1950. Individual practice law, Guthrie, Okla., 1950, county atty., Logan County, Okla., 1951-54, asst. U.S. atty., Oklahoma City, 1954-58; assoc. firm Butler, Rinehart and Morrison, Oklahoma City, 1958-61; partner Rinehart, Morrison and Cook, 1961-63; legal counsel and adviser to Gov. State of Okla., 1963-65; partner firm Cook and Ming, Oklahoma City, 1965, Cook, O'Toole, Ming and Tourtellotte, 1966-68, Cook, O'Toole and Tourtellotte, 1969-70, Cook and O'Toole, 1971; gen. counsel Shepherd Mall State Bank, Oklahoma City, 1967-71, pres., 1969-71, chmn. bd., 1969-71; dir. Bur. of Hearings and Appeals, Social Security Adminstrn., HEW, 1971-74; judge U.S. Dist. Ct., Tulsa, 1974-79; chief judge No. Dist. Okla., 1979—; mem. legal adv. council Okla. Hwy. Patrol, 1969-70; mem. magistrates com. Jud. Conf. U.S., 1980—; mem. indsl. adv. council Bur. Bus. and Econ. Research, U. Okla., 1970-71. First v.p. PTA, Sunset Elementary Sch., 1959-60; v.p. Parent-Tchrs. & Students Assn., John Marshall High Sch., Oklahoma City, 1970-71, pres., 1971; mem. Econ. Opportunity Com., Okla., 1963-65; tchr. Sunday sch. classes for coll., high sch. and adult ages Village Methodist Ch., Oklahoma City, 1959-65; mem. bd. of stewards First Meth. Ch., Guthrie, Okla., 1951-54. Served with USAF, 1943-45. Recipient Secretary's Spl. Citation HEW, 1973. Fellow Am. Bar Found.; mem. ABA, Fed. Bar Assn., Okla. Bar Assn. (del. to state bar convs.), Oklahoma City C. of C. Republican. Clubs: So. Hills Country, Shriners, Masons, Tulsa, Order Eastern Star (past worthy patron Okla.), Scottish Rite (hon. insp. gen.). Office: United States Court House Tulsa OK 74103

COOK, JAMES HOWELL, JR., electrical engineer, consultant; b. Anderson, S.C., Oct. 28, 1937; s. James H. and Louise (Goss) C.; m. Gail E. Baker, Mar. 26, 1960; children—Pamela, Sheri, Michelle. B.E.E., Ga. Inst. Tech., 1961, M.S. in Elec. Engring., 1970. Engr. Bendix Communication, Towson, Md., 1961-64; engr. Sci. Atlanta, Inc., Atlanta, 1964-68, engring. mgr., 1968-71, product line mgr., 1971-77, tech. dir. telecom group, 1977-84, prin. engr., 1977—; tech. cons. Research Inst., Ga. Inst. Tech., Atlanta, 1983-85; chmn. earth sta. working group FCC Adv. Com. on Reduced Satellite Spacing, 1984-85. Author: (with others) Microwave Antenna Measurements, 1968; (with Johnson and Jasik) Antenna Engineering Handbook, 1984. Editor: Principles of Satellite Communication, 1982. Contbr. articles to tech. mags. Recipient citation Armed Forces Communications and Electronics Assn., 1981; cert. of recognition IEEE-Microwave Theory and Techniques, 1983. Mem. IEEE (sr. mem.; chpt. chmn. profl. group antenna and propagation 1982-83, chpt. chmn. profl. group microwave theory and tech. 1982-83), AIAA, Assn. Old Crows. Republican. Methodist. Avocations: fishing; bowling; fly tying. Home: 4641 Westhampton Dr Tucker GA 30084 Office: Sci-Atlanta Inc 3845 Pleasantdale Rd Atlanta GA 30340

COOK, MICHAEL TAYLOR, corporate administrator; b. Apr. 1, 1956; s. Howard Taylor and Elaine (Whelen) C. Student Va. Wesleyan Coll., 1979. Merchandiser, Universal Brands Inc., Miami, Fla., 1980, salesman, 1980-81, supr., 1981-83, br. mgr., Key West, Fla., 1983—. Democrat. Catholic. Home: 8875 SW 147 Ave Miami FL 33196 Office: Universal Brands Inc 3325 NW 70th Ave Miami FL 33040

COOK, MIKI ANGLEA, psychology educator; b. Nashville, June 16, 1943; d. Pink Dews and Julia (Whittaker) Anglea; m. Albert Stanley Cook, Aug. 22, 1964; children—Richard Stanley, Margaret Angela, Sherri Michelle. A.S., Alexander City Jr. Coll., 1971; B.S., Auburn U., 1972, M.Ed., 1977; Ed.S. student U. Ala., 1981-83. Cert. secondary tchr., Ala. Bus. tchr. Coosa County Bd. Edn., Goodwater, Ala., 1972-73, Alex City State Jr. Coll., Ala., 1975-76; math. tchr. Alex City Bd. Edn., 1973-74; title I reading tchr. Tallapoosa Bd. Edn., Camp Hill, Ala., 1974-75; after-care coordinator E. Ala. Mental Health, Opelika, Ala., 1976-77; counselor, instr. psychology Gadsen State Community Coll., Ala. 1977—. Leader Alex City council Camp Fire Girls, Inc., 1967-68; den mother Alex City council Boy Scouts Am., 1973-74; bd. dirs. Etowah Parents and Children Together, Gadsden, 1984—. Mem. Etowah County Mental Health Assn., Am. Psychol. Assn. (assoc.), Etowah County LWV. Democrat. Episcopalian. Avocations: cooking; reading; bridge; tennis; golf. Office: Gadsden State Community Coll Wallace Dr Gadsden AL 35999

COOK, PEGGY JO, psychotherapist, consultant; b. Greenville, Miss., Jan. 2, 1931; d. Bertram R. Coffing and Mary Josephine (Rodgers) McCarthy; m. Jack Storey Cook, July 15, 1951 (div. 1969); children—Bill S., Paul K., Monte C., Carol Rose Doss. B.S. in Psychology, SUNY-Albany, 1979; M.Ed. in Counseling, North Tex. State U., 1980. Co-owner, mgr. Elec. Contracting, Co., Ft. Worth, 1952-68; co-founder, dir. Family Counseling Ctr., Ft. Worth, 1968—; psychotherapist, Co-dir. Ctr. Creative Living, Ft. Worth, 1982—. Mem. Am. Assn. Counseling and Devel., So. Assn. Counselor Edn. and Supervision, Tex. Assn. Counseling and Devel., North Central Tex. Assn. Counseling and Devel., Am. Mental Health Counselors Assn., Greater Fort Worth Bd. Realtors, Bus., Industry and Edn. Cons. Network. Mem. Seventh Day Adventist Ch. Avocations: grandchildren; antiques; skiing; landscaping. Home: 2401 Oakland Blvd Suite 200 Fort Worth TX 76103 Office: 2401 Oakland Blvd Suite 100 Fort Worth TX 76103

COOK, RONALD EMORY, dentist; b. Winston-Salem, N.C., Feb. 26, 1937; s. Claude Nathaniel and Mozelle (Agner) C.; m. Anne Samuels, June 4, 1960; children—Karen Elizabeth, Kelly Renee, Christopher Scott. B.S. in Chemistry, Washington Coll., 1959; D.D.S., Georgetown U., 1963. Intern U.S. Army, 1964; lab. instr. Georgetown U. Dental Sch., Washington, 1966-73; pvt. practice gen. dentistry, Springfield, Va., 1966—. Elder Kirkwood Presbyterian Ch., Springfield, 1967—; pres. Rolling Hills Swim Club, Springfield, 1977—. Served as capt. U.S. Army, 1963-66. Mem. ADA, Va. Dental Assn., No. Va. Dental Soc. (patient relations com. 1984—), Fairfax County Dental Soc., Omicron Kappa Upsilon, Delta Sigma Delta (life), Lambda Chi Alpha (life). Home: 8333 Carrleigh Pkwy Springfield VA 22152

COOK, SAMUEL EDWARD, oil company executive, philanthropist; b. Ft. Worth, Dec. 18, 1936; s. Sam and Haydie Marie Charlotte (Schultz) C.; m. Abigail Webb, Aug. 30, 1958; children—Cathy, Samuel Edward, Jr., Bonnie Marie. B.S.M.E., U. Miami, 1960; postgrad. Tex. Christian U., 1967-68. Pres., Cook Drilling Co., Ft. Worth, 1960—, Benbrook Oil Corp. Fellow Am. Soc. Petroleum Engrs., Am. Assn. Petroleum Geologists. Republican. Episcopalian. Clubs: Petroleum, Shady Oaks Country, Fort Worth Boat, Power Squadron (social chmn. 1983—) (Fort Worth). Avocations: sailing; scuba diving; horse racing. Home: 6244 Westover Dr Fort Worth TX 76107 Office: Cook Drilling Co 1003 Ridglea Bank Bldg Fort Worth TX 76116

COOK, STEPHEN L., state senator; b. Clinton, Iowa, Dec. 30, 1941; m. Carolyn A. Whitney; children—Craig, Matthew, Stephanie. Student U. Iowa, W.Va. U. Asst. bus. mgr. Laborers Dist. Council; commr. W.Va. Dept. Labor, 1977-79; apptd. W.Va. ho. of dels., 1980-82; mem. W.Va. senate, 1982—, chmn. energy industry and mining com. Del., Monongalia-Preston Labor Council. Mem. Indsl. Relations Research Assn., W.Va. Polit. Sci. Assn. Democrat. Methodist. Office: W Va Senate Charleston WV 25305*

COOK, TODD MCCLURE, medical center administrator; b. Frankfort, Ind., Nov. 3, 1962; s. Robert Eugene and Patricia (McKinney) C. Student Calif. State U., 1981-82, George Mason U., 1983. Lic. realtor. Asst. mgr. McDonalds Corp., Fresno, Calif., 1982-83, Stafford, Va., 1983-84; realtor Coldwell Banker, Alexandria, Va., 1983—; asst. dir. This Way House, Alexandria, 1984-85; dept. head Falls Church Med. Ctr., Va., 1985—; cons. St. Elizabeth's Hosp. Crisis Intervention Tng., Washington, 1985—, Alexandria's Child Safety Day, 1984; Bd. dirs. Help in Emotional Trouble, Fresno, 1982, v.p., bd. dirs., 1983; bd. dirs. Mental Health Assn., Alexandria, 1984, v.p. bd., 1985; del. Nat. Network of Runaway and Youth Services Symposium, Bethesda, Md., 1985. Fed. grantee Youth Devel. Bur., 1984, 85, Alexandria City grantee, 1985. Mem. Smithsonian Instn. Democrat. Presbyterian. Club: Entrepreneur Orgn. (Alexandria) (pres. 1985). Lodge: Demolay. Avocation: tennis. Home: 8817 Northern Spruce Ln Alexandria VA 22309 Office: 1506A Belle View Blvd Alexandria VA 22307

COOK, VICTOR JOSEPH, JR., marketing educator, consultant; b. Durant, Okla., June 25, 1938; s. Victor Joseph and Athelene Ann (Arduser) C.; m. Linda Lee Potter, June 6, 1960 (div. 1971); children—Victor Joseph III, William Randall, Christopher Phelps. B.A., Fla. State U., 1960; M.S., La. State U., 1962; Ph.D., U. Mich., 1965. Research assoc. Mktg. Sci. Inst., Phila., 1965-68, assoc. research dir., Boston, 1968-69; asst. prof. U. Chgo., 1969-75; pres., dir. Mgmt. & Design, New Orleans, 1975-78; prof. Freeman Sch. Bus., Tulane U., 1978—; cons. Ford Motor Co., Dearborn, Mich., 1964-67, IBM, N.Y.C., 1968-72, Sears, Roebuck & Co., Chgo., 1975-77, STC/ICL, London, 1981—. Author: Brand Policy Determination, 1967; designer, patentee furniture, Sud Möbel, 1976. Mem. Republican Presdl. Task Force, Washington, 1981—. Mem. Am. Mktg. Assn., Am. Econ. Assn., Inst. Mgmt. Scis., Assn. for Consumer Research, Beta Gamma Sigma, Phi Beta Kappa. Republican. Methodist. Avocations: golf; drawing; art collecting; travel. Office: AB Freeman Sch Bus Tulane U New Orleans LA 70118

COOK, WAYNE RALPH, lawyer; b. Danville, Ill., Aug. 13, 1912; s. Charles A. and Grace (Massey) C.; A.B., U. Ill., 1934; LL.B., Ind. U., 1944, J.D., 1945; M.A., Georgetown U., 1946; m. Maryla Karpin, June 4, 1934 (dec. Dec. 1969); 1 dau., Bonnie Karen (Mrs. Herbert L. Tallitsch); m. 2d, Irene G. Samuel, Apr. 17, 1976. Admitted to Ill. bar, 1945, Ind. bar, Ark. bar, 1977, U.S. Supreme Ct.; practiced in Danville, 1947-51, St. Charles, Ill., 1970-78; asst. atty. gen. Ill., Springfield, 1949-53; mem. firm Hubachek & Kelly, Chgo., 1953-59; spl. counsel Bankers Life & Casualty Co., Chgo., 1959-69; past pres., dir. Okla. Oil Co., Denver; former v.p., dir. Nat. Drilling Co., Inc., Property Investment Co., Inc., Ponderosa Paper Products, Inc., Ariz.; past dir. Forum Record Sales Corp., N.Y., Artia Records Corp., N.Y., Home Lockers, Inc., Parliament Records Corp.; asst. U.S. atty. No. Dist. Ill., Chgo., 1969-70; dep. atty. gen. State of Ind., 1970-71, asst. atty. gen. in charge environ. law, 1971-73, chief counsel depts., 1973-77; appeals referee Ark. Bd. Rev., 1977-80, chmn., 1980-81. Served to lt. col. AUS, 1941-43, 45-47. Decorated Purple Heart, Bronze Star, medialle de la France Liberèe; hon. Tex. citizen. Mem. Am., Ill., Ind., Ark., 7th Fed. Circuit, Chgo. (chmn. judiciary com. 1966-67), Indpls., Pulaski County bar assns., Am. Soc. Internat. Law, Am. Judicature Soc., Selden Soc., U.S. Armor Assn., 1st Armored Div. Assn. (pres. 1970-71), Sigma Delta Kappa. Clubs: Army and Navy (Washington); Capitol (Little Rock). Home: 8 Pinnacle Point Little Rock AR 72205

COOK, WILLARD FREDRICK, automobile company official; b. Ybor City, Fla., Nov. 6, 1922; s. Ernest Fredrick and Lyttie (Chauncey) C.; m. June Marie Yeluington, May 16, 1947; children—Charlene Louise Cook-Pyne, Lisa Marie Cook-Niebling. Salesman Chevrolet dealer's, So. Fla., 1946—; rep. Gen. Motors div. Motors Ins. Corp., So. Fla., 1950—. Mem. Orange Bowl Staging Com., Miami, 1981-83. Served with USCG, 1942-46; ETO, NATOUSA, PTO, CBI. Mem. Soc. Sales Execs. Democrat. Clubs: Legion of Honor. Lodges: Masons, Shriners.

COOK, WILLIAM WILBER, advertising agency executive; b. Evansville, Ind., Apr. 23, 1921; s. Wilburn Frederick and Mabel (Brookins) C.; student UCLA, 1940-42; B.A. in Bus., Evansville Coll., 1947; LL.D. (hon.), Bethune-Cookman Coll., 1976; m. Mary Andross Brewster, Nov. 2, 1963; children—William F., Constance C., Betty B., Jane R., Robert B. Sales rep. Sta. WIKY, Evansville, 1947-49, WMBR Radio and TV, Jacksonville, Fla., 1949-55; v.p. Dennis, Parsons & Cook Advt. Agy., Jacksonville, 1955-65; pres. William Cook Advt., Inc., Jacksonville, 1965-77, chmn. bd., 1977—. Former chmn. United Negro Coll. Fund; mem. lay adv. com. St. Vincent's Med. Center; trustee Jacksonville U.; former vestryman Episcopal Ch. Served as aviator USNR, 1942-46. Recipient CHIEF award Fla. Pvt. Higher Edn. Assn., 1977. Mem. Jacksonville C. of C. (gov., Com. of 100), Am. Assn. Advt. Agencies (past chmn. S.E. Council), Am. Advt. Fedn. (Silver medal), Fla. Public Relations Assn., Sales and Mktg. Execs. Assn. (Top Mgmt. award). Clubs: River, Univ., Selva Marina Country, Waynesville (N.C.) Country, Ponte Vedra Country, Seminole, Tournement Players. Lodges: Rotary (dir.), Masons. Home: 1325 Beach Ave Atlantic Beach FL 32233 Office: American Heritage Life Bldg Jacksonville FL 32202

COOKE, ANSON RICHARD, chemical company official; b. Lawrence, Mass., Jan. 12, 1926; s. Leonard Anson and Ruth (Livingstone) C.; m. Catherine Cecelia Murphy, June 5, 1948; children—Paula Ruth, Anson Douglas, James Richard, Dwayne Robert. B.S., U. Mass., 1949, M.S., 1950; Ph.D., U. Mich., 1953. Asst. prof. U. Hawaii, 1953-55, Okla. State U., 1955-56; research plant physiologist E.I. duPont, Wilmington, Del., 1957-63; dir. biol. research Amchem Products, Inc., Ambler, Pa., 1963-77; group leader Union Carbide Corp., Research Triangle, N.C., 1977—. Served with USMC, 1943-46. Mem. Am. Chem. Soc., Plant Growth Regulator Soc. Am. (exec. officer), Am. Soc. Plant Physiologists, Weed Sci. Soc. Am. Clubs: Chapel Hill Bird, Central N.C. Mineral. Editor: Procs. Plant Growth Regulator Soc., 1980-85; contbr. articles to profl. jours.; patentee in field. Home: 1210 Huntsman Dr Durham NC 27713 Office: Union Carbide Agricultural Products Co Inc PO Box 12014 Research Triangle Park NC 27709

COOKE, HELEN HEMLIN, editor, writer; b. N.Y.C.; d. Valentine and Katherine (Fischer) Hemlin; student U. N.Mex., 1925-26, Columbia U., 1927-29; m. Charles Cooke, Jan. 29, 1931 (dec. Sept. 1955); 1 son, Harris Craig. Mem. staff writers Lowell Thomas, 1929-33; reporter New Yorker Mag., N.Y.C., 1933-35; publicity dir. Douglas Leigh, Inc., N.Y.C., 1938-45, Monroe Dreher Advt. Agy., N.Y.C., 1941-45; free-lance editor, writer, Washington, 1948—; asst. to exec. v.p. Aerospace Med. Assn., Washington, 1960-61. Clubs: Am. Newspaper Women's, Nat. Press (Washington). Author: (with Evelyn D. Boyer) Distinguished Women of Washington, D.C., 1964. Contbr. articles to various newspapers, mags. including Washington Star Sunday mag., Balt. Sun, Aerospace Medicine, Cue mag., others. Patentee in field of toys. Home: 2244 N Nottingham St Arlington VA 22205

COOKE, PHILLIP CHARLES, office products company executive, mgr.; b. Balt., July 25, 1947; s. Cola Walma and Frances Elizabeth (Thomas) C.; B.S. in Personnel Mgmt., U. Md., College Park, 1970; M.B.A., Rochester Inst. Tech., 1975; m. Darlene Grace Engle, Nov. 7, 1970; 1 son, John Adam. Personnel rep. RCA, Cherry Hill, N.J., 1970-72; with Xerox Corp., Webster, N.Y., 1972—, placement mgr., 1973-75, compensation mgr., 1975-81, mgr. personnel ops. office products div., Dallas, 1981-83; v.p., officer Sunrise Systems, Inc., Dallas, 1983—. Pres., Highlands of McKamy Homeowners Assn., Dallas, 1977-81, 82—, North Dallas Homeowner's Coalition, 1982; mem. Dallas CATV Bd., 1983—. Mem. Am. Compensation Assn., Am.

Electronics Assn., Pi Kappa Alpha. Republican. Methodist. Clubs: Blackwall Racquet, So. Meth. U. Mustang, Md. Terrapin, 500. Contbr. articles to profl. jours. Home: 17208 Graystone Dr Dallas TX 75248 Office: 2209 Midway Rd Carrollton TX 75247

COOKE, RALPH GARY, safety inspector; b. Winston-Salem, July 6, 1943; s. John Ralph and Ellen Louise (Ragland) C.; m. Dorothy Carolyn Brewer, June 24, 1967; 1 child, Jonathan Gary. A.A.S., Gaston Coll., 1967; B.S., Memphis State U., 1971, M.S., 1972. Engring. technician N.C. Dept. Hwys., Winston-Salem, 1967-69; estimator Thompson-Arthur PavCo., Greensboro, N.C., 1972-73; sales rep. Spartan Equipment Co., Greensboro, 1973-74; maintenance crew leader N.C. Dept. Hwys., 1974-79; safety inspector, tng. specialist City of Roanoke, Va., 1979—. Named Marine of the Year, USMCR, 1983. Mem. Am. Soc. Safety Engrs., Am. Indsl. Hygiene Assn., Nat. Safety Mgmt. Soc., Southwest Va. Safety Soc. (pres. 1981-83). Republican. Avocations: camping, golf; basketball coaching. Home: 1820 Belleville Rd SW Roanoke VA 24015 Office: City of Roanoke 1802 Courtland Ave NE Roanoke VA 24015

COOKSEY, FRANK, city official. Mayor, City of Austin, Tex. Office: Office of Mayor PO Box 1088 Austin TX 78767*

COOKSEY, JOHN CHARLES, ophthalmic surgeon; b. Alexandria, La., Aug. 20, 1941; s. Henry Oscar and Ruth (Lee) C.; m. Dorothy Ann Grabill, Dec. 30, 1969; children—Karen, Carol Ann, Catherine. M.D., La. State U., New Orleans, 1966. Practice medicine specializing in ophthalmology, Monroe, La., 1972—; mem. teaching staff E.A. Conway Hosp., Monroe, 1972—; vis. lectr. Alton Ochsner Med. Found., New Orleans, 1978—; asst. clin. prof. La. State U., Baton Rouge, 1979—. Contbg. author: Cataract and Intraocular Lens Surgery, 1984. Lay leader St. Paul's United Meth. Ch., Monroe, 1978-80; mem. La. Republican Central Com., 1974-82; del. Rep. Nat. Conv., Kansas City, Mo., 1976. Served to capt. USAF, 1967-69. Mem. AMA, La. Med. Soc., Ouachita Parish Med. Soc. Methodist. Avocations: breeding quarter horses. Address: 1310 N 19th St Monroe LA 71201

COOL, THOMAS EDWARD, geophysicist; b. Auburn, Ind., Sept. 6, 1950; s. Philip and Suzanne Marian (Somers) C.; m. Iris Elaine Preas, Nov. 22, 1980; 1 child, Jack Philip. B.S. in Geology, Ind. U., Ft. Wayne, 1972; M.S. in Oceanography, Tex. A&M U., 1976, Ph.D., 1979. Petroleum geophysicist Gulf Oil Co., Houston, 1980-82, sr. geophysicist, 1982-84, project geophysicist, 1984—. Contbr. articles to profl. jours. Mem. Am. Assn. Petroleum Geologists, Houston Geol. Soc., fellow Geol. Soc. London. Methodist. Club: Houston A&M. Avocations: tennis; history; traveling. Home: 31A Gloucester Crescent London NW1 7DL England Office: Gulf Corp Attn: London Pouch PO Box 2227 Houston TX 77252

COOLER, KARL SANDERLIN, metallurgical engineer; b. Beaufort, S.C., June 27, 1950; s. Norman Burrell and Mary Frances (Russ) C.; student Clemson (S.C.) U., 1968-69; diploma ferrous metallurgy, Metals Engring. Inst., 1980; m. Rebecca Hewitt, Dec. 31, 1970; 1 dau., Courtney Rich. With Georgetown Steel Co. (S.C.), 1969-81, quality control steelmaking chief insp., 1979-80, product devel. engr., 1980-81; melt shop foreman Steel div. Hurricane Industries, Inc., Sealy, Tex., 1981-82, mgr. tech. services, 1982, supt. prodn. services, 1982—. Active local United Way, Heart Fund. Mem. S.C. N.G., 1969-75. Mem. Am. Soc. Metals, Wire Assn. Internat., AIME, Metals Engring. Inst., Nat. Mgmt. Assn. Baptist. Home: 515 Highmeadows Rd PO Box 984 Bellville TX 77418 Office: PO Box N Sealy TX 77474

COOLEY, FANNIE, counselor educator, consultant; b. Tunnel Springs, Ala., July 4, 1924; d. Willie P. Richardson and Emma Jean (McCorvey) Stallworth. B.S., Tuskegee Inst., 1947, M.S., 1951; Ph.D., U. wis., 1969. Cert. counselor. Asst. instr. Tuskegee U., Ala., 1947-48, prof. counseling, 1969—; instr. Alcorn A&M Coll., Lorman, Miss., 1948-51; asst. prof. Ala. A&M Coll., Normal, 1951-62, assoc. prof., 1964-65; grad. fellow Purdue U., West Lafayette, Ind., 1962-64; house fellow U. Wis., Madison, 1965-69; cons. VA Med. Ctr. Tuskegee, 1969—. Mem. Am. Assn. Counseling and Devel. (Disting. Service award 1985, bd. dirs.), Ala. Assn. Counseling and Devel. (pres. 1976-77, Service award 1978-79), Ala. Assn. for Counselor Edn. (pres. 1985-86), Internat. Platform Assn., AAUW, AAUP, Chi Sigma Iota. Episcopalian. Home: 802-C Ave A Tuskegee AL 36088 Office: Dept Counseling and Student Devel Tuskegee Inst Tuskegee AL 36088

COOLIDGE, EDWIN CHANNING, chemistry educator, consultant, researcher; b. Mt. Vernon, Ohio, Jan. 30, 1925; s. Walter Hatheral and Sarah Helen (Fay) C.; m. Bonita Mae Warner, May 1, 1953; 1 son, Edwin Channing. A.B., Kenyon Coll., Gambier, Ohio, 1941; Ph.D., Johns Hopkins U., 1949. Research chemist Procter & Gamble Co., Cin., 1949-54; asst. prof. chemistry Hamilton Coll., Clinton, N.Y., 1954-58; asst. prof. N.Mex. Inst. Mining and Tech., 1958-61; assoc. prof. chemistry Stetson U., Deland, Fla., 1961-64, prof., 1964—; dir. Assoc. Mid-Fla. Colls. Year Abroad program, 1968-69, Freiburg, Germany program, 1969-70; sr. Fulbright lectr., exchange prof. chemistry Paedagogische Hochschule, Freiburg, 1982-83. Served with Chem. Corps, U.S. Army, 1950-52. Mem. Am. Chem. Soc., Royal Soc. Chemistry, AAUP, Phi Beta Kappa, Sigma Xi, Omicron Delta Kappa, Gamma Sigma Epsilon. Episcopalian. Contbr. articles to profl. jours. Home: 2446 E New York Ave Deland FL 32724 Office: Box 8276 Stetson Univ Deland FL 32720

COOLIDGE, ROBERT CARL, medical administrator; b. Greeneville, Tenn., Aug. 29, 1948; s. Walter Everett and Ann Carolyn (Grier) C.; m. Lorraine Eleanor Cotton, Oct. 15, 1982. B.S., Middle Tenn. State U., 1972. Patients bus. mgr. Madison Hosp. (Tenn.), 1972-74; mfrs. rep. DePuy Mfg. Co., Warsaw, Ind., 1974-76; bus. office mgr. Pembroke Pines Gen. Hosp. (Fla.), 1977-78; adminstr. Southeastern Emergency Physicians, P.C., Chattanooga, 1978-80, Jewett Orthopaedic Clinic, P.A., Winter Park, Fla., 1980—; sec. health adv. com. Coll. Health, U. Central Fla., Orlando. Del., Republican Nat. Conv., 1980. Mem. Med. Group Mgmt. Assn., Am. Guild Patient Account Mgrs., Greater Orlando C. of C. (Orange Juice Forum com.). Republican. Club: Platinum Point Yacht (Punta Gorda, Fla.) Lodge: Rotary (sec.) (Winter Park). Office: Jewett Orthopaedic Clinic 1285 Orange Ave Winter Park FL 32789

COOMBES, LARRY EDWARD, research entomologist; b. Ft. Smith, Ark., Jan. 21, 1950; s. Hubert Spencer and Lola Edith (Smallwood) C.; m. Mary Jo Feltner, May 26, 1972; 1 son, Ryan Hunter. B.S. in Biology, Ark. Tech. U., 1972; M.S. in Entomology, U. Ark.-Fayetteville, 1973, Ph.D., 1977. With Union Carbide Corp., 1977—, mgr. Wayside Research Sta., Miss., 1980—. Mem. Entomol. Soc. Am., So. Weed Soc., Miss. Agrl. Chem. Assn., Soc. Nemotologists and Plant Pathologists, C. of C. (chmn. agr. bus. com.), Sigma Xi. Baptist. Clubs: Cypress Hills Tennis, Greenville Country (dir.). Contbr. articles to profl. jours. Home: 116 Gregory St Greenville MS 38701 Office: PO Box 2558 Hwy 1 S Wayside MS 38780

COON, JULIAN BARHAM, energy company executive; b. Jackson, Miss., Nov. 16, 1939; s. Morris Galloway and Dru Etta (Camp) C.; m. Barbara Schultz, Aug. 30, 1961; children—Julianne, Robert. B.S. in Physics, Tex. A&M U., 1961; Ph.D., La. State U., 1966. Asst. prof. physics U. Houston, 1968-73; with Conoco Inc., Ponca City, Okla., 1973—, mgr. mining and research, 1978-81, mgr. exploration research, 1981-84, v.p. petroleum research and devel., 1984—. Contbr. articles to profl. jours. Patentee in field. Mem. Soc. Exploration Geophysicists, Am. Assn. Petroleum Geologists, Soc. Petroleum Engrs., Phi Kappa Phi, Sigma Xi, Phi Eta Sigma, Sigma Pi Sigma. Republican. Episcopalian. Lodge: Rotary. Avocation: tennis. Home: 3636 Mistletoe St Ponca City OK 74604 Office: Conoco Inc PO Box 1267 Ponca City OK 74603

COONEY, RAY HOWARD, manufacturing company executive; b. Akron, Ohio, Dec. 14, 1921; s. Frederick B. and Myrtle A. (Young) C.; m. June H. Hawkins, June 13, 1947; children—Pamela J. Cooney Trent, Robbie L. Cooney Johansson, Mark R. B.A.E., U. Fla., 1943; postgrad., Georgtown U., 1946, Syracuse U., 1973-74. Asst. sales and advt. mgr. Adams Packaging Assn., Auburdale, Fla., 1946-48; v.p. Flag Sulphur & Chem. Co., Tampa, Fla., 1960-63, pres., 1963-67; sales mgr. Niagara Chem. div. Food Machinery, Tampa, 1967-68; mktg. dir. Scotty's Inc., Winter Haven, Fla., 1968-69, v.p., 1969-73, pres., chief exec. officer, 1973—; dir. Christian Towers, Fla. Guarantee & Trust Co., St. Petersburgh, Fla. Pres. Fla. Agrl. Research Inst., 1967-68; bd. govs. Lake Region YMCA. Served to sgt. inf. AUS, World War II. Decorated Purple Heart. Republican. Mem. Christian Ch. (Disciples of Christ). Lodges: Cypress Gardens Rotary (pres.); Masons; Shriners. Home: 5 Lake Link Dr SE Winter Haven FL 33880 Office: Scotty's Inc PO Box 939 Winter Haven FL 33880

COONS, RUNELL S., TV executive; b. Amarillo, Tex., July 11, 1944; d. Larry Burgie and LaRue (McCanne) Stitt; A.A., Amarillo Coll., 1963; B.S. cum laude, U. Houston, 1965; postgrad. West Tex. State U., 1966—; m. David Russell Coons, Aug. 23, 1968; children—Courtnay, Kevin. Copy writer McCormick Advt., Amarillo, 1965-67; continuity dir. KFDA-TV, Amarillo, 1967-73; continuity dir. KAMR-TV, Amarillo, 1973-75, traffic dir., 1975—; free lance advt. cons., 1975—; part-time instr. West Tex. State U., Canyon, 1977-79. Bd. dirs. Domestic Violence Council, Amarillo, sec., 1981-82, mem. speakers bur.; active Amarillo Little Theatre. Recipient Public Affairs award UP Internat., Amarillo Ad Club and Tex. Med. Assn., 1973; Addy award Amarillo Advt. Club, 1972, 74; named One of 12 Outstanding Women in Amarillo, Women's div. Amarillo C. of C. Mem. Tex. Press Women (state publ. chmn. 1979-80), Amarillo Advt. Club (chmn. speakers bur. 1980-81). Mem. Christian Ch. (Disciples of Christ). Club: Altrusa (v.p. 1982-84, pres. 1985-86) (Amarillo, Tex.). Home: 3505 Barclay St Amarillo TX 79109 Office: PO Box 751 Amarillo TX 79189

COOPER, ALLAN D., political science educator; b. Oklahoma City, Apr. 13, 1952; s. Morris Lawrence and Alice Joyce (Pearson) C.; m. Janet Mary Rogers, June 21, 1980; children—Justin, Alyssa. B.A., U. Okla., 1974; M.A., U. Wis., 1976; Ph.D., Atlanta U., 1981. Asst. prof. polit. sci. St. Augustine's Coll., Raleigh, N.C., 1981—. Author: U.S. Economic Power and Political Influence in Namibia, 1700-1982, 1982. Contbr. articles to profl. jours. Investigator Wake County NAACP, Raleigh, 1983-84; bd. dirs. Unitarian-Universalist Fellowship, Raleigh, 1982-84. Ford Found. grantee, 1978-79; U. Fla. grantee 1984; NEH grantee, 1984. Mem. Am. Polit. Sci. Assn., African Studies Assn., Assn. Concerned African Scholars (dir. 1982—), Acad. Polit. Sci., N.C. Polit. Sci. Assn. Home: 1408 Mordecai Dr Raleigh NC 27604 Office: St Augustine's Coll Raleigh NC 27611

COOPER, ARTHUR WELLS, forestry educator; b. Washington, Aug. 15, 1931; s. Gustav A. and Josephine W. (Wells) C.; m. Jean L. Farnsworth, Aug. 30, 1953; children—Paul A., Roy A. B.A., Colgate U., 1953, M.A., 1955; Ph.D., U. Mich., 1958. Asst. prof. botany N.C. State U., Raleigh, 1958-63, assoc. prof., 1963-68, prof., 1968-76, prof. forestry, 1976-80, head forestry dept., 1980—; asst. sec. N.C. Dept. Natural and Econ. Resources, Raleigh, 1971-76; instr. Biol. Sta., U. Mich., 1967-69, 71, 73. Recipient Conservation award Am. Motors, 1972; Sol Feinstone Environ. award SUNY-Syracuse, 1982; named Conservationist of Yr., N.C. Wildlife Fedn., 1982. Mem. Ecol. Soc. Am. (pres. 1981; Disting. Service award 1984), Soc. Am. Foresters, AAAS, N.C. Acad. Sci. Democrat. Contbr. articles to profl. publs. Office: Dept Forestry NC State U Raleigh NC 27695-8002

COOPER, B. LEE, college administrator, author, history educator; b. Hammond, Ind., Oct. 4, 1942; s. Charles Albert and Kathleen Marie (Kunde) C.; m. Jill Elizabeth Cunningham, June 13, 1964; children—Michael Lee, Laura Ellen, Julie Allison. B.S., Bowling Green State U., 1964; M.A., Mich. State U., 1965; Ph.D., Ohio State U., 1971; cert. Harvard U., 1980. Assoc. prof. history Urbana Coll., Ohio, 1965-73, dean student affairs, 1973-74, dean coll., 1974-76; v.p. acad. affairs Newberry Coll., S.C., 1976-85; curriculum cons. Concordia Luth. Coll., Austin, Tex., 1982, Tex. Wesleyan Coll., Fort Worth, 1983. Author: Images of American Society in Popular Music (ASCAP-Deems Taylor award 1983), 1982; Popular Music Handbook, 1984. Active Central United Methodist Ch., Newberry, 1976—, Newberry County Hist. Soc., 1977—, Champaign County Democratic Exec. Com., Urbana, 1972-74. Recipient Tchr. of Yr. award Urbana Coll., 1967; Outstanding Educator in Am. award, 1970, 73, 75. Mem. Am. Hist. Assn., Nat. Council Social Studies, Popular Culture Assn., Am. Culture Assn., Phi Alpha Theta (grad. scholar 1964), Omicron Delta Kappa. Home: 1812 Johnstone St Newberry SC 29108

COOPER, BERNARD RICHARD, physicist; b. Everett, Mass., Apr. 15, 1936; s. Edward and Florence (Solomon) C.; m. Sylvia Lenore Birman, Jan. 21, 1962; children—Jean Alane, David Jacob, Marilyn Clyta. B.S. in Physics, MIT, 1957; Ph.D. (NSF fellow), U. Calif.-Berkeley, 1961. Research assoc. Atomic Energy Research Establishment, Harwell, Eng., 1962-63; research fellow Harvard U., 1963-64; physicist Gen. Electric Research and Devel. Ctr., Schenectady, 1964-74; Claude Worthington Benedum prof. physics W.Va. U., Morgantown, 1974—; cons. Argonne Nat. Lab., MIT Nat. Magnet Lab.; collaborator Los Alamos Sci. Lab. NSF research grantee, 1977—; Dept. Energy grantee, 1980—; Air Force Office of Sci. Research grantee, 1986—. Fellow Am. Phys. Soc. (chmn. study on research planning for coal utilization and synthetic fuel prodn. 1980-81); mem. IEEE, Am. Vacuum Soc., Sigma Xi. Democrat. Jewish. Lodge: B'nai B'rith (pres. W.Va. council 1978-79). Editor: Scientific Problems of Coal Utilization, 1978; Chemistry and Physics of Coal Utilization, 1981; The Science and Technology of Coal and Coal Utilization, 1984; contbr. articles to profl. jours. Home: 102 Forest Dr Morgantown WV 26505 Office: Dept Physics W Va U PO Box 6023 Morgantown WV 26506

COOPER, CHARLES FRANKLIN, management consultant, real estate developer; b. Griffin, Ga., Sept. 11, 1939; s. Robert Franklin and Neva Beatrice (Fletcher) C.; m. Mary Esther Pender, Oct. 27, 1962; children—Angela Rain, Jeffrey Todd. B.S. in Indsl. Mgmt., Ga. Tech. U., Atlanta, 1961. Buyer dept. purchasing Lockheed-Ga. Co., Marietta, Ga., 1961-62; mgmt. cons. Arthur Young & Co., Atlanta, 1968-80; dir. mgmt. cons. service Draffin & Tucker, Albany, Ga., 1980-82; chief exec. officer C. Frank Cooper & Assocs. Inc., Albany, 1982—; developer, co-sponsor, presenter Fin. Mgmt. Seminar for Small Businesses, Albany, 1984; guest lectr. Ga. State U., Atlanta, 1974, Mercer U., Macon, Ga., 1976-79, 81-83; speaker, seminar leader Small Bus. Devel. Ctr., Albany, 1981-83; speaker Internat. Mgmt. Council, Albany, 1983. Bd. dirs. Dougherty County chpt. Am. Heart Assn., 1982—, council 97, Boy Scouts Am., 1984—. Served to capt. USAF, 1962-68. Named to Order of Ky. Col. Commonwealth Ky., 1973. Mem. Am. Assn. Individual Investors, Ga. Soc. C.P.A.s., Albany C. of C., Nat. Fedn. Ind. Bus. Baptist. Clubs: Berkeley Hills Golf, Doublegate Country. Home: 727 4th Ave Albany GA 31701 Office: C Frank Cooper & Assocs Inc PO Box 1634 Albany GA 31702

COOPER, CHARLES JASPER, lawyer; b. Tampa, Fla., Mar. 20, 1929; s. Harry Alva and Ruth (Smith) C.; m. Sally Ann Hill, Sept. 8, 1951; children—Carol, Douglas, Charles, Elizabeth, Kate. A.B., Brown U., 1951; J.D., Harvard U., 1954; Ph.D., Bryn Mawr Coll., 1967. Bar: Pa. 1955, Va. 1985. Assoc. counsel Montgomery, McCracken, Walker & Rhoads, Phila., 1954-55, Bellwoar, Rich & Mankas, Phila., 1956-60; lectr. polit. sci. U. Pa., Phila., 1964-67, asst. prof., 1967-68, vis. lectr., 1968-69; assoc. gen. counsel ARA Services, Inc., Phila., 1968-71; v.p., sec.-treas., dir. InterAx, Inc., 1971-72; sole practice, Bryn Mawr, Pa., 1972-83; legal counsel for devel. Randolph-Macon Coll., Ashland, Va., 1984—. Trustee, treas. Friends Central Sch., 1970-74; chmn. Harold and Ida Hill Charitable Fund, 1969—; bd. mgrs., treas. Friends Pub. Corp., 1972-79; bd. dirs. Phoenix House, 1973-79, 80-83, Phila. Child Guidance Clinic, 1981-84; trustee, treas. Ardmore Ave. Community Ctr.-Soul Shack, 1975-81; bd. dirs., treas. Family Support Ctr., 1976-79; treas. Friends Sch., Haverford, Pa., 1979-83; trustee Bryn Mawr Coll., 1978—; treas. Montgomery County Democratic Com., 1979-81. Mem. ABA. Pa. Bar Assn., Phila. Bar Assn., Am. Polit. Sci. Assn., Am. Acad. Polit. and Social Sci., Ams. for Democratic Action (bd. dirs. S.E. Pa. 1955-83, nat. bd. 1967—), Phi Beta Kappa. Home: 1516 Park Ave Richmond VA 23220 Office: Randolph Macon Coll Ashland VA 23005

COOPER, DAVID LAWRENCE, physician; b. Birmingham, Ala., Apr. 29, 1941; s. Harry Meyer and Pearl (Davidson) C.; m. Ann Norma Shapiro, Nov. 23, 1969 (div.); children—Steven, Amy, Jonathan, Avraham. B.S., Ga. Tech., 1963; M.D., Ind. U., 1967. Diplomate Am. Bd. Dermatology. Intern, Naval Regional Med. Ctr., N.Y.C., 1967-68; resident in dermatology Naval Regional Med. Ctr., Phila., 1968-71, Grad. Sch. Medicine, U. Pa., 1970-71; owner Forest Park (Ga.) Physicians Office, 1973-78; pres. D.L. Cooper, M.D., P.C., Riverdale, Ga., 1978—; asst. prof. Emory U. Med. Sch.; cons. Henry County Hosp., Clayton Gen. Hosp., Grady Hosp. Doctor for Day, Ga. State Legislature, 1982, 83, 84; active Ga. Med. Polit. Action Com., 1980—; bd. dirs. Jewish Nat. Fund, Zionist Orgn. Am. Served to lt. comdr. USN, 1967-73. Recipient Ga. Tech. Outstanding Alumni award, 1978, 83; spl. commendation Ga. Ho. of Reps., 1979. Mem. Am. Acad. Dermatology, AMA, Assn. Mil. Dermatologists, Royal Soc. Health, Royal Soc. Medicine, Israel Med. Assn., Southeastern Dermatology Soc., Ga. Dermatology Soc., Med. Assn. Ga., Century Club Dermatology Found. Clubs: Atlanta Track. Lodges: B'nai Brith, Kiwanis. Contbr. articles to profl. jours. Office: 150 Med Way C-2 Riverdale GA 30274

COOPER, EARL WALLACE, environmental scientist, hydrogeologist, petroleum geologist; b. Trenton, Tex., Jan. 31, 1925; s. Jack and Francis Imogene (Wallace) C.; m. Earlene Keeton, Aug. 9, 1951 (div. July 1975); m. Margaret Zoe Hall, Apr. 16, 1976; children—Don, Diane, Denise, Cydney, John, Sandra. B.S. in Petroleum Geology, Tex. Tech U., 1950. Exploration geologist Union Tex. Petroleum, 1950-54, Helmerich & Payne, Inc. Midland, Tex., 1954-58; dist. geologist J.M. Huber Corp., Midland, 1958-64; petroleum cons., 1964-65; hydrogeologist Tex. Dept. Water Resources, Austin, 1965-71; environ. scientist U.S. EPA, Dallas, 1971—; dir. Corpus Christi Oil Spill Assn., Tex., 1974—, Nat. Spill Control Sch., Corpus Christi, 1975-76. Recipient Gold medal EPA, 1973, Silver medal, 1979, Dir. award, 1979, Bronze medal, 1985. Mem. Am. Assn. Petroleum Geologists, Dallas Geol. Soc., Petroleum Engrs. Club. Lodge: Masons. Avocation: travel. Office: US EPA 1201 Elm St Dallas TX 75270

COOPER, FRED HANDEL, university administrator; b. Pontotoc, Miss., June 2, 1930; s. Fred Handel and Mattie Augusta (Bigham) C.; m. Shirley Jo Miller, Oct. 22, 1950; children—Fred H., Joe Richard. Student Tulane U., 1947-49; A.B., Am. U., 1952. With Times-Picayune, New Orleans, 1948-49, Washington Star, 1949-54, Sarasota (Fla.) Herald-Tribune, 1954-60, The Cooper Co., 1960-69, Powers Dr. Baptist Ch., Orlando, Fla., 1969-70; mem. adminstrn. Stetson U., DeLand, Fla., 1970—, asst. to pres. for athletics and dir. pub. relations/exec. dir. Coastal EdNl. Broadcast, 1983—. First v.p. Fla. Bapt. State Conv., 1974, vice chmn. state bd. mission, 1972-74. Recipient Freedoms Found. award, 1962; Orlando Press Club award, 1973; Fla. Mag. Assn. award, 1976; others. Mem. Pub. Relations Soc. Am., Planetary Soc., AAAS, Fla. Press Assn., Fla. Sportswriters Assn., Fla. Mag. Assn., Fla. Sportscasters Assn., Council Advancement and Support of Edn. Democrat. Clubs: Sertoma (internat. dir. 1960-63), Orlando Press (dir., sec.), Masons. Contbr. articles to profl. jours. Home: 6139 Pickering Ct Orlando FL 32808

COOPER, FREDERICK EANSOR, lawyer; b. Thomasville, Ga., Jan 18, 1942; s. Martin Milner and Margaret (Philips) C.; m. Helen Dykes, Dec. 10, 1966; children—Frederick Eansor, Johnson Joseph. B.A., Washington and Lee U., 1964; J.D., U. Ga., 1967. Bar: Ga. Partner firm Herndon & Cooper, Thomasville, 1972-73; gen. counsel Flowers Industries, Inc., Thomasville, 1973-74, gen. counsel, sec., 1974—, copr. v.p., 1978-83, exec. v.p., 1983-84, pres., 1984—, dir., 1975—. Chmn. Ga. Republican Com., 1981—. Served with JAGC AUS, 1967-72; mem. Res. Presbyterian. Club: Rotary. Home: 203 Junius St Thomasville GA 31792 Office: PO Box 1338 Thomasville GA 31792

COOPER, HAROLD HOMER, JR., lawyer; b. Tulsa, Aug. 3, 1940; s. Harold Homer and Marjorie (Burkett) C.; B.A., U. Tulsa, 1962, J.D., 1966; postgrad. So. Methodist U., 1958-60; div.; 1 son, Christopher Lee. Admitted to Tex. bar, 1968; corp. sec., gen. counsel Linbeck Constrn. Corp., Houston, 1967-72; asso. gen. counsel Mitchell Energy & Devel. Corp., Houston, 1972-74; v.p., gen. counsel, corp. sec. 1st Constrn. Group, Inc., Houston, 1974-77; v.p. and gen. counsel Houston div. Vantage Cos., 1978—. Bd. dirs. Houston Grand Opera Assn. Mem. Am., Okla. bar assns., State Bar Tex., Kappa Alpha, Phi Alpha Delta. Home: Houston TX Office: 10777 Westheimer St Suite 1000 Houston TX 77042

COOPER, HARRY EZEKIEL, educator; b. Kansas City, Mo., Dec. 10, 1897; s. Ezekiel and Helen (Moore) C.; Mus.B., Horner Inst. Fine Arts, 1920; Mus.D., Bush Conservatory, 1923; A.B., Ottawa U., 1937; m. Agnes Bickford, Nov. 18, 1926; children—Robert Ezekiel, Alice Caroline (Mrs. Theo Robert Potter). Supt. music Liberty (Mo.) Schs., 1917-19; prof. music, chmn. dept. William Jewell Coll., 1919-28; dean music Ottawa U., 1928-37; chmn. dept. music, prof. music Meredith Coll., 1937—. Organist, choirmaster Kansas City (Mo.) Chs., 1911-37, Christ Ch., Raleigh, N.C., 1937-47, 1st Bapt. Ch., 1948—; organist N.C. Symphony Orch., 1949. Condr., Raleigh Oratorio Soc., 1940-48. Fellow Am. Guild Organists; mem. N.C. Music Tchrs. Assn. (pres. 1943-44), Raleigh Chamber Music Guild (pres. 1942-43). Writer musical articles, various songs, others. Home: care Robert E Cooper 123 W Franklin St Suite 202E Chapel Hill NC 27514

COOPER, HOMER CHASSELL, sociology educator; b. Balt., Oct. 28, 1923; s. Homer Eber and Clara Frances (Chassell) C.; m. Patricia Montgomery Irvin, June 14, 1951; children—Alice Holmes, Ben Irvin, Marian Cooper Wilson. A.B., Oberlin Coll., 1949; M.A., U. Mich., 1953, Ph.D., 1957. Mem. faculty U. Mont., Missoula, 1956-59, Dartmouth Coll., Hanover, N.H., 1959-61, U. Pitts., 1961-64; prof. sociology U. Ga., Athens, 1964—; lectr., cons. to govtl., bus., indsl. orgns., 1956—. Author: (with Angus Campbell) Group Differences in Attitudes and Votes, 1956. Editor: (with Schabacker and Clark) Focus on the Future of Georgia, 1970. Contbr. articles to profl. jours. Commr., Clarke County, Ga., 1973-75; chmn. Clarke County Democratic Com., 1982-84, mem. 1970—; mem. Ga. State Dem. Com., 1974-82. Served with U.S. Army, 1944-46. Mem. Am. Sociol. Assn., So. Sociol. Soc., Ga. Sociol. Assn. (pres. 1969-70). Avocation: politics. Home: 145 Pendleton Dr Athens GA 30306 Office: Dept Sociology U Ga Athens GA 30602

COOPER, JAMES C., natural gas company executive; b. Richland, Tex., 1935; married. B.A., Tex. A&M U., 1956, M.S., 1958; Ph.D., U. Ill., 1966. Monetary economist Fed. Res. Bank, 1962-65; v.p., dir. econ. research Irving Trust Co., 1965-74; exec. v.p., chief fin. officer United Gas Pipe Line Co., 1974-77; exec. v.p. fin. United Energy Resources Inc., Houston, 1977—, also dir.; dir. United Gas Pipe Line Co., Interfirst Bank-Houston, United Tex. Transmission Co. Served to capt. USAR, 1956-64. Office: United Energy Resources Inc PO Box 1478 Houston TX 77251*

COOPER, JAMES HAYES SHOFNER, congressman, lawyer; b. Nashville, June 19, 1954; s. William Prentice Jr. and Horetense (Powell) C. B.A., U. N.C., 1975, Oxford U., 1977; J.D., Harvard U., 1980. Atty. Waller, Lansden, Dortch & Davis, Nashville, 1980-82; mem. 98th Congress from 4th Tenn. dist. Rhodes Scholar, 1975; Morehead scholar, 1972. Mem. Phi Beta Kappa. Democrat. Episcopalian. Home: 413 E Lane St Shelbyville TN 37160 Office: US Ho of Reps Washington DC 20515

COOPER, JEROME A., lawyer; b. Brookwood, Ala., Jan. 15, 1913; s. Marks Benjamin and Etta (Temerson) C.; A.B., Harvard U., 1933, LL.B., 1936; m. Lois Harriet McMillen, Aug. 16, 1938; children—Ellen Cooper Erdreich, Carol Cooper Sokol. Bar: Ala. 1936. Practice in Birmingham, 1946—; law clk. U.S. Dist. Judge Davis, 1936-37, U.S. Supreme Ct. Justice Hugo L. Black, 1937-40; regional atty. Solicitor's Office, Dept. Labor, 1940-41; ptnr. Cooper, Mitch & Crawford, 1950—; mem. Pres. Kennedy's Lawyers' Com. for Civil Rights Under Law, 1963; pres. adv. council Public Radio Sta. WBHM, 1980—. Mem. Birmingham Area Manpower Resource Devel. Planning Bd., 1969—, Gov.'s Task Force on Unemployment of Jefferson County, 1983; chmn. community devel. com. Operation New Birmingham; mem. Jefferson County Drug Abuse Coordinating Com., 1970-76; pres. Jefferson County Assn. Mental Health, Birmingham Jewish Community Ctr., United Jewish Fund; mem. Southeastern regional adv. bd. Anti-Defamation League, 1981; exec. bd. Birmingham Concentrated Employment Program; pres. Positive Maturity; sec., exec. bd. Jefferson County Com. Econ. Opportunity; pres. Crisis Center, 1976; Democratic candidate for Ala. Senate, 1966; bd. dirs. Birmingham Symphony Assn. Served to lt. comdr. USNR, 1942-45. Fellow Internat. Soc. Barristers; mem. Ala. Law Inst., Adminstrv. Conf. U.S. Jewish (trustee temple). Mem. editorial adv. bd. The Ala. Lawyer. Home: 42 Fairway Dr Birmingham AL 35213 Office: 409 N 21st St Suite 201 Birmingham AL 35203

COOPER, JEROME MAURICE, architect; b. Memphis, Jan. 24, 1930; s. Samuel and Bessie (Phillips) C.; m. Jean Kanter, Dec. 29, 1957; children—David Franklin, Samuel Randolph, Beth Lauren. B.S., Ga. Inst. Tech., 1952, B.Arch., 1955; postgrad. U. Rome, Italy, 1956-57. Fulbright fellow, Rome, 1956-57; pres. Cooper, Carry & Assocs. Inc., Atlanta, 1960—. Prin. works include: Coll. of Architecture Bldg., Ga. Inst. Tech., Siemens-Allis Hdqrs., Atlanta, Hickory Hollow Mall, United Am. Plaza, Green Hills Mall (AIA design award), Md. Casualty Hdqrs., Atlanta, Heritage Village at Sea Pines. Served to lt. (j.g.), USN, 1952-54. Fellow AIA (pres. chpt., nat. bd. dirs.). Home: 1070 Judith Way NE Atlanta GA 30324 Office: 3520 Piedmont Rd NE Atlanta GA 30305

COOPER, JERRY W., state senator; b. McMinnville, Tenn., Aug. 6, 1948; married; children—Sally Denise, Elisa Leigh, Faith Rae. B.S., U. Tenn., 1970.

Mem. Tenn. Senate, 1985—; dir. City Bank and Trust Co. Bd. dirs. Caney Fork Regional Library Assn. Served with USNG, 1970-76. Named Tenn. Outstanding Young Man Jaycees, 1983; Tenn. Small Businessman of Yr. SBA, 1983. Mem. Nat. Fedn. Ind. Bus., Nat. Assn. Mfrs., Jaycees (pres. Tenn. chpt. 1980-81, v.p. Tenn. Jaycee Found.), Alpha Phi Mu (hon. engring.), Phi Kappa Alpha. Democrat. Baptist. Office: Office of State Senate Legislative Plaza Room 7 Nashville TN 37219

COOPER, JIMMY LEE, pharmacist; b. Kirbyville, Tex., Mar. 22, 1942; s. Mitchell and Ocella (Simmons) C.; B.S. in Pharmacy, Tex. So. U., 1965; m. Diana Hightower, July 16, 1966; 1 son, James Sebestian Cabot. With Walgreen Drugs, Houston, 1962—, pharmacist, 1965—, store mgr., 1967—. Trustee, Variety Boys' Club; pres. Tex. So. Alumni Assn., Inc. Mem. Nat. Pharm. Assn., Tex. Pharm. Assn., Houston Pharm. Assn., Harris County Pharm. Assn., Am. Mgmt. Assn. Houston Jaycees, Chi Delta Mu. Baptist. Club: Rotary. Address: 9413 Bertwood St Houston TX 77016 Office: 5002 Tidwell Houston TX 77016

COOPER, LAWRENCE ALLEN, lawyer; b. San Antonio, Feb. 1, 1948; s. Elmer E. and Sally (Templkin) C.; m. Annie Nataf, Aug. 19, 1973; 1 child, Jonathan Alexander. B.A., Tulane U., 1970; J.D., St. Mary's U., San Antonio, 1974; LL.M., Emory U., 1980. Bar: Ga. 1975, Tex. 1975. Ptnr. Cohen, Pollock, Cooper & Comolli, Atlanta, 1979—. Mem. Atlanta Bar Assn., ABA, Ga. Bar Assn., Tex. Bar Assn., Ga. Trial Lawyers Assn., Assn. Trial Lawyers Am., Ga. Assn. Criminal Def. Lawyers. Office: 401 W Peachtree St NE Suite 1550 Atlanta GA 30308

COOPER, MELVIN DULEY, JR., educational administrator; b. Memphis, Aug. 12, 1940; s. Melvin Duley and Sydney Mae (Wilson) C.; A.B., Columbia U., 1962; M.Ed., Memphis State U., 1971; m. Eleanor Grace McCallie, Nov. 6, 1982. Tchr. English, Shelby County Schs., Memphis, 1963-65, Memphis U. Sch., 1965-69; account exec. Robert F. Sharpe & Co., Memphis, 1969-70; dir. devel. Hutchison Sch., Memphis U. Sch., Memphis, 1970-75, McCallie Sch., Chattanooga, 1975—. Bd. dirs. Memphis Opera Theater, 1974-75, Chattanooga Opera Assn., 1975-81, St. George's Day Sch., Germantown, Tenn., 1973-75, St. Andrew's-Sewanee Sch., 1981-85; Episc. Commn. of S.E. Tenn., 1981-83, English Speaking Union (Chattanooga branch), 1981-83, pres. alumni chpt. Coll. Edn., Memphis State U., 1974-75. Mem. Nat. Assn. Ind. Schs. (devel. com. 1976-79, chmn., 1977-79), Council Advancement and Support of Edn. (ind. schs. adv. com. 1973-75), Kappa Delta Pi. Episcopalian. Home: 112 Hilltop Dr Chattanooga TN 37411 Office: McCallie Sch Chattanooga TN 37404

COOPER, NAN ABBOTT, educator; b. Jacksonville, Tex., Mar. 25, 1947; d. Jack Mastin and Dorothy Geradline (Feagin) Abbott; m. Billy James Cooper, Dec. 25, 1966; children—Richard Alan, Ronald Wayne. Student Lon Morris Coll., 1965-66; B.S., Stephen F. Austin State U., 1969; M.Ed., U. Tex.-Tyler, 1980. Office mgr. Future Homes div. Triangle A Enterprises, Jacksonville, 1970-72; internat. sales and customs claims Wing Archery div. AMF, Jacksonville, 1972-75; tchr., coach Overston Ind. Sch. Dist. (Tex.), 1976-77; community liason dir., instr. Rusk County YMCA, Henderson, Tex., 1976-78; bookkeeper Lowe Tractor & Equipment Co., Henderson, 1978; tchr., athletic dir. Laneville Ind. Sch. Dist. (Tex.), 1978—. Dir. children's choirs 1st Baptist Ch., Laneville, 1982-84; mem. Laneville Vol. Fire Dept., 1983—. Recipient Chpt. Farmer degree Future Farmers Am. Mem. Assn. Tex. Profl. Educators (sec. 1981-82), Tex. High Sch. Girls' Coaches Assn., Tex. Basketball Coaches Assn., Beta Sigma Phi. Democrat. Baptist. Office: Laneville Ind Sch Dist PO Box 127 Laneville TX 75667

COOPER, NINA KELLY, salesperson b. Houma, La., May 21, 1949; d. Irvin John and Nina Mae (Nelms) Kelly; m. Barry James Cooper, May 21, 1968; children—Barry James, Wendy Ann. L.P.N., West Jefferson Vocat. Tech. Sch., 1976; A.A., U. Southwestern La., 1982, B.A., 1984. Lic. practical nurse La. Coordinator, dept. anesthesia West Jefferson Hosp., Marrero, La., 1976-78; staff nurse Our Lady of Lourdes, Lafayette, La., 1978-79; nurse Psychiatric Clinic, Lafayette, 1979-80; pvt. nursing care, Lafayette, 1980-82; med. salesperson Williams Physicians Surgeons Shreveport, La., 1983, UAD Labs., Jackson, Miss., 1983—; revenue officer La. Dept. Revenue, Houma, 1968-71; cons. U. Southwestern La., 1983; cons. United Givers Fund Am., 1983. Vol., Girl Scouts Am., Lafayette, 1978—; vol. Easter Seal, Lafayette, 1982; vol. Am. Heart Assn., Lafayette, 1981-82; mem. Council Exceptional Children, Lafayette, 1980-82; mem. Gov.'s Transition Team State La., Baton Rouge, 1983. Mem. League of Nurses, Kappa Delta Phi. Democrat. Roman Catholic. Clubs: City of Lafayette, Petroleum, Oakbourne Country. Office: UAD Labs PO Box 10587 6635 Hwy 18 West Jackson MS 39209

COOPER, RICHARD PAUL, project engineer; b. Attleboro, Mass., July 4, 1934; s. John and Ethel H. (Guest) C.; m. Madeleine Devaux, Oct. 21, 1960; children—Nicholas Richard, Barbara Madeline, Esther Madeline. B.S.M.E., CUNY, 1965. Marine engr. Standard Oil Co. N.J., 1952-60; power engr. Harrow Mgmt. Co., 1960-64; field constrn. mgmt. engr. Goldman Bros., 1964-68; supt. bldgs. and grounds Bd. Edn., City of N.Y., 1968-78; dir. engring. Lawrence Meml. Hosp. (Kans.), 1978-80; facilities engr. Ethicon Corp. subs. Johnson & Johnson Co., Cornelia, Ga., 1980—; mem. Elec. Industry Evaluation Panel. Mem. Habersham (Ga.) Sheriff Posse, 1981—; bd. dirs. local chpt. Am. Cancer Soc. Recipient Energy Engr. of Yr. award State of Ga., 1984. Mem. Assn. Energy Engrs. (pres. Ga. chpt. 1982-84, regional v.p. 1984—), Energy Mgmt. and Control Soc., Am. Soc. for Hosp. Engring. (award 1980), Nat. Assn. Power Engrs., Nat. Fire Protection Assn. Episcopalian. Club: Optimists. Lodge: Lions (past pres. Cornelia club). Contbr. articles to profl. jours.

COOPER, ROBERT ELBERT, state supreme ct. justice; b. Chattanooga, Oct. 14, 1920; s. John Thurman and Susie Inez (Hollingsworth) C.; B.A., U. N.C., 1946; J.D., Vanderbilt U., 1949; m. Catherine Pauline Kelly, Nov. 24, 1949; children—Susan Florence Cooper Hodges, Bobbie Cooper Martin, Kelly Ann Cooper Smith, Robert Elbert. Admitted to Tenn. bar; assoc. firm Kolwyck & Clark, 1949-51, Cooper & Barger, 1951-53; asst. atty. gen. 6th Jud. Circuit Tenn., 1951-53; judge 6th Jud. Circuit Tenn., 1953-60, Tenn. Ct. of Appeals, 1960-70; presiding judge Eastern Div., Tenn. Ct. of Appeals, 1970-74; justice Tenn. Supreme Ct., Chattanooga, 1974—, chief justice, 1976-78, 84-85; chmn. Tenn. Jud. Council, 1967—; mem. Tenn. Jud. Standards Commn., 1971-79; chmn. Tenn. Code Commn., 1976-78. Elder, Second United Presbyn. Ch., 1963—, chmn. bd. trustees, 1966-73; bd. dirs. St. Barnabas Nursing Home and Apts. for Aged, 1966-69; mem. exec. bd. Cherokee council Boy Scouts Am., 1960-64. Served with USN, 1941-46. Recipient Merit awards Alhambra Shrine Temple, Shrine Hosp. for Crippled Children, Lexington, Ky., 1966, Chattanooga Met. YMCA. Mem. Am., Tenn., Chattanooga bar assns., Conf. Chief Justices, Tenn. Jud. Conf., Am. Legion, Order of Coif, Phi Beta Kappa, Kappa Sigma, Phi Alpha Delta. Democrat. Clubs: Masons (33 deg.), KT; Shriners (potentate Alhambra Temple 1966); Royal Order Jesters. Home: 196 Woodcliff Circle Signal Mountain TN 37377 Office: Hamilton County Justice Bldg Chattanooga TN 37402

COOPER, WILLIAM EDWARD, private investor; b. Wichita, Kans., Oct. 16, 1921; s. Richard Percy and Natalie (Noel) C.; m. Mary Suzanne Blessington, June 2, 1947; children—William Patrick, Madelyn Cooper Abercrombie, Catherine Cooper Wilson, Thomas Edward. Grad. Wichita State U., 1948. With Beech Aircraft Corp., 1939-42; div. mgr. Western Lithograph Co., Tex., 1946-58; from v.p. to chmn. all related cos., Dallas Market Ctr. Co., 1958-83, chmn. emeritus, 1983—; dir. chmn. emeritus World Trade Ctr. Co., Trammell Crow Distbn. Co., 1st City Bank Dallas, BMC Fund., Inc., Fitz & Floyd, Inc. Past mem. Nat. Export Expansion Council; past chmn. Regional Export Expansion Council; mem. Dist. Export Council North Tex.; past chmn. Dallas Council World Affairs; chmn. aviation devel. com. North Tex. Commn.; voting mem., mem. exec. com. Dallas Citizens Council; chmn. Com. Minority and Women Econ. Devel., Tex. Sesquicentennial Air Race; past pres. Hope Cottage Children's Bur., Dallas Alliance Minority Enterprises, bd. dirs. Theatre Operating Co., Inc., Dallas Crime Commn.; Better Bus. Bur. Met. Dallas, Inc.; bd. dirs., exec. com., v.p. Dallas Health and Sci. Mus.; nat. trustee NCCJ and Jews; adviser Urban League Greater Dallas; active Greater Dallas Community Chs.; exec. com. Com. Qualified Judiciary; chmn. Jesuit Coll. Preparatory, 1983-84; adviser, vice chmn. Sch. Mgmt. and Adminstrn., U. Tex.-Dallas; chmn. policy com. City Dallas Econ. Devel. Bd. Served to capt. USAF, World War II. Recipient Shining Hours award Pub. Relations Soc. Am., 1973, Outstanding Alumni award Wichita State U. Achievement award, 1976, Brotherhood citation NCCJ, 1980; Pillar of Industry award Internat. Homefurnishings Reps. Assn., 1982. Mem. Dallas C. of C. (vice chmn., exec. com.), Dallas Council on World Affairs (H. Neil Mallen award for disting. service 1985), Knights of Malta. Republican. Roman Catholic. Clubs: Dallas Rotary (past pres.), St. Rita Men's (pres.). Office: 2700 Stemmons Freeway Suite 901 Dallas TX 75207

COPE, JOHN G(RAHAM), psychology educator, consultant; b. Savannah, Ga., Dec. 8, 1951; s. George Daffin and Enid (Graham) C.; m. Pamela Deborah Martin, Jan. 22, 1971. A.S., Armstrong State Coll., 1973, B.A., 1974; M.S., Augusta Coll., 1978; Ph.D., Va. Poly. Inst. and State U., 1982. Psychiat. social worker Ga. Regional Hosp., Savannah, 1974-76; grad. asst. testing ctr. Augusta (Ga.) Coll., 1976-78, dept. psychology, 1978; grad. teaching asst. dept. psychology Va. Poly. Inst. and State U., Blacksburg, 1979, lab. instr. in physiol. psychology, research asst., 1979-80; asst. prof. psychology East Carolina U., Greenville, N.C., 1981—; cons. Roanoka (Va.) Clean Valley Com., 1980-82, Burroughs Wellcome Co., Greenville, 1982; researcher indsl./organizational psychology and stats. Served with Air N.G., 1970-76. Mem. Am. Psychol. Assn., Southeastern Psychol. Assn., Am. Soc. Tng. and Devel., Soc. Psychol. Study of Social Issues, Sigma Xi. Methodist. Speaker profl. confs. Home: 802 Riverhills Dr Greenville NC 27834 Office: East Carolina Univ Speight 209 Greenville NC 27834

COPE, LAWRENCE GREGORY, power company executive; b. Savannah, Ga., Dec. 28, 1955; s. Edmond L. and Hildegarde (Wainwright) C. B.S., Ga. Inst. Tech., 1978; M.B.A., U. Miami, 1982. With Fla. Power & Light Co., Miami, 1979—, service planner, 1980-81, personnel adminstr., 1981, power service analyst, 1983—. Mem. Nat. Republican Senatorial Com. Mem. Soc. MBA Execs., Fla. Coll. Placement Assn., So. Coll. Placement Assn. Coconut Grove Jaycees, Good Govt. Assn. Miami, Ga. Tech. Alumni, U. Miami Alumni, Beta Theta Pi. Home: 18442 SW 92d Ct Miami FL 33157 Office: Fla Power & Light Co Box 390999 Miami Beach FL 33139

COPE, REBECCA BROWN, resort owner; b. Rabun County, Ga., Mar. 28, 1948; d. Harry and Estelle (Youngblood) Brown; student Reinhardt Coll., 1968, Western Carolina U., 1974; m. Jerry Cope, Oct. 26, 1968; 1 son, Marshall Andrew. Co-owner, co-mgr. Cope Crest Resort, Dillard, Ga., 1969—. Mem. Callerlab, Legacy, Ga. Callers Assn., Rabun County C. of C. (dir., pres. 1976), Nat. Restaurant Assn., Nat. Small Bus. Assn. Author: Square Dancers Treasure Chest of Ideas, 1979; Square Dance Resort Cookbook: Most Requested Recipes, 1979. Home: PO Box 129 Dillard GA 30537

COPELAND, EUGENE HERMAN, JR., architect, planner; b. Martinsville, Va., Apr. 7, 1934; s. Eugene Herman and Mary (Hurd) C.; m. Ann McColman, May 24, 1958; children—Allison, Sarah Lee, Letitia. B.S. in Bldg. Design, Va. Tech., 1955. Archtl. intern David L. Ragland, Danville, Va., 1956-58; asso. Albert C. Woodroof-A. C. Woodroof, Jr., Greensboro, N.C., 1958-62; architect and planner Odell Assos., Inc., Charlotte, N.C., 1962-80, pres., dir., 1978-80; founder, prin. E.H. Copeland, Jr., architect and planner, Charlotte, 1980—. Prin. works include: Hampton Va. Coliseum, Limestone Coll. Library, Camp Lejeune Marine Corps Base, Eastern Airlines, Crocker Nat. Bank San Francisco, Quinter, Inc. Active fund drive United Arts Council, 1974, United Way, 1979; mem. study commn. Charlotte Uptown Devel. Authority, 1977; pres., bd. dirs. Central Charlotte Assn., 1979—; bd. dirs. Myers Park Home Owners Assn.; chmn. bd. dirs. Myers Park Found., 1978—. Served to capt. U.S. Army, 1956. Registered architect, Va., N.C., S.C., Ohio, Ky. Mem. AIA (past pres. Charlotte chpt., v.p. N.C. assn. 1980), Am. Inst. Cert. Planners, Va. Tech. Alumni Assn. (past pres., dir. Carolina chpt., Alumni Service award Carolina chpt. 1973), Charlotte C. of C. (chmn. state legis. task force 1974-75). Methodist. Clubs: Commonwealth of Va., Charlotte Athletic (dir. 1975-79, 82, sec. 1979), Charlotte Country, Myrtle Beach Tennis. Home: 2044 Sherwood Ave Charlotte NC 28207 Office: 120 Brevard Ct Charlotte NC 28202

COPELAND, LARRY JAMES, gynecologic oncologist, educator; b. Brampton, Ont., Can., Dec. 1, 1947; s. Hugh Alexander and Frances Isabel (South) C. B.S., U. Waterloo, 1969; M.D., U. Western Ont., 1973. Diplomate Am. Bd. Ob-Gyn, Am. Bd. Gynecologic Oncology. Resident in ob-gyn McMaster U., Hamilton, Ont., 1973-77; fellow in gynecologic oncology U. Tex., M.D. Anderson Hosp., Houston, 1977-79; asst. prof. gynecology M.D. Anderson Hosp., Houston, 1979-84, assoc. prof., 1984—. Bobby Bauer Hockey scholar, U. Waterloo, 1966; Horner Gold medal U. Western Ont., 1973. Fellow Am. Coll. Ob-Gyn (Purdue Frederick award 1984), Royal Coll. Surgeons Can. ACS; mem. AMA, Soc. Obstetricians and Gynecologists of Can., Felix Rutledge Soc., Soc. Can. Gynecologic Oncologists, Am. Soc. Clin. Oncology, Soc. Surg. Oncology, Houston Gynecol. and Obstet. Soc., Soc. Gynecologic Oncologists, Houston Surg. Soc., M.D. Anderson Assocs., Internat. Soc. Gynec. Pathologists, Am. Med. Writers Assn., Am. Radium Soc., Soc. Surg. Oncology, Tex. Assn. Obstetricians and Gynecologists, Harris County Med. Soc., Tex. Med. Assn., AMA. Office: 6723 Bertner St Houston TX 77030

COPELAND, RALPH DAVID, broadcasting executive; b. San Angelo, Tex., Sept. 22, 1936; s. Gay Yates and Esther Lou (Hines) C. B.A., Kenyon Coll., Gambier, Ohio, 1959. Clin. editor Fisher Sci., Pitts., 1966-67; promotions mgr. Piper Aircraft, Lock Haven, Pa., 1967-69; account exec. Pobinson-Gerrard Advt., Houston, 1969-70; creative dir. PGC, Inc., Washington, 1970-73; pres. Triple R Broadcasting, Lockhart, Tex., 1975—; freelance writer, 1973—; v.p., dir. Sonora Aviation (Tex.), 1977-82. Bd. dirs. Mark Withers Trail Driver Mus., Lockhart, 1979-82; pres. Lockhart Community Theatre, 1981-82. Served with U.S. Army, 1960-63. Mem. Tex. Assn. Broadcasters, Nat. Assn. Broadcasters, Indsl. Advt. Assn., Mensa, Aircraft Owners and Pilots Assn. Republican. Baptist. Home: PO Box 85 Dale TX 78616

COPELAND, ROSANNA, teacher coach; b. Checotah, Okla., Jan. 19, 1948; d. August Dildy Copeland and Ina Marie (Hooker) Sorrels. B.S., Okla. State U., 1970; M.A., Tex. Woman's U., 1972. Cert. tchr. phys. edn. and visually impaired. Tchr., coach Prairie View A&M U. (Tex.), 1972-74, Okla. Sch. for Blind, Muskogee, 1975-85. Contbr. articles to profl. publs. Mem. Assn. Edn. Visually Handicapped, Am. Alliance Health, Phys. Edn., Recreation and Dance, Okla. Assn. Health, Phys. Edn., Recreation and Dance, U.S. Assn. Blind Athletes (1st internat. woman coach for U.S. women's goal ball), Okla. Assn. Blind Athletes (co-founder, sec.). Democrat. Mem. Assembly of God. Clubs: Okla. State U. Alumni Assn. (Stillwater, Okla.); Tex. Woman's U. Alumni Assn. (Denton, Tex.); Fosslwhack Investment (Muskogee) (treas. 1983-84). Home: 909 Autumn Oak Denton TX 76201 Office: PO Box 22055 TWV Station Denton TX 76204

COPENHAVER, JOHN THOMAS, JR., federal judge; b. Charleston, W.Va., Sept. 29, 1925; s. John Thomas and Ruth Cherrington (Roberts) C.; A.B., W.Va. U., 1947, LL.B., 1950; m. Camille Ruth Smith, Oct. 7, 1950; children—John Thomas III, James Smith, Brent Paul. Admitted to bar; law clk. to U.S. dist. judge Ben Moore, So. Dist. of W.Va., 1950-51; mem. firm Copenhaver & Copenhaver, Charleston, 1951-58; U.S. bankruptcy judge So. Dist. W.Va., Charleston, 1958-76, U.S. dist. judge, 1976—; adj. prof. law W.Va. U. Coll. Law, 1970-76; mem. faculty Fed. Jud. Center, 1972-76. Pres. Legal Aid Soc. Charleston, 1954, Municipal Planning Commn. City of Charleston, 1964; chmn., pres. W.Va. Housing Devel. Fund, 1969-72; chmn. vis. com. W.Va. U. Coll. Law, 1980-83; mem. adv. com. on bankruptcy rules Jud. Conf. U.S. Served with U.S. Army, 1944-46. Recipient Gavel award W.Va. U. Coll. Law, 1971. Mem. Am., W.Va., Kanawha County bar assns., Nat. Bankruptcy Conf., Nat. Conf. Bankruptcy Judges (past pres.), Phi Delta Phi, Beta Theta Pi. Republican. Presbyterian. Contbr. articles in fields of bankruptcy and comml. law to Bus. Lawyer, Am. Bankruptcy Law Jour., Personal Fin. Law Quar., W.Va. Law Rev., others. Office: US Courthouse Charleston WV 25329

COPENHAVER, WILLIAM PIERCE, chemical company executive; b. Tazewell, Va., Oct. 15, 1924; s. Henry Baker and Fern (Spencer) C.; B.S., Va. Poly. Inst. and State U., Blacksburg, 1948; grad. Advanced Mgmt. Program, Harvard U., 1966; m. Jane Foote Farrier, Mar. 1, 1946; children—Andrew, Paula, John, Elisabeth, David. Dir. planning, then plant mgr. Celanese Co. U.S., 1962-67; v.p., ops. mgr., then v.p., gen. mgr. Celanese Co. Can., Montreal, 1969-72; chmn. bd., pres., dir. Columbia Nitrogen Corp., also Nipco Inc., Augusta, Ga., 1972—; dir. Synres Chem. Co., Ga. R.R. Bank, Augusta, So. area of Arkwright Co., Boston. Vice pres. Augusta United Way; exec. bd. local Boy Scouts Am.; bd. dirs. St. John's United Methodist Ch., Augusta. Served with USAAF, 1942-45. Decorated Air medal. Mem. Augusta C. of C., Nat. Alliance Bus. (dir.), Mfg. Chemists Assn., Am. Mgmt. Assn., Fertilizer Inst., Petrochem. Energy Group. Clubs: West Lake Country, Augusta Country, Pinnacle. Home: 3531 Interlachen St Augusta GA 30907 Office: Nipco Inc PO Box 1483 Augusta GA 30913

COPLEY, SHARRON CAULK, educator; b. Columbia, Tenn., Oct. 2, 1947; d. Tom English and Beulah (Goodin) Caulk; children—Christopher, George English, Steffenee. B.A., George Peabody Coll., 1970; M.S., Vanderbilt U., 1980. Tchr. Fort Campbell Jr. High Sch., Ky., 1970-71, Whitthorne Jr. High Sch., Columbia, Tenn., 1977—. Edn. chmn. Homecoming 86, Columbia, 1984-86. Mem. Nat. Council Tchrs. English, Maury County Edn. Assn. (pres. 1983-84), Tenn. Edn. Assn., NEA, AAUW (Tenn. div. pres. 1983-85), Phi Delta Kappa. Mem. Ch. of Christ. Home: 1090 Rolling Fields Columbia TN 38401 Office: Whitthorne Jr High Sch Experiment Ln Columbia TN 38401

COPLIN, RAYE HARRIS, pharmacist, civic worker; b. Ocilla, Ga., July 8, 1952; d. Charles A. and Esther (Stein) Harris; m. Paul Robert Coplin, June 8, 1975; children—Brian, Arden, Elliot. B.Pharmacy, Mercer U., 1976. Registered pharmacist, Ga. Intern Dunwoody Prescription Ctr., Ga., 1973-75; sec. Psychiat. Assocs. of Middle Ga., 1980—. Contbr. articles to profl. jours. Fund raiser J. Roy Rowland Election Campaign, Macon, Ga., 1983, Reagan Republican Campaign, 1984; campaign worker Carter for Pres., 1976-80; bd. govs. Sherah Israel Synagogue, 1981-83, bd. dirs., 1983—; mem. exec. bd. Am. Heart Assn., 1985—, mem. health steering com., 1984—. Mem. Ga. Pharm. Assn., Am. Pharm. Assn., Mus. Guild of Arts and Scis., Peachbelt Med. Aux. (pres. 1982-84), Bibb County Med. Aux. (pres. 1984—), Aux. Med. Assn. Ga. (communications chmn. 1985—). Jewish. Club: Stratford Interested Parents. Lodge: Hadassah. Avocations: jogging; swimming; calisthenics; cooking. Office: 624 New St Macon GA 31201

COPP, EMMANUEL ANTHONY, oil company executive; b. San Antonio, Sept. 8, 1945; s. Nelson Gage and Aurora Gregoria (Saenz) C.; m. Monica Linda Harris, Nov. 2, 1972 (div. 1981); children—Tara Linda, Jacqueline Aurora; m. Kathryn Lynn Manson, June 18, 1983; 1 child, Alexander Anthony; stepchildren—Troy, Corey. B.A. in Internat. Relations, St. Mary's U., San Antonio, 1966, M.A. in Econs., 1967; Ph.D. in Econs., Tex. A & M U., 1974. Sr. economist Am. Petroleum Inst., 1970-74; v.p., mgr. Energy Resource and Devel. Group Salomon Brothers, 1974-80; v.p. corp. fin. Hunt Oil Co., Dallas, 1980—; pres., dir. Winona Corp., Winona Capital Corp. subs. Winona Corp. Mem. long-range planning com. Parish Day Sch., Dallas; bd. dirs. Dallas Opera, pres., 1986-87; bd. dirs. Dallas Symphony, Dallas Ballet. Served to capt. U.S. Army, 1969-70. Named most valuable staffer Am. Assn. Newspapers, 1964; NSF fellow, 1968-69. Mem. Soc. Petroleum Engrs., Am. Econ. Assn., Assn. Corp. Growth, Fin. Analyst Fedn., Nat. Assn. Bus. Economists. Roman Catholic. Club: Bent Tree Country (Dallas). Author: World Petroleum: The Economics of Supply and Price, 1975; Regulating Competition in Oil, 1976; contbr. articles to profl. jours.

COPPINS, RICHARD JAMES, management science educator, textbook author; b. Syracuse, N.Y., Mar. 21, 1946; s. Alan and Harriet (Ettelson) C.; m. Rosemarie Ferrara, Aug. 24, 1969; children—Janet Lynn, Ellen Elizabeth. B.S.E.E., Lehigh U., 1967, M.S. in Mgmt. Sci., 1968; Ph.D. in Ops. Research, N.C. State U., Raleigh, 1975. Indsl. engr. IBM, Endicott, N.Y., 1968-70; ops. analyst Research Triangle Inst., Research Triangle Park, N.C., 1974-75; asst. prof. Eastern Mich. U., Ypsilanti, 1975-78; asst. prof. Va. Commonwealth U., Richmond, 1978-81, assoc. prof., 1981—; cons. Sidall, Mater & Coughtus, Richmond, 1980, Reynolds Metals, Richmond, 1981. Author: (with others) Linear Programming & Extensions, 1981, College Mathematics, Applied Finite Mathematics, Applied Calculus, 1986. Vol., Am. Heart Assn., 1982, 83, 84, 85. Mgmt. sci. fellow Lehigh U., 1967-68. Mem. Am. Inst. Decision Scis., Math. Assn. Am., Ops. Research Soc. Am., Inst. Mgmt. Scis., Alpha Iota Delta (reg. v.p. 1981-84), Phi Eta Sigma, Eta Kappa Nu, Omega Rho, Beta Gamma Sigma, Sigma Alpha Mu. Avocations: reading; jogging; playing basketball. Home: 3800 McTyre's Cove Rd Midlothian VA 23113 Office: Va Commonwealth U Box 4000 1015 Floyd Ave Richmond VA 23284

COPPOCK, GLENN EDGAR, agricultural engineer; b. Cullman, Ala., May 18, 1924; s. John William and Dura Pearl (Braswell) C.; m. Barbara Ruth Hodges, Dec. 22, 1954; children—Deborah Ruth, Joyce Ann, Edward Glenn. B.S., Auburn U., 1949; M.S., Okla. State U., 1954. Research engr. dept. agr. Tillage Machinery Lab., Auburn, Ala., 1949-52; research engr. dept. agr. U. Okla., Stillwater, 1952-56, Shafter, Calif., 1956-57; profl. engr. IV Fla. Dept. Citrus, Lake Alfred, Fla., 1957—; researcher mech. harvesting farm crops. Served with Air Corps, U.S. Army, 1943-46. Chosen keynote speaker Internat. Hort. Congress, Sidney, Australia, 1978. Mem. Am. Soc. Agrl. Engrs. (tech paper award 1970), Fla. Soc. Agrl. Engrs., Fla. State Hort. Soc., Internat. Citrus Congress, Robotics Internat. Soc. Mfg. Engrs., Civitan Club (sec. 1960). Democrat. Methodist. Club: Kiwanis (chmn. agrl. com. 1982). Contbr. chpts. in books. Home: 1970 14th St NE Winter Haven FL 33880 Office: 700 Experiment Sta Rd Lake Alfred FL 33850

COPPRIDGE, ALTON JAMES, urological surgeon; b. Roanoke, Va., Dec. 8, 1926; s. William Maurice Coppridge and Ferrie (Patterson) Coppridge Choate; m. Helen Allen Burnett, June 24, 1950; children—William Allen, Virginia Choate. B.A., U. N.C., 1949; M.D., U. Va., 1953. Diplomate Am. Bd. Urology. Intern N.C. Meml. Hosp., Chapel Hill, 1953-54; surg. resident State U. of Iowa Hosp., Iowa City, 1954-56; urology resident U. Mich., Ann Arbor, 1956-59; mem. Coppridge Urologic Group, P.A., Durham, N.C., 1959—; dept. chmn. Durham County Gen. Hosp., 1978-84; asst. clin. prof. Duke Med. Ctr., Durham, 1970—; clin. instr. U. N.C. Med. Sch., Chapel Hill, 1960-75. Contbr. articles to urologic lit. Served with U.S. Army, 1944-46; Japan. Mem. Am. Urol. Assn. (exec. com. Southeast sect. 1983-86), Durham-Orange Med. Soc. (pres. 1978), N.C. Med. Soc. (pres. sect. urology 1978), Carolina Urol. Soc. (pres. 1985), ACS. Democrat. Presbyterian. Clubs: Hope Valley Country (Durham); Safari Internat. (Tucson) (pres. N.C. chpt. 1979-80); Kiwanis of Tobaccoland (Durham). Avocations: hunting; shooting; farm work. Home: 3605 Rugby Rd Durham NC 27707 Office: Coppridge Urologic Group PA 923 Broad St Durham NC 27705

CORAZZINI, JOHN GERALD, psychologist, counseling center executive, consultant; b. Boston, Dec. 15, 1938; s. Pasquale and Eileen Cecelia (Burke) C.; m. Agnes Elizabeth Kilduff, Mar. 20, 1971; children—Seth Aaron, Jeremy Luke. A.B., St. Johns Sem., 1961; S.T.B., Gregorian U., 1963; Ph.D., U. Notre Dame, 1974. Lic. clin. psychologist, Va.; lic. psychologist, Va. Asst. dir. U. Counseling Ctr., Colo. State U., Fort Collins, 1978-79; dir. U. Counseling Service, Va. Commonwealth U., Richmond, 1980—; cons. Midlothian, Va., 1981—. Contbr. articles to profl. jours. 2d v.p. PTA, Midlothian, 1984-86. Mem. Am. Psychol. Assn., Am. Coll. Personnel Assn., Va. Psychol. Assn., Am. Assn. Counseling and Devel. Home: 13430 Glendower Rd Midlothian VA 23113 Office: U Counseling Services Va Commonwealth U 913 W Franklin St Richmond VA 23284

CORBETT, ALLEN POWELL, univ. adminstr.; b. Camden, S.C., Apr. 17, 1939; s. Robert Allen and Melba Louise C.; B.S., Am. U., Washington, 1961; M.B.A., U. S.C., Columbia, 1969; Summer fellow Georgetown U. Med. Center, 1960; med. program asst., med. statistician FAA, Washington, 1961-65, lectr. computer sci., research cons., 1965-71; research supr. S.C. Employment Security Commn., 1971-73; dir. James C. Self Mgmt. Sci. Center, lectr. mgmt. sci. U. S.C., 1973—; cons. info. systems corp. and state agys. Research cons. S.C. Joint Legis. Com. to Study Problems of Handicapped, 1977—; chmn. fin. com., bd. dirs. S.C. Protection and Advocacy System for Handicapped, 1979—; pres. Citizens Advancement of Physically Handicapped, Inc., 1979-80; chmn. adv. com. S.C. Ind. Living Project of S.C. Vocat. Rehab. Dept.; research cons. S.C. Gen. Assembly. Recipient Meritorious Service award S.C. Vocat. Rehab. Assn., 1979; cert. data processor. Mem. Assn. Systems Mgmt. (sec. Midlands chpt.), S.C. Rehab. Assn., Assn. Computing Machinery, Omicron Delta Epsilon. Baptist. Home: 2809 Magnolia St Columbia SC 29204 Office: Coll Bus Adminstrn U SC Columbia SC 29208

CORBETT, H. STEWART, radio station executive; b. St. Augustine, Fla., Apr. 2, 1935; s. Harry Stewart and Rachel (Linscott) C.; B.A., U. Fla., 1957; postgrad. in bus. edn. Harvard U. Grad. Sch. Bus., 1972; m. Diane Donnell, May 16, 1980. Loan officer Trust Co. of Ga., Atlanta, 1960-64; v.p. Cox Broadcasting Corp., Atlanta, 1964-79; owner radio stas. WHHR, Hilton Head Island, S.C., 1979—, WKMK, WRTM, Blountstown, Fla., 1980—, WFMR, Menomonee Falls, Wis., 1983—. Served with U.S. Army, 1958-64. Mem. C. of C. (various coms.). Baptist. Clubs: Harvard N.Y.; Long Cove (Hilton Head Island); Cherokee Town and Country (Atlanta). Pub., Hilton Head-WHHR

Almanac, 1975. Home: 16 Nautilus Rd Hilton Head Island SC 29928 Office: 16 Nautilus Rd Hilton Head Island SC 29938

CORBETT, JAMES DANIEL (DANNY), state senator; b. Columbus, Ga., May 1, 1949; s. James Alphus and Alice (Hallmark) C.; m. Peggy Carter, Oct. 18, 1969; children—Chance Daniel, Heath Carter, James Brandon. With AT&T, Phenix City, Ala., 1969—; mem. Ala. State Senate from Dist. 22, 1982-83, Ala. State Senate from Dist. 28, 1983—. Mem. Communications Workers of Am., Ala. Cattlemen's Assn. (assoc.). Baptist. Home: Route 7 Box 821 Phenix City AL 36867

CORBETT, WILLIAM LYNNWOOD, clergyman; b. Springfield, S.C., Sept. 27, 1927; s. Albert S. and Margaret (Tarrant) C.; m. Hazel Clark Crosby, Feb. 12, 1949; children—Patricia Lynn, Robert Stokes. Cert. in Bible, Columbia Bible Coll., S.C., 1947. Ordained to ministry So. Methodist Ch., 1946. Pres. So. Meth. Ch., Orangeburg, S.C., 1955-66, minister, 1962-82, pres., 1982—. Recipient Christian Service award So. Meth. Coll., Orangeburg, 1966, 69, 70. Mem. Evangel. Tchrs. Tng. Assn., Am. Council Christian Chs. (officer 1956-66). Lodge: Lions (bd. dirs. Orangeburg 1985). Office: So Meth Ch 872 Broughton St Orangeburg SC 29115

CORBIN, CAROLYN PITTS, educational services company executive, management consultant; b. McKinney, Tex., Dec. 27, 1946; d. Walter Ben and Iva Orene (Craft) Pitts; m. Ray Wilburn Corbin, Jr., Oct. 16, 1976. B.A., North Tex. State U., 1969, M.A., 1971. Computer programmer/trainer LTV Corp., Grand Prairie, Tex., 1969-73; corp. officer, data processing Repub. Bank, Dallas, 1973-77; agt./supr. Northwestern Mut. Life Ins. Co., Dallas, 1977-80; founder, pres. Carolyn Corbin, Inc. (formerly Success Images), Dallas, 1979—. Author booklets: CAI: Education's New Frontier, 1970; MasterPlanning Your Future, 1983; Five Steps to Financial Success, 1984; Money Attitude Profile, 1985. Vol. counselor Denton (Tex.) State Sch., 1970-71; vol. instr. Dallas Pilot Home for Girls, 1975-78, Women's Ctr. of Dallas, 1978-80; vol. fund raiser Am. Heart Assn., Boy Scouts Am., 1975-79; mem. adv. bd. Athletes in Action, 1981—. Mem. Sales and Mktg. Execs. (dir. 1981—, v.p. 1982-83), Am. Soc. Tng. and Devel., Nat. Speakers Assn., Internat. Soc. Preretirement Planners. Club: Dallas Toastmistress. Office: Suite 114 4255 LBJ Freeway Dallas TX 75244

CORBIN, CLAIRE, marketing educator, consultant; b. N.Y.C., July 16, 1913; d. Herman and Anna (Kessler) Rothenberg; m. Arnold Corbin, Aug. 22, 1937; children—Lee Harrison, Karen Sue. B.S., NYU, 1933, M.S., 1941, Ph.D., 1956; postgrad. Yeshiva U. and NYU, 1957-60. Sales trainee Namm Store, Bklyn., 1929-30; merchandising trainee Macys, N.Y.C., 1930-32, buyer, 1939-40; asst. buyer Gimbels, N.Y.C., 1932-33; asst. prof. Long Island U., Bklyn., 1939-44; owner, mgr. Guildery Gifts, N.Y.C., 1944-45; dir. sales tng. Loft Candy Corp., N.Y.C., 1945-46; asst. prof. Baruch Sch. CCNY, 1946-49; dir. sales promotion and tng. Decorative Fabrics Inst., N.Y.C., 1948-57; dir. women's group activities Sta. WOR-TV, 1948-59; ptnr. Corbin Assocs., Delray Beach, Fla., 1949—; assoc. prof. Hofstra U., Hempstead, N.Y., 1949-57; prof. mktg. emeritus Fordham U., 1957-77; lectr. Hunter Coll., 1946-47. Namm scholar, 1929-33; N.Y. State Regents scholar, 1929-33. Mem. AAUP (sec.-treas. 1961-71), Am. Acad. Advt. (nat. finance chmn. 1966-67), Advt. Women of N.Y., Am. Soc. Interior Designers, Publicity Club of N.Y., Nat. Home Fashions League (v.p. 1955-56), Am. Mktg. Assn. (sec.-treas. 1970-73), Kappa Delta Pi, Beta Gamma Sigma, Eta Mu Pi, Pi Lambda Theta, Gamma Alpha Chi. Author: (with others) Principles of Retailing, 1955, Principles of Advertising, 1963, Decision Exercises in Marketing, 1964, New Trends in American Marketing, 1965, Implementing the Marketing Concept, 1973; editor Haire Publs., 1933-39, 2 to 6, 1946-47, Today's Woman, 1947-48; contbr. articles to profl. jours. Home and Office: 177 Waterford Crescent Delray Beach FL 33446 also 2 Margarita St Toms River NJ 08757

CORBIN, LAUREN L., association executive; b. Queens, N.Y., Apr. 20, 1959; s. Lowell Harvey and Barbara (Kruglansky) C. B.A. in Diplomacy and Fgn. Affairs, Miami U., Oxford, Ohio, 1981. Asst. mgr. Winkelman's Dept. Store, Cleve., 1981-82; adminstrv. asst. Am. Assn. Clin. Chemistry, Washington, 1983; program instr. Close Up Found., Arlington, Va., 1983-84, community coordinator, 1984—. Staff mem. Reagan-Bush re-election campaign com., Washington, 1984, 1984 Inaugural Com., Washington. Mem. Ind. Council for Social Studies, Nebr. Council Social Studies, Ohio Council Social Studies, Toastmasters Internat. (sec. 1982-83, v.p. 1981-82), Smithsonian Instn., Capitol Hist. Soc., Nat. Trust Historic Preservation, Friends of Nat. Zoo, World Wildlife, Miami U. Alumni Assn. (mem. council). Jewish. Avocations: racquetball; antiques. Home: 4520 King St Apt 301 Alexandria VA 22302 Office: Close Up Found 1235 Jeff Davis Hwy Arlington VA 22202

CORBIN, SCOTT DOUGLAS, architect; b. Seattle, Mar. 12, 1950; s. William Arthur and Nora Violet (McBride) C.; B.Arch., Va. Poly. Inst. and State U., 1973; m. Marissa Leigh Umberger, June 22, 1974; 1 dau., Kristen Leigh. Designer, draftsman Gresham & Smith, Nashville, 1973, project coordinator, 1975-77, project architect, 1977-80, sr. project architect, 1980-82, assoc. firm, 1982-86; ptnr. Floyd and Corbin, Architects, 1986—. Served to capt. USAR, 1974-81. Registered architect, Tenn. Mem. AIA (com. on architecture for health), Nat. Trust for Hist. Preservation. Lutheran. Works include: S. Austin Community Hosp., Detar Hosp., Victoria, Tex., Richmond Community Hosp., Richmond, Va., City Hosp., Martinsburg, W.Va., Lewis-Gale Hosp., Salem, Va., East Pointe Hosp., Leigh Acres Fla., Richmond Meml. Hosp., Harpeth YMCA, Brentwood, Tenn., Summerhill at Stony Point, Richmond, North Miss. Women's Health Ctr., Tupelo. Home: 408 Cotton Rd Franklin TN 37064 Office: 1602 21st Ave S Suite 201 Nashville TN 37212

CORBINO, MARCIA NORCROSS, writer, critic, consultant; b. Tulsa, June 12, 1927; d. Clelle Edward and Celeste Comorah (Corder) Norcross; m. Jon Corbino, Feb. 15, 1951 (des.); children—Lee, Christopher Jon, Michael Jon. B.A., Duke U., 1949; postgrad. Art Students League, 1951. Researcher Time, Inc., N.Y.C., 1949; fashion dir. Burlington Mills, N.Y.C., 1949-51; freelance writer Sarasota, Fla., 1951-74; writer, photographer Sarasota Jour., 1974-77; writer, critic Sarasota Herald-Tribune, 1977-82; freelance writer Sarasota, 1982—. Contbr. articles to profl. mags. Critics fellow Nat. Endowment for the Arts, Washington, 1980; Va. Ctr. for Creative Arts fellow, 1983; Atlantic Ctr. for Arts fellow, 1985. Mem. Internat. Assn. Art Critics, Am. Theatre Critics Assn., Dramatists Guild. Home: 1111 N Gulfstream Ave Apt 6B Sarasota FL 33577

CORBITT, ROBERT ALAN, civil engineer; b. Buffalo, Sept. 15, 1945; s. Hubert Wilson and Edith (Williamson) C.; m. Nancy Jean Waring, Sept. 10, 1977. B.C.E., Ga. Inst. Tech., 1966, M.S. in San. Engring., 1969. Environ. engr. Ga. Water Quality Control Bd., Atlanta, 1967-71; prin. engr. Teledyne Brown, Huntsville, Ala., 1971-72; municipal engring. service program mgr. Ga. Environ. Protection div., Atlanta, 1972-74; dept. mgr. Jordan Jones & Goulding, Atlanta, 1974—. Mem. Am. Acad. Environ. Engrs., Am. Water Works Assn., ASCE, Soc. Am. Mil. Engrs., Soc. Am. Value Engrs., Water Pollution Control Fedn. Home: 1415 Bunky Ln Atlanta GA 30338 Office: 2000 Clearview Ave Suite 200 Atlanta GA 30340

CORCORAN, DAVID HOWARD, journalist, educator, historian, historic preservationist; b. New Albany, Ind., May 27, 1942; s. Thomas Alvin and Iola Catherine (Moser) C.; m. Paula Nell Dorgay, Dec. 21, 1968; children—David Howard, Catherine Aileen, Patrick Dorgay. B.S., St. Louis U., 1964, M.A., 1965; Ph.D., U. Ky., 1977. Prof., Nazareth Coll. (Ky.), 1965-69; acting dir. Ky. Life Mus., Lexington, 1970-72; exec. dir. Pearl S. Buck Birthplace Found., Hillsboro, W.Va., 1972-76, dir., 1972—; dir. pub. relations-devel. W.Va. Sch. Osteo. Medicine, Lewisburg, W.Va., 1976-78; pub., editor Mullens Advocate (W.Va.), 1978—, Welch Daily News (W.Va.), 1981—, Oceana (W. Va.) Sun, 1984—. Mem. adv. bd. W.Va. Job Service, Welch, 1982—; dir. Pocahontas Coal Centennial, Bluefield, W.Va., 1981-83. Fulbright grantee, 1967, 68; Colonial Williamsburg fellow Nat. Trust Historic Preservation, 1970, Am. Assn. Higher Edn. fellow, 1978. Mem. W.Va. Press Assn. (editor News awards 1981-82, 83-84, 84-85), So. Newspaper Publishers Assn. (mem. editorial com. 1982—). Democrat. Roman Catholic. Lodges: Lions (pub. relations dir. 1981—), KC (dep. grand knight 1981—) (Welch). Home: 132 Riverside Dr Welch WV 24801 Office: PO Box 569 125 Wyoming St Welch WV 24801

CORCORAN, EUGENE FRANCIS, chemist, educator; b. Arthur, N.D., Nov. 28, 1916; s. Harold Alyn and Katherine Elizabeth (Zieg) C.; m. Aldoris Drevig; Aug. 29, 1940; children—Kathryn Ann Corcoran Edwards, Sheryl Jean Corcoran Alsbury. B.S., N.D. State Coll., 1940; postgrad. San Diego State Coll., 1946-49; Ph.D., UCLA, 1958. Cert. tchr., N.D., Calif. Tchr., Sanborn High Sch. (N.D.), 1940-41, Bowman High Sch. (N.D.), 1941-43; instr. math. San Diego State Coll., 1946-49; research asst. Scripps Inst. Oceanography (U. Calif.), 1949-50, biochemist II, 1952-57; asst. prof. U. Miami (Fla.), 1957-60, assoc. prof., 1960-67, assoc. program dir. NSF, 1967-68; assoc. dean Sch. Marine and Atmospheric Sci., 1972—, prof. Rosenstiel Sch. Marine and Atmospheric Sci., 1967-82, prof. emeritus and cons., 1982—. Contbr. articles to profl. jours. Served with USN, 1943-46, 50-52. Mem. Am. Chem. Soc., AAAS, Geochem. Soc., Am. Soc. Limnology and Oceanography, Sigma Xi. Presbyterian. Lodge: Masons. Home: 5990 SW 85 St South Miami FL 33143 Office: 4600 Rickenbacker Causeway Miami FL 33149

CORDELL, DORMAN EUGENE, newspaper publisher; b. Whitley City, Ky., Dec. 2, 1931; s. Ernest Rodney and Edith Mae (Trammell) C.; m. Frances Lowe, Nov. 18, 1978; 1 child, Elizabeth. B.A., U. Ky., 1952; postgrad. U. N.C., 1952-53, U. Ky.-Lexington, 1957-58; M.B.A., U. Dallas-Irving, 1981. Newsman, AP, Louisville, 1958-61, corr., Atlantic City, 1961-63, chief of bur., various cities, 1963-82; pres., pub. News-Texan Newspaper Group, Dallas, 1982—; pres. Freedom of Info. Found. of Tex., Dallas, 1982-83. Served to 1st lt. USAF, 1953-57; Far East. Mem. Soc. Profl. Journalists. Republican. Mem. Unity Ch. Clubs: Univ., Chaparral (Dallas). Avocation: skiing. Office: News-Texan Inc 4880 Alpha Rd Dallas TX 75244

CORDELL, JOE B., diversified corporation executive; b. Daytona Beach, Fla., Aug. 4, 1927; s. Joe Wynne and Ada Ruth (Wood) C.; m. Joyce Hinton, June 16, 1951; children—Joe B., Coleman Wynn, Lauren. Student, Yale U., 1945-46, Fla. So. Coll., 1946-47; B.S. in Bus. Adminstrn, U. Fla., 1949. C.P.A. Intern Price Waterhouse Corp., N.Y.C., 1948-49, staff acct., 1949-50, audit mgr., Atlanta, 1950-58; v.p. Jim Walter Corp., Tampa, Fla., 1958-70, sr. v.p., treas., 1970-74, pres., chief operating officer, dir., 1974—; dir. Royal Trust Bank of Tampa, Gen. Instrument Corp., Fla. Steel Corp., from 1978. Past pres., trustee U. Fla. Found.; trustee bus. adv. council U. Fla. Served with USNR, 1945-46. Mem. Am. Inst. C.P.A.s, Ga. Inst. C.P.A.s, Fla. Inst. C.P.A.s, Greater Tampa C. of C., Com. of 100, Alpha Kappa Psi, Alpha Tau Omega. Methodist. Clubs: Tower of Tampa, Tampa Yacht and Country, Palma Ceia Golf and Country, Wildcat Cliffs Country, University of Tampa, Ye Mystic Krewe of Gasparilla. Office: Jim Walter Corp 1500 N Dale Mabry Hwy Tampa FL 33607*

CORDELL, ROBERT JAMES, oil company executive, geologist; b. Quincy, Ill., Jan. 7, 1917; s. Vail R. and Gertrude Frances (Robison) C.; m. Frances Regina Sparacio, Sept. 20, 1942; children—Victor Vail, David Mark, Margaret Lynn. B.S., U. Ill., 1939, M.S., 1940; Ph.D., U. Mo., 1949. Instr. dept. geology Colgate U., Hamilton, N.Y., 1947-51; research paleontologist, research geologist, sr. research geologist Sun Oil Co., Abilene, Tex., 1951-55, mgr. geol. research, Richardson, Tex., 1955-63, sr. sect. mgr., 1963-70, sr. research scientist, sr. profl. scientist, 1970-77; pres. Cordell Reports, Inc., Dallas, Richardson, 1977—; mem. geol. domain com. Am. Petroleum Inst. hdqrs., Washington, 1955-64; mem. exec. com. Potential Gas Com. hdqrs., Golden, Colo., 1975—; cons. Sunmark Exploration Co., Irving, Tex., 1978-79, Basic Resources Co., N.Y.C., 1982-83. Bd. dirs., treas., v.p., pres. Richardson Community Concerts, Tex., 1958-70; bd. dirs., v.p., pres., chmn. bd. Richardson Symphony Orch., Inc., 1962-83; area chmn. Jim Collins Campaign for U.S. Senate, Richardson, 1982. Fellow AAAS, Geol. Soc. Am.; mem. Am. Assn. Petroleum Geologists (gen. chmn. nat. conv. 1974-76, disting. service award 1975), Soc. Econ. Paleontologists and Mineralogists, Dallas Geophys. Soc., Dallas Geol. Soc. (hon. life, pres. 1976-77, disting. service award 1975, research and publ. award 1980). Republican. Episcopalian. Clubs: Quarterback (treas. 1968-69), 1st Wednesday Book (Richardson). Avocations: music; jogging; bridge; travel; reading. Home: 305 W Shore Dr Richardson TX 75080 Office: Cordell Reports Inc 1633 Firman St Richardson TX 75081

CORDIN-SMITH, RUTH ANN, motor freight company executive, diversified company executive, fishing charter service executive; b. Chgo., Feb. 28, 1918; d. John Albert and Lucille Elizabeth (Kohl) Wolfe; m. Nicholas Cordin, Nov. 19, 1938 (dec. 1970); children—Walter Wolfe, J. Scott, Christine Ruth; m. Howard Walter Smith, Oct. 23, 1984. Student interior design, Art Inst. Chgo., 1941-43, Sch. Design, 1944-46; Diploma in bus. mgmt. Lagrange Jr. Coll., 1949. Owner, operator Spartan Interiors, Hinsdale, Ill., 1964-84, Top Drawer Antiques, Hinsdale, 1972-78; chief exec. officer, chmn. bd. dirs. Cordin Motor Freight Cos., Argo, Ill., 1970—; owner, operator R. Cordin Enterprises, Naples, Fla., 1985—, also chief exec. officer, chmn. bd. dirs.; owner, operator Fish Finders Charters, Naples, 1985—, also chief exec. officer, chmn. bd. dirs. Stage set designer Harold Dash Assoc., 1971. Food and travel editor DuPage Mag., 1974. Bd. dirs. Hinsdale Community House, 1968, Midwest Region Red Cross, Chgo., 1976; fin. chmn. Midwest Community Chest, Hinsdale, 1973; life mem. Art. Inst. Chgo. Republican. Clubs: Hinsdale Golf; Naples Sailing and Yacht; Quail Creek Country (Naples); Staniel Cay (Bahamas). Avocations: fishing; boating; cooking; painting; antiques.

COREY, ORLIN RUSSELL, publisher, editor; b. Nowata, Okla., May 4, 1926; s. Lue A. and Nada Gladys (Patton) C.; m. Irene Lockridge, Aug. 25, 1949 (div. 1974); m. Shirley Trusty, Nov. 27, 1975. B.A., Baylor U., 1950, M.A., 1952; cert. of directing and acting, Central Sch. Speech and Drama, London, 1956. Drama dir., asst. prof. Georgetown Coll., Ky., 1952-59; drama dir., assoc. prof. Centenary Coll., Shreveport, La., 1960-68; dir. Everyman Players, Pineville, Ky., 1958-80; producer John F. Kennedy Ctr., Washington, 1973-75; pub., editor Anchorage Press, Inc., New Orleans, 1977—; guest dir. U. N.H., Durham, 1968; lectr. Ohio State U., also other univs., 1968-75. Author: Theatre for Children, 1973; Towers of the Brazos. Adaptor for drama of the book of Job, 1960; producer Jennie Heiden Award, 1970. Producer La World Expo, World Theatre Festival, New Orleans, 1984; bd. dirs. New Orleans Ctr. Creative Arts, 1975—. Served with USN, 1944-46, PTO. Recipient Religious Drama award Nat. Catholic Theater Assn., 1968, Radius, London, 1974. Fellow Am. Theatre Assn.; mem. Children's Theater Assn. Am. (pres. 1971-73). Baptist. Avocations: photography; cooking; reading. Office: Anchorage Press Inc Box 8067 New Orleans LA 70182

CORKILL, JAMES MERRIC, engring. cons., mayor; b. Enid, Okla., Aug. 14, 1945; s. John Merric and Alyce Vinita (Mitchell) C.; B.S. in Environ. Design, U. Okla., 1975; student Ill. State U., 1964-65; m. Janice Gail Christy, Dec. 17, 1977; children—Shannon Merric, Christa Rhea, Kegan Merric. Commd. capt. U.S. Army, 1965, advanced through grades to maj., 1979; loss prevention cons. Factory Mut. Engring., Maryland Heights, Mo., 1975, resident cons., 1976; pres. Two Prairie Oil Co., Inc., Carlisle, Ark., 1977—; pres. Two Prairie Sales & Mktg., Inc., Corkill & Son Engring. & Design Co.; mayor City of Carlisle. Bd. dirs. Lonoke County Council on Aging. Decorated Air medal, Army Commendation medal, Bronze Star. Mem. Nat. Fedn. Ind. Businessmen (action council mem. 1978-79), Am. Mgmt. Assn., Ark. Oil Marketers Assn., So. Bldg. Code Congress Internat., Res. Officers Assn., Carlisle C. of C. (pres., dir.), VFW (post comdr. 1980), Am. Legion. Republican. Baptist. Club: Lions. Home: PO Box 604 Carlisle AR 72024 Office: Route 2 Box 15B Carlisle AR 72024

CORLEY, DEAN RICKEY, pharmaceutical company representative; b. Okla., Aug. 23, 1944; s. James Luther and Nora Lee (Hudson) C.; m. Jean Keeler, Jan. 22, 1965; children—Laura Luane, Ricky Dean Jr., Tolbert Hudson. B.S. in Math., Okla. State U. Tchr. Okla. High Schs., 1967-74; profl. field rep. Okla. Heart Assn., 1974-75, Ives Lab., Okla., 1975-83, Boehringer Ingleheim Ltd., Okla., 1983—. Chmn. Moore Park and Recreation Bd., Okla., 1978-85; pres. Moore Bd. Edn., 1983—. Mem. Okla. County Pharm. Soc., NEA, Okla. Edn. Assn. Republican. Mem. Ch. Christ. Avocations: hunting; fishing; camping; gardening. Home and Office: 1201 NE 20th St Moore OK 73160

CORLEY, JOE ALVIN, sheriff, rancher; b. Montgomery County, Tex., Jan. 12, 1939; s. Marshall Elbert and Annie Belle (Foster) C.; m. Judith Ann Sivley, July 3, 1959; children—Keith, Kimberly, April. Student, Sam Houston State Coll., 1956-60, Nat. Sheriffs Inst., 1983; basic peace officer cert. Tex. A&M U., 1979. Cert. peace officer, corrections officer, Tex. corrections officer Mobile Oil Co., Navasota, Tex., 1961-64, corrections officer Tex. Dept. Corrections, Huntsville, 1964-66; ranch foreman J-D Ranch and Quatro Ranch, Montgomery, Tex., 1966-77; county commr. Montgomery County, Tex., 1977-80, sheriff, 1981—; cons. Gondeck & Assocs., San Antonio, 1983—; rancher. Committeeman Montgomery County Agrl. Conservation Stabilization Bd., 1974-77; sch. bd. trustee Montgomery Ind. Sch. Dist., 1970-76. Recipient Appreciation award Woodlands Devel. Corp., Tex., 1980; Appreciation award Am. Legion, Conroe, Tex., 1981; Appreciation award March of Dimes, Conroe, 1982. Mem. Internat. Assn. Assn. Chiefs of Police, Tex. Sheriffs Assn., Nat. Sheriffs Assn., Am. Law Enforcement Officers Assn., Nat. Assn. Chiefs of Police, Future Farmers Am. (life hon.), Montgomery County Fair Assn. (life). Democrat. Baptist. Clubs: Walden Yacht, Woodlands Country (Montgomery County). Avocations: hunting; fishing; racquetball; softball; basketball. Home: 80 Bethel Rd Montgomery TX 77356 Office: Montgomery County Sheriff's Dept 300 Main Conroe TX 77301

CORMIER, FRANK ALEX, consulting petroleum engineer; b. Abbeville, La., Nov. 7, 1950; s. Alex and Verna (Petry) C.; m. Connie Marie LeGros, May 25, 1974; children—Suzanne, Rachel, Katie. B.S. in Petroleum Engring., U. Southwest La., 1972, M.S. in Engring. Mgmt., 1974, M.B.A. in Fin. Mgmt., 1977. Registered profl. engr., La. Field engr. trainee Halliburton Services, Lafayette, La., 1972; engring. asst. Union Tex. Petroleum, Lafayette, 1973; area engr. Am. Hess Corp, Lafayette, 1974-75, regional reservoir engr. 1975-77; cons. I.H. Delatte & Assocs., Lafayette, 1977-82; pres. Frank A. Cormier & Assocs., Lafayette, 1983—. Mem. Soc. Petroleum Engrs., Soc. of Profl. Well Log Analysts, Southwest La. Geophys. Soc., Am. Assn. of Profl. Geologists (assoc. mem.). Office: Frank A Cormier & Assocs Inc 319 Audubon Blvd Lafayette LA 70503

CORNELISON, RONALD FRANKLIN, defense services company executive, marketing and management consultant; b. Denver, Sept. 24, 1949; s. Charles Henderson and Margaret Hester (Peake) C.; m. 2d Lillian Jane Saunders, Jan. 31, 1981; 1 dau., Laura, 1 dau. by previous marriage, Jennifer. B.S., U.S. Naval Acad., 1971; M.S., U. So. Calif., 1978; M.B.A., Nat. U., San Diego, 1979. Vice pres. SEACOR, Arlington, Va., 1977-81; chmn. bd., pres. Waterbourne, Inc., Wilmington, Del., 1979-82; ptnr. C2GT Mgmt. Group, Arlington, 1982—; exec. v.p. Integrated Systems Analysts, Arlington, 1982—. Mem. Va. Republican Com., Alexandria, 1983. Served to lt. USN, 1971-76. Named Shiphandler of Yr., U.S. Pacific Fleet, 1974. Mem. Am. Soc. Naval Engrs., Arlington County C. of C. Home: 7732 Southdown Rd Alexandria VA 22308 Office: Integrated Systems Analysts 1225 Jefferson David Hwy Arlington VA 22202

CORNELL, KEITH ARTHUR, financial and marketing executive; b. Dhahran, Saudi Arabia, May 19, 1957; s. Vernon Arthur and Bonnie Lou (Richey) C.; m. Julie Jaye Lydon, May 3, 1980. B.S. in Engring., Harvey Mudd Coll., 1978; M.S. in Indsl. Engring., Carnegie-Mellon U., 1980. Mktg. coordinator United Controls div. Envirotech, Santa Fe Springs, Calif., 1978; cons. Mgmt. Adv. Services, Price Waterhouse & Co., Los Angeles, 1979, mgr. mgmt. adv. services, Ft. Worth, 1982-84; cons. Braxton Assocs., Boston, 1980; asst. to v.p. planning Western Co. of N.Am., Ft. Worth, 1981-82, controller Pacesetter Tool div., Houston, 1982; pres. DSA Fin. Corp., Dallas, 1984-85; dir. mktg. and product services Hall Fin. Group, Dallas, 1985—; dir. Planned Investments, San Francisco, M-Power Inc., Dallas, Med. Indsl. Capital, Inc., Mpls. Active Project Bus., Jr. Achievement, 1983—. Mem. Assn. M.B.A. Execs., Nat. Soc. Profl. Engrs. Home: 3200 Hilldale Rd Fort Worth TX 76116 Office: 10100 N Central Expressway Dallas TX 75231

CORNELSON, GEORGE HENRY, textile company executive; b. Spartanburg, S.C., July 12, 1931; s. George Henry and Elizabeth (Woodward) C.; student Davidson Coll., 1949-51; B.S., N.C. State U., 1953; postgrad. Harvard U. Grad. Sch. Bus. Adminstrn., 1953-54; m. Ann Martin Shaw, Oct. 6, 1956; children—George Henry, Martin S., Scott M., Elizabeth W. With Clinton Mills, Inc. (S.C.), 1954—, v.p., 1958, exec. v.p., 1970, pres., 1979—, dir. Clinton Mills, Inc., Clinton Mills of Geneva Inc., Geneva, Ala., 1979—; dir. M.S. Bailey Bankers, Clinton, S.C. Chmn. Greater Clinton Planning Commn., 1967; mem. exec. com. Blue Ridge Council Boy Scouts Am., 1974, chmn. Laurens dist., 1973; pres. Clinton United Fund, 1963-64; bd. dirs. N.C. Textile Found., 1982—, mem. exec. com.; trustee Presbyn. Coll., 1959-68; bd. trustees Thornwell Children's Home, 1968-76, sec., 1974, mem. exec. com., 1973-74; bd. trustees S.C. Found. Ind. Colls., 1971-83; elder First Presbyn. Ch., 1976—; bd. visitors Davidson Coll., N.C., 1986-88. Served with USAF, 1955-57. Named Outstanding Young Alumnus, N.C. State U., 1965; recipient Disting. Service award Jr. C. of C., 1962. Mem. Clinton C. of C. (pres. 1969, dir. 1966-68), S.C. C. of C. (dir. exec. com. 1975-78), S.C. Textile Mfrs. Assn. (pres. 1979—), Am. Textile Mfrs. Inst. Lodge: Lions (dep. dist. gov. 1969-70). Home: Merrie Oaks Clinton SC 29325 Office: Drawer 1215 Clinton SC 29325

CORNETT, JAMES CORBET, social worker, administrator; b. Banner Elk, N.C., Oct. 24, 1941; s. Glenn W. and Virginia (Aldridge) C.; m. Rosa Lee Cope, Aug. 1, 1964; children—Rusty, Tony, Jonathan. B.A., Tenn. Temple U., 1964; postgrad. U. Tenn., 1966-67. Welfare worker Dept. Human Services, Clinton, Tenn., 1965-72, field supr., 1972-78, county dir. IV, 1978—. Mem. Anderson County Sch. Bd., Clinton, 1979—; bd. dirs. United Way Anderson County, Oak Ridge, 1982—, Anderson County chpt. ARC, 1984-85, Anderson County Community Action, 1984—; pres. PTA, 1972-74. Named Young Man of Yr., Tenn. Jaycees, 1973. Mem. Tenn. Conf. Social Welfare, Am. Pub. Welfare Assn. Baptist. Avocations: metal detecting; coin collecting; hunting; fishing; gardening. Home: 22 Forest Rd Oliver Springs TN 37840

CORNFIELD, DANIEL BENJAMIN, sociology educator; b. Washington, Nov. 5, 1952; s. Melvin and Edith (Haas) C.; m. Hedy Merrill Weinberg, June 30, 1985. A.B., U. Chgo., 1974, A.M., 1977, Ph.D., 1980. Asst. prof. sociology Vanderbilt U., Nashville, 1980—. Appearances on various TV and radio programs. Contbr. articles to profl. jours. Grantee Russell Sage Found., 1985, Nat. Council Employment Policy, 1980. Mem. Am. Sociol. Assn., So. Sociol. Soc. Democrat. Jewish. Avocations: guitar; clarinet; saxophone; piano; labor union organizing. Office: Dept Sociology Vanderbilt U Nashville TN 37235

CORNISH, FRANK GARY, geologist; b. Yokohama, Japan, May 27, 1951 (parents Am. citizens); s. Lowell Jewell and Tsuyaka (Kimura) C.; m. Judith Sackett, May 18, 1975; children—Dante Alexander, Darian Sentaro. B.S., La. State U., 1973; M.A., U. Tex., 1975. Field asst. U.S. Geol. Survey, Denver, 1973; geologist devel., exploration Getty Oil, Midland, Tex., Oklahoma City, 1975-78; geologist exploration Tex. Oil & Gas, Oklahoma City, Corpus Christi, Tex., 1978—. Mem. Am. Assn. Petroleum Geologists, Oklahoma City Geol. Soc., Corpus Christi Geol. Soc., Coastal Bend Geophys. Soc. Office: Tex Oil & Gas 600 M Bank N Corpus Christi TX 78471

CORNYN, MICHAEL ROBERT, geophysicist; b. Dayton, Ohio, Sept. 11, 1951; s. Earl Robert and Josephine Marie (Szelagji) C.; m. Aprel Lynn Frye, June 26, 1976; children—Michelle Renee, Stephanie Anne. B.S., Wright State U., 1974, M.S., 1977. Geophysicist Union Oil Co. Calif., Jackson, Miss., 1977-80, area geophysicist, Lafayette, La., 1980-83, data processing coordinator, 1983—. Elder Trinity Lutheran Ch., Lafayette, 1984—. Mem. Soc. Exploration Geophysicists, Am. Assn. Petroleum Geologists. Avocations: woodworking; swimming. Office: Union Oil Co Calif PO Box 51388 OCS Lafayette LA 70503

CORONADO, JOSE RICARDO, hospital administrator; b. Benavides, Tex., Apr. 3, 1932; s. Pedro C. and Otila (Garza) C. B.S., Tex. Coll. Arts and Industry, 1957, M.S., 1959; M.Hosp. Adminstrn., Baylor U., 1973. Tchr. sci. Benavides Ind. Sch. Dist., 1955-56; asst. prin., tchr. Hebbronville High Sch. (Tex.), 1959-61; med. adminstrv. asst. for research Houston VA Med. Ctr., 1962-70; asst. dir. intern Kerrville VA Med. Ctr., 1971-72; asst. dir. Audie Murphy Vets. Hosp., San Antonio, 1973-75, dir., 1975—; mem. regional bd. VA-Dept. of Def. Civilian-Mil. Contingency Hosp. System; adv. council Council Teaching Hosps.; coordinating council VA Adminstrs. Health Care Adv. Forum. Div. chmn. Combined Fed. Campaign; bd. contbrs. United Way; vocat. adv. bd. council Edgewood Ind. Sch. Dist.; bd. dirs. Regional Blood Bank Bexar County, ARC. Mem. Am. Coll. Hosp. Adminstrs., Fed. Exec. Assn. (pres. 1978-80), Alamo Hosp. Div., San Antonio Med. Found., Am. Counselors Assn. (past state pres. and nat. v.p. Young Engrs. and Scientists). Office: Audie L Murphy Memorial Veterans Hospital 7400 Merton Minter Blvd San Antonio TX 78284

CORPOLONGO, JOHN D., osteopathic physician; b. Webb City, Okla., Mar. 29, 1931; s. Bennedetto Arturo and Ruby Gertrude (Moren) C.; m. Deloris Gean Alliett, July 11, 1953 (div. 1978); 1 child, John Michael; m. Barbara Jo Spencer, May 20, 1978. B.S., Pittsburg U., Kans., 1952; D.O., Kansas City Coll. Osteopathy, Mo., 1956. Lic. physician, Okla. Intern. Normandy Hosp., St. Louis, 1956-57; pvt. practice, St. Louis, 1957-59, Iola, Kans., 1959-81; coroner Allen County, Iola, 1974-81; chief of staff Allen County Hosp., Iola, 1974-76, 77-79. Mem. Am. Acad. Osteo. Surgery, Am. Acad. Gen. Practice, Am. Osteo. Assn., Okla. Osteo. Assn., Kans. State Osteo. Assn. (pres. 1977-78). Methodist. Club: Appaloosa Horse (Moscow, Idaho).

Avocations: Horseback trail riding; fishing. Home: Route 3 Box 234 Jay OK 74346

CORRADA, BALTASAR, mayor of San Juan, Puerto Rico; b. Morovis, P.R., Apr. 10, 1935; s. Romulo and Ana Maria (Del Rio) C.; m. Beatriz Betances, Dec. 24, 1959; children—Ana Isabel, Francisco Javier, Juan Carlos, Jose Baltasar. B.A. in Social Scis., U. P.R., 1956, J.D., 1959. Bar: P.R. 1959. Practiced in San Juan, 1959-76; chmn. Civil Rights Commn. of P.R., 1970-72; pres. editorial bd. P.R. Human Rights Rev., 1971-72; mem. 95th-98th congresses, 1977-85, as resident commr. from P.R.; mayor, San Juan, 1985—. Founder, dir. P.R. Teleradial Inst. Ethics. Mem. Am., Fed., P.R. bar assns. New Progressive. Roman Catholic. Club: Exchange. Home: 154 Tulipan St Rio Piedras PR 00927 Office: Mayor's Office PO Box 4355 San Juan PR 00905*

CORRADINO, JOSEPH CARMEN, civil engineer; b. Phila., Aug. 1, 1943; s. Anthony and Millie (D'Alessandro) C.; m. Vivian Mary Pomilio, Jan. 25, 1966; children—Joseph M., Guy A., Danielle M., Nicole A. B.C.E., Villanova U., 1965; M.S.C.E., Purdue U., 1966. Registered profl. engr., Pa., Ky., Fla., Mich., N.Y., Ill., Calif. Mng. prin. Schimpeler-Corradino Assocs., Louisville, 1970—; adj. asst. prof. Inst. Community Devel./Urban Studies Ctr., U. Louisville, 1973—; cons. Louisville and Jefferson County Air Bd., 1971-73; transp. engr. Simpson & Curtin, Inc., Phila., 1965-70. Chair, Louisville Mayor's Econ. Devel. Adv. Com., 1981-85; bd. dirs. St. Xavier High Sch., Sta. WKPC Pub. TV; bd. dirs. Louisville Community Design Ctr., since 1983—, chair, 1984-85; chair Commn. on New Charter for Louisville/Jefferson County, 1983—. Mem. ASCE, Inst. Traffic Engrs., Ky. Soc. Profl. Engrs., Nat. Soc. Profl. Engrs., Louisville C. of C. (v.p. econ. devel. steering com.), Chi Epsilon, Tau Beta Pi, Lodge: K/C. Home: 1505 Sylvan Ct Louisville KY 40205 Office: 1429 S 3d St Louisville KY 40208

CORRADO, BENJAMIN WILLIAM, marketing consulting; b. Bklyn., July 16, 1911; s. Anthony and Genevieve (La Guardia) C.; student Sch. Commerce, N.Y. U., 1930-32; m. Virginia M. McCormick, June 23, 1939. Chief statistician, investment counsellor Standard Statistics Co.; news editor, Washington editor Am. Machinist; Cleve. editor Iron Age mag.; metals and beverage specialist Poor's Pub. Co.; asst. pub. relations dir. Am. Iron and Steel Inst., 1946-48; coordinator advt., spl. asst. to pres. Market Research Dir., Publicker Industries, Inc., 1948-50; research cons., beverage Specialist, 1950-55; v.p. charge market research Nat. Distillers Products Co., 1955-66; v.p. industry relations Nat. Distillers & Chem. Corp., 1966-72; marketing cons., broker Benjamin W. Corrado Assos., 1972—. Jr. economist, munitions br. WPB, 1943; v.p. dir. Bourbon Inst.; v.p., dir. Ky. Distillers Assn.; v.p. Md. Distillers Assn.; author nat. liquor consumption estimate by states and by types, 1950-54; per diem cons. NPA, 1951-52. Recipient indsl. marketing award of merit for best pub. research Am. Machinist, 1945. Mem. Am. Legion, Nat. Assn. Bus. Economists, Am. Mktg. Assn. Assoc. Cooperage Ind. Am. Club: Nat. Press (Washington). Author: Distilled Spirits Industry-Public Revenues, 1943; Newsweek Liquor Advt. Exp. Mags., 1951, 52, 53, 54; Trne's Beer Consumption Report, 1952, 53; Am. Mag. Wine Consumption Report, 1952, 53; Liquor Marketing Handbook, 1954, 55; Alcoholic Beverage Control, 1973; U.S. News Wine and Spirits Mktg. Bull., 1974-85; contbr. articles to nat. mags. Home: 401 Briny Ave Pompano Beach FL 33062

CORREA, EILEEN ISRAEL, psychologist; b. New Orleans, Sept. 26, 1950; d. Norman Charles and Jeannette Augusta (Simison) Israel; B.S., U. Southwestern La., 1972; M.S., U. Ga., 1975, Ph.D., 1977; m. John Henry Correa, Jan. 28, 1978; 1 child, John Bernard. Lic. psychologist, MIss., La. Clin. psychologist Biloxi (Miss.) VA Med. Center, 1977-79; clin. psychologist New Orleans VA Center, 1979—, acting chief psychology service, 1980-81, dir. psychology tng. program, 1979-83. USPHS grantee, 1973-75. Mem. Am. Psychol. Assn., Southeastern Psychol. Assn. Roman Catholic. Contbr. articles to profl. jours. Home: 1144 Helios Ave Metairie LA 70005 Office: 1601 Perdido St New Orleans LA 70146

CORRELL, LOU PERKINS, library science educator; b. Hallsville, Tex., Mar. 5, 1921; d. Clement A. and Fannie A. (Martin) Perkins; m. Myron Bernard Correll, Jan. 7, 1943; children—Gay Correll Brown, Randy, Robin Correll Brooks. B.S., East Tex. State U., 1962, M.S. in L.S., 1966, Ed.D., 1974. Cert. tchr., librarian, Tex. Classroom tchr. Longview (Tex.) Ind. Sch. Dist., 1962-65, library coordinator, 1965-67; research asst. East Tex. State U., Commerce, 1967-68, instr., 1968-72, asst. prof., 1974—, assoc. prof. library sci.; ednl. media cons. Region Service Contest, San Antonio, 1972-74; pub. sch. ednl. cons., various sch. dists., Tex., 1972—. Author self instructional manual on use of books, libraries, 1981; contbr. articles in field to profl. jours.; producer sound-slide prodn., 1983. Mem. ALA, Tex. Library Assn., Tex. Assn. Sch. Librarians, Tex. Assn. Ednl. Tech., Tex. Assn. Coll. Tchrs., Tex. Soc. Coll. Tchrs. Edn., Tex. State Tchrs. Assn., Kappa Delta Pi. Republican. Baptist. Home: Route 1 Box 269 Mineola TX 75773 Office: East Tex State U East Texas State University Station Commerce TX 75428

CORRELL, NOBLE OTTO, JR., thoracic surgeon; b. Robinson, Ill., July 16, 1920; s. Noble Otto and Margaret (Hull) C.; B.S., Ind. State U., 1942; M.S., U. Ill., 1950, M.D., 1950; m. Violet Butler, June 25, 1944. Intern, U.S. Naval Hosp., San Diego, surg. resident VA Hosp., Hines, Ill., 1951-54; thoracic resident and fellow Presbyn.-St. Lukes Hosp., Chgo., 1955-57; chief-of-surgery Community Meml. Gen. Hosp., LaGrange, Ill., 1962-64, Luth. Gen. Hosp., Park Ridge, Ill., 1965-67, pres. med. staff, 1970-72; asso. clin. prof. U. Ill., 1973-75; dir. continuing med. edn. Cypress Community Hosp., Pompano Beach, Fla., 1975-78; mem. staff Martin Meml. Hosp., Stuart, The Hosp., Jupiter, Fla., Port St. Lucie Hosp. Pres., Margaret H. Correll Meml. Research Found. Served from ensign to lt. USNR, 1942-46. Fellow Am. Coll. Chest Physicians; mem. Soc. Thoracic Surgeons, So. Thoracic Surg. Assn., Midwest Surg. Soc., Pvt. Drs. Am. Inc. (v.p. 1972-80, pres. 1980-81, pres. No. Ill. chpt. 1971-73), Am. Council Med. Staffs, Ill. Thoracic Surg. Soc. (founder, pres. 1970). Contbr. articles to profl. jours. Home: 659 SE Saint Lucie Blvd Stuart FL 33494 Office: 501 E Osceola St Stuart FL 33494

CORRIERE, JOSEPH N., JR., urologist, educator; b. Easton, Pa., Apr. 3, 1937; s. Joseph N. and Rosa Ada (Poinsetta) C.; m. Evelyn Pavia Mossey, June 25, 1960 (div. July 1984); children—Joseph N., Christopher John, Gregory James, Evelyn Anne. B.A., U. Pa., 1959; M.D., Seton Hall Coll. Medicine, 1963. Diplomate Am. Bd. Urology. Intern Pa. Hosp., Phila., 1963-64; asst. instr. surgery, fellow in Harrison Dept. Surg. Research, Hosp. U. Pa., Phila., 1964-65, asst. instr. urology, 1965-68, USPHS urol. research trainee, 1967-68, instr. urology, 1968-69, assoc. in urology, 1969-71, asst. prof. urology, 1971-74; venereal disease trainee Phila. Dept. Pub. Health, 1965; radioisotope trainee William H. Donner Ctr. for Radiology, Phila., 1965-66; prof., dir. div. urology, dept. surgery U. Tex. Med. Sch., Houston, 1974—, interim chmn. dept. surgery, 1980-82, assoc. chmn. dept. surgery, 1984—; chief urology service Hermann Hosp., Tex. Med. Ctr., Houston; cons. Shriners Hosp. for Crippled Children, NASA, Spina Bifida Assn.; acad. staff St. Joseph Hosp., Houston. Contbr. numerous articles to profl. jours. Served to maj. USAF, 1969-71. Mem. Am. Urol. Assn., Soc. Univ. Surgeons, ACS, Soc. Univ. Urologists (sec.-treas. 1984-86), Am. Assn. Genitourol. Surgery, Am. Assn. for Surgery of Trauma. Roman Catholic. Club: Doctor's (Houston). Home: 7511 Morningside Dr Houston TX 77030 Office: U Tex Med Sch Urology Div 6431 Fannin Houston TX 77030

CORRIGAN, EUGENE PATRICK, JR., advertising agency executive; b. N.Y.C., July 15, 1930; s. Eugene Patrick and Alice Elaine (White) C.; Ph.B., Loyola Coll., Balt., 1951; M.A., U. S.C., 1986; accredited Pub. Relations Soc. Am., 1974; m. Mabel Chandler Johnstone, Mar. 2, 1956; children—Alice Jean Corrigan Tidd, Eugene Patrick, Ann Chandler. Mem. staff UP, Charleston, W.Va., 1951; advt. mgr. Am. Coolair Co., Jacksonville, Fla., 1953; account exec. Sta. WCSC-TV, Charleston, S.C., 1954, Sta. WTMA, Charleston, 1955; sales mgr. Sta. WTAL, Tallahassee, 1958, mgr., 1958; mgr. Sta. WMFJ, Daytona Beach, Fla., 1958; comml. mgr. Sta. WSAV-TV, Savannah, Ga., 1959; sales mgr. Sta. WOKE, Charleston, 1960; founder, pres. James Island News, Inc., Charleston, 1961; rep. Enterprise Promotions; dir. advt. and promotion Craver Industries, Charleston, 1963; founder, pres. Corrigan & Co. Advt. and Public Relations, Inc., Charleston, 1966; dir. communications Blue Cross-Blue Shield S.C., 1976; pres. Utilization, Inc., patent devel., Charleston, 1966—; partner Letters Perfect, telephone dictation, Columbia, 1980; founder, 1980, 1st v.p., pres. InTab, Inc., piggyback mailers, Columbia, 1980—. Mem. exec. com. Charleston County Republican Party, 1960-72. Mem. Public Relations Soc. S.C. Roman Catholic. Home: 109 Hillpine Rd 212 Columbia SC 29210-2456

CORRIGAN, GERARD MICHAEL, writer, consultant; b. N.Y.C., Dec. 14, 1946; s. Harold Joseph and Elizabeth (Yates) C.; children—Jessica, Casey, Erin. B.A., Holy Cross Coll., 1968. Tech. writer Courseware Inc., San Diego, 1976; instructional designer HBH Co./Hazeltine Corp., Arlington and Reston, Va., 1980—; free lance writer, San Diego, 1972-80. Contbr. articles to profl. jours. Served to lt. USN, 1968-75, Vietnam. Mem. Am. Soc. Tng. and Devel., Am. Legion. Avocations: swimming; writing. Home: 2610 N Franklin Rd Arlington VA 22201 Office: Hazeline Corp 10 800 Parkridge Blvd Reston VA 22091

CORRIGAN, HUGH, III, oil and gas producer; b. Duncan, Okla., Sept. 14, 1923; s. Hugh and Clementine (March) C.; m. Ann Ulmer, Mar. 27, 1947 (dec. 1978); children—Hugh, Patrick; m. Judith Edwards, June 10, 1984. Student Tex. Tech U., 1941-42, Tex. State U., 1946. Ind. oil and gas producer, Midland, Tex., 1946—. Served with USCG, 1942-45. Republican. Club: Shikar Safari Internat. (pres. 1965-66). Avocations: hunting; fishing. Home: 1926 Crescent Pl Midland TX 79705

CORRIGAN, PAUL JAMES, JR., hosp. adminstr.; b. Cleve., Nov. 11, 1933; s. Paul James and Lucille (Ryan) C.; B.S., U. Nebr., 1962; M.H.A., Baylor U., 1969; J.D., Nashville YMCA Night Law Sch., 1983; m. Dyann Robertson, Nov. 27, 1976; children by previous marriage—Michael Shaun, Patricia Colette. Commd., U.S. Air Force, 1952, advanced through grades to maj., 1972; adminstr. health services Med. Service Corps, Calif., Tex., Germany, 1952-72; hosp. adminstr. Western State Psychiat. Hosp., Bolivar, Tenn., 1972-76; asso. dir. Vanderbilt U. Hosp., Nashville, 1976—; mem. faculty div. med. adminstrn. Vanderbilt U. Sch. Medicine, 1977—; dir. Mid-south Med. Center Council; preceptor grad. program hosp. adminstrn. Med. Coll. Va. Decorated Meritorious Service medal. Recipient Service Testimonial, Chief Chaplains USAF. Mem. Tenn. Hosp. Assn. (council on edn. and profl. practice), Assn. Mental Health Adminstrs., Am. Coll. Hosp. Adminstrs., Ret. Officers Assn., Assn. Mil. Surgeons U.S., VFW. Clubs: Masons (32 deg.), Shriners. Address: 806 Fountainhead Ct Brentwood TN 37027

CORRON, DONALD RAY, mathematics educator; b. Clifton Forge, Va., June 22, 1935; s. Carl Daniel and Elizabeth (Hicks) C.; m. Lolene Hodges, Aug. 26, 1967; 1 child, David Alan. B.A., Emory and Henry Coll., 1958; M.S., Radford U., 1965; A.B.D., Va. Poly. Inst. State U., 1978; postgrad. Ind. U., U. Ga. Tchr., coach Marion High Sch., Va., 1960-61, Franklin County High Sch., Va., 1961-65, Floyd County High Sch., Va., 1965-66; assoc. prof. math. Ferrum Coll., Va., 1966—. Coach Little League Recreation Dept., Franklin County, teen and preteen golfers, Floyd County. Served with U.S. Army, 1958-60. Mem. Nat. Council Tchrs. Math., Math. Assn., Nat. Golf Assn. Avocations: golf; softball; volleyball. Office: Box 2655 Ferrum Coll Ferrum VA 24088

CORSO, GREGORY MICHAEL, psychology educator, researcher, consultant; b. Iowa City, May 6, 1947; s. John F. and Josephine A. (Solazzo) C.; m. Sondra Fergerson, June 12, 1971; children—Jennifer Jean, Rebecca Ann, Megan Elizabeth. B.S. in Psychology, SUNY-Cortland, 1974; M.A. in Exptl. Psychology, N.Mex. State U., 1976, Ph.D. in Engring. Psychology, 1978. Instr., SUNY-Geneseo, 1977-78; asst. prof. psychology Ga. Inst. Tech., Atlanta, 1978-84, assoc. prof., 1984—. Served with Air N.G., 1967-73, USAF, 1968-69. Fellow Southeastern Ctr. for Elec. Engring. Edn., 1982, Am. Soc. Engring. Edn., 1983; grantee Ga. Inst. Tech., 1979, 82, Air Force Office of Sci. Research, 1983-84, Biomed. Research Support, Ga. Inst. Tech., 1982. Mem. Human Factors Soc. (pres. Atlanta chpt.), AAAS, So. Soc. Philosophy and Psychology. Contbr. articles to profl. jours. Office: Sch Psychology Ga Inst Tech Atlanta GA 30332

CORSO, SAMUEL JOSEPH, artist, educator; b. Monroe, La., Jan. 11, 1953; s. Joseph Samuel and Angelena (Casamento) C. B.F.A., La. State U., 1975, M.F.A., 1977. Vice pres. Dufour Glass Studio, Ltd., Baton Rouge, 1977—; instr. La. State U., Baton Rouge, 1981-82, asst. prof., 1983-85; exhibitor in numerous shows throughout the U.S.; represented in numerous pub. and pvt. collections. Bd. dirs. La. Crafts Council, New Orleans, 1983—; bd. dirs., artist, mem. Baton Rouge Gallery, Inc., 1976—. La. State Arts Council fellow, 1982; recipient 1st place, purchase 40th Ann. Ala. Watercolor Soc./McWane Corp., 1980; 2d pl. Fragile Art '80, Glass mag., San Francisco, 1980; 1st pl. St. Tammany Art Assn., Covington, La., 1979. Mem. La. Crafts Council, La. Watercolor Soc., Glass Art Soc., Sigma Alpha Lambda. Democrat. Roman Catholic. Office: Dufour Glass Studio Ltd PO Box 336 Baton Rouge LA 70821

CORUM, JAMES F., electrical engineering educator, antenna consultant; b. Natick, Mass., Aug. 15, 1943; s. Fred T. and Lily E. (Holland) C.; m. Linda L. Bush, June 20, 1970; children—Heather, Joel, Rebekah, Judy. B.S.E.E., U. Lowell, 1965; postgrad., Tufts U., 1966; M.S.E.E., Ohio State U., 1967, Ph.D. in E.E., 1974. Lic. 1st class radio-telephone operator, FCC. Electronic technician, MIT, Cambridge, 1962-64; elec. engr. Nat. Security Agy., Fort Meade, Md., 1965-66; research assoc. Ohio State U., Columbus, 1967-70; prof. elec. engring. tech., Ohio Tech. U., Columbus, 1970-74; assoc. prof. dept. elec. engring W.Va. U., Morgantown, 1974—; cons. satellite video, antennas, comml. AM/FM/TV broadcasting, pvt. and govtl. orgns. Author: A Critical Analysis of Tesla's Colorado Springs Experiments, 1985; contbr. tech. articles to publs. including Jour. Math. Physics, Internat. Jour. Theoretical Physics; patentee toroidal helix antenna. Recipient Outstanding Teaching awards, W.Va. U., 1976, 77, 80, 82, 83, W.Va. U. Class of '49 award for Excellence in Teaching, Coll. Engring., 1981. Mem. IEEE (chmn. subsect. 1980-84, mem. Profl. Group on Antennas and Propagation 1967—), Soc. Motion Picture and TV Engrs., Sigma Xi. Office: Dept Elec Engring W Va Univ PO Box 6101 Morgantown WV 26506-6101

CORWIN, EDWARD STANLEY, legal administrator; b. Newark, Nov. 13, 1922; s. Morris H. and Jessamine W. Cohn; A.B., Lafayette Coll., Easton, Pa., 1942; LL.B., Columbia U., 1948; m. Patricia Goldman, June 18, 1949; children—Thomas M., Lawrence N., Elizabeth A. Admitted to N.J. bar, 1948; pvt. practice, Newark, 1948-50; various businesses, 1950-60; computer programmer-analyst Edwin T. Boyle & Co., C.P.A., Hackensack, N.J., 1960-66; head mgmt. adv. service Brach, Lane, Hariton & Co., C.P.A.s., N.Y.C., 1966-72; dir. adminstrn. Carlton, Fields, Ward, Emmanuel, Smith & Cutler, P.A., Tampa, Fla., 1972—. Pres. Gasparilla Sidewalk Art Festival, Tampa, 1982—. Served with USAAF, 1943-46. C.P.A., N.J. Mem. ABA, N.Y. State Soc. C.P.A.s. Home: 480 Lucerne Ave Tampa FL 33606 Office: Box 3239 Tampa FL 33601

CORWIN, JOYCE ELIZABETH STEDMAN, construction company executive; b. Chgo.; d. Cresswell Edward and Elizabeth Josephine (Kimbell) Stedman; student Fla. State U., U. Miami; m. William Corwin, May 1, 1965; children—Robert Edmund Newman, Jillanne Elizabeth Newman. Investment rep. A.M. Kidder & Co., N.Y.C., 1954-56; pres. Am. Properties, Inc., Miami, Fla., 1966-72; v.p. Stedman Constrn. Co., Miami, 1971—; owner Joy-Win Horses, Gray lady ARC, 1969-70; guidance worker Youth Hall, 1969-70; sponsor Para Med. Group of Coral Park High Sch., 1969-70. Hostess, Republican presdl. campaign, 1968; aide Rep. Nat. Conv., 1972. Mem. Dade County Med. Aux. (chmn. directory com. 1970), Fla. Psychiat. Soc. Aux., Vizcayans, Fla. Morgan Horse Assn., Fla. Thoroughbred Breeders Assn. Clubs: Coral Gables Junior Women's (chmn. casework com. 1959-63), Riviera Country, Coral Gables Country, Royal Palm Tennis. Home: 5780 SW 59 Ave Miami FL 33143 also Windrift Farm Route 1 Box 239 F Reddick FL 32686

CORWIN, LINDA WHIGHAM, geologist; b. Farmington, N.Mex., Aug. 1, 1956; d. Thomas Gordon and Roseland Virginia (McDonald) W.; m. Robert Vinton Corwin, Feb. 16, 1980. B.S., Baylor U., 1978; M.S., 1981. Clk., Northwest Pipeline Corp., Farmington, 1975; sr. research geologist Exxon Prodn. Research Co., Houston, 1981—. Author: Physical Geology Laboratory Supplement, 1979; Stratigraphy of the Fredericksburg Group North of the Colorado River Texas, 1982. Wendlandt scholar, 1978-80. Mem. Am. Assn. Petroleum Geologists, Geol. Soc. Am., Soc. Econ. Paleontologists and Mineralogists, Houston Geol. Soc., Baylor Alumnae Soc. Republican. Avocations: gardening; furniture refinishing. Home: 20 Ridgeline Ct The Woodlands TX 77381 Office: Exxon Prodn Research Co PO Box 2189 Houston TX 77001

CORWIN, WILLIAM, physician; b. Boston, Oct. 28, 1908; M.D., Tufts Coll., 1932; m. Frances M. Wetherell (dec.) m. 2d, Joyce S. Newman, 1965. Intern Wesson Meml. Hosp., Springfield, Mass., 1932-33; physician Met. State Hosp., Waltham, Mass., 1933-37, asst. supt., 1937-42; research fellow Harvard, 1937-46; practice medicine, specializing in psychiatry, Springfield, Mass., 1946-54, Miami, Fla., 1954—; mem. staff Jackson Meml. Hosp., Miami; instr. psychiatry Boston U., 1937-46, Tufts Coll., 1941-46; clin. asso. prof. psychiatry U. Miami, 1955-70, clin. prof., 1970—. Past mem. State Fla. Adv. Com. on Mental Health; agy. operations com. United Fund. Bd. dirs. Family and Childrens Services Miami. Served to lt. col. M.C., USAAF, 1942-46. Diplomate Am. Bd. Psychiatry and Neurology, Am. Bd. Forensic Psychiatry. Fellow Am. Psychiat. Assn. (life), Am. Coll. Psychiatrists; mem. AMA, S.Fla. Psychiat. Soc. (councillor). Contbr. articles on physiology of schizophrenia to profl. publs. Office: 5780 SW 59 Ave Miami FL 33143

CORY, WILLIAM EUGENE, research company executive; b. Dallas, Apr. 5, 1927; s. William Leroy and Maude (Cole) C.; m. Doris Garlington, Jan. 4, 1947; children—William Eugene II, Madeline K. B.S.E.E., Tex. A&M U., 1950; M.S., UCLA, 1959. Elec. engr. to supervisory elec. engr. Hdqrs. USAF Security Service, San Antonio, 1950-57; electronic systems engr., aircraft devel. engr. specialist Lockheed Aircraft Co., Burbank, Calif. and Marietta, Ga., 1957-59; sr. research engr., mgr. communications, dir., v.p. Electronic Systems Research div. S.W. Research Inst., San Antonio, 1959—. Served with U.S. Navy, 1945-46, to maj. USAF, 1951-52. Recipient Spl. Service award USAF Security Service, 1957. Fellow IEEE (dir. 1972-73, pres. 1974-75, dir. Electromagnetic Compatability Soc. 1971-75, 80—; award 1970, Laurence G. Cumming award 1983). Contbr. articles on communications theory, signal detection, extraction and processing, automation and electromagnetic compatibility to tech. jours. Patentee in field. Home: 4135 High Sierra St San Antonio TX 78228 Office: 6220 Culebra Rd San Antonio TX 78284

COSENZA, ARTHUR GEORGE, opera director; b. Phila., Oct. 16, 1924; s. Luigi and Maria (Piccolo) C.; student Ornstein Sch. Music Phila., 1946-48, Berkshire Music Festival, 1947, Am. Theater Wing, N.Y.C., 1948-50; m. Marietta Muhs, Sept. 16, 1950; children—Louis John, Arthur William, Maria leading baritone roles with opera cos. throughout U.S., Can., 1947-70; baritone New Orleans Opera, 1954-70, producer operas, 1960-74, resident stage dir., 1965-70, gen. dir., 1970—; asso. prof. Coll. Music, Loyola U. of South, 1954-84, dir. Loyola Opera Workshop, 1954-84; dir. Opera Program for City of New Orleans, 1955-73. Served with AUS, 1943-45. Decorated Purple Heart medal; cavaliere Order Star Italian Solidarity, cavaliere Ufficiale dell' Ordine al Merito (Italy); officier Ordre des Arts et des Lettres. Mem. Am. Guild Mus. Artists (hon. life), Blue Key. Home: 1720 Soniat St New Orleans LA 70115 Office: 333 St Charles Ave New Orleans LA 70130

COSGROVE, JOHN FRANCIS, lawyer, state legislator; b. Coral Gables, Fla., July 1, 1949; s. Francis Freheil and Vivia Adair (Rafferty) C.; m. Bernadine Elizabeth Cosgrove, Dec. 19, 1981; children—Michael, Tiffany, Colleen. A.A., U. Fla., 1969, B.S. in Journalism, 1971; J.D., Cumberland Sch. Law, 1975. Bar: Fla., U.S. Dist. Ct. (so. dist.) Fla., U.S. Ct. Appeals (5th cir.), U.S. Supreme Ct. Assoc., Hall & Hedrick, Miami, Fla., 1975-80; sole practice, Miami, 1980—; mem. Fla. Ho. of Reps., 1981—; gen. counsel Biscayne Coll.; columnist Miami Rev.—Juris Conspectus, 1975—. Chmn. Coral Gables Code Enforcement Bd.; mem. Coral Gables Econs. Devel. Bd.; mem. Jr. Orange Bowl Com.; chmn. Metro-Dade Econ. Devel. Bd., Miami Budget Rev. Com.; mem. South Miami Hosp. Assocs. Mem. ABA, Fla. Bar Assn. (jud. selection, adminstrn. and tenure com., vice chmn. jud. nominating com.), Dade County Bar Assn. (3d v.p.), Am. Judicature Soc., Assn. Trial Lawyers Am., Pvt. Industry Council of Dade County, Emerald Soc. of South Fla., Miami Springs-Hialeah C. of C., Coral Gables C. of C., Greater Miami C. of C., Blue Key, Phi Kappa Tau. Democrat. Roman Catholic (chmn. Cath. Service Bur.-50th anniversary). Clubs: Serra, Viscayans Civic, Le Lega Civic; Greater Miami Leadership Prayer Breakfast. Lodges: K.C. (grand knight Coral Gables; pres. Dade County chpt.), Kiwanis. Home: 1531 Ancona Ave Coral Gables FL 33146 Office: 19 W Flagler St Suite 215 Miami FL 33130

COSSIO-PINERO, ROSITA, psychotherapist, real estate broker; b. Havana, Cuba, Dec. 9, 1940; came to U.S., 1964, naturalized, 1970; d. Alejo and Rosa (Miralles) Cossio del Pino; B.A., Coll. of Sacred Heart, P.R., 1974; M.S., U. Bridgeport, 1976; postgrad. U. Miami (Fla.), 1977-79; m. Emilio R. Pinero, Feb. 11, 1966; children—Luis Alejo, Luis Orlando, Mayra Arrondo, Eileen B. Psychotherapist, Mentally Retarded Inst. of P.R., 1976-77, Miami (Fla.) Mental Health Center, 1978, aftercare clincian and psychotherapist, hypnotechnician, 1979—, day treatment program coordinator, info. specialist, 1979-80; hypnotherapist in pvt. practice, 1981-83; real estate broker, Miami; profl. cons., chmn. fin. com. Adaptación. Vice pres. Coll. Engrs., Architects and Surveyors, San Juan, P.R., 1968-76; mem. Dem. Com. of P.R. of Nat. Dem. Party, 1968-76; active Am. Cancer Soc., 1975—; pres. Cuban Anti-defamation League, 1980—; dir. social services Tent City, Miami, 1980; asst. adminstr. Cuban Haitian Task Force, State Dept., 1980—; v.p. Free Intellectuals and Writers Com. Mem. Am. Mental Health Counselors Assn., Am. Personnel and Guidance Assn., Am. Assn. Counselors. Democrat. Roman Catholic. Club: Dorado Beach (P.R.). Office: PO Box 651524 Miami FL 33165

COSTENBADER, WILLIAM BENJAMIN, JR., head and neck surgeon; b. Norfolk, Va., July 21, 1938; s. William Benjamin and Marian Virginia (Markle) C.; m. Carol Walton, June 23, 1962; children—Ann Katherine, William Benjamin III, Walton Rawls. B.S., Hampden-Sydney Coll., 1960; M.D., U. Va., 1964. Diplomate Am. Bd. Otolaryngology. Intern, U. Ky. Med. Ctr., Lexington, 1964-65, resident in gen. surgery, 1965-66; resident in otolaryngology U. Va. Hosp., Charlottesville, 1968-71; practice medicine specializing in otolaryngology Asheville Head, Neck and Ear Surgeons P.A., N.C., 1971—; mem. staff Meml. Mission Hosp., St. Joseph Hosp.; bd. dirs. Western N.C. Med. Peer Rev. Found., Asheville, 1977-85, pres., 1981-85. Participant Leadership Asheville, 1985. Served to lt. comdr. USN, 1966-68. Fellow Am. Acad. Otolaryngology-Head and Neck Surgery (bd. govs. 1982-85), ACS, Am. Soc. Head and Neck Surgery, Am. Acad. Facial Plastic and Reconstructive Surgery; mem. N.C. Soc. Otolaryngology (pres. 1977), N.C. Med. Soc. (exec. council 1984-85, commr. 1984-85). Republican. Episcopalian. Avocations: sailing; white water canoeing; gardening. Office Asheville Head Neck and Ear Surgeons PA 131 McDowell St Asheville NC 28801

COTHRAN, JOSEPHINE ANN, nurse; b. Hampton, Va., Apr. 25, 1926; d. William Edward Dewey and Josephine Louise (Weaver) D.; m. Charles Harrison Cothran, Jr., Feb. 19, 1948 (div. 1963); children—Diane Michelle Cothran Henry, Autumn Lynn Cothran Roberts. Student Bowling Green State U., Ohio, 1943-45; diploma St. Luke's Hosp. Sch. Nursing, Cleve., 1948. Cert. mobile intensive care nurse, N.C. Staff nurse, Premature Ctr., Rex Hosp., Raleigh, N.C., 1949-52; staff nurse, charge nurse obstetrics dept. Moses H. Cone Hosp., Greensboro, N.C., 1953-58; staff nurse med.-surg. Randolph Hosp. Inc., Asheboro, N.C., 1962-64, head nurse med.-surg., 1964-67, head nurse ICU, 1967-80, clin. coordinator critical care units, 1980—; instr. emergency med. technician and paramedic program Randolph Med. Res. Unit, Randolph Tech. Coll., Asheboro, N.C., 1970-73. Mem. council Central United Methodist Ch., Asheboro, 1983—; bd dirs. local chpt. Am. Diabetes Assn., Asheboro, 1984-85. N.C. regional program grantee N.C. Heart Assn., 1968; Fed. grantee U. N.C., Chapel Hill, 1970. Mem. Dist. 31 N.C. Nurses Assn. (dir. 1982-83, pres. 1968-69, 80-81, sec. 1978-80, treas. 1982-83, Nurse of Yr. 1984), Am. Nurses Assn., Council Cardiovascular Nurses, Am. Heart Assn., Old Salem Chpt. Assn. Critical Care Nurses, Am. Assn. Critical Care Nurses. Republican. Methodist. Club: Asheboro Country. Avocations: bridge; needlework; fishing; rock hunting. Home: 1405 Arrow Wood Rd Asheboro NC 27203 Office: Randolph Hosp Inc N Fayetteville St Asheboro NC 27203

COTNER, DONNA HARRISON, educator; b. Henderson, Tenn., Aug. 18, 1945; d. Sidney Russell and Tommie (Benson) Harrison; B.S., U. Tenn., 1964; M.Ed., Memphis State U., 1974, postgrad., 1978; m. Douglas MacArthur Cotner, Aug. 7, 1964. Tchr., Malesus Elem. Sch., 1964-65; tchr. math., physics, chemistry South Side High Sch., Jackson, Tenn., 1965-77; tchr. math. West Jr. High Sch., Denmark, Tenn., 1977-79, West Sr. High Sch., Denmark, 1979; mem. interim commn. on edn. reform Tenn. Dept. Edn., chmn. adv. council on tchr. edn. and cert. Bd. dirs. Madison County Polit. Action for Edn., 1976-77; advisor Sr. Girl Scout Troop, Madison County. Named Outstanding Student in Dept. Edn., U. Tenn., Martin, 1964. Mem. NEA (del. to rep. assembly), Nat. Council Accreditation Tchr. Edn., Tenn. Edn. Assn. (chmn. instructional and profl. devel. commn., pres.-elect bd. dirs. Task Force on Tchr. Excellence), W. Tenn. Edn. Assn. (v.p.), Madison County Edn. Assn. (past pres.), Delta Kappa Gamma (internation personal growth and services com, state 1st v.p.). Democrat. Mem. Ch. of Christ. Home: 128 W Grand Ave Jackson TN 38301 Office: West High Sch Route 1 Denmark TN 38391

COTONIO, THEODORE, III, school administrator, lawyer; b. New Orleans, Dec. 27, 1933; s. Theodore Jr. and Marian Elizabeth (Keighley) C.; m. Asta Augustine Viguerie, Apr. 24, 1965; children—Theodore IV, Philip Keighley Viguerie. B.A., Tulane U., 1956; J.D., Tulane U., 1962; M.Ed., U. S. Miss., 1972, Bar: La. 1962. Tchr. Jesuit High Sch., New Orleans, 1960-62, Rummel High Sch., Metairie, La., 1964-68; tchr. Newman Sch., New Orleans, 1968-80, chmn. English dept., 1971-73, head upper sch., 1972-77, headmaster, 1976—. Active Pvt. Sch. Commn., Baton Rouge, La., 1976—; pres. People Attached to Children's Hosp., New Orleans, 1982-83; exec. com. La. Children's Mus., New Orleans, 1982-85; bd. dirs. Jr. Achievement, New Orleans, 1983-85. Served with U.S. Army, 1956-58. Mem. Nat. Assn. Secondary Sch. Prins., Nat. Assn. Prins. Sch. Girls., Nat. Assn. Ind. Schs., Ind. Sch. Assn. S.W. (pres. 1984-86), La. Bar Assn. Roman Catholic. Clubs: Plimsoll, World Trade Ctr. Home: 49 Versailles Blvd New Orleans LA 70125 Office: Isidore Newman Sch 1903 Jefferson Ave New Orleans LA 70115

COTTER, DAVID JAMES, biology educator, artist; b. Glens Falls, N.Y., July 24, 1932; s. Harold Francis and Helen Marie (Maher) C.; m. Joann Wood, Aug. 21, 1953; children—David Barry, Mark Wood, John Walter. B.S., U. Ala.-Tuscaloosa, 1952, A.B., 1953, M.S., 1955; Ph.D., Emory U., 1958. Asst. prof., then assoc. prof. Ala. Coll., Montevallo, 1958-66; prof., chmn. dept. biology Ga. Coll., Milledgeville, 1966—; research assoc. Emory U., 1957-58, 63, U. Ga., summers 1966-68. Mem. Assn. Southeastern Biologists (pres. 1973), Ga. Acad. Sci., Ala. Acad. Sci., Ecol. Soc. Am. (cert.), Sigma Xi, Phi Sigma, Phi Kappa Phi, Beta Beta Beta. Contbr. articles to profl. jours. Home: 1652 Pine Valley Rd Milledgeville GA 31061 Office: Dept Biological and Environmental Sciences Georgia College Milledgeville GA 31061

COTTER, NORMAN ELWOOD, oil company executive, educator; b. Springfield, Ohio, Aug. 30, 1930; s. Robert Elwood and Anna (Athey) C.; m. Dorris Jane Steadman, Dec. 18, 1953; children—Robert Wayne, Linda Gail. B.S. in Geology, U. Fla., 1957, M.A. in Bus. Adminstrn., 1968. Cert. petroleum geologist. Geologist, Gulf Oil Corp., 1957-67; mgmt. tng. staff Amoco Prodn. Co., Houston, Tulsa, 1969-76; mgr. tng. devel. Christensen Diamond Prodn. Co., Salt Lake City, 1977-78; tng. cons. Standard Oil Co. of Ind., Chgo., 1978-82, supr. core curriculum, 1982-83, supr. info. service tng., Tulsa, 1983—; instr. mgmt. U. Fla., Gainesville, 1968-69; mgmt. cons., Houston, 1976-77. Author: (with others) A Study of Leadership Effectiveness, 1969. Corporate Core Curriculum, 1980. Sponsor, Jr. Achievement, Tulsa, 1970-71. Served as 1st class petty officer USCG, 1950-53. Mem. Am. Assn. Petroleum Geologists. Club: Thunderbird-Toastmasters (adminstrv. v.p. 1970-71) (Tulsa). Avocation: gardening Home: 6310 E 78th Pl Tulsa OK 74136 Office: Amoco Corp 519 S Boston St Tulsa OK 74103

COTTON, JERRY LEE, church administrator; b. Ardmore, Okla., Mar. 29, 1939; s. Victor Glenn and Marian Madeline (Haines) C.; m. Rhonda Lou Collins, Jan. 11, 1961; children—David, Deborah. B.B.A., S.W. Tex. State U., 1976. Cert. fellow in ch. bus. adminstrn. Instr., adminstr. San Marcos Bapt. Acad. (Tex.), 1967-76; asst. bus. mgr. E. Tex. Bapt. Coll., Marshall, 1977-81; ch. bus. adminstr. North Richland Hills Bapt. Ch. (Tex.), 1981—. Served with U.S. Army, 1959-67. Mem. Nat. Assn. Ch. Bus. Adminstrs., Tex. Bapt. Pub. Relations Assn. Baptist. Lodge: Lions. Home: 6708 Karen Dr North Richland Hills TX 76118 Office: 4001 Vance Rd North Richland Hills TX 76118

COUCH, JAMES HOUSTON, engineer, educator; b. Easley, S.C., June 5, 1919; s. A. Waverly and Gertrude (Foster) C.; B.S., Clemson U., 1941, M.S., 1952; grad. Inst. Materials Handling Tchrs., Northwestern U., 1969; grad. Materials Handling Inst., Purdue U., 1972; m. Sarah Crenshaw, Jan. 11, 1942; children—James F., Dorothy C. Couch Stafford. Asst. prof. indsl. engring. Clemson (S.C.) U., 1941-56, assoc. prof. indsl. engring., 1956-60, prof., 1960-84, prof. emeritus, 1984—; research engr. Lockheed Aircraft Corp., part time, Lockheed-Ga. Co., part-time 1955-69. Bd. dirs. Foundry Edn. Found., Cleve. Mem. Am. Welding Soc. (Meritorious award 1964, Adams Meml. membership award 1965), Am. Soc. Metals, Am. Foundrymen's Soc. Author: Manufacturing Processes and Materials, 1967; Engineering Manufacturing Processes, 1960. Home: 408 College Ave PO Box 826 Clemson SC 29633

COUCH, JOSEPH RICHARD, former government intelligence official; b. Kansas City, Mo., Apr. 21, 1916; s. William Morris and Eunice (Foster) C.; m. Mary Veronica Russell, Jan. 1, 1941; children—Elizabeth C. Arnow, Margaret C. Kammerer. A.S., Kansas City Jr. Coll., 1936; B.S., U.S. Mil. Acad., 1940. With CIA, various locations, 1947-73, bur. chief, Okinawa, Cyprus, 1952-64, div. chief, Washington, 1964-73, ret., 1973. Sreved to col. U.S. Army, 1940-47, ETO. Decorated Silver Star, Legion of Merit, Purple Heart (2); Croix de Guerre (France); Mil. Cross of Valor (Italy). Mem. Ret. Officers Assn., Mil. Order World Wars. Republican. Club: Army Navy Country (Arlington, Va.). Avocations: golf; swimming; travel.

COUCH, ROBERT CHESLEY, hospital administrator; b. Troy, Ala., Sept. 23, 1930; s. James Joshua and Margaret (White) C.; m. Barbara Allen Joyce, Sept. 3, 1952; children—Joyce, Gayle, Leslie, Karen. B.S., Auburn U., 1953; M.Hosp. Adminstrn., Ga. State U., 1957. Cons., Ga. State Health Dept., Atlanta, 1955-56; adminstr. Cherokee County Hosp., Centre, Ala., 1957-59; pres. Cumberland Med. Ctr., Crossville, Tenn., 1959—; cons. to surgeon gen. U.S. Air Force, 1973-83. Past pres. Cumberland County ARC, Tenn., 1960—, United Fund of Cumberland County, 1966—. Served to col. USAFR, 1953-83. Recipient Outstanding Service award USAF Hosp. and 97th Bomb Wing, Blytheville AFB, 1973-83; Meritorious Service award Tenn. Hosp. Assn., Nashville, 1983; Bus. Assoc. Yr., Am. Bus. Womens Assn., Crossville, 1984. Mem. Am. Coll. Hosp. Adminstrs., Healthcare Fin. Mgmt. Assn., Am. Hosp. Assn., Tenn. Hosp. Assn., Crossville C. of C. Club: Exchange (pres. 1963). Lodge: Rotary. Avocations: tennis; boating; fishing. Home: 1102 Scenic Dr Crossville TN 38555 Office: Cumberland Med Ctr 811 South Main St Crossville TN 38555

COUGHLIN, KATHLEEN, nun, hospital administrator; b. St. Louis, July 10, 1941; d. Thomas Carlyle and Lucille Marie (Baumker) C. B.S.N., Incarnate Word Coll., 1967; M.H.A., St. Louis U., 1972. Entered Sisters of Charity of Incarnate Word, Roman Cath. Ch., 1960. Dir. nurses St. Joseph's Hosp., Paris, Tex., 1967-70; nursing staff Mercy Hosp., Denver, 1971-72; asst. adminstr. St. Anthony's Hosp., Amarillo, Tex., 1972-73, adminstr., 1973-79; dir. Community and Apostolic Ministry, Provincial Council Sisters of Charity of Incarnate Word, St. Louis, 1978-81; pres. Spohn Hosp., Corpus Christi, Tex., 1981—. Diocesan coordinator health affairs Diocese of Corpus Christi, 1983—; bd. trustees Incarnate Word Health Services Corp., San Antonio, 1981—, chmn., 1985-87; trustee Incarnate Word Hosp., St. Louis, 1973—, chair., 1985; trustee Sisters of Charity Health System, Houston, 1984—; trustee Tex. Conf. Cath. Health Facilities, 1978-84, pres. 1983. Recipient Outstanding Leadership award Tex. Cath. Conf., 1983; named Woman of Year, Amarillo, Tex., 1976; Women in Careers award YWCA, Corpus Christi, 1984. Fellow Am. Coll. Healthcare Execs.; mem. Tex. Hosp. Assn. (trustee 1984-87), Cath. Health Assn. (trustee 1978-84), Corpus Christi C. of C. (trustee). Address: Spohn Hosp 600 Elizabeth St Corpus Christi TX 78404

COUGHLIN, RICHARD JAMES, sociology and anthropology educator; b. Buffalo, Dec. 12, 1917; s. Richard James and Mary (Eardley) C.; m. Margaret Morgan, Feb. 7, 1946; children—Kenneth, Elizabeth; Helene Yun-Sik Min, Aug. 15, 1981. B.S., Buffalo State Coll., 1941; M.A., Yale U., 1950, Ph.D., 1953. Vice consul Dept. State, Washington, 1946-48; asst. prof. sociology Yale U., 1954-60; assoc. prof. York U., Toronto, (Ont., Ca.), 1960-63; prof. U. Va., 1963—; vis. prof. Chinese U., Hong Kong, 1973-74; sr. rep. Asia Found., Hong Kong, 1951-59. Served with U.S. Army, 1942-45. Social Sci. Research Council grantee, 1951-52, 70. Wenner-Gren grantee, 1951-52, 61; U.S. govt. Fulbright grantee, 1951-52; USPHS grantee, 1960-61; Can. Council grantee, 1961; NSF grantee, 1964-65. Mem. Am. Sociol. Assn., So. Sociol. Soc., Assn. Asian Studies. Author: Position Women in Vietnam, Double Identity, Chinese in Modern Thailand, Vietnam Birth Customs, also articles. Home: 1204 Blue Ridge Rd Charlottesville VA 22903 Office: Dept Sociology Caisell Hall U Va Charlottesville VA 22902

COULIANOS, CONSTANTINOS HARALAMPOS, master mariner, marine surveyor; b. Greece, July 18, 1916; s. Haralampos Themistocles and Vassiliki Constantinou (Tsigonias) C.; came to U.S., 1940, naturalized, 1955; grad. Posidon Mcht. Marine Acad., 1938, Radar Sch., N.Y.C., 1957, N.Y. Meteorology Sch., 1957, N.Y. Mcht. Marine Sch., 1957; m. Franzi Siggelkow, Mar. 23, 1944; children—Harry, Katina. Chief officer, master Mcht. Marine during World War II for Western Shipping Corp., N.Y.C.; chief officer for Orion Shipping Corp., N.Y.C., 1950-54; harbour pilot V.I. Govt., 1955-57; master various cargo-tanker ships Global-Orion Shipping Corp., N.Y.C., 1957-65; dir. Coulianos Maritime Agy., St. Thomas, V.I., 1972—. Mgr. family's personal real estate. Chmn. fund raising A.R.C., 1972-73; mem. V.I. Taxicab Commn., 1972-74, V.I. Urban Renewal Bd., 1973-76. Pres. U.S.O., 1971-73; chmn. bd. Community Chest, 1968-74; hon. mem. bd. V.I. Port Authority. Served with inf., Greek Army, 1938-39. Recipient award P.R. League Against Cancer, 1970. Mem. St. Thomas-St. John C. of C. (dir.), U.S. Navy League (dir.), Andros Soc. N.Y., Mental Health Assn. St. Thomas, V.I. Hist. Soc., St. Thomas Pub. Info. Assn., Nat. Geog. Soc. Republican. Greek Orthodox. Club: V.I. Yacht (commodore 1966-68, 72-76). Lodge: Rotary (del. 1983). Author: Liquid Roads, 1961. Home: PO Box 236 Charlotte Amalie St Thomas VI 00801 Office: 23 Dronningens Gape 1 Levin Bldg Charlotte Amalie St Thomas VI 00801

COULIS, PAUL STEPHEN, medical company executive; b. Aug. 2, 1950; m. Diana Sue Harrer, Aug. 18, 1983; children—Dena Dae, Christian. A.B. in Biology, Linguistics, Ind. U.; M.B.A. Dir. First Bank, Las Colinas, Irving, Tex., 1984—. Office: Attention Med Co 3007 Skyway Circle North Irving TX 75038

COULSON, JESSIE EDWARD, counselor, minister; b. Davis, Okla., July 11, 1940; s. Ola and Eula Willie (Etherton) C.; m. Cunilla Birgitta Louise Jonsson, Sept. 3, 1960; children—Karen Louise Coulson Kobe, Nancy Sue, Linda Kay. Ministerial diploma Life Bible Coll., Los Angeles, 1963; B.A. in Psychology and Religion, Pacific Coll. Fresno, Calif., 1971; M.S. in Clin. Psychology, N. Tex. State U., 1974, postgrad. Lic. profl. counselor, Tex. Minister, Internat. Ch. of the Foursquare Gospel, Calif. and Oreg., 1963-71; clin. supr., staff psychologist Texoma Mental Health Ctr., Denison, Tex., 1974-82; pvt. practice counseling, Dallas and Denison, 1982—; pastor Mission United Meth. Ch., Gainesville, Tex., 1985—; Mem. leadership com. Sherman Area C. of C., 1983, mem. youth devel. com., 1982-84; mem. citizens road and subdiv. com. Grayson County Tex., Sherman, 1983. Mem. Am. Assn. Marriage and Family Therapy (clin.), Am. Assn. Counseling and Devel., Tex. Assn. Counseling and Devel. (bd. dirs. 1983—), Tex. Assn. for Measurement and Evaluation in Counseling and Devel. (bd. dirs. 1983—), Am. Acad. Behavioral Medicine, Texoma Counselors Assn. (pres. 1984-85), N. Central Tex. Assn. Counseling and Devel. (bd. dirs. 1985—). Democrat. Methodist. Avocations: raising small animals; gardening; painting; writing poetry. Home: Route 2 Box 514 Denison TX 75020 Office: Testing and Psychotherapy Ctr N Tex 12890 Hillcrest Suite 200 Dallas TX 75230

COULTER, EDWIN MARTIN, political science educator, author; b. Waynesboro, Va., July 18, 1937; s. Homer Preston and Eileen (Rader) C.; m. Aleta Holbrooks, June 22, 1963 (div. 1982); children—John Edwin, David Preston. B.A. in Polit. Sci., Furman U., 1962; Ph.D. in Fgn. Affairs, U. Va., 1965. Instr., U. Va., Charlottesville, 1964-65; assoc. prof. Ark. State U., Jonesboro, 1965-68, Okla. Coll. Liberal Arts, Chickasha, 1968-71; prof. Clemson U., S.C., 1971—. Author: Principles of Politics and Government, 1981, 2d edit. 1984. Served with USN, 1955-58. Woodrow Wilson fellow, N.Y., 1962. Mem. Am. Polit. Sci. Assn., So. Polit. Sci. Assn., Raven Soc., Phi Beta Kappa. Democrat. Episcopalian. Home: 207 Augusta Rd Clemson SC 29631

COUNCIL, JAMES EDWIN, insurance company executive; b. McRae, Ga., Feb. 2, 1923; s. Melton Downie and Virginia (Clark) C.; m. Diana Fulcher, Aug. 10, 1945; 1 child, Diana Leslie. B.S., Ga. Inst. Tech., 1946. Spl. agt. Ins. Co. N.Am., 1947-51; ptnr., then sr. ptnr. Hugh F. Dick & Co., mng. gen. agts., N.C. and S.C., 1951-68; v.p., mgr. Pilot and So. Fire & Casualty Cos., Greensboro, N.C., 1969-74; pres., dir. Jefferson-Pilot Fire & Casualty Co., Jefferson-Pilot Property Ins. Co., So. Fire & Casualty Co., Greensboro, 1974—; chmn. bd. N.C. Beach and Fair Plans. Served to lt. (j.g.) USNR, 1944-46. Democrat. Presbyterian. Clubs: City, Country (Greensboro, N.C.). Home: 3800 Cascade Dr Greensboro NC 27410 Office: 101 N Elm St PO Box 20967 Greensboro NC 27420

COUNCILOR, JAMES ALLAN, III, marketing/promotion company executive; b. Washington, Dec. 9, 1947; s. James Allan and Jane (Bronk) C.; m. Nancy Louise Fairbrother, Oct. 21, 1972; children—Katherine, Patricia. B.B.A., Roanoke Coll., 1970. Staff acct. Councilor, Buchanan & Mitchell, Washington, 1974; property acct., officer adminstr., disbursement mgr Ringling Bros. Barnum & Bailey, Washington, 1974-81; mgr. accounts payable MCI, Washington, 1981-85; dir. fin. Coffee Devel. Group, Washington, 1985—. Served with USN, 1970-74. Republican. Episcopalian. Lodge: Masons. Office: 1725 K St NW Washington DC 20006

COUNTISS, MARCUS LYNNDON, geophysicist, consultant; b. Norton, Va., Mar. 16, 1955; s. James L. and Catherine Neal (Madden) C.; m. Lisa Ann Aronstein, Sept. 27, 1980. Student U. Tenn., 1973; B.S. in Geophysics, U. Houston, 1978. Geophysicist Gulf Oil & Exploration & Prodn. Co., Houston, 1978-79, Strata Energy, Inc., Houston, 1979-80; pres., geophysicist M.L. Countiss Interests, Inc., Houston, 1980—; ptnr. Gulf Coast Exploration Cons., Houston, 1981—, Hitchock Exploration Co., Houston, 1981—. Mem. Nat. Tax Limitation Com., Washington, 1982—. Mem. Soc. Exploration Geophysicists, Am. Assn. Petroleum Geologists, Geophys. Soc. Houston, U. Houston Geol. Alumni Assn. Republican. Avocations: music, camping, hiking, electronics, golf, hunting. Office: Mil Countiss Interests Inc 12306 Ella Lee Ln Houston TX 77077

COUNTS, J. W., educational administrator. Supt. of schs. Arlington, Tex. Office: 1203 Pioneer Pkwy Arlington TX 76013*

COUPER, JAMES MAXWELL, painter, educator; b. Atlanta, Nov. 21, 1937; s. J. Maxwell and Frances (Ellis) C.; m. Carol Elaine Whitelaw, Apr. 1, 1960 (div. 1972); children—Sarah K., J. Maxwell. A.B. in English, Ga. State U., 1959, A.B. in Art, 1961; M.A. in Art, Fla. State U.-Tallahassee, 1963. Instr., U. Miami, Fla., 1963-64, Miami-Dade Community Coll., Miami, 1964-67; artist-in-residence Miami Art Ctr., 1967-69; prof. Fla. Internat. U., Miami, 1972—. Exhibitor numerous solo and group nat. and regional exhbns. Hand Hollow Found. fellow, 1982; State of Fla. Individual Artists' grantee, 1983; Fla. Internat. U. grantee, 1983. Office: Fla Internat U Tamiami Trail Miami FL 33156

COUPER, JAMES RILEY, chemical engineering educator; b. St. Louis, Dec. 10, 1925; s. James Galloway and Annetta (Riley) C.; m. Fanny D. Collins, Sept. 9, 1953 (div. May 1979); children—Geoffrey Collins, Kathleen Menzies; m. 2d, Maribelle Halverson, Aug. 11, 1979. Research chemist Presstite Engring. Co., St. Louis, 1950, Mol Portland Cement Co., St. Louis, 1950-51; sr. engr. Monsanto Co., St. Louis, 1952-58, prodn. supr., 1958-59; mem. faculty U. Ark., Fayetteville, 1959—, assoc. prof., 1959-65, prof., 1965—, head dept. chem. engring., 1968-79, adminstrv. asst. research coordinator, 1965-68; cons. in field. Served with USNR, 1944-46. Mem. Am. Inst. Chem. Engring., Am. Chem. Soc., Am. Soc. for Engring. Edn., Am. Assn. Cost Engrs., Soc. Rheology, Sigma Xi, Tau Beta Pi, Omicron Delta Kappa, Omega Chi Epsilon (nat. pres. 1982—), Alpha Chi Sigma, Sigma Chi. Episcopalian. Contbr. articles to profl. jours. Home: 2506 Sweetbriar Dr Fayetteville AR 72703 Office: Dept Chem Engring E-227 U Ark Fayetteville AR 72701

COURSEY, JOHN WILLIAM, anesthesiologist; b. Honolulu, Nov. 23, 1925; s. Richard Ray and Wilhelmina Antoinette (Hoffman) C.; children—John William, Timothy P., Michael P. B.S. in Animal Husbandry, U. Md., 1951, M.D., 1959. Diplomate Am. Bd. Anesthesiology. Intern, resident Lackland Air Force Hosp., Tex., 1959-63; commd. 2d lt., U.S. Air Force, 1958, advanced through grades to col., 1972; staff anesthesiologist USAF Hosp., Weisbaden, Germany, 1963-66, USAF Med. Center, Wright-Patterson AFB, Ohio, 1966-72, USAF Med. Ctr., Keesler AFB, Miss., 1972-76; ret., 1976; chief anesthesia service Gulf Coast Community Hosp., Biloxi, Miss., 1976—. Served with U.S. Army, 1944-47. Decorated Legion of Merit. Mem. Am. Soc. Anesthesiologists, Internat. Anesthesia Research Soc., Miss. Soc. Anesthesiologists, AMA. Republican. Roman Catholic. Address: 130 Alicia Dr Biloxi MS 39531

COURSON, JOHN EDWARD, state senator, insurance company executive; b. Augusta, Ga., Nov. 21, 1944; s. James W. and Mary C. (Harris) C.; m. Elizabeth Poinsett Exum, Apr. 1973; children—James Poinsett, Elizabeth Boykin. B.A., U. S.C., 1968. Exec. v.p. Keenan Ins. & Fin. Services. Fin. dir. S.C. Republican Party, 1969-75; sec., 1976-80, nat. committeeman for S.C. Rep. Nat. Committee, 1980—; chmn. campaign '80 for S.C.; Presdl. elector Rep., 1980, 1984; mem. S.C. Senate, 1984—; chmn. Re-elect Thurmond Com., 1984. Mem. United Way. Served with USMCR, 1968-74. Recipient Mounted Gold Elephant S.C. Republican Party, 1975, 80, 82; named Young Agt. of Yr., Ind. Ins. Agts. S.C., 1981. Mem. Am. Legion, Sigma Chi. Episcopalian. Clubs: Forest Lake, Tarantella, Columbia Ball, Palmetto. Avocations: tennis; politics. Office: Senate Office Bldg 606 Gressette Columbia SC 29202

COURT, LEONARD, lawyer, educator; b. Ardmore, Okla., Jan. 11, 1947; s. Leonard and Margaret Janet (Harvey) C.; m. JoAnn Dilleshaw, Sept. 2, 1967; children—Chris, Todd, Brooke. B.A., Okla. State U., 1969; J.D., Harvard U., 1972. Bar: Okla. 1973, U.S. Dist. Ct. (we. dist.) Okla. 1973, U.S. Dist. Ct. (no. dist.) Okla., 1978, U.S. Dist. Ct. (ea. dist.) Okla. 1983, U.S. Ct. Appeals (10th cir.) 1980, U.S. Ct. Mil. Appeals 1973., Assoc. Crowe & Dunlevy, Oklahoma City, Okla., 1977-81, ptnr., 1981—; adj. prof. Okla. U. Law Sch., Norman, 1984—; planning com. Annual Inst. Labor Law, S.W. Legal Found., Dallas, 1984—. Contbg. author: (supplement book) The Developing Labor Law, 1978, Employment Discrimination Law, 1983, Corporate Counsel's Annual, 1974. Chmn. bd. elders Meml. Christian Ch., Oklahoma City, 1980; cubmaster Last Frontier council Boy Scouts Am., 1984. Served to capt. USAF, 1973-77. Mem. Okla. State Univ. Bar Assn. (bd. dirs. 1980—), Oklahoma City C. of C. (mem. sports and recreation com. 1982—), Okla. State U. Alumni Assn. (bd. dirs. 1985—), Harvard Law Sch. Assn., ABA (labor and employment law sect. com. on devel. of law under Nat. Labor Relations Act, com. on EEO law, subcom. on substantive devels involving sex under Title VII, and subcom. of EEOC process Title VII coverage and multiple forums, litigation sect./employment and labor relations law com.), Okla. Bar Assn. (labor and employment law sect. council 1978-80, 82-84, chmn.-elect. 1984, labor law sect. speakers bur.), Okla. County Bar Assn., Fed. Bar Assn., Defence Research Inst. Okla. Assn. Defense Counsel. Office: Crowe & Dunlevy 20 N Broadway Oklahoma City OK 73102

COURTELIS, ALEC PANOS, real estate company executive; b. Alexandria, Egypt, Oct. 5, 1927, came to U.S., 1948; s. Panos John and Marie (Markidis) C.; m. Louise E. Hufstader, June 20, 1953; children—Pan Thomas, Kiki Lisa. B.S. in Civil Engring., U. Miami, 1955. Vice pres. Juriet & Assocs., Inc., Miami, Fla., 1955-59; pres., chmn. bd. Courtelis Co., Miami, Fla., 1959—; chmn. bd. TGIF Tex., 1979—, Courtelis Construction Co., Miami, Devcon Realty Corp., Miami, Ionian Corp., Miami, Univ. Lakes, Inc., Miami, Video Ventures Prodns., Inc.; pres. BriarWinds Corp., Courtelis Realty Co., Egholm Corp., Egholm Arabians, Inc., Town & Country Farms Corp., Ocala, Fla., Tennis Group, Inc., Miami, Falls Cts., Inc., Miami; dir. Skylake State Bank, Courtrust Assocs., Courtelis Capital Corp., Devcon Realty Corp., Devcon Internat. Corp., Cherry Grove, Ltd., Kislak Orgn., Gainesville Marketplace Assocs., Ltd., others; gen. ptnr. Reef Assocs. Ltd., Miami, Village Shoppes Assocs. Ltd., Miami. Trustee, Miami Children's Hosp. Found., 1982—; bd. dirs. Mercy Hosp. Found., 1982—, Arabian Horse Research Inst. and Hall of Fame; Armand Hammer United World Coll. of Am. West, 1983—; mem. pres. council U. Fla., 1977—; founder U. Miami, 1982—. Mem. Internat. Council Shopping Ctrs., ASCE, Fla. Engring. Soc., Nat. Assn. Home Builders, Mobile Home Mfrs. Assn., Greater Miami C. of C., South Dade C. of C., Ocala Arabian Breeders Soc. (dir.), Republican. Greek Orthodox. Clubs: Grove Isle, Ocala Jockey. Lodge: Elks. Home: 8880 SW 100 St Miami FL 33176 Office: 1101 Brickell Ave Suite 500 Miami FL 33131

COURTIN, ROBERT EDWIN, JR., banker, retired naval officer; b. New Orleans, Aug. 16, 1922; s. Robert Edwin and Sarah Elizabeth (Bartlett) C.; m. Margaret Elizabeth Baker, June 5, 1948; children—Amanda Margaret Courtin Myers, Sarah Baker Courtin-Hammond. B.A. in English, Tulane U., 1949; postgrad. Sch. Naval Intelligence, 1950-51. Commd. U.S. Navy, 1943, aviator, 1943; ret. capt., 1972; sr. v.p. Lakewood Bank and Trust Co., Dallas, 1972-82; sr. v.p. Energy Bank, Dallas, 1982—. Active, Dallas County Republican Men's Club, Men's Symphony Guild. Mem. Tex. Ind. Producers and Royalty Owners Assn., Phi Delta Theta. Presbyterian. Clubs: Army-Navy (Washington), Chapparal (Dallas). Office: Energy Bank 4849 Green Ville Ave Dallas TX 75206

COUTURE, JOHN ARNOLD, financial corporation executive; b. Adams, Mass., Apr. 28, 1943; s. Francis Euclid and Anne Mary (Chwalek) C.; m. Donna Goddard, Nov. 5, 1966; children—Heather Anne, John Goddard, Erin Amy. B.S. in Fin., Northeastern U., 1971; cert. Inst. Fin. Mgmt., Harvard Grad. Sch. Bus., 1973. With credit and loan div. State St. Bank and Trust Co., 1964-67; loan officer, v.p., exec. v.p., dir. Middlesex/Community Bank, Everett, Mass., 1967-73; v.p. fin. Amesbury Metal Div. Kendall Co. (Mass.), 1974-75; v.p. fin., treas., dir. U.S. Crane, Orlando, Fla., 1976-81; chmn., pres., chief exec. officer, dir. Triumph United Corp., Orlando, Fla., 1981—; dir. Media Brokers, Inc.; lectr. corp. fin. Am. Inst. Banking Sch. City councilman, Rochester, N.Y., 1974-75, co-chmn. Indsl. Devel. Commn., 1971-75. Mem. Constrn. Fin. Mgmt. Assn. Am. (del.). Republican. Roman Catholic. Home: 4909 Dorian Ave Orlando FL 32812 Office: 1217 McCoy Rd PO Box 30933 Orlando FL 32862

COUTURIAUX, PARIS, banker; b. Los Angeles, May 20, 1946; s. Clement and Marian (Bentley) C.; m. Helen Ruth McDonald, Apr. 17, 1947; children—Clay James, Zachary John, Wade Edward. Personnel officer Dekalb County Merit System, Decatur, Ga., 1970-73; personnel rep. Employers Ins. Tex., Dallas, 1973-74; dir. human resources Tex. Am. Bank, also Tex. Am. Bancshares Inc., Ft. Worth, 1974—; adj. prof. Tex. Christian U., Ft. Worth. Treas. Tarrant County chpt. Am. Heart Assn.; adult leader Boy Scouts Am. Served to 1st lt. U.S. Army, 1968-70; Vietnam. Decorated Bronze Star. Mem. Am. Soc. Personnel Adminstrn. (nat. dir.). Republican. Baptist. Author: Job Posting Guidebook, 1978.

COVENTON, EDWIN LLOYD, oil company executive, geological engineer; b. Ada, Okla., Oct. 11, 1928; s. William Telford and Daisy Hazel (Partain) C.; m. Dorothy Jean Stie, May 17, 1949 (div. Aug. 1981); 1 child, Cynthia Diane; m. Sharon Frances McCutchan, Oct. 2, 1982; children—Cyndy Holmes, Cathy Holmes, Brian Holmes. B.S., Okla. U., 1953. Registered profl. engr., Okla. Mgmt. trainee Western Co., Odessa, Tex., 1952, dist. engr., geologist Odessa, Wichita Falls and Ulysses, Kans., 1953-56; exploration geologist Eason Oil Co., Oklahoma City, 1957-66; sr. engr. Kerr-McGee, Oklahoma City, 1966-77; outside ops. mgr. Coastal Oil & Gas, Amarillo, Tex. and Denver, 1977-81; pres. Coventon Arrow Energy, Inc., Oklahoma City, 1981—. Co-inventor two zone hydraulic pumping unit, 1960. Curriculum adviser U. Kans., Liberal, 1956. Served as cpl. USMC, 1946-48. Republican. Baptist. Avocations: exotic and domestic birds; dog training; hunting; fishing; golf. Home: PO Box 868 1 Coventon Circle Blanchard OK 73010 Office: Coventon Arrow Energy Inc PO Box 868 Blanchard OK 73010

COVER, NELSON, JR., fund raising executive; b. Balt., July 31, 1947; s. Nelson and Isabel (Tunstall) C.; m. Gretchen Lee Chell, May 21, 1983. B.A., Johns Hopkins U., 1970, C.A.S., 1975; M.S., San Francisco State Coll., 1972. Assoc. dir. annual giving Johns Hopkins Instns., Balt., 1973-76, dir. annual giving, 1976-79; dir. med. ctr. devel. U. Chgo., 1979-80; dir. devel. The Washington Cathedral, Washington, 1980-82, The Am. Enterprise Inst., Washington, 1982-84; pres. The Sheridan Group, Arlington, Va., 1984—. Author: A Guide to Successful Phonathons, 1981 (best selling CASE Publ. 1981). Contbr. chpts. to books, articles to profl. jours. Mem. Nat. Soc. Fund Raising Execs. (v.p. for edn. 1982-84), Council for Advancement and Support of Higher Edn. (chmn. annual fund conf. 1978, 82), Nat. Assn. for Hosp. Devel. Episcopalian. Clubs: Johns Hopkins (Balt.); Princeton (N.Y.C.); St. Albans Tennis (Washington). Avocations: sailing, tennis, antique car restoration, creative writing, reading. Home: 2715 S Inge St Arlington VA 22202 Office: The Sheridan Group 2715 S Inge St Arlington VA 22202

COVER, NORMAN BERNARD, EDP adminstr.; b. Ephrata, Pa., Mar. 25, 1935; s. Barney Blainey and Chelta V. (Huff) C.; student Jacksonville U., 1955; m. Violet Hurmagene Winouski, Nov. 26, 1960; children—Brian Lee, Keith Alex. Tabulator operator State Farm Fire & Casualty Co., Bloomington, Ill., 1952-53, programming operator State Farm Mut. Auto Ins. Co., Jacksonville, Fla., 1954-56, shift supr., EDP, 1957-61, asst. supt. EDP, State Farm Ins. Co., Winter Haven, Fla., 1962-67, EDP supt., 1968-78, data processing mgr., 1979—. Chmn. data processing adv. com. Polk Community Coll., 1976—. Sponsor Winter Haven High Sch. Cotillion Club, 1982—. Cert. in data processing. Fellow Data Processing Mgmt. Assn. (S.E. regional treas. 1974-75, S.E. regional v.p. 1975-77, internat. v.p. 1977-78, dir. spl. interest group cert. data processors 1978-80, v.p. 1981, pres. 1982 internat. dir. Polk County chpt. 1982-83, chmn. by-laws com. 1983—, past presidents com. 1970—, Individual

Performance awards 1972-82), SAR. Democrat. Club: Elks, Cypress Gardens Sertoma (chmn. Stamp Out Crime com. 1975-80, dir. 1980-82, v.p. 1983-84, sec. 1984-85, pres. 1985-86), Winter Haven Rifle. Home: 1825 6th St SE Winter Haven FL 33880 Office: 3425 Lake Alfred Rd Winter Haven FL 33888

COVERDELL, PAUL D., state senator. Mem. Ga. Senate. Pres., Nat. Republican Legis. Assn. Office: Ga Senate State Capitol Atlanta GA 30334*

COVERT, J. A., educational administrator. Supt. of schs. Beaumont, Tex. Office: Box 672 Beaumont TX 77704*

COVINGTON, CECIL LYONS, management consultant, educator; b. Dallas, Nov. 21, 1911; s. William Roper and Mary Eliza (Lyons) C.; A.B. cum laude, Baylor U., 1933; LL.B., George Washington U., 1939, M.P.L., S.J.D., 1940; m. Phyllis Ruth McIntyre, Feb. 17, 1943 (dec.); 1 son, Mark Roper; m. 2d, Ruth Bratton Faust. Adminstrv. asst. PWA Washington, 1933-40; clk. to Senator Tom Connally of Tex., 1940-41; spl. asst. on contracts OSRD, 1941-43; spl. asst. to dir. tng., facilities service VA, in charge review contracts negotiated with all schs. and colls. Ark., La., Okla., Miss., Kans., Tex., Mo., 1946-53; contract adminstr. Texas Instruments, Inc., 1953-56, controller apparatus div., 1956-58, mgr. govt. contracts adminstrn., 1958-61, mgr. govt. contracts and banking relations, 1962-63, mgr. govt. relations, 1964-66, adminstrv. asst. to chmn. bd., 1967, contracts mgr. govt. products div., 1968, mgr. govt. relations equipment group, 1969-80; affiliate cons. Manco Realty-Investments, Inc., 1981; pres. Manco Bus. Mgmt. Services, Inc., 1982; vis. prof. Grad. Sch. Mgmt., U. Dallas, dir. M.B.A. program in acquisition and contract mgmt., 1983—. Served as lt. USNR, 1944-46. Mem. Am. Arbitration Assn. (comml. panel), Fin. Execs. Inst. (govt. bus. com.), Nat. Security Indsl. Assn. (procurement adv. com.), NAM (nat. def. com.), Sigma Nu Phi. Baptist. Clubs: Chandlers Landing Yacht, Dallas Woods and Waters, Dallas Flyfishers. (Dallas); Twin Points (Hot Springs, Ark.). Home: 6317 Pemberton Dallas TX 75230 Office: Grad Sch Mgmt Univ Dallas Irving TX 75061

COVINGTON, VICTOR THOMAS, corporate executive; b. Tampa, Fla., Feb. 4, 1919; s. Victor Thomas and Margaret Pearl (Browning) C.; m. Marcia Hughes, Sept. 5, 1949; children—Margaret Ann, Peter James, Scott Hughes, Mary Constance. B.S., U. Ala., 1946; M.B.A., Harvard U., 1950. Acct., Freeport Sulphur Co., New Orleans, 1946-48; credit analyst State St. Trust Co., Boston, 1950-52, asst. treas., 1952-55, comml. loan officer, 1955-56; credit mgr. Am. Enka Corp., Enka, N.C., 1956-57, asst. treas., 1957-66, adminstrv. asst. to div. v.p., gen. mgr., 1966-67, asst. controller, 1967-70; asst. controller Akzona Inc., Asheville, N.C., 1970-74, asst. treas., 1974—; instr. personal fin. mgmt. U.N.C., Asheville, 1981-83. Served with U.S. Army, 1942-46, ETO. Mem. Res. Officers Assn. U.S. (treas. Western N.C. chpt. 1961—), Ret. Officers Assn. Republican. Roman Catholic. Clubs: Harvard (N.Y.C.); Country (Asheville), Asheville Downtown City. Home: 53 Kingwood Pl Asheville NC 28804 Office: 1 Park Sq Asheville NC 28801

COWAN, CATHARINE LOUISE, psychology educator; b. N.Y.C., May 16, 1946; d. Rufus Bruce and Louise Catharine (Babel) Cowan. B.S. in Psychology, Western Ill. U., 1968; M.A. in Child Devel., U. Iowa, 1971, Ph.D. in Child Psychology, 1973. Research asst. dept. psychology Western Ill. U., 1967-68; research asst. Inst. Child Behavior and Devel., U. Iowa, 1968-69, 70-72; asst. prof. psychology U. Maine, Orono, 1972-76; faculty assoc. Exceptional Child Research Inst., Orono, 1974-76; editorial cons. Harper and Row Coll. Press, 1974-76; asst. prof. psychology Tex. Wesleyan Coll., Ft. Worth, 1976-80, assoc. prof., 1980—, chmn. dept., 1984—. Nat. Inst. Child Health and Devel. trainee, 1969; recipient Faculty Summer Research award U. Maine, 1975; Faculty Recognition award Tex. Wesleyan Coll., 1980. Mem. Am. Psychol. Assn., Soc. for Research in Child Devel., Psi Chi. Home: 3851 Meadowbrook Dr Fort Worth TX 76103 Office: Tex Wesleyan Coll Fort Worth TX 76105

COWART, D. R., insurance company executive; b. 1919. With Morrison Inc., Mobile, Ala., 1936—, exec. v.p., 1949, pres., chief exec. officer, 1968-79, chmn. bd., chief exec. officer, 1981—. Address: Morrison Inc 4721 Morrison Dr Mobile AL 36625*

COWART, SAMUEL, entrepreneur; b. New Orleans, Feb. 12, 1948; s. Kinder C. and Irmatine D. (Briddges) C.; B.S., So. U., 1973; M.B.A., Loyola U., New Orleans, 1981; m. Mary L. Frugé, May 1, 1967; 1 son, Roman S. Coordinator/counselor, career advisor Total Community Action, New Orleans, 1970-74; vocation counselor Orleans Parish Criminal Sheriffs Office, 1974-76; adminstrv. officer, div. youth services State of La., 1976-79; mgmt. analyst U.S. Dept. Commerce, 1979—; pres. Shamrock Prodns., Inc., 1979—; sr. personnel placement specialist New Orleans Ednl. Talent Search, 1981-82; tax examiner IRS, 1983—. Mem. La. Vo-Ed Adv. Council, 1978—, Metro Area Commn., 1972—. Recipient several awards. Mem. La. Econs. Assn., Met. Bankers Assn., So. U. Alumni Assn., Grambling U. Alumni Assn., Direct Sales Assn., New Orleans Bus. League, PUSH Internat. Trade Ctr., Black Music Assn., Advt. Specialty Inst., Specialty Advt. Assn. Democrat. Baptist.

COWDEN, WEBSTER LYTER, JR., apparel manufacturing company executive; b. Kansas City, Mo., Dec. 9, 1941; s. Webster Lyter and Callie (Taylor) C.; m. Susan Sawyer, Jan. 29, 1966; children—Webster Lyter, Catherine Taylor. Student Washington and Lee U., 1960-61; B.A., Transylvania U., 1964. Mfg. trainee Cowden Mfg. Co., Lexington, Ky., 1965-67, prodn. planner, 1967-70, v.p. merchandising and distbn., 1970-75, exec. v.p., 1975-80, pres., 1980—, also dir. Pres., Lexington Hearing and Speech Ctr., 1982. Served with U.S. Army N.G., 1964-65. Mem. Am. Apparel Mfrs. Assn. Republican. Presbyterian. Clubs: Lexington Country, Lexington; Idle Hour Country; Lafayette; Ducks Unlimited. Home: 2001 Hume Rd Lexington KY 40516 Office: 300 New Circle Rd Lexington KY 40505

COWELL, FRED J., hospital administrator; b. Louisville, May 22, 1939; s. and Nora C. C.; m. Jean Shafer, Nov. 23, 1972. B.S., W.Va. U., 1967. Asst. adminstr. Monongalia Gen. Hosp., Morgantown, W.Va., 1963-67; with Jackson Meml. Hosp., Miami, Fla., 1967—, dep. exec. dir., 1972, dir. hosp. ops., 1974—, exec. dir., 1976—; pres. Public Health Trust of Dade County, 1977—; bd. dirs. Health Systems Agy. South Fla., Inc. Mem. Fla. Hosp. Cost Containment Bd., 1979—, Fla. Task Force on Competition and Consumer Choices in Health Care, 1983. Mem. Am. Hosp. Assn., South Fla. Hosp. Assn. (dir.), Fla. Hosp. Assn., Council Teaching Hosps. (adminstrv. bd. 1980-82), Greater Miami C. of C. (trustee). Methodist. Home: 15920 Kingsmoor Way Miami Lakes FL 33014 Office: 1611 NW 12th Ave Miami FL 33136

COWGILL, BRUCE HAYDEN, ceramic engineer, electrical products company executive; b. Sewickley, Pa., Jan. 15, 1945; s. Bernard Francis and Lilye (Hayden) C.; m. Patricia Ann Diehl, Aug. 12, 1967; children—Bruce William, Michael Bernard. B.S. in Ceramic Engring., Alfred U., 1967. With Gen. Electric Co., Cleve., 1967—, various positions, 1967-69, project leader photoflash, 1969-70, shop ops. supr., 1970-73, supr. program planning, 1973-75, mfg. adminstr., 1975-79, plant mgr. electronics parts mfg. facility, 1979-81, plant mgr. components mfg. facility, 1981-83, mgr. mfg. base product line, 1983-84, mgr. ceramics products plant, 1984—. Mem. Am. Ceramic Soc., Elfun Soc., Delta Sigma Phi. Episcopalian. Clubs: Exchange, Jaycees. Lodge: Rotary. Office Gen Elec Ceramics PO Box 89 Laurens SC 29360

COWLES, ROGER WILLIAM, government audit executive; b. Ft. Madison, Iowa, July 5, 1945; s. Arthur William and Enid Francis (Smith) C. B.B.A. cum laude, Tex. Wesleyan Coll., 1968; M.A., Central Mich. U., 1980. Cert. cost analyst, Va. Contract auditor Def. Contract Audit Agy., Ft. Worth, 1967-76, course mgr., Memphis, 1976-78, program mgr. hdqrs., Alexandria, Va., 1978-80, chief mgmt. info. branch, 1980-81, chief spl. audits, 1982—; mem. congl. staff U.S. Congress, Washington, 1981-82. Creator toothpick sculpture (Spl. Merit award 1975). Contbr. articles to profl. jours. Mem. Assn. Govt. Accts. (facilitator 1985, Tng. Program award 1981), Inst. Cost Analysis, Mgmt. Devel. Program. Republican. Methodist. Avocations: bowling; golf; computer technology. Office: Def Contract Audit Agy Cameron Station Room 4A140 Alexandria VA 22304

COWLES, THOMAS CHARLES, manufacturing company executive; b. Grand Rapids, Mich., June 15, 1943; s. Newell Augustus and Marion Elizabeth (Wood) C.; m. Ruth Elaine Brown, Nov. 1, 1963 (div. 1982); children—Lynn Anne, Dennis Joseph; m. 2d, Dorothy Lu Voisey, Feb. 16, 1983. B.S. in Indsl. Edn. and Tech. with high honors, Tarleton State U., 1973, M.B.A., 1977. Mgr., Fibergrate Corp., Stephenville, Tex., 1975-79, mgr., 1980—; mgr. mfg. Norton Co., Stephenville, Tex., 1979-80. Served with USAF, 1961-71. Mem. Am. Soc. Tng. and Devel., National Rifle Assn. Republican. Methodist. Lodge: Toastmasters Internat. (pres.). Home: 303 Rosebud Dr Stephenville TX 76401 Office: PO Box 208 Stephenville TX 76401

COWLEY, ALFRED HILTON, JR., real estate developer; b. Miami, Fla., Mar. 3, 1945; s. Alfred Hilton and Doris Elaine (Smith) C.; m. Myra Anita Jane Miller, Jan. 30, 1977; 1 dau., Kristin Elaine. B.A., Columbia U., 1967. Investment banker Counts & Co., Atlanta, 1968-71, W.E. Hutton & Co., Atlanta, 1971-72; builder, developer Cowley & Assocs., Atlanta, 1972-77; developer CCL & Assocs., Atlanta, 1977— now mng. ptnr. devel. and investment fin.; chmn. bd. Dayton Bank & Trust, Dayton, Tenn. Bd. dirs. Adventist Adoption and Family Services, Portland, Oreg., 1981-83; trustee William Jennings Bryan Coll., Dayton. Republican. Seventh Day Adventist. Home: 9310 Huntcliff Trace NW Atlanta GA 30338 Office: CCL & Assocs 2060 E Exchange Pl Atlanta GA 30084

COWLING, DAN CAMPBELL, III, advertising executive; b. Fayetteville, Ark., Mar. 5, 1949; s. Dan Campbell and Carrolle (Hickman) C.; m. Marilyn Susan Webb, Mar. 17, 1973; 1 dau., Shannon Lee. B.A., U. Ark., 1971, M.A., 1973. Teaching asst. U. Ark., Fayetteville, 1971-72; account exec. S.M. Brooks Advt., Little Rock, 1973-75; v.p. Brooks/Pittman Advt., Hot Springs, Ark., 1975-76; v.p., dir. account services Cranford Johnson Hunt & Assocs., Little Rock, 1976-82; dir. client services Mangan Rains Ginnaven, Holcomb, Little Rock, 1983—; guest instr. U. Ark., Little Rock, 1980-81. Bd. dirs. Friends of KLRE, 1981-83, Pulaski County Literacy Council, 1980-83. Mem. S.W. Assn. Advt. Agys. (dir. 1981-82). Republican. Presbyterian. Office: 320 W Capitol Ave Suite 911 Little Rock AR 72201

COX, ARTHUR CHARLES, couture buyer; b. Wauseon, Ohio, Aug. 4, 1948; s. Casper Lee and Blanche Cecelia (Bornschlegell) C. A. Architecture, U. Toledo, 1968, B.B.A., 1971. Asst. buyer LaSalle's (Macy), Toledo, 1971-72; sales mgr. Bonwit Teller, N.Y.C., 1972-75; stores mgr. Courreges, N.Y.C., Palm Beach Fla., 1975-78; dir. couture Sakowitz Co., Houston, 1978-83; dir. fashion Esther Wolf Co., Houston, 1983-84; couture buyer, 1984—. Mem. The Fashion Group. Phi Kappa Psi (historian Toledo chpt. 1968-71), Phi Theta Kappa. Republican. Roman Catholic. Club: Greater Palm Beach Symphony (charter mem.) Office: 1702 S Post Oak Blvd Houston TX 77056

COX, BETSY, nurse, administrator; b. Houston, Aug. 26, 1951; d. Robert Earl and Marjorie (Domengeaux) C. L.V.N., Schreiner Coll., Kerrville, Tex., 1974; B.S. in Nursing, U. Tex.-Austin, 1977; cert. emergency med. tech., Kerr County Emergency Med. Services, Kerrville, 1983. Nurse ICU-CCU, Sid Peterson Meml. Hosp., Kerrville, 1974-75; nurse Camp Waldemar, Hunt, Tex., 1977; surgeon's asst. H.E. Kilgore, M.D., Kerrville, 1977-78; charge nurse operating room Bexar County Hosp., San Antonio, 1978; mem. open heart team Baptist Meml. Hosp., Little Rock, 1978; yacht tour dir. Viking of Kos, Athens, Greece, 1981; continuing edn. dir. emergency med. services Cynro, Inc., Kerrville, 1982—; nurse emergency room Sid Peterson Meml. Hosp., Kerrville, 1982—. Mem. Internat. Oceanographic Found., Emergency Dept. Nurses Assn., Kappa Alpha Theta. Republican. Episcopalian. Home: 1407 Vesper Dr Kerrville TX 78028 Office: Cynro Inc 501 Lois St Kerrville TX 78028

COX, CARSON CLAY, III, optometrist; b. Thomasville, N.C., Aug. 26, 1953; s. Carson Clay and Pauline Phillips (Walker) C.; m. Valerie Kay Townsend, June 24, 1984. B.A. in Zoology, U. N.C., 1975; M.Ed., U. N.C., 1981; B.S., O.D., Pa. Coll. Optometry, 1981. Cert. optometrist, Okla., N.C. Asst. prof. Northeastern State U. Coll. Optometry, Tahlequah, Okla., 1981-83, dir. pathology, 1981-83; practice optometry Eastern Okla. Eye Clinic, Inc., Tahlequah, 1982—; cons. council on clin. edn. Am. Optometric Assn., St. Louis, 1985; lectr. nat. continuing edn. confs. Mem. Tahlequah Arts council, 1985, 85. Fellow Am. Acad. Optometry; mem. Tahlequah C. of C., Cherokee Nat. Hist. Soc. Republican. Methodist. Lodge: Rotary. Avocations: bicycling; skiing; tennis; photography. Home: 1200 N Cedar Ave Tahlequah OK 74464 Office: Eastern Okla Eye Clinic Inc 200 Harris Circle Tahlequah OK 74464

COX, CLARK, journalist; b. Jefferson, N.C., Feb. 21, 1943; s. Scott Joseph and Jaunita Geneva (Weiss) C.; grad. high sch.; m. Brenda Sue Bowers, Oct. 30, 1971 (div.); m. 2d, Helen Jeanette Parks, June 9, 1979. Reporter, Watauga Democrat, Boone, N.C., 1963; editor Blowing Rocket, Blowing Rock, N.C., 1964, Marshville (N.C.) Home, 1965, Henry County Jour., Bassett, Va., 1966-67; reporter Messenger and Intelligencer, Wadesboro, N.C., 1969-71; sports editor Richmond County Daily Jour., Rockingham, N.C., 1971-73, investigative reporter, 1974-77, asst. editor, 1977—; freelance journalist, 1967-69, 73-74. Active Big Bros. Am. Recipient Sport reporting award N.C. Press Assn., 1971, 72, 1st place investigative reporting award, 1974, 1st place feature writing award, 1983, 1st place criticism award, 1985. Democrat. Author: (play) The Justice of Our Cause, 1976; (biography) Gen. Henry William Harrington, 1979; (history) Rockingham: 1784-1984, 1984. Home: 326 Curtis Dr Rockingham NC 28379 Office: PO Box 1056 Rockingham NC 28379

COX, DONALD EMERY, chemical engineer; b. Joplin, Mo., June 12, 1921; s. William Emery and Vera Leona (Hall) C.; B.S. in Chem. Engring., Okla. State U., 1943; m. B. Marie Chauncey, July 3, 1943; children—Albert Emery, Anita Emily, Raymond Emery. With chem. div. PPG Industries, Corpus Christi, Tex., 1943-78; v.p., gen. mgr. Refinery Terminal Fire Co., Corpus Christi, 1978—; cons. environ. engr., 1978—. Bd. dirs. Community Devel. Corp. of Corpus Christi, v.p., 1978-79; bd. dirs. Lower Nueces River Water Supply Dist., also pres., 1972—; mem. Coastal Bend Council Govts., 1966—, chmn., 1966-68, exec. com., 1966—; mem. Corpus Christi Zoning and Planning Commn., 1959-63; environ. quality com. Council Govts., 1972—, chmn., 1972-76, 78-83; adv. com. Nueces River Basin Water Planning, vice chmn., 1977-78; trustee Corpus Christi YWCA, 1970-76, pres., 1974-76; bd. dirs. Gulf Coast council Boy Scouts Am., 1985—. Recipient Community Service award PPG Industries, 1973, named Corporate Citizen of Year, 1976; registered profl. engr. Fellow Am. Inst. Chem. Engrs. (chmn. Coastal Bend sect. 1978, Service to Society award 1978); mem. Am. Chem. Soc., Tex. Soc. Profl. Engrs. (Outstanding Engr. for region 1985), Corpus Christi C. of C., Air Pollution Control Assn. Presbyterian. Clubs: Cactus and Succulent (pres. 1981), S. Tex. Engrs. Patentee in field. Home: 369 W Saxet Dr Corpus Christi TX 78408 Office: PO Box 4162 Corpus Christi TX 78469

COX, FLOYD BROOKS, JR., dentist; b. Gallipolis, Ohio, Feb. 23, 1920; s. Floyd Brooks and Mary Adele (Wallman) C.; student W.Va. U., 1938-41; D.D.S., U. Mich., 1944; postgrad. U. Ala., 1946-47; m. Marjorie Thomas Ballengee, Aug. 17, 1949; 1 dau., Mary Elizabeth. Staff dentist Manhattan Project, Oak Ridge, 1944-46; pvt. practice dentistry, Morgantown, W.Va., 1948—; mem. staff Monongalia Gen. Hosp., Morgantown. Bd. dirs. Monongalia chpt. ARC, 1954-62, chmn., 1961; bd. dirs. Park Hills Community Assn., 1962-63. Served with USPHS, 1946-48; capt. USAF, 1952-53. Mem. ADA (life), W.Va. Monongalia County dental assn. (pres. 1958), Am. Endodontic Soc., SR, U.S. Power Squadron (charter), U.S. Pony Clubs, No. W.Va. Automobile Assn. (dir., vice chmn.), Psi Omega. Roman Catholic. Clubs: Elks (life); Suncrest Garden. Home: 32 Bates Rd Morgantown WV 26505 Office: 344 Spruce St Morgantown WV 26505

COX, FRANK LEE, insurance agency executive; b. Dothan, Ala., July 13, 1952; s. Robert H. Cox, Curtis B. (stepfather) and Betty (Adams) Cox Williams. B.S., U. Ala., 1974; postgrad. Samford U., 1974-75. Owner, mgr. Cox Ins. Agy., Arab, Ala., 1976—; city dir. AmSouth Bank, N.A., Arab, 1984—. Bd. dirs. Marshall County ARC, Ala., 1980—. Mem. Ala. Ind. Agts. Assn., Arab C. of C. (v.p. 1985). Baptist. Lodges: Rotary (pres. 1984-85), Kiwanis (sec. 1977-79). Avocations: fishing; tennis; antiques. Home: 901 8th Ave NE PO Box 385 Arab AL 35016 Office: Frank Lee Cox Ins Agy 19 1st Ave NW Box 525 Arab AL 35016

COX, GLENN ANDREW, JR., petroleum company executive; b. Sedalia, Mo., Aug. 6, 1929; s. Glenn Andrew and Ruth Lonsdale (Atkinson) C.; m. Veronica Cecelia Martin, Jan. 3, 1953; children—Martin Stuart, Grant Andrew, Cecelia Ruth. B.B.A., So. Methodist U., 1951. With Phillips Petroleum Co., Bartlesville, Okla., 1956—, asst. to chmn. operating com., 1973-74, v.p. mgmt. info. and control, 1974-80, exec. v.p., 1980-85, pres., chief operating officer, 1985—, dir., 1982—; dir. Banc Okla. Corp.; exec. bd. Center Internat. Bus., Dallas. Bd. dirs. Cherokee Area council Boy Scouts Am., 1977—; bd. curators Central Meth. Coll., Fayette, Mo., 1985—. Served as pilot USAF, 1951-55. Mem. Am. Petroleum Inst. (dir., mem. budget adv. com.), Bartlesville Area C. of C. (pres. 1978). Methodist. Clubs: Hillcrest Country, Bartlesville Kiwanis. Office: 18 Phillips Bldg Bartlesville OK 74004

COX, HOLLIS UTAH, veterinarian, microbiologist; b. Holdenville, Okla., Mar. 4, 1944; s. Hollis Roy and Molinda Edline (Powell) C.; B.S., Okla. State U., 1965, D.V.M., 1967; Ph.D., La. State U., 1973; m. Debra Dawn Campbell, Dec. 4, 1976; children—Lindy Belle, Hollis Utah, Matthew Christopher, Lauren Dawn. Pvt. vet. med. practice, Choctaw, Okla., 1969-70; project veterinarian, instr. NIH-La. State U., Baton Rouge, 1970-73; asst. prof. microbiology Auburn (Ala.) U., 1973-75; asso. prof. vet. bacteriology La. State U., Baton Rouge, 1975-81, prof., 1981—, chief clin. diagnostic services, 1980—; cons. to pvt. vet. practices, 1975—. Campaign chmn. for vets. United Way, 1978. Served to capt. USAF, 1967-69; Vietnam. Diplomate Am. Coll. Vet. Microbiologists; cert. specialist in microbiology Am. Acad. Microbiology, Am. Soc. Clin. Pathologists. Mem. Am., La., Baton Rouge Area (pres. 1980), vet. med. assns., Am. Assn. Vet. Med. Colls., Am. Soc. Microbiology, Parklyn Chase Civic Assn., Vietnam Vets. Am., Sigma Xi, Phi Zeta, Phi Kappa Phi, Phi Eta Sigma, Alpha Psi. Episcopalian. Clubs: La. State U. Union, Masons, Shriners, Rosicrucian Order. Contbr. articles to profl. jours. Home: 5131 Butter Creek Ln #2d Baton Rouge LA 70809 Office: Dept of Veterinary Microbiology Sch Veterinary Medicine Louisiana State University Baton Rouge LA 70803

COX, J. B., geologist; b. Groesbeck, Tex., July 16, 1926; s. James Bradley and Mattie Golda (Prather) C.; m. Evelyn Dean Johnston, Sept. 5, 1948; children—Karen Evette, Trina Lynette. Student in Naval Sci., Okla. U., 1945-46; B.S. in Petroleum Geology, Tex. Tech. U., 1949. Cert. profl. geologist, Tex. Adminstrv. staff geologist So. Prodn., Midland-Ft. Worth, Tex., 1949-56; dist. geologist Oil Res. Corp., Houston, 1956-59; chief geologist Commonworth Oil Co., Houston, 1959-61; adminstrv. mgr. Fluor Corp., 1961-73; v.p. adminstrn. Lubbock Christian Coll., Tex., 1974; mgr. devel. INEXCO, 1974-77; chief geologist Transco Oil, 1977-80; mgr. exploration Coral Petroleum, 1980-82, Bill J. Barbee Petroleum Exploration, Houston, 1982—; cons., Houston, 1961-73; Served to lt. USN, 1943-46. Mem. Am. Assn. Petroleum Geologist, West Tex. Geol. Soc., Corpus Christi Geol. Soc., Am. Assn. Profl. Geologists, Administrv. Mgmt. Soc. (pres. 1972-73). Republican. Mem. Ch. of Christ. Home: 12834 Tennis St Houston TX 77099 Office: Bill J Barbee Petroleum Exploration 4120 Southwest Freeway Houston TX 77027

COX, J. MACKLIN, petroleum geologist; b. Richmond, Ky., Sept. 13, 1957; s. James M. and Betty D. (Pack) C.; m. Sharon Lee Pence, June 11, 1983. B.S. in Geology, Eastern Ky. U., 1981, M.S., 1983. Geologist in coal Alan K. Stagg & Assoc., Charleston, W.Va., 1981-82; geologist in petroleum Ohio Ky. Oil Corp., Lexington, 1984—. Contbr. articles to profl. jours. NSF research grantee, 1982; Service Assistantship grantee Eastern Ky. U., 1982. Mem. Am. Assn. Petroleum Geologists, Green River Archeol. Soc., Sigma Gamma Epsilon. Avocations: amateur archaeologist. Home: 3418 Greenlawn Lexington KY 40503 Office: Ohio KY Oil Corp 3060 Harrodsburg Rd Lexington KY 40503

COX, JAMES CLARENCE, hospital administrator; b. Milledgeville, Ga., Oct. 3, 1929; s. Clarence Goolsby and Mary Ruth (Edwards) C.; m. Avis Martin, July 5, 1952 (div. Jan. 1973); children—Laura Cathryn, Lisa Ruth Cox Conn, James Clarence, Jr.; m. Elaine Nichols, Nov. 29, 1975; stepchildren—Jan Stacks, Gregory Stacks. A.B., Mercer U., 1949; cert. in hosp. adminstrn. Ga. State U., 1964; M.P.A., Memphis State U., 1984. Hosp. adminstr. Coll. St. Hosp., Macon, Ga., 1968-74; staff adminstr. Charter Med. Corp., Macon, 1974-76; hosp. adminstr. Peninsula Ctr., Louisville, 1976-78; controller Howard Meml. Hosp., Biloxi, Miss., 1978-80; hosp. adminstr. Carolinas Hosp. and Health Services, Charlotte, N.C., 1980-81, Community Hosp. of Bolivar, Tenn., 1981—. Mem. adminstrv. bd. First United Meth. Ch., Bolivar, 1984—. Mem. Am. Coll. Hosp. Adminstrs., West Tenn. Hosp. Council (pres. 1984-86). Republican. Methodist. Lodge: Rotary (pres. 1984-85). Avocations: gardening; fishing; hunting; tennis. Office: Community Hosp of Bolivar PO Box C Bolivar TN 38008

COX, JAMES OLIVER, III, public relations agency executive; b. Houston, Nov. 13, 1946; s. James Oliver and Mary Jane (Byrd) C.; B.A. in Journalism, U. Houston, 1970; m. Barbara Ann Roose, Sept. 28, 1979; children—Ben, Chris. Vice pres. O'Neill Price Anderson Fouchard, Inc., Houston, 1972-74; v.p. S/C Communications, Houston, 1974-76; exec. v.p. Mel Anderson Communications, Inc., Houston, 1976-80; pres. James Cox, Inc., Houston, 1980-83; exec. v.p., gen. mgr. Daniel J. Edelman, Inc., Houston, 1983—; guest lectr. journalism, U. Houston, 1978-82. Mem. adminstrv. bd. 1st United Meth. Ch. Served with Army N.G., 1970-72; USAR, 1972-76. Mem. Public Relations Soc. Am. (accredited; mem. Counselor's Acad.), Forum Club. Republican. Club: Quail Valley Country. Home: 2014 Glenn Lakes Dr Missouri City TX 77459 Office: 9896 Bissonnet/Two Suite 490 Houston TX 77036

COX, JOHN CARROLL, engineering executive; b. Greenville, S.C., June 2, 1933; s. John Abner and Eva Lucille (Wrenn) C.; m. Jo Evelyn Snyder, Oct. 16, 1955; children—Faith, Lynn, Keith, Ken. B.S., in Archtl. Engring., Clemson U., 1955. Lic. profl. engr. S.C., N.C., Va., Ga., Fla., N.Y., Pa., N.H., Okla., Calif., Ariz. Structural designer Lockwood Greene Engrs., Inc., Spartanburg, S.C., 1955-60, structural group leader, 1960-66, structural dept. mgr., 1966-73, v.p., chief engr., 1973, corp. dir., 1980—. Mem. civil engring. adv. bd. Clemson U., 1976. Served with U.S. Army, 1957-58. Recipient AIA award as outstanding grad. in archtl. engring., 1955. Fellow ASCE; mem. Am. Concrete Inst. (pres. Carolinas chpt. 1976), Prestressed Concrete Inst., Cons. Engrs. S.C. Address: Box 491 Spartanburg SC 29304

COX, JOHN THOMAS, JR., lawyer; b. Shreveport, La., Feb. 9, 1943; s. John Thomas and Gladys Virginia (Canterbury) C.; B.S., La. State U., 1965, J.D., 1968; m. Tracey Lou Tanquary, Aug. 27, 1966; children—John Thomas III, Stephen Lewis. Asso. firm Sanders, Miller, Downing & Kean, Baton Rouge, 1968-70; asso. firm Blanchard, Walker, O'Quin & Roberts, Shreveport, La., 1970-71, partner, 1971—; dir. So. Saw Co., Inc., Shreveport; mem. adv. bd. La. Law Inst., 1969—; guest lectr. bus. law Centenary Coll. La., 1973-83. Served with AUS, 1963-70. Recipient Valley Forge Freedom Found. award, 1962. Mem. Am., La., Shreveport bar assns., La. Defense Lawyers Assn., Shreveport C. of C. (mem. com. on indsl. devel. 1975-—), Order of Coif, Phi Kappa Phi, Omicron Delta Kappa. Democrat. Presbyn. (elder 1977—). Clubs: Rotary (dir. 1979-80), Country, Shreveport, Pierremont Oaks, (Shreveport). Home: 555 Dunmoreland Dr Shreveport LA 71106 Office: PO Drawer 1126 Shreveport LA 71163

COX, JOHN WILLIAM, architect, educator; b. Cleve., Jan. 10, 1950; s. Nelson Henry and Margaret Elizabeth (Negrelli) C.; m. Mary Jo Tims, Dec. 17, 1977; children—Shaun William, Elyssa Marie. B.S., Kent State U., 1974; M.Arch., U. Mich., 1975. Design asst. Richard Fleischman Architects, Cleve., 1975-76; design asst. Don Hisaka and Assocs., Cleve., 1976-78; designer Caudill Rowlett Scott, Houston, 1979-81; sr. designer Pierce Goodwin Alexander, Houston, 1981-84; pres. John Cox Design Assocs., Inc., Houston, 1984—; lectr. U. Mich.; mem. faculty Sch. Architecture, U. Houston, 1983—; design juror Rice U., Kent State U., Tex. A&M U. Recipient Donaghy award excellence in design, 1974; Innovations in Housing citation of merit, 1981. Mem. Rice Design Alliance, AIA. Designer of housing projects, comml. and instnl. projects throughout the U.S. Home: 11811 S Little John Circle Houston TX 77071 Office: PO Box 61541 Houston TX 77208-1541

COX, LEWIS FRANKLIN, pharmacist, air force officer; b. Tallahassee, Dec. 26, 1949; s. William Franklin and Sara Frances (Lewis) C.; m. Stephanie Pamela Smiley, Dec. 27, 1980; 1 child, William Hunter. B.S. in Pharmacy, Auburn U., 1975; M.S. in Systems Mgmt., U. So. Calif., 1981. Mem. staff, clin. pharmacist Huntsville Hosp., Ala., 1976-78; commd. capt. U.S. Air Force, 1978, advanced through grades to maj., 1985; chief pharm. services U.S. Air Force Hosp. Loring, Maine, 1978-81, Kunsan, Korea, 1981-82, chief med. readiness, 1981-82; chief sterile products U.S. Air Force Hosp. Wilford Hall, Lackland AFB, Tex., 1982—. Mem. Central Tex. Soc. Hosp. Pharmacists, Am. Soc. Hosp. Pharmacists. Baptist. Avocations: coin collecting; diving.

COX, MARILYN ALLSBROOK, educator; b. Conway, S.C., Sept. 15, 1954; d. Albert Biscoe and Bobbie Marilyn (Hamilton) Allsbrook; m. Tony Keith Cox, Dec. 16, 1983; 1 son, Tony Keith. B.A., U. S.C., 1975, M.A., 1980. Tchr.

Horry County Schs., North Myrtle Beach, S.C., 1976-80; tchr. piano, Loris, S.C., 1980-82; tchr. adult edn. Horry County Schs., Loris, 1980-82, elem. tchr., 1980—; tutor in field. Pianist, Presbyterian Ch., 1970—; region coordinator Jenrette for Congress campaign, 1972; coordinator North Myrtle Beach council Girl Scouts Am., 1975, March of Dimes, 1976; mem. PTA. U. S.C. scholar, 1975. Mem. Horry County Edn. Assn., S.C. Edn. Assn., NEA. Democrat. Club: Women of Ch. (Loris) (historian 1984—). Lodge: Order Eastern Star. Home: Route 3 Box 435 B Loris SC 29569 Office: Loris Elem Sch Spring St Loris SC 29569

COX, RALPH FREDERICK, printing co. exec.; b. Boston, June 6, 1923; s. Edward J. and Hilda Catherine (Kunkel) C.; B.S., Babson Coll., 1949; m. Mary Eleanor Connelly, Feb. 4, 1950; children—Carolyn Louise, Ralph Frederick, Cynthia Ann. Sales rep. Lever Bros. Co., 1950-52, Westfield River Paper Co., 1952-57, Continetal Can Co., 1957-66; exec. v.p. Hibbert Co., 1966-72; pres. Hibbert-So., Inc., Houston, 1972-82, Printing Industries of Gulf Coast, 1982—, Retail Direct Corp., 1982—; v.p. The Premier Corp., 1982—; dir. Hibbert Co., Retail Direct Corp., Hibbert-Laman, Denver, Printing Industries of Gulf Coast. Served to capt. U.S. Army, 1942-45. Decorated Bronze Star medal. Mem. Am. Mgmt. Assn., Mail Advt. Service Assn. Internat. (chmn. bd. regents Inst. Continuing Edn., chmn. bd. 1985—), Internat., Houston Direct Mail/Mktg. Assn. Republican. Roman Catholic. Home: 6019 Coral Ridge St Houston TX 77069 Office: 6855 Wynnwood St Houston TX 77008

COX, ROBERT JOE, professional basketball executive; b. Tulsa, May 21, 1941; m. Pamela C.; children—Kami, Keisha. Student Reedley Jr. Coll., Calif. Baseball player Calif. League, Reno, 1960, N.W. League, Salem, 1961-62, Tex. League, Albuquerque, 1963-64, Pacific Coast League, Salt Lake City, 1965, Tacoma, 1966, Internat. League, Richmond, 1967, N.Y. Yankees, Am. League, 1968-69, Internat. League, Syracuse, 1970; mgr. Ft. Lauderdale State League, Fla., 1971, West Haven, Eastern League, 1972, Syracuse Internat. League, 1973-76, Atlanta Braves, Nat. League, 1978-81, Toronto Blue Jays, Am. League, 1982-85; gen. mgr. Atlanta Braves, Nat. League, 1985—. Office: care Atlanta Braves PO Box 4064 Atlanta GA 30302*

COX, TROY DWAIN, data processing company executive, consultant; b. Avon Park, Fla., Nov. 12, 1939; s. Troy Alphonso and Norma Lee (Barlow) C.; m. Diane B. Bryant, Apr. 26, 1963; children—Troy Dwain, Michael David, Angela Diane. B.S., Fla. So. Coll., 1962; M.A., Tulane U., 1972. Commd. 2d lt. U.S. Army, 1962, advanced through grades to lt. col., 1978; served as dep. dir. personnel and adminstrn. 2d Inf. Div., Tong DuChon, Korea, 1973-74, research and devel. coordinator Army Research Inst., Arlington, Va., 1974-84, exec. officer Orgn. Joint Chiefs of Staff, Pentagon, 1978-80, dir. personnel and adminstrn., Ft. Sill, Okla., 1980-83, ret., 1983; account mgr. Electronic Data Systems, Ft. Leavenworth, Kans., 1983, mgr. fin. and adminstrn., Alexandria, Va., 1983—; cons. various firms, Washington, 1974-83. Contbr. articles in field to publs. Athletic coach Chantilly Youth Assn., Fairfax, Va., 1974-78. Decorated Bronze Star. Mem. Am. Psychol. Assn., Assn. U.S. Army, Am. Mgmt. Assn. Home: 4441 Miniature Ln Fairfax VA 22033 Office: Electronic Data Systems 1600 N Beauregard St Alexandria VA 22311

COX, WILLIAM ANDREW, cardiovascular thoracic surgeon; b. Columbus, Ga., Aug. 3, 1925; s. Virgil Augustus and Dale Jackson C.; student Presbyn. Coll., 1942-43, Harvard U., 1944-45, Cornell U., 1945; B.S., Emory U., 1950, M.D., 1954; M.S. in Surgery, Baylor U., 1960; m. Nina Recelle Hobby, Jan. 1, 1948; children—Constance Lynn Cox Rogers, Patricia Ann Cox Brown, William Robert, Janet Elaine. Commd. 1st lt. M.C., U.S. Army, 1954, advanced through grades to col., 1969; intern Brooke Army Med. Center, San Antonio, 1954-55, resident in gen. surgery, 1956-60; resident in cardiovascular thoracic surgery Walter Reed Army Med. Center, Washington, 1960-62, staff cardiothoracic surgeon, 1962; asst. chief cardiothoracic surgery Letterman Gen. Hosp., 1962-65; chief dept. surgery and cardiothoracic surgery 121 Evacuation Hosp., Seoul, Korea, cons. cardiothoracic surgery Korean Theatre, 1965-66; asst. chief cardiothoracic surgery Brooke Army Med. Center, 1966-69, chief, 1969-73, bd. dirs. thoracic surgery residency programs, 1966-73, ret., 1973; clin. prof. cardio-thoracic surgery U. Tex. Sch. Medicine, San Antonio, 1971—; practice medicine specializing in cardiovascular thoracic surgery, Corpus Christi, Tex., 1973—; cons. cardio-thoracic surgery Brooke Army Med. Center, San Antonio, 1977—; chief staff Meml. Med. Center, 1980; dir. disaster med. care region 3A Tex. State Dept. Health, 1973—; mem. Coastal Bend council Gov.'s Emergency Med. Service Commn., 1979—; mem. adv. bd. on congenital heart disease Tex. Dept. Health, 1980—. Served to lt. USN, 1945-48. Decorated Legion of Merit; recipient A Prefix award Surgeon Gen. Army; diplomate Am. Bd. Surgery, Am. Bd. Thoracic Surgery. Fellow Am. Coll. Chest Physicians; mem. AMA, Soc. Thoracic Surgeons, Denton A. Cooley Cardiovascular Surgery Soc., Tex. Med. Assn., So. Thoracic Surgery Assn., Nueces County Med. Soc., Corpus Christi Surg. Soc., 38th Parallel Med. Soc. Republican. Presbyterian. Clubs: Yacht (past commodore presidio)(San Francisco); T-Bar-M Racquet Corpus Christi Country; Fort Sam Houston Officer's (San Antonio). Contbr. numerous articles in field to profl. jours. Home: 5214 Wooldridge Rd Corpus Christi TX 78413 Office: 2601 Hospital Blvd Corpus Christi TX 78405

COX, WILLIAM EDWARD, civil engineering educator, researcher, consultant; b. Pulaski, Va., Feb. 18, 1944; s. William Walker and Cora Lee (Davis) C.; m. Clara Sue Brown, Dec. 30, 1965; 1 dau., Wendy Jean. B.S., Va. Poly. Inst. and State U., 1966, M.S., 1968, Ph.D., 1976. Asst. prof. Va. Commonwealth U., Richmond, 1968-72; research assoc. Va. Water Resources Research Ctr., Blacksburg, 1972-77; asst. prof. civil engring. Va. Poly. Inst. and State U., Blacksburg, 1977-80, assoc. prof., 1980-86; prof., 1986—; cons. GKY and Assocs., Inc., 1981, Camp Dresser & McKee, Inc., 1985; lectr. Ferrum Coll., 1981, 83, 85. Mem. adv. com. N.C., Va. Water Resources Mgmt. Com., 1982-83. Grantee U.S. Office Water Research and Tech., 1975, 76, 79, 80, Va. Environ. Endowment, 1979, Va. Water Resources Research Ctr., 1983, 84, 85, Va. Dept. Conservation and Hist. Resources, 1985. Mem. ASCE, Am. Water Resources Assn., Internat. Water Resources Assn., Water Pollution Control Fedn., Va. Acad. Sci., UNESCO (working group on role of water in socio-econ. devel. 1982—), Sigma Xi. Baptist. Contbr. articles to profl. jours. Home: 1903 Shelor Ln Blacksburg VA 24060 Office: Va Poly Inst and State U Civil Engring Dept Blacksburg VA 24061

COZZENS, ROBERT F., chemistry educator, consultant; b. Alexandria, Va., Sept. 6, 1941; s. Marion A. and Francis H. (Thompson) C.; B.S., U. Va., 1963, Ph.D., 1966. Postdoctoral research assoc. NRC, 1966-67; asst. prof. chemistry George Mason Univ., Fairfax, Va., 1967-71, assoc. prof., 1971-75, prof., 1975—, dep. dir. Inst. Sci. and Tech. 1981—; cons. U.S. Naval Research Lab., Washington, several tech. corps. Mem. Am. Chem. Soc., Chem. Soc. Washington, Va. Acad. Sci., InterAm. Photochem. Soc., Sigma Xi. Methodist. Co-author books; contbr. articles to profl. jours. Home: 3009 N Tacoma St Arlington VA 22213 Office: George Mason U Fairfax VA 22030

CRABAUGH, MARJORIE WILLIAMS, retired radio commentator; b. Fort Smith, Ark., May 27, 1905; d. John Byron and Regina Cecilia (Scherer) W.; m. Alfred Jackson Crabaugh, Jan. 13, 1925; 1 dau., Dojelo Crabaugh Russell. Student U. Ark., 1922-25. Opinion researcher various orgs., Ark., Kans., Calif., 1943-46; reporter Ark. Recorder, Little Rock, 1943-64; radio commentator Ark Valley Broadcasting, Russellville, Ark., 1950-84; calendar clerk Ark. Senate, Little Rock, 1964-68. Legislator Silver-Haired Legislature, Little Rock, 1982-84; intern U.S. Congress Sr. Intern Program, Washington, 1981; del. White House Conf. Aging, Washington, 1980, Seminar on Employment (Rosalyn Carter conf.), Washington, 1978; sec., mem. Gov.'s Commn. on Aging, Little Rock, 1979—; mem. W. Central Ark. Area Council on Aging, Russellville, 1977-80; founder, chmn. United Charities of Russellville, 1947-84; chmn. bd. Pope County Hist. Found., Russellville, 1978—, Ark. Girls Tng. Sch., Alexander, 1957-64; bd. dirs. Ark. Valley Reg. Library, Dardanelle, 1970-73, Mid.-Ark. River Valley Abilities, Russellville, 1962—; active sr. citizens units. Named Citizen of Yr., Russellville C. of C. 1983; Woman of Yr. Ark. Democrat, 1979; recipient Exceptional Accomplishment award Ark. Community Devel. Program, State C. of C., 1979; Community award Human Services of W. Central Ark., 1979. Republican. Roman Catholic. Club: Jr. Auxiliary (Russellville) (founder, 1940). Avocations: bridge, gardening. Home: 2206 Red Hill Ln Russellville AK 72801

CRABB, JAMES WESLEY, SR., investment broker; b. Maud, Okla., Nov. 14, 1935; s. Roy Wesley and Cevella Mae (Hart) C.; m. Carol Ann O'Brien, Oct. 10, 1957; children—Tawanna Kay, James Wesley. B.A., U. Nebr., 1973; M.A., Central Mich. U., 1977; grad. Indsl. Coll. of Armed Forces, 1975. Enlisted U.S. Air Force, 1955, commd. 2d lt.; flew B-47, B-52 bombers; service in Vietnam, 1969-70; staff SAC Hdqrs., 1970-75; dep. comdr. maintenance, Kinchehoe AFB, Mich., 1975-77, Griffiss AFB, N.Y., 1977-79; chief of maintenance standardization SAC Hdqrs., 1979-81, aircraft div. chief, Tinker AFB, 1981-82, retired as col., 1982; investment broker Rauscher Pierce Refsnes, Inc., Kerrville, Tex., 1984—. Decorated Legion of Merit (2) Bronze Star, Meritorious Service medal (4); Air Force Commendation medal. Mem. Air Force Assn. (life); Retired Officers Assn. (life). Republican. Office PO Box 311 Kerrville TX 78028

CRABBS, JERRY RAY, physician; b. Rochester, Ind., Jan. 25, 1945; s. Lester F. and Nettie H. (Ray) C.; m. Glenna D. Venable, Dec. 23, 1978; children from previous marriage—Lynn, Donna, Jean, Dawn, Noell. B.S., Ind. State U., Terre Haute, 1967, M.D., Indpls., 1971. Intern, St. Elizabeth Med. Ctr., Covington, Ky., 1971-72; practice medicine specializing in family medicine, Covington, Ky., 1972—; mem. staff St. Elizabeth Med. Ctr.; dep. coroner Kenton County, Ky., 1974-83; part-time cons. family practice residency St. Elizabeth Med. Ctr., 1972-78. Served with USN, 1968-72. Mem. Ky. State Diabetes Assn. (bd. dirs.), Ky. Acad. Family Practice, Am. Acad. Family Practice, Ky. State Med. Assn., AMA, State Coroners Assn., Nat. Coroners Assn., Internat. Coroners Assn., Ky. Cols. Democrat. Baptist. Office: 1 W 43d St Covington KY 41015

CRABTREE, JOHN MICHAEL, college administrator, consultant; b. Fostoria, Ohio, Nov. 11, 1949; s. John Dwight and Opal Marie (Tate) C.; m. Cheryl Lynn Wallace, July 6, 1974. A.A. in Music Edn., Mt. Vernon Nazarene Coll., 1970; B.Mus. Edn., Bethany Nazarene Coll., 1972, M.A. in Edn., 1976; postgrad. U. Okla., 1976. Sports info. dir. Bethany Nazarene Coll., Okla., 1971-80, dir. pub. relations, 1974-80, assoc. dean student devel., 1974-78, dir. alumni and media relations, 1980—, adj. prof. mktg., 1979-82. Editor The Perspective, 1981—. Chmn. United Fund Drive, Bethany, 1983. Mem. Bethany Hist. Soc. (life), Bethany C. of C. (v.p.), Okla. Pub. Relations Assn. (bd. dirs.), Council for Advancement and Support of Edn., Sports Info. Dirs. Am. (com. 1974-80, ethics com. 1978-80 job attrition bd. 1980), Sigma Tau Delta. Republican. Club: Kiwanis (v.p.). Avocations: photography; philately; antique book collector. Office: Bethany Nazarene Coll 6729 NW 39th Expressway Bethany OK 73008

CRADDOCK, JACK, JR., transportation executive; b. Sylacauga, Ala., Oct. 26, 1942; s. Jack and Bessie Inez (Phurrough) C.; m. Dianne K. Beasley, June 1, 1963 (div. 1982); children—Dana Renee, Jacqueline Kay, Jack David; m. 2d, Judith A. Culver, Nov. 5, 1983. B.S. in Bus. Adminstrn., Auburn U., 1965. Mgr. prodn. control Avondale Mills, Stevenson, Ala., 1965-68; dir. safety Floyd & Beasley Transfer Co., Inc., Sycamore, Ala., 1968-73, v.p. safety and personnel, 1973-77, v.p. ops., 1977—; advisor Ala. Traffic Safety Com., 1973-77. Mem. United Givers, chmn. indsl. div., 1972-77, bd. dirs., 1972-77. Mem. Sylacauga C. of C. (v.p. transp. 1976-78), Ala. Trucking Assn. (vice chmn. council safety suprs. 1971, 73, chmn. 1974-75), Am. Trucking Assn. (chmn. southeastern region 1976, chmn. 1977), South Talladega County Auburn Club (v.p. 1975-77, pres. 1977-78). Clubs: Sylacauga Bass Anglers (v.p. 1981-84), Exchange (v.p. 1972—). Home: 811 Country Club Rd Sylacauga AL 35150 Office: Floyd and Beasley Transfer Co PO Drawer 8 Sycamore AL 35149

CRAFT, CHESTER LEE, JR., architect; b. Little Rock, Ark., Mar. 13, 1914; s. Chester Lee, Sr. and Malvina (Shipley) C. B.S. in Landscape Architecture, U. Fla., 1941, B.Arch., 1949. Registered architect, Fla. Prin., Craft and Assocs., Coral Gables, Fla., 1956-58, Tallahassee, 1971-82; zone architect Bd. Regents, Tallahassee, 1958-64; prin. Craft, Dade County, Fla., 1964-71; v.p. Poole Engring., Inc., Tallahassee, 1982—; cons. Com. Growth Mgmt., 1982—. Bd. dirs. Com. on Environment, Tallahassee, 1982. Mem. AIA (pres. Fla. North Central chpt. 1960-62), Beta Theta Pi. Democrat. Episcopalian. Home: 1111 Washington Ct Tallahassee FL 32303 Office: Poole Engring Co Inc 1641-A Met Circle Tallahassee FL 32308

CRAFT, DURWOOD, exploration geophysicist; b. Magee, Miss., Jan. 23, 1935; s. Gaddis and Arrese (McKinze) C.; m. Janna Craft, Aug. 8, 1957; children—Robert, Donald, Virginia, Michelle. B.S., U. So. Miss., 1957. Geophysicist, Seismograph Service Corp., Tulsa, 1960-63; geophysicist sr. Mobil Oil Corp., Dallas, 1963-76; geophysicist chief Arkla Exploration Co., Shreveport, La., 1976-79; cons. geophysicist, Shreveport, La., 1979-81; geophysicist dist. Hunt Energy Corp., Jackson, Miss., 1981-83, Placid Oil Co., New Orleans, 1983—. Served with U.S. Army, 1957-60. Mem. Soc. Exploration Geophysicists, Am. Assn. Petroleum Geologists. Baptist. Avocations: farming; outdoor sports. Home: 9696 Hayne Blvd Apt K-21 New Orleans LA 70127 Office: Placid Oil Co 1440 Canal St Suite 1900 New Orleans LA 70112

CRAFT, JAMES PRESSLEY, JR., educator, cons.; b. Louisville, Ga., Nov. 1, 1913; s. James Pressley and Edith (Galphin) C.; student Naval Postgrad. Sch., 1940-42; M.S., MIT, 1943; postgrad. Naval War Coll., 1952-53; Ph.D., U. Pa., 1969; m. Carolyn Crockett Martin, July 30, 1937; children—Carolyn Martin, James Pressley III, Frederick Galphin. Commd. ensign USN, 1934, advanced through grades to capt., 1952; head. contingency plans br. of Joint Staff of Joint Chiefs of Staff, 1960-62; comdr. U.S. Destroyers Mediterranean, 1959-60; dean men U. Pa., 1964-67, fellow, 1967-68; asst. prof. Ursinus Coll., Collegeville, Pa., 1968-69, assoc. prof. polit. sci., 1969-77, prof., 1977-80, asst. dean coll., 1970-77, exec. asst. to pres., 1977, v.p. for planning and adminstrn., 1977-80; pvt. cons., Austin, Tex., 1980—; vis. scholar U. Mich., summer 1971. Decorated Silver Star, Bronze Star with V, Purple Heart; recipient Letter of Commendation with V. NSF fellow Va. Poly. Inst. and State U., 1973. Mem. Pa. Polit. Sci. Assn. (pres. 1978-80), Northeastern Polit. Sci. Assn. (pres.-elect 1979-80), Am. Polit. Sci. Assn., Naval Inst., Pi Gamma Mu. Home: 7201 Montana Norte Austin TX 78731 Office: 313 E Anderson Ln Suite 316 Austin TX 78731

CRAFT, WILLIAM JACOB, engineer, university official; b. Gaffney, S.C., Oct. 14, 1941; s. William McElveen and Ruth Ann (Hord) C.; B.S. in Applied Math., N.C. State U., 1963, B.S. in Physics, 1963; M.S. in Engring. Mechanics (NSF fellow), Clemson U., 1969, Ph.D. in Engring. Mechanics (NSF fellow), 1970; m. Elizabeth Ann Fullerton, May 29, 1965; children—Lydia Elizabeth, Sonia Ann, Michael Jacob. Tutor dept. applied math. U. Sydney (Australia), 1964-66; instr. dept. engring. mechanics Clemson (S.C.) U., 1971; sr. engr. Structures div. Martin Marietta Corp., Orlando, Fla., 1971-72; group engr., vis. prof. mech. engring. N.C. Agrl. and Tech. State U., Greensboro, 1972-74, assoc. prof., 1974-77, dir. grad. engring. program, 1976—, asst. dean Sch. Engring., 1977-79, assoc. dean, 1979—; cons. So. Assn. Colls. and Schs., Registered profl. engr., N.C. Mem. Am. Acad. Mechanics, Am. Soc. Engring. Edn., Profl. Engrs. of N.C., Sigma Xi. Contbr. articles to profl. jours.; patentee in field. Office: Sch Engring NC Agrl and Tech State U 1601 E Market St Greensboro NC 27411

CRAFTON, THOMAS WARD, business executive, accountant; b. San Angelo, Tex., Oct. 6, 1947; s. Donald L. and Billie M. (Ward) C.; 1 dau., Cherish Leah. With E.F. Hutton, Houston and Chgo., 1968-72; self-employed acct., Houston, 1972-76, Omaha, 1976-78; controller Jones Lumber Co., Houston, 1973-75; controller Pepperdine U., Malibu, Calif., 1979-81; pres. The Coronado Group, Inc., Westlake Village, Calif.; pres. Defensive Security S.W., Jasper, Tex., 1981-83; controller Reynal Controls Inc., 1983—; cons. in field. Vol., Am. Cancer Soc., Republican Party; chmn. employer drive United Way. Mem. Nat. Assn. Accts. (pres. local chpt.), Nat. Assn. M.B.A.s, Delta Mu Delta. Mem. Ch. of Christ. Clubs: Lions, Rotary, Beverly Hills Men's. Office: 2659 Townsgate St Suite 109 Westlake Village CA 91361 also 10641 Haddington Dr Houston TX 77043

CRAFTON-MASTERSON, ADRIENNE, real estate executive; b. Providence, Mar. 6, 1926; d. John Harold and Adrienne (Fitzgerald) Crafton; student No. Community Coll., 1971-74; m. Francis T. Masterson, May 31, 1947 (div. Jan. 1977); children—Mary Victoria Masterson Bush, Kathleen Joan, John Andrew, Barbara Lynn Wickes. Mem. staff Senator T.F. Green of R.I., Washington, 1944-47, 54-60; mem. staff U.S. Senate Com. on Campaign Expenditures, 1944-45; asst. clk. Ho. Govt. Ops. Com., 1948-49; chief clk. Ho. Campaign Expenditures Com., 1950; asst. appointment sec. Office of Pres., 1951-53; with Hubbard Realty, Alexandria, Va., 1962-67; owner, mgr. Adrienne Investment Real Estate, Alexandria, 1968-83; pres. AIRE, Ltd., 1983-85, Century 21 AIRE, Ltd., 1986—. Incorporator, 1984, since pres., treas. Mt. Vernon-Lee Cultural Ctr. Found., Inc., Va. Mem. No. Va. Bd. Realtors (chmn. comml. and indsl. com. 1981-82, community revitalization com. 1983-85), Nat. Assn. Realtors, Va. Assn. Realtors, Internat. Orgn. Real Estate Appraisers (sr.), Nat. Assn. Indsl. and Office Parks, Internat. Platform Assn., Alexandria C. of C., Friends of Kennedy Center (founding), Nat. Hist. Soc., Nat. Trust Historic Preservation, Internat. Acad. Poets, Fairfax County Council Arts. Ind. Democrat. Home: Porto Vecchio 1250 S Washington St Alexandria VA 22314 Office: PO Box 1271 Alexandria VA also 7925 Richmond Hwy Alexandria VA 22306

CRAIG, DONNA MARIE, physician; b. Martinsville, Va., Nov. 13, 1951; d. Percy and Iris Natalie (Phillips) C.; m. Ronald Thomas Mason, Oct. 17, 1976. A.S. magna cum laude, Patrick Henry Coll., U. Va., 1972; B.A. cum laude, U. Va., 1974; M.D., Eastern Va. Sch. Medicine, 1978. Resident in internal medicine Eastern Va. Grad. Sch. Medicine, Norfolk, 1978-81, chief resident internal medicine, 1981-82; nephrology fellow Nephrology Research and Tng. Ctr., U. Ala., Birmingham, 1982-84, assoc. in medicine, 1982-84; internist, nephrologist West Paces Ferry Med. Clinic, Atlanta, 1984—. Contbr. articles and abstracts to profl. jours. Mem. patient care com. Med. Ctr. Hosps., Norfolk, 1980-81; mem. exec. com. residency program Eastern Va. Grad. Sch. Medicine, 1981-82. Named Resident of Year, Eastern Va. Med. Sch., 1981; Nat. Kidney Found. fellow, 1983—. Fellow Nat. Kidney Found.; mem. ACP, AMA, Phi Sigma, Phi Theta Kappa. Home: 124 Wood Hollow Dr Marietta GA 30067 Office: 3250 Howell Mill Rd NW Suite 305 Atlanta GA 30327

CRAIG, EUGENE ARNOLD, psychologist, book company executive; b. Wichita, Kans., Dec. 22, 1922; s. Ellis Aaron and Hazel Marie (Winters) C.; m. Mildred Ann Heard, Dec. 22; 1 child, Leanna. Student, Middlebury Coll., Vt., 1943-45, Brown U., 1945-46; B.A., Tulsa U., 1949; Ph.D., U. Colo., 1950. Assoc. prof. psychology Lehigh U., Bethlehem, Pa., 1960-66; prof. Pa. State Coll. System, 1966-69, New Eng. Coll. of Optometry, Boston, 1969-73; dir. research Insight, Inc., Ft. Myers, Fla., 1985—; pres. Parkway Books, Inc., Ft. Myers, 1975—; owner, mgr. Little Prof. Book Ctrs., Naples, Fla., 1973-83, Port Charlotte, Fla., 1976-80; dir. Gulf Point Books, Inc., Ft. Myers. Served with USN, 1942-46. Mem. Am. Psychol. Assn., N.Y. Acad. Scis., Am. Acad. Optometry, Sigma Xi, Psi Chi. Republican. Avocations: creative writing; cosmology. Home: 850 Hofstra Dr Fort Myers FL 33907 Office: Parkway Books Inc 3858 College Pkwy Fort Myers FL 33907

CRAIG, GEORGE DENNIS, economics educator, consultant; b. Geneva, Ill., Sept. 14, 1936; s. George S. and Alice H. (Childs) C.; m. Lelah Price, Aug. 21, 1984; children—R. Price Coyle, R. Nolan Coyle, Deborah L. Craig, W. Sean Coyle. A.B., Wheaton Coll., 1960; M.S., U. Ill., 1962, Ph.D., 1968. Asst. prof. econs. La. State U., Baton Rouge, 1965-69; assoc. prof. sch. bus. No. Ill. U., Dekalb, 1969-82; prof. econs., chmn. Oklahoma City U., 1982—; cons. AT&T, Oklahoma City, 1984—. Contbr. articles to profl. jours. Mem. Am. Econs. Assn., So. Econs. Assn. Nat. Assn. Bus. Economists, Internat. Inst. of Forecasting. Avocation: tennis. Home: 6915 Avondale Ct Oklahoma City OK 73116 Office: Dept Econs Oklahoma City U NW 23rd at N Blackwelder Oklahoma City OK 73106

CRAIG, MICHAEL EDWARD, mathematical statistician, consultant; b. Bluefield, W.Va., Aug. 22, 1951; s. Ether Opie and Dorothy Muriel (Blankenship) C.; m. Dorotha Elaine Musick, Jan. 16, 1973 (div. 1978); 1 child, Michael Troy. B.S. in Math. Edn., Va. Poly. Inst., 1973, M.S. in Math. Statis., 1974. Grad. teaching asst. Va. Poly. Inst., Blacksburg, 1973-74; math. statistician U.S. Dept. Agr., Richmond, Va., 1974-76, Washington, 1976-83, Charleston, W.Va., 1983—; free lance statis. cons. various locations including Central Am., S. Am., 1977—. Contbr. articles to profl. jours. Mem. Am. Statis. Assn., Phi Kappa Phi, Pi Mu Epsilon. Mem. Christian Ch. Club: YMCA (Charleston). Home: 1591 C Jackson St Charleston WV 25311 Office: Agrl Statistician US Dept Agr Charleston WV 25305

CRAIG, THOMAS FRANKLIN, electrical engineer; b. Indpls., Feb. 26, 1943; s. Robert Watson and Iris Evelyn (Evans) C.; B.S.E.E. (Charles M. Malott scholar), Purdue U., 1965, M.S.I.A., 1970; m. Ester Annelle Cantrell, Aug. 3, 1968; children—Amy Delynne, Josie Leigh. Engr., Boeing Mil. Airplace Co., Huntsville, Ala., sr. specialist engr., 1982—; Reliability engr. SCI Systems, Inc., Huntsville, 1968-71; components engr. Safeguard System Command, Huntsville, Ala., 1971-73; software engr. U.S. Army Guidance and Control Labs., Redstone Arsenal, Ala., 1973; systems engr. Pershing Project, 1974-77, communications equipment program mgr., 1977-81, chmn. Pershing II Communications Working Group; project engr. Stinger Project Office, 1981-82. Asst. treas., bd. dirs. Huntsville Depot Mus., 1976-84; chmn. bd. elders 1st Christian Ch., 1979-81; treas., trustee Helion Temple, 1978-84. Served to capt. ordnance, USAR, 1965-68. Engr.-in-tng., Ind., 1965. Mem. IEEE, IEEE Computer Soc., Armed Forces Communications and Electronics Assn., Am. Def. Preparedness Assn., AAAS, Ala. Acad. Sci., Assn. Old Crows, Mensa. Republican. Mem. Christian Ch. Clubs: Mountain Springs Swim, N. Ala. R.R., Sierra. Lodge: Masons (past master, York Rite Coll. Gold Honor award 1981). Editor, The North Star, 1979—. Ala. sec. Quatuor Coronati Corr. Circle, London, 1980—. Home: 1000 Lexington St Huntsville AL 35801 Office: PO Box 1470 Huntsville AL 35807

CRAIG, TODD ALEXANDER, research chemist; b. Springfield, Mass., Feb. 14, 1954; s. Gordon and Natalie Diane (Hall) C.; m. Rebecca Faith Hoffman, June 9, 1979. B.S. in Chemistry, State U. Coll. Arts and Scis., Geneseo, N.Y., 1975; Ph.D. in Organic Chemistry, Wesleyan U., 1980. Exploratory project scientist Union Carbide Agrl. Products Co., Research Triangle Park, N.C., 1981—. Regents scholar, 1971-75; Larry Cox scholar, 1975; NIH postdoctoral fellow, 1980-81 Mem. Am. Chem. Soc. (edn. chmn. N.C. sect. 1983—), N.C. Against Drunk Drivers, Sigma Xi. Presbyterian.

CRAIGO, OSHEL B., state senator; b. June 24, 1937; m. Joanna Parkins; children—Sabrina, Christina, Desiree, Shannon. Student W.Va. State Coll. Businessman; mem. W.Va. ho. dels., 1980-82, W.Va. Senate, 1982—, vice chmn. transp. com., vice chmn. natural resources com. Mem. Putnam Gen. Hosp. Bd. Mem. W.Va. Restaurant Licensed Beverage Assn. (past pres.). Democrat. Office: W Va Senate Charleston WV 25305

CRAIN, JAMES LARRY, university president; b. Franklinton, La., July 16, 1935; s. Henry and Birdie Von (Blackwell) C.; m. Jean Etta Lott, Oct. 15, 1955; children—Ricky Lynn, Rita Ann, Randall Henry. B.S. in Biology, U. So. Miss., 1957, Ph.D. in Zoology, 1966; M.A., Stephen F. Austin State U., 1963. Tchr. sci. Varnado High Sch., (La.), 1957-64; asst. prof., assoc. prof. Southeastern La. U., Hammond, 1966, 72, 72-76, cons., biologist, 1972-74, pres., 1980—; asst. sec. La. Dept. Culture, Baton Rouge, 1976-78; sec. La. Dept. Culture, Recreation and Tourism, 1978-80; genetic counsel Sickle Cell Anemia Program, Hammond, 1974-75; dir. Natural Sci. Mus., Hammond, 1967-76. Mem. Arts Council, Hammond, 1982, Cultural Found., 1982, Friends of Cabildo, New Orleans, 1982, La. Hist. Assn., Baton Rouge, Old State Capitol Assocs. Named Citizen of Yr. Kiwanis, 1982; recipient award of merit for preservation of material culture S.E. La. Hist. Assn., 1981. Mem. Am. Assn. State Colls. and Univs., Northlake Mus. and Nature Ctr.; mem. Am. Soc. Arms Collectors, Hammond C. of C. Democrat. Presbyterian. Club: Rotary. Home: 408 W Dakota St Hammond LA 70401 Office: Southeastern La U PO Box 784 Hammond LA 70402

CRAIN, JEFFREY LIN, data processing co. mgr.; b. Warren, Ohio, Aug. 2, 1943; s. Alfred Uno and Irene Yolanda (Kover) C.; B.S., Youngstown State U., 1970; M.B.A., City Coll. Seattle, 1980; m. Ruth Ann Lutsky, July 29, 1967. Ops./EDP auditor Evans Products Co., Portland, Oreg., 1974-76, ops. mgr., Grand Rapids, Mich., 1976-77, mfg. systems engr., cons., Portland, 1977-80; profl. services mgr./br. mgr. Digital Equipment Corp., Portland, 1980-83, ops. mgr., Atlanta, 1983—; instr. Seattle City Coll., 1980—; cons. Active United Fund, 1975. Served with USN, 1962-66. Youngstown Bd. Realtors scholar,

1968-69. Mem. Soc. Advancement of Mgmt., Am. Inst. Indsl. Engrs., Am. Prodn. and Inventory Control Soc., Omicron Delta Epsilon. Club: Pres.'s (City Coll. Seattle). Office: 360 Interstate N Pkwy Suite 600 Atlanta GA 30339

CRAIN, WILLIAM HENRY, curator; b. Victoria, Tex., July 19, 1917; s. William Henry and Margaret James (McFaddin) C.; student Tex. Mil. Inst., 1933-36; B.A., U. Tex., 1940, M.A., 1943, B.F.A., 1947, M.F.A., 1949, Ph.D., 1965. Resident playwright Artillery Lane Theatre, San Augustine, Fla., 1950-51; dir. David G. Benjamin Inc., Austin, Tex., 1957-59 Austin Mfg. Corp., 1957-59; publicity asst. drama dept. U. Tex., Austin, 1959-60; humanities research asso. II, 1965-70; curator Hoblitzelle Theatre Arts Library, Austin, 1970—, Harry Ransom Humanities Research Ctr.; dir. Waterloo Press, 1971—. Writer numerous plays produced including Brains and Eggs, 1948, The Muddled Magician, 1957, Sir Marmaduke Miles, 1976, Sweet Old Thing, 1961, The Reluctant Caesar, 1977, The Crossed Crescent, 1983. Bd. dirs. Austin Civic Theatre, 1961-64, Paramount Theatre for Performing Arts, 1976—. Served with AUS, 1941-45. Decorated Knight comdr. of Holy Sepulchre; recipient Cross of Mil. Service, U. D.C., 1961. Mem. Am. Theatre Assn., Sons Republic Tex., Serra Internat., Phi Eta Sigma, Phi Kappa Phi, Delta Kappa Epsilon. Roman Catholic. Clubs: Serra (treas. 1978-79), Austin, Players. Home: 2511 San Gabriel Austin TX 78705 Office: 7204 B Harry Ransom Center PO Drawer 7219 Austin TX 78713

CRAIS, THOMAS FLOYD, JR., plastic and reconstructive surgeon; b. New Orleans, Nov. 22, 1943; s. Thomas F. and Myrtle (Laresche) C.; m. Bonnie Mary Burke, Dec. 28, 1968; children—Vanessa, Hillary, Thomas III. Student Tex. A&M U., 1961-63; M.D., La. State U., 1968. Diplomate Am. Bd. Plastic Surgery. Rotating intern William Beaumont Hosp., El Paso, Tex., 1968-69; aerospace medicine fellow Naval Aerospace Med. Inst., Pensacola, Fla., 1969-70; chief outpatient clinic U.S. Army Hosp., Berlin, 1970-73; resident gen. surgery Boston U., 1973-77; resident plastic surgery NYU, N.Y.C., 1977-79, microsurgery fellow, 1979; practice medicine specializing in plastic and reconstructive surgery, New Orleans, 1980—; clin. instr. plastic surgery La. State U. Med. Ctr., New Orleans, 1980—; med. dir. microsurg. research and tng. lab. So. Bapt. Hosp., New Orleans, 1981—, course dir. ann. microsurgery symposium, 1981—. Contbr. articles to med. publs. Patentee microarterial bridge. Bd. dirs. Holy Cross Sch., New Orleans, 1983—. Served to maj. M.C., U.S. Army, 1968-73, Fed. Republic Germany. Mem. Am. Soc. Reconstructive Microsurgery, Am. Soc. Plastic and Reconstructive Surgery, AMA, La. Soc. Plastic and Reconstructive Surgery, La. State Med. Soc., Orleans Parish Med. Soc., Southeastern Soc. Plastic and Reconstructive Surgeons, So. Med. Assn., Surg. Assn. La., Internat. Soc. Reconstructive Microsurgery. Roman Catholic. Avocations: equestrian, jogger, languages. Office: 2626 Jena St New Orleans LA 70115

CRALL, JAMES MONROE, plant pathologist, plant breeder, educator; b. Monongahela, Pa., July 13, 1914; s. James Shelby and Margaret Bureau (Rabe) C.; m. Duronda Stanberry, Dec. 22, 1943; children—Cynthia Ann, James Stanberry. Student Washington and Jefferson Coll., 1934-35; B.S., Purdue U., 1939; M.A., U. Mo., 1941, Ph.D., 1948. Asst. prof. botany and plant pathology Iowa State U., Ames, 1948-52; mem. faculty Agrl. Research Center, Inst. Food and Agrl. Scis., U. Fla., Leesburg, 1952—, dir. Ctr., 1952-77, prof. plant pathology, 1954—, plant pathologist, 1954—. Pres., United Appeal, Leesburg, 1966, v.p., 1968, bd. dirs., 1960-68. Vestryman, Episcopal Ch. Served with USAAF, 1942-46 Mem. AAAS, Council Agrl. Sci. and Tech., Am. Phytopath. Soc., Mycol. Soc. Am., Am. Soc. Hort. Scis., Sigma Xi, Gamma Sigma Delta, Gamma Alpha. Lodge: Kiwanis (dir., v.p. 1965-66). Contbr. articles to profl. publs. Home: PO Box 321 Leesburg FL 32748 Office: PO Box 388 Leesburg FL 32748

CRAMER, GEORGE BENNETT, estate management executive; b. Swampscott, Mass., Aug. 15, 1903; s. Stuart Warren and Rebecca Warren (Tinkham) C.; student U. N.C., 1921-22; B.S., Harvard U., 1926; m. Elizabeth Crooks, Jan. 28, 1947; children—George Bennett, Richard Warren. Dir., Cramerton Mills, Inc., N.C., 1927-47, sec., 1927-46, asst. treas., 1927-31, treas., 1931-46; mill rep. Galey & Lord, N.Y.C., 1929-32; partner Cramer & Cramer investments & estate mgmt., Charlotte, N.C., 1947—; mem. adv. bd. Liberty Mut. Ins. Co., Charlotte, 1934-46; chief of textile div. Econ. Cooperation Adminstrn., Dept. State, Paris, 1949-51. Mem. Cramerton Sch. Bd., 1933-38; bd. dirs. Charlotte Symphony Orch., 1955-58, United Community Service Found., Charlotte, Charlotte United Community Fund, Charlotte Alcoholism Info. Center; v.p. Mint Mus. Art, Charlotte, 1930-40. Served from lt. to maj. USAF, 1940-46; ETO. Decorated Bronze Star. Mem. Charlotte C. of C. (aviation, fgn. trade and edn. com. 1968—), Soc. Mayflower Descs., SAR, Sons Colonial Wars, English Speaking Union (founding pres. Charlotte 1958-62), N.C. Hist. Assn., Soc. of Four Arts, Am. Legion. Republican. Episcopalian. Clubs: N.C. Wildlife, Rifle and Pistol, Charlotte Country, Quail Hollow Country, Myers Park Country, Charlotte City (Charlotte); Mchts., Harvard, Univ., Columbia Yacht (N.Y.C.); Palm Beach Yacht, Palm Beach Rifle and Pistol, Everglades, Bath and Tennis, Beach, Sailfish (Palm Beach); Hurlingham (London); Nantucket Yacht; Army and Navy, University (Washington); Anterlie (Paris). Home: Charlotte Midwood 2733 Country Club Ln Charlotte NC 28205 also One N Breakers Row PH462 Palm Beach FL 33480 Office: 1401 Commerce Center 129 W Trade St Charlotte NC 28202

CRAMER, HOWARD ROSS, geology educator, researcher, consultant; b. Chgo., Sept. 17, 1925; s. Don William and Esther Natalia (Johnson) C.; m. Ardis V. Lahann, Dec. 15, 1950 (dec. Sept. 1980); m. 2d, Themis Poulos, Dec. 5, 1982. B.S., U. Ill., 1949, M.S., 1950; Ph.D., Northwestern U., 1954. Registered geologist, Ga. Mem. faculty Franklin and Marshall Coll., 1953-58; asst. prof. geology Emory U., Atlanta, 1958-62, assoc. prof., 1962-76, prof., 1976—, chmn. dept., 1980—. Served with AUS, 1943-46. Decorated Bronze Star; recipient Holgate prize Northwestern U., 1953, cert. of commendation Am. Assn. State and Local History, 1974. Mem. Am. Assn. Petroleum Geologists, Geol. Soc. Am., Paleontol. Soc., Nat. Assn. Geology Tchrs., Ga. Acad. Sci. Greek Orthodox. Lodge: Ahepa. Contbr. articles sci. jours. Home: 2047 Deborah Dr Atlanta GA 30345 Office: Dept Geology Emory University Atlanta GA 30322

CRAMER, LAURA SCHWARZ, realtor; b. St. Louis, Aug. 13, 1925; d. Frederick William and Gertrude Margaret (Kipp) Schwarz; A.B., Duke U., 1947; M.A., Washington U., 1948; m. Robert R. Cramer, Oct. 29, 1949; children—Anne Randolph, Carol Parker, Laura Forster. Model, John Robert Powers Agy., N.Y.C., 1946; grad. asst. dept. psychology Washington U., St. Louis, 1947-48, instr., 1948-49; psychometrist Clayton (Mo.) pub. schs., 1961; dir. testing Columbia Sch., Rochester, N.Y., 1964-71; asst. registrar and counselor for women students St. John Fisher Coll., Rochester, N.Y., 1971-72, registrar, dean of women, 1972-76; sales exec. Sea Pines Real Estate Co., Hilton Head Island, S.C., 1976—; registered rep. Sea Pines Securities, 1983—. Bd. dirs. Vol. Service Bur., St. Louis, 1960-61, Monroe County Hosp. Aux., 1974-76, St. Louis Community Music Sch., 1959-61; bd. dirs. St. Louis Inst., chmn., 1960. Named Leading Sales Exec., 1981, 84, Leading Listing Exec., 1982, 83, 85. Jesse M. Barr fellow, 1947-48. Mem. Hilton Head Island Bd. Realtors (Million Dollar Club), Jr. League Savannah, Pres.' Roundtable of Leading Sales Execs., Phi Beta Kappa, Sigma Xi. Home: PO Box 3091 Hilton Head Island SC 29928 Office: Sea Pines Plantation Co Hilton Head Island SC 29948

CRAMER, ROXANNE HERRICK, educator; b. Albion, Mich., Apr. 24; d. Donald F. and Kathryn L. (Beery) Herrick; m. James Loveday Hofford, Jan. 29, 1955 (div.); children—William Herrick, Dana Webster, Paul Christopher; m. 2d Harold Leslie Cramer, Apr. 20, 1967. Student, U. Mich., 1952-55; B.A., U. Toledo, 1956; Ed.M., Harvard U., 1967; doctoral candidate Va. Poly. Inst. and State U., 1984—. Tchr. Wayland (Mass.) Pub. Schs., 1966-70, Fairfax County (Va.) Pub. Schs., 1970—; tchr./team leader Gifted/Talented program, 1975—; coordinating instr. Trinity Coll., Washington, 1978; nat. coordinator Gifted Children Programs, Am. Mensa, Ltd., 1981-84. Mem. Nat. Assn. Gifted Children, Am. Assn. Gifted Children, World Council Gifted and Talented Children, Va. Assn. Edn. Gifted, Intertel (chmn. Hollingworth award com.), Fairfax County Assn. Gifted, NEA, Va. Edn. Assn., Fairfax Edn. Assn., Mensa, Phi Delta Kappa. Club: Harvard (Washington). Contbr. articles to profl. jours. Home: PO Box 1145 Vienna VA 22180 Office: Louise Archer Gifted Ctr 324 Nutley St NW Vienna VA 22180

CRANDALL, LEE ALDEN, medical sociologist, medical educator; b. Alexandria Bay, N.Y., Aug. 27, 1947; s. Frank D. and Althea (Morse) C.; m. Terry Anne Russell, Aug. 26, 1967; children—Mark William, Timothy Russell. A.A., Jefferson Community Coll., 1967; B.A., SUNY-Potsdam, 1969; M.S., Purdue U., 1973, Ph.D. (USPHS fellow), 1976. Asst. research scientist U. Fla. Coll. Medicine, Gainesville, 1976-77, asst. prof. depts. community health and sociology, 1977-81, assoc. prof., 1981—, acting chief div. social scis. and humanities, assoc. prof., 1982-85; tchr.; research adminstr. Bd. dirs. Alachua County (Fla.) div. Am. Heart Assn., 1978—, chmn., 1983—. Mem. Am. Sociol. Assn., So. Sociol. Assn., Hastings Ctr. (assoc. mem.), Alpha Kappa Delta, Phi Kappa Phi. Episcopalian. Author: (with L.J. Beaulieu) Health in Rural Florida: A Statistical Profile, 1978; (with A. Oreglia, D.A. Klein, R.P. Duncan) A Guide to the Development of Health Resource Inventories, 1978; contbr. numerous articles in field to profl. jours. Home: 332 SW 77 Terr Gainesville FL 32607 Office: Box J 222 JHMHC U Fla Gainesville FL 32610

CRANDALL, ROBERT LLOYD, airline executive; b. Westerly, R.I., Dec. 6, 1935; s. Lloyd and Virginia B. Crandall; B.A., U. R.I., 1957; M.B.A., Wharton Sch., U. Pa., 1960; m. Margaret Jan Schmults, July 6, 1957; children—Mark, Martha, Stephen. Fin. mgr. Eastman Kodak, Rochester, N.Y., also Hallmark Cards, Kansas City, Mo.; v.p., controller TWA, 1967-73; sr. v.p. fin. Am. Airlines, Dallas, 1973-74, sr. v.p. mktg., 1974-80, pres., chief operating officer, 1980—; dir. Republic Bank of Dallas. Served as 2d lt. U.S. Army 1957-58. Office: PO Box 61616 DFW Airport TX 75261

CRANE, FRANCES HAWKINS, artist, educator; b. Johntown, Tex., July 8, 1928; d. Henry Cleo and Laura Elizabeth (Jenkins) Hawkins; ed. Del Mar Coll., 1948; studied under Frederic Taubes, N.Y.C.; m. Gene Calvin Crane, May 10, 1946; children—Cindie Crane Rogers, Cheryl Crane Garcia. Exhbns. include Highland Mall Gallery, Austin, Tex., Prichard Gallery, Houston, Heath and Brown Gallery, Houston, Salado (Tex.) Gallery, Bellas Artes Gallery, Kerrville, Tex., Jerry Smith Gallery, Alice, Tex., Corpus Christi Mus., M. and N. Originals, Corpus Christi; represented in permanent collections Corpus Christi Mus., Lyndon Baines Johnson Library. Recipient top awards local, state, nat., internat. shows. Mem. South Tex. Traditional Art Assn. (sec.-treas. Corpus Christi chpt. 1970-76), Nat. League Am. Pen Women, Internat. Platform Assn., Hill Country Arts Found., Internat. Soc. Artists. Home: 5058 Wingfoot St Corpus Christi TX 78413 Studio: 6600 S Staples Corpus Christi TX 78412

CRANE, GLENDA PAULETTE, educator; b. Orlando, Fla., June 29, 1946; d. James Author and Elizabeth Lorine (Johnson) C.; A.A. in Edn., Orlando Jr. Coll., 1966; B.A. in Elem. Edn., U. S. Fla., 1967; postgrad. So. Bapt. Theol. Sem., 1970; M.Edn., Rollins Coll., 1985. Tchr., Orange County Schs., Orlando, 1967-70, 79-80, Lake Highland Prep. Sch., Orlando, 1981—; tchr. Belle Glade (Fla.) Christian Sch., 1970-79, asst. prin., 1970-74, prin., 1975-79. State treas. Fla. Rainbow Girls., 1964. Mem. NEA, Fla. Edn. Assn., Orange County Tchrs. Assn., Assn. Supervision and Curriculum Devel., Fla. Council Social Studies, Alumni Assn. U. S. Fla., Alumni Assn. So. Bapt. Theol. Sem., Kappa Delta Pi. Democrat. Baptist. Clubs: Winter Park Pilot, Eastern Star, Winter Park Rainbow Girls. Home: 2406 S Bumby St Orlando FL 32806 Office: 901 N Highland Ave Orlando FL 32803

CRANE, JAMES GORDON, artist, writer, visual arts educator; b. Hartsborne, Okla., May 21, 1927; s. Gordon Turner and Naomi (Harrison) C.; m. Jeanette Marie Forgie, June 23, 1951 (div.); children—Lise Crane Tuley, Catherine Crane Knorpel, James Carey; m. Heidemarie Dhom Albright, June 26, 1982. A.A., Jackson Community Coll., Mich., 1949; B.A., Albion Coll., 1951; M.A., State U. Iowa, 1953; M.F.A., Mich. State U., 1962. Art tchr., Jackson, Mich., 1951-55; instr. art U. Wis., River Falls, 1955-57, St. Cloud State Coll., Minn., 1957-58; chmn. dept. art U. Wis., River Falls, 1958-63; coordinator art dept. Fla. Presbyn. Coll./Eckerd Coll., St. Petersburg, 1963-72, 75-85, chmn. collegium of creative arts Eckerd Coll., 1972-75, prof. visual arts, 1976—. Author: What Other Time, 1953; On Edge, 1965; GTM-The Great Teaching Machine, 1966; Inside Out, 1967; Parables, 1971. One-man show: Colombo Americano USIA, Cali, Colombia, 1983; exhibitor group shows: U.S. Embassy Art Collection, Katmandu, Nepal, 1967-75, Lima, Peru, 1975-80. Painter collage: Valley of Dry Bones, Ford Found. Walker Art Ctr., 1962. Contbg. artist Motive mag., 1950-70; feature cartoonist Ave Maria, 1964-69; polit. cartoonist The Mich. Democrat, 1961-62. Mem. edit. adv. bd. Motive mag., 1966-68. Founding bd. dirs. St. Petersburg Arts Commn., 1974-75; feature cartoonist United Church Herald, 1967-71. Danforth Found. grantee, 1960; recipient Disting. Alumni award Albion Coll., 1972, Outstanding Alumni award, 1974. Office: Art Dept Eckerd College PO Box 12560 St Petersburg FL 33733

CRANE, JAMES RALPH, mathematics educator; b. Saginaw, Mich., Apr. 11, 1941; s. Ralph Wendall and Mina Marjorie (Burcham) C.; m. Alice Cheng, June 10, 1965 (div. 1966); m. Ann Margaret Probst, May 28, 1977. B.S., Fla. State U., 1963, Grad. Cert., 1965; M.Ed., Fla. Atlantic U., 1967. Cert. tchr., adminstr., Fla.; cert. actuary. Data analyst S.T. Labs., Cocoa Beach, Fla., 1963-64; jr. engr. Philco Houston Ops., 1964; engr. L.T.V., Patrick AFB, Fla., 1965; math. instr. Brevard Community Coll., Cocoa, Fla., 1972—; U. Central Fla., Cocoa, 1983—, Rollins Coll., Patrick AFB, 1981—; math tchr. Rockledge High Sch., Fla., 1978—; math. tchr., comdt., headmaster pvt. sch., Melbourne, Fla., 1970-78; math tutor, 1982—. Data analyst Govt. Edn. Commn., Melbourne, 1983; counselor juvenile ct. Hillsborough Juvenile Ct., Tampa, Fla., 1964; mem. steering com. Sch. Evaluation for Accreditation, So. Assn. Colls. and Secondary Schs., 1983; vol. Melbourne Mcpl. Band, 1966-69. Grad. asst. Fla. State U., 1965, NSF, 1967; grantee Math. Inst., Brevard County Sch. Bd., summer 1985. Mem. Math. Assn. Am., AAUP, Phi Delta Kappa. Republican. Baptist. Lodges: Masons, Elks. Avocations: Plants, reading, sports, walking, good eating, mowing grass. Home: 731 Hickam Dr Melbourne FL 32901 Office: Rockledge High Sch 220 Raider Rd Rockledge FL 32955

CRANE, JOANNA BREEDLOVE, language specialist; b. Montgomery, Ala., Aug. 19, 1930; d. John William and Willora (Dixon) Breedlove; m. William Harry Crane, Sept. 15, 1970; stepchildren—Jean Adams, Ann Kelliher, Betsy Hornaday, Vickie Allen. B.A., Huntingdon Coll., 1952; M.A., So. Meth. U., 1953; postgrad. U. Miss., Aubigny-sur-Nere, France, 1958, La. State U., 1959, U. Ala., 1960-68. Cert. tchr., Ala. Tchr. French, English and history Montgomery County Bd. Edn., 1953-60; fgn. lang. cons. Ala. State Dept. Edn., Montgomery, 1960-76, asst. to dir. div. instrn., 1976-80, exec. sec. state courses of study program, 1980-84, fgn. lang. and English specialist, 1984—; reviewer NEH, Washington, 1977; mem. adv. council Montgomery Bd. Adult Basic Edn. Program, 1983—. Editor: Dimension: Languages '75: Lifelong Language Learning, 1975; div. editor newspaper; contbr. chpt. to book, articles to profl. jours. Pres. Soroptimist Internat. Montgomery, 1976-77; lay speaker United Meth. Ch. Recipient loyalty award Huntingdon Coll. Alumni Assn., 1985; NEH grantee, 1976. Mem. Am. Council on Teaching Fgn. Langs. (exec. council 1970-74, chmn. publicity com.), Nat. Council State Supervisors Fgn. Langs. (pres. 1969-70), So. Conf. Lang. Teaching (chmn. 1974-75), Ala. Assn. Fgn. Lang. Tchrs. (liaison coordinator 1965-76, 84—), Ala. Assn. Supervisors and Dirs. of Instrn. (liaison 1980—), Ala. Assn. Supervision and Curriculum Devel., Am. Assn. Supervision and Curriculum Devel., Soroptimist Internat. of Ams. Inc. (gov. So. region 1984-86), Alpha Delta Kappa, Kappa Kappa Iota (pres. 1971), Avocations: reading; piano, marimba; swimming. Home: 3300 Drexel Rd Montgomery AL 36106 Office: Ala State Dept Edn 111 Coliseum Blvd Montgomery AL 36193

CRANE, LAWRENCE L., JR., food stores executive. Pres. Piggly Wiggly Corp., Jacksonville, Fla. Office: Piggly Wiggly Corp PO Box 149 Jacksonville FL 32201*

CRANE, STEPHEN WALLACE, veterinary surgeon, educator; b. Modesto, Calif., Apr. 6, 1944; s. Paul Victor and Ora Mae (Wallace) C.; children—Scott Christian, Kevin Paul. B.S., U. Calif.-Davis, 1968, D.V.M., 1970. Intern, Angell Meml. Animal Hosp., Boston, 1970-71; resident surgery Animal Med. Ctr., N.Y.C., 1971-73; instr. surgery Ohio State U. Coll. Vet. Medicine, Columbus, 1973-75; staff surgeon Grand Ave. Pet Hosp., Santa Ana, Calif., 1975-77; chief small animal surg. services Coll. Vet. Medicine, U. Fla., Gainesville, 1977-79, acting chmn. dept. surg. services, 1979-80; prof., head companion animal, spl. species medicine Sch. Vet. Medicine, N.C. State U., Raleigh, 1980—; lectr. univs. Mem. Am. Coll. Vet. Surgeons (cert. splty. bd.), AVMA, N.C. Vet. Med. Assn., Am. Assn. Vet. Clinicians, Am. Assn. Vet. Med. Colls., N.Y. Acad. Scis., Sigma Xi, Alpha Zeta, Phi Zeta, Am. Animal Hosp. Assn. Democrat. Editor, Veterinary Clinics of North America; Symposium on Trauma, 1983; sect. editor: Soft Tissue Surgery: Current Techniques in Small Animal Surgery, 2d edit., 1984; editorial rev. bd. Jour. Vet. Surgery, 1981—, Jour. Am. Animal Hosp. Assn., 1978—; contbr. articles to publs., chpts. to books. Home: 3939 Glenwood Ave Apt 601 Raleigh NC 27612 Office: Sch Vet Medicine NC State U 4700 Hillsborough St Raleigh NC 27606

CRANE, STEVE, inventor; b. Buffalo Gap, Tex., May 21, 1945; s. Vergil and Beth C. B.A., U. Tex., 1967; M.A., Hardin Simmons U., 1968. Dist. mgr. Singer Corp., Dallas, 1967-71; regional mgr. Sight & Sound, Inc., Dallas, 1971-73; pres. Crane Assocs. Mfrs. Reps., Dallas, 1973-76, Creative Products & Mfg. Co., Dallas, 1976—. Bd. dirs. March of Dimes, Marganta Soc. Methodist. Patentee non-osmotic air evacuation container, others. Office: 9876 Chartwell Dr Dallas TX 75243

CRANE, WILLIAM HARRY, accounting educator; b. Montgomery, Ala., Mar. 21, 1925; s. Harold Curtis and Alvira (Landon) C.; student Clemson Coll., 1943, Duke U., 1946-47; B.S., M.S., U. Ala., 1950; m. Joanna Breedlove, Sept. 1970; children by previous marriage—Dorothy Jean Crane Adams, Lucy Anne Crane Kelliher, Mary Elizabeth Crane Hornady, Suzanne Victoria Crane Allen. Partner, Crane, Jackson & Thornton, C.P.A.s, Montgomery, 1953-64 Crane & Crane, C.P.A.s, Montgomery, 1964-67; pres. William H. Crane & Co., C.P.A.s, Montgomery, 1967-79; prof. acctg. Auburn U., Montgomery, 1979—. Budget dir., exec. com. United Appeal, Montgomery, 1962-64; bd. dirs. Montgomery chpt. ARC. Served with inf. AUS, 1943-45. Decorated Purple Heart with 2 clusters, Bronze Star, Silver Star, D.S.C., Combat Inf. badge; named Ky. col.; recipient Outstanding Univ. Faculty, 1985; C.P.A., Ala. Mem. Am. Inst. C.P.A.s, Ala. Soc. C.P.A.s (chmn. council 1964-65), Montgomery Assn. C.P.A.s (pres. 1961-62), Delta Sigma Pi. Methodist. Club: Rotary (dist. gov. 1969-70, Paul Harris fellow 1979). Home: 3300 Drexel Rd Montgomery AL 36106 Office: Auburn U Montgomery AL 36117

CRANK, CHARLES EDWARD, JR., clergyman; b. Richmond, Va., July 20, 1923; s. Charles Edward and Mary Frances (Cochran) C.; m. Melba Louise Cornett, June 7, 1947; children—Charles Edward III, Stephen Lee, Brian Cornett, Melba Kathryn. Student Hampden-Sydney Coll., 1940-42; B.A., Lynchburg Coll., 1947; B.D., Lexington Theol. Sem., 1950; D.D. (hon.), Bethany Coll., 1970. Ordained to ministry Christian Ch., 1947. Pastor, Ky. and Va., 1945-58; dist. minister N.E. Mo., 1958-65; assoc. prof. religion Culver-Stockton Coll., Canton, Mo., 1958-65; regional minister Christian Ch., Parkersburg, W.Va., 1965—; dir. Div. Homeland Ministries, 1971-80, W.Va. Council Chs., 1965—; chaplain Lions Club, 1952-55, Am. Legion, 1944-45. Dir. Hazel Green Acad., 1972-83; chmn. Shenandoah County (Va.) ARC, 1954; mem. PTA, 1955-73; worker Community Little League, 1959-65, Tb. Assn., 1956-58. Served with U.S. Army, 1943-44. Recipient Outstanding Alumni award Lexington Theol. Sem., 1971; Assoc. award Bethany Coll., 1969; Ch. Exec. Devel. Bd. scholar, 1968. Mem. Disciples Peace Fellowship, Council Christian Unity, Disciples of Christ Hist. Soc., Am. Philatelic Soc., Congress Disciples Clergy, Blennerhassett Hist. Found., Blennerhassett Stamp Soc. Democrat. Lodge: Masons. Editor W.Va. Christian Ch. News, 1965—. Office: Route 5 Box 167 Parkersburg WV 26101

CRANSTON, JOHN WELCH, historian; b. Utica, N.Y., Dec. 21, 1931; s. Earl and Mildred (Welch) C.; B.A., Pomona Coll., 1953; M.A., Columbia U., 1964; Ph.D., U. Wis., 1970. Asst. prof. history W. Tex. State U., 1970-74, U. Mo., Kansas City, 1970; asst. prof. Rust Coll., Holly Springs, Miss., 1974-80, asso. prof., 1980-83; historian U.S. Army Armor Ctr., Ft. Knox, Ky., 1983—. Served with U.S. Army, 1953-55. Nat. Endowment for Humanities fellow, summer 1976, summer 1981. Mem. Am. Hist. Assn., Phi Alpha Theta. Democrat. Episcopalian. Contbr. hist. articles to profl. lit. Home: PO Box 892 Radcliff KY 40160 Office: US Army Armor Center Fort Knox KY 40121

CRANTON, ELMER MITCHELL, physician; b. Haverhill, Mass., Sept. 17, 1932; s. Watson Hallet and Laura Mae (Mitchell) C.; children—John Allen, Anne Elizabeth, Catherine Louise, Jennifer Lynn. M.D., Harvard U., 1964; student U. Colo., 1957-59, U. Erlangen (W. Ger.), 1959-60. Rotating intern U.S. Naval Hosp., Pensacola, Fla., 1964-65, gen. surg. staff, 1965; gen. practice medicine, Encinitas, Calif., 1969-72, Arcadia, Calif., 1972-75; chief of staff USPHS Indian Hosp., Talihina, Okla., 1975-76; practice medicine specializing in family practice and preventive medicine, Trout Dale, Va., 1976—; med. dir. Mt. Rogers Clinic, Trout Dale, 1977—. Tchr., med. adv. Vol. Rescue Squads, Mt. Rogers, 1977—. Served with USN, 1951-58, 64-69; USPHS, 75-76. Diplomate Am. Bd. Family Practice. Fellow Am. Acad. Family Physicians, Am. Acad. Med. Preventics (pres.-elect 1985-87), Internat. Coll. Applied Nutrition; mem. Am. Holistic Med. Assn. (pres. 1980-82), Smyth County Med. Soc. (pres. 1980), AMA, Med. Soc. Va., S.W. Va. Med. Soc., Va. Acad. Family Physicians, Acad. Orthomolecular Psychiatry, Internat. Acad. Preventive Medicine, Internat. Acad. Parapsychology and Medicine, Am. Geriatrics Soc., Mensa, Alpha Epsilon Delta. Republican. Methodist (trustee 1979—). Home: Route 1 Box 13 Trout Dale VA 24378 Office: Mount Rogers Clinic Ripshin Rd PO Box 44 Trout Dale VA 24378

CRAPSE, LARRY MURDAUGH, ednl. adminstr.; b. Walterboro, S.C., Aug. 5, 1947; s. Murdaugh and Ida (Chisolm) C.; B.A., U. S.C., 1969; M.A.T., The Citadel, 1973; postgrad. Ind. U., 1975, Columbia U. Tchrs. Coll., 1978, Harvard U., summer 1981; cert. in lit. NYU, 1978; scholar Freedoms Found. at Valley Forge, summer 1982. English tchr. Southside High Sch., Florence, S.C., 1969-70; head English dept. Wilson High Sch., Florence, 1970-77; coordinator gifted programs Florence Dist. 1 Schs., 1977-79, coordinator secondary English, 1977—. Instr. rhetoric U. Ill., 1983-84; instr. cert. courses for tchrs. Active Young Democrats, del. state conv., 1974. Mem. NEA, S.C. Edn. Assn., Nat. Council Tchrs. of English, S.C. Council Tchrs. of English, Assn. Supervision and Curriculum Devel., Internat. Reading Assn. Mem. Christian Ch. (Disciples of Christ). Contbr. articles to profl. publs. Home: 410 1/2 B Cherokee Rd Florence SC 29501 Office: 319 S Dargan St Florence SC 29501

CRASILNECK, HAROLD BERNARD, clinical psychologist; b. San Antonio, Apr. 4, 1921; s. John and Kate (Wolfson) C.; m. Sherry Gold, Jan. 18, 1959; children—Rik, Candace, Jonathan. B.A., Trinity U., San Antonio, 1947; M.A., U. Houston, 1948, Ph.D., 1954. Diplomate Am. Bd. Examiners in Psychol. Hypnosis. Asst. prof. Trinity U., 1949-51; instr. U. Houston, 1951-53; intern in clin. psychology U. Tex. Southwestern Med. Sch., 1953-54, asst. prof., 1954-60, clin. prof. dept. anesthesiology, 1971—, dept. psychiatry, 1971—; pvt. practice clin. psychology and hypnotherapy, 1961—; staff Parkland Meml, Children's Med. Ctr., Baylor U. hosps. Served with USN, 1942-44. Recipient awards Soc. Clin. and Exptl. Hypnosis, 1958, 69, 71; Ben Raginsky award, 1965; Morton Prince award, 1968; Dorcus award, 1971, Best Book award, 1976, Milton Erickoon award, 1979, 81; cert. merit Nat. Coll. Criminal Def. Lawyers. Fellow Am. Soc. Clin. Hypnosis (v.p. 1985, pres. 1986-87, editorial bd.); mem. Australian Soc. Clin. Hypnosis (hon.), Royal Soc. Physicians and Surgeons (hon.)., Am. Psychol. Assn., Dallas Psychol. Assn. (pres. 1959-60), Southwestern Psychol. Assn., Soc. Clin. and Exptl. Hypnosis (pres. 1963-65, editorial bd.), Mensa, Sigma Xi, Phi Kappa Phi, Psi Chi. Author: Clinical Hypnosis: Principles and Applications, 2d edit., 1985. Contbr. articles to profl. jours. Home: 5635 Yolanda Circle Dallas TX 75229 Office: Barnett Tower 3600 Gaston Suite 901 Dallas TX 75246

CRAVENS, DENNIS CARL, structural engineer, construction company executive; b. Elmwood, Ohio, June 4, 1918; s. Ethridge M. and Ida Carolyn (Dosch) C.; m. Margaret Evelyn Johnson, Aug. 7, 1937; children—Dennis Wayne, Glenn Allen, Margaret Gayle. Student Mo. State Tchrs. Coll., 1944, U. Ky., 1951, Internat. Corr. Schs., 1965-69. Registered profl. engr., Ky., Tenn. Pres., Cravens & Cravens, Inc., Gen. Contractors, Lexington, Ky., 1947—, Dennis Cravens & Assocs., Lexington, 1970—; treas. Motel Developers Inc., 1966—. Scoutmaster, Bluegrass council Boy Scouts Am., 1962-66, post advisor, 1966-82; trustee Ky. Wesleyan Coll.; bd. dirs. Salvation Army, Lexington; trustee, mem. adminstrv. bd. Epworth United Meth. Ch., chmn., 1984. Served with USAF, 1943-45. Mem. Nat. Soc. Profl. Engrs. (v.p. profl. engrs. in constrn. 1975-76), Ky. Soc. Profl. Engrs. (chmn. profl. engrs. in constrn. sect. 1973, dir. Bluegrass chpt.; Engring. Achievement award 1975), Assoc. Gen. Contractors (past dir. Bluegrass chpt.), Greater Lexington C. of C. (dir. 1979-82), SAR, Soc. Boonesboro. Clubs: Masons, Lexington. Home: 423 Clinton Rd Lexington KY 40502 Office: 524 Lagonda Ave Lexington KY 40505

CRAVENS, MARGARET EVELYN JOHNSON, motel executive; b. nr. Versailles, Ky., May 11, 1919; d. Denny Johnson and Bethel (Goodpaster) Johnson Cox; student Draughn Bus. Coll., Springfield, Mo., 1943, U. Ky., 1951, Sch. Civil Def., 1959, Quality Inns, Inc. Motel Mgmt. Sch., 1969; m. Dennis Carl Cravens, Aug. 7, 1937; children—Dennis Wayne, Glenn Allen,

Margaret Gayle. Office mgr. Cravens & Cravens, Inc., Lexington, Ky., 1946-50; gen. mgr. Quality Inn, N.W. Lexington, 1968—; pres., dir. Motel Developers, Inc.; chmn. Quality Inns Internat. Operators Council, Region 9, 1973. Mem. Lexington-Fayette County Recreational, Tourism and Conv. Commn., 1971-79, chmn., 1975-77. Bd. dirs., Lexington Center, Inc., 1972-80, also past sec. Chmn. commn. on missions, mem. bd. stewards Epworth Methodist Ch., 1961-65, sponsor, counselor World Friendship Group of Girls, 1953-57. Bd. dirs. Nathanael Methodist Mission, Ky. Historic Mansions Preservation Found.; mem. Mayor's Sign Rev. Com., 1984. Mem. Greater Lexington C. of C. (dir. 1974-77), Am. (dir., exec. com. 1980-81), Ky. (pres. 1978-79), Lexington (pres. 1975) hotel-motel assns. Home: 423 Clinton Rd Lexington KY 40502 Office: Quality Inn NW 1050 Newtown Pike Lexington KY 40511

CRAVER, JENNIFER, association administrator; b. Marion, Ohio, Nov. 18, 1951; d. Ernest F. and Darlene (Hutchinson) Craver Shenefield; m. Larry M. Gipson, Aug. 20, 1974. Student Valparaiso U., 1970; B.S., Bowling Green State U., 1974. Dir., Ret. Sr. Vol. Program, Mansfield, Ohio, 1974-75; supr. social services Marion County Welfare Dept., Ohio, 1975-79; cons. options, Columbus, Ohio, 1979-81; v.p. human resources Met. Tulsa C. of C., Okla., 1982—. Bd. dirs. Street Sch., Tulsa, Leadership Tulsa. Mem. Am. Soc. Tgn. and Devel. Club: Moneymakers (pres. 1982-84) (Tulsa). Home: 1202 E 18th St Tulsa OK 74120 Office: Met C of C 616 S Boston St Tulsa OK 74119

CRAVER, ROGER MOORE, fundraising and marketing executive; b. Gettysburg, Pa., Aug. 8, 1941; s. Forrest Eugene and Dorothy (Meyer) C.; m. Paula Arnold Craver, Oct. 21, 1972; children—Christopher Moore, Caitlin Bailey. B.A., Dickinson Coll., 1963; J.D., George Washington U., 1970. Fundraising cons. Dickinson Coll., Carlisle, Pa., 1963-67; dir. devel. George Washington U., Washington, 1967-70, Common Cause, Washington, 1970-72; chmn., pres. Craver, Mathews, Smith & Co., Falls Church, Va., 1972—; chmn. Pub. Interest Communications, Falls Church, 1977—; prin. fundraising cons. to The Sierra Club, Common Cause, Democratic Nat. Com., Planned Parenthood, NOW, Costeau Soc., Handgun Control, Inc. Mem. Nat. Soc. Fundraising Execs., Direct Mail Mktg. Assn., Order of Coif. Democrat. Methodist. Home: 2039 Rhode Island Ave McLean VA 22101 Office: Craver Mathews Smith and Co 282 N Washington St Falls Church VA 22046

CRAWFORD, DAVID COLEMAN, diversified manufacturing company executive; b. Dixon, Ill., Mar. 7, 1930; s. Grace F. (Coleman) C.; B.S., Norwich U., 1952; M.S., U. Ill., 1954; m. Carolyn J. Morrow, Nov. 11, 1958; children—Eugene, Richard, Grace. Design engr. Freeport Sulphur Co., New Orleans, 1956-62; sr. engr. ETCO Engrs. & Assos., New Orleans, 1962-64; mgr. constrn. Offshore Co., Houston, 1964-70; asst. gen. mgr. Far East, Levingston Shipbldg. Co., Singapore, 1970-71; with Marathon Mfg. Co., Houston and Singapore, 1971—, sr. v.p., 1973-74, exec. v.p., 1974—, also dir.; dir. several subs. cos. Trustee Norwich U. Served with C.E., U.S. Army, 1954-56. Mem. ASCE, Am. Welding Soc., Sigma Xi, Chi Epsilon, Tau Beta Pi. Republican. Baptist. Clubs: Lakeside Country, Petroleum of Houston, Houston Engring., Heritage Research on brazed copper joints, 1952-54. Home: 611 Durley Rd Houston TX 77079 Office: 600 Jefferson St Houston TX 77002

CRAWFORD, FRED ALLEN, JR., cardiothoracic surgeon, educator; b. Columbia, S.C., Oct. 17, 1942; s. Fred Allen and Susan Valery Floyd C.; m. Mary Jane Dantzler, June 11, 1966; children—Fred Allen, III, Mary Elizabeth. M.D., Duke U., 1967. Diplomate Am. Bd. Surgery, Am. Bd. Thoracic Surgery. Intern, Duke U. Med. Ctr., Durham, N.C., 1967-68, resident in surgery, 1971-76, instr. surgery, 1975-76; asst. prof. surgery, chief div. cardiac surgery U. Miss., Med. Ctr., Jackson, 1976-79; prof. surgery pediatrics, chief div. cardiothoracic surgery Med. U. of S.C., Charleston, 1979—. Served to maj. U.S. Army, 1969-71. Decorated Bronze Star. Mem. Charleston County Med. Soc., S.C. State Med. Assn., Soc. Thoracic Surgeons, So. Surg. Assn., So. Thoracic Surg. Assn., Am. Heart Assn., Assn. for Acad. Surgeons, Am. Coll. Cardiology, ACS, Phi Beta Kappa, Alpha Omega Alpha. Presbyterian. Club: Ducks Unltd. Contbr. numerous articles to profl. jours. Home: 1012 Scottland Dr Mount Pleasant SC 29464 Office: Div of Cardiothoracic Surgery Med U of SC 171 Ashley Ave Charleston SC 29403

CRAWFORD, JOHN WILLIAM, English educator; b. Ashdown, Ark., Sept. 2, 1936; m. Kathryn Louise Bizzell; children—Jeffrey Wayne, Sonja Rene. B.A., B.S.E., Ouachita Bapt. U., 1959; M.S.E., Drake U., 1962; Ed.D., Okla. State U., 1968. Tchr. English East Greene High Schs., Grand Junction, Iowa, 1959-60; tchr. Eng. jr. high Jefferson schs., Ia., 1960-62; instr. Clinton Jr. Coll., Iowa, 1962-66; instr. Okla. State U., Stillwater, 1966-67; asst. prof. Henderson State U., Arkadelphia, Ark., 1967-68, assoc. prof., 1968-73, prof., 1973—, chmn. dept. English, from 1977. Author: Romantic Criticism of Shakespearean Drama, 1978 (Poetry awards 1966, 68); Early Shakespearean Actresses, 1984; author essay collections. Mem. South Central Coll. English Assn. (treas. 1978-80, pres. 1980-81), Coll. Eng. Assn. (nominating com. 1984-86), South Central MLA, Phi Delta Kappa (treas. local chpt. 1984-86), Theta Alpha Phi, Phi Sigma Epsilon. Republican. Baptist. Avocations: music; reading; gardening; first day cover collecting; drama. Home: 1813 Walnut Arkadelphia AR 71923 Office: Henderson State U Dept of English Arkadelphia AR 71923

CRAWFORD, RAYMON EDWARD, college administrator; b. Charlotte, N.C., July 1, 1939; s. Theodore and Georgetta (Bridgeforth) C. B.S., N.C. A&T U., 1961; M.S., Hampton Inst., 1973, Central Mich. U., 1978. Served to lt. col. U.S. Army, 1962-83; v.p. student affairs Morehouse Coll., Atlanta, 1983—; prof.-in-residence Atlanta Coll. Dental Med. Careers, 1983-84. Mem. Met. Atlanta Crime Commn.; mem. Atlanta Urban League. Decorated Purple Heart, Air medal, Joint Chief of Staff medal; named Man of Yr. U.S. Army, 1982. Mem. Southeastern Assn. for Housing Officers, Nat. Assn. for Personnel Workers (chmn. 1984-85), Nat. Assn. Student personnel Adminstrs., So. Assn. for Coll. Student Affairs, NAACP (exec. bd.), Nu Mu Lambda (Man Yr. award 1983). Democrat. Lodge: Rotary. Avocations: golf; football; basketball; baseball. Home: 4281 Greenvale Dr Decatur GA 30034 Office: Morehouse Coll 830 Westview Dr Atlanta GA 30314

CRAWFORD, RICHARD LEE, religious organization administrator; b. Maryville, Mo., Mar. 2, 1938; s. Pearl Oliver and Julia Helen (Stapler) C.; m. Arlene Cecilia Huerter, Sept. 15, 1962; children—Angela M., Jennifer T. Gay, Amy C., Andrews S. B.A., Oklahoma City U., 1981. Reporter, Topeka Capital Jour., Ottawa (Kans.) Herald, 1961-63; news editor Independence (Mo.) Examiner, 1963-65; city editor/mng. editor Pittsburg (Kans.) Headlight-Sun, 1965-71; staff editor Tulsa Tribune, 1971-77; v.p. Pub. Relations Internat. Ltd., Tulsa, Houston and London, 1977-79; diocesan exec. Episcopal Diocese Okla., Oklahoma City, 1979—; pub. relations and employee relations cons. Bd. dirs. Okla. Conf. Chs.; area v.p. S.W., Clan Lindsay Assn., 1975—. Served with U.S. Army Res., 1956-63. Recipient award Central Okla. Multi-Media Assn., 1981; Personal Column citation Mo. Press Assn., 1963; Excellence in Pub. Affairs Silver Anvil award Pub. Relations Soc. Am., 1978. Mem. Pub. Relations Soc. Am., Religious Pub. Relations Council (organizer, 1st pres. Sooner chpt.), Conf. Diocesan Execs., Oklahoma City U. Alumni Assn., Sigma Delta Chi. Episcopalian. Clubs: Masons. Editor Okla. Mission, 1979—. Home: 1220 Avondale Dr Norman OK 73069 Office: 1117 N Sharel St Suite 500 Oklahoma City OK 73103

CRAWLEY, SHARON JOYCE, educator; b. Waterbury, Conn., Aug. 18, 1946; d. Richard Lawrence and Marion Gladys (Rock) Crawley. B.S. in Elem. Edn., Central Conn. State Coll., 1968, M.S. in Reading, 1970, diploma in Reading, 1973; Ed.D. in Curriculum and Instrn., U. Houston, 1970. Tchr. pub. schs., Conn., 1968-71; cons. reading Simsbury, Conn., 1971-75; instr. Houston Community Coll., 1975; lectr. and teaching asst. Coll. Edn., U. Houston, 1976-78; assoc. prof. edn. Sch. Edn., Augusta (Ga.) Coll., 1979-86, U. Tex.-El Paso, 1986—; lectr. in field. Mem. task force Emergency Sch. Aid Act., 1979-80. Augusta Coll. Faculty Research and Devel. Com. grantee, 1982-83. Mem. Profl. Bus. Women's Orgn., Internat. Reading Assn., Nat. Council Tchrs. of English, Ga. Council Reading, Ga. Council Social Studies, Central Savannah River Area Reading Council, Kappa Delta Pi, Phi Delta Kappa. Lutheran. Author: (with Lee Mountain) Strategies: Teaching Reading in Content Areas, 1981, Teacher Guiding Students: Strategies for Content Learning; (workbooks) Cloze Attention to Comprehension, Book A, 1982, Cloze Attention to Comprehension, Book C, 1982; contbr. numerous edn. articles to profl. publs. Home: 840 El Parque El Paso TX 79912 Office: Coll Edn U Tex El Paso TX 79968

CRAYTON, GARY LEE, civic center official, accountant; b. Columbus, Ga., June 11, 1953; s. Samuel Elmo and Berter Lucille (Herrington) C.; m. Kathryn Miles Graham, Aug. 16, 1981; 1 son, Samuel Henry. B.S., Fla. State U., 1975, M.B.A., 1976. C.P.A., Fla. Asst. controller Tallahassee Meml. Regional Med. Ctr., 1979; acctg. services supr. Fla. Dept. Health and Rehab. Services, Tallahassee, 1979-82; bus. mgr. Tallahassee Leon-County Civic Ctr., 1982—; pvt. practice acctg., 1976—; cons. in field. Served with U.S. Army, 1977-79; to capt. USAR. Decorated Army Commendation medal with oak leaf cluster. Mem. Fla. Inst. C.P.A.s, Am. Inst. C.P.A.s, Fla. State U. Alumni Assn., Scabbard and Blade. Episcopalian. Home: 5531 Briarwood Cir Tallahassee FL 32301 Office: PO Box 10604 Tallahassee FL 32302

CREASY, ROBERT CLIFTON, petroleum exploration geologist; b. Lake Charles, La., Dec. 7, 1956; s. Ben Robert and Marlene Faye (Brame) C.; m. Sheri McInnis, April 8, 1984. B.S. in Geology, U. Southwestern La., 1978. Geologist The Wiser Oil Co., Houston, 1979-81, Vermilion Oil & Gas Co., Lafayette, La., 1982—. Mem. Am. Assn. Petroleum Geologists, Houston Geologic Soc., Lafayette Geologic Soc., Soc. Profl. Well Logistics Analysts, Soc. Paleontologists and Mineralogists. Baptist. Home: 702 Patrick St Broussard LA 70518 Office: Vermilion Oil & Gas Corp Brandywine 6 Suite 207 Lafayette LA 70505

CRECENTE, ELIZABETH LEVATO, psychologist, hospital program administrator, therapist; b. Chgo., Nov. 6, 1946; d. Ross Vincent and Carmella Theresa (D'ambrose) Levato; m. Joseph Wendell Crecente, May 28, 1966 (div. 1984); children—Joseph Andrew II, Brian David. B.A., U. Md.-College Park, 1973; M.A., U. Md.-Cantonsville, 1978; postgrad., Howard U., 1978—. Clin. psychologist U.S. Army, Seoul, Korea, 1980-82; cons. Foreigner's Community Service, Seoul, 1980-82; instr. U. Md. Far East Div., Seoul, 1980-82; program adminstr. Sun Valley Regional Hosp., El Paso, Tex., 1982—; pvt. practice therapy, El Paso, 1983—. Scholar Ga. State U., 1968, Seoul Am. Officer's Wives Club, 1981. Mem. Am. Psychol. Assn., El Paso Psychol. Assn. (chmn. bd. 1985-86), Am. Soc. Clin. Hypnosis (student affiliate), Psi Chi. Roman Catholic. Home: 6405 Los Robles El Paso TX 79912 Office: Sun Valley Regional Hosp 1155 Idaho El Paso TX 79902

CREECH, GLENWOOD LEWIS, educator, former university president; b. Middleburg, Ky., Dec. 31, 1920; s. Chester B. and Tennie (Estes) C.; student Centre Coll., 1937-38; B.S., U. Ky., 1941, M.S., 1950; Ph.D. (W.K. Kellogg Found. fellow), U. Wis., 1957; m. Martha Josephine Brooks, Apr. 4, 1942; children—Carolyn Ann (Mrs. Alan Grey), Walton Brooks. Tchr. Stanford (Ky.) High Sch., 1946-49; research specialist U. Ky., Lexington, 1951-54, editor, 1954-56, prof., v.p., 1965-73; prof. U. Wis. at Madison, 1957-59; dir. div. agr. W.K. Kellogg Found., Battle Creek, Mich., 1959-65; pres. Fla. Atlantic U., Boca Raton, 1973-83, prof. adminstrn., 1973—; vis. prof. Cornell U., 1958; cons. U.S. Dept. State, U.S. Dept. Agr. Bd. dirs. U. Ky. Devel. Council, 1965-73, U. Ky. Athletics Assn., 1965-73, Spindletop Hall, Inc., Lexington, 1965-73, Children's Theatre, 1966-73, Living Arts and Sci. Center of Central Ky., 1966-73, Boca Raton YMCA, 1975—, Fla. Endowment for Humanities, 1977-79; trustee St. Andrew's Sch., Boca Raton, 1975-77, Boca Raton Community Hosp.; public trustee Miami Ednl. TV Sta., 1974-79; mem. Historic Boca Raton Preservation Bd. Commrs., 1975-78; bd. dirs., pres. United Way of Greater Boca Raton, 1979-80; pres. Fla. Assn. of Colls. and Univs., 1980-81, Econ. Council of Palm Beach County. Served with AUS, 1941-46. Recipient Disting. Service award U. Ky. Alumni Assn., 1967; named to Hall of Disting. Alumni, U. Ky., 1975. Mem. Greater Boca Raton C. of C., Phi Delta Kappa, Omicron Delta Kappa, Delta Sigma Pi, Phi Kappa Phi, Phi Theta Kappa, Blue Key. Club: Rotary (hon.) (Boca Raton). Home: 700 S Ocean Blvd 605 Boca Raton FL 33432

CREEL, JOE MORTON, orthodontist; b. Gadsden, Ala., Apr. 9, 1940; s. Joseph and Nellie Jo (Morton) C.; m. Judith Ann Speece, Dec. 19, 1964 (div. Aug. 1978); children—Daniel Joseph, Scott Frederick; m. Dianne Elizabeth Billups, Sept. 13, 1980; chidren—Brian Robert, Andrew Stephen. D.D.S., Ohio State U., 1965; M.S., Washington U., St. Louis, 1969. Assoc. with George J. Coleman, D.D.S., Coral Gables, Fla., 1969-72; individual practice, Coral Gables, Fla., 1973-76, Melbourne, Fla., 1976—. Served as capt. Dental Corps., U.S. Army, 1965-67. Mem. ADA, Fla. Dental Assn., Central Dist. Dental Soc., Brevard County Dental Assn., Am. Assn. Orthodontists, So. Soc. Orthodontists, Fla. Assn. Orthodontists, South Dade Dental Soc. (past pres.), Greater Miami Acad. Orthodontists (past pres.). Republican. Methodist. Lodge: Kiwanis (past dir.). Home: 460 Rio Casa Dr S Indialantic FL 32903 Office: 1302 E New Haven Ave Melbourne FL 32901

CREESE, ROBERT CLAUDE, industrial engineering educator, consultant; b. Pitts., Nov. 24, 1941; s. Thomas Chalmers and Eleanor Maude (Smith) C.; m. Natalie Agnes Small, Dec. 14, 1962; children—Jennifer Lynn, Robert Eric. B.S.I.E., Pa. State U., 1963, Ph.D. in Metallurgy, 1972; M.S., U. Calif.-Berkeley, 1964. Registered profl. engr., Pa., W.Va. Indsl. engr. U.S. Steel Corp., Pitts., 1964-66; instr. Pa. State U., State College, 1966-72, asst. prof., 1976-79; asst. prof. Grove City (Pa.) Coll., 1972-76; assoc. prof. indsl. engring. W.Va. U., Morgantown, 1979—; part-time research engr. Ford Motor Co., Detroit, 1976, 78, David Taylor Naval Ship Research and Devel. Ctr., Annapolis, Md., 1982, Ft. Belvoir Research and Devel. Ctr., Va., 1984. Bd. dirs. Eastern Mercer County Home Health Care Agy., 1974-76. Alfred P. Sloan Found. fellow, 1963-64; Pa. State U. fellow, 1969-70. Mem. AIME, Am. Soc. for Metals, Am. Foundrymen's Soc., Inst. Indsl. Engrs., Am. Assn. Cost Engrs., Am. Soc. for Engring. Edn., Am. Numismatic Assn., Pa. State U. Alumni Assn. (life), Sigma Xi. Republican. Presbyterian. Contbr. articles to profl. jours. Home: 306 Oakland St Morgantown WV 26505 Office: WVa U 721 Engring Sci Bldg Morgantown WV 26506

CREIGHTON, JOSEPH RIGGS, electronic mfg. co. exec.; b. Canton, China, Jan. 5, 1920 (parents Am. citizens); s. John W. and Lois (Jameson) C.; m. Margaret Tyler Hitchner, 1942 (div. 1969); children—Howard, Jonathan, Richard; m. Claire Lorraine Poirier, Sept. 5, 1969. A.B., Oberlin Coll., 1941; J.D., Harvard U., 1947. Bar: Calif. 1949, Ill. 1958, Mass. 1960, Ohio 1969, Fla. 1983. Asso. law firm San Francisco, 1948-51; practiced in Oakland, Calif., 1951-55; atty. Gen. Electric Co., Plainville, Conn., 1955-57, Chgo., 1957-59; div. counsel Raytheon Co., Lexington, Mass., 1959-64; asst. gen. counsel, 1964-67; gen. counsel Harris Corp., Cleve., 1968-78, Melbourne, Fla., 1978—, v.p., 1975-85, sr. legal advisor, 1986—; chmn. law council Machinery and Allied Products Inst., 1981-84. Chmn., Orinda (Calif.) Planning Com., 1953-54; pres. Young Republicans Calif., 1954; chmn. Rep. Central Com., Contra Costa County, Calif., 1954-55; mem. Rep. State Central Com. Calif., 1955. Served to capt., Q.M.C., U.S. Army, 1942-46. Mem. ABA, Internat. Bar Assn., Fla. Bar Assn., Semicondr. Industry Assn. (chmn. law com. 1984—), Ohio State Bar (chmn. corp. counsel com. 1973-74). Home: 1601 S Miramar Ave Indialantic FL 32903 Office: 1025 Nasa Blvd Melbourne FL 32919

CREMERS, CLIFFORD JOHN, mechanical engineering educator; b. Mpls., Mar. 27, 1933; s. Christian Joseph and Marie Hildegard (Marshik) C.; m. Claudette Mae Humble, Sept. 25, 1954; children—Carla Ann, Rachel Beth, Emily Therese, Eric John, Melissa Joan. B.S. in M.E., U. Minn., 1957, M.S. in M.E., 1961, Ph.D., 1964. Instr. mech. engring. U. Minn.-Mpls., 1961-64; asst. prof. Ga. Inst. Tech., Atlanta, 1964-66; assoc. prof. U. Ky., Lexington, 1966-71, prof., 1971—, chmn. dept. mech. engring., 1975-84; vis. scholar Imperial Coll. Sci. and Tech., London, 1973; Lady Davis vis. prof. Technion, Israel Inst. Tech., Haifa, 1986; cons. in field. Served with U.S. Navy, 1953-55. Trane fellow, 1958; NSF grantee, 1965, 67, 71, 75, 78, 81; NASA grantee, 1968, 69, 70, 71, 72, 73; Western Golf Assn. scholar 1950, Maytag Scholar, 1956. Fellow ASME, AIAA (assoc. fellow); mem. AAAS, Am. Soc. Engring. Edn., Sigma Xi. Roman Catholic. Contbr. articles in field to profl. jours. Home: 3181 Lamar Dr Lexington KY 40502 Office: 242 Anderson Hall University of Kentucky Lexington KY 40506

CREMINS, JAMES SMYTH, political party official, lawyer; b. Washington, June 11, 1921; m. Mary Louise Gallagher (dec.); 5 children. A.B. with honors, U. Mo.-Columbia, 1943; J.D., U. Va., 1949. Treas. Democratic Com. Va., 1977—; of counsel CSX Corp., 1985—. Contbr. articles to legal jours. Lay minister St. Mary's Ch., Richmond; bd. visitors U. Va., St. Gertrude High Sch., Richmond, past instl. rep. Robert E. Lee council Boy Scouts Am.; mem. fin. council Richmond Catholic Diocese, 1978—; bd. dirs. Maymont Found., 1976—. Served to lt. USN, 1943-1946. Recipient Brotherhood citation NCCJ, 1983. Mem. Va. Soc. SAR (v.p.), Alpha Tau Omega, Phi Delta Phi. Lodges: Ancient Order Hiberians Am. (charter mem. Maj. James Dooley Div. 1); KC.

CRENSHAW, SALLY ANN, guidance counselor; b. Louisville, June 18, 1945; d. Lamar Jefferson and Helen Lorraine (Mercer) Allen; m. Donald Earl Crenshaw, Sept. 30, 1981; 1 stepchild, Jeremy Earl. B.A., Ky. Wesleyan Coll., 1967; M.Ed., Western Ky. U., 1975. Social worker Human Resources, Henderson, Ky., 1967-73; coordinator Ky. Dept. Edn., Frankfort, 1973-78, supr., 1978-81; guidance counselor, admissions officer Health Occupations Sch., Madisonville, Ky., 1981—; mem. accreditation vis. team So. Assn. Colls. and Schs. Named Outstanding Counselor, Vocat. Edn. Region 2, Ky., 1985. Mem. Ky. Vocat. Guidance Assn., Ky. Assn. Counseling and Devel., Am. Assn. Counseling and Devel., Ky. Vocat. Assn., Am. Vocat. Assn. Democrat. Mem. Ch. Christ. Avocations: home decorating; reading; bowling; swimming. Home: Rural Route 2 Robards KY 42452 Office: Madisonville Health Occupations Sch 701 N Laffoon Madisonville KY 42431

CRENSHAW, TENA LULA, librarian; b. Coleman, Fla., Dec. 15, 1930; d. Herbert Joseph and Nellie Jackson (Wicker) Crenshaw; B.S., Fla. So. Coll., 1951; postgrad. U. Fla., 1952-55; M.L.S. (Univ. scholar), U. Okla., 1960. Tchr. pub. schs., Coleman, Fla., 1952-55, St. Petersburg, Fla., 1955-57, Houston, 1957-59; tech. librarian Army Rocket & Guided Missile Agy., Redstone Arsenal, Huntsville, Ala., 1960-61; acquisitions librarian Martin Marietta Corp., Orlando, Fla., 1961-64; reader services librarian John F. Kennedy Space Center, NASA, Fla., 1964-66; research info. analyst, specialist Lockheed Missiles and Space Co., Palo Alto, Calif., 1966-68; head services to pub. A.W. Calhoun Med. Library, Emory U., Atlanta, 1969-78; with U. Fla. Edn. Library, Gainesville, 1980-84; with Westinghouse Electric Corp., Orlando, chmn. Fla. State Adv. Council on Libraries, 1980—. Mem. Spl. Libraries Assn. (treas. South Atlantic chpt. 1970-72, mem. com. on coms. 1983—, v.p. 1973-74, pres. 1974-75, mem. resolutions com. 1975-77, mem. archives com. 1978—, chmn. 1977-78, membership chmn. library mgmt. div. 1981—), Med. Library Assn., Southeastern Library Assn. (mem. new directions com. 1972-74), Ga. Library Assn. (careers in librarianship com. 1974-78, automation com. 1978-79), Fla. Library Assn., DAR, Alpha Delta Pi, Kappa Delta Pi. Democrat. Episcopalian. Contbr. to Spl. Libraries Assn. Newsletter. Office: Westinghouse Electric Corp Library-MC 235 The Quadrangle Orlando FL 32817

CRESIMORE, JAMES LEONARD, food broker; b. Statesville, N.C., Jan. 24, 1928; s. Fred Clayton and Cleo (Edison) C.; B.S. in Bus. Adminstrn., High Point Coll., 1949; m. Mary Josephine Conrad, June 3, 1956; children—James Conrad, Jennifer Cheryl, Joel Clayton. Gen. mgr. Home Service Stores, Inc., High Point, N.C., 1948-50; co-founder, sec. Red Dot Food Stores, Inc., 1952-56; sec. Consol. Wholesale Corp., 1952-56; owner Village Super Market, High Point, 1953-56; co-owner Bunker Hill Packing Corp., Bedford, Va., 1964—; chmn. bd., co-owner Assoc. Brokers, Inc., Raleigh, N.C., 1956—; founding dir., chmn. bd. State Bank Raleigh; chmn. bd. Smithfield Cos. Inc., Va.; past chmn. United Carolina Bank, Raleigh; dir. United Carolina Bank N.C. Chmn. Mayor's Manpower Com., Raleigh. Chmn. Wake County Republican Com., 1963—, del. nat. conv. San Francisco, 1964; 4th Congl. dist.; mem. platform com. Rep. Nat. Convention, Miami, Fla., 1968. Mem. advisory bd. Salvation Army; trustee Pheiffer Coll.; bd. dirs. Raleigh Community Hosp., N.C. Citizens for Bus. and Industry, Bapt. Children's Homes of N.C. Served with U.S. Army, 1950-52. Mem. Sales and Marketing Execs. Internat. (mem. bd., pres. Raleigh now v.p.), Raleigh Food Brokers Assn. (past pres.), Nat. Food Brokers Assn. (regional rep.), (lt. regional dir.) food brokers assns., Raleigh C. of C. (dir. 1973-74). Lodge: Rotary. Home: 3720 Williamsborough Ct Raleigh NC 27609 Office: 3309 Drake Circle Raleigh NC 27609

CRESS, ROBERT MENDENHALL, optometrist; b. Denton, N.C., Dec. 15, 1947; s. Robert Elias and Mary (Thayer) C.; m. Linda Ann Lorch, July 19, 1970; children—Kevin Robert, Steven Michael. B.S., Appalachian State U., 1970; O.D., So. Coll. Optometry, Memphis, 1975. Lic. optometrist, S.C., N.C. Practice optometry, Orangeburg, S.C., 1975—; ptnr. Mixson & Cress, Orangeburg, 1984—. Team chmn. Orangeburg United Way, 1978. Mem. Am. Optometric Assn., S.C. Optometric Assn. (sec.-treas. 1985-86), Central Midlands Optometric Soc., Orangeburg County C. of C., Beta Beta Beta. Lutheran. Lodge: Kiwanis (bd. dirs. 1985-86). Avocations: golf; gardening. Home: 1835 Taylor Blvd NE Orangeburg SC 29115 Office: Mixson & Cress ODs 605 Carolina Ave NE Orangeburg SC 29115

CRESSMAN, ARTHUR RAYMOND, JR., steel products company executive; b. Darby, Pa., Aug. 2, 1947; s. Arthur Raymond and Lorraine E. C.; student U. Kans., 1965-67, U. Md., 1972-74, U. Chgo., 1973-74, Harrow Inst., London, 1974-75; m. Constance A. Smith, Mar. 11, 1972; children—Arthur R., Jacqueline A. Mgr. ops. Itel Corp./Computer Dimensions Inc., Dallas, 1975-77; mgr. regional sales Dallas Pipe & Supply Inc., 1977-78; pres., chief operating officer Intercontinental Pipe & Steel Inc., Dallas, 1978-83; pres., chief operating officer Cressman Tubular Products Corp., Dallas, 1984—. Served with U.S. Navy, 1967-75. Mem. Nat. Assn. Steel Pipe Distbrs., Kans. Independent Oil and Gas Assn., Phi Kappa Tau. Clubs: Brookhaven Country (Dallas); Dallas County Republican Men's. Office: Cressman Tubular Products 2607 Walnut Hill Ln Suite 113 Dallas TX 75229

CRESWELL, LOYAL RAY, architectural executive; b. Lawton, Okla., Dec. 19, 1950; s. Loyal Bufford and Lena Faye (Flippin) C.; m. Karen Sue Force, June 10, 1978; children—Cortney Lynn, Kristin Rae. B.S.E.T. in Architecture, Memphis State U., 1975. Co-owner, v.p. R-Two Design Group, Inc., Dallas. Mem. AIA (assoc.), Tex. Soc. Architects, Constrn. Specifications Inst., Pi Kappa Phi. Republican. Baptist. Home: 209 Clay Ln Red Oak TX 75154

CREUZIGER, DONALD PHILLIP, professional services company executive, former army officer; b. Racine, Wis., Aug. 22, 1927; s. Charles Melford and Iva Hazel (Brandt) C.; m. Mary Louis Larsen, July 15, 1950; children—Karen; John. B.S., U.S. Mil. Acad., 1950; M.S., U. So. Calif., 1963. Lic. comml. helicopter pilot. Commd. 2d lt. U.S. Army, 1950, advanced through grades to col., 1970; staff officer Joint Chiefs of Staff, Washington, 1969-70; chief firepower div. Dept. Chief of Staff, Ops., Dept Army, Washington, 1971-72; chief of staff 1st Armored Div., Ansbach, Fed. Republic Germany, 1973-75; dep. asst. sec. of Army, Washington, 1975-76; asst. v.p. Jaycor, Alexandria, Va., 1977-79; chief exec. officer XMCO Inc., Reston, Va., 1979—. Decorated Legion of Merit with bronze oak leaf cluster, Air medal with 2 bronze oak leaf clusters. Mem. Nat. Trust Hist. Preservation, U.S. Senatorial Club, Fairfax C. of C., Assn. U.S. Army, Am. Def. Preparedness Assn., U.S. Armor Assn. (sec. 1978-82). Republican. Lutheran. Club: River Bend. Lodge: Masons. Avocations: golf; woodworking. Home: 10531 Brinham Rd Great Falls VA 22066 Office: XMCO Inc 11150 Sunrise Valley Dr Reston VA 22091

CREVOISIER, RALPH AARON, orthodontist, educator; b. Pitman, Ark., Dec. 10, 1932; s. Granville Adolph and Thelma Arline (Scates) C.; m. Sylvia Juanita Fernandez, July 14, 1955; children—Ralph Aaron Jr., Yvette Marie Crevoisier Harbour, Michael Vincent. B.A., St. Mary's U., San Antonio, 1960; D.D.S., St. Louis U., 1964, M.S.D., 1974. Pvt. practice gen. dentistry, San Antonio, 1964-72, orthodontics, San Antonio, 1974—; assoc. prof. U. Tex. Health Sci. Ctr., San Antonio, 1976—; cons. orthodontics Audie Murphy VA Hosp., San Antonio, 1981—. Singer San Antonio Symphony Mastersingers, 1965-82. Served with USAF, 1952-56. Mem. ADA, San Antonio Dist. Soc., Am. Assn. Orthodontists, Southwestern Soc. Orthodontists, Orthodontic Edn. and Research Found. (pres. 1984-85). Republican. Avocation: pilot. Home: 14060 Mint Trail San Antonio TX 78232 Office: 8647C Wurzbach Rd San Antonio TX 78240

CREWS, FREDA VONCILLE, pastoral and mental health counselor; b. Oleustee, Fla., Mar. 17, 1936; d. William Henry and Martha (Crawford) Green; m. William Robert Crews, Dec. 13, 1954; children—Terrie Wilkins, William Jr., Rachel Buckley. B. Religious Edn., Zion Coll., 1970; M. Religious Edn., Grace Bible Coll., 1973; M.A. in Counseling, N. Am. Bapt. Sem., 1979; D. Min., Trinity Evang. Divinity Sch., 1982. Counselor, adminstr. Bible Study Time Radio Broadcast, Spartanburg, S.C., 1970—; sec., treas. Grace Enterprises, Spartanburg, 1976—; pastoral assoc. McKennan Hosp., Sioux Falls, S.D., 1980-81; dir. pastoral care and counseling East Gaffney Baptist Ch., Gaffney, S.C., 1983—. Author: Comprehensive Introduction to Christian Lay Counseling, 1982. Counselor Good Samaritan Counseling Services, Gaffney. Mem. Am. Assn. for Counseling and Devel., S.C. Assn. for Counseling and Devel., Am. Mental Health Counselors Assn., S.C. Mental Health Counselors Assn., Nat. Assn. Marriage and Family Counselors. Avocations: cooking; flower gardening; flying. Home: 2206 Cherokee Ave Gaffney SC 29340 Office: Good Samaritan Counseling Services 2400 Cherokee Ave Gaffney SC 29340

CREWS, HAROLD RICHARDSON, clinical chemist; b. Sylvania, Ga., Aug. 31, 1934; s. George Mills and Eva Marie (Scott) C.; student South Ga. Coll., 1958-60, Ga. Southwestern Coll., 1960-62, U. Miami, 1966-67; Ph.D., Walden

U., 1984; m. Barbara McFarlane, Feb. 27, 1970; children—Karen Hope, Mark Richardson. Chemist, U.S. Naval Hosp., San Diego, 1953-55, Med. Coll. S.C., 1963-66; research asso. cardiovascular medicine Miami Heart Inst., Miami Beach, Fla., 1966-68; asso. dir. research and devel. cardiovascular medicine Parkway Gen. Hosp., North Miami Beach, Fla., 1968-71; gen. mgr., dir. Coulter Diagnostics div. research and devel. Coulter Electronics, Inc., Hialeah, Fla., 1971-82, div. mgr., 1982—. Served with USNR, 1953-57; Korea. NIH grantee, 1963. Mem. Am. Chem. Soc., Am. Assn. Clin. Chemists, Can. Soc. Clin. Chemists, AAAS. Research on arteriosclerosis and atherosclerosis; patentee in field. Home: 8960 NW 11th St Pembroke Pines FL 33024 Office: 740 W 83d St Hialeah FL 33014

CREWS, ROBERT NELSON, construction company executive; b. Texline, Tex., Feb. 28, 1924; s. John S. and Elizabeth L. (Shankle) C.; m. Joy Kleck, Aug. 17, 1946; children—Robert Nelson, Elizabeth Ann, M. Lesley. B.E.C.E., Tulane U., 1948. Registered profl. engr., Tex., La. Exec. v.p., dir. J. Ray McDermott, New Orleans, 1948-74; exec. v.p. Raymond Internat. Inc., Houston, 1975-78, pres., chief operating officer 1978—, also dir.; dir. 1st City Bank Highland Village; advisor Tulane U. Coll. Engring., 1970-72; chmn. offshore ops. com., 1965; mem. panel advisors to comdt. USCG, 1967-72. Bd. dirs. Greater Houston Area YMCA; mem. bus. sch. council Tulane U. Mem. editorial adv. bd. Offshore Mag. Served with USNR, World War II. Mem. The Moles, ASCE, La. Engring. Soc., Nat. Ocean Industries Assn. (bd. dirs., chmn.). Clubs: Petroleum, Tchefuncta Country. Home: 3617 Inwood Dr Houston TX 77019 Office: Raymond Internat Inc 2801 Post Oak Blvd Houston TX 77056

CRICK, PAUL ANTHONY, lighting company executive; b. Ridgetop, Tenn., July 10, 1922; s. Leonard Delos and Lera (Nell) C.; m. Anne Kinzle, Nov. 27, 1943; children—Anne Kinzle, Mary Eleanor, Barbara Lee, Paul A. B.S. in E.E., Vanderbilt U., 1948. Field engr. Gen. Elec. Co., Dallas, 1948-54, dist. mgr., 1954-56; owner Paul Crick Agy., Dallas, 1956-66; sales v.p. Lithonia Lighting, Conyers, Ga., 1966-69; owner Crick Illuminating Agy., Miami, Fla., 1969-74; pres. Fla. Lighting Assn., Miami, 1974—. Author: Living Aboard and Sailing, 1971. Pres. Methodist Men, Dallas, 1953. Served to 1st lt. USAF, 1942-45. Recipient Dist. Service award, Illuminating Engring. Soc., 1976. Lic. comml. pilot, capt. USCG. Mem. Illuminating Engring. Soc. (regional v.p. 1978-79; pres. 1964), Fla. Lighting Agts. (pres.). Republican. Presbyterian. Home: 180 Harbor Dr Key Biscayne FL 33149 Office: Florida Lighting Association Inc 660 NW 125th St North Miami FL 33168

CRIM, ALONZO A., superintendent of schools; b. Chgo., Oct. 1, 1928; s. George and Hazel (Howard) C.; B.A., Roosevelt Coll., 1950; postgrad. Chgo. Tchrs. Coll., 1953-54; M.A., U. Chgo., 1958; Ed.D., Harvard, 1969; m. Gwendolyn Motley, June 11, 1949; children—Timothy, Susan and Sharon (twins). Tchr. pub. schs., Chgo., 1954-63; prin. Whittier Elementary Sch., Chgo., 1963-65, Adult Edn. Center, Chgo., 1965, Wendell Phillips High Sch., Chgo., 1965-68; supt. dist. 27, Chgo. pub. schs., 1968-69, Compton (Calif.) Union High Sch. Dist., 1969-70, Compton Union Sch. Dist., 1970-73; supt. schs., Atlanta, 1973—; adj. prof. Atlanta U., 1973—, U. Ga., Athens, 1974—. Bd. dirs. Achievement Greater Atlanta, YMCA Met. Atlanta; adv. bd. Close Up; trustee Ga. Council Econ. Edn. Served with USNR, 1945-46. Recipient Vincent Conray award Harvard Grad. Sch. Edn., 1970, Eleanor Roosevelt Key award Roosevelt U., 1974. Mem. Am. Assn. Sch. Adminstrs., Nat. Alliance Black Sch. Educators, So. Council Internat. and Pub. Affairs, Edni. Program Assn. Am., Ga. Assn. Sch. Supts. Rotarian. Office: 210 Pryor St Atlanta GA 30335

CRIQUETTE, RUTH DUBARRY MONTAGUE, artist, lecturer, writer, educator; b. Paris; d. Roland Beauvais and Maria Violette (DuBarry) M.; student Ecole des Beaux Arts, pvt. ateliers, Paris, U. Nev., Lumis Art Acad., Prickett Sch. Painting, Ecole Marsan, Vernon, France. Dir. Prickett-Montague Studios of Painting, U.S.A., 1955-61; owner, dir. Montague Studio of Painting, New Orleans, 1962-63, Washington, 1964-69; asso. Ecole Marsan, 1970-72, Field Studio, Otter Rock, Oreg., 1974-76, Blue Ridge Mountains, Sterling, Va., 1976—; freelance writer, 1955—; tchr. oil painting, 1955—, color cons., 1955—exhibited Le Salon des Nations, Paris, 1983, 84, 85, 86. Recipient Lumis Art award, 1955. Life fellow Internat. Inst. Arts and Letters (Switzerland); hon. mem. Int. Com. Centro Studi E Scambi Internat. (Rome) (internat. award 1983), Internat. Acad. Leonardo da Vinci (Rome) (internat. award 1983), Internat. Arts Guild (Monaco), Women in Arts Mus. (charter). Author: 100 monographs in oil painting, 1961—; author-illustrator travel chronicle Bahamian Ah-h-h, 1969, Prose Poems, Sunburst Anthology, 1972, Internat. Bouquet of Poems, 1972; contbr. to anthology Today's Greatest Poems, 1983. Home: Blue Ridge Studio PO Box 344 Sterling VA 22170

CRISER, MARSHALL, lawyer, university president; b. Rumson, N.J., Sept. 4, 1928; s. Marshall and Louise (Johnson) C.; m. Paula Porcher, Apr. 27, 1957; children—Marshall III, Edward, Mary, Glenn, Kimberly, Mark. B.S. in Bus. Adminstrn., U. Fla., 1951, LL.B., 1951, (replaced by J.D., 1967). Bar: Fla. 1951; practiced in Palm Beach, 1953-84; partner Gunster, Yoakley, Criser & Stewart, 1955-84; pres. U. Fla., Gainesville, 1984—; atty. Palm Beach County Sch. Bd., 1958-64; dir. BellSouth Corp., City Fin. Corp. Flagler System, Inc., Perini Corp.; chmn. Installment Land Sales Bd., 1963-64. Bd. govs. Good Samaritan Hosp., West Palm Beach, pres., 1979-84; bd. dirs. Shands Teaching Hosp., Gainesville, pres., 1984—; bd. dirs. U. Fla. Found.; mem. Fla. Bd. Regents, 1965, 71-81, chmn., 1974-77. Served with AUS, 1951-53. Fellow Am. Bar Found.; mem. Fla. Council 100 (chmn. 1979-80), ABA (ho. dels. 1968-72), Fla. Bar (gov. 1960-68, pres. 1968-69), Fla. Blue Key, Phi Delta Phi, Sigma Lambda Chi, Sigma Nu. Home: 2151 W University Ave Gainesville FL 32601 Office: U Fla 226 Tigert Hall Gainesville FL 32601

CRISP, BRAULIA-NELIDA SORIANO, surgeon; b. Barceloneta, P.R., July 8, 1933; d. Rafael Soriano-Pintor and Virginia Soriano-Vega; m. George B. Crisp, Jr., June 13, 1959; 1 son, George Rafael. Pre-med, U. P.R., 1949-51; M.D., U. Madrid, 1955. Intern, Lebanon Hosp., N.Y.C., 1956; resident in surgery VA Hosp., Bklyn., 1957-59, 64-65; practice medicine specializing in gen. surgery, Bklyn., 1965-67, Atlanta, 1970-72, Fort Worth, 1974—; attending surgeon VA Adminstrn. Clinics, Bklyn., 1966-67, Atlanta, 1970-71; cons. Mem. AMA. Club: Petroleum (Ft. Worth). Office: 662 S Henderson St Fort Worth TX 76104

CRISPIN, MILDRED SWIFT (MRS. FREDERICK EATON CRISPIN), civic worker, writer; b. Branson, Mo.; d. Albert Duane and Anna (Harlan) Swift; student Galloway Woman's Coll., 1922-24; m. Herbert William Kochs, Dec. 1, 1928 (div. Mar. 1955); children—Susan Kochs Judevine (dec.), Herbert William, Judith Ann (Mrs. Nelson Shaw); m. 2d, George Walter King Snyder, Oct. 6, 1962 (dec. 1969); m. 3d, Frederick Eaton Crispin, May 20, 1972. Bd. dirs. Travelers Aid Soc., Chgo., 1936-68, nat. dir., 1948-71; bd. dirs. U.S.O., Chgo., 1944-65, nat. dir., 1951-57; bd. dirs. John Howard Assn., 1958-67, Community Fund Chgo., 1950-56, Welfare Council Met. Chgo., 1950-56; chmn. woman's div. Crusade of Mercy, Chgo., 1964. Mem. U.S. Women's Curling Assn. (co-founder 1947, pres. 1950, founder Indian Hill Women's Curling Club, Winnetka, Ill., 1945, chmn. 1945-46), DAR, Daus. Am. Colonists. Republican. Methodist. Clubs: Woman's Athletic, Saddle and Cycle, Town and Country Arts (pres. 1957-58) (Chgo.); Everglades (Palm Beach, Fla.); Venice (Fla.) Yacht; Coral Ridge Yacht (Ft. Lauderdale, Fla.). Home: PO Box 68 Osprey FL 33559

CRISSEY, DONALD REED, security products company executive; b. Livingston, Mont., Apr. 10, 1948; s. V.V. and Marjorie Constance (Heltenberg) C.; m. Peggy Bradshaw. B.S. in Aero. Engring., St. Louis U., 1971. Chief pilot Pautler Bros., contracters, Chester, Ill., 1972-76; mktg. and sales cons., 1976-81; pres., chief exec. officer Pembroke Techs., Cape Coral, Fla., 1981—; tchr. flight tng. Edison Jr. Coll., Ft. Myers, Fla., Parks Coll., Cakohia, Ill. Served as 2d lt. USAF, 1972-80. Mem. Greater Ft. Myers C. of C., Pi Mu Epsilon. Roman Catholic. Creator wrist-alert life saving system. Office: 411 Cape Coral Pkwy Cape Coral FL 33904

CRITCHLOW, DONALD EARL, educational psychologist, priest; b. Baker County, Oreg., Mar. 29, 1929; s. Lloyd Joseph and Alice Mae (Tucker) C.; B.S., Eastern Oreg. State Coll., 1953; M.A., Coll. of Idaho, 1956; Ph.D., U. Iowa, 1964; postgrad. Holy Trinity Sem., Irving, Tex., 1979-82; m. June Evelyn Naomi Rasmussen, Aug. 23, 1950 (dec. Apr. 24, 1978); children—Carmel Jeannien, Kevin Don. Ordained priest Roman Catholic Ch., 1982. Prin., tchr. Idaho Pub. Schs., Marsing and Meridian, 1951-52, 54-60; asst. prof., chmn. dept. edn. St. Ambrose Coll., Davenport, Iowa, 1960-64; prof. edn. Our Lady of the Lake U., San Antonio, 1966-70; prof. edn. and psychology, dir. reading-learning clinic Laredo (Tex.) State U., 1970-79; cons. testing, reading and spl. edn. to colls., univs., pub. sch. systems. Pres. Meridian (Idaho) Council PTA, 1956-60, hon. life mem. Idaho Congress PTA's. Served with USN, 1946-48. Mem. Am., Tex. psychol. assns., Internat. (pres. Tex. state council 1976-77), Tex. reading assns., Tex. Assn. Profs. of Reading (pres. 1975-76), Council Exceptional Children, Kappa Delta Pi. Roman Catholic. Club: Elks. Author: Dos Amigos Verbal Language Scales, 1973; Reading and the Spanish Speaking Child, 1973; Mainstreaming: Assessment and Referral, 1978; contbr. articles and book reviews to profl. jours.

CRITCHLOW, SUSAN MELISSA, public relations executive, graphic art consultant; b. Gainesville, Fla., Dec. 24, 1950; d. James Carlton and Mildred Estelle (Pringle) Barley; B.A., U. South Fla., 1972, M.A. in Speech Communication with honors, 1973; m. Warren Hartzell Critchlow, Jr., Aug. 18, 1973. Asst. dir. pub. relations Goodwill Industries of N. Fla., Inc., 1973-74; dir. pub. relations St. Luke's Hosp., Jacksonville, Fla., 1974; dir. informational services Greater Orange Park Community Hosp., Orange Park, Fla., 1974-82; pres. Susan Critchlow & Assocs., SC&A Pub. Co., Inc., Orange Park, 1976—. Named N.E. Fla. Bus. Communicator of Month, 1975, 78. Mem. Fla. Hosp. Assn. (bd. dirs. pub. relations council 1976-78, Gold award 1975, Silver award 1976, 78), Jacksonville Hosp. Pub. Relations Council (chmn. 1975-77), Fla. Pub. Relations Assn. (Golden Image award 1975, 76, 77, 78, 79, 80, 81, 82), Pub. Relations Soc. Am. Democrat. Episcopalian. Club: Pilot of Orange Park. Office: 2301 Park Ave Suite 208 Orange Park FL 32073

CRITTENDEN, RANDY LYNN, clinical psychologist; b. Sherman, Tex., Aug. 21, 1946; s. Clyde James and LaVerne (Keeton) C.; m. Tanya Denise Kincade, Dec. 28, 1968 (div. 1979); 1 child, Amy Beth; m. Linda Dale Martin, Mar. 4, 1982; 1 child, Teresa Lynn. B.A., Tex. Tech. U., 1969, Ph.D., 1973. Lic. psychologist, Tex. Clin. psychologist Psychol. Treatment Ctr., Prairie Village, Kans., 1973-76, Texoma Mental Health Ctr., Sherman, 1976-78, Texoma Psychol. Assn., Denison, 1978-81, Armando Desaloms M.D., Denison, 1981-83; pvt. practice clin. psychology, Paris, Tex., 1983—; cons. House of Hope, Sherman, 1984—, Paris Ind. Sch. Dist., 1983—, St. Joseph Hosp., Paris, 1984—, Dept. Human Resources, Paris, 1984—. Mem. Am. Psychol. Assn., Nat. Assn. Alcohol Counselors, Tex. Psychol. Assn., Nat. Register Health Services Providers. Lodge: Rotary. Home: 615 NE 34th St Paris TX 75460 Office: 3605 Loop 286 NE Suite 1400 Paris TX 75460

CROCKETT, EDWARD MERCER, retired state official; b. Austin, Tex., July 24, 1921; s. Cecil Leslie and Helen Gardner (Brown) C.; B.B.A., U. Tex., 1950; postgrad. Kans. State Coll., 1951; m. Ann Gertrude Wood, May 14, 1950; children by previous marriage—Edward Alexander, Patricia Joan. Template maker, prodn. clk., prodn. engr. Lockheed Aircraft Corp., Burbank, Calif., 1940-42; commd. 2d lt., U.S. Army Air Corps, 1942, advanced through grades to lt. col. U.S. Air Force, 1963; numerous positions including jet fighter pilot, aircraft comdr. in RC-121 Constellations; ret., 1965; dir. health referral program for med. rejectees Ga. Dept. Public Health, Atlanta, 1965-67, program mgr. Crippled Children's Program, 1967-81, adminstrv. cons. Child Health Program, 1981-85, med. adminstrn. cons., 1985-86; asst. prof. air sci. Kans. State Coll., 1949-53. Spl. nat. field commr. Boy Scouts Am., 1962-65. Served with USAAF, 1942-45. Decorated Air Force Commendation medal, Air medal; recipient Outstanding Service award Explorer Service Nat. Council Boy Scouts Am., 1965. Mem. Air Force Assn. (charter), Ret. Officers Assn., Ga. Public Health Assn. Methodist. Home: 4383 Beach View Dr SE Smyrna GA 30080

CROFT, VERNON DAVID, II, architect; b. Glendale, Ariz., June 7, 1953; s. Vernon David and Emma Sue (Hall) C.; B.Arch., U. Southwestern La., 1976; m. Susan Angel Coward, Oct. 3, 1981; 1 son, Vernon David, III. Designer/-prodn. mgr. archtl., engring. and devel. firms, 1972-78; project architect/mgr. Grimball/Gorrondona/Savoye, Metairie, La., 1978-81; project designer Ernest E. Verges & Assocs., New Orleans, 1981; project architect/mgr., assoc. Raymond C. Bergeron & Assocs., Metairie, 1981-83; ptnr. Bergeron Croft, Ltd., Metairie, 1983—. Mem. AIA, La. Architects Assn. (del. New Orleans chpt. 1982-84), Theta Xi. Democrat. Presbyterian (deacon 1984—). Home: 725 Old Metairie Dr Metairie LA 70001 Office: 1536 Sams Ave Metairie LA 70123 also 609 Texas St Suite 200 Shreveport LA 71101

CROLEY, DEBRA SUE, optometrist; b. Pineville, Ky., July 16, 1956; d. Willard and June (Cornelius) C. B.S., Cumberland Coll., 1978; O.D., U. Houston, 1982. Contract optometrist, Fort Worth, 1982-84; gen. practice optometry, Arlington, Tex., 1985—; cons. visual perception tng., Fort Worth, 1984-85. Mem. Republican Task Force; diplomate Smithsonian Instn., 1984-85. Mem. Tex. Assn. Optometrists, Arlington C. of C. Mem. Disciples of Christ. Home: 4612 Taos Dr North Richland Hills TX 76118 Office: 305A Forum 303 Arlington TX 76010

CROMER, ROBERT RUSSELL, systems analyst; b. El Paso, Tex., Apr. 13, 1933; s. Robert Russell and Zelma Blanche (Williams) C. Cert. Student Va. Poly. Inst. and State U., Blacksburg. Cert. in computer programming, data processing. Lead programmer ARBitron, Alexandria, Va., 1964-68; systems programmer S.S. Kresge Co., Detroit, 1968-69; systems programmer, analyst Computer Dimensions Co., 1969-73; with Taylor Pub. Co., Dallas, 1973-77, 78-79; mgmt. cons. R. Cromer Assocs., Irving Tex., 1977-78; sr. systems analyst NCR Comten Inc., Dallas, 1979-80; systems analyst Affiliated Food Stores, Inc., Dallas, 1980-81, First Tex. Computer Corp., Dallas, 1981-82; asst. STF mgr. Southwestern Bell, 1982-84; cons. SWB Corp., 1984-85; mgmt. cons., 1985—; tchr. classes in field. Served with AUS, 1955-56. Cert. in computer programming (CCP); cert. in data processing (CDP). Mem. Data Processing Mgmt. Assn., Inst. Cert. Computer Profls., others. Republican. Lutheran. Author books and articles in field. Home: 1022 E Grauwyler Rd Irving TX 75061 Office: 8267 Elmbrook Dallas TX 75247

CRONE, DAVID CHRISTIAN, JR., engineering consultant; b. Allentown, Pa., Nov. 17, 1948; s. David Christian and Jeanne (Ross) C.; m. Karen Kleppinger, June 21, 1969; children—Christina, Timothy. B.M.E., Le Tourneau Coll., 1972; postgrad. N.C. State U., 1977-80. Mfg. engr. Stemco Mfg. Co., Garlock Inc., Longview, Tex., 1971-72, indsl. engr., 1972-74; plant engr. AP Parts Co. div. Questor Corp., Goldsboro, N.C., 1974-80; pres. Engring. Cons., 1979-82, 84—; engring. mgr. Leslie-Locke Inc., Atlanta, 1982-84. Mem. Am. Inst. Indsl. Engrs. (sec. E. Tex. chpt. 1972-73), Soc. Mfg. Engrs., Am. Welding Soc. Baptist. Clubs: BMW Riders, Studebaker Drivers, Nat. Rwy. Hist. Home: 3236 Clearview Dr Marietta GA 30060 Office: 3329 Clovertree Ln Flint MI 48504

CRONHOLM, BEBRA TIDWELL, writer; b. Albertville, Ala., Nov. 6, 1952; d. Ollis Cleveland and DeMile Yvonne (Bobo) T. B.A., U. Ala., 1974. Copywriter, Gillis Advt., Inc., Birmingham, Ala., 1974-75; pub. service and continuity dir. KAUM Radio, Houston, 1975-76; copy dir. Point Communications, Inc., Houston, 1976-79; copy supr. Popejoy & Fischel Advt., Dallas, 1979-81; pub. relations account exec. Tracy-Locke/BBDO Advt., Dallas, 1981; owner, mgr. Bebra/Writer, Dallas, 1982—. Mem. Women in Communications, Internat. Assn. Bus. Communicators, Dallas Advt. League.

CRONK, JACK DILLON, pharmacy administrator, consultant; b. Highland Park, Mich., Dec. 5, 1943; s. Jack D. and Bernice M. (Cole) C.; m. Ruth Nanette Rizer, June 30, 1967; children—Bryan Lee, LeAnn B. B.S. in Pharmacy, Wayne State U., 1967, M.S. in Hosp. Pharmacy, 1972. Clin. pharmacist Botsford Gen. Hosp., Farmington, Mich., 1967-68; dir. drug info. and edn. USPHS, Gallup, N.Mex., 1968-70; dir. drug info. Grace Hosp., Detroit, 1970-71; dir. pharmacy Mercy Hosp., Jackson, Mich., 1971-75, Wyandotte Gen. Hosp., Mich., 1975-77, Holy Cross Hosp., Detroit, 1977-84, Mount Sinai Med. Ctr., Miami Beach, Fla., 1984—; clin. asst. prof. U. Mich., 1981-84; adj. asst. prof. Wayne State U., 1981-84; faculty Miami Dade Community Coll., Fla., 1984—; adj. asst. prof. U. Fla., 1984—; pharmacist cons. Internat. Health Council, Miami Beach, 1985—. Contbr. articles to profl. jours. Recipient Alumni citation Mich. Christian Coll., 1984. Mem. Mich. Soc. Hosp. Pharmacists (exec. sec. 1983-84, Pharmacist of Yr. award 1983), Fla. Soc. Hosp. Pharmacists (seminar chmn. 1985), Southeastern Mich. Soc. Hosp. Pharmacists (pres. 1979-80, lifetime hon. mem. award 1984), Am. Soc. Hosp. Pharmacists (ho. of dels. 1976), Am. Pharm. Assn. (student pres. 1967), Rho Chi. Republican. Mem. Ch. of Christ. Lodge: Rotary. Avocations: music; snorkeling. Home: 12010 NW 15th Ct Pembroke Pines FL 33026 Office: Mount Sinai Med Ctr 4300 Alton Rd Miami Beach FL 33140

CROOK, ROBERT LACEY, state senator, lawyer; b. Bolton, Miss., Apr. 22, 1929; s. Walter Barber and Louise (Lacey) C.; student U. Miss., 1952-53; LL.B., Jackson Sch. Law, 1965; m. Brigita Vija Nerings, Sept. 20, 1953; children—Robert Lacey II, Hubert William. Operator, Ruleville (Miss.) Dry Cleaners, 1953-60; Miss. dir. Civil Def., Jackson, 1960-64; admitted to Miss. bar, 1965, since practiced in Ruleville; mem. firm Robert L. Crook; mem. Miss. Senate, 1964—. Mem. Miss. Legis. Budget Com. Served with USMC, 1949-51. Named Ofcl. of Yr., Miss. chpt. Am. Soc. Pub. Adminstrn., 1981. Mem. State Civil Def. Dirs. Assn. (nat. v.p. 1962-63), Council State Govts. (past chmn. transp. com. So. Legis. Conf.), Am., Miss. bar assns., Miss. Bar Found., Am. Legion, S.C.V., Order Stars and Bars, Pi Alpha Alpha. Democrat. Home: 3615 Crane Jackson MS 39216 also 125 N Oak Ave Ruleville MS 38771 Office: 800 N Division Ave Ruleville MS 38771

CROOKE, PHILIP SCHUYLER, mathematics educator; b. Summit, N.J., Mar. 10, 1944; s. Philip Schuyler and Emma T. (Kaucky) C., Jr.; m. Barbara E. Carey, Aug. 31, 1968; children—Philip Alexander, Cornelia Elizabeth. B.S., Stevens Inst. Tech., 1966; Ph.D., Cornell U., 1970. Asst. prof. math. Vanderbilt U., Nashville, 1970-76, assoc. prof., 1976—; vis. fellow Cornell U., Ithaca, N.Y., 1982. Contbr. articles to profl. publs. Mem. Soc. Indsl. and Applied Math. Home: 611 Cantrell Ave Nashville TN 37215 Office: Vanderbilt U Box 6205 Sta B Nashville TN 37235

CROOKS, MARY ELIZABETH, city public health official; b. Picayune, Miss., May 14, 1948; d. Cornelius and Vivian Elizabeth (Palmer) Washington; m. Leonard W. Crooks, Nov. 9, 1968; 1 son, Leonard. B.S., Eureka Coll., 1971; M.P.H., Tulane U., 1981. Tchr. Acad. of Our Lady, Peoria, Ill., 1971-72; program dir. Peoria Health Dept., 1972-76; exec. dir. Harrison Homes Young Women's Ctr., Peoria, 1976-77; pub. health edn. supr. New Orleans Health Dept., 1978-85, clin. services coordinator, 1985—; instr. Phillips Jr. Coll., 1984—. Campaign sect. leader United Way of Greater New Orleans, 1979—; campaign organizer Cancer Soc.; active in campaigns for civic referenda. Mem. Health Edn. Council Greater New Orleans Area (pres. 1981, cert.), Am. Inst. Biol. Sci., Am. Pub. Health Assn. Home: 4554 Bonita Dr New Orleans LA 70126

CROOKS, THOMAS JACKSON, advertising executive; b. Franklin, Va., July 6, 1953; s. Robert Dils and Gloria (Ballengee) C.; m. Charlene Winans, Mar. 11, 1978; children—Thomas Jonathan, Sarah McColloch. B.A. in Polit. Sci. and Sociology, U. Richmond, 1975. Regional and nat. advt. account exec. Fahlgren & Ferriss, Inc., Parkersburg, W.Va., 1976-78; advt. account mgr. nat. and internat. accounts Ketchum McCloud & Grove, Inc., Pitts., 1978-79; account mgr., supr. Fahlgren & Ferris, Inc., Parkersburg, 1979—. Bd. dirs., v.p. Mid-Ohio Communicators, 1978-80; bd. dirs., v.p. Henry Logan Children's Home, Parkersburg, 1979—; bd. dirs. Mid-Ohio Valley chpt. ARC, 1981-83, Parkersburg YMCA; mem. com. Sour Mash Golf Tournament, Parkersburg, 1978-82, Kidfest Com., Parkersburg. 1978-81. Mem. Am. Mktg. Assn. Republican. Methodist. Home: 4504 3d Ave Vienna WV 26105 Office: Fahlgren & Ferris Inc PO Box 1628 Parkesburg WV 26101

CROOM, ALLEN BLAINE, educational administrator; b. Humboldt, Tenn., May 22, 1951; s. James Everett and Anne Marie (Landrum) C.; m. Patricia Joy Dunlap, June 18, 1972; children—Wendy Dawn, Allen B., II. B.S., U. Tenn.-Martin, 1973, M.Acctg., 1981. Purchasing agt. U. Tenn.-Martin, 1973-76, acct., 1976-79, dir. acctg. services, 1979-81, dir. bus. affairs, 1981—. Mem. Phi Kappa Phi. Baptist. Avocations: raising wild waterfowl and fancy bantams. Home: Box 434 Sharon TN 38255 Office: U Tenn Bus Office Martin TN 38238

CROOM, ROBERT EDWARD, criminal justice educator, social worker; b. Dillon, S.C., July 24, 1932; s. Archie Theodore and Lillian Carlisle (Burney) C.; m. Beverly Jo Eidson, Feb. 2, 1957; 1 child, Yashi Malenka Croom Warner. B.A. in Psychology, Mercer U., 1959; M.S.W., Atlanta U., 1970; M.S. in Urban Studies, Ga. State U., 1977; Ph.D. in Am. Studies, Emory U., 1983. Mem. faculty Ga. State U., Atlanta, 1971—, prof. criminal justice, 1984—, chmn. dept. criminal justice, 1980-82, chmn. dept. social work, 1982-84, asst. dean Coll. Pub. and Urban Affairs, 1981—. Exec. editor Criminal Justice Rev., 1983—. Adviser to Senate Com. on Children and Youth, Ga., 1975—. Served as sgt. USAF, 1950-54, Korea. Named Alumni Disting. Prof., Ga. State U., 1977. Mem. Ga. Juvenile Services Assn. (founder, chmn. 1969-70; Ables award 1970), Nat. Council Juvenile and Family Ct. Judges, Acad. Criminal Justice Scis., Am. Soc. Pub. Adminstrn., Urban Affairs Assn., Nat. Assn. Atomic Vets., Phi Kappa Phi. Office: Coll Pub and Urban Affairs Ga State U Atlanta GA 30303

CROOM, ROBERT EDWARD, JR., III, university official; b. Silver City, N.Mex., Oct. 23, 1942; s. Robert Edward and Evelyn Lee (Adams) C.; m. Linda June Campbell, Dec. 6, 1960; children—Janice L., Debra L., Daniel Edward (dec.). Student pub. schs. Tool and die maker Fred Allen Co., Houston, 1968-73; profl. musician, 1973-76; tool and die maker Don H. Boyer Co., Houston, 1976-80; supr. Oil Well Precision Machine, Inc., Lafayette, La., 1980-81; mfg. mgr. Oilwell Drilling Control, Lafayette, 1981-85; dir. computer automated mfg. with dept. mech. engring. U. Southwestern La., 1985—, co-chmn. indsl. relations com. Saturn project; owner BC Engring. and Research. cons. in field. Served with USN, 1960-63. Mem. Mfg. Engrs. Soc. (sr.), Nat. Computer Soc., Computer and Automated Systems Assn. (sr.), Instrument Soc. Am. (sr.), Am. Metals Soc. (sr.), ASCAP, Young Mens Bus. Club. Republican. Methodist. Contbr. articles to profl. publs. Patentee in field.

CROSBY, BETTY JEAN HALL, physician; b. Winston-Salem, N.C., Nov. 27, 1951; d. Walter Wayne and Sue (McLean) Hall; m. Jerry M. Crosby. B.A. with highest honors in Zoology, U. N.C.-Chapel Hill, 1974, M.D., 1978. Diplomate Am. Bd. Pediatrics. Intern, Med. U. S.C., Charleston, 1978-80; resident Children's Hosp., Nat. Med. Ctr., Washington, 1980-81; pediatrician Mecklenburg County Health Dept., Charlotte, N.C., 1981-84; pvt. practice Matthews Children's Clinic, N.C., 1984—; mem. staff Charlotte Meml. Hosp. Presby. Hosp., Vol., Handicapped Organized Women, Charlotte, N.C., 1982-84. Fellow Am. Acad. Pediatrics; mem. N.C. Pediatric Soc., Mecklenburg County Med. Soc., N.C. Med. Soc., AMA. Baptist. Office: Matthews Children's Clinic PO Box 338 Matthews NC 28105

CROSBY, CYRUS KELLER, pharmacist, medical center executive; b. Searcy, Ark., Oct. 27, 1930; s. Howard Billingsley and Ollie Pearl (Keller) C.; m. Martha Sylvia Rich, June 18, 1960; children—Carol, Amanda, Margaret. B.A., U. Ark., 1960, B.S., 1962. Cert. pharmacist, Ark. Pharmacist, Phillips Drug, Arkadelphia, Ark., 1962-65, Kellers Pharmacy, Batesville, Ark., 1965-73, City Drug, Lander, Wyo., 1973-75; dir. pharmacy White River Med. Ctr., Batesville, 1975—; mem. del. of pharmacists to People's Republic of China, 1985. Bd. dirs. Batesville Youth Ctr., 1971-72, Episcopal Day Sch. Commn., 1978-81, Independence County Fair Bd., Batesville, 1983—, N.E. Ark. Dist. Fair Bd., Jonesboro, 1984—; sr. warden St. Paul's Episcopal Ch.; dir., pres. Batesville Sch. Bd., 1977-83. Served to cpl. U.S. Army, 1954-56, Japan. Recipient High Stepper award Mo., Ark. Dist. Kiwanis Internat. 1982-83, Disting. Pres. with Honors Club Level Kiwanis Internat. 1982-83. Mem. Am. Pharm. Assn., Am. Soc. Hosp. Pharmacists, Ark. Pharmacist Assn. (dir. 1984, 85), Ark. Shared Purchasing (dir. 1979—). Lodge: Kiwanis (pres. 1982-83). Avocations: gardening; fishing; hunting; outdoor photography. Home: Rt 8 Box 536 Batesville AR 72501 Office: White River Med Ctr inc 1710 Harrison St Batesville AR 72501

CROSBY, GEORGE FREDERICK, JR., mechanical engineer; b. Bayonne, N.J., Mar. 11, 1912; s. George Frederick and Ida May (Evesson) C.; m. Josephine Boyd, Oct. 5, 1935 (dec. June 1966); children—Jean Ruth, Jo Ann, George Frederick III, Janice Lee; m. Florence June Perrilloux Mohn, Feb. 1, 1976. M.E., Stevens Inst. Tech., 1934. Research engr., engr. in charge ops. Internat. Nickel Co., Bayonne, 1934-42; mfg. and mgmt. cons. McKinsey Co., N.Y.C., 1942-48; mgr. operator tng. and mfg. reogn. programs Crosby & Assocs., 1948-71; div. mgr. mfg. engring. research and devel. Am. Mgmt. Assn., N.Y.C., 1971-77; mfg. and mgmt. cons. Crosby & Assocs., Westport, Conn., 1977-82, Bradenton, Fla., 1982—. Contbr. articles to profl. jours. Active Boy Scouts Am., 50 yrs., Community Relations Council, Leader Citizenship Forum, others. Recipient Silver Beaver award Boy Scouts Am. Mem. Nat. Soc. Profl. Engrs., ASME, Soc. Advancement Mgmt., Am. Mgmt. Assn., Am. Soc. Quality Control, Am. Inst. Indsl. Engrs.

CROSBY, JAMES M., hotel company executive; b. 1927. Student Georgetown U., 1949. With Internat. Paint Co., 1949-50, Harris Upham & Co., 1950-58; pres. Unexcelled Chem. Corp., 1958-66; with Resorts Internat. Inc.,

Miami, Fla., 1958—, chmn. bd., dir. Address: Resorts Internat Inc 915 NE 125th St Miami FL 33161*

CROSS, BETTY FELT, businesswoman; b. Newcastle, Ind., Jan. 8, 1920; d. Frank Ernest and Olive (Shock) Felt; m. Paris O. Cross, July 14, 1939 (div.); children—Ernest, Betty J., Robert D., Paris, Toni, Frank. Owner, mgr. Salon D'Or, Indpls., 1956-74; owner Bejon, Madison, Ind., 1974-78, Brass & Things, Madison, 1978—, Silver City USA, Madison, 1978—. Mem. Madison C. of C. Avocation: collecting dolls and art objects. Office: Silver City USA Olde Towne Village Madison TN 37115

CROSS, CLAUDE CHRISTOPHER, nuclear engineer; b. Washington, July 23, 1935; s. John Storrs and Ruth (Fuller) C.; m. Elaine Carolyn Franke, Jan. 4, 1958; children—Claude Fuller, Carolyn Lee, Thomas Christopher, John Storrs. B.S., U. Va., 1957. Registered profl. engr., Wis. Commd. ensign USN, 1957, advanced through grades to capt., 1975; exec. officer USS Von Steuben, 1967-71; comdg. officer USS Simon Bolivar, 1971-74; sr. mem. USN Nuclear Propulsion Examining Bd., 1974-77; comdr. Submarine Squadron 4, 1977-80; asst. to pres. Inst. Nuclear Power Ops., Atlanta, 1980—; dir. Bank Eureka Springs (Ark.). Decorated Legion of Merit. Mem. Am. Nuclear Soc., Pi Kappa Alpha. Club: Hibernian Soc. Home: 1 Stono St Charleston SC 29407 Office: Inst Nuclear Power Ops 1100 Circle 75 Pkwy Atlanta GA 30339

CROSS, DENNIS WARD, insurance company executive; b. Santa Barbara, Calif., Sept. 22, 1943; s. Ward H. and Durith Ann (Stonner) C.; B.S., Ill. Wesleyan U., 1965; M.B.A., Ind. U., 1967; C.L.U., Am. Coll., 1972; fellow Life Mgmt. Inst., 1980; m. Judith M. Marston, Feb. 5, 1967; 1 dau., Kimberly. Dir. consultation projects Life Ins. Mktg. and Research Assn., Hartford, Conn., 1970-75; asst. v.p. sales and service USAA Life Ins. Co., San Antonio, 1975-78, v.p. sales, 1978-81, sr. v.p. sales, 1981-82, sr. v.p. mktg., 1982-86, also dir.; pres. USAA Life Gen. Agy., 1984—; sr. v.p. USAA Fin. Services Group Mktg. Div., 1986—; dir. USAA Annuity and Life Ins. Co., USAA Investment Mgmt. Co.; instr., hon. faculty Army Logistics Mgmt. Center, Ft. Lee, Va., 1968-70; guest instr. U. Tex., San Antonio, 1978—, San Antonio Coll., 1978-81, St. Mary's U., 1982-85. Bd. dirs. San Antonio chpt. Am. Cancer Soc., 1983—; v.p., bd. dirs. San Antonio chpt. Jr. Achievement, 1983—. Served as capt. U.S. Army, 1967-70, Res., 1970-84. Mem. Am. Soc. C.L.U.s, Life Advertisers Assn., Life Ins. Mktg. and Research Assn. (bd. nominating com., 1982-83, market research com. 1981-83, mem. direct response mktg. com. 1982—, chmn. 1982-85), Am. Mgmt. Assn., Life Office Mgmt. Assn., Am. Mktg. Assn., Am. Advt. Fedn., Cattle Barons Assn., Ill. Wesleyan U. Alumni Assn. (class chairperson 1980-84). Home: 7206 Winterwood St San Antonio TX 78229 Office: 9800 Fredericksburg Rd San Antonio TX 78288

CROSS, EASON, JR., architect; b. Bisbee, Ariz., Nov. 14, 1925; s. Eason and Olive (Hardwick) C.; m. Diana Johnson, June 17, 1950; children—Ben, Becca, Amy, Susan. B.A., Harvard, 1949, M.Arch., 1951. With Prentiss Huddleston & Assos., Tallahassee, Fla., 1950-51, W.D. Compton, Cambridge, Mass., 1951-52, Deigert & Yerkes, Washington, 1952; asso. Charles M. Goodman, Washington, 1952-59, Keyes, Lethbridge & Condon, 1959-61; partner Cross & Adreon, Arlington, Va., 1961—; spl. instr. George Washington U., 1964-65. Pres. Hollin Hills Community Assn., 1978; chmn. Fairfax County Appeals Bd., 1970-80. Served with USNR, World War II. Recipient Ware prize, 1950, Washington Bd. Trade design award, 1965, Bethesda-Chevy Chase C. of C. design awards, 1966, 67; House and Home awards A.I.A., 1965-66; Mid-Atlantic Region design awards, 1967, 69; nat. honor award, 1968; Nat. honor award Am. Inst. Steel Constrn., 1967; 4 awards H.U.D.-Washington Center Urban Studies furniture competition, 1971. Fellow AIA (pres. N. Va. chpt., mem. com. on design, Va. Soc. energy award 1980); Mem. Fairfax County C. of C., Am. Arbitration Assn. (panelist). Democrat. Unitarian. Clubs: Harvard, Fox; Hasty Pudding-Institute of 1770 (Harvard). Patentee fastenings and furniture. Home: 2309 Glasgow Rd Alexandria VA 22307 Office: 950 N Glebe Rd Arlington VA 22203

CROSS, ELLEN DARE, artists' representative; b. Paris, June 21, 1956 (parents Am. citizens; d. Ralph James and Norma Annette (Evans) C.; m. Robert Artie Brown, Mar. 21, 1981. Student, L'Institut d'Etudes Européennes and Sorbonne, 1976-77; B.A., Randolph Macon Woman's Coll., 1978; postgrad. Ga. State U., 1981-82. Sales rep. Alan David Photography Studio, Atlanta, 1979-80; sales, mktg. dir. Allied Color Film corp., Atlanta, 1980-81; prin., propr. Ellen Cross Agy. for Comml. Artists, Atlanta, 1981—. Mem. Soc. Photographer and Artists' Reps., Inc. (founder, past sec., exec. council mem.), AAUW, Nat. Assn. Profl. Saleswomen, Nat. Assn. Female Execs.

CROSS, ELMO GARNETT, JR., lawyer, state senator; b. Richmond, Va., Feb. 19, 1942; m. Anne Geddy. B.S., U. Richmond, 1963; LL.B., T.C. Williams Sch. Law, 1966. Bar: Va. 1966. Staff acct. A.M. Pullen & Co., Richmond, 1968-71; ptnr. Cross & Cross, Mechanicsville, Va., 1972—; mem. Va. State Senate, 1976—. Mem. Hanover Democratic Com. Served with U.S. Army, 1966-68. Mem. Va. State Bar Assn., Hanover Bar Assn. Methodist. Office: 1125 Hanover Green Mechanicsville VA 23111

CROSS, JAMES MILLARD, educational administrator; b. Oneida, Tenn., Nov. 2, 1944; s. Millard and Edna (Posey) C.; student Cumberland Coll., 1961; B.S., East Tenn. State U., 1965; M.A.T., E. Tenn. State U., 1970; ednl. specialist, 1975; Ed.D., U. So. Miss., 1983. Tchr. intern Bristol City (Tenn.) City Sch., 1970; spl. edn. tchr. Elizabethton (Tenn.) City Schs., 1970-71; Washington County (Tenn.) work study coordinator Crockett High Sch., Jonesboro, Tenn., 1972-77; supr. spl. services Washington County Dept. Edn., Jonesboro, 1978—. Mem. Washington County Republican Exec. Com., 1977—. Served with U.S. Army, 1966-69. Decorated Army Commendation medal, Vietnam Campaign medal, Vietnam Service medal, Nat. Def. Service medal, others. Mem. Am. Assn. Sch. Adminstrs., Council for Exceptional Children, Nat. Rehab. Assn., Res. Officers Assn., Assn. Supervision and Curriculum Devel., Alpha Phi Omega, Kappa Delta Phi, Phi Delta Kappa. Baptist. Office: Washington County Dept Edn 405 W College St Jonesboro TN 37659

CROSS, JOFFRE JAMES, II, insurance agent; b. Houston, Apr. 25, 1951; s. Joffre James and Marjorie Iva (Berg) C.; m. Elise Compton Pritchett, Feb. 26, 1977. B.A., Washington and Lee U., 1973; M.B.A., U. Tex., Austin, 1975. C.P.C.U. Assoc., Langham Langston & Dyer, Houston, 1973-77, ptnr., 1978—; mem. adv. bd. Tanglewood Bank, 1986—. Author: (monograph) Managment of the Independent Insurance Agency, 1975. Mem. Soc. C.P.C.U. (bd. dirs. Houston chpt. 1984-85, treas. 1985—), Ind. Ins. Agts. Houston (bd. dirs., treas.). Clubs: Briar (bd. dirs. 1983—, treas. 1978-80), Inwood Forest Country. Avocations: golf; sailing; computers. Home: 1258 Fountainview Dr Houston TX 77057 Office: Langham Langston & Dyer 2400 Augusta Suite 422 Houston TX 77057

CROSS, LESLIE WILLIAM, human resources consultant, executive; b. Spring Lake, N.J., Sept. 18, 1919; s. Leslie Campbell and Ernestine Louise (Bachman) C.; m. Peggy Hauser, Oct. 5, 1957; children—William Leslie, Laura Leslie. B.S. in Bus. Adminstrn., Rutgers U. Coll., 1956. Tng. supr. Esso Bayway Refinery, Elizabeth, N.J., 1951-54; coordinator tng. and devel. Esso Standard Oil Co., N.Y.C., 1954-59, mgmt. and sales tng. specialist, 1959-62; tng. and communications coordinator Exxon Corp., N.Y.C., 1962-66, adv. personnel adminstrn. exec. devel., 1966-80; pres. Les Cross & Assocs., Inc., Wilmington, N.C., 1980—; instr. mgmt. program Inst. Mgmt. Labor Relations Rutgers U., New Brunswick, N.J., 1952-57; lectr. Mgmt. Inst. div. gen. edn. NYU, 1961-66. Contbr. articles to profl. jours. Served to capt. U.S. Army, 1943-46. Mem. Am. Soc. for Tng. Devel. (Outstanding Contbn. to Profession award 1973, pres., bd. dirs. N.Y. Met. chpt. 1964-65, chmn. bd. dirs. 1973-75, Outstanding Contbn. to Chpt. award 1979, dir. Cape Fear chpt. 1984-85). Clubs: Cape Fear Power Squadron, Shrewsbury River Yacht Club. Avocations: fishing; boating; music. Office: Les Cross & Assocs Inc PO Box 3415 Wilmington NC 28403

CROSS, LOUISE PORTLOCK, manufacturing company executive; b. Norfolk, Va., Jan. 20, 1907; d. William Seth and Mary Louise (Fanshaw) Portlock; grad. high sch.; m. James Byron Cross, July 17, 1929; 1 dau., Blanche Louise. With J.B. Cross, Inc., Norfolk, 1952—, exec. pres., 1959-60, pres., chief exec. officer, 1960—. Mem. Phi Sigma Alpha (charter). Episcopalian. Clubs: Order Eastern Star, Altrusa Internat., Ladies Oriental Shrine N.Am. Home: Atlantic Ave and 34th St Pacific Mayflower Tower Apt 1601 Virginia Beach VA 23451 Office: 3797 Progress Rd Norfolk VA 23502

CROSS, STEVEN JASPER, finance, economics educator; b. Hohenwald, Tenn., Apr. 19, 1954; s. Thomas Edward and Eula Mae (Mealer) C.; m. Martha Ellen Bradshaw, Aug. 23, 1974. B.S., Middle Tenn. State U., 1976, M.A.T., 1980, D.A., 1984. Sales rep. University Ford/Lincoln/Mercury Inc., Murfreesboro, Tenn., 1976; ins. underwriter Continental Ins. Inc., Nashville, 1976-77; credit rep. SunAm., Inc., Murfreesboro, 1977-78; instr. mgmt., bus. Dyersburg (Tenn.) State Community Coll., 1980-81; instr. Motlow State Community Coll., Tullahoma, Tenn., 1981-83, asst. prof. econs., bus., 1983-85; assoc. prof. Delta State U., 1985—. Contbr. articles to profl. jours. Mem. Am. Econ. Assn., Nat. Assn. Bus. Economists, Am. Fin. Assn., Eastern Fin. Assn., So. Fin. Assn., Southwestern Fin. Assn., Midsouth Acad. Econs. and Fin., Midwest Econs. Assn., Sigma Rho, Phi Beta Lambda, Delta Mu Delta, Gamma Beta Phi (faculty advisor 1982). Home: 25 Memorial Dr Boyle MS 38730 Office: Div Econ and Fin Sch Bus Delta State U Cleveland MS 38733

CROSS, WILLIAM HERBERT, fire control specialist; b. Salisbury, N.C., Feb. 18, 1945; s. John Herbert and Margaret Ruth (Kestler) C.; m. Linda Mariette Cauble, Mar. 7, 1969. Grad. high sch., Salisbury. Cert. fire control specialist. Stock mgr. Winn-Dixie Stores, Inc., Salisbury, 1963-67; fire control specialist Fire Dept., Salisbury, 1967—. Mem. Nat. Fire Protection Assn. (assoc.), N.C. State Fireman's Assn., Rowan County Fireman's Assn., Clan Ferguson Soc. N.Am. Republican. Methodist. Lodge: Order of DeMolay (life mem., chevalier). Avocations: hunting; Scottish activities. Home: 315 W 15th St Salisbury NC 28144 Office: Fire Dept 514 E Innes St Salisbury NC 28144

CROSSEN, FRANK MARVIN, diversified company executive; b. Dallas, 1923. Grad. So. Methodist U., 1949. Vice pres. Preston State Bank, 1940-55; with Centex Corp., Dallas, 1955—, v.p., 1955-71, chmn. bd., chief exec. officer, 1971—, also dir. Office: Centex Corp 4600 Rep Nat Bank Tower Dallas TX 75201

CROSSLAND, EDWARD JOHN, seismograph co. exec.; b. Okmulgee, Okla., Jan. 17, 1927; s. Samuel Hess and Iva (Jones) C.; B.S., U. Tulsa, 1954; m. Joyce Gardner, Dec. 27, 1963; children—Joy Lorraine, Iva Lynn, Lisa Pauline. Engr., Philco Corp., Phila., 1950-51; research engr. Seismograph Service Corp., Tulsa, 1951-56, mgr. new product devel., 1957-59, engring. mgr. voting machine div., 1959-65, nat. marketing mgr. voting products, 1966-68, exec. engring. cons. P.E.D./Seiscor Div., 1969—. Mem. Okla. State Bd. Registration for Profl. Engrs., 1962-67, chmn., 1966-67. Trustee Tulsa State Fair Bd., 1956-57. Served with USAAF, 1945-49. Registered profl. engr., Okla. Mem. Nat., Okla. socs. profl. engrs. Patentee in field. Home: 7022 E 64th Pl Tulsa OK 74133 Office: 6200 E 41st St PO Box 1590 Tulsa OK 74102

CROSSLIN, LOUISE, real estate broker; b. Sallisaw, Okla., May 29, 1927; d. Alvon A. and Maye M. (Burton) Diffee; student Oklahoma City U., 1949, 50; m. Paul L. Crosslin, July 18, 1943; children—Alvon Paul, Norman Randy. With CRE, Tahlequah, Okla., 1952—, owner, broker, 1955—. Mem. Rural Water Dist., Tahlequah, 1972-75. Mem. C. of C. (sec. 1952-82), Home Builders Assn., Okla. Real Estate Commn., Am. Legion Aux., VFW Aux., Beta Sigma Phi. Democrat. Baptist. Club: Sportsmen Acres Devel. Co. (pres. 1970-82). Home: PO Box 164 Tahlequah OK 74464 Office: 400 S Muskogee Tahlequah OK 74464

CROSSMAN, KENNETH CHARLES, clergyman; b. Toledo, Apr. 4, 1933; s. Elliott Andrew and Mabel Irene (Miller) C.; m. Cecily Riley, July 2, 1960; children—Catherine Ann, Scott Elliott, Sarah Elizabeth, John Mark. B.A., Wabash Coll., 1955; postgrad. Harvard Bus. Sch., 1955; M.Div., Candler Sch. Theology, Emory U., 1968. Regional sales mgr. Yardley or London, Inc., Ft. Lauderdale, Fla., 1958-65; student pastor United Methodist Ch., Atlanta, 1965-68, minister, Ft. Lauderdale, 1968-77, Orlando, Fla., 1977-81, Melbourne, Fla., 1981—, sr. minister St. Paul's United Meth. Ch., 1981—; host weekly local TV program; producer nat. TV commls. for United Meth. Ch.; chmn. TV and Radio Task Force, United Meth. Ch., Fla., 1980—; pres. Rebuild Found., Ft. Lauderdale, 1970-77; founder Specialized Urban Ministries, Ft. Lauderdale, 1970-77; v.p. Religion and Race Com. United Meth. Ch., Lakeland, Fla., 1977-80. Author: Questions Jesus Asked, 1981; producer various TV programs, 1983. Minister Orange County Commn., 1981, Orlando City Council, 1981; co-chmn. Broward County Community Relations Com., 1972-74; mem. Areawide Council on Aging, 1971-75; dir. Broward County Legal Aid Bd., pres., 1974-77; del. state Democratic Conv., 1981. Served with U.S. Army, 1956-58. Recipient Community Service award Broward Times, 1970; Outstanding Contbns. award Broward County Community Relations Commn., 1974; cert. of appreciation Broward County Commn., 1974-77; Human Relations award Fla. Edn. Assn., 1974; Community Service award Broward County Areawide Council on Aging, 1975; commendation Ft. Lauderdale City Commn., 1977; Human Relations award Broward County Classroom Tchrs. Assn., 1977; commendation Orlando City Council, 1981, Orange County Commn., 1981; named Outstanding Religious Leader, Melbourne Jaycees, 1981-82. Mem. United Meth. Assn. Ch. Bus. Adminstrs. (cert. ch. bus. adminstr.), Greater Ft. Lauderdale Ministerial Assn. (pres. 1974-75), Assn. Regional Religious Communicators. Office: St Paul United Meth Ch 1591 Highland Ave Melbourne FL 32935

CROUCH, CLIFTON WAYNE, utility company executive; b. Galveston, Tex., Aug. 19, 1951; s. Clarence L. and Iris L. (Pharis) C.; m. Debbie Belinda Pennington, June 17, 1979; children—Melissa Dawn, Scott Anthony. B.B.A. in Mktg., Central State U., Edmond, Okla., 1978; M.B.A. in Gen. Mgmt., 1980, M.A. in Urban Affairs, 1983. Mgr., Fashion Thimble Shoes, Lamarque, Tex., 1969-71; with Southwestern Bell, 1974—, sr. service cons., Shawnee, Okla., 1976-77, mgr., Oklahoma City, 1977-79, staff specialist, 1979-80, staff mgr., 1980—. Mem. Republican Congl. Com. Served with U.S. Army, 1971-74; Vietnam. Home: 8905 Kenny Circle Oklahoma City OK 73132 Office: 621 N Robinson Room 177 Oklahoma City OK 73102

CROUCH, RICHARD W., police official; b. Rockwood, Tenn., Nov. 15, 1950; s. Samuel Curtis and Marian (Johnson) C.; m. Mary Jean Hicks, Oct. 13, 1973; children—Allison, Bethany. B.S., Jacksonville State U., Ala., 1974, postgrad., 1975-82; postgrad. Miss. State U., 1984—. Cert. law enforcement officer, Ala., Miss. Police officer Anniston Police Dept., Ala., 1972-76, police sgt., 1976-77, police lt., 1977-80, police capt., 1980-82; chief of police Starkville Police Dept., Miss., 1982—; guest lectr. Miss. State U., Starkville, 1983—; accreditation assessor Commn. on Accreditation for Law Enforcement, Fairfax, Va., 1984—. Mem. campaign com. United Way, Starkville, 1982-84; vol. March of Dimes, Starkville, 1983—, Republican Presdl. Task Force, Washington, 1983-84. Mem. Internat. Assn. Chiefs Police, Miss. Assn. Chiefs of Police (mem. exec. com. 1984-85), Starkville Area C. of C. (membership drive vol. 1985). Republican. Lodge: Fraternal Order of Police. Avocations: tennis, numismatics. Home: 215 Hiawassee Dr Starkville MS 39759 Office: Starkville Police Dept 101 Lampkin St Starkville MS 39759

CROVITZ, ELAINE SANDRA, clinical psychologist; b. N.Y.C., Oct. 18, 1936; d. Sydney and Jennie (Papier) Kobrin; children—Gordon, Deborah, Sara Pi. B.A., Bklyn. Coll., 1956; M.A., Duke U., 1960, Ph.D., 1964. Instr. med. psychology, staff psychologist Duke U. Med. Center, Durham, N.C., 1963-64, assoc. med. psychology, supervising psychologist, 1964-67, asst. prof. med. psychology, 1967-75, assoc. prof., 1975—; tchr., cons., lectr., researcher. Mem. Am. Psychol. Assn., Southeastern Psychol. Assn., N.C. Psychol. Assn., Assn. for Advancement Psychology, Internat. Council Psychologists, Internat. Assn. Applied Psychology, Nat. Register Health Service Providers Psychology, AAUW. Author: (with Elizabeth Buford) Courage Knows No Sex, 1978; author research papers; contbr. articles to profl. jours. Home: 2745 Montgomery St Durham NC 27705 Office: PO Box 3895 Duke U Med Ctr Durham NC 27710

CROW, CYNTHIA ANN, counselor, administrator; b. Tulsa, Sept. 22, 1951; d. Joseph Jennings and Rosemary (Wright) C. B.S., Southeastern Okla. State U., 1973, M. Sch. Counseling, 1983; M.S., Okla. State U., 1975. Cert. tchr. Okla., Tex. Tchr., coach Ind. Sch. Dist., Mt. Vernon, Tex., 1975-76; instr., coach Grayson County Coll., Denison, Tex., 1976-82, Southeastern Okla. State U., Durant, 1982-83; dir., counselor So. Okla. Christian Counseling Ctr., Durant, 1983—. Mem. self-study steering com. Grayson County Coll., 1980-81, Baptist student union com., 1980-82; interim youth dir. First Bapt. Ch., Durant, Sunday Sch. tchr., 1979-84. Mem. AAHPERD, Nat. Assn. Girls and Women's Sports, Am. Assn. Counseling and Devel., Assn. Religious Values, Kappa Delta Pi. Democrat. Home: 623 N 3d St Durant OK 74701 Office: So Okla Christian Counseling Center 623 N 3d St Durant OK 74701

CROW, EVERETT G., publishing company sales representative; b. Mount Pleasant, Tex., Apr. 27, 1933; s. Lester C. and Lucy (Lee) C. B.B.A., East Tex. State Univ., 1957, M.B.A., 1958. Grad. teaching asst. East Tex. State Univ., Commerce, 1957-58; instr. Arlington State Coll., Tex., 1958-62; sales rep. South-Western Publishing Co., Cin., 1962—. Served to cpl. U.S. Army, 1953-55. Mem. Delta Pi Epsilon (pres. 1983-85). Democrat. Baptist. Lodge: Bordeaux Lions (pres. 1984-85). Avocations: photography; woodworking; bowling. Home: 5228 Whites Creek Pike Whites Creek TN 37189 Office: South-Western Publishing Co 5101 Madison Rd Cincinnati Ohio 45227

CROW, RICHARD VALJEAN, retired librarian; b. Threesands, Okla., June 17, 1924; s. Verne Elwell and Alta Marie (Cleeton) Elwell Crow; m. Lucy Emma Stuart, Dec. 21, 1952. Student Okla. A&M U., 1947-49; B.A. in English and Edn., Tex. Christian U., 1951; M.L.S., No. Tex. State U., 1954. Librarian, Patti Welder Jr. High Sch., Victoria Tex., 1954-56, Patti Welder High Sch., 1956-57, Hopkins Elem. Sch., Victoria, 1957-68, Stroman High Sch., Victoria, 1968-85. Mem. ALA, Tex. State Tchrs. Assn. (life), Tex. Assn. Sch. Librarians, Am. Assn. Sch. Librarians, Tex. Library Assn. (life), NEA (life), Teenage Library Assn. (chmn. state com. 1975-76), Internat. Platform Assn., Nat. Assn. for Deaf. Democrat. Mem. Christian Ch. (Disciples of Christ). Club: Executive Dinner (Victoria). Home: 2001 E Power Victoria TX 77901

CROW, SUE, nurse epidemiologist; b. Olla, La., Oct. 26, 1943; d. J.M. and Lessie (Hatten) Dearmon; m. Donald Crow, July 1, 1969. B.S. in Nursing, Northwestern State U., La., 1966, M.S. in Nursing, 1980. Staff nurse VA Med. Ctr., Shreveport, La., 1966-67, La. State U. Med. Ctr., Shreveport, 1967-72, nurse epidemiologist, 1972—; nursing practice advisor Nursing 85, 1983—; cons. infection control Surgeon Gen. U.S. Air Force, 1984—; lectr. at nat., internat. meetings. Assoc. editor Infection Control Jour., 1979—; mem. editorial staff Am. Jour. Infection Control, 1983—; clin. nurse reviewer RN, 1984—; assoc. editor Infection Control and Urol. Care, 1976-83; mem. edit. adv. bd. Jour. Hosp. Supply, Processing, and Distbn., 1984—. Contbr. chpts. in books, articles to profl. jours. Mem. Assn. Practitioners in Infection Control, (nat. v.p. 1978-80, pres. local chpt. 1981-82), Jr. League Shreveport. Democrat. Baptist. Club: Pierremont Oaks Tennis Ctr. (Shreveport). Avocations: tennis; reading. Home: 346 Berkshire Shreveport LA 71106 Office: Louisiana State U Med Ctr 1501 Kings Hwy PO Box 33932 Shreveport LA 71130

CROW, TERRY TOM, physics educator, physics researcher; b. Sapulpa, Okla., Sept. 16, 1931; s. John Terry and Era Kathryn (McLead) C.; m. Sara Frances Allen, Jan. 5, 1954; children—John Allen, Douglas Terry, David Brien. B.S., Miss. State U., 1953; M.A., Vanderbilt U., 1957, Ph.D., 1960. Asst. prof. Miss. State U., Miss. State, 1960-62, assoc. prof., 1964-67, prof. physics, 1967—, head physics dept., 1979—; physicist Lawrence Livermore Lab., Calif., 1962-64. Served to 1st lt. USAF, 1954-56. Mem. Am. Phys. Soc., Electromagnetics Soc. Home: 1111 Robinhood Rd Starkville MS 39759 Office: Miss State U Dept Physics Drawer 5167 Mississippi State MS 39762

CROW, WILLIAM CECIL, cons., former govt. ofcl.; b. Oneonta, Ala., Oct. 4, 1904; s. Mandeville McAlpin and Flora Jane (Brice) C.; A.B., Maryville Coll., 1924; A.M., U. Chgo., 1929; LL.D., Maryville College, 1969; m. Mary Lucille Johnson, July 5, 1935; 1 son, William Cecil. Asst. prof. econs., Ala. Poly. Inst., 1930-35; with U.S. Dept. Agr., 1935-72, successively with Bur. Agrl. Econs., 1935-42, War Food Adminstrn. and Prodn. and Marketing Adminstrn., 1942-53, dir. transp. and facilities research div., and liaison with state depts. of agr. Agrl. Marketing Service, 1953-63, dir. transp. and facilities research div. Agrl. Research Service, 1963-72; cons. food mktg. facilities, equipment, and systems, Africa, Asia, Australia, Europe, N.Am., Central Am., S.Am. Mem. Arlington (Va.) Com. of 100; chmn. Arlington County Pub. Utilities Commn. Trustee Presbytery of Washington. Decorated Chevalier de l'Ordre du Merite Agricole (France); Order of Long Leaf Pine (N.C.); recipient Achievement award Nat. Assn. Produce Market Mgrs., also plaque for exceptional service; Superior Service award U.S. Dept. Agr.; citation Greater Phila. Movement; named Ky. Col. Hon. life mem. Nat. Assn. Refrigerated Warehouses; mem. Am. Agrl. Econs. Assn., AAAS. Presbyterian. Club: Springfield Golf and Country. Author many publs. Home and office: 1258 N Buchanan St Arlington VA 22205

CROWDER, ASHBY BLAND, JR., English educator; b. Richmond, Va., June 29, 1941; s. Ashby Bland, Sr. and Margaret (Hughes) C.; m. Ann Lynn O'Malley, Mar. 10, 1973; 1 child, Ashby Bland, III. B.A., Randolph-Macon Coll., 1963; M.A., U. Tenn., 1965; Ph.d., U. London, England, 1972. Instr. English, Centre Coll., Danville, Ky., 1965-67; asst. prof. English Eastern Ky. U., Richmond, 1969-74; prof. English, Hendrix Coll., Conway, Ark., 1974—; mem. editorial staff The Complete Works of Robert Browning, Ohio-Baylor, 1972—; del. at large So. Humanities Conf., 1973-77. Contbr. articles to profl. jours. Mem. MLA, The Victorian Soc., Wallace Stevens Soc., S. Atlantic Modern Language Assn., S. Central Modern Language Assn., The Browning Inst., Convocation of The Univ. of London, Court of Electors of Birkbeck Coll. Democrat. Episcopalian. Home: 7 Fernwood Dr Conway AR 72032 Office: Hendrix Coll Conway AR 72032

CROWDER, ROBERT DOUGLAS, educator; b. Nashville, June 21, 1934; s. Noble Douglas and Eleanor Clare (Fulghum) C.; B.A., Vanderbilt U., 1956, M.A., 1960, Ph.D., 1967. Fulbright lectr. U. Lyon (France), 1958-59; instr. Vanderbilt U., 1960-64; dir. Vanderbilt U. in France, 1964-65; asso. prof. fgn. langs. N. Tex. State U., Denton, 1965—, chmn. dept. fgn. langs. and lits., 1979—. Fulbright scholar, U. Poitiers (France), 1957-58. Mem. AAUP, Am. Assn. Tchrs. French, Tex. Assn. Coll. Tchrs., Tenn. Hist. Soc., SAR, Sons Confederate Vets. Democrat. Home: 3710 Holland Dallas TX 75219 Office: Dept Fgn Langs and Lits N Tex State U Denton TX 76203

CROWE, JAMES OLIVER, insurance company executive; b. Tuskegee, Ala., May 22, 1946; s. Melvin and Gertrude (Tarver) Bronson; m. Sharon Graham, Sept. 17, 1968; 1 son, Brian Gerard. B.A., Tenn. State U., 1969; postgrad. Nashville Law Sch., 1969-70. Cert. casualty property claim law assoc. With Travelers Ins. Co., 1970—, claim rep., Nashville, 1970-71, spl. claim rep., Miami, Fla., 1971, asst. supr., Ft. Lauderdale, Fla., 1971-73, territorial examiner, Hartford, Conn., 1973-75, asst. mgr., Dayton, Ohio, 1975-76, assoc. mgr., Pitts., 1976-79, mgr. and officer of record, Jacksonville, Fla., 1979-84, claim mgr., officer of records, Tampa, Fla., 1984—. Author: Casualty Property Claims Manual, 1975. Fin. dir. Shawnee council Boy Scouts Am., Jacksonville, 1983—. Democrat. Baptist. Club: Sertoma (pres. elect NW Jacksonville chpt. 1983—, cert. appreciation 1983). Office: Travelers Ins Co 9485 Regency Sq Blvd Jacksonville FL 32211

CROWELL, GENTRY, state official; b. Chestnut Mound, Tenn., Dec. 10, 1932; married. Mem. 86th-89th Tenn. gen. assemblies; sec. state Tenn., 1977—; past pres. Nat. Assn. Secs. State. Democrat. Methodist. Clubs: Masons, Jaycees, Lions. Office: Office of Sec State State Capitol Nashville TN 37219

CROWLEY, LUCY ANN GRAMLING, educator, librarian; b. Gramling, S.C., Feb. 10, 1940; d. Ben Earle and Annie Lou (Petty) Gramling; m. James Carlton Crowley, June 15, 1963; 1 dau., Anna Carlton. B.A., Converse Coll., 1960; postgrad. U. Ga.-Athens, 1960-61; M.A., Furman U., 1969. Tchr. English, Spartanburg Day Sch. (S.C.), 1961-65, head librarian, 1970—; librarian Dist. 1 Sch., Spartanburg, 1965-70; realtor Jade Realty, Palmetto Realty, Diecy Gray Realty, Spartanburg, 1976-82. Bd. dirs., chmn. edn. com. Am. Heart Assn., Spartanburg, 1975—; bd. dirs., sec. S.C. affiliate Am. Heart Assn., 1980—; ward chmn. Democratic Party, Spartanburg County, Gramling, 1970-74. Mem. So. Assn. Colls. and Schs. (cons., vis. com. chmn. 1980—, chmn. S.C. liaison com. 1981—, mem. regional commn. 1980—, chmn. regional liaison com. 1982-83), ALA, S.C. Library Assn. (chmn. Children and Youth in Schs. 1983-84), Southeastern Library Assn., S.C. Sch. Librarians Assn., Spartanburg County Library Assn. (chmn.-elect 1984). Republican. Methodist. Clubs: Jr. League, Inman-Woman's, Debutante (Spartanburg). Office: Spartanburg Day School 1701 Skylyn Dr Spartanburg SC 29302

CROWN, BARRY MICHAEL, psychologist; b. Waukegan, Ill., June 23, 1943; s. Frank Edward and Sara (Babel) C.; m. Sheryl Joyce Lowenthal, Oct. 31, 1982. B.A., U. Miami, 1965; M.Ed., Fla. Atlantic U., 1966; Ph.D., Fla. State U., 1969. Diplomate Am. Acad. Behavioral Medicine. Research coordinator Gov. Office State Fla., 1967-69; postdoctoral fellow in psychology Mass. Gen. Hosp., Boston, 1969-70; asst. prof. psychiatry U. Ill. Med. Sch., Chgo., 1970-71, U. Miami Med. Sch., 1971-74; assoc. prof. psychology Fla. Internat. U., Miami, 1974-78; pvt. practice psychology, Miami, 1978—. NIMH postdoctoral fellow, 1969; recipient Disting. Sci. Contbn. award Nat. Council on Drug Abuse, 1975. Mem. Am. Psychol. Assn., Am. Coll. Psychology, Am. Psychology-Law Soc., Soc. Behavioral Medicine. Democrat. Jewish. Club: Tiger Bay (Miami).

CROXTON, THOMAS CLYBURN, JR., electronics and photographic company executive; b. Kershaw County, S.C., May 3, 1942; s. Thomas Clyburn and Willie Inez (Young) C.; student Clemson Coll., 1960-62; degree in Electronic Tech., Massey Tech. Inst., 1965; m. Sylvia Joan Newell, Mar. 4, 1967; children—Dawn, Tracie, Matt. Electronic maintenance technician Kinder Foto Internat., Charlotte, N.C., 1965-69, asst. plant engr., 1969-72; mgr. prodn. equipment PCA Internat., Matthews, N.C., 1972-75, dir. equipment mfg., 1975-81, asst. v.p. tech. ops., 1981-82, asst. v.p. corp. facilities and security, 1982—; bd. dirs. P.C.A. Internat. Fed. Credit Union, 1982—, pres., 1983—. Coordinator Neighborhood Crime Prevention, 1981—. Recipient Employer of Yr. award N.C. Assn. for Retarded Citizens, 1977. Mem. Soc. Mfg. Engrs., Am. Mgmt. Assn., Photo Mktg. Assn., Nat. Rifle Assn. (life). Republican. Presbyterian. Clubs: Woodmen of the World, Dutchman Creek Hunt (pres. 1982—). Office: 801 Crestdale Ave Matthews NC 28105

CROZAT, HELEN PERRIN, gift shop manager; b. New Orleans, Oct. 21, 1917; d. Emilien P. and Viola (Grosch) Perrin; m. Edwin Paul Crozat June 10, 1939; children—Judith, Helene, Suzanne, Corinne, Marie Louise, Lisette, Julie. Grad. high sch., New Orleans. Gift shop mgr. Houmas House Plantation, Convent, La., 1978—. Republican. Roman Catholic. Avocations: needlework, crafts. Office: Houmas House Gift Shop Route 1 Box 181 Convent LA 70723

CRUIKSHANK, THOMAS HENRY, financial executive; b. Lake Charles, La., Nov. 3, 1931; s. Louis James and Helene L. (Little) C.; B.A., Rice U., 1952; postgrad. U. Tex. Law Sch., 1952-53, U. Houston Law Sch., 1953-55; m. Ann Coe, Nov. 17, 1955; children—Thomas Henry, Kate Martin, Stuart Coe. Accountant, Arthur Andersen & Co., Houston, 1953-55, 58-60; admitted to Tex. bar; mem. firm Vinson & Elkins, Houston, 1961-69; exec. v.p. adminstrn. and fin., dir. Halliburton Co., Dallas, 1969-81, pres., chief exec. officer, 1980-81; pres. Halliburton Co., 1981—, chief exec. officer, 1983—; dir. Interfirst Bank, Dallas. Petroleum Equipment Suppliers Assn., Am. Petroleum Inst. Jr. Achievement, Dallas, 1974-76, chmn., 1976-78, mem. nat. bd., 1976—. Served to lt. (j.g.) USNR, 1955-58. C.P.A., Tex. Mem. Am., Tex. socs. C.P.A.s, Am., Tex. bar assns. Clubs: Dallas Petroleum River Oaks Country (Houston); Dallas Country (gov. 1977-79). Office: 400 N Olive LB 263 Dallas TX 75201

CRUM, DENNY EDWIN (DENZEL CRUM), university basketball coach; b. San Fernando, Calif., Mar. 2, 1937; s. Alwin Denzel and June (Turner) C.; m. Joyce Ellaine Lunsford, Sept. 15, 1951; children—Cynthia Lynne, Steven Scott, Robert Scott. B.A., UCLA, 1959; secondary teaching cert., San Fernando Valley State Coll., 1960. Asst., then head basketball coach Pierce Coll., Los Angeles, 1962-67; asst. coach UCLA, 1968-70; head basketball coach U. Louisville, 1971—. Author articles in field. Named Mo. Valley Conf. Coach of Year, 1973, 75, Coll. Coach of Year, 1974, Metro Conf. Coach of Year, 1979; winner NCAA Championship, 1980. Mem. Nat. Assn. Basketball Coaches. Office: 2301 S 3d St Louisville KY 40292

CRUM, WILLIAM PAUL, JR., financial planning and marketing executive; b. Tifton, Ga., Sept. 4, 1937; s. William Paul and Flora C.; m. Mary Wildes, June 14, 1959; children—William Paul III, Kenneth W. B.S., U. Ga., 1959; M.B.A., Brenau Coll., 1983. Cert. fin. planner. With Charter Capital Corp., 1973—, pres., 1978-83; sr. v.p., dir. mktg. Fin. Service Corp., Atlanta, 1983-84; pres. Chartered Fin. Services, Atlanta, 1984—. Chmn. bd. Psychol. Studies Inst., 1980-82; bd. dirs. Learning Labs., 1983—. Served with USAF, 1959-65. Mem. Internat. Assn. Fin. Planners (dir. 1965-69), Nat. Assn. Securities Dealers, Fellowship Christian Fin. Advisers (nat. bd. dirs.). Contbr. articles to nat. mags. Home: 2700 Mt Vernon Rd Dunwoody GA 30338

CRUMBLEY, DONALD LARRY, accounting educator, writer, consultant; b. Kannapolis, N.C., Jan. 18, 1941; s. Carl Donald and Velvia Leutte (Kelly) C.; m. Donna Darlene Loflin, Aug. 31, 1963 (div. 1983, remarried 1984); children—Stacey Lynn, Dana Lea, Heather Ann. B.S. cum laude, Pfeiffer Coll., 1963; M.S., La. State U., 1965, Ph.D., 1967. C.P.A., N.C. Grad. research asst. La. State U., Baton Rouge, 1963-65, teaching asst., 1965-66; asst. prof. acctg. Pa. State U., State College, 1967-69; staff acct. Arthur Andersen & Co., N.Y.C., 1969-70; adj. asst. prof. NYU Grad. Sch. Bus., spring 1970; faculty resident Laventhol & Horwath, summer 1972; assoc. prof., dir. master of bus. taxation program U. So. Calif., Los Angeles, 1973-74, U. Fla., Gainesville, 1970-73, 74-75; prof. Tex. A&M U., College Station, 1975—, Shelton taxation prof., 1984—; cons. First Coinvestor Inc., N.Y.C., 1974-76, Profl. Network System, N.Y.C. and Plainfield, N.J., 1983-84; editorial bd. Jour. ATA, Acctg. Rev.; editorial adv. bd. Advances in Acctg.; pension cons. Kagins Co., Des Moines, 1981-83; instr. Arthur Andersen & Co., Chgo., 1983-85. Author: (with Hoffman) West's Federal Income Taxation, 3 vols., 1980-86; (with McCarthy and Davis) Federal Income Tax, 1980-85 (with M. Davis) Organizing, Operating and Terminating Subchapter S Corporations: Tax and Accounting, 1980; Practical Guide to Preparing a Federal Gift Tax Return, 1981; Financial Management of Your Coin/Stamp Estate, 1978; (with R. Copeland and J. Wojdak) Advanced Accounting, 1972; (with C. Reese) Readings in the Crude Oil Windfall Profit Tax, 1982; (with D. Bandy) Tax Handbook on Corporate Distributions and Dividends, 1980; (with J. Curtis) Donate Less to the IRS, 1981; (with E. Milam) Estate Planning in the '80s, 1982; Readings in Selected Tax Problems of the Oil Industry, 1982; (with S. Grossman) Readings in Oil Industry Accounting, 1980; (with E.E. Milam) Estate Planning after the 1976 Tax Reform Act, 1978, Estate Planning: A Guide for Advisers and Clients; Handbook of Accounting for Natural Resources, 1986. Contbr. chpts. to books, articles to profl. publs.; editor Oil and Gas Tax Quar., 1977—; co-editor Tex. Tax Services, 1985—; co-author syndicated newspaper column Reluctant Taxpayer, 1971-72, also monthly column in Taxation for Accts.; cons. editor Lawyers and Judges Pub. Co., Tucson; contbg. editor Hard Facts and Tax Angles. Named to Alumni Hall of Fame, A.L. Brown High Sch., 1972; recipent Contbn. to Community award Sta. WRUF, 1972; Coll. Bus. Adminstrn. Research award Tex. A&M, 1976-77; Grad. Faculty Research fellow Tex. A&M, 1982; Ford Found. grantee, 1966-67; Disting. Alumni award Pfeiffer Coll., 1972. Mem. Am. Taxation Assn. (pres. 1974-75, trustee 1975-77; founder), Am. Inst. C.P.A.s, Am. Acctg. Assn., Nat. Taxation Assn., Tex. Soc. C.P.A.s, Numis. Lit. Guild, Order of Sundial, Phi Kappa Phi, Beta Gamma Sigma, Beta Alpha Psi. Republican. Methodist. Office: Dept Acctg Tex A&M Univ College Station TX 77843

CRUMBLISS, LAWRENCE EDWIN, health policy agency executive; b. Joplin, Mo., May 17, 1940; s. Grover Lawrence Crumbliss and Mildred Louis (Boucher) Crumbliss Christman; m. Ann-Groves McNeill, Apr. 20, 1974; 1 child, Marion Boucher. B.A. in Polit. Sci., U. Notre Dame, 1963. Dir. program Va. Tb and Respiratory Disease Assn., Richmond, 1972-78; exec. dir. Eastern Va. Med. Edn. Com., Norfolk, 1979-81; health systems analyst Cardinal Health Agy., Lumberton, N.C., 1981-84, exec. dir., 1984—; cons. med. edn.; farmer. Pres. council St. Mary's Roman Catholic Ch., Laurinburg, N.C. Mem. N.C. Health Systems Agy. Assn. (chmn.), Congl. Club. Republican. Avocations: golf; sailing. Home: 702 W Church St Laurinburg NC 28352 Office: Cardinal Health Agy 401 E 11th St Lumberton NC 28358

CRUMBO, MINISA, artist; b. Tulsa, Sept. 2, 1942; d. Woodrow and Lillian (Hogue) C.; student Tex. Western U., El Paso, 1961-62, U. Colo., Boulder, 1970-71, Taos (N.Mex.) Acad. Fine Arts, 1972-74, Sch. Visual Arts, N.Y.C., 1974-75; children—Woody Carter, Chris Carter. One-woman shows: Gilcrease Inst. Am. History and Art, Tulsa, 1976, Tulsey Town Gallery, Tulsa, 1975, USSR, 1978-79, Roy Clark Ranch Party-TV Spl., 1976, Pottawatomie Agy. and Cultural Center, Shawnee, Okla., 1977, Okla. Gov.'s Spl. Showing, 1976, Adobe Gallery, Las Vegas, 1977, Oklahoma City U., 1981, Independence (Kans.) Community Coll., 1981, Baker U., Baldwin, Kans., 1981; traveling exhbn. Indian Art Show, U. Oreg., 1977; exhibited Pushkin Mus., Moscow, 1979, Montreux (Switzerland) Jazz Festival, 1979; represented in permanent collections at Heard Mus., Phoenix, Gilcrease Inst. Am. History and Art, Philbrook Art Center, Tulsa, U. Tulsa Art Center, also pvt. collections in U.S. and Europe; guest artist instr. Taos Pueblo Day Sch. Center. Recipient Graphics award for pencil drawing Creek Woman, 29th Am. Indian Exhbn. at Philbrook Art Center. Mem. Native Am. Ch. Home: 515 N 2d St Independence KS 67301 Office: 3225 S Norwood St Tulsa OK 74135*

CRUME, WILLIAM DON, advertising agency executive; b. Farwell, Tex., Dec. 20, 1933; s. Charles Elmer and Jesse (Bell) C.; m. Caryetta Margurite Grissom, May 5, 1953 (div. Mar. 1973); children—Don, Carter, Olivia; m. 2d, Sandra Lahue, May 3, 1974. B.B.A., Tex. Technol. U., 1955. Vice pres., ptnr. Byrd Advt. Agy., Lubbock, Tex., 1958-69; v.p., gen. mgr. Aylin Advt. Agy., Dallas/Houston, 1969-71; pres., chmn., chief exec. officer Crume & Assocs., Inc., Dallas, 1971—; chmn. Crume Communications, Dallas, 1980—; pres. Emerald City Prodns., 1985—. Chmn. adv. bd. Dallas Met. YWCA, 1986—; bd. dirs. OPEN, Inc., 1986—; mem. adv. council Coll. Arts and Sci., Tex. Tech. U., 1986; mem. mass communications adv. bd. Tex. Technol. U., Lubbock, 1977—. Served to maj. USAF, 1955-58. Recipient Silver medal Lubbock Advt. League, 1968. Mem. Nat. Advt. Agy. Network (chmn. 1981-82), Dallas Advt. League. Clubs: Dallas Press, Dallas Athletic; Las Colinas Country (Irving, Tex.); Holly Lake Golf (Hawkins, Tex.). Office: Crume & Assocs Inc 1303 Walnut Hill Ln Irving TX 75038

CRUMP, CHARLES METCALF, lawyer; b. Memphis, Oct. 9, 1913; s. Dabney Hull and Mary Hadden (Metcalf) C.; m. Diana Temple Wallace, July 20, 1940; children—Charles Metcalf, Philip Hugh Wallace, Stephen Beard. B.A., Southwestern at Memphis, 1934; LL.B., U. Va., 1937; D. Canon Law (hon.), Seabury-Western Theol. Sem., 1983. Bar: Tenn. 1936, U.S. Supreme Ct. 1946. Assoc., Metcalf, Metcalf & Apperson, Memphis, 1937-40; ptnr. Apperson, Crump, Duzane & Maxwell, and predecessors, Memphis, 1940—; dir. Commerce Union Bank of Memphis, Ripley Industries, Inc., Elmwood Cemetery. Mem. Tenn. Gen. Assembly, 1939-43; sec. Shelby County Democratic Exec. Com., 1939-50; pres. Chickasaw council Boy Scouts Am., 1953; pres. Sheltered Occupational Shop, Memphis, 1963; v.p. United Fund, Memphis, 1955; mem. nat. exec. council Episcopal Ch., 1964-70, v.p. House of deps. Gen. Conv., 1967-70, chancellor Diocese of W. Tenn. Served with USNR, 1944-46; PTO. Recipient Outstanding Citizen award Memphis Jr. C. of C., 1943. Mem. ABA, Tenn. Bar Assn. (award of merit 1964), Shelby County Bar Assn. (dir., treas., sec. 1971-73), Memphis Bar Assn., Am. Coll. Probate Counsel, Estate Planning Council Memphis. Club: Memphis Country. Lodge: Rotary (pres. 1977-78). Contbr. notes and decisions to Va. Law Rev., 1935-37. Home: 4110 Tuckahoe Ln Memphis TN 38117 Office: 100 N Main Bldg Suite 2610 Memphis TN 38103

CRUMP, HAROLD CRAFT, broadcasting executive; b. Amory, Miss., Sept. 28, 1931; s. Harold W. and Eva Elizabeth (Craft) C.; m. Margaret Leigh Glenn, June 28, 1980; children by previous marriage—Harold T., William L., Laurie M. Crump Porter. B.B.A. in Advt., U. Miss., 1953. Asst. advt. mgr. Blythville (Ark.) Courier News Jour., 1955-56; with sta. WTVF (and predecessors), Nashville, 1956—, v.p., dir. sales, 1966-75, sta. mgr., 1969-75, exec. v.p., gen. mgr., 1975-81, 21st Century Prodns. (producers Hee Haw, Candid Camera and Hee Haw Honeys), Nashville, 1975-81; exec. v.p. and gen. mgr. Sta. KPRC-TV, Houston, 1981-84; pres. broadcast group H&C Communications, Inc., 1984—; dir. NBC affiliate, 1983—, TV Bur. Advt., 1984—, Broadcast Music, Inc.; mem. govt. relations com. CBS-TV, 1980-81. Bd. dirs. Nashville Jr. Achievement, 1965-71, Jr. Pro Football League, 1967-69, Nashville Drug Treatment Center, 1977, Nashville Salvation Army, 1978-80; vice chmn. Nashville Better Bus. Bur., 1974, chmn. adv. rev. com., 1967; TV chmn. fin. campaign United Givers Fund, 1963; exec. com. Nashville chpt. Muscular Dystrophy Assn., 1972-79; now mem. corp. nat. orgn. trustee Nashville Meml. Hosp., 1979-81. Served to 1st lt. USAF, 1953-55. Recipient Silver medal Am. Advt. Fedn.; named Man of Year in Advt. for Nashville Advt. Fedn., 1971. Mem. Sales and Mktg. Execs. Club Nashville (past dir.), Tenn. Assn. Broadcasters (past pres.), Nat. Assn. Broadcasters, Nat. Assn. TV Program Execs., Alpha Delta Sigma, Delta Kappa Epsilon. Presbyterian. Clubs: Houstonian, Rotary. Home: 2915 Quenby Houston TX 77005 Office: KPRC-TV 8181 Southwest Freeway Houston TX 77001

CRUMP, THOMAS FLETCHER, financial executive; b. Richmond, Va., Aug. 28, 1956; s. Charles H. and Madeline (Gerhardt) C. B.S., Va. Tech., 1978, M.B.A., 1980. C.P.A., Va.; cert. mgmt. acct. Fin. systems cons. Arthur Young & Co., Washington, 1979-80; sr. acct. Gary, Stosch, Walls & Co., Richmond, Va., 1980-83; sr. v.p., controller Investors Savs. & Loan Assn., Richmond, 1983—. Mem. Am. Inst. C.P.A.s, Va. Soc. C.P.A.s, Inst. Mgmt. Accts., Va. Tech. Alumni Assn., Kappa Sigma, Beta Gamma Sigma, Beta Alpha Psi. Baptist. Clubs: Bull and Bear, Hokie. Home: 10398 Iron Mill Rd Richmond VA 23235 Office: 9201 Forrest Hill Ave Richmond VA 23235

CRUMPTON, JOHN MABREY, JR., state government administrator; b. Gainesville, Fla., Sept. 24, 1934; B.S., Auburn U., 1959, M.Ed. (NSF fellow), 1962; Ed.D., N.C. State U., 1973; m. Anna Lee Waller; children—John M., Loren Ann. Tchr. sci., public schs., West Point, Ga., 1960-61; tchr. math. Muscogee County (Ga.) Bd. Edn., 1961-63; tchr. math. Brevard County (Fla.) Bd. Public Instrn., 1963-64, math. curriculum supr., 1964-65, data processing dir., 1965-67; with IBM, Sacramento, Calif., and Raleigh, N.C., 1967-75, account mgr., 1972, edn. mktg. rep., 1973-74, productivity rep., 1974-75; pres. Durham (N.C.) Tech. Inst., 1975-80; apprenticeship dir. N.C. Dept. Labor, 1980—. Cons., Dorothea Dix Hosp., Raleigh, 1972-73; bd. dirs. Durham Day Care Council, 1975-79, Durham Vol. Services Bur., 1975-80, Wake County (N.C.) Rehab. and Cerebral Palsy Center, 1976-81; bd. dirs. N.C. State U. Edn. Found., 1977-81; mem. conservation task force Nat. Energy, Edn., Bus. and Labor Conf., 1978-79. Served with U.S. Army, 1954-56. Recipient awards including Regional Mgrs.'s Productivity award IBM, 1974; named Boss of Yr., Bartlett Durham chpt. Am. Bus. Women's Assn., 1976. Mem. Greater Durham C. of C. (dir. 1976-79), N.C. Mfg. Apprenticeship and Tng. Assn. (dir. 1983—), Phi Delta Kappa. Author: Modern Mathematics for Parents, 1965; contbr. articles to profl. jours.; editor and contbr. Teleprocessing Newsletter, 1970-71. Office: 4 W Edenton St Raleigh NC 27601

CRUSE, BERNARD WILLIAM, JR., retired mechanical development company executive; b. Rowan County, N.C., July 14, 1927; s. Bernard William and Juanita (Boland) C.; m. Evelyn Davis, July 10, 1947 (dec. May 1984); children—Bernard William, Kathy Rebecca Cruse Parnell. Cert. dental technician McCarrie Sch. Mech. Dentistry, Phila., 1948. Pres., mgr. Metalcraft Mfg. Co., Inc., Concord, N.C., 1959-65; staff engr. Emle Mills, Monroe, N.C., 1965-69; mech. designer Celanese Corp., Charlotte, N.C., 1970-78; founder, pres., dir. CEM Corp., Indian Trail, N.C., 1971-84. Patentee; co-author, pub.: Descendants of Nicholaus Kress, 1975. Pres. Northeast Civic Assn., Livonia, Mich., 1952, Cruse Family Assn., Salisbury, N.C., 1976. Served with USMC, 1945-46; PTO. Recipient Indsl. Research award Research & Devel. Mag., 1982. Democrat. Lutheran. Home: 110 Beverly Dr Indian Trail NC 28079

CRUSE, IRMA BELLE RUSSELL, writer former telephone company supervisor; b. Hackneyville, Ala., May 3, 1911; d. Charles Henry and Nellie Dunn (Ledbetter) Russell; student Birmingham-So. Coll., 1927-28; corr. student U. Chgo., U. Wis., U. Minn., intermittently 1958-68; A.B. in Journalism, U. Ala.; M.A. in English, Samford U., 1981, M.A. in History, 1984; m. Jesse Clyde Cruse, Dec. 22, 1931; children—Allan Baird, Howard Russell. With So. Bell and successor S. Central Bell, Birmingham, Ala., 1928-44, 54-76, public relations supr., 1965-68, rate supr., 1968-76; freelance writer, 1956—. Vice pres. v.p. Birmingham Council Clubs, 1973-74; pres. Jefferson County Radio and TV Council, 1971-72; pres. Quota Club of Birmingham, 1976-77. Recipient numerous awards including Freedoms Found. award, 1967-69; Beautiful Activist, 1972; nominated Women of Yr., Birmingham, 1971, 72, 75, Woman of Achievement Met. Bus. and Profl. Women's Club, 1970-71; named to Ala. Voter Hall of Fame, 1986. Mem. Birmingham Bus. Communicators, Ala. Writer's Conclave (pres. 1973-74), Birmingham Council Clubs (sec. 1973-74, dir. 1979-80), Birmingham Met. Bus. and Profl. Women (pres. 1970-71), Women in Communications (pres. 1970-71), Nat. League Am. Pen Women (sec. Birmingham br. 1984-86), Birmingham Bus. Communicators (pres. 1968-69), Oral History Assn. Am., Am. Hist. Assn., Ala. Bapt. Hist. Soc. (pres. 1984-86), Women's C. of C., Freedoms Found. of Valley Forge, Telephone Pioneers Am. (editor newsletter 1970—), Ala. State Poetry Soc. (program chmn. 1972-74, editor Muse Messenger 1977—), AAUW (chmn. Women's issues 1985-86). Baptist. Contbr. articles to various publs. Home: 136 Memory Ct Birmingham AL 35213

CRUSE, JULIUS MAJOR, JR., physician, educator; b. New Albany, Miss., Feb. 15, 1937; s. Julius Major and Effie (Davis) C.; B.A., U. Miss., 1958, B.S. with honors, 1958; D.Microbiology with honors (Fulbright fellow), U. Graz, Austria, 1960; M.D., U. Tenn., 1964, Ph.D. in Pathology (USPHS fellow), 1966. USPHS postdoctoral fellow in pathology U. Tenn., 1964-67; faculty U. Miss., University, 1967—, research prof. immunology, prof. biology, Grad. Sch., 1967-74, asst. prof. pathology, Sch. Medicine, 1973-74, prof. pathology, 1974—, asso. prof. microbiology, 1974—, dir. grad. studies program in pathology, 1974—, dir. immunopathology sect. and tissue typing labs., 1980—; lectr. pathology U. Tenn. Coll. Medicine, Memphis, 1967-74; adj. prof. immunology Miss. Coll., 1977—. Recipient Coll. Am. Pathologists and Am. Soc. Clin. Pathologists award continuing edn., 1976; immunology book collection named in his honor at U. Wis., Madison. Fellow AAAS, Royal Soc. for the Promotion of Health, Am. Acad. Microbiology, Intercontinental Biographical Assn.; mem. Am. Assn. Pathologists and Bacteriologists, Am. Soc. for Exptl. Pathology, Am. Chem. Soc., British, Canadian socs. for immunology, Am. Soc. Microbiology, Internat. Acad. Pathology, Am. Assn. Immunologists, AMA (Physician's recognition award 1969, 75), Am. Inst. Biol. Scis., Am. Soc. Clin. Pathologists, Canadian Soc. Microbiologists, N.Y. Acad. Scis., Soc. for Experimental Biology and Medicine, Société Française d'Immunologie, Reticuloendothelial Soc., Transplantation Soc., Electron Microscopy Soc. Am., Am. Soc. Clin. Histocompatibility, Internat. Platform Assn., Am. Assn. for History of Medicine, Sigma Xi, Phi Kappa Phi, Phi Eta Sigma, Alpha Epsilon Delta, Gamma Sigma Epsilon, Beta, Beta, Beta. Episcopalian. Author: Immunology Examination Review Book, 1971, rev. edit., 1975; Introduction to Immunology, 1977; (with Schwartz) Basic Immunology, 1984. Editor: Survey of Immunologic Research; Survey and Synthesis of Pathology Research; Concepts in Immunopathology; Autoimmunity; Contributions in Microbiology and Immunology; contbr. articles to profl. jours. Home: 1000 E Northside Trail 352 Jackson MS 39206 Office: Dept of Pathology University of Miss Medical Center 2500 N State St Jackson MS 39216

CRUSOE, EDWIN EDGAR, IV, master mariner; b. Lakeland, Fla., Mar. 23, 1938; s. Edwin Edgar and Muriel Valerie (Christian) C. B.S. in Nautical Sci., Calif. Maritime Acad., 1960; M.A. in Bus. Mgmt., Central Mich. U., 1983. Served as lt. j.g. U.S. Navy, 1960-62; served from 3d mate to master U.S. Mcht. Marines, 1962-72; bar and harbour pilot Port of Key West, Fla., 1972—, harbor master, 1980—; marine surveyor, cons.; chmn. Monroe County Port Authority Adv. Com.; past mem. Key West Port and Transit Authority; pres. Key West Bar Pilots. Past chmn. Monroe County Career Service Council; past campaign chmn. Monroe County Democratic Party, 1976; mem. Monroe County Dem. Exec. Com., 1976-78. Mem. Masters, Mates and Pilots, Am., Fla. pilots assns., Propeller Club of Key West (past pres., commendation), Navy League, U.S. Naval Inst., Key West C. of C., Nat. Assn. Marine Surveyors (life), Key West Art and Hist Soc. Club: Wiccan Circle. Lodges: Masons; Shriners; Elks; Arcane Order, Jesters. Author: (poetry) Wanderings, 1970. Home: Route 2 Box 306 Summerland Key FL 33042 Office: PO Box 848 Key West FL 33040

CRUTCHFIELD, EDWARD ELLIOTT, JR., banker; b. Detroit, July 14, 1941; s. Edward Elliott and Katherine (Sikes) C.; m. Nancy Glass Kizer, July 27, 1963; children—Edward Elliott, III, Sarah Palmer. B.A., Davidson Coll., 1963; M.B.A., U. Pa., 1965. With First Union Nat. Bank, Charlotte, N.C., 1965—, head retail bank services group, 1970-72, exec. v.p. gen. adminstrn., 1972-73, pres., 1973—; dir. First Union Corp., Bernhardt Industries, Inc. Bd. deacons Myers Park Presbyn. Ch.; bd. dirs. United Community Services, Salvation Army, Charlotte Bd., Charlotte Latin Sch.; trustee Mint Mus. Art, N.C. Nature Conservancy; bd. mgrs. Charlotte Meml. Hosp.; bd. visitors Davidson Coll. Mem. Charlotte C. of C., Assn. Res. City Bankers, Am., N.C. bankers assns., Am. Textile Mfrs. Assn., Young Pres.'s Orgn. Clubs: Charlotte City, Charlotte Country, Linville (N.C.) Golf. Office: Jefferson-First Union Tower Charlotte NC 28288*

CRUTCHFIELD, JAMES ANDREW, writer, historian; b. Nashville, May 16, 1938; s. Sam Shaw Sr. and Frankie Alfreda (Whitworth) C.; m. Regena Arlene Hawkins, May 13, 1965. Student, U. Tenn., 1959, Vanderbilt U., 1960. Editor Tenn. Valley Hist. Rev., Nashville, 1972-74; hist. editor Muzzle Blasts Mag., Friendship, Ind., 1985—; freelance writer and historian, Franklin, Tenn. Author: The Harpeth River; A Biography (Commendation cert. 1973), 1972; Early Times in the Cumberland Valley, 1975; A Primer of Handicrafts of the Southern Appalachians, 1976; Footprints Across the Pages of Tennessee History, 1976; Williamson County: A Pictorial History, 1981; Yesteryear in Nashville, 1981; A Heritage of Grandeur, 1981; Timeless Tennesseans, 1984; The Natchez Trace: A Pictorial History, 1985; The Tennessee Almanac and Book of Facts, 1986; A Primer of the North American Fur Trade, 1986; also articles and maps. Past pres. Williamson County Hist. Soc., Franklin; past pres. Pioneers' Corner, Inc., Franklin, bd. dirs., 1976—. Served with USNG and U.S. Army, 1961-66. Mem. Western Writers Am. Republican. Lutheran. Home and Office: 1012 Fair St Franklin TN 37064

CRUTCHFIELD, SHARON LOUISE, librarian; b. San Antonio, Dec. 29, 1940; d. Bert Thurman and Helen Louise (Werner) Richey; m. Michael Paul Crutchfield, July 4, 1972. A.A., San Antonio Coll., 1963; B.A., U. Md., 1973, M.L.S., 1974. Catalog technician San Antonio Coll. Library, 1969-68; adminstrv. asst. Inst. Texan Cultures, 1968-72; librarian/cataloger Nat. Agrl. Library, Beltsville, Md., 1974-76; sec. JGSDF Liaison Office, U.S. Army, Camp Zama, Japan, 1976-77; office mgr. U. Alaska, Fairbanks, 1978-80; dir. D.R.T. Library, San Antonio, 1980—. Mem. ALA, Tex. Library Assn., Bexar Library Assn., Western History Assn., Tex. Folklore Soc., Spl. Libraries Assn., Soc. Am. Archivists, Soc. S.W. Archivists (mem. exec. bd. 1983—), Tex. State Hist. Assn. Home: 13743 Wilderness Point Dr San Antonio TX 78231 Office: Daughters of the Republic of Tex Library at the Alamo PO Box 2599 San Antonio TX 78299

CRUTCHFIELD, WILLIAM GAYLE, JR., retail executive; b. Charlottesville, Va.; s. William Gayle and Theresa Fredericka (Saltzseider) C.; m. Jana Kay Heischman, Dec. 5, 1981; 1 dau., Jennifer Anne. B.S. in Commerce, U. Va., 1965. Asst. to pres. Ridge Electronics Corp., Charlottesville, 1971-72; sec./treas. Haight Engring. Co., Inc., Charlottesville, 1972-75; pres. Crutchfield Corp. Charlottesville, 1974—, Crutchfield Electronics, Inc., Jacksonville, Fla., 1980—; vis. lectr. Darden Grad. Bus. Sch., U. Va., Charlottesville, 1983—. Chmn. adv. bd. McIntire Sch. Commerce, U. Va., 1981-84. Served to capt. USAF, 1966-70. Decorated Air Force Commendation medal; recipient SBA award, 1980; named Central Va. Marketer of 1983, Am. Mktg. Assn., Charlottesville, 1983. Mem. Charlottesville C. of C. (dir. 1984), Beta Gamma Sigma. Republican. Office: Crutchfield Corp 1 Crutchfield Park Charlottesville VA 22906

CRUZ, DINIA DELA, pediatrician; b. Mambusao, Capiz, Philippines, Sept. 12, 1948; came to U.S. 1977; d. Nicanor and Severina (Ticar) DeLa Cruz; m. Eduardo Vargas, Nov. 6, 1976; children—Andrew, Brian. B.S., U. East, Manila., 1969; M.S., 1974. Instr. pathology, microbiology, U. East Coll. Medicine, Manila, 1976; resident pediatrics Jewish Hosp. and Med. Center of Bklyn., N.Y.C., 1978-80; fellow ambulatory and community pediatrics Mercy Hosp. and Nassau County Med. Center, 1980-81; pediatrician Health Dept., Memphis, 1981-83; practice medicine specializing in pediatrics, Memphis, 1983—; attending physician Eastood Hosp., Lebonheur Hosp., Methodist Hosp., Memphis, 1983—. Bus. mgr. Philipino-Am. Assn., Memphis, 1983-84. Mem. Mid S. Pediatric Soc., Memphis. Roman Catholic. Home: 7825 Farindon Dr Germantown TN 38138 Office: 4453 Highway 61 S Memphis TN 38109

CRUZ, MIGUEL A., psychologist, educator; b. Mayaguez, P.R., July 8, 1952; s. Miguel A. Cruz and Carmen (Lopez) Cruz; m. Khyrsys Dominguez, Dec. 25, 1972 (div. 1982); 1 child, Synayzka. B.A. in Psychology, U. P.R., Mayaguez, 1973; M.Ed. in Counseling Psychology, Interamerican U., San German, P.R., 1975; Ph.D. in Psychology, Syracuse U., N.Y., 1979, Ph.D. in Gerontology, 1980. Licensed clin. psychologist, P.R. Prof. Catholic U., Ponce, P.R., 1972-75; coordinator youth community ctr. ACTION-D.C., Syracuse, 1977-79; psychologist, prof. psychology U. P.R., Mayaguez, 1980—; pvt. practice psychologist Weight Control Clinic, Mayaguez, 1980—, pres., 1983—; pres. Mayaguez Devel. Corp., 1984—; founder 1983, past pres. Hades Acad., Mayaguez. Author psychol. support system, 1984. Bd. dirs. Hades Acad. Handicapped Children, Mayaguez, 1983. Recipient Official State Assembly award, San Juan, P.R., 1977. HEW fellow, Syracuse U., 1978. Mem. Am. Psychol. Assn., P.R. Psychol. Assn. (coordinator 83—), Nat. Neuropsychologists Acad. Club: Sales Mktg. Exec. (San Juan). Home: 9A Nereida St Enshanche Martinez Mayaguez PR 00708 Office: U PR PO Box 5575 College Sta Mayaguez PR 00708

CSINOS, ALEXANDER STEPHEN, phytopathology educator, researcher; b. Tillsonburg, Ont., Can., Jan. 28, 1948; s. Alex J. and Elizabeth V. (Ribar) C.; came to U.S., 1972; m. Lucia Veronica Chadowski, June 23, 1973; 1 dau., Alexa Nicole. B.S. in Agr., U. Guelph (Ont., Can.), 1972; Ph.D., U. Ky., 1977, postdoctoral study, 1977. Asst. prof. U. Ga., Tifton, 1977-81, assoc. prof. phytopathology research, 1981—. Industry and commodity groups grantee, 1977-82. Mem. Am. Phytopathology Soc., So. Am. Phytopathology Soc., Sigma Xi. Contbr. numerous articles to profl. jours., abstracts, other publs. Office: Dept Plant Pathology Coastal Plain Sta U Ga Tifton GA 31793

CUCCINELLI, KENNETH THOMAS, trade assn. exec.; b. Jersey City, Aug. 12, 1945; s. Dominick and Josephine (Policastro) C.; B.Chem.Engring., Cath. U. Am., 1967; M.B.A., Marymount Coll. of Va., 1981; m. Maribeth Reilly, Sept. 16, 1967; children—Kenneth Thomas, Kevin James, Kristopher Devin. Sales engr. Trane Co., La Crosse, Wis. and East Orange, N.J., 1967-70; project engr. Shefferman & Bigelson Cons. Engrs., Silver Spring, Md., 1970-71; mgr. energy systems research and devel. Am. Gas Assn., Arlington, Va., 1971-73, v.p. mgr. energy systems, mktg. services, 1973-79, dir. mktg. services, 1979-80, staff v.p. mktg. services, 1980-83, v.p. mktg., 1983—; guest lectr. Cath. U. Am., Washington, 1974-76, Duke U., Durham, N.C., 1978. Program chmn. McLean Youth, Inc., 1973-75, coach, 1973, mgr. football, basketball, soccer, 1974-80; bd. dirs. Nat. Energy Found.; team mgr. McLean Little League, 1976—. Recipient Leadership award Dartmouth Coll., 1965; NSF grantee, 1965. Mem. ASHRAE (chpt. pres. 1980-81; award of merit 1975), Sales and Mktg. Execs., Am. Mktg. Assn., Delta Epsilon Sigma. Roman Catholic. Club: Chesterbrook Swim and Tennis (pres. 1984-86). Contbr. articles to profl. jours. Home: 1628 Linway Park Dr McLean VA 22101 Office: 1515 Wilson Blvd Arlington VA 22209

CUDAHY, WILLIAM BREWER, banker; b. Chgo., Jan. 23, 1912; s. Edward Ignacius and Leonore (Brewer) C.; B.A. magna cum laude, Harvard U., 1934; J.D., Northwestern U., 1937; m. Evelyn Wilkinson, Apr. 5, 1951; children—Victoria Fenton, Joseph Michael. Sec., dir. Callaghan & Co., Chgo., 1937-41; asst. sec. No. Trust Co., Chgo., 1945-51; v.p. Am. Nat. Bank & Trust Co., Chgo., 1951-60; v.p. First Nat. Bank, Palm Beach, Fla., 1960-70, dir., 1968—. Mayor, Palm Beach, Fla., 1977-78. Served with USCGR, 1941-45. Mem. Nat. Fedn. Fin. Analysts. Republican. Episcopalian. Clubs: Everglades, Bath and Tennis (dir.), The Beach. Address: 742 Slope Trail Palm Beach FL 33480

CUELLAR, DANN RAY, television journalist; b. Beeville, Tex., Apr. 12, 1954; s. Daniel Ray and Olga (Naranjo) C.; m. Marilyn Neal Blanton; children—Trinna Lee, Daniel Benjamin, Carley Marissa. Student, U. Houston, 1975, Victoria Coll., 1973. Radio personality KVIC and KTXN, Victoria, Tex., 1973-75; photographer, editor KXIX T.V., Victoria, 1975-78, anchorman, reporter, 1975-78; reporter, producer KHOU T.V., Houston, 1978-83, weekend anchor, 1980-83; news anchorman KMOL T.V., San Antonio, 1983—. Producer (documentary) Houston Warfare, 1980, (documentary) Lost Generation, 1984, (T.V. series) Hispanics: Dawn at New Hope, 1978. Bd. dirs. Greater San Antonio Credit Counseling, 1984-85; vol. Literacy Council, 1983-85; hon. chmn. Toys for Tots, 1984. Recipient Hispanic of Year award Lulac, 1979, Best News Story award Anti Defamation League, 1980, t.v. reporting award Houston Firefighters Assn., 1981, Best Creative Work award Sigma Delta Chi, 1982, Merit award Bexar County Hist. Soc. Fellow Ctr. Latin Am. Studies; mem. Am. Film Inst., Smithsonian Instn. (assoc.), Nat. Trust Historic Preservation, Sigma Delta Chi. Roman Catholic. Avocations: film making; racquetball; photography. Home: 4122 Shady Oak Dr San Antonio TX 78229 Office: KMOL TV Channel 4 PO Box 2641 San Antonio TX 78299

CUENOD, E. M., insurance company executive; b. 1929. B.B.A., U. Tex., 1955. With Am. Gen. Investment Co., 1953-59; with Southwestern Life Ins. Co., 1959-64; with Am. Nat. Ins. Co., Galveston, Tex., 1964—, supr. mortgage loans, 1964-68, asst. v.p. mortgage loans, 1968-70, v.p. mortgage loans, 1970-72, v.p. mortgage real estate investments, 1972-76, sr. v.p. investments, exec. v.p. fin., from 1976—; dir. The Tex. Bank & Trust Co., Houston, ANREM Corp., Securities Mgmt. and Research Inc. Office: Am Nat Ins Co 1 Moody Pl Galveston TX 77550*

CULBERSON, JESSIE WALLACE, fire chief; b. Williamson County Tenn., Mar. 9, 1929; s. Wallace Alexander and Robbie Ella (Hargrove) C.; m. Frankie Elsie Short, Feb. 14, 1958; 1 child, Michael Wallace. Grad. Bethesda High Sch., Williamson, Tenn. Cert. fire chief, cert. arson investigator, Tenn. Farmer, Williamson, 1947-54; laborer Tenn. Hwy. Dept., Nashville, 1954-58; salesman Interstate Ins. Co., Nashville, 1958-63; fireman Franklin Fire Dept., Tenn., 1963-69, fire prevention officer, 1969-72, asst. chief, 1972-76, chief, 1976—; bd. dirs. Tenn. Fire Chiefs, Nashville, 1980-82; commr. Tenn. Commn. Fire Fighting Standards Personnel, Nashville, 1976—. Baseball coach Franklin Optimist League, Tenn., 1970-77. Mem. Internat. Assn. Arson Investigation (pres. 1976-77), Tenn. Firemen Assn. Democrat. Baptist. Avocations: gospel singing; hunting; fishing. Home: 616 Eastview Dr Franklin TN 37064

CULBERTSON, CHARLES RICHARD, electrical engineer; b. Marysville, Kans., Aug. 30, 1946; s. Charles Hubert and Phyllis Evelyn (Swan) C.; m. Vicki Lynn Goodson, July 9, 1970 (div. June 1979); children—Steven Richard; m. Carol Ann Furr, Mar. 20, 1986. B.S., Okla. State U., 1970. Registered profl. engr., Okla. Tex., Field engr., apprentice lineman Indian Electric Coop., Cleveland, Okla., 1965-70; elec. engr. Okla. Gas & Electric Co., Western div., Oklahoma City, 1970-73; field engr. REA, U.S. Dept. Agr., Crescent, Okla., 1973-80; system engr., dept. head Central Rural Electric Coop., Stillwater, 1980-83; div. distbn. engr. S.E. div., Tex.-N.Mex. Power Co., Texas City, 1983—; mem. Texas City Elec. Bd., 1984—. Dep. comdr. cadets CAP, Stillwater, 1980-83; bd. dirs. Texas City Rebels Youth-Football, 1983—; youth coach football, baseball, Stillwater, 1981-82, Texas City, 1984-86, wrestling and baseball, Crescent, 1977-80. Served to capt. USAR, 1970-80. Eugene Tuttle scholar C.H. Guernsey & Co., 1967. Mem. Okla. Assn. Elec. Coop. Engrs. (co-founder; pres. 1979-80, parliamentarian 1981-83), Nat. Soc. Profl. Engrs., IEEE, Profl. Photographers Okla., Profl. Photographers Guild Houston, Tex. Profl. Photographers Assn. Republican. Lodge: Kiwanis (pres. 1979-80). Clubs: Crescent Takedown, Rebel Booster. Home: 2205 28th St N Texas City TX 77590 Office: 702 36th St N PO Box 2190 Texas City TX 77590

CULBERTSON, DOOLEY EWELL, holding company executive; b. Albany, Ga., June 29, 1936; s. Erwell Robert and Gertrude (Shemwell) C.; m. Ann Marcesta Frick, Apr. 2, 1937; children—Keith, Kay. B.S. in Mech. Engring., Auburn U., 1958. Group exec. product devel. staff Teledyne Corp., San Diego, 1972-74; pres. Pacemaker Corp., Egg Harbor City, N.J., 1974-78, Fuqua Homes, Arlington, Tex., 1978-84; exec. v.p. Fuqua Industries, Atlanta, Ga., 1984—. Republican. Episcopalian. Lodge: Rotary. Office: Fuqua Industries Inc 4900 Georgia-Pacific Ctr Atlanta GA 30303

CULBERTSON, JOHN DENNIS, counselor; b. Greenville, S.C., Aug. 18, 1947; s. John Bolt and Ellie (Barbare) C.; B.S., U. S.C., 1969; M.S., N.D. State U., 1978; Ph.D. (scholar), U. N.D., 1982; m. Eunice Virginia Watson, June 7, 1969; children—John David, Ellen Barbare. Cert. counselor Nat. Bd. for Cert. Counselors. Commd. 2d lt. U.S. Air Force, 1969, advanced through grades to capt., 1973; squadron exec. officer Minot AFB, N.D., 1975-77, resigned, 1977; grad. asst. U. N.D., Grand Forks, 1978; grad. asst., intern The Counseling Center, U. S.C., Columbia, 1978-79; pvt. practice counseling, Columbia, 1978, Florence, S.C., 1979—; elem. sch. counselor, Florence, 1979—, discussion leader students, staff, faculty. Vol. group leader Parenting Skills, Columbia Area Council on Child Abuse; vol. profl. leader Parents Anonymous, Florence. Mem. Am. Assn. Counseling and Devel., S.C. Assn. Counseling and Devel. (treas. elect 1984-85, Profl. Service award 1986), Am. Sch. Counselors Assn., S.C. Sch. Counselors Assn., Assn. for Specialists in Group Work, Nat. Council on Measurement in Edn., S.C. Assn. for Measurement and Evaluation in Guidance, Assn. for Non-White Concerns in Personnel and Guidance, S.C. Assn. for Non-White Concerns in Personnel and Guidance, S.C. Assn. for Humanistic Edn. and Devel., NEA, S.C. Edn. Assn., Am. Legion, others. Methodist. Home and Office: 1886 Westmoreland Dr Florence SC 29501

CULBREATH, HUGH LEE, JR., electric utility executive; b. Tampa, Fla., May 11, 1921; s. Hugh Lee and Daphne (Jackson) C.; m. Betty King, June 8, 1944; children—Betty Kay, Hugh Lee III. B.S., U.S. Naval Acad., 1944. Commd. officer USN, 1944, resigned, 1954; with Tampa Electric Co., 1957—, v.p. finance, sec. treas., 1966-71, exec. v.p., sec., treas., 1971, pres., 1971—, chief exec. officer, 1972—; dir. Transco Energy Co., Houston, NCNB Nat. Bank of Fla. Mem. Greater Tampa C. of C. (pres. 1972-73), Sigma Alpha Epsilon. Episcopalian (vestryman 1963-65, 67-69, treas. 1967). Clubs: Tampa Yacht and Country (commodore 1963), University, Exchange (pres. 1961), Palma Ceia Golf and Country, Ye Mystic Krewe of Gasparilla (Tampa). Home: 52 Bahama Circle Tampa FL 33606 Office: PO Box 111 Tampa FL 33601

CULBRETH, ALVIN ARCHIBALD, chiropractic physician; b. Valdosta, Ga., May 1, 1953; s. Alvin L. and Margaret Julia (McIntyre) C.; m. Julie Margaret Hubert, June 6, 1981; 1 son, Joshua Lamar. Student Valdosta State Coll., 1971-74; B.S., D.C., Palmer Chiropractic Coll., 1977. Lic. chiropractic physician, Ga. Chiropractor Stewart Clinic, Athens, Ga., 1977, assoc. with Dr. Earl P. Harris, Atlanta, 1978; owner, chiropractor Culbreth Family Chiropractic Clinic, Savannah, 1978—; v.p. Astro Exterminating Corp., 1978-83. Bible tchr. Bethesda Orphanage, 1979—, Vacation Bible Sch., Mt. Pilgrim Bapt. Ch., 1979-82; preacher Savannah Gospel Chapel, 1978-83; host Christian Radio program The Story of Jesus, 1981-83. Mem. Ga. Chiropractic Assn., Christian Chiropractic Assn., Better Bus. Bur. Address: 320 Montgomery Crossroads Savannah GA 31406

CULLEN, GEORGE EDWARD, JR., communications educator; b. Orange, Mass., Mar. 29, 1926; s. George Edward and Helen Rita (Congdon) C.; A.A., Boston U., 1949, B.S. in Journalism, 1951; M.S. in Journalism, W.Va. U., 1965, Ph.D., 1979; m. Hester Allen Nock, Apr. 30, 1955; children—Helen, Laura, Mary, George Edward III. Asst. prof. aerospace studies W.Va. U., Morgantown, 1961-65; mem. faculty Hampton (Va.) Inst., 1970—, prof. mass media arts, 1981—. Served with USAAF, 1944-46, USAF, 1951-69. Recipient Cert. of Merit, Spl. award for outstanding service Hampton Edn. Assn., 1970; Outstanding Tchr. award Women in Communications, Inc., 1982; State Dept. grantee, Ghana, 1975, So. Fellowships Fund fellow, 1978-79. Mem. Assn. Edn. in Journalism, Sigma Delta Chi (life), Kappa Tau Alpha. Author: Talking to a Whirlwind, 1980; editor Airlifter mag., 1956-58, Profiles in Communication mag., 1971. Home: 115 Culotta Dr Hampton VA 23666 Office: Box 6432 Hampton Inst Hampton VA 23668

CULLENS, JOHN FRANCIS, JR., marketing executive; b. Huntsville, Ala., Oct. 30, 1944; s. John Francis and Ruth (Kirkpatrick) C.; m. Charlotte Arlene Martin, Sept. 15, 1967; 1 dau., Alicia Anne. Student, U. Md., 1964; B.S. in Math., Fla. State U., 1966. Estimator, Atlantic Bldg. Systems Inc., Atlanta, 1966-70, salesman, 1970-71, dist. mktg. mgr., 1971-74, regional mktg. mgr., 1974-78, gen. mgr. sales, 1978-81, v.p. mktg., 1981—; dir. Atlantic Transp. Co., Atlanta. Contbr. articles to industry publs. Served to warrant officer USAF, 1962-66. U. Md. USAF spl. med. scholar, 1962. Mem. Metal Bldg. and Mfrs. Assn., Am. Iron and Steel Inst. Republican. Methodist. Club: Atlanta Athletic. Office: Atlantic Bldg Systems Inc PO Box 82000 Atlanta GA 30366

CULLENS, JOSEPH ROY, lawyer; b. Griffin, Ga., July 2, 1947; s. J.R. and Mary Ethel (Barfield) C.; m. Harriet Jane Hughes, Aug. 14, 1971; 1 dau., Melissa Erin. A.B. in Journalism cum laude, U. Ga., 1973; J.D., Emory U., 1977. Bar: Ga. 1979. Pub. relations specialist Ga. Dept. Natural Resources, Atlanta, 1973-75; assoc. Freeman & Hawkins, Atlanta, 1977-82, ptnr., 1982—. Contbr. articles to profl. jours. Mem. Am. Judicature Soc., State Bar Ga., ABA, Atlanta Bar Assn., Ga. Trial Lawyers Assn., Assn. Trial Lawyers Am. Democrat. Presbyterian. Home: 3944 Vinyard Way Marietta GA 30062 Office: Freeman & Hawkins 2800 First Atlanta Tower Atlanta GA 30383

CULLER, ROBERT RANSOM, furniture designing and product development company executive; b. High Point, N.C., Nov. 16, 1950; s. Roy Braxton and Dorthey Faye (Pegram) C.; m. Heidi Miller Maas, Feb. 24, 1969; children—Robert Ransom, John Byron, Kathrine Marie. Profl. degree in furniture design and interior design Kendall Sch. Design, Grand Rapids, Mich., 1974. Head of design La-Z-Boy Chair Co., Monroe, Mich., 1974-76; pres. R.R. Culler Assoc., High Point, 1976—, RCR Devel. Corp., High Point, 1978—; dir. The Color Works, Greensboro, N.C. Mem. Am. Furnitire Designers Assn., Am. Soc. Interior Designers. Democrat. Baptist. Club: Triad World Trade. Avocation: scuba diving. Office: RCR Devel Corp 1009 Finch Ave High Point NC 27261

CULLOM, WILLIAM OTIS, truck leasing company executive; b. Huntsville, Ala., Mar. 20, 1932; s. Otis McKinley and Elna Reese C.; B.S., Fla. State U., 1958; m. Caryl James, May 26, 1956; children—Cheryl Ann, Jennifer James. Finger-print expert FBI, 1950-52; asst. bus. mgr. Fla. State U., 1954-64; with Ryder Truck Rental Inc., Miami, Fla., 1964—, exec. v.p. Mem. cabinet United Way, Miami, 1974-79; vice chmn. bd. trustees Fla. State U., chmn., 1980-82; trustee Bethune Cookman Coll., Barry U.; bd. advs. Fla. Meml. Coll., Fla. Internat. U. Sch. Bus.; bd. dirs. Salvation Army, Goodwill Industry, Miami Free Zone Corp. Served with airborne inf. U.S. Army, 1952-54. Named Outstanding Alumni, Fla. State U., 1980, Outstanding Bus. Leader, Northwood Inst.; William O. Cullom chair of fin. established at Fla. State U., 1979. Mem. Am. Trucking Assn., Truck Leasing and Renting Assn. (pres. Fla. chpt. 1972-73), Fla. State U. Alumni Assn. (pres.), Greater Miami C. of C. (pres.), Miami Hist. Assn. Democrat. Methodist. Clubs: University, Miami, Bankers of Miami, Riviera Country (Miami); Coral Reef Yacht, Rotary; Kings Bay Yacht. Home: 8445 SW 151st St Miami FL 33158 Office: 1601 Biscayne Blvd Miami FL 33132

CULLUM, CHARLES GILLESP, corporate executive; b. Dallas, 1916. B.S., So. Methodist U., 1936. With Cullum Cos. Inc., Dallas, chmn. bd. chief exec., 1976, now chmn. bd., also dir. Served to lt. USN, 1943-46. Office: Cullum Cos Inc 14303 Inwood Rd Dallas TX 75234*

CULLUM, JIMMY RAY, software services company executive; b. Tulia, Tex., Nov. 23, 1947; s. Frank Henry and Gwyneth Deb (Bivens) C.; m. Jane Helen Figley, July 3, 1969; children—Michael Ray, Carol Beth. B.S., Tex. Tech. U. 1969; M.B.A., U. Dallas, 1977. Systems analyst Collins Radio Co., Richardson, Tex., 1969-72, Recognition Equipment, Irving, Tex., 1972-73; systems analyst, project mgr. Rockwell Internat., Richardson, 1973-83; mgr. corp. projects ADR Services, Vienna, Va., 1983—. Elder, St. Barnabas Presbyn. Ch., Richardson, 1973-75, 79-80, Burke Presbyn. Ch., Va., 1985—. Mem. Data Processing Mgmt. Assn., Armed Forces Communications Electronics Assn. Clubs: Lone Star Soc. (Washington); NOVATARI (Fairfax, Va.). Avocations: piano; photography; crossword puzzles. Home: 10914 Fox Sparrow Ct Fairfax VA 22032 Office: ADR Services 800 Follin Ln Vienna VA 22180

CULP, DELOS POE, univ. pres. emeritus, constrn. co. exec.; b. Clanton, Ala., July 26, 1911; s. Joseph Daniel and Lela (Popwell) C.; student Jacksonville State Coll., 1932-34; B.S., Auburn U., 1937, M.S., 1940; Ed.D., Columbia, 1949; m. Martha Edwardine Street, Dec. 23, 1934; children—Martha Jean, James David, John Stephen. Tchr., prin. Chilton, Butler counties, Ala., 1935-42; supt. Chilton County Schs., Ala., 1942-46; supr. pub. sch. trans., asst. dir. div. adminstrn. and finance State Dept. Edn., Montgomery, Ala., 1946-51; prof. edn. Ala. Polytech. Inst., 1951-54; pres. Livingston State Coll., 1954-63; pres. Ala. Coll., Montevallo, 1963-67; pres. E. Tenn. State U., Johnson City, 1967-77, pres. emeritus, 1977—; exec. v.p. Powell Constrn. Co., 1977—. Dir. First Peoples Bank. Mem. com. on studies Am. Assn. State Colls. and Univs., 1970—. Chmn. Nat. Commn. on Safety Edn., 1965—; mem. survey team for Philippine Sch. Bur. Survey, 1959-60; mem. bd. advisers Meth. Children's Home, Selma, Ala.; mem. nat. com. on exploring Boy Scouts Am., 1971—. Mem. Ala. Edn. Commn. (exec. dir. 1957-59), Ala. Edn. Assn. (chmn. policies commn. 1965—), Ala. Acad. Sci., Am. Assn. Sch. Adminstrs., Ala. Hist. Assn., Kappa Delta Pi, Kappa Phi Kappa, Phi Delta Kappa, Phi Kappa Phi. Democrat. Methodist. Rotarian. Home: 903 Beech Dr Johnson City TN 37601

CULP, FREDERICK L(YNN), physics educator; b. Duquesne, Pa., May 12, 1927; s. Elmer E. and Elizabeth M. (Rawlings) C.; m. Louise Zundell Overly, June 7, 1953; children—David Frederick, Diane Lynn. B.S., Carnegie-Mellon U., 1949, M.S., 1960; Ph.D., Vanderbilt U., 1966. Indsl. research U.S. Steel and Westinghouse Electric Corp., 1949-51, 53-55; research staff Carnegie-Mellon U., Pitts., 1956-59; mem. faculty Tenn. Tech. U., Cookeville, 1959—, prof. physics, 1965—, chmn. dept., 1965—. Served to lt. (j.g.) USN, 1945-46, 51-53. Recipient Outstanding Faculty award Tenn. Tech. U., 1983. Fellow Tenn. Acad. Sci.; mem. Am. Phys. Soc., Am. Assn. Physics Tchrs., Sigma Xi, Sigma Pi Sigma, Kappa Mu Epsilon, Phi Kappa Phi, Omicron Delta Kappa. Democrat. Presbyterian. Lodge: Rotary. Contbr. numerous articles to profl. publs. Home: 516 E 4th St Cookeville TN 38501 Office: Tenn Tech Univ Physics Dept Cookeville TN 38505

CULPEPPER, LUCY NELL, physician, pediatrician; b. Awin, Ala., June 11, 1951; d. L.C. and Lucy Lee (Davis) C. B.S., Ala. A & M U., 1973; M.D., Meharry Med. Coll., 1977. Med. lic. Calif., 1979, Ala., 1980. Intern in pediatrics Martin Luther King, Jr. Gen. Hosp., Los Angeles, 1977-78, resident pediatrics, 1978-80; gen. med. officer Nat. Health Service Corps, Tuscaloosa, Ala., 1980-82; practice specializing in pediatrics, Tuscaloosa, 1982—; pediatrician Tuscaloosa County Health Dept., 1982—; cons. Pickens County Hosp., Carrolton, Ala., 1983—. Mem. adv. bd. Christian Study Ctr. Child Abuse Prevention Program, 1982—; bd. dirs. Big Brothers/Big Sisters Tuscaloosa County, 1983—; Recipient 1973 Class Achievement award Ala. A&M U., 1978; named Woman of Yr., Christian Study Ctr. Ala., 1983. Mem. Druid City Hosp. Med. Staff (pediatric sect. sec. 1982-83), Tuscaloosa County Med. Soc., Ala. State Med. Soc., Hale Meml. Hosp. Med. Staff, Zeta Phi Beta (corres. sec. 1983-84). Baptist. Office: Pediatric and Adolescent Medicine 609 28th Ave Tuscaloosa AL 35401

CULPEPPER, MICHAEL IRVING, researcher, educator; b. Mobile, Ala., Sept. 28, 1951; s. Milton Irving and Betty Jean (Wimpee) C.; m. Cynthia Ann Langner, Mar. 11, 1972; children—Amber Joy, Amy Celeste, Amanda Kaye. Student Auburn U., 1969-71; B.S., U. Ala.-Birmingham, 1973, M.S., 1975, C.A.S.E., 1978; Ed.D., U. Ala., 1981. Cert. tchr., Ala. Asst. lab. technician div. orthopaedic surgery U. Ala.-Birmingham, 1971-72, lab. asst., 1972-73, research technician, 1973-74, research asst., 1974-75, research assoc., 1975-81, instr. stats., biomechanics/kinesiology, 1981—; dir. research Kerner-Quarterback Sports Medicine Inst., Children's Hosp., Birmingham, 1982—; lectr. to orgns. on sports medicine and health care. Athletic trainer Chelsea High Sch. (Ala.); bd. dirs. Dixie Softball Inc., Central Shelby League; chmn. long-range planning com. Chelsea Youth Club. Recipient M. Ray Loree research award U. Ala., Tuscaloosa, 1981. Mem. Ala. Acad. Sci., Am. Alliance Health Phys. Edn., Recreation and Dance, Am. Coll. Sports Medicine (chpt. membership com.), Nat. Athletic Trainers Assn., Soc. for Biomaterials, Sigma Xi, Kappa Delta Pi. Baptist. Contbr. articles to profl. jours.; developer U. Ala.-Birmingham sports injury/illness data storage and retrieval system. Home: Route 1 Box 127-J Chelsea AL 35043 Office: Kerner Quarterback Sports Medicine Inst Childrens Hosp 1600 7th Ave S Birmingham AL 35233

CULROSS, RITA ROMAINE, psychology educator; b. Monmouth, Ill., Jan. 31, 1950; d. Lee Acheson and Dorothy Julia (Baltz) Rodgers; m. Claude Culross, June 17, 1972. B.A. with highest distinction, Purdue U., 1972, M.S. in Edn., 1973, Ph.D., 1976. Asst. prof. psychology Marycrest Coll., Davenport, Iowa, 1976-78; instr. psychology N Harris County Coll., Houston, 1978-79; asst. prof. U. Houston-Clear Lake City, 1979-83, assoc. prof., 1983—; pvt. practice psychology, Houston, 1980—; cons. psychologist Clear Creek Schs. Gifted Program, 1980—. David Ross fellow, 1974-76; Purdue Research Found. grantee, 1974-76; U. Houston Organized Research grantee, 1982. Mem. Mental Health Assn. (edn. com. 1979-81, liaison to children's com. 1979-81, speaker's bur. 1979—), Am. Psychol. Assn., Am. Ednl. Research Assn., Houston Psychol. Assn., Tex. Psychol. Assn., Soc. for Pediatric Psychology, Presbyterian. Author: Counseling the Gifted: Developing the Whole Child, 1981. Home: 122 Red Bud Ln Baytown TX 77520 Office: 2700 Bay Area Blvd Houston TX 77058

CULVER, CHARLES DAVID, energy company executive; b. Hobbs, N.Mex., July 27, 1935; s. Charles V. and Cleo (Powers) C.; B.S. in Petroleum Engring., U. Tex., 1958; m. Eunice Elaine Cash, Apr. 20, 1963; 1 dau., Catherine Elaine. Engr., Pioneer Natural Gas Co., 1960-62, mgr. gas supply, Amarillo, Tex., 1971-73, v.p. gas supply, 1973-76; asst. supr. drilling and prodn. Amarillo Oil Co., 1962-65; v.p. Cons. Services, Inc., Amarillo, 1965-71; v.p., exec. asst. to pres. Pioneer Corp., Amarillo, 1976-79, exec. v.p., 1979-82, pres., 1982—, chief exec. officer, 1983—, also dir.; dir. Sharp Drilling Co., Inc., Tascosa Nat. Bank, Amarillo. Plains Machinery Co., Internat. Tool & Supply Co. Pres., Amarillo YMCA, 1975-76; bd. dirs. Panhandle Area Cancer Council, 1981. Served with AUS, 1959-60. Recipient Harry Mays Meml. award YMCA, 1979. Mem. Am. Assn. Petroleum Geologists, Soc. Petroleum Engrs., So. Gas Assn., Panhandle Geol. Soc., Panhandle Assn. Petroleum Landmen, Natural Gas Men Permian Basin, Natural Gas Men Okla., Natural Gas Men Houston, Tex. Soc. Profl. Engrs., U. Tex. Ex-Students Assn. (pres. Amarillo 1978), Ducks Unlimited (chmn. Tex. Panhandle chpt. 1975). Methodist. Clubs: Amarillo (pres. 1978), Amarillo Kiwanis (dir. 1972-74). Office: 301 Taylor St Amarillo TX 79163

CULVER, CHARLES MAURICE, manufacturing company executive; b. Howell, Mich., Dec. 29, 1935; s. Maurice Gale and Pearl May (Tuttle) C.; children—Julia Ann, Janet Marie, Laura Joann; m. 2d, Mary Delane Fletcher, Aug. 6, 1976. B.A., Mich. State U., 1960. Sales engr. Aeroquip Corp., Jackson, Mich., 1965-74; v.p. sales NRP Inc., Nephi, Utah, 1974-77; pres. Electric Hose & Rubber div. Dayco Corp., Ocala, Fla., 1977-82; pres. Trident Supply Co., Jacksonville, Fla., 1982—. Bd. dirs., founder Little League Assn.; trustee Golden Hills Theater. Served with AUS, 1955-57. Mem. Soc. Automotive Engrs., Rubber Mfrs. Assn., Jacksonville C. of C. Democrat. Methodist. Clubs: Golden Hills Golf and Turf. Home: 3501 SE 45th St Ocala FL 32670 Office: 609 N Lane Ave Jacksonville FL 32205

CULVER, JAMES CALVIN, wholesale grocery executive; b. Commerce, Tex., July 12, 1944; s. James C. and Elizabeth (Kvintus) C.; m. Sharon Lynn Nethers, July 30, 1972; children—Brandon Jacob, Taylor Brook. Student Ohio State U., 1963-66. Mgr. Big Bear Supermarkets, Columbus, Ohio, 1962-72; retail ops. mgr. Super Valu, Inc., Hopkins, Minn., 1972-76; v.p., gen. mgr. Fox, Wetterau, Inc., Milton, W.Va., 1976—. Served with USMC, 1966-72. Mem. W.Va. Wholesalers Assn. (chmn. 1984, pres. 1983), W.Va. Beverage Industry Recycling Assn. (dir. 1983-84), W.Va. Retail Grocers Assn. (sr. dir. 1982-84). Republican. Lutheran. Home: 128 Cheyenne Trail Ona WV 25545 Office: Davis Div Fox Industries Inc PO Box 386 Milton WV 25541

CULVERHOUSE, HUGH FRANKLIN, lawyer, football team owner; b. Birmingham, Ala., Feb. 20, 1919; s. Harry Georg and Grace Mae (Daniel) C.; m. Joy McCann, Nov. 14, 1942; children—Gay Culverhouse Gold, Hugh Franklin. B.S., U. Ala., 1941, LL.B., 1947; LL.D. (hon.), Jacksonville U., Stetson U. Bar: Fla. 1955, Ala. 1947 Asst. atty. gen. State of Ala., Montgomery, 1947-49; spl. atty., asst. regional counsel Office of Chief Counsel IRS, Atlanta and Jacksonville, Fla., 1949-56; mem. firm Culverhouse, Botts, & Culverhouse, Jacksonville, Tampa and Miami, Fla., 1956—; mem. adv. com. to commr. internal revenue, 1961-62; owner Tampa Bay Buccaneers, NFL, Tampa, Fla., 1974—; owner Mode, Inc.; dir. Am. Fin. Corp., Tampa Electric Co., partner, owner, developer various real estate projects, Fla., Ind., Ohio; Contbr. articles to legal jours. Mem. faculty U. Ala. Sch. Bus. Adminstrn.; Co-founder, 1st pres. Family Consultation Service, Jacksonville; vice chmn. bd. trustees Jacksonville U.; bd. visitors Coll. Commerce and Bus. Adminstrn., U. Ala.; bd. overseers Stetson U. Coll. Law; del., U.S. Ambassador 1976 Winter Olympics, Innsbruck, Austria; Served with USAAF, 1941-46; Served with USAF, 1951-53. Recipient Top Mgmt. award Sales and Mktg. Execs. of Jacksonville, Chief award Ind. Colls. and Univs. in Fla. Fla. Enterprise award. Mem. Am. Judicature Soc., ABA, Ala. Bar Assn., Fla. Bar Assn., Dade County Bar Assn., Miami Bar Assn., Jacksonville Bar Assn. (chmn. tax sect. 1957-59), Fla. Council of 100, Fla. Council on Econ. Edn., Fla. Speakers Adv. Com. on the Future, Am. Acad. Achievement, Knights of Malta. Republican. Episcopalian. Clubs: Fla. Yacht, Indian Creek Country, LaGorce Country, Surf, Palm Bay (Miami); Univ. (N.Y.C.), Palm Ceia Golf and Country (Tampa) Nat. Golf Links of Am. (Southampton), Devon Yacht (E. Hampton). Endowed chair in bus. adminstrn. Jacksonville U., chair in law Stetson U., scholar chair U. Fla., chair in accountancy, U. Ala. Address: PO Box 23688 Tampa FL 33623

CULVERHOUSE, JOY MCCANN, professional football team executive; b. Chgo., Mar. 6, 1920; married, Nov. 14, 1942; children—Gay Culverhouse Gold, Hugh. Student, La. State U., U. Ala. Formerly amateur golfer; v.p. Tampa Bay Buccaneers, NFL, Fla., 1981—. Bd. dirs. Found. for Eye Research, U. South Fla. Mem. Delta Delta Delta. State amateur golf champion, Ala., 1941, Fla., 1961. Office: c/o Tampa Bay Buccaneers One Buccaneer Pl Tampa FL 33607*

CUMBO, LAWRENCE JAMES, JR., business educator, consultant; b. Saltville, Va., June 22, 1947; s. Lawrence James and Mary (Martin) C.; m. Mary Lee Tuggle, Nov. 27, 1970; children—Tori Jill, Kolbi Lee, Benjamin James. B.S., E. Tenn. State U., 1970; M.B.A., Coll. William and Mary, 1975; Ph.D., Va. Polytech. Inst. and State U., 1981. Acct. Mason and Dixon Lines, Inc., Kingsport, Tenn., 1970-72; asst. bus. mgr. King Coll., Bristol, Tenn., 1972-74; acct. Appalachian Broadcasting Corp. Bristol, Va., 1974; assoc. prof. econs. and bus. Emory and Henry Coll., Emory, Va., 1975—; pres. Cumbo and Assoc., Inc., Emory, 1979—; cons., 1977—. Contbr. articles to profl. jours.; author software packages. Del. Democratic Congl. Nomination Meeting, Lebanon, Va., 1982. Recipient Excellence in Tchg. award Emory and Henry Coll., 1982, Hull Chair of Bus., 1984. Mem. Va. Assn. Economists, So. Mgmt. Assn., Southeastern Am. Inst. Decision Scis. Democrat. Presbyterian. Avocations: alpine skiing, tennis, golf. Home: Drawer QQ Emory VA 24327 Office: Emory and Henry Coll Emory VA 24327

CUMMINGS, FRANK C., bishop; b. Minter, Ala., Apr. 4, 1929; s. Edmond and Annie (Mouitrie) C.; B.A., Seattle Pacific Coll., 1949, 1952; B.D., D.D., Shorter Coll., 1970; m. Martha Coleen Colly, Mar. 5, 1954; 1 dau., Paschell Coleen. Ordained to ministry African Methodist Episcopal Ch. 1948; pastor A.M.E. Ch., Alridge, Ala., 1948-49, Bremerton, Wash., 1952-53, Santa

Barbara, Calif., 1954-60, St. Louis, 1960-68, sec.-treas. dept. ch. extension A.M.E. Ch., St. Louis, 1968-76; elected bishop A.M.E. Ch., 1976 assigned 8th Episc. Dist. (La.-Miss.), New Orleans, 1976—; pres. A.M.E. Mgmt. Agy., Inc., 1969-76. Vice chmn. St. Louis Civil Service Commn., 1965-71; pres. bd. dirs. West End Hosp. Assn. Mem. Alpha Phi Alpha. Office: 2138 St Bernard Ave New Orleans LA 70119

CUMMINGS, JEANETTE GLENN, social worker, gerontologist; b. Cyrene, Ga., Aug. 11, 1949; d. Asbery and Euzera (Humphrey) Glenn; B.S., Tuskegee Inst., 1972; M.S.W. (Univ. fellow), Atlanta U., 1973; cert. in gerontology Ga. State U.; m. Jesse Cummings, Dec. 30, 1978. Dir. resident services Wesley Homes Inc., Atlanta, 1973-78; sr. citizen planner/coordinator Central Savannah River Area Planning Commn., Augusta, Ga., 1979, dir. Area Agy. on Aging, 1979—; coalition/network devel. specialist, cons. on group work with elderly, organizing social service programs. Chmn. Mental Health/Mental Retardation Adv. Council; mem. Ga. Council on Aging; bd. dirs. Augusta chpt. ARC. Elected Employee of Yr., Central Savannal River Area Planning Commn., 1980; named Social Worker of Yr. Augusta unit Nat. Assn. Social Workers, 1982; Citizen of Yr. Sr. Enrichment Assn., 1982. Mem. Nat. Assn. Social Workers, Acad. Cert. Social Workers, Ga. Gerontology Soc. (pres.), Nat. Assn. Female Execs., LWV (bd. dirs.), Leadership Augusta Alumni Assn. (vice chmn.), Delta Sigma Theta. Democrat. Mem. Unity Ch. Club: Tuskegee Alumni. Home: 2715 Vernon Dr W Augusta GA 30906 Office: 2123 Wrightsboro Rd Augusta GA 30904

CUMMINGS, PETER THOMAS, chemical engineering educator; b. Wingham, New South Wales, Australia, Feb. 10, 1954; came to U.S., 1981; s. Henry St.John and Mary Clarence (McLeod) C.; m. Elizabeth June Way, May 17, 1975. B.Math. with 1st class honors, U. Newcastle, Australia, 1975; Ph.D., U. Melbourne, Australia, 1980. Postdoctoral research fellow dept. physics U. Guelph, Ont., Can., 1980; research assoc. dept. mech. engring. and chemistry SUNY-Stony Brook, 1981-83; asst. prof. dept. chem. engring. U. Va., Charlottesville, 1983—. Contbr. articles to profl. jours. Commonwealth Sci. and Indsl. Research Orgn. fellow, 1980; grantee Dreyfus Found., 1983, NSF, 1984, Petroleum Research Fund, 1984. Mem. Am. Inst. Chem. Engrs., Am. Math. Soc., Am. Phys. Soc., Sigma Xi. Congregationalist. Office: Dept Chem Engring Thornton Hall U Va Charlottesville VA 22901

CUMMINGS, ROBERT EUGENE, counseling psychologist; b. Honolulu, Aug. 15, 1930; s. Bernard J. and Mary (Moran) C.; m. Margit Castle, Mar. 16, 1973; children—Michael R., Caroline M. B.A., U. Calif.-Berkeley, 1953; M.A., U. Calif.-San Diego, 1963; D.Ed., U. Mo., 1969. Lic. counseling psychologist, Tenn. Exec. trainee Wells Fargo Bank, San Francisco, 1957-59; counseling psychologist Agnew State Hosp., Santa Clara, Calif., 1967-72, Mountain Home VA Med. Ctr., Johnson City, Tenn., 1972—. Author: Poems and Sculpture, 1977. Contbr. articles on veteran alcoholic treatment programs to profl. jours. Served to lt. (j.g.) U.S. Navy, 1954-57, Korea. Recipient 2d place sculpture award Sister Kenny Inst., 1984. Mem. Am. Psychol. Assn., Intermountain Psychol. Assn. Avocations: sculpture; swimming; walking. Office: Mountain Home VAMC Johnson City TN 37601

CUMMINGS, WILLIAM ROGER, international tax consultant, property management executive; b. Portland, Maine, Apr. 30, 1946. B.B.A., U. Miami, 1968, LL.M., 1973; J.D., Suffolk U., 1968; M.B.A., Fla. Atlantic U., 1978. Pvt. practice internat. tax mgmt., Palm Beach, Fla., 1971—; pres. Mgmt. Advantage, Palm Beach, 1972—, Computer Advantage, Palm Beach, 1981—. Bd. dirs., fund raising chmn. Am. Lung Assn. S.E. Fla., 1982-83; bd. dirs. March of Dimes, chmn. Palm Beach Golden Mile Walk, 1981-83; bd. dirs. Commerce and Industry Goldcoast chpt. Multiple Sclerosis; bd. govs. Hist. Soc. Palm Beach County, 1979—. Mem. Greater West Palm Beach C. of C., Palm Beach C. of C., Am. Mensa, Phi Delta Theta. Republican. Episcopalian. Office: PO Box 2705 Palm Beach FL 33480

CUMMINS, LIGHT TOWNSEND, historian, educator; b. Derby, Conn., Apr. 23, 1946; s. L.T. II and Roberta (Kelley) C.; m. Victoria Hennessey, Aug. 12, 1975; 1 child, Katherine Anne. B.A., S.W. Tex. U., 1968, M.A., 1972; Ph.D., Tulane U., 1977. Fulbright fellow Spanish Fulbright Com., Madrid, 1974-76; instr. Newman Sch., New Orleans, 1976; asst. prof. history Baldwin Coll., Tifton, Ga., 1976-78; prof. history Austin Coll., Sherman, Tex., 1978—; hist. cons. Georgia Agrirama, Tifton, 1976-79. Author: Guide to History of Louisiana, 1982; Guide to History of Texas, 1985; Spanish Diplomacy and Espionage in the American Revolution, 1985. Chmn. Grayson County Hist. Commn., Sherman, 1978-80. Served to 1st lt. USAF, 1967-71. Recipient Danforth Found. Assoc. award, 1979—; Mellon Found. fellow, 1980-84; NEH fellow, 1979. Mem. Am. Hist. Assn., So. Hist. Assn., Tex. Hist. Assn., La. Hist. Assn., SAR, Sons Republic of Tex.; assoc. mem. Colonial Williamsburg Found. Episcopalian. Home: 2402 Rex Cruse Dr Sherman TX 75090 Office: Austin Coll Dept History Sherman TX 75090

CUNHA, GEORGE MARTIN, emeritus conservator; b. Providence, Dec. 25, 1911; s. Anthony Martin and Augusta Elizabeth (Dwyer) C.; m. Dorothy Bourne Grant, Dec. 31, 1938; 1 stepson, James H. Ryan; children—George Martin, Suzanne Elizabeth. Student MIT, 1930-32, Lowell Inst., 1935-36, USN Line Sch., 1946-47, Naval War Coll., 1958-59. Control chemist Phillips Baker Rubber Co., Providence, 1932-34; devel. chemist Vultex Chem. Co., Cambridge, Mass., 1935-37; apptd. aviation cadet USN, 1938, advanced through grades to capt., 1957; conservator rare books, documents and works of art on paper Library of Boston Athenaeum, 1963-73; dir. New Eng. Document Conservation Center, 1973-78, dir. emeritus, 1978—; cons. in conservation, writer, lectr., 1963—. Author: The Conservation of Library Materials, 1967, rev. edit., 1971; Library and Archives Conservation, 1980s and Beyond, 1983; editor Procs. of Boston Athenaeum's 1971 Seminar on the Conservation of Library Materials, 1972, Seminar on Conservation Adminstrn., 1975. Mem. Ky. State Archives and Records Commn., 1981—; chmn. advancement com. Narragansett council Boy Scouts Am., 1956-59, pres. C.Z. council, 1960-61. Decorated D.F.C., Air medal with star; recipient Silver Beaver award Boy Scouts Am., 1958; cert. of merit Asociación de Scouts de Panamá, 1961. Fellow Royal Soc. Arts, Pilgrim Soc. (editorial com. 1972), Am. Inst. Conservation; mem. Internat. Inst. for Conservation Historic and Artistic Works, Guild of Book Workers (v.p.-at-large 1971-77), Colonial Soc. Mass. Republican. Club: Louisville Filson. Lodge: Masons. Home: 4 Tanglewood Dr Lexington KY 40505 Office: 4 Tanglewood Dr Lexington KY 40505

CUNLIFF, ALBERT EDWARD, JR., human resource developer; b. St. Louis, Apr. 1, 1947; s. Albert Edward and Elisabeth (Semple) C.; m. April Lynn Haulman, Oct. 13, 1978; children—Colin I., Ian C. Student U. Madrid, Spain, 1967-68; B.A., DePauw U., 1969; M.A. in Human Relations, U. Okla., 1974, Ph.D. in Adult and Community Edn., 1983. VISTA supr. Redland Community Action Found., Chandler, Okla., 1969-73; project mgr. Consultants in Community Devel., Norman, Okla., 1973-77; counselor Open Access Satellite Ednl. Systems, Oklahoma City, 1977-78; exec. dir. Ambulatory Health Care, Oklahoma City, 1979-80; grad. asst. U. Okla., Norman, 1980-81; dir. human resource devel. Okla. Teaching Hosp., Oklahoma City, 1981—. Editor Okla. Adult and Continuing Edn. Newsletter, 1980-83. Pres., bd. dirs. Human Relations Assn., Norman, 1976-78, Gatewood Neighborhood Assn., Oklahoma City, 1979-81; bd. dirs. Ann. Mexican Fiesta Orgn., Oklahoma City, 1979-80; mem. adv. com. Mental Health Planning Com., Oklahoma City, 1980; bd. dirs. Old House Fair, Neighborhood Devel. Ctr., Oklahoma City, 1985. Recipient cert. of appreciation Okla. Adult and Continuing Edn., 1983; Valuable Service award Okla. Nutrition Council, 1983. Mem. Am. Assn. Adult and Continuing Edn., Am. Ednl. Research Assn., Am. Soc. Tng. and Devel. (v.p. and treas. Oklahoma City 1981-84, Outstanding Bd. Mem. award Oklahoma City chpt. 1983), Internat. Community Edn. Assn., Okla. Group Process Soc. (bd. dirs. 1979), Phi Delta Kappa. Democrat. Congregationalist. Avocations: guitar; piano; soccer; tennis; jogging. Office: Okla Teaching Hosps PO Box 26307 Oklahoma City OK 73126

CUNNINGHAM, ATLEE MARION, JR., aeronautical engineer; b. Corpus Christi, Aug. 17, 1938; s. Atlee Marion and Carlos Dean (Shepherd) C.; B.S. in Mech. Engring., U. Tex., 1961, M.S. in Mech. Engring., 1963, Ph.D., 1966; m. Diana Wahl Bonelli, July 17, 1976; children by previous marriage—Christopher Atlee, Scott Patrick, Sean Michael. Research scientist Def. Research Lab., Austin, Tex., 1965; engring. specialist sr. Gen. Dynamics Corp., Fort Worth, 1965—; vis. indsl. prof. So. Meth. U. Inst. Tech., Dallas, 1969-70; vis. assoc. prof. aero. engring. U. Tex., 1978—; lectr. in aeroelasticity Nat. Cheng Kung U., Taiwan, 1984; cons. NASA, USAF, U. Tex. Vice pres. Tex. Fine Arts Assn., Fort Worth, 1972. Served with USN, 1962-64. Welding Research Assn. fellow, 1961-62; NATO fellow, 1964-65; recipient NASA Cert. of Recognition for tech. publ., 1980, Extraordinary Achievement award Gen. Dynamics, 1980, 83. Fellow AIAA (assoc.; tech. reviewer jours, structural dynamics tech. com. 1984—); mem. Sigma Xi. Contbr. articles to profl. jours.; inovator in subsonic, transonic and supersonic steady and oscillatory aerodynamics method; developer new methods for predicting high angle of attack aerodynamics in subsonic and supersonic flows. Pioneer in new technology development for unsteady separated flows at high angle of attack involving support of Air Force, Navy, NASA, National Aerospace Laboratory (Netherlands), General Dynamics and University of Texas at Austin. Home: 2212 Windsor Pl Fort Worth TX 76110

CUNNINGHAM, CAY, psychologist; b. Port Arthur, Tex., Sept. 8, 1939; d. Troy and Rachel (McGill) C. A.B. in Sociology, U. Calif.-Berkeley, 1967; M.A. in Psychology, U. Houston, 1973; Ed.D. in Psychology, 1982. Counselor, Neighborhood Ctrs., Houston, 1968-69; research asst. dept. psychiatry Baylor Coll. Medicine, Houston, 1969-70; assoc. program planner and coordinator early childhood projects, Harris County Dept. Edn., Houston, 1970-71; dir. early childhood div. Houston Child Guidance Ctr., 1970-84, dir. specialized services, 1984—. Mem. Am. Psychol. Assn., Nat. Assn. for Edn. of Young Children, Tex. Psychol. Assn., Houston Psychol. Assn. Office: Houston Child Guidance Ctr 3215 Austin Houston TX 77004

CUNNINGHAM, CHARLES BAKER, diversified company executive; b. St. Louis, 1941. B.S., Washington U., St. Louis, 1964; M.S., Ga. Inst. Tech., 1966; M.B.A., Harvard U., 1970. Staff engr. Prybylowski & Gravino, 1965-68; staff engr. R.W. Booker & Assocs., 1968-69; summer trainee Burlington Industries Inc., 1969-70; with Cooper Industries, Inc., Houston, 1970—, planning analyst, 1970-71, exec. asst. fin. and planning hardware group, 1971-72, dir. fin. Cooper Group, 1972-75, v.p. adminstrn. and fin. Cooper Group, 1975-77, v.p. corp. devel., 1977-79, pres. indsl. equipment group, 1979-80, corp. v.p. ops., 1980-82, exec. v.p. ops, 1982—. Served with U.S. Army, 1966-68. Office: Cooper Industries Inc PO Box 4446 Houston TX 77210

CUNNINGHAM, CLARENCE MARION, chemist, educator; b. Cooper, Tex., July 24, 1920; s. Willie Lee and Naomi Mae (Stokes) C.; B.S., Tex. A&M U., 1942; M.S., U. Calif., 1948; Ph.D., Ohio State U., 1954; m. Janet Ruth Kohl, Sept. 16, 1951; children—Elizabeth Jane, Daniel Marvin, Steven Charles, Margaret Helen. Asst. prof. Calif. Poly. State U., San Luis Obispo, 1948-49; cryogenic engr., cons. H.L. Johnston, Inc., Columbus, Ohio, 1951-53; vis. research prof. Ohio State U., Columbus, summer 1961; mem. faculty Okla. State U., Stillwater, 1954—, assoc. prof. chemistry, 1959-85, prof. emeritus, 1985—; cons. Arrow Machinery Inc., Oklahoma City, 1985—; cons. in field. Vice pres. Stillwater United Way, 1959-60, bd. dirs., 1958-62; v.p. Stillwater YMCA, 1958-61; bd. dirs. Payne Community Action Bd., 1965-69; bd. dirs., v.p. Stillwater Neighborhood Nursery, 1968-72, 78-85; sec. Payne County Dem. Central Com., 1964-67, 75-77. Served to capt. U.S. Army, 1942-46, to col. USAR, 1946-72. Recipient Silver Beaver award Boy Scouts Am., 1976; Research Corp. Am. grantee, 1955-56; NASA grantee, 1966-72. Mem. AAAS, Am. Phys. Soc., Am. Chem. Soc., AAUP (chpt. pres. 1964-65, state pres. 1965-67), Okla. Acad. Sci. Democrat. Quaker. Club: Kiwanis. Author: A Student's Guide for General Chemistry, 1977. Home: 924 Lakeridge Ave Stillwater OK 74075 Office: Dept Chemistry Okla State Univ Stillwater OK 74078

CUNNINGHAM, GUY ALLEN, retail home furnishings company executive; b. Longview, Tex., May 22, 1952; s. Basil William and Opal (Randle) C.; m. Jerri Shaw; 1 child, Carrie Noel; student Kilgore Coll., 1970-72, Tex. Tech. U., 1972, N. Tex. State U., 1973. Designer, salesperson Rick Furniture Co., Dallas, 1973-74; partner Trend Furniture & Interiors, Longview, 1974-78, operating partner, 1978—; tchr. interior design Kilgore Coll., 1975-76; dir., v.p. Downtown Devel. Corp. Chmn. Longview Planning and Zoning Commn. Mem. Am. Soc. Interior Designers, Interior Design Soc., Illuminating Engring. Soc. (affiliate), Longview C. of C., Kappa Alpha Order. Episcopalian. Clubs: Rotary, Masons. Office: 215 E Tyler St Longview TX 75601

CUNNINGHAM, RALPH SANFORD, oil company executive; b. Albany, Ohio, Oct. 16, 1940; s. Harold Sanford and Julia Marie (Lasch) C.; m. Deborah Elaine Brookshire, Dec. 23, 1976; children—Ralph Sanford, Susan Ellen, Stephen Earl, Jennifer Marie. B.S. in Chem. Engring., Auburn (Ala.) U., 1962; M.S., Ohio State U., 1962, Ph.D., 1966. With Exxon Co. U.S.A., 1966-80, refinery mgr., Benicia, Calif., 1977-80; exec. v.p. processing and mktg. Tenneco Oil Co., Houston, 1980—; dir. IT Corp., Petro-Tex Chem. Corp. Chmn. United Way Solano-Napa Counties, Calif., 1979; exec. council, v.p. Silverado council Boy Scouts Am., 1978-79. Mem. Am. Inst. Chem. Engrs., Am. Petroleum Inst., Sigma Xi. Republican. Presbyterian. Office: PO Box 2511 Houston TX 77001*

CUNNINGHAM, STEVEN RAY, research and consulting firm executive; b. St. Petersburg, Fla., Oct. 8, 1952; s. Henry George and Clara May Elizabeth (Huff) C.; m. Christine Marie Harris, June 20, 1981. B.A., U. South Fla., 1978. Mgr., Browns, Inc., 1974-75; fin. analyst Lincoln Nat. Corp., 1975-76; scientist ENSCO, Inc., 1979-81; sr. mathematician Harris Corp., Palm Beach, Fla., 1981-82; pres., chief prin. scientist mth. The Cunningham Group, Inc., Largo, Fla., 1982—. Mem. Math. Assn. Am., Am. Math. Soc., Am. Phys. Soc. Republican. Home: 8167 Hopewell Ct Largo FL 33543 Office: PO Box 1990 Largo FL 34294

CUNNINGHAM, WAYNE HUGH JACKSON, educator; b. Wilkinsburg, Pa., June 9, 1949; m. Karen Dannette Lavender, Mar. 21, 1983; children—Sarah, Heather. B.S., Pa. State U., 1971, M.B.A., 1973, Ph.D., 1981. Research asst. Pa. State U., State College, 1972-75, instr. continuing edn., 1975-76; instr. mgmt. Bucknell U., Lewisburg, Pa., 1976; asst. prof. transp. and logistics U. North Fla., Jacksonville, 1976-82, assoc. prof., 1982—. Mem. Am. Inst. Decision Scis., Am. Prodn. and Inventory Control Soc., Am. Soc. Traffic and Transp. Beta Gamma Sigma, Delta Nu Alpha. Contbr. articles to profl. jours. Address: 4628 Hearthstone Ct Jacksonville FL 32223

CUPPLES, JANET CUMMINGS, property company executive; b. Burnsville, Miss., Dec. 22, 1942; d. James Edwin and Juanita Ozene (Hale) Cummings; m. David Claudus Linton, May 21, 1961 (div. 1985); 1 child, Jeffory Mark; m. Thomas Gilbert Cupples, Mar. 5, 1985. Student Northeast Miss. Jr. Coll., 1960-61, Memphis State U., 1975-76, Sheffield Tech. Ctr. Computers, 1984-85. Owner, mgr. various properties, Burnsville, 1974—; chmn. adv. com. bus. dept. Sheffield Tech. Ctr., Memphis, 1984-85. Founder Memphis Rape Task Force, 1985; exec. com. Neighborhood Watches, Memphis, 1985; exec. com. Building Bridges for Better Memphis, 1985; vol. Memphis Brooks Mus. Art, 1981—, Met. Interfaith Assn., 1981—. Mem. NCCJ, Nat. Assn. Female Execs., Network Profl. Women's Orgn. Republican. Methodist. Avocations: Writing; community involvement; teaching. Office: Memphis Rape Task Force 3021 Eagle Dr Memphis TN 38115

CURETON, STEWART, JR., investment banker; s. Stewart and Lillian (Baldwin) C.; m. Lana Ruth Lee, May 25, 1968; children—Peter Stewart, Cameron John. A.B., Stanford U., 1967; M.B.A., Harvard U., 1973. Vice pres. corp. fin. Rotan Mosle Inc., Houston, 1973-78; v.p., dir. Curtin & Co., Inc., Houston, 1978—. Trustee Houston Ballet, 1981—, mem. exec. com., 1982—, v.p. mktg., 1983-84; ann. fund. drive capt. Houston Mus. Fine Arts, 1981-83; bd. dirs. Gulf Coast Conservation Assn., Houston Zool. Soc. Served to lt. USNR, 1968-71. Mem. Nat. Venture Capital Assn., Houston Venture Capital Assn. Clubs: Tex. Corinthian Yacht (Kemah); Athletic of Houston, Houston Country, Ramada. Office: Curtin & Co Inc 2050 Houston Natural Gas Bldg Houston TX 77002

CURLE, CHRIS, journalist, TV anchorwoman; b. Denver, Feb. 17, 1947; d. Fred W. and Claudia (Harding) C.; m. Don Farmer, Feb. 27, 1972. Student U. Calif.-Berkeley, 1965-67; B.S. with honors in Communications, U. Tex., 1969. News reporter Sta. KTRK-TV, Houston, 1969-72; freelance writer, photographer, radio reporter BBC/UPI/jours., Europe and Mideast, 1972-75; news anchor, program host Cable News Network, Atlanta, 1980—; news anchor Sta. WJLA-TV News, Washington, 1975-80. Office: Cable News Network Inc 1050 Techwood Dr NW Atlanta GA 30318

CURLEE, DOROTHY SUMNER, social worker; b. Coleman, Tex., July 31, 1921; d. Thaddeus Pickett and Lena (Pierson) Sumner; B.A., Howard Payne Coll., 1942; postgrad. Tulane U., 1944; M.S. in Social Work, Columbia U., 1963; m. A. Wesley Curlee; 1 dau., Lenae. Supr. child welfare Tex. Dept. Human Resources, 1944-54, 59-60; dir. adoptions Hope Cottage Children's Bur., Dallas, 1961-69; cons. Adoption Resource Exchange N.Am., Child Welfare League Am., 1969-70; asso. dir. Children's Home Soc. N.C., Greensboro, 1970-72; med. psychiat. social worker Tex. Dept. Mental Health and Mental Retardation, Denton, 1972-78; program mgr. crippled children's div. Tex. Dept. Health, Abilene, 1978—; field instr. social work U. Tex., 1950-52, 69. Mem. Acad. Cert. Social Workers, Nat. Assn. Social Workers, Tex. Assn. Mental Health (dir. 1957-59), Daus. Republic Tex. Office: Commerce Plaza Abilene TX 79604

CURNUTT, BARBARA, consultant; b. San Antonio, Mar. 25, 1950; d. Harry Otto and Esther (Clark) C. B.S. in Edn., Tex. Tech U., 1972; M.A. in Religious Edn., Southwestern Baptist Sem., 1976. Cert. tchr. lang. and/or learning disabilities and physically handicapped, Tex. Tchr. Northside Ind. Sch. Dist., San Antonio, 1972-74; cons. Woman's Missionary Union of Bapt. Gen. Conv. Tex., Dallas, 1977—; leade profl. confs. Author profl. publs. Vol. in probation Dallas County Juvenile Dept., Dallas, 1982—; vol. Republican Nat. Conv., 1984. Baptist. Office: Woman's Missionary Union Baptist Gen Conv Tex 511 N Akard Suite 1130 Dallas TX 75201

CURRIE, EDWARD JONES, JR., lawyer; b. Jackson, Miss., May 23, 1951; s. Edward J. and Nell (Branton) C.; m. Barbara Scott Miller, June 26, 1976; children—Morgan E., Scott E. B.A., U. Miss., 1973, J.D., 1976. Bar: Miss. 1976, U.S. Dist. Ct. (no. and so. dists.) Miss. 1976, U.S. Ct. Appeals (5th cir.) 1978, U.S. Supreme Ct. 1979. Assoc. Wise, Carter, Child, Steen & Caraway, Jackson, Miss., 1976-80; ptnr. Steen, Reynolds, Dalehite & Currie, Jackson, 1980—; adj. prof. Miss. Coll. Sch. Law, Jackson, 1977-81, 84—. Bd. dirs. Miss. chpt. Am. Diabetes Assn., Jackson, 1980-82. Mem. Miss. Bar Assn. (bd. dirs. young lawyers sect. 1981-82), Jackson Young Lawyers (bd. dirs. 1980-81), Fed. Bar Assn. (young lawyers liaison 1978, sec./treas. 1985-86), Miss. Def. Lawyers Assn., Hinds County Bar Assn., Am. Trial Lawyers Assn., Nat. Inst. Trial Advocacy, Phi Delta Phi, Sigma Alpha Epsilon (pres. Central Miss. alumni 1981). Presbyterian. Home: 1500 Northlake Circle Jackson MS 39211 Office: Steen Reynolds Dalehite & Currie PO Box 900 Jackson MS 39205

CURRIE, FERGUS GARDNER, producer, director, fine arts educator, writer, performer; b. Chgo., June 29, 1931; s. Neill Roswell and Ruth (Anderson) C. B.S., Davidson Coll., 1953; M.A., U. Mo., 1957; Ed.D., Columbia U., 1963. Instr. Columbia U., N.Y.C., 1957-61; instr. CUNY, 1961-64, asst. prof. speech and theatre, 1966-69; asst. exec. sec. Speech Assn. Am., N.Y.C., 1964-66; dir. theatre Ga. Inst. Tech., Atlanta, 1970-72, Emory U., Atlanta, 1972-82; pres. Atlantis Prodns., Inc., Atlanta, 1977—; assoc. producer Centauri Films, Washington, 1983-84; guest dir. Okla. Theatre Ctr., Oklahoma City, 1982, Fort Wayne Civic Theatre, 1984, Kanahwa Players, Charleston, W.Va., 1984; artist in residence Ga. Council for Arts, Atlanta, 1982-84; arts adminstr. U. South Fla., 1985—. Creator musical revues: From Harlem to Broadway, 1981; Harlem Nocturne, 1983, Sweet Auburn, 1985. Vice pres. DeKalb Council for Arts, Decatur, Ga., 1980-82. Served to 1st lt. inf. U.S. Army, 1954-56. Gregory scholar, 1956. Mem. Actors Equity Assn., AFTRA (treas. Atlanta chpt. 1977-79, 81-83, pres. 1984-85, nat. merger com. 1982—, chmn. caucus of locals 1984-85), Screen Actors Guild (pres. Ga. br. 1977-81), Am. Theatre Assn., Omega Delta Kappa. Presbyterian. Office: Dept Fine Arts Mgmt and Events USF Tampa FL 33620

CURRIE, LEONARD JAMES, architect-planner; b. Stavely, Alta., Can., July 28, 1913; s. Andrew and Florence (McIntyre) C.; m. Virginia M. Herz, Feb. 8, 1937; children—Barbara E. Joe, Robert G., Elizabeth Baumann. B.Arch., U. Minn., 1936; M.Arch., Harvard U., 1938, postgrad., 1940-41. Registered architect Va., N.C., Ill., Mass., Pa.; cert. Nat. Council Archtl. Registration Bds. Apprentice with Walter Gropius and Marcel Breuer, Cambridge, Mass., 1938-40; archeologist div. hist. research Carnegie Instn. Expdn. to Copan, Honduras, 1941; constrn. supt. Pan Am. Airways-U.S. Govt., Guatemala and Nicaragua, 1941-42; architect Architects' Collaborative, Cambridge, Mass., 1946-51; asst. prof. architecture Harvard U. Grad. Sch. of Design, Cambridge, 1946-51; dir. Inter-Am. Housing and Planning Ctr., Bogota, Colombia, 1951-56; prof., head dept. architecture Va. Poly. Inst., Blacksburg, 1956-62; architect, planner Atkins, Currie & Payne, Blacksburg, 1957-62; dean Coll. Architecture and Art, U. Ill., Chgo., 1962-72, prof., 1973-81; Fulbright sr. lectr., acting dean U. Sains Malaysia, Penang, 1972-73; architect, planner Leonard J. Currie & Assoc., Blacksburg, 1982—; cons. in field. Author, editor: Designing Environments for the Aging, 1977; co-author numerous books on architecture. Contbr. articles to profl. jours. Architect numerous bldgs. throughout the world. Served to lt. col. AUS, CE, 1942-46, World War II, ETO. Wheelwright travelling fellow Harvard U., 1940-41; decorated Medalla De Merito, Colombia, 1956; Fulbright sr. fellow, 1972-73; hon. prof. U. Nacional de San Antonio, Peru, U. Nacional Villareal, Peru, 1977; recipient disting. service award U. Ill. Alumni Assn., 1982. Fellow AIA (1st honor award 1963), Internat. Inst. Arts and Letters; mem. Am. Inst. Cert. Planners, Interam. Planning Soc., Soc. Archtl. Historians, Sociedad Colombiana de Arquitectos (hon.). Democrat. Clubs: Harvard (bd. dirs. Chgo. 1977-81); University (Blacksburg). Home: 1506 Carlson Dr Blacksburg VA 24060 Office: 200 N Main St Blacksburg VA 24060

CURRIE, WILLIAM NELSON, financial executive; b. Wadesboro, N.C., Aug. 14, 1940; s. Lum Bolton and Ruth (WinFree) C.; m. Carolyn Haywood, Nov. 29, 1963; children—Jocarole, Beth, Amy. A.B., Duke U., 1962; M.B.A., U. N.C., 1963. Loan officer Wachovia Bank, Winston Salem, N.C., 1966-68; fin. analyst Westinghouse Co., Lester, Pa., 1968-71; acctg. mgr., 1971-75, fin. mgr., South Boston, Va., 1975-76, div. controller, 1977—. Mem. budget com. United Way, South Boston, 1983; mem. fin. com. Methodist Ch., South Boston, 1983. Served to capt. U.S. Army, 1963-66. Mem. Nat. Assn. Accts. Methodist. Office: Westinghouse Co PO Box 920 South Boston VA 24592

CURRY, DONALD ROBERT, lawyer; b. Pampa, Tex., Aug. 7, 1943; s. Robert Ward and Alleith Elizabeth (Elliston) C.; m. Carolyn Sue Boland, Apr. 17, 1965; 1 son, James Ward. B.S., West Tex. State U., 1965; J.D., U. Tex., 1968. Bar: Tex. 1968, U.S. Dist. Ct. (no. dist.) Tex. 1970, U.S. Tax Ct. 1973. Assoc., Day & Gandy, Ft. Worth, 1968-69, ptnr., 1970-72; sole practice, Ft. Worth, 1972—; lectr. in field. Bd. regents West Tex. State U., Canyon, 1969-77, sec., mem. exec. com., 1972-75; mem. exec. bd. Longhorn council Boy Scouts Am., 1970—, dist. chmn., 1970-75; precinct chmn. Tarrant County (Tex.) Democratic Party, 1982—, election judge, 1982—. Mem. State Bar Tex., ABA, Fort Worth-Tarrant County Bar Assn., Ft. Worth Bus. and Estate Council, Tex. Ind. Producers and Royalty Owners Assn., Phi Alpha Delta. Methodist. Clubs: Ft. Worth, Petroleum of Fort Worth. Home: 3800 Tulsa Way Fort Worth TX 76107 Office: 905 Ft Worth Club Bldg Fort Worth TX 76102

CURRY, RALPH LEIGHTON, English educator; b. Bowling Green, Ky., Feb. 19, 1924; s. Daniel Preston and Ruby (Downey) C. A.B., W. Ky. State U., 1948; M.A., U. Pa., 1950, Ph.D., 1956. Assoc. prof. English Georgetown Coll., Ky., 1951-56, prof., 1956-70, dept. chmn., 1970—; dir. Stephen Leacock Meml. Mus., 1957-79. Served with U.S. Army, 1943-46. Fulbright prof., Iceland, 1965-66. Mem. AAUP, MLA, Am. Studies Assn., Ky.-Tenn. Am. Studies Assn., Ky. Philol. Assn., Conf. on Christianity and Lit. Baptist. Lodge: Rotary. Author: Stephen Leacock: Humorist and Humanist, 1959; Leacock Medal Treasury of Humor, 1978. Home: 407 Hollyhock Ln Georgetown KY 40324 Office: Georgetown Coll Georgetown KY 40324

CURRY, TONI GRIFFIN, counseling center executive, administrator, consultant; b. Langdale, Ala., June 23, 1938; d. Robert Alton and Elsie (Dodson) Griffin; m. Ronald William Curry, June 13, 1959 (div. 1972); children—Christopher, Catherine, Angela. B.A., Ga. State U., 1962; M.S.W., U. Ga., 1981. Cert. addictions counselor. Tchr. DeKalb County Bd. Edn., Atlanta, 1962-63; counselor Peachford Hosp., Charter Med. Corp., Atlanta, 1974-79; dir. aftercare, 1976-79; dir. aftercare and occupational services Ridgeview Inst., Atlanta, 1979-82; owner, dir., adminstr., counselor Atlanta Resource Ctr., 1982—; cons., lectr. to numerous cos. and orgns.; mem. adv. bd. Peachford Hosp., Atlanta, 1982—, Rockdale House, Conyers, Ga., 1981—, Outpatient Addictions Clinics Am., 1983—; bd. dirs. Southeastern Employee Assistance Programs Inst., 1981—; pres., mem. exec. bd. Ga. Employee Assistance Programs Forum, Atlanta, 1981—. Mem. Nat. Assn. Social Workers, Ga. Addiction Counselors Assn. (dir. 1982—), Ga. Citizens Council Alcoholism, Nat. Assn. Alcoholisms and Drug Abuse Counselors, Mems. Guild of High Mus. Art, Kappa Alpha Theta. Home: 2112 Bucktrout Pl Atlanta GA 30338 Office: Atlanta Resource Center 1655 Phoenix Blvd Atlanta GA 30349 also 5675 Peachtree-Dunwood Rd Atlanta GA 30349

CURTIS, GRANT R(ICHARD), beverage company executive; b. Elizabeth, N.J., Oct. 4, 1938; s. Philip and Rose (Freisinger) C.; m. Carol MacDougall, Dec. 30, 1967; children—James Andrew, Sarah Julia. A.B., Princeton U., 1960; M.B.A., Harvard U., 1966. Mgr. mktg. Coca-Cola Japan, Tokyo, 1969-71; mgr. new products Coca-Cola U.S.A., Atlanta, 1972-74, mgr. devel., 1974-76, mgr. plans and info., 1980—; v.p. mktg. Wine Spectrum, N.Y.C., 1977-80. Mgr., Buckhead Little League Team, Atlanta, 1983; advisor Jr. Achievement, 1983; vol. Arden Neighborhood Assn., 1983; fund raiser Pace Acad., Atlanta, 1983. Served with USN, 1960-64. Recipient Outstanding Vol. award Coca-Cola Co., 1983. Mem. Harvard Bus. Sch. Club Atlanta (program com. 1976). Republican. Episcopalian. Club: Brookwood Hills Community. Office: Coca-Cola Co PO Drawer 1734 Atlanta GA 30305

CURTIS-ROBINSON, NANCY REBECCA, publisher, real estate broker; b. Tampa, Fla., Aug. 27, 1955; d. George David, Jr., and Frances Katherine (Battey) Curtis; m. David L.B. Curtis-Robinson, Sept. 2, 1978 (dec. July 1982). B.A., U. South Fla., 1977, M.A., 1978. Account mgr. Fla. Service Ctr., Inc., 1978-79; sales rep. Moore Bus. Forms, Inc., Brevard County, Fla., 1979-80, Pubs. Press, Inc., 1980-82, mng. editor, 1981-82; pres., chief exec. officer The Publs. Group, Inc., Tampa, 1982—; broker Coach Realty, 1982—. Named Outstanding Young Career Woman, Dist. V, Fla. Fedn. Bus. and Profl. Women, 1980. Mem. Tampa Advt. Fedn., Jr. League Tampa, U. South Fla. Alumni Assn., Chi Omega. Republican. Episcopalian. Clubs: Tampa Yacht and Country, Downtown Tampa Bus. and Profl. Women's. Office: 115 S Dale Mabry Hwy Suite 400 Tampa FL 33609

CURTRIGHT, GLADYS STEELE, real estate broker; b. Evansville, Wis., May 13, 1904; d. Robert L. and Mamie L. (Haley) Steele; student Rockford (Ill.) Coll., Beloit (Wis.) Coll.; m. Walter L. Curtright, Dec. 22, 1923; children—Lois Rae Curtright Henderson, Jay B. Cosmotologist, Cin., 1922-28; agt. Prudential Ins. Co., Beloit, 1930-33; various acctg. positions, 1942-50; owner retail gift shop and real estate office, Beloit, 1950-64; broker, salesman J.R. Schuster Agy., Beloit, 1964-72, Exec. Services, Sanibel, Fla., 1974-78; v.p., broker Bluebill Properties, Inc., Sanibel Island, 1978—; past pres. Beloit Bd. Realtors. Mem. Nat. Assn. Realtors, Fla. Assn. Realtors, Ft. Myers Bd. Realtors, Naples Area Bd. Realtors. Methodist. Home: 896 Angel Wing Dr Sanibel Island FL 33597 Office: 2422 Periwinkle Way Sanibel Island FL 33957

CURVIN, KENYA JOYCE, energy executive, composer; b. Oklahoma City, June 15, 1938; d. T. Clinton and A. Jean (Coulter) Wallace; student Belhaven Coll., Jackson, Miss., 1957, Oklahoma City U., 1958, Okla. U., 1976-78; children—Derek Jerome Sanderson, Gina Rachelle Sanderson, Cimarron Trace Anthony Curvin. New accounts rep. Fidelity Bank N.A., Oklahoma City, 1964-68; geol. asst. G.B.K. Co., Oklahoma City, 1968-72; psychiat. unit mgr. Queens Hosp., Honolulu, 1972-74; exec. officer Standard of Wewoka, Inc., Oklahoma City, 1974—, also dir.; naturalist Okla. Tourism and Recreation Dept., 1977-78; pres., dir. Wildcat Mapping, Inc., Oklahoma City, 1979-85; owner M.W. Galaxy Music, Norman, Okla., 1981—; v.p. Scissortail Oil Corp., 1982-85; asst. v.p. G.B.K. Co., 1982; ecology and conservation lectr. Mem. Nat. Assn. Female Execs. (network dir.), Okla. Petroleum Drafting Assn., Internat. Platform Assn., Better Bus. Bur., Canadian River Park Assn. (life). Democrat. Author: Manna-Mana (poetry), 1977; composer: Redland (musical play), 1980 (Okla. Heritage award 1982); ballads; photographer.

CUSH, JOSEPH WILBUR, dentist; b. Natchitoches, La., Aug. 22, 1929; s. Samuel and Angeline Marie (Catanese) C.; student Centenary Coll., 1946-48; D.D.S., Loyola U. of So., 1953; m. Beverly Jean Burch, Aug. 21, 1954; children—Joseph Wilbur, Derrie Anne, Gregory Samuel, Bryan Stephan, Angela Marie. Intern oral surgery Charity Hosp., New Orleans, 1953-54; resident oral surgery Confederate Meml. Med. Center, Shreveport, La., 1956-58; pvt. practice oral surgery, Shreveport, 1958—; mem. staffs La. State Sch. Medicine Post Grad. Dept. Dir. United Merc. Bank. Pres. N.W. La. Cancer Soc., 1970. Bd. dirs. Doctor's Hosp., 1965-75, Downtown Shreveport Unltd., 1984. Served with USAF, 1954-56. Fellow Acad. Internat. Dentistry; mem. Am. Dental Soc. of Anesthesiology, Am., La., 4th Dist. (pres. 1965) dental assns., Pierre Fauchard Acad., Shreveport C. of C. (dir. 1976, 77, v.p. 1979), Delta Sigma Delta, Am. Legion. Roman Catholic. K.C., Rotarian. Clubs: Serra, Pierremont Oaks Tennis, East Ridge Country, University. Home: 307 Deborah St Shreveport LA 71106 Office: 915 Shreveport Barksdale Hwy Shreveport LA 71105

CUSHING, GEORGE HEREWARD, public relations executive; b. Detroit, July 5, 1915; s. George William and Clara Gertrude (Arkell) C.; m. Lucile Meredith Quail, Mar. 7, 1940. Student, Kenyon Coll., 1934-35. Newspaper editor various Wis. and Mich. papers, 1935-37; writer Campbell Ewald Advt. Agy., Detroit, 1937-40; various editorial and advt. agy. positions, incl. McCann-Erickson and Detroit editor of Motor Trend Mag., 1940-54; mgr. pub. relations ops. Chrysler Corp., N.Y., 1954-61; dir. pub. relations D.P. Brother & Co., 1961-64, Chrysler Internat., Geneva, Switzerland, 1964-70; dir. internat. pub. relations Am. Motors Corp., Detroit, 1971-76; U.S. editor and researcher Olyslager Orgn. Bv, Soesterberg, Holland and Misset Pub. Co., Doetinchem, Holland, 1976—; cons. in field. Mem. Am. Pub. Relations, Pub. Relations Soc. Am. (accredited). Democrat. Episcopalian. Club: Kiwanis. Address: 57 Blare Castle Dr PO Box 650 Palm Coast FL 32037

CUSHMAN, EDWARD CHARLES, JR., lawyer; b. Aiken, S.C., Sept. 21, 1918; s. Edward Charles and Mary Nagel (Swearingen) C.; m. Ruth Lecil Drummond, Nov. 15, 1943; children—Ruth Lecil Cushman Harden, Mary Nagel. A.B., Furman U., 1939; LL.B., U. S.C., 1942, postgrad., 1947-48. Bar: S.C. 1947, U.S. Dist. Ct. S.C. 1947. Sole practice, Aiken, S.C., 1947-51; ptnr. firm, Aiken, 1951-70; sole practice with assocs., Aiken, 1970—; U.S. commr., 1947-48; mem. S.C. Ho. of Reps., 1949-60, S.C. Senate, 1960-68; chmn. house com. on edn. and pub. works Aiken County (S.C.) Pub. Defender, 1970-77; lectr. in field. Trustee ex officio U. S.C. and Winthrop Coll., both 1955-60. Served with USMC, 1942-47. Decorated Bronze Star. Mem. ABA, S.C. Bar Assn., Aiken County Bar Assn. Democrat. Baptist. Clubs: Lions, The Outing, Masons (Aiken, S.C.). Home: 3434 Summit Dr Aiken SC 29801 Office: 623 Richland Ave W PO Box 270 Aiken SC 29802

CUSHMAN, PAUL, physician, educator; b. N.Y.C., Feb. 4, 1930; m. Paulette Bessire; children—Paul, III, Clare Hepburn. B.A., Yale U., 1951; M.D., Columbia U., 1955. Intern Barnes Hosp., St. Louis, 1955-56; asst. resident Strong Meml. Hosp., Rochester, N.Y., 1956-57, 1959-61; asst. resident attending physician St. Lukes Hosp., N.Y.C., 1961-77; instr. Columbia U., 1961-65, asst. prof. medicine, 1965-77; assoc. prof. medicine, pharmacology, psychiatry Med. Coll. Wis., Milw., 1977-81; assoc. prof. medicine, pharmacology and psychiatry Med. Coll. Va., Richmond, 1982—. Bd. dirs. Friends Va. Opera, Milw. Found. Served to capt. USAF, 1957-59. Recipient Caleb Fiske prize, 1967; Henry E. Sigerist prize Yale U., 1973. Fellow ACP, Am. Coll. Clin. Pharmacology; mem. Richmond Acad. Medicine, N.Y. Acad. Medicine, Endocrine Soc., Am. Physiol. Soc., AAAS, Am. Fedn. Clin. Research. Episcopalian. Clubs: Union (N.Y.C.); Westwood Rachet, Commonwealth (Richmond). Office: McGuire VA Hosp Richmond VA 32349

CUSTER, CAROL LEE, educator; b. Harrisonburg, Va., Aug. 7, 1945; d. Clarence Arvine and Margaret Kathryn (Fawley) C. B.A., Shepherd Coll., 1968; M.Ed., U. Va., 1971; postgrad James Madison U., Old Dominion U. Tchr., coach Frederick County Pub. Schs., Winchester, Va., 1968—, chmn. dept. phys. edn., 1974-80. Vol., ARC, 1968-82, Am. Heart Assn., 1981-83. Mem. NEA, Va. Edn. Assn., Frederick County Edn. Assn., AAHPERD, Va. Assn. Health, Phys. Edn. and Recreation. Republican. Methodist. Home: 342 Fairmont Ave Apt 2 Winchester VA 22601 Office: James Wood High Sch 1313 Amherst St Winchester VA 22601

CUSTODIO, JOSE ENRIQUE, mechanical engineer; b. Lares, P.R., Dec. 5, 1942; s. Jose M. and Rosa (Planell) C.; B.S.M.E., U. P.R., Mayaguez, 1965; m. Gloria C. Mendez, June 5, 1965; children—Glorimar, Cristina. Sales engr. A. Martinez & Co., San Juan, P.R., 1965-67; design engr. G. Ibarra & Assos., San Juan, 1967-69; sr. mech. engr. V.M. Garcia Assocs., San Juan, 1969-73, ptnr., dir. engring., 1973-77; v.p. R. Mediavilla & Sons, gen. contractors, San Juan, 1977-79; cons. engr., prin. Custodio & Assocs., San Juan, 1979-81; mng. ptnr. Custodio, Roe & Assocs., San Juan, 1981—; mem. P.R. Gov.'s Adv. Bd. on Constrn. Industry, 1978-80. Author: Energy Conservation Reduction of Outside Air in HUAC Systems; Analysis of the P.R. Energy Code; Quality Control in the Construction Industry; Principles of Cogeneration; Cogeneration in P.R.; Cogeneration in the Dominican Republic; Cogeneration in the Caribbean Basin Countries; Engineers and Architects, Design Compensation in P.R. Served with USAF, 1966. Mem. Colegio de Ingenieros y Agrimensores de Puerto Rico (pres. 1978-80), P.R. Soc. Mech. Engrs., P.R. Inst. Mech. Engrs., (pres. 1974-76), P.R. Soc. Profl. Engrs. (pres. 1983-84), Internat. Cogeneration Soc. (pres. P.R. chpt. 1983-84, dir. 1983—), ASME (pres. P.R. sect. 1970-71), ASHRAE, Phi Sigma Alpha. Roman Catholic. Clubs: Caparra Country, Bankers. Home: 5-24 Oviedo St Guaynabo PR 00657 Office: GPO Box 2397 San Juan PR 00936

CUSTURERI, RICHARD DOMENICK, lawyer; b. Jersey City, Nov. 14, 1957; s. Domenick and Mary (Foca) C.; m. Sherry Lynn Suereth, Aug. 30, 1980. B.S. in Chemistry, U. Fla., 1977, J.D., 1980. Bar: Fla. 1980, U.S. Dist. Ct. (mid. dist.) Fla. 1981, U.S. Ct. Claims 1982, U.S. Tax Ct. 1982, U.S. Ct. Appeals (11th cir.) 1985. Mem. Congressional staff, Washington, 1978; law clk. Student Legal Services, Gainesville, Fla., 1978-80; ptnr. Blanchard, Custureri & Merriam, Ocala, 1980—. Chmn. Am. Heart Assn., Marion County, Fla., 1983-86; charter bd. mem. Marion County CPR Program, Inc., 1983-86; precinct committeeman Marion County Republican Party, 1980—; pres. Marion County Young Reps., 1982—. Mem. Acad. Fla. Trial Lawyers, ABA, Assn. Trial Lawyers Am., Am. Judicature Soc., Phi Delta Phi, Omicron Delta Kappa, Jaycees (legal counsel 1981—). Roman Catholic. Lodges: K.C., Kiwanis, Elks. Home: 1309 SE 10th Ave Ocala FL 32671 Office: Blanchard Custureri & Merriam PO Box 24 Ocala FL 32678

CUTCHEN, BILLYE WALKER, accountant; b. Oklahoma City, Apr. 23, 1930; d. William Lafayette and Naomi (Armstrong) Walker; m. Walter Reed Brown, Sept. 2, 1949 (div. 1971); children—Susan M. Kresmer, Elizabeth A. Miles, Cynthia L. West; m. Paul Otto Cutchen, Apr. 18, 1974. B.A. magna cum laude, U. West Fla., 1981, M.A., 1985. C.P.A., Fla. Editor, Nat. Sci. Tchrs. Assn., Washington, 1962-64; free-lance writer, Va., Fla., India, Sri Lanka, Liberia, 1964-79; cashier U.S. Dept. State, Monrovia, Liberia, 1979-80; pub. accounts auditor Office of Auditor Gen. Fla., 1982-84; acct. Alexander Grant & Co., Pensacola, Fla., 1984-85; pvt. practice acctg., Milton, Fla., 1985—. Author: Floods, 1975, Earthquakes, 1974; Hurricanes and Tornadoes, 1972; Volcanoes, 1970; contbr. articles to profl. jours., Jack and Jill mag.; editor: The Legal System of Somaria, 1973; The Legal System of Lesotho, 1972; Modern Management of Myelomeningocele, 1972; The Black American, 1969; others. Mem. Nat. Assn. Accts., Am. Inst. C.P.A.s, Fla. Inst. C.P.A.s. Republican. Unitarian. Office: 416 Shell Rd Milton FL 32570

CUTCHINS, CLIFFORD ARMSTRONG, III, banker; b. Southampton County, Va., July 12, 1923; s. Clifford Armstrong and Sarah Penelope (Vaughan) C.; m. Ann Woods, June 21, 1947; children—Clifford A., William W., Cecil V. B.S. in B.A., Va. Poly. Inst. and State U., 1947; postgrad. Stonier Grad. Sch. Banking, Rutgers U., 1952. With Vaughan & Co. Bankers, Franklin, Va., 1947-62, pres., dir., 1960-62; sr. v.p., dir. Va. Nat. Bank, Norfolk, 1963-65, exec. v.p., 1965-69, pres., chief adminstrv. officer, 1969-72; pres., chief adminstrv. officer Va. Nat. Bankshares, Inc. and Va. Nat. Bank and dir., 1972-80, chmn. bd., chief exec. officer, dir., 1980-83; chmn. bd., chief exec. officer, dir. Sovran Fin. Corp. and Sovran Bank, N.A., 1983—; dir. Pulaski Furniture Corp., Franklin Equipment Co., Mid-Atlantic Exchange Inc.; mem. Assoc. Res. City Bankers Assn. of Bank Holding Cos. Bd. dirs. Alliance Health System; bd. dirs., pres. Va. Tech. Found., Inc. Served with U.S. Army, 1943-46. Baptist. Clubs: Commonwealth (Richmond, Va.); Cypress Cove Country (Franklin, Va.); Harbor, Norfolk Yacht and Country, Town Point (Norfolk). Office: 1 Commercial Pl Norfolk VA 23510

CUTIE, GUILLERMO ANTONIO, civil engineer, county administrator; b. Santiago, Cuba, Mar. 14, 1952; came to U.S., 1962; s. Guillermo Jose and Milagros O. (Duany) C.; m. Marta Isabel Garcia, July 12, 1974. A.A., Dade Community Coll., Miami, 1972; B.S., U. Miami-Coral Gables, 1975. Engr. technician City of Miami, 1973-78; engr. Metro-Dade County, Miami, 1978-82, adminstr., 1982—; engr. Carr Smith Assocs., Coral Gables, 1978; cons. Atlantic Services, Miami, 1977. Mem. Republican Nat. Com., Washington, 1983. Mem. Fla. Recreation and Park Assn. Roman Catholic. Club: Jr. Civitan (sec. 1969-70) (Miami). Office: Metro-Dade Park & Recreation 50 SW 32d Rd Miami FL 33129

CUTLER, LEROY RESPESS, clergyman; b. Washington County, N.C., Mar. 1, 1934; s. Leonard Leroy and Rosa Marie (Respess) C.; m. Eleanor Wilson Keech, July 20, 1952; children—Cynthia Elaine Cutler Biddle, Joseph Leroy, Gary LaVerne. B.D., Free Will Bapt. Bible Coll., 1958; M.Div., Luther Rice Sem., 1977, D.Min., 1979; postgrad. Tex. A. and M. U., 1965-66. Ordained to ministry Baptist Ch., 1955; pastor First Free Will Bapt. Ch., Jacksonville, N.C., 1958-64, First Free Will Bapt. Ch., Bryan, Tex., 1964-74, Immanuel Free Will Bapt. Ch., Jacksonville, Fla., 1974—; moderator Greater St. Johns River Assn.; mem. Fla. State Mission Bd., Nat. Home Missions Bd., 1984-85, Hymn Book Revision Com., 1985-86. Mem. Nat. Assn. Free Will Bapts., Aircraft Owners and Pilots Assn. Democrat. Baptist. Contbr. articles to Contact mag. Home: 10561 Villanova Rd Jacksonville FL 32218 Office: 6225 Norwood Ave Jacksonville FL 32208

CUTLER, ROGER THAYER, geophysicist; b. Washington, June 28, 1946; s. Addison Thayer and Ruth Ann (Jenks) C.; m. Carol Ellen Click, Feb. 12, 1982. B.A. with honors, U. Chgo., 1968, M.S., 1969; M.S., U. Ill., 1973, Ph.D., 1975. Postdoctoral fellow Argonne Nat. Lab., Ill., 1975-77; research geophysicist Gulf Research and Devel. Co., Harmarville, Pa., 1977-80, sect. dir., 1980-82; explorationist Gulf Oil Exploration and Prodn. Co., New Orleans, 1982-85; speaker in field. Contbr. articles to profl. publs., chpt. to book. Served with U.S. Army, 1969-71. U. Ill. fellow, 1974-75. Mem. Soc. Exploration Geophysicists, Am. Assn. Petroleum Geologists, Am. Phys. Soc. Home: 14627 Cindywood Houston TX 77079 Office: Chevron Geoscis Co Box 42832 Houston TX 77242

CUTTINO, GEORGE PEDDY, emeritus history educator; b. Newnan, Ga., Mar. 9, 1914; s. David Smith and Katie May (Peddy) C. B.A. with highest honors, Swarthmore Coll., 1935; M.A., U. Iowa, 1936; D.Phil., Oxford U., 1938. Instr., U. Iowa, Iowa City, 1939-42, asst. prof. history, 1946; asst. prof. history Bryn Mawr Coll., 1946-49, assoc. prof., 1949-52; asst. prof. Swarthmore Coll., 1946-49, assoc. prof., 1952-55, prof., 1955-80; Charles Howard Candler prof. medieval history Emory U., Atlanta, 1980-84, prof. emeritus, 1984—; vis. prof. Eckerd Coll. Summer Session, Sussex U. (Eng.), 1959; vis. honors examiner Swarthmore Coll., 1940, 41, 58, 61, U. Va., 1966; acad. cons. Bishop Coll., Dallas, 1963-65. Served with M.I., U.S. Army, 1942-46, 51-52. Decorated Bronze Star; Rhodes scholar, 1936-39; Guggenheim fellow, 1947-48, 53-54; recipient Haskins medal Medieval Acad. Am., 1979; membre correspondant Académie Européenne d'Histoire, 1981. Fellow Soc. Antiquaries (London), Medieval Acad. Am., Royal Hist. Soc., Brit. Acad. (Corr.); mem. Internat. Commn. on History of Parliamentary and Rep. Instns., Am. Hist. Assn., Conf. Brit. Studies, Brit. Records Assn., Huguenot Soc. S.C. Democrat. Club: Reform. Contbr. articles to profl. jours.; author: English Diplomatic Administration, 1259-1339, 1940, rev. edit., 1971; I Laugh Through Tears: the Ballades of François Villon, 1955; Le Livre d'Agenais, 1956; (with others) Civilization in the Western World, 1967, 2d edit., 1971; Gascon Register A (series of 1318-1319), 3 vols., 1976, 76; Saddle Bag and Spinning Wheel, being the Civil War Letters of G.W. Peddy, M.D., Surgeon and His Wife, 1981; History of the Cuttino Family, 1982; English Medieval Diplomacy, 1985. Home: 1270 University Dr NE Atlanta GA 30306 Office: Dept History Emory Univ Atlanta GA 30322

CUTTLER, SANDRA HARRIET, telecommunications marketing specialist; b. Albany, N.Y., Dec. 31, 1949; s. Abram Jackel and Norma Rose Cuttler; m. Gary Z. Lotner, Sept. 19, 1976; children—Jessica Beth, Daniel Eric. Research analyst Bell of Pa., Phila., 1976-77; staff mgr. in research and stats.-bus mktg. Mountain Bell, Denver, 1977-79; econometric forecaster So. Bell, Atlanta, 1979; dir. communications research Elrick & Lavidge div. Equifax, Atlanta, 1979-82; regional mktg. specialist MCI Telecommunications Corp., 1982—. Mem. Ga. Women's Polit. Caucus; network coordinator ERA Ga., 1979-80; mem. dual career conf. adv. bd. Women's Bur., U.S. Dept. Labor. Mem. Am. Mktg. Assn. (dir.), Women in Info. Processing, Atlanta Women's Network (dir.), Ga. Internat. Trade Assn. Democrat. Office: 4170 Ashford-Dunwoody Rd Suite 300 Atlanta GA 30319

DAANE, JAMES DEWEY, banking educator, financial executive; b. Grand Rapids, Mich., July 6, 1918; s. Gilbert L. and Mamie (Blocksma) D.; m. Blanche M. Tichenor, Apr. 28, 1941 (div. 1952); 1 child, Elizabeth Marie Daane Mallek; m. Onnie B. Selby, Jan. 23, 1953 (dec. Dec. 1961); m. Barbara W. McMann, Feb. 16, 1963; children—Elizabeth Whitney, Olivia Quartel. A.B. magna cum laude, Duke U., 1939; M.P.A., Harvard U., 1946, D.P.A. (Littauer fellow), 1949. With Fed. Res. Bank, Richmond, Va., 1939-60, asst. v.p., 1953-57, v.p., 1957-60, also cons. to pres. bank; assoc. economist Fed. Open Market Com., 1955-56, 58-59; chief IMF Fiscal Mission to Paraguay, 1950-51; adv. to pres. Fed. Res. Bank, Mpls., 1960; asst. to sec. treasury, 1960-61, dep. undersec. treasury for monetary affairs, 1961-63; bd. govs. Fed. Res. System, 1963-74; vice chmn. bd., dir. Commerce Union Bank, 1974-78; vice chmn. Tenn. Valley Bancorp., Inc., 1975-78; chmn. internat. policy com. Commerce Union Corp., 1978-84; vice chmn. trust bd. Commerce Union Bank, Nashville, 1984—; Frank K. Houston prof. banking Own Grad. Sch. Mgmt. Vanderbilt U., 1974—; dir. Whittaker Corp., Los Angeles, 1974—, Chgo. Bd. Trade, 1979-82, Nat. Futures Assn., 1983—. Bd. adv. Patterson Sch. Diplomacy and Internat. Commerce, U. Ky. Mem. J.F. Kennedy Sch. Govt. Assn. Harvard U., Am. Econ. Assn., Am. Fin. Assn. Clubs: Harvard (Washington), Harvard-Radcliffe, Cumberland, Belle Meade Country (Nashville). Office: Commerce Union Bank One Commerce Pl Nashville TN 37239

DABIRI, MASOUD TOGHRAI, mechanical engineer, educator; b. Shiraz, Fars, Persia, Apr. 20, 1954; s. Ali-Mohammed and Batoul D. Degree in Natural Scis., Mohammad Reza Shah Pahlavi High Sch. Shiraz, Fars, 1972; M.E., Old Dominion Univ., 1981. Mech. engr. H.R.D.S., Virginia Beach, Va., 1983—. Mem. ASME, Pi Tau Sigma. Home: 18111 SW 89 Court Miami FL 33157

DABNEY, TERRY MAURICE, mortician, funeral home executive; b. Campbellsville, Ky., July 16, 1952; s. Walter Maurice and Sarah Catherine (Gebehart) D.; m. Judy Diane Newton, Mar. 9, 1974; children—Tara Brooke, Traver Maurice. Diploma Ky. Sch. Mortuary Sci., 1973. Asst. Parrott & Ramsey Funeral Home, Campbellsville, Ky., 1969-81, pres., 1981—, also dir.; dep. coroner County of Taylor, Ky., 1978-81, coroner, 1982—. Treas., Good Hope Bapt. Ch., 1976; mem. Taylor County Bd. Health, Campbellsville, 1985. Named Outstanding Young Businessman Campbellsville Jaycees, 1981. Mem. Campbellsville-Taylor County C. of C. (bd. dirs. 1985), Nat. Funeral Dirs. Assn., Ky. Coroners Assn. (bd. dirs. 1986), Internat. Assn. Coroners and Med. Examiners, Ky. Funeral Dirs. Assn. Republican. Baptist. Lodges: Kiwanis (v.p. 1983-84, pres. 1985—), Masons. Avocations: boating; hunting; collecting coins and guns. Home and Office: 418 Lebanon Ave PO Box 426 Campbellsville KY 42718

DACEY, JANE GATES, educator; b. Biloxi, Miss., Apr. 21, 1936; d. Oliver Vivian and Pearl Vera (Gill) Dacey. B.A., La. State U., 1958; M.Ed., U. So. Miss., 1975; postgrad. U. South Ala., 1977-79. Claims adjuster Traveler's Ins. Co., New Orleans, 1958-59; tchr. Spanish, Biloxi Pub. Schs., 1960-62; tchr. Sci. and Spanish Davidson High Sch., Mobile, Ala., 1963-64; instr. English, Inst. Latin Am. Studies, Hattiesburg, Miss., 1964-65; tchr. elem. sch. Ocean Springs (Miss.) Pub. Schs., 1966—, tchr. gifted children, 1977-80; condr. workshops on gifted and learning centers; chmn. City Spelling Bee, 1980-82. Active New Orleans Mus. Art. Mem. Miss. Profl. Educators, Ft. Maurepas Reading Council (pres. 1973), Miss. Sci. Tchrs. Assn., PTA, Nat. Assn. Gifted Children, Miss. Wildlife Fedn., Nat. Wildlife Fedn., DAR, P.E.O., Phi Delta Kappa, Sigma Delta Pi, Delta Kappa Gamma (chpt. pres. 1978-80). Republican. Episcopalian. Author: Teacher's Guide to Mississippi's Past and Present, 1973; Involved in America, 1974. Home: 17 Cerro Verde Ocean Springs MS 39564 Office: PO Box 729 Ocean Springs MS 39564

DACHOWSKI, MARJORIE MCCORMICK, clinical psychologist; b. Chgo., Sept. 26, 1932; d. Harold Elmo and Irene Lillian (Fenn) McCormick; m. Lawrence W. Dachowski, Aug. 20, 1960; children—Elizabeth, David, Kathleen, Anne. Student Drury Coll., 1950-52; B.A. in Sociology, U. Ill., 1954, M.A. in Sociology, 1956, Ph.D. in Clin. Psychology, 1961. Counselor, Counseling Ctr. U. Ill., Urbana, 1959-62; psychologist Charity Hosp. Sch. Nursing, New Orleans, 1964-66; asst. prof. Dillard U., New Orleans, 1966-67, prof., 1968-74; dir. counseling Career Devel. and Placement Ctr., Loyola U., New Orleans, 1974—; cons. Tulane Counseling Ctr., 1979-80, Our Lady of the Cross, 1981-82, Charity Hosp. Sch. Nursing, 1966-70; vis. lectr. Tulane U. Mem. Am. Psychol. Assn., Am. Assn. Counseling and Devel., Assn. Univ. and Coll. Counseling Ctr. Dirs. (steering com. 1983-84), Democrat. Unitarian. Home: 366 Millaudon St New Orleans LA 70118 Office: PO Box 200 Loyola U New Orleans LA 70118

DACRE, ROBERT JOSEPH, construction company executive; b. Orlando, Fla., June 5, 1949; s. Arthur Paul and Laura (Brackett) D.; m. Carmelita Demetria, July 4, 1978; children—Stephen, Richard, Cassandra. B.S. in Bus. Adminstrn., U. S. Fla., 1970. Cert. gen. contractor, heavy constrn. estimator, Fla. Mgr. C.D.K. Constrn. Corp., Coral Springs, Fla., 1970-72; v.p. Arbo Devel. Corp., Orlando, Fla., 1972-74; gen. mgr. Romine Constrn. Co., Savannah, Ga., 1974-77; v.p. Pyramid Constrn. Co., Savannah and Detroit, 1974-82; pres. Fed. Constrn. Corp., Orlando (operating Fla., Ga., Caribbean, Nfld.), 1982—; dir. Leek Corp., Norcross, Ga., 1983, Demetrius Bldg. Corp., Orlando, 1983. Contbg. editor manual, 1982; author seminar, 1982; contbr. articles to publs. Councilman, Council for Minority Contracting Devel., Detroit, 1980; patron Council for Arts, Savannah, 1982; mem. Young Republicans, Winter Springs, Fla., 1983, Central Fla. council Boy Scouts Am., Savannah, 1983. Mem. Assoc. Gen. Contractors (dir. Young Exec. Com. Detroit 1980), Constrn. Specification Inst., Profl. Estimator's Soc., (presdl. adv. com. Orlando and Washington). Roman Catholic. Clubs: Plimsol (Savannah); Chatham (Orlando). Office: Fed Contracting Corp 235 Maitland Ave 215 Maitland FL 32751

DADISMAN, JOSEPH CARROL, newspaper publisher; b. Statesboro, Ga., May 24, 1934; s. Howard Dean and Mary Lou (Moore) D.; m. Mildred Jean Sparks, Aug. 19, 1956; children—David Carroll, Ellen Clarice. A.B. in Journalism, U. Ga., 1956; postgrad. Columbus (Ga.) Coll., 1979-80. Reporter, editorial writer, mng. editor Augusta (Ga.) Chronicle, 1956-66; editor Marietta (Ga.) Daily Jour., 1966-72; mng. editor Macon (Ga.) News, 1972-74; exec. editor, v.p. Columbus (Ga.) Ledger and Enquirer, 1974-80; gen. mgr. Tallahassee Democrat, 1980-81, pres., pub., 1981—. Mem. adv. bd. U. Ga. Sch. Journalism, 1977-83; pres. Jr. Achievement of Columbus-Phenix City, 1977; bd. dirs. United Way of Tallahassee-Leon County, 1980—, campaign chmn., 1984, pres., 1985; bd. dirs. So. Scholarship Found., 1981-84; mem. adv. bd. Sta. WFSU-TV, 1981—; pres. Funders, Inc., Tallahassee, 1982—. Served with U.S. Army, 1957-59. Named Young Man of Yr. Augusta, Ga., 1962. Mem. Am. Newspaper Pubs. Assn., Am. Soc. Newspaper Editors, Fla. Press Assn. (bd. dirs. 1984—), Fla. Econs. Club (bd. dirs. 1984—), Sigma Delta Chi. Methodist. Clubs: Forestmeadows Athletic, Governors (Tallahassee). Lodge: Rotary. Home: 1235 Live Oak Plantation Rd Tallahassee FL 32312 Office: PO Box 990 Tallahassee FL 32302

DAENECKE, ERIC, lawyer, former UN advisor; b. Bklyn., Jan. 24, 1914; s. August and Ida (Brosowski) D.; B.S., Am. U., Washington, 1944, M.A., 1947, Ph.D., 1950; J.D., U. Balt., 1954; LL.M. cum laude, U. Manila, 1964; D.C.L., U. Santo Tomas, Manila, 1966; m. G. Alma Schwenn, Apr. 5, 1936 (dec.); children—William Eric, Maryellen Daenecke Lawlor; m. 2d, Teresa Oakley Jones, Apr. 17, 1981. Chief of finance GAO and Dept. Labor, Washington, 1935-56; public adminstrn. adviser Dept. State, 1957-70; interregional advisor UN, N.Y.C., 1970-77; tchr. Strayer Coll., Washington, 1951-56, U. Md. Far East Br., 1967-70, grad. law U. Santo Tomas, Manila, 1964-66; minister Christian Ch., Washington, 1953-56. Mem. Am. Inst. C.P.A.s, Fed. Bar Assn., Am. Acctg. Assn., Rosicrucian Order. Club: Lawyers. Author: Tales of Mullah Nasr-Ud-Din, 1960; More Tales, 1961. Home: 5640 Wood St Port Orange FL 32019

DAGG, MICHAEL THOMAS, mathematician, educator; b. Bern, Gholimer, Germany, Apr. 11, 1949; came to U.S., 1949, naturalized, 1951; s. Carl Michael and Betty Louise (Holmes) D. B.S. in Math., Va. Polytech. Inst., 1971; Ph.D., Ind. U., 1975. Researcher, tchr. U. Calif., Berkeley, 1974-78, Calif. Inst. of Tech., Pasadena, 1978-79, Rice U., Houston, 1980—; undergrad. advisor Rice U., 1984—. Author: Harmonic Functions, 1980; (with others) Function Theory on Cn, 1983. Editor: Lebesque Integrals, 1984. Fellow Soc. Harmonic Analysis; mem. Am. Math. Soc., Math. Assn. Am., Collegiate Assn. Math. Democrat. Jewish. Avocations: electronics and mathematical electronic functions. Home: 294641 Wynne St Huntsville TX 77349 Office: Rice Univ University Dr Houston TX 77002

DAGGETT, MARSHA LEA, rancher, nutrition and foods educator; b. Fort Stockton, Tex., Feb. 10, 1917; d. Marsh and Artie (McLeod) Lea; m. Walter M. Daggett, June 19, 1938 (div. May 1964); 1 child, Walter Merrell. B.S., Tex. Woman's U., 1938, M.Ed., Sam Houston State U., 1957; Ph.D., Tex. Woman's U., 1972. Tchr. sci. Calvert High Sch., Tex., 1954-57; tchr. vocat. home econs.

Bremond High Sch., Tex., 1960-61; instr. home econs. Sam Houston State U., Huntsville, Tex., 1962-63, Stephen F. Austin State U., Nacogdoches, Tex., 1963-64; instr., asst. prof. Lamar U., Beaumont, Tex., 1964-70; asst. prof., assoc. prof. S.W. Tex. State U., San Marcos, 1971-77; rancher, Ft. Stockton, 1977—; mem. exec. council Tex. Nutrition Council, 1965-72; del. Internat. Fedn. Home Econs., Bristol, Eng., 1968, Ottawa, Can., 1975. Editor: History of Pecos County, 1979-84; sr. editor Census of Presido County 1870, 1979, Census of Pecos County 1880 and 1900, 1980. Mem. Pecos County Hist. Commn., Fort Stockton, 1978—; pres. Ft. Stockton Hist. Soc., 1980-81, bd. dirs., 1977-85; mem. Old Fort Restoration Com., Ft. Stockton, 1980-82. Named Tchr. of Yr., Kappa Lambda Kappa, San Marcos, 1974; Outstanding Mem. Pecos County Hist. Commn., Fort Stockton, 1981; recipient Teaching Excellence award S.W. Tex. State U., San Marcos, 1975, Appreciation award Kappa Lambda Kappa, San Marcos, 1977. Mem. Tex. Hist. Assn., Permian Basin Hist. Soc., Pecos County Livestock Assn., Pecos County Sheep and Goat Raisers Assn., Tex. Sheep and Goat Raisers Assn., Nat. Wool Growers Assn., Phi Upsilon Omicron, Delta Kappa Gamma, Kappa Omicron Phi. Republican. Presbyterian. Clubs: Pioneer (pres. 1979-80, sec. 1983-85), Ft. Stockton Literary (pres. 1984-85). Avocations: researching history of West Texas genetics in sheep and cattle; gardening. Home: PO Box 1545 Ft Stockton TX 79735

DAGGY, ROBERT EDWARD, literary archive curator, educator; b. New Castle, Ind., July 28, 1940; s. George Edward and Anna Louise (Linn) D.; B.A., Yale U., 1962; postgrad. Columbia U., 1962-63, Ball State U., 1965-66; M.A., U. Wis., 1968, Ph.D., 1971. Asst. to archivist Yale U. Archives, 1963-65; tchr. Darlington Sch. for Boys, Rome, Ga., 1965-67; asst. prof. ednl. policy studies and history U. Wis., Madison, 1971-73; chief research Thomas Merton Legacy Trust, Louisville, 1973-74; curator, dir. Thomas Merton Studies Center, coll. archivist Bellarmine Coll., 1974—, lectr. div. edn., 1975—; lectr. dept. ednl. founds. U. Louisville, 1974—; advisor, lectr. to various groups holding programs, seminars on Thomas Merton; mng. editor Merton Seasonal of Bellarmine Coll., Ky. Poetry Rev. Mem. Soc. Am. Archivists, Ky. Council on Archives, Am. Contract Bridge League, Louisville Bridge Assn., Yale Assn. Ky. Clubs: Yale of Ind., Filson. Contbr. articles to profl. jours.; editor: Introductions East and West: The Foreign Prefaces of Thomas Merton, 1981; Day of a Stranger, 1981; The Alaskan Journal of Thomas Merton, 1986; Thomas Merton: A Comprehensive Bibliography (with Marquita Breit), 1986; The Road to Joy: The Letters of Thomas Mertonto New and Old Friends, 1986. Office: Thomas Merton Studies Center Bellarmine Coll Newburg Rd Louisville KY 40205

DAGOSTINO, FRANK ROBERT, engineering technology educator, author; b. Schenectady, N.Y., Sept. 29, 1939; s. Andrew and Beryl D.; m. Joyce Marie Svetlik, Apr. 20, 1960 (div. 1984); children—Melissa, Laura. A.A.S., Hudson Valley Tech. Inst., 1961; B.Arch., U. Fla., 1965. Registered architect, Conn. Salesman, Dagostino Bldg. Blocks, Schenectady, 1958-59, mgr., 1968; chief draftsman E. Breitenback, Altamont, N.Y., 1965-67; instr. Hudson Valley Community Coll., Troy, N.Y., 1968-72; Sandhills Community Coll., Southern Pines, N.C., 1972-76; pvt. practice cons., Southern Pines, 1976-78; instr. Trident Tech. Coll., Charleston, S.C., 1978-80, dept. chmn., 1980—. Author: (textbooks) Estimating in Building Construction, 1977; Methods and Materials of Commercial Construction, 1974; Contemporary Architectural Drafting, 1975; Mechanical and Electrical Systems in Construction and Architecture, 1978; Mechanical Systems in Buildings, 1981; Materials of Construction, 1982; Handbook of Residential Construction, 1983; 3 audio-visuals. Recipient math. award Hudson Valley Tech. Coll., 1961. Mem. Am. Soc. Engring. Educators, S.C. Tech. Edn. Assn. Home: 309 Ashburne Ct Charleston SC 29418 Office: Trident Tech Coll 7000 Rivers Ave Charleston SC 29418

DAHLBERG, CARL FREDRICK, JR., holding company executive; b. New Orleans, Aug. 20, 1936; s. Carl Fredrick and Nancey Erwin (Jones) D.; B.S. in Civil Engring., Tulane U., 1958; M.B.A., Harvard U., 1964; m. Constance Weston, Dec. 30, 1961; children—Kirsten Erwin, Catherine Morgan. Regional mgr. bond dept. E.F. Hutton & Co., Inc., New Orleans, 1965-67; chmn. exec. com. Dahlberg, Kelly & Wisdom, Inc., New Orleans, 1967-71; pres. C.F. Dahlberg & Co., Inc., New Orleans, 1971—; co-organizer, dir. Charter Med. Corp., 1969-72; bd. dirs. Internat. Trade Mart, 1974—, mem. exec. com. 1981-85, treas., 1983-85; consul gen. of Monaco, New Orleans. Trustee, Metairie Park Country Day Sch., New Orleans, 1976—; treas., 1980-82, chmn., 1982-84; trustee, Eye, Ear, Nose and Throat Hosp., New Orleans, 1980—, mem. exec. com., 1980-83; trustee U. of the South, Sewanee, Tenn., 1984—; trustee Eye, Ear, Nose and Throat Found., 1980-83; vestryman Christ Ch. Cathedral, New Orleans. Served with U.S. Army, 1958-59. Registered profl. engr., La.; registered land surveyor, La. Mem. ASCE, Fin. Mgmt. Assn., New Orleans Council Bus. Economists, Nat. Assn. Corrosion Engrs., Am. Soc. Venerable Order Hosp. of St. John of Jerusalem, Mil. and Hospitaller Order of St. Lazarus. Republican. Episcopalian. Clubs: New Orleans Country, Pickwick; Knickerbocker (N.Y.C.). Co-author: Hydrochloric Acid Pickling, 1979. Home: 199 Audubon Blvd New Orleans LA 70118 Office: 601 Poydras St New Orleans LA 70130

DAHLGREN, MARY M. (MAGGI), retail specialty gift shop owner; b. San Antonio, Apr. 24, 1958; d. John Howard and Lucile (Yarborough). Student Georgetown U., 1976-77, Semester at Sea, spring 1979; B.A. in Sociology, Trinity U., San Antonio 1979, B.A. in Geology, 1982. Mapmaker Tobin Surveys, San Antonio, 1981; mgmt. sales staff Frost Bros., San Antonio, 1978-84; owner, mgr., buyer Just Fabulous! specialty gift shop, San Antonio, 1984—; researcher Mexican arts, crafts, customs, 1980—; creative cons. Irresistibles, Inc., San Antonio, 1984—. Contbr. recipes to Bon Apetit magazine, 1982. Asst. chmn. rummage sale Jr. League of San Antonio, 1983-84; bd. dirs. Young Art Patrons, 1983—; com. mem. Friends of McNay Museum, 1983—, San Antonio Museum Assn., 1983—; mem. Beautify San Antonio Assn., 1984—. Mem. Alamo Heights Bus. Assn., Am. Assn. Petroleum Geologists, South Tex. Geol. Soc. Republican. Episcopalian. Avocations: traveling; swimming; walking; movies; reading. Home: 119 Harrison San Antonio TX 78209 Office: Just Fabulous! 5929 Broadway San Antonio TX 78209

DAHLIN, ELIZABETH CARLSON, university administrator; b. Worcester, Mass., July 26, 1931; d. Alden Gustaf and Elizabeth Christine (Peterson) Carlson; B.A., Wellesley Coll., 1953; postgrad. Harvard U., 1953, 64; M.A., George Washington U., 1971; m. Douglas Gordon Dahlin, June 27, 1953; children—Christine Elizabeth, Cynthia Jean, Constance May. Substitute tchr. Fairfax County, Va., 1958-77; asst. folklife specialist, concessions mgr. Smithsonian Instn., Washington, 1976-77; asst. to exec. dir. Nat. Sch. Vol. Program, Alexandria, Va., 1978-80; asst. to v.p. devel. George Mason U., Fairfax, Va., 1980-83, dir. devel., 1983—. Treas., bd. dirs. Nation's Capital council Girl Scouts U.S.A., 1972-78, award, 1978; chief election judge Fairfax County Electoral Bd., 1967-75; mem. Fairfax County Com., chmn. Belle Haven precinct Mount Vernon dist.; deacon United Ch. of Christ; mem. alumni council Wellesley Coll., 1970, 81; bd. dirs. Alexandria Symphony. Brown U. grad. fellow, 1953. Mem. Va. Women's Polit. Caucus, Council Advancement and Support Edn., Profl. Women's Network, Textile Mus., Smithsonian Assos., Nat. Aviation Club, AAUW, George Washington U. Alumni Council (edn. council), Arlington C. of C. (bd. dirs.), Phi Delta Kappa. Clubs: Wellesley (bd. dirs. 1969—, treas. 1978-82, pres. 1980-82), Harvard (Washington); Fort Myer Officer's. Home: 6041 Edgewood Terr Alexandria VA 22307 Office: Devel House George Mason U 4400 University Dr Fairfax VA 22030

DAIGLE, EDWARD OSCAR, construction company executive; b. Grayville, La., Sept. 27, 1944; s. Edward Oscar and Leah (Schexnayder) D.; m. Susan Ayers, Aug. 3, 1963; children—Leslie, Rene, Matthew, Blythe. Foreman, J. Ray McDermott, Morgan City, La., 1965-77; supr. Shell Oil Co., New Orleans, 1977-80; pres. Tammco Unltd., New Iberia, La., 1980—. Mem. La. Polit. Action Council, Baton Rouge, 1981-83. Mem. La. Assn. Bus. and Industry, Am. Welding Soc. Republican. Roman Catholic. Office: Tammco Unltd Inc PO Box 10083 New Iberia LA 70560

DAIGLE, GERALD JOSEPH, JR., lawyer, accountant; b. New Orleans, Sept. 13, 1957; s. Gerald J. and Anna May (Chotin) D. B.S. summa cum laude in Acctg., U. New Orleans, 1978; J.D. cum laude, Loyola U., New Orleans, 1983. Bar: La. 1983; C.P.A., La. Tax sr. Arthur Andersen & Co., New Orleans, 1978-81; mng. editor Loyola Law Rev., New Orleans, 1982-83; assoc. Chaffe, McCall, Phillips, Toler & Sarpy, New Orleans, 1983—. Recipient Loyola Law Alumni award, 1982; medal for Excellence in Advocacy Am. Coll. Trial Lawyers, 1982-83; Corpus Juris Secundum award, 1982; Coll. Bus. Adminstrn. Faculty award Soc. La. C.P.A.s award, 1978. Mem. ABA, La. State Bar Assn., Am. Inst. C.P.A.s, Soc. La. C.P.A.s, Beta Gamma Sigma, Beta Alpha Psi, Phi Alpha Delta. Republican. Roman Catholic. Home: 6945 Canal Blvd New Orleans LA 70124 Office: 1500 First NBC Bldg New Orleans LA 70112

DAIL, HERMAN GRAHAM, safety engineer; b. Charlotte, N.C., Feb. 8, 1945; s. Herman Graham and Louise (Cato) D.; m. Carol Pratt, May 28, 1965; children—Richard Graham, Geoffrey Charles. B.A. in History and Geography, U. N.C.-Wilmington, 1967; M.A. in Rehab. Psychology, East Carolina U., 1973. Cert. hazard control mgr. Counselor N.C. Div. Vocat. Rehabilitation, Goldsboro, 1969-73; sr. cons. Behavioral Systems, Inc., Atlanta, 1973-76; asst. tng. dir. Cone Mills Corp., Greensboro, N.C., 1976-79, corporate safety mgr., 1979-84, mgr. safety and tng., 1984—. Bd. dirs. Nat. Found. March of Dimes, Greensboro, 1976-85, Am. Cancer Soc., Greensboro, 1979-80; mem. N.C. Referees Assn. Served with U.S. Army, 1967-69. Recipient John T. Haggard award U. NC-Wilmington, 1967. Mem. Am. Soc. Safety Engrs. (sec. N.C. chpt. 1984, pres.-elect 1985), Nat. Safety Council (gen. chmn. textile sect. 1984-85), Central Piedmont Safety Council (dir. 1979-84), Am. Soc. Tng. and Devel., Am. Soc. Indsl. Security, Am. Textile Mfrs. Inst. (mem. safety and health edn. task group 1981-82, chmn., 1982-83), Gate City Jaycees (pres. 1978-79; named Outstanding Local Pres. N.C. chpt. 1978-79, Outstanding Young Man of Am. 1980; life mem.). Democrat. Methodist. Lodge: Elks. Avocation: youth soccer. Office: Cone Mills Corp 1201 Maple St Greensboro NC 27405

DAILEY, JOHN HOWARD, draftsman; b. Montgomery County, Pa., Oct. 4, 1920; s. Samuel Brockway and Isobel Florence Dailey; student pub. schs.; m. Nadine Fountain, Mar. 5, 1960; 1 child, Patricia Ann; stepchildren: Robert Frances, Gary Louis. Various positions in mech. depts. in industry, 1940-52, 46-47; mgr. White Oak Lodge, Flats, N.C., 1957; registrar Surf Club, Miami Beach, Fla., 1947-48; body mechanic Puett Motors Co., Valdosta, Ga., 1948-50; machinist Metals Products Co., Valdosta, 1950-51; planning technician U.S. Civil Service, Moody AFB, Ga., 1951-80; draftsman Gold Kist Co., Valdosta, 1980—; cons. in field. Moderator Azalea City Bapt. Ch., 1969, chmn. bldg. com., 1969-70, trustee, 1984-86. Served with AUS, 1942-45. Mem. Am. Legion (past post sr. vice comdr.), Full Gospel Businessmen's Fellowship Internat. Democrat. Club: Masons. Home: 1204 Leone Ave Valdosta GA 31601 Office: Gold Kist Co Clay Rd Valdosta GA 31601

DAILEY, KURT CHARLES, safety engineer; b. Bayshore, N.Y., June 22, 1958; s. Joseph Benjamin and Carole June (Huber) D.; m. Emily Sue Chapman, July 26, 1980; children—Denise Louise, Anita Lynn. B.S. in Forestry, W.Va. U., 1980, M.S. in Safety Mgmt., 1981. Compliance officer Va. Electric Power Co., Richmond, Va., 1981-82; asst. safety mgr. Appalachian Power Co., Roanoke, Va., 1982—, Personnel asst., 1984—.Adviser, Jr. Achievement, Roanoke Valley, 1983—. Research grantee U.S. Dept. Labor, 1980; deacon Christian Ch. Mem. Am. Soc. Safety Engrs. (sect. chmn. 1984—), Am. Indsl. Hygiene Assn. Republican. Avocations: hunting; golf; photography; high fidelity. Home: 117 W Cleveland Ave Vinton VA 24179 Office: Appalachian Power Co PO Box 2021 Roanoke VA 24022

DAILY, LOUIS, ophthalmologist; b. Houston, Apr. 23, 1919; s. Louis and Ray (Karchmer) D.; B.S., Harvard U., 1940; M.D., U. Tex. at Galveston, 1943; Ph.D., U. Minn., 1950; m. LaVerl Daily, Apr. 5, 1958; children—Evan Ray, Collin Derek. Intern, Jefferson Davis Hosp., Houston, 1943-44; resident in ophthalmology Jefferson Davis Hosp., 1944-45, Mayo Found., Rochester, Minn., 1947-50; individual practice medicine, specializing in ophthalmology, Houston, 1950—; asso. prof. clin. ophthalmology U. Tex-Houston, 1972—, Baylor Med. Sch., Houston, 1950—. Vice pres. bd. dirs. Mus. Med. Sci., 1973-85, pres., 1980-82. Served as lt. (j.g.) USNR, 1945-46. Diplomate Am. Bd. Ophthalmology. Fellow A.C.S., Internat. Coll. Surgeons; mem. Soc. Prevention of Blindness (med. chmn. Tex. 1968-70), Contact Lens Assn. Ophthalmologists (exec. bd. 1976-78), Tex. Ophthal. Assn. (pres. 1963-64), Houston Ophthal. Soc. (pres. 1970-71), numerous other med. socs., Sigma Xi, Alpha Omega Alpha. Jewish. Clubs: Doctors, Harvard (dir. 1965-66) (Houston). Editorial bd. Jour. Pediatric Ophthalmology, 1964-68; asso. editor Eye, Ear, Nose and Throat Monthly, 1962-65, Jour. Ophthalmic Surgery, 1970; contbr. numerous articles to profl. publs., also contbr. to books. Home: 2523 Maroneal St Houston TX 77030 Office: 1517 Med Towers Houston TX 77030

DAJANI, MAHMOUD T., engineering company executive; b. Palestine, Jan. 6, 1932; s. Mohamed Tayeb and Subhia I. (Jabri) D.; m. Ninon Mehrez Sakr, June 2, 1955; children—Samir, Aida, Lina, Omar. B.S. in Chemistry, Roosevelt U., Chgo., 1957; M.S. in Phys. Chemistry, U. Chgo., 1959. Chemist and research chemist Nalco Chem. Co., Chgo., 1956-63, research group leader, 1963-66; tech. advisor UN Unido Libya, 1966-68; sales engr. Howe-Baker Engrs., Inc., Tyler, Tex., 1968-73, sales mgr. Middle East, 1973-77, v.p. Middle East Sales, 1977-79, v.p. sales, 1979—, also dir. Pres., Chgo. chpt. Arab Student Orgn., 1959. Mem. Am. Chem. Soc., Am. Mgmt. Assn., Nat. Assn. Arab Ams. Republican. Moslem. Club: Tyler (Tex.) Petroleum. Contbr. articles on corrosion, water and waste treatment to profl. jours. Patentee in field. Home: 512 Princeton Dr Tyler TX 75710 Office: Howe Baker Engrs 3102 E 5th St Tyler TX 75710

DAKE, MARCIA ALLENE, nursing educator, university dean; b. Bemus Point, N.Y., May 22, 1923; d. Earl B. and Bernice Delco (Haskin) D. Diploma, Crouse Irving Hosp., 1944; B.S., Syracuse U., 1951; M.A., Columbia U., 1955, Ed. D., 1958. Dean coll. nursing U. Ky., Lexington, 1958-72; dir. dept. nursing edn. Am. Nurses Assn., Kansas City, Mo., 1972-74; project dir. Milliken U., Decatur, Ill., 1974-75; dir. program devel. nursing ARC, Washington, 1975-79; prof., dean sch. nursing James Madison U., Harrisonburg, Va., 1979—. Served to 1st lt. U.S. Army Nurse Corp, 1945-46. Mem. Am. Nurses Assn., Va. Nurses Assn. (pres. dist. 9, 1983-85), Va. Soc. Profl. Nurses (treas. 1983—), Va. Assn. Colls. of Nursing (sec. 1980-82, pres. 1982-85). Delta Kappa Gamma.

DALBO, EUGENE JAY, advertising executive; b. Newark, Apr. 21, 1950; s. Peter J. and Mary E. (McDonnell) D.; m. Margaret Anne Craig, Sept. 8, 1973; children—Christine, Tracey, Ashley, Anthony. B.A. in Journalism, Seton Hall U., 1972. Asst. mktg. mgr. Fedders Corp., Edison, N.J., 1972-74; advt. account mgr. Oxy Metal Industries, Nutley, N.J., 1974-76; assoc. dir. mktg. Boy Scouts Am., Irving, Tex., 1976-80, nat. advt. mgr., 1980-86, nat. dir. advt. and printing prodn., 1986—. Mem. Direct Mktg. Assn., Direct Mktg. Guild, North Tex. Direct Mktg. Assn., Publicity Club N.Y. Office: 1325 Walnut Hill Ln Irving TX 75062

DALE, GEORGE WILLIAM, sales consultant; b. Coldwater, Kans., July 15, 1912; s. George William and Nellie (Haynes) Dale; B.A. in Bus., Fairmount Coll., 1936; postgrad. U. Kans., 1945-50; m. Mary Woodard, 1977; 1 son, Roger Dean. Tng. course planner N.Am. Aviation, Kansas City, Kans., 1941-44; ops. mgr. Consumers Co-op. Assn., Kansas City, Mo., 1944-54; pres. Pallister Mfg. Co., Wichita, Kans., 1954-57; pres. Hollidays Blueprint & Supply, Inc., Wichita, 1957-65; realtor, cons., Eureka Springs, Ark., 1966-81; pres., chmn. bd. Aramaic Bible Distbn. Soc., Charlotte, N.C., 1981—; counselor SCORE, SBA; pres. Eureka Springs Real Estate Bd., 1968-70. Methodist. Clubs: Masons, Shriners. Address: PO Box 25302 Charlotte NC 28212

DALE, SAM E., JR., ednl. adminstr.; b. Harmon, La., July 10, 1921; s. Sam E. and Willie Edith (Parr) D.; B.S. in Vocat. Agr., La. State U., Baton Rouge, 1947, M.S. in Vocat. Agr., 1954, Ph.D. in Vocat. Agr., 1972; m. Cathleen Trichel; 1 dau., Cathy Sue. With Catahoula Parish Sch. Bd., Jonesville, La., 1948—, supervising prin., 1969-72, dir. career and vocat. edn., 1973-79, supt., 1979—. Mem. adv. council La. State U.; mem. supts. council La. Bd. Elem. and Secondary Edn. Mem. La. (legis. com.), Catahoula Parish (pres.) tchrs. assns., La. Vocat. Assn., La. Agr. Tchrs. Assn., Am. Vocat. Assn., La. Supts. Assn., Gideons, Am. Legion, Phi Delta Kappa. Baptist. Lion. Home: PO Box 56 Sicily Island LA 71368 Office: PO Box 308 Jonesville LA 71343

DALEY, TIMOTHY PATRICK, police officer, security consultant; b. Little Rock, Jan. 15, 1947; s. Robert Patrick and Eloise Francis (Sisco) D.; m. Bettye Lou Cox, Oct. 14, 1967; 1 dau., Robyn Renae. B.S., U. Ark.-Little Rock, 1974; cert. FBI Nat. Acad., Quantico, Va., 1977. Patrolman, Little Rock Police Dept., 1969-75, sgt., 1975-79, lt., 1979-81, capt., 1981—; cons. Pleasant Valley Country Club, Little Rock, 1976—; chmn. Ark. Bd. Pvt. Investigators and Security Guard Agencies; lobbyist Ark. Mcpl. Police Assn.; dir. Fulfill a Dream, Inc. Pres. Pleasantree Property Owners Assn., 1981. Named Officer of the Month, Sertoma Club, 1971, 72, 75. Mem. Ark. Mcpl. Police Assn. (pres. 1983), Internat. Assn. Chiefs of Police, Nat. Assn. Crime Prevention, FBI Nat. Acad. Assocs. (sec.-treas. Ark. chpt. 1985, 2d v.p. 1986). Clubs: Black River Canoe (v.p. 1985-86), Big Lake (Little Rock). Lodge: Fraternal Order Police (recognition award 1983). Home: 15 Kings Ct Little Rock AR 72211 Office: Little Rock Police Dept 700 W Markham St Little Rock AR 72201

DALHOUSE, WARNER NORRIS, banker; b. Roanoke, Va., June 4, 1934; s. Jefferson William and Gay-Nell (Henley) D.; children—Ann Lauren Dalhouse Saunders, Julia Lea Dalhouse Caldwell. Student Roanoke Coll., 1952-54; B.S. in Commerce, U. Va., 1956. Vice pres. 1st Nat. Exchange Bank, Roanoke, Va., 1967-69; sr. v.p., 1969-73, exec. v.p., 1973-77, pres., chief adminstrv. officer, 1977-81; exec. v.p., chief adminstrv. officer Dominion Bankshares Corp., Roanoke, 1977-81, pres., chief exec. officer, 1981—. Pres. Roanoke Pub. Library Found.; dir. Western Va. Found. for Arts and Scis., Inc., Roanoke; bd. dirs. Washington-Dulles Task Force; trustee Roanoke Coll., Salem, Va.; mem. Va. Gov.'s Adv. Bd. Econ. Devel. Address: Dominion Bankshares Corp 213 S Jefferson St Roanoke VA 24040*

DALPES, LINDA FRANCES, management firm executive; b. New Orleans, Jan. 3, 1938; d. Walter James and Frances Katherine (Jordan) Fountain. A.A., Stephens Coll., 1957; B.A., U. Hawaii, 1959. Cert. dental asst. Sr. claims analyst Am. Gen. Life Ins. Co., Houston, 1960-64; mgr. claims Southwest region Calif. Western States Life Ins. Co., Houston, 1964-68; mgmt. cons. Met. Agy., Houston, 1968-70; clinic adminstr. Harris & Adams, Inc., Houston, 1970-75; founder, pres. Team Coordinators, Houston, 1975—; speaker, clinician major dental meetings; guest lectr. south, southwest univs.; exec. sec. Tex. Dental Hygienists Assn., 1972-75. Mem. LWV, Am. Mgmt. Assn., AAUW, Nat. Assn. Women Bus. Owners, Nat. Assn. Female Execs. Republican. Episcopalian. Home: 120 E Fork Rd Cleveland TX 77327 Office: PO Box 60744 Houston TX 77205

DALRYMPLE, DAVID EDWARD, physician; b. Elkhart, Ind., Nov. 10, 1936; s. Thurlow Edward and Irene Guinevere (Northrop) D.; A.B., DePauw U., 1958; M.S., Purdue U., 1960; postgrad. Ind. U., 1960-61; M.D., U. Chgo., 1965; m. Carol Mae Anderson, Aug. 2, 1959; children—David Northrop, Brian Anderson. Intern State U. Iowa, 1965-66, resident, 1966-68; NIH fellow Washington U. Sch. Medicine, St. Louis, 1968-69; practice medicine specializing in internal medicine and endocrinology, Atlanta, 1971—; chmn. patient care and dietary com., equipment com., exec. com., chmn. dept. medicine Northside Hosp., Atlanta. Vis. clin. instr. Med. Coll. Ga., Augusta, 1969-70. Mem. med. com. drug abuse Sandy Springs (Atlanta), Ga.; mem. North Fulton County Med. Care Program; mem. legis. com. Greater Atlanta Coalition for Health Care. Served with AUS, 1969-71; med. officer Specialized Treatment Center, Ft. Gordon. Recipient Resident award State U. Iowa, 1965. Diplomate Am. Bd. Internal Medicine, Am. Bd. Med. Examiners. Fellow ACP; mem. Am. Fedn. for Clin. Research, Med. Assn., Atlanta (trustee No. dist., past jr. trustee), Med. Assn. Ga. (splty bd. peer rev., trustee), Am., Ga. socs. internal medicine, AMA, Diabetes Assn. Atlanta (pres., chmn., dir.), Ga. Diabetes Assn. (dir.), Ga. Thoracic Soc., Ga. Wildlife Fedn., Sigma Xi, Alpha Tau Omega. Episcopalian. Club: Flying, Editorial bd. Atlanta Medicine. Contbr. articles to profl. jours. Home: 5515 Whitewood Ct Dunwoody GA 30338 Office: 6500 Vernon Woods Dr Atlanta GA 30328

DALTON, MARIE KALINEC, educational administrator, business educator; b. Midfield, Tex., Dec. 12, 1941; d. Henry Joseph and Tillie Marie (Cerny) Kalinec; m. Charles Dalton, Oct. 17, 1969 (div. Apr. 1985). A.A., Wharton County Jr. Coll., 1962; B.S., U. Houston, 1968, Ed.M., 1970, Ed.D., 1977. Tchr. bus. Dickinson High Sch., Tex., 1968-70; instr. Coll. of the Mainland, Texas City, 1970-75; div. chmn. Houston Community Coll., 1976-77; program mgr. U. Houston, 1977-78, program area chmn., 1978-81; div. chmn. San Jacinto Coll., Pasadena, Tex., 1981—; post secondary tchr. trainer Tex. Edn. Agy., Austin, Tex., 1978-79; cons. workshops and seminars, 1970—. Co-author word/info. processing textbooks. Contbr. articles to profl. jours. Editor: Integrating Microcomputers in Accounting Courses, 1983; Business Education's Response to the Changing Technologies, 1984. Grantee U.S. Dept. Energy, 1978, 1979; recipient Leader for the 80's award Inst. Leadership Devel., 1984. Mem. Tex. Bus. Edn. Assn. (pres. 1981, chmn. state edn. 1980-84), Nat. Bus. Edn. Assn., Am. Bus. Women's Assn., Deer Park C. of C., LaPorte C. of C., Delta Pi Epsilon. Republican. Roman Catholic. Avocations: traveling; collecting antiques. Home: 3245 Reba Dr Houston TX 77019 Office: San Jacinto Coll Central 8060 Spencer Hwy Pasadena TX 77505

DALTON, MARY MARTIN, nursing educator; b. Portsmouth, Va., June 8, 1952; d. Herbert Jordan and Violet Marie (Heptinstall) Martin; m. Gary Wayne Dalton, Apr. 7, 1973; children—Martin Alexander, Sally Martin, Katherine Anne. Student Longwood Coll., 1970-72, B.Nursing, U. Va., 1974; postgrad. Med. Coll. Va./Va. Commonwealth U., 1976-82. Staff nurse McGuire VA Med. Ctr., Richmond, Va., 1974-75, nursing instr., 1975-78; nursing instr. VA Med. Ctr., Hampton, Va., 1978-79, evening and night chief nurse rep., 1979-80, nursing instr., 1980-81, nursing instr. surg. units and intermediate care, chmn. nursing service procedure com., 1981—, staff developer surg. service, 1984—; mem. nurses alcohol task force Va. Commonwealth U., Richmond, 1978-79, mem. nurses alcohol task force, 1981-82. Recipient spl. advancement for performance award Hampton VA Med. Ctr., 1983; VA Adminstrs. Hands and Heart award, 1984. Republican. Episcopalian. Club: Carisbrooke Ladies (pres. 1981). Editor: Carisbrooke Community Assn. Directory, 1980, 81, 82, 83, 84. Home: 36 Nelson Maine Carrollton VA 23314 Office: 118A VA Med Center Hampton VA 23667

DALTON, ROBERT I., JR., textile executive, broker, consultant, researcher; b. Charlotte, N.C., Apr. 2, 1921; s. Robert I. and Edith (Gossett) D.; m. Gwin Barnwell, Nov. 16, 1946; children—Millie, Edith. B.S. in Textile Engring., N.C. State U. Vice pres. sales Whitin Machine Works, Whitinsville, Mass., 1946-67; pres. Cocker Machine and Foundry, Gastonia, N.C., 1967-70, Tech-Tex Inc., Charlotte, 1970—, Gossett-Dalton Co., Charlotte, 1973—, dir., 1955—; dir. Cadmus Communication Co., Richmond, Va., 1983—, Am.-Truetzschler, Charlotte, 1976—, Carter Furniture Co., Salisbury, N.C., 1983—; N.C. Nat. Bank, Charlotte, 1962—. Pres. Charlotte Symphony Orch., 1979-80; mem. bd. edn. Mecklenburg County, Charlotte, 1957-58. Served to maj. U.S. Army, 1943-46, ETO. Mem. Phi Psi. Methodist. Clubs: Charlotte City (pres. 1980-81), Charlotte Country. Avocations: tennis; photography. Home: 5900 Sardis Rd Charlotte NC 28226

DALY, JOHN AUGUSTINE, communication researcher and educator; b. Camp Adebury, Ind., June 30, 1952; s. John Augustine and Edith Winslow (Elliott) D.; m. Christine Walaity, Aug. 17, 1974; 2 children. B.A., U. Md., 1973; M.A., W.Va. U., 1974; Ph.D., Purdue U., 1977. Vis. lectr. W.Va. U., Morgantown, 1974—; asst. prof. communication U. Tex., Austin, 1977-82, assoc. prof., 1982—; cons. Nat. Assessment of Ednl. Progress, Denver, 1980-82. Editor: Avoiding Communication: Shyness, Reticence and Communication Apprehension, 1984; editor: Written Communication, 1983—; Communication Edn., 1985-87; Personality and Interpersonal Communication, 1986; editorial bd. Human Communication Research, 1977—, Communication Edn., 1979-81, Communications Monographs, 1983—, So. Speech Communication Jour., 1983—; adv. bd. Orgnl. Communication Abstracts, 1980—; contbr. articles sci. jours. Grantee Fund for Improvement Postsecondary Edn., 1980-82. Mem. Internat. Communication Assn. (v.p. 1979-81), Am. Psycho-. Assn., Am. Ednl. Research Assn., Speech Communication Assn. (chmn. commn. on communication avoidance 1984-86). Roman Catholic. Home: 2903 Kassarine Pass Austin TX 78704 Office: College of Communication University of Texas Austin TX 78712

DALY, KENNETH, meteorologist, psychologist; b. Jamaica, N.Y., Apr. 26, 1931; s. John Francis and Caroline Catherine (Pohl) D.; m. Barbara Louise Blackwell, Sept. 15, 1961; children—Connie Lynn, John Francis. A.A.S. in Meteorology, Community Coll. Air Force, 1974; B.A. in Bus. and Econs., Park Coll., 1974; M.A., U. No. Colo., 1977; Ph.D. in Psychology, U.S. Internat. U., 1981. Lifetime cert. in community coll. teaching and counseling, Calif.; lic. profl. counselor, psychologist, Ala.; nat. cert. counselor; nat. cert. career counselor. Chief master sgt. U.S. Air Force, 1951-76; asst. dir. communications Air Weather Service, Scott AFB, Ill., 1970-74, 1st Weather Wing, Hikam AFB, Hawaii, 1974-76; guidance counselor, Ft. Ord, Calif., 1980-81; program adminstr. Pope AFB, N.C., 1981-83; program specialist Community Coll. Air Force, Maxwell AFB, Ala., 1983-85, chief Air Force Jr. ROTC, 1985—; pvt. practice Homestead, Fla., 1976-77, Fayetteville, N.C., 1981-83. Decorated Bronze Star. Mem. Am. Assn. for Counseling and Devel., Mil. Edn. Counselors Assn., Ala. Assn. for Counseling and Devel. Avocation: competitive jogging.

Home: 2845 Old Orchard Ln Montgomery AL 36116 Office: Air Force ROTC/OTJ Maxwell AFB AL 36112

DAMANPOUR, FARAMARZ, finance educator; b. Tehran, Iran, Aug. 10, 1942; came to U.S., 1968; s. Ali and Afzal (Haji Ali Akbari) D.; m. Jill Veronica Card, July 20, 1973; 1 son, Jamshid Ali. B.S., Pahlavi U., Shiraz, Iran, 1966; M.A., SUNY-Albany, 1971; Ph.D., U. Tex., 1977. Research asst. Inst. Social Studies and Research, U. Tehran, 1967-68; instr. Fin. Sch. of Army, Tehran, 1967; fire rate adjustor Hartford Ins. Co. and Hutchinson-Rivinus Co., N.Y.C., 1968-69; research asst. dept. polit. economy SUNY, Albany, 1969-72, teaching assoc. ednl. opportunity programs, 1972-73, research asst. dept. econs., 1973; teaching assoc. dept. fin. U. Tex., Austin, 1975-76; asst. gen. mgr. Martell's Restaurant Corp., N.Y.C., 1973-74; lectr. fin. Coll. Bus. and Econs., Wash. State U., Pullman, 1977-79; instr. real estate fin. Corr. Study Office, U. Idaho and Idaho Real Estate Ednl. Council, 1979-83; asst. prof. fin. dept. bus. Coll. Bus. and Econs., U. Idaho, Moscow, 1976-80, dir. grad. studies, 1979-80; prof. and dir. fin. program Sch. Bus., James Madison U., Harrisonburg, Va., 1980—, dir. Small Bus. Inst., 1984-85; cons. and exec. mgmt. program Gen. Telephone, 1979, Comprehensive Employment Tng. Program, 1980; book reviewer Harper and Row Pubs., Inc., Dryden Press, 1978—. Contbr. articles to profl. jours. Served with Imperial Iranian Armed Forces, 1967-68. Recipient award Banking Symposium, Sch. Bus., Eastern Wash. U., 1980. Mem. Acad. Internat. Bus., Acad. Mktg. Sci., Southwestern Fin. Assn., Pacific N.W. Regional Assn. Moslem. Office: Fin and Bus Law Depts James Madison U Harrisonburg VA 22807

D'AMATO, KEITH ROCKY, psychologist; b. Paterson, N.J., July 28, 1952; b. Henry Joseph and Lillian Marie D'Amato. B.A., Newark State Coll., 1973; M.Ed., William Paterson Coll., 1978; M.A., Calif. Sch. Profl. Psychology, 1980, Ph.D., 1981. Tchr., counselor Paterson Pub. Schs., 1973-78; sch. psychologist Fresno (Calif.) Pub. Schs., 1979-80; intern Merced (Calif.) Dept. Mental Health, 1978-79, Madera (Calif.) Dept. Mental Health, 1981; chief psychologist Agy. for Children and Youth, Wellsboro, Pa., 1981-83; exec. dir. Mental Health Care Ctr. Monroe County, Key West, Fla., 1983—; chief psychologist Tioga County (Pa.) Superior Ct., 1981-83; adj. prof. dept. psychology William Paterson Coll., Fla. Keys Community Coll., 1983—. Contbr. articles to profl. jours. Named Outstanding Young Floridian, Fla. Jaycees, 1984; Clinician of Yr., Fla. Council for Community Mental Health, 1984. Mem. Am. Psychol. Assn., Calif. Assn. Sch. Psychologists and Psychometrists, Am. Assn. Marriage and Family Therapy (clin.), Acad. Psychologists in Marital, Sex and Family Therapy (clin.). Home: PO Box 1701 Key West FL 33040 Office: PO Box 488 Key West FL 33040

DAMIANI, MICHEL, physician, surgeon; b. Galveston, Tex., Aug. 16, 1921; s. Jules Vern and Anna (Sucich) D.; m. Dorthy Nell Pack, June 12, 1955 (dec. 1979); children—Michel, Renee Ann Damiani Kimball, Jules Murl, Anna Virginia; m. 2d, Norma Hardin, Nov. 29, 1980. Student, U. Tex.-Austin, 1946; M.D., U. Tex.-Galveston, 1950. Intern, Kaiser Permanente Hosp., Oakland, Calif., resident M.D. Anderson Hosp., 1951-52; gen. practice medicine and surgery, Houston, 1951—. Served to capt. USMC, 1942-45. Decorated Air medal. Fellow Alpha Omega Alpha. Methodist. Home: 934 Boros St Houston TX 77024

DAMP, HANS JUERGEN, steel company executive; b. Schwerin, Germany Mar. 14, 1938; came to U.S., 1981; s. Hans B. and Charlotte (Wendel) D.; m. Gertrud Heider, Mar. 29, 1963; children—Martin, Peter. B.A. equivalent, W.Ger. Mgmt. positions various cos., U.S., 1964-75; worldwide sales rep. Hoesch's major product groups, Germany, 1975-81, pres., chief exec. officer, dir. Hoesch Am. Inc., Atlanta, 1981—. Mem. Am. Inst. Imported Steel (exec. com.). Office: Suite 2470 3340 Peachtree Rd NE Atlanta GA 30026

DAMSEL, CHARLES H., JR., lawyer; b. Columbus, Ohio, Apr. 30, 1929; s. Charles H. and Dorothy Mae (Carter) D.; m. Margaret W. Damsel, Aug. 25, 1951; children—Charles H. III, Cherie Damsel Bicknell. B.S. in Bus. Adminstrn., U. Fla., 1950, J.D., 1956. Bar: Fla. 1956, U.S. Dist. Ct. Fla. 1956, U.S. Ct. Appeals (5th cir.) 1958, U.S. Supreme Ct. 1969, U.S. Ct. Appeals (11th cir.) 1981; cert. civil trial adv. Nat. Bd. Trial Advocacy. Assoc. Gurney, McDonald & Handly, Orlando, Fla., 1956-58; mem. Jones & Foster, P.A., West Palm Beach, Fla., 1958—. Contbr. articles to legal jours. Served with U.S. Army, 1951-53. Diplomate Am. Bd. Civil Trial Advs., Nat. Bd. Trial Advocacy. Mem. Palm Beach County Bar Assn. (pres. 1971), Fla. Def. Lawyers Assn. (pres. 1975-77), Fed. Bar Assn. (pres. local chpt. 1977), Fla. Bar (cert.; exec. council trial lawyers sect.), ABA, Fedn. Ins. Counsel (v.p. 1978-79), Am. Judicature Soc., Def. Research Inst. (area chmn.), Am. Arbitration Assn., Palm Beach County Econ. Council, Fla. Blue Key (pres. 1954), Phi Delta Phi, Alpha Kappa Psi, Alpha Phi Omega, Pi Epsilon Delta, Kappa Sigma. Republican. Presbyterian (ruling elder United Presbyn. Ch.). Lodge: Masons. Office: Jones & Foster PA 505 S Flagler Dr West Palm Beach FL 33402

DANCE, GLORIA FENDERSON, dance studio owner; b. Portsmouth, Va., Mar. 10, 1932; d. Charles Bournell and Ottillia Lavinia (Korn) Fenderson; m. Walter Forrest Dance III, June 4, 1951; children—Walter Forrest, Jon Marlon, Gloria Cherie. Student pub. schs., Petersburg, Va. Assoc. tchr. Boyer/Feaglor Dance Acad., Richmond, Va., 1952-60; founder, owner, dir. Gloria F. Dance Sch. Dancing, Petersburg, Va., 1960—; artistic dir. Petersburg Ballet, 1984—; prin. judge Miss America Preliminaries, Va., Md., N.C., Tenn., 1950's to 1980's. Black leader Ind. Voters, Walnut Hill, 1955—; chmn. Heart Fund, Petersburg; Va. chmn. Petersburg Dance Festival-White House Performance, 1984; Petersburg chmn. 1985 July 4 Festival. Recipient award best actress/actress-dancer Liot, South Pacific, Mosque, Richmond, 1950; hon. award Optimist Club, 1950-63; Va. Hon. award Va. Nat. Dance Week, 1984; Petersburg Pub. Service award Alumni Gloria F. Dance Sch., 1980, also others. Mem. Dance Educators Am., Profl. Dance Tchrs., Miss America Sorority. Presbyterian. Clubs: Country of Petersburg, Fort Lee Country, Battlefield Park and Racquet. Avocations: boating; swimming; snow skiing; dancing. Home: 1806 Brandon Ave Petersburg VA 23805 Office: 44 Goodwich Ave Petersburg VA 23805

DANCER, RICHARD EDWIN, chemical dependency psychotherapist, nursing educator; b. Toledo, July 4, 1930; s. Lloyd Russell and Margaret Loretta (Lafountain) D.; m. Mary Jane Watkins, Sept. 1, 1950 (div. Sept. 1978); children—John, Mark; m. 2d, Cynthia Ayres Fox, Jan. 8, 1979. B.A., U. Toledo, 1955; M.S., U. North Fla., 1980; postgrad., Columbia Pacific U., 1982-83. Cert. alcoholism counselor, Mich., Fla.; cert. social worker, Mich. Program dir. Flint Gen. Hosp. (Mich.), St. Joseph Hosp., Flint, Flint Osteo. Hosp., 1975-77; program dir. 4 county area St. Joseph Hosp., Tawas City, Mich., 1977-78; pres. Dancer & Assocs., Inc., Jacksonville, Fla., 1978-82; chief, aftercare services, alcoholism therapist Palm Beach Inst., Jupiter, Fla., 1982-84; program dir. Awareness Center for chem. and other stress creating dependencies, Tequesta, Fla., 1984—; chem. dependency nursing educator. Served with U.S. Army, 1952-54. Mem. Nat. Council Alcoholism Counselors, Mich. Assn. Alcoholism and Drug Abuse Counselors, Inc., Northeast Fla. Council on Alcoholism and Drug Abuse (dir.), Phi Kappa Phi. Lodges: Rotary (Tawas City), Masons. Home: 1004 Stillwater Dr Jupiter FL 33458

DANCZ, ROGER LEE, musician; b. Ludington, Mich., May 25, 1930; s. Roy Stanley and Viola Lenore (Boston) D.; B.Mus. cum laude, Stetson U., 1952; Mus.M., Peabody Coll., 1958; m. Phyllis Ann Jones, June 2, 1952; 1 son, Steven. Dir. instrumental music Martin County Schs., Stuart, Fla., 1952-53; profl. trumpet player, 1951-65; dir. bands, U. Ga., Athens, 1955—, asso. prof., 1971—; guest condr., adjudicator South and Southwest. Served with U.S. Army, 1953-55. Recipient Music in Sports award Broadcast Music Inc., 1976; Sandy Beaver award Superior Teaching, 1981. Mem. Nat. Assn. Jazz Educators (past pres. Ga. chpt.), Ga. Music Educators Assn. (past pres.), Coll. Band Dirs. Nat. Assn. (past pres. So. div.), Music Educators Nat. Conf., Gridiron Soc., Phi Beta Mu (past pres. Ga. chpt.), Phi Mu Alpha Sinfonia, Pi Kappa Lambda, Ye Mystic Krewe, Kappa Kappa Psi. Columnist Athens Banner-Herald, 1970—. Home: 680 Pinecrest Dr Athens GA 30605 Office: Dept Music U Ga Athens GA 30602

DANDRIDGE, WILLIAM SHELTON, orthopedic surgeon; b. Atoka, Okla., May 21, 1914; s. Theodore Oscar and Estelle (Shelton) D.; m. Pearl Sessions, Feb. 3, 1941; 1 dau., Diana Dawn. B.A., U. Okla., 1935, M.D., U. Ark., 1939; M.S., Baylor U., 1950. Intern, St. Paul's Hosp., Dallas, 1939-40; surg. residence Med. Arts Hosp., Dallas, 1940; commd. 1st lt. USAF, advanced through grades to lt. col., 1950; chief reconditioning service and reconstructive surgery Ashburn Gen. Hosp., McKinney, Tex., 1945-46; neurosurg. resident Brooke Army Med. Center, San Antonio, 1946-47; orthopedic surg. resident, 1947-50; chief orthopedic service and gen. surgery Francis E. Warren AFB, Cheyenne, Wyo., Travis AFB, Susan, Calif., 1950-51; chief orthopedic service and gen. surgery Shepherd AFB, 1951-52; comdg. officer, chief orthopedic service, chief gen. surgery Craig AFB Hosp., Selma, Ala., 1952-53; practice medicine specializing in orthopedic surgery, Muskogee, Okla., 1954-69, 72—; courtesy staff Muskegon Gen. Hosp.; orthopedic cons. McAlester (Okla.) Gen. Hosp., VA Hosp., Muskogee. Exec. mem. Eastern Okla. council Boy Scouts Am. Fellow ACS, Internat. Coll. Surgeons; mem. Am. Fracture Assn., Nat. Found. (adviser 1958-61), N.Y. Acad. Scis., Okla. State, Pan-Am., So., Aerospace med. assns., AMA, So. Orthopaedic Assn., Eastern Okla. Counties med. socs., S.W. Surg. Congress, Am. Rheumatology Soc., Air Force Assn. (life). Republican. Methodist. Mason (32 deg., K.T. Shriner, Jester), Lion. Club: Muskogee Country. Contbr. articles to profl. jours.; research and evaluation of various uses of refrigerated homogenous bone. Home: 3504 University Blvd Muskogee OK 74401 Office: 1601 W Okmulgee St Muskogee OK 74401

DANESHI, TAHEREH, mathematical sciences educator; b. Iran, Sept. 14, 1948; came to U.S., 1977; d. Mohamed Hassan and Robbabeh (Ghannadan) D.; m. Mohamed Soliman, Mar. 8, 1980; children—Shireen, Sameer. B.S., Tehran U., 1970; M.S., Okla. State U., 1973; Ph.D., Tex. Christian U., 1981. Instr. U. Sci. Tech., Tehran, Iran, 1974-77; asst. prof. dept. math. sci., Cameron U., Lawton, Okla., 1981-85, assoc. prof., 1985—, dir. math. colloquium, 1984—. Author paper in field. Scholar, Tex. Christian U., 1978-81, Ministry of Sci., Tehran, 1977. Mem. Am. Math. Soc., Math. Assn. Am. Avocations: Reading; racquetball; photography; sewing; cooking. Home: 3105 NE Brentwood Lawton OK 73505 Office: Cameron Univ 2800 W Gore Lawton OK 73505

DANFORTH, LARRY DENNIS, advertising agency executive; b. Independence, Mo., Mar. 10, 1952; s. James Edward and JoAnn Doris (Baker) D.; m. Celia Gail Littlefield, Dec. 17, 1977; 1 son, Jason Carl. B.F.A., U. Mo.-Kansas City, 1971; postgrad. Hardin Simmons U., 1975-76. Cert. mktg. cons. Cons., Sta. KFMN, Abilene, Tex., 1980; exec. producer radio-TV Zachry Assocs., Abilene, 1980-82; cons. state polit. campaigns Media S.W., Abilene, 1982; owner, pres. Media Mgmt. Cons., Inc., Abilene, 1982—. Pres. bd. dirs. Backdoor Theatre, 1979-82. Recipient Addy award Advt. Club, 1980, 3d place Internat. Radio Festival N.Y., 1981. Mem. Assn. Broadcast Execs. Tex., Assn. Ind. Radio Producers, Internat. Affiliation Theatrical Stage Employees. Mem. Ch. of Christ. Lodge: Rotary. Home: 3049 Crossroads Dr Abilene TX 79605 Office: Media Mgmt Cons 1052 N 5th St Suite 100 Abilene TX 79601

D'ANGELO, VINCENT RICHARD, JR., public service organization administrator; b. St. Petersburg, Fla., Jan. 26, 1948; s. Vincent Richard and Catherine Mary (Skripko) D'A.; m. Louise Hunnicutt, May 11, 1977; 1 child, Stephanie. B.A., U. South Fla., Tampa, 1972; postgrad. Sch. Bus., 1974. Dir. safety, disaster ARC, Charleston, S.C., 1977-78, dir. emergency service, St. Petersburg, 1980-81, exec. dir. Athens, Ga., 1981-83, exec. dir. Fort Worth, 1983—; exec. dir. Pinellas Epilepsy Found., St. Petersburg, 1979, pres. Pinellas Epilepsy Found., 1980-81; chmn. Pinellas Cardiopulmonary Resuscitation Council, 1980-81, bd. dirs. Pinellas County Heartsavers, Clearwater, Fla., 1980-81; chmn. Clarke County Hypertension Council, Athens, Ga., 1982-83. Mountaineering dir. Cherokee Dist. Boy Scouts Am. Ranger Camp, No. Georgia Mountains, 1981. Recipient Cert. Commendation, City St. Petersburg, 1967; Disting. Service Award, NE Ga. United Way, Athens, 1981; named best loaned exec., 1981, 2d disting. service award, 1982. Mem. Athens Jaycees (Christmas comm. 1982). Lodge: Rotary (Fort Worth). Home: 1713 Oakland Blvd Fort Worth TX 76103 Office: Tarrant County Chpt ARC 6640 Camp Bowie Blvd Fort Worth TX 76116

DANGLER, LEROY STOUT, retired educational administrator, retail store owner; b. Wayside, N.J., July 13, 1916; s. Charles Edmund and Joan (Stout) D.; m. Julia Ziccardi, Apr. 17, 1943 (dec.). B.A., Montclair State U., 1938; M.A., Middlebury Coll., 1946; postgrad. U. Pa., U. Va., Rutgers U., NYU, Cert. secondary sch. tchr., N.J. Tchr. Burlington City High Sch., N.J., 1939-46; instr. U. Pa., Phila., 1946-47, Lafayette Coll., Easton, Pa., 1947-49; civil engr. John Meehan & Son, Phila., 1949-53; engr. RCA Govt. Services, Cherry Hill, N.J., 1953-61; bus. adminstr. St. Mary's Hall-Doane Acad., Burlington, 1973-84; bus. adminstr., elder Presbyterian Ch., Burlington, 1966—; owner, operator Roy's Crafte Shoppe Ltd. Trustee Library Co. of Burlington, 1970-84, Snowden Naines Meml. Library, Burlington, 1975—; founder Julia Z. Dangler Meml. Scholarship, 1977—. Served with U.S. Army, 1942-45. Mem. Nat. Woldlife Fedn. (life), Smithsonian Instn. (donor), Am. Mus. Natural History, Franklin Inst., N.Y. Acad. Scis., Am. Hort. Soc., Oceanic Soc., Cousteau Soc., Audubon Soc., AAAS, Am. Forestry Assn., Nature Conservancy, Asia Soc. (assoc.), Va. Mus., Save the Bay Found., Woodworkers Assn. N.Am. Republican. Presbyterian. Home and Office: 3100 Able Ct Chesterfield VA 23832

DANIEL, CARL VENTRICE, JR., architect; b. Houston, Feb. 10, 1943; s. Carl Ventrice and Myrl Marguerite (Robberts) D.; m. Betty Lou Browning, June 9, 1962; children—M'Lissa Carlynn, Carla Michelle. B. Arch., U. Tex.-Austin, 1967. Registered architect. Designer 3D-1 Architects, Houston, 1967-72; lead designer CRS Architects, Houston, 1973-76; dir. design Lan Architects, Houston, 1977-85. Designer Hyatt Regency-West Houston, Hyatt Regency-Indpls. (AIA award 1977), Cameron Iron Office (TSA award 1971). Democrat. Mem. Ch. of Christ. Avocations: tennis; flying. Office: Brooks/Collier Architects 3131 Eastside Houston TX 77098

DANIEL, CORINNE TALLEY, artist, musician; b. Temple, Tex., Oct. 8, 1916; d. Lewis Robert and Madeline (Kyle) T.; m. John B. Daniel, Jr., June 8, 1940; children—Terry D. Fisher, Britt Talley, Kay Daniel Webster. Student Baylor U., 1934-36, Mary Hardin-Baylor U., 1936; B.A., U. Tex., 1938. One woman shows include Temple Jr. Coll., Temple Country Club, Temple Pub. Library, Temple Art Gallery, Arno Art Club, Temple, City Fedn. of Women's Clubs, Temple, Temple Nat. Bank, Cultural Activities Ctr., Temple; exhibited in group shows at Baylor U., Waco, Tex., McLennan County Community Coll., Waco, Cultural Activities Ctr., Temple, Visual Arts, Temple, Bettis Art Ctr., Waco, Waco Art Assn., Salado Art Galleries, Tex., Salado Mus. and Gallery; represented in numerous permanent collections throughout Tex., also Phoenix, Washington and Mpls.; has rendered piano selections and incidental music to various civic, church, club activities. Composer of popular and contemporary music and lyrics. Charter incorporator Cultural Activites, Ctr., Inc., Temple, 1958; pres. PTA, Lanier, Temple, 1950, Jefferson, 1955, Temple High Sch., 1965; local founder, organizer of first Girl Scout Troop, Temple, 1945; mem. ARC, 1944-46, Am. Cancer Soc., 1945-59, Temple Infantile Paralysis Assn., 1948-57; charter mem. Visual Arts div. Cultural Activities Ctr., 1979-85; mem. Contemporaries, 1970-86; trustee Friends of Temple Pub. Library, 1975-76; docent Cultural Activities Ctr. Recipient Disting. Alumnae award Mary Hardin-Baylor U., 1978. Mem. DAR, Bell-Lampasas-Mills Counties Bar Assn. Aux. (charter). Baptist. Clubs: Domestic Sci. (pres. 1978), Temple Music, Arno Art, Tuesday Study, City Fedn. of Women's of Temple, Nan Brown Garden (pres. 1943), Kappa Kappa Gamma Alumni Assn. Avocations: hunting; tennis, swimming; hiking; bicycling; aerobic dancing. Home: 1317 N 9th St Temple TX 76501

DANIEL, DAN, congressman; b. Chatham, Va., May 12, 1914; s. Reuben Earl and Georgia (Grant) D.; m. Ruby Gordon McGregor, Sept. 30, 1939; 1 son, Jimmie Foxx. Former asst. to chmn. bd. Dan River Mills, Inc., Danville, Va.; mem. 91st-99th congresses from 5th Dist. Va. Permanent mem. People-To-People Com.; Mem. Va. Ho. of Delegates, 1959-68. Served with USNR. Decorated Star of Solidarity, Italy, Croix de Merit; recipient Service to Mankind award; George Washington Honor medal. Mem. Am. Legion (past nat. comdr.), Va. C. of C. (past pres.). Office: 2368 Rayburn House Office Bldg Washington DC 20515

DANIEL, JOHN MONCURE, JR., state pollution control official, chemical engineer; b. Alexandria, Va., Mar. 2, 1928; s. John Moncure Daniel and Marguerite (Fitz-Gerald) Williams; m. Joy Anne Beam, June 13, 1951; children—John M. III, Joy Anne. B.Ch.E., U. Va., 1949; M.S., Ga. Inst. Tech., 1951. Registered profl. engr., Va. Chem. engr. Va.-Carolina Chem. Co., Richmond, 1954-56, sr. chem. engr., 1956-57, sect. leader (fertilizer), process and mech. devel., 1957-60, tech. asst., mfg. dept., 1960-63; asst. dir., quality control, mfg. dept. Mobil Chem. Co., 1963-66, supr., material control, research and tech. dept., 1966-68, mgr., tech. sect., 1968-69; asst. exec. dir. for enforcement Va. State Air Pollution Control Bd., Richmond, 1970—. Served with U.S. Navy, 1951-54. Mem. Am. Inst. Chem. Engrs., Air Pollution Control Assn. (past chmn. South Atlantic Sec., bd. dirs.; past chmn. Central Va. Chpt.), Tau Beta Pi. Episcopalian. Home: 102 Raven Rock Rd Richmond VA 23229 Office: State Air Pollution Control Bd 801 Ninth St Office Bldg Richmond VA 23219

DANIEL, JOSEPH CUNNINGHAM, training and development administrator; b. Birmingham, Ala., June 6, 1938; s. Herman Tooms and Rilla Jane (Whatley) D.; m. Lucy Jane Dunn, June 17, 1961; children—Joseph C., Jr., Melissa Jane. B.S., Samford U., 1960; M.S., So. Sem., 1963, 64. Dir. student activities Samford U., Birmingham, 1967-78; sr. tng. analyst Alabama Power Co., Birmingham, 1978-81, mgmt. devel. mgr., 1981—. Contbr. articles to profl. jours. Mem. exec. com. Red Cross Blood Program, Birmingham, 1972; assoc. commnr. Shades Mountain Community Park, Birmingham, 1973; treas. Berry High Sch. Athletic Assn., Birmingham, 1982. Mem. Am. Soc. Tng. and Devel., Southeastern Electric Exchange (chmn. planning com. 1985—), Nat. Mgmt. Assn. (adv. com.), Am. Mgmt. Assn. Democrat. Baptist. Avocations: tennis, racquetball, woodworking. Office: Alabama Power Co 600 N 18th St Birmingham AL 35291

DANIEL, JULIA ELLEN, home economics educator; b. Clanton, Ala., Jan. 15, 1940; d. Harlem Gresham and Annie Estelle (Bramlett) D. B.S., U. Montevallo, 1961; Ed.M., Auburn U., 1966; Ed.S., U. Ga., 1973, Ed.D., 1976. Secondary tchr. Clay County High Sch., Fort Gaines, Ga., 1961-65, Newton County High Sch., Covington, Ga., 1965-68, Talladega High Sch., Ala., 1968-69; asst. prof. home econs. Berry Coll., Mt. Berry, Ga., 1969-73; grad. asst. U. Ga., Athens, 1973-76; assoc. prof. U. Southwestern La., Lafayette, 1976—, interim dir. Sch. Home Econs., 1984. Mem. Am. Home Econs. Assn., La. Home Econs. Assn. (pres. 1981-82, v.p. annual meeting 1979-80), Am. Vocat. Assn., La. Vocat. Assn., Assn. Tchr. Educators, La. Home Econs. Tchr. Educators (chmn. 1985—). Democrat. Mem. Ch. of Christ. Home: 108 Bon Wier Ln Lafayette LA 70506 Office: U So La Box 40649 Lafayette LA 70504

DANIEL, MICHAEL ROLAND, lieutenant governor South Carolina; b. Gaffney, S.C., Apr. 13, 1940; s. Dewey B. and Ruth (Chaney) D.; m. Margaret Ann Carr, May 25, 1965; children—Becky, Shelly, Barbara. Student, The Citadel, 1958-59; B.A., U. S.C., 1962; J.D., 1966. Formerly assoc. Hall, Daniel, Winter & Clary, Gaffney; mem. S.C. Ho. of Reps., 1973-83, speaker pro tem, 1980-83; lt. gov. State of S.C., Columbia, 1983—. Trustee Limestone Coll. Served with U.S. Army, 1967-68; capt. JAGC Res. Mem. Cherokee County Bar Assn., S.C. Bar Assn., ABA, Assn. Trial Lawyers Am. Democrat. Methodist. Lodges: Masons; Rotary. Office: State House Columbia SC 29201*

DANIEL, ROBERT CARLTON, health care consultant; b. Miami, Fla., Dec. 26, 1919; s. Frederick Allen and Carrie Emma (King) D.; B.S., B.A., U. Fla., 1948; M.A., Trinity U., San Antonio, 1955; m. Ivy Lee, Apr. 30, 1949; children—Ivy Lenora, Roberta Katherine. Commd. 2d lt. U.S. Army, 1943, advanced through grades to col., 1963, exec. officer U.S. Air Force, Hosps., Bavaria, Germany, 1949-52, spl. cons. to Air Force surgeon gen., Washington, 1952-54, dir. adminstrv. services Wilford Hall Air Force Hosp., San Antonio, 1954-56, exec. officer U.S. Air Force Hosp., Tyndall AFB, Fla., 1956-59, Elmendorf AFB, Anchorage, 1959-62, Hunter AFB, Savannah, Ga., 1962-64; ret., 1964; asst. adminstr. Tallahassee Meml. Hosp., 1965-67, asso. exec. dir., 1967-79; exec. v.p. Tallahassee Meml. Regional Med. Center, Inc., 1979-84; pres. R.C. Daniel Health Cons., Inc., Tallahassee, 1985—; preceptor dept. grad. health adminstrn. U. Minn.; advisor Sch. Nursing, Tallahassee Community Coll., Sch. Allied Health Service, Fla. A&M U. Exec. dir. Sci. Fair Found. State of Alaska, 1955-56; deacon Presbyn. Ch. Decorated Legion of Merit. Mem. Am. Coll. Hosp. Adminstrs., Am. Hosp. Assn., Fla. Hosp. Assn., Am. Soc. Hosp. Mgmt., Ret. Officer Assn. Republican. Club: Rotary. Office: Profl Office Bldg 1401 Centerville Rd Tallahassee FL 32308

DANIEL, ROSS PRESTON, III, economics educator; b. Beckley, W.Va., July 6, 1951; s. Ross Preston and Ruth Irene (Roby) D. B.A., Marshall U., 1973, M.B.A., 1975; M.A., W.Va. U., 1979. Research fellow W.Va. U., Morgantown, 1976-77, teaching fellow, 1977-81, lectr., 1981-82; asst. prof. Nichols State U., Thibodaux, La., 1982-85; asst. prof. U. Southwestern La., Lafayette, 1985—; asst. mktg. mgr. Mountaineer Mall, Morgantown, W.Va., 1979-81; v.p. R.D. Software Inc., Thibodaux, 1983-84. Benedum research fellow, 1976. Mem. Am. Econ. Assn., Acad. La. Economists, Atlantic Econ. Soc., Tau Kappa Epsilon. Episcopalian. Home: #262 100 Bellefontaine Lafayette LA 70506 Office: U Southwestern La Lafayette LA 70504

DANIEL, WAYNE WENDELL, quantitative methods educator; b. Tallapoosa, Ga., Feb. 14, 1929; s. Lloyd Denver and Ora Viola (Cason) D.; m. Mary Elizabeth Yarbrough, June 2, 1956; children—Jean Elizabeth, Mary Carolyn, John Wayne. B.S. in Edn., U. Ga., 1951; M.P.H., U. N.C., 1959; Ph.D., U. Okla., 1965. Tchr., Villa Rica High Sch. (Ga.), 1954-57; statistician Ga. Dept. Pub. Health, Atlanta, 1957-68; prof. quantitative methods Ga. State U., Atlanta, 1968—. Served with U.S. Army, 1952-54. Mem. Am. Pub. Health Assn., Am. Statis. Assn., Am. Inst. for Decision Scis. Democrat. Baptist. Author: Essentials of Business Statistics, 1984; Biostatistics: A Foundation for Analysis in the Health Sciences, (3rd ed.) 1983; (with James C. Terrell) Business Statistics: Basic Concepts and Methodology, (4th edit.), 1986; Applied Nonparametric Statistics, 1978; Introductory Statistics with Applications, 1977. Home: 2943 Appling Dr Chamblee GA 30341 Office: Dept Decision Scis GA State U Univ Plaza Atlanta GA 30303

DANIEL, WILLIE FRED, health, physical education, and recreation educator; b. Shreveport, La., Dec. 6, 1947; s. Clarence and Mary (Davis) D.; m. Mary E. Smith, June 22, 1966; children—Yolanda M., LaNetra S. B.S., Grambling State U., 1971; M.S., U. Ill., 1972; Ed.D., U. Colo., 1977; M.S., Jackson State U., 1985. Teaching asst. U. Ill., Champaign, 1971-72, U. Colo., Boulder, 1975-77; assoc. dir., instr. Jackson State U., Miss., 1972-75, head dept. recreation, 1978-83, assoc. prof. health, phys. edn., 1983—; cons. Grambling State U., La., 1983-84, Humanics Assocs., Jackson, Miss., 1983-84, North Miss. Head Start Assn., Cleve., 1982. Vice pres. Brinkley Jr. High Sch., Jackson, Miss., 1979-80, pres., 1980-81; coach, judge Spl. Olympics, Jackson, 1980—; pres. Richwood Estates Homeowners Assn., Jackson, 1982—; v.p. Northwest Jackson Community Coalition, 1983-84. Recipient Mayor's award of merit Jackson, 1982; Outstanding service award Boy's Club Am., 1982; Outstanding Young Man of Am., Jaycees, 1979; grantee U.S. Dept. Edn., 1983, 84, 85. Mem. AAHPER, Nat. Recreation and Parks Assn., Miss. Alliance Health, Phys. Edn. and Recreation, Miss. Recreation and Parks Assn., Noon Optimist Club (chmn. fin. com., 1982-84), Kappa Alpha Psi. Democrat. Baptist. Avocations: tennis; fishing; reading. Home: 1827 Northwood Circle Jackson MS 39213 Office: Dept HPER Jackson State U 1325 John R Lynch Jackson MS 39217

DANIELS, ALLEN JERROLD, manufacturing company executive; b. Bklyn., June 4, 1946; s. Irving D. and Selma C. Daniels; A.A., Miami Dade Jr. Coll., 1967; B.A., Fla. Atlantic U., 1969, M.B.A., 1971; m. Peggy; children—Brian, Scott. Teller, Washington Fed. Savs. & Loan Assn., Miami Beach, Fla., 1966-67; sr. asst. mgr. Household Fin. Corp., Miami, 1967-68; loan officer and credit analyst Hialeah-Miami Springs (Fla.) First State Bank, 1968-70; credit mgr. Mary Carter Industries, Miami, 1970-72, Cain & Bultman Inc., Miami, 1972; regional mgr. Famco Services, Inc., Miami, 1972-73; fin. services mgr. Edward Don & Co., Miami, 1973-80; credit mgr. Moss Mfg., Inc., Miami, 1980-81; dist. sales mgr. Internat. Product Merchandising, Pompano Beach, Fla., 1981-82; credit mgr. Atlanta Textile Co., Inc., 1982—. Mem. Nat. Assn. Credit Mgmt. (chmn. internat. com.), So. Fla. Credit Mgmt. Assn. (pres. 1977-78). Democrat. Jewish. Office: 4505 Commerce Dr Atlanta GA 30336

DANIELS, ANN ELAINE, nursing educator; b. Rochester, N.Y., Apr. 26, 1941; m. Joseph W.C. Daniels; children—Douglas T., Michael R., Catherine A., Linda L., Susan E. R.N., Genesee Hosp. Sch. Nursing, 1961. Staff nurse Strong Meml. Hosp., Rochester, 1963-67; co-owner, mgr. Walnut Springs Bakery, Seguin, Tex., 1971-79; clin. instr. New Braunfels Sch. Vocat. Nursing, Tex., 1975-77, dir., instr., 1981—; staff nurse Warm Springs Rehab. Hosp., Gonzales, Tex., 1979-81. Mem. Nat. League Nursing, Tex. Assn. Vocat. Nurse Educators. Club: Zonta. Home: 65 Elm Creek Rd Seguin TX 78155-9329 Office: New Braunfels Sch Vocat Nursing 143 E Garzu New Braunfels TX 78130

DANIELS, AUBREY CLISE, psychologist; b. Lake City, S.C., May 17, 1935; S. Aubrey Oliver and Carrie Bell (Hanna) D.; m. Rebecca Tapp; children—Laura Lee, Joanna. B.A. Furman U., 1957; M.A., U. Fla., 1963, Ph.D., 1965. Lic. psychologist, Ga. Chief psychologist Ga. Mental Health Inst., Atlanta,

1965-68; dir. psychology Ga. Regional Hosp., Atlanta, 1968-71; pres. Behavioral Systems, Atlanta, 1972-78, Aubrey Daniels and Assocs., Atlanta, 1978—. Author: (with others) Performance Management, 1982. Editor Jour. Organizational Behavior Mgmt., 1976. Served to capt. U.S. Army, 1957-60. Mem. Am. Psychol. Assn., Assn. Advancement Behavior Therapy, Soc. Advancement Behavior Analysis. Republican. Baptist. Avocations: tennis; jogging; gardening; reading. Home: 2409 Castleridge Ct Tucker GA Office: Aubrey Daniels and Assocs 3531 Habersham at Northlake Tucker GA 30084

DANIELS, CAROLE ANGELA, metallurgical engineer; b. Phila., Nov. 10, 1945; d. Arthur Joseph and Angela Anita (Traveline) Daniels; m. Lewis Earl Sloter, June 2, 1978; 1 son, Lewis Earl. B.S. in Metall. Engring., Drexel U., 1968, M.S. in Materials Engring., (NSF fellow), 1973, Ph.D. in Materials Sci. (NSF grantee), 1977. Sr. engr. Westinghouse Electric Corp., Madison, Pa., 1974-77; vis. prof. mech. engring. U. Tex., Arlington, 1977-79; v.p. Data Processing div. John Lummus Co., Dallas, 1979-82; adj. prof. U. Tex., 1979; cons. in field. Vol. audio engr. N. Tex. Radio for Blind; mem. adv. com. Tex. Sect. Nuclear Energy Women, 1977—. Recipient cert. Service Dallas Ind. Sch. Dist., 1981. Mem. Am. Nuclear Soc., Am. Soc. Metals, The Metall. Soc. of AIME, Soc. Plastics Engrs., Alpha Sigma Mu. Contbr. articles in field to profl. jours.

DANIELS, FRANK ARTHUR, JR., newspaper publisher; b. Raleigh, N.C., Sept. 7, 1931; s. Frank Arthur and Ruth (Aunspaugh) D.; m. Julia Bryan Jones, June 4, 1954; children—Frank Arthur III, Julia Graham. A.B., U. N.C., 1953. With News and Observer Pub. Co., Raleigh, 1953—, bus. mgr., 1960-68, gen. mgr., 1968-71, pres., pub., 1971—; dir. A.P., Newspaper Advt. Bur., Mut. Ins. Co. Ltd., Hamilton, Bermuda, Bancshares of N.C., Inc., 1973-75. Bd. dirs., mem. exec. com., campaign chmn. United Way, 1964, pres., 1974-75; bd. dirs. Peace Coll., N.C. State U. Found., Rex Hosp., St. Mary's Coll.; chmn., pres. Am. Newspaper Pub. Assn. Found.; former mem. long-range planning com. Raleigh-Durham Airport.; past trustee Woodberry Forest Sch. Served with USAF, 1954-55. Named Outstanding Young Man of Yr. Raleigh Jaycees, 1963. Mem. So. Newspaper Pubs. Assn. (chmn. bd. 1973-74, pres. 1972-73, dir.), Am. Newspaper Pubs. Assn. (past bd. dirs., treas.), Eastern N.C. Press Assn. (pres. 1963-64), N.C. Press Assn. (past pres.), Delta Kappa Epsilon. Democrat. Presbyn. Clubs: Kiwanian., Capital City, Carolina Country, Sphinx (Raleigh). Home: 3514 Keats Pl Raleigh NC 27609 Office: 215 S McDowell St Raleigh NC 27601

DANIELS, HARRIET EARNESTINE, retired nurse, administrator; b. Shamrock, Fla., Oct. 10, 1937; d. Willie Lee and Carrie Elvira (Anderson) D.; B.S., Fla. A&M U., 1960; M.Nursing, U. Fla., 1971, postgrad., 1976. Sch. nurse Fla. A&M High Sch., Tallahassee, 1960-61; head nurse U. Fla. Med. Center, Gainesville, 1963-71, supr. obstetrics-gynecology, 1971-73, asst. dir. nurses, 1973-80. Bd. dirs. Upjohn Health Care Services. Fla. State Bd. Regents grantee, 1975-76. Mem. Zeta Phi Beta. Methodist. Clubs: Ebony Women's (treas. 1977-79), Order Eastern Star. Home: 1215 SE 13th St Gainesville FL 32601

DANIELS, JAMES WILLIAM, printing company executive; b. Orlando, Fla., June 13, 1936; s. Ernest William and Elizabeth (James) D.; m. Ellie Obiol, Aug. 24, 1974; children—Jennifer James, William MacNeill. Student St. Mary U., 1959-60, Asheville-Biltmore Coll., 1960-61. Chmn. bd., pres. Daniels Bus. Services, Inc., Asheville, N.C., 1961—. Vice pres. Asheville Area C. of C.; chmn. Bele Chere. Served with USAF, 1955-59. Recipient Disting. Service award Asheville Area C. of C. Mem. Printing Industry Am. (chmn. Region II), Printing Industries of the Carolinas. Democrat. Methodist. Home: 820 Town Mountain Rd Asheville NC 28804 Office: 15 Rankin Ave Asheville NC 28802

DANIELS, JOHN YADEN, textile research chemist; b. London, Ky., Feb. 12, 1950; s. Ollie P. and Louise (Yaden) D.; m. Marsha Robbs, Aug. 18, 1973; children—Laura Jill, Bonnie Leigh. B.S. in Textile Chemistry, N.C. State U., 1972, M.S. in Textile Chemistry, 1980; M.B.A., Winthrop Coll., 1984. Mgmt. trainee chemist Deering Milliken Research, Spartanburg, S.C., 1972-73; supr. zimmer flat bed carpet printing Deering Milliken Hillside Plant, La Grange, Ga., 1973-74; lab. mgr. Am. Assn. Textile Chemists and Colorists, Research Triangle Park, N.C., 1974-79; group leader dying research Springs Industries, Inc., Ft. Mill, S.C., 1979-85, research mgr., 1985—. Den father cub scout troop Moorehead Sch. Blind, 1977. Served with USAR, 1972-73, Ga. N.G., 1973-74, USAR, 1974-78. Recipient Outstanding Brother award N.C. State U., 1972, Outstanding Alumnus award, 1975; Cone Mills scholar, 1968-72, Outstanding Brother award Sigma Pi, outstanding alumnus award. Mem. Am. Assn. Textile Chemists and Colorists, Am. Chem. Soc. Republican. Home: 8229 Tifton Rd Pineville NC 28134 Office: Springs Industries Research and Devel Ctr Fort Mill SC 29715

DANIELS, L. ANN, health educator; b. Wilson, N.C., Nov. 25, 1950; d. James Roger and Myrtle Grace (Winstead) Daniels. B.S., N.C. Central U., 1973; M.Ed., U. NC., 1979. Registered health edn. specialist, N.C. Soc. Pub. Health Educators. Assoc. control biologist Cutter Pharm. Lab., Raleigh, N.C., 1973-75; dir. health edn. City of Eden (N.C.), 1975-77; dir. allied and pub. health edn. Bowman Gray Sch. Medicine, Winston-Salem, N.C., 1977—, instr. health edn., 1980—; adj. instr. health edn. U. N.C., Chapel Hill, 1980—; cons. on edn. and tng. VA Med. Ctr., Salisbury, N.C., 1981—. Bd. dirs. Am. Cancer Soc., Winston-Salem, 1982—, Battered Women's Services, Winston-Salem, 1983—, Consumer Counseling-Credit Services, Winston-Salem, 1984—. Recipient Outstanding Woman Achivement award Profl. Bus. League, Winston-Salem, N.C., 1982. Mem. ASTD, Nat. Assn. Profl. Cons., Nat. Assn. Female Execs., Nat. Soc. Prospective Medicine, Triad Trainers Guild (program dir. Winston-Salem 1982-83), Eta Sigma Gamma. Democrat. Baptist. Avocations: bowling; tennis; movies; self-development books. Home: 1825 N Liberty St Winston-Salem NC 27105

DANIELS, VINCENT S., mining equipment company executive; b. Plainfield, N.J., Mar. 22, 1945; d. Vincent G. and Anna Carmela (Spisso) D.; m. Marianne K.M. Klee, Aug. 30, 1968; children—Jonathan Vincent Klee, Sebastian Nickolas Klee. B.S., U. Tampa, 1973; M. Internat. Mgmt., Am. Grad. Sch. Internat. Mgmt., Glendale, Ariz., 1974. Pres., Hassdan Internat., Glendale, 1974; dist. mgr. Bucyrus-Erie, South Milwaukee, Wis., 1975-76; pres. Disc, South Plainfield, N.J., 1976-79, Minequip Corp. Miami, 1980—; cons., pres. Daniels Internat. Sales & Cons., Miami, 1983—; cons. Paranapanema S.A., Sao Paulo, 1982—; dir. Danico Inc., Miami, Minequip Ltda, La Paz, Bolivia, also Santiago, Chile, Lima, Peru and Rio de Janeiro, Brazil, 1983—. Contbr. articles to profl. jours. Mem. Republican Com. South Plainfield, 1976-79. Served to capt. U.S. Army, 1963-72; Vietnam, Greece, Ger. Decorated Air medal, Bronze Star, Purple Heart. Mem. Soc. Mining Engrs., Am. Mgmt. Assn., Mining Club, Inc., Internat. Center Fla., ARRL (life), Am. Legion. Home: 4180 El Prado Blvd Coconut Grove FL 33133 Office: Minequip Corp 7777 NW 54th St Miami FL 33166

DANIELSEN, ALBERT LEROY, economics educator, consultant; b. Council Bluffs, Iowa, May 26, 1934; s. Moroni Lloyd and Geneva Gale (Williford) D.; m. Eleanor Jean Gibson, June 7, 1958; children—Bartley Roland, Lea Anne, Albert William. B.S., Clemson U., 1960; Ph.D., Duke U., 1966. Dir. Office Internat. Market Analysis, U.S. Dept. Energy, Washington, 1977-78; from asst. prof. to prof. econs. U. Ga., Athens, 1963—; dir. Ga. Pub. Utilities Conf., Atlanta, 1980—. Author: Evolution of OPEC, 1982. Editor: Current Issues in Public Utilities Economics, 1983. Contbr. articles to profl. jours. Social Sci. Research Council grantee, 1982. Mem. Internat. Assn. Energy Economists (rep. Atlanta chpt., exec. com. 1981—), Am. Econs. Assn., So. Econs. Assn. Republican. Baptist. Avocations: swimming; golf. Home: 118 Spruce Valley Rd Athens GA 30605 Office: U Ga Athens GA 30602

DANIELSON, BRUCE JENSEN, telemarketing company executive, airline pilot; b. Denton, Tex., Apr. 8, 1939; s. Stanley Harold and Gertrude Marie D.; m. Jerrilyn Paula Donna Elizabeth Danielson, (dec. 1980); 1 son, Brian Lee. D.D., Universal Life Ch., 1976; student Iowa State U., 1957, Drake U., 1958, Am. Inst. Bus., 1960-61. Pilot, TransAm. Airlines, Oakland, Calif., 1965—; founder Troika Corp., pub. AG Trader; pres. Dan Jensen & Assocs., Inc., Dallas, 1979—. Served with USAF, 1961-65. Mem. Airline Pilots Assn., Am. Legion, YMCA, Aircraft Owners and Pilots Assn., Phi Theta Pi; American Contract Bridge League. Club: Turtle. Office: Box 59233 Northaven Dallas TX 75229

DANKS, DALE, mayor. Mayor of Jackson, Miss. Office: 219 S President St Jackson MS 39205*

DANNER, RAYMOND L., restaurant company executive; b. 1925. Ptnr. Moonlite Dreue Inc., 1950-52, with Commonwealth Realty Co. and Creder Restaurant, 1956-58; with Shoney's Inc., Nashville, 1958—, now chmn. bd., chief exec. officer. Address: Shoney's Inc 1727 Elm Mill Pike Nashville TN 37210*

DANNER, ROBERT LEA, SR., clergyman; b. Seattle, Dec. 12, 1929; s. Albert Lea and Stella (Bright) D.; m. Marilyn M. Davis, June 10, 1951; children—Deborah, Robert Lea, Mary, Steven. A.B., Chapman Coll., 1952; B.D., Lexinton Theol. Sem., 1955; postgrad. Calif. State U.-Northridge, 1961; Ph.D., Pacific Western U., 1979. Ordained to ministry Christian Ch., 1955; cert. tchr., Calif.; cert. coll. tchr., Va. Pastor, Christian Ch., Smithfield, Ky., 1952-55; assoc. minister Central Christian Ch., Van Nuys, Calif., 1955-57; minister edn. Hollywood-Beverly Christian Ch., Hollywood, Calif., 1957-59; pastor First Christian Ch., Reseda, Calif., 1959-62; tchr. Porter Jr. High Sch., Los Angeles City Schs., 1962-80; pastor Diamond Springs Christian Ch., Virginia Beach, Va., 1980-85; organizing minister Court House Christian Ch., Virginia Beach, 1984—; co-pastor Park View Christian Ch., Chesapeake, Va., 1985—; prof. St. Leo Coll., 1982—; marriage and family cons., 1981—. Bd. dirs. Bayside Jr. High Sch., Virginia Beach, Va., 1982-83; pres. Dist. 8 Christian Chs., Va., 1982-83; chmn. Ministers Assn., 1983-84, youth sponsor, 1984; mem. Capital Campaign for Christian Chs. Va., 1982-84, mem. clergy com., 1984—, mem. goals and promotion com., 1983-85. Radio host Deliberately Different, WCMS-AM, 1982-83. Mem. Soc. for Sci. Study Religion, Princess Anne County Hist. Soc., Internat. Assn. Near Death Studies, Mensa. Office: 5612 Haden Rd Virginia Beach VA 23455

DANSBY, MICKEY ROGERS, air force officer, research psychologist; b. Ozark, Ala., May 31, 1947; s. Rogers Oneal and Frances Burnice (Andrews) D.; m. Diane Marie Davis, Aug. 3, 1968; children—Julie Christine, Scott Edward. B.S., U. Fla., 1969, M.S., 1970, Ph.D., 1979. Commd. 2d lt. U.S. Air Force, 1969, advanced through grades to maj., 1982; tng. evaluator U.S. Air Force, Sheppard AFB, Tex., 1971-72, adminstr., Randolph AFB, Tex., 1972-74; assoc. prof. behavioral scis. U.S. Air Force Acad., Colorado Springs, Colo., 1974-83; dir. research Leadership and Mgmt. Devel. Ctr., U.S. Air Force, Maxwell AFB, Ala., 1984—. Dir. music Eden Hills Bapt. Ch., Wichita Falls, Tex., 1971-72, Camellia Bapt. Ch., Prattville, Ala., 1984—. Mem. Am. Psychol. Assn., Phi Beta Kappa, Phi Kappa Phi. Republican. Avocations: tennis; photography; music; computing. Home: 135 Quail Run Prattville AL 36067 Office: Air Univ Leadership and Mgmt Devel Ctr Maxwell AFB AL 36112

DANSER, MARY HELEN, pharmacist; b. Dawson Springs, Ky., Mar. 8, 1940; d. Maurice and Emma Louise (Thorn) Lisanby; m. Richard Allen Danser, June 8, 1963 (dec. Apr. 1976); 1 child, Richard Allen Jr. A.A., Lindsey Wilson Jr. Coll., 1961; B.S. in Pharmacy, U. Ky., 1965. Registered pharmacist, Ky. Intern. U. Ky. Med. Ctr., 1965; intern, pharmacist Hubbard & Curry Druggists, Lexington, Ky., 1965-66; chief pharmacist Ky. Dept. Mental Health, Frankfort, 1966-73, Ky. Bur. Health Services, 1973-84; pharmacy services program mgr. Ky. Dept. Mental Health Cabinet for Human Resources, Frankfort, 1984—; cons. in field; instr. Coll. Law Enforcement Dept. Traffic Safety, Eastern State U., 1968-84, Jefferson County Police Dept., Louisville, Ky., 1985—. Mem. pastor/parish com. 1st Meth. Ch., Lexington, 1971-77, adminstrv. bd., 1972-74; chmn. com. Troop 276, Boy Scouts Am., Lexington, 1984—; youth counselor Antioch Christian Ch., 1984—. Mem. Bluegrass Pharm. Assn., Ky. Soc. Hosp. Pharmacists (sec. 1970), Am. Soc. Hosp. Pharmacists (panelist 1975-77). Democrat. Methodist. Avocations: gardening; sewing. Home: 3175 Paris Pike Lexington KY 40511 Office: Dept Mental Health 275 E Main St Frankfort KY 40621

DANSEREAU, CHARLES PHILLIPPE, pharmacist; b. Labadieville, La., Oct. 19, 1938; s. Henry Charles and Jessie Josephine (Daigle) D.; m. Carole Anne Bergeron, Jan. 3, 1959; children—Charisse, Chelle, Carla. Student Nicholls State U., 1956-58; B.S. in Pharmacy, N.E. State U., Monroe, La., 1963. Pharm.D. (hon.), La. Pharmacy Assn., 1982, Nat. Assn. Druggists, 1981. Lic. pharmacist, La. Pharmacist, mgr. Choust Drug Store, Golden Meadow, La., 1963-64, Musso's Drug Store, Thibodaux, La., 1964-69, D&M Drug Store, 1969—; chmn. DMT, Inc., 1969—. Contbr. articles to profl. jours. Mem. La. Pharmacy Assn. (v.p. 1972), Nat. Assn. Retail Druggists, Acad. Gen. Practice Pharmacy, Thibodaux Jaycees (treas. 1973). Democrat. Roman Catholic. Avocations: boating; fishing; cooking; reading. Home: Hwy 308 Thibodaux LA 70301 Office: D&M Drug Store 1700 Canal Blvd Thibodaux LA 70301

DANSON, RALPH EMERSON, JR., credit company official; b. Jacksonville, Fla., May 30, 1941; s. Ralph Emerson and June Priscilla (Brunson) D.; m. Carolyn Delores Howard, Oct. 4, 1963; 1 son, Ralph David. Student Stetson U., 1959-60, Jacksonville U., 1960-63. With Gen. Electric Credit Corp., various locations, 1963—, internal control and procedures mgr., Atlanta, 1980—. Pres. Circle StoneSwim League; mem. council DeKalb County Swim League; deacon Indian Creek Baptist Ch.; instr. ARC; vol. worker Christian Service Corp. Served with US Army Res., 1966-67. Mem. Am. Mgmt. Assn., Bus. Forms Mgmt. Assn., Internat. 99 Computer Users Group, East Side Computer Users Group (pres.), Internat. Brotherhood of Magicians. Democrat. Baptist. Club: Circlestone. Office: General Electric Credit Corporation Box 1346 Atlanta GA 30301

DAPKUS, MARILYN ANNE, clinical psychologist; b. Linden, N.J., Feb. 11, 1954; d. Frank and Adelle (Paulauskus) D. B.A., Rutgers U., 1976; Ph.D., U. Tenn., 1982. Lic. psychologist, Tenn. Clin. psychologist Daniel Arthur Rehab. Ctr., Oak Ridge, 1982—, practice psychology, Knoxville, Tenn., 1982—. Contbr. articles to profl. jours. Mem. Am. Psychol. Assn., Tenn. Psychol. Assn., Phi Beta Kappa. Office: Daniel Arthur Rehab Ctr 728 Emory Valley Rd Oak Ridge TN 37830

DAPPRICH, JOHN WILLIAM, interior designer; b. Dearborn, Mich., Mar. 6, 1937; s. Elton and Ellen (Ketchum) D.; student Easter U., 1956-57; diploma Kendall Sch. Design, 1962. Interior designer Burdines Dept. Stores, Miami, Fla., 1963-64, Jordan Marsh Dept. Store, Miami, 1964-66; interior designer Waldo Perez Interiors, Coconut Grove, Fla., 1967-68; owner Dapprich Interiors, Coconut Grove, 1968-70; dir. interior design Deltona Corp., Miami, 1970—. Served with AUS, 1957-59. Mem. AID. Interior designer penthouse Joe Garagiola, Marco Island, 1970, also interior designer for Jack Paar, Key Biscayne, 1972, Henry Kissinger, Key Biscayne, 1972, Gene Sarazen, Marco Island, 1972, Ken Venturi, Marco Island, Adm. Rickenbacker, Senator George Smathers, Ara Parseghian, Naples Beach Club Hotel, Airport Regency Hotel, Quail Creek Country Club, Kings Bay Yacht and Country Club and Hotel, Jupiter Hilton Hotel (Fla.); TV commls. for Bob Griese of Miami Dolphins; hotels include Marco Beach Hotel, Marco Island, Fla., Key Biscayne (Fla.) Hotel, Tierra Verde Hotel, St. Petersburg, Fla., The Palace Hotel, Phila., J.F.K. Internat. Hotel, N.Y.C., Belmont Hotel, Bermuda, LAX Hotel, Los Angeles, Miami Spring Villas, Miami. Home: 3927 Douglas Rd Coconut Grove FL 33133

DARBEAU, JENNIFER JONES, elementary educator; b. Indpls., Nov. 1, 1951; d. Porter James and Bernice Albertra (Anderson) Jones; m. Don Douglas Darbeau, Feb. 17, 1979; children—Don Douglas, Chanel. B.S. in Elem. Edn., Knoxville Coll. (Tenn.), 1973; M.S. in Adminstrn., Nova U., Ft. Lauderdale, 1978; postgrad. in computer sci. Barry Coll. Cert. elementary edn., adminstrn., Fla., Mich. Tchr., Grand Rapids Sch. System (Mich.), 1973; tchr. Dade County Sch. System, Miami, 1974—; adminstrv. asst. Dade County Commn. Citizen Services Dept., Miami, 1981. Editor univ. program. Asst. dir. After Sch. program YMCA, Miami, 1983. Grantee Concordia Lutheran Coll., 1970; recipient Highest Service award Gamma Rho chpt. Eta Phi Beta, 1983. Mem. United Tchrs. Dade, Nat. Tchrs. Assn., Knoxville Coll. Alumni Assn., Nat. Inter-Alumni Council United Negro Coll. Fund. Democrat. Lutheran.

DARBY, EDWIN SYLVESTER, technical occupation educator, educational administrator; b. Wewoka, Okla., Oct. 11, 1932; s. Willis Foster and Bessie Deoria (Kerns) D.; m. Ramona Carolyn Taylor, Dec. 22, 1954; children—Charissa Lynn Darby Phipps, Chris Edwin, Michele Diane Darby Beard. Technician cert. Okla. A&M Coll., 1955; B.S. in Tech. Edn., Okla. State U., 1963, M.S. in Tech. Edn., 1970, Ed.D. in Tech. Occupational Edn., 1976. From instr. to asst. prof., dept. head Okla. State U., Stillwater, 1957-67, asst. prof., asst. dir. 1967-71, assoc. prof., assoc. dir., 1971-75, asst. dir., 1975, chief acad. officer, 1977—. Served with USN, 1951-53. EPDA Prof. Devel. fellow U.S. Office Edn., 1975. Mem. Okla. Tech Soc. (pres. 1974-75, Outstanding Service award 1976, life mem.), Inst. Cert. Engring. Techs., North Central Accreditation Assn. (cons. evaluator). Republican. Methodist. Avocation: mechanical systems design and development. Home: Route 2 Box 248 Beggs OK 74421 Office: Okla State Univ 4th & Mission Rd Okmulgee OK 74447

DARBY, JOSEPH JASPER, III, graphic arts company executive; b. Sherman, Tex., Mar. 31, 1942; s. Joseph Jasper, Jr. and Frances Addah (Rucker) D.; m. Vivian Marie Fantini, Aug. 18, 1979; children—D. Jennifer, Carrie Elizabeth Nelson. B.B.A., B.S., U. Okla., 1964. Vice pres. mfg. Eagle Internat./Overseas Inns, 1976-77, Classic Chem. Co., 1977-78; v.p. prodn. Pacesetters Graphic Typography Co., Dallas, 1978—. Mem. Printing Inst., Soc. Packaging and Handling Engrs., Packaging Inst. Republican. Methodist.

DARCY, GEORGE HARBRECHT, consulting company executive, researcher; b. Chgo., Aug. 16, 1951; s. George Robert and Martha Louise (Harbrecht) D.; m. Karen Alice Haynie, Aug. 10, 1974. B.A., U. Rochester, 1973; M.S., U. Miami, 1978; M.B.A., Fla. Internat. U., 1985. Asst. supr. Applied Marine Ecol. Services, Inc., Miami, 1976-77; fishery biologist Nat. Marine Fisheries Service, U.S. Dept. Commerce, Miami, 1978-79; research asst. Gulf and Caribbean Fisheries Inst., Miami, 1979-80; research asst. Coop. Inst. for Marine and Atmospheric Studies, Miami, 1980-82; pres. Marenco Inc., Miami, 1982—; fishery adminstr. Nat. Marine Fisheries Service, U.S. Dept. Commerce, Miami, 1985—; cons. Mariculture, Ltd., Deltona Corp., U.S. Navy, AT&T, Inderena Colombia, Dade County, Fla., Nat. Marine Fisheries Service, Fla. Internat. U., Applied Marine Ecol. Services. Maytag fellow, 1974-77; recipient U. Rochester Chester Dewey award, 1973. Mem. Am. Inst. Fishery Research Biologists (sec.-treas. Fla. div. 1982-83), Am. Soc. Ichthyologists and Herpetologists. Contbr. articles to profl. jours. Office: 17911 SW 92d Ct Miami FL 33157

DARCY, ROBERT E., political scientist, statistician, educator; b. Elizabeth, N.J., Feb. 25, 1942; s. John William and Jane (Alton) D.; m. Lynne C. Murnane, Sept. 1, 1975; children—Mary Francis, Catherine Rose. B.A., U. Wis., 1965; M.A., U. Ky., 1970, Ph.D., 1971. Asst. prof. George Washington U., Washington, 1971-77, Okla State U., Stillwater, 1977-80, assoc. prof. polit. sci., 1980-85, prof., 1985—; expert witness on ballot procedures Atty. Gen., State of Okla., Oklahoma City, 1984—; vis. guest prof. U. Conn., 1984; vis. research scholar Acad. Korean Studies, Seoul, 1983; European lectureship USIA, Sweden, Germany, 1983; vis. prof. U. New Orleans, 1985. Author: Barriers to Women in American Electoral Politics, 1986. Assoc. editor Jour. Women and Politics, 1980—, Social Sci. Jour., 1983—. Contbr. articles to profl. jours. Pres. Payne County Volunteers in Probation, Stillwater, 1985. Mem. AAUP (pres. 1984), Am. Polit. Sci. Assn., Am. Assn. Pub. Opinion Research, Western Social Sci. Assn., So. Polit. Sci. Assn., Midwestern Polit. Sci. Assn. Republican. Home: 2215 W 5th St Stillwater OK 74074 Office: Okla State U Dept Polit Sci Stillwater OK 74078

DARDEN, DAVID DOUGLAS, physician; b. Milner, Ga., Oct. 7, 1938; s. John Thomas Darden and Eva Imogene (Burbank) Rethron; divorced; children—David Dwight, Darice Darlyn. B.S. in Pharmacy, St. Louis Coll. of Pharmacy, 1960; D.O., Kirksville Coll. Osteo. Medicine, 1969. Diplomate Nat. Bd. of Examiners for Osteo. Physicians. Intern, Charles E. Still Hosp., Jefferson City, Mo., 1969-70, resident, 1970-71; resident in anesthesiology U. Ala. at Birmingham Med. Ctr., 1971-72; staff anesthesiologist Bradley Meml. Hosp., Cleveland, Tenn., 1972—, chmn. dept. anesthesiology, 1983-85; examining physician Shriners Crippled Children's Hosp., Cleveland, 1981—; pres. Cleveland Anesthesiologists, Inc., 1973—; dir. Tri-State Truss, Cleveland, 1977—, Tri-State Warehouses, Cleveland, 1980—; pharmacist Claxton-Hill Drugs, Macon, Ga., 1961-65. mem. Rep. Senatorial Inner Circle, Washington, 1984—; life mem. Rep. Nat. Com., Washington, 1979—. Mem. Am. Soc. Anesthesiologists, Am. Osteo. Assn., Internat. Anesthesia Research Soc., Tenn. Osteo. Med. Assn., Tenn. Soc. Anesthesiologists, Chattanooga Area Assn. Anesthesiologists (v.p., bd. dirs.). Baptist. Clubs: Cleveland Country, The Walden. Lodges: Masons, Alhambra Temple (Disting. Service award 1981-83). Avocations: earthwatching; certified tree farmer. Home: 1560 Ocoee St NE Cleveland TN 37311 Office: Cleveland Anesthesiologists Inc PO Box 3090 Cleveland TN 37311

DARDEN, GEORGE W., U.S. congressman; b. Hancock County, Ga., Nov. 22, 1943; m. Lillian Budd; children—Christy, George. A.B., U. Ga., 1965, J.D., 1967. Asst. dist. atty. Cobb County, Ga., 1968-72, dist. atty., 1973-77; sole practice law, from 1977; mem. Ga. Ho. of Reps., 1980-83; mem. 99th U.S. Congress from 7th dist. Ga., 1985—. Mem. Cobb County C. of C., Paulding County C. of C. Office: US House of Representatives Office of House Members Washington DC 20515*

DARDEN, JOHN WALDON, III, jewelry company executive; b. Conway, S.C., Dec. 15, 1945; s. John Waldon, Jr., and Hannah Ross (Smith) D.; B.S. in Bus., U. S.C., 1969; Diamond certificate Gemological Inst. Am., 1977; student Holland Sch. for Jewelers, 1976; m. Susan Ann Wright, Nov. 18, 1971; children—Stuart L., Elizabeth Ross. With Darden's Jewelers, 1969—, mgr., Lancaster, S.C., 1969-73. mgr., Conway, S.C., 1973-74, mgr., Myrtle Beach, S.C., 1974-75, pres. Darden's Jewelers of Conway, Myrtle Beach, Lancaster, and Georgetown, 1975—; pres. Jewelry Outlet, Goldcrafters Outlet, Spartansburg, S.C.; master jeweler Holland Sch. for Jewelers; cons. Nat. Profl. Jewelers Inst. Commr. housing Conway Housing Authority; bd. dirs. Conway Downtown Council. Mem. Conway C. of C., S.C. Mchts. Assn. (past pres.), Outlet Park Mchts. Assn. (pres.), S.C. Retail Jewelers Assn. (pres. 1975-76, 76-77), Retail Jewelers Am. (council of affiliated services), Am. Gem Soc. (registered jeweler), Lancaster Jaycees (bd. dirs., state dir.). Democrat. Methodist (chmn. adminstrv. bd., fin. com.). Clubs: Lancaster Toastmasters, Conway Lions (dir.). Home: 907 Lakeside Dr Conway SC 29526 Office: 331 Main St Conway SC 29526

DARDEN, SUE EAGLES, library executive; b. Miami, Fla., Aug. 13, 1943; d. Archie Yelverton and Bobbie (Jones) Eagles; m. Paul Fisher Darden, Jr., Aug. 24, 1969 (dec. 1978). B.A., Atlantic Christian Coll., 1965; M.L.S., U. Tex., 1970. Cert. librarian, N.C., Va. Instr. Chowan coll., Murfreesboro, N.C., 1966-68; librarian's asst. Albermarle Regional Library, Winton, N.C., 1968-69; br. librarian Multnomah County Pub. Library, Portland, Oreg., 1971-72; asst. dir. Stanly County Pub. Library, Albemarle, N.C., 1973-75, dir., 1976-80; asst. dir. Norfolk Pub. Library, Va., 1980-83, dir., 1983—. Mem. LAMA PRS Friends, Vols. and Advocates Com., 1986-87. Mem. ALA, Southeastern Library Assn. (sec. pub. library sect. 1982-84), Va. Library Assn. (conf. program chmn. 1984, council 1984, 86, chmn. conf. guidelines com. 1985-86). Office: Norfolk Pub Library 301 E City Hall Ave Norfolk VA 23510

DARE, MILTON LEE, development, public relations executive; b. San Benito, Tex., Aug. 13, 1954; s. Milton King and Dorothy Ann (Hahn) D.; m. Sandra Kay Wesch, Aug. 2, 1975; 1 son, Matthew Lee. B.B.A., Southwestern U., Tex., 1976; M.S., Trinity U., San Antonio, 1979. Adminstrv. resident SW Tex. Meth. Hosp., San Antonio, 1977-78, adminstrv. dir. clin. oncology program, 1978-80, dir. pub. relations, 1979-82, dir. devel./pub. relations, 1982—; cons. German Protestant Hosp. Assn., 1982. Mem. Am. Hosp. Assn., Tex. Hosp. Assn., Am. Soc. for Hosp. Mktg. and Pub. Relations (regional adv. council nat. membership com.), Tex. Soc. Hosp. Pub. Relations and Mktg. (Outstanding Ann. Report award 1980, chmn. ann. meeting 1984), Pub. Relations Soc. Am., Nat. Assn. Hosp. Devel., Internat. Assn. Bus. Communicators (award merit 1982, award of excellence 1985), Tex. Pub. Relations Assn., Nat. Soc. Fund Raising Execs. Methodist. Office: 7700 Floyd Curl Dr San Antonio TX 78229

DARENSBOURG, CYNTHIA PEPIN, educator; b. New Orleans, Jan. 29; d. Wendell E. and Mercedes A. (Marrero) Pepin; m. Ulysses J. Darensbourg; children—Christopher Joseph, Maria Angele. B.A., Xavier U., 1971. Mem. sales staff Sears, Roebuck and Co.; clerical and office worker; tchr. elem. sch., New Orleans. Mem. Am. Fedn. Tchrs., La. Fedn. Tchrs., Nat. Assn. Workshop Way Educators, United Tchrs. New Orleans, La. AFL-CIO, New Orleans AFL-CIO, Council Cath. Women.

D'ARIENZO, FREDERICK ANTHONY, mfg. co. exec.; b. Amsterdam, N.Y., Sept. 15, 1934; s. Anthony Ralph and Eva Mary (Slazer) D'A.; B.S. in Mech. Engring., U. Notre Dame, 1956; postgrad. in bus. adminstrn. N.Y. U., 1959-63; children from previous marriage—Peter, Kristina. With internat. mktg. and mgmt. depts., Gen. Electric Co., N.Y.C., San Juan, P.R., Johannesburg, South Africa, Rio de Janeiro, 1958-77, mgr. indsl. and power generation sales, Miami, Fla., 1977-82, mgr. Caribbean and Central Am., 1982—. Pres. Whispering Pines Lake Owners Assn. Served to 1st lt. U.S. Army, 1956-58. Mem. Navy League. Republican. Roman Catholic. Clubs: Emfalini,

Gavea, Dorado Beach. Home: 19420 SW 88th Ct Miami FL 33157 Office: 2801 Ponce De Leon Blvd Coral Gables FL 33134

DARITY, WILLIAM ALEXANDER, JR., economics educator; b. Norfolk, Va., Apr. 19, 1953; s. William Alexander and Evangeline (Royal) D.; m. Andrea Kirsten Mullen, Aug. 30, 1980; 1 child, Aden Lowell Mullen. B.A. magna cum laude, Brown U., 1974; Ph.D. in Econs., MIT, 1978. Instr. econs. Simmons Coll., Boston, 1977-78; asst. prof. econs. U. Tex., Austin, 1978-81, assoc. prof., 1981-83; assoc. prof. U. N.C., Chapel Hill, 1983—; disting. vis. prof. econs. U. Tulsa, 1984; vis. scholar Fed. Res., Washington, 1984; staff economist Nat. Urban League, Washington, 1980. Editor: Labor Economics; Modern Views, 1984. Contbr. articles to profl. jours. Marshall scholar, 1974; Danforth fellow, 1974. Mem. Am. Econ. Assn., Royal Econ. Soc., So. Econ. Assn. Avocations: black music, running, playing blues harmonica. Office: U NC Dept Econs Chapel Hill NC 27514

DARLAND, JAMES MARION, JR., educational administrator; b. Kingfisher, Okla., Aug. 12, 1930; s. James Marion and Luella Marian (Ball) D.; m. Dorothy Louise Adam, Nov. 24, 1950; children—Melanie Luann Darland Beu, Mark James. B.S. in Edn., Central State U., 1953; M.Ed., U. Tulsa, 1956, Ed.D., 1972. Tchr. Bell Jr. High, Tulsa, 1953-56; tchr., counselor Hamilton Jr. High, Tulsa, 1956-59; counselor Hale High Sch., Tulsa, 1959-64; asst. prin. Meml. Sr. High, Tulsa, 1964-72, prin., 1972-80, East Central Sr. High, Tulsa, 1980—; mem. communications com. Okla. Assn. Secondary Sch. Prins., 1975—. Served to cpl. U.S. Army, 1949-52, Korea. Mem. Tulsa Assn. Secondary Sch. Prins. (sec., treas., v.p., pres.), Okla. Assn. Secondary Sch. Prins. (Outstanding Adminstr. award 1982-83, v.p.), Nat. Assn. Secondary Sch. Prins. (mem. communications com. region 6), Phi Delta Kappa (sec., treas., v.p., pres., 1964-68), Kappa Delta Pi (sec., treas., v.p., pres. 1960-64). Lodge: Rotary (v.p. 1978-79). Avocations: gardening, woodworking, car restoration, fishing, reading, travel. Home: 10742 E 28th Pl Tulsa OK 74128 Office: East Central High Sch 12150 E 11th St Tulsa OK 74128

DARLING, JOHN ROTHBURN, JR., educator, university administrator; b. Holton, Kans., Mar. 30, 1937; s. John Rothburn and Beatrice Noel (Deaver) D.; A.A., Graceland Coll., 1957; B.S., U. Ala., 1959, M.S., 1960; Ph.D., U. Ill., 1967; m. Melva Jean Fears, Aug. 20, 1958; children—Stephen, Cynthia, Gregory. Divisional mgr. J.C. Penney Co., Kansas City, 1960-63; teaching asst. U. Ill., Urbana, 1965-66; asst. prof. mktg. U. Ala., Tuscaloosa, 1966-68; asso. prof. mktg. U. Mo., Columbia, 1968-71; prof. adminstrn., coordinator mktg. Wichita State U., 1971-76; dean, prof. mktg. Coll. Bus. and Adminstrn., So. Ill. U., Carbondale, 1976-81; v.p. acad. affairs and research, prof. internat. bus. Tex. Tech U, Lubbock, 1981—; mktg. research cons. Southwestern Bell, 1970; sr. v.p. Boothe Advt., Wichita, 1972; pres. Bus. Research Assos., Wichita, 1972-80, sr. research cons., 1976-81; spl. cons. FTC, Washington, 1972-75, Dept. Justice, 1973-74, Atty. Gen., State of Kans., 1972-76. Bd. dirs. Outreach Found., Inc., 1973-79, v.p., 1975-77; trustee Graceland Coll., Lamoni, Iowa, 1976-82; mem. mgmt. com. Park Coll., Kansas City, 1976-79. Mem. Am. Assn. Higher Edn., Assn. Research Adminstrs., Internat. Council Small Bus., Am. Mktg. Assn., Acad. Internat. Bus., Am. Econs. Assn., So. Bus. Adminstrn. Assn., So. Mktg. Assn., So. Econs. Assn., Midwest Bus. Adminstrn. Assn., Sales and Mktg. Execs. Internat., Beta Gamma Sigma, Alpha Kappa Psi, Chi Alpha Phi, Alpha Phi Omega, Phi Kappa Phi, Omicron Delta Kappa. Author: (with Harry A. Lipson) Marketing Fundamentals: Text and Cases, 1980. Contbr. articles to profl. jours. Home: 3302 41st St Lubbock TX 79413 Office: Office Acad Affairs Tex Tech U Lubbock TX 79409

DARLING, RICHARD HARRISON, international food service company executive, trust fund executive; b. Pomona, Calif., Feb. 19, 1925; s. Ralph MacIntire and Edith Isabel (Harrison) D.; m. Linda Leigh Truxall, Dec. 27, 1947 (div. 1973); children—Deborah Leigh Darling Blakeney, Susan Vickroy, Jennifer Louise Darling Folmer; Bruce MacIntire; m. 2d, Sybil Joyce Ruland, May 17, 1974. B.S. in Prodn. Mgmt., U. Calif.-Berkeley, 1949; postgrad. Sch. Law South Tex. U., 1956-58. Flanger Matson Nav. Co., 1943; dist. mgr. P.F. Collier & Son, 1947-52; asst. mgr. Rich Plan of Houston, 1952-55, v.p., 1955-67, chief exec. officer, 1955—, pres., chmn., 1967—; with Gen. Provisions Corp. Houston, 1952—, v.p., chief exec. officer, 1952-67, pres., chmn., chief exec. officer, 1967-75 (merged with Rich Plan 1975, now Rich Plan Internat. Corp.) pres., 1983—, also dir. Coach, mgr. Baseball League, Houston, 1964-67; mem. Jr. Dep. Sheriff Mounted Posse, Houston, 1965-75, pres., 1969-70; mem. U.S. Olympic Com. Served with inf. U.S. Army, 1943-46. Decorated 2 Bronze Arrowheads; recipient Gibson Sales award, 1980. Mem. Am. Legion (fin. officer 1966-69), Am. Assn. Meat Processors, U. Calif. Alumni Assn., Lambda Chi Alpha. Republican. Episcopalian. Club: 100 of Houston. Office: 6350 Brookhill Dr Houston TX 77087

DARNALL, LARRY J., petroleum company executive; b. Wichita Falls, Tex., Aug. 8, 1935; s. Joseph Henry and Thalia Alice (Fincher) D.; m. Sharon Kay Gary, Apr. 16, 1960; children—Julie Kay, Stephen Gregory. B.S., U. Tex., 1958. From geologist to v.p. geology Gulf Coast div. Gen. Am. Oil Co., Dallas, 1959-77; exploration mgr. Gulf Coast div. May Petroleum Inc., 1977-79; petroleum geologist, Dallas, 1979-82; pres., geologist Darnall Petroleum, Dallas, 1982—; cons. in field. Served with U.S. Army, 1958-62. Mem. Am. Assn. Petroleum Geologists, Am. Inst. Profl. Geologists, Soc. Ind. Petroleum Exploration, Dallas Geol. Soc., Lafayette Geol. Soc., New Orleans Geol. Soc., Alaska Profl. Hunters Assn. (assoc.), Sigma Gamma Epsilon. Republican. Baptist. Clubs: DAC Country, North Dallas Energy, Engrs. Avocations: hunting, fishing, tennis, golfing, boating. Office: Darnall Petroleum Inc 9400 N Central Expressway Suite 307 LB152 Dallas TX 75231

DARNALL, RAY O., diversified company executive; b. 1923; married. Dept. mgr. J.C. Penney Co., Inc., 1951-61; with Heck's Inc., Nitro, W.Va., 1961—, v.p. ops., 1969-72, asst. to pres., 1972-73, 1st v.p., 1973-79, pres., 1979—, also dir. Office: Heck's Inc Hub Indsl Park Box 158 Nitro WV 25143*

DARNELL, RILEY CARLISLE, state senator; b. Clarksville, Tenn., May 13, 1940; s. Elliott Sinclair and Mary Anita (Whitefield) D.; B.S., Austin Peay State U., 1962; J.D., Vanderbilt U., 1965; m. Mary Penelope Crockarell, June 2, 1963; children—Neil Whitefield, Duncan Edward, Mary Eve, Penelope Joy, Dawson Riley. Admitted to Tenn. bar, 1965; gen. practice, 1965-66, 69—; mem. Tenn. Ho. of Reps. from 67th Dist., 1971-80, treas. house-senate caucus, 1971—, sec. house com. ways and means, chmn. joint house-senate fiscal rev. com., 1975-80; mem. Tenn. State Senate, 1980—, chmn. transp. com., 1982—. Served to capt. JAGC, USAF, 1966-69. Democrat. Mem. ABA, Montgomery County Bar Assn., Tenn. Trial Lawyers, Nat. Conf. State Legislators (jud. task force), Clarksville C. of C. Mem. Ch. of Christ (deacon 1971—). Club: Clarksville Downtown Civitan. Home: 603 Waterloo Clarksville TN 37040 Office: 123 S 3d St Clarksville TN 37040

DARRAGH, WILLIAM ROLAND, JR., insurance executive; b. Middletown, Ohio, Feb. 20, 1929; s. William Roland and Sarah Ruth (Freeze) D.; M. Martha Neely, Feb. 4, 1948 (div. 1966); children—William Roland III, Barbara, Timothy, Lee Patrick; m. 2d Myrna Haines, Aug. 13, 1966; 1 dau., Sarah Maude. Student, So. Meth. U., 1947-48, U. Ala., 1948-50; M.B.A., Loyola Coll.-Balt., 1975. Vice pres. data processing Md. Casualty Ins. Co., Balt., 1967-76, sr. v.p., chief fin., 1976-81; sr. v.p. data processing Am. Gen. Corp., Houston, 1981-82; exec. v.p. Am. Gen., Nashville, 1982—; dir. Nat. Life & Accident Ins. Co., 1983, Life & Casualty Ins. Co. Mem. Mayor's 2000 Today Com., 1983. Served with U.S. Army, 1947-48. Mem. Life Office Mgmt. Assn., Fin. Execs. Inst. Clubs: Hillwood Country, Maryland, Heritage. Office: Am General Center Nashville TN 37250

DARST, WILLIAM MAURY, history educator, journalist; b. Galveston, Tex., Dec. 8, 1937; s. Homer William and Elisabeth (Robertson) D.; B.A., Stephen F. Austin State U., 1961, M.A., 1963; postgrad. Tex. Tech. U., 1970-75, U. Houston, 1975-82; m. Mary Lou Hughes, Apr. 20, 1963; children—Robert Maury, Catharine Fontaine. News reporter Galveston Daily News, 1963-65, religion writer, 1980—; tchr. journalism Ball High Sch., Galveston, 1965-67; instr. history Galveston Coll., 1967—. Mem. vestry Trinity Episcopal Ch., 1974-77; chmn. Galveston County Hist. Commn., 1966-67. Named Most Effective Tchr., Galveston Coll., 1972. Mem. E. Tex. Hist. Assn. (pres. 1974-75), So. Hist. Assn., Tex. Hist. Assn., Tex. Jr. Coll. Tchrs. Assn., Nat. R.R. Hist. Assn. Democrat. Episcopalian. Contbr. articles to profl. jours. Office: 4015 Ave Q Galveston TX 77550

DARTER, CLARENCE LESLIE, JR., education educator; b. Childress, Tex., June 18, 1929; s. Clarence Leslie and Alice Marie (Compton) D.; m. Ada Elizabeth Rogers, Mar. 11, 1950; children—David, Denise, Donna. B.S., Tex. Tech U., 1950, D.Ed., 1961; M.Ed., Trinity U., 1955. Tchr. Roosevelt Rural High Sch., Lubbock, Tex., 1955-56; tchr., counselor, prin. Lubbock pub. schs., 1956-63; staff assoc. Sci. Research Assocs., Lubbock, 1963-66; prof. edn. Midwestern State U., Wichita Falls, Tex., 1966—; mem. evaluating univs. Nat. Council Accreditation of Tchr. Edn., 1972—. Bd. dirs. North Tex. Rehab. Ctr., Wichita Falls, 1979—, Am. Heart Assn., Wichita Falls, 1981—. Served as sgt. USAF, 1951-55. Mem. NEA, Tex. State Tchrs. Assn., Phi Delta Kappa. Mem. Ch. of Christ. Home: 4606 Del Rio Trail Wichita Falls TX 76310

DARTEZ, LOUIS AVERY, typographer, rancher; b. Lafayette, La., Dec. 12, 1925; s. Joseph Avery and Marie (LeBlanc) D.; student in Journalism and Bus. Adminstrn., U. Houston, 1956-59, 62-63; m. Barbara Ann Jackson, Oct. 13, 1951. Engring. clk. Stone & Webster Engring. Corp., Houston, 1946-48; supr. non-tech. sect. Mathieson Chem. Co., Balt., 1949-52; adminstrv. asst. to v.p. dept. engring. Tellepsen Constrn. Co., Houston, 1952-59; founder, owner, operator Dart Type Co., Houston, 1959—; rancher Round Top Farm, Houston; owner Dart Aircraft Leasing & Chartering, Houston, Am. Manor Apts., Houston; partner Greenlea Land Devel., Houston; speaker on small bus. mgmt., typography and communications to sch. groups. Served with USAAF, 1943-46, USAF, 1948-49. Mem. Printing Industries Assn. Houston (pres. 1970-71, award of appreciation and recognition 1974), Nat., Houston (pres. 1974) composition assns., Printing Craftsmen Club, Houston Litho Club, Gen. Aviation Pilots Assn., Attakapas Hist. Soc. Republican. Roman Catholic. Contbr. articles on typography to tech. publs., newspapers; author copyfitting charts; contbr. editor Graphics S.W. Mag., 1968-70; geneal. research, including extensive travel, 1956—. Office: 3313 D'Amico St Houston TX 77019

DARVILLE, RAY LYNN, behavioral sciences educator; b. Port Arthur, Tex., May 1, 1955; s. Roy Brockley and Ruth Evelyn (Strickland) D.; m. Sandy Jean Moore, Oct. 23, 1982; 1 child, Christopher Zachery. B.A., East Tex. Baptist U., 1976; M.A., Stephen F. Austin State U., 1979; Ph.D., North Tex. State U., 1984. Teaching fellow North Tex. State U., Denton, 1979-82, research asst., 1979-84; lectr. U. Tex. at Dallas, Richardson, 1984; asst. prof. dept. behavioral scis. East Tex. Bapt. U., Marshall, 1984—. Author articles. Mem. Am. Sociol. Assn., So. Social Sci. Assn. Baptist. Avocations: golf; tennis. Home: 2209 George Gregg Marshall TX 75670 Office: East Tex Bapt Univ Dept Behavioral Sci Marshall TX 75670

DARWIN, FRED ARRANTS, bus. cons.; b. Chattanooga, May 28, 1913; s. Fred Perry and Alexandra Allen (Arrants) D.; student U. Chattanooga, 1929-31; B.S., U.S. Naval Acad., 1935; M.S., Harvard U., 1936; m. Hope Genung Sparks, Sept. 30, 1939; children—Hope Darwin Beisinger, Fred Arrants. Sr. supr. traffic dept. Western Union Telegraph Corp., Chgo., 1936-41; asst. dir. engring. Hazeltine Electronics Corp., N.Y.C., 1946-49; exec. dir. com. guided missiles research and devel. bd. Dept. Def., Washington, 1949-54; mgr. guided missiles Crosley div. Avco Mfg. Corp., Cin., 1954-56; mgr. missile electronics McDonnell Aircraft Corp., St. Louis, 1956-61, gen. mgr. electronic equipment div., 1961-63; asst. to pres. Librascope group Gen. Precision, Inc., 1963-65; bus. counselor, owner Gen. Bus. Services, Dallas, 1966—; mem. spl. com. radio tech. commn. for aeros. Dept. State, Dept. Navy, 1946; cons. del. UN Provisional Internat. Civil Aviation Orgn., 1946. Served to comdr. USNR, 1941-46. Recipient citations Sec. Navy, USAAF. Mem. IEEE, Aero. Weights Engrs., Harvard Grad. Soc., E. Dallas C. of C., Naval Acad. Alumni Assn., Alpha Lambda Tau. Conservative Democrat. Presbyterian. Club: Harvard. Contbr. articles to profl. jours.; originator word transponder; inventor multiple-coincidence mixer used in pulse-train coding. Home: 11805 Neering Dr Dallas TX 75218

DARWIN, JAMES GRANVILLE, manufacturing company official; b. McCaskill, Ark., Sept. 24, 1933; s. Jessie Granville and Sara Louise (Gentry) D.; m. Harriett Ann Wade, June 23, 1954; children—Stephen, Mark, Diane. B.S., U. Ark.-Fayetteville, 1955; postgrad. U. Ark. Med. Ctr., 1959-60. With Polyvend Inc., Conway, Ark., 1977—, adminstrv. mgr. contracts div., export mgr., 1980—, mktg. services mgr., 1983—. Served with U.S. Army, 1955. Home: 1905 Berry Pl Dr Conway AR 72032 Office: German Ln Conway AR 72032

DASGUPTA, AMIT, metallurgist; b. Patna, India, Oct. 29, 1939; s. Pramatha Nath and Indumati (Sen) DasG.; m. Gyllis Heine, July 6, 1968; 1 child, Hindola. B.Sc., Patna U., 1958; B.Tech. Met. Engr., Indian Inst. Tech., Kharagpur, 1962, M.Tech., 1963; Ph.D. in Materials Sci., Cornell U., 1971. Lectr. metall. engring. Indian Inst. Tech., Kharagpur, 1963-65; asst. prof. metal physics U. Goettingen (W.Ger.), 1971-74; sr. scientist Nuclear Research Center, Karlsruhe, W.Ger., 1974-75; vis. prof. physics U. Basel (Switzerland), 1980-81; scientist Oak Ridge Nat. Lab., 1975—; adj. prof. metallurgy and materials engring. Lehigh U., Bethlehem, Pa., 1980—. Indian Inst. Tech. fellow, 1958-63. Mem. Metall. Soc. AIME, Am. Phys. Soc. Contbr. articles to profl. jours. Home: 1233 Southbreeze Circle Knoxville TN 37919 Office: PO Box X Oak Ridge Nat Lab Oak Ridge TN 37831

DATTOLO, ALPHONSE ROBERT, lawyer, engineering consultant; b. Bklyn., Aug. 5, 1946; s. Carmine Louis and Anna (Cardile) D.; m. Virginia Eileen Lensch, Feb. 14, 1970; children—Bonnie Lynn, Jennifer Ann, Dianne Mari. B.S.I.E., Poly. Inst. Bklyn., 1968; M.S.I.E., Ga. Inst. Tech., 1977; J.D., Woodrow Wilson Coll. Law, 1980. Bar: Ga. 1980. Indsl. engr. JFD Electronics, Bklyn., 1968-69; safety engr. Gen. Services Adminstrn., Atlanta, 1972-80; ptnr. Davis & Dattolo, Riverdale, Ga., 1980—; asst. regional counsel GSA, Atlanta, 1982—; pres. S&D Assocs., Ltd., Ellenwood, Ga., 1977—; v.p., dir. Concepts VI, Inc., Doraville, Ga., 1984—. Coordinator ARC, Atlanta, 1984. Served to capt. U.S. Army, 1969-72. Mem. Am. Soc. Safety Engrs., ABA, Am. Trial Lawyers Assn., Ga. Bar Assn. Democrat. Roman Catholic. Lodge: Kiwanis (bd. dirs. 1984—). Home: 6192 Stillwater Dr Riverdale GA 30274 Office: GSA Office Regional Counsel 75 Spring St SW Atlanta GA 30303

DAUBENMIRE, REXFORD, botanist; b. Coldwater, Ohio, Dec. 12, 1909; s. George Franklin and Ethel Rebecca (Freidline) D.; m. Evelyn Jean Boomer, May 20, 1938; B.S., Butler U., 1930; M.S., U. Colo., 1932; Ph.D., U. Minn., 1935. Asst. prof. botany, U. Tenn.-Knoxville, 1935-36, U. Idaho, Moscow, 1936-46; asst. prof. to prof. botany Wash. State U., Pullman, 1946-75; cons. in field, lectr. numerous univs. Author: Plants and Environment, 1947; Plant Communities, 1968; Plant Geography, 1978. Recipient Barrington Moore Meml. award Soc. Am. Foresters, 1980. Mem. Assn. Southeastern Biologists, N.W. Sci. Assn. (hon. life mem.), Ecol. Soc. Am. (hon. life mem., pres. 1966-67), Sigma Xi, Phi Kappa Phi. Avocations: horticulture, fishing, jewelry making, square dancing. Home and Office: 626 Interlochen Dr Sorrento FL 32776

DAUGHDRILL, JAMES HAROLD, JR., college president; b. LaGrange, Ga., Apr. 25, 1934; s. James Harold and Louisa Coffee (Dozier) D.; student Davidson Coll., 1952-54; A.B., Emory U., 1956; D.D., Davidson Coll., 1973; B.D., M.Div., Columbia Theol. Sem., 1967; m. Elizabeth Anne Gay, June 26, 1954; children—James Harold, Louisa Risha, Elizabeth Gay. Ordained to ministry Presbyn. Ch. U.S., 1967; pres. Kingston Mills, Inc., Cartersville, Ga., 1956-64; minister St. Andrews Presbyn. Ch., Little Rock, 1967-70; sec. stewardship Presbyn. Ch. of U.S., 1970-73; pres. Rhodes Coll., Memphis, 1973—; dir. Buckman Labs., Inc. Trustee Frank E. Seidman Award Fedn.; past trustee Hutchison Sch. Brooks Meml. Art Gallery; past bd. dirs. Tenn. Student Assistance Corp.; bd. dirs. Memphis chpt. NCCJ, Liberty Bowl Football Classic, Memphis U. Sch. Mem. Econ. Club Memphis, Tenn. Council Pvt. Colls (past chmn.), Assn. Presbyn. Colls. (dir., past pres.), Assn. Am. Colls. (dir., vice chmn.), Tenn. Ind. Colls. Assn. (dir.), Coll. Athletic Conf. (past pres.), Young Pres. Orgn., So. Coll. Univ. Union (past chmn.), World Bus. Council, Chief Execs. Orgn. Omicron Delta Kappa. Clubs: Rotary of Memphis (past dir.), Memphis Country; Univ. (N.Y.C.). Author: Man Talk, 1972; assoc. editor Presbyterian Outlook, 1978. Home: 671 West Dr Memphis TN 38112 Office: 2000 N Parkway Memphis TN 38112

DAUGHERTY, BILLY JOE, banker; b. Timpson, Tex., Jan. 31, 1923; s. David Albert and Kate (Smith) D.; grad. Tyler Comml. Coll., 1942; postgrad. So. State Coll., 1945-47; grad. Southwestern Grad. Sch. Banking, So. Meth. U., 1969; student Nat. Credit Lending Sch., U. Okla., 1969; m. Martha Carroum, May 14, 1942; children—Stephen Michael, Tony Fares, Kathryn Love. Asst. v.p., asst. trust officer First Nat. Bank Magnolia (Ark.), 1947-52; plant acct. Republic Steel Corp., Magnolia, 1953-54; with Union Nat. Bank, Little Rock, 1954-70, v.p., cashier, 1965-70; exec. v.p., dir., sec. to bd. dirs. First State Bank & Trust Co., Conway, Ark., 1970-73, pres., dir., sec. to bd. dirs., 1973—. Dir. Ark. Banking Sch. Mem. adv. bd. Salvation Army, 1967-70; bd. dirs. Met. YMCA, Little Rock, 1966-70; chmn. Columbia chpt. ARC, Magnolia, 1952; mem. budget com. United Fund Pulaski County (Ark.), 1962-65; treas. City Beautiful Com. Little Rock, 1965-67; treas. Ark. br. Am. Assn. UN, 1965-67; pres. Heart of Ark. Travel Assn., 1971-74; pres., dir. United Fund of Faulkner County, 1972; state treas. Radio Free Europe, 1960-72; chmn. Faulkner County Heart Fund Campaign, 1971. Sec. to bd. dirs., trustee Union Nat. Found.; bd. dirs. Ark. Heart Assn., 1971-75, chmn. bd., 1975-77; trustee Ark. Baptist Med. Center, sec.-treas., 1965-69; bd. dirs. Am. Heart Assn., Goodwill Industries Ark., 1975—; treas. Goodwill Industries Ark., 1984—. Served with USAAF, 1943-46. Mem. Little Rock Clearing House Assn. (v.p. 1969, pres. 1965-66, sec.-treas. 1967-68), Ark. Bankers Assn. (pres. jr. bankers sect. 1950; bank dirs. adv. com. 1971-72, dir. 1979-82), Conway C. of C. (pres. 1975). Baptist (supt. Sunday sch.; chmn. bldg. com. 1964-66; chmn. bd. deacons 1962-63; mem. finance com. 1960-68, chmn. stewardship com. 1968). Clubs: Top of Rock (dir. 1969-70); Little Rock; Conway Country; Pleasant Valley Country; Western Hills Country (dir., sec. 1968-69). Home: 22 Riviera Dr Conway AR 72032 Office: First State Bank & Trust Co Harkrider Pl Conway AR 72032

DAUGHERTY, HARRY MALONE, business consultant; b. Columbus, Miss., Sept. 27, 1944; s. Harry Miller, Jr., and Oma Thankful (Everrett) D.; m. Margaret Jane Vice, Mar. 29, 1980; 1 dau., Hollie Anna. B.S.B.A., U. Tenn.-Knoxville, 1966; M.B.A., Emory U., 1967. Staff asst. to regional v.p. Texaco, Inc., Atlanta, 1967-68; v.p. dir. Gen. Oils, Inc., Chattanooga, 1969-78; spl. cons. agt. Northwestern Mut. Life, Chattanooga, 1978-81; pres. Wood Stores & Things Energy Store/Daugherty Energy Store, Chattanooga, 1981-83; spl. cons. Concrete Forms Corp., Chattanooga, 1982-84; owner, cons. Gen. Bus. Services/Daugherty Bus. Counselors, Chattanooga, 1984—; pres. Daugherty Mktg. Assocs.; pres. Heritage House Toys, 1984—, Windy Top Farms. Served with USAR, 1967-70, 76. Office: 4600 Hixson Pike Suite N Chattanooga TN 37343

DAUGHERTY, KENNETH EARL, research company executive, educator; b. Pitts., Dec. 27, 1938; s. Thomas Hill and Laura Elizabeth (Schuda) D.; B.S. in Chemistry, Carnegie-Mellon U., 1960; Ph.D. in Analytical Chemistry (DuPont, Shell Oil, Standard Oil, NSF fellow), U. Wash., 1964; M. Bus. Econs., Claremont Grad. Sch., 1971; m. Joan Kay Ogrosky, Dec. 22, 1961; children—Brian Earl, Kirsten Kay. Chemist, Marbon Chem.-Borg Warner, Washington, W.Va., 1960; research chemist Rohm and Haas Corp., Bristol, Pa., 1964; group leader, sr. staff Amcord, Riverside, Calif., 1966-71; assoc. prof. chemistry U. Pitts., 1971-73; dir. research and devel. Gen. Portland Inc., Dallas, 1973-77; dir. energy and materials sci. Inst. Applied Scis., North Tex. State U., Denton, 1977-79, prof. chemistry, 1979—, chmn. analytical div., 1980—, pres. KEDS Inc., KD Cons., 1977—; owner TRAC Labs., Denton, 1981—; adj. prof. chemistry U. Pitts., 1973—, N. Tex. State U., Denton, 1974—; adj. faculty Army Command and Gen. Staff Coll., 1983—; cons. in field. Served to col. AUS, 1964-66, Res., 1966—. Decorated Army Commendation medal, Army Achievement medal. Fellow Am. Inst. Chemists; mem. Research Soc. Am., ASTM, Rilem, Nat. (transp. research bd.), N.Y. acads. scis., Am. Ceramic Soc. (program chmn. 1986), Am. Chem. Soc. (chpt. pres. 1960, chmn. Dallas-Ft. Worth 1986), Applied Spectroscopy Soc., Soc. Petroleum Engrs., Soc. Plastics Engrs., Sigma Xi, Pi Kappa Alpha, Omicron Delta Epsilon, Phi Lambda Upsilon, Alpha Chi Sigma. Republican. Methodist. Clubs: Masons (32 deg.), Shriners, Rotary. Author numerous publs. in field. Patentee in field. Home: 317 Lakeland Dr Lewisville TX 75067 Office: Dept Chemistry North Tex State U Denton TX 76203 also TRAC Labs Inc 113 Cedar St Denton TX 76201

DAUGHTRY, JOHN PERSON, mathematics educator; b. Raleigh, N.C., Oct. 21, 1947; s. John Person and Margaret (Smith) D.; m. Sue Barden, May 23, 1970; B.S., U. N.C.-Chapel Hill, 1970; Ph.D., U. Va.-Charlottesville, 1973. Asst. prof. math. Sweet Briar Coll., Va., 1973-81, assoc. prof., 1981-83; assoc. prof. East Carolina U., Greenville, N.C., 1983—. Contbr. articles to profl. publs. Office: Dept Math East Carolina U Greenville NC 27834

DAUGHTRY, STEPHEN DARYL, publisher; b. Goldsboro, N.C., May 13, 1953; s. Thomas L. and Thelma Grace (Walston) D.; m. Mary Susan Allen, May 28, 1972; children—Margaux Erin, Robin Leah. Student pub. schs., Farmville, N.C. Profl. musician and singer, 1969-71, 78; pres. Praisentations, 1975-77; editor Leisure Guide Mag., 1972-77, Carolina Farmer Mag., 1979-80, Va. State Crime Clinic Mag., 1981-82, S.C. Law Enforcement Officers Assn. Mag., 1980-81; editor, pub. So. Sportsman Mag., 1982-84, Pitt-Greenville Times, 1981—, N.C. Law Enforcement Officers Assn. Jour., 1981-83; pres. Down East Pubs., Inc., Farmville, N.C., 1982-84; dir. Washington Daily News; pres. Daryl Daughtry Assocs., 1984—. Mem. So. Sporting Soc. (pres.). Rec. album Daryl Daughtry-Beauty for Ashes, 1978. Office: PO Box 8373 Greenville NC 27835

DAUSSMAN, GROVER FREDERICK, consulting engineer; b. Newburgh, Ind., May 6, 1919; s. Grover Cleveland and Madeline (Springer) D.; student U. Cin., 1936-38; Carnegie Inst. Tech., 1944-45, George Washington U., 1948-56; B.S. in Elec. Engring., U. Ala., 1963, postgrad., 1963-64, 77; postgrad. Indsl. Coll. Armed Forces, 1955, 63; Ph.D. (hon.), Hamilton State U., 1973; m. Elli Margrite Kilian, Dec. 27, 1941; children—Cynthia Louise Daussman Quinn, Judith Ann, Margaret Elizabeth Daussman Cooper. Coop. engr. Sunbeam Elec. Mfg. Co., Evansville, Ind., 1936-38; engr. draftsman Phila. Navy Yard, 1941-42; resident engr. supr. shipbldg. USN, Neville Island, Pa., 1942-45; engr. Pearl Harbor Navy Yard, 1945-48; with Bur. Ships, USN, Washington, 1948-56; head Guidance and Control Tech. Liaison Sect., Army Ballistic Missile Agy., Huntsville, Ala., 1956-58, chief program coordination Office Guidance and Control Lab., 1958-60; chief program coordination Office Astrionics Lab., Marshall Space Flight Center, Huntsville, 1960-62, staff asst. for advanced research and tech. Astrionics Lab., 1962-70; engring. cons., 1970—; project dir. fallout shelter surveys Mil. Dept. Tenn., 1971-73; head drafting dept. Alverson-Draughon Coll., Huntsville, Ala., 1974-77; instr. Ala. Christian Coll., 1977-79; engring. draftsman Reisz Engring. Co., Huntsville, 1979; chief engr. Sheraton Motor Inn, Huntsville, 1979; sr. engr. Sperry Support Services, 1980; assoc. Techn-Core Profls., Huntsville, 1980-81; elec. engr. Reisz Engring., Huntsville, 1981—. Recipient cert. Hon. Service, USN, 1945; Performance Award certificate U.S. Army, 1960; NASA Apollo Achievement award, 1969. Registered profl. engr., Ala., Va., D.C. Fellow Explorers Club; mem. U. Ala. Alumni Assn., Ala. (Engr. of Yr. award 1968, 82, chpt. pres. 1966-67, state dir. 1962-65, 68-71, 85-86), Nat. socs. profl. engrs., IEEE (life sr. mem., sect. chmn. N.Ala. sect. 1961-62, engring. mgmt. chpt. chmn. 1964-65, mem. adminstrv. com. engring. mgmt. soc. 1966—, sec. soc. 1969—, Engr. of Yr. award 1969, research com. 1965-67, dir. S.E. region, mem. inst. bd. dirs. 1972-73, Centennial medal), AAAS, Am. Def. Preparedness Assn. (post dir. Tenn. Valley), AIAA, Am. Soc. Naval Engrs., Missile, Space and Range Pioneers (life mem.), U.S. Naval Inst., Assn. U.S. Army, Internat. Platform Assn., Huntsville Assn. Tech. Socs. (sec. 1969-71, v.p., dir.), Marshall Space Flight Center Retirement Assn. (pres. 1974—), Hellenic Profl. Assn. Am. (hon.). Democrat. Mem. United Ch. of Christ (sec. ch. council 1965-66, vice moderator Ala-Tenn. Assn. 1965-68, bd. dirs. S.E. conv. 1965-66). Home: 1910 Colice Rd SE Huntsville AL 35801 Office: 2607 Leeman Ferry Rd Huntsville AL 35805

DAUTEN, DALE ALAN, research consultant, writer; b. Fairfield, Iowa, Sept. 30, 1950; s. Joel John and Geraldine Ann (Muck) D.; m. Sandra Kelley, Aug. 10, 1979; children—Hilary Michaela, Trevor Dale. B.S. in Econs., Ariz. State U., 1971, M.S. in Econs., 1972; postgrad. Stanford U., 1972-73. Research analyst AMERCO, Phoenix, 1973-75; research mgr. Armour-Dial Co., Phoenix, 1975-77; research dir. Consumer Behavior Ctr., Dallas, 1978; v.p. Hollander Assocs., Atlanta, 1978-80; pres. Research Resources, Atlanta, 1980—. Author: Quitting, 1980; Out of Line, 1984; contbr. articles to profl. jours., city mags., gen. interest pubs. Mem. Am. Mktg. Assn. Club: Mensa. Home: 336 Herrington Dr Atlanta GA 30342

DAVALL, SARAH DIANE, elementary educator; b. Asheville, N.C., Feb. 2, 1953; d. Ted Valentine and Martha Evageline (Sherlin) Davall. B.S. in Edn. magna cum laude, Western Caroline U., 1976. Tchr. elem. schs., Buncombe County, N.C., 1976—, also coach. Mem. NEA, Educators for Social Responsibility. Democrat. Mem. Episcopal Ch. of Redeemer. Club: Cumberland Women's Circle, Peace Links. Home: 82 Cumberland Ave Asheville NC 28801

DAVANI, BAHMAN FAGHAIE, telecommunication engineer; b. Abadan, Iran, Mar. 21, 1953; came to U.S., 1976; s. Mohammed Faghaie and Bomanjan (Piltan) D.; B.Sc. in Applied Math., U. Tehran, Iran, 1975; M.Sc. in Applied Math., Fla. Inst. Tech., 1977, M.Sc. in Computer Sci., 1978; Ph.D. (A.B.D.)

in Computer Sci., So. Meth. U., 1982. Instr. U. Tehran, 1975-76; research asst. So. Meth. U., Dallas, 1978-81; mem. tech. staff mem. Rockwell Internat., Richardson, Tex., 1979—. Free U. Iran scholar, 1976-79. Mem. IEEE, Assn. Computing Machinery, Math. Assn. Am., Nat. Mgmt. Assn. (cert. in mgmt. 1985). Avocation: soccer. Home: 4417 Denver Dr Plano TX 75075

DAVENPORT, FOUNTAIN ST. CLAIR, electronic engineer; b. Harmony, N.C., Jan. 16, 1914; s. Dennis F. and Margaret E. (Winfield) D.; B.S., U. Miami, 1950; postgrad. U. Miami, U. Balt., Johns Hopkins, U. Fla., Rollins Coll., Brevard Engring. Coll., 1952-64; M.S., Fla. Inst. Tech., 1970; m. Jane Helena Hermann, June 11, 1948 (dec. Sept. 1973); 1 dau., Sylvia Jane; m. Joyce Allen Huff, Mar. 16, 1974 (dec. 1983); m. 3d, Florence Cereceda Ryan, May 19, 1985. Engr., Bendix Aviation Corp., Towson, Md., 1951-53; project engr. Vitro Labs., Eglin AFB, Fla., 1953-55; engr. A, RCA Missile Test Project, Patrick AFB, Fla., 1955-60; supr. radar engring., guided missiles range div. Pan Am. World Airways, Inc., Patrick AFB, Fla., 1960-65, sr. systems engr. Aerospace Services Div., 1965-77; individual practice cons. engring., 1977-82; pres. Davenport Enterprises, Inc., 1982—. Cons. N.R.C., Churchill Research Range, Man., Can., 1966-67; faculty Fla. Inst. Tech., 1958-60, 62-63, mem. edn. com., 1964, adj. faculty physics and aerospace scis., 1979—. Mem. Friends Brevard Assn. for Advancement of Blind. Served with USN, 1934-37; with USNR, 1942-45. Life mem. Friends Melbourne Library. Mem. IEEE, Am. Defense Preparedness Assn., Assn. Physics Tchr., (life), Missile and Space Pioneers (life), Assn. Physics Tchrs., Soc. Wireless Pioneers (life). Lodge: Mason (32 deg.). Home: 2110 Shannon Ave Indialantic FL 32903

DAVENPORT, GEORGE KEEFE, computer company executive; b. N.Y.C., Dec. 30, 1937; s. Fred Morris and Dorothy Frances (Keefe) D.; B.A., Lehigh U., 1959; B.S. in Indsl. Mgmt., C.W. Post Coll., 1962; cert. orgn. devel. W. Ga. Coll., 1978; m. Phyllis Joan Dallin, Oct. 12, 1963; children—Dierdre Kirsten, Christopher Prescott. Indsl. engr., Grumman Aircraft Co., Bethpage, N.Y., 1955-62; sales rep. IBM, Jacksonville, Fla., 1962-67; prin. engr. Reliability Engring. Bendix Co., Cape Kennedy, Fla., 1967-70; area mgr. Xerox Data Systems, Jacksonville, 1970-76; br. mktg. mgr. energy Sperry Univac Co., Bellaire, Tex., 1976-80; partner Norr Davenport-World Wide Fin. Services; dir. Advanced Communications Inc.; chmn. West Main Corp., Site Improvers, Inc., G.K. Davenport, Inc., Haglund Boat Works, Inc.; asso. prof. indsl mgmt. U. Fla., Brevard Coll., 1967-72; mem. quality control and reliability adv. com. Brevard Jr. Coll., Cape Kennedy, 1967-72; mem. fund raising com. 5th Congl. Dist. Fla., 1970. Recipient New Technology Utilization award NASA, 1969. Mem. Am. Mgmt. Assn., Instrument Soc. Am., Data Processing Mgmt. Assn., Am. Inst. Indsl. Engrs., Soc. Am. Mil. Engrs. Methodist. Clubs: Ponte Vedra (Jacksonville, Fla.); Univ. (Houston). Author: Statistical Calibration, 1967; Reliability Objectives, 1970; Introduction to Data Processing, 1971, others; contbr. articles to profl. jours. Home: 11415 Beacon Dr Jacksonville FL 32225 Office: 38 E Union St Jacksonville FL 32202

DAVENPORT, JOHN WESLEY, life insurance company executive; b. Dallas, Apr. 26, 1941; s. Claude Franklyn and Nancy Belle Davenport; m. Alicia Ann Marshaus, July 15, 1978; children—Lea Michelle, Heather Kathleen. B.A. in Psychology, Tex. Tech U., 1963; M.Fin. Services, Am. Coll., 1980. C.L.U.; chartered fin. cons. Adminstrv. asst. Prudential Ins. Co., Houston, 1968-69; dept. mgr. Target Stores, Inc., Houston, 1969-70; salesman Am. Gen. Life Ins. Co., Houston, 1970-71, 2d v.p., dir. advanced underwriting, 1983-85, 2d v.p. agy. computer support, 1985—; div. mgr. Prudential Ins. Co., St. Louis, 1971-73; dir. advanced underwriting Gen. Am. Life Ins. Co., St. Louis, 1973-79; dir. mktg. Multiple Funding Corp., N.Y.C., 1979-82; dir. mktg. services Phila. Life Ins. Co., 1982-83; guest lectr. St. Louis U.; adj. faculty St. Louis Community Colls. Served with U.S. Army, 1963-68. Mem. Am. Soc. C.L.U.s, Nat. Assn. Life Underwriters, Nat. Space Inst., Assn. for Advanced Life Underwriting, Mensa. Presbyterian. Home: 2018 Ottawa Houston TX 77043 Office: 2727 Allen Pkwy Houston TX 77019

DAVENPORT, ROY WILLIS, health and safety company sales executive; b. Greenville, S.C., July 3, 1947; s. John Willis and Catherine Lucille (Browning) D.; m. Carolyn Tommie Moore, June 6, 1969; children—John Byars, Thomas Scott, Heather Laine. A.A. in Mgmt. Sci., Greenville Tech. Coll., 1975; B.A., Lander Coll., 1969. Tchr., coach Greenville County Sch. Dist., S.C., 1969-70; dir. community programs United Speech and Hearing Clinic, Greenville, 1972-76; v.p. sales and ops. ELB/Monitor, Inc., Greenville, 1976—. Songwriter; contbr. articles to profl. jours. Vice-pres. Young Republicans, Greenwood, S.C., 1967; chmn. fund raising com. Sertoma Internat., Greenville, 1974. Served with U.S. Army, 1970-72. Mem. Am. Soc. Safety Engrs., Council Accreditation Hearing Conservation. Methodist. Club: Songwriter (chmn. pub. relations com. 1984-85). Avocations: songwriting; guitar; sports; reading. Home: 7 Cavendish Close Taylors SC 29687 Office: ELB/Monitor Inc 110 Laurens Rd Greenville SC 29607

DAVENPORT, WILLIAM HAROLD, mathematics educator; b. Jackson, Tenn., Dec. 21, 1935; s. John Heron and Mary (Troutt) D.; m. Mary Janice Johnson, Mar. 18, 1960; children—Mark Edson, Amber Yvette; m. Sandra Elaine Holloway, July 30, 1973; children—William Harold II, David Carleton, Bennett John Joseph. B.S., U. Tenn., 1962; M.S., Tex. A&M U., 1966; Ph.D. in Math., U. Ala., 1971. Aerospace technologist NASA Manned Spacecraft Ctr., Houston, 1962-64; research mathematician Brown Engring. Co., Huntsville, Ala., 1966-67; teaching fellow, instr. math. U. Ala., University, 1967-71; mathematician U.S. Army Missile Command, Huntsville, 1971-72; asst. prof. math. U. Petroleum and Minerals, Dhahran, Saudi Arabia, 1972-77, Columbus Coll., Ga., 1977-81; assoc. prof. U. Ark., Little Rock, 1981—. Served with USN, 1954-58. Mem. Am. Math. Soc., Sigma Pi Sigma, Phi Kappa Phi, Pi Mu Epsilon. Roman Catholic. Avocation: tennis. Home: 7912 W 25th St Little Rock AR 72204 Office: U Ark Math Dept Little Rock AR 72204

DAVID, YADIN, biomedical engineer, health care technology consultant; b. Haifa, Israel, Nov. 25, 1946; came to U.S., 1972, naturalized, 1982; s. Bezalel and Ziona (Kovalsky) D.; m. Becky Lask, Jan. 23, 1968; children—Tal, Daniel. B.Sc., W.Va. U., 1974, M.Sc., 1975, Ph.D., 1983. Registered profl. engr., Tex. Dir. biomedical engring. W.Va. U. Hosp., Morgantown, 1976-82; asst. prof. W.Va. U. Med. Sch., Morgantown, 1979-82; pres. TALDAN Consultants, Houston, 1976—; dir. biomedical instrumentation St. Luke's Episcopal Hosp., Tex. Children's Hosp., Tex. Heart Inst., all Houston, 1982—; adj. assoc. prof. anesthesia dept. U. Tex. Med. Sci. Ctr., Houston, 1984—; program chmn. Clin. Engring. Symposium ann. confs., 1983, 84, 85. Contbr. articles to tech. jours. Patentee hand held server terminal. Advisor Bnai Brith Youth Orgn., Morgantown, 1981-82. Grantee W.Va. U., 1976. Mem. IEEE (rep. to standards com. 1978—), Engring. in Medicine and Biology (chmn. clin. engring. com. 1983—), Assn. Advancement Med. Instrumentation, Eta Kappa Nu. Office: Biomedical Instrumentation Dept St Luke's Episcopal Hosp PO Box 20269 Houston TX 77225

DAVIDS, ROBERT NORMAN, petroleum exploration geologist; b. Elizabeth, N.J., Apr. 27, 1938; s. William Scheible and Anna Elizabeth (Backhaus) D.; A.B. in Geology, U. Va., 1960; M.S., Rutgers U., 1963, Ph.D., 1966; m. Carol Ann Landauer, Apr. 20, 1957; 1 son, Robert Norman. With Exxon Co. USA, 1966—, micropaleontologist, New Orleans, 1965-71, uranium geologist, Denver, 1971-72, Albuquerque, 1972-78, supervisory geologist Tex. area exploration, Corpus Christi, 1978-80, N.W. area supr., 1981, dist. geologist so. dist., New Orleans, 1981-84, div. exploration tng. coordinator, spl. trades unit geologist, 1984—. Formerly active local Little League Baseball, Jr. Achievement. NSF grad. fellow, 1964-65. Mem. Geol. Soc. Am., AIME, Soc. Econ. Paleontologists and Mineralogists (treas. Gulf Coast sect. 1971), Am. Assn. Petroleum Geologists, Explorers Club, Sigma Xi, Beta Theta Pi. Author papers. Home: 18 Grand Canyon Dr New Orleans LA 70114 Office: PO Box 61812 New Orleans LA 70161

DAVIDSON, DAVID G., petroleum company executive; b. 1924. B.S., Stanford U., 1949, M.S., 1950. With Union Oil Co. of Calif., 1950-66; with Kern County Refinery, Inc., 1966-73; chmn. bd., chief exec. officer, pres. Edgington Oil Co., Inc., 1974-82; pres., chief operating officer, dir., Hill Petroleum Co., Houston. Served with USN, 1943-46. Address: Hill Petroleum Co 921 Main St Houston TX 77002*

DAVIDSON, DOROTHY ANN, educator; b. LaGrange, Ga., July 22 1947; d. Haywood and Mamie Catherine (Hubbard) D. B.S., Fort Valley State Coll., 1969, postgrad., 1976—. Tchr., Bellevue Elem. Sch., Macon, 1969—; math coordinator, tutor Hepzibath Children's Home. Mini-reading grantee State of Ga., 1972; recipient Exceptional Service awards Bibb Assn. Educators, 1974-76; award Mus. Arts and Scis., 1970, 75. Mem. NEA, Ga. Assn. Educators, Bibb Assn. Educators, Big Bros. and Big Sister Orgn. Methodist. Clubs: Usher Bd., Holsey Jr. Home: 3775 Houston Ave Apt 2-C Macon GA 31206

DAVIDSON, GLENN KIRK, management consultant; b. Cleve., May 31, 1954; s. Dalwyn Robert and Georganna Katherine (Sharp) D.; m. Carol Ann Bauer, Dec. 20, 1981. B.A., Am. U., 1975; M.A., George Washington U., 1983. Info. specialist, Joint Congl. Com. on Arrangements for Commemoration of Bicentennial, Washington, 1976; staff asst. to U.S. Rep. Yvonne Burke, Washington, 1976-77; legis. dir. to U.S. Rep. Ronald M. Mottl, Washington, 1977-80; dir. policy analysis and communications Santa Fe Corp., Alexandria, Va., 1980—; Mem. nat. advt. network John H. Glenn Presdl. Com. Named to Jaycee's Outstanding Young Men Am., 1983. Mem. Am. Polit. Sci. Assn., Pub. Relations Soc. Am., Am. Harp Soc. Editor: Santa Fe Abstract, 1982—. Office: 4660 Kenmore Ave Suite 900 Alexandria VA 22304

DAVIDSON, GORDON BYRON, lawyer; b. Louisville, June 24, 1926; s. Paul Byron and Elizabeth (Franz) D.; m. Geraldine B. Geiger, Dec. 21, 1948; children—Sally Burgess, Stuart Gordon. A.B., Centre Coll., 1949; J.D., U. Louisville, 1951; LL.M., Yale, 1952. Asst. Army staff judge advocate of First Army, Governors Island, N.Y., 1952-54; law clk. Sr. Justice Stanley Reed, U.S. Supreme Ct., Washington, 1954; mng. ptnr. Wyatt, Tarrant & Combs, 1955—; lectr. U. Louisville Law Sch., 1958—; dir. Courier-Jour. & Louisville Times Co., WHAS, Inc., Standard Gravure Co., Hermitage Farm, Inc. Pres. Louisville Central Area, Inc., 1971-73; chmn. River City Mall Com., 1973-74, Ky. Cultural Complex Com., 1977-78, Ky. Center for Arts Corp., 1979—, Louisville Devel. Com.; mem. Ky. Derby Festival Com.; mem. Louisville Commn. Fgn. Relations. Bd. dirs., chmn. Norton-Children's Hosps., Inc., Louisville Fund for Arts; trustee Centre Coll., Internat. Center of U. Louisville. Served as cadet midshipman U.S. Mcht. Marine Acad., 1944-45; 1st lt. AUS, 1952-54, Korea. Recipient Louisville Citizen of Yr. award, 1973-74, Mayor's Fleur de Lis award, 1974, Louisville Man of Yr. award, 1980. Fellow Am. Bar Found.; mem. Am. Law Inst., ABA, Ky. Bar Assn. (Outstanding Lawyer award 1984), Louisville Bar Assn., Fed. Bar Assn., Brandeis Soc., Louisville Area C. of C. (v.p., chmn. bd. 1986), Phi Delta Theta, Omicron Delta Kappa, Phi Kappa Phi. Democrat. Presbyn. Clubs: Harmony Landing Country; Jefferson (bd. govs.), Louisville Country (bd. govs.); Tavern; Lawyer's; Pendennis; Delray Beach. Home: 435 Lightfoot Rd Louisville KY 40207 Office: 28th Floor Citizens Plaza Louisville KY 40202

DAVIDSON, JAMES BLAINE, ocean engineering educator, acoustician; b. Oklahoma City, Nov. 10, 1923; s. Richard Blaine and Bessie Lowrance (Greene) D.; m. Anna Ruth Cox, Dec. 18, 1948; children—Annette Jan Davidson Board, Jeannette Ann Davidson McCallum, James Blaine. Student U. Okla., 1941-43; B.S. with distinction, U.S. Naval Acad., 1946; B.Engring. Electronics, U.S. Naval Postgrad. Sch., 1952; M.S. in Applied Phys. Acoustics, UCLA, 1953. Commd. ensign, U.S. Navy, 1946, advanced through grades to comdr. 1962, dir. undersea programs Office Naval Research, Washington, 1962-67, ret., 1967; prof. ocean engring., Fla. Atlantic U., Boca Raton, 1967—; vis. prof. Norwegian Tech. Inst., Trondheim, 1981-82; cons. Mettalgesellschaft AG, Frankfort, W. Ger., 1974-78, D.W.G. & Ptnrs. Internat., Tampa, Fla., 1984—. Participant Navy Advanced Sci. Program, 1952. Mem. Am. Soc. Engring. Edn. (chmn. ocean engring. 1978, sec. treas. engring. acoustics 1975—), Marine Tech. Soc., Acoustical Soc. Am. Republican. Presbyterian. Avocations: Golf; weightlifting; computer programming; bridge; stamp collecting; travel. Home: 1190 SW 11th St Boca Raton FL 33432 Office: Dept Ocean Engring Fla Atlantic Univ Boca Raton FL 33431

DAVIDSON, JERRY FRANK, music educator; b. Pine Bluff, Ark., July 26, 1942; s. Herman Jeremiah and Lalla Beth (Chidester) D.; m. Susan LaMothe, May 20, 1969; children—Douglas James, Colin Stuart. B. Mus., U. Ark., 1965; M. Sacred Mus., Union Theol. Sem. N.Y., 1969; Ph.D., Northwestern U., 1982. Asst. prof. music Harper Coll., Palatine, Ill., 1969-79; assoc. prof. La. State U., Baton Rouge, 1979-84, assoc. dean, 1984—. Composer of many choral works. Contbr. articles to profl. jours. Served to 1st lt. USAR, 1965-73, Korea. Mem. Am. Guild of Organists (assoc.), Phi Beta Kappa. Democrat. Anglican. Home: 9556 Goodwood Blvd Baton Rouge LA 70815 Office: Sch of Mus La State U Baton Rouge LA 70803

DAVIDSON, JOHN DARRELL, emergency medical educator, fire protection technology educator; b. Georgetown, Tex., Jan. 28, 1951; s. James Dickerson and Bettie (Goldberg) D.; m. Marilyn Rose Hillman, Dec. 18, 1971; children—Tiffany Lyn, Jodi Leah. Assoc. Applied Sci., Midland Coll., 1976, postgrad., 1978-80; B.S., Tex. A&M U., 1983. Firefighter, emergency med. technician Midland Fire Dept., Tex., 1973-78; instr. Midland Coll., 1983—. Served with U.S. Army. Named Firefighter of Yr., Downtown Lions Club, 1978. Mem. Am. Soc. Safety Engrs., Nat. Fire Protection Assn., Internat. Fire Service Tng. Assn., Nat. Rifle Assn., Phi Theta Kappa, Tau Alpha Pi. Republican. Avocations: inventing, fishing. Home: #1 Linda Ct Midland TX 79705 Office: Midland Coll 3600 N Garfield Midland TX 79705

DAVIDSON, JOHN RICHARD, consulting structural engineer; b. Derby, Conn., June 17, 1929; s. Le Roy Harold and Bertha Margaret (Kernick) D.; m. Leota Ruth Brown, Sept. 1, 1951 (div. 1984); children—John Eric, Richard Earle, John James. Sc.B., Brown U., 1951; M.S., Va. Poly. Inst., 1959, Ph.D., 1968. Registered prof. engr., Va., With NACA, 1951-57; research engr. NASA, Langley Research Ctr., Hampton, Va., 1951-65, head protective structures sect., 1965-70, asst. head structural integrity br., 1970-71, head fatigue and fracture br., 1971-85, ret., 1985; cons., 1985—; mem. structural integrity of aero. vehicles panel Tech. Coop. Program (English speaking countries), 1982—; aerospace panel chmn. for workshop on potential applications of aerospace tech. to marine transport industry, 1978; organizer 10th internat. meeting Soc. Engring. Sci., 1973. Flotilla comdr. U.S. Coast Guard Aux., 1983, mem., 1978—; mem. Amateur Radio Emergency Service, 1980—. Recipient achievement awards NASA, 1972, 81, 83. Mem. ASME, ASTM, Am. Radio Relay League, Sigma Xi. Episcopalian. Editor: Proc. 6th Internat. Meeting Internat. Com. for Aero. Fatigue, 1971; mem. editorial bd. Engring. Fracture Mechanics, 1978—; contbr. articles on engring. to profl. jours.; inventor electronically calibratable clock. Home: 114 Glenn Circle Williamsburg VA 23185

DAVIDSON, MICHAEL H., lawyer; b. N.Y.C., Nov. 5, 1947; s. Howard C. and Beulah Marie (Williams) D. B.A., U. Fla., 1970, J.D., 1974. Bar: Fla. 1975, U.S. Dist. Ct. (no. dist.) Fla. 1977, U.S. Ct. Appeals (5th and 11th cirs.), U.S. Dist. Ct. (so. dist.) Fla. 1986, Asst. atty. gen. State of Fla., 1975-78; gen. counsel Fla. Parole Commn., 1978-80; assoc. Wattles, Baker & Davidson, Tallahasee, 1981-82, ptnr., 1983-85; sole practice, Fort Lauderdale, 1983—. Republican. Roman Catholic. Home: 105 Lake Emerald Dr Apt 208 Oakland Park FL 33308 Office: Watson & Clark PO Box 11959 Fort Lauderdale FL 33339

DAVIDSON, ROBERT WAYNE, industrial textile company official; b. South Gate, Calif., Sept. 25, 1947; s. William Maynard and Barbara Jean (Terzenbach) D.; m. Alta Mae Barnes, July 23, 1966; children—Todd Edward, Trista Rene. Assoc.Sci., Moorepark Coll., 1977. Sales rep. United Textile & Supply Co., Los Angeles, 1971-79, nat. sales mgr., 1979-81, div. mgr., Ft. Lauderdale, Fla., 1983—; self-employed awning mfr., Simi Valley, Calif., 1981-83. Served with AUS, 1966-69. Methodist. Office: United Textile & Supply Co 820 NW 5th Ave Fort Lauderdale FL 33311

DAVIDSON, WILLIAM GEORGE, III, lawyer, accountant, financial and management consultant; b. Ft. Benning, Ga., Oct. 28, 1938; s. William George and Dorothea K. (Wright) D. B.S., U.S. Naval Acad., 1960; M.B.A. in Fin., U. Pa., 1970; J.D., Suffolk U., 1974. Bar: Ohio 1975, Md. 1980, U.S. Tax Ct. 1980, U.S. Supreme Ct. 1980, D.C. 1981, U.S. Ct. Claims 1983, U.S. Ct. Appeals (D.C. cir.) 1983, Va. 1985; C.P.A., Md. Electronics engr., systems analyst Phila. Naval Shipyard, 1968; fin. analyst Allied Chem. Corp., N.Y.C., 1969; fin. analyst, staff acct. Dennison Mfg. Co., Framingham, Mass., 1969-74; corp. controller Premix, Inc., North Kingsville, Ohio, 1974-78; owner, mgr. W.G. Davidson and Assocs., Inc., mgmt. and fin. cons., Rockville, Md., 1978—; mem. faculty Lake Erie-Garfield Coll., Painesville, Ohio, 1977-78; mem. faculty, dir. dept. acctg. and taxation Southeastern U., Washington, 1981—; mem. faculty Benjamin Franklin U., 1983—, Montgomery Coll., 1983—; del. White House Conf. on Small Bus., 1980. Active Vols in Tech. Assistance, 1970-75; mem. fiscal affairs com. Montgomery County, Md., 1983-84. Served to lt. comdr. USN, 1960-67. Mem. ABA, Am. Inst. C.P.A.s, Md. Bar Assn., Bar Assn. Montgomery County, Fairfax Bar Assn., D.C. Bar Assn., Va. State Bar Assn., Rockville C. of C., Fin. Execs. Inst., Nat. Assn. Accts., U.S. Naval Acad. Alumni Assn., Naval Res. Assn., Suffolk Law Sch. Assn. Washington. Roman Catholic. Lodges: Kiwanis (past dir. Ashtabula, Ohio); Civitan (Rockville). Home: 3601 Prince William Dr Fairfax VA 22031 Office: 4021 University Dr Fairfax VA 22030 also 27 W Jefferson St Rockville MD 20850

DAVIDSON, WILLIAM HAROLD, management consultant; b. Dayton, Ohio, Sept. 22, 1928; s. Oscar Roy and Anna Mary (Fisher) D.; student Miami U., Ohio, 1946-48; B.B.A., U. Dayton, 1954; M.B.A., Ind. U., 1955; m. Patricia Lucille Kernan, Apr. 23, 1949; children—Jill, Patricia, William Harold, Maribeth, Sally. Dir. mgmt. devel. Chrysler Corp., Detroit, 1955-63; v.p. Booz, Allen & Hamilton, Chgo., 1963-67; pres. Davidson-Kernan Corp., Ft. Worth, 1967—, also dir.; dir. Visa Travel, Inc.; tchr. U. Detroit, 1958-62. Pres., Warren (Mich.) Bd. Edn., 1961-62. Served with USNR, 1948-52. Republican. Roman Catholic. Clubs: Rivercrest Country, Ft. Worth. Home: 6009 Merrymount St Fort Worth TX 76107 Office: 5501 W Rosedale St Fort Worth TX 76107

DAVIE, ETHEL O., foreign language educator; b. Newark; d. Walter Francis O'Hara and Gertrude Isabel (Hancock) O'H.; m. Robert Park Davie, Mar. 27, 1942; children—Robert S., Thomas H., B.S., W. Va. State Coll., 1961, B.A., 1964; M.A. Columbia U., 1964; Ed.D., W. Va. U., 1976; postdoctoral Sorbonne U. Paris, Mem. faculty W. Va. State Coll. Inst., 1961—, prof., 1978—, chmn. dept. modern fgn. lang., 1974-84, adj. prof. Coll. Grad. Studies, 1980, 81; mem. W. Va. selection com. Fulbright, U.S. Dept. Edn.; mem. faculty adv. council. Bd. regents W.Va.; active Friendship Force, W.Va. Recipient U.S. State Dept. African Am. Inst. study award, summer 1973; Phelps Stokes Caribbean Am. Exchange prof., Guyana, 1977; NEH workshop award, 1979, 80; HEW Title III award, 1977. Mem. ALA, Am. Assn. Tchrs. French, Internat. Council Edn. Tchrs., AAUW, Am. Council Tchrs. Fgn. Lang., African Studies Assn., African Lit. Assn., So. Assn. Africanists (reviewer), W.Va. Fgn. Lang. Assn., Assn. Caribbean Studies. Republican. Methodist. Co-editor Caribbean sect. Handbook of Latin American Studies, 1982, 84; contbr. revs. and articles to profl. jours. Home: 2706 Knox Ave St Albans WV 25177 Office: W Va State Coll 222 Hill Hall Institute WV 25112

DAVIES, ARCHIBALD DONALD, clergyman; b. Pitts., Apr. 15, 1920; s. Archibald Decimus and Velma Mercedes (Harris) D.; m. Mabel Myrtle Roberts, Dec. 25, 1939; 5 children. B.A., U. Tulsa, 1944; S.T.B., S.T.M., Seabury-Western Theol. Sem., 1947. Ordained deacon Episcopal Ch., 1950, priest, 1951; deacon-in-charge Trinity Ch., El Dorado, Kans., 1950-51, rector, 1951-52; chmn. dept. ch. edn. Kans. State U., 1951-54; rector St. Paul Ch. and Chapel, 1952-54; asso. sec. adult div. dept. ch. edn. Exec. Council Epis. Chs., 1954-56, exec. sec., 1956-58; rector Grace Ch., Monroe, La., 1958-61; assoc. prof. ch. edn. Seabury-Western Theol. Sem., 1964-70; dean Trinity Cathedral, Omaha, 1968-70; bishop, Dallas, 1970—; Chaplain UAR, 1954—. Contbr. articles to mags. U.S. Army, 1962-64. Fellow Coll. Preachers. Office: The Episcopal Church 3572 Southwest Loop 820 Fort Worth TX 76133*

DAVIES, DONALD THOMAS, hospital administrator, air force officer; b. Chgo., June 12, 1948; s. Brettland Lloyd and Catherine (Dobesh) D.; m. Inta Eva Delmage, Apr. 20, 1968; children—Donald Thomas, Alicia, Melissa, Sebastian. B.B.A., Chaminade U., 1974; M.B.A., Philips U., 1984. Commd. 2d lt. U.S. Air Force, 1975, advanced through grades to maj., 1985; asst. adminstr. U.S. Air Force Hosp., Rantoul, Ill., 1975-78; chief med. placement U.S. Air Force, Chgo., 1978-81; adminstr. U.S. Air Force Clinic, Enid, Okla., 1981-83, U.S. Air Force Hosp., Lubbock, Tex., 1983—. Mem. West Tex. Hosp. Assn., Am. Coll. Hosp. Adminstrs. (presiding officer 1985—, cert.), Tex. Hosp. Assn., Am. Hosp. Assn., Delta Mu Delta. Republican. Roman Catholic. Avocations: camping; golfing; bowling. Home: 219 Mitchell Blvd Lubbock TX 79489 Office: US Air Force Hosp Reese AFB TX 79489

DAVIES, HENRY THOMAS, wholesale heating and air conditioning company executive; b. Franklin, Tenn., May 25, 1936; s. Harry Elmer and Sarah (Brown) D.; m. Carolyn Kennedy, June 26, 1955; children—Dottie, Tommy, Mike, Steve, Bob. Draftsman, Norfolk Naval Shipyard, Portsmouth, Va., 1954; estimator, sales Aaron Torch & Sons, Macon, Ga., 1955-58, salesman Associated Equipment Co. Inc., Geneva, Ala., 1958-63, mgr., Mobile, Ala., 1963—, now pres.; instr. heating and air conditioning course Auburn U., 1966-75; council mem. Westinghouse, Norman, Okla., 1967-79; instr. fin. course U. Tenn., Knoxville, 1976-83; mem. pres. council The Coleman Co., Wichita, 1981-84. Home: 3608 Linden Ln Mobile AL 36608 Office: Associated Equipment Co Inc 1230 N Beltline Hwy PO Box 7157 Mobile AL 36608

DAVIES, JAMES JUMP, investment consultant, actuary; b. Liverpool, Eng., June 25, 1941; came to U.S., 1966; s. Sydney Roderick and Freda Mary (Wright) D. B.A., U. Liverpool, Eng., 1961. Actuarial technician Duncan C. Fraser Co., Liverpool, 1961-66; cons. actuary Alexander & Alexander, Atlanta, 1966-71; investment cons. Hazlehurst & Assocs., Atlanta, 1971-84, Davies Investment Assocs., Inc., Atlanta, 1985—. Fellow Inst. Actuaries; mem. Inst. Chartered Fin. Analysts, Am. Acad. Actuaries, Conf. Actuaries in Pub. Practice, Soc. Actuaries (assoc.), Atlanta Actuarial Club, Atlanta Fin. Analysts Assn. Roman Catholic. Home: 215 Piedmont Ave NE 1009 Atlanta GA 30308 Office: Davies Investment Assocs Inc PO Drawer 56246 Atlanta GA 30343

DAVIES, RICHARD WALTER, state official; b. Little Rock, May 30, 1950; s. Samuel Ladd and Janice Marie (Goodbar) D.; m. Susan Elizabeth Blodgett, July 22, 1972; children—Katherine Ladd, Sarah Downing. B.A. in Journalism, U. Ark., 1972. Adminstrv. asst. Ark. Dept. Parks and Tourism, Little Rock, 1973-76, state parks dir., 1976—. Served to maj. U.S. Army Res., 1972—. Mem. Nat. Assn. State Parks Dirs. (v.p. 1983—), Res. Officers Assn., Southeastern Assn. State Park Dirs. (pres. 1983-84). Episcopalian. Office: Ark State Parks One Capitol Mall Little Rock AR 72201

DAVIS, A. DAN, grocery store chain executive. Student, Stetson U. With Winn-Dixie Stores Inc., Jacksonville, Fla., 1968—, corp. v.p., mgr. Jacksonville div., 1978-80, sr. v.p. and regional dir. Jacksonville and Orlando (Fla.) and Atlanta divs., 1980-82, pres., 1982—, dir. Office: Winn Dixie Stores Inc 5050 Edgewood Ct PO Box B Jacksonville FL 32203*

DAVIS, ANN GRAY, nurse, consultant; b. Phila., Jan. 18, 1932; d. Joseph Edward and Elaine (Wheaton) Gray; m. Herbert Paul Davis, Oct. 21, 1950 (div. June 1976); children—Debra Gianni, Paul, Derek, Megan. B.S., Roberts Wesleyan Coll., 1974; M.N., Emory U., 1978. Nurse, St. John's Home, Rochester, N.Y., 1974-75; instr. nursing Roberts Wesleyan Coll., Rochester, 1975-77; instr. nursing Lenoir-Rhyne Coll., Hickory, N.C., 1978-79, acting chmn. dept. nursing, 1979-80; psychiat. nurse clinician Frye Regional Med. Ctr., Hickory, N.C., 1980-81, dir. staff devel., 1981-82, asst. dir. nursing cons., assessment, research and evaluation, 1982-84, clin. specialist psychiatry, 1984—; guest faculty Lenoir-Rhyne Coll. and Northstate Acad., 1981—; adj. faculty N.C. U., Greensboro, 1985—; psychiat. nursing cons. Sec. treas. Catawba Valley Health Planning Council, 1978-82; mem. adv. council Health Occupations Edn., 1981-82; mem. Task Force on Edn., Catawba County, 1982—; mem. Family Life Task Force, Catawba County, 1982—; mem. Rape Task Force, N.C. Council on Status of Women, 1981—. NIMH grantee, 1977-78. Mem. Am. Nurses' Assn. (cert. clin. specialist in adult psychiat. mental health nursing, mem. council specialists in psychiat/mental health nursing), N.C. State Nurses' Assn., Catawba Valley Assn. Clin. Therapists, Sigma Theta Tau, Alpha Kappa Sigma. Democrat. Episcopalian. Office: 420 N Center St Nursing Adminstrn Frye Regional Med Ctr Hickory NC 28601

DAVIS, BARBARA FAYE, nurse; b. Stamford, Tex., Aug. 8, 1942; d. Dempsey and Mozelle (Johnson) Baker; m. Matthew Royal Davis, Mar. 31, 1964; children—Matthew Royal, Connye LaRue. A.A., Western Tex. Coll., 1976; B.S.N., West Tex. State U., 1978. Charge nurse Cogdell Hosp., Snyder, Tex., 1978-81, ICU/CCU coordinator, 1982-83, supr., 1983—; instr./trainer Am. Heart Assn., Snyder, 1982—. Mem. Nurses Coalition for Action in Politics, 1983—; mem. task force Am. Heart Assn., Abilene, 1983. Mem. Tex. Nurses Assn., Am. Nurses Assn., NAACP. Democrat. Baptist.

DAVIS, BARBARA HILLYER, women's studies administrator, educator; b. Creston, Iowa, Mar. 1, 1934; d. Murrell Newman and Wanda Laverne (Griswold) Hillyer; m. Robert Murray Davis, Dec. 28, 1958; (div.); children—Megan Elizabeth, Jennifer Anne, John Murray. B.A. in English, Rockford (Ill.) Coll., 1956, M.A. in English and Am. Lit., Claremont Grad. Sch., 1957, Ph.D. in English Lit., U. Wis., 1962. Instr., Mundelein Coll., Chgo.,

1962-64; instr. Loyola U., Chgo., 1964; acting instr. U. Calif.-Santa Barbara, 1967; vis. asst. prof. English, human relations U. Okla., Norman, 1973-76, dir. women's studies, 1976—, assoc. prof. women's studies, human relations, 1982—; project dir. Okla. Pub. Library Systems, 1974-75; evaluator Okla. Humanities Com., 1976. Chmn. Norman Okla. Women's Polit. Caucus, 1973-74; program cons., policy com. Women's Resource Ctr. Norman, 1975—; coordinator Equal Rights Coalition of Okla., 1972-73; adv. bd. Ctr. Displaced Homemakers, 1979-84; mem. task force on women Norman Alcohol Info. Ctr., 1980-83; mem. Norman Civic Improvement Council, 1974-76. Recipient Women of Eighties award Okla. Women's Polit. Caucus, 1980, Meritorious Service award, 1984; grantee Okla. Humanities Com., 1974, 78, 80, 82, Fund Improvement Post-secondary Edn., 1981-83. Mem. Nat. Women's Studies Assn., MLA, Phi Beta Kappa. Contbr. articles to profl. publs. Office: Women's Studies Program U Okla Norman OK 73019

DAVIS, BEATRICE ANNA KIMSEY, educator, civic worker; b. Oklahoma City, June 23, 1917; d. Carl Cleveland and Beatrice Mary (Rudersdorf) Kimsey; grad. Ward-Belmont Coll., 1938; m. Bruce A. Davis, Jan. 22, 1942; children—Belinda Anne Davis Pillow, Beatrice Annette Davis Orynawka, Beverly Anna Davis Steckler. B.A., Vanderbilt U., 1940; M.Ed., Lamar U., 1973. Personnel interviewer Ft. Sam Houston, San Antonio, 1942-43; advisor Jr. Achievement, 1974-80; asst. instr. drama Watkins Night Sch., Nashville, 1939-40; substitute tchr. Port Arthur (Tex.) Ind. Sch. Dist., 1964-85; high sch. English tchr. South Park Ind. Sch. Dist., Beaumont, Tex., head dept. English, 1982-84. Pres. Port Arthur Family Services Am., 1979-81 Women's Orgn. 1st Presbyn. Ch.; v.p. Jefferson High Sch. PTA; mem. bd. Hughen Sch. for Crippled Children, Gates Meml. Library, PTA of Tyrell Elem. Sch., Port Arthur, Parliamentarians of Port Arthur, Story League of Port Arthur; trustee, membership com., tchr. Presbyn. Ch. of Covenant; vol. docent McFaddin-Ward Hist. House and Mus., Beaumont, 1986—; mem. Beaumont Art Mus., Community Concert Assn. Port Arthur. Served as ensign USNR, 1942-43; lt. comdr. Res. Recipient numerous awards for outstanding civic service, various edn1. stipends and grants; named Tchr. of Yr. for South Park High Sch., Tex. A&M U., 1981-82. Mem. NEA, All Tchrs. Assn. Beaumont, Nat. Council Reading Tchrs., S.E. Tex. Council Reading Tchrs., Tex. Assn. for Specialists in Group Work, Sabine-Neches Personnel and Guidance Assn. AAUW (past pres. Port Arthur), Federated Women's Club (past pres. bd. Port Arthur), P.E.O. (chairperson Port Arthur chpt. 1986-87), Rosehill Bd. (past pres.), Panhellenic Assn. (past pres. Port Arthur), Women's Orgn. Symphony Club (pres pres.), Choral Club (past pres.). Thalian Drama Group (past v.p.), Heritage Soc., Tex. Gulf Hist. Soc., Reading, Knights of Neches Aux., DAR, UDC, SE Tex. Women's Commn., English-Speaking Union U.S. Sigma Kappa Alumni, Phi Lambda Phi, Phi Delta Kappa. Republican. Clubs: Port Arthur Country (past pres.), Hibiscus. Co-author Curriculum Guides for Reading, 1973, 81, for English, 1980; contbr. articles to mags. Home: 2816 35th St Port Arthur TX 77640

DAVIS, BRUCE GORDON, educational administrator; b. Fulton, Tex., Sept. 2, 1922; s. Arthur Lee and Clara Katherine (Rouquette) D.; B.A., U. Tex., 1950; M.Ed., U. Houston, 1965; m. Mary Virginia Jackson, Aug. 31, 1946; children—Ford Rouquette, Barton Bolling, Katherine Norvell Davis McLendon. Tchr., Edison Jr. High Sch., Houston, 1951; tchr. Sidney Lanier Jr. High Sch., Houston, 1957-60, asst. prin., 1966-74, prin., 1974—; tchr. Johnston Jr. High Sch., Houston, 1960-66; prin. Sidney Lanier Vanguard Sch., Houston, 1974-82. Served with USMC, 1942-45; with U.S. Army, 1951-57. Mem. Nat. Assn. Secondary Sch. Prins., Tex. Assn. Secondary Sch. Prins., Houston Profl. Adminstrs., U.S. Army Officers Res. Assn., Houston Congress Tchrs., Am. Legion. Republican. Presbyterian. Club: Masons. Home: 6614 Sharpview St Houston TX 77074 Office: 2600 Woodhead St Houston TX 77098

DAVIS, CALVIN DE ARMOND, history educator; b. Westport, Ind., Dec. 3, 1927; s. Harry R. and Abbie Jane (Moncrief) D. A.B., Franklin Coll., 1949; M.A., Ind. U., 1956, Ph.D., 1961. Tchr., Wilson Sch., Columbus, Ind., 1949-51, 53-54, Univ. Sch., Bloomington, Ind., 1954-55; asst. prof. history Ind. Central Coll., 1956-57; teaching assoc. history Ind. U., 1958-59; asst. prof. history U. Denver, 1959-62; asst. prof. Duke U., Durham, N.C., 1962-64, assoc. prof. history, 1964-76, prof. history, 1976—; vis. asst. prof. Ind. U., summer 1964; cons. NEH, 1974. Served with U.S. Army, 1951-52. Mem. Am. Hist. Assn. (Albert J. Beveridge award 1961), Orgn. Am. Historians, Soc. Historians Am. Fgn. Relations, Conf. Peace Research in History. Author: The United States and the First Hague Peace Conference, 1962; The United States and the Second Hague Peace Conference: American Diplomacy and International Organization, 1899-1914, 1976. Home: 907 Monmouth Ave Durham NC 27701 Office: Dept History Duke U Durham NC 27706

DAVIS, CALVIN GRIER, clergyman, college president; b. Wilmar, Ark., Sept. 15, 1906; s. Coleman Robert and Ollie Pearson (Hilliard) D.; m. Rebecca Spencer McDowell, July 6, 1935; children—Calvin Grier, James McDowell. B.A., Davidson Coll., 1927; B.Div., Union Theol. Sem., 1931, M.Th., 1933, Th.D., 1943; D.D. (hon.), Davidson Coll., 1943, Tusculum Coll., 1943. Ordained to ministry Presbyn. Ch., 1931. Asst. minister Grace Covenant Ch., Richmond, Va., 1931-33; minister Second Presbyn. Ch., Norfolk, Va., 1933-38, First Presbyn. Ch., Asheville, N.C., 1938-59; pres. Mt. Retreat Assn., 1959-72, Montreat-Anderson Coll., N.C., 1959-72; ret. 1972; trustee Davidson Coll., 1940-59, King Coll., Bristol, Tenn., 1950-59, Mt. Retreat Assn., Montreat, 1945-59, Montreat-Anderson Coll., 1945-59; bd. mgrs. Lords Day Alliance, U.S., Atlanta, 1940—; bd. dirs. Annuities and Relief of Presbyn. Ch. in U.S., Atlanta, 1948-58. Contbg. editor Presbyn. Outlook, 1938-60. Author: A Mountain Retreat, 1986; radio preacher The Protestant Hour, 1950. Mem. Ministers Assn. Asheville (pres. 1952). Club: Biltmore Forest Country. Lodge: Kiwanis. Avocations: golf; physical fitness. Home: 87 Shorewood Dr Asheville NC 28804

DAVIS, CARLOTTA JEAN, educator; b. Doddridge County, West Union, W.Va., Nov. 25, 1948; d. Carl Frederick and Pearl Oma (Phillips) Pratt; m. Frederick Cyde Davis, Jan. 12, 1963; children—Margaret Jean, Lorain Ann. B.S., Salem Coll., 1981. Cert. tchr., W.Va. With West Union Garment Factory (W.Va.), 1967-77; elem. tchr. Doddridge County Bd. Edn. (W.Va.), 1981—; owner Davis Dept. Store, West Union. Mem. W.Va. Edn. Assn. Mem. Ch. of Christ. Home: CP Star Route PO Box 19A West Union WV 26456 Office: 115 W Main St West Union WV 26456

DAVIS, CHERYL THISDALE, librarian; b. Memphis, Sept. 1, 1946; d. Glenn Francis and Iola (Bright) Thisdale; m. William Marsh Davis, Jr., Jan. 26, 1968; children—Patrick Glenn, Clinton Paul. B.S. in Edn., Memphis State U., 1968, M.S. in Library Sci., 1982. Cert., Tenn. Children's librarian Whitehaven Br. Library, Memphis, 1968-70; asst. librarian John Brister Library, Memphis State U., 1973; with Ridgeway Jr./Sr. High Sch., Memphis, 1974—, librarian, media specialist, 1975—. Mem. ALA, W. Tenn. Library Assn., Phi Kappa Phi. Baptist. Home: 6959 Briar Hill Dr Bartlett TN 38134 Office: 2009 Ridgeway Rd Memphis TN 38119

DAVIS, CLYDE WILLIAM, JR., insurance company executive; b. Blairsville, Ga., Mar. 24, 1940; s. Clyde William and E. Lee (Jackson) D.; m. Elinor Glenn Woodall, June 10, 1967; 1 dau., Lauren Woodall. B.A., West Ga. Coll., 1962; M.S., Auburn U., 1964, Ph.D., 1971. Instr. math. Auburn U., 1964-65; asst. prof. Columbus (Ga.) Coll., 1965-71, assoc. prof., 1971-76, prof. math., 1976-77; assoc. actuary Am. Family Life Assurance Co., Columbus, 1977, now sr. v.p. internat. ops.; dir. Am. Family Reins. Co., Am. Family Life Assurance (Thailand), Ltd., Am. Family (UK) Holdings Co., Ltd., Am. Health & Security Co., Ltd., Am. Family Life Assurance Co., Ltd., Credit Life Ins. Mgmt. Co., Ltd. Methodist. Office: American Family Life Assurance Co Columbus GA 31999

DAVIS, DIANE GAIL, nurse; b. Tappahannock, Va., Aug. 14, 1955; d. Warner Sandford and Juanita (Shackelford) D. Diploma, Richmond Hosp. Sch. Nursing, 1976. Staff nurse II, Richmond Meml. Hosp., 1976—. Mem. Assn. Operating Room Nurses. Home: 1575 Front Royal Dr Richmond VA 23278

DAVIS, DREXEL REED, treasurer State of Kentucky; b. Shelbyville, Ky., July 18, 1921; s. E. Forest and Myrtle Francis (Stacy) D.; m. Sarah Lillis, Oct. 15, 1947; children—Drexel R., Ann Lillis. Student, Georgetown Coll., 1940-42. Dep. clk. Ky.'s Ct. of Appeals, 1948-52, 56-63, clk., 1964-67; adminstrv. asst. Ky. Sec. of State, Frankfort, 1952-56; dist. mgr. Investors Heritage Life Ins. Co., Frankfort, 1969-72; treas. State of Ky., Frankfort, 1972-75, 79—, sec. of state, 1975-79. Served with Signal Corps U.S. Army, 1942-45. Mem. Southeastern Nat. Treas.'s Assn. (chmn.). Democrat. Clubs: Lions (dist. govt.), Am. Legion, VFW, Masons, Shriners. Office: Treasury Dept New Capitol Annex Frankfort KY 40601*

DAVIS, EDWARD BERTRAND, U.S. district judge; b. W. Palm Beach, Fla., Feb. 10, 1933; s. Edward Bertrand and Mattie Mae (Walker) D., J.D., U. Fla., 1960; LL.M. in Taxation, N.Y.U., 1961; m. Patricia Lee Klein, Apr. 5, 1958; children—Diana Lee Davis Gransden, Traci Russell, Edward Bertrand, III. Admitted to Fla. bar, 1961, pvt. practice, Miami, 1961-79, counsel firm High, Stack, Lazenby & Bender, 1978-79; U.S. dist. judge So. Dist. Fla., 1979—. Served with AUS, 1953-55. Mem. ABA, Fla. Bar Assn., Dade County Bar Assn. Office: PO Box 013189 Miami FL 33101

DAVIS, EDWARD EUGENE, contracting company executive; b. Memphis, Dec. 27, 1929; s. William Edward and Viola Edna (Freudenberg) D.; m. Colleen Eoff, June 23, 1951; children—Edward Eugene, Deborah Colleen. B.A. in Geology, U. Miss., 1954. With Delta Exploration, Inc., 1954; br. mgr. Adjustors, Inc., Meridian, Miss., 1955-58; owner, mgr. Edward E. Davis & Co., ins. adjusters, Ft. Walton Beach, Fla., 1958-69; chmn., pres. Edward E. Davis Contracting, Inc., Ft. Walton Beach, 1969-80, Gulf Coast Def. Contractors, Inc., Ft. Walton Beach, 1980—. Served with USAF, 1951-52. Mem. Assoc. Builders and Contractors, Alpha Tau Omega. Baptist. Club: Elks (Ft. Walton Beach). Home: 289 Miracle Strip Pkwy W Mary Esther FL 32569 Office: PO Drawer 3160 Fort Walton Beach FL 32548

DAVIS, EDWIN ADAMS, historian, archivist; b. Alba, Mo., May 10, 1904; s. Frank Byrd and Willie Belle (Greever) D.; B.S., Kans. State Tchrs. Coll., 1925; M.A., U. Iowa, 1931; Ph.D., La. State U., 1936; m. La Verna Mae Rowe, May 8, 1925 (dec. 1983); 1 son, Edwin Adams. High sch. tchr., asst. prin., Mo., Kans., Iowa, 1922-23, 25-31; asso. prof., acting head dept. history Drury Coll., Springfield, Mo., 1931-32; asst. history La. State U., 1932-34, instr., 1934-36. asst. prof., 1936-43, asso. prof., 1943-50, prof., 1950-73, prof. emeritus, 1973—, head dept., 1952-63, spl. asst. to pres. univ., 1962-67; founding editorial asso. Jour. So. History, 1935-36; founder, head dept. archives La. State U., 1935-46; vis. prof. U. Tex., summer 1937; state sponsor, editorial cons. publs. La. Hist. Records Survey, Works Project Adminstrn. La., 1937-43; spl. archival cons. various state depts. La. archives, govt. agys., 1937—; historian Acadian Bicentennial Celebration Assn., 1954-56; chief cons. La. Archives Survey, 1954-56, chief cons. State Archives and Records Service, 1956-83; historian laureate of State of La., 1975—. State chmn. com. conservation cultural resources Nat. Resources Planning Bd., World War II. Mem. com. on history source materials Am. Council Learned Socs., 1942-45. Mem. Am. (com. on hist. source materials 1942-45), So. (founding mem., exec. council 1947-50), Miss. Valley (exec. council tchrs. sect. 1952-55), La. (pres. 1958) hist. assns., Soc. Am. Archivists (founding mem., com. archival terminology 1937-39, com. on tng. archivists 1941-45), Soc. Am. Historians, Soc. Southwest Archivists (founding mem.) La., Miss. hist. socs., Phi Kappa Delta, Kappa Delta Pi, Sigma Mu Delta. Episcopalian. Author: Plantation Life in the Florida Parishes of Louisiana, 1943; Of the Night Wind's Telling, Legends from the Valley of Mexico, 1946; William Johnson's Natchez: the Ante-Bellum Diary of a Free Negro (with W.R. Hogan), 1951; The Barber of Natchez (with W.R. Hogan), 1954; Louisiana, The Pelican State, 1959; The Story of Louisiana, 1960; Louisiana, A Narrative History, 1961; Fallen Guidon, 1962; Heroic Years, Louisiana and the War for Southern Independence, 1964; Heritage of Valor: The Picture Story of Louisiana in the Confederacy, 1964; Louisiana, Its Horn of Plenty, 1968. Editor: (with M. H. Hall) A Campaign from Santa Fe to the Mississippi, 1961; founding editor Louisiana History 1960-63, 69-73; The Rivers and Bayous of Louisiana, 1968. Contbr. articles profl. gen. publs. Home: 506 Stanford Ave Baton Rouge LA 70808

DAVIS, ELOINE GREENE, interior decorator; b. Bartow County, Ga., Feb. 22, 1924; d. Eulus Llyallen and Vista (Thompson) Greene; student public schs., Cassville, Ga.; m. Jefferson Lee Davis, Apr. 1, 1942; children—Jefferson Lee, Sarah Grace. With Johnson-Davis Ins. Co., Cartersville, Ga., 1958-68, also sec.-treas.; owner, designer Eloine Interiors, Cartersville, 1961—. Chmn. exec. com. Bartow County Heart Unit, 1965-66; bd. dirs. Ga. Heart Assn., 1964-70, mem. public edn. com., 1966-67; bd. dirs. Etowah Valley Hist. Soc., 1977-81, pres., 1981-82; v.p. Cartersville Service League, 1960-62. Recipient Gold and Silver medallions, Ga. Heart Assn., 1967, 71. Episcopalian. Address: Route 1 Old Alabana Rd Cartersville GA 30120

DAVIS, FERD LEARY, JR., legal educator, lawyer; b. Zebulon, N.C., Dec. 4, 1941; s. Ferd L. and Selma Ann (Harris) D.; m. Joy Baker Davis, Jan. 25, 1963; children—Ferd Leary, III, James Benjamin, Elizabeth Joy. B.A., Wake Forest Coll., 1964; J.D., Wake Forest U. Sch. Law, 1967; LL.M., Columbia U. Sch. Law, 1984. Bar: N.C. 1967. Editor, Zebulon (N.C.) Record, 1958; tchr. Davidson County Schs., Wallburg, N.C., 1966; ptnr. Davis & Davis and related law firms, Zebulon and Raleigh, N.C., 1967-76; asst. prosecutor Wake County Dist. Ct., Raleigh, 1968-69; town atty., Town of Zebulon, 1969-76; dean Campbell U. Sch. Law, Buies Creek, N.C., 1975—, prof. law, 1975—; dir. Inst. for Study Practice of Law and Socioecon. Devel., 1985—; cons. U. Charleston, (W.Va.), 1979. Trustee Wake County Pub. Libraries, 1971-75, Olivia Raney Trust, 1969-71; mem. N.C. State Dem. Exec. Com., 1970-72; mem. N.C. Gen. Statutes Commn., 1977-79. Served with USAR, 1959-66. Babcock scholar Wake Forest U., 1963-67; Dayton Hudson fellow Columbia U., 1982-83. Mem. ABA, N.C. Bar Assn., N.C. State Bar, Phi Delta Phi, Delta Theta Phi. Democrat. Baptist. Assoc. editor Wake Forest Law Review, 1965-66. Office: Campbell Univ Sch of Law Box 158 Buies Creek NC 27506

DAVIS, FLOYD RUSSELL, mail order company executive; b. Richmond, Va., Nov. 14, 1951; s. George Amasa and Barbara Lou (Denzer) D. Student, John Tyler Comml. Coll., 1970-72. Bookkeeper, George A. Davis Co., Inc., Richmond, 1975-80, sec.-treas., gen. mgr., 1980—. Served with U.S. Army, 1972-74. Mem. Am. Mktg. Assn. Clubs: Va. Ski (Richmond).

DAVIS, FRED, fire department official. Fire chief, Nashville. Office: City Hall 107 Metropolitan Courthouse Nashville TN 37201*

DAVIS, GEORGE EDWARD, industrial designer; b. Hugo, Okla., July 3, 1928; s. Silas William and Florence Elva (White) D.; student U. Tex., Austin, 1946-49; B.A., Art Center Coll. Design, Los Angeles, 1956; m. Betty Sue Walker, July 21, 1951; children—Susan Elizabeth, Laura Ellen. Staff designer Friedrich Refrigeration Co., San Antonio, 1957; design dir. comml. div. Woodarts Co., Houston, 1958-59; staff designer Brede, Inc., Houston, 1960-61; designer, co-founder Concept Planners and Designers, Houston, 1962-64; mgr. archtl. dept. Lockheed-Calif. Co., NASA Manned Spacecraft Center, Clear Lake, Tex., 1965-66; staff designer Litton Industries, office products div., Austin, San Antonio, 1967-68; staff designer Clegg Design Group, San Antonio, 1969-76; ind. design cons., San Antonio, 1977—; dir. Systemics, Inc., San Antonio, Christian Bookmark, Inc., San Antonio. Trustee, San Antonio Christian Sch., 1973-82, chmn. bd., 1979-80; bd. elders Christ Presbyterian Ch., San Antonio; mem. Zoning Commn., City of Castle Hills, 1983—. Served with USAF, 1950-54. Decorated D.F.C., Air medal with 3 oak leaf clusters. Mem. AIA, Tex. Soc. Architects (award of merit 1968). Home: 205 Wisteria Dr Castle Hills TX 78213 Office: PO Box 13385 San Antonio TX 78213

DAVIS, GEORGE M., corporate executive. Pres., dir. Flint Industries, Inc. Office: PO Box 490 Tulsa OK 73101*

DAVIS, GILBERT KENNETH, lawyer, paralegal company executive; b. Waterloo, Iowa, Oct. 2, 1942; s. Dwight M. and Alice (Fredrickson) D.; m. Pamela Sue Saunders, Aug. 29, 1964. B.A., Cornell Coll., 1964; J.D., U. Va. Law Sch., 1969. Bar: Va. 1969, U.S. Dist. Ct. (ea. dist.) Va. 1969, U.S. Ct. Appeals (4th cir.) 1970, D.C. 1973, U.S. Dist. Ct. D.C. 1973, U.S. Dist. Ct. Md. 1973, U.S. Ct. Appeals (D.C. cir.) 1973, U.S. Supreme Ct. 1973, U.S. Dist. Ct. (we. dist.) Va. 1977. Asst. U.S. atty. ea. dist. Va., 1969-73; owner Gilbert K. Davis & Assocs. Law Firm; dir. Appalachian Mineral Devel. Corp.; commr. in chancery, judge pro tem Fairfax Circuit Ct. Vice-pres. Cornell Coll. Alumni Bd.; state chmn. Young Republican Fedn. Va., 1973-75; bd. dirs. Profl. Inst. Va. Mem. ABA, Va. State Bar, D.C. Bar, Assn. Trial Lawyers Am., Nat. Assn. Criminal Def. Lawyers, Fed. Bar Assn., Va. Trial Lawyers Assn., McLean Lawyers Assn. (past v.p.), Fed. Criminal Investigators Assn. (1st pres., founder D.C. chpt.), Delta Theta Phi. Presbyterian. Clubs: McLean Sporting, Commonwealth, Counselors. Assoc. editor Va. Lawyer Handbook, revised edit., 1969; also manual. Home: 2727 Wrexham Ct Herndon VA 22071 Office: Gilbert K Davis & Assocs 2579 John Milton Dr Suite 310 Herndon VA 22071

DAVIS, HAROLD GORDON, safety consultant; b. New Orleans, Aug. 17, 1931; s. John Rupert and Irene (Pierce) D.; m. Ruth Marie Jackson, Nov. 26, 1956; 1 child, Debra Gail. Student in Bus. Adminstrn., McNeese U., 1948-49; student in Engring., Lamar U., 1953-56, in Basic Electronics, 1957-58. Instrumentman, Texaco, Inc., Port Arthur, Tex., 1951-72; dist. mgr. OSHA, U.S. Dept. Labor, Beaumont, Tex., 1972-82; owner, safety cons. Harold G. Davis Cons. Safety Profl., Nederland, Tex., 1982—; safety instr. Lamar U. Sch. Tech. Arts, Beaumont, 1982-84. Served with U.S. Army, 1951-53, Germany. Football scholar, McNeese U., 1948. Mem. Am. Soc. Safety Engrs. Democrat. Baptist. Avocations: Fishing; golf. Home: 3603 Elgin Nederland TX 77627 Office: Harold G Davis Cons Safety Profl 3603 Elgin Nederland TX 77627

DAVIS, HARRY LOUIS, physician, educator; b. Crab Orchard, Ill., Mar. 8, 1921; s. Lyman Erastus and Augusta Motsinger D.; m. Edna Muriel McReynolds, June 25, 1949; children—Randall Lyman, Harry Craig. B.Ed., So. Ill. U., 1943, B.S., 1946; M.D., U. Ill. Coll. Medicine, Chgo., 1950; M.S., U. Minn., 1955. Diplomate Am. Bd. Internal Medicine, Am Bd. Pulmonary Disease. Intern, U.S. Naval Hosp., San Diego, 1950-51; resident Mayo Clinic, Rochester, Minn., 1952-55; asst. chief pulmonary disease sect. Baylor U., 1957-58; assoc. dir. cardiopulmonary lab. Bapt. Meml. Hosp., Memphis, 1958-64; with U. Tenn.-Memphis, 1964—, chief div. pulmonary medicine, 1971-83, prof. medicine, 1971—; dir. tng. in internal medicine St. Joseph Hosp., Memphis, 1968-71, med. dir. respiratory therapy dept., 1968—. Bd. dirs. Tenn. chpt. Am. Lung Assn. Served with USNR, 1942-46. Recipient J.P. Krantz award Tenn. chpt. Am. Lung Assn., 1981; U. Tenn. Disting. Service award, 1980. Mem. ACP, Am. Coll. Chest Physicians, Am. Thoracic Soc., AMA, IEEE, Soc. Med. Cons. to Armed Forces, Sigma Xi. Republican. Methodist. Contbr. chpts. to books, articles to sci. jours.

DAVIS, HARRY SCOTT, JR., banker; b. N.Y.C., July 3, 1943; s. Harry Scott and Elizabeth (Davidson) D.; m. Dale Franklin Abell, Dec. 21, 1965; children—William Davidson, Kimberly Abell. B.S.C., U. Louisville, 1965; M.B.A., Northwestern U., 1966; J.D., U. Louisville, 1980. Asst. to investment officer Liberty Nat. Bank, Louisville, 1966-69, asst. investment officer, 1969-70, asst. v.p., investment officer, 1970-71, v.p., investment officer, 1971-75, v.p., chmn. trust investment com., 1975-80, sr. v.p. treasury and money mgmt., 1980-84, exec. v.p. treasury and money mgmt. group, 1984—; lectr. U. Louisville, 1967-69, McKendree Coll., Lebanon, Ill., 1970—, Webster Coll., St. Louis. Active Arthritis Found. Ky., Louisville; mem. research com., grants subcom. Nat. Arthritis Found., Atlanta. Recipient Outstanding Alumni award U. Louisville; Nat. Vol. award Arthritis Found. Mem. ABA, Ky. Bar Assn., Louisville Bar Assn., Louisville Soc. Fin. Analysts (past pres., dir.), Cin. Soc. Fin. Analysts, Delta Upsilon (Outstanding Alumni award). Presbyterian. Clubs: Louisville Boat (treas., dir. 1967—), Pendennis. Lodges: Masons, Scottish Rite, Kosair Temple, Jefferson County Dep. Sheriff. Avocation: tennis. Home: 2100 High Ridge Rd Louisville KY 40207 Office: Liberty Nat Bank and Trust 416 W Jefferson Louisville KY 40202

DAVIS, HARRY WILLARD, JR., youth services administrator; b. Columbia, S.C., June 7, 1946; s. Harry Willard and Mary Texas (Watson) D.; children—Harry, Mary. B.S. in Econs., U. S.C., 1968, J.D., 1974. Bar: S.C., 1975. Asst. atty. gen. State of S.C., Columbia, 1974-76; state dir. S.C. Dept. Juvenile Placement and Aftercare, Columbia, 1976-81; adminstr. S.C. Interstate Compact on Juveniles, Columbia, 1976—; commr. S.C. Dept. Youth Services, Columbia, 1981—. Mem. Gov.'s Com. Criminal Justice, Crime and Delinquency, 1977—; cons. Gov.'s Adv. Council Juvenile Justice and Delinquency Prevention, 1977—; mem. Detention Standards Adv. Council S.C., 1978—; mem. policy council S.C. Continuum of Care Project, 1983—; vice chmn. Criminal Justice Tng. Task Force S.C., 1979—; adj. prof. Coll. Criminal Justice, U. S.C., 1981—; mem. adv. council Rehab. Tng. Services, Grad. Studies, U. S.C., 1979—; mem. corrections com. S.C. Law Enforcement Officers Assn., 1978—; chmn. penal modernization com. S.C. Bar, 1979-81; bd. dirs. S.C. Youth Workers Assn., 1976-78. Pres., Forest Lake Elem. Sch. PTO, 1979-80. Served to 1st lt. U.S. Army, 1969-72. Mem. ABA, S.C. Bar Assn., Am. Correctional Assn. Methodist. Club: Columbia Sailing (commodore). Lodge: Rotary. Home: 25 Arcadia Cove Columbia SC 29206 Office: PO Box 7367 Columbia SC 29202

DAVIS, HELEN GORDON, state legislator; b. N.Y.C., Dec. 25; m. Gene Davis; children—Stephanie, Karen, Gordon. B.A., Bklyn. Coll.; postgrad. U. South Fla. Mem. Fla. Ho. Reps., 1974—, vice chmn. appropriations com., 1982-83, chmn. com. on children andj youth. Pres., LWV Hillsborough County, 1966-69; mem. adv. council Fla. Motion Picture and TV, 1977—. Recipient Woman of Achievement in Arts award, 1975; Diana award NOW, 1975; Outstanding Woman in Govt. award Sorptomists, 1978; Community Service award Fla. Sch. Social Workers, 1979; Hannah G. Solomon award Nat. Council Jewish Women, 1979; Nelson Poynter Bill of Rights award, 1980; State of Arts award State of Fla., 1984; Humanitarian award Judeo-Christian Clinic., 1984. Democrat. Office: 178 E Davis Blvd Tampa FL 33606

DAVIS, HENRY EVAN, IV, insurance executive; b. Charleston, W.Va., Nov. 8, 1950; s. Henry Evan, III and Mary (VanBuren) D.; m. Melinda Cray, June 15, 1976; 1 son, Christopher Lynn White. B.A. with honors in Psychology, U. of South, Sewanee, Tenn., 1973. Research asst. in pharmacology U. Tex. Health Sci. Ctr., Dallas, 1972-73; athletic dir., instr. St. Michael's Sch., Episcopal Sch. of Dallas, 1973-76; athletic dir., coach, instr. psychology Northwood Inst., Cedar Hill, Tex., 1976-78; assoc. mgr. Gibraltar Life, Dallas, 1978-79; exec. v.p. Galaxia Life Ins. Co., sec. Bankers Preferred Life Ins. Co., exec. v.p. Galaxia Adminstrs., exec. v.p. Exec. Underwriters, Inc., Dallas, 1979—; sec. Galaxia Leasings, Inc., Galaxia Fin. Co., 1979—; cons.; dir. seminars. Mem. Am. Coll. Sports Medicine, Acad. Polit. Sci., various ins. groups. Episcopalian. Home: 2640 Beechmont Dallas TX 75228 Office: 17000 Dallas Pkwy Suite 205 Dallas TX 75248

DAVIS, I. G., JR., recreational company executive; b. 1924. Student, Harvard U. With Rheem Mfg. Corp., 1955-60; pres., dir. Resorts Internat., Inc., North Miami, Fla., 1960—. Address: Resorts Internat Inc 915 NE 125th St North Miami FL 33161*

DAVIS, JACKIE DOYLE, utility company executive; b. Bearden, Ark., Jan. 26, 1948; s. Doyle and Jackie Mary Christine (Yeager) D.; m. Linda Gayle Williams, Jan. 24, 1950; 1 child, Michael Laudell. Student, So. State Coll., Magnolia, Ark., 1966-67. Mgr. trainee ArkLa Gas Co., Camden, Ark., 1971-73, ops. supr., Hot Springs, Ark., 1973-79, ops. supt., 1979—. Served to staff sgt. USAF, 1967-71. Mem. Hot Springs C. of C. Baptist. Club: Lions. Avocations: fishing; hunting; gunsmithing; scouting. Home: 1910 Ridgeway Blvd Hot Springs AR 71901 Office: Ark La Gas Co 348 Malvern Ave Hot Springs AR 71901

DAVIS, JAMES LESLIE, geography educator; b. Trenton, N.J., July 13, 1936; m. Nancy M. Hightower; 1 son, Neal. B.A. in Geography magna cum laude, Marshall U., 1957, M.A. in Geography, 1957; Ph.D. in Geography, Northwestern U., 1964. Asst. prof., chmn. dept. geography, Elmhurst Coll. (Ill.), 1960-64; vis. prof. Marshall U., Huntington, W.Va., summer 1962; faculty Western Ky. U., Bowling Green, 1964—, assoc. prof. geography, 1964-67, prof. geography, head dept. geography and geology, 1967-70, assoc. dean of faculties, 1970-74, dean faculty programs, 1974-76, vice dean for acad. affairs, 1976-84, prof. geography, 1984—, mem. grad. faculty, 1966—, Fulbright program adviser, 1965-70, dir. seminars on higher edn. for profl. devel., 1973—, mem. acad. council, 1966-69, 70—; chmn., 1976—, Council Acad. Deans, 1970—, chmn., 1976—, bd. dirs. Wesley Found., 1972-77, chmn., 1976-77, transp. cons. U. Los Andes Project, 1976-77, univ. rep., spl. adviser Barren River Area Devel. Dist. Bd. Dirs., dir. Acad. Programs Evaluation Project; vis. lectr., cons. two Urban Mass Transit Insts. for Mgmt. Execs., 1967; participant nat. conf. Improvement of Instrn. for Geography Profs., 1971. Editor Faculty Research Bull., Western Ky. U., 1971. Author: The Elevated System and the Growth of Northern Chicago, 1965. Contbr. articles, monographs in field to publs. Apptd. mem. Citizens Task Force on Mass Transit Feasibility, Bowling Green, 1974-76. Served to 1st lt. M.I., U.S. Army, 1957-58, USAR, 1958-65. Woodrow Wilson fellow, 1957-58; Cokesbury fellow, 1958-60; Exxon fellow, 1974; named Boss of Yr., Am. Bus. Women's Assn., Bowling Green, 1978. Mem. Assn. Am. Geographers, Am. Assn. Higher Edn., Scabbard and Blade, Sigma Xi, Omicron Delta Kappa, Phi Eta Sigma, Pi Gamma Mu, Phi Alpha Theta, Gamma Theta Upsilon, Pi Delta Phi, Phi Kappa Phi, Lambda Chi Alpha. Democrat. Methodist. Home: 1321 Lois Ln Bowling Green KY 42101 Office: Western Ky U Dept Geography and Geology Bowling Green KY 42101

DAVIS, JAMES MERCER, trainer, educational administrator; b. Lakeland, Fla., July 11, 1952; s. Stanley H. and Ruth (Kahn) D. A.A., Miami-Dade Community Coll., 1973; B.S.B.A. U. Fla., 1975. Appraiser, Washington Federal Savs. and Loan, Miami Beach, Fla., 1976-77, First Federal of Miami, 1977-78; fee appraiser Larry Jones & Assocs., Houston, 1979-80; project mgr. Town Concepts, Houston, 1980-83; chief appraiser Citizens Mortgage, Houston, 1983-84; mgr., instr. Improved Reading Centre of Fla., Longwood, 1984—. Editor newsletter Network Orange, 1985—. Named Most Valuable Swimmer, Centre Coll., Danville, Ky., 1971. Mem. Am. Soc. Tng. and Devel. (chmn. exhibits Showcase '84, Central Fla. chpt., newsletter editor, 1985), Greater Orlando C. of C., Seminole County C. of C. Republican. Jewish. Avocations: boating; fishing; skiing; diving; powerboat racing. Home: 610 Montgomery Rd Altamonte Springs FL 32714 Office: Improved Reading Centres of Florida 2170 State Rd 434 Suite 250 Longwood FL 32779

DAVIS, JAMES ROYCE, microbiologist, educator; b. Rison, Ark., Apr. 6, 1938; s. Robert Hugh and Juanita (Pierson) D.; m. Barbara Ann Martin, May 29, 1959; children—Lezlie Dyan, Kimberly Nicole, Amy Suzanne. Student Miss. Delta Jr. Coll., 1956-57; B.S., Tex. A&I U., 1960; M.S. in Microbiology, U. Houston, 1962, Ph.D., 1965. Research asst. U. Houston, 1960-65, lab. teaching asst., 1960-62, teaching fellow in gen. biology, 1962-63, lectr. med. microbiology for nurses, 1963-64, instr. in microbiology, 1965; asst. prof. in microbiology Dental Br. U. Tex., Houston, 1965-68; dir. microbiology sect. clin. lab. Methodist Hosp., Houston, 1968—, assoc. dir. labs., 1983—; asst. prof. microbiology Baylor Coll. Medicine, Houston, 1968-84, asst. prof. pathology, 1973-84, assoc. prof. pathology, microbiology and immunology, 1984—; cons. clin. pathology service Harris County Hosp. Dist. Adv. bd. Bac/Talk newsletter; contbr. papers to sci. publs. and confs. Mem. Am. Soc. Microbiology (nat. and Tex. br.), Tex. Med. Ctr. Research Soc. (treas. 1967-68), Houston Soc. Clin. Pathologists, Southwestern Assn. Clin. Microbiologists, Sigma Xi, Beta Beta Beta. Office: Methodist Hosp 6565 Fannin St MS 205 Houston TX 77030

DAVIS, JAMES TAYLOR, college dean, education educator, consultant; b. Rogersville, Tenn., Aug. 25, 1928; s. Fred Franklin and Betty Esther (Horne) D.; m. Effie Gertrude Bridges, Aug. 1, 1953; children—Jamie A. Davis Rader, Tammie Lynette. B.S., East Tenn. State U., 1950; M.A., George Peabody Coll., 1956; Ed.D., U. Tenn.-Knoxville, 1972. Cert. tchr., Tenn. Tchr. chemistry, Church Hill, Tenn., Hebron, Md., and Kingsport, Tenn., 1952-68; asst. supt. curriculum devel., Kingsport, 1968-69; asst. dir. Kingsport U. Ctr. of East Tenn. State U., 1969-73, dir., 1973-80; program devel. specialist U. Va. S.W. Ctr., Abingdon, 1980-81; dean of continuing edn. and special services King Coll., Bristol, Tenn., 1981—; cons. Mem. Tenn. Gov.'s Bd. Merit Pay for Tchrs. Served to sgt. U.S. Army, 1950-52. Named hon. Ky. col.; NSF grantee, 1957, 59. Fellow Tenn. Acad. Sci.; mem. Sullivan County Hist. Soc., Assn. Continuing and Higher Edn., Tenn. Assn. Continuing and Higher Edn., Am. Chem. Soc., Internat. Platform Assn., Kingsport C. of C., Phi Delta Kappa. Republican. Presbyterian. Lodge: Allandale Kiwanis. Contbr. articles to profl. jours. Home: Route 6 Evergreen St Church Hill TN 37642 Office: Office of Continuing Education King College Bristol TN 37620

DAVIS, JIMMY FRANK, lawyer; b. Lubbock, Tex., June 14, 1945; s. Jack and Fern L. D.; m. Joyce Zelma Hart, Nov. 6, 1976. B.S. in Edn., Tex. Tech. U., 1968; J.D. U. Tex., 1972. Bar: Tex. 1972, U.S. Supreme Ct. 1975, U.S. Dist. (no. dist.) Tex. 1976, U.S. Ct. Appeals (5th cir.) 1976, U.S. Ct. Appeals (11 cir.) 1981. Asst. criminal dist. atty. Lubbock County, Tex., 1973-76, adminstrv. asst. for office, 1976-77; county and dist. atty. Castro County, Tex., 1977—. Pres. Am. Cancer Soc., Castro County unit, 1981-83. Mem. ABA, Nat. Dist. Attys. Assn., Tex. Dist. and County attys. Assn., Tex. Tech. Ex Students Assn. (dist. rep. 1981-84, bd. dirs. 1984-87), Coll. State Bar Tex., Lubbock County Jr. Bar (pres. 1977), Delta Theta Phi. Baptist. Club: Kiwanis of Lubbock (pres. 1977), Kiwanis of Dimmitt (pres. 1981). Office: Castro County Courthouse Dimmitt TX 79027

DAVIS, JOAN CARROLL, museum director; b. Binghamton, N.Y., Sept. 20, 1931; s. Homer Leslie and Ruby Isabelle (Stone) G.; m. Frederic E. Davis, Aug. 22, 1953; children—Timothy, Terri, Tami, Traci, Todd, Tricia. Student Bob Jones U., 1949-52. Supr. Day Care Ctr. Bob Jones U., Greenville, 1953-63; docent Univ. Art Gallery, Greenville, 1964-73, dir., 1974—. Republican. Baptist. Office: Bob Jones Univ 1700 Wade Hampton Blvd Greenville SC 29614

DAVIS, JOE WILLIAM, mayor; b. New Market, Ala., Oct. 22, 1918; s. Samuel Clifton and Sophie (Walker) D.; B.S. in Social Sci., E.Tenn. State Coll., 1941; M.A. in Edn. Adminstrn., Peabody Coll., 1953; m. Dorothy Allen, Dec. 21, 1951; children—Joe William, Jeffrey Clifton, Julia Evelyn. Tchr., prin. Huntsville (Ala.) schs., 1946-55; personnel mgr. U.S. Indsl. Chem. Corp., Tuscola, Ill., 1955-59, asst. mgr. indsl. relations and safety, also security adminstr., 1959-63; adminstrv. asst. to mayor Huntsville, 1964-68, mayor, 1968—. Served with USN, 1943-46. Mem. V.F.W., Am. Legion. Elk, Mason (Shriner), Lion, Moose, Eagle. Office: 308 Fountain Circle Huntsville AL 35804

DAVIS, JOHN SIDNEY, oil and gas company executive; b. Jonesboro, La., June 27, 1942; s. John W. and Venoil Y. Davis; m. Brenda Howell, Aug. 5, 1961; children—Scott, Shanna, Sonya. B.S. in Acctg., La. Tech. U., 1964, M.B.A., 1965. Traveling auditor Pennzoil Co., 1971-72; with United Gas Pipe Line Co., 1972-77, dir. fin. analysis, 1974-75, v.p. fin., 1975-77; v.p. fin. United Energy Resources, Inc., Houston, 1977-79, sr. v.p. fin., 1979-81, exec. v.p. planning and adminstrn., 1981—, also dir. Served with Audit Agy., USAF, 1965-70. Decorated Bronze Star. C.P.A., Tex., La. Mem. Am. Gas Assn., Am. Mgmt. Assn., Am. Inst. C.P.A.s, La. Soc. C.P.A.s, Tex. Soc. C.P.A.s, World Energy Conf. (U.S. nat. com.). Baptist. Clubs: Houston, Raveneaux Country. Office: United Energy Resources Inc 600 Travis Houston TX 77002*

DAVIS, JOHN VAUGHN, government official; b. Elmira, N.Y., Feb. 23, 1946; s. Vaughn Gleason and Louise (Kidder) D.; m. Merilyn Albritton, Feb. 15, 1969 (div.); children—Martha Louise, John Vaughn. B.A., SUNY-Brockport, 1969; M.A., U. Ga., 1970, postgrad., 1971. Instr. English, U. Ga., Athens, 1970-71; instr. English, U.S. Naval Acad., Bainbridge, Md., 1971-73; tng. officer IRS, Jacksonville, Fla., 1973-76; tng. ctr. adminstr. S.E. region U.S. Treasury Dept., Atlanta, 1976-78, sr. mgmt. analyst, 1978—. SUNY grantee, 1967; grad. asst. U. Ga., Athens, 1969; recipient Superior Performance award Dept. U.S. Navy, 1973; Spl. Achievement award IRS, 1984. Mem. Am. Mgmt. Assn. Republican. Episcopalian. Club: Atlanta City.

DAVIS, JUDITH EVELYN, nurse, consultant; b. Denison, Ohio, Dec. 19, 1939; d. Willard Albert and Lilyan E. (Thomas) O'Neil; m. Michael Kinney O'Heeron, July 24, 1960 (div. 1966); children—Michael Rollie, Patrick Todd, Peter Timothy; m. Maurice Eugene Davis, Aug. 19, 1966; 1 dau., Dawn Denise. Student Sam Houston U., 1957-60, Baylor Coll. Medicine, 1957-59, U. Houston, 1971; grad. Meth. Hosp. Sch. Nursing, 1960; B.S. in Nursing, U. Tex., 1979. Office nurse pediatrics, Bryan, Tex., 1960-62; charge nurse A&M Coll. Hosp., College Station, Tex., 1962-63; inservice instr. Meth. Hosp., Houston, 1963-64; dir. nursing Moody House, Galveston, Tex., 1964-65; sch. nurse Brazosport Ind. Sch. Dist., Freeport, Tex., 1966-78, supr. nurses, 1978-81; nurse cons. Infant Devel. Ctr., Brazoria County Activity Ctr. for Retarded, Lake Jackson, Tex., 1982-83; ednl. coordinator Intermedics Inc., Angleton, Tex., 1983-85; health educator Tex. Sch. for Deaf, Austin, 1985—; part-time surg. and med. ICU nurse Community Hosp., Freeport, 1966-71, part-time med. intensive care nurse and recruitment nurse, 1981-83; tchr. constrn. miniature dolls and plaques, owner The Calico Owl. Brazoria County Med. Aux. scholar, 1957-60; Good Samaritan scholar, 1957-60; Brazoria County Nurses Assn. scholar, 1978. Mem. Brazoria County Assn. for Prevention of Teenage Pregnancies. Baptist. Club: Miniature of Brazosport. Author nurse's manual for Tex. sch. dists.; co-author physicians manual for pub. law. Office: Tex Sch for Deaf Austin TX 78704

DAVIS, KATHLEEN DEE, psychologist; b. Corpus Christi, Tex., Sept. 13, 1940; d. Willie Roman and Dorothy Helen (Wollesen) Slovak; m. Early Clifford Davis, Jr., June 15, 1959 (div. Dec. 1979); children—Katrina Anne Ryan, Melissa Gaye. B.S., Tex. A. & I., 1967; M.A., Corpus Christi State U., 1979; Ph.D., Tex. A&M U., 1983. Lic. psychologist, Tex. Psychol. intern Nueces County Mental Health/Mental Retardation, Corpus Christi, 1981-82; psychologist Coastal Bend Wellness Ctr., Corpus Christi, 1983—; dir. Outpatient Alcoholic Rehab. Services, Corpus Christi, 1984-85. Bd. dirs. Nueces House, Corpus Christi, 1984-85. Mem. Am. Psychol. Assn., Am. Soc. Clin. Hypnosis, Nueces County Psychol. Assn. Democrat. Unitarian. Club: Exec. Women Internat. (Corpus Christi). Home: 304 S Morningside St Corpus Christi TX 78404 Office: Coastal Bend Wellness Ctr 1314 Santa Fe Suite B Corpus Christi TX 78404

DAVIS, KENNETH W., JR., oil and gas well supply executive; b. 1925. Chmn. bd. Mid-Continent Supply Co., Fort Worth, 1946—. Office: Mid Continent Supply Co PO Box 189 Fort Worth TX 76101*

DAVIS, LEONARD CHARLES, petroleum geologist, oil company executive; b. Alamo, Tex., Apr. 1, 1933; s. Leonard Cecil and Mary Helen (Martin) D.; m. Dolores Rankin; children—Elizabeth Danielle, Anita Marie; children by previous marriage—Brian Kelly, Michael Craig. B.S., Tex. A&M U., 1960. With Robert H. Ray. Co., Midland, Tex., 1960-62; geologist Atlantic Richfield Co., Houston, 1962-77; geol. engr. Tenneco Exploration, Houston, 1977-82; mgr. devel. geology Wainoco Oil & Gas Co., Houston, 1982—. Served with USN, 1951-55. Mem. Houston Geol. Soc., Am. Inst. Petroleum Geologists, Am. Assn. Petroleum Geologists, Soc. Paleontology and Mineralogy. Office: Wainoco Oil & Gas Co 1200 Smith St Suite 1500 Houston TX 77002

DAVIS, LINDA PEELER, mathematician, researcher; b. Milledgeville, Ga., May 2, 1947; d. Julian M. and Rita (Birk) Peeler; m. Carlos Clifford Davis Jr., June 12, 1971. B.A., U. Ga., 1969; M.A.T., Ga. State U., 1973, Ph.D., 1980. Tchr., DeKalb Bd. Edn., Decatur, Ga., 1969-71, Cobb Pub. Sch., Marietta, Ga., 1973-75; prof. So. Tech. Inst., Marietta, 1975-84; math. researcher DBA Systems, Inc., Melbourne, Fla., 1985—; cons. in field. Mem. Nat. Council Tchrs. of Math., Ga. Council Tchrs. of Math., IEEE (tech. com. for computers in edn.), Metro Atlanta Math Club (pres. 1982-83). Democrat. Methodist. Avocations: photography; reading. Home: 5035 Laguna Vista Dr Melbourne FL 32935 Office: DBA Systems Inc PO Box 550 Melbourne FL 32901

DAVIS, LOUIS, JR., advertising consultant; b. Ft. Benning, Ga., July 13, 1949; s. Louis and Fannie R. Davis; student Ala. A&M U., 1967-68, Columbus Coll. With Ledger-Enquirer newspaper, Columbus, Ga., 1974-76, account exec., asst. advt. mgr. Bayonet publ., 1976; advt. mgr. Montgomery Ward & Co., Columbus, 1977-81; freelance advt. cons., 1981—. Mem. Alpha Phi Alpha. Democrat.

DAVIS, LOURIE BELL, computer systems specialist; b. Las Vegas, N.Mex., Apr. 8, 1930; d. Currie Oscar and Irene Rodgers Bell; B.S. in Edn., W. Tex. State U., 1959; m. Robert Eugene Davis, Aug. 21, 1950; children—Judith Anne, Robert Patrick. Project leader Nat. Bank of Tulsa, 1968-71, Blue Cross/Blue Shield of Okla., Tulsa, 1971-75, 77—, project coordinator Corp. Data Base, 1977, mgr. systems support, 1977-78, mgr. planning and control, 1979-81, 82-83, dir. info. systems, 1981-82, plan rep. for info. ctr., 1983-84, mgr. info. ctr., 1984-85; mgr. profl. cons. and tng., 1985—; instr. computer sci. Tulsa Jr. Coll., 1975-76, mem. computer sci. adv. bd., 1976-83. Mem. steering com. U.S. Senatorial Bus. Adv. Bd., 1981; mem. U.S. Presdl. Task Force, 1982—; mem. budget com. Tulsa United Way, 1981—. Cert. data processing Inst. Cert. Computer Profls. Mem. Assn. Systems Mgmt. (chpt. award 1978, 84, Internat. Merit award 1980, Internat. Disting. Service award 1984; instr.), Am. Mgmt. Assn., Tulsa Area Systems Edn. Assn., Faculties of Okla. Colls. and Univs. Soc., Internat. Platform Assn., NEA, Okla. Edn. Assn., Alpha Chi. Republican. Presbyterian. Clubs: Mensa Internat., Intertel. Home: 2403 W Oklahoma St Tulsa OK 74127 Office: 1215 S Boulder St Tulsa OK 74102

DAVIS, M. G., lawyer, title company executive; b. Concho County, Tex., Nov. 11, 1930; s. Zack and Olive (Clifton) D.; m. Jeanne Focke, Feb. 7, 1959; children—Linda Jeanne, Lisbeth Dianne. Admitted to Tex. bar, 1957, U.S. Supreme Ct. bar, 1964; atty. Gen. Land Office, Austin, Tex., 1959-60, firm Smith, Porter & Caston, Longview, Tex., 1960-61; v.p. Am. Title Co. Dallas, 1961-67; owner, operator Security Land Title Co., Amarillo, Tex., 1967-69; pres. Dallas Title Co., Houston, 1969-70, Guardian Title, Houston, 1970-72, Collin County Title Co., Plano, Tex., 1972—; sole practice law, Plano, 1972-83; ptnr. firm Davis & Davis, Dallas, 1983—; dir. Allied Bank-Plano, 1985—; guest lectr. U. Houston, Richland Jr. Coll. Chmn. Selective Service Bd. 46, 1983—. Served to 1st lt. USAF, 1952-54; Korea. Recipient Involved Citizen award Dallas Morning News, 1980. Mem. State Bar Tex., Sons Republic Tex., Tex. Land Title Assn. (v.p. 1970-71), Tex. Tech. Ex-Students Assn. (dir. 1961-63), Collin County Title Assn. (pres. 1977), Collin County Bd. Realtors, Dallas Mortgage Bankers Assn., Collin County U. Tex. Ex-Students Assn. (pres. 1980), U. Tex. Ex-Students (exec. council 1983-86), Alpha Tau Omega. Democrat. Episcopalian. Home: 3708 Canoncita Ln Plano TX 75023 Office: Graystone Ctr 3010 LBJ Freeway Suite 1430 Dallas TX 75234

DAVIS, MARGARET CAUBLE, college administrator; b. Atlanta, June 28, 1929; d. Mark Waverly and Eva (Cheney) Cauble; m. Clinton Lee Davis, Aug. 29, 1953 (dec. Oct. 1968); children—Cheney, Mark, Andrew. A.B., Hollins Coll., 1949; M.A., U. Ga., 1951; student Temple U., 1973-74; Ed.D., U. Ga., 1981. Sch. librarian Sussex County Sch. Bd., Va., 1967-69; asst. dean students Beaver Coll., Glenside, Pa., 1969-73; dean students Harcum Jr. Coll., Bryn Mawr, Pa., 1974-78; grad. asst. U. Ga., Athens, 1980-81; dir. counseling Clayton Jr. Coll., Morrow, Ga., 1981—. Author: (with others) Higher Education Periodicals: A Directory, 1981. Trustee Clayton County Assn. Battered Women, Ga., 1984—. Mem. Ga. Coll. Personnel Assn. (sec. exec. bd. 1984—), Nat. Academic Advising Assn. (charter), Am. Coll. Personnel Assn., So. Assn. Coll. Student Affairs, Phi Delta Kappa. Methodist. Office: Clayton Jr Coll N Lee St Morrow GA 30260

DAVIS, MARGARET JEAN SEWELL, mathematics educator, consultant; b. Brisbane, Queensland, Australia, June 2, 1946; came to U.S., 1946; d. John Asbury and Jean (Pettett) Sewell; m. Phillip Norris Davis, Apr. 9, 1965; children—Phillip Lance, Christopher Shawn, Jonathon Clay. B.S. in Edn., Jacksonville State U., 1968; M.A. in Math., U. Ala., 1970, Ph.D. candidate in Stats., Birmingham, 1979—. Cert. tchr. Tchr. math Cherokee County High Sch., Centre, Ala., 1968-69, Trion High Sch., Ga., 1970-71; asst. prof. math. Floyd Jr. Coll., Rome, Ga., 1971—; adj. prof. Brenau Profl. Coll., 1985; sci. fair judge Northwest Ga. Sch. Tchrs., Rome, 1973—; speaker Floyd Jr. Coll. Bur., 1973—. Co-author: College Algebra, 1973. Mem. Am. Statis. Assn., AAUP (treas. local chpt. 1983—), Nat. Council Tchrs. of Math, Am. Math. Assn. of 2-Yr. Colls., Jaycettes (pres. Centre chpt. 1977, Outstanding Young Women in Am., 1970, 77). Democrat. Southern Baptist. Club: Baptist Student Union (sponsor Floyd Jr. Coll. 1972—) Avocation: piano. Home: PO Box 667 Cave Spring GA 30124 Office: Floyd Jr College Box 1864 Rome GA 30161

DAVIS, MARGARET MONTEITH, public schools administrator; b. Grenada, Miss.; d. Joe, Sr. and Vera (Hughes) Monteith; m. Hiram Davis, Jr., Feb. 6, 1982; stepchildren—Hiram, III, Carol. A.A., Holmes Jr. Coll., 1966; B.S. in Elem. Edn., Miss. State U., 1968; M. in Edn., U. Miss., 1972, Specialist in Edn., 1980. Cert. elem. tchr., Ala., Miss. Tchr., Huntsville Pub. Schs., Huntsville, Ala., 1968-69, Batesville Miss. Pub. Schs., 1969-74, Lizzie Horn Sch., Grenada Pub. Sch., 1974-78; prin. Lizzie Horn Sch., Grenada, 1978-82, prin. Grenada Jr. High Sch., 1982—. Mem., P.T.A., Grenada, 1978—. Named Woman of Achievement for 1984, Grenada Profl. Women. Mem. Miss. Assn. Sch. Administrs., U. Miss. Sch. Edn. Alumni Chpt. (bd. dirs. 1984—), Delta Kappa Gamma. Avocations: needlepoint; reading; travel. Office: Grenada Jr High Sch Jones Rd Grenada MS 38901

DAVIS, MARTHA H., librarian; b. Macon, N.C., Feb. 14, 1920; d. Raymond A. and Bessie M. (Satterwhite) Harris; A.B., Greensboro Coll.; B.S. in L.S., U. N.C.; m. William Edward Davis, II, Apr. 17, 1942; children—Harriet, Betsy Davis Cresenzo, William Edward, Allen Hunter. Asst. librarian Olivia Raney Library, Raleigh, N.C.; librarian Portsmouth (Va.) Public Library, Mary Bayley Pratt Children's Library, Chapel Hill, N.C., Hugh Morson High Sch., Raleigh, Ruffin (N.C.) High Sch., Reidsville (N.C.) Jr. High Sch.; instr. children's lit. Meredith Coll.; now dir. Rockingham County (N.C.) Public Library System. Bd. dirs. Rockingham County Fund, Inc.; chmn. Reidsville Library Commn., 1958-59, Piedmont Triad Library Council; bd. dirs. Girl Scouts U.S.A., 1959-60. Mem. ALA, Southeastern Library Assn., N.C. Library Assn. (sec. public library sect., chmn. 1979-81), Gen. Alumni Assn. Greensboro Coll. (pres. 1959-61). Democrat. Methodist. Clubs: Tuesday Afternoon Reading, Little Gardens Garden (pres.), Penrose Park Country. Office: 527 Boone Rd Eden NC 27288

DAVIS, MARTHA LOUCRETIA, insurance company official; b. Commerce, Tex., Nov. 10, 1952; d. Harold Lawayne and Mary Pearl (Duncan) Johnson; m. Jimmy Lee Davis, July 2, 1971. Student U. Tex., 1970. Cert. profl. ins. woman. Ins. rater Hartford Co., Dallas, 1971-72; ins. underwriter Ben Spurgin Ins., Dallas, 1972-78; regional systems analyst Comml. Union Ins., Dallas, 1978—; tchr. Richland Coll., Dallas, 1982—. Mem. Ins. Women Dallas, Nat. Assn. Ins. Women. Office: Commercial Union Ins Co 9330 Amberton Pkwy Dallas TX 75243

DAVIS, MARY ELIZABETH MOOREHEAD, teacher; b. Grafton, W.Va., Dec. 23, 1928; d. Lester Moorehead and Sadie Marquois (Lewis) Moorehead; m. Charles Cardwell, July 7, 1951 (div.); 1 dau., Karen Barbara Cardwell Poole; m. John Marshall Davis, Nov. 17, 1973. B.S., Bluefield State Coll., 1951. Tchr., Orange, Va., 1960-73, Buena Vista, Va., 1973-78, Roanoke, Va., 1978—; relief prin. Lincoln Terr. Sch., 1982—; art. cons. Head Start, 1973. Girl Scout U.S.A. leader, 1965-79. Mem. Roanoke Ednl. Assn., Va. Edn. Assn., NEA, Internat. Reading Assn., PTA (life), Blue Ridge Council Tchrs. of Math., Alpha Kappa Alpha. Baptist. Home: 625 Hanover NW Roanoke VA 24016

DAVIS, MAUREEN FLYNN, nursing educator; b. Syracuse, N.Y., Oct. 8, 1943; d. Paul V. and Laura C. (Fath) Flynn; m. Charles E. Davis, Jan. 6, 1978; children—Michael Briggs, Megan F. B.S.N., Creighton U., 1965; M.S.N., U. Nebr., 1976. R.N., cert. rehab. nurse. Staff nurse Gen. Rose Meml. Hosp., Denver, 1965-69; clin. instr. Methodist Hosp. Sch. Nursing, Omaha, 1969-70; asst. instr. U. Nebr., Omaha, 1970-74; staff nurse Clarkson Hosp., Omaha, 1974-75; instr. Coll. St. Mary, Omaha, 1976-77; asst. prof. Clemson (S.C.) U., 1977-85; staff nurse Roger C. Peace Inst. Rehabilitative Medicine, Greensville, S.C., 1981—. Vol. ARC, 1981—, Am. Cancer Soc., 1980 (both Greenville). Mem. ANA, Assn. Rehab. Nurses (bd. dirs. S.C. chpt. 1986), Oncology Nurses Soc., Sigma Theta Tau (chpt. counselor 1981-83, chmn. nominating com. 1980-81) Republican. Roman Catholic. Home: 14 Keowee Ave Greenville SC 29605

DAVIS, MORRIS SCHUYLER, astronomer, educator; b. Bklyn., Dec. 14, 1919; s. Nathan Samuel and Helen (Gross) D.; m. Dorothy Irene Hall, May 26, 1945; children—Glenn C., Elizabeth Nyblade, Cynthia, Deborah Toth, Katherine, Martha Werlen. B.A., Bklyn. Coll., 1946; M.A., U. Mo., 1947; Ph.D., Yale U., 1950. Instr. dept. math. and astronomy U. Ky., Lexington, 1950-52; asst. prof. astronomy U. N.C., Chapel Hill, 1952-56, Morehead prof. astronomy, 1970—; dir. Yale Computer Ctr., 1956-66; pres., dir. Triangles Univs. Computation Ctr., 1966-70; trustee Univ. Research Assocs., 1978-83. Fellow AAAS; mem. Internat. Astron. Union, Am. Astron. Soc. (chmn. div. dynamical astronomy). Unitarian. Editor: Celestial Mechanics. Home: 404 Estes Dr Chapel Hill NC 27514 Office: Dept Physics and Astronomy U NC Phillips Hall 039A Chapel Hill NC 27514

DAVIS, NEIL OWEN, newspaper executive, educator; b. Hartford, Ala., Aug. 15, 1914; s. Charles Francis and Katherine Anderson (West) D.; B.S., Auburn U., 1935; Nieman Found. fellow Harvard U., 1941-42; m. Henrietta Worsley, Nov. 5, 1938; children—Katherine Davis Savage, Henrietta Lee Davis Blackman, Neil Owen. Reporter, Dothan (Ala.) Jour., 1935; editor N. Ga. Jour., Rossville, 1936; editor Auburn (Ala.) Bull., 1937-75, editor, pub., 1937-75, editor emeritus, 1975—; prof. journalism Auburn U., 1976-80; pres. Bull. Pub. Co., Inc., 1939-75; sec. Auburn Broadcasting Co., Inc., 1947-76. Bd. dirs. United Fund, 1958, 70-74; sec. Lee County Democratic Com., 1952-68, mem. Ala. Dem. Exec. Com. 3d Dist., 1940-42, 48-56; mem. Ala. Bd. Pardons and Parole, 1951-55; mem. bd. Christian edn. Presbyterian Ch. in U.S., 1959-68, mem. ad interim com. to write New Confession of Faith, 1968-75, ruling elder 1st Presbyn. Ch., Auburn, Ala., moderator John Knox Presbytery, 1979, moderator Synod of Mid-South, 1980-81; trustee Agnes Scott Coll., Decatur, Ga., 1968-86, emeritus, 1986—; pres. Ala. Commn. for Better Schs., 1963; participant U.S. Presdl. Adv. Commn. on Rural Poverty, 1966-67; mem. So. Regional Council, 1968—; participant So. Regional Edn. Bd. coms., 1958-64; mem. Ala. Ethics Commn., 1980-83, chmn., 1983-84; chmn. com. to study Auburn Pub. Schs., 1976; mem. adv. council humanities Auburn U., chmn., 1981-83; bd. dirs. Council on Liberal Learning; vice chmn. Lee County Dept. Pension and Security. Served from 2d lt. to maj. USAAF, 1942-45. Recipient Pub. Service award Jaycees, 1941; numerous editorial awards Ala. Press Assn., 1938-75; Herrick Editorial award Nat. Editorial Assn., 1954, 59, 62; Auburn U. Alumni award for contbns. in humanities. Mem. Auburn C. of C. (dir. 1955-56, 1967-68), Ala. Press Assn. (pres. 1947), Sigma Delta Chi, Omicron Delta Kappa, Phi Kappa Phi, Lambda Chi Alpha. Author: (with others) Newsmen's Holiday, 1942; contbr. article to Nation Mag., 1947. Home: 241 Cary Dr Auburn AL 36830

DAVIS, NORMA JEAN, nurse; b. Seattle, Sept. 23, 1946; d. William Lamar and Norma Belle (Brantley) Rogers; m. Robert Howard Davis, 1967 (div. Nov. 1973); 1 child, Tia Telesa. Diploma, Meml. Hosp. Sch. Nursing, 1967; B.S. in Nursing, Armstrong State Coll., 1980. Cert. operating room nurse. Staff nurse operating nurse Candler Gen. Hosp., Savannah, Ga., 1967-73, 1976-80, head nurse operating room, 1980-84, coordinator surgery services, 1984—; staff nurse operating room Meml. Med. Ctr., Savannah, 1973-76; chmn. key mem. com. Internat. Mgmt. Council, Savannah, 1983—. Mem. Assn. Operating Room Nurses (bd. dirs. 1981-83, 1985—). Republican. Baptist. Avocations: aerobics; swimming; biking; reading; horseback riding. Office: Candler Gen Hosp 5353 Reynolds St Savannah GA 31405

DAVIS, PATRICIA LEE, special education educator; b. Madison, W.Va., Nov. 19, 1953; d. Patrick Henry and Mildred Louise (Hendricks) Goodwin; m. Stephen Paul Davis, Sept. 18, 1976. B.A. in Edn., Fairmont State Coll., 1975; M.A. in Spl. Edn., W.Va. Coll. Grad. Studies, 1979; postgrad. W.Va. U. Cert. tchr., W.Va. Tchr. specializing in learning disabilities Pub. Schs. Wirt County (W.Va.), 1977-79, Mason County (W.Va.), 1979-80, North Elem. Sch., Ravenswood, W.Va., 1980—. Mem. W.Va. Edn. Assn. (rep.), NEA, Alpha Delta Kappa, (chpt. sgt.-at-arms 1982-84). AAUP. Democrat. Presbyterian (elder). Home: 107 Fernwood Way Millwood WV 25262 Office: North Elem Sch Kaiser Ave Ravenswood WV 26164

DAVIS, PHILLIP EUGENE, oil field chemical manufacturing company executive, chemical engineer; b. Ft. Wayne, Ind., June 24, 1933; s. Ora Merle and Alice Louise (Fox) D.; B.S. in Chem. Engring., U. Mich., 1955; postgrad. Ind. State U., 1965-67, Marylhurst Coll., Portland, Oreg., 1979—; m. Patsy Ann Smith, July 28, 1985; 1 son, Alex Steven. Chemist, tech. engr., prodn. engr. Shell Chem. Corp., Deer Park, Tex., 1955-62; project engr., prodn. engr., plant engr. Velsicol Chem. Co., Marshall, Ill., 1962-70; project engr. Rhone Poulenc, Inc., New Brunswick, N.J., 1970-76, successively plant engr., prodn. supt., tech. mgr., Portland, Oreg., 1976-80; chief engr. Houston plant Baker Performance chems. div. Baker Internat., 1980-82, div. engr. mfg. div., 1982—, also cons. Served with AUS, 1955-57; maj. M.P. Res., 1957-76. Mem. Am. Inst. Chem. Engrs., Am. Inst. Plant Engrs., Res. Officers Assn. U.S., Alumni Assn. U. Mich. Republican. Mem. Christian and Missionary Alliance. Home: 1308 Town Circle Baytown TX 77520 Office: 3920 Essex Ln Houston TX 77027

DAVIS, RICHARD ALFRED, III, biomedical electronics technician; b. Portsmouth, Va., Sept. 9, 1953; s. Richard Alfred Jr. and Evelyn Anna (Witzmann) D. A.A.S., Tidewater Community Coll., 1977. Biomed. electronics technician Petersburg Gen. Hosp., Va., 1977—. Served with USN, 1971-75. Recipient God and Country award Boy Scouts Am., Virginia Beach, Va., 1967, Eagle award, 1968. Mem. Tidewater Biomed. Inst. Soc., Assn. Advancement of Med. Instrumentation. Club: Jordan Point Yacht (rear commodore 1984, vice commodore 1985) (Hopewell, Va.). Avocations: sailing; boating; swimming; hiking; hunting. Office: Petersburg Gen Hosp 801 S Adams St Petersburg VA 23803

DAVIS, RICHARD MACOMBER, aerospace executive; b. Fall River, Mass., Nov. 27, 1929; s. Richard Ordway and Doris Lucile (Macomber) D.; m. Sally Ann Patten; children—Brad Jeffrey, Kimberly Ann. B.S. in Aero. Engring., MIT, 1951; grad. Advanced Mgmt. Program, Harvard U., 1975. With Martin Marietta Corp., New Orleans, 1953—, various positions structures design, thermal heat shield design, nuclear crew compartment design, systems engr. for advanced re-entry vehicles, space sta. studies, skylab dir., to 1978, v.p. Space Shuttle External Tank Project, 1978—, dep. gen. mgr., 1979—, gen. mgr., 1984—. Served to 1st lt. USAF, 1951-53. Recipient Jefferson Cups, Martin Marietta, 1965, 70; Disting. Pub. Service medal NASA, 1981. Republican. Home: 100 Blackbeard Dr Slidell LA 70461 Office: PO Box 29304 New Orleans LA 70189

DAVIS, ROBERT, surgeon; b. Johannesburg, South Africa, Jan. 18, 1941; came to U.S., 1973; s. Simon and Sarah Ethel (Friedman) D.; m. Arlene M. Friedman, June 15, 1943; children—Garth, Toni, Kim. B.Medicine and B.Surgery, U. Witwatersrand, Johannesburg, 1963. Diplomate Am. Bd.

Surgery. Rotating intern internal medicine and surgery Johannesburg Gen. Hosp., 1964, sr. house surgeon, 1965; gen. practice, Florida, South Africa, mem. hemodialysis staff Discover's Meml. Hosp., 1965-71; surg. registrar Univ. Group Hosps., Johannesburg, 1972-73; resident in surgery Albert Einstein Coll. Medicine, N.Y.C., 1973-74, U. Tex. Med. Br., Galveston, 1974-76; practice gen., thoracic and vascular surgery, Houston, 1976—; mem. staff Meth. Hosp., Diagnostic Ctr. Hosp., Park Plaza Hosp.; mem. courtesy staff Tex. Children's Hosp., St. Luke's Hosp., Tex. Woman's Hosp., Twelve Oaks Hosp.; clin. instr. surgery U. Tex., Houston, Baylor Coll. Medicine. Pres. MacMedic Pubs. Author: (video) MacAnatomy. Fellow Royal Coll. Surgeons (Edinburgh), ACS; mem. Internat. Coll. Surgeons, Am. Soc. Abdominal Surgeons, AMA (Physician's Recognition award 1978, 83), Tex. Med. Assn., Harris County Med. Soc., Houston Surg. Soc., Houston Gastroent. Soc., Singleton Surg. Soc. Clubs: Doctors, Chancellors. Contbr. articles to med. jours. Office: 6560 Fannin Suite 738 Houston TX 77030

DAVIS, ROBERT, entomologist, educator; b. Delhi, N.Y., Feb. 22, 1931; s. Andrew Ferris and Frances Florence (Brown) D.; m. Marie Ann Mairholtz, July 2, 1966; children—Stephen R., Andrea M., Frances E. B.S. in Agr., U. Ga., 1956, M.S., 1961, Ph.D., 1963. Registered profl. entomologist. Entomologist, State of Ga., Atlanta, 1956, U.S. Army, Atlanta, 1956-59, U.S. Forest Service, Ashville, N.C., 1959-60, Agrl. Research Service, U.S. Dept. Agr., Tifton, Ga., 1963-65; supervisory research entomologist, lab. dir. Agrl. Research Service, U.S. Dept. Agr., Savannah, Ga., 1969—; adj. prof. U. Ga. Served to cpl. U.S. Army, 1952-54. Nat. Wildlife fellow, 1960; Sigma Xi research grantee, 1962. Mem. Entomol. Soc. Am., AAAS, Ga. Entomol. Soc., S.C. Entomol. Soc., Fla. Entomol. Soc., Sigma Xi. Contbr. articles to sci. jours., chpts. to books; author: Catalogue of Eriophyid Mites, 1982. Office: Agrl Research Service US Dept Agr PO Box 22909 Savannah GA 31403

DAVIS, ROBERT D., grocery company executive; b. 1931. B.A./B.S., U. Fla., 1953. With Winn-Dixie Stores, Inc., Jacksonville, Fla., 1955—, asst. sec., asst. treas., 1961-65, v.p. fin., 1965-82, vice chmn. bd., 1982, chmn. bd., 1983—. Address: Winn-Dixie Stores Inc 5050 Edgewood Ct Jacksonville FL 32205*

DAVIS, ROBERT ELLIOTT, chemist; b. Salt Lake City, Mar. 21, 1930; s. Mervin Wesley and Frances (Gilroy) D.; m. Marie DeNiro, July 6, 1955; children—Karen, Beth, Denise. A.B. in Chemistry, U. Utah, Salt Lake City, 1951, Ph.D. in Chemistry, 1954. Lic. profl. chem. engr., Calif. With Kerr-McGee Corp., Oklahoma City, 1969—, mgr. process engring., 1976-79, mgr. process technology, 1979-82, sr. tech. specialist, 1982-83, mgr. tech. ctr., 1983—. Mem. Am. Chem. Soc., Am. Inst. Chem. Engrs., Metall. Soc., AIME. Republican. Latter-day Saint. Office: Kerr McGee Corp Technology Div PO Box 25861 Oklahoma City OK 73125

DAVIS, ROBERT LLOYD, mathematician, educator; b. N.Y.C., May 23, 1919; s. Elmer Holmes and Florence (MacMillan) D.; m. Marian Hale, Mar. 18, 1949; m. Irene Jones, Mar. 21, 1967; 1 dau., Wendy. B.S., U. Chgo., 1949, M.S. in Math., 1951; Ph.D., U. Mich., 1957. Asst. prof. math. U. Va., Charlottesville, 1956-59; vis. asst. prof. math Stanford (Calif.) U., 1959-60; asst. prof. U. N.C.-Chapel Hill, 1960-61, assoc. prof., 1961-70, prof. math., 1970—; prof. associé U. Nice (France), 1966-67. Served to 1st lt., inf. AUS, 1941-42, 42-46. Decorated Silver Star, Purple Heart; fellow NSF, 1959-60; Fulbright fellow, 1966-67. Mem. Am. Math. Soc., Math. Assn. Am., Sigma Xi. Editor and co-author: Decision Processes, 1954; Modern Mathematical Methods and Models, 1958; editor: Elementary Mathematics of Sets, 1958. Home: 204 Glenhill Ln Chapel Hill NC 27514 Office: Dept Math U NC Chapel Hill NC 27514

DAVIS, ROBERT NORMAN, hospital administrator; b. Plainfield, N.J., July 30, 1938; s. Norman DuBois and Geraldine Elizabeth (Sliker) D.; B.S. civil engring., Pa. State U., 1960; M.S. in Mgmt., Rensselaer Poly. Inst., 1970; m. Elizabeth Ann Paine, June 15, 1985; children—Keith Robert, Kathryn Beth, Karl Thomas. Dir. plant ops. Am. Hosp. Assn., Chgo., 1964-68; dir. mgmt. engring. Hosp. Assn. of N.Y., Albany, 1968-72; asso. exec. dir. United Hosp., Portchester, N.Y., 1973-75; regional mgr. Arthur Young & Co., N.Y.C., 1975, Medicus Systems Corp., Nashville, 1976-79; pres. Resource Devel. Assos., Hendersonville, Tenn., 1979—; asso. adminstr. Vanderbilt U. Hosp., Nashville, 1979-81; adminstr. Meml. div. Charleston (W.Va.) Area Med. Center, 1981-83. Bd. dirs., treas. Middle Tenn. Youth Soccer Inc., 1979-82. Served with M.S.C., USAF, 1960-63. Mem. Hosp. Mgmt. Systems Soc. (dir. 1972-75, hon. fellow 1985), Am. Coll. Hosp. Adminstrs. Baptist. Contbr. articles to profl. jours. Home: Box 151 Hendersonville TN 37077

DAVIS, ROBERT SMOLIAN, builder, developer; b. Birmingham, Ala., Nov. 10, 1943; s. Laurance Barton Davis and Marcia (Smolian) Pruce; m. Sarah Robbins, 1966 (div. 1969); m. Daryl Rose, May 22, 1983. B.A., Antioch Coll., 1965; M.B.A., Harvard U., 1967. Pres. Seaside Community Devel. Corp., Fla., 1981—. Commr. South Walton Fire Dist., Walton County, Fla., 1984—. Recipient award Archtl. Record Houses, Apogee, Miami, Fla., 1977, Citation, Progressive Architecture, Seaside Town Plan, 1983, Honor award AIA, Seaside Town Plan, 1983, 84. Democrat. Jewish. Lodge: Lions. Avocations: cooking; boating; beach walking. Home: 105 Tupelo St Seaside FL 32454 Office: Seaside Community Devel Corp 103 Tupelo St Seaside FL 32454

DAVIS, S. ROBERT, business executive; b. Columbus, Ohio, Oct. 31, 1938; s. Herman and Minnie (Newman) D.; (m), 1955; 4 children. Student, Ohio State U. Founder, pres. S. Robert Davis & Co., Inc., Columbus, Ohio, 1958-68; founder, now pres. and chmn. bd. Orange Co. Inc., Columbus, 1968—; dir. M.I.F. Funds; chmn. bd. Buckeye Fed. Savs. & Loan Assn., Strata Corp. Clubs: Columbus Athletic, Scioto Country.

DAVIS, SYLVIA MAE, speech pathology educator; b. Port Arthur, Tex., Nov. 22, 1949; d. Giles A. and Bernice H. (Collins) Davis. B.S., Lamar U., 1971, M.S., 1972; Ph.D., Wichita State U., 1976. Cert. speech pathologist, La. Instr. dept. instructional services Wichita State U., 1974-75; speech/lang. pathologist Inst. Logopedics, Wichita, Kans., 1974-76; asst. prof. dept. audiology and speech pathology Sch. of Allied Health Professions, La. State U. Med. Ctr., New Orleans, 1976-79, assoc. prof. dept. communication disorders and otorhinolaryngology, 1979-83, prof., coordinator acads., 1983—. Mem. adv. bd. Adult Day Care program Assoc. Cath. Charities, New Orleans, 1982—, pres. elect, 1983. Hardin County (Tex.) grantee, 1973. Mem. Am. Speech-Lang.-Hearing Assn., Council for Exceptional Children, Soc. for Ear, Nose and Throat Advances in Children. Contbr. articles to profl. jours. Office: 1900 Gravier St New Orleans LA 70112

DAVIS, T. BOB, dentist, pianist; b. Luverne, Ala., Apr. 10, 1941; s. John Wilson and Vera Elizabeth (Willis) D.; m. Janis Margaret Murphy, Nov. 29, 1969; children—Shawn Timothy, Angie Beth, Creth Andrew. A.A., Mars Hill Coll., 1961; B.A., Samford U., 1963; D.M.D., U. Ala., 1967, Fellowship Acad. Gen. Dentistry, Chgo., 1981. Gen. practice dentistry, Dallas, 1969—; accompanist 1st Baptist Ch., Dallas, 1967—; staff pianist Prestonwood Bapt. Ch., Dallas, 1983—; pianist So. Bapt. Conv., Tex. Bapt. Evangelism Conf., Tex. Bapt. Conv. Super Summer Conf. Record albums include Gratefully T Bob, 1981, T. Bob-Piano, 1983. Vol. Buckner Childrens Home, Dallas, 1970—, Dallas County Juvenile Shelter, 1983—; deacon 1st Bapt. Ch., Dallas, 1976—; vol. dentist Matamoris Mexico Bapt. Orphanage, Mexico, 1977—; guest artist KCBI Radio Sharathon, Dallas, 1976—, Dino's 7 piano Pianorama Concerts, 1983—. Mem. ADA, Nat. Acad. Gen. Dentistry (del. 1981—), Tex. Dental Assn., Tex. Acad. Gen. Dentistry (pres. 1984-85), Dallas Acad. Gen. Dentistry (pres. 1982-83), Dallas County Dental Soc. (sec.-treas. 1983-84), Christian Med. Soc. Republican. Avocation: concert pianist. Home: 11925 Loch Ness Dr Dallas TX 75218 Office: 5510 Abrams Rd Suite 118 Dallas TX 75214 also 6959 Arapaho Suite 210 Dallas TX 75248

DAVIS, THEODORE ROOSEVELT, bishop, contractor; b. Hazelhurst, Miss., Mar. 28, 1903; s. Moses and Narcissus D.; m. Freddie Wilhemett, Aug. 30, 1923 (dec. 1984); children—Myrtle, Wilma, Dorothy, Connie, Frankie, Theo, Roosevelt; m. Emma Hawthrone, Jan. 12, 1985. Hon. degree Saints Acad., Lexington, Miss., 1969, Anthony Les Ctr., Hattiesburg, Miss., 1972. Ordained minister Pentecostal Ch., 1930. Contractor Wise Constrn., 1930-50; pastor Ch. of God in Christ, Bolton, Miss., 1930-45, Rankin, Miss., 1931-42, Vicksburg, Miss., 1937-47; sec. Jurisdiction So. Miss., 1940-55; dist. supt. 7th Dist., 1947-62; jurisdiction bishop So. Miss., 1962—; gen. contractor hdqrs. 1st jurisdiction Ch. of God in Christ, Jackson, Miss., 1972—, nat. treas., Memphis, 1980-85, also mem. bd. bishops; chaplain Westside Housing, Jackson, 1983—, Hinds County Republican Com., Jackson, 1977-85; cons. for housing Chisca Hotel, Memphis, 1978-85, chmn. bldg. commn., 1979-85; Bd. dirs. Saints Jr. Coll., Lexington, 1974-79; mem. Jackson Pub. Service Commn., 1984-85. Named Man of Yr., Religious Workers Guild, 1972; recipient Leadership award Ch. of God in Christ, 1984. Mem. Miss. Ministerial Allowance. Club: Millionaires (Memphis). Avocation: fishing.

DAVIS, THOMAS GARFIELD, utilities company executive; b. Waynesville, Mo., May 17, 1947; s. Nova Nelson and Erma Ruth (Reece) D.; B.B.A. in Acctg., North Tex. State U., 1969; m. Carolyn Gale Davis, Feb. 12, 1969; 1 dau., Katherine Deanna. With Dallas Power and Light Co., 1969-84; gen. acctg. supr. Tex. Utilities Electric Co., 1984—. Mem. Nat. Assn. Accts., Tex. Soc. C.P.A.s., Am. Soc. C.P.A.s. Lutheran. Home: 5718 Galaxie Rd Garland TX 75042 Office: 2001 Bryan Tower Dallas TX 75201

DAVIS, TINE WAYNE, JR., retail grocery chain executive; b. Miami, Fla., Sept. 16, 1946; s. Tine Wayne and Eunice (Chandler) D.; B.S., U. Ala., 1968, J.D., 1971; m. Mary Katherine Owen, Dec. 1, 1967; children—Catherine Rebecca, Elizabeth Ashley, Katherine Chase. Admitted to bar; joined Winn-Dixie Stores as lawyer, now v.p. public affairs, also dir.; dir. Barnett Bank of Jacksonville (Fla.), Central Bank of Montgomery (Ala.); chmn. Agribus. Inst. Fla., 1982. Chmn. Citizens Council on Budget Research, 1981-82; chmn. Retail Industry Polit. Action Com., 1981-82; chmn. bd. trustees Jacksonville Country Day Sch. 1985-86; bd. dirs. Jacksonville Wolfson Children's Hosp., Leadership Jacksonville; trustee Bolles Sch.; treas., Jacksonville Art Mus., 1985-86, bd. dirs.; chmn. Men's com. Cummer Mus. Art, 1986; v.p. govt. affairs Jacksonville C. of C., 1986, bd. dirs.; mem. Pres.'s Cabinet U. Ala.; mem. gov.'s Commn. Unitary Tax, 1984. Served with U.S. Army, 1971. Mem. Assoc. Industries Fla. (chmn. 1981-83), Fla. Supermarket Assn. (pres. 1980-82), Fla. Bar Assn., Fla. Retail Fedn. (chmn. 1983-85), Ala. Bar Assn., Am. Bar Assn., Food Mktg. Inst. (govt. relations com.), Phi Delta Phi. Republican. Episcopalian. Office: PO Box B Jacksonville FL 32203

DAVIS, W. E., clergyman. Bishop, Church of God in Christ, Southwestern Fla., Tampa. Office: Ch of God in Christ 2008 33d Ave Tampa FL 33610*

DAVIS, W. EUGENE, judge. Judge U.S. Ct. Appeals, Fifth Circuit, Lafayette, La. Address: PO Drawer W Lafayette LA 70130*

DAVIS, WILLIAM F., JR., insurance company consultant; b. Suffolk, Va., Mar. 13, 1955; s. William F. and Elaine (Leonard) D.; m. Susan Mackey, June 24, 1979; 1 child, Bryan. Student Va. Mil. Inst., 1973-75; B.S., Old Dominion U., 1977. Engineering cons. Aetna Casualty & Surety Co., Richmond, Va., 1978—. Mem. Am. Soc. Safety Engrs., Richmond Jaycees (publs. dir. 1983, membership dir. 1984). Republican. Methodist. Avocation: skiing. Home: 9502 Fordson Rd Richmond VA 23229 Office: Aetna Casualty & Surety Box 26283 Richmond VA 23260

DAVIS, WILLIAM GLENN, JR., orthodontist; b. High Point, N.C., June 28, 1938; s. William Glenn and Hazel (Hicks) D.; m. Ann Sherrill, July 29, 1961 (div. Mar. 1978); children—William Glenn III, Katherine, Ashlyn, Kelly; m. Deborah Fisher, Apr. 1, 1978; children—Hunter, Hillary. B.S., U. N.C., 1960, D.D.S., 1963, M.Sc., 1967. Diplomate Am. Bd. Orthodontics. Pvt. practice orthodontics, Chapel Hill, N.C., 1967—. Served to lt. USNR, 1960-65. Mem. ADA, Am. Assn. Orthodontists, So. Soc. Orthodontists, N.C. Assn. Orthodontists (pres. 1983-84), N.C. Dental Soc., U. N.C. Orthodontic Alumni Assn. (pres. 1971-72). Methodist. Lodge: Rotary (pres. 1971-72). Avocations: hunting; fishing; golf; tennis. Home: 802 Old Mill Rd Chapel Hill NC 27514 Office: Conner Drive Profl Bldg Conner Dr Chapel Hill NC 27514

DAVIS-JONES, CLAIRE CURTIS, meeting planner, consultant; b. Tucumcari, N. Mex., Aug. 3, 1938; d. Swep Taylor and Elizabeth (Curtis) Davis; m. Thomas Nelson Jones, Dec. 27, 1976. B.S., U. So. Miss., 1960; postgrad. U. So. Miss.-Jackson, 1967, George Mason U., 1980-81. Exec. v.p. Rivers and Harbors Assn. of Miss., Jackson, 1962-67; staff and press aide Congressman William M. Colmer, Washington, 1967-72; dir. women's programs Nat. Rural Electric Coop. Assn., Washington, 1972-80; pres. Davis-Jones & Assocs., Vienna, Va., 1980—. Recipient Outstanding Contbns. award Rivers and Harbors Assn. of Miss., 1967. Mem. Pub. Relations Soc. Miss. (sec./v.p. 1962-63, 64-65, 67), Am. Soc. Assn. Execs., Meeting Planners Internat., Greater Washington Soc. Assn. Execs., Washington Conv. and Visitors Assn. Baptist. Club: Hunter Valley Riding (treas. 1982-84, sec. 1985—). Avocations: stamp and coin collecting; relic hunting; gardening; horsebackriding. Address: Davis-Jones & Assocs 10411 Wickens Rd Vienna VA 22180

DAVISON, FREDERICK CORBET, university president; b. Atlanta, Sept. 23, 1929; s. Frederick Collins and Gladys (Carsley) D.; D.V.M., U. Ga., 1952; Ph.D., Iowa State U., 1963; L.H.D. (hon.), Presbyn. Coll., 1977; LL.D. (hon.), Mercer U., 1978, U. N.B., Can., 1985; m. Dianne Castle, Sept. 3, 1952; children—Frederick Corbet, William C., Anne. Pvt. practice vet. medicine, Marietta, Ga., 1952-58; research asso. Iowa State U., Ames, 1958-59, asst. prof., 1960-63, asso. inst. for atomic research, 1960; asst. dir. sci. activities Am. Vet. Med. Assn., Chgo., 1963-64; dean sch. vet. medicine U. Ga., Athens, 1964-66; vice chancellor Univ. System Ga., Atlanta, 1966-67; pres. U. Ga. at Athens, 1967—; dir. Fed. Savs. & Loan Assn. Mem. council Synod of Ga. Recipient Disting. Achievement award Iowa State U., 1978. Mem. Am. (council on biol. and therapeutic agts.), Ga. vet. med. assns., Inst. Lab. Animal Research of Nat. Acad. Scis., Nat. Com. on Pharmacy and Vet. Medicine, Sigma Xi, Phi Kappa Phi, Sigma Alpha Epsilon, Omega Tau Sigma, Alpha Zeta, Phi Zeta, Gamma Sigma Delta. Contbr. articles to profl. jours. Office: U Ga Athens GA 30601

DAVISSON, NELSON MARC, dentist, army officer; b. Winchester, Ind., Sept. 16, 1938; s. Ray Marcus and Garnet Rebecca (Addington) D.; A.B., DePauw U., 1960; D.D.S., Ind. U., 1964; m. Patricia Ann Crossen, Aug. 24, 1963; children—George William Tennis, Lani Catherine. Commd. capt. U.S. Army, 1964, advanced through grades to col., 1980; practice dentistry, Ft. Gordon, Ga., 1964-68, Viet-Nam, 1968-69, Fort Sam Houston, Tex., 1969-70; asst. chief crown and bridge service Walter Reed Hosp., Washington, 1971-72; chief crown and bridge service dental detachment, Ft. Leavenworth, Kans., 1972-77, 87th Med. Detachment, APO N.Y., 1977-81, Ft. Bliss, Tex., 1981-82; chief fixed prosthodontics service William Beaumont Army Med. Ctr., El Paso, Tex., 1982—. Decorated Bronze Star, Meritorious Service medal, Army Commendation medal. Diplomate Am. Bd. Prosthodontics. Fellow Am. Coll. Prosthodontists; mem. ADA, VFW, Psi Omega. Mem. Ch. of Jesus Christ of Latter-day Saints (elder 1971—). Home: 1020 De Leon Dr 303 Dunedin FL 33528 Office: USA Dentac El Paso TX 79920

DAVY, KAREN LEE, bank official; b. Columbus, Ohio, Dec. 2, 1952; d. Richard Lee and Janet Ruth (Seidel) D.; A.A., Manatee Jr. Coll., 1973; B.A., U. West Fla., 1975. Comml. loan note teller Nat. Bank of Sarasota (Fla.), 1973; fin. intern Office Comptroller of Currency, Atlanta, 1974-75, asst. nat. bank examiner, 1976-80, mem. EEO affirmative action com., region 6, 1977-80; consumer compliance asso. First City Bancorp. of Tex., Inc., Houston, 1980-81, consumer compliance rep., 1981-83, sr. consumer compliance rep., 1983, group mgr., 1983—. Active Sheltering Arms telephone reassurance program for elderly, Center for Retarded. Named Greek Woman of Yr. Panhellenic Assn., U. West Fla., Pensacola, 1974-75. Mem. Greater Houston Bankers Compliance Assn., Nat. Assn. Female Execs., Nat. Assn. Bank Women. Democrat. Mem. Ch. of Christ. Office: First City Bancorp of Tex Inc 1001 Fannin St Houston TX 77002

DAWES, CHARLES EDWARD, retired manufacturing company executive; b. Peoria, Okla., Feb. 7, 1923; s. Charles Gates and Lottie (Nonkesis) D.; A.A., Joplin (Mo.) Jr. Coll., 1950; B.S., U. Ark., 1953; m. Lorraine Mercer, Apr. 16, 1948; children—Charla Rene, Kevin Lawrence. Mgr. mfg. Vickers, Inc., Joplin, 1953-57; sales engr. Sebastian Diesel Co., Joplin, 1957-59; gen. mgr. Duplex Mfg. Co., Ft. Smith, Ark., 1959-77; v.p. Flanders Industries, Inc., from 1977, now ret. Chief, Ottawa Indians of Okla.; sr. counselor Inter-tribal Songchiefs Okla. Bd. dirs. Ark.-Okla. Regional Edn. and Promotion Assn., Old Fort Militia; trustee St. Edward Mercy Med. Center; bd. dirs., pres. Abilities Unlimited, Inc.; bd. dirs., mem. exec. com. Ft. Smith United Fund; mem. adv. bd. Seneca Indian Sch. Served with USAAF, 1943-46. Mem. Am. Soc. Tool and Mech. Engrs., Ft. Smith C. of C. (dir.), Personnel Assn. N.W. Ark., Western Ark. Purchasing Assn., Mfg. Execs. Assn. (pres. Ft. Smith), Nat. Congress Am. Indians, Okla. Inter-Tribal Council. Republican. Presbyterian. Mason. Home: PO Box 32 Quapaw OK 74363 Office: 318 Kentucky St Quapaw OK 74363

DAWES, RICHARD IRVING, retired aluminum company executive; b. Arlington, Mass., Nov. 24, 1919; s. Irving Desmond and Corinne Lee (Thies) D.; m. Elisabeth Hewitt Coffin, Apr. 2, 1949; children—Alan Stuart, Carol Winfield, Beverly Gail. A.B., Harvard Coll., 1940; M.B.A., Harvard U., 1942. With Reynolds Metals Co., Richmond, Va., 1946-84, adminstrv. asst. inventory control, 1946-48, scheduling mgr. printing div., 1948-53, staff asst. to gen. prodn. control mgr., 1953-57, asst. corp. sec., 1957-70, corp. sec., 1970-84, dir., 1972-77. Served to lt. USN, 1942-46. Mem. Am. Soc. Corp. Secs., Republican. Presbyterian. Clubs: Country of Va., Richmond Gentry, Harvard of Va. Home: 8900 Watlington Rd Richmond VA 23229

DAWKINS, DIANTHA DEE, librarian; b. McCamey, Tex., Oct. 6, 1942; d. Kirby Walls and Lucille (Watson) D. B.A. U. Tex., 1966, M.L.S., 1971. Cert. sch. librarian. Asst. librarian Lee High Sch., Midland, Tex., 1966-70, librarian, media coordinator Lee Freshman High, 1979—; asst. librarian, media coordinator Midland High Sch., 1970-73; librarian Austin Freshman Sch., Midland, 1973-79. Editor Communication Report, 1980-81. Bd. dirs. Meml. Christian Ch., Midland, 1980-82, sec. bd., 1982. Mem. ALA, Library and Info. Tech. Assn., Library Instrn. Round Table, Tex. Library Assn. (life; coms. 1981—, council 1984-86 dist. chmn. elect 1984-85, chmn. 1985-86), Am. Assn. Sch. Librarians (affiliate assembly 1979, 82), Tex. Assn. Sch. Librarians (chmn. 1979-80, council 1978-86), Tex. Classroom Tchrs. Assn., Midland Classroom Tchrs. (dir. 1976-84, pres. 1979-80), Tex. State Tchrs. Assn. (life; dir. ex-officio 1979-80), Grad. Sch. Library Sci. U. Tex. Ex-Students (life), U. Tex. Ex-Students (life), Freedom to Read Found., Delta Kappa Gamma. Mem. Disciples of Christ Ch. Clubs: Midland Community Theatre Hamhocks, French Heels (treas. 1968) (Midland). Home: Box 80459 Midland TX 79709 Office: Library Lee Freshman Sch 1400 E Oak Midland TX 79705

DAWKINS, IMOGENE, acct., income tax cons. and preparer; b. Edgefield County, S.C., May 8, 1938; d. Jack and Rebecca (Simmons) D.; B.S., S.C. State Coll., 1960; diploma Inst. Children's Lit., 1980. Adminstrv. asst. Greenwood (S.C.) Sch. Dist. 50, 1960-70; manpower devel. specialist Manpower Adminstrn., Dept. Labor, Washington, 1970-74; manpower devel. specialist Office Adminstrn., Office Gov. S.C., Columbia, 1974-76; magistrate, Edgefield County-Edgefield City, S.C., 1980; owner, operator Dawkins Income Tax and Acctg. Services, Edgefield, 1978—; owner Dawkins Janitorial Service. Candidate for Edgefield County Council. Mem. Am. Legion Aux., Alpha Kappa Alpha. Baptist. Home and Office: PO Box 304 219 Peachtree St Edgefield SC 29824

DAWSON, ALICE SHANKLE, wholesale company executive, travel agent; b. San Antonio, Oct. 6, 1938; d. Perry and Alice (Stratton) Shankle; m. Joseph Meadows Dawson, Jr., Sept. 10, 1960; children—Leslie Elizabeth, Susan Phillips. B.A., U. Tex., 1960; student Stanford U., 1982. Cert. travel counselor Inst. Cert. Travel Agts. Tchr. St. Mary's Hall, San Antonio, 1960-70, 71-73, Alamo Heights High Sch., San Antonio, 1969-70; office mgr. Bexar Insulation Co., San Antonio, 1970-74; mgr. Travel Boutique, San Antonio, 1975-78; travel counselor Sanborn's, San Antonio, 1979-80; sec. Perry Shankle Co., San Antonio, 1980-81, v.p., 1981-84; v.p., dir. Bexar Insulation Co., San Antonio, 1969—, South Tex. Insulation Co., San Antonio, 1970—, Polar Bear Insulation, San Marcos, Tex., 1975-84. Bd. dirs. Fiesta San Antonio Commn., 1979-85, San Antonio Charity Ball Assn., 1982—, Friends of San Antonio Pub. Library, 1986—; adv. bd. Sch. Bus. U. Tex., San Antonio, 1985—; v.p. Battle of Flowers Assn., 1983-84. Mem. Greater San Antonio C. of C. (task force on free enterprise). Republican. Episcopalian. Office: One Alamo Ctr Suite 710 San Antonio TX 78205

DAWSON, ALMA, librarian; b. Lecompte, La., Feb. 4, 1943; d. Joseph and Delia (Murphy) D. B.S., Grambling (La.) Coll., 1963; M.L.S., U. Mich., 1974; postgrad. Ind. U., summer 1966, Northwestern State U., Natchitoches, La., 1967-68, 74, Prairie View A&M U., 1970-72, 80. Cert. secondary English tchr., La. Tchr., librarian Natchitoches Parish Sch. System, 1964-69; library asst. Prairie View A&M U., 1969-72; library assoc. U. Mich., Ann Arbor, 1972-74; head serials dept. Prairie View A&M U., 1974-82; head Sch. Library and Info. Sci. Library, La. State U., Baton Rouge, 1982—; instr. ednl. tech. Prairie View A&M U., 1980-82; bibliographer. T.H. Harris scholar, 1959-63; Wortham Found. scholar, 1959-63; library assoc., 1972-74; Mellon-ACRL Mgmt. intern Mellon Found./ALA, 1978. Mem. ALA, La. Library Assn., Spl. Libraries Assn. (bus. mgr. La. chpt.), Phi Delta Kappa, Delta Sigma Theta. Democrat. Baptist. Clubs: Baton Rouge Area Library, La. State U. Woman's Faculty. Office: La State U 263 Coates Hall Baton Rouge LA 70803

DAWSON, BRUCE WARREN, exploitation geologist; b. Hutchinson, Kans., Oct. 15, 1958. B.S. in Geology, U. Kans., 1982. Sr. geologist Sun Exploration & Prodn. Co., Lafayette, La., 1982—. Mem. Am. Assn. Petroleum Geologists. Club: Spirit of Sun (Lafayette) (v.p. 1984, pres. 1985). Office: Sun Exploration & Prodn 3639 Ambassador Caffery Rd Lafayette LA 70503

DAWSON, EARL BLISS, educator; b. Perry, Fla., Feb. 1, 1930; s. Bliss and Linnie (Callaham) D.; B.A., U. Kans., 1955; student Bowman Gray Sch. Medicine, 1955-57; M.A., U. Mo., 1960; Ph.D., Tex. A. & M. U., 1964; m. Winnie Ruth Isbell, Apr. 10, 1951; children—Barbara Gail, Patricia Ann, Robert Earl, Diana Lynn. Research instr. dept. obstetrics and gynecology U. Tex. Med. br., Galveston, 1963-67, research asst. prof., 1967-70, research asso. prof., 1970—; cons. Interdeptl. Com. on Nutrition for Nat. Defense, 1965-68; cons. Nat. Nutrition Survey, 1968-69. Served with USNR, 1951-52. Nutrition Research fellow, 1960-61; NSF scholar, 1961-62; NIH Research fellow, 1962-63. Mem. Am. Chem. Soc., Tex., N.Y. acads. scis., AAAS, Am. Inst. Physicists, Am. Inst. Nutrition, Am. Soc. Clin. Nutrition, Soc. Environ. Geochemistry and Health, Sigma Xi, Phi Rho Sigma. Baptist. Mason. Club: Mic-O-Say (Kansas City, Mo.). Contbr. numerous articles to profl. jours. Home: 15 Chimney Corners LaMarque TX 77568 Office: Dept Obstetrics and Gynecology U Tex Med Br Galveston TX 77550

DAWSON, GARY LYNN, financial services company executive; b. Washington, Dec. 22, 1948; s. Harry Samuel and Gladys (Avey) D.; m. Carol Ann Heidegger, Oct. 13, 1967; children—Kimberlie Yvonne, Christopher Erin. Student Abilene Christian U., 1966-68, Southwestern State Coll., 1969-70; B. Liberal Sci., U. Okla., 1982; M.B.A. U. Houston, 1984. Photographer Altus Times Democrat, Altus, Okla., 1968-72; mgr. ops. GC Services Corp., Houston, 1972-75, nat. mktg. mgr., 1975-78, mktg. v.p., 1978—; v.p. Med. Center Hosp., Conroe, Tex., 1982-84; Montgomery County Health Devel. Corp., Woodlands, Tex., 1983—. Bd. dirs. Birnamwood Homeowners Assn., Spring, Tex., 1978; mem. fin. com. Med. Center Hosp., Conroe, Tex., 1982, v.p., 1982. Recipient 1st place award for photography USAF, 1977, Dept. Def., 1972; numerous photography awards Okla. Press Assn., 1971. Mem. Hosp. Fin. Mgmt. Assn., Am. Coll. Med. Adminstrs., Tex. Hosp. Assn., Am. Hosp. Assn., Houston Area Apple Users Group. Republican. Mem. Church of Christ. Home: 30 N Deerfoot Circle The Woodlands TX 77380 Office: GC Services Corp 6330 Gulfton St Houston TX 77081

DAWSON, H. C. BRYAN, geologist, oil company executive; b. Jackson County, Okla., Apr. 4, 1930; s. Henry Clay and Eula Mae (Griffin) D.; m. Norma Valjean, Oct. 15, 1952; children—Neil Clay, Cindy Jean Johny Bryan, Scott Allen, Christy Sue. B.S., Oklahoma City U., 1959. Subsurface geologist Crest Exploratory Co., Amarillo, Tex., 1959-66; pres. Crown Petroleum Inc., Amarillo, 1966-70, Dawson Operating Co., Inc., Amarillo, 1970—. Served to sgt. USAF, 1950-53. Mem. Am. Assn. Petroleum Geologists. Republican. Baptist. Avocations: flying, golf. Office: Dawson Operating Co Inc PO Box 7381 Amarillo TX 79114-7381

DAWSON, ROBERT EDWARD, ophthalmologist; b. Rocky Mount, N.C., Feb. 23, 1918; s. William and Daisy (Wright) D.; B.S., Clark Coll., 1939; M.D., Meharry Med. Coll., 1943; m. Julia Belle Davis, Mar. 10, 1950; children—Dianne Elizabeth, Janice Elaine, Robert Edward, Melanie Lorraine. Diplomate Am. Bd. Ophthalmology (examiner 1979-82). Intern, Homer G. Phillips Hosp., St. Louis, 1943-44, resident, 1944-46; preceptor Duke Hosp., 1946-50, clin. instr. ophthalmology, 1968-70; practice ophthalmology, Durham, N.C., 1946-55, 57—; mem. attending staff ophthalmology Lincoln Hosp., Durham, 1946-55; cons. ophthalmology N.C. Central U. Health Service, Durham, 1950-64; chief ophthalmology and otolaryngology Lincoln Hosp., Durham, 1959-76; mem. attending staff ophthalmology Watts Hosp., Durham, 1966-76; mem. attending staff ophthalmology Durham County Gen. Hosp., v.p. med. staff, 1976-78; med. dir. Lincoln Hosp., Durham, 1968-70; lectr. ophthalmology Lincoln Hosp. Sch. Nursing, 1948-56; clin. asso. Duke U., 1969-75, clin. asst. prof. ophthalmology, 1975-85; mem. N.C. Adv. Com. on Med. Assistance,

1972-85; mem. adv. bd. N.C. State Commn. for Blind, 1965-75; mem. Gov.'s Adv. Com. Med. Assistance; regional surg. dir. Eye Bank Assn. Am., Inc., 1968-79. Mem. Durham Council Human Relations, 1967-69; mem. Pres. Com. on Employment of Handicapped, 1971-79. Bd. dirs. Durham County Tb Assn., 1950-54, Better Health Found., 1960-66, Durham Community House, 1966-68, Lincoln Community Health Center, Am. Cancer Soc., Durham United Fund, Durham County Mental Health Center, 1976-79, Found. for Better Health of Durham County Gen. Hosp., 1975-79; bd. dirs., v.p. Nat. Soc. Prevention of Blindness; trustee Durham Acad., 1969-72; life trustee Meharry Med. Coll.; trustee emeritus N.C. Central U.; mem. bd. mgmt. Meharry Med. Coll. Alumni Assn.; bd. assocs. Greensboro Coll., N.C.; chmn. bd. dirs. Lincoln Pvt. Diagnostic Clinic; bd. visitors Clark Coll., Atlanta. Served as maj., M.C., USAF, 1955-57. Recipient Disting. Service award Clark Coll., 1984, Nat. Assn. Equal Opportunity in Higher Edn., 1985. Fellow A.C.S., Acad. Ophthalmology; mem. Am. Assn. Ophthalmology, Soc. Eye Surgeons, AMA, Nat. Med. Assn. (trustee 1971-80, pres. 1979-80, Disting. Service award 1983), Pan Am. Med. Assn. (diplomate), Old North State Med. Soc. (pres. 1966-67), Durham Acad. Medicine (pres. 1967-68), NAACP (life), Durham Bus. and Profl. Chain, C. of C., Meharry Nat. Alumni Assn. (past pres.), Alpha Omega Alpha, Alpha Phi Alpha (past pres.), Sigma Pi Phi (pres.), Chi Delta Mu. Democrat. Mem. A.M.E. Ch. (stewards bd. 1968—). Mason (32 deg., Shriner). Club: Toastmasters (pres. 1969-70). Home: 817 Lawson St Durham NC 27701 Office: 512 Simmons St Durham NC 27701

DAWSON, WILLIAM CRAIG, geologist; b. Streator, Ill., Apr. 17, 1952; s. Richard G. and Ina Gertrude (Sullivan) D.; m. Michele Ann Miller, May 28, 1977; children—Seth William, Eli Branz. B.S. in Geology, U. Ill., 1974; M.S., U. Tex., 1976; Ph.D., U. Ill., 1984. Staff geologist Fossil Petroleum Co., Dallas, 1976-77; exploration geologist Eason Oil Co., Oklahoma City, 1977-79; research assoc. Ill. Geol. Survey, Urbana, 1979-81; teaching asst. U. Ill., 1981-84; sr. geologist Texaco Research Ctr., Houston, 1984—. Contbr. articles to profl. jours. Mem. Am. Assn. Petroleum Geologists, Soc. Econ. Paleontologists and Mineralogists, Internat. Assn. Sedimentologists, Tex. Acad. Sci., Sigma Xi. Office: Texaco Research Ctr 3901 Briarpark Houston TX 77215

DAWSON, WILLIAM WALLACE, JR., lawyer, state legislator; b. Vinita, Okla., Aug. 13, 1943; s. William Wallace and Imogene Marie (Cagle) D.; m. Marie Theresa Rim, Aug. 15, 1970; children—William Anthony, Thomas Gregory. B.A., Okla. State U., 1966, M.A., 1968; J.D., U. Tenn., 1973; postgrad. Ohio State U., 1970. Methodist minister, Earlsboro, Cushing and Glencoe, Okla., 1962-66; instr. Central State U., Edmond, Okla., 1967-69; asst. prof. Pa. State U., Erie, 1970-71; staff Okla. Ct. Criminal Appeals, 1973; ptnr. Dawson, Cadenhead & Kite, Seminole, Okla., 1973—; mem. Okla. State Senate, 1974-78, 82—; real estate broker, auctioneer, 1981—. Recipient U. Okla. Pres.'s Leadership award; U. Tenn. Coll. Law Cert. Outstanding Achievement, Legal Clinic Cert. of Merit; Nat. Found. March of Dimes Disting. Vol. Leadership award, 1975. Mem. Seminole County Bar Assn., Okla. Bar Assn., ABA, Okla. Assn. Auctioneers, Nat. Assn. Auctioneers. Democrat. Methodist. Office: Dawson Cadenhead & Kite Attys 221 E Evans Seminole OK 74868 also Bill Dawson Realty Auctioneer 221 E Evans Seminole OK 74868

DAY, GEORGE MICHAEL, safety engineer, risk management professional; b. Iowa City, May 15, 1953; s. Homer Dale and Anna G. (Gianopolus) D.; m. Kimberly Ruth Holm, Aug. 20, 1983. B.S. in Occupational Safety and Health, Ill. State U., 1975. Loss prevention rep. St. Paul Ins. Co., Houston, 1976-78, state risk mgmt. rep., North Platte, Nebr., 1978-83, mgr. risk mgmt. services, Metairie, La., 1983—; driving instr. Nat. Safety Council, Chgo., 1978—; instr. Nebr. Hunters Safety, 1980-83. Bd. dirs. North Platte Gold Exchange, 1981-83. Mem. Am. Soc. Safety Engrs., Nat. Safety Council, Nat. Rifle Assn., Jaycees (dir. 1982). Democrat. Greek Orthodox. Avocations: radio-controlled aircraft; coin collecting; fishing. Home: 1816 Cinclair Loop LaPlace LA 70068

DAY, JAMES ORIEN, III, physician; b. Milledgeville, Ga., May 21, 1948; s. James Orien and Odessa (Bell) D.; m. Hannah Marie Barber, Aug. 21, 1971; 1 dau., Joanna Claire. A. Sci., Middle Ga. Coll., 1968; B.S., U. Ga., 1970; M.D., Med. Coll. Ga., 1974. Diplomate Am. Bd. Internal Medicine. Intern, U. Ark. Med. Ctr., Little Rock, 1974-75, resident in internal medicine, 1975-77; practice medicine specializing in internal medicine, Griffin, Ga., 1977—; mem. staff Griffin-Spalding County Hosp., chmn. dept. medicine, 1983-85, chief of staff, 1986-87. Mem. ACP, Am. Soc. Internal Medicine, Med. Assn. Ga., Am. Heart Assn., Ga. Thoracic Soc., Spalding County Med. Soc. (sec.-treas. 1983-85), Phi Theta Kappa, Alpha Epsilon Delta. Lodge: Rotary.

DAY, JAMES VINCENT, JR., sales promotion and marketing company executive; b. Portland, Maine, June 15, 1951; s. James Vincent and Delma Irene (McCormick) D.; m. Kerri Jolles, Sept. 29, 1979. B.S., U. Maine, 1973. Asst. buyer Drugfair, Inc., Alexandria, Va., 1973-77, buyer, 1978-79, sales promotion coordinator, 1979-80, sales promotions mgr., 1980-81; v.p. The Robb Report Mid Atlantic, Inc., Fairfax, Va., 1981-82, v.p. Impressions Mktg. Group, pres. The Robb Report Mid Atlantic, Inc., 1982—. Home: 13209 Dairymaid Dr Apt 202 Germantown MD 20874 Office: 7500 Fullerton Rd Springfield VA 22153

DAY, LEE ROSS, pharmacist; b. Ponca City, Okla., Sept. 28, 1948; s. Lee Forrest and Leora Evelyn (Lauver) D.; m. Kristin Weltge, Dec. 20, 1969 (div. 1978); children—Valerie Lynn, Traci Renee. B.S. in Pharmacy magna cum laude, Southwestern Okla. State U., 1971. Intern pharmacist Muskogee Gen. Hosp., Okla., 1971-72, staff pharmacist, 1972-75; asst. dir. pharmacy St. Joseph Regional Med. Ctr., Ponca City, 1975-79, dir. pharmacy, 1979—; cons. Henryetta Hosp., Okla., 1972-80, Fairfax Hosp., Okla., 1980-82. Contbr. articles to profl. jours. Sec., Ponca City Planning Commn., 1984-85, Regional Planning Commn., Ponca City., 1984-85. Mem. Am. Soc. Hosp. Pharmacists, Okla. Soc. Hosp. Pharmacists, Okla. Pharm. Assn. (chmn. intraprofl. relations com.), Health Adv. Bd.-Vocat. Tech., Rho Chi. Democrat. Presbyterian. Clubs: Ponca City Jaycees (dir. 1975-79), Am. Bus. (bd. dirs. 1979—). Lodge: Elks. Avocations: snow and water skiing; hunting; camping; fishing. Home: 2508 Oriole Ponca City OK 74601 Office: St Joseph Regional Med Ctr 14th & Hartford Ponca City OK 74601

DAY, MARSHALL PATRICK, optometrist; b. Clinton, Okla., Aug. 14, 1952; s. Bob G. and Betty Lee (Long) D.; m. Yvonne Suzanne Miller, May 20, 1972; children—Amanda, Kenneth. Student Okla. State U., 1970-73; O.D., So. Coll. Optometry, 1977. Optometrist Dr. G.W. Clay, Ardmore, Okla., 1977-78; gen. practice optometry, Clinton, 1978—. Bd. dirs. United Fund Clinton, 1982—. Fellow Am. Acad. Optometry (Recognition award 1984); mem. Am. Optometric Assn., Okla. Optometric Assn. (2nd v.p. 1985—, bd. dirs. 1982-83, 1985—), Am. Optometric Found., Clinton C. of C. (bd. dirs. 1982—). Democrat. Methodist. Lodge: Rotary (pres. 1985—). Avocation: hunting. Office: 517 S 30th PO Box 606 Clinton OK 73601

DAY, ROBERT ALAN, sociology educator, gerontology consultant; b. Oakland, Calif., June 26, 1944; s. Jack Edward and Jaine Rose (Craine) D.; m. JoAnne Victoria Chacko, Sept. 4, 1969; children—Christopher Robert, Matthew Patrick. B.A. in Sociology, U. Mont., 1966; M.A., Ohio State U., 1969; Ph.D., U. Mo., 1981. Asst. prof. U. Ky., Lexington, 1974-77, U. N.C.-Charlotte, 1981—; aging services specialist Lexington-Fayette County, Ky., 1978-79; asst. prof. U. Louisville, 1979-80. Contbr. articles to profl. jours. Aging specialist Lexington-Fayette County Govt., 1978-79; chmn. com. Council of Aging, United Way, Charlotte, 1982—; mem. Human Services Planning Bd., 1983—; bd. dirs. Adult Care and Share Ctr., Inc., Charlotte, 1983—; program chmn. U. Forum, U. N.C.-Charlotte, 1984—. Mem. Am. Sociol. Assn., So. Sociol. Soc., Midwest Sociol. Soc., Nat. Council Aging, Assn. for Gerontology in Higher Edn., Audubon Soc. Democrat. Methodist. Club: Philatelic Soc. (College Station). Avocations: reading; hiking; camping; sports; stamp and coin collecting. Home: 5501 Trossacks Ct Charlotte NC 28212 Office: Dept Sociology UNCC Station Charlotte NC 28223

DAYAN, MAURICE, psychologist; b. St. Petersburg, Fla., Apr. 6, 1930; s. Saul Hyman and Juliet (Schmidt) D.; m. Carole Barbara Haven, July 28, 1956; children—Juliet Rose, Esther Lea, Nathan Scott. B.A., U. Fla., 1955, M.Ed., 1956, Ed.D., 1962. Lic. psychologist, La. Tchr. Ft. Meyers Jr. High Sch., Fla., 1955-56; sch. psychologist Lee County Sch. Bd., Ft. Meyers, 1956-59; grad. research asst. U. Fla., Gainesville, 1959-60; chief psychologist Sunland Tng., Ft. Meyers, 1960-63, Marianna, Fla., 1963-64; dir. research Pinecrest State Sch., Pineville, La., 1964—; cons. St. Mary's Tng. Sch., Alexandria, La., 1976—, Pecan Grove Sch., Alexandria, 1975—, Holy Angels Sch., Shreveport, La., 1983—. Author: Communication Shaping, 1970. Contbr. articles to profl. jours. Bd. dirs. Rapides Parish Community Action, Alexandria, 1965-68; pres. B'nai B'rith, La., Lee County Assn. Retarded, Ft. Meyers, 1961-62, Family Counseling Agy., Alexandria, 1975-77. Served to 2nd lt. U.S. Army, 1951-54, Korea. Charles E. Dunbar career service award La. Civil Service, 1977. Fellow Am. Assn. Mental Deficiency (parliamentarian, Helen Thompson award 1983); mem. Am. Psychol. Assn., Council Exceptional Children. Democrat. Jewish. Avocations: fishing; painting; scuba diving; photography. Home: Box 191 Pineville LA 71360 Office: Pinecrest Box 191 Pineville LA 71360

DAYTON, BENJAMIN BONNEY, consultant, physicist; b. Rochester, N.Y., Feb. 25, 1914; s. Howard Hay and Helen (Thrall) D.; m. Irene Catherine Glossenger, Oct. 16, 1943; children—David Bonney, Glenn Charles. B.S. in Chemistry, MIT, 1937; M.S. in Applied Physics, U. Rochester, 1948; postgrad. Western Carolina U., 1973, 74, U. N.C., 1974, 77. Tchr. math. and sci. Livonia Central Sch., N.Y., 1938-40; supr. devel. and quality control Distillation Products Industries, Rochester, N.Y., 1940-53; dir. research Consol. Vacuum Corp., Rochester, 1953-55, tech. dir., 1955-62, chief physicist, 1962-68; tech. dir. Bendix Corp., Rochester, 1968-69, chief scientist SIED div., 1969-71, cons. SIED div., 1971-72; cons. Xerox Corp., Webster, N.Y., 1973, H.J. Ross Assocs., Inc., Miami, 1974-78, Babcock and Wilcox Co., Alliance, Ohio, 1982-84; tchr. phys. sci. Henderson County Sch., Hendersonville, N.C., 1973-79; tchr. physics and math. Blue Ridge Tech. Coll., Flat Rock, N.C., 1980-82; chmn. adv. com. Am. Nat. Standards Inst., 1964-71; mem. adv. panel Nat. Bur. Standards, Washington, 1965-71; staff lectr. vacuum techniques George Washington U., Washington, 1966-68; tech. dir. Internat. Union for Vacuum Sci, Tech. and Application, 1966-72. Editor: Glossary of Terms Used in Vacuum Technology, 1958; U.S. editor Vacuum, 1959-72; mem. editorial bd. Rev. Sci. Instruments, 1953-55. Contbr. articles to profl. jours. Patentee in field. Trustee Roberts Wesleyan Coll., North Chili, N.Y., 1951-61. Recipient bronze award Army Service Forces, C.E., Manhattan Dist., 1945. Mem. Am. Vacuum Soc. (pres. 1961, hon. life mem.), Am. Phys. Soc., Am. Sci. Affiliation, N.C. Assn. Educators (life). Home: 209 S Hillandale Dr East Flat Rock NC 28726

DAYTON, MARTIN, physician; b. Miami Beach, Fla., Aug. 7, 1944. B.S., Rutgers U., 1966; D.O., Kirksville Coll., 1970; M.D., Ross U., 1983. Diplomate Am. Bd. Internal Medicine, Ryodorak Research Inst. N.Am. Intern, Southeastern Med. Ctr., 1970-71; med. dir. Med. Ctr., Sunny Isles, Miami Beach, 1973—. Mem. Am. Osteo. Assn., Am. Acad. Family Physicians, Internat. Coll. Applied Nutrition, Fla. Acad. Family Physicians, Internat. Acad. Preventive Medicine, Am. Coll. Gen. Practitioners in Osteo. Medicine, Dade County Osteo. Med. Assn., Soc. Tchrs. Family Medicine, Soc. Healing Arts (pres. 1980-81). Office: Med Ctr Sunny Isles 18600 Collins Ave Miami Beach FL 33160

DEA, PETER ALLEN, geologist; b. Worcester, Mass., Aug. 28, 1953; s. Allen Pearson and Beverly Jane (Brown) D. B.A. in Geology, Western State Coll., Gunnison, Colo., 1976; M.S. in Geology, U. Mont., 1981. Geologist Novanda Exploration, Missoula, Mont., 1977, WGM, Inc., Anchorage, 1976-77, Converse Cons., Lakewood, Colo., 1980-81; prof. geology Western State Coll., Gunnison, 1980-82; sr. geologist Exxon Co., U.S.A., Corpus Christi, Tex., 1982—. Contbr. articles to profl. jours. Mem. Am. Assn. Petroleum Geologists, Corpus Christi Geol. Soc. Avocations: skiing; sailing; mountain climbing; kayaking; writing. Office: Exxon Co USA 4444 Corona St Corpus Christi TX 78411

DEAKTOR, DARRYL B., lawyer; b. Pitts., Feb. 2, 1942; s. Harry and Edith (Barnett) D.; m. Mary Ann Kelly, Apr. 27, 1973; children—Rachael Alexandra, Hallie Sarah. B.A., Brandeis U., 1963; LL.B., U. Pa., 1966; M.B.A., Columbia U., 1968. Bar: Pa., Fla., N.Y. Assoc. firm Goodis, Greenfield & Mann, Phila., 1968-70, ptnr., 1971; gen. counsel Life of Pa. Fin. Corp., Phila., 1972; asst. prof. U. Fla. Coll. Law, Gainesville, 1972-74, assoc. prof., 1974-80; assoc. firm Mershon, Sawyer, Johnston, Dunwody & Cole, Miami, Fla., 1980-81, ptnr., 1981-84, Walker Ellis Gragg & Deaktor, 1984—. Mem. Dist. III (Fla.) Human Rights Advocacy Com. for Mentally Retarded Citizens, 1974-78, chmn., 1978-80; mem. adv. bd. Childbirth Edn. Assn. Alachua County, Fla., 1974-80; mem. Resource Devel. Bd., Mailman Ctr. for Child Devel., 1981—. Mem. ABA, Fla. Bar, Club: City (Miami). Home: 13531 SW 77th Ct Miami FL 33156 Office: 4750 Southeast Fin Ctr 200 S Biscayne Blvd Miami FL 33131

DEAL, LARRY MICHAEL, geologist, biologist; b. Maryville, Tenn., Sept. 9, 1956; s. Ludell and Mary Elizabeth (Hill) D.; m. Sara Catherine Ham, June 23, 1979; 1 child, Marissa Catherine. Student, Enterprise State Jr. Coll., 1974-76; B.S. in Biology, Troy State U., 1979; B.S. in Geology, Auburn U., 1981. Project insp. USDA Soil Conservation Service, Ozark, Ala., 1976-78, engrng. asst., 1978-80, surveyor, 1980-81; land surveyor O'Neal Ham Inc., Ozark, 1978-82; sr. geologist Mountain Coals Inc., Bulan, Ky., 1982—; cons., London, Ky., 1984—. Mem. Am. Inst. Profl. Geologists (assoc.), Am. Assn. Petroleum Geologists (jr.). Republican. Baptist. Avocations: hunting; fishing; canoeing; backpacking. Home: Rural Route 5 Box 550 London KY 40741 Office: Mountain Coals Inc Bulan KY 41722

DEALY, MILTON DAVID, railroad executive; b. Sikeston, Mo., Feb. 10, 1954; s. Milton David and Lucy Jo (Aufdenburg) D.; m. Karen S. Graham, May 28, 1977; 1 dau., Dianna Jo. B.A., Central Meth. U., 1976. Asst. roadmaster Mo. Pacific R.R., North Little Rock, Ark., 1976-77, asst. trainmaster, New Orleans, 1977-78, market analyst, St. Louis, 1978-79, trainmaster, North Little Rock, Ark., 1979-81, div. supt., Chgo., 1981-82, North Little Rock, 1982-84; gen. supt. Union Pacific R.R., Omaha, 1984—. Mem. Am. Assn. R.R. Supts. Republican. Methodist. Club: Rotary (North Little Rock, Ark.). Lodge: Masons. Home: 7101 Sequoyah St North Little Rock AR 72116 Office: PO Box 5494 Mo Pacific RR North Little Rock AR 72119

DEAN, BOB WESLEY, mechanical engineer; b. Birmingham, Ala., Aug. 6, 1924; s. Robert Leon and Gertrude (Griffith) D.; B.Mech. Engrng., Auburn U., 1945; M.S. in Engrng., U. Ala., 1948; m. Martha Stone Grace, July 15, 1944; children—Robert Allbritton, Elizabeth Cary, Thomas Wesley, DeForest DeSha, David Bryant. Various positions, 1948-52; mfrs. rep. F. J. Evans Engrng. Co., Atlanta, 1952-57; design engr. Robert & Co., Atlanta, 1957-62; with Mallory & Evans, Inc., Scottdale, Ga., 1962—, v.p., project engr., dir. 1965—; asso. Mech. Engrng., Inc., Scottdale, Ga., 1965-70; mem. Bd. Examiners Warm Air Heating Contractors, State of Ga., 1970-80, mem. Constrn. Industries Bd., 1980—, chmn., 1985—, chmn. conditioned air div., 1982-85. Registered profl. engr., Ind., Pa., Calif., Miss., Ala., Ga., Fla., Tenn., S.C., N.C., Nebr., N.Y., Va., Ky., Del., Minn., Mo., Ark., Wash. Fellow ASHRAE, (chpt. pres. 1963-64); mem. ASME. Club: Ansley Golf. Patentee in field. Home: 760 Old Ivy Rd NE Atlanta GA 30342 Office: 646 Kentucky St Scottdale GA 30079

DEAN, CAROL LEE, nurse; b. Lynchburg, Va., May 10, 1949; d. Elymus Walter and Dorothy (Mills) D.; 1 foster dau., Bonnie G. Duggins. Diploma Ky. Mountain Bible Inst., 1970; student Morehead State U., 1970-71; B.S. in Nursing, U. Ky., 1974; M.Pub. Adminstrn. and Health Service Mgmt., 1986. Staff nurse, dorm parent, social worker Bethany Children's Home, 1974-83; staff nurse, asst. dir., dir. nursing Stanton (Ky.) Nursing Ctr., 1978-80; staff nurse, team leader Mary Childs Hosp., Mount Sterling, Ky., 1980-81; pub. health nurse Ky. River Dist. Health Dept., Wolfe County Health Ctr., Campton, Ky., 1981-83; Medicaid utilization rev. analyst Va. State Dept. Health, Richmond, 1983-85, Va. Dept. Med. Assistance Services, 1985—; mem. Home Health Adv. Council, 1981-83. Mem. Am. Pub. Health Assn., Ky. Home Health Assn., Ky. Pub. Health Assn. Republican. Nazarene. Home: 5720 Pony Farm Dr #201 Richmond VA 23227 Office: Va State Dept Med Assistance Services 109 Governor St Richmond VA

DEAN, CHARLES HENRY, government official; b. Knoxville, Tenn., Oct. 22, 1925; s. Charles Henry and Helen (Ford) D.; student U. Tenn., 1943-44; B.S., U.S. Naval Acad., 1947; m. Lottie Lavender, Dec. 30, 1947; children—Helen, James Miles, Camille. Sales rep. Knoxville Fertilizer Co., Dean-Planters Warehouses, 1950-59; with Knoxville (Tenn.) Utilities Bd., 1959-81, gen. mgr., 1971-81; chmn. bd. TVA, 1981—. Past pres. Knoxville Tourist Bur.; past chmn., Chancellors' Assos., U. Tenn.; trustee Knoxville Coll. Served with USMC, 1947-50. Recipient Profl. Mgrs. Citation, Soc. Advancement Mgmt., 1972. Mem. Am. Public Power Assn. (past dir.), Nat. Soc. Profl. Engrs., Tenn. Valley Public Power Assn. (past pres.). Republican. Presbyterian. Clubs: Civitan (past pres.), Racquet (past pres.) (Knoxville, Tenn.); Club LeConte (bd. govs.). Office: TVA Towers Knoxville TN 37902

DEAN, EDWIN BECTON, federal agency cost estimator; b. Danville, Va., Feb. 7, 1940; s. Edwin Becton and Lois (Campbell) D.; B.S. in Physics, Va. Poly. Inst. and State U., 1963, M.S. in Math., 1965; postgrad. George Washington U., 1974-77; m. Deirdre Anne Jacovides, Aug. 16, 1964; children—Jennifer E., Kristin R., Brian N. Technician, assoc. engr. Johns Hopkins U. Applied Physics Lab., Laurel, Md., 1959-64; physicist, mathematician, electronic engr., and ops. research analyst Naval Surface Weapons Center, Silver Spring, Md., 1964-79; owner Gen. Bus. Services and Beta Systems Virginia Beach, 1979-84; treas. Communique Inc., Virginia Beach, Va., 1980-81; registered rep. First Investors Corp., Arlington, Va., 1971-85; dir. Tips Club of Va. Beach, Inc., 1980-82; computer specialist Naval Supply Systems Command, Norfolk, Va., 1982-83; head cost modeling and control sect. NASA-Langley Research Ctr., Hampton, Va., 1983—. NASA fellow, 1963-65. Mem. IEEE, Internat. Soc. Parametric Analysts, Assn. for Computing Machinery, Inst. for Mgmt. Sci., AIAA, Sigma Pi Sigma, Pi Mu Epsilon, Phi Kappa Phi. Office: MS 444 NASA-Langley Research Ctr Hampton VA 23665

DEAN, H.R., utility company executive; b. 1926; married. B.S., Bowling Green Coll. Commerce, 1946. With Houston Light & Power Co., a Houston Industries Inc. Co., 1946—, comptroller, 1966-70, v.p., comptroller, 1970-73, group v.p., comptroller, 1973-78, group v.p. acctg. fin., 1978-81, exec. v.p. fin., 1981—, also dir. Office: Houston Light and Power Co 611 Walker Houston TX 77001*

DEAN, JACK PEARCE, insurance executive; b. Shreveport, La., Aug. 26, 1931; s. James A. and Nina (Smith) D.; B.S. in Acctg., La. Tech. U., 1951; m. Elizabeth Anne Tillman, June 5, 1952; children—Linda, Cynthia, James. With Peat, Marwick, Mitchell & Co., C.P.A.s, New Orleans, Jackson, Miss., 1958-63; with Lamar Life Ins. Co., Jackson, 1963—, dir., 1972—, pres., Lamar Life Corp., 1972-83, chmn., 1983—, also dir.; dir. 1st Capital Corp., Trustmark Nat. Bank, Central Miss. Growth Found., Inc., Lamar Leasing Co., Inc. Bd. dirs. Jackson Bus. and Indsl. Devel. Corp.; budget chmn. Capital Area United Way, 1968-69, advanced gifts chmn., 1970-71, assoc. campaign chmn., 1972, campaign chmn., 1973, v.p., 1974, pres., 1975; pres. Goodwill Industries Central Miss., 1972; trustee Miss. Found. Ind. Colls. Named Outstanding Alumnus of Yr., Coll. Adminstrn. and Bus., La. Tech. U., 1974; recipient Service to Humanity award Miss. Coll., 1978. Mem. Am. Inst. C.P.A.s, Am. Council Life Ins. (state v.p. 1975, 78, 82, 85, dir. 1978-81, chmn. life ins. polit. action com. 1982-84), Newcomen Soc. N.Am., Miss. soc. C.P.A.s, La. Soc. C.P.A.s, Life Ins. Assn. Miss. (pres. 1976, 81), Jackson C. of C. (dir. 1974-76, 81—, pres. 1986). Baptist. Clubs: 100, Country, Capital City Petroleum, Univ., Rotary. Home: 2241 Wild Valley Dr Jackson MS 39211 Office: PO Box 880 Jackson MS 39205

DEAN, JOHN AURIE, chemist, author, educator; b. Sault Ste. Marie, Mich., May 9, 1921; s. Aurie Jerome and Gertrude (Saw) D.; B.S. in Chemistry, U. Mich., 1942, M.S. in Chemistry, 1944, Ph.D., 1949; m. Elizabeth Louise Cousins, June 20, 1943 (div. 1981); children—Nancy Elizabeth, Thomas Alfred, John Randolph, Laurie Alice, Clarissa Elaine; m. 2d, Peggy DeHart Beeler, Oct. 23, 1981. Teaching fellow in chemistry, U. Mich., Ann Arbor, 1942-44, 45-46, lectr. in chemistry, 1946-48; chemist X-100 Phase Manhattan Project, Chrysler Corp., Detroit, 1944-45; assoc. prof. chemistry U. Ala., Tuscaloosa, 1948-50; asst. prof. chemistry, U. Tenn., Knoxville, 1950-53, assoc. prof., 1953-58, prof. chemistry, 1958-81, prof. emeritus, 1981—; sci. exchange lectr., Peoples Republic of China, 1985; cons. Union Car Nuclear Div., Oak Ridge, 1953-74, Stewart Labs., Knoxville, 1968-81. Mem. Am. Chem. Soc. (Charles H. Stone award Carolina-Piedmont sect. 1974), Soc. Applied Spectroscopy (past chmn. Southeast sect.; editor newsletter 1984—), Archeol. Inst. Am. (past pres. East Tenn. chpt.), Am. Schs. for Oriental Research, U.S. Naval Inst., Oriental Inst., Univ. Mus. (Pa.). Presbyterian. Author: Instrumental Methods of Analysis, 6 edits., 1948, 51, 58, 65, 74, 81; Flame Photometry, 1960; Chemical Separation Methods, 1969; Flame Emission and Atomic Absorption Spectrometry, vol. 1, 1969, vol. 2, 1971, vol. 3, 1975; Lange's Handbook of Chemistry, 11th edit., 1973, 12th edit., 1979, 13th edit., 1985; Handbook of Organic Chemistry, 1986; contbr. chpts. to books, articles to profl. publs. Home and Office: 201 Mayflower Dr Knoxville TN 37920

DEAN, JOSEPH ANTHONY, minister; b. Jamaica, West Indies, May 29, 1941; came to U.S., 1975; s. Francis and Doris (Ross) D.; m. Lucy Rebecca Dennis, Aug. 10, 1966; children—Mark, Daniel, Paul, Reba, Lydia, Wendy, Tracy. Ordained to ministry United Pentecostal Ch., 1966; pres. Native Constrn., Kingston, Jamaica, 1968-75, Allstate Bldg. Contractors, Miami, Fla., 1975-83, Gospelight Evang. Assn., Kingston, 1965-75, Apostolic Temple, Inc., Miami, 1975—, Carpenters of Fla., Inc., 1983—, Dean Investment Inc., Miami, Artistic Landscaping Inc., Miami.

DEAN, LINDA BARSOM, special education educator, writer; b. Biloxi, Miss., Oct. 29, 1950; d. George Kasper and Judith Buel (Reed) Barsom; m. John Edward Dean, June 15, 1974; children—Justin Ryan, Jeffrey Taylor. B.S., Fla. State U., 1972; postgrad. Valdosta State Coll., 1973-74; M.Ed., U. New Orleans, 1976; student Inst. Children's Lit., 1982-83. Cert. spl. edn. tchr., Ala. Tchr. for multi-handicapped Ochlocknee Children's Ctr., 1972-73; tchr. for emotionally disturbed North Andrews Gardens Elem. Sch., Ft. Lauderdale, Fla., 1973-75; dir. program for devel. delayed DePaul Hosp., New Orleans, 1975-76; free-lance writer children's stories and books, Mobile, Ala., 1983—; mem. core staff First Chance Project, Ochlocknee Children's Ctr., 1972-74, mem. curriculum devel. staff, 1973-74, coordinator Climax Children's Ctr., 1973-74; del. Internat. Council for Exceptional Children Conv. from Fla. State U., 1972, Southwest Ga., 1973. Sec., bd. dirs. Mobile area LWV, 1984-86, chmn. War Vets. Study, 1985—; treas., bd. dirs., 1985-86; v.p., co-founder Mobilians for Better Nutrition, 1982; active LaLeche League, 1977-81; tchr. confraternity on Christian doctrine St. Clements Ch., Ft. Lauderdale, 1974-75, St. Joan of Arc Ch., Mobile, 1981—; tutor learning disabled children Rotary Rehab. Ctr., 1984-85, Old Dauphin Way Sch., 1985-86. Named Tchr. of Yr. of Exceptional Children for Southwest Ga., Ga. Fedn. Council for Exceptional Children 1974. Mem. Nat. Trust for Hist. Preservation, Hist. Mobile Preservation Soc., Oakleigh Garden Soc., Spring Hill Food Coop., Aircraft Owners and Pilots Assn., Zeta Tau Alpha. Republican. Roman Catholic. Club: Port City Pacers Road Runners (Mobile).

DEAN, MARILYN FERWERDA, nursing consultant and administrator; b. Oak Park, Ill., Oct. 5, 1938; m. Frank Dean; children by previous marriage—Cathy Cree Denisco, Cliff Cree; stepchildren—Derek, Jeff Dean. B.S.N., U. Miami (Fla.), 1960; M.P.H., U. Mich., 1963. With Broward County Health Dept., Fort Lauderdale, Fla., 1960-65, supr., 1963-65; with Med. Personnel Pool, Fort Lauderdale, 1971-78; dir. nursing service North Beach Med. Center, Fort Lauderdale, 1978-79; regional dir. Med. Personnel Pool, Fort Lauderdale, 1979-82, nat. dir. profl. and consumer affairs, 1982-85, nat. dir., health care services, 1985—; instr. Broward Community Coll., 1975-78. Bd. dirs. Luth. High Sch., 1980-83. Mem. Am. Nurses Assn. (dir.), Nat. League Nursing, Am. Assn. Continuity of Care, Inservice Educators S. Fla. (pres. 1977-78), Assn. Care of Children's Health, Nat. Hospice Orgn. Lutheran. Home: 5521 NE 19th Ave Fort Lauderdale FL 33308 Office: 303 SE 17th St Fort Lauderdale FL 33316

DEAN, NATHAN D., state senator; b. Rockmart, Ga., May 9, 1934; s. Thomas James and Ellen (Brooke) D.; m. Norma Ann Carpenter, 1961. B.B.A., Shorter Coll., 1962. With Lockheed Aircraft Corp.; mem. Rockmart City Council, 1960—; now mem. Ga. Senate. Served to cpl. U.S. Army, 1956-58. Mem. Jaycees (dir.). Democrat. Baptist. Club: Touchdown (dir.). Lodge: Shriners. Office: Ga Senate State Capitol Atlanta GA 30334*

DEAN, NATHAN WESLEY, educational administrator, physicist; b. Johnson City, Tenn., Dec. 10, 1941; s. Everett Francis and Mary Ethel (Garvin) D.; m. Mary Dugger Fetzer, Apr. 11, 1963; 1 dau., Mary Ellen. Student, U. Tenn., 1959-61; B.S. with honors in Physics, U. N.C., 1963; Ph.D. (U.S. Churchill scholar, NSF fellow) in Elem. Particle Physics, Cambridge U., 1968. Vis. scientist CERN, Geneva, Switzerland, 1967-68; instr. Vanderbilt U., Nashville, 1968-69, asst. prof., 1969-70; asst. prof. Iowa State U., Ames, 1970-74, assoc. prof., 1974-78, prof., 1978-80, asst. dean Scis. & Humanities, 1974-80, asst. dir. Sci. & Human Research Inst., 1975-80; assoc. physicist Ames Lab. U.S. Dept. Energy, 1970-74, physicist, 1974-78, sr. physicist, 1978-80; adminstrv. staff High Energy Physics, AEC, Wash., D.C., 1973-74; asst. v.p. for research U. Ga., Athens, 1980-84, prof. physics, 1980—, acting v.p. for research, 1984—, dir. U. Ga. Indsl. Interface Program, 1983—dir. U. Ga. Program in Bioresources and Biotech., 1984—; Univ. System rep. to Ga. High Tech. Adv. Council, 1983—. Grantee, U.S. Dept. Energy, 1978, NSF, 1978, NIH, 1980-85,

NEH, 1980, U.S. Army, 1983, USPHS, 1981-85, Research Corp., 1971. Mem. Am. Phys. Soc., AAAS, Nat. Council of Univ. Research Adminstrs. (chmn. region 3 1984-85), Athens, Ga. C. of C. (econ. devel. com., 1983—), Phi Beta Kappa, Sigma Xi, Phi Kappa Phi. Author: Introduction to Strong Interactions, 1976; contbr. numerous articles to various physics jours. Home: 270 Skyline Pkwy Athens GA 30606 Office: 609 Grad Studies Univ GA Athens GA 30602

DEAN, RALPH JAMES, SR., law enforcement officer; b. Richmond, Va., Dec. 6, 1944; s. George Harry and Mildred Thelma (Franklin) D.; m. Valerie Gray, Apr. 23, 1973; children—Ralph James, Marie Regina, Kimberly Ann. Student Benedictine Coll. Mil. Acad., 1962. Cert. law enforcement officer, paramedic, tchr., Fla. Vice pres. Am. Investigation, Wilmington, Del., 1962-67; ops. mgr. Allied Stores, N.Y.C., 1968-73; with Broward County Sheriff's Office, Ft. Lauderdale, Fla., 1973—, sgt. road patrol div., 1979-83, sgt. community relations div., 1983—; mem. faculty Miami-Dade Community Coll., 1978. Mem. affiliate faculty Am. Heart Assn., Dallas, 1975-79; com. chmn. ARC, Richmond, Va., 1962-67. Named Ky. Col., 1982; recipient numerous awards Am. Heart Assn., Dallas, 1975-78. Mem. Fraternal Order Police (state officer 1982, dist. dir. 1982—, chmn. legis. com. 1983, chmn. labor com. 1983). Democrat. Roman Catholic. Office: Fraternal Order Police 5460 N State Rd 7 Fort Lauderdale FL 33319

DEAN, ROGER ALAN, administration educator, consultant; b. Melbourne, Victoria, Australia, Sept. 11, 1947; came to U.S., 1976; s. Alfred Ernest and Elizabeth Bruce (Skinner) D. B. Commerce, U. Queensland, Australia, 1974, M.B.A., 1976; Ph.D., Mich. State U., 1981. Lic. psychologist, Va. Tutor, U. of Queensland, 1975-76; instr. Mich. State U., East Lansing, 1976-80; asst. prof. So. Meth. U., Dallas, 1980-83; assoc. prof. Washington and Lee U., Lexington, Va., 1984—; cons. in field. Author: Study Guide for Personnel, 1985. Contbr. articles to profl. jours. Mem. Am. Physiol. Assn., Am. Soc. Personnel Adminstrn. (Research award 1982), Acad. of Mgmt., Pi Kappa Alpha. Republican. Baptist. Office: Washington & Lee Univ Sch of Commerce Econs & Politics Lexington VA 24450

DEAN, WILLIAM RUSSELL, geophysicist; b. Clovis, N.Mex., Mar. 8, 1954; s. George O. and Mary Elizabeth (Logan) D. B.S. in Geology, Steven F. Austin State U., 1981. Assoc. geophysicist Don W. Frazier, Inc., Houston, 1981-82; exploration geophysicist Columbia Gas Devel. Corp., Houston, 1982—. Mem. Soc. Exploration Geophysicists, Am. Assn. Petroleum Geologists, Houston Geol. Soc., Geophys. Soc. Houston, Steven A. Austin Geology Club (v.p. 1979-80, program dir. 1980-81), Sigma Gamma Epsilon. Republican. Avocations: drawing and painting; playing bass and cello. Home: 922 Merrill St Houston TX 77009 Office: PO Box 1350 Houston TX 77251

DEANDA, JAMES, U.S. district judge; b. Houston, Aug. 21, 1925; s. Javier and Mary Louise DeAnda; B.A., Tex. A&M U., LL.B., U. Tex., 1950; m. Joyce Anita DeAnda. Admitted to Tex. bar, pvt. practice, Houston, 1951-54, Corpus Christi, 1955-74, McAllen, 1974-79; U.S. dist. judge So. Dist. Tex., Houston, 1979—. Roman Catholic. Office: US Courts Bldg Houston TX 77002

DEANE, FREDERICK, JR., banker; b. Boston, Aug. 5, 1926; s. Frederick and Julia (Coolidge) D.; M.B.A. with distinction, Harvard U., 1951; m. Dorothy Legge, Dec. 21, 1948; children—Dorothy Porcher, Eleanor Dodds, Frederick III. With Bank of Va. and Bank of Va. Co. 1953—, now chmn. bd., chief exec. officer of both; dir. CSX Corp., Marriott Corp.; chmn. MasterCard Internat. Bd. dirs. Va. Mus. Found., Va. Found. Ind. Colls., Richmond Renaissance, Federated Arts Council Richmond (Va.), Va. Diocesan Center; trustee Funds of Protestant Episcopal Ch., Diocese of Va., Westminster-Canterbury Found., Served to 1st lt. U.S. Army, 1944-47, 51-53. Mem. Richmond Soc. Fin. Analysts (pres. 1963-64), Am. Bankers Assn., Assn. Bank Holding Cos. (chmn. 1979-80), Assn. Res. City Bankers (dir.), Fin. Analysts Fedn., Conf. Bd. (sr. mem., chmn. so. regional council). Republican. Episcopalian. Clubs: Harvard of Va. (pres. 1969-70, pres. Bus. Sch. sect. 1960); Brook, Harvard (N.Y.C.); Burning Tree (Bethesda, Md.); Commonwealth, Downtown. Country of Va. (Richmond); Met. (Washington); Hasty Pudding Inst. of 1770; Mid-Ocean (Bermuda); Country of Fla. Home: 110 W Hillcrest Ave Richmond VA 23226 Office: Bank of Va PO Box 25970 Richmond VA 23260

DEANGELIS, DAVID ANTHONY, artist; b. Balt., Dec. 31, 1950; s. James John and Anna May (Crusse) DeA. B.S., Loyola Coll., Balt., 1972. Art rep. Picture House, Inc., Atlanta, 1972-80. Artistic adv. Atlanta Humane Soc. Aux., 1983—, Alliance theatre Guild, 1985—, Henrietta Egleston Hosp., Atlanta, 1983—; decorations chmn. Beaux Arts Ball, Atlanta Coll. Art, 1985—. One man shows Creative Arts Guild, Dalton, Ga., 1983, Swan Coach House Gallery, Atlanta, 1986; exhibited in group shows Arts Festival of Atlanta, 1981-85, World's Fair, Knoxville, 1982, Arts Fair, Dalton, 1982-84, St. Joseph's Hosp., Atlanta, 1985; represented in permanent collection Creative Arts Guild, Dalton, 1982, Atlanta Ballet, 1984, Atlanta Bot. Garden, 1985, also corporate collections. Contbr. articles to mags. Mem. hon. staff Ga. Gov., 1985. Mem. Ga. Trust Historic Preservation (hon.), Forward Arts Found., High Mus. Art, Alliance Theatre Guild. Democrat. Roman Catholic. Avocations: Interior design; furniture design; fund raising; gardening. Address: Atlanta GA

DEARING, AUDREY TRAUGOTT, electronics company executive; b. San Antonio, Sept. 27, 1929; d. Arthur Charles and Ella Christine (Bartels) Traugott; m. Harry Leonard Dearing, Aug. 18, 1950; children—Denise Elaine, Harry Leonard, Linda Claire. A.A., San Antonio Coll., 1949. With Tracor, Inc., Austin, Tex., 1961—, asst. corp. sec., adminstrv. asst. to pres., 1970-73, corp. sec., adminstrv. asst. to chmn. and pres., 1973—; sec. Westronics Inc., Ft. Worth, 1971—, dir., 1972—; sec. numerous Tracor Inc. subs. cos. Trustee Capital Area United Way, Austin, 1978; sec. Dist. 10 Council 4-H Club, 1973-75, chmn. county council, 1972-74, sec.-treas., 1974-75, 85-86; pres. Friends of Plugerville Community Library, 1981-83. Recipient 4-H Club Leadership award, 1978, Silver Spur award, 1981. Mem. Am. Soc. Corp. Secs., Phi Theta Kappa. Office: Tracor Inc 6500 Tracor Ln Austin TX 78721

DEARING, ROBERT M., state senator; b. Natchez, Miss., Jan. 26, 1935; grad. Delta State U.; m. Shelley Ditzler; 2 children. Mem. Miss. Senate; ednl. cons. Sci. Research Assocs., U. So. Miss. Mem. Delta State Found., Delta State Alumni Assn., U. So. Miss. Alumni Assn., C. of C., Phi Delta Kappa. Democrat. Presbyterian. Lodge: Natchez Elks. Office: Miss State Senate Jackson MS 39205

DEARMON, THOMAS ALFRED, automotive industry financial executive, life insurance executive; b. Montgomery, Ala., Dec. 28, 1937; s. Thomas A. and Rose (Giardina) D.; m. Leigh Caroline Smith, Dec. 28, 1963; children—Jacob Thomas, Joshua Carter. B.B.A., U. Okla, 1961; J.D., Oklahoma City U., 1968. Bar: Okla. 1968. C.P.A., Okla. Audit mgr. Arthur Andersen & Co., Oklahoma City, 1961-68; account exec. F.I. DuPont, Oklahoma City, 1968-73; pres., dir. Century Life Assurance, Oklahoma City, 1983—; pres., dir. F.J. Mgmt. Corp., 1983—; exec. v.p., mem. investment com. Fred Jones Industries, Oklahoma City, 1985—; v.p. Fred Jones, Inc., 1973—, Fred Jones Mfg. Co., 1973—. Sec., dir. Historical Preservation, Inc., Oklahoma City, 1984—. Served with U.S. Army, 1963. Mem. Oklahoma Bar Assn., Oklahoma Soc. C.P.A.s, Fin. Execs. Inst. Democrat. Methodist. Lodge: Downtown Lions (pres. 1985—). Office: Fred Jones Industries 123 S Hudson St Oklahoma City OK 73102

DEASON, WILLIAM EDWARD, II, college administrator; b. Milledgeville, Ga., Nov. 2, 1949; s. William Edward, Sr. and Eva Mae (Humphrey) D.; m. Donna Delores Davis, Sept. 27, 1967; children—Christi Mechelle, Mary Kathryn. B.B.A., Ga. Coll., 1971; M.B.A., Valdosta State Coll., 1981. Bus. mgr. Ga. Mil. Coll., Milledgeville, 1968-71; asst. comptroller Middle Ga. Coll., Cochran, 1971-76; comptroller Waycross Jr. Coll., Ga., 1976-83, Dalton Jr. Coll., Ga., 1983—. Named Outstanding Alumni, Ga. Coll., 1983; Outstanding Young Man of Year, Jaycees, 1983. Mem. So. Assn. Coll. and Univ. Bus. Officers, Nat. Assn. Coll. and Univ. Bus. Officers. Baptist. Clubs: Exchange (v.p. 1984, treas. 1985, pres.-elect Ga. dist. 1986). Avocations: wood craft; fishing; skiing; camping. Home: 2202 Rocky Face Circle Dalton GA 30720 Office: Dalton Jr Coll 213 N College Dr Dalton GA 30720

DEASY, WILLIAM E., packaging company executive; b. Trenton, N.J., Jan. 10, 1920; s. Edward J. and Mary A. (Flanagan) D.; B.Ch.E., Villanova U., 1941; m. Bette M. Nedzbala, Sept. 13, 1947; children—Michael S., Mary Kay. Gen. mgr. Panelyte div. St. Regis Paper Co., N.Y.C., 1946-64; v.p. ops. Champion Packages Co., Chgo., 1965-69; pres., chief exec. officer RJR Archer, Inc., Winston-Salem, N.C., 1970—, dir. Served with USAAF, 1942-46. Mem. Flexible Packaging Assn. (vice chmn.), Aluminum Assn. (dir.), Winston-Salem C. of C. Republican. Roman Catholic. Office: RJ Reynolds Industries World Hdqrs Winston-Salem NC 27102

DEATON, FAE ADAMS, clinical social worker, counselor; b. Phila., Feb. 19, 1932; d. Charles Sizemore and Dorothea Lucia (Adams) Deaton; Mus.B., Salem Coll., 1953; postgrad. U. Alaska, 1968-69, Alaska Methodist U., 1969, Wright State U., 1971-73, Santa Clara U., 1980, others; M.S. in Edn., Old Dominion U., 1975; M.S.W., Norfolk State U., 1980; children—Dorothea Fae Stein, Caroline Louise Stein, Eric Charles Stein. Tchr. music, Mifflin, Ohio, 1953-54; supr. high sch. USN Dependents Sch., Argentia, Nfld., 1956-57; tchr. USAF Dependents Sch., Croughton, Eng., 1960-63, Upper Heyford, Eng., 1963-64; mag. editor Scott AFB, Ill., 1966-67; mem. staff Hist. and Fine Arts Mus., Anchorage, 1968-70; music and arts reviewer Anchorage Evening Times, 1968-70; publicity chmn., mem. publicity staff Alaska Council on Arts, 1969-70; counselor Youth Services Bur., Dayton, Ohio, 1973; engring. research aide Wright Patterson AFB Biophysics Lab., Dayton, 1973; writer Dayton Daily News, 1973; field research aide Am. Inst. Research, Palo Alto, Calif., 1974-75; counselor, patient advocate Norfolk (Va.) Free Clinic, 1975-76; adminstrv. asst. econs. dept. Old Dominion U., Norfolk, 1975-76; tchr., counselor Blessed Sacrament Sch., Norfolk, 1976-77; mem. mental health team, young adolescent unit, milieu therapist Portsmouth (Va.) Psychiat. Center, 1977-79, children's unit, 1979-80, child, adult, family and marital therapist sexual trauma treatment center Psychiatrists/Portsmouth Psychiat. Center, 1980-82; counselor children's services sexual trauma treatment unit Community Mental Health Ctr. and Psychiat. Inst., Norfolk, Va., 1983—. Mem. Tidewater Profl. Assn. on Child Abuse, 1978-82, pres., 1981-82; mem. Tidewater Rape Info. Services, Norfolk, 1978—; adminstr./author, bd. dirs. Sexual Abuse Helpline of Tidewater, 1979—; mem. VBDSS Sexual Abuse Treatment Team, 1979-82; mem. ad hoc com. Nat. Coalition on Sexual Abuse, 1980-81; bd. dirs. Tidewater Alliance on Sexual Abuse, 1981—, pres., 1984; mem. admissions/release bd. Norfolk Lakehouse Girls Detention Home, 1978-79; program chmn. Conf. Internat. Yr. of the Child, Norfolk, 1979; mem. Middle Atlantic Coalition on Sexual Victimization of Children, 1980—, sec., 1981-82; bd. dirs. Tidewater Assembly on Family Life, 1981-82, Va. chpt. Nat. Com. on Prevention of Child Abuse, 1981-82, Parents Anonymous of Va., 1982—; mem. Virginia Beach Dept. Social Services Multi Discipline Team, 1983—; mem. Norfolk Com. for Prevention of Child Abuse, 1983—. Chmn. task force spl. children Children's Art Center, Norfolk, 1979-81; bd. dirs. Norfolk Little Theater, 1977-78; co-chmn. Parents United Va., Inc., 1980—; sponsor/coordinator Virginia Beach chpt. Parents United, 1979—; historian Alaska Arts Club, 1969-70; mem. Elmendorf AFB Sch. Bd., 1967-68. Mem. Am. Assn. Counseling and Devel., Va. Assn. Counseling and Devel., Am. Orthopsychiat. Assn., Nat., Va. assns. specialists in group work, Nat. Public Offender Counselors Assn., Am. Sch. Counselors Assn., Va. Sch. Counselors Assn., Nat. League Am. Pen Women, Elem. Sch. Counselors Assn., Va. Elementary Sch. Counselors Assn., Va. Council Social Welfare (bd. dirs. Tidewater area 1978-81, membership chmn. 1979-80, presenter state conf. 1982), Tidewater Mental Health Assn., Va. Opera Assn. Guild, Chrysler Mus. Assn., Alaska Press Club. Contbr. papers and lectures various confs. and tng. programs in U.S., 1967—. Home: 1176 Pickett Rd Norfolk VA 23502 Office: Community Mental Health Center Assocs Suite C 205 Business Park Dr Virginia Beach VA 23462

DEAVER, FRANK, journalist, educator; b. Shawnee, Okla., Dec. 18, 1932; s. Anderson Franklin and Laura Raye (Isbell) D.; m. Mary Jo Tindol, Aug. 22, 1957; children—Lydia Jean, Paul Franklin. B.S., Sam Houston State U., 1958, M.A., 1959; Ph.D., U. Tex., 1969; postgrad. U. Okla., U. Oreg., U. Stockholm (Sweden). Instr., Sam Houston State U., 1959-62, Victoria Jr. Coll., 1962-69; asst. prof. U. Ala.-Tuscaloosa, 1969-74, assoc. prof., 1974-77, prof. journalism, 1977—; nat. archivist Coll. Media Advisers Inc.; TV producer for First Baptist Ch., Tuscaloosa, also radio programs; guest lectr., cons. mass media Univs. Stockholm, Linköping and Göteborg (Sweden), Univs. Helsinki, Tampere and Kommunalhögskolan (Finland), U. Moscow, London Coll. Journalism. Served with USAF, 1953-55. Newspaper Fund fellow; Rotary Internat. fellow; U. Ala. grantee. Mem. Assn. Edn. Journalism, Community Coll. Journalism Assn. (nat. archivist). Baptist. Author journalism textbooks, instruction manuals, revs.; editor journalism and media textbooks. Home: 1218 Northwood Lake Northport AL 35476 Office: PO Box 4135 University AL 35486

DEBAKEY, SELMA, educator, writer, editor, lecturer; b. Lake Charles, La.; B.A., Newcomb Coll. Tulane U., also postgrad. Dir. dept. med. communication Alton Ochsner Med. Found., New Orleans, 1942-68; prof. sci. communication Baylor Coll. Medicine, Houston, 1968—, editor Cardiovascular Research Center Bull., 1970-84; former editor: Ochsner Clinic Reports, Selected Writings from the Ochsner Clinic; former co-editor Bull. Am. Med. Writers Assn.; adv. com. International Angiology, 1985—. Mem. Soc. Tech. Communication, Assn. Tchrs. Tech. Writing, Am. Med. Writers Assn. (bd. dirs., various coms.), Council Biology Editors (com. on tng. in sci. writing), AAAS, Soc. Health and Human Values. Author: (with A. Segaloff and K. Meyer) Current Concepts in Breast Cancer, 1967; contbr. in field. Office: Baylor College Medicine One Baylor Plaza Houston TX 77030

DEBIE, ALEXIS IRÉNEÈ, educational psychologist; b. Bryn Mawr, Pa., Dec. 3, 1943; s. Johannes Cornelis and Marie Alexia duPont (Ortiz) deBie; m. Joan Farley, Mar. 7, 1980; children—Natacha Alexia, Denis Eglimez, Alexis Irénée. B.A., U. Paris, 1966; diploma psychiat. nursing, psychol. counseling Charenton Psychiat. Hosp., Paris, 1966-68; B.A., Goddard Coll., 1970, M.A., 1976; postgrad. Columbia Pacific U., 1982—. Lectr. tchr. edn. Ontario Inst. Studies in Edn., 1971-72; psychol. counsellor Ky. East/West Bluegrass Mental Health Comprehensive Care Ctr., Lexington, 1972-74; cons., tchr. Nat. Assn. for Gifted Children, Washington, 1964-76. Chmn., Psychosynthesis Found. Fla., Inc., Palm Beach, 1978—. Mem. Am. Assn. Gifted Children, Nat. Assn. Creative Children and Adults, Am. Geriatric Soc., Soc. Accelerated Learning, Fla. Assn. for Gifted, Nat. Psychiat. Assn., Assn. Humanistic Psychology, Internat. Freedom Found. Lodges: Kiwanis, Rotary. Avocation: Sailing.

DEBNAM, JOHN HANBY, real estate broker; b. Wilmington, N.C., Oct. 25, 1931; s. Frederick Archer and Adrienne Dudley (Hanby) D. B.A. in Polit. Sci., U. N.C., 1953. Grad. Realtors Inst. With Atlantic Coast Line R.R. Co., Wilmington, N.C., 1956-60; account exec. Reynolds & Co., Raleigh, N.C., 1960-68; Realtor assoc. Oleander Co., Inc., Wilmington, N.C., 1970-78, v.p., 1978—; v.p. Hanover Center, Inc., Wilmington, 1978—. Bd. dirs., sec. N.C. Ednl., Hist. and Sci. Found., 1971-80; sec.-treas. Bellamy Mansion, Inc., 1976—. Served to 1st lt. USAF, 1954-56. Mem. Nat. Assn. Realtors (Realtor assoc.), N.C. Bd. Realtors, Wilmington Bd. Realtors, Lower Cape Fear Hist. Soc. (pres. 1970-71), Soc. of Cincinnati, SAR. Republican. Home: 1423 Country Club Rd Wilmington NC 28403 Office: Hanover Center 3501 Oleander Dr PO Box 3145 Wilmington NC 28406

DEBNATH, NIRMALENDU, economics educator; b. Calcutta, India, Sept. 12, 1941; s. Lakshmi Narayan and Sumitra (Devi) D.; m. Rita Delal, July 30, 1969; children—Indranil, Indrajeet. B.A., Calcutta U., 1963; M.A., Ph.D., U. Kalyani, 1965; M.B.A., U. Bridgeport, 1973. Research assoc. U. Kalyani, India, 1967-70; assoc. prof. Lane Coll., Jackson, Tenn., 1974-78, prof. econs., 1979—; assoc. prof. econs. Tougaloo Coll., Miss., 1978-79. Contbr. articles to profl. jours. Mem. Indian Assn. Nashville. Research fellow U. Mo., Rolla, 1976, Northwestern U., Evanston, Ill., 1981, Howard U., 1982; Mellon scholar Vanderbilt U., 1983; U.S. Dept. Transp. grantee, 1982-83. Mem. Am. Econ. Assn., Midsouth Acad. Economists, Transp. Research Bd. Office: 545 Lane Ave Lane Coll Jackson TN 38301

DEBORDE, LINDA PLAYER, real estate broker, Realtor; b. Chester, S.C., June 20, 1939; d. Clyde Louis and Mary Janet (Gulledge) Player; m. Robert A. Wingate, Nov. 21, 1954 (dec. Apr. 1970); children—Cynthia, Tyna Lynn, Janetta; m. 2d Charles Norman DeBorde, Dec. 16, 1971. Student Daytona Community Coll., 1977-79; cert. Grad. Realtors Inst., 1980. Teller Bank of Warwick, Va., 1957-60; cashier Food Town, Salisbury, N.C., 1963-64; cashier, asst. mgr. 7-11 store, New Smyrna Beach, Fla., 1970-72; sec., ins. clk. Max Kreis Agy., New Smyrna Beach, 1975-77; salesman, mgr., appraiser Indian River Real Estate, New Smyrna Beach, 1977-79; broker-owner Nu-Day Realty, Inc., New Smyrna Beach, 1979—. Pres. New Smyrna Jr. High PTA, 1972, Chisholm Sch. PTA, New Smyrna Beach, 1973; treas. New Smyrna High Band Parents, 1973-75. Named to Million Dollar Circle, Nat. Assn. Home Builders, 1978; Fla. Assn. Realtors, Grad. Realtors Inst. scholar, 1981. Mem. New Smyrna Bd. Realtors (bd. dirs. 1978—, v.p. 1981-82, pres. 1982-83, Realtor of Yr. 1982), Fla. Assn. Realtors (bd. dirs. 1981-83), Nat. Assn. Realtors, Am. Bus. Women's Assn. (sec. 1978-79, treas. 1979-80, Woman of Yr. 1981), New Smyrna C. of C. (bd. dirs. 1984, 85), Beta Sigma Phi (corr. sec. 1977-78). Lodge: Elks Ladies (corr. sec. lodge 1974-75). Office: Nu-Day Realty Inc 406 N Orange St New Smyrna Beach FL 32069

DEBOSKEY, DANA STEPHENS, psychologist, hospital administrator, consultant; b. N.Y.C., Sept. 12, 1946; d. Valdane and Winifred Margaret (Rundlett) Stephens; m. William DeBoskey, Mar. 25, 1972; children—Kristina, Stephen, Christopher, Kari. B.A., U. South Fla., 1968, Ed.M., 1970, M.A., 1973; Ph.D., U. Tenn., 1982. Lic. psychologist, cert. sch. psychologist. Psychol., ednl. examiner Team Evaluation Ctr., Chattanooga, 1973-74, dir. psychol. services, 1974-75; psychol. examiner Drs. Bacon, Miller & Assocs., Knoxville, Tenn., 1975-79; sch. psychologist Hillsborough County Schs., Tampa, Fla., 1980-83; clin. coordinator U. S. Fla. Ctr. for Children, Tampa, 1983-84; chief of neuropsychology Tampa Gen. Hosp., 1984—; cons. psychology Douglas Cherokee Headstart, Alcoa, Tenn., 1976-78; cons. infant psychology Appalachian Regional Child Devel. Ctr., Knoxville, 1975-79; cons. neuropsychology Fla. Diagnostic and Resource Ctr., St. Petersburg, 1984—. Author: Manual for Management of Head Injury, 1985; articles, assessment tools in field. Mem. Temple Terrace Ladies Aux., 1985. U. South Fla. fellow, 1968-70, recipient Creative Scholar award, 1970. Mem. Am. Psychol. Assn., Nat. Assn. Sch. Psychologists, Suncoast Assn. Sch. Psychologists (sec. 1983-84), Acad. of Neuropsychology, Fla. Psychol. Assn. Democrat. Avocations: jogging; reading; youth sports. Home: 105 N Burlingame Ave Tampa FL 33617 Office: Tampa Gen Rehab Ctr Tampa Gen Hosp Tampa FL 33606

DEBUSK, RALPH EDWARD, statistician; b. Smyth County, Va., Jan. 26, 1922; s. Claude Tyler and Mabel (Litton) DeB.; m. Edith Maxine McCroskey; children—Betty DeBusk Yeatts, David F., Janet DeBusk Allen. B.S., Emory and Henry Coll., 1943; postgrad. in indsl. engring. and stats. U. Tenn., 1960-65. Jr. chemist Tenn. Eastman Co., Kingsport, 1946-47, asst. chemist, 1947-49, assoc. chemist, 1949-52, chemist, 1952-64, statistician, 1964-66, sr. statistician, quality control supr., 1966-75, sr. statistician, statis. cons., 1975-84; cons. Process Industries, 1984—; conf. chmn. Ann. Quality Control Clinic, U. Tenn., 1962. Mem. Sullivan County (Tenn.) Election Commn., 1971-75, sec., 1971-73. Served with U.S. Army, 1943-46. Fellow Am. Soc. Quality Control (chmn. chem. div. 1965-66, testimonial award in recognition of leadership and disting. service 1979); mem. Am. Inst. Indsl. Engrs., Republican. Lutheran. Patentee in field; author tech. papers; contbr. articles to profl. jours. Home: 4401 Timberlake Ln Kingsport TN 37664

DE BUYSSCHER, EDWARD VICTOR, veterinarian, immunologist, educator; b. Merksem, Belgium, July 26, 1946; s. Rene and Liza (Janssen) DeB.; m. Rose Marie Cnudde, Oct. 2, 1970; 1 son, Tristan Adriaan. D.V.M., State U. Ghent (Belgium), 1971; M.S., U. Wis., 1973, Ph.D., 1975. Lic. veterinarian Belgian Vet. Med. Assn. Research asst. U. Wis. Dept. Vet. Sci., Madison, 1971-75; asst. prof. immunology dept. med. microbiology Sch. Vet. Medicine, U. Ga., Athens, 1975-81; assoc. prof. dept. microbiology, pathology and parasitology N.C. State U. Sch. Vet. Medicine, Raleigh, 1981—, adj. assoc. prof. dept. microbiology; vis. researcher Internat. Inst. Cellular Pathology dept. exptl. medicine, U. Louvain, Brussels, Belgium, 1979; mem. nat. peer rev. panel U.S. Dept. Agr. nat. competitive grant com., 1980-83. Recipient Wis. Vet. Med. Assn. Burr A. Beach award, 1976; U. Ga. Sarah H. Moss fellow, 1979; recipient numerous research grants. Mem. AAAS, Am. Soc. Microbiology, AVMA, Conf. Research Workers in Animal Disease, Belgian Vet. Med. Assn., N.Y. Acad. Sci., Am. Assn. Vet. Immunologists, Am. Assn. Immunologists, Contbr. numerous articles to profl. pubs. Home: 6004 Misty Ridge Rd Holly Springs NC 27540 Office: North Carolina State U School Veterinary Medicine Raleigh NC 27650

DE CANIO, LETICIA MIRANDA, educator; b. Havana, Cuba, Sept. 19, 1929; came to U.S., 1948, naturalized, 1956; d. Angel and Maria-Teresa (De Urrutia) Miranda-Valcarcel; children—Salvatore M., Maria-Teresa. Grad. secretarial sci. Rider Coll., 1952; A.A. Palm Beach Jr. Coll., 1975; B.A. in Elem. Edn., Fla. Atlantic U., 1977, M.Ed., 1980. Kindergarten tchr. West Gate Elem. Sch., West Palm Beach, Fla., 1978—. Mem. Assn. Edn. of Young Children of the Palm Beaches (past pres.), So. Assn. Children Under Six, NEA, Assn. Childhood Edn. Internat., Classroom Tchrs. Assn, Internat. Reading Assn. (mem. Palm Beach County council), Nat. Assn. Female Execs. Democrat. Roman Catholic.

DE CARDENAS, CRISTINA, university administrator; b. Havana, Cuba, Mar. 12, 1938; d. Julio and Rosario (Lago) de Cardenas; divorced; children—Laureano, Cristina Ana. B.A., St. George Coll., Havana, 1955. Vice-pres., dir. internat. sales Ultimate Internat. Corp., Marietta, Ga., 1977-79; dir. Hispanic internat. affairs U. Miami/Jackson Meml. Med. Ctr., Coral Gables, Fla., 1979-82; dir. internat. affairs U. Miami, Coral Gables, 1982-83, exec. asst. to pres., 1983—; producer, host Sucesos TV talkshow, 1981-83. Pres., founder Internat. Childrens Fund, 1979—; bd. dirs. Ronald McDonald House, 1983. Mem. Greater Miami C. of C., Interam. Businessmen Assn., Latin Bus. and Profl. Women, Leadership Miami Alumnae Assn., Miami Forum (v.p. 1982-83), Coalition of Hispanic-Am. Women. Republican. Roman Catholic. Clubs: Country of Coral Gables, American. Home: 520 Brickell Key Drive Apt 1504 Miami FL 33131 Office: PO Box 248006 Coral Gables FL 33134

DECILLIS, DAVID MARK, dentist, pharmacist; b. Phoenix, Mar. 17, 1956; s. Thomas Donato and Martha Joan (Kusse) DeC.; m. Lynn Victoria Thompson, Jan. 9, 1981; 1 child, Katherine Ann. B.S. in Pharmacy, U. Md., 1979, D.D.S., 1983. Pharmacist Lykos Pharmacy, Balt., 1979-83; sole practice gen. dentistry, Heath Springs, S.C., 1983—; tchr. oral pathology York Tech. Coll., Rock Hill, S.C., 1985—. Active Boy Scouts Am.; chmn. Heath Springs Great Town Appearance Com., 1985; bd. dirs. Lancaster United Way, S.C., 1985-87. Recipient Service award Nat. Fedn. Dentistry for Handicapped, 1983. Mem. ADA, S.C. Dental Assn., Sand Hill Study Club (pres. 1985), Gorgas Odontological Soc. Baptist. Lodge: Lions, Moose. Avocations: tennis, boating, fishing, hunting. Address: PO Box 455 Heath Springs SC 29058

DECKER, GUY MILTON, petroleum geologist; b. Mason City, Iowa, Feb. 12, 1955; s. Ralph Waldo Emerson and Janice Colleen (Bowe) D.; m. Michal Margaret Bullock, Dec. 9, 1978; children—Lauren Elizabeth, Paige Colleen. B.S. in Geology, U. Tex.-El Paso, 1977, M.S. in Geology, 1981. Geotechnician, Chevron U.S.A., Denver, 1978-79; geologist Getty Oil Co., Oklahoma City, 1981-84, Petrocorp, Inc., Oklahoma City, 1984—. Mem. Am. Assn. Petroleum Geologists. Republican. Avocations: recquetball; woodworking; outdoor activities. Home: 2616 Keats Pl Oklahoma City OK 73120 Office: Petro Corp Inc 210 W Park Ave Suite 3131 Oklahoma City OK 73102

DECKER, JOSEPHINE I., clinic administrator; b. Barling, Ark., May 24, 1933; d. Ralph and Ada A. (Claborn) Snider; student public schs., Muldrow, Okla.; m. William Arlen Decker, Feb. 4, 1952; 1 son, Peter A. With Southwestern Bell Telephone Co., Ft. Smith, Ark., 1951-52; with Holt Krock Clinic, Ft. Smith, 1952—, bus. adminstr., 1970—. Bd. dirs. Sparks Credit Union, Adv. Council Northside and Southside high schs., Ft. Smith, Ft. Smith Girls Shelter, Ft. Smith Credit Bur. Mem. Credit Women Internat., Soc. Cert. Consumer Credit Execs. Office: Holt Krock Clinic 1500 Dodson Ave Fort Smith AR 72901

DECKER, KAREN, artist; b. Oceanside, Calif., Jan. 3, 1944; d. William Conway and Sylvia (Sundstrom) D. B.A. in English, Bucknell U., 1965. Represented by Oxford Gallery, Rochester, N.Y. and Tomlyn Gallery, Tequesta, Fla.; docent Norton Art Gallery, West Palm Beach, Fla., 1981—. Counselor Planned Parenthood, West Palm Beach, 1981—. Mem. Norton Artist Guild, Broward Art Guild, Lake Worth Art League, Fla. Ctr. Contemporary Art., Artists Equity Assn. Club: North Palm Beach Country. Home: 1070 Grand Bahama Singer Island FL 33404

DECOSMO, JOHN BAPTISTE, JR., physician; b. Ellwood City, Pa., Oct. 31, 1928; s. John Baptiste and Cristina (Pistachio) DeC.; m. Judith Jane Marshall, Jan. 11, 1973; children—John B. III, Elizabeth L., Gregory Paul, Valerie C., Courtney Marshall, Maria E., Cristopher R. B.A., Bklyn. Coll., 1953; D.O., Kirksville Coll. of Osteo. Medicine and Surgery, 1957; postdoctoral, U. South Fla., 1973. Intern Dallas Osteo. Hosp.; bd. mem., founder, treas., chmn. med. library Metro. Gen. Hosp., Pinellas Park, Fla., 1963—, chief of staff, 1964-65; founder, sec., bd. mem., chmn. med. library St. Petersburg Osteo. Hosp., Fla., 1975-82; founder, pres. West Coast Labs. Inc., St. Petersburg, 1975-82; founder Gateway Med. Arts Clinic, St. Petersburg,

1978—; dir., chmn. med. library Harborside Hosp., St. Petersburg, 1982—; dir., v.p. Madonna Ednl. Systems, Inc., St. Petersburg, 1985—; dir. 3-D Aluminum Extruders, Inc., St. Petersburg, 1984—, Organizer branch of N.Y. Pub. Library of Industry, N.Y.C., 1950; mem. Gov's. select Ombudsman Com., State of Fla., 1980-81. Mem. Am. Osteo. Assn., Fla. Osteo. Med. Soc. (pres. 1966-67, bd. govs. 1965), Fla. Osteo. Med. Assn., Pinellas County Osteo. Med. Soc. (gov. 1959-60), Am. Heart Assn. (dir. Suncoast chpt., Fla., 1979—), Avocations: civic activities; library functions; numismatics; boating; fishing. Office: Gateway Med Arts Clinic 8000 Fourth St N Saint Petersburg FL 33702

DEDHIA, HARAKH VASANJI, physician, educator; b. Bombay, India, Nov. 6, 1947; came to U.S., 1972, naturalized, 1982; s. Vasanji N. Shah and Sakarben Dedhia; m. Anuja Shah. Student, St. Xavier Coll., Bombay, 1964-66; M.B.B.S., Grant Med. Coll., 1970. Diplomate Am. Bd. Internal Medicine, 1977, lic. physician, India, 1970, Washington, 1975, Fla., 1977, W.Va., 1979. Intern J.J. Grant Bombay Hosps., 1970-71, Mt. Sinai Hosp., N.Y.C., 1972-73; resident Cath. Med. Ctr., N.Y.C., 1973-75, fellow, 1975-76; resident U. Pitts. Health Ctr., 1976-77; assoc. dir. intensive care unit W.Va. U. Med. Ctr., Morgantown, 1979-81, med. dir. intensive care unit, 1982—, assoc. prof. anesthesiology and medicine, 1982—; med. officer refugee camps, West Bengal, India, 1971, Barbuda, W.I., 1982. Fellow Am. Coll. Chest Physicians, ACP, Am. Soc. Lasers in Medicine and Surgery; mem. Am. Thoracic Soc., Soc. Critical Care Medicine, W.Va. State Med. Assn., Hindu. Contbr. articles profl. jours. Office: Dept Anesthesiology West Virginia Medical Ctr Morgantown WV 26506

DEDMON, DONALD NEWTON, university president; b. Mo., Aug. 13, 1931; s. Clarence R. and Ola Edith (Garner) D.; B.S. in Edn., S.W. Mo. State U., Springfield, 1953; M.A., U. Iowa, 1956. Ph.D., 1961; m. Geraldine Mary Sanders; children—Mary Elizabeth, Margaret Ann. Instr., dir. debate U. Iowa, 1955-59; asst., then asso. prof. speech, co-chmn. required communications courses St. Cloud (Minn.) State Coll., 1959-62; asso. prof., TV lectr. oral communications So. Ill. U., Carbondale, 1962-64, prof., chmn. dept. speech and arts Colo. State U., Boulder, 1964-66, communications cons., later head tng. and mgmt. devel. Smith, Kline & French Labs., 1966-68; dean Coll. Arts and Scis., then exec. v.p., v.p. acad. affairs, acting pres. Marshall U., Huntington, W.Va., 1968-72; pres. Radford (Va.) U., 1972—, also mem. found. bd. dirs. Dir. United Va. Bank, Radford. Mem. gen. profl. adv. com. Va. Council Higher Edn.; mem. Council Pres. of Commonwealth Va.; state rep. Am. Assn. State Colls. and Univs.; chmn. bd. dirs. St. Albans Psychiat. Hosp., Radford. Served with AUS, 1953-55. Mem. Va., Radford chambers commerce. Rotarian Contbr. numerous articles in field to profl. jours. Home: Radford U Radford VA 24142

DEE, PAUL TERRENCE, lawyer; b. Hoboken, N.J., Jan. 6, 1947; s. Paul Laurence and Anne D.; m. Elizabeth Hall, June 12, 1971; 1 son, Terrence Andrew. B.A., U. Fla., 1970; M.Ed., U. Miami, 1973, J.D., 1977. Tchr., athletic dir. Glades Central High Sch., Belle Glade, Fla., 1970-74; law clk. U.S. Dist. Ct. (so. dist.) Fla., 1976-78; atty. Dade County Sch. Bd., 1978-80; mem. Mershon, Sawyer, Johnston & Dunwody & Cole, Miami, Fla., 1980-81; gen. counsel, corp. sec. U. Miami, 1981—; ptnr. Mershon, Sawyer Johnston, Dunwoody & Cole, 1985—; dir. U. Miami Inn Corp.; instr. U. Miami Grad. Sch. Dist. committeeman South Fla. council Boy Scouts Am.; chmn. bd. Miami Cable Access Corp. Mem. ABA, Fla. Bar Assn., Dade County Bar Assn., Fed. Bar Assn., Nat. Assn. Coll. and Univ. Attys., Am. Acad. Hosp. Attys. Democrat. Roman Catholic. Clubs: Country (Coral Gables); Bankers (Miami). Home: 6260 SW 144th St Miami FL 33158 Office: 4500 Southeast Financial Ctr 200 S Biscayne Blvd Miami FL 33131

DEEN, LEIGH, store manager; b. Norfolk, Va., Nov. 4, 1946; d. Harry Lee and Fraustine (Yannone) D. B.A., U. Tampa, 1969. Cert. tchr., Fla. Sec. II, U. Tampa, Fla., 1970-71; draftsman Gen. Telephone Co., Tampa, 1971-75; Cashier I, U. South Fla., Tampa, 1976-79, clk typist III, 1979-82, bookstore mgr., 1982—. Bd dirs. Lamplighter-on-the-River Homeowners Assn., 1985—. Mem. Nat. Assn. of Coll. Stores (health sci. stores com. 1984—), Fedn. Mobile Home Owners Fla. (sec.-treas. 1985-86). Office: U South Fla Med Bookstore 12901 N 30th St Box 38 Tampa FL 33612

DEERING, FERDIE JACKSON, journalist; b. Denison, Tex., Oct. 24, 1910; s. Norman Henry and Hattie Elena (Brand) D.; m. Flora Mildred Jennings, May 3, 1935; children—Cheryl Beth Wilson, Robert Edward. Student East Central State U.; diploma of distinction, Okla. State U. Coll. Agr., 1972. Reporter Ada (Okla.) Evening News, 1931-33, night editor, 1934-37; advt. salesman Denison (Tex.) Daily Herald, 1933-34; assoc. editor The Farmer Stockman mag., Oklahoma City, 1937-42, editor, mgr., 1943-72; columnist, editorial writer, mag. editor Oklahoman & Times, Oklahoma City, 1943-85; dir. Okla. Pub. Co., Oklahoma City, 1958-75, asst. corp. sec., 1958-75; dir. The Farmer-Stockman Pub. Co., Dallas, 1972—. Vice-pres. Okla. Com. Nat. Cowboy Hall of Fame and Western Heritage Ctr., 1955-58; mem. Weather Modification Adv. Com., Okla. Water Resources Bd., 1972-74, 76-82. Recipient Disting. Alumnus award East Central State U., 1979; Henry G. Bennett Disting. Service award Okla. State U., 1983. Mem. Am. Agrl. Editors Assn. (v.p. 1950, pres. 1951), Agrl. Communicators in Edn. (Reuben Brigham award 1976), Oklahoma City C. of C. (v.p. 1961-62), Alpha Zeta. Republican. Baptist. Club: Men's Dinner (Oklahoma City). Author: USDA, Manager of American Agriculture, 1945; Look at Oklahoma, 1975; From the Grassroots Up, 1980. Home: Heritage Sq 11608 Susan Ln Oklahoma City OK 73120 Office: PO Box 25125 Oklahoma City OK 73125

DEERY, NORMA KIMREY, school counselor, counseling educator; b. Rock Hill, S.C., Oct. 16, 1946; d. Norman W. and Ruby L. (Leonard) Kimrey; children—Pride, Paige, Noel, Turner. B.A. in Early Childhood Edn. cum laude, U. S.C., 1978, M.Ed. in Elem. Counseling, 1980. Cert. elem. counselor. Grad. teaching asst., intern U. S.C., Columbia, 1979-80, supr. counseling practium, 1984—, adj. instr., 1985—; middle sch. counselor B-L Middle Sch., Batesburg, S.C., 1980-83; elem. counselor Pierce Terr. Elem. Sch., Fort Jackson, S.C., 1983—; presenter workshops, seminars and tng. programs. Tchr., coordinator elem. Ch. Sch., mem. kindergarten bd. dir., counselor youth camp, dir. vacation ch. sch. Asbury Methodist Ch. Sch.; sec., treas. Meth. Women, chmn. social concerns United Meth. Women, children's ministry coordinator, mem. commn. on edn., counsel on ministry, adminstrv. bd. Asbury Meth. Ch.; neighborhood vol. March of Dimes, Cystic Fibrosis, Cancer Soc., Heart Fund, Multiple Sclerosis; bd. dirs. YWCA Youth Task Force, Batesburg, 1980-83, Fort Jackson Family Adv. Council, 1983—; mem. health edn. commn. Lexington County Health Dept., 1981-83; bd. govs., parent edn. coordinator Fort Jackson Schs.; bd. dirs. S.C. Coalition for Concerned Children, Columbia. Recipient Ft. Jackson Crime Prevention award, 1985. Mem. S.C. Sch. Counselors Assn. (pres. 1986—, treas. 1980-82, bd. govs. 1980—, exec. council, human rights com. 1985—, S.C. Middle Sch. Counselor of Yr. 1979), S.C. Assn. for Childhood Edn. Internat. (bd. govs. 1981—, project chmn., parent edn. editor 1984—), Am. Sch. Counselor Assn., Am. Assn. of Counseling and Devel., S.C. Assn. of Counseling and Devel. (governing bd. 1986—), Am. Assn. Childhood Edn. Internat. Am. Assn. for Humanistic Edn. and Devel., S.C. Assn. for Humanistic Edn. and Devel., S.C. Adlerian Soc., U. S.C. Alumni Assn., Omicron Delta Kappa, Kappa Phi Kappa. Club: Palmetto Woman's (Columbia). Avocations: biking; camping; reading; painting; crafts. Home: 642 Planters Dr Columbia SC 20209 Office: Pierce Terrace Sch Adam's Ct Fort Jackson SC 20207

DEES, ANTHONY ROANE, historical society executive educator; b. Pikeville, N.C., Sept. 19, 1937; s. Claude Edward and Lois Winifred (Jackson) D.; m. Leslie Gray McNeill, Sept. 27, 1975. B.A., U. N.C., 1959, M.S. in L.S., 1964. Catalogue librarian Washington and Lee U., Lexington, Va., 1962-67; catalogue librarian to curator manuscripts U. Ga., Athens, 1967-77, mem. faculty, 1967-77; dir. Ga. Hist. Soc., Savannah, 1977—; mem. faculty Armstrong State Coll., Savannah, 1979—. Co-editor: Selected Eighteenth Century Manuscripts, Georgia Hist. Soc. Collection, Vol. XX, 1980. Contbr. articles to profl. jours. Mem. Soc. Am. Archivists, Soc. Ga. Archivists, Southeastern Library Assn., Ga. Library Assn. Democrat. Roman Catholic. Lodge: Rotary. Home: 2103 Springlake Dr NW Atlanta GA 30305 Office: 330 Capitol Ave SE Atlanta GA 30334

DEES, JAMES PARKER, bishop; b. Greenville, N.C., Dec. 30, 1915; s. James Earl and Margaret Burgwyn (Parker) D.; m. Margaret Lucinda Brown, Aug. 10, 1940; children—Margaret Lucinda, Eugenia Johnston Dees Osteen. B.A., U. N.C., 1938, postgrad., 1938-39; M.Div., Va. Theol. Sem., 1949; D.Div. (hon.) Bob Jones U., 1965. Ordained deacon Episcopal Ch., 1949, priest, 1950, resigned, 1963; ordained bishop Anglican Orthodox Ch., 1964. Shipping clk. Atlantic Coast Line R.R., Greenville, N.C., 1939-42; priest Protestant Episcopal Ch., Aurora and Beaufort, N.C., 1949-55, Episcopal Ch., Statesville, N.C., 1955-63; founder, presiding bishop Anglican Orthodox Ch., Statesville, 1963—; founder Cranmer Sem., Statesville, 1971; mem. Diocesan Exec. Council Episcopal Ch., 1951-60, sec., 1952-54, sec. conv., 1953-54, chmn. dept. youth, 1952-55, mem. dept. Christian edn., 1954-60, mem. dept. camps and confs., 1951-52. Author: Reformation Anglicanism, 1971, Runnymede, 1983. Founder, pres. N.C. Defenders of States' Rights; bd. dirs. Fedn. Constl. Govt., New Orleans, Independence Found., Portland, Ind.; mem. bd. policy Liberty Lobby, Washington; bd. dirs. Nat. Conservative Council, Richmond, Va.; mem. Com. to Restore the Constitution, 1976; pres. PTA, Statesville. Served with U.S. Army, 1943-45. Recipient Liberty award Congress of Freedom, 1968-74; Solidarity Freedom award Polish Freedom Fighters, Salem, Mass., 1983. Avocation: Historical reading. Office: Anglican Orthodox Ch PO Box 128 Statesville NC 28677

DEES, SALLY BICE, research microbiologist; b. Montgomery, Ala., July 5, 1933; d. Stoughton Nathaniel and Sibyl Carolyn (Simpson) Bice; B.A., Huntingdon Coll., 1955; M.S., Ga. State U., 1970; children—Deborah Diane Samuels, Laura Carolyn Wood, Marza Katherine Samuels. Microbiologist, Ala. State Health Dept., Montgomery, 1955-57, Ga. State Health Dept., Atlanta, 1957-61; research microbiologist Center for Disease Control, Atlanta, 1961-85, Emory U. Med. Sch., Atlanta, 1986—; lectr. in field. Trainer, scheduler Contact Teleministries, 24-Hour Crisis Line, 1977-78; mem. profl. clogging team Rainbow Connection, Hot Lanta Hoedowners. Cert. specialist in public health and med. lab. microbiology. Mem. Am. Soc. Microbiology, Sigma Xi. Research on DNA replication mechanisms using methods of molecular cloning and gene manipulation. Office: Microbiology (Immunology) Dept 561 Woodruff Meml Bldg Emory U Atlanta GA 30322

DE FÉE, BILL, def. contracting co. exec.; b. El Paso, Tex., Jan. 8, 1918; s. Emmette Lee and Meredith Elaine (Williams) de F.; ed. Tex. A&M Coll., 1941-43; cert. structural engring. Edison Tech. Inst., 1963; m. Frances Ann Doerr; children—Elaine, Peggy, James, Janet, Joan, Billy, Suzanne, David, Bonita. Chief liaison tool engr. Convair, Ft. Worth, 1941-43; engring. instr. Tex. A&M USESMDT Program, 1943; sr. mech. engr., then chief indsl. designer Brown Bigelow Corp., St. Paul, 1943; pres., chmn. bd. deSkal Engring. and Mfg. Corp., Gardena, Calif., 1951-57; chief mfg. project engr. Apollo project AVCO Corp., Wilmington, Mass., 1958-64; engring. div. mgr. Miss. Army Ammunition Plant, Mason Chamberlain, Inc. subs. Chamberlain & Mason Hanger, Bay St. Louis, 1965—. Weapons engring. cons. Task comdr. aircraft problems in combat, World War II. Recipient Army/Navy E award, World War II. Mem. Am. Def. Preparedness Assn., Assn. U.S. Army, Nat. Rifle Assn. (life). Democrat. Author, patentee in field. Home: Slidell LA 70458 Office: NSTL Station MS 39529

DE FOOR, MARJORIE KEEN, devel. co. exec.; b. West Palm Beach, Fla., Oct. 31, 1929; d. Stephen Wesley and Ada Mae Keen; student Stetson U., 1947; A.A., Stephens Coll., Mo., 1948; B.S., U. Ala., 1949; children—James Allison II, Stephen Charles, Sheila Keen Monaco. With Keen Fruit Corp., Frostproof, Fla., 1956—, v.p., 1980-83, pres., 1983—, also dir. Republican. Episcopalian. Club: Tower (Tampa, Fla.). Home: 1402 Olivia St Key West FL 33040

DE FRANK, VINCENT, conductor; b. L.I. City, N.Y., June 18, 1915; s. Nicholas and Della (Proudford) DeF.; m. Jean Marie Martin, Aug. 26, 1960; children—Vincent Nicholas, Philip Martin. Student, Juilliard Sch. Music, 1934-36; fellow Ind. U., 1952; D.Mus. (hon.), Southwestern U., Memphis, 1974. Cellist, Detroit Symphony Orch., 1939-40, St. Louis Symphony, 1947-50; founder, condr., Memphis Symphony Orch., 1952-84, condr. emeritus, 1984—; also Memphis Little Symphony, Memphis Chamber Orch.; music supr., Memphis-Hebrew Acad., 1969—; mem. adv. panel, Tenn. Arts Commn., 1970; guest condr., Memphis Civic Ballet, Memphis Opera Theatre, Tenn. All-State Orch., Sewanee Summer Music Center, Jackson (Miss.) Symphony, Nashville Symphony and Little Symphony, Quincy (Ill.) Symphony, Charlotte (N.C.) Symphony, Evansville (Ind.) Symphony; disting. vis. artist Rhodes Coll., Memphis; mem. Avery Fisher award recommendation bd. Served with AUS, 1940-45. Recipient Gov.'s Outstanding Tennessean award, 1984. Mem. Memphis Music Inc., Am. Symphony Orch. League, Violoncello Soc., Condrs. Guild, Nat. Acad. Rec. Arts and Scis. (Gov.'s award 1986), Nat. Rifle Assn. Clubs: Masons, Petroleum (Memphis). Home: 4748 Shady Grove Rd Memphis TN 38117 Office: Rhodes Coll Dept Music 2000N Parkway Memphis TN 38112

DEGEUS, STUART, restaurant company advertising executive; b. Saginaw, Mich., July 5, 1952; s. Henry and Helen Anne (Symons) deG.; m. Kathleen Ann Schaffer, Apr. 1, 1978; 1 son, David. B.S. in Edn., Central Mich. U., 1974. News dir. Sta.-WEYI-TV, 1974-78; account supr. Ross Ray Advt., Detroit, 1978-81; dir. advt. Spartan Food Systems, Inc., Spartanburg, S.C., 1981—. Recipient 3 Gold Addy awards Am. Advt. Fedn., 1980. Mem. Adcraft Club Detroit, Nat. Press. Photographers Assn. Roman Catholic. Office: PO Box 3168 Spartanburg SC 29304

DEGROOT, ROBERT PAUL, oil service company executive, professional counselor; b. Appleton, Wis., Aug. 9, 1947; s. Maurice Francis and Mary Jane (House) DeG.; m. Linda Karen Sterle, Sept. 14, 1968 (div. Feb. 1980); m. Kemba Dianne Koontz, Nov. 27, 1982. B.A., Southwest Tex. State U., San Marcos, 1975, M.Ed., 1976. Lic. profl. counselor, Tex.; cert. sch. psychologist, Tex. Asst. Inst. Psychology Southwest Tex. State U., San Marcus, 1975-76; assoc. sch. psychologist Temple Ind. Sch. Dist., (Tex.), 1976-78, editor, contbg. author in-house publication, 1976-78; supr. forensic clinic Mental Health Mental Retardation Assn. of Harris County, Houston, 1978-81; v.p. investment div. Bus. Title Co., Houston, 1981-82; mktg. mgr. Keystone Engring., Houston, 1982—. Recipient Service commendation Associated Students of Southwest Tex. State U., 1973, 75. Mem. Tex. Psychol. Assn. (Disting. Service award 1978). Home: 4040 San Felipe #210 Houston TX 77027 Office: Keystone Engring 6310 Sidney St Houston TX 77021

DEGUIRE, LILLIAN FRAZIER, media specialist, librarian; b. Charleston, S.C., Jan. 27, 1949; d. Eddie and Elizabeth (Howard) Frazier; m. Maxwell N. DeGuire, Aug. 16, 1969 (div. May 1973); children—Angela Yvonne, Andrea Yvette. B.A. in History, Coll. of Charleston, 1975; M.L., U. S.C., 1978. Kindergarten tchr. pub. schs. Charleston County (S.C.), 1975-77, media specialist, librarian, E.B. Ellington Elem. Sch., 1978—; tchr. upward bound students Coll. of Charleston. Del. Gov.'s Conf. on Library and Info. Services. Mem. S.C. Library Assn., S.C. Assn. Sch. Librarians, Am. Fedn. Tchrs., Southeastern Library Assn., Delta Sigma Theta. Baptist. Office: EB Ellington Sch 5600 Ellington School Rd Ravenel SC 29470

DE HURST, DINORAH ESCOBAR, government tourism office administrator; b. Mexico City, July 24, 1953; d. Salvador Escobar Santelices and Susana Perusquia Escobar; m. Thomas W. Hurst, Oct. 10, 1981. Asst. v.p. Construcciones Cimbracret, S.A., Mexico City, 1971-73; asst. gen. mgr. Preforzados del Istmo, S.A., Mexico City, 1973-75; promotion and control mgr. Procinemex, S.A., Mexico City, 1975-76; service and pub. relations mgr. Distribuidora Japay, S.A., Mexico City, 1977-78; regional dir. Mexican Govt. Tourism Office, Atlanta, 1978—. Mem. Travel Industry Assn. Ga., Pacific Area Travel Assn., Meeting Planners Internat., Ga. Soc. Assn. Execs., Am. Mktg. Assn., Ga. Internat. Trade Assn., Buckhead Bus. Assn., So. Ctr. for Internat. Studies, Young Matron's Circle. Club: West Paces Racquet.

DEICHMANN, DICK HENRY, graphics corporation financial executive; b. Durant, Iowa, Oct. 22, 1928; s. Carl W. and Amanda A. (Eriksen) D.; m. Arlene Ehrich, Aug. 13, 1950; children—Craig, Kurt, Janet. B.S.C. cum laude, U. Iowa, 1952. With Gen. Electric Co., 1952-70; v.p. fin., dir. Copperweld Corp., Pitts., 1970-74; v.p. fin. Victor Comptometer Corp., Chgo., 1975-77; v.p. fin. Visual Graphics Corp., Tamarac, Fla., 1978—. Served with U.S. Army, 1946-48. Mem. Fin. Execs. Inst. (pres. chpt.), Am. Fin. Assn. Clubs: Coral Springs Country, Patterson Country, Perry Park Country. Home: 2501 NW 112th Ave Coral Springs FL 33065 Office: 5701 NW 94th Ave Tamarac FL 33321

DEININGER, JAMES EDMUND, architect, educator; b. Trenton, Sept. 2, 1944; s. Charles E. and Ann Blades (Medhurst) D.; B.Environ. Design, Miami U., Oxford, Ohio, 1974, M.Arch., 1976; m. Janet A. Chieffalo, Jan. 24, 1970. Designer, J. Robert Hillier, Princeton, N.J., 1968-72; prof. architecture Tex. A&M U., College Station, 1976—, fgn. studies coordinator, Strasbourg, France, 1981; prin. Group 4 Architects/Planners, Bryan, Tex., 1982, James E. Deininger, Architect, 1983—; project architect Skidmore, Owings & Merrill, Chgo., 1979; project designer Pahlavi Nat. Library, 1976-77; designer housing in Egypt, 1983—. Served with AUS, 1966-68. Recipient spl. citation, 1979, Merit award, 1980. Home: 1818 Langford St College Station TX 77840 Office: Coll Architecture and Environ Design Tex A&M U College Station TX 77843 also 7607 Eastmark Dr Suite 250 College Station TX 77840

DEJOY, DAVID MICHAEL, occupational health and safety educator, researcher; b. Auburn, N.Y., Mar. 1, 1949; s. McLean Michael and Catherine (Kennedy) DeJ.; m. Elaine Marie Stahlman, Sept. 8, 1968 (div. 1979); 1 child, Katherine. B.A., SUNY-Geneseo, 1971, M.A., 1974; Ph.D., Pa. State U., 1978. Grad. asst. SUNY, Geneseo, 1971-73; grad. asst. Pa. State U., 1973-77, project assoc., 1977-78; psychologist EPA, Washington, 1978-80, environ. health scientist administr., 1980-81; asst. prof. dept. health and safety edn. U. Ga., Athens, 1981—, dir. grad. program, 1984—; speaker in field. Contbr. articles to profl. jours. Mem. Athens Wellness Council, Ga., 1983—. Recipient Certificate Meritorious Pub. Service EPA, 1981. Mem. Am. Psychol. Assn., Am. Soc. Safety Engrs., Southeastern Psychol. Assn., Eta Sigma Gamma. Roman Catholic. Office: Univ Ga Stegeman Hall Athens GA 30602

DEKEYSER, THOMAS LEE, exploration geologist; b. Green Bay, Wis., Nov. 30, 1945; s. Alphonse William DeKeyser and Frances Mildred (Nihil) Bohm; m. Lorraine Marie LaFreniere (div. Oct. 1973). B.S. in Geology, U. Wis.-Madison, 1972, M.S., 1974; Ph.D. in Geology, Oreg. State U., 1979. Asst. to mus. curator U. Wis., Madison, 1971-74; research scientist Amoco Prodn. Co., Tulsa, 1972-76; instr. geology Oreg. State U., 1977-79; asst. prof. Tex. Tech U., 1979-82; advanced exploration geologist Marathon Oil Co., Midland, Tex., 1982-84, sr. exploration geologist, Houston, 1984—. Contbr. articles to profl. jours. Served with U.S. Navy, 1967-71. Mem. Am. Assn. Petroleum Geologists, Geol. Soc. Am., Paleontol. Soc., Sierra Club, Sigma Xi. Republican. Avocations: backpacking, snow skiing, photography, reading, cycling. Home: 2607 Stoney Brook Dr Houston TX 77063 Office: Marathan Oil Co PO Box 3128 Houston TX 77253

DE LA CRUZ, JOSÉ GERARDO, professional building designer; b. México D.F., Mar. 2, 1956; came to U.S., 1964; naturalized, 1976; s. David Eliseo and Gloria Nicolasa-(Aguirre) De La C.; m. Juanita Sarmiento, Dec. 17, 1982; 1 child, Leslie. Student Tex. Tech. U., 1975-80. Cert. profl. bldg. designer. Bldg. designer Galo Investment Co., Laredo, Tex., 1980-83; field engr. Utley-James of Tex., Austin, 1983—; project supt. Joffko Internat., Marsa Elbrega, Libya, 1985—; bldg. constrn. cons., Laredo, 1982-84. Pres. United Mexican-Am. Student, Lubbock, Tex., 1977. Mem. Am. Inst. Bldg. Design, Tex. Inst. Bldg. Design. Republican. Roman Catholic. Avocations: horseback riding; writing poems. Office: Joffko Internat 6815 A Lindbergh Houston TX 77087

DE LA GARZA, E(KIKA), congressman; b. Mercedes, Tex., Sept. 22, 1927; s. Dario and Elisa (Villarreal) de la G.; student Pan Am. Coll., Edinburg, Tex., 1947-48; LL.B., St. Mary's U., San Antonio, 1951; m. Lucille Alamia, May 29, 1953; children—Jorge Luis, Michael Alberto, Angela Dolores. Admitted to Tex. bar, 1951; mem. Tex. Ho. of Reps., 1953-64; mem. 89th-98th Congresses from 15th Dist. Tex., chmn. agr. com. Served with USNR, World War II; with AUS, Korea. Democrat. Office: 1401 Longworth House Office Bldg Washington DC 20515

DE LA HORRA, PEDRO, architect; b. Havana, Cuba, Mar. 10, 1952, came to U.S., 1961, naturalized, 1975; s. Francisco and Emilia (Canaves) de la H.; m. Lillian Zoe Santiso, May 31, 1975; 1 child, Carolina. B. Arch., U. Miami-Fla., 1976. Registered architect, Fla. Draftsman Bleemer & Levine, Miami, 1977; asst. project mgr. Smith Korach Partnership, Miami, 1977-80; project mgr. H.J. Ross & Assoc., Miami, 1980-81; prin. De La Horra Assoc., Miami, 1981-83; project architect H.J. Ross & Assoc., Miami, 1983—; dir. Challenge Internat. Airlines, Miami, 1984—. Mem. AIA. Roman Catholic. Avocations: Travel; boating. Office: H J Ross & Assoc 8401 NW 53d Terr Miami FL 33166

DE LA MADRID HURTADO, MIGUEL, president of Mexico; b. Colima, Colombia, Dec. 12, 1934; law degree with hon. mention for thesis Nat. Autonomous U. Mex., 1957; M.P.A., Harvard U., 1965. With legal dept. Nat. Bank Fgn. Trade, 1953-57; adv. to mgmt. Bank of Mexico, 1960-65; asst. dir. gen. of credit Mexican Ministry of Treasury, 1965-70, gen. dir. credit, 1972-75, undersec. of treasury and public credit, 1975-79; asst. dir. fin. PEMEX, 1970-72; minister nat. planning and budget Govt. Mexico, 1979-82, pres. Mexico, Mexico City, 1982—; adv. Mexican Soc. Indsl. Credit, Mexican Ins. Co., Aeromexico, Nat. Bank Fgn. Commerce, Nat. Savs. Bank, Nat. Cinematographic Bank, Nat. Sugar Financing Commn., Nat. Public Works Bank; has represented Govt. Mexico at various internat. confs. on econ. issues, including those of IMF, World Bank, Interam. Devel. Bank and Interam. Econ. and Social Council. Office: Palacio Nacional Mexico City DF Mexico*

DELANEY, JOSEPH P., bishop Roman Catholic Ch.; b. Fall River, Mass., Aug. 29, 1934. Student Cardinal O'Connell Sem., Theol. Coll., Washington, Am. Coll., Rome, R.I. Coll. Ordained priest Roman Catholic Ch., 1960, consecrated bishop, 1981. Bishop of Ft. Worth, 1981—. Address: The Roman Cath Ch 100 SW Alsbury Blvd Burleson TX 76028*

DE LA PARTE, LOUIS ANTHONY, lawyer; b. Tampa, Fla., July 27, 1929; s. Louis and Dulce (Santa Cruz) de la P.; B.A., Emory U.; LL.B., U. Fla.; m. Helen C. White, Nov. 23, 1957; children—Louis David, Martha Ann. Admitted to Fla. bar; practice law, Tampa; spl. asst. atty. gen. State of Fla., 1953; asst. county solicitor, Hillsborough County, Fla., 1957-60; asst. state atty. 13th Jud. Circuit, 1960-61; mem. Fla. Senate, 1966—, senate pres. pro tempore, 1973-74, pres., 1974—. Mem. Fla. Ho. of Reps., 1962-66; del. Democratic nat. conv., 1964; mem. Gov.'s Commn. Capital Punishment, 1972, public employees rights com. Supreme Ct., 1973-74, Joint Legis. Uniform Probate Code Com. and Joint Legis. Criminal Code Com., 1973-74. Trustee, U. Tampa. Served to capt. USAF, 1953-56. Recipient Allen Morris award, 1967, 71, 73; Outstanding State Legislator award Fla. Young Dems., 1972; named Most Valuable Senator St. Petersburg (Fla.) Times, 1969, 70, 71, 74, Legislator of Year Fla. Assn. Retarded Children, 1969-74, Legislator of Year Fla. Vol. Health Assns., 1970, Legislator of Year, Pros. Attys. Assn., 1972. Mem. Am., Fla. bar assns., Am., Fla. trial lawyers assns., Greater Tampa C. of C. (past bd. govs.), Fla. Blue Key, Phi Delta Phi, Eta Sigma Phi, Sigma Alpha Epsilon. Roman Catholic. Home: 8003 N Rome St Tampa FL 33604 Office: 705 E Kennedy Blvd Tampa FL 33602

DE LA PAZ, EDWARD JOSEPH, shoe company executive; b. Gibraltar, Nov. 12, 1945; s. Joseph Henry and Hilda (Bottino) De La P.; m. Tessa Jane Masterton, Sept. 26, 1970; children—Nicola, Caroline, Alexandra. Chartered acct., U.K. Fin. controller Thomson Holidays, Palma Mallorca, Spain, 1972-74; mgr. Arthur Young & Co., Barcelona, Spain, 1974-76; fin. controller Bostitch div. Textron, Madrid, 1976-77; v.p. and gen. mgr. for Spain, Caressa, Inc., Miami, Fla., 1977—. Home: Urb La Huerta Tangel Alicante Spain Office: Caressa Inc 3601 NW 54th St Miami FL 33142

DE LA PENA, CORDELL AMADO, pathologist; b. Honolulu, Apr. 30, 1934; s. Eusebio de Guzman Awanan and Virginia Uyeno de Costa; M.D., U. Santo Tomas, Manila, 1958; m. Linda Laron Lapuz, Apr. 1, 1957; children—Leslie, Nina, Cordell Amado. Intern, St. John's Hosp., Lowell, Mass., 1960-61; resident New Britain (Conn.) Gen. Hosp., 1963-67; pathologist St. Mary's Hosp., Clarksburg, W.Va., 1967, Union Protestant Hosp., Clarksburg, 1967; pathologist United Hosp., Inc., Clarksburg, 1967-78, pres. med. staff, 1974-75, bd. dirs., 1974-75, chief pathologist, dir. lab. and blood bank, 1978—; cons. VA, St. Joseph's, Stonewall Jackson Meml. hosps.; asst. prof. pathology W.Va. Sch. Medicine, 1980-81; pres. Harrison County Cancer Soc., 1974-76. Diplomate Am. Bd. Anat. and Clin. Pathology (subcert. in hematology); cert. Am. Bd. Infection Control. Fellow Coll. Am. Pathologists (ho. of dels. 1982—), Am. Soc. Clin. Pathologists, Am. Soc. Hematology; mem. Internat. Acad. Pathology, Am., W.Va. (state councillor 1981—) med. assns., W.Va. Pathol. Soc. (treas. 1975-77, pres.-elect 1977-80, pres. 1980-81), Harrison County Med. Soc. (treas. 1977-78, pres. 1980-81), W.Va. State Soc. Hematology (pres. 1980-81), W.Va. Assn. Blood Banks (pres. 1982—), Assn. Philippine-Am. Pathologists (pres. 1981-83), Nat. Skeet Shooting Assn., W.Va. Bird Dog Club (pres. 1972), W.Va. Assn. Blood Banks (pres. 1982-83). Club: Masons. Contbr. articles to med. jours. Home: 209 Candlelight Dr Clarksburg WV 26301 Office: United Hosp Clarksburg WV 26301

DE LA PIEDRA, JORGE, orthopedic surgeon; b. Peru, Feb. 11, 1923; came to U.S., 1960; naturalized, 1963; s. Luis G. and Rosa M. (Quinones) de la P.; grad. Facultad de Ciencias, Universidad de San Marcos, Lima, Peru, 1942, M.D., 1950; m. June M. Daugherty, May 1, 1955; children—Ana Maria, Jorge Antonio, James Michael. Intern, Army Hosp., Lima, 1951-52; rotating intern Autustana Hosp., Chgo., 1952-53; resident in orthopedic surgery St. Francis Hosp., Peoria, Ill., 1953-54, Charlotte (N.C.) Meml. Hosp., 1954-57; acting chief orthopedic dept. Social Security Adminstrn. Hosp. #1, Lima, 1958-59; orthopedic Surgeon Mullens (W.Va.) Hosp., 1960-66; practice medicine specializing in orthopedic surgery, Princeton, W.Va., 1966—; mem. staff Princeton Community Hosp., 1966—, dir., 1974—. Served with Peruvian Army, 1951-52. Diplomate Am. Bd. Orthopedic Surgery. Mem. AMA physician's award 1969, 1972-74, 77. Fellow Internat. Coll. Surgeons; mem. W.Va. State Med. Assn., Mercer County Med. Soc., Am. Fracture Assn., So. Med. Soc., Latin Am. Soc. Orthopedic Surgeons, Orthopedic Research and Edn. Found. (life membership), Peruvian Acad. of Surgery. So. Orthopedic Soc., Peruvian Am. Med. Soc. Roman Catholic. Lodge: K.C. Office: Parkview Profl Bldg Morrison Dr Princeton WV 24740

DELASHMIT, WALTER HOWARD, JR., engineering researcher, engineering developer; b. Memphis, Dec. 14, 1944; s. Walter Howard, Sr. and Gertrude Marie (Scott) D.; m. Linda Fay Vaught, Aug. 20, 1967; children—Mark Robert, Rick Alan. B.S.E.E., Christian Brothers Coll., 1966; M.S.E.E., U. Ten., 1968. Registered profl. engr., Fla., Pa. Mem. tech. staff TRW Systems, Houston, 1969-72; sr. engr. Martin Marietta Aerospace, Orlando, Fla., 1972-76; research engr. Pa. State U. Applied Research Lab., State Coll., 1976-82; sr. staff engr. LTV Aerospace and Defense Co., Dallas, 1982—. Contbr. articles to profl. jours. Youth baseball coach Little League and Optimist Club, State College and Arlington, Tex., 1980-83, 85; youth soccer coach Centre Region Parks and Recreation Dept., State College, 1980-81; youth basketball coach ch. and YMCA, Bellefonte, Pa., Arlington, Tex., 1981, 83—; cubmaster Longhorn council Boy Scouts of Am., Arlington, 1982. Sr. mem. IEEE (chmn. Orland sect. aerospace and electronic systems group 1975-76, vice chmn. 1974-75); mem. Am. Statis. Assn., Advanced Target Recognizer Working Group. Republican. Baptist. Clubs: LTV Mgmt. (Dallas), LTV Employees (Dallas), Arlington Runners, Toastmasters Internat (Orlando). Lodge: Optimists (Arlington). Avocations: running; sports; coaching youth. Home: 3409 Woodside Dr Arlington TX 76016 Office: LTV Aerospace and Defense Co PO Box 650003 Dallas TX 75265-0003

DELATTE, BRIAN JOSEPH, pharmacist; b. Algiers, La., Mar. 19, 1952; s. Donald Paul and Cecelia (Waguespack) D.; m. Claire Rita Schexnayder, Aug. 20, 1975; children—Cristina, Jessica. Student Nicholls State U., 1973; B.S. in Pharmacy, N.E. La. U., Monroe, La., 1976. Registered pharmacist, La. Staff pharmacist Peoples Drugs, Houma, La., 1975-76, Family Drugs, Houma, 1976-78; mgr., pharmacist Lloyds Pharmacy, Houma, 1978-80, Kare Pharmacy, Houma, 1980-82, Terrebonne Drugs, Inc., Houma, 1982—; clin. preceptor La. Bd. Pharmacy, 1983—. Lector Roman Catholic Ch.; active Parke-Davis Child Care, Houma, 1985. Served with U.S. N.G., 1971-77. Club: Leisure Internat. (New Orleans). Avocations: gardening; physical fitness; fishing. Home: 108 Fence Row St Schriever LA 70395 Office: Eastside Pharmacy 1307 Grand Caillou Houma LA 70395

DE LA VINA, LYNDA YVONNE, economics educator, consultant; b. Edinburg, Tex., July 29, 1950; d. Juan Manuel and Herlinda (Cisneros) de la V.; B.A., Pan Am. U., 1972; M.A. Rice U., 1977, Ph.D., 1982. Asst. prof. U. Houston, 1978-79; asst. dir. Human Resources Program, U. Tex., San Antonio, 1979-82, asst. prof., 1982-85, assoc. prof. and dir. Inst. for Studies in Bus., 1985—; cons. Victoria Fin. Corp., San Antonio. Contbr. articles to profl. jours. Mem., com. chairperson Gov.'s Exec. Devel. Council, Austin, Tex., 1984—; area rep., United Way; mem. Steering com. Labor Market Info. Ctr.; Target 90 - Goals for San Antonio. Ford Found. fellow, 1972-77; Am. Assembly of Collegiate Schs. of Bus. grantee, 1983; Research grantee Mortgagse Bankers Assn. Am., 1984-85. Mem. Am. Econ. Assn., Southwestern Econs. Assn., Southwest Soc. Econs. Democrat. Avocations: tennis; sailing. Office: Inst for Studies in Business Univ Tex San Antonio TX 78285

DELAY, TOM DALE, congressman; b. Laredo, Tex., Apr. 8, 1947; s. Charles Ray and Maxine (Wimbish) DeL.; m. Christine Furrh, Aug. 26, 1967; 1 child, Danielle. B.S., U. Houston, 1970. Gen. mgr. Redwood Chem. Co., Houston, 1970-73; owner, operator Albo Pest Control, Stafford, Tex., 1973—; mem. Tex. Ho. of Reps., 1978-84; mem. 99th Congress from 22d Dist. Tex., mem. pub. works and transp. com., govt. ops. com., appropriations com., pub. health com.; vice chmn. adminstrn. com., chmn. budget and oversight of transp. com., mem. Grace Caucus, 1985—; mem. U.S.-Mex. Interparliamentary Del., Washington, 1985; mem. Republican study com. Sci. and Tech. Task Force, 1985; mem. Rep. research com. Regulatory Reform Caucus, 1985. Bd. dirs. Youth Opportunities Unltd., Houston; precinct chmn. Simonton Rep. Com., Tex., 1974-78. Named Legislator of Yr., Tex. Assn. To Improve Distbn.; ABC's Outstanding Legislator for 67th Session, Tex. Assoc. Builders and Contractors, 1984; recipient Nat. Security Leadership award Coalition Peace Through Strength, Washington, 1985; Leadership award Young Conservatives of Tex. Mem. Congl. Leaders for a Balanced Budget, Greater Houston Pest Control Assn. (former pres.), Tex. Pest Control Assn. (bd. dirs.), S.W. Energy Council, Am. Legis. Exchange Council, Nat. Conf. State Legislators, Fort Bend County Fair Assn. (life). Baptist. Clubs: Sweetwater Country (Sugar Land, Tex.); Fort Bend 100 (Rosenberg, Tex.). Lodge: Rotary. Avocations: hunting; skiing; golf. Office: 1234 Longworth House Office Bldg Washington DC 20515

DELCHAMPS, ALFRED FREDERICK, JR., retail grocery chain executive; b. Mobile, Ala., June 30, 1931; s. Alfred Frederick and Sara Lucile (Crowell) D.; student Duke U., 1948-50; B.S. in Commerce and Bus. Adminstrn., U. Ala., 1953; m. Carolyn Ann Weaver, Aug. 2, 1953; children—Alfred Frederick III, Thomas Weaver, Carolyn Delchamps Eichold. Supr., Delchamps, Inc., 1953-58, asst. sec., 1958-63, v.p. service ops., 1963-65, exec. v.p., 1965-76, pres., 1976—; v.p., dir. Topco Assocs., Inc.; dir. Van's Photo, Inc., 1st Nat. Bank, Mobile. Mem. bus. adv. council U. South Ala.; vice chmn. bd. trustees Huntingdon Coll., Montgomery, Ala.; past pres. Jr. Achievement Mobile, Inc.; past 1st v.p. Community Chest and Council of Mobile County; past pres. Mobile Symphony and Civic Music Assn., past disaster chmn. Mobile chpt. ARC; past gen. chmn. Group Aid for Retarded Children, Inc.; treas. Mobile Hist. Devel. Found., Mobile Track and Field Assn.; chmn. fin. com. Dauphin Way United Methodist Ch.; chmn. Ala. State Council Arts and Humanities; pres. Gulf Coast Pub. Broadcasting; bd. dirs. Mobile Area United Way; mem. Mobile United; chmn. fund dr. United Fund, 1980; chmn., mem. council budget com. Community Chest; mem. hon. fellows Mobile Coll. Mem. Am. Mgmt. Assn., Food Mktg. Inst., Mobile Area C. of C. (dir., v.p.). Republican. Clubs: Country of Mobile, Bienville, International Trade, Mobile Yacht, Mystic Socs. Home: 163 S Georgia Ave Mobile AL 36604 Office: PO Box 1668 Mobile AL 36633

DELCHAMPS, OLIVER H., JR., retail grocery company executive; b. 1900. Chmn. bd. Delchamps Inc., Mobile, Ala. Address: Delchamps Inc 305 Delchamps Dr Mobile AL 36633*

DELEEUW, SAMUEL LEONARD, engineering educator; b. Grand Rapids, Mich., Aug. 2, 1934; s. Samuel Bastion and Gertrude (Vanderploeg) DeL.; m. Nancy Kay Newton, Sept. 8, 1956; children—David, Daniel, Deborah. B.S. in Civil Engring., Mich. State U., 1956, M.S. in Applied Mechanics, 1958, Ph.D. in Applied Mechanics, 1961. Asst. prof. civil engring. Yale U., New Haven, 1960-65; prof., chmn. civil engring. U. Miss., University, 1965—. Trustee Polit. Action Com. Mem. ASCE, ASME, Am. Soc. Engring. Edn., Nat. Soc. Profl. Engrs., Miss. Engring. Soc., Sigma Xi, Tau Beta Pi, Chi Epsilon, Phi Lambda Tau. Episcopalian. Contbr. articles to profl. jours. Home: PO Box 1355 University MS 38677 Office: Dept Civil Engring U Miss University MS 38677

DE LEON, CIRA JANE, psychiatrist; b. Havana, Cuba, Dec. 27, 1949; d. Frank and Cira I. (De Leon) De Leon. B.S. magna cum laude, St. Thomas U., Houston, 1972; M.D., U. Tex. Med. Br., Galveston, 1976. Resident in psychiatry Timberlawn Hosp., Dallas, 1976-79; physician emergency room John Peter Smith Hosp., Ft. Worth, 1977-79; clin. dir. Mental Health Clinic, Houston, 1979-83; practice medicine specializing in psychiatry, Houston, 1979—; program med. dir. chem. dependency unit Belle Park Hosp., Houston, 1983-84, pres. med. staff, 1985, program med. dir. intensive care unit, 1985—; med. dir. Inst. Motivational Devel., 1983—; psychiat. cons. for other physicians, attys., 1979—. Mem. Am. Med. Polit. Action Com., 1982-85. St. Thomas U. scholar, 1968-72, Alliance Français scholar, Tours, France, 1970. Mem. AMA, Am. Psychiat. Assn., Am. Med. Women's Assn., Tex. Med. Assn., Houston Psychiat. Soc., Harris County Med. Soc., Houston Spanish Forum. Republican. Roman Catholic. Office: 7500 Beechnut St Suite 330 Houston TX 77074

DE LEON, LIDIA M(ARIA), editor; b. Havana, Cuba, Sept. 10, 1957; came to U.S., 1959; d. Leon J. and Lydia (Diaz Cruz) de L. B.A. cum laude, U. Miami, 1979. Staff writer Miami Herald (Fla.), 1978-79; editorial asst. Halsey Pub. Co., Miami, 1980-81, assoc. editor, 1981, editor, 1981—. Mem. Fla. Mag. Assn., Golden Key Nat. Honor Soc. Democrat. Roman Catholic. Home: 1805 Ixora Rd North Miami FL 33181 Office: Halsey Pub Co 12955 Biscayne Blvd North Miami FL 33181

DELEVETT, PETER CHRISTIAN, physician, anesthesiologist; b. Bridgeport, Conn., July 10, 1946; s. James Allen Fitzhugh and Jeanne (Sanders) D.; m. Molly Maloney, Oct. 25, 1969; children—Peter Christian II, Aimee Ellen Sanders. A.B. in Zoology, Ind. U., 1968, M.D., 1975. Intern in internal medicine Mt. Auburn Hosp., Cambridge, Mass., 1975-76; anesthesiology resident Mass. Gen. Hosp., Boston, 1976-78; staff anesthesiologist Med. Ctr. Clinic, W. Fla. Hosp., Pensacola, 1978—. Vice pres. Pensacola Arts Council, 1980-82; bd. dirs. Pensacola Symphony Orch., 1985—. Served with AUS, 1969-71. Mem. AMA, Fla. Med. Assn., Am. Soc. Anesthesiologists, Fla. Soc. Anesthesiologists, Soc. Cardiovascular Anesthesiologists, Am. Soc. Regional Anesthesiologists. Republican. Episcopalian. Home: 1660 Texar Dr Pensacola FL 32503 Office: Medical Center Clinic 8333 N Davis Hwy Pensacola FL 32504

DEL GADO, JOSEPH RAMON, business executive; b. Chgo., Mar. 4, 1932; s. Joseph Ramon and Florence (Nelson) D.; B.A. in English, U. Ill., 1958. With Campbell-Mithun Advt., Chgo., 1960-68, purchasing agent, dir. office services, 1960-66, purchasing agt., dir. office services, 1964-68; purchasing agt., asst. to pres. and treas. Maxant Button & Supply Co., Chgo., 1968-70; asst. purchasing agt., adminstrv. asst. Soiltest, Inc., 1970-82; v.p., asst. to pres. Southwest Chgo. Corp., 1982—. Mem. Lyric Opera Subscription Com., 1957. Observer, Joint Civic Com. on Elections, 1965, election-judge, 1968, 70. Served with AUS, 1952-54. Mem. Purchasing Agts. Assn. Chgo. (co-chmn. publicity and pub. relations com. 1963-64), U. Ill. Alumni, Illiniweks. Lutheran. Republican. Clubs: Whitehall, Barclay Ltd., Internat. (Chgo.). Dance choreographer for various groups and individuals. Home and office: 900 Lake Shore Dr Apt 905 Chicago IL 60611 also 3605 NE 32d Ave Fort Lauderdale FL 33308

DELGADO-PASAPERA, GERMAN ALBERTO, educator; b. Anasco, P.R., Apr. 14, 1928; s. Luis Mario Delgado-Lugo and Maria Pasapera-Tio; B.A., Poly. Inst. P.R., 1952; M.A., La. State U., 1964; Ph.D., U. Madrid, 1982; m. Maria del Pilar Acevedo-Defillo, Mar. 11, 1967. Tchr. secondary public schs., Mayaguez, 1953-54; research asst. Coll. Agr. and Mechanic Arts, U. P.R., Mayaguez, 1954-55, asst. registrar, 1955-59, acting registrar, 1959-60, dir. admissions, 1960-63, instr. history, 1962-63, 67-70, asst. prof., 1970-73, asso. prof., 1973-81, prof., 1981—; asst. dir. admissions Inter Am. U. P.R., San German, 1965-66, dir. fin. aid, 1966-67; lectr. geography, extension div. U. P.R., Rio Piedras, 1966, instr. humanities, 1967-69. Recipient plaque of merit, dept. social sci. U. P.R., Mayaguez, 1974; diploma Anasco Cultural Centre, 1974; plaque Festival Bellas Artes, Anasco, 1976; diploma of honor Festival Carnaval Mayaguez, 1976. Mem. Am. Acad. Polit. and Social Sci., Acad. Polit. Sci., Internat. Studies Assn., Caribbean Historians, Am. Assn. Tchr. Spanish and Portuguese, AAUP, Nat. Hist. Soc., Nat. Trust for Hist. Preservation, Sociedad Puertorriquena de Escritores, Asociacion Puertorriquena de Profesores Universitarios (dir. U. P.R., Mayaguez, 1973-75), World Acad., Internat. Platform Assn., Sociedad de las Letras Puertorriqueñas. Author: Desde el Fondo del Pecho (poems), 1964; (with F. Lluch-Mora and R. Torres-Delgado) Puerto Rico en la Geografia Universal de Malte-Brun, 1979; asso. editor Atenea Jour. of Sch. of Arts and Scis., U. P.R., Mayaguez, 1969-75; contbr. articles, short stories and poems to profl. publs. Home: 11 (altos) Nereidas PO Box 913 Mayaguez PR 00708 Office: G 334 C U PR Mayaguez Campus Mayaguez PR 00708

DELIA, CLAUDE WILLIAM, physician, pathologist; b. Medford, Mass., July 24, 1924; s. T. P. and Rose (Daiute) D.; m. Jeanne Wetmore, Aug. 2, 1949; children—Nancy Ann Delia Carpenter, Deborah Delia Webster, Pamela, Patricia J. Delia Glatfelter. Student, Harvard U., 1946; M.D., Yale U., 1950. Diplomate Am. Bd. Pathology. Dir. lab. Conway Hosp. (S.C.), 1960—; mem. adv. bd. First Citizens Bank, Conway. Served to maj. U.S. Army, 1950-60. Fellow Coll. Am. Pathologists, Am. Soc. Clin. Pathologists; mem. AMA, Japanese-Am. Soc. Pathologists, S.C. Med. Assn., N.Y. Acad Scis. Republican. Home: River Bend Star Route One Conway SC 29526 Office: PO Box 1599 Conway SC 29526

DELIONBACK, CHRISTIAN FOY, communications consultant, engineer, realtor; b. Durham, N.C., Oct. 11, 1936; s. Melvin Leon and Lottie Ellen (Cole) D.; m. Elizabeth Carter Lipford, July 11, 1959; children—Elizabeth Carter, Daniel Herbert. B.S. in Engring., N.C. State U.-Raleigh, 1962. Tech. asst. to prodn. mgr. Internat. Paper, Georgetown, S.C., 1962-65; engr. IBM, Raleigh, 1965-66; engr. new products design computer div. RCA Co., Palm Beach Gardens, Fla., 1966-71; sales agt. John Hancock Life Ins. Co., West Palm Beach, Fla., 1971-73; bldg. industry cons. So. Bell Co., West Palm Beach, 1973—; pilot. Served with USAF, 1953-57. Republican. Methodist. Recipient Outstanding Sales award John Hancock Life Ins. Co., 1972. Clubs: North Palm Beach Country, Quiet Birdmen. Lodges: Kiwanis, Moose. Office: Southern Bell Co 2021 S Military Trail West Palm Beach FL 33406

DE LISSER, STANLEY PEARSE, medical economics consultant; b. N.Y.C., Mar. 9, 1927; s. Horace Eloy and Loris (Harris) de L.; m. Donna Routh Parson, Apr. 24, 1982; children by previous marriage—Peter H. L., Andree Louise, Denise Anne. Student U. Del., 1945; B.A. cum laude, Williams Coll., 1949. Group ins. rep. Prudential Ins. Co., Newark, 1949, N.Y.C., to 1951; sr. cons. Johnson and Higgins, N.Y.C., 1951-58; v.p. Occupational Health Services, Inc., Asheville, N.C., N.Y.C., 1958; pres. The Exec. Health Examiners Group of Cos., Inc., N.Y.C., 1959-80, The de Lisser Orgn., Inc., N.Y.C., Washington, 1980; pres. The Ortho Molecular Nutrition Inst., Inc., N.Y.C., 1980-83; assoc. dir. Dallas/Ft. Worth Preventive Medicine Center, 1983—; mem. faculty AMR Internat.; speaker Am. Mgmt. Assn. Chmn. youth services com. Nassau County (N.Y.) Health and Welfare Council, 1964-65; pres. Freeport (N.Y.) Taconic Adv. Com. on Edn., 1961-62; mem. Freeport Bd. Edn., 1962-63. Served with USAAF, 1945-47. Fellow Am. Acad. Med. Adminstrs.; mem. Soc. Occupational and Environ. Health, Internat. Health Mgrs. Assn. (pres.), N.Y. Acad. Sci. Roman Catholic. Clubs: Town Tennis, Williams (N.Y.C.); Taconic Golf.

DELIZ-ALVAREZ, JOSE RINALDO, industrial engineering educator, consultant; b. Ponce, P.R., Dec. 19, 1941; s. Ramon Deliz and Josefina Alvarez; m. Luz N. Solis, Oct. 10, 1964. B.S.E.E. magna cum laude, U. P.R., 1964; M.S. in Indsl. Engring., NYU, 1966, Ph.D. in Indsl. Engring., 1971. Registered profl. engr., P.R. Engr. ITT Caribbean Mfg. Research and Devel. Lab., Rio Piedras, 1964; asst. prof. indsl. engring. U. P.R., Mayaguez, 1966-74, prof. indsl. engring., 1981—, assoc. prof. bus. adminstrn. U. P.R., Rio Piedras, 1974-80, dir. office of planning, 1974-76, asst. dir. office of Planning and Devel. Central Adminstrn., 1978, faculty fellow Am. Soc. Engring. Edn. NASA-Jet Propulsion Lab., Pasadena, Calif., 1980; cons. IBM, Poughkeepsie, N.Y., 1982, Endicott, N.Y., 1983, Digital Equipment Co., San German, P.R., 1984—; adviser info. systems Com. for Reorganizing Exec. Br., San Juan, P.R., 1978-79; pres. accrediting com. Council for Higher Edn., Polytech U., Bridgeport U., San Juan, 1978, 85; bd. dirs. Tech. Info. Ctr., U. P.R. and Econ. Devel. Adminstrn., Mayaguez, 1973, Quality Control Ctr. Econ. Devel. Adminstrn., San Juan, 1972-74. Recipient Founder's Day award NYU, 1971. Mem. Inst. Indsl. Engrs. (sr. mem., pres. local chapter 1974-76), Inst. Indsl. Engrs. Profl. Engrs. Assn. (pres. 1977-80), Am. Statis. Assn., Ops. Research Soc. Am., Am. Soc. Quality Control, Am. Soc. Engring. Educators, Engrs. and Land Surveyors Inst. (San Juan) (auditor 1978, Disting. indsl. engr. award 1985), Am. Prodn. and Inventory Control Soc. Avocations: reading, gardening. Home: Box 5709 College Station Mayaguez PR 00709

DELK, FANNIE MITCHELL, English language educator; b. Lexington, Miss., Dec. 13, 1933; d. Theodore R. and Inez (Logan) Mitchell; m. Frank Edward Delk, Oct. 12, 1957; children—Gregory Kevin, Gerald Keith. A.B. with distinction, Tenn. State U., 1956; M. Edn., Memphis State U., 1971. Tchr. Carver High Sch., Memphis, 1957-75; assoc. prof. LeMoyne Owen Coll., Memphis, 1975—; cons. in field. Contbr. articles to profl. jours. Vol. tchr. Memphis Vol. Placement Program, 1975—, bd. dirs., 1975—; bd. dirs. br. NAACP, Memphis, 1980-84. Recipient Woman of Year award Alpha Kappa Alpha, 1982, Vol. of Year award Memphis Vol. Placement Program, 1983; Humanities scholar West Tenn. Econ. Council, 1977. Mem. Nat. Council Tchrs. English, Southeastern Conf. Eng. in Two Year Colls., So. Assn. Coll. and Schs. (evaluator). Democrat. Roman Catholic. Avocations: reading; volunteer teaching. Home: 1556 S Wellington St Memphis TN 38106 Office: LeMoyne Owen Coll 807 Walker Ave Memphis TN 38126

DELK, JANE DARLING, nurse; b. Hooper, Nebr., Apr. 24, 1925; d. Benjamin Glenn Darling and Charlotte Martha (Monnich) D.; m. Mack B. Delk, Aug. 19, 1947; children—Denny D., Kerry K., Debby Ann Delk Karasek. Student Midland Coll., 1942-44, St. Louis City Hosp. Sch. Nursing, 1944-47; B.S.N., U. Tulsa, 1969, M.A. in Ednl. Adminstrn., 1975. Staff nurse St. Mary's Hosp., St. Louis, 1947-48; pvt. duty staff nurse, Tulsa, 1949-50; instr. Hillcrest Med. Ctr. Sch. Nursing, Tulsa, 1970-76; assoc. dir. Hillcrest Med. Ctr., 1976-80, dir. spl. nursing services, 1980—; v.p. Okla. League Nursing. Mem. Okla. Soc. Nursing Service Adminstrs. Presbyterian. Home: PO Box 286 Broken Arrow OK 74013

DELL, J. HOWARD, clergyman. Bishop, Ch. of God in Christ, No. Ga., Atlanta. Address: care Ch of God in Christ PO Box 6118 Knoxville TN 37914*

DELLINGER, VICKI SIGMON, nurse; b. Lincolnton, N.C., Sept. 18, 1941; d. Kenneth L. and Merlyn F. Sigmon; children—Walton Gene, Jr., Timothy W. Grad., Cleveland County Coll., Shelby, N.C., 1969; student, Catawba County Coll., 1981. Lic. practical nurse. Pvt. office nurse for Dr. G. C. Crowell, Lincolnton, 1969—. Council mem., St. Paul's Luth. Ch., Crouse, N.C., mem. Christian Edn., Youth Com., Sunday Sch. tch., chmn, Constrn. and Bylaws Com., sec. ch. council, mem. Luth. Ch. Women, choir mem., lay reader; dir. ACS, Lincoln County. Recipient Outstanding Student award Cleveland County Coll., 1969. Mem. N.C. Fedn. Bus. and Profl. Women's Clubs (mountain area rep. membership com., mem. dist. II nominating com.), Lincolnton Bus. and Profl. Women's Club (past pres.), Nat. Assn. Physicians' Nurses. Home: PO Box 88 Crouse NC 28033 Office: Dr G C Crowell 824 S Aspen St Lincolnton NC 28092

DELLO BUONO, PATRICIA, legal courier services company executive; b. Long Branch, N.J., Aug. 4, 1942; d. James U. and Emma Bertha (Strafel) Radichio; m. William L. Dello Buono, Feb. 26, 1963; children—Angelo, James, Todd. Student, Monmouth Coll., 1960-61, Fairleigh Dickinson U., 1961-62, Hudson Community Coll., 1975-76. Legal sec. various attys., N.J., N.Y.C. and Fla., 1960-76; owner, pres., chief exec. officer Legal Courier Services, Inc., West Palm Beach, Fla., 1977—, Action Courier, West Palm Beach, 1980—; instr. continuing edn. Palm Beach Jr. Coll., 1982—. Bd. dirs. Palm Beach County Child Advocacy Bd., 1982—, YWCA, 1984—; organizer Neighborhood Crimewatch, Cambridge Homes, West Palm Beach, 1983, Actors Workshop and Repertory Co., West Palm Beach, 1982—; del. White House Conf. on Small Bus. Recipient Small Bus. Person of Yr. award West Palm Beach C. of C., 1984. Mem. C. of C. Palm Beaches (dir. 1983—, chair small bus. council), Am. Bus. Women's Assn. (pres. chpt. 1982-83), Individual Career Advancement through Networking (Golden Girl award 1983), Better Bus. Bur. (dir.), Home Builders and Contractors Assn. Republican. Club: TIPS of Palm Beaches (pres.). Office: Legal Courier Services Inc 423 Clematis St West Palm Beach FL 33401

DE LOACH, CAMERON ELIZABETH CARPENTER, nurse; b. Vienna, Austria, Mar. 8, 1950; d. William Brunson and Mildred Mable (Clark) Carpenter; m. Ervin Daniel De Loach, Aug. 5, 1972; 1 son, Ervin Daniel II. B.S. in Nursing, Med. Coll. Ga., 1972, M.S. in Nursing, 1977. R.N., Ga. Staff nurse Med. Coll. Ga. Talmadge Hosp., Augusta, 1972-73; staff nurse Meml. Med. Ctr., Savannah, Ga., 1974-77, primary instr. obstetrics dept. allied health edn., 1977-78, cons. lic. practical nurse program, 1977; instr. in maternal child nursing U. Tenn.-Chattanooga, 1978-80; nursing adminstr. Savannah Plastic Surgery Assocs., 1980—, also researcher and developer teaching materials, 1980—; mem. vol. faculty to teach childbirth to unwed mothers through dept. psychology U. Tenn.-Chattanooga, 1979. Mem. Am. Nurses Assn., Ga. Nurses Assn., Am. Soc. Plastic and Reconstructive Nursing (chmn. southeastern region 1981-82, editor southeastern region newsletter 1982-84, program chmn. southeastern region 1983, chmn. Ga. chpt. 1983-84), Aux. to Ga. Med. Soc. (rec. sec. 1982-83, treas. Savannah 1984—), Sigma Theta Tau. Home: 8511 Kent Dr Savannah GA 31406 Office: Savannah Plastic Surgery Assocs 515 E 63d St Savannah GA 31406

DELOACH, COOPER JOE, insurance company executive; b. Vaiden, Miss., Oct. 5, 1931; s. Samuel Crawford and Grace (Turner) D.; m. Billie Ruth Todd, Nov. 16, 1956; children—Donna Ann, Cooper Joe, Yancy Todd. Student Miss. State U., 1951-55. With Nat. Life & Accident Ins. Co., Leland, Miss., 1960—, assoc. mgr., 1980-82, field tng. supr., 1982—. Served with U.S. Army, 1951-53. Mem. Washington County Life Underwriters, Nat. Life Top Hat Club. Baptist. Clubs: Lions, Deer Creek Town and Racquet. Home: 515 E 3d St Leland MS 38756 Office: 328 Main St Greenville MS 38701

DE LOACH, WILLIE ARNOLD, mining company representative, consultant; b. Gadsden, Ala., May 29, 1947; s. Lester and Louise (Gidley) De L.; m. Mary E. Kirkpatrick, July 3, 1970; children—William Christopher, Jonathan Lester. A.S. in Bus. Adminstrn., Gadsden State, 1966; B.S.M.E., Livingston U., 1968. In sales mgmt. Sherwin Williams Co., Gadsden, 1965-68; with machine errection staff Marion Power Shovel, Ohio, 1968-70; supr. prodn. Arch Minerals, Oakman, Ala., 1970-72; maintenance and prodn. staff Drummond Coal, Jasper, Ala., 1972-76; mine supr. Coal Systems Inc., Birmingham, Ala., 1976-80; equip. supr. Hobet Mining, Charleston, W.Va., 1980-84. Republican. Baptist. Lodge: Elks (sec. 1976-78). Avocations: golf; swimming; softball. Home: 5317 Glow Dr Charleston WV 25313

DELOATCH, SANDRA JEAN, computer science and mathematics educator, researcher; b. Suffolk, Va., July 28, 1949; d. David Wardell and Essie Mae (Riddick) DeL. B.S., Howard U., 1971; M.A., U. Mich., 1972; Ph.D., Ind. U., 1977. Mathematician Naval Ship Research and Devel. Ctr., Bethesda, Md., 1971; math. instr. Norfolk State Coll., Va., 1972-74; summer faculty fellow IBM, Armonk, N.Y., 1974; math. and computer sci. prof. Norfolk State U., Va., 1977—; researcher, cons. NASA Langley Research Ctr., Hampton, Va., 1980-81, 82—, summer research fellow, 1979, 82. Author (computer manual) MACSYMA Usage at Langley, 1985. Author: (with others) Mathematics for College Students, 1983. Mem. Fairmont Park Civic League, Norfolk, 1982—. Recipient Roy A. Woods Outstanding Tchr. award Norfolk State U., 1983. Mem. Assn. Computing Machinery, IEEE (mem. computer soc.), Math. Assn. Am., Phi Beta Kappa, Alpha Kappa Alpha (treas. 1983—). Democrat. Home: 2931 Dunkirk Ave Norfolk VA 23509 Office: Norfolk State Univ 2401 Corprew Ave Norfolk VA 23504

DE LONG, EDGAR EMILE, computer systems consultant; b. New Orleans, Aug. 15, 1928; s. Ormond Marx and Delta M. (Simoneaux) De L.; B.A., St. Leo (Fla.) Coll., 1979; m. Ruth Clare Bell, Sept. 12, 1953; children—Janelle Lynne, Thomas Edward, Gerianne Lee. Served as enlisted man, U.S. Navy, 1944-58; commd. ensign, U.S. Navy, 1958, advanced through grades to lt. comdr., 1966; project officer, long range missiles and space systems, operational test and evaluation, Norfolk, Va., 1962-65; dir. surface missile systems schs., Dam Neck, Va., 1966-69, ret., 1969; customer service mgr. Ednl. Computer Corp. subs. EDP Tech., Strafford, Pa., 1969-74; asso. mgr. advanced systems System Devel. Corp., Integrated Systems, Inc., Virginia Beach, Va., 1974-78; dep. mgr. Virginia Beach ops. Sperry Univac Corp., 1979-81, mktg. mgr., 1981-84; cons; in field; sec.-treas. London Bridge Fabric Barn Inc., Virginia Beach, 1976-79. Mem. various civic commns. City of Virginia Beach, 1961—; pres. numerous civic leagues City of Virginia Beach, 1964-77; bd. dirs. Council of Civic Orgns., Virginia Beach, 1974-77; pres. Eastern Va. Thorobred Assn., youth baseball, 1978-79. Recipient George Washington honor medal, Freedoms Found., Valley Forge, Pa., 1967, 68. Episcopalian. Club: Masons. Contbr. articles to mil. mags.; researcher effects of nuclear radiation on C-band radars. Home and office: 1500 Hidden Cove Virginia Beach VA 23454

DELONG, MARY ANN, educational administrator; b. Chester, Pa., July 11, 1944; d. John A. and Ann (Anthony) Fiduk; m. J. Thomas DeLong, Feb. 13, 1965. B.S., West Chester U., 1966; M.S., Kutztown U., 1970. Lic. mental health counselor, elem. tchr., adminstr., Fla. Tchr. Exeter Sch. Dist., Pa., 1966-68, Gov. Mifflin Sch. Dist., Shillington, Pa., 1968-71; guidance counselor Wilson Sch. Dist., West Lawn, Pa., 1971-73; guidance counselor Marion County Sch.

Bd., Ocala, Fla., 1973-75, coordinator, testing, 1975-79, supr., guidance, testing and research, 1979—. Bd. dirs. Marion Citrus Mental Health Ctr., Ocala, 1982—; chairperson Fla. Statewide Assessment Adv. Com., 1984-85; active Fla. Task Force Counselor Supervision, 1981-83; pres. Beta Phi chpt. Epsilon Sigma Alpha, Ocala, 1981-82. Named Educator of Yr., Mental Health Assn. Marion County 1984, Adminstr. of Yr., hon. mention award Fla. Sch. Counselors Assn. 1984. Mem. Fla. Assn. Counselor Educators and Suprs., Fla. Assn. Test Adminstrs. (bd. dirs.), Fla. Ednl. Research Assn. (bd. dirs.), Am. Assn. Suprs. and Adminstrs. Avocations: waterskiing; boating; reading; cats. Home: 514 Bahia Track Run Ocala FL 32672 Office: Marion County Sch Bd PO Box 670 Ocala FL 32678

DELOZIER, MAYNARD WAYNE, business educator, consultant; b. Newport News, Va., Apr. 21, 1945; s. Raymond Leo and Jean (Burton) D. Ph.D., U. N.C., 1971. Lectr., U. N.C.-Greensboro, 1969-70; asst. prof. Va. Poly. Inst. and State U., 1970-71; asst. prof. Wright State U., 1971-73; assoc. prof. U. S.C., Columbia, 1976—. Mem. Am. Mktg. Assn., Acad. Mktg. Sci. (gov.), Am. Acad. Advt., So. Mktg. Assn., Southwestern Mktg. Assn. Author: The Marketing Communications Process, 1976; Consumer Behavior Dynamics, 1977; Experimental Learning Exercises in Marketing, 1977; Marketing Management, 1978; Retailing, 1982; Retailing Casebook, 1982; Retailing Workbook, 1982. Home: 0-102 Hunts End Ct Columbia SC 29206 Office: Coll Bus Adminstrn U SC Columbia SC 29208

DEL PILAR, LETICIA QUETULIO, anesthesiologist; b. Laoag, Ilocos Norte, Philippines, Nov. 12, 1940; d. Apolinar Bitanga dna Paz Quismundo (Cawagas) Quetulio; came to U.S., 1964, naturalized, 1983; m. Jaime Velayo del Pilar, Mar. 5, 1966; children—Farah Trisha, Melinda Julita. B.S., U. Philippines, 1960, M.D., 1964. Diplomate Am. Bd. Anesthesiology. Intern Mercy Hosp., Hamilton, Ohio, 1964-65; resident in anesthesiology, Sinai Hosp. of Balt., 1965-67; mem. staff Prince William Hosp., Manassas, Va., 1972—, vice-chmn. dept. anesthesiology, 1973—. Mem. Prince William County Med. Soc., Va. Med. Soc., AMA, Va. Soc. Anesthesiologists, Am. Soc. Anesthesiologists, Internat. Anesthesia Research Soc., Philippine Soc. Anesthesiologists in Am., Va. Med. Polit. Action Com., Am. Med. Polit. Action Com. Republican. Roman Catholic. Club: Evergreen Country (Haymarket) Office: 8700 Sudley Rd Manassas VA 22110

DEL RE, ROBERT, civil engineer; b. N.Y.C., June 3, 1930; s. Nicholas and Virginia (Higginbotham) Del R.; B.S., Marietta Coll., 1952, B.S. in Petroleum Engring., 1973; m. Joyce Maley, Aug. 20, 1971. Engr., Greeley & Hansen, Chgo., 1957-71, assoc., 1971-83; engr. Camp Dresser & McKee Inc., Boston, 1983—, now South Region/Gulf Coast Area mgr. constrn. services, Tampa, Fla. Patron Tampa Bay Art Ctr. Served with C.E.C., USNR, 1952-55. Registered profl. engr., Calif. Mem. ASCE (vice-chmn. com. contract adminstrn.), Am. Acad. Environ. Engrs. (diplomate), Nat. Soc. Profl. Engrs., Fla. Engring. Soc., Fla. Pollution Control Assn., Soc. Am. Mil. Engrs., Am. Arbitration Assn., Earthquake Engring. Research Inst., Inter-Am. Assn. San. Engrs., Am. Water Works Assn., Tampa Hist. Soc., Tampa Preservation, Pi Epsilon Tau, Alpha Tau Omega. Clubs: University (Chgo. and Tampa). Contbr. articles to profl. jours. Home: 10130 White Trout Ln Tampa FL 33618 Office: One Tampa City Ctr Suite 1750 Tampa FL 33602

DEL-ROSARIO, ERNESTO, ins. co. exec.; b. Yauco, P.R., Nov. 17, 1911; s. Ulises and Josefa E. (Olivieri) Del-R.; student Yauco Comml. Coll., 1928-29; m. Josefina Masini, July 24, 1936; children—Elliette A. (Mrs. Jose H. Pico), Juan E. Asst. postmaster U.S. P.O., Yauco, P.R., 1929-37; income tax insp. P.R. Treasury Dept., San Juan, 1937-41; public acct. tax practice, San Juan, 1941-42; comptroller Coop. Azucarera Los Canos, Arecibo, P.R., 1942-62; br. mgr. Nationwide Ins. Cos., Hato Rey, P.R., 1962-77, resident v.p. for P.R., 1975-77, cons., 1977-78; pres. P.R. Ins. Guaranty Assn., 1975-78, exec. dir., also of Life, Disability and Health Ins. Guaranty Assn., 1978—. Hon. mem. Civic Crusade for Traffic Safety, 1975-76. Mem. P.R. Coll. C.P.A.s, Nat. Soc. Public Accts., Nat. Soc. Coop. Accts. Roman Catholic. Clubs: Elks, Casino De Puerto Rico, Bankers of Puerto Rico. Home: M-207 Villa Caparra Guaynabo PR 00657 Office: PO Box 272 Hato Rey PR 00919

DEL TORO, ILIA, educator; b. Ponce, P.R., July 17, 1918; d. Gerardo Gabriel and Angela (Robledo) del T.; B.A., U. P.R., Rio Piedras, 1940; M.A. in Edn., NYU, 1958. Elem. tchr. State Dept. Instrn., 1941-44; tchr. high sch. social studies, 1944-57; instr. high sch. social studies, Coll. Edn., U. P.R., 1957-59, asso. prof., coordinator student teaching, 1979—, officer external resources, 1975-76, supr. student teaching, methods in high sch. social studies, edn. sociology, elem. edn. in social studies, curriculum and teaching dept., 1959-81, coordinator Inst. Family Fin., 1962-69, coordinator EPDA/UR Project, 1970-75; exec. bd. leadership/mgmt. seminar U. Ill. Exec. Ctr., 1984. Mem. subcom. State Cert. of Tchrs. Com. P.R. del. Edith Macy Girl Scout Camp, 1947; v.p. Liceo Ponceño North Zone Ex Alumnae, mem. Ponce High Sch. Class 1936. Mem. Assn. Supervision and Curriculum Devel. (nat. bd.), Assn. Tchr. Educators., Nat. Council Social Studies, NEA, P.R. Tchr. Assn., Assn. Tchr. Educators (pres. Puerto Rican chpt.), Future World Soc., Smithsonian Instn., Phi Delta Kappa (pres. of ceremonials, 1978, 84, outstanding educator, San Juan chpt. Diamond Jubilee 1981), Delta Kappa Gamma (state founder 1976, chpt. pres. 1978-80, state pres. 1983—, mem. internat. exec. bd. 1984—, recipient Golden Gift Fund). Roman Catholic. Contbr. articles to profl. jours. Home: 506 Parque de Las Fuentes Hato Rey PR 00918 Office: Coll Edn U PR Rio Piedras PR 00931

DE LUGO, RON, congressman; b. St. Croix, V.I., Aug. 2, 1930; children—Maria Cristina, Angela Maria. Student, Colegio San Jose, P.R. Sta.-WIVI, St. Croix, 1950-55; mem. V.I. Territorial Senate, 1956-66; adminstr., St. Croix, 1961; rep. for V.I., Washington, 1968-72; mem. 93-98th Congress from V.I., Interior and Insular Affairs Com., Washington, Merchant Marine and Fisheries Co.; del. from V.I. U.S. Congress, 1972—. Founder V.I. Carnival, 1952; del. Democratic Nat. Convs., 1956, 60, 64, 68; mem. Dem. Nat. Com., 1959; del. V.I. Constl. Conv., 1971-72. Office: Room 2443 Rayburn House Office Bldg Washington DC 20515

DEMAREE, ROBERT GLENN, psychologist, educator; b. Rockford, Ill., Sept. 20, 1920; s. Glenn and Ethel Mae (Champion) D.; B.S., U. Ill., 1941, M.A., 1948, Ph.D. (univ. fellow 1949-50), 1950; m. Alyce Anisia Jones, Sept. 4, 1948; children—Dee Anne, Marta, James, David. Chief performance br. Personnel and Tng. Research Center, Lowry AFB, Denver, 1951-57; dir. human factors Martin Space Flight div. Bell Aircraft Corp., Balt., 1958-60; dir. programs Matrix Corp., Arlington, Va., 1960-61; dir. office instructional research U. Ill., 1961-63; projects dir. Life Scis., Inc., Hurst, Tex., 1963-66; mem. faculty Tex. Christian U., Ft. Worth, 1966-85, prof. psychology, prof. Inst. Behavioral Research, 1970-85, emeritus, 1985—; cons., 1985—. Served with AUS, 1941-46. Mem. Am. Psychol. Assn., Am. Statis. Assn., Psychometric Soc., Soc. Multivariate Exptl. Psychologists. Home: 4813 Eldorado Dr Fort Worth TX 76118

DEMAYO, MICHAEL JAMES, industrial contracting company executive; b. N.Y.C., Dec. 28, 1950; s. John Joseph and Theresa (Maroney) DeM.; m. Maryann Napolitano, Nov. 15, 1975; children—Gina Maria, Laura Elizabeth. B.S. in Acctg., Villanova U. (Pa.), 1974. Supt., Champion Constrn./Engrs., Huntington, N.Y., 1974-77; project mgr. Brooks Erection & Constrn., St. Louis, 1977-80; mgr. constrn. Central Rigging, Milford, Conn., 1980-81; gen. mgr. Riggers & Constructors, Houston, 1981-82; v.p. SOTEX Indsl. Contractors, Inc., Beaumont, Tex., 1982-83, pres., chief exec. officer, 1983-85; exec. v.p., chief exec. officer NOUN Indsl. Contractors, Inc., Beaumont, Tex., 1984. Mem. Republican Presdl. Task Force, Washington, 1982-83; bd. dirs. Jr. Achievement, Beaumont, Tex., 1983-85, Hope Sch.; trustee United Way. Mem. Beaumont C. of C. Roman Catholic. Club: Villanova Wildcat. Home: 4755 Chadwick St Beaumont TX 77706 Office: NOUN Indsl Contractors Inc 1675 Lindbergh Dr Beaumont TX 77707

DEMÉRÉ, ROBERT HOUSTOUN, oil company executive; b. Savannah, Ga., Feb. 15, 1924; s. Raymond McAllister and Josephine Elizabeth (Mobley) D.; m. Mary Elizabeth Bullock, Sept. 21, 1946; children—Robert Houstoun, John B., Raymond S., Sims B., Anne E. Student Yale U., 1941-43. Pres., chief exec. officer Colonial Oil Industries, Savannah, 1958—; pres., dir. Interstate Stas., Inc., Savannah, 1964—, Chatham Towing Co., Inc., Savannah, 1952—, Colonial Terminals, Inc., Savannah, 1977—; dir. Savannah Bank & Trust Co., First R.R. & Banking Co., Augusta, Ga. Bd. dirs. Coastal Empire council Boy Scouts Am., YMCA, Savannah; trustee United Way of Coastal Empire, Inc., Savannah. Served to lt. (j.g.) USN, 1942-45. Named Indsl. Man of Yr., Savannah chpt. Internat. Mgmt. Council, 1972. Mem. Ind. Fuel Terminal Operators Assn. (treas. 1979—), Ind. Liquid Terminal Operators Assn., Nat. Oil Jobbers Council, World Bus. Council, Sea Edn. Assn. (trustee 1982—), N.C. Oil Jobbers Assn., S.C. Oil Jobbers Assn., Ga. Oilmen's Assn., Savannah Dist. Export Council, Soc. of Cincinnati (v.p.), Soc. Colonial Wars (mem. standing com.). Clubs: Savannah Yacht, The Century, The Chatham, Cotillion, Oglethorpe, St. Andrew's Soc. (Savannah). Office: Colonial Oil Industries Inc PO Box 576 Savannah GA 31402-0576

DE MERE-DWYER, LEONA, med. artist; b. Memphis, May 1, 1928; d. Clifton and Leona (McCarthy) De Mere; B.A., Southwestern U., Memphis, 1949; M.Sc., Memphis State U., 1984; m. John Thomas Dwyer, May 10, 1952; children—John, DeMere, Patrice, Brian, Anne-Clifton DeMere Dwyer, McCarthy-DeMere Dwyer. Med. artist for McCarthy DeMere, Memphis, 1950-80; pres. Aesthetic Med. & Forensic Art, 1984—; speech therapist, Memphis, 1950-82; lic. embalmer, funeral dir., 1981; lectr. on med. art univs., conf., assns.; cons. in prostheses Vocat. Rehab. Services; bereavement counselor. Organizer Ladies of St. Jude, Memphis, 1960; active Brooks Art Gallery League of Memphis; leader Confraternity of Christian Doctrine, St. Louis Cath. Ch., 1966-67; vice dir. Tellico Hist. Found., 1980-80; active Republican campaign coms. Lic. Fedn. Internationale de'Automobile, (internat. car racing), 1972; recipient Disting. Service award Gupton-Jones Coll. Mortuary Sci., 1981; Silver Sons of the Am. Revolution medal, 1985. Mem. Assn. Med. Illustrators, Am. Assn. Med. Assts., Emergency Dept. Nurses Assn., Am. Physicians Nurses Assn., Am. Soc. Plastic and Reconstructive Surgeons Found. (guest mem., cons.), Women in Law (chmn. assos.), FORUM, Nat. Death Edn. Soc., Exec. Women Am., Brandeis U. Women, DAR (1st v.p. regent 1980), UDC (pres. Nathan Bedford Forrest chpt.), Cotton Carnival Assn. (chairperson children's ct. 1968-70), Pi Sigma Eta, Kappa Delta (adv.), Kappa Delta Pi. Club: Tennessee, Royal Matron Amaranth. (Faith Ct.) (Memphis). Contbr. articles to profl. jours. Home: 660 W Suggs Dr Memphis TN 38119

DEMERS, TONA MARIA, insurance executive; b. Little Rock, Aug. 27, 1957; d. Albert Nelson DeMers and Irma Louise (Ramsay) Blanton; m. Robert Edward Gorecke, Jr., Dec. 24, 1974 (div. Aug. 1977); 1 son, Jason Matthew. Student U. Ark.-Little Rock, 1980—. Lic. ins. agent, Ark. Vice pres., agt., underwriter E.W. Turner Co., Little Rock, 1974—. Pres. Young Democrats of U. Ark., 1981-83; mem. Pulaski County Dem. Com., Little Rock, 1982—. Mem. Ins. Women of Little Rock (named Rookie Ins. Woman of Yr. 1980), Mabelvale Bus. and Profl. Women (Young Careerist award for 1984), Nat. Assn. Ins. Women. Baptist. Home: 9643 Baseline Rd Little Rock AR 72209 Office: E W Turner Co Inc 4918 Baseline Rd Little Rock AR 72209

DEMILLO, RICHARD A., computer science educator; b. Hibbing, Minn., Jan. 26, 1947; s. Herman and Lorraine Kathryn (Edman) DeM.; m. Diane Hanson, Dec. 26, 1969 (div. Apr. 1984); children—Allan, Gina, Andrew. B.A., Coll. St. Thomas, 1969; Ph.D., Ga. Inst. Tech., 1972. Asst. prof. U. Wis., Milw., 1972-76; assoc. prof. Ga. Inst. Tech., Atlanta, 1976-80, prof. computer sci., 1980—, asst. dir. research, dept. computer sci., 1983—, dir. Software Engring. Research Ctr., 1985—; cons. IBM, Poughkeepsie, N.Y., 1984—, GTE Communications Systems Div., Phoenix, 1984, Inst. Def. Analyses, Alexandria, Va., 1983—, MSA, Atlanta, 1977—. Author: Foundations of Secure Computation, 1978; Applied Cryptology, Cryptographic Protocols and Computer Security, 1984. Grantee Naval Air Devel. Ctr., Warminster, Pa., 1984. Mem. Assn. Computing Machinery, Am. Math. Soc., Math. Assn. Am., Soc. Indsl. and Applied Math., Assn. for Symbolic Logic. Home: 2914 Lenox Rd #6 Atlanta GA 30324 Office: Ga Inst of Tech ICS Atlanta GA 30332

DEMONG, RICHARD FRANCIS, finance and investments educator, research director; b. Freeport, Ill., May 2, 1944; s. Maurice Dale and Ruth Jane (Kidwell) DeM.; m. Sue Ann Liddle, June 17, 1967 (div. Dec. 1983); children—Cheryl Ann, Lynn Ann. A.A., Orange Coast Coll., Costa Mesa, Calif., 1964; A.B., Calif. State U., 1966; M.B.A., Coll. of William & Mary, 1974; D.B.A., U. Colo., 1977. Cert. cost analyst; chartered fin analyst. Time keeper Douglas Aircrat Co., Long Beach, Calif., 1966; instr. U. Colo., Boulder, 1974-77; assoc. prof. U. Va., Charlottesville, 1977—; research dir. Fin. Analyst Research Found., Charlottesville, 1982-85; cons. Fin. Forecasting & Service, 1978—. Author: (with others) (monograph) New Financial Instruments: A Descriptive Guide, 1985. Editor: (with others) (monograph) Takeovers and Shareholders: The Mounting Controversy, 1985. Mem. Va. Small Bus. Council, Richmond, 1981-82; chmn. U. Va. ROTC com., Charlottesville, 1981-84; co-chmn. Central Va. Score and Ace Chpt., Charlottesville, 1981; dir. McIntire Small Bus. Inst., Charlottesville, 1978-82. Served to capt. USAF, 1966-72; Vietnam. Decorated DFC; named outstanding Air Force Mobilization Augmentee (reservest), Air Training Command, 1980. Fellow Richmond Soc. Fin. Analysts; mem. Inst. Chartered Fin. Analysts, Fin. Mgmt. Assn., Am. Fin. Assn., So. Fin. Assn. Roman Catholic. Avocations: gardening, tennis, racketball. Home: 2730 Leeds Ln Charlottesville VA 22901 Office: Univ of Va Monroe Hall Charlottesville VA 22903

DEMOPULOS, CHRIS, civil engineering executive, consultant, land developer; b. Texarkana, Tex., Oct. 30, 1924; m. Sophia Soteropulos, Nov. 12, 1950; children—Anastasia Elaine, Paul Chris. B.S. in Engring., Tex. A&M U., 1947. Registered profl. engr., La., Tex., Ark., Okla. Design Engr. E.M. Freeman & Assocs., Shreveport, La., 1947-52; partner, corp. officer Demopulos & Ferguson, Inc., Shreveport, 1953—. Bd. mgrs. Broadmoor YMCA, 1965-75; past bd. dirs. Metropolitan YMCA, Shreveport; active Shreveport Art Guild, La. State Fair Assn., Shreveport Hist. Soc. Served as lst lt. USAAF, 1943-45; ETO. Named Engr. of Yr., Engring. and Sci. Council, Shreveport, 1979, 1985; recipient A.E. Wilder award Consulting Engr. Council, 1980. Fellow ASCE, Am. Consulting Engrs. Council; mem. Nat. Soc. Profl. Engrs., La. Engring. Soc., Soc. Am. Mil. Engrs., Shreveport C. of C. (past dir.), Tex. Soc. Profl. Engrs. Clubs: A&M Alumni, Shreveport; Shreveport Country; City (Baton Rouge, La.). Lodge: Rotary (Shreveport).

DE MOSS, JERRY VAUGHN, executive search and management consultant; b. Los Angeles, Feb. 14, 1934; s. Lloyd Barrow and Ora May (Condon) DeM.; B.S. in Bus. Adminstrn., UCLA, 1956; m. Janet Ruth Brant, July 2, 1965; children—Suzanne Ruth, David Vaughn, Anne Marie. Dist. mgr. Caribbean Area Moore Bus. Forms de P.R., San Juan, 1960-66; franchisee Kelly Services, Inc., San Juan, 1966-71; founder, pres. CAREERS Inc., San Juan, 1971—; pres. Caribbean Horizons Group, cons. in mfg. activities. Bd. dirs. Better Bus. Bur. P.R., 1971—, Pvt. Investment Council of Govt. of P.R. bd. dirs., exec. com. United Fund P.R., San Juan, 1974—; bd. dirs. Traveller's Aide P.R., San Juan, 1972-74. Served to comdr. USN, 1956—. Recipient cert. of merit United Fund P.R., 1976. Mem. Naval Res. Assn. (founder, pres. San Juan chpt. 1967), P.R. Mfrs. Assn., Res. Officers Assn. Clubs: Rotary (pres. 1977-78), Bankers of P.R. Office: Suite 1919 Banco Popular Center Hato Rey PR 00918

DEMPSEY, BERNARD HAYDEN, JR., lawyer; b. Evanston, Ill., Mar. 29, 1942; s. Bernard H. and Margaret C. (Gallagher) D.; children—Bernard H., Matthew B., Kathleen N., Rose Maureen G., Alexandra C.T. B.S., Coll. Holy Cross, 1964; J.D., Georgetown U., 1967. Bar: Fla. 1968, D.C. 1979. Law clerk to presiding judge U.S. Dist Ct. (mid. dist.), Fla., 1967-69; asst. U.S. atty. Mid. Dist. Fla., 1969-73; assoc. Dixon, Shear, Brown & Stephenson, Orlando, Fla., 1973-75; sr. ptnr. Dempsey & Kelly, Orlando, 1975-77, Dempsey & Slaughter, P.A., Orlando, 1977-84; Dempsey & Goldsmith, P.A., 1984—. Contbr. articles to profl. jours. Recipient John Marshall award U.S. Dept. Justice, 1973; Outstanding Performance award, 1972. Mem. Fla. Bar Assn., ABA, Fed. Bar Assn., Acad. Fla. Trial Lawyers, Assn. Trial Lawyers Am., Delta Theta Phi. Republican. Roman Catholic. Clubs: Internat. (Washington); Univ. (Orlando); Winter Park (Fla.) Racquet. Office: 605 E Robinson St Suite 500 Orlando FL 32802

DEMPSEY, BRUCE HARVEY, museum director; b. Camden, N.J., July 4, 1941; s. Lawrence Aloysius and Esther Audrey (Harvey) D.; B.A., Fla. State U., 1964, M.F.A., 1966; m. Gabriele Katharina Heerling, July 12, 1969; children—Lawrence Maximilian, Gabriele Katharina. Faculty, Fla. State U., Tallahassee, 1966-75, gallery dir., 1969-75, instr. Fla. State U. Study Center, Florence, Italy, 1967-68; dir. Jacksonville (Fla.) Art Mus., 1975—. Mem. fine arts adv. bd. State of Fla. Fine Arts Council, 1974-76 (Visual ArtsIGrant Review Panel, 1981, Individual Visual Artist Grant Review Panel, 1982, 83), grant rev. panel, 1979; mem. adv. bd. Jacksonville Arts Assembly; visual arts adviser Fla. Div. Cultural Affairs, 1973-76; mem. Jacksonville Arts Assembly, 1975—; mem. art purchase panel Fla. Ho. of Reps., 1980; SECCA Southeast Seven VI Panel, 1981. Bd. dirs. Tallahassee Arts Council, 1973-77; mem. Fla. Bicentennial Com., 1974-76. U.S.-Chinese Relations travel-in-aid grantee, 1975. Mem. Fla. Art Mus. Dirs. Assn. (treas. 1977-79), Am. Assn. Museums, Internat. Council Museums. Office: Jacksonville Art Mus 4160 Boulevard Center Dr Jacksonville FL 32207

DEMPSEY, JOHN YOUNG, III, educator; b. Leesville, La., Jan. 16, 1936; s. John Young and Mattie Viola (Cain) D.; B.S., La. State U., Baton Rouge, 1957; D.Ed., McNeese State U. La., 1975. Tchr., Vernon Parish Schs., 1959-65, 66-67, dir. Title III ESEA program, 1971-73; tchr. Acad. Year Inst., Ohio State U., Columbus, 1965-66, Webster Parish Schs., Minden, La., 1967-71; tchr. Leesville (La.) High Sch., 1975—, chmn. sci. dept., 1976—. Named Tchr. of Yr., Vernon Parish, La., 1977-78; recipient Catalyst award Chem. Mfrs. Assn., 1978; Outstanding High Sch. Sci. Tchr. award La. Acad. Scis., 1982; La. Tchr. of Yr. award, 1982; Gov.'s award as La. Handicapped Citizen of Yr., 1983; Presdl. award for excellence in sci. and math. teaching; Faculty award for excellence in sci. instrn. U.S. Army Research Office Jr. Sci. and Humanities Symposium, 1983; Chem. Mfrs. Assn. Catalyst award for excellence in teaching, 1984; Presdl. award for excellence in sci. and math. teaching, 1985. Mem. Nat. Sci. Tchrs. Assn., Assn. Supervision and Curriculum Devel., Nat. Sci. Suprs. Assn., NEA, La. Assn. Educators, Vernon Parish Assn. Educators, Vernon Parish Sci. Tchrs. Assn., La. Jr. C. of C. (regional v.p. 1969-70, sec. 1970-71), Leesville Jr. C. of C. (life, pres. 1964-65), Phi Delta Kappa. Democrat. Baptist. Clubs: Masons, Shriners. Home: HC-79 Box 596 Leesville LA 71446 Office: Leesville High Sch PO Box 471 Leesville LA 71446

DEMPSEY, MARY STACY PUTNAM, speech, language and hearing consultant; b. Abbeville, La., Mar. 6, 1947; d. Richard Johnson and Dorethea Gooch Putnam; m. Alfred Brown Dempsey; children—John Putnam, Patrick Turner. B.A., Our Lady of Lake U., San Antonio, 1969, M.A., 1970. Teaching cert., Tex., La.; lic., La. Speech and lang. pathologist New Orleans Speech and Hearing Center, 1970-74; speech and lang. cons. Jefferson Parish Sch. Bd., 1974-78; pvt. practice speech, lang. and hearing cons., diagnostician, therapist, Metairie, La., 1981—. Mem. Am. Speech and Hearing Assn. (cert. clin. competence), La. Speech and Hearing Assn. Democrat. Roman Catholic. Home: 687 Bocage Ln Mandeville LA 70448 Office: 300 Codifer Blvd Metairie LA 70005

DEMPSEY, ROBERT DALE, safety engineer; b. Fort Smith, Ark., Mar. 4, 1947; s. Dale Rupert and Maude Lillian (Price) D.; m. Patricia Ann Thielemier, Dec. 28, 1969; children—Robert Dale, Gregory Price. B.S. in E.E., U. Ark., 1969; M.E. in Indsl. Engring., Tex. A & M U., 1970. Registered profl. engr., Calif.; cert. safety profl. Safety engr. Material Command U.S. Army, Alexandria, Va., 1970-73, safety mgr. Ammunition Plant, Shreveport, 1973-74, safety and health mgr. Troop Supply Command, St. Louis, 1974-76, safety engring. mgr. Engr. Div., Huntsville, Ala., 1976—. Ops chmn. March of Dimes Walkathon, Huntsville, 1978; mem. com. Tennessee Valley council Boy Scouts Am., Huntsville, 1983-84; pres. Camelot Recreation Assn., Huntsville, 1984-85. Recipient Engr. of the Year award U.S. Army Engr. Div., 1984; NSF fellow, 1967. Mem. Soc. Am. Mil. Engrs. (chmn. membership 1984-85), Am. Soc. Safety Engrs., Tau Beta Pi, Eta Kappa Nu, Alpha Pi Mu. Baptist. Avocations: coach basketball league, tennis, volleyball, fishing. Home: 2500 Willena Dr Huntsville AL 35803 Office: US Army Engr Div PO Box 1600 Huntsville AL 35807

DENFRUND, RICHARD JAMES, coach; b. Buffalo, June 28, 1957; s. John and Joan Catherine (Hoffman) D.; m. Robin Lee Ralston, May 28, 1983. B.S., U. Tampa, 1979. Coach swimming Chamberlain High Sch., Tampa, Fla., 1979-81; phys. edn. specialist Hillsborough County, Tampa, Fla., 1979-81; coach cross-country U. Tampa, 1982—, coach tennis, 1982—, dir. intramural athletics, 1981—; press box coordinator Tampa Bay Bandits, 1983—; race dir. Robinson's Symphony Classic, Tampa, Fla., 1982—; supr. events NCAA Men's Soccer Championship, Tampa, Fla., 1983. Merit scholar, 1976. Mem. Nat. Intramural and Recreational Sports Assn., U.S. Tennis Assn., Univ. Com. for Handicap Compliance. Home: 1812 Mill Run Circle Tampa FL 33612 Office: U Tampa 401 W Kennedy Blvd Tampa FL 33606

DENG, ROY FREDERICK, JR., architect; b. Saginaw, Mich., July 27, 1933; s. Roy Frederick and Mabel (Schott) D.; m. Eleanor Symonds, Sept. 4, 1958; children—Karen Marshall, Laura Brandreth, Tracy Stevens. B.Arch., U. Mich., 1956. Registered architect, Ala., Ill. Gen., structural drafter John A. Blume Assocs., Engrs., San Francisco, 1958-60; gen. drafter Harry Weese Assocs., Chgo., 1960; constrn. adminstr., field observer Bertrand Goldberg Assocs., Chgo., 1960-65; v.p., project architect Perkins & Will, Chgo., 1965-75; sr. project architect Mathhei & Colin, Chgo., 1975-78; v.p. health facility and instl. projects Blondheim, Williams & Golson, Birmingham, Ala., 1978-81; sr. project architect, studio head Gresham, Smith and Ptnrs., Birmingham, 1981—. Chmn. archtl. com. Hinsdale (Ill.) Plan Commn., 1971-78. Served with Combat Engrs., USAR, 1956-58. Mem. AIA, Constrn. Specifications Inst. Republican. Presbyterian. Clubs: Salt Creek Tennis, Glen Lake Yacht. Home: 1441 Panorama Dr Vestavia Hills AL 35216 Office: 504 A Brookwood Blvd Birmingham AL 35209

DENHAM, WILLIAM ERNEST, JR., clergyman, counselor; b. Louisville, Oct. 8, 1911; s. William E. and Myrtle (Lane) D.; m. Priscilla Kelley, June 27, 1941 (dec.); children—William Ernest III, James Kelley, Priscilla, Elizabeth Denham Thompson; m. 2d, Louise D. Yelvington, Nov. 23, 1974. A.B., Washington U., 1933; Th.M., So. Bapt. Theol. Sem., 1940, Ph.D., 1944; postgrad. U. Tex., Austin, 1971-73. Cert. counselor, Tex. Sec. Bapt. Student Union, Mo. Baptist Conv., 1933-35, Atlanta, 1935-37; pastor 1st. Bapt. Ch., Newport, Tenn., 1944-47, Macon, Ga., 1947-52, River Oaks Bapt. Ch., Houston, 1952-64, 1st. Bapt. Ch., Austin, 1964-75; dir. Counseling and Pastoral Care Ctr., Austin, 1975—; mem. bd. Bapt. Radio Commn., So. Bapt. Conv.; exec. com. mem. Bapt. Gen. Conv., Tex.; first bd. chmn. Houston Bapt. U. Mem. Family Meditation Assn. (cert.), Am. Assn. Marriage and Family Therapists, Am. Assn. Sex Educators, Counselors and Therapists, Am. Assn. Pastoral Counselors (diplomate), Omicron Delta Kappa. Democrat. Lodges: Rotary, Kiwanis. Contbr. articles to profl. jours. Office: Counseling and Pastoral Care Ctr 3701 N Lamar Ave Austin TX 78705

DENIUS, FRANKLIN WOFFORD, lawyer; b. Athens, Tex., Jan. 4, 1925; s. Samuel F. and Frances (Cain) D.; B.B.A., U. Tex., 1949, LL.B., 1949; m. Charmaine Hooper, Nov. 19, 1949; children—Frank Wofford, Charmaine. Admitted to Tex. bar, 1949; practice law, Austin, Tex., 1949—; partner firm Clark, Thomas, Harris, Denius & Winters, 1949-75; individual practice law, 1976—; pres., chief exec. officer So. Union Co., 1986—; dir. Tex. Commerce Bank, Austin, 1960—, Delhi Internat. Oil Corp., Dallas, 1952-81, So. Union Co., Dallas, 1955-75, 76—, Supron Energy Corp., Dallas, 1972-82; dir., sec., founder TeleCom Corp., Houston, 1958-85, Tex. Capital Corp., Houston, 1958—; chmn. bd. dirs. Aztec Oil and Gas Co., Dallas, 1954-76; gen. counsel Delhi-Taylor Oil Corp., Dallas, 1962-64, Delhi Pipeline Corp., Dallas, 1950-64, Pres. Young Men's Bus. League Austin; pres. United Way, 1972, chmn. bd., 1973; pres. Austin Ex-Students Assn., U. Tex., 1964-66; mem. U. Tex. System Devel. Bd., 1969—; mem., chmn. spl. gifts div., Devel. Bd., U. Tex., 1974-80; spl. counsel U. Tex., 1961-68; bd. dirs. Tex.-Ex Found., 1961-70; mem. U. Tex. Chancellor's Council, 1965—; mem. U. Tex. Pres.'s Assn., 1969—; bd. trustees Schreiner Coll., 1975-80, adv. trustee, 1980—; bd. trustees Austin Ind. Sch. Dist., 1970-73; bd. trustees, founder Austin Community Coll., 1970-73; sec., treas. Longhorn Edn. Found., 1978—; co-chmn. L.B.J. U. Tex. Library Found., 1979-80. Served with U.S. Army, 1943-45. Decorated Silver Star with three oak leaf clusters, Purple Heart, Croix de Guerre (France, Belgium). Named Outstanding Young Man of Austin, Jr. C. of C., 1959. Mem. Travis County Bar Assn. (dir.), State Bar Tex., Travis County Bar Assn. (dir.), Am. Bar Assn., Tex. Utilities Lawyers Assn. Presbyterian. (chmn. b. deacons; mem. bd. elders). Clubs: Longhorn (pres.), Optimist (dir., pres.) (Austin), Headliners (pres.), Burnt Orange (Austin). Home: 3703 Meadowbank St Austin TX 78703 Office: Texas Commerce Bank Bldg PO Box 2177 Austin TX 78768

DENMAN, JAMES BURTON, lawyer; b. Brownwood, Tex., Nov. 15, 1947; s. James Burton and Margaret Gwendolyn D.; m. Donna Van Tuyle, Feb. 18, 1978; children—Tuyle, Lindsay. A.A., Porterville Jr. Coll., 1968; B.S., Calif. State U.-Fresno, 1970; J.D., Samford U., 1973. Bar: Fla. 1974. Ptnr., assoc. Dolan, Denman & Gramling, P.A., Fort Lauderdale, 1975-78; prin. James B. Denman & Assocs., P.A., Fort Lauderdale, 1978-80; ptnr. Bunnell, Denman & Woulfe, P.A., Fort Lauderdale, 1980—; dir. Trans Air, Inc., Fort Lauderdale, 1984—. Bd. dirs. Bethany Christian Sch., Fort Lauderdale, 1984. Mem. Assn. Trial Lawyers Am., Acad. Fla. Trial Lawyers. Democrat. Lutheran. Clubs: Lauderdale Yacht, Tower. Home: 901 Cordova Rd Fort

Lauderdale FL 33316 Office: Bunnell Denman & Woulfe PA 1080 SE 3d Ave Fort Lauderdale FL 33316

DENMAN, JOE CARTER, JR., forest products company executive; b. Lufkin, Tex., Sept. 30, 1923, B.Arch., Tex. A. and M. U., 1950; m. Ginia Beth Cox, Jan. 10, 1948; children—Joe Carter, III, Elizabeth Anne, Ginia Geanette. With Temple Industries, Diboll, Tex., 1950—, corporate v.p., 1964-66, exec. v.p., 1966-72, pres., 1972—; exec. v.p. Temple-Eastex, Inc., 1974-77, pres., 1977—, also chmn., chief exec. officer; exec. v.p. Temple-Inland Inc., 1984—; v.p. Time, Inc., 1976-78, group v.p., 1978-84, dir., 1979-84; v.p. Angelina County Water Control and Improvement Dist. No. 2, 1963-68; v.p., dir. AFCO Industries, Inc., Alexandria, La., 1973—, Sabine Investment Co., Diboll; dir. Diboll State Bank, CRS Sirrine, Inc., Houston, Angelina Free Press Inc., Inland Container Corp., Indpls., Gt. Am. Res. Ins. Co., Dallas, Nat. Fidelity Life Ins. Co., Kansas City, Mo., Ga. Kraft Co., Rome, 1st Bancorp. of Cleveland, Tex. Lumbermens Investment Corp., Austin, Tex., South-Eastern R.R. Co., Diboll, Temple-White Co., Inc., Topaz Oil Co., Bd. dirs. Angelina County Community Fund, Inc., 1960-61, chmn. indsl. fund, 1965; pres., bd. dirs. Temple Industries Employees Fed. Credit Union, 1963-64; trustee Temple Pension Trust, 1964—; mem. adv. bd. Salvation Army, Lufkin; bd. dirs. Angelina Coll., 1980—, Tex. Forestry Mus., Lufkin; mem. devel. council Coll. Architecture and Environ. Design, Tex. A&M U. Served to lt. (j.g.), A.C., U.S. Navy, 1942-46. Named Disting. Alumnus, Tex. A&M U., 1981; registered profl. engr., Tex. Mem. Nat. (dir. 1968—), So. (pres. 1969-70) forest products assns., Tex. Forest Products Mfrs. Assn. (pres. 1967-69, dir.), Tex. Soc. Profl. Engrs., So. Pine Inspection Bur. (adv. bd.), So. Pines Plywood Standard (advisory com. 1961-64), Forest Products Research Soc. (dir. 1959-60), Am. Plywood Assn. (trustee 1973-74), Angelina County C. of C. (dir. 1966-68), Tau Beta Pi. Office: PO Drawer N Diboll TX 75941

DENMARK, LAWRENCE JAY, concrete products company executive; b. Miami Beach, Fla., Apr. 8, 1953; Irving J. and Evelyn (Kohn) D. B.S., Antioch Coll., Yellow Springs, Ohio, 1975; M.S., Univ. Coll. North Wales, 1975; Ph.D., Univ. Without Walls, Yellow Springs, 1980. Notary pub., Fla.; cert. tchr., Fla. Tchr., Dade County Pub. Sch. System, Miami, 1970, 75; research staff U. Miami, 1971, U. Calif.-San Diego, 1972, W. Indies Lab., St. Croix, 1973; v.p. Denmark Art Stone Co., Miami, 1975—, chief exec. officer, 1984—; dir. Denmark Cast Stone Co., Reil Advt., Denmark Synergisms, Oceana Lab., Tectona Industries; cons. in field.; bd. dirs. Alfred P. Sloan Found., Yellow Springs, Ohio, 1974-75. Mem. Am. Mgmt. Assn., S. Fla. Builders Assn., Nat. Precast Concrete Assn., AAAS, Fla. Nurseryman's Assn., Internat. Oceanographic Found. Lodge: Rotary. Office: Denmark Art Stone Co 12351 NW 7th Ave Miami FL 33168

DENNIS, CHARLES NEWTON, finance educator, economic consultant; b. Wichita Falls, Tex., Mar. 24, 1942; s. Homer Asbury and E. Pauline (Sessler) D.; m. Beverly Cattell, Oct. 2, 1964; children—Seeley Asbury, Andrew Whitfield. B.A. in Econs., So. Methodist U., 1964; M.A. in Econs. and Fin., Memphis State U., 1969; Ph.D. in Econs. and Fin., U. Ark., 1972. Chartered fin. analyst. Instr. econs. U. Ark., Fayetteville, 1970-71; prof. fin. U. So. Miss., Hattiesburg, 1971—; trustee Pub. Employees Retirement System, Miss., 1984—; cons. Bank N. Miss., Starkville, 1974—, Miss. Bankers Assn., Jackson, 1980, Ford Motor Co., New Orleans, 1983. Editor The Wall St. Review of Books Jour., 1982. Rep., Private Sector Action Council, Miss., 1984—. Served to capt. USAF, 1964-68. Am. Assembly Collegiate Schs. Bus. fellow, 1975-76; named Outstanding Bus. Sch. Prof., Coll. Bus. U. So. Miss., 1983. Fellow Fin. Analysts Fedn.; mem. Am. Econs. Assn., Am. Fin. Assn., Inst. Chartered Fin. Analysts, Miss. Fin. Analysts (v.p. 1983—), Omicron Delta Epsilon, Beta Gamma Sigma. Republican. Presbyterian. Avocation: sport cars. Home: 102 Darby Rd Hattiesburg MS 39401 Office: U So Miss PO Box 5076 So Sta Hattiesburg MS 39406

DENNIS, DIANE JACQUELINE, personnel and management executive; b. Phila., July 11, 1950; d. Leonard S. and Ruth Lipton; m. Warren L. Dennis, Dec. 28, 1968; children—Joanna, Seth. B.S., Temple U., 1970; M.S., George Mason U., 1975. Tchr., Phila. pub. schs., 1970; reading specialist Greenhedges Sch., Vienna, Va., 1975-77; from dir. to dist. mgr. Kindercare Learning Ctrs., 1977-81, dir. personnel and mgmt. tng. Eastern seaboard, Reston, Va., 1981-83, regional mgr. Mid-Eastern states, 1983—. Mem. Kindercare Execs. of Roundtable, LWV (chmn. Reston chpt. 1975-77). Home: 7113 Holyrood Dr McLean VA 22101 Office: Kindercare Falls Church VA 22070

DENNIS, GARY OWEN, clergyman; b. Waynesville, N.C., Feb. 17, 1946; s. Daniel Shaefer and Shirley Carlene (Owen) D.; m. Sara Bright, June 14, 1969. B.A., Taylor U., 1968; M.Div., Princeton Theol. Seminary, 1972, D.Min., 1986. Ordained to ministry Presbyterian Ch., 1972; assoc. pastor Second Presbyn. Ch., Memphis, 1972-73, Hollywood Presbyn. Ch., Los Angeles, 1973-76; pastor Westlake Hills Presbyn. Ch., Austin, Tex., 1976—; adj. prof. Fuller Theol. Sem., Pasadena, Calif., 1973-76; mem. stewardship com. Mission Presbytery, San Antonio, 1980-85, mem. edn. com., 1976-80; founder, dir. Youth Leadership Devel. Am., Los Angeles, 1973-76; cons. Lilly Endowment, Indpls., 1974-76. Contbr. articles to various publs. Bd. dirs. Central City Counseling Service, Austin, 1982-83, Ronald McDonald House, Austin, 1984, 85, 86. Democrat. Presbyterian. Lodge: Rotary.

DENNIS, JAMES LEON, state justice; b. Monroe, La., Jan. 9, 1936; s. Jenner Leon and Hope (Taylo) D.; B.S. in Bus. Adminstrn., La. Tech. Inst., Ruston, 1959; J.D., La. State U., 1962; LL.M. in Jud. Process, U. Va., 1984; m. Camille Smith; children—Stephen James, Gregory Leon, Mark Taylo, John Timothy. Bar: La. 1962. Assoc. firm Hudson, Potts & Bernstein, Monroe, 1962-65, ptnr., 1965-71; judge 4th Dist. Ct. La. for Morehouse and Ouachita Parishes, 1972-74; judge La. 2d Circuit Ct. Appeals, 1974-75; asso. justice La. Supreme Ct., 1975—; coordinator La. Constnl. Revision Commn., 1970-72; del., chmn. judiciary com. La. Constnl. Conv., 1973. Mem. La. Ho. of Reps., 1968-72. Served with AUS, 1955-57. Mem. ABA, La. 4th Jud. bar assns. Methodist. Club: Rotary. Office: Supreme Ct Bldg 301 Loyola Ave New Orleans LA 70112

DENNIS, PATRICK HARLEY, ophthalmologist, ophthalmology educator; b. Lynchburg, S.C., Dec. 10, 1932; s. James Alva and Ida Mae (Hodge) D.; m. Myrtle Ann Benton, Aug. 26, 1956; children—Patrick, Jr., Lisa, Jeffrey. B.S. in Natural Sci., Newberry Coll., 1954; M.D., Med. U. S.C., 1958, D. Ophthalmology, 1966. Diplomate Am. Bd. Ophthalmology. Intern Med. U. S.C., Charleston, 1958-59, resident in ophthalmology, 1963-66, teaching fellow, 1966, assoc. prof. ophthalmology, 1966—; practice medicine specializing in ophthalmology, Charleston, S.C., 1966—; cons. ophthalmology VA Hosp., Charleston, 1966-80. Served to capt. USAF, 1959-63. Fellow ACS, Am. Acad. Ophthalmology; mem. AMA, S.C. Med. Assn., Charleston Ophthal. Soc., Charleston County Med. Soc., S.C. Hist. Soc. Waring Library Soc. Presbyterian. Avocations: nature, history; photography; gardening Home: 899 White Point Blvd Charleston SC 29412 Office: 116 Ashley Ave Charleston SC 29401

DENNIS, VERLINE DIXON, educational counselor; b. Atlanta, Dec. 18, 1936; s. Clifton Cecil and Frieda Onevia (Allen) Dixon; m. George David Dennis, Dec. 26, 1955; children—Michael David, Deanna Lynn. B.S. in Edn., Oglethorpe U., 1965; M.Ed. in Guidance and Counseling, W. Ga. Coll., 1975, Ed.S. in Adminstrn. Supervision, 1985. Cert. tchr., Ga. Tchr., Douglasville Elem. Sch., Ga., 1963-68, Burnett Elem. Sch., Ga., 1972-73; tchr. Eastside Elem. Sch., Douglasville, 1973-75, counselor, 1975—; mem. citizens adv. panel Douglas County Dept. Family and Children's Services, Douglasville, 1986—; mem. staff devel. council Douglas County Sch. System, 1979—. Contbr. articles to profl. publs. Mem. Mental Health Assn. of Metropolitan Ga., Atlanta, 1976-85; sec. Douglas County Tipoff Club, 1983—. Mem. Douglas County Assn. Educators (legis. chmn. 1977—), Am. Sch. Counselor Assn., Ga. Sch. Counselors Assn. (chmn. govt. relations 1984—, 7th dist. Elem. Counselor of Yr. award 1980), NEA, Ga. Assn. Educators (Sch. Bell award 1976), Phi Delta Kappa, Delta Kappa Gamma, Kappa Delta Pi, Phi Kappa Phi. Democrat. Methodist. Avocations: music; reading. Office: Eastside Elem Sch 8266 Connally Dr Douglasville GA 30134

DENNIS, WILBURN DWAYNE, minister; b. Abilene, Tex., July 26, 1937; s. Wilburn Parker and Beulah Isabella (Dearing) D.; m. Marcia Ann Todd, June 23, 1959; children—Wilburn Todd, Sherrie Ann, Marcia Leigh. B.A., Abilene Christian U., 1958, M.A., 1959; M.Ed., West Tex. State U., 1975. Ordained to ministry Ch. of Christ. Minister, Crescent Park Ch. of Christ, Littlefield, Tex., 1959-62, Univ. Ch. of Christ, Canyon, Tex., 1967-75, Broadway Ch. of Christ, Paducah, Ky., 1975-78, Oakcrest Ch. of Christ, Oklahoma City, 1962-67, 78-84, Missouri St. Ch. of Christ, Baytown, Tex., 1984—; mem. adv. bd. Lubbock Christian Coll., Tex., 1959-62, Okla. Christian Coll., Oklahoma City, 1963-70, Freed-Hardeman Coll., Henderson, Tenn., 1975-80. Contbr. articles to religious jours. Republican. Lodge: Rotary. Avocations: jogging; travel; reading; music. Home: 4807 Burning Tree Dr Baytown TX 77521 Office: Missouri St Ch of Christ PO Box 4295 Baytown TX 77520

DENNISON, RAYMOND EVERETT, management consultant; b. Eureka, Calif., Dec. 25, 1938; s. Arthur Lloyd Dennison and Eva Florence (Quen) Dennison Haley; m. Judith Elaine Smith, July 25, 1969 (div. June 1982); children—Deidre, Erik, Astrid, Thaddeus, Thatcher. B.A., Pepperdine U., 1977; grad. Marine Corps Command and Staff Coll., 1979. Commd. 2d lt. U.S. Marine Corps, 1962, advanced through grades to lt. col., 1979, ret., 1982; tng. analyst Info. Spectrum Co., Arlington, Va., 1982-85; pres. AII, Arlington, 1985—. Contbr. articles to mil. jours. Mem. Marine Corps Aviation Assn. (life), Am. Helicopter Soc., Naval Aviation Assn., Naval Helicopter Assn., Assn. of Old Crows. Republican. Episcopalian. Avocations: Alpine skiing; woodworking. Home: 2429E S Walter Reed Dr Arlington VA 22206 Office: AII 4700 King St Suite 420 Alexandria VA 22302

DENSLOW, DAVID ALBERT, JR., economics educator; b. Eustis, Fla., Oct. 28, 1942; s. David Albert and Mary Sallie (Ashmore) D.; m. Nancy Mary Derrick, June 17, 1967; children—Sandra Jane, Sheri Ann. A.B., Earlham Coll., Richmond, Ind., 1964; M.A., Yale U., 1966, Ph.D., 1974. Asst. prof. U. Fla.-Gainesville, 1970-74, assoc. prof., 1975-85, prof. econs., 1985—; vis. prof. Fed. U. Ceará 0, Fortaleza, Brazil, 1972-73, 76-77; cons. World Bank, Washington, 1983. Contbr. articles to profl. jours. Named Tchr. of Yr., Omicron Delta Kappa, 1975, Coll. Bus. Adminstrn., 1974-75, 80-81, 83-84; recipient Disting. Faculty award Fla. Blue Key, 1983. Mem. Am. Econ. Assn., Econometric Soc., Econ. History Assn., Latin Am. Studies Assn., Western Econ. Assn. Methodist. Avocations: tennis, racquetball, running. Home: 3515 NW 7th Pl Gainesville FL 32607 Office: U Fla Dept Econs Gainesville FL 32611

DENSON, ROBERT J., architect; b. Cambridge, Eng., June 22, 1946; came to U.S., 1977; s. Wilfred and Stella Kathleen (Tomkinson) D.; m. Victoria Jane Neumann, May 11, 1985. B.Arch., Birmingham Sch. Architecture, Eng., 1970; M.Arch., Kingston Sch. Architecture, London, 1973. Registered architect, Ga., Tex. Designer, Design Research Unit, London, 1971-73; architect Mayorcas Guest, London, 1973-75; group leader Fitzroy Robinson, London, 1975-77; design architect Aeck Assocs., Atlanta, 1977-81; prin. Denson & Assocs., Atlanta, 1981—; v.p. for landscape, Inman Park Restoration, Atlanta, 1980-82, v.p. for zoning, 1982-84. Mem. Royal Inst. Brit. Architects, AIA, Nat. Trust Hist. Preservation, Downtown C. of C. Atlanta (exec. bd. 1980). Avocations: painting; gliding; trout fishing; archtl. restoration. Office: Denson & Assocs 741 Piedmont Ave Atlanta GA 30308

DENT, JOSEPH BAKER, JR., association executive; b. Portsmouth, Ohio, Oct. 16, 1931; s. Joseph Baker and Hilda (Carpenter) D.; m. Ella Sue Reasor, June 19, 1954; children—Carole Lee, Joe Baker, Kay Carpenter. B.S. with honors, Va. Commonwealth U., 1957; M.Ed., Coll. of William and Mary, 1964; Ph.D., Calif. Coast U., 1983. Personnel adminstr. Miller & Rhoads, Inc., Richmond, Va., 1956-58; tchr. counselor and adminstr. Va. Beach (Va.) pub. schs., 1958-65; asst. prof., chmn. dept. distributive edn. tchr. edn. sect. for B.S. and Merchandising sect. and hotel motel mgmt. sect. for A.A., Old Dominion U., Norfolk, Va., 1965-68; dir. bus., gov., treas. Va. Edn. Assn., Richmond, 1968—, also lobbyist in Va. Assembly, 1972—; cons. for NEA. Served with USAF, 1951-55. Mem. NEA, Va. Edn. Assn., Assn. for Ednl. Data Systems, AAUP, Va. Assn. Sch. Bus. Ofcls., Am. Soc. Assn. Execs., Parliamentary Law Club of Richmond, Phi Delta Kappa. Baptist.

DENTON, BOBBY E., state senator; b. Cherokee, Ala., Aug. 13, 1938; student Ala. public schs.; m. Barbara Jeffreys; children—Julie, Mike, Roger. Vice pres. bus. devel. Bank Ind., Sheffield, Ala.; former commr. Colbert County; mem. Ala. Senate from 1st Dist., 1979—. Mem. Muscle Shoals and Florence C. of C. Mem. Ch. of Christ. Office: Senate Chamber State Capitol Montgomery AL 36130

DENTON, CHARLES CLINTON, ophthalmologist; b. Waldron, Ark., Jan. 8, 1937; m. Jean Fry, Apr. 8, 1979. O.D., So. Coll. Optometry, 1960; M.D., U. Ark., 1970. Diplomate Am. Bd. Ophthalmology. Practice optometry, Ft. Smith, Ark., 1960-64; intern U. Ark. Hosp., Little Rock, 1971-72; resident in ophthalmology U. Tenn. Hosp., Memphis, 1972-75; fellow in disease and surgery of retina and vitreous Washington U. Sch. Medicine-Barnes Hosp., St. Louis, 1975-76; ophthalmologist Valley Eye Clinic and Outpatient Surgery Ctr., Harlingen, Tex., 1976—. Served as capt. USNG, 1970-74. Fellow Am. Acad. Ophthalmology; mem. Am. Soc. Contemporary Ophthalmologists, Internat. Soc. Reactive Surgery, Am. Intraocular Implant Soc., I.C.S., AMA, Tex. Med. Assn., Tex. Med. Found. Republican. Home: 3217 Clifford St Harlingen TX 78550 Office: Valley Eye Clinic & Outpatient Surgery Ctr 1515 Ed Carey Dr Harlingen TX 78550

DENTON, DAN NEAL, JR., petroleum and retail company executive; b. Shreveport, La., Nov. 16, 1954; s. Dan Neal and Joyce (Winn) D.; m. Linda Beth Roby, Apr. 28, 1979. B.B.A., Northeast La. U., 1975. Sr. acct. Peat, Marwick, Mitchell & Co., C.P.A.s, Shreveport, La., 1975-78, supr., Dallas, 1978-80; v.p. fin. JM Petroleum Corp., Dallas, 1980-83; sr. v.p. fin. Shanley Oil Co., Dallas, 1983—. Served to 1st lt. USAR, 1975—. Mem. Am. Inst. C.P.A.s, La. Soc. C.P.A.s, Tex. Soc. C.P.A.s, Ind. Producers Assn. Am. Republican. Methodist. Home: 5734 Brookstown Dallas TX 75230 Office: 2305 Cedar Springs Suite 300Dallas TX 75201

DENTON, JEREMIAH ANDREW, JR., U.S. senator, ret. naval officer; b. Mobile, Ala., July 15, 1924; s. Jeremiah Andrew and Irene Claudia (Steele) D.; student Spring Hill Coll., Mobile, 1942-43, L.H.D. (hon.), 1974; B.S. in Engring., U.S. Naval Acad., 1946; student Armed Forces Staff Coll., 1958-59, Naval War Coll., 1963; M.A. in Internat. Affairs, George Washington U., 1964; m. Kathryn Jane Maury, June 6, 1946; children—Jeremiah Andrew III, Donald, James, William, Madeleine, Michael, Mary Elizabeth. Commd. ensign U.S. Navy, 1946, advanced through grades to rear adm., 1973; aviator, flight instr., staff officer, 1946-65; combat pilot in U.S.S. Independence, 1965; prisoner of war, North Vietnam, 1965-73; research on prisoner of war behavior, attitudes and performance, 1973-74; comdt. Armed Forces Staff Coll., Norfolk, Va., 1974-77; ret., 1977; exec. asst. to pres. Spring Hill Coll., 1977-80; cons. to pres. Christian Broadcasting Network, 1978-80; Sol Feinstone lectr. U.S. Mil. Acad., 1975, U.S. senator from Ala., 1981—, mem. armed services com., judiciary com., labor and human resources com., veterans affairs, chmn., mem. various subcoms. Bd. regents, Spring Hill Coll.; founder Coalition for Decency. Decorated Navy Cross, D.S.M. (Def. Dept. and Navy), Silver Star with two oak leaf clusters, Bronze Star with five oak leaf clusters, D.F.C., Purple Heart with oak leaf cluster, Air medal with oak leaf cluster, Navy Commendation medal; recipient John Paul Jones award Navy League, 1973, Ct. of Honor award Ala. Nat. Exchange Club, Ala. Legislature resolution, 1973, awards Valley Forge Freedoms Found., 1974, 76, For God and Country award Capitol Hill First Friday Club, 1974, Cross of Mil. Service, UDC, 1975, Douglas MacArthur Meritorious Service award Norfolk chpt. Assn. U.S. Army, 1977. Mem. Ends of Earth Soc. (working com.), Am. Legion, VFW (Armed Forces award 1974), Catholic War Vets. (Celtic Cross award 1974). Res. Officers Assn. (hon. life). Roman Catholic. KC (Patriot of Yr. award Princeton, N.J. 1975, Lantern award 1981), Knights of Malta. Author: When Hell Was In Session, 1976. Office: US Senate Washington DC 20510

DENTON, ROGER MARIUS, lawyer; b. Galveston, Tex., Feb. 23, 1946; s. Dan N. and Frances Elizabeth (Hotopp) D. B.A., Loyola U., 1968, J.D., 1971. Bar: La. 1971, U.S. Dist. Ct. (ea. dist.) La. 1971, U.S. Ct. Appeals (5th cir.) 1971, U.S. Supreme Ct. 1976. Practice law, Metairie, La., 1972-75; pres. Roger M. Denton, P.C., Metairie, 1975—. Author: Louisiana Civil Practice Forms, 1985; assoc. editor Loyola Law Rev., 1970-71; editor Record, 1979-80. Vice-chmn. Jefferson Parish Charter Adv. Bd., 1980; chmn. East Jefferson Parish chpt. ARC, 1980-81; pres. Civic Council East Jefferson, 1975-76, Willowdale Civic Assn., 1973-74; mem. Chamber State Legis. Com., 1979—; bd. dirs. LaFreniere Park Found., 1982—, pres., 1984-85; trustee United Way Greater New Orleans, 1983—, exec. com., 1983—; bd. dirs. S.E. La. chpt. ARC, 1982—, exec. com., 1982-85; pres. Vets. Blvd. Bus. Assn., 1982-83. Served to capt. USAR, 1970-71. Recipient Nat. award of Merit, ARC, 1969; Silver Beaver award Boy Scouts Am., 1976; St. George Emblem, Roman Catholic Ch., 1972. Mem. ABA, Assn. Trial Lawyers Am., La. Bar Assn., New Orleans Estate Planning Council, Jefferson Parish Bar Assn., New Orleans and River Region C. of C. (dir. 1980-83). Clubs: Rotary (pres. 1978-79); City (New Orleans). Home: PO Box 73789 Metairie LA 70033 Office: 4900 Veterans Blvd Suite 904 Metairie LA 70006

DENYES, JAMES RICHARD, industrial engineer; b. Detroit, Oct. 9, 1948; s. Heyward Thornton and Rosalie (Blair) D.; B.S. in Indsl. Engring. and Ops. Research, Va. Poly. Inst. and State U., 1970; m. Mary Garcin, Aug. 1, 1970; children—Amy Cheryne, Laura Michelle. Indsl. engr., prodn. control engr., distbn. foreman Allied Chem. Corp., Moncure, N.C., 1970-72; quality control engr. Duke Constrn. Co., Norfolk, Va., 1972-75; command indsl. engr., staff indsl. engr. Navy Manpower and Material Analysis Center, Atlantic, Norfolk, 1975-84, head mgmt. engring. dept., 1981-84; dir. Navy Sch. Work Study, Navy Manpower Engring. Ctr., Norfolk, 1984—. Treas. Va. Orgn. To Keep Abortion Legal, 1977-79, bd. dirs., 1979-81; fin. adv. NOW, 1975-76; pres. B.M. Williams Elem. Sch. PTA, 1982-83, 1st v.p., 1983-84, 1st v.p./pres., 1984-85; mem. standards of quality planning council Chesapeake pub. schs., 1982-83. Mem. Am. Inst. Indsl. Engrs. (sr., bd. dirs. 1977—, pres. Southeastern Va. chpt. 1980-81), Improvement Inst. (trustee 1982-85), Pi Delta Epsilon (President's Cup 1985). Home: 1241 Kingsway Dr Chesapeake VA 23320 Office: NAVMEC Norfolk VA 23511

DE PÍNERO, EUROPA GONZÁLEZ GARRIGA (MRS. JOSE A. DE PINERO), educator; b. Aguadilla, P.R., Feb. 1, 1918; d. Juan C. Gonzalez Giocoechea and Maria Garriga Chacon; B.A. in Edn., U. P.R., 1938, profl. diploma, 1954; M.A. in Edn., N.Y. U., 1956, Ed.D., 1965; J.D., Inter-Am. U. P.R., 1978; m. Jose A. de Pinero, Dec. 22, 1939; children—Jose Juan, Luis Roberto, Europa Maria de Pinero del Valle, Imgard L. Tchr. elementary, jr. and high schs., prin. P.R. Dept. Pub. Instrn., 1938-58, asst. supt., supt. schs., 1960-65; instr. edn., supr. students U. P.R., 1958-60; prof., chmn. dept. edn. Inter Am. U. P.R., Hato Rey, 1966-70, dean acad. affairs, 1970-73, prof. grad. studies Sch. Edn., 1974—. Mem. cons. com. for devel. vocat. and tech. edn. P.R. Dept. Edn.; cons. P.R. Dept. Sch. Prins., 1968—; mem. sch. bd., pres. acad. com. Caribbean Consol. Schs. P.R., 1967-69. Recipient awards for outstanding ednl. work. Mem. Am. Assn. Colls. Tchr. Edn. (Distinguished Achievement award 1969), Assn. for Supervision and Curriculum Devel., Assn. for Childhood Edn. Internat., Am. Assn. for Higher Edn., Nat. Inst. for Advanced Study in Teaching Disadvantaged, Nat. Assn. for Edn. Young Children, Nat. Home Study Council, Am. Acad. Polit. and Social Sci., NEA (life), Tchrs. Assn. P.R., Am. Assn. U. Profs., N.Y. U. Alumni Assn. P.R. (past pres.). Author: Tendencias Ideas Pedagogicas: Su Aplicacion en Puerto Rico, 1971; Accountability and Change in Education, 1972; Schools in Transition, 1973; El Director de las Escuelas Publicas de Puerto Rico: Sus Problemas, Intereses y Necesidades, 1973; Del Quehacer Educativo Puertorriqueno, 1974; Evaluación del Maestro, Sistema de Mérito: Relación con el Derecho Administrativo, 1978; contbr. articles to ednl. jours. Home: 372 R Lamar St Hato Rey PR 00918

DEPLONTY, DUANE EARL, builder, real estate developer; b. Saginaw, Mich., June 1, 1923; s. Earl Edward and Ruth (Bond) DeP.; m. Larraine Sue Kerr, Nov. 23, 1962 (div. 1969); 1 dau., Stacey Sue; m. 2d, Joan Julia Wacker, Jan. 23, 1970; children—Ronald, David, Mary Ann. LL.B., LaSalle U., 1951; A.A., Delta Coll., 1968. Cert. gen. contractor. Pres., DePlonty Constrn., Inc., Punta Gorda, Fla., 1973—, DePlonty Realty, Punta Gorda, 1976—; dir., chmn. Heating, Air Conditioning, Refrigeration and Ventilation Bd., Charlotte County, 1976; mem. Charlotte County Bldg. Bd., 1976-78; pres. Olean Plaza Owners Assn., Port Charlotte, Fla., 1979-83, Sunshine Villas Owners Assn., Port Charlotte, 1977-81. Mem. Nat. Assn. Homebuilders, C. of C., John and Mable Ringling Mus. Art, Tournament Players Club of Prestancia. Republican. Presbyterian. Clubs: Kiwanis, Rotary, Elks, Sarasota Country (dir. 1982-83), Charlotte Harbour Yacht, Punta Gorda Country. Home: 3852 Spyglass Hill Rd Sarasota FL 33583 Office: Villas del Sol - DePlonty Constrn Inc 5656 Bermont Rd Punta Gorda FL 33950

DEPP, DAVID ALAN, thoracic and cardiovascular surgeon; b. New Orleans, Oct. 26, 1942; s. Oren Richard and Alma (Cates) D.; m. Karen Lee Deener, June 13, 1967; children—Kristin Elizabeth, Natalie Andrea. B.A., Tulane U., 1966, M.D., 1967. Diplomate Am. Bd. Surgery, Am. Bd. Thoracic Surgery. Intern U. Utah affiliated Hosps., Salt Lake City, 1967-68; resident in surgery and cardiovascular surgery, 1968-76; surgeon, ptnr. Thoracic and Cardiovascular Clinic, Baton Rouge, 1976—; clin. instr. dept. surgery La. State U. Sch. Medicine. Pres. Baton Rouge chpt. Am. Cancer Soc., 1976-77; pres. Baton Rouge unit Am. Heart Assn., 1981-82. Served to lt. comdr. USN, 1973-75. Mem. ACS, Am. Coll. Cardiology, Am. Coll. Chest Physicians, Soc. Thoracic Surgeons, So. Thoracic Surg. Assn. Republican. Episcopalian. Lodge: Rotary. Office: Thoracic and Cardiovascular Clinic 4750 North Blvd Baton Rouge LA 70806

DEPREE, CAROL MARGARET, psychologist; b. Dixon, Ill., July 6, 1948; d. John Wilkins and Margaret Emily (Minnihan) King; m. James Michael Kelly, June 27, 1970 (div.); m. James Arthur DePree, May 21, 1981; children—Gregory Lee, Sean Patrick, Jeffrey Todd. B.A., No. Ill. U., Dekalb, 1970, M.S., 1973; Ph.D., Pa. State U., 1982. Lic. psychologist, N.C. Case worker Dept. Pub. Aid, Joliet, Ill., 1970-73; researcher, tchr., adminstrv. asst. Pa. State U., 1974-77; instr. U. Wis., 1978-79; children's specialist Clearfield Jefferson Community Mental Health Ctr., DuBois, Pa., 1981-82; staff therapist Counseling Service, Bellefonte, Pa., 1982-83; dir. extended care program Cumberland Hosp., Fayetteville, N.C., 1985; pvt. practice psychology, Fayetteville, N.C., 1986—. Contbr. articles to profl. jours. Mem. Am. Psychol. Assn., Southeastern Psychol. Assn., Nat. Council Family Relations, Southeastern Council Family Relations. Democrat. Roman Catholic.

DEPRIEST, DOUGLAS JUNIOUS, statistician, scientific officer, lecturer; b. Sandston, Va., June 9, 1944; s. James Henry and Octavia (Christian) DeP.; m. Kerdene Mayo, Sept. 3, 1968; children—Marcia, Kraig, Delmar. B.S., Hampton Inst., 1966; M.S., U. Tenn., 1968; Ph.D., Am. U., 1976. Instr. Howard U., Washington, 1968-69; sci. officer Office Naval Research, Arlington, Va., 1971—, dep. for spl. programs, 1984—; lectr. Am. U., Washington, 1979—. Editor: Reliability in Acquisitions Process, 1983; Statistical Analysis of Weather Modification Experiments, 1980. Sec. YMCA, Fairfax, Va., 1983. Served with U.S. Army, 1969-71. Recipient Outstanding Performance award U.S. Navy, 1979, Merit Pay Performance award, 1982, 84. Fellow AAAS; mem. Am. Statis. Assn., Inst. Environ. Sci., Biometrics Soc., Alpha Kappa Mu, Beta Kappa Chi. Avocations: music, reading, sports. Office: Office Naval Research 800 N Quincy St Arlington VA 20017

DERKS, ROBERT ALLAN SCOTT, public relations director, writer; b. Belleville, Ill., Apr. 21, 1951; s. Wayne Gordon and Martha Hope (Lovell) D.; m. Alice Dillard Potter, May 10, 1975; children—Elizabeth Winfield, Marshall Kincaid. A.B. in Journalism, U. S.C., 1973. Reporter Rock Hill Evening Herald (S.C.), 1968-71, The State Newspaper, Columbia, S.C., 1971-73; environ. writer Ft. Myers (Fla.) News Press, 1973-76; dir. pub. info. Richland County Govt., 1976-81; v.p. pub. relations Citizens and So. Nat. Bank S.C., Columbia, 1981—; freelance writer. Pres. S.C. Crafts Assn.; vice chmn. Richland County Friends of the Library. Recipient S.C. AP award for feature writing, 1969; Ralph McGill fellow, 1971; Nat. Headliners award, 1975. Mem. Pub. Relations Soc. Am. Episcopalian. Contbr. numerous articles to mags. in field. Office: PO Box 727 Mktg Dept Citizens and So Nat Bank SC Columbia SC 29222

DE ROJAS, ARTURO, advertising agency executive; b. Matanzas, Cuba, Apr. 5, 1948; came to U.S., 1961, naturalized, 1972; s. Agustin Jose and E. Laura (de la Portilla) de R.; 1 son, Cristian Dale. B.F.A., Tex. Christian U., 1969. Copy dir. Group Three Advt. Corp., Ft. Lauderdale, Fla., 1974-76; v.p., creative dir. Group Two Advt., Inc., Ft. Lauderdale, 1976-78; freelance writer/producer J. Walter Thompson Co., Miami, Fla., 1978-80; copy dir. Posan, Lynn & Co., Ft. Lauderdale, 1980-83; sr. copywriter Steve Walker & Assoc., Ft. Lauderdale, 1983—. Recipient awards Am. Advt. Fedn., Art Dirs. Club N.Y.; Athena award, Telly award. Mem. Advt. Club Ft. Lauderdale, Sigma Phi Epsilon, Alpha Delta Sigma (past chpt. pres.). Home: 9892-C Boca Gardens Pkwy Baco Raton FL 33434

DERRICK, BUTLER CARSON, JR., congressman; b. Sept. 30, 1936; s. Butler Carson and Mary English (Scott) D.; m. Suzanne Mims, Dec. 29, 1960; children—Lydia Gile, Butler Carson, III. Student, U. S.C., 1954-58; LL.B., U. Ga., 1965; Hum.D. (hon.), Lander Coll., 1978. Bar: S.C. bar 1965. Partner firm Derrick & Byrd, Edgefield, S.C., 1970-75; mem. S.C. Ho. of Reps., 1969-74,

94th-98th Congresses from 3d S.C. Dist.; mem. house rules com., select com. on coms., exec. com. environ. study conf. 94th-97th Congresses from 3d S.C. Dist. Pub. study on Congl. Control of Expenditures. Pres. Edgefield County Fish and Game Assn. Named Outstanding Young Man of Year, 1971-72, S.C. Jaycees Assn.; Conservationist of Yr. S.C. Wildlife Fedn., 1977, Nat. Wildlife Fedn., 1977; one of Our Ten Best Friends in Congress Outdoor life mag.; Man of Yr. Anderson chpt. Ducks Unltd., 1980; recipient Disting. River Conservation award Am. Rivers Conservation Council, 1977. Mem. S.C. Bar Assn., ABA, Edgefield County Bar Assn. (past pres.). Democrat. Episcopalian. Home: Stonehenge Rd Edgefield SC 29824 Office: 201 Cannon House Office Bldg Washington DC 20515

DERRICK, CHARLES WARREN, JR., pediatrics educator, pediatrician; b. Mullins, S.C., Nov. 12, 1935; s. Charles Warren and Helen (Slaughter) D.; m. Ann Berry, Aug. 15, 1959; children—Andrea, Hope, Scott. A.B., Wofford Coll., 1958; M.D., Med. Coll. S.C., 1962. Diplomate Am. Bd. Pediatrics. Intern, Greenville Gen. Hosp., S.C., 1962-63; resident in pediatrics U. Ala. Med. Ctr., Birmingham, Ala., 1966-68, infectious disease fellow, 1968-71; dir. outpatient dept. Children's Hosp., Birmingham, 1971-76; from asst. prof. to assoc. prof. U. Ala. Sch. Medicine, 1971-76; practice medicine specializing in pediatrics, Sumter, S.C., 1977; prof., chmn. dept. pediatrics U. S.C. Sch. Medicine, Columbia, 1977—; dir. edn. pediatrics Children's Hosp. of Richland Meml. Hosp., Columbia. Served to capt. M.C., U.S. Army, 1963-65. Fellow Am. Acad. Pediatrics; mem. Infectious Diseases Soc. Am., Internat. Coll. Pediatrics, Ambulatory Pediatric Assn., Am. Fedn. Clin. Research. Methodist. Club: Lancefield Soc. Contbr. articles to profl. jours. Home: 2 Turnberry Ct Columbia SC 29223 Office: Dept Pediatrics University South Carolina 3301 Harden St Columbia SC 29203

DESAI, HARSHKUMAR CHIMANLAL, structural engineer; b. Hansot, Gujarat, India, Nov. 21, 1929; s. Chimanlal Pranvallabhdas and Savita Chimanlal (Vakil) D.; came to U.S., 1964, naturalized, 1974; B.Engring. in Civil Engring., Baroda U., 1954; M.S. in Civil Engring., Columbia, 1966, postgrad., 1966-67; postgrad. Vanderbilt U., 1968-70; m. Prafulla Rameshchandra Hansoty, May 21, 1957; children—Sujata, Amit. Asst. marine surveyor Bombay Govt., 1954-57; asst. civil engr. Kandla (India) Port, 1957-62, Gujarat Refinery, New Delhi, 1962; civil engr. Gujarat Fertilizers Co., Baroda, 1963-64; structural engr. ports Parsons, Brickerhoff, Quade & Douglas, N.Y.C., 1965-66; structural designer Frederic R. Harris, N.Y.C., 1966-67; structural designer bldgs. James Ruderman, N.Y.C., 1967, Weiskopf & Pickworth, N.Y.C., 1967-68; structural designer bridges Barge, Wagoner & Sumner, Nashville, 1968-69; structural designer marine works Van Houten Assos., N.Y.C., 1970-72; sr. structural engr. marine works Frederic R. Harris, Gt. Neck, N.Y., 1972-73; project engr. marine terminals Brown & Root, Houston, 1974-83; engring. div. Ft. Worth dist. U.S. Army C.E., 1983—. Registered profl. engr., N.Y., Tex., Calif. Fellow ASCE. Hindu. Contbr. articles to profl. jours. Home: 712 E Mitchell St Arlington TX 76010 Office: 819 Taylor St Fort Worth TX 76102

DESALVO, JOSEPH SALVATORE, economics educator, researcher; b. Jacksonville, Fla., Aug. 6, 1938; s. John S. and Mary (Costas) DeS.; m. Sandra Ann Birdseye, June 8, 1960; children—Debra Ellen, John Marion. B.A. in Econs., U. Fla., 1960, M.A. in Econs., 1961; Ph.D. in Econs., Northwestern U., 1968. Research economist The Rand Corp., Santa Monica, Calif., 1967-71; assoc. prof. U. Wis., Milw., 1971-75, dept. chmn., 1972-74; vis. research prof. Cath. U. Mons, Belgium, 1974-75; prof. U. Wis., Milw., 1975-83; U. South Fla., Tampa, 1983—; dir. Ctr. for Econ. & Mgmt. Research, U. South Fla., Tampa, 1984—. Author-editor: Perspectives on Regional Transportation Planning, 1975; contbr. articles to profl. jours. Econs.-in-Action fellow Case Inst. Tech., 1962; Univ. fellow Northwestern U., 1963-64. Mem. Am. Econs. Assn., Reg. Sci. Assn., Am. Real Estate & Urban Econs. Assn., Policy Studies Assn. Republican. Mem. Unitarian Universalist. Avocations: piano; jogging. Home: 3210 Stoneybrook Ln Tampa FL 33618 Office: Coll Bus Adminstrn Univ South FL Tampa FL 33620

DESANTIS, LYDIA ANN, nursing educator, anthropologist; b. Monongahela, Pa., Nov. 30, 1939; d. Frank and Albertina (Ferrari) DeS. R.N., Allegheny Gen. Hosp., 1960; B.S. in Nursing, U. Pitts., 1963, M. Nursing Edn., 1967; M.A., U. Wash., 1976, Ph.D., 1979. Staff nurse Allegheny Gen. Hosp., Pitts., 1960-61, instr., 1963-66; instr. U. Pitts., 1967-68, Duke U., Durham, N.C., 1968-69; asst. chief nurse edn. Project Hope, Jamaica, 1969-71; research assoc. U. Wash., Seattle, 1972-76; project coordinator Fred Hutchinson Cancer Research Ctr., Seattle, 1976-78; dir., dean Frontier Sch. Midwifery and Family Nursing, Hyden, Ky., 1979-81; assoc. prof. nursing U. Miami, Fla., 1982—. HEW grantee, 1974-75. Mem. Am. Anthropol. Assn., Am. Nurses Assn., Am. Pub. Health Assn., Nat. Council for Internat. Health, So. Anthropol. Assn., Am. Assn. for World Health, Council on Nursing and Anthropology, Transcultural Nursing Soc., Sigma Theta Tau. Office: U Miami Sch Nursing 1540 Corniche Ave Coral Gables FL 33124

DESHA, DORIS HOLLINGSWORTH, elementary educator; b. Pleasanton, Tex., Sept. 7, 1927; d. Carl and Sallie Jane (Burmeister) Hollingsworth; m. George K. Desha, Jr., May 12, 1951; children—Paul Alan, George K. III. Student U. Tex., 1944-46, 47-48, Sam Houston U., 1949, Tarleton U., 1961-62; B.S., U. N.Mex., 1969, postgrad., 1971-72; M.Ed., Tex. Christian U., 1980. Tchr., Jourdanton, Tex., 1946-47, Leming, Tex., 1949-50, Cost, Tex., 1951; substitute tchr., Big Spring, Tex., Albuquerque, Crowley, Tex., 1964-66, 76-77; tchr. McCollum Elem. Sch., Albuquerque, 1969-75, S.W. Christian Sch., Ft. Worth, 1975-76, St. Andrews Sch., Ft. Worth, 1977-80; elem. tchr. St. Andrews Interparochial Sch., Ft. Worth, 1980—. Mem. South Ft. Worth Bus. and Profl. Women's Club (rec. sec., co-chmn. com. on civic participation, co-chmn. music com.,1st v.p.), Soil Conservation Service Alumni, Am. Assn. Ret. Persons. Alpha Delta Kappa. Democrat. Mem. Ch. of Christ. Home: 1501 Linwood Ln Fort Worth TX 76134 Office: St Andrews Sch 3304 Dryden Rd Fort Worth TX 76109

DESJARDINS, CLAUDE, physiology educator; b. Fall River, Mass., June 13, 1938; s. Armand Louis and Marguerite Jean (Mercier) D.; m. Jane Elizabeth Campbell, June 30, 1962; children—Douglas, Marc, Anne. B.S., U. R.I., 1960; M.S., Mich. State U., 1964, Ph.D., 1967. Staff fellow The Jackson Lab., Bar Harbor, Maine, 1967; asst. prof. dept. physiology Okla. State U., Stillwater, 1968-69, assoc. prof., 1969-72; assoc. prof. physiology U. Tex., Austin, 1970-75, prof. Inst. Reproductive Biology, Patterson Labs., 1975—; research prof., NIH sr. fellow U. Va. Sch. Medicine, Charlottesville, 1983-84; cons. NIH, NASA, VA, FDA, U.S. Dept. Agr. Danforth Found. fellow, 1962; C.F. Wilcox Found. scholar, 1966. Mem. Am. Physiol. Soc., Soc. Exptl. Biology and Medicine, Soc. Neurosci., Soc. Study Reprodn. (pres. 1982-83), Endocrine Soc., Sigma Xi, Phi Kappa Phi, Phi Sigma. Editor: Am. Jour. Physiology: Endocrinology and Metabolism, 1982—; editorial bd. Biology of Reproduction, Endocrinology, Procs. Soc. Exptl. Biology and Medicine. Contbr.articles to profl. jours.; patentee in field. Office: Inst Reproductive Biology Patterson Labs U Tex Austin TX 78712

DESPAIN, JACK D., oil company executive; b. Altus, Okla., Dec. 25, 1936; s. Oscar James and Lois Emeline (Worrell) DeS.; m. Marion Ardena (Dena) Klock, Aug. 22, 1964; children—Heather, Clinton. B.S. in Geology, W. Tex. State U., 1966. Geologist, explorationist Texaco Co., Midland, Tex., 1966-71; regional geologist, explorationist Tenneco Co., Oklahoma City, 1971-72; div. geologist Southwest Gas Pipeline Co., Dallas, 1972-74; v.p. exploration and prodn. Crawford Energy Co., Dallas, 1974-76; ind. oil producer, cons. geologist, owner, pres. Jack DeSpain, Inc., DeSpain Energy Assocs., Inc., Piedmont, Okla., 1976—; cons. Mayor pro-tem, councilman, Murphy, Tex., 1972-76; vice-chmn. Canadian County Republican party, 1981-83; mem. Piedmont Bd. Edn., 1982—. Served with U.S. Army, 1959-62. Mem. Am. Assn. Petroleum Geologists, W. Tex. Geol. Soc., Dallas Geol. Soc., Oklahoma City Geol. Soc., N. Tex. Geol. Soc., Panhandle Geol. Soc. Lodges: Kiwanis (Piedmont); Sertoma (Oklahoma City); Moose (Yukon, Okla.). Home: 4120 Washington Ave W Piedmont OK 73078 Office: 113 Monroe Ave Piedmont OK 73078

DESPAIN, RONALD LEROY, college president; b. Laverne, Okla., Jan. 9, 1940; s. Ora and Opal (Adams) DeS.; m. Arvia Dee Smith, Aug. 25, 1961; children—Teri, Timothy, Todd, Tricia. B.A., Panhandle State U., 1963; M.S., Kans. State U., 1972. Tchr. Liberal High Sch., Kans., 1963-72; counselor Monte Vista High Sch., Colo., 1972-73; dir. student services San Luis Valley Area Vo-Tech., Monte Vista, 1973-76; mgr. student services Tex. State Tech. Inst., Amarillo, 1976, dean instruction, 1976-82, pres., 1982—. Bd. dirs. Llano Estacado council Boy Scouts Am., Amarillo, 1985—; ruling elder Covenant Presbyterian Ch., Amarillo, 1982—. Mem. Am. Vocat. Assn., Am. Tech. Edn. Assn., Tex. Assn. Post-Secondary Occupational Adminstrs., Tex. Vocat. Tech. Assn., Tex. Tech. Soc. (bd. dirs. 1982—), Amarillo C. of C. Lodges: Masons, Rotary. Office: Texas State Tech Inst PO Box 11035 Amarillo TX 79111

DESSAUER, HERBERT CLAY, biochemist, educator; b. New Orleans, Dec. 30, 1921; s. Herbert Andrew and Shirley Ross (Patin) D.; m. Frances Jane Moffatt, Dec. 10, 1949; children—Dan Winston, Rebecca Lynn, Bryan Clay. Cert. in Profl. Meteorology, Calif. Inst. Tech., 1945; B.S., La. State U., 1949, Ph.D., 1952. Instr., La. State U. Med. Ctr., New Orleans, 1951-63, prof. biochemistry, 1963—, acting head dept. biochemistry, 1977-78, research assoc. Mus. Zoology; research assoc. Am. Mus. Natural History, N.Y.C.; adj. prof. biology U. New Orleans. Mem. task force on fluoridation New Orleans Health Planning Council, 1971-72. Served to 1st lt. USAAF, 1943-46. NSF research grantee, 1960—; Am. Philos. Soc. research grantee, 1963. Mem. Am. Phys. Soc., Am. Genetic Assn., Soc. Exptl. Biology Medicine, AAAS, AMA, Am. Soc. Icthyology and Herpetology (pres. 1986), Herpetologists League, Soc. Study Amphibians and Reptiles, Soc. Systematic Zoology. Editor: (with M.S. Hafner) Collections of Frozen Tissues, 1984. Contbr. articles to profl. jours. Office: 1901 Perdido St New Orleans LA 70112

DETCH, ROSALIE STEWART, motel manager, museum manager; b. Parkersburg, W.Va., Oct. 8, 1916; d. John Lawrence and Ethel M. (Flesher) Stewart; m. John Lewis Detch, June 8, 1938 (div. 1972); children—John Lewis, Charlotte Dietz, Paul Stewart, Ethel R. A.B., U. W.Va., 1936; M.A. in Econ., U. Va., 1937. Instr. W. Va. U., Morgantown, 1937-39; legal sec. John L. Detch Atty., Lewisburg, W. Va., 1939-55; motel mgr. Fort Savannah Inn, Lewisburg, 1966—; mus. mgr. Fort Savannah Mus., Lewisburg, 1966—. Mem. Greenbriar County Bd. Edn., Lewisburg, 1950-62, pres., 1961-62. DuPont fellow, 1936-37. Mem. W. Va. Sch. Bds. Assn. (pres. 1958-59), AAUW. Clubs: Bus. and Profl. Women's, Garden. Home: PO Box 924 Lewisburg WV 24901

DETERING, CARL AUGUST, JR., real estate investment company executive; b. Houston, Oct. 28, 1952; s. Carl August and Phyllis (Childs) D. B.B.A., So. Meth. U., 1974. Mng. ptnr. Detering Bros. Investments, Houston, 1974—; chmn. bd. Tex. Am. Bank/Gulfway. Adv. dir. Park People, Inc.; mem. adv. bd. East End Progress Assn., chmn. Econ. Devel. Com.; bd. dirs. Orange Show Found., Sum Arts, Leadership Houston, 1982-83; chmn. bd. Miracle Farm for Children, Inc. Rotary Found. grantee, 1981. Mem. Urban Land Inst., Devel. Policies and Regulations Council. Republican. Presbyterian. Club: Forest Club of Houston. Office: 7007 Gulf Freeway Suite 200 Houston TX 77087

DETHLOFF, HENRY CLAY, historian, educator; b. New Orleans, Aug. 10, 1934; s. Carl Curt and Camelia (Jordan) D.; B.A., U. Tex., Austin, 1956; M.A., Northwestern State U. (La.), 1960; Ph.D., U. Mo., 1964; m. Myrtle Anne Elliott, Aug. 27, 1961; children—Clay, Carl. Mem. faculty dept. history U. Southwestern La., Lafayette, 1962-69, asso. prof., 1967-69; asso. prof. history Tex. A&M U., College Station, 1969-75, prof., 1975—; dir. Southwestern Archives and Manuscripts Collection, U. Southwestern La., 1964-68. Served with USNR, 1956-58. Mem. La. Hist. Assn. (dir. 1968-71), Econ. Hist. Assn., So. Hist. Assn., Agrl. History Assn., Tex. Hist. Assn., Phi Beta Phi, Phi Alpha Theta, Sigma Chi. Republican. Methodist. Author books in field including: Americans and Free Enterprise, 1979; (with others) A History of American Business, 1982. Office: Dept History Tex A&M Univ College Station TX 77843

DE TREVILLE, BRENDA CARTER, hospital official, marketing consultant; b. Sanford, Fla., Jan. 21, 1950; d. Jesse William and Ruby (Brewer) Carter; m. Richard H. de Treville, June 16, 1979. A.A., U. Fla., 1970; B.A. in Communications, U. Central Fla., 1972. Writer various newspapers, Fla., 1966-71; sr. publicist Walt Disney World Co., Lake Buena Vista, Fla., 1971-76; dir. pub. relations and publicity Ringling Bros. Barnum & Bailey Circus World, Haines City, Fla., 1976-78; dir. corp. communications and mktg. Fla. Cypress Gardens, Cypress Gardens, 1978-81; dir. mktg. Six Flags Stars Hall of Fame, Orlando, Fla., 1981-83; mktg. cons. Six Flags Atlantis, Ft. Lauderdale, Fla., 1983; chief mktg. officer AMI's Brookwood Community Hosp., Orlando, 1983—; former co-owner Image Mktg. Group, Orlando; adj. faculty Valencia Community Coll. Second v.p. Mid-Fla. Council Internat. Visitors; bd. dirs. Alumni Council U. Central Fla.; active Internat. Visitors Com. and Travel Action Team; mem. pub. relations adv. council bd. mem. Coll. Journalism and Pub. Relations U. Fla. Named Beauty in Action, Redbook mag., 1974; recipient Flying Orchid award Delta Airlines, 1978; recognition Six Flags Stars Hall of Fame, 1982; 2 Addy awards, 1981, 4 awards, 1982. Mem. Am. Mktg. Assn. (pres.), Fla. Travel Research Assn. (dir.), Pub. Relations Soc. Am., Fla. Pub. Relations Assn. (Fla. Golden Image award 1980, 84, 85), Am. Hosp. Pub. Relations Soc., Orlando Ad Fedn., Orlando Area Tourist Trade Assn. (speaker), Fla. Attractions Assn., Orlando C. of C. (past publicity chmn.), Zeta Tau Alpha. Democrat. Methodist. Lodge: Order Eastern Star. Columnist Tourist World News, Orlando, 1977-78. Home: 8227 Tansy Dr Orlando FL 32819 Office: 1800 Mercy Dr Orlando FL 32808

DEUEL, DEAN EDMOND, medical company executive, pharmacy consultant; b. Niles, Mich., Dec. 18, 1929; s. Frank Bell and Alice Margaret (Sachse) D.; m. Ardyce Elaine Kading, June 8, 1951; children—Scott, Jennifer, Stephanie, Matthew. B.S. in Pharmacy, U. Iowa, 1952. Vice pres. Swanson Super Stores, Cherokee, Iowa, 1960-62; pres. Desco Stores, Audubon, Iowa, 1962-70, Medicine Wagons, Harlan, Iowa, 1970-80; dir. pharmacy Kroger Co., Irving, Tex., 1980-84, Minyard Food Stores, Coppell, Tex.; dir. pharm. Attention Med. Co., Irving, 1984—; cons. Desco Inc., Boone, Iowa, 1960—. Artist creative advt. With publicity dept. Republican Party election of county atty., Harlan, 1975. Nile Kinnick scholar, Iowa Club scholar, U. Iowa, 1948. Mem. Am. Pharm. Assn., Tex. Pharm. Assn., Dallas County Pharm. Assn. Methodist. Clubs: Top O' Dallas (publicity com.), New Horizons (pres.)(Richardson, Tex.). Lodges: Masons, Order Eastern Star, York Rite, Scottish Rite, Shriners. Avocations: gardening; fitness; nutrition. Home: 1202 Huntington Dr Richardson TX 75080 Office: Attention Med Co 3007 Skyway Circle N Irving TX 75038

DEUPREE, JOE LEE, dentist; b. Edmond, Okla., Sept. 11, 1949; s. Clyde and Gloria Lee (Love) D.; m. Susan Van Burkleo, Mar. 24, 1968; children—Toby, Randy. B.S., Okla. State U., 1971; D.D.S., Creighton U., 1975. Pvt. practice dentistry, Paris, Tex., 1975—. Bd. dirs., asst. treas. NETSED Trails council Boy Scouts Am., Paris, 1977—, Bronze Bear award, 1985. Mem. ADA, Tex. Dental Assn., First Dist. Dental Soc. (pres. 1983, peer rev. com. 1981-85. Republican. Mem. Christian Ch. (Disciples of Christ). Club: Paris Golf and Country. Lodge: Elks. Avocation: hunting; golf; camping. Home: 1310 Sherwood Dr Paris TX 75460 Office: 2333 Lamar St Paris TX 75460

DEUTCH, JULIA FLUGER, dietitian; b. N.Y.C., Feb. 26, 1919; d. Max Lowenthal and Clara (Hoffman) Fluger; m. Samuel Deutch, Mar. 6, 1943; 1 dau., Reesa Joan. B.A., Hunter Coll., 1939; postgrad., 1944-45; postgrad. Columbia U., 1945-46. Dietetic intern City Home & Cancer Hosp., N.Y.C., 1939-41; dietitian Triboro Hosp., N.Y.C., 1941-43; with VA Hosp., Bronx, N.Y., 1943-62, asst. chief dietitian, to 1962; chief dietitian VA Hosp., Coral Gables, Fla., 1962-68, Miami, Fla., 1968-75; coordinator dietetic work experience Barry Coll., Miami, 1967-68; lectr. diet therapy U. Miami, 1968-69; mem. task force VA Personnel Utilization, Washington, 1969; chmn. curriculum planning adv. bd. Fla. Internat. U., Miami, 1969—, assoc. community prof., 1972-74; dir. Orientation in Hosp. Dietetics, Marymount Coll., Tarrytown, N.Y., 1970-72; chmn. ad hoc adv. com. VA, 1972-73; chmn. spl. edn. com. Dade County Vocat. Schs., 1968-74; dir. dietetic mgmt. job tng. Miami-Dade Community Coll., 1969-74. Author: Doctors Information Guide, 1970; (monthly pamphlets) Diet-Grams, 1970-74. Recipient Commendation U.S. VA, 1953, Outstanding Performance award, 1966, Superior Performance award, 1969, 71, 72, commendation, 1974; citation Fla. Rehab. Assn., 1968; Cert. of Merit, Jewish War Vets., 1970; Cert. of Appreciation, Lindsay Hopkins Vocat. Sch., Miami, 1974, Fla. Internat. U., 1974. Mem. Am. Dietetic Assn., Fla. Dietetic Assn., Miami Dietetic Assn. (dir. career guidance com. 1970-72, chmn. nominating com. 1971). Republican. Jewish.

DEUTERMAN, JOHN LYNDON, marketing research company executive; b. Elgin, Ill., Aug. 21, 1940; s. Joel LeRoy and Margaret Livingston (Johnston) D.; B.A. in Psychology, Northwestern U., 1962; M.S. in Counseling Psychology, George Williams Coll., 1973; m. Diane Vivienne Leloup, June 30, 1962; children—Joel Andre, Daniel Lyndon, Bradford John, William Fredrick. Project dir. Marplan div. McCann Erickson, Inc., Chgo., 1962-67, Container Corp. Am., Carol Stream, Ill., 1967-72; pres. Deuterman Research Services, Chgo., 1972-74; mgr. mktg. research Texize Chem. Co., Greenville, S.C., 1974-78; dir. mktg. research No Nonsense Fashions, Greensboro, N.C., 1978-83; v.p. Mktg. Workshop, Inc., 1983-84, Adult Ctr. for Creative Living, Inc., 1982-84; pres. Corp. Research Ctr., Inc., 1984—. Mem. Am. Mktg. Assn. (pres. N.C. chpt. 1983), Soc. Consumer Affairs Profls., Chi Phi, Alpha Phi Omega. Home: 106 Fairidge Ct Jamestown NC 27282 Office: 106 Fairidge Ct Jamestown NC 27282

DEUTSCH, ARTHUR, law enforcement official. Chief of police, Birmingham, Ala. Office: City Hall 710 N 20th St Birmingham AL 35020*

DEUTSCH, GARY MARTIN, safety consultant; b. Midland, Tex., June 30, 1953; s. Dayle Martin and Janice (Brown) D.; m. Tommy Joyce Hamilton, June 1, 1974; children—Jon Martin, David Dayle. Student Odessa Coll., 1971-73; indsl. fire fighting cert. Tex. A&M U., 1983. Fire extinguisher inspection lic., Tex. Crew mgr. McDonald's Restaurant, Odessa, Tex., 1970-73; roughneck Johnn Drilling Co., Odessa, 1977-78; route driver supr. Basin Welding Supply Co., Odessa, 1978-81; fire and safety salesman and cons. Thompson's Specialties, Odessa, 1981—. Served with USN, 1973-77. Mem. Am. Soc. Safety Engrs., Internat. Brotherhood Magicians. Mormon. Avocations: fishing; woodworking; magic. Home: 1528 Coronado Ave Odessa TX 79763 Office: Thompson's Specialties 411 W 2d St Odessa TX 79761

DEVENING, ROBERT RANDOLPH, wholesale food company executive; b. San Francisco, Mar. 8, 1942; s. John I. and Jean (Devening) Bolen; m. Susan Church Willis, Feb. 8, 1964; children—Jennifer McQueen, Brian Willis, Jason Bolen. A.B. in Internat. Relations, Stanford U., 1963; M.B.A., Harvard U., 1966. With Price Waterhouse & Co., C.P.A.s, 1963-64, Applied Power Industries, Inc., Milw., 1966-67, Jos. Schlitz Brewing Co., 1967-70, dir. distbn. planning and research, 1969-70; controller Fairmont Foods Co., Omaha, 1970-72; exec. v.p., treas. Ponderosa System, Inc., Dayton, Ohio, 1972-75; v.p. fin. Wilson Foods Co., Oklahoma City, 1975-79; sr. v.p. fin. and adminstrn. Fleming Cos., Inc., Oklahoma City, 1979-82, exec. v.p. fin. and adminstrn., 1982—, also dir.; advt. dir. Arkwright-Boston Ins. Co.; dir. Liberty Fin. Corp. Trustee Casady Sch. Mem. Fin. Execs. Inst., Stanford Alumni Club Wis. (pres. 1968), Harvard Bus. Sch. Club Milw. (sec.-treas. 1968-69). Home: 6921 Avondale Ct Oklahoma City OK 73116 Office: 6301 Waterford Blvd Box 26647 Oklahoma City OK 73126

DEVINE, PATRICK JAMES, psychology educator, consulting management psychologist; b. Milw., Mar. 11, 1952; s. Donald H. and Dee L. D.; m. Mary Ann Nancy Steck, Jan. 8, 1977. B.A. in Psychology, John Carroll U., 1974; M.Ed. in Counseling Psychology, Ga. State U., 1975; Ph.D. in Indsl.-Organizational Psychology, Ill. Inst. Tech., 1980. Lic. applied psychologist, Ga. Indsl.-organizational psychologist, Atlanta, 1977—; mgmt. cons. Donald Shepherd and Assocs., Chgo., 1978-80; asst. prof. psychology Kennesaw Coll., Marietta, Ga., 1980—. Chmn. study group program Leadership Cobb, Marietta, 1984-85. Mem. Am. Psychol. Assn., Southeastern Psychol. Assn., Soc. Indsl.-Organizational Psychology, Southeastern Indsl.-Organizational Psychol. Assn., Cobb C. of C. Roman Catholic. Lodge: KC. Avocations: athletics; model railroading; stained glass. Home: 5767 Shawn Terr Norcross GA 30092 Office: Kennesaw Coll Marietta GA 30061

DEVLIN, ROBERT MANNING, insurance company executive; b. Bklyn., Feb. 28, 1941; s. John Manning and Norma (Hall) D.; m. KatharineBareis, Sept. 13, 1961; children—Michael Hall, Matthew Bareis. B.A. in Econs., Tulane U., 1964. C.L.U. Various positions Mut. Life Ins. Co. N.Y., 1964-77; v.p., asst. to pres. Calif. Western States Life Ins. Co., Sacramento, 1977-80, sr. v.p., 1980; exec. v.p., dir. Life and Casualty Ins. Co. Tenn., Nashville, 1980—, Nat. Life and Accident Ins. Co., 1983—; dir. Am. Gen. Life Ins. Co. Okla., Am. Gen. Life Ins. Co. Del. Bd. dirs., mem. exec. com., v.p. Jr. Achievement, Nashville, 1981—; trustee, mem. exec. com. Father Ryan High Sch., Nashville, 1981—. Mem. Am. Soc. C.L.U.s, Nat. Assn. Life Underwriters. Roman Catholic. Clubs: Belle Meade Country, Nashville City. Home: 4417 Howell Pl Nashville TN 37205 Office: Life and Casualty Ins Co Tenn American General Center Nashville TN 37250

DEVRIES, WILLIAM CASTLE, cardiovascular surgeon; b. Bklyn., Dec. 19, 1943; m. Ane Karen Olsen, June 12, 1965; 7 children. B.S. cum laude, U. Utah, 1966, M.D., 1970. Diplomate Nat. Bd. Med. Examiners, Am. Bd. Surgery, Am. Bd. Thoracic Surgery. NSF fellow U. Utah Sch. Medicine, Salt Lake City, 1967, research assoc. div. artificial organs, 1967-84; intern in surgery Duke U. Med. Ctr., Durham, N.C., 1970-71, asst. resident, 1971-72, NIH scholar in acad. surgery, 1971-74, research fellow in surgery and physiology, 1972-74, sr. asst. resident in gen. and thoracic surgery, 1974-77, chief resident, 1977-78, teaching scholar cardiothoracic surgery, 1978-79; asst. prof. surgery U. Utah Sch. Medicine, Salt Lake City, 1979-83, chmn. div. cardiothoracic surgery, 1980-84, assoc. prof., 1983-84; dir. artificial heart project Humana Heart Inst. Internat./Heart Internat. Found., Inc., Louisville, 1984—; chief cardiothoracic service Salt Lake City VA Med. Ctr., 1979-84; Irvin Goldhart lectr., Toronto, Ont., Can., 1983; Alpha Omega Alpha vis. prof. Duke U., 1983; Francis Fisher Meml. lectr. Am. Dietetic Assn., 1983; Meadowbrook lectr., Oakland, Mich., 1984; Alpha Omega Alpha vis. prof. Mt. Sinai Med. Ctr., N.Y.C., 1984. Contbr. numerous articles to profl. jours., chpts. to books. Grantee N.C. Heart Assn., Am. Health Assistance Found., others. Physician, Nat. Ice Skating Championships, 1980; mem. exec. council Inst. Biomed. Engring., 1980-83; bd. dirs. Kolff Med. Inc.; mem. R&D com. Utah Heart Assn., 1981-84, bd. dirs., 1981-84; bd. dirs. Inst. Artificial Heart Research, Salt Lake City, 1983-84. Mem. Internat. Soc. Heart Transplantation, Am. Soc. Artificial Internal Organs, Assn. VA Surgeons, Soc. Thoracic Surg. Edn., Deryl Heart Surg. Soc., AMA, ACS, Alpha Epsilon Delta, Alpha Omega Alpha, Phi Eta Sigma, Phi Kappa Phi. Office: 718 Medical Towers N 624 S Floyd St Louisville KY 40202

DEW, JESS EDWARD, chemical engineering executive; b. Okemah, Okla., July 18, 1920; s. Jess Edward and Colleen Avara (Norman) D.; student Okla. Mil. Acad., 1939-41; B.S. in Chem. Engring., U. Okla., 1943; M.S. in Chem. Engring., MIT, 1948; m. Mary Ann Burns, Jan. 3, 1944; children—Anne, Stephen Dodson, David Burns; m. Sarah Shimoon Kelley, Feb. 4, 1984. Registered profl. engr., Okla. Asst. chem. engr. Exxon, Baytown, Tex., 1943-47; chem. engr. Amoco, Tulsa, 1948-52; v.p. engring. John Deere Chem. Co., Pryor, Okla., 1952-63; gen. supt. John Deere Planter Works, Moline, Ill., 1963-65; v.p. mfg. Arkia Chem. Corp., Helena, Ark., 1965-69; project mgr. Chem. Constrn. Co., N.Y.C. hdqrs., 1969-74, posts included Gt. Britain, 1969-71, Argentina, 1971, Saudi Arabia, 1971-72, Algeria, 1972-74; ind. cons. engr., 1974-78; constrn. mgr. W.R. Holway & Assocs., Tulsa, 1978-82; v.p., gen. mgr. R.L. Frailey, Inc., Tulsa, 1982—; pres., dir. Pryor Indsl. Conservation Co., 1961-63. Mem. Pryor Mcpl. Utility Bd., 1955-60, Pryor City Council, 1962-63, Rivers and Harbor Commn., Helena, 1966-70; adv. bd. Sacred Heart Acad., 1967-69; bd. dirs. Helena United Fund, 1969. Mem. Am. Inst. Chem. Engrs., ASME, Am. Chem. Soc., Nat. Eagle Scout Assn., Sigma Xi, Beta Theta Pi, Alpha Chi Sigma, Tau Beta Pi. Republican. Roman Catholic. Clubs: Tulsa, Okmulgee Country, Elks, Rotary. Contbr. articles to profl. jours. and books. Patentee in field. Home: 120 S Prairie Ave Okmulgee OK 74447 Office: 5200 S Harvard Ave Tulsa OK 74135

DEWAR, MILDRED (JO) ELLER (MRS. DONALD NORMAN DEWAR), librarian; b. Wilkesboro, N.C., Nov. 9, 1925; d. Charles Franklin and Golda (Velt) Eller; student Brevard Coll., 1942-44; diploma Jr. Coll., 1944; A.B., Berea Coll., 1946; B.S. in L.S., U. N.C., 1948; postgrad. Barry Coll., U. Fla., U. Miami; m. Donald Norman Dewar, Mar. 6, 1954; 1 dau., Heather. Tchr.-librarian Mountain View High Sch., Hays, N.C., 1946-47; chief librarian Tenn. Wesleyan Coll., Athens, 1948-50; dept. head U. Tex. Library, Austin, 1951; librarian U.S. Army Spl. Services, Ft. Jackson, S.C., 1951-52; chief post library system, Ft. Stewart, Ga., 1952-54; librarian Olsen Jr. High Sch., Dania, Fla., 1955-56; librarian Lauderdale Manors Sch., Ft. Lauderdale, Fla., 1956-63; head readers services Miami-Dade Jr. Coll. Library, Miami, Fla., 1963-70; library dir. Miami-Dade Community Coll., South, 1970—, chmn. library services steering com., 1983-84; chmn. library task force S.E. Fla. Consortium, 1982-83; mem. learning resources standing com. Fla. Council Instructional Affairs; vis. instr. library edn. U. Ga., summer 1967. Editorial bd. Community and Jr. Coll. Libraries, 1982—; contbr. articles to profl. jours. Co-exec. dir. Nat. Library Week Fla., 1966. Mem. AAUW (past br. v.p.), Am., Fla. library assns., Fla. Assn. Sch. Librarians (past pres.), Delta Kappa Gamma. Home: 3520 Crystal View Ct Coconut Grove FL 33133 Office: 11011 SW 104 St Miami FL 33176

DEWES, CRAIG ALLAN, training executive; b. Bklyn., May 17, 1954; s. Peter George and Harriet (Axthelm) D.; m. Laurie Studer, Aug. 11, 1979; 1 child,

Jennifer Lynn. B.A., Ramapo Coll. N.J., 1977; M.A., Towson State U., 1979. Tchr. aid Bergen Ctr., Englewood, N.J., 1976-77; grad. asst. Towson State U., Md., 1978-79; tng. specialist State Va. Southside Va. Tng. Ctr., Petersburg, 1979-81; mgr. tng. Merck, Sharp and Dohme, Elkton, Va., 1981—; cons. D.D. profl. com. Bethany Coll., Oak Brook, Ill., 1983-85. Mem. Am. Soc. Tng. and Devel. (program planning 1981-85, v.p., pres.-elect Blue Ridge chpt. 1986), Internat. Assn. Quality Circles. Methodist. Avocations: pilot; photography; woodworking. Home: 831 N Blue Ridge Dr Harrisonburg VA 22801 Office: Merck Sharp and Dohme PO Box 7 Elkton VA 22827

DEWHIRST, H(AROLD) DUDLEY, management educator, consultant; b. Balt., Oct. 25, 1931; s. Harold Hodgkins and Georgia Seymour (Harness) D.; m. Zara Beth Pape, May 25, 1968; children—William Gregory, Hillary Ellen. B.S. in Civil Engring., Va. Poly. Inst., 1953; M.B.A., Harvard U., 1957; Ph.D., U. Tex., 1970. Registered profl. engr., Va. Engr., econ. analyst Esso Standard Oil Co. (now Exxon Corp.), Baton Rouge, 1957-61; group head Humble Oil & Refining Co. (now Exxon Corp.), Houston, 1962-65; sr. analyst refining coordination Standard Oil of N.J. (now Exxon Corp.), N.Y.C., 1966-67; mem. faculty U. Tenn., Knoxville, 1969—, prof. mgmt., 1977—; cons. in field. Contbr. numerous articles on mng. engrs. and tech.-based orgns. to profl. jours., 1971—. Co-patentee two-stage hydrofining of light oils. Served to 1st lt. C.E., U.S. Army, 1953-55. Grantee NSF, 1974-77, Martin Marietta Energy Systems, 1983-84. Mem. Acad. Mgmt. Avocations: jogging; raising azaleas. Home: 2124 Indian Hills Dr Knoxville TN 37919 Office: U Tenn Dept Mgmt 409 SMC Knoxville TN 37996

DEWITT, CYNTHIA SUE CHAZARRA, geologist; b. Nashville, Mar. 11, 1957; d. Richard Anthony Ormand Chazarra and Margaret Mae (Stanfield) Penticuff; stepchild James Phillip Penticuff; m. Joseph Patrick DeWitt, May 26, 1984. B.A. in Geology, U. Tenn., 1980. Well logger Core Labs., Houston, 1981-82; asst. geologist Sohio Petroleum Corp., Houston, 1982—. Mem. Houston Geol. Soc., Am. Assn. Petroleum Geologists, Geol. Soc. Am., Nat. Assn. Female Execs., LWV. Democrat. Mem. Ch. of Christ. Home: 11618 Brook Meadows Ln Meadows TX 77477 Office: Sohio Petroleum Co 9401 SW Freeway Suite 1200 Houston TX 77074

DEWITT, FRANKLIN ROOSEVELT, lawyer; b. Conway, S.C., May 25, 1936; s. Matthew A. and Rebecca (Hughes) DeW., m. Willa Waylis Johnson, Aug. 20, 1960; children—Rosalyn Abravaya, Sharolyn Rene. B.S., S.C. State Coll., 1962; J.D., 1964; cert. urban affairs adminstrn. Ga. State U., 1974. Bar: S.C. 1964, D.C., 1966. Trial atty. CSC, Washington, 1965-67; sole practice law, Conway, S.C., 1967—. Mem. Conway City Council, 1968—; mem. Waccamaw Econ. Opportunity Council, 1968-81, treas. to 1981; del. Nat. Democratic Party Conv., 1972, 76, 80; sec. Dem. Precinct Com.; chmn. Waccamaw Mental Health Ctr. Served with USAF. Named Father of Yr., Cherry Hill Baptist Ch., 1972, Usher of Yr., 1978, recipient Disting. Service in Housing award Horry County. Mem. ABA, Nat. Bar Assn., Horry County Bar Assn., S.C. Bar Assn. Home: 1708 Hwy 378 Conway SC 29526 Office: 510 Hwy 378 Conway SC 29526

DEWITT, NANCY ELLEN, training coordinator; b. Baton Rouge, June 26, 1949; d. Paul L. and Martha E. (Russell) DeW. B.S., La. State U., 1971, M.Ed., 1976. Cert. pub. mgr. Tng. officer Villa Feliciana Hosp., Jackson, La., 1973-75; tng. coordinator La. Dept. Health and Human Resources, Baton Rouge, 1975-81; tng. dir. La. Dept. Revenue, Baton Rouge, 1981-82; training coordinator La. Dept. Civil Service, Baton Rouge, 1982—; mem. staff Gov.'s Com. of 100, Baton Rouge, 1984—. Instr., ARC, 1985. Mem. La. Intergovtl. Tng. Council, Am. Soc. Tng. and Devel. (cht. pres. 1985), La. Cert. Pub. Mgr. Soc. (past chpt. pres.), Am. Soc. Pub. Adminstrn. Democrat. Episcopalian. Avocation: photography. Office: La Dept Civil Service 5700 Florida St Baton Rouge LA 70806

DEWOLFE, JAMES PERNETTE, III, financial company executive; b. Carthage, Mo., Sept. 17, 1946; s. James Pernette and Doris Eliody (Monroe) DeW.; m. Peggy Ruth Ball, Sept. 26, 1970; children—Leah Lynette, Allison Pilar, James Pernette. Student, U. of South, 1964-67. With UNICO Holding Co., Ft. Worth, 1970-71; mgmt. DeWolfe Investment Co., Dallas, 1972-78; pres., chief exec. officer, chmn. bd. Universal Leasing Corp., Dallas, 1978—, 1978—; pres., chief exec. officer, chmn. bd. First U.S. Financial, 1983—. Mem. Am. Assn. Equipment Leasors, Phi Gamma Delta. Republican. Episcopalian. Clubs: River Crest Country, Century II, Fort Worth; University (Dallas). Home: 5 Shenandoah Pl Richardson TX 75080 Office: 8131 LBJ Freeway Suite 275 Dallas TX 75251

DEWS, JAMES KIRK, pharmaceutical company executive, laboratory technologist, rancher; b. Fort Worth, July 27, 1935; s. James Dacosta and Majorie Lenore (Black) D.; m. Barbara Ann Mims, May 20, 1955; children—Donna Sheree, Cheryl Deann, James Galen. Student U. Tex.-Arlington, 1956, Tex. Wesleyan Coll., 1960-62. Regional sales dir. Wampole Labs., Stamford, Conn., 1963-70; pres. Ion Labs., Hurst, Tex., 1970-71; pres., chief exec. officer Dews Co., Inc., Mineral Wells, Tex., 1971—; researcher in orthomolecular and preventive medicine fields. Served as pvt. U.S. Army, 1957-59. Mem. Am. Chem. Soc., Am. Assn. Bioanalysts, Tex. Assn. Bus., Mineral Wells C. of C. Republican. Methodist. Club: Petroleum (Fort Worth). Contbr. articles to sci. publs.; patentee in field.

DEY, DIPAK KUMAR, statistics educator, researcher; b. Calcutta, West Bengal, India, Aug. 12, 1953; came to U.S., 1975, naturalized, 1983; s. Debendra Nath and Renuka (Ghosh) D.; m. Rita Roy Chowdhury, June 3, 1977; 1 child, Debosri. B.A. in Stats. with honors, Indian Statis. Inst., Calcutta, 1974, M.Stats., 1975; M.S., Purdue U., 1977, Ph.D., 1980. Teaching asst., research asst. Purdue U., West Lafayette, Ind., 1975-79; vis. scholor Stanford U., Calif., 1979-80; vis. faculty U. Ky., Lexington, 1980-82, asst. prof. statistics Tex. Tech U., Lubbock, 1982—. Contbr. articles to profl. jours. David Ross fellow Purdue U., 1978. Mem. Inst. Math. Stats., Am. Statis. Assn. Home: 6402 Albany 1008 Lubbock TX 79424

DEZA, ERNESTO CABANGAL, psychiatrist; b. Iloilo City, Philippines, Aug. 6, 1923; came to U.S., 1953; s. Honorio Donasco and Ursula Diamante (Cabangal); m. Mary Brillantes, Nov. 12, 1949; children—Alfonso, Zenaida, Edmundo. A.A., U. San Agustín, 1946; M.D., U. Santo Tomás, 1951. Clin. dir. State Hosp. So., Blackfoot, Idaho, 1976-79; dir. clin. Western State Hosp., Hopkinsville, Ky., 1970-72; dir. Acute Intensive Services, Richmond, Ind., 1972-76; dir. Female Psychiat. Services of Tulsa, Vinita, Okla., 1978-83; dir. Gero-Psychiat. Services, Eastern State Hosp., Vinita, Okla., 1983—. Acting mayor Anilao, Philippines, 1942-43; pres. Vox Populi Civic Movement, 1942-43; chmn. Mental Health Com. of Idaho, 1969. Served with U.S. Armed Forces, 1941-45; Far East. Recipient Physician's Recognition award AMA, 1983. Mem. Am. Psychiat. Assn., Okla. Med. Assn., Philippine Med. Assn., World Med. News Panel, Miami Writer's Assn., Lyrical Guild of Iowa, Catholic Psychiatrist's Guild, Am. Cardiac Assn. Roman Catholic. Clubs: Lions, Holy Ghost Men's, ESH Jour., Auto of Okla. Author: Pay Back, 1951; Filipino Laugh Poems, 1969; New Laugh Poems, 1975; Philippine Psychiatry, 1968; The Psychiatrist, 1980; columnist: Our Health, 1960-70; artist: Search, 1969 (U. Phillipines prize winner). Home: 13 First ESH St Vinita OK 74301

DHALIWAL, SHER WINGH, economist, consultant; b. Pathereri J.S., Punjab, India, Apr. 15, 1937; came to U.S., 1962, naturalized, 1971; s. Sardar Jethasingh and Sharimati (Kauran) D.; m. Jan. 16, 1971 (div. Mar. 1980); children—Rajwant, Bhagwant, Herman Kaj, Michael S. B.A., Punjab U., 1957; M.A. in Sociology, Howard U., 1967; M.A. in Econs., Cath. U., 1976, Ph.D. in Econs. Research assoc. Far Eastern Econ. Rev., Hong Kong, 1961-62; fiscal officer Madison Mgmt., Washington, 1970-78; chief economist, energy Sterling Systems, McLean, Va., 1979-83; chief economist, prin. analyst Systems Planning Corp., Arlington, Va., 1984—. Author: (with Dick Wilson) Hong Kong Register, 1962; (with Kaiser Sung) Asian Textiles, 1962; econ. research studies for U.S. Postal Service, Jet Propulsion Lab., Pasadena, Calif., U.S. Army. Contbr. articles to profl. jours. Mem. Am. Econ. Assn., Inst. Cost Analysis (cert. cost analyst), Smithsonian Instn. Democrat. Home: 1625 Valencia Way Reston VA 22090

DHANDA, RAHUL, economics educator; b. Khartoum, Sudan, Aug. 31, 1956; came to U.S., 1969, naturalized, 1980; s. Roy Chand and Rani (Sood) D. B.A. in Econs., George Mason U., 1978, M.A. in Econs., 1980, Ph.D. in Econs., 1985. Economist J.W.K. Internat. Corp., Annandale, Va., 1979-81; lectr. econs. No. Va. Community Coll., Woodbridge, Va., 1981-83; researcher World Bank, Washington, 1983; asst. prof. econs. George Mason U., Fairfax, Va., 1984. cons. Enviro-Mgmt. & Research Springfield, Va., 1982; fellow Georgetown U., Washington, 1982-83. Contbr. articles to profl. jours. Soccer coach Alexandria Soccer Assn., 1973-75, Vienna Boys League, 1982. Mem. Am. Econ. Assn., Western Econ. Assn., Nat. Econs. Soc., Am. Statis. Assn. Hindu. Avocations: bridge, chess, movies. Home: 3139 Ellenwood Dr Fairfax VA 22031 Office: George Mason U 4400 University Dr Fairfax VA 22030

DIACON, FRANCES MARIE, educator for deaf; b. Davis, Okla., Dec. 16, 1933; d. Trice H. and Ruth (Thomason) Birch; m. Glen E. Diacon, May 5, 1956; 1 son, Glen E. B.S., East Central U., Ada, Okla., 1971; M.S., U. Okla., 1974. Cert. elem. edn., deaf and hard of hearing. With A.S. Barnhill, H.H. Earles & David Webb., 1954-59, Kermac Nuclear Fuels, Grants, N.Mex., 1959-60, Grants State Bank, 1962-63; jr. acct. Continental Divide Elec. Coop., Grants, 1964-66, Home Stake Sapien Ptnrs., Grants, 1966-67; tchr. Okla. Sch. for Deaf, Sulphur, 1971—. Active PTA, 1971—, High Sch. Wrestling Booster Club, 1973-80; tchr. Sunday sch. class for deaf children Bapt. Ch., 1975—. Mem. NEA, Okla. Edn. Assn., Conv. Am. Instrs. of Deaf, Phi Delta Kappa. Lodge: Order Eastern Star. Home: 26003 W 14th St Sulphur OK 73086 Office: Okla Sch for the Deaf Sulphur OK 73086

DIAMOND, HARVEY JEROME, machinery manufacturing company executive; b. Charlotte, N.C., Dec. 7, 1928; s. Harry B. and Jeanette R. (Davis) D.; B.B.A., U. N.C., 1952; m. Betty L. Ball, May 22, 1953; children—Michael A., Leah Beth, David A., Abby. Sales mgr. Dixie Neon Supply House, Charlotte, N.C., 1951-61; pres., sr. exec. officer Plasti-Vac, Inc., Charlotte, 1961—; pres., chmn. bd. Diamond Supply, Inc., Charlotte, 1971—; founder, pres. PVI Internat. Inc., internat. sales corp., 1981—; del. White House Conf. Small Bus., 1979, 80; mem. regional dist. export council Dept. Commerce, 1980—. Instr. Practical Politics in Action, Charlotte C. of C., 1966, 67, 68, 78; bd. dirs. OIC, Charlotte, Charlotte Fgn. Trade Zone No. 57, 1983—; mem. adv. bd. Phieffer Coll., Misenheimer, N.C., 1979—; vice chmn. Mecklenburg Democratic Com., 1970-72, chmn., 1974-75, treas., 1972-74, del. Dem. Nat. Conv., 1972. Served with U.S. Army, 1952-54. Recipient awards March of Dimes, 1966, U.S. Dept. Commerce, 1967; Gov.'s award for excellence in bus. exporting, 1981, 85. Mem. Soc. Plastic Engrs. (award 1970), Nat. Eelctric Sign Assn., Small Bus. Assn. S.E. (dir. 1979), C. of C. (internat. task force), N.C. World Trade Assn. (dir. 1983—, gen. chmn. ann. conv. 1984), Southeast Sign Assn. (dir. 1983—), Metrolina World Trade Club (v.p. 1982-83, pres. 1983-84). Jewish. Clubs: Charlotte Athletic, Cotswold Optimist, Metrolina World Trade (pres. 1983-84). Lodges: Masons, Shriners. Author: (manual) Introduction to Vacuum Forming, 1976; patentee in field of plastic thermoforming machinery. Home: 6929 Folger Dr Charlotte NC 28211 Office: PO Box 5543 Charlotte NC 28225

DIAZ, JULIO CESAR, computer science educator; b. Trujillo, Colombia, Dec. 3, 1948; came to U.S., 1970; s. Luis Eduardo and Josefina (Velasco) D.; m. Pamela Sue Jenkins, Aug. 19, 1978; children—Diana Cristina, Adriana Carolina. Lic. Math., U. de los Andes, 1970; M.A., Rice U., 1974, Ph.D., 1975. Prof., U. de Los Andes, Bogotá, Colombia, 1970; postdoctoral fellow U. Ky., Lexington, 1974-75, asst. prof., 1975-81; vis. asst. prof. U. Toronto, Ont., Can., 1978-79; sr. research mathematician Mobil Research and Devel., Dallas, 1981-84; assoc. prof. computer sci. U. Okla., Norman, 1984—. Contbr. articles to profl. jours. Scholar U. Andes, 1967-69; Rice U. fellow, 1970-74; summer faculty fellow U. Ky., 1975-76. Mem. Sociedad Colombiana de Matemáticas, Soc. Indsl. and Applied Math., Soc. Petroleum Engring., Soc. Exploration Geophysicists. Office: Univ Okla 202 W Boyd Room 219 Norman OK 73019

DIAZ-BUXO, JOSE A., internist, nephrologist educator; b. Caquas, P.R., June 2, 1946; s. Jorge Diaz and Mary R. (Buxo) D. B.S., U. P.R., San Juan, 1967. M.D., 1970; M.S. in Medicine, U. Minn., 1975. Diplomate Nat. Bd. Med. Examiners, Am. Bd. Internal Medicine, Am. Bd. Nephrology. Intern. Mayo Grad. Sch. Medicine, Rochester, Minn., 1970-71, resident in medicine, 1971-73, trainee nephrology, 1973-75; cons. nephrology Nalle Clinic Kidney Ctr., Charlotte, N.C., 1975-82, co-dir., 1978-81, med. dir., 1981-82; med. dir. Metrolina Kidney Ctr., 1982—; assoc. internal medicine, nephrology Charlotte Meml. Hosp., 1975-79, attending internal medicine, nephrology hosp., med. ctr., 1980—; clin. instr. dept. medicine U. N.C., Chapel Hill, 1975-76, clin. asst. prof., 1977-78, clin. assoc. prof., 1979—; com. Health Care Fin. Adminstrn. Study, 1978-79; cons. ESRD program Health Standards and Quality Bur., 1979-81, Franklin Research Ctr., Phila., 1981—; chmn. med. adv. bd. Nat. Kidney Found., N.C., 1980-81; med. rev. bd. N.C. Kidney Council, 1982—. Bd. visitors Charlotte Country Day Sch., 1983—; pres. nephrology div. Mayo Alumni Soc., 1981-83. Served to maj. M.C., USAR, 1971-83. Nat. Kidney Found. postdoctoral fellow, 1974. Fellow ACP, Internat. Soc. Artificial Organs, Am. Soc. Artificial Internal Organs, Internat. Soc. Nephrology, Am. Soc. Nephrology, AMA, Southeastern Regional Organ Procurement Found., Southeastern Dialysis, Transplantation Assn., Am. Soc. Internal Medicine, N.C. Med. Soc., Mecklenburg County Med. Soc. (N.C.), Renal Physicians Assn., N.C. Kidney Found. (med. adv. com. 1976-79, chmn. 1979-80, bd. mem. 1978—), Mecklenburg Kidney Found. (med. adv. com. 1975—, bd. dirs., 1978—, Network Coordinating Council N.C., N.Y. Acad. Scis., Minn. State Med. Assn. (1971-76), Alpha Omega Alpha, Sigma Xi. Club: Quail Hollow Country (Charlotte) Inventor Continuous Cyclic Peritoneal Dialysis; contbr. numerous articles, book chpts., abstracts to publs. editorial bd. dialysis publs. Office: 928 Baxter St Charlotte NC 28204

DIAZ-RIVERA, LUIS RAFAEL, educator; b. Santa Isabel, P.R., Nov. 8, 1940; s. Rafael and Matilde Diaz; A.S., U. P.R., 1962, B.A., 1964, profl. diploma, 1968, M.A., 1970; Ph.D., Lehigh U., 1976; m. Betty Vega, June 1, 1968. Tchr., counselor, prin., supr. pub. schs., Santa Isabel, 1964-70; prof. edn. Cath. U. P.R., 1970-77, Inter Am. U., Ponce, P.R., 1978-79, World U., Ponce, P.R., 1979-81; assoc. prof. edn., chmn. dept. Colegio Universitario Metropolitano, San Juan, P.R., 1981-82, dean acad. affairs, 1982—, faculty rep. Acad. Bd., Adminstrv. Council, 1981-86; dean acad. affairs U. Ponce, 1977-78; cons. to pvt. schs., 1970—; lectr. in field; mem. bd. Colegio ERGOS. Vol. counselor to community youth; adv. CREA (rehab. centers for drug addicts); cum and UMETcoordinator Institutional Self-Study for Accreditation, re-accr. processor, 1981-85. Named disting. educator Santa Isabel Sch. Dist., 1983; recipient Chancellor's plaque, 1983. Mem. Am. Personnel and Guidance Assn., Tchrs. Assn. P.R., Rehab. Counselors Assn. P.R., Phi Delta Kappa (founder, pres. 1974, Disting. Kappan award 1976). Author articles in field. Home: A-10 San Miguel Santa Isabel PR 00757

DIAZ-VERSON, SALVADOR, JR., insurance company executive; b. Havana, Cuba, Dec. 31, 1951; s. Salvador and Metodia Diaz-V.; m. Patricia Dianne Floyd, Apr. 24, 1976; 1 son, Salvador III. B.A. in Fin., Fla. State U., Tallahassee, 1973. Chief investment officer Am. Family Life Assurance, Columbus, Ga., 1977-79; exec. v.p. Am. Family Corp., Columbus, 1980-83, pres., 1983—, also dir.; dir. Phenix Girard, Phenix City, Ala., 1978—. Sec. Am. Family Polit. Action Com., 1983; bd. dirs. United Way, Columbus, 1983—; mem. vocat. tng. adv. com. Muscogee County Sch. Dist., Columbus, 1983—. Mem. Columbus C. of C. (dir. 1983—). Democrat. Roman Catholic. Clubs: Green Island Country, Country of Columbus. Office: American Family Corp 1932 Wynnton Rd Columbus GA 31999

DIBENEDETTO, ROBERT LAWRENCE, obstetrician-gynecologist, insurance company executive; b. New Orleans, Apr. 14, 1928; s. Salvador and Eunice Madeline (Frisch) DiB.; m. Mary Nathalie Roeling, June 20, 1951; children—Madeline E., Robert R., Lawrence W. Student Tulane U., 1945-47; B.S., La. State U., 1948, M.D., 1952. Diplomate Am. Bd. Ob-Gyn. Intern, Mercy Hosp., New Orleans, 1952-53; resident in pathology La. State U. Med. Sch., 1955-56, asst. clin. prof. ob-gyn, 1963; resident in ob-gyn Charity Hosp., New Orleans, 1956-59; practice medicine specializing in ob-gyn, Baton Rouge, 1959—; v.p. investment and audit La. Med. Mut. Ins. Co., New Orleans, 1981—; founding chmn. Mid-La. Health Systems Agy., 1976-77; pres. Capitol Area Health Planning, 1975-76. Bd. dirs. Woman's Hosp. Served with USPHS, 1953-55. Mem. South Central Ob-Gyn Soc., La. Med. Soc. (co-chmn. polit. action com., past pres.), AMA (alt. del.), East Baton Rouge Parish Med. Soc. (past pres.). Democrat. Roman Catholic. Clubs: City (Baton Rouge); So. Yacht (New Orleans); Pontchartrain Yacht (Mandeville, La.). Home: 6666 Pike's Ln Baton Rouge LA 70808 Office: 781 Colonial Dr Baton Rouge LA 70806

DICK, DEWAYNE, petroleum company executive; b. Marion, Kans., Apr. 20, 1951; s. Erwin Leonard and Sabrah Elizabeth (Priest) D.; m. Elizabeth Anne Sutton, May 23, 1972; children—April Chantel, Sondra Allison. B.B.A., Tex. Tech. U., 1973; M.A., Central Mich. U., 1981. Rate supr. T.I.M.E.-DC Trucking, Lubbock, Tex., 1971-75; transp. and dist. analyst Phillips Petroleum, Bartlesville, Okla., 1975-79, sr. regional distbn. rep., Kansas City, Kans., 1979-82, supr. transp. rep., Bartlesville, 1982—. Contbr. articles to profl. jours. Mem. Assn. I.C.C. Practitioners (pres. 1978-79), Council Logistics Mgmt., Assn. Transp. Practitioners (sec., treas. 1984—), Am. Soc. Transp. & Logistics (pres. 1984-86), Delta Nu Alpha (regional v.p. 1977-79). Republican. Baptist. Avocations: personal computing, book collecting. Office: Phillips Petroleum Co 832 AB Adams Bldg Bartlesville OK 74004

DICKE, CANDICE EDWARDS, bookseller; b. Elmhurst, Ill., Aug. 5, 1949; d. Frederick Francis and Bernice Pauline (Bartels) Cramer; m. Mark Edwin Edwards, June 19, 1971 (div. 1981); 1 dau., Kristin Paige; m. Timothy Lee Dicke, Aug. 5, 1984. B.A., U. Iowa, 1971; M.L.S., George Peabody Coll. Tchrs., 1974. Media specialist, Ga.; cert. librarian, tchr., Tex. Tchr., Durant (Iowa) Community Sch. Dist., 1971-72, Peabody Demonstration Sch., Nashville, 1972-75; reading tchr. Edgewood Ind. Sch. Dist., San Antonio, 1975-76; librarian Northside Ind. Sch. Dist., San Antonio, 1976-79; children's librarian DeKalb Library System, Decatur, Ga., 1979-80; media specialist DeKalb County Bd. Edn., Decatur, 1980-84; bookseller Everychild Bookstore, Duluth, Ga., 1984—; regional dir. S.E. Advocates of Lit. for Young People, Athens, Ga., 1983—. Author: The Reference Point, 1983. Mem. Am. Booksellers Assn., Booksellers Assn. Ga. (sec. 1986), Mall Corners Mchts. Assn. (pres. 1984-85), Beta Sigma Phi, Atlanta Mortar Board Alumni Club (treas. 1982-83, v.p. 1983-84). Episcopalian. Home: 4508 John Dr Norcross GA 30093 Office: Everychild Bookstore 3662 Satellite Blvd Duluth GA 30136

DICKENS, CHARLES ALLEN, petroleum company executive; b. Mount Gilead, N.C., Nov. 26, 1932; s. Alonzo Newton and Elizabeth Ann (Haywood) D.; B.S., N.C. State U., 1954; m. Helen Theresia Baudendistel, Jan. 4, 1958; children—Karen Ann, Constance Lynn, Pamela Jean, Kimberly Susan. Asst. chem. engr., chem. engr., sr. chem. engr., project chem. engr. Texaco, Inc., Beacon, N.Y., Port Arthur, Tex., 1954-63, sr. engr., London, 1963-65, project engr., Brussels, 1965-67, mgr. additive sales, Brussels, 1967-69, asst. sales mgr., additive div., Chgo., 1969-72, Houston, 1972-84, v.p. mktg. South Coast Terminals Inc., Houston, 1984—. Served with USAF, 1955-57. Fellow British Inst. Petroleum; mem. Am. Inst. Chem. Engrs., Am. Soc. Lubrication Engrs., Am. Mgmt. Assn., Soc. Automotive Engrs., Engrs. Council of Houston, Scabbard & Blade, Sigma Xi, Tau Beta Pi. Republican. Club: Westador Residents.

DICKENSON, KATHRYN TIPTON, learning disabilities educator; b. Memphis, June 22, 1937; d. Ralph Wynne and Ernestine (Johnson) Tipton; m. James Edward Dickenson, Aug. 23, 1958; children—James Edward, Forest Tipton. B.S., Memphis State U., 1959, M.Ed., 1981. Cert., Tenn. Dept. Edn. Spl. educator educationally mentally retarded Bartlett Elem. Sch., Shelby County, Tenn., 1959, Fairview Elem. Sch., Madison County, Tenn., 1960, Henrico County (Va.) Elem. Sch., 1961, Willow Oaks Elem. Sch., Memphis, 1961-62; music tchr. Emmanual Meth. Kindergarten, Memphis, 1973-78; spl. educator learning disabilities Kingsbury Elem. Sch., Memphis, 1978—. Leader handicapped troop Boy Scouts Am., 1980. Mem. NEA, Tenn. Edn. Assn., West Tenn. Edn. Assn., Memphis Edn. Assn., Memphis Assn. Learning Disabilities, Council for Exceptional Children, Alpha Gamma Delta Alumnae.

DICKERMAN, ALLEN BRIGGS, international business executive; b. Mt. Dora, Fla., Oct. 22, 1914; s. M. Marcellus and Emma (Dickerman) Javens; A.B., Hamilton Coll., 1936; M.B.A., Harvard U., 1941; Ph.D., Syracuse U., 1956; m. Stella M. Brower, May 15, 1943; children—Elizabeth (Mrs. Peter L. Thompson), Joanna (Mrs. Owen Parsons), Laura (Mrs. Jeff Dickerman-Rhodus); m. Luise E. Peake, July 23, 1985. Instr., Harvard Bus. Sch., 1941-42; instr. U. Rochester, 1946-49; assoc. prof. bus. adminstrn. Syracuse U., 1949-74, Internat. Bus. Research fellow, 1971, dir. internat. mgmt. devel. dept., 1960-74; prof. internat. bus., dir. Internat. Devel., Coll. Bus. Adminstrn., U. S.C., 1974-85; pres. Carolina Internat. Devel. Assocs., Inc., Columbia, 1985—; advisor to univs., Colombia, Brazil, Philippines, Costa Rica, Venezuela. Mem. S.C. Dist. Export Council, 1976-81. Served with USNR, 1942-46. Mem. Acad. Internat. Bus., Delta Upsilon. Republican. Episcopalian. Author: Training Japanese Managers, 1974. Home: 4828 Citadel Ave Columbia SC 29206 Office: PO Drawer 11486 Columbia SC 29211

DICKERSON, HELEN PAULINE, educator; b. Loudon County, Tenn., Jan. 16, 1929; d. Albert Carl and Martha Jane (Latham) Williams; m. Randolph Lee Plemons, Aug. 2, 1947 (dec. 1957); children—Russell Lee, Marsha Ann; m. Andrew Mizell Dickerson, Jr., Dec. 14, 1962. B.S., U. Tenn.-Knoxville, 1958; M.A., Middle Tenn. State U., 1959, Ed.S., 1977. Tchr. Murfreesboro (Tenn.) City Schs., 1959-61; tchr. Met. Nashville-Davidson County Schs., Nashville, 1961—; mem. council on tchr. edn. Middle Tenn. State U., 1976-77; team tchr. sci. methods course Fisk U., Nashville, 1974; alt. faculty rep. Met. Nashville Edn. Assn., 1966-67. Pres. Cumberland Presbyn. Women, 1974-75; tchr. Sunday sch. Vacation Ch. Sch. Camps, 1958-83. Met. Nashville Bd. Edn. grantee, 1976-77; recipient Nashville Tennessean award for Newspaper-in-the-Classroom program, 1976. Mem. NEA, Tenn. Edn. Assn., Middle Tenn. Edn. Assn., Met. Nashville Edn. Assn., Internat. Reading Assn., Tenn. Reading Assn., Pi Lambda Theta, Kappa Delta Pi. Home: 914 Dogwood Dr Murfreesboro TN 37130 Office: 455 Rural Hill Rd Nashville TN 37217

DICKERSON, ILSE AGNES, governmental agency executive; b. Schleitheim, Kanton Schaffhausen, Switzerland, Nov. 19, 1924; came to U.S., 1953; naturalized, 1957; d. Wilhelm and Katherina Franziska (Otto) Riedesel; widowed; children—Catherine Anne, William Andrew, Leslie Ann. Various secretarial positions, 1941-80; sr. exec. sec. Ky. Bd. of Claims and Crime Victims Compensation Bd., Frankfort, 1980-83, exec. dir., 1983—. Mem. Nat. Assn. Crime Victim Compensations Bds. (dir. 1984—), Internat. Assn. Crime Victim Compensation Bds., Nat. Orgn. for Victim Assistance. Democrat. Avocations: needlework; batik. Office: Bd Claims and Crime Victims Compensation Bd 113 E Third St Frankfort KY 40601

DICKERSON, LAWRENCE CLIFTON, III, lawyer; b. Shreveport, La., Aug. 12, 1951; s. Lawrence Clifton and Jean Kathleen (Smith) D.; m. Roberta Bollinger, June 5, 1976; children—Lawrence Clifton, IV, James Albert. B.A., La. State U., 1973; J.D., La. State U., 1977. Counsel Bollinger Machine Shop and Shipyard, Inc., Lockport, La., 1977—; dir., pres. Ocean Operators, Inc., Lockport; dir., sec. B & B Tug Corp., Lockport, Bollinger Workover, Inc., Lockport. Chmn. Lafourche Parish Republican Exec. Com., Thibodaux, La., 1984—; mem. Lafourche Parish Bd. Election Suprs., Thibodaux, 1984—; chmn. adminstrv. council Meml. United Meth. Ch., Mathews, La., 1982—. Lodge: Lions (pres. 1983—). Home: PO Box 241 Lockport LA 70374

DICKERSON, MARIE HARVISON, nurse anesthetist; b. Leaf, Miss., Oct. 14, 1946; d. Thurman C. and Mary C. (Jarrell) Harvison; m. George T. Dickerson, Sept. 2, 1978; children—George H., Kathryn Marie. A.A., Jones County Jr. Coll., 1967; B.S., U. Ottawa, Kansas City, Kans., 1976; M.Ed., U. S. Ala., 1978. Registered nurse; cert. registered nurse anesthetist. Operating room supr. George County Hosp., Lucedale, Miss., 1967-70; dir. Sch. Anesthesia, Mobile, Ala., 1972-79; chief anesthesia Wayne Gen. Hosp., Waynesboro, Miss., 1979-84; pres. Wayne Anesthesia, P.A., Waynesboro, 1984—. Mem. Am. Nurses Assn., Miss. Nurses Assn. (dist. pres. 1983), Am. Assn. for Counseling and Devel., Miss. Assn. Nurse Anesthetists (bd. dirs.), Miss Counseling Assn., Waynesboro Bus. and Profl. Women. Republican. Baptist. Club: Waynesboro Home and Garden. Avocations: piano; voice; computers; antiques. Home: Route 2 Box 1 Waynesboro MS 39367 Office: Wayne Anesthesia PA 718 Wayne St Waynesboro MS 39367

DICKERSON, OTHO THOMAS, engineer; b. Aransas Pass, Tex., June 7, 1933; s. Otho Arnold and Cleo Patra (McCormack) D.; m. Mary Elizabeth Duncan, June 16, 1957; children—Russell Thomas, Ginger Bernice. A.A., Del Mar Coll., 1957; B.S., Trinity U., San Antonio, 1959. Assoc. research engr. The Boeing Co., Huntsville, Ala., 1962-67; flight mechanics engr. NASA Marshall Space Flight Ctr., Huntsville, 1967; sr. flight mechanics engr. Chrysler Corp., New Orleans, 1967-68; sr. reliability engr. Kelly AFB, San Antonio, Tex., 1968-73; sr. reliability engr. Eglin Air Force Base, Fla., 1973-80, cons. for reliability mgmt., 1973-80; sr. quality engr. NASA Johnson Space Ctr., Houston, 1980—, cons. for quality mgmt., 1980—. Cubmaster Boy Scouts Am., Devine, Tex., 1972. Recipient Orgn. Excellence award USAF, Eglin AFB, 1975; Superior Performance award NASA Johnson Space Ctr., Houston, 1981, 83, Outstanding Performance award, 1983. Mem. Am. Soc. Quality Control (sr., cert. reliability engr., cert. quality engr.), System Safety Soc., Nat. Mgmt. Assn. Democrat. Avocations: artist; golfing; fishing; woodworking. Office: NASA Johnson Space Ctr Houston TX 77058

DICKERT, ANGELA KING, educator; b. Anderson, S.C., May 25, 1954; d. William Whitner and Margaret Louise (Turner) King; m. Marion Calvin Dickert, June 10, 1972 (div. Dec. 1978); 1 son, Marion Brian. B.A. in Elem. Edn., U. S.C., 1976, M.Ed. in Early Childhood Edn., 1980. Teaching cert., S.C. Elem. tchr. Halmark Sch., Columbia, S.C., 1977-78, Cherryvale Elem. Sch., Sumter, S.C., 1978-80; tchr. kindergarten Gilbert (S.C.) Elem. Sch., 1980—. Presbyterian. Home: 112 Thames Valley Ct Irmo SC 29063 Office: PO Drawer AE Gilbert SC 29054

DICKEY, BERT GERMAN, III, political adviser; b. Memphis, Feb. 14, 1949; s. Bert German Jr. and Alta Baer (Coldren) D.; m. Penny Farrar, Mar. 22, 1976; children—Cal, B.G. A.A., Wentworth Jr. Coll., 1969; B.S.E., U. Ark., 1973; B.S., Inst. Politics and Govt., Little Rock, 1980. Pres. B. G. Dickey Farms, Earle, Ark., 1973-84; trustee Fed. Bankruptcy Ct., Little Rock, 1981-85; polit. adviser, Earle, 1980-84. Commr. of housing City of Earle, 1983; dep. commr. state lands State of Ark., Little Rock, 1984; Chmn. Democratic Exec. Com., Little Rock, 1978-84; mem. Ark. Dem. Com., 1978-84; mem. Ark. Dem. Fin. Council, 1978-84; mem. Dem. Jud. Council, 1978-84; mem. adv. bd. Young Dems., 1978-84; del. 1980 Dem. Nat. Conv., N.Y.C., 1980, 1982 Dem. Conf., Phila., 1982. Served to 2d lt. U.S. Army, 1970-76. Methodist. Club: Safari Internat. (pres. 1979-80) (Memphis). Avocations: big game hunting; snow skiing; golf. Home: PO Box 993 Edwards CO 81632 Office: PO Box 206 Earle AR 72331

DICKEY, CATHARINE CLAUDE, foundation administrator, consultant; b. Quantico, Va., June 1, 1958; d. Robert Russell and Catharine Claude (Doolin) D. B.A. in Polit. Sci., Mary Washington Coll., 1980; M.A. in Pub. Adminstrn., U. Va., 1982. Research asst. Heritage Found., Washington, 1983-84; legis. asst. Nat. Def. Council Found., Alexandria, Va., 1984, legis. dir., 1984—; research cons. RIGHT PAC, Alexandria, 1984—; invited guest Asia and World Inst., Taiwan, Republic of China, 1984-85; mem. Conservative Network, Washington, 1985. Mem. Pi Sigma Alpha, Pi Gamma Mu. Republican. Episcopalian. Office: National Defense Council Found 108 S Columbus St Suite 101 Alexandria VA 22314

DICKEY, DAVID ALAN, statistics educator, consultant; b. Painesville, Ohio, Dec. 22, 1945; s. Lester L. and H. Ernestine (Pavey) D.; m. Barbara Sue Shell, Dec. 28, 1971; children—Michael, Susan. B.A., Miami U., Ohio, 1967, M.S., 1969; Ph.D., Iowa State U., 1976. Instr., William and Mary Coll., Williamsburg, Va., 1969-71, Randolph-Mason Coll., Ashland, Va., 1971-72; prof. N.C. State U., Raleigh, 1976-85; cons. Kilkelly Environmentalists, Raleigh, 1979—, SAS Inst., Raleigh, 1982—. Contbr. articles to profl. jours. Mem. Inst. Math. Stats., Am. Statis. Assn., Sigma Xi, Phi Kappa Phi. Republican. Methodist. Office: NC State U Dept Statistics Box 8205 Raleigh NC 27695-8203

DICKEY, EDWIN MILTON, JR., mathematics educator, computer educator, consultant, researcher; b. Rio de Janeiro, Brazil, Dec. 26, 1950; came to U.S., 1956; s. Edwin Milton and Heloisa (Costa Leite) D.; m. Karen Muriel Lauterbach, Jan. 4, 1975; 1 child, Isabel Marie. B.S., Georgetown U., 1973; M.S., U. S.C., 1975, Ph.D., 1982. Cert. math. tchr., S.C. Tchr., dept. chmn. Spring Valley High Sch., Columbia, S.C., 1977-81; asst. prof. math. Columbia Coll., 1981-84; asst. prof. edn. U. S.C., Columbia, 1984—; computer cons. Assn. Internat. Sch. in Africa, Nairobi, Kenya, 1983-84; math. cons. Lexington Sch. Dist. 5, Columbia, 1982-84, Lexington Sch. Dist. 1, 1984. Contbr. articles to jours. Named Tchr. of Yr., Spring Valley High Sch., 1981-82. Mem. Nat. Council Tchrs. of Math., Math. Assn. Am., Am. Assn. Colls. for Tchr. Edn., S.C. Council Tchrs. of Math., Assn. for Computers in Math. and Sci. Teaching. Avocations: tennis, gardening, computer programming, chess, photography. Home: 3540 Foxhall Rd Columbia SC 29204 Office: Coll of Edn Univ SC Columbia SC 29208

DICKHUT, HEINRICH BALDUIN, tool and die maker; b. Breslau, Germany, Apr. 12, 1937; s. Heinrich and Johanna (Gerd-to-Berens) D.; m. Karen J. Berns, May 2, 1964; children—Melanie, Cathy, Chris, Bill, Johanna. Grad. Berufschule. Apprentice, Berens Machine Tool & Die, Kankakee, Ill., 1957-66; tool and die maker Roger Corp., Kankakee, 1966-73; co-owner Bear Engrng. Machine Tool & Die, Bradley, Ill., 1973-77; owner Cullom Machine Tool & Die, 1977—. Mem. adv. bd. Kankakee Community Coll. Patentee in field. Served in U.S. Army, 1960-62. Mem. Soc. Mfg. Engrs., Nat. Fedn. Ind. Bus. Republican. Roman Catholic. Lodges: Moose, Masons. Home: Route 1 Box 587 Charleston TN 37310 Office: Cullom Machine Tool & Die 1701 Hardeman Ln Cleveland TN 37311

DICKIE, HERBERT GRASTY, JR., surgeon, educator; b. Wilmington, N.C., Sept. 20, 1916; s. Herbert Grasty and Kate Russell (DuRant) D.; m. Joyce Kingsbury, Feb. 9, 1943 (dec. July 1949); children—Katherine, Martha, Thomas; m. 2d, Margaret Gompers, Sept. 9, 1950; children—Helen, Elaine. A.B., Maryville (Tenn.) Coll., 1938; M.D., U. Va., 1942. Diplomate Am. Bd. Surgery. Intern, Albany (N.Y.) Hosp., 1942-43; resident Wheeling (W.Va.) Hosp., 1946-47; resident in surgery VA Hosp., Pitts., 1955-58; chief surg. resident Youngstown Hosp. (Ohio), 1958-59; practice medicine specializing in gen. surgery, Wheeling, 1959—; clin. asst. prof. surgery U. W.Va., 1980—. Served to maj. AUS, 1943-46. Fellow ACS (gov. 1980—), Southeastern Surg. Congress. Lodges: Masons, Shriners, Jesters. Home: PO Box 104 RD 4 Wheeling WV 26003 Office: 59 14th St Wheeling WV 26003

DICKINSON, CHARLES CAMERON, III, educator; b. Charleston, W.Va., May 13, 1936; s. Charles Cameron and Frances Ann (Saunders) D.; grad. Phillips Acad. (Andover), 1954; B.A. cum laude, Dartmouth Coll., 1958; student Chgo. Theol. Sem., 1962, U. Chgo. Divinity Sch., 1962-63; B.Div., Pitts. Theol. Sem., 1965; student Kirchliche Hochschule, West Berlin, 1965-66, Ernst Moritz Arndt Universitat, E. Ger., 1966; U. Pitts., 1966-68, Yale U. Divinity Sch., 1968-69, Union Theol. Sem., 1969-72; Ph.D., U. Pitts., 1973. Prof. English, Greek, N.T., Ecole de Theologie Kimbanguiste, Kinshasa, Zaïre, 1972; asst. prof. systematic theology and philosophy Union Theol. Sem. in Va., 1974-75; asst. prof. religion and philosophy Morris Harvey Coll., 1975-79; prof. religion and philosophy The Am. Coll. Rome, 1979; prof. theology and philosophy U. Charleston, 1980-81; curatorial asso. for manuscript collections Andover-Harvard Theol. Library, Harvard U., 1981—; prof. linguistics and lit. Hebei Tchrs. U., Shijiazhuang, Hebei Province, Peoples Republic of China, 1983-84, vis. scholar Christ Ch., Oxford (Eng.) U., 1979; vis. scholar Harvard Divinity Sch., 1980; dir. Univ. Press Edits., Mountain State Press, Charleston, W.Va., 1980—. Mem. ednl. council, bd. dirs. The River Sch., Charleston, W.Va., 1978—; bd. dirs. Kanawha Valley Youth Orchestra; Charleston Ballet; W.Va. Opera Theater; Kanawha Pastoral Counseling Center. Served with USMC, 1958-61. U. Chgo. Divinity Sch. Scholarship awardee 1962-63; Chgo. Theol. Sem. Entrance Fellow, 1962. Fellow Royal Soc. Arts; mem. Am. Acad. Religion, Soc. Bibl. Lit., Am. Theol. Soc., Am. Philos. Assn., Internat. Platform Assn., Am. Assn. Advancement of Humanities, AAAS, W.Va. Philos. Soc., W.Va. Assn. Humanities, Internat. Bonhoeffer Soc. Democrat. Presbyterian. Clubs: Charleston Rotary (chmn. student exchange com. 1978-79, mem. program com. 1981—), Edgewood Country, Wichita, University (Pitts.). Contbr. articles, revs. to profl. jours. Office: Andover-Harvard Theol Library Harvard Univ Cambridge MA 02138 also 111 City Nat Bldg Wichita Falls TX 76301

DICKINSON, CHARLES FREDERICK, III, steel company executive, oil and investment executive; b. Youngstown, Ohio, Sept. 21, 1934; s. Charles Frederick and Mary Elizabeth (McFadden) D.; m. Mary Elizabeth Edwards, Oct. 1, 1960; children—Charles Frederick IV, John Edwards, Sara Elizabeth. B.S., Carnegie-Mellon U., 1956, M.A., 1964. Dir. internat. Allegheny Ludium Steel Corp., Pitts., 1968-73; v.p., gen. mgr. Metalloy Corp., Phila., 1973-75; pres., Am. Mktg. Services Ltd., Houston, 1975—; cons. Berger and Co., San Francisco; dir. MPI Ventures Inc., Houston, IMI Inc., Houston. Served with USAR, 1957-63. Mellon fellow Carnegie-Mellon U., 1963. Republican. Roman Catholic. Clubs: Capital City (Raleigh, N.C.); Univ. (Houston). Avocations: boating; stamp collecting. Office: Am Mktg Services Ltd 5206 FM 1960 W #207 Houston TX 77069

DICKINSON, WILLIAM ANDREW, JR., hospital administrator; b. Atlanta, Aug. 25, 1945; s. William Andrew and Nancy McQuown (Ring) D.; m. Barbara Helen Griffin, June 13, 1970; children—William Andrew, III, Laura Craven. B.A. in Econs., U. Va., 1967; M.H.A., Ga. State U., 1973. Adminstrv. resident Ind. U. Hosps., Indpls., 1972-73; asst. adminstr. Med. Coll. VA Hosp., Richmond, Va., 1973-75; v.p. Baptist Hosp., Nashville, 1975-78; v.p. Roanoke Meml. Hosps., Va., 1978-84, sr. v.p., 1984—; dir. Roanoke Meml. Rehab. Ctr. Bd. dirs. Mental Health Assn. of Roanoke Valley, Va., 1979—, Soc. for the Crippled, Southwest Va., 1978—, Roanoke Neighborhood Partnership, Roanoke, 1983—, Burrell Home for Adults, Roanoke, 1983—. Served to lt. USNR, 1967-71. Mem. Va. Hosp. Assn., Am. Hosp. Assn., Am. Coll. Hosp. Adminstrs. Republican. Episcopalian. Lodge: Kiwanis. Office: Roanoke Meml Hosps PO Box 13367 Roanoke VA 24033

DICKINSON, WILLIAM ARTHUR, clinical psychologist, neuropsychologist; b. Hudson Falls, N.Y., Apr. 7, 1947; s. Frederick Joel and Marion Florence (Ash) D.; m. Joe Ann Marie Brandt; Apr. 4, 1981; 1 dau., Ashley Lauren Brandt. B.A., So. Ill. U., 1974, M.A., 1976, Ph.D., 1980. Lic. psychologist, Ga., Ala. Asst. prof. U. Ala. Med. Sch., Birmingham, 1979-81; pres. Savannah Psychol. Cons., PC, Ga., 1981—; v.p. Savannah Metabolic Clinics, Inc., 1985—, Savannah Midtown Properties, 1984—. Contbr. chpt. to Biological Foundations 1981. Contbr. articles to profl. jours. Vice pres. Citizens for Clean Air, Inc., Savannah, 1983-85. NIH fellow, 1979-80. Mem. Am. Psychol. Assn., Ga. Psychol. Assn., Nat. Acad. Neuropsychologists, Coastal Assn. Lic. Psychologists (pres. 1984—). Lodge: Savannah South Rotary. Home: 1 Mercer Rd Savannah GA 31411 Office: Savannah Psychol Cons 1 St Joseph's Professional Plaza Savannah GA 31419

DICKINSON, WILLIAM LOUIS, congressman; b. Opelika, Ala., June 5, 1925; s. Henry K. and Bernice (Lowe) D.; LL.B., U. Ala., 1950; m. Barbara Edwards, Mar. 10, 1977; children by previous marriage—Chris, Michael, Tara, Bill. Admitted to Ala. bar, 1950, practiced in Opelika, 1950-63; judge Opelika City Ct., 1951-53; judge Ct. Common Pleas, 1953-59; judge Juvenile Ct. Lee County, 1953-59; judge 5th Jud. Ct. Ala., 1959-63; asst. v.p. So. Ry. System, Montgomery, Ala., 1963-64; mem. 89th-98th Congresses from 2d Ala. Dist.; ranking Republican mem. com. on house armed services, mem. various subcoms. of house armed services com., mem. house adminstrn., mem. exec. com., com. on coms. of Rep. Conf. in the House. Chmn. Opelika Bd. Edn., 1960-61; mem. Gov.'s Indsl. Com. of 100, 1963-64; dir. Lee County Civil Def., 1961-62. Past pres. Ala. Mental Health Assn. Chmn. Ala. Rep. Congressional Del.; pres., bd. dirs. Lee County Mental Health Clinic; bd. dirs. Lee County Rehab. Center. Served with USNR, World War II. Named Man of Yr., Opelika Jr. C. of C., 1961, One of Four Outstanding Young Men in Ala., 1961; recipient Disting. Service award Ams. for Constl. Action; Watchdog of Treasury award Nat. Associated Businessmen; Statesman award Am. Conservative Union; Congressional Appreciation award Army Aviation Assn. Am.; Peace Through Strength medal Am. Security Council; Separation of Ch. and State award Ala. Christian Edn. Assn.; Jim Woodruff, Jr. award Assn. U.S. Army; Loyalty award D.C. dist. VFW. Mem. Ala. Bar Assn., U. Ala. Alumni Assn., Sigma Alpha Epsilon. Clubs: Shriners, Kiwanis, Elks. Methodist. Office: 2406 Rayburn House Office Bldg Washington DC 20515

DICKMAN, VIRGINIA MYERS, legal secretary; b. Tampa, Fla., Oct. 1, 1940; d. Thomas B. and Virginia Kathryn (Robinson) Kirby; student public schs. Sec. to lawyer, Tampa, 1958-61; sec. Hughes Aircraft Co., Newport News, Va., 1961-62; sec. Lifsey & Johnston, Attys., Tampa, 1962-66, Shackleford, Farrior, Stallings & Evans, Attys., Tampa, 1966—. Named Legal Sec. of Yr. Tampa Legal Secs. Assn., 1977-78. Mem. Profl. Secs. Internat., Nat. Assn. Legal Secs., Fla. Assn. Legal Secs. (del. state conv. 1979-81, 84, ways and means chmn. 1980-81, corr. sec. 1981-82), Tampa Legal Secs. Assn. (pres. 1978-79, gov. 1979-81, legal edn. co-chmn. 1980-81, historian 1982, public relations chmn. and parliamentarian 1983-84, fundraiser chmn. 1982-84), Greater Tampa C. of C. Presbyterian. Home: 121 Floral Dr Tampa FL 33612 Office: Shackleford Farrior Stallings & Evans PO Box 3324 Tampa FL 33601

DICKSON, ALAN T., textile, holding company executive; b. 1931. B.S., N.C. State Coll., 1953; M.B.A., Harvard U., 1955. With Amer & Efird Mills, Inc., 1957—, pres., 1957-69, chmn. bd., dir., 1969—; pres., dir. Ruddick Corp., 1968—; dir. NCNB Corp., Chatham Mfg. Co. Served with U.S. Army, 1955-57. Address: Ruddick Corp 2000 First Union Plaza Charlotte NC 28282*

DICKSON, ALEX DOCKERY, bishop, Episcopal Church; b. Alligator, Miss., Sept. 9, 1926. B.B.A., U. Miss., 1949; M.Div., U. of the South, 1958; M.E., Miss. Coll., 1972; m. Charlotte Perkins. Ordained to ministry, 1958. Rector, Chapel of the Cross, Rolling Fork, Miss.; vicar St. Paul's Ch., Hollandale, Miss., 1958-62; rector St. Columb's Ch., Jackson, Miss., 1962-68; rector, headmaster All Saints' Episcopal Sch., Vicksburg, Miss., 1968-83; first bishop Diocese of West Tenn., Memphis, 1983—. Address: The Episcopal Ch 692 Poplar Ave Memphis TN 38104*

DICKSON, CLARENCE, law enforcement official. Chief of police, Miami, Fla. Office: City Hall Police Dept 3500 Pan American Dr Miami FL 33133*

DICKSON, RICHARD LEE, dentist; b. San Antonio, Sept. 17, 1934; s. Richard Fomby and Geraldine (Henderson) D.; m. Peggy Cox, June 11, 1955; children—Cynthia Lee, Richard Stanley, Gregory Todd, Ronald Scott. Student Tex. U., Austin, 1953-54; A.S., San Antonio Coll., 1954; D.D.S., Baylor U., 1958. Gen. practice dentistry, San Antonio, 1960—. Bd. dirs. Youth Alternatives, Inc., San Antonio, 1978—; pres. Youth for Christ, 1977-79. Served to capt. USAF, 1958-60. Named Father of Yr. of San Antonio, Community San Antonio Businessmen, 1969. Mem. San Antonio Dist. Dental Soc., Tex. Dental Soc., ADA, Phi Psi Pi. Baptist. Clubs: Optimists (pres. 1968-69, dist. lt. gov. 1969-70), Knife and Fork (pres. 1981-82), Century. Home: 393 W Broadview Dr San Antonio TX 78228 Office: 1100 NW Loop 410 Suite 456 San Antonio TX 78213

DICKSON, ROBIN MARK, meeting and convention production executive; b. N.Y.C., Oct. 8, 1948; s. Charles E. and Joy (Sheinmark) D.; divorced; 1 son, Michael. Student Edward Williams Coll., 1966-68. Vice pres. Ray Bloch Prodns., N.Y.C., 1972—, v.p., gen. mgr., Atlanta, 1976—; cons., speaker in field. Contbr. article to profl. jour. Active Boy Scouts Am. Served with USAAF, 1968-72. Mem. Meeting Planners Internat., Am. Soc. Assn. Execs. (speakers platform), Sales and Mktg. Execs.; Hotel Sales and Mktg. Execs. Lodge: Masons (master). Home: 300 W Peachtree St Atlanta GA 30308 Office: Ray Bloch Prodns 230 Peachtree St NW Suite 1417 Atlanta GA 30303

DICKSON, RUSH STUART, holding company executive; b. Charlotte, N.C., Aug. 18, 1929; s. Rush Smith and Lake (Simpson) D.; grad. Davidson Coll., 1951; m. Joanne Shoemaker, Oct. 12, 1951; children—Rush Stuart, Thomas Walter, John Alexander, Laura Lake. With Am. & Efird Mills, Mt. Holly, N.C., 1951, Goldman, Sachs & Co., N.Y.C., 1951-52; pres. R.S. Dickson & Co., Charlotte, 1952-68; chmn. bd. Ruddick Corp., Charlotte, 1968—; dir. Am. & Efird Mills, Photo Corp. Am. Harris-Teeter Supermarkets, Piedmont REIT, Hemby Investments. Chmn. Charlotte-Mecklenburg Hosp. Authority; bd. dirs., officer Rush S. Dickson Family Found., The Dickson Found.; bd. visitors Davidson Coll.; trustee Wake Forest U.; bd. dirs. Found. U. N.C., Charlotte; trustee Arts and Sci. Council, Heineman Found.; bd. visitors Johnson C. Smith U. Served with USAR. Mem. Charlotte C. of C. (dir.), Newcomen Soc. N.C. Democrat. Boston. Clubs: Boston (New Orleans; Charlotte City, Charlotte Country, Quail Hollow Country (Charlotte); Capital City (Raleigh, N.C.); Country of N.C. (Pinehurst); Grandfather Golf and Country, Linville (N.C.) Country. Home: 2235 Pinewood Circle Charlotte NC 28211 Office: 2000 First Union Plaza Charlotte NC 28282

DICKSON, THOMAS INCHES, political science educator, researcher; b. N.Y.C., Oct. 17, 1923; s. Thomas I. and Isabel Anne (Kehoe) D.; m. Mona Faye Carroll, Sept. 28, 1979; 1 child, Francesanne. Ph.D., U. Texas, 1951. Research assoc. Texas Legis. Council, Austin, 1951-52; fgn. service officer U.S. Dept. State, Washington, 1952-68; from assoc. to prof. Auburn U., Ala., 1968—; project dir. Ala. Law Enforcement Planning Agy., Montgomery, 1973-74; project research dir. Office Pub. Service and Research, Auburn, 1976-80. Contbr. articles to profl. jours. Pres. Auburn-Guatemala City Ptnrs. Ams., 1978-79, bd. dirs. Ala.-Guatemala Ptnrs., 1980—; pres. Auburn United Way, 1980-82. Served to col. USMCR. NSF fellow, 1971. Mem. Am. Polit. Sci. Assn., Internat. Studies Assn., Southeastern Conf. Latin Am. Studies, Amateur Fencers League Am. (chmn. Ala. div. 1975-76). Avocations: fencing; tennis. Office: Auburn U Dept Polit Sci Auburn AL 36849

DICKSON-PORTER, CLAUDIA BLAIR, librarian; b. Memphis, Oct. 22, 1925; d. Walton Avery and Annie Laurie (Tate) Tucker; B.S., U. Nebr., Omaha, 1964; M.L.S., N. Tex. State U., Denton, 1971, Ph.D., 1979; m. Benjamin A. Dickson, June 5, 1945 (div.); children—Susan Dickson Morrison, Andrea Dickson Darby, Donna Dickson Stephens, Reid W., Bryan A.; m. 2d, William G. Porter, Feb. 8, 1978. Tchrs. schs. in Nebr. and Hawaii, 1964-71; librarian Nat. Assn. Retarded Citizens, Arlington, Tex., from 1971; dir. Regional Office TAS VI, Research and Tng Ctr. in Mental Retardation, Tex. Tech. U.; dir. planning Tex. Planning Council for Devel. Disabilities, Tex. Dept. Mental Health/Mental Retardation, 1979-80; program specialist Office of Devel. Disabilities, Office of Human Devel., Fed. Region VI, Dallas, 1980-82, grants mgmt. specialist Office of Fiscal Ops., 1982; community rep. for planning and evaluation Adminstrn. for Children, Youth and Families, Office Human Devel. Services, Fed. Region VI, Dallas, 1982—; tchr. community services courses El Centro Jr. Coll., Dallas. Mem. Spl. Libraries Assn., Southwestern, Tex. library assns., Am. Assn. Mental Deficiency, Council Exceptional Children, Soc. S.W. Archivists, Local History Soc., Phi Delta Kappa. Author, compiler in field. Home: 2413 Lakeside Dr Arlington TX 76013 Office: 1200 Main Tower Dallas TX 75202

DICLERICO, ROBERT EDMONDE, political science educator, consultant; b. Lynn, Mass., Nov. 15, 1943; s. Joseph Anthony and Ruth Adelle (Cummings) DiC. A.B., Hamilton Coll., 1966; Ph.D. (Earhart fellow), Ind. U., 1974. Asst. prof. polit. sci. W.Va. U., Morgantown, 1972-77, assoc. prof., 1977—; vis. prof. polit. sci. U. Houston, spring 1983; editorial cons. to Prentice-Hall, McGraw Hill, Addison Wesley pubs.; campus rep. for Truman and Rhodes scholarships. Author: The American President, 2d edit., 1982; (with Eric Uslaner) Few Are Chosen: Problems in Presidential Selection, 1983; editor: (with Allan Hammock) Points of View, 3d edit., 1986; Analyzing the Presidency, 1985. Recipient Amoco Outstanding Teaching award W.Va. U., 1975; Outstanding Teaching award Pi Sigma Alpha, 1977; Outstanding Teaching award Golden Key Nat. Honor Soc., 1983; Danforth fellow, 1976-82. Mem. Am. Polit. Sci. Assn., Ctr. for Study of Presidency, Midwest Polit. Sci. Assn., So. Polit. Sci. Assn., Western Polit. Sci. Assn., W.Va. Polit. Sci. Assn., Acad. Polit. Sci. Roman Catholic. Home: 529 Martin Ave Morgantown WV 26505 Office: Dept Polit Sci W Va Univ Morgantown WV 26505

DIECCHIO, RICHARD JOSEPH, geology educator; b. Yonkers, N.Y., Aug. 13, 1948; s. Richard Rocco and Lucille Ann (Consula) D.; m. Janet Ann Avery, Nov. 29, 1975; children—Katherine Avery D., Michael Joseph, James Jacob. B.S. in Geology, Rensselaer Poly. Inst., Troy, N.Y., 1970; M.S. in Geology, Duke U., 1974; Ph.D. in Geology, U. N.C., 1980. Cert. profl. geologist, Va. Field geologist Dunn Geosci. Corp., Latham, N.Y., 1970, 72; geol. engr. Stone & Webster Engrng. Corp., Boston and N.Y.C., 1974-76; mem. geology faculty George Mason U., Fairfax, Va., 1980—. Contbr. articles, maps to profl. jours. NSF grantee, 1982. Mem. Geol. Soc. Am., Am. Assn. Petroleum Geologists, Nat. Assn. Geology Tchrs., Va. Acad. Sci. (vice chmn. geology sect. 1985-86), Geol. Soc. Wash., W.Va. Geol. Survey (cooperating geologist 1982-84). Office: Dept Geology George Mason U 4400 University Dr Fairfax VA 22030

DIEDRICH, RICHARD JOSEPH, architect; b. South Bend, Ind., May 8, 1936; s. Arthur Joseph and Lucille D.; Diploma in Architecture, Ecole Des Beaux Arts Americaines, Fountainbleau, France, 1960; B.Arch., U. Ill., 1961, M.Arch., 1962; m. Linda P. Diedrich; children—Dawn Marie, Lisa Lee, Andrea Lynn. Archtl. designer Richardson Severns Scheeler & Assos., Champaign, Ill., 1961-62; design critic U. Ill. Sch. Architecture, 1961-62; archtl. designer Swensson & Kott, Nashville, 1963-64; architect, v.p. Miller Waltz Diedrich, Architects, Milw., 1965-77; pres. MWD Architects, Atlanta, 1978-80, Diedrich Architects, Atlanta, 1980—. Mem. Whitefish Bay Bd. Appeals, 1968-71; v.p. North Decatur Youth Assn., 1975-76. Margaret T. Biddle scholar, 1960. Mem. AIA (past pres. Milw. chpt., six design awards, regional award, Ga. AIA award), Wis. Architect (past pres.). Club: Druid Hills Country. Archtl. works include: Avondale Sta., Atlanta Rapid Transit, S. Miami Sta. of Miami Rapid Transit, Student Center, U. Ga., Bloomingdale's Store, Boca Raton. Home: 8 Brookhaven Dr Atlanta GA 30319 Office: 235 Peachtree St NE Suite 1101 Atlanta GA 30303

DIEFENDERFER, CAREN, mathematics educator, consultant; b. Allentown, Pa., Jan. 18, 1952; d. Carson F. and Nancy N. (Ross) D. A.B., Dartmouth Coll., 1973; M.A., U. Calif.-Santa Barbara, 1975, Ph.D., 1980. Asst. prof. math. Hollins Coll., Va., 1977—; vis. assoc. prof. math. Va. Poly. Inst. and State U., Blacksburg, 1983-84. Recipient Suzan Rose Benedict Prize in Math., 1971. Mem. Am. Math. Soc., Math. Assn. Am. (sec. Md.-D.C.-Va. sect. 1982-85), Assn. Women in Math., Phi Beta Kappa, Sigma Xi, Pi Mu Epsilon. Contbr. articles to jours. in field. Office: PO Box 9562 Hollins Coll Hollins College VA 24020

DIEFFENBACH, CHARLES MAXWELL, emeritus law educator, lawyer; b. Westfield, N.Y., July 9, 1909; s. Arthur Warren and Mary Bertha (Meyer) D.; m. Gladys Ethel Gray, June 29, 1935; children—Gretchen Dieffenbach Gehlbach, Roxann Huschard. B.S. in Civil Engrng., U. Ala., 1934; postgrad. Bus. Sch., Harvard U., 1934-35; M.A. in Econs., U. Cin., 1948; J.D., Ohio No. U., 1957. Bar: Ohio 1957. Meat packing exec. H.H. Meyer Packing Co., Cin., 1935-55; from asst. prof. to prof. law Chase Coll. Law, Cin., 1957-65; prof. bus. adminstrn. N.Mex. State U., Las Cruces, 1965-68; prof. law Chase Coll. Law, No. Ky. U., Highland Heights, 1968-79, prof. law emeritus, 1980—; vis. prof. law Detroit Coll. Law, 1979-80. Served to maj. U.S. Army, 1942-46, ETO. Republican. Episcopalian. Club: University (Cin.). Home: 710 Ivy Ave Cincinnati OH 45246 Office: No Ky U Chase Coll Law 508 Nunn Hall Highland Heights KY 41076

DIERCKS, JOHN HENRY, music educator; b. Montclair, N.J., Apr. 19, 1927; s. John Henry and Ann Marie (Boschen) D.; m. Thelma Lai-Keam Chock, June 16, 1958; children—Lisa, Amanda. B.Mus., Oberlin Coll., 1949; M.Mus., Eastman Sch., Rochester, N.Y., 1950; Ph.D., U. Rochester, 1960. Instr. Coll. Wooster, Ohio, 1950-54; from instr. to prof. music Hollins College, Va., 1954—, chmn. dept., 1962—; pub. Crystal Springs Music Pubs., Inc., Roanoke, Va., 1980—; free lance cons., editor, arranger. Composer over 100 works, 1956—; contbr. articles to profl. jours. Chmn. Bicentennial Music Com., Roanoke, 1976; mem. adv. bd. pub. radio sta. WVWR-FM, Roanoke, 1980-83; mem. program com. Roanoke Symphony Orch., 1980—. Served with USN, 1945-46. Grantee Mellon Found., 1974, 75, 78-84, Danforth Found., 1960, 62, NEH, 1977. Mem. ASCAP (serious music awards 1968, 69, 82, 83, 84), Am. Music Ctr., Music Library Assn., Va. Composers Guild, MacDowell Colony (exec. bd. 1983—). Home and Office: Hollins Coll Dept Music Hollins College VA 24020

DIERKING, DANNY LEE, financial executive; b. Higginsville, Mo., Dec. 27, 1948; s. Walter Eugene and Dorothy Lee (Hanneman) D.; m. Mary Ann Green, Nov. 27, 1971; children—Howard, Leah Anne. B.S. in Bus., Central Mo. State U., Warrensburg, 1970. C.P.A., Tex. Acct., Armco Steel, Kansas City, Mo., Houston, 1970-71; controller Cablevision Constrn., Houston, 1971-74; cost acctg. mgr. Hycel, Inc., Houston, 1974-78; controller Coastal Transport, Houston, 1978-79; asst. controller F.H. Maloney Co., Houston, 1979-81, controller, 1981-83; controller Zeno Systems of Houston, 1983-85, Vetco Offshore, Inc., Houston, 1985—. Mem. Nat. Assn. Accts., Am. Inst. C.P.A.s, Tex. Soc. C.P.A.s, Am. Prodn. and Inventory Control Soc. Republican. Baptist. Address: 8002 Twin Hills Dr Houston TX 77071

DIESEL, JOHN PHILLIP, multinational corporation executive; b. St. Louis, June 10, 1926; s. John Henry and Elsa A. (Poetting) D.; m. Rita Jan Meyer, June 12, 1949; children—Holly, Gretchen, John, Dana. B.S., Washington U., St. Louis, 1951. Exec. asst. div. mgr. McQuay-Norris Mfg. Co., St. Louis, 1951-57; partner Booz, Allen & Hamilton, Inc., Chgo., 1957-61; v.p. ops. Ops. Research, Inc., Santa Monica, Calif., 1961-62; v.p., treas., dir. Mgmt. Tech., Inc., Los Angeles, 1962-63; dir. mktg. and planning A.O. Smith Corp., Milw., 1963-65, dir. mfg. and engring., 1965-67, v.p. mfg. and planning, 1967-70, group v.p., 1970-72; chmn. bd. Armor Elevator Can., Ltd., 1970-72; chmn. bd., pres. Armor Elevator Co., Inc., 1970-72; pres., chief exec. officer Newport News (Va.) Shipbldg. & Dry Dock Co., 1972-78, chmn. bd., 1976-78; exec. v.p. Tenneco Inc., 1976-79, pres., 1979—, also dir.; dir. Cooper Industries, Inc., First City Nat. Bancorp. Tex., Inc., Aluminum Co. Am., Allied Stores Corp. Served with USNR, 1944-47. Methodist. Clubs: Pine Valley Golf, Seminole Golf, Houston Country. Home: 327 Longwoods Ln Houston TX 77024 Office: Tenneco Inc PO Box 2511 Houston TX 77001

DIETZ, JESS CLAY, environmental consultant, civil engineer; b. Fond du Lac, Wis., Oct. 10, 1914; s. Jesse Clay and Mayme Lucille (Duerschmidt) D.; m. Ellen Davison, Apr. 24, 1942; children—Dorothy Dietz Bonnett, Gail Dietz Conley, John D. B.C.E., U. Wis., 1939, M.C.E., 1941, Ph.D. in Civil Engring., 1947. Instrn., research asst. U. Wis., Madison, 1940-42, 1945-47; prin. sanitary engring. U. Ill., Urbana, 1947-57; sr. v.p. Clark Dietz Engrs., Inc., Sanford, Fla., 1957-79; environ. cons., Longwood, Fla., 1979—. Served to col. C.E., U.S.

Army, 1942-45; ETO. Decorated Bronze Star; Croix de Guerre (France); recipient Disting. Service citation U. Wis., 1976; Raindrop award Wabash Valley Assn., 1972. Fellow ASCE, Am. Pub. Health Assn.; mem. Am. Water Works Assn. (life), Water Pollution Control Fedn. (life), Fla. Engring. Soc., Nat. Soc. Profl. Engrs., Am. Pub. Works Assn., Scabbard and Blade, Sigma Xi, Tau Beta Pi, Chi Epsilon, Gamma Alpha, Pi Mu Epsilon. Author: (with Noth Kessler) Effect of Sewage on Sewer Pipe, 1940. Researcher in water and waste area. Home and Office: 12 Horseman Cove Longwood FL 32750

DI FAVAZE, ALESSANDRO, (COUNT), language educator, author; b. Firenze, Italy, June 19, 1937; came to U.S., 1960, naturalized, 1974; s. Michele and Montana (Brazzi) di F. B.B.A., B.A., Am. U. Beirut, 1957, B.S., 1960; Baccalaureat francais Première et deuxième parties, Université Saint-Joseph, Beirut, 1957; M.A., Ind. U., 1962; postgrad. U. Denver, 1963-64; U. Colo., 1965—. Instr. Tchr.'s Tng. Coll., Tripoli, Libya, 1958; linguist, protocol officer U.S. embassies, North Africa, 1958-59; instr. Colo. Women's Coll., Denver, 1962-63; asst. prof. Bellarmine Coll., Louisville, 1965-68; instr. U. Louisville, 1968-72; lectr. in modern langs. div. French and Italian, Baylor U., Waco, Tex., 1979—. Ind. U. fellow, 1961-62. Mem. AAUP, Honor Soc. Fgn. Langs. Author: French Grammar Review, 1967; Les Domaines Généraux, Les Tendances, Idées et Doctrines du XVIIème Siècle, 1967; Italian Grammar Review, 1972. Home: 1519 Washington Ave Apt 11 Waco TX 76702 Office: Dept Modern Langs Div French and Italian Baylor U Waco TX 76798

DIGGS, CHARLES ALBERT, pathologist, county official, consultant; b. Emporia, Va., Jan. 7, 1943; s. Kermit Hunter and Ruth Ophelia (Winstead) D.; m. Mary Elstak, June 2, 1971; children—Charlotte, Angela. B.S., Morehouse Coll., 1964; M.D., Meharry Med. Coll., 1968. Diplomate Am. Bd. Pathology. Intern, Norfolk Gen. Hosp. (Va.), 1968-69; resident in surgery Columbia U. and Harlem Hosp., N.Y.C., 1969-70; resident in pathology U.S. Naval Hosp., Portsmouth, Va., 1971-75; resident in forensic pathology U. Miami (Fla.), 1976-77; asst. med. examiner Dade County, Miami, Fla., 1977-80; dep. med. examiner Hillsborough County, Tampa, Fla., 1980—; clin. asst. prof. pathology U. South Fla. Coll. Medicine; lectr. schs., colls., civic groups on effects of alcohol and drugs. Researcher alcohol and the victim participated homicide. Served to comdr. M.C., USN, 1970-76. Mem. Nat. Assn. Med. Examiners, Am. Acad. Forensic Scis. Baptist. Office: 401 S Morgan St Tampa FL 33607

DIGGS, WILLIAM EDWARD, oil company executive; b. Fredricksburg, Va., July 1, 1931; s. Charles Douglas and Elizabeth (Macy) D.; m. Wauhilla Adkins, Mar. 9, 1957; children—Charles Edward, Charlotte Lynn, William Douglas. B.Sc. in Geology, Va. Poly. Inst., 1953, M.Sc. in Geology, 1955. Geologist Carter Oil Co., Ft. Smith, Ark., 1954-62; pvt. practice cons. geologist, Ft. Smith, 1962-68; gen. mgr. Alliance Oil Devel., Melbourne, Australia, 1968-76; mgr. Bates Oil Co., Tulsa, 1977-79; v.p. exploration Heston Oil Co., Tulsa, 1979-83, ONEOK Exploration Co., Tulsa, 1983—; mem. Australian Inst. Mining and Metallurgy, Melbourne, 1970-75. Mem. Am. Assn. Petroleum Geologists (sec. Ho. of Dels. 1985, cert.), Tulsa Geol. Soc., Oklahoma City Geol. Soc., Sigma Xi. Presbyterian. Home: 6521 S Jamestown St Tulsa OK 74136 Office: ONEOK Exploration Co 100 W 5th St Tulsa OK 74102

D'IGNAZIO, FRED, writer, editor, computer, robotics consultant; b. Bryn Mawr, Pa., Jan. 6, 1949; s. Silvio Frederick and Elizabeth Owsley (McComas) D'I.; m. Janet Letts, Sept. 5, 1969; children—Catherine Shum, Frederick Letts. B.A. in Internat. Relations, Brown U., 1970, M.A. in Internat. Relations, Tufts U., 1971; postgrad. Am. U. Washington Sch. Law, 1971-72; postgrad. dept. computer sci. U.N.C., 1975-82. Program dir. The Inst., Dickerson, Md., 1971-74; reviewer AAAS Sci. Books and Films, Washington, 1972-83; asst. editor The Futurist Mag., Washington, 1973-74; mgalyst. Mgmt. Systems Corp., Bowie, Md., 1973; instr. adult continuing edn. on computers, U.N.C. Sch. Continuing Edn., Chapel Hill, 1974—, asst. dir. Study Efficacy of Nosocomial Infection Control Project dept. biostats., 1976-77; analyst John Hamburg & Assoc., Chapel Hill, 1976-77, Computer Scis. Corp., Washington and Chapel Hill, 1974-76; assoc. editor, columnist Compute!, Greensboro, N.C. 1982—, Compute!'s Gazette, 1983—, Compute!'s PC & PC jr., 1984—. contbg. editor, columnist Enter, Children's TV Workshop, N.Y.C. 1983—, Softside, Turtle News, Richardson, Tex., 1981-83, Video Movies, Chgo., 1984—; mem. ednl. adv. bd. Terrapin, Inc., Cambridge, Mass., 1981—; edn. adv. bd. Tar Heel (N.C.) Computer Camps, 1982; lectr. Internat. Robotics Literacy Course, London, 1983; numerous TV and radio appearances; regular commentator Good Morning Am. on ABC-TV, also computer programs PBS, Nat. Pub. Radio and CBS: cons. E.P. Dutton Co., electronic pub. div., Enter, Consumer Guide. Author: Messner's Introduction to the Computer, 1983; The Star Wars Question and Answer Book About Computers, 1983; Chip Mitchell: The Case of the Stolen Computer Brains, 1983; Electronic Games, 1982, The New Astronomy: Probing the Secrets of Space, 1982; Working Robots 1982; Small Computers: Exploring Their Technology and Future, 1981; The Creative Kid's Guide to Home Computers: Super Games and Projects to Do with Your Home Computer, 1981; Atari in Wonderland, 1983; The Atari Playground, 1983; Chip Mitchell: The Case of the Robot Warriors, 1984; The Science of Artificial Intelligence, 1984; The Computer Parade, 1983; The Crazy Robot, 1984; How to Get Intimate with Your Computer, 1984; Computing Together: A Parents and Teachers Guide to Computing with Young Children, 1984. (picturebook) Katie and the Computer, 1983.

DI JAMES, PASCAL, union exec.; b. Buffalo, Aug. 1, 1926; s. Daniel and Agnes DiJ.; student Chown Sch. Bus., 1948-50; m. Lenora, 1967; children—Daniel, Leonard. Mem. Local 8, Internat. Assn. Tile, Marble, Terrazzo, Finishers, Shopworkers and Granite Cutters Internat. Union, 1952—, fin. sec. Local 8, Marble State & Stone Polishers, 1952-54, bus. agt., 1954-71, internat. union rep., 1971-75, gen. pres.-sec.-treas., Alexandria, Va., 1975—. Served with U.S. Army, 1945-47. Office: 801 N Pitt St Alexandria VA 22314

DILKS, KENNETH ROWLAND, aviation computer systems company executive; b. Woodbury, N.J., Dec. 30, 1937; s. Rowland Ware Dilks and Iva (Newkirk) Freshwater; m. Irene Jennifer Stagg; children—Calvin P., Julien K., Sonja S. B.S. in Math., U. N.C., 1959. Site programmer Litton Industries, Giebelstadt, Fed. Republic Germany, 1965-67; mem. tech. staff Hughes Aircraft, Feltham, Middlesex, Eng., 1967-68; sr. programmer analyst Control Data Corp., Arden Hills, Minn., 1968-74; program dir. Computer Sci. Corp., Falls Church, Va., 1974-77; pres. Dilks Co., Virginia Beach, Va., 1977—. Contbr. articles to profl. jours. Chmn. State Citizens for Jackson, 1972. Mem. Air Traffic Control Assn., Radio Tech. Commn. Aeronautics, Aircraft Owners and Pilots Assn., Nat. Bus. Aircraft Assn., Confederate Air Force (hon. col.) Avocation: flying. Home: 528 Vanderbilt Ave Virginia Beach VA 23451-3667 Office: Dilks Co Inc 1711 First Colonial Ct Virginia Beach VA 23454-3109

DILL, DALLAS CHARLES, dentist; b. San Angelo, Tex., Sept. 17, 1943; s. Dallas Carlisle and Annie Ora (Harris) D.; m. Darla Ann Gloff, June 11, 1966; children—Shannon Diane, Devin Shawn. A.A., San Angelo Coll., 1964; B.S. in Pharmacy, U. Tex., 1967; D.D.S., Baylor U., 1971. Intern USPHS, Seattle, 1971-72; gen. practice dentistry, Cleburne, Tex., 1974—. Pres. local chpt. Am. Cancer Soc., Cleburne, 1974-75, local chpt. Family Services, Cleburne, 1982-83. Served with USPHS 1971-72, to lt. comdr. USCG, 1972-74. Named to Outstanding Young Men Am., U.S. Jaycees, 1977. Mem. ADA, Tex. Dental Assn., Ft. Worth Dist. Dental Soc., Baylor Dental Alumni Assn., Omicron Kappa Upsilon. Mem. Ch. of Christ. Lodge: Rotary (bd. dirs. local club 1980-81). Avocations: tennis; auto racing; photography. Office: 209-A N Ridgeway Cleburne TX 76031

DILL, RONALD LEE, engineer, oil supply company executive, consultant in health physics; b. Neosho, Mo., June 9, 1945; s. Roger Lewis and Betty Jo (McGee) D.; m. Kathleen Loraine Latimer, Aug. 10, 1969; children—Meredith Kathleen, Lizabeth Elaine. B.S. in Chemistry and Biology, Tex. Tech. U., 1970, B.S. in Edn., 1972; A.S., La. State U., 1974. Cert. tchr., Tex. Dental technician Ratliff Dental Lab., Dr. William McCauley, Lubbock, Tex., 1968-72; instr. and chmn. sci. dept. Ropesville (Tex.) High Sch., 1971-73; drilling fluids engr. Baroid of N.L. Industries, Odessa, Tex., 1973-74; gen. mgr. Gamma Industries, Midland, Tex., 1974-76; pres., owner Tracer Lab. of Midland, Inc. (Tex.), 1976—; cons. and instr. health physics Dept. Transp. Active United Way, 1979-83; mem. local com. Republican party; bd. dirs. Christmas in April, 1974-83. Mem. Soc. Petroleum Engrs., Am. Soc. Non-Destructive Testing (charter mem. West Tex. chpt.), West Tex. Well-Logging Assn., West Tex. C. of C., Tex. Tchrs. Assn., Permian Basin Petroleum Assn., Phi Epsilon Kappa. Baptist. Club: Kiwanis (dir.). Contbr. articles to profl. lit.

DILLARD, EARLE STERLING, insurance executive; b. Man, W.Va., Apr. 24, 1925; s. Andrew Sterling and Margaret Grace (Keiffer) D.; student Marshall U., 1953-54; m. Naomi Ruth Ferrell, Aug. 31, 1947; children—Dan Earle, Cherilyn Ruth, David Ferrell, Kevin Andrew, Kerry Paul, Julie Beth. Supr. agts. Security Ins. Co., Huntington, W.Va., 1948-54; pres. Dollar Stores Corp., Huntington, 1971-79, Harlo Corp., Huntington, 1971-82; pres., treas. Bloss & Dillard, Inc., Huntington, 1954—; pres. Ins. Mgrs., Inc., Columbus, Ohio, 1977—, Agts. Ins. Markets, Inc., Richmond, Va., 1979—; dir. Huntington Fed. Savs. Loan Assn. Chmn., Huntington Mayor's Adv. Com., 1967-69; pres. Huntington YMCA, 1969-71; pres. Marshall U. Big Green Scholarship Found., 1981-83. Served with USCG, 1943-46; ETO. W.Va. Ins. Agts. Co. Man of Yr., 1977; YMCA Layman of the Yr., 1964. Mem. W.Va. Ins. Assn. (pres. 1969), Am. Assn. Mng. Gen. Agts. (pres. 1974-75), W.Va. Surplus Lines Assn. (pres. 1979-80), U.S.A. Alliance (pres. 1985—), Am. Legion, VFW, C. of C. Baptist. Clubs: Guyan Country, Masons, Lions (pres. 1964-65). Home: 1934 S Englewood Rd Huntington WV 25701 Office: 1925 Adams Ave Huntington WV 25704

DILLARD, JOHN MILTON, counselor, educator, author; b. Prenter, W. Va., July 25, 1936; s. John Milton and Lucy (Martin) D.; divorced; 2 children—Scott Maurice, Brian Milton. Student W. Va. State Coll., 1957-58; B.S. in Elem. Edn., Wilberforce U., 1964; Ed.M. in Sch. Counseling, SUNY-Buffalo, 1971, Ph.D. in Counselor Edn., 1975; postgrad. in higher edn. adminstrn. Okla. State U., 1981-82. Tchr. elem. sch., Buffalo, 1964-72; tchr. basic adult edn., 1966-69; elem. sch. guidance counselor, 1972-76; clin. teaching asst. dept. counseling and ednl. psychology SUNY-Buffalo, 1974-75, adj. asst. prof., 1975-76; vis. asst. prof. U. Carabobo (Venezuela), summer 1978; assoc. prof. counseling and student personnel, dept. applied behavioral studies in edn. Okla. State U., Stillwater, 1976-85, also coordinator higher edn. counseling and student personnel adminstrn. programs; prof. ednl. psychology and ednl. adminstrn., Tex. A&M. U., College Station, 1985—, coordinator univ. lecture series, 1985-86, also coordinator of coll. student personnel program; cons. devel. workshop presentation; speaker in field. Mem. Internat. Assn. Cross-Cultural Psychology, Am. Psychol. Assn., Am. Assn. Counseling and Devel., Am. Ednl. Research Assn. (chmn. career counseling and vocat. devel. panel), Am. Psychol. Assn., So. Assn. Coll. Student Affairs, Am. Sch. Counselor Assn., Okla. Sch. Counselor Assn. (past v.p.), Phi Delta Kappa, Kappa Alpha Psi. Author: Multicultural Counseling: Toward Ethnic and Cultural Relevance in Human Encounters; Lifelong Career Planning. Adv. editor Jour. Ednl. Psychology; cons. editor, bd. dirs. Jour. Ednl. Internat. Student Personnel, 1979-80; editorial bd. mem. Jour. Voc. Behavior. Contbr. articles to profl. jours. Office: Dept Ednl Psychology 704 Harrington Edn Ctr Tex A&M U College Station TX 77843

DILLARD, MAX MURRAY, diversified energy executive; b. Lueders, Tex., Nov. 21, 1935; s. Alva C. and Effie Carroll (Murray) D.; B.S. in Petroleum Engring., U. Tex., 1958; m. Carol Gayle Jenkins, Dec. 28, 1957; children—Denise Gayle, Pamela Deanne, Julie Ann. Ops. mgr. Peter Bawden Drilling Co., Long Beach, Calif., 1967-69; pres. Bandera Drilling, Inc., Dallas, 1969-73; pres., dir. Garvey Drilling, Inc., Wichita, Kans., 1973-75; pres., chief operating officer Progress Drilling, Inc., Houston, 1975-78; pres., chmn. bd., chief exec. officer Drillers, Inc., Houston, 1978—; pres. Di Energy Inc., 1982—; dir. Dillco, Inc. Mem. Republican Pres.'s Com. Registered profl. engr., Tex. Mem. Internat. Assn. Drilling Contractors (dir.), Am. Petroleum Inst., Tex. Ind. Producers Assn., Nat. Soc. Profl. Engrs. Republican. Mem. Ch. of Christ. Clubs: Houston, Wichita Petroleum, Raveneaux Country. Author articles in field. Office: 450 Gears Rd Suite 625 Houston TX 77067

DILLARD, TOM W., historical agency administrator, state official; b. Sims, Ark., Dec. 24, 1948; s. Thomas O. and Hattie (Baggs.) D.; m. Donna Atwood, June 1, 1968 (div. 1980); 1 child, Neil Q.; m. Mary Frost, Jan. 4, 1982. B.S., U. Central Ark., 1970; M.A., U. Ark., 1974. Tchr., Little Rock Pub. Schs., 1974-77; historian Ark. Park Dept., Little Rock, 1977-80; dir. Dept. Ark. Heritage, Little Rock, 1980—; adj. prof. U. Ark. at Little Rock, 1983—. Co-author: Researching Arkansas History, 1979. Co-compiler: Arkansas History: A Selected Bibliography, 1984. Contbr. articles to hist. jours. Named Ark. Humanist of Yr., Ark. Endowment for Humanities, 1985. Mem. Ark. Hist. Assn. (pres. 1983-84), Ark. Mus. Assn. (pres. 1980-81), So. Hist. Assn., Am. Assn. for State/Local History, Soc. Am. Archivists. Lutheran. Avocations: gardening; book collecting. Office: Dept of Arkansas Heritage 225 E Markham Suite 200 Little Rock AR 72201

DILLARD, WILLIAM T., department store chain executive; b. 1914; married. B.S.B.A., U. Ark., 1935; M.S., Columbia U., 1937. With Dillard Dept. Stores Inc., Little Rock, chmn. bd., pres., chief exec. officer, until 1977, chmn. bd., chief exec. officer, 1977—, also dir.; dir. First Nat. Bank, Little Rock. Office: Dillard Dept Stores Inc 900 W Capitol Little Rock AR 72201*

DILLEHAY, DAVID ROGERS, pyrotechnic engineer; b. Shreveport, Sept. 21, 1936; s. Thomas Jefferson, Jr. and Rachel (Todd) D.; B.A. in Chemistry, Rice U., Houston, 1958; Ph.D. in Chemistry, Clayton U., St. Louis, 1983; m. Marilyn Heath, Nov. 23, 1957; children—David, Janet. With Morton Thiokol Corp., Marshall, Tex., 1958—, research and devel. projects supr., 1979—. Recipient award U.S. Army Material Command, 1969. Mem. Am. Mgmt. Assn., Am. Def. Preparedness Ass-. (1st v.p. La. chpt. 1981, pres. Ark.-La.-Tex. chpt. 1982, rep. nat. council 1983), Internat. Pyrotechnics Soc. (sec. 1980-84, v.p. 1984-86, pres. 1986—), R Assn., Thiokol-Longhorn Mgmt. Club, Ark.-La.-Tex. Wireless Assn. Roman Catholic. Author, patentee in field. Home: 107 Ashwood Terr Marshall TX 75670 Office: PO Box 1149 Marshall TX 75670

DILLEHAY, RONALD CLIFFORD, psychology educator; b. Malvern, Iowa, Nov. 2, 1935; s. Clifford Marvin and Lela May (Raines) D.; m. Valerie Ruth Sherbourne, Dec. 22, 1954; children—Pamela Ann, Ronald Clifford Jr., Darin Raines. Student, Calif. State U.-Fresno, 1953-55; A.B., U. Calif.-Berkeley, 1957, Ph.D., 1962; postgrad. in law U. Ky., 1976. Research behavioral scientist, lectr. U. Calif.-Berkeley, 1960-64; from asst. prof. to assoc. prof. dept. behavioral sci. and psychology U. Ky., Lexington, 1964-66, assoc. prof., 1969-71, prof., 1971—, chmn. dept. psychology, 1973-80, research assoc. Social Welfare Research Inst., 1970-73; assoc. prof. dept. psychology, Tex. Christian U., Ft. Worth, 1966-69; cons. pub. health agys., Calif. and Ky., 1960-70, various pvt. legal firms, Ky., Calif., Oreg., Ga., Ala., Md., S.C., 1978—. Author: (with John P. Kirscht) Dimensions of Authoritarianism, 1967; (with Michael T. Nietzel) Psychological Consultation in the Courtroom, 1985. Contbr. chpts. to books, articles and papers to profl. publs. Fulbright-Hays sr. fellow La Pontificia Universidad Católica, Lima, Peru, 1973-74; fellow james McKeen Cattell Found., 1980-81. Mem. Am. Psychol. Assn., Soc. for Psychol. Study Social Issues, Midwestern Psychol. Assn., Southeastern Psychol. Assn., Soc. Exptl. Social Psychology, Sociedad Interamericana de Psicologîa, Sigma Xi. Club: Ky. Kickers Soccer (bd. dirs. 1983-85) (Lexington). Home: 1848 McDonald Rd Lexington KY 40503 Office: Dept Psychology U Ky 220A Kastle Hall Lexington KY 40506

DILLER, THOMAS EUGENE, mechanical engineering educator; b. Orrville, Ohio, Sept. 10, 1950; s. Ray E. and Ruth Virginia (Johnson) D.; m. Sharon Leigh Street, Apr. 23, 1977; children—Nathanael John, Peter Ray, Elizabeth Grace. B.S., Carnegie Mellon U., 1972; S.M., MIT, 1974, Sc.D., 1977. Sr. engr. Polaroid Corp., Waltham, Mass., 1976-79; assoc. prof. mech. engring. Va. Poly. Inst. and State U., Blacksburg, 1979—; engring. cons. dir. Hertz Found. fellow, 1972-76; NIH grantee, 1980-81, 82-83, Whitaker Found. grantee, 1981-84; Dept. Energy grantee, 1982—. Mem. ASME, Am. Inst. Chem. Engrs., AAAS, Sigma Xi, Pi Tau Sigma, Tau Beta Pi. Contbr. articles to profl. jours.

DILLEY, JERRY DALE, diversified industry executive; b. Dallas, Nov. 24, 1931; s. Loniel Elmer and Mary Magdeline (Graves) D.; student Crozier Tech. Sch., Dallas, 1948-49, Dallas Art Inst., 1946-50; m. Carol Parker, Apr. 5, 1974; children—Marilyn Smith, Paul E., Lori White, Wesley C., Trey D., Cassandra K. Shopman, Welding Lab., Dallas, 1948-50, designer, 1950-51, chief engr., 1951-53; v.p., chief engr. Metal Structures Corp., Grapevine, Tex., 1954-58, v.p., gen. mgr., 1958-62; v.p., gen. mgr., dir. Rollform Corp., Dallas, 1961-63; pres., dir. Dilley Corp., 1961-65; exec. v.p., dir. Omega Industries, Inc., Grapevine, 1965—. Recipient award for painting Dallas Mus. Fine Arts, 1941. Mem. Nat. Coil Coaters Assn., Soc. Mfg. Engrs., Am. Mgmt. Assn., Order Foresters. Office: Grapevine TX

DILLMAN, GEORGE FRANKLIN, financial and management consultant; b. Coronado, Calif., Sept. 5, 1934; s. Wilbur Mitchell and Meadie (Ables) D.; student Abilene Christian Coll., 1952; B.S., B.B.A., U. Tex., 1958; m. Virginia Gayle Yeary, Sept. 1, 1961; children—Leesa Gayle, Mitchell Lynn, Virginia Louise, Laura Lynn. Asso., Bus. Research Corp. Tex., Austin, 1957-61; dir. econ. research Pacific Western Properties, Inc., Los Angeles, 1961; dir. corp. relations, econ. research Diversa, Inc., Dallas, 1961-62, corp. sec., 1962-65, v.p., corp. sec., dir., 1965-67; chmn. bd., pres. Bonanza Internat. (Bonanza Steak House), 1965-67; chmn., mng. ptnr. Dillman & Assos. (formerly Dillman-Berry & Assos.), Dallas, 1968—; chmn. exec. com., dir. Richardson Savs. & Loan Assn., 1965-76; chmn. Security Savs. Assn., 1974-75; chmn. exec. com. Dallas Internat. Bank, 1974-76, Preferred Prop. Corp., 1982—, Caprock Savs., 1983—. Mem. bd. assos. Pepperdine U., Malibu, 1967-77; mem. bd., past pres. Dallas Assembly; chmn. Tex. Tourist Devel. Agy., Pub. Health Services Bd. Dallas County, 1972-79; vice chmn. Child Welfare Bd. Dallas County; mem. Citizens/Police Rev. Bd. City of Dallas. Served with USNR, 1952-60. Democrat. Mem. Ch. of Christ. Contbr. articles to profl. and ch. jours. Home: 13361 Peyton Dr Dallas TX 75214 Office: 4230 LBJ Freeway Dallas TX 75234

DILLON, LINDA SUSAN, vocational education educator, consultant; b. Berwyn, Ill., Aug. 11, 1948; d. Robert and Alvanell (Riddle) Schnulle; m. David Austin Dillon, May 15, 1979. B.S., Iowa State U., 1970; M.S., U. N.C.-Greensboro, 1976; Ph.D., Ohio State U., 1979. Acad. advisor Ohio State U., Columbus, 1976-78; grad. research assoc. Nat. Ctr. Research in Vocat. Edn., Columbus, 1978-79; assoc. prof. occupational edn. N.C. State U., Raleigh, 1979—. Office: N C State U 502 Poe Hall Raleigh NC 27695-7801

DILLON, MARYE BRIDGET, nurse manager, consultant; b. N.Y.C., Apr. 27, 1948; d. Patrick and Bridget (Callaghan) D.; m. Raymond H. Abbott, Nov. 5, 1977; 1 dau., Carolyn. R.N., Misericordia Hosp., Bronx, N.Y., 1970; B.S. in Nursing, Spalding Coll., 1980; M.S. in Nursing, Ind. U.-Purdue U.-Indpls., 1984. Staff nurse Meml.-Sloan Kettering Inst. for Cancer, N.Y.C., 1970-72; staff nurse med. intensive care Mass. Gen. Hosp., Boston, 1973-74; staff nurse ICU/CCU Anna Jaqes Hosp., Newburyport, Mass., 1974-76; staff nurse Surg. Intensive Care Unit, VA Med. Ctr., Louisville, 1977-78, adminstrv. coordinator, 1978-81, nurse mgr. Surg. Intensive Care Unit, 1981-85, surg. splty. mgr., 1985—; cons. in field. Bd. dirs. Haverhill-Newburyport Human Services Inc., 1975. Recipient Catherine Zollinger award for leadership, Spalding Coll., 1980, Heart and Hands award VA Med. Ctr., 1983. Mem. Am. Nursing Assn., Am. Assn. Critical Care Nurses, Am. Heart Assn., Sigma Theta Tau. Democrat.

DILWORTH, BILLY D., newspaperman; b. Martin, Ga., Oct. 4, 1934; s. B.Q. and Pearl (Davis) D.; student journalism U. Ga. Ga. editor Anderson (S.C.) Ind., 1953-63; state editor Atlanta Times, 1964-65; state editor Athens (Ga.) Daily News, 1967-72, roving editor, columnist, 1975—; state editor Anderson Independent, 1972-75; host programs radio sta. WLET, Toccoa, Ga., 1960—, sta. WSPA-TV, Spartanburg, S.C., 1968—. Mem. Ga. Scholarship Commn., 1971—. Recipient A.P. award reporting and news photo, 1963; nominee Disk Jockey of Yr., Country Music Assn., 1974-75, 75-76, 77-78, 78-79. First newsman to announce Presdl. candidacy of Jimmy Carter. Home: Box 117 Carnesville GA 30521

DIMBATH, MERLE F., economic consultant, business educator; b. Dayton, Ohio, Mar. 21, 1939; s. Merle S. and Zella (Shadowens) D.; children—Merle, Richard, Sesilie, Eric. B.S. in Commerce, U. Va., 1961; M.A. in Mktg., U. Fla., 1962, Ph.D. in Econs. and Bus. Adminstrn., 1964. Qualified econ. expert witness state and fed. cts., Fla. Chmn. dept. econs. and bus. Fla. So. Coll., Lakeland, 1967-77; supt. pub. instrn. Polk County, Fla., 1968-69; exec. dir. Fla. Pub. Sch. Bd., Tallahassee, 1969; land developer, real estate and mortgage broker, investments, Lakeland, Fla., 1971-80; pres. Dimbath Devel. Co., Lakeland, 1971—; econ. research and cons. Dimbath & Assocs., Stuart, Fla., 1980—; assoc. prof. Coll. Bus. and Pub. Adminstrn., Fla. Atlantic U., Boca Raton, 1981—; money reporter sta. WPEC-TV, West Palm Beach, Fla., 1982—. DuPont scholar, 1957-61; Ford Found. fellow, 1963-64. Mem. Am. Econ. Assn., Nat. Assn. Bus. Economists, So. Econ. Assn. Address: PO Box 2910 Stuart FL 23495 Home: 72 S River Rd Stuart FL 33495 Office: Suite 202 3601 E Ocean Blvd Stuart FL 33494

DIMICK, ALAN ROBERT, surgeon, educator; b. Birmingham, Ala., Sept. 30, 1932; s. Daniel Baker and Jennie Rose (Coplon) D.; m. Eleanor Hamilton, July 17, 1954; children—Susan Elaine, Robert Marshall, Richard Neil. B.S., Birmingham So. Coll., 1953; M.D., Med. Coll. Ala., 1958. Diplomate Am. Bd. Surgery. Intern, U. Ala. Hosps., Birmingham, 1958-59, resident, 1959-63; assoc. prof. surgery U. Ala.-Birmingham, 1963—; dir. Burn Ctr., U. Ala. Hosps.; chmn. adv. com. Emergency Med. Services City of Birmingham, 1967—; chmn. adv. bd. Emergency Med. Services, State of Ala., 1972—. Recipient Service to Mankind award Birmingham Sertoma Club, 1981. Mem. Med. Assn. State of Ala. (Samuel Buford Word award 1978), AMA (com. on emergency med. services 1974—), Am. Burn Assn., Am. Coll. Surgeons, Southeastern Surg. Congress, Am. Assn. for Surgery of Trauma, Surg. Infection Soc., Alpha Omega Alpha. Contbr. publs. to profl. lit. Home: University Station Birmingham AL 35294 Office: Dept Surgery University Station Birmingham AL 35294

DIMSDALE, PARKS B., marketing educator; b. Atlanta, Nov. 23, 1934; s. Parks and Eugenia Paris Dimsdale; m. Bonnie M. Trinka, July 25, 1974. B.B.A., Ga. State U., 1961; M.B.A., Emory U., 1962; Ph.D., U. Fla., 1969. Cert. mgmt. cons. Assoc. prof. La. State U., Baton Rouge, 1969-71; exec. v.p. Purcell Cons., Decatur, Ga., 1971-73; prin. Dimsdale Assocs., Atlanta, 1973-78; dir. bus. programs U. W. Fla., Panama City, 1978-82; chmn. mktg. dept., 1982—, prof., 1985—; dir., Reg Files, Inc., Tallahassee; cons. Bapt. Hosp., Pensacola, Artline Graphics, Atlanta, Dimsdale Assocs., Gulf Breeze, Fla., 1982—. Author: A History of Cotton Producers Association, 1971; (with John Wright) Pioneers in Marketing, 1974. Vice pres., bd. dirs. Atlanta Assn. Retarded Citizens, 1975-78; campaign coordinator Mary Hitt for Lt. Gov. of Ga., 1974. Served with USN, 1956-58. Recipient Outstanding Prof. award U. W. Fa., 1980, 81. Mem. Am. Mktg. Assn. (v.p elect, bd. dirs.), N.W. Fla. Mktg. Assn. (founder, pres. 1984—), Pensacola C. of C. (com. chmn. 1983—), So. Mktg. Assn., Acad. Mktg. Sci. Republican. Avocations: travel; biking. Office: Dept Mktg and Econs Univ W Fla Pensacola FL 32514

DINGFELDER, STEVEN PETER, clinical psychologist, mental health service administrator; b. Mpls., May 9, 1944; s. Sigbert and Elizabeth (Neu) D.; B.A., U. Minn., 1966; M.A., Ind. State U., 1968, Ph.D., 1971; cert. mental health adminstrn. U. Minn., 1981; m. Claire Elaine and Shechter, Dec. 19, 1965; children—Jennifer Ann, Scott Allen, Heidi Lynn. Psychologist, Moore-Porter Evaluation Clinic, Terre Haute, Ind., 1968; sch. psychologist Vigo County (Ind.) Sch. Corp., Terre Haute, 1969-70; clin. psychologist Katherine Hamilton Mental Health Center, Terre Haute, 1970-72, program dir., 1972-74; chem. dependency coordinator No. Pines Unified Services Center, Cumberland, Wis., 1973—; exec. dir. Sandhills Mental Health Devel. Found., 1980-83; adj. prof. psychology Ind. State U., Terre Haute, 1972, adj. prof. U. Minn., 1981—; cons. psychologist Gibault Sch. for Boys, Terre Haute, 1974; area dir. Sandhills Mental Health Center, Pinehurst, N.C., 1977-83; pres., practitioner Growth Inst., Inc., Pinehurst, 1982-83; dir. Matanzas Bay Pavilion for Health Resources, St. Augustine, Fla., 1983-84. pvt. practice, St. Augustine, 1984—; pres. Enrichment Tng. Assocs., 1985—. Mem. Ind. Gov.'s Adv. Council on Alcohol and Drug Abuse, 1974; treas. St. John's Interagy. Council. Recipient Becker award Ind. State U., 1968. Mem. Am. Psychol. Assn., Ind. Psychol. Assn. (chmn. div. sch. psychology 1973-74), Fla. Psychol. Assn., Ind. Assn. Counselors Alcohol and Drug Abuse (v.p. 1973-74), Wis. Assn. Community Human Services Program, Wis. Assn. Chem. Abuse Coordinators (chmn. 1976), Area Dirs. Assn. N.C. (sec.-treas. 1979, v.p. 1982), Lambda Psi Sigma, Phi Delta Kappa. Address: Corp Sq Suite A6 Saint Augustine FL 32084

DINI, RICHARD FRANCIS, fund raising company executive; b. Medford, Mass., May 7, 1935; s. Louis Paul and Alice (Cecconi) D.; m. Jeanne Fowler, Dec. 18, 1960; children—Mark Edwin, David Walker. B.S., Boston U., 1959. Devel. officer Harvard U., Cambridge, Mass., 1962-65; asst. to pres. Rice U., Houston, 1965-69; pres. R.F. Dini & Assocs., Houston, 1970-83, chmn., 1983—. Div. mgr. United Fund of Boston, 1960-62. Served with U.S. Army, 1954-55. Knighted Royal Order of St. George, 1979. Mem. Am. Assn. Fund-Raising Counsel, Nat. Soc. Fund Raising Execs. Roman Catholic. Club: Brae-Burn Country (Houston). Home: 5235 Loch Lomond Houston TX 77096 Office: R F Dini & Assocs Inc Suite 630 600 Jefferson St Houston TX 77002

DINKEL, ROBERT MILLER, concrete products company executive; b. Cin., Mar. 17, 1908; s. Nicholas Stephen and Amelia (Miller) D.; m. Eileen V. Bass, Sept. 8, 1940; children—Tara Jane, Sanne, Rebecca, John. B.A., U. Notre

Dame, 1930; M.A., U. Minn., 1940; Ph.D., U. N.C.-Chapel Hill, 1950. Instr. sociology DePauw U., 1940-41; with U.S. Govt., Washington, 1942-46; founder, pres. Carolina Quality Block Co., Greensboro, N.C., 1946—; faculty sociology Guilford Coll., Greensboro, 1950-72. Pres., Greensboro Community Council, 1959-60; bd. dirs. Nathanial Greene council Boy Scouts Am., 1965-69. Served with USMCR, 1944-45. Mem. Nat. Concrete Masonry Assn., Am. Sociol. Assn., Am. Anthrop. Assn., Population Assn. Am., Internat. Union Sci. Study Population. Club: Greensboro Country. Home: 1209 Lakewood Dr Greensboro NC 27410 Office: Carolina Quality Block Co 1100 S Elm St Greensboro NC 27406

DINKINS, JANE POLING, management consultant; b. Van Wert, Ohio, Oct. 11, 1928; d. Doyt Carl and Kathryn (Sawyer) Poling; B.B.A., So. Methodist U., 1974. Stewardess, instr. Am. Airlines, 1946-50; exec. sec., adminstrv. asst. Southland Royalty Co., 1956-63; exec. sec. Charles E. Seay, Inc. and C.W. Goyer, Jr., Dallas, 1963-68; systems analyst, programmer Southland Life Ins. Co., Dallas, 1968-69, 1st Nat. Bank, Dallas, 1969-72, Occidental Life Ins. Co., Los Angeles, 1972-73; systems analyst, programmer Pacific Mut. Life Ins. Co., Newport Beach, Calif., 1973-74, mgr. mut. fund subs., 1975; systems analyst, programmer, info. services div. TRW, Orange, Calif., 1975-79; EDP auditor Union Bank, Los Angeles, 1979; sr. EDP auditor Security Pacific Nat. Bank, Glendale, Calif., 1979-80, asst. v.p., Los Angeles, 1981; mgmt. cons. Fed. Res. Bank, Automation Program Office, Dallas, 1982-85; pres. Poling & Assocs., Inc., 1985—. Mem. Am. Mgmt. Assn., Quality Assurance Assn., EDP Auditors Assn. Club: Bachelors, Sigma Kappa (Newport Beach, Calif.); University (Dallas). Republican. Methodist. Home: 4820 Westgrove Dr Apt 606 Dallas TX 75248

DINTINGER, ROBERT WESTNEY, oil service company executive; b. Phila., Sept. 6, 1932; s. Norman R. and Laura M. (Chase) D.; m. Bernadette R. Pollick, Mar. 31, 1934; children—Lois M., Donna L., Robert W., Mark N., Matthew R. Diploma, Pa. State U., 1963; B.A. in Bus. Adminstrn., Calif. Western U., 1976. With John J. Nesbitt Inc., 1955-63; mgmt. cons. Naus & Newlyn Inc., 1963-66; prodn. mgr. Singer Co., 1966-68; mgmt. cons., Auburn, N.Y., 1968-70; dir. mgmt. services Londontown Corp., 1970-73, Olga Inc., Van Nuys, Calif., 1973-74; dir. mgmt. info. services MSI Data Inc., Costa Mesa, Calif., 1974-76; dir. material Pyke Mfg. Inc., Salt Lake City, 1976-78; mfg. cons. Sperry Univac, 1978-79; v.p. material and mfg. Best Industries Inc., Houston, 1979—. Served with U.S. Navy, 1950-53. Mem. Am. Prodn. Inventory Control Soc., Am. Mgmt. Assn. Republican. Lutheran. Lodge: Masons. Office: 12800 Aldine-Westfield Houston TX 77019

DIRKS, KENNETH RAY, pathologist, retired army officer, educator; b. Newton, Kans., Feb. 11, 1925; s. Jacob Kenneth and Ruth Viola (Penner) D.; M.D., Washington U., St. Louis, 1947; m. Betty Jean Worsham, June 9, 1946; children—Susan Jan, Jeffrey Mark, Deborah Anne, Timothy David, Melissa Jane. Rotating intern St. Louis City Hosp., 1948, asst. resident in gen. surgery, 1948-49; resident in pathology VA Hosp., Jefferson Barracks, Mo., 1951-53, resident in pathology, asst. chief lab. service, Indpls., 1953-54; resident in pathology Letterman Army Hosp., San Francisco, 1956-57; fellow in tropical medicine and parasitology, La. State U., Central Am., 1958; asst. in pathology Washington U. Sch. Medicine, St. Louis, 1952-53; asst. chief, lab. service, VA Hosp., Jefferson Barracks, Mo., 1953; instr. pathology U. Ind. Med. Center, Indpls., 1953-54; commd. capt. M.C., U.S. Army, 1954, advanced through grades to maj. gen., 1976; dir. research, Med. Research and Devel. Command, Washington, 1968-69, dep. comdr., 1969-71, comdr., 1973-76; dep. comdr. Med. Research Inst. Infectious Diseases, Ft. Detrick, Frederick, Md., 1972-73, comdr., 1973; comdr. Med. Research and Devel. Command, Washington, 1973-76, Fitzsimons Army Med. Center, Denver, 1976-77; supt. Acad. Health Scis., Fort Sam Houston, 1977-80; ret., 1980; prof. Coll. Medicine, Tex. A&M U., College Station, 1980—, asst. dean, 1980—. Decorated D.S.M., Legion of Merit with oak leaf cluster, Meritorious Service medal, Army Commendation medal with oak leaf cluster; diplomate Am. Bd. Pathology. Fellow Coll. Am. Pathologists, Internat. Acad. Pathology; mem. AMA, Am. Soc. Clin. Pathologists, Assn. Mil. Surgeons U.S., Sigma Xi. Contbr. articles to med. jours. Office: Coll Medicine Tex A&M Univ College Station TX 77843

DI SABATO, LOUIS ROMAN, zoo director; b. Columbus, Ohio, Oct. 7, 1931; s. Roman John and Lucille Katherine (Bernard) DiS.; m. Phyllis Ann Thompson, July 8, 1953; children—Christopher R., Julie Ann, Maura L., Carol N., Kathleen. Student, Ohio State U., 1949-52. With Columbus Municipal Zoo, 1955-63, dir., 1961-63, Seneca Park Zoo, Rochester, N.Y., 1963-68, San Antonio Zool. Gardens and Aquarium, 1968—. Mem. Nat. Mus. Services Bd. Served to 1st lt. U.S. Army, 1952-55. Fellow Am. Assn. Zool. Parks and Aquariums; mem. Internat. Wild Waterfowl Assn., Internat. Union Dirs. Zool. Gardens. Roman Catholic. Club: Rotary (sec.).

DI SANTO, GRACE JOHANNE DEMARCO (MRS. FRANK MICHAEL DI SANTO), poet, civic worker; b. Derby, Conn., July 12, 1924; d. Richard and Fannie (DeMarco) De Marco; student N.Y. U. Sch. Journalism, 1941-43; A.B. in English, Belmont Abbey Coll., 1974; m. Frank Michael Di Santo, Aug. 30, 1946; children—Frank Richard, Bernadette Mary, Roxanne Judith. Newswriter, Australian Asso. Press, N.Y.C., 1942-43; staff reporter Ansonia Sentinel, Derby, 1943-45; feature writer, drama critic Bridgeport Herald, New Haven, 1945-46; editor monthly bull. Pa. State Coll. Optometry, Phila., 1947-48; free-lance writer, 1949-54; founder, pres. Broad Investors Ltd., Morganton, N.C., 1966-67. Pres. Burke County chpt. N.C. Symphony Soc., 1968-70; mem. exec. bd. Community Concerts Assn., 1962-73; Burke County chmn. nat. humanities series Woodrow Wilson Fellowship Found., 1971-73. Bd. dirs. Burke county chpt. March of Dimes, 1966-72; trustee N.C. Symphony Soc., 1965-73; trustee, bd. dirs. North State Acad., Hickory, N.C., 1973—; bd. advisors Belmont Abbey Coll., N.C. Mem. Am. Acad. Poets, Poetry Council N.C., N.C. Poetry Soc., Delta Epsilon Sigma. Republican. Roman Catholic. Clubs: Grandfather Golf and Country (Linville, N.C.); Mimosa Hills Golf. Author: (poems) The Eye Is Single; Portrait of the Poet as Teacher: James Dickey. Address: 218 Riverside Dr Morganton NC 28655 also Grandfather Golf and Country Club Linville NC 28646

D'ISERNIA, BRIAN RAPHAEL, lawyer, shipbuilding company executive; b. N.Y.C., Dec. 30, 1943; s. Alfred Louis and Mary M. D'Isernia; B.A., Georgetown U., 1965; J.D., Fordham U., 1968; m. Miriam Eastburn Apuzzo, June 26, 1971; children—Kathleen, Miriam, Brian, Luke, Daisey, Joseph, Bridgett. Admitted to N.Y. State bar, 1969; pres. Key Largo Fisheries, Inc., White Plains N.Y., 1972-80, Capt. Fritz, Inc., White Plains, 1972-80, Kathmir, Inc., White Plains, 1972-78, Miss Penny, Inc., Panama City, Fla., 1976-80; pres., chief exec. officer Eastern Marine, Inc., Panama City, 1976—. Bd. dirs. Tom P. Haney Vocat.-Tech. Sch., Pamama City. Mem. N.Y. Bar Assn., Soc. Naval Architects and Marine Engrs. Roman Catholic. Club: St. Andrew Bay Yacht. Office: 2200 Nelson St Panama City FL 32401

DISNEY, JANELLE, counselor, educator; b. Tuscaloosa, Ala., June 15, 1946; d. Arthur Lee and Sara Evelyn (Sullivan) D.; m. Richard Carico Davenport, Sept. 15, 1967 (div. 1977); children—Richard B., Adrienne L. B.A., U. Ala.-Tuscaloosa, 1979, M.A., 1975, Ph.D., 1979. Sch. liaison Griffin Area Child Devel. Ctr., Ga., 1977-78; counselor, evaluator Charles Cox & Assocs., Lake Charles, La., 1980-83; assoc. prof. McNeese State U., Lake Charles, 1979—, dir. counseling and scholarship, testing, 1981-82; counselor, evaluator Univ. Assocs. in Psychology, Lake Charles, 1984—. Bd. dirs. Etc., orgn. for treating psychol. and drug problems of youth, Lake Charles, 1984—. Mem. La. Psychol. Assn. (sec. 1984—), Southwest La. Psychol. Assn. (organizer conf. 1983, 84, sec. 1984, pres. 1985), Am. Psychol. Assn. Republican. Baptist. Avocations: water skiing; snow skiing; bike riding. Home: 508 Dolby St Lake Charles LA 70605 Office: Dept Psychology McNeese State U Lake Charles LA 70609

DISPENNETTE, SARA ANNE MARIE, nurse; b. Memphis, June 23, 1953; d. Florian Emile and Maggie Etolia (Lindsey) Jabour; m. Michael Henry Thompson, Jan. 13, 1969 (div. Sept. 1976); m. 2d, John William Dispennette, June 4, 1977; children—John Michael, Sandra Marie, Jennifer Lee. A.S. in Nursing, Troy State Sch. Nursing, Montgomery, Ala., 1983. Secretarial position, Montgomery, Ala., 1966-72; floral designer CCC Assocs., Montgomery, 1970-77; kindergarten tchr. Gantt's Pvt. Sch., Montgomery, 1974-76; sec., store mgr. Convenience Marketers, Inc., Montgomery, 1977-78; with Technicolor Graphics, Montgomery, 1978-79; sec.-treas. Slush Puppie, Montgomery, 1977-83; staff nurse Bapt. Med. Ctr., Montgomery, 1983—. Methodist. Home: 5906 Carmel Dr Montgomery AL 36117

DISSTON, HARRY, author, business executive, horseman; b. Red Bank, N.J., Nov. 23, 1899; s. Eugene John Kauffmann and Frances Matilda Disston; A.B., Amherst Coll., 1921; m. Valerie Ivy Duval, Mar. 26, 1930 (dec. 1951); children—Robin John Duval, Geoffrey Whitmore; m. Catherine Sitler John, Aug. 26, 1960. With N.Y. Telephone Co., 1921-32, with AT&T, N.Y.C., 1932-60, exec. tng. student, dist. traffic supt., sales engr., dist. mgr., adv. staff engr., adv. staff exec. ind. co. relations, 1951-60; coordinator devel. activities, placement dir. Grad. Sch. Bus. Adminstrn., U. Va.; v.p. Equine Motion Analysis, Ltd., 1979—; horse dir. AMVEST Leasing Corp., Charlottesville, Va. Aide-de-camp to gov. Va.; chmn. Louisa County Electoral Bd.; mem. Va. Bd. Mil. Affairs; chmn. finance com. Republican party Va.; chmn. Louisa County Rep. Com. Vice pres., dir. Park Ave. Assn. Mem. exec. com. Episcopal Diocese of Va., also pres. council, region 15; trustee Grant Monument Assn., Va. Outdoors Found.; bd. dirs. Atlantic Rural Expn., Lee-Jackson Found.; chmn., bd. dirs. Charlottesville-Albemarle Clean Community Commn., 1978—. Served from maj. to col., cav. and gen. staff corps, 1941-46; PTO; comdg. officer 107th Regtl. Combat Team, N.Y.N.G., 1947-57; brig. gen. ret. Awarded Legion of Merit, Bronze Star with oak leaf cluster; comdr. Order of Boliver; Philippine Liberation Medal; Medal of Merit with Swords, Free Poland. Mem. Am. Horse Shows Assn. (judge, steward, tech. del.), Vets. 7th Regt., N.Y. Soc. Mil. and Naval Officers World Wars (past pres.), Vet. Corps Arty., Mil. Order Fgn. Wars, Mil. Order World Wars, Am. Legion, Res. Officers Assn. (chpt. pres.), St. Georges Soc., St. Andrews Soc., Va. Thoroughbred Assn., U.S. Pony Clubs (gov.), Phi Beta Kappa, Phi Kappa Psi. Clubs: Torch (pres. Charlottesville-Albermarle); Union; Amherst; Church of New York; Farmington Country, Greencroft, Jack Jouett Bridle Trails (pres.) (Charlottesville, Va.); The Pilgrims of the U.S.; Keswick Hunt, Keswick of Va. Author: Equestionnaire, 1947; Riding Rhymes, 1951; Know About Horses, 1961; Young Horseman's Handbooks, 1962; Elementary Dressage, 1971; Beginning Polo, 1973; Beginning the Rest of Your Life; columnist Charlottesville Daily Progress; several mag. articles on mil., equine and bus. subjects; contbr. to Ency. Brit. Home: Hidden Hill Farm Keswick VA 22947 Office: 1 Boar's Head Pl Charlottesville VA 22901

DISTELHORST, CRAIG TIPTON, savings and loan executive; b. Pitts., Nov. 3, 1941; s. Carl Frederick and Josephine Harris (Smith) D.; m. Judith Ann Harrill, Oct. 6, 1979. B.S., Washington and Lee U., 1963; J.D., George Washington U., 1966. Bar: N.Y. 1969, D.C., 1967. Sr. v.p., sec. Home Fed. Savs., Greesboro, N.C., 1976-79; v.p. Mortgage Guaranty Ins. Corp., Milw., 1979-82; exec. v.p., chief operating officer Benjamin Franklin Savs. and Loan, Houston, 1982-84, pres., dir., 1984-85, chmn. exec. com., 1985—; dir. Security Capital Credit Corp. Hartford, Conn., Foster Ins. Mgrs., Inc., Houston, Lloyds Mgmt. Corp., Houston, Security Capital Lloyds, Houston. Mem. corp. bd. dirs. Milw. Sch. Engring., 1980-82; vol. steering com. United Craftsman, Bedford-Stuyvesant, N.Y., 1968-69; chmn. support program, George Washington U. Law Sch., 1969; mem. Mo. Republican State Com., 1972-74; adv. Ret. Sr. Citizens Vol. Program, Nevada, Mo., 1975-76; vol. Junenile Probation Officer, Nevada, 1974-76; bd. dirs. Mo.-Kans. Regional council Boy Scouts Am., 1975-76; bd. dirs. Greater Greensboro Housing Found., N.C., 1978-79; state fin. chmn. for election Gov. Kit Bond of Mo., 1972; chmn. Vernon County United Fund, Nevada, 1975, Nevada City Planning Comm., 1973-75, Mo. Mcpl. Bond Com., 1978-79; vice chmn., bd. dirs. United Arts Council Greensboro, 1979; mem. Nevada City Council, 1975-76. Mem. Phi Delta Phi. Presbyterian. Club: Kingwood Country. Lodge: Elks, Rotary (bd. dirs. 1975-76, chmn. program 1974-76). Avocations: jogging; swimming; sailing; snow skiing. Home: 4615 Breezy Point Dr Kingwood TX 77345 Office: Benjamin Franklin Savings Assn 5444 Westheimer St Houston TX 77056

DI TROLIO, ROBERT R., court administrator; b. Los Angeles, Nov. 26, 1948; s. Vito Rocco and Carmela (Torvarelli) Di T.; m. Corinne Jane Colombo, June 2, 1979; children—Lisa Joy, Tara Lynn. A.A., El Camino Coll., 1973; B.S., U. So. Calif., 1975, M.P.A., 1977. Research assoc. Fed. Jud. Ct., Washington, 1976-77; records mgmt. cons. Adminstrv. Office of Cts. Atlanta, 1977; mgmt. analyst U.S. Dist. Ct. Western Dist. Pa., Pitts., 1977-79; dir. adminstrv. services U.S. Bankruptcy Ct., Los Angeles, 1979-80; gen. mgr. Bon Appetit, Inc., Huntington Beach, Calif., 1980-83; asst. ops. mgr. U.S. Dist. Ct. So. Dist. Fla., 1983—, adminstrv. mgr., cons. County Chief Adminstrs. Office, Los Angeles, 1975; researcher/analyst Dept. Fin. Calif., Sacramento, 1976; adj. prof. Barry U., Miami, Fla., 1985—. Pres. bd. dirs. Community Services, Hunting Ridge, Pa., 1979; bd. dirs. Community Merchants Assn., Huntington Beach, Calif., 1981-82. Served with U.S. Army, 1969-71; Ger., Vietnam. Fellow Inst. Ct. Mgmt.; mem. Am. Soc. Pub. Adminstrn., Am. Judicature Soc. Republican. Office: US Dist Ct 301 N Miami Ave Miami FL 33128

DITTMER, JAMES HAROLD, retail food company executive; b. Cook County, Ill., July 9, 1951; s. Harold and Petro (Einersen) D.; student So. Ill. U., 1969-70; B.S. in Bus. Edn., Western Mich. U., 1974; M.B.A., 1983. Public adminstr. Dundee (Ill.) Park Dist., 1974-75; v.p., gen. mgr. Interstate GMC, Elgin, Ill., 1975-76; pres., founder J. H. Dittmer & Co., Daytona Beach, Fla., 1976—; retail mgr. Super Foods, Inc., Orlando, Fla., 1981-82; retail mgr. Gt. So. Foods, Inc., 1982-83; co-mgr. Super X Food and Drug div. Kroger Co., 1983—; founder computer listing div. J.H. Dittmer & Co., 1983. Recipient Eagle Scout award Boy Scouts Am., 1967; Service award YMCA, Athletic Letters award, AAU, 1972. Mem. Nat. Grocer's Assn., Retail Grocer's Assn. Republican. Episcopalian. Home: 145 Orchid Ln Port Orange FL 32019 Office: PO Box 5701 Daytona Beach FL 32018

DIXIT, AJIT SURESH, research chemist; b. Nadiad, India, Sept. 30, 1950; naturalized, 1981; s. Suresh Chaturlal and Narendra Suresh (Yajnik) D.; m. Darshana J. Desai, Oct. 27, 1981; M.S., U. Maine, 1976; Ph.D., U. Miss., 1980. Research assoc. U. Kans., 1980-81; sr. research chemist Olin Corp., Pisgah Forest, N.C., 1981—. Nat. Sci. Talent scholar, 1967-72. Mem. Am. Chem. Soc., Royal Chem. Soc., TAPPI, Sigma Xi. Republican. Hindu. Home: PO Box 1706 Brevard NC 28712 Office: Olin Corp PO Box 200 Pisgah Forest NC 28768

DIXON, DONNA SUE, educator, learning resources specialist; b. Beaumont, Tex., Nov. 26, 1945; d. Jackson Daries and Wanda Melvo (Brown) Beasley; m. Raymond Douglas Dixon, Aug. 27, 1966. B.A. in History, Lamar U., Beaumont, 1966, M.A. in History, 1970; M.L.S., North Tex. State U., 1979. Cert. learning resources specialist, Tex. Instr. Spanish, Bridge City (Tex.) Ind. Sch. Dist., 1968-70, Streator (Ill.) Twp. High Sch., 1970-71, Blackhorse Pike Schs., Blackwood, N.J., 1971-73; instr. social studies Trinity Heights Acad., Shreveport, La., 1973-77; learning resources specialist Irving (Tex.) Ind. Sch. Dist., 1978-81, Carrollton (Tex.)-Farmers Branch Ind. Sch. Dist., 1981; instr. social studies and sci. Ft. Bend Ind. Sch. Dist., Missouri City-Tex., 1981-82; learning resources specialist John Foster Dulles High Sch., Stafford, Tex., 1982—. Alpha Delta Kappa scholar, 1963-66; Woodrow Wilson fellowship nominee, 1966; NDEA fellow, 1966-67; recipient Audio-Visual Prodn. award Tex. Assn. Sch. Librarians, 1979. Mem. ALA, Tex. Library Assn., North Tex. State U. Sch. Library Sci. Alumni Soc., Phi Kappa Phi, Beta Phi Mu, Alpha Lambda Sigma. Methodist. Author: (with Sherry DeBorde) Library Skills Handbook, Grades 6-8, 1981. Office: John Foster Dulles High School 500 Dulles Ave Stafford TX 77477

DIXON, ERNEST THOMAS, JR., clergyman; b. San Antonio, Oct. 13, 1922; s. Ernest Thomas and Ethel Louise (Reese) D.; m. Lois Brown, July 20, 1943 (dec. 1977); m. Ernestine Gray Clark, May 18, 1979; children—Freddie Brown, Ernest Reese, Muriel Jean, Leona Louise. B.A. magna cum laude, Samuel Huston Coll., 1943; B.D., Drew Theol. Sem., 1945; D.D. (hon.), Huston-Tillotson Coll., 1962; L.H.D. (hon.), Southwestern Coll., 1973; LL.D. (hon.), Baker U., 1973; Litt.D. (hon.), Westmar Coll., 1978; H.H.D. (hon.), Kans. Wesleyan Coll., 1980. Ordained to ministry Methodist Ch., 1946; pastor Meth. Ch., Brackettville, Tex., 1943; asst. pastor E. Calvary, Harlem, N.Y.C., 1943-44, Wallace Chapel A.M.E. Zion, Summit, N.J., 1944-45; dir. religious extension service Tuskegee Inst. (Ala.), 1945-51; exec. sec. West Tex. Conf. Bd. Edn., 1951-52; staff mem., div. local ch., bd. edn., 1952-64; pres. Philander Smith Coll., Little Rock, 1965-69; asst. gen. sec. program council, div. coordination, research and planning United Meth. Ch., 1969-72; consecrated bishop United Meth. Ch., 1972; bishop Kans. area, 1972-80, San Antonio area, 1980—; pres. gen. bd. higher edn. and ministry United Meth. Ch., 1972-76; pres. BOD Bethlehem Ctr., Nashville, 1953-64; trustee Gulfside Assembly, Waveland, Miss., 1978—; Ala. del. Midcentury White House Conf. Children and Youth, 1950, del. gen. conf., 1964-72. Citizens adv. com. Gov. Ark., 1967-69; bd. dirs. Little Rock C. of C., 1967-69; active San Antonio chpt. ARC; pres. Tex. Conf. Chs., 1984-86; trustee Gammon Theol. Sem., Houston-Tillotson Coll., Holding Inst., Lydia Patterson Inst., Meth. Mission Home, San Antonio, Mission Home, Waco, Tex., Morningside Manor, Mt. Sequoyah Assembly, S. Meth. U., Southwestern U., Southwest Meth. Hosp. Mem. Alpha Phi Alpha. Home: 9507 Burwick San Antonio TX 78230 Office: 535 Bandera Rd San Antonio TX 78228

DIXON, EVA CRAWFORD JOHNSON, librarian; b. Evinston, Fla., Aug. 28, 1909; d. William Alpheus and Willie (Crawford) Johnson; A.B. in Edn. with honors, U. Fla., 1937, M.A., 1948; postgrad. Fla. State U., 1950, Appalachian State Tchrs. Coll., 1955; m. Thomas Gordon Dixon, Dec. 14, 1935 (div. 1944). Tchr. English, librarian Jefferson High Sch., Monticello, Fla., 1945-47; audio-visual dir. Jefferson County Schs., 1948-50; tchr. English, librarian Maigs (Ga.) High Sch., 1954-55; librarian Chipola Jr. Coll., Marianna, Fla., 1955-57, dir. library services, 1958-80, emeritus, 1980—, chmn. student aid and scholarship com., 1961-65. Elder, 1st Presbyterian Ch. Marianna, 1976—, chmn. witness/evangelism com., 1978-80, parliamentarian Fla. Presbytery, 1979—. Mem. Jefferson County Edn. Assn. (pres. 1948-50), Fla. Edn. Assn. Honor Socs. (chmn. 1950-51), Bus. and Profl. Women's Club (pres. 1958-59, 62-63), Fla. Fedn. Bus. Profl. and Women's Clubs (dist. dir. 1962-63), Women of 1st Presbyn. Ch. (pres. 1962-65), Nat. Assn. Parliamentarians (v.p., program chmn. Jacksonville Mace unit 1983-84), Am. Inst. Parliamentarians (sec. Jacksonville area 1984), Kappa Delta Pi. Contbr. articles to profl. jours. Home: 6621 Shindler Dr Jacksonville FL 32222

DIXON, FRANK ALOYSIUS, JR., oil company executive; b. Phila., Oct. 18, 1928; s. Frank Aloysius and Helen (Iversen) D.; m. Patricia Riley, Feb. 24, 1967. B.A., Brown U., 1950. Pres. Pengo Petroleum Co., Houston. Bd. dirs. Oklahoma City Symphony, 1969, Alley Theatre Houston, 1969-72. Republican. Roman Catholic. Clubs: River Oaks Country (Houston); Tex. Corinthian Yacht, Sleepy Hollow Country; N.Y. Doubles; Racquet, Tavern, Chgo. Yacht (Chgo.). Home: 3215 Avalon Pl Houston TX 77019 Office: Two Shell Plaza Houston TX 77002

DIXON, JOHN ALLEN, JR., state justice; b. Orange, Tex., Apr. 8, 1920; s. John A. and Louella (Stark) D.; B.A., Centenary Coll., 1940; LL.B., Tulane U., 1947; m. Imogene K. Shipley, Oct. 20, 1945; children—Stella (Mrs. Paul Shepard), Diana (Mrs. L.C. Morehead, Jr.), Jeannette (Mrs. Michael Downing). Tchr., coach Tallulah High Sch., 1940-42; admitted to La. bar, 1947; pvt. practice law, Shreveport, La., 1947-57; asst. dist. atty., Shreveport, 1954-57; judge 1st Dist. Ct., 1957-68, La. Ct. Appeal, Shreveport, 1968-70; asso. justice La. Supreme Ct., 1971, now chief justice. Served with AUS, 1942-45. Democrat. Methodist. Mason. Office: Supreme Ct La 301 Loyola Ave New Orleans LA 70112

DIXON, JOHN WAINWRIGHT, business executive; b. Lexington, Ky., Mar. 12, 1920; s. Thomas H. and Mary (Edmonds) D.; student George Washington U., 1948-49; A.B., U. Houston, 1948; M.A., U. Miami (Fla.), 1951; m. Doris I. Sowell, May 13, 1961; children—Jacqueline P., Frederick D.R., Clinton M. Asst. prof. So. Miss. Coll., 1952-53; asst. to v.p. planning Convair Gen. Dynamics, San Diego, 1956-61; asst. comptroller, dir. systems planning Office Asst. Sec. Def., Washington, 1961-62; dir. planning Ling Temco Vought, Inc., Dallas, 1962-67, v.p. planning, 1967-69; chmn., pres. E-Systems, Inc., 1969—; dir. MKT R.R., Katy R.R. Mem. Dallas Citizens Council; mem. nat. adv. council Inf. Museum Assn. Bd. dirs. Christmas Pageant of Peace, 1973—, Center for Internat. Bus. S.W., Dallas Civic Opera, Dallas Community Coll. Dist. Found., Dallas Symphony Assn., Nat. Park Found., United Way, U.S.O., Wolf Trap Found., So. Meth. U. Found. for Sci. and Engring.; mem. adv. com. Honor Am.; chmn. Dallas County U.S. Savings Bonds, 1975-81. Named to Honor Role Inf. Officer Candidate Hall Fame, Ft. Benning, Ga. Served with AUS, 1941-46. Mem. Air Force Assn., Aerospace Industries Assn. (bd. govs.), Am. Def. Preparedness Assn. (bd. dirs.), U.S. Army Assn. (chmn. 1979-80), Armed Forces Communications and Electronics Assn. (bd. dirs.), U.S. C. of C., Dallas Council World Affairs, Nat. Security Indsl. Assn. (trustee, exec. com.), Assn. for Unmanned Vehicle Systems (hon. trustee), Phi Beta Kappa. Club: Dallas Economists (pres. 1968). Office: PO Box 6030 Dallas TX 75266

DIXON, LARRY DEAN, state official; b. Nowata, Okla., Aug. 31, 1942; s. Chesley Lafayette and Charlene (Walker) D.; m. Gaynell Kimbrough, Dec. 23, 1967; children—Katherine Kimbrough, Elizabeth Walker. A.A.Scis., Columbia Basin Jr. Coll., 1966; B.S. in Police Sci., Wash. State U., 1968, M.A. in History, 1970. Cons., Ala. State Dept. Edn., 1970-72; dir. dept. edn. Med. Assn. State of Ala., Montgomery, 1972-76; dir. Montgomery Family Practice Residency Program, 1976-78, Jackson Hosp. Found., Montgomery, 1978-81; exec. dir. Ala. Bd. Med. Examiners, Montgomery, 1981—. Mem. Montgomery City Council, 1975-78, Ala. Ho. of Reps., 1978-82, Ala. Senate, 1982; mem. steering com. Nat. Clearinghouse on Licensure, Enforcement and Regulation; bd. dirs. Fedn. State Med. Bds. Served with U.S. Army, 1961-64. Mem. Nat. Conf. State Legislatures, Adminstrs. in Medicine Soc. (pres.), Ala. Ex POWs (hon.) Republican. Methodist. Clubs: Young Men's Bus., Blue Gray Assn. Lodge: Lions (Montgomery). Home: 820 E Fairview Ave Montgomery AL 36106 Office: PO Box 946 Montgomery AL 36102

DIXON, RICHARD DEAN, lawyer; b. Columbus, Ohio, Nov. 6, 1944; s. Dean A. and Katherine L. (Currier) D.; m. Kathleen Manfrass, June 17, 1967; children—Jennifer E., Lindsay K. B.S. in E.E. (Cooper Industries Engring. scholar), Ohio State U., 1967, M.S. in E.E., 1968; M.B.A., Fla. State U., 1972, J.D. (fellow), 1974. Bar: Fla., 1975. Systems engr. PAA Aerospace Services Div., Patrick AFB, Fla., 1968-72; pvt. practice, 1975-80; sr. counsel govt. systems sector Harris Corp., Melbourne, Fla., 1980-84; corp. counsel Ford Microelectronics Inc., Colorado Springs, Colo., 1985—; adj. prof. bus. law Fla. Inst. Tech., 1980—; legal advisor Fla. Ho. of Reps., 1976-78. Recipient Nathan Burkan Legal Writing award, 1974. Mem. Am. Intellectual Property Law Assn., ABA, Lic. Execs. Soc., Am. Corp. Counsel Assn.

DIXON, ROBERT BEATTIE, investment banker; b. North Hoboken, N.J., Oct. 9, 1908; s. James Monroe and Anna Louise (Sawyer) D.; m. Mary Florence Gilmore, May 20, 1935; children—Robert Beattie Jr., Marion Monroe. B.P.H., Emory U., 1931. With Am. Service Bur., Atlanta, 1931-33; state mgr. Hooper Holmes Bur., Inc., S.C., 1933-36, N.C., 1936-45; mng. ptnr. McDaniel Lewis & Co., Greensboro, N.C., 1945-55; pres., dir. United Securities Co., Greensboro, 1955-66; sr. v.p., dir. Interstate Securities Co., Charlotte, N.C., 1966—; dir. Wysong Miles Co., Greensboro; mem. Phila.-Balt. Exchange, 1955-66; assoc. mem. N.Y. Securities Exchange. Fin. chmn. Grace United Meth. Ch., Greensboro. Mem. Securities Dealers of Carolinas, (pres. 1952-53), Securities Traders (pres. 1952-53), Nat. Assn. Securities Dealers (bus. conduct com. 1955-58), Greensboro C. of C. (bd. dirs. 1960). Democrat. Clubs: Greensboro Country, Greensboro City. Lodges: Woodmen of the World (state pres.), Civitan (pres.). Home: 202 Homewood Ave Greensboro NC 27403

DIXON, RONALD MEREALL, principal; b. Hazlehurst, Ga., Nov. 19, 1944; s. John and Birdie Mae (Simmons) D.; m. Patia Jones, Jan. 28, 1966; children—Niles C., Carl J. A.S., South Ga. Coll., 1964; B.S., Ga. So. Coll., 1967, M.Edn., 1974, Ed.S., 1985. Cert. secondary tchr. Tchr., Jefferson Davis County Bd. Edn., Hazlehurst, Ga., 1966-77, asst. prin., 1977-79, secondary sch. prin., 1979—; cons. So. Accrediting Commn. Schs. and Colls., Atlanta, 1985—. Mem. Jefferson Davis County Assn. Educators (pres. 1976-77), Ga. Assn. Educators, Nat. Assn. Secondary Sch. Prins., Ga. Assn. Sch. Prins. Avocations: boating; fishing; hunting; reading Home: Route 2 Box 1685 Hazlehurst GA 31539 Office: Jefferson Davis High Sch Broxton Rd Hazlehurst GA 31539

DIXON, THELMA ANNETTA, educational counselor; b. Beatrice, Ala., Oct. 25, 1945; d. Henry Clifton Dixon and Idell (Stallworth) Brackett. B.S., Ala. State U., 1967, M.Ed., 1975. Bus. tchr. W.J. Jones High Sch., Pine Apple, Ala., 1967-77, counselor, 1977—, asst. prin., 1980-84; cheerleader advisor Jones High Mustangs, 1969-84. Active NAACP. Recipient certs. Soc. Disting. Am. High Sch. Students, Birmingham, Ala., 1982-83, Cystic Fibrosis Found., Birmingham, 1980; mem. Ala. Guidance and Counseling Adv. Com. Mem. NEA, Ala. Edn. Assn., Wilcox County Edn. Assn., Kappa Delta Pi. Democrat. Baptist. Lodge: Order Eastern Star. Home: PO Box 21 Beatrice AL 36425 Office: WS Jones High Sch Pine Apple AL 36768

DIXON, WARREN ARTHUR, architect, educator; b. Tallahassee, Mar. 11, 1934; s. Coleman Sweeting and Madie Leo (Peavy) D.; B. Arch., U. Fla., 1958; m. Alice Gay Pound, July 12, 1969; 1 dau., Heloise Leonora. Draftsman, Huddleston & Assos., Albert Woodward, Barrett & Marshall, Architects, James Stripling, Architect, Barrett, Daffin & Bishop, to 1961; architect Fla. Bd. Parks and Hist. Memls., 1963-66; assoc. Robert Maybin, 1963-68, Robert

Maybin & Warren Dixon, Architects, 1968-71; prin. Warren A. Dixon, Architect, 1971—; head drafting and archtl. tech. program Lewis Lively Vocat-Tech. Center; works include Tallahassee Police Dept. Hdqrs., Providence Pl. Housing for Elderly. Deacon, Tallahassee Bible Ch. Served with U.S. Army Res., 1958-64. Mem. Constrn. Specifications Inst., Nat. Trust Historic Preservation. Democrat. Club: Springtime Tallahassee. Home: 1817 Ivan Dr Tallahassee FL 32303 Office: 308 E Park Ave Tallahassee FL 32301

DIXON, WILLIAM MERRITT, JR., college administrator; b. Dayton, Ohio, June 3, 1937; s. William Merritt and Dorthey (Brawner) D.; m. Rita Hurt, Aug. 28, 1960; 1 child, William Merritt III (Chip). A.B., Georgetown Coll., 1959; M.B.A., Xavier U., 1964. Store supr. Monsanto-Moundlab, Miamisburg, Ohio, 1962-67; mgr. materials Leland Airborne, Vandalio, Ohio, 1967; plant mgr. Elano Corp., Xenia, Ohio, 1967-71; plant mgr. Koehring, Dayton, 1971-73; v.p., div. mgr. Inland Motor, Radford, Va., 1973-76; dean fin. and adminstrv. services Wytheville Community Coll., Va., 1976—. Pres., Scott Meml. PTA, Wytheville, 1979-80; chmn. Wytheville Recreation Commn., 1981; bd dirs. Wythe County Selective Service Bd., 1982—; active community info. com. Indsl. Devel. Authority, Wytheville, 1983—, fin. adv. com. State Council Higher Edn., Richmond, Va., 1984—. Served with U.S. Army, 1960-62. Recipient Layman of Yr. award Kiwanis, 1983. Mem. Nat. Assn. Coll. and Univ. Bus. Officers, So. Assn. Coll. and Univ. Bus. Officers, Va. Community Coll. Assn. (sec./treas. fin. commn. 1982-83). Methodist. Club: Soiree (v.p. 1985). Lodge: Lions (v.p. 1984-85). Avocations: tennis; choir director; participation in drama productions, softball, basketball. Home: 880 Mount View Dr Wytheville VA 24382 Office: Wytheville Community Coll 1000 E Main St Wytheville VA 24382

DO, Y HOANG, ophthalmologist; b. Hanoi, Vietnam, June 14, 1951; came to U.S., 1975, naturalized, 1981; s. Vinh Thuc and Chau An (Hoang) D.; m. Quy Linh, Jan. 30, 1977; children—Dakao, Linh Thu, Linh Thi, Linh Dan. APM, U. Saigon (Vietnam), 1969, M.D., 1975. Diplomate Am. Bd. Ophthalmology. Internship BinhDan Gen. Hosp., Saigon, 1974-75; resident Tex. Tech., Lubbock, 1978-81; ophthalmologist, Plainview, Tex., 1981—; asst. clin. prof. ophthalmology Tex. Tech. Sch. Medicine, Lubbock, 1981—. Mem. Tex. Med. Assn., Hale, Floyd and Briscoe Med. Soc., Am. Acad. Opthalmology. Office: 812 W 8th St Suite 1 B Plainview TX 79072

DOAN, PATRICIA NAN, librarian; b. Fayetteville, Ark., Oct. 27, 1930; d. William Rader and Olga (White) Rogers; B.A., U. Ark., 1951; m. John Cannon Doan, Apr. 2, 1950; children—William Curtis, Sarah Cannon, Mary Virginia. Librarian, Okmulgee (Okla.) Public Library, 1967—. Treas. Okmulgee Art Guild, 1969-71; sec. Okmulgee County Devel. Council, 1971—, Creek Nation Council House Bd., 1975—. Mem. Okmulgee Meml. Hosp. Found.; mem. Okmulgee Task Force, county chmn. Okmulgee County History Book Com. Mem. ALA, Okla. Library Assn. (sec. public library div. 1970), Okmulgee County Geneal. Soc. (v.p. 1970), Sigma Alpha Iota, Zeta Tau Alpha. Democrat. Episcopalian. Compiler: Index of the 1907 Census of Okmulgee, Oklahoma, 1971. Home: 540 N Morton St Okmulgee OK 74447 Office: 218 S Okmulgee St Okmulgee OK 74447

DOANE, HAROLD EVERETT, record company executive; b. N.Y.C., Oct. 17, 1904; s. Thomas J. and Mary S. (Blaisdell) D.; student Edison Sch. Arts, 1919-23, Columbia, 1924; m. Mary G. Gardner, Dec. 20, 1936 (div. 1941); m. 2d, Faith S. Tracy, Oct. 17, 1943 (div. 1966); children—Priscilla Clare (Mrs. Ramiro Tello-Saldano), Richard Henry Tracy; m. 3d Vivian Dillon Dunn, May 3, 1966. Asst. cameraman D.W. Griffith Orienta Point Studios, Mamaroneck, N.Y., 1921-22; radio announcer sta. WGBU, Fulford, Fla., 1925-26, WBNY, N.Y.C., 1926-27, WMCA, 1927 WKBQ, 1927-28; owner radio sta. WCOH, Mt. Vernon, N.Y., 1928-29; research engr., N.Y.C., 1929-35; dir. Gramercy Pictures Corp., N.Y.C., 1935-37; producer Spotlight Prodns., Inc., 1940-41; tech. operations dir. War Finance Com., N.Y. State div. U.S. Treasury Dept., N.Y.C., 1941-44; gen. mgr. Art Records, Miami, Fla., 1945-59, pres., 1959—. Mem. nat. adv. bd. Am. Security Council. Mem. Nat. Acad. Rec. Arts and Scis., N.Y. Advt. Club. Republican. Home: 5800 SW 17th Ct Plantation FL 33317 Office: PO Box 15032 Ft Lauderdale FL 33318

DOAR, WILLIAM WALTER, JR., lawyer, state legislator; b. Rock Hill, S.C., Mar. 9, 1935; s. William Walter and Julia (Poag) D.; B.S., U. S.C., 1957, LL.B.; m. Louise D. Doar, Aug. 24, 1957; children—Elizabeth, Julia, Amaryllis. Admitted to S.C. bar; practice law; mem. S.C. State Legislature. Served with JAGC, USAF.

DOBBINS, GEORGE, JR., maintenance and pest control company executive; b. Hernando, Miss., Aug. 14, 1940; s. George and Eddye Joy (William) D.; m. Jean E. Gordon, Aug. 13, 1966; children—Alondas, Ashley. B.S., Miss. Indsl. Coll., 1965; postgrad. U. Tenn. Head football coach Hernando High Sch. (Miss.), 1965-70; stock broker Investor Diversified Co., 1970-73; spl. account rep. 3M Co., 1973-80; pres. Dobbins & Co., Memphis, 1980—. Mem. Memphis and Shelby County Planning Commn., 1974-79, chmn., 1978; cons. City Beautiful Commn., Memphis, 1982; mem. polit. selection com. Shelby County Republican Com., 1979—; mem. Shelby County Port Commn., Memphis, 1983. Named Sales Person of South Region, IDS Brokers, 1972. Mem. Nat. Maintenance Assn., C. of C., New South Media (bd. dirs.), Nat. Assn. Security Dirs. Baptist. Club: Kiwanis. Home: 3781 Shady Hollow Memphis TN 38116 Office: 4466 Elvis Presley Blvd Suite 258 Memphis TN 38116

DOBBINS, JAMES GREGORY, engineer, mathematician; b. Ashland, Ky., June 30, 1943; s. James E. and Opal J. (Hall) D.; m. Susan J. Culver, Dec. 18, 1971; children—Julia, Stephen, Elizabeth. B.A., U. Ky., 1965, M.A., 1966, Ph.D., 1969. Asst. prof. Marshall U., Huntington, W.Va., 1969-70; assoc. prof. Wheaton Coll., Ill., 1970-76; prof. Mt. Vernon Coll., Ohio, 1976-81; sr. prin. engr. NCR Corp., Columbia S.C., 1981—; teaching assoc. Ohio State U. and U. S.C., 1977-81, 81—. Contbr. articles to profl. jours. Research Corp. Am. grantee, 1973. Mem. Am. Soc. Quality Control, Am. Statis. Assn. Republican. Presbyterian. Club: Toastmasters. Avocations: camping; woodworking; remodeling. Office: NCR 3325 Platt Springs Rd West Columbia SC 29169

DOBBINS, ROBERT CRAIG, church musician; b. Parkersburg, W.Va., June 20, 1951; s. Robert Moore and Emma Jean (Clem) D. B.Mus., Baldwin-Wallace Coll., 1973; M.Mus. in Organ Performance, U. Mich., 1976, M. Mus. in Mus. History, 1976. Tchr., City Pub. Schs., Marietta, Ohio, 1977-78; asst. musical dir. Ohio Showboat Drama, Inc., Marietta, 1978; dir. music First Presbyn. Ch., Greenville, Miss., 1978-84, First Presbyn. Ch., Jacksonville, Fla., 1984—; bd. dirs. Greenville Symphony Orch., Miss., 1979-82, chmn. personnel com., 1980-83, chmn. program com., 1980-84. Bd. dirs. Delta Music Assn., Greenville, Miss., 1980-84; vol. Greenville Boys' Club, 1978-79. Recipient Acad. award, Dayton C. Miller Honor Soc., Berea, Ohio, 1973. Mem. Am. Guild Organists (sub-dean 1985, dean), Presbyn. Assn. Musicians, Hymn Soc. Am., Choristers Guild, Am. Orff-Schulwerk Assn., Phi Mu Alpha Sinfonia (chpt. sec. 1971-73). Republican. Presbyterian. Avocations: racquetball; biking; swimming; reading. Home: 2731 Apache Ave Jacksonville FL 32210 Office: First Presbyn Ch 118 E Monroe St Jacksonville FL 32202

DOBBS, GEORGE ALBERT, retail corporation executive; b. Atlanta, Oct. 16, 1943; s. Albert F. and Ruby Lee (Haynes) D.; B.A., Cornell U., 1966, M.B.A., 1972; Retail store mgr. Alterman Foods, Atlanta, 1960-72; ind. mng. cons. George A. Dobbs & Assos., Decatur, Ga., 1972-78; retail mgr. K-Mart Corp., Decatur, 1978—; notary public, 1976—. Named Small Bus. Mgr. of Year, Dekalb Businessman's Assn., 1974. Mem. Ga. Small Bus. Mgrs. Assn. (Recognition cert. for contbns. 1976), Dekalb Businessmen's Assn., Dekalb Sheriff's Posse, Ga. Sheriff's Assn. Republican. Baptist. Clubs: Capital City, Masons, Shriners. Mailing Address: PO Box 399 Antioch TN 37013 Office: K-Mart Corp 2901 Clairmont Rd NE Atlanta GA 30033

DOBES, WILLIAM LAMAR, JR., dermatologist; b. Atlanta, Apr. 16, 1943; s. William Lamar and Sara (Wilson) D.; B.A., Emory U., 1965, M.D., 1969; m. Martha Husmann, June 16, 1966; children—Margaret Alison, William Shane. Intern Grady Meml. Hosp., Atlanta, 1969-70; fellow dermatology Mayo Clinic, 1970-71; fellow U. Miami, 1971-73; clin. instr. Emory U. Sch. Medicine, Atlanta, 1973-77, asst. prof. dermatology, 1977-83, assoc. prof., 1983—, dir. immunofluorescense lab.; mem. staff Crawford Long, West Paces Ferry, Grady Meml., Ga. Bapt., Piedmont hosps. (all Atlanta). Past chmn. profl. edn. unit Atlanta unit Am. Cancer Soc., also bd. dirs.; mem. Ga. med. bd. Lupus Found.; bd. dirs. Am. Cancer Soc. Diplomate Am. Bd. Dermatology. Mem. Soc. Investigative Dermatology, Am. Acad. Dermatology (chmn. com. quality assurance 1981-84), So. Med. Assn. (vice-chmn. sect. 1982-83), Ga. Med. Soc., Pan Am. Med. Assn., ACP, AMA, Am. Soc. Dermatologic Surgery, Atlanta Dermatol. Assn. (pres. 1979), N.Am. Clin. Dermatologic Soc., Soc. Tropical Dermatology, Atlanta Clin. Soc., Emory U. Med. Alumni Assn. (pres. 1980), Phi Delta Theta (pres. 1965), Phi Chi (pres. 1968). Club: Cherokee Town & Country (Atlanta). Contbr. articles to profl. jours. and texts. Home: 2898 Rivermead Dr Atlanta GA 30327 Office: 478 Peachtree St Atlanta GA 30308 also Dept Dermatology Emory U School Medicine Atlanta GA 30308

DOBEY, CHARLES MICHAEL, oil company executive; b. Shawnee, Okla., Mar. 19, 1951; s. Charles Bennett and Tresa Rose (Binning) D.; B.S., Okla. State U., 1974; m. Mary Kathryn Newkumet, Jan. 17, 1976; children—Heidi Anne. Programmer, analyst City of Stillwater (Okla.), 1972-74; programmer, analyst Grace Petroleum Corp., Oklahoma City, 1974-75, systems and ops. supr., 1975-76, programming and systems mgr., 1976-78, tech. services mgr., 1978-79; mgr. data processing ITT-Eason Oil, Oklahoma City, 1979-80, dir. mgmt. info. systems, 1980-83; mgr. info. systems Wagner & Brown, Midland, Tex., 1983—; cons. Hertz Corp., Scrivner Foods, Inc., Church Systems, Inc., Oklahoma City. Vol., Am. Cancer Soc., Vols. for Animal Welfare. Mem. Assn. Systems Mgmt. (treas. 1980-81), Data processing Mgmt. Assn., Tex. Archeol. Soc. Republican. Baptist. Lodge: Rotary (dir. 1985-86). Home: 4502 Stillmeadow Midland TX 79707 Office: 300 N Marienfeld St Suite 1100 Midland TX 79702

DOBOS, RONALD THOMAS, industrial hygienist; b. Cleve., Sept. 22, 1953; s. Andrew Stephen and Mary (Plavac) D.; m. Linda Joanne Wolski, Aug. 22, 1981; children—Elizabeth Dianne, Andrew Craig. B.S., U. Ga., 1975; B.S.N., Emory U., 1978. Lic. registered nurse, Fla. Staff nurse Henrietta Egleston Hosp. for Children, Atlanta, 1978-79; charge nurse Peachford Hosp., Dunwoody, Ga., 1979; safety engr. Liberty Mutual Ins., Orlando, Fla., 1979-84, indsl. hygienist, 1984—. Mem. Am. Indsl. Hygiene Assn., Am. Soc. Safety Engrs. (v.p. 1981-82), Am. Assn. Occupational Health Nurses. Democrat. Roman Catholic. Address: Liberty Mutual Ins Co 988 Woodcock Rd Orlando FL 32814

DOBROVOLSKY, NICHOLAS WASIL, counseling psychologist; b. Beaver Meadows, Pa., Feb. 19, 1935; s. Nicholas and Theresa (Goida) D.; B.S. summa cum laude, Troy State U., 1973, M.S., 1974; Ph.D., Tex. A&M U., 1977; m. Edna Arlean Smith, June 1, 1957; children—Michael J., Pamela A., Janice L., Thomas E., David A., Laura J. Commd. airman U.S. Air Force, 1954, advanced through grades to maj., 1966; aviation cadet, Houston, 1955; navigator/bombadier, Salina, Kans., 1956-58; instr. navigator, Wichita, Kans., 1958-61; student pilot, Enid, Okla., 1962; pilot, Waco, Tex., 1962-66; combat pilot, Vietnam, 1966-67; flying safety officer, Oklahoma City, 1967-70; maintenance officer/squadron comdr. Maxwell AFB, Montgomery, Ala., 1970-74; ret., 1974; counseling psychologist personal counseling service Tex. A&M U., 1974—. Decorated D.F.C., Meritorious Service award, Air medal with 5 oak leaf clusters, Air Force Commendation medal; lic. psychologist, Tex.; lic. profl. counselor, Tex. Mem. Am. Assn. Family and Marriage Therapy, Am. Soc. Clin. Hypnosis, Nat. Register Health Service Providers, Am. Psychol. Assn., Brazos Valley Psychol. Assn. (past pres., bd. govs.), Internat. Soc. Hypnosis, Phi Delta Kappa. Roman Catholic. Office: Student Counseling Service 300 YMCA Bldg Tex A&M U College Station TX 77843

DOBSON, BOBBY WAYNE, floor covering company executive; b. Texarkana, Tex., Mar. 1, 1940; s. Ernest Harold and Emma Louise (Flynt) D.; m. Sharon Lee Murawski, Aug. 10, 1963; children—Damon Duane, Richard Ian; 1 dau. by previous marriage, Ruby Earlene. Pres., Dobson Floors, Inc., Garland, Tex., 1968-76, Floors Unltd., Inc., Dallas, 1979—. Served with Tex. N.G., 1957-59. Baptist. Lodges: Masons, Shriners. Office: First Floors 10771 Estate Ln Dallas TX 75238

DOBSON, DONALD ALFRED, elec. engr.; b. Evanston, Ill., Feb. 19, 1928; s. Alfred Topping and Agnes Lucille (Park) D.; B.S. in Elec. Engring., Northwestern U., 1950, Ph.D., 1955; M.S.E.E., M.I.T., 1951. Research asso. Northwestern U., Evanston, 1951-54; engr. Indsl. Research Products, Franklin Park, Ill., 1952; sr. engr. Sperry Gyroscope Co., Great Neck, N.Y., 1954-59; sr. tech. specialist N. Am. Aviation, Columbus, Ohio, 1959-63; research staff mem. Inst. Def. Analyses, Arlington, Va., 1963—; instr. physics Adelphi Coll., Garden City, N.Y., 1956. Mem. IEEE, Sigma Xi, Tau Beta Pi, Eta Kappa Nu, Pi Mu Epsilon. Home: 6800 Fleetwood Rd Apt 420 McLean VA 22101 Office: 1801 N Beauregard St Alexandria VA 22311

DOBY, MARY CATHERINE, marriage and family counselor, health facility administrator; b. Corbin, Ky., Sept. 15, 1946; d. John Thomas and Rose Catherine (Hopper) Doby; m. Stephen N. Holloman, Dec. 14, 1985. B.S. in Psychology, Ga. Coll., 1973; M.Ed. in Counseling and Psychol. Services, Ga. State U., 1979. Psychology technician Central State Hosp./Regional Devel. Ctr., Milledgeville, Ga., 1973-74, mental retardation unit team leader, 1974-76; psychologist I, Yarbrough Rehab. Ctr., Central State Hosp., Milledgeville, 1976-77; coordinator day treatment program Central DeKalb Mental Health Ctr., Decatur, Ga., 1979-81; dir. child and family counseling ctr. Peachbelt Mental Health Ctr., Warner Robins, Ga., 1981-85; cons. and tng. in child sex abuse cases; pvt. practice family therapy, therapy with child sex abuse victims. Office: 119 Carl Vinson Pkwy PO Box 1864 Warner Robins GA 31099

DOBYNS, AUDREY HARRIDGE, retired accountant, dog breeder; b. Antioch, Ill., Apr. 1, 1905; d. Harrison Lynn and Maude Eva (Cheshire) Kepner; m. Clinton R. Harridge, Oct. 12, 1923 (div.); m. William T. Dobyns, Dec. 6, 1952 (div. 1960). Grad. trade sch. Acct. Marshall Field & Co., then Am. Can Co., Indsl. Constrn. Co. and University Club, Evanston, Ill.; ret., 1968. Author: Gene's Jeans N' Dog Gone Gene's-By-Clinaude, 1985. Contbr. articles on dog breeding to hobby mags. Sustaining mem. Republican Nat. Com., 1976—; Fla. state rep. U.S. Congl. Adv. Bd., Am. Security Council, 1984—; charter mem. Ronald Reagan Trust. Recipient Outstanding Service award Dog World, 1971. Mem. Mid-west Boxer Club (life, pres. 1966). Avocations: breeding, exhbtg. Clinaude Boxers; current events; reading. Home: The Forest Club 543 Club Ct Lake Mary FL 32746

DODD, BRUCE C., JR., educational administrator; b. Akron, May 23, 1931; s. Bruce Corwin and Wuanita Esta (Dye) D.; m. Carolyn Anne Pim, Feb. 17, 1956; children—Dann Bruce, Scott James, Kimberly Ann, Robb Jon (dec.), Robynne Beth, James William. B.S., U Pa., 1954; M.P.S., N.Y. Theol. Sem./NYU, 1982; postgrad U. Mass., U. Ga., SUNY-Stony Brook Ordained to ministry Presbyterian Ch., 1985. Tchr., coach Stony Brook Sch., 1958-62, adminstr. 1965-82; tchr. Setauket Pub. Schs., N.Y., 1962-64; prs. Rabun Gap Nacoochee Sch., Ga., 1983—; interim pastor Cutchogue Presbyn. Ch., N.Y., 1978-82; dir. Habersham Fed. Savs. Bank. Author: Poe, 1969; also articles, hymns; patentee sublimerselfballasting swim grip. Christian edn. asst Setauket Presbyn. Ch., 1963-66; commr., 188th Assembly Presbyn. Ch. U.S.A., 1976; trustee Hambidge Ctr., 1983-85, Clayton Hist. Soc., 1984—; bd. advisers Northeast Ga. council Boy Scouts Am. Served to lt. USN, 1954-58. Recipient Outstanding Young Man of Yr. award Stony Brook/Setauket Jaycees, 1968, Jefferson Davis medal UDC, Atlanta, 1983. Mem. Rabun County C. of C. (bd. dirs. 1985—), Rabun County Ministerial Assn. Clubs: Princeton N.Y.C., U. Ga. Track Ofcls. Lodge: Rotary. Avocations: Jogging; swimming, sailing, fishing. Home: Rabun Gap Nacoochee Sch Rabun Gap GA 30568

DODD, ROBERT HARRY, stock broker; b. Detroit, Sept. 14, 1923; s. Harry and Velma E. (Lyon) D.; m. Marjorie Menshardt, Apr. 17, 1948; children—Deborah J., Robert Harry. B.S., U. Mich., 1947. Owner, pres. Detroit City Electrotype Co., 1950-69; broker Merrill Lynch, Pierce, Fenner & Smith, North Palm Beach, Fla., 1969-80, asst. v.p., mgr., 1980-84, v.p., 1984—. Mem. Riviera Beach (Fla.) City Council, 1974-82. Served to 1st lt. USAAF, 1943-45. Decorated D.F.C. Mem. Mensa. Republican. Episcopalian. Clubs: Sailfish, Old Port Yacht. Lodges: Kiwanis. Office: Merrill Lynch Pierce Fenner & Smith 741 US Hwy 1 North Palm Beach FL 33408

DODD, ROGER JAMES, lawyer; b. Sewickley, Pa., Sept. 15, 1951; s. Carl Roger and Dorothy Maude (Barley) D.; m. Emily Elizabeth Lilly, June 9, 1974; children—Matthew A., Andrew J. B.A. in Econs., Bucknell U., 1973; J.D., U. Pitts., 1976. Ga. 1976, Fla. 1977, U.S. Ct. Appeals (5th cir.) 1976, U.S. Ct. Appeals (11th cir.) 1981, U.S. Dist. Ct. (mid. dist.) Ga. 1976, U.S. Dist. Ct. (no. dist.) Ga. 1983, U.S. Dist. Ct. Fla. 1983, U.S. Supreme Ct. 1981. Ptnr., Blackburn, Bright, Edwards & Dodd, Valdosta, Ga., 1976—; spl. asst. atty. gen. State of Ga., 1979-85; mem. faculty Nat. Criminal Defence Coll., 1986—. Contbr. articles to legal publs. and newspapers. Bd. dirs. Lowndes Country Assn. Retarded Citizens, Valdosta, 1977, Valwood Sch., Valdosta, 1984—. Named Outstanding Law Day Chmn., State Bar Ga., 1977. Mem. Ga. Assn. Criminal Def. Lawyers (v.p. 1982-83, bd. dirs. 1982—, Pres.'s award 1982, exec. v.p. 1984, pres. elect 1985, pres. 1986), State Bar Ga. (mem. exec. com. family law sect.), Ga. Trial Lawyers Assn. (contbr. articles), Assn. Trial Lawyers Am., Nat. Assn. Criminal Def. Lawyers, Valdosta Bar Assn. (sec.-treas. 1977-78), Nat. Inst. Trial Advocacy (Advance Trial Advocacy Skills 1985), Ga. Inst. Trial Advocacy (faculty 1986), Mensa. Libertarian. Presbyterian. Clubs: William Pitt (Pitts.), William Bucknell Assn. Lodge: Elks. Home: 1415 Williams St Valdosta GA 31601 Office: Blackburn Bright Edwards & Dodd 1008 N Patterson St Valdosta GA 31601

DODD, TED BYRON, environmental scientist; b. Tyler, Tex., Oct. 1, 1952; s. James Byron and Roxie Fayne (Mitchum) D.; B.S., Sam Houston State U., 1979; m. Cynthia Ann Duren, June 12, 1971; children—Justin Tyler Jackson, Kristin Nicole Jane. Chemist, City of Huntsville (Tex.), 1977-79, City of Conroe (Tex.), 1979; plant chemist Pilot Industries Tex., Houston, 1979-80; ops. mgr. People's Nat. Utilities, Houston, 1980—; owner Republic Water Systems Tex., Houston, 1977—; div. head environ. dept. Demar/Republic; environ. scientist Coe Utilities, Inc., 1980—; gen. mgr. H&J Water Co., B&B Sewer Co.; pres. Am. Utility Co., Crest San. Corp., Crest Utility Co., Tex. I.O.U. Inc.; cons. Champ's Utilities, West Montgomery Utilities Corp. Served with USAF, 1971-75. Mem. Am. Chem. Soc., Am. Water Works Assn., Sam Houston Water Utilities Assn. (2d v.p.), Green Forest Water Utilities Assn. Republican. Baptist. Home: 10706 MacKenzie St Houston TX 77086

DODDER, RICHARD A., sociology and statistics educator; b. Overbrook, Kans., July 22, 1941; s. Albert M. and Alta S. (Heffner) D.; m. Gearaldine Gunther, Aug. 30, 1964; children—Christian Erik, Elizabeth Greenfield. B.A., B.S., U. Kans., 1963, M.A., 1966, Ph.D., 1969. Instr. Math. Secondary Sch., East Lyme, Conn., 1964-65; sociology instr. U. Kans., Lawrence, 1968-69; prof. sociology and stats. Okla. State U., Stillwater, 1969—; cons. Langston U., Okla., 1979-81, U.S. Dept. Energy, Washington, 1981, U.S. Dept. Edn., Washington, 1983. Author: Treatment Strategies, 1982. Assoc. editor Sociol. Spectrum, Birmingham, Ala., 1984—. Contbr. articles to profl. publs. Bd. dirs. Payne County Youth Services, Stillwater, 1978—, Child Welfare Adv. Com., Stillwater, 1983—. Named Outstanding Grad. Prof., Grad. Student council, 1973, Tchr. of Yr., Okla. State U. Alumni Assn., 1980. Mem. Southwest Soc. (membership com. 1984, program com. 1985), Am. Sociol. Assn., Am. Soc. Criminology, Alpha Kappa Delta, Pi Mu Epsilon. Democrat. Presbyterian. Home: 2110 W 3d Stillwater OK 74074 Office: Okla State U Dept Sociology Stillwater OK 74078

DODDS, ALVIN FRANKLIN, emeritus pharmaceutical chemistry educator; b. Starkville, Miss., Jan. 20, 1919; s. Charles Richey and Cora Frances (Floyd) D.; m. Annie Ruth Arnold, Sept. 7, 1943; children—Kenneth A., Carolyn R., William R. B.S., Miss. State U., 1940; M.S., Northwestern U., 1942, Ph.D., 1943; B.S. in Pharmacy, Med. U. S.C., 1949. Registered pharmacist, S.C. Research chemist Pan Am. Refining Corp., Texas City, Tex., 1943-45; asst. prof. Loyola U. of South, New Orleans, 1945-47; assoc. prof. pharm. chemistry Med. U. S.C., Charleston, 1947-53, prof., 1953-81, prof. emeritus, 1981—. Mem. Am. Pharm. Assn., Sigma Xi. Presbyterian. Home: 425 Geddes Ave Charleston SC 29407

DODEN, RUSSELL LEE, computer explorationist; b. Anamosa, Iowa, July 2, 1947; s. Willis Frederick and Rita Ann (Nehl) D.; m. Beverly Ann Hitchens, Oct. 4, 1975. B.S., U. Nev., 1974. Well logging engr. Birdwell, Las Vegas, Nev., 1973-74; store mgr. Radio Shack, Tulsa, Okla., 1975-76; jr. programmer Seismograph Service, 1976-78; computer explorationist Cities Service Oil, 1978-83, Santa Fe Minerals, Tulsa, 1983—; cons. Micro-Sci Services, Broken Arrow, Okla., 1983—. Served with USN, 1966-70. Mem. Am. Assn. Petroleum Geologists, Soc. Exploration Geophysicists, Tulsa Geol. Soc., Computer-Oriented Geol. Soc. Avocations: astronomy; amateur radio; camping. Home: 4208 S 200 East Ave Broken Arrow OK 74014 Office: Santa Fe Minerals 4500 One Williams Ctr Tulsa OK 74172

DODGE, CHARLES FREMONT, III, geologist, corporation executive, educator, consultant; b. Dallas, May 28, 1924; s. Hale Barbour and H. C. (Clark) D.; m. Kathryn Charlyne Pond, Aug. 4, 1950; children—Deborah Kathryn, Rebecca Lee. B.S., So. Meth. U., 1949, M.S., 1952; Ph.D., U. N.Mex., 1966. Registered profl. geologist, Calif. With Pickette Engring., Dallas, 1947-48; instr. Arlington State Coll. (Tex.), 1948-50; geologist Concho Petroleum Co., Dallas, 1950-51; geologist Intex Oil Co., Corpus Christi, Tex., 1951-53; dist. geologist Am. Trading and Prodn. Co., Midland, Tex., 1953-57; assoc. prof. U. Tex., Arlington, 1957-66, prof., 1966-77, chmn., 1972-77; pres. Regal Exploration Co., 1973-79; v.p. Arkoma Gas Co. (Tex.), 1978—; cons., geologist Core Lab., Mobil Research & Devel., Arco Research & Devel., McCord Engring., Lewis Engring., U.S. Dept. Agr., U.S. EPA, Sun Oil Research & Devel., Marathon Research & Devel.; Murchison Oil; Palo Petro; pres. C.F. Dodge & Assocs., Inc., Arlington; adj. prof. geology So. Meth. U., Dallas. Served with USAAC, 1943-46; USAR, 1946-66; ret. capt. USACE. NSF sci. faculty fellow, 1965-66; HEW mining and mineral fuel fellow, 1974-81; recipient Disting. Service award Dallas Geol. Soc., 1976; Disting. Alumni award U. Tex., 1977. Mem. Dallas Geol. Soc. (hon. life mem., pres. 1981-82), Dallas Geophys. Soc., West Tex. Geol. Soc. Am. Assn. Petroleum Geologists (pres. Southwest sect. 1985-86), Am. Inst. Profl. Geologists, Soc. Econ. Paleontologists and Mineralogists, Soc. Exploration Geophysicists, Soc. Ind. Profl. Earth Scientists, Ind. Petroleum Assn. Am., Tex. Ind. Producers and Royalty Owners, Sigma Gamma Epsilon, Sigma Xi. Republican. Unitarian. Clubs: Dallas Petroleum; Dallas Energy. Co-editor: Enhanced Oil Recovery; author 7 field trip guide books; contbr. articles to profl. jours.

DODGE, JOHN HOPKINS, II, lawyer; b. Beaumont, Tex., July 16, 1939; s. John and Mary Velma (Robichaux) D.; m. Ethel Lowden Wiley, Dec. 18, 1965; children—Elizabeth, John Hopkins, III, Alice Anne. B.S. in Mech. Engring., Tex. A&M U., 1961; postgrad. Baylor U. Sch. Law, 1961-62; J.D., U. Houston, 1968. Bar, Tex., 1967; registered profl. engr., Tex. Engr. Sinclair Oil Corp./Arco Chem., Channelview, Tex., 1964-69; patent examiner U.S. Patent Office, Washington, 1969-70; assoc. Pravel, Wilson & Matthews, 1970-73; ptnr. Pravel & Wilson and successor firms, Houston, 1973-82, Dodge & Bush, Houston, 1982—. Pres. U. Houston Law Alumni, 1979-80. Served to 1st lt. U.S. Army, 1962-64. Mem. ABA, Houston Bar Assn., Houston Patent Law Assn., ASME. Democrat. Methodist.

DODGE, RICHARD KENNETH, biostatistician, statistical programmer; b. Springfield, Vt., Mar. 28, 1946; s. Kenneth Clarence and Bertha Belle (Gordon) D.; m. Carol Ann Demeritt, Sept. 10, 1977. B.S. in Math., U. Vt., 1973, M.S. in Stats., 1979. Statistician U. Vt., Burlington, 1979-82; biostatistician St. Jude Children's Research Hosp., Memphis, 1982—. Served with U.S. Army, 1967-70. Mem. Am. Statis. Assn., Am. Philatelic Soc., Shelby County Chess Club. Avocation: chess. Office: St Jude Children's Research Hosp 332 N Lauderdale St Memphis TN 38101

DODGE, TERRY LEE, anesthesiologist; b. Callaway, Nebr., June 11, 1947; s. Ernest Clyde and Rose Agnes (Sladky) D.; m. Vickey Jayne Pierce, Aug. 20, 1967; children—Jeffrey Lynn, Mark Erin. Student Kearney State Coll., 1965-68; B.S., U. Nebr., 1970, M.D., 1972. Intern, St. Elizabeth Hosp., Covington, Ky., 1972-73; resident in anesthesiology U. Ky. Hosp., Lexington, 1973-74; resident, fellow in anesthesiology Med. U. S.C., Charleston, 1974-76; staff anesthesiologist, bd. dirs. Piedmont Med. Ctr., Rock Hill, S.C., 1978—. Served to lt. comdr. M.C., USNR, 1976-78. Recipient Rotary Internat. award, 1980. Mem. AMA, York County Med. Soc. (pres.), Am. Soc. Anesthesiologists (S.C. del. 1981-86), S.C. Med. Assn. (trustee), S.C. Soc. Anesthesiologists, Internat. Anesthesia Research Soc. Contbr. articles to profl. jours. Office: Anesthesia Assocs Rock Hill 1631 Ebenezer Rd Rock Hill SC 29730

DOERR, ARTHUR HARRY, educational administrator; b. Johnston City, Ill., Aug. 28, 1924; s. Arthur Harry and Nettie Ester (Felts) D.; m. Dale A. Lantrip, Aug. 15, 1947; 1 son, Marc M. B.A., So. Ill. U., 1947; M.A., Ind. U., 1948; Ph.D., Northwestern U., 1951. From asst. prof. to regents prof., dept. chmn. U. Okla., Norman, 1951-70, asst. dean Grad. Coll., 1960-61, dean, 1961-65; prof. U. Pa., Phila., 1966-67; leader AID devel. project, Pahlavi U., Iran, 1966-67; mem. faculty U. West Fla., Pensacola, 1970—; v.p. acad. affairs, 1970—, prof. earth/atomspheric scis., 1970—. Served to 2d. lt. USAAF, 1943-46. Recipient Teaching award U. Okla., 1955; Alumni award for Disting. Profl. Achievement, So. Ill. U., 1965; Am. Assn. Middle Eastern Affairs fellow, Israel, 1965. Fellow Okla. Acad. Sci.; mem. Assn. Am. Geographers, Southwestern Social Sci. Assn., Okla. Edn. Assn., AAAS, Nat. Council Geog.

Edn., Phi Kappa Phi, Sigma Xi. Author: (with Lee Guernsey) Principles of Geography, 1959, 2d edit., 1975, Principals of Physical Geography, 1960, 2d edit., 1976; An Introduction to Economic Geography, 1969; Coal Mining in Oklahoma and Landscape Modification, 1969. Contbr. articles to various publs. Home: 66 Blithewood Dr Pensacola FL 32514 Office: U West Fla Pensacola FL 32514

DOERR, ROBERT WAYNE, nursing administrator; b. New Castle, Pa., Mar. 21, 1947; s. Richard Leroy and Garnet Mae (McCandless) D.; m. Suellen Lewis, Nov. 9, 1969 (div. Nov. 1976); m. Alicia Fay Galloway, May 10, 1980; children—Ross William, Ryan Wesley. B.S. in Psychology, U. Ala., 1973; B.S. in Nursing, Capstone Coll. Nursing, Tuscaloosa, 1979. R.N. Patient activity specialist Bryce Hosp., Tuscaloosa, 1972-73, psychologist, 1973-78; supr. Jackson Hosp., Montgomery, Ala., 1979-80; dir. nursing service Tarwater Devel. Ctr., Wetumpka, Ala., 1980-83, Bryce Hosp., Tuscaloosa, 1983—; mem. adj. faculty U. Ala., Tuscaloosa, 1984. Formerly active Boy Scouts Am. Served to capt. USAFR, 1968—. Mem. Assn. Mil. Surgeons U.S. (nursing div.), W. Ala. Council Nursing Service Adminstrs., Res. Officers Assn. Democrat. Methodist. Avocations: swimming, softball, woodworking. Home: 92 Hawthorne Pl Northport AL 35476 Office: Bryce Hosp 200 University Blvd Tuscaloosa AL 35401

DOERRING, PAUL LUTHER, psychologist; b. Andrew, Iowa, Apr. 26, 1931; s. Elmer and Elsa (Bredow) D.; m. Gerry Birdsell, Aug. 15, 1953; children—Erik, Susan, David. B.S. in Bus. Administrn., Macalester Coll., 1954; M.A. in Ednl. Psychology, Stanford U., 1957, Ph.D. in Psychology, 1960. Lic. psychologist Mich., S.C. Staff clin. psychologist Des Moines Child Guidance Ctr., Iowa, 1960-62; mem. faculty Merrill Palmer Inst., Detroit, 1962-67; pres. Psychol. Inst. Mich., Birmingham, 1967-79; practice psychology, Hilton Head Island, S.C., 1979—; cons. Hilton Head Island Youth Ctr., 1982—, Cranbrook Acad., Kingswood Sch., Birmingham, 1968-79; staff Hilton Head Island Hosp., 1980—. Columnist Hilton Head Island newspaper, 1981—. Author: (monograph) Meaning of Death to the Young Child, 1976. Bd. dirs. Hilton Head Youth Ctr., 1982—; v.p., bd. dirs. Coast Jazz Assn., 1984—. Served with U.S. Army, 1954-56. Stanford U. scholar, 1958-59; Sloan fellow, 1958. Fellow Am. Orthopsychiat. Assn. (com. 1970-72); mem. Am. Psychol. Assn., Am. Assn. Marriage and Family Therapy (clin.) Presbyterian. Lodge: Rotary. Avocations: tennis; jazz music; landscaping; auto restoration. Home: 42 Misty Cove Hilton Head Island SC 29928 Office: 38C Bow Circle PO Box 5547-29938 Hilton Head Island SC 29928

DOGBE, KORSI, sociologist; b. Aflao, Ghana, Dec. 4, 1940; came to U.S., 1977; s. Avornor Werwerzi and Yaovi Martha (Amenya) D.; B.A., U. Ghana, 1966; M.A., M.Sc., Ph.D., U. So. Calif.; m. Akosua Tess Asante, Aug. 14, 1977; children—Kelali Kordzo, Mawuse Abla. Peace Corps vol. to U.S., 1967-69; asst. prof. edn. Chapman Coll for World Campus Afloat, Orange, Calif., 1972-73; lectr. African sociology, sociology of edn. U. Cape Coast, Ghana, 1973-77; assoc. prof. sociology Hampton Inst., 1978-83, prof., 1983—; Fulbright-Hayes curriculum cons. Dept. State, Norfolk State U., 1977-78; dir. Group Projects Abroad, U.S. Dept. Edn., 1984. Chmn., Christian edn. com., supt. vacation Bible sch. Messiah Presbyn. Ch., 1983-84. Fulbright-Hayes Educators' grantee, 1967, 77; UN U. Research grantee, 1980; U.S. Dept. Edn. grantee, 1983-84. Mem. Am. Sociol. Assn., Am. Acad. Polit. and Social Scis., Am. Assn. Tchr. Educators, Internat. Sociol. Assn., Internat. Soc. Comparative Study Civilizations (council 1983—), Am. Council UN U., African Studies Assn., Phi Delta Kappa, Phi Kappa Phi. Author: Reflection on African Culture, 1978; Endogenous Creations in Africa, 1980; contbr. articles to profl. jours. Home: 533D E Queen St Hampton VA 23669 Office: Dept Sociology Hampton Inst Hampton VA 23668

DOGRU, ALI HAYDAR, petroleum engineer, researcher, mathematical model builder; b. Ardahan, Turkey, Sept. 29, 1945; came to U.S., 1970; s. Mehmet and Sidret (Bilgin) D.; m. Sevgi Aydin, Aug. 24, 1971; children—Mehmet Ulgar, I. Pinar, Altay. M.S., Tech. U. Istanbul, 1968; Ph.D., U. Tex.-Austin, 1974. Lectr., Norwegian Inst. Tech., Trondheim, 1975-76; asst. prof. Tech. U. Istanbul, Turkey, 1976-79; petroleum cons. specialist Core Labs. Inc., Dallas, 1979-82; assoc. in petroleum engring. Mobil Research and Devel. Inc., Dallas, 1982—; vis. assoc. Calif. Inst. Tech., Pasadena, 1977-78; asst. prof. U. Tex., Austin, 1974-75; cons. Turkish Petroleum Corps., Core Labs. Inc. Europe, mining industry, oil corps., Kuwait, 1977-79. Prin. author articles in profl. publs. Pres., Turkish-Am. Assn. Dallas, 1981. NATO doctoral scholar, 1970, postdoctoral scholar, 1977. Mem. Soc. Petroleum Engrs., ASME (assoc.), Soc. Indsl. Applied Math. (assoc.), Pi Epsilon Tau, Pi Eta Sigma. Office: Mobil Research and Devel Corp DRD PO Box 819047 Dallas TX 75381

DOLGORUKY, MICHAEL SCHACHT, computer company executive, lawyer; b. Berlin, Nov. 25, 1921; s. Simeon Schacht Count of Kasan and H.I.M. Princess Yeratharina Aleksandrova Dolgoruky Countess of Kasan; m. Isabel Arevalo Salas, Feb. 19, 1872; children—Ilona-Maria, Udo-Michael. B.A., Jesuit Coll., Breslau, Germany, 1938; J.D., U. Breslau-Munich, 1950; C.E., Tech. Sch., Munich, 1952; D. in Polit. Sci., Sorbonne, 1953; postdoctorate London Sch. Econs., 1953-54. Bar: Munich 1954, Paris 1957, The Hague 1961. Negotiating del. Krupp Co., Essen, Germany, and Africa, 1955-60, legal and fin. cons., 1960-65; legal and fin. cons. Stockfis, Netherlands, and Africa, 1960-65; legal adviser Govt. Ivory Coast, Abidjan, 1965-70; pres., chief exec. officer PROSACA Inc., Pensacola, 1970—, INTRAG Inc., Dallas, 1983—; pres. Multilingual Communication Ctr. Inc., Pensacola, 1983—. Author: Encyclopedia of Commercial Correspondence, 8 vols., 1970-80; Computerized Commercial Correspondence; Co-author: Guia de la Redaccion Legal (English/Spanish), 2 vols., 1978. Served to lt. comdr. German Navy, 1940-45. Conservative Russian Orthodox Catholic. Mem. Omicron Delta Kappa. Avocations: polo; snow and water skiing; deep sea fishing. Address: Prosaca Inc 3193 W Nine Mile Rd Pensacola FL 32506

DOLIN, RICHARD ALAN, business educator, clergyman; b. Greensboro, N.C., Dec. 10, 1944; s. David Alan and Doris Marie (Smittle) D.; m. Jacqueline Adams, Sept. 1, 1968; children—Amanda Whitney, Miriam Garrett. B.S., Ohio State U., 1970; J.D., U. Louisville, 1973; M.Div., Louisville Presbyn. Sem., 1974; M.B.A., Bellarmine Coll., 1979. Bar: Ky. 1973, U.S. Dist. Ct. (we. dist.) Ky. 1973, Ind. 1975, U.S. Supreme Ct. 1976, U.S. Tax Ct. 1975, U.S. Dist. Ct. (so. dist.) Ind. 1975, U.S. Dist Ct. (ea. dist.) Ky. 1979; ordained to ministry Presbyn. Ch. U.S.A., 1976. Technician, Mt. Carmel Hosp., Columbus, Ohio, 1965-70; assoc. Lohman, Diamond & Dolin, Louisville, 1973-78, Frederick & Dolin, Louisville, 1978—; asst. prof. bus. adminstrn. Bellarmine Coll., Louisville, 1980—, chmn. dept., 1984—; cons. Nomos, Ltd., Louisville, 1980—. Bd. dirs. Presbyn. Homes for Sr. Citizens, 1980—; sec. bd. dirs. Westminster Terr., 1980—; sec. bd. dirs. Presbyn. Homes and Services of Ky., Inc., Westminster Woods, Inc., bd. dirs. Helmwood Services, Inc., 1984—, Bellwood Children's Home, 1985—. legal advisor Presbytery of Louisville, 1976—, mem. exec. council, 1978—, rec. clk., 1976-79, stated clk., 1983—; mem. council Synod of Mid-South, 1979—, chmn., 1981—; mem. Ky. Council Econ. Advisors, 1984—; mem. Gov.'s Fin. Planning Council, 1985—. Mem. Am. Mgmt. Assn., ABA, Evaluation Research Soc., Evaluation Network, Fed. Bar Assn., Fin. Mgmt. Assn., Ky. Bar Assn., Ind. Bar Assn., Southwestern Fin. Assn., So. Fin. Assn., Ky. Econs. Assn. (bd. dirs.), Midwest Fin. Assn., Louisville Bar Assn., Phi Alpha Delta, Delta Sigma Pi, Beta Gamma Sigma, Alpha Delta Epsilon. Democrat. Presbyterian. Contbr. articles to profl. jours. Home: 1306 Old Taylor Trail Goshen KY 40026 Office: Bellarmine Coll Newburg Rd Louisville KY 40205

DOLINER, NATHANIEL LEE, lawyer; b. Daytona Beach, Fla., June 28, 1949; s. Joseph and Asia (Shaffer) D.; m. Debra Lynn Simon, June 5, 1983. B.A., George Washington U., 1970; J.D., Vanderbilt U., 1973; LL.M. in Taxation, U. Fla., 1977. Bar: Fla. 1973, U.S. Tax Ct. 1973, U.S. Dist. Ct. (mid. dist.) Fla. 1974. Assoc. Smalbein, Eubank, Johnson, Rosier & Bussey, P.A., Daytona Beach, Fla., 1973-76; vis. asst. prof. law U. Fla., Gainesville, 1977-78; assoc. Carlton, Fields, Ward, Emmanuel, Smith & Cutler, P.A., Tampa, Fla., 1978-82, ptnr., 1982—, chmn. tax, corp. and securities dept., 1984—, treas., 1985-86. Dist. commnr. Gulf Ridge council Boy Scouts Am., 1983; bd. dirs. Big Bros./Big Sisters of Greater Tampa Inc., 1981-83, child Abuse Council, Inc., 1986-87; bd. dirs. Tampa Jewish Fedn., 1984-86, chmn. community relations com., 1985-86. Mem. ABA (tax sect., vice chmn. continuing legal edn. com. 1986-87), Fla. Bar Assn. (mem. exec. com. tax sect. 1980-83); Greater Tampa C. of C. (chmn. Ambassadors target task force of Com. of 100, 1984-85). Democrat. Clubs: Tampa, Carrollwood Village Golf and Tennis. Lodge: Rotary (bd. dirs. 1986—). Home: 3207 Tarabrook Dr Tampa FL 33618 Office: Carlton Fields Ward Emmanuel Smith & Cutler PA 777 S Harbour Island Blvd 5th Floor Tampa FL 33602

DOLL, PADDY ANN, psychologist, educator; b. Shreveport, La., July 31, 1928; d. Charles and Helen (D'Artois) D. B.A., Centenary Coll., 1948; M.A., La. State U., 1952; Ph.D., U. Houston, 1969. Lic. psychologist, La. Personnel dir., pres. Doll Bros., Shreveport, 1948—; asst. prof. McNeese State U., Lake Charles, La., 1956-61; teaching fellow U. Houston, 1961-64; asst. prof. dept. psychology Loyola U., New Orleans, 1964-71, assoc. prof., 1971—, chmn. dept., 1966-69, 76-78, 81-85; psychol. dir. St. Mary's Residential Sch. for Mentally Retarded, Clarks, La., 1953-56; prof. Notre Dame Sem., New Orleans, 1968-71; cons. in field; mem. La. State Bd. Examiners Psychology, 1978-82, sec.-treas., 1978-79, vice-chmn., 1979-82. Author: Toplevel Executives, 1965. Contbr. articles to profl. jours. Bd. dirs. La. Assn. Retarded Children, 1952-56; bd. dirs. Magnolia Sch., New Orleans, 1966-69. Mem. Am. Psychol. Assn., Southwestern Psychol. Assn., La. Psychol. Assn., Southeastern Psychol. Assn., AAAS, Phi Sigma Iota, Sigma Pi Sigma, Psi Chi, Delta Omicron, Delta Phi Alpha. Republican. Roman Catholic. Home: Psychology Dept Loyola U 6363 Saint Charles Ave New Orleans LA 70118

DOLLARD, JOHN DAY, educator; b. New Haven, Jan. 19, 1937; s. John and Victorine (Day) D.; m. Joan Ganis. B.A., Yale U., 1958; M.A., Princeton U., 1960, Ph.D., 1963. Research assoc. Princeton U., N.J., 1963-65; asst. prof. U. Rochester, 1965-69; assoc. prof. U. Tex.-Austin, 1969-79, prof. math., 1979—, chmn. dept. math., 1983—. Author: (with Charles N. Friedman) Product Integration, 1979. Mem. Am. Phys. Soc., Am. Math. Soc., Math. Assn. Am. Home: 1827 Westlake Dr Austin TX 78746 Office: Dept Math U Tex Austin TX 78712

DOMI, TANYA LESLIE, army officer; b. Indpls., July 24, 1954; d. John Thomas Domi and Louise Joan Edwards. B.A., Central Mich. U., 1981; postgrad., 1981-82. Grad. asst. Central Mich. U., 1981-82; commd. 2d lt. U.S. Army, 1982; now sta. Ft. McClellan, Ala. Mem. exec. bd. Isabella County Democratic Com. (Mich.), 1979-82; mem. Mich. Women's Dem. Caucus, 1981; bd. dirs. Glenn Civic Center, 1978-79. Mem. Res. Officers Assn., ACLU, Assn. U.S. Army, Sigma Delta Chi, Mu Sigma, Chi Gamma Iota. Contbr. Soldier's mag., Trailblazer, Ft. McClellan News. Home: PO Box 5133 Fort McClellan AL 36205 Office: CoA 1st BN (BT) Fort McClellan AL 36205

DONAHUE, MARY KATHERINE, library consultant; b. Dallas, Jan. 14, 1942; d. Joseph W. and Ellen (Onan) D.; B.A., Our Lady of the Lake U., 1963; M.L.S., U. Calif.-Berkeley, 1965; M.A., Tex. A&M U., 1983, postgrad, 1983—; m. John Patrick Hooker, July 29, 1976. Librarian, Dallas Public Library, 1963-64; 1st asst. Lubbock (Tex.) City-County Libraries, 1965-66, asst. dir., 1966-68, acting dir., 1968-69; librarian U. Tex., Arlington, 1969; corp. librarian Univ. Computing Co., Dallas, 1969-72; sr. librarian Corpus Christi (Tex.) Public Libraries, 1973-75, adminstrv. coordinator, 1975-76; coordinator Hidalgo County (Tex.) Library System, McAllen, 1976-80; asst. prof. Tex. A&M U., College Station, 1981-84; library cons., 1983—; grant writer. Recipient Disting. Service award Tex. Hist. Commn. Home: 504 S Dexter St College Station TX 77840

DONALD, GEORGE LYNWOOD, university financial officer; b. Macon, Ga., Nov. 29, 1945; s. Paul Roger and Mary Mabel (Hadaway) D.; m. Dayle June Rowland, Apr. 15, 1966; children—DeeDee Lyn, Alexander Damon, Hollie Miranda. Assoc. B.S., Middle Ga. Coll., 1965; B.S., Ga. Southwestern Coll., 1968. Groups claims trainee Life of Ga., Atlanta, 1968-69; jr. acct. Gen. Motors Corp., Atlanta, 1969-71; asst. comptroller, internal auditor Mercer U., Macon, Ga., 1971-73, chief acct., 1973-77, univ. comptroller, 1977-84, asst. v.p. for fin., univ. comptroller, 1984—, comptroller Penfield/Rowland Printing subsid. Mercer U., 1982—, asst. v.p. fin., 1985—. Mem. Nat. Assn. Accts. (v.p. ednl. programs Middle Ga. chpt. 1975). Avocations: hunting; fishing; Little league baseball and softball. Home: 5481 Cascade Ave Macon GA 31206 Office: Mercer Univ 1400 Coleman Ave Macon GA 31207

DONALDSON, CHARLES WILLIAM, university official and dean, educator; b. Newport, Ark., Mar. 8, 1947; m. Mable L. Noel, Jan. 25, 1970; 1 child, Andrea Nicole. B.A., Philander Smith Coll., 1968; M.S., State Coll. Ark., 1971; Ed.D., U. Ark., 1982. Lic. profl. counselor. Tchr., counselor, asst. prin. Pulaski County Spl. Sch. Dist., Little Rock, 1968-73; counselor U. Ark., Little Rock, 1973-77, dir. career planning and placement, 1977-83, assoc. vice chancellor ednl. services, 1983—, dean Univ. Coll., 1985—. Bd. dirs. Central Ark. Mental Health Services, 1980-82, Little Rock Job Corp, 1984-85. Mem. Am. Assn. for Counseling and Devel., Am. Coll. Personnel Assn., Nat. Assn. Student Personnel Adminstrs., So. Assn. Student Personnel Adminstrs., Ark. Coll. Personnel Assn. (exec. com. 1984-85), Alpha Phi Alpha. Democrat. Methodist. Avocations: jogging; photography; coin collecting. Home: 3006 Lennox Dr Little Rock AR 72204 Office: U Ark at Little Rock 33rd and University Ave Little Rock AR 72204

DONALDSON, ROBERT BRUCE, oil company executive; b. Balt., Mar. 27, 1932; s. Lennox Bruce and Gladys Sydelle (Durham) D.; m. Betty Ellen Roy, June 10, 1955; children—Debborah Leigh Cantrell, Grant Bruce. B.B.A., U. Ga., 1957. Warehouse mgr. Ofcl. Products Co., Atlanta, 1955-57; account exec. mktg. Gulf Oil Corp., Houston, 1959-85, Gulf Products div. BP Oil, Inc., Cleve., 1985—; vital source speaker Gulf Oil Corp., Birmingham, Ala., 1979-82; mem. speakers bur. Ala. Petroleum Council, Birmingham, 1979-82. Advisor Vulcan Dist. Boy Scouts Am., 1975. Served to 1st lt. U.S. Army, 1957-59. Republican. Baptist. Club: Civitan (Birmingham) (pres. 1973-74, lt. gov. 1974). Avocations: swimming; fishing; painting. Home: 613 Cox Ave Hattiesburg MS 39401

DONALDSON, TERRENCE LEE, biochemical engineer; b. Franklin, Pa., Apr. 20, 1946; s. Winston G. and Ruby (Pryor) D.; m. Catherine Huheey. B.S., Pa. State U., 1968; Ph.D., U. Pa., 1974. Registered profl. engr., Tenn. Asst., asoc. prof. U. Rochester, N.Y., 1974-80; research engr., group leader Oak Ridge Nat. Lab., Tenn., 1980—, biotech. coordinator, 1985—; assoc. prof. U. Tenn., Knoxville, 1982—; ad hoc visitor for accreditation of chem. engr. programs Accreditation Bd. Engring. and Tech., N.Y.C., 1982—. Contbr. articles to profl. jours.; patentee in field. Served with U.S. Army, 1968-70, Vietnam. Recipient teaching award U. Rochester, 1980. Mem. Am. Chem. Soc., Am. Inst. of Chem. Engrs. Office: Oak Ridge Nat Lab PO Box X Oak Ridge TN 37831

DONALDSON, WILLIS LYLE, electrical engineer; b. Cleburne, Tex., May 1, 1915; s. Charles Lyle and Anna Belle (Willis) D.; B.S. in Elec. Engring., Tex. Tech. U., 1938; m. Frances Virginia Donnell, Aug. 20, 1938; children—Sarah Donaldson Seaberg, Susan Donaldson Pollock, Sylvia Donaldson Nelson, Anthony Lyle. Distbn. engr. Tex. Elec. Service Co., Wichita Falls, 1938-42, supervisory engr., 1945-46; asst. prof. elec. engring. Lehigh U., 1946-51, asso. prof., 1953-54; sr. research engr. dept. physics S.W. Research Inst., San Antonio, 1954-55, mgr. communications sect. dept. electronics and elec. engring., 1955-59, dept. dir., 1959-64, v.p., 1964-72, v.p. planning and program devel., 1972-74, sr. v.p. planning and program devel., 1974-85, sr. cons., 1985—; mem. adv. coms. engring. div. St. Mary's U., elec. engring. dept. Tex. Tech. U. Served to capt. USNR, 1942-45, 51-53. Bd. dirs. San Antonio Chamber Music Soc., 1962-72. Named Disting. Engr., Tex. Tech. U., 1969; registered profl. engr., Tex., Pa. Fellow IEEE (life), Am. Soc. Nondestructive Testing; mem. Nat. Soc. Profl. Engrs., Tex. Soc. Profl. Engrs., Am. Optical Soc., Armed Forces Communications and Electronics Assn., Am. Mgmt. Assn., Sigma Xi, Tau Beta Pi, Eta Kappa Nu, Alpha Chi. Mem. Disciples of Christ Ch. Contbr. publs. in electronics field; patentee in field. Home: 104 Pontiac Ln San Antonio TX 78242 Office: Southwest Research Inst 6220 Culebra Rd San Antonio TX 78284

DONATELLI, BRUCE EDMUND, manufacturing executive; b. Los Angeles, May 26, 1942; s. Victor Edmund and Margaret Doris (MacCormick) D.; m. Julie Elizabeth Guziel, Jan. 29, 1966; children—Christine, Amy, Paul. B.S., UCLA, 1965, M.S., 1967. Faculty, U. Md., European Div., Fed. Republic Germany, 1968-70; planning analyst, mgr. bus. analysis Babcock & Wilcox Co., Beaver Falls, Pa., 1971-76, mgr. fittings and forgings ops. 1977-81; gen. mgr. ops. Edgewater Mfg. Co., York, S.C., 1981—. Vice pres. planning div. United Way, Beaver County, Pa., 1980-81. Served to capt. U.S. Army, 1967-71. Mem. Forging Industry Assn., Assn. Iron and Steel Engrs., Tau Beta Pi. Presbyterian. Lodge: Rotary (pres.). Home: 4405 Wood Forest Dr Rock Hill SC 29730 Office: 500 Edgewater Rd York SC 29745

DONATO, DAVID IVAN, operations research analyst, scientific software developer; b. San Mateo, Calif., Dec. 11, 1951; s. Dewey Francois Donato and Lillian Ruth (Herrington) Sheets; m. Liberte Amiedevie, Mar. 21, 1980; 1 child, Verite Amidevie. Student MIT, 1970-72; B.S. in Math. with honors, U. So. Colo., 1975; postgrad., Tulane U., 1977-78, U. New Orleans, 1979-81. Student worker MIT, Cambridge, 1971-72; copyboy Pueblo Chieftain, Colo., 1973-76; statistician U.S. Dept. Interior, New Orleans, 1976-85, ops. research analyst, Reston, Va., 1985—; free-lance sci. software designer, Kenner, La., 1982—. Editor: OCS Statistical Summary, 1977-83. Contbr. articles to govt. publs. Mem. Math. Assn. Am. Avocations: music; bicycling. Home: 307 Aaron Ct Sterling VA 22170 Office: U S Geol Survey MS 508 12201 Sunrise Valley Dr Reston VA 22092

DONCASTER, JOHN DEMPSTER, educational administrator; b. Macclesfield, Eng., Dec. 16, 1931; came to U.S., 1955; s. Clarence Frederick and Honor (Collins) D.; m. Robin Lavinia Ramsay, Mar. 18, 1965; children—Thomas Mellen, Angela, Peter. B.A., Oxford U., Eng., 1955, M.A., 1957. Dean of boys Graham-Eckes Sch., Palm Beach, Fla., 1955-56; instr. So. Meth. U., Dallas, 1956-57; headmaster Selwyn Sch., Denton, Tex., 1957—. Bd. govs. Southwest Outward Bound Sch., Santa Fe, 1973-82, Colo. Outward Bound Sch., Denver, 1982—; v.p. trustee Shreveport Country Day Sch., La., 1985—; trustee Ind. Edn. Fund, Washington, 1985—. Served to lt. Brit. Inf., 1950-52. Mem. Headmasters Assn., Country Day Sch. Headmasters Assn., Nat. Assn. Ind. Schs. (trustee 1983—, pres. Southwest chpt. 1974-75). Episcopalian. Clubs: United Oxford and Cambridge (London). Home: 3333 University Dr West Denton TX 76201 Office: The Selwyn Sch 3333 University Drive West Denton TX 76201

DONCHIAN, RICHARD DAVOUD, econ. analyst; b. Hartford, Conn., Sept. 21, 1905; s. Samuel B. and Armenouhi A. (Davoud) D.; A.B., Yale U., 1928; C.F.A., U. Va., 1964; Inst. Chartered Fin. Analysts; m. Alma C. Gibbs, Feb. 9, 1957. Market technician Hemphill Noyes & Co., N.Y.C., 1933-35; Samuel Donchian Rug Co., Hartford, 1935-38; pres. Fin. Supervision, Inc., 1938-42; Statis. control officer, USAAF, 1942-45. econ. analyst, marker letter writer, Shearson-Hammill & Co., N.Y.C., 1946-48; investment advisor, 1948-60; pres., Futures Inc., N.Y.C., 1948-60; dir. commodity research, account exec. Hayden, Stone & Co. (now Shearson Am. Express Inc.), N.Y.C., 1960-69, v.p., 1970-76, sr. v.p. investments, 1976—; sr. advisor Shearson Commodity Trend Timing Fund, 1979—; dir. Donchian Mgmt. Inc., Ft. Lauderdale, Fla., Fin. Supervision Inc., Greenwich, Conn. Mem. N.Y. Cotton Exchange, Commodity Exchange, Inc., N.Y. Futures Exchange; N.Y. Soc. Security Analysts, Am. Statis. Assn., Inst. Chartered Fin. Analysts, Fin. Forum N.Y. Rug Soc. Republican. Presbyterian (elder). Clubs: Yale, N.Y.C. Down Town Assn.; Yale (Ft. Lauderdale, Fla.); Univ. (Hartford); Scarsdale Golf; Deerfield Country (Fla.). Author articles and monographs. Home: 133 Pompano Beach Blvd Pompano Beach FL 33062 also Country Club Apts Hartsdale NY 10530 also Bomoseen VT 05732 Office: 2 Greenwich Plaza Greenwich CT 06830 also 2400 E Commercial Blvd Fort Lauderdale FL 33308

DONDA, RUSSELL SCOTT, retail executive; b. Cleve., Mar. 14, 1955; s. Joseph Stanley and Julie (Dolhancyk) D.; m. Margaret Marie O'Boyle, Oct. 11, 1975. B.B.A., Cleve. State U., 1978. Mgr. trainee Fishers Big Wheel Stores, Inc., Streetsboro, Ohio, 1979, asst. mgr. soft lines, 1980; mgr. trainee Schwartz Klines Dept. Stores, New Philadelphia, Ohio, 1980; asst. mgr. Wilson's Dept. Stores, Gainesville, Fla., 1980-81, gen. mgr., 1981—, v.p., 1983—; treas., dir. Schwartz Apparel; dir. Oaks Mall Merchants Assn., Gainesville, 1980—, Palatra Mall Merchants Assn., (Fla.), 1982. Head retail div. United Way, Alachua County, Gainesville, 1982. Mem. Gainesville C. of C. (mem. com. 100 econ. devel. 1983). Republican. Mem. Unity Ch. Office: Wilson's Dept Stores Inc 6324 Newberry Rd Gainesville FL 32605

DONEHUE, JOHN DOUGLAS, newspaper executive; b. Cramerton, N.C., July 5, 1928; s. John Sidney and Annie (Shepherd) D.; student Am. Press Inst., Columbia U., 1965, 71-73; H.H.D., Bapt. Coll. at Charleston, 1985; m. Mary Phelps, Jan. 9, 1952 (dec. 1964); children—Teresa Jean, Marilyn Phelps; m. Sylvia Louise McKenzie, Feb. 11, 1966 (dec. Nov. 1971); children—Hayden Shepherd, John Douglas; m. Virginia Kirkland, June 28, 1975; children—Ann Mikell, Robertson Carr. Sports writer Charleston, S.C. News and Courier, 1947, copy editor, 1956, state editor, 1959-62, city editor, 1962-68, mng. editor, 1968-71, promotion dir., 1971—, v.p. for corp. public relations, 1975—, compiler News and Courier Style Book, 1969; sports editor Orangeburg (S.C.) Times and Democrat, 1948-50; polit. reporter Montgomery (Ala.) Advertiser, 1954-55; faculty advisor Bapt. Coll. at Charleston Student Newspaper. Spl. adviser comdt. 7th USCG dist. for establishment dist.-wide pub. info. program, 1960-61; journalism lectr. Bapt. Coll., Charleston, sec. 1st bd. founders, 1969; lectr. Am. Press Inst. Seminars, Reston, Va. Chmn. adv. bd. Salvation Army; chmn. regional adv. council S.C. Dept. Youth Services; chmn. United Way Planning Bd.; bd. dirs. S.C. Tricentennial Parade Com., 1969—; v.p. Greater Charleston Safety Council; pres. Palmetto Safety Council; mem. exec. com. Charleston Higher Edn. Consortium; mem. Charleston Waterfront Commn. Served with S.C. N.G., 1948-50, USAF, 1950-54, USMCR, 1955-56, USAR, 1956-59, USCGR, 1959-66, USNR, 1966-75. Recipient Freedoms Found. award, 1969, 71. Mem. John Ancrum Soc. of Soc. Prevention Cruelty to Animals, Carolina Art Assn., YMCA, Internat. Newspaper Promotion Assn., S.C. Press Assn. (pres. 1985), Air Force Assn. (dir. Charleston council), Navy League (v.p. Charleston council), Charleston Trident C. of C. (pres. 1983), Toastmasters Internat. (charter mem. Okinawa club), Okinawa Soc. Episcopalian (lay reader, vestryman). Clubs: Country, Rotary (pres. 1974-75) (Charleston). Guest commentator Nat. Pub. Radio. Home: 66 Bull St Charleston SC 29401 Office: 134 Columbus St Charleston SC 29401

DONELAN, WILLIAM JOSEPH, hospital administrator; b. Washington, Oct. 2, 1946; s. William Joseph and Anna Grayson (Curtice) D.; m. Mary Anne McGuinness, Aug. 17, 1968. B.A., Wheeling Coll., 1968; M.S., Duke U., 1974. Asst. bus. mgr. Duke U. Med. Ctr., Durham, N.C., 1969-70, adminstrv. asst., 1970-74, bus. mgr., 1974-81; chief operating officer Duke U. Hosp., Durham, N.C., 1981—; adj. asst. prof. Duke U., 1982—. Trustee Kidney Found. N.C., Chapel Hill, 1971-78, Nat. Kidney Found., N.Y.C., 1973-76; bd. dirs. Lincoln Community Health Ctr., Durham, 1977-82. Recipient pres.'s award Kidney Found. N.C., 1976. Democrat. Roman Catholic. Club: Duke Mgmt. (Durham) (pres. 1981-82). Home: 150 Dixie Dr Chapel Hill NC 27514 Office: Duke U Hosp Durham NC 27710

DONIA, TOM EARL, public relations administrator; b. Houghton, Mich., Aug. 30, 1949; s. Robert A. and Angeline A. (Dornbos) D. B.A., Hope Coll., 1971. Reporter Kalamazoo (Mich.) Gazette, 1971-76; dir. pub. relations Nat. Trust Hist. Preservation, Washington, 1976-80, Transp. Inst., Washington, 1980-81; dir. communications South Fla. Blood Service, Miami, 1981—; freelance writer, photographer. Mem. pub. relations com. Epilepsy Found. S. Fla., Assn. Retarded Citizens, Dade County (Fla.). Mem. Internat. Assn. Bus. Communicators, S. Fla. Hosp. Pub. Relations Assn., Pub. Relations Soc. Am., Am. Assn. Blood Banks, Fla. Assn. Blood Banks, Dade Heritage Trust, Miami Design Preservation League. Home: 735 14th Pl Apt 2 Miami Beach FL 33139

DONKIN, ROBERT GORDON, mgmt. cons.; b. Cleve., Apr. 16, 1923; s. Robert Forster and Louise (Hess) D.; B.S.M.E., Case Inst. Tech., 1944; postgrad. U.S. Naval Acad., 1944; m. Marilyn Ann Mitzel, Dec. 23, 1944; children—Marilyn Ann Donkin Walters, Elizabeth Louise Donkin Ayers, Diana Jeanne Donkin Grigg. Design engr. Towmotor Corp., 1946-47; chief engr. Webster Products Corp., 1947-48; chief mech. designer Swartwout Co., 1949-50, asst. gen. supt., 1951-54, mgr. steam specialties mfg., 1955-56; gen. supt. Rockwell Mfg. Co., Chgo., 1957-58, works mgr., 1959-62, gen. mgr., Tulsa, 1962-63; mng. asso., gen. mgmt. cons. div. mgmt. services Arthur Young & Co., Tulsa, 1964-66, prin., 1967-68, dir., partner, 1969-73; pres. Indsl. Relations Services, Inc., Tulsa, 1973-83; exec. v.p. Selindex, Inc., 1976-84; pres. ABC Systems, Tulsa, 1983—; designer, author ABC Systems Software. Served to ensign USNR, 1942-46. Mem. Am. Prodn. and Inventory Control Soc. (pres. Tulsa chpt. 1975-76), Phi Delta Theta. Republican. Methodist. Club: Mason. Patentee centrifuge. Home: 5408 E 38th St Tulsa OK 74135 Office: 2300 E 14th St Suite 302 Tulsa OK 74104

DONNAHOE, ALAN STANLEY, newspaper executive; b. Asheville, N.C., Aug. 27, 1916; s. Paul Albert and Kate (Stanley) D.; student pub. schs.; m. Elsie Pitts, 1938; children—Kate Stanley Donnahoe Vaughan. Admitted to Va., N.C. bars; dir. research Richmond (Va.) C. of C., 1936-46, asst. exec. mgr., 1946-50; exec. sec. Richmond Inter-Club Council, 1938-41, Va. Soc. Pub. Accountants, Richmond, 1946-50; dir. research Richmond Newspapers, Inc.,

1950-55, v.p., 1956-59, exec. v.p., asst. pub., 1959-65, pres., also dir.; pres., chief exec. officer, dir. Media Gen., Inc., 1969—; pres., dir. Southeast Media, Inc., Richmond Newspapers, Inc., (all Richmond, Va.), Cablevision of Fredericksburg, Inc. (Va.), Tribune Co., Tampa, Fla., Piedmont Pub. Co., Winston-Salem, N.C., dir. Security Fed. Savs. & Loan Assn. and subs.'s, United Va. Bank, United Va. Bankshares, Inc., Beacon Press, Media Gen. Fin. Services, Inc., Garden State Paper Co. (all Richmond), WXFL, Inc., Tampa, FSC Paper Corp., Chgo. Purolator, Inc., Piscataway, N.J. Cliggott Pub. Co., Greenwich, Conn., Pronapade. Mexico City, Onduline-USA, Fredericksburg, Va., Highlander Publs. Inc., Hacienda Heights, Calif.; mem. bus. adv. com. U.S. Bur. Labor Statistics, 1948-49, U.S. Bur. Census, 1948-49; lectr. statistics U. Richmond, 1948-49; mem. Tax Study Commn., 1963-64, Va. Met. Area Study Commn., 1966-67; mem. fiscal study com. Va. Adv. Legis. Council, 1956-58; mem. adv. com. to sec. edn. State of Va., 1973; mem. listed co. adv. com. Am. Stock Exchange. Former mem. bd. dirs. Richmond Meml. Hosp.; bd. dirs. Nat. Center for Resource Recovery, Inc., Washington, Richmond Area Community Council, 1972—. Citizens Study Council, 1973—; bd. govs. United Givers Fund., 1960-63, 66-69; pres. Collegiate Schs., 1967-68; bd. dirs., past pres. Richmond Eye Hosp., RPI Found., Va. Commonwealth U., Richmond; mem. Nat. Commn. on Taxes and IRS, 1979—, chmn. Bus. Adv. Commn. on White Collar Crime, 1980—. Served from pvt. to 1st lt., C.E., AUS, 1943-46; ETO; as 1st lt. Gen. Staff, U.S. Army, 1950-52. Recipient Good Govt. award Richmond First Club, 1967. Distinguished Service award Richmond Urban League, 1969. Mem. Am. Statis. Assn., Am. Newspaper Pubs. Assn. (newsprint com. 1976—), Am. Mktg. Assn. (pres. Va. chpt. 1954-55), C. of C. U.S. (communications com. 1970-75, chmn. postal service panel 1976-80), Richmond C. of C. (pres. 1968), Beta Gamma Sigma. Presbyterian. Clubs: Commonwealth (dir. 1972—), Country of Va., Downtown (Richmond). Home: 8912 Alendale Rd Richmond VA 23229 Office: 333 E Grace St Richmond VA 23219

DONNALLEY, MARY JANE, behavioral science center executive, realtor-broker; b. Denver, July 11, 1922; d. Albert West and Anne Porter (Kolb) Metcalf; m. Kenneth G. Donnalley (dec. May 1979); children—Ken Donnalley, Jr., Eryn Anne, James E. Donnalley (dec.). B.A., Rollins Coll., 1943; M. Ed., U. Va., 1958, Ed.D., 1966. Various acad. positions, Va., N.Mex., Tenn., 1959-73; dir. civic environment City of Roanoke, Va., 1973-76; asst. state dir., asst. v.p. U.S. Dept. Labor Green Thumb Programs, 1976-79; asst. prof. human services Pan Am. U., Edinburg, Tex., 1979-83; pres. M.J.D. & Assocs., McAllen, Tex., 1979-83; realtor-broker Action Real Estate, McAllen, 1979-83; v.p. human resources and pub. relations Wooden Consol. Industries, Dallas, 1983-84; pres. Behavioral Sci. Ctr., Dallas, 1984—; realtor-broker cons. Ebby Halliday Realtors, Dallas, 1983—; vis. prof. Western N. Mex. U., Silver City, 1969,80; adj. faculty mem. Grad. Sch. Bus., Dallas, Dallas Bapt. U., Brookhaven Colls., Tex. Woman's U., Anglican Sch. Theology; cons. Def. Adv. Com., Washington, 1971—; pres. Internat. Orgn. Women Execs., McAllen, 1979-83; cons. Zonta Internat., Dallas, 1984—. Author: Net Results, 1955; Group Teaching, 1959. Contbr. articles to profl. jours. Presbyn. Ch. fellow 1959; Sloan Found. fellow, 1971. Mem. Dallas C. of C., Women's Council Realtors, Dallas Bd. Realtors, Am. Mgmt. Assn., Am. Inst. Counseling and Psychotherapy (diplomate), Nat. Speakers Assn., U.S. Profl. Tennis Assn., Nat. Assn. Realtors, Am. Soc. Tng. and Devel. Republican. Episcopalian. Club: Northwood Rep. Women's. Avocations: swimming; golf; piano. Home: 15211 Preston Rd Dallas TX 75248 Office: 16000 Preston Rd Suite 100 Dallas TX 75248

DONNELL, WILLIAM TINSLEY, architect; b. Lebanon, Tenn., Jan. 7, 1930; s. Ralph Tinsley and Loy Evelyn (Drinnen) D.; m. Ruby Carolyn Little, Mar. 18, 1953; children—David Tinsley, Rebecca Ann. B.A. in Architecture, Auburn U., 1953. Registered architect, Ala., Miss. Draftsman Parrish & Smith Architects, Jackson, Tenn., 1953-56, various archtl. firms, Mobile, Ala., 1956-57; architect, designer Platt Roberts & Co., Mobile, 1957-65; architect, v.p. A.B. Benson & Co., Mobile, 1965-68; architect, ptnr. Donnell, Froom & Rogers, Mobile, 1968-83, Donnell & Froom, Mobile, 1983—; mem. State Bd. for Registration of Architects, Mobile, 1980-84; grader Nat. Council Archtl. Registration Bds. Exams., Chgo., 1981-82, state coordinator, Milw., Dallas, 1983-84. Pres. Civitan Club, Spanish Fort, Ala., 1970-71. Mem. AIA. Republican. Baptist. Club: Lake Forest Yacht and Country. Avocations: reading; golf. Home: 113 Spanish Main Spanish Ft AL 36527 Office: Donnell & Froom Architects 1407 Mchts Nat Bank Bldg Mobile AL 36602

DONNELLAN, THOMAS A., archbishop; b. N.Y.C., Jan. 24, 1914; s. Andrew and Margaret (Egan) b. A.B., Cathedral Coll., 1933; student, St. Joseph's Sem., 1933-39; J.C.D., Catholic U. Am., 1942. Ordained priest Roman Catholic Ch., 1939; synodal judge Marriage Tribunal, 1950-58; vice chancellor Archdiocese N.Y., 1947-50, chancellor, 1958-62, vocation dir., 1957-62; rector St. Joseph's Sem., 1962-64; bishop of, Ogdensburg, N.Y., 1964-68, archbishop of, Atlanta, 1968—, also chaplain del., vicar gen., mil. ordinariate for, Ga., Fla., N.C., S.C., 1972—; Treas., chmn. region, com. hispanic affairs Nat. Conf. Catholic Bishops; Treas., com. capitalism and Christianity, com. pro-life activities U.S. Catholic Conf.; mem. exec. bd. Catholic Near East Relief.; bd. govs. Cath. Ch. Extension Soc. Decorated knight comdr. Knights Holy Sepulchre. Address: Chancery Office 680 W Peachtree St NW Atlanta GA 30308*

DONNELLY, ANDREA (MARY KATHRYN), sister, educator, counselor; b. Muskegon, Mich., July 7, 1937; d. Andrew John and Valeria Janet (Gregory) D. B.A., Marquette U., 1960; M.Ed., Duquesne U., 1972. Joined Pallottine Missionary Sisters, Roman Catholic Ch. Tchr. St. Mary's Sch., Laurel, Md., 1964-66, Holy Family Sch., Richwood, W.Va., 1966-68, St. Mary's Sch., Spring Lake, Mich., 1968-71; guidance dir., counselor Pallotti High Sch., Laurel, 1971-75, Cath. Central, Muskegon, 1975-76; pastoral care asst. St. Mary's Hosp., Huntington, W.Va., 1977-84; tchr. St. Joseph Central High Sch., Huntington, 1984—. Mem. Am. Assn. Counseling and Devel., Assn. Religious Value in Issues s in Counseling, W.Va. Counseling Assn. Roman Catholic. Avocations: stamp collecting; reading; water skiing. Home: 2900 1st Ave Huntington WV 25701

DONNELLY, JOSEPH, corporate executive; b. 1929. B.S., U. Scranton, 1950; J.D., U. Pa., 1953. Law sec. Chief Justice of Pa., 1953-55; dep. atty. gen. Commonwealth of Pa., 1955-58; v.p. fin. Pa. Power & Light Co., 1958-79; with Gulf States Utilities Co., Beaumont, Tex., 1979—, now exec. v.p.; dir. InterFirst Bank Beaumont. Office: Gulf States Utilities Co 350 Pine Beaumont TX 77704

DONNELLY, SISTER KATHLEEN, nun, educational administrator; b. West Palm Beach, Fla., Oct. 7, 1921; d. Charles Henry and Kathleen Marie (O'Hare) D. B.A., Barry Coll., 1949, M.A., 1957; postgrad. U. Fla.; Mich. State U., Fla. Atlantic U., Cath. U. Am. Joined Adrian Dominican Sisters, 1937. Tchr. St. Matthew Sch., Chgo., 1939-43, St. Dominic Sch., Detroit, 1943-44, St. Patrick Sch., Miami Beach, Fla., 1944-52; prin. Sacred Heart Sch., Pensacola, Fla., 1952-58; asst. prin., tchr. St. Matthew Sch., Jacksonville, Fla., 1958-61, Little Flower Sch., Hollywood, Fla., 1961-66, Holy Family Sch., St. Petersburg, Fla., 1966-67; prin. Our Lady Queen of Martyrs Sch., Fort Lauderdale, Fla., 1967-74, St. Hugh Sch., Coconut Grove, Fla., 1974—; superior Sacred Heart Convent, Pensacola, 1952-58. Leader Girl Scouts U.S.A., Detroit, 1943. Mem. Nat. Catholic Edn. Assn., Nat. Assn. Elem. Sch. Prins., Internat. Platform Assn., Fla. Assn. for Supervision and Curriculum Devel., Fla. Cath. Conf. (chmn.), Kappa Delta Pi. Office: St Hugh Sch 3460 Royal Rd Coconut Grove FL 33134

DONOFF, GAIL SHARON, psychotherapist; b. Dayton, Ohio, July 20, 1942; d. Herman Fred and Louise Slavin (Goodman) Slutzky; m. Ronald Harvey Donoff, Aug. 4, 1963; children—Heather Michelle, Marlo Lynn. B.A. in Psychology cum laude, U. Tex., 1980, M.S. in Social Work, 1982. Cert. social worker, Tex.; lic. profl. counselor, Tex. Sales staff Rike's, Dayton, Ohio, 1972-75; v.p. Tower Research, Dallas, 1978-80; sales exec. Universal of St. Louis, 1980-82; psychotherapist Family Guidance Center, Dallas, 1982-84; psychotherapist in pvt. practice Human Affairs, Internat., 1984—. Chmn. Women's Am. ORT, Dayton, 1970, Hadassah, Dayton, 1972. Mem. Nat. Assn. Social Work, Orthopsychiat. Assn., Acad. Cert. Social Workers, Sigma Delta Tau. Republican. Jewish. Home: 6115 La Cosa Dr Dallas TX 75248 Office: Human Affairs Internat 12700 Hillcrest Rd Dallas TX 75230

DONOGHUE, WILLIAM THOMAS, antiques company executive; b. Houston, Nov. 13, 1932; s. Gerald Thomas and Louise (Huggins) D.; m. Christa Neidhardt, Apr. 6, 1957; children—Charlotte Luisa, Hilary. B.A. in Econs., U. Va., 1954. Ptnr., Christy Donoghue Antiques, Inc., Bad Nauheim, W. Ger., 1957-61, Victoria, Tex., 1961-69, pres., Victoria, 1969—. Bd. dirs. Victorial Regional Mus. Assn., 1976-82. Served to 1st lt. U.S. Army, 1954-57; ETO. Mem. Appraisers Assn. Am., Internat. Soc. Appraisers, Am. Soc. Appraisers (assoc.). Office: Christy Donoghue Antiques Inc 2424 N Navarro Victoria TX 77901

DONOHUE, JOHN WILLIAM, JR., insurance sales company executive; b. El Paso, Tex., Feb. 3, 1935; s. John W. and Marie R. D.; B.S. in Geology, U. Tex., El Paso, 1957; m. M. Elaine Abbott, Sept. 14, 1957; 1 dau., Lori Elaine. Agt., Aetna Life Ins. Co., El Paso, 1962-63, supr., 1963-66; life partner Rogers & Belding Ins. Co., El Paso, 1966-77; pres. John W. Donohue, Jr. Assocs., Inc., ins. and investment sales cons. firm, El Paso, 1977—; dir. West El Paso Nat. Bank; participating partner Exec. Life Ins. Co. Ariz.; mem. adv. bd. Exec. Life of Ariz. Founder, 1st chmn. Leadership El Paso, 1977-79; pres. El Paso Mental Health Assn., 1966-67; founder, chmn. bd. Casa Blanca Halfway House for mentally ill, El Paso, 1966-67. Served to 1st lt. U.S. Army, 1957-58. Life mem. Million Dollar Round Table. Mem. U. Tex. El Paso Alumni Assn. (pres. 1967-68), Tex. Assn. Life Underwriters (pres. 1971-72), El Paso Assn. Life Underwriters (pres. 1966-67, Man of Yr. 1975), Assn. Advanced Life Underwriters, El Paso C. of C. (past bd. dirs.), Texas Leaders Round Table (bd. dirs.). Republican. Roman Catholic. Home: 1815 E Robinson El Paso TX 79902 Office: 4849 N Mesa Suite 208 El Paso TX 79912

DONOHUE, PEGGY JEAN, marriage and family counselor, educator, consultant; b. West, Tex., Sept. 11, 1942; d. Henry A. and Agnes (Kral) Urbanovsky; m. Wendell Glenn Donohue, Nov. 11, 1961; children—Lori Dianne, Lance Jason. Student Richland Coll., 1977-79; B.A. in Psychology, U. Tex.-Dallas, 1980; M.A. in Psychology, Tex. Woman's U., 1983. Lic. profl. counselor. Computer operator William Cameron Co., Waco, Tex., 1961-65; field dir. Girl Scouts U.S.A., Colorado Springs, Colo., 1975-77; adj. prof. Richland Coll., Dallas, 1983-85; marriage and family counselor Profl. Counseling Services, Dallas, 1985—; personal career counselor Every Woman Program, Dallas, 1982-85. Rep. Dallas Women's Coalition, 1983-85. Mem. Am. Assn. for Counseling and Devel., Am. Assn. Marriage and Family Therapists. Democrat. Roman Catholic. Avocations: travel; jogging; reading; sewing. Office: Profl Counseling Services 1450 Preston Forest Sq Dallas TX 75230

DONOVAN, HERBERT ALCORN, JR., bishop; b. Washington, July 14, 1931; s. Herbert Alcorn and Marion Mitchell (Kirk) D.; m. Mary Gertrude Sudman, July 7, 1959; children—Mary Ellen, Herbert Alcorn III, Jane. B.A., U. Va., 1954; M.Div., Va. Theol. Sem., 1957, D.Div. (hon.), 1981; D.Div. (hon.), U. of the South, 1985. Ordained to ministry Episcopal Ch., 1957. Rector St. John's Ch., Green River, Wyo., 1957-59; vicar, rector St. Andrew's Ch., Basin/Greybull, Wyo., 1959-64; exec. officer Diocese Ky., Louisville, 1964-70; rector St. Luke's Ch., Montclair, N.J., 1970-80; bishop Diocese Ark., Little Rock, 1980—; chmn. adv. council Ark. Conf. Chs. and Synagogues, Little Rock, 1983-84. Co-author: God Willing: Decision in the Church, 1973; author: Forward Day-by-Day, 1983. Chmn. bd. Heifer Project Internat., Little Rock, 1985—; bd. dirs. All Saints' Sch. Vicksburg, Miss., 1980—; trustee U. of the South, Sewanee, Tenn., 1980—. Served as capt. USNR, 1955—. Named Hon. Canon, Christ Ch. Cathedral, Louisville, 1966. Coll. of Preachers fellow, 1976. Office: Episcopal Diocese Ark 300 W 17th St PO Box 6120 Little Rock AR 72216-6120

DONOVAN, JAMES ALBERT, professional fund raiser; b. Utica, N.Y., Jan. 20, 1949; s. James Hubert and Esther (Moretti) D.; m. Janet Ann Liesch, Apr. 19, 1974; children—Kelly, Katie. B.A., Wadhams Hall Sem. Coll., 1972. Dir. campaign United Way Utica, N.Y., 1972-74; dir. devel. United Negro Coll. Fund, N.Y.C., 1975-77, Tusculum Coll., Greenville, Tenn., 1977-78; asst. dir. devel. East Tenn. State U., Johnson City, 1978-80; dir. devel., exec. dir. U. Central Fla. Found., Orlando, 1980-84; assoc. v.p. devel. Clemson U., S.C., 1985—; cons. in field. Contbr. articles to profl. jours. Recipient Gov.'s award Am. Legion Boys State, 1967. Mem. Nat. Soc. Fund Raising Execs. (founder Central Fla. chpt. 1982), Orlando C. of C. (Leadership award 1983, 84). Republican. Roman Catholic. Club: Keowee Country. Avocations: photography; golf; jogging. Home: 118 E Brookwood Dr Clemson SC 29631 Office: Clemson U Office Devel 110 Daniel Dr Clemson SC 29631

DOODY, BARBARA PETTETT, computer specialist; b. Cin., Sept. 18, 1938; d. Philip Wayne and Virginia Bird (Handley) P.; student Sinclair Coll., Tulane U.; m. Louis C. Doody, Jr.; 1 son by previous marriage, Daniel Frederick Reasor, Jr. Owner, mgr. Honeysuckle Pet Shop, Tipp City, Ohio, 1970-76; office mgr. Doody & Doody, C.P.A.s, New Orleans, 1976-77, computer ops. mgr., 1979—; office mgr. San Diego Yacht Club, 1977-79. Mem. DECUSERS Assn., DAR, UDC, Jamestowne Soc., Colonial Dames of XVII Century, U.S. 1812, So. Dames, Daus. Am. Colonists. Republican. Lutheran. Home: 16 Cypress Covington LA 70433 Office: 1160 Commerce Bldg New Orleans LA 70112

DOODY, JOHN ROBERT, oil and natural gas company executive; b. Joplin, Mo., Nov. 21, 1930; s. Patrick John and Anna Margaret Doody; m. Mary Ann Goold, Nov. 24, 1962; children—John Robert, Jr., Gregory Lawrence, Elizabeth Ann, Lisa Marie. B.S., U. Mo., 1957. With Ernst & Ernst, St. Louis, 1957-66; with Brown Group, Inc., St. Louis, 1966-74; exec. v.p. fin. and adminstrn. Sonat Inc., Birmingham, 1974—; dir. So. Natural Gas Co., Sonat Offshore Drilling, Sonat Marie and Sonat Exploration. Served with USAF, 1951-55. Mem. Fin. Exec. Inst., Am. Inst. C.P.A.s. Republican. Roman Catholic. Home: 4441 Fredericksburg Circle Mountain Brook AL 35213 Office: PO Box 2563 Birmingham AL 35202

DOODY, LOUIS CLARENCE, JR., accountant; b. New Orleans, Feb. 5, 1940; s. Louis Clarence and Elsie Clair (Connors) D.; m. Mary Evelyn Barba, Nov. 13, 1965 (div. 1982); children—Dana Lori, Mary Lyn, Kathleen Louise; m. 2d, Barbara Virginia Pettett, Oct. 9, 1982. B.C.S., Tulane U., 1963. C.P.A., La., Tex., Miss. Acct., Louis C. Doody, C.P.A., 1963-68, ptnr. Doody & Doody, C.P.A.s, New Orleans, 1969—. Mem. Am. Inst. C.P.A.s, La. Soc. C.P.A.s. Republican. Lutheran. Home: 16 Cypress Covington LA 70433 Office: 821 Gravier St Suite 1160 New Orleans LA 70112

DOOLEY, CHARLES CORBET, pharmacist; b. Campbellsville, Ky., July 23, 1948; s. Vernon Lee and Vernice Jean (Brown) D.; m. Martha Jane Gee, Dec. 26, 1970; children—Meredith Noel, Charles Christopher, David Corbett. B.S. in Pharmacy, U. Ky., 1975. Pharmacist Taylor Drugs, Louisville, 1975-76, pharmacist, asst. mgr., Lexington, 1976-80, pharmacist, mgr., 1980-81; pharmacist, mgr. Warehouse Drugs, Lexington, 1981—. Served with U.S. Army, 1967-70. Mem. Bluegrass Pharmacists Soc. Republican. Baptist. Avocations: chess; metal detecting.

DOOLIN, JOHN B., state supreme court justice; b. Alva, Okla., May 25, 1918; s. John B. and Leo M. (Museller) D.; m. Katherine E. Bruck, June 7, 1946; children—John William, Mary L. Doolin Trembley, Katherine, Carole and Colleen (twins), Martha. B.S. in Bus. Adminstrn., Okla. U., 1941, LL.B., 1947. Bar: Okla. bar 1942. Practiced in, Alva, 1947-53, Lawton, 1963-73; justice Okla. Supreme Ct., 1973—; mem. Okla. Hwy. Commn., 1959-63. Trustee Comanche County (Okla.) Meml. Hosp., 1967-73, chmn., 1968-73. Served to capt. AUS, 1941-45. Mem. Phi Delta Phi. *

DOOM, JAMES LANIER, architectural consultant; b. Knoxville, Tenn., June 29, 1914; s. James Murphy and Marion (Sease) D.; m. Emma Moffett McMullen, July 9, 1942; children—Martha Johnston, David Stuart, William Moffett, Nancy Marion. B.S. in Architecture, Georgia Tech., 1936; B.D., M.Div., Columbia Theol. Sem., 1943. Ordained to ministry Presbyn. Ch. Archtl. draftsman Robert & Co., Inc., Atlanta, 1937-40; pastor Jacksonville Presbyn. Ch., Ala., 1943-48, Hartsville Presbyn. Ch., S.C., 1948-55, Hamlet Presbyn. Ch., N.C., 1955-58; dir. dept. ch. architecture Presbyn. Ch., Atlanta, 1958-73; cons. ch. architecture, Decatur, Ga., 1974—. Recipient Elbert Conover award Guild Religious Architecture, 1973. Mem. Interfaith Forum Religion, Art and Architecture. Clubs: Exchange, Rotary. Avocations: gardening; wood working. Home: 2266 Tanglewood Rd Decatur GA 30033

DORMAN, MALCOLM JOEL, cardiovascular surgeon; b. Bklyn., Aug. 6, 1942; s. Edward and Lillian D. B.S., Fairleigh Dickinson U., 1963; M.D., Chgo. Med. Sch., 1967. Intern, Nassau County Med. Ctr., L.I., 1967-68; resident gen. surgery L.I. Jewish-Hillside Med. Ctr., New Hyde Park, N.Y., 1968-71, chief resident, 1971-72; resident thoracic and cardiovascular surgery Baylor Coll. Medicine, Houston, 1972-73, chief resident, 1973-74; asst. research scientist, clin. fellow cardiovascular surgery NYU Sch. Medicine, Univ. Hosp., N.Y.C., 1974-76; pvt. practice cardiovascular surgery Miami Heart Inst., South Miami Hosp., 1976—. Mem. ACS, Nat. Bd. Med. Examiners, Am. Thoracic Soc., Am. Bd. Gen. Surgery, Am. Heart Assn., Tex. Thoracic Soc., AMA, Fla. Med. Assn., Dade County Med. Assn., Greater Miami Heart Assn., Michael DeBakey Internat. Cardiovascular Soc., So. Thoracic Surg. Assn., So. Med. Assn., Am. Bd. Thoracic Surgery, Mended Hearts, Am. Coll. Chest Physicians, Fla. Soc. Thoracic and Cardiovascular Surgeons, AAAS, Am. Coll. Cardiology. Contbr. chpts. to books, articles to profl. jours. Home: 2333 Brickell Ave Apt 2601 Miami FL 33139 Office: 1150 NW 14th St Suite 207 Miami FL 33136

DORMINEY, HENRY CLAYTON, JR., physician; b. Tifton, Ga., May 15, 1949; s. Henry Clayton and Virginia (Petty) D.; B.S., Davidson Coll., 1971; M.D., U. Iowa, 1975; m. Diane Louise Thiel, Sept. 29, 1978. Med. intern, U. Iowa Hosps. and Clinics, Iowa City, 1975-76, med. resident, 1976-78, allergy and immunology fellow, 1978-80; practice medicine specializing in allergy and clin. immunology Allergy and Dermatology Assos. Tifton, P.C. (Ga.), 1981—. Recipient Physician's Recognition award AMA, 1979, 85; diplomate Am. Bd. Internal Medicine, Am. Bd. Allergy and Immunology; lic. physician, Ky., Ga., Iowa; VA grantee, 1978-80; Am. Coll. Allergy grantee, 1980. Mem. ACP, Am. Acad. Allergy (travel grantee 1980), Tift County Med. Soc. (sec.-treas. 1983-84, v.p., pres. elect 1984-85), N.Y. Acad. Scis., Med. Assn. Ga. Democrat. Asso. editor Vital Signs, 1969-71, contbg. author, 1970-71. Home: 1001 N Ridge Ave Tifton GA 31794 Office: 1409 B Tift Ave Tifton GA 31794

DORNENBURG, PETER RAYMOND, orthopaedic surgeon; b. Pitts., Apr. 13, 1943; s. Delbert Donald and Theodora Catherine (Kearns) D.; B.A., St. Vincent Coll., 1965; M.D., U. Pitts., 1969. Intern, Vanderbilt U. Hosp., Nashville, 1969-70, resident in gen. surgery, 1970-71, resident in orthopaedic surgery, 1971-74; practice medicine specializing in orthopaedic surgery, Little Rock, 1976—; clin. instr. dept. orthopaedic surgery U. Ark. for Med. Scis., Little Rock, 1976—; cons. Spina Bifide Clinic, Ark. Children's Hosp., 1976-80. Served to lt. comdr., M.C., USNR, 1974-76. Diplomate Nat. Bd. Med. Examiners, Am. Bd. Orthopaedic Surgery. Fellow Am. Acad. Orthopaedic Surgeons, Internat. Coll. Surgeons, A.C.S. (chmn. Ark. com. on trauma 1979-83); mem. Ark. Orthopaedic Soc. (sec.-treas. 1977-78, pres. 1978-79), Ark. Med. Soc., Pulaski County Med. Soc., Internat. Arthroscopy Assn., Am. Coll. Legal Medicine, Mid-Central States Orthopaedic Soc., Ark. Hand Club (treas. 1982-83, sec. 1983-84). Home: Route 1 Box 15 Roland AR 72135 Office: Suite 210 1 St Vincent Circle Little Rock AR 72205

DOROUGH, H. WYMAN, toxicologist, biological sciences educator; b. Notasulga, Ala., Dec. 23, 1936; s. J.D. and Audie H. Dorough; div.; children—Hendley, Keith, Gary, Melinda, Melissa; m. 2d, Mary Elaine Davenport, Jan. 29, 1977; 1 stepson, Bradley. B.S., Auburn U., 1959, M.S., 1960; Ph.D., U. Wis., 1963. Diplomate Acad. Toxicological Scis. Asst. prof. Tex. A&M U., College Station, 1963-67, assoc. prof., 1967-68; prof. toxicology and enotmology U. Ky., Lexington, 1969-85, assoc. dean grad. sch., 1974-76, dir. Grad. Ctr. Toxicology, 1977-83; prof. head dept. biol. scis. Miss. State U., Mississippi State, 1985—. Recipient research award, 1974, outstanding contbn. to grad. edn., 1980. Mem. Soc. Toxicology, Entomol. Soc. Am. (outstanding research in pesticide chemistry and toxicology award 1981), Am. Coll. Toxicology, Soc. Environ. Toxicology and Chemistry, Am. Chem. Soc., Sigma Xi, Phi Kappa Phi, Gamma Sigma Delta. Co-author: Carbamate Insecticides-Chemistry, Biochemistry and Toxicology, 1976; co-editor: Fate of Pesticides in Large Animals, 1977; contbr. articles to profl. jours. Office: Miss State U Dept Biol Scis Mississippi State MS 39762

DORR, DARWIN ALFRED, clinical psychologist; b. Rochester, N.Y., Apr. 1, 1940; s. Joseph Frank and Catherine Joanna (LaRock) D.; children—Benjamin Paul, Christopher Joseph. B.A., Alfred U., 1962, M.A., 1965; Ph.D., Fla. State, 1969. Diplomate Am. Bd. Clin. Psychology. Research assoc. U. Rochester, 1969-72; asst. prof. Washington U., 1972-75; assoc. prof. Highland Hosp., Duke U., Asheville, N.C., 1975-81, chief psychologist, 1981—; clin. prof. med. psychology Duke U. Med. Sch., 1984—. Contbr. numerous articles to profl. jours. Bd. dirs. Community Ctr. for Arts, Asheville, N.C., 1980—, founding mem. Fellow Am. Psychol. Assn., N.C. Psychol. Assn. Avocations: study of voice and performing. Home: 67 Maple Ridge Ln Asheville NC 28806 Office: Highland Hosp PO Box 1101 Asheville NC 28802

DORRIS, PEGGY RAE, biologist, educator; b. Holly Bluff, Miss., Feb. 27, 1933; d. Hugh Baskerville and Alta Eugenia (Stampley) D. B.S. with distinction, Miss. Coll., 1956; M.S., U. Miss., 1963, Ph.D., 1967. Tchr. biology pub. schs., Benton, Miss., 1956-57, Wilmot, Ark., 1957-60, Pontotoc, Miss., 1960-61; grad. asst. U. Miss., Oxford, 1961-66; prof. Henderson State U., Arkadelphia, Ark., 1966-72, chmn. dept. biology, 1972—; mem. AAUW, 1967-80, Ark. Edn. Assn., 1967-78, AAUP, 1968-78, Delta Kappa Gamma, 1967-80. Contbr. articles to jour. Miss. Acad. Sci., trans. Am. Micros. Soc., Procs. Ark. Acad. Sci., other publs. Bd. dirs. Arkadelphia Water and Sewer Commn., 1978—, Soil and Water Conservation Commn., Arkadelphia, 1983—, Clark County Fair Assn., 1983—. NSF grantee, 1961-63; C.E. grantee, 1978-79. Mem. Audubon Soc., Herpetology Soc., Arachnology Soc., Ark. Acad. Sci. (mem. constl. com. 1984-85), Ark. Simmental Soc. (bd. dirs., treas. 1978-85). Avocations: reading; cycling; hunting; fishing; ranching. Home: 125 Evonshire Arkadelphia AR 71923 Office: Henderson State U H-7544 Arkadelphia AR 71923

DORSETT, ANTHONY DREW (TONY), professional football player; b. Aliquippa, Pa., Apr. 7, 1954. Ed., U. Pitts. Profl. football player Dallas Cowboys, NFL, 1977—. Recipient Heisman Trophy, 1976; named to NFL All-Star Team, Sporting News, 1981, Coll. Player of Yr., Sporting News, 1976, Rookie of Yr., 1977; established NFL record for longest run from scrimmage (99 yds.), 1983. Office: care Dallas Cowboys 6116 N Central Expy Dallas TX 75206*

DORSETT, CHARLES IRVIN, mathematics educator; b. Lufkin, Tex., Sept. 25, 1945; s. C.B. and Dorothy Alice (Smith) D. B.S., Stephen F. Austin State U., Nacogdoches, Tex., 1967, M.S., 1968; Ph.D., N. Tex. State U., 1976. Cert. secondary sch. tchr., Tex. Instr. Stephen F. Austin State U., 1968-71; lectr. N. Tex. State U., Denton, 1976-77, 78-79; asst. prof. La. Tech U., Ruston, 1977-78, assoc. prof., 1982—; lectr. Tex. A&M U., College Station, 1979-82; reviewer Zentralblatt Für Mathematic and ihre Grenzgebrite, 1983—; referee Indian Jour. Pure and Applied Math., 1984—. Contbr. articles to profl. publs. Recipient Cert. for Excellence in Research, La. Tech U., 1984-85. Mem. Am. Math. Soc., Sigma Xi. Baptist. Avocations: mathematical research, farming. Home: Route 9 Box 4290 Lufkin TX 75901 Office: La Tech U Dept Math and Statistics Ruston LA 71272

DORSETT, CORA MATHENY, librarian; b. Camden, Ark., July 15, 1921; d. Walter Stanton and Cora (Smith) Matheny; B.S. in Edn. summa cum laude, Centenary Coll. La., 1963; M.L.S., U. Miss., 1965, Ph.D., 1972; postdoctoral study U. Okla., 1974. Tchr. pub. schs., Shreveport, La., 1963-64; dir. Pine Bluff and Jefferson County Pub. Library, Pine Bluff, Ark., 1965—. Editor: Mississippi Delta. Contbr. articles to profl. jours. Alpha Chi fellow, 1962-63; recipient Social Sci. award Chi Omega, 1963. Mem. ALA, Ark. Library Assn., Southeastern Library Assn., Jefferson County Hist. Assn., Kappa Delta Pi, Phi Delta Kappa. Episcopalian. Home: 1305 W 35th Ave Pine Bluff AR 71603 Office: 200 E 8th Ave Pine Bluff AR 71601

DORSETT, HERBERT FRANKLIN, hospital administrator; b. Branford, Fla., Oct. 21, 1933; s. Alford Owen and Georgia Willard (Howell) D.; m. Nettie A. Sharrock, Nov. 12, 1955; children—Jerry, Carol, Jon Andrew, Johanna. B.M. in Music, Stetson U., 1955; postgrad. U. Md. (Europe), 1957; M.H.A., Baylor U., 1965. Commd. 2d lt. U.S. Army, 1955, advanced through ranks to maj., 1965; dir. personnel and adminstrn. 44th Med. Brig., Saigon, Vietnam, 1966-67; adminstr. dept. medicine Walter Reed Gen. Hosp., Washington, 1967-68; dept. head, program dir. ITT Sheraton Corp., Boston, 1968-72; dept. head Multivest Internat., Inc., Indpls., 1972-73, pres., 1973-74; pres., part-owner Aegis Corp., Indpls., 1974-75; chief exec. officer Fawcett Meml. Hosp., Port Charlotte, Fla., 1975-81; exec. dir. Ft. Myers Community Hosp., Fla., 1981-84, pres., 1985—. Decorated Bronze Star, Army Commendation medal. Mem. Fla. League Hosps. (dir. 1976-86, chmn. 1979-80), Fedn. Am. Hosp. (dir. 1979-86), Am. Coll. Hosp. Adminstrs., Fla. Hosp. Assn. (sec.-treas. 1980-81, bd. dirs. 1980-86, chmn. 1986), Charlotte County C. of C. (dir. 1978-81, pres. 1979-80), Lee County C. of C. (dir. 1985-86), Omicron Delta Kappa, Pi Kappa Phi. Republican. Presbyterian. Club: Royal Palm Yacht.

Lodge: Rotary (pres. Port Charlotte 1978-79, dir. Fort Myers 1982-86). Office: Fort Myers Community Hosp 3785 Evans Ave Box 7146 Fort Myers FL 33901

DORSEY, ELY ALFRED, mathematician, educator, consultant; b. N.Y.C., Sept. 27, 1943; s. Ely Alfred Dorsey and Julia (Cruz) Odierna; m. Lynnetta Bell, July 18, 1966 (div. 1972); 1 child, Ely; m. Barbara Ann Crosby, Sept. 14, 1972; children—Anthony, Tashamee. B.A., CUNY, 1970. Asst. prof. U. of D.C., Washington, 1979-80, Montgomery Coll., Rockville, Md., 1982-83; researcher NASA, Greenbelt, Md., 1980-82; trn. supr. Lockheed Corp., Greenbelt, 1983-84, prin. scientist, 1984—; assoc. prof. William and Mary Coll., Williamsburg, Va., 1984—; expert witness Com. for Equitable Telephone Rates, Washington, 1983, NSF, Washington, 1982; cons. Blacks United for Excellence in Edn., Silver Springs, Md., 1983. Producer radio, TV series, 1981, ednl. TV program, 1985. Contbr. articles to profl. jours. Mgr. Carter Campaign, N.Y.C., 1976; coordinator Nat. Alliance of Third World Journalist, Washington, 1983; worker Jackson Campaign, Montgomery County, Md., 1984; chmn. polit. action com. First Baptist Ch., Williamsburg, Va., 1985; chmn. labor and industry com. NAACP, Williamsburg, 1985. Fellow Grad. Profls. Opportunities Program Howard U., 1979-81, NASA, 1980-81, NASA/ASEE, 1982. Served with U.S. Army, 1962-65. Mem. Am. Math. Soc., Math. Soc., Math. Assn. Am., AAAS. Baptist. Home: 327 Merrimac Trail 9A Williamsburg VA Office: Sch Bus Adminstrn Coll William Mary Williamsburg VA 23185

DORSEY, HAZEL DORTCH, educator; b. Danville, Ga., Apr. 7, 1942; d. Jesse and Thomasine (Underwood) Dortch; m. Billy Frank Dorsey, Nov. 3, 1959; children—Darrell, Everett, B.S., Tex. Wesleyan Coll., 1974; M.Ed., North Tex. State U., 1978. Tchr. kindergarten Everman (Tex.) Pub. Schs., 1974-78, Fort Worth Pub. Schs., 1978—; workshop presenter. Mem. Nat. Assn. Edn. of Young Children, Ft. Worth Assn. Edn. of Young Children, So. Assn. Children Under Six, Tex. State Tchrs. Assn., NEA, Phi Delta Kappa. Methodist. Home: 1163 Kirkwall Dr Fort Worth TX 76134

DORSEY, MICHAEL ANTHONY, art educator, artist; b. Findlay, Ohio, July 31, 1949; s. Dwight L. and Betty Jane (Mischke) D.; m. Susan L. Chaplin, Aug. 21, 1971; children—Shea, Nicholas. B.S. in Edn., Eastern Ill. U., 1971; M.A., Bowling Green State U., 1972; M.F.A., 1973. Instr. Miss. State U., 1973-77, asst. prof., 1977-81, assoc. prof., 1981—, acting head dept. art, 1982-83, head dept. art, 1983—; bd. regents Miss. Mus. Art, Jackson, 1984-85. One-man shows include Meridian Mus. Art, Miss., Miss. Mus. Art, Jackson, Miss. State U., Starkville; numerous group shows include Eastern Ill. U., Charleston, Minot State Coll., N.D., U. of South Sewanee, Tenn., U. Ala., Tuscaloosa Northeast La. U., Monroe; represented in permanent collections Bowling Green State U., Ohio, Art Inst. Chgo., Tweed Mus., U. Minn.-Duluth, Southeast Ark. Arts and Scis. Ctr., Pine Bluff. Recipient 3 awards for art. Democrat. Roman Catholic. Home: 108 Cedar Ln Starkville MS 39759 Office: Miss State U Dept Art Box 5182 Mississippi State MS 39762

DOSS, CHRISS HERSHEL, county official, lawyer; b. Cullman, Ala., May 28, 1935; m. Faye Williams, July 5, 1957; children—William, Reuben, Nonna, Dorothea. B.A., Howard Coll., 1957; B.D., Eastern Bapt. Theol. Sem., 1962; M.L.S., Drexel U., 1962; J.D., Cumberland Sch. Law, 1968. Bar: Ala. 1968. Asst. librarian, assoc. prof. history Eastern Bapt. Theol. Sem., 1962-64; law librarian Samford U., Birmingham, Ala., 1964-67; exec. dir. Ala. Democratic Exec. Com., 1967-69; ptnr. Doss, Gorham & Natter, Birmingham, 1969-75; mem. Ala. Ho. of Reps., 1970-74; mem. Jefferson County Commn., Birmingham, Ala., 1975—, pres., 1982—. Democrat. Baptist. Office: Jefferson County Alabama 716 N 21st St Birmingham AL 35263

DOSS, ERICE ELAINE, psychologist; b. Nashville, July 29, 1952; d. Woodrow Wilson and Birdie Mae (Northington) D. B.S., Tenn. State U., 1973; M.S., U. Tenn., 1975; Ed.D., Vanderbilt U., 1985. Team coordinator Tenn. Dept. Mental Health Retardation, Arlington, 1975-77; outreach social worker, Nashville, 1977-78, adminstrv. rev. officer, 1978-80, program specialist, 1980-84; counseling intern Ga. State U., Atlanta, 1984-85; counseling psychologist Ga. Inst. Tech., Atlanta, 1985—; cons. Personal Resource Design, Inc., Atlanta, 1985—; writer Nat. Baptist Pub. Bd., Nashville, 1982-83, 85—. T.B. Boyd fellow Nat. Bapt. Pub. Bd., 1983. Mem. Am. Assn. Counseling Devel., Assn. Mental Health Counselors, Atlanta Mental Health Assn. Assn. Non-White Concerns, Assn. Black Psychologists, Southeastern Psychol. Assn., Assn. Social and Behavioral Scientists, Kappa Kappa Gamma (scholar), Alpha Kappa Alpha. Avocations: reading; writing; singing; sports; public speaking. Home: 3626F Clubhouse Circle East Decatur GA 30032 Office: Ga Inst Tech 225 North Ave Atlanta GA 30332

DOSS, JUDITH HARRIS, country club executive; b. Memphis, Dec. 7, 1934; d. Wiley Chasteen and Irene Randle (Hodges) Harris; m. Leslie Walter Doss, Jr., Oct. 3, 1953 (div. Jan. 1973); children—Leslie Walter III, Randle Elizabeth. Student Memphis State U., 1952-53, exec. seminar Vanderbilt U., 1982, Gourmet's Oxford, 1982, Lo Scaldavivande, Rome, 1983. Dir. food services The Webb Sch., Bell Buckle, Tenn., 1976-83; mgr. Plantation Country Club, Pharr, Tex., 1983—. Co-chmn. The Webb Cook Book, 1977. Pres. Hillwood Presbyterian Ch. Women, Nashville, 1968-70; life mem. Ladies Hermitage Assn., Nashville; del. Nat. Nutrition Conf., Washington, 1980, 82. Mem. Nat. Assn. Female Execs., Orgn. Women Execs., Wine Assn. Am. (charter 1985), Zonta Internat., Tex. Restaurant Assn., Tex. Club Mgrs. Assn., Club Mems. Assn. Am., Pharr C. of C., Alpha Gamma Delta Alumni Assn., Colonial Dames Am. (chpt. dir. 1981-83), Assn. Tenn. Antiquities, DAR. Avocations: gourmet cooking; travel; music; theatre; art. Home: 2729 Ashley Ct Pharr TX 78577 Office: Plantation Country Club 2503 Palmer Dr Pharr TX 78577

DOSS, MARION KENNETH, lawyer; b. Wildwood, Fla., Sept. 25, 1939; s. Marion D. and Clide (Maxwell) D.; m. Addren Taylor, July 8, 1977; children—M. Kenneth Jr., Lisa Marie. B.S., Ga. Inst. Tech., 1961; LL.B., U. Ga., 1963. Bar: Ga. 1965, N.C. 1979, U.S. Dist. Ct. (no. dist.) Ga. 1977, U.S. Ct. Apls. (5th cir.) 1976, U.S. Sup. Ct. 1978. Ptnr., Northcutt, Edwards & Doss, Atlanta, 1963-71; v.p., gen. counsel Roy D. Warren, Atlanta, 1971-73; ptnr. Doss & Sturgeon, Atlanta, 1973-75; atty. Rollins, Inc., Atlanta, 1975-78; assoc. gen. counsel, asst. sec. Fieldcrest Mills, Inc., Eden, N.C., 1978—. Pres., bd. dirs. Eden YMCA; pres., bd. dirs. Rockingham County Arts Council. Mem. Assn. Trial Lawyers Am., Def. Research Inst., Ga. Assn. Plaintiffs Trial Attys., Corp. Counsel Assn. Greater Atlanta, Atlanta Bar Assn., N.C. Trial Lawyers Assn., ABA, N.C. State Bar, Ga. Bar Assn., Rockingham County Bar Assn., Am. Textile Mfrs. Assn., N.C. C. of C. (past dir.). Club: Meadow Greens Country. Office: Fieldcrest Mills Inc 326 E Stadium Dr Eden NC 27288

DOSS, MARTHA MERRILL, city official, editor; b. Grand Rapids, Mich., Jan. 2, 1941; d. Raymond Oneil and Imogen (Merrill) D. Cert., Katharine Gibbs Secretarial Sch., 1962; B.S. in Bus. Adminstrn., Ferris State Coll., Big Rapids, Mich., 1963. Presdl. campaign asst., Mich., Washington, 1967-68; adminstrv. asst. The White House, Washington, 1969-73; freelance editorial, conv. mgmt., speakers bur. cons., Washington, 1974-78; dir. speakers bur. Consumer Product Safety Commn., Washington, 1978-80; editorial asst. Army Mag., Arlington, Va., 1980-82; dir. Visitors Bur., City of Lexington, Va., 1982—; editor Garrett Park Press, Md., 1980—. Editor: The Directory of Special Opportunities for Women, 1981; Women's Organizations: A National Directory, 1986. Treas., No. Va. Women's Polit. Caucus, Arlington, 1980-81; bd. dirs. Shenandoah Valley Travel Assn., 1985—. Republican. Christian Scientist. Avocations: photography; writing; travel. Office: Lexington Visitors Bur Visitor Visitor Ctr 107 E Washington St Lexington VA 24450

DOSTER, JEROME BROWN, airline exec.; b. Macon, Ga., Mar. 8, 1950; s. Norman Brown and Lily Lorraine (Crum) D.; B.S., Ga. Inst. Tech., 1973; M.B.A., Tulane U., 1975. Indsl. engr. Am. Airlines, Inc., N.Y.C., 1975-79, fin. analyst div. mktg. automation, Arlington, Tex., 1979—; fin. cons. to N.Y.C. Ballet, 1978-79, Opera Orch. of N.Y., 1978-79. Chmn., Glen Pines Assn. Mem. Ga. Inst. Tech. Alumni Assn., Tulane U. Alumni Assn., Chi Phi, Omega Trust Assn. Methodist. Club: N.Y. Athletic. Home: 3610 Travis St Dallas TX 75204 Office: Am Airlines Mktg Automation 601 Ryan Plaza Arlington TX 76011

DOSTER, JOSEPH C., newspaper publisher; b. Rutherford County, N.C., Aug. 4, 1928; s. Joseph C. and Estelle (Lawter) D.; m. Ann Lee Howard, Mar. 27, 1951; children—Joseph Michael, David Anthony, Scott Eric. Successively reporter, polit. writer, state editor Charlotte (N.C.) Observer, 1956-68; capital corr., then mng. editor Winston-Salem (N.C.) Jour., 1968-77; pub. Winston-Salem Jour. & Sentinel, 1977—; pres. Journalism Found., U. N.C. Sch. Journalism. Served with AUS, 1950-52. Mem. Am. Newspapers Pubs. Assn., So. Newspaper Pubs. Assn., N.C. Press Assn. (past pres.). Democrat. Episcopalian. Clubs: Rotary, Twin City, Forsyth Country. Home: 130 Billie Sue Dr Winston-Salem NC 27104 Office: 418 N Marshall St Winston-Salem NC 27102

DOTSON, GEORGE STEPHEN, drilling company executive; b. Okemah, Okla., Dec. 25, 1940; s. Hilmer C. and Alma Lucille (McGee) D.; m. Phyllis A. Nickerson, Aug. 17, 1963; children—Sarah, Grant. B.S., M.I.T., 1963; M.B.A., Harvard U., 1970. Asst. to pres. Helmerich & Payne, Inc., Tulsa, 1970-73; v.p. Helmerich & Payne (Peru) Drilling Co., 1974-75, Helmerich & Payne Internat. Drilling Co., 1976-77, pres., chief operating officer, 1977—; v.p. drilling Helmerich & Payne, Inc., 1977—; dir. Buruch Foster Corp. Served to capt. U.S. Army, 1964-68. Decorated Bronze Star. Office: Helmerich & Payne Internat Drilling Co Utica at 21st Sts Tulsa OK 74114

DOTSON, MARILYN DENESE KNIGHT, mathematics educator, administrator, information development consultant; b. Auburn, Ala., May 22, 1952; d. Charlie McKinnley and Mildred Joyce (Jones) Knight. B.S. in Math., Ga. So. Coll., 1975; M.S. in Ednl. Math., Ga. Southwestern U., 1976; postgrad. U. Ga., 1977-78, U. Charlotte, 1982—. Tchr. math. Am. City Bd. Edn., Americus, Ga., 1975-78; instr. math. Belmont Abbey Coll., N.C., 1979-80, chairwoman math. dept., 1980—, dir. dual degree program, 1982—; cons. info. devel. Sykes Enterprises, Inc., Charlotte, N.C., 1984—. Mem. 2005 Generalized Land Use Plan Charlotte-Mecklenburg Planning Commn., 1984—, Site Rev. Com. Zoning Ordinance, 1983, Transp. Task Force Mayor of Charlotte, 1980. Recipient Cert. Merit City of Charlotte, 1980, Cert. Appreciation Leadership Charlotte Urban Inst., 1983. Mem. Math. Assn. Am. (regional rep.), Bus. and Profl. Women's Club (pres. 1980-81, outstanding young careerist 1982), Nat. Council Tchrs. Math., Charlotte Women's Polit. Caucus. Democrat. Office: Belmont Abbey Coll Belmont NC 28012

DOTY, CATHERINE PEDEN, educational counselor; b. Belen, Miss., July 12, 1926; d. Clausen and Virginia (Cooper) Peden; m. Willis P. Veazey III, Dec. 31, 1950 (div. June 1964); children—Willis P. IV, Virginia S.; m. Horace Ray Doty, Jan. 15, 1965; step-children—Horace Ray Jr., Lynn Doty Edwards, Charles Ray. B.A. in Edn., U. Miss., 1948; M.Ed., Houston Bapt. U., 1980. Cert. tchr., counselor, Miss. Tchr. Tate County Schs., Senatobia, Miss., 1948-50, 61-69, Ocean Springs Elem. Sch., Miss., 1969-70, St. Martin Sch., Ocean Springs, 1971-72, Coldwater Jr. High Sch., Miss., 1980-81; alternative learning ctr. counselor Hernando High Sch., Miss., 1981-82; counselor Middle Sch., Senatobia, 1983—. Vice pres. Ocean Springs Hosp. Aux., 1974. Mem. Am. Assn. for Counseling and Devel., Miss. Counseling Assn., Miss. Sch. Counselors Assn., Kappa Delta Pi, Psi Chi. Methodist. Home: PO Box 1 649 Peyton Rd Coldwater MS 38618 Office: Senatobia Middle Sch 303 College St Senatobia MS 38668

DOTY, COY WILLIAM, agricultural engineer, educator; b. Cleveland, Ala., Sept. 18, 1931; s. Marcenia Wilson and Lula Ann (Standridge) D.; m. Marian Irene Bryant, Feb. 10, 1951; children—Joan Doty Springs, Kevin William, Dwight Wilson, Lynda Anne. B.S. in Agrl. Engring., Auburn U., 1958; M.S. in Agrl. Engring., S.D. State U., 1968. Registered profl. engr., S.C. Agrl. engr. U.S. Sedimentation Lab., Holly Springs, Miss., 1958-64, Agrl. Research Service, USDA, Brookings, S.D., 1964-68, Coastal Plains Research Ctr., Agrl. Research Service, Florence, S.C., 1968—; adj. instr. S.D. State U., Brookings, 1964-68; adj. asst. prof. Clemson U., S.C., 1975—. Served with U.S. Army, 1952-54. Mem. Am. Soc. Agrl. Engrs., Soil Conservation Soc. Am., U.S. Com. on Irrigation, Drainage and Flood Control. Clubs: Toastmasters (pres. Florence 1975), Civitan (pres. Holly Springs, Miss. 1967). Home: Route 3 Box 34 Florence SC 29501 Office: USDA Agrl Research Service Coastal Plains Research Ctr PO Box 3039 Florence SC 29502

DOTY, WILLIAM JASPER, JR., real estate executive; b. Pasadena, Tex., Nov. 4, 1943; s. William Jasper and Sonia (Rasi) D.; B.B.A., Rice U., 1967; m. Patsy Ruth Corley, Sept. 7, 1962; 1 dau., Dona Chemine. Systems analyst Eastern Airlines, Miami, Fla., 1967-68, sr. systems analyst, 1968-73, mgr. mktg. info. systems, 1973-74; sr. cons. Arthur Young & Co., Houston, 1974-75, mgr., 1975-78, prin., dir. fin. planning cons. services, 1978-81; treas. Kilroy Co. of Tex., Inc., Houston, 1981-82; v.p. fin. and adminstrn., treas. Joe A. McDermott, Inc., Houston, 1982—. Mem. Nat. Assn. Accts., Am. Prodn. and Inventory Control Soc., Planning Execs. Inst., Inst. Mgmt. Cons., N. Am. Soc. Corp. Planners, Am. Petroleum Inst., Tex. Mid-Continent Oil and Gas Assn. Roman Catholic. Home: PO Box 829 Seabrook TX 77586 Office: PO Box 1589 Houston TX 77001

DOUB, EUGENE MCKINLEY, real estate executive, contractor; b. Winston-Salem, N.C., June 8, 1934; s. William Earnest and Flora Alice (Allgood) D.; m. Anna Mae Beroth, Feb. 2, 1958 (div. Oct. 1978); 1 child, Peggy Sue; m. Kelly Denise Smith, May 28, 1983. Chem.E., Tulane U., 1957. Lic. gen. contractor. Constrn. estimator R.J. Reynolds Tobacco Co., Winston-Salem, 1957-60; pres. Gene's Concessions, Winston-Salem, 1960-75, Heather Hills, Inc., Winston-Salem, 1975—, Dowat, Inc., Winston-Salem, 1975—. Mem. Assoc. Gen. Contractors. Democrat. Methodist. Home: 5505 N Ocean Blvd Box 7191 Myrtle Beach SC 29577 Office: Heather Hills Inc 3801 Heathrow Dr Winston-Salem NC 27107

DOUECK, NORMAN BRUCE, utility company executive; b. N.Y.C., Apr. 22, 1947; s. Morris and Rachel Doueck; m. Lynne Ellen Bryan, Mar. 5, 1982; children—India, Leslie. B.A., Fla. State U., 1969. Tchr., Duval County Sch. Bd., Jacksonville, Fla., 1969-71; mgr. Edge City Corp., Jacksonville, 1972-74; energy analyst Mayor's Energy Office, Jacksonville, 1975-78; energy conservation coordinator Jacksonville Electric Authority, 1978-81, chief energy conservation div., 1982—. Coordinator Sun Day, Jacksonville, 1978; mem. steering com. Leadership Jacksonville, 1980; chmn. program and devel. Preservation Assn. for Tree Hill, Jacksonville, 1983-84. Named Environmentalist of 1980, Lee and Mimi Adams Award Bd., Jacksonville, 1980; recipient President's award for energy efficiency Pres. Jimmy Carter, Washington, 1980. Mem. Assn. Energy Engrs., Northeast Fla. Solar Energy Assn., Am. Pub. Power Assn. (chmn. energy services com. 1984-85), Fla. Jr. Coll. Community Instructional Services (chmn. environ. video 1984-85), Jacksonville Jaycees (Jaycee of Mo. 1977). Avocations: photography; skin diving. Home: 11863 Tumbling Oaks Ln Jacksonville FL 32223 Office: Jacksonville Electric Authority 1055 N Main St Jacksonville FL 32206

DOUGHERTY, CARY MCCONNELL, JR., hospital executive; b. New Orleans, July 17, 1946; s. Cary McConnell and Jean Percy (Highfill) D.; m. Patricia Elaine Skyring, Aug. 24, 1968; children—Jeannette Cary, Elizabeth Stewart, Cary McConnell. B.S., La. State U., 1969; M.P.H., Tulane U., 1975. Asst. adminstr. Ochsner Found., New Orleans, 1974-78; adminstr. Eye, Ear, Nose and Throat Hosp., New Orleans, 1978-82, Union Med. Ctr., El Dorado, Ark., 1982—. Pres. men's club St. Mary's Episcopal Ch., El Dorado, 1983-84; dist. committeeman DeSoto Area council Boy Scouts Am., 1982—; mem. adv. com. Oil-Belt Vo-Tech Sch., El Dorado, 1982—; mem. residency adv. com. U. Ark. Med. Sch., 1982—; v.p., bd. dirs. Union Med. Found., 1983—; trustee S. Ark. Symphony, S. Ark. Devel. Council. Mem. Am. Coll. Hosp. Adminstrs., Am. Hosp. Assn., Ark. Hosp. Assn., El Dorado C. of C. (trustee 1982-84), L.R. Jordan Mgmt. Soc. (bd. dirs.), Ark. Shared Purchasing Assn. (bd. dirs. 1984—). Lodge: Rotary. Home: 1330 N Madison St El Dorado AR 71730 Office: Union Med Ctr 700 W Grove St El Dorado AR 71730

DOUGHERTY, CHARLES EDWARD, retired government official; b. Shawnee, Okla., Jan. 12, 1921; s. William Estil and Catherine Beatrice (McCoy), D.; m. Billie Bess Sunday, Nov. 4, 1983. Student, U. Okla., 1938-41. Spl. asst. Office of Personal Rep. of Pres. of U.S., New Delhi, India, 1945-46; dir. pub. relations Consol. Producers Corp., Hollywood, Calif., 1946-47; cons. pub. relations, Beverly Hills, Calif., 1947-50; chief Korean Br., U.S. Army Psychol. Warfare Div., Tokyo, 1955-59; dir. pub. relations Office Internat. Trade Fairs, Washington, 1962-66; fgn. affairs analyst, cons. psychol. warfare USIA, Washington, 1966-73. Commr. Bicentennial Commn., Alexandria, Va., 1977-82; sustaining mem. Republican Nat. Com., 1975—. Served with U.S. Army, 1942-45, CBI, 1950-53, Korea. Mem. Am. Legion, VFW, Nat. Rifle Assn. Presbyterian. Avocations: military and diplomatic history. Home: PO Box 3306 Shawnee OK 74802

DOUGHERTY, DAVID E., agricultural research scientist; b. Canton, Ohio, Nov. 4, 1946; s. Cyril Edward and Gladys Helene (Bennett) D.; m. Jenelle Louise Shover, Dec. 30, 1977. B.A., Denison U., 1968; M.S., Ohio State U., 1973; Ph.D., U. Ga., 1976. Asst. plant pathologist U. Fla., Immokalee, 1977-80; field research scientist BASF Corp., Raleigh, N.C., 1980—. Contbr. articles to profl. jours. Served with U.S. Army, 1968-71. Mem. Am. Phytopathol. Soc., So. Weed Sci. Soc., U.S. Jr. C. of C. (pres. 1979-80). Lodge: Rotary (Immokalee). Avocations: gardening; computers. Home: 1321 Hickory Hollow Ln Raleigh NC 27610 Office: BASF Corp Raleigh NC 27610

DOUGHERTY, DAVID MALCOLM, computer science educator, consultant; b. Muskegon, Mich., Sept. 20, 1939; s. Ralph P. and Jane (Sproat) D.; m. Karen S. Heckmann, July 2, 1977 (div. Nov. 1983); 1 son, David Henry Ralph. M.E., Colo. Sch. Mines, 1961; M.B.A., Case Western Res. U., 1969. Registered profl. engr., Tex. Quality control engr., process engr., sr. mfg. engr. Gen. Electric Co., Cleve., 1961-67; advanced projects engr., mgr. planning and systems dept. Chase Brass & Copper, Cleve., 1968-71; pres. Nat. Systems Co., Cleve., 1971-74; asst. prof. Cleve. State U., 1971-76; instr. U. Md., College Park, 1976-79; asst. prof. computer science U. Tex., El Paso, 1979—; prin. Harris-Eaton Corp., El Paso, 1983—, also dir.; ind. computer cons., 1974-82; dir. Urban Small Bus. Cons., Inc., Delphi Assocs. Inc.; cons. City of Cleve., 1974-76, City of El Paso, 1980-81. Bd. dirs. Kern Place Assn., 1980-82; trustee Help for Retarded Children, 1972-76; vol. SBA, 1968-74. Served from 2d lt. to capt. U.S. Army, 1961-66. Named Top Grad., Case Western Res. U., 1969; recipient Active Corps Execs. award SBA, 1971. Mem. Am. Nat. Standards Inst. (com. X3J4), Ind. Computer Cons. Assn., Am. Inst. Decision Scis., Am. Prodn. and Inventory Control Soc., Assn. Ednl. Data Systems, Assn. Computing Machinery, Assn. Computer Users, Ops. Research Soc. Am., Inst. Mgmt. Scis., IEEE. Mem. Soc. of Friends. Lodge: Masons. Contbr. articles to profl. jours.; patentee in field. Home: 411 E New York Ave El Paso TX 79902 Office: Mgmt Dept U Tex El Paso TX 79968

DOUGHERTY, F(RANCIS) KELLY, systems engineer; b. Lubbock, Tex., May 15, 1953; s. Francis Kelly and Mary Ann (Odell) D.; B.A. in Math. and Physics summa cum laude, U. Dallas, 1975; m. Bonnie Lee Burch, June 14, 1975; children—Anne Katherine, Margaret Erin, Mary Bridget. Actuarial trainee Ranger Nat. Life Ins., Houston, 1976-77; mgr. time sharing services Phila. Life Ins. Co., Houston, 1977-81; systems engr. Electronic Data Systems, Dallas, 1981—. U. Dallas scholar, 1971-75; Rice U. fellow, 1975-76. C.L.U.; cert. in data processing; cert. in computer programming; chartered fin. cons. Fellow Life Mgmt. Inst. Republican. Roman Catholic. Club: KC. Home: 4007 Latham Plano TX 75023

DOUGHERTY, J(OHN) CHRYS(OSTOM), lawyer; b. Beeville, Tex., May 3, 1915; s. John Chrysostom and Mary V. (Henderson) D.; B.A., U. Tex., 1937; LL.B., Harvard U., 1940; diploma Inter-Am. Acad. Internat. and Comparative Law, Havana, Cuba, 1948; m. Mary Ireland Graves, Apr. 18, 1942 (dec. July 1977); children—Mary Ireland, John Chrysostom IV; m. 2d, Bea Ann Smith, June 1978 (div. Apr. 1981); m. 3d, Sarah B. Randle. Admitted to Tex. bar, 1940; atty. Hewit & Dougherty, 1940-41; partner firm Graves & Dougherty, 1946-50, Graves, Dougherty & Greenhill, Austin, Tex., 1950-57, Graves, Dougherty & Gee, 1957-60, Graves, Dougherty, Gee & Hearon, 1961-66, Graves, Dougherty, Gee, Hearon, Moody & Garwood, 1966-73, Graves, Dougherty, Hearon, Moody & Garwood, 1973-79, Graves, Dougherty, Hearon & Moody, 1979-80, Graves, Dougherty, Hearon, Moody & Garwood, 1980-81, Graves, Dougherty, Hearon & Moody, 1981—; spl. asst. atty. gen., 1949-50; dir. InterFirst Bank Austin, N.A.; hon. French consul in Austin, 1971—; lectr. tax, estate planning, probate code, community property problems. Mem. Tex. Submerged Lands Adv. Com., 1963-72, Tex. Bus. and Commerce Code Adv. Com., 1964-66, Gov.'s Com. Marine Resources, 1970, Colo. River Basin Water Quality Mgmt. Study Com., 1972-73, Tex. Legis. Property Tax Com., 1973-75; bd. dirs. Grenville Clark Fund at Dartmouth Coll., 1976—; trustee St. Stephen's Episcopal Sch., 1969-83, U. Tex. Law Sch. Found., 1971—. Served as capt. C.I.C., U.S. Army, 1941-44, JAGC, 1944-46, maj. Res. Decorated Medaille Francaise, Medaille d'honneur en Argent des Affairs Etrangeres (France). Fellow Tex. Bar Found., Am. Bar Found., Am. Coll. Probate Counsel, Am. Coll. Tax Counsel, Tex. State Bar Coll.; mem. Am. Arbitration Assn. (S.W. adv. council 1965—), Internat. (patron), Inter-Am., Travis County (pres. 1976-77) bar assns., ABA (ho. of dels. 1982—, chmn. spl. com. lawyers pub. service responsibility 1982-84), State Bar Tex. (chmn. sect. taxation 1965-66, pres. 1979-80), Internat., Am. fgn. law assns., Internat. Acad. Estate and Trust Law, Am. Law Inst., Am. Soc. Internat. Law (exec. council 1959-62), Inter-Am. Bar Assn., World Assn. Lawyers, Cum Laude Soc. (hon.), Phi Beta Kappa, Phi Eta Sigma, Beta Theta Pi (dir. Tex. Beta Students Aid Fund 1949-85). Presbyterian. Club: Rotary. Co-editor Texas Appellate Practice, 1964, 2d edit., 1977; contbr.: Bowe, Estate Planning and Taxation; Texas Lawyers Practice Guide, 1967, 71; How to Live and Die with Texas Probate, 1968, 4th edit., 1983; Texas Estate Administration, 1975, supplement, 1980; bd. editors Appellate Procedure in Texas, 1964, 2d edit., 1982. Contbr. articles to profl. publs. Home: 6 Green Lanes Austin TX 78703 Office: InterFirst Bank Tower PO Box 98 Austin TX 78767

DOUGHERTY, RALPH CLIFFORD, chemistry educator, consultant; b. Dillon, Mont., Jan. 31, 1940; s. Clifford Alonzo and Virginia Ring (Ferguson) D.; m. Judith Jeanne Stringfellow, Dec. 27, 1960; children—Erika Jeanne, Tara Michelle, Deirdra Harriette. B.S. in Chemistry, Mont. State U., 1960; Ph.D., U. Chgo., 1963. Asst. prof. chemistry Ohio State U., 1965-69; assoc. prof. Fla. State U., 1969-77, prof., 1977—. Grantee NIH, NSF, U.S. EPA; fellow Woodrow Wilson, NSF. Mem. Am. Chem. Soc., Am. Phys. Soc., Am. Soc. Mass Spectrometry. Democrat. Presbyterian. Author: (with M.J.J. Dewar) PMO Theory of Organic Chemistry, 1977; contbr. numerous articles to profl. jours. Home: 1006 Waverly Rd Tallahassee FL 32312 Office: Dept Chemistry Fla State Univ Tallahassee FL 32306

DOUGHERTY, WILLIAM JOHN, architect; b. Louisville, Ohio, Feb. 28, 1933; s. William A. and Maxine J. (Polen) D.; m. Helen T. Parker, Mar. 15, 1957; 1 son, William Reid. B.S. in Architecture, Ga. Inst. Tech., 1960. Prin., William J. Dougherty, Architect, Atlanta, 1966-74, 82—; pres. Dougherty Assocs., P.C., Atlanta, 1974-80, Dougherty, Fernandez, Marchant, Inc., Atlanta, 1980-82, Custom Structures, Inc., Atlanta, 1980—; prin. archtl. works include residential and comml. bldgs. Del. community devel. citizens adv. com. Atlanta Regional Commn., 1973-75, chmn., 1976-77; mem. Atlanta Mayor's Task Force for New Grand Mus. Park, 1975; mem. energy com. Atlanta Bd. Edn., 1976-77; bd. dirs. Druid Hills Arts Council, 1973-75, pres., 1972-73; trustee Atlanta Outdoor Activity Ctr., 1976-82, vice chmn., 1979-82; trustee Arts Festival of Atlanta, 1968-69, pres., 1969-70. Served with U.S. Army, 1953-55. Fellow AIA (Ivan Allen Sr. award for service to community Atlanta chpt. 1975, pres. Atlanta chpt. 1977-78, commr. urban planning, housing, human relations and hist. preservations coms. 1975-76); mem. Ga. Planning Assn. Contbg. author: Land Use, 1974. Home: 4303 Davidson Ave NE Atlanta GA 30319 Office: PO Box 9727 Atlanta GA 30319

DOUGLAS, CLYDE (JERRY) G(ERALD), JR., flooring company executive; b. Wichita Falls, Tex., Dec. 19, 1939; s. Clyde Gerald and Rachel (Dea) D.; m. Joyce Darlene Parker, Sept. 14, 1958 (div. dec. 1977); children—Dennis, Stephen; m. Ruby Faye Shepard Masters, Dec. 20, 1977; stepchildren—Jo Anne Masters, Felicia Masters, Dena Masters Cozby. Student pub. schs., Wichita Falls. With Douglas Floor Co., Wichita Falls, 1955—, warehouse man, 1965-70, estimator, 1970-74, ptnr., 1975-85, owner, 1985—. Mem. com. on ch. and community First United Methodist Ch., Wichita Falls, 1983-85. Mem. Wichita Falls Bd. Commerce and Industry, Small Bus. Council, Air Force Assn., Constrn. Specifications Inst. (charter mem. chpt.). Lodge: Rotary (dir. vocat. services Wichita Falls 1981-83). Home: 2725 Darwin Dr Wichita Falls TX 76308 Office: Douglas Floor Co 2301 Holliday Wichita Falls TX 76301

DOUGLAS, EDDIE DILWORTH, college counselor; b. Yoakum, Tex., Aug. 20, 1919; s. Emmitt and Emma (Dilworth) D.; m. Ethel Lucille Douglas, May 15, 1955; children—Vera, Grace, Roy. B.S., Prairie View A&M U., 1941; M.A., Stanton U., 1964. Tchr. pub. schs., Yoakum, Tex., 1941-42, Hearne, Tex., 1942-44, Hardin, Tex., 1947-54; meat insp., San Francisco, 1944-46; tchr., missionary Nat. Baptist Conv., Jamaica, B.W.I., 1955-63; counselor Houston Community Coll., 1963—. Author: Bare Facts, 1963; The Closed Door, 1967. Active North McGregor Oak Civic Assn., Houston, Community Devel. Assn. Mem. Am. Soc. Notaries, Tex. Notary Assn., Profl. Counselors Assn. (treas. Houston 1976-82), Nat. Tchrs. Assn. (parliamentarian Washington 1973-74). Democrat. Lodge: Masons. Home: 3220 Calumet Houston TX 77004

DOUGLAS, ELI, educational administrator. Supt. of schs. Garland, Tex. Office: 720 Stadium Dr Garland TX 75040*

DOUGLAS, JAMES WALTER, pharmaceutical auditing company executive, consultant pharmacist; b. Clarendon, Tex., Feb. 10, 1929; s. Clyde James and Dorinda (Tatum) D.; m. Mary Sanders, July 21, 1961. B.S. in Pharmacy, U. Tex., 1949. Registered pharmcist, Tex. Owner, operator Douglas Pharmacy, Irving, Tex., 1961-69; pres. Family RX Systems, Irving, 1970-74, PAS, Irving, 1982—; v.p. Meyers & Rosser Pharmacies, Dallas, 1975-82. Served with USN, 1950-54; Korea. Mem. Dallas County Pharm. Soc., Tex. Pharm. Assn., Am. Pharm. Assn. Republican. Lodge: Optimist. Avocations: fly fishing; quail hunting; tennis. Home: 1941 Standish St Irving TX 75061 Office: PAS PO Box 154145 Irving TX 75015

DOUGLAS, JOHN EDWARD, law enforcement agency administrator, crime analyst; b. Bklyn., June 18, 1945; s. Jack and Dolores (Holmes) D.; m. Pamela Elizabeth Modica, June 24, 1972; children—Erika, Lauren. B.S., Eastern N.Mex. U., 1970; M.S., U. Wis.-Milw., 1975, Ed.S., 1976. Spl. agt., FBI, Detroit, 1971-72, Milw., 1972-77, supervisory spl. agt., Quantico, Va., 1977-83. Supervisory spl. agt. criminal profiling program, 1980—, program mgr., 1980—, case cons., Washington, 1977—, cons. local, state, fed. police agys., 1977—. Served with USAF, 1966-70. Mem. Am. Correctional Assn., Am. Humane Assn., Am. Orthopsychiat. Assn., Am. Legion. Contbr. numerous articles to law enforcement and psychiat. bulls. Office: FBI Acad-Behavioral Sci Unit Quantico VA 22135

DOUGLAS, LINDSEY RUSSELL, oral and maxillofacial surgeon; b. Lexington, Ky., Sept. 23, 1950; s. Lindsey Russell and Madge Culver (Johns) D.; m. Debra Jane Ely, July 26, 1975; 1 child, Lindsey Russell IV. B.A., Centre Coll., 1972; D.M.D., U. Ky., 1977. Diplomate Am. Bd. Oral and Maxillofacial Surgery. Resident VA Hosp., Lexington, Ky., 1977-78; intern U. Ky. Med. Ctr., Lexington, 1978-79, resident, 1979-80; chief resident, 1980-81; assoc. Oral and Maxillofacial Surgery Assocs., Ashland, Ky., 1981-83, pres., 1983—; vol. Marshall U. Med. Sch., Huntington, W.Va., 1981—; cons. VA Hosp., Huntington, 1981—; assoc. prof. W.Va. U., Morgantown, W.Va., 1985—. Recipient Anesthesiology award U. Ky. Coll. Dentistry, Lexington, 1977. Fellow Am. Assn. Oral and Maxillofacial Surgeons, Am. Bd. Oral and Maxillofacial Surgery, ADA, Am. Soc. Dental Anesthesia. Club: Tri-City Rugby (Ashland) (founder and pres.). Lodge: Elks. Avocations: rugby; scuba diving; oceanography, skiing; stamp collecting. Office: Oral & Maxillofacial Surgery Assocs 2301 Lexington Ave 100 Ashland KY 41101

DOUGLAS, RICHARD COLEMAN, Air Force officer; b. Delhi, N.Y., June 23, 1959; s. Harold Lindsay and Barbara Lee (Tigue) D.; m. Beth Ellen Amundson, July 11, 1981. A.A.S. in Edn., Community Coll. of the Air Force, Montgomery, Ala., 1980; B.A. in Sociology, USNY-Albany, 1981, B.S. in Bus., 1980; M.B.A., Nat. U., 1984. Enlisted as airman basic U.S. Air Force, 1977, advanced through grades to 1st lt., 1985; edr. adv. U.S. Air Force, Boston, 1977-80; cons./owner Douglasystems, San Diego, 1981-83; chief special projects U.S. Air Force Occupational Measurement Ctr., San Antonio, 1984—. Mem. Phi Delta Kappa. Avocations: tennis; karate. Home: 221 E Perimeter Dr San Antonio TX 78227 Office: DET 1 USAFOMC Lackland AFB TX 78236-5000

DOUGLAS, THOMAS JACKSON, veterinarian; b. Brunswick, Ga., Dec. 14, 1926; s. Charles Jackson and Susan Earline (Loftin) D.; m. Dorothy Elizabeth Walker, May 30, 1953; children—Charles Walker, James Thomas. D.V.M., Auburn U., 1948. Gen. practice vet. medicine, Greenville, S.C., Claxton, Ga., 1948-49; dir. Gen. Disease Diagnostic Lab., Gainesville and Canton, Ga., 1953-57; field cons., field researcher Am. Cyanamid, Princeton, N.J., 1962-66; dir. vet. services Goldkist, Atlanta, 1966—. Scoutmaster, Boy Scouts Am., Canton, 1975-83. Served to capt. U.S. Army, 1951-53. Recipient Legion of Merit award Atlanta council Boy Scouts Am., 1981. Mem. Am. Assn. Swine Practitioners, Am. Assn. Avian Pathologists, AVMA, Poultry Sci. Assn. Contbr. articles to profl. publs.

DOUGLASS, EDWARD TRENT, JR., industrial furnace company executive; b. Birmingham, Ala., Feb. 18, 1906; s. Edward Trent and Clara Holmes (Cotten) D.; m. Florence Nicholson, Dec. 2, 1936; children—Florence Douglass Williams, Marguerite Trent Douglass Caddis; m. Margaret Davidson Sizemore, Jan. 14, 1983. With Douglass Bros. Wholesale Produce Co., Birmingham, 1929-31, Douglass-Murray Fuel Co., Birmingham, 1931-50; pres. Indsl. Furnace Co., Inc., Birmingham, 1950—. Warden emeritus Episcopal Cathedral Ch. of the Advent, Birmingham. Mem. Birmingham-Jefferson Hist. Soc. (pres. 1981-83), S.R. (past pres. Ala.), St. Andrews Soc., Newcomen Soc. N.Am., Soc. Coloniel Wars, Soc. War of 1812, Sigma Alpha Epsilon. Republican. Clubs: Birmingham Country, Mountain Brook Country, The Club, Redstone (past pres.), Birmingham Downtown Kiwanis. Patentee in field. Home: 3084 Sterling Rd Birmingham AL 35213 Office: 2709 5th Ave S Birmingham AL 35233

DOUGLASS, HARRY ROBERT, hospital and health care consultant, architect, educator; b. McCook, Nebr., Mar. 27, 1937; s. Harry William and Irma Ruth Douglass; m. Mary Laurel Rigg, Dec. 14, 1964; 1 son, William Robert. B.Arch., U. Nebr., 1963; M.Arch. in Hosp. Planning, U. Minn., 1965; grad. exec. devel. program Harvard U. Bus. Sch., 1983. Chmn., chief exec. officer Robert Douglass Assocs. Inc., Hosp. Cons., Houston, 1973—; chmn. bd. MJ Software Inc., Houston, 1983—; chmn. Mktg. Research Cons., Inc., Sacramento, Calif., 1984—; assoc. prof. Rice U., U. Tex. Sch. Pub. Health, 1973-75; adj. prof. health care planning Rice U., 1975—. AIA-Am. Hosp. Assn. Joint fellow, 1964-66. Fellow Am. Assn. Hosp. Cons.; mem. Soc. Hosp. Planners, AIA (nat. com. on architecture for health), Am. Assn. Hosp. Planning (dir. 1975-80), Am. Mgmt. Assn., Houston C. of C. (health com.). Episcopalian. Contbr. articles to profl. jours.; rep. exec. bd. WHO, Managua, 1972; organizer, dir. internat. seminar in hosp. and health care Panamanian Orgn., U. San Martin, Buenos Aires, 1971; designer, planned of numerous archtl. projects; recipient numerous design awards, including Presdl. Silver medal for Charles River Project, Boston, 1984. Home: 1741 Albans Houston TX 77005 Office: 1020 Holcombe Suite 1600 Houston TX 77030

DOUGLASS, MARGARET SIZEMORE, university official, civic worker; b. Birmingham, Ala.; d. Julius Weston and Ruth (Lee) Davidson; m. James Middleton Sizemore, June 19, 1937; children—James Middleton, Ruth Lee Sizemore House; m. 2d Edward Trent Douglass, Jr., Jan. 14, 1983. A.B., M.A., Samford U.; normal degree U. Paris; postgrad. Western Res. U., U. Ala., Sorbonne, Paris; LL.D. (hon.) Jacksonville State U., 1979. Assoc. prof. modern lang. Howard Coll., 1947-58, dean of women, 1950-70; asst. to pres. Samford U., Birmingham, 1970—, dir. adult edn., 1975-78, dir. paralegal studies, 1975—; tchr. community class in antiques, 1970—; 1st French classes on Ala. Ednl. TV, 1st TV series on antiques. Co-author: The Amazing Marriage of Marie Eustis and Josef Hofmann, 1965; author: Collecting Antiques, 1977; author hist. sketches; contbr. articles on antiques and travel to periodicals. Adv. com. women in services Dept. of Def., 1965-68; mem. Birmingham Centennial Commn., 1971, Ala. Sesquicentennial Commn., 1969, U.S. Bicentennial Commn., 1974-76, Ala. Constl. Commn., 1969—; mem. Tannehill Furnace and Foundry Commn., 1969—, past chmn.; chmn. speakers' bur. Birmingham Civic Opera Bd., 1959-60; adv. bd. Birmingham Mus. Art; mem. woman's com. Birmingham Symphony.; co-chmn. Com. to Refurbish Gov.'s Mansion; bd. dirs. Ala. Pops Orch.; chmn. Birmingham Festival of Arts, 1960-61, hon. chmn., 1962, sec., 1962-63; bd. visitors Monterey Tech. U. (Mex.), 1957-63; co-founder Freedom Ednl. Found.; bd. dirs. Am. Scholars, Library Ala. Lives; co-founder, past pres. Women's Com. 100 for Birmingham; pres. Jefferson County Hist. Commn.; mem. Birmingham Mayor's Adv. Bd., 1972-76; adv. bd. Ala. Hist. Commn.; mem. Ala. Commn. on Ethics and Morals in Edn., 1971-77; mem. Ala. Gov.'s Com. for Employment of Handicapped, 1971-77; chmn. Ala. Women's Commn., 1972—; bd. dirs. Jefferson-Shelby Lung Assn., 1970-76; goodwill ambassador Birmingham (Ala.), to Birmingham (Eng.), 1953, 78. Named Ami de France, City of Paris, 1951; recipient scroll from Archbishop of Canterbury (Eng.), 1951; ofcl. guest City of Birmingham (Eng.), 1953; citation as Woman of Achievement in Edn., 1956, 57; named Birmingham Woman of Yr., 1962; recipient award Freedoms Found., Valley Forge, Pa., 1963, Vigilant Patriot award, 1963, award for civic service Birmingham Jaycees, 1965, Community Service award Religious Heritage of Am. Assn., 1979, award for outstanding family life Family Found. Am., 1980; named Ala. Merit Mother, 1964. Life Fellow Royal Soc. Arts; mem. Nat. Assn. Women Deans, Ala. Assn. Women Deans (sec. 1951-53), Nat. League Am. Penwomen (pres. Birmingham br. 1966-68, state pres. 1973-75, nat. dir. 1976-80), Antiquarian Soc. (pres. 1960-61), Nat. Soc. Arts and Letters (hon. mem.), Ala. Hist. Assn., Birmingham Hist. Soc., Arlington Hist. Soc. (life trustee, pres. 1970-71), Forney Hist. Soc. (pres. 1975—), English Speaking Union, Pres. and Deans Am. Colls., Brit. Am. Soc. Am., Ala. Guidance Assn. (pres. 1955-57), AAUW, Am. Decorative Arts Trust (charter), Ala. Writers Conclave (pres. 1962-63), Daus. Colonial Wars, Colonial Dames Am., Daus. Barons of Rennemede, DAR (chpt. regent 1975-77), Daus. Am. Colonists (state regent 1964-67), Soc. Lees of Va., UDC (pres. 1966-67), English Ceramic Circle, Am. Ceramic Circle, Am. Hist. Print Collectors Assn., Furniture History Soc. London, Royal Oak Soc., Internat. Platform Assn., Newcomen Soc., Alpha Delta Pi. Clubs: Bibliophiles, The Club, Country of Birmingham, Mountain Brook, New Era, Concordia, Faculty Woman's, Altrusa (pres. Birmingham 1955-56), Overseas (pres.), Scottish Clan (Chattan). Address: Samford U Birmingham AL 35229

DOUMAR, ROBERT G., U.S. district judge; b. 1930; m. Dorothy Ann Mundy; children—Robert G., Charles C. B.A., U. Va., 1951, LL.B., 1953. Assoc. firm Venable, Parsons, Kyle & Hylton, 1955-58; sr. ptnr. Doumar, Pincus, Knight & Harlan, 1958-82; U.S. dist. judge Eastern Va., Norfolk, 1981—. Office: 306 US Courthouse 600 Granby St Norfolk VA 23510

DOVE, GRANT ALONZA, electronics company executive; b. Sycamore, Va., 1928; married. B.S.E.E., Va. Poly. Inst., 1951. With Sperry Gyroscope Co., 1951-52, Maxson Elec. Corp., 1952-59; with Tex. Instruments Inc., 1959—, mgr. Washington sales office, 1962-63, mktg. mgr., 1963-65, project mgr., 1965-67, asst. v.p., dept. mgr., 1967-68, v.p., mgr. corp. devel., 1968-72, group v.p., mgr. services group, 1972-77, group v.p., mgr. govt. electronics and services, 1977-80, sr. v.p., mgr. corp. mktg., 1980-82, exec. v.p., Dallas, 1980—; dir. Western Co. N.Am. Served with USN, 1946-48. Mem. Nat. Security Indsl. Assn. (trustee, vice chmn. exec. com.). Office: Tex Instruments Inc PO Box 225474 Dallas TX 75265

DOVEL, JOHN RUSSELL, construction company executive; b. Takoma Park, Md., May 23, 1948; s. Claude Vernon and Violet Louise (Harris) D.; m. Tatiana Christina Lansing, Feb. 11, 1984. Assoc. degree in bus. No. Va. Community Coll., 1976; Assoc. degree in gen. studies, 1982; B.S. in Bus. Adminstrn., Am. U., 1983. Pres., Mgmt. Services, Fairfax, Va., 1977—; v.p. Structural Concepts, Fairfax, 1984—. Del. Va. Republican Conv., 1980; mem. exec. com. Men of All Saints Episcopal Ch., Chevy Chase, Md., 1983—, mem. bldg. and grounds com., outreach com., 1985—; mem. steering com. Samaritan Ministry, Washington, 1985; job counseling vol. St. Stephen and Incarnation Ch., Washington, 1983; vol. Martha's Table Soup Kitchen, Washington, 1983—, Calvery Shelter for Homeless Women, Washington, 1984, So Others Might Eat Soup Kitchen, Washington, 1984. Served with U.S. Army, 1969-72. Univ. scholar Am. U., 1982-83; recipient 1st place photography award Women in Communication, 1980-81, 2d place photography award U.S. Army, Okinawa, 1972. Mem. Am. Inst. Constructors, Nat. Trust for Hist. Preservation. Avocations: golf; tennis; photography; water sports; chess. Home: 3042 Cedar Ln Fairfax VA 22031 Office: PO Box 692 Merrifield VA 22116

DOVER, JANINE GAMBILL, educator; b. St. Petersburg, Fla., June 25, 1944; d. George Washington and Dorcas Harriett (Darling) Gambill; m. Dale Kermit Dover, Aug. 21, 1965; children—Deidre, Dale Kermit. B.A., LaGrange Coll., 1965; postgrad. U. Ga., 1967-68; M.Ed., Ga. Southwestern Coll., 1974. Tchr. phys. edn., coach Stephens County High Sch., Toccoa, 1965-66; tchr. math, phys. edn. Randolph County High Sch., Cuthbert, Ga., 1966-67; head health and phys. edn., coach Mitchell Baker High Sch., Camilla, Ga., 1967—; founder, dir. Flying Eagles gymnastics group, 1976—. Tchr. Sunday sch. Camilla United Methodist Ch., 1967-75, adminstrv. bd., 1969-70, youth counselor, 1976-79. Mem. Ga. High Sch. Coaches Assn., Ga. Edn. Assn., NEA, U.S. Gymanastics Fedn., Ga. Health, Phys. Edn. Recreation Assn. Club: Pinecrest Country (bd. govs. 1983-85). Office: Mitchell Baker High Sch Rt 3 Box 510 Camilla GA 31730

DOVER, VERNON EUGENE, engineering technologist; b. Asheville, N.C., Apr. 4, 1949; s. Wayne Vernon and Clara (Massey) D.; m. Cheryl Chambers, Sept. 1, 1967; children—Lynette, Bryan. Student Western Carolina U., 1969-72. Material man Carolina Power & Light Co., Asheville, N.C., 1967-68, lineman, 1968-69, right-of-way agt, 1969-72, engring. technologist, 1972—. Chmn., Buncombe County Bd. Edn., Asheville, 1982—; mem. Buncombe County Indsl. Facilities and Pollution Control Fin. Authority, Asheville, 1981—; mem. West Buncombe Vol. Fire Dept., Asheville, 1965-83, chief, 1980-83. Democrat. Baptist. Avocations: golfing; camping. Home: Route 1 Box 348-E Leicester NC 28748 Office: Carolina Power & Light Co PO Box 1601 Asheville NC 28748

DOW, ANDREW NISBET, JR., college administrator; b. Jacksonville, Fla., Apr. 26, 1920; s. Andrew Nisbet and Rebecca (Peavy) D.; m. Grace E. Ullman, Apr. 25, 1959 (dec. Nov. 18, 1980); 1 dau., Rebecca. B.A., U. Fla., 1941, M.A., 1943, Ed.D., 1977; student U. Minn., 1946-47, U. Pa., 1945. Head dept. psychology and edn., coordinator of testing Miami-Dade Community Coll., 1960-64; project dir. Automated Selection for Enlisted Tng., Navy-Wide, NPRDC, San Diego, 1964-67, Navy-wide spl. examiner for sr. and master chief petty officer candidates, Great Lakes, Ill. and Pensacola, Fla., 1967-80, nat. dir. evaluation Naval ROTC, Chief Naval Edn. Tng. Staff, Pensacola, Fla., 1980-83; evening coordinator Pensacola Jr. Coll.; research cons. New Pride of Pensacola, 1983-84; adj. prof. psychology Pensacola Jr. Coll., 1977-78, U. Fla., 1964. Mem. personnel and tng. bd. San Diego council Girl Scouts U.S.A., 1965-67; mem. adv. bd. Internat. Order Rainbow for Girls, 1976-81; assoc. Meals on Wheels program, 1985-86; bd. dirs. Reading is Fundamental, 1985-86. Served with USNR, 1943-46. Mem. Am. Psychol. Assn., Am. Ednl. Research Assn., Northwest Fla. Psychol. Assn., Phi Delta Kappa. Mason. Home: 4237 Futura Dr Pensacola FL 32504 Office: PJC 5555 W Hwy 98 Pensacola FL 32507

DOWBEN, CARLA LURIE, lawyer, educator; b. Chgo., Jan. 22, 1932; d. Harold H. and Gertrude (Geitner) Lurie; m. Robert Dowben, June 20, 1950; children—Peter Arnold, Jonathan Stuart, Susan Laurie. A.B., U. Chgo., 1950; J.D., Temple U., 1955; postgrad. cert., Brandeis U., 1968. Bar: Ill. 1957, Mass. 1963, Tex. 1974, fed. cts., 1957, U.S. Supreme Ct., 1974. Assoc. firm Conrad and Verges, Chgo., 1957-62; exec. officer MIT, Cambridge, Mass., 1963-64; legal planner, Mass. Health Planning Project, Boston, 1964-69; assoc. prof. Life Scis. Inst., Brown U., Providence, 1970-72; asst. prof. health law U. Tex. Health Sci. Ctr., Dallas, 1973-78, assoc. prof., 1978—; cons. Bd. dirs. Mental Health Assn., 1958—, Ft. Worth Assn. Retarded Citizens, 1980-83, Advocacy, Inc., 1981-85. Mem. ABA, Tex. Bar Assn., Dallas Bar Assn., Nat. Health Lawyers Assn., Hastings Inst. Ethics, Tex. Family Planning Assn. Quaker. Contbr. articles to profl. jours.; active in drafting health, mental health legislation, agency regulations in several state, local govts. Home: 7150 Eudora Dr Dallas TX 75230 Office: 2900 Turtle Creek Plaza Suite 500 Dallas TX 75219

DOWDA, ROBERT ELLIS, educational administrator; b. Bradford, Ala., June 10, 1942; s. Robert Jack Dowda and Agnes Juanita (Peoples) Burger; m. Elizabeth Mae Striplin, June 15, 1963; children—Robert, Richard. A.B., Birmingham So. Coll., 1963; B.D., Duke U., 1966, Th.M. summa cum laude, 1968, Ph.D., 1972. Cert. tchr., adminstr., Ga. Chmn. dept. history and religion Valwood Sch., Valdosta, Ga., 1971-72, asst. headmaster, 1972-73; headmaster Southwood Sch., Waycross, Ga., 1973-82, Pulaski Acad., Little Rock, 1982—. Vice-pres. Waycross United Way, 1976; div. dir. Little Rock United Way, 1983; dir. Little Rock Community Theatre, 1984—. Danforth fellow, 1967. Mem. Ark. Assn. Ind. Schs. (pres. 1985—), Ind. Schs. Assn. Central States (state rep. and legis. liaison 1983—), SE Assn. Ind. Schs. (pres.-elect Macon, Ga. 1981-82), Omicron Delta Kappa. Methodist. Lodge: Rotary. Avocations: music, theatre, sports. Home: 1508 Jennifer Dr Little Rock AR 72212 Office: Pulaski Acad 12701 Hinson Rd Little Rock AR 72212

DOWDELL, JOSEPH EDWARD, university bookstore manager; b. Elyria, Ohio, Mar. 6, 1950; s. Richard William and Jane Gertrude (Obringer) D.; children—Christopher J., Melissa S., Kyle E. B.S. in Edn., Kent State U., 1973. Textbook mgr. Kent State U., Ohio, 1974-78; asst. bookstore mgr. Stetson U., DeLand, Fla., 1978-82; bookstore mgr., Embry Riddle Aeros. U., Daytona Beach, Fla., 1982—. Coach Youth Soccer Volusia County Recreation Dept., DeLand 1980-84, West Volusia YMCA, 1984. Served with USCGR, 1971—. Mem. Nat. Assn. Coll. Stores (com. mem. 1985), Fla. Assn. Coll. Stores (governing bd. 1981, pres. 1985—). Avocations: sports; fishing; woodwork; reading. Office: Embry Riddle Bookstore DB Regional Airport Daytona Beach FL 32015

DOWDLE, JOAN GATES, principal, educator, consultant; b. Helena, Ala., Jan. 2, 1934; d. John and Hattie (Cook) Gates; m. Joseph Clyde Dowdle, Aug. 26, 1956; children—Barbara Jan, Jeanne Olive, Joanna Gates. B.S., Ala. Coll. Women, 1954; M.A., U. Ala., 1973, Ed.D., 1980. Cert. in adminstrn., Ala. Tchr. Montgomery Schs., Ala., 1954-56, Auburn Schs., Ala., 1956-57, Raleigh Pub. Schs., N.C., 1958-62; tchr., staff developer Huntsville City Schs., Ala., 1967-74, prin., 1974-85; prin. Tuscaloosa Middle Sch., Ala., 1985—; adj. prof. adminstrn. and ednl. leadership U. Ala., University, 1984—; pvt. cons., Ala., 1980—; chmn., cons. Southeastern Assn. Colls. and Schs., Ala., 1978—. Grade level author: New Zaner Blosser 7th Grade Spelling Book, 1983. Presentor Computer Use in Schs., 1982-83. Mem., officer Community Ballet Assn., Huntsville, 1964-67; bd. dirs., officer Soroptimist Club, Huntsville, 1978-85; bd. dirs. Multiple Sclerosis Soc., Huntsville, 1970-75. Recipient Leadership award Ala. Council Sch. Adminstrs., 1981. Mem. Nat. Assn. Middle Schs., Nat. Assn. Middle Schs., Nat. Assn. Elem. Prins., Nat. Assn. Secondary Prins., Delta Kappa Gamma, Phi Delta Kappa. Club: Univ. Women's (pres. Huntsville 1980-81). Home: Tuscaloosa AL 35401

DOWDY, BILLY VERNON, English educator; b. Whitehouse, Tex., Jan. 8, 1937; s. Vernon and Myrtle D. B.A., Stephen F. Austin U., 1958; M.A., East Tex. State U., 1960; postgrad. Tex. Tech. U., 1966, Mary Hardin-Baylor U., 1969-71, Baylor U., 1972-73, Howard Payne Coll., 1973, Idaho State U., 1975-76, Tex. A&M U., 1979. Tchr. English, Trinidad (Tex.) Ind. Sch. Dist., 1958-60, all-level sch. prin., 1960-66; prof. dept. English McLennan Community Coll., Waco, Tex., 1966—; area collegiate-level English text reviewer Holt, Rinehart and Winston, CBS Inc., N.Y.C., 1981, Little, Brown and Co. Pubs., Boston, 1981, Macmillan Pub. Co., Inc., N.Y.C., 1981. Author: English 311 Study Aids: A Sequenced Approach to Writing All College Papers Persuasively, 1981; English 312 Study Aids: A Sequenced Approach to Writing All Multi-Paragraph Collegiate Papers Persuasively, 1981; contbr. articles to profl. jours. Recipient Master Tchr. award McLennan Community Coll., 1983. Mem. NEA, AAUP, Coll. Council Tchrs. English, Tex. Jr. Coll. Tchrs. Assn., Tex. State Tchrs. Assn., Tex. Secondary Prins. Assn., Waco Jaycees. Methodist. Lodges: Rotary, Masons. Home: 1425 Chattanooga St Waco TX 76704 Office: McLennan Community Coll 1400 College Dr Waco TX 76708

DOWDY, WAYNE, congressman; b. Fitzgerald, Ga., July 27, 1943; m. Susan Tenney; children—Dunbar, Charles, Eloise. B.A., Millsaps Coll., Jackson, Miss., 1965; LL.B., Jackson Sch. Law, 1968. Mayor, McComb, Miss., 1978-81, city judge, McComb, 1970-74; mem. 97th-98th congresses from 4th Dist. Miss. Pres. Pike County Indsl. Found.; past mem. state bd. Easter Seal Soc., United Way, Salvation Army. Mem. Am. Trial Lawyers Assn., Miss. Trial Lawyers Assn., Miss. Bar Assn., Pike County Bar Assn. Democrat. Methodist. Office: 210 Cannon House Office Bldg Washington DC 20515

DOWE, WILLIAM EMMETT, hospital administrator; b. Victoria, Tex., Oct. 29, 1926; s. Emmett Lee and Mary Elizabeth (Clark) D.; m. Louise Allen, Sept. 10, 1947; children—William A., Barbara Jean Dowe Bailey. B.A., U. Louisville. Mgmt. trainee Sears Roebuck & Co., Louisville, 1949-56; personnel dir. CIT Fin. Corp., Louisville, 1956-71; from personnel dir. to assoc. adminstr. Our Lady of Peace Hosp., Louisville, 1971-83; adminstr. Jane Todd Crawford Meml. Hosp., Greensburg, Ky., 1983—. Served with USN, 1944-46. Baptist. Club: Rotary. Avocations: oil painting; golf; fishing; gardening. Office: Jane Todd Crawford Meml Hosp 202 Milby St Greensburg KY 42743

DOWELL, RICHARD PATRICK, professional services company executive; b. Washington, Apr. 21, 1934; s. Cassius McClellan and Mary Barbara (McHenry) D.; m. Eleanor Craddock Halley, Dec. 23, 1957 (div. Sept. 1973); children—Richard Patrick Jr., Robert Paul, Christopher Lee; m. Sandra Susan Humm, June 16, 1974. B.S., U.S. Mil. Acad., 1956; M.A., Stanford U., 1961, postgrad., 1962; postgrad. Am. U., 1974-80. Commd. 2d lt. U.S. Air Force, 1956; advanced through grades to lt. col., 1974; asst. ops. officer 555th Tactical Fighter Squadron, Ubon/Udorn, Thailand, 1967-68; air staff rep. Joint Chiefs of Staff, Trust Territory of Pacific Islands Planning Group, 1968-72; grad. Nat. War Coll., 1974-75; joint staff ops. planning officer, 1975; ret., 1976; mgr. BDM Corp., Fairfax, Va., 1977-79; sr. analyst Analytic Services, Inc., Arlington, Va., 1979-81, div. mgr., 1981-84; v.p., 1984—; asst. prof. U.S. Air Force Acad., 1962-66; adj. faculty Am. U., 1978-80. Pres. Alexandria Taxpayers Alliance, 1983. Decorated D.F.C. with one oak leaf cluster, Air medal with 13 oak leaf clusters, Bronze Star, Air Force Commendation medal. Mem. Mil. Ops. Research Soc., Air Force Assn. Republican. Roman Catholic. Avocations: running; swimming; squash; bridge. Home: 414 Franklin St Alexandria VA 22314 Office: Anser Inc 1215 Jefferson Davis Hwy Suite 800 Arlington VA 22202

DOWIAK, DANIEL JOSEPH, restaurant company executive; b. Passaic, N.J., Jan. 5, 1950; s. Benjamin J. and Helen (Serafin) D.; Electronic technician, R.E.T.S., Nutley, N.J., 1969-71; B.S., N.J. Inst. Tech., 1978; m. Susan Ann McManus, June 17, 1972; children—Jennifer, Jason. Installation technician Western Electric, Union, N.J., 1970-75; environ. engr. Am. Cyanamid, Wayne, N.J., 1975-78; environ. cons. Trinity Cons., Dallas, 1978-79; adminstr. environ. engring. Tex. Oil & Gas Corp., Dallas, 1979-82; project mgr. TERA Corp., Dallas, 1982-84; real estate devel. mgr. S&A Restaurant Corp., Dallas, 1984—. Mem. Water Pollution Control Fedn., Air Pollution Control Assn. Russian Orthodox. Office: 6606 LBJ Freeway Dallas TX 75240

DOWLING, JACQUES MACCUISTON, sculptor, painter, juror, writer; b. Texarkana, Tex., Oct. 19, 1906; d. Charles Edward and Viola John (Estes) MacCuiston; tchrs. cert. Coll. Marshall, 1923; art student Loyola U., Frolich's Sch. Fine Art, Los Angeles, NAD, Art Students League, N.Y.C.; Ph.D., Colo. State Christian U. One-woman shows: Fedn. Dallas Artist, 1950, Rush Gallery, 1958, Sartor's Gallery, Sheraton-Dallas, Dallas Auditorium, 1960; exhibited in group shows: Dallas Mus. Fine Arts, Mus. N.Mex., Fedn. Dallas Artists, Sartor's Galleries, Ney Art Mus., Oak Cliff Soc. Fine Arts, Sheraton-Park, Washington, Phillips Mill Fall Exhbn., New Hope, Pa., 1967-74, others; selected sculpture, 1st S.W. ann. show Mus. N.Mex., 1957; represented in permanent collections: corps., pvt. homes; former columnist En Passant for newspaper chain. Recipient 1st place in sculpture, 2 best in show, 1st in oil painting Fedn. Dallas artist, 1954, awards in sculpture, 1950, 51, 52, 53, 54, 55, 56; Sweepstakes award for sculpture 1st S.W. Ann. Arts and Crafts Show, 1954; 3 journalism awards, 1963; hon. certificate award Dallas Fed. Bus. Assn., 1964; Gold medal Internat. Acad. Lit., Arts and Sci., Tommaso Campanello, Rome, 1972; 1st in profl. sculpture 4th dist. N.J. Fedn. Women's Club, 1972-74, 1st in profl. sculpture state exhbn., 1972-74; 3d in sculpture Yardley Art Assn. Spring Show, 1972, 2d, 1973; Acad. of Italy with gold medal Accademia Italia, Parma, 1979, Gold medal, 1980; diploma of Merit Universitàdelle Arti, Parma, Italy, 1982; Golden Centaur award Accademia Italia, Parma, 1983, gold medal Internat. Parliament Safety and Peace, 1983; Statue of Victory, Cert. of Distinction, Centro Studi e Ricerche delle Nazioni (Italy), 1984, Academia Italia Premio, 1985, numerous others. Fellow Internat. Inst. Arts and Letters (life); mem. Nat. Soc. Arts and Letters, St. Catherine's Bus. and Profl. Guild (past pres.), Cousteau Soc. (founding), Sr. Citizens Delaware Valley (past pres.), Am. Contract Bridge League, U.S. Chess Fedn., Woodmere Art Gallery (life), Internat. Acad. Lit., Arts and Sci. (life golden album mem.), C. of C. South Hunterdon (hon.). Republican. Episcopalian. Clubs: Order Eastern Star (grand officer 1959-68), Solebury Farmers (past pres.), Kalmia (past pres.); Middle Bucks Chess (charter). Former pub., editor-in-fact Anchor News. Home: 723 Tam O'Shanter Ave Sun City Center FL 33570

DOWLING, JESSIE P., psychiatric social worker; b. Sturgills, N.C., June 15, 1918; d. Rohe V. and Stella (Eller) Pennington; A.B., Berea Coll., 1939; M.S.W., Columbia, 1945. Social work assignments WPA, Ky., 1939-43; social worker ARC, New Orleans, Bklyn., 1943-45, VA, Huntington, W.Va., also Washington, 1946-56; instr. Sch. Social Work, W.Va. U., Morgantown, 1953-54; cons. W.Va. Dept. Mental Health, Charleston, 1954-55; program supr. USPHS Clin. Center, Bethesda, Md., 1956-62; cons. social work NIMH, Chgo. and N.Y.C., 1962-66; asso. regional health dir. Mental Health Programs, N.Y.C., 1966—. Mem. adv. council Columbia U. Sch. Social Work. Mem. Nat. Assn. Social Workers (exec. bd. 1968-70), Columbia U. Sch. Social Work Alumni Assn. (pres. 1979—), Columbia U. Alumni Fedn. Bd. Mem. editorial adv. bd. Social Casework, 1968—. Home: 504 Kildee Dr Lexington NC 27292 Office: 26 Federal Plaza New York NY 10007

DOWLING, WILLIAM P., banking executive; b. 1933. With Liberty Nat. Bank & Trust Co., Oklahoma City, 1954—, now exec. v.p., treas., dir. Address: Liberty Nat Bank & Trust Co of Oklahoma City 100 Broadway Oklahoma City OK 73102*

DOWLING, WINIFRED BAUMER, aging specialist; b. West Point, N.Y., Apr. 1, 1939; d. William Henry and Alice Hull (Brough) B.; m. Thomas

William Dowling, Jan. 20, 1979; 1 child, Valerie. Student Marymount Coll., 1956-57, U. Paris, 1957-60, 64-65; M.A., U. Tex.-El Paso, 1984. Copy editor Washingtonian Mag., 1965-69; writer/editor VISTA, Washington, 1969-74; indirect recruitment mgr. ACTION, Washington, 1974-79; freelance writer, El Paso, 1979-81; grad. teaching asst. U. Tex.-El Paso, 1981-82; dir. ret. sr. vol. program, El Paso, 1983—; adv. com. mem. for sr. adult program El Paso Community Coll.; ombudsman task force Area Agy. on Aging. Mem. Nat. Assn. RSVP Dirs. (bd. dirs.), Soc. Profls. in Aging (past. pres.), Tex. Assn. Ret. Sr. Vol. Program Dirs., Assn. Vol. Dirs., Leadership El Paso, Exec. Forum. Democrat. Author: Guide to El Paso, 1980; contbg. author articles in field. Home: 2917 Rocky Ridge El Paso TX 79904 Office: City Hall 2 Civic Center Plaza El Paso TX 79999

DOWNER, MICHAEL G., psychologist, family service program administrator; b. Indpls., Dec. 12, 1949; s. Harry E. and Katherine A. (Broderick) D.; m. Kathy J. Sanford, Apr. 19, 1980; 1 child, Kristin M. B.S., Xavier U., 1971; M.S., E. Ky. U., 1973; Ed.D., Ind. U., 1982. Lic. psychologist, Ky. Psychologist. supr. No. Ky. Comprehensive Care Ctr., Covington, 1973-75, psychologist, mgr., 1977—; pvt. practice as psychologist, Ft. Thomas, Ky., 1984—; cons. Excelsior Enterprises, Cin., 1983—. Bd. dirs. Women's Crisis Ctr., Newport, Ky., 1985—; speaker's bur. Mental Health Assn., Covington, 1983—. Mem. Am. Psychol. Assn., Ky. Psychol. Assn. Avocations: racquetball; basketball. Home: 3046 Magnolia Court Edgewood KY 41017 Office: Family and Children's Counseling Ctr PO Box 549 Burlington KY 41005

DOWNEY, J. SIDNEY, college administrator; b. Anderson, Ind., Dec. 13, 1947; s. Bert Lee and Naomi Irene (Conner) D.; student Franklin Coll., 1966-67; B.S., High Point Coll., 1970; M.B.A., Ind. U., 1975; postgrad. Western Mich. U., 1978-80, U. Tenn., 1980—; m. JoEtta Davenport, Aug. 30, 1968; children—Rachele Lorraine, Andrea Sue, Elizabeth Gail, Mary Leigh. Asst. dir. bus. placement office Ind. U., Bloomington, 1972-75; instr. econs. and bus. adminstrn. Hope Coll., Holland, Mich., 1975-77, asst. prof., 1977-80, acting dept. chmn., 1980; asst. prof. bus. adminstrn. Maryville (Tenn.) Coll., 1980-82; fiscal officer Coll. Edn., U. Tenn. at Knoxville, 1982-83; v.p. adminstrn., treas. Maryville Coll. (Tenn.), 1983—. Dist. chmn. Western Mich. Shores council Boy Scouts Am., 1979-80, dist. commr., 1977-79, dist. tng. chmn., 1975-77, dist. award of merit, 1979, dist. com. Great Smoky Mountain Council, 1981—; pres. Charry Ln. Nursery Sch., 1976-78; center dir. Jr. Achievement, 1976-77; pres. United Meth. Men, 1982, youth coordinator, 1981-83, chmn. fin. com., 1984—. Served with AUS, 1970-72. Recipient Mellon Faculty Devel. grant, 1976, Disting. Service award Jaycees, 1978. Mem. Am. Soc. Personnel Adminstrn., Assn. MBA Exec., Ind. U. Alumni Assn. (life), Mich. Acad. Sci., Arts and Letters, Nat. Eagle Scout Assn., Sigma Iota Epsilon. Home: 127 Periwinkle Ln Maryville TN 37801 Office: Anderson Hall Maryville Coll Maryville TN 37801

DOWNEY, WILLIAM GERALD, JR., lawyer, farmer, retired banker, retired army officer; b. Bklyn., June 20, 1914; s. William Gerald and Mary Veronica (Ryder) D.; m. Ellen Wagle, Apr. 17, 1942 (dec.); 1 son, William G. III (dec.); m. Laufey Arnadottir, June 5, 1947; children—Robert, Richard, Elizabeth, Mary, Catherine, William, Gerald IV, Karen. B.S.S., CCNY, 1937; M.A., Catholic U., 1938; J.D., Georgetown U., 1951; cert. internat. law U. Mich., 1937, Latin Am. area tng., 1946; student U. Iceland, 1941-42; grad. Command and Gen. Staff Coll., 1962; diploma Anglo-Irish Lit., Trinity Coll., Dublin, 1976. Commd. 2d lt. inf. Res., 1936, advanced through grades to col. JAGC, 1964, ret., 1969; chief internat. law br., 1946-50, Group Judge Adv., Formosa, 1952-54; sr. ptnr. Downey & Lennhoff, Springfield, Va., to 1985; now of counsel Duvall, Blackburn, Hale & Downey, Fairfax, Va.; practice law, Va. and Washington; commr. in chancery Circuit Ct. Fairfax County (Va.); acting chmn. bd. Greene Communications, Inc., Standardsville, Va., 1984-86; founder, past chmn. bd. No. Va. Bank; fellow internat. law Cath. U., 1936-37; fellow internat. law Georgetown U., 1937-38, instr. govt., 1939-40; prof. internat. law Soochow U. Law Sch., 1952-54. Mem. Fairfax County Democratic Com.; del. Va. Dem. Conv., 1960, 64, 68; candidate Va. State Senate, 1963. Mem. Springfield C. of C. (pres. 1961-62, dir.), Washington, Va. bar assns., Am. Angus Assn. Clubs: Kiwanis (pres. Springfield 1961-62, 78-79; lt. gov. 10th div. Capital dist. 1974-75, dist. chmn. internat. relations 1976-77, ofcl. rep., dist. chmn. Va. 1977-78, chmn. past lt. govs. com., dist. chmn. long range planning com. 1982-83); Army-Navy, Army-Navy Country; Morgan Horse. Author articles on mil. and internat. law. Contbr. to Ency. Brit. Home: Crest View 1005 Crest Ln McLean VA 22101 also Kinderhook Farms Greene County VA 22973 Office: PO Box 6 Springfield VA 22150 also 4130 University Dr Suite 202 Fairfax VA 22030

DOWNEY-PRINCE, ELEANOR PAULINE LONG, psychological counselor, medical researcher; b. Birmingham, Ala., Nov. 27, 1942; d. Roger Winston and Ruby Pauline (King) Long; A.B., Birmingham So. Coll., 1964; postgrad. U. Ala., 1965-67, 68—; m. Stanford H. Downey, Jr., July 4, 1964 (div.); children—Stanford Harmon III, Jonathan Michael; m. 2d, Daniel Scott Prince, May 27, 1977. Lab. asst. Seale Harris Clinic, 1959-60; cancer research technologist. Meml. Inst. Pathology, Birmingham, Ala., 1960-64, anthropology and clin. pathology research asso., 1963—, now coordinator research activities; lectr. Silva mind control, 1981—; statis. cons. Gravlee Labs, 1972-73; bd. dirs. Info. and Document Mgmt. Inc., 1974—; cons. Ga. Hosp. Assn., 1972; med. sec. to dr., 1960-62; high sch. tchr., Trussville, Ala., 1963-64. Mem. A.A.A.S. (award 1960), Internat. Cancer Congress, Internat. Acad. Pathology, Ala. Acad. Sci., Am. Assn. Phys. Anthropologists, Am. Statis. Assn., Caucus for Women in Statistics, Nat. Orgn. Women, Nat. Audubon Soc., Nat. Wildlife Assn., Ala. Tng. Network, Alpha Chi Omega (adv. bd. 1964—), Kappa Delta Epsilon. Unitarian (Sunday sch. tchr., pianist, mid-south coordinator camp and conf. center). Co-author book. Contbr. numerous articles to profl. jours. Home: 373 Laredo Dr Birmingham AL 35226 Office: 1222 14th Ave S Suite 212 Birmingham AL 35205

DOWNING, EVERETT RAPHAEL, architect, designer; b. New Orleans, Sept. 7, 1938; s. James Mitchell and Bertricia (Morris) D.; m. Adelle Marie Johnson, June, 1968; children—Yvette Rachel, Everett Raphael, Nicole Terese. B.S. in Indsl. Arts Edn., Xavier U., New Orleans, 1962; B.S. in Architecture, U. Colo., 1973. Tchr. indsl. arts Peabody High Sch., Alexandria, La., 1967-68, Hahnsville (La.) High Sch., J.B. Martin Jr. High Sch., Paradise, La., 1968-69, Baseline Jr. High Sch., Boulder, Colo., 1969-70; architect GSA, Denver, 1973-74, Heery and Heery, Architects, Atlanta, 1974-75; project rep. Cimini/Meric, Architects and Planners, Hahnville Courthouse and Jail Facilities, New Orleans, 1975-77; sr. draftsman Roger/Nagel/Langhart, Denver, Craddock's Devel. Co., Lakewood, Colo., 1977-78, Ellerbe Assocs., Architects, Planner Hosp. Facilities, New Orleans, 1978-79; draftsman Caudill/Rowell/-Scott, Houston, 1979-80; sr. draftsman, job capt., architecture designer Meurer/Serafini/Meurer, Inc., Denver, from 1980; co-founder/organizer Urbtec Corp., 1980—; pres., owner Designers Internat. Ltd.; organizer, co-ptnr. Bailey/Downing Constrn. Co. Inc., Hahnville, La. Prin. artistic or archtl. works include: Lake Buena Vista Shopping Ctr., Walt Disney World, Orlando, Fla., 1974, Hahnville Courthouse and Jail Facilities, 1976, housing facilities, Saudi Arabia, 1978, Sheridan Savs. and Loan and Office Bldg., Lakewood, 1980, expansion Meurer Serafini Meurer Cons. Office Bldg., Denver, 1980, Ponderosa Med. Office Bldg., Aurora, Colo., 1980, Savs. and Loan Bldg., Haxtun, Colo., 1980. Community rep., coordinator Vista Community Housing Project, Killona, La., 1968-69; community athletics coordinator summer programs, Killona, 1968, 78. Served with U.S. Army, 1962-65. Assoc. mem. AIA; mem. Urban League Met. Denver, Constrn. Specifications Inst. (jr.). Democrat. Roman Catholic. Address: PO Box 533 Killona LA 70066

DOWNING, JAMES TERRELL, geologist; b. Corpus Christi, Tex., Apr. 3, 1956; s. William Robert and Iona Susie (Terrell) D.; m. Anna Ree Hamlin, Apr. 28, 1984. B.S., Sul Ross State U. Uranium geologist Anaconda Copper Co., Corpus Christi, Tex., 1979-80; Coastal Uranium, Inc., Corpus Christi, 1980-81; dist. petroleum geologist Sage Energy Co., Midland, Tex., 1981—. Mem. Am. Assn. Petroleum Geologists, West Tex. Geol. Soc. Republican. Roman Catholic. Avocations: hunting; fishing. Home: 3601 W Michigan Ave Midland TX 79703

DOWNING, M. SCOTT, government official; b. Enid, Okla., Aug. 20, 1942; s. K.F. and Maurine (Melvin) D.; m. Ina M. Herrington, June 16, 1963; 1 dau., Cynthia Ann. B.A., Phillips U., 1964; M.A., U. Okla., 1966. Budget analyst Bur. Census, Washington, 1966-67, U.S. Dept. Agr., Washington, 1970-73; instr. U. Md., 1967-69; budget systems analyst Dept. State, Washington, 1973-74; sr. budget analyst FEA, Washington, 1974-77; budget analyst Dept. Energy, Washington, 1977-80; budget systems analyst GSA, Washington, 1980—; guest lectr. in field; referee internat. conf., 1983, 84. Author: The TVA and the Courts, 1966; Dollars and Sense, 1976; contbg. fin. editor Govt. Exec., 1972-80. Served with U.S. Army, 1967-69; PTO. Recipient Superior Service award FEA, 1976; Outstanding Service citation GSA, 1983. Methodist.

DOWNS, ANTHONY, urban consultant, economist; b. Evanston, Ill., Nov. 21, 1930; s. James C. and Florence G. (Finn) D.; m. Katherine Watson, Apr. 7, 1956; children—Kathy, Christine, Tony, Paul, Carol. B.A., Carleton Coll., 1952; M.A. in Econs., Ph.D., Stanford U., 1956. With Real Estate Research Corp., Chgo., 1959-77; faculty econs. and polit. sci. depts. U. Chgo., 1959-62; with Rand Corp., Santa Monica, Calif., 1963-65; sr. fellow Brookings Instn., Washington, 1977—. Active Nat. Commn. Urban Problems, 1966-68. Served with USN, 1956-59. Mem. Am. Econ. Assn., Urban Land Inst., Am. Real Estate and Urban Econs. Assn. Democrat. Roman Catholic. Clubs: Commercial, Economics (Chgo.). Author: Economic Theory of Democracy 1957; Inside Bureaucracy, 1967; Opening Up the Suburbs, 1973; Racism in America, 1968; Federal Housing Subsidies, 1973; Urban Problems and Prospects, 1970, 76; Neighborhoods and Urban Development, 1981; Rental Housing in the 1980s, 1983; The Revolution in Real Estate Finance, 1985; (with others) Urban Decline and the Future of American Cities, 1982. Home: 8483 Portland Pl McLean VA 22102 Office: 1775 Massachusetts Ave NW Washington DC 20036

DOWNS, CLARA FAYE, speech pathologist; b. Obion, Tenn., Jan. 31, 1940; d. Vernon Cleatus and Ina Jerlene (Bogard) Douglas; children—Ronald Keith, Michael Douglas, Mark Bradley. B.S. in Elem. Edn., Murray State U., 1963, M.A. in Elem. Edn., 1971, postgrad., 1979. Cert. elem. tchr., supr. instrn., elem. prin., Ky.; lic. speech pathologist, Ky. Tchr., Paducah (Ky.) Pub. Schs., 1963-68, speech correctionist, 1968—; support trainer Project ENRICH, Ky. Dept. Edn. Recipient Cert. Appreciation, Ky. Dept. Edn., 1983. Mem. Paducah Edn. Assn. (Cert. Appreciation 1983), 1st Dist. Edn. Assn., Ky. Edn. Assn., NEA, Assn. for Childhood Edn. Internat., Forest Hills PTA, Ky. Congress of Parents and Tchrs. (life), Ky. Assn. for Retarded Citizens, Kappa Delta Pi, Alpha Delta Kappa. Democrat. Baptist. Home: 3941 Laura Ct Paducah KY 42001 Office: Paducah Pub Sch Walter C Jetton Blvd PO Box 2550 Paducah KY 42001

DOWNS, JON FRANKLIN, drama educator, director; b. Bartow, Fla., Sept. 15, 1938; s. Clarence Curtis and Frankie (Morgan) D.; student Ga. State Coll., 1956-58; B.F.A., U. Ga., 1960, M.F.A., 1969. Dir. The Beastly Purple Forest (marionettes) U. Ga., 1968, Dracula: A Horrible Musical, DeKalb Coll., 1971, Streetcar Named Desire, DeKalb, 1974, Brigadoon, DeKalb, 1981, others; actor Wedding in Japan, N.Y.C., 1960, Dark at the Top of the Stairs, N.Y.C. and tour, 1961, A Life in the Theatre, DeKalb Coll., 1981, numerous others; designer Sweeney Todd, DeKalb Coll., 1970, Romulus, 1971, Grass Harp, 1972, others; author, dir. Gold, tour, summer 1974-75, The Vigil, tour, summer 1975, 76; drama dir. DeKalb Coll., Clarkston, Ga., 1969—. Writer, dir. plays Tokalitta, Gold!, The Vigil; on tour of Ga., summers 1973, 74, 75, 76. Ga. Dept. Planning and Budget arts sect. grantee, 1973, 74. State and Nat. Bicentennial Commn. grantee, 1975. Mem. Southeastern Theatre Conf. (state rep. 1971-73), Ga. Theatre Conf. (exec. bd. 1970-73 79-83). Author: The Illusionist, 1979. Home: 1124 Forrest Blvd Decatur GA 30030 Office: DeKalb Coll 555 N Indian Creek Dr Clarkson GA 30021

DOYAL, LINDA E., clinical pharmacist; b. Villa Rica, Ga., Sept. 10, 1957; d. Wilbur Joe and Charlotte Maize (Moon) D. B.S. with honors in Pharmacy, U. Ga., 1980; Pharm.D. with honors, Med. U. S.C., 1983. Registered pharmacist, Ga., Tenn. Staff pharmacist Parkway Regional Hosp., Lithia Springs, Ga., 1980-81; faculty Coll. Pharmacy U. Ga., 1983-84; clin. pharmacist Dede Wallace Mental Health Ctr., Nashville, 1984—, also dir. med. services; cons. in field. Contbr. articles to profl. jours. Choir mem. Green Acres Bapt. Ch., Athens, Ga., 1984. Mem. Mental Health Assn., Am. Soc. Cons. Pharmacists, Am. Soc. Hosp. Pharmacists, Ga. Pharm. Assn., Am. Pharm. Assn., Am. Assn. Colls. Pharmacy, Rho Chi. Avocations: snow skiing; water skiing; hiking; camping; traveling. Home: 5025 Hillsboro Rd Unit 21-B Nashville TN 37215 Office: Bapt Hosp Pharmacy Dept 200 Church St Nashville TN 37236

DOYLE, EDWARD WINDSOR, school counselor; b. Jan. 3, 1937; s. Albert Nathaniel and Ethel Rose (Buchanan) D. B.A., Xavier U., 1958; M.S., Barry Coll., 1972. Cert. guidance counselor Fla. Tchr. Dade County schs., Miami, Fla., 1962-73, secondary sch. counselor, 1974—. Sec., Holy Name Soc., Miami, 1962-70, St. Vincent De Paul Soc., Miami, 1973-83; mem. NAACP, Black Archives History and Research Found. Served with AUS, 1960-62; Korea. Mem. Xavier Univ. Alumni Club Miami (pres. 1979-81, historian 1981-83), Cath. Educators Guild (v.p. 1981-82, outstanding service award 1982), Dade County Personnel and Guidance Assn. (parliamentarian 1982-83, outstanding service award 1983), Fla. Assn. Counseling and Devel. Democrat. Home: 802 NW 55th Terr Miami FL 33127 Office: Cutler Ridge Jr High Sch 19400 Gulfstream Rd Miami FL 33157

DOYLE, FREDERICK JOSEPH, government research scientist; b. Oak Park, Ill., Apr. 3, 1920; s. John Frederick and Mary Elizabeth (Meyers) D.; m. Mary Blaskovich, June 18, 1955; children—Frederick J., Margaret, Mary Ellen, George. B.C.E., Syracuse U., 1951; postgrad. (Fulbright fellow) Internat. Tng. Ctr. Aerial Survey, Delft, Netherlands, 1952; D.Eng. (h.c.), Tech. U., Hannover, W.Ger., 1976. Assoc. prof. geodetic scis. Ohio State U., 1952-60, chmn. dept., 1959-60; chief scientist Raytheon Autometric Co., Alexandria, Va., 1960-69; research scientist Nat. Mapping div. U.S. Geol. Survey, Reston, Va., 1969—, dir. earth resources observation systems program, 1978-80; mem. geodesy cartography adv. com. Nat. Acad. Scis., 1967-69; chmn. NASA Apollo Orbital Sci. Photo Team, 1969-73; mem. exec. com. Div. Earth Sci., NRC, 1973-76. Served with C.E., AUS, 1943-48; PTO. Recipient Fairchild Photogrammetric award Am. Soc. Photogrammetry, 1968, Alan Gordan award, 1985; Exceptional Sci. Achievement medal NASA, 1971; Meritorious Service award Dept. Interior, 1977, Disting. Service medal, 1981; Silver medal City of Paris, 1978. Fellow AAAS; mem. Am. Soc. Photogrammetry (pres. 1969-70), Internat. Soc. Photogrammetry and Remote Sensing (pres. 1980-84, Brock Gold medal 1984), Am. Congress Surveying and Mapping, Am. Geophys. Union. Contbg. author, editor Am. Soc. Photogrammetry publs. Home: 1591 Forest Villa Ln McLean VA 22101 Office: US Geol Survey Nat Ctr 516 Reston VA 22092

DOYLE, IRENE ELIZABETH, electronic sales executive, nurse; b. West Point, Iowa, Oct. 5, 1920; d. Joseph Deidrich and Mary Adelaide (Groene) Schulte; m. William Joseph Doyle, Feb. 3, 1956. R.N., Mercy Hosp., 1941. Courier nurse Santa Fe R.R., Chgo., 1947-50; indsl. nurse Montgomery Ward, Chgo., 1950-54; rep. Hornblower & Weeks, Chgo., 1954-56; v.p. William J. Doyle Co., Chgo., 1956-80, Ormond Beach, Fla., 1980—. Served with M.C., U.S. Army, 1942-46. Mem. Electronic Reps. Assn. Republican. Roman Catholic. Club: Oceanside Country (treas. women's golf assn. 1983) (Ormond Beach).

DOYLE, JOHN ROBERT, JR., author; b. Dinwiddie County, Va., Jan. 22, 1910; s. John Robert and Marian Stickley (Binford) D.; B.A., Randolph-Macon Coll., 1932; M.A., U. Va., 1937, Bread Loaf Sch. English, 1941; postgrad. U. N.C., 1944-45; m. Clarice Alise Slate, June 13, 1942; 1 child, Gwendolen Binford Doyle Hurst. Head dept. English, Dinwiddie (Va.) High Sch., 1932-40; instr. English, Clemson U., 1940-41; asst. prof. English, The Citadel, 1941-44, asst. prof., 1946-57, assoc. prof., 1957-63, prof., 1963-75, prof. emeritus, 1975—, dir. Fine Arts Series, 1965-75. lectr. in physics U. N.C., 1944-45; lectr. lit. Stephens Coll., 1945-46; vis. prof. Am. lit. Univs. Cape Town and the Witwatersrand, 1958; author books including: The Poetry of Robert Frost, 1962; William Plomer, 1969; Francis Carey Slater, 1971; Thomas Pringle, 1972; Arthur Shearly Cripps, 1975; William Charles Scully, 1978; founding editor of The Citadel Monograph Series; contbr. articles and essays to periodicals. Pres. Charleston Civic Ballet, 1963-65; chmn. fine arts events S.C. Tri-Centennial, 1970. Recipient Smith-Mundt grant to S. Africa, 1958; Daniel Disting. Teaching award, 1968; Algernon Sidney Sullivan award, The Citadel, 1971. Mem. Poetry Soc. S.C. (past pres., dir. writing group 1947-75, award of merit 1971), Modern Lang. Assn. Am. (chmn. conf. So. lit. 1965, world lit. written in English 1967), Am. Studies Assn. (past dir.), Coll. English Assn., Va. Writers Club, Phi Beta Kappa. Home and Office: Rives Ave McKenney VA 23872

DOYLE, PAULA MARIE, government food program specialist; b. Johnson City, N.Y., Feb. 3, 1953; d. Paul and Anne Dervay; m. Gerard F. Doyle, May 14, 1983. B.S. cum laude in Home Econs., SUNY-Plattsburgh, 1975. Lic. pvt. pilot. Coll. intern FDA, Rockville, Md., 1974-75; nutrition aide Coop. Extension Service, Binghamton, N.Y., 1976; adminstrv. asst. Action Agy., Washington, 1976-78; food program specialist Spl. Supplemental Food Program for Women, Infants and Children, Dept. of Agr. Food and Nutrition Service, Alexandria, Va., 1978—; caterer. Recipient Cert. of Merit, Dept. of Agr., 1979. Mem. Psi Upsilon Omicron. Republican. Club: Washington Golf and Country (Arlington, Va.). Home: 6304 Stoneham Ln McLean VA 22101 Office: 3101 Park Center Dr Alexandria VA 22302

DOZIER, ROSALYN SKELTON, educator, consultant; b. Roanoke, Va., Jan. 27, 1942; d. Enoch Jones and Illamae (Smith) Skelton; m. Lewis Bryant Dozier, Nov. 1, 1980; children—Robyn, Keith. A.A. in Lit. Arts and Drama, Mars Hill Coll., 1962; B.S. in Edn., Radford Coll., 1964; M.Ed. in Reading, U. Va., 1967, postgrad., 1968-85. Tchr. dramatics, tchr. 8th grade reading and study skills William Byrd High Sch., Vinton, Va., 1964-66, tchr. English, 1964; reading specialist Thomas Jefferson Jr. High Sch., Arlington, Va., 1966-67; tchr. 4th grade, leader 4th grade team Beverly Farms Elem. Sch., Potomac, Md., 1967-69; rapid reading tchr. Montgomery County Schs., Md., summers 1969-74; reading and career edn. cons., 1969-78; reading specialist Cameron Elem. Sch., Fairfax County, Va., 1978-81, Bush Hill Elem. Sch., Fairfax County, 1981-83, Hughes Intermediate Sch., Fairfax County, 1983—; cons. reading and career selection; owner, dir. No. Va. Reading Lab., Vienna, 1972-80. Active Jr. Achievement, Inc., 1962—, now mem. vol. conf. staff; team mother Vienna Recreation League; vice chmn. bd. trustees Vienna Wesleyan Meth. Ch., 1975-76, dir. high sch. Sunday Sch. dept., 1978-81; mem. nominating com. Vienna Bapt. Ch., 1984-87. Mem. Internat. Reading Assn., Va. Reading Assn., Greater Washington Reading Council, Fairfax Edn. Assn., Fairfax Edn. Assn., Fairfax County Reading Tchrs., NEA, Va. Edn. Assn., Assn. Children with Learning Disabilities, Middle Sch. Assn. Home: 8535 Aponi Rd Vienna VA 22180

DOZIER, WELDON GRADY, real estate development marketing company executive; b. Gainesville, Tex., Oct. 21, 1938; s. Weldon G. and Dorothy M. (Woods) D.; B.A., Union U., 1962; postgrad. N. Tex. State U.; m. Pamela Kay Kerns, Dec. 15, 1978. Mgr., Hybrid Computer Center sponsored by NASA, Denton, Tex., 1962-69; EDP mgr. Continental Ins. Cos., Atlanta, 1970-72; dist. systems mgr. 14 states for TRW Data Systems, Inc., 1973-75; pres. Property Mktg., Inc., Denison, Tex., 1976—; cons. in field. Mem. Nat. Speakers Assn., Internat. Platform Assn., Am. Land Developers Assn., Lake Texoma Assn., Denison C. of C. Republican. Baptist. Clubs: Woodlawn Country (Sherman, Tex.); Rod and Gun Country (Denison); Toastmaster (sec., treas., v.p., pres.). Author: The Bell, 1982; False Echoes, 1983. Home: 800 Crestview Dr Sherman TX 75090 Office: 330 W Chestnut St Denison TX 75020

DOZIER, WILLIAM EVERETT, JR., newspaper editor/publisher; b. Delhi, La., June 12, 1922; s. William Everett and Harriet E. (Miles) D.; m. Eleanor Ruth Roye, Sept. 1, 1944; children—Martha Carolyn Dozier Hunnicutt, Sarah Rebecca. B.A. in Journalism, La. Tech. U., 19—. Assoc. editor Delhi Dispatch, 1936-39; reporter, state editor New Orleans Times-Picayune, 1946-50; editor Courier-Times-Telegraph, Tyler, Tex., 1952-65; pres., editor, pub. Kerrville (Tex.) Daily Times, 1965—; pres. Hills o'Texas Publs., Inc., 1982—; gen. ptnr. Frio-Nueces Publs., Ltd., 1976—. Vice-pres., Kerrville Music Found. and Performing Arts Soc., 1978-84; bd. dirs. Adm. Nimitz Ctr. Found., Fredericksburg, Tex., 1976—; chmn. United Fund campaign, Kerrville, 1967; v.p. Tex. State Arts & Crafts Fair Assn., 1980—. Served with USN, 1943-46, 50-52; ret. comdr., 1973. Lay leader First United Methodist Ch., Kerrville, 1984-86, past chmn. bd. trustees, chmn. adminstrv. bd. Mem. Am. Soc. Newspaper Editors, Am. Newspaper Pubs. Assn., Nat. Newspaper Assn., Tex. AP Mng. Editors Assn. (pres. 1964-65), Tex. Press Assn. (pres. 1979-80), Tex. Daily Newspaper Assn. (dir. 1984—), Tex. Press Found. (pres. 1982—), So. Newspaper Pubs. Assn. (chmn. smaller newspaper com. 1983-84, dir. 1984—), Kerr County C. of C. (pres. 1973-74), W. Tex. C. of C. (regional v.p. 1981-84, pres. 1985-86), Sigma Delta Chi. Lodges: Masons (Tyler); Kiwanis (lt. gov. div. 5 Tex.-Okla. dist. 1974, pres. Kerrville 1973; Disting. Club Pres. 1973, Disting. Lt. Gov. 1974). Home: 376 Englewood Dr Kerrville TX 78028 Office: PO Box 1428 Kerrville TX 78028

DRAGAN, IRINEL CHIRIL, mathematics educator; b. Iasi, Romania, July 8, 1931; came to U.S., 1981; s. Chiril and Cecilia (Stoicescu) D.; m. Maria Pricop, Oct. 13, 1978. M.S. in Math., U. Iasi, 1954, Ph.D. in Math., 1961. Prof. math. U. Iasi, 1969-80, U. Tex., Arlington, 1984—; tchr. U. Pisa, Italy, 1981, U. Kassel, W. Ger., 1981, U. Tirane, Albania, 1973. Author: (textbook) Basic Techniques in Linear Programming, 1976. Mem. Ops. Research Soc. Am., Am. Math. Soc., Math. Programming, Inst. Mgmt. Sci. Greek Orthodox. Home: 121 Turtle Creek Arlington TX 76010 Office: U Tex Arlington TX 76019

DRAKE, JOHN BRYANT, mathematician; b. Demorest, Ga., Jan. 29, 1953; s. Richard Bryant and Julia Leland (Angevine) D.; m. Frances Laing Strickler, Aug. 20, 1974; children—Susanna, Emma, Paul. B.A. in Math., U. Ky., 1977; M.S. in Applied Math., Purdue U., 1979. Research asst. and numerical cons. Martin-Marietta, Oak Ridge, 1979—. Mem. Soc. Indsl. and Applied Math. Democrat. Presbyterian. Home: 100 Pelham Rd Oak Ridge TN 37830 Office: Math and Statistics Sect PO Box Y 9207A Oak Ridge TN 37830

DRAKE, LYNN ANNETTE, physician; b. Albuquerque, Aug. 4, 1945; d. Olen Lester and Lucille Susan (Henry) Drake; B.A., Adams State Coll., 1966, M.A., 1967; M.D., U. Tenn., 1971. Instr. math. Adams State Coll., Alamosa, Colo., 1966-67; intern City of Memphis Hosp., 1971-72, resident in dermatology, 1972-75, chief resident, 1974-75; mem. faculty dept. medicine, div. dermatology U. Tenn. Center Health Scis., also Med. Practice Group, Inc.; asst. prof. dermatology Emory U., Atlanta; chief dermatology VA Med. Center, Atlanta; chmn. chemosurgery tag group VA; instr. advanced cardiac life support Am. Heart Assn.; mem. emergency room com. St. Joseph Hosp. Vol., Am. Cancer Soc., 1973-75. Diplomate Am. Bd. Dermatology. Fellow Am. Acad. Dermatology (chmn. com. on health care and quality assurance, council on govt. liaison); mem. Soc. for Investigative Dermatology, Am. Acad. Dermatology (com. on health planning), AMA, Tenn., Women's, Memphis, Shelby County med. assns., ACP, Ga. Dermatology Soc., Atlanta Dermatology Soc. (program chmn.), Am. Assn. Med. Colls., Council Acad. Scis., Women's Dermatology Soc. (pres. 1984—), Dermatology Found. Home: 2270C Dunwoody Crossing Atlanta GA 30338 Office: Emory U Clinic 1365 Clifton Rd NE Atlanta GA 30322

DRAKE, VAUGHN PARIS, JR., cons. elec. engr., ret. telephone co. exec.; b. Winchester, Ky., Nov. 6, 1918; s. Vaughn Paris and Margaret Turney (Willis) D.; student U. Ky., 1936-41; m. Lina Louise Wilson, May 5, 1946; 1 son, Samuel Willis. With Gen. Telephone Co. Ky., Lexington, 1945-81, asst. engr., 1945-50, field engr., 1950-54, dist. engr., 1954-56, div. engr., 1956-57, depreciation engr., 1957-62, gen. valuation and cost engr., 1962-81. Mem. profl. adv. bd. Zoning Commn., Lexington and Fayette County (Ky.), 1955-57. Served with AUS, 1941-45. Registered profl. engr., Ky. Mem. Nat., Ky. (chmn. engrs. in industry sect. 1967-68, Outstanding Engr. in Industry award 1979) socs. profl. engrs., IEEE (sr.), Ind. Telephone Pioneer Assn., Ky. Hist. Soc. Author: (manual) Conduit Engineering for Telephone Engineers, 1958. Home and Office: 633 Portland Dr Lexington KY 40503

DRAPER, BRUCE, architect; b. Gainesboro, Tenn., July 28, 1927; s. Herbert Ridley and Hallie Mae (Reeves) D.; m. Jane Helen Caplinger, Dec. 11, 1953; children—Cynthia, Christopher, Elizabeth. Student, U. Chgo., 1947-48. Architect, Nashville, 1954—. Frank Lloyd Wright Found. fellow, 1948-50. Episcopalian. Office: 170 4th Ave N Nashville TN 37219

DRAPER, COLIN J., machinery supplies company executive. Chmn. N.W.S. Supply Group, Inc., Houston. Office: NWS Supply Group Inc 16825 N Chase Houston TX 77060*

DRAPER, E. LINN, electric utility executive; b. Houston, Feb. 6, 1942; s. Ernest L. and Marcia Lee (Saylor) D.; m. Mary Deborah Doyle, June 9, 1962; children—Susan, Robert, Barbara, David. Student Williams Coll., 1960-62; B.A., Rice U., 1964, B.S., 1965; Ph.D., Cornell U., 1970. Registered profl. engr., Tex. Asst. prof. U. Tex., Austin, 1969-72, assoc. prof. mech. engring., 1972-79; tech. asst. to chmn. bd. Gulf States Utilities, Beaumont, Tex., 1979-80, v.p. nuclear tech., 1980-81, sr. v.p. engring. and tech., 1981-82, sr. v.p. external affairs, 1982-84, vice chmn. bd., exec. v.p. external affairs and prodn., 1985-86, vice chmn., pres., chief operating officer, 1986—; cons. in field; cons. Congl. Office of Tech. Assessment, Washington, 1982—; mem. com. on radioactive waste mgmt. Nat. Acad. Sci., Washington, 1975-80; mem. Com. on Radioactive Waste Mgmt.; mem. Tex. Energy and Natural Resources Adv. Com., Austin, Tex., 1979-82. Fellow NSF, 1965, 66, AEC, 1967, 68; recipient Faculty award U. Tex. Mem. Am. Nuclear Soc. (exec. com., bd. dirs. 1983—, pres. 1985-86, chmn. ad hoc com. on regulatory reform 1982-83, pub. info. com. 1976—, pres. 1985—), Am. Phys. Soc. Contbr. numerous articles on nuclear tech. to profl. jours.; editor Tex. Symposium Procs., Procs. of Implications of Nuclear Power for Tex. Home: 1190 Dowlen Beaumont TX 77706 Office: 350 Pine St Beaumont TX 77704

DRAPER, JAMES (JIMMY) THOMAS, clergyman; b. Hartford, Ark., Oct. 10, 1935; s. James T. D.; m. Carol Ann Floyd, 1956; children—Randy, Bailey, Terri. B.A., Baylor U., 1957; B.D., Southwestern Bapt. Theol. Sem., M.Div.; hon. degree, Howard Payne U., Brownwood, Tex., Dallas Bapt. Coll.; D.D. hon., Campbell U., Buies Creek, N.C. Ordained to ministry Baptist Ch.; pastor Steel Hollow Bapt. Ch., Bryan, Tex., Iredell Bapt. Ch., Tex., Temple Bapt. Ch., Tyler, Tex., Univ. Park Bapt. Ch., San Antonio, Tex., Red Bridge Bapt. Ch., Kansas City, Mo., First So. Bapt. Ch., Del City, Okla.; assoc. pastor First Bapt. Ch., Dallas, pastor, Euless, Tex., 1975—; mem. adminstrv. com. Bapt. Gen. Conv., Tex., mem. exec. bd., mem. missions funding com., mem. exec. dir. search com.; pres. So. Bapt. Conv., 1982-84, So. Baptist Conv. Pastors Conf., 1979—; trustee So. Bapt. Conv. Annuity Bd.; preacher numerous convs., confs. Author 16 books. Contbr. articles to religious jours. Office: First Baptist Ch PO Box 400 Euless TX 76039

DRAPER, KATHRYN GRACE, educational consultant; b. Amarillo, Tex., Apr. 30, 1950; d. Atha Edwin and Faith (Boyd) D.; m. Neil Rufus Osgood, July 8, 1983; children: Scott, Toby. B.S. in Edn., Tex. Tech U., 1973, M.S. in Edn., 1977. Cert. tchr.-elem., mental retardation, learning disabilities, emotional disturbance. Spl. edn. resource specialist Meadow Schs., Tex., 1974-76; reading specialist Lubbock State Sch., Tex., 1976-78; tchr. early childhood spl. edn., Guymon, Okla., 1978-81; resource instr. Canadian County Schs., El Reno, Okla., 1981-82; tchr. spl. edn.-learning disabilities, Moore, Okla., 1982-84; ednl. cons. Profiles, Moore, 1982—. Mem. Am. Soc. for Tng. and Devel., Bus. and Profl. Women's Orgn., Okla. Edn. Assn. Democrat. Clubs: Toastmasters, Zonta. Avocations: reading, writing, gardening, drawing. Home: 1149 Elmhurst St Moore OK 73160

DRAPER, WILLIAM LEONARD, physician; b. Atlanta, Jan. 18, 1925; s. William Loyt and Belva (Ducote) D.; student Birmingham-So. U., 1942-43, Emory U., 1943-44; M.D., Baylor U., 1948; m. Beverly Blue Steele, Aug. 21, 1947; children—Diane, Kerry, Laura, Steven. Intern, Jefferson Hillman Hosp., Birmingham, Ala., 1948-49; resident Baylor U. Coll. Medicine Affiliated Hosps., Houston, 1951-54; practice medicine specializing in otolaryngology, Houston, 1954—; clin. asso. prof. otolaryngology Baylor Coll. Medicine and U. Tex. Med. Sch., Houston. Served to lt. (j.g.) USNR, 1942-45, 49-51. Mem. Harris County Med. Soc., Tex. Med. Assn., AMA, Tex. (past pres.), Houston (past pres.), otolaryngol. assns., Tex. Soc. Otolaryngology, Am. Soc. Ophthalmol. and Otolaryngol. Allergy (past pres.), Am. Rhinol. Soc. Presbyterian. Home: 2131 Brentwood St Houston TX 77019 Office: 1400 Hermann Profl Bldg Houston TX 77030

DRASEN, RICHARD FRANK, manufacturing company executive; b. Chgo., Jan. 16, 1930; s. Frank Bernard and Margaret Louise (Lindsteadt) D.; student Mich. State U., 1948-49, Northwestern U., 1954-55, UCLA, 1956-58, 1960-61, Calif. State U., Northridge, 1961-63. Teacher, dir. The Acad., Los Angeles, 1959-61; mgr. communications United Parcel Service, Los Angeles also N.Y.C., 1961-68; mgr. public relations and communications Signal Oil & Gas Co., Los Angeles also Houston, 1968-74; mgr. public affairs Burmah Oil, Inc., N.Y., 1974-75, Burmah Oil & Gas Co., Houston, 1975-77; mgr. public relations—energy R.J. Reynolds Industries, Inc., Winston-Salem, N.C., 1977-78; v.p. corp. affairs Howell Corp., Houston, 1978-80; mgr. public relations MAPCO, Inc., Tulsa, 1980-81; v.p. corp. relations Geosource Inc., Houston, 1981-84; corp. relations cons., 1984—. Pres., Tara Homeowners Assn., 1960. Served with AUS, 1951-53. Mem. Internat. Assn. Bus. Communicators, Nat. Investor Relations Inst., Public Relations Soc. Am., Tex. Pub. Relations Soc. Clubs: Houston, Warwick. Office: 12447 Honeywood Trail Houston TX 77077

DRAUGHON, SCOTT, lawyer, financial advisor, stockbroker, financial planner. Bar: Okla.; sr. registered fin. planner. Founder, exec. dir. Fin. Hotline; fin. columnist The Single Spirit mag.; gen. counsel, sec.-treas. Latin Am. Distbg. Co.; gen. counsel Oilbond, Ltd., Southwestern Fin. Group; feature writer Minority Times; columnist Mushogee Daily Phoenix; columnist Cherokee Tribe. Leader Fin. Freedom Seminar. Contbr. articles to profl. jours. Mem. adminstrv. bd. Asbury United Methodist Ch., 1982—; founder Christian Fin. Planning Seminar; mem. adv. bd. Tulsa Minority Bus. Devel. Ctr.; mem. Pvt. Industry Council, Okla. Tribal Assistance Program; mem. Native Am. Voter Registration Com. Mem. Nat. Assn. Accts. (bd. dirs. Tulsa chpt., dir. community responsibility), Tulsa County Bar Assn. (various coms.), Tulsa C. of C. (goals for tomorrow com.), Phi Delta Phi. Lodges: Shriners, Masons, Rotary (sgt.-at-arms). Address: PO Box 471280 Tulsa OK 74147

DRAYER, BURTON PAUL, neuroradiologist, neurologist, educator; b. N.Y.C., Mar. 19, 1946; s. Alexander and Marion Horowitz; m. Michaele Gerri Cohen, June 13, 1968; children—Aron Stuart, Alex Nathan. A.B., U. Pa., 1967; M.D., Chgo. Med. Sch., 1971. Diplomate Am. Bd. Psychiatry and Neurology, Am. Bd. Radiology. Intern, U. Vt. Med. Center, Burlington, 1971-72, resident in neurology, 1972-75; fellow, resident in radiology, U. Pitts. Health Center, 1975-78; asst. prof. neurology, U. Pitts., 1977-79, assoc. prof. radiology, 1978-79; dir. neuroradiology Children's Hosp. U. Pitts., 1978-79; assoc. prof. radiology and asst. prof. neurology, Duke U. Med. Center, Durham, N.C., 1979—, chief sect. neuroradiology, 1981—. Grantee, Squibb Research Inst., 1981-82, 82-83, Nat. Heart, Lung, and Blood Inst., 1983—. Fellow Am. Acad. Neurology; mem. Soc. Magnetic Resonance in Medicine, Am. Soc. Neororadiology (outstanding paper award 1981), Soc. for Neuroscis., Am. Roentgen Ray Soc., Am. Heart Assn. (exec. com. stroke council), Radiol. Soc. N.Am., Am. Acad. Neurology, Sigma Xi, Alpha Omega Alpha. Editorial bd. Neuroradiology, 1980—; contbr. articles to books and jours. Home: 4011 Nottaway Rd Durham NC 27707 Office: Dept Radiology Box 3808 Duke Univ Durham NC 27710

DREKMANN, RALPH ALEXANDER, training and development executive, human resources consultant; b. Cuxhaven, Fed. Republic Germany, Feb. 14, 1928; came to U.S., 1950, naturalized, 1953; s. Karlhermann Drekmann and Gerhardine (Zimmermann) Bueckmann; m. Freya Lange, June 3, 1953; children—Diane, Denis. B.B.A., CCNY, 1959; M.B.A., NYU, 1962; C.L.U. Dir. learning systems Equitable Soc. of U.S., N.Y.C., 1963-71; free-lance tng. cons., Dallas, 1971-74; dir. tng. ITT Fin. Group, Denver, 1974-75; tng. mgr. Frito Lay Corp., Dallas, 1975-79; dir. tng. Gen. Reins., Greenwich, Conn., 1979-80, human resources cons., 1982-84; sr. cons. Hay Group, Dallas, 1980-82; dir. corp. tng. and devel. INTECOM, Inc., Allen, Tex., 1984—. Contbr. articles to profl. jours., chpt. to handbook, audio and video cassettes. Vol. instr., cons. Nat. Assn. Business JOBS Program, Dallas, 1974. Served to cpl. MPC, 1951-53, Berlin. Mem. Am. Soc. for Tng. and Devel., Nat. Soc. for Performance Instrn. (chpt. officer), Alumni Assn. NYU, Alumni Assn. CCNY, Programmed Instrn. Assn. (past pres.). Avocations: woodworking; boating; travel; photography; antique tools. Office: INTECOM Inc 601 Intecom Dr Allen TX 75002

DRENNAN, DAVID LEE, mathematics educator; b. Ft. Worth, Mar. 24, 1940; s. Arvil Otis and Lois Lee (Stephenson) D; m. Sandra Kay Cole, Aug. 29, 1965; children—David Daniel, Leigh. B.A. in Math., Tex. Christian U., 1963, M.A. in Math., 1965, Ph.D. in Math., 1968. Tchr. Jarvis Christian Coll., Hawkins, Tex., 1968; asst. prof. math. U. Okla., Norman, 1968-75, adj. prof., 1980—; tchr. Norman Pub. Schs., 1975—, dir. inst. computing, 1979—. Recipient Presdl. award NSF, 1984; Rickover Sci. Inst. fellow, 1985. Mem. Nat. Council Tchrs. Math., Math. Assn. Am. Avocations: softball; tennis; computers. Home: 809 Annie Ct Norman OK 73069 Office: Norman High Sch 911 W Main Norman OK 73069

DRENNAN, DOROTHY ELIZABETH CARTER, composer, opera house administrator, author; b. Hankinson, N.D., Mar. 21, 1929; d. Albert Janes and Ruth Pearl (Morris) Carter; m. Robert Adrian Drennan, Jan. 15, 1949 (dec. May 1966); children—Mark, Michael, Grace, Gladys. B.Mus. Edn. cum laude, Barry Coll., 1969; Mus.M., U. Miami, 1971, Ph.D., 1975. Instr. music U. Miami, Coral Gables, Fla., 1971-75; v.p. Coral Gables Civic Opera, 1984-85; dir. Fla. Opera Repertory, Coral Gables, 1975-84. Composer cantata, concerto, various compostions for solo voice, chorus, and instrumental ensembles. Mem. Am. Musicological Soc., Am. Soc. Univ. Composers, Coll. Music Soc. Home and Office: 7880 SW 12 St Miami FL 33144

DRERUP, JOHN WILLIAM, shoe company executive; b. Brookfield, Mo., May 22, 1922; s. Alphonse Lawrence and Mary (Killion) D.; B.S., Murray State U., 1947; postgrad. U. S.D., 1943, Washington U. Law Sch., 1946-47; m. Margaret Burrus, Oct. 9, 1948; children—Patricia, John William. Salesman, Bay Bee Shoe Co., Inc., Dresden, Tenn., 1949-51, sales mgr., v.p., 1951-62, pres., 1962-78, chmn. bd., 1978—; pres. First Realty Co., 1969—; partner Venture Investment Co.; dir. First Am. Bank, Jackson and Union City, Benton Co. Broadcasting, DCM Co. Mem. U. Tenn. Devel. Council, U.S. Jaycees (past nat. dir.). Served with Signal Corps, U.S. Army, 1943-46. Named Young Man of Year, Jr. C. of C., 1956, Civitan award for outstanding work in community, 1978. Mem. Shoe Travlers Assn., Am. Legion. Roman Catholic. Lodges: Rotary, Moose. Home: 1015 Woodlawn St Union City TN 38261 Office: 140 Hillcrest St Dresden TN 38225

DRESKIN, JEANET STECKLER, painter, medical artist, educator; b. New Orleans, Sept. 29, 1921; d. William Steckler and Beate (Burgas) Steckler Gureasko; m. E. Arthur Dreskin, May 9, 1943; children—Richard B., Stephen C., Janet Dreskin Haig, Rena Dreskin Schoenberg. B.F.A., Newcomb Coll., 1942; grad. cert. in med. art Johns Hopkins U., 1943; M.F.A., Clemson U., 1973; student Art Students League, N.Y.C., Art Inst. Chgo., 1946, Balt. Mus. Fine Art, 1943, Staff artist Am. Mus. Natural History, N.Y.C., 1943-45, U. Chgo. Med. Sch., 1945-50; mem. faculty Mus. Sch. Art, Greenville, S.C., 1950-52, 62—, dir., 1968-75; adj. prof. art U. S.C. at Mus. Sch. Art, 1973—; mem. faculty Govs. Sch. for Arts, Greenville, 1980—; condr. workshops, lectr. in art edn., 1970; mem. arts adv. bd. S.C. State Mus., Columbia, 1984-87; workshop leader art dept. U. Ga., 1985; rep. by Fay Gold, Atlanta, Hampton III, Taylors, S.C., also by Etchings Internat. group shows Butler Inst. Am. Art, Youngstown, Ohio, 1974, 83, Chataugua Exhbn. Am. Art, N.Y., 1970; represented in permanent collections Nat. Mus. Am. Art, Washington, S.C. State Art Collection, Columbia, Ga. Mus. Art, Greenville County Mus. Art, Guild Hall Mus., East Hampton, N.Y., Gibbes Art Gallery, Charleston, S.C., Columbia Mus. Art, Tex. Fine Art Assn., Laguna, Sunrise Valley Mus., Charleston, W.Va., Beaufort Mus., S.C., Kate Shipworth Mus. at U. Miss. Contbr. med. drawings to various publs. Com. mem. community Found. Greenville, 1968-84, chmn. projects com., 1976-79; historian Rose Ball, Greenville, 1972-86. Recipient Kaplan award Nat. Assn. Painters in Casein, 1969, 71; Keenen award Am. Contemporary Exhbn., Palm Beach, Fla., 1970; So. Watercolor-Mabry award La. Tech. U., 1981. Mem. Guild S.C. Artists (pres. 1970-71, bd. dirs. 1981-86), S.C. Watercolor Soc. (pres. 1983-84, bd. dirs. 1985—), Nat. Assn. Women Artists (S.C. membership chmn. 1970-86), Nat. Assn. Med. Illustrators, Am. Contemporary Artist, Greenville Artists Guild (pres. 1956-58, 63, bd. dirs. 1954-83). Home: 60 Lake Forest Dr Greenville SC 29609 Office: Mus Sch Art 420 College St Greenville SC 29601

DRESSER, RICHARD NEWELL, safety professional; b. Eureka, Calif., Dec. 12, 1944; s. Kenneth Richard and Christine (Hagberg) D.; m. Sylvia Louise Ebin, Aug. 22, 1976; 1 child, Donald Samuel. B.S., U. Vt., 1972; M.Ed., Tex. A&M U., 1975. Cert. safety profl. Driver edn. instr. Plymouth Area High Sch., N.H., 1975-77; loss control rep. Liberty Mut. Ins. Co., Greensboro, N.C., 1977-78; sr. loss control rep. Am. Gen. Fire and Casualty Co., Little Rock, 1979—. Co-compiler Suggested K-12 Safety Curriculum, 1974. Served with U.S. Army, 1968-70. Mem. Am. Soc. Safety Engrs. (sec. Ark. chpt. 1981-82), Am. Driver and Traffic Safety Edn. Assn. Democrat. Avocations: running; swimming; biking; skiing; triathlon. Home: 323 N Walnut St Little Rock AR 72205 Office: Am Gen Fire and Casualty Co PO Box 8501 Little Rock AR 72215

DRESSLER, ROBERT ANTHONY, lawyer, city official; b. Ft. Lauderdale, Fla., Aug. 20, 1945; s. R. Philip and Elizabeth (Anthony) D.; m. Patricia K. Toth, Nov. 7, 1981; 1 son, James Philip. A.B. cum laude, Darthmouth Coll.; J.D. cum laude, Harvard U. Bar: Mass. 1973, Fla. 1974, D.C. 1980, U.S. Dist. Ct. (so. dist.) Fla., U.S. Dist Ct. Mass., U.S. Ct. Appeals (1st and 5th cirs.), U.S. Supreme Ct. Assoc. Goodwin, Proctor and Hoar, Boston, 1973-75; ptnr. Dressler & Dressler, P.A., Ft. Lauderdale, 1975-82; ptnr. English, McCaughan & O'Bryan, Ft. Lauderdale, 1982—; mayor City of Ft. Lauderdale, 1982—. Vice chmn. Broward Tng. and Employment Adminstrn., Ft. Lauderdale, 1982—; bd. dirs. Broward County League of Cities, 1985—. Served to capt. USMC, 1969-72. Mem. ABA, Broward County Bar Assn. (legis. com. 1983-85), Fla. Bar, D.C. Bar, Estate Planning Council Broward County, Vietnam Vets Am., Phi Beta Kappa. Republican. Presbyterian. Clubs: Drummers, Tower (bd. govs. 1983—). Lodge: Kiwanis. Avocations: jogging; scubadiving; hiking. Home: 1608 NE 6th St Fort Lauderdale FL 33304 Office: PO Box 14098 Fort Lauderdale FL 33302

DREW, HORACE RAINSFORD, JR., lawyer; b. Jacksonville, Fla., Jan. 1, 1918; s. Horace Rainsford and Margaret Louise (Phillips) D.; B.S. in Bus. Adminstrn., U. Fla., 1940, LL.B., 1941, J.D., 1967; m. Rae Berger, Oct. 28, 1944; children—Shelley Louise, Robert Fairbanks, Horace Rainsford III. Bar: Fla. 1941. Estate tax examiner Office Internal Revenue Agt. in Charge, Jacksonville, 1946-50; practice law, Jacksonville, 1951—; ptnr. Buck, Drew, Ross & Short, 1951-84, Buck, Drew & Ross, 1985—. Bd. dirs. Childrens Home Soc. Fla., Family Consultation Service, Duval County unit Am. Cancer Soc., 1962-71; founder, trustee Episcopal High Sch., Jacksonville; trustee Frank Lubbock Miller, Jr. Enl. Found.; founding mem. So. Acad. Letters, Arts and Scis. Served to maj. F.A., AUS, 1941-45; ETO; lt. col. Res. (ret.). Mem. Am., Fla. (chmn. estate and gift tax com. 1956-58, chmn. tax sect. 1959-60), Jacksonville (chmn. spl. liaison tax com. Southeastern region 1962-63, chmn. com. on taxation 1955-56, 64-65) bar assns., Am. Judicature Soc., Am. Security Council (nat. adv. bd.), Sons of Confederate Vets., Fairbanks Family in Am. (life), Internat. Order Blue Gavel, Phi Delta Phi, Sigma Alpha Epsilon. Episcopalian. Clubs: River; San Jose Country, San Jose Yacht (commodore 1978); Officers U.S. Naval Air Sta. (Jacksonville). Home: 861 Waterman Rd N Jacksonville FL 32207 Office: 8186 Bay Meadows Way W Jacksonville FL 32216

DREW, LAWRENCE JAMES, geologist, statistician; b. Astoria, N.Y., Dec. 18, 1940; s. James Joseph and Olive Virginia (McAfee) D.; m. Sheila Moore Collins, Oct. 16, 1965; 1 child, Michael C. B.S., U. N.H., 1962; M.S., Pa. State U., 1964, Ph.D., 1966, postdoctoral studies, 1966-67. Statistician, Geotech., Inc., Alexandria, Va., 1967-69; geologist Cities Service Oil Co., Tulsa, 1969-72; geologist U.S. Geol. Survey, Reston, Va., 1972-82, br. chief, 1982—. Contbr. more than 65 articles to profl. jours., encys. Mem. Internat. Assn. Math. Geologists, Am. Statis. Assn. Presbyterian. Avocation: gardening. Home: 12663 Magna Carta Rd Herndon VA 22071 Office: US Geol Survey Mail Stop 920 Reston VA 22092

DREWER, MILTON LEE, JR., banker; b. Saxis, Va., Mar. 10, 1923; s. Milton Lee and Georgie (Seward) D.; B.A. in Econs. and Govt., Randolph-Macon Coll., 1949; M.A. in Sch. Adminstrn., U. Va., 1951; m. Sarah Elizabeth Coshatt, Dec. 17, 1949; children—Milton Lee, III, Alan G., Carol Lynn, William D. High sch. tchr., So. Va., 1952-57; head football coach, athletic dir. Coll. William and Mary, Williamsburg, Va., 1957-64; with First Am. Bank Va., and predecessor, McLean, 1964—, pres., chief exec. officer, 1978—; dir. Va. Electric & Power Co.; mem. Gov. Va. Adv. Bd. Revenue Estimates, 1977-80, Gov. Va. Electricity Costs Commn. Bd. visitors Coll. William and Mary; trustee Randolph Macon Coll.; bd. dirs. Arlington Hosp. Served with AUS. Mem. Am. Gas Assn. (banking adv. council) Am. Bankers Assn. (regional dir. elect), Va. Bankers Assn., (past pres.), Va. C. of C. (past pres.), Sigma Phi Epsilon, Omicron Delta Kappa. Methodist. Clubs: Washington Golf and Country (past pres.), Farmington Country (past pres.), Lago-Mar Country (past pres.). Office: 1970 Chain Bridge Rd McLean VA 22102

DREWRY, WILLIAM ALTON, civil engineer, educator; b. Dyess, Ark., Oct. 23, 1936; s. Charles Clarence and Cathleen (Ford) D.; Asso. Sci., Ark. Poly. Coll., 1956; B.S. in Civil Engring., U. Ark., 1959, M.S., 1961; Ph.D., Stanford U., 1968; m. Nancy Gray Miller, Jan. 4, 1981; children by previous marriage—William Boyd, Bette Cathleen, Leslie Ann. Instr., U. Ark., Fayetteville, 1960-62, asst. prof., 1965-68; research asst. Stanford U., Palo Alto, Calif., 1962-65; assoc. prof. dept. civil engring. U. Tenn., Knoxville, 1968-73, prof., 1973-76; prof., chmn. dept. civil engring. Old Dominion U., Norfolk, Va., 1976-84, prof., 1985—; cons. numerous industries and govt. agys.; mem. sewerage adv. com. Va. Water Control Bd. and Dept. Health, 1977—. Registered profl. engr., Ark., Tenn., Va. Mem. ASCE (pres. Va. sect. 1983-84), Am. Soc. Engring. Edn., Nat. Soc. Profl. Engrs. (PEE bd. govs. 1978-81, 82—, trustee ednl. found. 1981-84), Va. Soc. Profl. Engrs. (pres. 1984-85), Engrs. Club Hampton Roads, Ark. Acad. Civil Engrs., Sigma Xi, Tau Beta Pi, Chi Epsilon. Contbr. articles on wastewater treatment and environ. research to profl. jours. Office: Dept Civil Engring Old Dominion U Norfolk VA 23508

DREY, EDNA W., medical foundation executive; b. Corpus Christi, Tex., Sept. 11, 1950; d. Samuel Johnson and Marie Bernadette (Smith) D. B.A., U. Tex., 1972; M.S. in Mgmt., Tex. Women's U., 1975. Mgr. various physician's offices, Amarillo, Tex., 1972-74; supr. office staff Johnson Med. Supply Co., Ft. Worth, 1975-78; exec. sec. Werik Med. Found., Dallas, 1978-80, exec. dir., 1980—; cons. various pub. agys., cos. Fund raiser United Way, Ft. Worth, 1977-78. Contbr. articles on office mgmt. to profl. jours. Mem. Assn. Women Execs., AAUW, NOW. Republican. Roman Catholic. Club: University. Office: Werik Med Found 5635 Yale Blvd 1st Floor Dallas TX 75206

DREYFOOS, WALLACE DAVID, aerospace manufacturing company executive; b. Atlanta, Aug. 28, 1923; s. Samuel L. and Rose (Liebermuth) D.; m. Jeanne Pinkerson, Jan. 18, 1950; children—William W., Dale L. B.S. in Indsl. Engring., Ga. Inst. Tech., 1947, postgrad., 1947, Emory U., 1955. Prodn. engr. Scripto Inc., 1947-48; indsl. engr./mgmt. Rich's Inc., Atlanta, 1948-51; with Lockheed-Ga. Co., Atlanta, 1951—, tool engring. mgr., 1955-62, asst. tool shop supt., 1962-65, C-141 planning mgr., 1965-66, C5A planning mgr., 1966-70, sheet metal methods mgr., 1970-71, assembly planning mgr., 1971-82, corp. mgr. robotics, 1977-82, mfg. research mgr., 1982-83, chmn. mfg. tech. sub-com., 1982-83, chief planning engr., 1983—; cons. to U.S. Air Force for B-1 producibility; speaker internat. conf. on robotics, 1977—. Served with USAF, 1943-46. Mem. Robot Inst. Am. (bd. dirs. 1977-82, charter), Nat. Mgmt. Assn., Soc. Mfg. Engrs., Soc. for Advancement Mgmt. (pres. Atlanta chpt. 1952-55), Atlanta Audubon Soc. (pres. 1972-76), Ga. Ornithol. Soc. (pres. 1978), Ga. Conservancy (sec./trustee 1978-82). Republican. Jewish. Club: Lockheed Management (Man of Yr. 1962, pres. 1963). Contbr. articles on robotics, ornithology to profl. jours. Home: 4627 Tall Pines Dr Atlanta GA 30327 Office: Lockheed-Ga Co 86 S Cobb Dr Marietta GA 30063

DRIESSEL, KENNETH R., oil company applied mathematician; b. Milw., 1940; s. Richard H. and Margaret (Otto) D. B.S., U. Chgo., 1962; M.S. Oreg. State U., 1965, Ph.D., 1967. Asst. prof. U. Colo., Denver, 1967-71; research scientist Amoco Research, Tulsa, 1971-85. Mem. Am. Math. Soc., Soc. for Indsl. Applied Math., Assn. for Symbolic Logic, Assn. for Computer Machinery. Avocation: bicycling. Office: care G Landman 1921 S Boston Tulsa OK 74119

DRIEVER, CARL WILLIAM, pharmacology educator; b. Chgo., Mar. 4, 1938; s. Carl L. and Myra M. (Haegele) D.; m. D. Suzanne Haslanger, June 6, 1964; children—Deborah Sue, Scott Andrew. B.S. in Pharmacy, Purdue U., 1961, M.S. in Bionucleonics, 1963, Ph.D. in Pharmacology, 1965. Lic. pharmacist, Ind., Tex. NIH fellow Purdue U., 1962-65; asst. prof. U. Md., Balt., 1965-67; asst. prof. pharmacology U. Houston, 1967-68, assoc. prof., clin. pharmacy, 1968—; pres. D&H Cons., Inc., Houston, 1983—. Author: Working in Pharmacies, 1982; also many jour. articles, book chpts. Pres. Sharpstown Swim Team, Houston, 1980-84; active Boy Scouts Am., 1981—. Teaching grantee VA, 1977-82. Mem. Am. Soc. Hosp. Pharmacists, Am. Assn. Colls. of Pharmacy, Sigma Xi, Rho Chi. Methodist. Avocations: computers, short wave radio, fishing, hunting. Home: 9230 Roos Rd Houston TX 77036 Office: U Houston Coll of Pharmacy 1441 Moursund St Houston TX 77030

DRILL, BARBARA ANN, music educator, organist; b. Duncan, Okla., Nov. 11, 1933; d. John Knox and Lula Ann (Hatley) Bowling; m. James Lawrence Kiniry, Nov. 15, 1957 (div. Dec. 1966); children—Daniel Knox, John Michael; m. Lewis Stewart Drill, June 12, 1971. B.Mus., So. Methodist U., Dallas, 1955. Cert. tchr. music edn., Tex. Tchr. music Dallas Ind. Schs., 1955-58, 67-70; pvt. piano and organ tchr., Dallas, 1955, 84; tchr. music Hockaday Sch., Dallas, 1983—; organist Casa View Christian Ch., Dallas, 1978—, dir. Children's Choir, 1982—, Dallas Girls' Chorus, 1982—; accompanist numerous festivals, recitals and performances including Dallas Bapt. Coll. prodn. of Oliver, 1981; accompanist/organist European concert tour Tex. Ch. Chorale, 1985. Recipient Recognition for Outstanding Contbn. to Program for Talented and Gifted, Dallas Ind. Sch. Dist., 1977. Mem. Dallas Music Tchrs. Assn., Tex. Music Tchrs. Assn., Music Tchrs. Nat. Assn., Choristers Guild, Assn. Disciple Musicians, Tex. Music Educators Assn., Am. Guild Organists, Gamma Phi Beta. Republican. Home: 8635 Hackney Ln Dallas TX 75238 Office: Hockaday Prep Sch 11600 Welch Rd Dallas TX 75229

DRISCOLL, DENNIS LAWRENCE, financial consultant; b. Lynn, Mass., Mar. 4, 1943; s. Leo Francis and Eda Christine (Lawrence) D.; m. Donna Jeanne Reinhart, Jan. 29, 1971; children—Elizabeth Ellen, Rebecca Ruth. B.S. in Bus. Adminstrn., U. Fla., 1964; postgrad. U. Tenn., 1967-68. Ter. mgr. Container div. Internat Paper Co., St. Petersburg, Fla., 1965-69; buyer Burdines Dept. Store, 1970; gen. mgr. Gen. Wholesale, Atlanta, 1971-75; ind. contractor fin. instn. premiums, 1975-77; div. mgr. Atlanta PIC, E.F. MacDonald div. Carlson Co., Atlanta, 1977-82; v.p. bus. devel. div. Fin. Instn. Services, Inc., Nashville, 1982—; condr. bank mktg. assn. bus. devel. workshops; lectr. in field. Served with USCG, 1960-62. Mem. Bank Mktg. Assn., Am. Mktg. Assn., Alpha Kappa Psi, Phi Delta Theta. Republican. Methodist. Club: Masons. Contbr. articles to profl. jours. Home: 1613 Gordon Petty Dr Brentwood TN 37027 5d 5600 Home: 1613 Gordon Petty Dr Brentwood TN 37027 Office: 49 Music Sq W Nashville TN 37203

DRISCOLL, MICHAEL HARDEE, lawyer; b. Houston, Mar. 24, 1946; s. Victor Amadale and Inez (Hardee) D.; m. Betti Rose McNamara, Apr. 7, 1978 (dec. 1984). B.B.A., U. Houston, 1969, J.D., 1972. Bar: Tex. 1972. Precinct judge Harris County, Houston, 1969-73, justice of peace, Clear Lake, Tex., 1973-78; pres. judge Friendswood, Tex., 1978-80; now atty. Harris County, Houston; ptnr. Burge, Shults & Driscoll, Houston, 1978-80; hearing judge Tex. Edn. Agy., Austin and Houston, 1978-80. Mem. adv. council Houston Salvation Army Boys Club, 1985. Recipient Pres.'s award for Disting. Service U. Houston Law Alumni, 1976-77. Mem. Houston Bar Assn., Tex. Bar Assn., Tex. Dist. and County Attys. Assn. (dir. 1983), Houston C. of C. Democrat. Baptist. Lodges: Masons, Shriners. Avocations: travel; golf; tennis. Office: County Atty Suite 634 1001 Preston St Houston TX 77002

DRISCOLL, ROBERT LLOYD, college administrator; b. Hornell, N.Y., Oct. 17, 1935; s. Lloyd M. and Martha (Dunham) D.; m. Martha Sikaras, Aug. 16, 1964; children—Tanya, Elizabeth, Stephanie. B.S. in Edn., State Univ. Coll., Brockport, 1958; M.S. in Edn., Alfred U., 1961; student U. Rochester, 1961-65; Ph.D., Mich. State U., 1970. Cert. elem. and jr. high sch. tchr., N.Y. Tchr., Newark Central Schs., N.Y., 1958-63; history tchr. Williamson Central Schs., N.Y., 1963-66; instr., ctr. coordinator State Univ. Coll., Oswego, N.Y., 1966-67, dir. field experiences, Fredonia, N.Y., 1969-72; dir. edn. field experience Ga. State U., Atlanta, 1972-78; dean sch. edn. Kennesaw Coll., Marietta, Ga., 1978—. Editor: Ga. Jourl. of Tchr. Edn., 1980—. Contbr. articles to profl. jours. Coordinator group learning experience Cobb County Leadership Project, Edn. Cobb County C. of C., Ga., 1983-84; mem. Gov.'s Task Force on Edn., 1977-82, Elem. Com. of Ga. So. Assn. of Colls. and Sch., Atlanta, 1981—. Mem. Ga. Assn. Colls. for Tchrs. Edn. (pres. 1983—), Ga. Adv. Council on Edn. (chmn. 1983-84), Am. Assn. Colls. for Tchr. Edn., Assn. Supervision and Curriculum Devel. Adv. Council of State Reps. Avocations: tennis; reading; jogging; baroque music. Home: 1228 Sherlock Dr NE Marietta GA 30066

DRIVER, CHARLOTTE ANN, insurance executive; b. Norton, Mass., Mar. 13, 1935; d. James Clinton and Esther Mary (Lincoln) Watson Henning; m. James W. Driver, Nov. 23, 1959 (div. May 28, 1982); 1 dau., Alison Esther; m. Hoyt K. Chandler, June 21, 1983. Notary public, Ga. Personnel mgr. Armor Bronze and Silver, Taunton, Mass., 1953-58; social sec. Mansion House Inc., Vineyard Haven, Mass., 1958-60; adminstrv. asst. to pres. Johnson & Higgins Ga. Inc., Altanta, 1960-75, bond account exec., 1975—. Recipient award Wheaton Coll., 1952. Mem. Nat. Secs. Assn. Internat., Altanta Assn. Ins. Agts., Nat. Assn. Ins. Women (treas. 1982-83), Henry County Tax Assn. Republican. Presbyterian. Home: 973 Fairview Rd Stockbridge GA 30181 Office: Johnson & Higgins of Georgia Inc 25 Park Pl NE Atlanta GA 30371

DRIVER, PAMELA JEAN, seminar presenter, trainer, consultant; b. Louisville, June 30, 1957; d. Stanley L. and Dorothy (Meador) Keen; m. Jesse E. Driver, June 18, 1976; children—Cliff, Jennifer. B.S. U. Tenn., 1978, M.S., 1982. Dietary supr. Fort Sanders Hosp., Knoxville, Tenn., 1977-78; grad. asst.

U. of Tenn., Knoxville, 1979-80; food service supr. Loudon County Schs., Tenn., 1980-83; pres. Driver and Assoc., Philadelphia, Tenn., 1983—. Chairperson, March of Dimes, Heart Fund. Recipient Commendation award Loudon County Bd. Edn., 1983, Citation award USDA, 1983. Mem. Nat. Restaurant Assn., Soc. for Tng. and Devel., Am. Mgmt. Assn., Omicron Nu. Club: Jr. Womans (arts chairperson). Avocations: reading; sports; gourmet cooking and dining. Home: Route 1 Philadelphia TN 37846 Office: PO Box 139 Philadelphia TN 37846

DRODDY, MARVIN JACKSON, geologist; b. Houston, Nov. 4, 1946; s. Marvin Jackson and Florence Mildred (Loofs) D. B.Sc. in Geology, U. Houston, 1970, M.Sc. in Geology, 1974; Ph.D. in Geology, U. Tex., 1978. Geologist IV, Bendix Field Engring Co., Austin, Tex., 1978-81; sr. geologist Texaco Inc., Bellaire, Tex., 1981-82; sr. sedimentary petrologist Atlantic Richfield Corp., Houston, 1982-85, cons., 1985—. Author: (with others) A Geologic Excursion of Central Texas, The Llano Uplift through the Austin Cretaceous, 1978. Mem. Am. Assn. Petroleum Geologists, Houston Geol. Soc. Baptist. Avocations: auto mechanics, camping, choral music. Home: 8734 Wind Stream Dr Houston TX 77040

DROHAN, FRANCIS PIERCE, JR., optometrist; b. Jacksonville, Fla., July 31, 1922; s. Francis Pierce and Helene (Cook) D.; m. Elizabeth Hancock, May 4, 1952 (div. 1964); children—Cheryl Helene, Michael Pierce, Deidre Elaine, Lisa Marian. A.A., Williams Coll., 1944; O.D., No. Ill. Coll. Optometry, 1949. Pvt. practice, Jacksonville, Fla., 1955—. Served to lt. comdr. USNR, 1942-72. Recipient Will Wasson award, N.E. Fla. Soc. Prevention of Blindness, 1975. Fellow Am. Acad. of Optometry; mem. N.E. Fla. Optometric Assn. (past pres. 1956-57, 1971-72). Republican. Roman Catholic. Club: Les Amis Du Vin (Jacksonville) (dir. 1985). Lodge: Lions (vice chmn. 1957). Office: 6834 Arlington Expressway Jacksonville FL 32211

DROHAN, WILLIAM MICHAEL, association executive; b. Providence, R.I., Feb. 22, 1954; s. William Joseph and Helen Ann (Kazin) D.; m. Sally Riddick, Nov. 10, 1984. B.S., Bryant Coll., 1976; M.B.A., George Washington U., 1981. Research assoc. Mass. Energy Policy Office, Boston, 1975, Atty. Gen. of R.I., Providence, 1975-76; pub. info. specialist Consumer Product Safety Commn., Washington, 1976; legis. rep. Solar Energy Industry Assn., Washington, 1977; exec. dir. Nat. Assn. of State Credit Union Suprs., McLean, Va., 1978—. Author: (with others) Use of Solar Energy in Space Heating and Hot Water, 1976. Editor: (with others) Report on Credit Unions Monthly Magazine, 1982—. Mem. Orgn. of Young Democrats, Arlington, Va., 1981—. Mem. Am. Soc. Assn. Execs. (com. mem. 1980—, cons., evaluator 1984-85, membership devel. com., 1984), Greater Washington Soc. of Assn. Execs. (com. mem. 1980—, chief exec. officer Roundtable Devel. 1984), Exchequer Club. Democrat. Roman Catholic. Avocations: skiing; fishing; running. Home: 11837 Brockman Ln Great Falls VA 22066 Office: Nat Assn of State Credit Union Suprs 1477 Chain Bridge Rd Suite 200 McLean VA 22101

DRONKERS, AREND JOHANNES, geologist; b. Eindhoven, Netherlands, Nov. 13, 1952; came to U.S., 1984; s. Pieter Leendert and Digna Cornelia (Teunis) D.; m. Josefa Lucilla Keeman, June 12, 1981; children—Bodil Louise, Barend Pieter. Candidaats, State U. Earth Sci. Dept., Utrecht, Netherlands, 1976, Doctoraal, 1980. Asst. tchr. in structural geology State U., Utrecht, 1976-80; profl. geologist, sr. geologist Mobil Producing Netherlands, Inc., The Hague, Netherlands, 1980-84; sr. geologist, staff geologist Mobil Oil Exploration and Producting South-East Inc., New Orleans, 1984—; pres. Personnel Club Mobil Producing Netherlands, Inc., The Hague, 1980-84. Editor mag. Dept. Earth Sci., 1973-77. Mem. Royal Dutch Geol. and Mining Soc., Am. Assn. Petroleum Geologists, Petroleum Geol. Circle. Avocations: photography, musician/composer, sailing, skiing. Home: 1301 Chimneywood Ln New Orleans LA 70126 Office: Mobil Oil Exploration and Producing South East Inc 1250 Poydras Plaza New Orleans LA 70113

DROPEK, KENNETH STANLEY, JR., petroleum geophysicist; b. Ottawa, Ill., Dec. 17, 1951; s. Kenneth S. and Margaret Ann (Farmer) D.; m. Gail Snyder Blocher, Oct. 2, 1982; 1 child, Stephanie. B.A. in Polit. Sci., U. Kans., 1973; B.S. in Geology, 1976. Cert. petroleum geologist. Geophys. technician Western Geophys., Houston, 1976-77; geophysicist Fairfield Industries, Houston, 1977-79, Conoco Oil Co., Houston, 1979-81; dist. geophysicist J. M. Huber Co., Houston, 1981—. Mem. Soc. Exploration Geophysicists, Am. Assn. Petroleum Geologists (1st place photo contest 1984), Houston Geophys. Soc. Republican. Methodist. Avocations: photography; racketball; baseball; tennis. Office: J M Huber Corp 2000 W Loop South Houston TX 77027

DROPP, CYNTHIA JEAN, learning disabilities educator; b. Delhi, N.Y., Mar. 4, 1948; d. George P. and Doris (Truscott) D. B.A. in Elem. Edn., Fredonia State U. Coll., 1970; M.A. in Edn., Va. Poly. Inst. and State U., 1974. Tchr. elem. edn. grade 3 Schuylerville (N.Y.) Central Sch., 1970-72; specific learning disabilities tchr. Christiansburg (Va.) Elem. Sch., 1973-77, 79, Belview Elem. Sch., Radford, Va., 1980—. Recipient Tchr. of the Handicapped award Rotary Club, 1977; William Cadbury grantee Aston U., Birmingham, Eng., 1978. Mem. NEA, Va. Edn. Assn., Montgomery County Edn. Assn., Nat. Assn. for Children and Adults with Learning Disabilities, Va. Assn. for Children and Adults with Learning Disabilities. Home: 90A Ellett Rd Christiansburg VA 24073 Office: Belview Elem Sch Route 4 Box 229 Radford VA 24141

DROSSOS, ANGELO JOHN, investment company executive; b. San Antonio, Oct. 31, 1928; s. John Angelo and Demetra (Rigopoulos) D.; m. Lillie Fontenopulos, Dec. 4, 1960; children—Debra, John. Student, U. Tex., 1946-47, St. Mary's U., San Antonio, 1950, postgrad. in law, 1956-57. With Shearson, Hammill & Co. (merged with Shearson Hayden, Stone, Inc. 1974, now Dean Witter Reynolds, Inc.), San Antonio, 1963—; now sr. v.p. Dean Witter Reynolds, Inc.; pres. San Antonio Spurs; chmn. exec. com. SLM Corp. Chmn. bd. dirs. YMCA; pres. bd. dirs. St. Sophia Greek Orthodox Ch., San Antonio; trustee St. Mary's U., San Antonio, 1983—. Served with U.S. Army, 1950-52. Mem. Nat. Basketball Assn. (dir., Exec. of Year 1978). Home: 7614 Woodhaven St San Antonio TX 78209 Office: 700 N St Mary's St Suite 412 San Antonio TX 78205

DROST-HANSEN, WALTER, chemistry educator, water research laboratory administrator; b. Chgo., Sept. 29, 1925; s. Andreas Hans Kristian Hansen and Anna Johanne (Drost) D.-H.; m. Bee Madsen, Apr. 1, 1950 (div. 1983); children—Christine E., Cathryn L.; m. Martha L. Harrington, Apr. 23, 1983. Magister Scientiarum, Copenhagen U., Denmark, 1950. Teaching asst. Denmark Tech. U., Copenhagen, 1945-46; collaborator jr. sci. Niels Bohr's Inst., Copenhagen, 1946-50; assoc. prof. N.Mex. Inst. Mining Tech., Socorro, 1953-56; sr. research chemist Jersey Prodn. Research Co., Tulsa, 1961-64; prof. chemistry U. Miami, Coral Gables, Fla., 1964—; dir. Lab. Water Research, Coral Gables, 1971—. Author: (with others) Cell-Associated Water, 1979. Contbr. articles to profl. jours. Carlsberg Found. fellow, 1950. Mem. Am. Chem. Soc., N.Y. Acad. Scis., AAAS, Math Assn. Am., Internat. Assn. Colloid Interface Scientists. Avocations: travel; painting. Home: 6701 SW 116th Ct Miami FL 33173 Office: Lab Water Research Dept Chemistry U Miami Coral Gables FL 33124

DROTMAN, D. PETER, physician, federal health official, educator; b. Scarsdale, N.Y., Sept. 18, 1947; s. Myron and Florence D.; m. Carolyn N. Arakaki, Feb. 14, 1979. B.S., Union Coll., 1969; student U. Hawaii, 1969-71; M.D., U. So. Calif., 1973; M.P.H., UCLA, 1975. Intern, Los Angeles County/U. So. Calif. Med. Ctr., 1973-74; resident UCLA, 1974-77, fellow, 1977-79; smallpox officer WHO Smallpox Eradication Program, Rangpur Dist., Bangladesh, 1975; dep. dist. health officer Los Angeles County Health Dept., 1976-79; epidemic intelligence service officer environ. health Ctrs. for Disease Control, Atlanta, 1979-81, clin. services cons. div. venereal disease control, 1981-83, med. epidemiologist AIDS program, 1983—; clin. asst. prof. community health Emory U., 1983—; lectr. in pub. health and epidemiology. Served with USPHS, 1979—. Named to Order of the Bifurcated Needle, WHO, 1975; recipient USPHS Commendation medal, 1984. Fellow Am. Coll. Preventive Medicine; mem. Am. Pub. Health Assn., Am. Heart Assn., Commd. Officers Assn. of USPHS, Am. Diabetes Assn., Fla. Pub. Health Assn., Cousteau Soc., Audubon Soc., Sun Coast Sea Bird Sanctuary, Am. Mus. Nat. History. Club: Sierra. Contbr. articles to profl. jours., chpts. to books. Office: Centers For Disease Control Atlanta GA 30333

DRUMHELLER, JOE CARROLL, geologist; b. Roanoke, Va., Dec. 2, 1946; s. John Lewis and Mary Snow (Tune) D.; m. Susan Sheldon, May 16, 1982; children—Kasey Marie, Samuel Joseph. B.S. in Geology, Va. Poly. Inst., 1968. Registered profl. geologist, Va., Ga., Idaho. Geophysicist, U.S. Naval Oceanographic Office, Washington, 1968-73; engr. Bechtel Assocs., Washington, 1973; geologist Law Engring. Testing Co., Washington, 1973-77, sr. geologist, Atlanta, 1977-84, mgr., Anchorage, 1981-82; v.p. GeoSystems, Inc., Sterling, Va., 1984—; chmn. Hazardous Waste Symposium, Atlanta, 1982. Contbr. papers to tech. lit. Mem. Assn. Engring. Geologists. Methodist. Home: 13160 Lazy Glen Ln Herndon VA 22071 Office: GeoSystems Inc 101 Holly Ave Sterling VA 22170

DRUMMOND, BOYCE ALEXANDER, JR., university administrator; b. Little Rock, Sept. 21, 1921; s. Boyce Alexander and Carmeta (Sanders) D.; m. Gene Thornton Oct. 24, 1944; children—Boyce III, David, Carol, Robert. A.B., Baylor U., 1943; A.M., U. Chgo., 1949, Ph.D., 1957. Chmn. dept. social scis. Henderson State U., Arkadelphia, Ark., 1961—, dean Sch. Liberal Arts, 1969—. Assoc. editor Ark. Hist. Quar. Democrat. Methodist. Home: 1614 Evans St Arkadelphia AR 71923 Office: Henderson State U Box 7546 Arkadelphia AR 71923

DRUMMOND, GARRY N., mining company executive. Chmn. Ala.-By-Products Corp., Birmingham. Office: Ala By-Products Corp PO Box 10246 Birmingham AL 35202*

DRUMMOND, GARY DAVID, business executive, writer; b. Toronto, Ont., Can., May 4, 1944; s. David Bogie and Margaret Lillian (Thompson) D.; student Kent State U., 1963-64, Cerritos Coll., 1965-66; m. Dorothy Elaine Bush, Mar. 4, 1967 (div.); children—Jeffrey David, Jay Charles; m. 2d, Bridgett A. Brennan, Aug. 4, 1979; 1 child, Gretchen Bridget. Salesman, Sears Roebuck and Co., Los Angeles, 1965-67, Addressograph Multigraph Corp., San Francisco, 1967-71, San Bernardino, Calif., 1971-72, Las Vegas, Nev., 1972-73; founder, pres., chief exec. officer Spl. Service Systems, Inc., Tulsa, 1973—; pres. Spl. Service Systems Inc., Fullerton, Calif. Served with USMCR, 1975. Mem. Data Processing Mgmt. Assn., Nat. Assn. Accountants, Okla. Bankers Assn., Independent Bankers Assn. Okla., Okla. Hosp. Assn., Okla. Writers Fedn., Pres.'s Assn. Republican. Office: 10514 E Pine St Tulsa OK 74116

DRUMMOND, GEORGE WAYNE, consulting company executive; b. Spartanburg, S.C., Aug. 17, 1956; s. George Madison and Rachel (Magness) D. B.S., The Citadel, 1978; M.B.A., U. Ky., 1980. Grad. asst., athletic trainer athletic dept. U. Ky., Lexington, 1978-80; territory mgr. Gulf Coast area food service div. Carnation Co., Mobile, Ala., 1980-83; pres., owner Achievement Cons., Mobile, 1983—; distbr. Leadership Mgmt., Inc., Waco, Tex., 1983—; sales exec. TVC Pre Paid Legal, Inc., 1986—; profl. speaker, humorist, 1985—. Unit commr. Boy Scouts Am., Mobile, 1980—; youth advisor Jr. High, Springhill Presbyn. Ch., Mobile, 1981—, deacon, 1984—. Named Outstanding Young Man of Am., Jaycees, 1981; recipient Arrowhead honor, Masters degree of Commr. Sci., Boy Scouts Am., Choctaw dist., Mobile, 1983, Scouter's Key. Mem. Mobile Area C. of C. (membership com. 1983, co-chmn. seminar com. 1986), Nat. Speakers Assn. Presbyterian. Club: Toastmasters (cert. toastmaster, ednl. v.p. 1985, pres. 1986), Fellow Investors (pres. 1985—). Home and Office: 6401 Cedar Bend Ct #8 Mobile AL 36608

DRUMMOND, JUDITH DARLENE, assistant principal; b. Mt. Clemons, Mich., Dec. 3, 1946; d. Francis Farrow and Esther JO (Grant) Watkins; m. Willie Hinton Drummond, Jr., Aug. 10, 1978. B.S. in Elem. Edn., Jacksonville State U., 1969, M.S., 1974. Tchr., Attalla (Ala.) Elem. Sch., 1969—, librarian, asst. prin., 1981—. Mem. Ala. State Textbook Com., Montgomery, 1981-82; Sunday Sch. tchr. Dwight Baptist Ch., Gadsden, Ala., 1969—. Mem. NEA, Ala. Edn. Assn., Profl. Assn. Attalla Educators. Office: 812 N 4th St Attalla AL 35954

DRUMMOND, PAULA GRIER, lawyer; b. Ft. Lauderdale, Fla., Dec. 8, 1950; d. John P. and Jeanne C. (Bottomley) Grier; m. Michael A. Fruchey, (div. Oct. 1972); 1 child, Cecily Noelle; m. Richard W. Drummond, June 17, 1978; 1 child, John Edward. A.A. with honors, Brevard Community Coll., 1973; B.A. summa cum laude, U. Central Fla., 1975; J.D., Fla. State U., 1978. Bar: Fla. 1978, U.S. Dist. Ct. (no. dist.) Fla. 1978, U.S. Ct. Appeals (11th cir.) 1982, U.S. Supreme Ct. 1984. Law clk. to U.S. magistrate, Pensacola, Fla., 1978-80; asst. county atty. Escambia County, Pensacola, 1980-81, county atty., 1982-83; sole practice Pensacola, 1983—. Mem. Ct. of 1984, Mayoki Indians Fiesta of Five Flags, Pensacola, 1984; bd. dirs. YWCA, Pensacola, 1984—. Mem. ABA, Escambia-Santa Rosa Bar Assn. (exec. com. 1984-85, chmn. bar found. com.), Network of Exec. Women, Fla. Bar (exec. council local govt. law sect. 1982-83), Pensacola Profl. Women's Assn. Democrat. Roman Catholic. Club: Panhandle Tiger Bay. Office: PO Box 9518 Pensacola FL 32513

DRURY, JOHN E., chemical waste disposal company executive; b. 1944. Pres., owner Lakeville Sanitary Services, 1964-68; with Atlas Disposal Service (now Browning-Ferris Industries Inc.), 1967—, exec. v.p. waste systems div., 1972-82, pres., chief operating officer, 1983—, also dir. Office: Browning-Ferris Industries Inc 14701 Saint Marys Ln Houston TX 77079*

DRURY, LLOYD LEONARD, business executive; b. New Orleans, Oct. 12, 1925; s. John Joseph and Evelyn (Nebel) D.; student U.S. Mcht. Marine Acad., 1946; B.S., La. State U., 1949; M.B.A., Loyola U., 1961; Ph.D., Rochdale Coll., 1972; D.D., Ch. Universal Brotherhood, 1975; Ph.D., Pacific So. U., 1976; m. Betty Bray Byrne, July 10, 1946; children—Lloyd Leonard, David Bray, Susan Joan, Denise Ann. Marine engr. Grace Lines, Inc., N.Y.C., 1945-46; field engr. Calif. Co., New Orleans, 1949; various tech. and mgmt. positions Gen. Electric Co., 1949-59, corp. exec., New Orleans, 1959—; mgmt. cons.; lectr. La. State U., Tulane U.; cons. psychologist. Div. leader United Fund, New Orleans, 1960; leader Jr. Achievement, New Orleans, 1969-71; mem. Alumni council La. State U.; v.p. First Evang. Ch., 1972. Served with USN. Named hon. La. State Senator; recipient Gen. Electric managerial achievement awards. Registered profl. engr. Mem. Nat. Soc. Profl. Engrs., Soc. Naval Architects and Marine Engrs., Am. Soc. Indsl. Security, La. Engring. Soc., La. State U. Engring. Alumni Assn. (pres. 1984—). Clubs: Metairie Country, Beau Chene Golf and Raquet. Home: 4465 Bancroft Dr New Orleans LA 70122

DUBARD, CLARA SPRY, educator; b. Columbia, S.C., June 20, 1944; d. Bernard David and Sallie Henrietta (Corley) Spry; m. Melvin DuBard, Dec. 27, 1975; 1 son, Melvin. B.A., Benedict Coll., 1966; M.Ed., U. S.C., 1975. Cert. early childhood tchr., spl. edn. tchr., reading and elem. sch. prin., S.C.; registered cosmetologist, S.C. Tchr., Florence (S.C.) Sch. Dist. 3, 1966-67, Fairfield County (S.C.) Schs., 1968-74; cons. Midlands Regional Ctr., S.C. Dept. Mental Retardation, Columbia, 1974-76, dir. childhood devel. tng. unit, 1976-77; staff devel. and tng. specialist S.C. Dept. Social Services, Columbia, 1977-78, child devel. specialist, 1978-81; supervising tchr. Midlands Regional Ctr., S.C. Dept. Mental Retardation, Columbia, 1981-83; tchr. Richland County Schs., 1983—. Named Tchr. of Yr., John R. Thomas Elem. Sch., Richland Sch. Dist., 1985. Mem. Am. Bus. Women's Assn. (Inner Circle Title award 1982, Woman of Yr. 1983), Riverbanks Zool. Soc., Greater Columbia Literacy Council, Inc., S.C. State Employees Assn., S.C. Edn. Assn., Richland County Edn. Assn., NEA. Democrat. Baptist (missionary). Clubs: Benedict Coll. Alumni, U. S.C. Alumni. Office: Gordon Elem Sch Box 542 Fairfield St Winnsboro SC 29180

DUBAY, ROLAND CHARLES, public affairs director; b. Unterreichenbach, Ger., Mar. 7, 1949; s. Charles John and Alice Gisela (Burke) D.; B.A., U. S.C., 1971, M.A., 1980. State project developer Title I Programs, Higher Edn. Act of 1965, Columbia, S.C., 1979-83; pub. affairs dir., editor Emergency Mgmt. Rev., Nat. Coordinating Council on Emergency Mgmt., Columbia, 1983—. Polit. campaign mgr., Richland County Young Rep. Club, 1977, sec., 1977-78, chmn., 1978, newsletter editor, 1978-79; committeeman, Lykesland Precinct and exec. com. mem. Richland County Rep. Party, 1978-81, del. to state conv., 1978, 82, chmn., editor newsletter, 1979, chmn. speakers com., 1979, 3d vice chmn., 1980—. Active, Easter Seal Soc. S.C., 1979-80. Served with USN, 1971-76; to lt. comdr. USNR, 1976—. Recipient S.C. State Legis. internship, 1978. Mem. Columbia Jaycees, Columbia Navy League, Naval Res. Assn., Res. Officers Assn., U. S.C. Alumni Assn., Columbia Soc. for Prevention of Cruelty to Animals, VFW (adj. post 641, 1979-80, newsletter editor, 1979-80, chmn. post 641, polit. action com., 1979-80, sr. vice comdr. 1981, comdr. 1981-83; comdr. dist. 2 Dept. S.C. 1983—), U. S.C. Soc. Pub. Adminstrn. (program chmn. 1978), S.C. Assn. Higher Continuing Edn., Internat. Platform Assn. Presbyterian. Clubs: Columbia First Tuesday, Jonathan Maxcy. Office: 3126 Beltline Blvd Suite 101 Columbia SC 29204

DUBERG, JOHN EDWARD, educator, research scientist; b. N.Y.C., Nov. 30; s. Charles Augustus and Mary(Blake) D.; B.S. in Engring., Manhattan Coll., 1938; M.S. in Engring., Va. Poly. Inst., 1940; Ph.D., U. Ill., 1948; postgrad. Fed. Exec. Inst., 1971; m. Mary Louise Andrews, June 11, 1943; children—Mary Jane, John Andrews. Engr., Cauldwell-Wingate Builders, N.Y.C., 1938-39; research asst. U. Ill., 1940-43, prof. structures, 1957-59; research engr. Langley Labs., NACA, Langley Field, Va., 1943-46, chief structures research, 1948-56, asst. to chief theoretical mechanics div. Langley Research Center, NASA, Langley AFB, Va., 1959-61, tech. asst. to asso. dir., 1961-64, asst. dir., 1964-68, asso. dir., 1968-79; research Standard Oil Co. (Ind.), Chgo., 1946-48; mgr. aero mechanics Aeronutronics, Glendale, Calif., 1956-57; instr. U. Va. Extension, 1944-45; adj. prof. George Washington U., then prof., 1980—; dir. Newport News Savs. and Loan Assn., Joint Inst. for Advancement of Flight Scis., George Washington U., 1971-79; mem. NACA/-NASA adv. coms., 1950-63; mem. materials adv. bd. Nat. Acad. Sci., 1950; mem. subcom. profl., sci. and tech. manpower Nat. Manpower Adv. Com., Dept. Labor, 1971. Trustee Peninsula United Fund, 1963—; campaign chmn., 1965-66; sci. adv. bd. Va. Assoc. Research Center; pres. Greater Tidewater Fed. Exec. Assn., 1975-76; bd. dirs. Peninsula Jr. Nature Mus.; mem. Pres.'s Adv. Council Christopher Newport Coll., 1973-75, vice chmn., council, 1976; chmn. Hampton Rds. chpt. ARC, 1984—; mem. vestry Episcopalian Ch. Recipient NASA Outstanding Leadership award. Fellow AIAA (recipient DeFlorez award), AAAS, Va. Acad. of Sci.; mem. N.Y. Acad. Scis., Am. Soc. Engring. Edn. (dir. 1982—), Soc. of Engring. Scis. (dir.), Sigma Xi, Tau Beta Pi, Phi Kappa Phi. Clubs: James River Country, Rotary (pres. 1967-68), Engrs. (pres. Va. Peninsula 1955). Contbr. numerous articles on flight scis. to profl. jours. Office: George Washington U/JIAFS NASA Langley Research Center M/S 269 Hampton VA 23665

DUBOSE, JAMES DAULTON, dentist; b. Turbeville, S.C., July 14, 1938; s. Robert Alvin and Olive (Dennis) DuB.; B.S., U. S.C., 1961; D.M.D., U. Louisville, 1965; m. Kathy Elizabeth Johnson, Mar. 14, 1974; children—Olive Elizabeth, Dixie Dawn. Practice dentistry, Bishopville, S.C., 1965-70, Aiken, S.C., 1970-72, Manning, S.C., 1972—; staff mem. Clarendon Meml. Hosp., Manning; pres. D.M.D. Enterprises; owner Bluff Plantation, Colleton County, S.C.; v.p. R.A. DuBon, Inc. Chmn. Heart Fund, Lee County, S.C., 1966; trustee Summerton Bapt. Ch. Mem. ADA, Am. Soc. Dentistry for Children, Augusta Dental Soc., Pee-Dee Dist. Dental Soc., Delta Sigma Delta. Baptist. Clubs: Century (Columbia, S.C.); Sertoma (Aiken, S.C.); Lions (Summerton, S.C.); Masons. Home: Church St Summerton SC 29148 Office: Mill and Hospital Sts Manning SC 29102

DUBUC, CARROLL E., lawyer; b. Burlington, Vt., May 6, 1933; s. Jerome J. and Rose M. (Bessette) D.; m. Mary Jane Lowe, Aug. 3, 1963; children—Andrew, Steven, Matthew. B.S., Cornell U., 1955; J.D., Boston Coll., 1962; postgrad. NYU Grad. Sch. Bus. Bar: N.Y. 1963, U.S. Ct. Appeals (2d cir.) 1965, D.C. 1972, D.C. Ct. Appeals 1972, U.S. Supreme Ct. 1970, U.S. Ct. Appeals (D.C. Cir.) 1975, U.S. Ct. Appeals (4th cir.) 1984, U.S. Ct. Appeals (9th cir.) 1985, U.S. Ct. Appeals (7th cir.), U.S. Ct. Appeals (5th cir.). Assoc. Haight, Gardner, Poor & Havens, N.Y.C., 1962-70, ptnr. N.Y. office, 1970-75, resident ptnr., Washington, 1975-83; ptnr. Finley, Kumble, Wagner, Heine, Underberg, Manley & Casey, Washington, 1983—; gen. counsel internat. airlines; trial counsel aircraft mfrs. and airlines; dir. aviation-oriented cos. Contbr. articles to profl. jours. Served with USN, 1953-59; to capt. USNR, 1959-79, ret. Mem. Assn. Navy Aviators, Naval Res. Assn., ABA, Aviation Com. (chmn.), N.Y. Bar Assn. (past chmn. aviation com.), D.C. Bar Assn., Fed. Bar Assn., Transp. Law Counsel, Internat. Assn. Ins. Counsel, Fedn. Ins. Counsel, Res. Officers Assn., Mil. Order World Wars, Navy Aviation Commandery (vice comdr.). Clubs: Congressional Country, Capital Hill (Washington); University, Aero, Wings, World Trade (N.Y.C.).

DUBUC, GERARD PIERRE, JR., beverage industry executive; b. Versailles, France, Jan. 18, 1941; came to U.S., 1962, naturalized, 1973; s. Gerard P. and Claire E. (Dobes) D.; Baccalaureat, Academie Nationale Française, 1960, B.S. in Bus. Adminstrn., 1962; LL.B., LaSalle U., 1969. Mgr. data processing Young's Market Co., Los Angeles, 1966-72; v.p. ops., dir. Joseph J. Battle Corp., Oakland, Calif., 1973-74; dir. ops. Automatic Data Processing Co., San Francisco, 1974-75; dir. systems, gen. office mgr. Nat. Distbg. Co., Los Angeles, 1975-81; adminstr. Anaheim Eye Med. Group, Inc., and mng. dir. Anaheim Profl. Services, Inc., 1981-83; v.p., dir. Mis. Nat. Distbg. Co., Atlanta, 1983—. Served with JAGC, U.S. Army, 1964-66. Mem. Data Processing Mgmt. Assn. (dir. 1969-72), Am. Mgmt. Assn., Townhall of Calif., Med. Group Mgmt. Assn., Am. Group Practice Assn. Republican. Home: 1699 Withmere Way Dunwoody GA 30338 Office: 1 National Dr SW Atlanta GA 30336

DUCEY, DONNA Y., nurse, nursing adminstrator; b. Camden, N.J., June 28, 1952; d. George Henry and Joan Shirley (Fennell) Young; m. Kevin Francis Ducey, Sept. 12, 1981. B.S. in Nursing, U. Del., 1974; M.S., Va. Commonwealth U., 1978. Nurse Med. Coll. Va. Hosps., Richmond, 1974-79, asst. dir. nursing, 1979-84; v.p. profl. services Radford Community Hosp., Va., 1984—; bd. dirs. Outpatient Nursing Services, Christiansburg, Va., 1984—; mem. adj. faculty Med. Coll. Va. Sch. Nursing, Richmond, 1982-84. Mem. Am. Assn. Critical Care Nurses, Am. Nurses Assn., Sigma Theta Tau (chpt. v.p.). Avocations: piano; gardening; tennis. Office: Radford Community Hosp PO Box 3527 Radford VA 24143

DU CILLE, CHRISTINE MARIE, educator; b. Pompano Beach, Fla., Dec. 3, 1952; d. Henry and Marie Edwards; m. Carl Basworth du Cille, May 10, 1976; children—Eric Pierre, Yolanda Monique, Kimberly Michelle. B.S. cum laude, Fla. Meml. Coll., 1974; postgrad. Fla. Atlantic U. Teaching cert. in elem. and early childhood edn., Fla. Kindergarten tchr. Miami Gardens Elem. Sch., Miami, Fla., 1974, Norland Elem. Sch., Miami, 1976, Crestview Elem. Sch., Miami, 1975, Highland Oaks Elem. Sch., Miami, 1974-76; 2d grade tchr. Tamarac (Fla.) Elem. Sch., 1977; kindergarten tchr. Walker Elem. Sch., Ft. Lauderdale, Fla., 1978—; pre-sch. music tchr. Sheridan Vocat. Ctr., Hollywood, Fla., 1979; aftersch. program dir., summer day camp dir. YMCA, 1983; dir./owner Future Generations Pre-Sch. Ctr., Ft. Lauderdale, 1983—. Mem. NEA, Classroom Tchrs. Assn., Fla. Teaching Profession, Delta Sigma Theta. Democrat. Mem. Ch. of God in Christ. Home: 1744 NW 55th Ave Apt 204 Lauderhill FL 33313 Office: Walker Elem Sch 1001 NW 4th St Fort Lauderdale FL 33311

DUCKWORTH, PAUL EDWARD, fire chief; b. Dallas, July 30, 1935; s. George Edward and Orpha Mae (Cain) D.; m. Ola Maye Sanstrom, Dec. 16, 1954; children—Paul Michael, Paula Maye Wilcox, Tamie Lynn. Student Dallas County Jr. Coll., 1967-72, Kilgore Jr. Coll., 1982—, E. Tex. Police Acad., 1985. Cert. arson investigator. Fire fighter Richardson Fire Dept., Tex., 1958—, driver, engr., 1960—, lt., 1964, 75-79, tng. officer, adminstrv. asst. to chief of dept., 1970—; guard Pinkerton Detective Agy., 1960; fire chief Kilgore Fire Dept., Tex., 1979—; instr. Richardson Fire Sch., 1962-79, Tex. A & M Fire Sch., College Station, 1975—, NE Tex. Fire Sch., Tex. Eastman, Longview, 1979—, Henderson County Fire Sch., Athens, Tex., 1980—; cert. class A instr. Tex. Commn. Fire Protection Personnel Standards and Edn., 1983—. Asst. scoutmaster Boy Scouts Am., Richardson. Named Fireman of Yr., Richardson Jaycees, 1963, Hon. Fire Chief, Richardson Fire Dept., 1979; recipient Cert. Merit, Muscular Dystrophy Assn. and Jerry Lewis, 1978. Mem. Internat. Fire Chief's Assn., Tex. Soc. Fire Service Instrs., Tex. Fire and Arson Investigators Assn., Richardson Fire Fighters Assn. (sec.-treas. 1974-79), NE Tex. Fire Chief's Assn. (pres. 1979—; fire chief of yr. 1985), Tex. Fire Chief's Assn., State Firemen's and Fire Marshal's Assn. Tex. (chmn. resolutions com. 1981—, mem. legis. com.), NE Firemen's and Fire Marshal's Assn. (pres. 1982, 1st v.p. 1985), Rusk County Fire Fighter's Assn. (bd. dirs. 1983—). Democrat. Baptist. Lodges: Masons, Shriners. Avocations: fishing; hunting; football; baseball; woodworking. Home: 604 Ridge Ln Kilgore TX 75662 Office: Kilgore Fire Dept 724 Harris St Kilgore TX 75662

DUCLOZ, MARC, textile company executive; b. France, Aug. 16, 1945; came to U.S., 1971; m. Margot Lee, May 1, 1976; children—Cecilia, Christopher. Grad. Ecole Superieur de Commerce, Marseilles, France, 1968. Asst. mgr. Pavailler, Stockholm, 1969-71; sales mgr. IMC, N.Y.C., 1971-72; gen. mgr. Vie de France, Washington, 1972-74, v.p., 1974-76; gen. mgr. Phildar, Hartford, Conn., 1977-79, pres., Atlanta, 1980—; French trade counselor fgn. affairs, 1982—. Republican. Roman Catholic. Home: 3775 Woodsong Ct Dunwoody GA 30338

DUCOFFE, KEITH RICH, advertising/design executive; b. Atlanta, June 13, 1950; s. Arnold Lionel and Emily (Rich) D.; m. JoAnn Cardon, May 6, 1984; stepchildren—Lauren S., Caroline P. B.F.A., U. Ga., 1973; M.Product Design, N.C. State U.-Raleigh, 1978. Designer, Schuss Design, Columbus, Ohio, 1975-76; instr. Sch. of Design, N.C. State U., Raleigh, 1976-78; free lance designer, 1977-78; account exec. Alpha Bet Group, Atlanta, 1978-80; v.p. account services Creative Services, Inc., Atlanta, 1981—; mem. faculty N.C. State U., Art Inst. of Atlanta, 1978-80; dir. Southeast Wholesale Furniture Co. Bd. dirs., v.p. Forrest Place Condominium Assn., Atlanta, 1980-82. Mem. Soc. for Photog. Edn., Friends of Photography, Orchid Soc. Am. Jewish. Clubs: Porsche of Am., Mercedes Benz. Contbr. articles to profl. jours. Home: 5455 Errol Pl Atlanta GA 30327 Office: 7 Piedmont Ctr Suite 500 Atlanta GA 30305

DUCOTE, CHARLOTTE GESINA, psychologist; b. New Orleans, Feb. 3, 1944; d. Charles and Gesina Mary (Picone) Ducote; m. Richard Alan Melancon, Nov. 24, 1979. B.A., La. State U., 1967; M.S., Northwestern State U., La., 1973; Ph.D., U. So. Miss., 1980. Lic. psychologist. Therapist, DePaul Hosp., New Orleans, 1967-68; instr. Nicholls U., Thibodaux, La., 1972-74; psychometrist Hannie Clinic, Metairie, La., 1975-77; supervising psychologist St. Charles Parish Pub. Schs., Luling, La., 1978-83; pvt. practice psychology, Jefferson, La., 1982—. Editor: La. Sch. Psychologist newsletter, 1982. Mem. awards and scholarship com. U. New Orleans, 1985. Mem. Orleans Psychol. Soc. (pres. 1985), La. Psychol. Assn., Am. Psychol., Assn., IBM Computer Users Group (New Orleans), U. New Orleans Alumni Assn. (chmn. awards and scholarship com.), Psi Chi. Roman Catholic. Avocations: using computers; pottery making; dog obedience training. Home: 134 Brooklyn Ave Jefferson LA 70121 Office: 134 Brooklyn Ave Jefferson LA 70121

DUCOTE, WILLIE JOHN, educational administrator; b. Cottonport, La., Oct. 24, 1944; s. Curtis Joseph and Brenda Grace (Landry) D. B.S.B.A., U. Southwestern La., 1967. Bus. edn. instr. Avoyelles Parish Sch. Bd., Simmesport, La., 1967-69; dir. fin. aid Delta Coll., Baton Rouge, La., 1971—; pvt. cons. fin. aid assistance, 1978—. Served with U.S. Army, 1969-71, Vietnam. Mem. La. Assn. Fin. Aid Adminstrs. (pres. 1982-83). Democrat. Roman Catholic. Avocations: deep sea fishing; ski instructor. Home: 9358 S Tigerbend Rd Baton Rouge LA 70817 Office: Delta Coll 7290 Exchange Pl Baton Rouge LA 70806

DUCY, PATRICIA CORNELIA, computer software consulting company executive; b. Bklyn., July 17, 1945; d. Clement Ambrose and Ellen Catherine (O'Brien) D. Student Ottumwa Heights Jr. Coll., 1963-64, George Washington U., 1967-69, No. Va. Community Coll., 1980—, U.S. Dept. Agr. Grad. Sch., Washington, 1983—. Staffing mgr. audit div. Arthur Andersen & Co., Washington, 1973-75; comptroller The Co. Inkwell, Arlington, Va., 1976-78; registrar Antioch Sch. Law, Washington, 1978-79; dir. fin. and adminstrn. SRA Corp., Arlington, Va., 1979-81; mem. staff com. govt.-univ. relations Nat. Acad. Scis., Washington, 1981-83; dir. fin. and adminstrn. Advanced Systems Devel. Inc., Arlington, 1983—; cons. in field. Vol. J.F. Kennedy Campaign, Bethesda, Md., 1960, Georgetown U. Hosp., Washington, 1960-63; sec. D.C. chpt. Am. Jr. Red Cross, 1962; prodn. coordinator Am. Light Opera Co., Washington, 1964-67. Recipient 500-hour award Georgetown U. Hosp., 1961, Mem. Am. Mgmt. Assn., Nat. Contracts Mgmt. Assn., Tech. Mktg. Soc. Am. Democrat. Roman Catholic. Office: Advanced Systems Devel Inc 1701 N Ft Myer Dr Suite 1101 Arlington VA 22209

DUDA, EDWIN, mathematics educator; b. Donora, Pa., Oct. 15, 1928; s. John and Julia (Widuch) D.; m. Emma Lou Cheney, Sept. 6, 1955; children—Mark, Kent, Wendy, Amy, Heather. B.A., Washington-Jefferson Coll., 1951; B.S., W.Va. U., 1953; Ph.D., U. Va., 1961. Instr. W.Va. U., Morgantown, 1955-57, U. Va., Charlottesville, 1960-61; prof. math. U. Miami, Coral Gables, Fla., 1961—. Author: (with others) Dynamic Topology, 1979. Contbr. articles to profl. jours. Served as cpl. U.S. Army, 1953-55. NSF grantee, 1965-71. Mem. Am. Math. Soc., Math. Assn. Am. (chmn. Fla. sect. 1980-81), Polskie Towarzystwo Matematyczne. Democrat. Avocations: fishing, lobstering, biking, jogging, tropical fruits. Office: U Miami Coral Gables FL 33124

DUDIK, ROLLIE M., hospital administrator; b. Hartford, Conn., Sept. 29, 1935; s. Martin and Iola Maxine (Hamilton) D.; Ph.D., Am. U., 1981. Gen. mgr. Freedman Artcraft Engring., Charlevoix, Mich., 1970-73; exec. v.p. Harrison Community Hosp., Cadiz, Ohio, 1973-77; dir. institutional rev. Dade Monroe PSRO, Miami, Fla., 1977-78; exec. dir. Fla. Keys Meml. Hosp., Key West, 1978-82; exec. v.p. Eisenhower Hosp., Colorado Springs, 1982-83; v.p. South Fla. Med. Mgmt., Inc., Miami, 1982—; pres. R.M. Dudik & Assocs., Inc., 1983—; med. projects cons. Orah Wall Med. Enterprises, Inc., San Antonio, 1985—; dir. Lahaina Inn Resort, Inc., 1985—; pres. Caribbean Diagnostic Ctrs., Inc., 1986—. Served with U.S. Army, 1956-62. Mem. Am. Inst. Indsl. Engrs., Am. Acad. Med. Adminstrs., Am. Coll. Hosp. Adminstrs., Hosp. Fin. Mgmt. Assn., Hosp. Mgmt. Systems Soc., Am. Soc. Law and Medicine, Nat. Assn. Flight Instrs., Nat. Assn. Accts., Nat. Counterintelligence Corps Assn. Clubs: Rotary, Kiwanis. Address: 8420 SW 102d Ave Miami FL 33173

DUDLEY, BROOKE FITZHUGH, educational consultant; b. East Orange, N.J., Oct. 22, 1942; s. Benjamin William and Jean (Peeples) D.; A.B. in Econs., Colgate U., 1966; 1 dau., Catherine Sanford. Sales mgr. De La Rue Instruments, Phila., 1968-71; comml. banker Bankers Trust Co., N.Y.C., 1966-68, Provident Nat. Bank, Phila., 1972-74; dir. admissions/financial aid St. Stephen's Episcopal Sch., Austin, Tex., 1974-78; exec. dir. U. Tex. Law Sch. Found., Austin, 1978-85; ednl. cons., 1982—. Chmn. bd. trustees Austin Evaluation Center; trustee Austin Repertory Theater; chmn. bd. dirs. All Saints Episcopal Day Sch., Austin; bd. dirs. Symphony Sq., Austin Child Guidance and Evaluation Ctr. usher, mem. stewardship com. St. David's Episcopal Ch.; Republican campaign mgr., N.Y.C., 1966-68. Served with U.S. Army, 1962-64. Mem. Ind. Ednl. Counselors Assn. (treas. bd. trustees), Hill Sch. Alumni Assn. (mem. exec. com. 1968-71), Edna Gladney Austin Aux. (past pres.). Episcopalian. Office: 3432 Greystone St Suite 210 Austin TX 78731

DUDLEY, GARY EDWARD, clinical psychologist; b. Columbus, Ohio, July 19, 1947; s. Ray Leonard and Mary Virginia (Russi) D.; B.S., Ohio State U., 1969; M.S. (NIMH fellow, 1971, VA fellow, 1971), U. Miami, 1972, Ph.D. (NIMH fellow, 1973), 1975; m. Linda Jean Patterson, June 21, 1969; children—Michelle Denise, Karen Elizabeth. Tchr. Columbus (Ohio) pub. schs., 1969-70; intern in clin. psychology Mt. Zion Hosp. and Med. Center, San Francisco, 1972-73; clin. psychologist Met. Dade County Jail, Miami, Fla., 1974-76, Southeast Inst. Criminal Justice, Miami, 1974-76, Ga. So. Coll., Statesboro, 1976-80; pvt. practice clin. psychology, Marietta, Ga., 1980—; cons. Child Devel. Ctr., Ga. Psycho-Ednl. Network, Atlanta. Lic. psychologist, Ga., Fla. Mem. Am. Psychol. Assn., Southeastern Psychol. Assn., Ga. Psychol. Assn., Nat. Honor Soc. in Psychology, Sigma Xi. Contbr. articles to profl. jours. Home: 592 Cupelo St Marietta GA 30064 Office: Doctors Bldg/Windy Hill 2520 Windy Hill Rd Suite 101 Marietta GA 30067

DUDLEY, GEORGE WILLIAM, JR., state education board administrator; b. Mullins, S.C., Apr. 21, 1931; s. George William and Annie Grace Bethea D.; m. Katherine Clark, Aug. 7, 1957 (div. 1980); children—Kari, Leigh, Skip. B.A. in Econs., 1953; M.A. in Guidance and Counseling, 1962. Assoc. dir. Florence-Darlington Tech. Edn. Ctr., S.C., 1963-66; dir. Horry-Georgetown Tech. Edn. Ctr., Conway, S.C., 1966-74; assoc. exec. dir. State Bd. for Tech. and Comprehensive Edn., Columbia, 1974-76, interim exec. dir., 1976, exec. dir., 1976—; lectr. in field. Served to 2d lt., U.S. Army, 1953-54. Recipient Presdl. medallion Horry-Georgetown Tech. Coll., 1984; named Tech. Educator of Yr., S.C. Tech. Edn. Assn., 1980; Boss of Yr., Midlands Am. Bus. Women's Assn., 1979. Mem. Am. Indsl. Devel. Council, S.C. Indsl. Council (bd. dirs.), So. Indsl. Devel. Council, Nat. Assn. Industry-Edn. Cooperation, S.C. Pvt. Industry Council. Presbyterian. Office: SC State Bd Tech and Comprehensive Edn 111 Executive Center Dr Columbia SC 29210

DUDLEY, JAMES SAMUEL, manufacturing company executive; b. St. Petersburg, Fla., June 5, 1934; s. Jerrold F. and Jacqualine L. (Yon) Jacob; A.A., Palm Beach Jr. Coll., 1956; postgrad. U. Fla., 1956-58; m. Florence Delores Howarth, Apr. 15, 1956; children—Lisa, Tracy, James, Julie, David. Owner, Dudley Mfg., Lantana, Fla., 1964-66; project supr., chief pilot Perry Submarine Builders, Riviera Beach, Fla., 1966-77; program mgr. Perry Oceanographics, Riviera Beach, 1977-84; facilities mgr. Perry Offshore, Inc., 1984—. Served with USMC, 1951-54. Home: 3225 Thunderbird Dr Lake Worth FL 33463 Office: 275 W 10th St Riviera Beach FL 33404

DUDLEY, MERLE BLAND, clergyman; b. Norfolk, Va., Feb. 19, 1929; s. Harry Roy and Merle (Garrett) D.; B.A., Lynchburg Coll., 1950; M.Div., Union Theol. Sem., 1954; M.A., Presbyn. Sch. Christian Edn., 1969; Ph.D., Glasgow (Scotland) U., 1973; m. Lillie M. Pennington, Oct. 12, 1950; children—Carter Bland, Jane Merle. Ordained to ministry Presbyterian Ch., 1954; pastor McQuay Meml. Presbyn. Ch., Charlotte, N.C., 1954-56, Holmes Presbyn. Ch., Cheriton, Va., 1956-59; asst. pastor First Presbyn. Ch., Roanoke, Va., 1959-60; pastor Christ Presbyn. Ch., Virginia Beach, Va., 1960-67; asso. pastor First Presbyn. Ch., Winston-Salem, N.C., 1967-70; pastor Westminster Presbyn. Ch., Waynesboro, Va., 1971—; mem. adj. faculty dept. philosophy and religion Blue Ridge Community Coll., Weyers Cave, Va., 1977—. Mem. Am. Acad. Religion, Soc. Bibl. Lit., Ch. Service Soc., Am. Schs. Oriental Research, Waynesboro Ministers' Assn. (pres. 1978-79), Va. Hist. Soc., Va. Soc. Sons of Am. Revolution (3d v.p.), Jamestowne Soc. Republican. Presbyterian. Club: Rotary (pres. 1974-75) (Waynesboro, Va.). Author: New Testament Preaching and Twentieth Century Communication, 1973. Home: 1900 Mount Vernon St Waynesboro VA 22980 Office: 1904 Mount Vernon St Waynesboro VA 22980

DUDLEY, ROBERT HAMILTON, state supreme court justice; b. Jonesboro, Ark., Nov. 18, 1933; s. Denver Layton and Helen (Paslay) D.; children—Debbie, Kathy, Cindy, Bob. J.D., U. Ark., 1958. Bar: Ark. 1958, U.S. Surpeme Ct. 1959. Dep. pros. atty., Randolph County, Ark., 1958, spl. mcpl. judge, 1959; pros. atty. 16th Jud. Dist. Ark., 1965-70; chancery judge 3d Jud. Dist. Ark., 1971-80; justice Ark. Supreme Ct., Little Rock, 1981—. Dist. chmn. Boy Scouts Am., 1960; mem. Ark. State Crime Commn., 1970-80. Mem. Ark. Jud. Council (chmn. exec. com. 1978-79); Am. Bar Assn. Ark. Bar Assn., U. Ark. Alumni Assn. (dir. 1972-75). Democrat. Office: Justice Bldg Little Rock AR 72201

DUDLEY, ROY LEE, cemetery executive; b. Norfolk, Va., Aug. 21, 1927; s. Roy Wilson and Marceline (Lilliston) D.; m. Elizabeth McRae, Dec. 22, 1951; children—Roy Lee, Jr., Marsha McRae, Armistead Wilson. B.S. in B.A., Va. Poly. Inst., 1949. Project adminstr. Bush Orgn., Norfolk, Va., 1952-54, project mgr., 1954-64, gen. mgr., 1964-68; v.p. Meadowbrook Meml. Gardens, Inc., Suffolk, Va., 1968-71, owner, pres., 1971—. Mem. Va. Cemetery Assn. (dir.), So. Cemetery Assn., Am. Cemetery Assn. Clubs: Exchange (pres. 1957), Norfolk Yacht and Country (commodore 1973, 74; sec. 1981, 82). Home: 1425 Monterey Ave Norfolk VA 23508 Office: PO Box 5128 Suffolk VA 23435

DUDNEY, EMILE ELIZABETH, educator, business executive; b. Chattanooga, Aug. 13, 1928; d. John Alfred and Rose Mariah (Sullivan) D. B.A., Southwestern U., 1949; M.A., E. Tenn. State U., 1971. Tchr. sci. City of Kingsport (Tenn.), 1949-85, girls' track coach Dobyns-Bennett High Sch., 1973-81; owner, operator Dieudonne Farms, Piney Flats, Tenn., 1967—; pres. Fert'l Green, Inc., Church Hill, Tenn., 1983—; chmn. bd. Dieudonne Enterprises, Inc., 1982—; mem. Kingsport City Bd. Edn. Developed fertile mulch process, 1982. Audiovisual coordinator First Baptist Ch., Kingsport, 1960-68; active United Fund Kingsport, 1968-69. Named Track Coach of Yr., Big Nine Conf., 1975, 76, 78, 79, 80, Upper E. Tenn. Coach of Yr., 1979, Track Coach of Yr., Region I, 1979, 80, 81, Outstanding Sci. Tchr., Applachian Region, 1970. Mem. Nat. Sch. Bds. Assn., Tenn. State Sch. Bds. Assn., Kingsport C. of C. Democrat. Baptist. Club: Ridgefields Country. Home: 1514 Waverly Rd 1 Kingsport TN 37664 Office: Dieudonne Farms Rt 2 Box 195 Piney Flats TN 37686

DUER, THOMAS C., banker. Exec. v.p. Sun Banks Inc., Orlando, Fla. Office: Sun Banks Inc Sun Bank NA Bldg Orlando FL 32802*

DUERER, ALBERT WOODROW, JR., roofing company executive; b. Houston, Oct. 30, 1945; s. Albert Woodrow and Cevilla Mae (Dickens) D.; m. Sharron Kaye Dunnam, Mar. 24, 1983; 1 child, Lloyd Wayne. B.B.A., Tex. A&M U., 1968; M.B.A., Sam Houston State U., 1972. Asst. mgr. Abbey Rents, Houston, 1972-74; sales rep. So. Components, Houston, 1974, Stahlman Lumber Co., Stafford, Tex., 1974-75, Trussway, Inc., Houston, 1975-85; mgr. sales Tex. Truss, Inc., Houston, 1985-86; sales and office mgr. Timber Tech Inc., Tomball, Tex., 1986—. Mem. com. Sam Houston Area council Boy Scouts Am., 1984; mem. Athletic Booster Club, Spring, Tex., 1985; asst. coach softball, 1981. Served to lt. USNR. Recipient Outstanding Dir. award Bryan Jaycees, 1968. Mem. Houston Apartment Assn., Greater Houston Builders Assn., Toastmasters Internat., North Houston Toastmasters. Baptist. Avocations: hunting; fishing; camping.

DUERKSEN, ERWIN, grain company executive; b. 1923. With Union Equity Co-op Exchanges, 1944—, now pres. Office: Union Equity Co-op Exchange 10th and Willow St Enid OK 73701*

DUES, THEODORE ROOSEVELT, JR., lawyer; b. Montgomery, W.Va., June 23, 1953; s. Theodore Roosevelt and Mary Lucille (White) D.; m. Mona Lisa Day, Aug. 25, 1979; 1 child, Theodore Roosevelt III. B.S.B.A., W.Va. U., 1975, J.D., 1978. Bar: W.Va. 1978, U.S. Dist. Ct. (no. and so. dist.) W.Va. 1978, U.S. Ct. Appeals (4th cir.) 1978. Sole practice, Fayetteville, W.Va., 1978-79, Charleston, W.Va., 1979-81; sr. ptnr. Dues, Tyree & Hicks, Charleston, 1981-83, Dues & Tyre, Charleston, 1983-85; sole practice, Charleston, 1985—, hearing examiner W.Va. Human Rights Commn., Charleston, 1981—; bd. govs. W. Va. State Bar, 1985—. Bd. dirs. Family Services United Way Agy., Charleston, 1983—, Appalachian Research and Def. Fund, Charleston, 1979-83, Legal Aid Soc., 1981-84; commr. Kanawha County Dep. sheriffs, 1984—. Named Most Outstanding Black Atty., Black Am. Law Students, 1982. Mem. NAACP (W.Va. legal redress com. 1978—, chmn. Charleston legal redress com. 1983—), Mountain State Bar Assn., W.Va. State Bar Assn. (jud. improvement com. 1983—). Club: Civitan. Office: Daniel Boone Bldg 405 Capitol St Charleston WV 25301

DUFF, WILLIAM GRIERSON, electrical engineer; b. Alexandria, Va., Dec. 16, 1936; s. Johnnie Douglas and Annetta Osceola (Rind) D.; B.E.E., George Washington U., 1959, postgrad., 1959-72; M.S., Syracuse U., 1969; D.Sc. in Elec. Engring., Clayton U., 1977; m. Sandra K. Via, June 25, 1983; children—Warren David, Valerie Lynn, Dawn Elizabeth, Deborah Arleen, Kelly Juanita. Mgr. advanced systems tech. dept. Atlantic Research Corp., Alexandria, 1959—; asst. prof. Capitol Inst. Tech., Greenbelt, Md., 1972—; instr. Interference Control Technologies, Don White Cons., Inc., Gainesville, Va. Counselor, Meth. Sr. High Youth Group, 1965-73. Recipient Good Citizenship award DAR, 1955; Math. award George Washington High Sch., Alexandria, 1955. Fellow IEEE (pres. EMC Soc., assoc. editor group newsletter 1970—); mem. AIEE (Best Paper award 1961), George Washington U. Engring. Alumni Assn. (pres. 1963-64, Engring. Alumni Service award 1980), Sigma Tau, Theta Tau. Clubs: Springfield Golf and Country; Occoquan (Va.) Water Ski (pres. 1976). Author: EMI Handbook, vol. 5, EMI Prediction and Analysis Techniques, 1972; Mobile Communications, 1976; contbr. articles to profl. jours. Home: 11684 Havenner Rd Fairfax Station VA 22039 Office: 5390 Cherokee Ave Alexandria VA 22314

DUFFEY, PAUL ANDREWS, bishop; b. Brownsville, Tenn., Dec. 13, 1920; s. George Henderson and Julia Griffin (McKissack) D.; m. Anna Louise Calhoun, June 20, 1944; children—Melanie Duffey Hutto, Paul Andrews Jr. Student, U. Ala., 1938-40; A.B., Birmingham-So. Coll., 1942, D.D., 1966; B.D., Vanderbilt U., 1945. Ordained to ministry as deacon United Meth. Ch., 1944, elder, 1946; pastor Chapel Hill Ch., Tenn., 1944-46, Abbeville, Ala., 1946-50, Marion, Ala., 1950-54, Dexter Ave United Meth. Ch., Montgomery, Ala., 1954-61, First Ch., Pensacola, Fla., 1961-66, Dothan, Ala., 1966-70, Montgomery, Ala., 1970-76; supt. Montgomery dist. United Meth. Ch., 1976-80, mem. jud. council, 1976-80; bishop United Meth. Ch., Louisville, 1980—. Trustee Birmingham-So. Coll., 1956—, chmn. bd., 1956-73. Office: United Meth Ch 4010 Dupont Circle Louisville KY 40207

DUFFIELD, GARY OTIS, computer company executive; b. Acme, W.Va., Feb. 25, 1932; s. William I. and Fern (Boggess) D.; m. Coralie Estep, Aug. 26, 1956 (div. Feb. 1974); children—Kelly Dawn, Gary Otis, Todd Alan; m. 2d, Lois M. Blood, Jan. 18, 1975. B.S. in Elec. Engring., W.Va. Tech. U., Montgomery, 1960. Engr., Philco Corp., Phila., 1960-66; sr. engr. Honeywell, St. Petersburg, Fla., 1966-69; v.p. Navigate Inc., Clearwater, Fla., 1969-76; pres. Morg Controls, Clearwater, 1976—; dir. Lite Cart Corp., Largo, Fla. Mem. Com. of 100 Pinellas County, Fla., 1984. Served with U.S. Army, 1952-55. Recipient Profl. in Material Handling award Internat. Material Mgmt. Soc., 1977. Mem. Material Handling Inst., Ga. Tech. Material Handling Research Ctr., Fla. C. of C., Clearwater C. of C. Lodge: Masons. Home: 1664 Sheffield Dr Clearwater FL 33546 Office: Morg Controls 13900 49th St N Clearwater FL 33520

DUFFNER, LEE R., ophthalmologist; b. Milw., June 3, 1936; m. Alvina Bross, Aug. 31, 1957; children—Fay, Rachel, Tamar. B.S. in Engring., Purdue U., 1957; M.S. in Physiology, Marquette U., 1961; M.D., Med. Coll. Wis., 1962. Diplomate Am. Bd. Ophthalmology. Intern, Stanford U., 1962-63; resident U. Miami, Fla., 1966-69; practice medicine specializing in ophthalmology, Hollywood, Fla., 1969—; clin. assoc. prof. ophthalmology U. Miami Sch. Medicine, 1969—. Pres. town council Town of Golden Beach, Fla., 1983—. Served to capt. USAF, 1963-66. Fellow Am. Acad. Ophthalmology, ACS; mem. Miami Ophthal. Soc. (pres. 1983-84). Republican. Jewish. Avocation: marathon running. Home: 185 Ocean Blvd Golden Beach FL 33160 Office: 2740 Hollywood Blvd Hollywood FL 33020

DUFFY, R. LORETT, advertising and public relations executive; b. Scranton, Pa., May 23, 1936; d. John R. and Loretta (Walsh) Williams; divorced; children—Kathleen, Patrick, Noreen, Sharon, Irene. Adminstrv. asst. Decair Helicopters, Inc., Spring Valley, N.Y., 1970-76; controller asst. Lone Star Industries, Inc., West Nyack, N.Y., 1977-80; pub. relations, advt. sales rep. Broward Cablevision, Dovie, Fla., 1980—. Recipient Media award Dania Democratic Club. Mem. Dovie-Cooper City C. of C., Dania C. of C. (dir.; Extraordinary Service award), Movie Picture and TV Industry Assn., Ft. Lauderdale C. of C. Democrat. Roman Catholic. Club: Soroptimist Internat. Home: 3150 W Rolling Hill Circle Apt 505 Dovie FL 33328 Office: 5001 S University Dr Dovie FL 33314

DUFLOT, LEO SCOTT MELLOO, physician; b. Mayfield, Ky., June 24, 1919; s. Joseph Leo and Elizabeth Shanklin (Melloo) D.; m. Rosemary Collins, Mar. 24, 1951; children—Rene, Jeanne, Carol, Merrie, Joseph. Student West Tex. State Coll., 1935-37; B.A., U. Tex., Austin, 1940, M.D., Galveston, 1943. Intern, Parkland Hosp., Dallas, 1943-44; gen. practice medicine, Canyon, Tex., 1946-48; resident in anesthesiology U. Tex., Galveston, 1949-51; mem. faculty U. Tex. Med. Br., Galveston, 1952—, prof. anesthesiology, 1973—; dir. dept. anesthesiology Driscoll Found. Childrens Hosp., Corpus Christi, 1979—. Served with U.S. Navy, 1944-46. Fellow Am. Coll. Anesthesiology; mem. Tex. Med. Assn., Am. Soc. Anesthesiologists, Tex. Soc. Anesthesiologists (past pres.), Internat. Anesthesiology Research Soc. Democrat. Club: Pharaoh Country (Corpus Christi). Office: 3533 S Alameda St Corpus Christi TX 78411

DUGAN, JAMES F., III, architect; b. Murray, Ky., Nov. 10, 1943; s. James F. Dugan II and Virginia Lee (Lesser) Dugan Fenton; m. Tere Otero, Sept. 16, 1978; 1 child, James F. IV. B.Arch., N.C. State U., 1968. Staff mem. Cosanti Found., Arcosanti, Ariz., 1975; designer Summers & Gardner, Orangeburg, S.C., 1976-77; architect Shields-Wyatt Assocs., Rocky Mount, N.C., 1977-80, Hardee's Food Systems, Rocky Mount, 1980-83, prin. James F. Dugan III, AIA, Rocky Mount, 1983—; chmn. Rocky Mount Energy Bd., 1983-85, mem., 1979-85; mem. archtl. rev. bd. Downtown Revitalization Com., Rocky Mount, 1978-80. Served to capt. CE, U.S. Army, 1968-72; Vietnam. Mem. AIA (pres. eastern sect. N.C. 1984-85, dir. N.C. chpt. 1986—), Twin County Jaycees (fin. v.p. 1979), U.S. Power Squadron (exec. officer Rocky Mount 1985, comdr. 1986); Neuse Sailing Assn. (treas. 1985-86). Methodist. Lodge: Lions, Rocky Mount Luncheon. Avocation: sailing. Home and Office: James F Dugan III AIA 105 S Kirkwood Ave Rocky Mount NC 27801

DUGAN, JOSEPH PATRICK, JR., geoscientist, researcher; b. San Antonio, Oct. 5, 1954; s. Joseph Patrick and Lucille (Tomlinson) D. B.S. in Geophysics, U. Okla., 1976; M.S. in Geology, No. Ill. U., 1978; Ph.D. candidate So. Meth. U., 1981—. Grad. teaching asst. No. Ill. U., DeKalb, 1976-77, head teaching asst., 1977-78; research asst. La. State U., Baton Rouge, 1978-79; grad. teaching asst. Purdue U., West Lafayette, Ind., 1979-81; dist. geologist Placid Oil Co., Dallas, 1981-83; geophysicist TLC Data Processing Co., Richardson, Tex., 1983—. Contbr. articles to profl. jours. Bd. dirs. Wesley Found., Norman, Okla., 1974-76, DeKalb, 1976-78; mem. adminstv. bd. Lovers Lane United Meth. Ch., Dallas, 1983-85, pres. Roaring 20's, 1984. Served with USNR, 1972-75. Eagle Scout, 1971; mem. Skylab Project, AAAS, 1972; grantee So. Meth. U., 1984. Mem. Soc. Exploration Geophysicists (scholar 1973-76), Dallas Geol. Soc. (scholar 1973-76), Geophys. Soc. Oklahoma City (scholar 1975-76), Am. Assn. Petroleum Geologists, Dallas Geophys. Soc. Avocations: mineral collecting, mountaineering; photography; philetaley; numismatist. Home: 8511 Flower Meadow Dr Dallas TX 75243

DUGAN, KIMIKO HATTA (MRS. WAYNE ALEXANDER DUGAN), anatomist, educator; b. Kyoto City, Japan, Oct. 21, 1924; naturalized U.S. citizen, 1956; d. Shinzo and Sano (Hatta) Hatta; student U. Md., 1957-58; B.A., Okla. Coll. Women, 1961; M.S., U. Okla., 1965, Ph.D., 1970; m. Wayne Alexander Dugan, Aug. 18, 1947 (dec. Aug. 1971). Grad. fellow dept. anatomy Sch. Medicine, U. Okla., Oklahoma City, 1964-69, instr. dept. anat. sci. Coll. Medicine, 1969-71, asst. prof., 1971-78, assoc. prof., 1978—. Recipient Undergrad. Chemistry Achievement award Okla. Coll. Women, 1960; elected to U. Sci. and Arts Okla. (formerly Okla. Coll. Women) Alumni Hall of Fame, 1977. Mem. Am. Assn. Anatomists, AAAS, AAUW, Am. Chem. Soc., Am. Soc. Zoologists, Electron Microscopy Soc. Am., Internat. Soc. for Devel. Comparative Immunology, N.Y. Acad. Scis., Okla. Acad. Sci., Sigma Xi. Episcopalian. Home: 1139 NW 63d St Oklahoma City OK 73116 Office: Dept Anat Scis Coll Medicine U Okla Health Scis Center PO Box 26901 Oklahoma City OK 73190

DUGAN, RICHARD FRANKLIN, retired fish and wildlife biologist; b. Sugar Grove, Ill., July 27, 1916; s. Ralph Emory and Nettie Frances (Bunnel) D.; student Aurora (Ill.) Coll., 1934-35; B.S. in Agr., U. Ill., 1938; B.S. in Forestry/M.F. in Wildlife Mgmt., U. Mich., 1941; postgrad. in outdoor recreation Tex. A and M U., 1967-68; m. Lucile Helen Shoger, June 19, 1941; children—Richard, Mary, Phyllis, Carol. Timber surveyor U.S. Forest Service, Ore., 1940; agrl. aide Soil Conservation Service, U.S. Dept. Agr., Mich., 1941, biologist/woodland conservationist, N.J., 1958-59, biologist/recreation specialist, Va., 1960-77; asst. prof. forestry and wildlife mgmt. W.Va. U., 1942-57. Mem. Wildlife Soc., Soil Conservation Soc. Am. (life), Am. Fisheries Soc., Nat. Recreation and Parks Assn., Am. Forestry Assn., Nat. Audubon Soc., Smithsonian Instn., Izaak Walton League (life), Nat. Wildlife Fedn. (life), Nat. Rifle Assn. (life), Alpha Zeta, Xi Sigma Pi. Baptist (deacon). Lion. Contbr. articles profl. jours. Home: 4306 Chickahominy Ave Richmond VA 23222

DUGGAN, CAROL COOK, researcher; b. Conway, S.C., May 25, 1946; d. Pierce Embree and Lillian Watkins (Eller) Cook; m. Kevin Duggan, Dec. 29, 1973. B.A., Columbia Coll., 1968; M.S., U. Ky., 1970. Reference asst. Richland County Pub. Library, Columbia, S.C., 1968-69, asst. to dir., 1970, chief adult services, 1971-82; dir. Maris Research, Columbia, 1982—. Mem. Friends of Richland County Pub. Library, 1977—, Greater Columbia (S.C.) Literacy Council, 1973—. Recipient Sternheimer award, 1968. Mem. ALA (councilor 1980-82, chmn. state membership com. 1979-83), S.C. Library Assn. (sec. 1976, exec. bd. 1976, 78-82), S.C. Pub. Library Assn. (pres. 1980-81), Beta Phi Mu. Methodist (exec. bd. United Methodist Women 1983—). Club: PEO (pres. 1983-85, chmn. amendments and recommendations com. 1983-85). Home: 2101 Woodmere Dr Columbia SC 29204

DUGGAN, KEVIN, data processor; b. St. Louis, Feb. 29, 1944; s. Leo Patrick and Jean Claire (McHenry) D.; B.A., U. S.C., 1977; m. Lillian Carol Cook, Dec. 29, 1973. With S.C. Nat. Bank, Columbia, 1970-79, mgr. tech. support, 1978-79; dir. data processing Midlands Tech. Coll., Columbia, 1979—; cons. electronic data processing. Mem. Richland County Friends of Library, Literacy Council S.C. Served with USMC, 1963-67. Decorated Bronze Star (3). Mem. Assn. Systems Mgr., IBM Users Group, Data Processing Mgmt. Assn., Palmetto Fencing Soc., Amateur Fencing League Am. Methodist. Office: PO Box 2408 Columbia SC 29202

DUHE, JOHN M., JR., U.S. district judge; b. Iberia Parish, La., Apr. 7, 1933; s. J. Malcolm and Rita (Alexander) D.; children—Kim, Richard, Jeanne, Edward, M. Bofill. B.B.A., Tulane U., 1955, LL.B., 1957. Atty. firm Helm, Simon, Caffery & Duhe, New Iberia, La., 1957-58; state dist. judge, New Iberia, 1979-84; U.S. dist. judge Western La. dist., Lafayette, 1984—. Office: Room 249 Federal Bldg Lafayette LA 70501*

DUKE, BILLY WAYNE, university administrator, b. Shongaloo, La., Jan. 4, 1938; s. Avis (Walker) D.; m. Judith Anne Lenox, Sept. 2, 1972; children—Angela, Amy. B.S. in Sci. and Math., La. Tech. U., 1960, M.A. in Counseling

Psychology, 1963; Ed.D., U. Mo., 1970. Dean students Southside Va. Community Coll., Alberta, 1970-71; v.p. student affairs U. Tex., Arlington, 1971—. Contbr. articles to profl. jours. Participant Leadership Ft. Worth, 1977—; bd. dirs. N. Tex. Higher Edn. Authority, Arlington, 1984—. NDEA fellow, 1968-70. Mem. Nat. Assn. Student Personnel Adminstrs., Am. Assn. Counseling and Devel. (chmn. task force on student athletics 1982-85), Southwest Assn. Student Personnel Adminstrs., Tex. Assn. Student Personnel Adminstrs. (chmn. legis. comm. 1982, 83, 85). Baptist. Avocations: hunting; fishing; camping. Home: 4604 Woodstone Ct Arlington TX 76016 Office: U Tex PO Box 19115 Arlington TX 76019

DUKE, CHARLES IRVING, development corporation executive; b. Rosedale, N.Y., Aug. 28, 1928; s. Charles Irving and Adele Louise (Muller) D.; m. Joan Mary Davis, June 16, 1951; children—Susan Jean Duke McAlpin, Stephen Charles, Patrice Joan, David Lindsay, Elizabeth Jane. B.S. in Bus. Adminstrn., NYU, 1951. Sr. contract adminstr. Grumman Aircraft Corp., Bethpage, N.Y., 1954-60; v.p. Henry C. Muller Co., N.Y.C., 1961-68; v.p. Zimco Housing Corp. div. Zimmer Homes, Pompano Beach, Fla., 1968-72; v.p. Kings Point West, Sun City, Fla., 1972-75; v.p. Connestee Falls Devel. Corp., Brevard, N.C., 1975—, Connestee Falls Realty Corp., Fordco, Inc., Brevard; v.p. Transylvania Elec. Co., Brevard; pres. Evergreen Investment Corp. Vice pres. Ford's Colony at Williamsburg, Inc. (Va.). Served to capt. USMCR, 1951-53. Mem. Nat. Home Builders Assn., N.C. Home Builders Assn. (dir.), Transylvania Home Builders Assn. (pres., dir.), Brevard Bd. Realtors, C. of C., Tau Kappa Epsilon. Republican. Christian Scientist. Clubs: Glen Cannon Country, Racquet (Brevard); Asheville Rifle and Pistol. Home: Route 2 Box 44 Pisgah Forest NC 28768 Office: Fordco Inc Box 512 Brevard NC 28712

DUKE, KATHERINE B., counselor, psychologist; b. Prattville, Ala., Dec. 22, 1930; d. Malfus Porter and Adele (Weldon) Billingsley; m. Donald Edward Duke, Aug. 10, 1958; 1 child, Don Jr. A.B., U. Ala.-Tuscaloosa, 1952; M.A., Columbia U., 1961; Ed.S., U. Ga., 1973; Ph.D., Vanderbilt U., 1980. Counselor, gen. practice psychologist, Greenville, N.C., 1984—. Mem. Am. Assn. for Counseling and Devel., Kappa Delta Pi. Republican. Baptist. Address: PO Box 1581 Greenville NC 27834

DUKE, LOIS LOVELACE, government educator, public relations consultant; b. Bessemer City, N.C., Feb. 13, 1935; d. Fred R. and Pearl (Kiser) Lovelace; children—Bruce F., Mary Louanne. B.A., U. S.C., 1976, M.A., 1979, Ph.D., 1986. Instr. Am. govt. and polit. theory U. S.C., 1980—; pub. relations cons. Pub. Relations/Mktg. Assocs., Charlotte, N.C., 1982-83; chief pub. info. and community relations officer, pub. affairs office, Fort Jackson, S.C. Organist and choir dir. United Meth. Ch.; officer PTO; leader Indian Waters council Boy Scouts Am.; leader Girl Scouts Am. Mem. Pub. Relations Soc. Am. (pres. chpt.), Am. Women in Radio and TV (pres. Palmetto Chpt.), Gamma Tau Alpha, Sigma Delta Chi., Pi Sigma Alpha, Beta Sigma Phi. Clubs: Columbia Media (pres.); Columbia Advt. Home: 129 Garden Springs Rd Columbia SC 29209 Office: Dept Govt & Internat Studies U SC Columbia SC 29208

DUKES, JAMES HENDERSON, economics educator; b. Charleston, S.C., Apr. 30, 1919; s. Clifton Abraham and Martha May (Bellinger) D.; m. Thelma Chance, Nov. 28, 1953; children—Teresa Patton, Cecilia Smith, James H., Jr. B.S. in Ceramic Engring., Ga. Sch. Tech., 1940; M.A. in Econs., Emory U., 1953; Ph.D. in Econs., U. Fla., 1963. Ops. lube engr. Texaco, Inc., Cuba, P.R. and N.Y.C., 1940-47; sales, field engr. Tenn. Eastmen, Latin Am. and N.Y.C., 1947-51; econ. analyst FoA, ICA, Rio de Janeiro, Brazil, 1954-58; teaching asst., instr. U. Fla., Gainesville, 1960-63; asst. prof. U.S. Naval Acad., Annapolis, Md., 1964-68; assoc. prof. econs. U. W. Fla., Pensacola, 1968—; field reviewer U.S. Census Dept., Decatur, Ga., 1960. Served with U.S. Navy, 1943-46, 50-53. Fulbright grantee, 1967, 71, 73. Mem. Am. Econ. Assn., So. Econ. Assn., Atlantic Econs. Assn., Keramos, U.S. C. of C. (chmn. indsl. com. 1976), Sigma Chi. Democrat. Roman Catholic. Lodge: Kiwanis. Avocations: tennis; international travel; classical music; ballet. Home: 309 Conecuh St Milton FL 32570 Office: U W Fla Econs Dept Pensacola FL 32514

DUKES, JEFF ALBERT, automotive parts warehouse company executive; b. Jackson, Miss., Oct. 7, 1954; s. Wilbur Chapman and Mildred Ann (McDaniel) D.; B.S. in Bus. Adminstrn., Miss. Coll., Clinton, 1977, M.B.A., 1979. Lic. pilot, Miss. Founder, owner Dukes A/C, Jackson, Miss., 1972—; assoc. prof. econs. Miss. Coll., 1983—. Dep. sheriff Hinds County Sheriff's Dept., Jackson, 1975—. Mem. Jackson Jaycees (chmn. ops. Walk for Mankind 1981, dir. 1981-82, named outstanding Jaycee 1981), Delta Sigma Pi (v.p. 1975, chmn. profl. activities 1975, 76). Baptist. Office: Dukes A/C 360 Culbertson Ave Jackson MS 39209

DUKES, PHILIP DUSKIN, plant pathologist, educator; b. Reevesville, S.C., Jan. 16, 1931; s. Henry L. and Roberta E. (Reeves) D.; B.S., Clemson U., 1953; M.S., N.C. State U., 1960, Ph.D., 1963; student Colo. State U., 1957; m. Marlene Hart, July 28, 1956; children—MarLa Hart, Philip Duskin. Plant chief clk. Davison Chem. Corp., Savannah, Ga., 1953-54; asst. county agt. S.C. Extension Service, Saluda, 1956-58; research asst. N.C. State U., Raleigh, 1958-62; asst. prof. U. Ga., Tifton, 1962-67, asso. prof. plant pathology, 1967-70, research plant pathologist U.S. Vegetable Lab., U.S. Dept. Agr., Charleston, S.C., 1970—; mem. Tobacco Variety Adv. Com., 1967-70; adj. prof. Clemson U.; chmn. Tobacco Disease Evaluation Com., 1969-70, Sweetpotato Disease Com., 1970-80. Mem. local bd. SSS. Served with Signal Corps, U.S. Army, 1954-56. Recipient Ware research award for excellence in horticultural research, 1979. Mem. Internat. Soc. Plant Pathology, Soc. Nematologists, Am. Phytopath. Soc., Internat. Soc. Tropical Root Crops, So. Assn. Agrl. Scientists, Nat. Sweetpotato Collaborator Group, (vice chmn. 1985, chmn. 1986), Sigma Xi, Phi Kappa Phi, Alpha Zeta. Methodist (lay speaker). Research on physiology of phytopathogenic fungi, physiology of parasitism of root and stem pathogens, breeding disease resistant vegetables. Address: US Vegetable Lab 2875 Savannah Hwy Charleston SC 29407

DUKES, WILLIAM WALTER, JR., engineering executive; b. Orangeburg, S.C., Mar. 28, 1917; s. William Walter and Ethel Donaldson (Chambers) D.; m. Margaret Crevensten, Oct. 3, 1942; children—Peggy Dukes Dickinson (dec.), Susan Dukes Woodard, William W. B.S.E.E., Clemson U., 1938. Turbine engr. Gen. Electric Co., Lynn, Mass., 1939-41; v.p. Applied Engring. Co., Orangeburg, 1946-74, pres., chief exec. officer, 1974-80, chmn., chief exec. officer, 1980-83, ret., 1984; vice chmn., dir. Blu Surf Inc., Parma, Mich.; dir., mem. exec. com. 1st Fed. Savs. & Loan S.C., Greenville; vice chmn., dir. Surfinco, Inc., Albion, Mich.; dir. numerous cos. Bd. dirs., pres. Clemson U. Found.; chmn. Orangeburg Aviation Commn.; trustee St. Mary's Coll., Raleigh, N.C., 1964-85; bd. dirs. Orangeburg-Calhoun Tech. Coll. Found., S.C. Episcopal Ministry to the Aging. Recipient Clemson Univ. Disting. Alumni award, 1979; named Orangeburg Citizen of the Yr., 1980. Served to major U.S. Army, 1941-46, to col. USAR. Mem. Nat. Soc. Profl. Engrs., ASME (life), AIEE (life), Gas Appliance Mfrs. Assn. (past dir.), Midwest Gas Assn. (past dir.), Southeastern Gas Assn. (past dir.), Am. Gas Assn. (assoc.), Gild of Ancient Suppliers, S.C. Forestry Assn.,Tau Beta Pi. Episcopalian. Clubs: Orangeburg Country. Lodges: Kiwanis (past pres., lt. gov.), Elks, Am. Legion. Address: 140 Livingston Terr Orangeburg SC 29115

DULA, ARTHUR MCKEE, III, lawyer; b. Arlington, Va., Feb. 6, 1947; s. Arthur McKee D.; m. Tamea A. Smith, Dec. 27, 1971. B.S., Eastern N.Mex. U., 1970; J.D., Tulane U., 1975. Bar: Tex. 1975. Assoc. firm Butler & Binion, Houston, 1975-79; mem. firm Dula, Shields & Egbert, Houston, 1979—; cons. space law various orgns. including NASA, Gen. Dynamics, 1979-83; faculty med. physics Cancer Ctr., U. Tex. System, Houston, 1975-84; faculty law U. Houston, 1977-80. Author reports in field. Bd. dirs. U. Houston Law Rev., 1978-84. Fellow Brit. Interplanetary Soc.; mem. ABA (sci. and tech. sect. chmn. 1982-83, award 1982), AIAA, Internat. Inst. Space Law (Paris). Home: 3102 Beauchamp St Houston TX 77009 Office: Dula Shields & Egbert 6960 Texas Commerce Tower Houston TX 77002

DULAN, JEANNETTE EUGENIA ROGERS, educator, consultant; b. Charlotte, N.C., July 28, 1945; d. Ernest Eugene and Mildred Octavia (Strachan) Rogers; m. Claude Garland Dulan, Jan. 29, 1967; children—Stanton Cavell, Stacia Ginneh, Sherian Jeanine. B.S., Union Coll., 1966; M.Ed., U. Tenn.-Chattanooga, 1979. Tchr., Flint (Mich.) Community Schs., 1966-68; dir.-tchr. Tot Lot Project, Mott Found., Flint, Mich., 1967; tchr. Riverside (Calif.) Unified Schs., 1968-69; tchr. Prince George County Schs., Hyattsville, Md., 1969-70; dir. supr. summer park program Prince George County, Rockville, Md., 1970; tchr. Riverside (Calif.) Unified Schs., 1970-75; clin. reading instr. Inst. Devel. Studies, Chattanooga, 1975-79; tchr. Chattanooga Pub. Schs., 1975-76, 80-81; instr. ednl. test and measurement So. Coll., Collegedale, Tenn., 1981; asst. prof. elem. edn. Oakwood Coll., Huntsville, Ala., 1981—. Radio and TV broadcasting host LWV, Chattanooga, 1976-77. Mem. Am. Ednl. Research Assn., Assn. Tchr. Educators, NAACP, Kappa Delta Pi. Seventh-day Adventist. Office: Dept Edn Oakwood Coll Huntsville AL 35896

DULANEY, JAMES PATRICK, petroleum geologist; b. Haskell, Tex., Aug. 27, 1955; s. James Barry and Betty Jo (Toliver) D.; m. Robin Gayle Wheatley, June 12, 1977 (div. Apr. 1983); 1 child, James Robert. B.S., Tex. Tech. U., 1980, M.S., 1982. Research asst. Clay Lab., Tex. Tech. U., Lubbock, 1979-80, teaching asst. geosci. dept., 1980-82; geologist Superior Oil Co., Midland, Tex., 1982-84, petroleum geologist, 1984-85; prodn. geologist Mobil Producing, Midland, Tex., 1985—. Mem. West Tex. Geol. Soc., Am. Assn. Petroleum Geologists. Democrat. Clubs: Austin Healey Am., Acad. Model Aeronautics (Reston, Va.). Avocations: Austin Healey restoration; and rallyeing; model aviation; bird hunting. Home: 3117 Barkley Midland TX 79701 Office: Mobil Producing Tex and N Mex 500 W Illinois St Midland TX 79702

DULING, FRANK SAMUEL, JR., city ofcl.; b. Richmond, Va., Dec. 9, 1923; s. Frank Samuel and Margaret Sarah (Rotruck) D.; student Richmond Police Tng. Sch., Va. Central Police Tng. Sch., U. Louisville, Md., Mich. State U.; m. Mary Irene Maiden, Sept. 18, 1948; 1 dau., Vanessa Irene Duling Preston. Bookkeeper, First & Merchants Nat. Bank, Richmond, 1941-44; with Richmond Bur. Police, 1944—, capt., 1957-60, maj., 1960-67, col., 1967—, insp. police, 1960-65, comdr. investigative ops., 1965-67, chief of police, 1967—; mem. Va. State Crime Commn. Active ARC; dir. Richmond mem. Robert E. Lee council Boy Scouts Am., Richmond; mem. exec. com. Nat. Found. March of Dimes. Recipient Meritorious Police medals Richmond Bur. Police; ARC Service to Mankind award; Richmond Profl. Inst. Law Enforcement Edn. award; U.S. Jaycees cert. of merit; VA award; J. Edgar Hoover Meml. award. Mem. Fraternal Order of Police (pres. 1959-60, pres. Va. State lodge 1964-70, chmn. Va. legis. com. 1970-74, dir. John Marshall Lodge #2 Youth Camp), Va. Assn. Chiefs Police (past pres.), Internat. Assn. Chiefs of Police, Va. Soc. Safety Engrs., Assn. Public Safety Communications Officers Inc., Safety Town Inc. (dir.), Alumni Assn. So. Police Inst. U. Louisville, Richmond Police Benevolent Assn. Baptist. Club: Mason. Office: 501 N 9th St Richmond VA 23219

DULY, GILDA RIZZUTO, former Am. foreign service officer; librarian; b. Rome, N.Y., Jan. 2, 1910; d. Joseph and Catherine (Elia) Rizzuto; divorced. Grad. Rome Free Acad., 1928, Fgn. Service Inst., 1945. Asst. librarian Jervis Library, Rome, N.Y., 1928-29; joined Fgn. Service, Dept. State, Washington, 1945, ret., 1960; librarian Honolulu YWCA, 1970-73; writer, archivist. Author of poetry and short stories. Mem. Rep. Nat. Com. Recipient Loyal and Meritorious Service award U.S. Dept. State, 1960. Mem. The Asia Soc. Home: 51 Island Way #602 Island Estates Clearwater FL 33515

DUMARS, GARY JAMES, real estate broker; b. Meadville, Pa., July 3, 1948; s. Donald and Nan Jean (Taylor) D. B.S., U. N.C.-Chapel Hill, 1969; M.S., Cornell U., 1971; Ph.D., Northwestern U., 1973. With Abelson, Inc., Morton Grove, Ill., 1965-79, pres., 1979-82; pres., owner DuMars Home Repair & Landscape, Inc., Vero Beach, Fla., 1979-82; real estate broker, Fellsmere, Fla., 1982—. Councilman, City of Fellsmere, 1981-83, chmn. ways and means com., 1982-83. Mem. Fla. Assn. Home Builders, Nat. Bd. Realtors, Nat. Assn. Broadcasters.

DUMAS, BONNIE PLEASANTS, biometrician; b. Siler City, N.C., Apr. 21, 1944; d. George David and Gwendolyn (MacMullin) Pleasants; m. David Lang Dumas, Aug. 30, 1969; children—David Lang, Jr., Michael Christopher. B.S. Math., U. S.C.-Columbia, 1969; M.S. in Biometry, Med. U. S.C.-Charleston, 1978. With Southeastern Newspapers, Augusta, Ga., 1970-72; instr. Med. U. S.C., Dept. Biometry, 1974-82; scientist-biometrician Westvaco Corp., Timberlands Div., Charleston, S.C., 1982—; adj. instr. dept. biometry Med. U. S.C. Mem. Am. Statis. Assn. (pres. S.C. chpt.), AAUW, Assn. Computing Machinery, IEEE, Biometrics Soc., Mu Sigma Rho, Sigma Xi. Office: I-26 and 17A PO Box 1950 Summerville SC 29484

DU MAS, DOROTHY JONES, banking officer; b. Richmond, Va., Mar. 1, 1922; d. Russell Edward and Etta May (Thompson) Jones; student U. Denver, U. Mont., N.Mex. State U.; m. Frank Maurice du Mas, Nov. 20, 1941; children—Donald Edward, Michael Earl, Mark Maurice, Douglas Frank, Dorothy Mae. Engaged in banking, 1952—; personnel dir. central info. file Ga. RR Bank, Augusta, 1966-69; officer, plan mgr. bank credit card dept. First Nat. Bank & Trust Co., Augusta, 1969-82; with Peachtree Bank and Trust Co., Atlanta, 1982-83; asst. br. mgr. Trust Co. Bank, Atlanta, 1983—. Named Outstanding Lady Banker of Yr., Am. Inst. of Banking, 1971. Mem. Am. Inst. Banking (mem. faculty; speaking award 1970), Nat. Assn. Bank Women, Credit Women Internat. Baptist. Contbr. articles to profl. jours. Office: 5008 Buford Hwy Atlanta GA 30341

DUNAGEN, HUBERT LEE, architect, consultant, publisher; b. Atlanta, Jan. 22, 1951; s. Charles Edward and Mary Louise (Lawrence) D. B.Arch., Ga. Tech. Inst., 1974, M.S.I.E., 1978; M.F.A., Princeton U., 1977. Registered architect. Instr., Coll. Architecture, Ga. Tech. Inst., 1974-79; design architect Abreu & Robeson, Inc., Atlanta, 1976-78, dir. mktg. and bus. devel., 1978-80; architect RFM Group, San Diego and Atlanta, 1980-81; v.p. Med. Design Atlanta, 1981—; pres. H.L. Dunagen, Inc., Bus. Cons. and Pubs., Atlanta, 1982—; cons. med. office design, hist. preservation. Exec. dir. Atlanta Landmarks, Inc., 1977-79. Recipient Golden Shovel award, 1982. Mem. AIA, AAUP, Nat. Trust Hist. Preservation, Soc. Archtl. Historians, Am. Hosp. Assn., Fedn. Am. Hosps. Republican. Roman Catholic. Club: Atlanta City. Author: Enrico Zuccalli, 1978; The Architecture of Adolf Hitler, 1980; Coming Out, 1982; patentee Electronic Christmas Tree, 1982; designer Piedmont Internal Medicine Ctr., Greenwood, S.C., 1981; Glamorgan Med. Ctr., Alliance, Ohio, 1982; Palmetto Med. Ctr., New Smyrna Beach, Fla., 1983; Computer Dr. Assn. Bldg., Raleigh, N.C., 1982; The Miller Clinic, Charlotte, N.C., 1981; others. Office: Med Design Internat 1945 Cliff Valley Way Suite 240 Atlanta GA 30329

DUNAVANT, LEONARD CLYDE, state senator; b. Ripley, Tenn., Oct. 29, 1919; s. Harvey Maxie and Chloris Earl (Akin) D.; student Union U., Tenn., Memphis State U.; m. Deloris Anderson, Jan. 5, 1940; children—Janene Dunavant Pennel, Leonard Clyde, Susanne Dunavant Ripski. Alderman City of Millington (Tenn.); mem. Tenn. Ho. of Reps., chmn. fin., ways and means com.; mem. Tenn. Senate, chmn. legis. council pensions and retirement. Served with USNR, World War II. Mem. So. Regional Edn. Bd. Republican. Methodist. Club: Rotary (past pres.). *

DUNAVIN, LEONARD SYPRET, research agronomist; b. Algood, Tenn., Dec. 17, 1930; s. Leonard Sypret and Odell (Cornwell) D.; m. Willie Mae Payne, Dec. 22, 1962; children—Sheri Patricia, Juliana Kathleen. B.S., Tenn. Tech. U., 1952; M.S. in Agr., U. Fla., 1954, Ph.D., 1959. Asst. agronomist West Fla. Expt. Sta., Jay, 1959-67; assoc. prof. agronomy Agr. Research and Edn. Ctr., U. Fla., Jay, 1967—. Contbr. articles to profl. jours. Served with U.S. Army, 1954-56. Mem. Am. Soc. Agronomy, Crop Sci. Soc. Am., Soil and Crop Sci. Soc. Fla., Am. Forage and Grassland Council, Gamma Sigma Delta. Methodist. Avocation: hunting. Home: 912 Berryhill St Milton FL 32570 Office: U Fla Agr Research and Edn Ctr Route 3 Box 575 Jay FL 32565

DUNAWAY, DONNA ELIZABETH KASTLE, computer scientist, real estate developer; b. Ft. Worth, Mar. 16, 1935; d. Joseph A. and Susie (Garrett) Kastle; B.A., Tex. Christian U., 1956; M.S., So. Meth. U., 1969, Ph.D., 1972; children—Diane Elizabeth Dunaway Pitcher, Thomas Kastle. Owner, pres. Ditrec Corp., Dallas, 1971—, Dunaway Group Inc., Dallas, 1982—; computer sci. researcher Tex. Instruments, Inc., 1973-79; mgr. software devel., 1979-81. Mem. Math. Assn. Am., Assn. Computing Machinery, Kappa Kappa Gamma. Presbyterian. Home: 7 Cavendish Court Dallas TX 75225

DUNAWAY, DONNA LEE, physical education educator; b. Birmingham, Ala., Sept. 22, 1948; d. John D. and Frances (Lovelady) D. B.S., U. Montevallo, 1970; M.A.Ed., U. Ala., Birmingham, 1973, Ed.D., Tuscaloosa, 1982. Tchr. Hueytown Elemen. Sch. (Ala.), 1970-77, 78-79; cons. elem. sch. phys. edn. U. Ala., Tuscaloosa, 1977-78; asst. prof. health and phys. edn. Samford U., Birmingham, 1979—. Mem. AAHPERD, Ala. Assn. Health, Phys. Edn., Recreation, Dance (publs. editor 1980-81, treas. 1981-82, v.p. recreation 1983-84), Kappa Delta Pi. Office: Samford Univ 800 Lakeshore Dr Birmingham AL 35209

DUNAWAY, JAMES CRAWFORD, safety engineer; b. Franklinton, La., June 29, 1949; s. Clifton C. and Dorothy M. (James) D.; m. Whilemena Mullins, Feb. 18, 1966; children—Shannon Lynn, Monica Hope. A.A., Meridian Jr. Coll., Miss., 1981; B.S. in Health Scis., George Washington U., 1982; postgrad. U. So. Miss., 1985—. Enlisted U.S. Navy, 1968, resigned, 1981; safety engr. Diamond M. Drilling Co., Morgan City, La., 1982-84, Tranworld Drilling Co., Lafayette, La., 1984—. Scoutmaster Boy Scouts Am., Pensacola, Fla., 1976, Tidewater, Va., 1978; instr. ARC, McComb, Miss. Mem. Am. Soc. Safety Engrs. Republican. Mormon. Club: Beta (Monticello, Miss.). Avocations: jogging; camping; reading; writing. Home: Route 2 Box 147 Jayess MS 39641

DUNAWAY, LEAH DECKER, training specialist; b. Repton, Ala., Aug. 6, 1940; d. John Benjamin and Mildren (Jennings) Brown; children—Andrea, Caroline. Student Baylor U., 1958-60; B.S., U. Houston, 1961, M.S., 1970, Ed.D., 1983. Tchr. Tex. Pub. Schs., 1961-70; ednl. cons. State of Tex., Houston, 1979-82; instructional technologist NL Petroleum Services, Houston, 1982-83; sr. tng. analyst Exxon Prodn. Research, Houston, 1983—. Writer, editor, cons. for various tech. tng. manuals for petroleum industry, 1982—. Vol. St. Luke's Emergency Room, Houston, 1980, St. Joseph Hosp. Psychiatric div., Houston, 1978; mem. Tex. Sesquicentennial Com. Mem. Am. Soc. Tng. and Devel. (com. mem.), Jr. League Houston, Nat. Soc. for Performance and Instrn., Park People. Avocations: gardening; travel; restorations of houses and furniture. Office: Exxon Production Research Co 3104 Edloe St Houston TX 77001

DUNAWAY, MILTON, educational adminstrator, educator; b. Lumpkin, Ga., July 11, 1938; s. John Maxie and Harriette Evelyn (Parker) D.; m. Evalyn Thaxton, Mar. 30, 1957; children—Kerry Milton, John E., Angela Suzann. B.Ed. in Math., U. Ga., 1959; M.Ed. in Math., Mercer U., 1966; Ed.D. in Adminstrn. and Supervision, Auburn U., 1969. Cert. Adminstrn. and Supervision, Ga. Registrar, dir. Adminstrn. Ga. Southwestern Coll., Americus, 1961-67; dept. head Auburn U., Montgomery, Ala., 1968-70; headmaster Beechwood Sch., Marshallville, Ga., 1970-73; v.p. devel. Tift Coll., Forsyth, Ga., 1973-78; acad. dean Crandall Coll., Macon, Ga., 1978-79; supervising prin. Northeast High Sch., Macon, 1979—; adj. prof. Mercer U., Macon, 1973—. Active Macon Red Cross; bd. dirs. Vol. Macon., 1983-84. Recipient Star Tchr. award Crawford County Bd. Edn., Roberts, Ga., 1964. Mem. Profl. Assn. Ga. Educators. Republican. Methodist. Lodge: Lions. Avocations: golf; tennis. Home: 1194 River North Circle Macon GA 31210 Office: Northeast High Sch 1646 Upper River Rd Macon GA 31211

DUNBAR, JAMES V., JR., lawyer, educator, real estate broker, broadcaster; b. Union, S.C., June 4, 1937; s. James V. and Hatten (Crawford) D.; m. Nancy Mayer, Feb. 26, 1960; children—Nancy Phillips, Katherine Crawford. B.S. in Bus., U. S.C., 1959; J.D., U. Va., 1965. Bar: S.C. 1965, Va. 1965, Colo. 1965, U.S. Supreme Ct. 1980. Assoc. Holme, Roberts & Owen, Denver, 1965-68; v.p. Cosmos Broadcasting Corp., Columbia, S.C., 1969-74; mng. ptnr. Berry Dunbar & Woods, Columbia and Atlanta, 1974—; pres. Mid-Carolina Communications, Inc., 1978—, Selected Brokerage Realty, 1975—; grad. prof. U. S.C.; lectr. corp. structure and immigration, U.S. and abroad. Chmn. S.C. Lawyers for Reagan, 1980; pres. Columbia Philharm. Orch., 1981-82, Trinity Cathedral Men's Club, 1979-80, Mid-Carolina Council on Alcohol and Drug Abuse, 1974-78; gen. counsel S.C. Broadcasters Assn., So. Edn. Communications Assn. Served to lt. col. USMCR, 1959—. Named Young Man of Year, S.C. Jaycees, 1970. Mem. ABA, Colo. Bar Assn., S.C. Bar Assn., Va. Bar Assn., Fed. Communications Bar Assn., Am. Immigration Lawyers Assn., London C. of C., Belgian Am. C. of C., Kappa Alpha Order, Phi Alpha Delta. Episcopalian. Clubs: Forest Lake Country, Belle Isle, Summit, Kiwanis, World Trade (Atlanta); Commerce (Greenville, S.C.). Contbr. articles to profl. publs. Office: 1325 Laurel St Columbia SC 29201

DUNBAR, PAUL EDWARD, music educator; b. Gasville, Ark., Mar. 31, 1952; s. Charles Edward and Ruby Lain (Morris) D.; m. Pamela Jill Sowers, June 14, 1980; children—Katherine Anne (dec.), Kara Elisabeth. Mus. B., Henderson State U., 1974; Mus.M., La. State U., 1975, D. Musical Arts, 1980. Teaching asst. La. State U., Baton Rouge, 1977-78; head organ dept. Bob Jones U., Greenville, S.C., 1978—, chmn. div. music, 1981—; organist Westminster Presbyterian Ch., Hot Springs, Ark., 1972-74; organist, choirmaster Ch. of the Way Presbyn. Ch., Baton Rouge, 1975-78. Mem. Am. Guild Organists (dean 1979-81, sub-dean 1983-85), Phi Mu Alpha Sinfonia, Pi Kappa Lambda. Republican. Presbyterian. Office: Bob Jones U Box 34533 1700 Wade Hampton Blvd Greenville SC 29614

DUNBAR, PRESCOTT NELSON, investment co. exec.; b. New Orleans, Feb. 22, 1942; s. Lewis D. Prescott and Eleanor (Nelson) D.; B.A., U. of South, 1964; M.A., La. State U., 1967; M.A. (Ford fellow), Harvard U., 1969; m. Sarah W. Blodgett, Feb. 10, 1969; children—P. Hayden, Lander G. Financier, New Orleans. Trustee, New Orleans Mus. Art, 1974—, 1st. v.p., 1979, treas., 1978, chmn. of accessions, 1977, sec., 1982, 2d v.p, 1984, 85; trustee New Orleans Ballet; bd. dirs. Save Our Cemeteries, 1975—, Anglo-Am. Mus. Friends, 1985; trustee Friends of French Market, 1984, pres., 1985. Mem. La. Hist. Soc., Friends of Cabildo, Friends of Winterthur, Provincetown Art Assn., Am. Assn. Mus. Trustees. Republican. Episcopalian. Clubs: Stage Harbor Yacht, Chatham Beach and Tennis; Harvard of N.Y.; New Orleans Country, Internat. House (New Orleans). Home and Office: 2423 Prytania New Orleans LA 70130

DUNCAN, ARDINELLE BEAN, author; b. Berlin, N.H., Dec. 6, 1913; d. Sylvester James and Mary Ellen (Connors) Bean; m. Robert Leon Duncan, Nov. 23, 1950; children—Carole, Robert Leon, James Bean. Student pub. schs., Iroquois Falls, Ont., Can. Research librarian Abitibi Power and Paper Co., Iroquois Falls, 1930-32; researcher FBI, Washington, 1943-47; editorial staff TV Digest, Washington, 1946-47, Broadcasting-Telecasting Mag., 1947-50; editor Fla. Keys News, Homestead, 1957-58; producer Talk of the Town, Findlay, Ohio, 1969; tchr. creative writing, pub. speaking Catawba Valley Community Coll., Hickory, N.C., 1965-66; guest lectr in field. Mem. Columbia County (Pa.) Bd. Pub. Assistance, 1972-79, sec., 1975; mem. com. of one hundred to provide YMCA facility, Bloomsburg, 1976; editor The Record Mental Health Assn. Columbia/Montour counties, 1976-78. Recipient citation for service to mental health, 1977. Mem. Nat. League Am. Penwomen. Clubs: Bloomsburg State U. Woman's, Fairway Springs Woman's (pres. 1986-87). Author: Twirly Hurly, the Helicopter Rabbit, 1962. Contbr. articles, stories to ednl. mags., jours. Home: 3136 Crenshaw Ct New Port Richey FL 33553

DUNCAN, BUELL GARD, JR., banker; b. Orlando, Fla., July 31, 1928; s. Buell Gard and Elizabeth Phillips (Parks) D., B.A., Emory U., 1950; postgrad. BMA Sch. Bank Mktg., 1959; m. Patricia Ann Jones, Mar. 25, 1952; children—Buell Gard III, Patricia Ann, Allan Griffin, Nancy Elizabeth. With Sun Bank, N.A., Orlando, 1953—, asst. cashier, 1956-60, asst. v.p., 1960-61, v.p., 1961-68, sr. v.p., 1968-72, exec. v.p., 1972-75, pres., 1975-76, chmn. bd., chief exec. officer, 1977—, also dir., sr. exec. v.p., chmn. sr. mgmt. council Sun Banks Inc.; dir. Nat. Standard Life Ins. Co., Orlando. Bd. dirs. United Way of Orange County (Fla.), 1966—, pres., 1973; chmn. Downtown Devel. Bd., 1979-81; treas., dir. Central Fla. Blood Bank, 1962—; pres. U. Central Fla. Found., 1982-83; active Valencia Community Coll. Found.; mem. Com. of 100 of Orange County. Served with USAF, 1951-53. Mem. Fla. Bankers Assn., Bank Mktg. Assn. (pres. 1971-72), Fla. C. of C. (pres. 1984-85), Orlando C. of C. (pres. 1970-71), Navy League (dir. central Fla. council 1969—), Fla. Blue Key, Phi Delta Theta. Kiwanian (past pres.). Clubs: Country of Orlando (pres., dir.), Citrus, Univ. (Orlando). Home: 1200 Country Ln Orlando FL 32804 Office: Sun First Nat Bank 200 S Orange Ave Orlando FL 32801

DUNCAN, CHESTER EUGENE, army officer; b. Dallas, Oct. 6, 1940; s. Chester Otto Duncan and Ruth Elizabeth (Oliver) Duncan Woods; m. Virgie Lee Teague, Jan. 20, 1963; children—Tammy Lynn (dec.), Lori Anne, Deborah K. Assoc. of Bus., Texarkana Jr. Coll., 1961; B.Bus., So. State Coll., Magnolia, Ark., 1963; M.A., Ball State U., 1977. Enlistedman U.S. Army, 1963-64, warrant officer aviator, 1965-67, commd. 2d lt., 1967, advanced through grades to lt. col., 1985; comdr. 3d bn. Acad. Health Sci., Fort Sam Houston, Tex., 1985—. Vice pres. Cole High Sch. PTO, Fort Sam Houston, 1984. Decorated D.F.C., Bronze Star, Air medal with 20 oak leaf clusters. Mem. U.S. Army Aviation Mus. Found. (charter), U.S. Army Aviation Assn. Am. (v.p. 1985—), U.S. Army Assn. Democrat. Methodist. Avocations: fishing; hunting; woodworking; gardening. Home: 551 Graham Rd San Antonio TX 78234 Office: Acad Health Sci 3d Bn Fort Sam Houston TX 78234

DUNCAN, HARRY ERNEST, educator; b. Hartford, W.Va., Nov. 20, 1936; s. William Robert and Margaretta (Harris) D.; B.S., W.Va. U., 1959, M.S., 1961, Ph.D., 1966; m. Carmela Rose Mangano, June 14, 1958; children—Deborah Ann, Pamela Sue, Harry Ernest. Asst. prof. plant pathology N.C. State U., Raleigh, 1965-70, asso. prof., specialist-in-charge, Plant Pathology Extension, 1970-77, prof., specialist-in-charge plant pathology extension, 1977—. Mem. Pesticide Assn. N.C. (bd. dirs. from 1972), Corn Growers Assn. N.C. (bd. dirs. from 1977), Am. Phytopathol. Soc., Sigma Xi, Epsilon Sigma Phi, Gamma Sigma Delta. Roman Catholic. Home: 201 Chatterson Dr Raleigh NC 27609 Office: PO Box 7616 NC State Univ Raleigh NC 27695

DUNCAN, JAMES RUSSELL, industrial executive; b. Tucson, Apr. 17, 1917; s. Bradford and Mattielee (Josey) D.; m. Mimi Galloway; children—Joanne, Robert, Lance. Student, U. Ariz., U. Wis. Extension, Milw. Vice pres., gen. mgr. Peerless Machine Co., Racine, Wis., 1940-45; gen. mgr. Moore Machinery Co., Los Angeles, 1945-46; sec.-treas. McCulloch Motors Corp., Los Angeles, 1946-48; chief of capital goods ECA Mission to Italy, 1948-50; indsl. cons., Italy, 1950-52; pres. Electric Sprayit Co. (and subs.), Sheboygan, Wis., 1952-53; asst. to pres. Stewart-Warner Corp. (cons.), Chgo., 1954-55; v.p. Misco Corp., also Consol. Founderies & Mfg., Chgo., 1955-57; chmn., pres., dir. Mpls.-Moline Co., Hopkins, Minn., 1957-60; cons., dir. Bowser, Inc., 1960-62, United Board & Carton Corp., 1960-62; chmn. bd., chief exec. officer, treas. Steego Corp. (formerly Sterling Precision Corp.), 1962—; chmn. bd. Resource Exploration, Inc., Shreveport, La., Milw. Western Corp., Milw. Recipient Recognition award U. Ariz. Clubs: Memphis Country, Memphis Hunt and Polo, Delray (Fla.) Beach Yacht; Everglades, Bath and Tennis (Palm Beach, Fla.). Office: Suite 900 319 Clematis St West Palm Beach FL 33401*

DUNCAN, JOHN JAMES, congressman; b. Scott County, Tenn., Mar. 24, 1919; married; four children. Asst. atty. gen., 1947-56; dir. law, Knoxville, Tenn., 1956-59, mayor, 1959-64; mem. 89th-98th congresses from 2d dist. Tenn. Served with U.S. Army, 1942-45. Mem. Am., Tenn., Knoxville bar assns., Am. Legion (comdr. Tenn. 1954), V.F.W. Presbyn. Republican. Office: 2458 Rayburn House Office Bldg Washington DC 20515

DUNCAN, KIT, social worker; b. Anderson, Ind., Jan. 1, 1956; s. Leo and Theda (Robinson) Craig; A.A., Freed-Hardeman Coll., 1975; B.A., Lubbock Christian Coll., 1978; M.S. in Social Work, U. Tex., 1985. Caseworker Smithlawn Maternity Home, Lubbock, Tex., 1978-79; campus caseworker Christ's Haven for Children, Keller, Tex., 1979-82; VA, Temple, Tex., 1982-83; dir. family services AGAPE of N.C., Inc., 1983-85; program dir. Lutheran Family Services, 1985—. Recipient Psychology/Sociology award Lubbock Christian Coll., 1978-79. Mem. Nat. Assn. Social Workers. Mem. Ch. of Christ. Home: 4100 North O'he Greensboro NC 27405

DUNCAN, NORMA HEFNER, nurse practitioner; b. Altapass, N.C., Sept. 24, 1937; d. Roy Leo and Dora Lou (Biddix) Hefner; m. Charles Pippin Duncan, Aug. 3, 1957; children—Brynne Charles, Constance Leigh. Student Grace Hosp. Sch. Nursing, 1955-57; diploma Rowan Hosp. Sch. Nursing, 1961; cert. family nurse practitioner U. N.C., 1974; cert. in Nursing Adminstrn., Duke U., 1978. Office nurse, Killeen, Tex., 1958-62; operating room supr. Spruce Pine (N.C.) Community Hosp., 1963-64; operating room staff, supr. York Gen Hosp., Rock Hill, S.C., 1964-70; sch. nurse Mitchell County Bd. Edn., Bakersville, N.C., 1971-73; family nurse practitioner Rural Health Clinic, Burnsville, N.C., 1974-75; dir. nursing Blue Ridge Hosp., Spruce Pine, 1975-82; asst. dir. nursing, inservice educator Madison Manor Nursing Ctr., Mars Hill, N.C., 1983, dir. nursing, 1983—; tchr. nurse asst. classes Asheville Biltmore Tech., Ashville, N.C. Past dist. rep. for revision of N.C. Nurse Practice Act and Ednl. Standards. Bd. dirs. Baptist Women's Missionary Union; past pres. Jr. Woman's Club, PTA; past sec. Children's Services Council. Recipient N.C. Gov.'s grant, 1973; Humanitarian award Optimist Internat., 1980; named Best Nurse, Rowan Meml. Hosp., 1961. Mem. Am. Nurses Assn., Nat. League Nursing, N.C. League Nursing (past sec.), Santa Filomena Hon. Soc. Democrat.

DUNCAN, PAUL, printmaker, communications consultant, educator; b. Columbia, S.C., July 10, 1909; s. William Whiteford and Myrtle Frances (Gibson) D.; B.A., U. Ala., 1934; postgrad. Corcoran Sch. Art, 1967-75, Georgetown U., 1973-74; m. Gwendolyn Margaret Drolet, Feb. 6, 1937; children—Paula D. Hereford, Denis D. Hasty, Jean Laurens D. Lott. With Montgomery (Ala.) Advertiser, 1926-30, Anniston (Ala.) Star, 1934, Knoxville News-Sentinel, 1935-36, AP, Montgomery and Birmingham, Ala., 1937-42; with Office of Govt. Reports, Nat. War Labor Bd., Office Economic Stabilization of Exec. Office Pres., Washington, 1942-46; adminstrv. asst. U.S. Senator Lister Hill, Washington, 1946-51; dir. information and reports Tech. Coop. Adminstrn. Dept. State, Washington, 1951-53; information cons. Pres.'s Com. on Scientists and Engrs., Washington, 1956-58; owner, cons. on mass communications and pub. affairs co., Washington, 1953-77. Prints exhibited in Corcoran Gallery Art, 1969-71. Bd. dirs. Performing Arts Assn., Foley, Ala. Decorated Comdr. Most Noble Order Crown, King of Thailand, 1960. Recipient First prize printmaking, Corcoran Sch. Art, 1971. Mem. Phi Gamma Delta. Democrat. Presbyterian. Author: Motivate, Teach, Train, 1952 (handbook). Editor: The Scientific Revolution: Challenge and Promise, 1959. Home and Studio: Magnolia Springs AL 36555

DUNCAN, PAUL EUGENE, college dean; b. Starkville, Miss., Feb. 4, 1937; s. Belton Youngblood and Elizabeth (Taylor) D.; m. Tannis Marie Alford; children—Angela Lyn, Paul Eric. B.A., Miss. State U., 1959; M.S.S.W., U. Tenn., 1962. Child welfare supr. Miss. Dept. Welfare, Jackson, 1962; dir. social work Ch. of God Home for Children, Sevierville, Tenn., 1962-68; dir. cure corps Teen Challenge, N.Y.C., 1968-70; dean students Lee Coll., Cleveland, 1970—. Author: On Campus, 1977; contbr. articles to mags., jours. Bd. dirs. Cleveland YMCA, 1984—, Boys Club Cleveland, 1980—; v.p. Contact, 1972—. Mem. Acad. Christian Deans, Tenn. Tchrs. Edn. Assn. Democrat. Mem. Ch. of God. Club: Optimist (pres. 1978). Avocations: tennis; racquetball. Home: 2760 Greenbrier Dr NW Cleveland TN 37311 Office: Lee Coll N Ocoee St Cleveland TN 37311

DUNCAN, PHYLLIS ANGIE, nurse, administrator; b. Crossnore, N.C., Jan. 14, 1942; d. Theodore Rosevelt and Gwendolyn Aileen (McKinney) Burleson; m. Roger Dale Duncan, Aug. 30, 1964; children—Ed, Ted, Meg. Diploma in nursing arts Presbyn. Hosp. Sch. Nursing, Charlotte, N.C., 1964; B.S., Appalachian State U., 1975. R.N., N.C. Staff nurse Johnson City Eye Hosp., 1965-66, pub. health nurse, 1966-67, 69-70, operating room/recovery room nurse, 1967-68, asst. dir. nursing, 1968-69; instr. nursing Mayland Tech. Coll., Spruce Pine, N.C., 1974-80; dir. nursing Blue Ridge Hosp. System, Spruce Pine and Burnsville, N.C., 1982—. Mem. adv. com. Mountain Area Health Edn. Ctr.; co-edn. chmn. Am. Cancer Soc. Recipient Bedside Nursing award Presbyn. Hosp. Sch. Nursing, 1964. Mem. N.C. Nursing Adminstrs. Soc. Baptist.

DUNCAN, PHYLLIS ANN, manufacturing company executive; b. Pawhuska, Okla., July 22, 1946; d. Ray Garrett and Darlene Genevia (Frazier) Lewis; m. Larry Joe Duncan, Aug. 17, 1962 (div. July 1982); children—Daniel Alan, Sheryl Lynne; m. 2d. Robert Brian Battaglia, Aug. 13, 1983; stepchildren—David Battaglia, Julie Battaglia. A.A. in Bus. Adminstrn., Westark Community Coll., 1979, A. Applied Sci. Transp., 1982; B.S. in Bus. Adminstrn., Coll. of Ozarks, 1980; M.B.A., U. Ark., 1982. Inventory control clk. Am. Can-Dixie Products, Fort Smith, Ark., 1966-68, customer service order clk., 1968-70, customer service sales asst., 1970-80, mfg. assoc., 1980, dept. supr. shipping, warehousing, distbn., 1980-82; gen. supr. tech. ops. James River-Dixie/No Inc., Fort Smith, 1982-83, mgr. quality and process control, 1984—; instr. bus. Coll. of Ozarks, Clarksville, Ark., 1982—. Loaned exec. United Way-United Fund Drive, Fort Smith, 1980; choir dir. Phoenix Village Baptist Ch., Fort Smith, 1968—, ch. organist, 1970—. Named Women of the Day Bus. and Profl. Women Assn., 1980. Mem. Am. Soc. for Quality Control, Women M.B.A.s (U. Ark. chpt.), Nat. Assn. Female Execs. (network dir.), Am. Guild Organists, Coll. of Ozarks Alumni Assn., U. Ark. Alumni Assn. Republican. Home: PO Box 1531 Fort Smith AR 72902 Office: James River-Dixie/No Inc 4411 Midland Blvd PO Box 428 Fort Smith AR 72902

DUNCAN, POPE ALEXANDER, college president; b. Glasgow, Ky., Sept. 8, 1920; s. Pope Alexander and Mabel (Roberts) D.; B.S., U. Ga., 1940, M.S., 1941; Th.M., So. Bapt. Theol. Sem., 1944, Ph.D., 1947; postgrad. U. Zurich (Switzerland), 1960-61; m. Margaret Flexer, June 30, 1943; children—Mary Margaret Duncan Jones, Annie Laurie Duncan Kelly, Katherine Maxwell. Instr. physics U. Ga., 1940-41; fellow So. Bapt. Theol. Sem., 1944-45; dir. religious activities Mercer U., 1945-46, Roberts prof. church history, 1948-49; prof. religion Stetson U., 1946-48, 49-53; prof. ch. history Southeastern Bapt. Theol. Sem., 1953-63; dean Brunswick Coll., 1964; pres. South Ga. Coll., Douglas, 1964-68; v.p. Ga. So. Coll., Statesboro, 1968-71, pres., 1971-77; pres. Stetson U., Deland, Fla., 1977—; chmn. council pres.'s So. Consortium for Internat. Edn., 1974-75; mem. coll. commn. So. Assn. Colls. and Schs., 1978-82; bd. dirs. Nat. Assn. Ind. Colls. and Univs., 1980-83; chmn. Fla. Ind. Coll. Fund, 1980-81; mem. president's commn. Nat. Collegiate Athletic Assn., 1984—. Pres. Wake Forest Civic Club, 1959-60, Ga. Assn. Colls., 1968-69; pres. Coastal Empire council Boy Scouts Am., 1973-74; bd. dirs. Deland Com. of 100, 1981-85. Mem. Fla. Assn. Colls. and Univs. (pres. 1982-83), Ind. Colls. and Univs. of Fla. (chmn. 1982-84), Assn. So. Bapt. Colls. and Schs. (pres. 1980-81), Am. Hist. Assn., Am. Soc. Ch. History, Assn. Ch.-Related Colls. and Univs. of South (v.p. 1982-83, pres. 1983-84), Douglas-Coffee County C. of C. (dir. 1966-68), Statesboro-Bulloch County C. of C. (dir. 1971-77), Deland C. of C. (dir. 1977-81, v.p. 1980-81), Fla. Council of 100, Phi Beta Kappa, Omicron Delta Kappa, Phi Kappa Phi, Phi Delta Kappa, Kappa Delta Pi, Pi Mu Epsilon, Phi Eta Sigma, Sigma Phi Sigma. Democrat. Baptist. Rotarian (dir. 1965-66, 1970-72, pres. 1967-68). Author: Our Baptist Story, 1958; The Pilgrimage of Christianity, 1965 Hanserd Knollys, 1965; bd. dirs. S.B.C. Today, 1983—. Home: 418 N Woodland Blvd Deland FL 32720

DUNCAN, ROBERT TYUS, computer industry executive; b. Jacksonville, Fla., Dec. 23, 1937; s. Joseph Elvin and Antoinette Talmadge (Tyus) D.; m. Helen Murray, July 17, 1965; children—Tonya Lynne, Cindy Rochelle. B.B.A., U. Ga., Athens, 1959. Sales rep. Sperry (Univac div.), Atlanta, 1965-66; industry mktg. mgr. Honeywell, Atlanta, 1967-70; dir. industry mktg. Internat. Group, Wellesley Hills, Mass., 1971-72; account exec. Sperry Corp., Atlanta, 1973-82; chief exec. officer, pres. Catronix Corp., Atlanta, 1982—, also dir. Served to lt. U.S. Navy, 1959-64. Episcopalian. Home: 4590 Millbrook Dr NW Atlanta GA 30327 Office: Catronix Corp 120 Ralph McGill Blvd NE Atlanta GA 30308

DUNCAN, THOMAS ALTON, editor; b. Staunton, Va., Mar. 30, 1942; s. Walter Alton and Anna Wallace (Ramsey) D.; m. Claudette Judith Gilbert, Apr. 23, 1966; children—Lissa Annette, Daniel Alton, Robert Keith. B.G.S., Wichita State U., 1980. Ordained to ministry Baptist Ch., 1971. Enlisted U.S. Navy, 1961, resigned, 1969; dir. radio dept. New Tribes Mission, Jackson, Mich., 1969-74; minister Bible Baptist Ch., Newton, Kans., 1974-77; advt. writer Sta. KOEZ, Newton, 1977-80; tech. editor GTE Service Corp., Lexington, Ky., 1981—. Author: (with others) The Write Design, 1984. Mem. Am. Soc. for Tng. and Devel. (editor 1984-85). Republican. Avocations: camping; gardening. Home: 1824 Traveller Rd Lexington KY 40504 Office: GTE Service Corp 3050 Harrodsburg Rd Lexington KY 40503

DUNGAN, RONALD TROY, electrical contractor executive, consultant; b. Austin, Tex., July 28, 1943; s. Clarence Vernon and Agnes Pauline (Weidebusch) D.; m. Patricia Ann Marburger, Apr. 25, 1964; children—Rhonda Ann, Brian Keith. Student Nixon Clay Coll., 1961-63. Journeyman electrician, Austin, 1966-70; electrician Tecapa Electric Co., Austin, 1967-69; sec.-treas., estimator Mark Electric, Austin, 1970-84; pres. Sun*Tech Electric, Austin, 1984—. Trustee Liberty Hill Ind. Sch. Dist. Bd. Trustees, Tex., 1982-84, pres. 1984—. Served with N.G., 1966-72. Methodist. Avocations: hunting; fishing; golf; swimming. Home: 2705 Cedar Hollow Rd Georgetown TX 78628 Office: Sun*Tech Elect Contractors Inc PO Box 15181 Austin TX 78761

DUNHAM, DONALD HARRISON, insurance executive; b. Davies County, Mo., Sept. 15, 1913; s. Emory H. and Zula (Crain) D.; A.A., Pomona Coll., 1935; LL.B., Nat. U., Washington, 1941, LL.M., 1942; J.D., George Washington U., 1968; m. Lillian Mae Ingram, Aug. 21, 1941; 1 dau., Carol-Lynn Shirley. Instr. ins., office mgmt. Nat. Inst. Tech., Washington, 1946-47, dist. mgr. group dept. Mass. Mut. Life Ins. Co., 1947-48; regional mgr. group dept. U.S. Life, N.Y.C., 1948-50; region and group dir. Eastern Seaboard, Minn. Mut. Life Ins. Co., 1950-51; dir. retirement, safety and ins. dept., also contbr. editor Rural Electrification mag. Nat. Rural Electric Coop. Assn., 1951-58; asst. v.p. Church Life Ins. Corp., 1958-59, adminstrv. v.p., 1959-64, v.p., mgr., 1964-72, dir., 1962-72, mem. exec. com., 1964-72; sec. Ch. Agy. Corp., Ch. Finance Corp., 1966-72; asst. v.p. govt. relations Ch. Pension Fund P.E. Ch., 1959-72; dep. asst. adminstr. Tex. State Bd. Ins., 1972-74; dep. asst. adminstr., ins. contract specialist Tex. Dept. Human Resources, 1974-77, adminstr. contractual devel., compliance rev., purchased health services, 1977—, HMO specialist, 1975—; ins. cons., 1950—; ins. cons. Nat. Telephone Coop. Assn.; mem. Gov.'s Com. on Nat. Health Ins. and Com. on Aging, 1977-78. Chmn. adv. com. problems aging to Borough Council, 1959-72; vice chmn. planning bd. Borough of New Providence, 1966-72; chmn. New Providence Indsl. Devel. Com., 1970-72; mem. Md. Gov.'s Citizens Com. Traffic Safety, 1951-72, Pres.'s Conf. Traffic Safety, Indsl. Safety; nat. safety counsel Ins. Conf. of Coop. League U.S. Served with USNR, 1944-46. Mem. A.I.M. (fellow pres.'s council), Am. Legion (post comdr.), Minn. State Soc. (past pres.), V.F.W., D.A.V., Nat. Assn. Ins. Commrs. (Episcopal Ch. rep. 1958-72), Group Health Fedn. Am., Group Health Assn. Am., Nat. Assn. HMO Regulators, Nat. Health Lawyers Assn., U.S. Power Squadron (No. N.J. safety com.), Kappa Sigma Kappa, Sigma Delta Kappa, Delta Psi Omega (mem. bishop's com. 1959-72). Mason (32 deg.). Clubs: Kenwood Golf and Country (Chevy Chase, Md.); Lucaya Golf and Country (Freeport, Grand Bahamas); Craftsman. Home: 4213 Endcliffe Dr Austin TX 78731 Office: Tex Dept Human Resources PO Box 2960 Mail Code 611E Austin TX 78769

DUNLAP, GLADYS FLORENCE, nurse; b. Mt. Croghan Twp., S.C., Feb. 17, 1921; s. Kirby Spofford and Martha Elizabeth (Gulledge) Gulledge; m. Leeton Cornelius Dunlap, Aug. 24, 1942; children—Margie, Martha, Marcia, James (dec.), John (dec.). Cosmotologist Sch. of Beauty, Salisbury, N.C., 1959; practical nurse Rowan Tech., Salisbury, 1967; with Cannon Mills, Kannapolis, N.C., 1941-47; owner, operator East 19th Beauty Shop, Kannapolis, 1960-64; nurse Cabarrus Meml. Hosp., Concord, N.C., 1965—. Mem. Lic. Practical Nurses Assn. N.C. Baptist.

DUNLAP, JOE EVERETT, dentist, writer, editor; b. Delaware, Ohio, May 11, 1930; s. Arthur Calvin and Mary Irene (Jones) D.; student Ohio Wesleyan U., 1949-50, 54; D.D.S., Ohio State U., 1959; m. Mary Susan King, June 17, 1959; children—Marlene, Todd, David, Sherrie, Dru. With Fla. Instl. Dental Service, Gainesville, Ft. Myers, 1959-60; individual practice dentistry, Clearwater, Fla., 1961-81; gen. mgr. ops. corp. hdqrs. Sheppard Dental Centers, Tampa, Fla., 1981-84; editor PennWell Books, Tulsa. Author: Surviving in Dentistry; The Beginning Dental Practice; Stress, Change & Related Pains; Keeping the Fire Alive; contbr. articles to dental jours., articles and photographs to regional publs. Served to 2d lt. Med. Service Corps, AUS, 1950-53. Mem. ADA, Fla., West Coast Dist. dental assns. Home: 1816 Lombardy Dr Clearwater FL 33515

DUNLAP, LOUIS TEMPLETON, mud logger; b. Ponca City, Okla., May 2, 1947; s. Oral Preston and Hayesenne (Little Bear) D.; m. Susan E. Cromling, Dec. 23, 1975 (div. May 1976). B.S., Okla. State U., 1969. Mud logging engr. Midwest Well Logging Co., Oklahoma City 1969-74, Universal Well Log Co., Elk City, Okla., 1974-76; contract mud logger Profl. Well Loggers, Oklahoma City, 1976-78; owner, mgr. L.T.D. Mud Logging Co., Midwest City, Okla., 1978—. Mem. Okla. State U. Alumni Assn. (life), NRA, Oklahoma City Geol. Soc., Tex. Panhandle Geol. Soc., Am. Assn. Petroleum Geologists. Democrat. Roman Catholic. Lodge: Moose. Avocations: hunting; fishing; prospecting; legalized gambling. Office: LTD Mud Logging PO Box 10779 Midwest City OK 73140

DUNLAP, NAOMI GIBSON, psychologist; b. Meridian, Tex., Oct. 10, 1911; d. John Wheat and Callie Jane (Taylor) Gibson; B.A., Baylor U., 1949; M.A., U. Tex. at Austin, 1950, Ph.D., 1961; m. Artie Reynolds Dunlap, Nov. 24, 1932 (dec.); 1 dau., Norma Dell (Mrs. Jack Thomas Harris). Clin. psychologist VA Center, Temple, Tex., until 1975; part-time pvt. practice clin. psychology, Austin, Tex., 1976—. Mem. Am. Psychol. Assn., Southwestern Psychol. Assn., Tex. Psychol. Assn. Home: 3204 W Ave T Temple TX 76501

DUNLAP, RICHARD FREEMAN, railway executive; b. Roanoke, Va., Mar. 24, 1922; s. Albert Christian and Helen (Meals) D.; ed. Hampden Sydney Coll., 1939-42; m. Marie Fallwell, Nov. 22, 1946; children—Richard Freeman, Anne Fallwell Dunlap Kanady. With N.&W. Ry., 1942—, asst. trainmaster, Portsmouth, Ohio, 1953-54, Williamson, W.Va., 1954-55, trainmaster, Portsmouth, 1955-56, asst. supt., Norfolk, Va., 1956-57, supt., Crewe, Va., 1957-58, Bluefield, W.Va., 1958-60, gen. supt. Eastern gen. div., Roanoke, 1960-62, regional mgr. Eastern region, 1962-64, gen. mgr. Lake region, Cleve., 1964-65, asst. v.p. ops., 1965-66, v.p. ops., 1966-73, sr. v.p. ops., 1973-80, exec. v.p., 1980-82, pres., 1982—; chief exec. officer, dir. Norfolk, Franklin & Danville Ry. Co.; pres., dir. C.W. Ry., Wheeling & Lake Erie Ry. Co., v.p., dir. Va. Holding Corp.; dir. Belt Ry. Co. of Chgo., High Point, Thomasville & Denton R.R., Lake Erie Dock Co., Norfolk & Portsmouth Belt Line R.R. Co., Pocahontas Land Corp., Terminal R.R. Assn. St. Louis, Wabash R.R. Co., Dereco, Ill., So. Ry., Dominion Bankshares Corp. Winston-Salem Southbound Ry. Co., Winston-Salem Terminal Co., Winston Land Corp.; Bd. dirs. Community Hosp. Roanoke Valley, Inc., W.Va. Found. Arts and Scis., Roanoke Symphony Soc., Roanoke Valley Devel. Corp.; mem. bus. adv. council Va. Poly. Inst. and State U. Served to capt. inf. AUS, 1942-46. Decorated Silver Star, Bronze Star, Purple Heart, Combat Infantryman's badge. Mem. Assn. Am. R.R.'s (past chmn. gen. com. operating-transp. div.), Am. Ry. Engrs. Soc., Ohio, Va., Roanoke chambers commerce, Kappa Alpha Frat. Episcopalian. Clubs: Shenandoah, Little Scorpions, Roanoke German. Home: 323 Cassell Ln SW Roanoke VA 24014 Office: 8 N Jefferson St Roanoke VA 24042

DUNLAP, STANTON PARKS, naval officer; b. San Diego, Sept. 18, 1934; s. Stanton Baldwin and Abby V. (Parks) D.; m. Dorothy Joan Denon, June 22, 1957; children—Stanton P., Christopher D. B.S.M.E., U.S. Naval Acad., 1957; M.S.S., U. So. Calif., 1983; Ph.D., Calif. Western U., 1985. Cert. hazard control mgr.; cert. profl. safety cons. Commd. ensign U.S. Navy, advanced through grades to capt., 1979; ops. officer, exec. officer Reconnaissance Attack Squadron 3, 1971-73; comdg. officer Tng. Squadron 86, 1973-74; safety officer USS America, 1974-77; force safety officer Naval Air Force-Atlantic Fleet, 1977-80; dir. naval aviation safety programs Naval Safety Ctr., Norfolk, Va., 1980—. Contbr. articles to profl. jours. Mem. choir St. Peter's Episcopal Ch., Norfolk, 1974-85, also lay reader; mgr., coach, umpire Little League, Albany, Ga., 1969-75; scoutmaster Boy Scouts Am., Albany, 1969-75. Decorated Meritorious Service medal, Air Medal with 4 clusters, others. Mem. Am. Soc. Safety Engrs., Nat. Safety Mgmt. Soc., System Safety Soc., Naval Inst., Naval Acad. Alumni Assn. (v.p. 1982-83). Republican. Lodge: Masons. Avocations: jogging; woodworking; gardening. Home: 1331 Acredale Rd Virginia Beach VA 23464 Office: Naval Safety Ctr Norfolk VA 23511

DUNLOP, BURTON DAVID, sociologist; b. Skowhegan, Maine, Jan. 26, 1944; s. Burton David and Marion Ada (Dickinson) D.; m. Sandra Lee Savage, Aug. 30, 1965; children—Kimberly Lynn, Kristin Lee. B.A., Eastern Nazarene Coll., 1966; M.A., U. Ill., 1970, Ph.D., 1973. Research assoc. Urban Inst., Washington, 1972-77, sr. research assoc., 1977-80; sr. policy analyst Abt Assocs., Inc., 1980-81, Project Hope Ctr. for Health Affairs, Millwood, Va., 1982—; cons. in field. Author: The Growth of Nursing Home Care, 1980. Editor: New Federalism and Long Term Health Care of the Elderly, 1985. Contbr. articles to profl. jours. and chpts. to books. Bd. dirs., v.p. Fair Oaks Estates Homeowners Assn., Va., 1984—. Served with USAF, 1966-68. Ford Found. fellow, 1971-72. Mem. Am. Sociol. Assn., Gerontol. Soc. Am., Phi Delta Lambda. Baptist. Avocations: landscaping; singing. Office: Project Hope Ctr for Health Affairs Millwood VA 22646

DUNLOP, LINDA LEDBETTER, school counselor, consultant; b. Asheville, N.C., Nov. 13, 1944; d. Lauice Bryan and Donnie Mae (Ray) Ledbetter; m. Joseph Clayton Dunn, June 26, 1966 (div. 1974); m. 2d, Charles Smith Dunlop, Jr., Dec. 31, 1976. B.A., U. N.C.-Greenville, 1966; M.Ed., Memphis State U., 1971; Ed.S., Western Carolina U., 1982. Biology tchr., sr. advisor Ahrens Trade High Sch., Louisville, 1966-70; sch. counselor, vocat. devel. coordinator, guidance dir. North Buncombe High Sch., Weaverville, N.C., 1972—; dist. VIII resource counselor N.C. State Dept. Pub. Instrn., vocat. guidance div., 1982—; mem. N.C. Guidance and Counseling Govt. Network System, 1981-83; mem. N.C. Statewide Interagy. Sch. Discipline Program and Inst., 1982, 83; mem. Buncombe County Schs. Task Force Interagy. Discipline Team, 1982, 83; mem. Buncombe County Health Occupation/Students of Am. Adv. Council, 1977-83; advisor Children's Welfare League, Asheville, N.C., 1975-83; mem. Buncombe County Schs. Com. on Grading, 1979-83; mem. Buncombe County Master Plan Com., 1980-83. Ambassador to USSR, N.C. Friendship Force, 1982; mem. N.C. Friendship Force, 1982, 83; mem. Asheville Friendship Force, 1983; mem. Apple Dumpling Clog Team. Recipient Hon. Admissions award U.S. Naval Acad., 1973; Cert. of Appreciation USAF Acad., 1983; 3d place trophy Carolina Canter Road Race, 1983. Mem. Am. Personnel and Guidance Assn., Am. Sch. Counselor Assn., Am. Vocat. Assn., NEA, N.C. Personnel and Guidance Assn., N.C. Sch. Counselor Assn., N.C. Vocat. Guidance Assn. (mem. exec. bd. 1983-84), N.C. Vocational Assn. (Vocat. Counselor of Yr. 1983), N.C. Occupational Info. and Guidance Div., N.C. Assn. Educators, N.C. Assn. Classroom Tchrs., Kappa Delta Pi, Phi Kappa Phi. Democrat. Methodist. Club: Asheville (N.C.) Track; Pearl Harbor Marine Base 50 Mile Swim. Home: Route 2 Box 275 Weaverville NC 28787 Office: Route 2 Box 102 North Buncombe Weaverville NC 28787

DUNN, BARBARA HURST, mathematics educator; b. New Kensington, Pa., Apr. 21, 1938; d. Thomas Marion and Helen (Whitesell) Hurst; m. Jerry Olin Yarborough, May 4, 1956 (div.); children—Jerry L., Bryan K., David A.; m. John Howard Dunn, May 7, 1982. A.A. with high honors, Fla. Jr. Coll., 1971; B.A. with honors, U. No. Fla., 1975; M.S. in Math. with high honors, Troy State U., 1979. Tchr. Duval County Sch., Jacksonville, Fla., 1976-82; lectr. math. U. Fla., Gainesville, 1983—, U. No. Fla., Jacksonville, 1983—, Fla. Jr. Coll., Jacksonville, 1983—, St. John's Jr. Coll., Palatka, Fla., 1983—. Area v.p. Am. Cancer Soc., Clay County, Fla., 1984—; pres. Innerwheel, Keystone Heights, Fla., 1985—. Mem. Nat. Council Tchrs. Math., Math. Assn. Am. Republican. Methodist. Home: PO Box 663 Springlake Keystone Heights FL 32656 Office: U Fla 324 Walker Hall Gainesville FL 32611

DUNN, BYRON G., engring. cons.; b. Ft. Worth, Feb. 4, 1928; s. William O. and Maude (Parker) D.; student Wayland Coll., 1948, Tex. Tech. U., 1948-50; m. Jo Ann Alexander, Aug. 31, 1950; children—Margaret Ann, W. Byron, Mary Kathleen. With Firestone Tire & Rubber Co., 1950-55; owner Byron Dunn & Assos., Muskogee, Okla., 1956-61; pres. Continental Mfg. & Engring. Co., Muskogee, 1961-66; exec. v.p. Sonics Internat Inc., Dallas, 1967-70; pres. Pyrotech, Inc., Dallas, 1970—, Byron Dunn Engring. Co., 1979—; chmn. bd. Delta Fine Wire Co., 1979—. Mem. adv. bd. Am. Security Council; mem. Rep. Nat. Com., 1978—. Served in USNR, 1946-48. Mem. Nat. Fire Protection Assn. Patentee. Home: 6831 Orchid Ln Dallas TX 75230

DUNN, CHARLES DEWITT, political science educator; b. Magnolia, Ark., Dec. 2, 1945; s. Charles Edward and Nora Lucille (Bailey) D.; m. Donna Jane Parsons, Apr. 9, 1966; children—Aimee, James, Joseph. B.A., So. Ark. U., 1967; M.A., North Tex. State U., 1970; Ph.D., So. Ill. U., 1973. Instr. polit. sci. U. Ark.-Monticello, 1969-72, asst. prof., 1972-75; assoc. prof. U. Central Ark., Conway, 1975-80, prof., 1980—, chmn. dept. polit. sci., 1976-82, dir. govt. relations, 1982—; cons. Survey Research Assn., Ark., 1976—. Committeeman, Democratic County Com., Conway, 1984. Mem. Ark. Polit. Sci. Assn. (pres. 1976-77), So. Polit. Sci. Assn., Conway C. of C. (bd. dirs. 1984—, v.p. 1985—). Methodist. Lodge: Rotary. Office: U Central Ark Box U943 Conway AR 72032

DUNN, CHARLES WYTHE, political science educator; b. Bloomington, Ill., Oct. 8, 1940; s. Charles Gleaves and Teresa (Goodrich) D.; m. Carol Nelson, Nov. 25, 1967; children—Charles W., Joshua M., Teresa C., Maria E. B.S., Ill. State U., 1962; M.S., Fla. State U., 1965, Ph.D., 1965. Spl. asst. to gov. State of Wash., Olympia, 1965-66; spl. asst. to Rep. Leslie C. Arends, Washington, 1966-67; dep. dir. Republican conf. U.S. Ho. of Reps., Washington, 1967-68; adminstrv. asst. U.S. Senator Charles Goodell, Washington, 1968-70; counsel, mem. legis. com. Ill. Constl. Conv., Springfield, 1970; asst. prof. polit. sci. U. Ill., Urbana, 1970-72; prof., head dept. polit. sci. Clemson U., S.C., 1972—. Author: American Democracy Debated, 1978, 2d edit., 1982; American Political Theology, 1984. Editor: The Future of the American Presidency, 1975. Contbr. articles to profl. jours. Del., Rep. Nat. Conv., Dallas, 1984. Recipient Alumni Achievement award Ill. State U., 1982. Mem. Am. Polit. Sci. Assn., So. Polit. Sci. Assn. Home: 100 Brookwood Ln Clemson SC 29631 Office: Clemson U Dept Polit Sci 408 Strode Tower Clemson SC 29631

DUNN, CHARLETA JESSE, psychology educator; b. Clarendon, Tex., Jan. 18, 1927; d. James A. Sisk and Ruby Roberta (Burcham) Sisk Rice; m. Roy E. Dunn; children—Thomas A., Roy E, III, Sharleta E. B.S., West Tex. U., 1951, Ed.M., 1954; Ed.D., U. Houston, 1966; postgrad. U. Tex.-Galveston,

1970. Tchr. Amarillo Pub. Schs., Tex., 1954-62; asst. prof. psychology U. Houston, 1966-69; psychologist Goose Creek Ind. Sch. Dist., Baytown, Tex., 1971-74; prof. Tex. Woman's U., Houston, 1974—; cons. pub. schs., Houston area, 1966—. Author: Songs of Sharleta, 1969; World of Work, 1971; 5 monographs. Grantee Gusreda, 1965, Hogg Found. for Mental Health, 1966-69, Regional Edn. Service Ctr., 1928, ORGA, 1982-83. Mem. Am. Psychol. Assn., Tex. Psychol. Assn., Southwestern Psychol. Assn., Am. Assn. Marriage and Family Therapy. Avocations: reading; sewing; cooking.

DUNN, DANNY LEROY, chemist; b. Wichita, July 12, 1946; s. Delmer L. and LeEtta (Johnson) D.; m. Nancy H. Helson, Aug. 5, 1967; children—Wendy E., Andrew D. B.S., Wichita State U., 1968; M.S., 1970; Ph.D., N. Tex. State U., 1976. Postdoctoral fellow U. Tex. Health Sci. Ctr., Dallas, 1976-78; sr. scientist Alcon Labs., Fort Worth, 1978—. Contbr. articles to profl. jours. Judge, Regional Sci. Fair, 1978—. Served to 2d lt. USAF, 1970-72. Mem. Am. Chem. Soc. Home: 1003 Yvonne St Joshua TX 67058 Office: Alcon Labs 6201 S Fwy Fort Worth TX 76134

DUNN, DEAN ALAN, oceanography educator; b. Groton, Conn., Nov. 11, 1954; s. Edward Daniel and Margaret Elizabeth (Smillie) D.; m. Jana Marie Adams, May 24, 1986. B.S. in Biology, U. So. Calif., 1976, B.S. in Geology, 1977; Ph.D. in Oceanography, U. R.I., 1982. Lab. techician geology dept. U. So. Calif., Los Angeles, 1975-77; geophys. asst. Union Oil Co., Santa Fe Springs, Calif., summer 1976; grad. teaching asst. geology dept. Fla. State U., Tallahassee, 1977-78; grad. research asst. oceanography U. R.I., Kingston, 1978-82; staff scientist deep sea drilling project U. Calif., San Diego, 1983—; asst. prof. geology U. So. Miss., Hattiesburg, 1983—; cruise scientist oceanography cruises U. So. Calif., 1976-77; shipboard scientist oceanography cruise U. R.I., 1979; shipboard sedimentologist deep sea drilling project, 1982; shipboard sci. rep., sedimentologist, 1983. Author: (with others) Initial Reports of the Deep Sea Drilling Project, vol. 85, 1985. Contbr. articles to profl. jours. Nat. Merit scholar, 1972-77. Mem. Am. Assn. Petroleum Geologists, Geol. Soc. Am., Am. Geophys. Union, Soc. Econ. Paleontologists and Mineralogists, Sigma Xi, Sigma Gamma Epsilon. Presbyterian. Club: Am. Mensa. Avocations: photography; bicycling; raquetball; reading; music. Home: PO Box 8506 Hattiesburg MS 39406 Office: U So Miss Dept Geology S Sta Box 5044 Hattiesburg MS 39406

DUNN, DELMER DELANO, political science educator; b. Lone Wolf, Okla., Oct. 31, 1941; s. Robert Patrick and Mildred Marion (Morris) D.; m. Ann Gregg Swinford, May 15, 1971; children—John Swinford, Kielly McKee. B.A., Okla. State U., 1963; M.S., U. Wis., 1964, Ph.D., 1967. Asst. prof. polit. sci. U. Ga., 1967-71, assoc. prof., 1971-77, prof., 1977-82, Regents prof., 1982—, dir. Inst. Govt., 1973-82; research assoc. The Brookings Instn., Washington, 1969-70. Trustee Leadership Ga., 1976-82; pres. Clarke/Oconee unit Am. Cancer Soc., 1981-82, chmn., 1982-83. Mem. Am. Polit. Sci. Assn. (Congressional fellow 1968-69), So. Polit. Sci. Assn., Midwestern Polit. Sci. Assn., Am. Soc. Pub. Adminstrn., AAAS, Pi Alpha Alpha. Presbyterian. Author: Public Officials and the Press, 1969; Financing Presidential Campaigns, 1972; contbr. articles to profl. jours. Office: Dept Polit Sci Univ Ga Athens GA 30602

DUNN, EDGAR M., JR., state senator; b. Daytona Beach, Fla., Feb. 14, 1939; s. Edgar M. and Charlotte (Galloway) D.; B.A., U. Fla., 1962, J.D., 1967; m. Margaret McCurry, 1960; children—Wesley R., Kathleen S., Christine M., Julie E. Admitted to Fla. bar; practice in Ormond Beach; asst. city atty., prosecutor, Daytona Beach, Fla., 1967-70; gen. counsel to gov. Fla., 1971-73; asst. states atty. 7th Jud. Circuit Fla., 1973-74; mem. Gov. Fla. Council Criminal Justice, 1973—; chmn. Fla. Organized Crime Coordinating Council, 1974-77; mem. Fla. Senate, 1974—; mem. council Law Center, U. Fla. Sch. Law, 1974—. Served to capt. USAR, 1962-64. Recipient Furtherance of Justice award Fla. Pros. Attys. Assn., 1973; also various young man of yr. awards. Mem. Am. Bar Assn., Fla. Bar Assn., Volusia County Bar Assn., Am. Legion, Civic league Halifax Area. Roman Catholic. Office: Fla State Senate Tallahasse FL 32301

DUNN, EDWIN RAY, JR., corporate affairs executive; b. Maryville, Tenn., Apr. 9, 1948; s. Edwin Ray and Doris E. (McGaughey) D.; m. Karen Kimbrough Dunn, Aug. 18, 1970; 1 son, Andrew Bradley. B.S., U. Tenn.-Knoxville, 1970; M.A., U. South Fla., 1974; M.B.A., Ga. State U., 1984. Instr., Pinellas Sch. Systems, St. Petersburg, Fla., 1970-73; project mgr. Human Research & Devel., St. Petersburg, 1974-75; asst. dir. So. Office, Council State Govts., Atlanta, 1975-78; head govt. programs/corp. affairs So. Solar Energy Ctr., Atlanta, 1978-82; v.p. ESG Inc., Atlanta, 1982-84; coordinator corp. sec. services So. Co. Services, Atlanta, 1984—; sec. bd. dirs. SSEC, Inc., Atlanta, 1978-82. Author: Energy Sourcebook for Southern Legislators, 1974; contbr. articles to profl. jours. Bd. govs. Fla. Conf. Concerned Democrats, Miami, 1973, pres. Pinellas County chpt., 1973; mem. govt. com. Suncoast Consumer League, St. Petersburg, 1974; mem. Region IV Child Abuse Project, Atlanta, 1975. Recipient cert. of recognition Gov. of Va., 1975. Mem. Am. Mgmt. Assn., Internat. Solar Energy Soc., SCS Profl. Devel. Soc. Presbyterian. Home: 3102 Olde Canton Ct Marietta GA 30067 Office: So Co Services Inc 64 Perimeter Center E Atlanta GA 30346

DUNN, HENRY HAMPTON, editor; b. Floral City, Fla., Dec. 14, 1916; s. William Harvey and Nannie L. (Hemrick) D.; student Mercer U., Macon, Ga., U. Tampa (Fla.); m. Charlotte Rawls, Aug. 16, 1941; children—Janice Kay, Henry Hampton, Dennis Harvey. Mem. staff Tampa (Fla.) Times, 1936-58, city editor, 1946-51, mng. editor, 1951-58; polit. analyst and newscaster WCKT-TV, Miami, 1958-59; public relations dir. Peninsula Motor Club, 1959—, also sr. v.p.; editor Fla. Explorer. Adv. council Gordon Keller Sch. Nursing, 1955-72, chmn. 1956-59; adv. bd. Salvation Army, 1953—, chmn., 1955-56; dir., past pres. United Cerebral Palsy of Tampa, state pres.; dir., treas. Tampa ARC; selections com. Girl Scouts; dir., v.p. Vis. Nurses Assn. Greater Tampa 1956—, pres., 1973-74, also life mem.; mem. Nat. AAA Traffic and Safety Com., Nat. AAA Public Relations Com., Nat. AAA Hwy. Com.; mem. West Central Fla. Com. Mil. Assistance to Safety and Traffic; chmn. Citizen's Adv. com. Tampa Urban Area Transp. Study. Charter trustee Historic Pensacola Preservation Bd., Historic Tallahassee Preservation Bd.; trustee Historic Tampa/Hillsborough County Preservation Bd., chmn., 1980—; past pres., dir. emeritus DWI Counterattack Tampa-Hillsborough County; mem. Carrollwood Civic Assn.; bd. dirs. Sunshine Post Card Club, Girl's Club of Tampa, Hillsborough County unit Am. Cancer Soc., Hillsborough Community Mental Health Center, Inc., Rough Riders Inc.; adv. com. Hillsborough Community Coll.; pres. Friends of Library, Tampa/Hillsborough County Public Library; life mem. Pres.'s Council, U. S.Fla. Served to maj. USAF, World War II; MTO. Decorated Bronze Star, Battle Star (5); recipient award for best news story AP, 1946; Torch award Citrus County C. of C., 1969; Jefferson Davis medal United Daus. Confederacy; Outstanding Service award Dick Pope chpt. Fla. Public Relations Assn., 1973; Fla. History award Peace River Valley Hist. Soc., 1974; Cooper-Taylor award Jaycees, 1974; Disting. Public Service award U. Tampa, 1975, Achievement medal, 1978; Outstanding Alumnus award U. Tampa, 1976; Chase award Hwy. Users Fedn., 1978; citation Am. Assn. State and Local History, 1981, award of excellence and merit Internat. Assn. Bus. Communicators, 1982, award of merit Fla. Mag. Assn., 1982, outstanding citizen's library award Fla. Library Assn., 1983; Golden Image award Fla. Pub. Relations Assn., numerous others; named Fla. Patriot, Fla. Bicentennial Commn., 1976. Mem. Am. Legion, Tampa C. of C. (tourist com., mem. hwy. com.), Fla. Hist. Soc. (bd. dirs., award of merit), Hist. Assn. So. Fla., U. Tampa Alumni Assn. (past pres.), AP Assn. Fla. (pres. 1955-56), Internat. Platform Assn., Tampa Hist. Soc. (pres. 1973-74, D.B. McKay award 1978, pres.' award 1982, editor Sunland Tribune), Old Timers Assn. Hillsborough County (pres. 1975-76, dir.), Sigma Delta Chi (pres. Fla. West Coast chpt. 1954-55, 81-82). Baptist. Clubs: Masons, Rotary (public relations chmn., bd. dirs., pres. Tampa, dist. gov., dist. rep. to R.I. legis. council 1977, 80, Paul Harris fellow); mem. Order Eastern Star. Author: Re-Discover Florida; WDAE, Florida's Pioneer Radio Station; Yesterday's Tampa; Yesterday's St. Petersburg; Yesterday's Clearwater; Yesterday's Tallahassee; Florida Sketches; Accent Florida; Yesterday's Lakeland; Back Home-The History of Citrus County; Wish You Were Here; Tampa—A Pictorial History; Fla. Hist. writer Fla. Trend mag., Tampa Tribune, Tampa Times; writer syndicated hist. column. Home: 10610 Carrollwood Dr Tampa FL 33618 Office: 1515 N Westshore Blvd Tampa FL 33607

DUNN, HERBERT DEIGHTON, editor; b. Salt Lake City, July 3, 1924; s. Samuel Benjamin and Alice (Deighton) D.; A.B., Westminster Coll., Utah, 1948; B.J., U. Mo., 1955; m. Mary Frances Lyon, June 28, 1961; 1 son, Samuel Thomas. Reporter, Blytheville (Ark.) Courier News, 1955; writer, asst. sports editor Ala. Jour., Montgomery, 1955-64; editor Ala. Conservation Mag., Montgomery, 1964—. Mem. Montgomery Assn. Bus. Communicators (past pres.). Presbyterian. Clubs: Kiwanis (pres. South Montgomery 1975-76), Masons (montgomery). Home: 4337 Sussex Dr Montgomery AL 36116 Office: 64 N Union St Montgomery AL 36130

DUNN, JAMES ANDREW, JR., marine construction company executive; b. Pitts., Oct. 7, 1944; s. James Andrew and Antonette Marie (Zeibel) D.; m. Judith Raye King, July 17, 1965 (div. Aug. 1972); children—David Anthony, Andrew Daniel; m. 2d, Peggy Branning, Apr. 6, 1973; children—Holly Colleen, Machelle Marie. Student Lafayette Coll., 1961-63, Am. Coll. of Switzerland, Leysin, 1963-64, Italian U. for Foreigners, Perugia, 1964; B.S. in Civil Engring., U. Tex.-Arlington, 1968. Registered profl. engr., La. Office clk. Am. Bridge div. U.S. Steel Corp., Pitts., summer 1962; steel detailer Thornton Industries, Inc., Fort Worth, 1965-67; jr. design engr. R.R. Lacey & Assocs., Cons. Engrs., Arlington, Tex., 1967-68; offshore engr. J. Ray McDermott & Co., Inc., New Orleans and Warri, Nigeria, 1968-70; asst. office engr. Carter & Burgess, Inc., Cons. Engrs., Ft. Worth, 1970; sr. project engr. Santa Fee U.K. Ltd., London, 1971-72, project coordinator Santa Fe Engring. Services Co., Orange, Calif., 1973-74, project mgr., 1975-76, engring. and equipment mgr. Santa Fe Engring. & Constrn. Co., Houma, La., 1976-77, project mgr., 1978; asst. chief estimator marine div. Morrison-Knudsen Co., Inc., New London, Conn., 1979; v.p. offshore ops. Ingram Marine Constructors, Lafayette, La., 1979—. Sustaining mem. Republican Nat. Com., 1978—. Mem. Nat. Soc. Profl. Engrs., Soc. Petroleum Engrs., Am. Welding Soc. (Acadiana sect.), ASCE, Am. Petroleum Inst., La. Engring. Soc. (sec. Bayou chpt. 1977-78, state vice chmn. profl. engrs. in constrn.). Presbyterian. Contbr. presentations to engring. socs.; patentee pipelaying and jetting ops. Home: 100 Steve St Lafayette LA 70503 Office: Ingram Marine Constructors PO Drawer 53475 Lafayette LA 70505

DUNN, JAMES OWEN, financial consultant; b. Quincy, Mass., Dec. 5, 1918; s. James J. and Julia T. (Flood) D.; m. Millie-Rue Romney, Mar. 6, 1945; children—James Owen, Jr., Christopher Romney, Michelle Dunn Morgan, Philip Stephen. B.S. magna cum laude, Boston Coll., 1947; M.B.A., Harvard U., 1949; D.C.S. (hon.), Merrimack Coll., 1968; LL.D. (hon.), St. Anselm's Coll., 1968. C.P.A., Mass. Instr. through prof., Boston Coll., 1949-66; fin., bus. cons. to Roman Catholic Archbishop of Boston, 1966-76; exec. dir. ACH, 1966-83; former dir. Greenwich Gas Co., FWD Corp., Bay Bank Newton, Waltham Trust Co., Boott Mills. Trustee Hammond Mus., Joseph P. Kennedy Meml. Hosp., St. Elizabeth's Hosp., Nazareth, Inc., Cushing Rehab. Ctr., Cardinal Cushing Hosp., St. Sebastian's Country Day Sch., St. John's Sem., Pope John Sem.; bd. govs. Harvard Bus. Sch. Assn. of Boston; bd. dirs. Archdiocesan Sch. Bd., Greater Boston Hosp. Council; mem. gov.'s adv. bd. State Comprehensive Health Planning Council; Greater Boston Hosp. Council; Council on Blue Cross Affairs. Recipient Alpha Kappa Psi faculty award Boston Coll., 1960; decorated knight of St. Gregory, 1967; named Papal Chamberlain, 1978. Mem. Fin. Execs. Inst., Am. Inst. C.P.A.s, AAUP, Am. Acctg. Assn., Am. Hosp. Assn., Beta Gamma Sigma. Clubs: Smyrna Yacht, Halifax, Harvard, Algonquin. Contbr. articles to profl. jours. Home: 405 Quay Assisi New Smyrna Beach FL 32069

DUNN, RICHARD EUGENE, chiropractor; b. Louisville, Dec. 6, 1927; s. William Hubert and Ida Mildred Dunn; m. Martha Graham Cardwell, May 3, 1947 (dec.); children—Richard Allen, Phyllis Ann Cox, Rosemary Springer; m. 2d, Beverly Joan Schmidtt, June 4, 1977; stepchildren—Charles Ware Vaught, Lauren Ann Eason, William David Vaught. D.Chiropractic, Lincoln Chiropractic Coll., Indpls., 1950. Cert. Ky. State Bd. Examiners. Practice, Jeffersontown, Ky., 1950—, pres. owner Richard E. Dunn, P.S.C., 1980—; cons. chiropractic legal relations and ins. relations Ky. Chiropractic Soc. Past. pres. Lincoln Chiropractic Coll. Athletic Assn.; past mem. Jeffersontown Planning and Zoning Commn.; past mem. Jeffersontown Vol. Fire Dept. Served with USN, 1946. Mem. Am. Chiropractic Assn. (charter), Ky. Chiropractic Soc. (charter; Dr. of Year award 1982, ins. relations com.), Ky. Assn. Chiropractors (pres. award 3d dist. 1969, Dr. of Year award 1970), Am. Chiropractic Assn. Council Roentgenology, Jeffersontown C. of C. (charter), Found. Chiropractic Edn., Research, Commonwealth Ky. Dept. Transp., Delta Tau Alpha (past fin. sec.). Democrat. Roman Catholic. Club: Old Grand Dad Am. Contbr. articles to profl. publs. Home: 6301 Dillard Ct Prospect KY 40059 Office: 9500 Taylorsville Rd Jeffersontown KY 40299

DUNN, RONALD HOLLAND, engineering company executive; b. Balt., Sept. 15, 1937; s. Delmas Joseph and Edna Grace (Holland) D.; student U. S.C., 1956-58; B.S. in Engring., Johns Hopkins U., 1969; m. Verona Lucille Lambert, Aug. 17, 1958; children—Ronald H., Jr. (dec.), David R., Brian W. Field engr. Balt. & Ohio R.R., Balt., 1958-66; chief engr. yards, shops, trackwork DeLeuw, Cather & Co., D.C., 1966-73; mgr. engring. support Parsons Brinckerhoff-Tudor-Bechtel, Atlanta, 1973-76; dir. railroad engring. Morrison-Knudsen Co., Inc., Boise, Idaho, 1976-78; v.p. Parsons Brinckerhoff CENTEC, Inc., McLean, Va., 1978-83; v.p., tech. dir. ry. engring., profl. assoc., area mgr. Parsons Brinckerhoff Quade & Douglas, Inc., McLean, 1983, Pitts., 1983-84; dir. transp. engring. R.L. Banks & Assocs., Inc., Washington, 1984; pres. R.H. Dunn & Assocs., Inc., Oakton, Va., 1984—. Mem. adv. com. track engrs. U.S. Dept. Transp. Chmn., Cub Scout Pack, 1972-73, committeeman, 1973-75; troop committeeman Boy Scouts Am., 1978-85. Mem. Am. Mgmt. Assn., Am. Ry. Engring. Assn., ASCE, Can. Soc. Civil Engring., Am. Pub. Transit Assn., Soc. Am. Mil. Engrs., Roadmasters and Maintenance of Way Assn. of Am., Am. Ry. Bridge and Bldg. Assn., Ry. Tie Assn., Inst. of Rapid Transit, Can. Urban Transit Assn., Inst. Transp. Engrs., Constrn. Specifications Inst., Nat. Soc. Profl. Engrs., Transp. Research Bd., Soc. Profl. Mgmt. Cons., Phi Kappa Sigma. Methodist. Author tech. publs., profl. articles. Guest of Japan Ry. Civil Engring. Assn. observing, inspecting railroad and rail rapid transit facilities in Japan, 1972, Europe, 1980, 82, 84, Hong Kong and China, 1985. Office: 2840 Rifle Ridge Rd Oakton VA 22124

DUNN, SHIRLEY ANN, nurse; b. Wichita, Kans., Mar. 18, 1934; d. Harry Herbert, Sr. and Zella Ethel (Davis) Brown; m. Lloyd Warren Verbeck, Jr., Mar. 22, 1952 (div. Nov. 1968); children—Janice Robyn, Byron Ted, Joni Lynn, Karie Kristen; m. 2d Alvin Wilford Dunn, Jan. 23, 1981. Student Wichita Practical Nursing Sch., 1975; student pharmacology Wichita Vocat. Sch., 1976. Lic. vocat. nurse. Key punch operator Farmers & Bankers Life, Wichita, 1952-55; medication nurse Osteo. Hosp., Wichita, 1975-78; charge nurse Hillhaven, Wichita, 1978-81; lic. vocat. nurse staff Meml. Hosp. of Galveston County, Texas City, Tex., 1981-82; now staff Nurses Coop., Texas City, Tex. Mem. Assembly of God Ch.

DUNN, THOMAS TINSLEY, lawyer; b. Petersburg, Va., Aug. 27, 1901; s. George White and Emma (Tinsley) D.; B.S., U. Va., 1925, LL.B., 1926; m. Elizabeth E. Campbell, Dec. 31, 1927; children—Janet Dunn Tillery, Thomas Churchill. Admitted to Va. bar, 1925, Fla. bar, 1926; asst. trust officer 1st Nat. Bank, St. Petersburg, Fla., 1926-30; v.p., trust officer United Savs. Bank, Detroit, 1930-35; asst. v.p. Public Nat. Bank and Trust Co. (merged into Bankers Trust Co.), N.Y.C., 1935-36; dir. estate and trust planning Citizens and So. Nat. Bank, Atlanta, 1938-41; v.p., trust officer 1st Nat. Bank (now Fla. Nat. Bank), St. Petersburg, 1941-54; of counsel firm Dunn & Dunn, P.A., St. Petersburg, 1954—. Co-founder Goodwill Industries-Suncoast, Inc., Sunny Shores Villas, Suncoast Manor, St. Petersburg. Mem. Am. Bar Assn., Fla. Bar (50-yr. cert. 1976), Mayflower Descs., SAR, Huguenot Soc., Epps Soc., Newcomen Soc., Phi Alpha Delta, Alpha Chi Rho. Episcopalian. Clubs: St. Petersburg Yacht, Bath, Shriners, Masons (32 deg.). Author: A Lawyer's Advice to Retirees, 1981. Home: 7400 Sun Island Dr Apt 201 South Pasadena FL 33707 Office: Dunn & Dunn 3023 Central Ave PO Box 12669 Saint Petersburg FL 33733

DUNN, WESLEY ASBURY, clinical psychologist, child psychologist; b. Winchester, Ind., Dec. 20, 1922; s. Francis W. and Florence (Goodrich) D.; m. Elsie Ann Locke, Apr. 5, 1952 (div. Jan. 1968); children—George, Stephanie, Francis, Elizabeth; m. Sandra L. Toneman, Oct. 13, 1973; children—J. Todd Aschleman, Jane Ann Aschleman. A.B., Harvard U., 1946, M.S., Purdue U., 1947; postgrad. Columbia U., 1948-50; Ph.D., Purdue U., 1951. Diplomate Am. Bd. Profl. Psychology. Asst. dir. Marion County Child Guidance Clinic, Indpls., 1951-62; cons. Marion County Juvenile Ct., 1958-74; pvt. practice psychology, 1960-74, Punta Gorda, Fla., 1980—. Bd. dirs. NAACP, Indpls., 1958-62, Ind. Civil Liberties Union, 1963-71. Served to 1st lt. USAF, 1944-47, Japan. Mem. Am. Psychol. Assn., Fla. Psychol. Assn., Ind. Psychol. Assn. (bd. dirs.). Avocations: sailing, golf, tennis, scuba diving. Home and Office: 57 Ocean Dr Punta Gorda FL 33950

DUNN, WILLIAM PAUL, naval officer, oral and maxillofacial surgeon, educator; b. Louisville, Aug. 2, 1942; s. William Paul and Molly Jane (Walker) D.; m. Patsy Truitt Estes, June 9, 1965; 1 child, Ashley Catherine. D.D.S., Emory U., 1967. Diplomate Am. Bd. Oral and Maxillofacial Surgery. Commd. lt., U.S. Navy, 1967, advanced through grades to capt., 1982; dept. head USS America, Norfolk, Va., 1975-77; chief oral surgery Naval Hosp., Cherry Point, N.C., 1977-81; clinic dir. Camp Hansen Dental Clinic, Okinawa, Japan, 1981-82; oral surgeon Naval Dental Clinic, Little Creek Amphibious Base, Norfolk, 1982-83; command cons., dept head oral-maxillofacial surgery Naval Dental Clinic Norfolk, 1983—. Deacon First Bapt. Ch., Havelock, N.C., 1978-81; dir. Casualty Treatment Tng. Course, Norfolk, 1984-85. Fellow Am. Coll. Oral Maxillofacial Surgeons, Am. Assn. Oral Maxillofacial Surgeons, Am. Dental Soc. Anesthesiology; mem. Tidewater Soc. Fed. Oral Maxillofacial Surgeons (sec.-treas.), Tidewater Fed. Soc. Oral Maxillofacial Surgeons (pres. 1985—), Tidewater Striders, Tidewater Triathlon Club, Alpha Tau Omega, Zi Psi Phi. Republican. Baptist. Avocations: running; triathlons; salt water fishing; boating; skiing. Home: 1026 Graydon Ave Apt A Norfolk VA 23507 PO Box 1124 Swansboro NC 28584 Office: Naval Dental Clinic Oral Surgery Dept Taussing Blvd Norfolk VA 23511

DUNNING, ROBERT LEE, university official; b. San Antonio, Dec. 30, 1943; s. Raymond Manuel and Gladys Mae (Barnett) D.; m. Ruverna Francis Hopper, 1964; 1 son, Robert Lee. B.B.A., Sam Houston State U., 1965. Acct. Pennzoil United, Houston, 1966-68; asst. registrar Sam Houston State U., Huntsville, Tex., 1968—. Deacon, 1st Christian Ch., Huntsville, 1979-81, bd. dirs., 1980-81, chmn. evangelism and membership com., 1979-80, v.p. Christian Men's Fellowship, co-sponsor Christian Youth Fellowship. Mem. Am. Assn. Collegiate Registrars and Admissions Officers, Tex. Assn. Collegiate Registrars and Admissions Officers, Delta Sigma Pi (alumni), Phi Theta Kappa (co-sponsor). Home: 3657 Youpon Ln Huntsville TX 77340 Office: Sam Houston State Univ Registrar's Office Huntsville TX 77341

DUNSTON-THOMAS, FRANCES JOHNSON, pediatrician, public health official; b. Richmond, Va., Mar. 12, 1943; d. John R. and Ruth E. (Reeves) Johnson; m. George A. Dunston Sr., Aug. 20, 1966 (dec.); m. Gustave R. Thomas, Aug. 16, 1980; children—George Dunston, Karla Dunston. B.A. in Chemistry summa cum laude, Fisk U., 1964; M.S. in Chemistry, Rutgers U., 1972; M.D., Coll. Med. and Dentistry of N.J.-Rutgers Med. Sch., 1978; M.P.H. candidate U. N.C., 1982—. Diplomate Am. Bd. Pediatrics. Research chemist Am. Cyanamid Corp., Bound Brook, N.J., 1964-71; research chemist Colgate Palmolive Co., Piscataway, N.J., 1972-73; instr. N.J. Med. Sch., Newark, summers 1973-74; resident Med. Coll. Va., Richmond, 1978-81; dep. health dir. Richmond Health Dept., 1981-83, health dir., 1983—. Bd. dirs. Richmond Area High Blood Pressure Ctr., 1983—, Richmond Urban League, 1982—. Mem. Richmond Acad. Medicine, Richmond Med. Soc., Va. Pub. Health Assn., Richmond Pediatrics Assn., Phi Beta Kappa, Alpha Omega Alpha, Delta Sigma Theta. Clubs: Jack and Jill, Links, Inc. (Richmond). Office: Richmond Health Dept 600 E Broad St Richmond VA 23217

DUNTEN, DIANA DENTON, psychologist, mental health administrator; b. Balt., Sept. 22, 1945; d. Monroe Albert Denton, Sr. and Naomi Lee (Hoeflich) Denton; m. Nicholas Steinmetz Dunten, May 30, 1969 (div. Apr. 1981). A.B., Mercer U., 1967; M.S., U. Tenn., 1972, Ph.D., 1977. Lic. psychologist, Ga. Psychologist, Central DeKalb Mental Health Ctr., Decatur, Ga., 1976-78; dir. Adult Counselling Ctr., Savannah, Ga., 1979; exec. dir. Human Resources Ctr., Daytona Beach, Fla., 1980; forensic psychologist N.W. Ga. Regional Hosp., Rome, 1981-84; inpatient unit dir. Physicians & Surgeons Hosp., Altanta, 1984; dir. substance abuse treatment unit Greenleaf Ctr., Valdosta, Ga., 1985—. Fin. sec. Holy Trinity Lutheran Ch., Rome, 1983-84. Mem. Am. Psychol. Assn., Ga. Psychol. Assn., Am. Assn. Psychodrama Group Psychotherapy, Atlanta Bus. and Profl. Guild, Sigma Mu, Cardinal Key. Avocations: renovations, reading, racquetball. Home: 205 W Park Ave Valdosta GA 31602 Office: Greenleaf Ctr Valdosta GA 31602

DUNTON, JAMES GERALD, association executive; b. Circleville, Ohio, Nov. 10, 1899; s. Oscar Howard and Florence (Nightengale) D.; A.B., Harvard U., 1923, M.Ed., 1928; m. Dorothy Winfough, Oct. 10, 1944. Free lance author, 1925-34; Fed. Projects dir., Ohio, 1935-37; spl. rep. Fed. N.W. Ter. Sesquicentennial Commn., 1938; editor Ohio Democracy, 1939-40; Ohio field rep. Office Govt. Reports, Exec. Office of Pres., 1940-41; dir. spl. activities Office Sec. Def., 1950-61; exec. dir. Va. Health Care Assn., 1965-75, spl. rep., 1975—; Washington rep. Am. Chess Found., 1962-81, adv. bd., 1982—; adv. council Oliver Wendell Holmes Assn., 1966—. Mem. vets. com. Presdl. Inaugurations, 1965, 69, 77; pres. Nat. Capital USO, Washington, 1966-67, mem. nat. council, 1966—; mem. Va. State Adv. Com. Adult Services, 1972; disting. sponsor 100th Anniversary 1st Battle of Bull Run, 1961. Served with Ambulance Corps, A.E.F., U.S. Army, 1918-19, to maj. AUS, World War II, Korea. Recipient cert. of appreciation Nat. Press Club, 1955, Commendation award Pres.'s Com. on Employment of Handicapped, 1963; decorated Army Commendation medal; hon. fellow Truman Library Inst. Mem. Nat. Assn. Execs. (life), U.S. Army Hon. Ret. Res., SAR, Am. Legion (Nat. Comdr.'s award 1975), Vets. World War I, DAV, VFW, Res. Officers Assn., U.S. Army Ambulance Service Assn., Mil. Order World Wars, Ohio Soc. Washington, Soc. of Va. (pres.). Presbyterian (elder). Club: Harvard (Washington); Jefferson of Va. (founding mem. 1983). Author: Wild Asses, 1925; Murders in Lovers Lane, 1927; Maid and a Million Men, 1928; Counterfeit Wife, 1930; Honey's Money, 1933; Queen's Harem, 1933; (anthology) C'est La Guerre, 1927. Contbr. articles to mags., newspapers. Address: 2820 Bisvey Dr Falls Church VA 22042

DUNWELL, ROBERT R., educational administration educator; b. Kansas City, Kans., May 13, 1930; d. Albert L. and Mollie O. D.; m. Janice C. Alcorn, Dec. 21, 1977; children—Nancy Carol, Judith K. Nichols, Erich Jon. B.S. in Edn., U. Kans., 1952, M.S. in Edn., 1956, Ed.D., 1961. Tchr. jr. high sch. English, Kansas City, Mo., 1956-58; tchr. high sch. English and journalism, Lawrence, Kans., 1958-60; dir. curriculum and instrn., Leavenworth, Kans., 1960-62; head dept. edn. Hanover Coll., Ind., 1962-65; chmn. dept. cirruculum and instrn. U. No. Colo., Greeley, 1965-69; chmn. dept. ednl. adminstrn., U. Hawaii, Honolulu, 1969-77; chmn. dept. edn. Southeast Mo. State U., Cape Girardeau, 1977-81; chmn. dept. ednl. leadership and counseling U. Tex., El Paso, 1981—. Served to lt. USN, 1952-55. Mem. Assn. for Supervision and Curriculum Devel., Phi Delta Kappa. Author (with Robert L. Wendel): Foundations for Teaching and Learning, 1977. Office: Edn Bldg 712 Univ Tex El Paso El Paso TX 79968

DUPLANTIER, ADRIAN GUY, federal judge; b. New Orleans, Mar. 5, 1929; s. F. Robert and Amelie (Rivet) D.; J.D. cum laude, Loyola U., New Orleans, 1949; m. Sally Thomas, July 15, 1951; children—Adrian G., David L., Thomas, Jeanne M., Louise M., John C. Admitted to La. bar, 1950, U.S. Supreme Ct., 1954; practiced law, New Orleans, 1950-74; judge Civil Dist. Ct. Parish of Orleans, 1974-78, U.S. Dist. Ct., New Orleans, 1978—; part-time prof. code of civil procedure Loyola U., 1951—, lectr. dental jurisprudence, 1960-67, lectr. English dept., 1948-50; mem. La. State Senate, 1960-74; 1st asst. dist. atty., New Orleans, 1954-56. Del., Democratic Nat. Conv., 1964; pres. Associated Cath. Charities New Orleans, Social Welfare Planning Council Greater New Orleans; mem. adv. bd. St. Mary's Dominican Coll., 1970-71, Ursuline Acad., 1968-73, Mt. Carmel Acad., 1965-69; chmn. pres.'s adv. council Jesuit High Sch., 1979—; active Assn. Retarded Children, Cystic Fibrosis Found. Recipient Meritorious award New Orleans Assn. Retarded Children, 1965; Gov.'s Cert. of Merit, 1970. Mem. Am. Bar Assn. (award 1960), La. Bar Assn., New Orleans Bar Assn., Order of Coif, Alpha Sigma Nu. Editorial bd. Loyola Law Rev., 1947-48, editor-in-chief, 1948-49. Office: 500 Camp St Chambers C-205 New Orleans LA 70130

DUPLANTIS, D. DAVID, personnel executive; b. New Orleans, Nov. 20, 1939; s. DeWelder David and Sadie Marie (Pellegrin) D.; m. Barbara Lynn Lawson, Jan. 16, 1965; 1 child, Courtney. B.A., Nicholls State U., 1970; postgrad. U. New Orleans. Personnel technician Jefferson Parish, Jefferson, La., 1970-72, personnel supr., 1972-76, dir. tng. and devel., 1976-80, dir. employee mgmt., 1980—. Mem. adv. bd. U.S. Nat. Park Service, New Orleans, 1979—; chmn. Jefferson Parish Community Arts Commn., 1980-81; mem. W. Jefferson Cultural and Civic Ctr. Com., Jefferson Parish, 1983—; mem. Jefferson Parish World's Fair Com., 1981-84. Named Boss of Yr., Westbank Bus. and Profl. Women's Club, 1981. Mem. Am. Mgmt. Assn., Internat. Personnel Mgmt. Assn., Am. Soc. Tng. and Devel., Am. Assn. Adult and Continuing Edn., La. Intergovtl. Tng. Council. Democrat. Roman Catholic. Clubs: Visitation Coop (Marrero, La.); Jefferson Hist. Soc. (La.); New Orleans

Mus. Art. Avocations: art; music; cooking. Office: Jefferson Parish Employee Mgmt Room 521 Gretna Courthouse Gretna LA 70053

DUPLANTIS, DANIEL JAMES, financial executive; b. Port Arthur, Tex., Feb. 25, 1948; s. Joseph C. and Laura Elaine (Englehardt) D.; m. Patricia Elain Bond, Mar. 7, 1972 (div. Mar. 6, 1979); children—Bryan D., Amy L.; m. Jenny Rhodes, Jan. 5, 1980; 1 child, Matthew P. Grad. electronic technician, Port Arthur Coll., 1969; student in real estate Lamar U., 1966-68, 75-77. Realtor, mgr. Zodiac Real Estate, Newark, Ohio, 1973-74; realtor Dal Sasso Real Estate, Nederland, Tex., 1975-77; asst. v.p., br. mgr. First Fed. Savs. and Loan, Beaumont, Tex., 1977-81; v.p. real estate InterFirst Bank Nederland, 1981-82; pres. First Mortgage Investment Co., Nederland, 1982—, exec. v.p. First Mortgage Investment Assn. Chmn. Nederland Ind. Community Chest, 1982. Lutheran. Clubs: Port Arthur Jaycees (pres.); Rotary (Port Neches, Tex.) (dir.). Home: 14823 Charlmont Houston TX 77083 Office: First Mortgage Investment Co 2901 Wilcrest Suite 500 Houston TX 77042

DUPONT, JOSEPH BENTON, JR., surgeon; b. Thibodaux, La., July 2, 1948; s. Joseph Benton and Frances Rose (Breaux) D.; m. Carolyn Jane Robertson, Mar. 16, 1974; children—Joseph Benton III, Elizabeth Bolin. Student Tulane U., 1966-69; M.D., La. State U., 1973. Diplomate Am. Bd. Surgery. Intern, Grady Meml. Hosp., Atlanta, 1973-74; resident in surgery Charity Hosp., La. State U. Service, New Orleans, 1974-79; fellow in surgery Anderson Tumor Inst., Houston, 1977-78; chief adminstrv. surg. resident Charity Hosp., New Orleans, 1978-79; staff surgeon Baton Rouge Clinic, 1981—; asst. prof. surgery La. State U. Med. Ctr., New Orleans, 1981—; mem. staff E.K. Long Meml. Hosp., Baton Rouge; practice surgery specializing in surg. oncology andj head and neck surgery Baton Rouge Gen. Hosp. (La.), Our Lady of Lake Hosp., Baton Rouge. Am. Cancer Soc. jr. faculty clin. fellow, 1979. Fellow ACS; mem. La. Surg. Soc., James D. Rives Surg. Soc., La. Med. Soc., Soc. Surg. Oncology, East Baton Rouge Parish Med. Soc. Republican. Roman Catholic. Contbr. articles to profl. jours. Office: 8415 Goodwood Blvd Baton Rouge LA 70806

DUPONT, RANDOLPH THOMAS, clinical psychologist; b. Passaic, N.J., June 17, 1951; s. Harry Louis and Marilyn (Lahare) D.; m. Elizabeth Ann Montegut, May 25, 1974. B.A. cum laude, Loyola U., New Orleans, 1973; Ph.D. with distinction, U. Tex., 1980. Lic. Psychologist, Tenn. Intern, U. Tenn. Med. Sch., Memphis, 1976-77; counselor, dir. Southwestern Coll. (now Rhodes Coll.), Memphis, 1977-78; therapist, psychologist Frayser Mental Health Ctr., Memphis, 1978-81; pvt. practice psychology, Memphis, 1981—; cons. Memphis State U. Ctr. for Nuclear Studies, 1979-81, Bapt. Meml. Hosp. Employee Assistance Program, Memphis, 1985. NIMH fellow, 1973-77. Mem. Tenn. Psychol. Assn. (pres.-elect 1985—), Memphis Area Psychol. Assn. (pres. 1984-85), Am. Psychol. Assn., Am. Orthopsychiat. Assn. Office: 3606 Austin Peay Suite 320 Memphis TN 38128

DUPONT, WILLIAM DUDLEY, biostatistician, educator; b. Montreal, Que., Can., Nov. 6, 1946; came to U.S., 1971; s. Charles Thomas and Jean White (Peters) Dupont; m. Susan Miller McChesney, July 20, 1974; children—Charles Thomas, Peter William. B.Sc., McGill U., 1969, M.Sc., 1971; Ph.D., Johns Hopkins U., 1976. Lectr., U. Md., Balt., 1976-77; asst. prof. biostats. Vanderbilt U. Sch. Medicine, Nashville, 1977—. Nat. Cancer Inst. grantee, 1982. Mem. Am. Statis. Assn., Biometric Soc., Soc. Clin. Trials, Soc. Epidemiol. Research, Sigma Xi. Office: Dept of Preventive Medicine Vanderbilt U Med Sch Nashville TN 37232

DUPRE, MAURICE JOSEPH, mathematician; b. Albany, Calif., Nov. 28, 1943; s. Albida Joseph Dupre and Inez (Gilliland) Boswell; m. Brigitta Wermuth, Sept. 11, 1971; children—Adrienne, Marielle, Juliette. B.S., U. Fla., 1965; M.A., U. Pa.-Phila., 1969, Ph.D., 1972. Asst. prof. math. U. Hawaii, Honolulu, 1972-73; asst. prof. Tulane U., New Orleans, 1973-79, assoc. prof., 1980—. Author: Banach Modules and Automorphisms, 1984. Contbr. articles to profl. pubs. Ford Found. fellow, 1963-66; NSF grantee, 1974-83. Mem. Am. Math. Soc., N.Am. Soc. Research Scientists. Avocations: music; piano. Office: Tulane U Dept Math New Orleans LA 70118

DUPREE, SUSAN HARRELSON, transit authority executive; b. Mullins, S.C., Aug. 7, 1948; d. Billy Hoover and Annie Irene Harrelson; m. James Reid Dupree, Dec. 31, 1966 (div. May 1971); 1 dau., Cynthia Irene. Student pub. schs., Mullins. Legal sec., Florence, S.C., 1970-73; coordinator Pee Dee Regional Council Govts., Florence, 1973-79; asst. dir. Pee Dee Regional Transp. Authority, Florence, 1979-82; mgr. Retro-Tran, Mullins, 1982-83; exec. dir. Coastal Rapid Pub. Transit Authority, Conway, S.C., 1983—. Mem. Gov.'s Com. on Hwy. Safety, 1978—; bd. dirs. Marion County Council on Aging, 1982. Democrat. Baptist. Home: PO Box 775 Mullins SC 29574 Office: PO Drawer 1740 Conway SC 29526

DUPREE, THOMAS RANDALL, writer; b. Norfolk, Va., Nov. 27, 1949; s. Harry Randall Dupree and Betty Jean (Luper) Bearss; B.A. in Polit. Sci. and Theatre, Millsaps Coll., 1971; M.A. in Journalism, U. Ga., 1974; m. Mary Elizabeth Narrow, Sept. 18, 1971 (div. 1974). Mem. Sunday staff Clarion-Ledger/Jackson (Miss.) Daily News, 1965-71; newsman UPI, 1969-71; info. specialist Coll. Agr. Expt. Stas., U. Ga., Athens, 1971-75; copy chief, broadcast prodn. mgr. Gordon Marks & Co., Jackson, 1975-79; assoc. creative dir. Advt. & Mktg., Jackson, 1979-82; ptnr. The Millennium Co., Jackson, 1982—, Compleat Gamer, Jackson, 1983—; freelance scriptwriter Miss. Authority Ednl. TV, 1977—; freelance rock writer, 1971-77; contbr. to Rolling Stone, Playboy, Oui, Creem, Billboard, Record World, Fusion, Changes, Circus, Game News; contbr. The Rolling Stone Record Review, 1974; co-author: (play) Oh, Mr. Faulkner, Do You Write?, 1981; actor New Stage Theatre. Named Copywriter of Year, Greater Jackson Advt. Club, 1977. Mem. Mensa (state chmn. 1985—), Intertel, Lambda Chi Alpha. Methodist. Home: PO Box 16113 McWillie Station Jackson MS 39236 Office: PO Box 16002 Jackson MS 39236

DUPUY, GEORGE MCVICAR, consulting company executive; b. Bronxville, N.Y., Apr. 26, 1943; s. Trevor Nevitt and Jean (McVicar) D.; m. Peggy King Hicks, Aug. 26, 1966; children—David, Deborah, Ashley. B.A. cum laude, Coll. William and Mary, 1965; M.B.A., U. N.C., 1966, Ph.D. in Bus. Adminstrn., 1974. Vice pres. Lighthouse Point Bank, Pompano Beach, Fla., 1969-71; assoc. prof. U. Va., Charlottesville, 1975-80; prof., assoc. dean Old dominion U., Norfolk, Va., 1980-81; dean bus. sch. Lynchburg Coll., Va., 1981-83; v.p. Drake Beam Morin, Inc., Atlanta, 1983—; cons. to numerous firms, Va., 1975-83. Contbr. articles to profl. jours. Recipient Excellence award Drake, Beam, Morin, Inc., 1984. Mem. Am. Mktg. Assn. Home: 5019 Mt Vernon Way Dunwoody GA 30338 Office: Drake Beam Morin Inc 2200 Century Pkwy Atlanta GA 30345

DURALD, MARY MAGDELENE, psychiatric nurse; b. Gurley, La., Mar. 16, 1929; d. Dave Ernest Williams and Sadie Bell (Sample) Green; m. George DeBlanc m. Emmanuel Lombard (dec.); m. Edward Melvin Durald, July 1, 1968. M.N., La. State U., 1976. Cert. nurse adminstr. Staff nurse obstets. Flint Goodridge Hosp., New Orleans, 1951-52; charge nurse obstets. U. Calif.-San Francisco, 1952-53; staff nurse psychiatry Charity Hosp., New Orleans, 1953-54, shift supr. psychiat unit, 1954-68, supr. crisis intervention unit, 1968-76, clin. dir. neuropsychiatry, 1976—. Recipient Dunbar award La. Civil Service League, 1980. Mem. Am. Nurses Assn., Nurses Book Soc., New Orleans Dist. Nurses Assn., Sigma Theta Tau. Contbr. articles to profl. jours. Home: 111 Alden Pl New Orleans LA 70119 Office: 1532 Tulane Ave New Orleans LA 70140

DURAN, ELVA, special education educator; b. Canutillo, Tex., July 12, 1946; s. Juan P. and Petra M. D. Ph.D. in Edn., U. Oreg., 1978. Asst. prof. spl. edn. U. Tex.-El Paso, 1978—, dir. spl. edn. clinic, 1978—; cons. Ysleta and El Paso Ind. Sch. Dist., El Paso, Tex. Hightower Found. grantee, 1981-82. Mem. Am. Ednl. Research Assn., Assn. for Severely Handicapped, Nat. Soc. for Children And Adults with Autism. Roman Catholic. Contbr. articles to numerous jours.

DURAN, MICHAEL WYNN, nurse; b. Fort Sam Houston, Tex., June 23, 1953; s. Raymond Ray and Evelyn (Fuselair) D.; m. Wanda Fruge, Apr. 10, 1976; 1 child, Jason. B.S. in Nursing, McNeese State U., 1977. Staff nurse U.S. Army Walter Reed Army Med. Ctr., Washington, 1977-80; shift change nurse emergency room U.S. Army, Fort Polk, La., 1980-81; house supr. Dr. W.O. Olin Moss Regional Hosp., Lake Charles, La., 1981-82, med. surg., infection control supr., 1983—. Served with Nurse Corps, U.S. Army 1977-81. Mem. Lake Charles Dist. Nurses' Assn. (Notable Accomplishment award 1984). Republican. Roman Catholic. Avocations: tennis; sailing. Office: Dr Olin Moss Regional Hosp 1000 Walters St Lake Charles LA 70601

DURAN, MIGUEL HERRERA, engineering educator; b. Ysleta, Tex., Sept. 30, 1934; s. Matilde and Feliciana (Herrera) D.; student N.Mex. State U., 1954, Capitol Engring. Inst., 1971, Upper Iowa U., 1978, Southwestern U., 1983; m. Emma G. Luna, Aug. 3, 1955; children—Edsel Lee, Wyatt Ross, Mary Lynn, Michael. Electronics field engr. RCA Service Co., Cherry Hill, N.J., 1959-67; telemetry systems engr. Lockheed Electronics Co., Houston, 1967-72; tech. tng. supr., systems engr. E-Systems, Inc., Garland, Tex., 1972-84, Tech. Devel. Corp., 1984—; prof. elec. engring. tech., evening div. Nat. Inst. Tech., Dallas, 1979-86. Served with USAF, 1955-59. Cert. mfg. engring. technologist. Mem. Am. Soc. Tng. and Devel., IEEE, Am. Soc. Mfg. Engrs. (sr.). Democrat. Roman Catholic. Home: 1202 Carroll Dr Garland TX 75041 Office: Tech Devel Corp Def Systems Group 621 Six Flags Dr Arlington TX 76011

DURAN, REGINALD JOSEPH, oil well drilling contractor engineer; b. Bear Valley, Wis., Mar. 21, 1915; s. Peter J. and Frances M. (Weitzel) D.; m. Mildred V. Seaman, Oct. 21, 1939; children—Craig, Brenda. Student U. Wis.-Madison, 1934-36, Northeastern State Coll., 1946-47, Centenary Coll., 1949-50. Dist. supt., well logger Baroid div. NL Industries, 1943-59; drilling fluid supr. Loffland Bros., 1959-84; ret., 1984; cons. in field. Mem. Am. Petroleum Inst., Soc. Petroleum Engrs. of AIME. Republican. Roman Catholic. Author, illustrator manual Mud Engineering, 1961; author drilling engring. software programs HYDANL and RECHYD, 1982. Home: 3121 S Utica Ave Tulsa OK 74105

DURBETAKI, PANDELI, mechanical engineering educator, researcher; b. Istanbul, Turkey, May 31, 1928; s. John Anthony and Angeliki (Vidalis) D.; m. Elisabeth F. Megerle, Aug. 28, 1954; children—N. John, Peter E., Christina E. B.S.M.E., Robert Coll. Engring. Sch., Istanbul, 1951; M.S., U. Rochester, 1954; Ph.D., Mich. State U., 1964. Grad. asst. mech. engring. U. Rochester, 1951-52; draftsman, designer Anstice Co., Rochester, 1952, Capital Plastics, Rochester, 1952-53; instr. U. Rochester, 1953-56, asst. prof., 1956-60; instr. mech. engring. Mich. State U., 1960-61, 63-64; assoc. prof. mech. engring. Ga. Inst. Tech., Atlanta, 1964-77, prof., 1977—; cons.; coordinator grad. studies Ga. Inst. Tech. Sch. Mech. Engring. Recipient 2 NSF Sci. Faculty awards, 1961-63; research grantee N.O. Broderson, 1954-60, NSF, 1965-66, 72-76, Nat. Bur. Standards, 1977-78, Dept. Energy, 1978-80, Ga. Inst. Tech., 1982-83. Mem. ASME, Combustion Inst., Sigma Xi. Greek Orthodox. Lodge: Order of AHEPA. Contbr. articles to profl. jours. Office: School of Mechanical Engineering Georgia Institute of Technology Atlanta GA 30332

DURBIN, KENNETH C., accountant; b. Clanton, Ala., June 24, 1921; s. Mack C. and Etta (Headley) D.; m. Marian Simmons, Sept. 10, 1949; children—Brent L., John Brandon. B.B.A., Tex. Tech. U., 1950. C.P.A., Tex. Staff acct. Edwin Merriman, Lubbock, Tex., 1949-52, ptnr., C.P.A., 1955-81; mgr., C.P.A., Heard, McElroy & Vestal, Shreveport, La., 1952-54; comptroller M. Levy Co., Shreveport, 1954-55; C.P.A., Lubbock, Tex., 1981—. Served to lt. USAF, 1940-45. Mem. Am. Inst. C.P.A.s, Tex. Soc. C.P.A.s (chpt. pres. 1963-64; treas. 1967-68, dir. 1963-67, 78-81), Nat. Assn. Accts., Accts. for Coops. Republican. Episcopalian. Home: 4717 22d St Lubbock TX 79407

DURHAM, FLOYD WESLEY, JR., economist, educator; b. Yuma, Ariz., Feb. 9, 1930; s. Floyd Wesley and Inez (Irvin) D.; B.A., N. Tex. State U., 1951, M.A., 1952; Ph.D., U. Okla., 1963; m. Patricia Keehan, May 24, 1973; children—Mark Kipling, Ronald Chappell. Claimsman, Liberty Mutual Ins. Co., Boston and Ft. Worth, 1955-58; mem. faculty dept. econs. Tex. Christian U., Ft. Worth, 1960—, prof., 1971—; cons., 1964—. Pres., Suicide Prevention Tarrant County, 1968-69. Bd. dirs. Ft. Worth Literacy Council, 1963-70. Served with AUS, 1953-55. Danforth Found. grantee, 1969-70. Mem. Am., So. econ. assns., Southwestern, Western social sci. assns., AAUP, Beta Gamma Sigma, Omicron Delta Epsilon, Lambda Chi Alpha. Author: A Pilot Methodological Study to Determine Dibilitating Conditions, 1967; The Trinity River Paradox; Flood and Famine, 1976. Contbr. articles to profl. jours. Home: Durham Ranch Route 1 Box 75 Aledo TX 76008

DURHAM, RONALD DALE, lawyer; b. Albuquerque, Jan. 25, 1953; s. Billie Jack and Annie Liberia (Ward) D.; m. Joy Lynn Miller, Sept. 4, 1976; children—Christopher Eric, DeAnna Marie. Student, U.S. Coast Guard Acad., 1971-73; B.A., Okla. Bapt. U., 1976; J.D., U. Tulsa, 1981. Bar: Okla. 1981, U.S. Dist. Ct. (ea., we., no. dist.) Okla. 1982, U.S. Ct. Appeals (10th cir.) 1982. Staff law librarian U. Tulsa, 1977-81; assoc. atty. Jones, Gungoll, Jackson, Collins & Dodd, Enid, Okla., 1981-83; atty., ptnr. Jones, McNaughton & Blakeley, Enid, 1983—. Served with USCG, 1971-73. Mem. Okla. Bar Assn. (mineral, real property and bankruptcy sect.), ABA (mineral and banking law sect.). Home: 2310 W Broadway Enid OK 73701 Office: Jones McNaughton & Blakley 1100 Broadway Tower Enid OK 73701

DURHAM, THENA MONTS, microbiologist, researcher; b. Bradenton, Fla., July 10, 1945; d. Turner Monts and Silverrene (Taylor) M.; m. Millard Durham, Aug. 30, 1969; children—Bryce Vincent-Barnard, Brittanie Yvonne. B.A., Fisk U., 1966; M.S. Purdue U., 1968. Research microbiologist Ctrs. for Disease Control, Atlanta, Ga., 1968—, cons. FDA. Rec. sec. Hillside Acad. PTA, 1982; mem. NAACP, Neighborhood Planning Unit. Recipient Superior performance award Ctrs. for Disease Control, 1972. Mem. Sci. Research Soc., AAAS, Am. Soc. Microbiologists, Sigma Xi. Democrat. Author numerous tech. papers; contbr. articles to profl. jours.

DURKEE, JEAN KELLNER, cooking school executive, author; b. Chgo., Feb. 7, 1932; d. Herbert Ernest and Lucy (Stevens) Kellner; B.S. in Home Econs., U. Tex., Austin, 1953; m. Robert Rosswell Durkee, Jr., Oct. 3, 1953; children—Robert III, Mark, Todd. Dir., First Presbyn. Nursery Sch. and Kindergarten, Lafayette, La., 1954-56; dir. Grace Presbyn. Nursery Sch. and Kindergarten, Lafayette, 1965-67; pres. Tout de Suite à la Microwave, Inc., Lafayette, 1978—; tchr. microwave cooking. Pres., Lafayette Natural History Mus. Mem. Am. Home Econs. Assn., Home Economists in Bus., La. Home Econs. Assn., Internat. Assn. Cooking Schs., Internat. Microwave Power Inst., P.E.O. (pres. chpt. 1961-62). Republican. Methodist. Clubs: Jr. League (pres. club 1959-60) (Lafayette); Chez Amis Women's (pres. 1957-58). Author, pub.: Tout de Suite a la Microwave, I, 1977, II, 1980; author: Voilà! Lafayette Centennial Cookbook 1884-1984, 1984; co-author Waves and Blades column 1978-82. Office: PO Box 30121 Lafayette LA 70503

DURKEE, JOHN MICHAEL, oil company executive, engineer; b. Tulsa, Sept. 16, 1946; s. George Alfred Durkee and Lois Etta (Autry) McFarlane; m. Linda Sue Jones, Dec. 21, 1968 (div. 1974); 1 child, Ron Michael; m. Judy Lynn Cope, May 10, 1979; children—Angela Kim, Michael Todd. B.S. in Math., Northeastern State U., 1974; M.S. in Engring. Mgmt., Tulsa. Registered profl. engr., Okla. Project engr. Burtek, Inc., Tulsa, 1974-77; plant engr. Southwest Tube Mfg., Sand Springs, Okla., 1977-78; v.p. chief engr. Interco, Inc., Tulsa, 1975-80; pres. Oilwell Completion, Inc., Tulsa, 1976—; dir. Brass Ring Devel. Corp., Tulsa, 1982—; Virgo Energy, Tulsa, 1981—. Served to sgt. U.S. Army, 1968-72. Mem. Nat. Soc. Profl. Engrs., Okla. Soc. Profl. Engrs., Tulsa Engring. Soc., Am. Assn. Petroleum Geologists, Kappa Mu Epsilon. Republican. Roman Catholic. Club: Tulsa Computer Soc. Avocations: reading; gun collecting; coins; stamps; swimming. Home: Office: Oilwell Completion Inc 3726 S Peoria Suite 26 Tulsa OK 74105

DURLACH, MARCUS RUSSELL, mech. engring. cons., artist; b. Bklyn., Jan. 27, 1911; s. Marcus Russell and Nellie Kinard (Schureman) D.; M.E., Stevens Inst. Tech., 1933; M.Sc., Cornell U., 1946; m. Jeannette Vivian Lorber, June 29, 1941; children—Marcus Russell, Richard Stevens. Tchr. Bklyn. Tech. High Sch., 1934-41; test engr., supr. U.S. Navy, Charleston, S.C., 1941-45; asso. prof. engring. U. S.C., Columbia, 1945-52; cons. engr., sr. partner Durlach, O'Neal & Jenkins, Columbia, 1946—. Mem. S.C. Bd. Engring. Examiners. Exhibited in one-man shows at Columbia Coll., Ft. Jackson Gallery, Columbia Mus. Art; exhibited in group shows at Columbia Gallery, Columbia Mus. Art; represented in permanent collections. Chmn. curriculum com. Midlands Tech. Inst., Columbia, 1969-78. Recipient various art awards. Registered profl. engr., N.C., S.C., Ga., Nev., Wis. Fellow Am. Soc. M.E. (profl. practice com. 1972—), Am. Soc. Heating Ventilation Air Conditioning Engrs.; mem. Artists Guild Columbia (pres. 1973-74), S.C. Guild of Artists, Nat. (dir. 1966-69), S.C. (pres. 1964), Columbia (pres. 1957) socs. profl. engrs., S.C. Watercolor Soc. (pres.), So. Watercolor Soc. (pres. 1979—), S.A.R. Rotarian (pres. club 1963-64). Home: 6025 Lakeshore Dr Columbia SC 29206 Office: 2119 Santee Ave Columbia SC 29205

DURM, MARK WENDELL, educator; b. Winchester, Tenn., May 17, 1950; s. Darwin Lee and Edna Odell (Hatchett) D. B.A., Middle Tenn. State U., 1972, M.A., 1976; A.A., Martin Coll., 1970, M.A., 1974; Ph.D., U. Miss., 1983. Dir. student affairs Martin Coll., Pulaski, Tenn., 1972-76; asst. prof. psychology Columbia State Community Coll., 1976-81; asst. prof. psychologist Athens State Coll., Ala., 1982—; adj. faculty Cumberland U., Lebanon, Tenn., 1984—. Author: General Psychology Handbook, 1980-81. Contbr. articles to profl. jours. Mem. Exec. Com. Giles County, Pulaski, 1973-76; chmn. Young Dems., 1974-76; bd. dirs. Big Bros./Big Sis., Columbia, 1979-81. Mem. Am. Psychol. Assn. Home: Blue Springs Subdivision Elk River AL 35611 Office: Athens State Coll Athens AL 35611

DURNIL, DONALD EARL, occupational safety and health director; b. Hammond, Ind., May 23, 1947; s. Earl Lester and Marion Louise (Morgan) D.; m. Janis Marie Buff, Mar. 8, 1969; children—Jason Bryon, Cherie Elizabeth. B.S. in Engring. Ops., N.C. State U. Cert. safety profl. Safety engr. Naval Air Rework Facility, Cherry Point, N.C., 1975-81, occupational safety and health dir., 1982—. Speaker profl. symposium, civic group. Sunday Sch. tchr. Faith Evangelistical Bible Ch., Newport, N.C., 1981—. Served with USN, 1968-72, Philippines, Spain. Mem. Am. Soc. Safety Engrs. (chmn. 1982, sec.-treas. Eastern Sect. N.C. chpt. 1983), Fed. Mgmt. Assn., Cherry Point Employees Assn. Republican. Avocations: marathon running; music. Home: 5 Chattawka Dr Havelock NC 28532 Office: Naval Air Rework Facility Code 01500 Marine Corps Air Station Cherry Point NC 28533

DURRENBERGER, BRUCE BAKER, insurance company public relations executive; b. Houston, Oct. 22, 1934. B.B.A., U. Tex., 1957, postgrad. Grad. Sch. Bus., 1958. Group sales mgr. Am. Gen. Life Ins. Co. subs. Am. Gen. Corp., Pitts., 1960-63, v.p. pension mktg., Houston, 1963-68, 71-77, asst. to pres., 1970-71; v.p. mktg. Equity Annuity Life Ins. Co. subs. Am. Gen. Corp., Washington, 1968-70; dir. investment counseling Am. Gen. Capital Mgmt. Co. subs. Am. Gen. Corp., Houston, 1977-78; dir. pub. relations Am. Gen. Corp., Houston, 1978—; dir. Bankers Property Trust, Washington, Stockholders of Am., Inc.; bd. dirs. Stockholders Am. Found., Washington. Trustee Houston Arboretum and Bot. Gardens, Crisis Intervention Houston, Crisis Hotline Houston, Concert Chorale of Houston, Harris County Ct. Vols.; bd. adminstrs. St. Paul's Methodist Ch., Houston; mem. adv. com. Hogg Found. for Mental Health; active St. Joseph's Hosp. Women's Pavillion Campaign, 1982-83, numerous polit. campaigns; sustaining mem. Republican Nat. Com.; charter mem. Rep. Presdl. Task Force. Served to 1st lt. U.S. Army, 1958-60; ETO. Mem. Am. Soc. Pension Actuaries (assoc.), Pub. Relations Soc. Am., Nat. Investor Relations Inst., Main Event Mgmt. Inst. (cert. instr.). Clubs: Forest, Regency (Houston); Aspen (Colo.).

DURST, MARCIA LYNETTE, nurse; b. Bryan, Tex., June 12, 1955; d. Harold Frank and Anita Geraldine (McLain) Blinka; m. Roger Don Durst, Apr. 22, 1978; children—Brandon Roger, Eric Michael. A.S.N., Angelo State U., 1977. Nurse, St. Joseph's Hosp., Bryan, 1977-78, Sid Peterson Meml. Hosp., Kerrville, Tex., 1979-81 1982—. Address: 1104 Donna Kay Kerrville TX 78028

DURYEA, EDWARD RUSSELL, real estate developer, community planner; b. Passaic, N.J., Mar. 28, 1935; s. James Edward and Priscilla Eleanor (Larlham) D.; m. Edna Anne Hahn, Sept. 9, 1955; children—Russell Duane, Lynn Allison, Susanne Michele, Kim Elizabeth. B.Landscape Architecture, U. Ga., 1957. Landscape architect Div. Architecture, State of N.Y., 1957-59; assoc. landscape architect H. Boyer Marx, Atlanta, 1959-60; sr. city planner City of Syracuse (N.Y.), 1960-62; founder, pres. Duryea & Wilhelmi Profl. Corp., Syracuse, 1962-80; v.p. 1208 James Property Ltd., 1971-80; pres. Chatham Woods, Ltd., 1978—, The Windloch Corp., Punta Gorda, Fla., 1980—. Active Vols. in Tech. Assistance. Mem. Am. Soc. Landscape Architects (accreditation bd. 1976), Am. Arbitration Assn. (mem. panel 1970—). Author: Unit Cost Index, 1970. Home: 568 NW Susan Ave Port Charlotte FL 33952 Office: 11195 Tamiami Trail Punta Gorda FL 33955

DUSKY, JOAN AGATHA, weed scientist, educator; b. Tacoma, Wash., Aug. 13, 1951; d. Albert Robert and Josephine Ann (Gawelek) D. B.S., Baldwin Wallace Coll., 1973; M.S., N.D. State U., 1975, Ph.D., 1978. Research fellow U.S. Dept. Agr., Agrl. Research Service, Metabolism and Radiation Research Lab., Fargo, N.D., 1978-80; weed scientist, asst. prof. dept. vegetable crops Agrl. Research and Edn. Ctr., U. Fla., Belle Glade, 1980—. Mem. Weed Sci. Soc. Am., Am. Soc. Plant Physiologists, Am. Soc. Hort. Sci., AAAS, So. Weed Sci. Soc., Sigma Xi. Home: 360 Azalea St Palm Beach Gardens FL 33410 Office: Agr Research and Edn Center PO Drawer A Belle Glade FL 33430

DUTHU, DAVID BATCHELOR, engring. corp. exec.; b. Houma, La., Jan. 29, 1950; s. Robert John and Wanda LaVern (Batchelor) D.; B.S. in Mech. Engring., Tex. A&M U., 1977; cert. in piping drafting La. State U. Piping draftsman H.E. Wiese Engrs. and Constructors, Baton Rouge, 1969-70; retail merchandiser, Houma, La., 1970-72; draftsman DeFraites & Assos., Houma, 1971-72; mech. designer Castagnos, Richard & Gaudet, Cons. Engrs., Houma, 1972-74; mech. and solar designer R.L. Patrick Inc., Cons. Engrs., Bryan, Tex., 1974-77; mech. engr. R.L. Patrick, Inc., Cons. Engrs., Bryan, 1977-79, Northway Engring., Latham, N.Y., 1979; project mgr., engr. Bernard Johnson, Inc., Houston, 1979-81; prin., v.p. computer tech. Tex. Energy Engrs., Inc., 1981—; solar researcher Tex. A&M U., 1975-79; reviewer Tex. Gov.'s Energy Council, 1978. Research co-grantee Center for Energy and Mineral Resources, Tex. A&M U., 1975, 76; grantee designer Housing and Urban Dept., 1978. Cert. energy auditor State of Tex. Mem. ASME, ASHRAE, Assn. Energy Engrs. (chmn. alt. energy com. Houston chpt., 1981, Energy Engr. of Yr. Houston chpt. 1981), Internat. Solar Energy Soc., Tex. Solar Energy Soc., Brazos Solar Energy Soc. (vice chmn., 1979). Inventor flat plate vacuum environ. solar energy collector; co-inventor flexible coupling. Home: PO Box 1455 Bellaire TX 77401 also 4014 Glenshire Dr Houston TX 77025 Office: 5645 Hillcroft Suite 503 Houston TX 77036

DUTTON, ARTHUR MORLAN, statistics educator; b. Des Moines, July 28, 1923; s. Arthur William and Letta Sarah (Morlan) D.; m. Joanne McHenry, Sept. 3, 1945; children—David, Margaret. B.S., Iowa State U., 1945, Ph.D., 1951. From instr. to assoc. prof. U. Rochester (N.Y.), 1951-68; prof., chmn. math. sci. U. Central Fla., Orlando, 1968-74, prof. stats., 1974—; cons. Dawson Research Corp., Orlando, 1976—. Served with USNR, 1942-51. USPHS spl. postdoctoral fellow, 1965-66. Fellow Am. Statis. Assn., AAAS; mem. Biometric Soc. Contbr. articles to profl. jours. Home: 9953 Lake Georgia Dr Orlando FL 32817 Office: Univ Central Fla Orlando FL 32816

DUTTON, JANICE ISBELL, educator; b. Haskell, Tex., Nov. 21, 1950; d. Allen and Lyla Mary (Mickler) Isbell; m. Willerford Frank Dutton, Jan. 9, 1975; children—Kristina Ann, Willerford Frank. B.S., Tex. Tech. U., 1973; postgrad. Midwestern State U. Cert. tchr., Tex. Tchr. kindergarten, home econs. Weinert (Tex.) Rural Sch. Dist., 1973-75; tchr. early childhood and spl. edn. Munday (Tex.) Ind. Sch. Dist., 1975—. Mem. Assn. Tex. Profl. Educators (pres.). Methodist. Home: 640 West B Munday TX 76371 Office: Main St Munday TX 76371

DUTY, TONY EDGAR, lawyer, judge, historian; b. Golinda, Tex., May 14, 1928; s. Tony and Glennie Mae (Butler) D.; m. Kathleen Lou Lear, July 20, 1934; children—Valerie Ann, Barbara Diane, Dan Richard. Student U.Colo., 1947-49; B.B.A., Baylor U., 1952, J.D., 1953. Bar: Tex. 1954, U.S. Dist. Ct. (we. dist.) Tex. 1970, U.S. Ct. Appeals (5th cir.) 1978, U.S. Ct. Appeals (11th cir.) 1981, U.S. Supreme Ct. 1982. Sole practice, Waco, Tex., 1954-56, 64—; 1st asst. atty. City of Waco, 1957-63; mcpl. judge City Woodway, Tex., 1963-80, City of Lacy-Lakeview, Tex., 1976-78, City of Beverly Hills, Tex., 1976-78, City of Waco, 1957—, City of Bellmead, Tex., 1964—; prof. bus. law, corps. and real estate Baylor U., 1976-78; ptnr. Indian Creek Estates; dir. Shannon Devel. Co., Telco Systems Inc., Sun Valley Water and Devel. Co., Inc., Hewitt Devel. Co., Susans, Inc., Woodway Seed and Garden Co., Inc. Mem. Waco Plan Commn., 1966-69, Waco-McLennan County Library Commn., 1968-72, chmn., 1971-72; mem. Waco Fire and Police Civil Service Commn., 1975-81, chmn., 1980-81; mem. Waco Am. Revolution Bicentennial Commn., 1974-76; chmn. Waco Heritage '76, 1974-76; mem. McLennan County Hist. Survey Commn., 1970—; chmn. Ft. House Mus., Waco, 1968-72, bd. dirs. Waco Heritage Soc., 1960—. Served with USAF, 1946-49. Mem. State Bar Tex., Waco-McLennan County Bar Assn., Waco-McLennan County Def. Lawyers Assn. (v.p.), Delta Theta

Phi. Democrat. Baptist. Clubs: Masons, KP. Author: The Coronado Expedition, 1540-1542, 1970; James Wilkinson: 1757-1825, 1971; Champ D'Asile, 1972; The Home Front: McLennan County in the Civil War, 1974; contbr. articles to historical jours. Home: 613 Camp Dr Waco TX 76710 Office: 2309 Austin Ave Waco TX 76701

DUVAL, MILES P., JR., ret. naval officer; b. Portsmouth, Va., Apr. 19, 1896; s. Miles P. and Minnie Lee (Chalkley) DuV.; B.S., U.S. Naval Acad., 1918, student U.S. Naval War Coll., 1925-26; U.S. Naval Postgrad. Sch., 1930-31; M.F.S., Fgn. Service Sch., Georgetown U., 1937. Commd. ensign USN, 1918, advanced through grades to capt., 1945; comdg. officer U.S.S. Dupont, 1933-35, participated in naval demonstration off Cuban ports, 1933-34; sec. Shore Sta. Devel. Bd., Navy Dept., Washington, 1936-38; comdg. officer U.S.S. Antares, 1939-40; capt. of port, Balboa, C.Z., in charge marine ops. of Pacific subdiv. of Panama Canal, 1941-44; planned and coordinated enlargement of Balboa Harbor, 1942-43; developed high level terminal lake 3d locks plan for major modernization of Panama Canal, 1943; comdg. officer U.S.S. Dade, 1944-46, participated in Okinawa campaign, 1945; designated as Navy Dept. liaison officer and coordinator for modernization studies of Panama Canal by Sec. Navy, 1946; ret. active service, 1949. Vice pres., gen. cons. John F. Stevens Hall of Fame com., 1969—. Bd. dirs. Gorgas Meml. Inst. Tropical and Preventive Medicine; trustee James Monroe Meml. Found.; mem. nat. adv. bd. MacArthur Meml. Found. Decorated Legion of Merit (Army), 1945, World War I Victory medal with Atlantic and Grand Fleet clasps, 1918, Am. Def. with Fleet and Base clasps, 1939-41, Am. campaign, 1941-44, Aslatic-Pacific campaign with bronze star, 1945. Recipient Roger Brooke Taney award Md. div. SCV; medal of honor Nat. Soc. DAR; Gold medallion Am. Revolution Bicentennial Commn. Fellow AAAS; mem. Va. Hist. Soc., Naval Hist. Found., Soc. of Va. in Washington (past v.p.), Permanent Internat. Assn. Nav. Congresses (life), U.S. Naval Inst., U.S. Strategic Inst., Soc. Am. Mil. Engrs., Panama Hist. Soc. (corr. mem.), Panama Canal Soc. of Washington (pres.), Panama Canal Natural History Soc. (past v.p.), Baronial Order Magna Charta, Mil. Order Crusades, Jamestowne Soc., Phi Alpha Theta (hon.). Clubs: Explorers; Cosmos, Army and Navy (Washington); Yacht (N.Y.C.). Author: Series on Panama Canal: Cadiz to Cathay, 4th edit., 1975; And the Mountains Will Move, 2d edit., 1969; Let the Waters Rise; Matthew Fontaine Maury: Benefactor of Mankind, 1964; Sam Houston: The Washington of the Vast Southwest, 1966; George Rogers Clark: Conqueror of the Old Northwest, 1970; John Frank Stevens: Civil Engineer, Explorer, Diplomat and Statesman, 1976; James Monroe—An Appreciation, 1982; also papers on interoceanic canal history and problems.

DUVALL, CHARLES FARMER, Episcopal bishop; b. Cheraw, S.C., Nov. 18, 1935; s. Henry and Elizabeth Phoebe (Farmer) D.; m. Nancy Warren Rice, June 2, 1957; children—Ann Rice, Charles Farmer, Theodore Wannamaker. B.A. with honors in History, The Citadel, 1957; M.Div., Va. Theol. Sem., 1960; D.D. (hon.), Va. Theol. Sem., 1982. Ordained priest Episcopal Ch., 1960, consecrated bishop, 1981. Served at various chs. in Diocese of S.C., 1960-70; rector Holy Trinity Ch., Fayetteville, N.C., 1970-77, Ch. of the Advent, 1977-80 bishop, Mobile, Ala., 1981—. Address: Episcopal Diocese of Central Gulf Coast PO Box 8547 Mobile AL 36689

DUVALL, LINDA STUDDERT, educator; b. Beaumont, Tex., Dec. 15, 1950; d. John Adam and Juanita Louise (Emery) Studdert; m. Robert Carlton Duvall, Aug. 11, 1980; children—John Lee, Jenna Lee. B.S. in Elem. Edn., Lamar U., 1973; M.Ed., North Tex. State U., 1978. Lic. tchr., Tex. Tchr. primary spl. edn. Warren (Tex.) Ind. Sch. Dist., 1973-74, jr. high math. tchr. 1974-75; tchr. math. Grapevine-Colleyville (Tex.) Ind. Sch. Dist., 1975-80, Mineral Wells (Tex.) Ind. Sch. Dist., 1980-81; tchr. math, reading, English, Garner (Tex.) Ind. Sch. Dist., 1981-84; condr. workshops in field. Named Colleyville Middle Sch. Tchr. of Yr., Grapevine Edn. Assn., 1978-79. Mem. Tex. Tchrs. Assn., Tex. Classroom Tchrs. Assn., Warren Edn. Assn., Grapevine-Colleyview Edn. Assn., Garner Edn. Assn., Cap and Gown, Delta Kappa Gamma (World Fellowship chmn.), Kappa Delta, Alpha Lambda Delta, Phi Kappa Phi. Home: Route 1 PO Box 84A Poolville TX 76076

DUVALL, LORETTA MARYANN, child abuse specialist; b. Cleve., Jan. 8, 1949; d. Aloysius Joseph and Natalie Maryann Mysliwczyk; m. Stephen Goodwin Duvall, Jan. 8, 1983. B.A., U. Fla., 1970. With State of Fla., 1970—, formerly child abuse specialist, now program analyst Program Serving Handicapped or Chronically Ill children. Mem. Juvenile Officers Assn. Democrat. Roman Catholic. Clubs: South Fla. Gourmet, Supper (Ft. Lauderdale). Home: 10650 NW 43d Ct Coral Springs FL 33065 Office: 201 W Broward Blvd Fort Lauderdale FL 33301

DVORETZKY, ISAAC, petroleum company executive; b. Houston, Jan. 24, 1928; s. Max and Anna (Greenfield) D.; B.A., Rice U., 1948, M.A., 1950, Ph.D. in Chemistry, 1952; children—Rachel Leah, Aaron Benjamin, Rebecca Esther. With Shell Oil Co., various locations, 1952—, mgr. unconventional raw materials dept., Emeryville, Calif., 1969-72, mgr. profl. recruitment, univ. relations Shell Devel. Co. div., Houston, 1972—. Exchange scientist Royal Dutch/Shell Lab., Amsterdam, 1958-59; mem. council Gordon Research Confs., 1972—. Bd. dirs. San Francisco Bay Area Sci. Fair, 1971-72; mem. grad. council Rice U., 1977-79; mem. Houston Commn. for Jewish Edn., 1976-78; v.p. Houston Kashruth Assn., 1979-81; bd. dirs. Nat. Consortium for Grad. Degrees for Minorities in Engring., 1980—. Mem. Am. Chem. Soc., Phi Beta Kappa Alumni Assn. Greater Houston (dir. 1976-78), Phi Beta Kappa, Sigma Xi, Phi Lambda Upsilon. Jewish (synagogue officer, trustee). Contbr. articles to profl. jours.; editorial bd. Rice U. Studies, 1981-83. Patentee hydrocarbon chemistry and catalysis. Home: 11025 Larkwood #1221 Houston TX 77096 Office: PO Box 1380 Houston TX 77001

DWIGGINS, CLAUDIUS WILLIAM, JR., chemist; b. Amity, Ark., May 11, 1933; s. Claudius William and Lillian (Scott) D.; B.S., U. Ark., 1954, M.S., 1956, Ph.D. (Am. Oil Co. fellow, Coulter-Jones scholar), 1958. With U.S. Dept. of Energy, Bartlesville (Okla.) Tech. Center, 1958-84, chemist, 1958-60, project leader surface physics project, 1960-65, project leader petroleum composition research project, 1965-80, supervisory research chemist, thermodynamics div., 1980-84; cons., 1984—. Mem. Am. Chem. Soc., N.Y. Acad. Scis., AAAS, Am. Crystallographic Assn., Am. Inst. Physics, Sigma Xi (sec. 1966-67), Alpha Chi Sigma, Delta Sigma Phi (treas. 1952). Contbr. articles to profl. jours. Home: 1211 S Keeler St Bartlesville OK 74003

DWORKIN, ANTHONY GARY, sociologist, educator; b. Los Angeles, Nov. 22, 1942; s. Harry Arnold and Dorothy (Dropkin) D.; m. Rosalind Jean Barbagallo, Mar. 21, 1966; 1 child, Jason Peter. A.B., Occidental Coll., 1964; M.A., Northwestern U., 1966, Ph.D., 1970. From instr. to asst. prof. U. Mo., Columbia, 1968-73; prof. U. Houston, 1973—. Co-editor: The Blending of Races, 1972; author: When Teachers Give Up, 1985; Teacher Burnout in the Public Schools, 1986; co-author: The Minority Report, 1976, 82; The Female Revolt, 1986. Recipient Bobbs-Merrill award, 1966; Woodrow Wilson fellow, 1964, 67; grantee NSF, NIMH, Hogg Found., Nat. Inst. Edn. Mem. Am. Sociol. Assn., S.W. Social Sci. Assn., S.W. Sociol. Assn. (parliamentarian 1982—, assoc. editor 1969-73), Midwest Sociol. Soc., Soc. Study Social Problems, Soc. Psychol. Study Social Issues, Phi Beta Kappa. Avocations: astronomy; golf; computers. Office: U Houston Dept Sociology 4800 Cullen Blvd Houston TX 77004

DWYER, GERALD PAUL, JR., economics educator, consultant; b. Pittsfield, Mass., July 9, 1947; s. Gerald Paul and Mary Frances (Weir) D.; m. Katherine Marie Lepiane, Jan. 15, 1966; children—Tamara K., Gerald P. III, Angela M., Michael J.L., Terence F. B.B.A., U. Wash., 1969; M.A. in Econs., U. Tenn., 1973; Ph.D. in Econs., U. Chgo., 1979. Economist, Fed. Res. Bank, St. Louis, 1972-74, Fed. Res. Bank, Chgo., 1976-77; asst. prof. Tex. A&M U., College Station, 1977-81, Emory U., Atlanta, 1981-84; assoc. prof. U. Houston, 1984—; sr. research assoc. Law and Econ. Ctr. Emory U., Atlanta, 1982-84; vis. scholar Fed. Res. Bank, Atlanta, 1982-84; cons. FTC, Washington, 1983-84, Arthur Bros., Corpus Christi, Tex., 1980-81. Contbr. articles to profl. jours. NSF trainee U. Tenn., 1970-72; Weaver fellow Intercollegiate Studies Inst., 1974-75, Earhart Found. fellow 1975-77. Mem. Am. Econ. Assn., Econometric Soc., Econ. History Assn., We. Econ. Assn., So. Econ. Assn., Beta Gamma Sigma, Phi Kappa Phi. Avocation: computers. Home: 3417 Northline Oaks St Conroe TX 77384 Office: Dept Econs U Houston Houston TX 77004

DYAL, JERRY EDWARD, marketing executive; b. Orlando, Fla., June 7, 1951; s. Edmund Clarence and Betty Ann (Mercer) D.; m. Debbie Jean Overstreet, Oct. 7, 1969 (div. 1983). Student Jacksonville U., 1973. Abstractor, Fla. Title Guaranty, Jacksonville, 1973-75; salesman Fashee Realty, Jacksonville, 1975-77; sales mgr. Lawyers Title Ins. Corp., Jacksonville, 1977-82; account exec. LTISA (Continental Group), Jacksonville, 1982—; title liaison Mortage Bankers Assn., 1981-83. Active Boy Scouts Am., 1982-83. Served with USMC, 1970-73. Recipient Outstanding Service award Westide Businessmen's Club, 1980; Presdl. award Lawyers Title 1980; Outstanding Grad., 1979; Affiliate of Yr., Jacksonville Bd. Realtors, 1981; others. Mem. Fla. Land Title Assn., Young Title People, N.E. Fla. Home Builders, Clay, Beaches and Jacksonville Bd. Realtors, Sales and Mktg. Execs. Jacksonville, Women's Council Realtors, Mortgage Bankers Assn., Mortgate Brokers Assn., West Duval Jaycees (dir. 1980—), Am. Legion, S.W. Council C. of C. (dir. 1980—). Democrat. Baptist. Club: Westside Businessmen's. Home: 5215 Quan Dr Jacksonville FL 32205 Office: 1800 Independent Dr Suite 1800 Jacksonville FL 32202

DYCK, ROBERT GILKEY, university official, educator; b. Blacksburg, Va., Nov. 20, 1930; s. Paul Benjamin and Cornella Jane (Gilkey) D.; m. Franciska Kertesz, June 25, 1960; children—Henrika, Sara Jane. A.B., Oberlin Coll., 1952; B. Arch., MIT, 1955; M.C.P., U. Pa., 1959; Ph.D., U. Pitts., 1970. Registered architect, N.Y. Architect-planner Pitts. Regional Planning Assn., 1957-59; assoc. R.C. Weinberg & Assocs., Architects and Planners, N.Y.C., 1960-63; asst. prof. planning and assoc. dir. Office Research and Devel., W. Va. U., Morgantown, 1963-68; prof. urban affairs and planning Va. Poly. Inst. and State U., Blacksburg, 1970—, dir. internat. programs, 1976-84; trustee S.E. Consortium Internat. Devel.; dir. Council Internat. Ednl. Exchange. Contbr. articles to profl. jours. Chmn. New River Valley Health Council, 1976-80; active Montgomery County Democratic Party, 1972-83. Recipient Fulbright-Hays Faculty Research award, Yugoslavia, 1973, group project in India, 1980. Home: 2905 Ashlawn Dr Blacksburg VA 24060 Office: Va Tech Inst 218 Hutcheson Hall Blacksburg VA 24061

DYE, BRADFORD JOHNSON, JR., lieutenant governor Mississippi; b. Tallahatchie County, Miss., Dec. 20, 1933; married; 3 children. B.B.A., LL.B., U. Miss. Bar: Miss 1959. Practiced law, Grenada, Miss., 1959-61, later in Jackson, Miss.; mem. Miss. Ho. of Reps., 1960-64, Miss. Senate, 1964-68; dir. Agrl. and Indsl. Bd., 1968-71; treas., State of Miss., 1972-76, lt. gov., 1980—; formerly served with U.S. Senate Judiciary Com. Staff; pres. Jackson Fed. Savs. Assn., 1976-79. Mem. Pi Kappa Alpha. Methodist. Office: Office Lt Gov New Capitol Bldg Jackson MS 39205*

DYE, LOWELL DELANO, JR., navy petty officer; b. Columbus, Ohio, Mar. 7, 1955; s. Paul Edward and Elsie Alice (Shepard) Hulbert; m. Linda Fay Burns, Aug. 4, 1974; 1 son, Adrian Young. A.A., U. Md., 1981; B.S., SUNY-Albany, 1982; postgrad. U. Ark., 1983. Enlisted U.S. Navy, 1973, advanced through grades to petty officer 1st class, 1979; weapons supr., fire control div. supr. USS James Monroe, Charleston, S.C., 1976-78; weapons module test shop supr. USS Holland AS-32, Holy Loch, Scotland, 1978; weapons quality assurance div. supr., 1978-81; instr. leadership and mgmt. edn. and tng. Navy Human Resource Mgmt. Sch., Memphis, 1981—; mem. faculty Fogelman Coll. Bus. and Econs., Memphis State U., 1984—; founder Mgmt. Enterprises, Memphis, 1983—. Mem. Resolve, Inc., 1979, Memphis Council on Adoptable Children, 1981; bd. dirs. Full Gospel Businessmen's Fellowship, Internat., Memphis chpt. Baptist.

DYE, PATRICK FAIN, college football coach, athletic director; b. Augusta, Ga., Nov. 6, 1939; s. Frank Wayne Dye and Nell Slaughter; m. Sue Ward; children—Patrick Fain, Missy, Brett, Wanda. Student U. Ga., 1962. Profl. football player Edmonton Eskimoes, Can. Football League, 1963-65; asst. football coach U. Ala., University, 1965-73; head football coach East Carolina U., Greenville, 1974-79; football coach U. Wyo., Laramie, 1980; head football coach Auburn U., Ala., 1981—. Served to 1st lt. AUS, 1963-64. Office: Auburn U Athletic Dept Auburn University AL 36849

DYE, W. SCOTT, JR., architect, developer; b. Tulsa, Nov. 25, 1945; s. Worley Scott, Sr. and Bella L. (Wallace) D.; children—Nataly Daun, Amber Lynn. B. in Architecture, Okla. U., 1973, B. in Environ. Design, 1973; postgrad., Richland Coll., 1976, Central State U. Registered architect, Tex., Okla., Fla. Project architect Envirodynamics, Dallas, 1973-74; v.p. Omegaplan, Dallas, 1974; project mgr. Zale Corp., Dallas, 1974-77; prin. Scott Dye Architects, Dallas, 1977—. Pres., Yale Elem. PTA, Richardson, Tex., 1981-82; mem. Dallas Zool. Soc., 1985—; mem. Dallas Zoning Ordinance Adjustment Bd; local adviser Boy Scouts Am; deacon Richland Bible Fellowship Ch. Mem. Tex. Soc. Architects, AIA, Nat. Assn. Home and Apartment Builders, Nat. Council Archtl. Registration Bds., Jr. C. of C., Richardson C. of C., North Dallas C. of C. Club: Okla. U. Alumni (Dallas) Office: Scott Dye Architects 5025 Arapaho Suite 110 Dallas TX 75248

DYE, WILLIAM MERCER, JR., construction executive, building design consultant; b. Atlanta, Feb. 7, 1950; s. W. Mercer and Florence (Jackson) D.; m. Mary Atherton, Mar. 20, 1971; 1 dau., Jennifer Atherton. Student Mercer U., Macon, 1968-71; B.A., West Ga. Coll., Carrollton, 1972. Asst. dir. Scott Gallery, Atlanta, 1972-74; project mgr. Brice Bldg. Co., Atlanta, 1974-76; v.p. Dye Constrn. Co., Atlanta, 1976—; chmn. ops. Fulton County Airport Assn., Atlanta, 1984—; dir. Delta Info. Systems, Atlanta, Springlake Properties Inc., Lawrenceville, Ga. Trustee Trinity Sch., Atlanta, 1982—; contbr., campaigner Harold Dye for Gov. campaign, Ga., 1978. Mem. Assoc. Gen. Contractors, Kappa Sigma. Republican. Presbyterian. Club: Cherokee. Office: Dye Constrn Co Inc 550 Pharr Rd NW Atlanta GA 30305

DYER, DOLORES, psychologist; b. Ft. Worth; d. William Leon and Frances Louise (Cargill) D.; B.A. with highest honors, N. Tex. State U., 1963; grad. (scholar) So. Meth. U. Grad. Sch., 1964-65; Ph.D. (fellow), Southwestern Med. Sch., U. Tex., Dallas, 1973; m. Mark Howard Perkins; children—Michael Dexter Allen, Benjamin Seth, Eden Dyer Perkins. Adminstr., Child and Adolescent Community Mental Health Center, Dallas, 1969-70; asst. to dir. Dallas County Mental Health and Mental Retardation Center, 1970-73, project dir. Dallas County Comprehensive Child Care Program, 1973; dir. Dallas Commn. on Children and Youth, 1974; pvt. practice psychology, Dallas, 1975—; former tchr. Adult Sch. Continuing Edn., So. Meth. U.; mem. clin. adv. bd., trainer Suicide Prevention Center of Dallas; trainer group tng. program Dallas Group Psychotherapy Soc. Mem. children and youth adv. com. Dallas Office of Human Devel., 1974-76; bd. dirs. Dallas County Mental Health Assn., Dallas Area Women's Polit. Caucus, 1982—; mem. steering com. Dallas Women's Issues Congress; mem. adv. bd. Women's Ctr. of Dallas; mem. Health and Human Services Commn. of Dallas. Mem. Am. Psychol. Assn., Dallas Psychol. Assn., Tex. Psychol. Assn., Am., Southwest, Dallas group psychotherapy assns., Am., Dallas socs. clin. hypnosis, Women's Coalition Dallas. Democrat. Clubs: The 500 Inc. Home: 4031 Inwood Rd Dallas TX 75209 Office: 2505 Wycliff Dallas TX 75219

DYER, ELEANOR ANN, educator; b. Temple, Tex., May 5, 1941; d. J.C. and Viola Gertrude (Greener) D.; B.A., Sam Houston State U., Huntsville, Tex., 1963, M.A., 1972; Ed.D., Tex. A&M U., 1983. Tchr. sci. Tex. public schs., 1973-79; lectr., lab. instr. Tex. A. and M. U., 1978-79; curriculum cons. Region XVI Edn. Service Center, Amarillo, Tex., 1980—; judge Jr. High Sch. Sci. Fair, 1970-80. Mem. St. Thomas Apostle Roman Cath. Alter Guild, Amarillo, 1981-82. Alpha State scholar Delta Kappa Gamma, 1978-79, Internat. scholar, 1981-82; grantee NSF, 1970, 73, 75. Mem. Assn. Supervision and Curriculum Devel., Nat. Sci. Tchrs. Assn., Sci. Tchrs. Assn. Tex., Tex. Sci. Suprs. Assn., Tex. Tchrs. Assn. (life), Delta Kappa Gamma. Democrat. Author articles in field, curriculum materials. Editor STATellite, 1979—; co-editor Focus, 1981—. Office: PO Box 30600 Region XVI Edn Service Center Amarillo TX 79120

DYKES, LILLIAN ELISE LEVY, lawyer; b. New Orleans, Sept. 30, 1946; d. Lewis Harris and Phyllis Marie-Louise (Williams) Levy; m. Osborne Jefferson Dykes III, Dec. 31, 1965 (div. 1970). B.A., Memphis State U., 1973, J.D., 1975. Bar: Tenn. 1975, U.S. Dist. Ct. (we. dist.) Tenn. 1979. Atty., Tenn. Dept. Mental Health, Memphis, 1975-78; assoc. James F. Schaeffer, Memphis, 1978-79, Wilson, McRae, Ivy, McTyre, Sevier, Strain, Memphis, 1979-84; sole practice, Memphis, 1985—; assoc. prof. U. Tenn. Ctr. for Health Scis., Memphis, 1976-77; actress Berlin Internat. Theatre, 1966-67, Memphis Little Theatre, 1969—, Am. Community Theatre Conf., 1973. Mem. adv. bd. Lowenstein House, Memphis, 1979-81; jud. candidate Circuit Ct. Shelby County, Tenn., 1982; pres. Cooper-Young Community Assn., Memphis, 1984-85; bd. dirs. Theatre Memphis, 1986—. Mem. ABA, Assn. Trial Lawyers Am., Memphis Trial Lawyers Assn., Memphis-Shelby County Bar. Democrat. Roman Catholic. Clubs: American Businesswomen's, Zonta Internat., Tennessee (Memphis). Home: 2076 Evelyn Memphis TN 38104 Office: 60 N 3d Memphis TN 38103

DYMACEK, WAYNE MARSHALL, mathematics educator; b. Richmond, Va., June 25, 1952; s. Joseph Marshall and Beulah Ann (Stanley) D.; m. Elizabeth Diana Ruth, Dec. 21, 1973; children—Ivy Ida, Julian Marshall. B.S. in Math., Va. Poly. Inst. 1974, Ph.D. in Math., 1978. Crypt-analytic mathematician Nat. Security Agy., Ft. Meade, Md., 1978-81; asst. prof. math. Washington and Lee U., Lexington, Va., 1981—; reviewer Math. Revs., Ann Arbor, Mich., 1980—. Contbr. articles to profl. jours. Mem. Am. Math. Soc., Math. Assn. Am. Libertarian. Home: 103 Monticello Rd Lexington VA 24450 Office: Washington and Lee U Lexington VA 24450

DYRKACZ, W. WILLIAM, metallurgical engineer, consultant; b. Arnold, Pa., Apr. 17, 1919; s. Elias and Stella (Sabram) D.; m. Mary Scheller, Oct. 2, 1943. B.S. in Metall. Engring., Carnegie Inst. Tech., 1942. Metallurgist, Gen. Electric Co., Schenectady, N.Y., 1942-46; chief metallurgist Cameron Mfg. Co., Emporium, Pa., 1946-49; assoc. dir. research, chief metallurgist, dir. product devel. Allegheny Ludlum Steel Co., Watervliet, N.Y., 1949-66; v.p. ops. Teledyne Titanium Co., Monroe, N.C., 1966-68; metall. cons. in mfg. tech., expert witness, Waxhaw, N.C., 1968—; cons. U.S. govt. Recipient Lounsberry award Allegheny Ludlum Steel, 1955. Fellow Am. Soc. Metals; mem. AIME, Am. Vacuum Soc. Introduced vacuum arc remelting process for superalloys and steels; patentee innovations superalloys, stainless steels. Contbr. articles to profl. jours. Office: Lochaven Rd Route 3 Waxhaw NC 28173

DYSON, FRANK, law enforcement official. Chief of police, Austin, Tex. Office: PO Box 1088 Austin TX 78767*

DYSON, JAMES LAFAYETTE, JR. (JIM), internat. and marine safety adminstr.; b. Little Rock, Nov. 8, 1944; s. James L. and Frances M. (Blevins) D.; student East Tex. Coll., Duke U., Tex. A. and M. U.; m. Barbara L. Gillespie, Oct. 30, 1971; children—Elizabeth Ineta, Jill Danielle. With Meyer's Bakery, 1970-73, Ben Hogan Constrn. Co., 1973-76, Duckett Constrn. Co., 1976-77, Brown & Root, Inc., 1977-79; Dolphin Internat., 1980; safety adminstr. internat. and marine ops. Blocker Internat., Houston, 1980—; fgn. experience includes Vietnam, Kulalampur, Peru, Argentina, Brazil, Venezuela, Mex., Tanzania, Kenya. Lic. pvt. detective, N.Mex. Served with U.S. Army, 1965-70. Mem. Am. Soc. Safety Engrs., Am. Nat. Standard Inst., VFW. Author: What You Should Know About Marijuana. Home: Route 3 Box 147-A Hope AR 71801

DZIERBA, STEVEN HENRY, hospital pharmacist, college educator; b. Buffalo, Oct. 28, 1956; s. Henry M. and Helen A. (Yaczniczs) D.; m. Lauren McCormick, Aug. 15, 1981. A.A. in Journalism Tech., SUNY-Morrisville, 1976; B.S. in Pharmacy, Mass. Coll. Pharmacy, 1980; M.S. and resident in Hosp. Pharmacy, Ohio State U. and Univ. Hosps., 1983. Resident, undergrad. teaching asst. Mass. Coll. Pharmacy, Boston, 1978-79; pharmacy intern Harvard Community Health Plan, Cambridge, Mass., 1979-80; staff pharmacist Mass. Eye and Ear Infirmary, Boston, 1980-81; pharmacy resident Ohio State U. Hosps., Columbus, 1981-83; asst. dir. pharmacy Thomason Hosp., El Paso, 1983-85; dir. pharmacy Northwest Tex. Hosp., Amarillo, 1985—; faculty El Paso Community Coll., Tex., 1983-85. Contbr. articles to profl. jours. Mem. Am. Soc. Hosp. Pharmacists (adminstrv. spl. interest group), Tex. Soc. Hosp. Pharmacists (newsletter editor 1984—), El Paso Area Soc. Hosp. Pharmacists (sec./treas. 1984-85, pres. 1985—), Am. Pharm. Assn. Republican. Roman Catholic. Avocations: reading; weight training, running; woodwork and carpentry. Home: 7049 Westwind #6014 El Paso TX 79912 Office: Northwest Tex Hosp Amarillo TX

EACHUS, JOSEPH JACKSON, computer scientist, consultant; b. Anderson, Ind., Nov. 5, 1911; s. Lewis and Irene (Rogers) E.; m. Ruth Porter, 1938 (div. 1946); children—Alan C., W. James; m. O. Barbara Abernethy, 1947. A.B., Miami U., Oxford, Ohio, 1933; M.A., Syracuse U., 1936; Ph.D., U. Ill., 1939. Instr., Purdue U., West Lafayette, Ind., 1939-42; civil servant Dept. Defense, Washington, 1946-55; scientist Honeywell EDP, Waltham, Mass., 1955-76; cons., Cambridge, Mass., 1977-78; engr. Raytheon Co., Sudbury, Mass., 1979-80; cons., Sarasota, Fla., 1980—. Contbr. articles to math. and engring. jours. Served to lt. comdr. USNR, 1942-46; ETO. Fellow IEEE, AAAS; mem. Am. Math. Soc. (emeritus), Assn. Computing Machinery (mem. nat. council 1960-62). Patentee in field. Home: 4935 Stevens Dr Sarasota FL 33580 Office: Eachus EDP Cons 4935 Stevens Dr Sarasota FL 33580

EACHUS, PATRICIA LOUISE, physician; b. Rockwood, Tenn., Jan. 14, 1951; d. Fred Jr. and Alpha Amelia (Burnette) Eachus. B.S. in Biology, Tenn. Tech. U., 1972, M.A. in Guidance and Counseling, 1973; M.D., U. Tenn. Center for Health Scis., 1976. Diplomate Am. Bd. Family Physicians; lic. physician, Tenn. Intern, U. Tenn. Meml. Research Center and Hosp., Knoxville, 1973-74, resident in family practice, U. 1973-76, now mem. staff, clin. instr.; practice medicine specializing in family practice, 1976—; pvt. practice, Harriman, Tenn., 1979-80; physician primary care clinic, med. dir.; Knox County Health Dept. (Tenn.), 1980-83; physician student Health Clinic, U. Tenn., Knoxville, 1984—; mem. courtesy staff Harriman Gen. Hosp. (Tenn.). Mem. Am. Acad. Family Physicians, Tenn. Med. Assn., Knoxville Acad. of Medicine, Phi Kappa Phi. Episcopalian. Office: Andy Holt Ave Knoxville TN 37996

EADS, LYLE WILLIS, retired government inspector; b. Ida Grove, Iowa, June 29, 1916; s. David J. and Bertha E. (McGonigle) E.; m. Betty Boles, Dec. 22, 1946; children—Diane, Mary Ellen. Enlisted U.S. Navy, 1934, advanced through grades to comdr., ret., 1964; asst. inspector gen. Naval Sea Systems Command, Washington, 1966-84, ret. 1984—. Author: Survival Amidst the Ashes, 1978. Decorated Merito Naval Degree of Knight, Republic of Brazil, Rio de Janeiro. Mem. DAV, Am. Legion, Mil. Order of Purple Heart, Am. Ex-Prisoners of War, Inc., Ret. Officers Assn., Am. Security Council Found. Methodist. Lodge: Masons. Avocation: writing. Home: 401 S Carlyn Spring Rd Arlington VA 22204

EAGER, EUGENE MOREHEAD, financial consultant; b. Valdosta, Ga., Sept. 6, 1925; s. William Goronwy and Eugene Morehead (Johnston) E.; m. Frances Jean Andrews, Dec. 3, 1947; children—Karen Eager Wallmeyer, Rebekah Eager Daniel, Eugene Morehead, Virginia W. B.S. in Indsl. Mgmt., Ga. Inst. Tech., 1948. Vice pres., sales mgr. Eager Bros. Inc., Valdosta, 1952-72; v.p., fin. cons. Robinson-Humphrey/Am. Express, Albany, Ga., 1972—. Fin. chmn. Thronateeska Heritage Found., 1975; elder Covenant Presbyterian Ch., 1980-82; dir. adv. bd. Salvation Army, 1981-83. Served to lt. USNR, 1943-46. Mem. Sigma Alpha Epsilon. Lodge: Dougherty County (Ga.) Kiwanis (pres. 1983-84). Home: 2323 Bristol Rd Albany GA 31707 Office: Robinson-Humphrey/Am Express 235 Roosevelt Ave Suite 410 Albany GA 31701

EAKER, JOHN HYSHAM, lawyer, free-lance photographer; b. Pittsburg, Kans., Mar. 2, 1946; s. J. Gordon and Marjorie H. Eaker; m. Susan Cook, July 24, 1971; children—David, Meredith. B.B.A., So. Meth. U., 1968; J.D., U. Tex.-Austin, 1971. Bar: Tex. 1971; cert. in comml. real estate law Tex. Bd. Legal Splzn. Asst. city atty. City of Houston, 1971-73; corp. counsel Marvin E. Leggett & Assocs., Inc., Houston, 1973-81; sr. v.p., gen. counsel Regency Devel. Co., Houston and Dallas, 1981-85; v.p., gen. counsel Tanglewood Corp., Houston, 1985—. Pres., Rustling Oaks Civic Assn., Inc., 1977-79. Mem. State Bar of Tex., Houston Bar Assn.; life mem. Houston Livestock Show and Rodeo Assn. (breeder greeter com.). Republican. Presbyterian. Photographs pub. in Tierra Grande Mag. Office: 1661 Tanglewood Rd Houston TX 77056

EAKINS, JOHN LEROY, food and wine executive; b. Jacksonville, Fla., Aug. 30, 1943; s. Duane LeRoy and Mary Augusta (Quinn) E. Student pub. schs., Clarksburg, W.Va. Founder, Mr. John Enterprises, 1969-82; founder, operator Fancy's Food & Wine Group, 1981—; realtor Stadler Assocs.; builder, developer. Served with USN, 1960-64. Mem. Chaine des Rotisseurs (maitre rotisseurtraitur), Les Amis de Vin (life). Republican. Roman Catholic. Clubs: Jockey, Grove Isle (Miami, Fla.). Office: Fancy's Food & Wine 7382 SW 56th Ave Miami FL 33143

EARHART, EILEEN MAGIE, human development educator; b. Hamilton, Ohio, Oct. 21, 1928; d. Andrew Joseph and Leah Martha (Waldorf) Magie; m. Paul Gordon Earhart, July 28, 1950; children—Anthony Gordon, Bruce Paul,

Daniel Thomas. B.S. in Edn., Miami U., 1950, H.H.D. (hon.), 1980; M.A., Mich. State U., 1962, Ph.D., 1969. Cert. tchr., Ohio, Mich. Tchr. West Alexandria Schs., Ohio, 1950-51; tchr., specialist Waterford Schs., Pontiac, Mich., 1959-67; sr. research assoc. Mich. State U., 1968-69, from asst. prof. to prof., 1969-84, chairperson dept., 1974-83; prof., head dept. Fla. State U., Tallahassee, 1984—; cons. in field. Editor Jour. Issue of Family Relations, 1984. Contbr. articles to profl. jours. and chpt. to book. Mem. Mich. Gov.s Task Force for Children and Youth, 1981; bd. dirs. Lansing Com. Children's TV, 1973-78, Women's Resource Ctr., Grand Rapids, Mich., 1976-81. Recipient Danforth Found award Miami U., 1947; NSF scholar, 1961; Delta Kappa Gamma Soc. fellow, 1967-68. Mem. Am. Home Econs. Assn. (del., coms., honored as one of nat. leaders 1984), Mich. Home Econs. Assn. (pres. and other offices 1975-84), Fla. Council Family Relations (pres. elect 1985—), Nat. Council Family Relations (assoc. editor 1980—), Am. Ednl. Research Assn. (task force, com.), AAUW (organized bd. 1964), Delta Kappa Gamma (sec.). Methodist. Avocations: reading; sewing. Home: 3717 Galway Dr Tallahassee FL 32308 Office: Fla State U 222 Sandels Bldg Tallahassee FL 32306

EARHART, PHILIP CHARLES, banker; b. New Orleans, Sept. 10, 1954; s. Robert Hailes and Esther Ruth (Dorhauer) E.; m. Lucie Hagood Bethea, Nov. 27, 1976; 1 child, Carolyn Frances. B.A., U. of South, 1976; M.B.A., U. New Orleans, 1981; postgrad. Nat. Comml. Lending Sch., Am. Bankers Assn., Norman, Okla., 1983. Mgmt. trainee Nat. Bank Commerce, Metairie, La., 1977-80, credit mgr.-banking officer, 1980-81, lending officer, asst. v.p., 1981-83; sect. mgr., v.p. Hibernia Nat. Bank, New Orleans, 1983—. Jr. warden St. Augustine Episcopal Ch., Metairie, 1985—; bd. dirs. Salvation Army, New Orleans, 1982-83, Metairie Central Bus. dist., 1983—, Vol. and Info. Agy. of United Way, New Orleans, 1984—. Mem. Robert Morris Assn., La. Bankers Assn., Am. Mgmt. Assn., Am. Bankers Assn., Internat. House, Order Gownsmen. Republican. Clubs: Ambassador, Round Table (New Orleans); Metairie Country. Avocations: golf; tennis; reading; swimming. Home: 4105 Tartan Dr Metairie LA 70003 Office: Hibernia Nat Bank 313 Carondelet New Orleans LA 70161

EARL, CHARLES RILEY, chemical consultant, educator; b. San Diego, Oct. 27, 1933; s. Charles Edward and Helen Cecilia (Riley) E.; m. Josephine Robins Lippard, June 4, 1960; children—Edward Arthur, James David. Student San Diego State Coll., 1951-54; A.B., Whittier Coll., 1955; Ph.D. Poly. Inst. Bklyn., 1970. Chemist, FDA, Los Angeles, 1955-56, Aerojet Gen. Corp., Azusa, Calif., 1955-60; sr. research fellow Poly. Inst. Bklyn., 1961-68; sr. research chemist Milliken Research Corp., Spartanburg, S.C., 1968-72; dept. head chemistry and textiles Spartanburg Tech. Coll., 1972-81; vis. assoc. prof. Clemson U., 1981-82; chem. cons. Spartanburg, 1981—; gen. mgr. S&C Chem. Co., Spartanburg, 1983-85; vis. prof. Anderson Coll. (S.C.), 1984—. Mem. Am. Chem. Soc. (sect. sec. 1977-78, chmn. 1980), Appalachian Trailway Conf., Sigma Xi. Republican. Episcopalian. Address: 440 Harrell Dr Spartanburg SC 29302

EARL, LEWIS HAROLD, lawyer, association administrator; b. Guthrie, Tex., Dec. 17, 1918; s. Henry W. and Martha Ruth (O'Neal) E.; m. Patricia Miller, Mar. 5, 1943 (dec. 1973); children—William Lee, Patricia Lewis, Robert Charles, James Michael; m. Maxine Marks, Jan. 31, 1981. B.A., Tex. Tech U., 1939; postgrad. in econs. and govt. U. Tex., 1939-40, Am. U., 1942; J.D., Georgetown U., 1950; postgrad. George Washington U., 1942-61; Bar: D.C., 1950, U.S. Supreme Ct., 1972, Tex. 1983. Student asst. dept. govt. Tex. Tech U., Lubbock, 1937-39; grad. asst. dept. govt. U. Tex.-Austin, 1939-40; jr. economist Bur. Labor Stats., U.S. Dept. Labor, Washington, 1940-42, industry economist, 1946-51; industry-commodity economist Nat. Prodn. Authority, U.S. Dept. Commerce, Washington, 1951-53; productivity devel. specialist U.S. Tech. Coop. Program in Brazil, 1953-54; asst. program officer U.S. Ops. Mission, Rio de Janeiro, Brazil, 1954-57, program officer, Buenos Aires, Argentina, 1957-59, San Salvador, El Salvador, 1959-61; internat. relations officer AID, Washington, 1961-63; chief fgn. manpower and automation research Manpower Adminstrn., U.S. Dept. Labor, Washington, 1963-66, chief fgn. manpower policy staff, 1966-70; tech. dir. OAS seminar for tng. coordinators from Panama, C.Am. and Mex., summer 1970; manpower planning officer Houston Mayor's Office, 1970-74; cons. Gov.'s Div. Planning Coordination, Austin, Tex., 1974; program devel. assoc. Ctr. for Human Resources, U. Houston, 1970-75; instr. econs., dir. human resources program U. Mo., Columbia, 1975-78; expert cons. Bur. Internat. Labor Affairs, U.S. Dept. Labor, Washington, 1978-79; sr. cons. Nat. Inst. Pub. Mgmt., Washington, 1978-80; sr. assoc. (part-time) Kramer Assocs., Inc., Washington, 1979-80; staff adv. Am. Productivity Ctr., Houston, 1980; expert cons. UNIDO, Cairo, 1981; lectr. mgmt. Coll. Bus. Adminstrn., Tex. Tech U., 1982-83; sec. Post Econ. Devel. Corp.; mgr. C. of C., Post, Tex., 1984—; chmn. U.S. del. ILO Chem. Industries Conf., Geneva, 1969; pres. Southwest Manpower Planners, 1974. Author: Manpower Factbook for Energy Industries, 1980; contbr. articles on productivity and human resources to profl. publs. Pres. Bethesda Neighborhood council Cub Scouts Am., 1967-68; del. Tec. conf. White House Conf. on Aging, 1981. Served to lt. USNR, 1942-46. Mem. Am. Acad. Polit. and Social Sci., Acad. Polit. Sci., Indsl. Relations Research Assn., Soc. Internat. Devel., Population Assn., Nat. Economists Club, Nat. Planning Assn., Am. Soc. Tng. and Devel., Internat. Assn. Personnel of Employment Security, ACLU, VFW, Houston Personnel Assn., Pi Sigma Alpha, Alpha Chi, Omicron Delta Epsilon, Sigma Iota Epsilon. Democrat. Congregationalist. Club: Rotary Internat. Home: 601 W Main St Post TX 79356 Office: 106 S Broadway Post TX 79356

EARLE, (EDWARD) BEN, JR., environmental sciences educator; b. McBee, S.C., July 17, 1949; s. Edward B. and Sara (Freeman) E.; m. Lynn Patterson, June 6, 1970; 1 child, Jody. B.S., Clemson U., 1971, M.Agr., 1972. Research herdsman U. Ga., Eatonton, 1972-74; asst. mgr. Ridgeview Farms, McBee, 1974-76; instr. agri-bus. Catawba Valley Tech. Coll., Hickory, N.C., 1976-83, div. chmn., 1983—. Vice-chmn. Police Citizens Adv. Com., 1984-85. Mem. Nat. Cattleman's Assn., N.C. Cattlemen's Assn. (bd. dirs. 1980-85, chmn. membership com. 1985), Catawba Valley Cattlemen's Assn. (bd. dirs. 1983-87), N.C. Farm Bur. Baptist. Avocations: fishing; horses; travel. Home: 208 Shannonbrook Dr Newton NC 28658 Office: Catawba Valley Tech Coll Hwys 64 and 70 Hickory NC 28601

EARLE, JULIUS RICHARD, physician; b. Walhalla, S.C., Apr. 1, 1928; s. Harry Utley and Allie Mae (Woolbright) E.; m. Myrtle Vivian Corbitt, June 5, 1953; children—Julius Richard, Suzanne E., Dennis P., Helen B., Rhetta M. B.S., Clemson A&M Coll., 1949; M.D., Med. Coll. S.C., 1953. Intern, White Cross Hosp., Columbus, Ohio, 1953-54; gen. practice medicine, Walhalla, S.C., 1954—; mem. staff Oconee Meml. Hosp., chief staff, 1971-73, Mem., vice chmn. Oconee County Sch. Bd., 1961-75; mem., vice chmn. Oconee County Council, 1978—; mem., sec. treas., vice chmn. S.C. Appalachian Council Govt., 1979—. Served to lt. M.C., USN, 1956-58. Mem. N.Y. Acad. Sci., AMA, S.C. Med. Assn., So. Med. Assn., Oconee County Med. Soc. (v.p. 1972-73). Democrat. Methodist. Lodge: Masons (32 deg.). Home: Earlestead Walhalla SC 29691 Office: Earlestead Walhalla SC 29691

EARLES, THOMAS DREW, social worker; b. Waycross, Ga., Feb. 25, 1942; s. Edgar and Gertrude (Spence) E.; m. Gracelyn Hawkes, Aug. 30, 1964; children—Julie Lynn, John Allen. A.B., U. Ga., 1964; M.S.W., Fla. State U., 1966; Ph.D., Ga. State U., 1982. Cons. mental health Ga. State Health Dept., Atlanta, 1968-72; dir. adult family care Ga. State Mental Health Div., Atlanta, 1972-76; family and child therapist Ga. Mental Health Inst., Atlanta, 1976—; psychotherapist, Clarkston, Ga., 1982—; chmn. state family task force, Atlanta, 1969; asst. clin. prof. psychiatry Emory U., Atlanta, 1971—; field instr. U. Ga. Sch. Social Work, Atlanta, 1980-83; instr. Atlanta U. Sch. Social Work, 1984—. Vice pres. Clarkston Methodist Mens Club. Served to maj. Med. Service Corps, USAR, 1966-85. Recipient State Residential Service award Ga. Assn. Retarded Citizens, 1976; Fla. State U. fellow, 1964; Title XX grantee U.S. Dept. HEW, 1973. Mem. Nat. Assn. Social Workers (state bd. dirs. 1976-77), Am. Psychol. Assn., Ga. Soc. Clin. Social Work, Physicians for Social Responsibility (assoc.), Phi Beta Kappa. Sigma Chi, Democrat. Clubs: YMCA Soccer Coachs, Atlanta Tennis Assn. Lodge: Optimist. Avocations: tennis; poetry. Home: 1083 Nielsen Dr Clarkston GA 30021 Office: 4112 E Ponce de Leon Ave Clarkston GA 30021

EARLOUGHER, ROBERT CHARLES, petroleum engineer; b. Kans., May 6, 1914; Petroleum Engr., Colo. Sch. Mines, 1936; m. Jeanne Delight Storer; children—Robert Charles, Janet Craven, Anne o'Connell. With Sloan and Zook Co., Bradford, Pa., 1936-38; co-owner Geologic Standards Co., Tulsa, 1938-45; owner Earlougher Engring, Tulsa, 1945-73; chmn., sr. cons. Godsey-Earlougher, 1973-76; chmn. Godsey-Earlougher Div., Williams Bros. Engring. Co., 1976—. Recipient citation for ser Am. Petroleum Inst., 1964; Disting. Achievement award Colo. Sch. Mines, 1960; Disting. Service award Soc. Petroleum Engrs., 1973; Anthony F. Lucas Gold medal AIME, 1980. Registered profl. engr., Okla., Kans., Tex., Calif. Mem. Okla. Soc. Profl. Engrs., Nat. Soc. Profl. Engrs. AIME (hon. mem.), Am. Petroleum Inst., Ind. Petroleum Assn. Am., Interstate Oil Compact Commn. Republican. Episcopalian. Clubs: Tulsa, So. Hills Country, Masons. Contbr. articles to profl. jours. Home: 2135 E 48th Pl Tulsa OK 74105 Office: 6600 S Yale Tulsa OK 74136

EARLY, ANN MARIE, university lecturer, women's studies coordinator; b. Cleve., Apr. 16, 1925; d. William Dillon and Josephine Ann (Sullivan) McKenny; m. James Early, Aug. 20, 1949; children—Mark, Edward, Joanne. A.B., Clark U., 1946; M.A., Harvard U., 1947. Tchr., Concord High Sch., Mass., 1947-53, New Haven Coll., Conn., 1953-57; Dutchess Community Coll., Poughkeepsie, N.Y., 1959-64; faculty So. Meth. U., Dallas, 1966—, coordinator women's studies, 1980—. Mem. Dallas Mus. Art, Colophon, Friends of Dallas Pub. Library, Historic Preservation League. Named Outstanding Prof., So. Meth. U., 1977, 79, recipient M award, Merit Award for Outstanding Teaching, Concord, 1953. Mem. Modern Lang. Assn., Coll. Art Assn., Nat. Women's Studies Assn. Roman Catholic. Home: 7015 Lake Shore Dr Dallas TX 75214 Office: So Meth U 227 Dallas Hall Dallas TX 75275

EARLY, JOHN LEVERING, lawyer; b. Staunton, Va., Dec. 19, 1896; s. Charles E. and Ida (Clark) E.; A.B., Washington and Lee U.; LL.B., U. Va., 1923; m. Maebelle C. Brooks, June 2, 1924; 1 son, Charles Edward; m. Myrta P. Early, Apr. 27, 1981. Admitted to Va. bar, 1923, W.Va. bar, 1924, Fla. bar, 1924; practice law, Welch, W.Va., 1923-24, Sarasota, Fla., 1924—; cattleman, breeder thoroughbred Shorthorns. Mem. Sarasota-Bradenton (Fla.) Airport Authority, 1951-53. Mem. Ho. Reps., 1933-39; mcpl. judge, 1944-46; mayor City Sarasota, 1951-53. Served as pvt., inf., 1918-19. Recipient Pres.'s Disting. service award Asbury Coll., 1980; Ky. col. Mem. Sarasota County Bar Assn. (pres.), Am. Legion, DAV, Helping Hands (pres.), Rodeheavers Boy's Ranch Assn., Founders Club, Fla. Sheriffs Boys Ranch, Order of Coif. Methodist. Clubs: Masons, Odd Fellows. Home: 1841 Oak St Sarasota FL 33577 Office: 920 1st Fed Bldg Sarasota FL 33577

EARLY, JOHN WESLEY, II, pharmacist; b. Rome, Ga., July 6, 1946; s. John Wesley and Louise Sybil (Pritchett) E.; m. Sherry Denise Summerville, Dec. 16, 1967; children—John Wesley, Charles Matthew. B.S. in Pharmacy, Auburn U., 1968. Staff pharmacist Floyd Hosp., Rome, 1966-68, Ward's Pharmacy, Rome, 1968-69; instr. Dalton Jr. Coll., Rome, 1968-69; staff pharmacist Redmond Park Hosp., Rome, 1969-70; pres. Ealy Drug Co., Fairmont, Ga., 1972—; dir. First Fed. Savs. and Loan, Calhoun, Ga. Mayor pro tem Fairmont, 1972-84; bd. dirs. Gordon County Bd. Edn., Calhoun, 1973-76, chmn., 1980-85. Mem. Nat. Assn. Retail Druggists, Ga. Pharm. Assn. Democrat. Baptist. Lodge: Kiwanis (Disting. Pres. award 1980-81). Avocations: reading; military history; snow skiing; rafting; backpacking. Home: Route 1 Box 39 Fairmont GA 30139 Office: Early Drug Co Hwy 411 Fairmont GA 30139

EARLY, STEPHEN BARRY, lawyer; b. South Gate, Calif., Apr. 8, 1945; s. Charles Nelson and Hilma Mae (Mumaw) E.; m. Janice Ann Webb, Aug. 20, 1966 (div. Feb. 1978); m. Jill Michael Wells, Feb. 5, 1983; children—Christian Webb, Jana Kay. B.A., Tex. Christian U., 1967; M.B.A., U. Dayton, 1970; J.D., So. Meth. U., 1975. Bar: Tex. 1975, Ky. 1982, U.S. Supreme Ct., various fed. cts. appeal and dist. cts. Assoc. atty. Roberts, Harbour Smith, Harris, French & Ritter, Longview, Tex., 1975-77; sole practice, Longview, 1977-80; gen. counsel, sec., dir. Shakey's Inc., Dallas, 1980-81; v.p., gen. counsel KFC Corp., Louisville, 1981—. Served to capt. USAF, 1968-72. Mem. ABA, Tex. Bar Assn., Ky. Bar Assn., Soc. Mayflower Descs., SAR. Republican. Mem. Christian Ch. Home: 7215 Sunset Ln Crestwood KY 40014 Office: KFC Corp 1441 Gardiner Ln Louisville KY 40232

EARNHART, THOMAS PATRICK, investment management company executive; b. Van Nuys, Calif., Mar. 28, 1947; s. Milton Gerard and Mary Elizabeth (Robben) E.; m. Jo Courtney Harris, July 27, 1968; children—Kristen, Bryan. Student U. Americas, Mexico City, 1965; B.S., U. Ark., 1969. Account exec. Beals Advt., Fort Smith, Ark., 1969-70; founding ptnr. Bedill-Earnhart Inc., Fort Smith, Ark./Oklahoma City, 1970-73; dir. mktg. Ark. Best Corp., Fort Smith, 1973-74; v.p., pres., chmn. bd. Armbruster/Atageway, Inc., Fort Smith, 1974-83; owner, chmn. bd. Superior Coaches, Lima, Ohio, S&S Coach Co., Lima, Car Craft Corp., Lima, 1980—, Earnhart Inc., Fort Smith, Ark., Commerce Park, Ark. Vice-pres. Fort Smith Art Ctr., 1982; v.p. pub. relations Fort Smith Air Port Commn., 1977-82; justice of the peace, 1974; pres. Fort Smith-Van Buren Advt. Fedn., 1975-76; v.p. pub. relations Fort Smith United Way, 1974; v.p. pub. relations Fort Smith Heart Fund, 1973. Recipient awards of merit Fort Smith and Tulsa Advt. Fedn. Addy awards, 1973, 74, 75; Outstanding Achievement award Fort Fort Smith Advt. Fedn., 1974; Outstanding Service award City of Fort Smith, 1982. Mem. Fort Smith C. of C. (mem. aviation devel. com., mem. indsl. devel. com. 1982, dir. 1983—). Roman Catholic. Club: Elks (Fort Smith). Patentee in field. Home: 9809 Essex Pl Fort Smith AR 72903 Office: 8501 Hwy 271 S Suite D Fort Smith AR 72093

EARP, EUGENE FREDRICK, safety engineer; b. Detroit, June 7, 1927; s. Eugene Thadious and Ida Myrtle (Rodgers) E.; m. Ann Lois Johnson, Aug. 15, 1948; children—Rebecca Jo, Polly Ann. A.A., East Central Jr. Coll., Decatur, Miss., 1948; B.S., U. So. Miss., 1950. Registered profl. safety engr., Calif.; cert. safety profl. Fire control tng., safety officer Miss. Forestry Commn., Jackson, 1950-60; loss control supr. Zurich Am. Ins. Co., Jackson, 1960-72, zone loss control mgr., 1974-79; v.p. loss control Hewitt Coleman & Assoc., Jackson, 1972-74; safety dir. La. State U., Baton Rouge, 1979—; instr. safety, fire protection U. So. Miss., Hattiesburg, 1973; cons. in field. Served with USN, 1944-46, PTO. Recipient Award of Merit Nat. Safety Council Colls. and Univs., La. State U., 1980, Award of Honor Nat. Safety Council Colls. and Univs., La. State U., 1982, Staff Outstanding Service award La. State U., 1984. Mem. Am. Soc. Safety Engrs. (pres. Miss. chpt. 1970-71, presdl. plaque 1970-71), La. Colls. and Univs. Safety Assn. (pres. 1985-86). Methodist. Home: 6026 Chattanooga Baton Rouge LA 70816 Office: La State U Office Campus Safety Pleasant Hall Baton Rouge LA 70803

EARP, HERBERT MANSFIELD, internal audit supervisor; b. Montgomery, Ala., Oct. 2, 1951; s. Joseph Redding and Sarah Mattiel (Thomas) E.; m. Lettia Ramsay Simmons, Aug. 21, 1971 (div. 1978); children—Bert Jr., Sarah. B.S. in Acctg., Fla. State U., 1975. Ops. officer Flagship Bank, Talahassee, 1975-76; internal auditor Flowers Industries Inc., Thomasville, Ga., 1976-79, State of Fla., Tallahassee, 1980-82; div. acct. State of Ala., Montgomery, 1982-83; internal audit supr. Vanity Fair Mills Inc., Monroeville, Ala., 1984—. Served with USCGR, 1970-75. Mem. Inst. Internal Auditors. Republican. Roman Catholic. Avocations: raquetball; golf; skiing; swimming. Home: 712 Bigger St Monroeville AL 36460 Office: Vanity Fair Mills Inc 624 S Alabama Ave Monroeville AL 36460

EARP, JAMES FRANCY, civil engineer; b. Spencer, W.Va., Feb. 11, 1935; s. Fogle Francy and Hettie Catherine (Langford) E.; B.S. in Civil Engring., W.Va. U., 1958; divorced; children—James Kevin, Gregory Allen, Jennifer Lynn. Sec., mgr. F.F. Earp & Son, Inc., Fairmont, W.Va., 1958-60; pres. Laurel Materials & Engring., Inc., Fairmont, 1960-65; engr. Anderson's Black Rock, Inc., Charleston, W.Va., 1965-68, Polk County Engring. Dept., Bartow, Fla., 1969-70; owner J.F. Earp Assocs., cons. engrs., Lakeland, Fla., 1970—, P.R.M. Sales, Lakeland, 1976—; internat. mktg. cons. PRMS Internat., Lakeland, 1980—; cons. transactional analysis, 1973—; tchr. adult continuing edn. Polk Community Coll., Winter Haven, Fla.; also freelance writer and photographer. Mem. ASCE (past pres. Ridge chpt.), Fla. Engrs. Soc., Nat. Soc. Profl. Engrs., Internat. Transactional Assn. Methodist (tchr., mem. choir). Home: PO Box 620 Lakeland FL 33802 Office: PO Box 620 Lakeland FL 33802

EARP, ORSON KELLOGG, JR., real estate company executive; b. Memphis, Oct. 21, 1934; m. Claudia Elizabeth Willins; 3 children. B.A., Washington & Lee U., 1956. Cert. property mgr.; registered apt. mgr.; cert. real estate broker, ins. agt., Tenn. With bond dept. U.S. Fidelity and Guaranty Co., 1956; salesman Galbreath Ins. Agy., Memphis, 1959-62, v.p., 1962-67, exec. v.p., 1967-73; v.p. Percy Galbreath & Son, Inc., Memphis, 1967-73; pres., chief exec. officer Galbreath Co., Inc., Memphis, 1973-77, chmn. bd., 1977; v.p. Marx & Bensdorf, Memphis, 1977-79, exec. v.p., 1979-80, chmn. Marx & Bensdorf Real Estate and Investment Co., pres. Marx & Bensdorf Leasing and Mgmt. Co., Memphis, 1980—. Pres. Phoenix Club, 1964-65, Tenn. Club, 1977-78; chmn. ins. adv. com. Memphis/Shelby County, 1970-71; pres. Insurors of Memphis, 1968; mem. Downtown Council, Memphis Area C. of C.; bd. dirs. exec. com. Memphis/Shelby County Unit Am. Cancer Soc.; Boys' Clubs of Memphis; bd. dirs., exec. com. Memphis Regional Cancer Ctr. Mem. Internat. Real Estate Fedn. (life mem., Am. chpt.), Memphis Bd. Realtors Million Dollar Club, Nat. Inst. Real Estate Mgmt. (pres. Memphis 1972, exec. com. 1973-76, regional v.p. 1972-73, sr. v.p. 1975, treas. 1976), Omega Tau Rho, Sigma Alpha Epsilon (pres. student chpt.). Lodge: Rotary (officer 1978-79). Home: 2938 Garden Ln Memphis TN 38111 Office: 1407 Union Ave Memphis TN 38104

EARVIN, LARRY LEE, social science educator, consultant; b. Chattanooga, Feb. 23, 1949; s. William Lee and Clara (Ware) E.; m. Valerie Belinda Johnson, Dec. 8, 1974; children—William Jarrett, Allyson Valeria. B.A., Clark Coll., 1971; M.S., Ga. State U., 1973; Ph.D., Emory U., 1982. Planning intern DeKalb County, Decatur, Ga., 1972-73; research assoc. Clark Coll., Atlanta, 1973-75, research exec., 1975-80, social sci. dept. chmn., 1980—; cons. So. Edn. Found., Atlanta, 1978-83, So. Assn. Colls. and Schs., Atlanta, 1983—, U.S. Dept. Edn., Washington, 1976-80. Author: Housing in Atlanta, 1975; Transit Development and Neighborhood Viability, 1978; Transit-Linked Development, 1981. Chmn. bd. Metro Atlanta Fair Housing Services, Atlanta, 1980-82; bd. dirs. Butler St. YMCA, Atlanta, 1983—; pres. Peyton Forest PTA, Atlanta, 1985—; bd. dirs. Alpha Phi Alpha Bldg. Found, Chgo., 1971-84. Fellow Transp. Systems Ctr. 1978, U.S. Dept. Commerce 1979, United Negro Coll. Fund, 1976. Mem. Am. Planning Assn, Pi Gamma Mu (Ga. Iota founder 1982), Alpha Phi Alpha (pres. 1984—). Democrat. United Methodist. Home: 154 Peyton Rd SW Atlanta GA 30311 Office: Clark Coll 240 Brawley Dr SW Atlanta GA 30314

EASOM, RUBY LEE, interior decorator; b. Lake City, S.C., Nov. 1, 1930; d. Luther and Ruth (Baker) Ward; m. Durwood William Easom, Apr. 18, 1953 (div. 1978); 1 dau., Tanya Lee. Student Mary Washington Coll., 1949-50; U.S.C., 1950-52, St. Petersburg Jr. Coll., 1982. Bookkeeper Easom Machinery Co., Columbia, S.C., 1953-59; owner, operator Easom Mack Truck Sales, Inc., Asheville, N.C., 1960-68; Easom Truck Sales, Inc., 1968-78, Truck Accessories of Asheville, 1979-81; freelance interior decorator, St. Petersburg Beach, Fla., 1981—. Mem. Ninety Nines, Inc. Lodge: Order of Eastern Star.

EASON, ALLEN WENDELL, wood products company executive, safety engineer; b. Golden, Okla., Jan. 25, 1943; s. George Emmitt and Weacie E. (Ruth) E.; m. Margaret Louise McGowen, Oct. 13, 1962; children—Jessie Allen, Jimmy DeWayne. Grad. pub. schs., Broken Bow, Okla. Registered emergency med. technician; cert. safety profl. Mem. personnel/safety staff Dierks Forests, Inc., Wright City, Okla., 1963-69; safety engr. Weyerhaeuser Co., Wright City, 1969-83, safety/loss control mgr., 1983—. Sec., Town Council, Wright City, 1966-68. Mem. Am. Soc. Safety Engrs. (chmn. wood products Ark. chpt. 1984, sect. chmn. 1983-85). Home: PO Box 36 Wright City OK 74766 Office: Weyerhaeuser Co Star Route Box 100 Wright City OK 74766

EASON, HELGA RUTH HALVORSEN, former librarian; b. Nebraska City, Nebr.; d. Lee Roy and Luella (Strong) Halvorsen; student Evansville (Ind.) Coll., 1924-25; A.B., Ohio Wesleyan U., 1927; B.S. in L.S., Simmons Coll., 1929; m. Morris Jackson Eason, Nov. 23, 1947. Circulation asst. N.Y. Pub. Library, 1930-39; br. librarian Evansville Pub. Library, 1941-45; head reference dept. Miami (Fla.) Pub. Library, (became Miami-Dade Pub. Library System 1971—), 1947-52, head community relations dept., 1952-77, now hon. life mem.; mem. Region 12 steering mature com. White House Conf. on Libraries and Info. Scis., 1977-78. Mem. program com. WTHS-TV Community TV Found. South Fla., 1955-70. Bd. dirs. Miami Fin. Welfare Employees Fed. Credit Union, 1949-72, sec., 1963-72; bd. dirs. Miami LWV, 1952-53. Recipient cert. of merit Fla. Fedn. Women's Clubs, 1964; John Cotton Dana Publicity awards for library, 1952-54. Mem. ALA (past dir., com. chmn., 2d. vice pres. adult services div. 1968-69; reference and adult services rep. to membership com. promotion task force 1972-74), Reference and Subscription Books Alumni, Fla. (Nat. Library Week award 66, sect. pres., com. chmn.), Dade County (past pres.) library assns., City Miami Pub. Library Staff Orgn. (past pres.), Nat. League Am. Pen Women (sec., dir., past v.p. Greater Miami br., editor Owls Feather 1970-72, 76-78, 80-84, 1st v.p. 1972-74, pres. 1974-76, dir. 1976-78, conv. chmn. state orgn. 1972, 78—, workshop chmn. 1974-76, mem. nat. bylaws com. 1977-78, regional chmn. mature women's scholarship com. 1978-80, nat. librarian 1982-84), Fla. State Poetry Assn. (chpt. pres. 1982-86), Laramore Rader Poetry Group (pres. 1959-61), Fla. Pub. Relations Assn. (hon.), Women in Communication (chmn. hospitality and friendship com. Greater Miami chpt.), NOW. Contbr. articles to profl. jours., book and film revs. to mags., also Pen Woman Mag.; mem. editorial bd. Her Story, 1978-82. Home: 330 NW 144th St Miami FL 33168

EASON, JAMES, mayor. Mayor of Hampton, Va. Office: 22 Lincoln St Hampton VA 23669*

EASON, SHARON GREENE, psychologist, educator; b. Princeton, W.Va., Oct. 12, 1953; d. Vernon Edward and Elizabeth (Stafford) Greene. B.A., E. Carolina U., 1974, M.A., 1977, cert. advanced study, 1978. Lic. psychologist, N.C.; cert. sch. psychologist, N.C. Sch. psychologist Elizabeth City-Pasquotank Bd. Edn., Elizabeth City, N.C., 1977—; instr. Coll. of the Albemarle, 1978-79, Elizabeth City State U., 1982—; cons.; speaker nat., state, community orgns. Mem. NEA, Nat. Assn. Sch. Psychologists, Council Exceptional Children, N.C. Assn. Educators, N.C. Sch. Psychologists Assn., Am. Orthopsychiat. Assn. Episcopalian. Home: Box 1751 Elizabeth City NC 27909 Office: 1400 Halstead Blvd Elizabeth City NC 27909 also 1004 Parkview Ave H L Trigg Elem Sch Elizabeth City NC 27909

EAST, CHARLES E., JR., advertising executive; b. Baton Rouge, La., Dec. 5, 1949; s. Charles Elmo and Sarah (Simmons) E.; B.A. in Journalism, La. State U., 1971; m. Patrice Ann Prats, Apr. 19, 1980; children—Rachel Elizabeth, Catherine Mae. Successively state desk copy editor, gen. assignment reporter, edn. writer Times-Picayune, New Orleans, 1971-73; co-founder, editor Gris-Gris, Baton Rouge, 1973; successively advt. and pub. relations copywriter Weill/Strother, Inc., Baton Rouge, 1973-74, exec. v.p., 1974-79; ptnr. Weill/-Strother/East, Inc., 1979-81; ptnr. Weill & East, Inc., 1981—, pres., 1984—. Recipient Journalism awards La. State U., 1969, 70, 71, Hodding Carter award, 1971, Mpls. Star award, 1970. Mem. La. Assn. Advt. Agys. (dir. 1983, v.p. 1984, pres. 1985), Advt. Club Baton Rouge. Democrat. Lodge: Rotary. Home: 4436 Broussard St Baton Rouge LA 70808 Office: Weill & East Inc PO Box 14476 Baton Rouge LA 70898

EAST, DOROTHY GAIL, school counselor; b. Atlanta, Oct. 16, 1940; d. Robert Leon and Verna Dorothy (Bryce) Gordon; A.B., Emory U., 1962; M.Ed., Ga. State U., 1972; m. Donald Paul East, July 15, 1962. Tchr. English, then tchr. remedial reading Forest Park (Ga.) Jr. High Sch., 1962-69; tchr. English, Morrow (Ga.) Jr. High Sch., 1969-70, guidance counselor, 1970—, chmn. English dept., 1966-70. Mem. Am., Ga. sch. counselors assns., Am. Personnel and Guidance Assn., PTA. Episcopalian. Home: 166 Foster Dr McDonough GA 30253 Office: Morrow Jr High Sch Maddox Rd Morrow GA 30260

EAST, JOHN PORTER, U.S. senator; b. Springfield, Ill., May 5, 1931; s. Laurence J. and Virginia (Porter) E.; m. Priscilla Sherk, Sept. 26, 1953; children—Kathryn, Martha. B.A. in Polit. Sci., Earlham Coll., 1953; LL.B., U. Ill., 1959; M.A. in Polit. Sci., U. Fla., 1962, Ph.D., 1964. Bar: fla. bar 1959. Prof. polit. sci. E. Carolina U., Greenville, N.C., 1964-80; mem. U.S. Senate from N.C., 1980—; Del. to Republican Nat. Conv., 1976, 80, nat. committeeman, 1976—. Author: Council-Manager Government: The Political Thought of Its Founder, Richard S. Childs, 1965; contbr. numerous articles on American polit. thought to scholarly jours., book revs. in field to lit. jours.; mem. editorial bd.: Polit. Sci. Reviewer, 1970—, Modern Age, 1975—. Served to lt. USMC, 1953-55. Nat. Def. fellow, 1961-64. Mem. Am. Polit. Sci. Assn., Fla. Bar Assn., So. Polit. Sci. Assn., Am. Legion, Phi Beta Kappa. Republican. Methodist. Home: 5901 Mount Eagle Dr Apt 1418 Alexandria VA 22303 Office: US Senate Washington DC 20510

EASTER, YVONNE KUNCIS, public relations specialist, singer, writer; b. Boulder, Colo., Aug. 25, 1930; d. Peter Kuncis and Ethel (Haines) Kuncis; m. Donald P. Easter, Feb. 17, 1950 (div.); children—James, Anita, Brian, Lise. Student Am. U. Singer opera, concert, oratorio, Washington Opera, Nat. Symphony, Arlington Symphony, New Haven Chorale; solo appearances Corcoran Art Gallery, Washington, N.Y.C. Met. Mus. Art; specialist pub. relations Easter Communications, Reston, Va., 1976—; freelance writer; cons.

pub. relations. Nat. bd. gov.s Am. Guild Musical Artists. Mem. Am. Guild Musical Artists, Internat. Assn. Bus. Communicators, Pub. Relations Soc. Am. (accredited), Am. Soc. Assn. Execs., N.Y. Publicity Club. Author: Glimpse at American History/John F. Kennedy Ctr. for the Performing Arts, 1972; contbr. articles to jours. in field.

EASTERLIN, JAMES FINNEY, oil company executive; b. Montezuma, Ga., Nov. 11, 1949; s. William M. and Florence F. Easterlin. B.A., B.S. summa cum laude, Washington and Lee U., 1971; postgrad. U. Cologne, (W.Ger.), 1971-72; M.B.A., Harvard U., 1974. With Charter Oil Co. div. Charter Co., Jacksonville, Fla., 1974-77, v.p. info. services gasoline mktg. div., 1977-79, v.p. ops. econs., 1979-81, sr. v.p. supply and distbn., fuel oil div., 1981-83, pres. fuel oil div., 1983—. Mem. Phi Beta Kappa. Club: Fla. Yacht. Home: 5106 Pirates Cove Rd Jacksonville FL 32210 Office: 21 W Church St Jacksonville FL 32232

EASTERLING, CHARLES ARMO, lawyer; b. Hamilton, Tex., July 22, 1920; s. William Hamby and Jenny Arilla (Jackson) E.; B.B.A., Baylor U., 1950; LL.B., 1951, J.D., 1969; m. Irene Alice Kelm, Apr. 25, 1943; children—Charles David, Danny Karl, Jan Irene Easterling Petty. Bar: Tex. 1950. Sr. asst. city atty. City of Houston, 1952-64; ptnr. firm Easterling & Easterling, Houston, 1964—; city atty. City of Pasadena (Tex.), 1969—; instr. South Tex. Coll. Law, 1954-69. Served to lt. col. USAAF, 1943-46. Mem. State Bar Tex., Houston-Harris County Bar Assn., Res. Officers Assn., Phi Alpha Delta. Democrat. Methodist. Clubs: Kiwanis (pres. club 1958) Masons, Shriners (potentate 1971, chmn. bd. trustees Shriners Hosps. for Crippled Children-Galveston, (Tex., unit 1978-84). Home: 5103 Sleepy Creek St Houston TX 77017 Office: 1018 Preston 6th Floor Houston TX 77002

EASTLAKE, CHARLES NELSON, II, engineering educator; b. Wilmington, Ohio, July 31, 1944; s. Charles Nelson and Jeanne Marie (Bowen) E.; m. Linda Jean Woodrow, June 10, 1967; children—Thomas Michael, Pamela Jean. B.Aero. and Astron. Engring., Ohio State U., 1967, M.S., 1968. Registered profl. engr., Fla. Wind tunnel test engr. N.Am. Aviation, Columbus, Ohio, 1968-69; chief engr. Vertak Corp., Troy, Ohio, 1972; sr. research scientist Systems Research Labs., Dayton, Ohio, 1969-77; aerospace engr. Modification Design div. 4950th Test Wing, Wright Patterson AFB, Ohio, 1977-79; assoc. prof. aero. engring. Embry Riddle Aero. U., Daytona Beach, Fla., 1979—; cons. in field. Mem. AIAA, Am. Soc. Engring. Edn., Exptl. Aircraft Assn. Contbr. articles to profl. jours. Office: Embry Riddle Aeronautical U Daytona Beach FL 32014

EASTMAN, ALAN DAN, chemist; b. San Francisco, Oct. 10, 1946; s. Dan M. and E. LaVelle (James) E.; m. Robyn Le Gillis, Sept. 14, 1970; children—Daniel, Giselle, Krista, Evan, Jonathan. B.A. cum laude, U. Utah, 1971, Ph.D., 1975. Research chemist Phillips Petroleum, Bartlesville, Okla., 1975-79, sr. research chemist, 1979-81, mktg. research specialist, 1981-83, mktg. research sr. specialist, 1983—. Patentee in oxidation catalysts, hydrodesulfurization and hydrodenitrogenation catalysts. Mem. Am. Chem. Soc., Sigma Xi, Phi Kappa Phi. Republican. Mormon. Lodge: Lions. Avocations: piano, organ, voice; carpentry. Home: 3209 Wilson Rd Bartlesville OK 74006 Office: Phillips 66 Co 11 B 11 AB Bartlesville OK 74004

EASTMAN, CHARLES THOMAS (TOM), cable contracting company executive, consultant cable television; b. Tulsa, Feb. 4, 1947; s. John Thomas Eastman and Mary Jane (Weeks) Eastman Pasley; m. Donna S. Smith, Sept. 7, 1968; 1 son, Thomas Anthony. B.S. in Psychology and Sociology, Northeastern State U., Tahlequah, Okla., 1970; M.A. in Human Relations, U. Okla., 1976. Asst. to city mgr. for personnel City of Norman (Okla.), 1976; gen. mgr. Am. TV & Communications, Okla., La., Tex., 1977-80; v.p., gen. mgr. Golden West Broadcasters, Dallas, 1980-81; cons. cable TV to cable and appraisal cos., C.Am. and S.Am., 1981—; pres. Summit Cable Contractors, Inc., Arlington, Tex., 1983—; owner E & M Cable assocs., Inc., Arlington, 1983—. Served with USAF, 1970-74. Mem. Tex. Cable Assn. (assoc.), Sigma Tau Gamma (pres. 1969). Republican. Methodist. Office: Summit Cable Contractors Inc 1106 W Pioneer Pkwy Suite 100 Arlington TX 76013

EASTMAN, WILLIAM MICHAEL, coast guard officer; b. Seaford, N.Y., Jan. 22, 1953; s. William Raymond and Ethel Elizabeth (Wesson) E.; m. Judith Ann Richards, Mar. 23, 1975; children—Dylan James, Justin Scott, Kaitlin Ann. B.S. in Organizational Behavior, U. San Francisco, 1981; M.S. in Mgmt., Calif. Am. U., 1982. Enlisted U.S. Coast Guard, 1975, advanced through enlisted grades to lt. (j.g.), 1984; oceanographic technician U.S. Coast Guard Cutter Ingham, Portsmouth, Va., 1976-77; chief technician Oceanographic unit U.S. Coast Guard, Washington, 1977-79, trainer, leadership sch., Petaluma, Calif., 1979-82, dir. research, leadership sch., Yorktown, Va., 1982-85, chief, leadership sch., Yorktown, 1985—; pres., owner Leadership Devel. Programs, Yorktown, 1981—; assoc. Creative Mgmt. Assocs., Seaford, Va., 1983—; adj. prof. Hampton Inst., Va., 1984—, Thomas Nelson Community Coll., Hampton, 1984—. Mem. Am. Soc. Tng. and Devel., Nat. Soc. Performance and Instrn., Am. Mgmt. Assn., Va. Community Colls. Assn., Tidewater C. of C. Libertarian. Avocations: running; computers. Home: S-R Box 404A Gloucester Point VA 23062 Office: Leadership Devel Programs PO Box 600 Yorktown VA 23690

EASTON, ROGER CONANT, international and domestic consultant; b. Bklyn., Apr. 13, 1930; s. Glenn Herman and Cornelia (Hanson) E.; B.B.A., U. Mich., 1953, M.B.A., 1953; postgrad. Wharton Sch. Bus., U. Pa., 1949-50; m. Roberta Calhoun Clark, Aug. 16, 1952; children—Roger Conant, George Sawyer. C.L.U. Mgmt. research cons. Met. Life Ins. Co., N.Y.C., 1953-54; asst. export advt. mgr. Procter & Gamble Distbg. Co., N.Y.C., 1955-58; with Avon Products, Inc., 1959-68, 71-75, internat. merchandising mgr., N.Y.C., 1959-61, merchandising mgr. Avon Cosmetics, Ltd., Northampton, Eng., 1962-64, divisional sales mgr., 1965, mktg. mgr., 1966, dir. sales promotion, advt., merchandising, 1967-68; v.p. Dart Industries, Direct Selling Group, Orlando, Fla., 1969-70; dir. market research-spl. projects Avon Products, Inc., N.Y.C., 1971-72, dir. internat. sales promotion and incentive mktg., 1973, dir. internat. market planning, 1974-75; internat. and domestic bus. cons. The Profit Adviser, Orlando, 1976—; spl. agt. Northwestern Mut. Life Ins. Co., 1977-81; sr. life rep. Amica Life Ins. Co., Orlando, 1982-84; sales mgr. The Acacia Group, Orlando, 1985, account mgr., 1986; registered rep., investment adv. assoc. Calvert Securities Corp., Orlando, 1986; adj. prof. internat. mktg. Crummer Grad. Sch. Bus., Rollins Coll., 1981—; lectr. sales mgmt. Pace U., 1975; adj. lectr. internat. mktg. U. Central Fla., 1981. Pres., Class of 1953, U. Mich. Sch. Bus., 1952-53. Served with U.S. Army, 1950. Mem. Nat. Assn. Life Underwriters (Nat. Sales Achievement awards 1978—), Central Fla. Assn. Life Underwriters (dir. 1980-81, Agt. of Year 1977, Million Dollar Round Table 1977-79), Phi Delta Theta, Delta Sigma Pi. Republican. Office: 400 S Osceola Ave Orlando FL 32801

EASTRIDGE, CHARLES EDWIN, surgeon, educator, administrator; b. Oakdale, Tenn., Feb. 18, 1921; s. Charles Zenith and Lillie May (Taylor) E. Student Memphis State U., 1947, M.D., U. Tenn., 1950. Diplomate Am. Bd. Surgery, Am. Bd. Thoracic Surgery. Intern John Gaston Hosp., Memphis, 1950-51; practice medicine, Catlettsburg, Ky., 1952-55; gen. surgery, thoracic surgery resident VA Hosp., Memphis, 1955-62, asst. chief thoracic surgery, 1962-72, chief, 1972—; prof. gen., thoracic surgery U. Tenn. Coll. Served with USN, 1944-46. Mem. ACS, So. Thoracic Surg. Assn. (pres' award best sci. paper 1971, 2d place pres's award exhibit 1981), Soc. Thoracic Surgery, Am. Assn. Thoracic Surgery, So. Med. Assn., Bowers Surg. Soc., Assn. VA Surgeons, Alpha Omega Alpha. Republican. Baptist. Clubs: Masons, Shriners. Contbr. numerous articles to med., surg. publs. Home: 57 N Somerville Apt 514 Memphis TN 38104 Office: 1030 Jefferson Ave Memphis TN 38104

EASTRIDGE, MICHAEL DEAN, pharmacist; b. Huntington, W.Va., Dec. 5, 1950; s. Robert Dean and Sue (Layne) E. B.G.S., U. Ky., 1973, B.S. in Pharmacy, 1978. Pharmacist Taylor Drugs, Frankfort, Ky., 1978-79; pharmacist-mgr. Taylor Drugs, Lexington, Ky., 1979-84, Taylor Drugs, Danville, Ky., 1984—. Mem. Bluegrass Pharm. Assn. Republican. Baptist. Home: 434 Patrician Pl Apt 4 Danville KY 40422 Office: Taylor Drugs US Hwy 127 Danville KY 40422

EASTWOOD, DAVID BALLARD, economist; b. Mahoning Twp., Pa., Sept. 16, 1944; s. Walter Holmes and Ruth (Ballard) E.; m. Judith Morison, June 17, 1967; children—Heather, David, Jr. A.B., Hanover Coll., Ind., 1966; M.A., Brown U. 1968; Ph.D., Tufts U., 1972. Asst. prof. econs. U. Lowell, Mass., 1971-76; assoc. prof. U. Tenn.-Knoxville, 1977—; agrl. economist U.S. Dept. Agr., Washington, 1979-80; cons. to various local govts. and bus., 1971—. Author: The Economics of Consumer Behavior, 1985. Editor Jour. Consumer Affairs, 1984—. Contbr. articles to profl. jours. Mem. Christian edn. com. Westminster Presbyn. Ch., Knoxville, 1984—; chmn. fin. com. Gulfwood Recreation Assn., Knoxville, 1984—. Grantee fed. and state orgns., 1972—; named to Outstanding Young Men Am., Jaycees, 1977; Am. Council Edn. fellow, 1979-80. Mem. Am. Econ. Assn., Am. Council on Consumer Interests, So. Agrl. Econs. Assn., Am. Agrl. Econs. Assn. Avocation: squash. Home: 806 Sunnydale Rd Knoxville TN 37923 Office: Dept Agrl Econs and Rural Sociology U Tenn Knoxville TN 37901

EATON, CHARLES EDWARD, author, educator; b. Winston-Salem, N.C., June 25, 1916; s. Oscar B. and Mary (Hough) E.; m. Isabel Patterson, Aug. 16, 1950. Student Duke U., 1932-33; A.B., U. N.C., 1936; M.A., Harvard U., 1940; postgrad. Princeton U., 1936-37. English instr. U. Mo., Columbia, 1940-42; prof. creative writing U. N.C., Chapel Hill, 1946-51; Am. vice consul Rio de Janeiro, Brazil, 1942-46. Recipient Ridgely Torrence Meml. award Poetry Soc. Am., 1951; Ariz. Quarterly award, 1956, 77, 79, 82; Roanoke-Chowan Poetry Cup, N.C. Lit. and Hist. Soc., 1970; Oscar Arnold Young Meml. award N.C. Poetry Soc., 1971; Golden Rose, New Eng. Poetry Club, 1972; Alice Fay di Castagnola award Poetry Soc. Am., 1974; Arvon Found. Internat. Poetry Competition award, 1981; Zoe Kincaid Brockman Meml. award, 1984; Hollins critic award, 1984; others. Mem. Am. Acad. Poets, Poetry Soc. Am., New Eng. Poetry Club, N.C. Poetry Soc., N.C. Art Soc., Provincetown Art Assn., Phi Beta Kappa, Sigma Nu. Poems include: The Bright Plain, 1942; The Shadow of the Swimmer, 1951; The Greenhouse in the Garden, 1956; Countermoves, 1963; On the Edge of the Knife, 1970; The Man in the Green Chair, 1977; Colophon of the Rover, 1980; The Thing King, 1983; The Work of the Wrench, 1985; short stories include: Write Me from Rio, 1959; The Girl from Ipanema, 1972; The Case of the Missing Photographs, 1978, others. Address: 808 Greenwood Rd Chapel Hill NC 27514

EATON, JANE EMRICH, educational diagnostician, therapist; b. Boston; d. Alfred John and June (Toolas) Emrich; children—Robert Marc, Shelley June, Carter Eric. A.A., Blinn Coll., 1974; B.A. magna cum laude, Sam Houston U., 1976; M.Ed., Lamar U., 1979. Cert. provisional tchr. speech therapy, mentally retarded, lang./learning disabilities; cert. supr. spl. edn., profl. supr.; cert. ednl. diagnostician, 1982. Tchr. mentally/phys. handicapped, 1976-77; tchr., speech therapist Silsbee Ind. Sch. Dist. (Tex.), 1977-78; speech therapist, 1978-79; tchr. learning disabled Channelview (Tex.) Ind. Sch. Dist., 1979-81, speech therapist, ednl. diagnostician, coordinator dist. speech therapists, 1981—; dir. Bay Area Edn. and Diagnostic Ctr., Baytown, 1982—; G.E.D. tchr. Mem. Tex. Ednl. Diagnostician's Assn. (Met. Houston chpt.), Council Exceptional Children, Assn. Tex. Profl. Educators, Tex. Speech-Lang.-Hearing Assn., Houston Area Assn. Communication Disorders. Author: Time for Txmes, 1982. Home: 107 Morrell St Baytown TX 77520

EATON, JOE O., judge; b. Monticello, Fla., Apr. 2, 1920; s. Robert Lewis and Mamie (Gireadeau) E.; A.B., Presbyn. Coll., 1941, LL.D. (hon.), 1979; LL.B., U. Fla., 1948; practiced in Miami, Fla., 1948-51, 55-59; asst. state atty. Dade County, Fla., 1953; circuit judge, Miami, 1954-55, 59-67; mem. Fla. Senate, 1956-59; mem. law firm Eaton & Achor, Miami, 1955-58, Sams, Anderson, Eaton & Alper, Miami, 1958-59; judge U.S. Dist. Ct. So. Dist. Fla., 1967—, now chief judge. Instr. law U. Miami Coll. Law, 1954-56. Served with USAAF, 1941-45, USAF, 1951-52. Decorated D F C, Air medal. Methodist. Kiwanian. Office: US Dist Ct PO Box 014941 Miami FL 33101

EATON, PRESCOTT, computer scientist; b. Seattle, Jan. 29, 1930; s. Harrison George and Eleanor Jean (McCormick) E.; m. Gretchen White, June 4, 1955; children—Brigid Eleanor, Kimberly Linhart. B.A., U. Wash., 1953; M.S., Eastern Wash. U., 1967. Commd. 2d lt. U.S. Army, 1953, advanced through grades to lt. col., 1968; assoc. dir. mgmt. programs Nat. Ctr. Def. Mgmt., Washington, 1975-77; mem. adv. staff Computer Scis. Corp., Washington, 1978-81; systems application scientist PL Research Corp., McLean, Va., 1981—; vis. instr. Nat. Coll. Criminal Def. Lawyers and Pub. Defenders, Bates Coll. Law, U. Houston, 1976-77; vis. instr. U.S. Dept. Agr. Grad. Sch., Washington, 1977. Contbr. articles to profl. jours. Decorated Legion of Merit, Bronze Star, Army Commendation medal (3), Air medal. Mem. Assn. Legal Adminstrs. (chmn. tng. and liaison com. 1976-77), Am. Psychol. Assn., Data Processing Mgmt. Assn., Assn. Computing Machinery, World Future Soc. Episcopalian. Home: 45 Florida Blvd Merritt Island FL 32953 Office: PRC 1303 Kennedy Space Center FL 32899

EATON, THOMAS ELDON, consulting engineer; b. Ironton, Mo., Nov. 27, 1948; s. Russell Lee and Shelia Maxine (Fitzgerald) E. B.S. in Mech. Engring., U. Mo.-Rolla, 1970, M.S. in Mech. Engring., 1970; M.S. in Nuclear Engring. (AEC fellow), MIT, 1974, Nuclear Engr., 1974, Sc.D., 1975. Registered profl. engr., Ky., Ind., Ohio, W.Va., Va., Colo., Calif. Asst. prof. U. Ky., Lexington, 1975-78; cons. engr., accident investigation specialist, Eaton Engring. Co., Nicholasville, Ky., 1978—. Mem. ASME, ASHRAE, Am. Inst. Chem. Engrs., Am. Nuclear Soc., Am. Ry. Engring. Assn., Am. Soc. Lubrication Engrs., Soc. Mining Engrs. Office: Box 1100 Nicholasville KY 40356

EAVES, GLENN PATRICK, geophysicist; b. Grass Valley, Calif., Sept. 21, 1936; s. Lucian and Melba Marie (Roe) E.; m. Katie Rector, July 26, 1959; children—Craig S., Krist D. B.S. in Chemistry, Sul Ross State U., Alpine, Tex., 1959, B.S. in Geology, 1958; M.S. in Geology, Tex. A&M, 1965. Sr. geophysicist Exxon Co., USA, Houston, London, Midland, Tex., 1964-75; dist. geophysicist Getty Oil Co., Midland, 1975-84; geophysicist RK Petroleum Corp., Midland, 1984-85, Valero Producing Co., Midland, 1985—. Served to 1st lt. U.S. Army, 1960-63. Mem. Am. Assn. Petroleum Geologists, Soc. Exploration Geophysicists, Perman Basin Geophys. Soc. Republican. Methodist. Avocations: guitar, woodworking. Home: 2912 Northtown Pl Midland TX 79705 Office: Valero Producing Co 400 Claydesta Midland TX 79705

EBAUGH, FRANK WRIGHT, consulting industrial engineer, investments exec.; b. New Orleans, July 31, 1901; s. John Lynn and Mary (Wright) E.; B.Chem. Engring., Tulane U., 1923; m. Elizabeth Brown, Feb. 22, 1930; 1 dau., Betty Jane Ebaugh McFarland. Engr., asso. mgmt. Texas Co., 1923-34; partner retail firm, Jacksonville, Tex., 1934-54; mgr., partner Ebaugh & Brown Investments, Jacksonville, 1955-62; prin. Frank W. Ebaugh, Profl. Engr.; dir. Superior Savs. Assn. Pres., Upper Neches River Municipal Water Authority; dir. Tex. Indsl. Devel. Council; vice chmn. Tex. Mapping Adv. Com.; sec. Tex. Coordinating Water Com.; pres. Neches River Devel. Assn.; panel chmn. Cherokee County (Tex.) War Price and Ration Bd., 3 years; mem. regional com. Girl Scouts Am.; mem. Jacksonville Bicentennial Bd.; bd. dirs. Neches River Conservation Dist., Jacksonville Pub. Library. Named Man of Month, East Tex. C. of C., 1953; Man of Year, Lions Club, 1953; Disting. Visitor, Tex. Senate; Appreciation Plaque erected in Jacksonville Library, 1969; honored for preservation of hist. home Clean Community System of Jacksonville. Mem. Nat. Soc. Profl. Engrs. (life), Tex. Soc. Profl. Engrs. (chmn. water com., life mem.), E. Texas C. of C., Jacksonville C. of C. (past pres., dir., chmn. water resources com.), Am. Chem. Soc. (life mem.), AAAS, Tex. Acad. Sci. Presbyn. (elder, trustee). Clubs: Headliners (Austin); Rotary, Country of Jacksonville (past pres.). Patentee Ebaugh Mixer. Home: 428 S Patton St Jacksonville TX 75766 Office: Box 1031 Jacksonville TX 75766

EBAUGH, RICHARD WAYNE, controller; b. Hanover, Pa., May 20, 1946; s. Marvin Homer and Virginia Lee (Ecker) E.; m. Mary Louise Weaver, July 3, 1971 (div. 1979); m. 2d, Regina June Welch, Jan. 9, 1980; 1 dau., Tamara Christina. B.S. in Bus. Adminstrn., U. Balt., 1971; M.A. in Mgmt., Central Mich. U., 1983; cert. in mgmt. info. systems U. So. Calif. Chief quality control Continental Can Corp., Balt., 1969-71; budget and operating acct. Marine Corps Exchange Service, Quantico, Va., 1975-76, controller Exchange 0121, 1976—; pvt. practice bus. and tax cons. Served with USAF, 1971-75. Mem. Assn. Govt. Accts., U.S. Assn. Mil. Comptrollers, Am. Legion, Sigma Iota Epsilon. Republican. Methodist. Lodge: Elks. Home: 65 Hidden Spring Ln Stafford VA 22554 Office: PO Box 229 Quantico VA 22134

EBELHAR, ANN JEANETTE, insurance agency executive, commercial lines agent; b. Owensboro, Ky., Aug. 6, 1944; d. Robert Preston, Sr., and Frances Elizabeth (Aud) O'Bryan; m. Charles Leo Ebelhar, Apr. 25, 1970; children—Beth Marie, Lori Ann. Ed. parochial schs., ins. courses. Lic. ins. agt., Ky. Ins. clk. McAlister Agy., Owensboro, 1964-68; ins. clk. Horn's Ins. Agy., Inc., Owensboro, 1968-73, office mgr., 1973-82, corp. exec., 1982—, bookkeeper, agt., 1982—. Chmn., Precious Blood Sch. Bd., Owensboro, 1983—; vol. Owensboro Crime Prevention Unit, 1980—. Recipient Key to City, City of Owensboro, 1979. Mem. Ohio Valley Ins. Women (pres. 1982-84, Ins. Woman of Yr. 1978, cert. of achievement 1981, Lace award 1980), Nat. Assn. Ins. Women, Ky. Assn. Ins. Women (treas. 1984—). Democrat. Roman Catholic. Home: 913 Marianna Dr Owensboro KY 42301 Office: Horns Insurance Agency Inc 2212 Frederica St Owensboro KY 42301

EBERHARDT, RONALD ROBERT, printing company executive; b. Cedarburg, Wis., Nov. 27, 1946; s. Milton Frederick Otto and Maria Irene (Klauser) E.; m. Mary Elizabeth Irwin, June 18, 1977; children—Catherine Marie, William Daniel; children by previous marriage—Todd David, Amy Beth. Cert. lithographic stripper. Preparation foreman W.A. Krueger Co., Brookfield, Wis., 1977-78; preparation foreman Desaulniers, Milan, Ill., 1978-79, preparation supt., 1979-80; plant supr. Schultz Wack Weir, Portland, Oreg., 1980-81; plant mgr. R.F. Rodgers Litho, Tulsa, 1981-82, v.p. mfg., 1982—. Pres., Gideons, Ozaukee, Wis., 1976-77, chaplain, Moline, Ill., 1979; treas. 1st Evang. Free Ch.-Tulsa Area, Okla. 1983-84, fin. chmn., 1985-86; treas. Midsouth dist. Evang. Free Ch. Am., 1983, 84, trustee, 1985-88, mem. nat. ch. ministries bd., 1985-88. Mem. Graphic Arts Tech. Found., Internat. Assn. Quality Circles, Adminstrv. Mgmt. Soc. Republican. Home: 1524 S Delaware St Tulsa OK 74104 Office: RF Rodgers Lithographing Co Inc 2211 S Jackson St Tulsa OK 74107

EBERHART, MARY ANN PETESIE, wholesale company executive; b. Baton Rouge, Aug. 20, 1940; d. Wilford Malvern and Mary Gordon (Davidson) E.; B.S., McNeese State U., 1963. With United Service Warehouse, Inc., Baton Rouge, 1963-82, v.p., 1974-82, sales mgr., 1979-82; v.p. United Engine Service, Inc., Baton Rouge, 1980-83, pres., 1983—, gen. mgr., 1981—. Recipient Worlds Champion Cutting Horse award Womens Profl. Rodeo Assn., 1971. Mem. Automotive Wholesalers Assn. La. (credit com. chair, sec. fed. credit union), Women's Profl. Rodeo Assn. (v.p. 1978-83), McNeese State U. Alumni Assn., NOW, Delta Zeta. Democrat. Episcopalian. Club: Baton Rouge Country. Home: 4070 Stumberg Ln Baton Rouge LA 70816 Office: 11923 Cloverland Ave Baton Rouge LA 70809

EBERLE, BRUCE WAYNE, advertising executive; b. St. Joseph, Mo., Dec. 14, 1943; s. Adolph Herman and Emma (Reinert) E.; m. Katherine Lee Mitchem, Aug. 25, 1973; children—Elizabeth Ann, Matthew Carl. B.S. Mech. Engring., U. Mo., Rolla, 1966. Engr., Gulf Oil Co., Port Arthur, Tex., 1966-71; exec. v.p. Potomac Arts Ltd., McLean, Va., 1971-74; pres. Bruce W. Eberle & Assocs., Vienna, Va., 1974—; pres., dir. Computer Communications, Omega List Co., Omni Direct Mail Services Ltd., Direct Response Telecommunications Inc. Alt. del. Republican Nat. Conv., 1980. Served with AUS, 1968-70. Mem. Direct Mktg. Assn. (Echo award 1980, 82), Direct Mktg. Assn. Washington (past dir.), Am. Assn. Polit. Cons., Assn. Direct Mktg. Agencies. Lutheran. Home: 1449 Montague Dr Vienna VA 22180 Office: 8330 Old Courthouse Rd #700 Vienna VA 22180

EBERLEIN, PATRICK BARRY, mathematics educator; b. San Francisco, Mar. 3, 1944; s. William Frederick and Mary (Barry) E.; m. Jennifer Pedlow, July 13, 1968; children—Michael Douglas, Nicholas Patrick. B.A., Harvard U., 1965; M.A. in Math., UCLA, 1967, Ph.D., 1970. Lectr. math. U. Calif., Berkeley, 1970-71, 72-73; asst. prof. math. U. N.C., Chapel Hill, 1973-75, assoc. prof., 1975-81, prof., 1981—; guest researcher U. Bonn/Max Planck Inst., W.Ger., 1971-72, 83-84. Contbr. articles to profl. jours. Mem. Am. Math. Soc. Democrat. Avocations: chess, tennis, piano. Home: 1607 Fountain Ridge Rd Chapel Hill NC 27514 Office: Dept Math U NC Chapel Hill NC 27514

EBERSTEIN, ISAAC WARREN, sociology educator, demography researcher; b. Palestine, Tex., Nov. 16, 1952; s. Leon Joseph and Mary Grace (Edwards) E.; m. Nancy Irice Stern, Dec. 26, 1973; children—Jason, Rachel. B.A. in Sociology, U. Tex., 1974, M.A. in Sociology, 1976, Ph.D. in Sociology, 1979. Asst. prof. Sociology U. Miss., University, 1979-81; asst. prof. Fla. State U., Tallahassee, 1981-85, assoc. prof., 1985—. Contbr. articles to profl. jours. Mem. Population Assn. Am., Am. Sociol. Assn., Internat. Union for Sci. Study Population, Am. Pub. Health Assn. Office: Ctr for Study of Population FL State U Tallahassee FL 32306

EBERT, RICHARD PHILIP, insurance company executive; b. Chgo., Oct. 6, 1939; s. Charles Philip and Mildred Evelyn (Ciske) E.; m. Deeane Mae Crater, Jan. 20, 1969 (div. Nov. 1974); 1 child, Lori Michelle; m. Betty Euilene Miller Walworth, Aug. 21, 1980. Assoc. in Electronics, Allegheny Tech. U., 1964; B.S. in Bus., U. Pitts., 1975. Technician, H.R.B. Singer Inc., State College, Pa., 1964-69; research technician U.S. Steel, Monroeville, Pa., 1969-73; buyer Koppers Corp., Pitts., 1974-77; restaurant mgr. Sambo's Corp., Janesville, Wis., 1977-79; ins. mgr. Bankers Life & Casualty Co., Lawton, Okla., 1979—; Served with USN, 1958-62. Fellow Life Underwriting Tng. Council; mem. Nat. Assn. Life Underwriters. Republican. Masons. Avocations: hiking; bicycling; camping; fishing; golf. Home: 7903 NW Folkstone Way Lawton OK 73505 Office: Bankers Life and Casualty Co 1303 W Gore Suite B Lawton OK 73505

EBERT, VELINA GAIL HAMMOND, counselor; b. Laurinburg, N.C., June 8, 1954; d. Guilford Fritzer and Mary Ellen (Hunt) Hammond; m. Steve Lester Ebert, Aug. 7, 1976. A.B., Guilford Coll., 1976; M.Ed., U. N.C.-Greensboro, 1983. Nat. cert. counselor. Evening admissions coordinator N.C. Bapt. Hosp., Winston-Salem, 1979-81; counselor Guilford Tech. Community Coll., Jamestown, N.C., 1983—. Mem. Am. Assn. Counseling and Devel., Am. Coll. Personnel Assn., Nat. Vocat. Guidance Assn. Democrat. Moravian. Avocations: sports; reading; music. Office: Guilford Tech Community Coll PO Box 309 Jamestown NC 27282

EBERWEIN, VALERY DONALD, electrical engineer, consultant; b. Ponca City, Okla., June 17, 1940; s. Leo E. and Mary Lou (Marshal) E.; m. Charlotte Lee Hefner, Mar. 21, 1963 (div. May 1977); 1 dau., Lisa Dawn. B.S.E.E., Okla. State U., 1963; postgrad. U. Houston, 1963-68. Registered profl. engr., Tex. Elec. engr. NASA Manned Spacecraft Ctr., Houston, 1963-66, Texas Instruments, Houston, 1966-69, Paragon Systems, Houston, 1969-71; cons. engr., pres. Eberwein and Assocs., Houston, 1971—. Mem. Aircraft Owners and Pilots Assn. Patentee in field.

EBERWINE, JAMES ALLEN, hospital director, former army officer; b. Birmingham, Ala., Aug. 26, 1933; s. Ralph H. and Edna E. E.; m. Joy Dennison, Sept. 3, 1954; children—Mark A., David B., Kyle C., Brian K., Julie A. B.A., U. Akron, 1956; M.H.A., Baylor U., 1971; M.A. in Edn., Pepperdine U., 1976; grad. Army Command and Gen. Staff Coll., Indsl. Coll. Armed Forces. Commd. 2d lt., U.S. Army, 1957, advanced through grades to lt. col., 1971; officer Army Med. Dept., 1957-78; helicopter medevac, Vietnam; ret., 1978; asst. supt. Massillon State Hosp. (Ohio), 1978-79; assoc. adminstr. Marion Gen. Hosp., 1979-81; dir. Oaks Psychiat. Hosp. of The Brown Schs., Austin, Tex., 1981—. Involved in youth activities; campaign chmn. Combined Fed. Campaign, United Way. Decorated Silver Star, DFC, Bronze Star Medal with V and Oak leaf cluster, 23 Air Medals, Purple Heart, Army Commendation Medal with oak leaf cluster, Meritorious Service Medal with oak leaf cluster (U.S.), Cross of Gallantry (Vietnam); designated Disting. U.S. Internat. Shooter, 1962; recipient Gold medal Pan-Am. Games, 1959, George Washington Honor medal Freedoms Found., 1974. Mem. Am. Coll. Hosp. Adminstrs., Assn. Mental Health Adminstrs., Am. Hosp. Assn., Tex. Hosp. Assn. (del. 1983-86). Presbyterian. Club: Optimist. Lodges: Masons, Kiwanis. Mem. U.S. World Championship Shooting Team to Moscow, 1958. Home: 4903 Trail West Dr Austin TX 78735 Office: The Oaks 1407 Stassney Ln Austin TX 78745

EBY, JOHN WILMER, business educator; b. Lancaster, Pa., Apr. 23, 1940; s. Wilmer Martin and Arlene (Bomberger) E.; m. Joyce Lavonne Rutt, June 29, 1963; children—Carol Lavonne, Scott Lamar. B.A. in Chemistry, Eastern Mennonite Coll., 1962; M.S. in Sociology, Cornell U., 1970, Ph.D., 1972. Faculty Eastern Mennonite Coll., Harrisonburg, Va., 1982—, prof. bus., 1983—, chmn. dept., 1983—; bd. dirs. Mennonite Econ. Devel. Assocs., Akron, Pa., 1984—. Author: Mokatlho wa Badumedi Mo Pitseng: A Church Related Development Project in Botswana, 1982. Mem. Acad. Mgmt., Am. Sociol. Assn., Am. Mgmt. Assn., Mennonite Econ. Devel. Assn. Avocation: woodworking. Home: 1623 N College Ave Harrisonburg VA 22801 Office: Eastern Mennonite Coll Harrisonburg VA 22801

ECCLES, WILLIAM JAMES, electrical engineering educator, consultant; b. Owatonna, Minn., Apr. 18, 1932; s. William Edmund and Marion Lucille (Adair) E.; m. Patricia Mae Paschal, May 6, 1967; children—William Noble, Julia Katherine. S.B.E.E., MIT, 1954, S.M., 1957; Ph.D., Purdue U., 1965.

Registered profl. engr., S.C. Dir. ComputereCtr. U. S.C., Columbia, 1965-71, organizer, head dept. computer scis., 1967-73, head dept math., computer sci., 1973-76, assoc. prof. computer sci., 1971-79, assoc. prof. engring., 1965-71, 79-82, prof. engring., 1982—; cons. UN Central Water and Power Research Sta., Pune, India, 1981-84. Author: (textbook) Microprocessor Systems: A 16-Bit Approach, 1985. Served to 1st lt. Signal Corps U.S. Army, 1957-59. Recipient Litman award Coll. Engring., 1984; Danforth Found. assoc., 1970-86. Mem. IEEE (sr., microprocessor workshops 1976-81, 84), Assn. for Computing Machinery, Am. Assn. Engring. Edn. Episcopalian. Lodge: Masons (master 1972). Home: 2413 Wilmot Ave Columbia SC 29205 Office: Coll Engring U of S C Columbia SC 29208

ECHEVARRIA, LUIS CRUZ, public relations and marketing educator, consultant; b. Santurce, P.R., Sept. 11, 1952; s. Fernando Luis Cruz and Lydia Echevarria (Rodriguez) E. B.S., Cath. U., Ponce, P.R., 1973; M.A., Ball State U., 1976, M.B.A., 1977. Accredited pub. relations and mktg. educator. Coordinator pub. relations Tourism Co., Hato Rey, P.R., 1973-75; dir. pub. relations U.S. div. Tourism Co., N.Y.C., 1977; pres. Communications Cons., Inc., Pueblo Viejo, P.R., 1978-79; dir. dept. communications Univ. Sacred Heart, Santurce, P.R., 1979-81; asst. prof. pub. relations U. Sacred Heart, Santurce, P.R., 1981—; cons. various cos. and hosps.; prof. mktg. Interamerican U., Rio Pierras, P.R., 1983—. Named Pub. Relations Educator of Yr., San Juan Civic Club, 1982. Mem. Pub. Relations Soc. Am. (accredited), Am. Mgmt. Assn., Internat. Assn. Bus. Communicators, Assn. Relacionistas Profesionales, Kappa Tau Alpha. Clubs: Pan-American Gun (Bayamon, P.R.); Exchange (Hato Rey, P.R.). Home and Office: Cond Aranjuez Apt 101 Hato Rey PR 00917

ECHOLS, JENNIE LOUISE, nursing administrator; b. Hartselle, Ala., Sept. 24, 1955; d. Sherman Davis and Blanche (Stone) Echols. B.S.N., U. Ala., 1977, M.S.N., 1980. Lic. nurse, Ala. Staff nurse U. Ala. Hosp., Birmingham, 1977; charge nurse East End Meml. Hosp., Birmingham, 1977-78; patient care dir. Home Health Care Agy., 1978-79; hosp. adminstrn. resident Oschsner Found. Hosp., New Orleans, 1980; psychiat. nursing dir. Brookwood Med. Ctr., Birmingham, 1981-83, adminstrv. dir. psychiatric services, 1983—; adj. faculty Birmingham So. Coll., 1983—. Mem. Jefferson County Mental Health Authority, 1983—. Fed. trainee for grad. work in psychiatric nursing, 1979-80. Mem. Ala. Council Psychiat. Mental Health Clin. Nurse Specialists, Ala. Soc. Nursing Services Adminstrs., Am. Hosp. Assn., Alpha Lambda Delta. Republican. Baptist. Home: 1508 Primrose Pl Birmingham AL 35209 Office: 2010 Brookwood Med Center Dr Birmingham AL 35209

ECHOLS, RALPH GORDON, architect, urban and regional planner; b. Bluefield, W.Va., Sept. 12, 1929; s. Ralph and Rowena Lee (Carper) E.; m. Patton Alexander, chpt., 13, 1953; children—Ralph James, Gordon Alexander, Annette Lee, Stuart Patton. B.S., Va. Poly. Inst., 1953, M.S., 1954; M.Arch., Harvard U., 1960; M.City Planning, U. Pa., 1966. Architect, Thomas T. Hayes, AIA, Southern Pines, N.C., 1954-58, Architects Collaborative, Cambridge, Mass., 1958-59, Atkins, Currie & Payne, Architects Planners, Blacksburg, Va., 1960-71; assoc. prof. Va. Poly. Inst., Blacksburg, 1960-71; prof., chmn. dept. Miami U., Oxford, Ohio, 1971-75; prof., assoc. dean Tex. A&M U., College Station, 1975-81, prof. urban and regional planning, 1981—; pvt. practice architecture, 1960—. Served with USAF, 1954-56. Mellon fellow U. Pa., 1966. Mem. AIA (past pres. chpt., chmn. historic resources com.) Tex. Soc. Architects, Am. Inst. Cert. Planners. Democrat. Episcopalian. Contbr. articles to profl. jours. Home: 2508 Faulkner Dr College Station TX 77840 Office: Coll Architecture and Environmental Design Tex A&M U College Station TX 77843

ECKBERG, DOUGLAS LEE, sociology educator; b. San Antonio, Dec. 4, 1948; s. Orville E. and Wandalene (Paullins) E.; m. Rose-Ellen May, Aug. 8, 1971; children—Hilary Grace, Paula Denise. B.A. in Psychology, U. Tex., 1971, Ph.D. in Sociology, 1978; M.A. in Sociology, U. Mo.-Columbia, 1973. Vis. asst. prof. Tex. Christian U., Forth Worth, 1978-79; asst. prof. U. Tulsa, 1979-85, assoc. prof., 1985—. Active NCCJ, ACLU. Fellow, U. Tex.-Austin, 1977-78, W.H. Webb Chair History and Ideas, 1977-78; NEH grantee, 1980. Me. Am. Sociol. Assn., Soc. Study Social Problems, S.W. Social Sci. Assn., So. Sociol. Soc., Okla. Sociol. Assn., Western Social Sci. Assn., Soc. Study Symbolic Interaction, Soc. Social Studies Sci., AAUP (pres. Tulsa U. chpt.). Author: Intelligence and Race, 1979; assoc. editor Social Sci. Jour., 1979—, Youth and Society, 1983—, Free Inquiry in Creative Sociology, 1984—; contbr. articles to profl. jours. Home: 798 N Zenith Ave Tulsa OK 74127 Office: Sociology Faculty University of Tulsa Tulsa OK 74104

ECKELS, ROBERT ALLEN, state legislator; b. Houston, Mar. 14, 1957; s. Robert Young and Carolyn (Bickley) E.; m. Tammy Lynn Howard, May 16, 1981. B.S., U. Houston, 1979. Sales counselor General Homes, Houston, 1979-82; assoc. TCI, Houston, 1982—; mem. Tex. Ho. of Reps., Austin, 1983—. Republican. Episcopalian. Office: Tex House of Representatives PO Box 2910 Austin TX 78769

ECKHART, JAMES MILTON, lawyer; b. Miami, Fla., Mar. 13, 1944; s. Joseph W. and Elsie M. E. A.B., U. Miami (Fla.), 1965, J.D., 1968. Bar: Fla. 1968, D.C. 1979, U.S. Dist. Ct. (so. dist.) Fla. 1969, U.S. Ct. Appeals (11th cir.) 1981. Assoc., C.P. Lantz, Miami, 1968-70, Carey, Dwyer, Austin, Cole & Selwood, P.A., Miami, 1970-76; ptnr. Carey, Dwyer, Cole Selwood & Bernard, P.A., Miami, 1976-78, dir., 1978-81; dir., ptnr. Carey, Dwyer, Cole, Eckhart, Mason & Spring, P.A., Miami, 1981—; arbitrator, lectr. Am. Arbitration Assn.; guest lectr. U. Miami. Dade County Democratic committeeman, 1970-74. Served with U.S. Army, 1968-76. Mem. ABA, Fla. Bar Assn., D.C. Bar Assn., Dade County Bar Assn. (dir.), Am. Judicature Soc., Def. Research Inst., Fla. Def. Lawyers Assn., Delta Theta Phi, Phi Delta Theta. Roman Catholic. Clubs: Rod and Reel, Coral Reef Yacht (Miami). Office: 2180 SW 12th Ave Miami FL 33129

ECKL, WILLIAM WRAY, lawyer; b. Florence, Ala., Dec. 2, 1936; s. Louis Arnold and Patricia Barclift (Dowd) E.; m. Mary Lynn McGough, June 29, 1963; children—Eric Dowd, Lynn Lacey. B.A., U. Notre Dame, 1959, LL.B., U. Va., 1962. Bar: Va. 1962, Ala. 1962, Ga. 1964. Law clk. Supreme Ct. of Ala., 1962; ptnr. Gambrell, Harlan, Russell & Moye, Atlanta, 1965-68, Swift, Currie, McGhee & Hiers, Atlanta, 1968-82, Drew, Eckl & Farnham, Atlanta, 1983—. Served to capt. JAGC, USAR, 1962-65. Mem. Def. Research Inst., State Bar of Ga. Roman Catholic. Clubs: Lawyers of Atlanta, Brookwood Hills. Home: 348 Camden Rd Atlanta GA 30309 Office: 1400 W Peachtree St PO Box 7600 Atlanta GA 30357

ECKMAN, CARL EARL, JR., electronics co. exec.; b. Houston, June 18, 1928; s. Carl Earl and Lois W. Eckman; B.S. in Elec. Engring., U. Tex., Austin, 1958; m. Marva Jean Anderson, Feb. 26, 1947; children—Carla Jean, Dale Ferman, Sherry Gail, Marni Lois. Elec. engr. Temco Aircraft Co., Greenville, Tex., 1959-63; chief program mgr. LTV Electro Systems Co., Greenville, 1963-67, dir. programs, 1967-68; dir. programs E Systems Inc., Greenville, 1968-70, dir. requirements, 1970-73, v.p. requirements and market devel., 1973-77, v.p. Mid East ops., 1977-80, v.p., gen. mgr. subs. Serv Air Inc., 1980—. Mem. adv. bd. Greenville Salvation Army, 1971-72. Served with U.S. Mcht. Marine, 1945-47. Registered profl. engr., Tex. Mem. Assn. U.S. Army, Air Force Assn. (past chpt. pres.), Aerospace Industries Assn., Electronic Industries Assn., Nat. Security Indsl. Assn., Armed Forces Communications and Electronics Assn., Army Aviation Assn., Am. Def. Preparedness Assn. Republican. Episcopalian. Clubs: Masons. Address: PO Box 1669 Greenville TX 75401

ECKMAN, STEVEN WILLIAM, college administrator; b. Eau Claire, Wis., Aug. 30, 1951; s. William Charles and Beverly Elizabeth (Kruschke) E.; m. LaRee Scroggin, Aug. 14, 1971; children—Jarred, Jeremy. A.A., York Coll., 1971; B.A., Harding U., 1973; M.A., Abilene Christian U., 1984. Admissions counselor York Coll., Nebr., 1973, dir. admissions, 1973-78, dir. fin. aid, 1974-79; asst. dir. admissions Lubbock Christian Coll., Tex., 1979, dean of student services, 1980—. Contbr. articles to profl. jours. Coll. chmn. Greenlawn Ch. of Christ, Lubbock, 1983—; vol. youth minister East Hill Ch. of Christ, York, 1975-77. Recipient Staff Service award Lubbock Christian Coll., 1981; named Staff Mem. of Month, Lubbock Christian Coll., 1985. Mem. Tex. Assn. Coll. and Univ. Student Personnel Adminstrs., Southwest Assn. Student Personnel Adminstrs., Alpha Chi. Republican. Office: Lubbock Christian Coll 5601 W 19th St Lubbock TX 79407

ECKOLS, HOWARD LOYD, banker; b. Luling, Tex., Mar. 23, 1930; s. Lewis Vernard and Gladys (Colwell) E.; student Tex. Tech., 1947-48; B.B.A., S.W. Tex. State U., 1954; m. Martha Lynn Wilson, Jan. 29, 1954; children—Timothy, Linda. State auditor State of Tex., Austin, 1954-55; mgr. data processing Shell Oil Co., Houston, 1956-62, Tex. Commerce Bank, 1962-69; mgr. data processing Houston Nat. Bank, 1969-73, corr. banking dept., 1973—, asst. v.p., 1965-75, v.p., 1975-82; v.p., mgr. fin. instns. RepublicBank Houston, 1982—. Bd. dirs. S.W. Tex. State U. Ex-Students Assn. Served with USN, 1948-49. Mem. Data Processing Mgmt. Assn. (dir. Houston chpt. 1965—). Home: 7219 Bayou Forest Dr Houston TX 77088 Office: Republic-Bank Houston Box 299001 Houston TX 77299

ECKSTEIN, EUGENE CHARLES, biomedical engineering educator; b. Bucyrus, Ohio, Oct. 31, 1946; s. Robert Frederick and Catherine C. (Pessefall) E.; m. Jane Foster Bernstein, Sept. 1, 1968; children—Matthew, Sarah, Adam. S.B., M.I.T., 1970, S.M., 1970, Ph.D., 1975. Assoc. in bioengring. Peter Bent Brigham Hosp./Harvard Sch. Medicine, Boston, 1974-75; asst. prof. mech. and biomed. engring. U. Miami, Coral Gables, Fla., 1975-81, assoc. prof., 1981—; cons. in field. Mem. ASME, Internat. Soc. for Artificial Organs, Am. Soc. Artificial Internal Organs., Sigma Xi. Contbr. articles to profl. jours. Office: Dept Biomed Engring Univ Miami PO Box 248294 Coral Gables FL 33124

ECONOMEDES, JOHNNY GEORGE, city fire chief; b. Brownsville, Tex., Nov. 14, 1932; s. George John and Despina (Kontos) E.; divorced; 1 son, Andrew John; m. Hermelinda Casas, May 27, 1967; 1 child, Despina Anastasia. B.A., Pan Am. Coll., Edinburg, Tex., 1952, 57, cert. in parks and recreation, 1952. Tchr. phys. edn. Edinburg Schs., 1957-58; with parks and recreation dept. City of Edinburg, 1958-73, fire chief, 1983—; with Fibercrafters of Edinburg, 1973-83; Bd. dirs. Tex. Parks and Recreation Soc., 1968-70, Tex. Athletic Assn. Fedn., Austin, 1968-74; chmn. state firemen's pumper races, 1980-84. Named Outstanding Fireman of Yr., Edinburg Vol. Fire Dept., 1975, Outstanding Fireman of Yr., Am. Legion, 1975; recipient cert. of achievement 50th Anniversary People Helping People, 1980. Mem. Lower Rio Grande Valley Fireman's and Firemarshall's Assn. (pres. 1983-84), Tex. Fire Chief's Assn., Internat. Fire Chief's Assn., S.W. Fire Chief's Assn., State Firemen's and Firemarshall's Assn., Edinburg C. of C. (chmn. bandido com. 1970-85, pres. 1983-84, pres. red coat com. 1983-85), Beta Eta Omega. Democrat. Greek Orthodox. Avocations: hunting; fishing; cooking.

EDDIN, M(ARY) EDNA, economist; b. Daisy, Tenn., Nov. 8, 1941; d. Tip and Floretta Wright; B.A., Berea Coll., 1965; M.A., Am. U., 1969; Ph.D., U. S.C., 1976; m. M. Shehab Eddin, Oct. 1, 1964. Research asst. Am. Council Edn., Washington, 1963-66; economist Dept. Commerce, Washington, 1966-67; instr. econs. Gardner-Webb Coll., Boiling Springs, N.C., 1969-73; planning and devel. cons., Columbia, S.C., 1973-75; asso. prof. econs. Brescia Coll., 1976-78; sr. economist HUD, Louisville, 1978-80, dir. econ. and market analysis div., 1980—. Mem. AAUP, Am. Econ. Assn., So. Econ. Assn., Am. Polit. Sci. Assn., ACLU, Pi Sigma Alpha, Omicron Delta Epsilon, Phi Delta Kappa. Author: Attitude Toward Business in Relations to Economic Knowledge, 1976; contbr. articles to profl. jours. Office: HUD Louisville Area Office Louisville KY 40201

EDDINGS, DAVID WENDELL, law enforcement officer, movie actor; b. Columbia, Tenn., Jan. 21, 1939; s. James Elzie and Mattie Harris (Hewitt) E.; m. Barbara Jeunelle Huggins, Sept. 12, 1964; children—Karen R., Donna L., Michelle D. Cert. Central Mo. State U., 1974, U. Tenn., 1975. With production dept. Sta. WLAC-TV, Nashville, 1957-64; police officer Met. Police, Nashville, 1964-73, police sergeant, 1973-82, police lt., 1982—; actor MGM-United Artist movie Marie, 1985. Mem. Fraternal Order of Police, Nashville Police Supervisor's Assn. Democrat. Baptist. Lodge: Masons. Avocations: hunting; antique guns; reading. Home: 1229 Apache Ln Madison TN 37115 Office: Met Police Tactical Sect 3718 Nolensville Rd Nashville TN 37211

EDDY, MELISSA JANE, counseling and consulting firm executive; b. Medina, Ohio, Dec. 27, 1951; d. Ernest DeRhone and Jane Anne (Lose) E.; m. Tracy Schiemenz, Jan. 17, 1981. B.A. magna cum laude, Kalamazoo Coll., 1974; M.A. with honors, Western Mich. U., 1976. Psychologist Battle Creek (Mich.) Community Mental Health Clinic, 1976-77; coordinator program services Center for Battered Women, Austin, Tex., 1978-81; pvt. practice counseling and cons., Austin, 1981—; owner women's bridal and formal-wear consignment bus., Austin, 1982—1982-85; mem. alcohol services adv. com. Austin Travis County Mental Health/Mental Retardation, 1980-83; mem. Austin Family Violence Diversion Network Adv. Com., 1980-84; program assoc. Tex. Council on Family Violence, 1985—. Bd. dirs. Mediation Ctr. of Travis County, 1983—, pres., 1984—; campaign vol. Democratic candidates, 1980-82. Mem. Am. Psychol. Assn. Tex. Psychol. Assn., Assn. Women in Psychology, Tex. Council Family Violence (dir. 1978-85), Nat. Coalition Against Domestic Violence, Phi Beta Kappa, Alpha Lambda Delta. Research on burnout among family-violence workers, treatment programs for spouse abusers. Home and office: PO Box 9802-654 Austin TX 78766

EDELMAN, ROBERT MARC, real estate agency executive; b. Dallas, Jan. 17, 1946; s. William and Claire (Portney) E.; m. Mary Linda Desilva, June 1, 1968; children—Stephen Andrew, Jenny Kathleen. B.A., U. Okla., 1967. With Citicorp., 1969-72; founder, pres., chief exec. officer Robert Edelman Co., Dallas, 1972—; founder, dir. Good Earth Devel. Co., Welmarc Corp.; dir. Sherry Douglas Inc. Mem. Nat. Assn. Home Builders, Bldg. Owners Mgmt. Assn. Republican. Jewish. Club: City (Dallas). Office: 8222 Douglas St Suite 880 Dallas TX 75225

EDELMAN, STEVEN ROI, psychologist; b. N.Y.C., Nov. 6, 1948; s. Arthur and Roberta (Weisfeld) E.; m. Rita Anne Mandell, Aug. 27, 1972; 1 child, Dara. B.A. in Polit. Sci., Fairleigh U., 1970; M.A. in Ednl. Psychology, Jersey City State U., 1978. Lic. psychol. assoc., N.C. Psychol. assoc. Bklyn. Developmental Ctr., N.Y.C., 1975-77; psychologist O'Berry Ctr., Goldsboro, N.C., 1977-78, Cherry Hosp., Goldsboro, 1978-80, practice psychology, Wilson, N.C., 1980-82, Goldsboro, 1982—; dir. Psychology Howells Child Care, LaGrange, N.C., 1985—; assoc. Goldsboro Psychol. Services, 1983—; cons. Our Homes, Inc., Kinston, N.C., 1984—; chmn. conf. Computers in Psychology, 1983. Author: (poetry) Pegasus, 1968. Developer treatment procedure Stereotypic Behavior, 1978. Pres. Congregation Oheb Shalom, Goldsboro, 1984—; campaign worker Hunt for Senate, 1984; pres. Young Democrats, 1968. Regents Coll. scholar N.Y. State Bd. Regents 1966. Mem. Assn. Eastern N.C. Psychologists (v.p. 1984—), N.C. Psychol. Assn., Am. Psychol. Assn. (assoc.), Psi Chi (pres. 1982-83). Home: 105 Lou Dr Goldsboro NC 27530 Office: Howells Child Care Ctrs Inc Rt 4 LaGrange NC 28551

EDELSON, RICHARD I., neuropsychologist; b. Bklyn., June 3, 1947; s. David and Miriam (Osnovitz) E.; m. Ann Bridges, Aug. 17, 1969; children—Aaron, Benjamin. B.S. in Psychology with high honors, U. Ill., 1969, Ph.D. in Clin. Psychology, 1975; M.S. Ed., Ill. State U., 1972. Tchr. pub. schs., Champaign, Ill., 1969-71; intern in psychology Portland (Oreg.) VA Med. Ctr., 1974-75; staff psychologist Louisville VA Med. Ctr., 1975-80; pvt. practice, Louisville, 1980—; practicum supr. dept. psychology U. Louisville. Mem. Am. Psychol. Assn., Ky. Psychol. Assn., Am. Acad. Neuropsychologists, Internat. Assn. Study Chronic Pain, Behavioral Medicine Soc., Phi Beta Kappa. Jewish. Home: 8919 Lippincott Rd Louisville KY 40222 Office: 107 St Mary's Med Plaza 1900 Bluegrass Ave Louisville KY 40215

EDELSTEIN, STEPHEN GEORGE, cardiologist; b. Bklyn., Jan. 10, 1938; s. Moe and Helen (Klahr) E.; m. Karen Mae Moss, Sept. 3, 1961; children—Ellen, David. A.B. magna cum laude, NYU, 1957; M.D., Harvard U., 1961. Diplomate Am. Bd. Internal Medicine. Intern, Cin. Gen. Hosp., 1961-62, resident in medicine, 1962-63; resident in medicine, U. Ky., 1965-66, fellow in cardiology, 1966-67, clin. instr., 1967-70, asst. prof. clin. medicine, 1970-76, assoc. prof., 1977-81, prof., 1982—; cons. cardiologist, Lexington; pres. Cardiac Data Services, Inc.; cons. cardiologist Ky. State Dept. Health. Served with USPHS, 1963-65. Recipient Josephine Munson Mactavish medal NYU, 1957; Physician's Recognition award AMA, 1982. Fellow ACP, Am. Coll. Cardiology, Am. Heart Assn.; mem. Boylston Med. Soc. Address: 1517 Nicholasville Rd Lexington KY 40503

EDELSTEIN, STEVEN A(LLEN), lawyer; b. Newark, Nov. 18, 1943; s. Edwin M. and Frances R. (Rosenbloom) E.; m. Mary Lou Eisnor, June 4, 1973; 1 son, Adam Craig. B.A., Fairleigh Dickinson U., 1969. Bar: Fla. 1973, U.S. Dist. Ct. (so. dist.) Fla. 1974, U.S. Ct. Appeals (5th cir.) 1975, U.S. Ct. Appeals (11th cir.) 1981, U.S. Supreme Ct. 1977. Assoc. Hilery F. Silverman, Miami, Fla., 1973-74, Walton, Lantaff Schroeder & Carson, Miami, 1974-78, Storace, Hall & Hauser, Miami, 1978-79; asst. city atty. City of Miami Law Dept., 1979-83; assoc. Ress, Gomez, Rosenberg & Howland, P.A., North Miami, Fla., 1983—. Co-editor: Handbook for Dade County Lawyers, 1979. Served with U.S. Army, 1965-66. Mem. Fla. Bar, ABA, Assn. Trial Lawyers Am., Am. Judicature Soc. Home: 2720 Country Club Prado Coral Gables FL 33134 Office: Res Gomez Rosenberg Howland & Mintz PA 1700 Sans Souci Blvd North Miami FL 33181

EDENFIELD, BERRY AVANT, federal judge; b. Bulloch County, Ga., Aug. 2, 1934; s. Perry and Vera E.; B.B.A., U. Ga., 1956, LL.B., 1958; m. Vida Melvis Bryant, Aug. 3, 1963. Admitted to Ga. bar, 1958; partner firm Allen, Edenfield, Brown & Wright and predecessors, Statesboro, Ga., 1958-78; judge U.S. Dist. Ct., So. Dist. Ga., 1978—; mem. Ga. Senate, 1965-66. Chmn. Statesboro Regional Library. Served with Army N.G., 1957-63. Office: US Dist Ct Federal Bldg 125 Bull St Room 116 Savannah GA 31401

EDENS, EMILY SANDERS, marketing executive; b. Columbia, S.C., Jan. 15, 1953; s. Manley Conway and Emily Lenoir (Burrows) Sanders; m. John Benjamin Edens, June 16, 1974; children—Emily Sanders, John Benjamin. B.A., U. S.C., 1973, M.A., 1975. Sales, pub. affairs staff WDXY, WFIG Radio, part-time, 1972-74; pub. info. dir. Sumter (S.C.) Area Tech. Coll., 1974-78; v.p., dir. mktg. and pub. relations Nat. Bank of S.C., Sumter, 1978—; mem. faculty Golden Gate U., 1979-80; cons. in field. Bd. dirs. Boys Club, Sumter, 1982—. Named Young Careerist, Sumter, Bus. and Profl. Women, 1978. Mem. S.C. Bankers Assn., Pub. Relations Soc. Am., Bank Mktg. Assn., Greater Sumter C. of C. (v.p., mem. exec. com.). Club: The Forum. Home: 7 Richardson St Sumter SC 29150 Office: 207 N Main St Sumter SC 29150

EDGAR, MARGARET ANN DEVAUGHAN, special education educator; b. Geneva County, Ala., Mar. 1, 1937; d. Wesley Hugo and Irene (Cox) DeVaughan; m. Jerry Wilburn Edgar, Dec. 23, 1956; children—Marcella Faith Edgar Scurlock, David Marcus. A.A. (with honors), Gordon Coll., 1970; B.A. (with honors), Tift Coll., 1972; postgrad. Fla. State U., 1975—. Cert tchr., Fla. Coll. prep. hist. tchr. Calhoun County Bd. Instrn., Altha (Fla.) High Sch., 1971-76; tchr. Jackson Christian Sch., Marianna, Fla., 1976-77, substitute tchr., 1978-79; tchr. basic academics Jackson County Assn. Retarded Citizens, Greenwood, Fla., 1980-81; tchr. handicapped pre-schoolers Child Devel. Ctr., Greenwood, 1981—. Active community awareness programs on handicapped and devel. delayed children; coach Bible Quiz team, 1977; coach TV Quiz Bowl team Altha High Sch., 1976; Sunday sch. tchr. Assembly of God, Heritage Cathedral, Marianna, 20 yrs.; youth vol. Assembly of God chs. in Ala., Ga. and Fla. Selected Beta Tchr. of Yr., Altha High Sch., 1976. Mem. Phi Theta Kappa. Home: PO Box 25 Altha FL 32421 Office: PO Box 98 Greenwood FL 32443

EDGAR, THOMAS RAY, professional services company executive, consultant; b. Boston, Aug. 30, 1940; s. Ernest Earl and Joan Margaret (Reamy) E.; children—Alison, Steven. B.A. in Sociology, Boston U., 1963. Br. mgr. Workingmens Coop. Bank, Boston, 1964-66; personnel mgr. Addison-Wesley Pub. Co., Reading, Mass., 1966-68; v.p., cons. Cole & Assocs., Boston, 1969-72; prin., cons. Stanton Assocs., St. Paul, 1972-73; v.p. personnel Bank Va. Potomac, Falls Church, 1973; asst. v.p. human resources The BDM Corp., McLean, Va., 1973-81; exec. dir. human resources Advanced Tech., Inc., 1981—; adj. prof. Am. U., Marymount Coll. Mem. Am. Compensation Assn. (cert.), Am. Soc. for Personnel Adminstrn. (cert.), Am. Mgmt. Assn. Home: 1917 Batten Hollow Rd Vienna VA 22180 Office: 12005 Sunrise Valley Dr Reston VA 22091

EDGE, JOHN NELSON, oil company executive; b. Shawnee, Okla., Feb. 6, 1929; s. Elmer Faye and Alice (Euvea) E.; m. Ann Goodpasture, Aug. 13, 1953; children—Leslie Rene, Gary Nelson, Randall Wayne. B.S., U. Okla., 1952. Registered geologist. With Conoco, 1952—, div. mgr. exploration, Midland, Tex., 1980-83, coordinator industry environ. affairs, Houston, 1983—. Served with USN, 1946-48, ETO. Mem. Midland C. of C., Am. Assn. Petroleum Geologists (edn. com. 1983—), Am. Petroleum Inst. (com. mem.), Nat. Ocean Industries Assn. (safety and environ. com. 1983—), Western Oil and Gas Assn. (exploration com. 1983—), Houston Geol. Soc., W.Tex. Geol. Soc. Republican. Club: Theta Xi (pres. 1951-52). Avocations: walking; swimming; gardening. Home: 18202 Oakhampton Dr Houston TX 77084 Office: Conoco Inc PO Box 2197 Houston TX 77252

EDGE, RONALD DOVASTON, physics educator; b. Bolton, Eng., Feb. 3, 1929; came to U.S., 1958, naturalized, 1968; s. James and Mildred (Davies) E.; m. Margaret Skulina, Aug. 14, 1956; children—Christopher James, Michael Dovaston. B.A., Cambridge U., 1950, M.A., 1952, Ph.D., 1956. Research fellow Australian Nat. U., Canberra, 1954-58; asst., then assoc. prof. U. S.C., Columbia, 1958-63, prof., 1964—; research assoc. Yale U., New Haven, 1963-64; vis. prof. Stanford U., Calif. Tech. Inst., U. Munich, U. Sussex, U. Witwatersrand, Oak Ridge Nat. Lab., Los Alamos Nat. Lab. Recipient Russell award, U. S.C. Fellow Am. Physical Soc. (James B. Pegram award 1979), Am. Assn. Physics Tchrs. (apparatus award 1973). Unitarian (past pres. Columbia fellowship). Author: String and Sticky Tape Experiments, 1978, Physics in the Arts, 1973; contbr. articles to profl. jours. Home: 1515 Lilly Ave Columbia SC 29204 Office: Physics Dept USC Columbia SC 29208

EDGE-BOYD, SANDRA KAY, social worker; b. Ft. Cobb, Okla., June 26, 1950; d. Roland Hildreth and Doris Lorene (Meek) Edge; m. Bruce Wayne Boyd, Sept. 4, 1983. B.A., Okla. Bapt. U., 1972; M.S.W., U. Okla., 1975; M.R.E., Southwestern Bapt. Theol. Sem., 1975. Lic. social worker, Okla. Psychiat. social worker Taliaferro Community Mental Health Ctr., Lawton, Okla., 1975-76, Anadarko br. coordinator, 1976-79; asst. county dir. Red Rock Mental Health Ctr., Stroud, Okla., 1979-80, dir. emergency services, Oklahoma City, 1980-82; dir. Kingfisher County, North Central Okla. Community Mental Health (Okla.), 1982-83, dir. Kingfisher/Logan County, 1983—; cons. Sunbeam Family Services, Oklahoma City, 1982. Bd. dirs. Contact-Kingfisher, 1982-83. Mem. Nat. Assn. Social Workers, Acad. Cert. Social Workers, Okla. Health and Welfare Assn. Democrat. Baptist. Office: PO Box 736 406 N Main St Kingfisher OK 73750

EDGELL, WALLACE ALAN, college dean; b. Fairmont, W.Va., July 27, 1949; s. John W. and Edith (Hostutler) E.; m. Nancy Ann Oates, Feb. 29, 1976; children—Jeremy, Jenny. B.A., Fairmont State U., 1970, A.B. cert., 1974; M.A., W. Va. U., 1976; Ph.D., Tex. A&M U., 1983. Tchr., Grant County Sch., Petersburg, W. Va., 1971-74, asst. prin., 1973-76, prin., 1976-82; adminstrv. asst. Tex. A&M U., College Station, 1982-83; dean Blinn Coll., Brenham, Tex., 1983—. Author: Beyond the Crib, 1982. Contbr. articles to profl. jours. Coach, Little League Basketball/Football, Petersburg, 1972-78; bd. dirs. Little League Football, Petersburg, 1978-81, Valley View Golf Course, Petersburg, 1978-81. Recipient Coll. scholarship Benedum Found., 1967; All Conf. Golf award W. Va. Intercollegiate Athletic Conf., 1968; Outstanding Elem. Tchr. Am. award, 1973. Mem. Council Univs. and Colls. Am. Assn. Community and Jr. Colls., Phi Kappa Phi, Phi Delta Kappa. Democrat. Methodist. Lodge: Kiwanis (spl. emphasis chmn.). Avocations: golf; fishing; hunting. Office: Dean of Men Blinn Coll 902 College Ave Brenham TX 77833

EDGERTON, A. FREEMAN, lawyer; b. Coushatta, La., Oct. 22, 1919; s. Clarence Eugene and Daisy Bell (Gardner) E.; B.A., La. State U., 1940, J.D., 1976; C.L.U., C.P.C.U.; m. Kerttu Sofia Maria von Ammondt Friman, Feb. 26, 1946. Ins. sales E.T. Edgerton Agy., Asheville, N.C., 1940-42; owner, operator ins. agy., Charlotte, N.C., 1948-73; admitted to La. bar, 1977, N.C. bar, 1977; legal research asst. to judge La. Ct. Appeal, Baton Rouge, 1977-78; asso. firm Watson, Blanche, Wilson & Posner, Baton Rouge, 1978—; pres., chief exec. officer, dir. State Nat. Capital Corp., State Nat. Life Ins. Co., Delta Nat. Life Ins. Co.; chmn., dir. State Nat. Title Guaranty Co., State Nat. Fire Ins. Co., State Nat. Life Agy., Inc., State Nat. Loan Corp., State Nat. Gen. Ins. Agy., Inc.; pres., dir. Champion Capitol Corp., Champion Ins. Co.; v.p., sec., dir. H. & J. Capital Corp., Goudchaux/Maison Blanche Life Ins. Co.; treas., dir. La. Ins. Guaranty Assn.; dir. Met. Bank & Trust, 1st Met. Fin. Corp., 1st Met. Mortgage Corp., Met.-Sherwood Investment Corp.; underwriting mem. Lloyd's of London. Pres., Charlotte br. English-Speaking Union, 1962-72; chmn. dept. fin. Diocesan Council, Episcopal Diocese N.C., 1957-66; bd. dirs. Greater Carolinas chpt. ARC, 1962-70. Served with U.S. Army, 1942-46. Mem. N.C., La., Am., Baton Rouge bar assns., Phi Alpha Delta, Phi Kappa Phi, Omicron Delta Kappa, Kappa Alpha. Democrat. Clubs: Charlotte City; Camelot, City (Baton Rouge); Blowing Rock (N.C.) Country. Home: 7982

Brandon Dr Baton Rouge LA 70809 Office: 505 North Blvd PO Box 2995 Baton Rouge LA 70821

EDGERTON, RICHARD, restaurant/hotel owner; b. Haverford, Pa., May 2, 1911; s. Charles and Ida Bonner E.; m. Marie Lytle Page, Oct. 24, 1936; children—Leila, Margaret, Carol. Pres./owner, Lakeside Inn Properties, Inc., Mt. Dora, Fla., 1935—; co-owner 24 Burger King restaurants, Pa., 1966—; gen. mgr., pres. Buck Hill Falls (Pa.) Co., 1961-65; pres., chief exec. officer Eustis Sand Co., Mt. Dora; founding dir. Fla. Service Corp., Tampa; v.p., dir. First Nat. Bank, Mt. Dora. Mem. Gov.'s Little Cabinet, 1955-61. Trustee Lake Sumter Coll.; trustee emeritus Berry Coll.; bd. dirs. Mt. Dora Community Trust Fund. Served to lt. USNR, 1944-46; ETO. Mem. Am. (dir.), Fla. (past pres.), NH. (past pres.) hotel and motel assns., Newcomen Soc., Welcome Soc., Pa. Soc. Clubs: Miami; Mt. Dora Yacht, Mt. Dora Golf Lodge: Kiwanis. Home: 3d and McDonald Sts Mount Dora FL 32757 Office: 234 W 3d Ave Mount Dora FL 32757

EDGERTON, WALTER LEE, hospital administrator, consultant, pharmacist; b. Battle Creek, Mich., Aug. 6, 1943; s. Walter L. and LaVinna J. (Baker) E.; m. Sandra L. Van Riper, Dec. 20, 1969; children—Todd W., Allison N., Jodi A. B.S. in Pharmacy, U. Mich., 1967, D.Pharmacy, 1968; M.B.A., U. South Fla., 1985. Dir. pharmacy services Bascom Palmer Eye Inst., U. Miami, Fla., 1978-79, Fort Myers Community Hosp., 1979-82; dir. pharmacy services Basic Am. Med. Inc., Ft. Myers, 1982-84, dir. support services, 1984-85; v.p. med./support services Englewood Community Hosp., Englewood, Fla., 1985—; guest lectr. IBM Exec. Health Lecture Series, Dallas, Chgo., Los Angeles, San Francisco, N.Y.C., Atlanta, 1981-84. Contbr. articles to profl. publs. Bd. dirs. Royal Palm Players, Fort Myers, 1983, Fort Myers Diabetic Assn., 1982. Mem. Fla. Soc. Hosp. Pharmacists (regional pres. 1982, chmn. legal com. 1984-85, bd. dirs. 1983-84), Fla. Pharmacy Assn. (legis com. 1984-85), Am. Soc. Hosp. Pharmacists (adminstrv. sig group 1975—), So. Gulf Soc. (pres. 1982), Nat. Intravenous Therapy Assn. Office: Englewood Community Hosp 506 N Indiana Ave Englewood FL 34295

EDGINGTON, WALTER ROY, electronics company executive; b. Guthrie Center, Iowa, Apr. 26, 1925; s. Thomas William and Helen Violet (Schrader) E.; B.S., M.S., Georgetown U., 1954; m. Florence Mary Kowaleski, Nov. 9, 1949; children—Eric Michael, Bruce Edward. Various civilian positions U.S. Army, 1949-66, intelligence specialist, 1954-62, ops. analyst, 1962-66, program mgr. Communications Projects, 1966-69; mgr. Monmouth Engring. Center GTE Sylvania Inc., New Shrewsbury, N.J., 1969-71, mgr. office Springfield, Va., 1967-71, v.p. mktg., Arlington, Va., 1972—. Mem. Pres.'s Export Council. Served with U.S. Army, 1946-49. Mem. Armed Forces Communications and Electronics Assn. (dir. 1977—, pres. Washington chpt.), Am. Def. Preparedness Assn., Assn. U.S. Army, Electronic Industries Assn. (chmn. export/import com. 1976—), Navy League U.S., Nat. Security Indsl. Assn. (dir. 1977—, chmn. internat. com.), Air Force Assn. Clubs: International, Capitol Hill, Aviation. Home: 4843 Dodson Dr Annandale VA 22003 Office: 1777 N Kent St Arlington VA 22209

EDINGER, JACK DONALD, clin. psychologist; b. Lehighton, Pa., July 24, 1951; s. Norman Donald and Edith Ellen E.; B.A., Lafayette Coll., 1973; M.S., Va. Commonwealth U., 1975, Ph.D., 1977; m. Wanda F. Hood, May 12, 1979. Staff psychologist Butner Fed. Correctional Inst. (N.C.), 1977-80, VA. Med. Center, Durham, N.C., 1980—; asst. prof. dept. med. psychology Duke U., Durham, 1980—. Mem. Am. Psychol. Assn., Southeastern Psychol. Assn., Internat. Differential Treatment Assn. Lutheran. Contbr. articles, papers to profl. lit. Home: 8312 Polaris Dr Bahama NC 27503 Office: VA Med Center 508 Fulton St Durham NC 27705

EDINGER, WARD MUNSON, petroleum engineer, consultant; b. Elizabeth, N.J., Nov. 5, 1912; s. Harry Munson and Helen (Bauer) E.; m. Lucille H. Edinger, Oct. 26, 1940 (dec. Mar. 1978); children—Ronald, Eileen, Susan, Robert; m. Janice Beatty, Oct. 7, 1978. B.S., U. Mo., 1935. Chemist, technician Sinclair Prairie Oil Co., Tulsa, 1935-39; div. engr.-head engring. dept. Core Labs. Inc., Dallas, 1939-46; chief engr. Harper-Turner Oil Co., Oklahoma City, 1946-47; pres., chmn. bd. Edinger Inc., Oklahoma City, 1954—; dir. Equity Benefit Life, Blackwell, Okla., 1974-78; trustee Hales Estate Trust, Oklahoma City, 1968—. Contbr. articles to profl. jours. Bd. dirs. Oklahoma City Symphony Soc., 1977,78,79; chmn. Radio Free Europe, Oklahoma City, 1965-66. Served to lt. U.S. Army, 1935-39. Recipient Disting. Service award Sertoma Club. Mem. AIME, Am. Petroleum Inst. (pres. Oklahoma City chpt. 1948-49), Soc. Ind. Earth Scientists, Alpha Chi Sigma (pres. 1933-34). Republican. Christian Scientist. Lodge: Sertoma (pres. 1972-73). Avocations: traveling; sports fishing. Home: 3325 Robin Ridge Rd Oklahoma City OK Office: Edinger Inc 510 Hightower Bldg Oklahoma City OK 73102

EDLEY, LAURA JEAN, librarian; b. Orange, N.J., Mar. 28, 1957; d. Gaspar G. and Jacqueline (Clementi) Bellitti; m. Richard Michael Edley, June 28, 1980. B.A., Kean Coll. N.J., 1979; M.L.S., U. So. Miss., 1982. Circulation clk. Springfield (N.J.) Pub. Library, 1976-79; sch. librarian/media supr. Sandshore Sch., Budd Lake, N.J., 1979-80; substitute tchr. Biloxi Pub. Schs. (Miss.), 1980-82; tchr. Lopez Elem. Sch., Biloxi, 1982-83; children's librarian, asst. dir. Harrison County Gulfport Library, Gulfport, Miss., 1983-84, Riverhead Free Library, N.Y., 1984—. cons. Our Lady of Fatima Cath. Sch., 1983-84. Publicity capt. Neighborhood Watch Club, Biloxi, 1981-84. Recipient Citizenship award LWV, 1974; Honor and Spanish awards Jonathan Dayton High Sch., 1974, 75. Mem. ALA, Miss. Librarians Assn., Children's Librarians of Middlesex County (pes.), Suffolk County Children's Librarians Assn., Coastal Miss. Library Coop., Am. Assn. Sch. Librarians, Gulf Coast Italian Am. Soc., Kappa Delta Pi. Republican. Roman Catholic.

EDMOND, DALE BARBAREE, educator; b. Bodcaw, Ark., Jan. 2, 1926; s. Thomas Jackson and Edna Viola (Jordan) Barbaree; B.A., Henderson State U., Arkadelphia, Ark., 1946; M.A., Tulsa U., 1953; Ed.D., Okla. State U., Stillwater, 1974; m. Clay Manning Edmond, Dec. 24, 1949; children—Kobe Clay, Rebebekah Barbaree. Classroom tchr., Okla., 1947-61; lang. arts supr., Tulsa, 1961-64; supr. elem. math., Okla., 1964-67; dir. Learning Resource Center, Okla., 1967-70; prin. Carnegie Elem. Sch., Okla., 1970-71; dir. elem. curriculum Tulsa Ind. Sch. Dist. I, 1971-73, dir. elem. schs., 1973—; cons. in field. Mem. Assn. Supervision and Curriculum Devel., Nat. Assn. Elem. Sch. Prins., Nat. Assn. Gifted/Talented, Nat. Assn. Tchrs. Math. Democrat. Methodist. Author curriculum materials; editor: Math Tapes, 1968; adv. bd. Instructor mag., 1975-78. Home: 6044 S Lakewood St Tulsa OK 74135 Office: 3027 S New Haven St Tulsa OK 47145

EDMOND, MARY ELIZABETH, special education administrator; b. Raleigh, Miss., Aug. 12, 1940; d. Whitman Barney and Gladys Cleo (Craft) Headrick; m. Paul Eugene Edmond, Oct. 31, 1965; children—Miriam Elizabeth, Paula Eugenia. B.A., Asbury Coll., 1962; M.A., William Carey Coll., 1975. Tchr. music, Christian edn., Karachi, Pakistan, 1962-65; vice-prin. Trinity Grade Sch., Karachi, 1964-65; tchr. pub. schs., Pittsburg, Calif., 1971-73; tchr. Smith County Sch. Dist., Raleigh, Miss., 1973-78, spl. edn. tchr., 1978-81, spl. edn. supr., 1981—. Mem. Miss. Orgn. Spl. Edn. Services, Miss. Assn. Talented and Gifted, Miss. Assn. Children with Learning Disabilities. Democrat. Methodist. Office: PO Box 308 Raleigh MS 39153

EDMONDS, JAMES ALBERT, economist; b. Chgo., Nov. 3, 1947; s. Albert James and Mary (Foley) E.; m. Frances Chevarley, Aug. 28, 1971. B.A., Kalamazoo Coll., 1969; M.A., Duke U., 1972, Ph.D., 1974. Instr. econs. Greensboro Coll., N.C., 1973-74; asst. prof. Centre Coll. of Ky., Danville, 1974-78; scientist Inst. Energy Analysis, Washington, 1978—; cons. in field. Author: Global Energy, 1985. Mem. AAAS, Am. Econ. Assn., So. Econs. Assn., Internat. Assn. Energy Economists. Roman Catholic. Avocations: tennis; cooking; cabinet making.

EDMONDS, VERNON H., sociology and psychology educator; b. Clinton, Okla., Dec. 18, 1927; s. Clarence Lee and Mary Jane (Hurd) E.; A.A., Okla. State U., 1952, B.A., 1954; M.S., Purdue U., 1955; Ph.D., U. Mo., 1960; m. Gloria Graves King, Aug. 26, 1955; 1 son, Kevin. Instr. psychology and sociology Cottey Coll., Nevada, Mo., 1956-58; asst. prof. sociology U. South Fla., Tampa, 1960-63, Fla. State U., Tallahassee, 1963-67; prof. sociology Coll. William and Mary, Williamsburg, Va., 1967—. Pres. ACLU of Fla., 1966-67; chmn. ACLU Tallahassee, 1964-67; mem. nat. bd. dirs. ACLU, 1965-67. Served with USAAF, 1946-49. NSF grantee, 1970-72. Mem. Am. Sociol. Assn., Nat. Council Family Relations, So. Sociol. Soc. Asso. editor Jour. Marriage and Family; prin. author: Social Behavior, 1967. Home: 2 Travis Ln Williamsburg VA 23185 Office: College of William and Mary Williamsburg VA 23185

EDMONDSON, JEANNETTE B., sec. state Okla.; b. Muskogee, Okla., June 6, 1925; d. A. Chapman and Georgia (Shutt) Bartleson; m. J. Howard Edmondson, May 15, 1946 (dec.); children—James H. (dec.), Jeanne E. Watkins, Patricia E. Zimmer. B.A., U. Okla., 1946. Sec. of state State of Okla., Oklahoma City, 1979—. Chmn. bd. Okla. affiliate Am. Heart Assn., 1979. Democrat. Methodist. Office: Office of Sec of State 101 State Capitol Oklahoma City OK 73105

EDMONSON, WILLIAM FRED, college dean; b. Nashville, Jan. 16, 1938; s. Fred and Annie Myra (Cox) E.; m. Brenda Joyce Jones, June 17, 1965; children—Christina Noel, William Bryan. B.S., U. So. Miss., 1961, M.B.A., 1965; D. Edn., U. Miss., 1973. Coordinator distributive edn. Mt. Vernon High Sch., Alexandria, Va., 1966-68; instr. bus. adminstrn. N. Fla. Jr. Coll., Madison, 1968-71; asst., then dean U. Miss. Grad. Sch., University, 1971-73; adminstrv. asst. to dean instrn. Rockingham Community Coll., Wentworth, N.C., 1973-74; dean instructional affairs Itawamba Jr. Coll., Fulton, Miss., 1974—. Contbr. articles to profl. jours. Mem. Itawamba County Camp Gideons; pres., chmn. fundraising United Way; bd. deacons; moderator First Baptist Ch., Fulton; bd. dirs. Tupelo Symphony, 1983-85. Mem. Miss. Pub. Jr. Coll. Acad. Deans Assn., Am. Assn. Community Jr. Colls., So. Assn. Colls. and Schs., (del. various confs.), Kappa Delta Pi, Omicron Delta Kappa, Phi Delta Kappa. Lodge: Rotary (bd. dirs.). Avocations: fishing; swimming; tennis; music. Home: Box 481 Fulton MS 38843 Office: Itawamba Jr Coll Fulton MS 38843

EDMUND, RICHARD KENNETH, manufacturing company executive; b. Whiteville, N.C., Nov. 5, 1955; s. Howard Jackson and Alice Nelson (Ivey) Edmund; m. Lisas Marie Stallcup, Sept. 19, 1982; m. Deborah Bullard, Aug. 19, 1978 (div. Sept. 1982). Student, Southeastern Community Coll., Whiteville, N.C., 1973-77, Western Carolina U., 1977. Golf profl. Surf, Golf and Beach Club, Myrtle Beach, S.C., 1976-78; salesman Oakwood Homes Corp., Greensboro, N.C., 1978-80, gen. mgr. sales, 1980—. Republican. Baptist. Home: 720 Howe Springs Rd Florence SC 29501

EDNEY, JIMMY LISH, fuel services corp. ofcl.; b. Erwin, Tenn., Aug. 14, 1944; s. William Lish and Mildred Gertrude (Hensley) E.; student Steed Coll., 1974-75; m. Nellie L. Linville, Apr. 3, 1965; children—Diane, Shirley, Melissa Chadwick. Civil engr. trainee Trammel Constrn. Co., Bristol, Tenn., 1965-66; operator Nuclear Fuel Services, Inc., Erwin, Tenn., 1966, surveillance technician, 1967, surveillance shift supr., 1967-68, data processor, 1968-71, prodn. control clk., 1971-73, materials supr., 1973-74, materials supr. ops. spl. nuclear material, 1974-79, nuclear materials supr., ops., 1979-80, records control mgr., 1980—; operator Tenn. Eastman Co., Kingsport, 1966-67; owner Jim's Dairy Clippers, Erwin, 1967. Served with USN, 1962-65. Mem. Am. Prodn. and Inventory Control Soc. Clubs: Masons, Elks. Home: 104 Fanning St Erwin TN 37650 Office: PO Box 218 Erwin TN 37650

EDWARDS, ANNE FOX, psychologist, consultant; b. Baton Rouge, Mar. 1, 1953; d. Ernest Greenwood and Martha Louella (Strange) F. B.A., Furman U., 1975; M.S., N.C. State U., 1981, postgrad., 1981—. Lic. psychol. assoc. Staff illustrator, mgmt. asst, Baptist Theol. Sem., Ruschlikon, Switzerland, 1975-76; staff psychotherapist Raleigh Adolescent Counseling Ctr., N.C., 1981, Family Therapy Ctr., Raleigh, 1981-82; staff psychologist Ctr. for Growth and Devel. (Burroughs Wellcome Co. employee assistance program), Raleigh, 1982—; cons. diagnostician Bd. Edn., Cumberland County, N.C., 1984; cons. psychologist Bd. Edn., Cumberland County, Burlington City, N.C., Johnston County, N.C., 1985. Mem. Am. Psychol. Assn. (student affiliate), Can. Psychol. Assn., Am. Assn. Counseling and Devel., AAUW, Psi Chi (treas. 1980-81). Presbyterian. Avocations: painting; ballet theatre. Office: Ctr for Growth and Devel 3700 Computer Dr Raleigh NC 27609

EDWARDS, CARLA FAYE, university administrator; b. West Palm Beach, Fla., May 9, 1955; d. Freeman and Esther (Cargill) E. B.A., Jacksonville U., 1977; M.S., Fla. State U., 1978. Head resident, residence student devel. Fla. Stat. U., Tallahassee, 1977-78; asst. residence hall coordinator U. Tex., Austin, 1978-80; asst. dir. housing for residence life, div. of housing, U. Fla. Gainesville, 1980—. Vol. big sister Big Bros./Sisters, Gainesville, 1981—. Mem. Am. Assn. for Counseling and Devel., Am. Coll. Personnel Assn., Am. Soc. for Tng. and Devel., Assn. Coll. and Univ. Housing Officers. Democrat. Mem. Ch. of Christ. Avocations: piano; reading; sewing. Home and Office: Broward Area Office U of Fla Gainesville FL 32612

EDWARDS, CHARLES EDWARD, educator; b. Charleston, S.C., July 19, 1930; s. Edward and Elizabeth (Orr) E.; B.S., Ga. Inst. Tech., 1952, M.S., 1953; Ph.D., U. N.C., 1961; m. Carol Latimer Little, Apr. 28, 1951; children—Mary Lynn, Charles Edward, Betty Ann, John Orr. Part time instr. Ga. Inst. Tech., Atlanta, 1952-53, U. N.C., Chapel Hill, 1955-58; asst. prof. U. S.C., Columbia, 1959-63, asso. prof., 1963-68, prof. bus. adminstrn., 1968—; bd. dirs. Child Centers, Inc., Columbus, Ga. Served with USAF, 1953-55. Faculty fellow for advanced research and study So. Fellowships Fund, 1958-59, Ford Found. regional seminar in econs., summer 1962. Mem. Am. Fin. Assn., Fin. Mgmt. Assn., Eastern Fin. Assn., Western Fin. Assn., So. Fin. Assn. Presbyterian. Author: Dynamics of the U.S. Automobile Industry, 1965; contbr. articles to profl. jours. Home: 4615 Limestone St Columbia SC 29206 Office: Univ South Carolina Columbia SC 29208

EDWARDS, CHARLES WEAVER, programmer; b. Elizabethtown, N.C., Feb. 24, 1955; s. Robert Lee and Frances Inez (Hair) E. A.A.S., Gaston Coll., 1978; diploma in machine tool tech. York Tech. Coll., 1975. Cert. engring. technician Nat. Inst. Certification in Engring. Tech. Machinist Duff-Norton Co., Charlotte, N.C., 1975-76; numerical control programmer Textile div. Warner & Swasey, 1976-81, Metrology Products div. Jones & Lamson-Textron, York, S.C., 1981—. Mem. Soc. Mfg. Engrs. Republican. Baptist. Home: 2303 Kingsburry Rd York SC 29745 Office: 501 Kings Mountain St York SC 29745

EDWARDS, DARRELL JERI, construction company executive; b. Marshall, Tex., Oct. 27, 1943; s. William Osband and Velma Floriene (Scholars) E.; m. Deborah Roberts, Apr. 5, 1969; children—Darrell Jeri Jr., Dana Clair. B.B.A., North Tex. State U., 1966. Estimator, LTV Aerospace Co., Dallas, 1966-68, W.T. Hall Constrn. Co., Marshall, 1968-69; supt. Norwood Homes, Houston, 1969-71; purchasing agt. L.O.G. Devel. Co., Houston, 1972-74; owner, chief exec. officer Darrell Edwards, Inc., San Antonio, 1974—. Mem. Greater San Antonio Bldgs Assn. Methodist. Lodge: Kiwanis. Avocations: importing European sport horses; cattle ranching; fishing. Home: 706 Garraty Rd San Antonio TX 78209 Office; Darrell Edwards Inc 173 Ira Lee San Antonio TX 78218

EDWARDS, DEL M(OUNT), business executive; b. Tyler, Tex., Apr. 12, 1953; s. Welby Clell and Davida (Mount) E.; m. Susan Alicia Pappas, Apr. 28, 1984. A.A. cum laude, Tyler Jr. Coll., 1974; B.B.A., Baylor U., 1976. Corp. coordinator Dillard Dept. Stores, Inc., Fort Worth, Tex., 1976-77; exec. v.p. W. C. Supply, Inc., Tyler, 1977—; pres., owner Walker Auto Spring, Inc., Shreveport, La., 1978—, Edwards & Assocs., Inc., Tyler, 1984—; v.p. W. C. Square, Inc., 1976—; dir. So. Automotive Show, Dallas, 1981-84. Chmn. Rose Garden Trust Fund, 1981—; originator designers showcase house Connally-Musselman House, Tyler, 1983—. Bd. dirs. Camp Tyler Found., 1984—, East Tex. Fair Assn., 1984—, Carnegie History Ctr., 1984-85. Mem. Council Fleet Specialists, Tyler Area C. of C., Smith County Hist. Soc./Hist. Commn. (pres., chmn. bd. govs. 1984-85), Tyler Jaycees (bd. dirs. 1981-85), SCV (treas. camp 124, 1978-80). Baptist. Clubs: Tyler Petroleum, Willow Brook Country (Tyler). Home: 3415 S Keaton Ave Tyler TX 75701 also Mountwood Ranch Route 2 Box 213 Tyler TX 75704 Office: WC Square Front at Bonner Sts Tyler TX 75710 also 1041 Jordan St Shreveport LA 71101

EDWARDS, EDWIN WASHINGTON, governor of Louisiana; b. Marksville, La., Aug. 7, 1927; s. Clarence W. and Agnes (Brouillette) E.; J.D., La. State U., 1949; m. Elaine Schwartzenburg, Apr. 5, 1949; children—Anna Edwards Edmonds, Victoria Elaine Edwards Arledge, Stephen Randolph, David Edwin. Admitted to La. bar, 1949; practiced in Crowley, La., from 1949, Baton Rouge, La., 1980-84; sr. partner firm Edwards, Edwards & Broadhurst; mem. Crowley City Council, 1954-62, La. Senate from 35th dist., 1964-66; mem. 89th-92d Congresses from 7th La. dist.; gov. La., 1972-80, 84—. Chmn. Interstate Oil Compact Commn., Ozarks Regional Commn., So. Govs.' Conf., So. Regional Energy Adv. Bd. Served with USNR, World War II. Mem. Internat. Rice Festival, Greater Crowley C. of C., Crowley Indsl. Found., Am. Legion. Democrat. Roman Catholic. Lion. Office: Office of Governor PO Box 44004 Baton Rouge LA 70804

EDWARDS, ELTON, lawyer; b. Wayne County, N.C., Aug. 14, 1923; s. Charles Henry and Lillie Estelle (Thornton) E.; B.A., U. N.C., 1943, J.D., 1948; postgrad. Auburn U., 1943-44, U. Nebr., 1944; m. Jessie Macon Sapp, Mar. 27, 1954; children—Elton Thornton, Ruth Macon. Bar: N.C., U.S. Ct. Appeals (4th cir.), U.S. Ct. Mil. Appeals; sole practice, 1949-54; assoc. Moseley and Edwards, Greensboro, 1954-69, Moseley, Edwards and Greeson, 1969-71, Edwards, Greeson and Toumaras, 1971-77, Edwards, Greeson, Weeks and Turner, 1977-82, Edwards and Weeks, 1982-83; sole practice, Greensboro, 1983—; sec. Handi-Clean Products, Inc., Greensboro, 1965—, Triad Bank, 1982—. Mem. N.C. Bd. Juvenile Correction, 1955-65; mem. N.C. Senate, 1969-71, 83-84, N.C. Ho. of Reps., 1965-69. Served with U.S. Army, 1943-45; col. USAF ret. Decorated Legion of Merit. Mem. ABA, N.C., Bar Assn., Greensboro Bar Assn. Democrat. Presbyterian. Clubs: Greensboro City; Army-Navy (Washington). Lodges: Masons, Shriners. Home: 3815 Madison Ave Greensboro NC 27403 Office: PO Box 448 Greensboro NC 27402

EDWARDS, EUGENE, electronic engineer; b. Fairfield, Ala., June 9, 1953; s. Robert and Henrietta (Bennett) E. B.S. in Engring. Tech., Ala. A&M U., 1974; M.S. in E.E., Howard U., 1976. Engring. fellow NASA-MSFC, Huntsville, Ala., summers 1979, 80; prof./engr. Ala. A&M U., Huntsville, 1977-81; electronic engr. U.S. Army Primary Standards Lab., Huntsville, 1981—; prof. engring. Oakwood Coll., Huntsville, summer 1979; engring. and ednl. cons. Advisor/cons. Boys Club of Am., 1976—; music dir. ch. groups, 1971—. Whirlpool fellow Howard U., 1974; NASA fellow, 1980, 79. Mem. IEEE, Am. Soc. Engring. Edn., Am. Nuclear Soc., Nat. Tech. Assn., Internat. Assn. for Hydrogen Energy, Sigma Xi, Pi Theta Gamma. Democrat. Baptist. Contbr. articles to profl. jours. Home: 6220 Sandia Blvd NW Huntsville AL 35810 Office: SEPD US Army Missile Command Attn AMSMI-EE Redstone Arsenal AL 35898

EDWARDS, GEORGE CHARLES, III, political science educator, author; b. Rochester, N.Y., Jan. 3, 1947; s. George Charles Jr. and Mary Elizabeth (Laing) E.; m. Carmella Rose Pierce, May 22, 1981; 1 child, Jeffrey Allan. B.A., Stetson U., 1969; M.A., U. Wis., 1970, Ph.D., 1973. Asst. prof. polit. sci. Tulane U., New Orleans, 1973-78; assoc. prof. polit. sci. Tex. A&M U., College Station, 1978-81, prof., 1981—; vis. asst. prof. U. Wis.-Madison, 1976; vis. prof. U.S. Mil. Acad., West Point, N.Y., 1985—; pres. Presidency Research Group, 1984—; lectr. U.S. Info. Service, Europe, 1985; cons. NSF, Washington, 1977—. Author: Presidential Leadership 1985; The Public Presidency, 1983; Presidential Influence In Congress, 1980; Implementing Public Policy, 1980; The Policy Predicament, 1978; Editor: The Presidency and Public Policy Making, 1985; Studying The Presidency, 1983; Public Policy Implementations, 1984; Perspectives on Public Policy-Making, 1976. Mem. editorial bd. Am. Jour. Polit. Sci., 1985—, Am. Politics Quar. 1981—, Presdl. Studies Quar., 1978—, Congress and the Presidency, 1981—, Policy Studies Jour., 1981-83. Contbr. articles to profl. jours. Pres., Greenfield Plaza Condominium Assn., Bryan, Tex., 1980-81; mem. East Tex. 2000 Commn., 1980-81. Served to capt. USAR, 1971-79. Woodrow Wilson fellow 1969, Ford Fellow 1970-73. Mem. Am. Polit. Sci. Assn. (sect. pres. 1984—), So. Polit. Sci. Assn., Midwest Polit. Sci. Assn., Policy Studies Orgn., Ctr. Study of Presidency (bd. dirs. 1978—), Phi Beta Kappa, Pi Sigma Alpha, Phi Alpha Theta, Pi Alpha Alpha. Avocations: collecting art, skiing, tennis, travel. Home: 2317 Bristol Bryan TX 77802 Office: Tex A&M U Dept Polit Sci College Station TX 77843

EDWARDS, GEORGE JOHN, researcher, consultant; b. Jackson Center, Pa., June 27, 1921; s. John C. and Marie Emily (Falkenstine) E.; m. Helen Clair Dahlgren, May 6, 1949; children—Patty, Jane, Carol, Christie. B.A., Bridgewater Coll., 1946. Geophysicist U.S. Geol. Survey, Washington, 1947-51; jr. chemist Internat. Mineral and Chems., Mulberry, Fla., 1951-52; asst. prof. remote sensing U. Fla. Citrus Research and Ednl. Ctr., Lake Alfred, Fla., 1952—. Recipient Best Paper award Fla. Hort. Soc., 1972; Civic Service award Am. Chem. Soc., 1977. Mem. Am. Photogrammetric Soc., Remote Sensing Soc. Can., Am. Soc. Photogrammetry and Remote Sensing (bd. dirs. Fla. sect.), Remote Sensing Soc. (London), Research Soc. N.Am. (sec.). Democrat. Presbyterian. Clubs: Ridge Model Railroad, Masons. Office: 700 Experiment Station Rd Lake Alfred FL 33850

EDWARDS, GERALD, geophysicist; b. Denton, Md., July 31, 1951; s. Harold Harrison and Helen Ana (Shia) E.; m. Alicia Maria Gonzalez, Sept. 30, 1983; m. Diane Marie Brooks, Aug 31, 1976 (div. Sept. 1983). B.S., U. Nev., 1973; M.S., N.E. La. U., 1975; D. Geol. Scis., U. Tex., El Paso, 1985. Vis. prof. Peace Corps, Polytechnic U., Guayaquil, Ecuador, 1975-77, U. Costa Rica, San Jose, 1977-78; geophysicist Texaco Latin Am./West Africa, Coral Gables, 1980—. Mem. Am. Assn. Petroleum Geologists, Soc. Econ. Geologists, Miami Geol. Soc. Republican. Avocations: photography; horse riding; reading; classical music. Office: Texaco Latin Am/West Africa 150 Alhambra Circle Coral Gables FL 33134

EDWARDS, HARRY LAFOY, lawyer; b. Greenville, S.C., July 29, 1936; s. George Belton and Mary Olive (Jones) E.; m. Suzanne Copeland, June 16, 1956; 1 dau., Margaret Peden. LL.B., U. S.C., 1963, J.D., 1970. Bar: S.C. 1963, U.S. Dist. Ct. S.C. 1975, U.S. Ct. Appeals (4th cir.) 1974. Assoc. Edwards and Edmunds, Greenville, 1963; v.p., sec., dir. Edwards Co., Inc., Greenville, 1963-65; atty. investment legal dept. Liberty Life Ins. Co., Greenville, 1965-67, asst. sec., asst. v.p., head investment legal dept., 1967-70; asst. sec. Liberty Corp., 1970-75; asst. v.p. Liberty Life Ins. Co., 1970-75; sec. Bent Tree Corp., CEL, Inc., 1970-75; sec., dir. Westchester Mall, Inc., 1970-75; asst. sec. Libco, Inc., Liberty Properties, Inc., 1970-75; sole practice, Greenville, 1975—. Com. mem. Hipp Fund Spl. Edn., Greenville County Sch. System; mem. Boyd C. Hipp, II Scholarship Com. Wofford Coll., Spartanburg, S.C., B. Calhoun Hipp Scholarship, U. S.C. Served with USAFR, 1957-63. Mem. ABA, S.C. Bar Assn., Greenville County Bar Assn., Phi Delta Phi. Baptist. Clubs: Greenville Lawyers, Poinsett (Greenville). Home: 106 Ridgeland Dr Greenville SC 29601 Office: PO Box 10350 Federal Station Greenville SC 29603

EDWARDS, JACK, retail department store company executive; b. 1933. Student, U. N.C., 1953; B.A., Harvard U., 1955, M.B.A., 1959. Vice pres. mktg. Jewel Co. Chgo., 1959-77; pres., chief operating officer Cornwall Equities Ltd., 1977-79; sr. v.p., gen. merchandise mgr. Ames Dept. Stores, 1979-82; with Rose's Stores, Inc., Henderson, N.C., 1982—, exec. v.p. sales, merchandising ops., 1982-84, pres., chief operating officer, dir., 1984—. Served with U.S. Army, 1955-57. Address: Rose's Stores Inc PO Box 947 Henderson NC 27536*

EDWARDS, JAMES BENJAMIN, accountant, educator, data processor, researcher, consultant; b. Atlanta, Apr. 27, 1935; s. James T. and Frances L. (McEachern) E.; m. Virginia Ann Reagin, Feb. 21, 1958; children—James Benjamin II, Chad Reagin, Calli Ann, Judy Clair. B.B.A., U. Ga., 1958, M.B.A., 1962, Ph.D., 1971. C.P.A., Tenn., Ga., S.C. Controller Better Maid Dairy Products, Inc., Athens, Ga., 1958-62; auditor Max M. Cuba & Co., C.P.A.s, Atlanta, 1962-63; ptnr. Wilson, Edwards & Swang, C.P.A.'s, Nashville, 1964-66; instr. David Lipscomb Coll., Nashville, 1963-66; instr. U. Ga., Athens, 1966-71; asst. prof. acctg. U. S.C., Columbia, 1971-73, assoc. prof., 1973-77, prof., 1977—, U. S.C.-Bus. Partnership Found. fellow, 1979; internal cons. J.W. Hunt & Co., C.P.A.s, Columbia, 1983—; cons. in field, 1966—; speaker in field. Served with USMCR, 1954-62. Recipient 8 nat. awards for outstanding contbns. to acctg. lit. Pres. Ga. Christian Found., Inc., 1968-69; coach, officer Little League Baseball, 1972-77; treas. Spring Valley Band Boosters Club, 1975-83; v.p. Spring Valley Edn. Found., 1983-85; bd. dirs. Atlanta Bible Camp, Inc. Mem. Am. Inst. C.P.A.s, S.C. Soc. C.P.A.s, Am. Acctg. Assn. (nat. profl. cert. com. 1982-83), Nat. Assn. Accts. (cert. mgmt. acctg.; pres. Columbia chpt. 1973-74, pres. Carolinas Council 1976, nat. v.p. 1980-81, Disting. Service award Columbia chpt. 1975, named to Stuart Cameron McLeod Soc. for Leadership), S.C. Assn. Acctg. Instrs. (founding pres. 1972), Inst. Internal Auditors (chmn. Palmetto profl. cert. com. 1980-81, chmn. coll. and univ. relations com. 1982-83, Outstanding Mem. award of Palmetto chpt. 1980, cert internal auditor), Planning Execs. Inst. (asst. editor Managerial Planning mag. 1971-77), Am. Inst. Decision Scis. (v.p. Southeastern region 1975-76), Inst. for Cert. Computer Profls. (cert. data processing), Inst. Cost Analysis, (cert. cost analyst), Delta Sigma Pi, Beta Alpha Psi,

Omicron Delta Epsilon, Beta Gamma Sigma, Sigma Chi. Mem. Ch. of Christ. Home: 38 E Branch Ct Columbia SC 29223 Office: U SC Coll Bus Adminstrn Columbia SC 29208

EDWARDS, JAMES BURROWS, university president, oral surgeon; b. Hawthorne, Fla., June 24, 1927; s. O.M. Edwards; m. Ann Norris Darlington, Sept. 1, 1951; children—James B., Catharine Edwards Wingate. B.S., Coll. of Charleston, 1950, Litt.D., 1975; D.M.D., U. Louisville, 1955, D.Social Sci., 1982; postgrad. Advanced Corrolated Clin. Scis., U. Pa. Grad. Med. Sch., 1957-58; LL.D., U.S.C., 1975, Bob Jones U., 1976, The Citadel, 1977; D.Sc., Erskine Coll., 1982, Georgetown U., 1982; D.Hum., Francis Marion Coll., 1978, Bapt. Coll. at Charleston, 1981; others. Diplomate Am. Bd. Oral and Maxillofacial Surgery. Resident in oral surgery, Henry Ford Hosp., Detroit, 1958-60; practice dentistry specializing in oral and maxillofacial surgery, Charleston, S.C., 1960—; clin. assoc. in oral surgery Coll. Dental Medicine, Med. U. S.C., 1970-77, clin. asst. prof. oral surgery and community dentistry, 1977-82, prof. oral and maxillofacial surgery, 1982—, pres. univ., 1982—; gov. State of S.C., 1975-78; U.S. sec. of energy, 1981-82; First Nat. Bank of S.C., Columbia, First Bankshares Corp., Columbia, J. P. Stevens & Co., Inc., N.Y.C., Phillips Petroleum Co., Bartlesville, Okla., Burris Chem., Inc., Charleston, William Benton Found., Chgo., Support Systems Internat., Inc., Charleston. Trustee Baker Hosp., Charleston, Coll. of Charleston Found.; bd. dirs. Harry Frank Guggenheim Found., N.Y.C.; past bd. dirs. Coastal Carolina Council Boy Scouts Am.; past trustee Charleston County Hosp., Greater Charleston YMCA, Coll. Preparatory Sch., Charleston, Baker Meml. Hosp., Charleston; chmn. Charleston County Republican Com. 1964-69; del. to Nat. Rep. Convs., 1968, 72, 76, 80; chmn. 1st Congl. Dist. Rep. Com., 1970; mem. S.C. State Senate, 1972-74; chmn. subcom. on nuclear energy Nat. Govs. Assn., 1978; chmn. So. Govs. Conf., 1978; Fellow Am. Coll. Dentists, Internat. Coll. Dentists; mem. ADA, S.C. Dental Soc., Coastal Dist. Dental Soc. (past pres.), Chalmers J. Lyons Acad. Oral Surgery, Southeastern Soc. Oral and Maxillofacial Surgeons, Am. Soc. Oral and Maxillofacial Surgeons, Brit. Assn. Oral and Maxillofacial Surgeons, Internat. Soc. Oral and Maxillofacial Suregons, Fedn. Dentaire Internationale, S.C. Soc. Oral and Maxillofacial Surgeons (founder, charter mem., past pres.), Navy League U.S. (Charleston hosp. council), Oral Surgery Polit. Action Com. (founder, charter mem., chmn. bd. dirs. 1971-73), Pi Kappa Phi, Delta Sigma Delta, Omicron Delta Kappa. Served with U.S. Mcht. Marines, 1944-47, to lt. comdr. USNR, 1955-57. Clubs: Ahepa, Rotary, Masons. Office: Med U SC 171 Ashley Ave Charleston SC 29425

EDWARDS, JAMES EDWIN, lawyer; b. Clarkesville, Ga., July 29, 1914; s. Gus Calloway and Mary Clara (McKinney) E.; student U. Tex., 1931-33; B.A., George Washington U., 1935, J.D. cum laude, 1946; m. Frances Lillian Stanley, Nov. 22, 1948; children—Robin Anne, James Christopher, Clare (Mrs. Ronald C. Wilkson). Bar: to Fla. 1938, D.C. 1981. Practiced in Cocoa, Fla., 1938-42; divisional asst. Dept. State, 1945-50; practice law, Ft. Lauderdale, 1951-77, Coral Springs, 1977-81, 84-85; mem. firm Edwards & Leary, 1981-84; asst. city atty., Ft. Lauderdale, 1961, 63-65; city commr., Coral Springs, Fla., 1970-76, mayor, 1972-73; arbitrator Am. Arbitration Assn., 1984—. Chmn., Ft. Lauderdale for Eisenhower, 1952; Republican county parliamentarian, 1954-59; pres. Rep. Attys. Club Broward County, 1960-64. Served to lt. USCGR, 1942-45; lt. col. USAF Res. ret. Mem. Fla. Fla. Bar Assb., Sportsmen's Assn. (pres. 1967-68), Broward Sportsmen's Soc. (pres. 1983-84), Fla. Conservative Union (chpt. pres. 1976), Broward Sportsmen's Soc. (pres. 1983-84), Delta Sigma Rho, Pi Gamma Mu, Phi Delta Phi, Phi Sigma Kappa. Clubs: Rotary, Gold Coast Dressage Assn. Author: Myths About Guns, 1978. Home and Office: PO Drawer 88 Keswick VA 22947

EDWARDS, JAMES MELVIN, wholesale company executive; b. N.Y.C., Feb. 25, 1942; s. Jackson A. and Natalie E.; B.S. in Bus. Adminstrn., Boston U., 1963; m. Debra Edwards, Aug. 2, 1981; children—Jon Stuart, Meredith Joy. Mgr., dist. mgr., asst. treas., treas. Associated Ind. Theatres, N.Y.C., 1963-65; with Tujax Electric Supply Co., 1965-73, v.p., 1970-73, br. mgr., 1965-73; v.p., br. mgr. Consol. Electric Supply Co., Hollywood, Fla., 1973-76, v.p. hdqrs., Miami, 1976—, pres. Internat. div., 1981-85. Bd. dirs. Temple Solel, Hollywood, 1976-82, mem. adv. bd., 1983-86; sustaining mem. Republican Nat. Com., 1976-80; bd. dirs. South Broward High Sch. Band Patrons Assn., 1981-82, v.p., 1982-83, pres., 1983; life mem. Rep. Party, 1979—. Mem. Illuminating Engring. Soc. N.Am., Young Execs. of Today div. Nat. Assn. Elect. Distbrs. Club: Lions (1st v.p. 1977-78). Office: 7000 NW 52d St Miami FL 33166

EDWARDS, JOAN ARNOLD, pharmacist; b. Austin, Tex., July 21, 1947; d. Olice and Mary Alice (Hill) Arnold; m. Kenneth Ralp Edwards, Jan. 26, 1969 (div. Jan. 1975); children—Kenneth, Rondal. B.S. in Pharmacy, Tex. So. U., 1970. Staff pharmacist Meml. NW Hosp., Houston, 1970-72, Meml. SE Hosp., 1972-74, Meml. SW Hosp., 1974—. Baptist. Avocation: tennis. Home: 8505 Ariel St Houston TX 77074 Office: Meml Hosp System 7600 Beachnut St Houston TX 77074

EDWARDS, JOHN DAVID, geologist; b. Hackensack, N.J., June 17, 1925; s. David and Helen (Davidson) E.; m. Joan Fessenden, July 4, 1946; children—David, Charles, Heather, Hope, Helen. B.S. in Mech. Engring., Cornell U., 1946; M.A., in Geology, Columbia U., 1950, Ph.D. in Geology, 1952. Mgr. exploration ops. Latin Am., Pecten Internat. Co., Houston, 1980—. Fellow Geol. Soc. Am.; mem. Am. Assn. Petroleum Geologists (editorial bd.). Home: 11711 Memorial Dr Apt 197 Houston TX 77024 Office: Pecten Internat Co PO Box 205 Houston TX 77001

EDWARDS, JOHN RAYMOND, JR., real estate developer, resorts owner; b. New Haven, June 18, 1944; s. John Raymond and Christina (Forsyth) E.; m. Margaret S. Salomone, July 16, 1983; children—Jennifer, John Raymond. B.B.A., Hofstra U., 1970. Pres., America Outdoors, Key Largo, Fla., 1970—; v.p. Rock Harbor Devel. Corp., Key Largo, 1973—; gen. ptnr. Resort Enterprises, Tavernier, Fla., 1978—, Sheraton Hotel, Key Largo; Fund raiser ARC, Key Largo, 1975-80, Upper Keys Guidance Clinic, Tavernier, 1983. Served to 1st lt. U.S. Army, 1966-69. Decorated Purple Heart, Bronze Star, others; Vietnamese Cross of Gallantry. Democrat. Clubs: Islamorada Fishing, The Forest (Ft. Myers). Home: 21 N Bounty Ln Key Largo FL 33037 Office: America Outdoors PO Box 420 Tavernier FL 33070

EDWARDS, J(OSEPH) D(ANIEL), JR., chemist, educator; b. Alexandria, La., Nov. 25, 1924; s. Joseph Daniel and Florence Coral (Hoell) E.; 1 child, Lauresia Catherine. B.S. with spl. distinction, La. Coll., Pineville, 1944; M.A., U. Tex., 1948, Ph.D., 1950; postdoctoral U. Ill., 1950-51. Chemist, Fercleve Corp., Oak Ridge, 1944, U.S. Naval Research Lab., Phila., 1945; sr. research scientist VA Research Lab., Houston, 1951-59; asst. prof. Baylor U. Coll. Medicine, Houston, 1951-59; assoc. prof. Clemson U., S.C., 1959; assoc. prof. Lamar U., Beaumont, Tex., 1960-65, prof., 1965-67; prof. chemistry U. Southwestern La., Lafayette, 1967—, head chemistry dept., 1967-72; sr. research chemist Monsanto Chem. Co., Texas City, Tex., 1959; invited lectr. Clemson U., 1958, U.S. Dept. Agr. Conf., 1959, Carl M. Lyman Meml. Symposium, Am. Oil Chemists Soc., 1970, Baylor U., 1968. Robert A. Welch Found. grantee, Univ. grantee Lamar U., 1962-67; Cotton Research Commn. fellow, Austin, Tex., 1947-50; Coop. Coll.-Sch. Sci. Program grantee NSF, 1969-70. Fellow Chem. Soc. (London); mem. Am. Chem. Soc., Phytochem. Soc. N.Am., Phi Lambda Upsilon, Sigma Xi, Alpha Chi. Democrat. Baptist. Avocations; travel, coin collecting, Boys Club work. Home: 401 Brentwood Blvd Lafayette LA 70503 Office: 130 Montgomery Hall Univ of Southwestern La Lafayette LA 70504

EDWARDS, LATRELLE NIX, educator; b. Hall County, Ga., Jan. 19, 1945; d. J. L. and Sarah Frances (Highsmith) Nix; m. Billy Wayne Edwards, July 30, 1963; children—John Christian, Sarah Frances. Student Truett-McConnell Jr. Coll., 1963-64; A.B., Piedmont Coll., 1964-67. Tchr., White County Elem. Sch., Cleveland, Ga., 1967—. Mem. NEA, Ga. Assn. Educators, White County Assn. Educators. Democrat. Baptist. Home: PO Box 458 Cleveland GA 30528

EDWARDS, MARVIN H. MICKEY, congressman; b. Cleve., July 12, 1937; s. Edward A. and Rosalie (Miller) E.; m. Lisa Reagan. B.J., Okla. U., 1958; J.D., Oklahoma City U., 1969. Dir. pub. relations Beals Advt. Agy., Oklahoma City, 1964-68; editor Pvt. Practice mag., 1968-73; spl. legis. cons. Republican Steering Com., Washington, 1973-74; tchr. law and journalism Oklahoma City U., 1975-76; mem. 95th-98th Congresses from 5th Okla. Dist., House Appropriations com. (various subcoms.); asst. House Rep. whip, vice chmn. Nat. Rep. Congressional Com.; organizer, supr. congressional adv. com. to Reagan presdl. campaign.; Chmn. Am. Conservative Union. Editor: Muskogee (Okla.) Daily Phoenix, 1958-59; reporter, editor: Oklahoma City Times, 1959-63; Author: Hazardous to Your Health, 1972, Behind Energy Lines, 1983. Recipient Freedom Founds. medal (3); named Outstanding Young Man Am., 1973. Mem. Sigma Delta Chi, Phi Delta Phi. Clubs: Masons (32 deg.), Kiwanis. Address: Office of House Members House of Representatives Washington DC 20515*

EDWARDS, MICHAEL DEREK, dentist; b. Birmingham, Ala., May 13, 1953; s. Hyman Monroe and Patricia Ann (Coburn) E.; m. Terri Lynn Earley, Dec. 14, 1973; 1 child, Michael Brent. B.S., U. Ala., 1975, D.M.D., 1979. Extern, U.S. Dept. Health, St. Ignatius, Mont., 1979; pvt. practice dentistry, Wedowee, Ala., 1979—; pres. Profl. Corp., Wedowee, 1980—; mem. staff Wedowee Hosp., Randolph County Hosp.; advisor Randolph County Health Council, 1981—. Served with USPHS, 1978-79. Recipient Outstanding Achievement award Acad. Operative Dentistry, 1979; State Ala. scholar, 1975. Mem. ADA, Internat. Assn. Orthodontics (mem. study-teaching group), Am. Assn. Functional Orthopedics, Ala. Dental Assn., Ala. Implant Study Group, Ala. 5th Dist. Dental Soc., U.S. C. of C., Wedowee Jaycees, Omicron Kappa Upsilon. Methodist. Club: 150 Flying (Roanoke, Ala.). Home: 65 Ester Circle Wedowee AL 36278 Office: 605 N Main St Wedowee AL 36278

EDWARDS, PHYLLIS HALL, teacher; b. Altavista, Va., Aug. 1, 1950; d. James Thomas Hall and Ruby Inez (Roberts) H.; m. Joseph Elwood Edwards, Jr., Mar. 27, 1971; children—Joseph Gordon, Heather Marie. B.S. in Elem. Edn., Campbell U., 1973. Children's librarian Oxford (N.C.) Pub. Library, 1972; tchr., Bunnlevel, N.C., 1973-75, Harnett Middle Sch., Dunn, N.C., 1975-85, Dunn Middle Sch., 1985—; mentor tchr., 1985—. Rec. sec. Dunn Homemakers Club, 1978-79, pres., 1979-80; den leader Cub Scout Pack 719, Dunn, 1983-84; dir. children's handbell choir First Bapt. Ch., Dunn, 1984—, also mem. choir, mission friends leader. Mem. NEA (sec. local chpt. 1979-80). Baptist. Office: Dunn Middle Sch N Orange Ave Dunn NC 28334

EDWARDS, RAOUL DURANT, writer, editor, consultant; b. N.Y.C., Nov. 3, 1928; s. Louis Durant and Gloss Edwards; student NYU, 1957-58, U. Chgo., 1970-72; m. Jean Guthrie, Nov. 22, 1958; children—Guthrie Hamilton, Jonathan Valentine. Asst. mng. editor Am. Banker, N.Y.C., 1953-62, Washington bur. chief, 1962-63; asst. to bd. FDIC, Washington, 1963-66; dir. pub. relations Bank Adminstrn. Inst., Park Ridge, Ill., 1966-70; prin. R.D. Edwards & Assocs., Park Ridge, 1971-73, Falls Church, Va., 1973—; assoc. editor U.S. Banker mag., 1977-80, sr. editor, 1981-83, editor, 1983—; sr. editor Issues and Innovations, 1982—; editorial dir. Fin. Computing, 1984-85; guest lectr. Va. Commonwealth U., Richmond, 1977—. Del., Va. Rep. State Conv., 1978, 80, 81. Mem. N.Y. Fin. Writers Assn., Electronic Banking Econs. Soc., World Future Soc., Exchequer Club Consumer/Bus. Fin. Services Forum (chm. exec. com. 1985—). Republican. Baptist. Gen. editor ATM Program Success. Author: NOW Account Planning Strategies; co-author: The Changing World of Banking. Contbr. articles to newspapers, mags., jours. Home and Office: 5927 Merritt Pl Falls Church VA 22041

EDWARDS, RICHARD PAUL, JR., chiropractor; b. Cherry Point, N.C., Jan. 22, 1955; s. Richard Paul and Marilyn Joyce (Drewry) E.; m. Cindy Lou Edwards, May 27, 1978; children—Richie, Ryan. A.S., York Christian Coll. (Nebr.), 1976; D.Chiropractic, Palmer Coll. Chiropractic, Davenport, Iowa, 1980. Diplomate Nat. Bd. Chiropractic Examiners. Chiropractor, corp. pres. Edwards Clinic, P.C., Edmond, Okla., 1983—. Mem. Am. Bus. Men's Assn. (2d v.p., weekly dir. programs 1983-84, sponsorship chmn. 1982-83), Parker Chiropractic Research Found., Am. Chiropractic Assn., Okla. Chiropractic Assn. (chmn. state legis. com.), Chiropractic Assn. Okla., Edmond C. of C. (acting ambassador 1983-84, named Ambassador of Month 1983), Internat. Chiropractic Assn., Chiropractic Mgmt. Assn. (named baron of chiropractic). Republican. Mem. Ch. of Christ. Lodges: Kiwanis, Masons. Home: 1213 Bluff Creek Edmond OK 73034 Office: Edwards Clinic of Chiropractic PC 163 SE 33d St Edmond OK 73034

EDWARDS, RICHARD WAYNE, architect; b. Jonesboro, Ark., Apr. 3, 1947; s. John Richard and Tuleet Hester (Tarpley) E.; B.Arch., U. Ark., 1971; m. Cynthia Janet Russo, Apr. 6, 1974; children—Erica Elizabeth, Jilla Alissa. With Langwith, Wilson, King Assos., Houston, 1971—, project architect, 1976-78, asso., 1978—, project mgr.. 1979—; prin. works include: Agrl. Research Farm, Tex. Tech. U., 1974-78; Internat. Goat Research Facility, Prairie View A&M U., 1980-82, phys. plant/transp. ctr. complex, 1982-84; restoration First United Meth. Ch., Huntsville, Tex., 1978; Intercontinental Terminals Co. office bldg., Deer Park, Tex., 1981; Sercel, Inc. office bldg., Houston, 1979; Westheimer Oaks Office Park, Houston, 1976; Westheimer Oaks Shopping Complex, Houston, 1976. Mem. AIA (chmn. internship and licensing com. 1977-80, co-chmn. intern devel. program 1979-81), Nat. Council Archtl. Registration Bds., Tex. Soc. Architects, Constrn. Specifications Inst., U. Ark. Alumni Assn. (past pres., dir.). Methodist. Club: Century (U. Ark.). Home: 7014 Pyron Way Houston TX 77036 Office: 17 S Briar Hollow Suite 100 Houston TX 77027

EDWARDS, ROBERT LEE, educational administrator; b. Slocomb, Ala., Jan. 30, 1939; s. Joseph Colley and Elsie Lee (Dunn) E.; B.S., Bethune-Cookman Coll., 1965; Leadership cert. Platt Inst., 1966; M.S., CCNY, 1973; Achievement cert. Opportunities Acad. Mgmt. Tng., 1974; m. Barbara Jean Spalding, Aug. 26, 1967; children—Randy Keith, Robert Corey. Tchr., Dade County Public Schs., Miami, Fla., 1965-66, prin., 1974—, prin. Jan Mann Opportunity Sch., 1977-83, prin. Charles R. Drew Jr. High Sch., Miami, 1983—; dir. Brownsville Community Council, Bklyn., 1966-70; br. mgr. Opportunities Industrialization Center, N.Y.C., 1970-74; cons., lectr. in field. Bd. dirs. Family Planning Center, N.Y.C., 1968-70; pres. Lexia Sch. for Young Adults, Lee, Mass., 1973-74; bd. dirs. Orgn. United for Regional Service, 1968-74; coordinator Brownsville Black Solidarity Day, 1968-69; rep. N.Y. Tenant Council, 1966-68; co-chmn. Bicentennial Football Classic, 1975-76; mem. coordinator evaluation team, nat. convocation Opportunities Industrialization Centers, 1973-74, edn. rep., 1970-74, recipient Supreme Dedication award, 1974, Disting. Service award, 1972; active YMCA. Served with inf. AUS, 1961-63. Recipient numerous awards from civic orgns., colls., ednl. instsn., groups. Mem. Nat. Assn. for Study Afro Am. Life and History (exec. council 1968-70, pres. Brownsville chpt. 1972-74), Adult Edn. Soc., Nat. Alliance Black Sch. Educators, NAACP (dir. Miami chpt. 1978—), Nat. Assn. for Public Continuing and Adult Edn., Nat. Assn. Elem. Sch. Prins., Nat. Assn. Secondary Sch. Prins., Assn. for Supervision and Curriculum Devel., Dade County Sch. Adminstrn. Assn., Bethune-Cookman Coll. Alumni Assn., Urban League Greater Miami, Kappa Alpha Psi (life). Home: 17241 NW 9th Pl Miami FL 33169 Office: Charles R Drew Jr High Sch 1801 NW 60th St Miami FL 33142

EDWARDS, ROBERT WILLIS, infectious disease researcher, educator, consultant; b. Paintsville, Ky., Feb. 4, 1950; s. Lloyd Ronald and Vera Velma (Conry) E. B.S., U. Ky.-Lexington, 1974; M.S., Eastern Ky. U., 1976; Ph.D., U. Ark., Fayetteville, 1980. Research asst. Eastern Ky. U., 1974-76; grad. asst. U. Ark., 1976-80; cons. Southeast Consortium for Internat. Devel., 1981; NIH/WHO postdoctoral fellow U. N.C., 1981—; cons. Dept. Health and Human Service, 1983, dir. Migrant Worker Parasitology Study; cons. pub. health and infectious disease in 3d world countries. Vol. paramedic, Prestonburg, Ky., 1972-76. Mem. AAAS, Am. Soc. Trop. Medicine and Hygiene, Am. Soc. Parasitologists, Soc. Protozoologists, U. Ky. Alumni Assn., Sigma Xi., Phi Sigma. Democrat. Baptist. Contbr. articles in field to profl. jours. Home: 3 Silver Cedar Ln Chapel Hill NC 27514 Office: U NC Dept Parasitology and Lab Medicine SPH Rosenau Hall 201-H Chapel Hill NC 27514

EDWARDS, RONNIE PHILIP, psychology educator; b. Tulsa, Apr. 8, 1943; s. James Price Edwards and June (Lisle) Bishop; m. Carol Jean, Jan. 11, 1964 (div. 1973); children—Michael, Alicia; m. Jean Louise Stevens, Jan. 11, 1974. B.S., Okla. State U., 1966; M.A., U. Iowa, 1968, Ph.D., 1970. Dir. grad. study, asst. prof. dept. psychology Western Carolina U., Cullowhee, N.C., 1970-75; asst. prof. U. S.C., Columbia, 1975-78, U. So. Miss., Hattiesburg, 1978-79, assoc. prof., 1978-84, prof. psychology, 1984—, dir. sch. psychology tng., 1981—. Contbr. articles to profl. jours. Mem. Am. Psychol. Assn., Nat. Assn. Sch. Psychologists (del. 1982—), Miss. Assn. Psychology in the Schs. (charter, pres. 1981-82, Disting. Service award 1984). Republican. Avocations: computer programming; reading; music; travel. Home: PO Box 288 Purvis MS 39475 Office: Dept Psychology U So Miss Southern Station Box 5025 Hattiesburg MS 39406

EDWARDS, SCOTT ELROY, airline pilot; b. Athens, Ohio, Aug. 6, 1947; s. Thomas E. and Vera J. Edwards; m. Sandra L. Karczmarek, June 29, 1974; children—Randy L., Kimberley J. B.A. in History, Allegheny Coll., 1969; M.A. in Indsl. Mgmt., Central Mich. U., 1974. Pres. Stanley Printing, Inc., Marathon, Fla., 1974-79; capt. B-737 Air Florida, Miami, 1979—. Served to capt. USAF, 1969-74. Mem. Am. Legion. Republican. Methodist. Lodge: Rotary. Home: 17781 SW 52d Ct Fort Lauderdale FL 33331

EDWARDS, SCOTT SAMUEL, JR., lawyer; b. Atlanta, Apr. 16, 1915; s. Scott Samuel and Maggie (Harris) E., Sr.; J.D., Woodrow Wilson Coll., 1941; m. Jeanette Victoria Smith, Nov. 14, 1945; 1 son, David Scott. Bar: Ga. 1941. Practice law, Marietta, Ga., 1946—; ptnr. firm Edwards, Friedewald & Grayson; asst. county atty., Cobb County, 1948-53; atty. City of Marietta, 1948-60, Kennestone Hosp., Marietta, 1948-73; bar examiner State of Ga., 1972-73; Amicus Curiae of Supreme Ct. Ga., 1980. Served with Signal Corps, AUS, 1941-45; PTO. Mem. ABA, Ga., Cobb County (pres. 1955-56) bar assns., Am. Legion. Presbyterian. Club: Civitan (pres. 1952-53; Honor Key 1973). Home: 330 S Woodland Dr Marietta GA 30064 Office: 272 Washington Ave Marietta GA 30060

EDWARDS, STEVE, physics educator, dean; b. Quincy, Fla., June 16, 1930; s. Steve and Sarah Frances (Ryan) E.; m. Helen Wallace Carothers, Dec. 17, 1964; children—Ashley Lynn, Leigh Holladay. B.S., Fla. State U., 1952, M.S., 1954; Ph.D. (Gen. Motors fellow), Johns Hopkins U., 1960. Grad. asst. Fla. State U., Tallahassee, 1952-55, asst. prof. physics, 1960-65, assoc. prof., 1965-69, prof., 1969—, dean of faculties, dep. provost, 1985—, assoc. chmn. physics, 1965-73, chmn. physics, 1973-79, chmn., athletic bd., 1980, pres. faculty senate, 1983-85; jr. qnstr. Johns Hopkins U., 1955-57; dir. Recon, Inc., Tallahassee, 1960-65, staff coms., 1965-70. Author: Lectures on the Theory of Direct Reactions, 1961; General Physics, 1968; Physics-A Discovery Approach, 1971, paperback edition 1982. Contbr. articles to profl. jours. Recipient Coyle E. Moore award Fla. State U., 1965; named Ky. Col. Mem. Am. Assn. Physics Tchrs., Am. Phys. Soc. (chmn. Southeastern sect. 1982-83), Order De Molay, (chevalier degree 1949, legion of honor 1963), Sigma Xi, Sigma Pi Sigma (zone supr. Southeastern U.S. 1962-65), Gamma Alpha, Kappa Sigma, Phi Mu Alpha Sinfonia, Omicron Delta Kappa, Order Omega. Democrat. Episcopalian. Home: 5026 Barfield Rd Tallahassee FL 32308

EDWARDS, THOMAS HENRY, JR., retired construction company executive; b. Montgomery, Ala., Feb. 16, 1918; s. Thomas Henry and Florence Virginia (Cameron) E.; m. Marilyn Rae Myers, Nov. 18, 1943; children—Thomas Henry III, Mary Lynn Edwards Angell. B.S. in Civil Engring., Auburn U., 1939; postgrad. U. Mich., 1940-41. Registered profl. engr., Ala.; registered land surveyor, Ala. San. engr. W.K. Kellogg Found., Battle Creek, Mich., 1939-40; estimator Algernon Blair Constrn. Co., Montgomery, 1946-47; engr. Tenn. Coal and Iron div. U.S. Steel Corp., Birmingham, Ala., 1947-53; project mgr. Sullivan, Long, Hagerty, Birmingham, 1953-73, v.p., 1973-83; ret., 1983. Served with U.S. Army, 1942-45. Mem. Sigma Nu. Republican. Methodist. Lodge: Lions. Home: 3628 Kingshill Rd Birmingham AL 35223

EDWARDS, WANDA RUSHING, law education specialist, sociology educator, media consultant; b. Charlotte, N.C., July 30, 1952; d. John Leroy and Fair (Pinion) R.; m. Joel L. Edwards, Dec. 23, 1972; children—Benjamin, William. B.A. in History, U. N.C.-Greensboro, 1974, M.A. in Sociology, 1981. Facilitator sch. arts Winston Salem-Forsyth County Schs., N.C., 1974; teaching houseparent Juvenile Justice, Winston-Salem, 1974-78; instr. sociology Community Coll., Statesville, N.C., 1981—; researcher-law edn. N.C. Dept. Justice, Raleigh, 1981—; staff conf. planning State Conf. Delinquency Prevention, 1983-84. Author: Social Studies-Learning the Law, 1983; The PYD PILOT: A Guide to Public Awareness for Delinquency Prevention, 1982. Mem. Mocksville Appearance Commn., 1984-85; treas. Friends of the Library, Davie County, 1984; pres. PTA Mocksville Elem., 1984-85; mem. Davie County Democratic Exec. Com., 1985—. Recipient Sch. Vol. award N.C., 1984. Mem. Nat. Assn. Attys. Gen. (staff state com., 1983, N.C. junvenile justice clearing house planning com. 1985—), Eastern Sociol. Soc., So. Sociol. Soc., So. Legislators Conf. Children. Baptist. Avocations: photography, jogging, swimming, water skiing. Home: PO Box 381 Mocksville NC 27028

EDWARDS, WILLIAM EVERETT, dentist; b. Spartanburg, S.C., Mar. 19, 1928; s. James Baxter and Cora (Stone) E.; m. Margaret Alice Carlton, July 28, 1951. B.S., Wofford Coll., 1951; D.D.S., Emory U., 1965. Gen. practice dentistry, Spartanburg, S.C. Mem. Spartanburg County Health Planning Commn., 1979—. Fellow Acad. Gen. Dentistry; mem. ADA, S.C. Dental Assn., Spartanburg County Dental Soc. (pres. 1979-80), Delta Sigma Delta, Omicron Kappa Upsilon. Club: Sertoma (pres. Spartanburg 1983-84, chmn. bd. 1984—). Avocation: golf. Home: 140 Bellwood Ln Spartanburg SC 29302 Office: 301 N Pine St Spartanburg SC 29302

EDWARDS, WILLIAM FRANK, communications research analyst, photographer; b. Harrison, Ark., Feb. 3, 1946; s. William Frank and Leota Mae (Atchley) E.; B.A., UCLA, 1968, M.A., 1970; Ph.D. in Communications, U. Tex.-Austin, 1979. Staff writer Walt Disney Prodns., Burbank, Calif., 1970-72; instr. U. Ark., Fayetteville, 1973-76; prof. English and communications U. Tex., 1977-82; research analyst Dallas Communications Complex, 1982—; freelance photographer; cons. to Film Sch., U. Tex. U. Zurich (Switzerland) grantee, 1975. Mem. Am. Film Inst., AAUP, Tex. Ex-Students Assn., Young Republicans Tex., Sigma Chi. Home: 3507 University Blvd Dallas TX 75205

EDWARDS, WILMA DEALVA, social worker; b. Olden, Tex., Dec. 21, 1939; d. William Price and DeAlva Maud (McCune) E. B.A., East Tex. State U., 1963, M.A., 1969; M.S.S.W., U. Tex.-Arlington, 1983. Cert. social worker, Tex. Tchr., coach Ranger (Tex.) High Sch., 1963-64, Carlsbad (N.M.) Sr. High Sch., 1965-70; tchr., coach Temple (Tex.) High Sch., 1970-81; social worker Family Services, Inc., Arlington, Tex., 1983—. Mem. Nat. Assn. Social Workers, Alpha Delta Mu. Democrat. Methodist. Contbr. articles to profl. jours. Office: 3212 W Park Row Suite E Arlington TX 76013

EFFINGER, GEORGE ALEC, writer; b. Cleve., Jan. 10, 1947; s. George Paul and Ruth Carolyn (Uray) E.; student Yale U., 1965-66, 69-70, N.Y. U., 1968-69. Free-lance writer, 1970—; novels include: What Entropy Means to Me, 1972, Relatives, 1973, Those Gentle Voices, 1976, Felicia, 1976, Death in Florence, 1978, Heroics, 1979, The Wolves of Memory, 1981; The Nick of Time, 1985, The Bird of Time, 1986, When Gravity Fails, 1986, Shadow Money, 1986; short story collections include Mixed Feelings, 1974, Irrational Numbers, 1976, Dirty Tricks, 1978, Idle Pleasures, 1982; tchr. sci. fiction Tulane U., New Orleans, 1974. Mem. Sci. Fiction Writers Am., Authors Guild, PEN. Address: Box 15183 New Orleans LA 70175

EFFRON, ALAN MICHAEL, diagnostic radiologist; b. Chgo., June 16, 1942; s. David Vernon and Hylda Rose E.; m. Nancy Diane Epstein, June 20, 1964; children—Brenda Laura, Erika Denise. Diplomate Am. Bd. Radiology. M.D., U. Tenn., 1966. Intern, City of Memphis Hosps., 1966-67; resident in radiology Letterman Army Med. Ctr., San Francisco, 1971-74; pvt. practice Las Cruces, N.Mex., 1975-76; staff radiologist Oklahoma City Clinic, 1976—, Presbyterian Hosp., Oklahoma City, 1976—; vis. lectr. U. Okla. Coll. Medicine, 1976—; chmn. adv. com. Presbyn. Hosp. Sch. Radiologic Tech., 1984—. Served to lt. col. AUS, 1968-75. Decorated Bronze Star. Mem. Radiol. Soc. N.Am., Am. Coll. Radiology, AMA. Clubs: Oklahoma City Dinner, U.S. Power Squadron. Office: 701 NE 10th St Oklahoma City OK 73104

EFRON, MARVIN, optometrist, educator; b. Aiken, S.C., May 30, 1930; s. Harry H. and Mary (Fadem) E.; m. Sara Timmerman, June 20, 1956; children—Leslie Kay, Susan Frances. O.D., So. Coll. Optometry, 1951; M.A., U. S.C., 1965, Ph.D., 1969. Optometrist West Columbia Optometric Group, S.C., 1958—; lectr. U. S.C., Columbia, 1970—; adj. faculty So. Coll. Optometry, Memphis, 1982—. Author: Vision Guide for Teachers of Deaf-Blind Children, 1974. Creator visual acuity test. Inventor prism device. Vice-pres. S.C. Ptnrs. of Ams., Columbia, 1985, S.C. Nat. Soc. to Prevent Blindness, Columbia, 1985; trustee Wil Lou Gray Opportunity Sch., West Columbia, 1970—. Recipient Disting. Alumnus award Coll. Edn. U. S.C., 1984, Optometrist of Yr. award S.C. Optometric Assn., 1970, Outstanding Young Man of Yr. award West Columbia Jaycees, 1966, Outstanding Vision Research award So. Council Optometry, 1970, 66. Mem. Am. Optometric Assn., Am. Psychol. Assn., Nat. Rehab. Assn. (bd. dirs., citation 1983). Avocations: travel; photography. Home: 1212 Canary Dr West Columbia SC 29169 Office; West Columbia Optometric Group 1205 D Ave PO Box 4045 West Columbia SC 29171

EGAN, EILEEN MARY, university administrator; b. Boston, Jan. 11, 1925; d. Eugene O. and Mary B. (Condon) E. B.A., Spalding U., 1956; M.A., Cath. U. Am., 1963; Ph.D., U. Louisville, 1966, J.D., 1981. Tchr. secondary schs., Wakefield, Mass., 1956-60, Memphis, 1960-62; mem. faculty English dept. Cath. U. Am., Washington, 1963-66; chmn. dept. English, Spalding U., Louisville, 1966-67, v.p., 1968-69, pres., 1969—; adminstrv. intern Smith Coll., 1967-68; prof. U. Louisville, 1982; chmn. bd. Louisville br. Fed. Res. Bank St. Louis. Exec. com., chmn. bd. dirs. Kentuckiana Metroversity; bd. dirs., trustee Ky.-Ind. Coll. Fund; bd. dirs., pub. edn. com. Louisville C. of C.; bd. dirs. Louisville Central Area Inc., Metro United Way, U. Louisville Internat. Ctr.; mem. Louisville Com. Fgn. Relations; exec. bd. Old Ky. Home Council Boy Scouts Am.; bd. trustees Jewish Hosp. Systems, Jewish Hosp Found; mem. Louisville Mayor's Adv. Com. on Ethics. Cath. U. Am. Bd. Trustees scholar, 1963-66; recipient Louisville Urban League Equality award, 1978, Louisville Jewish Community Center Blanche B. Ottenheimer award, 1978, NCCJ Brotherhood award, 1979. Mem. Council Ind. Colls. (dir., com. membership), Council Ind. Ky. Colls. and Univs. (research and coop. programs com.), So. Assn. Colls. and Schs. (commn. colls., com. admission to membership insts. at Levels II-V), Nat. Assn. Ind. Colls. and Univs. (govt. relations adv. com.), Am. Assn. Higher Edn., AAUW, English-Speaking Union, Ky. Bar Assn., ABA. Mem. Sisters of Charity of Nazareth. Office: 851 S Fourth St Louisville KY 40203

EGAN, MICHAEL JOSEPH, lawyer; b. Savannah, Ga., Aug. 8, 1926; s. Michael Joseph and Elsie (Robider) E.; m. Donna Cole, Apr. 14, 1951; children—Moira, Michael, Donna, Cole, Roby, John. B.A., Yale U., 1950; LL.B., Harvard U., 1955. Bar: Ga. 1955, D.C., 1961. Assoc. firm Sutherland, Asbill & Brennan, Atlanta, 1955-61, ptnr., 1961-77, 79—; mem. Ga. Ho. of Reps., 1966-77, minority leader, 1971-77; assoc. atty. gen. U.S. Dept. Justice, Washington, 1977-79. Served with U.S. Army, 1945-47, 50-52. Mem. Atlanta Bar Assn., State Bar Ga., Atlanta Lawyers Club., Am. Law Inst. Am. Coll. Probate Counsel. Republican. Roman Catholic. Home: 97 Brighton Rd NE Atlanta GA 30309 Office: 3100 1st Atlanta Tower Atlanta GA 30383 also 1666 K St NW Washington DC 20006

EGEDE-NISSEN, THOR, truck-trailer manufacturing executive; b. Oslo, Norway, Feb. 26, 1936; came to U.S., 1945, naturalized, 1955; s. Dag and Dorothea (Christensen) Egede-N.; m. Ruth Elizabeth Dixon, Dec. 30, 1964; children—Ingrid Lise, Thor Olav. B.S. in Indsl. Engring., Columbia U. Sch. Engring., 1963. Registered profl. engr., Calif. Indsl. engr. unbleached div. Union Camp Corp., Savannah, Ga., 1963-68; indsl. relations mgr. Great Dane Trailers, Inc., Savannah, 1968-74, corp. dir. indsl. relations, 1974-84, v.p. indsl. relations, 1984—. Vice pres. United Way of Coastal Empire, Savannah, 1984-85; nat. pres. Internat. Mgmt. Council, King of Prussia, Pa., 1977-78; pres. Parent Child Devel. Services, Inc., Savannah, 1977-78. Served with U.S. Army, 1957-60. Recipient Service award Internat. Mgmt. Council, 1983, Savannah Indsl. Man of Yr. award Savannah Indsl. Mgmt. Club, 1976. Mem. Am. Inst. Indsl. Engrs. (pres. 1968-69), Truck Trailer Mfg. Assn. (indsl. relations com. chmn. 1981-82), Am. Soc. Personnel Adminstrs. (dist. dir. 1971-72). Club: Ogelthorpe. Avocation: marine tropical fish genealogy. Home: 1531 Whitfield Park Circle Savannah GA 31406 Office: Great Dane Trailers Inc 600 E Lathrop Ave Savannah GA 31401

EGG, ROBERT C., construction manager, engineer; b. Cuero, Tex., Feb. 14, 1951. B.S. in Engring., Tex. A&M U., 1973. Research assoc. Tex. Agrl. Expt. Sta., College Station, 1973-74; sect. engr. Alaska Resource Scis., Fairbanks, 1974-77; camp mgr. Holmes & Narver, Inc., Orange, Calif., 1977-78, asst. project mgr., Prudhoe Bay, Alaska, 1984—; field engr. Williams Bros. Engring. Co., Tulsa, 1979; constrn. engr. Northwest Alaska Pipeline, Fairbanks, 1980-82. Darnell scholar Tex. A&M U., 1969; recipient Antarctic Services medal NSF, 1978. Mem. Am. Soc. Agrl. Engrs. (assoc.), AAAS, Tex. Farm Bur. Assn. Address: Gen Delivery Meyersville TX 77974

EGGEBRAATEN, GARY BRUCE, senior software engineer, consultant; b. Key West, Fla., Oct. 21, 1958; s. Bradley Delaine and Pearl Ottilee (Roberts) E.; m. Debra Yvonne Sloneker, July 26, 1980. B.S. in Math., Fla. State U., 1979, B.S. in Math. Edn., 1979. Cert. tchr., Fla. Student programmer Fla. State U., Tallahassee, 1980-81; computer systems analyst, 1981-84; part-time tchr. Lincoln High Sch., Tallahassee, 1983-84; mem. tech. staff Found. Computer Systems, Cary, N.C., 1984-85; sr. software engr. No. Telecom, Inc., Raleigh, N.C., 1985—. Co-author computer software KEY2DISK, 1983. Mem. Assn. Computing Machinery, Math. Assn. Am., Internat. Council for Computers in Edn., Nat. Council Tchrs. Math. Democrat. Methodist. Avocations: softball; baseball; music. Home: 115 Rose St Cary NC 27511 Office: 4018 Patriot Dr 1 Park Ctr Durham NC 27703

EGGEN, JOHN ALBERT, JR., architect; b. Granada, Miss., Mar. 21, 1934; s. John A. and Gladys (Lord) E.; B.Arch., Rensselaer Poly. Inst., 1957; m. Gayle Aycock McGrew, June 22, 1963 (div. 1986); children—Christine A., Jennifer E. Draftsman, Cooper, Robison & Carlson, Kansas City, 1951-59; job capt. Kivett & Myers, Kansas City, 1959-61; partner Coombs & Eggen, Kansas City, 1961-62; architect John A. Eggen, Jr., Kansas City, 1962-66; partner Seligson/Eggen, 1966-72; v.p. planning Fin. Corp. N. Am., 1972-73; pres. Shelter Equities Corp., 1973-75; assoc. H.N.T.B., 1975-85; v.p. Allen Morris Co., Miami, 1985—; instr. Kansas City Met. Jr. Coll., 1961-66. Mem. Kansas City Bd. Bldg. Code Appeals, 1970-79; bd. trustees Barry U. Mem. Miami C. of C., AIA (chpt. honor award for design 1966, 68, treas. 1970, sec. 1971), Delta Kappa Epsilon, Pi Delta Epsilon. Episcopalian. Clubs: Riviera Country, Miami, University (Miami). Lodge: Rotary. Important works include Center City Med. Plaza (AIA Honor award 1970), Fire Sta. 30, (AIA medal award 1970, AIA Nat. Am. Inst. Steel Constrn. Design award 1970), Grove Swimming Pool Bath House (AIA medal award 1972), Maple Woods Community Coll. (AIA medal award 1974), Bartle Conv. Center, 1976, Performing Arts Center, U. Mo., 1979, United Telephone Office Bldg., Orlando, Fla., 1983. Home: 725 Tizians Coral Gables FL 33143 Office: 2 S Biscayne Miami FL 33131

EGGERS, PAUL WALTER, lawyer; b. Seymour, Ind., Apr. 20, 1919; s. Ernest H. and Ottile (Carre) E.; B.A., Valparaiso U., 1941; LL.B., U. Tex., 1948; m. Virginia McMillin Streeter, Feb. 23, 1974; 1 son, Steven Paul. Bar; Tex. 1948. Practiced in Wichita Falls, 1948-69; mem. firm Eggers, Sherrill & Pace, 1952-69; gen. counsel U.S. Treasury Dept., Washington, 1969-70; practice law, Dallas, 1971-78; pres. Eggers & Greene, P.C., 1978—. Pres., Wichita Falls Symphony, 1960-62; chmn. Wichita County Republican party, 1966-67; chmn. Rep. State Task Force on Revenue and Fiscal Policy, 1967; Rep. candidate for gov. Tex., 1968, 70; mem. Pres. Assay Comm., 1972; trustee Episcopal Ch. Bldg. Fund, St. Mark's Sch. Tex., 1974-80; bd. dirs. Student Loan Mktg. Assn., 1973-78; adv. council St. Paul Hosp., 1974—; bd. dirs. Dallas County ARC, 1974-81; mem. profl. adv. com. Home Hospice, 1980-82; bd. dirs. Vis. Nurse Assn., 1982—; pres. corp. Episc. Diocese of Dallas, 1984—. Served to maj. AUS, 1941-46. Mem. State Bar Tex., ABA, Am. Judicature Soc. Episcopalian (chancellor diocese Dallas 1979—, sr. warden 1983—). Home: 3131 Maple St Apt 1D Dallas TX 75201 Office: 1999 Bryan St Suite 3220 Dallas TX 75201

EGGLESTON, DANIEL MAURICE, computer scientist, educator; b. Ancon, Republic of Panama, June 17, 1939; s. Daniel Maurice and Carmen Rita (Hele) E.; m. Deborah Aken, June 19, 1965; children—Stasie, Daniel, Amalia, William. B.S.E.E., Va. Polytech. Inst., 1961; M.S., Naval Postgrad. Sch., 1970; grad. Army Command & Gen. Staff Coll., 1976. Commd. officer U.S. Army, 1961, advanced through grades to lt. col., 1977; assoc. prof. math. U.S. Mil. Acad., 1977-81; exec. officer 2d Inf. Div., Camp Casey, Korea, 1982-83; sr. ops. researcher U.S. Readiness Command, Tampa, Fla., 1983-84; computer scientist Computer Scis. Corp., St. Petersburg, Fla., 1984—; adj. faculty C.W. Post Ctr., 1979-81, Fla. Inst. Tech., St. Petersburg, 1983—. Tech. editor: Combat Effectiveness Study Wartime Support, Europe, 1975. Contbr. articles to profl. jours. Coach, youth soccer, Washington, 1975-76, Ft. Leavenworth, Kans., 1976-77, West Point, N.Y., 1977-80; sec. Korean Am. Friendship Council, Camp Casey, Korea, 1982-83. Decorated Legion of Merit. Home: 14444 87th Ave N Seminole FL 33542 Office: Computer Scis Corp 801-94th Ave N Suite 200 St Petersburg FL 33702

EGLOFF, JULIUS, III, geologist; b. Washington, Sept. 19, 1946; s. Julius and Cassandra Mary Sue (Adreon) E.; m. Cassie LeAnn Tumlin, Feb. 17, 1980; children—Cassandra Desiree, Julius Tristan. B.S. in Geology, U. Miami, 1969. With Nautical Chart div. Cartographic Br., U.S. Naval Hydrographic Office, Suitland, Md., 1965; with Deep Ocean Surveys div. Geology and Geophysics Br., U.S. Naval Oceanographic Office, Washington, 1966, with Deep Ocean Vehicle Br., 1967, oceanographer Global Ocean Floor Analysis Research Project Code 038, 1968-76; geologist, oceanographer Seafloor Geoscis. div. Code 361, U.S. Naval Ocean Research and Devel. Activity, Bay St. Louis, Miss., 1976—; chief exec. officer Re-Evaluations Co., Pass Christian, Miss., 1980—; chief geologist, pres. Deep Ventures, Ltd. Oil and Gas and Minerals Exploration Co., Inc., 1983—. Contbg. author: Atlantis: The Eighth Continent, 1984. Contbr. articles to profl. publs. Fellow Explorers Club; mem. Am. Assn. Petroleum Geologists, Baton Rouge Geol. Soc., New Orleans Geol. Soc. Republican. Avocations: research of historical and undiscovered shipwrecks and archaeological subjects. Home: PO Box C Pass Christian MS 39571

EGUES, RANDY JULIAN, city official, newscaster, program moderator; b. Habana, Cuba, June 19, 1949; s. Antonio and Berta (Diaz) E.; m. Mercedes L. Egues, Sept. 2, 1972; children—Randy A., Javier A.; m. Vivian Lugo, Jan. 15, 1983. A.A., Miami Dade Community Coll., 1971, A.S., 1973; B.S., Fla. Internat. U., 1982, M.P.A. candidate. Human resources coordinator Metro-Dade Police, Miami, Fla., 1972—; newscaster WQBA Radio, Miami, 1979—; moderator WLRN Channel 17, Miami, 1979—; security cons. Miami Herald, 1975, S.E. Data Processing, Miami, 1976, Am. Hosp., Miami, 1980. Contbr. articles to various newspapers. Mem. adv. com. Spanish League Against Discrimination, 1982-83. Republican. Roman Catholic. Lodge: Kiwanis (Miami). Office: Metro-Dade Police 1320 NW 14th St Miami FL 33125

EHLEN, JUDY, geologist; b. Portland, Oreg., June 27, 1944; d. E.A. and Mina J. (Cowgill) Ehlen. B.A. in German, U. Oreg., 1966, B.A. in Geology, 1969, M.A. in Geology, 1969; M.A. in History, George Mason U., 1980; postgrad. U. Birmingham, Eng., 1985—. Teaching asst. U. Oreg., Eugene, 1966-68; service rep. Mountain Bell, Great Falls and Billings, Mont., 1969-71; cartographic aide U.S. Army Topographic Command (name changed to Def. Map Agy. Hydographic/Topographic Center 1972), Washington, 1971-72; geologist U.S. Army Engr. Topographic Labs., Ft. Belvoir, Va., 1972—. Mem. Geol. Soc. Am., Geol. Soc. Washington, Brit. Geomorphological Research Group, Ussher Soc., Sigma Xi. Contbr. articles to profl. publs. Office: US Army Engr Topographic Labs Center for Remote Sensing Fort Belvoir VA 22060

EHRHARDT, MARGARET WRIGHT, librarian; b. Orangeburg, S.C., Sept. 17, 1918; d. Harry Alison and Florence Olive (Black) Wright; B.A., Duke U., 1939; B.A.L.S., Emory U., 1949; postgrad. Furman U., 1970, U. S.C., 1978, U. Pitts., 1978; m. Benedict Groseclose Ehrhardt, Oct. 27, 1951; 1 son, Benedict Glen. High sch. librarian, library supr. Orangeburg (S.C.) Public Schs., 1945-51; children's librarian Richland County (S.C.) Public Library, Columbia, 1952-58; asst. order librarian U. S.C., Columbia, 1960-64; order librarian Wofford Coll., 1964-65; library cons. S.C. Dept. Edn., Columbia, 1965—. Mem. ALA, Southeastern Library Assn., S.C. Library Assn. (sec. 1971-72, pres. 1977), Delta Kappa Gamma. Lutheran. Editor: Media Services Newsletter, 1965-77, contbr. articles, revs. to S.C. Librarian, Media Center Messenger. Home: 227 Lawand Dr Columbia SC 29210 Office: 810 Rutledge Bldg Columbia SC 29201

EHRLICH, GRANT C(ONKLIN), corporation executive; b. Chgo., Aug. 16, 1916; s. Howard and Jenese (Conklin) E.; m. Gretchen Woerz, Sept. 14, 1940; children—Galen Matthews, Gretel Stephens. B.S. in Adm. Engring. and mech. Engring., Cornell U., 1938. Sales and engring. mgr. New Eng. Tape Co., Hudson, Mass., 1938-44; pres. Resin Industries, Inc., Santa Barbara, Calif., 1944-56, Industrial de Resinas. S.A., Mexico City, 1953—; chmn. Templock Corp., Carpinteria, Calif., 1977—; chmn., chief exec. officer Flow General Inc., McLean, Va., 1983—; dir. Diversion Dynamics, Inc., Santa Barbara, Gen. Research Corp.-Flow Gen., Inc. Chmn. Young Republicans of Calif., 1950. Club: Valley Club of Montecito (treas., dir. 1980-82). Office: Flow General Inc 7655 Old Springhouse Rd McLean VA 22102

EHRLICH, MARC IRA, psychologist; b. Bklyn., July 14, 1952; s. Sidney and Janet (Kaiser) E.; m. Maria de Lourdes Velasquez, June 28, 1980; 1 child, Sandra. B.A. in Edn., Bklyn. Coll., 1974; M.S. in Sch. Psychology, Pace U., 1977; Ph.D., U. Tex., 1980. Cert. sch. psychologist, N.Y., Tex., psychotherapist, Family Inst. Mex., Adj. prof. Nat. Univ. Mex., Mexico City, 1981-83, Internat. U., 1984—; dir. masters program Anahuac U., Mexico City, 1981-84, dir. clin. services, 1980-84; pvt. practice psychotherapy, Mexico City, 1981—; psychol. trainer Inst. for Creative Leadership, Mexico City, 1985—; cons. Jr. League of Mex., Mexico City, 1984—; spl. columnist The News, Mexico City, 1981—. Author: Husbands, Wives and Their Children, 1983; author articles. Mem. Am. Psychol. Assn., Psi Chi. Jewish. Avocations: reading; photography; travel. Home: Fuente de Etiopia #27 Tecamachalco Mexico 53950

EHRLICH, MORTON, airline executive; b. N.Y.C., Dec. 1, 1934; s. Milton and Anne (Tannenbaum) E.; B.B.A. cum laude, City Coll. N.Y., 1960; Ph.D. in Economics (Ford Found. fellow), Brown U., 1965; m. Rosalind, Feb. 7, 1960; children—Bruce, Ellen, Wendy. Economist, Fed. Res. Bank of N.Y., 1965-67, Nat. Indsl. Conf. Bd., N.Y.C., 1967-68; v.p. Eastern Airlines, Miami, Fla., 1968-76, sr. v.p. planning, 1976—, also dir., dir. Eastern Airlines, S.A., IBM World Trade Ams./Far East Corp. Trustee, U. Miami; bd. dirs. Nat. Bur. Econ. Research. Served with U.S. Army, 1953-56. Mem. Am. Econ. Assn., Nat. Assn. Bus. Economists, Econ. Soc. South Fla. (dir.), Downtown Econs. Club New York, U.S. C. of C. Author: Discretionary Income, 1967; A Weekly Index of Business Activity, 1967; U.S. Foreign Trade, 1968; Computer Application in the Allocation of Airline Resources, 1975; An Integrated System for Airline Planning and Management Information, 1977. Home: 7541 SW 114th St Miami FL 33156 Office: Eastern Airlines Miami Internat Airport Miami FL 33148

EHRLING, ROBERT F., real estate company executive; b. N.Y.C., Dec. 7, 1939; s. John Robert and Kathleen (Clarke) E.; m. Cheryl M. Vogt, Aug. 6, 1966; children—Michael, John, Robert. B.S., Fordham U., 1961; M.B.A., St. John's U., 1967. Dir. Levitt & Sons Inc., N.Y.C., 1968-72; v.p. Larwin Group, Beverly Hills, Calif., 1973-74; various positions Gen. Devel. Corp., Miami, Fla., 1974-80, pres., 1980—. Vice-pres. Big Bros.-Big Sisters, Miami, 1982-83; chmn. Gov.'s Adv. Council-H.R.S., Fla., 1982; panel chmn. United Way of Miami, 1982. Roman Catholic. Home: 14600 SW 79th Ct Miami FL 33158 Office: Gen Devel Corp 1111 S Bayshore Dr Miami FL 33131

EICH, WILBUR FOSTER, III, physician; b. Tuskegee, Ala., June 26, 1938; s. Wilbur Foster and Lula Olivia (Dudley) E.; B.A., Huntingdon Coll., 1960; M.D., Tulane, 1964; m. Eugenia Glass Graves, May 31, 1963; children—Paul Foster, Mark Samuel, Donna Eugenia. Intern, Lloyd Noland Hosp., Fairfield, Ala., 1964-65; resident in pediatrics U.S. Naval Hosp., Portsmouth, Va., 1967-69; pediatrician Infants' and Children's Clinic, Florence, Ala., 1971—; pres. med. staff Eliza Coffee Meml. Hosp., 1980-81; ordained priest Episcopal Ch., 1981. Vol., Project Hope, Brazil, 1973; trustee Huntingdon Coll., Montgomery, Ala., 1977—. Served with USN, 1965-71. Diplomate Am. Bd. Pediatrics. Fellow Am. Acad. Pediatrics, Am. Acad. Cerebral Palsy and Devel. Medicine; mem. AMA, So. Med. Assn., Med. Assn. Ala., Lauderdale County Med. Soc., Christian Med. Soc. Home: 201 Flurnoy Ave Florence AL 35630 Office: 412 Cedar St S Florence AL 35630

EICHENBAUM, BARRY ALLAN, optometrist; b. Bklyn., Jan. 23, 1953; s. Albert W. and Alice (Silverman) E.; m. Shelli Dee Meligan, May 22, 1977 (div. 1984); 1 child, Aaron Michael; m. Lisa Ellen Schomer, Feb. 16, 1985. A.A., U. Fla., 1973, B.S., 1974; O.D., Pacific U., 1979. Optometrist, Coral Gables, Fla., 1979—. Bd. dirs. Coral Gables Jaycees, 1982. Mem. Dade County Optometric Assn. (treas. 1984-85, sec. 1982-83, trustee 1983-84, service awards 1982-84). Democrat. Jewish. Lodge: Lions (sec. 1982-83, pres. 1983-84, zone chmn. 1983-84, sec. 1985—). Avocations: swimming, racquetball. Office: 327 Alhambra Circle Coral Gables FL 33134

EICHORN, JOHN FREDERICK GERARD, JR., utility executive; b. Boston, Mar. 3, 1924; s. John Frederick Gerard and Hazel (Morris) E.; m. Mary Louise MacIsaac, Oct. 11, 1952; children—Christine Louise, Elisabeth Anne (dec.), Ellen Marie. B.S. in Mech. Engring, U. Maine, 1949; postgrad., Northeastern U., 1963-64. Registered profl. engr., Mass. With New Eng. Elec. System (various locations), 1949-71; v.p., regional exec. New Eng. System (Mass. Electric div.), North Andover, Mass., 1968-71; exec. v.p. Eastern Utilities Assos., Boston, 1971-72, pres., chief exec. officer, 1972—, also trustee; pres., dir. Montaup Electric Co., Somerset, Mass., 1971—, EUA Service Corp., Boston, 1971—; chmn., dir. Blackstone Valley Electric Co., Lincoln, R.I., 1971—, Eastern Edison Co., Mass., 1971—; dir. Yankee Atomic Power Co., Rowe, Mass., Conn. Yankee Atomic Power Co., Haddem Neck, Conn., Maine Yankee Atomic Power Co., Wiscasett, Vt. Yankee Nuclear Power Corp., Vernon.; Chmn. exec. com. New Eng. Power Pool. Served with AUS, 1942-45. Mem. Edison Electric Inst. (dir.), Electric Council New Eng. (dir.). Clubs: Algonquin, Fed. (Boston).

EINSPRUCH, BURTON CYRIL, psychiatrist; b. N.Y.C., June 27, 1935; s. Adolph and Mala (Goldblatt) E.; B.A., So. Meth. U., 1956, Sc.B., 1958; M.D., Southwestern Med. Sch., Dallas, 1960; m. Barbara Standen Traeger, Oct. 9, 1960; children—Julia Moat, Alexander Louis, Robert Sands. Intern, Montefiore Hosp., N.Y.C., 1960-61; resident Nat. Hosp. Inst. Neurology, London, 1962, U. Tex., Dallas, 1961-64 (also fellow); sr. resident Parkland Meml. Hosp., Dallas, 1964; instr. psychiatry U. Pa., 1964-66; pvt. practice psychiatry, Dallas, 1966—; mem. staff Presbyn. and Parkland hosps., Timberlawn Psychiat. Hosp.; clin. asst. prof. U. Tex., Health Sci. Center, Dallas, 1966-70, dir. psychiat. div. Student Health Service, 1966-72, clin. assoc. prof., 1970—; dir. Southwestern Adult Psychiat. Clinic, Dallas, 1966-74; dir. psychiat. service Dallas Home for Jewish Aged, 1966-82, now cons. staff; research cons. Dallas Geriatric Research Inst., 1974—; adj. prof. sociology N. Tex. State U., Denton, 1975—; cons. staff Baylor U. Hosp., Golden Acres Hosp.; clin. asso. prof. psychiatry U. Tex. Health Scis. Center, Dallas, 1971—. Bd. dirs. Mental Health Assn. Dallas, 1960-69, Jewish Family Service, 1969-71, 73-75. Served to lt. comdr. M.C., USNR, 1964-66. Diplomate Am. Bd. Psychiatry and Neurology (examiner, 1974—). Fellow Am. Psychiat. Assn., Am. Coll. Psychiatrists, Am. Soc. Adolescent Psychiatry, N. Tex. Soc. Adolescent Psychiatry (past pres.); mem. Royal Coll. Psychiatry London, AMA, Tex. Med. Assn., Gerontol. Soc., Am. Geriatric Soc. Contbr. profl. jours. Home: 5411 Meaders Ln Dallas TX 75229 Office: 8330 Meadow Rd Suite 117 Dallas TX 75231

EISELE, GARNETT THOMAS, judge; b. Hot Springs, Ark., Nov. 3, 1923; s. Garnett Martin and Mary (Martin) E.; m. Kathryn Freygang, June 24, 1950; children—Wendell A., Garnett Martin II, Kathryn M., Jean E. Student, U. Fla., 1940-42, Ind. U., 1942-43; A.B., Washington U., 1947; LL.B., Harvard U., 1950, LL.M., 1951. Bar: Ark. Practiced in Hot Springs, 1951-52, Little Rock, 1953-69; asso. firm Wootten, Land and Matthews, 1951-52, Owens, McHaney, Lofton & McHaney, 1956-60; asst. U.S. atty., Little Rock, 1953-55, individual practice, 1961-69; U.S. dist. judge Eastern Dist. Ark., 1970—, chief judge, 1975—; Legal adviser to gov. Ark., 1966-69. Del. Ark. 7th Constl. Conv., 1969-70; Trustee U. Ark., 1969-70. Served with AUS, 1943-46; ETO. Mem. Am., Ark., Pulaski County bar assns., Am. Judicature Soc., Am. Law Inst. Office: PO Box 3684 Little Rock AR 72203*

EISELE, WILLIAM DAVID, insurance agency executive; b. Iron Mountain, Mich., July 31, 1927; s. David Christian and Muriel Elizabeth (Ockstadt) E.; B.S., U. Mich., 1950; m. Helen Jeanne Holmberg, Dec. 27, 1953; children—David, Meg. Ins. agt. Employers Mut. of Wausau, Milw., 1951, West Bend, Wis., 1952-53, Watertown, Wis., 1953-56, Orlando, Fla., 1957, Tampa, Fla., 1958; pres. William D. Eisele & Co., Clearwater, Fla., 1959—. Charter pres. Heritage Presbyn. Housing Project, 1971-72; elder Presbyn. Ch. Recipient disting. alumni service award U. Mich., 1975. Mem. Fla. Assn. Ins. Agts., Clearwater-Largo-Dunedin Insurors (past pres.), U. Mich. Alumni Assn. (dir., v.p.). Clubs: Clearwater Rotary; U. Mich. (organizer, past pres. Pinellas County, Fla.). Office: 1012 E Druid Rd Clearwater FL 33516

EISENBACH, ROBERT LEONARD, JR., chemical engineer; b. N.Y.C., Aug. 21, 1929; s. Robert Leonard and Helen Louise (Aronsohn) E.; m. Jean Rose London, Apr. 5, 1952; children—Janice London, Robert Leonard III. B.S., U. Ala., 1950; B.S. in Ch.E., Ga. Inst. Tech., 1956. Process engr. Ethyl Corp., Baton Rouge, 1956-60; project engr. Tenn. Products & Chem. Corp., Chattanooga, 1960-62; project engr. Kaiser Aluminum & Chem. Corp., Baton Rouge, 1962-67, area engr., 1967-69, staff environ. engr., 1969-82, staff environ. engr., Gramercy, La., 1982-85; sr. program mgr. G&E Engring., Inc., Baton Rouge, 1985—. Served with AUS, 1951-54. Mem. Air Pollution Control Assn. (past pres., past bd. dirs.), Phi Lambda Upsilon. Home: 3063 Yorktown Dr Baton Rouge LA 70808 Office: PO Box 45212 Dept 186 Baton Rouge LA 70895

EISENBACK, JONATHAN DAVID, nematologist, educator; b. Columbia, S.C., June 30, 1952; s. Samuel Jacob and Frances Maye (Sallee) E.; m. Marilyn Lee Hawkins, May 6, 1974; children—Brian Matthew, Justin David. B.A., Bryan Coll., 1974; Ph.D., N.C. State U., 1979. Layout artist Word Systems, Dayton, Tenn., 1973-74; tchr. gen. sci. Rhea County Consolidated High Sch., Evensville, Tenn., 1974-75; grad. research asst. N.C. State U., Raleigh, 1975-79, research assoc., 1979-84; asst. prof. Va. Poly. Inst. and State U., Blacksburg, 1985—. Recipient Biology Dept. award Bryan Coll., 1974; First prize Nikon's Internat. Small World Photo Contest, 1982, 85. Mem. Soc. Nematologists (best student paper award 1978), Southeastern Electron Microscopy Soc., N.C. Assn. Plant Pathologist and Nematologists, Sigma Xi, Gamma Sigma Delta. Republican. Baptist. Co-author: A Guide to the Four Common Species of Root-Knot Nematodes, 1981; contbr. articles in field to profl. jours. Office: Dept Plant Pathology Va Poly Inst and State U Blacksburg VA

EISENBERG, LAWRENCE AVRUM, fund raiser; b. Oak Park, Ill., Feb. 16, 1954; s. Harry H. and Sophie (Kanter) E.; m. Christine Marie Halpin, June 17, 1979; 1 son, Andrew Lawrence. B.B.A. in Fin. and Acctg., U. Iowa, 1976; M.A. in Guidance and Counseling, Oakland U., 1980. Teller First Nat. Bank, Rock Island, Ill., 1970-72; night mgr. Sheraton Motor Inn, Rock Island, 1972-73; br. mgr. Am. Fed. Savs., Iowa City, 1973-74; coll. agt. Northwestern Mut. Life, Iowa City, 1974-75; exploring dir. Clinton Valley council Boy Scouts Am., 1977-81, past nat. pres. Am. Explorers, past mem. nat. exec. bd.; 1977-81, regional dir. U.S. Olympic Com., Dallas, 1981—; cons. in field. Author: Fund Raising Materials, 1978, 4th edit., 1984. Mem. White House Conf. on Youth, 1973-74, Nat. Health and Safety Commn., 1974-75, Pres.' Youth Adv. Council, 1973-76, Nat. Drug Abuse Council, 1974-77, Nat. Revolution Bicentennial Commn., 1975-76; nat. youth ambassador U.S., 1973-75; past pres. World Youth Forum, InterAm. Youth Conf.; Mem. Nat. Soc. Fund Raising Execs. cert. fund raising exec.; dir.), Phi Beta Kappa, Sigma Nu. Clubs: Rotary, Las Colinas Sports. Home: 6215 Mimosa Ln Dallas TX 75230 Office: US Olympic Com 901 W Walnut Hill Ln Irving TX 75038

EISENSTEIN, SAM, pediatric dentist; b. Montreal, Que., Can., Jan. 12, 1936; came to U.S., 1964; s. Isaac and Eva (Katz) E.; m. Esther Benjamin, June 24, 1962; children—Sandra Toby, Lana Rachel, Jeffrey Joshua. B.Sc., Sir George Williams Coll., 1957; M.Sc., McGill U., 1959, Ph.D., 1963; D.M.D., Tufts U., 1973. Research asst. Royal Victoria Hosp., Montreal, 1962-64; postdoctoral trainee Wistar Inst., Phila., 1964-65; research assoc. Albert Einstein Med. Ctr., Phila., 1965-66, Variety Children's Research Found., Miami, Fla., 1966-69; dental resident Children's Hosp., Boston, 1973-75; pvt. practice pediatric dentistry, South Weymouth, Mass., 1975-81, Miami, 1975—; clin. asst. in pedodontics Boston Children's Hosp., 1976-80; clin. instr. Harvard Sch. Dental Medicine, Boston, 1978-80, Tufts Sch. Dental Medicine, Boston, 1980-81; mem. attending staff Miami Children's Hosp., 1982—. Mem. ADA, Am. Soc. Dentistry for Children (cert. of merit 1973), Am. Acad. Pediatric Dentistry, Sigma Xi, Alpha Omega Delta, Omicron Kappa Epsilon. Jewish. Avocations: photography; model railroading; stamp collecting. Home: 5023 Grant St Hollywood FL 33021 Office: Dental Health Group 17301 NW 27h Ave Miami FL 33055

EISLER, DAVID LEE, university dean, music educator; b. Camden, N.J., Nov. 15, 1951; s. Jacob and Sarah Elizabeth (Korman) E.; m. Patricia Ann Johnson, Jan. 6, 1973; children—Heather Leigh, Lindsay Suzanne. Mus.B., U. Mich., 1972; Mus.M., Yale U., 1975; D.M.A., U. Mich., 1978. Teaching fellow Yale U., New Haven, 1974-75; instr. music Troy State U. (Ala.), 1975-77, asst. prof., 1978-85, assoc. prof., 1985—; asst. dean Sch. Fine Arts, 1982—, coordinator instrumental music, dir. grad. studies in music, 1978—; teaching fellow U. Mich., Ann Arbor, 1977-78; exec. dir. Southeastern U.S. Band Clinic. Mem. dean's adv. bd. Yale U., 1974-75. Boston Symphony fellow, 1972. Mem. Coll. Band Dirs. Nat. Assn., Internat. Clarinet Soc., Nat. Assn. Coll. Wind Percussion Instrs., Pi Kappa Lambda, Kappa Kappa Psi, Phi Mu Alpha, Tau Beta Sigma. Methodist. Author: A Bass Clarinet Orchestral Excerpt Book, 1972. Home: 201 Norfolk Ave Troy AL 36081 Office: 3 Long Hall Troy State U Troy AL 36082

EISMA, JOSE ALBARRACIN, physician; b. Jolo, Sulu, Philippines, Oct. 18, 1939; came to U.S., 1964, naturalized, 1973; s. Marcelo L. and Rosa A.

(Albarracin) E.; A.A., Silliman U., Philippines, 1958; M.D., U. Santo Tomas (Manila), 1963; m. Lenora Womack, Sept. 14, 1977; children—Joseph, Greg, John, Teri, Lori, Juli. Rotating intern Wilson Meml. Hosp., Johnson City, N.Y., 1964-65, med. resident, 1965-67; med. resident Kingsbrook Jewish Med. Center, Bklyn., 1967-68; gen. internist Reynolds Army Hosp., Ft. Sill, Okla., 1971-73; resident in pulmonary disease Brooke Army Med. Center, Ft. Sam Houston, Tex., 1973-74; chief of medicine, med. dir. respiratory therapy dept. West (Tex.) Community Hosp., 1976—, also bd. dirs. Served to col., Army N.G., 1975-85. Diplomate Am. Bd. Family Practice. Fellow Am. Acad. Family Physicians; mem. ACP, Am. Soc. Internal Medicine, Am. Thoracic Soc. Clubs: Res. Officers Assn., Tex. N.G. Assn., Assn. U.S. Army, Assn. Mil. Surgeons of U.S. Home: 1406 N Reagan St West TX 76691 Office: 300 N Reagan St West TX 76691

EISNER, I. TONI, educational administrator; b. Bklyn., June 21, 1944; d. Samuel A. and Lillian R. (Meyer) Margulies; m. Jerry Eisner, Jan. 21, 1973; children—Miriam, Beckah. B.S. in Edn., SUNY-New Paltz, 1965; M.A., Tchrs. Coll. Columbia U., 1968; Ed.D., U. Miami, 1972. Tchr. N.Y.C. pub. schs., 1965-68; asst. dean student affairs Fla. Atlantic U., Miami Beach, 1970-72, asst. dir. Cultural and Human Interaction Ctr., 1973-78, dir. Ctrs. and Insts. Univ. Outreach, 1978-80, dir. grant contracts and personnel, Sch. Edn., 1980-84; dir. equal opportunity programs Fla. Internat. U., 1984—; program officer Dade County Community Relations Bd., Miami, 1972-73; trainer, cons. in human relations, affirmative action. Mem. Dade County Fair Housing and Employment Appeals Bd., 1976—, chmn., 1979—; bd. dirs. Hemispheric Congress for Women, 1977-78; mem. Dade County Housing Planning Adv. Com., 1977-78. NDEA fellow, 1968-69. Mem. Am. Personnel and Guidance Assn., Assn. Specialists in Group Work, Assn. Humanistic Psychology, Nat. Com. Sch. Desegregation. Democrat. Jewish. Office: OEO Programs Div Human Resources Fla Internat Univ Miami FL 33199

EISNER, JEROME ALLAN, service company executive; b. Sheboygan, Wis., July 6, 1945; s. Harold Frederick and Frieda (Diener) E.; m. Eileen Ann Dixon, Aug. 17, 1968; children—Elizabeth Ann, Kimberly Jinmee. B.S., U.Wis.-Oshkosh, 1968; Edn. Cert. Alverno Coll., 1970. Tchr. Pius XI High Sch., Milw., 1968-71; sales rep. R.L. Polk & Co., Kansas City, Mo., 1971-72; mem. sales, mktg. staff 3M Co., St. Paul, 1972-78; program developer Golle & Holmes, Minnetonka, Minn., 1978-82; exec. dir. U.S. Jaycees, Tulsa, Okla., 1983; pres., owner Servpro of So. Hills, Tulsa, 1983—; sec. Nat. Found. for Volunteerism, Tulsa, 1982-83; mem. nat. adv. bd. Am. Family Soc., Washington, 1983. Author: Member's Guide to Speak Up, 1976; You Can Be Whatever You Want to Be, 1978. Bd. dirs. Project Concern, Minn., 1980-82; bd. dirs. Minnesota Jaycees, 1977-82, pres., 1980-81; bd. dirs. Minn. Jaycees Charitable Found., 1980-82. Named Jaycees Internat. Senator, 1980, U.S. Jaycees Ambassador, 1982, Minn. Jaycees Statesman, 1981, Outstanding Young Men of Am., 1978,79,81; recipient Clayton Frost Meml. award U.S. Jaycees, 1981, Cert. Merit award 3M Chmn. of Bd., 1975; Greek Man of Yr. award, 1968. Mem. Am. Soc. Tng. and Devel., Am. Entrepreneurs Assn., Personal Dynamics Assn., Am. Inst. of Maintenance, Tulsa C. of C., Pi Kappa Delta, Alpha Epsilon Rho. Club: St. Benedicts Men's (Broken Arrow, Okla.). Lutheran. Avocations: reading; weightlifting; karate. Home: 2217 W Memphis St Broken Arrow OK 74012

EKDAHL, RICHARD WILLIAM, association executive; b. Worcester, Mass., Feb. 25, 1930; s. Harold Gustavus and Hildur Marianne (Nordlander) E.; B.Mus., Boston U., 1951, A.M., 1954; Ed.D., U. Houston, 1970; m. Mary Edgerton Hazard, Nov. 22, 1956; 1 dau., Lauren Lee. Choral dir. St. Bernard's Sch., Gladstone, N.J., 1954-55, Cushing Acad., Ashburnham, Mass., 1955-57; tchr., asst. dean St. John's Sch., Houston, 1957-68; tchr., dir. admissions Holland Hall Sch., Tulsa, 1968-72; exec. dir. Ind. Schs. Assn. Southwest, Tulsa, 1965—; trustee, treas., vice chmn. trustees Town and Country Sch., Tulsa; trustee, sec. Inst. Study Pvt. Schs., Los Angeles, Tex. Assn. Nonpublic Schs. Treas., trustee Concertime, Inc., Tulsa; trustee Winston Sch., Dallas; mem. Tex. Pvt. Sch. Accreditation Commn. Mem. Assos. for Research Pvt. Edn. (trustee), Am. Ednl. Research Assn., Assn. Supervision and Curriculum Devel., Nat. Council Tchrs. Math. Episcopalian. Home: 3632 S Yorktown Pl Tulsa OK 74105 Office: PO Box 52297 Tulsa OK 74152

ELAM, ANDREW GREGORY, II, insurance company executive; b. Winchester, Va., Feb. 6, 1932; s. Andrew Gregory and Francis Clayton (Gold) E.; A.B., Presbyn. Coll., 1955; m. Rebecca Rhea Cole, Oct. 26, 1958; children—Andrew Gregory III, Philip Cole, Dawna Francis. Adminstrv. asst. Citizen's and So. Nat. Bank, Columbia, S.C., 1955-56; nat. exec. dir. Pi Kappa Phi, Sumter, S.C., 1956-59; pres. Carolina Potato Co., Inc., West Columbia, S.C., 1959-61; mem. pub. relations staff Kendavis Industries Internat., Inc., Ft. Worth, 1961-63; dir. sales promotion Pioneer Am. Ins. Co., Ft. Worth, 1963-64, dir. pub. relations and sales promotion, 1964-66, asst. v.p., 1966-68, v.p., mem. exec. com., 1968-71, dir., 1970-71; v.p. public relations and sales promotion Gt. Am. Res. Ins. Co., Dallas, 1972— J.C. Penney Life Ins. Co., Dallas, 1978-82; mem. pub. relations adv. council Am. Council Life Ins., Washington, 1971—; mem. pub. relations com. Tex. Life Conv., 1970-78. Mem. pub. info. adv. com. Am. Cancer Soc., Tex. div., 1969-80, chmn., 1972-77, exec. com., bd. dirs., 1972-77; vice-chmn. public relations com. Tarrant County United Fund, 1967; campaign leader Community Pride Campaign Performing Arts, 1969; bd. dirs. Ft. Worth Community Theatre, 1971-72; bd. dirs., treas., vice-chmn. Tarrant County unit Am. Cancer Soc., 1963-71, bd. dirs. Dallas County unit, 1972—; bd. dirs. Baylor U. Med. Center Found., 1979—; adv. bd. Charles A. Sammons Cancer Ctr. Mem. Life Ins. Advertisers Assn. (dir. communications workshop 1970-71, exec. com. 1973-75, chmn. So. Round Table 1972), Public Relations Soc. Am., Tex. Public Relations Assn. (dir. 1966), Indsl. Editors Ft. Worth (pres. 1968), Meeting Planners Internat. (nat. conv. program chmn. 1979, pres. chpt. 1980-81, internat. dir. 1981-83, internat. edn. com. 1983-85; named Planner of Year, 1985), Ft. Worth C. of C. (chmn. publ. com. 1970), Dallas Advt. League, Soc. Preservation and Encouragement of Barbershop Quartet Singing in Am. (chpt. pres. 1978, chmn. southwestern dist. charity drive 1979-83; treas. 1983-85, exec. v.p. 1985—; Barbershopper of Yr. Southwestern dist. 1982). Presbyterian (deacon 1966-68; stewardship chmn. 1980; ruling elder 1969—). Clubs: Chaparral, Rotary (Dallas). Home: 7730 Chattington Dr Dallas TX 75248 Office: 2020 Live Oak Dallas TX 75221

ELAM, GEORGIA JONES, day center executive; b. Hartsville, S.C.; d. George W. and Fannie C. (Chapman) Jones; m. Leon Mansfield Elam, Dec. 24, 1955; 1 dau., Loretta Elam Taylor. B.S., S.C. State Coll., 1942; M.A., Columbia U., 1949. Tchr. C.A. Johnson High Sch., Columbia, S.C., 1950-51, 55-80, Carver Jr. High Sch., Columbia, 1946-50; instr. S.C. State Coll., Orangeburg, 1952-55; owner, dir. Kinder World Day Care, Columbia, S.C., 1974—. Named Boss of Yr., Am. Bus. Women, 1979; Tchr. of Yr. in Home Econs., S.C., 1975. Mem. NEA, NOW, Am. Home Econs. Assn., S.C. Home Econs. Assn. (pres. 1952-54), Am. Bus. Women's Assn., Am. Vocat. Assn., S.C. Edn. Assn., S.C. Vocat. Assn., Delta Sigma Theta. Home: 1909 McFadden St Columbia SC 29204 Office: Kinder World Day Care 2460 Barbanville Rd Columbia SC 29204

ELAM, MICHAEL ANTHONY, college administrator; b. Henderson, N.C., Jan. 28, 1956; s. John and Ella (Ward) Cornish; m. Maxine Marie St. Helena Walcott, June 6, 1981. B.S., Howard U., 1979, M.Ed., 1981. Asst. to residence counselor Howard U., Washington, 1979-81; residence hall coordinator residence hall Ill. State U., Normal, 1981-83; counselor Eastern Ky. U., Richmond, 1983-85, acting dir. minority affairs, 1984—. Mem. NAACP. Recipient Outstanding Adv. award Black Student Union Eastern Ky. U., 1985, Outstanding Young Man of Yr. award Jaycees, 1984, Outstanding and Dedicated Service award Howard Residence Life, 1980-81, Outstanding Tutor award Upward Program, 1978, 79, 80. Baptist. Avocations: jogging; music; sports. Office: Eastern Ky U Powell 130 Richmond KY 40475

ELDER, IVAN RODNEY, psychologist; b. Salt Lake City, Dec. 27, 1946; s. Ivan and Charlotte (Bacon) E.; m. M. Gail Dutton, Sept. 15, 1978; children—Natalie, Alex; 1 stepson, Peter. B.A., Vanderbilt U., 1969; M.A., U. Ala.-Tuscaloosa, 1975, Ph.D., 1977. Staff psychologist VA Hosp., Tuscaloosa, Ala., 1977-79; coordinator addictions treatment unit VA Hosp., Columbia, S.C., 1979—. Patentee in field of baby products. Contbr. articles to profl. jours. Mem. Am. Psychol. Assn., Phi Beta Kappa, Nova Psi. Republican. Avocation: computers. Home: 116 Greengate Dr Columbia SC 29223 Office: Psychiatry Service VA Hosp Garners Ferry Rd Columbia SC 29201

ELDER, JOAN ELIZABETH, music educator; b. Huntington, W.Va., June 15, 1954; d. Lonnie Carl and Edith Elizabeth (Ellis) Bartee; m. Charles Roy Elder, June 30, 1973; children—Angela Marie, Charles Jeffrey. A.A. with honors, Miami Dade Jr. Coll., 1972; B.M.E. magna cum laude, Fla. State U., 1975. Tchr.'s cert., Fla. Exec. sec. Rose Printing Co., Tallahassee, 1975-76; music dir. First Presbyn. Ch. of Havana (Fla.), 1975-80; tchr., music dir. Gadsden Christian Acad., Havana, 1979—; state dir. Sunburst U.S.A. Beauty Pageant, Inc., Tenn. and Pa., 1984—; music dir. Whispering Pine Camp, Havana, 1980, 84; Faith Christian Fellowship, Quincy, Fla., 1982-83, Quincy chpt. Aglow Fellowship, 1983-84; co-organizer, music dir. Community Christmas Program, Havana, 1978; video tape minister Kenneth Copeland Ministries, 1982-84. Organizer, mem. bd. Shekinah Christian Center, Havana, 1979—; organizer, dir. Community Youth Group, 1976. Mem. Am. Inst. Fgn. Study, Planetary Soc., Nat. Geog. Soc., Moral Majority. Democrat. Office: PO Box 918 Havana FL 32333

ELDER, WILLIAM JOSEPH, government administrator; b. Altoona, Pa., Jan. 27, 1945; s. Walter Joseph and Margaret Regina (Beigle) E.; m. Catherine Glenda Arrowood, Nov. 13, 1971; children—William Walter, Catherine Elizabeth. Grad. in Indsl. Mgmt., Tidewater Community Coll., 1974; A.S. in Hazard Control, Ind. U., 1976, B.S. in Hazard Control, 1978. Cert. hazard control mgr. With Dept Navy, Norfolk, Va., 1967—, safety and occupational health profl., 1974—. Contbr. articles to navy mag. Served with U.S. Army, 1962-65. Recipient Civilian Logistics Intern award Navy Dept., 1977. Mem. Am. Soc. Safety Engrs., Navy Field Safety Assn. Club: Newport News Soccer (bd. dirs. 1984—). Avocations: woodworking, little league coaching.

ELDERS, PAULA FITTS, home health care administrator, nurse; b. Linden, Tex., Mar. 27, 1955; d. Otis Wayland and Doris Faye (Knight) Fitts; m. Terry Hugh Elders, Oct. 23, 1976; 1 child, Tyler Hugh. A.A.S., in Nursing, Texarkana Community Coll., 1976. Charge nurse, Linden Mcpl. Hosp., Linden, 1976-80, ICU supr., 1979-82, inservice edn. dir., 1980-82, instr. CETA sponsored nurse aide course, 1980, quality assurance coordinator, 1980-81, asst. dir. nurses, 1981, dir. nurses, 1981-82, clin. instr. Sch. Vocat. Nursing, 1982, dir. Sch. Vocat. Nursing, 1982-83, shift supr., 1983-84, asst. dir. nurses, 1984, dir. Linden Mcpl. Hosp. Home Health System, 1984—; nurse cons. Oak Manor Nursing Home, Linden, 1980-81. Sunday sch. tchr. Linden United Meth. Ch., 1983-85; mem. Cave Springs Community Club, Linden; instr. ARC, Linden, 1982—; vol. Am. Cancer Soc., Linden, 1985; vol. facilitator As Parents Grow Older/Family Eldercare Inc., Linden, 1985. Avocations: reading; fishing; piano. Home: 401 Crow St Linden TX 75563

ELDREDGE, H. RICHARD, television broadcasting executive. Exec. v.p. Knight-Ridder Broadcasting, Inc., Miami, Fla. Office: Knight-Ridder Broadcasting Inc 1 Herald Plaza Miami FL 33101*

ELENBURG, CAROLYN MORRIS, early childhood educator; b. Pell City, Ala., July 13, 1947; d. Kenneth and Vera Ruth (Hyde) Morris; m. Gaines Elenburg, Jr., July 1, 1967; 1 dau., Amy Darlene. Student Jefferson State Jr. Coll., 1965-67, U. Ala.-Birmingham, 1968. Faculty Oak Hill Pvt. Sch., Inc., Birmingham, Ala., 1976—, now five yr. old kindergarten tchr., asst. prin. Presbyterian. Home: 2939 Ave Z Birmingham AL 35208 Office: 4716 Ave I Birmingham AL 35208

ELEQUIN, CLETO, JR., physician; b. Antique, Philippines, Oct. 18, 1933; s. Cleto and Enriqueta (Tengonciang) E.; M.D., Far Eastern U. (Philippines), 1957; m. Nancy Johnson, May 14, 1958; children—Tracy, Thomas Kyle, Stuart Scott. Rotating intern Good Samaritan Hosp., Lexington, Ky., 1957-58; gen. practice resident Central Bapt. Hosp., Lexington, 1958-59; psychiat. resident State Hosp., Danville, Pa., 1959-60, 61-62; psychiat. resident with child psychiatry State Hosp., New Castle, Del., 1962-63; staff physician Eastern State Hosp., Lexington, 1960-61, dir. Fayette County Project, dir. intensive treatment service, 1964-67, supt., 1969-71; dep. commr. Dept. Mental Health, State Ky., 1967-69; practice medicine, specializing in family practice, Pecos, Tex., 1971-72, Austin, Tex., 1974—; asst. dep. commr. Tex. Dept. Mental Health and Mental Retardation, Austin, 1973-74, dep. commr. mental health, 1974; attending psychiatrist U. Ky. Med. Center, 1964-71, Good Samaritan Hosp., 1969-71, Central Bapt. Hosp., 1966-71; cons. psychiatrist U. Ky. Student Health Service, 1965-71, Peace Corps, 1966-68, Bur. Rehab., State Ky., 1965-71, Blue Grass Community Care Center, 1967-71, Covington (Ky.) Community Care Center, 1969-71, Hazard Community Care Center, 1969-71, Danville (Ky.) Community Care Center, 1969-71, Maysville (Ky.) Community Care Center, 1969-71; clin. instr., asst. clin. prof. dept. psychiatry U. Ky. Med. Center, 1964-69, asso. clin. prof., 1969-71. Mem. Profl. Adv. Council Community Mental Health-Retardation Center, Lexington, 1967-71; mem. Lexington Hosp. Council, 1969-71. Mem. AMA, Am. Psychiat. Assn., Tex. Med. Assn., Travis County Med. Soc., Austin Psychiat. Soc., Assn. Med. Supts. Mental Hosps., Am. Acad. Family Physicians. Home: 7109 Montana Norte Austin TX 78731 Office: 942 Peyton Gin Rd Austin TX 78758

ELEUTERIUS, LIONEL NUMA, botany educator; b. Biloxi, Miss., Dec. 25, 1936. A.S., Perkinston Jr. Coll., 1958; student Miss. State U., 1958-59; B.S., U. So. Miss., 1966, M.S. in Botany, 1968; Ph.D. in Botany, Miss. State U., 1974. Biol. technician Plant Pathology Lab., U.S. Dept. Agr. Forest Service, Gulfport, Miss., 1961-65; lab. instr., research asst. U. So. Miss., Hattiesburg, 1965-68, instr. botany and genetics U. So. Miss. Resident Ctr., Keesler AFB, Biloxi, 1969-70; prof. botany, head botany sect. Gulf Coast Research Lab., Ocean Springs, Miss., 1968—, instr. summer session, 1976—; adj. assoc. prof. botany Miss. State U., 1976—; adj. asst. prof. biology U. Miss., 1977—, U. So. Miss., 1981—; mem. Deer Island Study Com., 1978-79; mem. Nat. Wetlands Tech. Council, Washington; mem. Miss. Gov.'s Conf. on Coastal Zone Mgmt., 1974. Served with U.S. Army, 1959-60, to maj. Army N.G., 1960-77. Mem. Am. Inst. Biol. Scis., Am. Bot. Soc., So. Appalachian Bot. Club (v.p. 1979-80), Am. Soc. Limnology and Oceanography, AAAS, Am. Soc. Naturalists, Soil Sci. Soc. Am., Am. Soc. Plant Taxonomists, Ecol. Soc. Am., Internat. Assn. Aquatic Plant Biologists, Miss. Acad. Sci. (chmn. botany sect. 1970-71), Torrey Bot. Club, Soc. Wetland Scientists, Internat. Assn. for Plant Taxonomy, Phi Theta Kappa, Beta Beta Beta. Contbr. articles on botany to profl. jours.; reviewer manuscripts for jours. Office: Gulf Coast Research Lab Ocean Springs MS 39564

ELEUTERIUS, NANCY LEA, hospital administrator; b. Biloxi, Miss., Aug. 19, 1943; d. Leo and Mary (Cochrane) E.; m. Nick Cefalu, Sept. 9, 1961 (div. Oct. 1975); children—Deborah, Cindy. Student Thomas Nelson Coll., 1972-73, U. Ind., 1975-76. Dir. patient adminstrv. services Riverside Hosp., Newport News, Va., 1970-80, Norfolk Gen. Hosp., Va., 1980—; workshop leader Eastern Va. Med. Sch., Norfolk, 1981. Contbr. articles to profl. jours. Bd. dirs. local unit Am. Cancer Soc., 1979-80. Named Outstanding Dept. Head of Yr., Norfolk Gen. Hosp., 1983, recipient Dept. Head Leadership award, 1984. Mem. Nat. Assn. Hosp. Admitting Mgrs. (accredited; regional facilitator 1984, regional rep. to edn. com. 1983—), Tidewater Assn. Hosp. Admitting Mgrs. (pres., founder 1979, bd. dirs. 1979—, v.p. 1981—), Va. Hosp. Assn. (prin. speaker 1980), Am. Hosp. Assn., Norfolk Gen. Hosp. Vols. Roman Catholic. Avocations: music, theatre, sailing. Home: 2217 Sun Vista Dr Virginia Beach VA 23455 Office: Norfolk Gen Hosp 600 Gresham Dr Norfolk VA 23507

EL-FAYOUMY, SAAD G. A., economist, banker, accountant, consultant; b. Cairo, Egypt, June 10, 1926; came to U.S., 1962, naturalized, 1973; s. Guirguis Awad El-Fayoumy and Labiba Youssef Boustarous (El-Sissi) El-F.; m. Joanne Patricia (Quinn), Sept. 8, 1963. B.A., Cairo U., 1949, M.A., 1960; Ph.D., NYU, 1972. Cert. acct., Egypt; C.P.A., Va. Chief insp., mgr., chief auditor, chief acct. Banque Misr, Egypt, 1949-61; under sec. econ. planning President's Council for Econ. Planning, Cairo, 1962; economist Egyptian interest section UN, N.Y.C., 1962-67; cons. to World Bank, Agrl. Bank of Sudan, Khartoum, Sudan, 1982-84; prof. Norfolk State U., Va., 1967—; dir. Banking Edn. Ctr., Norfolk State U., 1974—; dir., vice-chmn. Hirschfeld Bank of Commerce, Virginia Beach, Va., 1976-78. Author: New Accounting Systems, 1984; New Budgeting Systems, 1984; Agriculture and Commercial Banking Techniques, 1984. Founder-pres. Arab-Am. Assn. Va., Hampton Roads, Va., 1970; bd. dirs. World Affairs Council, Norfolk, 1970—; chmn. Faculty Benefits Commn., Faculty Senate of Va., 1969-81. Recipient Founders Day award, NYU, 1973. Fellow Va. Soc. C.P.A.s, mem. Am. Econ. Assn., Atlantic Econ. Soc., Am. Fin. Assn. Mem. Coptic Orthodox of Alexandria. Republican. Home: 652 Greentree Dr Virginia Beach VA 23452 Office: 650 Greentree Dr Virginia Beach VA 23452

ELFSTROM, DOROTHY LILLIAN BETTENCOURT (MRS. WALTER WILLIAM ELFSTROM), author; b. Galveston, Tex.; d. Henry Joseph and Margaret (Rowan) Bettencourt; grad. Draughon's Bus. Coll.; m. Walter William Elfstrom (dec.); children—Dorothy Elfstrom Bailey, Bill, Henry. Weekly columnist Texas City Sun; poet laureate Galveston County; poet laureate State of Tex.; contbr. poetry to Galveston mag., Travelhost mag., IDEALS mag. Recipient 1st pl. awards Nat. Fedn. Press Women, 1963, Tex. Press Women, 1963. Author: Challenge of the Seasons, 1963; Fireside Fancies, 1960; Voyager on the Sea of Life, 1971; Seeker, 1974. Writer various songs including But I Just Can't Say Goodbye; You're Way Behind the Beat, Lovely Galveston; What Are you Trying to Find; At Taps Time I Have a Date With You; Not for Keeps; You Have Shaken Up My World; I Know You've Got to Go; Now You Won't Let Me Be; No Plastic Heart for Me; I Have Captured an Old-Fashioned Christmas; I Fell in Love with You in Old San Antonio; That Good Old-Fashioned 14 Karat Band. Contbr. to numerous mags., newspapers. Home: 3815 Ave S Galveston TX 77550

ELGUINDI, AHMED SABRI, physician, educator; b. Egypt, Nov. 11, 1938; came to U.S., 1972; m. Jutta Ehlhert, Dec. 30, 1980; children—Laila; children from previous marriage—Nader, Nellie. M.D., Alexandria U., 1964. Diplomate Am. Bd. Internal Medicine and Pulmonary Medicine. Intern, resident Alexandria U. Hosp., 1963-67; med. house officer, registrar Foubourne, Rochford and Hillcrest hosps., Eng., 1969-72 resident Allegheny Gen. Hosp., Pitts., 1972-74; pulmonary fellow Med. Coll. Ga., Augusta, 1977-79; lectr. Alexandria U., 1967-69; dir. ambulatory care Allegheny Gen. Hosp., 1974-77; asst. prof. medicine med. Coll. Ga. and VA Med. Ctr., Augusta, 1979-84, assoc. prof., 1984—; med. dir. respiratory and pulmonary diagnostic lab., 1980-85. Contbr. articles to profl. jours. Grantee VA. Fellow Am. Coll Chest Physicians, A.C.P.; mem. Am. Thoracic Soc., Ga. Thoracic Soc., AMA. Avocations: jogging; growing roses. Office: Pulmonary Disease Sect VA Med Ctr 2460 Wrightsboro Rd Augusta GA 30910

ELIEL, ERNEST LUDWIG, chemist, educator, author; b. Cologne, Germany, Dec. 28, 1921; came to U.S. 1946; s. Oskar and Luise (Tietz) E.; m. Eva Schwarz Dec. 23, 1949; children—Ruth Louise, Carol Susan. D.Phys. Chem. Sci., U. Havana, Cuba, 1946; Ph.D., U. Ill, 1948; D.Sc. (hon.), Duke U., 1983. Instr. to prof. U. Notre Dame, 1948-72, prof., 1960-72, head dept. chemistry, 1964-66; W.R. Kenan Jr. prof. chemistry U. N.C., Chapel Hill, 1972—. Chmn. Internat. Relations Council, St. Joseph County, South Bend, Ind., 1961-63; trustee Stanley Clark Sch., South Bend, 1962-67; chmn. United Jewish Appeal drive, Chapel Hill, 1985-86. Recipient Coll. Chemistry Tchrs. award Chem. Mfgrs. Assn., 1965, Laurent Lavoisier medal French Chem. Soc., 1968; NSF fellow, 1958-59, 67-68; Guggenheim fellow, 1975-76, 83-84. Fellow AAAS; mem. Nat. Acad. Sci., Am. Acad. Arts, Scis., Am. Chem. Soc. (medal Cleve. sect. 1965, Mosher award 1983, dir. 1985—), Chem. Soc. London, AAUP, Sigma Xi. Author: Stereochemistry of Carbon Compounds, 1962; (with others) Conformational Analysis, 1965; Elements of Stereochemistry, 1969. Co-editor Topics in Stereochemistry, 16 vol. series, 1967—; also more than 200 articles, revs. to publs. Office: Dept Chemistry 045A U NC Chapel Hill NC 27514

ELISHA, WALTER Y., textile manufacturing company executive; b. 1932; student Wabash (Ind.) Coll., Harvard U. Sch. Bus.; married. Vice chmn. bd., dir. Jewel Cos., 1965-80, chmn. pres., chief exec. officer Springs Industries, Inc., Ft. Mill, S.C., 1980—; dir. Jack Eckerd Corp. Office: Springs Industries Inc PO Box 70 205 N White St Fort Mill SC 29715*

ELISSALDE, GWENDOLYN SCHEUERMANN, veterinary microbiologist; b. Suyoc, Luzon, Philippines, Oct. 7, 1939; d. Gustav John and Helen Grace (Friday) Scheuermann; B.S., S.W. Tex. State U., 1973; B.S. in Vet. Sci., Tex. A&M U., 1976, D.V.M., 1977, Ph.D., 1980; m. Marcel Howell Elissalde, Jr., Dec. 19, 1967; children—Kitty Lynette, Daniel Paul, Nora Elena, Morgan Christian. Electronics technician Tex. A&M U., 1964, lab. mechanic, 1964-66, marine geophysics technician, 1967-69, parasitology student worker, 1975-77, vet. clin. asso., 1977-80, asst. prof. dept. vet. microbiology-parasitology Coll. Vet. Medicine, 1980—, also dir. Clin. Immunology Lab. Faculty adv. women's service orgn., 1980—. Contbr. articles to sci. jours. Served with USN, 1958-59. Recipient Charles Spurgeon Smith award in biology, 1974. Mem. Am. Assn. Vet. Immunology, Am. Soc. Microbiology, AAUP, Am. Assn. Women in Sci., Am. Assn. Vet. Parasitologists, Am. Assn. Vet. Med. Colls. Council Educators, Alpha Chi, Beta Beta Beta, Phi Sigma. Unitarian. Home: 1507 Medina College Station TX 77840 Office: Coll Vet Medicine Tex A&M U College Station TX 77843

ELKINS, DARRELL THOMASON, aviation insurance company executive; b. San Mateo, Calif., Jan. 11, 1946; s. Stacy Byron and Helen (Cantrel) E.; m. Pamela JoAnn Obriotti, Aug. 1, 1970; children—Jason, Jeffrey, Jonathan. B.B.A., North Tex. State U., 1969; Ph.D., Pacific Western U., 1984. Regional rep. Nat. Aviation Underwriters, Dallas, 1969-70; v.p. Airbanc of Am., Inc., St. Louis, 1969-70; mgr. Internat. Aviation Underwriters, Dallas, 1970-78; chmn., chief exec. officer Darrell Elkins & Co., Inc., Houston, 1972—; v.p., sec., treas. John Nichols Ins. Co., Houston, 1978—, Worldwide Aircraft Sales Co., Houston, 1981—; chief exec. officer J.A. Elkins Bros. Pub. Co., 1984—; ptnr. Montgomery County Investment Co.; dir. Intercontinental Ins. Co., Houston, Intercontinental Techs., Houston. Author: Aviation Insurance-An Introduction to General Aviation Insurance in the United States, 1983. Columnist, Houston Aviation Jour., 1985. Chmn., Montgomery County Polit. Action Com., Porter, Tex., 1982. Mem. Aviation Ins. Assn., Helicopter Operators of Tex. (treas. 1983-85), Confederate Air Force (col. 1969), Montgomery County C. of C., Houston C. of C. (mem. rotocraft subcom. of aviation com. 1984-85), Mitsubishi Owners Assn. (co-founder, dir.). Methodist. Office: Darrell Elkins & Co Inc PO Drawer 785 Porter TX 77365

ELKINS, HOWARD FREDERIC, financial company executive; b. N.Y.C., Mar. 4, 1934; s. Frank F. and Flora (White) E.; m. Helen Grace Elkins, Dec. 21, 1960; children—Gordon, Douglas, Alexandra. B.A., St. Lawrence U., 1956. Exec. v.p. Travel-Wide Syndicate, N.Y.C., 1957-60; pres., R.E.T. Internat., N.Y.C., 1960-62, Lloyd's Industries Ltd., N.Y.C., 1962—; chmn. Overseas Trade & Devel. Corp., Del., 1967-76; dep. sec.-gen. Metra Internat., London and Paris, 1966-76; pres. Hormel Internat. Corp., 1968-76; chmn., chief exec. officer Holt Lloyd Americas Ltd., Atlanta, 1976—, pres. Holt Lloyd Corp., from 1976, now chmn., chief exec. officer; chmn. Holt Lloyd Ltd., Can., Toronto, 1984—; joint mng. dir. Holt Lloyd Internat. PLC, 1984—; chmn. L.P.S. Export, 1980—, Kert Chem. Industries, Toronto, 1984—, Holt Lloyd Australasia Ltd., Sydney, Holt Lloyd Ltd., Aukland, N.Z.; dir. O.P.F. Corp., Okinawa, Japan, Wis., Inter-Holding Co., Del., Lloyd's Trading Corp., N.Y.C., L.I. Internat. Holdings Pty. Ltd., Sydney, Australia; guest lectr. internat. mktg. Aoyama-Gakuin U. Tokyo, 1960. Dir., officer Atlanta Civic Opera Assn. Served to lt. AUS, 1956. Mem. Am. Mgmt. Assn., Brit.-Am. C. of C. N.Y., Can.-Am. Soc. World Trade Club Atlanta (dir.), Brit.-Am. Bus. Group (dir.), Omicron Delta Kappa. Club: Naval and Mil. (London). Contbr. articles to internat. mktg. and world trade bus. jours. Home: 2867 Wyngate Dr NW Atlanta GA 30305 Office: 4647 Hugh Howell Rd Tucker GA 30084

ELKINS, JAMES ANDERSON, JR., banker; b. Galveston, Tex., Mar. 24, 1919; s. James Anderson and Isabel (Mitchell) E.; B.A., Princeton U., 1941; m. Margaret Wiess, Nov. 24, 1945; children—Elise, James Anderson III, Leslie K. With First City Nat. Bank, Houston, 1941—, v.p., 1946-50, pres., 1950-60, chmn. bd., 1960-79, also dir.; chmn. bd. First City Bancorp., Inc., 1970—, also dir.; dir. Eastern Airlines, Cameron Iron Works, Am. Gen. Ins. Co., Houston, Freeport McMoran, Inc., N.Y.C. Trustee U. Houston, Baylor Coll. Medicine, Princeton U. Episcopalian. Home: 101 Farish Circle Houston TX 77024 Office: First City Nat Bank Houston TX 77001

ELKINS, JAMES ANDREW, JR., lawyer; b. Little Rock, Jan. 24, 1940; s. James Andrew and Doris (O'Neal) E.; A.B., U. of South, 1962; J.D., U. Ga., 1965; m. Martha Lee Allen, Nov. 11, 1963; children—James Andrew, Allen Lee, Martha Lee. Admitted to Ga. bar, 1965; asso. firm Roberts and Thornton, Columbus, Ga., 1965-69, Roberts, Elkins & Kilpatrick, Columbus, 1969-71, Grogan, Jones & Layfield, Columbus, 1971-72; individual practice law, Columbus, 1972-73; ptnr. firm Elkins & Flournoy, P.C., Columbus, 1973-83, Elkins & Gemmette, 1983—. Bd. dirs. Pioneer Little League Columbus, Inc., 1977-79, sec., 1978-79; mem. Com. on Drug Abuse Control, 1971-75. Mem. Am. Trial Lawyers Assn., Ga. Trial Lawyers Assn., Ga. Assn. Criminal Def. Lawyers, State Bar Ga., Chattahoochee Bar Assn., Nat. Orgn. Social Security Claimants Reps. Republican. Episcopalian. Club: Columbus Lawyers. Home: 6130 Canterbury Dr Columbus GA 31904 Office: PO Box 1736 Columbus GA 31902

ELKINS, THOMAS WAYNE, public administrator; b. Whiteville, N.C., Mar. 18, 1950; s. Roscoe Edison, Sr. and Lillian Hazel (Hayes) E.; m. Anne Marie

Hickson, July 12, 1975. B.A. in Internat. Studies, U. N.C., 1973. Lic. county adminstr. N.C. Inst. Govt.; real estate broker. Personnel technician N.C. Dept. Human Resources, Raleigh, 1974; adminstrv. asst. N.C. Div. Health Services, Raleigh, 1974-75, adminstrv. officer, 1975-78, pub. health program mgr., 1978-80; exec. dir. Region L Council of Govts., Rocky Mount, N.C., 1980—; dir. Emergency Med. Services Systems, Inc., Greenville, N.C., Devel. Evaluation Ctr. Adv. Bd., Rocky Mount; vice chmn. N.C. Regional Dirs. Assn., Raleigh, 1983-84; mem. Internat. Personnel Mgmt. Assn., Raleigh, 1974-76. Author newspaper articles (Golden Star Journalism award southeastern N.C. 1968). Mem. Internat. City Mgmt. Assn., N.C. City and County Mgmt. Assn., Eastern N.C. Devel. Assn., Nash County Migrant Council, Nash County Community and Rural Devel. Com., Sir Walter Jaycees (external v.p. 1976-78), Gen. Alumni Assn.-U. N.C. Democrat. Presbyterian. Club: Fairfield Harbour Country (New Bern, N.C.). Avocations: fishing; reading; basketball; dancing. Home: 3305 Jason Dr Rocky Mount NC 27801 Office: Region L Council of Govts PO Drawer 2748 Rocky Mount NC 27802

ELKS, JEANNE FARABOW, educator, basketball and softball coach; m. Fuquay-Varina, N.C., June 2, 1944; d. Willie Grey and Mary Joyce (Mann) Farabow; m. James H. Elks, Dec. 20, 1969; 1 dau., Julia Anne. B.S., East Carolina U., Greenville, N.C., 1966, M.Ed., 1967. Cert. in health and phys. edn., N.C. Tchr. health and phys. edn., coach girls basketball and softball Plymouth (N.C.) High Sch., 1967—; tchr. Kay Yow Basketball Camp, N.C. State U., 1979—. Grad. teaching fellow, 1966; named Most Outstanding Sr., Women's Recreation Assn., 1966, Basketball Coach of Yr., Northeastern Athletic Conf., 1982, 83, 84, Tchr. of Yr., Washington County, N.C., 1984. Mem. AAHPERD, NEA, N.C. Edn. Assn., N.C. Coaches Assn., Community Schs. Assn. (dir.). Democrat. Methodist. Home: PO Box 254 Plymouth NC 27962 Office: Box 827 Plymouth NC 27962

ELLEFSON, GEORGE EDWIN, JR., cons. elec. engr.; b. Ft. Smith, Ark., June 19, 1929; s. George Edwin and Cecil (Soard) E.; B.S.E.E., U. Ark., 1954; m. Claire Stannus, Aug. 28, 1952; children—Dorothy Lyn, Jane Ann. Staff engr. Sandia Corp., Albuquerque; project engr. Reynolds Metal Co., Jones Mills, Ark.; elec. engr. Erhart, Eichembaum, Ruach and Blass, Architects, Little Rock; now owner cons. elec. engring. firm; dir. Brock, Ellefson and Assos. Served with Armed Forces, 1947-50; mem. Res., 1954-56. Mem. IEEE (sr.), AAAS, N.Y. Acad. Sci., IES, NFPA, Am. Arbitration Assn. (panel arbitrators), Am. Mgmt. Assn., Assn. Energy Engrs. (charter). Presbyterian. Home and Office: 1617 N Harrison St Little Rock AR 72207

ELLENDER, STEPHEN ERNEST, JR., orthodontist; b. Houma, La., Oct. 21, 1939; s. Stephen Ernest and Ernestine (Boudreaux) E.; m. Sandra Catherine Schmedtje; children—Stephen, Catherine, Ernest, Brian. D.D.S., Loyola U., 1964; Orthodontic Degree, U. Pa., 1985. Diplomate Am. Bd. Orthodontists. Practice orthodontics, Houma La. Mem. La. Orthodontic Assn. (pres. 1973-74), Bayon Dist. Dental Assn. (pres. 1983), Terrebomme Dental Assn. Coll. Diplomates of Am. Bd. Orthodontists. Avocations: marlin fishing; duck hunting. Home: 1111 Bayon Black Dr Houma LA 70360 Office: 808 Belanger St Houma LA 70360

ELLER, DAVID GALLAWAY, agricultural executive, oil and gas exploration and development executive; b. Mexia, Tex., Mar. 13, 1938; s. James Marion and Myrtis (Gallaway) E.; m. Margaretha Sallen, Mar. 5, 1956 (dec. Nov. 1973); children—David Erik, Dirk Gustaf; m. 2d, Linda Schmuck, June 28, 1980. B.S. in Bus. Adminstrn., Tex. A&M U., 1959; Exec. Program, Stanford U., 1977, 84. Mgr. Western Union, Warren & Co., Frankfurt, W.Ger., 1962-65; pres. Becco, Inc., N.Y.C., 1965-72; chmn., chief exec. officer Alcorn Internat., N.Y.C. and London, 1967-72; chmn., chief exec. officer Granada Corp., Houston, 1972—, Am. Nat. Petroleum Co., Houston, 1979—; dir. Allied Bank of Tex., Houston. Founding patron Tex. Bus. Hall of Fame, Houston; co-chmn. Mark White for Gov., Houston, 1982; chmn. Granada Gala, Am. Cancer Soc., Houston, 1982-83; bd. regents Tex. A&M U., 1983—; trustee Baylor Coll. Medicine, Houston. Served to capt. U.S. Army, 1960-62. Mem. Houston Engring. and Sci. Soc., ASME. Methodist. Clubs: Houston Raquet, The Houstonian, Plaza, University. Lodge: Tejas Vaqueros (dir. 1983—). Office: Granada Corp 10900 Richmond Ave Houston TX 77242

ELLINGSWORTH, HUBER WINTON, communications educator; b. Corydon, Iowa, Aug. 13, 1928; s. Arthur J. and Helen Marguerite (Kirk) E.; m. June Gray Davis, Aug. 14, 1952 (dec. 1981); children—Claudia, Denise (dec.), Nancy; m. Sue Marie Young, May 25, 1983. B.A., Pacific U., 1949; M.A., Wash. State U., 1950; Ph.D., Fla. State U., 1955. Asst. prof. communications Mich. State U., East Lansing, 1956-63; prof. Md. State Coll., Frostburg, 1963-66, U. Hawaii, Honolulu, 1966-81; prof., dept. chmn. U. Tulsa, 1981—; cons. Internat. Agrl. Devel. Assn., Rosslyn, Va., 1983—, UNESCO Research Project on new communication techs., Paris, 1984—. Author: Speech and Social Action, 1967; Effective Speech Communication, 1968. Contbr. articles to profl. jours. East-West Ctr. scholar, 1971-72. Mem. Internat. Communication Assn. Democrat. Methodist. Avocations: painting; tennis; travel. Home: 2102 E 25th Pl Tulsa OK 74114 Office: Dept Communications U Tulsa Tulsa OK 74104

ELLINGTON, JOHN DAVID, state official; b. Cramerton, N.C., Dec. 24, 1935; s. Joseph Randolph and Lyda Eva (Skidmore) E.; m. Mary Frances Powell, June 14, 1959; children—Susan Gail, John David, Michael Jon. A.A., Mars Hill Coll., 1956; A.B., U. N.C., 1958, M.Ed., 1961. Tchr. social studies Chapel Hill High Sch., N.C., 1958-65; cons. social studies N.C. Dept. Pub. Instrn., Raleigh, 1965-72, asst. dir. social studies, 1972-76, dir. div. social studies, 1976—; mem. adv. bd. Mini-Page Inc., Washington, 1973-82. Mem., chmn. Enloe Area Adv. Council, Raleigh, N.C., 1981-85; precinct officer Precinct 28, Raleigh, 1981-82; mem. U.S.-Japan Conf. Cultural and Ednl. Interchange, U.S. Office Edn., Tokyo, 1977. Reynolds fellow in econs. U. N.C., Chapel Hill, 1961. Mem. Nat. Council Social Studies (com. chmn. 1984-85), N.C. Council Econ. Edn. (trustee-exec. com. 1975-85), Council State Social Studies Specialists. Democrat. Baptist. Avocations; baseball coach; recreational sports. Home: 1517 N King Charles Rd Raleigh NC 27610 Office: Div Social Studies NC Dept Pub Instrn Raleigh NC 27603

ELLINGTON, REX TRUESDALE, chemical engineer; b. Gunnison, Colo., Apr. 20, 1921; s. Rex Truesdale and Weltha Almeda (Brown) E.; m. Carol Louine Grasmoen, July 15, 1949; children—Lisa Carol, Rex. T. III. B.S. in Chem. Engring., U. Colo., 1943; M.S. in Chem. Engring. and Gas Tech., Ill. Inst. Tech., 1950, Ph.D., 1952. Registered profl. engr., Tex., Okla. Engr., Boston Gas Co., 1950, Chattanooga Gas Co., 1952-54; assoc. dir. Inst. Gas Tech., 1954-63, chmn. edn. program, 1956-63; gen. mgr. mineral resources devel. Sinclair Oil and Gas Co., 1963-69; mgr. syncrude devel. ops. Arco, Dallas, 1969-71; synfuels cons., Denver, 1972; mgr. tech. services Transco, Energy Co., Houston, 1972-74; sr. mgr. projects Fluor Engrs. and Constructors, Inc., Houston, 1974-79; v.p. engring. and tech. devel. Occidental Oil Shale, Grand Junction, Colo., 1979-82; v.p. engring. Cathedral Bluffs Oil Shale Co., Grand Junction, 1981-82; prof. chem. engring. and material scis., U.Okla., Norman, 1982—, co-dir. integrated energy systems project; cons. synfuels, thermodynamics, process control, project mgmt.; v.p., dir. Calumet Creek Oils, Ltd.; dir. Syncrude Can. Ltd. Bd. dirs. Mesa Coll. Devel. Found. Colo., 1981-82. Served with USNR, 1944-46. Named to Hall of Flame, Am. Gas Assn., 1961; recipient Disting. Service award Gas Processors Assn., 1976. Fellow Am. Inst. Chem. Engrs.; mem. Soc. Petroleum Engrs. (disting. lectr. 1972), Am. Mgmt. Assn., Am. Soc. Engring. Edn., Am. Petroleum Inst., Exptl. Aircraft Assn. Contbr. numerous articles on chem. engring. to profl. jours. Patentee in field. Office: 202 W Boyd Room 23 Norman OK 73019

ELLIOT, ROBERT M., furniture company executive. With Levitz Furniture Corp., 1914—, chmn., chief exec. officer, 1983—. Office: Levitz Furniture Corp 1317 NW 167th St Miami FL 33169*

ELLIOTT, ALAN CURTIS, microcomputer specialist, statistician; b. Dallas, July 10, 1952; s. Tom Sanford and Ida Elizabeth (Scirrat) E.; m. Annette Gail Bertrand, Jan. 3, 1974; children—Mary Elizabeth, William Curtis. B.A., Dallas Bapt. U., 1974; M.Applied Stats., So. Meth. U., 1976. Microcomputer cons. So. Meth. U., Dallas, 1982-85; stat. cons. U. Tex. Health Sci. Ctr., Dallas, 1979-82, microcomputer cons., 1985—; v.p. program devel. TexaSoft, Inc., Dallas, 1979—; pres. N. Tex. IBM PC Users Group, Inc., Dallas, 1981-84. Author: On Sunday the Wind Came, 1980; PC Programming Techniques, 1985; (with others) Directory of Microcomputer Statistical Programs, 1985. Mem. Am. Stats. Assn. Republican. Methodist. Club: Old Oak Cliff Conservation League (Dallas). Avocation: woodwork. Home: 812 Penn Pl Cedar Hill TX 75104

ELLIOTT, CAROL S(USIE), human resource generalist; b. Enid, Okla., Oct. 31, 1950; d. Kenneth Lee Baker and Gladys L. Mack; m. Richard R. Elliott, Jan. 31, 1969 (div. Aug. 1978); children—Jeff, Jennifer. Student Draughon Sch. Bus., Oklahoma City, 1969, Central State U., Okla., 1969-72. Accredited human resources profl. Human resource specialist S&A Restaurant Corp., Dallas, 1978-81, dir. corp. personnel, 1981-83, dir. corp. tng., 1983—. Mem. Am. Soc. Tng. and Devel., Am. Soc. Personnel Adminstrs., Dallas Personnel Assn. (v.p. publicity 1985). Republican. Lutheran. Club: Toastmasters (chpt. sec. 1983). Office: S&A Restaurants 6606 LBJ Freeway Dallas TX 75240

ELLIOTT, EDWARD, investment executive, financial planner; b. Madison, Wis., Jan. 11, 1915; s. Edward C. and Elizabeth (Nowland) E.; B.S. in Mech. Engring., Purdue U., 1936; m. Letitia Ord, Feb. 20, 1943 (div. Aug. 1955); children—Emily, Ord; m. Melita Uihlein, Jan. 1, 1958; 1 dau., Deborah. Engr., Gen. Electric Co., Schenectady, 1936-37; engr. Pressed Steel Tank Co., Milw., 1937-38, N.Y.C., 1939-41, dist. sales mgr., Cleve., 1946-48, N.Y.C., 1949-54, sales mgr., Milw., 1954-58; v.p. sales Cambridge Co. div. Carrier Corp., Lowell, Mass., 1958-59; mgr. indsl. and med. sales Liquid Carbonic div. Gen. Dynamics Corp., Chgo., 1959-61; v.p. Haywood Pub. Co., Chgo., 1961-63; pres. Omnibus, Inc., Chgo., 1963-67; gen. sales mgr. Resistoflex Corp., Roseland, N.J., 1967-68; investment exec. Shearson, Hammill & Co., Inc., Chgo., 1968-74; v.p. McCormick & Co., Inc., 1974-75; v.p. Paine, Webber, Inc., Naples, Fla., 1975—. Bd. govs. Purdue U. Found. Served with USAAF, 1941-46. Decorated officer Order Brit. Empire. Mem. Inst. Cert. Fin. Planners, Internat. Assn. Fin. Planning, ASME, Air Force Assn., Phi Delta Theta. Republican. Episcopalian. Clubs: Mid-Day, Racquet (Chgo.); Shore Acres Golf (Lake Bluff, Ill.); Onwentsia (Lake Forest, Ill.); Milwaukee Country, University (Milw.); Chenequa Country (Hartland, Wis.); Lake (Oconomowoc, Wis.); Army-Navy Country (Arlington, Va.); Lafayette (Ind.) Country; Coral Beach (Paget, Bermuda); Rotary, Royal Poinciana Golf, Hole in the Wall Golf, Naples Yacht, Naples Athletic, Olympiad (Naples). Home: 1285 Gulf Shore Blvd N Naples FL 33940 Office: Paine Webber Inc 1400 Gulf Shore Blvd N Naples FL 33940

ELLIOTT, ELLEN LEE BRIDEWELL, educator, counselor; b. Beauregard, Miss., Apr. 18, 1917; d. Nathaniel and Bettie (Duncan) Bridewell; m. Edwin Powers Elliott, Sept. 10, 1946; children—Edwin Powers Jr., Francis Moxom. Student Montreal Coll., 1935-37; A.B., Northwestern State U., 1939; M.R.E., Presbyterian Sch. Christian Edn., 1945; postgrad. Pa. State U., Coll. William and Mary, U. Va., Commonwealth U., George Washington U., Tchr., Ascension Parish, La., 1938-42; missionary North Ga. Presbyn. Ch., 1942-43; dir. Christian edn. Clifton Forge Presbyn. Ch., Va., 1945-46; Bible tchr., Brunswick County, Va., 1946-48; dir. Christian edn. First Presbyn. Ch., Utica, N.Y., 1954-57; tchr., counselor Eichelberger High Sch., Hanover, Pa., 1958-59, Biglerville High Sch., Pa., 1959-62; counselor Prince William County Pub. Schs., Va., 1962—. Active Republican Party. Mem. No. Va. Personnel and Guidance Assn. (pres. 1969), Am. Sch. Counselors Assn., Va. State Counselors Assn., Nat. Vocat. Guidance Assn., Va. Vocat. Guidance Assn., D.A.R., United Daus Confederacy. Avocations: creative writing; gardening; grandchildren. Home: 8902 Center St Manassas VA 22110 Office: Parkside Middle Sch 8602 Mathis Ave Manassas VA 22111

ELLIOTT, FRANK WALLACE, lawyer, foundation executive; b. Cotulla, Tex., June 25, 1930; s. Frank Wallace and Eunice Marie (Akin) E.; m. Winona Trent, July 3, 1954 (dec. 1981); 1 dau., Harriet Lindsey; m. Kay Elkins, Aug. 15, 1983. B.A., U. Tex., 1951, LL.B., 1957. Bar: Tex. 1957, U.S. Supreme Ct. 1962, U.S. Ct. Mil. Appeals 1974. Asst. atty. gen. State of Tex., 1957; briefing atty. Supreme Ct. Tex., 1957-58; prof. U. Tex. Law Sch., 1958-77; dean, prof. law Tex. Tech. U. Sch. Law, 1977-80; pres. Southwestern Legal Found., 1980—; parliamentarian Tex. Senate, 1969-73; dir. research Tex. Constl. Revision Commn., 1973. Author: Texas Judicial Process, 2d edit., 1977; Texas Trial and Appellate Practice, 2d edit., 1974; Cases on Evidence, 1980; West's Texas Forms, 18 vols., 1977—. Served with U.S. Army, 1951-53, 73-74. Decorated Purple Heart, Meritorious Service medal, Army Commendation medal. Mem. Inter-Am Bar Assn., ABA, Judge Advs. Assn., Am. Judicature Soc., Res. Officers Assn., Am. Bar Found., Am. Law Inst., Tex. Bar Found. Home: 7710 Scotia Dr Dallas TX 75248 Office: PO Box 830707 Richardson TX 75083

ELLIOTT, JERRY CHRIS, engineer, physicist; b. Oklahoma City, Feb. 6, 1943. B.S. in Physics, U. Okla., 1966. Guidance engr. NASA, Houston, 1966-67, systems engr., 1967-68, trajectory engr., 1968-72, ops. mgr., 1972-74, project engr., 1974-85, tech. mgr. space sta. configuration design, 1985—; founder, dir. Nat. Soc. Am. Indian Engrs., 1976-77, Am. Indian Sci. and Engring. Soc., Oklahoma City, 1977-79. Contbr. articles to profl. jours. Nat. chmn. Native Am. Awareness Week, 1976; emergency care technician ARC, Houston, 1983—. Recipient Presdl. Medal of Freedom, Pres. Nixon, 1970, Sci. and Engring. Nat. Achievement award Am. Indian Art and Cultural Exchange, 1976, Bronze Halo Humanitarian award So. Calif. Motion Picture Council, 1983. Mem. Nat. Mgmt. Assn., Fed. Bus. Assn., Poetry Soc. Tex. Clubs: Intertribal Council Houston, Bay Area Classical Guitar Soc. Avocations: jewelry design and crafting; guitar; outdoors guide. Home: PO Box 58182 Houston TX 77258 Office: NASA Johnson Space Ctr Houston TX 77058

ELLIOTT, JOHN FRANKLIN, clergyman; b. Neosho, Mo., June 11, 1915; s. William Marion and Charlotte Jeanette (Crump) E.; student Maryville Coll., 1933-35; A.B., Austin Coll., 1937; postgrad. Louisville Presbyn. Sem., 1937-38, U. Tenn., 1938, Dallas Theol. Sem., 1939-40; B.D., Columbia Theol. Sem., 1942, M.Div., 1971; D.Litt. (hon.), Internat. Acad., 1954; m. Winifred Margaret Key, July 6, 1939; children—Paul Timothy, Stephen Marion, Andrew Daniel. Ordained to ministry Presbyterian Ch., 1942; founder Emory Presbyn. Ch., Atlanta, 1941, Wildwood Presbyn. Ch., Salem, Va., 1950; pastor Wylam Presbyn. Ch., Birmingham, Ala., 1942-47, Salem Presbyn. Ch., 1947-51, Calvary Presbyn. Ch. Ind., Fort Worth, 1952—; founder, pastor Grace Presbyn. Ch. Ind., Roanoke, Va., 1951-52; founder headmaster Colony Christian Sch., Ft. Worth, 1968—; sometime chaplain Dallas Cowboys, Tex. Rangers, 1985, 86. Bd. dirs., pres. Salem (Va.) Nursing Assn., 1949; charter mem. Fellowship Independent Evang. Chs., 1950—, pres., 1967, nat. sec., 1971; founder, dir. Ft. Worth Home Bible Classes, 1954—; dir. Spanish Publs., Inc., 1969—; bd. dirs. Ind. Bd. for Presbyn. Home Missions, 1956-74; dist. committeeman Longhorn council Boy Scouts Am., Ft. Worth, 1960-66; bd. dirs. Union Gospel Mission, Ft. Worth, 1965-70, pres., 1968; mem. U.S. Coast Guard Aux., Ft. Worth, 1967—; pilot, chaplain, col. CAP, Ft. Worth, 1970—, chmn. nat. chaplain com., 1979-80, chief of chaplains, 1980-82; mem. Tex. State CAP Commn., 1978-83; ministerial adviser bd. dirs. Reformed Theol. Sem., Jackson, Miss., 1973-82; chaplain Tex. Constl. Conv., 1974; bd. dirs. Scripture Memory Fellowship Internat., 1979-83, Graham Bible Coll., 1966-74. Fellow Philos. Soc. Gt. Britain (Victoria Inst.), Royal Geog. Soc., Huguenot Soc. of London. Clubs: Ft. Worth, Ridglea Country, Ft. Worth Boat, Rotary. Home: 3980 Edgehill Rd Fort Worth TX 76116 Office: 4800 El Campo Ave Fort Worth TX 76107

ELLIOTT, LEO BOYD, JR., petroleum geologist; b. Tyler, Tex., Feb. 4, 1957; s. Leo Boyd and Frances Bernice (Fulford) E.; m. F. Carol McMahon, Aug. 18, 1979; 1 child, Jordan Lewis. B.S., Ark. Tech. U., 1979. Mining geologist Homestake Mining Co., Grants, N.Mex., 1979-81; petroleum geologist Ricks Exploration Co., Oklahoma City, 1981—. Mem. Am. Assn. Petroleum Geologists (jr.), Oklahoma City Geol. Soc. Republican. Baptist. Club: Jaycee's (Edmond, Okla.). Avocations: athletics; hunting; fishing; bowling; golf. Office: Ricks Exploration Co 5600 N May St Suite 350 Oklahoma City OK 73112

ELLIOTT, LILLY MAE, oil company executive, consultant; b. Jackson, Miss., July 15, 1909; d. William Scott and Mary (Tucker) Hill; m. Donald Dwight Elliott, July 22, 1925 (dec. 1981); children—Martha Elliott Ramsey, Mary Elliott Harlan (dec.). Student Kidd Key Women's Coll., Sherman, Tex., 1924-25. Chmn., v.p., dir. Don Elliott, Inc., Sherman, 1959—. Bd. dirs. Sherman Service League, 1969—, Dallas Civic Opera Guild, 1971—, Met. Opera Guild Dallas, 1972—, Preservation League, Sherman, 1973—, Sherman Hist. Museum, 1980—; mem. woman's guild bd. Sherman Musical Arts, 1973—. Mem. Woman's Guild Dallas, Woman's Guild Sheman, So. Meth. U. Alumni Assn.; hon. mem. Grayson County Guidance Clinic, Child Guidance Clinic. Republican. Methodist. Clubs: Sherman Garden (pres. 1946), Woodlawn Country, Mr. L's, Pompanos, Current Rev. (pres. 1976), Rejebian Rev., Tuesday Lit., 200 (sec. 1960) Sherman; Tanglewood (Dallas). Home: 709 W Washington Sherman TX 75090 Office: Don Elliott Inc M & P PLaza Bldg Suite 4 Sherman TX 75090

ELLIOTT, MARGARET HENDERSON, reading educator, clinical diagnostician, consultant; b. Pittsylvania County, Va., Oct. 28, 1942; d. David Lawson and Louise (Puryear) Henderson; m. Lauriston Kennerly Elliott, Nov. 15, 1963; children—Alice Marilyn, David Kennerly. Diploma Phillips Bus. Coll., Lynchburg, Va., 1961; student U. Va., 1970-71, Stratford Coll., 1972; B.A. in Edn., Averett Coll., 1974; M.S. in Edn. summa cum laude, Longwood Coll., 1982. Cert. tchr., reading specialist, supr., Va. Stenographer, Va. chpt. Arthritis and Rheumatism Found., Lynchburg, 1962; sec., office mgr. Riverside Constrn. Co., South Boston, Va., 1963-68; pvt. piano tchr., Halifax, Va., 1968-71; adminstrv. tchr. Cluster Springs Acad. (Va.), 1971-74; resource tchr. Charlotte County Pub. Schs. Reading Ctr., 1974-76; reading specialist, diagnostician, resource tchr. Chase City Acad. (Va.), 1976-82, master tchr., cons., 1982-85; lang. arts supr., asst. supr. Mecklenburg Acad., 1985—; cons. Mecklenburg Ednl. Found., 1982-83. Bd. dirs. Dan River Youth; Dan River Assn. Mission Action dir., 1979-81, Acteen dir., 1981-83. Recipient Community Service Program award Southside Community Coll., 1975, Superior Instrn. award State AAA. Mem. Averett Alumni Assn., Longwood Alumni Assn., Assn. Va. Acads., Kappa Delta Pi. So. Baptist. Club: Lakewood Homemakers (Halifax). Home: Route 2 Box 522 Halifax VA 24558 Office: 449 Dodd St Chase City VA 23924

ELLIOTT, ROBERT BURL, orthopaedic surgeon; b. Kirksville, Mo., Dec. 30, 1919; s. Burl Dennis and Beatrice (Corbin) E.; A.B., U. Iowa, 1941, M.D., 1943; M.S., U. Minn., 1951; m. Georgia Anne Lindley, Aug. 24, 1950; children—Robert Burl, Stephen Corbin, Gregory Taylor. Intern, Md. Gen. Hosp., Balt., 1944; Cole fellow in orthopaedic surgery U. Minn., Mayo Clinic, 1944-47; practice orthopaedic surgery, Houston, 1948—; instr. orthopaedic surgery Lillie Jolly Sch. Nursing, Meml. Hosp.; former chmn. orthopaedic sect., former chief surgery, dir. acad. orthopaedics Meml. Hosp.; instr. clin. faculty Baylor U. Med. Sch.; prof. U. Tex. Med. Sch. Diplomate Am. Bd. Orthopaedic Surgery, Am. Acad. Orthopaedic Surgery. Recipient Residents Outstanding Tchr. award, 1984; Spl. Outstanding Service award U. Tex. Family Practice Residents, 1985. Fellow ACS, Internat. Coll. Surgeons (v.p. U.S. sect. 1980, pres. Tex. 1970-71, regent for Tex. 1972-76, U.S. regent 1976-80, chmn. U.S. bd. regents 1981-83, chmn. bd. trustees 1984-85, recognition award 1983); mem. Am. Fracture Assn. (pres. 1969-71; bd. govs.), Tex. Orthopaedic Soc., So., Pan-Am. med. assns., Houston Surg. Soc., ASTM (F-4 award merit 1977, hon. fellow and soc. award merit 1979, exec. bd. 1968—, chmn. osteosynthesis sect. 1968-80, chmn. orthopedics subcom. 1974-80, chmn. long-range planning and devel. commn. 1982—, bd. dirs. 1982-84), Royal Soc. Medicine, Am. Nat. Standards Inst. (med. devices tech. adv. bd. 1973-86), Internat. Standards Orgn. (tech. com. surg. implants, U.S. tech. adv. group), Western Orthopaedic Assn., Pan Am. Assn. Orthopaedics and Traumatology (founding), Houston Orthopaedic Club, Am. Orthopaedic Foot Soc. (chmn. ednl. com. 1978-82), Sam Houston Trail Assn. (hon. life; dir., pres. 1971-73), Sociedad Latino-Americana de Ortopedía y Traumatología, Spectators Orthopaedic Club, Sigma Alpha Epsilon, Phi Rho Sigma. Clubs: Masons, KT, Shriners, Elks. Editorial bd. Health Devices, 1974—. Home: 10902 Wickwild Dr Houston TX 77024 Office: Memorial Hospital Profl Bldg Suite 414 7777 Southwest Freeway Houston TX 77074

ELLIOTT, RODNEY GORHMAN, urologist; b. Middleburg, Ky., June 27, 1935; s. James Lloyd and Myra (Taylor) E.; m. Ann Walker, June 21, 1958; children—Karen Gregory, Rodney Bain. B.S., Coll. of William and Mary, 1957; M.D., Med. Coll. Va., 1961. Diplomate Am. Bd. Urology. Intern USPHS Hosp., Seattle, 1961-62; resident in urology USPHS Hosp., Staten Island, N.Y., 1962-66; dep. chief urology USPHS Hosp., Seattle, 1966-69; practice medicine specializing in urology, Memphis, 1969—; assoc. clin. prof. urology U. Tenn. Coll. Medicine. Adv. med. bd. Planned Parenthood; v.p., trustee Mid-South Found. Med. Care; chief staff Bapt. Hosp. Mem. AMA, Am. Urol. Assn. (S.E. sect.), Memphis Urol. Soc., Phi Beta Kappa, Omicron Delta Kappa, Alpha Omega Alpha. Unitarian. Contbr. articles to profl. jours. Home: 1958 Old Lake Pike Memphis TN 38119 Office: 920 Madison St Suite 420N Memphis TN 38103

ELLIOTT, RONALD DOUGLAS, psychologist; b. Elkhart, Ind., Sept. 13, 1941; s. C. Don and Marilyn E.; B.A., Manchester Coll., 1963; M.S., Ind. U., 1966, Ph.D., 1970; m. Lynn Burns, Aug. 21, 1976; 1 child. Pvt. practice clin. psychology, 1975-76; clin. psychologist Wabash Valley Hosp. Mental Health Center, West Lafayette, Ind., 1976-77; mgmt. cons. Rohrer, Hibler & Replogle, Waltham, Mass., 1977-78, Hay Assos., Atlanta, 1978-80; mgr. mgmt. devel. Frito-Lay, Dallas, Tex., 1980-81; sr. v.p. in charge Dallas office Drake Beam Morin, Inc., 1981—; instr. U. Calif., Santa Cruz, 1972-73, Calif. Sch. Profl. Psychology, 1974-75; pvt. practice clin. psychology, Dallas, 1980—. Served to capt. U.S. Army, 1968-75. USPHS fellow, 1966-67; lic. psychologist, Tex., Ga., Calif. Mem. Am. Psychol. Assn., Tex. Psychol. Assn., Nat. Register Health Service Providers in Psychology, Dallas Psychol. Assn. Methodist. Home: 926 Reno St Lewisville TX 75067

ELLIOTT, SHIRLEY RAE, medical technologist; b. Binghamton, N.Y., Oct. 21, 1922; d. John Rook and Carrie Marie (Keeney) Reynolds; student Duke U., 1940-42, U. Tex., 1942-43; m. Floyd S. Elliott, Nov. 13, 1943; children—Linda Rae, Teresa Marie, Rita Kay, Susan Irene, John Roger, Katherine Claire, Floyd S. With VA Med. Center, Nashville, 1956—, supervisory med. technologist, 1972—; instr. med. technology Vanderbilt U.-VA, 1972-81. Mem. Am. Soc. Clin. Pathologists, Am. Soc. Med. Tech., Royal Soc. Health, Internat. Soc. Lab. Tech., Tenn. Soc. Clin. Microbiology. Methodist. Club: Toastmasters Internat. Home: 1007 Bentley Circle Gallatin TN 37066 Office: 1310 24th Ave S Nashville TN 37203

ELLIS, CAROLYN SUE, sociology educator; b. Luray, Va., Oct. 13, 1950; d. Arthur Cleveland and Mary Katherine (Good) E.; m. Eugene A. Weinstein, Dec. 25, 1984 (dec. 1985). B.A., Coll. William and Mary, 1973; M.A., SUNY, 1977, Ph.D., 1981. Assoc. prof. sociology U. South Fla., Tampa, 1981—. Author: Fisher Folk: Two Communities on Chesapeake Bay, 1985. Contbr. articles to profl. jours. Office: Dept Sociology U South Fla Tampa FL 33620

ELLIS, CLARENCE LEE, police official; b. Willis, Tex., Feb. 13, 1937; s. Omer William and Allie (Pratt) E.; m. Mariann English, Apr. 24, 1959 (div. Apr. 1985); children—Robert Lee, Charles David. Student Howard Payne U., 1955-59. Instr. Cert. Tex. Commn. on Law Enforcement Standards and Edn., 1969, advanced cert., 1970, peace officers license, 1984. Police officer San Angelo Police Dept., Tex., 1960-64; sgt. Pasadena Police Dept., Tex., 1964-70; narcotic agt. Tex. Dept. Public Safety, Austin, 1970-71; lt. Pasadena Police Dept., 1971-81, dep. chief, 1981—. Mem. Internat. Assn. Chiefs Police, Tex. Assn. Chiefs Police, Tex. Narcotic Officers Assn., Tex. Crime Prevention Assn., Tex. Law Enforcement Intelligence Assn. Recipient Meritorious award Optimist Club, 1968, 72; Merit cert. K.C., 1980. Democrat. Baptist. Lodge: Masons. Avocation: Motorcycle touring. Office: Pasadena Police Dept PO Box 3209 Pasadena TX 77501

ELLIS, CLAUDE ALEXANDER, planning consultant, housing manager, evangelist; b. New Orleans, Mar. 26, 1932; s. Claude Alexander and Jeannette (Taylor) E. B.S., Prairie View A&M U., 1951; postgrad. Lamar U., 1962. Asst. exec. dir. Urban Renewal Agy., Port Arthur, Tex., 1958-62; sr. archtl. planning cons. Planning Cons. Port Arthur, 1962—; real estate broker, housing mgr. Prince Hall Village Trust, Port Arthur, 1962—; pub. Angela News, Angela News Publs., Port Arthur, 1958-68; pastor of evangelism 1st 6th St. Bapt. Ch., Port Arthur, 1969—; evangelist Revelation Resurrection Evang. Assn., Port Arthur, 1976—. Pub., editor Civil Rights, 1960, (Meritorious award Port Triangle Voters League 1962). Organizer Council of New Dimension, Port Arthur, 1964, Revelation Resurrection, Inc., 1972; chmn. 7th St. Br. YMCA, Port Arthur, 1977. Served to 1st lt. air borne inf. U.S. Army, 1951-53. Decorated Silver Star, Bronze Star, Purple Heart; recipient citation for establishing city bus system City of Port Arthur, 1963. Mem. Kappa Alpha Psi. Democrat. Lodge: Masons. Home: PO Box 4175 Port Arthur TX 77641

ELLIS, DAVID PHELPS, management consultant; b. Pasadena, Calif., Aug. 15, 1953; s. Frederick Joseph and Marjorie Victoria (Beaman) E.; m. Susan Gale Beddingfield; 1 son, J. Christopher Stansell. B.S., Va. Poly. Inst. and State U., 1975; M.B.A., Ga. State U., 1979. Dir. Decision Scis. Lab., Ga. State U., Atlanta, 1978-79; dir. corp. planning info. Baddour, Inc., Memphis, Tenn., 1979-82; asst. to pres. Sun Life Group Am., Atlanta, 1982-84, dir. adminstrv. methods, 1982-84; cons. Touche Ross & Co., 1984—. Rep., Hawaii State Republican Conv., 1975-76. Recipient Outstanding Merit award Ga. State U., 1979. Mem. Planning Execs. Inst., Am. Mktg. Assn. Republican. Episcopalian. Office: 225 Peachtree St NE Suite 1400 Atlanta GA 30043

ELLIS, GEORGE SABA, SR., ophthalmologist; b. Almonsif, Lebanon, May 30, 1923; came to U.S., 1923; s. Sam Saba and Jamelle (Assaf) E.; m. Lorraine Doris Haik, Mar. 19, 1950; children—George Saba, Robert G., Joan Ellis Green. B.A., U. Tex., 1943; M.D., Tulane U., 1946. Diplomate Am. Bd. Ophthalmology. Intern Charity Hosp., New Orleans, 1946-47, resident, 1950-53; from asst. prof. to prof. ophthalmology La. State U., New Orleans, 1956-77; prof. Tulane U., New Orleans, 1977—; mem. staff Hotel Dieu Hosp., New Orleans, 1951—, pres. med. staff, 1978-79. Contbr. articles to profl. jours. Served to lt. (j.g.) USN, 1947-49. Fellow ACS, Internat. Coll. Surgeons; mem. AMA, Am. Acad. Ophthalmology, (cert. merit 1975), Am. Opthalmol. Soc., So. Med. Assn. (councilor 1978-83, Ophthalmologist of Yr. 1976), New Orleans Acad. Ophthalmology (pres. elect 1984-86, cert. appreciation 1976). Orleans Parish Med. Soc. (pres. 1985-86). Episcopalian. Clubs: Metairie Country (La.); Bienville (New Orleans). Lodge: Rotary. Home: 42 Pelham Dr Metairie LA 70005 Office: George M Haik Eye Clinic 812 Maison Blanche Bldg 921 Canal St New Orleans LA 70112

ELLIS, JAMES JOLLY, resort official; b. Meadville, Pa., Mar. 3, 1937; s. Walter Harmon and Nerea Isabel (Farver) E.; A.A., Orlando Jr. Coll., 1959; B.S. in Bus. Adminstrn. and Econs., Rollins Coll., 1981. With Orlando (Fla.) Parks and Forestry Dept., 1961-70; supt. landscape dept. Walt Disney World, Fla., 1970-78, 81-82, Epcot Ctr., 1982—, Walt Disney Village Communities, Orlando, 1978-81. Served with U.S. Army, 1959-60. Mem. Am. Mgmt. Assn., Fla. Turf Grass Assn. Republican. Lutheran. Home: 705 S Summerlin Ave Orlando FL 32801 Office: PO Box 35 Lake Buena Vista FL 32830

ELLIS, JANET, psychologist, consultant; b. N.Y.C., June 27, 1930; d. Joseph Nathan and Ruth (Glass) Koch; m. Edward Lowell Ellis, July 25, 1964; David Hershel, Joshua Nathan, Noah Ari. B.F.A. in Radio-TV, U. Tex., 1950; M.A., So. Meth. U., 1968; M.A. in Clin. Psychology, N. Tex. State U., 1974, Ph.D. in Counseling Psychology, 1981. Program coordinator, instr. Ctr. for Behavioral Studies N. State Tex. U., Denton, 1973-83; indsl. cons. Performance Cons., Denton, 1984—; program coordinator Behavioral Clin. Intervention, Kalamazoo, 1983. Author: (with others) Training the Severely Behaviorally in the Classroom, 1977. Contbr. articles to profl. jours. Bd. dirs. Denton Assn. Citizens for Edn., 1981-82; mem. spl. edn. adv. com. Denton County Spl. Edn. Services, 1981-83; bd. dirs. ACLU; mem. spl. events com. Lewisville C. of C., 1982; mem. exec. bd. LWV, Denton, 1985. Mem. Am. Acad. Behavioral Medicine (life), Am. Psychol. Assn., Assn. Behavior Analysis, Dallas Psychol. Assn., Tex. Psychol. Assn. Democrat. Club: Assn. Women Entrepeneurs (Dallas). Home and Office: Performance Cons 2145 Pembrooke Suite 205 Denton TX

ELLIS, JOHN, educational administrator; b. Amherst, Ohio, Sept. 15, 1929; s. Edward Pierson and Jean (Scott) E.; m. Carolyn Elizabeth Collier, Dec. 29, 1951; children—Linda Ellis Wieand, Jeanine Fay, Jeanette Kay Ellis Hale, John Edward. B.S., Bowling Green State U., 1953; M.A., Case-Western Res. U., 1958; Ed.D., Harvard U., 1964. Tchr. pub. schs., Lorain, Ohio, 1953-54, prin., 1957-61, asst. supt. schs., Massillon, Ohio, 1963-64, supt. schs., 1964-66, Lakewood, Ohio, 1966-71, Columbus, Ohio, 1971-77; adj. prof. ednl. adminstrn. Ohio State U., 1971-77; exec. dep. commr. edn. U.S. Office Edn., Washington, 1977-80; supt. schs., Austin, Tex., 1980—. Served with USAF, 1947-49, 54-57. Recipient Massillon Young Man of Yr. award, 1965; named to Saturday Rev. Honor Roll, 1977. Mem. Phi Delta Kappa, Pi Kappa Alpha, Phi Alpha Theta, Kappa Delta Pi, Gamma Theta Upsilon. Presbyterian (elder). Lodge: Rotary. Home: 7007 One Oak Rd Austin TX 78749 Office: PO Box 1088 Austin TX 78767*

ELLIS, JOSEPH ELLSWORTH, dentist; b. Huntingburg, Ind., Feb. 28, 1940; s. Eugene Ellsworth and Elizabeth Anice (Renner) E.; m. Marilyn Elise Clay, Dec. 8, 1961; 1 child, Mary Kathryn. D.D.S., Ind. U., 1964. Sr. asst. dental surgery USPHS, Redlake, Minn., 1964-66; gen. practice dentistry, North Vernon, Ind., 1966-84, Venice, Fla., 1984—. Bd. dirs. Jennings Community Hosp., North Vernon, 1974-84; examiner Bd. Dentistry State of Ind., Indpls., 1981-84. Recipient Sagamore of the Wabash award Gov. of Ind., 1984. Mem. ADA, Fla. Dental Assn., Acad. Gen. Dentistry (bd. dirs. 1975-82), Acad. Operative Dentistry, Am. Assn. Dental Examiners. Republican. Lodge: Sertoma. Avocation: fabrication of stained glass panels. Office: 1776 S Tamiami Trail Venice FL 33595

ELLIS, LESTER NEAL, JR., lawyer; b. Washington, Aug. 1, 1948; s. Lester Neal and Marie (Brooks) E.; m. Rhoda Goheen, June 14, 1970; children—Patrick Neal, Bret Hamilton, Ryan Renyer. B.S. U.S. Mil. Acad., 1970; J.D., U. Va., 1975. Bar: Va. 1975, N.Y. 1985, U.S. Ct. Appeals (5th cir.) 1977, D.C. 1978, U.S. Ct. Appeals (4th and D.C. cirs.) 1979, U.S. Ct. Appeals (11th cir.) 1982. trial atty. litigation div. office JAG, Dept. Army, Washington, 1975-78; assoc. Hunton & Williams, Richmond, Va., 1978-84, ptnr., Raleigh, N.C., 1984—. Contbr. articles to profl. jours. Served to maj. U.S. Army, 1970-78. Recipient Judge Paul W. Brosman award U.S. Ct. Mil. Appeals, 1975. Mem. ABA, Va. Bar Assn. (spl. issues com. 1982—), D.C. Bar Assn. (ct. rules com. 1981—), Phi Kappa Phi. Republican. Episcopalian. Home: 7204 Willmark Ct Raleigh NC 27612 Office: Hunton & Williams One Hannover Sg St Mall Raleigh NC 27602

ELLIS, LONNIE CALVERT, educator; b. Oneida, Tenn., Sept. 18, 1945; s. Lewis Calvert and Alma Gean (Goad) E.; m. Karen Chambers, Dec. 16, 1967; children—Lonnie Christopher, James Gregory, Megan Lynn. B.S., Cumberland Coll., 1968; M.A., Tenn. Tech. U., 1974, Ed.S., 1985. Tchr. math, coach Oneida Ind. Sch. Dist., Tenn., 1968-72, Scott County Sch. System, Huntsville, Tenn., 1972-78, 1979—; mgr. personnel Tibbals Flooring Co., Oneida, 1978-80; instr. Roane State Community Coll., 1985—, State Tech. Inst., Knoxville, 1985—. Chmn. Cissy Baker for Senate campaign, Huntsville, 1980; vice chmn. Scott County Recreation Com., 1984—. Recipient Dist. Coach of Yr. award Coca Cola Bottling Co., 1985, recognition award Tenn. Ho. of Reps., 1985, Citizens award E. Tenn. chpt. Nat. Football Found., 1978. Mem. Scott County Edn. Assn. (chmn. welfare com., state contact person, pres. elect), E. Tenn. Edn. Assn., Tenn. Edn. Assn., NEA. Baptist. Avocations: computers; golf; fishing; hunting; bowling. Home: Route 1 Box 44 Helenwood TN 37755 Office: Scott County High Sch Scott High Dr Huntsville TN 37756

ELLIS, SUSAN GOTTENBERG, psychologist; b. N.Y.C., Jan. 24, 1949; d. Sam and Sally (Hirschman) Gottenberg; m. David Roy Ellis, July 23, 1972; children—Sharon Rachel, Dana Michelle. B.S., Cornell U., 1970; M.A., Columbia U., 1971; M.A., Hofstra U., 1975, Ph.D., 1976. Cert. sch. psychologist, Fla., N.Y., N.J. Cert. health edn tchr., Fla., N.Y. Cert. jr. coll. tchr., Fla. Instr. Nassau Community Coll., N.Y.C., 1971-73; sch. psychologist spl. edn. Lafayette Sch., Somerville, N.J., 1976-77; clin. psychologist Somerset County Community Mental Health Ctr., 1976-77; sch. psychologist Pinellas County, Fla., 1977-78; psychologist Learning Assessment Program Morton Plant Hosp., Clearwater, Fla., 1978-79; instr. assertiveness tng. women's program St. Petersburg Jr. Coll., Clearwater, Fla., 1978; pvt. practice psychology, Largo, Fla., 1977—. Author publs. in field. N.Y. State Regents scholar; Home Econs. Alumnae Martha Van Rensselaer scholar, 1968-70; Homemakers Council scholar, 1969-70; Tchrs. Coll. Tuition scholar, 1970-71. Mem. Am. Psychol. Assn., Fla. Psychol. Assn., Pinellas Psychol. Assn. (interim treas. 1978, polit. action chmn. 1979), Kappa Delta Pi. Avocations: swimming; bicycling; reading; nutrition; playing piano and guitar. Office: 2499 E Bay Dr Suite 103 Largo FL 33541

ELLISON, BONNIE BIGSBY, school administrator; b. Kirksville, Mo., May 15, 1943; d. Edgar Lorenz and Roberta (Phelps) B.; m. Donald Richard Ellison, Aug. 29, 1965; children—Sims Edgar, Kyle Richard. B.J., U. Mo., 1965. With Pub. Relations div. U. Mo.-Rolla., 1965; with ABC-TV and KOCO-TV, Oklahoma City, 1963-65; with Sta. KIOX, Bay City, Tex., 1965-68; with Pitluk Advt. Agy., San Antonio, 1972-73; pub. info. dir. Northside Ind. Sch. Dist., San Antonio, 1973—. Mem. membership com. Alamo council Boy Scouts Am., 1981—; mem. publicity com. Am. Heart Assn., 1982; publicity chmn. 5th Dist. Tex. PTA, 1983. Named Educator of Month, Tex. Sch. Bus. Mag., 1981; Today's Woman, San Antonio Light newspaper, 1982. Mem. Internat. Assn. Bus. Communicators (v.p. San Antonio chpt. 1981), Nat. Sch. Pub. Relations Assn. (pres. Tex. chpt. 1979, pres. 1984-85). Author: Internal Communications-Basic School Public Relations Guide, 1980; contbg. author: School Finance Kit: You Can Win at the Polls, 1981; contbr. articles to profl. jours. Office: Northside Ind Sch Dist 5900 Evers Rd San Antonio TX 78238

ELLISON, JAMES OLIVER, judge; b. St. Louis, Jan. 11, 1929; s. Jack and Mary (Patton) E.; student U. Mo., Columbia, 1946-48; B.A., U. Okla., 1951, LL.B., 1951; m. Joan Roberts Ellison, June 7, 1950; 1 son, Scott. Admitted to Okla. bar; individual practice, Red Fork, Okla., 1953-55; partner firm Boone, Ellison & Smith, Davis & Minter, 1955-79; U.S. dist. judge No. Dist. Okla., Tulsa, 1979—. Trustee, Hillcrest Med. Center, Institution Programs, Inc.; elder Southminster Presbyterian Ch. Served to capt., inf. AUS, 1951-53. Mem. ABA, Okla. Bar Assn., Tulsa County Bar Assn., Alpha Tau Omega. Home: 2767 S Utica Tulsa OK 74114 Office: 333 W 4th St Fed Bldg Room 4-500 Tulsa OK 74103

ELLISON, JERRY LEROY, editor; b. Gilmer, Tex., Aug. 31, 1938; s. Robert Leonard and Editha Ann (Tutor) E.; m. Katherine Ruth Green, May 14, 1977; Student, Kilgore Coll., 1957-59, Tex. A&I U., 1960-62, U. Del., 1965, U. Tex.-Austin, 1975-77. Photo lab mgr. Tex. A&I U., Kingsville, Tex., 1969-71; news photographer KZTV, Corpus Christi, Tex., 1971-72; dir. publs. Assn. and Society Mgmt., Inc., Austin, 1973-76; trainee Upshur Rural Electric Coop., Gilmer, Tex., 1980—. Field sec. Friends Gen. Conf., 1983—. Served with USAF, 1960-69. Mem. New Pictorialist Soc. fellow, 1971-83. Mem. New Pictorialist Soc. (librarian 1982—), Photographic Soc. Am., U.S. Chess Fedn., Nat. Com. on Indian Affairs. Mem. Soc. Friends. Contbr. articles, poems, photographs to various mags.; editor: Telectronics, 1976-77, Tex. Surveyor, 1976-77, New Pictorialist Quar. Bull., 1978-82, AVISO Photography Jour., 1978-82. Address: Route 3 PO Box 377 Gilmer TX 75644

ELLISON, MICKEY DON, association executive; b. Clovis, N.Mex., Apr. 29, 1950; s. Howard Levern and Melba June (Jester); E.; m. Shirley Jean Reynolds, Aug. 14, 1970; 1 child, Kimberly Michelle. B.S., Tex. Tech U., 1973; M.Ed., U. Fla., 1980. Tng. program mgr. Dr. Pepper Co., Dallas, 1980-82; tng. cons. Action System Inc., Dallas, 1982-83; profl. devel. mgr. Soc. Petroleum Engrs., Richardson, Tex., 1983—. Author: Norton-MWD Training System, 1982. Mem. edn. com. Waterview Ch. of Christ, Richardson, 1983—. Served with USNR, 1973—. Mem. Am. Soc. Tng. and Devel. Republican. Avocations: microcomputers; fishing; Bible instruction; singing. Home: 2912 Mulberry Ln Plano TX 75074 Office: Soc Petroleum Engrs 222 Palisades Creek Dr Richardson TX 75080

ELLISON, OSCAR, III, physician; b. Phila., Aug. 23, 1953; s. Oscar and Pauline Ellison. Grad. Lawrenceville Sch., 1971; A.B., Harvard U., 1975; M.D., Georgetown U., 1980. Teaching fellow Harvard U., Cambridge, Mass., 1975; intern Georgetown U. Hosp., Washington, 1980-81, resident in family medicine, 1981-82; practice medicine specializing in gen. medicine, Falls Church and McLean, Va., 1982—; mem. staffs Arlington Hosp., Va., No. Va. Doctors' Hosp., Arlington; mem. Johnson & Ellison Ltd., Falls Church, 1982—, McLean Family Practice, 1982—. Named an Outstanding Young Man of Am., U.S. Jr. C. of C., 1980. Mem. AMA, Va. Med. Soc., Arlington County Med. Soc., U.S. Rowing Assn., Internat. Shotokan Fedn., Am. Med. Triathlon Assn. Clubs: Potomac Boat, Harvard (Washington). Office: Johnson & Ellison Ltd 2767 Annandale Rd Falls Church VA 22042

ELLISON, RICHARD PERHAM, corporation executive, association executive; b. Mpls., Nov. 14, 1930; s. Perham M. and Elizabeth Catherine (Turner) E.; m. Martha J. Steiger, Oct. 17, 1981; children—Richard Jr., Terry, Sarah. B.A., Trinity Coll., 1952. Communications engr. AT&T, N.Y. and Washington, 1957-59; pres., chief exec. officer Foley Electronics Co., College Park, Md., 1959-61, Sound Corp. Am., Worchester, Mass., 1961-63; pres., chmn. bd. Dynatron Mfg. Corp., Silver Spring, Md., 1964-75; mng. dir. Boat Owners Assn. U.S., Alexandria, Va., 1966—; pres. Boat Am. Corp., Alexandria, 1983—. Served to lt. USN, 1953-57. Mem. Soc. Assn. Execs. Republican. Episcopalian. Home: 5009 N 25th St Arlington VA 22207 Office: Boat Am Corp 884 Pickett St Alexandria VA 22304

ELLISON, SAMUEL PORTER, JR., geology educator, consultant; b. Kansas City, Mo., July 1, 1914; s. Samuel Porter and Mary Frances (Edwards) E.; m. Dorothy Mabel Cannady, June 9, 1940; children—Samuel David, John Robert, Stephen Paul. B.A., U. Kansas City, Mo., 1936; M.A., U. Mo.-Columbia, 1938, Ph.D., 1940. Instr. geology U. Mo. Sch. Mines, Rolla, 1939-43, asst. prof., 1943-44; geologist Standard Oil and Gas Co., Midland, Tex., 1944-47, dist. geologist, Wichita Falls, Tex., 1947-48; prof. geol. sci. U. Tex., Austin, 1978-79, Deussen prof. energy resources, 1972-79, emeritus prof., 1979—, acting dean Coll. Arts and Scis., 1970-71, dean Coll. Natural Sci., 1971-73; cons. in field, 1953—. Contbr. articles to prof. publs. Named Alumnus of Yr., U. Kansas City, 1955; recipient Pander medal Pander Soc., 1977. Fellow Geol. Soc. Am. (councilor 1963-66); mem. Am. Assn. Petroleum Geologists (v.p. 1972-73, hon. mem. 1982, Disting. Service award 1977), Soc. Econ. Geologists and Minerologists (sec.-treas. 1953-56, pres. 1959-60), Soc. Petroleum Engrs., Am. Inst. Profl. Geologists (pres. Tex. chpt. 1968-69). Methodist. Avocations: photography, golf, hiking. Home: 5948 Highland Hills Dr Austin TX 78731 Office: Dept Geol Sci U Tex Austin TX 78713

ELLISON, THORLEIF, consulting engineer; b. Lyngdal, Norway, May 13, 1902; s. Andreas Emanuel and Gemalie (Svensen) E.; C.E., Christiania Coll. Tech., 1924; postgrad. George Washington U., U. Va.; m. Reidun Ingeborg Skonhoft, Jan. 1, 1932; children—Earl Otto, Thorleif Glenn, Sonja Karen. Came to U.S., 1928, naturalized, 1933. Supervising engr. GSA, Washington, 1948-57; supervising airport and airways service engr. FAA, 1957-61; chief airways engring. AID, Iran, West Pakistan, Turkey, 1961-67; cons. engr., Washington and Va., 1971-82; supervising structural engr. for reconstrn. of The White House, 1949-52; mission dir. Bethlehem, Israel, Holy Land Christian Mission, Kansas City, 1968-71. Active Christian Bus. Men's Com., Washington, Boy Scouts Am. Registered profl. engr. Mem. Nat. Soc. Profl. Engrs. (dir.), Sons of Norway (pres. Washington chpt.), Norwegian Soc. (treas.). Presbyterian (ruling elder). Home: Svennevik Rosfjord 4580 Lyngdal Norway also 6324 Telegraph Rd Alexandria VA 22310

ELMORE, BARBARA JEANNE, educator; b. Shattuck, Okla., July 26, 1932; d. Walter Conner and Lura Faye (Hart) Harris; grad. high sch.; m. Donald Lee Elmore, June 7, 1953 (div. 1966); children—Debra Kay Elmore Whitworth, Donald Duane, Dana Denise Elmore Fielder. B.S., Northwestern Okla. State U., 1973, M.S., 1983. Dep. county clk. Woodward County, Okla., 1950-52; dep. dist. ct. clk. Ochiltree County, Perryton, Tex., 1963-67; legal sec. Eldred Harmon, Alva, Okla., 1968-73; 2d grade tchr. Ames (Okla.) Pub. Sch., 1973—. Mem. NEA, Okla. Edn. Assn., Ames Edn. Assn. Republican. Baptist. Home: Box 169 Ames OK 73718 Office: Ames Pub Sch Ames OK 73718

ELMORE, CHARLES JEROME, college administrator; b. Savannah, Ga., Apr. 17, 1945; s. Norman Brokenshire and Pauline Elizabeth (Williams) E.; m. Juanita Washington, Aug. 10, 1968; children—Charles Jerome Jr., Brandi Elizabeth. B.S. in Biology, Savannah State Coll., 1967; M.A. in Journalism, U. Mich., 1972, Ph.D. in Higher Edn. Adminstrn., 1979. Sci. tchr. Chatham County Bd. Edn., Savannah, 1967-71; instr. English Savannah State Coll., 1972-74, dir. pub. relations, 1974-76, asst. to pres., 1979—; grad. asst. U. Mich., Ann Arbor, 1978-79; dir. So. Regional Press Inst., Savannah, 1975—, Coll. Publs., Savannah, 1979—; cons. publs. Jasper County Sch. Bd., Ridgeland, S.C., 1981. Active Clean Community Adv. Council, Savannah, 1981-86, Savannah chpt. ARC, 1984, Communications Commn. Diocese of Savannah, 1983-84. Recipient Man of Yr. award Savannah State Coll., 1967; U. Mich. fellow, 1976-79; Men of Achievement award Internat. Biol. Assn., 1980. Mem. Sigma Delta Chi, Phi Delta Kappa, Alpha Kappa Mu, Omega Psi Phi. Democrat. Roman Catholic. Club: Blood Donors. Avocations: swimming; amateur historian; collecting jazz records and books; writing; skating. Home: 11400 White Bluff Rd Apt 34 Savannah GA 31419 Office: Savannah State Coll PO Box 20427 Savannah GA 31404

ELMORE, JAMES LEWIS, aquatic ecologist, researcher; b. Chattanooga, Tenn., May 28, 1948; s. Charles Scott and Myrtle Louise (Bryant) E.; m. Barbara Victoria Bouquard, Aug. 26, 1972; 1 son, Joseph Charles. B.A., U. Tenn.-Chattanooga, 1971; M.S., U. Tenn.-Knoxville, 1973; Ph.D., U. South Fla., 1980. Grad. teaching asst. U. Tenn.-Knoxville, 1971-73; grad. teaching asst. U. South Fla., Tampa, 1974-76, project dir., 1979-80; research assoc. Oak Ridge (Tenn.) Nat. Lab., 1980—; cons. Biol. Research Assocs., Tampa, 1974-79. Dept. Health and Rehab. Services State of Fla. grantee, 1979. Mem. Am. Soc. Limnology and Oceanography, Ecol. Soc. Am., Societas Internationalis Limnologiae, N.Am. Benthological Soc., Assn. Southeastern Biologists, Am. Orchid Soc., Bromeliad Soc., Sigma Xi (research grantee 1976), Phi Sigma (v.p. 1978), Beta Beta Beta. Contbr. articles to profl. lit. Home: 1700 Huntwood Ln Knoxville TN 37923 Office: Environ Scis Div Oak Ridge Nat Lab Oak Ridge TN 37831

ELMS, DAVID TATUM, clergyman; b. Gorman, Tex., Apr. 7, 1943; s. Finley Milton and Pauline Estelle (Gressett) E.; m. Linda Marlene Benson, Jan. 8, 1943; children—Melody Lynn, David Timothy, Nathan Joel. A.A., San Diego City Coll., 1967; B.A., San Diego State U., 1971. With Naval Air Rework Facility, San Diego, 1964-73; evangelist United Pentecostal Ch. Internat., 1973-74, campus evangelism coordinator South Central States, 1974-75; ordained to ministry United Pentecostal Ch., 1978; pastor First United Pentecostal Ch., Charlotte, N.C., 1975—; dir. N.C. Dist. Youth Orgn., 1977-78. Bd. dirs. N.C. Sunday Sch. Dept., 1978-80, N.C. Dist. Fgn. Missions Div., 1982—; pres. Personal Growth Inst., 1982—. Recipient Sheaves for Christ award, 1978. Author: Revival Churches for the Rapture Generation, 1977; contbr. articles to profl. jours.

ELMSTROM, GARY WILLIAM, horticulture educator, director research center; b. Chgo., Jan. 10, 1939; s. Rudolph Eric and Edna Katherine (Koepke) E.; m. Mary Frances Moffitt, June 24, 1967; children—Michael Eric, Kristin Kathleen, Jennifer Mae. B.S., So. Ill. U.-Carbondale, 1963, M.S., 1964; Ph.D., U. Calif.-Davis, 1969. Asst. prof. U. Fla. Agrl. Research Center, Leesburg, 1969-74, assoc. prof., 1974-78, Center dir. and assoc. prof., 1978-81, Center dir. and prof., 1981—. Mem. Am. Soc. Hort. Sci., So. Assn. Agrl. Scientists, Fla. State Hort. Soc. Republican. Presbyterian. Club: Kiwanis (pres. Leesburg 1977-78, Outstanding Pres. award Kiwanis Internat. 1978). Contbr. articles to World Book Ency. and profl. publs. Home: 1621 Normandy Way Leesburg FL 32748 Office: PO Box 388 Leesburg FL 32749

ELMY, RAYMOND LOUIS, manufacturing company executive, mechanical engineer; b. Cleve., Nov. 19, 1938; s. Raymond Merle and Agnes Wilma (Kazmersky) E.; m. Delores Ann Rohling, May 7, 1960; children—Raymond William, Susan Michelle. Student Cast Inst. Tech., 1956-57; B.S. summa cum laude in Mech. Engring., U. Tenn.-Nashville, 1974; postgrad. U. Tenn., 1974-77. Apprentice tool and die maker Murray Ohio Mfg. Co., Lawrenceburg, Tenn., 1957-61, tool designer, Nashville, 1963-69, project engr., 1969-75, mgr. devel. engring., Brentwood, Tenn., mgr. riding mower engring., 1978-80, asst. v.p. engring., 1980-84, v.p. design engring., 1984—; mem. lawn mower safety standards com. Am. Nat. Standards Inst. Served with U.S. Army, 1961-63. Mem. Soc. Automotive Engrs., Williamson County Hist. Soc. Roman Catholic. Patentee clutch and braking systems. Home: Route 1 Lake Colonial Ct Arrington TN 37014 Office: PO Box 268 Brentwood TN 37027

ELROD, JEAN CRAIG, educator; b. Little Rock, Apr. 18, 1930; d. Joseph Marion and Lula Bessie (Couch) Craig; m. Tullis Craig Elrod, Aug. 23, 1947; children—Steven Craig, John Stanley. A.A. in Early Childhood Edn., U. Ark., 1978. Pre-kindergarten tchr. Children's Ctr., U. Ark., Little Rock, 1979—; vol. tchr. ESL. Mem. Nat. Assn. for Edn. Young Children, So. Assn. Children under Six, Ark. Assn. Children under Six. Democrat. Methodist.

ELSON, EDWARD ELLIOTT, distribution/retail executive; b. N.Y.C., Mar. 8, 1934; s. Harry and Esther (Cohn) E.; m. Suzanne Wolf Goodman, Aug. 24, 1957; children—Charles Myer, Louis Goodman, Harry Elson II. B.A. with honors, U. Va., 1956; J.D., Emory U., 1959. With Atlanta News Agy., 1959—, chmn. 1979—, pres., 1961-82; pres. Airport News Corp., Atlanta, 1961-82, chmn., 1982—; pres. Elson's Atlanta, 1963-82, chmn. 1982—; mem. publ. com. Commentary Mag., 1967—, chmn., 1975-80; chmn. Gordon County Bank, 1976-81; dir. Citizens and So. Ga. Corp. Bd. govs. Am. Jewish Com., 1966—, trustee, 1977—, v.p., 1982-84, treas., 1984; bd. dirs. So. Regional Council, 1966—; mem. Presdl. Commn. on Obscenity and Pornography, 1967-71; mem. pres.'s council Brandeis U., 1967; mem. City of Atlanta Fund Appeals Rev. Bd., 1971-73; mem. corp., 1973-74; mem. Atlanta Fulton County Recreation Authority, 1973-80, vice chmn., 1975-80; bd. visitors Clark Coll., 1973—, chmn., 1982—; bd. visitors U. Va.; mem. alumni council Phillips Acad., Andover, Mass., 1973-76; mem. pres.'s council Agnes Scott Coll., 1973—, chmn., 1975—; trustee Talladega Coll., 1973—, U. Mid-Am., 1979-82, Am. Fedn. Arts, 1985—; fellow Brandeis U., 1979—; chmn. Ga. Adv. Com. to U.S. Commn. Civil Rights, 1974-82, mem., 1974—; bd. dirs. Reading Is Fundamental, 1975—, Atlanta Urban League, 1978-79; chmn. adv. bd. Southeastern Ctr. for Contemporary Art, 1976—; mem. Nat. Adv. Commn. Pub. Edn. and Desegregation, 1976-77; chmn. bd. Nat. Pub. Radio, 1977-80; chmn. So. Regional Adv. Com. to U.S. Commn. Civil Rights, 1978; mem. presdl. del. returning crown of St. Stephen to Hungary, 1978. Recipient Robert B. Dons award Grad. Sch. Library Sci., U. Ill., 1971; Human Relations award Am. Jewish Com., 1975; Nat. Pub. Radio's Disting. Service award, 1979; Inst. Human Relations award, 1982. Mem. Ga. Bar Assn., Atlantic Coast Distbrs. Assn. (bd. dirs. 1963-76), Lucius Quintus Cincinnatis, Lamar Soc. (v.p. 1973-74, chmn. bd. dirs. 1974—), Jewish Publs. Soc. (trustee 1974-82), Am. Jewish Hist. Soc. (exec. com., 1980—, v.p. 1982-85), U. Va. Alumni Assn. (bd. mgrs. 1982-84). Jewish. Club: Commerce, Standard, Town and Country (Atlanta); University (N.Y.C.); Farmington Country (Charlottesville, Va.). Home: 65 Valley Rd NW Atlanta GA 30305 Office: 4070 Shirley Dr SW Atlanta GA 30336

ELWART, STEVEN PHILLIP, chemical engineer; b. Evanston, Ill., July 5, 1953; s. Richard Joseph and Fern Adell (Dusold) E.; B.S. in Chem. Engring., Okla. State U., 1975; postgrad. U. So. Miss., U. Okla.; m. Inez P. Ashley, Aug. 25, 1980; children—Joseph Thomas Barrett, Brandy A., Paul Frederick, Jason Timothy Barrett, Richard W. Environ. coordinator Cities Service Co., Tulsa, 1975-76; area process engr. Cities Service Oil Co., Lake Charles, La., 1976-77; process engr. Champlin Petroleum Co., Enid, Okla., 1977-79; process control supr. Amerada Hess Corp., Purvis, Miss., 1979-80, sr. process engr., 1980-81, process engring. supr., 1981, asst. refinery mgr., 1982; sr. process engr. Kerr McGee Refining Corp., Wynnewood, Okla., 1982-85; chief processing engr. Ergon Refining Corp., Vicksburg, Miss., 1985—. Bd. dirs. Hattiesburg Youth Found.; mem. adv. com. Hattiesburg council Boy Scouts Am. Registered profl. engr., Miss., Okla. Mem. Am. Inst. Chem. Engrs. (chmn. govt. interaction com.), Nat. Soc. Profl. Engrs., Am. Mensa Soc. (sci. and edn. council), Hattiesburg Jaycees (v.p. 1980—, nat. dir. 1978-80, dist. dir. 1977-78, Disting. Service award 1981). Office: Ergon Refining Co PO Box 305 Vicksburg MS 39180

ELWICK, MARY KAY, educator; b. San Antonio, Jan. 18, 1945; d. Arthur Dee and Ellen Mildred (Mulherin) Shepard; m. Vernon Lamar Coy, Oct. 30, 1965 (div. May 1969); m. 2d, Donald Carwin Elwick, June 15, 1969; children—Donald Dee, Stephanie Kay. B.A., U. No. Colo., 1966; M.A., Northeastern Okla. State U., 1983. Tchr., Johnstown Pub. Sch. Dist. (Colo.), 1966-67, Platteville, Colo., 1967-69, Jewel Pub. Schs. (Kans.), 1969-70, Ponca City Pub. Schs. (Okla.), 1970-71, Van Buren Pub. Schs. (Ark.), 1972-80, Sallisaw Pub. Schs. (Okla.), 1980—. Recipient awards Fedn. Women's Clubs, 1981. Mem. NEA, Okla. Edn. Assn., Eastern Okla. Reading Council (sec. 1982). Democrat. Methodist. Club: Onawa Study (pres. 1981). Home: 38 Redwood Dr Sallisaw OK 74955 Office: 603 E Choctaw St Sallisaw OK 74955

ELY, HIRAM, III, lawyer; b. Lexington, Ky., May 14, 1951; s. Hiram and Buena E. (Wright) E.; m. Deborah A. Johnson, Oct. 22, 1977. B.A., Centre Coll. Ky., 1973; J.D., Washington and Lee U., 1976. Bar: Ky. 1976. U.S. Dist. Ct. (we. dist.) Va. 1976, U.S. Dist. Ct. (we. dist.) Ky., 1976. U.S. Dist. Ct. (ea. dist.) Ky. 1979, U.S. Supreme Ct. 1979, U.S. Ct. Appeals (6th cir.) 1979, U.S. Ct. Claims, 1979, U.S. Tax Ct. 1984. Clk. to presiding justice U.S. Dist. Ct. Va., Roanoke, 1976-77; assoc. Ewen, MacKenzie & Peden, P.S.C., Louisville, 1977-81; assoc. Greenebaum, Doll & McDonald, Louisville, 1981-84, ptnr., 1984—. Fund raising capt. Old Ky. Home council Boy Scouts Am., 1984; fund raiser profl. div. Metro United Way, Louisville, 1983-85; bd. dirs. Goodwill Industries, 1985—, Louisville C. of C., 1985—. Legal Research Assn. grantee, 1974; named among Top Ten Outstanding Young Kentuckians, Ky. Jaycees, 1969. Mem. Young Lawyers Club (v.p. 1982-83, pres. 1983-84), Louisville Bar Found. (chmn. continuing legal edn. sect. 1985—, bd. dirs. 1985—), Louisville Bar Assn. (subcom. chmn. 1983—, spl. subcom. SP mem. 1983-84, mem. litigation, internat. law, young lawyers, fed. practice sects.) Ky. Bar Assn., ABA (discovery com. litigation sect. 1981—), Ky. Acad. Trial Atty's., Ky. Def. Counsel, Def. Research Inst., Sigma Chi. Club: Jefferson, Harmony Landing Country (Louisville). Office: Greenebaum Doll & McDonald 3300 First Nat Tower Louisville KY 40202

ELY, JOSEPH BUELL, II, corporate executive; b. Boston, Nov. 5, 1938; s. Richard and Louise (Ludwick) E.; m. Barbara Kurzina, Aug. 5, 1967; children—Joseph Buell, III, Christina, Peter Douglas, Sarah Ann. B.S., Boston U., 1965, Ph.D., 1981. Dir. Amoskeag Co., Boston, 1977—, pres., chief exec. officer, 1978—; dir. Fieldcrest Mills, Inc., Eden, N.C., 1976—, chmn. bd., 1982—, chief exec. officer, 1985—; chmn., chief exec. officer Fanny Farmer

Candy Shops, Inc., Bedford, Mass., 1980-84, also dir.; chmn., chief exec. officer Bangor & Aroostook R.R. Co., Bangor, Maine, Westville Homes Corp., 1974—, also dir. Office: Fieldcrest Mills Inc 326 E Stadium Dr Eden NC 27288

ELZA, CHARLES ERNEST, land developer, coal company executive; b. Oneida, Ky., Feb. 15, 1949; s. Willard E. and Ruby (Harrison) E.; m. Carol Ann Anderson, Mar. 13, 1971; children—Christina, Brian, Heather. B.S., Eastern Ky. U., 1971. Asst. cashier Corbin Deposit Bank, Ky., 1973-74, asst. v.p., 1974-75, v.p., 1975; v.p. London Bank and Trust Co., Ky., 1975-77, pres., 1977-85, bd. dirs., 1977-85; pres., bd. dirs. London BancShares Inc., 1983-85; bd. dirs. Computer Bank Services, Lexington, Ky., 1977-85. Pres. Laurel County Basketball League, 1975-78; v.p. Kiwanis, Laurel County, 1976, pres., 1977; bd. dirs. Laurel County Agrl. Com., 1983-84; adv. bd., fin. advisor Calvary Worship Ctr., London, 1979—. Recipient Outstanding Young Businessman award London Jaycees, 1978; Outstanding Young Man Am. award U.S. Jaycees, 1978; Ky. Col. award Gov. of Ky., 1979. Mem. Ky. Bankers Assn. (sec. 1982, v.p. 1983, pres. 1984). Republican. Home: Route 1 PO Box 136 London KY 40741 Office: Ruby Coal Co Route 11 Box 54 London KY 40741

EMBERTON, WALLACE AARON, automotive manufacturing company executive; b. Louisville, Oct. 27, 1933; s. Huey Denzmore and Lola Mae (Smith) E.; student Western Ky. U., 1966, Ariz. State Coll., 1974, Stanford U., 1975, Air U., U. N.C., 1978, Air Force Acad., 1980; grad. Contract Law Sch. Harvard U., 1984; m. Mary D. Reagan, July 6, 1953; children—Jacqueline, Joyce, Janet. Served as enlisted man U.S. Air Force, 1952-56; commd. 2d lt. U.S. Air Force, 1962, advanced through grades to 1st lt.; now col. USAR, Ret. with Sorensen Mfg. Co. also Am. Parts Co., Houston, Guranteed Parts Co., Seneca Falls, N.Y., all Gulf & Western Cos., Glasgow, Ky., 1962—, procurement mgr., 1974—, now dir. purchasing; page Ky. Senate, 1972. Decorated Bronze Star with 3 oak leaf clusters, others; commd. Ky. col., 1968; named Outstanding Air Force Res. Man for Material Airlift Command, 1982; recipient Gulf & Western Disting. Achievement award, 1984. Mem. Nat. Assn. Purchasing Mgmt. Mem. Churches of Christ. Home: 105 Lyon Ave Glasgow KY 42141 Office: Sorensen Mfg Co 1115 Cleveland St Glasgow KY 42141

EMBRY, IRMAGENE W., educator; b. Carrollton, Ga., Sept. 11, 1934; d. Square Thomas and Charligene W. (Ridley) Williams; m. Elroy Embry, Dec. 21, 1963 (dec.); 1 son, Michael LeRoy. B.A., Morris Brown Coll., 1966; M.A., Atlanta U., 1972. Cert. tchr., Ga. Tchr. elem. schs., Atlanta, 1966—; tutor for disadvantaged youths, Atlanta, 1966-70, summers 1974-76; cons. Early Learning Ctrs., Harralson County, Ga., 1970-82; tchr. reading and math. E. Rivers Elem. Sch., Atlanta, 1972-83, supr. reading-math. program, 1976—. Bd. dirs. spl. projects Ga. State Coll., Atlanta, 1977-80; vol. Atlanta City Parks and Recreation Dept., 1974-76. Named Nat. Disting. Educator, NASA, 1983. Mem. NAACP, United Negro Coll. Fund, Atlanta Assn. Educators, Internat. Reading Assn., Women for Morris Brown Coll., Atlanta U. Cultural Arts Club. Methodist. Lodge: Nat. Squaws. Home: 2924 Pine Valley Circle East Point GA 30344 Office: 8 Peachtree Battle Ave NW Atlanta GA 30344

EMENER, WILLIAM GEORGE, dean, psychologist, rehabilitation educator; b. N.Y.C., June 10, 1943; s. William George and Rose (Donner) E.; m. Rae Dorothy Torgesen, June 25, 1965; children—Kare, Barbara, Scott. Student Tusculum Coll., 1961-62; B.A., Trenton State Coll., 1965; M.A., NYU, 1968; Ph.D., U. Ga., 1971. Lic. psychologist, Fla., Ky. Resident asst., Trenton State Coll., N.J., 1964-65; tchr. high sch. English No. Burlington County Regional Sch., 1965-66; internship vocat. guidance counselor E.R. Johnstone Tng. and Research Ctr., Bordentown, N.J. 1967-68, rehab. counselor, 1968-69; teaching assistanship U. Ga., 1970, instructorship, 1971; asst. prof. rehab. edn. Murray State U., Ky., 1971-84; pvt. practice psychology, Murray, 1972-74; coordinator Fla. State U., 1976-77; research cons. Fla. Office Vocat. Rehab., Tallahassee, 1977; assoc. prof. rehab. Fla. State U., 1977-78; dir. U. Ky., 1978-80; prof. U. South Fla., 1980—, assoc. dean, 1983—. Author: (with others) Rehabilitation Administration and Supervision, 1982; Selected Rehabilitation Issues and their Impact on People, 1984. Served on numerous editorial bds. and cons. positions for profl. jours. Contbr. chpts. to books and articles to profl. jours. Recipient Gold medal U.S. govt., 1959, Citizenship award N.J., 1961, Cert. Appreciation Inst. on Deafness, 1978. Mem. Am. Personnel and Guidance Assn., Assn. Counselor Edn. and Supervision, So. Assn. Counselor Edn. and Supervision, Am. Rehabilitation Counseling Assn. (bd. editors, 1975-78, Outstanding Contbn. award 1978), Nat. Rehab. Assn., Nat. Rehab. Counseling Assn. (cert. appreciation 1979), Nat. Council Rehab. Edn. (bd. editors. 1976-79), Nat. Rehab. Adminstrn. Assn. (pres. 1983-84, Advancement of Research award 1982), Am. Psychol. Assn., Fla. Assn. Practicing Psychologists. Home: 16404 Shagbark Pl Tampa FL 33618 Office: U South Fla Coll Social and Behavioral Sci 4202 Fowler Ave Tampa FL 33620

EMERSON, DAVID EDWIN, chemist, researcher; b. Checotah, Okla., May 15, 1932; s. David Ervin and Della Elizabeth (Fennell) E.; m. Ermyne Faith Snodgrass, Aug. 21, 1953; children—Joe David, Sally Gayle, Terry William, Carrie Leigh. B.S. in chemistry, Southeastern State Coll., 1955. Civilian instr. U.S. Air Force, Amarillo, Tex., 1955-57; chemist U.S. Bur. Mines Helium Research Ctr., Amarillo, Tex., 1957-59, supr. chemist, 1959-62, chief br. of lab. services, 1962-71, chief tech. services, Heliam Field Ops., 1971—; owner, glassblower Southwest Glassblowing Lab., Amarillo, 1965-76. Patentee in field. Dir. Amarillo Fed. Credit Union, 1980—. Served to sgt. U.S. Army, 1956-62. Mem. First Christian Church. Home: Rt 7 Box 891 Amarillo TX 79118

EMERSON, K(ARY) C(ADMUS), scientific consultant; b. Sasakwa, Okla., Mar. 13, 1918; s. Earle Evans and Diva Elisabeth (Wilkins) E.; B.S., Okla. State U., 1939, M.S., 1940, Ph.D., 1949; m. Mary Rebecca Williams, Aug. 13, 1939; children—William K., James B., Robert E. Commd. officer U.S. Army, 1940, advanced through grades to col.; ret. from active duty, 1966; asst. prof. Okla. State U., 1946-49, adj. prof., 1971—; staff Armistice Commn., Korea, 1958-59; tech. liaison Office Chief Research and Devel., Army Dept., Washington, 1959-60; asst. for research Office Sec. Army, Washington, 1961-78, acting dep. asst. sec. Army, 1973-75, acting asst. sec. Army, 1975-76, dep. for sci. and tech., 1974-78; mem. Army Sci. Bd., 1978-83. Research assoc. Smithsonian Instn., 1960—, Fla. Dept. Agr. and Consumer Service, 1981—, Seminole Nation Museum, 1975—, B.P. Bishop Mus.; collaborator U.S. Dept. Agr., 1959—; instr. Far East br. U. Md., 1959; mem. Def. Com. on Research, 1967-78; U.S. Panel Systematics and Taxonomy, 1968—, NATO Panel I Long-term Sci. Studies, 1970-78. Bd. dirs. Sanibel-Captiva Conservation Found., 1982-85; chmn. adv. com. J.N. Darling Nat. Wildlife Refuge; pres. Care and Rehab. of Wildlife, Inc., 1984-85. Decorated Legion of Merit, Bronze Star, Purple Heart; recipient 2 Exceptional Civilian Service awards Army; Outstanding Civilian Service award Dept. Def. Fellow Entomol. Soc. Am., Washington Acad. Sci., Explorers Club; mem. Biol. Soc. Washington (exec. bd. 1969-72), Soc. Tropical Medicine and Hygiene, Soc. Systematic Zoology, Wildlife Disease Assn., Entomol. Soc. Am., Entomol. Soc. Washington, Am. Soc. Parasitology, AAAS, Sanibel Captiva Audubon Soc. (bd. dirs.), Care and Rehab. of Wildlife (bd. dirs.), Internat. Osprey Found., Sigma Xi, Alpha Zeta, Phi Sigma. Club: Cosmos (Washington). Author or co-author numerous books; mem. editorial bd. 2 sci. jours.; contbr. articles to profl. jours. Home: 560 Boulder Dr Sanibel FL 33957

EMERSON, WILLIAM PRESTON, college administrator; b. La Grange, N.C., Aug. 21, 1932; s. William Clarence and Effie Jane (Pool) E.; m. Doris Rose Bryan, Dec. 29, 1959; children—Karen Michelle, Michael Preston, Claudia Deane. B.S., East Carolina U., 1954, M.A., 1963; Ph.D., Mich. State U., 1971. Counselor Kinston City Schs., N.C., 1963-64; dean student affairs Lenoir Community Coll., Kinston, 1964—. Precinct chmn. Democratic Party, La Grange, 1974—; vice chmn. Airport Commn., Kinston, 1984—; mem. Lenoir County Bd. Commrs., Kinston, 1984; bd. dirs. Neuse River Council Govt., New Bern, N.C., 1984. Served to 1st lt. USAF, 1954-57. Mem. Nat. Assn. Student Personnel Adminstrs., Phi Delta Kappa. Episcopalian. Lodges: Elks, Rotary.

EMERY, DURWARD LESLIE, process engineering and management consultant; b. Mercedes, Tex., June 24, 1924; s. Carl L. and Margaret (Huff) E.; m. Helen Redding, Dec. 23, 1944; children—Glynda Wilkins, Richard Emery, Carol Bowers. B.S., Tex. A&I U., 1947; M.S., U. Houston, 1953. Registered profl. engr., Tex. Engr., Pan Am. Refining, Texas City, Tex., 1947-51; chief physicist Sinclair Rubber Co., Pasadena, Tex., 1951-54; engr. Alcoa, Pitts., 1954-58, plant mgr., 1958-77, tech. mgr., 1977-83; cons. Durward Emery Engring., Inc., McDade, Tex., 1983—; chmn. bd. Crawford Mfg. Co., Inc., Brenham, Tex., 1984—; dir. Brenham Home Improvement Co. Contbr. articles to profl. jours. Inventor in lignite carbonization. Mayor pro-tem Point Comfort, Tex., 1962-68; deacon Baptist Ch. Served with USN, 1944-46. Mem. Am. Inst. Chem. Engrs. Democrat. Lodge: Kiwanis (pres. 1963, 65, 80, Outstanding Kiwanian of Yr. 1967), Masons. Home and office: Route 1 PO Box 235 McDade TX 78650

EMERY, JANICE JOY, obstetrician, gynecologist; b. Adair, Iowa, Apr. 16, 1947; d. Lawrence Irvin and Eva Harriet (Hanshaw) Zimmerman; m. Mark Haney Emery, June 19, 1971; children—Cathleen Alyssa, Matthew Ryan. B.S. with highest distinction, U. Iowa, 1970; M.D., 1975. Diplomate Am. Bd. Ob-Gyn. Intern, resident in ob-gyn Maimonides Med. Ctr., 1975-79; practice medicine specializing in ob-gyn, Washington and Gaithersburg, Md., 1979-82, Burke, Va. 1982—; mem. staff Columbia Hosp. for Women, Washington, Fairfax Hosp., Falls Church, Va.; clin. instr. ob-gyn Georgetown U., 1980-82. Fellow Am. Coll. Obstetricians and Gynecologists; mem. Washington Gynecologic Soc., No. Va. Obstetric Soc., Fairfax County Med. Soc., Phi Beta Kappa. Democrat. Roman Catholic. Home: 9122 Christopher St Fairfax VA 22031 Office: 9004 Crownwood Ct Burke VA 22015

EMERY, JARED MAURICE, physician; b. St. Johnsbury, Vt., Mar. 4, 1940; s. Charles Edward and Myrtle (Stanhope) E.; m. Juliet Morrison Bergan, June 29, 1963; children—Jessica, Clare, Sarah, Nicolas. B.A., U. Vt., 1962; M.D., Yale U., 1966. Intern, U. Colo. Med. Ctr., Denver, 1966-67; resident in ophthalmology Johns Hopkins U., 1970; instr. ophthalmology The Wilmer Inst., Balt., 1970-71, asst. prof. ophthalmology, 1971; asst. prof. ophthalmology Baylor Coll. Medicine, Houston, 1971-74, assoc. prof., 1974—; chief ophthalmology Ben Taub Gen. Hosp., Houston, 1972-78; dep. chief ophthalmology service The Methodist Hosp., Houston, 1983—. Author: Phacoemulsification and Aspiration of Cataracts, 1979, Extracapsular Cataract Surgery, 1983. Editor: Current Concepts in Cataract Surgery, 1974, 76, 78, 80, 82, 84. Contbr. articles to sci. jours. Served with U.S. Army, 1957-65. Mem. Internat. Ophthalmic Microsurgery Study Group, Internat. Coll. Surgeons, A.C.S., Am. Acad. Ophthalmology, AMA. Episcopalian. Office: Baylor Coll Medicine 6501 Fannin St NC200 Houston TX 77030

EMERY, ROBERT EDGAR, JR., psychologist, educator; b. Athol, Mass., Aug. 30, 1952; s. Robert Edgar and Margaret Josephine (Girardi) E.; m. Jean Margaret Younger, June 10, 1978; 1 child, Margaret Elizabeth. B.A., Brown U., 1974; M.A., SUNY-Stony Brook, 1980, Ph.D., 1982. Lic. psychologist, Va. Research analyst Mass. Gen. Hosp., Boston, 1974-77; clin. intern SUNY, Stony Brook, 1980-81; asst. prof. U. Va., Charlottesville, 1981—; pvt. practice clin. psychology Charlottesville, 1981—; cons. in field. Contbr. articles to profl. jours. Grantee Guggenheim Found., 1983-84, W.T. Grant Found., 1983-86. Mem. Am. Psychol. Assn., Assn. Advancement Behavior Therapy, Nat. Council Family Relations. Home: 405 Allen Dr Charlottesville VA 22903 Office: U Va Dept Psychology Gilmer Hall Charlottesville VA 22901

EMGE, THOMAS MICHAEL, electrical engineer; b. Milw., Apr. 7, 1957; s. Thomas Ray and Bernice Margaret Emge. B.S. in Elec. Engring., U. Evansville, 1981; postgrad. Fla. Inst. Tech., 1982. Engr. analog digital and microprocessor circuit design, aerospace services div. Pan Am. World Airways, Patrick AFB, Fla., 1981-84; engr., nav/attack radar systems group Tex. Instruments Inc., McKinney, 1984—. Roman Catholic. Home: Apt 272 1300 N Redbud Blvd McKinney TX 75069 Office: Tex Instruments Inc PO Box 801 MS 8037 McKinney TX 75069

EMICK, DUDLEY JOSEPH (BUZZ), JR., state senator; b. Sept. 17, 1939; m. Martha Louise Elliott. Mem. Va. Ho. of Reps., 1972-74, Va. Senate, 1976—. Democrat. Office: Va Senate Gen Assembly Bldg 9th and Broad Sts Richmond VA 23219*

EMKEN, ROBERT ALLAN, diversified company executive; b. Portland, Oreg., June 13, 1929; s. Cecil Wheeler and Grace (Hill) E.; m. Constance Cook, May 1, 1954; children—Judith, Janice, Robert A. B.S., U. Md., 1951; M.A., George Washington U., 1957. Staff accountant Stoy, Malone & Co., Washington, 1956-58; comptroller R.J. Reynolds Tobacco Co., Winston-Salem, N.C., 1958-70, R.J. Reynolds Industries, Winston-Salem, 1970-75; exec. v.p. Sea-Land Service subsidiary, Edison, N.J., 1975-79; v.p. fin. and adminstrn. R.J. Reynolds Tobacco Co., Winston-Salem, N.C., 1979-83, exec. v.p. fin. and adminstrn., 1983—; dir. N.W. region Wachovia Bank. Trustee Winston-Salem State U. Served with USCGR, 1951-54. Mem. Am. Inst. C.P.A.s, Find. Execs. Inst., Nat. Assn. Accountants. Home: 305 Banbury Rd Winston-Salem NC 27104 Office: RJ Reynolds Tobacco Co Winston-Salem NC 27102

EMLER, DONALD GILBERT, clergyman, educator; b. Kansas City, Mo., June 1, 1939; s. Earl Cecil and Esther Margaret (Brier) E.; m. Lenore Suzanne Plummer, Aug. 9, 1968; children—Matthew Kirk, David Earl. B.A. in History and Govt., U. Mo.-Kansas City, 1960; M.Div., Garrett-Evang. Theol. Sem., 1963; M.S. in Edn., Ind. U., 1972, Ed.D., 1973. Ordained to ministry Methodist Ch., 1961; minister Broadway United Meth. Ch., Kansas City, Mo., 1963-66; chaplain and instr. Central Meth. Coll., Fayette, Mo., 1966-68; minister Platte Woods U. Meth. Ch., Kansas City, 1968-70, Gosport-Quincy United Meth. Ch., Gosport, Ind., 1970-73, St. John's United Meth. Ch., Kansas City, Mo., 1973-76; prof. Christian edn. and chmn. religion dept. Centenary Coll. of La., Shreveport, 1976—, dir. ch. careers program, 1980-81; cons. to local chs. in Christian edn.; video-tape instr. First Meth. Ch., Shreveport. Bd. dirs. Interfaith Com. on Human Dignity and Social Justice, 1981; bd. dirs. Lameco Credit Union, 1980-84; mem. Parents Coalition, 1981-82; chmn. Shreveport Ecumenical Lecture Series, 1985—. Mem. Christian Educators Fellowship, Religious Edn. Assn., United Meth. Assn. Profs. of Christian Edn. (sec.-treas. 1982-84), Assn. Profs. and Researchers in Religious Edn., Am. Assn. Adult and Continuing Edn., Nat. Council on Religion and Pub. Edn. Contbr. articles to religious jours. Home: 136 Adger Shreveport LA 71105 Office: Centenary Coll PO Box 41188 Shreveport LA 71134

EMLET, HARRY ELSWORTH, JR., systems analysis company executive, researcher; b. New Oxford, Pa., Sept. 21, 1927; s. Harry Elsworth and Mary Jane (Myers) E.; m. Elinor Kathryn Stolee, Oct. 3, 1951; children—Mark David, Susan Jennifer Emlet Furst. Tech. degree Mercersburg Acad., 1945; A.B., Princeton U., 1952; postgrad. Luth. Theol. Sem., 1953-55. Systems reviewer Prudential Ins. Co., Trenton, N.J., 1955-56; engr. Martin Co., Balt., 1956-57; research analyst Melpar, Inc., Alexandria, Va., 1957-58; systems analyst Analytic Services, Inc., Alexandria, 1958-64, mgr., v.p., Falls Church, Va., 1965-84, dir., Arlington, Va., 1984—. Editor: Operations Research and National Health Policy Issues, 1977; Challenges and Prospects for Advanced Medical Systems, 1978; Systems Approach to Strokes and Heart Disease, 1980. Mem. editorial bd. Jour. Med. Systems, 1976—. Served with U.S. Army, 1945-47. Mem. Am. Assn. for Med. Systems Informatics (bd. dirs., v.p. 1985—), AAAS, AIAA, Ops. Research Soc. Am. (sect. chmn. 1976-77), Washington Ops. Research Mgmt. Sci. Council, Soc. for Advanced Med. Systems (bd. dirs., pres.), Symposium for Computer Applications in Med. Care (bd. dirs.), Alliance for Engring. Medicine and Biology (bd. dirs., treas.). Democrat. Lutheran. Club: Princeton. Avocations: skiing; tennis; music; reading. Office: ANSER Crystal Gateway 3 Suite 800 1215 Jefferson Davis Hwy Arlington VA 22202

EMMETT, WALTER CHARLES, business brokerage firm executive; b. Lawrence, Mass., July 6, 1925; s. Walter Thornton and Agnes (Owens) E.; student Dartmouth Coll., 1942-43, 46-47; m. Laurel Stinnett Emmett, Nov. 21, 1975; children—Jeffrey, Nancy, Scott; stepchildren—Wayne, Victoria Dammier. Past owner, pres. Panhandle, Tex., 1978—; past owner Your Graphics Are Showing, Amarillo, 1977-79; salesman Ada Realtors, Amarillo, 1976-78; salesman Stevenson Motor, 1969-74, Russell Buick, 1974-76; past pres. Bus. Appraisal Service div. Emmett Bus. Brokers, Inc.; bus. broker Boston/Chamblin Realtors; small bus. cons.; lectr. Amarillo Coll. Trustee Amarillo Found. for Health and Sci. Edn.; mem. art com. Conv. and Visitors Council City of Amarillo; mem. adv. com. Amarillo Coll. Fine Arts; mem. adv. com. on comml. art Amarillo Coll.; lay reader St. Andrew's Episcopal Ch., Amarillo. Served with A.C., USN, 1943-46. Lic. real estate broker, Tex., Okla. Mem. Nat. Fedn. Ind. Bus., Nat. Panel Consumer Arbitrators, Inst. Cert. Bus. Counselors, Center Entrepreneurial Mgmt., Tex. Assn. Bus. Brokers, Am. Soc. Profl. Cons., Inst. Bus. Appraisers, Amarillo C. of C. (chmn. commerce and indsl. relations). Clubs: Amarillo, Masons, Downtown Kiwanis (dir. 1979-80, 2d v.p., program chmn.), K.T. Home: 2611 Henning St Amarillo TX 79106 Office: 3131 Bell Suite 201 Amarillo TX 79106

EMORY, EMERSON, psychiatrist, physician; b. Dallas, Jan. 29, 1925; s. Corry Bates and Louise (Linthecum) E.; m. Peggy Lillian Herald, Sept. 1, 1951; children—Sharon, Karon Bailey, Emerson, Jr. Student Prairie View U., 1940-42; B.A. cum laude, Lincoln U., Pa., 1948; M.D., Meharry Med. Coll., 1952. Intern, St. Paul's Hosp., Dallas, 1952-53, resident in internal medicine, 1953-54, City of Hope, Duarte, Calif., 1954-55, VA Ctr., Los Angeles, 1955-56; fellow in psychiatry U. Tex. Southwest Med. Sch., Dallas, 1966-69; staff physician VA Hosp., Dallas and McKinney, Tex., 1957-60; staff psychiatrist Terrell State Hosp., Tex., 1969-71; chief psychiatric services Fed. Correctional Inst., Seagoville, Tex., 1971-72; vol. physician State Dept. AID program, Vietnam, 1966; practice medicine specializing in psychiatry and internal medicine, Dallas, 1973—. Editor, pub. weekly newspaper Freedom's Jour., 1979-81; host TV program Freedom Jour., 1985—. Ind. candidate for mayor City of Dallas, 1975, 77, Tex. State Legislature, 1974, 76. Recipient Humanitarian Service award AMA Com. of 100, 1966, Cert. Appreciation, Republic of Vietnam, 1966. Fellow Acad. Psychosomatic Medicine; mem. Acad. Psychiatry and Law, Black Psychiatrists Am., Nat. Naval Officers Assn. (founder, past pres.), Washington/Lincoln Alumni Assn. (founder, past pres., Outstanding Alumni award Lincoln U. 1968). Roman Catholic. Club: Prometheans (Washington) (chaplain 1976-78). Lodges: Elks (asst. grand med. dir. 1961-81, exalted ruler 1985), K.C. Avocation: writing; publishing. Home: 4931 W Mockingbird Ln Dallas TX 75209 Office: 2524 Martin L King Blvd Dallas TX 75215

EMSHOFF, JAMES GORDON, psychology educator; b. Chgo., May 5, 1952; s. William G. and Jeanne A. (Shupp) E.; B.S., U. Ill., 1974; M.A., Mich. State U., 1978, Ph.D., 1980. Asst. prof. Mich. State U., East Lansing, 1980-82, Ga. State U., Atlanta, 1982—; cons. in field. Author: (with others) Social Support and Agression, 1981, Applied Social Psychology Annual, 1984. Contbr. articles to profl. jours. Mem. membership and coordinating coms. Fund for Southern Communities, Atlanta, 1982—. Research grantee NSF, 1980, Nat. Inst. Justice, 1980, Nat. Inst. Alcoholism and Alcohol Abuse, 1985. Mem. Am. Psychol. Assn. (recipient First prize student competition div. 35, 1981), Southeastern Psychol. Assn. Avocation: professional pianist. Home: 918 St Charles Atlanta GA 30303 Office: Dept Psychology Ga State U University Plaza Atlanta GA 30303

EMSWILLER, ELLA MAE CUSTER, elementary educator; b. Beckley, W.Va., Aug. 2, 1939; d. Lyle Letcher and Ora Lee (Crotty) Hudson; m. Derwood Carlton Custer, June 3, 1962 (dec. Mar. 1978); children—Adrian, Carlton; m. 2d, Fred R. Emswiller, Jr., June 14, 1980; stepchildren—Mitchel, Martin, Lynn. B.S. in Edn., Concord Coll., 1961; M.Ed., U. Va., 1978. Tchr. home econs. Hillsboro (W.Va.) High Sch., 1961-64; tchr. home econs. Elkton (Va.) High Sch., 1964-71; tchr. 4th grade Elkton (Va.) Elem., 1978-82, Ashby Lee Primary, Mt. Jackson, Va., 1981—. Bd. dirs. Harrisonburg Rockingham Day Care. Mem. Va. Edn. Assn., Shenandoah County Edn. Assn., Shenandoah Valley Reading Council, Internat. Reading Assn. Methodist. Club: United Meth. Women (Elkton). Home: 483 Eastover Dr Harrisonburg VA 22801 Office: Ashby Lee Primary PO Box 68 Mount Jackson VA 22842

ENFINGER, BENJAMIN FRANKLIN, retail executive; b. Skipperville, Ala., June 16, 1928; s. Benjamin F. and Verna (Wetherington) E.; m. Martha DeFord Hays, Jan. 19, 1950 (div. Mar. 1973); 1 son, Jeffrey Wade; m. 2d, Mary Evelyn Bramblett, Apr. 6, 1973; 1 stepson, Kenneth L. Colston. B.S. in Econs., Auburn U., 1951. With Sears, Roebuck and Co., various locations, 1954-81, store mgr., Baton Rouge, La., 1973-77, gen. merchandise mgr. So. ter., Atlanta, 1977-80, So. catalogue group mgr., 1980-81; pres., chief exec. office Am. Agronomics Distbg. Co., Tampa, Fla., 1981-82; v.p. ops. Great Atlantic Mgmt. Co., Newport News, Va., 1982-83; v.p. Am. Cable Connection Inc., Atlanta, 1983—. Served to lt. (j.g.), U.S. Navy, 1946-47, 51-54. Unitarian. Clubs: Selma Country (Ala.); Anniston (Ala.); Horseshoe Bend Country (Roswell, Ga.); City (Baton Rouge); Stadium (Atlanta); Tampa.

ENGELHARDT, HUGO TRISTRAM, JR., medical ethics educator; b. New Orleans, Apr. 27, 1941; s. Hugo Tristram and Beulah (Karbach) E.; m. Susan Gay Malloy, Nov. 25, 1965; children—Susan Elisabeth, Christina Tristram, Dorothea. B.A., U. Tex.-Austin, 1963, Ph.D., 1969; M.D. with honors, Tulane U., 1972. Asst. prof. U. Tex. Med. Br., 1972-75, assoc. prof., 1975-77, mem. Inst. Med. Humanities, 1973-77; Rosemary Kennedy prof. philosophy of medicine Georgetown U., 1977-82; sr. research scholar Kennedy Inst. Ctr. for Bioethics, Washington, 1977-82; prof. Ctr. for Ethics, Medicine and Pub. Issues, Baylor Coll. of Medicine, Houston, 1983—. Mem. bioethics com. Nat. Found. March of Dimes, 1975—; bd. dirs. Masters and Johnson Inst., 1977-82, mem. dirs. adv. council, 1983—; bd. dirs. Internat. Studies in Philosophy and Medicine, 1979—. Fulbright grad. fellow, 1969-70. Fellow Inst. Soc. Ethics and the Life Scis.; mem. Am. Philos. Assn. Author: Mind-Body: A Categorial Relation, 1973; Foundations of Bioethics, 1986. Assoc. editor Ency. of Bioethics, 1973-78; assoc. editor Jour. Medicine and Philosophy, 1974-84, editor, 1984—; contbg. editor Lit. and Medicine, 1982—; mem. editorial bd. Teaching Philosophy, 1975—; mem. editorial adv. bd. Theoretical Medicine, 1980—, Social Sci. and Medicine, 1981—, Bioethics Reporter, 1982—; editor: (with others) Philosophy and Medicine Series, 1974—; Evaluation and Explanation in the Biomedical Sciences, 1975; Philosophical Dimensions of the Neuro-Medical Sciences, 1976; Philosophical Medical Ethics, 1977; Mental Health, 1978; Clinical Judgment, 1979; Mental Illness: Law and Public Policy, 1980; Law-Medicine Relation, 1981; Concepts of Health and Disease, 1981; New Knowledge in the Biomedical Sciences, 1982; Abortion and the Status of the Fetus, 1983; Scientific Controversies. Home: 2802 Lafayette St Houston TX 77005 Office: Center for Ethics Medicine and Pub Issues Baylor Coll of Medicine Houston TX 77030

ENGELHARDT, MARY VERONICE, educational psychologist, nun; b. Syracuse, Mar. 29, 1912; d. Herman Joseph and Ella Marguerite (Collins) E. B.S.Ed., Cath. U., 1937, M.A., 1938, Ph.D., 1962. Joined Third Franciscan Order Roman Catholic Ch., 1929; tchr. elem. and secondary schs., 1933, 38-52; instr. edn. St. Francis Normal Sch., Syracuse, 1942-56, diocesan and community sch. supr., 1952-56; dean women, head dept. edn. and psychology Chaminade Coll. Honolulu, 1957-60; clin. instr. Child Ctr. Catholic U., Washington, 1961, supr. student teaching, 1962; instr. edn., 1961-62; head dept. edn. and psychology Maria Regina Coll., Syracuse, 1962-68, founder, dir. Reading and Speech Clinics, 1962-68; founder, dir. Franciscan Learning Ctr., Franciscan Acad., Syracuse, 1968-85; asst. mother gen. Third Franciscan Order, 1965-71, chmn. personnel bd., 1972-75, chmn. communications bd., 1972-78, also editor community newsletter. Author: Looking at God's World, Creatures in God's World, Learning More About God's World; editor: Creative Arts, 1981-83. Mem. Am. Psychol. Assn., Am. Ednl. Research Assn., Internat. Reading Assn., Nat. Soc. Poets, Nat. League Am. Pen Women (1st v.p. Central N.Y. br. 1981-83). Address: 304 E Linebaugh Ave Tampa FL 33612

ENGERRAND, DORIS DIESKOW, educator; b. Chgo., Aug. 7, 1925; d. William Jacob and Alma Wilhelmina (Cords) D.; B.S. in Bus. Adminstrn., N. Ga. Coll., 1958, B.S. in Elementary Edn., 1959; M. Bus. Edn., Ga. State U., 1966, Ph.D., 1970; m. Gabriel H. Engerrand, Oct. 26, 1946; children—Steven, Kenneth, Jeannine. Tchr., dept. chmn. Lumpkin County High Sch., Dahlonega, Ga., 1960-63, 65-68; tchr., Gainesville, Ga., 1965; asst. prof. Troy (Ala.) State U., 1969-71; asst. prof. bus. Ga. Coll., Milledgeville, 1971-74, assoc. prof., 1974-78, prof., 1978—, chmn. dept. bus. info. systems and communications, 1978—. Named Outstanding Tchr. Lumpkin County Pub. Schs., 1963, 66, Outstanding Educator bus. faculty Ga. Coll., 1975; Exec. of Yr., Milledgeville, 1983; Post Secondary Tchr. of Yr., Ga. Bus. Edn. Assn., 1983; Bus. Edn. Educator of Yr., Ga. Vocat. Assn., 1983. Mem. Assn. Bus. Communication (nat. dir., v.p. Southeast), Office Systems Research Assn., Soc. Tech. Communication, Ga. Assn. Educators, Acad. Mgmt., So. Mgmt. Assn., Nat., Ga. bus. edn. assns., Am., Ga. vocat. assns., Nat. Secs. Assn., Ninety-nines Internat. (chmn. N. Ga. chpt. 1975-76, named Pilot of Year N. Ga. chpt. 1973), AAUW, Delta Pi Epsilon, Beta Gamma Sigma. Methodist. Contbr. articles on bus. edn. to profl. publs. Home: 1674 Pine Valley Rd Milledgeville GA 31061 Office: Ga Coll Milledgeville GA 31061

ENGIN, ANN W., psychology educator; b. Fremont, Ohio, July 28, 1940; d. Jack Frank Wonzer and Lillian (Cushman) W.; m. Ali E. Engin, Feb. 14, 1971 (div.); children—Jack, Timur. Ph.D., U. Mich., 1970. Lic. psychologist, Ohio. From asst. prof. to assoc. prof. Ohio State U., Faculty for Exceptional Children, 1970-79; prof. psychology dept. U. S.C., Columbia, 1979—. Fellow Am. Psychol. Assn., Nat. Assn. Sch. Psychologists (pres. 1978-79), Council Exceptional Children, Am. Ednl. Research Assn., Phi Delta Kappa. Contbr.

chpts. to books, articles to profl. jours. Home: 27 Foxhill Ct Columbia SC 29223 Office: Dept Psychology U SC Columbia SC 29208

ENGLAND, ELLEN MCGORDY (ELZA), librarian; b. New Brunswick, N.J., Sept. 5, 1944; d. James Henry and Elsie (Varga) McGordy; m. James T. England, Jr., June 20, 1970. B.A. in English Lit., Am. U., 1966; M.A. in Social Sci. and Asian Studies, Montclair State Coll., 1977; M.L.S., Rutgers State U., 1979. Cert. librarian, N.J., Va. Librarian, Sparta High Sch. (N.J.), 1971-79, Northern Va. Community Coll., Woodbridge, 1979—. Book reviewer Libr. Jour., 1979-81, Reprint Bulletin, 1981—, Law Books in Rev., 1982—. Mem. ALA (community and jr. coll. sects., communications com. 1980—, bibliography com. 1985—), Phi Delta Kappa. Lodge: Order Eastern Star. Office: Northern Va Community Coll Woodbridge Campus Learning Resources Ctr 15200 Smoketown Rd Woodbridge VA 22191

ENGLAND, LYNNE LIPTON, lawyer, speech pathologist; b. Youngstown, Ohio, Apr. 11, 1949; d. Sanford Yale and Sally Lipton; B.A. cum laude, U. Mich., 1970; M.A., Temple U., 1972; J.D. cum laude, Tulane U., 1981; m. Richard E. England, Mar. 5, 1977. Sr. speech therapist Rockland Children's Hosp., Orangeburg, N.Y., 1972-74; clin. audiologist Rehab. Inst. Chgo., 1974-76; childhood aphasia therapist Jefferson Parish Sch. System, Gretna, La., 1977-78; pvt. practice speech pathology, New Orleans, 1973—; atty. Trenan, Simmons, Kemker, Scharf, Barkin, Frye & O'Neill, 1981-84; asst. U.S. atty., Tampa, 1984—. Mem. ABA, Fla. Bar Assn., Am. Speech and Hearing Assn., Am. Congress Physical Medicine and Rehab., Tulane Law Women's Assn., Hillsborough County Bar Assn., Order of Coif, Phi Delta Phi. Jewish. Home: 3054 Wister Circle Valrico FL 33594

ENGLE, FRED ALLEN, JR., economics educator, author; b. Louisville, Nov. 14, 1929; s. Fred Allen and Susan Kathryn (Johnson) E.; m. Mary Jean Purves, May 25, 1953; children—Susan E. McCool, Allen D., F. Bruce. B.S., Eastern Ky. U., 1951; M.B.A., U. Ky., 1954, Ed.D., 1966. Mgr., Gen. Electric Co., Lexington, Ky., 1955-57; prof. Coll. William and Mary, Williamsburg, Va., 1957-59. prof. econs. Eastern Ky. U., Richmond, 1959—. Served to 1st lt. U.S. Army, 1951-53. Recipient Cert. of Recognition, Phi Delta Kappa, 1970, 80. Mem. SAR, Ky. Econs. Assn. (mem. labor com.). Republican. Baptist. Lodge: Masons. Author: (with others) Madison's Heritage, 1985. Contbr. weekly column on local history and periodic columns on econs. to Richmond Register. Home: Hickory Hills Richmond KY 40475 Office: Eastern Ky U Richmond KY 40475

ENGLE, KAREN KAY, special education resource teacher; b. Detroit, Apr. 5, 1943; d. Richard Melvester and Bessie Virginia (Woodruff) Shaffer; m. Jon Karshner Engle, June 24, 1967; children—Cheri Tabitha, Jon Anthony, Kimberly Kay. B.S. in Edn., Capital U., 1965; postgrad. Miami U., Oxford, Ohio, 1970-72, Memphis State U., 1983. Tchr. Franklin Elem. Sch., Royal Oak, Mich., 1965-67, Monta Vista Elem. Sch., Vista, Calif., 1967-70, Madison Jr. Sch., Middletown, Ohio, 1970-73; tchr. spl. edn. resources Adamsville Elem. Sch. (Tenn.), 1974—. Vice pres. Adamsville Band Boosters, 1980—; room mother Adamsville Elem. PTO, 1975, 77-82. Recipient Presdl. Achievement award Republican Nat. Com., 1982. Named Woman of Yr., McNairy County charter chpt. Am. Bus. Women's Assn., 1982. Mem. So. Assn. Colls. and Schs. (chmn. com.), McNairy County Edn. Assn. (treas. 1983-84), Tenn. Edn. Assn. (del. to rep. assembly 1981—). Lutheran. Lodge: Lioness (treas. 1983-84). Home: PO Box 140 Adamsville TN 38310 Office: Elm St Adamsville TN 38310

ENGLER, MARTIN R(USSELL), JR., natural gas company executive; b. 1924; married. B.S.M.E., Calif. State Poly. U., 1950. Exec. v.p. San Diego Gas & Electric Co., 1950-75; exec. v.p. El Paso LNG Co., 1975-81; exec. v.p. El Paso Natural Gas Co., an El Paso Co. co., 1981—, also dir. Office: El Paso Natural Gas Co Texas and Stanton St El Paso TX 79978*

ENGLESMITH, TEJAS, television executive, art consultant, actor; b. London, Nov. 28, 1941; s. George and Lydia Julia (Johnson-Briet) E. Student U. St. Thomas, Houston, 1959-63. Asst. dir. Whitechapel Art Gallery, London, 1963-69; curator contemporary art Jewish Mus., N.Y.C., 1969-70; dir. Leo Castelli Gallery, N.Y.C., 1970-75; art cons., N.Y.C. and Houston, 1975—; exec. producer sta. KUHT-TV, Houston, 1980—. Recipient Silver award Assn. for Community TV, 1981, Gold award, 1982. Club: —TLC— Four Seasons Houston Center. Office: 4513 Cullen Blvd Houston TX 77004

ENGLISH, GLENN LEE, JR., congressman; b. Cordell, Okla., Nov. 30, 1940; s. Glenn and Marcella (Rainbolt) C.; B.A. in Gen. Bus., Acctg. and Econs., Southwestern State Coll., 1964; m. Jan Pangle, 1970. Petroleum landman, Cordell, 1973-74; mem. 94th-97th congresses from Okla. 6th Dist., 1974—. Staff worker Calif. State Assembly, 1967-68, U.S. Ho. of Reps., 1965; exec. dir. Okla. Democratic Com., 1969-73; Office: 2235 Rayburn House Office Bldg Washington DC 20515

ENGLISH, JOHN RIFE, ednl. adminstr.; b. Barney Brooks, Ga., Mar. 22, 1926; s. Andrew James and India Mariah (Williams) E.; A.B., U. Ga., 1949, M.Ed., 1950, postgrad., 1957-75; postgrad., Ga. So. Coll., 1972-73; m. Helen Marie Langford, June 7, 1947; children—Julianne, Helen Marie, Kathleen, John Cornelius. Prin., Midville (Ga.) High Sch., 1950-56; asso. prin. Comml. High Sch., Savannah, Ga., 1956-59, Groves High Sch., Savannah, 1959-60; prin. Chatham Jr. High Sch., Savannah, 1960-62, Mercer Jr. High Sch., Garden City, Ga., 1962-64, Robert W. Groves High Sch., 1964-70; purchasing mgr. 1st Dist. Coop. Ednl. Services Agy., Statesboro, Ga., 1970-72; headmaster Bulloch Acad., Statesboro, 1972-74; prin. Appling County High Sch., Baxley, Ga., 1974-75, Norris Middle Sch., Thomson, Ga., 1975—; mem. Ga. Adv. Council Title III ESEA. Bd. dirs. Burke County Library, 1954-56; mem. bd. registrars Garden City, 1961-70. Served with USNR, 1942-44. Mem. Nat. Assn. Secondary Sch. Prins., Assn. Curriculum Devel., Ga. Assn. Educators, NEA, Profl. Assn. Ga. Educators, Burke County Edn. Assn. (pres. 1952-53), Chatham County Edn. Assn. (pres. 1960-61), McDuffie Edn. Assn. (pres. 1978-79), Internat. Platform Assn., Pi Sigma Alpha, Kappa Delta Pi. Methodist. Clubs: Lions (pres. Midville 1952-53, Garden City 1967-68), Kiwanis (pres. Thomson 1978-79). Home: Route 3 Box 427 Thomson GA 30824 Office: PO Box 1087 Harrison Rd Thomson GA 30824

ENGLISH, LLOYD CARTER, art educator; b. Altus, Okla., July 4, 1944; s. Lloyd H. and Owene (Carter) E.; m. Phyllis Kay; children—Deborah Jan, Kevin Radcliffe. Cert. standard tchr., Okla., N.J. Chmn. art dept. Elk City High Sch., Okla., 1967-68, Bound Brook High Sch., N.J., 1969-72, Sayre Jr. Coll., Okla., 1972-75, Western Okla. State Coll., Altus, 1975—. Republican. Baptist. Avocations: musician; camping; fishing. Office: Western Oklahoma State Coll 2801 N Main St Altus OK 73521

ENGLISH, NORMA JEAN, bookstore executive, writer; b. Mishawauka, Ind., Apr. 19, 1934; d. Ernest LaVerne and Gladys Pearl (Thomas) Casper; m. Ransom James English, Oct. 4, 1952; children—Michael, Eric, Robert. Grad. high sch. Owner, Noran's Co., Repton, Ala., 1952—; coop advt. dir. Vanity Fair, Monroeville, Ala., 1983—. Editor: Self Esteem, 1983. Pres., Women For Political Action, Greenfield, Ind., 1969. Named Woman of Year, Bessemer Community Theatre 1971. Mem. Ala. Antique Dealers Assn. (v.p. 1981—), Beta Sigma Phi (v.p. 1980-82). Club: Duplicate (pres. 1983—) (Monroeville). Avocations: master play; contract bridge. Home: 101 Front St Repton AL 36475-0066 Office: Noran's Book Exchange US 84 at AL 41 PO Box 66 Repton AL 36475-0066

ENGLISH, ROY, pharmacist, wholesale distributor; b. Paducah, Ky., Oct. 3, 1931; s. Roy C. and Cora B. (Rudolph) E.; m. Nancye A. Jones, Nov. 4, 1957 (div. 1966); children—Lisa Kay, Dana Ann. B.S. in Pharmacy, U. Ky., 1958. Med. service rep. E.R. Squibb Co., Princeton, N.J., 1960-64; pharmacist, owner Holland Drugs, Murray, Ky., 1964-77, Safert Discount Pharmacy, Murray, 1962-77; pres. Murray Drug Corp., Murray, 1964—; nursing home cons., Murray, 1964—. Served with USN, 1951-55; Korea. Democrat. Baptist. Avocation: breeding race horses. Office: Murray Drug Corp 415 S 4th St Murray KY 42071

ENGLISH, TIMOTHY JOSEPH, real estate executive; b. Atlanta, Feb. 8, 1957; s. Joseph Lindsey and Helen Marian (Cochran) E.; m. Sarah Elizabeth Bryant, Mar. 14, 1981. B.Engring., Vanderbilt U., 1979; M.B.A., Columbia U., 1982. Engr., Procter & Gamble, Memphis, 1979-81; pres. English Properties, Atlanta, 1982—; v.p. Bryant Properties, Atlanta, 1982—, Key Devel. & Constrn., Atlanta, 1982—; treas. Sports Realty Co., Inc., 1982—; pres. Southland Devel. Corp., Atlanta, 1985—. Recipient Stein Stone award Vanderbilt U. Sch. Engring., 1979. Mem. DeKalb Developers Assn., Columbia U. Real Estate Club. Presbyterian. Home: 3218 Bolero Way Atlanta GA 30341 Office: English Properties Inc 2015 B Montreal Rd Tuckor GA 30341

ENGLISH, WILLIAM DESHAY, lawyer; b. Piedmont, Calif., Dec. 25, 1924; s. Munro and Mabel (Michener) E.; m. Nancy Ames, Apr. 7, 1956; children—Catherine, Barbara, Susan, Stephen. A.B. in Econs., U. Calif., 1948, J.D., 1951. Bar: Calif. 1952, D.C., 1972. Trial atty., spl. asst. to Atty. Gen., Dept. Justice, Washington, 1953-55; sr. atty. U.S. AEC, Washington, 1955-62; legal advisor U.S. Mission to European Communities, Brussels, Belgium, 1962-64; asst. gen. counsel internat. matters COMSAT Gen. Corp., Washington, 1965-73, v.p., gen. counsel, dir., 1973-76; sr. v.p. legal and govtl. affairs Satellite Bus. Systems, McLean, Va., 1976—. Served with USAAF, 1943-45. Decorated Air medal. Mem. Am. Corp. Counsel Assn. (dir., past pres.), Am. Council for Competitive Telecommunications, ABA, D.C. Bar Assn., State Bar Calif., Fed. Communications Bar Assn., Fgn. Policy Discussion Group. Club: Metropolitan (Washington). Home: 7420 Exeter Rd Bethesda MD 20814 Office: 8283 Greensboro Dr Mc Lean VA 22102

ENGSTROM, RICHARD LEE, political science educator, political consultant; b. Grand Rapids, Mich., May 23, 1946; s. Elmer Franklin and Louise Clare (Bogerd) E.; m. Carol Lynn Verheek, June 7, 1968; children—Richard Neal, Mark Andrew, Brad Alan, Amy Min. B.A., Hope Coll., 1968; M.A., U. Ky., 1969, Ph.D., 1971. Asst. prof. U. New Orleans, 1971-74, assoc. prof., 1974-79, prof. polit. sci., 1979—; Fulbright lectr. Nat. Taiwan U., Taipei, 1981-82; vis. scholar Academia Sinica, Taipei, 1981-82. Contbr. articles profl. jours. Mem. Am. Polit. Sci. Assn., So. Polit. Sci. Assn., Midwest Polit. Sci. Assn. Presbyterian. Home: 4910 Redwood New Orleans LA 70127 Office: U New Orleans Dept Polit Sci New Orleans LA 70168

ENGUM, ERIC STANLEY, psychology administrator, lawyer; b. N.Y.C., Oct. 31, 1949; s. Silas H. and Gertrude (Brown) E. B.S., Wagner Coll., Staten Island, N.Y., 1971; M.S., Tulane U., 1973; Ph.D., U. S.D., 1977; J.D., U. Tenn., 1982. Bar: Tenn. 1983, U.S. Dist. Ct. (ea. dist.) Tenn. 1983; U.S. Ct. Appeals (6th cir.) 1983. Clin. intern U. Ala. Med. Ctr., Birmingham, 1977; clin psychologist Iowa Methodist Med. Ctr., Des Moines, 1977-79; dir. clin. psychology Ft. Sanders Regional Med. Ctr., Knoxville, Tenn., 1982—; cons. in field. Contbr. articles to profl. jours. Recipient LeTourneau award Am. Coll. Legal Medicine, 1982. Mem. Am. Psychol. Assn., ABA, Nat. Health Lawyers Assn., Tenn. Bar Assn., Nat. Register Health Service Providers in Psychology. Republican. Lutheran. Avocations: golf, tennis, scuba diving, cycling. Home: 1705 Cherry Oak Pl Knoxville TN 37909 Office: Fort Sanders Regional Med Ctr 1901 Clinch Ave SW Knoxville TN 37919

ENIS, THOMAS JOSEPH, lawyer; b. Maryville, Mo., July 2, 1937; s. Herbert William and Loretta M. (Fitzmaurice) E.; m. Harolyn Gray Westhoff, July 24, 1971; children—Margaret Elizabeth, David Richard, John Anthony, Brian Edward. B.S., Rockhurst Coll., 1958; J.D., U. Mo.-Columbia, 1966. Bar: Mo. 1966, Okla. 1973. Law clk. U.S. dist. Ct. (we. dist.) Mo., 1966-67; prof. law U. Okla. Coll. Law, Norman, 1967-74, assoc. dean, 1970-74; atty. Southwestern Bell Telephone Co., Oklahoma City, 1974-79; ptnr. Bulla and Enis, Oklahoma City, 1979-81; sole practice, Oklahoma City, 1981—; lectr. Insts. for Energy Devel., Okla. Bar Rev. Bd. dirs. Okla. Symphony Orch., 1978—, legal counsel, 1981—. Mem. ABA, Okla. Bar Assn., Mo. Bar Assn., Oklahoma County Bar Assn., Order of Coif, Phi Delta Phi. Democrat. Roman Catholic. Editor-in-chief Mo. Law Rev., 1965-66. Home: 3016 Stoneybrook Rd Oklahoma City OK 73120 Office: 1203 First Nat Center W Oklahoma City OK 73102

ENLOE, REBECCA LYNN, educator; b. Magnolia, Ark., Apr. 11, 1949; d. Russell Paul and Jamie Minette Eshenbaugh; 1 son, Bryan Michael. A.S., N.Mex. Jr. Coll., 1969; B.S., Coll. Southwest, Hobbs, N.Mex., 1971; M.Ed., Pan Am. U. at Brownsville (Tex.), 1980. Cert. tchr., Tex., N.Mex. Tchr., Lovington (N.Mex.) Schs., 1971-73, Brownsville, Tex., 1973—, tchr. Egly Elem. Sch., 1977—; adj. faculty Pan Am. U., Brownsville, Tex. Rotary scholar, 1967. Mem. NEA, Tex. State Tchrs. Assn., Assn. Brownsville Educators, Phi Delta Kappa, Alpha Delta Kappa (chpt. officer, dist. officer). Republican. Methodist. Home: 107 Huisache PO Box 886 Los Fresnos TX 78566 Office: Egly Elem Sch 445 Land O'Lakes St Brownsville TX 78521

ENOCH, JACK MARTIN, JR., investment banker; b. Knoxville, Tenn., Jan. 24, 1948; s. Jack Martin and Betty Gene (Boyd) E.; m. Nita Carlson, Apr. 7, 1984. B.A., Randolph-Macon Coll., 1970; M.B.A., U. Pa., 1975. Comml. lending officer Phila. Nat. Bank, 1975-78; asst. v.p. Phila. Capital Advisors, Phila., 1978-80; asst. v.p. Trust Co. Ga., 1980-81; v.p. fin., chief fin. officer Healthcare Venture Corp., Richmond, Va., 1981-83; with corp. fin. dept. Branch, Cabell & Co., Richmond, 1984—. Mem. exec. com. of bd. assocs. Randolph-Macon Coll. Served to lt. (j.g.) USN, 1970-73. Republican. Episcopalian. Mem. Omicron Delta Kappa, Pi Gamma Mu, Phi Delta Theta. Clubs: Commonwealth, Merion Cricket, Orpheus of Phila. Home: 10012 Joppa Ct Richmond VA 23233 Office: 919 E Main St Richmond VA 23219

ENOUEN, WILLIAM ALBERT, paper corporation executive; b. Columbus, Ohio, Nov. 7, 1928; s. John J. and Bertha (Thiry) E.; m. Joan Claire Batsche, June 20, 1953; children—William A., Robert, Kathryn, James, Patricia. B.S., U. Dayton, 1952; student advanced mgmt. program, Harvard U., 1975. Various acctg. positions Touche, Ross & Co., Dayton, Ohio, 1952-59; asst. to controller, asst. to group v.p. and fin. cons. affiliated cos. Mead Corp., Dayton, 1959-68, controller, 1969-72, v.p., controller, 1972-81, v.p. fin. resources and control, 1981—; v.p. Brunswick Pulp & Paper Co., 1968-69; dir. Northwood Forest Industries, Ltd., Brunswick Pulp & Paper Co., Mead Re Inc., Westbury Ins. Co., B.C. Forest Products Ltd., Morris Bean. Served with AUS, 1946-47. Mem. Ohio Soc. C.P.A.s (v.p. Dayton chpt. 1959-60). Home: 4617 Ackerman Blvd Dayton OH 45429 Office: Brunswick Pulp & Paper Co PO Box 1438 Brunswick GA 31520*

ENSENAT, LOUIS ALBERT, physician; b. Merida, Mexico, Oct. 24, 1916; s. Frank and Guadalupe F. (Ensenat) E.; B.S., Tulane U., 1938, M.D., 1941; M.Sc. in Medicine, U. Pa., 1953; m. Ruth Ogden, July 9, 1943; children—Gloria Louise, Tinita Ruth, Louis Albert, Rita Joan, Barbara Jean, Michael Monroe. Intern, Charity Hosp., New Orleans, 1941-42; resident surgery Charity Hosp., Monroe, La., 1942, Lakeshore Hosp., New Orleans, VA hosp., New Orleans, Batavia, N.Y.; fellow in surg. pathology Tulane U. Sch. Med.; preceptorship in surgery Biloxi (Miss.) VA Hosp.; staff surg. VA Hosp., Montgomery, 1946-52; pvt. practice surgery, Pasadena, Tex., 1952-63, New Orleans, 1963—; adminstr. Mercy Hosp. Pasadena, 1954-63, chief surgery, 1954-63; founder, dir. Gulf Coast Home Builders, Inc. Trustee, Big State Factors Corp. Served from lt. (j.g.) to lt. comdr. USN, 1942-46. Decorated Purple Heart, Bronze Star. Diplomate Am. Bd. Surgery, Am. Bd. Abdominal Surgery. Fellow French Soc. Phlebology, Am. Coll. Angiology (pres.); mem. Hawthorne Surg. Soc., Am. Soc. Abdominal Surgeons, N.Y. Acad. Scis., Am. Med. Writers Assn. Author articles in field. Home and Office: 7630 Jeannette Pl New Orleans LA 70118

ENTREMONT, PHILIPPE, conductor, pianist; b. Rheims, France, June 7, 1934; s. Jean and Renée (Monchamps) E.; m. Andree Ragot, Dec. 21, 1955; children—Félicia, Alexandre. Student, Conservatoire National Superieur de Musique, Paris, Jean Doyen. Profl. debut at 17, in Barcelona, Spain, Am. debut at 19, at Nat. Gallery, Washington, 1953, performs throughout world; pianist-condr. debut at, Mostly Mozart Festival, Lincoln Center, N.Y.C., 1971; rec. artist Epic, Concert Hall and Columbia records; music guest condr., Royal Philharm., Orch. Nat. de France, Montreal Symphony, San Francisco Symphony, Vienna Chamber Orch., numerous others; music dir., prin. condr., New Orleans Philharm. Symphony Orch., 1981—. Decorated chevalier de l'Ordre National du Merite.; A finalist Queen Elizabeth of Belgium Internat. Concours, 1952; Grand Prix Marguerite Long-Jacques Thibaud Competition, 1953; Harriet Cohen Piano medal, 1953; 1st prize Jeunesses Musicales; Grand Prix du Disque, 1967, 68, 69, 70; Edison award, 1968; Nominee Grammy award, 1972. Former mem. Academie Internationale de Musique Maurice Ravel (pres. 1975-80). Office: New Orleans Philharm Symphony Maritime Bldg Suite 903 203 Carondelet St New Orleans LA 70130*

EPNER, MARCIA GORNICK, college administrator, reading and education educator; b. N.Y.C., Mar. 7, 1933; d. Julius and Ann Gornick; m. Martin Epher, June 19, 1954; children—Maury, Susan, Daniel, Paul. B.A., Bklyn. Coll., 1954; M.A., NYU, 1966, Ph.D., U. Tex.-Austin, 1975. Tchr., Old Country Rd. Sch., Hicksville, N.Y., 1954-56, Pub. Sch. #199, N.Y.C., 1956-57; reading specialist Battle Hill Clinic, White Plains, N.Y., 1966-67; clinician U. Tex.-Austin, summer 1974; prof. reading and edn. San Antonio Coll., 1968-77, chmn. dept. reading and edn., 1977—. Author: Fundamental Facts for the Reading Instructor, 1975, Innovative Reading Strategies, 1980; also articles. Judge Tex. Forensic Assn., San Antonio, 1972—; evaluator Ednl. Testing Service, Princeton, N.J., 1978; active reading skills task force San Antonio C. of C., 1979; bd. dirs. Early Childhood Sch. Bd., San Antonio, 1979—. Piper Prof. nominee Minnie Stevens Piper Found., 1980. Mem. Internat. Reading Assn. (membership chmn. 1979), NEA, Assn. Curriculum Devel., Tex. Jr. Coll. Tchrs. Assn. (v.p. devel. reading sect. 1977-78). Jewish. Avocations: swimming; gardening; walking; reading. Home: 403 Squires Row San Antonio TX 78213 Office: San Antonio Coll 1300 San Pedro Ave San Antonio TX 78284

EPPERLY, JOHN DAVID, lawyer; b. Floyd, Va., Oct. 14, 1920; s. Issac Lafayette and Melinda (Wheddle) E.; m. Judy Martin, Oct. 4, 1968; children—Carolyn, Elizabeth, John David, Anne. B.S., U. Va., 1941, LL.B., 1947. Bar: Va., U.S. Ct. Appeals (4th cir.), U.S. Supreme Ct. Practice, Martinsville, Va., 1947—; ptnr. Broaddus, Epperly, Broaddus & Hankins. Served to lt. USAAF. Mem. Am. Coll. Trial Lawyers, Am. Judicature Soc., Supreme Ct. of U.S. Hist. Soc., Order of Coif, Omicron Delta Kappa. Baptist. Office: Broaddus Epperly Broaddus & Hankins 106 E Main St Martinsville VA 24112

EPPERSON, DAVID ROSS, architect, planner, photographer; b. Miami, Fla., May 27, 1939; s. Thiel Otis and Helen Amanda (Ross) E.; m. Merrie-Jayne Tallamy, Apr. 9, 1965; 1 son, David Ross. B.Arch., U. Fla., 1965; M.S., Fla. State U., 1972, Ph.D., 1978. Registered architect, Fla., Ga., Tex. Project architect KBJ Architects, Jacksonville, Fla., 1965-69; sch. cons. architect State of Fla., Tallahassee, 1969-73; project mgr. Eoghan Kelley Assocs., Architects, Sanford, Fla., Atlanta, 1973-75; state research architect State of Fla. Dept. Edn., Tallahassee, 1975-80; dir. facilities planning Escambia Dist. Schs., Pensacola, Fla., 1980—; archtl. planning and program cons. David R. Epperson, A.I.A. Architect, Pensacola, 1980—. Author of monographs. Mem. jour. editorial bd. Council of Ednl. Facilities Planners Internat., Columbus, Ohio, 1984—. Mem. Pensacola Mus. Art, State of Fla. Gov.'s Design awards jury, Tallahassee, 1983; mem. select com. drafting constrn. legis. Fla. Sch. Bds. Assn., Tallahassee, 1980. Recipient 2nd place photo award Arts and Design Soc. Ft. Walton Beach, Inc., 1984, numerous other photo awards; Kappa Delta Pi scholar, 1972; Fla. Bd. Regents grantee, 1979, 81. Mem. AIA, Fla. Assn. AIA, Northwest Fla. Chpt. AIA (pres. 1984-85), Council of Ednl. Facilities Planners Internat. (regional service citation 1984, alt. dir. Southeast Region 1985-86), Fla. Facilities Planners Assn. (pres. 1985—), ASHRAE, Constrn. Specifications Inst., U. Fla. Alumni Assn., Fla. State U. Alumni Assn., Phi Delta Kappa, Theta Chi. Democrat. Episcopalian. Lodge: Rotary. Avocations: photography; antique toy trains; guitar. Office: Escambia Dist Schs 215 W Garden St Pensacola FL 32501

EPPERSON, JEAN WARNER, rancher; b. Waco, Tex., July 7, 1919; d. Asa W. and Annie Mae (Bell) Warner; m. Clinton W. Breeding, Feb. 20, 1942 (div. Nov. 1958); children—Bayard, Webb, Leanna; m. Robert Julius Epperson, June 5, 1965. B.A., Baylor U., 1941; cert. Gulf Park Coll., Miss., 1939; postgrad. So. Meth. U., 1970-71. Mng. dir. Baylor U. Sch. Drama, Waco, 1943; rancher, Satin, Tex., 1954—. Nat. Museum House chair Nat. Soc. Colonial Dames Am., 1980—; pres. Brazos Forum, 1985—, Greater Waco Beautification Assn., 1984; bd. dirs. Dallas Garden Ctr., 1967-69, Dallas Theatre Ctr., 1965-75. Editor: Guidelines for Museum Houses, 1984. Named Woman of Yr., Kappa Alpha Theta, 1985. Mem. Phi Theta Kappa. Clubs: Dallas Garden (v.p. 1979), Jr. League Garden (pres. 1970) (Dallas). Home: PO Box 110 Windsong Satin TX 76685

EPPERSON, JOEL RODMAN, lawyer; b. Miami, Fla., Aug. 29, 1945; s. John Rodman and Ann Louise (Barrs) E.; m. Gretchen Jean Meyer, Apr. 16, 1968; children—Joel Rodman, David Michael, Sandra Elizabeth. B.S., U. South Fla., 1967; J.D., South Tex. Coll., 1976. Bar: Fla. 1976, U.S. Dist. Ct. (mid. dist.) Fla. 1976, U.S. Ct. Appeals (5th cir.) 1976, U.S. Supreme Ct. 1979. Asst. states atty. State of Fla., Tampa, 1976-79; mem. firm Bryant & Epperson, 1979—. Served to capt. USMC, 1968-72. Mem. ABA, Assn. Trial Lawyers Am., Fla. Criminal Def. Lawyers Assn., Fla. Trial Lawyers Assn., Hillsborough County Bar Assn. Democrat. Home: 10905 Cliff Dr Temple Terrace FL 33617 Office: Bryant & Epperson 1107 E Jackson St Tampa FL 33602

EPPLEY, FRANCES FIELDEN, educator, author; b. Knoxville, Tenn., July 18, 1921; d. Chester Earl and Beulah Magnolia (Wells) Fielden; m. Gordon Talmage Cougle, July 25, 1942; children—Russell Gordon Eppley, Carolyn Eppley Horseman; m. Fred Coan Eppley, Mar. 8, 1953; 1 dau., Charlene Eppley Sellers. B.A. in English, Carson Newman Coll., 1942; M.A., Winthrop Coll., 1963. Tchr., East Corinth (Maine) Acad., 1942-43; tchr. pub. schs., Charlotte, N.C., 1950-53, 59—, Greenville, S.C., 1954-56, Spartanburg, S.C., 1957-58; head start tchr., summers 1964-68. Mem. hist. com. N.C. Bapt. Conv., 1985-86. Alpha Delta Kappa grantee, 1970. Mem. NEA, N.C. Social Studies Conf., Writers Assn., Alpha Delta Kappa, Pi Kappa Delta, Alpha Psi Omega. Baptist. Author: First Baptist Church of Charlotte, North Carolina: Its Heritage, 1981; History of Flint Hill, 1983; The First Astrologer, 1983; Sammy's Song, 1984; No Show Dog, 1985; Sun Signs for Christians, 1985; mus. drama: The Place To Be, 1982; mus. show: Songs of The People, 1983; song: Katie, 1985.

EPPS, JAMES HAWS, III, lawyer; b. Johnson City, Tenn., Sept. 15, 1936; s. James H. and Anne (Sessoms) E.; m. Jane Mahoney, Oct. 9, 1976; children by previous marriage—James Haws IV, Sara Stuart. B.A., U. N.C., 1959; J.D., Vanderbilt U., 1962. Bar: Tenn. 1962, ICC 1962, U.S. Supreme Ct. 1967, U.S. Ct. Appeals (6th cir.) 1971. Assoc. Cox, Taylor, Epps, Miller & Weller, Johnson City, 1962, Epps, Powell, Weller, Taylor & Miller, 1962-69, ptnr. 1969-72; ptnr. Epps, Powell, Weller & Epps, 1972-73, Epps, Powell, Epps & Lawrence, 1973-76, Powell & Epps, 1976-84; sole practice, Johnson City, 1984—; city atty. Johnson City, 1967—; atty. Johnson City Bd. Edn., 1967—; spl. counsel State of Tenn., 1966-70; past dir., E. Tenn. & Western N.C. Transp. Co., E. Tenn. & Western N.C. R.R., Tennolina Corp., Appalachian Air Lines, Inc., Farmers and Mchts. Bank of Limestone, Tenn., Appalachian Flying Service, Inc. Mem. Tenn. Law Revision Commn., 1970-71. Mem. budget com. United Fund, Johnson City, 1964-68, former mem. bd. dirs.; former legal adviser Appalachian council Girl Scouts Am.; mem. adv. bd. Salvation Army, 1974—; charter mem. Johnson City/Washington County Boys' Club, Inc.; mem. Civil Def. Adv. Bd., 1967—; mem. county exec. com. Democratic party; past bd. dirs., counsel Tenn. Mental Health Assn., Washington County Mental Health Assn. Mem. Fed. Bar Assn., ABA, Tenn. Bar Assn. (mem. continuing legal edn. com. 1971-74), Washington County Bar Assn. (past pres.), Am. Judicature Soc., Am. Trial Lawyers Assn., Tenn. Trial Lawyers Assn., Tenn. Sch. Bd. Attys. Assn., Nat. Sch. Bd. Attys. Assn., Assn. ICC Practitioners (former mem. com. profl. ethics and grievances), Motor Carrier Lawyers Assn. (bd. govs. Transp. Law Jour.), Am. Counsel Assn., Nat. Assn. R.R. Trial Counsel, Lawyers Com. for Civil Rights Under Law, World Peace Through Law Ctr., Def. Research Inst., Nat. Orgn. on Legal Problems of Edn. Tenn. Mcpl. Attys. Assn., Supreme Ct. Hist. Soc., Nat. Inst. Mcpl. Law Officers, C. of C. (govtl. affairs com., Disting. Service award 1968), Tennesseans for Better Transp., Tenn. Taxpayers Assn. (past dir.), Internat. Platform Assn., Nat. Legal Aid Defender Assn., Transp. Lawyers Assn., Tenn. Correctional Assn., Tenn. Lung Assn., Nat. Rifle Assn., Tipton Haynes Hist. Assn. (dir.), Phi Delta Phi, Phi Delta Theta. Episcopalian (vestryman, 1965-68, 70-71, clk. 1968-71, layreader). Clubs: North Johnson City Business (dir., pres. 1966-67), Hurstleigh, Johnson City Country, Nat. Lawyers, Unaka Rod and Gun, Highland Stable, Leconte, E. Tenn. State U. Century. Lodges: Elks (legal counsel 1963-67), Masons. Home: 705 Judith Dr Johnson City TN 37601 Office: 115 E Unaka Ave Johnson City TN 37601

EPRIGHT, CHARLES JOHN, engineer; b. Bklyn., Jan. 11, 1932; s. Charles and Margaret Mary (Tripoli) E.; m. Mary Lucy Bono, May 29, 1954; children—Daniel John, Michael James, Marisa Epright Brimblecom, Victoria Ann, Maria Carmela. B.S. in Math., U. Nev., 1965; M.S. in Engring. Mgmt., Northeastern U., 1971. Sr. engr. Raytheon, Andover, Mass., 1970-78, Delmo-Victor, Belmont, Calif., 1978-79; advanced systems engring. specialist Lockheed Missile & Space Co., Austin, Tex., Sunnyvale, Calif., 1979—; cons. Colo. Electronic Training Course, Colorado Springs., 1968-69. Civic advocate Salem-in-Action, N.H., 1977-79; dir. Reachout, Salem, 1976-79; community action com. mem. N.H. Com. for Adopted and Foster Children, Manchester,

1978-79, Runaway Hotline, Austin, 1984-85. Served with USAF, 1950-70. Decorated Legion of Merit, 1969; recipient Family of Yr. award Sons of Italy, 1968, 69. Mem. Internat. Assn. Elec. and Electronic Engrs., Air Force Assn. (life), Assn. Old Crows, Am. Inst. Am. Scientists, DAV. Roman Catholic. Lodge: KC (grand knight 1968-69). Avocations: stamp collecting; photography; collecting old books. Home: 7500 Bender Dr Austin TX 78749 Office: Lockheed Missile and Space Co Inc 2124 E St Elmo Rd Austin TX 78749

EPSTEIN, DAVID CARLIN, physician; b. Chgo., Oct. 26, 1950; s. Chester M. and Florence Elaine (Carlin) E. B.S., Tulane U., 1972; M.D. Chgo. Med. Sch., 1976. Resident in gen. surgery Baylor Coll. Medicine, Houston, 1976-78; emergency physician EMSCO, Ltd., Chgo., 1978-81; clin. instr. emergency medicine Northwestern U., U. Ill.-Chgo., 1980-81; med. dir. emergency dept. Shallowford Hosp., Atlanta, 1981-83; gen. practice medicine, Atlanta, 1983—; instr. advanced cardiac life support Am. Heart Assn., 1980; instr. advanced trauma life support ACS. Mem. Am. Coll. Emergency Physicians. Home: 6857 C Glenlake Pkwy Atlanta GA 30328 Office: 3475 Lenox Rd NE Atlanta GA 30326

EPSTEIN, EDWARD STEVEN, motion picture producer and director, sales and marketing executive; b. Balt., Oct. 3, 1948; s. Leon Stuart and Claire (Miller) E.; divorced; children—Ivy Marin, Stefanie Arlin. B.A., U. Md., 1971, B.S., 1971. Vice pres., producer Screenscope, Inc., Washington, 1972-77; producer, dir. Fla. Prodn. Ctr., Jacksonville, 1977-85; sr. ptnr. Woolfe-Miller Communications, Jacksonville, 1985—. Assoc. producer T.V. series First Tuesday (Emmy award 1971); producer, dir. film documentary In the Year of Our Lord (Emmy award 1971). Sr. advisor United Syynagogue Youth, Jacksonville, 1982—; sr. cons. P.E.C. Internat., Charleston, S.C., 1985—; bd. dirs. Beth Shalom Congregation, Jacksonville, 1982—. Recipient Moscow Film Festival award Moscow Ednl. Film Body, 1969, Most Honored Film award Bus. Screen Mag., 1969. Mem. Nat. Press Club, Nat. Acad. TV Arts and Scis., Am. Advt. Fedn. (bd. dirs. 1977-80, numerous Addy awards). Democrat. Jewish. Avocations: scuba diving; photography. Home and Office: 3379 Maiden Voyage Circle N Jacksonville FL 32217

EPSTEIN, LOUIS ALLEN, entertainment company owner; B. Bklyn., July 12, 1957; s. Gerald and Eleanor Augusta (Brown) E.; m. Penelope Richards, July 31, 1983; 1 dau., Anna Rose. Student U. Houston, 1977—. Mime performer U. Houston Mime Troupe, 1978-82; mime performer, co-dir. Tex. Mime Troupe, Houston, 1980-83; co-dir., owner mgr. Best Entertainers, United, Houston, 1980—; actor, mime Mad Hatter Talent Agy., Houston, 1980-81; puppeteer, writer Royal Puppet Theatre, Houston, 1983—; actor, writer Houston Children's Theatre Festival, 1979-81; co-owner Humoreske, music, comedy, variety nightclub; sec. Zinneppers, Inc. Co-author play: Ruby Ring, 1983; author puppet show: The Dragon with a Complex, 1983; co-author mime shows and comedy workshop tour company shows. Mem. Houston Council Conv. and Visitors Bur., 1982—. Mem. AFTRA, Screen Actors Guild. Jewish. Home: 1411 Kipling St Apt 1 Houston TX 77006 Office: 3321 Entertainers Unltd 3309 W Lamar St Houston TX 77019

EPSTEIN, SAMUEL ABRAHAM, geologist; b. N.Y.C., Sept. 14, 1956; s. Isidor and Mamie (Kosofosky) E.; m. Peggy Ann Eisenberg, July 4, 1979; children—David Solomon, Daniel Moses. B.S., Bklyn. Coll., 1977; M.S., Rensselaer Poly. Inst., 1979. Geologist Cities Service, Houston, 1979-82; petroleum geologist sr. grade Texaco, Inc., Houston, 1982-85; ind. geologist, Houston, 1985—. Bd. dirs. Rensselaer Alumni Assn., Houston, 1984, Young Israel Houston Synagogue, 1984; laison Bklyn. Coll. Geol. Alumni Assoc., 1980. Mem. Am. Assn. Petroleum Geologists, Houston Geol. Soc. Home: 6027 Dawnridge Houston TX 77035

ERB, LEE HARVEY, aeronautical engineer; b. Conneaut, Ohio, Aug. 12, 1929; s. John Irvin and Edith Anise (Harvey) E.; m. Mary Alice Stewart, July 16, 1954; children—Robert Irvin, Russell Earl. B.S. in Aero. Engring., St. Louis U., 1951; M.S., U. Colo., 1958. With design and devel. dept. McDonnell Aircraft, St. Louis, 1951-53; with Bell Helicopter, Ft. Worth, 1953-82, sr. design engr., 1979-82; owner, cons. Omni Innovations, Arlington, Tex., 1982—. Scoutmaster, Boy Scouts Am., 1970—; sec. bd. dirs. Ft. Worth Regional Sci. Fair, 1979-83. Served to 1st lt. USAF, 1954-56. Fellow AIAA (assoc.); mem. Am. Helicopter Soc., Air Force Assn., Soc. Flight Test Engrs. Methodist. Home and Office: 832 S Collins St Arlington TX 76010

ERBELE, LEO ALBERT, physician; b. Mandan, N.D., Jan. 8, 1927; s. Albert Frederick and Anna (Goldmann) E.; student Creighton U., 1944-45; B.A., U. N.D., 1949, B.S., 1950; M.D., Bowman Gray Sch. Medicine, 1952; m. Josephine Phelps Matthews, Apr. 26, 1973; children by previous marriage—John, Olivia, Peter, Mary. Intern City Hosp., Winston-Salem, N.C., 1952-53; gen. practice medicine, Clover, S.C., 1953-54, Marion, N.C., 1954-55; residency tng. Bowman Gray Sch. Medicine, Winston-Salem, 1955-59; asso. pathologist Macon (Ga.) Hosp., 1959-61, dir. labs., 1961-65; now engaged in pvt. practice. Served as sgt. USAAF, 1945-47. Diplomate in anatomic pathology and clin. pathology Am. Bd. Pathology, Am. Bd. Nuclear Medicine. Fellow Am. Soc. Clin. Pathologists, Coll. Am. Pathologists; mem. So. Med. Assn. Home: 3379 Osborne Pl Macon GA 31204 Office: 630 Orange St Macon GA 31208

ERBER, JOAN T., psychology educator; b. Rochester, N.Y., June 21, 1943; d. Milton and Harriet (Frank) Tatelbaum; children—Stephanie Lynn, Melanie Gail. B.A. in Psychology, Washington U., St. Louis, 1965; M.S. in Psychology, St. Louis U., 1969, Ph.D. in Exptl. Devel. Psychology, 1971. Postdoctoral fellow aging and devel. Washington U., St. Louis, 1972-74, research assoc. in aging/psychology, 1977-82, 74-75; assoc. prof. psychology Fla. Internat. U., Miami, 1982—. Contbr. articles to profl. jours.; chpts. to books. Fellow Gerontol. Soc. Am., Am. Psychol. Assn., Phi Beta Kappa, Sigma Xi. Office: Fla Internat U Tamiami Campus Psychology Dept Miami FL 33199

ERBY, KENNETH WYATT, business educator; b. Wadesboro, N.C., June 11, 1946; s. Benjamin Hooper and Wilma Lea (Smith) E. A.A., Sandhills Community Coll., 1967; B.S., Pembroke State U., 1969; M.S. in Econs. and Bus., Appalachian State U., 1972. With mgmt. J.P. Stevens Co., Rockingham, N.C., 1969-70; tchr. math. Marlboro County Sch., Bennettsville, S.C., 1970-71; city acct. City of Rockingham, 1971-72; instr. bus. Chesterfield-Marlboro Tech. Coll., Cheraw, S.C., 1973—, chmn. bus. div., 1975—. Mem. Am. Bus. Law Assn., Am. Acctg. Assn., S.C. Tech. Ednl. Assn. Republican. Baptist. Avocation: all sports. Home: 2015 Brookbank Rd Rockingham NC 28379 Office: Chesterfield-Marlboro Tech Coll PO Drawer 1007 Cheraw SC 29520

ERDREICH, BEN, congressman; b. Birmingham, Ala., Dec. 9, 1938; s. Stanley and Corinne E.; m. Ellen Cooper, 1965; children—Jeremy C., Anna B. B.A., Yale U., 1960; J.D. with honors, U. Ala., 1963. Bar: Ala. 1963. Pvt. practice, Birmingham, 8 yrs.; mem. 98th-99th congresses from 6th Dist. Ala. Mem. Ala. Ho. of Reps., 1970-74, Jefferson County Commn., 1974-80. Served to 1st lt. U.S. Army, 1963-65. Mem. Ala. Bar Assn., Birmingham Bar Assn., ABA. Democrat. Jewish. Office: 439 Cannon House Office Bldg Washington DC 20515

ERESHEFSKY, LARRY, psychopharmacologist, educator, consultant; b. Bklyn., Mar. 10, 1952; s. Sam and Claire (Geller) E.; m. Elke S. Weisburd, Sept. 1, 1974; children—Benjamin Jacob, Sabrina Hope. Pharm.D., U. So. Calif. 1976. Cert. psychiat. pharm. practice, Calif. Research asst. UCLA, 1970-73; clin. instr. U. So. Calif., 1976-77; asst. prof. U. Tex.-Austin, 1977-82, assoc. prof., 1982—, Regents chair in psychopharmacology, 1985—, assoc. prof. pharmacology and psychiatry, Health Sci. Ctr., San Antonio, 1982—, program dir., 1983—; cons. in field. Contbr. articles to profl. jours. Mem. Am. Coll. Clin. Pharmacy (chmn. clin. practice affairs), Am. Soc. Hosp. Pharmacists (SIG officer 1980-82, mem. council edn. affairs 1982-83, chmn. psychopharmacology 1982), AAAS, Am. Assn. Colls. of Pharm., Phi Kappa Phi, Rho Chi. Jewish. Avocations: sailing; snorkeling; hiking; reading. Office: U Tex Health Sci Ctr 7703 Floyd Curl Dr San Antonio TX 78284

ERFFT, KENNETH REYNDERS, educational consultant; b. Chgo., Nov. 14, 1908; s. Victor Athen and Ethel (Reynders) E.; A.B., No. Mich. U.; 1932; M.A., U. Richmond, 1936, D.S.C., 1967; Litt.D., Maclean Coll., 1947; LL.D., No. Mich. U., 1961; m. Nancy Fontaine Creath, June 8, 1940. Instr. Ironwood (Mich.) High Sch., 1932-34; clk. bd. edn. Petersburg (Va.) pub. schs., 1936-42; bus. mgr. Furman U., Greenville, S.C., 1946-54; comptroller Pa. State U., 1954-57; v.p., treas. Rutgers State U., 1957-62, Thomas Jefferson U., 1962-64; pres. Kenneth R. Erfft Assocs., Inc., ednl. cons., Phila. 1964-66; v.p. Duquesne U., Pitts., 1966-72; exec. dir. Nationwide Conf. Edn. Centers, Inc., Atlanta, 1972-74; pres. Univ. Center in Va., Richmond, 1974-78; ret., 1978; chmn. bd. dirs. Afuture Fund, Carlisle-Asher Enterprises. Mem. adminstrv. com. for Calif. and Western Conf. Cost and Statis. Study, 1955-57. Served from lt. (j.g.) to comdr. USNR, 1942-46. Decorated knight Sacred Order Constantinian of St. George; recipient Disting. Alumnus award No. Mich. U., 1979. Mem. Eastern Assn. Coll. and U. Bus. Officers (pres.), AAUP, Middle States Assn., Delta Sigma Phi, Phi Epsilon, Tau Kappa Alpha, Omicron Delta Kappa, Theta Omicron Rho. Clubs: Engineers (Richmond); Internat. Torch. Co-author: Administrators in Higher Education, 1962. Editorial com. College and University Business Administration, rev. edits. Home: 1600 S Ocean Dr Apt 3-D Hollywood FL 33019

ERICKSON, BRUCE RAYMOND, university administrator, photographer; b. Lindsborg, Kans., July 4, 1947; s. Eugene D. and Ruth V. (Nelson) E.; m. Mary Escher; children—Bret, Kirsten, Christopher. B.S. in Journalism, Kans. U., 1971, M.S. in Journalism, 1976. Dir. pub. info. Culver-Stockton Coll., Mo., 1976-80; asst. dir. continuing edn. Kans. U., Lawrence, 1980-82; dir. pub. info. Pan Am. U., Edinburg, Tex., 1982—. Served with USNR, 1969-70. Mem. Council Advancement and Support Edn. Roman Catholic. Lodge: Rotary. Office: Pan Am U 1201 W University Dr Edinburg TX 78539

ERICKSON, DAVID THEODORE, petroleum engr.; b. Delta, Colo., June 1, 1951; s. Carl John and Mary Bancroft (Wortham) E.; B.S., Colo. Sch. Mines, 1973. Assoc. engr. Continental Oil Co., Hobbs, N.Mex., 1974, engr., 1975; social coordinator AIME, Hobbs, 1975-76; prodn. engr. Continental Oil Co., Oklahoma City, 1977-78, supervising reservoir engr., Lake Charles, La., 1978-80, coordinator gas sales Mid-Continent and Rocky Mountain regions, Houston, 1980-81; sr. petroleum engr. internat. exploration and prodn. Union Tex. Petroleum, Houston, 1981—; propr. Erickson Arabians, 1981—. Registered profl. engr., N.Mex., Okla., La. Mem. Soc. Petroleum Engrs., AIME, Gulf Coast Arabian Horse Club, Arabian Riders and Breeders Assn., Am. Horse Show Assn., Arabian Horse Show Registry Am., Internat. Arabian Horse Assn., Nat. Horse Show Registry. Republican. Home: Route 1 Box 412-E Office: 1 Riverway Houston TX 77001

ERICKSON, JAMES RICHARD, psychologist; b. Mpls., June 21, 1934; s. Clarence Gustav and Lillie Mae (Evenson) E.; m. Shirley Warren, Dec. 21, 1957 (div. 1978); children—Kenton R., Marcus R., Stuart R. B.S., U. Minn.-Mpls., 1959, Ph.D., 1963. Asst. prof. to prof. Ohio State U., Columbus, 1962-75; vis. assoc. prof. U. Colo., Boulder, 1968-69; prof. psychology U. Tex., Arlington, 1975—, chmn. dept. psychology, 1975-82. Contbr. articles to profl. jours. Fellow Am. Psychol. Assn.; mem. Psychomomic Soc., Psychometric Soc., Midwestern Psychol. Assn., Soc. for Math. Psychology. Office: Dept Psychology Univ Tex Box 19528 Arlington TX 76019

ERICKSON, JOHN ALBIN, architect, planner; b. Tacoma, Apr. 17, 1946; s. Carl Albin and Frances Elizabeth (Stitt) E.; student U. Tex., Arlington, 1964-65, U. Tex., Austin, 1966-72; m. Susan Margaret Hurley, Sept. 27, 1969; children—Derek, Jason, Jeremy. Draftsman, Fehr & Granger, Architects and Planners, Austin, Tex., 1967-69; designer/draftsman Roger Erickson, Architect, Engr., Austin, 1969-70; designer Walter Carrington Bldg., Austin, 1970-72; asso. in charge design Environ. Design Group, Austin, 1972-74; design and prodn. coordinator Architects Partnership, Dallas, 1974-75; dir. design Killebrew/Rucker/Asso., Inc., Wichita Falls, Tex., 1975-81; owner, prin. John A. Erickson AIA, Wichita Falls, 1981-82; pres. Erickson/Lebow/-Morrison, Inc., Architects, Engrs., and Planners, 1982—; design cons. Image Advt., 1979-80, All Saints Episcopal Ch., 1979-80. Recipient First Place awards in residential single family design Tex. Inst. Bldg. Design, 1972; registered architect, Tex. Mem. AIA, Tex. Soc. Architects. Episcopalian. Archtl. works include The Bluffs at Lakeway, 1972, Patient Services Bldg., Wichita Falls State Hosp., 1978, S.W. Nat. Bank Complex, 1981—. Home: 5306 Pyrenees St Wichita Falls TX 76310 Office: 1106 1/2 Brook Ave Wichita Falls TX 76301

ERICSON, ROGER DELWIN, forest products company executive, lawyer; b. Moline, Ill., Dec. 21, 1934; s. Carl and Linnea (Challman) E.; A.B., Stetson U., 1958, J.D., 1958; M.B.A., U. Chgo., 1971; m. Norma F. Brown, Aug. 1, 1957; children—Catherine Lynn, David. Bar: Fla. 1958, Ill. 1959, Ind. 1974. Atty. Brunswick Corp., Skokie, Ill., 1959-62; asst. sec., asst. gen. counsel Chemetron Corp., Chgo., 1962-73; asst. v.p. law, corp. sec. Inland Container Corp., Indpls., 1973-75, v.p., gen. counsel, sec., 1975-84, dir., v.p., sec., 1984—; gen. counsel, sec. Temple-Inland Inc., 1984—; v.p., sec., dir. Ga. Kraft Co., Rome, Ga., 1981—; vice chmn., pres., dir. Kraft Land Services, Inc., Atlanta, 1981—, GK Investments, Inc., Atlanta, 1981—; dir. Temple-Eastex, Inc.Trustee, Chgo. Homes for Children, 1971-74; mem. alumni council U. Chgo., 1972-76; mem. Palatine Twp. Youth Commn., 1969-72; sect. chmn. Chgo. Heart Assn., 1972, 73; mem. alumni bd. dirs. Stetson U. Mem. ABA, Ill. Bar Assn., Ind. Bar Assn., Fla. Bar Assn., Chgo. Bar Assn., Indpls. Bar Assn. (profl. responsibility com. 1982-83), Am. Soc. Corp. Secs., Am. Paper Inst., Indpls. C. of C. (govt. affairs com.), Omicron Delta Kappa, Phi Delta Phi. Republican. Methodist. Clubs: Plum Grove (pres. 1969 Chgo.); Crooked Stick Golf (Carmel, Ind.); Crown Colony Country (Lufkin, Tex.). Recipient West Pub. Co. award, 1957; Nichols Trial Practice award, 1958. Home: 4 Cypress Point Lufkin TX 75901

ERICSON, RUTH ANN, psychiatrist; b. Assaria, Kans., May 15; d. William Albert and Anna Mathilda (Almquist) Ericson; student So. Meth. U., 1945-47; B.S., Bethany Coll.; M.D., U. Tex., 1951. Intern, Calif. Hosp., Los Angeles, 1951-52; resident in psychiatry, U. Tex. Med. Br., Galveston, 1952-55; psychiatrist Child Guidance Clinic, Dallas, 1955-63; clin. instr. Southwestern Med. Sch., Dallas, 1955-68; practice medicine specializing in psychiatry, Dallas, 1955—; cons. Dallas Intertribal Council Clinic, 1974-82, Dallas Ind. Sch. Dist., U.S. Army, Welfare Dept., Tribal Concerns, alcoholism, Adv. Bd. Intertribal Council. Fellow Am. Geriatric Soc.; mem. Am. Med. Women's Assn. (corr. sec. 1980-81), Paleopath. Soc., So., Tex., Dallas med. assns., Am. Psychiat. Assn. (life), Dallas Area Women Psychiatrists, Alumni Assn. U. Tex. (Med. Br.), Navy League (life), Air Force Assn., Tex. (life), Dallas (life, pres. 1972-73, 82-84, pres. 1982-84) archaeol. socs., Alpha Omega Alpha, Delta Psi Omega, Alpha Psi Omega, Pi Gamma Mu, Lambda Sigma, Alpha Epsilon Iota. Lutheran. Home: 4007 Shady Hill Dr Dallas TX 75229 Office: 2915 LBJ Freeway Suite 135 Dallas TX 75234

ERLANDSON, RAY SANFORD, educator; b. Wausau, Wis., May 3, 1893; s. Paul and Torgine (Olson) E.; A.B., U. Wis., 1918; M.A., George Washington U., 1921; m. Margery McKillop, Aug. 22, 1919; children—Paul McKillop, Ray Sanford, William. Sch. adminstr. Chippewa Falls, Wis., 1913-16; asst. sec., bus. mgr. NEA, 1919-24; bus. mgr. Internat. Council Religious Edn., 1924-27; sales exec. John Rudin & Co., 1927-29, Grigsby Grunow Co., 1929-32, Zenith Radio Corp., 1932-35; v.p. Rudolph Wurlizer Co., 1935-45; v.p. San Antonio Music Co., 1945-50, pres., 1950-53; pres. Bledsoe Furniture Co. 1950-53; chmn. dept. bus. adminstrn. Trinity U., 1953-64, prof. emeritus, 1964—; pres., chief exec. officer Children's Fund, San Antonio, 1964-70; pres. Am. Inst. Character Edn., 1970-74, chmn. bd., chief exec. officer, 1970—; dir. 1st Fed. Savs. & Loan Assn.; founder Am. Sch. of Air, 1929; pres. Am. Music War Council, 1942-44; chmn. nat. trade practice code com., music industry, 1944-53. Nat. vice chmn. ARC, 1959-60; past bd. dirs. San Antonio chpt.; past bd. dirs. San Antonio Symphony Soc., Taxpayers League, Community Welfare Council; bd. dirs., mem. exec. com. S.W. Research Inst., chmn. bd. of control, 1961-64. Served as lt., F.A., U.S. Army, World War I; cons. joint Army-Navy com. on welfare, recreation, World War II. Named Father of Year, San Antonio, 1951; Disting. Alumnus award Wis. State U., 1969. Mem. NEA, San Antonio Chamber Music Soc. (pres. 1950-56), Research and Planning Council (pres. 1957), AAUP, Nat. Mcpl. League, San Antonio Council Pres. (pres. 1951), Nat. Assn. Music Mchts. (pres. 1950-52, hon. life). Republican. Presbyterian. Clubs: Rotary (gov. dist. 584 internat. 1958-59, Paul Harris fellow 1981, hon. life mem.), Knife and Fork (pres. 1954), Breakfast (pres. 1953), San Antonio. Author: (with others) Principles of Retailing, 1955; Principles of Marketing 1958; Principles of Advertising. Home: 401 Shook Ave San Antonio TX 78212 Address: Am Inst for Character Edn Box 12617 San Antonio TX 78212

ERNEST, DORA PAGE, educator; b. Stanton, Ala., July 23, 1926; s. George L. and Lillie Mae (Mull) Grover; m. Gerald R. Page, Apr. 20, 1946 (dec.); children—Sarah Bowles Page Schisel, Allen Page, Ann Page Gafford; m. 2d, Jimmy F. Ernest, July 31, 1959. B.A., Troy State U., 1958. Tchr., Brewton Elem. Sch., 1958-59, Parker Elem. Sch., Bay County, Fla., 1959-69, Northside Elem. Sch., Panama City, Fla., 1969—. Mem. Assn. Bay County Educators, Fla. Teaching Profession, Nat. Tchrs. Assn., NEA. Democrat. Baptist.

ERNOUF, ANITA BONILLA, educator; b. Santurce, P.R., Feb. 22, 1920; d. John and Dolores (Asencio) Bonilla; B.A., Hunter Coll., 1944; M.A., Columbia U., 1946, Ph.D., 1970; m. Edward Ernouf, Feb. 8, 1946; children—Edward, Roderic. French, Spanish and Portuguese examiner U.S. Postal Service, N.Y.C., 1942-44; research asst., librarian Hispanic Inst. Columbia U., 1945-47; asst. prof. Spanish, Hollins Coll., Va., 1947-60; prof. Longwood Coll., Farmville, Va., 1960—, chmn. dept. fgn. langs., 1972-79. Mem. NEA, Longwood Edn. Assn. (v.p. 1981-82), AAUW (br. pres. 1980-81), Am. Assn. Tchrs. Spanish and Portuguese, Tchrs. French, Tchrs. German, Am. Council on Teaching Fgn. Langs., Va. Fgn. Lang. Assn. (pres. 1972-73, pres. elect 1978, pres. 1979). Office: Longwood College Farmville VA 23901

ERNST, RICHARD JAMES, college president; b. Niagara, Wis., Feb. 3, 1933; s. Seymour and Rose Marie (Berger) E.; B.S. with high honors, U. Fla., 1956, M.Ed. (univ. fellow), 1959; Ed.D., Fla. State U., 1965; m. Elizabeth Lyle McGeachy, Dec. 23, 1959; children—Marie Elizabeth, Theresa Ann, Richard James. Tchr., Pinellas and Hillsborough County pub. schs., Fla., 1958-62; adminstrv. intern Pinellas County Pub. Schs., 1962-63; instr., asst. dean instrn. St. Petersburg (Fla.) Jr. Coll., 1963-65, dean acad. affairs, 1965-68; pres. No. Va. Community Coll., Annandale, 1968—. Bd. dirs. Consortium for Continuing Higher Edn. in No. Va., 1972—, chmn. bd., 1978; mem. extension and pub. service adv. com. Va. Council Higher Edn., 1972-73, mem. gen. profl. adv. council, 1978—; mem. nat. commn. on acad. affairs Am. Council on Edn., 1972-74, mem. commn. on mil.-higher edn. relations, 1978—; mem. adv. com. nat. orgns. Corp. for Pub. Broadcasting, 1972-74; mem. Va. Adv. Council Vocat. Edn., 1976—; mem. Va. adv. com. Nat. Identification Program for Advancement of Women in Higher Edn. Adminstrn., 1977—; mem. Va. Forum on Edn., 1978—; chmn. fin. com., chmn. personnel com., mem. exec. com., adv. council pres.'s, mem. research and edn. com. Va. Community Coll. System; adv. bd. Jr. Service League No. Va., 1969-71; v.p. bd. trustees Fairfax Hosp., 1972—, also mem. exec. com., chmn. planning and program devel. com., chmn. joint conf. com.; mem. fin. com., mem. adv. panel on hosp.-physician contracts Fairfax Hosp. Assn., 1978—; bd. dirs. Interfaith Center on Corp. Responsibility, 1975—. Coop. for Advancement Community-Based Community Coll. Edn., 1975—; chmn. acad. affairs com., trustee Mary Baldwin Coll., 1976—; mem. exec. com. bd. trustees; mem. gen. assembly misson bd. Presbyterian Ch. in U.S., 1974—, chmn. investment com., 1974—, chmn. long-range planning task force, vice chmn. div. central support services, chmn. fiscal and data sub-div.; mem. trustees' assembly United Way Nat. Capitol Area; mem. Washington Dulles Task Force Adv. Com., 1983-84, Gov.'s Task Force Sci. and Tech., 1982-83; founding mem. Congl. award Council; bd. dirs. Am. Cancer Soc. Served with AUS. 1956-58. Fla. Ho. of Reps. scholar, 1952-56. Mem. No. Va. Ednl. TV Assn., So. Assn. Colls. and Schs. (com. on standards and reports, chmn. commn. on colls., chmn. accrediting comns.), Am. Assn. Jr. Colls. (nat. commn. on instrn.), Phi Eta Sigma, Phi Kappa Phi, Kappa Delta Pi, Phi Delta Kappa. Presbyterian (deacon, elder). Home: 8524 Pappas Way Annandale VA 22003

ERNST, WILLIAM JOEL, III, community planner; b. Chgo., Aug. 11, 1945; s. William Joel and Lelia Ruth (McMurphy) E.; m. Annette Mae Blower, Aug. 19, 1972; children—Margel Lea, William Joel, IV. B.A. cum laude, Westminster Coll., 1967; M.A., U. Va.-Charlottesville, 1968, Ph.D., 1978; M.U.R.P., Va. Commonwealth U., 1978. Zoning inspector, Chesterfield County, Va., 1979-80, planner, 1980-83; community planner Office of Policy Analysis and Research, Va. Dept. Housing and Community Devel., Richmond, 1983-85, sr. planner, 1985—. Served with U.S. Army, 1968-70. Woodrow Wilson fellow, 1967-68, Va.-Danforth Teaching fellow, 1970-74. Mem. Am. Planning Assn. Democrat. Episcopalian. Editor: Chesterfield County: Early Architecture and Historic Sites, 1983; contbr. articles to jours.

ERNSTER, CLETUS PHILLIP, SR., mfg. co. exec.; b. Caledonia, Minn., Apr. 11, 1923; s. Math P. and Matilda A. (Schwebach) E.; grad. high sch.; m. Kathleen A. Hiller, June 15, 1944; children—Cletus Phillip, Timothy Wayne, Sharon Marie. Organizer, Tex. Air U., Cuero, 1946; founder Gulf Coast Kitchens (now Gulf Coast Wood Products Inc.), Cuero, 1956—, Timco Industries, Cuero, 1973—; dir. Am. Bank of Commerce, Victoria, Tex.; comml. pilot. Founder, past pres. Turkeyfest Assn., Cuero. Served as officer USAF, 1944-46. Decorated D.F.C., Air medal with two oak leaf clusters; named Outstanding Citizen of Cuero, 1977; Small Businessman, State of Tex., 1980 Nat. Small Businessman award Pres. Carter, 1980. Mem. Tex. Millwork Assn. (past pres.), Nat. Archtl. Woodwork Inst. (pres.), Cuero C. of C. (past pres.), Sheriffs Assn. Tex., Hump Pilots Assn. (life), Am. Legion, VFW. Roman Catholic. Clubs: Lions, Cuero Country; Victoria Country. Home: 201 E Prairie St Cuero TX 77954 Office: 115 E South Railroad St Cuero TX 77954

ERSKINE, BOBBY FRANK, school principal; b. Jackson, Miss., June 13, 1928; s. Andrew Frank and Norma (Law) E.; m. Catherine Workman, Dec. 23, 1961; children—Robert Michael, Charles Patrick. B.A., U. Tex., 1949, M.Ed., 1957. Tchr. Victoria Ind. Sch. Dist., Tex., 1949-51; prin. Victoria Jr. High Sch., 1954-65; doctoral candidate intern Highland Park Sch. Dist., Tex., 1966; prin. Victoria High Sch., 1967—. First aid chmn. Red Cross, Victoria, 1958-65; bd. chmn. Salvation Army, Victoria, 1960-64; evaluator Boy Scouts Am., Victoria, 1970-75. Served to 2nd lt. U.S. Army, 1951-53. Mem. Tex. Assn. Secondary Sch. Prins., Nat. Assn. Secondary Sch. Prins., Phi Delta Kappa, Phi Kappa Phi, Alpha Phi Sigma. Mem. Bible Ch. Lodge: Lions (Victoria) (pres. 1984-85). Avocations: reading; history. Office: Victoria High Sch 1110 Sam Houston Dr Victoria TX 77902

ERSKINE, WILLIAM CRAWFORD, university business executive, accountant; b. Seattle, Feb. 29, 1924; s. Alwin Crawford and Emilie Hildred (Davies) E.; m. Mary Jean Hopkins, Feb. 28, 1946; children—Scott Crawford, Nancy Page. B.A. in Bus. Adminstrn., U. Wash., 1950. Sr. auditor Ansell Johnson & Co., C.P.A.s, Seattle, 1956-59; controller Food Giant Stores, Seattle, 1959-64; comptroller U. Wash., Seattle, 1964-70; v.p. bus. U. Colo., Boulder, 1970-74; exec. v.p. U. Nebr. system, Lincoln, 1974-80; v.p. bus. affairs U. Tex., El Paso, 1980—; dir. West Tex. Higher Edn. Authority, El Paso, 1982—; cons. Educator Cons. Panel GAO, 1978—. Revision com. Coll. and Univ. Bus. Adminstrn., 1971-75. Mem. Wash. State Soc. C.P.A.s, Western Assn. Colls. and Univ. Bus. Assn., Nat. Assn. Colls. and Univ. Bus. Officers, Tex. Assn. Colls. and Univ. Bus. Officers, Nat. Assn. State Univ. and Land Grant Colls. (exec. com. 1977-80). Club: Coronado Country. Home: 6109 Sierra Valle Ln El Paso TX 79912 Office: Univ Tex El Paso University at Hawthorne El Paso TX 79968

ERVIN, JERALD DEE (SAM), city police chief; b. Kress, Tex., Jan. 13, 1938; s. Robert Lee and Byrdie Dee (Skipworth) E.; m. Rozella Wiliams, Oct. 17, 1958 (div. 1978); children—Jerald Dwayne, Shelly Dawn Ervin McMartery, Stuart Grant; m. Wanetta Josephine Potter, May 10, 1979. Cert. Okla. Hwy. Patrol Acad. Water plant operator City of El Reno, Okla., 1958-62, police officer, 1962-64; trooper Okla. Hwy. Patrol, 1964-65; dep. sheriff Canadian County Sheriff's Dept., Okla., 1966-70; chief of police Yukon Police Dept., Okla., 1970—. Served with U.S. Army, 1956-57. Named Police Officer of Yr., Yukon Police Dept., 1970; recipient Service award Am. Legion, Yukon, 1974, Ingenuity award City of Yukon, 1979. Mem. Internat. Assn. Chiefs of Police, Okla. Assn. Chiefs of Police, (treas. 1976-78), Okla. Sheriffs and Peace Officers Assn., Okla. Res. Law Officers Assn. (life mem., pres. 1978-82, Outstanding Service award 1978, 79, 80, 81), Oklahoma City Metro Chiefs Assn. (chmn. 1972). Democrat. Baptist. Lodge: Rotary (bd. dirs. local club 1973-74). Avocations: bowling; sportscars; landscaping. Office: Yukon Police Dept 100 Ranchwood Dr S Yukon OK 43099

ERVIN, SAMUEL JAMES, III, federal judge; b. Morganton, N.C., Mar. 2, 1926; s. Sam E.; B.S., Davidson Coll., 1948; LL.B., Harvard U., 1951. Admitted to N.C. bar; pvt. practice law, Morganton, 1952-57; mem. firm Patton, Ervin & Starnes, and predecessors, Morganton, 1957-67; judge Superior Ct. 25th Jud. Dist. N.C., 1967-80; now judge U.S. Ct. Appeals 4th Circuit, Morganton; solicitor Burke County (N.C.) Criminal Ct., 1954-56. Pres., Davidson Coll. Nat. Alumni Assn., 1973-74; trustee Davidson Coll., 1983—. Mem. Burke County C. of C. (pres. 1962). Named Young Man of Year, Morganton Jaycees, 1954. Office: PO Drawer 2146 Morganton NC 28655

ERVIN, THOMAS JOSEPH, exploration manager, geologist; b. Rantoul, Ill., Aug. 14, 1953; s. Schley Odell and Charlotte (Miklethun) E.; m. Susan Germany, Mar. 17, 1984; children by previous marriage—Jason Thomas, Amanda Elizabeth. B.S. in Geology, U. Ala., 1977. Geologist, Getty Oil Co., New Orleans, 1978-80; exploration geologist Sunmark Exploration Co., Dallas, 1980-81, Calto Oil Co., Dallas, 1981-84; dist. exploration mgr. Germany Exploration Co., Dallas, 1984—, also adv. dir., 1985—. Mem. Am. Assn.

Petroleum Geologists, Miss. Geol. Soc., Dallas Geol. Soc. Clubs: University, Energy (Dallas). Avocations: skiing, theater, racquetball. Office: Germany Exploration Co PO Box 25025 Dallas TX 75225

ERWIN, J(OHN) D(AVID), service merchandise executive; b. Harrison, Ark., Oct. 26, 1935; s. Jethro Tom and Donna Clayton (Owens) E.; m. Judith Ann Merriweather, June 18, 1954; children—Linda, John. Br. mgr. Pepsi-Cola Bottling Co., Springdale, Ark., 1951-56; salesman, supr. Sav-A-Stop, Springfield, Mo., 1956-61; asst. dir. sales Mass Merchandisers, Inc., Harrison, 1961-63, v.p., dir. sales, 1963-75, exec. v.p. sales, 1975-80, exec. v.p. trade relations, 1980-81, pres. service sales, 1981-82, pres., 1983—. Mem. Nat. Assn. Service Merchandisers (dir.), Harrison C. of C. (dir.). Methodist. Home: Route 1 PO Box 152 Harrison AR 72601 Office: Mass Merchandisers Inc PO Box 790 Hwy 43 E Harrison AR 72601*

ERWIN, JOHN SEYMOUR, writer, editor, composer; b. Vicksburg, Miss., Aug. 2, 1911; s. Victor Flournoy and Margaret Preston (McNeily) E. Student Sch. Contemporary Arts and Crafts, 1929-31, Columbia U., 1939-40; student of Alexander Siloti, 1934, of Serge Rachmaninoff, 1938. Feature editor The Am. mag., N.Y.C., 1954-56; mus. editor World and Its Peoples, Greystone Press, N.Y.C., 1959-61; co-founding editor SHOW mag., N.Y.C., 1962-63; sr. editor Natural History mag., N.Y.C., 1964-66; ency. project editor The Reader's Digest, N.Y.C., 1966-67; med. editor Media Medica, N.Y.C., 1968-70; contbr. Ency. Americana. Served with RCAF, 1940-44. Decorated George VI medal, Vol. Service medal; Tiffany Found. fellow, 1934-35; Gloucester Sch. fellow, 1935. Mem. Authors Guild. Episcopalian. Author: Like Some Green Laurel: The Life and Letters of Margaret Johnson Erwin, 1821-1863, 1981; composer: The Trojan Women Suite, 1942; Sappho in Levkas, 1940; Bermuda Sketches, 1979.

ERWIN, RICHARD C., federal judge; b. McDowell County, N.C., Aug. 23, 1923; s. John Adam and Flora (Cannon) E.; B.A., Johnson C. Smith U., 1947; LL.B., Howard U., 1951; m. Demerice Whitley, Aug. 25, 1946; children—Richard Cannon, Jr., Aurelia Whitley. Admitted to N.C. bar, U.S. Supreme Ct. bar; practice law, Winston-Salem, N.C., 1951-77; judge N.C. Ct. Appeals, 1978, U.S. Dist. Ct. Middle Dist. N.C., 1980—; rep. N.C. Gen. Assembly, chmn. hwy. safety com. Trustee, Forsyth County Legal Aid Soc., Amos Cottage, Inc.; chmn. bd. trustees Bennett Coll.; bd. dirs. N.C. 4-H Devel. Fund, Inc.; bd. visitors Div. Sch., Duke U.; trustee Children's Home Winston-Salem; mem. steering com. Winston-Salem Found.; bd. dirs. United Fund; bd. dirs., pres. Citizens Coalition Forsyth County and Anderson High Sch. PTA. mem. N.C. Bd. Edn., 1971-77, N.C. State Library Bd. Trustees, 1968-69; mem., chmn. personnel com. Winston-Salem/Forsyth County Sch. Bd.; chmn. bd. trustees St. Paul United Methodist Ch. Mem. N.C. Bar Assn. (v.p. 1983-84), N.C. Assn. Black Lawyers, Forsyth County Bar Assn. (pres.), N.C. State Bar. Office: PO Box 89 Greensboro NC 27402

ESCHNER, THOMAS RICHARD, exploration geologist; b. Wilkes-Barre, Pa., Apr. 21, 1956; s. Arthur Richard and Jean Marie (Scheuerle) E.; m. Marie Sharon Germain, Aug. 19, 1978; children—Adam Kathan. B.S. in Geology/German, Syracuse U., 1978; M.S. in Geology, Colo. State U., 1981. Hydrologist, geologist U.S. Geol. Survey, Denver, 1979-82; geologist Arco Exploration Co., Lafayette, La., 1982-85, Plano, Tex., 1985—. Recipient Outstanding Service award U.S. Geol. Survey, Denver, 1982. Mem. Geol. Soc. Am., Am. Assn. Petroleum Geologists, Lafayette Geol. Soc. (editor 1984-85), Phi Beta Kappa, Sigma Xi. Avocations: backpacking; music. Home: 3608 Marlborough Dr Plano TX 75075 Office: Arco Exploration Co 2300 W Plano Pkwy Plano TX 75075

ESCUE, WILLIAM BURKE, construction equipment company executive; b. Brownsville, Tenn., June 8, 1942; s. James Henry and Hazel (McConnico) E.; m. Kathy Smith, Aug. 14, 1960; 1 child, Adrina Christine. Student Ferris Inst., 1961. Sales rep. Williams Equipment Co., Memphis, 1966-71, Albert Equipment Co., Tulsa, 1976-77; Southwestern dist. rep. Allied Steel Co., Cleve., 1971-76; sales rep. Moody-Day, Inc., Dallas, 1977-80, gen. sales mgr., 1981—; dist. sales mgr. Duff-Norton Co., Inc., Charlotte, N.C., 1980-81. Served with USAF, 1962-66. Mem. Assoc. Equipment Distbrs., So. Indsl. Distbrs. Assn., Assoc. Gen. Contractors, Assoc. Bldg. Contractors, Am. Subcontractors Assn., VFW. Republican. Episcopalian. Club: Engineers. Home: 548 Ave J East Grand Prairie TX 75050 Office: Moody-Day Inc 2323 Irving Blvd Dallas TX 75207

ESHBAUGH, ROHE NEIL, psychologist; b. South Boston, Va., Sept. 5, 1939; s. John Seitz Eshbaugh and Jane (Meyer) Eshbaugh McDonough; m. Claudia Marie Hunter, July 26, 1978; children—Edith Elizabeth, Rohe Neil. B.A. in Psychology, Presbyterian Coll., Clinton, S.C., 1961; M.A. in Psychology, U. Louisville, 1963, Ph.D. in Psychology, 1969. Licensed psychologist, N.Mex., Tex., Calif. Chief psychologist, dir. youth services Southwest Mental Health Ctr., Las Cruces, N.Mex., 1969-70; ind. psychologist, Las Cruces, 1970-77, El Paso, Tex., 1970—; vis. lectr. U. Tex.-El Paso, N.Mex. State U., Las Cruces; corporate cons., El Paso, 1976—; adviser, profl. resource person parenting and child abuse prevention groups, El Paso. Contbr. articles to profl. jours. and gen. interest publns. Author, producer cassette tapes. Chmn. bd. dirs. Las Cruces Council for Youth, 1969-71. Mem. Am. Psychol. Assn. Presbyterian. Avocations: flying, skiing, writing, desert riding. Office: Affiliated Psychol Services Summit Pl 5752 N Mesa St El Paso TX 79912

ESHLEMAN, CHARLENE HUMPHRIES, church association administrator; b. Richmond, Va., July 19, 1955; d. Bernard Rawles and Margaret Ruth (Durvin) Humphries; m. David Martin Eshleman, June 14, 1980. B.S. in Mass Communications, Va. Commonwealth U., 1977, also postgrad. Procedures analyst Miller and Rhodes, Richmond 1978-81; systems mgmt. coordinator SEC Computer Co., Richmond, 1981-83; tng. coordinator Life of Va. Ins. Co., Richmond, 1984; staff devel. mgr. Fgn. Mission Bd. So. Baptist Conv., Richmond, 1984—; cons. Mary Kay Cosmetics, 1984—. Mem. ASTD, Assn. Psychol. Type. Baptist. Office: Foreign Mission Bd So Baptist Conv 3806 Monument Ave Richmond VA 23111

ESKEW, RHEA TALIAFERRO, publisher, company executive; b. Lebanon, Tenn., Nov. 16, 1923; s. Robert Edward and Sammie (Taylor) E.; m. Nancy Hall, June 13, 1953; children—Rhea Taliaferro, Jr., Elizabeth Vaughan Eskew Landers, Tucker Alexander, Hall Edward. Student U. Tenn., 1941-42; B.A. in English, Emory U., 1948. With UP/UPI, Atlanta, Tallahassee and Miami, 1948-54; staff corr. So. Bell Pub. Relations, Atlanta, 1954-56; div. mgr., gen. mgr. communications UPI, Atlanta and N.Y.C., 1956-73; gen. mgr., pres., co-pub., pub. Greenville (S.C.) News-Piedmont, 1973-84; v.p. newspapers, dir. Multimedia, Inc., Greenville, 1978—; dir. First Fed. S.C. Mem. journalism adv. bd. U. Ga.; pres. Goodwill Industries of Upper S.C., 1976; gen. campaign mgr. United Way, 1978. Served with AUS, 1942-45. Mem. Greenville C. of C. (v.p. 1977), S.C. Press Assn. (past pres.), So. Newspaper Publishers Assn. (pres. 1982-83). Methodist. Clubs: Greenville Country, Greenville City, Poinsett; Commerce (Atlanta). Home: 400 Huntington Rd Greenville SC 29615 Office: 305 S Main St Greenville SC 29601

ESKRIDGE, JESS BOYD, optometry educator; b. Green River, Wyo., June 29, 1928; s. Clyde Martin and Mahala Lavon (Wright) E.; m. Beth LaPreal Ferre, Aug. 20, 1950; children—Chris Wayne, Cheryl Ann. B.Sc., U. Calif.-Berkeley, 1953, O.D., M. Optometry, 1954; M.Sc., Ohio State U., 1959, Ph.D., 1964. Lic. optometrist, Calif., Utah, Ala. Asst. prof. optometry Ohio State U., Columbus, 1963-67, assoc. prof., 1967-71; assoc. prof. Ind. U., Bloomington, 1971-72; prof. optometry U. Ala., Birmingham, 1972—; cons. panel on ophthalmic devices FDA, 1976-80; cons. Nat. Bd. Optometry, Washington, 1970—; bd. dirs. Optometric Research Inst., 1978-82. Contbr. articles to sci. jours.; referee sci. jours. Am. Optometric Found. fellow, 1958-61; recipient Disting. Faculty award Epsilon Psi Epsilon, 1968, Spurgeon Earl award Am. Optometric Found., 1984. Fellow Am. Acad. Optometry. Mormon. Avocation: hiking. Home: 3427 Sage Brook Ln Birmingham AL 35243 Office: U of Ala Sch of Optometry Birmingham AL 35294

ESPARZA, THOMAS, SR., university sports director; b. Edinburg, Tex., May 21, 1921; s. Greg and T.R. (Tirsa) E.; m. Esther La Madrid, June 1, 1949; children—Tommy Jr., Steven, Teylene. Student Allen Mil. Acad., 1943; B.S., Tex. A. & I. U., 1948, M.S., 1951, Ph.D., 1977. Coach Edinburg (Tex.) Consol. Ind. Sch. Dist., 1948-68, adminstrv. asst., 1963-65, instructional media cons., 1963-65, athletic events mgr., 1957-68, health, phys. edn. cons., 1950-68; dir. intramurals dept. phys. edn., Pan Am. U., Edinburg, 1968—, univ. chmn. steering com. Nat. Phys. Edn. and Sports Week; pres. Leo Najo Amateur Baseball League, 1985; v.p. Rio Grande Valley Sports Hall of Fame; mem. steering com. Met. Bank, 1973—; cons. edn. City Park bd., 1968—; coordinator dist. I, Spl. Olympics, 1968-78; workshop cons. health and phys. edn. to various schs., 1968—; lectr. to phys. edn. and athletic dirs., Mexico, 1981—; pres. Edinburg Tchrs. Credit Union, 1958-65, Pan Am. U. Credit Union, 1970, Leo Najo Amateur Baseball League, 1985—. Bd. dirs. Am. Cancer Soc., 1948-73, v.p. Edinburg unit, 1976, ednl. dir. Edinburg unit, 1977—; originator Panocha Bread Cook-Off, 1979; v.p. Rio Grande Valley Sports Hall of Fame; cons. baseball reunions. Served with USNR, 1946-48. Mem. Tex. High Sch. Coaches Assn., Tex. Assn. Health, Phys. Edn., Recreation and Dance (emeritus), NEA, AAHPER, Tex. State Tchrs. Assn., N.I.A., Edinburg C. of C., Hidalgo County Hist. Soc. (bd.), Am. Legion (comdr. post 1970-75, post 408, 1982—, 15th dist. baseball chmn. 1975—, 3d div. baseball chmn. 1975—, state baseball chmn. 1980—, mem. state Americanism, constn. and by-laws, credentials coms. 1976—, nat. legis. council 1983—), DAV (life). Author numerous publs. in field. Home: 811 S 16th Ave Edinburg TX 78539

ESPINOZA-GALA, LILLIAN RUTH, offshore oil and gas technologist, technical writer; b. Des Moines, Dec. 5, 1948; d. Charles N. and Marjorie R. (Hammons) Miller; A.A. in Petroleum Tech., Nichols State U., Thibodaux, La., 1977; m. Carlos Y. Espinoza-Gala, July 5, 1975 (div.). Galley hand Offshore Foods & Service Co., Houma, La., 1973-74; with Ocean Drilling & Exploration Co., New Orleans, 1974—, jr. gauger, 1975-77, gauger, 1977-81, project coordinator offshore field tng. com., 1979—; Vol. counsellor Prison Fellowship; outreach leader First Baptist Ch., Houma, La., also publicity chmn. Together We Build Program; publicity com. Thibodaux Playhouse. Mem. Nichols State U. Alumni Assn., La. Writers Guild, Bayou Writer's Guild, Friends of Library (publicity chmn. Lafourche Parish), Capt. Daniel Little Family, DAR (Conservation medal; chpt. conservation chmn.), Soc. Mayflower Descendants (Iowa chpt.). Republican. Baptist. Contbr. article to Acadiana Profiles. Home: 1414 W Main St Houma LA 70360 Office: PO Box 956 Gray LA 70359

ESPOSITO, ALBERT CHARLES, ophthalmologist, educator; b. Pitts., Nov. 9, 1912; s. Charles Micali and Elizabeth Ellen (Cuda) E.; m. V. Elizabeth Dodson, July 17, 1940; children—Bettina Kelly, Gregory, Mary Alice Tartler. B.S., U. Pitts., 1933; M.D. cum laude, Loyola U., Chgo., 1939; D.Sc., Marshall U., 1977. Intern St. Francis Hosp., Pitts., 1938-39; resident Ohio State U. Med. Coll. Hosp., Columbus, 1943-45, assoc. prof., 1945-47; chmn. dept. ophthalmology St. Mary's Hosp., Huntington, W.Va., 1950—, pres. staff, 1966-67; attending ophthalmologist Cabell-Huntington Hosp., 1962—, Morris Meml. Hosp., Huntington, 1950-70; clin. prof., chmn. dept. ophthalmology Marshall U. Sch. Medicine, Huntington, 1976—; ophthal. cons. C&O R.R., VA Hosp.; chmn. bd. So. W.Va. Blue Shield; mem. W.Va. Ho. of Dels., 1974-82. Mem. exec. com. State Republican Com. Served to maj. AUS, World War II. Recipient Outstanding Ophthalmologist in the South award, 1972; Disting. Service award Marshall U., Appreciation award City of Huntington, 1974; Stritch Medal award Loyola U., Chgo., 1976; Honor award Am. Acad. of Ophthalmology. Mem. So. Med. Assn. (past pres.), Cabell County Med. Assn., Am. Assn. Ophthalmology (past pres.), Am. Acad. Ophthalmology (past councilor, Key M.D. Teaching faculty, 1967—), Internat. Coll. Surgeons, W.Va. Acad. Ophthalmology (past pres.), Am. Intra-Ocular Implant Soc., W.Va. State Med. Assn. (past pres.), Am. Diopter and Decible Soc. (past pres.), Greater Huntington C. of C. (bd. dirs.), Alpha Omega Alpha. Roman Catholic. Clubs: Guyan Golf and Country, Lions Internat., City (Huntington). Contbr. numerous articles to profl. jours.; patentee in field of intra ocular lens. Home: 171 Woodland Dr Huntington WV 25705 Office: 420 11th St Huntington WV 25701

ESPOSITO, FREDERICK WILLIAM, insurance company executive; b. New Haven, Feb. 6, 1931; s. Frederick F. and Dorothy Ruth (Sheehy) E.; m. Evelyn Piscitelli, Jan. 12, 1951; children—Carla, Frederick William, Cynthia, William, Dorothy. B.S., Quinnipiac Coll., 1957; C.L.U., Am. Coll., 1969; student Mgmt. Inst., Purdue U., 1979. C.L.U. Agt., John Hancock Mut. Life Ins. Co., 1958-61, sales mgr., 1961-67, founding mgr. Appleton, Wis., 1967-69, mgr. agy. Hartford, Conn., 1969-74; 2d v.p. Life of Va., Richmond, 1974-81, v.p. mktg. resources, 1981—, dir. manpower, 1975—, dir. agencies, 1977—; regional dir. Mutual Benefit, 1985—; bd. govs. Regional Fin. Planners, 1986. Chmn. bd. Am. Trauma Soc.; chmn. Task Force to Lessen Disability in State of Va.; mem. Nat. Head Injury Found. Served to 1st lt. C.E. U.S. Army, 1950-54. Recipient Life of Va. Community Service award, 1981, Am. Trauma Soc. div. award, 1982. Mem. Life Underwriter's Assn. Roman Catholic. Lodge: KC.

ESPOSITO, JOHN VINCENT, lawyer; b. Logan, W.Va., Dec. 25, 1946; s. Vito T. and Mary Frances (Lamp) E. B.A. magna cum laude, W.Va. U., 1968, J.D., 1971. Bar: W.Va. 1971, S.C. 1980, U.S. dist. ct. (no. and so. dists.) W.Va., S.C. Legis. aide to Congressman Ken Hechler, 4th Dist. W.Va., 1971; counsel to Hans McCourt, Pres. W.Va. State Senate, 1972; instr. So. W.Va. Community Coll., 1972-74; sr. ptnr. Esposito & Esposito, Logan, W.Va. and Hilton Head Island, S.C., 1972—; arbitrator United Mine Workers Am.-Coal Operators Assn.; spl. judge Cir. Ct. Logan County (W.Va.); commr. in chancery Cir. Ct. Logan County; judge Mcpl. Ct. City of Chapmanville (W.Va.). Served to 2d lt. U.S. Army. U. Calif. Hastings Coll. Law Coll. Advocacy scholar. Mem. ABA, Assn. Trial Lawyers Am., Am. Judicature Soc., W.Va. State Bar, S.C. Bar, Internat. Platform Assn. Co-author: Laws for Young Mountaineers, 1973-74. Office: One Saint Augustine PO Drawer 5705 Hilton Head Island SC 29938 also 401 Stratton St PO Box 1680 Logan WV 25601

ESPOSITO, VITO T., school principal; b. Cenadi, Italy, Mar. 1, 1915; came to U.S., 1927, naturalized, 1930; s. Vito N. and Rosa (Roselli) E.; married; children—Vito Jr., John, Patrick, Tom, Rosemarie, Michael. A.A., Bowling Green U., 1942; A.B. in Mktg., San Diego U., 1943; M.B.A., Marshall U., 1958, M.A. in Guidance, 1959, M.A. in Sch. Administrn., 1960. Retail bus. Veto Mkt., Logan, W. Va., 1943-60; educator, prin. Logan County Bd. Edn., 1953—. Home: PO Box 1022 Logan WV 25601

ESSENWANGER, OSKAR MAXIMILIAN KARL, army research physicist, educator; b. Munich, Germany, Aug. 25, 1920; s. Oskar and Anna (Ritzinger) E.; came to U.S., 1956; m. Katharina Dorfer, June 17, 1947. B.S., Tech., U. Danzig, 1941; M.S., U. of Vienna, 1943; Ph.D., U. Würzburg, 1950. Cert. cons. meteorologist, cert. quality engr. Instr., meteorologist German Air Force, 1944-45; research meteorologist German Weather Service, 1946-57; project assoc. U. Wis.-Madison, 1956; prin. investigator Nat. Weather Record Center, Asheville, N.C., 1957-60; supr. research physicist, aerophysics, research directorate, U.S. Army Missile Command, 1961—, adj. prof. environ. sci. U. Ala., Huntsville, 1961—; affiliated prof. Colo. State U., 1968-72. Recipient Missile Command Sci. Achievement award, 1965; Hermann Oberth award AIAA Ala.-Miss. Sect. 1981. Fellow Intercontinental Biog. Assn., assoc. fellow AIAA; mem. Am. Soc. Quality Control (sr.), Ala. Acad. of Sci. (v.p. physics), Bernoulli Soc. (Holland), Am. Meteorol. Soc., German Meteorol. Soc., Am. Statis. Assn., Sigma Xi (pres. 1978-82). Roman Catholic. Editor: Applied Statistics in Atmospheric Science, Vol. A (Elsevier), 1976; contbr. articles in field to Am. and European sci. jours.

ESSMYER, MICHAEL MARTIN, lawyer; b. Abilene, Tex., Dec. 6, 1949; s. Lytle Martin Essmyer and Roberta N. Essmyer Nicholson; m. Cynthia Rose Piccolo, Dec. 27, 1970; children—Deanna, Mike, Brent Austin. B.S. in Geology, Tex. A&M U., 1972; student Tex. Christian U., 1976; J.D. magna cum laude, South Tex. Coll. Law, 1980. Bar Tex. 1980, U.S. Ct. appeals (5th cir.) 1981, U.S. Dist. Ct. (no., so., ea. dists.) Tex. 1982. Briefing atty. Supreme Ct. Tex., Austin, 1980-81; ptnr. Haynes & Fullenweider, Houston, 1981—. Lead article editor south Tex. Law Jour., 1979. Democratic candidate for state rep., Bryan, Tex., 1972; del. Dem. Party, Houston, 1982, 84; precinct chmn. Harris County Democratic Exec. Com., Houston, 1983—. Served to capt. USAF, 1972-78. Nat. Merit Scholar, 1968-72. Mem. Houston Bar Assn., ABA, Houston Young Lawyers Assn., Tex. Young Lawyers Assn., Assn. Trial Lawyers Am., Tex. Criminal Def. Lawyers Assn., Harris County Criminal Lawyers Assn. (dir. 1986—). Roman Catholic. Club: Metropolitan Racquet (Houston) Home: 15634 Fern Basin Dr Houston TX 77084 Office: Haynes & Fullenweider PLC 4300 Scotland Houston TX 77007

ESTABROOK, RONALD WINFIELD, biochemistry educator; b. Albany, N.Y., Jan. 3, 1926; s. George Arthur and Lillian Florence (Childs) E.; m. June Elizabeth Templeton, Aug. 23, 1947; children—Linda Estabrook Gilbert, Laura Estabrook Verinder, Jill, David. B.S., Rensselaer Poly. Inst., 1950, Ph.D., U. Rochester, 1954, D. Sc. (hon.), 1980; M.D. (hon.), Karolinska Inst., Stockholm, 1981. Johnson Research Found. fellow U. Pa. Sch. Medicine, 1955-58; research assoc. U. Cambridge (Eng.), 1958-59, asst. prof. phys. biochemistry, 1959-61, assoc. prof., 1961-65, prof., 1965-68; Virginia Lazenby O'Hara prof. biochemistry U. Tex. Health Sci. Ctr., Dallas, 1968—, chmn. dept., 1968-82, dean, 1973-76; chmn. basic sci. rev. com. VA, 1972-74; cons. in field; chmn. bd. toxicology and environ. health Nat. Acad. Sci., 1980-84; mem. Atlantic Richfield Sci. Adv. Council, 1981—. Bd. sci. advisers St. Jude's Hosp., Memphis, 1978-81. Served with USNR, 1943-46. Recipient Disting. Scientist award Fedn. Am. Socs. Exptl. Biologists, 1977; Claude Bernard medal U. Montreal, 1969. Mem. Inst. Medicine, Nat. Acad. Scis., Pan Am. Assn., Biochem. Socs. (sec.-gen. 1972-75), Am. Assn. Med. Schs., (adminstrv. bd. council acad. socs.; task force cost med. edn. 1971-72, liaison com. med. edn. 1975-80), Am. Soc. Biol. Chemists, Am. Soc. Pharmacology and Exptl. Therapeutics, Sigma Xi. Exec. editor: Archives of Biochemistry and Biophysics, 1966-73, 82—; editor Jour. Pharmacology and Exptl. Therapeutics, 1969-74, Xenobiotica, 1970—, Life Scis., 1973-84; contbr. articles on biochemistry to profl. jours. Home: 5208 Preston Haven Dallas TX 75229 Office: U Tex Health Sci Center 5323 Harry Hines Blvd Dallas TX 75235

ESTEB, ADLAI ALBERT, retired clergyman, author; b. La Grande, Oreg., Nov. 17, 1901; s. Lemuel Albert and Addretta (Koger) E.; B.Th., Walla Walla Coll., 1931; M.A., Calif. Coll., Peiping, China, 1953; Ph.D., U. So. Calif., 1944; m. Florence Edna Airey, Feb. 5, 1923; children—Adeline, Lucille. Ordained to ministry Seventh-day Adventist Ch., 1923; missionary to China, 1923-37; pastor Seventh-day Adventist Ch., Long Beach, Calif., 1938-40; sec. home missionary dept. So. Calif. Conf. Seventh-day Adventist Ch., 1940-46, Pacific Union Conf. Seventh-day Adventist Ch., Glendale, Calif., 1946-50; editor Go, Jour. for Adventist Laymen, gen. conf. Seventh-day Adventist Ch., Washington, 1950-70; vis. prof., lectr. Christian ethics Andrews U., Berrien Springs, Mich., 1955-75, ret. Cited as poet laureate of denomination by pres. World Conf., 1966; named Alumnus of Yr., Walla Walla Coll., 1979. Mem. China Soc. of So. Calif. (pres. 1946-50), Oriental Fellowship (pres. 1963), Phi Beta Kappa, Phi Kai Phi, Phi Kappa Phi. Author: Driftwood, 1947; Firewood, 1952; Sandalwood, 1955; Morning Manna, 1962; Rosewood, 1964; Scrapwood, 1967; (poetry) Redwood, 1970; Kindle Kindness, 1971; The Meaning of Christmas, 1972; When Suffering Comes, 1974; Straight Ahead, 1974. Home: Pisgah Estates Condominium Candler NC

ESTES, ARMAND WILLIAM, investment counselor; b. Chgo., Aug. 24, 1926; s. Harry Arthur and Onesta (Otto) E.; B.A., George Washington U., 1952; m. Rosemary Niner, Feb. 23, 1952; children—Michael, Suzanne. Sr. acct. Ernst & Ernst, Balt., 1953-56; gen. acctg. supr. Kaiser Aluminum & Chem. Corp., Balt., Ravenswood, W.Va., 1956-59; controller Overseas Nat. Airways, Balt., 1959-62; regional comptroller Pa. R.R. Co., Buffalo, Phila., 1963-65; v.p., treas. Exec. Jet Aviation, Inc., Columbus, Ohio, 1965-69; v.p. Wachovia Corp., Winston-Salem, N.C., 1969-71; partner Trade Mgrs. Internat., Winston-Salem, 1971-75; v.p. H.E. Crawford Co., Kernersville, N.C., 1975-81; pres. Franwill Corp., Winston-Salem, 1981—. Served with USNR, 1944-46. C.P.A., Washington. Mem. Am. Inst. C.P.A.s. Republican. Club: Wake Forest U. Tennis. Home: 125 Lamplighter Circle Winston-Salem NC 27104

ESTES, CARL L., II, lawyer; b. Fort Worth, Tex., Feb. 9, 1936; s. Joe E. and Carroll E.; B.S., U. Tex., 1957, LL.B., 1960; m. Gay Gooch, Aug. 29, 1959; children—Adrienne Virginia, Margaret Ellen. Admitted to Tex. bar, 1960; law clk. U.S. Supreme Ct., 1960-61; assoc. firm Vinson & Elkins, Houston, 1961-69, partner, 1970—. Bd. dirs. St. Lukes Meth. Ch., Houston, 1978—. Mem. Am. Law Inst., Am. Coll. Probate Counsel, Am. Bar Assn., Internat. Bar Assn., Tex. Bar Assn., Internat. Fiscal Assn., Internat. Acad. Estate and Trust Law. Clubs: Allegro, Houston, Ramada, Houston County, Houston Center. Home: 101 Broad Oaks Circle Houston TX 77056 Office: 3400 1st City Tower Houston TX 77002

ESTES, HILDA JEANETTE, librarian; b. Dubach, La., Apr. 23, 1942; d. John Nolan and Nancy George (Smith) Brazzel; m. Mack Ross, Feb. 7, 1970. B.A., La. Tech. U., 1964; M.S. in L.S., La. State U., 1970. Tchr., Vernon Parish Sch., Leesville, La., 1964-65; librarian Port Arthur (Tex.) Ind. Sch., 1965—. Bd. dirs. Port Arthur Community Concert Assn. Mem. Tex. Library Assn., ALA, Jefferson County Library Assn. (sec. 1979-80), Beta Phi Mu, Alpha Delta Kappa. Democrat. Baptist. Home: 4220 Ferndale Dr Port Arthur TX 77642 Office: 2200 Jefferson Dr Port Arthur TX 77642

ESTES, JACOB THOMAS, JR., pharmacist; b. Dallas, Sept. 2, 1944; s. Jacob Thomas and Burgenia Mae (Kelly) E.; m. Susan Jean Rader, Mar. 7, 1980; 1 child, Amy Dianne. B.S. in Pharmacy, U. Tex., 1967. Hosp. pharmacist St. Joseph Hosp., Ft. Worth; pharmacist Park Row Pharmacy, Arlington, Tex., Plaza Pharmacy, Ft. Worth; pharmacist in-charge Whitten Pharmacy, K-Mart Pharmacy, Ft. Worth; dist. intervenor Pharmacy Helpline for Impaired; dir. Tex. Bd. Pharmacy, Ft. Worth. Bd. dirs. Mother and Unborn Baby, Ft. Worth, 1983—, Unborn Child Clinic Care, 1984—. Served to capt. USAFR, 1968-74. Name Employee of Month, K-Mart Pharmacy, 1985. Mem. Tex. Pharm. Assn., Tarrant County Pharm. Assn., U. Tex. Ex Students Assn. Roman Catholic. Club: Holy Family Chor. Lodge: K.C. Avocation: golfing. Home: 6865 Chickering Rd 434 Fort Worth TX 76116 Office: K-Mart 4346 Pharmacy 1701 S Cherry Ln Fort Worth TX 76108

ESTES, JAMES RUSSELL, botanist; b. Burkburnett, Tex., Aug. 28, 1937; s. Dow Worley and Bessie (Seidlitz) E.; B.S. in Biology, Midwestern State U., 1959; Ph.D. in Systematic Botany, Oreg. State U., 1967; m. Nancy Elizabeth Arnold, Dec. 21, 1962; children—Jennifer Lynn, Susan Elizabeth. Mem. faculty U. Okla., Norman, 1967—, asst. prof., 1967-70, assoc. prof., 1970-82, prof. botany, 1982—, dir. Okla. Natural Heritage Program, 1981-82, curator Bebb Herbarium, 1979—; cons. in environ. work, 1979—. Bd. govs. United Campus Christian Found., 1976-80; mem. adv. bd. Sutton Urban Wilderness Park, 1980—; mem. steering com., asst. editor Flora Okla. Project, 1984—; trustee Flora Okla., Inc., 1985—. Served with U.S. Army, 1960-63. Grantee NSF, 1968-70, 81-86; NSF fellow, 1963, 65-67; Ortenburger award Phi Sigma, 1975; Baldwin Study Travel award Okla. U. Alumni Found., 1976. Mem. Am. Soc. Plant Taxonomists (sec. 1980-83; program chmn. 1980-83, pres. elect 1984-85, pres. 1985-86), Bot. Soc. Am., Southwestern Assn. Naturalists (bd. govs. 1980-83, assoc. editor 1980-82). Democrat. Presbyterian. Co-editor Grasses and Grasslands: Systematics and Ecology, 1981. Contbr. articles to sci. books and jours. Home: 1906 Burnt Oak Norman OK 73071 Office: 770 Van Vleet Oval Norman OK 73019

ESTES, ROBERT EDMUND, psychology educator; b. Los Angeles, Mar. 11, 1931; s. Edmund Grady and Mary May (Schlatter) E.; m. Maridon Castonguay, June 29, 1952 (div.); children—Megan, Peter; m. Janet Carolyn Stewart, Nov. 23, 1977. B.A., U. Calif.-Santa Barbara, 1954; M.A., U. So. Calif., 1960; Ph.D., U. Iowa, 1963. Lic. psychologist, Tex. Assoc. prof. Hampden-Sydney Coll., Va., 1965-66; asst. prof. psychology So. Meth. U., Dallas, 1967-71; asst. prof. pediatrics Southwestern Med. Sch., Dallas, 1971-74; asst. prof. spl. edn. U. Tex.-Dallas, Richardson, 1974-77; assoc. prof. psychology East Tex. State U., Commerce, 1977—; psychologist Children's Med. Ctr., Dallas, 1968-70; pvt. therapist to hospitalized drug abusers, Dallas, 1977-80; sch. psychology cons. Hopkins-Franklin Spl. Edn. Coop., Sulphur Springs, Tex., 1981—, Ennis Sch. Dist., Tex., 1980—. Contbr. articles to profl. jours. Served as 1st lt. U.S. Army, 1954-57, Fed. Republic Germany. Mem. Am. Psychol. Assn. Republican. Episcopalian. Home: Route 2 Box 119 Celeste TX 75423 Office: Psychology Dept E Tex State U Commerce TX 75428

ESTES, SUSAN DIANE, government official; b. Sioux City, Iowa, Dec. 24, 1944; d. Norman Thomas and Mary Hedwig (Freeman) Lynberg; children—Evan Allen, Eric Thomas, Erin Diane. Student Okla. State U., 1976—. With Bur. Prisons, Dept. Justice, Atlanta, 1963-65; with Dept. Def., U.S. Army, Fayetteville, N.C., 1965-76; with contracting and procurement depts. Soil Conservation Service, U.S. Dept. Agr., Stillwater, Okla., 1976—. Recipient Outstanding Merit Performance award U.S. Army, 1967, 74, Dept. Agr., 1981. Mem. Soil Conservation Soc. Am., Gold Key, Delta Gamma Sigma, Phi Kappa Phi. Roman Catholic. Club: Okla. State U. DustBowl Divers.

ESTES, THOMAS GLENVALL, JR., business and finance executive, accounting educator; b. Natchez, Miss., Jan. 13, 1940; s. Thomas Glenvall Sr. and Lorene Lois (Lauderdale) E.; m. Frances Carol Beard, Aug. 22, 1964; children—Carol Ann, Michael, Robert. B.S. in Acctg., U. So. Miss., 1963; M.S. in Acctg., Okla. State U., 1964; Ph.D. in Bus., U. Ark., 1971. C.P.A., Tex., Miss. Auditor, Arthur Young & Co., Dallas, 1964-66; asst. prof. U. So. Miss., Hattiesburg, 1966-67, assoc. prof., 1969-71; 71-73; asst. dir. Continuing Profl. Edn. Div., Am. Inst. C.P.A.'s, N.Y.C., 1974-76; v.p. bus., fin. U. So. Miss.,

Hattiesburg, 1976—; dir., chmn. fin. com. So. Ctr. for Research and Innovation, Hattiesburg, 1982-84; dir. Miss. Higher Ednl. Assistance Corp., Jackson. Author: An Audit Manual, 1969. Contbr. articles to profl. jours. Pres., bd. dirs., Forrest-Lamar United Way, Hattiesburg, 1978; chmn. county membership com. Miss. Economic Council, Jackson, 1983; mem. Hattiesburg City Planning Commn. Served with U.S. Army, 1961-72. Recipient Outstanding Young Man Yr. award Hattiesburg Jr. C. of C., 1976. Mem. So. Assn. Coll. Univ. Bus. Officers (mem. profl. devel. com., mem. membership com.), Nat. Assn. Coll. Univ. Bus. Officers (mem. acctg. principles com.), Miss. Soc. C.P.A.s, Am. Inst. C.P.A.s, Miss. Economic Council Com. Membership Services, Beta Gamma Sigma, Omicron Delta Kappa, Beta Alpha Psi. Baptist. Lodge: Rotary (pres. 1981-82). Avocations: football; spectator of baseball, basketball; real estate investments. Office: U So Miss So Station Box 5005 Hattiesburg MS 39406

ESTES, WILLIAM CHAPMAN, pump manufacturing company executive; b. Waxahachie, Tex., Mar. 30, 1937; s. Ted Gent and Ruth (Chapman) E.; m. Sally Ross Risser, Mar. 19, 1960; children—Kris Risser, Risser Chapman. B.B.A., U. Tex.-Austin; M.B.A., Stanford U. Asst. to pres. S.W. Pump Co., Inc., Bonham, Tex., 1961-78, chmn. bd., 1978—. Mem. nat. council Camp Fire Girls Am., Bonham. Methodist. Clubs: Bonham Golf (pres. 1973-75); Dallas Petroleum. Office: SW Pump Co Inc 1300 Bicentennial Dr Bonham TX 75418

ESTESS, TED LYNN, English educator; b. Jackson, Miss., Oct. 29, 1942; s. Ansel and LaVerne (Simmons) E.; m. Sybil Pittman, Aug. 20, 1966; 1 child, Benjamin Barrett Pittman. B.A., Baylor U., 1964; M.Div., So. Bapt. Sem., 1968; Ph.D., Syracuse U., 1971. Dir. honors program, assoc. prof. English U. Houston, 1977—. Author: Elie Wiesel, 1980. Bd. dirs. Houston Ctr. for Humanities, 1980—. Mem. Am. Acad. Religion, MLA. Office: U Houston-University Park Honors Program Houston TX 77004

ESTEVES-VELAZQUEZ, MABEL ROSAURA, elec. engr.; b. San Sebastian, P.R., Mar. 21, 1950; d. Esteban Figueroa-Andujar and Rosaura Velázquez-Del Rio; B.S. in Elec. Engring., U. P.R., Mayaguez, 1976. Registered profl. engr., P.R. Instr. physics U. P.R., Mayaguez, 1975-76; chmn. electronic technology dept. Inst. Tech. P.R., Manati, 1976-77; design engr. GTE Sylvania, Canovanas, P.R., 1977-79, sr. design engr. 1979-81; materials and reliability engr. Hewlett Packard P.R., Aquadilla, 1981-82, product regulations/reliability engr., 1982—. Mem. Soc. Women Engrs. P.R. (pres. 1981-83, Disting. New Engr. award 1980), P.R. Inst. Elec. Engrs. (dir. 1980-81), IEEE, IEEE Edn. Soc., Soc. Elec. Engrs. P.R. Patentee apparatus for variably adjusting magnetic level with translating spring force. Home: PO Box 3887 Aquadilla PR 00605 Office: PO Box H Aquadilla PR 00605

ESTEVEZ, ROBERTO, cardiologist; b. Montevideo, Uruguay, Aug. 24, 1942; came to U.S., 1974; s. Alfonso and Alicia (Carmona) E.; m. Elizabeth Goodson, Oct. 31, 1967; children—Laura, Leonardo, Anahid. M.D., Montevideo Sch. Medicine, 1970. Diplomate Am. Bd. Internal Medicine. Intern Upstate Med. Ctr., Syracuse, N.Y., 1974-75; fellow cardiology Guthrie Clinic, Sayre, Pa., 1975; resident in internal medicine Guthrie Clinic and Robert Packer Hosp., Sayre, Pa., 1976-77; practice medicine specializing in cardiology, Amarillo, Tex., 1979—; mem. staff, dir. cardiac rehab. St. Anthony Hosp., Amarillo; chief of medicine North West Tex. Hosp., Amarillo, 1983-85. Fellow Am. Coll. Cardiology (cert.); mem. AMA, ACP. Home: 6402 Palacio St Amarillo TX 79109 Office: 301 Amarillo Blvd W Suite 111 Amarillo TX 79107

ESTRADA, DOLORES, educator; b. Newcastle, Tex., Aug. 6, 1932; d. Rodrigo and Antonio (Hernandez) Estrada. B.A., Midwestern U., 1956, M.A., 1962; postgrad. U. Tex.-Austin, summer 1969, U. Ariz. summer 1974. Lic. tchr., Tex. Tchr. first grade Edcouch-Elsa Ind. Sch. System, 1956-61; tchr. Wichita Falls (Tex.) Ind. Sch. System, 1961—, 1st grade bilingual tchr.; participant bilingual workshops. Publicity chmn. Huey PTA, 1982—. Recipient AAUW scholar, 1952-56; named Tchr. of Yr., Wichita Falls Classroom Tchrs. Assn., 1976-77. Mem. Assn. Childhood Edn., Wichita Falls Area Reading Council, Assn. Tex. Profl. Educators, AAUW, Delta Kappa Gamma. Democrat. Baptist. Office: Wichita Falls TX 76301

ETCHISON, ANNIE LAURIE, librarian, artist; b. Cana, N.C., Dec. 5, 1908; d. John W. and Nana (Cain) Etchison; A.B., Western Res. U., 1939, B.L.S., 1940. Librarian, Cleve. Pub. Library, 1941-42; chief librarian Langley AFB, Va., 1942-44; supervisory librarian U.S. Army, Hawaii, 1945; chief librarian Armed Forces Western Pacific, Phillipines, Okinawa 1945-46; command librarian 2d Mil. Dist. U.S. Army, Europe, 1947-48, Hdqrs. U.S. Air Force, Alaska, 1950-52; librarian recruitment Dept. Army, Washington, 1952-54; staff librarian U.S. Army Hdqrs. KCOMZ, Korea, 1954-55; librarian Dept. Navy, Washington, 1956; chief librarian Ft. Bragg, N.C., 1957-63; staff librarian Hdqrs. 3d U.S. Army, Atlanta, 1963-72; library dir. U.S. Army Europe, 1972-78; cons. automation of libraries and library design. Awarded U.S. Army Meritorious Service medal, Armed Forces Achievement citation ALA, 1978. Pioneer in library service for armed forces; designed 1st computer-based library system for U.S. Army post libraries, 1968. Home: RFD 5 Box 58 Mocksville NC 27028

ETGEN, ANN, ballet teacher, artistic director, choreographer; b. Dallas; d. Eddy R. and Myrtle (Applegate) Etgen; m. Bill Atkinson, Aug. 16, 1961; Dancer, Met. Opera Ballet N.Y.C., 1958-60, Broadway musicals Brigadoon, Carousel; guest dancer Omnibus History of Dance for Agnes De Mille, 1957; artistic dir. Etgen-Atkinson Sch. of Ballet, Dallas, 1962—, Dallas Met. Ballet, 1964—; host S.W. Regional Ballet Festival, 1973. Dance panel Tex. Fine Arts Com., 1978-79; active Arts Magnet Sch., 1980, 81, 82, 83. NEA choreography grantee, 1976; Tex. Fine Arts Commn. grantee, 1973, 76-77; Mobile Oil grantee, 1979; 500 Inc. grantee, 1978-79; recipient choreography plan award Nat. Assn. Regional Ballet, 1983. Mem. Nat. Assn. Regional Ballet. Presbyterian. Creator ballets for Dallas Met. Ballet. Office: Dallas Met Ballet 6815 Hillcrest Ave Dallas TX 75205

ETHEL, DOUGLAS LYNN, pharmacist, consultant; b. Clinton, Okla., June 12, 1951; s. Lowell M. and Lois L. (Taylor) E. B.S. in Biology, Southwestern Okla. State U., 1973, B.S. in Pharmacy, 1975. Registered pharmacist, 1976. Intern pharmacist Southwestern Hosp., Lawton, Okla., 1976; dir pharmacy Broken Arrow Med. Ctr., Okla., 1976—; medication cons. Country View Chem. Dependency Ctr., Broken Arrow, 1983—. Mem. Okla. Pharm. Assn., Okla. Soc. Hosp. Pharmacists, Am. Soc. Hosp. Pharmacists, Profl. Rodeo Cowboys Assn. (contestant), Beta Beta Beta, Rho Chi. Democrat. Methodist. Lodge: Masons. Avocations: golf, rodeo, softball. Home: 701 W Albuquerque Broken Arrow OK 74011 Office: Broken Arrow Med Ctr 3000 S Elm Pl Broken Arrow OK 74012

ETHERIDGE, KENNIETH SAWYER, lawyer; b. Norfolk, Va., Jan. 3, 1936; s. Kennieth Sawyer and Caroline Amelia (Smith) E.; m. Rebecca Anne Schweistris, Aug. 23, 1958; children—Kennieth S. III, John Andrew, Jeffrey Thomas, Elizabeth Anne. B.S., Wake Forest U., 1958, J.D., 1960. Bar: N.C. 1960. Research asst. N.C. Supreme Ct., Raleigh, 1960-61; with Etheridge, Moser & Garner, P.A., Laurinburg, N.C., 1961—. Chmn., Scotland County Bd. Edn., N.C., 1976—. Mem. Scotland County Bar Assn., 16th Jud. Dist. Bar Assn., N.C. Bar Assn., Internat. Assn. Ins. Counsel, Assn. Ins. Attys., Laurinburg Jaycees (pres. 1964-65, Young Man of Yr. award 1964), N.C. Jaycees (v.p., legal counsel 1965-67). Lodge: Rotary (pres. 1966-67). Home: 500 Forest Rd Laurinburg NC 28353 Office: Etheridge Moser & Garner P A 600 E S Main St Laurinburg NC 28352

ETHIER, C. JAMES, canning company executive; b. Spencer, Mass., Apr. 29, 1915; s. Henry O. and Maude O. (Langlois) E.; m. Lena Maye Bush, May 30, 1939; children—James Bush, Camille Frances. With TVA, 1936-39; distbn. engr. Bonneville Power Adminstrn., Portland, Oreg., 1939-40; valuation engr. Beck Metcalf Cons. Engrs., Seattle, 1940-43; with Bush Bros. & Co., Dandridge, Tenn., 1946—, chmn. bd., 1978—; dir. First Am. Bank. Served with USN, 1943-46. Home: Route 4 Dandridge TN 37725 Office: Bush Brothers & Co Route 4 Dandridge TN 37725

ETHRIDGE, F(RANKLIN) MAURICE, sociology educator, minister; b. Ft. Worth, Dec. 26, 1933; s. Frank Lusk and Ruth Blanche (Hadsell) E.; m. Nola Gail DesChamps, Nov. 19, 1956; children—Rebecca Leigh, Mona Lynn, John Montgomery, Clifford Dean. B.A. in History, N. Tex. State U., 1959, M.A. in Sociology, 1963; Ph.D. in Sociology, U. Tex., 1973. Ordained to ministry Ch. of Christ, 1956. Assoc. minister Preston Rd. Ch. of Christ, Dallas, 1964-66; minister Ch. of Christ, Glenwood Springs, Colo., 1966-68; asst. prof. sociology Pepperdine U., Los Angeles, 1968-70; teaching asst. U. Tex., Austin, 1962-64, 70-72; prof. sociology Tenn. Tech. U., Cookeville, 1972—. Contbr. articles to profl. publs. Mem. Am. Sociol. Assn., So. Sociol. Soc., Southwestern Sociol. Assn. Mid-South Sociol. Assn., Assn. Sociology/Religion, Soc. for Sci. Study of Religion. Democrat. Avocations: jogging, golf, tennis. Home: Route 5 Box 84 Cookeville TN 38501 Office: Tenn Tech U Dixie Ave Cookeville TN 38505

ETHRIDGE, VELMA STREET, educator; b. Sanford, N.C., Sept. 4, 1938; d. Eugene Weldon and Bessie Catherine (Johnson) Street; m. Arthur Theotis Ethridge, Aug. 15, 1962; 1 dau., Jeanine Kaye. B.S. cum laude, Fayetteville State Tchrs. Coll., 1960; postgrad. Augusta Coll., 1980—. Tchr. elem. schs. Williamsburg-James-City County (Va.), 1960-64; tchr. elem. schs. Newport News, Va., 1966-71, Columbia County, Ga., 1971—; tchr. career edn. resources. Bd. dirs. Bible Sch.; active Girl Scouts U.S., Assn. for Better Columbia County, 1983. Mem. NEA, Ga. Assn. Educators, Columbia County Assn. Educators (sec. 1976), Alpha Kappa Mu, Alpha Kappa Alpha. Baptist. Home: Rural Route 2 PO Box 211-A Appling GA 30802 Office: N Columbia Elem Sch Appling GA 30802

ETTER, JOSEPH WESLEY, III, construction company safety director, personnel director; b. Long Island, N.Y., June 19, 1957; s. Joseph Wesley and Rita Anne (Robusto) E.; m. Carol Anne Stouffer, May 1, 1983. B.A., U. Maryland, 1981; M.A., W.Va. U., 1982. Psychiatric counselor Brook Ln. Ctr., Hagerstown, Md., 1979-82; safety dir. Oman, Fischbach, Amcat, 1982-84; safety dir., personnel dir. Oman Construction Co., Largo, Fla., 1984—. Mem. Nat. Safety Mgmt. Soc. (cert.), Am. Soc. Safety Engrs. (cert.), Equal Employment Opportunity Commn., Biology Club (pres. 1977), Chemistry Club (pres. 1977). Home: 2183 Briar Way Dr Clearwater FL 33575 Office: Oman Construction Co PO Box 2200 Largo FL 34294

ETTLING, JOHN, history educator; b. Poplar Bluff, Mo., Oct. 30, 1944; s. Albert John and Emily (Tucker) E.; m. Jennifer Beth Tarlin, Sept. 30, 1974; children—Sarah Isabel, Rachel Anne. B.A., U. Va., 1966; A.M., Harvard U., 1972, Ph.D., 1978. Assoc. prof., chmn. dept. history U. Houston, University Park, 1979—. Author: The Germ of Laziness: Rockefeller Philanthropy and Public Health in the New South, 1981. Served to capt. USAF, 1966-71. Recipient Allan Nevins prize Soc. Am. Historians, 1979; Friends of the Dallas Pub. Library prize Tex. Inst. Letters, 1982. Mem. Am. Hist. Assn., Orgn. Am. Historians, So. Hist. Assn., Am. Assn. for History of Medicine, Phi Beta Kappa. Home: 4616 Rockwood Houston TX 77004 Office: Dept of History Univ of Houston University Park Houston TX 77004

EUBANKS, BOBBY WAYNE, chemical company executive; b. Palestine, Tex., Jan. 29, 1943; s. Harvey Lee and Willie Mae (Lafitte) E.; m. Elizabeth Ellen Jackson, Aug. 28, 1965; 1 dau., Melissa. B.B.A., Sam Houston State U., 1965, M.B.A., 1967. Transp. analyst Shell Oil Co., Houston, 1967; systems analyst NCH Corp., Irving, Tex., 1968-69, exec. adminstr. ops. Europe, Birmingham, Eng., 1969-73, asst. plant mgr., Princeton, N.J., 1974, Indpls., 1974-78, internat. dir. ops., Irving, Tex., 1979-80, v.p. internat. ops., 1981—. Served with USAF, 1967-68. Sam Houston State U. teaching fellow, 1965-67; recipient award Wall St. Jour., 1965. Mem. Delta Sigma Pi, Omicron Delta Epsilon. Republican. Mem. Christian Ch. Home: 1013 Sean St Hurst TX 76053 Office: 2727 Chemsearch Blvd Irving TX 75060

EUBANKS, GARY LEROY, lawyer; b. North Little Rock, Ark., Nov. 22, 1933; s. Herman and Gertrude (Carmack) E. children—Gary L., Jr., Bobby Ray; m. Beverly Gayle Mauldin, Apr. 21, 1971 (div. 1983); 1 child, Shane Mauldin. J.D., U. Ark., 1960. Bar: Ark. 1970, U.S. Dist. Ct. Ark. 1970, U.S. Supreme Ct. 1970. Ptnr. Bailey, Jones, and Eubanks, Little Rock, 1960-63, Eubanks and Deane, Little Rock, 1963-65, Eubanks, Hood, and Files, Little Rock, 1965-69, Eubanks, Files and Hurley, Little Rock, 1969-76, Haskins Eubanks and Wilson, Little Rock, 1976-79, Gary Eubanks and Assocs., Little Rock, 1979—. Mem. Ark. Ho. of Reps., 1963-66; mem. Pulaski County (Ark.) Sch. Bd., 1967. Served with USN, 1952-54. Mem. ABA, Ark. State Bar Assn., Pulaski County Bar Assn., Ark. Trial Lawyers Assn., Assn. Trial Lawyers Am., Am. Bd. Trial Advocacy (civil trial advocate). Republican. Methodist. Home: #4 Wayside Dr North Little Rock AR 72116 Office: 708 W 2d St Little Rock AR 72201

EUBANKS, LORRAINE YANCEY, employee benefits manager; b. San Antonio, Apr. 19, 1927; d. John Harvey and June Coulter Yancey; m. Lewis Benton Eubanks, Nov. 25, 1944; children—John Dewey, Elizabeth Wright Pyatte. Clk., Automobile Agy., 1949-51, sec. to gen. mgr., 1952-57; bookkeeper Thompson & Jones, 1962-65, office mgr., 1966-69; asst. to personnel dir. S.W. Research Inst., San Antonio, 1969-72, mgr. employee benefits, 1972—, dir. Fed. Credit Union, 1979—, supr. com., 1979-80. Mem. Am. Mgmt. Assn., San Antonio Employers Alliance Assn. Baptist. Clubs: Turtle Creek Country, Order Eastern Star. Home: 7426 Brandyridge San Antonio TX 78250 Office: PO Drawer 28510 San Antonio TX 78284

EUBANKS, LOUANN MORGAN, optometrist; b. Borger, Tex., Mar. 16, 1955; d. John William and Wilma Lee (Smith) Morgan; m. George E. Eubanks Jr., Apr. 26, 1983. B.S. in Optometry, U. Houston, 1978, O.D., 1980. Lic. optometrist, Tex. Gen. practice optometry specializing in pediatric vision, Hereford, Tex., 1980-81, Lubbock, Tex., 1981-84, Amarillo, Tex., 1985—. Mem. Mensa, Beta Sigma Phi. Republican. Club: Pilot Internat. Avocations: antique furniture restoration; yoga; aerobics. Home: Box 1107 Hereford TX 79045 Office: Optometry Practice 7701 West I-40 #708 Amarillo TX 79121

EUBANKS, LUTHER BOYD, U.S. judge; b. Caprock, N.Mex., July 31, 1917; s. J.P. and Evelyn (Downs) E.; B.A., U. Okla., 1940; m. Lois Stevens, Sept. 5, 1942; children—Nancy Eubanks McClaran, Carolyn Eubanks Bryan, Stephen. Admitted to Okla. bar, 1944; county atty. Cotton County, Okla., 1946-49; mem. Okla. House Reps. from Cotton County, 1949-53; district judge, Lawton, Okla., 1956-65; U.S. dist. judge Western Dist. Okla., 1965—, now chief judge. Served with AUS, World War II; ETO. Rotarian. Address: 3301 Fed Courthouse Bldg 200 NW 4th St Oklahoma City OK 73102

EUBANKS, MARY WALTINE BANKS, educator; b. Esmont, Va., May 21, 1941; d. Walter Earl Banks and Madolia (Scott) Banks Chambers; m. Jack Junior Eubanks, July 3, 1982. B.S., Va. State Coll., 1964; M.Ed., U. Va., 1972. Tchr., Nelson County, Va., 1964-77, B.F. Yancey Elem. Sch., Esmont, Va., 1977—. Editor New Hope Ch. Yearbook, 1976. Pres. bd. dirs. Southside Health Ctr.; active Albermarle Democratic Com., Southside Albemarle NAACP, Albemarle City Parks and Recreation Commn.; lead soprano singing group Echoes. Recipient Recognition award Va. Edn. Jour., 1981. Mem. Va. Edn. Assn. (del.), NEA, Albemarle Edn. Assn. Baptist. Club: Greencroft Garden. Lodge: Household of Ruth. Home: Route 1 Box 277 Esmont VA 22937 Office: Route 1 PO Box 285 Esmont VA 22937

EUBANKS, MICHAEL RAY, lawyer, circuit court judge; b. Lumberton, Miss., Sept. 21, 1940; s. Michael Joseph and Nell Elizabeth (Bass) E.; student Phillips Acad., 1954-58; B.B.A., Tulane U., 1962, J.D., 1965; m. Sue Ellen Griffin, Aug. 10, 1968; children—Michelle, Christy Leigh, Mark Webster. Admitted to La. bar, 1965, Miss. bar, 1966; individual practice law, Lumberton, Miss., 1966-71; partner firm Eubanks Temple & Hudson, Purvis, Miss., 1971-82, sr. partner, 1971-82; atty. Lamar County Bd. Suprs., 1972-79, City of Lumberton, 1970-82; circuit judge 15th Judicial Dist. Miss., Purvis, 1983—; served as judge City of Lumberton, 1968-70. Exec. dir. Lumberton C. of C., 1973-77. Mem. gov.'s staff State of Miss., 1971-79. Recipient Regional Improvement award Tulane Alumni Fund, 1976; Miss. alumni rep. Philips Acad., 1973—. Mem. Am., Miss., La., S. Central Miss., Lamar County bar assns., Am., Miss. trial lawyers assns. Democrat. Methodist. Clubs: T, Tulane U. Home: 702 W Main Ave Lumberton MS 39455 Office: PO Box 488 Courthouse Sq Purvis MS 39475

EURE, THAD, state official; b. Gates County, N.C., Nov. 15, 1899; s. Tazewell A. and Armecia (Langstun) E.; student U. N.C., 1917-19, Law Sch., 1921-22; LL.D., Elon Coll., 1958; m. Minta Banks, Nov. 15, 1924; children—Armecia (Mrs. J. Norman Black, Jr.), Thad. Lawyer; mayor City of Winton, N.C., 1923-28; atty. Hertford County, N.C., 1923-31; prin. clk. N.C. Ho. of Reps., 1931, 33, 35, 36; sec. state State of N.C., Raleigh, 1936—. Mem. N.C. Ho. of Reps., 1929; keynote speaker N.C. Democratic Conv., 1950, permanent chmn., 1962. Chmn. bd. trustees Elon Coll. Mem. Nat. Assn. Secs. of State (pres. 1942; dean 1961), Am. Legion, 40 and 8, Theta Chi. Mem. United Ch. of Christ. Elk. Office: State Capitol Bldg Raleigh NC 27611

EUTON, MICHAEL FRED, landscape architect, farmer, intelligence consultant; b. Houston, Aug. 10, 1938; s. William Robert and Lillie Bertha (Wisher) E. Student U. Tex., Austin, 1956-59, Massey Bus. Coll., Houston, 1972. Sales mgr. Civic Reading Club, Houston and San Antonio, 1960-62; designer Davis Landscape Service, Houston, 1962-66; landscape architect Mike Euton Landscape Service, Barker, Tex., 1966—, City of Katy (Tex.), 1975-80; founder, pres. Teutonic Internat., 1985—; lectr. in field. Exec. com. Harris County Democratic Com., 1966-68; del. Harris County Dem. Conv., 1960, 62, 64, 66, 68, 70, 72, 74, 76, 78, 80, 84, Tex. Dem. Conv., 1960, 64, 68, 72, 74; precinct election judge, 1976; active numerous polit. campaigns for gov. of Tex., U.S. Ho. of Reps., U.S. Senate, Presdl. campaigns, 1956—, Jesse Jackson campaign, 1984, Ronald Reagan campaign, 1984; mem. U.S. Olympic Com., 1980; ex post facto mem. Katy Horizons Com., 1980, 81; mem. horizons com. Tri County Am. Revolution Bicentennial Commn., 1976; mem. Statue of Liberty-Ellis Island Centennial Commn., 1983. Recipient U.S. Presdl. Achievement award, 1983; cert. of appreciation, Vietnam Vets. Meml. Fund, 1983. Mem. Tex. Soc. Landscape Architects, Tex. Farm Bur., Barker Heritage and Preservation Soc. (charter mem., sec. 1976, pres. 1977-78, chmn. bd. 1979-80), Native Plant Soc. Tex. (charter), Katy C. of C., U. Tex. Ex-students Assn. (life mem.), Citizens for the Republic. Club: One-Hundred (Houston). Address: 3506 Greenhouse Rd Barker TX 77413

EVAINS, ALTHEA EVELYN, educator; b. St. Petersburg, Fla., Apr. 8, 1954; d. Clarence and Rosa Mae (Davis) E.; 1 son, Andre Lavaughn Butler. B.A. in Edn., U. South Fla., 1977. Cert. tchr., Fla. Family service aide Health and Rehabilitative Services, St. Petersburg, 1977-78; remedial reading tchr. Pinellas County schs., St. Petersburg, 1978-80; elem. tchr., Arcadia, Fla., 1980-83; lang. arts and reading tchr. Southside Fundamental Middle Sch., St. Petersburg, Fla., 1980—; summer youth coordinator, Arcadia, summer 1981—. Mem. Desota County Tchrs. Assn. Democrat. Baptist.

EVANOFF, SUSAN MARIE, educator; b. Milw., May 1, 1947; d. Robert James and Dolores Joan (Leque) Tietz; m. Larry Lee Evanoff, June 15, 1968; children—Mark Andrew, Laura Christine. B.S. in Elem. Edn., Lowell State U., 1972; postgrad. The Citadel, 1982—. Cert. elem. tchr., S.C. Profl. model Hart Agy., Boston, 1969-72; dir. pub. relations, fashion coordinator Montgomery Ward Co., Colorado Springs, Colo., 1974-76; tchr. pub. schs. Ft. Walton Beach, Fla., 1978, Guam, 1978-80, Berkeley County, S.C., 1981—. Adult counselor, leader local ch. fellowship group; speaker various bus. women's forums. Recipient community service award Ter. of Guam, 1980; elected to Ancient Order of Chammori, Guam, 1980. Republican. Home: 109 Queensbury Circle Goose Creek SC 29445 Office: Howe Hall Elementary School O Howe Hall Rd Goose Creek SC 29445

EVANS, ALBERT LOUIS, surgeon; b. Sandersville, Ga., July 10, 1914; s. Albert Louis and Mary Gainer (Warthen) E.; m. Lena Louise Lovett, Dec. 27, 1940; children—Albert Louis, John Sanford, Leon Lovett, Benjamin Gainer, William Postell. Student Mercer U., 1931-33; M.D., Emory U., 1937. Diplomate Am. Bd. Surgery. Intern, Grady Hosp., Atlanta, 1937-38; resident in surgery St. Joseph's Hosp., Balt., 1938-41; practice medicine specializing in surgery, Atlanta, 1945—; mem. staff Ga. Bapt. Hosp., Crawford W. Long Hosp., Drs. Meml. Hosp., West Paces Ferry Hosp. Mem. home mission bd. So. Bapt. Conv.; 1st v.p., also mem. exec. com. Ga. Bapt. Conv.; chmn. Bapt. Host Commn., 1983-86; mem. exec. com. So. Bapt. Conv., 1973-81. Served to maj. U.S. Army, 1941-45. Mem. Med. Assn. Atlanta, Med. Assn. Ga., AMA, ACS, Southeastern Surg. Congress, Ga. Surg. Soc. Republican. Club: Cherokee Town and Country. Lodge: Masons. Home: 3392 Woodhaven Rd NW Atlanta GA 30305 Office: 735 Piedmont Ave NE Atlanta GA 30308

EVANS, ALFRED CLEVELAND, accountant, minister; b. Potts Camp, Miss., Aug. 8, 1919; s. A.B. and Maude E. (Garrett) E.; m. Kathryn J. Shipman, June 1945; children—Elizabeth Jenelle, Alan B., Helene Carrol. Student Union U., 1955-56, So. Bapt. Coll., 1957-58, Oklahoma City U., 1945, Hills Bus. U., Oklahoma City, 1946-47; Ordained to ministry Bapt. Ch., 1958. Pastor, Salem Bapt. Ch., Potts Camp, 1959-60; bookkeeper and acct., Potts Camp, 1970—. Served with USAF, 1941-45. Lodges: Lions (pres. 1984-85), Masons. Avocations: music. Home: Route 1 Box 326 Potts Camp MS 38659

EVANS, A(NDREW) JAY, hospital administrator; b. N.Y.C., Feb. 7, 1943; s. Andrew J. and Claire (Bickerton) E.; m. Georgianna LeGrand, May 20, 1972; children—Jennifer, Ashley, Andrew. B.S. in Bus. Adminstrn., Trinity U., 1968, M.S. in Health Care Adminstrn., 1973. Various Hosp adminstrn. positions Humana, Inc., 1974-78; regional v.p. Brookwood Health Services, Birmingham, Ala., 1979-80; sr. v.p. Hosp. Mgmt. Assn., Ft. Myers, Fla., 1980-81; cons. hosp. adminstrn., Birmingham, 1981-83; adminstr. Highland Hosp., Asheville, N.C., 1983-85; regional mgr. Am. Healthcare Mgmt., Inc., The Woodlands, Tex., 1985—. Pres., Mental Health Assn. Buncombe County, Asheville, 1985—; mem. Area Health Edn. Ctr. Mental Health Adv. Council, 1985—; mem. Leadership Asheville, 1985—; bd. dirs. Assn. Children with Learning Disabilities 1985—. Mem. Na. Assn. Pvt. Psychiatric Hosps., Fedn. Am. Hosps., Central Neuro-Psychiatric Hosp. Assn., N.C. Hosp. Assn., Tex. Hosp. Assn. Republican. Roman Catholic. Club: Woodlands Athletic Ctr. Avocations: tennis; family outings. Office: Am Healthcare Mgmt Inc 14160 Dallas Pkwy Dallas TX 75240

EVANS, BENJAMIN HAMPTON, architect, educator, consultant; b. Premont, Tex., Oct. 27, 1926; s. Clyde Allen and Grace Ruth (Pierce) C.; m. Gwendolyn Jones, July 29, 1950; children—Ann Elizabeth, Sara Lynn, Gail Leigh. B.Arch., Tex. A&M Coll., 1952, M.Arch., 1960. Research architect Tex. Engring. Experiment Sta. and asst. prof. Tex. A&M Coll., 1952-61, head archtl. research lab., 1960-63; dir. edn. and research programs AIA, 1963-69; asst. dir. Bldg. Research Adv. Bd., Nat. Acad. Scis., Washington, 1969-75; prof. architecture Coll. Architecture and Urban Studies, Va. Tech. U., Blacksburg, 1975—; prin. Daylighting/Energy, Design Assocs.; cons. in field. Served with U.S. Army, 1944-46. Recipient Owens-Corning Fiberglas Energy Conservation award, 1980; Men of the Quarter Century award, Bldg. Research Adv. Bd., Nat. Acad. Scis., 1976. Fellow AIA (corp.); mem. Illuminating Engring. Soc. (chmn. daylighting com.). Mem. Disciples of Christ Ch. Lodge: Lions. Author: Daylight in Architecture, 1981; contbr. various research reports and articles to publs. Home: 2504 Capistrano Blacksburg VA 24060 Office: Coll Arch Va Poly Inst and State U Blacksburg VA 24061

EVANS, BOYD ALEXANDER, JR., educator, university administrator; b. New Orleans, Sept. 27, 1939; s. Boyd Alexander and Lois (Natal) E.; m. Patricia Owen; children—Carolyn Elizabeth, Boyd Alexander. B.S., Lynchburg Coll., 1962; M.B.A., Auburn U., 1964. Instr., Auburn U., Ala., 1963-65; asst. prof. Middle Tenn. State U., Murfreesboro, 1965-69, assoc. dean of students, 1969-70, dir. devel., 1970—. Recipient Outstanding Tchr. award Middle Tenn. State U., 1966, Mem. Council for the Advancement and Support of Edn., Pi Kappa Pi (trustee of found., 1975-81). Republican. Methodist. Lodges: Kiwanis (pres., 1965-71), Rotary, Moose. Avocations: sailing; flying; tennis. Office: Dir of Devel Middle Tenn State U Murfreesboro TN 37132

EVANS, CAROLYN DIAN, medical technologist; b. Marshall, Tex., Mar. 26, 1942; d. Harold Wade and Dorothy B. (Green) Spencer; m. Edmond Cecil Evans, Jr., June 5, 1965; children—Edmond Cecil III, Michael Jeremy. B.S., East Tex. State Coll., 1963, Tex. Christian U., 1964. Med. technologist St. Mary's Hosp., Kansas City, Mo., 1964-69, Evans Clinic, Mineral Wells, Tex., 1969-71, part-time technologist, 1971—. Trustee Mineral Wells Ind. Sch. Dist., 1978—; Mem. Tex. Assn. Sch. Bds., Am. Soc. Med. Technologists, Am. Soc. Clin. Pathologists, Mineral Wells C. of C. (chmn. ed. com. 1984-85, bd. dirs. 1985—), Phi Delta Kappa (Friend of Edn. award 1985). Methodist. Club: Zonta. Avocations: reading; travel; gardening; swimming. Home: PO Box 1248 Mineral Wells TX 76067 Office: Mineral Wells Sch Dist 102 NW 6th Ave Mineral TX 76067

EVANS, CHARLES WAYNE, II, research biologist; b. Athens, Ohio, Aug. 9, 1929; s. Charles Wayne and Florence Louise (Sheets) Evans Claypool; m. Jo F. Burt, 1948 (div. 1959); children—Charles Wayne III, James Friedrich (dec.), John Burns, Elizabeth Burt; m. Patricia Anne Baker, 1971; children—Debbie Jo, Caralyn Michelle. Student, Tex. A&M U., 1947-51, B.A., 1957, postgrad., 1963-65; postgrad., U. Houston, 1969-70. Seismologist, Universal Seismic Expt., Beaumont, Tex., 1958-65; marine biologist CRI/VIERS, St. Thomas, U.S. Virgin Islands, 1965-71; geologist Dr. C. B. Claypool, Beaumont, 1971-76;

research biologist Panthera-Marine-Internat., Ltd., Belize, C.A., Beaumont, 1976-79, pres., chief exec. officer, 1976—; research biologist Synectics, Inc., Las Vegas, 1979-82, bd. dirs., treas., 1979—; research biologist SAC Research Ctr., Beaumont, 1982—; pres. Jordhammer, Inc., Las Vegas, 1980—; bd. dirs. Ant Fire, Inc., Beaumont, 1985—. Co-inventor Jordhammer, 1982, Earthfire Injection System, 1983. Sus. mem. Rep. Nat. Com., Washington, 1982—; charter mem. Ellis Island Found., N.Y.C., 1983—; pres. Caribbean Inst. Natural Sci., St. Thomas, 1967-70. Served with N.G., 1945-47. SAC Research Ctr. grantee, 1983, Dr. C. B. Claypool grantee, 1963, 78. Mem. AAAS, Smithsonian Assocs., Am. Mus. Natural History (assoc.), Internat. Oceanographic Found., World Wildlife Fund. Clubs: Aggie, Century (Tex. A&M U.). Lodge: Lions. Avocations: music; chess; big game fishing. Office: SAC Research Ctr 5000 Belmont St Beaumont TX 77707

EVANS, DARDANELLA LISTER, nurse, writer; b. Vernon, Tex., Jan. 26, 1921; d. Jack and Jenna Ferol (Bradley) Lister; grad. U. Okla. Sch. Nursing, 1943; grad. Nat. Landscape Inst., 1959; m. Kent E. Evans, May 21, 1946; children—Karen Louise Evans Ulehla, Sharon Jean Evans Wilson. With Okla. Pub. Co. and Sta. WKY, 1939-40; nurse U. Hosp. and Crippled Childrens' Hosp., Oklahoma City, 1940-43; vol. nurse Sch. Immunization Community Program, Dallas, 1958-69; key market editor for N.Y. publs. including Radio & TV Weekly, 1964-71, U.S. Tobacco Jour., 1964-71; v.p. Atlas Engring. Services, Inc., Atlanta, 1976-83, now dir.; free lance writer health and safety, 1939—. PTA room rep. Lakewood, Long and Woodrow Wilson high schs., Dallas, 1953-69; girl scout leader Lakewood Sch. council Girl Scouts U.S., 1956-63; Sunday sch. tchr. Skillman Ave. Ch. of Christ, 1962-65; mem. dir.'s com. U.S. Senatorial Bus. Adv. Bd., 1981. Served with U.S. Army Nurse Corps, 1943-46. Mem. Women in Communications, Nutrition Today Soc., Nat. Writers Club, Associated Bus. Writers Am., Smithsonian Nat. Assn., Am. Trauma Soc., Ret. Army Nurse Corps Assn., DeKalb North Art Alliance, Riverview Civic Assn., Ret. Officers Assn. Republican. Mem. Ch. of Christ. Club: Atlanta Athletic. Author: Nest Not in My Hair!, 1978; contbr. poetry to various lit. publs. Home: 4324 Ridgegate Dr Duluth GA 30136

EVANS, DAVID HUDSON, zoology educator; b. Chgo., June 9, 1940; s. Ronald George and Margaret Virginia (Ketchum) E.; m. Jean Margaret Rose, Aug. 18, 1962; children—Andrew William, Matthew Richard. B.A., DePauw U., 1962; Ph.D., Sanford U., 1967. Asst. prof. biology U. Miami, Fla., 1969-73, assoc. prof., 1973-78, prof., chmn. dept. biology, 1978-81; prof. zoology U. Fla., Gainesville, 1981—, chmn. dept. zoology, 1982-85; cons. Office of Sci. and Tech. Policy, Washington, 1982-84; dir. Mt. Desert Island Biology Lab., Maine, 1982—. Contbr. articles to profl. jours., chpts. to books. NSF grantee, 1970—. Mem. Am. Soc. Zoologists, Soc. for Exptl. Biology, Am. Physiol. Soc., European Soc. for Comparative Physiology and Biochemistry, Sigma Xi, Omicron Delta Chi, Phi Kappa Phi. Democrat. Methodist. Avocations: running, tennis, golf.

EVANS, DAVID HUHN, JR., music educator; b. Boston, Jan. 22, 1944; s. David Huhn and Anne Marie (Kunze) E.; m. Cheryl June Thurber, Sept. 19, 1971; children—Phoebe, Chloe. A.B., Harvard U., 1965; M.A., UCLA, 1967, Ph.D., 1976. Lectr., asst. prof., assoc. prof. anthropology Calif. State U., Fullerton, 1969-78; assoc. prof., prof. music Memphis State U., 1978—; cons. Mississippi River Mus., Memphis. Mem. Memphis and Shelby County Music Commn., 1981-82, chmn., 1981. Nominee Grammy award, 1981; recipient W. C. Handy award, 1981; Chgo. Folklore prize U. Chgo., 1981-82; grantee: NEA, 1979-80, 82-83, Tenn. Arts/Humanities Support Program, 1980. Mem. Am. Folklore Soc., Soc. for Ethnomusicology, Friends of the John Edwards Meml. Found., Tenn. Folklore Soc., Miss. Folklore Soc., Ozark States Folklore Soc., Calif. Folklore Soc., Internat. Soc. for Jazz Research, Music Industries of Memphis, Nat. Acad. of Rec. Arts and Scis. Author: Tommy Johnson, 1971; Big Road Blues: Tradition and Creativity in the Folk Blues, 1982; contbr. numerous articles on Am. folk and popular music and folklore to profl. jours. Home: 2441 Forrest Ave Memphis TN 38112 Office: Dept Music Memphis State U Memphis TN 38152

EVANS, ERNEST COLSTON, program advisor, researcher; b. N.Y.C., July 19, 1920; s. Harold Thomas Colston and Violet (White) E.; m. Odile Ricci, Dec. 5, 1942; children—Edward E., Thomas C., Robert J. Cert. in bus. adminstrn. N.J. Coll. Commerce, 1940; cert. in elec. engring., MIT, 1944; B.S. in Engring., U. Tenn., 1954, M.S. in Physics, 1957. Registered profl. engr., Tenn. Engr., Union Carbide Corp., Oak Ridge, 1946-54, dept. head, 1954-65, div. dir., 1965-83; sr. program advisor Martin Marietta Energy Systems, Inc., Oak Ridge, 1983—. Developer gas centrifuge for comml. scale isotope separation, 1960-83; patentee measurement and controls; author tech. publs. Pres. Morgan Pl. Homeowners Assn., Solway, Tenn., 1985. Served with U.S. Army, 1942-46. Fellow Instrument Soc. Am. (pres. Oak Ridge sect. 1965-66); mem. Nat. Soc. Profl. Engrs. (Outstanding Service award 1982). Avocation: fishing. Home: 11413 Berry Hill Dr Knoxville TN 37931 Office: Martin Marietta Energy Systems Inc PO Box P MS-434 Oak Ridge TN 37831

EVANS, FREDERICK ELBER (FRITZ), III, financial consultant; b. Winston-Salem, N.C., Sept. 22, 1942; s. Frederick Elbert and Nancy Marguerite (Stoltz) E.; m. Judy Patricia Smith, Nov. 11, 1962; children—Frederick Stuart, Patricia Dawn, Frederick Christian. B.S. in Psychology, Gardner-Webb Coll., 1978; postgrad. Southwestern Baptist Theol. Semn., Ft. Worth, 1981—. Front end mgr. Ingles Markets, Inc., Shelby, N.C., 1974-78; with Pangburn Mfg. Co., Ft. Worth, 1978-81; agt. Jefferson Standard Life Ins., Norfolk, Va., 1981-82; sales cons. Ins. Cons. Inc., Virginia Beach, Va., 1982—; pres. Positive Mgmt. Systems, Virginia Beach, 1985—; Mem. Sandbridge Civic League, Virginia Beach. Served with USMC, 1960-68. Named Man of Yr., Ins. Cons., Inc., Virginia Beach., 1984; recipient Leaders Club award Guardian Life Ins., N.Y.C., 1983, 84; Centurian Club award, 1983. Mem. Nat. Assn. Life Underwriters. Baptist. Avocations: golfing; tennis; water sports. Home: 4949 Admiration Virginia Beach VA 23464 Office: Ins Cons Inc 3090 Brickhouse Ct Virginia Beach VA 23452

EVANS, GARY LYNN, building company executive; b. Houston, Aug. 20, 1951; s. Robert Bryant and Floydell (Cotten) E.; m. Sharon Margaret Voiles, Mar. 22, 1972; 1 son, Gary Lynn. Exec. v.p. Evans Constrn. Co., Houston, 1972—. Dir. Tex. Commerce Bank, Sugarland. Bd. dirs. Cystic Fibrosis Orgn., Acapulco Children's Home; deacon Sugar Creek Baptist Ch. Mem. Aircraft Owners and Pilots Assn., Helicopter Operators Tex. Republican. Lodges: Masons, Shriners. Home: 1207 Sugar Creek Blvd Sugarland TX 77478

EVANS, GEORGE THAMES, chiropractic physician; b. Birmingham, Ala., Sept. 19, 1936; s. George Turnell and Dorothy Hester (Thames) E.; m. Patricia Grace Byers, June 19, 1961 (div.); m. 2d, Diane Grace Davidson, Nov. 19, 1978; children—Jana, Scott, Sherrie. B.S., U. So. Miss., 1963; D.Chiropractic, Logan Chiropractic Coll., St. Louis, 1977. Diplomate Nat. Bd. Chiropractic Examiners. Manuscript evaluator Little Brown Pub. Co., Boston, 1968-70; with cardiac unit St. Joseph's Hosp., St. Charles, Mo., 1975-77; gen. practice chiropractic medicine Horseshoe Bend Chiropractic Clinic, Atlanta, 1977—; sec./treas. V.M. Nutri, S.E. Served with M.C., U.S. Army, 1958-60, 61-62. Recipient Inventive Achievement award Ga. Sci. Fair, 1969. Mem. Am. Chiropractic Assn., Ga. Chiropractic Assn., Parker Chiropractic Research Found., Internat. Health Inst., Price-Pottinger Research Inst., Cobb C. of C., Assn. for Total Health. Democrat. Mormon. Club: Optimist. Lodge: Lions. Author: Nutritional Physicians Cookbook, 1979. Inventor disposable pallets.

EVANS, HAZEL ATKINSON, political party official; b. Atlanta, Aug. 16, 1931; d. Alex P. and Hazel (Thomas) Robert; student Marjorie Webster Jr. Coll., Washington, 1951; m. W. Reed Talley, Sept. 11, 1951; children—W. Reed Talley, Alex R.; m. 2d, Robert Winfield Evans, Nov. 30, 1968. Mem. State Democratic Com. Manatee County, 1962-64, Pinellas County, 1966-84; mem. Dem. Nat. Com., 1968-84, mem. exec. com., 1973-84; mem. State Central Com. Dem. Exec. Com., Fla., 1966-84; sec. Young Dem. Clubs Fla., 1962-63, v.p., 1963-64; del. Dem. Nat. Conv., 1964, 68, 72, 76, 80, mem.-at-large exec. com., 1976; del. Nat. Dem. Mid-Term Conf., Kansas City, 1974, Memphis, 1978; co-chmn. arrangements com. Dem. Nat. Conv., 1976, 1980; chmn. arrangements com. Dem. Nat. Conv., 1984; chmn. 6th Congressional dist. Dem. com., 1976—; del. Fla. Dem. Conv., 1975, 77, 79, 81, 83; vice-chmn. Dem. party Fla., 1980-84; bd. dirs. Fla. Opera, Deaf Service Ctr. Pinellas County. Mem. Gov.'s Adv. Com. Pinellas County; commr. Pinellas County Housing Authority, 1972-76, vice chmn., 1975; bd. dirs. Fla. Heart Assn., Fla. Mental Health Assn., Ringling Mus. Art, United Fund Manatee, Pinellas County. Recipient Meritorious award Am. Heart Assn., 1960, 64, 66; Pres.'s award Young Dems. Fla., 1963, 64. Mem. Beta Sigma Phi. Home: 1146 41st Ave NE Saint Petersburg FL 33703

EVANS, HOWARD TASKER, JR., research physicist; b. Ancon, Panama Canal Zone, Sept. 9, 1919; s. Howard Tasker and Ruth Mildred (Dutton) E.; m. Eloise Humez, June 21, 1942 (div. 1966); 1 dau., Cecily Ruth; m. 2d, Grace Ethel Dressler, Apr. 23, 1966. S.B., MIT, 1942, Ph.D., 1948. Instr. sect. graphics MIT, Cambridge, 1945-48, research assoc. Lab. for Insulation Research, 1947-49; Research physicist Philips Labs., Irvington-on-Hudson, 1949-52; physicist U.S. Geol. Survey, Reston, Va., 1952—. John Simon Guggenheim fellow, 1960-61. Mem. Am. Crystal Assn. (sec. 1950-51, pres. 1964), Mineral. Soc. Am., Am. Chem. Soc., AAAS, Sigma Xi. Democrat. Unitarian. Contbr. papers and articles to profl. lit. Home: 6107 Roseland Dr Rockville MD 20852 Office: US Geol Survey Nat Ctr 959 Reston VA 22092

EVANS, JAMES S., media-related holding company executive; b. 1921. B.S., Purdue U., 1942. With Media General, Inc., 1974—, v.p., 1974-77, sr. v.p. newsprint ops., 1977-80, exec. v.p. ops., 1980-82, pres., chief operating officer, dir., 1982-85, pres., chief exec. officer, dir., 1985—. Address: Media General Inc 333 E Grace St Richmond VA 23219*

EVANS, JAMES WILLIAM, computer software expert; b. Fulton, Ky., Dec. 5, 1929; s. Sebra and Roberta (Thurmond) E.; B.S., Memphis State Coll., 1955; postgrad. Memphis Law Sch., 1955; m. Anne Talbot, Dec. 26, 1954; children—Carol Glynn, William Talbot. Ops. mgr. Westinghouse Co., Tampa, Fla., 1968-70; pres. ASM, Clearwater, Fla., 1970-72; sales mgr. Burroughs Corp., Tampa. 1955-68, 72-77; chmn. bd., chief exec. officer Southeastern Computer Corp., Clearwater, Fla., 1977—, J. Evans Assocs., Inc., Clearwater, 1985—; pres., chief exec. officer, chmn. bd. St. Clair Software Services, Inc., Clearwater, 1985—; cons. tax adminstrn. and election mgmt. systems to state and local govts., corps. Served to capt. AUS, 1950-53. Decorated Silver Star, Purple Heart. Mem. Internat. Assn. Assessing Officers, Assn. Computing Machinery, Inst. Property Taxation, Data Processing Mgmt. Assn., Kappa Alpha. Clubs: Countryside Country. Patentee in field. Home: 2951 Meadow Hill Dr Clearwater FL 33519 Office: 2536 Contryside Blvd Suite 501 PO Box 4400 Clearwater FL 33519

EVANS, JO BURT, rancher; b. Kimble County, Tex., Dec. 18, 1928; d. John Fred and Sadie (Oliver) Burt; B.A., Mary Hardin-Baylor Coll., 1948; M.A., Trinity U., 1967; m. Charles Wayne Evans II, Apr. 17, 1949; children—Charles Wayne III, John Burt, Elizabeth Wisart. Owner, mgr. Sta. KMBL, Junction, Tex., 1959-61; real estate broker, Junction, 1965-74; staff economist, adv. on 21st Congl. Dist., polit. campaign Nelson Wolff, 1974-75; asst. mgr., bookkeeper family owned ranches and rent property, Junction, 1948—; gen. mgr. TV Translator Corp., Junction, 1968—, sec.-treas., 1980—. Treas., asst. to coordinator Citizens for Tex., 1972; mem. Com. of Conservation Soc. to Save the Edwards Aquifer, San Antonio, 1973; treas., asst. coordinator New Constn., San Antonio, 1974; homecoming chmn. for Kimble County Schs.; mktg. chmn. Tex. Sesquicentennial. Recipient commendation Tex. Senate, 1973. Mem. Nat. Translator Assn., AAUW (scholarship named in her honor Kerrville br. 1972), Daus. Republic Tex., Junction Bus. and Profl. Women (sec. 1979-81, pres. 1981-82), Junction High Sch. Execs. (chmn.), Nat. Platform Soc., Tex. Sheriff's Assn. Democrat. Mem. Ch. Divine Sci. Home: PO Box 283 Junction TX 76849 Office: 618 Main St Junction TX 76849

EVANS, JOHN CALVIN, program manager, former army officer; b. West Chester, Pa., Mar. 14, 1930; s. Luther W. and Alma L. Evans; m. Paula Patricia Hale, Dec. 27, 1955. B.A. in Polit. Sci., The Citadel, 1952. Commd. U.S. Army, 1952, advanced through ranks to lt. col., 1976; ret., 1976; program mgr. Sci. Applications, Inc., Arlington, Va., 1976-79, BDM Corp., McLean, Va., 1979—. Decorated Legion of Merit (2), Vietnamese Cross of Gallantry with Palm. Mem. Am. Soc. Indsl. Security (com. safeguarding proprietary info.; chmn. com. privacy and info. mgmt. 1982), Am. Def. Preparedness Assn., U.S. Naval Inst., Smithsonian Resident Assocs., Nat. R.R. Hist. Soc. Methodist.

EVANS, JOHN DERBY, telecommunications company executive; b. Detroit, June 3, 1944; s. Edward Steptoe and Florence (Allington) E.; A.B., U. Mich., 1966; m. Susan Blair Allan, Apr. 7, 1973; children—John Derby, Courtenay Boyd. Pres., Evans Communications Systems, Inc., Charlottesville, Va., 1970-72; v.p., gen. mgr. Capitol Cablevision Corp., Charleston, W.Va., 1972-76; regional mgr. Am. TV & Communications Corp., Denver, 1974-76; telecommunications cons. to asst. sec. for planning and devel. Dept. HEW, Washington, 1976; exec. v.p., chief ops. officer Arlington (Va.) Tele Communications Corp., 1976-83; pres. Arlington Cable Ptnrs. Ltd., 1983—, Evans Telecommunications, Inc., 1983—; pres. Suburban Cablevision Co., 1985—, Montgomery County Cablevision Co., 1986—, North Central Cablevision, Hauser Communications Inc., N.Y.C., 1985—; dir. Cable Satellite Public Affairs Network (C-Span), 1978—. Served to lt. USN, 1966-70. Mem. Nat. Cable TV Assn. (pres.'s award 1979, Challenger award 1984, nat. chmn. awards com. 1981, dir. 1982—), Va. Cable TV Assn. (dir. 1979—, v.p. 1982, pres. 1983-84), Soc. Motion Picture TV Engrs. Republican. Episcopalian. Clubs: Farmington Country, Boars Head Sports (Charlottesville); Old Dominion Boat (Alexandria, Va.); Wintergreen (Va.) Sports; Washington Golf and Country (Arlington, Va.). Home: 1530 N Key St #1210 Arlington VA 22201 Office: 2707 Wilson Blvd Arlington VA 22201

EVANS, JUDI S., nurse; b. New Haven, Aug. 26, 1938; d. Morris and Marion Ruth (Root) Senderoff; m. Richard W.C. Evans, III, Aug. 15, 1959; children—Victoria Lee, Richard W.C. Student U. Conn., 1956-58, Ariz. State Coll., summer 1957, Coll. Boca Raton, 1971-74; A.S. in Nursing, Broward Community Coll., 1977. R.N., Conn., Fla. Asst. microbiol. lab. Yale U. Med. Sch., New Haven, 1958-59; staff nurse Boca Raton (Fla.) Hosp., 1977; spl. duty nurse Upjohn Health Care, Inc., Boca Raton, 1977-83; dir. T.L.C. Clinic, Inc., Boca Raton, 1983-84; dir. Jeri Jacobus of Dallas, 1985—; tchr. vols.; counselor; substitute tchr. Putnam Valley (N.Y.) Pub. Schs., 1968-70; instr. children with learning disabilities, 1970. Bd. dirs. YMCA Boca Raton, 1975-76, Hospice, 1975-76. Named Employee of Month, Upjohn Health Care. Mem. Fla. Nurses Assn., Am. Nurses Assn. Republican. Presbyterian. Club: Christian Business Women. Designer furniture. Address: 6120 Via Tierra Boca Raton FL 33433

EVANS, MARY ELIZABETH, educator; b. Baytown, Tex., Oct. 26, 1940; d. Joseph Augustus and Elizabeth Stephana (Helpert) Kubica; m. Rand Boyd Evans, June 22, 1963; children—Victoria Anne, Karl Michael, Veronica Marie. Student Tex. Women's U., 1959-61; B.S. in Elem. Edn., Southwest Tex. State U., 1963. Cert. tchr., Tex. Tchr., Brook Elem. Sch., Austin, Tex., 1963-65; Title I tutor Chandler Sch., Somersworth, N.H., 1974-76; tchr. Crockett Elem. Sch., Bryan, Tex., 1977—. Docent, Christmas in Olde Bryan Homes Tour, Citizens for Hist. Preservation, 1980-82. Recipient award Arts Council Brazos County, 1982. Mem. Assn. Tex. Profl. Educators. Democrat. Roman Catholic. Home: 609 E 30th St Bryan TX 77803

EVANS, NORENE RUSSELL, writer, publisher, trainer; b. Deming, N.Mex., June 30, 1935; d. Theodore Hoy and Dorothy Gertrude (Baker) Russell; m. Robert Hill Evans, Oct. 7, 1955; children—Lauralyn Lee, Robert Hill, Dana Shawn. Student N.Mex. State U., 1954-56; A.S., U. SUNY, 1978. Profl. writer, Ft. Huachuca, Ariz., 1975-77; self-employed in pub. relations, Ft. Huachuca, 1977-79; founder, dir. Milcom & Chapel Publicity, Springfield, Va., 1980—, Sharing Assocs., Springfield, 1984—, Publicity Press, Springfield, 1984—; v.p. Religious Pub. Relations Council, Washington, 1983-84, pres., 1985-86, mem. Wilbur Awards com., 1984-86. Author/editor, pub. Going Public, 1980, Publicity Patterns, 1983, A New Ministry, 1985. Contbr. articles to profl. jours. Pub. relations/pub. coordinator Officers & Civilians Wives Club, Ft. Huachuca, 1964-67. Mem. Internat. Assn. Bus. Communicators, Am. Soc. Tng. and Devel. Avocations: walking; bowling. Address: 8611 Burling Wood Dr Springfield VA 22152

EVANS, ORINDA D., federal judge; b. Savannah, Ga., Apr. 23, 1943; d. Thomas and Virginia Elizabeth (Grieco) Evans; B.A., Duke U., 1965; J.D. with distinction, Emory U., 1968; m. Roberts O. Bennett, Apr. 12, 1975; 1 son, Wells Cooper. Admitted to Ga. bar, 1968; assoc. Alston, Miller & Gaines, Atlanta, 1969-74, ptnr., 1974-79; U.S. dist. judge No. Dist. Ga., Atlanta, 1979—, adj. prof. Emory U. Law Sch., 1974-77; counsel Atlanta Crime Commn., 1970-71. Bd. dirs. Ansley Park Civic Assn., 1975-76. Mem. State Bar Ga., Atlanta Bar Assn. (dir. 1979). Democrat. Episcopalian. Home: 200 The Prado NE Atlanta GA 30309 Office: 1988 US Courthouse 75 Spring St SW Atlanta GA 30303

EVANS, PETER KENNETH, advertising executive, playwright; b. Brighton, Sussex, Eng., Apr. 18, 1935; came to U.S., 1968; s. Percy Edward and Doris (McCoy) E.; m. Juana Santana Ramirez, Mar. 31, 1956; children—Luis Miguel, Linda Rosa Del Rocio, Pilar de Los Angeles. Ed. in Brighton. Creative group head Goodis, Goldberg, Soren, Toronto, Ont., Can., 1961-63; v.p., creative dir. Baker/BBDO, Toronto, 1963-65; creative dir. Kenyon & Eckhardt, Toronto, 1965-67, Mexico City, 1967-68; exec. v.p., creative dir. Vladimir & Evans, Miami, Fla., 1968-72; pres., creative dir. Evans & Ciccarone, Miami, 1972—; judge ADDY awards Greater Miami Advt. Fedn., 1976; instr. advt. Fla. Internat. U., Miami, 1974. Author play: Ruiz, 1982. Leader Jr. Achievement, Miami, 1968; asst. Boy Scouts Am., Miami, 1970. Named one of 100 Top Creative Men Ad Day/USA, 1974, Art Dir. of Yr., Miami Advt. Fedn., 1972; recipient Gold medal Art Dirs. Club, 1968; 8 Gold medals Miami Advt. Fedn., 1973. Mem. Dramatists Guild, Nat. Assn. Underwater Instrs. Anglican. Club: Key Biscayne Beach (Fla.). Home: 285 W Mashta Dr Key Biscayne FL 33149 Office: Evans & Ciccarone 420 NW 42d Ave Miami FL 33126

EVANS, RALPH AIKEN, physicist, consultant; b. Oak Park, Ill., Feb. 2, 1924; s. Durward Randall and Hazel Agnes (Aiken) E.; m. Catherine Mary Martin, 1967; children—Paul A., Ann M. B.S., Lehigh U., 1944; Ph.D. in Physics, U. Calif.-Berkeley, 1954. Dir. Link-Belt Research Lab., Indpls., 1959-61; research physicist Research Triangle Inst., Durham, N.C., 1961-72, cons., 1972—; mng. editor IEEE Transactions on Reliability; editor Am. Soc. Quality Control Reliability Rev. Served to ensign USNR, 1944-45. Fellow Am. Soc. for Quality Control, IEEE. Home and office: 804 Vickers Ave Durham NC 27701

EVANS, RALPH LAFAYETTE, JR., designer, draftsman; b. Tuscaloosa, Ala., Oct. 23, 1949; s. Ralph LaFayette and Jean Marie (Koertner) E.; m. Norma Thomas, Jan. 24, 1970; children—Ashley Christine, Kelly Rochelle, Bradley LaFayette. Owner, mgr. Royal Carpets Ltd., Dade City, Fla., 1974-76, Evans Residential Design, Dade City, 1976-84; ptnr. Paul E. Hagler Engr., Dade City, 1982; corporate dir. Excel Assoc., Dade City, 1984—. Mem. Dade City Jaycees (pres. 1982), Dade City C. of C. (pres. 1985). Republican. Lutheran. Avocations: classical guitar; jogging. Home: 1607 Grant Ave Dade City FL 33525 Office: Excel Assoc Inc 306 E 5th St Dade City FL 33525

EVANS, RICHARD MARTIN, forester; b. Nashville, July 26, 1945; s. William Hubert and Estelle (Hefflin) E. m. Carole Clinton, Feb. 18, 1969; children—Nathan Clinton, Ashley Elizabeth. B.S., U. Tenn., 1968, M.S., 1971. Survey party chief U.S. Forestry Service, Burns, Oreg., 1965; asst. geneticist Tex. A&M U., College Station, 1970-73; supt., dir. Forestry Experiment Sta. and Arboretum, U. Tenn., Oak Ridge, Oliver Springs and Tullahoma, 1973—; owner Newstead Farm, Wartburg, Tenn., 1981—; cons. Velsicol Chem. Co., 1983; dir. MidSouth Christmas Tree Assn., Sewanee, Tenn., 1984—. Author articles. Mem. Soc. Am. Foresters (chmn., mem. exec. com Ky.-Tenn. chpt. 1984-85; Outstanding Service award 1984), MidSouth Christmas Tree Assn. (bd. dirs.), Natural Resource Conservation Soc. Tenn. (bd. dirs. 1982—), Tenn. Forestry Assn., Morgan County Forestry Devel. Assn. (bd. dirs. 1981—), Tenn. Native Plant Soc. (bd. dirs. 1980-84), U Tenn Arboretum Soc. (bd. dirs. 1973—), Oak Ridge C. of C. Methodist. Avocations: hiking; camping; wood crafts. Home: 901 Kerr Hollow Rd Oak Ridge TN 37830 Office: Forestry Experiment Sta U Tenn Oak Ridge TN 37830

EVANS, ROBERT ARTHUR, neuroradiologist, psychiatrist; b. San Francisco, Apr. 6, 1928; s. Arthur Thomas and Hazel (Bronson) E.; m. Vicki L. Greiff. A.B. with great distinction, Stanford U., 1947, A.M., 1948; M.D., Columbia U., 1952. Intern, Columbia-Presbyn. Med. Center, N.Y.C., 1952-53, asst. resident in medicine, 1953-54, asst. resident in radiology, 1954-59; trainee Nat. Cancer Inst., 1957-59; instr. radiology Columbia U., N.Y.C., 1959; research fellow Nat. Heart Inst., 1959-60; instr. radiology Stanford U., 1960-61, instr. pediatrics, 1960-61; Nat. Inst. Neurol. Disease and Blindness spl. fellow in neuroradiology Neurol. Inst. N.Y., Columbia-Presbyn. Med. Center, N.Y.C., 1962-64; asso. prof. radiology Baylor Coll. Medicine, Houston, 1964-82, resident dept. psychiatry, 1983-85; mem. staff Meth. Hosp., Ben Taub Gen. Hosp., Tex. Children's Hosp., VA Hosp., all Houston. Served in USNR, 1956-57. Recipient Zabriskie prize Columbia U., 1951. James Picker Found. grantee, 1961-63. Mem. AMA, Am. Soc. Neuroradiology, Am. Coll. Radiology, Am. Acad. Neurology, Am. Assn. Neurol. Surgeons, Rocky Mountain Neurosurg. Soc., Tex. Med. Assn., Harris County Med. Soc., Houston Neurol. Soc., Am. Psychiat. Assn., Soc. for Psychoanalytic Psychotherapy, Houston Group Psychotherapy Soc., Phi Beta Kappa, Alpha Omega Alpha, Phi Chi. Office: Dept Psychiatry Baylor Coll Medicine Houston TX 77030

EVANS, SARAH FRANCES HINTON, nurse; b. Athens, Ga., July 19, 1924; d. Charles Jackson and Bessie Marie (Hickman) Hinton; m. Omer Fountain, Oct. 9, 1948 (div. 1964); children—Anita Francine, Sarah Alice; John Duggan Evans, Feb. 14, 1969. (dec. Apr. 1971). R.N., Macon Hosp. Sch. Nursing, 1945; B.S. in Nursing, Med. Coll. Ga., 1975. Cert. Bd. Infection Control. Night supr. Ware County Hosp., Waycross, Ga., 1946-47; staff nurse nursery and obstetrics Macon Hosp., Ga., 1952-54, 1955-56, head nurse colored labor and delivery, 1956-64, obstet. staff nurse, 1964-65; head nurse newborn nursery Med. Ctr. Central Ga., Macon, 1965-74, infection control nurse, 1974—; mem. Ga. Bd. Nursing, 1977-80. Mem. Am. Nurses Assn., Assn. Practitioners in Infection Control, Ga. Heart Assn., Ga. Pub. Health Assn., Sixth Dist. Ga. Nurses Assn., Med. Ctr. Central Ga., Med. Coll. Ga. Alumnae Assn., Ga. Infection Control Network (charter, 1st vice chmn.). Baptist. Home: 6375 Houston Rd Macon GA 31206 Office: Med Ctr Central GA Box 6000 Macon GA 31208

EVANS, THOMAS MARTIN, lawyer; b. Athens, Ala., Nov. 20, 1914; s. Henry Bugg and Betty (Ross) E.; m. Virginia Richey, June 26, 1941 (dec.); children—Dorothy E., Thomas Martin. LL.B., Cumberland U., 1937. Bar: Tenn. 1937, U.S. Dist. Ct. (mid. dist.) Tenn. 1937. Sole practice, Nashville, 1937—. Served with USNR, 1942-46. Mem. Nashville Bar Assn., Tenn. Bar Assn., ABA. Methodist. Office: 18th Floor 3d Nat Bank Bldg Nashville TN 37219

EVANS, THOMAS PASSMORE, educator, licensing consultant; b. West Grove, Pa., Aug. 19, 1921; s. John and Linda (Zeuner) E.; B.S. in E.E., Swarthmore Coll., 1942; M.Engring., Yale U., 1948; m. Lenore Jane Knuth, June 21, 1947; children—Paula S., Christina L., Bruce A., Carol L. Engr., Atomic Power div. Westinghouse Electric Corp., Pitts., 1948-51; dir. research and devel. AMF, Inc., N.Y.C., 1951-60; dir. research O.M. Scott & Sons Co., Marysville, Ohio, 1960-62; v.p. research and devel. W.A. Sheaffer Pen Co., Ft. Madison, Iowa, 1962-67; dir. research Mich. Technol. U., Houghton, 1967-80; dir. research, mem. faculty Berry Coll., Mt. Berry, Ga., 1980—, prof. bus. adminstrn., 1980—. Served to lt. USN, 1943-46. Registered profl. engr., Pa. Mem. Am. Forestry Assn., Am. Def. Preparedness Assn., Am. Phys. Soc., IEEE, Soc. Plastics Engrs., Am. Mgmt. Assn., Yale Sci. and Engring. Assn., Nat. Council Univ. Research Adminstrs., Licensing Execs. Soc., Air Force Assn., Am. Legion, AAAS, Art Inst. Chgo., Community Concert Assn., Ga. Friends of Humanities, High Mus. Art, Hunter Mus. Art, Japan-Am. Soc. Ga., Nat. Trust Historic Preservation, Nat. Ret. Tchrs. Assn./Am. Assn. Ret. People, Assn. Pvt. Enterprise Edn., Rome Little Theatre, Rome Symphony, VFW, Sigma Xi, Tau Beta Pi. Clubs: Yale of Ga., Rotary. Home: PO Box 97 Mount Berry GA 30149 Office: Dept Research Berry College Mount Berry GA 30149

EVANS, TIMOTHY CRAIG, family therapist, clergyman; b. Waynesboro, Pa., June 20, 1958; s. John Edwin and Ruth Marie (Kriner) E. A.A., Hagerstown Jr. Coll., 1978; B.S., Oral Roberts U., 1979, M. Div., 1983; postgrad. Tex. Christian U., 1983-84; M.S., East Tex. State U., 1986. Ordained to ministry Assemblies of God Ch., 1985; cert. counselor Tex. Rehab. Commn. Asst. research technician Oral Roberts Med. Sch., Tulsa, 1977, jr. adj. instr. Oral Roberts U., 1979-82; psychol. aide County View Hosp., Broken Arrow, Okla., 1983; substance abuse counselor Help Is Possible, Dallas, 1985; family therapist H.E.B. Harris Hosp., Euless, Tex., 1984—; chaplain intern Hillcrest Med. Ctr., Tulsa, 1981-82, Baylor U. Med. Ctr., Dallas, 1983-84; spiritual care intern City of Faith Med. and Research Ctr., Tulsa, 1983; vol. assoc. pastor Christian Chapel, Tulsa, 1982-83. Mem. social action com. St. Mary's Catholic Ch., Tulsa, 1979; mem. nursing home ministry Christian Service Council, 1977-78; mem. bus ministry Maranatha Brethren Ch., Hagerstown, Md., 1975. Named Outstanding Young Man Am., U.S. Jaycees, 1981; Oral Roberts U. scholar, 1977-79, grantee, 1980-82. Mem. Assn. Clin. Pastoral Edn., Am. Assn. Counseling and Devel., Tex. Assn. Counseling and Devel., Assn. Chaplains of Tex., Tex. Mental Health Counselor Assn., Nat. Employment Counselor Assn., Assn. Religious and Value Issues in Counseling, Assn. Specialists in Group

Work, Am. Mental Health Counselors Assn., Am. Rehab. Counseling Assn., Nat. Assn. Alcoholism and Drug Abuse Counselors, Tex. Assn. Alcoholism and Drug Abuse Counselors. Democrat. Avocations: restoring classic cars and antique furniture; bicycling; writing poetry; table and board games. Home: 2106 Bennett Ave Apt 122 Dallas TX 75206 Office: HEB Harris Hosp Addiction Treatment Ctr 2219 W Euless Blvd Euless TX 76040

EVANS, TIMOTHY PAUL, accountant; b. Barnesville, Ga., Feb. 21, 1953; s. William Edgar and Sara Imogene (Wilson) E.; m. Deborah Jean Scarborough, Nov. 22, 1973; 1 dau., Jennifer Elizabeth. B.B.A. in Acctg., U. Ga., 1976, M.A.C.C. in Taxation, 1977. C.P.A., S.C. Tax supr. Ernst & Whinney, Greenville, S.C., 1977-82; tax mgr. Price Waterhouse Co., Atlanta, 1982-83, Peat, Marwick, Mitchell & Co., Greenville, 1983-85, Kidder, Peabody & Co. Inc., Atlanta, 1985—. Served to sgt. N.G., 1971-77. Mem. Am. Inst. C.P.A.s, S.C. Assn. C.P.A.s. Home: 3268 N Creekview Dr Lawrenceville GA 30245 also PO Box 1913 Lilburn GA 30247 Office: Kidder Peabody & Co Inc 2700 First Atlanta Tower Atlanta GA 30383

EVANS, TODD EDWIN, physicist, consultant physicist; b. Jackson, Mich., June 3, 1947; s. Harold Merel and Jane Nanette (Mounteer) E.; m. Michele Simone Deroulez, Aug. 20, 1981; 1 dau., Cassandra Nanette. B.S. with honors in Physics, Wright State U., 1978, B.S.E. in Engring., 1978; M.S. in Physics, U. Tex., 1979, Ph.D. in Physics and E.E., 1984. Research scientist Fusion Research Ctr., U. Tex., Austin, 1978-84, research engr. Electronics Research Ctr., 1978-83; instr. physics Austin (Tex.) Community Coll., 1979-80; research physicist Wright Patterson AFB, Dayton, Ohio, 1978; project engr. ITT, Springfield, Ohio, 1972-75; research scientist Fusion research Ctr. and Fusion Engring. Ctr. U. Tex., Austin, 1978—; cons. U. Tex., Austin, various high tech. firms, Austin. Mem. World Future Soc. Recipient Profl. Devel. award, U. Tex., 1982, H.L. Book Scholarship, 1979-81. Mem. IEEE, Am. Phys. Soc., Sigma Pi Sigma, Phi Kappa Phi. Contbr. articles to various publs. Office: Fusion Research Center U Tex Austin TX 78712

EVANS, VAN HOLLAND, minister; b. Danville, Ark., Feb. 18, 1924; m. Lenora Hanley, 1949; children—Linda, Joyce, Janet, Stephen. B.S. in Elec. Engring., La. Tech. U., 1949; M.R.E., New Orleans Bapt. Theol. Seminary, 1958. Dist. mgr. Cities Service Oil Co., 1949-53; ordained to ministry Baptist Ch., 1959; minister music and edn. First Bapt. Ch., Monticello, Ark., 1953-54, Sheffield, Ala. 1954-56; minister edn. and adminstrn. First Bapt. Ch., Gulfport, Miss., 1957-60; assoc. pastor in edn. and adminstrn. First Bapt. Ch., Bossier City, La., 1960-63; minister edn. and adminstrn. First Bapt. Ch., El Dorado, Ark., 1963—; v.p. Ark. Bapt. Family and Child Care Agy., 1976, pres., 1977, chmn. personnel com., 1979-84. Bd. dirs. United Way of Union County, Ark., 1981-84, chmn. budget allocations, 1981, 1st v.p., 1982, pres., 1983, mem. agys. relation bd., 1978-80; bd. dirs. and instr. Ark. Bapt. Coll. Extension Center, 1974-80. Mem. So. Bapt. Bus. Officers Conf., Ark-La-Tex chpt. Nat. Assn. Ch. Bus. Adminstrs., Liberty Bapt. Assn. (budget, fin., personnel, stewardship coms. 1978-83). Served with USN, 1943-46. Co-author: The El Dorado Plan; contbr. to religious mags. Home: 109 Stroud St El Dorado AR 71730 Office: 200 W Main St El Dorado AR 71730

EVANS-CLOUD, LINDA SUE, business educator; b. Bridgeport, Ala., Mar. 8, 1956; d. Ted Eugene and Betty Jean (Matthews) C.; m. Russell M. Evans, Jr., Mar. 17, 1984. B.S., U. North Ala., 1978; M.Ed., Memphis State U., 1979, postgrad., 1979—. Grad. teaching asst. Memphis State U., 1979-80; instr. office adminstrn. dept. Coll. Bus., Austin Peay State U., Clarksville, Tenn., 1980-83, asst. prof., 1983—; office occupations instr. Summer Youth Employment program, 1981-82; cons. publs. div. Tenn. Sec. of State Dept., 1981. Bd. dirs. Cumberland River March of Dimes, 1983—. Mem. AAUW (scholar 1983—), Nat. Bus. Edn. Assn., So. Bus. Edn. Assn., Tenn. Bus. Edn. Assn., Am. Bus. Communication Assn., Delta Pi Epsilon. Mem. Ch. of Christ. Clubs: Univ. Women's. Office: PO Box 4477 Austin Peay State Univ Clarksville TN 37044

EVATT, PARKER, state representative, association executive; b. Greenville, S.C., Aug. 27, 1935; s. H.D. and Ruby (Parker) E.; m. Jane Mangum, Sept. 2, 1960; children—Katherine, Alan. B.S., U. S.C., 1958, M.Criminal Justice, 1978; LL.D. (hon.), Presbyterian Coll., 1977. Exec. dir. Alston Wilkes Soc., Columbia, S.C., since 1966—; mem. S.C. Ho. of Reps., 1975—. Mem. adminstrv. bd. Virginia Wingary Meml., United Methodist Ch., del. to gen. conf., 1972, del. to jurisdiction confs., 1972, 76, 80, 84; past lay leader Columbia Meth. Dist. Served with USN, 1958-60. Recipient numerous awards and citations from civic, religious and profl. orgns. Mem. S.C. Youth Workers Assn. (past pres.), Christian Action Council (bd. govs. 1968-71), St. Andrews Jaycees (life), Nat. Assn. Social Workers (named Citizen of Yr. S.C. chpt. 1978), Internat. Halfway Assn. (v.p. 1973-76), Res. Officers Assn. (v.p. Columbia chpt.), Naval Res. Assn. (past pres. Carolina chpt.), Pi Kappa Alpha. Lodge: Rotary. *

EVERETT, ANN NEVAREZ, religious educator; b. Uvalde, Tex., Aug. 10, 1915; d. Severo Nevarez and Dorothy (Canales) N.; m. Howard Devire Everett, Oct. 16, 1947; children—Howard Devire Jr., Mary Ann, James Joseph. Student Sch. Ministry, 1974-77. Chmn. internat. affairs Archdiocesan Council Catholic Women, San Antonio, 1979-81; Western Deanery Cath. Women, San Antonio, 1976-81; chmn., counselor of Respect Life, San Antonio, 1979-85; local chmn. Telethon Navideno, San Antonio, 1983-84; instr. religious edn. Confraternity Christian Doctrine, San Antonio, 1973-85. Recipient Archbishop Francis Furey medal Archdiocese of San Antonio, 1977, Leadership Course award Our Lady of Angels Ch., San Antonio, 1982, Vol. Dedication award Elizabeth Seton Home, San Antonio, 1984. Republican. Roman Catholic. Avocations: swimming; bowling; crocheting. Home: 2034 Bronte San Antonio TX 78207

EVERETT, KARL MENOHER, JR., health policy administrator, educator; b. Latrobe, Pa., Aug. 13, 1935; s. Karl Menoher and Nell Irene (McCullough) E.; R.N. with honors, div. nursing, Coll. Medicine, N.Y. U., 1958; grad. U.S. Fgn. Service Inst., Washington, 1970-71; B.A. cum laude, U. Md., 1974; M.A., U. Okla., 1982, doctoral studies, 1982—; m. June Kay Lenz, Dec. 10, 1960; children—Dianna Lynn, Christopher Douglas. Instr. clin. urology Coll. Medicine, div. nursing N.Y. U., N.Y.C., 1958-59; mem. staffs N.Y. U.-Bellevue Med. Center, N.Y.C., 1955-59, N.Y. U. Postgrad. Hosp., N.Y.C., 1958-59; commd. 2d. lt. U.S. Army, 1959, advanced through grades to maj., 1967; served Brooke Army Med. Center, San Antonio, 1959, Walter Reed Army Med. Center, Washington, 1959-60, Vets. Hosp. Center, Norman, 1977-82; intelligence officer Dept. Def., apptd. mem. ad hoc com. Nat. Security Council, 1968-69; pvt. negotiator UN Command, Korea, with People's Republic of China and Dem. People's Republic Korea, 1971-75; dir. Directorate of Security F.A. Center and Ft. Sill, Okla., 1975-77, ret., 1979; pres., chmn. bd. dirs. Okla. World Cons., Inc., Norman, 1977-78; sr. assoc. Karl M. Everett & Assocs., Norman, 1979—; cons. N.E. Asian bus. affairs Am. U., Washington, 1975-80; lectr. comparative internat. jud. systems overseas br. Los Angeles City Coll., 1975; mem. vis. faculty John F. Kennedy Center, Fayetteville, N.C., 1977-80; bd. dirs. SEC LTD, Rockville, Md., 1974-77. Mem. Cleveland County Christmas Store, Norman, 1977-80; bd. dirs. Cleveland County Mental Health Assn., 1979-82, chmn. public affairs com., 1979-80, pres., 1981-82; del. Okla. White House Conf. on Aging, 1981; mem. exec. com. Cleveland County Republican Com., 1981; presenter paper Mid-Am Congress on Aging, 1981; chmn. bd. dirs. Citizens for Honest and Responsive Govt., 1982-84. Decorated Bronze Star, Joint Services Commendation medal; recipient Ogden D. Mills scholarship award, 1958, various U.S. mil. awards, ministerial level awards Govt. Republic of Korea. Mem. N.Y. Acad. Scis., Am. Acad. Polit. and Social Scis., Am. Soc. Pub. Adminstrn., Am. Soc. Law and Medicine. Pi Alpha Alpha, Alpha Kappa Delta. Lodges: Masons (Mystic Circle, Lawrence, Ind.), Scottish Rite, Shrine (Everett, Wash.), Shrine Club of Korea (life). Researcher hemodialysis and cardiac catheterization, 1955-58; contbr. articles on socio-polit.-econ. problems Cambodia and S.E. Asia to publs. Home: 1305 Spruce Dr Norman OK 73072

EVERETT, MICHAEL, seafood company official; b. Miami, Fla., Dec. 9, 1940; s. Hobart Robley and Lillian Bernice (Farwig) E.; m. Barbara Blank Feb. 14, 1962; children—Katherine, Michael R., Richard. B.Acctg., U. Tampa, 1967. Controller, Seabrook Internat. Foods, Tampa, Fla., 1967-78, gen. mgr., 1978-80; asst. v.p. Kitchen Ready Foods, Tampa, 1981; controller Reilly Dairy Foods, Tampa, 1981-82; plant mgr. Nat. Sea Products, Tampa, 1983—. Served with U.S. Army, 1959-61. Mem. Nat. Assn. Accts. (dir. 1983-84). Republican. Lutheran. Home: 4409 Sevilla St Tampa FL 33629 Office: Nat Sea Products US Corp Ltd 1356 Shoreline Ave Tampa FL 33605

EVERETT, MICHAEL DAVID, marketing and transportation educator; b. Cin., Jan. 30, 1938; s. Rollin H. and Eleanor (Sutermeister) E.; m. Caryl Ann Reed, May 24, 1964; children—Eric Reed, Alexander Myer. A.B., Washington U., St. Louis, 1960, Ph.D. in Econs., 1967. Instr. El Colegio de Mex., 1967-68; asst. prof. Fla. State U., Tallahassee, 1968-73; assoc. prof. U. So. Miss., Hattiesburg, 1973-77, East Tenn. State U., Johnson City, 1977—; mem. Transp. Research Bd., Washington, 1973-84; cons. on bicycle transp. and recreation systems; lectr. in field. Contbr. articles to profl. jours. Active civil rights movement, early 1960s; set up workshops studying peasant economies central Mex., late 1960s, early 1970s; analyst, cons. econ. impact of mil. build-up. Served with U.S. Army, 1956. NDEA fellow, 1962-67; Washington U. fellow; winner age group Warriors Path Triathlon, Tenn., 1983, 84. Mem. Am. Econ. Assn., Am. Soc. Traffic and Transp. (cert. examination com. 1978-84), Am. Mktg. Assn., So. Mktg. Assn. (award for outstanding paper on edn. 1982), Tri Cities Road Club. Democrat. Home: 5 Horseshoe Bend Johnson City TN 37601 Office: East Tenn State U Dept Mktg and Mgmt Johnson City TN 37601

EVERETT, ROBERT NATHAN, hotel purchasing manager; b. Oak Grove, La., Nov. 28, 1950; s. William Freeman and Rose Lee (Smith) E.; m. Pamela Joy Perkins, Nov. 20, 1980 (div. 1982). B.S., U. Ala., 1972; postgrad., Jacksonville U., 1972-73. Owner, mgr. Ind. Restaurants, Birmingham, Ala., 1973-76; project devel. officer Holiday Inns Inc., Memphis, 1976-79; food and beverage dir. Sheraton Hotels, Atlanta, 1979-83; cons. Piccadilly Cafeterias, Baton Rouge, 1983-85; purchasing mgr. Hilton Hotels Corp., New Orleans, 1985—. Sec. Young Republicans, Tuscaloosa, Ala., 1972; treas. Civitans Internat., Birmingham, 1976. Recipient Outstanding Menu award Diners Club Internat., 1974, Best Restaurants of Southwest award Travel Holiday Mag., 1975. Fellow Le Comite Nat. des Vins de France; mem. Internat. Food Service Execs. Assn., Atlanta Jaycees. Episcopalian. Avocation: international competition in horse show jumping events. Office: Hilton Hotels Corp 2 Poydras St New Orleans LA 70140

EVERHART, ROBERT LEE, accountant, financial and tax planner; b. Thomasville, N.C., Oct. 31, 1951; s. Arthur Lee, Jr. and Mary Grey (Ward) E.; m. Sandra Kay Yokeley, Aug. 15, 1971; 1 child, Kristen Michelle. Student U. N.C.-Chapel Hill, 1969-70; B.S., U. N.C.-Greensboro, 1973. Sr. acct. Bruce Hall & Co., Winston-Salem, N.C., 1973-78; ptnr. Booker Everhart & Co., P.C., Winston-Salem, 1978—; instr. taxation seminars, Winston-Salem, 1978-83; instr. acctg. Patrick Henry Community Coll., Martinsville, Va., 1980. Active Congl. Club, Raleigh, N.C., 1980—. Fellow N.C. Assn. C.P.A.s, Va. Soc. C.P.A.s; mem. Am. Inst. C.P.A.s. Republican. Baptist. Avocations: family; sports; travel. Home: Route 12 Box 158 Winston-Salem NC 27107 Office: Booker Everhart & Co PC PO Box 11004 4680 Brownsboro Rd Winston-Salem NC 27116

EVERS, JANELLA MAGEE (JAN), nurse educator; b. Tylertown, Miss., Sept. 29, 1938; d. Wade Lampton and Lena Mae (Walters) Magee; m. Carl Gustav Evers, July 10, 1960; children—Karen Alicia, Julie Anne, Carl Gustav. B.S. in Nursing, U. Miss., 1960, M.Nursing, 1973. R.N., Miss. Staff nurse Univ. Hosp.-U. Miss. Med. Ctr., Jackson, 1960-62, adminstrv. asst., 1962-72, asst. dir., 1972-73, clin. nurse specialist, 1973; dir. continuing edn. Sch. Nursing, U. Miss., Jackson, 1975-77, asst. dean, 1977-78, assoc. dean, 1978—; mem. So. Council Collegiate Edn. for Nursing. Bd. dirs. Miss. div. Am. Cancer Soc.; mem. profl. edn. com. Miss. affiliate Am. Heart Assn.; ch. organist. Named Alumnae of Yr., U. Miss. Nursing Chpt., 1976; named to U. Miss. Sch. Nursing Honor Soc., 1983. Mem. Am. Nurses Assn., Guardian Soc. of U. Miss. Miss. Nurses Assn., State Instns. Higher Learning Deans and Dirs. Council, Univ. Med. Ctr. Women, Miss. State Med. Assn. Aux., U. Miss Alumni and Guardian Soc., Jackson Symphony League, Am. Guild Organists (subdean). Lutheran. Club: Revelers (Jackson). Home: 4458 Wedgewood St Jackson MS 39211 Office: 2500 North State St Jackson MS 39216

EVERSON, STEVEN DONALD, veterinarian; b. Cin., Jan. 16, 1950; s. Charles Donald and Laura Perrin (Wilson) E.; m. Debra Ann Gisclair, Sept. 9, 1972; children—Bradley, Jeffrey. B.A., La. State U., 1972, D.V.M., 1979; postgrad. La. State U.-Shreveport, 1973-75. Assoc. veterinarian Summer Grove Animal Hosp., Shreveport, 1979-84; ptnr. Kingston Rd. Animal Clinic, Shreveport, 1984—; lab. animal cons. La. State U. Med. Sch., Shreveport, 1979-84. Mem. Northwest La. Vet. Med. Assn. (sec.-treas. 1982-83), La. Vet. Med. Assn. (Meml. scholar 1977), AVMA, Phi Kappa Phi, Phi Zeta. Democrat. Roman Catholic. Lodge: Elks. Avocations: yachting; tennis; fishing.

EVETT, RUSSELL DOUGHERTY, physician; b. Norfolk, Va., Feb. 1, 1932; s. Edward Hall and Elizabeth (Dougherty) E.; B.S., Randolph-Macon Coll., 1953; M.D., Med. Coll. Va., 1957; M.S. in Medicine, Mayo Clinic and U. Minn., 1963; m. Mary Gail Kirby, Aug. 18, 1956; children—Stephen, Anne, Gail, John. Intern, DePaul Hosp., Norfolk, 1957-58; fellow in internal medicine Mayo Clinic, Rochester, Minn., 1960-63; pvt. practice internal medicine, Norfolk, 1964—; pres. med. staff Leigh Meml. Hosp., Norfolk, 1970-72; chmn. dept. internal medicine Norfolk Gen. Hosp., 1972-74; asso. prof. medicine Eastern Va. Med. Sch., 1974—; mem. staff Med. Center Hosps., Chesapeake Gen. Hosp., DePaul Hosp. Served with USNR, 1958-60. Diplomate Am. Bd. Internal Medicine. Fellow ACP; mem. Va. Gastroenterol. Soc. (pres. 1975-77), Norfolk Acad. Medicine (pres. 1976-77), Med. Soc. Va., AMA, So. Med. Assn., Phi Beta Kappa, Omicron Delta Kappa, Alpha Omega Alpha. Methodist. Clubs: Norfolk Yacht and Country, Harbor. Home: 6147 Studeley Ave Norfolk VA 23508 Office: 530 Wainwright Bldg Norfolk VA 23510

EWALT, GEORGE W., electrical contracting company executive; b. Balt., May 25, 1935; s. George W. E. and Lilly (Harrison) Floyd Ewalt; m. Patricia C. Ewalt, Sept. 30, 1961; children—Gretchen Walther, Paige Noel. B.S., U. Md.; postgrad., George Washington U. Contract adminstr., program coordinator Melpar, Inc., Washington, 1969-71; v.p. facilities mgmt. Dynalectron Corp., McLean, Va., 1971-73, group v.p., 1973-77, sr. v.p., 1977-85, exec. v.p., chief operating officer, 1985—. Mem. Am. Mgmt. Assn., Nat. Elec. Contractors Assn., Nat. Joint Apprenticeship and Tng. Com. for Elec. Industry. Home: Route 4 Box 518 Leesburg VA 22075 Office: Dynalectron Corp 1313 Dolley Madison Blvd McLean VA 22101

EWELL, BARBARA CLAIRE, literature and English language educator; b. Baton Rouge, Mar. 10, 1947; d. Dave Haas and Ruth Chloe (Guidry) E.; m. Jerry Lane Speir, May 20, 1979. B.A. summa cum laude, U. Dallas, 1969; Ph.D., U. Notre Dame, South Bend, Ind., 1974. Asst. prof. Loyola U., New Orleans, part-time, 1974-75; instr. English, Newcomb College, Tulane U., New Orleans, 1975-76, asst. prof. English, Univ. Coll., 1976-79; asst. prof. English, U. Miss., Oxford, 1979-84; assoc. prof. English, City Coll., Loyola U., New Orleans, 1984—; cons. to pub. relations firms; tech. writing instr. for programs Tulane U. Grad. Sch. Bus., 1977-79. Woodrow Wilson fellow, 1969, 72-73; NDEA fellow, 1969-72; Monticello Coll. Found. fellow, Newberry Library, 1982-83; Am. Council of Learned Socs. grantee, 1983. Mem. MLA, South Central MLA, S.E. Women's Studies Assn., Renaissance Soc. Am., South Central Renaissance Conf., MLA Women's Caucus. Democrat. Roman Catholic. Home: 1024 Dante St New Orleans LA 70118 Office: City College Loyola Univ 6363 St Chas Ave New Orleans LA 70118

EWELL, BOBBY EARL, health care administrator, financial advisor; b. Little Rock, Sept. 5, 1939; s. Boyce Henry Ewell and Mable Lee (Taylor) Simms; m. Eldora Marie Gary, Sept. 5, 1980; 1 child, Summer Melody. B.S., Ark. Poly., 1971. Commd. hospitalman E-1 U.S. Navy, 1956; advanced through grades to hosp. corpsman 2d class, 1966; field rep. Gen. Elec. Credit Corp., Little Rock, 1971-72; credit mgr., br. mgr. Borg-Warner Acpt. Lafayette, La., Houston, 1971-77; fin. mgr., adminstr. Humana Inc., Erath, La., 1977-80; chief exec. officer, adminstr. Erath Gen. Hosp., 1980—; cons., adminstr. Regent Health System, Colorado Springs, Colo., 1984—; cons. Epsilon Sigma Alpha, Abbeville, La.; sec. of governing body, bd. dirs. Erath Gen. Hosp., 1980—. Mem. Am. Coll. Hosp. Adminstrs., La. Fedn. Hosp. (bd. dirs. 1984, sec. 1984—); Republican. Roman Catholic. Avocations: golf; deer hunting. Address: Erath Langlinais Ln Abbeville LA 70510 Home: 329 Langlinais Ln Abbeville LA 70510 Office: Erath Gen Hosp 504 N Broadway Erath LA 70533

EWIN, GORDON OVERTON, lawyer, farmer; b. New Orleans, June 1, 1923; s. James Perkins and Lucille Havard (Scott) E.; m. Katharine Elise Keller, Sept. 6, 1947; 1 dau., Katharine Adair. B.A., Tulane U., 1943, J.D., 1948; postgrad. Faculté de Droit, U. Paris, 1948-49. Bar: La. 1948, U.S. Dist. Ct. (ea. dist.) La. 1949, U.S. Ct. Appeals (5th cir.) 1949. Assoc. Milling, Saal, Saunders, Benson & Woodward, New Orleans, 1949-52; ptnr. Ewin & Robertson, New Orleans, 1952-55; staff atty. Humble Oil & Refining Co., New Orleans, 1955-59; ptnr. Chaffe, McCall, Phillips, Toler & Sarpy, New Orleans, 1959—; pres. Greenwood Planting Co., 1979—; dir. Farmers Bank & Trust Co., Cheneyville, La. Bd. dirs. New Orleans Philharm. Orch., 1961; mem. Young Life Adv. Council, 1972; bd. dirs. Garden Dist. Assn., 1967-74, pres., 1973-74; bd. dirs. Friends of the Cabildo, 1976-82, pres., 1981-82. Served to lt. (j.g.) USNR, 1943-46; PTO. Mem. New Orleans Bar Assn. (treas.), La. Bar Assn., ABA. Republican. Episcopalian. (vestryman Trinity Ch. 1976-80). Clubs: La., Boston (New Orleans); Soc. Colonial Wars (past gov.). Home: 1220 Antoine St New Orleans LA 70115 Office: 210 Baronne St 1500 First NBC Bldg New Orleans LA 70112

EWING, GEORGE H., transmission company executive; b. San Antonio, June 11, 1925; s. H.L. and Miriam (Galloway) E.; B.C.E., Tex. A. and M. U., 1948; m. Doris Ann Cannan, May 31, 1947; children—Susan, Beverly, Mary, Bryan. With Tex. Eastern Transmission Corp., Houston, 1948—, chief plans and research div., 1956-58, supervising engr., 1958-64, v.p., chief engr., 1965-71, v.p. engring. and supplemental fuels, 1971-76, sr. v.p. gas supply, 1976; pres., chief exec. officer Tex. Eastern Gas Pipeline Co., 1979—, Transwestern Pipeline Co., 1979—. Served with USNR, 1943-46. Registered profl. engr., La. Mem. ASME, Am. Gas Assn., Ind. Natural Gas Assn. Houston. Presbyterian. Club: Petroleum (Houston). Home: 502 W Forest St Houston TX 77079 Office: PO Box 2521 Houston TX 77252

EWING, JOHN KIRBY, realtor, independent oil operator, investor; b. Mercedes, Tex., Apr. 23, 1923; s. Emile Kelty and Edna Lillian (Olson) E.; student U.S. Naval Acad., 1941-42; B.A., U. Tex., 1946; m. Virginia Wilson, Oct. 2, 1970; children—Steven Calder, Charlotte Kelty, Robin Virginia, Holly Hammond. Staff asst. to gov. of Tex., 1943-46; asst. purchasing agt. Estate of John H. Shary, Mission, Tex., 1946-47; mortgage banker David C. Bintliff & Co., Inc., Houston, 1947-52; self-employed bldg. contractor and residential subdiv. developer, Houston, 1952-54; mortgage loan mgr. Ringer Properties, Inc., Houston, 1954-57; partner Curtis & Ewing, realtors, Houston, 1957—; sales cons. Wilson Mfg. Co., Inc., oilwell drilling and servicing equipment, Wichita Falls, Tex., 1970-74, dir., 1973-77, v.p., 1974-75, pres., 1975-76; pres. Wichita Clutch Co., 1975-76; pres., dir. Mt. Royal Mining & Exploration Co., 1973—, Old Ontario Mining Co., 1973-77. Active local Boy Scouts Am., 1935-63, chmn. Buffalo Dist. Friends of Scouting, 1962-81, Western div. show chmn., 1977, bd. dirs. Sam Houston Area council, 1980—, div. B chmn., 1980-82, chmn. orgn. council ops., 1983, v.p. fin., mem. exec. com., 1984; active fund raising United Way, 1950-51, 55. Election judge Harris County, 1958-64; sec. credentials com. Tex. Democratic Com., 1952, mem. Harris County exec. com., 1958-65, del. convs., 1952-64; bd. dirs. Mental Health Assn. Houston, 1969-74, pres., 1970-73; bd. dirs. Tex. Assn. Mental Health, 1970—; chmn. NBC-ARC CPR Race for Life Project, 1981; chmn. safety services com. Greater Houston chpt. ARC, 1981-84, bd. dirs., del. conv., 1982, spl. events chmn. Health Awareness Week with Harris County Med. Soc., Shell Oil Co., and Channel KTR-TV, 1982. Recipient Disting. Service award Nat. Assn. Mental Health, 1973, Silver Beaver award Boy Scouts Am., 1983. Mem. Houston Bd. Realtors, Nat. Assn. Real Estate Bds., Am. Foundrymen's Soc., Tex. Assn. Realtors, U.S. Naval Acad. Alumni Assn. (past pres., dir. Houston chpt., nat. trustee 1981—, v.p. central region 1983—), Nat. Rifle Assn. (life), Am. Legion, Bayou Rifles, Silver Spur, Kappa Alpha Order, Pi Sigma Alpha. Methodist (ofcl. bd. 1966-68, 69-71, 72-74, 78-80, 82—). Clubs: Masons, Kiwanis (dir. Houston 1967-69). Home: 1508 Kirby Dr Houston TX 77019 Office: 616 Southwest Tower 707 McKinney Ave Houston TX 77002

EWING, MARTHA MCCRACKEN, counselor, psychology educator; b. Little Rock, July 29, 1952; d. Mark Maurice and Dorothy (Carson) McCracken; m. George E. Ewing, Jr., Apr. 17, 1981. B.A. magna cum laude, Am. Christian Coll., 1974; M.S., U. Tex.-Dallas, 1979; postgrad. Columbia U., 1984—. Asst. prof. psychology, Am. Christian Coll., Tulsa, 1975-77; grad. asst. Univ. Tex.-Dallas, Richardson, 1978-79; assoc. registrar Eastfield Coll., Mesquite, Tex., 1979-81, adj. prof., 1979—; counselor, prof. DeVry Inst. Tech., Dallas, 1984—. Author: Evaluation of Counseling Program, 1979; (with others) Assessment of Prior Learning, 1981. Recipient Outstanding Employee award DeVry Inst. Tech., 1985. Mem. Am. Assn. for Counseling and Devel., Assn. for Measurement and Evaluation in Counseling; Tex. Assn. for Counseling and Devel., North Tex. Council of Coll. Registrar's and Admission Officers, Nat. Assn. for Women Deans, Adminstrs. and Counselors. Republican. Avocations: swimming; needlepoint. Home: PO Box 190912 Dallas TX 75219 Office: DeVry Inst Tech 4250 N Beltline Rd Irving TX 75038

EWING, THOMAS EDWARD, petroleum consulting executive, geologist; b. Elgin, Ill., Aug. 6, 1954; s. Galen Wood and Alice (Sipple) E.; m. Linda Anne Lewis Son, Oct. 6, 1984; 1 child, Christina Anne. B.A., Colorado Coll., 1975; M.S., N.Mex. I.M.T., 1977; Ph.D., U. B.C., Can., 1980. Research scientist assoc. U. Tex.-Bur. Econ. Geology, Austin, 1980-81, research assoc., 1981-85; pres., dir. research Frontera Exploration Services, San Antonio, 1985—; lectr. Profl. Seminar Group, Midland, Tex., 1984. Author: Hackberry Sandstone Reservoirs, 1984. Editor: Gulf Coast Association of Geological Societies Transactions, 1985. Contbr. articles to profl. jours. Mem. Austin Choral Union, Tex., 1981-84. Nat. Merit scholar, 1971. Mem. Am. Assn. Petroleum Geologists (A.I. Levorsen award Gulf Coast sect. 1982). Geol. Soc. Am., Geol. Assn. Can., Am. Geophys. Union, Assn. Geoscientist Internat. Devel., Phi Beta Kappa. Baha'i. Club: Nature Conservancy (Tex.). Avocations: choral music, history, geography. Home: 1403 Aylsbury St San Antonio TX 78216 Office: Frontera Exploration Services 900 NE Loop 410 Suite D303 San Antonio TX 78209

EWTON, LELIA CHRISTIE, educator; b. Ringgold, Ga., Dec. 7, 1949; d. LeLand Leonidas and Ruth (Dills) Christie; children—Michael Farrell, Leland Clay, Justin Heath. A.A. in Edn., Dalton Jr. Coll., 1968; B.S., U. Tenn.-Chattanooga, 1971; M.Ed., Berry Coll., 1975; Ed.S., W. Ga. Coll., 1982; Ed.D. candidate U. Ga. Tchr., Whitfield County Schs., Dalton, Ga., 1971—; part-time lectr. Chattanooga State Tech. Community Coll., 1983—. Dalton Jr. Coll. Found. scholar, 1967; Regent's scholar, 1968. Mem. Whitfield Edn. Assn., Ga. Assn. Educators, NEA, Am. Fedn. Tchrs., Ga. Fedn. Tchrs., Whitfield Fedn. Tchrs., Kappa Delta Pi, Alpha Delta Kappa, Phi Delta Kappa. Democrat. Episcopalian. Home: 217 Lakeview Dr Rossville GA 30741 Office: 1815 Utility Rd Rocky Face GA 30740

EWY, MARVIN ROY, insurance company executive; b. Newton, Kans., Nov. 18, 1934; s. Waldo and Sarah Alma (Dirks) E.; m. Rebecca May Springer, Nov. 27, 1955 (div. 1982); children—Duane Dee, Janice Lynn; m. 2d Diana Rae Simpson, June 10, 1983. B.S.E., Kans. State Tchrs. Coll., 1959, M.S., 1960, postgrad., 1960-63. C.L.U. Asst. prof. history East Central State U., Ada, Okla., 1963-66; agt., gen. agt. then regional mgr. Nat. Educator Life Ins. Co., Ft. Worth, 1966-70; with Am. Fidelity Assurance Co., Oklahoma City, 1970—, asst. sec., 1974-75, asst. v.p., 1975-79, 2d v.p., 1979-82, v.p., 1982—; adj. prof. bus. Oklahoma City Community Coll. Bd. dirs., mem. exec. com. Okla. Council on Econ. Edn., 1978—, treas., 1979-82, pres., 1986—; bd. dirs. Community Health Centers, Inc., 1975-81, sec.-treas., 1979-81. Mem. Am. Soc. C.L.U.s, Nat. Assn. Life Underwriters, Pi Kappa Alpha. Author: Charles Curtis of Kansas: Vice President of the United States, 1929-1933, 1961. Home: 4916 McMillan Ave Bethany OK 73008 Office: 2000 Classen Center Oklahoma City OK 73106

EXELBERT, MICHAEL MARK, educational administrator; b. Bklyn., Nov. 30, 1948; s. Fred and Eva Vilma (Singer) E.; m. Lois Maxine Love, June 21, 1970; children—Eric, Janet, Ian, Brian. B.Ed., U. Miami (Fla.), 1970, M.Ed., 1975. Tchr., Dade County Public Schs. (Fla.), 1970-75, dist. adminstrv. coordinator exceptional student edn., 1975-77, ednl. planner, 1977-79, dist. budget specialist exceptional student edn., 1979-82; dist. supr. Home Hosp. and Alternative Telecommunication Instrns. Ctr., Dade County Pub. Schs., Miami, 1982—; coordinator spl. programs Fla. Internat. U., Miami, 1973-75; dir. habilitation program for exceptional adults Miami Dade Community Coll. North, Miami, 1972-74; chmn. Fla. Com. for Home and Hospitalized, 1975—; mem. Metro Dade Local Rev. Panel for Services and Demonstration Project for Paratransit Devel.; co-chmn. Occupational Inst. Handicapped, Fla. Internat. U.; mem. adv. bd. Metatherapy Inst. regional commr. Am. Youth Soccer Orgn.; past pres. South Dade Hebrew Acad.; mem. exec. bd. Temple Zion; mem. Pres.'s Com. for Employment Handicapped. Recipient McDonald award Fla. Rehab. Assn., 1973; citation Fla. Gov.'s Com. for Employing Handicapped, 1975. Mem. Assn. Devel. Exceptional (past pres., chmn. bd.), Assn. Retarded Citizens, Miami U. Alumni Assn., Council Exceptional Children (past pres. state div. physically handicapped, dir.), Fla. Home Hosp. Tchrs. and

Adminstrs. Assn. (past pres.), Phi Delta Kappa. Democrat. Lodges: Masons (past master), B'nai B'rith. Author: How to Travel By Bus, 1975. Home: 9405 SW 89th St Miami FL 33176 Office: 47 Zamora Ave Coral Gables FL 33124

EXUM, JAMES GOODEN, JR., state supreme court justice; b. Snow Hill, N.C., Sept. 14, 1935; s. James Gooden and Mary Wall (Bost) E.; B.A., U. N.C., Chapel Hill, 1957; LL.B., N.Y. U., 1960; m. Judith McNeill Jamison, June 29, 1963; children—James Gooden, Steven Jamison, Mary March Williams. Bar: N.C. 1960. Law clk. to Chief Justice Emery Denny, N.C. Supreme Ct., 1960-61; assoc. firm Smith, Moore, Smith, Schell & Hunter, Greensboro, N.C., 1961-67; resident judge Superior Ct., 1967-74; assoc. justice N.C. Supreme Ct., Raleigh, 1975—; adj. faculty Law Sch. U. N.C., 1977, 81, 82, 83, 85; chmn. N.C. Jud. Council, 1979-81. Rep. N.C. Gen. Assembly, 1967; vice chmn. central selection com. Morehead Scholarships; parliamentarian Episcopal Diocese N.C., 1978-83. Served to capt. USAR, 1963-67. Recipient Disting. Service award Greensboro Jaycees, 1969, Psi Disting. Achievement and Service award Psi chpt. Sigma Nu, 1974; Morehead Scholar; Root Tilden Scholar. Mem. ABA (council criminal justice sect. 1981-85, chmn. death penalty cost study com.), N.C. Bar Assn. Wake County bar assns. Democrat. Clubs: Raleigh Racquet, Capital City; Milburnie Fishing. Home: 2240 Wheeler Rd Raleigh NC 27607 Office: PO Box 1841 Raleigh NC 27602

EYBERG, SHEILA MAXINE, psychology educator; b. Omaha, Nebr., Dec. 31, 1944; d. Clarence George and Geraldine Elizabeth (Gilbert) E. B.A., U. Omaha, 1967; M.A., U. Oreg., 1970, Ph.D., 1972. Lic. psychologist, Oreg., Fla. Intern in med. psychology Oreg. Health Scis. U., Portland, 1971-72, resident in pediatric psychology, 1972-74, asst. prof. med. psychology, 1974-81, assoc. prof., 1981-85, dir. child psychology outpatient clinic, 1974-85; prof. clin. psychology U. Fla., Gainesville, 1985—. Mem. editorial bd. Jour. Pediatric Psychology, 1977—, Jour. Clin. Child Psychology, 1982—. Contbr. articles to profl. jours. Fellow Am. Psychol. Assn. (pres.-elect sect. 1, div. 12, 1986); mem. Alpha Lambda Delta, Phi Kappa Phi. Clubs: Multnomah Athletic, Mountain Park Raquet (Portland). Office: Dept Clin Psychology U Fla Box J-165 JHMHC Gainesville FL 32610

EYZAGUIRRE, RAMON CESPEDES, manufacturing engineer; b. Santa Cruz, Bolivia, Aug. 31, 1943; came to U.S., 1975, naturalized, 1979; s. Armengol and Edith E.; m. Leticia M. Carrillo, June 10, 1967; children—Alan, Sherry, Yvette. B.S. in Mech. Engring., U. Major San Andres, Bolivia, 1967. Cert. mfg. engr. Tool designer Jet Avion Corp. div. Heinicke Instruments Co., Hollywood, Fla., 1976-79, tooling and mfg. engr., 1979-81, chief engr. Jet Avion Corp. and Heinicke Instruments Co., 1981-83, v.p. engring., 1983—. Mem. Soc. Mfg. Engrs. (sr. mem). Republican. Office: Heinicke Instruments Co PO Box 7209 Hollywood FL 33021

EZELL, JEFF DON, psychologist; b. Corpus Christi, Tex., Oct. 4, 1954; s. Dee Earl and Eileen (Day) E. B.A. in Psychology, U. Tex., 1975; M.S. in Psychology, Tex. Christian U., 1978, Ph.D. in Psychology, 1981. Lic. psychologist, Tex. Psychol. assoc. Tarrant County Mental Health-Mental Retardation, Ft. Worth, 1977-80; staff psychologist Colo. West Regional Mental Health Ctr., Grand Junction, 1980-82; psychologist Ft. Worth Ind. Sch. Dist., 1982-84; dir. adolescent treatment Beaumont Neurol. Hosp., Tex., 1984—; cons. Tex. Dept. Human Resources, Tarrant County, 1978-80, 82-84, Child Protection Team, Grand Junction, 1981-82, Placement Alternative Commn., Grand Junction, 1981-82. Editor: Classroom Management with Handicapped Students, 1984. Mem. Am. Psychol. Assn., Am. Acad. Behavioral Medicine (diplomate), Southeast Tex. Psychol. Assn. Democrat. Anglican. Office: Beaumont Neurol Hosp 3250 Fannin St Beaumont TX 77701

FABER, CHARLES PHILIP, investment company executive; b. Sheboygan, Wis., Aug. 1, 1941; s. Charles W. and Bernetta P. (Metscher) F.; m. Jane E. Schneider, Dec. 22, 1962; children—Charles R., David R. B.B.A. (Dow-Corning scholar), U. Wis., 1966, M.B.A., 1967. Field rep. Caterpillar Tractor Co., Peoria, Ill., 1967-68; mktg. mgr. Apache Corp., Mpls., 1969-72, sales rep., 1973-74; gen. mgr. Apache Programs, Inc., Mpls., 1974-76, br. mgr., Milw., 1976-77; exec. v.p., dir. Investment Search, Inc., Annapolis, Md., 1978-82; chmn., dir. Samson Securities Co., 1983—; pres., dir. Samson Properties, Inc., Tulsa, 1984—; dir. Samson Resources Co. Served with U.S. Army, 1961-63. Mem. Internat. Assn. Fin. Planners, Assn. for Continuing Edn. in Bus., Nat. Assn. Securities Dealers (lic. prin.), Beta Gamma Sigma. Home: 4540 E 85th St Tulsa OK 74137

FABER, CORDELIA HANNER, bookseller; b. Toledo, Oct. 9, 1929; d. Julius Carroll and Winona Bernice (Lam) Hanner; m. Charles Thomas McLees, June 12, 1955 (div. 1968); children—Cordelia Elise, Charles Thomas Jr., Michael Blake, Winona Dawn; m. John Albert Faber, Mar. 21, 1969; stepchildren—Scott, Susan. Student Clemson U., 1955-57; A.B. in Edn., Greensboro Coll., 1959. Dir., Univ. Kindergarten Nursery, Chapel Hill, N.C., 1959-60; tchr. Hope Valley Sch., Durham, N.C., 1960-65, Seven Pines Sch., Richmond, Va., 1965-71; owner, operator The Book Trader, Greensboro, N.C., 1971-85. Active, Old Greensborough Preservation Soc., Greensboro, 1979—, Friends of the Carolinas, Greensboro, 1980—, The First Baptist Ch., Greensboro, 1979—; tchr. Ginter Park Baptist Ch., Richmond, Va., 1972. Served with USN, 1953-55. Republican. Office: The Book Trader 312 S Elm St Greensboro NC 27401

FABIAN, ELISSA ANN, nurse, administrator; b. Bronx, N.Y., Dec. 9, 1937; d. Julius and Betty (Tischelman) Rothholz; m. Leslie Howard Zackowitz, Jan. 22, 1956 (dec. 1974); children—Jodi Zackowitz Sohl, Corey Bruce; m. Herbert Raymond Fabian, Dec. 18, 1977; stepchildren—Michael, Cheryl Fabian Styck. B.A., Hunter Coll., 1960; L.P.N., Montefiore Hosp., 1965; R.N., County Coll. Morris, 1974. Staff nurse Montefiore Hosp., Bronx, 1965-66; office nurse R. Selznick, M.D., Bronx, 1965-66, P. Newman, M.D., Short Hills, N.J., 1966-74; staff and charge nurse St. Barnabas Hosp., Livingston, N.J., 1974-76; head nurse intensive care unit and cardiac care unit Coral Gables Hosp., Fla., 1976-79; asst. dir. nursing Hanover House Nursing Ctr., Miami, 1979-80; dir. nursing LaPosada Convalescent Ctr., Miami, 1980, Jackson Heights Skilled Care Ctr., Miami, 1980-82; head nurse intensive care unit and cardiac care unit James Archer Smith Hosp., Homestead, Fla., 1982-84, nursing supr., 1984-85, infection control nurse, employee health nurse, relief supr., 1985—. Recipient Employee of Yr. award Unicare Health Facilities, Inc., 1978. Mem. Am. Nurses Assn. (cert. nursing adminstr.), Fla. Nurses Assn., Assn. Practioners of Infection Control, Am. Assn. Critical Care Nurses, Am. Heart Assn. Democrat. Jewish. Club: Hadassah. Home: 11820 SW 170th Terr Miami FL 33177 Office: James Archer Smith Hosp 160 NW 13th St Homestead FL 33030

FABRE, FRED RUFFIN, automobile repairman; b. Baton Rouge, Sept. 22, 1939; s. Joseph Ruffin and Bessie S. (Solomon) F.; student La. State U. Engaged in automobile repair, 1961—; owner Carriage House Garage, Baton Rouge, 1978—; cons. Rolls-Royce restorations, 1971—. Bd. dirs., trainer, coordinator drug end., counsellor Genesis House, crisis center, Baton Rouge, 1970-71. Recipient various service awards. Mem. Antique Automobile Club Am. (officer; award for article 1978), Rolls-Royce Owners Club, Rolls-Royce Enthusiasts Club, Rolls-Royce Heritage Trust, Bentley Drivers Club, Phanton III Tech. Soc., BMW Owners Assn., Vintage BMW Owners Club, Capital Area Health Planning Council. Newsletter and tech. editor, tech. cons. R-R Owners Club. Home: 4063 Mohican St Baton Rouge LA 70805 Office: 3745-A Prescott Rd Baton Rouge LA 70805

FABRY, PAUL ANDREW, internat. assn. exec.; b. Budapest, Hungary, June 19, 1919; s. Andrew and Ilona (Gombos) F.; B.A., Godollo Jr. Coll., 1937; Ph.D., U. Budapest, 1942, J.D., 1943; m. Louise Hitchcock Fair, May 15, 1958 (div. 1968); children—Lydia Louise, Alexa Fair; m. 2d, Angela Andrews Rutledge, May 8, 1971 (div. 1979). Came to U.S., 1949, naturalized. War corr. Central European Press Service, Warsaw, Poland, Berlin, Vienna, Austria, Zurich, Switzerland, Budapest, 1943-44; sec. Fgn. Office, Budapest, 1945; head Prime Minister's Cabinet, Budapest, 1945-46; charge d'affaires of Hungary, Ankara, Turkey 1946-47; fgn. corr. Istanbul, Turkey, 1948-49; sect. chief Radio Free Europe, N.Y.C., 1950-53; free lance writer, lectr., N.Y.C., 1954; pub. relations adviser E.I. du Pont de Nemours & Co., Wilmington, Del., 1955-62; mng. dir. Internat. House, New Orleans 1962-84; cons., dir. New Orleans World Trade Ctr., 1985—; hon. consul of Belgium, 1983—. Rep. Internat. Red Cross, Vienna-Budapest, 1945-46; adv. bd. Istanbul U., 1948-49, Internat. Econ. Cooperation Com., N.Y.C.; v.p. Cultural Services, Inc., N.Y.C., 1953-54; moderator Fact and Opinion, WYES-TV, 1965-74. Active United Fund, Wilmington, 1955-60. Trustee, mem. exec. com. New Orleans Ednl. TV Found., 1970-75. Served as capt. Royal Hungarian Arty., 1943. Mem. Pub. Relations Soc. Am., World Trade Centers Assn. (v.p., treas. 1969—), Fgn. Press Assn., New Orleans Bd. Trade, C. of C. Home: 1127 Bourbon St New Orleans LA 70116 Office: 607 Gravier St New Orleans LA 70130

FACINOLI, JOHN FRANKLIN, osteopathic physician; b. Pitts., Feb. 20, 1948; s. Bert Winston and Helen Irene (Grubb) F.; m. Sallie Ann Dixon, May 12, 1973 (div.). B.S. in Biology, Morris Harvey Coll., 1974; D.O., W.Va. Sch. Osteo. Medicine, 1978. Intern Richmond Heights Gen. Hosp (Ohio), 1978-79; resident in emergency medicine Mt. Sinai Med. Ctr., Cleve., 1980-83; dir. emergency services Putnam Gen. Hosp., Hurricane, W.Va., 1983—. Mem. AMA, Am. Coll. Emergency Physicians.

FACKLER, WILLIAM MARION, banker; b. Canton, Ga., June 24, 1938; s. Newman Eidson and Mary Edna (Williams) F.; m. Judith Virginia Tomme, June 27, 1965; children—William Marcus, Michael Tomme. B.A., Emory U., 1960; M.B.A., Ga. State U., 1967; Grad. degree, Comml. Banking, Stonier Grad. Sch. of Banking, 1970. V.P. market research, product devel. The First Nat. Bank of Atlanta, 1960-75; sr. v.p. AmSouth Bank N.A. (formerly The First Nat. Bank of Birmingham), 1975-83; exec. v.p. Barnett Banks of Fla., Inc., 1983—; dir. Barnett Banks Trust Co. N.A.; mem. faculty Stonier Grad. Sch. Banking, Ga. Banking Sch. Served with USAF, 1961. Mem. Bank Mktg. Assn. (dir., exec. com.), Am. Mktg. Assn., Birmingham chpt. (Mktg. Person of the Yr., 1980), Am. Inst. Banking (pres. Atlanta chpt.), Sales and Mktg. Execs., Consumer Bankers Assn. (communications com.) Methodist. Clubs: Timuquana Country, River. Mem. editorial review bd. Journal of Retail Banking. Home: 3809 Timuquana Rd Jacksonville FL 32210 Office: 100 Laura St Jacksonville FL 32202

FACUSSÉ, ALBERT SHUCRY, lawyer; b. Tegucigalpa, Honduras, Feb. 10, 1921; s. Nicholas and Maria (Barjum) F.; m. May Bandak, Dec. 22, 1946 (dec.); children—Vivian Neuwirth, Denise Lentz. J.D. cum laude, Loyola U., New Orleans, 1943. Bar: La. 1957. Sole practice, New Orleans, 1957—; pub. speaker. Mem. La. State Bar Assn., ABA, Internat. Platform Assn. Democrat. Roman Catholic. Comment editor Loyola U. Law Rev., 1943. Home: 6731 Manchester St New Orleans LA 70126 Office: 234 Loyola Ave Suite 832 New Orleans LA 70112

FADEL, HOSSAM ELDIN, obstetrician, gynecologist, educator; b. Cairo, Oct. 15, 1940; came to U.S., 1970; s. Ahmed and Dorreya Mohammad (Aly) F.; m. Skina Ibrahim Fuoad, Aug. 26, 1965; children—Mohammad, Ayman. M.D., Ain Shams U., 1960, diploma ob-gyn, 1963, diploma gen. surgery, 1964. Diplomate Am. Bd. Obstetrics and Gynecology, Am. Bd. Maternal-Fetal Medicine. Intern Ain Shams Univ. Hosps., Cairo, 1961-62, resident in ob-gyn, 1962-64, clin. demonstrator, 1965-68; lect., 1968-70; fellow family planning program dept. ob-gyn U. Chgo., 1970-71; chief resident in ob-gyn Passavant Meml. Hosp., Northwestern U., Chgo., 1971-72; fellow maternal-fetal medicine Rush Presbyn. Hosp., St. Luke's Med. Ctr. Rush Med. Coll., Chgo., 1972-74; asst. prof. dept. ob-gyn, asst. dir. perinatal medicine sect., 1974-75; asst. prof. dept. ob-gyn Med. Coll. Ga., Augusta, 1975-76, assoc. prof., 1976-81, prof., 1981—; med. dir. maternal and infant care project Med. Coll. Ga., 1975-84, dir. maternal-fetal medicine fellowship program, 1980-84, chief maternal-fetal medicine sect., 1977-84; mem. staff Med. Coll. Ga. Hosp. and Clinic; cons. Univ. Hosp., Augusta, Med. Ctr. Central Ga., Macon, Meml. Med. Ctr., Savannah, Ga., Dwight David Eisenhower Army Med. Ctr., Ft. Gordon, Ga.; Rush Presbyn.-St. Luke's Med. Ctr. grantee, 1975; Nat. Found. March of Dimes grantee, 1977; Fred A. Moss Charity Trust grantee, 1978; Med. Research Found. grantee, 1980; 82-83; NIH grantee, 1980; Syntex Corp. grantee, 1980; others. Fellow Am. Coll. Obstetricians and Gynecologists; mem. Richmond County Med. Soc., Med. Assn. Ga., AMA, Ga. State Ob-Gyn Soc., Ga. Perinatal Assn., So. Perinatal Assn., Nat. Perinatal Assn., Soc. Obstetric Anesthesiologists and Perinatologists, Am. Fertility Soc., Soc. Perinatal Obstetricians, Islamic Med. Assn. U.S. and Can. (pres. 1985—), Internat. Assn. for Maternal and Neonatal Health, Assn. Profs. of Gynecology and Obstetrics, Internat. Soc. for Study of Hypertension in Pregnancy, Soc. for Gynecologic Investigation, Islamic Soc. N.Am., Sigma Xi. Club: West Lake Country. Contbr. articles, papers, chpts. to profl. lit. Office: Dept OB-Gyn Med Coll Ga Augusta GA 30912

FAGAN, (MARGARET) JOEN, psychology educator; b. Atlanta, Sept. 5, 1933; d. Joseph Poley and Elizabeth Bryant (Pruden) F. A.B., Agnes Scott Coll., 1954; M.S., Pa. State U., 1956, Ph.D., 1958. Successively asst. prof., assoc. prof., prof., Regent's prof. psychology Ga. State U., Atlanta, 1958—. Fellow Am. Psychol. Assn., Am. Acad. Psychotherapists. Author: Gestalt Therapy Now, 1970. Office: Georgia State U 33 Gilmer St SE Atlanta GA 30303

FAGAN, MAURICE JAMES, JR., dentist; b. Coventry, R.I., Dec. 4, 1921; s. Maurice James and Ellen Louisa (Albro) F.; B.S., Providence Coll., 1943; student Balt. Coll. Dental Surgery, 1944-47; D.D.S., U. Md., 1947; m. Ruth Pearl Mcdonald, June 28, 1947; children—Maurice James III, Malford, Mark, Mitchell, Laurie Anne, Margo Jean. Practice dentistry, Wakefield, R.I., 1947, Atlanta, 1956—; assoc. in geriatrics, cons. Malford Thewlis Geriatric Clinic, 1947-56, Dental Masters, Inc.; founder dental health program South Kingston (R.I.) Sch. Dept., 1948, dir., 1948-50; instr. USAF Med. Service, Atlanta, 1959-64; pres. Dental Practice Plan Inc. Founder, 1960, since pres., chmn. bd. dirs., trustee Maurice J. Fagan Meml. Dental Hosp., Dentistry for Aged and Handicapped, Atlanta; cons. Gale Clinic, Narragansett, R.I., 1957—; lectr. and tchr.; sec. Internat. Research Com. for Oral Implantology. Served to lt. col. USAF, 1942-72. Decorated knight of Malta with title of Sir by Queen Juliana of Netherlands, 1975; officier Ordre de la Ville de Paris; grand hospitaler Venerable Sovereign Order of St. John, Knights of Malta; knight of justice Knights of Malta; knight comdr. of grace Knights of Malta; Grand Cross of Justice recipient Silver medal of Honor, Paris, 1973, Vermeil medal, 1981, Gold Medal of Honor, Republic of France, 1973. Fellow Am. Acad. Gen. Dentistry, Internat. Congress Oral Implantologists (a founder 1972, pres. 1982—, dir.), Royal Soc. Health, Acad. Implants and Transplants; mem. Royal Soc. Medicine (asso.), So. Acad. Oral Implantology (founder; pres. 1969-70, sec. 1982—), So. Acad. Implant Dentistry (pres. 1983), Am. Prosthodontic Soc., Am. Acad. Implant Dentistry, Am. Acad. Implant Prosthetics (pres. 1982—), ADA, Ga. Dental Assn., No. Dist. Dental Soc., Am. Geriatric Soc., Am. Soc. Geriatric Dentistry, Assn. Advance Ethical Hypnosis, Res. Officers Assn., Am. Soc. Clin. Hypnosis, Acad. Gen. Dentistry, Am. Inst. Advanced Dentistry (dir.), Brit. Assn. for Dental Implant Research, Unione della Legion d'Oro of Accademia Tiberina (Rome), Venezuela Implant Dental Soc. (hon.), Associazone Nazionale Implantoprotesi Orale, Greek Implant Soc. (hon.), Portuguese Dental Soc. (hon.), Le College International de Recherchen Implantaires (hon.), Psi Omega. Author: Dental Practice Planning; How to Succeed in Dentistry; New Concepts in Implant Dentistry; Treatment of Severe Alveolar Atrophy, Vol. I.; The Interplant Techniques Manual; asst. editor Jour. Oral Implantology; contbr. articles to profl. jours.; inventor dental implants. Home: 5360 Peachtree-Dunwoody Rd NE Atlanta GA 30342 Office: 960 Johnson Ferry Rd NE Atlanta GA 30342

FAGAN, RAYMOND, epidemiologist; b. Bklyn., Dec. 27, 1914; s. Louis J. and Bertha Fagan; m. Esther Fried, Sept. 20, 1936; children—Susan Barbara, Kathleen Ellen, Deborah Jill. B.A., NYU, 1935; D.V.M., Cornell U., 1939; M.P.H., Harvard U., 1949. With U.S. Dept. Agr., 1939-42, USPHS, 1946-54; assoc. prof. U. Pa. Sch. Vet. Medicine, 1954-56; sr. virologist Wyeth Labs., 1956-67; prin. scientist Philip Morris Research Ctr., Richmond, Va., 1967-85; adj. prof. epidemiology Drexel U., Phila., 1964-67; adj. assoc. prof. epidemiology Med. Coll. Va., Richmond, 1975—; chmn. adv. com. on environ. health Phila. Dept. Health, 1964-67; mem. Richmond Air Pollution Control Bd., 1975-80. Served to capt. AUS, 1942-46. Mem. Am. Pub. Health Assn., AVMA, Am. Soc. for Microbiology, AAAS, N.Y. Acad. Scis. Home: 8554 Old Spring Rd Richmond VA 23235 Office: Philip Morris Research Ctr PO Box 26583 Richmond VA 23261

FAGAN, THOMAS JOSEPH, clinical psychologist; b. N.Y.C., Oct. 5, 1949; s. Thomas J. and Francis M. (DeFabiis) F.; m. Kathleen M. Sampson, June 10, 1972; children—Kimberly Erin, Amy Elizabeth. B.A., Rutgers U., 1971; M.S., Va. Poly. Inst. and State U., 1973, Ph.D., 1977. Lic. clin. psychologist, Va. Staff psychologist Fed. Bur. Prisons, Petersburg, Va., 1977-82, chief psychology services, 1982-84, N.E. regional psychology services adminstr., 1984—; dir. Psychology Services Ctr., Colonial Heights, Va., 1984—. Contbr. articles to profl. jours. Mem. Am. Psychol. Assn., Am. Assn. Correctional Psychologists. Office: Fed Correctional Instn Psychology Services Petersburg VA 23803

FAGAN, THOMAS KEVIN, psychology educator; b. Warren, Ohio, Feb. 25, 1943; s. Paul Francis and Ruth Ione Fagan; m. Susan Reuter; children—Shannon, Lance, Colleen. B.S. in Edn., Kent State U., 1965, M.A., 1966, Ph.D., 1969. Asst. prof., then assoc. prof. psychology Western Ill. U., Macomb, Ill., 1969-76; assoc. prof., then prof. Memphis State U., 1976—. Mem. Tenn. Assn. Sch. Psychologists, Nat. Assn. Sch. Psychologists. Republican. Roman Catholic. Lodge: Elks. Home: 1855 S Rainbow Rd Memphis TN 38107 Office: Memphis State U Psychology Dept Memphis TN 38152

FAHEY, WILLIAM FRANCIS, naval officer, organization development consultant; b. Washington, Oct. 8, 1934; s. William Hiliard and Emily (Glynn) F.; m. Constance Jean Quamme, June 27, 1959; children—Jean Inger, Colleen Elizabeth. B.S. U.S. Mcht. Marine Acad., 1956; grad. Def. Intelligence Coll., 1967; grad. with highest distinction, Naval War Coll., 1978; M.A. in Psychology, Cath. U. Am., 1981. Registered orgn. devel. profl. Commd. ensign, U.S. Navy, 1957, advanced through grades to capt., 1978; comdg. officer USS Badger, Pearl Harbor, Hawaii, 1973-75; chief of staff for ops. S. Atlantic Force, P.R., 1975-77; br. chief Joint Chiefs of Staff, Washington, 1978-81; dir. Navy Family Service Ctr., Washington, 1981-84; comdr. Organizational Effectiveness System, Norfolk, Va., 1984—. Contbr. article to Naval War Coll. Rev. 1978 (Colbert Meml. award). Bd. dirs. Urban League of Tidewater, Norfolk, 1984—. Decorated Bronze Star with V, Def. Meritorious Service Medal; recipient Profl. Achievement award, Mcht. Marine Acad. Alumni Assn., 1981. Mem. Am. Soc. Tng. and Devel., Am. Assn. Counseling and Devel., Acad. of Mgmt., O.D. Network. Republican. Roman Catholic. Avocations: Salt water fishing. Home: 4645 Lakewood Dr Virginia Beach VA 23464 Office: Organizational Effectiveness System Atlantic 5621 Tidewater Dr Norfolk VA 23509

FAHR, LINDA MEYERS, radiologist; b. N.Y.C., Sept. 20, 1942; d. Paul Tabor and Jessie V. (Jones) Meyers; B.A., Barnard Coll., 1964; M.D., U. Iowa, 1968; m. James Dwight Watson, Mar. 29, 1980; children—John Pearson Fahr, Bruce Tabor Fahr. Resident in radiology U. Iowa, Iowa City, 1971-74; staff radiologist VA Hosp., Houston, 1974-77, chief dept. radiology, 1977-79; chief radiologist MacGregor Med. Clinic, Houston, 1980—; clin. asst. prof. Baylor Coll. Medicine, Houston, 1974-79. Mem. Am. Assn. Women Radiologists (pres. 1983, past pres. 1984), Am. Coll. Radiology, Radiol. Soc. N.Am., Tex. Radiol. Soc., Houston Radiol. Soc. (treas. 1982, sec. 1983), Tex. Med. Assn., Harris County Med. Assn., Women's Profl. Assn. (exec. bd. 1984). Office: 8100 Greenbriar Houston TX 77054

FAHRINGER, CATHERINE HEWSON, retired savings and loan association executive; b. Phila., Aug. 1, 1922; d. George Francis and Catherine Gertrude (Magee) Hewson; grad. diploma Inst. Fin. Edn., 1965; m. Edward F. Fahringer, July 8, 1961, 1 child by previous marriage, Francis George Beckett. With Centrust Savs. Bank (formerly Dade Savs. and Loan Assn.), Miami, Fla., 1958-85, v.p., 1967-74, sr. v.p., 1974-81, sec., 1975-79, head savs. personnel and mktg. div., 1979-83, exec. v.p. office of chmn., 1984, dir., 1984, chmn. nominating com., co-chmn. audit com. of bd. dirs. Trustee, co-chmn. panel D. mem. priorities and allocations com., 1982, chmn. audit com., 1983, fin. com. United Way of Dade County (Fla.); trustee Public Health Trust, Dade County, 1974-84, sec. 1976, vice chmn., 1977-78, chmn. bd., 1978-81; hon. bd. govs. U. Miami, Soc. for Research in Med. Edn.; trustee South Fla. Blood Service, Miami, 1979-84, vice chmn., 1980, chmn., 1981-84; trustee Dade County Vocat. Found., 1977-81; trustee Fla. Internat. U. Found., 1976—, v.p. bd., 1978-81, pres., 1982-84; bd. dirs. WPBT, 1985. Named Woman of Yr. in fin. Zonta Internat., 1975, ambassador Air Def. Arty., U.S. Army Air Def. Command, 1970; recipient Trail Blazer award Women's Council of 100, 1977, Community Headliner award Women in Communication, 1983; Outstanding Citizen of Dade County award, 1984. Mem. U.S. League of Savs. Assn., Nat. League Savs. and Loan Assn., Fla. Savs. and Loan League, Am. Soc. Personnel Adminstrs., Dade Bus. and Profl. Women's Club (past pres., Woman of Yr. 1974), Inst. Fin. Edn. (life; nat. dir., past pres. Local Greater Miami chpt.), Savs. and Loan Mktg. Soc. South Fla. (past pres.), Savs. and Loan Personnel Soc. South Fla. Democrat. Congregationalist. Clubs: Coral Gables Country, Fla. Women's Network (dir. 1983—). Contbr. articles to profl. jours. Office: 1470 NW 139th Miami FL 33167

FAIGEL, MARTIN JOSEPH, librarian, univ. adminstr.; b. Lawrence, Mass., May 14, 1938; s. Thomas Maxwell and Anne (Cantor) F.; B.A. magna cum laude, Harvard U., 1959; M.L.S., U. Calif., Berkeley, 1972. Asst. to dir. collection devel. Widener Library, Harvard U., 1960-61, asst. to dir. Houghton Library, 1962-64, chief librarian Villa I Tatti. Harvard U. Center Italian Renaissance Studies, 1964-66; researcher Ency. World Art, McGraw Hill, Rome, 1966-67; tchr. Centro di Studi Americani, Rome, 1967-68; teaching asst. U. Calif., Berkeley, 1968-71; French and Italian bibliographer U. Va., 1972-77; univ. bibliographer, dir. collection devel. U. Ala., 1977—, prof., 1983—. Woodrow Wilson fellow, 1959-60; John Harvard scholar, 1959. Mem. Ala. Library Assn. (mem.-at-large coll. and univ. sect. 1983-84). ALA (resources and tech. services div.), Library and Info. Tech. Assn., Assn. Coll. and Research Libraries, Phi Beta Kappa, Beta Phi Mu. Democrat. Translator: Ippolito and Lionora (attributed to Leon Battista Alberti), 1970; mem. editorial bd. Library Resources and Tech. Services. Office: U Ala Library PO Box S University AL 35486

FAIN, REBECCA ANN, nurse; b. Rupert, W.Va., Jan. 8, 1951; d. Virgil William and Helen Rose (Surbaugh) F. B.S. Nursing, Tex. Woman's U., 1973; M.S. in Nursing, W.Va. U., 1985. Staff nurse Winter Park (Fla.) Meml. Hosp., 1973-74, Lucerne Hosp., Orlando, Fla., 1974-75; nurse clinician Fla. Hosp., Orlando, 1975; charge nurse Charleston Area Med. Ctr. (W.Va.), 1975-77, head nurse, 1979-83, quality assurance coordinator, office patient affairs, 1983-85; dir. quality assurance/utilizationj mgmt., 1985—; instr. basic life support Am. Heart Assn., 1977-82, nurse cons., 1983. Mem. W.Va. Nurses Assn. Polit. Action Com., Charleston, 1983. Mem. Am. Nurses Assn. (membership com. 1982—, ho. dels. 1986), Nat. Orthopedic Nurses Assn. (pres. 1981-83), Nat. League Nursing. Democrat. Episcopalian. Home: Apt A-604 2106 Kanawha Blvd E Charleston WV 25311 Office: Office Legal Services Charleston Area Med Ctr PO Box 1547 Charleston WV 25326

FAIR, DONALD WAYNE, university administrator, accountant; b. East Liverpool, Ohio, Apr. 17, 1947; s. Wayne Allen and Dorothy Eileen (Garner) F.; m. Catherine Irene Rhenish, July 13, 1975; children—John William, Elizabeth Anne. B.B.A., Youngstown (Ohio) State U., 1970; M.Acctg., Bowling Green State U., 1971. C.P.A., Fla. Instr., Bowling Green (Ohio) State U., 1971-74; instr. Fla. Internat. U.-Miami, 1974-76, asst. dean Coll. Bus. Adminstrn., 1976—. Mem. Am. Inst. C.P.A.s, Fla. Inst. C.P.A.s, Am. Acctg. Assn. Republican. Office: Fla Internat Univ Coll Bus Miami FL 33199

FAIR, MORRIS HARLEY, investment banker; b. Tyronza, Ark., Nov. 12, 1929; m. Diane Mack, Jan. 21, 1954; children—Ronald Harley, Gregory Mack, Lance Turner, Jason Johnson. B.S.B.A. in Acctg., U. Ark., 1956. Acctg. supr. Southwestern Bell Telephone Co., Little Rock, 1956-58; asst. to pres. First Pyramid Life Ins. Co., Little Rock, 1959-60, planning and systems mgr., 1960-61, asst. comptroller, 1961-62; comptroller First U.S. Corp., Memphis, 1962-66; v.p. UMIC Inc., subs. UMIC Securities Corp., Memphis, 1966-68, exec. v.p., 1968-74, pres., 1974—, chief exec. officer, 1981—; pres. UMIC Govt. Securities, Inc., subs. UMIC Securities Corp., Memphis, 1978—, also dir.; mem. Com. on Investment Ark. State Funds, 1972. Served to sgt. USAF, 1950-53. Mem. Nat. Assn. Securities Dealers (vice chmn. dist. bus. conduct com. 1975), Little Rock Assn. Ins. Accts. (pres. 1961), Pub. Securities Assn., Securities Industry Assn. (vice chmn. so. dist. 1980-81), Jaycees Internat. (senator 1965—). Clubs: Holy Cross Episcopal Ch. Men's (pres. 1981-82), Meadowbrook Country (dir. 1969-71, 73). Office: UMIC Inc 959 Ridgeway Loop Rd Memphis TN 38119

FAIR, OWEN WAYNE, mathematics educator; b. Oakland City, Ind., Oct. 30, 1933; s. Randall Owen and Bessie (Ayers) F.; m. Faye Leavern O'Neal, Feb. 21, 1954; children—Leonard Owen, Debra Elaine. B.S. in Edn., Oakland City Coll., 1957; M.A.T. in Math., Ind. U., 1961. Cert. math. tchr., Ind., Fla. Math, physics tchr. Orleans High Sch., Ind., 1957-59; math. tchr. Francesville High Sch., Ind., 1959-61, Arlington High Sch., Indpls., 1961-69, Piper High Sch., Ft. Lauderdale, Fla., 1971-78; instr. math. N.W. Mo. State U., Maryville, 1969-71, Coastal Carolina Community Coll., Jacksonville, N.C., 1978—; part time instr. Broward Community Coll., Ft. Lauderdale, 1972-78. Asst. scoutmaster Broward County council Boy Scouts Am., 1972-76; Sunday sch. tchr. Merrill United Meth. Ch., Ft. Lauderdale, 1974-78, chmn. adminstrv. bd., 1976-78, chmn. bldg. com., 1977-78; Sunday sch. tchr. Trinity United Meth. Ch., Jacksonville, 1981—. Served with USNR, 1952-54. Mem. Nat. Councils Tchrs.

of Math. Republican. Avocations: camping; gardening. Home: Route 3 Box 421-C Jacksonville NC 28540 Office: Coastal Carolina Community Coll 444 Western Blvd Jacksonville NC 28540

FAIRBROTHERS, CATHERINE WILSON, oil company executive, geologist; b. Edmonton, Alta., Can., Aug. 30, 1958 (mother Am. citizen); d. John Lauchlin and Nora Jane (Dale) W.; m. Gregg Everett Fairbrothers, July 30, 1983. B.S., U. Tulsa, 1980. Geologist, Harrell & Bradshaw Exploration, Tulsa, 1978-80, Phillips Petroleum, Bartlesville, Okla., 1980-81; exploration geologist Samson Resources Co., 1981-83; pres. Green Mountain Exploration, Inc., Tulsa, 1983—, also dir. Named State Champion, Okla. Hunter and Jumpers Assn., 1978. Mem. Am. Assn. Petroleum Geologists, Tulsa Geol. Soc. Methodist. Avocations: training and breeding thoroughbred horses; farming; computer programming. Office: Green Mountain Exploration Inc PO Box 521028 Tulsa OK 74152

FAIRBROTHERS, GREGG EVERETT, geologist; b. Jersey City, N.J., Oct. 30, 1954; s. David Earl and Marguerite Elaine (Freitag) F.; m. Catherine Lynn Wilson, July 30, 1983. B.S., Dartmouth Coll., 1975; M.S., Rutgers U., 1977; M.B.A., U. Tulsa, 1983. Teaching research asst. Rutgers U., 1975-77; asst. dist. geologist Texaco, Inc., New Orleans, 1977-80; v.p. Exploration Samson Resources Co., Tulsa, Okla., 1980—. Author: (novel) A Biography of the deFreepe Brothers, 1978; contbr. articles to profl. jours. Mem. fin. com. 1st United Meth. Ch., Tulsa, 1983—. Mem. Am. Assn. Petroleum Geologists, Tulsa Geol. Soc., Sigma Xi, Beta Gamma Sigma. Avocations: novelist; restoration of old homes; gardening; classical music. Office: Samson Resources Co Samson Plaza 2 W 2d St Tulsa OK 74103

FAIRCHILD, JOHN PHILLIP, physician; b. Washington, Dec. 25, 1918; s. Iler James and Vera Fae (Ward) F.; A.B., George Washington U., Washington, 1940, M.D., 1943; m. Julia Pearl Printz, Sept. 12, 1945; children—Jean Printz Fairchild DeTarnowsky, John Phillip, Jacqueline Patricia Fairchild Auxt, James Patrick, Jerome Paul, Jeffrey Preston. Enlisted U.S. Army, 1944, resigned, 1946, re-enlisted 1948, commd. 1st lt., 1944, advanced through grades to col.; intern Gallinger Mcpl. Hosp., Washington, 1943, resident pediatrics, 1948-50; chief pediatric services U.S. Army Hosp. Ft. Bragg, N.C., 1950-53, Brooke Gen. Hosp., Ft. Sam Houston, Tex., 1953-58, Tripler Gen. Hosp., Honolulu, 1958-62, Walter Reed Gen. Hosp., 1963-66; dir. HEW U.S. Civil Adminstrn. Ryukyu Islands, 1966-69; dep. comdr. Walter Reed Hosp., 1969-71, ret., 1971; gen. practice medicine Garnett, Kans., 1946-48; dir. field services div. Montgomery County (Md.) Health Dept., 1971-75; chief surgeon U.S. Soldiers and Airmen's Home Hosp., Washington, 1975-79; staff dept. pediatrics Regional Med. Clinic/Mountain Health Services, McDowell, Ky., 1979—, active staff McDowell Appalachian Regional Hosp., 1979—; asst. to asso. clin. prof. pediatrics Baylor U., 1954-58; asso. clin. prof. pediatrics Georgetown U., 1963-66, clin. prof., 1973-75; clin. prof. U. Louisville, 1981—; cons. in field. Decorated Legion of Merit; recipient Supreme award Japanese Med. Assn., 1969. Mem. AMA, Med. and Chirurg. Faculty State Md., Ky. Med. Soc., Floyd County Med. Soc., Assn. Mil. Surgeons, Am. Public Health Assn., Sigma Chi. Presbyterian. Contbr. articles to profl. publs. Home: PO Box 239 McDowell KY 41647

FAIRCHILD, RAYMOND EUGENE, oil company executive; b. Bowling Green, Ohio, June 25, 1923; s. Ira Ethalbert and Bessie Louise (Gearhart) F.; m. Eleanor Faith Vaughn, Sept. 1, 1973. B.S., Ohio U., 1948; M.S., U. Mo., 1950. Dist. geologist Pan Am. Prodn. Co., Houston, 1950-56; gulf coast div. exploration mgr. Pan Handle Eastern subs., Houston, 1956-72; mayor City of Hunter Creek, Tex., 1967-71; exploration cons. Houston, 1972-73; exploration mgr. A.P. Moller, Copenhagen, 1973-80; v.p. Hunt Oil Co., Dallas, 1980—. Alderman, City of Hunter Creek, 1962-67; commr. Spring Br. Fire Dept., 1962. Fellow Geol. Soc. London; mem. Petroleum Exploration Soc. Great Britain, Dansk Geologisk Forening, Gulf Coast Assn. Geol. Socs., Houston Geol. Soc., Dallas Geol. Soc. Republican. Club: Dallas Petroleum. Office: Hunt Oil Co 1401 Elm St 2900 InterFirst One Bldg Dallas TX 75202

FAIRFAX, LAURA MAY, pediatric psychologist; b. Otterville, Mo., Dec. 11, 1943; d. Hugh Reed and Lena Irene (Conrad) F. Ph.D., U. Mo., 1971. Lic. psychologist, Fla., Kans., Mo. Psychologist, Kansas City Mental Health Found., Mo., 1971-73; research psychologist Psychol. Corp. Wechsler Intelligence Scale for Children, 1974; community psychologist Western Mo. Area Health Edn. Ctr., Kansas City, Mo., 1973; pvt. practice clin. psychology Kansas City, 1972-74; cons. psychologist St. Johns River Psychiat. Hosp., Jacksonville, Fla., 1978—; pvt. practice clin. psychology, Jacksonville, 1975—; asst. prof. dept. psychology U. N. Fla., 1974-79; guest prof. Stress Mgmt. Course, Jacksonville U., 1984; presenter mental health TV program Sta. WJCT-TV; speaker at mental health forums. Editor: Preschool Screening Handbook, Greater Kansas City Mental Health Found., 1973. Mem. Fla. State Atty.'s Youth Mediation Program (4th Jud. Circuit), 1985—; mem. legis. network Mental Health Assn. Jacksonville, 1976—; judge Kiwanis Ann. Sci. Fairs, 1976—. Fellow Menninger Found.; mem. Am. Psychol. Assn., Fla. Psychol. Assn. (membership chmn. 1977-79), Jacksonville Assn. Women in Psychology (charter mem.), Fla. Psychol. Assn. (Northeast chpt. pres.), Kappa Epsilon Alpha, Alpha Chi Omega, Jacksonville Alumnae Panhellenic Assn. (chmn. scholarship 1984-85). Presbyterian. Clubs: Ponte Vedra Country (Fla.). Avocations: tennis; swimming; jogging. Office: Arlington Profl Ctr 1331 Bellemeade Blvd Jacksonville FL 32211

FAIRHURST, WILLIAM, exploration geologist; b. Royal Oak, Mich., Feb. 11, 1957; s. Thomas Johnston and Nancy Ruth (Rulketter) F.; m. Patricia Elizabeth Hughes, Aug. 15, 1981. B.A., Ohio Wesleyan U., 1979; M.S., U. Mo., 1984. Teaching asst. Ohio Wesleyan U., Delaware, 1978-79, U. Mo., Columbia, 1980-81; exploration geologist Marathon Oil Co., Houston, 1981—. Mem. Big Bros., Delaware, Ohio, 1975. U. Mo. grantee, 1980, Atlantic Richfield Co. grantee, 1981. Mem. Am. Assn. Petroleum Geologists, Soc. Econ. Paleontologist and Mineralogist, Houston Geol. Soc., Sigma Gamma Epsilon. Avocations: running; aerobics, soccer; sailing. Office: Marathon Oil Co 5555 San Felipe Rd Houston TX 77253

FAIRLEIGH, JAMES PARKINSON, music educator; b. St. Joseph, Mo., Aug. 24, 1938; s. William Macdonald and Mable Emily (Parkinson) F.; m. Marlane Alberta Paxson, June 25, 1960; children—William Paxson, Karen Evelyn. B. Mus., U. Mich., 1960; M. Mus., U. So. Calif., 1965; Ph.D., U. Mich., 1973. Instr., asst. prof. Hanover Coll., Ind., 1965-75; assoc. prof. R.I. Coll., Providence, 1975-80; head, music dept. Jacksonville State U., Ala., 1980—; dir. of music First Presbyterian Ch., Anniston, Ala., 1981—. Served to 1st lt. U.S. Army, 1960-62. Mem. Am. Musicol. Soc., Ala. Mus. Tchrs. Assn. (cert., treas. 1982—), Coll. Music Soc., Music Educators Nat. Conf., Music Tchrs. Nat. Assn. (cert.), Riemenschneider Bach Inst., Phi Beta Kappa, Phi Kappa Phi, Pi Kappa Lambda, Phi Eta Sigma, Phi Mu Alpha Sinfonia. Republican. Avocations: waterskiing; swimming. Home: 70 Fairway Dr Jacksonville AL 36265 Office: Dept of Music Jacksonville State U Jacksonville AL 36265

FAIRLEY, EDWARD LEE, foreign affairs consultant; b. Hannibal, N.Y., Dec. 4, 1917; s. Edward James and Helen (Hewitt) F.; m. Katherine Marie Spradlin, Apr. 30, 1944 (dec. Apr. 1956); children—Alan, Carol; m. Gisela Elsa Hensel, Mar. 30, 1957; 1 child, Helen. Mus. B., Eastman Sch. Music, 1939, Mus. M., 1941. Asst. reference librarian Library of Congress, Washington, 1941-48; music specialist Dept. State, Washington, 1948-53; fgn. affairs info. officer USIA, Paris, 1952-54, Bonn, 1955-57, Kampala, 1960-65, Rabat, 1966-69, Washington, 1969-75; dir. internat. affairs Am. Pub. Works Assn., Washington, 1976-79; fgn. affairs cons., McLean, Va., 1979—; program annotator Nat. Symphony Orchestra, Washington, 1942-52. Author of essays. Editor Jour. Notes, 1946-52. Pres. Potomac Hills Civic Assn., McLean, 1984—. Mem. Am. Fgn. Service Assn., Am. Music Library Assn., Am. Musicological Soc. Democrat. Presbyterian. Clubs: Dacor, Friday Morning Music (Washington). Avocations: reading, travelling, playing chamber music. Home and Office: 6134 Tompkins Dr McLean VA 22101

FAIRWEATHER, GLADSTONE HENRY, health center exec.; b. Jamaica, W.I., Nov. 30, 1935; s. Arnold Darrell and Miriam Loretta Fairweather; B.A., William Jewell Coll., 1960; M.S., So. Ill. U., 1962; M.H.A., U. S.C., 1970; 1 child. Asso. dir. tng. and devel. N.Y.C. Health and Hosp. Corp., 1970-72; exec. dir. Greensborough Neighborhood Health Center, Westchester County (N.Y.) Health Dept., 1972-75; dir. ambulatory services Meharry Med. Coll., Nashville, 1974-78; exec. dir. Matthew Walker Health Center, Nashville, 1979—; instr. health care adminstrn. Belmont Coll., 1978-78. Elder Lord's Chapel, Nashville. Mem. Nat. Assn. Health Execs. (pres. Nashville chpt. 1975-79), Am. Coll. Hosp. Adminstrn., Nat. Assn. Community Health Centers, Am. Hosp. Assn., Tenn. Hosp. Assn., Nat. Assn. Health Services Execs., Am. Public Health Assn. Home: 1701 Primrose St Nashville TN 37212 Office: 1501 Herman St Nashville TN 37208

FAJARDO-ORTIZ, GUILLERMO, physician; b. Mexico City, Jan. 20, 1931; s. Guillermo and Otilia Fajardo-Tapia (Ortiz); m. Olga Dolci, Jan. 28, 1960; children—Guillermo Antonio, Giovanni Martin, German Enrique. M.D., Universidad Nacional Autonoma de Mex., Mexico City, 1954; M.H.A., U. Minn., 1959. Resident, Mt. Sinai Hosp., Mpls., 1958-59; prof. health adminstrn. U. Mex., Mexico City, 1960—; head tech. services Mexico City Med. Services, 1967-69, Inst. Social Security Services for Fed. Employees, Mexico City, 1973-74; cons. health adminstrn. Mex. Inst. Social Security, 1973-85; cons. health adminstrn. and planning WHO, Pan Am. Health Orgn. Mem. Internat. Hosp. Fedn. (mem. Rene Sand Conf., Oslo 1979, v.p. 1981-83, pres. 1983, 85-87), Mex. Hosp. Assn. (pres. 1973-76), Latin Am. Hosp. Fedn. (bd. dirs. 1977-81), Academia Nat. Medicine, Mex. Acad. Surgery. Author: Teoria y Practica de la Atencion Medica y de Hospitales, 1968; Las Relaciones Publicas en Los Servicios Medicos, 1970, La Atencion Medica en Mexico, 1979; contbr. over 50 articles to profl. publs. Home: Sur 75-4352 Mexico City DF 08200 Mexico Office: Queretaro 210 Mexico City DF 06700 Mexico

FAKO, WANDA LEE, writer, producer educational programs, clinical researcher; b. Chardon, Ohio, July 26, 1949; d. Thomas Edgar and Wanda Marie (Bard) Beattie; m. Gary Lee Fako, July 8, 1972. B.S. in Nursing, Kent State U., 1972; M.S., Ohio State U., 1978. R.N., Ohio. Staff nurse Fairview Gen. Hosp., Cleve., 1972-73; instr. ob-gyn Fairview Gen. Hosp. Sch. Nursing, Cleve., 1973-77, asst. prodn. coordinator, 1977-78, patient edn. coordinator, 1978-79; sales rep. Critikon, Inc., Tampa, Fla., 1979-82, clin. research assoc., 1982-83, profl. relations adminstr., 1983-85; ter. mgr. Hyper Scan Dallas, Inc., Tex., 1985—; cons. Beckton-Dickinson, Rutherford, N.J., 1977-79, Auto-Syringe, Hooksett, N.H., 1977-79, Ancer, Columbus, Ohio, 1979-82. Trustee Far West Center, North Olmsted, Ohio, 1978-82, 1st v.p. bd. trustees, 1980-82; mem. Rep. Assembly for Community Planning, Cuyahoga County, Ohio, 1980-82, Author (16mm films) Central Venous Pressure Part I, 1977, Central Venous Pressure Part II, 1977, Bathing Your Baby, 1977, Infant Nutrition Part I, 1977, Infant Nutrition Part II, 1977, Problem Oriented Nursing Part I, 1978, Problem Oriented Nursing Part II, 1978, The Teaching Learning Process, 1978, Writing Behavioral Objectives, 1978, The Evaluation Process, 1978; author, producer slide tape program Dinamap 1846 Inservice Program, 1983, Simplicity Plus Infusion Pump Inservice Program, 1984. Mem. Nurses Assn. Am. Coll. Obstetricians and Gynecologists, Soc. Clin. Trials, Nat. Assn. Female Exec., Inc., Ohio State U. Alumni Assn. Republican. Roman Catholic. Home: 12610 Jupiter Place #626 Dallas TX 75238 Office: Hyper Scan Dallas Inc 4809 Cole Ave Suite 330 Box 120 Dallas TX 75205

FALCON, TERESITA, architect, landscape architect; b. Bauta, Cuba, July 9, 1947; came to U.S., 1961, naturalized, 1972; d. Pedro Francisco and Carmelina (Martin) Falcon; m. Juan Antonio Bueno, July 29, 1972. A.A., Miami-Dade Community Coll., 1968; B.Arch., U. Miami, 1972. Registered architect, Fla.; registered landscape architect, Fla. Designer, Hudson & Root, Coral Gables, Fla., 1968-71; designer Connell, Pierce, Garland & Friedman, Miami, Fla., 1972; planner, designer Berkus Assocs., Coral Gables, Fla., 1972-74; v.p. Planners & Designers, Inc., Coconut Grove, Fla., 1974-77; ptnr. Falcón & Bueno, Coconut Grove, 1978—. Recipient design awards Am. Soc. Landscape Architects. Mem. AIA, Archtl. Club of Miami. Democrat. Roman Catholic. Contbr. articles to profl. jours. Home and Office: 4061 Battersea Rd Coconut Grove FL 33133

FALK, CHARLES FREDERICK, college administrator; b. Evanston, Ill., Sept. 26, 1937; s. Irving Frederick and Inez Simpson (Price) F.; m. Joan Marie Stout, Oct. 8, 1960; children—Laura Sue Falk Hamilton, Bryan Eric, Scott Kristofer, Keith Frederik. B.S. in Bus. Adminstrn., Elmhurst Coll., 1959; M.S., No. Ill. U., 1965, Ed.D., 1975. Asst. prof., then assoc. prof. bus. adminstrn. William Rainey Harper Coll., Palatine, Ill., 1967-79, chmn. dept., 1969-76, dean continuing edn., 1976-78; dir. bus. outreach No. Ill. U., DeKalb, Ill., 1979-80; dir. continuing edn. Tex. Christian U., Fort Worth, 1980—. Contbr. articles to profl. jours. Served with U.S. Army, 1960-62. Recipient Lyle Maxwell award No. Ill. U., 1979. Mem. Assn. Continuing Higher Edn. (bd. dirs. 1985—), Nat. U. Continuing Edn. Assn., Am. Assn. Adult and Continuing Edn., Am. Vocat. Assn., Am. Soc. Tng. and Devel., Tex. Assn. Community Service and Continuing Edn. (bd. dirs. 1984—). Lutheran. Avocations: tennis; sporting dogs; photography; specialty automobiles. Office: Div Continuing Edn Tex Christian U PO Box 32927 Fort Worth TX 76129

FALK, LAWRENCE CLASTER, publisher, editor; b. Birmingham, Ala., Oct. 6, 1942; s. August Lawrence and Mildred (Claster) F.; student U. Ala. Law Sch., 1963-64, B.A., U. Ala., 1978, postgrad., 1978-79; m. Willo Ella Niebow, Mar. 16, 1974; children—Wendy Rebecca, Laura Davida. Reporter, Birmingham Post-Herald, 1964-65; newsman UPI, Raleigh, N.C., 1965-67, mgr., Charlotte, N.C., 1967-68, Birmingham, 1968-70, nat. editor, Chgo., 1970-74; news bur. editor AMA, Chgo., 1973-74; news mgr. Northwestern U., 1974-75; dir. info. services U. Ala., Tuscaloosa, 1975-78; asst. v.p. U. Louisville, 1978-82; pres., chief exec. officer Falsoft, Inc., 1981—; pub., editor Rainbow mag., 1981—, PCM mag., 1982—; pub. ScoreCARD mag., 1983—; pub. Soft Sector mag., 1984—, Rainbow Books, 1983—; pub. VCR Mag., 1985—, Voice Newspaper, 1986—, Louisville Skyline Newspaper, 1986—; pres., chief exec. officer FPSS, Ag., 1963—; chief exec. officer, chmn. Posh Travel Assistance, Inc., 1985—; instr. public relations, 1979—; cons. Gadsden Community Coll.; speaker, seminar leader Council for Advancement and Support Edn. Recipient Louisville Creative Competition award, 1980, 81, Council for Advancement and Support of Edn. award, 1980, 81, citation Ala. Legislature, 1971. Mem. Public Relations Soc. Am., Sigma Delta Chi (Investigative Reporting award 1970). Jewish. Clubs: B'nai B'rith (Outstanding Adv. to Youth citation 1971), Jewish Community Center, The Temple; Jefferson. Home: 5803 Timber Ridge Dr Prospect KY 40059 Office: Falsoft Bldg 9509 US Hwy 42 Prospect KY 40059

FALKENBERG, JOAN BARBARA, geologist; b. Uvalde, Tex., Aug. 10, 1951; d. Wil G. and Barbara Lee (Davenport) Falkenberg. A.S., San Antonio Coll., 1972; B.S. in Geology, St. Mary's U., 1978; M.S. in Environ. Resources, U. Tex.-San Antonio, 1986. Geologist Montgomery's Stratigraphic Service, San Antonio, 1979—. Author: (field trip guide book) Seven Mile Hill, 1985. Mem. S. Tex. Geol. Soc. (chmn. field trips 1982-85, chmn. pub. relations 1985-86), Assn. Engring. Geologists, Soc. Petroleum Engrs. (nat. chmn. publicity 1982), San Antonio Conservation Soc., Am. Petroleum Inst., Am. Assn. Petroleum Geologists. Ch. Christ. Home: 431 Lively St San Antonio TX 78213 Office: Montgomery's Stratigraphic Services 1134 Milam Bldg San Antonio TX 78205

FALKOWSKI, HENRY STEVEN, chemistry educator; b. Nanticoke, Pa., Oct. 8, 1951; s. Henry Leonard and Katherine (Uhas) F.; m. Terry Gae Harman, May 16, 1981. Assoc. Sci., Luzerne County Community Coll., Wilkes-Barre, Pa., 1971; B.S. in Chemistry, King's Coll., Wilkes-Barre, 1973; M.S. in Analytical Chemistry, W.Va. U., 1976, Ed.D. in Chemistry Edn., 1983. Lab. technician Luzerne County Community Coll., 1971; lab. instr., teaching asst. W.Va. U., Morgantown, 1973-76, instr. chemistry Potomac State Coll., Keyser, W.Va., 1976-84, asst. prof., 1984—. Recipient Sch. and Community Service award VFW, 1969; acad. scholar State of Pa., 1970-73. Mem. Internat. Naval Research Orgn., U.S. Naval Inst., W.Va. Acad. Sci., Am. Chem. Soc., Two-Yr. Coll. Chemistry Conf., Nat. Sci. Tchrs. Assn., Internat. Union, Pure and Applied Chemistry (assoc.). Democrat. Roman Catholic. Author lab. manuals, 1980, 82; contbr. articles to profl. jours. Home: 76 1/2 James St Keyser WV 26726 Office: Box 533-FO Potomac State Coll Keyser WV 26726

FALLON, DANIEL, college dean, psychology educator; b. Cartagena, Colombia, Aug. 24, 1938; came to U.S., 1941; s. Carlos and Maureen Bligh (Byrne) F.; m. Christine Frances Laird, June 20, 1964; children—Kathleen Maria, Sylvia Maureen. B.A., Antioch Coll., 1961; M.A., U. Va., 1963, Ph.D., 1965. Asst. prof. psychology SUNY-Binghamton, 1965-72, assoc. prof., 1972-76, asst. dean arts and scis., 1969-71, assoc. dean, 1971-76; prof. psychology, dean Coll. Liberal Arts and Scis., U. Colo., Denver, 1976-84; prof. psychology, dean Coll. Liberal Arts, Tex. A&M U., College Station, 1984—; cons. NEH. Author: The German University: A Heroic Ideal in Conflict with the Modern World, 1980 (Kayden prize 1981). Contbr. articles to profl. jours. Founder, pres. Friends of Opera in Colo., Denver, 1982. Mem. AAAS, Am. Psychol. Assn., Council Colls. Arts and Scis., Conf. Urban Colls. Arts, Letters and Scis. Democrat. Congregationalist. Home: 1014 Madera Circle College Station TX 77840 Office: Office of Dean Coll Liberal Arts Tex A & M U College Station TX 77843

FALLON, RICHARD GORDON, university dean, theater director; b. N.Y.C., Sept. 17, 1923; s. Perlie Peter and Margaret Elizabeth & Julia F.; student Brown U., 1941-42; B.A., M.A., Columbia U., 1951; cert. excellence Old Vic Theatre Sch., 1945; m. Suzanne Constance Bowkett, Jan. 7, 1945; children—Diane Elizabeth Fallon Tomasi, Richard Wiley. Radio-stage actor, dir., N.Y.C., 1940-46; dir. theatre Hartwick Coll., 1946-50, Md. State Coll., 1950-54; founder, exec. dir. Asolo State Theatre, Sarasota, Fla., 1961—; dean Sch. Theatre, Fla. State U., Tallahassee, 1973—, Lawton disting. prof., 1975—. Chmn. bd. chancellors MacArthur Center for Am. Theatre; chmn. bd. dirs. Burt Reynolds Found. for Theatre Tng. Served with AUS, 1942-45. Recipient Harbison award, 1971. Mem. Am. Theatre Assn. (pres.-elect 1981), Nat. Theatre Conf. (pres. 1975), The Players, Southeastern Theatre Conf., Fla. Theatre Conf. Home: 2302 Delgado Dr Tallahassee FL 32304 Office: Sch Theatre Fla State Univ Tallahassee FL 32306

FANCHER, CHARLES EDWARD, JR., utility company executive; b. Miami, Fla., Jan. 22, 1950; s. Charles Edward and Jean Margaret (Bramlett) F.; m. Barbara Johns Fancher, Dec. 20, 1971. B.S.B.A., U. Fla., 1972; M.B.A., U. Miami, 1979. Acctg. dept. Fla. Power Light, Miami, various positions, 1973-77, acct., 1977-78; rate case coordinator Gen. Devel. Utilities, Miami, 1978-79, various positions, 1980-83, v.p. ops. and fin., 1984—; dir. C.R. Lee & Assocs., Miami, 1976—. Trustee, Better Govt. Polit. Action Com., Miami, 1982—. Mem. Fla. Waterwork Assn. (dir. 1984—), Phi Delta Theta. Club: University (Miami, Fla.).

FANDRICH, ROBERT THOMAS, JR., engineering executive; b. Milw., Mar. 10, 1939; s. Robert Thomas and Erika (Gilomen) F.; B.S., U. Wis., Madison, 1961; M.S., Purdue U., 1964; m. Judith Ellin Fieschko, Oct. 28, 1961; children—Robert Thomas III, Laura Judith, Christopher Grant; m. 2d, Christine Androsko, Sept. 11, 1982; children—Kristin Day, Lamar Day. Designer Torrington Bearing Co. (Conn.), 1961-63; project engr. A. C. Electronics Co., Milw., 1964-67; mgr. dept. environ. engring., materials engring., product design mech. engring. Harris Electronic Systems div., Melbourne, Fla., 1967—; lectr. in field. Instr. Marquette U., 1965, Milw. Sch. Engring., 1966. Mem. Inst. Environ. Scis. (panel on cost effectiveness in dynamic testing 1974), Mensa, Internat. Meditation Soc. Unitarian. Contbr. articles to profl. jours. Home: 1754 Brookside St NE Palm Bay FL 32907 Office: PO Box 8000 Melbourne FL 32901

FANNIN, TROY EDWARD, optometrist, educator; b. Sandy Hook, Ky., Jan. 19, 1925; s. Floyd Mitchell and Elizabeth (Hayes) F.; B.S., U.S. Mcht. Marine Acad., 1945; B.S., O.D., Ohio State U., 1952; m. Cecile Mae Owen, Nov. 24, 1949; 1 dau., Heather Fay. Marine engr. Isthmian S.S. Co., 1945-46, Coastwise S.S. Co., 1946-47; instr. U. Houston Coll. Optometry, 1954-56, asst. prof., 1965-68, asso. prof., 1968-73, prof., 1973—, chmn. dept. clin. scis., 1974-79, optics tract coordinator, 1979—; vis. asso. prof. U. Calif. at Berkeley, summer 1969; pvt. practice optometry, Houston, 1956-65. Served to lt. USNR. Diplomate Nat. Bd. Optometry. Mem. Am. Acad. Optometry (past chmn. sect. meetings), Am., Tex., Harris County optometric assns., AAUP, Tex. Assn. Coll. Tchrs., Editorial Council Am. Acad. Optometry, Assn. Optometric Educators, Beta Sigma Kappa. Unitarian. Home: 13334 Bretagne Dr Houston TX 77015

FANSHIER, CHESTER, metal products mfg. exec.; b. Wilson County, Kans., Mar. 2, 1897; s. Thomas J. and Nora Bell (Maxwell) F.; m. Ina Muriel Goens, Apr. 12, 1918; 1 dau., Norma Elaine (Mrs. Robert B. Rice). Gen. mgr. Bart Products Co., 1932-39; pres., gen. mgr. Metal Goods Mfg. Co., 1939—. Commr. Tulsa Presbytery to 156th Gen. Assembly, Presbyn. Ch. U.S.A., 1944; pres. Sunday Eve. Fedn. (chs.), 1937-38. Recipient Wisdom award Honor, 1970; Gutenberg Bible award; Ring of the Order of Engrs.; Paul Harris fellow, 1981. Registered profl. engr., Okla. Mem. ASME (life), ASTM, Am. Def. Preparedness Assn. (life), Nat. Rifle Assn. (life), Nat., Okla. (charter) socs. profl. engrs., Okla. Rifle Assn. (life), Profl. Photographers Am., SAR, Bartlesville C. of C. Presbyn. (elder). Clubs: Rotary (pres. 1956-57), Engrs. Bartlesville (charter mem.; past dir.). Home: 1328 Cherokee Ave Bartlesville OK 74003 Office: 309 W Hensley Blvd Bartlesville OK 74003

FANTLE, SHELDON W., retail chain drug store executive. Student, Ohio State U.; B.S., U. Cin. Exec. v.p. and gen. mgr. Schuman Drug Co., 1951-70; pres., chief exec. officer, Lane Drug Co., 1970-75; pres., chief exec. officer Lane Drug Corp., 1973-75; with Peoples' Drug Stores, Inc., Alexandria, Va., 1975—, chmn. bd., pres., chief exec. officer and dir.; dir. Am. Security Corp. Office: Peoples' Drug Stores Inc 6315 Bren Mar Dr Alexandria VA 22312*

FARABEE, RAY, state senator, lawyer; b. Nov. 22, 1932; student Midwestern U.; B.B.A., U. Tex., LL.B. Admitted to Tex. bar; mem. Tex. Senate, 1975—. Office: PO Box 12068 Austin TX 78711 also PO Drawer S & P Wichita Falls TX 76307

FARAGHER, THOMAS JAMES, banker; b. Seattle, May 20, 1941; s. Thomas Robert and Mary Jane (Mueller) F.; m. Ana Cristina Cabrera, July 16, 1966; 1 son, Robert. B.B.A., U. Wash., 1963; M.B.A., Stanford U., 1975. Credit officer Wells Fargo Bank, San Jose, Calif., 1965-67; stockbroker Dean Witter & Co., San Mateo, Calif., 1967-70; stockbroker Reynolds Securities, San Mateo, 1970-73; regional mgr. Tex. Commerce Bank, Houston, 1975-79; chmn. bd., dir. Tex. Commerce Bank, Dallas, 1979—; dir. Tex. Commerce Bank, Quorum. Bd. dirs. Dallas Clearing House Assn., Theatre Arts Ctr. Assn., Inc.; mem. CBD Hist. Bldg. Preservation Commn., CBD Task Force, Mayor's Task Force on Historic Bldgs., City of Dallas Landmark Com. bd. dirs. Theatre Three; trustee Dallas/Ft. Worth Leukemia Soc.; bd. dirs. Dallas Soc. Crippled Children, Central Bus. Dist. Assn., Better Bus. Bur. Served to lt. comdr. USN, 1963-65. Mem. Stanford Bus. Sch. Alumni Assn. Republican. Episcopalian. Clubs: Rotary of Dallas, Northwood, Plaza Athletic, Chaparral (Dallas); Westside Tennis (Houston). Home: 13732 Hughes Ln Dallas TX 75240 Office: PO Box 222265 Dallas TX 75222

FARBER, GEORGE ALLAN, dermatologist; b. Miami, Fla., Jan. 4, 1934; s. Charles R. and Clara M. (Milman) F.; B.S., La. State U., 1955, M.D., 1959; m. Nancy Graves, Dec. 26, 1955; children—George Allan, Michael G., Jeffrey N., Guy C., Scott O. Intern So. Bapt. Hosp., New Orleans, 1959-60; resident Charity Hosp. of New Orleans, 1963-66; pvt. practice dermatology, 1970—; commd. 2d lt. M.C., U.S. Air Force, 1955, advanced through grades to lt. col., 1965; chief aviation medicine and mil. pub. health Luke AFB, Phoenix, 1960-63; flight surgeon, chief dermatology and syphilology Cam Ranh Bay, Viet Nam, 12th U.S. Air Force Hosp., 1966-67; chief dermatology service and cons. to Surgeon Gen. for S.E. region U.S. Air Force Med. Referral Center, Keesler AFB, Miss., 1967-70, ret., 1970; mem. staff Charity Hosp. New Orleans, East Jefferson Hosp., So. Bapt. Hosp.; asst. prof. medicine Tulane U. Sch. Medicine, New Orleans, 1970-75, assoc. prof., 1976—, clin. asso. prof. dermatology, 1975—; pres. Burks Dermatology & Dermatologic Surgery Clinic, P.C.; mem. profl. staff Kenner Dermatology Clinic; chmn. bd., pres. Zenith Polyfactoring Corp., 1963-81; dir. Fairground Corp., New Orleans. Decorated Air medal with 3 oak leaf clusters, Bronze Star; diplomate Am. Bd. Dermatology. Mem. Am. Acad. Dermatology, Am. Soc. Dermatologic Surgery (pres. 1978-79), Am. Assn. Physicians and Surgeons, Assn. Mil. Dermatologists (life), So. Med. Assn., Am. Assn. Cosmetic Surgeons (dir.), Internat. Soc. Dermatologic Surgery, Air Force Soc. Internists and Allied Specialists, AMA, Kenner Dermatol. Soc. (dir.), VFW, Alpha Tau Omega, Phi Chi. Democrat. Methodist. Club: Chateau Golf and Country. Contbr. articles to med. jours. Home: #5 Chateau Petrus Ct Kenner LA 70065 Office: 144 Elk Pl Suite 1604 New Orleans LA 70112 also 3701 Williams Blvd Suite 301 Kenner LA 70065

FARBER, JIMMIE DELOSS, English educator; b. Lyons, Nebr., July 25, 1927; s. Leo Deloss and Anna La Vena (Pounds) F.; m. Elsie Margaret Schumacher, Aug. 7, 1947; children—Anne Louise, Steven Michael. B.A. summa cum laude, Midwestern State U., Wichita Falls, Tex., 1968, M.A., 1970; Ed.D., Tex. Tech. U., 1979. Self-employed in agrl., Munday, Tex., 1949-65; English instr. Lamar U., Beaumont, Tex., 1970-72; English tchr. Vernon Regional Jr. Coll., Tex., 1972—, chmn. communications dept., 1982—. Active county agrl. coms., farmer's co-op, 1949-65; chmn. subcom. Vernon Ind. Sch. Dist., 1983. Served to staff sgt. USAF, 1944-48. Mem. Nat. Council Tchrs. of English, Tex. Jr. Coll. Tchrs. Assn., Phi Kappa Phi, Alpha Chi. Roman Catholic. Avocations: carpentry; gardening. Home: 2902 Sunset Circle Vernon TX 76384 Office: Vernon Regional Jr Coll 4400 Coll Dr Vernon TX 76384

FARBER, SCOTT PHILLIP, advertising executive; b. Chgo., Dec. 18, 1951; s. Seymour and Lenore Miriam (Pitalis) F.; m. Marilyn Sue Higgins, Aug. 31, 1974 (div. Feb. 1981); 1 dau., Kelly Ann. B.A., Okla. U., 1974. Account exec., program dir. Sta. WRMN, Elgin, Ill., 1974-76; sports dir., anchor Sta. KTIV-TV, Sioux City, Iowa, 1976-78, Sta. WPTA-TV, Ft. Wayne, Ind., 1978-79; sr. account exec. Sta. KTVT-TV, Ft. Worth and Dallas, 1980-83; dir. Farber & Stephens Inc., Advt., Syndication and Pub. Relations, Dallas, 1983—. Jewish. Office: North Central Plaza Suite 226 12655 N Central Expressway Dallas TX 75243

FARENTHOLD, FRANCES TARLTON, lawyer, former college president; b. Corpus Christi, Tex., Oct. 2, 1926; d. Benjamin Dudley and Catherine (Bluntzer) Tarlton; A.B., Vassar Coll., 1946; J.D., U. Tex., 1949; LL.D., Hood Coll., 1973, Boston U., 1973, Regis Coll., 1976, Lake Erie Coll., 1979; children—Dudley Tarlton, George Edward, Emilie, James Dougherty, Vincent Bluntzer (dec.). Admitted to Tex. bar, 1949; mem. Tex. Ho. of Reps., 1968-72; dir. legal aide Nueces County, 1965-67; asst. prof. law Tex. So. U., Houston; pres. Wells Coll., Aurora, N.Y., 1976-80. Mem. Tex. adv. com. to U.S. Commn. on Civil Rights, 1968-76; mem. nat. adv. council ACLU; Democratic candidate Gov. Tex., 1972; del. Dem. nat. conv., 1972, 1st woman nominated to be candidate v.p. U.S., 1972; nat. co-chmn. Citizens to Elect McGovern-Shriver, 1972; chairperson Nat. Women's Polit. Caucus, 1973-75, chmn. adv. com., 1975-76; adv. bd. Schlesinger Library Radcliff Coll., 1974-76; trustee Vassar Coll., 1975-82; bd. dirs. Mex. Am. Legal Def. and Ednl. Fund, 1980-84, Women's Advocacy Project, Ctr. for Devel. Policy, adv. bd. 3d World Women's Project. Recipient Lyndon B. Johnson Woman of Year award, 1973. Mem. State Bar Tex. Office: 2100 Travis St Suite 1203 Houston TX 77002

FARGO, ROBERT RAY, shipbuilding executive, retired naval officer; b. Springfield, Ill., Mar. 1, 1926; s. Col. Wells and Betty (Ray) F.; m. Martha Moore Turner, July 2, 1964; children—Leslie Vance, Sandra Leigh, Robert Ray, Stephanie Hepburn. B.S. in Engring., U.S. Naval Acad., 1947; Nav.E. in Naval Architecture and Marine Engring., MIT, 1952. Commd. ensign, 1947, advanced through grades to capt., 1968; served on U.S.S. Rupertus, 1947-49; asst. design officer Supervisor of Shipbuilding and Naval Insp. Ordnance, Groton, Conn., 1952-53; resident supr. shipbuilding Fairchild Aircraft Corp., Farmingdale, N.Y., 1954-55; sr. ship supr. submarines Pearl Harbor Naval Shipyard, Hawaii, 1955-58; asst. for POLARIS shipbuilding Bur. of Ships, Dept. Navy, Washington, 1958-60; asst. inspection officer submarines Supr. Shipbuilding and Naval Insp. Ordnance, U.S. Navy, Newport News, Va., 1960-61, submarine project officer, 1962-63; head Deep Recovery Sect., Deep Submergence Systems Rev. Group, 1963; sr. ship supt. U.S.S. John Adams, asst. shipbuilding supt. Portsmouth Naval Shipyard (N.H.), 1963-64, quality assurance officer, 1964-68; supr. shipbuilding conversion and repair U.S. Navy, Pascagoula, Miss., 1968-70; exec. dir. prodn. Naval Ship Systems Command, Washington; comdr. Phila. Naval Shipyard, 1973-75; fleet maintenance officer, asst. chief staff for maintenance and material readiness U.S. Atlantic Fleet, Norfolk, Va., 1975-77; retired U.S. Navy, 1977; asst. to elec. dir. Ingalls Shipbuilding Div., Pascagoula, 1978, mgr. life cycle support destroyer programs, 1979-82, dir. prodn. standards and ops. adminstrn., 1982—; exec. v.p. Naval Systems Support, Inc., 1978-79. Decorated Legion of Merit (2), Iranian Order of Lion and Sun. Mem. Am. Soc. Naval Engrs., U.S. Naval Acad. Alumni Assn., Navy League U.S. Republican. Episcopalian. Clubs: Pascagoula Country, Rotary Internat. Contbr. articles to profl. jours. Home: 3703 Crosby Dr Pascagoula MS 39567

FARIA, EDWARD CYRINO, health care administrator; b. Peabody, Mass., Aug. 12, 1924; s. Celestino and Laura (Lucio) F.; student U. S.C., 1948-50, 1956-60, U.S. Armed Forces Inst., 1957-58, So. Ill. U., 1961-65; certificate USAF Sch. Aviation Medicine Air U., 1955; m. Gloria Jewel Harrison, Jan. 15, 1944; children—Gloria Dawn, Evelyn Celeste, Elizabeth Vermel. Served as enlisted man USAAF, 1942-46, USAF, 1950-67, advanced through grades to chief master sgt. USAF, 1960; med. adminstrv. specialist USAAF, 1942-46; chief storekeeper VA Regional Office, S.C., 1946-50; med. adminstrv. supt. Lawson AFB Hosp., Ga., 12th Air Force Surgeons' Office, Wiesbaden, Germany, Spangdahlem Air Base, Toul-Rosier Air Base, France, 1950-67; adjutant Spandahlem Air Base, 1951-54; exec. officer Mil. Air Transport Service, Scott AFB, Ill., 1961-62, chief adminstrv. services, 1965-66; asst. adminstr. Myrtle Beach (S.C.) AFB Hosp., 1966-67; sr. instr. med. adminstr. USAF Med. Service, USAF Med. Sch., Gunter AFB, Ala., 1954-60; ret., 1967; loan guarantee analyst VA Regional Office, Columbia, S.C., 1967; personnel statistician U.S. Army Hosp., Ft. Jackson Hosp., S.C., 1967-68; adminstr. Columbia (S.C.) Area Mental Health Center, 1968—; cons. in community mental health; instr. healthcare adminstrn., psychiat. residency Hall Psychiat. Inst., Columbia. Chmn. deacons Seventh Day Adventist Ch., Montgomery, Ala., 1957-58, supt. Sabbath Sch., Columbia, 1966-67, asst. supt. Sabbath Sch., Orangeburg, S.C., 1975-76, ednl. sec., 1975-76. Fellow Am. Acad. Med. Adminstrs.; mem. Adminstrv. Mgmt. Soc., Assn. Mental Health Adminstrs., Soc. Personnel Adminstrn., USAF Assn., S.C., Am. hosp. assns., Am. Cancer Soc., Heart and Lung Assn., Southeastern Statisticians, Smithsonian Inst. Assos. Clubs: Armed Forces, Am. Legion, DAV, VFW, Elks (hon.), Optimists (v.p. internat. 1971-72). Author: Medical Services Financial Management, 1959; Base Level Medical Checklist for Self Inspection, 1954, 3d rev. edit., 1956. Home: Route 2 Box 351 Saint Matthews SC 29135 Office: 1618 Sunset Dr Columbia SC 29203

FARISH, JAMES MATTHEW, accountant; b. Monroe, Va., Dec. 18, 1946; s. Robert Franklin and Josephine Elizabeth (Dudley) F.; m. Martha Ann Sawyers, Aug. 11, 1972; 1 child, Robert Joseph. B.S., Va. Commonwealth U., 1975, M.B.A., 1978. Pres. Farish Pub. Acctg., Richmond, Va., 1975—. Pres. Bethlehem Little League, Richmond, 1976-80; treas. Lakeside Little League, Richmond, 1982-85, v.p., 1986. Mem. Va. Soc. Pub. Accts. Republican. Baptist. Lodge: Lions (treas. 1977-81, 85-86). Avocation: Golf. Home: 2317 Carr Ln Richmond VA 23230

FARLEY, CHARLES RICHARD, JR., policy analyst, consultant; b. Wheeling, W.Va., July 16, 1947; s. C. Richard and Fritzi Jolene (Hobbs) F.; student W.Va. U., 1965-68; diploma Divers Tng. Acad., Ft. Lauderdale, Fla., 1969; m. Lucia Earle Crawford, May 26, 1979. Underwater instr. and dive master, Cousteau's Project Ocean Search expdns., 1976; journalist Island Packet Newspaper, Hilton Head Island, S.C., 1977-78; dir. program devel. and research Jean-Michel Cousteau Inst., Hilton Head Island, 1978-80; coordinator Cousteau Ops. Center, Norfolk, Va., 1980-81; coordinator info. and policy analysis Cousteau Soc., Norfolk, 1981-83; cons., 1983—; environ. policy analyst, sci. writer. Mem. citizen rev. com. Hilton Head Island Environ. Impact Statement, 1979; mem. S.C. Gov.'s Commn. for Yr. of the Coast, 1980. Mem. Marine Tech. Soc., Profl. Assn. Diving Instrs., World Future Soc., Cousteau Soc. Contbr. investigative, environ. and feature articles to various publs.; contbg. editor Calypso Log mag., Ocean Realm mag.

FARLEY, GAIL CONLEY, librarian; b. Mead, Okla., July 9, 1936; s. William Conley and Marguerite Gaines (Austin) F.; B.S. in History, Sul Ross State U., Alpine, Tex., 1957; M.S. in L.S., East Tex. State U., Commerce, 1970. Served with U.S. Army, 1957-60; tchr. San Felipe Ind. Sch. Dist., Del Rio, Tex., 1963-64; tchr. Natalia (Tex.) Ind. Sch. Dist., 1964-65; librarian Medina Valley Ind. Sch. Dist., Castroville, Tex., 1965-77, La Pryor (Tex.) Ind. Sch. Dist., 1977-78, McCamey (Tex.) Ind. Sch. Dist., 1978—. Reporter Medina County Sheriff's Res., 1973-75, pres., 1975-77. Mem. Tex. Library Assn., Acad. Polit. Sci., Tex. Assn. Sch. Librarians, Assn. Tex. Profl. Educators, Nat. Rifle Assn. (life), Tex. Rifle Assn. (life). Home: PO Box 965 McCamey TX 79752 Office: PO Drawer 1069 McCamey TX 79752

FARLEY, JOSEPH MCCONNELL, electric utility executive; b. Birmingham, Ala., Oct. 6, 1927; s. John G. and Lynne (McConnell) F.; student Birmingham-So. Coll., 1944-45; B.S. in Mech. Engring., Princeton, 1948; student Grad. Sch. Commerce and Bus. Adminstrn., U. Ala., 1948-49; LL.B., Harvard, 1952; L.H.D., Judson Coll., 1974; m. Sheila Shirley, Oct. 1, 1958 (dec. July 1978); children—Joseph McConnell, Thomas Gager, Mary Lynne. Admitted to Ala. bar, 1952; asso. firm Martin, Turner, Blakey & Bouldin, Birmingham, 1952-57; partner successor firm Martin, Balch, Bingham & Hawthorne, 1957-65; exec. v.p., dir. Ala. Power Co., 1965-69, pres., dir., 1969—; v.p. So. Electric Generating Co., 1970-74, pres., 1974—, also dir.; pres., dir. Ala. Property Co.; dir., pres. Columbia Fuels, Inc.; dir. Am.South Bancorp., The So. Co., So. Co. Services, Inc., Associated Industries Ala., So. Electric Internat., AmSouth Bank N.A., Torchmark Corp.; dir. Inst. Nuclear Power Ops. Mem. adv. bd. Salvation Army; vice chmn., trustee Gorgas Scholarship Found.; mem. exec. bd. Southeastern Electric Reliability Council, chmn., 1974-76. Mem. Jefferson County Republican Exec. Com., 1953-65; counsel, mem. Ala. Rep. Com., 1962-65; permanent chmn. Ala. Rep. Conv., 1962; alternate del. Rep. Nat. Conv., 1956. Bd. dirs. Edison Electric Inst., 1976-79, Ala. Safety Council, Inc., Kidney Found. Ala., Ala. Bus. Hall of Fame, Birmingham Area YMCA, Operation New Birmingham, Warrior-Tombigbee Devel. Assn., Jefferson County Community Chest; pres. Southeastern Electric Exchange, 1984; chmn. bd. trustees So. Research Inst.; trustee Thomas Alva Edison Found., Ala. Symphony Assn., Tuskegee Inst.; trustee, pres. bd. trustees Children's Hosp. Birmingham; mem. pres.'s council U. Ala., Birmingham; mem. pres.'s cabinet U. Ala., Tuscaloosa; bd. visitors U. Ala. Sch. Commerce; mem. bus. adv. council Sch. Bus., U. Ala., Birmingham. Mem. Naval Res., 1948; now lt. ret. Mem. Ala., Birmingham bar assns., Ala. Assn. Ind. Colls. (bd. govs.), Ala. C. of C. (dir., pres. 1984), Birmingham Area C. of C. (dir., pres. 1974), Newcomen Soc. N.Am., Phi Beta Kappa, Kappa Alpha, Tau Beta Pi, Beta Gamma Sigma (hon). Episcopalian (vestryman). Clubs: Birmingham Country, Relay House, Downtown (gov.), Princeton of New York, Mountain Brook (gov.), The Club, Inc. Lodge: Rotary. Office: 600 N 18th St Birmingham AL 35291

FARLEY, LINDA NELL, chem. co. exec.; b. Charleston, W.Va., Nov. 24, 1941; d. Frederick Paul and Frances Eloise (Hale) Farley; student Eastern Mont. Coll. of Edn., 1959-60, W.Va. State Coll. Instr. gymnastics Lawrence Frankel Inst., Charleston, 1960-61; sec. Union Carbide Corp., Institute, W.Va., 1961-73, office services supr., 1973-76, sr. office supr., pub. relations adminstr., non-exempt tng. adminstrn., now tng. asso. Mem. Nat. Assn. Female Execs., ASTD. Club: Altrusa (corr. sec. 1976-77) (Charleston). Home: 4 Sitting Bull Dr Saint Albans WV 25177 Office: PO Box 2831 Charleston WV 25330

FARMER, CHARLES DUDLEY, nephrologist; b. Indpls., Nov. 22, 1933; s. Charles R. and Margaret (Shouse) F.; m. Lois Kay Poffenbarger, May 17, 1958; children—Stuart, Douglas, Randall, Suzanne. B.A., Ind. U., 1955, M.D., 1958; M.S., U. Minn., 1965. Diplomate Am. Bd. Internal Medicine. Intern, U. Calif. Hosp., San Francisco, 1959; resident in internal medicine Mayo Clinic, Rochester, Minn., 1961-65; practice medicine specializing in nephrology, Charlotte, N.C., 1966—; nephrologist Nalle Clinic Kidney Ctr., Charlotte, 1975—; dir. dialysis unit Charlotte Meml. Hosp., 1970-82; clin. prof. medicine U. N.C. Sch. Medicine, Chapel Hill. Bd. dirs. Charlotte Opera Assn., Meckenburg County Kidney Found. Served to capt. USAF, 1959-61. Mem. ACP, N.C. Med. Soc., Am. Soc. Nephrology, Am. Soc. Artificial Internal Organs, AMA, Phi Beta Kappa, Alpha Omega Alpha. Office: 928 Baxter St Charlotte NC 28107

FARMER, DAVID JOHN, criminal justice educator, consultant; b. Barnstaple, Eng., July 1, 1935; came to U.S. 1965, naturalized 1970; s. Joseph and Gladys Eva (Bowden) F.; children—Damien, Mark, Gregory, Elizabeth; m. Rosemary Lee Baker, Apr. 16, 1978. B.S., London Sch. Econ. and Polit. Sci., U. London, 1956; M.A. U. Toronto, Ont., Can., 1965; D.P.A., Nova U., 1980; Ph.D., U. London, 1984. Cons., Pub. Adminstrn. Service, Chgo., 1965-70; prin. assoc. Jacobs Co. (Planning Research Corp.), Chgo., 1970-71; spl. asst. to police commr. N.Y.C. Police Dept., 1971-74; dir. police div. Nat. Inst. Justice U.S. Dept. Justice, Washington, 1974-80; chmn., assoc. prof. dept. adminstrn. justice and pub. safety Va. Commonwealth U., Richmond, 1980—; cons. to numerous cities, counties, states, also N.Y. State Conf. Mayors, Am. Pub. Works Assn., Nat. Adv. Commn. on Civil Disorders. Author: Crime Control: The Use & Misuse of Police Resources, 1984; Civil Disorder Control, 1969. Contbr. articles to profl. jours. and chpts. to books. Bd. dirs. Offender Aid and Restoration of Richmond, 1982-85, Human Resources Inc., Richmond, 1982-83, Rubicon Inc., Richmond, 1982-83. mem. Pub. Safety Commn. Park Forest South, Ill., 1968-70. Mem. Acad. Criminal Justice Sci., Am. Econ. Assn., Pub. Choice Soc., Am. Soc. Criminology, Va. Assn. Criminal Justice Educators, Am. Criminal Justice Assn., Internat. Assn. Chief of Police, Am. Soc. Profl. Law Enforcement. Office: Dept Adminstrn Justice and Pub Safety Va Commonwealth Univ 816 W Franklin St Richmond VA 23284-0001

FARMER, ELIZABETH BAILEY, fundraising consultant; b. Durham, N.C., June 18, 1946; d. William Dempsey and Elizabeth (Sellars) F. B.A., Duke U., 1968. Instl. trader Fin. Service Corp., Atlanta, 1970-75, Robinson-Humphrey Co., Inc., Atlanta, 1975; trader, office mgr. Weeden & Co., Atlanta, 1976-77; asst. v.p. Wall, Patterson, McGrew & Hamilton, Inc., Atlanta, 1978-83; cons. Allen MAC Inc., Winston-Salem, N.C., 1984—. Trustee, Chatham Hall, Va., 1980—, pres. Alumnae Assn., 1980-82; active Jr. League Atlanta; mem. Duke U. Council on Women's Studies, 1986—. Mem. Assn. Women in Securities (co-founder, pres. 1977-78, exec. bd. 1978-79), Kappa Alpha Theta. Presbyterian. Office: 114B Reynolda Village Winston-Salem NC 27106

FARMER, JOE SAM, petroleum consultant; b. Hot Springs, Ark., Mar. 2, 1931; s. Walter L. and T. Naomi (Ewalt) F.; student Ohio State U., 1950-51; B.Sc., Tex. A&M U., 1955; m. Elizabeth Jean Keener, Dec. 27, 1952; children—J. Christopher, David E., Kathryn L. Geologist, Lion Oil Co., Shreveport, La., 1955; geologist, asst. chief geologist Placid Oil Co., New Orleans, Shreveport and Dallas, 1958-68; exploration mgr. Union Carbide Petroleum Corp., Houston, 1968-71; v.p. domestic exploration and prodn. Ashland Exploration, Inc., Houston, 1971-73, exec. v.p., Houston, 1973-77; adminstrv. v.p. Ashland Oil, Inc. (Ky.), 1977-79; v.p. Mesa Petroleum Co., Houston, 1979-81; pres., chief oeprating officer Union Tex. Petroleum Corp., Houston, 1981-83; pres. JSF Interests, Inc.; petroleum and bus. cons., 1983—; dir. Bank of S.W., Houston, DeKalb Agresearch, Inc., Ill., Midhurst Corp., Houston. Served with USAF, 1955-58. Cert. petroleum geologist. Mem. Am. Assn. Petroleum Geologists, Am. Petroleum Inst., Mid-Continent Oil and Gas Assn., Houston Geol. Soc., Ind. Producers Assn. Am. (dir.) Clubs: Petroleum (dir., pres.) (Houston); April Sound Country. Home: 9033 Briar Forest Dr Houston TX 77024 Office: Interfirst Plaza Suite 3410 1100 Louisiana Houston TX 77002

FARMER, ROBERT ALAN, advertising executive; b. Orlando, Fla., June 28, 1950; s. Charles Woodrow and Gladys T. (Thompson) F.; m. Jo Ann Scott, Aug. 1, 1970; children—Scott Alan, Brian Anthony. B.A., U. Ky., 1972. Asst. sec. Avery Fed. Savs. & Loan, 1973-79; mktg. dir. Future Fed. Savs. & Loan, Louisville, 1979-82; owner Robert Farmer Communications, Advt. Agy., Louisville, 1982—; dir. Beaux Arts mag. Bd. dirs. Louisville Autistic Children Sch. Recipient 1st Pl. award Ky. League Savs. Assns. Speech Contest, 1979. Mem. Savs. Instns. Mktg. Soc. Am., Pub. Relations Soc. Am., Ad Club Louisville, Nat. Speakers Assn., Ky. Speakers Assn. Democrat. Clubs: Jefferson, Executives (Louisville); Rotary Masons. Contbr. articles to profl. jours. Home: 2213 Bashford Manor Ln Louisville KY 40218 Office: 6100 Dutchman's Ln Louisville KY 40205

FARMER, THOMAS SHELBY, investor; b. New Orleans, Sept. 2, 1931; s. John Walter and Elizabeth Shelby (Buck) F.; B.S. in Chem. Engring., Tulane U., 1952; M.S.E. in Chem. Engring., Princeton U., 1953; m. Ann Wood, Aug. 27, 1955; children—Jeanne, John, Thomas. Various tech. managerial positions Standard Oil of N.J. affiliates, 1953-67; mgr. planning Esso Chem., Inc., N.Y.C., 1967-68; v.p. EssoChem Europe, Brussels, 1968-71; pres. Borg-Warner Chems., Chgo., 1971-77; pres. internat. group Hooker Chem. Co., Houston, 1978-83; ind. investor, 1984—; dir. Winnebago Industries; pres. Chem. Industries Council Midwest, 1976-78. Mem. pres.'s council Tulane U. Served to cpl. U.S. Army, 1953-55. Recipient Harold Levy Alumni award Tulane U., 1962; registered profl. engr., Tex. Mem. Am. Chem. Soc., Am. Inst. Chem. Engrs., Mfg. Chemists Assn. (dir. 1964-67), AAAA, Sigma Alpha Epsilon, Alpha Chi Sigma. Republican. Presbyterian. Club: Chicago Yacht. Home: 327 Florida Blvd New Orleans LA 70124 Office: 719 Napoleon Ave New Orleans LA 70115

FARNSWORTH, DAVID EDWIN, refining company executive; b. Ranger, Tex., Sept. 8, 1920; s. Madison and Martha F.; B.S. in Chem. Engring., Rice U., 1942. Founding officer Eddy Refining Co., Houston, 1946, pres., 1958-83, chief exec. officer, 1970-83; ret., 1983; founding pres. Key Oil Co., 1950-79; dir. Tex. Commerce Med. Bank. Bd. govs. Rice U.; dir. Farnsworth Library and Art Mus., Rockland, Maine; past pres. English Speaking Union, Houston; chmn. bd. Houston Youth Symphony and Ballet; officer United Methodist Found. of Tex. Ann. Conf.; bd. dirs. Soc. Performing Arts, Scurlock Found.; trustee St. Paul's United Meth. Ch., chmn. bd., 1965-66. Served to lt. USN, 1943-46. Recipient Brotherhood award NCCJ, Houston, 1981; named Outstanding Engring. Alumnus, Rice U., 1981; Houston Cultural Leader of Yr., 1983. Mem. Am. Inst. Chem. Engrs. Club: River Oaks Country. Home: 2 Sunset Blvd Houston TX 77005

FARNSWORTH, T BROOKE, lawyer; b. Grand Rapids, Mich., Mar. 16, 1945; s. George Llelwyn and Gladys Fern (Kennedy) F.; m. Cherrill Kay Bowers, Aug. 24, 1968; children—Leslie Erin, T Brooke. B.S. in Bus., Ind. U., 1967; J.D., Ind. U.-Indpls., 1971. Bar: Tex. 1971, U.S. Dist. Ct. (so. dist.) Tex. 1972, U.S. Tax Ct. 1972, U.S. Ct. Appeals (5th cir.) 1977, U.S. Ct. Appeals D.C. Cir. 1977, U.S. Supreme Ct. 1978, U.S. Ct. Appeals (11th cir.) 1982. Adminstrv. asst. to treas. State of Ind., Indpls., 1968-71; assoc. Butler, Binion, Rice, Cook & Knapp, Houston, 1971-74; counsel Damson Oil Corp., Houston, 1974-78; ptnr. Farnsworth & Martin, Houston, 1978—; pres., chmn. bd. TME, Inc., 1983—; corp. sec. Lomax Oil & Gas Co.; dir. Citizens Nat. Bank-West, Dorill Enterprises, Inc., F&L Ventures, Inc. Mem. State Bar Tex., Houston Bar Assn., ABA, Fed. Energy Bar Assn., Comml. Law League Am., Am. Pub. Power Assn. Republican. Mem. Christian Ch. (Disciples of Christ). Clubs: Petroleum of Houston, Champions Golf (Houston); Greenspoint. Contbr. articles on law to profl. jours. Home: 5903 Bermuda Dunes Dr Houston TX 77069 Office: 333 N Belt Suite 800 Houston TX 77060

FARR, ABE ROWSHANI, petroleum engineer, energy consultant; b. Kermanshah, Iran, Jan. 18, 1948, came to U.S., 1975, naturalized, 1984; s. Nasser and Taban Rowshah; m. Song Sun Kim, Feb. 24, 1979; children—Samuel, Farah. B.S. in Geology, Pahlavi U., Iran, 1974; M.S. in Engring., Tulsa U., 1976, M.S. in Geophysics, 1978, Ph.D. in Geophysics, 1983. Cons., Associated Resource Cons., Tulsa, 1978-82, Regent Oil & Gas, Tulsa, 1983-84; geologist Clyde Petroleum, Tulsa, 1982-83; petroleum engr. Oneok Exploration, Tulsa, 1984—. Author: Pressure Buildup Analysis, 1976. Mem. Assn. Petroleum Geologists, Soc. Petroleum Engrs., Soc. Exploration Geophysicists, Tulsa Geol. Soc., Soc. Profl. Well Log Analysts. Avocations: swimming; travelling. Home: 8521 E 78th Place Tulsa OK 74133

FARR, PATRICIA HUDAK, librarian; b. Youngstown, Ohio, Mar. 10, 1945; d. Frank Francis and Anna Frances (Tylka) Hudak; m. William Howard Farr, Aug. 28, 1971; 1 dau., Jennifer Anne. B.A., Youngstown State U., 1970; M.L.S., U. Md., 1980. Children's librarian Pub. Library Youngstown and Mahoning (Ohio), 1970-71; asst. Fla. State U. Library, Tallahassee, 1971-73; research asst. John Hopkins U. Sch. Hygiene and Pub. Health, Balt., 1974-76; asst. Mary Washington Coll. Library, Fredericksburg, Va., 1976-79; children's librarian Central Rappahannock Regional Library, Fredericksburg, 1980-84, young adult librarian, 1984—. Revision editor HEW pub. Thesaurus of Health Education Terminology, 1976; compiler Health Edn. Monographs, 1974-76. Youngstown State U. scholar, 1963-64; R.V. Lowery Meml. scholar, 1979-80. Mem. ALA, Va. Library Assn. Democrat. Roman Catholic. Club: Rappahannock Twirlers Square Dance. Home: Route 11 Box 1634 Fredericksburg VA 22405 Office: Central Rappahannock Regional Library 1201 Caroline St Fredericksburg VA 22401

FARR, RUSSELL HAYNES, investment consultant; b. Blytheville, Ark., Feb. 20, 1923; s. Russell Carter and Mabel Anna (Haynes) F.; B.S. in Bus. Adminstrn., U. E.Fla., 1950; B.A., Shaw U., 1975, Edison Coll., 1976; Ph.D. in Humanities (hon.), Calif. Western U., 1975; m. Mary Sue Piercy, July 22, 1944; 1 son, Gary Russell. Ptnr., then owner R.C. Farr & Sons Oil Co., Blytheville, 1946-78; ptnr., then owner Delta Propane Co., Blytheville, 1955-78; ind. investment cons., Blytheville, 1978—; dir. Blytheville Fed. Savs. & Loan Assn. Past pres. Chickasawba chpt. ARC, Blytheville Bowling Assn.; pres. Blytheville United Way, 1980-81; mem., sec.-treas. Blytheville Sewer Commn., 1980—; county Democratic committeeman, 1978—; trustee Mississippi County Community Coll., 1983—; mem. Ark. State L-P Gas Adv. Bd., 1983—. Served with AUS, 1942-46, 51-52. Decorated Bronze Star, Purple Heart. Mem. Ind. Cons. Am. (gov. 1979-82), Blytheville C. of C. (past pres.), Am. Soc. Quality Control, Nat. Assn. Accountants, Nat. Mgmt. Assn. (cert. profl. mgr.), U. Ark. Alumni Assn., 11th Armored Div. Assn., Air Force Assn., VFW (life), Am. Legion, Sigma Alpha Epsilon. Baptist. Clubs: Nat. Sojourners (past pres. Blytheville), Blytheville Country (past pres.), Masons. Home: 1805 Eastgate Ln Blytheville AR 72315 Office: 398 S 3d St Blytheville AR 72315

FARRAR, JOEL PHILLIP, insurance executive; b. El Dorado, Ark., May 19, 1943; s. Clyde L. and Zada (Trull) F.; m. Helen E. Farrar, Oct. 29, 1965 (div. 1984); children—Kim Lanette, Christopher Eric. B.S., La. Inst. Tech., 1966, postgrad., 1966-71; grad. Life Underwriter Tng. Council, 1981. Deptl. bus. mgr. La. Inst. Tech., Ruston, La., 1966-71; asst. bus. mgr. Wharton County (Tex.) Jr. Coll., 1971-74; comptroller Galveston Coll. (Tex.), 1974-76; owner Gulf Coast Office Products, Texas City, Tex., 1976-80; spl. agt. Prudential Ins. Co., Houston, 1979-82; pres. CKF, Inc., Texas City, 1982—; gen. agt., owner J. Phillip Farrar & Assocs., Texas City, 1982—. Contbr. articles to profl. jours. Pres., Galveston County Children's Protective Services Bd., 1978; bd. dirs. Tex. Jaycee Hosp. Found., Grand Prairie, 1973-81. Recipient Cert. of Commendation, Tex. Ho. of Reps., 1973; Outstanding Service award La. Peach Festival, 1969; Disting. Service award ARC, 1967; others. Mem. Nat. Assn. Life Underwriters, Tex. Assn. Life Underwriters, Mainland Assn. Life Underwriters (pres. 1982-83), S.W. Football Ofcls. Assn., Nat. Assn. Sports Ofcls. Jaycees (internat. senator 1976; Outstanding Adminstrv. Nat. Dir. and Presdl. award of Honor 1976-77; Outstanding Apptd. Officer 1975-76). Lodge: Kiwanis. Office: 922 14th St N PO Box 2536 Texas City TX 77592

FARRAR, SIDNEY BOB, music producer, composer; b. Dallas, June 16, 1928; s. Simon Bowden and Gladys (Reynolds) F.; m. Carolyn Sue Belton, June 21, 1956 (div. Oct. 1970); children—Stephen Martin, Suzanne Margaret, Scott Bowden. B.Mus., So. Meth. U., 1951; postgrad. North Tex. State U., 1985—, Northwestern U., summer 1952. Music dir. Liberty Broadcast System, Dallas, 1951-52; program dir. KENS-TV, San Antonio, 1952-55; co-owner Charles Meeks Advt., Dallas, 1956-58; asst. music dir. Comml. Rec. Corp., Dallas, 1958-62; co-owner Radio Sta. KVIL, Dallas, 1958-62; creative dir. Pams Music Prodns., Dallas, 1962-68; pres. Bob Farrar Music Prodns., Dallas, 1971—; music cons. to advt. agys., film producers. Bd. dirs. 1st Meth. Ch., Dallas, 1960-62. Served with Tex. Nat. Guard, 1948-60. Recipient San Antonio Journalism TV award San Antonio Evening News, 1953; Peabody award, 1979; awards Columbia Film Festival, Am. Film Festival, Internat. Film Festival on Human Environ., N.Y. Film Festival; CINE Golden Eagle, CHRIS award, Eudora Welly award. Mem. Am. Fed. Musician, AFTRA, ASCAP, Blue Key, Phi Mu Alpha Sonfonia. Republican. Methodist. Composer music for film series Human Dimensions, So. Bapt. Radio/TV Commn., 1971, Christian Athletes, 1973; music for PBS-TV series Profiles in Am. Art, 1982-83; music for U.S. Air Force film A Strong America; music for feature film A Father, A Son, A Three Mile Run, Play Dead, 1983, The Angel of Sardis, 1985, Terror at Ten Killer; Music for PBS miniseries Lone Star.

FARRELL, ANNE DOYLE, communications company executive; b. South Bend, Ind., June 22, 1948; d. Vincent T. and Isabel (Molloy) Doyle; m. Michael J. Farrell, Sept. 21, 1985. student U. Madrid, 1968-69; B.A. in Spanish, U. Mich., 1972. Intern TV news Northwestern U., summer 1973; news reporter Sta. WJIM, Lansing, Mich., 1972-73; news anchor/reporter Sta. WDEE, Detroit, 1973, Sta. WZZM-TV, Grand Rapids, Mich., 1973-77; anchor Sta. KHJ-TV, Los Angeles, 1977-78; sports reporter, anchor Sta. WJBK-TV, Detroit, 1978-83; news editor UPI, Atlanta, 1984-85; pres. Doyle-Farrell & Assocs., bus. communications, Atlanta, 1985—; lectr. George Washington U., AAUW, others. Recipient awards UPI, AP, others. Mem. Sportswomen in Detroit (pres. 1980-83), Detroit Sports Broadcasters Assn., Women in Communications, Nat. Acad. TV Arts and Scis., AFTRA. Office: Doyle-Farrell & Assocs Atlanta GA

FARRELL, EDMUND JAMES, English language educator, author; b. Butte, Mont., May 17, 1927; s. Bartholomew J. and Lavinia H. (Collins) F.; A.B., Stanford U., 1950, M.A., 1951; Ph.D., U. Calif., Berkeley, 1969; m. Jo Ann Hayes, Dec. 19, 1964; children—David, Kevin, Sean. Chmn. English dept. James Lick High Sch., San Jose, Calif., 1954-59; supr. secondary English, U. Calif. at Berkeley, 1959-70; field rep. Nat. Council Tchrs. English, 1970-71, asst. exec. sec., 1971-73, asso. exec. dir., 1973-78; adj. prof. English, U. Ill., Urbana, 1973-78; prof. English edn. U. Tex., Austin, 1978—; pres. Farrell Ednl. Services; speaker at local, state and nat. confs. of English tchrs., 1954—; cons. to NDEA Insts., 1965-68; reader compositions for advanced placement program Rider Coll., Princeton, N.J., 1969, 72-77; participant revision of lit. objectives Nat. Assessment of Ednl. Progress, Denver, 1972-73, 78-82; chmn. English discipline com. Coll. Entrance Exam. Bd., 1974-79. Served with USNR, 1945-46. Fellow Nat. Conf. Research on English; mem. Nat. Council Tchrs. English (disting. service award 1982), Coll. Composition and Communication Assn., Calif. Assn. Tchrs. English (pres. 1962-63), Tex. Joint Council Tchrs. English (pres. 1986-87), Phi Delta Kappa. Unitarian. Co-author: Exploring Life Through Literature, 1964; Counterpoint in Literature, 1967;

Projection in Literature, 1967; Outlooks in Literature, 1973; Fantasy: Forms of Things Unknown, 1974; Science Fact/Fiction, 1974; Comment, 1976; Myth, Mind, and Moment, 1976; I/You, We/They, 1976; Traits and Topics, 1976; Up Stage/Down Stage, 1976; To Be, 1976; Conflict in Reality, 1976; Arrangement in Literature, 1979; Purpose in Literature, 1979; Album U.S.A., 1979; Discoveries in Literature, 1985; Patterns in Literature, 1985. Home: 6500 Sumac St Austin TX 78731 Office: Dept Curriculum and Instruction U Texas Austin TX 78712

FARRELL, JOHN MARSHALL, architect; b. Poplar Bluff, Mo., Nov. 2, 1942; s. Marshall Dee and Frieda Mae (Burk) F.; m. Susan Martha Garbett, Dec. 7, 1968; children—Kevin, Elizabeth. B.Arch., Tex. Tech U., 1965. Registered architect Tex., N.Mex., Calif., Fla. Designer Skidmore Owings & Merrill, Chgo., 1968-70; project architect Bernard Johnson Inc., Houston, 1970-72; project architect NSHD Inc., Houston, 1972-73; prin., corp. dir., project mgr. Golemon & Rolfe Assocs. Inc., Houston, 1973-83; pres. Farrell-Robson Architects Inc., 1983—. Mem. zoning and planning comm. City of West University Place (Tex.), 1980-82; v.p. West University Little League, 1981-83; mem. adminstrv. bd. St. Luke's United Methodist Ch., Houston, 1982-84. Served as officer USNR, 1965-68; Vietnam. Mem. AIA (past dir. Houston chpt.), Tex. Soc. Architects, NCARB (cert.), Council Ednl. Facility Planners. Club: Briar. Archtl. works: U. Houston at Clear Lake City, 1975; Riverwalk Marriott Hotel, San Antonio, 1978; Oak Ridge High Sch., Conroe, Tex., 1981; Saida Hilton Condominium, South Padre Island, 1982; Crowne Plaza West Loop Hotel, Houston, 1983. Home: 3028 Wroxton Rd Houston TX 77005 Office: 3000 Post Oak Suite 1330 Houston TX 77056

FARRER-MESCHAN, RACHEL (MRS. ISADORE MESCHAN), physician; b. Sydney, Australia, May 21, 1915; came to U.S., 1946, naturalized, 1950; d. John H. and Gertrude (Powell) Farrer; m. Isadore Meschan, Sept. 3, 1943; children—David, Jane Meschan Foy, Rosalind Meschan Weir, Joyce Irene. M.B., B.S., U. Melbourne (Australia), 1940; M.D., Wake Forest U., 1957. Intern Royal Melbourne (Australia) Hosp., 1942; resident Women's Hosp., Melbourne, 1942-43, Bowman-Gray Sch. Medicine, Wake Forest U., Winston-Salem, N.C., 1957-73, asst. clin. prof. dept. ob-gyn, 1973—. Co-author (with I. Meschan): Atlas of Radiographic Anatomy, 1951, rev., 1959; Roentgen Signs in Clinic Diagnosis, 1956; Synopsis of Roentgen Signs, 1962; Roentgen Signs in Clinical Practice, 1966; Radiographic Positioning and Related Anatomy, 1968; Analysis of Roentgen Signs in General Radiology, 1973; Roentgen Signs in Diagnostic Imaging, Vol. III, 1985, Vol. IV, 1986. Home: 305 Weatherfield Ln Kernersville NC 27284

FARRINGER, JOHN LEE, JR., surgeon, educator; b. Bowling Green, Ky., Sept. 4, 1920; s. John Lee and Zora (Lawson) F.; B.A., Vanderbilt U., 1942; M.D., U. Tenn., 1945, M.S., 1950; m. Mary Margaret Smith, Mar. 8, 1947; children—John Lee, III, Janice Ann, Mary Jill. Intern, Harris Meml. Meth. Hosp., Ft. Worth, 1946; resident John Gaston and U. Tenn. Hosp., Memphis, 1949-54; practice surgery, Nashville, 1954—; asst. clin. prof. surgery Vanderbilt U. Sch. Medicine, 1956-84, assoc. clin. prof. surgery, 1984—; chief surgery Baptist Hosp., Nashville, 1966-69, pres. staff, 1971, vice chief staff, 1973-75, chief of staff, 1976-78; assoc. clin. prof. Surgery U. Tenn., 1983-85. Coordinator, Battle Nashville Centennial Commemoration, 1964—; chmn. Met. Hist. Commn., Nashville, 1966-73; exec. bd. Middle Tenn. council Boy Scouts Am., 1961—; pres. Davidson County Found. for Med. Care, 1973-75; mem. Statewide Health Coordinating Council, 1977-81. Bd. dirs. Davidson County unit Am. Cancer Soc., Davidson County Council Retarded Children, Police Assistance League, Profl. Systems Nashville, Tenn., Middle Tenn. Health Systems Agy.; trustee Parkview Hosp., 1970-73. Served with AUS, 1943-45. Diplomate Am. Bd. Surgery. Fellow Soc. for Surgery of Alimentary Tract, A.C.S. (pres. Tenn. chpt. 1983-84), Southeastern Surg. Congress, Collegium Internationale Chirurgiae Digestivae, Société International de Chirurgie, So. Surg. Assn., Am. Geriatric Soc.; mem. Nashville Acad. Medicine (dir. 1970-73), Davidson County Med. Soc. (dir. 1970-73), So. Med. Assn., Nashville Surg. Soc. (pres. 1973), Harwell Wilson Surg. Soc. (pres. 1977-78), Co. Mil. Historians, Nashville Area C. of C., Alpha Kappa Kappa. Clubs: Richland Country, Nashville City, University (Nashville). Contbr. articles to surg. jours. Home: 2325 Golf Club Lane Nashville TN 37215 Office: 1919 Hayes St Nashville TN 37203

FARRINGTON, JERRY S., utility holding company executive; b. Burkburnett, Tex. B.B.A., North Tex. State U., 1955, M.B.A., 1958. With Tex. Electric Service Co., 1957-60; v.p. Tex. Utilities Co. (parent co.), 1970-76, pres., Dallas, 1983—, Dallas Power & Light Co., chief exec. officer, 1976-83; chmn. Tex. Electric Co. Office: Tex Utilities Co 2001 Bryan Tower Dallas TX 75201*

FARRIS, JAMES RUSSELL, geologist; b. Ft. Worth, Tex., Apr. 23, 1937; s. Maldon Floyd and Mary Helen (Anderson) F.; student Baylor U., 1955-57, M.A., 1965; student Am. Inst. Banking, Los Angeles, 1957, Hardin Simmons U., B.A., 1963; postgrad. Mesa Coll., 1973-75, Ohio U., 1976-79; m. Mava Janeece Johnston, Aug. 3, 1962; children—Gwendolyn Camille, Elizabeth Renee, Allison Nicole. Chief geologist First Worth Corp., Denton, Tex., 1965-69; sr. petrologist, mgr. mineralogy petrology lab. Lucius Pitkin Inc., Grand Junction, Colo., 1969-73; pres. Ventucross Corp., Grand Junction, 1973-74, also dir.; regional staff geologist Coastal States Energy Corp., Houston, 1974-75; chief geologist, mgr. logging div. Mineral Service Co., Grand Junction, 1975-76; sr. geologist Am. Electric Power Corp., Lancaster, Ohio, 1976-79; pres., chmn. bd., dir. Ventio Co., 1979-80; sr. geologist Tex. Pacific Oil Co., 1980-81, Sun Oil Co., Abilene, 1981-82; chmn. bd., pres. Ventucross Corp.; pres. Geotex Land and Exploration Co., 1982—; dir. Vanguard Industries Corp., 1982—, Crystal Minerals Corp., 1979—. Active Boy Scouts Am., Abilene, Tex., 1960-63, 80—, Waco, Tex., 1963-64, Grand Junction, Colo., 1970-72; advisor 4H, Athens, Ohio, 1978-80. Recipient Abilene Geol. Soc. award, Most Outstanding Geology Student, 1961-62, 62-63. Mem. Am. Mgmt. Assn., Internat. Platform Assn., Am. Geol. Inst., Soc. Petrol. Engrs. and Soc. Mining Engrs. of AIME, Soc. Advancement Mgmt., Clay Minerals Soc., Am. Soc. Photogrammetry, ASTM, Mineral. Soc. Am., N. Am. Thermal Analysis Soc., The Coblentz Soc., Colo. Mining Assn., Soc. Profl. Well Log Analysts, Houston Geol. Soc., Ariz. Small Mine Operators Assn., Am. Assn. Petroleum Geologists, AAUP, Internat. Assn. Study of Clays, Geol. Soc. Am., Soc. Eco Paleo & Min., Nat. Eagle Scout Assn. Baptist. Club: Masons. Home: 2318 Greenbriar Abilene TX 79605 Office: PO Box 2817 Abilene TX 79604

FARVER, LINDA LOUISE, educator; b. Balt., July 30, 1948; d. Roby Thomas and Ethel LaRue (Waddell) Farver. B.S., Frostburg State Coll., 1970; M.Ed., Middle Tenn. State U., 1973. Phys. edn. tchr. Carroll County Bd. Edn., S. Carroll High Sch., Sykesville, Md., 1970-72; grad. asst. Middle Tenn. State U., Murfreesboro, 1972-74; instr. phys. edn. Salisbury State Coll., Md., 1974-76, Cent. Va. Community Coll., Lynchburg, 1976-77; asst. prof. phys. edn. Liberty U., Lynchburg, 1977—, head coach women's basketball, 1977—. First aid instr. ARC, Lynchburg, 1977—. Named Outstanding Female Athlete, Frostburg State Coll. Women's Athletic Assn., 1970; Outstanding Phys. Edn. Major, Frostburg State Coll., 1970. Mem. AAHPERD, Va. Assn. Intercollegiate Athletics for Women (pres. 1980-81). Office: Liberty U Box 20000 Lynchburg VA 24506

FASCELL, DANTE B., congressman, lawyer; b. Bridgehampton, L.I., N.Y., Mar. 9, 1917; s. Charles A. and Mary (Gullotti) F.; J.D., U. Miami, 1938; m. Jeanne-Marie Pelot, Sept. 19, 1941; children—Sandra-Jeanne Fascell Diamond, Toni F. Strother, Dante J. (dec.). Admitted to Fla. bar, 1938; practiced in Miami, 1938-41, 46—; legal attache state legis. del. Dade County, 1947-50; mem. Fla. Ho. of Reps., 1950-54; mem. 84th-99th Congresses from 19th Dist. Fla., chmn. com. fgn. affairs, chmn. subcom. internat. security and sci. affairs, mem. select com. on narcotics abuse and control, mem. commn. security and cooperation in Europe; mem. U.S.-Can. Inter-Parliamentary Group; mem. U.S. del. 24th UN Gen. Assembly, 1969; chmn. Ho. del. N. Atlantic Assembly. Served as capt. U.S. Army, 1942-46; ETO. Named one of ten outstanding legislators Fla. Legislature, 1951, 53; one of five outstanding men in Fla., Fla. Jr. C. of C., 1951. Mem. Miami Jr. C. of C. (pres. 1947-48), Am., Dade County, Fed., D.C. bar assns., Fla. Bar, Am. Legion, Kappa Sigma. Democrat. Clubs: Lions, Italian-Am. (pres. 1947-48), Dade County Young Democratic (pres. 1947-48) (Miami). Home: 6300 SW 99th Terr Miami FL 33156 Office: House Office Bldg Washington DC 20515 also 7855 SW 104th St Suite 220 Miami FL 33156 also Blackwell Walker Fascell & Hoehl 1 SE 3d Ave Suite 2400 Miami FL 33131

FASH, WILLIAM LEONARD, architecture educator; b. Pueblo, Colo., Feb. 9, 1931; s. James Leonard and Jewel Dean (Rickman) F.; m. Maria Elena Shaw, June 5, 1982; children—Cameron, Lauren Victoria; children by previous marriage—Victoria Ruth, William Leonard. B. Arch., Okla. State U., 1958, M. Arch., 1960; postgrad. Royal Acad. Fine Arts, Copenhagen, 1960-61. Asst. prof. U. Ill., Urbana, 1961-64, assoc. prof., 1967-70, prof., 1970-76; assoc. prof. Okla. State U., Stillwater, 1964-66, U. Oreg., Eugene, 1966-67; vis. prof. Chulalongkorn U., Bangkok, Thailand, 1973-74; prof., dean coll. architecture Ga. Inst. Tech., Atlanta, 1976—; bd. dirs. Nat. Archtl. Accreditation Bd.; mem. edn. com. adv. bd. Nat. Council Archtl. Registration Bds.; profl. cons. U.S. Navy Trident Submarine Base, Kings Bay, Ga.; mem. adv. bd. Atlanta Urban Design Commn.; cons. Atlanta High Mus. Art bldg. com. Author, editor monographs; Chmn. bd. Southeast Energy Tech. Group; chmn. tech. adv. com. Gov.'s Commn. State Growth Policy. Recipient awards for design; Fulbright-Hays fellow, Copenhagen, 1960-61. Mem. Assn. Collegiate Schs. Architecture, AIA (award juries 1968, 75, 76, 79), Phi Kappa Phi, Sigma Tau, Pi Mu Epsilon, Alpha Rho Chi. Clubs: Snapfinger Woods Golf (Atlanta); Bent Tree Country (Jasper, Ga.). Home: 2854 Ridgemore Rd NW Atlanta GA 30318 Office: Ga Inst Tech Coll Architecture Atlanta GA 30332

FASHBAUGH, HOWARD DILTS, JR., lawyer; b. Monroe, Mich., Jan. 31, 1922; s. Howard Dilts and Ninetta Esther (Greening) F.; B.S.E. in Chem. Engring., U. Mich., 1947, M.S.E., 1948, M.B.A. with high distinction, 1960; J.D. cum laude, Wake Forest U., 1972; M.Law and Taxation, Coll. William and Mary, 1983; m. Joyce Dallas MacCurdy, Dec. 25, 1946; children—James Howard, Linda Carol, Patricia Lee. Mgr. engring. and mfg. Dow Corning Corp., Midland, Mich., 1952-70; admitted to Va. bar, 1973, Mich. bar, 1975; asso. firm Williams, Worrell, Kelly & Greer, Norfolk, Va., 1972-76, partner firm, 1976-77; corp. counsel Va. Chems., Inc., Portsmouth, 1977-83; ptnr. firm Williams, Worrell, Kelly & Greer, Norfolk, 1983-85; sole practice law, 1985—; gen. counsel CEP, Inc., 1985—. Chmn. adv. bd. Salvation Army, Midland, 1967-69, Portsmouth, 1975—. Served to lt. USNR, 1943-46, 50-52. Decorated Bronze Star. Mem. Am. Bar Assn., Va. Bar Assn., Portsmouth Bar Assn., Norfolk-Portsmouth Bar Assn., Beta Gamma Sigma. Presbyterian. Clubs: Kiwanis (past pres.). Home and office: 3905 Stonebridge Ct Chesapeake VA 23321

FASSIE, PIERRE FERNAND, foreign language educator; b. Vaison-la-Romaine, France, Sept. 14, 1950; came to U.S., 1973; s. Noël F. and Fernande Louisette (Jouvent) F.; m. Mary-Jo Downing, June 22, 1974; children—Vanessa Laure, Nathalie Claire. Student, Université de Provence, 1968-73, Maîtrise d'Histoire, 1973; M.A., U. Ill., 1976, Ph.D., 1983. Grad. teaching asst. U. Ill., Urbana, 1975-78; instr. French, Hollins Coll., Roanoke, Va., 1978-83, asst. prof., 1983-85; tchr. French, Roanoke City Pub. Schs., 1985—. U. Ill. fellow, 1974-75; Nat. Endowment Humanities fellow, summer 1984, Mem. Am. Assn. Tchrs. French, MLA, Fgn. Lang. Assn. Va. Pi Delta Phi. Author short stories: Bories (in Ecriture), 1981, Dans la lumière (in La Revue de Belles-lettres), 1982; book of short stories: Voix d'Exécution, 1984; contbr. articles to profl. jours.

FATE, MARTIN EUGENE, JR., utility executive; b. Tulsa, Jan. 9, 1933; s. Martin Eugene and Frances Mae (Harp) F.; B.S.E.E., Okla. State U., 1955; grad. Advanced Mgmt. Program, Harvard U., 1981; m. Ruth Ann Johnson, Aug. 28, 1954; children—Gary Martin, Steven Lewis, Mary Ann. With Public Service Co. of Okla., Tulsa, 1955—, v.p. power, 1973-76, exec. v.p., 1976-82, pres., chief exec. officer, 1982—; dir. Central & South West Services, Inc., Energy Fuels Devel. Corp., Tulsa, First Nat. Bank & Trust of Tulsa; chmn., chief exec. officer Ash Creek Mining Co. Trustee, U. Tulsa, Phillips U., Enid, Okla., U. Tulsa, Okla. Osteo. Hosp.; dir. Energy Fuel Devel. Corp., Tulsa. Served to capt. USAF, 1955-57. Mem. Met. Tulsa C. of C., Phi Kappa Phi, Eta Kappa Nu, Tau Beta Pi. Mem. Christian Ch. Club: Tulsa Summit. Office: PO Box 201 Tulsa OK 74102

FAUGHT, IRVING LEE, lawyer; b. Oklahoma City, Apr. 17, 1940; s. Irving H. and Dorothy (Damron) F.; m. Sandra Jane Stephens; children—September Jann, Heather, Jill Alistar. Student Columbia U., 1958-59; B.A., U. Okla., 1962; J.D., U. Va., 1965. Bar: Okla. 1965, U.S. Supreme Ct. 1969. Asst. mpcl. csl. City of Oklahoma City, 1965-70; ptnr. Andrews, Davis Legg, Bixler Milslen & Murrah, Oklahoma City, 1970—; mem. select com. on pvt. offerings Okla. Securities Commn., 1982. Bd. dirs. Okla. Theatre Center, 1981—, UN Assn. Okla., 1973—; gen. counsel Daily Living Centers, Inc., 1977—, also dir. ACLU Okla., 1977-79; mem. Oklahoma City Mayor's Adv. Council, 1985. Served to lt. cmdr. JAG, USNR, 1966-83. Mem. ABA. Lodge: Rotary. Office: 500 W Main Oklahoma City OK 73102

FAULKNER, CLAUDE WINSTON, educator; b. Barbourville, Ky., Apr. 24, 1916; s. James Edward and Eulah (Swearingen) F.; A.B., Union Coll., Ky., 1936, Litt.D., 1962; M.A., U. Ky., 1938; Ph.D., U. Ill., 1947; m. Nancy Isabel McCallum, Dec. 9, 1944; children—Linda Jo, Keith Edward, Sally Ann, Charles Douglas. Instr. English, U. Ill., 1947; faculty U. Ark., 1947—, prof. English, 1953—, chmn. dept., 1953-74. Served to capt. USAAF, 1942-46; lt. col. Res. Named Distinguished Alumnus, Union Coll., 1954. Mem. Modern Lang. Assn., Phi Beta Kappa, Phi Kappa Phi. Author: Writing Good Sentences, 1950, 3d edit., 1981. Co-author: Writing Good Prose, 1961, 4th edit., 1977. Home: 306 W Prospect St Fayetteville AR 72701

FAULKNER, HELEN JEAN, travel company executive; b. Columbus, Ga., Oct. 13, 1934; d. Tally Monroe and Marguerite (Carroll) Faulkner. B.A., Mercer U., 1956; M.Ed., Ga. Coll., 1968. Sales rep. State Mut. Ins., Atlanta, 1972-74; sales rep., planning dir. Your Tour World, Atlanta, 1974-75; dir. tours Days Inns Am., Atlanta, 1975-77; mgr., v.p. Goodtimes Travel, Atlanta, 1977-80; mgr. br. Corp. Travel, Atlanta, 1980-84, mgr. employee devel., 1984—. Mem. Travel Industry Assn. Ga., Am. Soc. Travel Agts., Am. Soc. Tng. and Devel. Republican. Baptist. Avocations: sports; travel; music; arts. Home: 3257 Lynnray Dr Doraville GA 30340 Office: Corp Travel Inc/Amex 3867 Roswell Rd Atlanta GA 30342

FAULKNER, WILLIAM R(AY), real estate development executive, restaurateur; b. Ft. Worth, Sept. 1, 1946; s. Brock H. and Vera (Thompson) F.; m. Martha Burgoon, Aug. 4, 1973; children—Charles Warren, William Brock. B.S., Tex. A&M U., 1968, M.Urban Planning, 1970. Gen. mgr. South/West Planning Assocs., Bryan, Tex., 1970-71; commd. 2d lt. U.S. Army, 1971, advanced through grades to capt., 1974; served C.E., U.S., Vietnam, Korea, project officer and dep. dist. engr. civil works Ft. Worth, 1974-77, ret., 1981; pres., chief exec. officer Brazos Valley Gen. Devel., Inc., also A Bldg. Co., Inc., Bryan, 1981—. Bd. dirs. Brazos Valley Better Bus. Bur., Bryan, 1983—. Decorated Bronze Star. Mem. Am. Inst. Planners, Am. Planning Assn., Urban Land Inst. (assoc.), Center for Entrepreneurial Mgmt., Alpha Phi Omega (pres. 1966-67, disting. service key 1967, state chmn. 1967-68), Tau Sigma Delta, Phi Kappa Phi. Baptist. Office: 4444 Carter Creek Pkwy Suite 110 Bryan TX 77802

FAUST, ROBERT JOSEPH, physician; b. Ft. Worth, Mar. 23, 1938; s. Charles Fredrick and Kathleen (Singler) F.; m. Lynn Griffin, June 14, 1958; children—Wendy Elizabeth, Allison Marie. B.A. in Biology, Tex. Christian U., 1960; M.D., U. Tex.-Galveston, 1964. Diplomate Am. Bd. Internal Medicine. Resident in internal medicine and cardiology John Sealy Hosp., Galveston, 1964-68; pvt. practice medicine, specializing in internal medicine and cardiology, Lubbock, Tex., 1968—; assoc. clin. prof. internal medicine Tex. Tech. U.; dir. cardiopulmonary labs. South Park Hosp., Inc., Lubbock, also trustee. Mem. Lubbock C. of C., Am. Heart Assn. (chpt. pres. 1975-76), Lubbock, Crosby and Garza Med. Soc., AMA, Tex. Med. Soc., Tex. Club Internists, Alpha Omega Alpha. Republican. Roman Catholic. Clubs: Univ. City, Sports Car of Am., Corvette. Home: 9102 Vicksburg Apt 27 Lubbock TX 79424 Office: 6630 Quaker Ave Suite B Lubbock TX 79413

FAVARO, MARY KAYE ASPERHEIM (MRS. BIAGINO PHILIP FAVARO), pediatrician; b. Edgerton, Wis., Sept. 30, 1934; d. Harold Wilbur and Genevieve Catherine (Hyland) Asperheim; B.S., U. Wis., 1956; M.S., St. Louis Coll. Pharmacy, 1965; M.D., U. Wis., 1969; m. Biagino Philip Favaro, May 31, 1969; children—Justin Peter, Gina Sue. Instr. pharmacology St. Louis U. and St. Mary's Hosp. Sch. Practical Nurses, 1959-64; staff pharmacist U. Hosps., Madison, Wis., 1964-65; intern Albany (N.Y.) Med. Center, 1969-70, resident, 1970-71; resident in pediatrics U. S.C., Charleston, 1971-72, asst. prof. pediatrics, 1973-75; pvt. practice pediatrics, 1974—. Mem. A.M.A., Am. Med. Women's Assn. Roman Catholic. Author: Pharmacology, an Introductory Text, 1986; The Pharmacologic Basis of Patient Care, 1985. Home: 1866 Capri Dr Charleston SC 29407 Office: 5390 Dorchester Rd Charleston Heights SC 29418

FAWCETT, ROBERT EARL, JR., banker; b. San Antonio, Nov. 28, 1931; s. Robert E. and Blanche Annette (Johnson) F.; B.B.A., U. Tex., 1952; m. Ann Ingrum, Dec. 6, 1952; children—Lynn Allen Fawcett Russell, Elizabeth Langston Fawcett Pritchard, Ann Ingrum. Registered securities broker, 1952-54; with comml. real estate mgmt. and sales co., 1954-57; with Frost Nat. Bank of San Antonio, 1957—, sr. exec. v.p., 1974—; chmn. bd. North Frost Bank, N.A., San Antonio, 1981—; pres. Liberty Frost Bank, 1982—; alderman City of Alamo Heights (Tex.), 1977-83. Served with USAF, 1951. Mem. Am. Bankers Assn., San Antonio C. of C., Mil. Order Loyal Legions, San Antonio Econ. Devel. Found., Tex. Cavaliers, Order of Alamo, Kappa Sigma. Republican. Episcopalian. Clubs: San Antonio Rotary, Conopus, Town, San Antonio Country, Argyle, Merry Knights of King William, German. Home: 140 Grant Ave San Antonio TX 78209 Office: PO Box 1600 San Antonio TX 78296

FAWCETT, THOMAS F., prefabricated housing company executive. Pres. Rondesics Home Corp., Asheville, N.C. Office: Rondesics Home Corp 527 McDowell St Asheville NC 28803*

FAWVER, DARLENE ELIZABETH, music librarian; b. Arlington, Va., June 28, 1952; d. William Garrett and Hannah (Johnson) Fawver. B.A., Coll. of William and Mary, 1974; B. Mus., Westminster Choir Coll., 1976; M.S. in Library Sci., Ind. U., 1980, M. Mus. cum laude, 1983. Assoc. instr. Ind. U., Bloomington, 1977-80; music librarian, instr. Ky. State U., Frankfort, 1980-81, instr. music, 1981; music librarian Wichita Pub. Library, Kans., 1982-83; Converse Coll., Spartanburg, S.C., 1983—. Organist, Martinsville United Methodist Ch., N.J., 1976, Princeton U. Brass and Percussion Ensemble, N.J., 1975-76; substitute organist for various churches, 1974—. Mem. Am. Musicological Soc., Music Library Assn. (editor Breve Notes 1984—), Beta Phi Mu, Delta Omicron (chpt. pres. 1973-74, chpt. advisor 1986—, Star award, 1972). Republican. Presbyterian. Avocations: racquetball; sewing; swimming; needlepoint; musicological research. Home: 1514 Fernwood Glendale Rd #302 Spartanburg SC 29302 Office: Gwathmey Library Converse Coll 580 E Main St Spartanburg SC 29301

FAY, PETER THORP, judge; b. Rochester, N.Y., Jan. 18, 1929; s. Leston Thorp and Jane (Baumler) F.; B.A., Rollins Coll., 1951, LL.D., 1971; J.D., U. Fla., 1956; LL.D., Biscayne Coll., 1975; m. Claudia Pat Zimmerman, Oct. 1, 1958; children—Michael Thorp, William, Darcy. Admitted to Fla. bar, 1956, U.S. Supreme Ct. bar, 1961; partner firm Nichols, Gaither Green, Frates & Beckham, Miami, Fla., 1956-61, Frates, Fay, Floyd & Pearson and predecessors, Miami, 1961-70; judge U.S. Dist. Ct. for So. Fla., Miami, 1970-76; judge U.S. Ct. Appeals for 11th Circuit (formerly 5th Circuit), 1976—; prof. Fla. Jr. Bar Practical Legal Inst., 1959-65; lectr. Fla. Bar Legal Inst., 1959—; faculty Fed. Jud. Center, Washington, 1974—. Mem. Jud. Conf. Com. for Implementation Criminal Justice Act, 1974—, Adv. Com. on Codes of Conduct, 1980—; mem. Orange Bowl Com., 1974—; dist. collector United Fund, 1957-70; mem. adminstrv. bd. Biscayne Coll., 1970—. Served with USAF, 1951-53. Mem. Law Sci. Acad., Fla. Acad. Trial Attys., Am., Fla., Dade County, John Marshall (past pres.) bar assns., Fla. Council of 100, U. Fla. Alumni Assn. (dir.), Miami C. of C., Medico Legal Inst., Order of Coif, Phi Delta Phi (past pres.), Omicron Delta Kappa (past pres.), Pi Gamma Mu (past pres.), Phi Kappa Phi, Phi Delta Theta (past sec.). Republican. Roman Catholic. Clubs: Wildcat Cliffs (N.C.), Snapper Creek Lakes, Coral Oaks (Miami). Home: 11000 Snapper Creek Rd Miami FL 33156 Office: US Court of Appeals 300 NE 1st Ave Miami FL 33132

FAY, TEMPLE H., mathematics educator, researcher; b. Washington, Aug. 12, 1940; s. Leroy Edwin and Dorothy Elizabeth (Byrne) F. B.S., Guilford Coll., 1963; M.A., Wake Forest U., 1964; Ph.D., U. Fla., 1971. Asst. prof. math. Hendrix Coll., Conway, Ark., 1970-76; vis. sr. lectr. U. Cape Town, S. Africa, 1976-77; vis. asst. prof. N.Mex. State U., Las Cruces, 1978-79; prof. math. U. So. Miss., Hattiesburg, 1977—; vis. assoc. prof. Tulane U., New Orleans, 1983; NASA summer faculty fellow, 1980, 81; Naval Oceanographic Research and Devel. Activity fellow, summer 1983. U. So. Miss. research grantee, 1982. Mem. Am. Math. Soc., Math. Assn. Am., S. African Math. Soc., Sigma Xi, Pi Mu Epsilon. Quaker. Clubs: Chamale (Slidell, La.); Hattiesburg Racquet Ball. Editor Jour. of Undergrad. Math., 1974-81; reviewer math revs.; contbr. articles to profl. jours.

FEAGANS, ROBERT GEARY, mechanical engineer; b. Ashland, Ky., July 5, 1924; s. Guy and Hazel Edna (McIntyre) F.; B.S., U. Ky., 1948; m. Anna Louise McCalvin, Sept. 14, 1924; children—Deborah Louise Feagans Buckner, Pamella Feagans Graves. Self-employed as mech. contractor, Ironton, Ohio and Frankfort, Ky., 1948-63; mech. engr. Rust Engring. Co., Calhoun, Tenn., 1965-68; chief mech. engr. Patchen, Mingledorff & Asso., cons. engrs., Augusta, Ga., 1969-80; pvt. practice, Aiken, S.C., 1980—; pecan grower, Aiken County, S.C., 1971—. Served with U.S. Mcht. Marine, 1944-45. Registered profl. engr., Tenn., Ga. Mem. ASHRAE, Ga. Soc. Profl. Engrs. (pres. Augusta chpt. 1976-77). Home: Route 1 Box 494 Aiken SC 29801

FEAGIN, JOE RICHARD, sociology educator; b. San Angelo, Tex., May 6, 1938; s. Frank Joe and Hanna (Griffin) F.; m. Clairece Booher, Sept. 1, 1959; children—Michelle, Trevor. B.A., Baylor U., 1960; Ph.D., Harvard U., 1966. Asst. prof. sociology U. Calif.-Riverside, 1966-70; assoc. then full prof. U. Tex., Austin, 1970—; scholar-in-residence U.S. Commn. Civil Rights, 1974-75. Mem. Am. Sociol. Assn. Democrat. Unitarian. Author: Ghetto Revolts, 1973 (nominated for Pulitzer Prize); Discrimination American Style, 1978; The Urban Real Estate Game, 1983; Modern Sexism, 1986. Office: Burdine 436 Univ Tex Austin TX 78712

FEAGIN, ROY CHESTER, chemist, consultant; b. Andersonville, Ga., July 23, 1914; s. James Gordon and Willie Frances (Wicker) F.; m. Lillian Elizabeth Joyner, Feb. 25, 1938; children—Diane Elizabeth, Susan Louise. B.S., Auburn U., 1936, M.S., 1937. Chemist Gen. Electric Co., Schenectady, 1937-39; chemist Austenal Co., N.Y.C., 1939-48, chief chemist, 1948-53; mgr. chem. research Howmet Corp., Dover, N.J., 1953-68, mgr. internat. ops., Muskegon, Mich., 1968-73; v.p. research and devel. Remet Corp., Pompano Beach, Fla., 1975-81; cons. Feagin Enterprises, Pompano Beach, 1981—. Contbr. articles to profl. jours. Patentee investment casting, waxes, coatings, plastics. Am. Chem. Soc., Am. Ceramic Soc. Mem. ASTM, Internat. Assn. Dental Research (life mem. Dental Materials Group). Republican. Congregationalist. Lodge: Masons. Avocation: mineral and coin collecting. Home: 750 NE Marine Dr Boca Raton FL 33431 Office: Feagin Enterprises Inc 1971 W McNab Rd Pompano Beach FL 33069

FEAGIN, TERRY, computer science educator; b. Houston, Mar. 27, 1945; s. Frank Joe and Hanna (Griffin) F.; m. Diane Parmley, Sept. 14, 1968; children—Russell Austin, Kyle Jefferson. B.A., Rice U., 1967; M.A., U. Tex., 1969, Ph.D., 1972. Postdoctoral research assoc. NASA, Greenbelt, Md., 1972-73; asst. prof. computer sci. U. Tenn., Knoxville, 1973-78, assoc., 1978-82, prof., 1982-84, assoc. dir. computing ctr., 1978-79; prof. U. Houston-Clear Lake, 1984—. Contbr. articles to profl. jours. Ford Found. scholar, 1970; NASA grantee, 1973-75. Mem. Assn. for Computing Machinery, Am. Assn. for Artificial Intelligence. Office: U Houston-Clear Lake 2700 Bay Area Blvd Houston TX 77058

FEAREY, MARY ESTILL (MRS. PORTER FEAREY), club woman; b. Corpus Christi, Tex., Mar. 30, 1917; d. Richard Gentry and Mary Henrietta (King) Estill; student Columbia Coll., 1936-37, U. Mo., 1937-39; m. Porter Fearey, May 14, 1944; 1 dau., Mary (Mrs. John A. Storie). With Trans World Airlines, 1941-43. Flower show life judge Nat. Council State Garden Clubs, 1964—, flower show master judge, 1965—; hon. internat. flower show judge, 1963—; instr., demonstrator flower arranging; lectr. mobiles, also cultivation and uses of gourds, Central Tex., 1968-77; lectr. pictorial slide programs with emphasis on bot. aspects of internat. travel, 1958—; co-creator Mary Henrietta King Estill scholarship Columbia (Mo.) Coll., 1970—; bd. dirs. New Braunfels Mental Health-Mental Retardation, 1981. Served as pilot Women's Airforce Service, 1943-44. Mem. Nationally Accredited Flower Show Judges (pres. San Antonio 1966-67, v.p. 1970-71), Tex. Garden Clubs (state chmn. judges councils 1965-67, state chmn. pilgrimages 1967-69, state chmn. bonsai 1969-71, state chmn. bonsai and gourds 1971-78), Am. Gourd Soc., Am. Horticulture Soc. (state chmn. geraniums 1981-83), Nat. Wildlife Fedn., Aircraft Owners and Pilots Assn., Ninety-Nines, Columbia Coll. Alumni Assn., New Braunfels Conservation Soc., Innerwheel, Colonial Dames Am., Dames Mil. Order Loyal

Legion U.S. Republican. Episcopalian. Clubs: Sierra (life), Easter Island Exchange (Alexandria, Va.); St. Anthony, Women's of Ft. Sam Houston, Argyle (San Antonio); Giraud, Club at Retama. Home: PO Box 633 New Braunfels TX 78130

FEAREY, PORTER, rancher, investor; b. Albany, N.Y., June 27, 1918; s. Porter and Elizabeth B.W. (Martin) F.; student Williams Coll., 1938-39, S.W. Tex. State U., 1946-48; m. Mary King Estill, May 14, 1944; 1 dau., Mary King Estill (Mrs. John A. Storie). Began career as salesman Westchester Pubs., Inc., Noel Macy Chain, Yonkers, N.Y., 1940-41; mktg. supr. Gulf Oil Corp., N.Y.C., 1941-45, Tex. Co. (Texaco, Inc.), Houston, 1945-46; owner, pres. Water Service Co., San Antonio, 1948-82; rancher, real estate investor, 1982—; pres., dir. Apartimientos S.A., Monterrey, Mexico, 1958-68; owner, pres. Ice Service, Inc., San Antonio. Mem. central exec. com. Episcopal Diocese West Tex., 1960—, mem. dept. fin., 1963—, mem. exec. bd., 1963-66, 69-72, mem. central exec. com. Episc. Advance Fund; del. Tex. Council Chs., 1968, 69-72, 73-74, 75-76, 77-78, 78-79; del. Tex. State Republican Conv., 1960, 74; del. Comal County (Tex.) Rep. Conv., 1956, 74; bd. dirs. Tex. State Guard Assn., 1975-78. Served with USAAF, World War II; ret. Mem. Comal County (dir.), New Braunfels (dir.), S. Tex. chambers commerce, Good Govt. League (dir.), Episc. Churchmen's Assn., Williams Coll. Alumni Assn., Am. Legion, Mil. Order Loyal Legion U.S. (comdr. Tex. commandery 1965—), Mil. Order World Wars, Res. Officers Assn. Ret. Officers Assn., Armed Forces Communications and Electronics Assn., Am. Ordnance Assn., San Antonio Zool. Soc., Comal County Hist. Soc. (dir.), New Braunfels Conservation Soc. (dir.), Mil. Order Fgn. Wars U.S., St. Nicholas Soc. N.Y.C., N.Y. So. Soc., St. Georges Soc. N.Y., S.R., Soc. Colonial Wars, SAR, Vets. Assn. 7th Regiment N.Y. N.G., Assos. Engr. Corps 7th Regiment N.Y. N.G., Mil. Order World Wars, Am. Georg. Soc., Tex. Rangers Assn. Found., Kappa Alpha. Republican. Episcopalian (vestryman, sr. warden; diocesan exec. bd.). Clubs: Rotary Internat. (Paul Harris fellow), Elks; Explorers (N.Y.C.); St. Anthony (San Antonio); Williams (N.Y.C.); Corpus Christi Yacht. Home: 100 Paseo Encinal San Antonio TX 78212 Office: PO Box 633 New Braunfels TX 78130

FEARING, WILLIAM KELLY, art educator, artist; b. Fordyce, Ark., Oct. 18, 1918; s. George David and Frankie (Kelly) F. B.A., La. Tech. U., 1941; M.A., Columbia U., 1950. Classroom tchr. Windfield Pub. Schs., La., 1942-43; prodn. illustrator Consolidated Vultee Aircraft, Fort Worth, 1943-45; prof. art Tex. Wesleyan Coll., Fort Worth, 1945-47, U. Tex.-Austin, 1947—, Ashbel Smith prof., 1983—. Author: (with C.I. Martin and E. Beard) Our Expanding Vision, 1960, The Creative Eye, 1969, 2d edit., 1979; (with E. Beard, N. Krevitsky, C.I. Martin) Art and the Creative Teacher, 1971, (with E. L. Mayton, B. Francis, E. Beard) Helping Children See Art and Make Art, 1982; (with E.L. Mayton and R. Brooks) The Way of Art Inner Vision Outer Expression, 1986. One-man shows include El Paso Mus. Art, Esther Bear Gallery, Santa Barbara, 1964, Gallery Visual Arts, La. Tech. U., Ruston, 1966, U. Tex. Art Mus., Austin, 1967, Fort Worth Art Ctr., 1969, Witte Meml. Mus., San Antonio, 1969, U. Tex. Art Mus., Austin, 1974, Mary Moore Gallery, La Jolla, 1975, Mary Moffett Gallery, La. Tech. U., Ruston, 1976, DuBose Gallery, Houston, 1977, L and L Gallery, Longview, 1975, 78, Retrospective Spencer Gallery, Fine Arts Ctr., U. Ark.-Monticello, 1981, Mary Moffett Gallery, Sch. Art and Architecture, La. Tech. U., Ruston, 1981, Old Jail Art Ctr., Albany, Tex., 1985, Marion Koogler McNey Art Mus., San Antonio, 1986; exhibited in group shows at Carnegie Inst., Pitts., 1955, Pa. Acad. Art, Phila., 1954-56, Carnegie Inst., Pitts., 1956-57, Mus. Fine Arts, Houston, 1956-57, Dallas Mus. Fine Art, 1956-57, Munson-Williams-Proctor Inst., Utica, 1956-57, Edwin Hewitt Gallery, N.Y.C., 1957, Dallas Mus. Fine Art, 1958, Am. Fedn. Art, 1958, Mus. Fine Arts, Little Rock, 1961, Colorado Springs Art Ctr., 1961, 63 Philbrook Art Ctr., Tulsa, 1963, Fort Worth Art Ctr., 1963, U. Ill., Urbana, 1955, 59, 63, Denver Art Mus., 1963, U. Ariz. and Ark. Art Ctr., 1964-65, N.Y. World's Fair, Tex. Pavilion, 1964, Tex. Pavillion Hemistair, San Antonio, 1968, Tex. Tech. U. Mus. Art, Lubbock, 1978, U. Tex.-Austin, 1979, Art Gallery Sch. Art and Architecture, La. Tech. U., Ruston, 1984, Archer M. Huntington Art Gallery, U. Tex.-Austin, 1983, Longview Mus. and Arts Ctr., Tex., 1962, 63, 75, 85. Mem. Nat. Art Edn. Assn., Tex. Art Edn. Assn., Phi Kappa Phi, Phi Delta Kappa. Home: 914 Calethea St Austin TX 78746

FEARN, ROBERT MORCOM, economics and business educator, consultant; b. Paterson, N.J., Oct. 10, 1928; s. William and Violet Emily (Bray) F.; m. Priscilla Anne Southard, Sept. 15, 1951; children—Diane C. Fearn Desrosiers, Deborah A. Sears, Priscilla L., Robert W. A.A., Boston U., 1950; B.S. in Commerce, Ohio U., 1952; M.A. in Econs., Wash. State U., 1955; Ph.D. in Econs., U. Chgo., 1968. Grad. asst. Wash. State U., Pullman, 1952-54; intelligence officer CIA, Washington, 1954-63; from asst. to prof. econs. and bus. N.C. State U., Raleigh, 1965—; vis. prof. Duke U., Durham, N.C., 1982; expert witness NLRB, Winston-Salem, N.C., 1981-83; cons. Research Triangle Inst., Research Triangle Park, N.C., 1968—, Pres.'s Commn. Income Maintenance, Washington, 1970; mem. econ. study and ad hoc wage bd. City Raleigh, 1974, others. Author: Labor Economics: The Emerging Synthesis, 1981. Contbr. articles to profl. jours. Pres., v.p., bd. dirs. West Raleigh Civic Assn., 1968-80; vice chmn. Free Alliance for Improvement Raleigh, 1968-81; scoutmaster, asst. scoutmaster, committeeman Occoneechee council Boy Scouts Am., Raleigh, 1970-80. Served with U.S. Army, 1946-48. Noyes-Ford-Hillman fellow, 1963-65. Mem. Am. Econ. Assn., So. Econ. Assn. (mem. bd. editors 1975-77), Indsl. Relations Research Assn., N.C. Faculty Senate (chmn. 1984-85, vice chmn. 1983-84), U. Chgo. Club of N.C. (sec. 1982-83, 83-84, bd. dirs. 1981—), Raleigh Area Masters Swimming, Phi Kappa Phi, Beta Gamma Sigma, Acad. Outstanding Tchrs., Alpha Kappa Lambda. Democrat. Unitarian-Universalist. Avocations: swimming; long distance backpacking; camping; sailing. Home: 1202 Kent Rd Raleigh NC 27606 Office: N C State U Dept Econs Bus Box 8109 Raleigh NC 27695

FEATHERSTON, CHARLES HENRY, III, Realtor; b. Wichita Falls, Tex., Jan. 6, 1925; s. Solon Richmond and Lillie Beall (Reeves) F.; B.B.A., U. Tex., Austin, 1947; m. Florence Emily Harding, Oct. 26, 1947; children—Solon Richmond III, Randall Mason, David Harding, Molly Kay. Salesman, Crestview Meml. Park, Wichita Falls, 1947-49; sales dir. Crestview Meml. Park and Mausoleum, Wichita Falls, 1949-51; realtor, developer, homebuilder, Wichita Falls, 1954-66; evangelist Billy Graham Evangelistic Film Ministry, East Tex. region, 1966-72; prin. Charles Featherston Assos., Realtors, Tyler, Tex., 1972—; v.p., dir. Village Mortgage Co., Wichita Falls; co-founder, charter chmn. Multiple Listing Service of Wichita Falls Bd. Realtors; mng. ptnr. real estate joint ventures; dir. Shamgar, Inc. tchr. real estate courses Midwestern U. Bd. dirs. Ednl. Radio Found. E. Tex.; elder Grace Community Ch. Served to lt. (jg.), USNR, 1943-46, to lt. (s.g.), 1951-53; PTO. Mem. Nat. Assn. Real Estate Bds., Tex. Assn. Real Estate Bds., Tyler Bd. Realtors. Home: 3200 Silverwood St Tyler TX 75701 Office: 3923 S Broadway Tyler TX 75701

FEATHERSTON, CHARLES RONALD, energy consulting company executive; b. Doniphan, Mo., Dec. 30, 1938; s. Charles Henry and Ellen Inez (O'Brien) F.; children—Deri Lynn, Lara Andrea. B.S. in Petroleum Engring., Mo. Sch. Mines, 1961. Registered profl. engr., Tex. With Magnolia Petroleum, Healdton, Okla., 1959; laborer, draftsman Mo. Natural Gas Co., Poplar Bluff, 1960; petroleum engr. Texaco, Inc., 1961-70, offshore dist. drilling engr., 1970-71, foreman drilling and prodn., Morgan City, La., 1971-73, div. drilling engr., New Orleans, 1973-76; sr. drilling engr. Southwestern div. Eastern Houston Oil and Minerals Corp., 1976-77, sr. ops. engr. Tex. div., 1977-78, ops. mgr. Eastern div., 1978-80; v.p. engring. Eaton Industries, Houston, 1980—. Served with U.S. Army, 1961-64. Decorated Army Commendation medal. Mem. Am. Legion, Am. Petroleum Inst., Soc. Petroleum Engrs., Sigma Gamma Epsilon. Mem. Christian Ch. Club: Houston Underwater. Office: 1980 Post Oak Blvd Suite 2000 Houston TX 77056

FEATHERSTON, JOSEPH FRANCIS, aviation logistics company executive; b. Phila., Sept. 26, 1939; s. Joseph Francis and Rosemary Agnes (Smith) F.; m. Carol Anne Williams, July 22, 1961 (div. Feb. 1980); children—William Joseph, Diane Michele, Janet Lynn; m. 2d, Jeanenne Gayle McMillen, Oct. 8, 1983. B.Tech., Fla. Internat. U., Miami, 1980. Enlisted as pvt. U.S. Marine Corps, 1956, advanced through grades to maj., 1978; head aviation support improvement group Navy Aviation Supply Office, Phila.; group supply officer Marine Aircraft Group 12, Iwakuni, Japan, also Combat Crew Readiness Tng. Group 20, Cherry Point, N.C., ret., 1978; supr. inventory plan Nat. Airlines, Miami, 1978-80; supr. logistics control Pan Am., Miami, 1980-82; dir. purchasing/supply Air Fla., Miami, 1982; dir. materials mgmt. Aviation Sales Co., Miami, 1982—, dir. ops., 1984—, v.p. ops., 1985—. Decorated numerous mil. decorations. Mem. Soc. Logistics Engrs., Marine Corps Aviation Assn. (squadron comdr. 1983-86), Fla. Internat. U. Alumni Assn. (exec. com., bd. dirs. 1982-86), Am. Legion. Republican. Roman Catholic. Home: 8804 SW 150th Pl Circle Miami FL 33196 Office: Aviation Sales Co Ryder Systems Inc 6905 NW 25th St Miami FL 33122

FEATHERSTONE, PHILIP BRYAN, chiropractor; b. Indpls., Jan. 6, 1949; s. Bryan Richard and Aileen Litton (Leyman) F. B.S. in Chemistry, U. Fla., 1971; B.S. in Human Biology, Nat. Coll. Chiropractic, Lombard, Ill., 1976, D.Chiropractic, 1979. Diplomate Am. Bd. Chiropractic Examiners. Research asst. Coll. Medicine, Gainesville, Fla., 1972-74; chiropractic physician, Port St. Lucie, Fla., 1980—. Mem. Am. Chiropractic Assn., Fla. Chiropractic Assn., Treasure Coast Chiropractic Soc. (pres. 1982-83), Port St. Lucie C. of C. (com. chmn. 1982-83). Republican. Clubs: Sertoma (dir. Martin County 1981-83), Port St. Lucie Exchange (dir. 1982-83). Home: 210 S Albany Ave Stuart FL 33494 Office: 8380 S US 1 Port Saint Lucie FL 33452

FEDELE, ANTHONY JOSEPH, communications company executive; b. Bklyn., Sept. 9, 1943; s. Thomas Michael and Philomena (Soldano) F.; m. Kay Ann Williams, June 27, 1965; children—Skae, Anthony, Gaetano, Brianna. B.S., U. Fla., 1967. With Campbel-Dickey Advt., Ft. Lauderdale, Fla., 1967-69, Bloom Advt., Dallas, 1969-71; writer, producer Tracy-Locke/BBDO Advt., Dallas, 1971-76; with Houston-Fedele, Dallas, 1976-78; pres. Fedele, Inc., Dallas, 1978-83; sr. v.p., creative dir. Point Communications, Dallas, 1983—; tchr. Actors Workshop, KD Studios, Dallas; judge Clio Awards, Internat. Broadcast Awards. Cons., Democratic Forum, 1981-82, Dallas Soc. Visual Communications, 1978, Italian Club Dallas, 1982. Recipient Internat. Film Festival of N.Y. Gold medal, 1982; Clio TV and Radio finalist, 1979, 81, 83; Addy Gold medal, 1981, 82. Democrat. Roman Catholic. Home: 117 Westshore Dr Richardson TX 75080 Office: 1700 South Tower Plaza of the Americas Dallas TX 75201

FEDOR, ROBERT PAUL, physician and surgeon; b. Erie, Pa., May 17, 1948; s. Alexander J. and Janet C. (Mordski) F. B.S., Pa. State U., 1974; postgrad.; U. Miami, 1974-76; D.O., Kirksville Coll. Osteo. Medicine, 1976-80. Diplomate Nat. Bd. Examiners. Intern, Suncoast Hosp., Largo, Fla., 1980-81; gen. practice osteo. medicine, Madeira Beach, Fla., 1981—. Profl. group leader United Fund Pinellas County, Fla., 1982. Served to 1st lt. USAR, 1968-74. Recipient Gold award United Fund 1982. Mem. Madeira Beach C. of C., Am. Osteo. Assn., Am. Coll. Gen Practitioners, Fla. Osteo. Med. Assn., Am. Coll. Sports Medicine (bd. dirs. 1984—). Republican. Lodge: Rotary. Avocations: fishing, diving, snow skiing, traveling. Home: 388 150th Ave Madeira Beach FL 33708

FEE, DOROTHEA LILLIAN, nurse; b. Wheeling, W.Va., Aug. 17, 1929; d. Harvey Gorrell and Elva (Borck) F. Diploma, Wheeling Hosp., 1950; B.S. in Nursing Edn., U. Steubenville, 1954; M.A. in Nursing Adminstrn., U. Pitts., 1961. R.N. Dir. nursing Meml. Hosp., Charleston, W.Va., 1963-71, Northwestern Meml. Hosp., Chgo., 1971-73; asst. v.p. Children's Hosp., Chgo., 1973-75; v.p. nursing Jewish Hosp., Cin., 1975-81; v.p. nursing High Plains Baptist Hosp., Amarillo, Tex., 1982—. Served to col. U.S. Army Res. Mem. Am. Nurses Assn., Tex. Soc. Nursing Adminstrn., Am. Orgn. Nursing Execs., Bus. and Profl. Women's Club (chmn. legis. com. Amarillo 1984-85), Sigma Theta Tau. Methodist. Club: Pilot (Amarillo). Office: High Plains Baptist Hosp 1600 Wallace Blvd Amarillo TX 79106

FEE-FULKERSON, KATHERINE CYNTHIA, psychologist, consultant; b. Knoxville, Iowa, Jan. 4, 1948; d. James Russell and Bernice Helen (Pastovich) Fee; m. Conrad Carnes Fee-Fulkerson, Aug. 13, 1977. B.A., Clarke Coll., Dubuque, Iowa, 1970; M.A., U. N.C., 1976, Ph.D., 1982. Lic. psychologist, N.C. Editor, Central Carolina Farmers, Durham, N.C., 1971-72; editorial asst. Inst. of Govt., Chapel Hill, N.C., 1972-76; dir. GRITS project U. N.C., Chapel Hill, 1978-80; psychologist Duke U., Durham, 1980-81; practice psychology, Durham, 1980—. Author: Becoming, 1980. Contbr. articles to profl. jours. Recipient W.D. Perry award U. N.C., 1980; Mary Gervase scholar Clarke Coll., 1970. Mem. Am. Psychol. Assn., N.C. Psychol. Assn., N.C. Assn. Advancement of Psychology. Democrat. Roman Catholic. Avocations: horseback riding, weightlifting. Home: 2712 Legion Ave Durham NC 27707 Office: 3001 Academy Rd Durham NC 27707

FEHRENBACH, T(HEODORE) R(EED), author, businessman; b. San Benito, Tex., Jan. 12, 1925; s. T. R. and Rose Mardel (Wentz) F.; m. Lillian Breetz, Aug. 22, 1951. B.A. magna cum laude, Princeton U., 1947. Field supr. Travelers Ins. Co., San Antonio, 1954-56; owner ind. ins. agy., San Antonio, 1956-69; mng. trustee Fehrenbach Trusts, 1970—; pres. Royal Poinciana Corp., San Antonio, 1971—; chmn. bd. San Antonio Pub. Corp., 1982-85; author: This Kind of War, 1963; This Kind of Peace, 1966; Lone Star (PBS TV series 1985-86), 1968; Fire and Blood, 1973; Comanches, 1974; Seven Keys to Texas, 1983; Texas: A Salute from Above, 1985, others; contbr. numerous articles, stories to mags., U.S., fgn. periodicals. Mem., Tex. 2000 Commn., 1981-82; mem. Tex. Hist. Commn., 1983—. Served to 1st lt. AUS, 1943-46, to lt. col., 1950-53. Recipient Freedoms Found. award, 1965; Evelyn Oppenheimer award, 1968; citations Tex. Ho. of Reps., 1969, 73, Tex. Legislature, 1977; T.R. Fehrenbach Book awards created in his honor Tex. Hist. Commn., 1986; named Disting. Citizen, San Antonio, 1973; Knight of San Jacinto. Fellow Tex. State Hist. Assn. (T.R. Fehrenbach Book awards 1986); mem. Philos. Soc. Tex., Authors Guild, Sci. Fiction Writers Am. Republican. Episcopalian. Clubs: Conopus, Torch, Princeton. Home: 131 Mary D Ave San Antonio TX 78209 Office: 5108 Broadway San Antonio TX 78209

FEIBLEMAN, JAMES KERN, philosophy educator, writer; b. New Orleans, July 13, 1904; s. Leopold and Nora (Kern) F.; m. Dorothy Steinman; 1 son, Peter; m. Shirley Ann Grau, Aug. 4, 1955; children—Ian, Nora, William, Katherine. D.Litt., Rider Coll., 1973; L.H.D., U. Louisville, 1976; LL.D., Tulane U., 1977. Poet, short story writer, novelist; asst. mgr. dept. store; ptnr. investment co.; mem. faculty Tulane U., New Orleans, prof. philosophy, to 1975, chmn. dept., 1951-56, W.R. Irby prof. philosophy, 1968-74, Andrew W. Mellon prof. humanities, 1974-75, emeritus prof. philosophy, 1975—; Barry Bingham prof. humanities U. Louisville, 1975-76; spl. lectr. dept. psychiatry La. State U. Med. Sch., 1958-67. Mem. Am. Philos. Soc., Southwestern Philos. Soc. (pres. 1980-81), Phi Beta Kappa; fellow Charles S. Peirce Soc. (past pres.), New Orleans Acad. Scis. Republican. Jewish. Clubs: Southern Yacht; Metairie Country (New Orleans). Author 45 books, including: Great April, 1971; The Revival of Realism, 1972; Scientific Method: The Hypothetico-Experimental Laboratory Procedure of the Physical Sciences, 1972; The Quiet Rebellion: The Making and Meaning of the Arts, 1972; Understanding Philosophy: A Popular History of Ideas, 1973, paperback edit., 1975; Collected Poems, 1975; Understanding Civilizations: The Shape of History, 1975; The Stages of Human Life: A Biography of Entire Man, 1975; Understanding Oriental Philosophy: A Popular Account for the Western World, 1976, paperback edit., 1977; Adaptive Knowing, 1977; The Reach of Politics, 1969; Understanding Human Nature: A Popular Guide to the Effects of Technology on Man and His Behavior, 1978; New Proverbs for Our Day, 1978; Assumptions of Grand Logics, 1978; Ironies of History, 1980; Technology & Reality, 1982; Conversations, 1982; From Hegel to Terrorism, 1984; Justice, Law and Culture, 1985; (anthology) The Two-Story World, 2 vols., 1966; double edit. of jour. Studium Generale devoted to his work, 1971; contbr. over 175 articles to profl. jours.; founder, past editor Tulane Studies in Philosophy.

FEICK, THOMAS WILLIAM, JR., army officer; b. Columbus, Ohio, Mar. 20, 1952; d. Thomas William and Harriet (Eaton) F. B.S., John Carroll U., 1974; M.S., Fla. Inst. Tech., 1979. Commd. 2d lt. U.S. Army, 1974, advanced through grades to capt., 1979; logistics officer Hdqrs. NCEUR, Stuttgart, Germany, 1979-82; comdr. 62d Transp. Co., Fort Bliss, Tex., 1983—. Mem. Nat. Def. Transp. Assn., Res. Officers Assn., El Paso Jaycees. Home: 8500 Viscount Blvd El Paso TX 79925 Office: 62 Transportation Co Fort Bliss TX 79916

FEIG, EVA, automotive import company executive, civic worker; b. Havana, Cuba, June 17, 1947; came to U.S., 1961, naturalized, 1965; d. Herman and Elisa (Gerskes) Feldenkreis; m. R. Steven Feig, Jan. 22, 1972; children—Ryan Oliver, Clayton Ross. A.A., Miami Dade Jr. Coll.; B.A., Bernard Baruch Coll., 1970; Cert. in Spl. Edn., Barry U., 1980. Sec.-treas., Fgn. Parts Distbrs., Inc., Hialeah, Fla., 1985—. Mem. Cuban div. com. Greater Miami Jewish Fedn.; mem. Cuban div. com. Israel Bonds; mem. edn. com. Mus. of Sci., Miami, Fla.; co-chmn. women's div. luncheon Nat. Parkinson Found., Inc., Miami, 1984-85; mem. hon. com. Pentland Hall, Miami; bd. dirs. Miami Gran Prix Gala Com., 1986, Found. Jewish Philanthropies, 1985—; mem. organizing com. for benefit of Ptnrs. for Youth, 1985; hon. bd. dirs. Deed Club Children's Cancer Clinic, 1985—; mem. Share Zedek Hosp., Israel; mem. com. Miami's for Me; mem. Ballet Concerto; hon. chmn. Leukemia Soc. Luncheon, 1986; active Nat. Colitis and Illeitis Found., Mailman Ctr. of U. Miami, Hope Sch. for Mentally Retarded, Hebrew Acad., Easter Seal for the Handicapped, Lubavitch Youth Ctr., Weissman Inst. Sci., Los Ninos del Deed of Deed Club, Soc. Humanity, Inc.-SOJO, Miami Ballet Soc. Named to Legendary Women of 1984, San Juan de P.R. Ctr., Miami; active numerous other civic and charitable orgns. Named Ms. Charity, 1986. Republican. Jewish. Office: Fgn Parts Distbrs Inc FPD 545 W 18th St Hialeah FL 33010

FEIGE, ROBERTO JUAN, geophysicist, consultant; b. Madrid, Spain, May 21, 1943; came to U.S., 1963, naturalized, 1982; s. Karl Rudolf and Pilar (Ron) F.; m. Marcella Leonor Martinez, Apr. 10, 1965; children—Mariela Katherine, Eric Hans. Bachillerato, Liceo Aplicacion, Caracas, Venezuela, 1960, UCV, Caracas, 1962; postgrad., St. Michael's Coll., Vt., 1963; Cert. in Geophysical Engring., Colo. Sch. of Mines, 1966. Reservoir engr. Shell, Lagunillas, Venezuela, 1966-67; staff geophysicist Phillips Petroleum, Bartlesville, Okla., 1967-71; sr. geophysicist Gulf Oil, San Tomé, Venezuela, 1971-78; resident geophysicist Monsanto, Oklahoma City, 1978-81; owner Integral Geophysics, Oklahoma City, 1982—. Mem. Am. Assn. Petroleum Geologists, Soc. Exploration Geophysicists, Oklahoma City Geol. Soc., Geophys. Soc. Oklahoma City. Republican. Roman Catholic. Club: The Greens (Oklahoma City). Avocations: chess; tennis; fishing; travel. Home: 6400 Kensington Ct Oklahoma City OK 73132

FEIGEN, LARRY PHILIP, physiologist, pharmacologist; b. Everett, Mass., Mar. 27, 1942; s. Robert and Celia (Beecher) F.; m. Judy Lee Segel, Dec. 26, 1965; children—Scott Harris, Sharon Jean. B.A. in Physics, Northeastern U., Boston, 1964, M.S. in Physics, 1966; Ph.D. in Physiology and Biophysics, Chgo. Med. Sch., 1974. Research assoc. Chgo. Med. Sch., 1968-74; asst. prof. Tulane Med. Sch., New Orleans, 1974-81, assoc. prof. physiology, 1981—; cons. to various drug cos. Contbr. chpts. to books. Recipient numerous travel awards; grantee NIH, 1981-84, Am. Heart Assn., 1983—. Mem. Am. Physiol. Soc., Am. Soc. for Pharmacology and Exptl. Therapeutics, Am. Heart Assn., La. Heart Assn., N.Y. Acad. Sci., AAAS. Jewish. Home: 2157 La Salle Ave Gretna LA 70053 Office: Dept Physiology Tulane Med Sch 1430 Tulane Ave New Orleans LA 70112

FEIGERT, FRANK BROOK, political science educator, author; b. N.Y.C., Nov. 10, 1937; s. Morris Samuel Feigert and Anna (Frank) Spelke; m. Frances Goodside, June 17, 1961; children—Benjamin, Daniel. B.A., Allegheny Coll., 1959; M.A., U. Md., 1965, Ph.D., 1968. Instr. to asst. prof. Knox Coll., Galesburg, Ill., 1966-70; asst. to prof. SUNY, Brockport, 1970-77; prof. polit. sci. N. Tex. State U., Denton, 1977—. Author: (with others) Political Analysis, 1972, 76; Parties and Politics in America, 1976; Politics and Process of American Government, 1983; American Political Parties, 1984; American Party System and The American People, 1985. Chmn. Supts. Adv. Com., Denton, 1983—; precinct leader Monroe County Democratic Com., N.Y., 1972-77, registration chmn., 1972; campaign chmn. State Assembly Campaign, Monroe County, 1974. Served to capt. USAF, 1959-64. Fulbright-Hays sr. fellow 1977-78. Recipient Wright Teaching award Knox Coll., 1969; Chancellor's Teaching award SUNY-Brockport, 1973; Honor Prof. Teaching award N. Tex. State U. 1980. Mem. Am. Polit. Sci. Assn., Southwestern Polit. Sci. Assn., So. Polit. Sci. Assn., Midwestern Polit. Sci. Assn., Northeastern Polit. Sci. Assn. Jewish. Clubs: Dallas Corinthian Yacht (Oak Point, Tex.) (treas. 1983—), U.S. Yacht Racing Union. Avocations: sailing, photography, travel. Home: 1404 Wellington Denton TX 76201 Office: N Tex State U Dept Polit Sci Denton TX 76203

FEIGHNER, J.W., mayor; b. Marion, Ind., Sept. 17, 1916; s. H.W. Feighner; m. Margaret Richards, Aug. 23, 1941 (dec.); children—Barrett Feighner Crawford, Katherine Feighner Reeves, J.W. Jr. B.S. in Mech. Engring., Purdue U., 1939; postgrad. Harvard U., 1955. Pres., chief exec. officer Tom's Foods, Columbus, Ga., 1959-79; exec. v.p. Gen. Mills Co., Mpls., 1966-80; mayor Columbus, Consol. Govt., Ga., 1983—. Bd. dirs. Water Bd. Columbus, 1983—, Dept. Pub. Health Columbus, 1983—. Trustee, St. Francis Hosp., Columbus, Columbus Coll. Found.; pres. United Way. Served to capt. USAAF, 1942-46. Mem. C. of C. Columbus (bd. dirs. 1983—). Presbyterian. Clubs: Columbus Country; Green Island Country, Big Eddy. Avocations: fishing.

FEIGON, JUDITH TOVA, physician, medical educator; b. Galveston, Tex., Dec. 2, 1947; d. Louis and Ethel (Goldberg) Feigon; m. Nathan C. Goldman. A.B., Barnard Coll., Columbia U., 1970; postgrad. in sci., Rice U. and U. Houston, 1970-71; M.D., U. Tex.-San Antonio, 1976. Diplomate Am. Bd. Ophthalmology. Intern, Mt. Auburn Hosp., Cambridge, Mass. Intern and clin. teaching fellow, Harvard U. Med. Sch., 1976-77; resident in ophthalmology, Baylor Coll. Medicine, Houston, 1977-80, fellow in retina, 1980-82, clin. instr., 1982—; asst. prof. ophthalmology U. Tex. Med. Br., Galveston, 1982-85, clin. asst. prof., 1985—; practice medicine specializing in ophthalmology, vitreoretinal diseases and surgery, Houston, 1983—; mem. staff Methodist, St. Lukes/Tex. Children's, John Sealy, Rosewood hosps. Bd. dirs. Houston br. Tex. Soc. To Prevent Blindness. Mem. Am. Acad. Ophthalmology, Tex. Med. Assn., Harris County Med. Soc., Barnard Club of Houston, U. Tex.-San Antonio Alumni Assn., Harvard Med. Sch. Associate Alumni, Vitreous Soc., AMA. Contbr. article to profl. publs. Office: 6410 Fannin Suite 404 Houston TX 77030

FEIN, LEAH GOLD, psychologist; b. Minsk, Russia; d. Jacob Lyon and Sarah Freda (Meltzer) Gold; B.S., Albertus Magnus Coll., 1939; M.A., Yale U., 1942, Ph.D. (Marion Talbot fellow), 1944; m. Alfred Gustave Fein, June 10, 1944; 1 son, Ira Hirsch. Health educator New Haven Schs., 1930-43; instr. psychology Carleton Coll., 1944-45; research asso. Conn. Interracial Commn., 1946; chief psychologist Seattle Psychiat. Clinic, 1947-48; prof. U. Bridgeport, 1946-47, 52-58; ind. clin. practice, specializing in clin., child consultation, Seattle, 1948-52, Stamford, Conn., 1952-64, N.Y.C., 1967-81, West Palm Beach, Fla., 1982—; dir. Research Ctr. for Group Counseling, Boca Raton, Fla., 1983-85; clin. cons. Conn. Commn. on Alcoholism Clinic, 1952-60; research asso. Soc. for Investigation Human Ecology; therapist Norwalk Psychiat. Clinic, 1952-64; cons. Child Edn. Found., 1953-56; dir. research Sch. Nursing Norwalk Hosp., 1961-64; dir. clin. services cerebral palsy and mental retardation, Waterbury, Conn., 1964-65; asso. prof. Quinnipiac Coll., Hamden, Conn., 1965-66; cons., instr., med. staff N.Y. Hosp.-Cornell Med. Center, White Plains, 1966-67; dir. psychology Psychiat. Treatment Center, N.Y., 1967-68; research asso. Roosevelt Hosp. Child Psychiatry, 1968-69; supr., cons. research psychologist Bur. Child Guidance, N.Y.C. Board Edn., 1969-72; faculty Greenwich Inst. Psychoanalytic Studies, 1971-79; sr. research scientist Postgrad. Center for Mental Health, N.Y.C., 1980-82; mem. program com. Internat. Congress Social Psychiatry, 1974; research cons. N.Y.C. Mayor's Vol. Action Com., Human Resources Adminstrn., N.Y.C. Study of Delinquency and Study Abused and Neglected Children; cons., inservice trainer Center Group Counseling, Boca Raton, Fla., 1982-85; manuscript reviewer Perceptual Motor Skills, Profl. Psychology. Diplomate clin. psychology Am. Bd. Profl. Psychology. Fellow Soc. Personality Assessment, Am. Psychol. Assn. (council of reps. 1983-86), Am. Acad. Psychotherapists, Internat. Council Psychologists (v.p. 1961-62, 71-73, pres. 1973-75), Am. Orthopsychiat. Assn., N.Y. Acad. Sci.; mem. Nat. Assn. Gifted (v.p. 1961-62), Internat. Council Women Psychologists (chmn. profl. relations among psychologists), Psychologists in Pvt. Practice (treas. 1972-78, bd. dirs. 1979-83), Am. Psychol. Assn. (sec. div. psychotherapy 1966-69; council of reps.), N.Y. State, Fla., psychol. assns., Am. Assn. Group Psychotherapy and Psychodrama (council 1973-75), World Fedn. Mental Health, Nat. Council Jewish Women, Hadassah. Club: Yale (N.Y.C.). Author: The Three Dimensional Personality Test—Reliability, Validity and Clinical Implications, 1960; The Changing School Scene: Challenge to Psychology, 1974; editor Jour. Internat. Understanding, vol. 9-10, 1974; Jour. Psychology Div. Am. Friends Hebrew U.; guest editor Jour. Clin. Child Psychology, 1975; cons. editor Jour. Psychotherapy in Pvt. Practice; others; contbr. Jour. Clin. Psychology, other profl. jours. Address: 213 29th St West Palm Beach FL 33407

FEIN, LOUIS IRA, speech pathologist; b. N.Y.C., Apr. 9, 1941; s. Saul N. and Sally F.; B.A., L.I. U., 1966; M.S., Bklyn. Coll., 1969; Ph.D., Elysion Coll., 1980; m. Carla Ginsburg, Apr. 25, 1965; children—Marc, Tracy; m. 2d, Rebecca Spoor, Oct. 15, 1983; children—Brooke, Erin. Sr. staff therapist Bklyn. Coll. Speech and Hearing Clinic, 1966-69; dir. speech pathology Miami Dade Community Coll., 1970-74; dir. South Miami Speech Clinic, 1970—; supr. speech clinic, instr. Grad. Sch. U. Miami, 1974-75, adj. asst. prof. dept.

otolaryngology Med. Sch. U. Miami, 1975—; exec. dir. United Testing Service, Inc., 1976—. Cert. speech pathologist N.Y., Fla. Mem. Am. Speech Hearing Assn., Fla. Speech and Hearing Assn., Fla. Cleft Palate Assn., Nat. Stutterers Found. Developed FAST Fein Articulation Screening Test. Office: 12390 SW 82d Ave Miami FL 33156

FEINMAN, MINDY ANN, educational administrator; b. Chgo., Mar. 29, 1958; d. Jerome and Leah Joanne (Schafer) F. B.A., U. Va., 1980; M.Ed., Kent State U., 1983. Head tchr. Westminister Child Care Ctr., Charlottesville, Va., 1979-80; resident asst. U. Va., 1978-80; admissions officer Kent State U., 1980-83; asst. dean acad. services U. New Orleans, 1983—. Corresponding sec. Women's Am. ORT, 1985—, honor roll chmn., 1984—. Mem. Am. Coll. Personnel Assn. (conf. planning com.), La. Assn. High Sch. Relations Personnel (zone coordinator 1983—), Nat. Assn. Women Deans, Administrs. and Counselors, Nat. Orientation Dirs. Assn. (state chair program presentor), So. Assn. Collegiate Registrars and Admissions Officers (program presentor), Phi Beta Kappa. Jewish. Avocations: cooking; aerobics. Home: 4147 State St Dr New Orleans LA 70125 Office: Univ New Orleans 256 Business Administrn New Orleans LA 70148

FEINSCHREIBER, ROBERT ANDREW, lawyer, accountant; b. N.Y.C., Apr. 18, 1943; s. Selven Frederick and Maxine (Borodkin) F.; B.A., Trinity Coll., Hartford, Conn., 1964; M.B.A., Columbia U., 1967; LL.B., Yale U., 1967; LL.M. in Taxation, NYU, 1973. Bar: N.Y. 1971, Fla. 1983; C.P.A., Fla. children—Steven, Kathryn. Bar: N.Y. 1971, Fla. 1983. Asst. prof. Wayne State U. Law Sch., Detroit, 1967-69; taxation supr. Chrysler Corp., 1969-70; dir. taxation and fin. analysis NAM, N.Y.C., 1970; asst. chief accountant Seagrams Co., N.Y.C., 1970-72; asso. Oppenheim Appel Dixon & Co., 1972-74; pvt. practice law Robert Feinschreiber & Assos., N.Y.C., from 1972, now Feinschreiber & Assos., Miami, N.Y.C.; with Feinschreiber & Co., C.P.A.s, Key Biscayne, Fla.; v.p. Harrison Internat., Inc., 1979-82; dir. Internat. Bus. Seminars, Inc.; guest lectr. in field. Mem. Am., N.Y. State bar assns., N.Y. County Lawyers Assn., Internat. Tax Inst. (dir. 1972-79), Key Biscayne C. of C., Pi Gamma Mu. Author: Tax Depreciation, 1975; Tax Incentives for U.S. Exports, 1975; International Tax Planning Today, 1977; Allocation and Apportionment of Deductions, 1978; Domestic International Sales Corporations, 1978; co-author: Fundamentals of International Taxation, 1977; editor: Internat. Tax Jour., 1974-82, Bus. Operation Tax Jour., 1976-77, Interstate Tax Report, 1981—, Inventory Tax Report, 1981-82, Export Tax Report, 1983—. U.S. editor Tax Haven and Shelter Report, 1977-78; mem. editorial adv. bd. Internat. Tax Report, 1977-78, Export Tax Report, 1983—. Office: Suite 300 Key Executive Bldg 104 Crandon Blvd Key Biscayne FL 33149

FEINSILVER, PAUL, municipal bond dealer; b. Maplewood, N.J., Jan. 10, 1949; s. Irwin Charles and Claire (Goldberg) F.; grad. U. Md., 1971; m. Denise Schilling, Nov. 24, 1971; children—Corey Blaire, Zachary Evan. Exec., J.B. Hanauer & Co., Livingston, N.J., 1971-78; founder First Miami Securities, Inc., North Miami Beach, Fla., 1978, chmn. bd., 1978—. Mem. Fla. Mcpl. Bond Club. Office: First Miami Securities Inc 1001 NE 163d St North Miami Beach FL 33162

FEINSMITH, PAUL LOWELL, lawyer; b. N.Y.C., July 30, 1941; s. Sydney William and Esther (Gell) F.; m. Sherry Raphael, May 28, 1967 (div. 1972); children—Jeremiah R., Deborah R.; m. Alicia Goldstein, Nov. 18, 1979; 1 child, Sylvie G. B.A., U. Pa., 1962; J.D., NYU Sch. Law, 1965. Bar: N.Y., 1965, Ill., 1969, Fla., 1981. Assoc. Platoff, Heftler, Harker & Nashel, Esqs, Union City, N.J., 1965-69; v.p., gen. counsel Elgin & Waltham Watch Cos., Chgo., 1969-79, N.Y.C., 1972-76, Miami, Fla., 1979-82; ptnr. Hoffman, Larin & Feinsmith, Ft. Lauderdale, Fla., 1982—. Pres. Nat. Kidney Found. Fla., 1981-85; mem. exec. com. Renal Network, 1982—; pres. NAPHT, 1984—. Mem. ABA, Chgo. Bar Assn., Fla. Bar Assn. Democrat. Jewish. Club: New York University (N.Y.C.). Lodge: B'nai B'rith. Home: 4101 Jefferson St Hollywood FL 33021 Office: 3661 W Oakland Park Blvd 202 Ft Lauderdale FL 33309

FELDER, RICHARD MARK, chemical engineering educator; b. N.Y.C., July 21, 1939. B.Chem. Engring., CCNY, 1962; Ph.D. in Chem. Engring., Princeton U., 1966. With Atomic Energy Research Establishment, Harwell, Eng., 1966-67, Brookhaven Nat. Lab., 1967-69; mem. faculty N.C. State U., Raleigh, 1969—, Alumni disting. prof. chem. engring., 1983-85; condr. seminars and courses in field, U.S., Europe, S.Am. Co-author: Elementary Principles of Chemical Processes, 1978, 2d edit., 1986. Contbr. tech. papers to publs. in field; patentee continuous in-stack pollutant monitoring system. Recipient Outstanding Tchr. award N.C. State U., 1978, 81, award for excellence in teaching, research and extension R. J. Reynolds Industries, Inc., 1982, Sigma Xi Faculty Research Achievement award, 1973, award for excellence in engring. edn. AT&T Found., 1985. Mem. Am. Chem. Soc., Am. Inst. Chem. Engrs., Am. Soc. Engring. Edn. Home: 2417D Weswill Ct Raleigh NC 27607 Office: Dept Chem Engring NC State Univ Raleigh NC 27695

FELDMAN, JACK MICHAEL, psychologist, educator; b. Chgo., Sept. 4, 1944; s. Daniel Roy and Lauretta G. (Zaslaw) F.; B.S., U. Ill., Urbana, 1966, M.A., 1968, Ph.D., 1972; m. Susan Jane Pfeifer, Aug. 26, 1967; children—Joshua David, Zachary William. Prof. mgmt. U. Fla., Gainesville, 1972-85, U. Tex.-Arlington, 1985—. Fulbright sr. research fellow, 1977. Mem. Am. Psychol. Assn., Am. Inst. Decision Scis., Am. Motorcyclist Assn. Jewish. Contbr. articles in field to profl. jours.

FELDMAN, JACOB, diversified metals company executive; b. 1906. B.B.A., So. Meth. U. With Comml. Metals Co., Dallas, 1932—, chmn., 1970—. Address: Comml Metals Co 7800 Stemmons Freeway Dallas TX 75221*

FELDMAN, MARTIN L. C., federal judge; b. St. Louis, Jan. 28, 1934; s. Joseph and Zelma (Bosse) F.; m. Melanie Pulitzer, Nov. 26, 1958; children—Jennifer Pulitzer, Martin L.C. Jr. B.A., Tulane U., 1955, J.D., 1957. Bar: La., Mo. 1957. Law clk. to Hon. J.M. Wisdom, U.S. Ct. Appeals, 1958-59; asso. firm Bronfin, Heller, Feldman & Steinberg, New Orleans, 1959-60, partner firm, 1960-83; U.S. dist. judge, New Orleans, 1983—; trustee, former chmn. Sta. WYES-TV. Contbr. articles to profl. jours. Former nat. sec. Anti-Defamation League; former pres. bd. mgrs. Touro Infirmary; bd. dirs. Public Broadcasting Service. Mem. ABA, La. Bar Assn. (chmn. law reform com. 1980-82), Mo. Bar Assn., Am. Law Inst., Order of Coif. Republican. Jewish. Home: 12 Rosa Park New Orleans LA 70115 Office: 500 Camp St New Orleans LA 70130

FELDMAN, NANCY GOODMAN, lawyer, sociology educator; b. Chgo., Oct. 4, 1922; d. Benedict Kay and Irene (Kesner) G.; m. Raymond G. Feldman, Mar. 2, 1946; children—Richard Goodman, Elizabeth Kay, John Kesner. B.A., Vassar Coll., 1944; J.D., U. Chgo., 1946. Asst. prof. sociology U. Tulsa, 1954-50, assoc. prof., 1954-64, prof., 1968-72; prof. mgmt. and sociology Tulsa Univ. Ctr., 1980—; mem. vis. com. U. Chgo. Law Sch.; mem. exec. com. Nat. Space Inst. Vice-chmn. Sangam Internat. Ctr., World Assn. Girl Guides and Girl Scouts; bd. dirs. Planned Parenthood Fedn. Am.; regional chairperson Family Services Assn. Am., Tulsa Psychiat. Ctr.; trustee Simon's Rock of Bard Coll. Named Woman of Yr., Okla. Newsmedia, 1976; recipient Pub. Service award U. Chgo., 1974. Mem. Okla. Bar Assn., Celebrate Women (pres.), Women's Sports Found. (adv. bd.). Club: Tulsa Tennis. Contbr. articles to profl. jours. Home and Office: 2120 E 46th St Tulsa OK 74105

FELIX, ROBERT LOUIS, law educator; b. Detroit, Apr. 7, 1934; s. Camille Herbert and Rosalie (Le Floch) F.; m. Judith Joan Grossman, Aug. 25, 1962; children—Marie, Bridget, Robert, Conan. A.B., U. Cin., 1956, LL.B., 1959; M.A., U. B.C., 1962; postgrad. Oxford U. 1962-63; LL.M., Harvard U., 1967. Asst., assoc. prof. law Duquesne U., Pitts., 1963-67; assoc. prof. law U. S.C., 1967-72, prof., 1973—; prof. S.C. Legal History Inst., 1984—; faculty assoc. Inst. Internat. Studies. Served with U.S. Army, 1960. Ford fellow Harvard Law Sch., 1966-67; Fulbright vis. lectr. U. Clermont-Ferrand, France, 1975-76; lectr. Program on Internat. Legal Coop., Free U., Brussels, Belgium, 1976. Mem. Assn. Am. Law Schs. (sect. on Conflict of Laws), Southeastern Fulbright Alumni Assn. (pres.). Roman Catholic. Author: (with R. Leflar, L. McDougal) Cases and Materials on American Conflicts Law, 1982; (with others) New Directions in Legal Education, 1969, The Vanity Fair Gallery, 1979. Contbr. articles to profl. jours. Home: 6233 Macon Rd Columbia SC 29209 Office: Sch Law U of SC Columbia SC 29208

FELLERS, (DAVE) JAMES DAVISON, trade association executive; b. Oklahoma City, Sept. 14, 1948; s. James Davison and Margaret Ellen (Randerson) F.; m. Janice Kay Kilfoy, Dec. 19, 1969; children—Stacia, Andrea. B.A. cum laude, Central State U., 1971; postgrad. U. Okla., 1971-73. Cert. assn. exec. Reporter, Okla. Jour. Daily, 1968-71; asst. to dir. Central State U., Edmond, Okla., 1970-71; account exec. Ray Scales Assocs. Advt. & Pub. Relations, 1971, v.p., ptnr., 1972-73; dir. mem. services Okla. Oil Marketers Assn., 1971-73, editor Okla. Oil Marketer, 1971-78, exec. v.p., 1974-78; exec. v.p., chief staff officer Tex. Oil Marketers Assn., Austin, 1978—, editor Tex. Oil Marketer, 1978—, Marketers Report, 1979—, co-adminstr. co. ins. trust, 1980—, sec./treas. marketers polit. action com., 1981—. Contbr. articles to profl. jours. Mem. fund-raising drive Salvation Army; mem. Symphony Sq. Com., Assn. Execs. for Reagan-Bush, 1980, 84; mem. emergency planning com. Tex. Energy and Natural Resources Adv. Council; mem. indsl. adv. com. Tex. Air Control Bd.; steering com. Permanent Fund for Neighborhood Parks. Recipient Disting. Service award Okla. Petroleum Council, 1975, Spl. Recognition award Okla. Oil Marketers Assn., 1977, Industry Recognition award Tex. Tourist Council, 1980, Distinction award Am. Petroleum Inst., 1981, Disting. Former Student award Central State U., 1982. Mem. Petroleum Marketers Assn. Am. (chmn. assn. execs. conf., chmn. ins. adv. com.), Am. Soc. Assn. Execs. (Grand award for mgmt. achievement 1984), Tex. Soc. Assn. Execs (chmn. edn. com., pres. 1984-85), Tex. Hwy. Users Fedn. (bd. dirs.), Central State U. Journalism Alumni Assn. (pres.), Bldrs. of Tex. Assn. (steering com.), Austin C. of C., U.S. C. of C., Tex. Assn. Bus., Associated Research. Methodist. Clubs: Capital (bd. dirs.), Austin, Westover Hills, Westwood Country, University. Office: Tex Oil Marketers Assn 701 W 15th St Austin TX 78701

FELLERS, JAMES DAVISON, lawyer; b. Oklahoma City, Apr. 17, 1913; s. Morgan S. and Olive R. (Kennedy) F.; m. Margaret Ellen Randerson, Mar. 11, 1939; children—Kay Lynn (Mrs. Fred A.) Grieder, Lou Ann (Mrs. James B.) Street, J. Dave. A.B., U. Okla., 1936, J.D., 1936; LL.D. (hon.), Suffolk U., 1974, William Mitchell Coll. Law, 1976, San Fernando Valley U., 1976; D.H.L. (hon.), Okla. Christian Coll., 1974. Bar: Okla. 1936, U.S. Supreme Ct. 1948. Practice in Oklahoma City, now sr. mem. Fellers, Snider, Blankenship, Bailey & Tippens. Mem. U.S. Com. Selection of Fed. Jud. Officers, 1977-79; bd. dirs. Nat. Legal Aid and Defender Assn., 1973-76, Am. Bar Endowment, 1977—; mem. adv. bd. Internat. and Comparative Law Ctr.; trustee Southwestern Legal Found., 1949—; hon. consul Belgium for Okla., 1972—. Served to lt. col. USAAF, 1941-45; ETO, MTO. Decorated Bronze Star, Knight of Order of Crown (Belgium) 1984; recipient Hatton W. Sumners award Southwestern Legal Found., 1975. Fellow Am. Coll. Trial Lawyers, Am. Bar Found., Okla. Bar Found., Nat. Jud. Coll. (dir. 1967-70); mem. ABA (pres. 1974-75, chmn. ho. of dels. 1966-68), Barra Mexicana (hon.), Can. Bar Assn. (hon.), Internat. Bar Assn., Inter-Am. Bar Assn., Minn. Bar Assn. (hon.), Okla. Bar Assn. (pres. 1964), W.Va. Bar Assn. (hon.), Am. Judicature Soc., Am. Law Inst. (life), Inst. Jud. Adminstrn., Internat. Assn. Ins. Counsel (v.p. 1955), Nat. Conf. Bar Presidents, World Peace through Law Ctr., Oklahoma City C. of C., Phi Kappa Psi. Episcopalian. Clubs: Beacon, Petroleum. Inducted in Okla. Hall of Fame, 1982. Office: 2400 First National Ctr Oklahoma City OK 73102

FELLOWS, RUSSELL COLEMAN, retail chain executive; b. Rentz, Ga., Sept. 26, 1938; s. Rufus C. and Myrtice Lucille (Brown) F.; m. Patsy Patterson, June 26, 1960. Student pvt. schs., Macon, Ga. With Scott's Supermarket, Macon, 1946-60; asst. mgr.; mgr. Handy Andy Food Stores, Macon; also partner, gen. mgr.; gen. mgr. food stores Munford, Inc., Atlanta, then v.p., gen. mgr., sr. v.p., pres. food stores, 1974-76, sr. v.p. corp. devel., 1976-81, sr. v.p. petroleum mktg., 1978, sr. v.p. mktg., 1979-81, pres., 1981—, chief operating officer, 1982—, also dir. Mem. Nat. Assn. Convenience Stores (dir.), Ga. Retail Food Dealers Assn. (past dir.). Baptist. Home: 649 Old Club Rd S Macon GA 31210 Office: Munford Inc 1860-74 Peachtree Rd NW Atlanta GA 30309*

FELNER, ROBERT DAVID, psychology educator, researcher, consultant; b. Norwich, Conn., June 3, 1950; s. Joseph and Roslyn (Aptaker) F.; m. Tweety J. Yates. B.A., U. Conn., 1972; M.A., U. Rochester, 1975, Ph.D., 1977. Lic. psychologist. Clin. psychology intern Convalescent Hosp. for Children, Rochester, N.Y., 1973-74, Center for Community Studies, Rochester, 1974-75, U. Rochester Med. Ctr., 1975-76; asst. prof. psychology, Yale U., New Haven, 1976-81; assoc. prof., dir. doctoral program in clin./community psychology Auburn U. (Ala.), 1981—; mem. NIMH Small Grants Panel, NIMH Child/Family/Prevention Panel, 1983; NSF grants reviewer, 1983; cons. Conn. Bar Assn., 1978-82, Charles Henderson Child Health Ctr., 1981—, Office for Prevention, NIMH, 1983. NSF research grantee, 1980-82, 83-85; grantee NIH, 1976-77, Edward W. Hazen Found., 1978-81. Fellow Am. Psychol. Assn., Am. Orthopsychiat. Assn.; mem. Soc. for Research in Child Devel. Democrat. Jewish. Author: Preventive Psychology: Theory Research and Practice, 1983; contbr. chpts. to books, articles to profl. publs. in field; mem. editorial bd. Jour. Clin. Child Psychology, Jour. Divorce, Am. Jour. Community Psychology, Jour. Social and Clin. Psychology, Profl. Psychology: Theory and Research. Office: Dept Psychology Auburn Univ Auburn AL 36849

FELPS, WADE HENRY, social worker; s. Childress, Tex., Mar. 13, 1926; s. Henry and Eva (Erwin) F.; m. Emma Jesse Peterson, June 4, 1949; children—Henry Andrew, Kelly Erwin, Jenni Lynn, Sarah Leigh. B.A. in Psychology, Tex. Tech. U., 1953; M.S.W., U. Tex.-Austin, 1959; postgrad. U. Detroit, 1981. Licensed child care adminstr., Tex. Pub. assistance worker Tex. Dept. Pub. Welfare, Breckenridge, 1954-55, Borger, 1956, pub. assistance supr., 1957, regional dir. child welfare Tex. Dept. Pub. Welfare, Houston, 1959, regional child welfare Panhandle region, 1960-62; dir. social work and adoptions Christ's Haven for Children, Keller, Tex., 1962-81, supt., 1981—; cons. in field. Served with U.S. Army, 1944-45. Mem. Acad. Cert. Workers, Nat. Assn. Social Workers, Southwestern Assn. Child Care Adminstrs., Nat. Right to Life Orgn. Democrat. Mem. Ch. of Christ. Contbr. articles to profl. jours. Office: Route 1 Box 467 Keller TX 76248

FELTON, CHARLES ANTHONY, correctional administrator; b. Omaha, Feb. 28, 1944; s. Willie and Myrtis (Brown) F.; B.S., U. Nebr., 1968; M.A., U. Chgo., 1971; m. Carletha Wells Marshall, Nov. 27, 1965; children—Charles Anthony, Tamara Anette, Cary Marshall. Probation officer Cook County Juvenile Ct., Chgo., 1968-70; counselor Stateville Penitentiary, 1970-71; dir. social services Ga. Dept. Corrections, Atlanta, 1971-73; supt. Joliet (Ill.) Penitentiary, 1973-74; asst. dir. youth and correctional services Chgo. Dept. Human Services, 1974-78; supt. reception, diagnostic and classification Cook County Dept. Corrections, Chgo., 1978-80; dir. corrections Pinellas County (Fla.), 1981—; assoc. prof. social work Atlanta U., 1971-73; asst. prof. George Williams Coll., 1973-76, Fla. A&M U., 1980; assoc. prof. St. Petersburg Jr. Coll., 1983. cons. in field. Active Democratic party; co-chmn. St. Petersburg Community Alliance, 1983-84, St. Petersburg Human Relations Bd., 1983. Served with USAF, 1962-64. Mem. Am. Corrections Assn., Nat. Assn. Blacks in Criminal Justice (dir. 1980-81), Fla. Sheriffs Assn. (hon. life), St. Petersburg C. of C. (bd. govs. 1983-84), Omega Psi Phi. Home: 2501 Madrid Ways St Petersburg FL 33712 Office: 14400 49th St N Clearwater FL 33520

FENERTY, MARJORY RODGERS, educator, historical researcher; b. Manila, Feb. 18, 1912; d. George William and Anna Hendricks (Rodgers) Wright; m. Harold Franklin Fenerty, June 26, 1936. Student Wooster Coll. (Ohio), 1928-29; A.B., Mt. Holyoke Coll., 1932; A.M., Ohio Wesleyan U., 1933. Tchr. sci. Mt. Holyoke Coll., St. Agnes Sch., Albany, N.Y., Winsor Sch., Boston, Lincoln Sch., Providence, 1933-47; editor Am. Dir. Water Utilities, 1964-70; research assoc. H.M. Baker Assocs., 1970—; freelance hist. and geneal. researcher. Trustee library, Westwood, Mass., 1955-63, Bethel Park, Pa., 1963-65, Edison, N.J., 1971-74; past dir. Soc. for Preservation of Old Mills; hon. life mem. First Parish of Westwood United Ch., also ch. historian. Mem. Westwood Hist. Soc., New Eng. Hist. Geneal. Soc., Manasota Geneal. Soc. (librarian 1976-80), Chgo. Hist. Geneal. Soc., Western N.Y. Geneal. Soc.. Author: The Meeting House on a rock, 1959; West Dedham-Westwood, 300 Years, 1972; contbr. articles to newspapers, mags., jours. Home and Office: 361 Tampico Palmetto FL 33561

FENN, ORMON WILLIAM, JR., furniture company executive; b. Tyler, Tex., Mar. 13, 1927; s. Ormon William F.; m. Lucille Kelley; children—Miles, Andrea, Kelly, Mike. Student Yale U., 1945-49. Vice pres., gen. sales mgr. Thomasville Furniture Industries, Inc. (N.C.), 1969-77; exec. v.p. sales and mktg. Stanley Furniture Co., Stanleytown, Va., 1977-78, pres., chief operating officer, 1978-81; pres. Am. Drew, 1982; pres., chief operating officer LADD Furniture Co., High Point, N.C., 1982—, dir., 1982—; chmn. bd. govs. Western Mdse. Mart, San Francisco; past chmn. market adv. bd. High Point So. Furniture Market Center. Home: 510 Emerywood Dr High Point NC 27262 Office: Box HP3 High Point NC 27261

FENNELL, EILEEN BRENNAN, clinical psychologist, educator; b. Massillon, Ohio, Aug. 5, 1942; d. Daniel Joseph and Margaret Helen (O'Connell) Brennan; m. Aug. 1984; children—Shannon Elizabeth, Christopher Brian. B.A., U. Fla., 1964, M.S., 1975, Ph.D., 1978. Lic. psychologist, Fla. With U. Fla., Gainesville, 1964—, asst. prof., 1978-83, assoc. prof. clin. psychology, 1983—, also dir. psychology clinic; cons. in field. Contbr. articles to profl. jours. Field official Fla. AAU-Swimming, 1978-80. Mem. Am. Psychol. Assn., S.ea. Psychol. Assn., Fla. Psychol. Assn. (chpt. pres. 1982-84), Internat. Neuro Psychol. Soc. (bd. govs. 1985—), Soc. Personality Assessment (assoc.), Phi Beta Kappa, Sigma Xi. Democrat. Episcopalian. Club: Jazz Soc. Avocations: music; theater. Home: 2530 NW 68th Ter Gainesville FL 32601 Office: Dept Clin Psychology Univ Florida Box J-165 MSB Gainesville FL 32610

FENNELL, TERRESA ANN, counselor, consultant; b. Norfolk, Va., Feb. 18, 1955; d. Robert Wallace and Patricia Louise (Riley) F.; m. Duncan Marshall, Nov. 11, 1978 (div.). B.A. in Spanish, Erskine Coll., 1976; M.A. in Counseling Psychology, U. Pacific, 1982. Registered marriage, family, child counselor intern, Calif. Counselor Valley Community Counseling Services, Stockton, Calif., 1981-85; exec. dir. Parents Anonymous Ala., Inc., Anniston, 1985—. Active San Joaquin County Sexual Abuse Treatment Providers, Mem. Assn. Measurement and Evaluation in Guidance, Am. Mental Health Counselors Assn., Am. Personnel and Guidance Assn., Nat. Vocat. Guidance Assn., Assn. Religious and Value Issues in Counseling, Assn. Specialists in Group Work. Democrat. Presbyterian. Home: 904 Isabel Ave Anniston AL 36201 Office: PO Box 2638 Anniston AL 36202

FENNER, ANN (CLELAND), real estate agency executive; b. Pensacola, Fla., Mar. 17, 1941; d. John Belton and Thelma Freed (Martin) Cleland; m. William Orien Fenner II, June 9, 1959 (div. Mar. 1981); children—Kathleen Fenner Laird, William Orien III, Kenneth Lawrence, Shirley Ann. Student pub. schs., Fernandina Beach, Fla. Lic. in real estate, Fla.; lic. pvt. pilot. Vice pres. Batura & Fenner, Inc., Orlando, Fla., 1980—. Mem. Indsl. Devel. Commn. Mid-Fla. Mem. Orlando-Winter Park Bd. Realtors, Fla. Assn. Realtors, Nat. Assn. Realtors, West Orange C. of C., Orlando C. of C. (aviation com.), Downtown Orlando Inc. Republican. Episcopalian. Clubs: Citrus (Orlando); Bay Hill.

FENTRISS, GRAYSON GOLDZIER, insurance marketing firm executive, legal and business consultant; b. Danville, Va., Oct. 1, 1929; s. Robert Bernard and Janie (Thompson) F.; m. Oct. 20, 1950 (div. June 1972); children—Stephen R., Laurence C., Cynthia L. Fentriss Dixon. B.A. in Econs., U.Va., 1951; J.D., Coll. William and Mary, 1969. Bar: Va. 1969; C.L.U. Agt., Underwriter Acacia Ins. Co., 1951-53; home office life underwriter Prudential Ins. Co., 1953-58; chief underwriter Fidelity Bankers Life, 1958-60; state sales mgr. Peoples Home Life, 1960-64; pres., chmn. bd. Williamsburg Life Ins. Co., 1964-67; pres. Flexibility Unltd., Inc., Williamsburg, Va., 1967—; dir. Human Resources, Inc., Comprehensive Human Resources, Inc. Past pres. Richmond Assn. Internat. Health Underwriters; past v.p. Williamsburg Life Underwriters Assn.; past v.p. Am. Inst. Mgmt. Presbyterian. Office: Flexibility Unltd Inc PO Drawer GF Williamsburg VA 23235

FERAYORNI, JULIAN JOHN, ophthalmic surgeon; b. N.Y.C., Aug. 14, 1942; s. Julius Joseph and Theresa Florence (Rocchetti) F.; m. Elizabeth Mary Farruggio; Oct 9, 1971; children—Justin John, Lauren Beth. A.B., Brown U., 1964; M.D., N.Y. Med. Coll., 1968. Intern, Albany Med. Ctr., North Ridge, N.J.; resident N.Y. Eye and Ear Infirmary; practice medicine specializing in ophthalmic surgery, Fort Lauderdale, Fla., 1974—; surg. staff Holy Cross Hosp., North Ridge Hosp., Bascom-Palmer Eye Inst. Served to maj. M.C., USAF, 1972-74. Mem. AMA, Broward County Ophthalmology Assn. Lodges: Elks, K.C. Avocation: boating. Office: 1960 NE 47th St Fort Lauderdale FL 33308

FERDON, JACOB FERRIS, III, publishing company executive; b. Indpls., Dec. 3, 1948; s. Jacob Ferris and Frances (Pittman) F.; m. Camby Brann, Oct. 23, 1971; children—Judson Ferris, Camby Noelle. B.S., Ball State U., 1973. Mem. sales staff Heftel Broadcasting, Pitts., 1973-76; sales mgr. Am. Broadcasting Co., Houston, 1976-77; with Tex. Monthly Mag., Houston, 1977, sales mgr., Dallas-Ft. Worth, 1977-79; advt. dir., co-founder Dallas Digest Mag., 1979—, Ft. Worth Digest Mag., 1981—; with Hayden Pub. Co., pubs. Personal Computing mag., Personal Software mag., Hasbrouck Heights, N.J., 1981—, regional mgr., Richardson, Tex., 1981—. Served with USAFR. Mem. Dallas Advt. League, Mag. Advt. Sales Assn. Dallas (founding sec. 1979), Culver Acad. Alumni Assn. (life), Phi Delta Theta. Republican. Presbyterian. Home and Office: 325 Lookout Dr Richardson TX 75080

FERGUSON, CHARLES AUSTIN, newspaper editor; b. New Orleans, Mar. 16, 1937; s. Austin and Josephine Hayes (Gessner) F.; B.A., Tulane U., 1958, LL.B., 1961; m. Jane Pugh, Dec. 21, 1961; children—Elizabeth Hayes, Caroline Pugh. Admitted to La. bar, 1961; from reporter to editor States-Item, New Orleans, 1961-80; editor Times-Picayune/States-Item, New Orleans, 1980—; anchor TV program City Desk, New Orleans, 1971-78. Trustee, Dillard U., New Orleans, 1972—, chmn. exec. com., 1978—; trustee Inst. Politics, Loyola U., New Orleans, 1968-75, pres., 1971-75; co-chmn. Louis Armstrong Meml. Park Com., New Orleans, 1971-79. Recipient Torch of Liberty award Anti-Defamation League of B'nai B'rith, 1984; Nieman fellow, 1965-66. Mem. Am. Soc. Newspaper Editors, La. Bar Assn. Club: New Orleans Lawn Tennis. Home: 1448 Joseph St New Orleans LA 70115 Office: 3800 Howard Ave New Orleans LA 70140

FERGUSON, CHARLES RAY, management consultant; b. Duncanville, Tex., Jan. 15, 1925; s. John H. and Inez (Brandenburgh) F.; m. Billie Lucille Benson, Nov. 11, 1945; children—Ben, Becky, Rachel. B.S., So. Meth. U., 1945, M.S., 1955. Registered profl. engr., Tex.; cert. mgmt. cons. Founder, chmn., chief exec. officer LWFW Group, Inc., Dallas, 1956—; dir. Pacific Constrn. Co., Fibergrate Corp. Author: Measuring Corporate Strategy, 1974; co-author Handbook for Corporate Directors, 1984. Hon. chmn. bd. govs. Dallas Symphony Assn.; past pres. bus. adv. council U. Tex.-Arlington. Served with USNR, 1943-47. Mem. Assn. Mgmt. Cons. (bd. dirs.). Clubs: City, University. Office: 12700 Park Central 1805 Dallas TX 75251

FERGUSON, DAVID L., church administrator; b. Pampa, Tex., June 6, 1947; s. Roy William and Ragina Francis (Lockard) F.; m. Teresa Jean Carpenter, June 29, 1963; children—Terri, Robin, Eric. B.S., U. Tex., 1969, M.S., 1972. Ordained to ministry Baptist Ch., 1981. Systems analyst J.M. Huber Corp., Borger, Tex., 1964-65; dir. info. system mgmt., dep. dir. adminstrn. Tex. Dept. Water Resources/Tex. Interagency Natural Resource Council, Austin, 1969-81; adminstr. Allandale Bapt. Ch., Austin, 1981—. Mem. Presdl. Space Council, 1980-81; mem. exec. bd. Alpha Omega Ministries; pres. Capitol City Community Interests. Recipient Outstanding Merit award NASA, 1979. Mem. Nat. Govs. Assn. (data council chmn. 1980-81), Metro Austin 2000, Leadership Austin, Bapt. Assn. (exec. bd.). Author: Meeting Your Spouse's Seven Basic Needs, 1975; Discipleship in Christ-Likeness, 1979; Discipleship in Life Issues, 1981; Family Discipleship Ministry, 1984. Office: 2615 Allandale Rd Austin TX 78756

FERGUSON, DONALD LEE, auditor, consultant; b. Lebanon, Pa., Dec. 21, 1954; s. Franklin Lawrence and Edith Mary (Feeman) Smith; m. Phyllis Louise Wilbanks, Dec. 31, 1973 (div. May 1981); children—Patrick Wayne, Donna Jean; m. 2d, Beverly Joan Anderson, May 21, 1981 (div. Apr. 1984); 1 son, Jack M. Brown. B.A. in Bus. Mgmt., Va. Intermont Coll.; Assoc. in Acctg., Va. Highlands Community Coll. Notary pub., Va., Tenn. Auditor, Quality Inn, 1980-81; auditor, cons. Howard Johnson, Inc., Bristol, Va., 1981—; cons. research and devel. Mem. Senatorial Adv. Com., Republican Presdl. Task Force. Served to sgt. USMC, 1972-80. Author handbooks and catalogs.

FERGUSON, DOUGLAS GORDON, interior design executive; b. McKeesport, Pa., Sept. 10, 1949; s. Douglas Eber and Gladys May (Carpenter) F.; m. Eileen Fay McGuinness, July 29, 1972; children—Kelly Eileen, Derek Douglas. Student Kent State U., 1967-69, Art Inst. Pitts., 1969-70, Art Inst. Ft. Lauderdale, 1971-72. With William Maler & Assocs., Ft. Lauderdale, Fla., 1973-76; ptnr. Design 300, Inc., Coral Springs, Fla., 1976-79; pres. Planning Group, Inc., Boca Raton, Fla., 1979—; adv. bd. Interior Giants, N.Y.C., 1984-85. Mem. adv. bd. Caldwell Playhouse, Boca Raton, 1983—. Served with USMC, 1970-72. Recipient Nation's Top Interior Firm award Interior Design

Mag., 1983, 84. Mem. ASID (bd. dirs. 1983, exec. bd. 1984, 86, Outstanding Service award 1983), Inst. Bus. Designers, Boca Raton C. of C. Republican. Methodist. Clubs: Boca Hotel, Boca Pointe Country. Avocations: swimming; racquetball; boating; camping. Office: Planning Group Inc 1699 S Federal Hwy Boca Raton FL 33432

FERGUSON, EDWARD CLIFTON, medical educator, ophthalmologist; b. Beaumont, Tex., Mar. 11, 1926; married. B.S., Northwestern U., 1946, B.M., 1949, M.D., 1950; postgrad. Harvard U., 1953-54. Diplomate Am. Bd. Ophthalmology; lic. physician, Iowa, Ill., Tex., Colo., Wash. Rotating intern Evanston Hosp., Ill., 1949-50; gen. practice intern Cook County Hosp., Chgo., 1950-51; resident Ill. Eye and Ear Infirmary, U. Ill., Chgo., 1954-56; fellow in neuro-ophthalmology Howe Lab., Boston, 1956-57; fellow in strabismus Columbia U., N.Y.C., 1957; fellow dept. ophthalmology U. Iowa, Iowa City, 1957, chief retina service, asst. prof., 1957-63; assoc. prof. U. Tex. Med. Br., Galveston, 1964-69, prof. dept. ophthalmology, 1969—, chmn. dept., 1969-81; cons. St. Mary's Hosp., Galveston. Contbr. articles to profl. jours. Served with USNR, 1944-45; to capt. M.C. USAFR, 1952-53. Mem. Am. Acad. Ophthalmology, AMA, ACS, Am. Intraocular Implant Soc., Am. Soc. Contemporary Ophthalmology, Contact Lens Assn. Ophthalmology, Internat. Glaucoma Congress, Pan Am. Ophthal. Assn., Assn. for Research in Vision and Ophthalmology, Tex. Ophthal. Assn., Tex. Soc. Ophthalmology and Otolaryngology, Sigma Xi, Alpha Omega. Alpha. Office: Dept Ophthalmology U Tex Med Br Galveston TX 77550

FERGUSON, ELIZABETH LEIGH, nurse; b. Grenada, Miss., Dec. 16, 1956; d. Richard James and Mary Leigh (Garner) Stoker; m. John David Ferguson, Nov. 19, 1976; 1 son, William Jonathan. L.P.N., Holmes Jr. Coll., 1976. Lic. practical nurse Care Inn, Grenada, 1982—. Democrat. Baptist. Lodges: Order Eastern Star, Women of Moose, Rosicrucian Order.

FERGUSON, FRANCES MCCARTY, marketing communications executive, consultant; b. Kansas City, Mo., Oct. 17, 1952; d. Jack Russell and Elizabeth Louise (Gloyd) McCarty; m. Boyd Neal Ferguson, June 8, 1974. B.J., U. Mo., 1974. Staff reporter, feature writer The Columbia Missourian, 1973-74; dir. mail and retail copywriting specialist Mo.-Kans. div. Macy's, Kansas City, 1974-76; freelance retail copywriter Woolf Bros., Kansas City, 1975; advt. and adminstrv. asst. Kroh Bros. Realty Co., Kansas City, 1976-78; freelance copywriter and layout artist Builders' Promotional Service, Dallas, 1978; communications asst. Henry S. Miller Cos., Realtors, Dallas, 1978, dir. advt. and pub. relations, 1978-80, asst. v.p. corp. communications, 1980-83; mktg. cons. SilverTree Prodns., Inc., Dallas, 1982-84; adminstrv. cons. Balcones Computer Corp., Austin, Tex., 1983; owner Corporate Communications, Dallas, 1984-85; regional mktg. dir. Coopers & Lybrand, C.P.A.s, Dallas, 1985—. Mem. Joske's Consumer Adv. Bd., Dallas, 1981, Young Women of the Arts, 1982-83. Recipient First Place award Inst. Real Estate Mgmt., 1981. Mem. Internat. Assn. Bus. Communicators (job bank counselor and competition judging coordinator Dallas), Dallas Advt. League, Dallas Soc. Visual Communications, Pi Beta Phi. Presbyterian. Home: 2205 Mill Pond Rd Garland TX 75042 Office: 1999 Bryan St 30th Floor Dallas TX 75201

FERGUSON, JACK H., power company executive; b. 1931. M.E., U. Colo., 1960. Vice pres. J.A. Jones Constrn. Co., 1974-79; with Houston Power & Light Co., 1979-80; with Virginia Electric & Power Co., 1980—, exec. v.p. power, 1980-83, pres., chief operating officer, 1983—; also pres., dir. Dominion Resources, Inc. Address: Virginia Electric & Power Co PO Box 2666 Richmond VA 23261*

FERGUSON, JOHN LEWIS, state historian; b. Nashville, Ark., Mar. 1, 1926; s. Clarence Walter and Nannye Nell (McCrary) F.; m. Oris Brandon, June 9, 1956; children—Clay Walt, Ora Lee. B.A., Henderson State Tchrs. Coll., 1950; M.A., U. Ark., 1952; Ph.D., Tulane U., 1960. Head dept. social studies Conway Bapt. Coll., Ark., 1952-58; asst. prof. history Ark. Poly. Coll., Russellville, 1958-60; state historian Ark. History Commn., Little Rock, 1960—. Editor: Arkansas and the Civil War, 1965; author: Arkansas Lives, 1965; co-author: Historic Arkansas, 1966. Republican. Baptist. Home: 12 Pilot Point Little Rock AR 72205 Office: Ark History Commn 1 Capitol Mall Little Rock AR 72201

FERGUSON, LESLIE RAYMOND, petroleum geologist; b. Dallas, Oct. 3, 1941; s. Leslie Raymond and Mildred Lee (Deaton) F., Sr. B.S. in Geology, U. Tex.-Arlington, 1980. Stock broker C.A. Pittman Inc., Bellevue, Wash., 1968-72; regional sales rep. Consol. Foods, Denver, 1973-77; exploration geologist Ark. Western, Oklahoma City, 1980-82; prodn. geologist Southwestern Energy Prodn. Co., Oklahoma City, 1982—. Mem. Am. Assn. Petroleum Geologists, Oklahoma City Geol. Soc., Tulsa Geol. Soc., U. Tex.-Arlington Geol. Soc. (v.p. 1979-80), Sigma Gamma Epsilon, Alpha Chi. Avocations: computers, fishing, gardening. Office: Southwestern Energy Prodn Co 1001 NW 63d Suite 200 Oklahoma City OK 73116

FERGUSON, MARLA KAYE, university athletic administrator; b. Baton Rouge, Feb. 4, 1955; d. Homer William and Myrtle Ruth (Newman) F. B.S., La. State U., 1976; M.S., U. N.C.-Greensboro, 1979. Tchr./coach Baker High Sch. (La.), 1976-77; tchr. Plaquemine High Sch. (La.), 1977-78, U. N.C.-Greensboro, 1978-79; women's athletic dir. Southeastern La. U., Hammond, 1979—; dir. aquatics K.C., Plaquemine, 1973-80. Vice pres. Capitol City Bd. Ofcls., Baton Rouge, 1974-75. Named Knight of Round Table, Episcopal High Sch., Baton Rouge, 1979. Mem., Nat. Volleyball Coaches Assn., Assn. Intercollegiate Athletics for Women, U.S. Tennis Assn., Nat. Assn. Coll. Tennis Coaches, AAHPERD, Democrat. Baptist. Lodge: Eastern Star. Office: Athletic Dept Southeastern La State U PO Box 309 Hammond LA 70402

FERGUSON, RONALD DALE, mathematics and computer science educator, consultant; b. San Antonio, Nov. 19, 1942; s. William P. and Martha Ophelia (McKinney) F.; m. Cecilia Kinsel, Dec. 28, 1970; children—Julie Michelle, Lara Denise. B.A., Baylor U., 1965; M.S., N. Tex. State U., 1969; Ph.D., Tex. A&M U., 1982. Prof. math. and computer sci. San Antonio Coll., 1969—. Author (with others) An Algebra Primer, 1975. Mem. AAUP, Math. Assn. Am. (local rep. 1981-83), Tex. Jr. Coll. Assn. Baptist. Club: Health User's Group (pres. 1984). Avocations: micro computers; reading; sailing; carpentry. Office: San Antonio Coll 1300 San Pedro Ave San Antonio TX 78284

FERGUSON, THOMAS CAMPBELL, lawyer; b. Roswell, N.Mex., Sept. 3, 1906; s. William Marion and Martha Ann (Harvey) F.; grad. high sch.; m. Vera Elizabeth Foster, Apr. 20, 1930. Owner-editor Liberty Hill Index, 1921-23, Blanco Courier, 1923-24; pub. Burnet (Tex.) Bull., 1924-26; floor foreman, advt. mgr. Superior (Ariz.) Sun, 1926-27; dep. dist. clk. Burnet County, 1927-28; admitted to Tex. bar, 1929, also U.S. Supreme Ct.; practiced in Burnet, 1929—; city atty. Burnet, 1932-36, Marble Falls (Tex.), 1930-42, 63-66, Johnson City (Tex.), 1963-68; spl. counsel County of Burnet, 1932-38; atty. Home Owners Loan Corp.; county judge Burnet County, 1945-47; dist. judge 33d Jud. Dist. Tex., 1947-60, ret.; now sr. dist. judge; chmn. State Bd. Ins., 1961-62. Mem. Burnet County Sch. Bd., 1934-41; chmn. Def. Bond sales Burnet County, 1941-42; county officer U.S.O., 1940-42; county chmn. ARC, 1946-47; adult scouter Boy Scout program, 1940-80. Chmn. Burnet County Democratic Com., 1928-30; mem. Tex. Ho. of Reps., 1931-32; mem. State Dem. Exec. Com. from 10th Dist., 1933-34; mayor, Burnet, 1939-43. Bd. dirs. Lower Colorado River Authority, 1935-37, 45, 65-71; chmn. adv. bd. to registrants SSS for Burnet County, 1939-47. Served with AUS, 1942-45. Mem. State Bar Tex., Burnet County Bar Assn., Tex. Bar Found., Nat. Hist. Assn., Tex. State Hist. Soc., Tex. Hist. Found., Supreme Ct. Hist. Soc., Burnet County Hist. Commn., Sons of Republic of Tex., Sons of Confederacy, Am. Legion, 40 and 8, various geneal. and hist. assns. and family fellowships. Mem. Christian Ch. Lodge: Masons. Home: 208 E Post Oak St Burnet TX 78611 Office: PO Box 38 Burnet TX 78611

FERGUSON, THOMAS MORGAN, avian physiologist; b. Burnet, Tex., Nov. 8, 1915; s. Thomas Anthony and Ruth Pauline (Morgan) F.; B.A. in Chemistry, Southwestern U., Georgetown, Tex., 1936; M.S. in Biology, Tex. A&M U., 1946, Ph.D. in Zoology, 1954; m. Grace Evelyn Barnett, Aug. 28, 1938; children—Thomas M., John F., Letitia R., Leonard P. Tchr., coach, prin. A&M Consol. High Sch., College Station, Tex., 1936-41; high sch. biology tchr., Corpus Christi, Tex., 1941-42; civilian instr. AAFTTC, Chanute Field, Ill. and Lincoln, Nebr., 1942-43; instr., then asst. prof. biology Tex. A&M U., 1946-52, asso. prof. poultry sci., 1955-65, prof., 1965-79, prof. emeritus, 1979—; biochemist Interdeptl. Com. on Nutrition for Nat. Def. nutrition survey team, Libya, 1957, Ethiopia, 1958, Uruguay, 1962. Active Little League, 1951-61, Boy Scouts, 1954-65; mem. adminstrv. bd. A&M United Methodist Ch., 1978-79. Served in USNR, 1943-46. USPHS postdoctoral research fellow Nat. Cancer Inst., 1953-55. Mem. Poultry Sci. Assn., Am. Inst. Nutrition, Soc. Exptl. Biology and Medicine, AAAS, Fedn. Am. Socs. Exptl. Biology, Sigma Xi, Phi Kappa Phi, Gamma Sigma Delta. Contbr. articles to sci. jours. Home: 4217 Nagle St Bryan TX 77801 Office: Tex A&M U College Station TX 77843

FERGUSON, VIRGINIA CAMPBELL, college administrator, human resource manager; b. Hazard, Ky., Mar. 6, 1949; d. Denver Curtiss and Geraldine Ruth (Morgan) Campbell; m. Robert William Ferguson, Oct. 20, 1973; 1 child, Morgan Slater. B.A., Georgetown Coll., Ky., 1971. Tng. officer, personnel specialist Ky. Dept. Transp., Frankfort, 1971-76; state dir. Ky. Supportive Service, Frankfort, 1976-77; personnel dir. E. Ky. Power Coop., Winchester, 1977-80; community edn., community service coordinator Jefferson Community Coll., Louisville, 1983—. Vol. Mothers' March Dimes, Louisville, 1982-85; bd. dirs. Clark County United Way, Winchester, 1979-80. Mem. Am. Soc. Tng. and Devel. Republican. Office: Jefferson Community Coll 109 E Broadway Louisville KY 40202

FERMAN, RAY, JR., designer; b. Northwebster, Ind., July 8, 1925; s. Ray Levi and Ruth Emily (Pontious) F.; student Miss. State Coll., 1943, Okla. State U. Tech. Inst., 1976; m. Anita Faye Brewer, June 3, 1946; children—Roger B., Richard L., Ray D., Renita F. Commd. 2d lt. USAAF, 1945, advanced through grades to maj. USAF, 1963; served with Berlin Airlift, 1946-49; assigned March AFB, Calif., 1950, Korea, 1951-52, Langley AFB, Va., 1953-55, Chaumont, France, 1956-59, Lowry AFB, Denver, 1960-63; ret.; electro-mech. designer Collins Radio Co., Dallas, 1966-72; program and site mgr. Rockwell Internat. Collins Internat. Service Co., Oklahoma City, 1973-78; designer Rockwell Internat., Dallas, 1979—. Decorated D.F.C., Air medal with oak leaf cluster. Mem. AIAA, Soc. Mfg. Engrs. (sr. mem.), Ret. Officers Assn. Home: 411 W Middleton St Sherman TX 75090 Office: Rockwell Internat 1110 Commerce Richardson TX 75081

FERNANDEZ, ERIC, cardiologist; b. Havana, Cuba, Sept. 19, 1944; s. A.C. and Dolores (Navarro) F.; B.S., U. Md., 1965; M.D., U. Salamanca (Spain), 1972; children—Katrina Lorenne, Candice Ann, Lorene Carin. Chief of medicine Palm Spring Gen. Hosp.; clin. asst. prof. U. Miami Med. Sch., 1978—. Mem. A.C.P., Am. Soc. Internal Medicine, Fla. Med. Assn., Dade County Med. Assn. Home: 18852 NW 64th Ct Miami FL 33015 Office: 2140 W 68th St Suite 402 Hialeah FL 33016

FERNANDEZ, ROBERTO ISAAC, management consultant; b. Havana, Cuba, June 3, 1956; s. Enrique and Guillermina (Villar) F. B.S. cum laude in Spanish, Bus. Edn. and Acctg., Vanderbilt U., 1974-78. C.P.A., Tex. Sr. acct. audit Deloitte Haskins & Sells, Fort Worth, 1978-82; cons. mgmt. adv. services Price Waterhouse, Fort Worth, 1982-83, mgr. mgmt. adv. services, 1983—. Mem. Assn. Retarded Citizens, 1981—; mem. adv. com. Tarrant County Mental Health Mental Retardation Assn., 1983—, v.p., 1986-87; bd. dirs. Ft. Worth Girls Club, 1984—; mem. allocations subcom. United Way Tarrant County, 1985—. Mem. Tex. Soc. C.P.A.s (membership com. 1985—), Petroleum Accts. Soc. Fort Worth, Fort Worth Jaycees (bd. dirs. 1983—, pres. 1984-85). Roman Catholic. Home: 6604 Chestnut Ct Fort Worth TX 76137 Office: 1600 Two Tandy Center Fort Worth TX 76102

FERNANDEZ, SERGIO C(RESCENCIO), construction executive; b. Havana, Cuba, Sept. 14, 1951; came to U.S., 1960; s. Jose and Ofelia (Hernandez) F.; m. Herminia Raquel Moreno, Dec. 13, 1980. A.A. in Arch., Miami Dade Community Coll., 1972; B.A. in Archtl. Engring., U. Miami, 1974. Project mgr. Berard Constrn. Co. Inc., Miami, Fla., 1974-76, Atlantic Coast Devel. Corp., Miami, 1976-79; constrn. mgr. Group III Gen. Contractors, Miami, 1979-81, U.S. Lend Lease Inc., Ft. Lauderdale, Fla., 1981-82; v.p. Terrinvest Inc., Miami, 1982—; constrn. cons. Bldg. Cons. & Assocs., Miami, 1977-81; dir. Abaci Bldg. Col., Miami, 1982—. Contbr. articles to publs. in field (hon. mention awards 1977, 79). Mem. AIA, Constrn. Specificiations Inst., Am. Concrete Inst. Republican. Roman Catholic. Clubs: Optimists, Kiwanis. Home: 9331 SW 6th Ln Miami FL 33174 Office: Terrinvest Inc 8585 Sunset Dr #80 Miami FL 33143

FERNÁNDEZ, TELESFORO, JR., clothing industry executive; b. San Juan, P.R., Nov. 25, 1942; s. Telesforo and Luisa (Martinez) F.; B.S. in Econs., U. Pa., 1965; m. Awilda A. Rodriguez, Nov. 23, 1967; children—Telesforo, Andrés Alexis, Cristina Alexandra. Vice pres., treas. La Esquina Famosa, San Juan, 1965-68, v.p., treas., 1969-77, pres., 1977—; account exec. Young & Rubicam P.R., Inc., San Juan, 1968-69; dir., v.p., treas., prin. Telesforo Fernández & Hermano, Inc.; dir. Caribbean Bus., Mem. Menswear Retailers Am., P.R. C. of C., Plaza las Americas Mchts. Assn., Sales and Mktg. Assn. San Juan (mgmt. award 1972), AFDA Frat. Republican. Roman Catholic. Club: N.Y. Athletic. Office: GPO Box G 2624 San Juan PR 00936

FERNANDEZ-MAITIN, ANIA, physician; b. Havana, Cuba, Nov. 14, 1944; came to U.S., 1961; d. Rene Fernandez and Grace Maitin; children—Ayna Beatriz, Ehren Dayne, Anya Kareni. A.A., Miami Dade Jr. Coll., 1964; B.S., U. Miami, 1967, M.D., 1980; M.S., Fla. Internat. U., 1975. Diplomate Am. Bd. Family Practice. Research asst. Inst. Molecular and Cellular Evolution, Coral Gables, Fla., 1966-73; tchr. pub. schs., Miami, Fla., 1974-76; resident physician Jackson Meml. Hosp., Miami, 1980-83; chief of staff, attending physician Cigna Health Plan, Miami, 1983—. Mem. Am. Acad. Family Physicians, AMA, Fla. Med. Assn., Dade County Med. Assn. Democrat. Roman Catholic.

FERNEA, ELIZABETH WARNOCK, author, film-maker, educator; b. Milw., Oct. 21, 1927; m. Robert A. Fernea; children—Laura Ann, David, Laila. B.A., Reed Coll., 1949; postgrad. in English, Mt. Holyoke Coll., 1949-50, U. Chgo., 1954-56. Lectr. dept. English and Ctr. Middle Eastern Studies U. Tex., Austin, 1975—; cons. Nat. Pub. Radio, 1982—, Ind. Broadcasting Assoc., Concord, Mass., 1981—, Mellon Found. Project on Women and Social Change, Smith Coll., 1978—; lectr. Smithsonian Study Tour Morocco, 1982, 84; contributing editor Texas Books in Review, Dallas; bd. dirs. Am. Near East Refugee Aid, Washington, Am.-Mideast Ednl. and Tng. Services, Washington; speaker Tex. Union Ideas and Issues Com., 1977, 82, Liberal Arts Coll. Forum, 1979. Author: (with Robert A. Fernea) The Arab World, 1985; A Street in Marrakech, 1975; A View of the Nile, 1970; Guests of the Sheik, 1965. Editor: Women and the Family in the Middle East: New Voices of Change, 1984; (with Marilyn Duncan) Texas Women in Politics, 1977. Co-editor and translater: (with Basima Qattan Bezirgan) Middle Eastern Muslim Women Speak, 1977. Writer, producer films on Middle East; contbr. articles to profl. jours.; translater short shories, poems from Arabic; book reviewer; presenter of lectures, forums and film showings to confs. and symposia, U.S. and abroad. Grantee Ford Found., 1983, NEH, 1978, 80; named Outstanding Woman in Lit., Tex. AAUW, 1978. Mem. Tex. Inst. Letters, Middle East Studies Assn. N.Am. (pres. elect 1984—).

FERNER, JACK DENNIS, management educator; b. Rochester, N.Y., May 22, 1930; s. John T. and Dorothy F. (Seel) F.; m. Sara Wilford Boyd, June 11, 1960 (div. 1981); children—Scott G., Jeffrey T., Clayton S., Kendal B. B.S., U. Rochester, 1953; M.B.A., Harvard U., 1955. Mem. adminstrv. staff Eastman Kodak Co., Rochester, N.Y., 1948-54; mem. adminstrv. sales staff Burlington Industries, N.Y.C. and Greensboro, N.C., 1955-57; sr. mgmt. cons. Bromfield Assocs., Boston, 1957-62; v.p. Formulast Corp., Boston, 1959-63; pres., treas., chief exec. officer Chem. Separations Corp., Oak Ridge, 1963-71; dean Babcock Sch., Winston-Salem, N.C., 1971-74, lectr. mgmt. Wake Forest U., 1971—; dir. Santek, Inc., Sun Sports, Inc., L.A. Reynolds Co. Mem. Am. Assn. Accts., Internat. Council Small Bus., Fin. Mgmt. Assn., Inst. Mgmt. Acctg., Winston-Salem C. of C. Episcopalian. Author: Successful Time Management, 1980. Home: 1203 Aspenwood Ct Winston-Salem NC 27106 Office: Box 7659 Reynolds Sta Winston Salem NC 27109

FERNS, CHESTER KIPP, JR., geologist; b. Trenton, N.J., Aug. 24, 1930; s. Chester Kipp and Easter (Watson) F.; m. Dolores Feeler, Oct. 19, 1952; children—Donna Dee, Rebecca Kipp. B.S. in Mining Engring. with Petroleum Engring. Option, U. Mo.-Rolla, 1952. With Cities Service Oil Co., 1953-80; dist. devel. geologist Coastal Oil & Gas Corp. (name formerly ANR Prodn. Co.), Jackson, Miss., 1980-82, dist. exploration mgr., 1982-84, regional exploration mgr., 1984-85, dist. exploration mgr., 1986—. Sec.-treas. Mornin' Lord Ministries, Inc., Jackson, 1977—; arbitrator Better Bus. Bur., Jackson, 1985. Served to cpl. U.S. Army, 1953-55. Mem. Am. Assn. Petroleum Geologists (del. 1982-85), Gulf Coast Assn. Geol. Socs. (del. 1984-85), Miss. Geol. Soc. (pres. 1984-85). Republican. Baptist. Club: Toastmasters (Jackson) (pres. 1980-81). Avocations: photography; officiating basketball and football. Home: 576 Dryden Ave Jackson MS 39209 Office: Coastal Oil & Gas Corp 111 E Capitol St Suite 400 Jackson MS 39201

FERRAN, HARRY AVERY, engineering company executive, mechanical engineer; b. Orlando, Fla., Nov. 28, 1936; s. Edgar Loraine and Laura Fair (Morrow) F. B.M.E., U. Fla., 1964; postgrad. Advanced Mgmt. Program, Harvard U., 1974. Registered profl. engr., Fla. Field sales engr. Trane Co., 1964-67; owner, pres. Ferran Air Conditioning, 1967-69; owner, pres. Ward Air Conditioning, Orlando, Fla., 1967—, Harry A. Ferran & Assocs. Cons. Engring., Orlando, 1967—, Avtech Corp., Orlando, 1971—, Johnson Electric Co., 1981—, Avery Plumbing, Orlando, 1981—. Mem. exec. com. mgmt. efficiency adv. com. City of Orlando, 1976; pres. John Young Sci. Ctr.; chmn. Code Enforcement Bd. Orlando; vice-chmn. Orlando County Airports Bd. Zoning Adjustments, 1983. Mem. ASHRAE, Nat. Soc. Profl. Engrs., Soc. Automotive Engrs., Fla. Engring. Soc., Com. of 100 of Orange County, Inc., Orlando Area C. of C. (v.p., dir. 1973), Leadership Fla., Blue Key, Mensa. Republican. Presbyterian. Club: Economics (pres. 1982). Home: 576 S Osceola Ave Orlando FL 32801 Office: 530 Grand St Orlando FL 32805

FERRARA, JOHN CIRO, landscape nursery executive; b. Boston, June 12, 1920; s. Philip and Angelina (LoForte) F.; m. Madeline Boyd, Aug. 16, 1947; 1 child, John Michael. Student Northeastern U., 1938; B.A., Boston Tchrs. Coll., 1941. With Boston Pub. Library, 1937-41; substitute tchr. Boston Sch. System, 1945; ptnr., pres. Campbell & Ferrara, Inc., Alexandria, Va., 1945—; sec.-treas., dir. Ferrabell Corp., Va.; dir. First Va. Banks. Contbr. to Landscape Guide and Manual. Served to capt. USAAF, 1941-45. Mem. Am. Assn. Nurserymen (rep. to Council Tree and Landscape Appraisers 1979—), Internat. Soc. Arborculture, Va. Soc. Landscape Designers, Air Force Assn., Jr. C. of C. (pres. 1952), Alexandria C. of C. (bd. dirs., sr. v.p. 1964), U.S. Senatorial Club, Capitol Hill Club. Republican. Methodist. Club: Belle Haven Country (Alexandria) (pres. 1974). Lodges: Rotary (pres. 1969), Masons, Shriners. Avocations: golf; fishing; hunting. Home: 1211 Burtonwood Ct Alexandria VA 22307 Office: Campbell Ferrara Nurseries Inc 6651 Little River Turnpike Alexandria VA 22312

FERRÉ, FREDERICK POND, philosopher, educator; b. Boston, Mar. 23, 1933; s. Nels F.S. and Katharine L. (Pond) F.; m. Marie Booth, June 8, 1954 (div. July 18, 1980); 1 dau., Katharine Marie; m. 2d, Barbara Meister, June 12, 1982. Student Oberlin Coll., 1950-51; A.B. summa cum laude Boston U., 1954; M.A., Vanderbilt U., 1956; Ph.D., U. St. Andrews (Scotland), 1959. Cert. flight instr., FAA. Vis. asst. prof. Vanderbilt U., 1958-59; asst. prof. Mt. Holyoke Coll., 1959-62; assoc. prof. Dickinson Coll., 1962-67, prof., 1967-80, Charles A. Dana prof. philosophy, 1970-80; prof., head dept. philosophy and religion U. Ga., Athens, 1980-84, prof., head dept. philosophy, 1984—; vis. prof. So. Meth. U., Bucknell U., Pitts. Theol. Sem., Princeton Theol. Sem., Purdue U., Vanderbilt U., Iliff Theol. Sem.; cons. Nat. Humanities Faculty. Boston U. Prof. Augustus Howe Buck scholar, 1951-54; Fulbright fellow, 1956-58; Soc. Religion in Higher Edn. Kent fellow, 1957-59; NEH Younger Scholar fellow, 1969-70, nat. humanities fellow, 1978-79. Mem. Am. Philos. Assn., Philosophy Sci. Assn., Metaphys. Soc. Am., Am. Theol. Soc. Democrat. Author: Language, Logic and God, 1961; Exploring the Logic of Faith, 1962; Basic Modern Philosophy of Religion, 1967; Shaping the Future, 1976; contbg. editor The Challenge of Religion, 1982. Office: Dept Philosophy U Georgia Athens GA 30602

FERRE, MAURICE ANTONIO, former mayor, corporate consultant; b. Ponce, P.R., June 23, 1935; s. Jose Antonio and Florence (Salichs) F.; m. Maria Mercedes Malaussena, Aug. 25, 1955; children—Mary Isabel, Jose Luis, Carlos Maurice, Maurice Raimundo, Francisco Antonio, Florence. Grad. Lawrenceville (N.J.) Sch., 1953; B.S. in Archtl. Engring., U. Miami (Fla.), 1957. Mem. Fla. Ho. of Reps., 1967—; mayor of Miami, 1973-85. Mem. City of Miami Commn., 1967-70. Trustee U. Miami. Home: 1747 Espanola Dr Miami FL 33133 Office: PO Box 451033 Miami FL 33145*

FERREE, PAUL KIRKPATRICK, industrialist; b. Morganton, N.C., Apr. 5, 1906; s. Charles Eugene and Jeanette (Kirkpatrick) F.; m. Louise Hyder, Oct. 10, 1925; children—Gwen Ferree Brown, Jeanette Ferree Davis, Barbara Ferree Tarver, Yvonne Ferree Sell, Paula Ferree Baron. A. in Bus. Law and Acctg., Kings Bus. Coll., Charlotte, N.C., 1928. Exec., Bolton Leather Co., Knoxville, Tenn., 1927-45, pres., 1945-56; pres. Pekay Leather Products, Knoxville, 1945-56; chmn. Saddlecraft, Inc., Cherokee, N.C., 1956—; chmn. 1st Union Nat. Bank, Cherokee, 1968—; pres. Shoe Service Inst. Am., 1949-51. Trustee Montreat-Anderson Coll., Montreat, N.C., 1974-83; moderator Asheville Presbytery, Presbyn. Ch., 1981-82, elder, 1965—. Recipient Disting. Service award Montreat-Anderson Coll., 1983. Democrat. Lodges: Rotary, Masons. Office: Saddlecraft Inc Acquoni Rd Cherokee NC 28719

FERRELL, JOE EDWARD, theatre arts educator; b. Lewistown, Mont., Mar. 30, 1940; s. Harold E. and Ann L. (Songer) F.; m. Georgia Ann Benton, Aug. 20, 1966; 1 son, Lane; 1 adopted son, Terry. B.A. in English, U. Mont., 1962, M.A. in Theater, 1966; postgrad. U. Iowa, 1968-69, Ind. U., 1972-73. Instr., Newberry (S.C.) Coll., 1966-68; asst. prof. Georgetown (Ky.) Coll., 1970-83; asst. prof. dept. theatre arts U. Ky., Lexington, 1983—; guest dir. Theatre Downunder, U. Ky., Lexington, Junkyard Players, Lexington, various community theatres; theatre cons. Ky. Arts Commn. Served to 1st lt., arty. U.S. Army, 1963-65. Mem. Am. Theatre Assn., Southeastern Theatre Assn. (chmn. coll. and univ. div.), Ky. Theatre Assn., Ky. Arts in Edn. Home: 106 Clay Ave Georgetown KY 40324 Office: Dept Theatre Arts U Ky Lexington KY 40506

FERRELL, NANCY KAREN, human resource specialist; b. Charleston, W.Va., Apr. 24, 1946; d. Armel Ferrell and Maxine (Fugate) Dellinger. B.A., Fla. State U., 1969; M.R.E., Southwestern Bapt. Theol. Sem., 1972; M.S. in Edn., E. Tex. State U., 1984, doctoral candidate, 1983—. Assoc. dir. Baptist Student Union, U. Tulsa, 1972-75; asoc. dir. Woman's Missionary Union, Louisville, 1976-79; owner/pres. Profl. Services & Edn., Dallas, 1980—. Vol. trainer Restart, Dallas, 1985; deacon, Sunday sch. tchr. Royal Ln. Baptist Ch., Dallas, 1982-85. Tallhassee Bus. and Profl. Women scholar, 1968-69; Woman's Missionary Union scholar, 1978; Josephine Proctor Jones scholar, 1979; So. Bapt. Conv. grantee, 1979. Mem. Am. Soc. Tng. and Devel., Phi Delta Kappa. Republican. Avocations: quilting; bicycling. Office: Profl Services & Edn 5622 Vickery Blvd Dallas TX 75206

FERRELL, STEPHANIE ELAINE, architect, consultant; b. Phoenix, Feb. 11, 1948; d. Charles Wayne and M. Elaine (Manning) F.; m. Stephen Paul Morrill, Sept. 1, 1979. Student Wake Forest Coll., 1966-67; B.Arch., U. Fla., 1972. Registered architect, Fla. Architect Hist. Tampa/Hillsborough Preservation Bd., Fla., 1978-80, dir., 1980—; cons. hist. preservation. Contbr. articles to profl. jours. Bd. dirs., pres. Tampa Community Design Ctr., 1976-80; bd. dirs. Ybor City Mus. Soc., Tampa, 1983—. Recipient cert. of recognition Fla. Sec. of State's Office, 1985. Mem. AIA (sec. Tampa sect. 1984-85, v.p. Tampa sect. 1986, pub. communications award, article award 1984), Nat. Trust Hist. Preservation, Fla. Trust: Alliance Preservation Bds. and Commns. (steering com. 1983—, pres. 1985-86), Tampa Writer's Alliance, Ybor City C. of C. (dir. 1985—), Tampa Architecture Club (founding). Democrat. Home: 2105 Watrous Ave Tampa FL 33606 Office: Hist Tampa/Hillsborough County Preservation Bd 452 W Kennedy Blvd Tampa FL 33606

FERRER, EDWIN, architect; b. N.Y.C., Dec. 2, 1928; s. Juan and Rosaura (Lopez) F.; B.S., U. Houston, 1957, B. Arch., 1958; m. Nadene Joan Reinders, Oct. 13, 1961 (div.); 1 dau., Andrea; m. 2d, Barbara Sue Gibson, May 29, 1979. Designer-project architect firm Rustay Martin & Vale, Houston, 1962-69; project architect Neuhaus & Taylor, Houston, 1969-71, Wyatt C. Hedrick, Houston, 1971-72, Koetter Tharp Cowell & Bartlett, Houston, 1973-76; design supr. C.E. Lummus Co., Houston, 1976-78; prin. Edwin Ferrer AIA, 1978—; works include schs., comml., residential, chs. Served with AUS, 1946-48. Mem. AIA (mem. residential architecture com. Houston), Tex. Soc. Architects. Home: 10738 Hazen Rd Houston TX 77072 Office: 5633 Richmond Ave Suite 201 Houston TX 77072

FERRER, ESTEBAN A., lawyer; b. Cuba, Sept. 20, 1925; s. Esteban A. and Carola (Ruiz) F.; m. Susan W. Stone, Apr. 15, 1970; children—Esteban, Cristina, Carlos, Geoffrey. LL.D., U. Havana, 1947; Cert. of Law, U. Fla., 1976. Ptnr. Salaya y Casteleiro, Havana, 1948-60; v.p., sr. advisor Council of the Americas, N.Y.C., 1961—; ptnr. Shutts & Bowen, Miami, Fla., 1977—. Pres., Internat. Ctr. of Fla., 1977, 84; bd. dirs. St. Thomas Sch. Law. Mem. ABA, Interam. Bar Assn., Cuban-Am. Bar Assn. Roman Catholic. Clubs: Key

Biscayne Yacht, Bankers, American (Miami); Larchmont Yacht (N.Y.). Office: Shutts & Bowen 100 Chopin Plaza Miami FL 33131

FERRISS, ABBOTT LAMOYNE, retired sociology educator; b. Jonestown, Miss., Jan. 31, 1915; s. Alfred William Overby and Grace Childs (Mitchell) F.; m. Ruth Elizabeth Sparks, Dec. 21, 1940; children—John Abbott, William Thomas. B.J., U. Mo., 1937; M.A., U. N.C., 1943, Ph.D., 1950. Asst. prof. sociology Vanderbilt U., 1949-51; research social scientist Human Resources Research Inst., Air U., 1951-54; chief unit effectiveness br. Air Force Personnel and Tng. Rev. Ctr., 1954-57; chief health survey br. Bur. of Census, 1957-59; supervisory survey statistician Outdoor Recreation Resources Rev. Commn., 1959-62; asst. study dir. NSF, 1962-67; research sociologist Russell Sage Found., 1967-70; prof. sociology Emory U., 1970-82, chmn. dept., 1970-76; lectr. George Washington U., 1958-59, U. Md., 1959-61, No. Va. Ctr. of U. Va., 1960-70. Served with USAAF, 1943-46; CBI. NSF grantee, 1976-78. Mem. Am. Sociol. Soc., Sociol. Research Assn., So. Sociol. Soc. (pres. elect 1985-86), So. Regional Demographic Group, Population Assn. Am. (sec.-treas. 1968-71), Ga. Sociol. Assn., D.C. Sociol. Soc. (sec.-treas. 1965-68, pres. 1969-70). Democrat. Episcopalian. Club: Cosmos (Washington). Author: National Recreation Survey, 1962; Indicators of Trends in the Status of American Women, 1971; Indicators of Change in the American Family, 1970; Indicators of Trends in American Education, 1969; Attitudes of Far Eastern Air Force Personnel Toward Natives, 1953; editor: Research and the 1970 Census, 1971; (with J.C. Glidwell) Reducing Traffic Accidents by Use of Group Discussions-Decision: An a priori Evaluation, 1957; editor, pub. SINET (Social Indicators Network News), 1984—; editor So. Sociologist, 1981-84; assoc. editor Social Forces, 1976-79; editor PAA Affairs, 1968-71, The Sociologist, 1965-68; mem. editorial bd. Social Indicators Research, 1980—. Home: 1273 Oxford Rd NE Atlanta GA 30306

FERRITER, JOHN RICHARD, administrator physical education center; b. Muskogee, Okla., Aug. 7, 1942; s. Paul Thomas and Kathryn Mary F.; m. Mary Jo Williams, Apr. 4, 1964. B.S., U. S.C., 1971, 78. Mgr., Asst. facilities dir. Solomon Blatt Phys. Edn. Center, U. S.C., Columbia, 1971-80, facility dir., 1980—, instr., 1971—; cons. swimming pool and facilities. Race dir. S.C. State Fair, 1978—; merit badge counselor Boy Scouts Am., also cubmaster, 1964-66. Served with USMC, 1961-66. Mem. AAHPER, Am. Assn. Leisure and Recreation, Nat. Assn. Sport and Phys. Edn., Am. Mktg. Assn., U. S.C. Adminstrv. Employees (pres. 1979-80). Republican. Roman Catholic. Clubs: Columbia Ski (dryland ski sch. dir. 1979—, pres. 1979-80). Lodge: KC (grand knight 1983-84). Home: 103 Ashridge Ct Columbia SC 29210 Office: Rm 201 Blatt Phys Edn Center U SC Columbia SC 29208

FERTIG, STEVEN ALLEN, dentist; b. New Brunswick, N.J., Oct. 24, 1947; s. Joel Robert and Barbara Roslyn (Caplan) F.; m. Janet Muna Silber, June 29, 1969; 1 child, Marni Katherine. Student Stetson U., 1965-68; D.M.D., U. Ky., 1971. Diplomate and Past Bd. Examiner Fed. Services Bd. Gen. Dentistry. Resident in comprehensive dentistry Nat. Naval Dental Ctr., Bethesda, Md., 1975-77; commd. officer U.S. Navy, 1972, advanced through ranks to comdr., 1980; dental dept. head U.S. Naval Air Sta., Guantanamo Bay, Cuba, 1972-74; dental br. head Naval Dental Clinic, Washington, 1974-75; asst. dental dept. head U.S.S. Canopus, Rota, Spain and Charleston, S.C., 1977-80; exec. officer, dir. clin. services 12th Dental Co., Cherry Point, N.C., 1980-84; resigned, 1984; gen. practice dentistry New Bern, N.C., 1984—; staff mem. dept. oral surgery Naval Hosp., Cherry Point, 1985—. Project chmn. Sertoma Internat., Summerville, S.C., 1979-80; campaign capt. United Way Fund Dr., New Bern, 1984; co-chmn. Nat. Safe Boating Week, New Bern, 1984. Recipient Research award Nat. Naval Dental Ctr., 1975-76; Merit Mark award U.S. Power Squadron, 1982. Mem. ADA, Am. Acad. Oral Medicine (Oral Medicine award 1972), Acad. Operative Dentistry, Acad. Gen. Dentistry, Assn. Mil. Surgeons of U.S., N.C. Dental Soc., Coastal Carolina Dental Soc., Craven County Dental Soc. (sec./treas. 1985-86), Beta Beta Beta, Mu Alpha Theta. Clubs: Eastern Carolina Yacht (treas. 1983-84, rear commodore 1984-85), Cape Lookout Power Squadron (auditor 1983-84). Avocations: boating; fishing; auto and boat mechanics. Home: 804 Arcane Circle New Bern NC 28560 Office: 1917 Trent Blvd New Bern NC 28560

FETKO, PAUL, electronics and building materials executive; b. Central City, Pa., Apr. 12, 1931; s. Charles and Pearl (Doban) F.; m. Eleanore Salamanchuk, June 7, 1955; children—Linda Louise, Debra Marie, Laura Jean. B.S., U.S. Mil. Acad., 1955; M.B.A., Harvard U., 1959; postgrad. NYU, 1960-63. Engr. Arabian Am. Oil Co., N.Y.C., 1955-59; engring. adminstr. Bendix Corp., Teterboro, N.J., 1959-61; fin. adminstrn. mgr. Gen. Precision Corp., Little Falls, N.J., 1961-64; with Avion Electronics and Cardion Electronics units Gen. Signal Corp., N.Y.C., 1964-68; adminstrv. mgr., 1964-66, v.p., gen. mgr., 1966, pres., gen. mgr., 1966-68; exec. asst. to pres. Paul Venze Assocs. (GAC), Miami, Fla., 1968-70; exec. asst. to pres. Cavanagh Communities Corp., Miami, 1970-71; v.p. ops. Am. Agronomics, Inc., Miami, 1971; exec. v.p. Transworld Realty Corp., Miami, 1971-75; pres., dir., prin. Preferred Equities Corp., Miami, 1972—, Aerotronics, Inc., Miami, 1981—; v.p., dir., prin. Puritan Mills, Inc., Atlanta, 1982—; cons. Martin Marietta Corp., Orlando, Fla., 1982. Served with USAF, 1949-51; with U.S. Army, 1955. Mem. U.S. Mil. Acad. Assn. Grads., Am. Def. Preparedness Assn., Phi Kappa Phi. Home: 6200 Rivercliffe Dr NW Atlanta GA 30328 Office: 1424 Hills Pl NW Atlanta GA 30318

FETNER, CHARLES ANTHONY, hospital administrator; b. Lineville, Ala., Feb. 12, 1951; s. Leon and Doris (Proctor) F.; m. Lynne Walker, Apr. 26, 1975; children—Matt, Molly, B.S., U. Ala.-Tuscaloosa, 1972; J.D., Jones Law Inst., Montgomery, Ala., 1976. Bar: Ala. 1977. Pub. auditor State Examiners, Montgomery, 1974-75; budget mgr. Ala. Dept. Mental Health, Montgomery, 1975-77; asst. dir. Bryce Hosp., Tuscaloosa, 1977-81, hosp. dir., 1981—. Bd. dirs. United Way, Tuscaloosa, 1983—. Mem. ABA, Ala. Bar Assn. Home: 93 Heritage Hills Tuscaloosa AL 35406 Office: Bryce Hosp University Blvd Tuscaloosa AL 35403*

FETT, THOMAS H., petrophysicist, consultant; b. Canton, Ohio, Dec. 1, 1943; s. John Crosby and Marjorie (Hatchett) F.; m. Kristina M. Stephens, Apr. 24, 1965; children—Ralph (dec.), Carol, Neil. B.S. in Engring. Sci., Trinity U., 1966. Registered profl. engr., Tex. Engr. field Schlumberger Well Services, Pharr, Tex., 1966-73, mgr. dist., Graham, Tex., 1973-76, sr. sales engr., Corpus Christi, 1976-80, specialist dipmeter, 1980-85; asst. vis. prof. Tex. Coll. Arts & Indsl., Kingsville, 1978—. Mem. Am. Petroleum Inst. (local bd. dirs. 1984—), Am. Assn. Petroleum Geologists, Soc. Econ. Paleontol. & Mineralogists, Soc. Profl. Well Log Analysts (internat. sec. 1983-84, internat. bd. dirs. 1982-83), Corpus Christi Geol. Soc., Houston Geol. Soc., San Antonio Geol. Soc., Soc. Petroleum Engrs. (local bd. dirs. 1978-80). Republican. Presbyterian. Avocations: travel; photography; golf; tennis. Home: 4134 Sierra St Corpus Christi TX 78410 Office: Schlumberger Well Services 400 Wilson Tower Corpus Christi TX 78476

FETTER, FRANKLIN CLAYTON, JR., geologist; b. Phila., May 13, 1946; s. Franklin Clayton and Eleanor Bragg (Scott) F.; m. Barbara Ann Heinicke, Nov. 26, 1970; 1 child, Jennifer Anne. B.S., U. Miami, 1968; postgrad. Eidgenössiche Technische Hochschule, Zurich, Switzerland, 1969-70; M.S., Fla. State U., 1973. Ops. geologist Amoco, New Orleans, 1974-78; geologist chief exploitation geologist McMoRan Exploration Co., New Orleans, 1978—. Mem. Am. Assn. Petroleum Geologists, Marine Tech. Soc. (chmn. 1976-78). Avocations: raising cattle and horses. Office: McMoRan Exploration Co 1615 Poydras St New Orleans LA 70112

FETZER, HOMER DONALD, physics educator, consultant; b. San Antonio, Oct. 19, 1932; s. W. J. and Gertrude L. (Lamm) F.; m. Laura Sue Gorrell, June 19, 1954; children—Donald, Jeffrey, Susan, Patrick, Mark. B.S. in Physics, St. Mary's U., San Antonio, 1954; M.A., U. Tex., 1959, Ph.D., 1965. Instr. St. Mary's U., San Antonio, 1959-63, assoc. prof. physics, 1965-72, prof., 1972—, Minnie Stevens Piper prof., 1983; research physicist S.W. Research Inst., San Antonio, 1966-83, cons., 1983—. Served to 1st lt. U.S. Army, 1954-57. NSF sci. faculty fellow U. Tex., Austin, 1962; NSF summer inst. fellow Am. U., Washington, 1967, Oak Ridge, 1969; AEC summer inst. fellow, Oak Ridge, 1971. Mme. Am. Assn. Physics Tchrs. Office: St Mary's U Dept Physics One Camino Santa Maria San Antonio TX 78284

FEW, MELINDA MULLINIKS, stock brokerage company executive; b. Memphis, Oct. 13, 1938; d. Robert Curlee and Hallie Agnas (Marshall) Mulliniks; m. Robert Pierce Few, Jan. 13, 1962 (div.); 1 son, Marshall Read. Student, Memphis State U., 1956-58, v.p. Henderson, Few & Co., Atlanta, 1963-67; broker Robinson-Humphrey Co., Inc., Jacksonville, Fla., 1978-81; v.p. Blackstock & Co., Inc., Jacksonville, 1981—; sec.-treas., dir. Nat. Health Care Systems, Denticare, Inc. Active Ponte Vedra Woman's Club (bd. dirs., past pres.). Republican. Presbyterian. Home: 215 Pablo Rd Ponte Vedra Beach FL 32082 Office: Blackstock & Co 10 W Adams St Jacksonville FL 32202

FIALLOS, ALEJANDRO, food and beverage company executive; b. Managua, Nicaragua, Sept. 13, 1956; came to U.S., 1981; s. Francisco and Celia (Navarro) F.; m. Ivonne Lacayo, Dec. 27, 1977; children—Alejandro Jose, Carlos Alberto. B.S. in Bus. Adminstrn., U. Centroamericana, Nicaragua, 1978; cert. total quality control inspection U.S. Dept. Agr., 1982. Asst. v.p. mktg. Indsl. Cervecera S.A., Managua, Nicaragua, 1977-81; plant mgr. Nat. Food Industries, Miami, 1981-84; gen. mgr. Blue Mountains Co., Miami, 1984—. Gen. dir. commerce Nicaraguan Reconstruction Govt., Managua, 1979, exec. dir., 1980. Mem. Bus. Adminstrs. Assn., Potato Chips Snack Food Assn. Roman Catholic. Home: 14909 SW 104th St Apt 13 Miami FL 33196 Office: Blue Mountains Co SA 8278 NW 66th St Miami FL 33166

FICARA, ANTHONY JOHN, periodontist; b. N.Y.C., Sept. 8, 1943; s. Paul and Mary (Lerario) F.; m. Jane Ellen Hightower, Aug. 17, 1968; children—Paula L., Kristen M. B.A., Hofstra U., 1965; D.D.S., Fairleigh Dickinson, U., 1969; M.S., George Washington U., 1974. Diplomate Am. Bd. Periodontology. Commd. 2d lt. U.S. Army, 1965; advanced through grades to col. Dental surgeon Oakland Army Base, Calif., 1970-72; mentor dental resident programs, Fort Hood, Tex., 1974-79; preventive dentistry officer U.S. Army, Fort Hood, 1977-79; preventive dentistry officer Tripler Army Med. Ctr., Hawaii, 1979-81, chief peridontology, 1979-82; dir. Army Peridontics Residency program, Fort Gordon, Ga., 1982—; clin. prof. Med. Coll. Ga., Augusta, 1984—; cons. periodontics Surgeon Gen., Washington, 1984. Recipient Order of Mil. Med. Merit, U.S. Army Med. Dept., 1983; Profl. Designator award, 1984. Mem. ADA, Am. Acad. Periodontology, Ga. Soc. Peridontists, Am. Acad. Periodontology (advanced edn. and accreditation com., Chgo. 1983—), Omicron Kappa Upsilon. Club: Italian Am. Avocations: tennis; jogging; clarinet; classical music. Home: 8115 Sir Galahad Dr Evans GA 30809

FICHTER, JOHN L., business executive; b. Kobe, Japan, 1924. B.S., U. So. Calif., 1948, M.S. in Chem. Engring., 1949. With Anderson Clayton & Co., Houston, 1949—, process engr. paymaster div., v.p. agrl. and indsl. ops., mem. exec. com., 1964-74, exec. v.p., 1974—, also dir. Served with U.S. Navy, 1944-46. Office: Anderson Clayton & Co 1100 Louisiana St Houston TX 77002

FICKLING, WILLIAM ARTHUR, JR., health care company executive; b. Macon, Ga., July 23, 1932; s. William Arthur and Claudia (Foster) F.; m. Neva J. Langley, Dec. 30, 1954; children—William Arthur III, Jane Dru, Julia Claudia, Roy Hampton. B.S., Auburn U., 1954; LL.D. (hon.), Mercer U., 1983. Exec. v.p. Fickling & Walker Co., Macon, Ga., 1957-69; chmn., chief exec. Charter Med. Corp., Macon, 1969-85, pres., chmn., 1985—; dir. Ga. Power Co., C&S Ga. Corp., Atlanta, Live Oak, Perry & So. Ga. R.R.; gov. Am. Stock Exchange, N.Y.C. Trustee Wesleyan Coll., Macon, U. Ga. Found., Athens. Served to 1st lt. USAF, 1955-57. Recipient Gold award-Best Chief Exec. Wall St. Transcript, 1985; named Bus. Exec. of Yr., Ga. Security Dealers Assn., 1982; Disting. Alumnus award Auburn U. Sch. Bus., 1980. Mem. Am. Bus. Conf., Fedn. Am. Hosps. Methodist. Club: Macon Civic. Office: Charter Med Corp PO Box 209 577 Mulberry St Macon GA 31298

FIDDLER, THOMAS ROBERT, retail executive; b. N.Y.C., Mar. 24, 1921; s. Earl Thomas and Margaret (Martsolf) F.; m. Jane Carol Sundlof, Sept. 12, 1942; children—Martha J., Thomas N. (dec.), Kathryn A. A.B., Princeton U., 1942. With Marshall Field & Co., Chgo., 1945-51, buyer, 1950-54; with Rich's Inc., Atlanta, 1954-60, gen. mgr., Tenn., 1955-60; with Frederick Atkins, N.Y.C., 1960-67, pres., 1963-67; with D.H. Holmes Co. Ltd., New Orleans, 1967—, pres., 1972—; dir. Hibernia Nat. Bank, Delchamps, Inc.; tchr. mktg. U. Ga., evenings 1952-54; bd. dirs. Internat. Trade Mart, 1983—; mem. council advisers Tulane U. Grad. Sch. Bus. Bd. dirs., exec. com. New Orleans Econ. Devel. Council, 1974—; chmn. maj. gifts United Way, 1974-75; sr. v.p. Council for a Better La., 1983; bd. dirs. New Orleans Met. Area Com., 1970—, New Orleans Symphony, 1974, 79, New Orleans Tourist Commn., 1969—; pres. New Orleans Tourist Commn., 1977-78, chmn., 1979; trustee King Sch., Stamford, Conn., 1962-66, Low Heywood Sch., Stamford, 1964-67, Xavier U., 1979; bd. dirs., exec. mgmt. com., v.p. La. World Expn., 1980—. Served to lt. comdr. USNR, 1942-45. Mem. Nat. Retail Mchts. Assn. (dir. 1974—), Am. Retail Fedn. (dir. 1981—), New Orleans Retail Mchts. Council (pres. 1972-73), New Orleans C. of C. (dir., exec. com.), Internat. House (dir., exec. com.). Republican. Episcopalian. Clubs: Univ. (N.Y.C.); New Orleans Country, Boston, Plimsoll (New Orleans); Pass Christian Golf, Pass Christian Yacht (Miss.); Diamondhead. Home: 5418 Dayna Ct New Orleans LA 70124 Office: DH Holmes Co Ltd 819 Canal St New Orleans LA 70160

FIDEL, EDWARD ALLEN, clinical psychologist; b. Tyler, Tex., May 25, 1943. B.S.F.S., Georgetown U., 1966; Ph.D., Tex. Tech U., 1974. Lic. psychologist, La. Clin. instr. dept. neurology La. State U. Med. Ctr., New Orleans, 1973; staff clin. psychologist inpatient psychiatry VA Med. Ctr., New Orleans, 1974-79, coordinator clin. biofeedback program, 1979—; staff clin. psychologist VA Mental Hygiene Clinic, New Orleans, 1979—; asst. prof. U. New Orleans, 1979. Mem. Am. Psychol. Assn., Biofeedback Soc. Am., Southeastern Psychol. Assn. Author research publs. Office: Psychology Service VA Med Ctr 1601 Perdido St New Orleans LA 70146

FIELD, ELIZABETH ASHLOCK, former historic site administrator; b. Little Rock, Nov. 27, 1915; d. Jesse Vernon and Felecia Irene (Bruner) Ashlock; grad. Little Rock Jr. Coll., 1934; student Washington U., St. Louis, 1934-35, U. Ark., 1962-63; m. Henry Lamar Field, Sept. 8, 1938 (dec. Nov. 1960); 1 dau., Elizabeth Field Wassell. Dir. historic house mus. Angelo Marre House, 1965-71; dir. Ark. Commemorative Commn., Little Rock, 1972-74. Former spl. advisor Coral Gables House-Home of George Merrick, founder of Coral Gables; vol. Hist. Assn. So. Fla.; former chmn. St. Joan's chpt. St. Thomas Ch., former mem. women's bd.; bd. dirs. Coral Gables House. Mem. Nat. Trust for Historic Preservation, Fla. Trust for Historic Preservation, Decorative Arts Trust, Lowe Art Mus., Am. Clan Gregor Soc., Dade Heritage Trust (trustee 1975-76), Vizcayans, Hist. Assn. So. Fla. (sec. 1980-81), Quapaw Quarter Assn. (pres. 1972-74), Internat. Research Assn. (life), Phi Theta Kappa. Episcopalian. Home: 5520 Maggiore Coral Gables FL 33146

FIELD, JULIA ALLEN, environmental planner, writer; b. Boston, Jan. 5, 1937; d. Howard Locke and Julia (Wright) Allen; A.B. cum laude, Harvard U., 1960; postgrad. Pius XII Art Inst., Florence, Italy, 1961, Harvard Grad. Sch. Design, 1964-65, Walden U. Inst. Advanced Studies, 1983—. Founder, v.p. Black Grove Inc., Fla., 1970—; pres. AMAZONIA 2000, Colombia, S.Am., 1971—; prepared environ. poster exhbn. Writing on the Wall for internat. conf. Cities in Context, U. Notre Dame, 1968; mem. Symposium Tropical Biology, Leticia, Colombia, 1969; cons. to Forestry Dept., Simla, Himachal Pradesh, N. India, 1969; mem. Presdl. Adv. Group of Year 2000, Republic of Colombia, 1972-74, also Man and Biosphere Com., UNESCO, Colombia, 1974-78; del. from AMAZONIA 2000 to Nat. Seminar on Ecology and Urbanization, Bogotá, Colombia, 1973. Mem. City of Miami Bicentennial Commn., 1974; pres. Acad. Arts and Scis. of the Ams., Miami, 1979—; coordinator Community of Man Task Force Horizons '76 Project, Miami; dir. La Manigua Center for Amazon Research, Colombia, 1976—; coordinator AMAZONIA 2000 Task Force, Colombia, 1977-78; designer Amazon Pavilion, Feria Internacional, Bogotá, Colombia, 1978; Nat. U. Colombia del. to 2d Latin Am. Bot. Congress, Brasilia, 1978; planner 1st Internat. seminar Amazon Desting, 1983. Winner Rachel Carson Story award, 1967. Author: Essays on American Culture, 1961; (film) Man Against Nature, 1966. Editor: Game and Wild Life Preserves in the USSR, 1965; Amazonia 2000, 1978. Office: 3551 Main Hwy Coconut Grove FL 33133

FIELD, MARGARET ANN (PUNKIN), artist; b. Tulsa, Aug. 15, 1924; d. Earl Faye and Lena Wilhelmina (Pittenger) Ammons; m. Eric Edward Field, Oct. 27, 1945; children—Suzanne Field Lawson, Eric Edward II. Student U. Ark., 1942-44. Editor, Glen Laker mag., Dallas, 1954-72; mem. sales staff, furniture dept. Sanger Harris, Dallas, 1972; owner, operator Punkin Field Gift Shop, Dallas, 1973-77; custom artist designer, needlepoint, other mediums, Dallas, 1978—; designer, owner Polly Wogg Designs, 1978-85; owner Fabri Chic, 1982-85; owner, designer Comfy Critters, Dallas, 1986—. Bd. dirs., v.p. Kidney Found. Tex., 1965-82; co-chmn. ann. mother dau. style show Kidney Found. Tex., 1967-76; chmn. sales com. Byron Nelson Golf Classic, 1968-82; co-chmn. Tex. State Seniors Golf Tournament, 1967. Republican. Mem. Kappa Kappa Gamma. Presbyterian. Clubs: Royal Oaks Country (pres. golf assn. 1972), Glen Lakes Golf Assn. (v.p.). Home: 15928 Coolwood Ln Dallas TX 75248

FIELD, PAUL STEPHEN, advertising executive; b. Norwalk, Conn., Nov. 20, 1940; s. Reginald and Pauline (Stempler) F.; m. JoAnne Dee, Sept. 18, 1971; children—Anne Lorigan, David Robbins. B.A., Yale U., 1963. Asst. account exec. Young & Rubicam, N.Y.C., 1966-69; mktg. mgr. Computer Mktg. Corp., N.Y.C., 1969-70; sales promotion mgr. Avon Products, Inc., N.Y.C., 1970-72; account supr., mgr. Washington office Grey Advt. Inc., 1972-77; v.p., account supr. Kal, Merrick & Salan, Inc., Washington, 1977-81; exec. v.p. Myers & Assocs., Stuart, Fla., 1981-83; account supr. Smith, Burke & Azzam, Balt., 1983-84; v.p., account supr. Richardson, Myers & Donofrio, Inc., Balt., 1984—. Served with USMCR, 1963-66. Home: 2463 Springlake Dr Timonium MD 21093

FIELDS, DAIL LESLIE, telecommunications company executive; b. Milw., Apr. 14, 1946; s. Ernest C. and Evalyn M. (Schlitz) F.; m. Mary Kathleen Mitchell, Aug. 24, 1968; children—Jill, D. Thomas. B.A. with honors, Johns Hopkins U., 1968; postgrad. George Washington U., 1969-70. Cons. Dept. Def., Washington, 1968-71; mgr. Costley, Miller & Assocs., Washington and Atlanta, 1971-74; v.p. CMI Investment Corp., Madison, Wis., 1974-77; mgr. Touche Ross & Co., Washington, 1977-80; dir., v.p. MCI Telecommunications Co., Atlanta, 1980-85; treas. DMW, Inc.; owner, operator small print shops. Roman Catholic. Home: 545 Bridgewater Dr Atlanta GA 30328 Office: 6303 A Barfield Rd Atlanta GA 30328

FIELDS, DAVID JON, clergyman; b. Miami, Fla., Nov. 29, 1959; s. Samuel H. and Virginia (Swift) F.; m. Teresa Gayle Bayliss, June 27, 1981. B.S., Tenn. Temple U., 1980; M.R.E., So. Bapt. Theol. Sem., 1982. Ordained to ministry Southern Baptist Ch., 1982. Minister youth and music Fordsville Bapt. Ch., Ky., 1980-82; minister edn. and youth First Bapt. Ch., Covington, Ga., 1982-84, Southside Bapt. Ch., Dothan, Ga., 1984-85; minister edn. and youth Ft. Mitchell Bapt. Ch., Ft. Mitchell, Ky., 1985—. Mem. So. Bapt. Religious Edn. Assn., Religious Edn., Assn. Democrat. Avocations: music; running; computers. Home: 142 Grace Ct Apt 3 Fort Mitchell KY 41017 Office: Ft Mitchell Bapt Ch 2323 Dixie Hwy Fort Mitchell KY 41017

FIELDS, JACK MILTON, congressman; b. Houston, Feb. 3, 1952; s. Jack Milton and Jessie Faye F.; m. Roni Sue Haddock, Mar. 10, 1979. B.A., Baylor U., 1974, J.D., 1977. Bar: Tex. Practiced in Humble, Tex., 1977-79; v.p. Rosewood Meml. Park Cemetery, 1977-79; mem. 97th-99th congresses from 8th dist. Tex. Republican. Baptist. Lodge: Masons. Office: 4B Cannon House Office Bldg Washington DC 20515*

FIELDS, NANCY LOIS, counselor, lecturer, researcher, author; b. Baytown, Tex., Sept. 9, 1946; d. John Henry and Edna Lois (Phillips) Tompkins; m. James Albert Kitchens, Oct. 2, 1964 (div. 1974); children—Jimmy, Johnny; m. Roy Alan Fields, July 9, 1977; 1 child, Daniel Alan. B.S., U. Houston, 1982, M.A., 1983. Owner, dir. Gingerbreadhouse Day Care Ctr., Webster, Tex., 1973-76; pastoral counselor Christian Counseling Assocs., Houston, 1981-85; owner, dir., pastoral counselor Broadway Counseling Ctr., Houston, 1985—. Author: Pentecostal Charismatic Experiences, 1985. Mem. Am. Assn. for Counseling Devel., Am. Assn. Pastoral Counselors, Assn. Clin. Pastoral Edn., Assn. for Religious Value Issues in Counseling, Assn. for Specialists in Group Work, Am. Coll. Personnel Assn., Christian Counseling Assocs., Christian Counselors Tex. Democrat. Pentecostal. Avocations: interior decorating; carpentry; printing design; computers. Office: PO Box 263285 Houston TX 77207

FIELDS, ROBERT ASHLEY, television company sales manager; b. Houston, Oct. 11, 1947; s. Franklyn Thomas and Dorothy Elaine (Haines) F. B.S., Tex. Tech. U., 1970. Advt. sales exec. Houston Radio, KRBE, KAUM, 1970-72, Turner Broadcasting's Atlanta TV Sta., WTCG, 1972-79, NBC-TV, WLWT, Cin., 1979-80, NBC-TV Dallas, KXAS, 1980-83; sales mgr. KTBC-TV, CBS, Austin, Tex., 1983-84; S.E. regional mgr. TV ratings Arbitron div. Control Data Co., Atlanta, 1984-86; gen. sales mgr. Sta. WNFT-TV, Jacksonville, Fla., 1986—; sales and mktg. broadcast advt. comml. sales Atlanta Braves, Atlanta Hawks, Cin. Reds, Bengals, Tex. Rangers, Dallas Mavericks and Cowboys. Mem. Soc. Am. Baseball Research, Authors Guild, Atlanta Broadcast Execs. Club, Inter Fraternity Council, Sigma Chi. Baptist. Author: Take Me Out to the Crowd, 1977. Office: Sta WNFT-TV 2117 University Blvd S Jacksonville FL 32216

FIESE, JON S., building products company sales executive; b. Davenport, Iowa, m. 10, 1944; s. S.E. and Mary Aileen (Roege) F.; m. Charlotte Joan Neeves, June 6, 1965; children—Stephanie, Kimberly, Bryan, Douglas. Student Western Ill. U., 1962-64; B.S. in Indsl. Adminstrn., U. Ill., 1966, M.S., 1967. Indsl. engr. John Deere, Des Moines, 1967-70; salesman Standard Register Co., Des Moines, 1970-71; salesman Masonite Corp., Des Moines, 1971, mgr. sales tng., Chgo., 1971-73, regional mgr., Los Angeles, 1975-79, gen. sales mgr., 1979-80, dir. mktg. and sales, Ukiah, Calif., 1980-82; dir. sales Masonite Corp., Laurel, Miss., 1982-84; v.p. mktg., sales Elk Corp. Am., Dallas, 1984—. Vice pres. Ukiah Valley Youth Soccer, 1979-80, dir. coaches, 1979. Named Regional Mgr. of Yr., Masonite Corp., 1978. Mem. Am. Mgmt. Assn. Roman Catholic. Home: 6705 Leslie Ct Plano TX 75075 Office: 6750 Hillcrest Plaza Dr Dallas TX 75230

FIFE, JAMES HENRY, mathematics educator; b. Atlanta, July 14, 1949; s. James Alexander and Ernelle Ruth (Blair) F.; m. Elaine Elizabeth Schilf, Apr. 7, 1979. B.S., Tulane U., 1971; M.Phil., Yale U., 1979, Ph.D., 1982. Instr. U. New Haven, 1979-80; asst. prof. Oberlin Coll., Ohio, 1980-83; asst. prof. U. Richmond, Va., 1983—. Contbr. articles to publs. Recipient Prize Teaching fellowship, Yale U., 1975; summer research grantee U. Richmond, 1985. Mem. Am. Math. Soc., Math. Assn. Am., Phi Beta Kappa, Pi Mu Epsilon (faculty dir. U. Richmond 1985—). Democrat. Mem. United Ch. of Christ. Avocations: swimming; reading; trains. Home: 6909 Everview Rd Richmond VA 23226 Office: Dept Math and Computer Sci U Richmond Richmond VA 23173

FIGG, ROBERT MCCORMICK, JR., lawyer; b. Radford, Va., Oct. 22, 1901; s. Robert McCormick and Helen Josephine (Cecil) F.; grad. Porter Mil. Acad., Charleston, S.C.; A.B., Coll. Charleston, 1920, Litt.D., 1970; student law Columbia, 1920-22; LL.D., U. S.C., 1959; m. Sallie Alexander Tobias, May 10, 1927; children—Robert McCormick III, Emily (Mrs. Richard A. Dalla Mura), Jefferson Tobias. Admitted to S.C. bar, 1922; practiced in Charleston, 1922-61, mem. firm Rutledge, Hyde, Mann & Figg; circuit solicitor 9th Jud. Circuit S.C., 1935-47, spl. circuit judge, 1957, 75, 76; dean Law Sch., U. S.C., 1959-70; sr. counsel firm Robinson, McFadden, Moore, Pope Williams, Taylor & Brailsford, Columbia, 1970—. Mem. S.C. Ho. of Reps., 1933-35; mem. S.C. Reorgn. Commn., 1948—, chmn., 1951-55, 71-75; gen. counsel S.C. State Ports Authority, 1942-72. Pres., Coll. Charleston Found., 1970-74, hon. life chmn., 1975—. Recipient Durant Disting. Service award S.C. Bar Found., 1982; Founders medal Coll. of Charleston, 1986. Fellow Am. Coll. Trial Lawyers; mem. ABA (ho. dels. 1970-72, mem. fair trial-free press com. 1965-69, mem. spl. com. study legal edn. 1974-77), Inter-Am., Charleston County (pres. 1953) bar assns., Am. Law Inst., Am. Judicature Soc., Inst. Jud. Adminstrn., World Assn. Lawyers, S.C. State Bar (pres. 1970-71, ho. of dels. 1975—), Blue Key, Phi Beta Kappa, Phi Delta Phi. Lodge: Masons 33 deg., grand master S.C. 1972-74. Co-author: Civil Trial Manual, 1974. Home: 1522 Deans Ln Columbia SC 29205

FIGHTMASTER, MICHAEL, safety engineer; b. Oklahoma City, Mar. 9, 1948; s. Clarence Wallace and Lois Maxine (Wiggins) F.; m. Donna Sue Stotts, Mar. 21, 1969 (div. 1980); 1 child, Eric. B.S., Central State U., 1973, M.S., 1975; A.D. in Environ. Safety, Okla. State U., 1980. Safety engr. USF&G Ins. Co., Oklahoma City, 1976-78, Western Ins. Co., Fort Scott, Kans., 1978—. Bd. mem.-at-large Edmond Art Assn., 1985; mem. Wilderness Soc., Sierra Club. Served with U.S. Army, 1969-70, Vietnam. Mem. Am. Soc. Safety Engrs. (edn. and scholarship chmn. 1984-85). Republican. Unitarian. Club: Metro Camera (Oklahoma City). Avocations: Nature photography; woodworking. Home: 901-939 Brook Forest Edmond OK 73034 Office: Western Ins PO Box 12993 3716 NW 36th St Oklahoma City OK 73157

FIGUEROA-TORRES, JUAN, psychologist; b. Santurce, P.R., Apr. 14, 1938; s. Juan and Carmen L. Figueroa-Torres; widower 1970; children—Carmen, Juan. B.A., U. P.R., 1960, M.A. in Pub. Adminstrn., U. Minn., 1961;

TQ

STAPLE HERE

NO POSTAGE
NECESSARY
IF MAILED
IN THE
UNITED STATES

BUSINESS REPLY MAIL

First Class Permit No. 4577 Chicago, Illinois

POSTAGE WILL BE PAID BY ADDRESSEE

MARQUIS Who's Who
200 East Ohio Street
Chicago, Illinois 60611

Ph.D., Syracuse U., 1978. Dir. managerial tng. program P.R. Electric Power Authority, Santurce, 1962-74; dir. continuing edn. Inst. Hispanic Family, Hartford, Conn., 1978-79; cons. psychologist Carolina Mental Health Ctr. Dept. Health and Mental Health, Carolina, P.R., 1979—; prof. clin. and counseling psychology P.R. InterAm. U., Rio Piedras, 1979-82. Mem. Am. Psychol. Assn., Am. Personnel and Guidance Assn., Assn. P.R. Psychologists. Roman Catholic. Contbr. articles to profl. jours., poetry, essays and short stories to literary jours. Home: 462 10th St Santurce PR 00915 Office: Carolina Mental Health Ctr Carolina PR 00630

FIKE, MARGARET SUE, educator; b. Charleston, S.C., Nov. 14, 1946; d. Frank Edward and Lillian Sue (Patterson) F.; A.B. in Religion and Elem. Edn., Coker Coll., Hartsville, S.C., 1968; postgrad. U. No. Colo., U. N.Mex.; M.Spl. Edn., The Citadel, 1983. Elem. sch. tchr. Bur. Indian Affairs, Dzilth-na-o-dith-hle Sch., Navajo Reservation, N.Mex., 1969-77; tchr. Cherokee (N.C.) Elem. Sch., 1977-81, Trident Acad., Mt. Pleasant, S.C., 1981-82, James B. Edwards Sch., Mt. Pleasant, 1982-85, Buist Acad., 1985—; mem. math. guidelines team NSF; math. resource tchr. Eastern Navajo Agy. Sunday sch. tchr. Navajo Mission, 1970-73, Bethel Meth. Ch., Charleston, S.C.; leader Boy Scouts Am., 1970-73, Girl Scouts U.S.A., 1974; coordinator Children Inc., 1970-77, career edn. com., 1977-78; v.p. Clyburn Guild, 1982—; v.p. United Meth. Women; mem. schedule com., chmn. gifted and talented com., readiness com. PTA. Cert. tchr., N.C., S.C., N.Mex. Mem. Iota (pres. 1978). Democrat. Methodist. Home: 1154 Culpepper Circle Charleston SC 29407 Office: Buist Academy Charleston SC

FILAK, DAVID FRANCIS, psychology educator; b. Joliet, Ill., Feb. 26, 1952; s. Frank and Elizabeth K. (Sabina) F.; m. Janet E. Palmer. B.A. in Psychology with honors, Lewis U., 1973; M.A. in Psychology, Roosevelt U., 1975; Ph.D. in Psychology, Ill. Inst. Tech., 1985. Adj. instr. psychology Lewis U., Lockport, Ill., 1976-77, Joliet Jr. Coll., 1977-78, Ill. Benedictine Coll., Lisle, 1979-80; asst. prof. Coll. St. Francis, Joliet, 1977-82; psychology instr. El Paso Community Coll., Tex., 1982—; dir. psychology lab. Coll. St. Francis, Joliet, 1979-82; program coordinator psychology, 1980-82. Roosevelt U. scholar, 1974-75. Mem. Am. Psychol. Assn. (assoc.), El Paso Psychol. Assn. (chmn. research com. 1984-85). Republican. Roman Catholic. Club: El Paso Community Coll. Ski Assn. (pres. 1984—). Avocations: snow skiing; scuba diving; jogging; weight lifting. Home: 4800 N Stanton 172 El Paso TX 79902 Office: El Paso Community Coll Box 20000 El Paso TX 79998

FILIPS, NICHOLAS JOSEPH, management consultant, medical equipment supplier; b. Garrett, Ind., June 10, 1925; s. John and Elizabeth (Grigore) F.; student U. Detroit, 1942-45, Ind. U., 1945-47; B.S. in Biology, Am. U., 1948; postgrad. Ind. U., 1979; m. Lucille N. Baker, July 5, 1947; children—Steven, Mary Beth, Fred John. Vice pres., mgr. Wayne Pharmacal Supply Co., Ft. Wayne, Ind., 1949-67, pres., chmn. div. Bendway, Inc., South Bend, Ind., 1955-67; v.p., gen. mgr. Karel First-Aid Supply Co., Chgo., 1967-71; pres., gen. mgr. Amedic Surg. Supply Co., Miami, 1971-78; pres., chief exec. officer Med. Supply Co., Inc., Jacksonville, Fla., 1978-81, Exec. Mgmt. Cons. Assocs., Coral Gables, Fla., Peoria, Ill., 1981—; pres., gen. mgr. KNF Med. Enterprises, Inc. Recipient Am. Legion Leadership award, 1939. Mem. Am. Surg. Trade Assn. (recipient Distinctive Service award 1960), Fla. Sheriffs Assn. Democrat. Roman Catholic. Club: Lions. Benefactor hosps. and clinics, S.Am.; contbr. articles in field to profl. jours.

FILLER, WILLIAM HOWARD, dentist, educator; b. Miami, Fla., Feb. 15, 1935; s. Charles Lee and Mildred Leona (Stratton) F.; m. Edelize Willhite, Aug. 14, 1962; 1 child, James Stratton. A.A., U. Fla., 1956; D.D.S., Emory U., 1960, cert. in prosthetics, 1971. Gen. practice dentistry, Winter Garden, Fla., 1963-67; assoc. prof. dentistry Emory U., Decatur, Ga., 1967-73; prof. Baylor Coll. Dentistry, Dallas, 1973—, course dir. for removable prosthodontics, 1973—. Served to capt. U.S. Army, 1960-63. Recipient Tchr. of Yr. award Baylor Coll. Dentistry, 1985. Mem. Dallas County Dental Soc., Tex. Dental Assn., ADA, Southwest Soc. Prosthodontists, Am. Assn. Dental Schs., Internat. Assn. Dental Research. Republican. Baptist. Avocations: oil painting; fishing; gardening; arts and crafts. Home: 1108 S Delaware Irving TX 75060 Office: Baylor Coll Dentistry 3302 Gaston Ave Dallas TX 75246

FILSTRUP, SCOTT HOGENSON, marketing, planning and venture capital executive; b. Evanston, Ill., Apr. 4, 1942; s. Alvin William, Jr., and Elaine H. (Hogenson) F.; B.S.C.E., Northwestern U., 1965, M.B.A., 1967; m. Margaret McGinnis, Dec. 21, 1967; children—Laura Leigh, Scott Douglas. Comml. devel. supr. Monsanto Co., St. Louis, 1973-74; dir. industry planning Agrico Chem. Co., The Williams Co., Tulsa, 1974-76, mgr. planning Edgcomb Metals Co. div., 1977-78, mgr. bus. and market devel., 1978-80, exec. adminstr. The Williams Cos., 1980-81; mgr. strategic planning MAPCO, Inc., Tulsa, 1981-82; pres., chief exec. officer EPM Industries, Inc., Tulsa, 1982-84; v.p., gen. mgr. Polyvoltac, Inc., 1984-86; pres. Consultants Ltd., Tulsa, 1986—; nat. speaker mkgt., planning, chem. and metals industries. Mem. adv. council mktg. Tulsa U.; bd. dirs. Jr. Achievement of Tulsa, 1979-82, exec., adv. and nat. awards; adv. bd. Tulsa Econ. Devel. Commn., 1978-82; bd. dirs., treas. Community Services of Tulsa, Met. Tulsa Transit Authority; trustee Kirk of the Hills Presbyterian Ch. Recipient Alumni award Northwestern U., 1980. Mem. Am. Mktg. Assn. (pres. Tulsa chpt. 1979-80, nat. v.p. indsl. mktg. 81-83), Auto Parts and Accessories Assn. (bd. dirs., chmn. mktg. com.), Tulsa Econs. Club (pres. 1977-79). Republican. Clubs: Rotary, Univ., Northwestern U. Alumni of Okla. (pres. 1976-84). Contbr. articles to Am. Mktg. Jour., Econs., Tulsa, others. Home: 7412 E 67th Pl Tulsa OK 74133 Office: Tulsa OK

FINCH, HUGH EDSEL, real estate agency executive; b. Spartanburg, S.C., June 21, 1928; s. Robert Lewis and Rosalee (Wyatt) F.; A.B., Wofford Coll., 1952; m. Geraldine Green; children—Deborah Elaine, Susan Denise. m. Sharon K. Smith, 1971; children—Michael Alan, Hugh Edsel, Alice Michelle. Newspaper reporter Spartanburg (S.C.) Herald Jour., 1952-55; tchr. Pacolet (S.C.) High Sch., 1955-56; operator, owner Hugh E. Finch Agy., Spartanburg, 1958. Mem. S.C. Ho. of Reps., 1956-66, 69-72. County chmn. March of Dimes, 1968. Democrat. Methodist. Clubs: Masons, Shriners, Lions, Ruritan (past pres.). Home: 100 Vanderbilt Ln The Bluffs Apt E-1 Spartanburg SC 29301 Office: 1265 Asheville Hwy Spartanburg SC 29303

FINCH, RICHARD INGE, dentist; b. Mobile, Ala., Sept. 6, 1934; s. Gregory Bernard and Anna Kanarens (Luenberg) F.; m. Shirley Jean Jordan, Jan. 2, 1965; 1 child, Caroline Camille. B.S., Springhill Coll., Mobile, 1956; D.M.D., U. Ala., 1960. Gen. practice dentistry, Mobile, 1962—. Served to capt. U.S. Army, 1960-62. Mem. ADA Ala. Dental Assn., Am. Equilibration Soc., Am. Acad. Craniomandibular Disorders, Pierre Fauchard Acad., 1st Dist. Dental Soc. (sec.-treas. 1970-71, v.p. 1971-72, pres.-elect 1972-73, pres. 1973-74). Roman Catholic. Avocations: hunting; fishing. Home: 4352 Stein St Mobile AL 36609 Office: 515 Azalea Rd Mobile AL 36609

FINCH, SAMUEL THOMAS, fin. cons. co. exec.; b. Port Huron, Mich., Sept. 24, 1945; s. Clarence John and Florence Mary (Finch) Schatzline; B.B.A., Eastern Mich. U., 1968; A.A., St. Clair County Community Coll., 1966; postgrad. Wayne State U., 1970-71. Asst. to officer in charge Nat. Bank of Detroit, 1968-74; asst. cashier S.C. Nat. Bank, Columbia, 1974-78; asst. v.p. Bank of New Orleans & Trust Co., 1978-80; owner, cons. Fin. Mgmt. Services Group, Houston, 1981—; pres. Productivity Mgmt. Techs.; dir. FUTURE Bank Consortium, 1978—, pres., 1979-81. Bd. dirs. Deerfield Inst., 1976—. Registered profl. engr., Tex. Mem. Am. Inst. Indsl. Engrs., MTM Assn. Standards and Research, Assn. Systems Mgmt., N. Am. Modapts Assn., U.S. Ski Assn. Democrat. Episcopalian. Clubs: Mason. Author: Optimum Staffing in the Clerical Environment, 1976; Staffing Your Office Personnel with Microprocessors, 1978; Motivational Management for the 80's, 1982. Office: Financial Management Services PO Box 772353 Houston TX 77015

FINDLEY, CHARLES H., manufacturing company executive; b. Saegertown, Pa., Jan. 14, 1924; s. Homer L. and Marian L. (Luce) F.; A.B., Baldwin-Wallace Coll., 1947; LL.B., Cleveland-Marshall Law Sch., 1952; m. Helen Fyler, June 17, 1949; children—Robin, Susan, Alison. With Gen. Electric Co., N.Y., 1951-57, Ill. and Tenn., 1957-61, supt., employee relations mgr., 1961-63, plant mgr., 1964-69; gen. mgr. Clyde and St. Paul divs. Whirlpool Corp., 1971-78; pres., chief exec. officer Heil-Quaker Corp., Nashville, 1978—; dir. Clyde Savs. Bank, Northwestern Bank. Bd. dirs. Fremont Hosp., 1971-76, Better Bus. Bur., Mpls./St. Paul, 1976-78; mem. Sch. Bd. Murfreesboro (Tenn.), 1968-71, Water Bd., 1967-71. Served with USNR, 1943-46. Mem. C. of C., Gas Appliance Mfrs. Assn. (bd. dirs.), Air Conditioning and Refrigeration Inst. (bd. dirs.). Republican. Methodist. Clubs: Kiwanis, Rotary. Home: 1136 Heil-Quaker Blvd LaVergne TN 37086 Office: 635 Thompson Ln Nashville TN 37204

FINDLEY, EUGENE MILTON, educator; b. Shelby County, Ala., Apr. 15, 1918; s. William Joseph and Viola (Phillips) F.; Ed.D., David Lipscomb Coll., 1940; B.S., Abilene Christian U., 1950; M.Ed., Trinity U., 1953; Ed.D., Baylor U., 1973; m. Emma Sue Guthrie, May 21, 1943; children—Jean Madelon Findley Harrison, Jerry Wayne, LaJuana Sue Findley Peeples. Sci. tchr. Devine (Tex.) High Sch., 1950-51; prin. Natalia (Tex.) Elem. Sch., 1951-53, Briggs-Coleman Elem. Sch., Rio Hondo, Tex., 1953-54, Los Fresnos (Tex.) High Sch., 1954-59, Colorado (Tex.) Jr. High Sch., 1959-60, Colorado (Tex.) High Sch., 1960-63, Mountain View Sch. for Boys, Gatesville, Tex., 1963-68; faculty Abilene Christian U., Tex., 1968—, prof., chmn. dept. edn., 1977—. Served with USAAF, 1941-45. Mem. Tex. Assn. Tchr. Educators, Tex. Assn. Colls. Tchr. Edn., Tex. Soc. Coll. Tchrs. Edn., Tex. Assn. Profs. Sch. Adminstrn., Phi Delta Kappa. Republican. Mem. Ch. of Christ. Club: Kiwanis. Home: 2425 Campus Ct Abilene TX 79601 Office: Abilene Christian Univ Education Dept Box 7962 Abilene TX 79699

FINDLEY, JOHN ALLEN, JR., newspaper executive; b. Fulton, Mo., Feb. 25, 1951; s. John Allen and Naomi Joan (Reker) F.; m. Sharon Lynn Starr, Nov. 27, 1976. student U. Calif.-Berkeley, 1972, U. Mo., 1973; A.B., Westminster Coll., 1973. Sales rep. Kingdom Daily News, Fulton, 1973-74; advt. dir. Colo. Daily, Boulder, 1974-76; cons. advt. Boulder, 1976-77; advt. sales mgr. Dallas Times Herald, 1977-80, dir. consumer mktg., 1981-83, dir. circulation, 1983, dir. retail advt., 1983—. Mem. Dallas Advt. League, Internat. Newspaper Circulation Mktg. Execs., Internat. Newspaper Advt. and Mktg. Execs., Internat. Newspaper Promotion Assn., Collie Club of Am., Sigma Chi.

FINDLEY, JOHN SIDNEY, dentist; b. Bryan, Tex., Oct. 3, 1942; s. Sidney Albert and Leila Mae (Reading) F.; m. Patricia Ann Reep, June 10, 1967 (div. 1977); children—John Brett, Sidney Alan; m. 2nd Judith Ann Smith, May 22, 1981. Student U.S. Air Force Acad., 1961-62, N. Tex. State U., 1963-65; D.D.S., Baylor U. Coll. Dentistry, 1970. Practice dentistry, Plano, Tex., 1970—; mem. staff Meml. Hosp. of Garland, Tex., 1971—, Plano Gen. Hosp., 1978—. Contbr. articles to profl. jours. Bd. dirs. Plano YMCA, United Way of Plano, Park Bd. City of Plano, Charter Rev. Commn. City of Plano; chmn. advancement com. North Trail Dist. Boy Scouts Am.; campaign chmn. Plano YMCA Fund Dr., 1978. Recipient Cert. of Recognition Am. Acad. Dental Radiology, 1970; Paul Harris fellow Rotary Internat., 1979. Mem. Am. Dental Assn., Tex. Dental Assn., Dallas County Dental Soc., Acad. Gen. Dentistry. Methodist. Lodge: Rotary (Plano) (bd. dirs., pres. 1977-78). Home: Rt 3 Box 498 Aubrey TX 76227 Office: John S Findley DDS Inc 1410 14th St Plano TX 75074

FINDLEY, WILLIAM EARLE, former mayor; b. Pickens County, S.C., Aug. 20, 1911; s. William Elbert and Essie (Earle) F.; ed. high sch.; m. Mary Louise Penland, Oct. 6, 1940; children—William Earle, Mary Ann. Mem. Pickens City Council, 1953-55, mayor, 1955-77; dir. Pickens Savs. & Loan Assn., Bankers Trust Co., Pickens, Laurel Hill Nursing Center. Vice chmn. Pickens County Planning and Devel. Commn., 1956—. Mem. Pickens County Mcpl. Assn. (pres. 1957, 64, 69). Methodist. Clubs: Masons, Shriners. Named Citizen of Year, Pickens, 1960. Home: 206 Hampton Ave Pickens SC 29671 Office: Town Hall Pickens SC 29671

FINE, DAVID JEFFREY, hospital executive, consultant, lecturer; b. Flushing, N.Y., Oct. 10, 1950; s. Arnold and Phyllis Fine. B.A., Tufts U., 1972; M.H.A., U. Minn., 1974. Asst. to dir. U. Calif. Hosp., San Francisco, 1974-76, asst. dir., 1976-78; sr. assoc. dir. U. Nebr. Hosp. and Clinic, Omaha, 1978-83; adminstr. W.Va. Univ. Hosp., Morgantown, 1983-84; pres. W.Va. Univ. Hosps., Inc., Morgantown, 1984—; cons. Merck, Sharp & Dohme, West Point, Pa., 1983—, Eli Lilly & Co., Indpls., 1984; bd. dirs. Univ. Hosp. Consortium, Atlanta, 1983—. Editorial bd. Hospital Formulary, 1982—; co-author jour. articles, book chpts., films. Bd. trustees Monongalia Arts Council, 1984—. Recipient James A. Hamilton prize, U. Minn., 1974. Fellow Am. Coll. Hosp. Adminstrs. (Robert S. Hudgens Young Adminstr. of Yr. award 1985); mem. Morgantown C. of C. Jewish. Club: Fgn. Affairs (Omaha). Lodge: Rotary. Office: West Va Hosps Inc Medical Center Dr Morgantown WV 26506

FINE, KENNETH, psychotherapist, biofeedback therapist, musician; b. Phila., May 9, 1949; s. Bernard Fine and Harriet (Brier) Glick. B.A. in Exptl. Psychology, Fla. Atlantic U., 1979; M.A. in Psychology, Antioch U., 1980; Ph.D. in Clin. Psychology, U. Humanistic Studies, Las Vegas, 1982. Lic. marriage and family counselor, Nev., mental health counselor, Fla. Studio musician, Sigma Sound Studio, Phila., 1973-78; psychotherapist Do It Now Found., Los Angeles, 1979-80, Stress Mgmt. Ctr., Las Vegas, 1981-83; mental health counselor Counseling Affiliates, Fort Lauderdale, 1981—; psychotherapist North Miami Community Mental Health Ctr., 1985—; lectr. in field; writer, producer, host radio talk show, Las Vegas, 1981-83. Writer/producer: (ednl. film) A Record is Born, 1979. Contbr. articles to profl. jours. Mem. Am. Psychol. Assn. (assoc.), Am. Mental Health Counselors Assn., Am. Assn. for Counseling and Devel., Biofeedback Soc. Am., Fla. Mental Health Counselors Assn. Office: Modern Health Care Services Inc 2845 Aventura Blvd North Miami Beach FL 33180

FINERTY, JOHN CHARLES, retired university administrator, anatomist; b. Chgo., Oct. 20, 1914; s. John Lawrence and Hulda (Schulte) F.; m. Mildred King, Dec. 28, 1940; children—Olivia Lou Finerty Moore, Donna Elizabeth Finerty Gatewood. A.B., Kalamazoo Coll., 1937; M.S., Kans. State U., 1939; Ph.D., U. Wis., 1942. Instr. anatomy U. Mich., 1943-46; asst. prof. Washington U. St. Louis, 1946-49; from assoc. prof. to prof. U. Tex. Med. Br., Galveston, 1949-56; prof., head dept. anatomy, assoc. dean U. Miami, 1956-66; dean Sch. Medicine, La. State U., New Orleans, 1966-71, vice chancellor, dean grad. studies, 1971-84. Rackham Found. fellow, 1942-43. Mem. Am. Assn. Anatomists (pres. 1975-76), Am. Physiol. Soc., Radiation Research Soc., Soc. Exptl. Biology and Medicine, Tex. Acad. Sci. (pres. 1955-56). Clubs: Nicolet Country (Laona, Wis.); Inwood Forest Golf (Houston). Author: (with Cowdry) Textbook of Histology, 1960; contbr. articles to sci. jours. Home: 1110 Bethlehem St Houston TX 77018

FINGER, JERRY ELLIOTT, banker; b. Houston, Oct. 11, 1932; s. Hyman Elliott and Bessie Kaplan F.; B.S. in Econs., Wharton Sch., U. Pa., 1954; m. Nanette Breitenbach, June 20, 1954; children—Richard Breitenbach, Jonathan Samuel and Walter Goodman. Asst. controller Finger Furniture Co., Houston, 1956-59; partner Finger Interests, Houston, 1959—; pres. Republic Nat. Bank, Houston, 1963-75, chief exec. officer, dir., chmn., 1975—; chmn. Beaumont Savs. & Loan Assn. (Tex.), 1968-76, adv. chmn., 1976-79; chmn. exec. com. Reagan Commerce Bank, Houston, 1968-77; pres. Charter Ins. Co., Houston, 1971-84, chmn.,1984—; chmn. bd. trustees SW Mortgage & Realty Investors, Houston, 1972-82; chmn. exec. com. Gulf Republic Fin. Corp., Houston, 1972-81; chmn., dir. Colonial Nat. Bank (now Charter Nat. Bank-Colonial), Houston, 1975—, Charter Nat. Bank-Houston, 1981—, Charter Nat. Bank-Willowbrook, 1981-85, chmn. exec. com., 1985—; dir. Charter Nat. Bank-Westheimer; adv. chmn. exec. com., The Standard Bank, Houston, 1981—, adv. dir., 1979-80; dir. Gulf Resources & Chem. Corp., Houston, 1977-81. Trustee, Meml. Hosp. Systems, 1971—; bd. dirs. Houston Clearing Assn., 1977-82, Coastal Ind. Water Authority, 1968-72, Contemporary Arts Mus., 1980—. Served to lt. (j.g.) USN, 1954-56. Mem. Am. Bankers Assn., Robert Morris Soc., Tex. Bankers Assn. (legis. com. 1980-82). Republican. Jewish. Clubs: Houston Racquet, Univ., Houston Yacht, Houstonian, Houston City. Office: 2600 Citadel Plaza Dr Suite 600 Houston TX 77008 also 5200 N Shepherd St Houston TX 77091

FINK, CHARLES AUGUSTIN, behavioral systems scientist; b. McAllen, Tex., Jan. 1, 1929; s. Charles Adolph and Mary Nellie (Bonneau) F.; A.A., Pan-Am. U., 1948; B.S., Marquette U., 1950; postgrad. No. Va. Community Coll., 1973, George Mason U., 1974; M.A., Cath. U. Am., 1979; m. Ann Heslen, June 1, 1955 (dec. June 1981); children—Patricia A., Marianne E., Richard G., Gerard A. Journalist, UP and Ft. Worth Star-Telegram, 1950-52; commd. 2d lt. U.S. Army, 1952, advanced through grades to lt. col., 1966, various positions telecommunications, 1952-56, teaching, 1956-58, exec. project mgmt., 1958-62, def. analysis and research, 1962-65, fgn. mil. relations, 1965-67, def. telecommunications exec., 1967-69, chief planning, budget and program control office Def. Satellite Communications Program, Def. Communications Agy., 1969-72; ret., 1972; pvt. practice cons. managerial behavior, Falls Church, Va., 1972-77; pres. Behavioral Systems Sci. Orgn., and predecessor, Falls Church, 1978—; leader family group dynamics, 1958-67. Adv. bd. Holy Redeemer Roman Cath. Ch., Bangkok, Thailand, St. Philip's Ch., Falls Church, 1971-73. Decorated Army Commendation medals, Joint Services Commendation medal; recipient Behavior Modeling award 1980 Internat. Congress on Applied Systems Research and Cybernetics; named to Fink Hall of Fame, 1982. Mem. Soc. Gen. Systems Research, Am. Soc. Cybernetics, Internat. Assn. Cybernetics, Cybernetics Acad. Odobjeja. Am. Assn., Counseling and Devel., Assn. Counselor Edn. and Supervision, Internat. Network for Social Network Analysis, Armed Forces Communications and Electronics Assn., Assn. U.S. Army, Ret. Officers Assn. Club: KC; Finks Internat. (v.p. 1981—). Developed hierarchial theory of human behavior, uses in behavioral, social and biol. sci. and their applications, behavioral causal modeling research methodology, systems nesting organizational theory, computer aided behavior system coaching. Pioneer in home kidney dialysis treatment and research. Home: 3305 Brandy Ct Falls Church VA 22042 Office: PO Box 2051 Falls Church VA 22042

FINK, CHESTER WALTER, pediatric educator, pediatric rheumatologist; b. N.Y.C., May 6, 1928; s. Murray and Estelle (Halbfinger) F.; m. Dorothy Wiletts Crate, Dec. 3, 1955; children—Ellen L., Curtis M., Murray G. B.A., Duke U., 1947, M.D., 1951. Intern, King's County Hosp., N.Y.C., 1952; resident in pediatrics Upstate Med. Ctr., Syracuse, N.Y., 1953, Univ. Hosp. Cleve., 1954, 57; from instr. to prof. pediatrics U. Tex. Southwestern Med. Sch., Dallas, 1957—; dir. pediatric rheumatology Tex. Scottish Rite Hosp. Crippled Children, 1959—. Served to capt. U.S. Army, 1954-56. Mem. Am. Pediatric Soc., Soc. Pediatric Research, Am. Rheumatism Assn., Sigma Xi. Contbr. articles to profl. jours. Home: 4432 Hockaday Dr Dallas TX 75229 Office: U Tex 5323 Harry Hines Blvd Dallas TX 75235

FINK, JANE LOUISE, bookstore manager; b. East Liverpool, Ohio, Nov. 17, 1929; d. Charles Cyril and Nelle Alice (Aken) Taylor; m. John Burr Fink, June 30, 1949; children—John, Rebecca, Daniel. Student Bethany Coll., 1947-49, Meredith Coll., 1978-79. Swimming tchr. YWCA, East Liverpool, 1945-49; clk. Elizabeth Knipes Children's Store, Raleigh, N.C., 1959-60; supr. Roses Dept. Store, Raleigh, 1971-72, Thalhimers Store, Raleigh, 1972-80; mgr. Will's Book Store, Raleigh, 1981—. Leader Illinois council Girl Scouts U.S.A., 1960-62, Occoneechee council Boy Scouts Am., 1957-59; tchr. Sunday Sch., Good Shepherd Ch., 1958-62; pres. Air Force Officer's Wives Club, Tucson, 1964-65. Mem. Am. Bus. Women's Assn. (Woman of Yr. award 1984, v.p. 1983, pres. 1984, program chmn. Wake County ABWA Exchange Com. 1984—). Democrat. Episcopalian. Clubs: Cary Gourmet, Friday Night Dance, Esquire Dance. Avocations: golfing; ballroom dancing; reading; cooking. Home: 1013 Manchester Dr Cary NC 27511 Office: Will's Book Store North Hills Mall Raleigh NC 27609

FINK, LESTER HAROLD, electric systems engineering company executive, educator; b. Phila., May 3, 1925; s. Harold D. and Edna B. (Hopkins) F.; m. R. Naomi Veit, Dec. 10, 1955; children—Lois Hope, Carol Anne. B.S.E.E., U. Pa., 1950, M.S.E.E., 1961. Supr. engr. research div. Phila. Electric Co., 1950-74; asst. dir. Electric Energy Systems div. Dept. Interior, Washington, 1974-75, ERDA, 1975-77, Dept. Energy, 1977-79; pres. Systems Engring. for Power, Inc., Vienna, Va., 1979-83; chmn. Carlsen & Fink Assocs., Inc., 1983—; adj. prof. Drexel U., 1961-74, U. Md., 1979-80. Served with U.S. Army, 1943-46. Recipient Meritorious Service award U.S. Dept. Energy, 1979. Fellow IEEE, Instrument Soc. Am.; mem. Conf. Internationale de Grande Reseaux Electrique, AAAS, Sigma Tau, Eta Kappa Nu, Tau Beta Pi. Presbyterian. Patentee underground power transmission and automatic generation control; contbg. author: Large Scale Systems, 1982; Power System Analysis and Planning, 1983; contbr. chpt. to electronics engring. handbook, 1982. Home: 11304 Full Cry Ct Oakton VA 22124

FINK, MICHAEL ARMAND, music educator, composer, writer; b. Long Beach, Calif., Mar. 15, 1939; s. Lee and Lillian Florence (Gardner) F.; m. Jo Ann Brister; children—Ian Michael, Leigh Michelle. B. Mus., U. So. Calif., 1960; M. Mus. New England Conservatory, 1962; postgrad. Columbia U., 1962-63; Ph.D. in Music, U. So. Calif., 1977. Lectr. Calif. State U., Fullerton, 1970; mem. profl. staff S.W. Regional Lab. for Edn. Research, Los Alamitos, Calif., 1971-75; assoc. prof. of music U. Tex., San Antonio, 1975—. Composer of 26 published musical works, 1964—. Contbr. articles to music jours. and computer mags. Mem. Coll. Mus. Soc. (adv. council 1980-83, student affairs chmn. 1982-84), Music Industry Educators Assn. (treas. 1983—). Avocations: computer programming, golf. Home: 4826 Bucknell St San Antonio TX 78249 Office: Div of Mus U of Tex at San Antonio San Antonio TX 78285

FINKEL, GERALD MICHAEL, lawyer; b. N.Y.C., July 29, 1941; s. Abraham B. and Elizabeth B. (Michaels) F.; m. Beverly Lynne Jaffee, Aug. 26, 1962; children—Bruce Daniel, Judith Michelle. B.A., NYU, 1962; J.D., U. S.C., 1970. Bar: S.C. 1970, U.S. Dist. Ct. S.C. 1970, U.S. Ct. Appeals (4th cir.) 1973, U.S. Supreme Ct. 1973, D.C. 1973. Prin., Finkel, Georgaklis, Goldberg, Sheftman and Korn, P.A., Columbia, S.C., 1970—; adj. prof. trial advocacy U. S.C.; faculty mem. fed. trial practice Am. Law Inst., ABA; lectr. S.C. Bar, S.C. Trial Lawyers Assn., Richland County Bar and Profl. Insts. Spl. judge Richland County Family Ct., 1974-78, Ct. Gen. Sessions 5th jud. cir., 1976; hearing officer S.C. Dept. Health and Environ. Control, 1979-84; mem. S.C. Appellate Def. Commn., 1982-83, Gov.'s Sentencing Guidelines Commn., 1982-83. Served to capt. U.S. Army, 1962-67. Recipient Internat. Outstanding Alumni cert. Phi Alpha Delta, 1972. Mem. ABA, Richland County Bar Assn., Am. Judicature Soc., Assn. Trial Lawyers Am., Am. Law Inst., S.C. Trial Lawyers Assn. (pres. 1982-83), S.C. Bar (chmn. ins., negligence and worker's compensation sect. 1979-80, bd. govs. 1985—), Phi Alpha Delta (justice dist. XIX 1974-76). Democrat. Jewish. Author: (with Ralph C. McCullough, II) A Guide to South Carolina Torts, 1981. Office: Finkel Georgaklis et al PO Box 1799 Columbia SC 29202

FINKEL, KAREN EVANS, school transportation association executive, lawyer; b. New Orleans, Dec. 30, 1952; d. Wilbur Bowen and Geneva Wilma (Lauterbach) Evans; m. William Samuel Finkel, Apr. 28, 1979. B.A., U. Cin., 1975; J.D., U. Dayton, 1978. Bar: Conn. 1978, Va. 1979. Assoc., Billings & Billings, Wallingford, Conn., 1978-79; spl. asst. Congressman Tom Luken, Washington, 1979-80; asst. to exec. dir. Nat. Sch. Transp. Assn., Springfield, Va., 1981-82, exec. dir., 1982—; sec., treas. Inst. Sch. Bus Safety Inc., Springfield, 1984—. Editor mag. Nat. Sch. Bus Report, 1982—; newsletter Nat. Sch. Transp. Assn., 1982—. Mem. Am. Soc. Assn. Execs., Nat. Safety Council, Nat. Assn. Pupil Transp. Avocations: sailing, tennis, reading, travel. Office: Nat Sch Transp Assn 6213 Old Keene Mill Ct Springfield VA 22152

FINKENSTAEDT, ELIZABETH, archaeologist, educator; b. Rockford, Ill., Aug. 13, 1930; d. Kimball Lawrence and Artena (Phillips) F. A.B., Wellesley Coll., 1952; M.A., U. Mich., 1955; student U. Utrecht (Netherlands), 1960-61, 62-63; Ph.D., Harvard U., 1963. Instr., U. Oreg., 1959-60, 61-62; asst. prof. Mount Holyoke Coll., South Hadley, Mass., 1965-70; assoc. prof. U. Ky., Lexington, 1970—; asst. registrar Agora, Athens, Greece; excavator Idalion, Cyprus, Pollensa, Majorca. osteologist Ky. Indian excavations. Frank L. Weill fellow, 1968; Sachs fellow, 1960-61. Mem. AAAS, Am. Research Ctr. in Egypt, Soc. Field Archaeologists, Phi Beta Kappa. Republican. Episcopalian. Contbr. articles to profl jours. Home: 1153 Lane Allen Rd Lexington KY 40504 Office: 203 Fine Arts Bldg Rose St Lexington KY 40506

FINKL, CHARLES WILLIAM, II, geologist; b. Chgo., Sept. 19, 1941; s. Charles William and Marian L. (Hamilton) F.; m. Charlene Bristol, May 16, 1965 (div.); children—Jonathan William Frederick, Amanda Marie. B.Sc., Oreg. State U., 1964, M.Sc., 1966; Ph.D., U. Western Australia, 1971. Instr. natural resources Oreg. State U., 1967; demonstrator U. Western Australia, 1968; staff geochemist for S.E. Asia, Internat. Nickel Australia Pty. Ltd., Perth, 1970-74; chief editor Ency. Earth Sci., N.Y.C., 1974—; dir. Inst. Coastal Studies, Nova. U., 1980-83; pres. Resource Mgmt. & Mineral Exploration Cons., Inc., Ft. Lauderdale, Fla., 1974-85 Info. Mgmt. Corp. (IMCO), 1985—; exec. dir., v.p. Coastal Edn. and Research Found., Ctr. Coastal Research, Ft. Lauderdale, 1983—; prof. dept. geology Fla. Atlantic U., Boca Raton, 1983—; corr. mem. Internat. Geog. Union Commn. on Geomorphol. Survey and Mapping and Sub-commn. on Morphotectonics, Internat. Geol. Correl. Program; mem. Internat. Geog. Union Commn. on River and Coastal Plains; corr. mem. Internat. Geog. Union Commn. on Coastal Environment; radio and TV appearances. Mem. AAAS, Am. Assn. Petroleum Geologists, Am. Geophys. Union, Am. Geog. Soc., Am. Quaternary Assn. Am. Littoral Soc., Am. Shore and Beach Preservation Assn., Assn. So. Agrl. Scientists, Australian Soc. Soil Sci., Australasian Inst. Mining and Metallurgy, Brit. Geomorphological Research Group, Brit. Soc. Soil Sci., Can. Geophys. Union, Coastal Soc.,

Deutsche Bodenkundlichen Gesellschaft, Deutsche Geologische Vereininung, European Assn. Earth Sci. Editors, Estuarine and Brackish-Water Scis. Assn., Fedn. Am. Scientists, Fla. Acad. Sci., Fla. Shore and Beach Preservation Assn., Geol. Assn. Can., Geol. Soc. Am., Geol. Soc. Australia, Geol. Soc. London, Geol. Soc. Miami, Geol. Soc. South Africa, Geologists Assn., Geosci. Info. Soc., Inst. Australian Geographers, Internat. Soil Sci. Soc., Internat. Union Geol. Scis., Mineral. Assn. Can., Nature Conservancy, Nat. Parks and Conservation Assn., N.Y. Acad. Scis., Soil Sci. Soc. Am., Société de Belgede Pedologie, Soc. Econ. Paleontologists and Mineralogists, Soc. Mining Engrs., Am. Registry Cert. Profls. in Agronomy, Crops and Soils (cert. profl. soil scientist), Gamma Theta Upsilon. Republican. Presbyterian. Contbr. articles, revs. to profl. publs., newspapers. Author: Soil Classification, 1982. Vol. editor, contbg. author: The Encyclopedia of Soil Science, Part I: Physics, Chemistry, Biology, Fertility, and Technology, 1979. Editor, contbg. author: The Encyclopedia of Applied Geology, 1983. Editor-in-chief Jour. Coastal Research: An Internat. Forum for the Littoral Scis., 1984—. Series editor Benchmark Papers in Soil Sci., 1982—. Editor: Current Titles in Ocean, Coastal, Lake and Waterway Sciences, 1985—. Home: 1808 Bay View Dr Fort Lauderdale FL 33305 Office: Dept Geology Fla Atlantic U Boca Raton FL 33431

FINLAY, JOEL S., organization development executive; b. Waterbury, Conn., Feb. 7, 1944; s. George Glen and Eleanor Marie (Helgaas) F.; Ph.B., U. N.D., 1968; M.A. (scholar), U. Cin., 1969; m. Belinda Lee Henderson, Dec. 27, 1975; 1 son, Sean Patrick Harrison. Instr., Kent State U., 1969-71, U. Mo., St. Louis, 1972-73; dir. European ops. MIND, Inc., N.Y.C., 1973-75; dir. IMPAC communications Integrated Control Systems Co., Litchfield, Conn., 1975-80; mgr. tng. and devel. Pic 'N Pay Stores, Inc., Charlotte, N.C., 1980-81; mgmt. and orgnl. devel. exec. Vulcan Materials Co., 1981—; v.p., dir. mgmt. devel. Ga. Fed. Bank; guest lectr. Samford U., Birmingham So. Coll. Author: The Creative Process, 1983; contbr. numerous articles to profl. jours. Served with USAR, 1962-63. Mem. Am. Soc. Tng. and Devel., Orgn. Devel. Inst., Speech Communication Assn., Mensa, World Future Soc., Ala. Zool. Soc., Sigma Nu. Republican. Methodist. Club: Moose. Home: 13 Old Decatur Circle Decatur GA 30030 Office: PO Box 105370 Atlanta GA 30348

FINLEY, GEORGE ALVIN, III, hardware distribution and government contracting executive; b. Aurora, Ill., Apr. 25, 1938; s. George Alvin, II, and Sally Ann (Lord) F.; B.B.A., So. Meth. U., 1962; postgrad. Coll. Grad. Program, Ford Motor Co., 1963; m. Sue Sellors, June 20, 1962; children—Valerie, George Alvin IV. Rep. for Europe, Finco Internat., 1959-61; trainee Ford Motor Co., Dearborn, Mich., 1962-63; v.p. mktg. Internat. Motor Cars, Oakland, Calif., 1963-64, Sequoia Lincoln lease mgr., 1965; regional mgr. Behlen Mfg. Co., Dallas, 1965-67; pres., chmn. bd. C.C. Distbrs., Inc., Corpus Christi, Tex., 1967—; pres. Taurgo Industries, Inc.; guest instr. Sch. Bus., So. Meth. U.; mem. exec. com. Pro Hardware Inc., Stamford, Conn. Apptd. bd. mem. Nueces River Authority, 1976—, v.p. bd.; pres. Coastal Bend Alcoholic Rehab. Ctrs., Inc. Mem. Nat., Tex. (past v.p.) wholesale hardware assns., Nat. Retail Hardware Assn., So. Hardware Assn., Phi Delta Theta. Democrat. Unitarian. Clubs: Rotary Internat, Corpus Christi Yacht (bd. dirs.). Asst. in design, engring., production, mktg. Apollo Automobile, 1963-64. Home: 3360 Ocean Dr Corpus Christi TX 78411 Office: PO Box 9153 210 McBride Ln Corpus Christi TX 78469

FINLEY, GORDON ELLIS, psychology educator; b. Evanston, Ill., July 30, 1939; married. B.A., Antioch Coll., 1962; M.A., Harvard U., 1965, Ph.D., 1968. Asst. prof. U. B.C., 1967-69, U. Toronto, 1969-71; vis. asst. prof. U. Calif.-Berkeley, 1971-72; assoc. prof. psychology, Fla. Internat. U., Miami, 1972-76, prof., 1976—; exec. sec. U.S. and Can. Interamerican Soc. Psychology, 1974-76; sec. gen. XVI Interamerican Congress Psychology, 1976; cons. Fla. Occupational Therapy Assn., City of Miami Beach, 1980, Latin Am. Research and Exchange Program Devel. Group U. South Fla., 1983—; Southeast Fla. Ctr. Aging, 1985—; AID, 1984—; numerous coms. Fla. Internat. U., Miami, 1972—. Contbr. articles to profl. jours., chpts. to books. Consulting editor Jour. Cross-Cultural Psychology, 1974—, Revista Interamericana de Psicologia/Interamerican Jour. Psychology, 1983—. Bd. editorial commentators Behavioral and Brain Scis., 1978—. Grantee U. Chgo., 1965, Ednl. Research Inst. B.C., 1968-69, Can. Council, 1969-71, Fla. Internat. U., 1972-76, NIMH 1975-76, Fla. Internat. U. Found., 1975-80, Nat. Inst. Aging 1977, Fla. Internat. U./Fla. Atlantic U., 1980-81, Fla. Internat. U. Latin Am. and Caribbean Ctr. 1981-84, Fla. Internat. U. Coll. Arts and Scis. 1981-84, AID, 1982—, Southeast Fla. Ctr., 1985. Fellow NIMH 1963-67. Mem. Am. Psychol. Assn., Assn. Anthropology and Gerontology, Gerontol. Soc., Interamerican Soc. Psychology (v.p. for U.S. and Can. 1983—), Internat. Assn. Cross-Cultural Psychology (treas. 1981-82), Soc. Cross Cultural Research. Office: Dept Psychology Fla Internat U Miami FL 33199

FINLEY, JEAN BOND, librarian, registered nurse; b. Pittsylvania County, Va., May 1, 1935; d. Elvin Haywood Bond, Sr. and Vada Katherine (Motley) Bond; m. Sidney William Finley, June 17, 1958; children—Sidney William, John Clifton. A.A., Averett Coll., 1954; B.S. in Nursing, Med. Coll. Va., 1957; M.L.S., La. State U., 1979. R.N. Staff nurse Richmond Meml. Hosp., Richmond, Va., 1957-58; nurse Anesthesia Dept. Med. Coll. Va., Richmond, 1958-61; clin. instr. Practical Nursing, 1961-65; librarian La. Dept. Urban and Community Affairs, Baton Rouge, 1980—. Mem. ALA, La. Library Assn., Baton Rouge Library Club, La. Govt. Info. Network Com., La. State Agys. Interest Group Coordinator, Council of Planning Librarians. Home: 1735 Marilyn Dr Baton Rouge LA 70815 Office: La Dept Urban Community Affairs PO Box 44455 Baton Rouge LA 70804

FINLEY, RICHARD GAYLE, chemical company executive; b. Abilene, Tex., Feb. 22, 1944; s. Jeffery Donald and Esther Bessie (Strickland) F.; B.A., Howard Payne Coll., 1966; postgrad. Rice U., 1966-68; M.A. (Robert A. Welch research asst.), U. Tex., Austin, 1971; postgrad. U. Tex., Permian Basin, 1979-80. Sr. mfg. chemist Champion Chemicals, Inc., Odessa, Tex., 1973-74; dir. quality control lab. Champion Chemicals, 1974-77, mgr. mfg., 1977-80, asst. to v.p. tech. ops., 1980—. Rice U. fellow, 1966-68. Mem. Soc. Petroleum Engrs., Nat. Assn. Corrosion Engrs., Blue Key, Alpha Chi, Beta Gamma Phi. Baptist. Club: Odessa Country. Home: 521 N Alma St Goldsmith TX 79741 Office: 115 Proctor St Odessa TX 79760

FINLEY, WAYNE HOUSE, medical educator; b. Goodwater, Ala., Apr. 7, 1927; s. Byron Bruce and Lucille (House) F.; m. Sara Will Crews, July 6, 1952; children—Randall Wayne, Sara Jane. B.S., Jacksonville State U., 1948; M.A., U. Ala.-University, 1950; M.S., U. Ala.-Birmingham, 1955, Ph.D., 1958, M.D., 1960. Diplomate Am. Bd. Med. Genetics. Intern, U. Ala. Hosps., Birmingham, 1960-61; trainee med. genetics U. Uppsala, Sweden, 1961-62; mem. faculty U. Ala.-Birmingham, 1962—, prof. pediatrics, 1970—, dir. Lab. Med. Genetics, 1966—. Served with USAR, 1945-46, 51-53. Recipient Disting. Alumni award U. Ala. Sch. Medicine Alumni Assn., 1978; Disting. Faculty lectr. Med. Ctr. U. Ala., 1983. Mem. Am. Soc. Human Genetics, Am. Physiol. Soc., N.Y. Acad. Sci., So. Med. Soc., AAAS, AMA, Ala. Med. Soc., Jefferson County Med. Soc., Sigma Xi. Baptist. Contbr. articles to profl. jours. Home: 3412 Brookwood Rd Birmingham AL 35223 Office: Dept Pediatrics U Ala University Sta Birmingham AL 35294

FINNEGAN, MARK ALAN, geologist; b. Tulsa, Jan. 23, 1954; s. Hugh I. and Betty L. (Perry) F.; m. Stephanie A. Kouri, Sept. 6, 1980; children—Paul Michael, Anthony Sean. Student U. Okla., 1972-74, Tulsa Jr. Coll., 1974, 76; B.S., Okla. State U., 1978. With Seismograph Service Corp., Tex., Miss., Ark., Nev., summer 1977; geol. asst. info. services div. U. Tulsa, 1979, geologist, 1980—. Mem. Am. Assn. Petroleum Geologists, Geol. Soc. Am., Geosci. Info. Soc., Tulsa Geol. Soc. Roman Catholic. Avocations: sailing; fishing; backpacking; reading; camping and hiking. Office: Info Services Div U Tulsa 600 S College St Tulsa OK 74104

FINNEGAN, RICHARD PAUL, bank executive; b. Pitts., May 8, 1950; s. Regis Patrick and Edna Ann (Jesteadt) F. B.A., Pa. State U., 1972, M.Ed., 1974. Resident dir. Duquesne U., Pitts., 1974-76; asst. dir. residence halls U. Miami, Coral Gables, Fla., 1976-78; personnel interviewer Sun Bank of Miami, Fla., 1978-79, asst. v.p., personnel dir., 1979-80; asst. v.p. employee relations Sun Banks, Inc., Orlando, 1980-81; v.p., personnel dir. Sun Bank, N.A., Orlando, 1981-84, sr. v.p., personnel dir., 1985—. Pres. bd. dirs. Green House Family Counseling Ctr., Orlando, 1985. Mem. Am. Soc. Tng. and Devel. Office: Sun Bank NA 200 S Orange Ave PO Box 3833 Orlando FL 32897

FINNEY, JOYCE LEE, university administrator, librarian; b. Nashville, Aug. 18, 1940; d. William J. Finney and Helen L. (Hopper) Finney Isaacs. B.A. in English, David Lipscomb Coll., Nashville, 1975; M.L.S., U. Tenn., 1976. IBM teamleader Nat. Life and Accident Ins. Co., 1958-65; traveling cons. agy. mgmt. Mut. N.Y., 1965-68; agy. cashier New Eng. Life, Buffalo, 1968-70; adminstrv. asst. to pres., pension cons. Retirement Plans, Inc., Buffalo, 1971; in various positions David Lipscomb Coll., 1971-75; student asst. Grad. Library, U. Tenn., Knoxville, 1975-76, librarian Energy, Environment, and Resources Ctr., 1976-77, ctr. info. specialist, 1977-78, ctr. research assoc., 1979-81, asst. dir. ctr., head ctr. communications and coordination div., 1981-84, assoc. dir., 1984—. Cons. in field; participant profl. activities. Author numerous bibliographies. Mem. Am. Soc. Info. Scis. Mem. Ch. of Christ. Home: 1169 Keowee Ave Apt F-5 Knoxville TN 37919 Office: Energy Environment and Resources Ctr U Tenn Knoxville TN 37999

FINNEY, STANLEY CHARLES, geology educator, researcher; b. Chula Vista, Calif., Oct. 14, 1947; s. Samuel Shirley Finney and Ida (Valpredo) Zakula; m. Linda Anne Massie, Oct. 14, 1977; 1 child, Matthew. B.S., U. Calif.-Riverside, 1969, M.S., 1971; Ph.D., Ohio State U., 1977. Postdoctoral fellow Meml. U., St. John's, Newfoundland, Can., 1977-78, Field Mus. Natural History, Chgo., 1978-79; instr. Ohio State U., Columbus, 1979-80; asst. prof. No. Ariz. U., Flagstaff, 1980-81; assoc. prof. Okla. State U., Stillwater, 1981—. Research grantee Nat. Geographic Soc., 1981, NSF, 1982, Am. Chem. Soc., 1982. Mem. Am. Assn. Petroleum Geologists, Geol. Soc. Am., Paleontol. Soc., Paleontol. Assn., Internat. Paleontol. Assn. Office: Sch Geology Okla State U Stillwater OK 74078

FIORENTINO, CARMINE, lawyer; b. Bklyn., Sept. 11, 1932; s. Pasquale and Lucy (Coppola) F. Student ct. reporting Hunter Coll., 1951; student radio announcing Columbia Broadcasting Sch., N.Y.C., 1952; LL.B., Blackstone Sch. Law, Chgo., 1954, John Marshall Law Sch., Atlanta, 1957; student fiction and non-fiction writing Famous Writers Sch., 1962. Bar: Ga. 1958, D.C. 1971, U.S. Dist. Ct. D.C. 1971, U.S. Dist. Ct. (no. dist.) Ga. 1959, U.S. Ct. Appeals (2d cir.) 1971, U.S. Ct. Appeals (5th cir.) 1959, U.S. Supreme Ct. 1970. Legal stenographer N.Y. State Workmen's Compensation Bd., N.Y. State Dept. Labor, 1950-53; ct. reporter, hearing stenographer Gov. Thomas E. Dewey's Com. State Counsel and Attys., 1953; pub. relations sec. Indsl. Home for Blind, Bkly., 1953-55; legal stenographer, researcher, law clk. various law firms, Atlanta, 1955, 57-59; sec. for import-export firm, Atlanta, 1956; sole practice, Atlanta, 1959-63, 74—; atty.-adviser trial atty. HUD, Atlanta and Office HUD Gen. Counsel, Washington, also legal counsel Peachtree Fed. Credit Union, 1963-74; acting dir. Elmira Disaster Field Office, HUD (N.Y.), 1973; appearances on network and local TV and radio broadcasts; mem. Atlanta Lawyer Reference Panel, 1959-63. Contbr. articles to Evening Star, Nat. Observer; composer, lyricist songs, hymns. Mem. Republican Nat. Com., Rep. Presdl. Task Force; dir. HUD Elmira Disaster Field Office, 1972. Recipient commendation U.S. House Un-Am. Activities Com., 1951, U.S. Crusade for Freedom, 1951. Mem. ABA, Fed. Bar Assn., Atlanta Bar Assn., Decatur-DeKalb Bar Assn., Am. Judicature Soc., Old War Horse Lawyers Club, Assn. Trial Lawyers Am., Jr. C. of C. of Atlanta, Internat. Platform Assn., Smithsonian Instn., Life Dynamics Fellowship, Nat. Hist. Soc., Atlanta Hist. Soc., AAAS, Am. Mus. Natural History, Atlanta Bot. Gardens, Nat. Audubon Soc., AAAS, Planetary Soc., Sierra Club, Mus. Heritage Soc. Clubs: Toastmasters, Gaslight, U.S. Senatorial. Home: 2164 Medfield Tr NE Atlanta GA 30345

FIORENZA, JOSEPH A., bishop Roman Catholic Ch.; b. Beaumont, Tex., Jan. 25, 1931. Student St. Mary's Sem., LaPorte, Tex. Ordained priest Roman Catholic Ch., 1954, consecrated bishop, 1979. Bishop Diocese of San Angelo, Tex., 1979—. Address: The Roman Cath Ch Chancery Office Box 1829 San Angelo TX 76901*

FIREBAUGH, GLENN ALLEN, sociology educator; b. Charleston, W.Va., Oct. 23, 1948; s. George Lawrence and Rosanelle (Grose) F.; m. Judy Rae Thompson, Nov. 21, 1970; children—Heather, Joel, Rose Marie. B.A., Grace Coll., 1970; M.A., Ind. U., 1974, Ph.D., 1976. Asst. prof. Vanderbilt U., Nashville, 1976-82, assoc. prof., 1982—. Author chpts. in books, 1980, 85. Mem. editorial bd. Sociol. Quarterly, Sociol. Methods and Research, Social Forces, Am. Jour. Sociology. Contbr. articles to profl. jours. NIMH fellow, 1972-76; NSF grantee, 1983-84. Mem. Am. Sociol. Assn., Population Assn. Am. Home: 3622 Meadowbrook Ave Nashville TN 37205 Office: Dept Sociology Vanderbilt Univ Box 3 Station B Nashville TN 37235

FIRESTONE, GEORGE, state official; b. N.Y.C., May 13, 1931; m. Nola A. Nissenson. Ins. broker, 1952-61; with Gray Security Service, Miami, Fla., 1961-72; sec.-treas. Investco, Inc., Miami, 1972—; mem. Fla. Ho. of Reps., 1966-72, chmn. com. house adminstrn. and conduct, 1971-73; mem. Fla. Senate, 1972-78, chmn. legis. auditing and legis. mgmt. coms., vice chmn. rules com.; co-chmn. Fla. Energy Com., 1973-74; chmn. Dade County Personnel Adv. Bd., 1962-64; sec. of state Fla., 1979—; past mem. Miami Econ. Adv. Bd. Served with U.S. Army, 1948-52. Recipient Good Govt. award Miami Jaycees, 1972. Mem. Nat. Conf. State Legislators (past pres.), Miami Jaycees (past pres.), N.W. Miami Property Owners Assn. (past pres.), Dade County Council Civic Orgns. (past pres.). Democrat. Club: Tiger Bay (Miami).

FIRNBERG, JAMES WALLACE, university administrator; b. Alexandria, La., Mar. 25, 1935; s. Erle Albert and Dorathea (Kidd) F.; m. Ancy Cruse, June 3, 1958; children—James W. Jr., William, Timothy, Edward. B.A., U. Southwestern La., 1956; M.Ed., La. State U., 1959, Ed.D., 1969. Tchr. East Baton Rouge Parish Sch., 1956-59; counselor La. State U., Baton Rouge, 1959-63; asst. registrar instl. research La. State U., Baton Rouge, 1963-66; coordinator instl. research La. State U. System, 1966-68, asst. prof., coordinator instl. research, 1969-73, assoc. prof., coordinator instl. research, 1973-78, prof., coordinator instl. research, 1978-80, dir. system office instl. research, 1980-82, asst. v.p. acad. affairs, dir. system office instl. research, 1982-84; chancellor, prof. La. State U., Alexandria, 1984—; cons. La. Higher Edn. Facilities Commn., also several sch. systems, various colls. and univs. mem. Gov.'s Edn. Study Com., La., 1974-75; cons. to sec. HEW, 1976; mem. tchr. certification adv. council La. State Bd. Elem. and Secondary Edn., 1975-78; mem. adv. panel on univ. sci. statistics NSF, 1977-82. Co-editor: New Directions for Institutional Research, 1983. Contbr. articles to profl. jours. Bd. dirs. Indsl. Devel. Bd. Central La., Alexandria, 1984—, St. Frances Cabrini Hosp., Alexandria, 1984—; bd. trustees Alexandria Mus., 1984—; mem. exec. com. Boy Scouts Am., Alexandria, 1984—; bd. dirs. YMCA, 1986. Served with U.S. Army, 1961-62. Mem. Am. Assn. Collegiate Registrars and Admissions Officers, Assn. Instl. Research (pres. 1976-77), So. Assn. Instl. Research, So. Assn. Colls. and Schs., Alexandria/Pineville C. of C. (bd. dirs. 1985—, v.p. 1986). Methodist. Lodge: Rotary (Alexandria) (bd. dirs. 1986). Office: Chancellor La State U Alexandria LA 71302

FISCHER, DANIEL EDWARD, psychiatrist; b. New Haven, Apr. 22, 1945; s. Alexander and Miriam (Kramer) F.; m. Linda Lee Bradford, June 12, 1969; children—Meredith Tara, Alexis Anne. B.A., Boston U., 1969, M.D., 1969; J.D., Coll. William and Mary, 1986. Intern in medicine Baylor Affiliated Hosps., Houston, 1969-70; resident in psychiatry Washington U. Sch. Medicine, St. Louis, 1970-73; practice medicine specializing in psychiatry, Virginia Beach, Va., 1975—; chmn. dept. psychiatry DePaul Hosp., Norfolk, Va., 1978-79, Bayside Hosp., Virginia Beach, 1980-81. Contbr. articles to profl. jours. Bd. dirs. Tidewater Pastoral Counseling Service, Norfolk, 1976—, Kempsville Conservative Synagogue, Virginia Beach, 1982—. Served as maj. U.S. Army, 1973-75. Decorated Army Commendation medal. Fellow Acad. Psychosomatic Medicine; mem. AMA, Am. Psychiat. Assn., Va. Med. Soc., Va. Psychiat. Assn., Virginia Beach Med. Soc., Tidewater Acad. Psychiatry. Democrat. Jewish. Avocation: Stamp Collecting. Office: Hearst Fischer & Schreiber Ltd Pembroke 5 Suite 331 Virginia Beach VA 23462

FISCHER, EDWARD ALLAN, insurance executive; b. Bronx, N.Y., Mar. 14, 1942; s. Leonard Selwyn and Lillian (Brickman) F.; m. Susan Raber, Dec. 11, 1976 (div. July 1978); m. Anne B. Freedman, May 20, 1979. Student Rockland Coll., 1959-62. Sales mgr. Caribbean Internat. Corp., San Juan, P.R., 1970-74, ESJ Towers, Inc., San Juan, 1974-76; state trainer Combined Ins. Co. of Am., Miami, Fla., 1976-79; agt. Mass. Mut. Life Ins. Co., Miami, 1981—; v.p. Exec. S.O.S., Inc., Miami, 1980—, sales cons., 1980—; dist. sales mgr. Combined Ins. Co. Am., 1976-79. Served with U.S. Army, 1966-68; Vietnam. Mem. Miami Assn. Life Underwriters, So. Miami-Kendall C. of C. (membership chmn. 1982-83, dir. 1984—, v.p. 1985—); cert. of appreciation 1982-83). Democrat. Jewish. Clubs: S. Dade Toastmasters (pres. Miami 1982), S. Dade Founders. Lodges: B'nai B'rith, Rotary. Home: 6721 SW 113 Pl Miami FL 33173 Office: Exec SOS Inc 10850 SW 113 Pl Suite 117 Miami FL 33176

FISCHER, JEROME MORTON, consulting engineer; b. N.Y.C., Mar. 15, 1924; s. Lester and Hilda (Schwartz) F.; m. Rhoda Barsha, Sept. 2, 1946; children—Steven, Karen, Michael, Marion. B.C.E., N.C. State U., 1948; postgrad., Tex. A&M U., 1942-43. Registered profl. engr., N.Y., Vt.; chartered engr., U.K. With Parsons, Brinckerhoff, Hall & MacDonald, N.Y.C., 1948-52, Tippets-Abbett-McCarthy-Stratton, 1952-60; v.p., then sr. v.p. Frederic R. Harris, Inc., The Hague, Netherlands, 1960-66, exec. v.p., N.Y.C., 1966-72, chmn. bd., 1972—; also dir.; v.p. Internat. Planning Research Corp., 1974—; dir. Planning Research Corp., 1974—, exec. v.p., 1977—; pres. PRC Engring., Inc., 1981—. Author numerous papers in field. Served with C.E. AUS, 1942-46. Decorated Order of Crown (Belgium); recipient Medal of Honor, Spanish Ministry Pub. Works. Fellow ASCE, Inst. Civil Engrs. (Gt. Britain); mem. Am. Cons. Engrs. Council, Am. Inst. Cons. Engrs., Am. Concrete Inst., Internat. Rd. Fedn., Internat. Toll Rd., Tunnel and Turnpike Assn., Nat. Soc. Profl. Engrs., Permanent Internat. Congress Rds., Royal Netherlands Inst. Engrs., Soc. Flemish Engrs., Soc. Am. Mil. Engrs., U.S. C. of C. in Netherlands (past dir.). Clubs: Petroleum (London); Scarsdale (N.Y.) Golf. Home: 18 Hampton Rd Scarsdale NY 10583 Office: Planning Research Corp 1500 Planning Research Dr McLean VA 22102*

FISCHER, JOHN ARTHUR, financial analyst; b. Mpls., Oct. 23, 1929; s. Carl Frederick and Kathryn Dorothy (Gehrenbeck) F.; m. Betty Louise Christopher, May 23, 1953; children—Mark Alan, Cris Lynn. B.G.S., U. Nebr., 1969. Customer engr. IBM, Jacksonville, Fla., 1956, Poughkeepsie, N.Y., 1956-57, systems engr., Kingston, N.Y., 1957-58, Kansas City, Mo., 1958-60, programmer, project mgr., Omaha, 1960-69, site mgr. Lowry AFB, Denver, 1969-71, Leesburg, Va., 1971-72, project mgr., Manassas, Va., 1972-76, staff programmer, 1976-79, staff bus. controls analyst fed. systems div., 1979—, chmn. supervisory com. Employees Credit Union, 1979—, dir., 1983—. Mem. county and state com. Va. Republican party. Served with USN, 1947-56; ETO. Mem. Assn. Computing Machinery, Prince William County Beekeepers Assn. (treas. 1977—). Home: 4407 Sanders Ln Catharpin VA 22018 Office: IBM Corp 9500 Godwin Dr 101/082 Manassas VA 22110

FISCHER, NORMAN, JR., media broker, appraiser, broadcast consultant; b. Washington, Mar. 14, 1924; s. Norman and Agnes Columbia (May) F.; m. Ela Cecile Ragland, Mar. 28, 1959; 1 son, Norman Terrill. B.S., Washington and Lee U., 1949. Lic. real estate salesman, Tex. Owner, operator radio stas. KUKA-AM, San Antonio, 1961-67, WEBB-AM, Balt., 1967-70, KBER-AM, Abilene, Tex., 1976-82; account exec. radio stas. KTSA-AM, San Antonio, 1957-60, KONO-AM, San Antonio, 1960-61; ptnr. Holt-Fischer, Austin, Tex., 1970-72; v.p. R. Miller Hicks Co., Austin, 1972-75; pres. Advance Inc. owners KRMH, Austin, 1972-75; pres. Norman Fischer & Assocs., Inc., Austin, 1974—; guest instr. U. Tex. Sch. Communications, 1979. Mem. Bexar County Democratic Com., 1966; active Austin chpt. March of Dimes, 1973-77, chpt. chmn., 1976. Served with Signal Corps, AUS, 1943-46. Mem. Nat. Assn. Broadcasters, Tex. Assn. Broadcasters, La. Assn. Broadcasters, Nat. Radio Broadcasters Assn., Nat. Media Brokers Assn., Austin C. of C. Democrat. Episcopalian. Clubs: Tarry House, Capitol (Austin). Lodge: Downtown Rotary. Office: Norman Fischer & Assos Inc 1209 Parkway Box 5308 Austin TX 78763

FISCHER, PATRICK CARL, computer scientist, educator; b. St. Louis, Dec. 3, 1935; s. Carl Hahn and Kathleen (Kirkpatrick) F.; B.S., U. Mich., 1957, M.B.A., 1958; Ph.D., M.I.T., 1962; m. Linda Loomis, Dec. 22, 1956 (div. Jan. 1967); 1 son, Carl; m. 2d, Charlotte Froese, Apr. 2, 1967; 1 dau., Carolyn. Asst. prof. applied math. Harvard U., Cambridge, Mass., 1962-65; asso. prof. computer sci. Cornell U., Ithaca, N.Y., 1965-68; prof. computer sci. U. Waterloo (Ont., Can.), 1968-74, chmn. dept. applied analysis and computer sci., 1972-74; prof. dept. computer sci. Pa. State U., 1974-79, head dept., 1974-78; prof., chmn. computer sci. dept. Vanderbilt U., Nashville, 1980—; cons. actuary, 1962-75; vis. asso. prof. U. B.C., 1967-68. Woodrow Wilson fellow, 1958-59; NSF grad. fellow, 1959-62, research grantee, 1964-68, 79-84; grantee Nat. Research Council Can., 1968-75. Fellow Soc. Actuaries; mem. Assn. Computing Machinery (founder, chmn. spl. interest group 1968-73, editor-in-chief spl. publs. 1971—, chmn. constn. and bylaws com. 1978-84), IEEE, IEEE Computer Soc., Phi Beta Kappa, Sigma Xi, Phi Kappa Phi, Beta Gamma Sigma. Republican. Asso. editor Jour. Computer and System Scis., 1968-74, editor, 1974—; editor SIAM Jour. Computing, 1974-84; editorial adv. bd. Jour. Computer Langs., 1974—; contbr. to profl. jours. Office: Box 6026 Sta B Vanderbilt U Nashville TN 37235

FISCHER, PETER HEINZ, public affairs specialist; b. Nuremberg, Ger., Feb. 17, 1942; came to U.S., 1950, naturalized, 1956; s. Hans and Helen (Müller) F.; m. Marianne Dee, Apr. 22, 1964; children—Christopher, Melanie. B.A. in English and Journalism, Stephen F. Austin U., 1964. Editor, Shell Oil Co., Houston and Deer Park, Tex., 1964-69, regional editor, New Orleans, 1969-71, pub. relations rep., 1971-78, sr. pub. relations rep., 1978-81, mgr. community relations southeast, 1981-82, mgr. nat. news media relations, Houston, 1982-83, sr. staff pub. affairs rep., 1983—. Republican. Contbr. articles to profl. jours. Home: 27310 Blueberry Hill Dr Conroe TX 77385 Office: 1558 One Shell Plaza PO Box 2463 Houston TX 77001

FISH, A. JOE, U.S. district judge; b. Los Angeles, Nov. 12, 1942; s. John Allen and Mary Magdalene (Martin) F.; m. Betty, Jan. 23, 1971; 1 child, Abigail. B.A., Yale U., 1965, LL.B., 1968. Atty. firm McKenzie & Baer, Dallas, 1968-80; state dist. judge, 1980-81; assoc. judge Tex. Appeals Ct., 1981-83; U.S. dist. judge No. dist. Tex., Dallas, 1983—. Mem. ABA, State Bar of Tex., Dallas Bar Assn. Office: Room 15-A-3 US Courthouse 1100 Commerce St Dallas TX 75242*

FISH, BILL EDWIN, manufacturing company executive; b. Nitro, W.Va., Sept. 2, 1949; s. Frank Archer and Francis Margaret (Walker) F.; m. Beverly Billingslea, Oct. 3, 1970. B.S., W.Va. Inst. Tech., 1972. With Fruhauf div. Fruehauf Corp., Charleston, W.Va., 1972-75; gen. mgr. So. div. Power Brake div. R.M. Wilson Co., Wheeling, W.Va., 1975-79; sales mgr. Browning Ferris Industries, Phila., 1979-82; pres. Indsl. Forumations Corp., Poca, W.Va., 1982—. Served as lt. Army NG, 1970-76. Presbyterian. Club: Masons. Office: Rock Branch Indsl Bank PO Box 568 Poca WV 25159

FISH, ROBERT JAY, dental surgeon, diversified entrepreneur exec.; b. Zanesville, Ohio, June 4, 1947; s. Sidney and Sara Mae (Rogovin) F.; B.S., Ohio State U., 1969, D.D.S., 1973; m. Lana Joy Halperin, May 24, 1981. Extern dept. oral surgery Jackson Meml. Hosp.; practice gen. dentistry and dental reconstruction, Ft. Lauderdale, Fla., 1973—; chmn. bd. Flying Fish Inc., RJF Assocs., Royal Rents Inc., Royal Resources Inc.; pres., chmn. Cosmetic Dental Assocs. Inc., Profl. Software Applications Inc.; pres., dir. Sidereal Investment Group Inc.; dir. Royal T Travel Inc.; chmn. bd., pres., chief exec. officer Tevere Inc. (OTC), advt./mktg. imported wines and spirits; dir. Dental Health Services Inc., 1975-78; assoc. prof. microbiology Broward Community Coll., 1974; mem. staff Pa. Hosp. Inst., Fla. Med. Center Hosp.; guest speaker; weekly radio program Ask the Dentist; importer Domaine de Saint Jean wine under name Robert Jay Fish & Co. Designer, U.S. rep. for Sandri Dental Program, SRL, Genoa, Italy high-tech. dental delivery system. Mem. AAAS, Am. Soc. Clin. Hypnosis, Aircraft Owners and Pilots Assn., Am. Analgesia Soc., Am. Soc. Anesthesiologists, Alpha Omega. Author: Cosmetic and Reconstructive Dentistry, 1975. Home: 10237 NW 2d St Coral Springs FL 33065 Office: 4850 W Oakland Park Fort Lauderdale FL 33313

FISHER, ALTON SELTON, JR., healthcare company executive; b. Lebanon, Tenn., Nov. 20, 1943; s. Alton Selton and Ocie (Jewell) F.; B.S., Middle Tenn. State U., 1970; postgrad. U. Minn., 1979-82; m. Janet Laraine Morgan, Sept. 8, 1967; children—Amy Katherine, Stephanie Laraine. With Ernst & Ernst, Nashville, 1970-73, North Fla. Regional Hosp. and Hosp. Corp. Am., Gainesville, 1973-77; v.p. Alachua Gen. Hosp., Inc., Gainesville, 1977-82; v.p., asst. treas. Santa Fe Healthcare Systems, Inc. and Wellness, Inc., Gainesville, 1982-83, v.p. diversified group ops., 1983-84; v.p. profl. and health provider relations Blue Cross Blue Shield of Fla., Inc., Jacksonville, 1984—; lectr., cons. Mem. U. Fla. Campus/Community Council, 1983-84. Served in USAF, 1961-65. Recipient Follmer award Healthcare Fin. Mgmt., 1980, Reeves award, 1983. Mem. Gainesville C. of C. (mem. Com. 100 and membership task force chmn.; dir. 1983—), Healthcare Fin. Mgmt. Assn. (chpt. pres. 1981-82, nat. bd. dirs. 1985—), Am. Coll. Hosp. Adminstrs., Fla. Hosp. Assn., U. Minn. Alumni Assn., Am. Inst. C.P.A.s, U.S. Power Squadron. Methodist. Club: Gainesville Offshore Fishing. Editor: Healthcare Financial Management Handbook, 1981, 82. Home: 2434 Castellon Dr Jacksonville FL 32217 Office: 532 Riverside Ave Jacksonville FL 32202

FISHER, ANITA JEANNE, English educator; b. Atlanta, Oct. 22, 1937; d. Paul Benjamin and Cora Ozella (Wadsworth) Chappelear; m. Kirby Lynn Fisher, Aug. 6, 1983; 1 child by previous marriage, Tracy Ann. B.A., Bob Jones U., 1959; post grad. Stetson U., 1961, U. Fla., 1963; M.A.T., Rollins Coll., 1969; Ph.D. in Am. Lit., Fla. State U., 1975; postgrad. Writing Inst., U. Central Fla., 1978, NEH Inst., 1979. Chmn. basic learning improvement program, secondary sch. Orange County, Orlando, Fla., 1964-65; chmn. compositon Winter Park High Sch., Fla., 1978-80; chmn. English depts. Orange County Pub. Schs., Fla., 1962-71; reading tchr. Woodland Hall Acad., Reading Research Inst. (Found.), Tallahassee, 1976; instr. edn., journalism, reading, Spanish, thesis writing Baptist Bible Coll., Springfield, Mo., 1976-77; prof. English, SW Mo. State U., Springfield, 1980-84, instr. continuing edn. courses in music and creative writing, 1981-82, editor LAD Leaf. Vol.; Greene County Action Com., 1977, Heart Fund, 1982. Contbr. articles to profl. jours. Fellow Writing Program, U. Central Fla., 1978. Mem. AAUP, Internat. Reading Assn., MLA, Nat. Council Tchrs. of English, Volusia County Council Tchrs. English, Fla. Council Tchrs. English, Kappa Delta Pi. Republican. Presbyterian. Home: 812 Victoria Circle W Ormond Beach FL 32074

FISHER, ANN DOROTHY, company executive, lawyer; b. Governor Island, N.Y., Apr. 5, 1939; d. William Parker and Dorothy (Douglas) Fisher; m. William J. Danaher, Feb. 22, 1958 (div. 1963); children—Dorothy Lynn, Jo Ann Danaher Chitty. Student Barnard Coll., 1956-58; M.B.A. (valedictorian), U. Miami, 1976, J.D. cum laude, 1981. Bar: Fla. 1981. Sales promotion mgr. Aristar Mgmt., Inc., Miami, 1965-71; dir. instl. sales Terner's of Miami, 1971-80; atty. Jorden, Melrose & Schuette, Miami, 1981-83; co-owner Now Courier, Inc., Hialeah, Fla., 1983-84; pres. Cannon & Fisher Corp., Fisher & Benson, 1984-85. Mem. ABA, Nat. Assn. Women Bus. Owners, Nat. Assn. Women Lawyers, Fla. Bar Assn., Fla. Assn. Women Lawyers, Dade County Bar Assn. Republican. Home and office: 1514 Zuleta Ave Coral Gables FL 33146

FISHER, CHARLES J., holding company executive; b. 1920; (married). B.S., MIT, 1946. Jr. engr Hamilton Paper Co., 1947-56; v.p., gen. mgr. Wyemissing Corp., 1956-64; v.p., gen. mgr. splty. chems. div. Reliance Universal Inc., Louisville, 1969-78, pres., 1978—, chief operating officer, 1979—. Office: Reliance Universal Inc 1930 Bishop Ln Louisville KY 40218*

FISHER, CONSUELO (CONNIE), telecommunications company executive; b. Oakland, Calif., Dec. 30, 1933; d. George T. and Laura K. (Koski) Carmona; m. Russell C. Fisher, June 4, 1967; children—Laura, Landrum, Belinda, Nadine. Student Mexico City Coll., 1952-55. Columnist, El Excelsior, Mexico City, 1949; reporter, columnist The News, Mexico City, 1950-54; travel agt. Redwood Travel Advisors, San Rafael, Calif., 1962-67, GTS Travel, 1967-72; writer The News-Times, Danbury, Conn., 1972-74; owner, dir. Connie Fisher Communications, Wilton, Conn., 1974-78; dir. community relations Vitan Center, Inc., 1975, 78; writer The Hour, Norwalk, Conn., 1978-80; pub. affairs coordinator Continental Telephone Tex., Dallas, 1980-83; mgr. mktg. publs. No. Telecom Inc., 1983—. Press officer Democratic party, Wilton, Conn., 1976; mem. adminstrv. bd. All Saints Cath. Ch., Dallas, 1983-84. Mem. Internat. Assn. Bus. Communicators (Bronze Quill award 1982, 83; dir.), Tex. Pub. Relations Assn. Democrat. Roman Catholic. Club: Brookhaven Country (Dallas). Home: 6533 Clearhaven Circle Dallas TX 75248 Office: 1001 E Arapaho Richardson TX 75080

FISHER, ESTELLA MARIE, school nurse, consultant; b. Houston, Oct. 21, 1939; d. William Edward and Maudesta (Hardison) Hooks; m. Constance James Fisher, 1969; 1 child, James Henry. B.S. in Nursing Edn., Prairie View A&M, 1961; M.S. in Nursing Edn., Ind. U., 1963; M.S.W., U. So. Calif., 1968. Cert. social worker; lic. profl. nurse. Social worker Calif. Youth Authority, Norwalk, 1968-69; nursing instr. Prairie View A&M, Tex., 1961-62, 63-66, 69-70; lead instr. med. surg. instrn. Alvin Jr. Coll., Tex., 1972-74; psychiat. nursing instr. Tex. Women's U., Houston, 1974-81; elem. sch. nurse R.P. Harris Elem. Sch., Houston, 1981—; cons. Prairie View Coll. Nursing, Houston, 1985; bd. dirs. Tex. Lupus Soc., Houston, 1977-79, program chmn., 1978—; coordinator workshop for nurses on lupus, 1978. Life mem. Roland P. Harris PTA, Houston, 1985; elect lady God Deliverance Ch., Houston, 1985; publicity chmn. for black media Metro. Organ., Houston, 1985; dep. registrar Harris County, Houston, 1985. NIMH scholar, 1966-68; USPHS trainee, 1962-63; recipient Leadership award St. Philip Neri Catholic Ch., 1980-83, All Around Dedication award, 1982, Black Cath. Concerned award Houston Galveston Diocese, 1978. Mem. Am. Nurses Assn., Nat. Black Nurses Assn., Nat. Black Social Workers Assn., Am. Assn. for Counseling and Devel. Democrat. Roman Catholic. Avocations: reading; swimming; travel. Home: 5223 Bungalow Ln Houston TX 77048 Office: Roland P Harris Elem Sch 1262 Mae Dr Houston TX 77015

FISHER, FLOYD LEE, lawyer, consultant; b. Rittman, Ohio, Nov. 27, 1951; s. Donald Paul and Hazel Jean (Whitney) F.; m. Nedra Kay Anders, Aug. 2, 1980; 1 child, Ashley Kent. Student, Cedarville Coll., 1970-72; B.S., U. Akron, 1974, J.D., 1980; postgrad., Ohio No. U., 1976-77. Bar: Ohio 1980, Tex. 1981, U.S. Dist. Ct. (no. dist.) Tex. 1982. Dispatcher, Rittman Police Dept., Ohio, 1972-75; customer service Morton Salt Co., Rittman, 1976-79; sole practice, Garland, Tex., 1981-85; corp. atty. LGM Enterprises, 1985—; cons. Am. Christian Acad., Colleyville, Tex., 1982—, Tex. Coalition Home Schs., Richardson, 1983—. Republican. Baptist. Home: 5008 Lake Ridge Dr Garland TX 75154 Office: PO Drawer E Lancaster TX 75146

FISHER, JAMES ARTHUR, history educator; b. Takoma Park, Md., June 8, 1942; s. Kenneth Frank and Stella Elizabeth (Blose) F.; B.A., Fla. So. Coll., 1964; M.A., Wake Forest U., 1972; Ph.D. (grad. asst.), Middle Tenn. State U., 1974; m. Delores Ann King, Dec. 11, 1976; children—Elizabeth Ann, James Arthur, Alice Jeanne. Tchr., Mulberry (Fla.) High Sch., 1965-70, Bartow (Fla.) High Sch., 1970-72; researcher Center for Advanced Internat. Studies, Washington, 1974; prof. history DeKalb Coll., Dunwoody, Ga., 1974—; hist. cons. Coastal Petroleum Co., 1980—. Del. Ga. Rep. Conv., 1984. Named Tchr. of Yr., DeKalb Coll., 1983; Outstanding Young Men in Am., 1975; Fulbright fellow, Korea, 1984. Mem. Orgn. Am. Historians, So. Hist. Soc., Eastern Community Coll. Social Sci. Assn., Profl. Assn. Ga. Educators, Polk County Hist. Soc., Assn. for Improvement of Community Coll. Teaching, SAR, Omicron Delta Kappa, Pi Gamma Mu, Phi Alpha Theta, Kappa Alpha. Republican. Baptist. Author: The History of Mulberry, Florida, 1974; editor Jour. Assn. for Improvement of Community Coll. Teaching, 1983-85. Home: 2525 N Brook Rd Snellville GA 30278 Office: DeKalb College 2101 Womack Rd Dunwoody GA 30338

FISHER, JAMES WILLIAM, medical educator, pharmacologist; b. Startex, S.C., May 22, 1925; s. Ernest Amaziah and Mamie V. (Turner) F.; m. Carol Barbara Brodarick, June 5, 1947; children—Candis, Patricia, Richard, William, John, Elaine. B.S. in Chemistry, U. S.C., 1947; Ph.D. in Pharmacology, U. Louisville, 1958. Pharmacologist Armour Pharm. Res. Labs., Chgo., 1950-53, Lloyd Bros. Inc. Pharm. Res. Labs., Cin., 1954-56; instr. dept. pharmacology U. Tenn. Med. Units, Memphis, 1958-60, asst. prof., 1960-62, assoc. prof., 1962-66, prof., 1966-68; prof., dept. pharmacology Tulane U., New Orleans, 1968—, chmn. dept., 1968—, mem. numerous univ. coms.; guest investigator Argonne Cancer Res. Hosp., U. Chgo. Med. Sch., 1960; guest investigator, vis. prof. dept. pharmacology Christie Hosp. and Holt Radium Inst., U. Manchester (Eng.) Med. Sch., 1963-64; guest investigator, vis. prof. Pharmacology Inst., U. Freiburg (W.Ger.) Med. Sch., 1963-64; guest investigator, vis. prof. to other instns.; mem. numerous nat. coms. and directorships to profl. orgns. and instns.; chmn. session on regulation of Erythropoisis, 2d Internat. Congress Pathol. Physiology, Prague, 1975; chmn. session on hematopharmacology 6th Internat. Pharmacol. Congress, Helsinki, 1975; chmn. fall meeting Am. Soc. Pharmacology and Exptl. Therapeutics, New Orleans, 1976; chmn. Symposium on the Kidney and Erythropoiesis, 16th Internat. Congress of Hematology, Kyoto, Japan, 1976; chmn. symposium Internat. Congress Hematology, Budapest, Hungary, 1982; cons. and lectr. in field; lectr. numerous symposia, workshops and profl. confs. throughout the world. Served to lt. USNR, 1943-46. Recipient Purkinje medal Czech Med. Soc., 1975; Golden Sovereign award U. Louisville Med. Sch., 1976; USPHS fellow in pharmacology U. Louisville Med. Sch., 1956-58; USPHS career devel. award, 1960-65. Mem. Am. Soc. Pharmacology and Exptl. Therapeutics, Soc. Exptl. Biology and Medicine, Am. Soc. Nephrology, Am. Soc. Hematology, Assn. Med. Sch. Pharmacology, AAAS, Internat. Soc. Nephrology, AAUP, N.Y. Acad. Scis., Kidney Found. La. (med. adv. bd. 1977—), Am. Fedn. Clin. Research, Sigma Xi. Editor: Kidney Hormones, Vol. I, 1971, Vol. II, 1977, Vol. III, 1986; Renal Pharmacology, 1971; co-editor: Erythropoiesis, 1975; cons. editor N.Y. Acad. Sci., Erythropoietin, 1968; mem. editorial rev. bd. Blood, 1969—, Jour. Lab. Clinical Medicine, 1967—, Sci., 1969—; Soc. Exptl. Biol. Medicine, 1971—; Yugoslavica Physiologica et Pharmacologica Acta, 1979; co-editor; Monograph on Internat. Conf. on Erythropoiesis, Tokyo, 1975; contbr. chpts. to books and encys., articles to profl. jours.; patentee potent anti-inflammatory agt., radio immunoassay for Erythropoietin. Home: 4025 Pin Oak Ave New Orleans LA 70114 Office: 1430 Tulane Ave New Orleans LA 70112

FISHER, JIMMIE LOU, state official. Treas. State of Ark., Little Rock. Office: State Treas 220 State Capitol Bldg Little Rock AR 72201*

FISHER, JOHN EDWIN, lawyer; b. Lincoln, Nebr., Feb. 2, 1941; s. Edwin Dorrington and Clarissa (Flansburg) F.; m. Thellie S. Fisher, Aug. 11, 1977; m. Beverly C. Diebold, Dec. 28, 1963; children—Mark Dorrington, Bradford D. B.A., Yale U., 1962, LL.B., 1965. Bar: Fla. 1965. Assoc. Akerman Senterfitt & Eidson, Orlando, Fla., 1965-69, ptnr., 1969-83; ptnr. Fisher, Rushmer, Werrenrath, Keiner, Wack & Dickson, P.A., 1984—. Mem. ABA, Fla. Bar Assn., (chmn. trial lawyers sect. 1977-78), Orange County Bar Assn. (exec. council 1982-85, v.p. 1985-86), Fla. Def. Lawyers Assn. (pres. 1978-79), Fedn. Ins. Counsel, Fla. Bar Found. Office: PO Box 712 Orlando FL 32802

FISHER, JOHN RICHARD, construction company executive; b. Columbus, Ohio, Dec. 28, 1924; s. Don Alfred and Katherine Buchanan (Galigher) F.; m. Kitson Overmyer, Oct. 2, 1946; children—Scott Owen, Lani Kitson. B.S., U.S. Naval Acad., 1946; B.S. in C.E., Rensselaer Poly. Inst., 1950, M.S. in C.E., 1950; A.M.P. Harvard U., 1971. Registered profl. Engr., S.C. Commd. ensign U.S. Navy, 1946, advanced through grades to rear adm., 1972; comdr. Pacific div. Naval Facilities Engring. Command, 1973-77; ret., 1977; v.p. Raymond Internat. Inc., Houston, 1977-81, sr. v.p., 1981-83, exec. v.p., 1983—. Bd. dirs., pres. Community Hosp. Assn. Mid-Am., Columbus. Decorated D.S.M., Legion of Merit with Combat V. Fellow Soc. Am. Mil. Engrs.; mem. ASCE, Navy League U.S. (nat. dir.), Mil. Order Carabao, Sigma Xi, Tau Beta Pi. Clubs: Outrigger Canoe, Army-Navy Country. Home: 10615 E Arabian Park Dr Scottsdale AZ 85259 Office: 2801 S Post Oak Blvd Houston TX 77056

FISHER, JOSEPH OLAN, chemical company loss prevention engineer, consultant; b. Marshall, Tex., Jan. 22, 1925; s. Eli Franklin and Sadie (Terry) F.; m. Martha Caroline Frierson, Aug. 15, 1952; children—Martha Leigh, Phylis Frierson Fisher White. Student Centenary Coll., 1946-47; student La. State U., 1947-50, B.S. in Indsl. Engring., 1953. Profl. safety engr. Safety engr. Chemstrand Corp., Pensacola, Fla., 1953-67; sr. safety engr. Monsanto Co., Luling, La., 1967—; organizer, chmn. St. Charles Indsl. Mut. Aid System, Luling, 1968-82; mem. exec. com. Nat. Safety Council, Fertilizer and Agrl. Chems. Sect., 1969-85, gen. chmn., 1980-81; cons. Bordon Co., Pensacola, 1965, City of Gulf Breeze, Fla., 1964-66, Monsanto Co., St. Louis, 1968, Delta Services, Houma, La., 1971, Monsanto Co., Fayetteville, N.C., 1981. Contbr. articles to profl. publs. and confs.; co-chmn. Intermountain Fertilizer and Agrl. Chems. Safety and Health Schs., 1983, 85. Pres. PTA, Gulf Breeze, 1959, 60, 62. Citizens for Better Edn., Gulf Breeze, 1965-67; mem. Fla. State PTA, 1961-62; advisor Jr. Achievement, Pensacola, 1964-67, organizer, advisor, Hahnville, La., 1968-75. Served with USN, 1942-46, PTO, with USNR, 1950-51, Korea. Mem. Am. Soc. Safety Engrs. (co-organizer Tri-Parishes chpt. 1983-84), Epsilon Pi Tau, Delta Sigma Phi. Republican. Episcopalian. Avocations: golf; gardening; fishing; swimming; bicycling. Home and Office: 9 W Levert Dr Luling LA 70070

FISHER, KING, marine contracting co. exec.; b. Port Lavaca, Tex., Jan. 14, 1916; s. Charles Everett and Kittie (Moss) F.; student pub. schs., Port Lavaca; m. Jewel Tanner, Aug. 13, 1937; children—Ann Fisher Boyd, Linda Fisher LaQuay. Pres. King Fisher Marine Service, Inc., Port Lavaca, 1941—; corp. sec. Fisher Channel & Dock Co., Port Lavaca, 1954—; dir. First Nat. Bank of Corpus Christi, First Nat. Bank of Port Lavaca. Bd. dirs. Indsl. Found. of South. Mem. Tex. Mid-Coast Water Devel. Assn., Port Lavaca C. of C. Home: Hillcrest Chocolate Bay Port Lavaca TX 77979 Office: PO Box 183 Port Lavaca TX 77979

FISHER, PATRICIA HAWKINS, health physical education teacher; b. Portsmouth, Va., July 12, 1948; d. Jack Clinton and Beatrice (Hall) Hawkins; m. Tony Alfred Fisher, Jr., Sept. 6, 1969; children—Nichol Tonette, Shanetta Sherice. B.S., Norfolk State U., 1971; M.S., Old Dominion U., 1983. Comptroller asst. Norfolk Naval Shipyard, Portsmouth, Va., summers 1968, 69; health and phys. edn. tchr. John Yeates High Sch., Suffolk, Va., 1971-72, Harry Hunt Jr. High Sch., Portsmouth, 1973-76; health and phys. edn. specialist Parks and Recreation Dept., Portsmouth, summers 1976, 77, dance specialist, summer 1975; health and phys. edn. tchr. Cradock High Sch., Portsmouth, 1975—, girls' basketball coach, 1975-82. Sec. tennis assn. Cavalier Manor Forum, Portsmouth, 1980; mem. Portsmouth chpt. Jack and Jill Am. Inc., 1980—. Recipient Homeroom Tchr. of Yr. award Cradock High Sch., 1980-81; Dance Choreography awards Norfolk State U. (3). Mem. Portsmouth Edn. Assn., Va. Edn. Assn., NEA. Democrat. Presbyterian.

FISHER, ROBERT HENRY, yacht and ship broker and, builder; b. Boston, May 20, 1925; s. Milton and Mae (Gurson) F.; m. Peggy von Lindenmayer, Aug. 3, 1954. Student, M.I.T., 1948; B.S., Boston U., 1948. Vice pres., gen. mgr. Gloucester Marine Rys. Corp. (affiliate Rocky Neck Shipyards, Inc.), Mass., 1950-59; v.p. Breen-Fisher & Assos. (yacht brokers), Ft. Lauderdale, Fla., 1960-63; pres., chief exec. officer Northrop & Johnson, Inc. (yacht and ship brokers), Ft. Lauderdale, 1964—; marine cons. Bd. dirs., mem. marine adv. com. Fla. Atlantic U.; bd. dirs. Fla. Ocean Scis. Inst. Served with USMC, 1941-46. Mem. North Am. Yacht Racing Union, So. Yacht Brokers Assn. (pres. 1964-65, v.p. 1977-80). Clubs: Storm Trysail (fleet capt. So. sta.); Royal Norwegian Yacht (Oslo); Propellor, Gulfstream Sailing (Ft. Lauderdale); Boston Yacht (Marblehead, Mass.); Indian Harbor Yacht (Greenwich, Conn.). Home: 401 Idlewyld Dr Fort Lauderdale FL 33301 Office: 1300 SE 17th St Fort Lauderdale FL 33316

FISHER, STEPHEN LYNN, political science educator; b. Charleston, W.Va., Aug. 22, 1944; s. John Lynn and Mary Margaret (Pollitt) F.; m. Elizabeth Anne Campbell, June 1, 1968 (div. Apr. 1981). B.A., Wake Forest U., 1966; M.A., Tulane U., 1969; Ph.D., 1972. Instr. Tulane U., New Orleans, 1970-71; prof. polit. sci. Emory and Henry Coll., Emory, Va., 1971—, chmn. dept. polit. sci., 1972-77, 1979-80, 1982-85. Author: The Minor Parties of the Federal Republic of Germany: Toward a Comparative Theory of Minor Parties, 1974. Editor: A Landless People in a Rural Region: A Reader on Land Ownership and Property Taxation, 1979. Contbr. articles to profl. jours. Recipient Excellence in Teaching award Emory & Henry Coll. 1978, 80; James Still fellow 1981, 85. Mem. Am. Polit. Sci. Assn., So. Polit. Sci. Assn. Avocation: tennis. Home: PO Box BBB Emory VA 24327 Office: Emory and Henry Coll PO Box BBB Emory VA 24327

FISHER, WILLIAM MORRISON, mechanical engineer, scientist; b. Frankfort, Ind., June 18, 1940; s. Lawrence Levaun and Esther Alice (Morrison) F.; m. Solveig Greibesland; children—Ruth Ingrid, Elizabeth Morrison. B.S.M.E., Purdue U., 1962, M.S. in Engring., 1966; M.A. in Linguistics, U. Chgo., 1971, Ph.D. in Linguistics, 1973. Systems engr. R. R. Donnelley & Sons, Inc., Chgo., 1968-72, 75-80; research assoc. Central Inst. for the Deaf, St. Louis, 1972-75; mem. tech. staff Tex. Instruments, Inc., Dallas, 1980—. Contbr. articles to profl. jours. Mem. Linguistic Soc. Am., Assn. Computing Machinery, AIAA, Assn. Computational Linguistics, Sigma Xi. Club: Norwegian Soc. Tex. (Dallas). Lodge: Masons. Avocations: photography; music; model building. Home: 1920 Boulder Dr Plano TX 75023 Office: Tex Instruments Inc PO Box 226015 MS 238 Dallas TX 75266

FISHMAN, BARRY STUART, lawyer; b. Chgo., June 14, 1943; s. Jacob M. and Anita (Epstein) F.; B.A., U. Wis., 1965; J.D., DePaul U., 1968; m. Meredith Porte, Mar. 27, 1976; 1 child, Janna. Admitted to Ill. bar, 1968, Fla., Calif. bars, 1969; partner firm Fishman & Fishman, Chgo., 1968-72; counsel real estate fin. dept. Baird & Warner, Inc., Chgo., 1972-75; counsel firm Cohen & Angel, North Miami, Fla., 1976; gen. counsel Biscayne Fed. Savs. & Loan Assn., Miami, Fla., 1977-84; mem. firm, Eastern regional council Logs Nationwide Representation of Lenders and Wiener, Shapiro & Rose, North Miami Beach, Fla., 1984—; mem. firm Pallot, Poppell, Goodman & Slotnick, Miami, 1977—; dir. investment div. Cushman and Wakefield of Fla., 1978—. Mem. big gifts com. Greater Miami Jewish Fedn., 1977—; dir. Neighborhood Housing Services, Dade County, Fla., 1977—. Mem. Fla., Calif., Ill., Chgo., Dade County bar assns., Nat. Assn. Realtors, Real Estate Securities and Syndication Inst., Mortgage Bankers Assn. Jewish. Clubs: Turnberry Isle Yacht & Racquet, Aventura Country, Covennant. Home: 1025 NE 203d Ln Miami Beach FL 33179 Office: 1031 Ives Dairy Rd Miami FL 33629

FISHMAN, LAWRENCE MARTIN, endocrinologist, educator; b. Bklyn., Dec. 20, 1933; s. Matthew and Ruth Janet (Frank) F.; m. Suzanne Marian Rubenstein, Oct. 16, 1955; children—Matthew Edward, Charles Neal, Betsy Rachel, Andrew Klein. A.B. magna cum laude Harvard Coll., 1955; M.D., Harvard U., 1960. Diplomate Nat. Bd. Med. Examiners, Am. Bd. Internal Medicine, subsplty. in Endocrinology and Metabolism. Intern, Peter Bent Brigham Hosp., Boston, 1960-61, asst. resident in medicine, 1961-62; clin. assoc. endocrinology Nat. Cancer Inst., NIH, Bethesda, Md., 1962-65; fellow in diabetes and endocrinology Vanderbilt U. Sch. Medicine, Nashville, 1965-67; asst. prof. medicine U. Miami Sch. Medicine, 1967-72, assoc. prof., 1972-75, prof., 1975—; chief endorinology and metabolism sect. VA Med. Center, Miami, assoc. chief staff for research. Contbr. articles to profl. jours., chpts. to books. Fellow ACP; mem. Endocrine Soc. (chmn. postgrad. com.), Am. Fedn. Clin. Research, So. Soc. Clin. Investigation, Phi Beta Kappa, Sigma Xi, Alpha Omega Alpha. Office: VA Medical Center (111) 1201 NW 16th St Miami FL 33125

FISHMAN, MARK BRIAN, computer scientist, educator; b. Phila., May 17, 1951; s. Morton Louis and Hilda (Kaplan) F.; m. Alice Faber, Feb. 20, 1977. A.B. summa cum laude, Temple U., 1974; postgrad. Northwestern U., 1974-76; M.A., U. Tex., 1980. Bilingual tchr. Wilmette Pub. Schs., 1974; research assoc., programmer, asst. instr. U. Tex., Austin, 1976-80; instr. computer and info. scis. U. Fla., Gainesville, 1980-85; asst. prof. computer sci. Eckerd Coll., St. Petersburg, Fla., 1985—. U. Tex. univ. fellow, 1978-80; F.C. Austin scholar, 1975; Nat. Def. Fgn. Lang. fellow, 1974. Mem. Assn. Computing Machinery (Tchr. of Yr. award U. Fla. 1984), IEEE Computer Soc., Am. Assn. Artificial Intelligence, Assn. Computational Linguistics, Phi Beta Kappa, Phi Kappa Phi, Upsilon Pi Epsilon. Home: 6166 Lynn Lake Dr S Saint Petersburg FL 33712 Office: Eckerd Coll Computer Sci Dept Saint Petersburg FL 33733

FISHMAN, NOAH, geologist; b. Bklyn., Dec. 26, 1949; s. Marvin and Rose (Worshbo) F.; m. Sheryl Ann Hoffman, Nov. 24, 1973; children—Maya Jenny, Seth Aaron. Student CUNY Grad Ctr., 1969; B.Sc. in Geology, Queens Coll., 1975. Gen. mgr. Data Office Services, Jerusalem, Israel, 1971-72; geologist Zimco Ltd., Lusaka, Zambia, 1975-78; geologist, assoc. ptnr. Peppard & Assoc., Midland, Tex., 1978-80; ind. petroleum geologist, Midland, 1980—; gen. ptnr. TNO Ltd., Midland, 1984—; cons. VF Petroleum Inc., Midland, 1980-81, Govt. Israel, Tel Aviv, 1983—. Discoverer emerald, hydrocarbon deposits. Bd. dirs. Temple Beth El, Odessa, Tex., 1979—, pres., 1982, 85—; bd. dirs. Midland County Library, 1984—; pres. B'nai Brith, Midland, 1983—. Mem. Am. Assn. Petroleum Geologists, Permian Basin Geol. Soc., Mensa. Avocation: public speaking. Home: 3201 Marmon Dr Midland TX 79705 Office: TNO Ltd 605 W Ohio St Midland TX 79701

FISHMAN, RICHARD E., investment adviser; b. N.Y.C., July 31, 1933; s. Joseph and Lea (Penzel) F.; m. Harlene Birnbach, Mar. 20, 1955; children—Deborah, Andrew, Susan. B.B.A., CUNY, 1963; Cert. fin. planner Coll. Fin. Planning, 1979. With Merrill Lynch Pierce Fenner & Smith, Inc., N.Y.C. and Miami, 1967-80, v.p., Miami, 1979-80; v.p., fin. cons., Boca Raton, Fla., 1982—; v.p. Oppenheimer & Co., Inc., Miami, 1980-82. Pres., Friends of Boca Pops, 1983. Mem. Boca Raton Estate Planning Council (sec. 1984—), Fin. Analysts Fedn., Internat. Found. Health Welfare and Pension Funds, Fla. Govt. Fin. Officers Ass., Ednl. Conf. Health, Welfare and Pension Funds, Fla. Assn. Public Employee Pension Trustees. Clubs: Boca West, Boca Raton Hotel; Ocean Reef (Key Largo). Lodge: B'nai B'rith (pres. 1979-80, 84-85). Office: Merrill Lynch 6100 Glades Rd Boca Raton FL 33434

FISK, RAYMOND PAUL, marketing educator; b. Yuma, Ariz., Sept. 27, 1953; s. Elwin Lee and Verleen Thelma (Rafferty) F.; m. Marsha L. Hansberry, Oct. 16, 1976 (div. July 1979); m. Jamie Tucker, Aug. 8, 1980. B.S., Ariz. State U., 1976, M.B.A., 1977, Ph.D., 1980. Faculty assoc. Ariz. State U., Tempe, 1977-80; instr. Am. Grad. Sch. Internat. Mgmt., Glendale, Ariz., 1978; asst. prof. mktg. Okla. State U., Stillwater, 1980-84, assoc. prof. mktg., 1984—; mktg. analyst Nat. U. Teleconf. Network, 1983; dir mktg. Teleconf. Consortium, 1984-85. Dissertation research grantee dept. mktg. Ariz. State U., 1980; Dean's excellence fund summer grantee Okla. State U., 1981-82; research grantee Okla. State U./Asian Inst. Mgmt. Coop. Research Program, 1983; Summer Bus. Extension grantee Okla. State U., 1983. Mem. Am. Mktg. Assn. (doctoral consortium fellow 1979, editor mktg. newsletter 1984—), AAAS, Assn. Consumer Research, So. Mktg. Assn., Southwestern Mktg. Assn., Beta Gamma Sigma. Editor: (with Stephen W. Brown) Marketing Theory: Distinguished Contributions, 1984; (with Patriya S. Tansuhaj) Services Marketing: An Annotated Bibliography, 1985; cons. editor Mktg. News, 1981-82; editorial rev. bd. Jour. Health Care Mktg., 1983—; contbr. articles to profl. jours. Office: Coll Bus Adminstrn Okla State U Stillwater OK 74078

FITCH, HOWARD MERCER, lawyer, labor arbitrator; b. Jeffersonville, Ind., Dec. 23, 1909; s. J. Howard and Kate Orvis (Girdler) F.; B.M.E., U. Ky., 1930, M.S., 1936, M.E., 1939; J.D. magna cum laude, U. Louisville, 1942; m. Jane Rogers McCaw, Dec. 25, 1930; children—Catherine Mercer (Mrs. Charles E. Druitt), Jane Rogers (Mrs. Fitch Butterworth); m. Nancy Langley, Apr. 28, 1984. Bar: Ky. Engr., Western Electric Co., Kearny, N.J., 1930-32; joined Am. Air Filter Co., Inc., as sales engr., 1936, successively prodn. mgr., mgr. legal and patent dept., asst. to exec. v.p., became mgr. Herman Nelson div., 1953, dir. ops., 1958-63, v.p., 1954-72; admitted to Ky. bar, 1942, Ill. bar, 1954, also U.S. Patent Office, 1943; practiced in Louisville, 1942—; ptnr. Hunt & Fitch, 1945-58. Patentee in field. Mem. nat. com. Atlantic Union Com., mem. Louisville Labor-Mgmt. Council; bd. dirs. Louisville Urban League, Louisville Better Bus. Bur., Consumers Adv. Council. Registered profl. engr., Ky. Mem. ASME, ASHRAE, Am. Arbitration Assn. (panel arbitrators), Nat. Acad. Arbitrators, Am., Ky., Louisville bar assns., Hon. Order Ky. Cols., SAR, Louisville C. of C., Asso. Industries Quad Cities (past pres.), Am. Soc. Personnel Adminstrn., Louisville Personnel Assn. Episcopalian (vestryman). Clubs: Filson, Pendennis, Arts (pres. 1985-86). Lodge: Rotary. Home and Office: 1704 Spruce Ln Louisville KY 40207

FITE, JUDGE BROWN, realty company executive, real estate educator; b. Dallas County, Mar. 7, 1917; s. Judge Andrew and Leona (Moran) F.; m. Modenia Earle Dene Long, Apr. 12, 1941; children—Linda Kay Fite Myers, Jan Earle Fite Miller, Judge Carl, James Robert. Student Rosemont Sch., Dallas. Realtor, Dallas County, 1937—, present chmn. bd. Judge Fite Co., Inc., Dallas, owner, mgr. Judge Fite Land Assocs., Dallas, pres. Judge Fite Enterprises, Inc., Dallas; mem. faculty, lectr. real estate sales techniques at various schs., colls., univs. in Tex.; cons. Internat. Linguistics Ctr. Served with U.S. Army, World War II. Mem. Internat. Real Estate Fedn., Greater Dallas Bd. Realtors (dir. 1956-70, pres. 1968-69, named Realtor of Yr. 1970), Tex. Assn. Realtors (pres., dir.), Nat. Assn. Realtors (cert. farm and land mem., dir., mem. exec. com., (trustee Realtors Found. 1979-82, pres. Farm and Land Inst. 1981, named Tex. Farm and Land Broker of Yr. 1979, Farm and Land Realtor of Am. of Yr. 1984), Tex. and Southwestern Cattle Raisers Assn., Oak Cliff C. of C., Dallas C. of C., U.S. C. of C., Mensa, Intertel, Omega Tau Rho. Episcopalian. Home: 2044 Marydale St Dallas TX 75208 Office: Judge Fite Co Inc 2744 W Davis St Dallas TX 75211

FITSKO, MICHAEL JOHN, educational administrator; b. Leicester, Eng., June 4, 1945; came to U.S., 1954; s. John and Elsie May (Stacey) F.; m. Deborah Ann White, Apr. 12, 1980; children—Tiffany, Matthew. B.S., Ohio State U., 1967, M.A., 1973, postgrad., 1975-78. Tchr. English/sociology Springfield Ind. Sch. Dist. (Ohio), 1968-69, Worthington Ind. Sch. Dist. (Ohio), 1969-76; dean of students Worthington High Sch., 1976-79; prin. Homestead High Sch., S.W. Allen County Schs., Ft. Wayne, Ind., 1979-81, Jasper (Tex.) High Sch., 1981-83, Palestine (Tex.) High Sch., 1983—; weekly radio show Sta. KTXJ, Jasper, 1981-83; cons. CADRE, Vail, Colo., 1982, Ohio State U., 1979, Elyria Pub. Schs., 1973-74. Contbr. articles to profl. jours.; bi-weekly columnist "Principal Ponders", 1981-83. Coordinator Central Ohio Lung Assn., Columbus, 1978, Worthington Schs. Bicentennial Com., 1975-76; activities sponsor Ohio Hist. Soc., 1972. Mike Fitsko Day proclaimed by PTA Ft. Wayne, 1981; Martha Holden Jennings scholar, 1971-72, 68-69. Mem. Nat. Assn. Secondary Sch. Prins., Tex. Assn. Secondary Sch. Prins., Sabine-Neches Sch. Bds./Sch. Adminstrs. Assn., Collegial Assn. Advancement and Renewal of Educators, Palestine C. of C. (dir.), Phi Delta Kappa. Democrat. Baptist. Clubs: Rotary, Lions. Home: Route 8 Box 418 Palestine TX 75801 Office: Palestine Ind Sch Dist Loop 256 Palestine TX 75801

FITTON, GARVIN, lawyer; b. Harrison, Ark., Oct. 5, 1918; s. David Edwards and Lulu Vance (Garvin) F.; LL.B., U. Ark., 1941, J.D., 1969; m. Martha Ann Hamilton, Sept. 22, 1941; children—John, Thomas, Ann. Admitted to Ark. bar, 1941; practice in Little Rock, 1945-52; partner Fitton & Adams, Harrison, Ark., 1952-62, Fitton & Meadows, Harrison, 1962-76; dir. Harrison Security Bank, 1952-73, Commonwealth Theatres, Inc., Harrison, 1952-76. Pres. Harrison Sch. Bd., 1959, 64, sec., 1957, 67-69; mem. Ark. Bd. Law Examiners, 1971-73; civilian aide sec. of Army, 1981-82. Served to maj. U.S. Army, 1941-45, col. Res. ret. Mem. Am., Ark., Boone County bar assns., SAR. Democrat. Methodist (past trustee). Clubs: Masons, Shriners, Rotary. Home: 921 W Nicholson St Harrison AR 72601 Office: PO Box 249 Harrison AR 72602

FITTS, E. GRANT, insurance company executive. Chmn., chief exec. officer Gulf United Corp., Jacksonville, Fla. Office: Gulf United Corp Gulf Life Tower Jacksonville FL 32207*

FITZGERALD, DAVID PATRICK, advertising agency executive; b. Rockville Centre, N.Y., Feb. 19, 1949; s. John Francis and Katherine (Crosby) F. B.S., U. Dayton, 1971, M.B.A., 1973. Account exec. Tucker Wayne & Co., Atlanta, 1973-75; v.p. McDonald & Litte, Atlanta, 1975-80; exec. v.p. Green & Ptnrs., Atlanta, 1980—, gen. mgr., 1982—. Mem. Am. Advt. Fedn., High Mus. Art. Democrat. Roman Catholic. Club: Atlanta Advt. (bd. dirs. 1982-84). Home: 933 Beaver Brook Dr Atlanta GA 30318 Office: 100 Colony Square Suite 1700 Atlanta GA 30361

FITZGERALD, JOSEPH MICHAEL, JR., lawyer; b. Norfolk, Va., Oct. 9, 1943; s. Joseph Michael and Grace Elizabeth (Finegan) F.; B.S., Mt. St. Mary's Coll., 1965; J.D., Cath. U. Am., 1970; LL.M., U. Miami, 1973; m. Lynne Marie Leslie, May 3, 1974. Investigator, Retail Credit Co., Miami, Fla., 1965-66; intelligence analyst Def. Intelligence Agy., Washington, 1966-70; admitted to Fla. bar; mem. firm Wood, Lucksinger & Epstein, Miami, 1970—; dir. Alexander Hamilton Nat. Bank, 1979—; lectr. environ. law and health law at various symposiums and univs.; advisor to Office Environ. Affairs, Fla. Dept. State, 1971; spl. counsel Broward County Environ. Quality Control Bd., 1973-82; spl. prosecutor for environ. crimes Broward County, 1975-76. Trustee, Fla. Ind. Coll. and Univs. Found., 1977-81; trustee Seton Shrine Center, 1980-81, chmn., 1981; adv. bd. St. Francis Hosp., 1981—; trustee Inst. on Man and the Oceans, 1973-81, chmn., 1976-77; trustee Boystown of Fla., 1978-83, Kiwanis Youth Found., 1980-81. Recipient award of merit Dade County Bar Assn., 1975, 76. Mem. Am., Fla., Dade County bar assns., Am. Judicature Soc., Nat. Health Lawyers Assn., Cath. Lawyers Guild (pres. 1976-79), Serra Internat. (trustee 1979-80, pres. 1984—). Democrat. Roman Catholic. Clubs: Fla. Jaycees (dir. 1971-72), Kiwanis, Miami, Univ., Surf, Bath. Home: 12300 SW 68th Ave Miami FL 33156 Office: 1501 Venera Ave Miami FL 33146

FITZGERALD, KERRY P., lawyer; b. Washington, Jan. 25, 1942; s. John L. and Genevieve W. FitzGerald; m. Kathleen Purcell; children—Klaire, Kyran, Kristina, Kerry, Kathleen. Student Georgetown U.; B.B.A., So. Methodist U., 1963; LL.B., U. Tex., 1966. Bar: Tex. 1966, U.S. Dist. Ct. (no. dist.) Tex. 1967, U.S. Ct. Appeals (5th cir.) 1969, U.S. Ct. Appeals (11th cir.) 1981, U.S. Supreme Ct. 1976. With trial and appellate sects. Dallas County Dist. Attys. Office, 1966-69; practice, Dallas. Mem. ABA, State Bar Tex. (chmn. criminal law sect. 1982), Tex. Criminal Def. Lawyers Assn. (dir. 1977-79), Dallas Bar Assn. (chmn. criminal law sect. 1976), Dallas County Criminal Bar Assn., Assn. Trial Lawyers Am. Roman Catholic. Contbr. articles in field. Office: 3503 Fairmount St Dallas TX 75219

FITZGERALD, MICHAEL GARRETT, accountant, author; b. El Dorado, Ark., Dec. 14, 1950; s. Johnny Fotch and Tommye Mae (Murphy) F.; B.B.A., So. State Coll., Magnolia, Ark., 1972. Acct., Southwestern Electric Power Co., Shreveport, La., 1972—; works include: Universal Pictures—A Panoramic History in Words Pictures and Filmographies, 1977; American Movies—The Forties, vol. I, 1940-44, 1980, vol. II, 1945-49, 1981. Democrat. Baptist. Home: 1310 Harold Ellen St El Dorado AR 71730 Office: 428 Travis St Shreveport LA 71104

FITZ GERALD-BUSH, FRANK SHEPARD, historian, poet; b. Hialeah, Fla., Oct. 11, 1925; s. Frank Shepard and Lady Irene (Coburg-FitzGerald) Bush; A.B., U. Miami (Fla.), 1953, M.A., 1964. Instr. Ransom Sch., Coconut Grove, Fla., 1957-58, St. Johns Country Day Sch., Orange Park, Fla., 1959-61; instr. in history Homestead AFB Extension, Fla. State U., 1961-64; reference librarian, curator Floridiana, John F. Kennedy Meml. Library, Hialeah, 1966-71; historian City of Opa-locka (Fla.), 1975—; dir. South Fla. Archaeol. Museum, 1975; instr. Vivian Laramore Rader Poetry Group, 1973—; author: (poetry) Native Treasure, 1943, Sonnets In Search of Sequence, 1968, Remembered Spring, 1974; Memories of a Golden Land, 1985; (history) A Dream of Araby: Glenn H. Curtiss and the Founding of Opa-locka, 1976; contbr. numerous articles, revs. and poems to profl. jours. in Gt. Britain, France, U.S., 1942—; trustee Friends of Opa-locka Library, 1976—; mem. bd. advisers South Fla. Poetry Inst., 1975. Served with RCAF, 1943-44, USMCR, 1948-51 Am. Field Service, 1944-45, USAF, 1951-55. Recipient Recognition award Laramore Rader Poetry Group, 1975, 76. Mem. Fla. Hist. Soc., Hist. Assn. So. Fla., Dade Heritage Trust, Irish Georgian Soc., County Kildare Archaeol. Soc. (life), Fla. Anthropol. Soc., RAF Assn. (life), Opa-locka C. of C. (asso.), S.R., SAR, Magna Charta Barons, English-Speaking Union, Viscayans, DAV (life). Author: Young Alfred: The Forgotten Prince, 1979. Home: 3030 NW 171st St Opa-locka FL 33056

FITZHARRIS, TIMOTHY P., scientist, corporation executive; b. N.Y.C., Oct. 31, 1944; s. Timothy P. and Mildred M. (Heim) F.; m. Linda L. Hummel, Nov. 4, 1945; children—Jeffrey Scott, Kelly Anne. B.S., SUNY-Potsdam, 1966; M.S., SUNY-Albany, 1969, Ph.D., 1971; postgrad. (postdoctoral fellow), U. Colo., 1971-72. Asst. prof. dept. anatomy Med. U. S.C., Charleston, 1972-77, assoc. prof., 1977-83, prof., 1983-84; assoc. dir. sci. and clin. affairs Litton Bionetics, Charleston, 1984—, dir. clin. affairs, 1985—; dir. research and devel. Organon Teknika Corp., Charleston, 1985—; affiliate marine scientist S.C. Wildlife & Marine Research Ctr., Charleston, 1973—; condr. workshops/seminars in field; established investigator Am. Heart Assn., 1980-84. Trustee Moultrie Sch. Dist. #2, 1980-84; bd. dirs. S.C. Heart Assn., 1983—; co-chmn. fund drive Charleston chpt. S.C. Heart Assn., 1982-83. NIH fellow, 1969; N.Y. State Regents scholar, 1962-66; NSF summer fellow, 1967, postdoctoral fellow, 1971; NIH grantee, 1974-77; Am. Heart grantee, 1979-82, 82-84; vis. exchange scientist Nat. Acad. Scis., Prague, Czechoslovakia, 1980. Mem. S.C. Electron Microscopy Soc. (pres.), S.E. Electron Microscopy Soc. (pres.), Am. Soc. Cell Biology, Soc. Devel. Biology, Am. Assn. Anatomists, Sigma Xi. Club: Snee Farm Country. Contbr. articles to profl. jours. Home: 1021 Planters Curve Mount Pleasant SC 29464 Office: Organon Teknika Corp 2020 Bridgeview Dr Charleston SC 29405

FITZ-HUGH, SUSAN HARRISON, state official; b. Charlottesville, Va., Dec. 21, 1943; d. William Wright and Janet (Phillips) Harrison; m. Glassell Slaughter Fitz-Hugh, Jr., May 11, 1963; children—Glassell Slaughter, III, Meredith Harrison. Student Salem Coll., 1961-63. Kindergarten tchr. Baptist Day Care Ctr., Martinsville, Va., 1973-77; com. clerk Va. Senate, Richmond, 1979-82; exec. sec. Va. Bd. Elections, Richmond, 1983—. Mem. Nat. Assn. Secs. State (assoc.). Episcopalian. Home: 3805 Sulgrave Rd Richmond VA 23221 Office: State Bd Elections 101 Ninth St Office Bldg Richmond VA 23219

FITZHUGH, WILLIAM AYLETT, beer company executive; b. Erie, Pa., Jan. 5, 1926; s. William Bullitt and Sue Kathrene (McKnight) F.; m. Marguery Anne Ingalls, Aug. 1, 1951; children—Kathy, Bullitt, Patricia, Elizabeth, Anne. B.B.A., U. Tex., 1949. With Central Beverage, Inc., Dallas, 1949—, now chmn. bd. Served with U.S. Army. Club: Brook Hollow Golf. Office: Central Beverage Inc 2601 Perth St Dallas TX 75230

FITZPATRICK, HUGH, physician; b. Richmond, Va., Dec. 6, 1921; s. Hugh and Ruby Amoretta (Gilliam) F.; B.S., Hampden Sydney Coll., 1943; M.D., Med. Coll. Va., 1950; m. Rachel Anne Lewis, Dec. 21, 1948; children—Hugh E., Stuart L., Julia L., Anne L. Intern, U.S. Naval Hosp., Phila., 1950-51; practice medicine, Asheboro, N.C., 1951-70; emergency room physician High Point (N.C.) Meml. Hosp., 1970-83, chief emergency dept. staff, 1973-78; health dir. Randolph County, N.C., part-time 1970-78; pres. Triad Emergency Assos.; med. adv. Rampon Products, 1976—; mem. staff High Point Meml. Hosp.; cons. Randolph County Health Dept., 1978—; county coroner, 1954-58; pres. Vanguard Emergicare Assocs., 1983—; dir. Jung Products Inc., Cin. Pres. bd. Randolph County Tb. and Health Assn., 1956-58; mem. Asheboro City Sch. Bd., 1962-68; bd. dirs. Randolph Center for Exceptional Children, United Fund; mem. Asheboro-Randolph County Vocat. Adv. Council, 1975-84. Served to lt. (j.g.) USNR, 1943-46, 50-51. Mem. N.C., Randolph County (pres. 1957) med. socs., Am. Acad. Gen. Practice, Am. Coll. Emergency Physicians (dir. N.C. chpt. 1974-80), Theta Chi, Alpha Kappa Kappa. Presbyterian (ruling elder 1957). Democrat. Lodge: Kiwanis (bd. dirs. 1956-58). Home: 117 S Main St Asheboro NC 27203

FITZPATRICK, JAMES RALPH, investment company executive; b. Auburn, Ala., Oct. 5, 1952; s. James Ward and Ruth (Horn) F.; m. Judith Nicoletti, Sept. 24, 1976 (div. Apr. 1982); m. 2d, Deborah Ann Fitzpatrick, Aug. 14, 1982; 1 dau., Allison Vogtle. B.S., Auburn U., 1974. Vice-pres. MICS, Inc., Auburn, Ala., 1972-74; pres. Inland Metals, Inc., Charlotte, N.C., 1975-78, Continental Commodities, Inc., Charlotte, 1978-83; chmn., chief exec. officer Metalex Corp., Charlotte, 1983—, also dir.; ptnr. Fitzpatrick Assocs., Charlotte, 1982—, Continental Properties, Charlotte, 1982—, Fitzpatrick Properties, Charlotte, 1982—; micro-computer cons.; dir. Quality Ventures, Inc., Charlotte. Campaign dir. T.D. Little for State Rep., Auburn, Ala., 1973; mem. bldg. fund Good Shepherd Presbyterian Ch., Charlotte, N.C., 1983. Mem. Nat. Assn. Recycling Industries, Inst. Scrap Iron and Steel, Phi Gamma Delta. Republican. Presbyterian. Office: Metalex Corp PO Box 13008 Charlotte NC 28226

FITZPATRICK, JOHN J., clergyman; b. Trenton, Ont., Can., Oct. 12, 1918; ed. Propaganda Fide Coll. (Italy), Our Lady of Angels Sem. (U.S.) Ordained priest Roman Catholic ch., 1942; named titular bishop of Cenae and aux. of Miami (Fla.), 1968, consecrated, 1968; named bishop of Brownsville, 1971, installed, 1971. Address: PO Box 2279 Brownsville TX 78522

FITZPATRICK, J(OSEPH) F(ERRIS), JR., scientist, educator, consultant; b. New Orleans, Mar. 8, 1932; s. Joseph Ferris and Ethel Beatrice (Sanders) F.; m. Sarah Lynn Ebersole (div.); children—Joseph Ferris, Kathleen Anne, Eileen Elizabeth, Daniel Thomas; m. 2d, Barbara Ann Laning. B.S., Tulane U., 1959, M.S., 1961; Ph.D., U. Va., 1964. Instr. zoology U. Ky., Lexington, 1964; asst. prof. zoology Miss. State U., State College, 1964-69; assoc. prof. biology Randolph-Macon Woman's Coll., Lynchburg, Va., 1969-73; assoc. prof. biology U. South Ala., Mobile, 1973-78, prof., 1978—. Served with U.S. Army, 1952-54. NSF grantee; Philip Francis DuPont fellow, Henry Clay Marchant fellow, 1961-64. Fellow AAAS, Internat. Assn. Astacology (founder), Crustacean Soc. (founder), Phi Sigma, Sigma Xi. Author: How to Know the Freshwater Crustacea, 1983; contbr. articles to sci. jours. Office: U S Ala Dept Biol Scis Mobile AL 36688

FITZPATRICK, PETER B., lawyer; b. New Orleans, June 30, 1945; s. William W. and Frances (Westfeldt) F.; m. Anne Wallace, Aug. 24, 1968; children—Bryan W.W., Lydia W.C. B.A., Princeton U., 1968; M.A., Stanford U., 1969; J.D., U. Va., 1973; postgrad. St. Antony's Coll., 1976. Bar: Va. 1974, N.Y. 1977, D.C. 1978. Assoc. Winthrop, Stimson, Putnam & Roberts, N.Y.C., 1976-80; asst. counsel Newsweek Inc., N.Y.C., 1980-83; assoc. Hunton & Williams, Norfolk, Va., 1983—. Trustee St. Antony's Coll Trust, Pembroke Coll. Found., Oxford; bd. advisors Va. Ctr. World Trade, Norfolk, 1984; communications com. Campaign U. Va. Mem. ABA, D.C. Bar Assn., Va. Bar Assn., Assn. Bar City N.Y. (com. human rights). Home: 1220 Brandon Ave Norfolk VA 23507 Office: Hunton & Williams 101 St Paul's Blvd Norfolk VA

FITZSIMMONS, FRANKIE JUNE, nursing administrator; b. Jasper, Ga., June 1, 1935; d. John Cyrus and Nacie Allifair (Simmons) Darnell; m. John William Fitzsimmons, Sept. 19, 1960 (div. 1980); children—Nacie Susan, Julie Amber, Beverly Elizabeth. Student North Ga. Coll., Dahlonega, 1953-55; B.S. in Nursing, Emory U., Atlanta, 1958. Dir. nursing Tate Community Clinic (Ga.), 1958-60, 1962-63, 65-66; charge nurse Bay Meml. Hosp., Panama City, Fla., 1961-62; charge nurse Southwestern Gen. Hosp., El Paso, Tex., 1963-64; supr. obstetrics Williamburg Community Hosp. (Va.), 1964-65; supr. obstetrics Rose DeLima Hosp., Henderson, Nev., 1966-67; charge nurse Providence Hosp., Anchorage, 1968-72; dir. nursing Pickens Gen. Nursing Ctr., Jasper, Ga., 1973—; cons. Pickens County Home Health Adv. Bd., Jasper, 1983—. Sec., treas. Pickens Primary Care Authority Bd., Jasper, 1980-83. Mem. Ga. Nursing Adminstrs., Ga. Assn. Nurses in Long Term Care (chmn. pub. relations 1980-82). Baptist. Lodge: Eastern Star. Home: 221 Indian Forest Rd Jasper GA 30143 Office: Pickens Gen Nursing Ctr 1319 Church St Jasper GA 30143

FITZSIMMONS, LOWELL COTTON, professional basketball coach; b. Hannibal, Mo., Oct. 7, 1931; s. Clancy and Zelda Curry (Gibbs) F.; m. Jo Ann D'Andrea, Feb. 2, 1978; 1 child, Gary. B.S., Midwestern U., 1956, M.A., 1957. Coach Moberly Jr. Coll., 1957-67; tchr., coach Kans. State U., 1967-70; profl. NBA coach, Phoenix, 1970-72, Atlanta, 1972-76, Buffalo, 1977-78, Kansas City, 1978-84, San Antonio, 1984—. Address: Hemisfair Arena San Antonio Spurs PO Box 530 San Antonio TX*

FITZWATER, ROBERT LEE, II, human resources administrator; b. Coral Gables, Fla., July 7, 1950; s. Robert Lee and Susan (Marcum) F.; m. Catherine Elizabeth Anderson, Dec. 18, 1971; children—William Ryan, Camille Marie, Sarah Jane. B.S. in Mgmt., Park Coll., Parkville, Mo., 1981. Staff x-ray technologist Miami Valley Hosp., Dayton, Ohio, 1974-76, coordinator materials mgmt., personnel adminstrn., 1978-82; coordinator Def. Electronics Supply, Civilian Health Service, Dayton, 1975-76; asst. adminstr. human resources Highlands Gen. Hosp., Sebring, Fla., 1982—, mem. speakers bur., 1982—. Served with U.S. Army, 1971-74. Mem. bd. advisers Montgomery County Vocat. Schs. (Ohio), 1978-82. Recipient cert. appreciation Montgomery County Vocat. Schs., 1981, Outstanding Merit award USAF, 1975. Mem. Am. Soc. Personnel Adminstrs., Fla. Hosp. Assn. for Personnel Adminstrs., Highlands County Personnel Assn., Am. Compensation Assn., Fla. Soccer Coaches Assn., U.S. Soccer Assn., Am. Legion, Lake Placid Jaycees. Democrat. Roman Catholic. Lodge: Lions (v.p.) (Sebring). Office: PO Drawer 2066 Sebring FL 33870

FITZWATER, SIDNEY ALLEN, judge; b. Olney, Md., Sept. 22, 1953; s. Ivan Welton and Kathleen Elizabeth (Schroeder) F.; B.A., Baylor U., 1975, J.D., 1976; m. Nancy Jane Ware, Aug. 6, 1976; children—John Welton, Joseph Leon, James Sidney. Admitted to Tex. bar, 1977, U.S. Supreme Ct. bar, 1981; assoc. Vinson & Elkins, Houston, 1976-78, Rain Harrell Emery Young & Doke, Dallas, 1978-82; judge 298th Jud. Dist. Tex., Dallas, 1982—. Bd. dirs. Dallas Services for Visually Impaired Children, 1980-85; mem. exec. com. Dallas County Republican Party, 1981-82; state del. Tex. Rep. Conv., 1980, 82, 84; candidate Dallas City Council, 1981; mem. exec. com. Tex. Young Reps., 1981-82; bd. dirs. Dallas County Rep. Men's Club, 1984-85. Recipient Baylor U. award of merit, 1983, also named Outstanding Young Alumnus, 1985. Fellow Tex. Bar Found.; mem. Nat. Conf. State Trial Judges, State Bar Tex., ABA, Dallas Bar Assn., Nat. Order of Barristers, Phi Alpha Delta, Omicron Delta Kappa. Co-author: School Law Simplified, 1980. Office: Dallas County Courthouse Dallas TX 75202

FIX, JOHN, engineer, land developer, contractor; b. Pitts., June 16, 1934; s. John William and Virginia F.; B.S. in Mech. Engring., U. Miami, 1960; postgrad. U. Fla., 196i-62, U. Calif., 1969-71; m. Beverly Berry, Apr. 9, 1960; children—Tracey Ayn, John William. Aerospace engr., regional mgr. Pitney Bowes Controls, Laguna Niguel, Calif., 1960-69, regional mgr., 1969-72; land developer, profl. engr., gen. contractor, Stuart, Fla., 1972—, cons. govt. agys.; chmn. Contractors Bd. Martin County (Fla.); apptd. mem. Constrn. Industry Licensing Bd. Fla.; apptd. mem. Fla. Solar Research Center Adv. Bd.; dir. Barnett Bank of Martin County Pres., Tri-County Rehab. Ctr.; mem. Martin County Airport Adv. Bd., Martin County Film and TV Bd.; mem. State Park Blue Ribbon Com., Martin County Beach Acquisition Com.; chmn., chief exec. officer Fla. Engring. Devel. Corp.; mem. Martin County Water System Adv. Bd. Served with USMC, 1953-56. Recipient Yellow Feather award Martin County Press Club, 1983; Builder of Yr. award Treasure Coast Builders Assn., 1983. Mem. Nat. Soc. Engrs., Nat. Assn. Home Builders (nat. dir., 1978-79, state dir., 1978-81, local dir., 1977-81), Fla. Homebuilders Assn., Fla. Engring. Soc., C. of C. (dir.). Patentee aerospace field; contbr. articles to profl. publs. Office: PO Drawer 2800 Stuart FL 33495

FIX, RONALD EDWARD, civil engineer; b. Dallas, Dec. 27, 1941; s. Robert Eugene and Ida Fay (McGuire) F.; B.S. in Civil Engring., Tex. A. and M. U., 1963; postgrad. U. Tex., 1963-65. Engring. asst. Tex. Water Rights Commn., 1963-65; process engr. EIMCO Corp., Dallas, 1965-68; owner Ronald E. Fix & Assos., Tyler, Tex., 1969—. Registered profl. engr., Tex. Mem. Am., Tex. (chmn. publs. and registration com.) socs. profl. engrs., Am. Water Works Assn., Tex. Water Pollution Control Fedn., ASCE (dir. Tex. sect., state chmn. C & I sect., past pres. E. Tex. chpt.), Assn. Former Students Tex. A. and M. U. Mem. Christian Ch. Clubs: South Tyler Rotary; Smith County A. and M.; Aggie; Diamond Century. Home: Box 1015 Tyler TX 75701 Office: 120 S Broadway Suite 209 Tyler TX 75702

FLAGG, WALLY, educational administrator, psychology educator; b. Worcester, Mass., July 29, 1947; s. Wallace Dexter and Margaret (Heywood) F. B.S., Springfield Coll., 1969, M.Ed., 1972. Asst. Dir. Keystone Jr. Coll., LaPlume, Pa., 1972-74; employment counselor Dept. of Labor, Springfield, Mass., 1974-78; admissions rep. Tampa Coll., Fla., 1978-80; asst. basketball coach Tampa Cath. High Sch., 1980-82; asst. dir. St. Leo Coll.-MacDill Ctr., Tampa, 1981—, psychology instr., 1981—. Served with U.S. Army, 1969-71; Vietnam. Mem. Am. Assn. Counseling Devel., Am. Coll. Personnel Assn. Club: Bayshore Runners (Tampa). Avocations: running, gardening. Office: St Leo Coll MacDill Ctr PO Box 6063 MacDill AFB FL 33608

FLAHERTY, DAVID THOMAS, JR., lawyer; b. Boston, June 17, 1953; s. David Thomas and Nancy Ann F. B.S., U. N.C., 1974, J.D., 1978. Bar: Mass. 1979, N.C. 1979, U.S. Dist. Ct. (we. dist.) N.C. 1979, U.S. Dist. Ct. (cen. dist.) N.C. 1981, U.S. Ct. Appeals (4th cir.) 1981, U.S. Tax Ct. 1982. Legal intern U.S. Dept. Commerce, Washington, 1975; law clk. Turner, Enochs, et al, Greensboro, N.C., 1976; assoc. Wilson & Palmer, Lenoir, N.C., 1979-81, Ted West, P.A., Lenoir, 1981-82; ptnr. Robbins, Flaherty & Lackey, Lenoir, 1982—. Mem. Caldwell County Council on Alcoholism, 1982, Caldwell County Friends, Inc., 1984, Caldwell County Republican Men's Club, 1983, Caldwell County Young Republicans, Lenoir, 1979. Mem. N.C. Bar Assn., N.C. Acad. Trial Lawyers, Assn. Trial Laywers Am., ABA, Catawba Valley Estate Planning Council, Lenoir Jaycees (Jaybird 1980). Methodist. Home: 228 Pennton Ave SW Lenoir NC 28645 Office: Robbins Flaherty & Lackey 204 Main St Lenoir NC 28645

FLAIG, NENO PEARL, college dean; b. Arkadelphia, Ark., Jan. 25, 1921; d. Edgar and Pearl (Adams) Nowlin; m. Edward G. Flaig, Mar. 25, 1944. B.A., Ouachita Bapt. U., 1943; M.Ed., Henderson State U., 1965. Counselor for women Ouachita Bapt. U., Arkadelphia, 1964-66, dean of women, 1966—. Mem. Nat. Assn. for Women Deans, Adminstrs., and Counselors, Am. Council on Edn. Nat. Identification Program for the Advancement of Women in Higher Edn. Adminstrn., Southwest Assn. of Student Personnel Adminstrn., Nat. Assn. of Student Personnel Adminstrs. Office: Ouachita Baptist U Arkadelphia AR 71923

FLAKES, LARRY JOSEPH, civil engineer; b. Birmingham, Ala., Jan. 27, 1947; s. John W. and Lurlene (Patton) F. B.S. in Civil Engring., Howard U., 1969. Registered profl. engr., Ga. Ala. Structural mass properties engr. Lockheed Ga. Co., Marietta, Ga., 1969-70; traffic engr. I, City of Atlanta, 1970-71; contract engr. Ala. Power Co., Birmingham, 1972-74; tax engr. So. Ry. Co., Atlanta, 1976-81; project engr. Norfolk & So. Corp., 1981—; pres. Flakes Engring. Co., cons. engrs., 1983—. Recipient Presdl. Merit award, 1982; Howard U. scholar, 1964-65. Mem. ASCE (Student Newsletter award 1967), NAACP, Am. Ry. Engrs. Assn. Baptist. Home: PO Box 87522 College Park GA 30337 Office: 99 Spring St Room 103 Atlanta GA 30303

FLAMMER, HAROLD RICHARD, chemical company executive; b. Bronxville, N.Y., Sept. 19, 1942; s. Harold and Patricia (Bevier) F.; m. Julia K. Martin, Jan. 12, 1964 (div. 1970); children—Lisa M., Kristen B.; m. 2d, Suzanne C. McCord, Apr. 17, 1982. B.S. in Chemistry, Dickinson Coll., 1964; P.M.D., Harvard U., 1978. With Conoco, Inc., Houston, 1964-84, product mgr., 1969-71, dir. market devel., 1971-73, bus. area mgr. surfactant chems., 1973-76, gen. mgr. polyvinylchloride, 1976-84; v.p. Vista Polymers, 1984—. Mem. Conoco Polit. Action Com., 1980-82; mgr. East Harlem (N.Y.) Little League, 1972-75. Mem. Vinyl Inst. (sec. 1983-85, vice chmn. 1986—, dir. 1983—), Mfg. Chemists Assn., Soc. Plastics Industries. Republican. Episcopalian. Clubs: Houston Yacht, Valley Lodge. Contbr. articles to profl. publs.

FLANDERS, FRANKLIN BENJAMIN, banker; b. Gretna, La., July 16, 1942; s. Robert Seal and Louise Vivian (Ferguson) F.; m. Judith Arlene Riche, Oct. 17, 1964; children—Franklin Benjamin, Christopher M., Bernadette L. Student U. Southwestern La., Lafayette, 1961-63. Adjuster, United Credit, New Orleans, 1965-66; mgr. Gulfco Fin., Bunkie, La., 1967-69; credit mgr. Devillier Furniture, Cottonport, La., 1969-70; asst. v.p., sec. treas. Central La. Bank & Trust, Marksville, 1970—; dir. Am. Inst. Banking, 1980-82; sec. treas. Avoyelles Agr. Credit Corp., Marksville, 1983—. Sec.-treas. Cen-Pac, Marksville, 1983. Named Outstanding Citizen, Woodmen of the World, 1983; Hon. Chpt. Farmer, Future Farmers Am., 1983. Mem. Avoyelles Parish Bankers Assn. (sec. treas. 1980—). Roman Catholic. Lodge: KC (dist. dept. 1979-81). Home: Route 1 Box 486 Hessmer LA 71341 Office: Central La Bank & Trust PO Box 5 Marksville LA 71351

FLANDERS, HENRY JACKSON, JR., religion educator; b. Malvern, Ark., Oct. 2, 1921; s. Henry Jackson and Mae (Hargis) F.; B.A., Baylor U., 1943; B.D., So. Bapt. Theol. Sem., 1948, Ph.D., 1950; postgrad. U. Tenn., 1943, Union Theol. Sem., 1963, Hebrew Union Coll., 1948; m. Tommie Lou Pardew, Apr. 19, 1944; children—Janet, Jack III. Ordained to ministry Bapt. Ch., 1940; prof., chmn. dept. religion, chaplain Furman U., 1950-62; pastor First Bapt. Ch., Waco, Tex., 1962-69; prof. religion Baylor U., Waco, 1969—, chmn. dept., 1980—. Chaplain, Tex. Rangers Commn. Trustee Baylor U., Hillcrest Bapt. Hosp.; chmn. bd. Golden Gate Bapt. Theol. Sem.; mem. exec. bd. Bapt. Gen. Conv. Tex.; pres. bd. dirs. Econ. Opportunity Advancement Corp.; bd. dirs. Heart of Tex. Red Cross; adv. Christian Life Commn. Served with USAAF, 1943-45. Decorated Air medal with clusters. Mem. Baylor Alumni Assn. (pres.), Waco Bapt. Ministerial Assn. (pres.), Assn. Bapt. Profs. Religion (pres.), Soc. Bibl. Lit., Soc. for Religion and Ethics, Council on Religion and Law, AAUP (chpt. pres. 1971-72), Am. Acad. Religion. Clubs: Masons, Rotary (dir.); Western S.C. Torch (Greenville, S.C.). Author: People of the Covenant, 1963; Introduction to the Bible, 1973; also numerous articles. Home: 3820 Chateau St Waco TX 76710

FLANNAGAN, WILLIAM HAMILTON, hospital executive; b. Trevillians, Va., Sept. 14, 1920; s. Henry Alexander and Hanna Mae (Hamilton) F.; B.S., Hampden-Sydney Coll., 1940, LL.D. (hon.), 1976; m. Kathryn Elizabeth Middleton, June 22, 1942; children—William Hamilton, Patricia Lyle Flannagan Sarver and John Michael (twins). Asst. librarian Library of Congress, Washington, 1940-43; dir. hosp. services McGuire VA Hosp., Richmond, Va., 1946-49; adminstr. Bur. Hosps. and Nursing Home Services, Va. Dept. Health, Richmond, 1949-51, Franklin Meml. Hosp., Rocky Mount, Va., 1951-54; pres. Roanoke (Va.) Meml. Hosps., 1954—; preceptor Va. Commonwealth U., Med. Coll. Va. and other schs. health care adminstrn.; hosp. cons.; chmn. adv. bd. so. div. brs. Colonial Am. Nat. Bank, 1975-76; pres. Roanoke Hosp. Found., Commonwealth Health Services Co., Roanoke Meml. Services Corp., RMH Air, Ltd., Syndicated Collection Agy., Ltd., Emerald Property Mgmt., Inc., Burrell Health Care Ctr. Corp., Health East, Inc., Healthcare Interiors, Inc., Roanoke Wellness and Fitness Ctr., Sterile Concepts, Inc. Elder, Presbyn. Ch., 1951-54; active Va. Mental Health Study Commn., 1961-64; mem. Gov.'s Adv. Hosp. Council, 1955-59, 61-65; vice chmn. Gov.'s Med. Facilities Commn., 1969-73; pres. Roanoke Area Hosp. Council, 1965-66; bd. dirs. Hosp. Bur., Va. Regional Med. Programs, Va. Council on Health and Med. Care, Blue Cross of S.W. Va., Colonial Am. Nat. Bank, Roanoke Valley Regional Health Services Planning Council, YMCA; past trustee Franklin Meml. Hosp., Burrell Meml. Hosp., Roanoke. Served to 1st lt., Med. Adminstrn. Corps, AUS, 1943-46. Named One of Ten Most Prominent Men in Roanoke Area, 1977, One of A Dozen Who Make A Difference, 1982. Hon. alumni Va. Commonwealth U., Med. Coll. Va., Sch. Hosp. Adminstrn. Fellow Am. Coll. Hosp. Adminstrs. (regent), Royal Soc. Health; mem. Am., Va. (dir., past pres.), Roanoke (pres., trustee), Carolinas-Virginias (past pres.) hosp. assns., Southeastern Hosp. Conf. (dir., past chmn.), Hosp. Fin. Mgmt. Assn., Am. Soc. Hosp. Public Relations Dirs., Va. Soc. Hosp. Public Relations Dirs., Joint Underwriters Assn. State Corp. Commn. (hosp. adv. com.), Kappa Alpha, Omicron Delta Kappa. Clubs: Shenandoah, Roanoke Country, Jefferson (Roanoke); Downtown (Richmond); Contbr. articles in health field to profl. pubs. Chili Cookoff champion of Va., 1980. Home: 2532 S Jefferson St Roanoke VA 24014 Office: Belleview at Jefferson St PO Box 13367 Roanoke VA 24033

FLANNERY, VIRGIL LANCE, safety consultant; b. Prestonsburg, Ky., Oct. 20, 1947; s. Virgil and Della Edith (Newsome) F.; m. Anna Marie Flannery, Mar. 16, 1984. B.S., U. Ky., 1975. Cert. safety profl. Mgr., instr. Parker Shelton

Karate, Fort Wayne, Ind., 1972-73; sr. loss control rep. Am. Mutual Ins. Co., Louisville, 1973-77; sr. loss control rep. Meridian Ins. Co., Louisville, 1977-78; instr. U. Ky., Louisville, 1983—; sr. loss control rep. Alexsis Risk Mgmt. Services Inc., Louisville, 1978—. Mem. Am. Indsl. Hygiene Assn. (dir. 1984-86), Am. Soc. Safety Engrs. (pres. 1982-83, Safety Profl. of Yr. region VII 1984-85, Louisville chpt. 1983-84), Cert. Safety Profls. Am. (mem. bd. 1985—). Republican. Lodge: Order Blue Goose. Avocations: karate; volleyball; guitar; plants; family. Home: 2613 Drayton Dr Louisville KY 40205 Office: Alexsis Risk Mgmt Services Inc 29th Floor First Nat Tower Louisville KY 40202

FLATOW, JEFFREY HOWARD, psychiatrist; b. N.Y.C., May 18, 1943; s. Jack and Mary (Rubin) F.; m. Felicia Madelaine Spondrey, Sept. 20, 1964 (div. Feb. 1973); 1 son, Kevin J.; m. 2d, Pamela Ellen Schilifka, Sept. 25, 1977. B.A., Bkyn. Coll., 1964; M.D., U. Louvain, 1970. Intern, McGill U., Montreal, Que., Can., 1970-71; psychiatrist Nassau County Med. Ctr., East Meadow, N.Y., 1971-74; unit chief day hosp. L.I. Jewish-Hillside Med. Ctr., 1974-75; chief liaison psychiatry and dir. day hosp. St. Vincent's Med. Ctr., S.I., N.Y., 1975-76; cons. Pinellas County Mental Health Services, St. Petersburg, Fla., 1977-78, Manatee County Mental Health Services, Bradenton, Fla., 1977-78; practice medicine specializing in adolescent and adult psychiatry, N.Y.C., 1974-76, St. Petersburg, 1978—; cons. Pinellas County Sch. Bd., Fla. Health and Rehab. Services, Gulfcoast Jewish Family Services, Pinellas Assn. Retarded Children; supr. for sr. med. students. Pres. Bay Mus. Arts Co., St. Petersburg. Recipient AMA Physicians' Recognition cert., 1981—. Mem. Am. Psychiat. Assn., Pinellas County Psychiat. Assn. (chmn. community psychiatry), Fla. Med. Assn., Pinellas County Med. Soc., Am. Assn. Adolescent Psychiatrists. Democrat. Jewish. Office: St Anthonys Profl Office Bldg St 1201 5th Ave N Suite 508 Saint Petersburg FL 33705

FLAWN, PETER TYRRELL, businessman, emeritus university president, educator; b. Miami, Fla., Feb. 17, 1926; s. Stanley Charles and Laura Carolyn (Rotz) F.; m. Priscilla Bernice Pond, June 28, 1946; children—Tyrrell Flawn Hill, Laura. B.A., Oberlin Coll., 1947; M.S. (Cooksey fellow), Yale U., 1948; Ph.D. (Binney fellow), Yale U., 1951. Jr. geologist mineral deposits br. U.S. Geol. Survey, 1948; research scientist, geologist Bur. Econ. Geology, U. Tex., Austin, 1949-60; dir. Bur. Econ. Geology, prof. geology, 1960-70, dir. div. natural resources and environment, prof. geol. scis. and pub. affairs, 1970-72, v.p. acad. affairs, 1970-72, exec. v.p., 1972-73; pres. U. Tex.-San Antonio, 1973-77; Leonidas T. Barrow prof. mineral resources U. Tex.-Austin, 1978-85; pres. univ. U. Tex., 1979-85, pres., emeritus, 1985; vice chmn. Rust Group, Inc., Austin, 1986—; dir. Tenneco, Inc., Harte-Hanks Communications, Radian, Tex. Commerce Bank, Gearhart Industries; mem. Tex. Interagy. Council on Natural Resources and Environment, 1969-73; served various coms. Nat. Acad. Scis.-NCR; mem. Nat. Sci. Bd., 1980—. Author: Basement Rocks of Texas and Southeast New Mexico, 1956, The Ouachita System, 1962, Mineral Resources, 1966, Environmental Geology in Landuse Planning Resource Management and Conservation, 1970; contbr. articles to profl. jours. Vice chmn. edn. com. Tex. Constl. Revision Commn.; Bd. govs., adv. trustee S.W. Found. for Research and Edn., 1973-78, bd. govs., 1974-78; trustee Southwest Research Inst., 1973—, Tex. Mil. Inst., 1974-77, St. David's Hosp., 1981—; bd. dirs. S.W. Tex. Ednl. TV Council, 1973-78. Served with USAAF, 1944-45. Recipient Wilbur Cross medal Yale U., 1985. Mem. Nat. Acad. Engring., Am. Inst. Mining, Metall. and Petroleum Engrs., Assn. Profl. Geol. Scientists, Am. Assn. Petroleum Geologists, Assn. Am. State Geologists (hon. mem.; pres. 1969-70), Soc. Econ. Geologists (trustee 1971-76), Sociedad Geologica Mexicana, Am. Geol. Inst. (dir. 1967-70), Geol. Soc. Am. (councilor 1972-77, v.p. 1977, pres. 1978), Conf. Bd., Greater San Antonio C. of C. (dir. 1975-78). Clubs: Headliners, Metropolitan, Tarry House (Austin); Rotary; Cosmos (Washington). Home: 3718 Bridle Path Austin TX 78703 Office: Rust Group Inc One Am Ctr Suite 3200 600 Congress St Austin TX 78701

FLECK, MARIANN BERNICE, health scientist; b. San Francisco, June 19, 1922; d. Erwin and Grace B. (Fisher) Kahl; m. Jennings McDaniel, June 1946; m. Jack Donald Fleck, Mar. 28, 1980; children—Gary, Eugene. B.Vocat. Edn., Calif. State U., 1965, B.A., 1965, M.A., 1968; Ph.D., Laurence U., 1975. Prof. life sci. div., adminstr. Fullerton Coll., Calif., 1960-75; profl. adminstr. Cypress Coll., Calif., 1975-80, prof. emeritus, 1980—; dir., owner Profl. Services Assoc. Counseling, Santa Ana, Calif., 1977-80, Hypnosis Ctr., La Mirada, Calif., 1975-80; producer Dr. Mariann Health Program, Sta. KJON Boonville, Ark., 1980-85; dir. Jack Fleck Golf and Health Acad., Magazine, Ark., 1980—. cons., lectr. in field. Mem. Am. Assn. Counseling and Devel., Assn. Univ. Radiologic Technologists (sec. 1973-75, pres. 1975-76), Am. Guild Hypnotists, Am. Assn. Guidance and Devel, Epsilon Sigma Alpha. Republican. Presbyterian. Club: Total Fitness Internat. Home: Route 1 Box 15A Magazine AR 72943 Office: H&P Internat Magazine AR 72943

FLEER, JACK DAVID, political science educator; b. Washington, Mo., Sept. 21, 1937; s. Daniel William and Viola (Scherman) F.; A.B., Okla. Bapt. U., 1959; M.S., Fla. State U., 1961; Ph.D., U. N.C.-Chapel Hill, 1965. Research asst. Inst. Govtl. Research, Fla. State U., 1959-60; research asst. Inst. for Research in Social Sci., U. N.C.-Chapel Hill, 1960-61, part-time instr. dept. polit. sci., 1961-64, research asst. Inst. Govt., summers 1962, 63; asst. prof. Wake Forest U., 1964-69, chmn. dept. politics, 1969-77, 85—, assoc. prof., 1969-79, prof., 1979—, chmn. dept. politics, 1985—; intern congl. staff, Washington, summer 1961; cons. 5th Congl. Dist. Campaign, 1966, 68; dir. police-community relations tng. program City of Winston-Salem, 1968, lectr., 1969-70. Cons., Project Community, Winston-Salem/Forsyth County Sch. System, 1968-70; mem. Citizens Adv. Com., Gov.'s Conf. on Libraries and Info. Services, 1978; mem. N.C. Govtl. Evaluation Commn., 1978-81; bd. dirs. N.C. Boys' State, N.C. dept. Am. Legion, Wake Forest U., 1965—. Mem. Am. Polit. Sci. Assn., So. Polit. Sci. Assn., N.C. Polit. Sci. Assn. Democrat. Episcopalian. Author: North Carolina Politics: An Introduction, 1968; contbr. articles to profl. jours., book revs., book notes to profl. jours. Home: 100 Aaron Ln Winston-Salem NC 27106 Office: Wake Forest U Dept Politics Box 7568 Reynolds Sta Winston-Salem NC 27109

FLEISCHAKER, MARTIN, mental health counselor, educator; b. Savannah, Ga., June 25, 1941; s. Jack and Eva (Nathan) F.; m. Laurice Koudsi, Dec. 17, 1967; children—Lara, Natasha, Thomas. A.A., Armstrong Coll., 1959-61; B.S. in Edn., M.Ed., Ga. So. Coll., 1964; postgrad. Johns Hopkins U., 1971-73, Towson State U., 1972-73, Southeastern Mo. U., 1980-81. Instr. math. Edison Twp., N.J., 1965-68; asst. prof. Embry Riddle U., Daytona Beach, Fla., 1968-71; instr. math. Anne Arundel Co., Annapolis, Md., 1971-79; sch. psychologist Counseling Services, Saint Genevieve, Mo., 1979-82; dir., therapist Ministry for Christ, Mental Health Counseling Services, Ladson, S.C., 1982—; cons. testing Charleston Bd. Edn., S.C., 1983-84. Chmn. Saint Genevieve Mental Health Bd. Trustees, 1981-82. Mem. Am. Assn. Counseling and Devel., Am. Mental Health Counselors Assn., S.C. Assn. Counseling and Devel., S.C. Mental Health Counselors Assn. Republican. Lutheran. Avocations: Christian ministry; creative writing; guitar; tennis; gardening. Office: Ministry for Christ Mental Health Counseling Services 215 Elliot Dr Ladson SC 29456

FLEISCHER, BARBARA JANE, organizational psychologist, consultant, researcher; b. N.Y.C., July 10, 1948; d. Francis Joseph and Dolores (Pietri) F. A.B. cum laude, St. Louis U., 1970, M.S., 1975, Ph.D., 1978. Lic. in indsl. and organizational psychology, La. Evaluation cons. Change in Liberal Edn., Washington, 1974-75; evaluation coordinator St. Louis CETA office, 1975-76; dir. research services U. So. Miss. Sch. Nursing, Hattiesburg, 1976-78; organizational cons. S. Miss. Home Health, Hattiesburg, 1979-80; staff psychologist Wellness Inst., New Orleans, 1981-84; dir. tng. Associated Catholic Charities, New Orleans, 1980—; cons. New Orleans, 1980—. Contbr. articles to profl. jours. Grantee Nat. Ret. Tchrs. Assn.-Am. Assn. Ret. Persons Andrus Found., 1977, German Protestant Orphan Asylum, 1984. Mem. Am. Psychol. Assn., Am. Assn. Tng. Dirs. Roman Catholic. Avocations: music, church service, tennis. Office: Associated Catholic Charities 1231 Prytania St New Orleans LA 70130

FLEISCHER, PETER, marine geologist; b. Coburg, Bavaria, Ger., Sept. 10, 1941; came to U.S., 1948, naturalized, 1962; s. Heinrich Rudolf and Else Antonie (Kellersch) F.; m. Virginia Ann Thomas, Dec. 27, 1972. B.A. cum laude, U. Minn., 1963; Ph.D., U. S. Calif., 1970. Asst. prof. Old Dominion U., Norfolk, Va., 1971-78; geologist Naval Ocean Research and Devel. Activity, Nat. Space Tech. Labs., Miss., 1978—. Contbr. articles to profl. jours. NSF fellow Duke U. Marine Lab., 1970. Mem. Geol. Soc. Am., Am. Assn. Petroleum Geologists, Soc. Econ. Paleontologists and Mineralogists, Internat. Assn. Sedimentologists, Miss. Acad. Scis. Home: 113 Palm Ave Pass Christian MS 39571 Office: NORDA Code 361 NSTL MS 39529

FLEISCHMAN, SOL JOSEPH, retired television broadcasting executive; b. Hawkinsville, Ga., Sept. 12, 1910; s. Joseph Simon and Alma (Rockman) F.; Hon. degree U. Tampa (Fla.), 1954; m. Helen Elsberry; children—Sol Joseph, Martin Paul. Profl. musician, Tampa, 1926-32; announcer, control operator WDAE Radio, Tampa, 1928, chief announcer, 1950-57; sports dir., outdoor editor Tampa Daily Times, 1946-57; asst. to gen. mgr. L.S. Mitchell, 1956-57; sports dir., public relations dir. WTVT-TV, Tampa, 1957-75. Mem. Fla. Gov.'s Conservation Com., 1969-72, Tampa Mayor's Bd. Public Recreation, Public Relations and Conv. Centers, 1968—; trustee Land's For You, Inc. Served with USCG, 1942-46. Named Tampa's Outstanding Citizen, Tampa Sports Club, 1969-70; recipient Disting. Service award U. Tampa, 1975; Merit award Fla. Boxing Assn.; Fightin' Gator award U. Fla., 1975, Achievement Gold medal U. Tampa; named to U. Fla. Sports Hall of Fame, Tampa Sports Hall of Fame; Fla.'s Outstanding Conservationist, Fla. Wildlife Fedn., also other awards. Mem. Outdoor Writers Am., Fla. Outdoor Writers Assn., Fla. League Outdoor Writers, Fla. Lunkers Assn., Fla. Sportscasters Assn. (dir. 1970-73), Internat. Fishing Hall of Fame, Greater Tampa C. of C., Manatee C. of C., Sigma Delta Chi. Clubs: Palma Ceia Golf and Country, Sword and Shield, Tampa University Quarterback, Touchdown (Tampa); Santa Rosa Golf; Palma Sola Golf (Bradenton); Highlands Country (N.C.); Bradenton Country, Sun City North and South Golf, Caloosa Golf and Country. Lodges: Masons, Shriners, Rotary. Home: 1508 Cloister Dr Sun City Center FL 33570 also 801 Fern St Anna Maria Island FL 33501

FLEMENBAUM, ABRAHAM, psychiatrist, educator; b. Cali, Colombia, Sept. 17, 1942; came to U.S., 1966; s. Moises R. and Ana (Safirstein) F.; m. Lily Gorenstein, Apr. 3, 1965; children—Arieh M., Joel N., Judith S. Pre-med. degree magna cum laude, U. Andes, 1960; M.D., U. Del Valle, 1964; M.S., U. Minn., 1973; Ph.D., 1974. Diplomate Am. Bd. Psychiatry. Intern, Mt. Sinai-Chgo. Med. Sch., 1966-67; resident in psychiatry U. Minn., 1967-70, research fellow in psychiatry, 1970-73; asst. to assoc. prof. Tex. Tech U. Sch. Medicine, Lubbock, 1973-78; prof. La. State U., Shreveport, 1978-79; clin prof. psychiatry U. Miami, 1979—; practice medicine specializing in psychiatry and psychopharmacology, Hallandale, Fla., 1980—; mem. staff Bd. dirs. Hineni, Jewish Family Services. Recipient Alfredo Correa Henao Basic Scis. award U. Del Valle, 1962; William C. Menninger award Central Neuropsychiat. Assn., 1970. Mem. Am. Psychiat. Assn. (past pres. West Tex. chpt.), Soc. Biol. Psychiatry, South Fla. Psychiat. Soc. Lodge: B'nai B'rith. Contbr. numerous articles to profl. jours. Office: 2500 E Hallandale B Blvd Suite 508 Hallandale FL 33009

FLEMIG, ERNEST R., aeronautical engineer; b. Jamaica, N.Y., Apr. 26, 1937; s. Ernest August and Isabelle Elinore (Schmidt) F.; m. Claudia Ann Stevens, June 14, 1958; children—Steven Brian, David Gerard, Cristy Ann. B.S. in Aero. Engring., MIT, 1958. Various positions Morton Thiokol, Inc., Huntsville, Ala., 1961—, dir., 1982—. Author tech. papers. Served to capt. USAF, 1958-61. Fellow AIAA (assoc.); mem. Assn. U.S. Army, Huntsville C. of C. Roman Catholic. Club: Exchange (past pres. Ala.). Avocations: Flying; fishing. Home: 818 Baylor Dr Huntsville AL 35802 Office: Morton Thiokol Corp Redstone Arsenal Huntsville AL 35807

FLEMING, CHRISTOPHER PAUL, ophthalmologist; b. Cleve., July 3, 1948; s. Matthew John and Mary Catherine (Smith) F.; m. Leslie Courtney, May 7, 1977; children—Abigail Courtney, Christopher Paul, Jr., Katherine Courtney. B.S., Loras Coll., 1971; M.D., Case Western Res. U., 1977. Diplomate Am. Bd. Ophthalmology. Intern Los Angeles County-U. So. Calif. Med. Ctr., Los Angeles, 1977-78; resident Jules Stein Eye Inst., UCLA, 1978-81; practice medicine specializing in ophthalmology Lumberton Eye Clinic, P.A., Lumberton, N.C., 1981—. Sec., treas. Robeson County Med. Soc., Lumberton, 1984-85. Mem. AMA, N.C. Soc. Ophthalmology, Am. Acad. Ophthalmology. Republican. Roman Catholic. Lodge: Rotary. Avocations: scuba diving; snow skiing. Home: 202 Oxford Dr Lumberton NC 28358 Office: 202 W 28th St Lumberton NC 28358

FLEMING, DOUGLAS RILEY, journalist, publisher, public affairs consultant; b. Fairmont, W.Va., Jan. 25, 1922; s. Douglas Riley and Sarilda Artemes (Short) F.; m. Irene Stachowicz, Oct. 28, 1944 (dec. 1979). B.S., Georgetown U., 1953. Commd. ensign U.S. Navy, 1944, advanced through ranks to comdr.; naval aviator; chief protocol NATO, Naples, 1962-67, ret. 1967; with Francis I. DuPont & Co., Investment Banking, Rome, 1968-70; exec. editor, gen. mgr. Daily American, Rome, 1970-75; pres. Stampa Generale, S.R.L., Pubs., Naples, Italy, 1975—; mng. dir. Italo-Am. Assn., Naples; dir. Am. Studies Ctr., Naples, 1975-80; pres. Gen. Press Services, Washington, 1979—; dir. Va. Winery Coop., Inc., Culpeper, 1985—; proprietor, operator Campicello Vineyards, Madison, Va., 1982—. Active Nat. Trust Hist. Preservation, Smithsonian Assocs., Assn. Naval Aviation. Mem. Associazione Della Stampa Estera in Italia, Georgetown U. Alumni Assn. (pres. Italy 1972-80), Am. C. of C. in Italy, Retired Officers Assn., Navy League of U.S., Nat. Press Club, Vinifera Wine Growers Assn., Jeffersonian Wine Grape Growers Soc., Va. Vineyards Assn. Clubs: Naval and Mil., Royal Aero (London); Circolo Canottieri (Naples); N.Y. Athletic. Home: 515 S Fairfax St Alexandria VA 22314 also Campicello Box 589 Madison VA 22727

FLEMING, FREDERICK JOSEPH, library director; b. Chickamauga, Ga., July 18, 1941; s. Elston and Margaret (Sims) F. B.A., U. Chattanooga, 1963, postgrad., 1965; postgrad. U. N.C., 1964; M.L.S., U. Tenn.-Knoxville, 1984. Tchr., Walker County Bd. Edn., Rossville, Ga., 1963-72; critic-reviewer Nat. Sch. Yearbook Assn., Memphis, 1968-73; writer Catoosa County News, Ringgold, Ga., 1973-74; head librarian Rossville Pub. Library (Ga.), 1974-84; dir. Cherokee Regional Library, 1985—. Contbr. articles to profl. jours. Poll officer City of Rossville, 1981-83; vol. press sec. 7th Dist. congl. election, Rossville, 1983. R.J. Reynolds fellow, 1964; NDEA fellow, 1965; named Exchangite of Yr., Exchange Club, 1980, Disting. Sec. award, 1978. Mem. Chattanooga Area Library Assn. (pres. 1980-81), Southeastern Library Assn. (state membership chmn. 1981-82), ALA, Walker County Hist. Soc., Tenn. Library Assn., Ga. Library Assn., Am. Guild Organists, John Ross House Assn., Phi Alpha Theta. Episcopalian. Clubs: Chattanooga Music, Exchange (pres. 1981-82). Home: 153 Mission Ridge Rd Rossville GA 30741 Office: Cherokee Regional Library 305 S Duke St PO Box 707 LaFayette GA 30728

FLEMING, PARTEE AUGUSTUS, furniture company executive, author; b. Memphis, Nov. 4, 1916; s. Partee Augustus and Frances (Green) F.; A.B. cum laude, Vanderbilt U., 1939; grad. war course U.S. Coast Guard Acad., 1942; m. Marie Anita Tiblier, June 24, 1943; children—Geraldine Frances, James Partee, Anita Marie. Reporter, Nashville Tennessean, 1938-41; editor Inglewood (Calif.) Citizen, 1941-42; founder, 1947, owner, pres., chmn. bd. Fleming Fine Furniture, Memphis, 1947-80, owner, chmn. bd., 1980—. Democratic candidate for mayor of Memphis, 1959. Served to lt. (j.g.) USCGR, 1942-47. Recipient Man of Yr. award Memphis Gavel Club, 1974. Mem. Tenn. Home Furnishings Assn., Memphis Home Furnishings Assn. (pres. 1976-77, dir. 1970—), Irish Soc. Memphis (pres. 1970-71, 79-80), VFW (comdr. Memphis and Shelby County 1973-74, dir. 1955—, Jim Poole award 1974), Ret. Officers Assn., Am. Legion (vice comdr. Memphis 1970-71, chaplain 1971-75), Alpha Tau Omega (Thomas Arkle Clark award 1939). Episcopalian. Club: Moose. Author: God's Book of Remembrance, 1965; God and the Devil, 1965; Is God's Bible the Greatest Murder Mystery Ever Written?, 1980. Home: 6763 Wild Berry Ln Memphis TN 38119 Office: 3560 Mendenhall S Memphis TN 38118

FLETCHER, ALLAN STUART, energy investment company executive; b. Springfield, Mass., June 22, 1926; s. Samuel and Ann (Bradsnyder) F.; B.S. cum laude, Am. Internat. Coll., 1957. Cryptographic analyst U.S. State Dept., 1948-52; bus. trainee Gen. Electric Corp., Bridgeport, Conn., 1957-58; acct. Cities Service Co., N.Y.C., 1958-64, asst. mgr., mgr., N.Y.C., Bartlesville, Okla., 1964-73, asst. controller, Houston, 1973-81, sr. adv. acctg. ops. Europe/Africa/Mid-East region, Houston, 1981-83, asst. controller various corp. and fgn. subs., 1973-83; controller Merrill Lynch Energy Investments, Inc., Houston, 1983—. Vol. instr. English in Action, N.Y.C., 1962-66. Served with AUS, 1952-54; Korea. Decorated Army Commendation medal. Mem. Petroleum Accts Soc. (dir. Houston 1976-79), Nat. Field Archery Assn., Tex. Field Archery Assn., Buffalo Field Archery Club. Congregationalist. Home: 201G Avondale St Houston TX 77006 Office: 100 Waugh Dr Suite 200 Houston TX 77007

FLETCHER, JAMES NORRICE, retail executive; b. Tipton County, Tenn., June 18, 1928; s. Harold Clarence and Ivie Myrtle (Turnage) F.; student Lambuth Coll., 1946-48; m. Georgia LaVerne Lamb, May 27, 1951; children—Cheryl Christine, Victoria Jane (twins) Julia Ellen, Amy Elizabeth. Trainee, Sears Roebuck & Co., Paducah, Ky., 1948-54, mdse. mgr., Fayetteville, N.C., 1954-59, zone mdse. mgr., 1959-65, mgr., Orlando, Fla., 1965-66, mgr., Roanoke, Va., 1965-69, mgr. Pembroke Mall, Virginia Beach, Va., 1969—; dir. United Va. Bank. Chmn. bd. trustees Bayside Hosp.; chmn. pastoral parish com. Haygood United Methodist Ch.; crusade chmn. Am. Cancer Soc., 1973; chmn. friends drive Va. Wesleyan Coll., 1974; chmn. Norfolk Met. br. Nat. Alliance Bus., 1971; mem. Virginia Beach Sch. Bd., 1981—, chmn., 1986—; bd. dirs. Four Cities United Way, Hampton Roads, Va., 1982—. Served with AUS, 1950-51. Recipient Boss of Yr. award Virginia Beach Jaycees, 1972, Virginia Beach br. Nat. Secs. Assn., 1971. Mem. Va. C. of C. (dir., pres. 1975). Republican. Lodges: Masons, Rotary. Office: 4588 Virginia Beach Blvd Virginia Beach VA 23462

FLETCHER, LEROY STEVENSON, engineering educator; b. San Antonio, Oct. 10, 1936; s. Robert Holton and Jennie Lee Fletcher; m. Nancy Louise McHenry, Aug. 14, 1966; children—Laura, Daniel. B.S., Tex. A&M U., 1958; M.S., Stanford U., 1963, Engr., 1964; Ph.D., Ariz. State U., 1968. Research scientist NASA-Ames Research Ctr., Moffett Field, Calif., 1958-62; instr., research assoc. Stanford U., 1962-64, Ariz. State U., 1964-68; mem. faculty Rutgers U., New Brunswick, N.J., 1968-75, U. Va., Charlottesville, 1975-80; prof. mech. engring. Tex. A&M U., College Station, 1980—, assoc. dean Coll. Engring., 1980—; assoc. dir. Tex. Engring. Expt. Sta., 1985—; bd. dirs. Accreditation Bd. for Engring. and Tech., 1983—. Author: Introduction to Engineering Including FORTRAN Programming, 1977; Aerodynamic Heating and Thermal Protection Systems, 1978; Heat Transfer and Thermal Control Systems, 1978; Introduction to Engineering Design with Graphics and Design Projects, 1980; Problems in Engineering Design Graphics, 1981; contbr. articles to profl. jours. Recipient Aerospace Edn. Achievement award Am. Soc. for Engring. Edn./AIAA, 1982. Fellow ASME (gov. 1983—, pres. 1985-86, Charles Russ Richards award 1982), AAAS, AIAA (dir. 1981-84, assoc. editor Jour. Energy 1979-83), Am. Soc. for Engring. Edn. (dir. 1974-80, George Westinghouse award 1981, Ralph Coates Roe award 1983, Donald E. Marlowe award 1986), Am. Astronautical Soc., Inst. Mech. Engring. London; mem. Sigma Xi, Tau Beta Pi, Pi Tau Sigma, Sigma Gamma Tau, Phi Kappa Phi. Office: Dept Mech Engring Tex A&M U 9007 Sandstone Dr College Station TX 77840

FLETCHER, MARION LOUISE, insurance agent, office administrator; b. Washington, Oct. 7, 1922; d. John Wilson and Susan Ida (Smith) Sparkman; m. Robert T. Graham, May 18, 1945 (div. 1951); children—Juanita, Robert T.; m. 2d, Beauford Burnell Fletcher, Feb. 22, 1952; 1 son, John Wayne. Student Columbia Tech. Art Inst., Washington, 1944; Lake-Sumter Community Coll., Leesburg, Fla., 1970—. Sr. stenographer pub. works dept. U.S. Navy Yard, Washington, 1941-44; interviewer Fla. State Unemployment Office, Leesburg, 1949-50; office mgr., gen. lines agt. Lassiter-Ware, Inc., Leesburg, 1950—. Mem. Lake-Sumter Ind. Ins. Agts., Ins. Women's Assn. Lake County (sec. 1979-80), Leesburg Art Assn. (Best of Show oil painting, hon. mention oil painting, 1974). Democrat. Baptist. Home: 706 Miller St Leesburg FL 32748 Office: Lassiter-Ware Inc 1317 Citizens Blvd Leesburg FL 32749

FLETCHER, (MARTHA) ANN MESSERSMITH, counselor, educator; b. Indpls., June 9, 1935; d. Lloyd Lowell and Fae Elizabeth (Houston) Messersmith; m. Lindsay Bruce Smith, Dec. 28, 1957 (div. 1974); children—Montgomery Bruce, Jean Elizabeth; m. 2d, Robert Rolph Fletcher, May 16, 1976; 1 dau., Nancy Roberta. B.A., DePauw U., 1956; M.Ed., U. Houston, 1967. Cert. tchr., Tex., Ind.; lic. counselor, Tex. Coordinator elem. phys. edn. programs Cities of Clarendon Hills and Hinsdale (Ill.), 1957-61; tchr., speech therapist Tex. Sch. for Cerebral Palsied, Galveston, 1961-64; developer, dir. social services Moody House, Galveston, 1962-67; missionary Global Missions Methodist Ch., LaPaz, Bolivia, 1968-74; coordinator, instr., trainer ednl. paraprofls. program Mountain View Coll., Dallas, 1974-82, counselor, 1982—. Mem. adv. bd. Dallas Community Coll. Ministry; bd. dirs. Highland Park United Meth. Ch. Mem. Tex. Educators Ednl. Paraprofls. (state dir. 1982-83), Tex. Jr. Coll. Tchrs. Assn., Council Exceptional Children. Contbr. articles to profl. jours. Home: 3513 Purdue St Dallas TX 75225 Office: 4849 W Illinois St Dallas TX 75211

FLETCHER, MARY ANN, immunologist, educator; b. Little Rock; d. William T. and Myrtle P. (Jernigan) Sharp; divorced; 1 son, William T. B.S., Tex. Tech. Coll., 1959; M.A., U. Tex., 1961; Ph.D., Baylor U., 1966. Asst. prof. Northwestern U., Evanston, Ill., 1968-69; adj. asst. prof. Ill. Inst. Tech., Chgo., 1970-71; asst. prof. U. Miami (Fla.) Sch. Medicine, 1972-75, assoc. prof., 1975-80, prof. medicine, microbiology and immunology, 1980—, dir. clin. immunology lab. NIH grantee, 1971-85. Mem. AAAS, Am. Assn. Immunologists, Am. Assn. Microbiologists, Soc. for Complex Carbohydrates, NOW. Democrat. Contbr. articles to sci. jours.; holder 2 patents.

FLETCHER, MARY JEANNE, mathematics educator; b. Louisville, Nov. 2, 1935; d. Edward Eugene and Della Ruth (Jones) Fisher; m. Ford Clayton Fletcher, June 18, 1966 (dec. 1976). B.A. summa cum laude, Ursuline Coll., 1958; M.A., U. Louisville, 1962. Cert. tchr., Ky. Tchr. Jefferson County Bd. Edn., Louisville, 1958-68; prof. Jefferson Community Coll., Louisville, 1968—, cognitive tchr., 1984—, cognitive tchr. trainer, 1984—; part-time tchr. U. Louisville, 1962-72, Spalding Coll., Louisville, 1966-67, Bellarmine Coll., Louisville, 1968-69, Ind. U.-New Albany, 1972-78. Author texts: Mathematics for Nurses, 1977; Geometry for Teachers, 1978; Mathematics for Elementary Teachers, 1978; Workbook for Basic Algebra, 1983. Recipient Great Tchr. award Jefferson Community Coll., 1971, Outstanding Tchr. award for adj. faculty Ind. U., 1972, 73, 74, Tchr. of Yr. award Westport High Sch., 1967, Cert. of Recognition for Scholarly Achievement in Math. dept. math. and astronomy, U. Ky., 1963. Mem. Ky. Math. Assn. for Two-Yr. Colls., Am. Math. Assn. for Two-Yr. Colls., Am. Math. Assn., Ky. Assn. Community Coll. Profs., Profl. Devel. Assn. Avocations: dancing, fishing. Home: 2324 Tyler Ln Louisville KY 40205 Office: Jefferson Community Coll 109 E Broadway Louisville KY 40202

FLETCHER, MINOS L., III, metal finishing company executive; b. Nashville, Mar. 21, 1923; s. Minos L. and Emma B. (Shwab) F.; A.B., Harvard U., 1945; m. Gayle S. Jones, 1982; children—Minos IV, Laura, Barry. Treas., So. Finishers Inc., 1954-58; v.p. Delta Plate Inc., Nashville, 1958-60, Master Plate Inc., Nashville, 1958-65; pres. Metal Plate, Inc., Nashville, 1965—. Mem. Nat. Assn. Metal Finishers (dir. 1979—, pres. 1986-87), Nashville C. of C. Republican. Clubs: Fly, Harvard of Nashville, Nashville Exchange, Belle Meade Country. Served to capt. USAAF, 1944-51. Home: 55 Revere Park Nashville TN 37205 Office: 7121 Cockrill Bend Rd Nashville TN 37209

FLETCHER, RILEY EUGENE, lawyer; b. Eddy, Tex., Nov. 29, 1912; s. Riley Jordan and Lelih (Gill) F.; B.A., Baylor U., 1950, J.D., 1950; m. Hattie Inez Blackwell, June 11, 1954. Admitted to Tex. bar, 1950; asst. county atty. Navarro County, Tex., 1951-52, county atty., 1952-54; pvt. practice law, Corsicana, Tex., 1955-56; asst. atty. gen. Tex., 1956-62, chief law enforcement div., atty. gen.'s dept., 1958-61; chief taxation div., atty. gen.'s dept., 1961-62; asst. gen. counsel Tex. Mcpl. League, 1962-63, gen. counsel, 1963-78, spl. counsel, 1978—. Mem. counsellors Baylor Law Sch. Lt. col. AUS ret. Recipient Disting. Service award Tex. Mcpl. Cts. Assn., 1980; Appreciation award Tex. City Attys. Assn., 1982, Assn. Mayors, Council Mems. and Commrs., 1984. Mem. Am., Travis County bar assns., State Bar Tex., Am. Judicature Soc., Res. Officers Assn. (chpt. pres. 1979-80), Assn. U.S. Army (chpt. pres. 1965-66), Am. Legion, Judge Advs. Assn., Austin World Affairs Council, Mil. Order World Wars. Baptist. Mason. K.P. Home: PO Box 1762 Austin TX 78767 Office: 1020 Southwest Tower TX 78701

FLETER, WALTER HENRY, business services company executive; b. Milw., Aug. 10, 1920; s. Gustav and Emma (Stenske) F.; B.S., Marquette U., 1947; postgrad. U. Chgo., 1948-49; children by former marriage—William, Marcia, Kurt, James. Office mgr. Inland Steel Co., Chgo., 1947-53; asst. to div. mgr. Milprint Co., Milw., 1953-54; underwriter bus. ins. Phoenix Mut. Life Ins. Co., Milw., 1954-58; mgmt. cons. A.L. Osmundson & Assos., Milw., 1957-59; sales rep. Curtis 1000 Inc., Smyrna, Ga., 1959-62, office mgr., 1962-65, sales mgr., 1965-71, mgr. sales promotion, 1971-74; mgr. mktg. Speedi-Print Co., subs., 1974-76, nat. research and devel. mgr. Curtis, 1976-82, nat. sales promotion mgr., 1982—; lectr. in field. Served to 1st. lt., U.S. Army, 1941-46. Mem. Sales/Mktg. Execs., Word Processing Assn., Alpha Kappa Psi (pres. Gamma Delta chpt. 1947-49). Lutheran. Home: 557 Little Rd SE Marietta GA 30067 Office: Curtis 1000 Inc 2100 River Edge Pkwy Atlanta GA 30328

FLICKINGER, WAYNE J., aerospace company executive; b. Fort Wayne, Ind., Nov. 27, 1923; s. Lawrence Edwin and Clura Viola (Powell) F.; m. Doris Ella Lockwood, Jan. 23, 1945; children—Andrea R., Maralyn F., Brenda J., Shirley A. Student Purdue U., 1954-56, Ariz. State U., 1958-60, Phoenix Coll., 1960; B.S. in E.E., Pacific Internat. Coll., 1966. Supr. Magnavox Co., Ft. Wayne, 1943-51; research and devel. technician Farnsworth Electronics, Ft. Wayne, 1951-57; group supr. Motorola, Inc., Scottsdale, Ariz., 1957-60; elec. design engr. Gen. Dynamics, San Diego, 1960-62; staff engr. Chrysler Space Div., New Orleans, 1962-67; reliability engr. Gen. Electric, Houston, 1967-70; engring. sect. head Control Data Corp., Omaha, 1970-71; quality mgr. A.M. Multigraphics Div., Mt. Prospect, Ill., 1971-78; quality supr. Siemens Allis Corp., New Orleans, 1978-80; sr. quality engr. Martin Marietta, New Orleans, 1980-82, dept. mgr., Orlando, Fla., 1984—; product assurance mgr. Litton Data Systems, New Orleans, 1982-84; cons. Delf Enterprises, Orlando. Mem. Ochsner Found., 1983—. Served to cpl. U.S. Army, 1943-46. Decorated Bronze Star. Mem. IEEE (sr.), Am. Soc. Quality Control (sr.); mem. Am. Soc. for Metals. Club: American Radio Relay League (Newington, Conn.). Home: 10025 Gramerly Ln Orlando FL 32821 Office: Martin Marietta 5600 Sand Lake Rd Orlando FL 32855

FLINCHBAUGH, PATRICE LYNNE, journalist, graphics firm executive; b. York, Pa., Aug. 1, 1957; d. Glenn Dale and Patricia Ann (Frey) Flinchbaugh. B.A. in Polit. Sci., Dickinson Coll., 1978; M.A. in Journalism, U. Mich., 1980. Intern, Modern Media Inst., St. Petersburg, Fla., 1979, Capitol Hill, Washington, 1976; graphics asst. Pa. Bar Assn., Harrisburg, Pa., 1978; teaching asst. U. Mich., Ann Arbor, 1980; reporter York Daily Record, Pa., 1980-81; polit. editor Tampa Tribune, Fla., 1981—; v.p. Glenn's Designs Inc. Researcher, trade jour. Columbia Journalism Rev., 1979; editor-in-chief internat. grad. sch. mag. Mich. Journalist, 1980. Club: Tampa Bay Press (program com. and charter mem.). Address: Tampa Tribune 202 Parker St Tampa FL 33606

FLINDT, FLEMMING, ballet master; b. Copenhagen, Denmark, Sept. 26, 1936; came to U.S., 1981; s. Charles and Elly Flindt; m. Vivi Gelker, Jan. 28, 1967; children—Tina, Bernadette, Vanessa. Student Royal Danish Ballet, Copenhagen, 1945-46; prin. dancer London Festival Ballet, London, Eng., 1955-58; danseur etoile Paris Opera Ballet, France, 1960-65; balletmaster, artistic dir. Royal Danish Ballet, Copenhagen, 1966-78; artistic dir. Dallas Ballet, Tex., 1981—. Choreographer, stage dir. (ballet) The Lesson, 1963 (Prix Italia 1963); The Young Man Must Marry, 1964; The Three Musketeers, 1966; Triumph of Death, 1971; The Toreador, 1978; Salome, 1977; Marriage in Hardanger, 1981; Texas on Point, 1982; Quartet For Two, 1983; Tarantelle Classique, 1985; Cinderella, 1985; Children's Songs, 1986. Decorated chevalier Order Arts and Letters, knight 1st degree Dannebrog, knight Swedish Order of Vasa. Office: Dallas Ballet Assn Inc 1925 Elm St Suite 300 Dallas TX 75201

FLINT, BENNY, architect, real estate developer, consultant; b. Miami Beach, Fla., May 6, 1954; s. Israel and Frida (Lelental) F. Grad. prep. sch. U. Haifa, Israel, 1973; B.Arch., U. Miami, 1978; grad. real estate course, 1982. Project coordinator Superconstrucciones, Bogota, Colombia, 1978-79, 9 Island Ave., Miami Beach, 1980-81; designer/ptnr. Architectum, Inc., Miami Beach, 1981—; pres. B. Flint & Assocs., Haim, Flint & Assocs., 1985—; real estate developer F.G.F. Corp., Miami Beach, 1981—, pres., 1985—; v.p. Architectum, Inc., 1985—. Contbr. chpts. to books, articles to Fla. Design Quar., On Design, Donde Mag., Preservation Today, others. Recipient 1st place award for S. Fla., Interior Design Guild, 1985; award Miami Design Preservation League for Art Deco, 1982-85. Mem. Am. Soc. Interior Design (assoc.), Archtl. Club Miami, Miami Beach Jaycees. Republican. Jewish. Club: Hebraica (Miami, Fla.). Home: 100 Bayview Dr Apt 1816 North Miami Beach FL 33160 Office: Haim Flint & Assocs 21338 W Dixie Hwy North Miami Beach FL 33180

FLINT, C. W., JR., corporate executive. Chmn., dir. Flint Industries, Inc. Office: Flint Industries Inc PO Box 490 Tulsa OK 73101*

FLIPPO, RONNIE GENE, congressman; b. Florence, Ala., Aug. 15, 1937; s. Claude and Esther (McAfee) F.; B.S., Florence State U., 1965; M.A., U. Ala., 1966; m. Faye Cooper, Nov. 27, 1958; children—Ronnie Gene, Linda Gail, Brenda Faye, Lea Ella, Kelly Reid, Ryan Cooper. Accountant, Flippo & Robbins, C.P.A.'s, Florence, Ala., 1972-76; mem. Ala. Senate, 1975-76; mem. 95th-97th Congresses from 5th Ala. Dist. Chmn. March of Dimes, 1969. Mem. Am. Inst. C.P.A.'s, Ala. C.P.A.'s Soc., Nat. Assn. Accountants. Democrat. Mem. Ch. of Christ. Club: Elks. Office: 2334 Rayburn House Office Bldg Washington DC 25015

FLOCA, CHARLES VINSON, JR., development company executive, architect; b. Temple, Tex., July 1, 1947; s. Charles Vinson and Barbara (Stewart) F.; m. Priscilla Haines, June 14, 1970; 1 child, Melissa Haines. B.A., U. Tex., 1969; M.Arch., Tex. A&M U., 1979. Registered architect, Tex. Constrn. rep. 3D/Internat., Houston, 1979-80; project mgr. Tex. Commerce Bancshares Inc., Houston, 1980-81; exec. v.p. Poydras Services Inc., New Orleans, 1981-85; v.p. design and constrn. Joseph C. Canizaro Interests, New Orleans, 1985—. Served to capt. USMC, 1971-75. NDEA fellow HEW, Tulane U., 1969. Mem. AIA, Marine Corps Res. Officers Assn., Tex. Soc. Architects, Internat. Arabian Horse Assn., Arabian Horse Assn. La., Delta Kappa Epsilon. Club: Lettermen's T Assn. Avocations: breeding, training and showing purebred Arabian horses. Home: Route 2 Box 113F Covington LA 70433 Office: Joseph C Canizaro Interests 300 Poydras St Suite 2201 New Orleans LA 70130-3297

FLOM, EDWARD LEONARD, steel company executive; b. Tampa, Fla., Dec. 10, 1929; s. Samuel Louis and Julia (Mittle) F.; m. Beverly Boyett, Mar. 31, 1956; children—Edward Louis, Mark Robert, Julia Ruth. B.C.E., Cornell U., 1952. With Fla. Steel Corp., Tampa, 1954—, v.p. sales, 1957-64, pres., dir., 1964—; dir. NCNB Nat. Bank Fla., Teco Energy, Inc., Tampa Electric Co., Gen. Portland, Inc. Bd. dirs., exec. com. United Fund Tampa; adv. com. St. Joseph's Hosp., Tampa; bd. dirs. Family Service Assn. Tampa, Jewish Welfare Fedn. Tampa; exec. com. Com. of 100, Tampa. Served with C.E., U.S. Army, 1952-54. Mem. Am. Iron, Steel Inst. (dir.), Young Pres.'s Orgn., Fla. Engring. Soc. Jewish (bd. dirs. temple). Club: Palma Ceia Golf, Country, Tampa Yacht, Gasparilla Krowo. Lodge: Rotary (bd. dirs. Tampa). Home: 4936 Saint Croix Dr Tampa FL 33629 Office: 1715 Cleveland St Tampa FL 33606

FLOM, JULIA MITTLE, civic worker; b. Bowman, S.C., Aug. 2, 1906; d. Edward Nathan and Minnie Josephine (Jackson) Mittle; m. Samuel Louis Flom (dec.); children—Joann Flom Greenberg, Edward L., Mary Sue Flom Rothenberg. Student Randolph-Macon Women's Coll., 1924-26, So. Sem., Buena Vista, Va., 1923. Bd. dirs. Univ. Community Hosp., Tampa, Fla., 1982—, Hillsborough Mental Health Assn., Tampa, 1965—, Vis. Nurses, Tampa, 1970-84, Temple Schaarai Zedek Sisterhood, Tampa, 1929—; chmn. bldg. com. Suncoast council Girl Scouts U.S.A., 1930-60; founding mem. U. South Fla., 1956—, pres.'s council, 1984-85; mem. Salvation Army, Easter Seal Guild, 1970—; Fla. Orch. and Guild, 1968—; bd. fellows U. Tampa, 1983—; mem. Jewish Welfare and Community Ctr.; mem. Council Jewish Women. Democrat. Lodge: Hadassah. Avocations: golf; painting. Address: 2403 Ardson Pl Apt 501B Tampa FL 33629

FLOOD, CHARLES F., JR., solid waste service company executive; b. Mt. Vernon, N.Y., Feb. 20, 1946; s. Charles F. and Janet Ann (Byrne) F.; m. Polly Ann Mishoe, Dec. 31, 1966; children—Kimberley Ann, Christopher Michael. B.Ed., U. Miami, 1968. Asst. to pres. SCA Services, Inc., Boston, 1976-77, dist. mgr., Ft. Worth, 1977-80, regional mgr. Tex. region, 1980-82, v.p., So. div. mgr., 1982-84; sr. v.p., gen. mgr. GSX Solid Waste Services Inc., 1984—. Mem. North Richland Hill (Tex.) Charter Com., 1980. Roman Catholic. Lodge: Ft. Worth Lions. Home: 6500 Spring River Ln Fort Worth TX 76118 Office: GSX Solid Waste Services Inc 669 Airport Freeway Suite 400 Hurst TX 76053

FLOOD, JOAN MOORE, law librarian; b. Hampton, Va., Oct. 10, 1941; d. Harold W. and Estalena (Fancher) M.; B.Mus., North Tex. State U., 1963, postgrad., 1977; postgrad. So. Meth. U., 1967-68, Tex. Women's U., 1978-79, U. Dallas, 1985-86; 1 dau. by former marriage, Angie. Clk., Criminal Dist. Ct. Number 2, Dallas County, Tex., 1972-75; reins. librarian Scor Reins. Co., Dallas, 1975-80, Assocs. Ins. Group, 1980-83, Akin, Gump, Strauss, Hauer & Feld, 1983—. Mem. Spl. Libraries Assn., Am. Assn. Law Librarians, Tex. Libraries Assn., S.W. Libraries Assn., Dallas County Library Assn., Dallas Assn. Legal Assts., State Bar Tex. (charter mem. legal assts. div.), Dallas Assn. Law Librarians, other orgns. Republican. Episcopalian. Home: 4609 Southern Ave Dallas TX 75209 Office: 4100 First City Ctr Dallas TX 75201-4618

FLOOD, WALTER A., electrical engineer; b. N.Y.C., Apr. 27, 1927; s. Walter A. and Lillian E. (Peterson) F.; m. Joan C. Cruthers, Sept. 6, 1954; children—Peter, Amanda, Timothy. B.E.E., Cornell U., 1950, M.E.E., 1952, Ph.D., 1954. With Cornell Aero. Lab., Buffalo, 1954-67, prin. engr., 1961-63, staff scientist, 1963-67; prof. elec. engring. N.C. State U.-Raleigh, 1967-81; dir. geoscis. div. Army Research Office, Research Triangle Park, N.C., 1981—; cons. in field. Served with U.S. Army, 1944-46. Mem. IEEE, Am. Geophys. Union, Optical Soc. Am., N.Y. Acad. Scis., Sigma Xi, Eta Kappa Nu. Roman Catholic. Office: PO Box 12211 Research Triangle Park NC 27709

FLORA, JOSEPH MARTIN, English educator; b. Toledo, Ohio, Feb. 9, 1934; s. Raymond Dwight Flora and Frances (Ricica) Neumann; m. Christine Lape, Jan. 30, 1959; children—Ronald James, Stephen Ray, Peter Joseph, David Benjamin. B.A., U. Mich., 1956, M.A., 1957, Ph.D., 1962. Instr. U. Mich., Ann Arbor, 1961-62; U. N.C., Chapel Hill, 1962-64, asst. prof., 1964-66, assoc. prof., 1966-77, prof. English, 1977—, asst. dean Grad. Sch., 1967-72, assoc. dean, 1977-78, acting chmn. dept. English, 1980-81, chmn., 1981—. Author: Vardis Fisher, 1965; William Ernest Henley, 1970; Hemingway's Nick Adams, 1982, (Mayflower award 1982). Editor: The English Short Story 1880-1945, 1985. Recipient Faculty Research award U. N.C. 1963, 75, Cooperative Program in Humanities Research award Duke U., U. N.C. 1966, Kenan Research leave U.N.C., 1978. Mem. MLA, South Atlantic Modern Lang. Assn., Western Lit. Assn. (exec. council 1979-81), Soc. Study So. Lit. (exec. council 1984—), South Atlantic Assn. Depts. English (v.p. 1985-86). Home: 505 Caswell Rd Chapel Hill NC 27514 Office: U NC Dept English Greenlaw Hall 066A Chapel Hill NC 27514

FLORA, WALTER, III, optometrist; b. Hobbs, N.Mex., July 6, 1943; s. Walter and Mildred (Stivers) F.; m. Gloria Gay Peacock, June 17, 1967; children—Stephanie Ann. B.S., O.D., So. Coll. Optometry, Memphis, 1966. Practice optometry, Belleair Bluffs, Fla., 1969—; clin. investigator Burton Parsons & Co., 1976-78, Acu-gel Soft Lens for Strieter Labs., Collinsville, Ill., 1974-75, Sherman Labs., Abita Springs, La., 1980-82, Biomed. Labs., Anaheim, Calif., 1982—. Served to capt. AUS, 1966-68, Vietnam. Fellow Am. Acad. Optometry, Internat. Orthokeratology Soc. (pres. 1984—, diplomate cornea and contact lens sect.); mem. Am. Optometric Assn., Fla. Optometric Assn. (trustee 1980-84), Pinellas County Optometric Assn. (pres. 1979-80, optometrist of yr. 1982), So. Orthokeratology Soc. (pres. 1980-82). Club: Sertoma. Republican. Avocations: Sports; cooking. Home: 2937 Landmark Way Palm Harbor FL 33563 Office: 432 Indian Rocks Rd Belleair Bluffs FL 33540

FLORENCE, MIKE E., III, economist; b. Dallas, Sept. 7, 1949; s. Mike E. Jr. and Barbara Ann (Whitman) F. B.A., Tex. A&M U., 1971; M.S., U. Dallas, 1975. Unit collection mgr. Nat. Bank Commerce, Dallas, 1973; fin. analyst Lone Star Gas Co., Dallas, 1975-78, research specialist, 1978-79, dir. rate research, 1979-81, dir. rate adminstrn. and research, 1982—; expert witness R.R. Commn. Tex., Okla. Corp. Commn., 1979—. Cons., Jr. Achievement, Dallas, 1977-78, Project Bus., Dallas, 1979-80; del. Dallas 2000 Conf., 1982-83, Goals Dallas, 1983—. Mem. Nat. Soc. Rate Return Analysts, Dallas Assn. Investment Analysts. Club: Engrs. (Dallas). Avocations: reading; travel. Home: 6441 Orchid Ln Dallas TX 75230 Office: Lone Star Gas Co 301 S Harwood Dallas TX 75201

FLORES, ELIZANDRO ALEX, produce company executive; b. Edinburg, Tex., May 2, 1945; s. Alfredo and Maria (Elizondo) F.; m. Elma Estella Cavazos, Mar. 14, 1969; children—Aliza Marie, Mark Alexander, Rosanna Lynn. Student Pan Am. U., 1964-66. Owner, pres. Houston Avocado Co., Inc., 1974—. Served with U.S. Army, Vietnam, 1967-68. Roman Catholic. Office: Houston Avocado Co Inc 2520 Airline St Houston TX 77009

FLORES, MANUEL C., JR., editor; b. Laredo, Tex., July 29, 1948; s. Manuel and Maria Luisa (Chapa) F.; B.S. in Edn., Tex. A&I U., 1970, M.S. in Polit. Sci. and Journalism, 1981; postgrad. N. Tex. State U., to 1972; m. Rosa Lydia Acevedo, Dec. 19, 1970; children—Mario, Marcos Teresa Marisol. Sports editor Irving (Tex.) Daily News, 1970-72; sports writer, columnist Corpus Christi Caller-Times, 1972-73; public relations asst. Central Power and Light Co., Corpus Christi, 1973, editor co. mag., 1972—; instr. polit. sci. Del Mar Jr. Coll. Mem. Corpus Christi Buccaraders Parade Assn.; cubmaster Boy Scouts Am.; mem. peace and justice commn. Roman Catholic Diocese of Corpus Christi. Served to capt. inf. U.S. Army, 1970; capt. Tex. Army N.G. Mem. Internat. Assn. Bus. Communicators, Res. Officers Assn., N.G. Assn. Tex., N.G. Assn. U.S., Leadership Corpus Christi, Corpus Christi C. of C. (edn. com., community devel. com.). Democrat. Club: Corpus Christi Press. Home: 5837 Llano St Corpus Christi TX 78407 Office: Box 2121 Central Power and Light Co Corpus Christi TX 78403

FLORES, PATRICK F., archbishop; b. Ganado, Tex., July 26, 1929. Ed. St. Mary's Sem., Houston. Ordained priest Roman Catholic Ch., 1956; ordained titular bishop of Itolica and aux. bishop of San Antonio, 1970, apptd. bishop of El Paso, 1978, archbishop of San Antonio, 1979. Office: Roman Catholic Ch 309 N Alamo St San Antonio TX 78205*

FLOREZ, LEOPOLDO, architect, real estate broker; b. Pinar Del Rio, Cuba, Oct. 15, 1945; came to U.S., 1962; naturalized, 1972; s. Emilio and Juliana (Alvarez) F. A.A., Miami-Dade Community Coll., 1967; B.Arch., U. Fla., 1970; M.S. in Urban and Regional Planning, Fla. State U., 1972. Registered architect, Fla.; registered real estate broker, Fla. Archtl. designer, constrn. supr. Cook, Reiff & Assoc., Architects/Engrs., Miami, Fla., 1969-70; planner intern Metro-Dade Dept. HUD, Miami, 1970-72; assoc. planner Fla. Div. State Planning, Tallahassee, 1972-75; community planner Metro-Dade Office of Community and Econ. Devel., Miami, 1975-78, dir. community planning div., 1978—. Pres. Fla. Community Devel. Assn., Tallahassee, 1981—; bd. dirs. New Century Devel. Corp., Miami, 1983—; mem. United Way Area Agy. on Aging Com. Recipient Silent Achiever award Nuestro mag., 1980. Mem. Am. Planning Assn. (Gold Coast chpt.), Nat. Trust for Hist. Preservation, Coral Gables Bd. Realtors, Greater Miami C. of C. (new trade and opportunities com.). Roman Catholic. Home: 511 SW 21 Rd Miami FL 33129 Office: Metro-Dade Office Community and Econ Devel 90 SE 8th St Suite 309 Miami FL 33130

FLORY, ROBERT MIKESELL, computer systems analyst, personnel management specialist; b. Bridgewater, Va., Feb. 21, 1912; s. John Samuel and Vinnie (Mikesell) F.; m. Thelma Thomas, Sept. 14, 1942; 1 child, Pamela. B.A., Bridgewater Coll., 1932; M.A., U. Va., 1938; postgrad. U. Chgo., 1946-51. Job/methods analyst United Air Lines, Chgo., 1945-47; job analyst Julian Baer, Chgo., 1948; asst. to v.p. Fairbanks, Morse, Chgo., 1949-60; mgmt. cons. Yarger & Assocs., Falls Church, Va., 1961; computer systems analyst, various fed. agys., Washington, 1962-82; tchr. Roosevelt U., Chgo., 1956-61; seminar leader U. Chgo., 1960-61; cons. Va. Gov.'s Commn. for Reorgn. State Govt., 1961. Served to lt. comdr. USN, 1942-45, PTO. Mem. Inst. Mgmt. Scis. Home: 5501 Seminary Rd Apt 1204-S Falls Church VA 22041

FLOURNOY, JANIE DAVIS, public relations specialist, college official; b. Shreveport, La., Mar. 15, 1950; d. Paul Robert and Dorothy Jane (Schmied) Davis; m. T. Cole Flournoy, Mar. 27, 1971; 1 dau., Frances Miller. Student, Mary Baldwin Coll., 1968-70, U. Reading, Eng., 1970-71; B.A., Centenary Coll., 1972. Writer, Shreveport Times, 1972-79; dir. pub. relations Centenary Coll. of La., 1979—. Chmn. 4th dist. adv. bd. La. Pub. Broadcasting, 1981-84; pres. Shreveport Opera Guild, 1983-84; bd. dirs. Jr. League, 1979, 81-82. Mem. Pub. Relations Soc. Am. Presbyterian. Home: 18 Dudley Sq Shreveport LA 71106 Office: Centenary Coll 2911 Centenary Blvd Shreveport LA 71104

FLOWERS, AUREATHA WILLIS, educator; b. Albany, Ga., Aug. 22, 1936; d. R.L. and Susie Mae (Miller) Willis; m. Eallie Flowers, July 22, 1959 (dec. Oct. 1969). B.S. in Elem. Edn., Albany State Coll., 1954; M.Ed., Tuskegee Inst., 1968; Ed.S., Atlanta U., 1981. Cert. tchr., Ga. Tchr. LaGrange Bd. Edn., Ga., 1954-65, Cobb County Bd. Edn., Ga., 1965-69; tchr., dept. chairperson Atlanta Bd. Edn., 1969-81; interrelated spl. end. specialist Atlanta U., 1981—. Editor activity manual Love Them, 1982. Fundraiser Am. Cancer Soc., Atlanta, 1980-83; tchr. sponsor Spl. Olympics, Atlanta, 1981-84; explorer adviser Carver High Sch. council Boy Scouts Am., 1982; tchr. Close Up, Atlanta, 1982. Recipient cert. award George Washington Carver Comprehensive chpt. Jr. Civitan, Atlanta, 1982, Youth Leadership in Am. award Boy Scouts Am., 1983. Mem. AFT (local 1565), Council Exceptional Children (chpt. cert. merit 1973), NEA, Ga. Assn. Educators, Atlanta Tchr.'s Assn., Phi Delta Kappa. Democrat. Baptist. Home: 1355 Beecher St SW Atlanta GA 30310 Office: Atlanta City Bd Edn PO Box 10754 Atlanta GA 30310

FLOWERS, JUANZETTA SHEW, nursing educator; b. Gadsden, Ala., Aug. 8, 1941; d. Shelly Jerome and Pluma Lee (Odom) Shew; m. Charles Ely Flowers, Jr., Sept. 25, 1972. B.S.N., U. Ala., 1966; M.A., U. Ala.-Birmingham, 1978, M.S.N., 1983, postgrad., 1983—. Pub. health nurse, Birmingham, Ala., 1966-68; sch. nurse, New Ulm, Germany, 1970; head nurse, cons., instr. U. Ala. Sch. Medicine-Birmingham, 1974-78, assoc. prof. dept. ob-gyn, 1978—, asst. prof. Sch. Nursing, 1985—. Pres., Birmingham Humane Soc., 1975-77. Mem. NOW, AAUW, Am. Nurses Assn., Soc. Sci. Study Sex, Nurses Assn. of Am. Coll. Obstetricians and Gynecologists (chmn. Ala. sect. 1977-81), Nat. League Nursing, Am. Assn. Sex Educators, Counselors and Therapists, Sigma Theta Tau, Phi Kappa Phi. Republican. Methodist. Home: 3757 Rockhill Rd Birmingham AL 35223 Office: Dept Ob-Gyn U Ala Birmingham Sch Nursing University Station Birmingham AL 35294

FLOWERS, LANGDON STRONG, retired foods company executive; b. Thomasville, Ga., Feb. 12, 1922; s. William Howard and Flewellyn Evans (Strong) F.; m. Margaret Clisby Powell, June 3, 1944; children—Margaret Flowers Rich, Langdon Strong, Elizabeth Powell Flowers McKinney, Dorothy Howard Flowers Swinson, John Howard. B.S., MIT, 1944, M.S., 1947. Engr., Douglas Aircraft, Los Angeles, 1947; supr. Flowers Baking Co., Thomasville, 1947-50, sales mgr., 1950-58, v.p. sales, 1958-65; pres., chief operating officer Flowers Industries, Inc., Thomasville, 1965-76, vice chmn. bd., chief exec. officer, 1976-81, chmn. bd., 1981-85, ret., 1985; dir. Am. Heritage Life Ins. Co., Ga. Power Co. Pres. Thomasville YMCA, 1958-62; past trustee Presbyn. Coll., Clinton, S.C., Archbold Meml. Hosp., Thomasville. Served as lt. (j.g.) USNR, 1943-46. Named Man of Year, Thomas County C. of C., 1974. Mem. Am. Bakers Assn. (exec. com. 1974-75, chmn. 1975-76), So. Bakers Assn. (chmn. bd. 1969-70), NAM (dir., exec. com.), Thomasville C. of C. (pres. 1953-54), Sigma Alpha Epsilon. Presbyterian (chmn. bd. deacons 1952-56, elder 1956—, rep. Gen. Assembly 1966). Club: Rotarian. Home: 819 Blackshear St Thomasville GA 31792 Office: PO Box 1338 Thomasville GA 31799

FLOYD, BRENDA CAROL, optometrist; b. Sacramento, Calif., Jan. 8, 1955; d. Louis Carrell and Catherine Louise (Hawkins) F.; m. Richard Joseph Brochetti, June 22, 1985. A.A. summa cum laude, Gaston Coll., 1973; B. in Chemistry summa cum laude, U. N.C.-Charlotte, 1975; B.S. in Physiol. Optics cum laude, U. Ala.-Birmingham, 1979, O.D. cum laude, 1981. Lic. optometrist, Tex. Research asst. U. Ala., Birmingham, 1977-79, researcher, 1980-81; optometrist Optical Clinic, Dallas, 1981-85; pvt. practice optometry, Lewisville, Tex., 1985—; clinician, intern Diabetes Hosp., Birmingham, 1980-81, Ctr. Devel. and Learning Disorders, Birmingham, 1980-81. Sustaining mem. Republican Nat. Com., 1983—. Mem. Tex. Assn. Optometrists, Am. Optometric Found., Women in Optometry, Gamma Beta Phi. Baptist. Avocation: piano compositions. Home: 3745 Casa Del Sol Dallas TX 75228 Office: 724 W Main St Suite 200 Lewisville TX 75067

FLOYD, DAVID NEVILLE, geologist, geophysicist; b. Rockdale, Tex., Jan. 17, 1935; s. Nofsinger and Lois Maurine (Neville) F.; m. Betty Ruth Schroeder, June 17, 1962; children—Brenda Ruth, Michael David. B.S. in Geology, U. Houston, 1962, postgrad., 1962-63. Geophysicist, M.L. Randall Explorations, Houston, 1961-63; geologist, draftsman Ashland Oil Corp., Houston, 1963-67; dist. geophysicist Apache Corp., Lafayette, La., 1967-72; cons. geophysicist R. Brewer & Co., 1972-74, sr. geophysicist, 1972-74; advance geophysicist Pennzoil Co., Houston, 1974-78; sr. geophysicist Hamilton Bros. Oil Corp., Houston, 1978-81; sr. geologist Damson Oil Corp., Houston, 1981-83, acting exploration mgr., chief geologist, 1983-84; pres. DNF Cons., Inc., 1984—. Served as 1st lt. USAR, 1959-61. Mem. Am. Assn. Petroleum Geologists. Lutheran.

FLOYD, EMMETT OWEN, clergyman, administrator; b. Griffin, Ga., Mar. 21, 1928; s. Henley Beale and Mary Elizabeth (Owen) F.; m. Katherine Holmes, June 5, 1948; children—Marian, Elizabeth, David, Karen and Karyl (twins). A.B., Mercer U., 1948; M.Div., So. Sem., 1951; M.A., Emory U., 1956; S.T.D., San Francisco Theol. Sem., 1973. Ordained to ministry United Ch. of Christ. Sr. minister Clairmont Hills Ch., Atlanta, 1954-62, Windermere Union Ch. (Fla.), 1964-67, 1st Congl. Ch., Greensboro, N.C., 1967-80; exec. minister S.E. Conf., United Ch. of Christ, Atlanta, 1980—; adj. prof. religion Greensboro Coll., 1972-80. Trustee, Catawba Coll., Salisbury, N.C., 1975-80. Served as chaplain USN, 1952-54, Korea, 1962-64, Cuba, to rear adm. Res. Recipient Man of Yr. award Atlanta Jr. C. of C., 1959. Mem. Mil. Chaplains Assn., Naval Res. Assn., Res. Officer Assn., Blue Key. Lodge: Rotary. Home: 2085 Imperial Dr Atlanta GA 30345 Office: 2676 Clairmont Rd Atlanta GA 30320

FLOYD, JOHN B., JR., surgeon; b. Louisville, Sept. 18, 1917; s. John B. and Barbara Lois (Lanahan) F.; children—Lynne Egge, John B., III, Lucy Floyd Rosson, Lanahan Max, William C.L. m. Margaret Feeback; 1 stepson, Michael Feeback. A.B., U. Ky., 1938; M.D., U. Louisville, 1941; M.S., Tulane U. 1949. Intern, St. Elizabeth Hosp., Covington, Ky.; jr. asst. resident in medicine City Hosp., Louisville, 1942-43; resident in surgery Lexington (Ky.) Clinic and Ochsner Found., 1943-49; individual practice medicine specializing in surgery Lexington, Ky., 1949—; clin. instr. vol. faculty U. Ky. Med. Ctr., from 1967, now ret. Contbr. articles to profl. jours. Served as maj. M.C., USAF, 1955. Recipient Distinguished Service award, Ky. div. Am. Cancer Soc., 1950, Disting.Am. Cancer Soc., 1967; pres. sr. class U. of Louisville Sch. Medicine, 1940-41; diplomate Am. Bd. Surgery. Fellow ACS; mem. Southeastern Surg. Congress, Lexington Surg. Soc., Ky. Surg. Soc., Fayette County Med. Soc., Ky. Med. Assn., Ky. Hist. Soc., So. Med. Assn. Democrat. Episcopalian. Clubs: Kiwanis, Filson. Home: 1890 Parkers Mill Rd Lexington KY 40504 Office: 119 E Maxwell St Lexington KY 40508

FLOYD, WILLIAM ANDERSON, psychology educator; b. Akron, Ohio, Dec. 5, 1928; married. A.B., Eastern Ky. U., 1949; M.A., U. Akron, 1953; B.D. with honors, So. Methodist U., 1956; D.Ed. in Counseling Psychology, North Tex. State U., 1962. Lic. psychologist, Ky., S.C. Asst. prof. psychology and religion Columbia Coll., 1959-61, assoc. prof. psychology, 1961-65, dir. Community Psychol. Service Ctr., 1959-65; assoc. prof. edn. and psychology Appalachian State U., 1965-68; prof. psychology Western Ky. U., Bowling Green, 1968—, prof. child devel. and family living, 1969—, head dept. home econs. and family living, 1969—, counseling psychologist VA, S.C. State and Baptist Hosps., S.C. Dept. Vocat. Rehab., numerous other instns. NIMH postdoctoral fellow U. Minn., 1967-68. Mem. Am. Assn. for Marriage and Family Therapy (clin. mem.; supr.), Am. Personnel and Guidance Assn. (life), Am. Psychol. Assn., Ky. Psychol. Assn., Am. Home Econs. Assn., Ky. Home Econs. Assn. (bd. dirs.), Nat. Vocat. Guidance Assn. (profl.), Soc. Police and Criminal Psychology, S.C. Psychol. Assn., Phi Delta Kappa, Kappa Delta Pi, Phi Upsilon Omicron. Lodge: Masons. Author: A Definitive Study of Your Career As A Minister, 1969; contbr. chpts. to books, articles to profl. jours. Home: 320 Windsor Cir Bowling Green KY 42101 Office: Dept Home Econs and Family Living Western Ky U Bowling Green KY 42101

FLUME, EILEEN DUGAN, lawyer; b. Springfield, Ohio, Jan. 15, 1951; d. Thomas P. and Mary (Conroy) Dugan; m. Richard A. Flume, June 1, 1979; 1 child, Gabrielle. B.A. in History and English Writing, Notre Dame U. and St. Mary's Coll., Ind., 1973; J.D., St. Mary's U., San Antonio, 1978. Bailiff, asst. jury commr. Dist. Ct. of Common Pleas, Hancock County, Ohio, 1967-72; trial asst. Sawtelle, Goode, Davidson & Troilo, San Antonio, 1974-77; ptnr. Flume & Flume, San Antonio, 1979—; adj. prof. bus. law San Antonio Coll., 1979-81. Bd. dirs. Women's Law Ctr., San Antonio, 1981-84, voter registration project Tex. Women of 80's, 1984-85. Mem. Am. Trial Lawyers Assn., Tex. Trial Lawyers Assn., San Antonio Trial Lawyers Assn. Democrat. Club: Chaine de la Rouisseurs. Home: 213 Briarcliff San Antonio TX 78216 Office: Flume & Flume 7103 Blanco Rd San Antonio TX 78216

FLYNN, PATRICK JOSEPH, opera guild administrator; b. N.Y.C., Sept. 28, 1950; s. Frank Joseph and Gladys Eliza (Grotz) F.; m. Karen Anne Rumbaugh, July 29, 1977. B.A., Manhattan Coll., 1972; M.Mus., U. Miami, 1978. Mktg. rep. IBM, N.Y.C., 1972-73; asst. dir. music Cardinal Gibbons High Sch., Ft. Lauderdale, 1973-78; chmn. dept. music Stranahan High Sch., Ft. Lauderdale, 1978-80; gen. mgr. The Opera Guild, Inc., Ft. Lauderdale, 1980—; mem. music panel Fla. Arts Council, 1982, 84. Vice-chmn. Broward Arts Council, Ft. Lauderdale, 1980—, Broward Cultural Arts Awards, Ft. Lauderdale, 1985—. Mem. Am. Symphony Orch. League, Assn. Coll. Univ. and Community Arts Adminstrs., Am. Fedn. Musicians. Republican. Roman Catholic. Clubs: Mensa, Tower. Avocations: music; photography; theatre; films; travel. Home:

700 SE 14th St Fort Lauderdale FL 33316 Office: The Opera Guild Inc 1040 Bayview Dr Suite 610 Fort Lauderdale FL 33304

FLYNN, PAUL BARTHOLOMEW, newspaper publisher; b. Quincy, Mass., Sept. 17, 1935; s. Bartholomew Joseph and Katherine Marie (Coleman) F.; m. Aline Therese Nicholson, Feb. 11, 1961; children—Bonnie Marie, Laureen P., Elizabeth A., Bernadette J. A.B., Stonehill Coll., 1957; LL.D. (hon.), Allentown Coll. St. Francis, 1985. Sportswriter Patriot Ledger, Quincy, 1955-63, community relations dir., 1963-65; dir. pub. relations Mass. Tchrs. Assn., Boston, 1965-66; asst. dir. pub. service Rochester Democrat (N.Y.) and Chronicle and The Times-Union, 1966-71, dir. pub. service and research, 1971-72; dir. advt. Huntington Herald-Dispatch and Advertiser (W.Va.), 1972-74; dir. advt. Binghamton Press and Sun-Bull. (N.Y.), 1974-76; dir. mktg. services Gannett Co., Rochester, N.Y., 1976-77; gen. mgr. Jour.-News, Nyack, N.Y., 1977; pres., pub. Fort Myers News-Press (Fla.), 1977-84; exec. v.p. USA Today, 1983-84, interim pres. USA Today, 1984; pres. Gannett Southeast Newspaper Group, 1984—; v.p. Gannett South, 1985—; pres., pub. Pensacola News-Jour., 1984—; Southeast regional v.p. Gannett Co., 1981-83; v.p. Gannett Newspaper Advt. Sales, N.Y.C., 1976-77; dir. Landmark Banks, Inc. Co-editor: Promoting the Total Newspaper, 1977. Pres. Lend-a-Hand Fund of Southwest Fla., 1977-83; pres. Southwest Fla. council Boy Scouts Am., 1981; bd. dirs. Lee County United Way, 1978-84, campaign chmn., 1981; bd. dirs. Edison Community Coll. Endowment Found., 1978-84, Sr. Friendship Ctrs., Inc., 1981-82; mem. adv. bd. U. South Fla., Fort Myers; bd. advisers Stonehill Coll., 1985—; bd. dirs. Sacred Heart Hosp. Found., United Way of Escambia Country, Pensacola Jr. Coll. Found. Served with U.S. Army, 1957-58. Recipient Disting. Service award B'nai B'rith of Cape Coral, Fla., 1979; Gold medal for good citizenship SAR, 1980; Outstanding Alumnus award Stonehill Coll., 1984. Mem. Am. Newspaper Pubs. Assn., Internat. Newspaper Promotion Assn. (dir. 1977-78), So. Newspaper Pubs. Assn., Fla. Press Assn., Fla. C. of C. (bd. dirs. 1978-80), Stonehill Coll. Alumni Assn. Roman Catholic. Club: Scenic Hills Country. Office: One News-Journal Plaza Pensacola FL 32501

FLYNN, THOMAS BROWN, neurosurgeon; b. Dyersburg, Tenn., Sept. 15, 1936; s. Thomas T. and Helen (Brown) F.; m. Joan Y. Kuebel, Dec. 19, 1959 (div. Dec. 1979); m. Pamela Noriea, July 25, 1980; children—Sean, Heidi, Rhys. B.S., U. South, 1958; M.D., Tulane U., 1962. Diplomate Am. Bd. Neurol. Surgeons. Straight surg. intern Charity Hosp. La., New Orleans, 1962-63; fellow neurol. surgery Ochsner Found., New Orleans, 1963-65; resident neurol. surgery Tulane U. Med. Sch., New Orleans, 1965-67, instr., 1967-68, asst. clin. prof. div. neurosurgery, 1979; chief resident neurol. surgery Charity Hosp. La. Tulane Service, New Orleans, 1966-67; practice medicine specializing in neurol. surgery, Baton Rouge, 1967—; assoc. prof. neurol. surgery La. State U. Med. Sch.; cons. neurol. surgery Karl K. Long Meml. Hosp., Baton Rouge; chief neurosurg. service Baton Rouge Gen. Hosp., 1974, 75, 76, chief surg. services, 1975, 76, 77, vice-chief staff, 1978-79, sec. staff, 1979-80, chief med. staff, 1980; vice-chief neurosurgery Our Lady of the Lake Hosp., 1982, chief neurosurgery, 1983; chief neurosurgery Baton Rouge Gen. Hosp., 1983; mem. adv. council alcohol and drug abuse prevention program Baton Rouge Sch. System, 1981—; chmn. bd. ESI, Inc. Contbr. articles to profl. jours. Fellow Internat. Coll. Surgeons, ACS; mem. Congress Neurol. Surgeons, Am. Assn. Neurol. Surgeons (continuing edn. award in neurosurgery 1976, 79), AMA (physician's recognition awards 1973-75, 75-78, 79-81, 82-84, 86—), Am. Soc. Stereotatic and Functional Neurosurgery, So. Med. Assn., So. Neurosurg. Soc., La. Neurosurg. Soc., (pres. 1977), La. State Med. Soc., Houston Neurol. Soc., Baton Rouge Surg. Soc. (pres. 1983), East Baton Rouge Parish Med. Soc. Home: 3913 Churchill Baton Rouge LA 70808 Office: 2237 S Acadian Baton Rouge LA 70808

FLYNT, THOMAS HENRY, clinical pharmacist; b. Greensboro, Ga., July 25, 1952; s. Reuben Henry and Patricia (McCollough) F.; m. Edith Amanda May, Apr. 9, 1983; children—Eileen May Fowler. B.S. in Pharmacy, U. Ga., 1976; Pharm.D., Mercer U., 1982. Lic. pharmacist, Ga., S.C. Staff pharmacist Union Pharmacy, Union Point, Ga., 1976-79; pharmacist-in-charge Oconee Area Mental Health/Mental Retardation Program, Milledgeville, Ga., 1979-81; psycho pharmacy resident William S. Hall Psychiat. Inst., Columbia, S.C., 1982-83, teaching pharmacist, 1983-84; clin. asst. prof. pharmacy U. S.C., Columbia, 1983-84; staff pharmacist Med. Coll. Ga. Hosp. and Clinics, Augusta, 1984—; advanced emergency med. technician Greene County Emergency Med. Service, Union Point, 1978-81. Bd. trustees 1st United Meth. Ch., Union Point, 1981-83, pres. mens club, 1977-81; scoutmaster Troop 306 Boy Scouts Am., Union Point, 1976-79; co-chmn. Gov's Community Project Program, Union Point, 1978. Recipient cert. appreciation Green County Emergency Med. Service, 1981. Mem. Am. Pharm. Assn., Am. Soc. Hosp. Pharmacists (spl. interest group on psychopharmacy practice), Ga. Pharm. Assn., Ga. Soc. Hosp. Pharmacists, S.C. Soc. Hosp. Pharmacists. Avocations: golfing; camping; fishing; reading. Home: 2211 Woodbluff Way Augusta GA 30909 Office: Dept Pharmacy Med Coll of Ga Hosp and Clinics Augusta GA 30912

FOCKLER, DOUGLAS D., fabricated metal products executive; b. Defiance, Ohio, Jan. 24, 1942; s. Delbert and Isabelle (Dreher) F.; B.S., Ohio State U., 1965, postgrad., 1978; m. Christine M. Spires, Oct. 25, 1969; children—Drew D., Cortney L. Prodn. supr. Cummins Engine Co., Columbus, Ind., 1965-67; acct. Babcock & Wilcox Co., Lancaster, Ohio, 1967-69, mgr. cost acctg., 1969-72; mgr. mfg. Mirror insulation unit, 1972-74; mng. dir. Diamond Power GmbH, Oberhausen, W. Ger., 1975-78; gen. mgr. Belfab unit Babcock & Wilcox Co., Daytona Beach, Fla., 1979-81; pres. Belfab div. Pacific Sci. Co., Daytona Beach, 1981—; v.p., dir. Volusia County Bus. Devel. Corp., 1985—; corp. v.p. Pacific Sci. Co., 1984—; dir. Fla. Nat. Bank of Daytona Beach. Chmn. indsl. div. United Way Volusia County, 1980, 81, unit A chmn., 1982, bd. dir., 1982—; bd. dirs. Daytona Beach Econ. Devel. Council, 1980, 81—, pres.-elect, 1982, pres., 1983-84; bd. counselors Bethune-Cookman Coll., 1980—; pres. Volusia Spl. Events; host Miss Teen U.S.A., 1986. Named Employer of Yr., Easter Seal Soc. Volusia County, 1979. Mem. Volusia County Mfrs. Assn. (founding dir. 1980, pres. 1981, 82), Theta Tau. Republican. Baptist. Patentee in field. Home: 29 Choctaw Trail Ormond Beach FL 32074 Office: 305 Fentress Blvd Datona Beach FL 32018

FOCKLER, JOHN KEEDY, foundation executive; b. Hagerstown, Md., Jan. 6, 1926; s. Samuel Mitchell and Mary Stitt (Keedy) F.; B.S. in Mgmt. Engring., Carnegie Mellon U., 1949; postgrad. U. Pitts., 1949-50, U Oslo, 1950, U. Del., 1955-56; M.B.A., Case Western Res. U., 1961; J.D., Memphis State U., 1982; m. Barbara Ann Rossland, Apr. 24, 1954; children—John Keedy, Robert Mitchell, Anne Chandlee, Ellen Rossland. Bar: Tenn. 1982. Asst. indsl. prodn. editor Bus. Week mag., N.Y.C., 1952-53, research editor, 1953-54, asst. bur. mgr., Pitts., 1956-57, bur. mgr., Cleve., 1957-62; v.p. Cleve. Devel. Found., 1963-68, exec. v.p., 1968-69; regional dir. Nat. Corp. Housing Partnerships, Washington, 1969-70; prin. John K. Fockler & Assos., housing cons., Cleve., 1970-74; exec. dir. Memphis-Plough Community Found., 1974-82, pres., 1982—; tchr. bus. Ohio State U., 1963-64; tchr. econs. Cuyahoga Community Coll., 1964-67, Cleve. State U., 1967-69; tchr. bus. communications Baldwin-Wallace Coll., 1972-74. Treas., Mid-South Med. Center Council, 1976-78; v.p. Gemantown (Tenn.) Arts Assn., 1976-78; pres. Memphis Conf. United Methodist Found., 1975—; conf. lay leader Memphis Conf. United Meth. Ch., 1982—; mem. city council, Bay Village, Ohio, 1960-61, 64; mem. budget, accounting and fin. adv. com. City of Germantown, 1976-78; chmn. council on ministries Germantown United Meth. Ch., 1976-78; bd. dirs. Mid-South Regional Blood Center, 1978-82, Lausanne Sch., 1978-81. Served with U.S. Army, 1954-56. Mem. ABA, Tenn. Bar Assn. Clubs: Summit, Delta. Lodge: Kiwanis. Home: 7101 Corsica Dr Germantown TN 38138 Office: Suite 249 1755 Lynnfield Rd Memphis TN 38119

FODIMAN, AARON ROSEN, restaurant chain executive; b. Stamford Conn., Oct. 10, 1937; s. Yale J. and Thelma F.; B.A., Tulane U., 1958; LL.B., N.Y. Law Sch., 1960; M.B.A., NYU, 1961. Bar: N.Y. 1960, D.C. 1964, Va. 1965. Trial atty. FTC, Washington, 1961-65; practiced in Arlington, Va., Washington, N.Y.C., 1965-78; pres. Fast Food Operators, Inc., N.Y.C., 1978-84, Franchised Food Operators, Inc., Washington, 1978-84, Kapok Corp., Clearwater, Fla., 1984—; dir. Hayloft Dinner Theatre, Inc., Mannassas, Va. Bd. dirs. Washington Ballet, Manhattan Punch Line Theatre; mem. adv. bd. Am. Film Inst.; spl. envoy U.S. Dept. State to Iran, Poland, Russia, Senegal, 1964-78; chmn. People for Ford Campaign, 1976; advisor Ford Adminstrn., 1974-76. Recipient I Speak for Democracy award, 1954. Mem. Phi Beta Phi. Clubs: B'nai B'rith (pres.), Barrister Inn (pres.) (Washington). Home: 2864 Pheasant Run Clearwater FL 33519 Office: 923 McMullen Booth Rd Clearwater FL 33519

FOELKER, GEORGE ALBERT, JR., clinical psychologist; b. Washington, July 21, 1951; s. George Albert and Clara F. B.A., Angelo State U., 1973; M.A., N. Tex. State U., 1975; Ph.D., U. South Fla., 1985. Cert. psychol. assoc., Tex. Staff psychologist mental retardation program Mexia, Tex., 1975-77, diagnostic team supr., San Antonio, 1977-79; mental health counselor Horizon Hosp., Clearwater, Fla., 1981-82, psychol. examiner, 1982-83; intern Baylor Coll. Medicine, Houston, 1983-84; clin. psychology fellow gerontology ctr. Tex. Research Inst. Mental Scis., Houston, 1984-85; coordinator geriatric services Dallas County MHMR. Contbr. articles to profl. jours. Mem. subcom. Mental Health Assn. Harris County, 1985. Angelo State U. scholar, 1970-73. Mem. Am. Psychol. Assn., Am. Assn. Mental Deficiency, So. Gerontol. Soc., Gerontol. Soc. Am., Southwestern Psychol. Assn., Phi Kappa Phi. Home: 3214 Bowen St 111 Dallas TX 75204 Office: Dallas County MHMR Geriatric Services Program 329 Centre St Dallas TX 75208

FOERCH, JOSEPH HENRY, JR., retired social scientist; b. Milford, Conn., Nov. 6, 1916; s. Joseph Henry and Mary Jane (Hubbell) F.; grad. Refrigeration and Air Conditioning Inst., Chgo., 1939; student Texarkana Jr. Coll., 1947-49, U. Md., 1952-56, Consol. U. N.C., 1957-60, B.A., N.C. State U., Raleigh, 1967, M.Ed., 1974; postgrad. Nova U., 1978; m. Althea Elizabeth Hoadley, Aug. 31, 1941; 1 dau., Bonnie Elizabeth Foerch Timperley. Drafted into U.S. Army, 1941, advanced through grades to lt. col., 1957, ret., 1961; chmn. dept. electronics Fayetteville (N.C.) Tech. Inst., 1961-73, chmn. dept. social sci., 1979-81, ret., 1981. Decorated Legion Merit (U.S.); Legion Merit (Korea). Mem. N.C. Sociol. Assn., Am. Assn. Ret. Persons, Ret. Officers Assn., Res. Officers Assn., N.C. Assn Ret. Mil., Smithsonian Assos. Democrat. Club: Shriners.

FOGARTY, ELIZABETH RUMMANS, retired librarian, researcher; b. Portsmouth, Ohio, Nov. 1, 1916; d. George Rummans and Mattie Belle (Shaver) Jordan; m. Joseph Christopher Fogarty, Oct. 6, 1945 (dec. Jan. 1977); children—Patricia C., Michelle., Josephine S. B.A. magna cum laude, Ohio Wesleyan U., 1938; M.L.S., U. Ill., 1939. Post librarian U.S. Army, Camp Atterbury, Ind., 1942-45; organizer of library Legis. Auditor's Calif. Capitol Office, Sacramento. 1952-53; med. research librarian U.S. Army Med. Ctr., Ryukyu Islands, Japan, 1967-70, U.S. Army Hosp., Ft. Polk, La., 1970-72; librarian pub. services McAllen Pub. Library, Tex., 1974-76. Researcher for Calif. state legislators and physicians. Chmn. council on ministries, mem. adminstrv. bd. St. Mark United Methodist Ch., McAllen, 1975—; Germany country commr. North Atlantic Girl Scout Bd. Europe, 1961-63. Mem. AAUW (pres. McAllen br. 1977-81, dir. internat. relations Tex. state div. bd. 1981-84, conductor internat. relations workshops at Tex. state and nat. convs. 1981—, Outstanding Woman of yr. award 1980), DAR (regent Sam Maverick chpt. 1983-85), Colonial Dames 17th Century (pres. Capt. Thomas Jefferson chpt. 1985—, Tex. state bd. 1985—), United Daus. Confederacy (treas. Palo Alto chpt. 1982-84), ALA, LWV, Mortar Board; Phi Beta Kappa, Delta Delta Delta, Delta Sigma Rho, Phi Sigma Alpha. Methodist. Club: Hidalgo County Republican Women. Home: 405 Vermont St McAllen TX 78503

FOGELMAN, AVRON B., real estate executive; b. Mar. 1, 1940; s. Morris F.; grad. Tulane U., Memphis State U. Law Sch.; m. Wendy Mimeles, Dec. 24, 1961; children—Hal David, Richard Louis, Mark Alan. Pres., Fogelman Properties; co-owner Kansas City Royals; owner Memphis Chick's Baseball Team; chmn. bd. Wendy's of New Orleans. Former chmn. bd. Mud Island Park, Memphis; mem. Pres.'s exec. bd. Tulane U.; chmn. Memphis and Shelby County Land Use Control Bd., 1978-79; chmn. bus. adv. council Memphis State U., 1978; bd. dirs. Tenn. Sports Hall of Fame; vice chmn. bd. Future Memphis; chmn. awards banquet NCCJ, 1981; mem. bd. adminstrn. Tulane U.; bd. dirs. Gov.'s Tech. Found. for Tenn.; bd. dirs. Memphis Jobs Conf., Tenn. Gov.'s Residence Found.; mem. president's council Southwestern Coll.; mem. Gov.'s Adv. Council on Better Schs. Recipient Outstanding Citizen award East Memphis Civitan Club; Liberty Bell award Memphis Bar Assn.; Best Ten of a Decade award Comml. Appeal; Outstanding Community Salesman of Yr. award Sales and Mktg. Execs. Memphis, Inc.; Disting. Service award Memphis State U.; Memphis State U. Bus. Sch. named Fogelman Coll. Bus. and Econs. in his honor; entreprenurial fellow Memphis State U., 1980. Mem. Memphis C. of C. (pres.). Home: 5491 Shady Grove Rd Memphis TN 38117 Office: 1000 Brookfield Memphis TN 38119

FOGELMAN, STEVEN, psychologist, psychotherapist; b. Bklyn., Nov. 4, 1950; s. Joseph and Rose (Okun) F.; m. Marsha Fogelman, Apr. 4, 1978 (div. 1982); 1 dau., Jamie Beth. B.Psychology, SUNY-Buffalo, 1974; M.Rehab. Counseling, U. South Fla., 1978. Dir. South County, Storefront, Sarasota, Fla., 1976-79; health services supr. II Metro-Dade Alcohol and Drug Abuse Program, Miami, Fla., 1979—; pvt. practice psychotherapy Miami, 1979—. Bd. dirs. Big Bros./Sisters, Venice, Fla., 1976-78; bd. dirs. Peppermill Homeowners Assn., Miami, 1983; mem. Task Force on Youth and Alcohol, Task Force on Chem. People North Miami. Mem. Phi Theta Kappa. Democrat. Home: 8004 SW 149th Ave Apt C108 Miami FL 33193 Office: Met Dade County Alcohol Drug Abuse Program 600 NE 27th St Miami FL 33137

FOGLE, RONALD EDWIN, safety engineer, communications company executive; b. Salem, Ill., May 1, 1946; s. Joe Roy and Alvena L. (Starwalt) F.; m. Linda Elaine Carter, Dec. 4, 1965; children—Cherie Lyn, Michelle Dawn. A.S., Kaskaskia Coll., 1971; B.S. in Indsl. Engring., U. Ill., 1973. Cert. protection profl. Am. Soc. Indsl. Security. Asst. plant indsl. engr. Anaconda Co., Harrisonville, Mo., 1973-74, plant indsl. engr., 1974-76; safety engr. FMC Corp., South Charleston, W.Va., 1976-77; mgr. safety-security ITT Corp., Kernersville, N.C., 1977-82; mgr. safety-security-health services No. Telecom Inc., Research Triangle Park, N.C., 1983—; pres., dir. Fogle Enterprises, Inc., Frisco, Colo., 1985—. Served with USN, 1966-68. Mem. Am. Soc. Safety Engrs., Am. Soc. Indsl. Security (chmn. 1986). Baptist. Avocations: golf; camping; snow skiing; photography. Home: 1413 Laughridge Dr Cary NC 27511 Office: Northern Telecom Inc PO Box 13010 Research Triangle Park NC 27709

FOGLIA, STEVEN KENT, regional sales executive; b. DuQuoin, Ill., Mar. 1, 1947; s. Louis Leslie and Lena Patricia (O'Hara) F. Student pub. schs. Laborer, Firestone Tire & Rubber Co., Decatur, Ill., 1967-76; dist. mgr. R.C. Cobb Theatres, Ala., Fla., 1976-80; shipper/print control Atlanta Film Service, 1980-83, R. S. Films, Inc., Atlanta, 1983—. Home: PO Box 13828 Atlanta GA 30324 Office: R S Films Inc 1455 Tullie Circle #101 Atlanta GA 30329

FOLEY, EDWARD JOSEPH, association executive, editor; b. Wakefield, Mass., June 4, 1928; s. James and Clara Mary (Grenier) F.; m. Barbara Ruth Findlay, Nov. 23, 1958; 1 dau., Loretta Ann. B.S., B.A., Northeastern U., 1954. Vice pres. Manning Pub. Relations, N.Y.C., 1954-58; pres. Sutton Place Publs., Inc., N.Y.C., 1959-75; exec. dir. Nat. Assn. Franchise Cos., N.Y.C. and Miami, 1970-80; owner, mgr. Foley Pub. Relations, N.Y.C. and Miami, 1958-80; v.p., sec. treas. Amateur Golfers Assn. Am., Inc., Hollywood, Fla., 1981—. Served with USAAF, 1946-48. Mem. Gulf Writers Assn. Am., South Fla. Assn. Execs., Bus. Writers Assn. Democrat.

FOLEY, JOSEPH HENRY, III, financial executive; b. Teaneck, N.J., Nov. 3, 1951; s. Joseph Henry and Dolores Loretta (Woods) F.; m. Alexandra Hughes, Apr. 23, 1983. B.S., Seton Hall U., 1973. C.P.A., N.J. Audit supr. Coopers & Lybrand, Newark, 1973-78; audit supr. Johnson & Johnson, New Brunswick, N.J., 1978-80; corp. cost. acctg. mgr. Ethicon, Inc., Somerville, N.J., 1980-82, controller, San Angelo, Tex., 1982—. Treas. Inst. for Cognitive Devel., San Angelo, 1982-83. Fellow N.J. Soc. C.P.A.s; mem. Am. Inst. C.P.A.s. Roman Catholic. Office: Ethicon Inc PO Box 511 San Angelo TX 76902

FOLEY, LINDA ANDERSON, psychology educator, educational administrator; b. Stamford, Conn., June 3, 1941; d. Harry Carl and Ethel (Regan) A.; children—Timothy James, Maureen Elizabeth. B.A., Western Conn. State U., 1971; M.A., U. Fla., 1972, Ph.D., 1974. Asst. prof. U. North Fla., Jacksonville, 1974-1978, assoc. prof., 1978-1984, prof. psychology, chmn., 1983—; assoc. prof. U. Md., Germany, 1982-83; cons. in field, 1978—; condr. workshops Blue-Cross-Blue Shield, Jacksonville, 1976-78; cons. Naval Air Sta., Jacksonville, 1981-82. Contbr. articles to profl. jours. Bd. pres. Job Readiness Program, Jacksonville, 1977-78; v.p. bd. Parents Resource Ctr., Jacksonville, 1979-80, Probation Restitution Ctr., Jacksonville, 1977—; bd. dirs. YWCA, Jacksonville, 1975-78. Grantee Dept. Labor 1978, 79, Mott Found. 1981. Recipient Disting. Faculty award U. North Fla. 1982. Mem. Am. Psychol. Assn., Soc. Psychol. Study Social Issues, Am. Soc. Criminology, Nat. Council Crime and Delinquency, Southeastern Psychol. Assn., Acad. Criminal Justice Scis. Avocations: jogging; racquetball; reading; bicycling. Home: 4138 Tradewinds Dr Jacksonville Beach FL 32250 Office: U North Fla Dept Psychology 4567 St Johns Bluff Jacksonville FL 32216

FOLGER, JEFFREY BENJAMIN, actor; b. Durham, N.C., Aug. 22, 1947; s. Worth Barnard and Helen (Saunders) F. B.S. in Bus., Western Carolina U., 1969. Announcer, Sta. WAGA-TV, Atlanta, 1969-72; freelance comml. performer, Atlanta, 1972—. Mem. AFTRA (past pres. Atlanta chpt.), Screen Actor's Guild, Nat. Acad. TV Arts and Scis. (bd. govs. Atlanta chpt.), Am. Film Inst. Club: Willow Springs Country (Roswell, Ga.). Office: PO Box 52303 Atlanta GA 30355

FOLK, SHARON LYNN, printing company executive; b. Bellefontaine, Ohio, June 13, 1945; d. Emerson Dewey and Berdena Isabelle (Brown) F.; A.B., Belmont Abbey Coll., 1968; L.H.D. (hon.), Sacred Heart Coll., 1985. Exec. v.p. Nat. Bus. Forms Inc., Greeneville, Tenn., 1968-73, pres., chmn. bd., 1973—; pres., chmn. Nat. Forms Co. Inc., Gastonia, N.C., 1973-79; dir. Andrew Johnson Bank, Greeneville, Internat. Bus. Forms Industries, Arlington, Va. Active YMCA Community Orch.; bd. dirs. Greeneville YMCA, 1977-80, United Way, 1980—; mem. presdl. steering com. U.S. Senator Howard Baker, 1979-80; mem. Republican Presdl. Com., 1981—, Rep. Presdl. Task Force, 1981—; chmn. parish com. Notre Dame Catholic Ch., Greeneville, 1985-86; life mem. Rep. Nat. Com., 1981—; charter mem. Com. 200, 1982—; mem. bd. advisors Belmont Abbey Coll., 1984—, trustee, 1986-89; trustee Sacred Heart Coll., Belmont, N.C., 1985—; 2d lt. CAP, 1984—. Mem. Internat. Bus. Forms Industry (chairperson indsl. relations com. 1978-80). Nat. Bus. Forms Assn., Tuesday Night Bus. Women's Bowling League, Am. Mgmt. Assn., Tenn. Bus. Roundtable (bd. dirs.), Greeneville Women's Bowling Assn., U.S. Tennis Assn. (life), Airplane Owners and Pilots Assn. Home: 1131 Hixon Ave Greeneville TN 37743 Office: Nat Bus Forms Co Inc 100 Pennsylvania Ave Greeneville TN 37743

FOLKER, MARK STEPHEN, pharmacist, nutrition consultant; b. Savannah, Ga., Sept. 20, 1956; s. John Ashton and Catherine (Brigdon) F.; m. Karen Deadwyler, Oct. 3, 1981; children—Stephen Andrew, John Mark. B.S. in Edn., Ga. So. U., 1978; B.S. in Pharmacy, U. Ga., 1981. Registered pharmacist, Ga., S.C. Cons. pharmacist Instl. Pharmacy Cons., Griffin, Ga., 1981-82; pharmacist Eckerd Drugs, Thomaston, Ga., 1982-84; cons. pharmacist Ga. Geriatrics, Smyrna, Ga., 1984-85, Griffin-Spalding County Hosp., Griffin, Ga., 1985—. Recipient Eagle Scout-Bronze Palm award Boy Scouts Am., 1973. Fellow Am. Soc. Cons. Pharmacists; mem. Ga. Pharm. Assn. Republican. Baptist. Lodge: Kiwanis. Avocations: private pilot; golf. Home: 1362 Zebulon Rd Griffin GA 30223 Office: Griffin-Spalding County Hosps 8th St Griffin GA 30223

FOLLRATH, KRISTINA LANPHEAR, computer programmer, conductor; b. Springfield, Ohio, Nov. 29, 1951; d. Jack Kirchwehm and Barbara Anne (Botsford) Follrath; m. Frank L. Wilson, Jr., June 29, 1984. B.A., Washington U., St. Louis, 1975; Mus.M., Northwestern U., 1977. Hostess, supr. Internat. Olympic Com., Munich, W.Ger., summer 1972; condr. Northeastern Ill. U., Chgo., 1977; lectr., condr. Lake Forest Coll. (Ill.), 1977-79; travel dir. Intrav, St. Louis, 1979-81; condr., mus. tchr. Lovett Sch., Atlanta, 1981-82; computer programmer Delta Airlines, Atlanta, 1982—; condr., mus. dir. Gilbert & Sullivan Guild, Chgo., 1976-78; mem. Chgo. Symphony Chorus, 1976-79; choral asst. auditor Chgo. Lyric Opera, 1978-79; mem., rehearsal asst. Atlanta Symphony Chorus, 1981-84; mus. editor PBS Broadcast, Sing-Along Messiah, 1978. Vice pres. Young Republicans Springfield, 1968. Recipient Antoinette Dames award Washington U., 1974. Mem. Chimes, Alpha Lambda Delta (v.p. 1970-71). Office: Delta Airlines Adminstrv Center Atlanta GA 30331

FOLMAR, EMORY, mayor. Mayor of Montgomery, Ala. Office: PO Box 1111 Montgomery AL 36192*

FOLWELL, WILLIAM HOPKINS, clergyman, bishop; b. Port Washington, N.Y., Oct. 26, 1924; s. Ralph Taylor and Sara Ewing (Hopkins) F.; m. Christine Elizabeth Cramp, Apr. 22, 1949; children—Ann, Mark, Susan. B.C.E., Ga. Inst. Tech., 1947; B.D., Seabury Western Theol. Sem., 1953, D.D., 1970; D.D., U. of South, Sewanee, 1970. Ordained to ministry Episcopal Ch., 1952; priest Plant City and Mulberry, Fla., 1952-55; asst. chaplain St. Martin's Sch., New Orleans, 1955-56; vicar St. Augustine Ch., New Orleans, 1955-56; rector St. Gabriel's Ch., Titusville, Fla., 1956-59, All Saints Ch., Winter Park, Fla., 1959-70; bishop Diocese Central Fla., Winter Park, 1970—; asst. traffic engr. City of Miami, 1947-49. Trustee U. of South, Seabury-Western Theol. Sem., Evanston, Ill. Lt. j.g. USNR, 1943-46. Home: 458 Virginia Dr Winter Park FL 32789 Office: The Episcopal Ch 324 N Interlachen Ave PO Box 790 Winter Park FL 32789*

FOLZ, ALAN LORCH, JR., investment company executive; b. Dallas, Apr. 20, 1955; s. Alan Lorch and Ann (Jacobus) F. B.A. magna cum laude, Dartmouth Coll., 1976. Fin. analyst Windsor Assn., Inc., Dallas, 1977-79, investment counselor, 1979-80; account exec. E.F. Hutton, Dallas, 1980-83, portfolio mgr., 1983—. Jewish.

FONDREN, HERBERT RAY, glass company executive, real estate investor; b. Corpus Christi, Tex., Dec. 2, 1929; s. Walter Silas and Evy Lenora (Roper) F.; m. Joyce Ann Herron, Sept. 7, 1956; children—Patti, Denise, Raelene, Misty. Student schs. Corpus Christi, Tex. Glazier, Pitts. Plate Glass, Corpus Christi, 1946-51, 55-59; glazing supt. Horton Glass Co., Corpus Christi, 1959-62; v.p. Thurman Fondren Glass, Corpus Christi, 1962-80, pres., 1980—; pres. Thurman Fondren Properties, Corpus Christi, 1967—; ptnr. Padre Weber MiniStorage, Crosstown MiniStorage, Padre Palms Office Bldg.; sec. F.D.C. Devel., Corpus Christi. Bd. dirs. Christian Edn. Activities Corp., Corpus Christi, 1979-83; deacon Gardendale Baptist Ch., 1963-83. Served with USN, 1951-55. Mem. Assoc. Gen. Contractors (exec. bd., polit. action com. 1982-83), Nat. Glass Dealers Assn., Home Builders Assn., Nat. Assn. Small Bus., Nat. Assn. Home Builders, U.S. C. of C., Corpus Christi C. of C. Republican. Home: 7301 Wooldridge Corpus Christi TX 78415 Office: Thurman Fondren Glass Co Inc 4233 S Padre Island Dr Corpus Christi TX 78411

FONDREN, WILLIAM MERLE, JR., hardware and floor covering distribution company executive; b. Cleveland, Miss., Jan. 16, 1940; s. William Merle and Evelyn (Baird) F.; m. Sondra Warmack, Dec. 18, 1965; children—William Merle III, Susan Marie. B.S., Miss. State U., 1961; M.S., MIT, 1963. Mktg. rep. data processing div. IBM Corp., Birmingham, Ala., 1965-73; in mktg. and sales dept. E.L. Bruce Co., Inc., Memphis, 1973-77; gen. mgr. appliance div. Orgill Bros. & Co., Inc., Memphis, 1977-79, v.p., gen. mgr. hardware div., 1981, pres., 1981—, also dir., 1981—; v.p. corp. devel.-mktg. Miller Industries, Inc., Memphis, 1979-80; vice chmn. Liberty Distbrs., 1984—. Bd. dirs. Mueller Found., 1983-84. Bd. dirs. Chickasaw Council Boys Scouts Am., Tenn.-Ark.-Miss. Council Girl Scouts U.S.A. Served to 1st lt. U.S. Army, 1963-65. Mem. Pres. Assn. Am. Mgmt. Assn., Nat. Wholesale Hardware Assn. (mem. exec. bd. 1983—). Club: Farmington Country. Avocations: hunting; golf; music; playing guitar. Office: Orgill Bros & Co Inc 2100 Latham St Memphis TN 38109

FONES, WILLIAM HARDIN DAVIS, state supreme court justice; b. Friendship, Tenn., Oct. 6, 1917; s. Roy Revelle and Kitty (Davis) J.; student Memphis State U., 1934-37; J.D., U. Tenn., 1940; m. Rebecca Logan Barr, July 26, 1946; children—Jere, William Hardin Davis. Admitted to Tenn. bar, 1942, practiced in Memphis, 1945-71; judge div. 3 15th Jud. Circuit Ct. Tenn., Shelby County, Memphis, 1971-73; assoc. justice Supreme Ct. Tenn., 1973-74, 76-82, chief justice, 1974-76, 82-84; mem. exec. council Conf. Chief Justices, 1976-79. Active local Boy Scouts Am., ARC, Shelby United Neighbors fund drives; bd. dirs. Nat. Ctr. for State Cts., Williamsburg, Va., 1982-85. Served with USAAF, 1942-45. Decorated Air medal with 3 oak leaf clusters. Office: Supreme Ct Tenn 1103 State Office Bldg Memphis TN 38103

FONTENOT, BENNETT PAUL, dentist; b. Crowley, La., Oct. 18, 1948; s. Bennett and Mary Myrtle (Leblanc) F.; m. Karen Marie Karre, June 9, 1979; children—Bennett Boustany, Katherine Karre, Elizabeth Marie. Cert. med. tech. Confederate Meml. Med. Ctr., Shreveport, La., 1973; B.S., U. Southwestern La., 1970, M.S., 1972; D.D.S., La. State U., 1977. Practice dentistry, Breaux Bridge, La. Author: Histochemical Studies of The Trematode Parasites of South Louisiana Amphibians and a Lung Fluke From Mexico, 1972. Mem. ADA, La. Dental Assn., La. State Bd. Dentistry, Acadiana Dist. Dental Assn., Clin. Found. of Orthopedics and Orthodontists, Acad. Gen. Denistry, Clin. Research Assocs. Phi Kappa Phi. Democrat. Roman Catholic. Avocations:

tennis; hunting. Home: 702 Robert Lee Circle Lafayette LA 70506 Office: 1329 Grand Point Rd Breaux Bridge LA 70517

FOORMAN, BARBARA ROBINS, educational psychologist, researcher; b. St. Louis, Feb. 6, 1948; d. George Kenneth and Marjorie (McCarthy) Robins; m. David Carl Foorman, May 16, 1970 (div. 1979); m. Justin Fritz Leiber, June 18, 1983; 1 child, Katherine Caitlin. Cert. life elem. and secondary tchr., Calif. Instr. Tennoji English Acad., Osaka, Japan, 1970-71; assoc. in human devel. U. Calif., Davis, 1977-78; assoc. prof. ednl. psychology U. Houston, 1978—; vis. lectr. Universidad Autonoma, Guadalajara, Mex., 1979; vis. scholar Oxford U., Eng., 1981, 83; vis. prof. Miyazaki U., Japan, 1983, 84; cons. in field. Reviewer Child Devel. Jour., 1980—. Editor: Acquisition of Reading Skills, 1985. Chmn. Japan Am. Soc. Com., Houston, 1984-85; bd. dirs. Japan Am. Soc., Houston, 1983-85, Asia Soc., Houston, 1984—, Roblee Found., St. Louis, Mo., 1973—. Grantee U. Houston, 1979, 80, 82, 83. Mem. Am. Ednl. Research Assn. (reviewer), Am. Am. Psychol. Assn., Internat. Reading Assn., Soc. for Research Child Devel., Phi Delta Kappa. Democrat. Presbyterian. Avocations: swimming; hiking; skiing. Home: 528 Bayland Houston TX 77009 Office: Univ Houston Dept Ednl Psychology Houston TX 77004

FOOSE, ROBERT JAMES, art educator, painter, printmaker, graphic designer; b. York, Pa., Oct. 17, 1938; s. Clarence Norman and Rebecca Gillam (Gorsuch) F.; m. Roxanne Richardson, Mar. 16, 1985; children—Alice Katherine, Megan Anne. B.A., U. Ky., 1963. Art dir. Univ. Press of Ky., Lexington, 1964-82; prof. art U. Ky., Lexington, 1983—; dir. Living Arts Sci. Ctr., Lexington; pres. Lexington Art League, 1969-71, Ky. Guild Artists and Craftsmen, Berea, 1972-74. Illustrator: Byron's Natural Man-Daniel Boone, 1980; A Bestiary, 1974. Recipient first place painting awards Blue Grass Painting Exhibition, 1984, Watercolor Soc., 1977. Mem. Ky. Watercolor Soc. (first place painting award 1983), So. Watercolor Soc. (1st place painting award, 1981, Gold Medallion 1981), Ky. Arts Commn., Nat. Soc. Arts and Letters. Republican. Home: PO Box 22541 Lexington KY 40522 Office: Univ Ky Room 209 Fine Arts Bldg Lexington KY 40506

FOOTE, AVON EDWARD, communications scientist, educator; b. Burnsville, Miss., Sept. 24, 1937; s. Avon Ruble and Lila Frances (Broughton) F.; B.S., Florence State U., 1963; M.S., U. So. Miss., 1968; Ph.D., Ohio State U., 1970; m. Dorothy Veronica Gargis, Mar. 15, 1960; children—Anthony E., Kevin A., Michele. Announcer, Sta. WJOI, Florence, Ala., 1958-60; prodn. mgr. Sta. WOWL-TV, Florence, 1960-64; advt. coordinator Plough Inc., Memphis, 1964-66; faculty adviser Sta. WMSU, U. So. Miss., Hattiesburg, 1966-67; producer-dir. telecommunications Ohio State U., Columbus, 1967-69; assoc. prof. broadcasting U. Miss., Oxford, 1971-72; project dir. Ohio Valley TV System, Columbus, 1972-74; mem. faculty, coordinator grad. studies Sch. Journalism and Mass Communication, U. Ga., Athens, 1974-80; prof. broadcasting U. North Ala., Florence, 1980—; awards judge Ohio State Awards, 1968-73; chmn. screening com. Peabody Radio-TV Awards, 1976-79. Bd. dirs. Florence YMCA, 1982—. NDEA fellow, 1967, Nat. Acad. TV Arts and Scis. Meml. fellow, 1970; recipient Community Service award Florence Civitan Club, 1985; regional 1st pl. award, Nat. 3d pl. award Univ./Student Emmy award Hollywood Acad. TV Arts and Scis., 1984. Mem. Broadcast Edn. Assn., Alpha Epsilon Rho. Republican. Methodist. Club: Exchange (bd. dirs. 1984—), Lodge: Elks. Editor: The Challenges of Educational Communications, 1970; CBS and Congress: "The Selling of the Pentagon" Papers, 1972. Author: (with Koenig and others) Broadcasting and Bargaining, 1970; Chotankers, 1982. Editor Ednl. Broadcasting Rev., 1969-73. Producer ednl. TV programs. Home: 222 Shirley Dr Florence AL 35630 Office: Media Center Box 5063 Florence AL 35630

FOOTE, EDWARD THADDEUS, II, lawyer, university president; b. Milw., Dec. 15, 1937; s. William Hamilton and Julia Stevenson (Hardin) F.; B.A., Yale U., 1959; LL.B., Georgetown U., 1966; LL.D. (hon.), Washington U., 1981; m. Roberta Waugh Fulbright, Apr. 18, 1964; children—Julia, William, Thaddeus. Reporter, Washington Star, 1963-64, Washington Daily News, 1964-65; exec. asst. Pa. Ave. Commn., 1965-66; admitted to Mo. bar, 1966; asso. firm Bryan, Cave, McPheeters & McRoberts, St. Louis, 1966-70; vice chancellor, gen. counsel Washington U., St. Louis, 1970-73, dean Sch. Law, 1973-80, spl. adv. to chancellor and bd. trustees, 1980-81; pres. U. Miami (Fla.), 1981—; fed. ct.-apptd. chmn. citizens com. and desegregation monitoring com., St. Louis sch. desegregation case, 1980-81. Author: An Educational Plan for Voluntary Cooperation Desegregation of School in the St. Louis Met. Area, 1981. Mem. Council on Fgn. Relations, St. Louis, 1966-69; bd. dirs. Expt. in Living, St. Louis, 1966-69, Legal Services Eastern Mo., 1973-78; mem. steering com. Gov.'s Conf. on Edn., 1974-76; pres. bd. New City Sch., St. Louis, 1967-73; bd. dirs. St. Louis City and County Legal Aid Soc., 1973-78; bd. advs. to pres. Naval War Coll., 1979-82; mem. edn. com. Fla. Council 100; mem. South Fla. Coordinating Council, Miami Com. on Fgn. Relations, Met. Miami Action Plan; mem. exec. com. Miami Citizens Against Crime. Served with USMCR, 1959-62. Decorated Order of Sun (Peru). Mem. Am. Bar Assn., Greater Miami C. of C. (bd. govs.), Order Coif. Democrat. Office: Univ Miami Office of Pres Coral Gables FL 33124

FORBES, EDWARD COYLE, diversified company executive; b. Bangalore, India, Sept. 5, 1915 (parents Am. citizens); s. Sherman Guy and Bertha (Coyle) F.; grad. Phillips Exeter Acad., 1934; B.S. in Elec. Engring., Auburn U., 1938; M.S. in Aero. Engring., Air Force Aero. Inst., 1945; m. Anne Fromm Forbes, June 28, 1980; children—Christina, Lucien, Alexandra, Edward, Alvaro. With Gen. Electric Co., 1939-41, Internat. Gen. Electric Co., Paris, 1946-51, pres. Gen. Electric Portugal, 1951-55, gen. mgr. Gen. Electric Argentina, 1955-63; v.p. corporate planning Worthington Corp., Harrison, N.J., 1963-64, v.p., group exec., 1964-67, chmn., chief exec. officer, 1971-74; pres., chmn. Alco Products, Inc., 1967-69; v.p., group exec. Studebaker-Worthington, Inc., 1967-74; chmn., dir. MLW-Worthington, Ltd., Can., 1967-74; pres. Liberia Mining Co., 1974-78; pres. Am. Ship Bldg. Co., Tampa, Fla., 1978-83; dir. Sentinel Group Fundings Inc., Sentinel Cash Mgmt. Fund Inc. Mem. exec. com. Engring. Council Auburn U.; lectr. on mgmt. to profl. assns. U.S., Argentine War Coll. Bd. dirs., founder Argentine Inst. for Devel. Execs., 1953-64; bd. dirs., treas. Centro de Estudios Sobre Libertad, Argentina, 1957-63; trustee Eaglebrook Sch., Deerfield, Mass., 1945-61. Served to maj. USAAF, 1941-46. Registered profl. engr. N.J., Ohio Mem. ASME, Am. Mgmt. Assn., Eta Kappa Nu, Kappa Alpha. Clubs: Univ.; N.Y. Yacht; Two Rivers Hounds; Shinnecock Hills Golf and Country. Home: PO Box 3056 2036 Windward Way Vero Beach FL 32963

FORBES, MICHAEL SHEPARD, research scientist, cell biologist, electron microscopist; b. Washington, Jan. 21, 1945; s. Alan Conrad Forbes and Mary Charles (McMackin) Forbes Layne; m. Janie Ann Eli, Nov. 8, 1970; children—Daniel Alan, Amy Elizabeth. B.A. in Biology, U. Va., 1966, Ph.D. in Biology, 1971. Postdoctoral fellow dept. physiology U. Va., Charlottesville, 1971-73, research assoc. depts. physiology and biology, 1973-74, research asst. prof. dept. physiology, 1979-85, research assoc. prof. dept. physiology, 1985—; participant cell and molecular program, 1982—, governing com. central electron microscope facility, 1983—; instr. dept. neurology U. Md., Balt., 1974-76, asst. prof., 1976-78. Contbr. chpts. to books, articles to profl. jours. Nat. Heart/Lung/Blood Inst. grantee, 1982-85, Research Career Devel. award, 1979-84; Am. Heart Assn. grantee, 1978-81; NIH grantee, 1982-84. Mem. Am. Soc. Zoologists, Am. Heart Assn. (basic sci. council), Electron Microscopy Soc. Am., Chesapeake Soc. Electron Microscopy, Sigma Xi. Republican. Avocations: gardening; recipe invention; automobile restoration. Home: Route 1 Box 268 Troy VA 22974 Office: U Va Sch Medicine Dept Physiology Charlottesville VA 22908

FORBES, PETER CAIRNEY, energy company executive; b. Colombo, Sri Lanka, Apr. 16, 1945; came to U.S., 1975; s. James and Jean (Cairney) F.; m. Alayne Norma Deas, July 29, 1967; children—James, Andrew, Kirsty. A.M.P., Harvard U., 1983; M.A., U. Edinburgh (Scotland), 1966. Chartered acct., Scotland. Acct., Deloittes & Co., Edinburgh, 1966-70; lectr. acctg. and fin. U. Edinburgh, 1970-72; investment mgr. Ivory & Sime, Edinburgh, 1972-74; mgr., officer treasury div. Tex. Eastern Corp., Houston, 1975-85; sr. v.p., chief fin. officer Zapata Corp., Houston, 1985—. Founding pres. Familytime Found., Humble, Tex., 1977-80. Mem. Inst. Chartered Accts. Scotland, Fin. Execs. Inst. Methodist. Clubs: Houston, Houston Center. Office: PO Box 2521 Houston TX 77252

FORBIS, JOHN W., city official. Mayor, City of Greensboro, N.C. Office: City of Greensboro Drawer W-2 Greensboro NC 27402*

FORCH, JOHN JOSEPH, accountant; b. N.Y.C., Sept. 21, 1949; s. Joseph Edward and Josephine Winifred (McNamara) F.; m. Joanne Collier, May 4, 1954. B.S. in Acctg., Va. Poly. Inst., 1971. C.P.A., Va., Fla. Staff acct. Becker, Weinstein & Kaufman, Washington, 1971-73; partner Peat Marwick Mitchell & Co., Miami, Fla., 1973—. Chmn. bd. trustees Coconut Grove Playhouse, Coconut Grove, Fla., 1982-83. Mem. Am. Inst. C.P.A.s, Fla. Inst. C.P.A.s, Fla. Council Internat. Devel., Miami Com. Fgn. Relations, Greater Miami C. of C., Va. Tech. Alumni Assn. Roman Catholic. Club: Courts at the Falls (Miami, Fla.). Home: 9838 SW 106 Terr Miami FL 33176 Office: Peat Marwick Mitchell & Co 800 Brickell Ave Miami FL 33176

FORD, BETTE HEATH, nursing educator; b. Nassawadox, Va., Aug. 1, 1939; d. Thomas James and Sabrina Lee (Hallett) H.; m. William Howard Ford, Mar. 25, 1961; children—Sabrina Ruth, Mary Heath. Diploma, Grace Hosp., 1960; B.S. in Nursing, Hampton Inst., 1969, M.A. in Guidance and Counseling, 1972, M.S. in Advanced Adult Nursing, 1983. R.N., Va. Staff nurse Hampton (Va.) VA Hosp., 1963-65, 66-67; instr. Thomas Nelson Community Coll., Hampton, 1969-72; asst. prof. Sch. Nursing, Hampton Inst., 1972—, clin. coordinator, 1980—; cons. in devel. learning modules. Mem. Nat. League for Nursing, Sigma Theta Tau. Democrat. Episcopalian. Home: 4 Pin Oak Rd Newport News VA 23601 Office: Hampton Inst Hampton VA 23668

FORD, CATHY ZOE, dentist; b. Knoxville, Tenn., June 2, 1953; d. Lester Smith and Velma (Dyer) Ford; m. James Tate McClung, Jr., June 17, 1978; 1 child, Lindsay Hunter. B.A., U. Tenn., 1974; D.D.S., La. State U., 1979. Med. rep. Arnar-Stone Labs., New Orleans, 1974-75; gen. practice dentistry, Rocky Mount, Va., 1980—; cons. Eldercare, Rocky Mount, 1982-84. Vol. Jr. League of Roanoke Valley, Roanoke, Va., 1982—. Recipient Achievement in Oral Surgery award La. Soc. Oral and Maxillofacial Surgeons, 1977-79. Mem. Alpha Lambda Delta. Republican. Presbyterian. Avocations: golf; tennis. Home: 322 Cassell Ln Roanoke VA 24014 Office: 40 West Route 4 Box 4 Rocky Mount VA 24151

FORD, CHARLES REED, state senator; b. Tulsa, Aug. 2, 1931; s. Juell Reed and Marzee (Lane) F.; m. Patricia Ann Ojers, 1951; children—Christopher Reed, Roger Howard, Karin Rebecca, Robyn Ann. Student Okla. State U., 1949-51. Engr., aide C.E., 1951-53; designer Sunray-DX, 1953-55, asst. mktg. engr. Tidewater Oil Co., 1955-58, real estate investor Charles Ford Co.; pres. Gothic Investments, Inc.; mem. Okla. Ho. of Reps., 1967-81, minority floor leader, 1970-76, former asst. minority leader; mem. Okla. Senate, 1981—, caucus chmn., 1982-83, caucus whip, 1984; mem. Southwest region adv. com. Nat. Park Service, 1982—. Trustee, Tulsa Expn. and Fair Corp., 1955-67; vice chmn. Tulsa Met. Area Planning Commn., 1960-65; former officer Tulsa County Young Republicans; del. Rep. Nat. Conv., 1972. Served with USNR, 1948-53. Mem. Jaycees (Okla. pres. 1959-60, U.S. v.p. 1960-61, internat. v.p. 1963), Alpha Sigma Eta. Republican. Office: Okla Senate Room 527A Oklahoma City OK 73105

FORD, CYNTHIA ANN, psychology educator; b. Natchez, Miss., Sept. 4, 1955; d. James and Rosie (Barnes) Seals. B.S. cum laude, Jackson State U., 1972-75; M.S., So. Ill. U., 1977, Ph.D., 1979. Grad. asst. So. Ill. U., 1975-77, grad. teaching asst., 1977-78, grad. research asst., 1978-79; asst. prof. psychology Jackson State U., Miss., 1980—. Contbr. articles to profl. jours. Solicitor, United Way, Jackson, 1980-81; v.p. United Methodist Women, 1982-85. Named Outstanding Young Woman Am., 1981, 82; Air Force Office of Sci. Research grantee, 1984-85. Mem. Miss. Psychol. Assn. (com. mem.), Am. Psychol. Assn., Miss. Acad. Scis., Miss. Assn. Women in Higher Edn., Psi Chi (treas. 1980-81). Avocations: reading; bike riding. Home: 904 Eastview St Jackson MS 39203 Office: Dept Psychology Jackson State Univ 1500 Lynch St Jackson MS 39217

FORD, DAWN SHEELER, consumer and public affairs executive; b. Balt., Dec. 15, 1944; d. Norman C. and Betty A. (Larsh) Sheeler; m. Richard Ford, June 1, 1969; 1 son, Christopher Norman. B.S., U. Md., 1966. Staff assoc. pub. relations hdqrs. Chesapeake and Potomac Telephone Co., 1968; asst. chief info. office Land Between the Lakes, TVA, Ky., 1969-73, chief info. office Land Between the Lakes, TVA, 1973-76, info. officer TVA, Knoxville, 1976-78, adminstrv. asst. to chmn. bd., 1978, chief citizen action office, 1978-84; pres. Consumer Awareness Mgmt., 1984—. Bd. dirs. Knoxville LWV. Recipient Best Ann. Report award Internat. Assn. Broadcast Communicators, 1977. Mem. Pub. Relations Soc. Am. (pres.-elect., dir. vol. chpt.; Pub. Relations Practitioner of Yr. 1982), Issues Mgmt. Assn., Exec. Women's Assn., Knoxville C. of C. (diplomat), Federally Employed Women (co-chmn. regional tng. conf. 1977—), Beta Sigma Phi (Woman of Yr. 1974), Pi Beta Phi (province pres.). Office: PO Box 30121 Knoxville TN 37930

FORD, FRANCES COTTON, pharmacist; b. Panama City, Fla., Mar. 11, 1945; d. Bernice Newton and Theresa Louise (Pledger) Cotton; m. Ralph E. Ford, Oct. 1962 (div. 1970); children—Ralph E. II, Catherine Renee. B.S. in Pharmacy, U. Fla., 1971. Intern Bay Med. Ctr., Panama City, 1971-72, staff pharmacist, 1972-75, dir. pharmacy, 1975—. Mem. Fla. Soc. Hosp. Pharmacists, Fla. Pharm. Assn. (exec bd. 1986—), Am. Soc. Hosp. Pharmacists, Am. Pharm. Assn., Bay County Pharm. Assn. (v.p. 1983-84). Democrat. Baptist. Avocations: reading; swimming; music. Home: 1214 W 12th St Panama City FL 32401 Office: May Med Ctr 615 N Bonita Ave Panama City FL 32401

FORD, FRANCES LANELLE, psychotherapist; b. Plainview, Tex., Nov. 17, 1924; d. Albert Carroll and Eula Theresa (McPherson) Brigance; m. Dennis B. Ford, Sept. 11, 1943; children—Betty Kathryn, Linda Frances. B.B.A., Tex. A&I U., 1948, M.S., 1972; Psy.D., Fielding Inst., 1978. Lic. profl. counselor, Tex. Tchr. secondary sch., Olton, Tex., 1944-45; exec. sec. Tex. A&I U., 1946-48, Tex. Tech U., 1948-49; exec. dir. and therapist Kleberg County Family Guidance Services, Kingsville, Tex., 1973-78; psychotherapist Psychol. Service Ctr., Corpus Christi, Tex., 1978-80; pvt. practice, Austin, Tex., 1980—. Mem. Am. Psychol. Assn., Internat. Transactional Analysis Assn., Am. Assn. Marriage and Family Therapists, Am. Group Psychotherapy Assn., Am. Assn. Sex Educators, Counselors and Therapists, (cert. sex therapist). Baptist. Clubs: Kingsville Women's; A&I U Faculty Women (pres. 1966-67). Office: 5524 W Bee Caves Rd Suite I-2 Austin TX 78746

FORD, GEORGE DUDLEY, biophysicist; b. Morgantown, W.Va., Aug. 18, 1940; s. O. Rex and Eleanor Mayo (Barnett) F.; m. D. Margaret Shrader, 1965; children—Laura Ellen, Timothy Rex. B.S. in Physics, W.Va. U., 1961; M.S. in Physics, Iowa U., 1964; Ph.D. in Pharmacology, W.Va. U., 1967. Phys. testing engr. Allegheny Ballistics Lab., Cumberland, Md., 1961, design engr., 1962; postdoctoral fellow U. Rochester, N.Y., 1967-69; asst. prof. Med. Coll. Va., Richmond, 1969-76, assoc. prof. physics, 1976—. cons. in field. Contbr. articles to profl. jours. Basketball scorekeeper Va. Commonwealth U., Richmond, 1978—. Fulbright scholar, 1982-83. Mem. Am. Phys. Soc., Biophys. Soc., AAAS, Mill Quarter Golf Assn. (pres. 1981, 1983-86), Sigma Xi, Phi Beta Kappa, Rho Chi. Avocations: golf; duplicate bridge. Home: 7641 Yarmouth Dr Richmond VA 23225 Office: Med Coll Va MCV Box 551 Richmond VA 23298

FORD, GERALD EUGENE, ins. co. mktg. exec.; b. Plainview, Tex., Sept. 8, 1933; s. Herman Weldon and Fern (Callaway) F.; student Tex. Tech. U., North Tex. State Coll.; B.A. in Econs. and Fin., So. Meth. U.; m. Rue Campbell, Aug. 25, 1956; children—Gerald Herman, Caren Rue, Michael Callaway. Salesman, Connecticut Mut. Life, Dallas, 1957-59; sales mgr. Gt. Am. Res. Ins., Amarillo, Abilene, Tex., 1959-66; with Southland Life, 1966-75, Am. Nat. Life, Galveston, Tex., 1975-80; v.p. div., chief mktg. officer First Pyramid Life Ins., Little Rock, 1980—; dir. Computronics Corp. Served with USMC, 1954-56. Mem. Nat. Assn. Life Underwriters, Gen. Agts. and Mgrs. Assn., Am. Soc. Life Underwriters. Republican. Methodist. Club: Pleasant Valley Country. Home: 3 Williamsburg Circle Little Rock AR 72207 Office: 650 Shackleford Rd Little Rock AR 72212

FORD, HAROLD EUGENE, congressman; b. Memphis, May 20, 1945; s. Newton Jackson and Vera (Davis) F.; B.S., Tenn. State U.; M.B.A., Howard U.; m. Dorothy Jean Bowles, 1949; children—Harold Eugene, Newton Jake, Sir Isaac. Mem. Tenn. Ho. of Reps., 1971-74, majority whip, to 1974; mem. 94th-98th congresses from 9th Tenn. dist., chmn. subcom. on pub. assistance and unemployment compensation ways and means com., select com. on aging. Del. Democratic Nat. Conv., 1972. Trustee Rust Coll., Fisk U.; mem. nat. adv. bd. St. Jude Children's Research Hosp.; bd. dirs. Mid-South Fair, Met. YMCA. Hon. fellow Harvard U.; named Outstanding Young Man of Year, Memphis Jaycees, 1976, Tenn. Jaycees, 1976. Mem. Pi Omega Pi, Alpha Phi Alpha. Baptist. Home: 2773 Unicorn Ln NW Washington DC 20015 Office: 2305 Rayburn House Office Bldg Washington DC 20515

FORD, JOHN N., state senator, funeral director; b. Memphis, May 3, 1942; m. Maxine Foster; children—Michelle, Sean, Kemba, Autumn. B.S. in Bus. Adminstrn., Tenn. State U., 1964; M.A. in Pub. Adminstrn. and Fin., Memphis State U., 1978. With N.J. Ford and Sons Funeral Parlors, Memphis, 1969—, now pres.; pres. J.F. Assocs.; former mem. Memphis City Council, mem. Tenn. Senate, chmn. gen. welfare, health and human resources com., mem. fin., ways and means com. Past chmn. Shelby County Legislative Del.; bd. dirs. Regional Sickle Cell Anemia Council; mem. Council of Pensions and Retirements, Council of State Govts., Adv. Council of Vocat. and Tech. Edn.; mem. Adv. Council of Youth, Inc., South Memphis Devel. Corp., Leadership Memphis Selection Com.; exec. dir. Concerned Citizens for a Combined Community. Recipient Outstanding Citizens award Mallory Knights Charitable Orgn., 1971; award Civic Liberty League of Chgo., 1976; Community Achievement award Lutheran Bapt. Ch., 1976; also others. Mem. Nat. Black Caucus of State Legislators, Tenn. Black Caucus State Legislators (treas.), State-Fed. Assembly of Nat. Conf. State Legislatures (health and human resources com.), So. Legis. Conf. (human resources and urban affairs com.), NAACP (life), Nat. Black Caucus Local Elected Ofcls., Alpha Phi Alpha. Democrat. Office: PO Box 9443 12 S Parkway W Memphis TN 38109

FORD, JOHN SUFFERN, psychiatrist; b. Waterville, Maine, July 7, 1939; s. Elsford Q. Ford and Florence Helen Weeks; B.A., Tex. A. and M. U., 1961; M.D., U. Tex., 1965; m. Mary Ann Campbell, July 27, 1963 (div. 1979); children—Cynthia Ann, John Christopher, Curtis Alexander; m. 2d, Elizabeth Lee, 1980; 1 child, Elysia Lee. Intern, John Sealy Hosp., Galveston, 1965-66, resident, 1966, 69-72; practice medicine specializing in psychiatry Clear Lake Psychiat. Assos., Nassau Bay, Tex., 1972—; mem. staff West Oaks, St. John, Clear Lake hosps.; mem. staff Houston Internat. Hosp., pres. med. staff, 1985, also rep. to AMA hosp. staff sect., 1985. Bd. dirs. Bay Area Com. on Drug Abuse, Houston, 1975-77; bd. dirs., v.p. Bay Area Hosp. Authority, Nassau Bay, 1975. Served with AUS, 1966-69. Decorated Army Commendation medal; recipient Physician Recognition award AMA, 1983; diplomate Am. Bd. Psychiatry and Neurology. Mem. Tex. Med. Assn., Am. Psychiat. Assn., Am. Soc. for Adolescent Psychiatry, Phi Rho Sigma. Home: 18240 Nassau Bay Dr Houston TX 77058 Office: 1120 NASA Rd 1 Suite 444 Nassau Bay TX 77058

FORD, JOSEPH DILLON, composer, educator; b. Americus, Ga., Feb. 6, 1952; s. William Lamar and Julia King (Dillon) F. B.F.A., Fla. Internat. U., 1975; A.M., Harvard U., 1978. Tchrs. asst. Dade County Pub. Sch. System, Miami, Fla., 1979-80; music prof. Miami-Dade Community Coll., 1980-82; tchr. The Am. Sch. Tangier (Morocco), 1982-83; former mem. acad. music faculty South campus Miami-Dade Community Coll. Bd. dirs., sec. S. Fla. Chamber Ensemble, 1979-80. Variell scholar Harvard U., 1976, 77. Author: Cosmic Strings, 1978; Chromatic-1: A New Technique for Instrumental Speech, 1983; Sidi Mustafa: A Fable, 1984; composer: Two Ancient Dances, 1980; Capriccio in D minor, 1980; Capriccio in G Major, 1981. Home: 9060 SW 187th Terr Miami FL 33157

FORD, JOSEPH MAURICE, museum administrator; b. Owensboro, Ky., Feb. 8, 1925; s. Maurice Hampton and Mary Ethel (Crabtree) F.; m. Nancy Helen Boyle, Nov. 18, 1949; 1 child, Nancy Dianne. Student U. Ky.; D.Sc. (hon.), Ky. Wesleyan Coll., 1978. Curator Owensboro Mus., Ky., 1966-69, dir., 1969—; editor Ky. News Central States Archeol. Soc., 1961-70. Author: Haunts to Hookers, 1981. Active Owensboro Arts Comn., 1980-84, Daviess County Hist. Soc., 1975—; bd. dirs. Audubon Econ. Edn., 1982—; editor League Ky. Sprotsmen, 1977-85. Recipient Ky. Colonel award, Gov. Bert Combs, 1961, Gov. Wendell Ford, 1974. Mem. Am. Assn. Mus., Nat. Rifle Assn., Ky. Ornithol. Assn., Central States Archeol. Soc., Nat. Audubon Soc. Democrat. Baptist. Club: Daviess County Fish and Game. Avocation: herpetology. Home: 3415 Marycrest W Owensboro KY 42301 Office: Owensboro Area Mus 2829 S Griffith Owensboro KY 42301

FORD, KATHERINE L., public relations/advertising agency executive; b. Waco, Tex., June 19, 1945; d. E.L. and Lillie P. (Gibson) F.; 1 dau., Laurie Dee Ford. Student, Baylor U., 1967-69; B.A., U. Houston, 1973. Account exec. A.R. Busse & Assocs., Houston, 1974-76; dir. pub. relations Howell Corp., Houston, 1976-78; owner, mgr. Katherine Ford Pub. Relations/Advt. Agy., Houston, 1978-83, Miami, Fla., 1983—. Mem. Pub. Relations Soc. Am. Republican. Episcopalian. Office: Katherine Ford Pub Relations/Advt Agy 9325 Park Dr and NE 6th Ave Miami Shores FL 33138

FORD, LINDA LAVENDER, ballet director; b. Canton, Miss., June 9, 1941; d. Edward Warf and Johnnye (Drane) Lavender; m. Joseph Albert Ford Jr., Aug. 20, 1960; children—Joe, Johnnye, Linda Lou. Student Northeast La. U., 1960-61. Artistic dir., ballet mistress Twin City Ballet, West Monroe, La., 1978—; dancer, choreographer; dir. Linda Lavender Sch. of Dance. Mem. So. Assn. Dance Masters (prin.), Southwest Regional Ballet Assn. (bd. dirs.), Nat. Assn. Regional Ballet. Democrat. Methodist. Home: Route 8 Box 158A West Monroe LA 71291 Office: 214 Haynes West Monroe LA 71291

FORD, LISA ANN, training consultant; b. Knoxville, Tenn., Nov. 12, 1956; d. Lester Smith and Velma (Dyer) F. B.A., U. Tenn., 1977; student Alliance Française (Paris), 1976. Energy edn. specialist Oak Ridge Assoc. U., Tenn., 1977-78; tng. cons. Vernine & Assocs., Knoxville, 1978-83; tng. cons., owner Ford & Assocs., Atlanta, 1983—. Vol. High Mus. Art/Young Careers, Atlanta. Mem. Am. Soc. Tng. and Devel. (treas. 1978-79, bd. dirs. 1979-84), Nuclear Energy Women, Atlanta Womens Network. Republican. Baptist. Avocations: tennis; sailing; travel. Home and Office: 6849 D Glenlake Pkwy Atlanta GA 30328

FORD, MICHAEL ARNO, pharmacist; b. Parkersburg, W.Va., June 30, 1955; s. Arno Wade and Helen Margaret (Kirsch) F.; m. Susan Nichols, May 28, 1978 (div. 1980); m. Richa Angel, Mar. 10, 1984; 1 stepson, Jeremiah. B.S., U. Richmond, 1977; B.S. in Pharmacy, Mercer So. Sch. Pharmacy, 1981. Lic. pharmacist, Ga., Va. Chief pharmacist Northwest Prescription Ctr., Atlanta, 1981-83, pharmacist Prucare Pharmacy, Atlanta, 1983—, Prudential Health Care Plan Inc., Atlanta, 1983—; pharmacist Prucare of Atlanta, 1983—, pharmacist-in-charge, 1984—; pharmacy preceptor Mercer U. So. Sch. Pharmacy, Atlanta, 1982—. Mem. Spina Bifida Assn., 1981—. Mem. North Fulton County Pharm. Assn., Ga. Pharm. Assn. Republican. Episcopalian. Home: 2310 Brookstone Dr Lithia Springs GA 30057

FORD, MICHAEL RAYE, lawyer; b. Blackwell, Okla., Sept. 1, 1945; s. Oscar Raye and Lucille (Belton) Ray; B.A., U. Okla., 1967, J.D., 1970; LL.M. in Taxation, George Washington U., 1974; m. Carol Annette Naylor, June 17, 1972; children—Seth Michael, Jared Raye. Admitted to Okla. bar, 1970; asso. firm Gable, Gotwals, Rubin, Fox, Johnson & Baker, Inc., Tulsa, 1974-77; partner firm Baker, Baker, Wilson, Selph & Ford, Oklahoma City, 1977-79, McKnight, Gasaway, Beck, Seals, Ford & Smith, Enid, Okla., 1979-84, Ford & Brown, Enid, 1984—; pres. Enid Estate Planning Council. Deacon, bd. dirs. First Christian Ch., Falls Church, Va.; deacon, bd. dirs., chmn. com. First Christian Ch., Tulsa; class pres., tchr. Putnam City Christian Ch., Oklahoma City; deacon, vice chmn. bd. dirs. Central Christian Ch., Enid. Served to capt. Judge Adv. Gen., U.S. Army, 1970-74. Mem. ABA, Okla. Bar Assn. (chmn. sect. taxation 1984; program dir. and lectr. seminar 1984, mem. bar/media relations com.), Garfield County Bar Assn., Greater Enid C. of C. (dir. 1983—), Order of Coif, Phi Delta Phi. Club: Kiwanis (pres. 1984-85 dir.) (Enid). Articles editor Okla. Law Rev.; contbr. articles to profl. jours. Home: 1516 Tahlequah St Enid OK 73701 Office: PO Box 6155 102 S Van Buren Enid OK 73702

FORD, RAMONA LOUISE, Sociology educator; b. Kansas City, Mo., July 29, 1937; d. Claude Gilbert and Anna Louise (Synder) Owen; m. Arthur Morton Ford, Dec. 23, 1955 (dec. June 1977); 1 child, Owen Lewis Anthony. A.B., Baker U., 1959; M.A., Ind. U., 1962, New Sch. Social Research, 1971; Ph.D., So. Ill. U., 1978. Librarian Columbia U., N.Y.C., 1967-68, Bklyn. Coll., 1968-70; instr., tchng. asst. So. Ill. U., Carbondale, 1972-78; instr. Pan Am. U., Edinburg, Tex., 1978-79; asst. prof. Southwest Tex. State U., San Marcos, 1979—; mem. bd. Nat. Ctr. Employee Ownership. Mem. Am. Sociol. Assn., So. Sociol. Soc., Southwestern Sociol. Assn., AAUP, High Plains Applied Anthropologists. Avocation: camping. Home: 116 Laurel Ln San Marcos TX 78666 Office: Dept Sociology Anthropology Southwest Tex State U San Marcos TX 78666

FORD, ROBERT BRUCE, psychiatrist; b. Easley, S.C., Feb. 7, 1931; s. Enos Walker and Ruby (Berryman) F.; B.A., Furman U., 1953; M.D., Med. Coll. S.C., 1957; m. Daphne Berry, Sept. 13, 1958; children—Robert, Donald, Steven, James. Intern, Med. Center Hosps., Charleston, S.C., 1957-58, resident in psychiatry, 1958-61; postgrad. in mental retardation Letchworth Village, N.Y., 1961; practice medicine specializing in psychiatry, Spartanburg, S.C., 1963—; chmn. dept. psychiatry Spartanburg Gen. Hosp.; mem. med. staff Mary Black Meml. Hosp., Spartanburg, Drs. Meml. Hosp.; psychiatrist Spartanburg Area Mental Health Clinic, 1963-68; asst. clin. prof. psychiatry Med. U. S.C.; mem. People to People med. del. to China, 1981. Bd. dirs. Lawrence D. McCarthy Sch. for Handicapped Children, Spartanburg, 1964-71, chmn. bd., 1970-71; instrumental in concept and design, mem. bldg. com., mem. personnel com., bd. dirs. Charles Lee Center for Spl. Edn. and Rehab., Spartanburg, 1971—; elder emeritus Routh Meml. Presbyn. Ch., Spartanburg. Served with M.C., USAF, 1961-63. Fellow Am. Psychiat. Assn. (pres. S.C. dist. br. 1980-81), Acad. Orthomolecular Psychiatry; mem. AMA, S.C. Med. Assn. (chmn. com. mental health 1971-76), Spartanburg County Med. Soc., U.S. Power Squadron. Home: 2471 Country Club Rd Spartanburg SC 29302 Office: 943 N Church St Spartanburg SC 29303

FORD, ROGER JULIAN, SR., clergyman; b. Esmont, Va., Oct. 2, 1934; s. Fleming Vaughn and Frances Catherine (Copeland) F.; m. Velma Lee Gray, Mar. 1, 1958; children—Lori, Nadine, Francine, Robin, Wendy, Roger Julian. D.D. (hon.), Va. Sem. & Coll., 1985. Pastor Chestnut Grove Baptist Ch., Esmont, Va., 1962-70, Mt. Zion Bapt. Ch., Greenwood, Va., 1963-69, Wake Forest Bapt. Ch., Slate Hill, Va., 1969-74, Mt. Sinai Bapt. Ch., Madison Heights, Va., 1971—; exec. dir. Monticello Community Action Agy., Charlottesville, Va., 1970-74, Opportunity Industrialized Ctr., Lynchburg, Va., 1978-80; manpower dir. Total Action Against Poverty, Roanoke, Va., 1974-78; mgr. Ebonaire Ch. Supply, Madison Heights, 1980—. Co-chmn. Amherst County Dem. Party, Va., 1980-82; pres. Va. State Conf. NAACP, 1978-80, Amherst County Br. NAACP, 1975-78, 1980—. Served to sgt. USMC, 1954-58. Recipient Community Achievement award Lynchburg Nationwide Ins. Co., 1980; named Minister of Year Community Advancement and Achievement Movement, 1977; Leader of Year Amherst County NAACP 1979. Lodge: Odd Fellows. Home: Route 6 Box 535 Madison Heights VA 24572 Office: PO Box 707 Dixie Airport Rd Madison Heights VA 24572

FORD, THOMAS JEFFERS, indsl. developer; b. Charleston, S.C., Sept. 9, 1930; s. Rufus and Mildred (Jeffers) F.; A.B., Wofford Coll., 1952; postgrad. U. N.C., 1956-58, 59-61, U. Okla., 1965-67; m. Barbara Jean Jackson, Dec. 28, 1954; children—Thomas Jeffers, Edward Rufus. Asst. mgr. Albany (Ga.) C. of C., 1956; mgr. Rock Hill (S.C.) C. of C., 1957-58; dir. trade devel. Greenville (S.C.) C. of C., 1959-60, dir. bus. and indsl. relations, 1961; exec. dir. Marlboro County Devel. Bd., Bennettsville, S.C., 1962-65, Lakeland (Fla.) Indsl. Bd., 1966-67; dir. Chesterfield-Marlboro Tech. Edn. Center, Cheraw, S.C., 1968-72; dir. area devel. dept. 6th Congl. Dist. S.C., Florence, 1973-74; dir. bus. devel. Eskridge & Long Constrn. Corp., Sanford, N.C., 1975; chief exec. officer Greater Orangeburg (S.C.) C. of C.; chief exec. officer Orangeburg County Devel. Commn., 1976-79, exec. dir., 1979—. Served with USN, 1952-53. Cert. indsl. developer. Fellow Am. Econ. Devel. Council (past mem. internat. certified indsl. devel. bd.; regent edn. programs); mem. S.C. Indsl. Developers Assn. (past pres.), So. Indsl. Devel. Council (past dir.), Blue Key, SAR, Sigma Alpha Epsilon. Methodist. Lodge: Rotary (past club pres.). Home: 2978 Lakeside Dr NE Orangeburg SC 29115 Office: PO Box 1303 Orangeburg SC 29116

FORD, WENDELL HAMPTON, U.S. senator; b. Owensboro, Ky., Sept. 8, 1924; s. Ernest M. and Irene (Schenk) F.; m. Jean Neel, Sept. 18, 1943; children—Shirley Jean Ford Dexter, Steven. Partner Gen. Ins. Agy., Owensboro, 1959-67; chief asst. to Gov. Ky., 1959-61; mem. Ky. Senate, 1965-67; lt. gov. Ky., 1967-71, gov., 1971-74; mem. U.S. senate, mem. coms. on commerce, sci. and transp., energy and natural resources; rules and adminstrn. chmn. Democratic Senatorial Campaign Com., 1976-82. Served with U.S. Army, 1944-46; Ky. N.G., 1949-62. Mem. Ky. Jaycees (state pres. 1954-55, nat. pres. 1956-57, internat. v.p. 1958-59), U.S. C. of C. (bd. dirs.). Democrat. Baptist. Home: Bethesda MD 20816 Office: US Senate Washington DC 20510

FORDHAM, CHRISTOPHER COLUMBUS, III, physician, university chancellor; b. Greensboro, N.C., Nov. 28, 1926; s. Christopher Columbus and Frances Clendenin F.; m. Barbara Byrd, Aug. 16, 1947; children—Pamela Fordham Richey, Susan Fordham Crowell, Betsy Fordham Templeton. Cert. medicine U. N.C., 1949; M.D., Harvard U., 1951. Diplomate Am. Bd. Internal. Medicine. Intern, Georgetown Univ. Hosp., Washington, 1951-52; resident Boston City Hosp., 1952-53; resident N.C. Meml. Hosp., Chapel Hill, 1953-54, fellow, 1954-55; instr. U. N.C. Sch. Medicine, Chapel Hill, 1958-60, asst. prof. medicine, 1960-64, assoc. prof., 1964-68, asst. dean, 1965-68, assoc. dean, 1968-69, dean, 1971-79, vice chancellor, 1977-80, chancellor, 1980—; dean, v.p. medicine Med. Coll. Ga., Augusta, 1969-71. Served to capt. USAFR, 1955-57. Recipient Disting. Service awards N.C. Hosp. Assn., 1980, N.C. Acad. Gen. Dentistry, 1980. Fellow ACP, AAAS; mem. Inst. Medicine of Nat. Acad. Scis., Am. Assn. Med. Colls. (disting. service mem.; chmn. council of deans 1977), Inst. Medicine of Nat. Acad. Scis. (council 1985—). Office: South Bldg U NC Chapel Hill NC 27514

FORDIK, KENNETH JACK, retail store executive; b. Glasgow, Mont., Jan. 13, 1939; s. Jack and Edna Anna (Quandt) F.; m. Vera Ann Crosley, June 15, 1963; children—Chrisanne, Scott, Diane. B.S., U. Mont., 1962; M.B.A., Calif. State U.-Long Beach, 1971. Compensation adminstr., recruiter McDonnell, Douglas & N.Am. Aviation, Los Angeles, 1962-67; personnel mgr. Bissett-Berman, Santa Monica, Calif., 1967-70; labor relations mgr. Amcord, Inc., Riverside, Calif., 1970-74; personnel dir. Warner Lambert, Morris Plaines, N.J., 1974-81; v.p. personnel Burdines, Miami, Fla., 1981—. Chmn.-elect Pvt. Industry Council Dade County, 1981—; mem. exec. com. Bus. Assistance Com., 1982—; mem. mgmt. adv. bd. Fla. Internat. U., 1982—; asst. troop leader Boy Scouts, 1980—. Mem. Miami C. of C., Pvt. Industry Council S. Fla., Am. Soc. Personnel Adminstrn., Greater Miami Personnel Assn. Republican. Lutheran. Office: 7100 NW 32d Ave Miami FL 33147

FORDYCE, HOMER EDMUND, civil engr.; b. Ridgeway, Mo., Aug. 1, 1916; s. Orey Francis and Mabel Edna (Baxter) F.; B.C.E., U. Wyo., 1941; m. Mary Louise Gilbert, Mar. 25, 1948; 1 son, Jerry Edmund; 1 stepdau., Mary Lee Sooter Phillips. Cons. in gen. design Marley Co., Mission, Kans., 1945-78. Mem. Mo. Republican Com., Clay County. Served with USAF, 1942-45. Mem. ASCE, Am. Concrete Inst. (v.p. Kans. chpt. 1977-78, pres. Kans. chpt. 1978). Patentee in cooling tower designs. Home: 146 El Cielo Circle Harlingen TX 78550

FORE, BRYAN DOUGLAS, oil company executive, geologist; b. Beaumont, Tex., Nov. 22, 1950; s. William Lewis and Vivian Clair (Broussard) F.; m. Donna Annette Perricone, Aug. 5, 1972; children—Bryan Douglas, John Daryl. B.S. in Geology, Lamar U., 1976. Sta. mgr., Schlumberger Well Service, Gainesville, Tex., 1981-82, sales engr., Woodward, Okla., 1982; ind. petroleum geologist, San Angelo, Tex., 1982-83; v.p. Murley-Hobbs-Fore Geol. Cons., San Angelo, 1983-85; sec. treas. MHF Operating Co., San Angelo, 1983-85; pres., chief exec. officer Fore Exploration, San Angelo, 1984—. Mem. Am. Assn. Petroleum Geologists, San Angelo Geol. Soc., Soc. Profl. Well Log Analysts, Sigma Phi Epsilon. Republican. Roman Catholic. Avocations: flying, sailing, snow skiing, hunting, fishing. Home: PO Box 60014 San Angelo TX 76906 Office: Fore Exploration Inc 2702 Loop 306 Suite 311 San Angelo TX 76904

FORE, ROBERT CLIFFORD, medical society executive; b. Jacksonville, Fla., Feb. 23, 1948; s. Clifford Roy and Annie Laurie (Wiltshire) F.; m. Rorie Elizabeth Smith, Aug. 8, 1970; children—Dorian Brooke, Jessica Allison. B.A., U. South Fla., 1969; M.Ed., U. Fla., 1972; Ed.D., U. Ga., 1976. Cert. in ednl. adminstrn., mental retardation, dir. spl. edn. and ednl. supervision, Fla. Tchr., coordinator Duval County Sch. Bd., Jacksonville, 1969-72; asst. prof. edn. Jacksonville U., 1975-77; edn. supr. program for multi-handicapped Ga. Acad. for the Blind, Macon, 1977-79; field underwriter N.Y. Life Ins. Co., Macon, 1979-82; dir. sci. activities Fla. Med. Assn., Jacksonville, 1982-84, assoc. exec. dir. programs, adminstrn., 1984—. coordinator Spl. Olympics, Jacksonville, 1976-77; adj. prof. Mercer U., Macon, 1978-79. Bd. dirs. N. Fla. chpt. Am. Diabetes Assn., Jacksonville, 1983. Recipient Eagle Scout and God and Country award Boy Scouts Am., 1962; U.S. Office Edn. fellow, 1973-75. Mem. Am. Assn. Med. Soc. Execs., Alliance Continuing Med. Edn., Council for Exceptional Children, Nat. Eagle Scout Assn., Phi Delta Kappa, Kappa Delta Pi, Sigma Alpha Epsilon. Democrat. Methodist. Clubs: U. Ga. Bulldog Alumni (v.p.), Sertoma Internat. (life mem., v.p., sec.). Exec. editor Jour. Fla. Med. Assn., 1982—. Office: Fla Med Assn 760 Riverside Ave Jacksonville FL 32203

FORE, WILLIAM WHATELY, physician, educator; b. Lynchburg, Va., May 27, 1936; s. William Henry and Rosalie (Reeves) F.; m. Judy O'Neal, Feb. 28, 1981; children—William Whately, Thomas Butler, Mary Tyler Reeves. Student Duke U., 1953-56, M.D., 1960. Diplomate Am. Bd. Internal Medicine, Am. Bd. Nuclear Medicine. Intern Osler med. service Johns Hopkins Hosp., Balt., 1960-61; jr. asst. resident in medicine, Duke U. Med. Ctr., Durham, N.C., 1961-62, sr. asst. resident in medicine, 1963-64; fellow in endocrinology and metabolism, 1962-63; practice medicine specializing in internal medicine, Greenville, N.C., 1966-84; instr. Lincoln Hosp., Durham, 1963-64; assoc. clin. prof. medicine East Carolina U. Sch. Medicine, Greenville, 1971-84; assoc. prof. medicine Sch. Medicine, E. Carolina U., Greenville, 1984—; co-dir. Nuclear Medicine Lab., Pitt County Meml. Hosp., Greenville. Former chmn. Heart Fund; campaign mgr. Richard Nixon for Pitt County. Served to lt. comdr., M.C., USNR, 1964-66. Recipient Physician's Recognition award AMA, 1969, 75, 79, 83, 86. Fellow ACP (pres. N.C. chpt. 1984, gov. for N.C. 1986—), mem. AMA, N.C. Med. Soc. (2d v.p., chmn. sect. internal medicine, chmn. hosp. and profl. liaison com. task force third-party liaison commr., chmn. com. on practice variations), Pitt County Med. Soc. (pres. 1981), N.C. Soc. Internal Medicine (pres. 1979-80, exec. council), Soc. Nuclear Medicine, Am. Diabetes Assn., (bd. dirs. Pitt County chpt.), Greenville C. of C. Republican. Episcopalian. Club: Greenville Golf and Country. Contbr. articles to profl. pubis. Home: 207 Fairlane Rd Greenville NC 27834 Office: Brody Bldg 3514 East Carolina U Sch Medicine Greenville NC 27834

FOREMAN, EDWIN FRANCIS, broker; b. Syracuse, N.Y., July 24, 1931; s. Herve Joseph and Ruth Margaret F.; m. Colleen Frances Tapp, July 7, 1962; children—Lisa C., Eric E. B.A.E. in Econs. and Fgn. Trade, U. Fla., 1957; postgrad. in real estate Fla. Internat. U., 1974-75. Owner, prin. Edwin F. Foreman, Mortgage Broker, Hollywood, Fla., 1974—; with Consol. Energy Corp., Hollywood, 1977—, pres., chmn. bd., 1977—; v.p. Aljon Securities, Inc., 1977—; owner, prin. Edwin F. Foreman, Real Estate Broker, 1978—; pres., chmn. One-Fore-Devel., Inc., 1985, Three-Fore-Devel., Inc., 1985, L&E Communications Inc., 1985; dir. Med. Imagery Corp. Served with USAF, 1950-53. R.J. Reynolds fellow U. N.C., 1961. Mem. Hollywood C. of C., Ft. Lauderdale World Trade Council. Democrat. Unitarian. Clubs: Palm Bay, Jockey (Miami). Office: 1747 Van Buren St Suite 840 Hollywood FL 33020

FORER, DANIEL BENJAMIN, photographer; b. N.Y.C., Feb. 7, 1940; s. Samuel and Lillian (Rabinowitz) F.; m. Loretta Rosen, May 25, 1982; children—Christine, Jeremy. Student Brandeis U., 1957-60. Freelance theatrical lighting designer, 1959-65; v.p. Eiger and Forer, Inc., P.R., 1965-72; owner Dan Forer, Photography, Miami, Fla., 1972-81; pres. Forer, Inc. (doing bus. as Dan Forer, Photographer), Miami, 1981—. Recipient Archtl. Photography award Fla. Assn. of AIA, 1985. Served with U.S. Army, 1963-65. Mem. Am. Soc. Mag. Photographers, Inst. Bus. Designers (press affiliate). Home: 4941 SW 71st Pl Miami FL 33155 Office: 1970 NE 149th St North Miami FL 33181

FORESTER, JEAN MARTHA BROUILLETTE, educator, librarian; b. Port Barre, La., Sept. 7, 1934; d. Joseph Walter and Thelma (Brown) Brouillette; B.S., La. State U., 1955; M.A. (Carnegie fellow 1955-56), George Peabody Coll. Tchrs., 1956; m. James Lawrence Forester, June 2, 1957; children—Jean Martha, James Lawrence. Librarian Howell Elementary Sch., Springhill, La., 1956-58; asst. post librarian Fort Chaffee, Ark., 1958; command librarian Orleans Area Command, U.S. Army, Orleans, France, 1958-59; acquisitions librarian Northwestern State U., Natchitoches, La., 1960; serials librarian La. State U., New Orleans, 1966-66; mem. faculty La. State U., Eunice, 1966—, asst. librarian, 1972-85, assoc. librarian, 1985—, asst. prof., 1972-85, faculty senator, 1978-80, 85-86. Active Eunice Assn. Retarded Children. Mem. La. Library Assn. (sect. sec. 1971-72, coordinator serials interest group 1984-85), UDC, Delta Kappa Gamma (chpt. parliamentarian 1972-74, rec. sec. 1984-86), Alpha Beta Alpha, Phi Gamma Mu, Phi Mu. Democrat. Baptist. Mem. Order Eastern Star. Co-author: Robertson's Bill of Fare. Contbr. articles to profl. jours. Home: 1351 Gregg Ave Eunice LA 70535

FORESTIERI, FELIX ERNESTO, corporate communications specialist; b. Santo Domingo, Dominican Republic, July 7, 1937; s. Pascual and Fedora (Sanabia) F.; m. Anthea B. Monterotti, Sept. 5, 1959 (div. Apr. 1967); children—Alex, Marco; m. Aleida A. Bello, Aug. 10, 1968; children—Cristina, Claudia. Ph.D. in Polit. Sci. magna cum laude, Universita Internazionale Degli Studi Sociali, Rome, 1962, postgrad. in pub. relations, 1962. Asst. to pres. Universita Internazionale degli Studi Sociali, Rome, 1958-59; dir. pub. relations Notre Dame Internat. Sch., Rome, 1959-62; pub. relations dir., cons. advt. Corporación de Fomento Industrial, Santo Domingo, 1962-65; mktg., advt. and pub. relations cons., Santo Domingo, 1965-72; v.p. tng. Leadership Dynamics Inst., Inc., San Juan, P.R., 1972-73; v.p. mktg. Computer Systems P.R., Inc., 1973-74; regional mgr. pub. relations (Caribbean), Eastern Airlines, San Juan, 1974-81; corporate communications mgr. for Latin Am., Eastern Airlines, Miami, 1981—; mem. Fla. Trade in Services Com., Miami, 1982-84. Co-founder, organizer Instituto Tecnológico de Santo Domingo, 1972. Mem. Dominican Am. C. of C. (dir. 1982-84), Pub. Relations Soc. P.R. Republican. Roman Catholic. Club: Overseas Press of Puerto Rico. Home: 1136 Partridge Ave Miami Springs FL 33166 Office: Eastern Airlines Miami FL 33148

FORGIE, GEORGE BARNARD, history educator; b. Phila., May 31, 1941; s. James William and Mary (Barnard) F. B.A., Amherst Coll., 1963; LL.B., Stanford U., 1967, M.A., 1967, Ph.D., 1972. Lectr. history Princeton U. (N.J.), 1969-72, asst. prof., 1972-74; asst. prof. U. Tex., Austin, 1974-80, assoc. prof., 1980—. Recipient Allan Nevins prize Soc. Am. Historians, 1973; Harry H. Ransom award for teaching excellence in liberal arts U. Tex., 1979, Pres.'s Teaching award 1984. Mem. Am. Hist. Assn., Orgn. Am. Historians. Author: Patricide in the House Divided: A Psychological Interpretation of Lincoln and His Age, 1979. Home: 1119 Red Bud Trail Austin TX 78746 Office: Dept History U Tex Austin TX 78712

FORGY, LAWRENCE E., JR., lawyer; b. Aug. 4, 1939. A.B., George Washington U, 1961, J.D., 1964. Mem. staff U.S. Congress, Washington, 1960-67, aide to Sen. Thruston B. Morton and asst. sgt.-at-arms, 1960-65, legal counsel Joint Com. on Internal Revenue Taxation, 1965-67; state budget dir., dep. commr. fin., dir. fiscal mgmt. State of Ky., Lexington, 1967-70; v.p. bus. affairs, treas. U. Ky., 1970-75; ptnr. Wyatt Tarrant & Combs, Lexington, to present; pres. Southeast Coal Sales Co., Lexington, to present. Mem. Republican Nat. Com.; chmn. Ky. Reagan-Bush Campaign, 1980; former mem. Ky. Mental Health Manpower Commn.; former bd. dirs. Spindletop Research Ctr., Lexington; former bd. dirs. and treas. U. Ky. Athletics Assn. Mem. Ky. C. of C., Omicron Delta Kappa. Office: 1100 Kincaid Towers Lexington KY 40508

FORMAN, SUSAN GREENBERG, psychology educator; b. Bklyn., Dec. 28, 1948; d. George J. and Mildred (Weber) Greenberg. B.A., U. R.I., 1969, M.S., 1971; Ph.D., U. N.C., 1975. Sch. psychologist Washington pub. schs., 1971-72; dir. pupil personnel services Chapel Hill pub. schs., 1974-77; asst. prof. dept. psychology U. S.C., Columbia, 1977-82, assoc. prof. 1982—. Ednl. and Profl. Devel. Act fellow 1970-71. Fellow Am. Psychol Assn.; mem. Nat. Assn. Sch. Psychologists (S.E. regional dir. 1981-83), S.C. Assn. Sch. Psychologists. Contbr. articles to profl. jours. Home: 1716 Stillwater Dr Columbia SC 29210 Office: Dept Psychology University of South Carolina Columbia SC 29208

FORMAN, WILLIAM WAYNE, natural resource company executive; b. Baton Rouge, Oct. 30, 1944; s. W. H. and V.B. Forman; B.S., La. State U., 1966, M.S., 1968; postgrad. Tulane U., 1971-78. Student biol. aide La. Dept. Wildlife and Fisheries, Grand Terre Marine Lab., 1962; grad. teaching asst. zoology dept. La. State U., Baton Rouge, 1966-68, Gulf Coast Research Lab., Ocean Springs, Miss., 1968; marine biologist Freeport Sulphur Co., Belle Chasse, La., 1968-79, mgr. environ. services, New Orleans, 1979-85; asst. dir. corp. environ. affairs Freeport-McMoRan, Inc., 1985—. Fund raiser United Fund New Orleans, 1972; advisor Jr. Achievement New Orleans, 1972-73. Mem. Water Pollution Control Fedn. (program com. 1980), Air Pollution Control Assn. (program com. 1983), Am. Fisheries Soc. (cert. fisheries scientist), Am. Soc. Ichthyologists and Herpetologists, Gulf States Council on Wildlife, Fisheries and Mosquito Control (pres. 1972), Gulf Estuarine Research Soc., La. Acad. Scis., La. Environ. Profls. Assn. (cert. environ. profl.; v.p. 1980-81), La. Water Pollution Control Assn. (chmn. pub. affairs com.), La. Air Pollution Control Assn. (dir.), La. Wildlife Biologists Assn. (mem. publs. awards com. 1976, 80), Am. Inst. Fishery Research Biologists (elected mem.), La. Univs. Marine Consortium Found. Inc. (pres.). Home: 4411 Copernicus St New Orleans LA 70114 Office: PO Box 61520 New Orleans LA 70161

FORMANEK, PETER, food products company executive; b. 1943. B.A., U. N.C., 1966; M.B.A., Harvard U., 1968. Adminstrv. asst. to pres., asst. prof. bus. adminstrn. LeMoyne-Owen Coll., Tenn.; exec. v.p. Super Drugs, 1969-72, pres. 1972; with Malone & Hyde, Inc., Memphis, 1968—, asst. to pres., 1968-73, v.p. drugs and rock service, 1973-79, group v.p. retailing 1979-81, exec. v.p. specialty retailing 1981—. Address: Malone & Hyde Inc 1991 Corporate Ave Memphis TN 38132*

FORMBY, JOHN PAUL, economics educator; b. Carrollton, Ga., Feb. 12, 1940; s. Albert Spencer and Mary Clyde (Brown) F.; m. Nita Sewell, May 3, 1958; children—Jana, Jeffery. B.A., Colo. Coll., 1962; Ph.D., U. Colo., 1965. Asst. prof. U. Ark., Fayetteville, 1965-66; asst. prof. U. N.C., Greensboro, 1966-70, assoc. prof., 1970-74, prof., head dept. 1974-82; sr. economist Council of Wage and Price Stability, Washington, 1979-80; prof., chmn. dept. U. Ala., Tuscaloosa, 1983—. Contbr. articles to porfl. publs. Fellow NSF, NDEA, Woodrow Wilson. Mem. Am. Econ. Assn., Atlantic Econ. Assn. So. Econ. Assn., Royal Econ. Soc., Pub. Choice Soc. Home: 11-M Northwood Lake Northport AL 35476 Office: The Univ of Ala PO Box J Dept of Econs Fin and Legal Studies University AL 35486

FORNADEL, DAVID JOSEPH, health care adminstrator, army officer; b. Sharon, Pa., Jan. 30, 1952; s. Joseph Andrew and Maryanne Theresa F.; m. Martha Sue Moll, Sept. 8, 1974; children—Lenora Catherine, Todd David. B.A., Ohio State U., 1975; M.S. in Health Care Adminstrn., U. No. Colo., 1980. Commd. 2d lt. U.S. Army, 1975, advanced through grades to capt., 1980; med. platoon leader 52d Engr. Bn., Ft. Carson, Colo., 1976-77, exec. officer D Co. 4th Med. Bn., 1977-78, asst. chief patient adminstrn. div. U.S. Army Hosp., Ft. Carson, 1978-79; exec. officer U.S. Army Dental Activity, Ft. Huachuca, Ariz., 1979-81; comdr. Hdqrs 2d Med. Bn., 1981-82; br. med. advisor U.S. Army Readiness Group, Ft. Sill, Okla., 1982-84; asst. dir. patient adminstrn. Brooke Army Med. Ctr., Ft. Sam Houston, Tex., 1984—; mgmt. cons. Exec. com. Boy Scouts Am.; instr. ARC, Am. Heart Assn. Cert. emergency med. technician, instr. CPR. Mem. Am. Hosp. Assn., Assn. U.S. Army, Am. Coll. Health Care Execs., (affiliate). Home: 12906 El Sendero San Antonio TX 78233 Office: Brooke Army Med Ctr Fort Sam Houston TX 78234

FORNEY, JOHN EDGAR, microbiologist; b. Waterloo, Iowa, June 22, 1917; s. Isaac M. and Mary Elizabeth (Eikenberry) F.; m. Joann K. Donnell, Jan. 8, 1944 (div.); children—Susan Jo, David Lowell, Sharon Jane; m. Martha E. Mason, Dec. 22, 1976. A.B., Manchester Coll., 1938; M.A., Stanford U., 1948, Ph.D., 1949. Assoc. prof. microbiology U. So. Calif. Sch. Medicine, Los Angeles, 1949-55; asst. dir. City of Los Angeles Health Dept. Lab., 1955-63, dep. dir. lab. consultation and devel. sect., 1963-68, dir. lab. licensure sect., 1968-72, microbiologist cons. lab. tng. and consultation div., 1972-82; acting dir. tech. evaluation and assistance div., 1982-83; microbiologist cons. Ctrs. for Disease Control, Atlanta, 1963-85; adj. prof. microbiology U. N.C. Sch. Pub. Health, 1973-85; cons. in lab. biosafety, WHO, Pan Am. Health Orgn., Peoples Republic of China; editor Health Lab. Sci., 1973-78. Served to capt. U.S. Army, 1941-46. Mem. Am. Soc. Microbiology. Am. Soc. Clin. Pathologists, Am. Acad. Microbiologists, Conf. Pub. Health Lab. Dirs., Sigma Xi. Contbr. articles to profl. jours.

FORNOS, PEDRO GENARO, internist; b. Havana, Cuba, Sept. 19, 1922; s. Pedro J. and Maria Angeles (Palencia) F.; came to U.S., 1965, naturalized, 1971; M.D., U. Havana, 1946; m. Caridad Lopez, Dec. 21, 1950; children—Pedro, Emma Maria. Intern, Univ. Hosp., Havana, 1947-49; resident Austin (Tex.) State Hosp., 1968-69, Meth. Hosp., Dallas, 1969-71; dir. pulmonary function dept. Univ. Hosp., Havana, 1961-65; dir. respiratory therapy dept., Bapt. Meml. Hosp. System, San Antonio, 1973—; pvt. practice internal medicine, San Antonio, 1971—. Diplomate Am. Bd. Internal Medicine. Fellow Am. Coll. Chest Physicians; mem. AMA, Tex., Bexar County med. assns., San Antonio Club Internal Medicine. Roman Catholic. Home: 3038 Oneida St San Antonio TX 78230 Office: 201 Med Sq Med Bldg 311 Camden St San Antonio TX 78215

FORREST, HUGH SOMMERVILLE, science educator, editor; b. Glasgow, Scotland, Apr. 28, 1924; came to U.S., 1951; s. Archibald and Margaret Wilson (Peden) F.; m. Rosamond Scott Baker, Jan. 12, 1954; children—Eleanor Scott, Anne Sommerville, Hugh Watson. B.Sc. with honors, U. Glasgow, 1944; Ph.D., U. London, 1947, D.Sc., 1970; Ph.D., U. Cambridge, 1951. Mem. staff Med. Research Council of Gt. Britain, London, 1945-48, Dept. Sci. and Indsl. Research fellow, 1948-51; USPHS fellow Calif. Inst. Tech., Pasadena, 1951-53; sr. research fellow, 1953-54; Carnegie scholar U. Glasgow, 1945 research scientist U. Tex.-Austin, 1955-56, assoc. prof., 1956-63, prof. zoology, 1963—, chmn. zoology dept., 1974-78; USPHS fellow MIT, 1973-74. Editor: Biochem. Genetics, 1970—. Recipient numerous NIH, NSF, Robert A. Welch Found. (Houston) research grants. Fellow Royal Soc. Edinburgh, Royal Soc. Chemistry; mem. Am. Chem. Soc., Soc. Biol. Chemists. Discoverer biopterin and methoxatin; contbr. numerous sci. articles to profl. publs. Home: 3302 River Rd Austin TX 78703 Office: U Tex Dept Zoology Austin TX 78712

FORRESTER, J. OWEN, U.S. district judge; b. 1939. B.S., Ga. Inst. Tech., 1961; LL.B., Emory U., 1966. Staff atty. for gubernatorial candidate, 1966-67; assoc. firm Fisher & Phillips, Atlanta, 1967-69; asst. U.S. atty. No. Ga. Dist., 1969-76, U.S. magistrate, 1976-81; U.S. dist. judge No. Dist. Ga., Atlanta, 1981—. Office: 2367 US Courthouse 75 Spring St Atlanta GA 30303*

FORSBERG, CARL EARL, musician, retired educator; b. Rochelle, Ill., Apr. 12, 1920; s. Karl Eskil and Laura Julia (Dewey) F.; m. Clara Mae Eadler, Aug. 24, 1957. B.Mus., B.S., U. Ill., 1943; M.A., State U. Iowa, 1944; Ph.D., Ind. U., 1964. Instr., Northwestern State U., Natchitoches, La., 1944-46; asst. prof. Midland Coll., Fremont, Nebr., 1946-49; prof. music U. Central Ark., Conway, 1949-84, chmn. music dept., 1970-80; violinist Ark. Symphony, Little Rock, 1949-84. Co-condr. Conway Civic Orch., 1983, 84. Recipient Pres.'s Achievement award U. Central Ark., 1972; Outstanding Coll. Tchr. award Ark. State Music Tchrs. Assn., 1981. Mem. Am. Musicol. Soc., Music Tchrs. Nat. Assn., Music Educators Nat. Conf., Am. String Tchrs. Assn., Ark State Music Tchrs. Assn., Ark. Music Educators Assn. Democrat. Episcopalian. Lodge: Rotary. Avocations: stamp collecting; gardening.

FORSYTHE, CHARLES BRAD, advertising executive; b. Detroit, June 5, 1953; s. John W. and Ann (McGhee) F. B.S., Central Mo. State U., 1975. Account exec. KWKI-FM, Kansas City, Mo., 1976-78, KSHE-FM, St. Louis, 1978-79, KRBE-FM, Houston, 1979-80; successively dir. new bus. devel., account supr., v.p. account services Gray O'Rourke Susman, Houston, 1980-82, sr. v.p. Gray Communications, 1982-83; pres. Forsythe & Butler Advt. & Mktg., Houston, 1983—. Mem. Southwestern Assn. Advt. Agencies, Houston Advt. Fedn. Office: 8401 Westheimer Suite 180 Houston TX 77063

FORSYTHE, ROGER SCOTT, geologist; b. Osceola, Ark., Aug. 9, 1955; s. Richard Lewis and Martha Evelyn (Williams) F.; m. Vicki Loraine McCullough, Aug. 11, 1979. B.A. in Edn., Ark. State U., 1977; M.S. in Geology, U. Ark., 1982. Cert. secondary tchr., Ark. Tchr., Strawberry High Sch., Ark., 1978, Woodland Jr. High Sch., Fayetteville, Ark., 1978-82; geologist Geomap Co., Houston, 1982-83, Plano, Tex., 1983—. Mem. Dallas Geol. Soc., Am. Assn. Petroleum Geologists. Republican. Baptist. Avocations: athletics; gardening. Home: 2517 Majestic Dr Plano TX 75074 Office: Geomap Co 1100 Geomap Lane Plano TX 75074

FORT, EDWARD BERNARD, university chancellor; b. Detroit, Apr. 14, 1932; s. Edward Clark and Inez Corrine (Baker) F.; B.A., Wayne State U., 1954, M.A., 1958; Ph.D., U. Calif., Berkeley, 1964; m. Lessie Covington, Dec. 5, 1960; children—Clarke, Lezlie. Supt., Inkster (Mich.) Schs., 1967-71; adj. prof. adminstrn./urban edn. U. Mich., Ann Arbor, 1968-71; supt., dep. supt. schs., Sacramento, 1971-74; chancellor U. Wis. Center System, Madison, 1974-81, N.C. A&T State U., Greensboro, 1981—, vis. prof. Mich. State U., East Lansing, 1974. Bd. dirs. Sacramento Urban League, 1973-74. Madison Urban League, 1979—; bd. advisors Fund for Improvement Post Secondary Edn., 1979—. Served with AUS, 1954-56. Bd. editorial cons.'s Phi Delta Kappa, 1980—. Office: NC A&T State U Chancellor's Office 312 N Dudley St Greensboro NC 27411

FORTENBERRY, ROBERT, educational administrator. Supt. of schs. Jackson, Miss. Office: PO Box 2338 Jackson MS 39225*

FORTINO, THEODORE LEE, lawyer, devel. agy. exec.; b. Poughkeepsie, N.Y., Aug. 29, 1943; s. Theodore and Helene Patricia (Couse) F.; B.A., Marist Coll., 1966; LL.B., Atlanta Law Sch., 1973, LL.M., 1974; m. Nancy Lee Silliman, May 10, 1969; 1 dau., Marianne C. Community devel. specialist State of Ga., 1970-74; asst. exec. dir. N.E. Ga. Area Planning and Devel. Commn., Athens, 1974-78; exec. dir. Altamaha Ga. So. Area Planning and Devel. Commn., Baxley, 1978—; mem. Gov.'s Adv. Com. on Area Planning and Devel. Recipient Disting. Service award N.E. Ga. Area Planning Commn., 1978. Mem. Navy League (chpt. sec.-treas. 1975-78), Appling County C. of C., Nat. Assn. Devel. Orgns., Am. Planning Assn. Methodist. Home: Appling County GA 31513 Office: 505 W Parker St Baxley GA 31513

FORTNEY, DOYLE WRIGHT, association executive; b. Louisville, Dec. 11, 1933; s. Karle Wright and Bertha Mae (Westerfield) F.; m. Carolyn Miller Farr, Aug. 18, 1955 (div. 1974); children—Lawrence Doyle, Kenneth Paul; m. Loretta Jean Harding, Aug. 17, 1974; children—Justin Wright, Stefani Andrea. B.A. with honors, Pepperdine U., 1981; M.Divinity, Louisville Presby. Sem., 1982; M.A., Spalding U., Louisville, 1985. Ordained to ministry. Commd. seaman, U.S. Navy, 1952, advanced through grades to cmdr., 1977, ret., 1981; comdr. ROTC, Louisville, 1982-83; dir. personnel Christian Appalachian Project, Lancaster, Ky., 1983-84, dir. religious programs and planning, 1985—; project mgr. Universal Energy Systems, Dothan, Ala., 1984-85. Crisis counselor Suicide and Crisis Intervention, Memphis, 1977. Mem. Christian Ministries Mgmt. Assn. (sec. 1984), Am. Soc. Personnel Adminstrn., Am. Assn. Tng. and Devel., Am. Assn. Counseling and Devel., Am. Mgmt. Assn. Democrat. Mem. Ch. of God. Avocation: flying. Home: Route 2 Clubside Dr Dix River Estates Stanford KY 40484 Office: Christian Appalachian Project 322 Crab Orchard Rd Lancaster KY 40466

FORTSON, DEWEY CHARLES, SR., safety and hygiene specialist; b. Anderson, S.C., July 25, 1946; s. Hoke Smith and Zelma (Hulme) F.; m. Frances Youmans Heath, Aug. 31, 1968; children—Dewey, Jr., Stacy, Valerie. A.B. in Polit. Sci., U. Ga., 1968. Math. tchr. Elbert County Bd. Edn., 1968-69, sci. tchr., 1972-73, asst. indsl. engr., 1973-76, personnel and tng. mgr., 1979-82; indsl. safety and hygiene specialist United Merchants, Greenville, S.C., 1983—. Cand. Elbert County Bd. Commrs., 1980; mem. adv. bd. Am. Security Council Elberton, 1976-82. Served to capt. U.S. army, 1969-72, Vietnam. Decorated Bronze Star; Nat. Police Honor medal Nat. Police, Republic Vietnam, 1970. Mem. Am. Soc. Safety Engrs., Indsl. Hygiene Assn. Carolinas. Republican. Baptist. Club: Key Men's (Elberton) (pres. 1980-81). Lodge: Lions (pres. 1979). Avocations: coin collecting; hiking. Home: 118 Hartsville St Taylors SC 29687 Office: United Merchants 108 Frederick St Greenville SC 29602

FORTUNE, MAURICE PATRICK, JR., forensic chemist; b. Richmond, Va., Sept. 13, 1948; s. Maurice Patrick and Mary Virginia (Hewitt) F.; m. Irene Regina Wilson, Mar. 18, 1972; children—Athena Michelle, Michael Sean, Kathleen Marie, Maurice Patrick III, Mathew Terence. Student Va. Poly. Inst., 1966-67, John Tyler Community Coll., 1968; B.S. in Chemistry, Belmont Abbey Coll., 1970; postgrad. Va. Commonwealth U., 1975-81. Analytical chemist Commonwealth of Va., Bur. Forensic Sci., 1972-77, forensic scientist, 1977—; sr. instr. Va. Army N.G. NCO Acad. Vol., Friends of 23 Pub. TV, 1976—, Sci. Mus. Va., 1980—. Served with Va. Army N.G., 1970—. Decorated Va. Commendation medal with Gold Dogwood Blossom, Va. Service medal with Gold Dogwood Blossom, CSM Leadership award. Mem. Internat. Assn. Arson Investigators, Mid-Atlantic Assn. Forensic Scientists, Belmont Abbey Alumni Assn. (pres. Richmond chpt. 1974-75, v.p. 1973-74), Va. Nat. Guard Enlisted Assn., Vol. Assn. Sci. Mus. Va. (v.p. 1981-82, pres. 1982-84), Delta Epsilon Sigma. Roman Catholic. Home: 7338 Springleaf Ct Richmond VA 23234 Office: PO Box 999 Richmond VA 23208

FORTUNE, PORTER LEE, JR., educational administrator; b. Old Fort, N.C., July 2, 1920; s. Porter and Eunice (Ross) F.; m. Mary Elizabeth Cummings, Oct. 15, 1944; children—Philip Lee, Peggy Jean, Janet Cummings, Carey Ross. B.A., U. N.C., 1941, Ph.D., 1949; M.A., Emory U., 1946. Instr., Emory U., 1946; teaching asst. U. N.C., 1946-47; faculty Miss. So. Coll., 1949-61, successively asst. prof. history, asso. prof., dean Basic Coll., 1948-57, prof., dean Coll. and Grad. Sch., 1957-61; nat. exec. v.p. Nat. Exchange Club, 1961-68; chancellor U. Miss., 1968-84, chancellor emeritus, 1984—. Civilian aide to sec. army for Miss., 1971-79; past chmn. Miss. Com. for Humanities; past pres. Southeastern Conf., So. Univ. Conf., Miss. Assn. Colls., So. Assn. Land-Grant Colls. and State Univs.; former chmn. awards jury Freedoms Found. Served as lt. (s.g.), USNR, 1942-46; adv. council Naval Affairs. Decorated Bronze Star, Navy Disting. Public Service award; recipient John R. Emens Nat. award for a Free Student Press; Gov.'s Outstanding Mississippian award; Freedoms Found. George Washington honor medal, 1966, Leadership award, dist. 43 Toastmasters Club, 1974; Miss. Disting. Civilian Service medal, 1980; U.S. Disting. Civilian Service medal, 1980; Disting. Pub. Service award U.S. Navy, 1981. Mem. NEA, Miss. Hist. Soc. (past pres.), Miss. Council Devel. Marine Resources, So. Regional Edn. Bd. So. Assn. Com. on Colls., Miss. Art. Assn. (trustee), Orgn. Am. Historians, So. Hist. Assn., C. of C., Miss. Com. for Humanities (past chmn.), Phi Alpha Theta, Phi Kappa Delta, Omicron Delta Kappa. Phi Kappa Phi, Pi Gamma Mu, Delta Theta Pi, Alpha Phi Omega, Delta Sigma Pi, Phi Delta Kappa, Pi Tau Chi, Kappa Alpha. Kappa Delta Pi, Delta Pi Epsilon. Methodist. Clubs: Masons (32 deg). Shriners. Exchange (past pres. Hattiesburg, past pres. Miss. chpt. nat. regional v.p., chmn. nat. edn. com., nat. bd. control, past nat. pres. Golden award for service 1968; named to Nat. Ct. of Honor 1983). Address: Office of Chancellor Emeritus U Miss University MS 38677

FORTUNE, ROBERT JONES, textile chemist, chemical products executive; b. King's Mountain, N.C., Aug. 12, 1921; s. William Lavender and Tempie Ellen (Jones) F.; m. Hazel Marian Falls, Oct. 24, 1943; children—Jennifer Ellen Fortune Johnson, Elizabeth Falls Fortune Witt. Student Wake Forest U., 1940-42; B.S. in Textile Chemistry, N.C. State U., 1949. Jr. chemist Eastman Chem. Products, Inc. div. Eastman Kodak Co., Kingsport, Tenn., 1949-51, chemist, 1952-59, sr. chemist, 1960-76, mgr. customer service for dyes, 1976—. Contbr. articles to tech. jours. Served with U.S. Army, 1943-45; ETO. Vice pres. Kingsport Symphony Chorus, 1985; pres. East Camp of Gideons, 1984-85. Mem. Am. Assn. Textile Chemists and Colorists (sr.). Republican. Baptist. Avocations: furniture refinishing; flower growing; golf. Home: 2616 Brighton Ct Kingsport TN 37660 Office: Eastman Chem Products Inc PO Box 431 Kingsport TN 37662

FOSBACK, NORMAN GEORGE, stock market econometrician, editor, researcher, author, analyst; b. Astoria, Oreg., July 15, 1947; s. Oscar George and Lucy (Hoagland) F.; m. Myrna Liebowitz, June 13, 1982. B.S. in Bus. Adminstrn., Portland State U., 1969, postgrad., 1970-71. Pres. Inst. for Econometric Research, Ft. Lauderdale, Fla., 1971—. Author: Stock Market Logic, 1976. Editor several investment newsletters. Mem. Am. Fin. Assn., Am. Statis. Assn., Econometric Soc., Am. Econ. Assn., Ops. Research Soc. Am., ACLU, Common Cause. Home: 2600 NE 30th Ave Fort Lauderdale FL 33306 Office: Inst for Econometric Research 3471 N Federal Hwy Fort Lauderdale FL 33306

FOSDICK, FRANKLIN LAWRENCE, aircraft company manager; b. Ansonia, Conn., Sept. 12, 1919; s. Horace George and Maude Percy (Buck) F.; student New Haven U., 1946-48; B.B.A. with highest honors, So. Meth. U., 1962; M.B.A., Pepperdine U., 1978; m. Bette H. Burns, Sept. 19, 1940; 1 son, Franklin Lawrence, Jr. With Vought Corp., 1946—, mgr. material services, purchasing and ops. control Mich. div., Warren, 1963-70, mgr. traffic, transp. and shipping Vought Systems div., Dallas, 1970-74, mgr. material control Vought Corp., 1974—; instr. Mountain View Coll., Dallas; chmn. liability and claims task force, mem. exec. com. traffic service div. Aerospace Industries Assn. Am., 1970-74; pres., prin. owner Bali Hi Apts., Dallas, 1958—; dir., sec. LTV Missiles & Space Credit Union, Warren, 1964-70; mem. freight adv. bd. Am. Airlines, N.Y.C., 1970-74. Served to 1st lt. U.S. Army, 1944-46. Mem. Purchasing Mgmt. Assn. Detroit (dir. 1969), Nat. Assn. Purchasing Mgmt. (dist. vice chmn. pub. relations 1970), Dallas Apt. Assn., Nat. Property Mgmt. Assn. (certified property mgr. 1978). Methodist (chmn. adminstrv. bd. 1973-75). Clubs: Masons (32 deg.), Shriners (Dallas); Village Players (Birmingham, Mich.). Home: 1639 Whitedove St Dallas TX 75224 Office: Vought Corp PO Box 226114 Dallas TX 75266

FOSS, DONALD WALLACE, geochemist, analytical laboratory executive, geologist, consultant; b. Portland, Maine, Nov. 3, 1941; s. Ernest Carroll and Gertha Amanda (Wallace) F.; m. Mary Jean Flanagan, July 1, 1967; children—Jennifer Ann, Martha Jane. B.S. Ed. in Chemistry, U. Maine, 1966; postgrad. in geology U. Va., 1971. Tchr. pub. schs., Glastonbury, Conn., 1967-68; sr. geochemist N. Am. Exploration, Inc., Charlottesville, Va., 1969-71, v.p., 1971-80; pres. Blue Ridge Analytical Lab., Inc., Charlottesville, 1980—. mem. campus ministry com. Lutheran Ch. Am., Charlottesville, 1978—, mem. youth ministry com., 1980—, mem. Va. Synod Campus Ministry Mng. Group, 1981—; scoutmaster Stonewall Jackson council Boy Scouts Am., 1979-84, council commr., 1984—, adviser Order of Arrow, 1982—, mem. council camping com., 1982—, mem. nat. council; mem. council camp site com. Va. Skyline council Girl Scouts U.S.A., 1982-83, treas. 3 units, 1980—. Recipient Dist. award of Merit, Boy Scouts Am., 1982. Mem. Am. Inst. Profl. Geologists (cert. profl. geologist; bd. dirs. Va. sect. 1983), Soc. Mining Engrs. (chmn. Va. sect. 1982-84), Am. Chem. Soc., Soc. Exploration Geochemists, Geochem. Soc., Assn. Ofcl. Analytical Chemists, Nature Conservancy, U.S. C. of C., Sigma Xi (assoc.), Sigma Gamma Epsilon. Republican. Author profl. papers. Home: 109 St Ives Rd Charlottesville VA 22901 Office: 2116 Berkmar Dr PO Box 7545 Charlottesville VA 22906

FOSS, EDWARD WILBUR, agricultural engineer, educator, consultant; b. Laconia, N.H., Dec. 4, 1914; s. Robert Alfred and Grace Mabelle (Hill) F.; m. Elizabeth Howard Peabody, Aug. 13, 1938; children—Joan, John, Linda. B.S. in Agr., U. N.H., 1936; M.S. in Agrl. Engring., Cornell U., 1947. Instr. vocat. agr. and indsl. arts Averill Park, N.Y. and Walpole, N.H., 1936-42; instr. agrl. engring. U. N.H., 1942-45; extension agrl. engr. Coll. Agr., U. Maine, Orono, 1945-49; prof. agrl. engring. Cornell U., Ithaca, 1949-80; prof. agrl. engring. U. Ibadan, Nigeria, 1968-70, U. Hawaii, Hilo, 1977-78; energy cons. Vol. Devel. Corps., Washington; mem. adv. com. Palm Beach Solid Waste, 1983—. Trustee Village of Lansing, N.Y., 1974-77; v.p. Ithaca City Expanded Sch. Dist., 1963-68. Recipient N.Y. State Assn. County Agrl. Agts., 1976. Mem. Am. Soc. Agrl. Engrs. (life; 11 blue ribbon awards), Nat. Fire Protection Assn. (James F. Lincoln-Arc Welding award 1950). Republican. Inventor tree delimber, 1957; contbr. articles to profl. jours. Home and Office: Quay S 1026 126 Lake Shore Dr North Palm Beach FL 33408

FOSSUM, ROBERT ROSS, academic administrator, engineer; b. El Paso, Tex., Nov. 17, 1928; s. Ragnar Magnus and Dorothy Faye (Ross) F.; m. Ellen Carson, Sept. 20, 1951; children—Susan Elizabeth, Jane Ann, Robert Ross. B.S., U. Idaho, 1951; M.S., U. Oreg., 1956; Ph.D., Oreg. State U., 1969. Dir. Def. Advisory Research Project Agy., Arlington, Va., 1977-81; v.p. Systems Labs. ESL, Inc., Sunnyvale, Calif., 1969-74; mgr., systems engr. GTE Sylvania, Mountain View, Calif., 1956-69; dean Sch. of Engring., So. Methodist U., Dallas, 1981—; bd. trustees Southwest Research Inst., San Antonio, 1983—; cons. various cos. Mem. exec. panel Chief of Naval Ops., Alexandria, Va., 1983; mem. com. on engring. tech./systems NRC, Washington, 1983. Served to lt. USN, 1951-54. Recipient Disting. Pub. Service Medal Def. Dept., 1981; Jerome C. Lee award Oreg. State U., 1968; Carol Howe Foster award U. Idaho, 1951, U. Idaho Hall of Fame award, 1985. Mem. IEEE, Am. Soc. for Engring. Edn., Sigma Xi, Phi Beta Kappa, Tau Beta Pi. Club: Engrs. (Dallas). Avocations: skiing. Home: 8555 Fair Oaks Crossing Apt 502 Dallas TX 75243 Office: Office of Dean Sch of Engring and Applied Sci So Methodist U Dallas TX 75275

FOSTER, BOBBY LYNN, financial executive; b. Temple, Tex., Aug. 18, 1946; s. James Leonard and Ramona LaVerne (Wilhelm) F.; m. Judith Ellen Knott, Oct. 25, 1966; 1 child, Jennifer Lynn. B.B.A., U. Tex.-Arlington, 1973; M.B.A., East Tex. State U., 1975. Auditor, Defence Contract Audit Agy., Greenville, Tex., 1973-77, auditor-in-charge, Houston, 1977-80; govt. contracts auditor Lockwood, Andrews & Newnam, Houston, 1980-81, controller, 1981-82, controller, treas., 1982—; instr. San Jacinto Jr. Coll., Pasadena, Tex., 1978-82. Served with USN, 1963-67. Named Auditor Trainee of Yr., Def. Contract Audit Agy., Greenville, 1975. Mem. Assn. Govt. Accts. (dir. 1978-79, pres. Houston chpt. 1984-85), Nat. Contract Mgmt. Assn. (dir. 1982-83). Republican. Lutheran. Home: 10614 Sagetrail Houston TX 77089 Office: Lockwood Andrews & Newnam 1500 Citywest Blvd Houston TX 77042

FOSTER, EARL MASTERS, investment advisor, investment consultant; b. Boston, May 28, 1940; s. John Jacob and Etta (Masters) F.; m. Nancy Ruth Hall, Sept. 20, 1964; children—Tamar Lynne, Elana Faye, Dara Kate. B.A., Tufts U., 1962; M.B.A., Boston U., 1964; Ph.D., NYU, 1969. Asst. prof. Boston U., 1969-72; sr. v.p. Southeast Banks Trust Co., Miami, Fla., 1974-79; cons., dir. Fla. Div. of Land Sale, Tallahassee, 1979-80; corp. economist Southeast Banking, Miami, 1980-82; prin. Earl M. Foster Assocs., Miami, 1982—; also cons. Author: Common Stock Investment, 1974. Contbr. articles to profl. jours. Mem. S. Fla. Fin. Analysts Soc. Office: Earl M Foster Assocs 14301 SW 75th Ct Miami FL 33158

FOSTER, EUGENE HOWARD, psychologist; b. Cin., Jan. 21, 1947; s. Eugene Lewis and Mavis Estelle (Howard) F.; m. Paula Dianne Dolly, Nov. 10, 1984; 1 child, Nicole Mavis. B.A., Barrington Coll., 1969; M.A., R.I. Coll., 1972, cert. advanced grad. study, 1973; Ed.D., Boston U., 1975. Lic. psychologist, R.I., W.Va. Dir. spl. edn. North Smithfield Schs., R.I., 1974-76; asst. prof. Providence Coll., 1976-80; v.p. U.T.D., Inc., Elkins, W.Va., 1980-83; exec. dir. Tygart Valley Counseling Ctr., Elkins, 1983—; cons. W.Va. Children's Home, 1984—. Contbr. articles to profl. jours. Chmn., Davis Meml. Presbyterian Ch., Elkins, 1985. Mem. Am. Psychol. Assn. Presbyn. Avocation: boating. Home: 109 Davis St Elkins WV 26241 Office: Tygart Valley Counseling Ctr Elkins WV 26241

FOSTER, FERN ALLEN (MERONEY), sex counselor, administrator, consultant; b. Ranger, Tex., Sept. 19, 1921; d. Jess and Grace (Bradley) Meroney; m. Austin Foster; children—Gayanne, Stuart, Ann, William, David. A.A., Ranger Coll., 1941; B.A., Newport U., 1981. Cert. social worker, Tex. Sex counselor Marriage Counseling Assocs., Fort Worth, 1964-69, The Edna Gladney Home, Fort Worth, 1971-83; psychotherapist VA Hosp. and Clinic, New Orleans, 1969-71; sex counselor Fort Worth Counseling Ctr., 1971-84, dir., 1984—; fellow in human sexuality Tex. Sch. of Profl. Psychology, Fort Worth, 1985—; cons. human sexuality Blackwell Counseling Ctr., Fort Worth, 1985—. Mem. Am. Assn. Sex Educators, Counselors and Therapists (cert.), Sex Info. and Edn. Council of U.S., Nat. Council on Adoption, Am. Assn. Counseling and Devel., Am. Mental Health Counselors Assn. Club: Century II (Fort Worth). Home: 166 Victorian Dr Fort Worth TX 76134 Office: Fort Worth Counseling Ctr PO Box 6242 Fort Worth TX 76115

FOSTER, GEORGE JAMES, security director; b. Chgo., June 23, 1928; s. George Joseph and Marion (Shields) F.; m. Rita Thomas, Nov. 29, 1952; children—Susan, Thomas, William, Elizabeth, Patricia. B.S. in Bus. Adminstrn., U. Notre Dame, 1952; M.S. in Forensic Sci., George Washington U., 1976. With FBI, 1954-79, squad supr., Chgo., 1968-69, supervisory spl. agt., Washington, 1969-79; security mgr. distbn. div. Ga. Pacific Corp., Portland, Oreg., 1979-81, corp. security dir., Atlanta, 1981—. Served to lt. (j.g.) USN, 1952-54; Korea. Mem. Soc. Former Spl. Agts. FBI, Am. Soc. Indsl. Security. Club: Exchange. Lodges: Elks, KC. Office: 133 Peachtree St NE Atlanta GA 30303

FOSTER, JAMES ROBERT, architect, planner; b. Beaumont, Tex., Jan. 4, 1944; s. Robert Lee and Harietta (Mayo) F.; m. Jane Marie Roby. B.Arch., Tex. A&M U., 1968, M.Arch., 1969. Registered architect, Tex; cert. Nat. Council Archtl. Registration Bds. Asst. dean Tex. A&M U., College Station, Tex., 1969-72; project mgr. Marmon Mok Partnership, San Antonio, 1972-75, project architect, 1975-77; ptnr. Marmon, Barclay Souter Foster Hays, San Antonio, 1978—. Author: (with others) Housing Early Childhood Education in Texas, 1969. Editor: Architecture Plus, 1967. Design team San Antonio Airport Terminal complex (Honor award). Bd. dirs. San Antonio Youth Literacy, 1984—; adv. trustee St. Mary's U., San Antonio, 1984—. Mem. Tex. Soc. Architects (pres. 1985, cert. of appreciation, 1982, 83), AIA (pres. San Antonio chpt. 1980, cert. of merit 1968), Am. Planning Assn. Methodist. Avocations: canoeing; gardening; backpacking. Home: 101 Lindell San Antonio TX 78212 Office: Marmon Barclay Souter Foster Hays 700 N St Mary's Suite 1600 San Antonio TX 78205

FOSTER, JOE B., company executive; b. Arp, Tex., July 25, 1934; s. William R. and Ruth D. (Knox) F.; B.S. in Petroleum Engring., Tex. A. and M. U., 1957, B.B.A. in Gen. Bus., 1957; m. Mary Alice Warren, Feb. 1, 1958; children—Warren, Ken, Jennifer, Jr. petroleum engr. Tenneco Oil Co., Oklahoma City, 1957-59, petroleum engr., Lafayette, La., 1959-62, dist. engr., 1962-66, adminstrv. asst. to exec. com., Houston, 1966-68, chief econ. planning and analysis, 1968-70, mgr. exploration, 1970-72, v.p., 1972-74, sr. v.p., 1974-76, exec. v.p., 1976-78, pres. Tenneco Oil Exploration and Prodn., 1978-81; exec. v.p. Tenneco, Inc., 1981—; dir. Tenneco Inc., Interfirst Bank, Houston. Mem. geoscis. devel. Council Tex. A&M U. Served to 2d lt. U.S. Army, 1958. Mem. Soc. Petroleum Engrs. of AIME, Nat. Gas Supply Assn. (exec. com.), Am. Petroleum Inst. Methodist. Clubs: Heritage, The Houstonian, Met. Racquet (Houston). Office: Box 2511 Houston TX 77001

FOSTER, JOYCE GERALDINE, research biochemist; b. Farmville, Va., Oct. 10, 1951; d. James Monroe and Fannie Louise (Torrence) F. B.S., Longwood Coll., 1974; M.S., Va. Tech. U., 1976. Ph.D., 1979. Grad. teaching/research asst. dept. biochemistry and nutrition Va. Tech. U., Blacksburg, 1974-79, research assoc. dept. biochemistry and nutrition, 1979; research assoc. dept. horticulture U. Wis., Madison, 1979-80; research assoc. dept. botany Wash. State U., Pullman, 1981; agrl. scientist div. plant and soil sci. W.Va. U., Morgantown, 1982; research biochemist U.S. Dept. Agr. Appalachian Soil and Water Conservation Research Lab., Beckley, W.Va., 1982—; adj. asst. prof. dept. biochemistry and nutrition, dept. plant pathology and physiology and weed sci. Va. Tech. U., 1983—. Mem. alumni bd. dirs. Longwood Coll., 1983-86. Recipient Sr. acad. award Alpha Lambda Delta, 1974; Longwood Coll. Acad. Achievement scholar, 1974; Mary White Cox Coll. scholar, 1970. Mem. Am. Chem. Soc. (sr. chemistry award), Am. Soc. Plant Physiologists, Japanese Soc. Plant Physiologists, Australian Soc. Plant Physiologists, Am. Inst. Biol. Scis., Am. Soc. Agronomy, Crop Sci. Soc. Am., Plant Growth Regulator Soc. Am., AAAS, N.Y. Acad. Sci., Am. Soc. Biol. Chemists, Scandinavian Soc. Plant Physiology, Agrl. Chem. Soc. Japan, Phytochem. Soc. N. Am., Va. Acad. Sci. (J. Shelton Horsely research award), Sigma Xi, Phi Lambda Upsilon, Phi Sigma, Phi Tau Sigma, Phi Kappa Phi, Omicron Delta Kappa, Kappa Delta Pi, Alpha Lambda Delta. Contbr. articles to profl. jours. Home: 109 Cherry Hill Beaver WV 25813 Office: PO Box 867 Airport Rd Beckley WV 25802

FOSTER, MARY ELIZABETH, real estate broker; b. Beloit, Wis., June 27, 1924; d. William Perry and Lelah Ferne (Coffin) Kissick; student Earlham Coll., 1941-45; B.A. in Bus. Adminstrn., Columbia Pacific U., 1980, M.A., 1980, Ph.D. in Bus. Adminstrn. and Real Estate, 1981; m. Russell E. Grant; 1 son, Gerald B.; m. 2d, LeRoy Quintin Foster, Feb. 11, 1966. Sec. to pharmacologist, Phila., 1946; asst. cataloguer Coll. Physicians Med. Library, Phila., 1946-47; dental asst., sec. bookkeeper, Boyertown and Malvern, Pa., and Bonita Springs, Fla., 1949-64; med. sec. Naples (Fla.) Community Hosp., 1965; sec., office mgr., Lee Foster, Gen. Contractor, Bonita Springs, 1966-70; real estate salesman Carmen Reahard, Bonita Springs, 1966-68; real estate broker, owner Foster Real Estate, Bonita Springs, 1968—; pres. Bonita Springs Bd. Realtors and Multiple Listing Service, 1971, 72, 77, 79. Active S.W. Fla. Symphony Orch. and Chorus Assn., charter mem. chorus, 1962—, bd. dirs. Symphony, 1976—, exec. com., 1976-77, pres. chorus, 1976-77; co-organizer Bonita Springs-Ft. Myers Friends Worship Group (Quakers), 1975—; co-founder, bd. dirs. Politically Active Property Owners of Lee County, 1972—, pres., 1975; mem. chorus Bonita Players, 1974-76; mem. Bonita Springs Dem. Club, sec., 1981, pres., 1982; mem. Coalition for Positive Growth, Inc.; founder Bonita Improvement Group, 1969, sec., 1983, pres., 1984, 86; charter mem. Bonita-Estero Bay Coastal Conservancy, Inc., 1983—, sec., 1983-84; bd. dirs. Montessori Sch., Bonita Springs, 1980-83; mem. Pvt. Industry Council, 1984—, Southwest Fla. Regional Planning Council Citizens Adv. com., 1984—. Mem. Nat. Assn. Realtors, Fla. Assn. Realtors (dir. 1971, 72, 77, 79, Diamond Pin Club 1973—), Bonita Springs C. of C. (dir. 1968-80, v.p. 1976). Author: Florida Women in Real Estate and Their Historical Background, 1981; contbr. poetry to books and mags., articles to newspapers and publs. Home and Office: 27301 Foster Ln SE Bonita Springs FL 33923

FOSTER, RALPH SHELL, JR., advertising and marketing executive; b. Montgomery, Ala., Sept. 19, 1957; s. Ralph Shell and Clara Virginia (Hodnette) F. B.S. in Bus. Adminstrn., Auburn U., 1979. Advt. mgr. Renfroe's Shoppe, Inc., Montgomery, Ala., 1979-81; gen. mgr. The Ad Agy., Inc., Montgomery, 1981; dir. ops. Ad/Mar, Montgomery, 1981-84; self-employed cons., 1984—. Mem. Soc. Advancement Mgmt. (pres. 1986-87), Am. Mktg. Assn., Am. Advt. Fedn., Delta Nu Alpha. Baptist. Home and Office: 3131 Whitney Dr Montgomery AL 36106

FOSTER, RITA DORN, government official, computer specialist; b. Winona, Minn., Mar. 24, 1933; d. Herbert H. and Katherine Mary (Zenk) Dorn; m. Ralph W. Merritt, Jan. 2, 1956 (div. May 1974); children—Maury Lynne, Karen Jeanne, Keith Alan; m. Walter A. Blanks, Jan. 7, 1977 (dec. Feb. 1981); m. Perry Gaston Foster, Jr., Apr. 24, 1983. B.S., U. Nebr., 1955; M.B.A., Columbia Pacific U., Mill Valley, Calif., 1980. Stewardess, United Airlines, Chgo., 1955-56; mgmt. analyst Ft. Eustis, Va., 1967-68, computer specialist Computer Systems Command, 1968-74, chief Mgmt. Analysis div., 1975-78, chief Force Mgmt. div., 1978-80, chief Mgmt. Services div. Applied Tech. Lab., 1980-82, chief Comml. Activities div., 1983-84, chief mgmt. div. Army Tng. Spt. Ctr., 1984—; chief network br. U.S. Army Mgmt. Systems Support Agy., Pentagon, 1982-83. Bd. dirs. Ft. Eustis Fed. Credit Union. Recipient cert. of achievement Applied Tech. Lab., Ft. Eustis, 1983. Mem. Fed. Women's Program (former chmn./mgr. chpt.) Am. Soc. Mil. Comptrollers (former sec.), Am. Helicopter Soc., Army Aviation Assn. Am., Assn. U.S. Army, Peninsula Women's Network, Beta Gamma Sigma. Clubs: Ft. Eustis Officers; Hampton (Va.) Yacht. Home: 21 Edwards Rd Poquoson VA 23662 Office: Ch Mgmt Div ATSC Fort Eustis VA 23604

FOSTER, TERRY LYNN, microbiologist, researcher, consultant; b. Mt. Pleasant, Tex., Apr. 4, 1943; s. Clarence and Marguerite (Rogers) F.; m. Vickey Stroman, Feb. 1, 1964; children—David Charles, Christopher Todd. B.A. in Biology, N. Tex. State U., 1965, M.A. in Microbiology, 1967; Ph.D. in Microbiology, Tex. A&M, 1973. Prof. biology Hardin-Simmons U., Abilene, Tex., 1967-78, research prof., 1978—, sr. research sci. Sci. Research Ctr., 1980-84, dir. research, 1981-84; mng. dir. Fairleigh Dickinson Labs., Abilene, 1984—; dir.-sec. Fairleigh Dickinson Labs., 1985; cons. in field, 1981—. Contbr. articles to prof. jours.; patentee in field. Active Taylor County Child Welfare, Abilene, 1982-84. Recipient NASA Cert. of Merit, Viking Program, 1975; 9 NASA grants, 1972-80; USDA grantee. Mem. AAAS, Am. Soc. Microbiology. Baptist. Avocations: skiing; sailing; hunting; home improvement projects. Office: Fairleigh Dickinson Labs Inc 1249 Ambler Ave Abilene TX 79601

FOSTER, WALTON ARTHUR, broadcasting executive; b. San Angelo, Tex., Aug. 26, 1927; s. Arthur Rambo and Katie Pearl (Walton) F.; A.A., San Angelo Coll., 1948; m. Arla Vee Bishop, Feb. 17, 1950; 1 son, Walton Arthur II. Comml. mgr. sta., then gen. mgr. Sta. KTXL, San Angelo, 1948-54; comml. mgr., then gen. mgr. Sta. KTXL-TV, 1952-54; mem. staff Sta. KGKO, Dallas, 1954; mem. staff Sta. KTRK-TV, Houston, 1955; mem. staff Sta. KLIF, Dallas, 1956; founder, KIXY and KIXY-FM, pres. Solar Broadcasting Co. Inc., 1954-78; founder, pres. Sta. KVRN and KVRN-FM, Foster Broadcasting Co. Inc., 1975—; pres., chmn. bd. Foster Communications Co., Inc., 1981—; owner stas. KIXY and KQSA, San Angelo, Tex., 1984—; 1st violin San Angelo Symphony Orch., 1947. Mem. S.A.R., San Angelo Advt. (v.p. 1952-53), Assn. Broadcasting Execs. Tex., Phi Theta Kappa (chpt. pres. 1945). Clubs: Optimist (charter mem., dir. 1948, v.p. 1949-50), 20-30 (charter mem., pres. 1950-51). Home: 3002 Oak Mountain Trail San Angelo TX 76904 Office: KIXY-KQSA Foster Communications Co Inc City Hall Plaza at W 1st St San Angelo TX 76903

FOUNTAIN, HENRY FRANCIS, JR., architect; b. Biloxi, Miss., Nov. 26, 1924; s. Henry F. and Edmee L. (Thensted) F.; m. Gloria S. Swetman, June 15, 1950; children—Valri, Kim, Craig, Sean, Dama, Wendy, Kelly, Taylor, Lori. B.S. in Archtl. Engring., La. State U., 1951. Registered architect, Miss., La., Ala., Fla. Draftsman, Ewing Engring. Corp., Mobile, Ala., 1951-52, Smith & Dawson, Gulfport, Miss., 1952-55; architect, owner H.F. Fountain Jr. & Assoc., Biloxi, 1955—; prin. works include Miss. Coast Coliseum and Conv. Ctr., Our Lady of Fatima Ch. (AIA award). Mem. Biloxi Planning Commn., 1958-61; mem. Diocese Bldg. Commn., Biloxi, 1983—. Served with USN, 1942-46. Recipient Design award Miss. Pine Assn., Ocean Springs, 1970. Mem. AIA (design award 1976, service award Miss. chpt. 1970, past Miss. chpt. pres.). Roman Catholic. Club: Biloxi Bus. Mens (pres. 1965). Avocations: sailing; fishing; golfing; music. Office: Fountain Lamas & Fields Architects Ltd 137 Magnolia St Biloxi MS 39530

FOUNTAIN, TROY WILLIAM (BILL), development organization executive; b. Shreveport, La., Aug. 13, 1948; s. Troy W. and Jean (Prothro) F.; m. Virginia Leah Remm, Dec. 20, 1969; 1 child, Shawn Dylan. B.S., La. State U., 1971. Exec. dir. Shreveport Bicentennial Commn., 1973-76; asst. dir. parks and recreation City of Shreveport, 1977-78, staff asst. to mayor, 1978-79; exec. dir. Downtown Devel. Authority, Downtown Shreveport Devel. Corp., Downtown Shreveport Unltd., 1979-82; pres. Downtown Tulsa Unlimited, Okla., 1982—. Bd. dirs. Tulsa Sales Tax Review Com., 1985; chmn. Citizens for a Better Shreveport, 1979, Citizens for Better Govt., 1978; active mem. Com. for Sales Tax Extension, Tulsa, 1985. Mem. Internat. Downtown Assn. (bd. dirs.), Building Owners and Mgrs. Assn., Urban Land Inst., Nat. Assn. Housing and Redevel. Ofcls., Nat. Parking Assn. Home: 2229 S Rockford Tulsa OK 74114 Office: Downtown Tulsa Unlimited Inc 6 E 5th St Suite 200 Tulsa OK 74103

FOURCARD, INEZ GAREY, foundation executive, artist; b. Bklyn.; d. George W. and Frances E. (MacDonald) Garey; student Pratt Inst., 1946-48; B.F.A., McNeese State U., 1963; m. Waldren Arthur Fourcard, Aug. 7, 1948; children—Chrystal Frances, Sharon Lynn, Waldren Arthur, Andrea Renee, David Marquard, Anita Lynn. Exhibited in numerous one man shows throughout U.S., also in Eng., France and Spain; mem. gifted and talented sect. of Spl. Edn. State of La., 1971-73; mem. adv. council Child Centered/Parent Tutored Kindergarden Program, 1974—; mem. La. Task Force for Community Edn., 1974-75; v.p. La. Assn. for Sickle Cell Anemia, 1974—; mem. Calcasieu Parish Bicentennial Com., 1974—; exec. dir. Southwestern Sickle Cell Anemia Found., Lake Charles, La., 1973—; del. Democratic Nat. Conv., 1980, 84. Roman Catholic. Important works include The Widow in pvt. collection Berlrand Russell Peace Found., London. Home: 1414 Saint John St Lake Charles LA 70601 Office: PO Box 3254 118 Enterprise Blvd Lake Charles LA 70601

FOURNELLE, THOMAS ALBERT, research mathematician, educator, consultant; b. St. Paul, Apr. 24, 1946; s. Clarence John and Kathryn Adrienne (Schweizer) F.; m. Kathleen Rose O'Brien, June 17, 1978. B.A., St. John's U.-Collegeville, Minn., 1969; M.S., St. Louis U., 1972; Ph.D., U. Ill., 1978. Teaching and research asst. dept. math U. of Ill.-Urbana, 1972-78; postdoctoral instr. dept. math. Mich. State U., East Lansing, 1978-80; asst. prof. Univ. Ala., University, 1980—; vis. faculty U. Wis.-Parkside, 1983-85; reviewer Jour. Math. Revs., 1979—. U. Ala. Research grantee, 1981, 83; U. Wis. research grantee, 1984; NSF grantee, 1985. Mem. Am. Math. Soc., Sigma Xi, Phi Kappa Phi, Pi Mu Epsilon. Contbr. articles in field to profl. jours. Office: Dept Math Univ of Wisconsin Parkside Kenosha WI 53141 Office: Dept of Math U of Alabama University AL 35486

FOUTS, ELIZABETH BROWNE, psychologist, metals company executive; b. New Orleans, July 5, 1927; d. Donovan Clarence and Mathilde Elizabeth (Hanna) B.; m. James Fremont Fouts, June 19, 1948; children—Elizabeth, Donovan, Alan, James. B.A., Tulane U., 1948; M.S., N.E. La. U., 1973, postgrad., 1984. Cert. sch. psychologist, La.; cert. reality therapist, La. Instr. spl. ed., psychol. cons. N.E. La. U., Monroe, 1971-73; sch. psychologist Ouachita Parish Schs., Monroe, 1973—; sec.-treas Fremont Corp., Monroe, 1967—, Auric Metals Corp., Salt Lake City, 1975—. Bd. dirs. Assn. for Retarded Citizens, Monroe, 1982—, treas., 1984; mem. exec. bd. Episcopal Diocese of Western La., 1983—. Mem. Nat. Assn. Sch. Psychologists, Council for Exceptional Children, La. Sch. Psychologists Assn. (pres. 1979-80, Outstanding Woman Sch. Psychologist 1984). Avocations: biking; skiing; swimming. Home: PO Box 7070 Monroe LA 71211 Office: Ouachita Parish Sch Bd 100 Bry St Monroe LA 71201

FOUTS, JAMES FREMONT, consulting chemical engineer; b. Port Arthur, Tex., June 3, 1918; s. Horace Arthur and Willie (Edwards) F.; B.S. in Chem. Engring., Tex. A&M U., 1940; m. Elizabeth Hana Browne, June 19, 1948; children—Elizabeth, Donovan, Alan, James. Div. supt. Baroil div. Nat. Lead Industries, Rocky Mountains and Can., 1940-60; pres. Riley-Utah Co., Salt Lake City, 1960-67, Fremont Corp., Monroe, La., 1967—, Auric Metal Corp., 1972—, Lowe DE Analyzer Co., 1982—; dir. LaFonda Hotel, Santa Fe, N.Mex., High Plains Natural Gas Co. Mem. Republican Presdl. Task Forces, 1981-82, adv. bd. Rep. nat. com., 1981-82. Served to lt. col. AUS, 1942-46. Mem. Am. Assn. Petroleum Geologists, Wyo. Geol. Assn. (past v.p.), Mont. Geol. Assn., Utah Geol. Assn., Ind. Petroleum Assn. Republican. Episcopalian. Clubs: Univ. (Salt Lake City), Elks. Home: 4002 Bon Aire Dr Monroe LA 71203 Office: PO Box 7070 Monroe LA 71211

FOUTS, LOUIS MILNER, III, lawyer, real estate investor; b. Dallas, Mar. 3, 1944; s. Fredric Clark and Dorothy Jean (Frey) F.; m. Sondra Sue Tally, Jan. 25, 1969 (div. 1977); children—Molly Anne, Paul Louis. B.B.A., So. Meth. U., 1966; J.D., U. Tex., 1970. Bar: Tex., 1969. Assoc., Ramey, Brelsford, Flock, Devereux & Hutchins, Tyler, Tex., 1969-72; gen. counsel Southwestern Dynamics, Inc., Dallas, 1972-74; ptnr. Benners & Fouts, Dallas, 1974-83; sole practice, Dallas, 1983—; lectr. Dallas Bd. Realtors seminars; mem. Bar Candidate Admissions Bd.; dir. Child Welfare Bd.; co-chmn. Law Day Com. Mem. 500, Inc., Young Republicans, Fourth Session Club; bd. dirs. vestry Christ Episcopal Ch. Mem. Dallas Bar Assn., Phi Delta Theta, Phi Alpha Delta. Home: 9125 Drumcliffe Dallas TX 75231 Office: 2522 McKinney Ave Suite 102 Dallas TX 75201

FOWLER, BRUCE ANDREW, toxicologist; b. Seattle, Dec. 28, 1945; s. Andrew and Dolores Yvonne F.; B.S. in Fisheries, U. Wash., 1968; Ph.D. in Pathology, U. Oreg., 1972; m. Mary Glenn Oler, June 9, 1968; children—Glenn Andrew, Randall Bruce. Staff fellow Nat. Inst. Environ. Health Scis., Research Triangle Park, N.C., 1972-74, sr. staff fellow, 1974-77, research biologist, 1977—, sr. scientist, 1978—; adj. assoc. prof. pathology and toxicology curriculum U. N.C.; temporary adv. WHO; mem. work group Internat. Agy. Research Against Cancer; mem. Permanent Com. and Internat. Assn. on Occupational Health, Sci. Com. on Toxicology of Metals; chmn. Dahlem Workshop on Mechanisms of Cell Injury: Implications for Human Health, Berlin, 1985. Mem. AAAS, Am. Soc. Cell Biology, Am. Soc. Pharmacology and Exptl. Therapeutics, Am. Assn. Pathologists, Soc. Toxicology (councilor mechanisms of toxicity sect.), Sigma Xi, N.Y. Acad. Sci. Editor: Biological and Environmental Effects of Arsenic, 1983; editorial bd. Chemico-Biol. Interactions, 1980-85, Environ. Health Perspectives, 1981; Toxicology and Applied Pharmacology, 1985, Jour. Toxicology and Environ. Health, 1986, Internat. Archives Environ. Health, 1986. Contbr. articles to profl. jours., chpts. to books. Office: Nat Inst Environ Health Scis PO Box 12233 Research Triangle Park NC 27709

FOWLER, BRUCE WAYNE, physicist; b. Gadsden, Ala., Dec. 10, 1948; s. James Kenneth and Helen Christine (Towers) F.; B.S. in Chemistry (Gorgas fellow), U. Ala., Tuscaloosa, 1970; M.S., U. Ill., Urbana, 1972; Ph.D., U. Ala., Huntsville, 1978. Systems analyst Teledyne Brown Engring. Co., Huntsville, Ala., 1972-74; physicist Advanced Systems Concepts Office, U.S. Army Missile Command, Huntsville, 1974—, chief theoretical physicist smoke ad hoc group, 1975. Certified profl. chemist. Mem. Am. Phys. Soc., Am. Chem. Soc., Ala. Acad. Sci., Sigma Xi, Sigma Pi Sigma, Pi Mu Epsilon, Alpha Chi Sigma. Contbr. articles to profl., indsl., govtl. publs. Home: 1996 Marinawoods Dr Huntsville AL 35803

FOWLER, DELBERT MARCOM, staff building systems engineer; b. Ladonia, Tex., Sept. 14, 1924; s. Robert Delbert and Floy Ethel (Marcom) F.; B.S., U.S. Mil. Acad., 1945; M.S. in Civil Engring., Tex. A. and M. U., 1954; M.S. in Internat. Affairs, George Washington U., 1965; grad. Indsl. Coll. Armed Forces, 1965; m. Betty Alouise Reichey, Dec. 11, 1948; children—Kathryn Lewis (Mrs. David Irwin), John D. Marcom, Francine Floy (Mrs. James Zion). Commd. 2d lt. C.E., U.S. Army, 1945, advanced through grades to col., 1966; assigned Austria, 1945-48, Korea, 1950-52, W. Ger., 1958-61, policy and planning positions, Washington, 1961-67, 70-72, Vietnam, 1968-69, ret., 1972; project mgr. Urban Systems Devel. Corp., Arlington, Va., 1973; regional adminstr. Fed. Energy Adminstrn., Dallas, 1973-77; sr. assoc. Planergy Inc., Austin, 1978-79; pres. Blum Building Automation, Security, and Communications, Dallas, 1979-85; coord. architect engr. services Dallas Ind. Sch. Dist., 1985—. Mem. energy task force Goals for Dallas, 1976-77; mem. Austin Energy Conservation Commn., 1979. Decorated Legion of Merit, Bronze Star, Air medal. Fed. Exec. fellow Brookings Instn., 1971-72. Registered profl. engr., Tex.; cert. energy mgr. Mem. Nat., Tex., Dallas socs. profl. engrs., Am. Soc. Mil. Engrs., Soc. Energy Engrs., ASHRAE, Illuminating Engring. Soc., Internat. Platform Assn., SAR, Sons Confederate Vets. Presbyterian. Author articles, papers. Home: 5708 Willow Ln Dallas TX 75230 Office: 3700 Ross Ave Dallas TX 75204

FOWLER, DONALD WAYNE, engineer; b. Grand Prairie, Tex., Aug. 18, 1944; s. Benjamin Thomas and Leola Augusta (Butterworth) F.; m. Elaine Louise Danielson, Aug. 25, 1968; children—James, Thomas. B.S. in Mech. Engring., Tex. A&M U., 1966; M.S. in Mech. Engring., U. Tex.-Austin, 1968. Registered profl. engr., Tex. Engr., scientist Tracor, Inc., Austin, 1968-69; v.p., co-founder Lace Engring. Co., Austin, 1969-75; pres., co-founder Napp, Inc., Austin, 1969-75, Tex. Gas Transport Co., Austin, 1975—, Pressure Transport, Austin, 1975—; chmn. bd. dirs. Novacorp Pressure Transport Inc., Calgary, Alta., Can., 1984—. Contbr. articles to profl. jours. Inventor or co-inventor high volume vacuum slide valve, method and system for producing and transporting natural gas, distributing natural gas, transporting natural gas to a pipeline, method and apparatus for producing natural gas from tight formations. Dir., treas. Austin Assn. Retarded Citizens, 1974-76; mem. indsl. adv. bd. Tex. Tech U., 1983—. Served with Army N.G., 1969-75. Mem. ASME (sect. chmn. 1973-75, J. George H. Thompson award 1975, Founder's award, 1973-75), Soc. Petroleum Engrs. Office: Tex Gas Transport Co 5407 N IH-35 Austin TX 78723

FOWLER, EARL BEALLE, engineering consultant, retired navy officer; b. Jacksonville, Fla., Sept. 29, 1925; s. Earl Beall and Veva May (Carpenter) F.; m. Helen Marie Jorgenson, Feb. 2, 1948; children—Mary Helen, Joan Ann. B.S. in Mech. Engring., Ga. Inst. Tech. 1946; B.E.E., MIT, 1949; postgrad. Harvard U., 1971. Commd. ensign U.S. Navy, 1943, advanced through grades to vice admiral, ret., 1985, project mgr. Naval Ships Systems Command, Washington, 1967-71, dep. comdr. Naval Electronic Systems Command, Washington, 1972-75, vice comdr., 1975-76, comdr., 1976-80; comdr. Naval Sea Systems Command, Washington, 1980-85; cons., Washington, 1985—; mem. vis. com. ocean engring. dept. MIT, Cambridge, Mass., 1980—; mem. tech. com. Am. Bur. Shipping, N.Y.C., 1980—. Decorated Legion of Merit, Meritorious Service medal, Disting. Service medal. Mem. IEEE, Am. Soc. Naval Engrs., ASHRAE, Soc. Naval Architects and Marine Engrs. Democrat. Episcopalian. Clubs: N.Y. Yacht; Army Navy Country (Arlington, Va.); Cosmos (Washington). Avocation: golf. Home and Office: 1008 Dalebrook Dr Alexandria VA 22308

FOWLER, ELIZABETH MILTON, real estate executive; b. Watertown, Fla., Jan. 11, 1919; d. Arthur Wellington and Mattie Jean (Hodges) Milton; student Bowling Green Bus. U., 1938-39; m. Albert L. Fowler, Jr., Aug. 6, 1948; children—Patricia Dawn Cecilia, Richard Gordon Sean. Sec. to dir. Workmen's Compensation Div., Fla. Indsl. Commn., Tallahassee, 1940-41; sec. to supt. div. Gibbs Ship Yard Repair, 1942-44; sec. to elec. engrs. Reynolds, Smith & Hills, Architects and Engrs., 1946-49; sec. to pres. Aichel Steel Corp., Jacksonville, Fla., 1949-50; adminstr. office mgr. for prin., vice-prin. Am. Dependent Sch., Moron Air Base, Spain, 1961-63; owner, mgr. Elizabeth Properties, Jacksonville, 1956—. Chmn. ways and means com. Chattanooga High Sch. PTA, 1956-57; asst. den mother Cub Scout Troop, 1970; block worker Gov. Reagan's Presdl. Campaign. Recipient Spl. Appreciation award Eglin AFB, Fla., 1969. Mem. Nat. Assn. Female Execs., Am. Security Council (nat. adv. bd.), Dade County Crimewatch Orgn. Republican. Home and Office: 20101 SW 92d Ave Miami FL 33189

FOWLER, FRANK EISON, artists representative; b. Chattanooga, June 2, 1946; s. Richard Calvin and Mamie Craig (Howell) F.; B.B.A., U. Ga., 1969; m. Mary Zimmermann, Feb. 5, 1972; children—Christopher Andrew. Thomas Weston. Artists rep., Chattanooga, 1970—; mem. adv. com. arts John F. Kennedy Center Performing Arts; dir. Commerce Union Bank, Chattanooga. Bd. dirs. Children's Home, Chattanooga, 1979—; mem. alumni bd., chmn. sustaining fund, bd. dirs. Baylor Sch., Chattanooga; bd. dirs. Ga. Mus. Art, Retirement Services Am. Mem. Internat. Soc. Appraisers, Appraisers Assn. Am. Episcopalian. Address: 1213 Fort Stephenson Oval Lookout Mountain TN 37350

FOWLER, GUY ANTHONY, home center company executive; b. Greenville, S.C., July 8, 1944; s. Guy Nathanial and Mabel Irene (Hawkins) F.; m. Gloria Lynn Wolff, Nov. 12, 1967; children—Lori Dawn, Rhett Anthony. Student Greenville Tech. Sch., 1966. Customer service rep. Dan River Carpets, Greenville, 1966-71; salesman Lowe's Cos., Charleston, S.C., 1971-73, store mgr., Spartanburg, and Atlanta, 1973-81; dir. leadership sch., North Wilkesboro, N.C., 1981—. Bd. dirs. Merchants Bur., Spartanburg, S.C., 1975-78; bd. advisers Sch. Bus. Adminstrn., Wilkes Community Coll., Wilkesboro, 1983—. Mem. Am. Soc. Tng. and Devel., Home Builders Assn. (bd. dirs. 1973-79, Mem. of Yr. 1977). Republican. Baptist. Avocation: golf. Office: Lowe's Cos Inc 268 East Box 1111 North Wilkesboro NC 26856

FOWLER, H. RAMSEY, college dean, English educator; b. Bklyn., June 18, 1938; s. Mortimer A. and Irene H. (Ramsey) F.; m. Lynda Harris Bearden, Dec. 21, 1963 (div. 1967); m. Joan Alice Dheere, Mar. 21, 1980; 1 child, Jessica. B.A., Princeton U., 1959; M.A.T., Harvard U., 1961; M.A., U. Mich., 1963, Ph.D., 1969. Instr. English, U. Mich., Ann Arbor, 1967-68; asst. prof. English, Memphis State U., 1968-74, assoc. prof., 1974—, dean Univ. Coll., 1980—. Author: Little, Brown Handbook, 1980, 83; also articles. Mem. Memphis Alcohol and Drug Council. Mem. Am. Assn. Higher Edn., Assn. Am. Colls. (instl. liaison), Council Advancement of Experimental Learning (instl. liaison), The Alliance. Democrat. Episcopalian. Club: Faculty U. Tenn. Home: 1682 Lawrence Pl Memphis TN 38152 Office: Univ Coll Memphis State U Memphis TN 38152

FOWLER, HAROLD GORDON, entomologist, educator; b. Roswell, N.Mex., Aug. 25, 1950; s. Hubert G. and Ruby L. (Lain) F.; m. Vilma Elena Martinez, Jan. 11, 1975; children—Aileen Nicole, Hayden Gabriel. B.A., SUNY-Brockport, 1971; M.S., Rutgers U., 1978, Ph.D., 1982. Prof., Cath. U., Arequipa, Peru, 1972-74; research entomologist Paraguayan Ministry Agr., Asunción, 1974-76; prof. grad. sch. Hermanos Escobar, agrl. univ., Juárez, Mex., 1979; vis. prof. Universid Estadual Paulista, Rio Claro, São Paulo, Brazil, 1983; research assoc. biol. control U. Fla., Gainesville, 1982—; cons. in field. Active, Nat. Council Returned Peace Corps Vols., Xerces Soc., Vols. in Tech. Assistance. N.J. Pest Control Assn. grantee, 1980, 81, 82; C.C. Compton award Rutgers U., 1981, 82. Mem. AAAS, Am. Soc. Naturalists, Entomol. Soc. Am. (Eastern br. award 1978, doctoral thesis award 1980), Ecol. Soc. Am., Sigma Xi. Methodist. Contbr. articles to profl. jours. Office: Entomology Dept Univ Fla Gainesville FL 32611

FOWLER, JAMES WILEY, III, minister, educator; b. Reidsville, N.C., Oct. 12, 1940; s. James Wiley and Lucile May (Haworth) F.; m. Lurline Locklair, July 7, 1962; children—Joan S., Margaret. B.A., Duke U., 1962; B.D., Drew U., 1965; Ph.D., Harvard U., 1971. Ordained to ministry Methodist Ch., 1968. Assoc. dir. Interpreters House, Lake Junaluska, N.C., 1968-69; minister United Meth. Ch., 1968—; asst. prof. to assoc. prof. Harvard U. Div. Sch., Cambridge, Mass., 1969-76; assoc. prof. Boston Coll., Chestnut Hill, Mass., 1976-77; prof. theology and human devel. Emory U., Atlanta, 1977—, founder, dir. Ctr. Faith Devel., 1980—. Author: To See the Kingdom, 1974; (with Sam Keen) Life Maps, 1978; (with others) Trajectories in Faith, 1980; (with others) Toward Moral and Religious Maturity, 1980; Stages of Faith, 1981; Becoming Adult, Becoming Christian, 1984; Faith Development and Pastoral Care, 1986. Mem. Am. Acad. Religion, Religious Edn. Assn., Assn. Profs. and Researchers in Religious Edn. Democrat. Home: 2740 Janellen Dr NE Atlanta GA 30345 Office: Emory U Sch of Theology Atlanta GA 30322

FOWLER, JOHN BALLARD, lawyer; b. Berea, Ky., Oct. 4, 1949; s. John Thomas and Imogene (Ballard) F.; m. Jennifer Jan Johnson, July 10, 1976. B.A., Berea Coll., 1971; J.D., U. Ky., 1974. Bar: Ky. 1974, Tenn. 1977, U.S. Dist. Ct. (ea. dist.) Ky. 1974, U.S. Dist. Ct. (ea. dist.) Tenn. 1977, U.S. Supreme Ct. 1980. Atty. Dept. of Transp., Lexington, Ky., 1974-76; assoc. Ambrose, Wilson & Grimm, Knoxville, Tenn., 1976-80, ptnr., 1980—; instr. banking law State Tech. Inst., Knoxville, 1982; mem. Tenn. Lawyers Profl. Liability Ins. Com., 1984—. Recipient Alumni Leadership and Service award U. Ky. Alumni Assn., 1982. Mem. Ky. Bar Assn., Tenn. Bar Assn., Knoxville Bar Assn., ABA. Clubs: City, LeConte, Ft. Loudoun Yacht. Home: 1825 Nantasket Rd Knoxville TN 37922 Office: Ambrose Wilson & Grimm 9th Floor VFB Bldg Knoxville TN 37901

FOWLER, MEL, marble sculptor, retired U.S. Air Force officer; b. San Antonio, Nov. 25, 1921; s. Walter James Fowler and Thelma Anne (Hays) Gregory; m. Catherine Oeland Childs, May 9, 1981; by previous marriage—James Everett, Robert Michael, William Wade. Student Southwestern U., U. Tex., U. Md., Norfolk Sch. Art. One man shows include Tex. Luth. Coll., 1975, McCann-Wood Gallery, Lexington, Ky., 1975, Southwestern U., Georgetown, Tex., 1976, Art League, Galveston, Tex., 1976, Congl. Exhibition, U.S. House Reps., Washington, 1976, Art Council, Port Washington, N.Y., 1976, Galerie im Savoy, Kaiserslautern, Fed. Republic Germany, 1977, State Capitol Rotunda, Austin, Tex., 1977, Galerie Beck, Homburg, Fed. Republic Germany, 1977, Abilene Fine Arts Mus., Tex., 1977, Galerie Beck, Homburg, 1978, Art Mus., Abilene, Tex.; 1977, Internat. Art Mus., McAllen, Tex., 1983, Art Mus., Wichita Falls, Tex., 1985; exhibited in 14th internat. exhbns. in Europe, 15 nat. and regional exhbns., 1974-86. Served to lt. col. USAF, 1941-71; ETO, Vietnam. Decorated DFC with two silver oak leaf clusters, Bronze star, 13 air medals, Purple Heart, British Air medal, Vietnam medal of gallantry. Mem. Accademia Internazionale di Lettere, Scienze and Arte (Florence, Italy). Home and office: PO Box 255 Liberty Hill TX 78642 also Molino di Pomezzana Stazzema-Pomezzana-Lucca Italy 55040

FOWLER, RAYMOND PAULETTE, JR., broadcast sales and marketing executive; b. Suffolk, Va., July 21, 1948; s. Raymond P. and Norma L. (May) F.; m. Deborah Anne Busekist, Oct. 11, 1968; children—Raymond Patrick, Canda Shea, Aaron William. Student, U. Richmond, 1967, Art Instrn. Schs. Minn., 1967-78, U. Md., 1968-70. Gen. mgr. Cert. Leasing Corp., Norfolk, Va., 1970-73; mgr. retail mktg. Drug Fair Va. Inc., 1973-74; owner, pres. Diversified Mktg. Services, Suffolk, 1974-77; mgr. sales and programming CBN-Continental Broadcasting Network-WXRI Radio, Portsmouth, Va., 1978—; owner, pres. Diversified Media Cons., Inc., 1977—; sr. v.p., ptnr. Media Cons. Internat., Virginia Beach, Va.; pres. Satellite Syndication Services Inc., Norfolk; field tng. dir. NOVAR-Corp., 1977-78. Pres., founder Christian Bus. Alliance, 1978; bd. counsel Tidwater TV Adv. Council, 1980. dist. coordinator Am. Freedom Council. Served with U.S. Army, 1968-70. Mem. Nat. Religious Broadcasters, Greater Tidewater C. of C., Soc. Profl. Radio Broadcasters, Va. Assn. Broadcasters. Baptist. Contbr. articles to various periodicals. Office: 1318 Spratley St Portsmouth VA 23704

FOWLER, ROBERT GLEN, exploration company executive; b. Mart, Tex., Apr. 29, 1930; s. J.H. and Elizabeth F.; m. Bonita Fay Conner, Mar. 22, 1955; children—Becky Ann, Robert Glen. B.S. in Petroleum Engring., Okla. U., 1958; grad., Advanced Mgmt. Program, Harvard U., 1975. With Enserch Exploration, Inc. and predecessor 1958—, v.p., then exec. v.p., Dallas, 1972-78, pres., chief operating officer, 1978—, also dir.; dir. Reunion Bank, Dallas, Mem. Am. Petroleum Inst., Ind. Petroleum Assn. Am., Am. Petroleum Landmen's Assn., Permian Basin Natural Gas Men's Assn., Soc. Petroleum Engrs., Okla. Natural Gas Men's Assn., Dallas Petroleum Landmen's Assn., Houston Natural Gas Men's Assn., Harvard Advanced Mgmt. Assn. Baptist. Club: Dallas Petroleum. Address: Enserch Exploration Inc 1817 Wood St Dallas TX 75201*

FOWLER, ROBERT WALTER, architect; b. Kearney, Nebr., July 16, 1949; s. Gerald Byrum and Ruth E. (Nicholas) F.; B.Arch., U. Nebr., Lincoln, 1972; m. Beryl Jean Henry, July 10, 1976; children—Joshua John, Laura Anne. Draftsman, Dana, Larson, Roubal & Assocs., Omaha, 1971; intern architect Sheetz & Bradfield Architects, Atlanta, 1972-73; designer/project capt. Fin. Bldg. Cons., Atlanta, 1973-75; designer, project capt. Milton E. Sweigert, Architect, Atlanta, 1975-76; project architect Tipton Masterson Assocs. Architects, Atlanta, 1976-82, v.p., 1980-82, sr. v.p., 1982—. Deacon, First Alliance Ch., 1976-79, mem. exec. bd., 1978-82, elder, 1980-81, mem. long-range planning com., 1983—. Recipient Merit award Masonry Inst. Atlanta, 1979. Mem. AIA. Home: 5048 Winding Branch Dr Dunwoody GA 30338 Office: 2030 Powers Ferry Rd Atlanta GA 30339

FOWLER, WILLIAM WYCHE, JR., congressman; b. Atlanta, Oct. 6, 1940; s. William Wyche and Emelyn (Barbre) F.; B.A., Davidson Coll., 1962; J.D., Emory U., 1969; 1 dau., Katherine Wyche. Bar: Ga. 1970. Chief asst. to Congressman Charles Weltner, 1965; assoc. Smith Cohen Ringel Kohler & Martin, Atlanta. mem. Atlanta Bd. Aldermen, 1969-73; pres. Atlanta City Council, 1974-77; mem. 95th-99th Congresses from 5th Dist. Ga. Served with U.S. Army. Recipient Myrtle Wreath award, 1972. Mem. State Bar Ga. Democrat. Home: 894 Dean Dr NW Atlanta GA 30318 Office: 1210 Longworth House Office Bldg Washington DC 20515

FOWLES, CARL STEVEN, insurance company and health maintenance organization executive; b. Salt Lake City, Nov. 24, 1948; s. George Donald and Lavee (Brady) F.; m. Martha Ann Fellows, Apr. 24, 1974; children—Jordan Thomas, John Brandon, Jenaree, Aaron Spencer, Adam Carl. B.A., Brigham Young U., 1974, M.P.A., 1978, Ed.D. ABD, 1981. Tng. cons. Gen. Telegraph, Coeur d'Alene, Idaho, 1978-79; tng. coordinator First Security Bank, Salt Lake City, 1980; coordinator career and orgn. devel. Conoco, Inc., Houston, 1981; mgr. manpower and planning devel. LTV, Dallas, 1982; dir. human resources Trammell Co., Dallas, 1982-83; dir. orgn. devel. Cigna Health Plan, Inc., Dallas, 1983—. Chmn. Utah County Adminstrv. Republican Com., 1977-78; pres. Inter Mountain EDP Systems Trainers, Salt Lake City, 1980; mem. com. Dallas Art Mus., 1983. Brigham Young U. fellow, 1978. Mem. Brigham Young U. Mgmt. Soc. (bd. dirs. 1983—), Orgn. Devel. Network, Group Health Assn. Am. (bd. dirs. for edn. 1984—), Am. Soc. Tng. and Devel., Am. Soc. Personnel Adminstrn., Human Resources Planning Soc., Brigham Young U. Alumni Assn. (chmn. Dallas-Ft. Worth region). Mormon. Avocations: research; sports; literature. Office: Cigna Health Plan Inc 4975 Preston Park Blvd Plano TX 75075

FOWLIS, WILLIAM WEBSTER, fluid dynamicist, physicist; b. Baillieston, Scotland, Jan. 21, 1937; came to U.S., 1962; s. David and Christina Miller (Fleming) F.; m. Mary Duncan Knopp, Dec. 4, 1970; 1 child, David. B.S. in Physics with honors, U. Glasgow, 1959; Ph.D. in Physics, U. Durham, Eng., 1964. Research assoc. MIT, Cambridge, 1962-64; research assoc., asst. prof., assoc. prof. dept. meteorology Fla. State U., Tallahassee, 1965-76; assoc. program dir. for meteorology Nat. Sci. Found., Washington, 1974-76; aerospace engr. fluid mechanics, Marshall Space Flight Ctr., NASA, Huntsville, Ala., 1976—; com. mem. adv. group Microgravity Sci. Div. NASA, 1984—; cons. Office Naval Research, EPA. Author, co-author articles and conf. proceedings. Active Caledonian Soc. Ala., Clan Munro Assn. of U.S.A., 1984—. Recipient Tunnock Gold Medal for Sci., Uddingston Grammar Sch., Scotland, 1954, Medal for Exceptional Sci. Achievement, NASA, 1982, cert. of recognition, NASA, 1983, various achievement awards, 1977—; research grantee NSF, Office Naval Research, 1967-74. Mem. Am. Meteorol. Soc., Am. Geophys. Union, Am. Phys. Soc., Glasgow U. Grads. Assn. Avocations: Music; philosophy. Office: NASA Mail Code ES75 Marshall Space Flight Ctr Huntsville AL 35812

FOWLKES, JENNIFER YVONNE, pediatrician; b. Birmingham, Ala., May 29, 1955; d. B.A. and Katie Louise (Thomas) F. B.S., Clark Coll., 1976; M.D., Meharry Med. Coll., 1980. Resident in pediatrics Emory U. Affiliated Hosps., Atlanta, 1980-83; pediatrician W.T. Brooks Clinic, East Point, Ga., 1983—; cons. East Point Health Ctr., 1983—. Campaign vol. Billy McKinney Senate, Atlanta, 1982. Jr. fellow Am. Acad. Pediatrics; mem. Beta Kappa Chi, Delta Sigma Theta. Democrat. Baptist. Home: 3788 Holy Cross Dr Decatur GA 30034 Office: WT Brooks Clinic 1636 Connally Dr East Point GA 30344

FOX, BETTE DANEMAN, political science educator; b. Akron, Ohio, Apr. 6, 1925; d. Peter C. and Mary P. (Englezoff) Daneman; m. James Walker Fox, Jan. 20, 1962; children—Michael Peter, James Walker, Jr. B.A. summa cum laude, Western Res. U., 1947; M.A., Brown U., 1949; Ph.D., Case Western Res. U., 1961; postgrad. Soviet studies Harvard U., 1959-60. Cert. tchr. Inst., asst. prof. U. Akron, Ohio, 1949-51, 56-67; fgn. affairs officer UN Affairs, U.S. Dept., of State, Washington, 1952-53; youth dir. Council on World Affairs, Cleve., 1953-54; prof. polit. sci. Madison Coll., Harrisonburg, Va., 1967-74; prof. police adminstrn. Eastern Ky. U., Richmond, 1974—. Coordinator Workshop on Women in Criminal Justice, Richmond, 1975, Conf. on Women Who Work, Richmond, 1980, Workshop on Critical Issues in Criminal Justice, Richmond, 1977; adv. com. GROW Conf. for Women Researchers, Lexington, Ky., 1982-83; chmn. neighborhood com. Am. Cancer Soc., Harrisonburg, 1972; site coordinator Bluegrass Health Fair, Richmond, 1983; mem. adv. bd. Pattie A. Clay Community Hosp., Richmond, 1983—; mem. Madison County Spouse Abuse Adv. Bd., Richmond, 1985—. Fulbright sr. scholar; research grantee to Bulgaria, Council for Internat. Exchange, 1984; Ford Found. research grantee Russian Research Ctr., 1960-61. Mem. Am. Polit. Sci. Assn., Am. Soc. Criminology, Acad. Criminal Justice Scis., AAUP, LWV, Mortar Board. Phi Beta Kappa. Democrat. Unitarian. Club: Altrusa. Avocations: cooking, reading, walking. Home: 129 Buckwood Dr Richmond KY 40475 Office: Coll Law Enforcement Eastern Ky U Richmond KY 40475

FOX, CAROLYN ELAINE, registered nurse; b. Swannanoa, N.C., Aug. 28, 1933; d. William Marion and Sereptha (West) F. Diploma in Nursing, Rutherford Hosp., 1955; B.S. in Nursing, Western Carolina U., 1978, M.A. in Edn., 1981. Staff nurse Highland Hosp., Asheville, N.C., 1955-64, head nurse, 1964-71, supr., 1972-73, acting dir. of nursing service, 1974-75, 84-85, asst. dir. of nursing service, 1975-79, clin. coordinator, 1979-84, assoc. dir. nursing service, 1985—. Contbr. articles to profl. publs. Mem. Am. Nurses Assn., N.C. Nurses Assn., Dist. #1 Nurses Assn. (bd. dirs., v.p.), Council of Specialists in Psychiatric/Mental Health Nursing, Sigma Theta Tau. Baptist. Avocations: crafts; spectator sports; bowling; music; art. Home: 219 Richmond Ave Swannanoa NC 28778 Office: Highland Hosp Box 1101 Asheville NC 28802

FOX, CARROLL LAWSON, electric utility company executive; b. Sevierville, Tenn., June 23, 1925; s. Grady Bascom and Aura Rebecca (Lawson) F.; m. Mildred Grace Perryman, Sept. 1, 1951; children—Lawson Alan, Shauna Carol Fox Oden. Engr. substa. design Chattanooga Electric Power Bd., 1947-64, asst. sec., 1964-66, sec., comptroller, 1966-72, sec.-treas., 1972—, pres., co-founder employees credit union. Active United Way. Served with USNR, 1944-46. Democrat. Baptist. Club: Rotary. Home: 540 N Crest Ct Chattanooga TN 37404 Office: 537 Cherry St Chattanooga TN 37402

FOX, CINDY KATZ, public relations specialist; b. Houston, June 19, 1957; d. Gerald Lee and Doris Betty Ostrow; m. Leslie Brian Fox, Nov. 28, 1982. B.A. in Communications and Pub. Relations, Newcomb Coll., Tulane U., 1979. Intern, Sta. WQUE-FM, New Orleans, 1978-79; pub. relations and mkgt. rep. St. Luke's Episcopal Hosp., Tex. Children's Hosp. and Tex. Heart Inst., Houston, 1979—. Active Sisterhood Temple Beth Israel, Houston. Mem. Internat. Assn. Bus. Communicators, Pub. Relations Soc. Am., Tex. Soc. Hosp. Pub. Relations and Mktg., Tex. Hosp. Assn., Houston Area Hosp. Pub. Relations Soc. Office: PO Box 20269 Houston TX 77225

FOX, ELLIOT MILTON, publisher, consultant; b. Deer Lodge, Mont., Aug. 30, 1920; s. Charles Adin and Beulah (Churchill) F.; A.B., Washington U., St. Louis, 1942; M.A., Columbia, 1954, Ph.D., 1970; m. Byrdann Sachs, Mar. 8, 1943; children—John, Catherine, James, Jeffrey. Investigator, Personnel Survey Bur., N.Y.C., 1950-53; lectr. govt. City Coll. N.Y., 1953-56; tng. coordinator, mgmt. and supervisory devel. Union Carbide Corp., Linde div., 1956-69; asso. dir. industry mgmt. services Am. Gas Assn., Arlington, Va., 1969-79; ind. cons., 1979—; exec. dir. Alexandria (Va.) Bldg. Industry Assn., 1980—; editor, pub. Conflict Resolutions Newsletter, 1986—. Chmn., Stevenson-Kefauver Com., Astoria, N.Y., 1956; Democratic candidate for town supr., Cortlandt, N.Y., 1963; pres. Wessynton Homes Assn., 1978. Mem. Authors Guild, Assn. Humanistic Psychology, Am. Soc. Tng. and Devel., World Future Soc. Methodist (ofcl. bd. 1966-68). Co-editor: Dynamic Administration—The Collected Works of Mary Parker Follett, 1973. Home: 3404 Wessynton Way Alexandria VA 22309

FOX, GEORGE EDWARD, molecular biology educator; b. Syracuse, N.Y., Dec. 17, 1945; s. Charles Dainer and Henrietta L. (Carpentier) F.; m. Carolyne Ann Tordiglione, Sept. 1, 1973; children—Brian Trevor, Kevin William. B.S. in Chem. Engring., Syracuse U., 1967, Ph.D. in Chem. Engring., 1974. Research assoc. U. Ill., Urbana, 1973-77; asst. prof. molecular biology U. Houston, 1977-82, assoc. prof., 1982—. Contbr. chpts. to books, articles to profl. jours. Mem. editorial bd. Jour. Molecular Evolution, 1978—, Molecular Biology and Evolution, 1984—. Grantee NSF, 1983—, NASA, 1977—. Mem. Am. Soc. Microbiologists, AAAS, Am. Chem. Soc., Sigma Xi, Theta Tau. Avocations: bridge; chess. Office: Dept Biochem Scis U Houston TX 77004

FOX, GERALD LYNN, oral surgeon; b. Asheboro, N.C., Mar. 4, 1942; s. Clarence William and Jane Marie (Brock) F.; B.S., U. Tenn., 1964, D.D.S., 1967; m. Ellen Carol Smith, Mar. 18, 1961; children—Angela Carol, Michael Lynn, Lisa Elaine. Rotating intern Wilford Hall USAF Hosp., San Antonio, 1968-69; intern and resident in oral surgery U. Tex. Med. Sch., San Antonio, 1974; mem. teaching staff U. Tex. Sch. Dentistry and VA Hosp., San Antonio; practice dentistry specializing in oral and maxillofacial surgery; mem. staff Holston Valley Hosp. and Med. Center, Indian Path Hosp., Kinsport Hosp., Tenn.; apptd. by gov. to Mal-Practice Rev. Bd., Tenn., 1975-81; dir. Indian Hills Med. Complex. Pres., Sullivan County chpt. Am. Cancer Soc., 1975-77; med. missionary, Honduras, 1980, 83, 85; People-to-People ambassador to Japan, Malaysia and Korea, 1985—. Served to capt. USAF, 1968-72. Recipient Marion Fuller award, 1967; award Am. Cancer Soc., 1977; award So. Bapt. Missionary Bd., 1980; diplomate Am. Bd. Oral & Maxillofacial Surgery. Fellow Am. Coll. Oral and Maxillofacial Surgeons (a founder); mem. ADA Am. Assn. Oral and Maxillofacial Surgeons, Internat. Assn. Oral Surgeons, Tenn. Dental Assn., Tenn. Soc. Oral and Maxillofacial Surgeons, Am. Assn. Hosp. Dentists, 1st Dist. Dental Soc., Kingsport Dental Soc. & Study Club, Flying Dentists Assn., Tex. Bd. Dentistry, Fla. Bd. Dentistry, Airplane Owners and Pilots Assn., Xi Psi Phi. Methodist. Clubs: LeConte (Knoxville, Tenn.), Ridgefield Country. Contbr. articles to profl. jours. Home: 2525 Essex Dr Kingsport TN 37660 Office: 2008 Brookside Rd Kingsport TN 37660

FOX, JAMES CARROLL, lawyer, judge; b. Atchison, Kans., Nov. 6, 1928; s. Jared Copeland and Ethel (Carroll) F.; m. Katharine deRosset Rhett, Dec. 30, 1950; children—James Carroll, Jr., Jane Haskell Fox Brown, Ruth Rhett Fox Jordan. B.B.A., U. N.C., 1950, J.D. with honors, 1957. Bar: N.C. Vice-pres. and gen. mgr. Dillard Paper Co., Wilmington, N.C., 1951-55; clerk to presiding justice U.S. Dist. Ct., Wilmington, 1957-58; assoc. Carter & Murchison, Wilmington, 1958-59; ptnr. Murchison, Fox & Newton, Wilmington, 1960-82; judge U.S. Dist. Ct. (ea. dist.) N.C., Fayetteville, N.C., 1982—; lectr. N.C. Bar Assn., 1964; New Hanover County atty, 1967-81. Contbr. articles to profl. jours. Adv. com. U. N.C. Sch. Medicine div. edn. and research in community med. care., 1970; bd. dirs. Family Service Soc., 1961-65, Opportunities, Inc. of New Hanover County, 1968-69, New Hanover Sch. Mentally Retarded Children, 1968-71, St. John's Art Gallery, 1974; pres. United Fund N.C., 1969-70. Served with U.S. Army, 1951. Recipient Block award, 1957, Clark award, 1957; Conservation Service award Ducks Unltd., 1975. Mem. New Hanover County Bar Assn. (pres. 1967-68), 5th Jud. Dist. Bar Assn. (sec. 1960-62), N.C. Dist. Bar Assn., ABA, N.C. State Bar, N.C. Acad. Trial Lawyers, Order of Coif. Republican. Episcopalian. Clubs: Wilmington Civitan, Ducks Unltd. Office: PO Box 1148 Fayetteville NC 28302

FOX, JOANNE BLYTHE, beverage company official, accountant; b. Vancouver, B.C., Can., Feb. 5, 1951; came to U.S., 1980; d. John Walden and Marie Edith Fox; m. James A. Moring, Feb. 28, 1970 (div. 1980). Cert. gen. acct. U. B.C., Vancouver, 1980. Head teller Yorkshire Fin. Corp., Vancouver, 1970-73; fin. mgr. Can. Assn. C.G.A.s, Vancouver, 1973-78; asst. controller Merck, Hamilton, Bermuda, 1978-80; systems rep. Gen. Electric/Software Internat., Atlanta, 1981-83; project mgr. Coca-Cola Co., Atlanta, 1983-84, tng. cons., 1984—. Mem. Can. Cert. Gen. Accts. Assn. Avocations: art, music. Office: Coca-Cola Co 310 N Ave Atlanta GA 30301

FOX, JOHN MICHAEL, fresh produce company executive; b. Esher, U.K., Dec. 26, 1912; came to U.S., 1913, naturalized, 1918; s. James and Grace E. (Blott) F.; m. Floy B. George, Mar. 16, 1938; children—Byron, Susan, Stephen. A.B., Colgate U., 1934. Chief exec. officer Minute Maid Corp., 1945-60; chief exec. officer United Fruit Co., Boston, 1962-72; chief exec. officer H.P. Hood Inc., Boston, 1972-78; pres., dir. Natural Pak Produce Inc., Closter, N.J.; dir. Narragansett Capital, Harvey Group, Internat. Signals & Controls, Cissell Mfg. Republican. Clubs: Algonquin (Boston); Rotary (Orlando). Home: 2666 Lakeshore Dr Orlando FL 32803

FOX, JOSEPH CARTER, pulp and paper manufacturing company executive; b. Petersburg, Va., Sept. 8, 1939; s. William Tarrant and Virginia (Newell) F.; B.S., Washington and Lee U., 1961; M.B.A., U. Va., 1963; m. Carol Spaulding Fox, June 16, 1962; children—Carol Faulkner, Lucy Carter, Baylor Tarrant. With Chesapeake Corp. of Va., 1963—, controller, 1969-71, controller, asst. treas., 1971-74, v.p. corp. planning and devel., asst. treas., 1974-79, sr. v.p., asst. treas., 1979-80, pres., chief exec. officer, 1980—, dir. affiliate cos. Chmn. ann. fund Washington and Lee U., 1973-75. Episcopalian. Clubs: West Point Country (past pres.), Ware River Yacht, Commonwealth. Home: PO Box 461 West Point VA 23181 Office: Chesapeake Corp Va PO Box 311 West Point VA 23181*

FOX, JUDITH ELLEN, personnel executive; b. N.Y.C., Aug. 2, 1941; d. Murray A. and Harriette Schneider; student Pa. State U., 1959-60; m. Jerry Fox, Aug. 16, 1964; children—Brian Spencer, Jennifer Leslie. Asst. personnel dir. Miles Shoe Co., N.Y.C., 1961-63; freelance writer, photographer Coronet, The Progressive, U.S. Catholic, numerous local and state periodicals, 1962-77; asst. personnel dir. Wallachs, Inc., N.Y.C., 1963-64; co-owner, photographer J. Fox Photographers, Stony Brook, N.Y., 1968-72; mgr. Forbes Temporaries, Richmond, Va., 1975-78; pres. Fox-Huber Temporaries, Inc., Richmond, 1978—, Fox-Huber Permanent Placements, Richmond, 1985—, Rosemary Scott Temps., N.Y.C., 1983—; adv. bd., chmn. women in bus. com. Women's Bank, 1981-83; chmn. customer adv. bd. Va. Electric Power Co., 1981-84; cons. to pvt. industry, 1980—. Dist. chmn. Va. gubernatorial campaign, 1977; charter mem. Businesses Who Care; bd. dirs. Multiple Sclerosis Soc., Central Va. chpt., 1979-80; mem. exec. com. Gov.'s Adv. Com. Small Bus.; 1982-86; bd. dirs. Met. Richmond YMCA, 1982-86, Pvt. Industry Council, 1983—; vice-chmn. Richmond area U.S. Olympic Com., 1983—; mem. fundraising com. Hampton Inst.; bd. dirs. Sci. Mus. Va., 1985—. Mem. Profl. Orgn. Temporary Services, Va. C. of C. (small bus. com. 1983-85), Richmond C. of C. (chmn. small bus. council 1982-84, dir. 1983—, exec. bd. 1984—, mem. legis. affairs com. 1981—), Va. Assn. Temp. Services (v.p. 1981—), Nat. Assn. Female Execs., Richmond Assn. Women Bus. Owners, Internat. Platform Assn. Office: 5006 Monument Ave Richmond VA 23230 also 515 Madison Ave New York NY 10022

FOX, KENNETH RICHARD, ophthalmologist, surgeon; b. N.Y.C., Apr. 20, 1947; s. Lester and Frances Fox; m. Wendy Richter, Nov. 29, 1975; children—Kimberly Anne David Eric. B.A., U. Pa., 1967; M.D., Georgetown U., 1972. Diplomate Am. Bd. Ophthalmology. Resident in opthalmology Case Western Res. U., Cleve., 1973-76; fellow in retinal/vitreous surgery, U. Tenn., Memphis, 1976, Inst. Ophthalmology, U. London, 1977; practice medicine specializing in ophthalmology and eye surgery, Falls Church, Va., 1977—. Fellow Internat. Coll. Surgeons, Am. Acad. Ophtalmology, Am. Soc. Laser Medicine and Surgery; mem. Internat. Ophthal. Council, Royal Soc. Medicine, World Medicine Assn., AMA, So. Med. Assn. Contbr. articles to profl. jours. Office: 6051-C Arlington Blvd Falls Church VA 22044

FOX, RAYMOND GRAHAM, educational technologist; b. Portland, Oreg., May 31, 1923; s. George Raymond and Georgia Dorothy (Beckman) F.; B.S., Rensselaer Poly. Inst., 1943; m. Harriet Carolyn Minchin, Apr. 17, 1948; children—Susan, Christine, Ellen, Laura, John. Salesman IBM Corp., N.Y.C., 1946-48, br. mgr., 1949-56, systems mgr., 1957-65, edn. systems devel. mgr., 1965-76; cons. tech. and industry relations Va. Council for Deaf, Warrenton, Va., 1976-78, mem., 1978-84; chmn. bd. Learning Tech. Inst., Warrenton, 1975—; pres. Instrn. Delivery Machines Corp., 1985—. Mem. Va. Council for Deaf, 1978-84; chmn., 1980-83; mem. Sec. of Navy Adv. Bd. on Edn. and Tng., 1972-77; cons. for tech. Va. Legis. Adv. Com. on Handicapped, 1970; mem. Nat. Def. Exec. Reserve, 1970-83; mem. emeritus, 1983—. Served with USNR, 1943-46. Mem. Soc. Applied Learning Tech. (pres. 1972—), Nat. Security Indsl. Assn. (chmn. tng. group 1974-76). Anglican. Clubs: Army & Navy (Washington); Fauquier (Warrenton); Columbia Country (Chevy Chase, Md.); Moorings (Vero Beach, Fla.). Patentee interactive audio visual instruction device. Home: Reynwood PO Box 376 Warrenton VA 22186 Office: 50 Culpeper St Warrenton VA 22186

FOX, RICHARD LAUMAN, II, publishing company official; b. Fayetteville, N.C., Sept. 1, 1946; s. George C. and Mary Elizabeth (Corbett) F.; m. Ashton Wilson Lilly, Nov. 13, 1971; children—Ashton, Noel, Richard, Corbett. B.A. in English, Meth. Coll., 1968. With Fayetteville Pub. Co., 1971—, maj. account and nat. advt. mgr., 1976—; owner Fayetteville Aviation, Inc., 1980-82; dir. Cannon Aircraft Co. Asst. treas. YMCA, 1980-81; pres. adv. bd. Fayetteville Little Theatre, 1977-78; Democratic precinct officer, 1975-76. Served with U.S. Army, 1969-71. Mem. Fayetteville Area Advt. Fedn. (dir.), Internat. Newspaper Advt. and Mktg. Execs. Assn., Mid-Atlantic Newspaper Advt. and Mktg. Assn. Episcopalian. Clubs: Highland Country, Seapath Boatominium, Exchange.

FOX, THEODORE BERT, educator, city official; b. Jacksonville, Ala., Oct. 25, 1912; s. Cass and Jennie Magnolia (Taylor) F.; student Selma U., 1929-30, Gen. Motors Inst., 1935-36; certificate Ala. State U., 1954, Allen Electric Co. Sch., 1950, Ala. A. and M. U., 1956; m. Agnes Marshall Watley, Apr. 7, 1933; children—Sydney (Mrs. Eugene Reid, Jr.), June (Mrs. J. Mason Davis), Barbara (Mrs. Franklin Todd), Sandra (Mrs. Thomas Sudduth). Supr., Anniston (Ala.) Army Ordnance Depot, 1940-46; vocational instr. Anniston City Bd. Edn., 1946-80, tchr. Anniston Area Vocational Tech. Sch.; asso. pastor 1st Bapt. Ch.; mem. City Council Jacksonville, 1968—, mayor pro-tem, 1977—; bd. dirs. Ala. Democratic Com., 1970—. Pres. Jacksonville Civic League; bd. dirs. Jacksonville Child Care Center; mem. exec. bd. Choccolocco council Boy Scouts Am.; bd. dirs. Cottaquilla council Girl Scouts U.S. Recipient Silver Beaver award Boy Scouts Am., 1962; Outstanding Citizen award Delta Sigma Theta, 1975; Disting. Service award Ala. Vocat. Assn., Ala. NAACP. Mem. NEA, Anniston Edn. Assn. (pres.), NAACP. Baptist. (pres. Sunday sch., Bapt. tng. Union Congress 1937-80). Home: 157 Spring Ave SW Jacksonville AL 36265 Office: City Hall Jacksonville AL 36265

FOX, VICTORIA, public relations consultant; b. Chgo., Oct. 21; d. Louis and Rose (Posnak) F.; m. Ira Jay Druckman, June 24, 1955 (div. June 1977); children—Daniel Scott, Eric Steven, Michael Adam. B.S. with honors in Communications, Fla. Internat. U., 1979; postgrad. in film and video U. Miami. Mgmt. tng. asst. Jerome Barnum Assocs., White Plains, N.Y., 1975-80; with Hunt/Meyer Community Relations, Miami, 1979; internat. pub. relations and mktg. Lodding Engring., Auburn, Mass., 1979; tng. and devel. supr. Burdines, Miami, 1980-81; community relations coordinator Miami Lighthouse for the Blind, 1981-82; freelance pub. relations cons./coordinator, Key Biscayne, Fla., 1982—; facilitator, developer Success Seminars. Mem. docent com. Zool. Soc., 1976-79; chmn. port of entry com. Council for Internat. Visitors, 1974—; Southeast regional asst. coordinator The Hunger Project, 1979; active worker nat. Democratic presdl. and vice presdl. campaign, 1976. Mem. Pub. Relations Soc. Am., Coral Gables C. of C. (mem. TV and film com.), Coral Gables Bd. Realtors, Assn. Humanistic Psychology (So. regional bd. dirs.). Democrat. Home and Office: 155 Ocean Lane Dr Apt 1204 Key Biscayne FL 33149

FOX, WILLIAM MCNAIR, organizational behavior educator, consultant; b. New Orleans, Nov. 1, 1924; s. Frederick Hewitt and Lorena Grace (Bates) F.; m. Else Carola Collett-Muller, Sept. 10, 1949; children—Jane Inge, William Bates. B.B.A., U. Mich., 1948, M.B.A., 1948; Ph.D., Ohio State U., 1954. Asst. to personnel dir. Peerless Woolen Mills, Rossville, Ga., 1948-49; asst. prof. mgmt. Tex. Tech. Coll., Lubbock, 1950-52, U. Wash., Seattle, 1952-54; asst. prof. mgmt. U. Fla., Gainesville, 1954-57, prof. organizational behavior, 1963—; cons. numerous orgns. and advanced mgmt. programs. Asst. dir. civil def. Alachua County, Fla., 1957-63. Served with AUS, 1943-45. Research grantee Office Naval Research, 1970-74; Fulbright lectr., 1957-58; sr. Fulbright research scholar, 1974-75. Fellow Acad. Mgmt.; mem. Am. Psychol. Assn., So. Mgmt. Assn. (pres. 1963-64). Club: Gainesville Golf and Country. Author: The Management Process, 1962; editor: Readings in Personnel Management From Fortune Rev., 1957, 63. Home: 1726 SW 8th Dr Gainesville FL 32601 Office: Dept Mgmt and Adminstrv Scis Coll Bus Adminstrn U Fla Gainesville FL 32611

FRABEL, HANS GOOB, glass sculptor; b. Jena, East Germany, June 9, 1941; came to U.S., 1965; s. Willy E. and Lisa (Falke) F. Student Mainzer Kunstscule Mainz, W. Germany, 1956-59. Sci. glassblower Jena Glas Works, Mainz, 1956-65, Ga. Inst. Tech., Atlanta, 1965-68; founder, dir. Frabel Studio, Atlanta, 1968—; dir. Callanwolde Fine Arts Ctr., Atlanta, 1977-83; cons. artist Penland Sch. Art, N.C., 1979, R.I. Sch. Design, Providence, 1980. Works exhibited in museums around the world, including the Smithsonian Inst., and Corning Mus. of Glass, N.Y. R.I. Sch. Design grantee, 1979-81. Mem. Am. Sci. Glassblowers Soc., Glass Art Soc. Lutheran. Avocations: gardening; horticulture; collector of art and sculpture. Office: The Frabel Studio 695 Antone St Atlanta GA 30318

FRACKER, ROBERT GRANGER, librarian; b. Spout Spring, Va., Sept. 29, 1928; s. Dudley Granger and Ruby Walker (Page) F.; student Va. Poly. Inst. and State U., 1946-49, Roanoke Coll., 1948; B.S., E. Tenn. State U., 1954; M.A., Appalachian State U., 1957; postgrad. U. Ill., 1957-59, Duke U., 1962-65, U. N.C., Chapel Hill, 1977, N.C. Central U., 1978; m. Sandra Elizabeth Snyder, June 5, 1965; 1 dau., Mary Susan. Coach, tchr. English, social studies Beaver Creek High Sch., West Jefferson, N.C., 1954-56; counselor Univ. Council on Tchr. Edn., U. Ill., Urbana, 1957-59; mem. faculty Meredith Coll., Raleigh, N.C., 1962—, reference librarian, media coordinator Carlyle Campbell Library, 1977—. Campus chmn. United Way of Wake County, 1976. Served with U.S. Army, 1951-53. Mem. N.C. Assn. Tchr. Educators (pres. 1975-76), Internat. Phenomenological Soc., Assn. Tchr. Edn., Philosophy of Edn. Soc., Am. Soc. Mil. Insignia Collectors, Kami Kaze, Kappa Komma Kappa, Kappa Delta Pi, Phi Delta Kappa, Order Silver Sunset. Democrat. Presbyterian. Home: 307 Oak Ridge Rd Cary NC 27511 Office: Carlyle Campbell Library Meredith Coll Raleigh NC 27611

FRAICHE, DONNA DIMARTINO, lawyer; b. New Orleans, Dec. 8, 1951; d. Anthony and Rose Mary (Batchelona) DiMartino; student St. Mary's Dominican Coll., New Orleans, 1971, La. State U., 1972; J.D., Loyola U., New Orleans, 1975; m. John F. Fraiche, Dec. 27, 1974; 1 son, Geoffrey Michael. Bar: La. 1975, U.S. Ct. Claims 1979, U.S. Tax Ct. 1977, U.S. Supreme Ct. 1979 U.S. Ct. Appeals (5th, 4th, 11th, 10th cirs.). Practiced in New Orleans, Baton Rouge, 1975—; assoc. Martzell & Montero, 1972-76, McCollister, McCleary, Fazio, Mixon, Holliday and Jones, 1976-78; individual practice law, from 1978; ptnr. Wyllie & Fraiche, P.C.; pres., dir. Wyllie, Fraiche & Sullivan, P.C., New Orleans, from 1982; now ptnr. Broadhurst, Brook, Mangham & Hardy. Mem. pres.'s adv. com. to bd. Our Lady of Holy Cross Coll., New Orleans, 1979; council mem. La. State Arts Council, 1984—; bd. dirs. Louise Davis Devel. Ctr. Recipient cert. of merit Loyola U. Sch. Law, 1975. Mem. ABA (mem. forum com. on health law, co-chmn. New Orleans forum com. on health law), Nat. Health Lawyers Assn. (dir. 1982-85, exec. com. 1985, sec., chmn. med. staff legal issues program), Am. Soc. Hosp. Attys., Am. Coll. Legal Medicine (asso.), Assn. Trial Lawyers Am., La. Trial Lawyers Assn., Am. Women Lawyers Assn., Mortar Bd., Phi Delta Phi. Past editor-in-chief Delta mag. La. State U. Contbr. articles to profl. publs. Democrat. Roman Catholic. Home: 3924 St Charles Ave New Orleans LA 70115 Office: 400 Poydras Suite 2600 New Orleans LA 70130

FRALEY, BILLY PAUL, II, oil company executive; b. Borger, Tex., June 7, 1951; s. Billy Paul and Jackie Irene (Stewart) F.; m. Brenda Gail Allison, Mar. 6, 1982; children—Shelly Elaine, Allison Heather. A.A., Frank Phillips Coll., 1972; B.S., West Tex. State U., 1979. Exploration geologist Amarala Petroleum, Amarillo, Tex., 1979-80; staff geologist Baker & Taylor Drilling Co., 1980-82; geologist Bill Fraley II-Cons., 1982; v.p. D&B Petroleum, 1983; pres. Fraley Energy Corp., Amarillo, 1983—. Coach, Kids Inc., Amarillo, 1981-83. Mem. Amarillo C. of C., Am. Assn. Petroleum Geologists, Soc. Petroleum Engrs., Soc. Exploration Geophysicists, West Tex. Geol. Soc., Alpha Chi, Sigma Gamma Epsilon. Republican. Lodge: Elks. Avocations: astronomy, music, reading. Home: 6404 Cromwell Amarillo TX 79109 Office: Fraley Energy Corp 1616 S Kentucky St Bldg D Suite 220 Amarillo TX 79102

FRAME, HELEN DUNN, public relations executive, Realtor; b. N.Y.C., Nov. 10, 1939; d. Edward and Eunice Elizabeth (Harvey) Dunn; 1 son, Dana Edward. B.A. (scholar) Syracuse U., 1960; M.A., N.Y. U., 1967; cert. in German, Volkhochshule, Nurnberg, Germany, 1969. Writer, mgmt. trainee Consol. Edison N.Y., Inc., N.Y.C., 1960-64; mgr. Amer-Mac Assocs., Am. Mayflower Moving & Storage Services, Dallas, 1971-74; freelance pub. relations/mktg. communicator, London, Nürnberg and Munich (Ger.), Dallas, 1967—; assoc. Lou Smith, Inc., resdl. real estate sales, 1984-86; gen. mgr., Realtor, Kennedy, Phillips & Calumet Real Estate, 1986—. Chmn. dinner com. Dallas Com. for Fgn. Visitors; chmn. publ. relations English Speaking Union. Grantee in field. Mem. Women in Communications, Dallas C. of C. (internat. bus. forum), Tex. Internat. Bus. Assn. Episcopalian. Contbr. articles to Southern Living mag., Travel, Boston Globe, Los Angeles Times, Open Road, Greek Accent, The Trader, and others; author: Positively Single. Address: 2214 Nantucket Valley Circle Dallas TX 75227

FRAMPTON, WILLIAM BURWELL, architect; b. Huntington, W.Va., Aug. 9, 1926; s. William Ray and Erma Estella (Bowser) F.; B.Arch., Va. Poly. Inst., 1950; m. Janice Callaway, June 10, 1950; children—Linda Dianne, Martha Louise, Laura Elizabeth. Draftsman, Frampton & Bowers, Huntington, 1952-57, head draftsman, 1958-64, architect, 1958-64; pvt. practice architecture, 1964—. Mem. Mayor's Com.; bd. dirs. Salvation Army; chmn. adv. bd. Huntington Hist. Soc., 1975-82; treas. Fifth Ave. Baptist Ch. Served with USN, 1945-46. Registered architect, W.Va., Ohio, Ky. Mem. AIA, Soc. Am. Registered Architects, Am. Legion, Navy League. Club: Rotary (past pres. Huntington 1978-79). Home: 522 13th Ave Huntington WV 25701 Office: 501 6th Ave Huntington WV 25701

FRANCFORT, ALFRED JOHN, JR., educator; b. Washington, June 28, 1939; s. Alfred John and Lucille Joan (Wall) F.; m. Elisabeth A. Dey, Aug. 5, 1968. B.S., Monmouth Coll., 1964; M.A., U. Pitts., 1969, Ph.D., 1972. Instr. econs. Chatham Coll., Pitts., 1970-72; teaching fellow U. Pitts., 1966-70, asst. prof. econs., 1972-77, assoc. prof., 1977-83; prof. fin. James Madison U., Harrisonburg, Va., 1983—; mem. mediation panel Labor-Mgmt. Participation Com., Johnstown Regional Industries, 1982-83; cons. on electric utility rate cases and regulation, 1977—; lectr. corp. mgmt. tng. programs, 1973—; mem. U. Pitts. Steering Com. on Regional Econ. Devel., 1973-75. Mem. editorial bd. Jour. Econ. Lit., 1970-83. Contbr. articles to profl. jours. MIT scholar, 1974; fellow Univ. Chgo., 1977; faculty fellow U.S. Gen. Acctg. office, Washington, 1979-80. Mem. Am. Econ. Assn. (transp. and pub. utility group), Am. Fin. Assn., Eastern Fin. Assn., Fin. Mgmt. Assn. So. Fin. Assn. Home: 1115 Chestnut Dr Harrisonburg VA 22801 Office: James Madison Univ Dept Fin Harrisonburg VA 22807

FRANCH, KENNETH DAVID, structural engineer, architect; b. Oak Park, Ill., Aug. 5, 1950; s. Victor John and Jennie (DeStefano) F.; m. Beatrice Susan Stremich, June 19, 1971; children—Kimberly Ann, Stacy Marie. B.Arch., U. Ill., 1973, M.S. in Archtl. Engring., 1975. Registered architect, Ill., Wis., Tex.; registered structural engr., Ill.; registered profl. engr., N.Mex., Tex., Va. With Phillips Swager Assocs., Inc., Peoria, Ill., 1975-83, project engr., 1976, assoc., 1978, chief structural engr., 1980-83, v.p., Dallas, 1983—. Scoutmaster, Boy Scouts Am., 1976-83, dist. mem. at large, 1979-83; adviser Order of the Arrow, 1980-83; participant Leadership Plano, 1985. Recipient Dist. Award of Merit, Boy Scouts Am., 1981, others. Mem. AIA (chmn. Peoria sect.), ASCE (sec.), Structural Engrs. Assn. Ill., Constrn. Specifications Inst., Am. Inst. Steel Constrn., Am. Concrete Inst., Nat. Council Archtl. Registration Bds. (cert.), Plano C. of C. Republican. Roman Catholic. Lodge: K.C. (officer). Office: One Oaks Plaza Suite 1175 6750 LBJ Freeway Dallas TX 75240

FRANCIS, JOHN ELBERT, university dean; b. Kingfisher, Okla., Mar. 14, 1937; s. John Amos and Virginia Lorain (Mitchell) F.; m. Susan Ruth Bentley, June 2, 1962; children—John Carl, Steven Michael. B.S., U. Okla., 1960, M.S., 1963, Ph.D., 1965. Engr., Allis Chalmers Mfg. Co., Springfield, Ill., 1960; asst. prof. U. Mo.-Rolla, 1964-66; asst. prof. aerospace, mech. and nuclear engring. U. Okla., Norman, 1966-69, assoc. prof., 1969-74, prof., 1974—, asst. dean Grad. Coll., 1968-71, assoc. dean Coll. Engring., 1981—. Mem. AIAA, ASME, Am. Soc. Engring. Educators, N.Y. Acad. Sci., Optical Soc. Am., Pi Tau Sigma, Sigma Xi. Democrat. Roman Catholic. Contbr. articles to tech. jours. Home: 1406 Greenbriar Dr Norman OK 73069 Office: 202 W Boyd St Norman OK 73019

FRANCK, WILLIAM FRANCIS, textile company executive; b. Fayetteville, N.C., July 29, 1917; s. William Francis and Martha Elizabeth (Lawhon) F.; m. Carolyn Ann Pannill, Nov. 29, 1941; children—Martha (Mrs. Overman Rollins), William Francis III, Carolyn Ann (Mrs. Alex Gordon), John M. B.A., Duke U., 1939. Salesman Belk Leggett Co., Durham, N.C., 1935-40; cost clk. DuPont Co., Martinsville, Va., 1940-43; personnel mgr. Pannill Knitting Co., Martinsville, 1946-50; v.p. gen. mgr. Sale Knitting Co., Martinsville, 1950-53; pres., chief exec. officer Tultex Corp., Martinsville, 1953—; v.p. Tulstar Factors, Inc., N.Y.C.; dir. Piedmont Bank Group, Inc., Am. Furniture Co., Martin Processing Co. Inc., all Martinsville. Bd. mem. Martinsville YMCA, 1969-78; fund drive chmn. Meml. Hosp., 1966-67, bd. mem., 1963-77; mem. Martinsville Sch. Bd., 1956-61, Blue Ridge Airport Authority, 1962—. Served to 1st lt. Q.M.C. AUS, 1943-46, ETO. Mem. Martinsville C. of C. (1st pres. 1959-61). Presbyterian (elder 1954-76). Club: Chatmoss Country. Lodge: Kiwanis. Home: 1105 Plantation Rd Martinsville VA 24112 Office: Tultex Corp PO Box 5191A Martinsville VA 24115*

FRANCO, JOHN ALBERT, insurance holding company executive; b. N.Y.C., Apr. 1, 1942; s. Dominick and Theresa (DiBlasi) F.; A.B., Columbia U., 1963; LL.B., NYU, 1967; m. Mary Elizabeth Drake, May 27, 1967; children—John Albert, Susan, Margaret, Carol. Bar: N.Y. 1967. With Westvaco Corp., N.Y.C., 1970-79, comptroller, 1979; exec. v.p., chief fin. officer Capital Holding Corp., Louisville, 1979-84, pres. agy. group, 1984—; dir. Capital Enterprise Ins. Group, Commonwealth Life Ins. Co., Ga. Internat. Life Ins. Co., Home

Security and Peoples Life Ins. Cos., Nat. Liberty Corp., Capital Ventures Corp., First Deposit Corp.; past chmn. pension com. Am. Paper Inst. Served with U.S. Army, 1967-69; Vietnam. Decorated Bronze Star. Office: Capital Holding Corp Louisville KY 40232

FRANK, BENJAMIN BERMAN, estate planner; b. Stonewall, Miss., Dec. 28, 1932; s. Aaron Clarence and Eugenia Mae (Brumfield) F.; m. Catherine Barnes Dempsey, Apr. 19, 1958; children—Elizabeth Randolph, Rebecca Brumfield, Benjamin Berman. B.S., U. So. Miss., 1955. With Crown-Headlight Mfg. Co., Cin., 1955-59, Ortho Pharm. Corp., New Orleans, 1959-63, Fidelity Union Life Ins., New Orleans, 1963-64; with Home Life Ins. Co., New Orleans, 1964—, estate planner, 1984—. Bd. dirs., vice chmn. Lakeside Hosp., Metairie, La., 1969-73; fin. chmn. Senator Ken Hollis, Metairie, 1983, Councilman Ken Hollis, 1982. Named Co. Man of Yr., Friedler-Leyens Agy., 1971, Man of Yr., 1968; Top Salesman Eastern Region, Ortho Pharm. Corp., 1961. Mem. Nat. Assn. Life Underwriters (Nat. Quality award 1966-83), Million Dollar Round Table, Am. Coll. C.L.U.s. Republican. Home: 5033 Bissonet Dr Metairie LA 70003 Office: Home Life Ins Co Suite 300 415 Lafayette St New Orleans LA 70130

FRANK, GEORGE WILLARD (WILL), petroleum engineer, oil company executive; b. Beloit, Kans., Mar. 25, 1923; s. George Nicklas and Catherine Cecelia (Wideman) F.; m. Dorothy Elaine Wells, June 22, 1947; children—Barbara Beth Frank Doherty, Janis Henry. B.S. in Petroleum Engring., U. Kans., Lawrence, 1946; postgrad. South Tex. Law Coll., Houston, 1950. Exec. v.p. Austral Oil Co., Houston, 1956-78; pres. Houston Oil Internat., 1978-81, dir. and officer all fgn. subs., 1981—; v.p., gen. mgr. E & P Internat. div. Tenneco Oil, Houston, 1981—, dir. and officer all fgn. subs., 1983—. Served to lt. USNR, 1942-46. Republican. Presbyterian. Clubs: Lakeside Country, Petroleum (Houston). Office: 1100 Louisiana St Suite 2400 Houston TX 77002

FRANK, GORDON DAVID, ophthalmologist; b. Pine Bluff, Ark., Nov. 11, 1925; s. Alexander and Bertha (Levine) F.; m. Paula Feldman, Dec. 15, 1955; children—Cynthia Frank Birne, Margaret Jill. B.S., The Citadel, 1952; M.D., U. Ark., 1952. Diplomate Am. Bd. Ophthalmology. Intern, U. Chgo., 1952-53; resident ophthalmology Michael Reese Hosp., Chgo., 1953-55, U. Ill. Hosp., Chgo., 1955-56; clin. instr. Northwestern U. Med. Sch., Chgo., 1956-58, Ill. Eye and Ear Infirmary, U. Ill., Chgo., 1956-58; mem. attending staff Baylor Hosp., Dallas, 1960—; attending physician Presbyn. Hosp., Dallas, 1966—; asst. clin. instr. U. Tex. Southwestern Med. Sch., Dallas, 1958—. Mem. nat. bd. Am. Jewish Com., Dallas, 1964—. Served to lt. (j.g.) USNR, 1943-46, ETO. Mem. AMA, Pan Am. Med. Assn., Tex. Med. Assn., Tex. Ophthalmol. Assn., Dallas Acad. Ophthalmology (program chmn. 1979—), Sdns Confederate Vets. Republican. Jewish. Club: The Citadel (Dallas). Lodges: Masons, Shriners. Avocations: backpacking; cycling; sailing. Home: 7123 Currin Dr Dallas TX 75230 Office: 8210 Walnut Hill Ln Suite 710 Dallas TX 75231

FRANK, JOE LEE, III, naval officer; b. Norfolk, Va., Feb. 11, 1947; s. Joe Lee Jr. and Barbara Olive (Bloxam) F.; m. Nancy Ellen Bruce, May 4, 1974; children—Joe Lee IV, Brian Wallace. B.S., U. S. Naval Acad., 1964, M.S. in Physics, 1975. Commd. U.S. Navy, 1968, advanced through ranks to comdr., 1983; asst. combat info. officer USS Mahan, 1969-70, U.S. liaison officer Fed. German Navy Destroyer Rommel, 1970-71, weapons officer USS Cook, 1971-73, ops. officer USS Sacramento, 1976-78; staff chief of naval ops., 1978-80, exec. officer USS Scott, 1981-83, ops. officer USS Iowa, 1983—. Guest lectr. Peninsula Nature and Sci. Ctr. Mem. Am. Astron. Soc., U.S. Naval Inst., Internat. Planetarium Soc., Sigma Xi. Contbr. articles to profl. jours. Home: 9 Madison Ln S Newport News VA 23606 Office: USS Iowa (BB-61) FPO New York NY 09546

FRANK, MILTON, III, physician, educator; b. Huntsville, Ala., Apr. 19, 1938; s. Milton and Zimmie (Wise) F.; m. Cookie Arnovitz, June 11, 1961; children—Amy Sue, Milton IV, Steven Jay. B.S., U. Ala., 1960; M.D., Vanderbilt U., 1964. Diplomate Am. Bd. Internal Medicine. Intern, Vanderbilt U. Hosps., Nashville, 1965; resident in internal medicine U. Wash. Hosps., Seattle, 1966-67; fellow in cardiology U. Ala. Hosps., Birmingham, 1967-68, 70-71; practice medicine specializing in cardiology and internal medicine, Atlanta, 1971—; asst. clin. prof. Emory U. Med. Sch., Atlanta, 1973—; cons. Cardiac Rehab. Clinic, Atlanta Jewish Community Ctr., 1976—; cardiac cons. Ga. State U. Phys. Fitness Inst., 1983—. Past chmn. med. div. United Way Atlanta. Served to maj. M.C., AUS, 1968-70. Fellow ACP, Am. Coll. Cardiology; mem. Med. Assn. Atlanta (bd. dirs. 1980-83), Med. Assn. Ga. (membership chmn.), Am. Soc. Internal Medicine (pres. 1971-73 Ga. chpt.), U. Ala. Alumni Assn. (pres. Atlanta chpt. 1979-80), Phi Beta Kappa, Omicron Delta Kappa, Zeta Beta Tau. Jewish. Office: 1372 Peachtree NE Suite 301 Atlanta GA 30309

FRANK, PATRICIA ANNE, state senator; b. Cleve., Nov. 12, 1929; d. Paul Conrad and Mildred Patricia (Roane) Collier; B.S. in Fin. and Taxation, U. Fla., Gainesville, 1951; postgrad. Georgetown U. Law Sch., 1951-52; m. Richard H. Frank, Dec. 21, 1951; children—Stacy, Hillary, Courtney. Bus. economist anti-trust div. Dept. Justice, Washington, 1951-53; mem. staff U.S. Congressman John R. Foley, 1959-60; mem. Hillsborough County (Fla.) Sch. Bd., 1972-76, chmn., 1975-76; past mem. Hillsborough County Tax Bd., Tampa Election Bd.; mem. Fla. Ho. of Reps. from 67th Dist., 1976-78; past mem. adv. council dist. VI, Fla. Health and Rehab. Services; mem. Fla. Senate from 23d Dist., 1978—, past chmn. Senate edn. com.; vice chmn. policy com. Nat. Assessment Ednl. Progress; mem. task group on govts. of Nat. Sci. Bd. Com. on Precoll. Edn. in Math., Sci. and Tech., NSF; mem. nat. planning com. Advanced Leadership Program Services; spl. ambassador to Independence of St. Vincent's Island, 1979. Mem. So. Regional Edn. Bd. Bd. dirs. Tampa Bay Com. Fgn. Relations. Recipient numerous service and community service awards. Home: 825 1/2 Bayshore Blvd Tampa FL 33606 Office: 401 S Albany Ave Tampa FL 33606

FRANK, PETER, physician, director; b. Vineland, N.J., Mar. 24, 1944; s. Ulrich Anton and Ruth (Esser) F.; m. Jane Littwin, June 14, 1964 (div.); m. Patricia Frank, Jan. 11, 1974; 1 child, Alexis J. B.A. in Psychology, Temple U., 1964; D.O., Chgo. Coll. of Osteo. Medicine, 1968. Diplomate Nat. Bd. of Osteo Examiners. Intern, Lakeview Hosp., Milw., 1968-69; gen. practice osteo. medicine, Phila., 1971-81, Hardeeville, S.C., 1981—, Bluffton, S.C., 1981—, Daufuskie Island, S.C., 1981—; med. dir. Coastal Med. Assocs., 1981—; pres. Continental Med. Services, 1971-76; cons., stockholder, HMO Diversified, 1971—; emergency med. cons. Western Eastern Roadracers' Assn., 1974-84; dir. of emergency room services Jasper County Gen. Hosp., Ridgeland, S.C., 1981-83; emergency room physician Hilton Head Hosp., Hilton Head Island, S.C., 1981; med. control officer Jasper County Emergency Med. Services, 1981-84; mem. Low County Regional Emergency Med. Services Council, 1981—; sch. physician May River Acad., Bluffton, S.C., 1981—; vis. lectr. dept. family practice Med. U. of S.C., Charleston, 1985, Meml. Med. Ctr., Savannah, Ga., 1985; mem. staff St. Joseph's Hosp., Phila., 1971-76, Jasper County Gen. Hosp., 1981—, Hilton Head Hosp., 1981-84; Served as capt. MC, U.S. Army, 1969-71; Vietnam. Mem. S.C. Osteo. Assn. (v.p. 1984-85, Am. Heart Assn. (advanced cardiac life support cert. 1981), Am. Cancer Soc. (pres. Jasper County chpt. 1981—), Beaufort County Med. Soc., Am. Acad. Family Physicians, Am. Osteo. Assn., S.C. Med. Assn., S.C. Acad. Family Physicians, Lambda Omicron Gamma. Republican. Unitarian. Club: Bluffton Men's (v.p. 1982-83). Avocations: motorsports; music; travel. Office: 43 Coastal Hwy Hardeeville SC 29927

FRANKEL, FREDERIC ALAN, exploration geologist, musician; b. Chgo., Feb. 20, 1955; s. Jay and Violet (Dunlin) F.; m. Mary Margaret Clay, July 3, 1982. Student, U.S. Internat. U., 1972-74; B.S. in Geology, Western State Coll., 1977. Cons., Mobil Oil Corp, Milan, N.Mex., 1978-79; cons. geologist, Denver, 1979; energy landman Cempco, Inc., Denver, 1979-80; exploration geologist Dome Petroleum, Denver, 1980-81, Oklahoma City, 1981-84; petroleum geologist Texaco, Inc., New Orleans, 1984—; lectr. to high schs., 1985—. Mem. New Orleans Geol. Soc. (edn. com. 1984—), Am. Assn. Petroleum Geologists (conv. judge 1984—), Oklahoma City Geol. Soc., Geophys. Soc. Okla. Clubs: Craven Country (soc. dir. 1970-72) (Gunnison); Okla. Doers (vice chmn. 1981-84) (Oklahoma City). Avocations: volleyball; downhill skiing; scuba diving; guitar; miniature lead soldier collecting. Home: 1201 Hall Ave Metairie LA 70003

FRANKLIN, BILLY JOE, university president; b. Fannin County, Tex., Jan. 30, 1940; s. John Asia and Annie Mae (Castle) F.; m. Sonya Kay Erwin, June 1, 1958; children—Terry Daylon, Shari Dea. B.A., U. Tex.-Austin, 1965, M.A., 1967, Ph.D., 1969. Instr. sociology S.W. Tex. State U., 1967-68; asst. prof. sociology Baylor U., Waco, Tex., 1968-69; asst. prof. sociology U. Iowa, Iowa City, 1969-71; assoc. prof., chmn. dept. sociology and anthropology Western Carolina U., 1971-73; prof., chmn. dept. sociology Wright State U., Dayton, Ohio, 1973-75; prof. sociology dean Sch. Liberal Arts, S.W. Tex. State U., 1975-77; prof. sociology, v.p. acad. affairs Stephen F. Austin State U., Nacogdoches, Tex., 1977-81; pres. Texas A&I U., Kingsville, 1981-84, Lamar U., Beaumont, Tex., 1984—. Commr., Bd. Zoning Appeals, Wayne Twp., Dayton, 1973-75, Community Devel. Bd., San Marcos, Tex., 1975-77; bd. dirs. Nacogdoches County United Way, 1977—. Mem. Am. Sociol. Assn., Southwestern Sociol. Assn., Am. Assn. Higher Edn., Tex. Acad. Sci. Southwestern Social Sci. Assn. Democrat. Presbyterian. Lodge: Rotary. Author: Research Methods: Issues and Insights, 1971; Social Psychology and Everyday Life, 1973; contbr. articles to profl. jours. Office: President's Office Lamar Univ Beaumont TX 77710*

FRANKLIN, DAWSON CLEVELAND, JR., exec. search cons.; b. Lake End, La., June 13, 1922; s. Dawson Cleveland and Mary Elizabeth (McCann) F.; B.A., La. Coll., 1942; m. Cecilia Joy Pate, July 27, 1965; children—Dawson Cleveland III, Cecilia Elizabeth Angelita Althea. Partner, Franklin & Lee Tractor Co., Shreveport, La., 1947-59; sales mgr. U.S. Massey-Ferguson, Inc., Toronto, Ont., Can., 1959-64; v.p. internat. Fed. Services Fin. Co., Inc., Washington, 1964-66; group v.p. ISC Fin. Corp., Kansas City, Mo., 1966-77; pres. Mgmt. Recruiters Baton Rouge, Inc., 1977—. Trustee, mem. exec. com. William Jewell Coll., Liberty, Mo., 1972—, Baton Rouge Gen. Hosp., 1978—. Served with USN, 1942-46. Mem. Nat. Assn. Personnel Cons., Cert. Personnel Cons. Soc., Inc. (treas.), La. Assn. Personnel Cons. (pres.). Republican. Baptist. Clubs: Rotary, Sherwood Forest County, Camelot; Army and Navy (Washington). Home: 1303 Ted Dunham Ave Baton Rouge LA 70802 Office: 2762 Continental Dr Suite 201 Baton Rouge LA 70808

FRANKLIN, LARRY DANIEL, newspaper publishing company executive; b. Commerce, Tex., July 16, 1942; s. John Asia and Annie Mae (Castle) F.; m. Charlotte Anne Walker, Aug. 18, 1962; children—Kelly Leigh, Kristi Lynn. B.B.A., East Tex. State U., 1965; M.B.A., Tex. Tech U., 1966. Mem. audit staff Arthur Andersen Co., Dallas, 1966-67; controller, treas. Paris Milling Co., Tex., 1967-69; mem. audit staff Price Waterhouse Co., Dallas, 1969-71; asst. corp. dir. acctg. Harte-Hanks Communications Inc., San Antonio, 1971, corp. dir. fin. services, 1971-72, chief fin. officer, treas., 1972-74, v.p. fin., treas., 1974-75, v.p. fin., sec.-treas., 1975-78, sr. v.p., pres. newspaper ops., 1978-80, exec. v.p., 1980—, dir.; dir. Interfirst Bank, San Antonio. Mem. mass communication adv. com. Tex. Tech U., Lubbock, St. Thomas Episcopal Ch., San Antonio; mem. adv. council Sch. Bus. Incarnate Word Coll.; mem. program ops. com. United Way; past mem. graphic arts adv. com. Rochester Inst. Tech.; bd. dirs. East Tex. State U. Found., Commerce. Mem. Am. Inst. C.P.A.s, Fin. Execs. Inst. (founding dir., past pres. South Tex. chpt.), Am. Newspaper Pubs. Assn. (newsprint com.), So. Newspaper Pubs. Assn. (bd. dirs.), Am. Press Inst. (bd. dirs.), Tex. Daily Newspaper Assn. Home: 16451 Lost Cabin St San Antonio TX 78232 Office: Harte-Hanks Communications Inc PO Box 269 San Antonio TX 78291*

FRANKLIN, SIDNEY, computer company specialist; b. London, Apr. 21, 1942; came to U.S., 1959, naturalized, 1966; s. John Herbert and Joan Sarah (Barber) F.; m. Charlotte Ann Summers, Feb. 15, 1964; children—Mary Ann, John Christopher. Ops. supr. Nat. Life Ins. Co., 1963-65, Aladdin Industries, Nashville, 1965-67; sci. systems analyst Lockheed Aircraft Corp., Houston, Atlanta, 1967-70; systems analyst State of Tenn., Nashville, 1970-72, Commerce Union Bank, Nashville, 1972-74; asst. mgr. data processing Tenn. Wholesale Drug Co., Nashville, 1974; dist. systems mgr. Mohawk Data Sci. Corp., Nashville, 1974-80; corp. systems coordinator Ingram Industries, Inc., Nashville, 1980-81; sr. tech. specialist Schering Plough, Memphis, 1981-82; sr. systems engr. Storage Tech. Corp., Nashville, 1982—. Named Systems Analyst of Yr. for So. Region, Mohawk Data Sci. Corp., 1978. Mem. Sports Car Club Am. (sec., treas., regional exec. 1964-67), Data Processing Mgmt. Assn., Assn. Computing Machinery. Home: 1105 Greenleaf Ct Franklin TN 37064 Office: 301 S Perimeter Park Dr Suite 116 Nashville TN 37211

FRANKLIN, WILLIAM WEBSTER, congressman; b. Greenwood, Miss., Dec. 13, 1941; s. Webster Cromwell and Mary Elizabeth (Irby) F.; m. Edna Green Lott, June 12, 1965; children—Webster Cromwell, Melissa Lansdale. B.A., Miss. State U., 1963; J.D., U. Miss., 1966; grad., Nat. Jud. Coll., 1979. Bar: Miss. Practice law, Greenwood, Miss., 1970-82; asst. dist. atty. 4th Dist. Miss., 1972-78; judge Miss. Circuit Ct. 4th dist., 1978-82; mem. 98th Congress from 4th Miss. Dist. Served to capt. JAGC U.S. Army, 1966-70. Recipient Meritorious Service City of New Orleans, 1968; fellow Miss. Inst. Politics, 1971. Mem. ABA, Miss. Bar Assn., Leflore County Bar Assn. Republican. Episcopalian. Home: 613 River Rd Greenwood MS 38930 Office: Room 508 Cannon Office Bldg Washington DC 20515

FRANKNECHT, ROBERT HOWARD, industrial hygienist; b. Chgo., Apr. 20, 1955; s. Kenneth J. and Mary-Ellen (Marsh) F.; m. Joanne Cowan, Jan. 24, 1981; 1 child, Sheryl Elaine. B.S., Tex. A&M U., 1977, M.S., 1979. Indsl. hygienist Exxon Co., U.S.A., Houston, 1979-80, Baton Rouge, 1980—. Bd. dirs. La. Arts and Sci. Ctr., Baton Rouge, 1983, 84, 85, Avalon Recreation Assn., Baton Rouge, 1985; chmn. youth industry com. Internat. Mgmt. Council, Baton Rouge, 1984—. Mem. Am. Indsl. Hygiene Assn., (sec./treas. local chpt. 1983-84; bd. dirs. 1985—), Am. Soc. Safety Engrs. Club: Toastmasters. Avocations: tennis; swimming; jogging. Home: 14737 Avalon Baton Rouge LA 70816

FRANKS, BURNETT, broadcasting executive; b. St. Louis, Aug. 21, 1949; s. Arthur Franks, Jr. and Betty Franks Partain. B.S., So. Ill. U., 1972. Cert. radio mktg. cons. Gen. mgr. Harrisburg Broadcasting Co. Inc., Harrisburg, Ill., 1975-76; account exec. Plough Broadcasting Co. Inc., Atlanta, 1976-78; programming cons. TM Programming Inc., Dallas, 1978-79; account exec. Plough Broadcasting, Tampa, St. Petersburg, Fla., 1979-80; programming cons. Noble Broadcast Cons., San Diego, 1980-81; account exec. Plough Broadcasting Co., Inc., Atlanta, 1981—. Mem. Atlanta Broadcast Advt. Club, Sigma Tau Gamma. Home: 1135 Morningside Pl Atlanta GA 30306

FRANKS, CHARLES LESLIE, banker; b. Columbus, Miss., Jan. 21, 1934; s. Leslie J. and Almeda (Morris) F.; m. Cece Alice Cronovich, Feb. 7, 1959; children—Carolyn, Chris. B.S. summa cum laude, Miss. State U., 1956. C.P.A., Tex. Acct., Arthur Andersen & Co., Houston, 1959-61; internal audit mgr. Bank of the Southwest, Houston, 1961-71; gen. auditor Southwest Bancshares, Inc., Houston, 1972-79; sr. v.p., auditor Mercantile Nat. Bank, Dallas, 1979—; speaker bank adminstrn. inst. seminars, meetings, conv. Served to capt. USAF, 1956-59. Mem. Tex. Soc. C.P.A.s (sec. local chpt. 1971-72), Bank Adminstrn. Inst. (v.p. local chpt. 1971-72, pres. 1973-74), Am. Inst. Banking, Inst. Internal Auditors (pres. local chpt. 1974-75), Houston C. of C., Phi Eta Sigma, Chi Lambda Rho, Phi Kappa Phi, Alpha Kappa Psi. Home: 6022 La Cosa Dr Dallas TX 75248 Office: Mercantile Nat Bank PO Box 225415 Suite 520 Dallas TX 75265

FRANKS, JOAN LOOPE, writer; b. New Tazewell, Tenn., June 2, 1935; d. G. Dewey and Eunice G. (Hopper) Loope; A.B., U. Tenn., 1962, M.Ed., 1964; postgrad. U. Edinburgh (Scotland), 1964, Am. U., 1966, U. Tenn., 1967, U. So. Ill., 1969; m. Herschel P. Franks, June 2, 1957; 1 dau., Ramona. With Knoxville (Tenn.) Utilities Bd., 1957-59, Electric Power Bd., Chattanooga, 1959-64; faculty U. Tenn., Chattanooga, 1964-70. Mem. John Ross Pk. Adv. Bd., 1972-80, Hamilton County-Chattanooga Hist. Adv. Bd., 1977-80, French Store Adv. Bd., 1977-80. Mem. Chattanooga Audubon Soc. (pres. 1972, 77-78), Chattanooga Art Hist. Assn. (pres. 1970-72, 77-80), Tenn. Hist. Soc. v.p. 1977-79), Chattanooga Opera Assn. (dir. 1972-78), Chattanooga Opera Guild (dir. 1973), John Ross Assn. (dir. 1972-80), So. Hist. Assn., Tenn. Hist. Commn., Am. Acad. Polit. Sci., Ga. Hist. Assn., Hamblen County Hist. Assn., James County Hist. Assn., Sullivan County Hist. Assn., Nat. Hist. Assn., East Tenn. Hist. Soc., West Tenn. Hist. Soc., Rugby Hist. Soc., Freedoms Found. at Valley Forge (pres. Chattanooga chpt. 1981-82), others. Democrat. Congregationalist. Author: Holdings of the John Storrs Fletcher Library, 1968; editor: Walk with History, 2 edits., 1976, 77; editor publs., Opti-Mrs. News, 1963, Chattanews, 1973-75, Audubon Flyer, 1977; contbr. articles to profl. jours.; preservationist Spring Frog's Cabin, circa 1754, John Browns Tavern, circa 1803. Address: 703 Browns Ferry Rd Chattanooga TN 37419

FRANKS, PAUL TAYLOR, real estate executive; b. Laurens, S.C., May 6, 1934; s. Paul A. and Elizabeth (Taylor) F.; m. Margaret McKay, May 27, 1961; children—Paul McKay, Linda Margaret. B.B.A., U. Ga., 1956, postgrad., 1956-57; postgrad. Ga. State U., 1965-66. Cert. real estate broker, S.C. Mgr. distbn. and devel. Texaco Inc., Miami, Fla., Atlanta, 1957-66; pres., dir. Petro-Wash, Inc., Atlanta, 1966-78; v.p. Sea Pines Real Estate Co., Hilton Head Island, S.C., 1978-85, pres., 1985—; dir. Sea Pines Securities, Hilton Head Island, Mariners Inn Assocs., Hilton Head Island. Served with U.S. Army, 1956-57. Mem. Hilton Head Bd. Realtors (bd. dirs. 1981-82), S.C. Assn. Realtors (bd. dirs. 1982-83), Kappa Alpha. Republican. Baptist. Clubs: Hilton Head Cotillion, Cherokee Town and Country, Sea Pines, Wexford. Lodge: Rotary. Home: 5 Oyster Landing Hilton Head Island SC 29928 Office: Sea Pines Real Estate Co Sea Pines Circle Hilton Head Island SC 29928

FRANTZ, PHARES ALBERT, architect; b. New Orleans, Nov. 1, 1923; s. Roy Florestan and Marie Lucile (O'Kelley) F.; m. Elinor Mae McCloskey, Feb. 20, 1954; children—Ninette Marie, Colleen Marie, Melinda Marie. B.Arch., Tulane U., 1950. Registered architect, La., Miss. Draftsman, Richard Koch Architect, New Orleans, 1950-52, architect, 1952-55; assoc. Richard Koch & Samuel Wilson Jr. Architects, New Orleans, 1955-72; ptnr. Koch and Wilson Architects, New Orleans, 1972—. Mem. Citizens Adv. com. Studying Revisions to City Zoning Ordinance, 1969; bd. dirs. Incarnate Word Parish Sch. Bd., 1971-80, pres., 1977-80; bd. dirs. France Amerique, 1981; pres. La. Polit. Com. Design Profls., 1984. Decorated Order of St. Louis Archdiocese of New Orleans. Mem. La. Inst. Bldg. Scis. (dir. 1980), AIA (mem. hist. resources com. 1975-79, 83—, pres. New Orleans chpt. 1968-69, dir. 1970-71, state preservation coordinator 1982), La. Architects Assn. (pres. 1980), Construction Specifications Inst. (pres. New Orleans chpt. 1960), Friends of Cabildo, La. Landmarks Soc., SAR, Nat. Trust, Mag. St. Bus. Assn. (v.p. 1981), Delta Tau Delta. Republican. Roman Catholic. Club: Pendennis. Home: 8427 Pritchard Pl New Orleans LA 70118 Office: Koch and Wilson 1100 Jackson Ave New Orleans LA 70130

FRANTZ, THOMAS RICHARD, lawyer; b. Waynesboro, Pa., Sept. 10, 1947; s. J. Richard and Janet (Donnelly) F.; B.A., Coll. William and Mary, Williamsburg, Va., 1970, J.D., 1973, M.Law and Taxation, 1981; m. Dianne L. Boffa; children—Thomas Richard, Lindsey Amore. Supr. tax dept. Peat, Marwick & Mitchell, C.P.A.s, Norfolk, Va., 1973-74; atty., officer, dir. firm Clark & Stant, P.C., Norfolk and Virginia Beach, Va., 1974—; adj. prof. law Marshall-Wythe Sch. Law, Coll. William and Mary, 1981-82; dir. Sovran Bank N.A.; chmn. planning com. tax conf. Old Dominion U., Norfolk, 1981; lectr. in field. Trustee William and Mary Coll. Athletic Ednl. Found., 1977-82, Old Dominion U. Edn. Found.; chmn. participants com. Va. Republican Conv., 1981; chmn. Virginia Beach Marathon, 1977; bd. dirs., exec. com. Va. Mus. Marine Scis.; chmn. capital funds drive Virginia Beach United Way, 1985. Served as capt. USAR, 1973-81. C.P.A., Va. Mem. Am. Inst. C.P.A.s, ABA, Am. Assn. Attys.-C.P.A.s, Va. Bar Assn. (chmn. cooperation with C.P.A.s 1980—), Va. Soc. C.P.A.s, Norfolk-Portsmouth Bar Assn. (exec. com.), Virginia Beach Bar Assn. Lutheran. Club: Virginia Beach Rotary. Author articles in field. Home: 3756 Little Neck Point Virginia Beach VA 23452 Office: One Columbus Center Suite 900 Virginia Beach VA 23462

FRANZ, JERRY LOUIS, cardiac surgeon; b. Decatur, Ind., Aug. 5, 1943; s. Lyle D. and Helen J. (Martin) F.; B.S. in Chemistry, Ohio No. U., 1965; M.S. in Bacteriology, U. Fla., 1967; M.D., U. Ky., 1971; m. Jennie Rose Heim, June 20, 1970. Intern surgery U. Ky. Hosps., Lexington, 1971-72; jr. asst. resident surgery Bexar County Hosp., San Antonio, 1972-73, resident surgery, 1973-76, adminstrv. resident surgery, 1975-76, resident cardiothoracic surgery, 1976-78. Diplomate Am. Bd. Surgery, Am. Bd. Thoracic Surgery. Mem. Am. Coll. Chest Physicians, Bexar County Med. Soc., AMA, Tex. Med. Assn., Assn. for Acad. Surgery, J. Bradly Ansr Surg. Soc. (pres. 1983-84), Cooley Cardiovascular Soc. Contbr. articles to profl. jours. Home: 106 Painted Post Ln San Antonio TX 78231 Office: 350 Methodist Plaza San Antonio TX 78229

FRASE, CLARENCE CAESAR, educational administrator; b. Moody, Tex., May 11, 1926; s. Robert and Rosa (Bredthauer) F.; m. Kathryn Merle Satterwhite, June 23, 1951; children—Steven, Nancy. B.Ed., U. Tex., 1951, M.Ed., 1957. Cert. tchr., prin., supt., Tex. Credit sales mgr. Sears, Roebuck & Co., Temple, Tex., 1954-55; tchr. Seguin Ind. Sch. Dist., Tex., 1955-58, asst. supt. schs., 1958-81, supt. schs., 1981—. Served to sgt. U.S. Army, 1944-46; PTO. Mem. Am. Assn. Sch. Adminstrs., Tex. Assn. Sch. Adminstrs., Assn. Supervision and Curriculum Devel., Seguin C. of C. Lutheran. Lodge: Kiwanis (local pres. 1967). Avocations: photography; reading. Home: 1464 Robin Ln Seguin TX 78155 Office: Seguin Ind Sch Dist 1227 E Cedar St Seguin TX 78155

FRASER, WILLIAM BRIAN, geophysicist, researcher; b. N.Y.C., Jan. 14, 1952; s. John Harold and Roberta Madlyn (Fleck) F.; m. Melanie Mason, Aug. 4, 1982; 1 child, Virginia Elizabeth. B.S., U. S.C., 1973; M.S., Old Dominion U., 1982. Commd. 2d lt. U.S. Marine Corps, 1973, advanced through grades to capt., 1980; geophysicist Exxon Co. U.S.A., New Orleans, 1982-84, sr. geophysicist, 1984—. Vol. Big Bros. Program of New Orleans, 1984. Old Dominion U. grantee, 1981. Mem. Am. Assn. Petroleum Geologist, Soc. Econ. Geophysicists. Republican. Lutheran. Avocations: running; scuba diving. Home: 5801 Rhodes Ave New Orleans LA 70114

FRATAR, THOMAS JOSEPH, civil engineer; b. May 26, 1913; s. John N. and Bridget (Gibbons) F.; m. Mary Jean Small, June 5, 1948; children—Stephen, Frederick. C.E., Rensselaer Poly. Inst., 1936; M. Engring. Yale U., 1942. Registered profl. engr., N.Y., Alaska, Ariz., Calif., Fla., Hawaii, Mass., P.R., D.C., Malawi. Field engr. Madigan Hyland, Engrs., 1937-41; research analyst Yale U., 1941-42; structural designer Shreve, Lamb & Harmon, Architects, 1942; assoc., then assoc. ptnr., Tippetts Abbett McCarthy Stratton, Engrs., Architects and Planners, N.Y.C., 1946-56, ptnr., 1956-75, cons., 1975—; bd. cons. Eno Found. Transp., 1961-70, 73-75; bd. dirs. Engring. Found., 1959-63; trustee United Engring. Trustees, Inc., 1961-75; mem. N.Y. State Bd. Engring. and Land Surveying, 1966-75, chmn., 1971-72. Served to 1st lt. U.S. Army, 1942-46. Fellow ASCE (nat. dir. 1958-61), Am. Cons. Engrs. Council, Inst. Transp. Engrs.; mem. Nat. Soc. Profl. Engrs., N.Y. State Soc. Profl. Engrs., Am. Arbitration Assn., Sigma Xi, Chi Epsilon (hon. mem.). Contbr. articles to profl. jours. Club: Yale (N.Y.C.). Lodge: Rotary. Republican. Roman Catholic. Home: 1985 Compass Cove Dr Vero Beach FL 32963

FRATE, DENNIS ANTHONY, epidemiologist, research consultant; b. Cleve., Oct. 26, 1948; s. Carl Angelo and Elizabeth (Sunday) F.; m. Juliet Deborah Bielawski, Dec. 28, 1979; 1 dau., Elizabeth Julia. B.A., Miami U., Oxford, Ohio, 1970, M.A., U. Ill.-Urbana, 1974, Ph.D., 1978. Dir. Office Community Health Research, Rockford Sch. Medicine, U. Ill., 1977-79; prin. investigator and research assoc. prof. Research Inst. Pharm. Scis., U. Miss., Goodman, 1980—; cons. Nat. Heart, Lung and Blood Inst. NIH, 1980—. Nat. Heart, Lung and Blood Inst., NIH grantee, 1980—. Fellow Council Epidemiology, Am. Heart Assn.; mem. Am. Pub. Health Assn., Sigma Xi. Co-editor: The Extended Family in Black Societies, 1978; author: (with Wolstadt, Meyer) Medical Education in the Ambulatory Setting: An Evaluation, 1982. Home: Route 1 Box 249X Canton MS 39046 Office: U Miss Research Inst Pharm Scis PO Box 283 Goodman MS 39079

FRATELLO, MICHAEL ROBERT, professional basketball coach; b. Hackensack, N.J., Feb. 24, 1947. Student, Montclair State Coll., R.I. Asst. coach U. Rhode Island, 1971, James Madison U., 1972-75, Villanova U., 1976-78, N.Y. Knicks, NBA, 1982-83, Atlanta Hawks, NBA, 1978-82, head coach, 1983—. Office: care Atlanta Hawks 100 Techwood Dr NW Atlanta GA 30303*

FRAZEE, PAMELA WALKER, business executive; b. New Brighton, Pa., July 8, 1947; d. Ralph Wayne and Pearl Armour W.; B.S., Edinboro State Coll., 1969; M.Ed., Memphis State U., 1975; postgrad. San Antonio Coll., 1977, U. Mex., 1977, U. Tex., Austin, 1978-80, Trinity U., 1979; children—Tasha Jane, Nikki Mila. Tchr., Erie (Pa.) City Schs., 1969, Norton (Ohio) City Schs., 1969-73, Trenors Day Sch., Memphis, 1973-74; project dir. Stanford Research Inst., Menlo Park, Calif., 1978; ednl. cons. Learning About Learning, San Antonio, 1978-80; sales dir. Colonial Life & Accident, San Antonio, 1980-82, dir. mktg., 1982-83; v.p. mktg. Infotech Systems, Inc., San Antonio, 1983—. Mem. NOW, Nat. Art Edn. Assn., Nat. Assn. Profl. Saleswomen, Nat. Assn. Exec. Females, Ind. Automotive Service Assn., Phi Kappa Phi, Phi Mu Phi. Home: 14203 Ridgemeadow St San Antonio TX 78233 Office: 2135 NW Military Hwy Suite 2 San Antonio TX 78213

FRAZIER, ALICE MARIA, psychotherapist; b. Midland, Tex., Feb. 6, 1945; d. Howard Edward and Ihna Bell (Reid) Muskopf; m. Marvin Richard Tawwater, Mar. 16, 1963 (div.); children—Kimberly M., Andrea D., Nicole L.;

m. Charles Edward Frazier, May 21, 1983. B.A., U. Tex., 1977, M.S., 1979. Pschotherapist, biofeedback therapist Dallas Diagnostic Assocs., 1979-85; pvt. practice psychotherapy, Dallas, McKinney, Tex., 1984—; bus. cons. for stress mgmt., Dallas, 1983—. Staff counselor Suicide Prevention Crisis Line, Dallas, 1978-80. Chmn. public edn. Am. Heart Assn., Irving, Tex., 1971-74. Recipient Meritorious Service award, 1972, Disting. Service award, 1974. Mem. Am. Assn. Counseling and Devel., Am. Mental Health Counselors Assn., Biofeedback Soc. Am., Biofeedback Soc. Tex. (bd. dirs. 1984-86), Assn. Humanistic Psychology. Democrat. Mem. Unity Ch. Avocations: historical restoration; bicycling. Office: 12810 Hillcrest Rd Suite 218 Dallas TX 75230

FRAZIER, CHARLES O., educational administrator. Supt. of schs. Davidson County, Tenn. Office: 2601 Bransford Ave Nashville TN 37204*

FRAZIER, JOHN RICHARD, psychiatrist, consultant; b. Gary, Ind., Nov. 21, 1935; s. Richard and Marion (Ludlum) F.; m. Anne Marie Rieget, Sept. 23, 1961; children—Richard, Arthur, David, Walter, Robert. B.S., St. Joseph's Coll., 1958; M.D., Coll. Medicine and Dentistry N.J., 1962. Diplomate Am. Bd. Psychiatry and Neurology. Pediatric intern Jersey City Med. Ctr., 1962-63, resident pediatrics, 1963-65; resident gen. psychiatry N.Y. Met. Hosp., 1967-69, resident child and adolescent psychiatry, 1969-70; practice medicine specializing in child and adolescent psychiatry, Salem, Va.; chmn. utilization rev. com. Roanoke Valley Psychiat. Ctr.; sec. med. staff Roanoke Valley Psychiat. Ctr.; cons. Mental Health Services Roanoke Valley, Roanoke City Sch., Mercer County Bd. Edn., Princeton, W.Va., Radford Mental Health Ctr. (Va.). Mem. adv. com. spl. edn. Roanoke County Schs. Served with USAF, 1965-67. Staten Island Mental Health Soc. child psychiatry fellow, 1970, 70-71. Mem. Am. Psychiat. Assn., AMA, Assn. Child and Adolescent Psychiatry, Neurospychiat. Soc. Va., Peer Standards Rev. Orgn., Roanoke Acad. Medicine. Office: 1902 Braeburn Dr Salem VA 24153

FRAZIER, WALTER RONALD, real estate investment company executive; b. Dallas, Mar. 3, 1939; s. Walter and Gracie Neydene (Bowers) F.; m. Bertina Jan Simpson, May 10, 1963; children—Ronald Blake, Stephen Bertram. B.S. in Civil Engring., Tex. A&M U., 1962, B.S. in Archtl. Constrn., 1962. Tech. dir. Marble Inst., Washington, 1965-68; dir. mktg. Yeonas Co., Vienna, Va., 1969-72; pres. McCarthy Co., Anaheim, Calif., 1972-76, The Frazier Group, Annandale, Va., 1977-79; chmn. Equity Programs Investment Corp., Falls Church, Va., 1980—; pres., dir. Community Constrn. Co., Falls Church, 1982—; dir. Community Ventures Inc., Falls Church. Pres., bd. dirs. Annandale Jaycees, 1967-69, Annandale Nat. Little League, 1983-85. Served to 1st lt. U.S. Army, 1963-65. Named to Outstanding Young Men Am., U.S. Jaycees, 1973. Republican. Methodist. Avocations: golf; boating. Home: 4203 Elizabeth Ln Annandale VA 22003 Office: Equity Programs Investment Corp 5113 Leesburg Pike Falls Church VA 22041

FRAZIER, WINFRED CLARENCE, television station official; b. Houston, Sept. 15, 1950; s. Albert and Emmola F.; m. Johnnie Jeanne Paris, Dec. 22, 1973; children—Denise Tatum, Winfred Taylor. B.B.A., Tex. So. U., 1972. Account exec. Sta. KTRK-TV, Houston, 1972-80, sales mgr., 1980—. Trustee, Juvenile Ct. Vols. of Harris County, Inc., 2d Cavalcade Baptist Ch. Mem. Omega Psi Phi, Phi Beta Lambda. Home: 11918 Stanwood Dr Houston TX 77031 Office: 3310 Bissonnet St Houston TX 77005

FREDE, MARTHA CHAMBERS, clinical psychologist; b. Marvell, Ark., June 18, 1926; d. Landon Benjamin and Marie (Quinelly) Chambers; B.A. cum laude, U. Tex., Austin, 1945; Ph.D., U. Houston, 1970; m. Ralph Edward Frede, Dec. 25, 1946; children—Phyllis Marie, Bethann, Gretchen (dec.), Ellen Claire, Sarah Jane. Diagnostic bacteriologist Tex. State Dept. Health, Austin, 1945-48; pre-sch. tchr. St. Francis Episcopal Day Sch., Houston, 1961-65; center program coordinator Parent-Child Devel. Center, U. Houston, 1970-72, psychologist, Counseling Center, 1972-75; pvt. practice clin. psychology, Houston, 1974—; instr. Houston Community Coll., 1974-75; cons. Children's Mental Health, Alternative Drug Abuse Program, New Community Services Orgn., Criminal Justice Council. Mem. Assocs. of Mus. Fine Arts, Houston, 1980—, Houston Ballet Guild, 1980—, Houston Zool. Soc., 1981—; bd. dirs., mem. exec. com. Can-Do-It. Mem. Am. Psychol. Assn., Tex. Psychol. Assn., Houston Psychol. Assn. (sec.-treas. 1974-75), Mental Health Assn., Am. Assn. Sex Educators, Counselors, and Therapists (cert. sex therapist), Assn. for Advancement Behavior Therapy, Houston Behavior Therapy Assn. (pres. 1977-78), Family Mediation Network, Phi Kappa Phi. Episcopalian. Home: 849 Hickorywood Ln Houston TX 77024 Office: 2650 Fountainview Suite 210 Houston TX 77057

FREDE, RALPH EDWARD, college official; b. Floydada, Tex., Sept. 28, 1921; s. Elmer Fred and Marjorie (King) F.; B.J., U. Tex., 1943, M.A., 1947; m. Martha Camilla Chambers, Dec. 25, 1946; children—Phyllis Frede Patrick, Bethann Frede Walmus, Ellen, Sarah Jane Jenkins. Mgr. pub. relations and edn. Austin (Tex.) C. of C., 1947-48; dir. student employment bur. U. Tex., Austin, 1948-50; state rep. Nat. Found. Infantile Paralysis, Austin, Tex. and Jefferson City, Mo., 1950-56; dir. devel., exec. dir. U. Houston Found., 1956-70; lectr. pub. relations U. Houston, 1956-70; dir. devel. and pub. relations, v.p. pub. affairs Baylor Coll. Medicine, Houston, 1970—. Pres. bd. dirs. Protestant Charities Houston, 1966-67; bd. dirs. Houston United Fund, 1968; sr. warden Christ Ch. Cathedral, 1985. Served to lt. USNR, 1943-46. Recipient Silver Beaver award Boy Scouts Am., 1950. Mem. Pub. Relations Soc. Am. (accredited; past dir.; Silver Anvil award 1965, Gold Anvil award 1972), Am. Coll. Pub. Relations Assn. (dist. chmn. 1969; Exceptional Achievement award 1964, 65), Found. Pub. Relations Research and Edn. (pres. 1975-77), Sigma Delta Chi. Clubs: Friars (U. Tex.); Houston, The Noustonian, Doctors. Lodge: Rotary (pres. Houston 1977-78). Home: 849 Hickorywood Ln Houston TX 77024 Office: One Baylor Plaza Houston TX 77030

FREDERIC, THOMAS PAUL, construction company executive; b. Baton Rouge, Dec. 3, 1948; s. Vernon Joseph and Lorraine Marie (Moran) F.; m. Mary Virginia Watts, July 17, 1970; 1 dau., Monique. B.S. in Polit. Sci., La. State U., 1970. Project mgr. Moran Electric, Baton Rouge, 1972-76, Toomer Elec., Baton Rouge, 1976-77; project mgr. Service Painting Co., Baton Rouge, 1977-82, pres., chief exec. officer, 1982—; comml. arbitrator Am. Arbitration Assn., Baton Rouge, 1980—. Served to 1st lt. U.S. Army, 1970-74. Mem. Nat. Assn. Corrosion Engrs., Am. Subcontractors Assn. (nat. dir. 1979-81, regional dir. 1979-81). Democrat. Roman Catholic. Club: Gonzales Country (treas.). Home: 1330 S Vista Ave Gonzales LA 70737 Office: Service Painting Co PO Box 2547 Baton Rouge LA 70821

FREDERICK, DELORAS ANN, artist, educator; b. Fletcher, Okla., Jan. 25, 1942; d. Delbert Clyde and Hazel May (Baxter) Dodson; m. John George Frederick, Jan. 22, 1958; children—John Dale, James Craig. Student Central State U., 1975. Tchr. beginning watercolor Rick's Arts & Crafts, Oklahoma City, 1975-79; tchr. gifted and talented students Nichels Hills Elem. Sch., Oklahoma City, 1981; demonstrator art guilds. Parent contact Nat. Found. Sudden Infant Death, 1976-78. Recipient numerous art awards. Mem. Okla. Art Guild (1st v.p. 1977-78), Mid-Dell Art Guild (1st v.p. 1977), Okla. Watercolor Assn. (1st v.p. 1977-78, show chmn. 1979-82, pres. 1984—), Nat. League Am. Pen Women, So. Watercolor Assn., Southwest Watercolor Assn., Norman Art Guild, S. Okla. Art Assn. Democrat. Baptist. Contbr. Okla. Art Gallery mag., Art Voices South mag. Home and Office: 7301 NW 13th St Oklahoma City OK 73127

FREDERICK, DONALD J., architect, engineer; b. Cleve., May 30, 1931; s. Sam and Lenore F.; m. Arlene Davis, Jan. 23, 1955; children—David, Alan, Steven, Tracy. B.Arch., U. Fla., 1954; B.S. in Civil Engring., U. Ill., 1957. Pvt. practice architecture and engring., Miami, 1964-67; v.p., chief architect Rader & Assocs., Miami, 1974-78; chief architect Met. Dade County, Fla., 1978—. Served to capt. USAF, 1954-60. Mem. AIA (bd. dirs. So. Fla. chpt.), Nat. Acad. Sci. (pub. facility com.), Constrn. Specifications Inst., Am. Pub. Works Assn., Republican. Home: 19731 NE 10th Ct North Miami Beach FL 33179 Office: 140 W Flagler St Suite 1204 Miami FL 33130

FREDERICK, NATHAN CASEY, college official; b. Asheville, N.C., Oct. 7, 1944; s. N.C. and Robbie Grey (Elmore) F.; m. Joyce Ellen Gaylor, June 5, 1966 (div. 1982); 1 child, Nathan Brent; m. Helen Lundy Byrd, Oct. 8, 1983. B.S., Mars Hill Coll., 1965; M.A., Appalachian State U., 1967; postgrad. in bus. adminstrn. Miss. State U., 1967. Instr. Mars Hill Coll., N.C., 1967-70; asst. bus. mgr. Francis Marion Coll., Florence, S.C., 1970-73, asst. bus. mgr., 1973-74, bus. mgr., v.p. adminstrv. services, 1974-76, v.p. bus. and fin., 1976—. Vice-pres. Pee Dee Area council Boy Scouts Am., 1976-83; treas. Francis Marion Coll. Found., 1976—. Recipient Silver Beaver award Boy Scouts Am., 1981. Mem. Nat. Assn. Coll. and Univ. Bus. Officers, So. Assn. Coll. and Univ. Bus. Officers. Democrat. Presbyterian. Lodge: Kiwanis (bd. dirs. Florence 1981-84). Avocations: tennis; gardening. Home: 333 Bayberry Circle Florence SC 29501 Office: Francis Marion Coll PO Box 7500 Florence SC 29501

FREDERICK, WILLARD DRAWN, JR., city official; b. Winter Haven, Fla., July 6, 1934; s. William D. and T. Lucille (Adams) F.; m. Joanne Race, July 12, 1957; children—Charles, Virginia, John. A.B., Duke U., 1956; J.D., U. Fla., 1961. Bar: Fla. 1961. Pub. defender State of Fla., Orlando, 1963-68; ptnr. Frederick, Wooten & Honeywell, Orlando, 1968-80; mayor City of Orlando, 1980—. Mem. Greater Orlando Aviation Authority, Orlando Utilities Commn., Orlando-Seminole-Osceola Transit Authority, 1980—. Served to lt. (j.g.) USNR, 1956-58. Mem. ABA, Fla. Bar Assn. (bd. govs. young lawyers sect. 1965-69), Fla. Council 100, Fla. State Pub. Defenders Assn. (pres. 1966-67). Democrat. Baptist. Home: 105 W New Hampshire St Orlando FL 32804 Office: Mayor's Office City of Orlando 400 S Orange Ave Orlando FL 32801

FREDRICKS, RICHARD THEODORE, real estate executive; b. Calgary, Alta., Can., Apr. 25, 1944; came to U.S., 1978; s. Richard and Adeline Ruth (Kuch) F.; m. Carolyn Anne Parks, June 12, 1965. B.S. in Bus. Adminstrn., U. Tulsa, 1969. Property adminstr. Trizec Corp., Calgary, Alta., 1974-75; mgr. property mgmt. div. Toole & Cote Real Estate, Calgary, 1975-78; mgr. comml. div. H. Anderson Real Estate, Ft. Lauderdale, Fla., 1978-80; mktg. coordinator Home Owners Warranty, Palm Beach, Fla., 1980-82; v.p. Landsing Property Corp., Tulsa, Okla., 1982—. Mem. Ft. Lauderdale Bd. Realtors, Calgary Real Estate Bd. Home: 8223 N 167th E Ave Owasso OK 74055 Office: Landsing Property Corp 6128 E 38th St Suite 305 Tulsa OK 74135

FREDRICKSEN, CLEVE LAURANCE, thoroughbred horse farm owner, real estate investor; b. Bklyn., Nov. 28, 1941; s. Cleve John and Harriet (Johnson) F.; m. Beverly Janice Simon, Dec. 28, 1963; children—Cristi Louise, Cleve Matthew. B.B.A., Bucknell U., 1963. With comml. lending dept. Bankers Trust, N.Y.C., 1964-66, investment advisory dept., 1966-68; acct. exec. Kidder Peabody, N.Y.C., 1968-71; owner, mgr. Ore Hill Farm, Spottswood, Va., 1972—. Served to E-5 USCGR, 1963-69. Mem. Va. Thoroughbred Assn., Va. Horse Council. Avocations: tennis; swimming; running; horseback riding. Home and Office: Ore Hill Farm Route 1 Box 364 Spottswood VA 24475

FREEDMAN, ARNOLD MICHAEL, historian; b. N.Y.C., June 21, 1918; s. William Solomon and Ida (Mandel) F.; B.A., Fla. State U., 1963; M.A., U. Fla., 1964, Ph.D., 1978; m. Frederica Morris, Dec. 29, 1956 (dec. Dec. 1975). Sales mgr. Peterkin Co., N.Y.C., 1936-41; enlisted in U.S. Army, 1941, commd. 2d lt., 1943, advanced through grades to lt. col., 1962; service in Far East, Panama, C. Am., S. Am.; ret., 1962; mem. faculty Palm Beach (Fla.) Jr. Coll., 1964—, prof. history, 1964—; adv. nat. def. Am. Security Council. Decorated Combat Inf. badge (2) with silver star, Bronze Star with V (5), Army Commendation medal (4), Purple Heart (3), also presdl. citations U.S., Philippines, Korea. Mem. Am. Hist. Assn., Hispanic Am. Historical Assn., Assn. U.S. Army, Ret. Officers Assn., Mil. Order World Wars, Phi Alpha Theta. Club: Masons (32 deg.). Home: 7978 Edgewater Dr West Palm Beach FL 33406 Office: 4200 S Congress Ave Lake Worth FL 33460

FREEDMAN, JACK IRVING, oil company executive; b. Atlanta, Apr. 26, 1921; s. Morris and Annie (Zion) F.; m. Phyllis B. Freedman, Jan. 19, 1947; children—Douglas S., Robyn G. Spizman. Student, Emory U., 1940-41, U. Ga. System, 1941. Vice pres. Greyshaw, Inc., 1950-63, Norris Lake Shore Devel. Corp., 1963—; exec. v.p. Guernsey Petroleum, Atlanta, 1969—. Bd. dirs. Jewish Home, 1978—; exec. and nat. orgn. com. Am. Men's ORT, 1975—; pres. Atlanta Jewish Community Ctr., 1985; v.p. Ahavath Achim Synagogue, 1979-82. Served to lt. USN, 1942-46. Recipient Disting. Service award B'nai B'rith, 1979; Hillel award, 1980; ORT Achievement award Am. Men's ORT, 1974; Enternal Light award Jewish Theol. Sem., 1984; ORT Past Pres. award 1984. Mem. Atlanta Jewish Fedn. (gen. campaign chmn. 1979, bd. dirs., 1972—. Address: 1470 Wesley Pkwy Atlanta GA 30327

FREEDMAN, LEON DAVID, chemistry educator; b. Balt., July 19, 1921; s. Samuel and Jennie (Greenberg) F.; m. Myrle Florence Neistadt, June 23, 1945; children—Carl Howard, Jean Rose. B.A., Johns Hopkins U., 1941, M.A., 1947, Ph.D., 1949. Analytical chemist USPHS, Balt., 1941-44, organic chemist, Chapel Hill, N.C., 1949-61; assoc. prof. N.C. State U., Raleigh, 1961-65, prof. chemistry, 1965—. Author: Organometallic Compounds of Arsenic, Antimony and Bismuth, 1970. Editor: Organic Electronic Spectral Data, Vol. VI, 1970; editorial bd. Organic Electronic Spectral Data, Inc., Silver Spring, Md., 1962—, Phosphorus and Sulfur, Cos Cob, Conn., 1976—. Served with USN, 1944-46. Recipient Outstanding Tchr. award N.C. State U., 1984; USPHS fellow, 1949; Merit scholar Johns Hopkins U., 1938-41. Fellow AAAS; mem. Am. Chem. Soc., Phi Beta Kappa, Sigma Xi. Avocation: travel. Home: 2006 Myron Dr Raleigh NC 27607 Office: Dept Chemistry NC State U Box 8204 Raleigh NC 27695

FREELAND, CHARLES JOHNSTON, III, clergyman; b. Rayne, La., Sept. 8, 1940; s. Charles Johnson and Mary Alice (Wynn) F.; m. Sandra Lee Dean, May 31, 1964; children—Charles Johnston IV, Mary Kay. B.A., Davidson Coll., 1962; M.Div., Austin Presbyn. Theol. Sem., 1965, D.Min., 1979. Ordained to ministry Presbyterian Church U.S., 1965. Pastor, First Street Presbyn. Ch., New Orleans, 1965-71, Highland Presbyn. Ch., Hot Springs, Ark., 1971-81; organizing pastor United Presbyn. Ch., Owasso, Okla., 1981-83, pastor, 1983—; dir. La. Irrigation & Milling Co., Crowley, La., 1975—. Pres. Irish Channel Action Found., New Orleans, 1970, Office of Econ. Adminstrn., Hot Springs, 1972-76. Mem. C. of C. Owasso. Democrat. Club: Lions (Owasso).

FREEMAN, BILLY DAN, oil co. exec.; b. Strawn, Tex., Dec. 21, 1936; s. Jewel Elvis and Ida Inez F.; student Sul Ross State Coll., 1954-55, West Tex. State U., 1955, Odessa Jr. Coll., 1965-67; B.S., Internat. Corr. Schs., 1972; m. Glenda Jaquess, May 23, 1959; children—Kimberly, Kent. With Shell Oil Co., various locations, 1965—, staff environ. engr., Traverse City, Mich., 1976-79, New Orleans, 1979—. Contbr. articles to profl. jours. Served with USMC, 1956-59. Mem. Mid Continent Oil and Gas Assn., La., Miss., Ala. oil and gas assns. Republican. Baptist (deacon, Sunday sch. tchr.). Home: 213 Camden St Slidell LA 70458 Office: PO Box 61555 New Orleans LA 70161

FREEMAN, CORINNE, mayor; b. N.Y.C., Nov. 9, 1926; d. Sidonie Daxe Lichtenstein; R.N., Adelphi Coll. Sch. Nursing, 1948; m. Mar. 14, 1948; children—Michael L., Stephan J. Mayor, City of St. Petersburg, Fla., 1977—. Mem. Fla. League Cities (1st v.p. 1981-82, pres. 1982-83), U.S. Conf. Mayors, Nat. League Cities. Republican. Home: 2101 Pelham Rd N St Petersburg FL 33710 Office: PO Box 2842 St Petersburg FL 33731

FREEMAN, COY, urologist; b. McAlester, Okla., Sept. 19, 1942; s. Coy and Verna Edith (Monroe) F.; m. Wilma Catherine Baker, Jan. 5, 1962; children—Marion Grant, Andrew Coy. B.S., Okla. State U., 1964; M.D., U. Okla., 1967. Intern, Johns Hopkins Hosp., Balt., 1967-68, resident in surgery, 1970-71, resident in urology, 1971-75; practice medicine specializing in urology, 1975—; mem. staff St. Mary's Med. Ctr., East Tenn. Children's Hosp., Ft. Sanders Presbyn. Hosp. Served to lt. comdr. USPHS, 1968-70. Fellow ACS; mem. Am. Urol. Assn., AMA. Republican. Methodist. Contbr. articles in field to med. jours. Office: 939 Emerald Ave Knoxville TN 37917

FREEMAN, CYNTHIA JO, nutritionist; b. Los Angeles, Dec. 1, 1947; d. Harry J. and Joan I. Freeman. B.S., U. Del., 1969; R.D., U. Hosps., Cleve., 1971; M.S., Case Western Res., 1971. Therapeutic dietitian Anaheim Meml. Hosp., Anaheim, Calif., 1971-72; clin. dietitian, adminstrv. dietitian, asst. food service dir. St. Jude Hosp., Fullerton Calif., 1972-76; nutritionist Lake County Health Dept., Tavares, Fla., 1976—. Del. Central Fla. chpt. Am. Heart Assn.; pres. Lake Service Council. Recipient scholarship Del. Dietetic Assn. Mem. Am. Dietetic Assn., Fla. Pub. Health Assn. (chmn. nutrition sect.; service award, nutrition sect.), Fla. Nurses Assn. (nutrition rep.), Fla. Dietetic Assn. (chmn. Fla. dist. pres's.; pres., E. Central Dietetic Assn. chpt.; recipient Recognized Young Dietitian award). Roman Catholic. Office: PO Box 1305 Tavares FL 32778

FREEMAN, DAVID ALLEN, phonograph records manufacturing executive; b. N.Y.C., May 22, 1939; s. Mark and Pauline (Allen) F.; m. Andrea Lee Viola, July 17, 1972; children—Mark, Kyle, Connie, Whitney. B.A., Columbia Coll., 1962. Founder, owner Country Records, N.Y.C., 1964-73, Floyd, Va., 1973—. Recipient Blue Ridge Inst. award, 1985. Office: Country Records/Record Depot PO Box 3057 Roanoke VA 24015

FREEMAN, DONALD WILFORD, real estate developer, horse breeder; b. Brooksville, Fla., Sept. 25, 1929; s. Fred Maxwell and Dovie (Keef) F.; B.S., U. Ala., 1953, LL.B., 1953; LL.M., N.Y. U., 1957; m. Ruby Jane Lewis, Feb. 25, 1956; children—Clifton Lewis, Susan Anne. Accountant Ernst & Ernst, Atlanta, 1953-55; admitted to Ala. bar, 1953; tax atty. Office Chief Counsel, U.S. Treasury Dept., N.Y.C., 1955-57, West Point Mfg. Co. (Ga.), 1957-58; asst. treas. Ryder System, Inc., Miami, Fla., 1958-61; v.p., dir. Henderson's Portion Pak, Inc., 1961-63; pres. Biscayne Capital Corp., 1963-66; asso. Lazard Freres & Co., N.Y.C., 1967-69; pres. James A. Ryder Corp., Miami, 1969-78; owner Continental Country Club, Inc., Leesburg, Fla., 1978—, Kiyara Arabians, Ocala, Fla., 1978—. Served with AUS, 1946-48; PTO. C.P.A., Ga. Mem. Fla. Inst. C.P.A.'s, Phi Kappa Sigma, Beta Gamma Sigma. Episcopalian. Home: Rt 1 Box 239 AA Reddick FL 32684 Office: PO Box 5000 Leesburg FL 32748

FREEMAN, FRANK RAY, counselor; b. French Lick, Ind., Sept. 16, 1936; s. William Stanford and Amanda Victoria (Fentress) F.; student Ball State U., 1954-55; A.B., Bellarmine Coll., 1958; postgrad. Georgetown U., 1958-60; M.Ed., Spalding Coll., 1967; postgrad. Cath. U., 1977-79. Head social studies Providence High Sch., Clarksville, Ind., 1960-64; tchr. DeSales High Sch., Louisville, 1964-66; prin. Carr Twp. Elementary Schs., Clark County, Ind., 1966-67; instr. U. Va., Falls Church, 1967-70; counselor, asso. prof. counseling No. Va. Community Coll., 1970—; pvt. profl. counselor, Springfield, Va., 1977—. Lic. profl. counselor. Mem. Am. Personnel and Guidance Assn., No. Va. Personnel and Guidance Assn., Va. Edn. Assn., NEA, AAUP, ACLU, Assn. Measurement and Evaluation in Guidance. Democrat. Home: 6905 Edgebrook Dr Springfield VA 22150 Office: 8333 Little River Turnpike Annandale VA 22003

FREEMAN, HAROLD STANLEY, textile chemistry educator; b. Raleigh, N.C., Apr. 7, 1951; s. Raymond Perry F. and Dorothy Freeman Nelson; m. Ruby Dorothine Williams, May 5, 1973; children—Rodney Gerard, Jeramy Lanier. B.S. in Chemistry, N.C. A&T State U., 1972; M.S., N.C. State U., Raleigh, 1978, Ph.D. in Chemistry, 1981. Sr. chemist Burroughs Wellcome Co., Research Triangle Park, N.C., 1973-82; adj. asst. prof. textile chemistry N.C. State U., Raleigh, 1981-82, assoc. prof. textile chemistry, 1982—. Active NAACP, Wake County Black Democratic Caucus of N.C.; bd. deacons First Cosmopolitan Baptist Ch. Recipient Man of Yr. award N.C. Assn. Alphamen, 1980. Mem. Am. Chem. Soc., Am. Assn. Textile Chemists and Colorists, Nat. Tech. Assn., Sigma Xi, Alpha Phi Alpha. Home: 10521 Leafwood Pl Raleigh NC 27612 Office: PO Box 5666 NC State U Raleigh NC 27560

FREEMAN, MARY ANNA, librarian; b. Sentinal, Okla., July 24, 1943; d. Wylie Lee and Thelma Anna (Elam) Johnson; m. Charles Edward Freeman, Jr., Aug. 26, 1963; children—Charles Edward III, Juliana Elizabeth, Mark Adrian, Lee Agustin. B.S., Abilene Christian U., 1963; M.L.S., Tex. Woman's U., 1981. Tchr. 4th grade Las Cruces Pub. Sch. (N.Mex.), 1963-64; tchr. 2d grade, 1964-67; head audiovisual dept. El Paso Pub. Library (Tex.), 1972; head librarian Guillen Jr. High Sch., El Paso, 1974—. Treas., Guillen PTA, El Paso, 1983-85. Mem. ALA, Tex. Library Assn. Office: Guillen Library 900 S Cotton St El Paso TX 79901

FREEMAN, RICHARD C., judge; b. Atlanta, Dec. 14, 1926; A.B., Emory U., 1950, LL.B., 1952. Admitted to Ga. bar, 1953, since practiced in Atlanta; mem. firm Haas, Holland & Blackshear, 1955-58, partner Haas, Holland, Freeman, Levison & Gibert, 1958-71; judge U.S. Dist. Ct., 1971—. Alderman City of Atlanta, 1962-71; pres. Atlanta Humane Soc., 1981. Mem. Ga., Atlanta bar assns., Lawyers Club Atlanta, Chi Phi, Phi Delta Phi. Office: 2121 US Courthouse 75 Spring St SW Atlanta GA 30303

FREEMAN, ROBERT L., lieutenant governor of Louisiana; b. Washington, Apr. 27, 1934; m. Marianne Drago; children—Lisa Freeman Koch, Robert L., Jr. Student La. State U., Baton Rouge, La. State U.-New Orleans, 1960; J.D., Loyola U., 1965. Bar: La. Mem. La. Ho. of Reps., 1968-80; now lt. gov. State of La., Baton Rouge. Chief adminstrv. floor leader to Gov. Edwin W. Edwards; mem. Gov.'s Commn. on Uniform Indigent Defense System; mem. Spl. Joint Legis. Com. on Reorgn. of Exec. Br.; bd. govs. La. Jud. Coll.; mem. legis. budget com.; alt. del. Nat. Democratic Conv., 1968, chmn. dels., 1968; bd. dirs. Iberville Assn. Retarded Children. Served with CIC, U.S. Army, 1956-59. Recipient award A. Phillip Randolph Inst., La. Cross of Merit, State Adj. Gen., Martin Luther King award, recognition award Cath. Daus. Am., United Am. Indian appreciation award, 1979, 80, Silver Anniversary award Nat. Collegiate Athletic Assn., 1981. Mem. La. Bar Assn., 18th Jud. Dist. Ct. Bar Assn. Roman Catholic. Clubs: St. John Father's, Woodmen of World, Ducks Unltd., Order of Alhambras, La. State U. Nat. L. Lodges: K.C., Lions. Office: PO Box 44243 State Capitol Baton Rouge LA 70804

FREEMAN, ROBERT MALLORY, banker; b. Richmond, Va., 1941; grad. U. Va., 1963, Stonier Grad. Sch. Banking, 1971. Pres., chief exec. officer, dir., vice chmn. Bank of Va., Richmond, dir. Va. Indsl. Devel. Corp. Adv. bd. Robert E. Lee council Boy Scouts Am.; trustees United Way of Greater Richmond, 1984, pres. Mem. Va. Bankers Assn. (pres.-elect), Assn. Res. City Bankers, Assn. Bank Holding Co., Young Pres. Orgn. Office: Bank of Virginia 7 N 8th St Richmond VA 23219

FREEMAN, STEPHEN WALLACE, psychologist; b. Bronx, N.Y., Aug. 8, 1941; s. Henry and Rosylind Freeman; B.Ed., U. Miami, 1963; M.A. in Counseling and Psychology, Appalachian State U., 1965; Ed.D. in Cons. Psychology, U. Tenn., 1970; m. Amy Lydia Thornton, Dec. 19, 1965; children—Amy Alecia, Kristine Dawn. Instr. psychology Sweet Briar Coll., 1966-68; supervising clin. psychologist Birth Defects Center, Knoxville, Tenn., 1970-72; cons. psychologist Community Mental Health Center, Pensacola, Fla., 1974-76, U.S. Navy, Corry Sta., Pensacola, 1978; sr. psychologist Greene Valley Devel. Center, Greeneville, Tenn., 1978—; bd. dirs. Escambia County Assn. Retarded Citizens, 1975-78, N.W. Fla. Assn. Children with Learning Disabilities, 1975-78, United Cerebral Palsy of N.W. Fla., 1975-78, Epilepsy Soc. N.W. Fla., 1975-77; mem. profl. adv. bd. Fla. Assn. Children with Learning Disabilities, 1975-78. Recipient Humanitarian award United Cerebral Palsy Assn. N.W. Fla., 1976; Brotherhood award Fla. Assn. Retarded Citizens, 1977; named Outstanding Educator, Fla. Assn. for Children with Learning Disabilities, 1978. Mem. Am. Psychol. Assn., Am. Assn. Mental Deficiency, Council for Exceptional Children, Epilepsy Found. Am., Nat. Assn. Children with Learning Disabilities, Nat. Assn. Retarded Citizens. Democrat. Unitarian. Author: Does Your Child Have A Learning Disability, 1974; The Epileptic in Home School and Society, 1979; contbr. articles to profl. jours. including Jour. Mental Retardation, Sch. Counselor, Sch. Health. Home: 1505 Brentwood Dr Greeneville TN 37743 Office: Thomas Rehab Hosp One Rotary Dr Asheville NC 28813

FREEMAN, TINA, photographer, studio executive, consultant; b. New Orleans, May 5, 1951; d. Richard W. and Montine (McDaniel) F.; m. Philip M. Woollam, May 31, 1979. B.F.A. in Photography, Art Ctr. Coll. Design, Los Angeles, 1972; student history of photography, Helmut Gernsheim (France), 1978, 79, Beaumont Newhall, Carmel, Calif., 1981. Freelance photographer, Los Angeles, 1972-74; owner, mgr. Tina Freeman Photography, New Orleans, 1974-82, Freeman-Anacker Gallery, New Orleans, 1975-77; curator photography New Orleans Mus. Art, 1977-82, cons. curator, 1982-85; pres. Decatur Studio, New Orleans, 1982—; lectr. Free U., New Orleans, 1980. Mem. admissions com. Met. Leadership Forum, New Orleans, 1981-84; mem. mayor's task force Iberville Cemeteries Area, 1981-82; bd. dirs. Gallier House Mus., New Orleans, 1974-77, Traveler's Aid, New Orleans, 1974-77, Ella West Freeman Found., 1977—, New Orleans Philharm. Symphony Soc., 1978-82, La. Council for Music and Performing Arts, 1980—, Met. Area Com., 1982—, Save Our Cemeteries, New Orleans, 1982-84; bd. dirs. Contemporary Arts Ctr., 1984—, v.p., 1985-86; bd. dirs. Planned Parenthood of La., 1984—, sec., 1984-85. Mem. Am. Soc. for Mag. Photographers, Soc. for Photog. Edn. Solo shows include: Cuningham-Ward Gallery, N.Y.C., 1977, Galerie Simonne Stern, New Orleans, 1978, 80, 83, Betty Cuningham Gallery, N.Y.C., 1981, Newcomb Art Gallery, Tulane U., New Orleans, 1983; group shows include: Cuningham-Ward Gallery, 1978, Contemporary Arts Ctr., New Orleans, 1979, Nat. Arts Club, N.Y.C., 1979, Galerie Simonne Stern, 1979-85, Los Angeles Art Assn. Gallery, 1982. Editor: Diverse Images, 1979; The Photographs of

Mother St. Croix, 1982; Leslie Gill: A Classical Approach to Photography, 1983; contbr. articles to Arts Quar., 1978-83.

FREESE, RALPH FRANCIS, card and party shop executive, retired naval officer; b. Hugoton, Kans., May 8, 1930; s. Ralph Francies and Pearl (Parker) F.; m. Trianne Ruth Lampkin, Dec. 11, 1954; children—Ralph, Timothy, Elizabeth. B.S., U.S. Naval Acad., 1953; M.A., George Washington U., 1964. Commd. ensign U.S. Navy, 1953, advanced through grades to comdr., 1973; served in USS Roberts, USS Magoffin, USS F. Marion; with office Chief Naval Ops., Naval Activities, London, Naval Supply Systems Command, Alaskan Command, Naval Base Charleston, Portsmouth Naval Shipyard; ret., 1973; owner, operator Card & Party Shop, Ltd., Falls Church, Va., 1973—. Mem. Mchts. Assn. 7 Corners Shopping Ctr. (pres.), Mchts. Assn. Georgetown Park, (pres. 1981-83), Theta Tau Omega. Republican. Episcopalian. Club: Army-Navy Country. Lodge: Masons. Home: 2065 Kedge Dr Vienna VA 22180 Office: Card & Party Shop Ltd 6201 Arlington Blvd Falls Church VA 22044

FREESE, RONALD EUGENE, tax and financial consultant; b. Marion, Ohio, Dec. 11, 1934; s. Roy J. and Verna M. F.; m. Margo E. Dodds, June 7, 1957 (div. Sept. 1965); m. Margaret R. Brewer, Oct. 14, 1966; 1 son, Steven R. B.S. in Bus. Adminstrn., Ohio State U., 1959; postgrad. in Finance, U. Toledo, 1966-67. Enrolled agt. IRS. Economist, Fed. Res., Cleve., 1959-61; portfolio mgr. Ohio Nat. Bank, Columbus, 1961-65; controller U. Toledo, 1966-67, Fla. State U., 1968-69; portfolio mgr. and trust adminstrn. officer banks in Fla., 1969-80; owner, operator Freese's Fin. Services, Lake Worth and Boca Raton, Fla., 1980—; lectr. estate planning and trusts. Trustee, Colonial Hills Civic Assn., 1964. Served with U.S. Army, 1953-55. Mem. N.Y. Soc. Security Analysts, Columbus Soc. Security Analysts, Miami Soc. Security Analysts. Republican. Lutheran. Home: 3125 NE 48th Ct Apt 221 Lighthouse Point FL 33064 Office: Freese's Fin Services 516 S Dixie Hwy Lake Worth FL 33460

FREITAG, HERTA THERESE, mathematics educator, researcher; b. Vienna, Austria, Dec. 6, 1908; came to U.S., 1944; d. Joseph Heinrich and Paula Caroline (Roth) Taussig; m. Arthur H. Freitag, Dec. 26, 1950 (dec. 1978). M. Rerum Naturalium, U. Vienna, 1934; M.A., Columbia U., 1948, Ph.D., 1953. Prof. math. Realgymnasium, Vienna, 1934-35; chmn. dept. math. Mount Sch., Amberley, Stroud, Eng., 1942-44, The Greer Sch., Hopefarm, N.Y., 1944-48; prof. math. Hollins Coll., Va., 1948-71, dept. chmn., 1979-81, prof. emeritus, 1981—; mem. People-to-People Univ. Math. Edn. del. People's Republic of China, 1983; lectr., cons. profl. assns., colls., schs., orgns., 1948—. Author monograph, articles. Recipient Americanism Medal, DAR, Roanoke, 1967; Cert. of Merit, Va. Fedn. Women's Clubs, 1967; Hollins Coll. Medal, 1979, named Hon. Alumna, 1967; recipient Algernon Sidney Sullivan award N.Y. So. Soc., 1977; named Va. Math. Coll. Tchr. of Yr., Va. Coll. Tchrs. of Math., 1980. Fellow AAAS, Chinese Assn. Sci. and Tech., Nat. Council Tchrs. of Math.; mem. Am. Math. Assn. (pres. 1962-63), Am. Math. Soc., Chinese Math. Soc., Central Assn. Sci. and Math. Tchrs., Kappa Lambda Pi. Avocations: Mathematics; painting; swimming. Home: B 40 FM 320 Hershberger Rd NW Roanoke VA 24012 Office: Hollins College Hollins College VA 24020

FREMMING, MIKE DOUGLAS, engineering company executive; b. Omaha, Dec. 11, 1932; s. Morris Adolph and Patricia Dorothy (Morgan) F.; m. Shirley Ann Graves, Dec. 30, 1951; children—Michele, Sheridan, Mike, Pat. B.S., U. Tex.-Arlington, 1961; M.S., Tex. Wesleyan U., 1962. Engrng. specialist IBM, Dallas, 1961-62; v.p. mktg. University Computing Co., Dallas, 1962-70; chmn. bd. Sayre-Fisher Co., N.Y.C., 1970-72; pres. Reville Engring. Co., Dallas, 1972—. Author: Use of Computers as Teaching Machines, 1961; Time Sharing Strategies, 1966. Mem. Assn. for Computing Speaker (nat. speaker (1966-70), Data Processing Mgrs. Assn. (nat. speaker 1966-69), Methodist.

FREMONT, WALTER GILBERT, university dean; b. Terre Haute, Ind., July 20, 1924; s. Walter G. and Muriel Margarette (Carson) F., Sr.; m. Gertrude M. Reed, Aug. 12, 1947; children—Gail Marlene Fremont Berger, Elaine Marie, Walter G., III. B.S., U. Dayton, 1949; M.S., U. Wis.-Madison, 1950; Ed.D., Pa. State U., 1961; L.H.D. (hon.), Hyles-Anderson Coll., Hammond, Ind., 1977. Prof. edn. Bob Jones U., Greenville, S.C., 1950-53, dean Sch. Edn., 1953—. Co-author: Formula for Family Unity, 1980; Formula for Youth Leadership, 1986. Served to lt. U.S. Army, 1943-46, ETO. Mem. exec. bd. Gospel Fellowship Assn., Greenville, 1962—; speaker family seminars, 1964—; bd. dirs. Children's Gospel clubs, Greenville, 1961—, Wilds Camp and Conf., Brevard, N.C., 1969—. Mem. NEA (life), S.C. Assn. Coll. Tchrs. Edn. (pres. 1960-61), S.C. Adv. Council Tchrs. Edn., S.C. Assn. Student Teaching (pres. 1959-60). Republican. Baptist. Home: 105 Stadium View Dr Greenville SC 29609 Office: Bob Jones U Wade Hampton Blvd Greenville SC 29614

FRENCH, THOMAS DANIEL, chemical oceanographer, environmental chemist; b. Phoenix, Oct. 14, 1950; s. George Daniel and Margaret Strembel F. B.S., Ariz. State U., 1972; M.S., Fla. Inst. Tech., 1980. Research asst./assoc. Med. Research Inst., Fla. Inst. Tech., Melbourne, 1977-80; sr. chemist/analyst Post, Buckley, Schuh & Jernigan, Inc., Orlando, Fla., 1980-83, lab. supr., 1984—. Mem. Sigma Xi.

FRENGER, PAUL FRED, medical computer consultant, physician; b. Houston, May 9, 1946; s. Fred Paul and Frances Mae (Mitchell) F.; m. Sandra Lee Van Schreeven, Aug. 17, 1979; 1 child, Kirk Austin. B.A. in Biology, Rice U., 1968; M.D., U. Tex.-San Antonio, 1974. Licensed physician, Tex., Colo. Pediatric intern Keesler USAF Med. Ctr., Biloxi, Miss., 1974-75; course dir. U.S. Air Force Physician Assistant Sch., Sheppard AFB, Tex., 1976-78; spl. projects cons. Med. Networks, Inc., Houston, 1979-81; dir. med. products Microprocessor Labs., Inc., Houston, 1983; chief med. officer, dir. Mediclinic, Inc., Houston, 1984-85; pres., cons. Working Hypothesis, Inc., Houston, 1981-83, 85-86. Contbr. 7 articles to profl. jours. Served to lt. col. USAF, 1969-78. Decorated Air Force Commendation medal. Mem. Am. Assn. Med. Dirs., Am. Assn. Med. Systems and Informatics, Nat. Model R.R. Assn., Mensa. Episcopalian. Avocations: model engring. and railroading. Home: 12502 Boheme Dr Houston TX 77024-4932 Office: A Working Hypothesis Inc 2323 S Voss Rd #110 Houston TX 77057

FRETWELL, ELBERT KIRTLEY, JR., university chancellor; b. N.Y.C., Oct. 29, 1923; s. Elbert Kirtley and Jean (Hosford) F.; m. Dorrie Shearer, Aug. 25, 1951; children—Barbara Alice (Mrs. Peter Cooke), Margaret Jean (Mrs. John C. Cross), James Leonard, Katharine Louise (Mrs. Robert Saul). A.B. with distinction, Wesleyan U., Middletown, Conn., 1944; M.A. in Teaching, Harvard U., 1948; Ph.D., Columbia U., 1953; hon. doctorate, Tech. U. Wroclaw, Poland, 1976; LL.D., Wesleyan U., 1981. Corr. AP, 1942-44; staff writer ARC, 1944-45; vice consul Am. embassy, Prague, Czechoslovakia, 1945-47; tchr. Brookline (Mass.) Pub. Schs., 1948, Evanston (Ill.) Twp. High Sch. and Community Coll., 1948-50; adminstrv. sec. John Hay Fellowships, John Hay Whitney Found., 1951-53; asst. prof., asst. to dean Tchrs. Coll., Columbia U., 1953-56, assoc. prof., 1956; asst. commr. for higher edn. N.Y. State Dept. Edn., 1956-64; summer faculty U. Calif. at Berkeley, 1964; dean acad. devel. City U. N.Y., 1964-67; pres. State U. N.Y. Coll. at Buffalo, 1967-78; chancellor U. N.C., Charlotte, 1979—; Organizer N.Y.C. meeting White House Conf. Edn., 1955; cons. Pres.'s Com. Edn. Beyond High Sch., 1956; assisted in James B. Conant Study Edn. Am. Tchrs., 1962; mem. commn. higher instns. Middle State Assn., 1965-71; mem. Am. Council Edn. Nat. Commn. on Higher Edn. Issues, 1981-82; trustee Carnegie Found. for Advancement Teaching, 1968-77, chmn., 1975-77; mem. Carnegie Council on Policy Studies in Higher Edn., 1973-79; trustee N.C. Council Econ. Edn., 1979—; chmn. planning com. 17th Nat. Conf. Higher Edn., 1962; bd. dirs. Microelectronics Ctr. N.C., 1981—; trustee Wesleyan U., 1967-70, Nichols Sch., Buffalo, 1969-78, Canisius Coll., 1969-76; bd. dirs. Found. of U. N.C. at Charlotte, 1981—, Mint Mus., Charlotte, N.C.; bd. visitors Johnson C. Smith U.; exec. dir. com. on edn. N.Y. State Constl. Conv., 1967. Author: Founding Public Junior Colleges, 1954, also articles, chpts. in yearbooks. Vice chmn. N.Y. State Am. Revolution Bicentennial Commn., 1969-76; bd. dirs. Am. Assn. State Colls. and Univs., 1973-76, 77-80, pres., 1978-79; mem. del. to Peoples Republic of China, Peking, 1975, to Republic of China, Taiwan, 1976, to Cuba, 1978, to UNESCO/Paris Conf., 1979, to India, 1980; pres. Middle States Assn. Colls. and Secondary Schs., 1973-74; adv. commr. Edn. Commn. of States, 1975-76, 79-80; bd. dirs. Am. Council on Edn., 1979-82, chmn., 1980-81; v.p. Univ. Research Park, Charlotte, 1979—; bd. dirs. Mecklenburg council Boy Scouts Am., 1979, United Community Services, 1979—. Decorated Order of Cultural Merit, Poland, recipient alm. award N.Y. State Assn. Jr. Colls., 1962; Distinguished Alumnus awards Wesleyan U., 1974; Carnegie Corp. grantee, 1964, 74. Mem. Am. Assn. Higher Edn. (exec. com. 1962-66, nat. pres. 1964-65), Am. Acad. Polit. Sci., Nat. Ry. Hist. Soc., Greater Charlotte C. of C. (dir. 1979-84). Clubs: Harvard (N.Y.C.); Adirondack Mountain, Charlotte City, Charlotte Country, Rotary. Home: 3066 Stonybrook Rd Charlotte NC 28205 Office: Univ NC at Charlotte Charlotte NC 28223

FREUND, EMMA FRANCES, medical technologist; b. Washington; d. Walter R. and Mabel W. (Loveland) Ervin; B.S., Wilson Tchrs. Coll., Washington, 1944; M.S. in Biology, Catholic U., Washington, 1953; cert. in mgmt. devel. Va. Commonwealth U., 1975; student SUNY, New Paltz, 1977, J. Sargeant Reynolds Community Coll., 1978; m. Frederic Reinert Freund, Mar. 4, 1953; children—Frances, Daphne, Fern, Frederic. Tchr. math. and sci. D.C. Sch. System, 1944-45; technician in parasitology lab., zool. div., U.S. Dept. Agr., Beltsville, Md., 1945-48; histologic technician dept. pathology Georgetown U. Med. Sch., Washington, 1948-49; clin. lab. technician Kent and Queen Anne's County Gen. Hosp., Chestertown, Md., 1949-51; histotechnologist surg. pathology dept. Med. Coll. Va. Hosp., Richmond, 1951—, supr. histology lab., 1970—; mem. exam. council Nat. Cert. Agy. Med. Lab. Personnel. Asst. cub scout den leader Robert E. Lee council Boy Scouts Am., 1967-68, den leader, 1968-70. Cert. Nat. Cert. Agy. for Clin. Lab. Personnel. Mem. Am. Soc. Med. Technology (rep. to sci. assembly histology sect. 1977-78, chmn. histology sect. 1983-85), Va. Soc. Med. Technology, Richmond Soc. Med. Technologists (corr. sec. 1977-78, dir. 1981-82, pres. 1984-85), Va. Soc. Histology Technicians (dir. 1979—, pres. 1982-85), N.Y. Acad. Scis., Am. Soc. Clin. Pathologists (cert. histology technician), Nat. Geog. Soc., Va. Govtl. Employees Assn., AAAS, Nat. Soc. Histotech. (by-laws com. 1981—; C.E.U. com. 1981—, program com. regional meeting 1984, 85), Am. Mus. Natural History, Smithsonian Instn., Am. Mgmt. Assn., Clin. Lab. Mgmt. Assn., Nat. Soc. Historic Preservation, Am. Biog. Inst. Research Assn. (life), Sigma Xi, Phi Beta Rho, Kappa Delta Pi, Phi Lambda Theta. Home: 1315 Asbury Rd Richmond VA 23229 Office: Surgical Pathology Dept Med Coll Va Hosp 12th and Broad Sts Richmond VA 23298

FREVERT, JAMES WILMOT, financial planner; b. Richland Twp., Iowa, Dec. 19, 1922; s. Wesley Clarence and Grace Lotta (Maw) F.; m. Jean Emily Sunderlin, Feb. 12, 1949; children—Douglas James, Thomas Jeffrey, Kimberly Ann. B.S. in Gen. Engrng., MIT, 1948. Prodn. mgr. Air Reduction Chem. Co., Calvert City, Ky., 1955-61; plant mgr. Air Products & Chems., West Palm Beach, Fla., 1961-62; pres. Young World HWD, Ft. Lauderdale, Fla., 1962-66; v.p. Shareholders Mgmt. Co., Los Angeles, 1966-73; v.p. cert. fin. planner Thomson McKinnon Securities, Inc., North Palm Beach, Fla., 1973—. Founder, past pres. MIT Club Palm Beach County, dir., 1976—, ednl. council mem., 1977-81. Served to 1st lt. USAF, 1943-46. Mem. Internat. Assn. Fin. Planning (dir. Gold Coast chpt. 1968—), Inst. Cert. Fin. Planners, Registry Fin. Planning Practitioners. Republican. Presbyterian. Clubs: Palm Beach Pundits, Old Port Yacht. Home: 883 Country Club Dr North Palm Beach FL 33408 Office: Thomson McKinnon 713 US Hwy 1 North Palm Beach FL 33408

FREW, WILLIAM MICHNER, oil company executive, consultant; b. Tarentum, Pa., Feb. 21, 1931; s. William Michener and Isabel (Cook) F.; m. Madge Pumroy, Sept. 4, 1951; children—William Michael, Marna Lynn, Erik Boyd. B.S., U. Mich., 1954, M.S., 1955. Cert. petroleum geologist. Geologist Conoco, Casper, Wyo., Shreveport, La., Roswell, N.Mex., Jackson, Miss., Corpus Christi, Tex., Houston, 1955-68, Cockrell Corp., Houston, 1968-71, Hamilton Brothers Oil Co., Houston, 1971-73; chief geologist Transco Exploration, Houston, 1973-76; dist. mgr. Southland Royalty Co., Houston, 1976-78; gen. mgr. Pamale, Houston, 1978-80; sr. v.p. Cenergy Exploration Co., Houston, Dallas, 1981-84; pres. Aegean Petroleum Co., Houston, Dallas, 1980—; dir. Aegean Petroleum Co., Dallas. Served to cpl. USMC, 1951-52. Mem. Am. Assn. Petroleum Geologists (mem. house of dels. 1981-83), Am. Assn. Petroleum Landmen, Houston Geol. Soc., Houston Assn. Petroleum Landmen, Rocky Mountain Assn. Geologists, Dallas Geol. Soc. Lodge: Rotary. Home: 16509 Amberwood Rd Dallas TX 75248

FREY, GERARD LOUIS, clergyman; b. New Orleans, May 10, 1914; s. Andrew and Marie Therese (DeRose) F.; D.D., St. Joseph's Sem. at St. Benedict's, La., 1933; postgrad. Notre Dame Sem., New Orleans. Ordained priest Roman Catholic Ch., 1938, consecrated bishop, 1967; asst. pastor, Taft, La., 1938-46, St. Leo The Great Ch., 1946-47; asst. dir. Confraternity Christian Doctrine, Archdiocese New Orleans, 1946, dir., 1946-47; pastor St. Frances Cabrini Ch., New Orleans, 1952-63, St. Frances DeSales Ch., Houma, La., 1962-67; bishop Diocese of Savannah, Ga., 1967-72, Diocese of Lafayette, La., 1972—; clergy rep. 2d Vatican Council, 1964; dir. Diocesan Friendship Corps, New Orleans, 1966; Episcopal moderator Theresians Am., from 1968. Recipient Bishop Tracy Vocation award St. Joseph's Sem. Alumni Assn., 1959. Address: PO Drawer 3387 Lafayette LA 70502

FREY, HERMAN S., publishing company executive; b. Murfreesboro, Tenn., Apr. 19, 1920; s. Saleem McCool and Minnie May (Felts) F.; m. Daisy Rook Corlew, Apr. 3, 1946; 1 child, Pamela Anne. Cert. Commerce, U. Va., 1958; Cert. Internat. Law, Internat. Ct. Justice, Netherlands, 1959; B.A., Am. U., 1964; M.B.A., George Washington U., 1965; Cert. Constl. History, Oxford U., 1974, Cert. Fgn. and Imperial Policy, 1975. Commd. navigator USN, 1937-61; advanced through grades to lt. comdr., 1955; with navigation dept. USS Quincy, 1937-41, navigator USS Sagamore, 1941-42, asst. navigator USS Iowa, 1942-44, with Naval Schs., Norfolk, Va., N.Y.C., Miami, 1944-45, navigation and gunnery officer USS Zuni, 1945-46, exec. officer USS Chickasaw, 1946-47, comdg. officer, 1947-48; instr. Naval Sch., Boston, 1948-51; comdg. officer USS Sisken, 1951-52; comdr. mine div., task unit, 1952-54; exec. officer USS McClellan, 1954-55; officer detailer Bur. Naval Personnel, Washington, 1955-58; advisor, liaison Am. Embassy, Netherlands, 1958-61; stock broker Auchincloss, Parker & Redpath, Arlington, Va., 1966-67; asst. prof. Georgetown U., Washington, 1967, U. Va., Charlottesville, 1967-69; freelance journalist Europe, U.S., 1972-76; pres. Frey Enterprises, 1976—; faculty U. Md., College Park, 1978; mem. bd. govs. Am. Sch. of Hague, Netherlands, 1959-61; cons. State of Tenn., 1969-70. Author: Jefferson Davis, 1977. Ran for U.S. Senate, Tenn., 1970, 72; bd. govs. Methodist Ch., Arlington, 1962-64, Mem. Soc. Advancement Mgmt. (pres. 1964), U.S. Naval Inst., Tenn. Hist. Soc., Tenn. Sheriff's Assn., Retired Officers Assn., Nat. Assn. Uniformed Services. Am. Legion. VFW, Phi Alpha Theta. Democrat. Club: Mil. Dist. Washington Officer's. Avocations: collecting history and literature and rare books; travel; amateur cooking; collecting recipes. Office: Frey Enterprises 2120 Crestmoor Rd Nashville TN 37215

FREY, (MILTON) WILLIAM, contracting company executive; b. Chestnut Hill, Pa., June 23, 1934; s. C. Elmer and Mary (Starke) F.; m. Doris Wenger, June 23, 1956; children—Eric C., Roger J., Barry E. B.S., Pa. State U., 1956, Ph.D., 1963; M.S., U. Conn., 1957. Asst. to assoc. prof. Pa. State U., University Park, 1958-68; assoc. prof., dir. master programs, asst. dean Sch. Bus., U. Mass., Amherst, 1968-71; founder, pres. N. Am. Contracting Corp., Sanibel, Fla., 1971—; dir. Bay Bankshares, Clearwater Oaks Bank, others. Pres., Eastern Acad. Mgmt., 1972-73; bd. dirs. Nat. Acad. Mgmt.; pres., council chmn. Sanibel Community Ch., 1977-78, pres., 1980-82. Mem. Sanibel Captiva C. of C. Republican. Contbr. articles to profl. jours.

FREY, ROBERT THOMAS, chiropractor; b. Dayton, Ohio, Feb. 27, 1931; s. Montello Lee and Hazel Julia F.; m. Phyllis Kirby, Feb. 14, 1978. Student U Dayton, 1949-50, U. Fla., 1950-51; D. Chiropractic, Lincoln Chiropractic Coll., Indpls., 1959. Practice chiropractic, Riviera Beach, Fla., 1959—. Served with med. dept. USN, 1951-55; Korea. Mem. Am. Chiropractic Assn., Fla. Chiropractic Assn., Palm Beach County Chiropractic Soc. (pres. 1962, ethics chmn. 1982, legis. chmn. 1983-84). Republican. Roman Catholic. Lodge: Exchange. Home: 4200 N Ocean Dr Singer Island FL 33404 Office: 25 E Blue Heron Blvd Riviera Beach FL 33404

FREYMEYER, ROBERT HOWARD, sociology educator, researcher; b. Wadsworth, Ohio, Dec. 9, 1951; s. John Henry and Edith May (Hilder) F. B.A., Vanderbilt U., 1973; M.A., Coll. William and Mary, 1976; Ph.D., U. Cin., 1979. Vis. asst. prof. Lander Coll., Greenwood, S.C., 1979-81; asst. prof. Gettysburg Coll., Pa., 1981-84, Presbyn. Coll., Clinton, S.C., 1984—; cons. Gettysburg Area Sch. Dist., 1982-83, Adams County Family Planning and Health Ctr., Gettysburg, 1983-84. Contbr. articles to profl. jours. Plan devel. com. Three Rivers Health Service Agy., Columbia, S.C., 1980-81; bd. dirs. Adams County Family Planning and Health Ctr., 1983-84. Nat. Endowment for Humanities fellow, 1980, 83; Lander Found. grantee, 1980; Gettysburg Coll. grantee, 1982, 83. Mem. Am. Sociol. Assn., Population Assn. Am., So. Sociol. Soc., North Central Sociol. Soc., So. Regional Demographic Soc. Methodist. Avocations: sailing; running. Home: 208 Belmont Stakes St Clinton SC 29325 Office: Presbyn Coll Clinton SC 29325

FRIAS, JAIME LUIS, pediatrics educator; b. Concepción, Chile, Mar. 20, 1933; came to U.S., 1970; s. Luis Humberto and Olga Ana (Fernandez) F.; m. Jacqueline May Steel, Apr. 8, 1961; children—Jaime Arturo, Juan Pablo, Patricio Andres, Maria Josefina. M.D., U. Chile, 1959. Diplomate Am. Acad. Pediatrics, Am. Bd. Human Genetics. Intern, Hosp. Regional, Concepcion, 1958-59; resident in pediatrics Calvo Mackenna Hosp., Santiago, Chile, 1960-62; clin. genetics and dysmorphology fellow U. Wis.-Madison, 1965-66, U. Wash., Seattle, 1966-67; asst. prof. pediatrics U. Concepcion, 1967-69, prof., 1969-70; asst. prof. pediatrics U. Fla. Coll. Medicine, Gainesville, 1970-74, assoc. prof., 1974-77, prof., 1977—, chief div. genetics, 1977—, chmn. med. sch. admissions com., 1983—; chmn. Com. for Protection of Human Subjects, 1975-78; chmn. Fla. Com. on Prevention of Developmental Disabilities, 1979-82, chmn. infant hearing screening adv. council, 1982—. Mem. Fla. Assn. Retarded Citizens. Named Tchr. of Yr., U. Fla. Coll. Medicine, 1978-79. Mem. Am. Acad. Pediatrics, Am. Pediatric Soc., ACP (affiliate; W.K. Kellogg fellow 1965-67), Am. Soc. Human Genetics, Assn. Clin. Scientists. Democrat. Roman Catholic. Club: 300 (Gainesville). Author chpts. in books, articles in profl. jours. Office: JHM Health Ctr U Fla PO Box J-296 Gainesville FL 32610

FRIBOURGH, JAMES HENRY, university official; b. Sioux City, Iowa, June 10, 1926; s. Johann Gunder and Edith Katherine (James) F.; B.A., U. Iowa, 1949, M.S., 1949, Ph.D., 1957; m. Cairdenia Minge, Jan. 29, 1955; children—Cynthia, Rebecca, Abbie. Instr., Little Rock Jr. Coll., 1949-56; assoc. prof. biology Little Rock U., 1957-59, prof., 1959-69, chmn. dept., 1959-69; vice chancellor for acad. affairs U. Ark., Little Rock, 1969-78, interim chancellor, 1972-73, 82, exec. vice chancellor, 1978—, provost, 1983-84, Disting. prof., 1984-84, univ. disting. prof., 1984—; research biologist Dept. Interior, 1959-69, Charles Pfizer and Co., Inc., 1968-69; assoc. Marine Biol. Lab., Woods Hole, Mass.; cons. VA Hosp. Co-author spl. sci. report Fisheries Bur. of Sport Fisheries and Wildlife, research, publs. in field; editor: A Course of Study for Biology, 1959. Fellow Coll. Preceptors, AAAS, Am. Inst. Fisheries Research Biologists, Coll. of Preceptors (London); mem. Am. Fisheries Soc. (cert. fisheries scientist), Electron Microscopy Soc. Am., Am. Soc. Swedish Engrs. (corr.), AAUP, Sigma Xi, Phi Kappa Phi. Episcopalian. Clubs: Rotary, Vasa Order Am., Swedish of Chgo. Office: 33d and Univ Ave Little Rock AR 72204

FRIDAY, JENNIFER CORINNE, educational administrator; b. Codrington, Barbuda, W.I., Oct. 8, 1954; came to U.S., 1962; s. Clement E. and Lillian E. (Sebastian) F. B.A., Millikin U., 1977; M.A., U. Tenn., 1982, Ph.D., 1983. Personnel technician V.I. Govt., St. Thomas, 1978; assessment ctr. dir. Knoxville Coll., Tenn., 1982, asst. prof., 1982-84; asst. prof. U. Tenn., Knoxville, 1983-84; project dir. So. Regional Edn. Bd., Atlanta, 1984—; cons. Knoxville Area Urban League, 1982-85. Bd. dirs. Knoxville Rape Crisis Ctr., 1981-84; mem. adv. bd. Phyllis Wheatley YWCA, Knoxville, 1983. Advanced Research in Edn. fellow Nat. Instn. Edn., U. Tenn., 1982. Mem. Am. Psychol. Assn. (minority fellow 1979-82), Assn. Social and Behavioral Seis., Nat. Council Black Studies, Southeastern Psychol. Assn. (minority interest group coordinator 1984-85), Internat. Assn. Rsychosocial Rehab. Workers, Delta Sigma Theta (social action chair 1982-83). Episcopalian. Avocations: athletic activities; gardening. Home: 4159 Church St Apt 4D Clarkston GA 30021 Office: So Regional Edn Bd 1340 Spring St NW Atlanta GA 30309

FRIDAY, WILLIAM CLYDE, university president; b. Raphine, Va., July 13, 1920; s. David L. and Mary E. (Rowan) F.; student Wake Forest Coll., 1937; B.S., N.C. State Coll., 1941; LL.B., U. N.C., 1948; LL.D., Belmont Abbey Coll., Wake Forest Coll., 1957, Duke, Princeton, 1958, Elon Coll., 1959, Davidson Coll., 1961, U. Ky., 1970, Mercer U., 1977; D.C.L., U. of South, 1976; m. Ida Howell, May 13, 1942; children—Frances H., Mary H., Ida Elizabeth. Admitted to N.C. bar, 1948; asst. dean students U. N.C., 1948-51, asst. to pres., 1951-55, sec. of univ., 1955-56, acting. pres., 1956, pres., 1956—. Mem. Nat. Com. for Bicentennial Era; past chmn. Am. Council on Edn.; chmn. Pres.'s Task Force on Edn., 1966-67; vice chmn. So. Regional Edn. Bd., 1967-69, mem. exec. com., 1969—; mem. nat. council Boy Scouts Am. Trustee Carnegie Found. for Advancement Teaching; bd. visitors Davidson Coll.; mem. Carnegie Commn. on Higher Edn.; mem. Commn. to Study SUNY; trustee Urban Inst., 1968-73, Am. Bd. Med. Spltys., 1975—, Howard U., 1975—, Citizen Involvement Network. Served as lt. USNR, World War II. Mem. Assn. Am. Univs. (pres. 1971). Democrat. Baptist. Home: 402 E Franklin St Chapel Hill NC 27514

FRIEDBERG, HAROLD DAVID, cardiologist; b. Johannesburg, S. Africa, June 7, 1927; s. Samuel and Violet (Grodzen) F.; M.D., U. Witwatersrand, Johannesburg, 1949; postgrad. U. London (Eng.), 1949-51, U. Manchester (Eng.), 1956-58; m. Patricia Ann Barnett, June 27, 1954; children—Mandy Violetta, Adrienne Valinda, Richard Charles, Adam Seth. Came to U.S., 1964. Intern, Baragwanath Hosp., Johannesburg, 1949-50; resident Royal Coll. Physicians Affiliated Hosps., London, 1950-54, Christie Hosp., Manchester, Eng., 1956-58; cons. cardiologist, Salisbury, Rhodesia, 1959-63; fellow medicine Johns Hopkins Med. Sch., Balt., 1964-65; mem. staff Milw. VA Hosp., chief cardiology, 1966-73, cons., 1973-79; cons. cardiology St. Luke's Hosp., 1968—, dir. coronary care unit and pacemaker clinic, 1972-79; asso. clin. prof. medicine Med. Coll. Wis.; prof. medicine U. South Fla., Tampa, 1979—; sci. adviser to several med. tech. cos. Fellow A.C.P., Am. Coll. Chest Physicians, Am. Coll. Cardiology, Am. Heart Assn. Council Clin. Cardiology, Royal Coll. Physicians (London); mem. Am. Heart Assn. (dir. Wis. 1970-78, pres. 1973), N.Am. Soc. Pacing and Electrophysiology (founding mem.), AAAS, Sociedad Argentina de Estimulacion Cardiaca (corr.). Assoc. editor Jour. Electrocardiology. Contbr. articles to profl. jours., chpts. to med. books. Home: 2000 Webber St Sarasota FL 33579 Office: PO Box 522 Longboat Key FL 33548

FRIEDHEIM, STEPHEN BAILEY, public relations executive, secretarial school executive; b. Joplin, Mo., Nov. 13, 1934; s. Robert Wray and Virginia Grace (Bailey) F.; m. Jan V. Eisenhower, Sept. 1, 1984; children—Neenah Marie Friedheim Gray, Stephen Bailey II, Robert William. B.A., U. Ark., 1956; D.B.A. (hon.), Johnson and Wales Coll., Providence, 1978; D.A.M. (hon.), Central New Eng. Coll., Worcester, Mass., 1984. Announcer, Sta. KBRS, Springdale, Ark., 1956-57; newsman Sta. KFSB, Joplin, 1957; dir. pub. relations Am. Personnel and Guidance Assn., Washington, 1961-66; exec. v.p. Am. Soc. Med. Tech., Houston, 1966-76; pres. Assn. Ind. Colls. and Schs., Washington, 1976-84; sr. v.p. Campbell Communications, Bethesda, Md., 1984—; pres. Exec. Secretarial Sch., Dallas, 1984—; mem. task force on transfer credit Council on Postsecondary Accreditation, 1977-78, bd. dirs., 1980-82; mem. Nat. Task Force on Image of the Sec., 1980—; cons. Profl. Secs., Inc., 1980-82. Bd. dirs. St. Aidan's Sch., Alexandria, Va., 1979-82; trustee Dollars for Scholars, 1982—; vestry man Ascension Ch., Houston, 1973-76, sr. warden, 1976; narrator Minn. Symphony Orch., 1972. Served with U.S. Army, 1957-61. Recipient Freedoms Found. award, 1960, 62; Broadcasting award Am. Legion Aux., 1963. Fellow Australasian Coll. Bio-med. Scientists; mem. Am. Soc. Assn. Execs. (cert.), Washington Soc. Assn. Execs., Southwestern Pvt. Sch. Assn. (bd. dirs. 1985—), Dallas-Fort Worth Met. Assn. Career Schs. (bd. dirs. 1985—), Am. Assn. Higher Edn., Nat. Assn. Execs., Nat. Assn. Concerned Vets, U.S. C. of C. (edn., employment and tng. com. 1980—). Club: Torch. Home: 6450 Patrick Dr Dallas TX 76214 Office: 2829 W Northwest Hwy Suite 226 Dallas TX 75220

FRIEDL, ERNESTINE, anthropology educator, college administrator; b. Cegled, Hungary, Aug. 13, 1920; came to U.S., 1922; d. Nicholas and Ethel (Heindorfer) F.; m. Harry L. Levy, Sept. 27, 1942 (dec.). B.A., Hunter Coll., 1941; Ph.D., Columbia U., 1950. Lectr., Bklyn. Coll., 1942-44, 46-47; instr. Wellesley Coll., 1944-46; from lectr. to prof. Queens Coll., 1947-73, dir. 1st honors program, 1963-64, chmn. dept. anthropology and sociology, 1965-68, chmn. dept. anthropology, 1968-69; exec. officer Ph.D. program in anthropology CUNY, 1970-71; prof. anthropology Duke U., Durham, N.C., 1973—, chmn. dept., 1973-78, dean Arts and Scis. and Trinity Coll., 1980-85; vis. prof. anthropology Harvard U., spring 1980, Princeton U., 1986-87. mem. Com. on Advanced Anthropology Test, Ednl. Testing Service, 1970, adv. screening com. in anthropology Com. on Internat. Exchange of Persons (Fulbright program), 1972-75, spl. fellowship panel Am. Council Learned Socs., 1973-75, social sci. panel NEH, 1973-76; cons. N.Y. State Edn. Dept., 1978-79; mem. Nat. Sci. Bd., 1979-84. Recipient Disting. Tchr. award Queens Coll. Alumni Assn., 1974; named to Hunter Coll. Hall of Fame, 1975. Fellow Am. Acad. Arts and Scis., Am. Anthrop. Assn. (pres. 1974-75), AAAS; mem. Modern Greek Studies Assn., Soc. for Applied Anthropology, Am. Ethnological Soc. (pres. 1967), Northeastern Anthropological Assn. (pres. 1971), Phi Beta Kappa. Author:

Vasilika: A Village in Modern Greece, 1962; Women and Men: An Anthropologist's View, 1975. Mem. bd. adv. editors Human Nature, 1977-78; mem. editorial bd. Sex Roles, 1977—; editor Jour. Modern Greek Studies, 1985—. Contbr. articles to profl. jours. Home: 21 Stoneridge Circle Durham NC 27705 Office: Duke U Dept Anthropology Social Sci Bldg Durham NC 27706

FRIEDLANDER, JEROME PEYSER, II, lawyer; b. Washington, Feb. 7, 1944; s. Mark Peyser and Helen (Finkel) F.; m. Irene Bluethenthal, Apr. 23, 1972; children—Jennifer R., Tyler Weil. B.S., Georgetown U., 1965; L.L.B., U. Va., 1968. Bar: Va. 1968, U.S. Dist. Ct. (ea. dist.) Va. 1968, D.C. 1968, U.S. Dist. Ct. D.C. 1968, U.S. Ct. Appeals (4th and D.C. cirs.) 1978, U.S. Supreme Ct. 1978. Ptnr. Friedlander, Friedlander & Brooks, P.C., Arlington, Va., 1972-85; substitute judge Arlington County Gen. Dist. Ct., 1985—; dir. Artech Corp., Fairfax, Va. Author: Handbook for Auto Accident Victims, 1980. Served to capt. U.S. Army, 1969-71. Mem. ABA, Assn. Trial Lawyers Am., Internat. Bar Assn., Inter-Am. Bar Assn., Va. Trial Lawyers Assn., Fed. Bar Assn. (treas. No. Va. chpt.), Office: Friedlander Friedlander & Brooks 2018 Clarendon Blvd Arlington VA 22201

FRIEDLANDER, SHERRY LYNN, publisher; b. New Orleans, Nov. 16, 1938; d. Andrew W. and Thelma M. (Sturgeon) Cannava; m. George E. Olsen, June 4, 1983. Pres. C/F Communications, Ft. Lauderdale; pres. Prism Mag., Inc. Pres., Multiple Sclerosis Soc., Ft. Lauderdale; del. White House Conf. on Small Bus., 1986. Mem. Sales and Mktg. Execs. Internat. (v.p.), Nat. Assn. Women Bus. Owners, Women in Communications. Republican. Office: 1040 Bayview Dr Fort Lauderdale FL 33304

FRIEDMAN, ALLYN STANFORD, mental health executive, psychologist; b. Akron, Ohio, Jan. 24, 1942; s. Frank E. and Hilda (Rosenberg) F.; m. Natalie J. Goldberg, Oct. 14, 1969; children—Maria, Nicole. B.A., U. Akron, 1964, M.A., 1965; postgrad. Clark U., 1965-70. Cert. mental health adminstr., real estate broker. Psychologist, Fallsview Mental Health Ctr., Cuyahoga Falls, Ohio, 1966, PMD Clinic, Worcester, Mass., 1968-70; psychologist, intern Worcester State Hosp., 1967-68; dir. Southwest Guidance Ctr., Oklahoma City, 1970-74, Red Rock Mental Health Ctr., Oklahoma City, 1974—; cons. Hosp. Corp. Am., Nashville, 1984—. Editor: Readings for General Psychology, 1965. NIMH fellow, 1965-68. Mem. Oklahoma City C. of C., Southwestern Psychol. Assn., Okla. Assn. Community Mental Health Ctrs. (sec. 1981-82, pres. 1983-84), Assn. Mental Health Adminstrs., Am. Soc. for Tng. and Devel., Soc. for Personality Assessment. Office: Red Rock Mental Health Ctr 214 E Madison St Oklahoma City OK 73105

FRIEDMAN, ARNOLD S., health care executive; b. N.Y.C., June 13, 1932; s. Lawrence D. and Frances (Dansyear) F.; m. Dorothy Oshlag Weinstein, Apr. 6, 1984. B.A., U. Miami (Fla.), 1966; M.S., Fla. Internat. U., 1978. Audio engr. Peekskill Enterprises, 1964-70; author, producer syndicated radio show Black Athlete in Am., 1970; mgr. Olson Electronics, Hialeah, Fla., 1970-72; account exec. Walston and Co., Miami, Fla., 1972-73, Merrill Lynch, Pierce, Fenner & Smith, Miami, 1973-75; asst. to pres. Hoxie Bros. Circus, 1975-76; v.p., adminstr. St. Johns Home Health Agy., Hialeah, 1976—. Pres., Epilepsy Found. S. Fla., 1979-82; chmn. minority Bus. enterprise policy com. State I, Rapid Transit Metro-Dade County, 1978—; bd. dirs. N.W. Dade Com. 100, Pvt. Industry Council; founding bd. dirs. Citizens Improved Transp., 1978. Served with AUS, 1952-54. Recipient Robert W. Laidlaw Humanitarian award. Fellow Am. Acad. Med. Adminstrs.; mem. Am. Pub. Health Assn., Am. Coll. Hosp. Adminstrs., Fla. Assn. Home Health Agys. (dir.), Health Systems Agy. South Fla., Fla. Assn. Home Health Agys. Polit. Action Com. (pres.), U. Miami Alumni Assn. (dir.), Coral Gables C. of C., Hialeah Miami Springs C. of C. (pres. 1984-85). Clubs: Rotary (past pres.; dist. conf. com.); Spotlight (dir.). Home: PO Box 2335 Hialeah FL 33012 Office: 551 W 51st Pl Hialeah FL 33012

FRIEDMAN, BARRY ALLEN, lawyer; b. Mobile, Ala., June 21, 1950; s. Louis and Grace Katherine (Ladezensky) F.; m. Eleanor Ann Capeloto, Dec. 26, 1971; children—Joshua Daniel, Scott David. B.S., U. Ala., 1972, J.D., 1975. Bar: Ala. 1975, U.S. Dist. Ct. (so. dist.) Ala. 1975, U.S. Ct. Appeals (11th cir.) 1981, U.S. Supreme Ct. 1979. Staff atty. Mobile County Legal Aid Soc., 1975-76, dir., 1976-78; ptnr. Copeland & Friedman, Mobile, 1978-79, Hall & Friedman, Mobile, 1979-83; sole practice, Mobile, 1983—. Trustee, U.S. panel trustees So. Dist. Ala. Served with USAFR, 1970-76. Mem. ABA, Ala. State Bar, Mobile County Bar Assn., Assn. Trial Lawyers Am., Comml. Law League. Jewish. Lodge: B'nai B'rith (v.p.). Home: 1621 Norwich Ct Mobile AL 36609 Office: 3004 La Clede 150 Government St Mobile AL 36602

FRIEDMAN, BARRY LEE, finance company executive; b. Memphis, Apr. 26, 1950; s. Sidney Joe and Zelda Rose (Person) F.; B.S. in Mktg., U. Mo., Columbia, 1972; m. Brenda Crain, Apr. 10, 1981. Ter. mgr. Dow Chem. Co., Dallas, 1973-75; dist. sales mgr. Stephens Industries, Inc., Dallas, 1975-77; pres. 1st Continental Leasing Corp., Dallas, 1977-82; pres. 1st Continental Fin. Corp., Dallas, 1982—; lectr. and cons. in field. Named Ambassador of Good Will, State of Tex., 1979, hon. Ky. col., Constrn. Man of Yr., Engring. News Record, 1986. Mem. Am. Assn. Equipment Lessors, Dallas C. of C., Am. Pub. Works Assn., U. Mo. Alumni Assn. (bd. dirs. Dallas chpt.), Hotchkiss Alumni Assn. Republican. Jewish. Home: 7826 Ridgemar St Dallas TX 75231 Office: 6500 Greenville Ave Suite 500 Dallas TX 75206

FRIEDMAN, EMMA FLEISCHMAN, editor, publisher; b. Chgo., Feb. 16, 1904; d. Max Louis and Rose (Plofsky) F; m. Samuel David Friedman, July 3, 1927 (dec.); children—Howard Irwin, Sandra. Student U. Ill., 1922-24, 25-26, Moser Shorthand Sch., 1921. Legal sec. Cavanagh & Pakenham, Attys., Chgo., 1921-22; sec. No. Trust Co. Safe Deposit Vaults, Chgo., 1924-25; editor/pubr. The Southwest Jewish Chronicle, Oklahoma City, 1933—; pvt. French tchr., Springfield, Ill., 1930-31. Contbg. author: Henry Cohen, Messenger of the Lord, 1954. Sec., Temple Sisterhood, Springfield, 1928-31; Sunday sch. tchr. Springfield Temple, 1928-31. Lewis Inst. scholar, 1921.

FRIEDMAN, MELVIN, university dean, geology educator; b. Orange, N.J., Nov. 14, 1930; s. Leonard and Hannah Lillian (Sholk) F.; m. Deborah Friedman, June 13, 1954; children—Barry David, Cheryl Anne. B.S. (Henry Rutgers scholar), Rutgers U., 1952, M.S., 1954; Ph.D., Rice U., 1961. Field geologist Geologic Survey of Nfld., 1952-54; geologist Shell Devel. Co., Houston, 1954-58, project leader, 1958-65, research assoc., sect. leader, 1965-67; assoc. prof. geology Tex. A & M U., College Station, 1967-69, prof., 1969—, dir. Ctr. for Tectonophysics, 1979-82, assoc. dean Coll. Geoscis., 1982-83, dean, 1983—; researcher, cons. in field; co-editor in chief Tectonophysics (internat. jour.). Past pres. Congregation Beth Shalom College Station; bd. dirs. B'nai-B'rith Hillel Found. (Tex. A & M U.). Recipient Research award Intersociety Com. on Rock Mechanics, 1968-69; Faculty Disting. Achievement award Tex. A&M U., 1975. Fellow: Geol. Soc. Am., AAAS; mem. Am. Geophys. Union, Sigma Xi. Phi Kappa Phi. Club: Briarcrest Country (Bryan, Tex.). Contbr. numerous articles to profl. jours. Office: Office of the Dean Coll Geosciences Tex A&M Univ College Station TX 77843

FRIEDMAN, PHYLLIS TERRY, psychologist; b. Glendale, Calif., Feb. 6, 1950; d. Deane Stanley and Grace Elizabeth (Floyd) T.; m. Lawrence Carl Friedman, Sept. 9, 1984. B.A., UCLA, 1972; Ph.D., Calif. Sch. Profl. Psychology, 1977. Lic. psychologist, Mass. Psychologist, Corrigan Mental Health Ctr., Fall River, Mass., 1977-81; pvt. practice psychology, writer, lectr., Fall River and Arlington, Va., 1981—; cons. Lifeline, Fall River, 1978-80. Contbr. articles to profl. jours. Mem. Am. Psychol. Assn., Soc. Psychoanalytic Psychotherapy.

FRIEDMAN, ROBERT MICHAEL, lawyer; b. Memphis, June 19, 1950; s. Harold Samuel and Margaret (Siegel) F.; m. Elaine Freda Burson, Dec. 21, 1975; children—Daniel Justin, Jonathan Aaron. B.S., U. Tenn., 1973, J.D., 1975; postgrad., Exeter U., Eng., 1974. Bar: Tenn. 1976, U.S. Dist. Ct. (we. dist.) Tenn. 1977, U.S. Dist Ct. (no. dist.) Miss. 1979, U.S. Ct. Appeals (5th cir.) 1979, U.S. Supreme Ct. 1983. Assoc., Cassell & Fink, Memphis, 1976-78; pres., sr. ptnr. Friedman & Sissman, P.C., Memphis, 1978—; legal counsel, dir. Tenn. Interpreting Service for Deaf, Memphis, 1981—, Mid-South Hospitality Mgmt. Ctr., Inc., Memphis, 1984—, United Service Advt., Inc. Mem. staff, contbr. Tenn. Law Rev., 1974-75, recipient cert., 1975. Bd. dirs. Project 1st Offenders, Shelby County, Tenn., 1976-78; bd. dirs., legal counsel Memphis Community Ctr. for Deaf & Hearing Impaired, 1980-81; bd. dirs. Eagle Scout Day, Chickasaw council Boy Scouts Am., 1978—. Served with USCG, 1971-72. Recipient Outstanding Service award and Key Alpha Phi Omega, 1972, Am. Jurisprudence award Lawyers Co-op. Pubg. Co. and Bancroft-Whitney Co., 1973-74, Chancellor's Honor award George C. Taylor Sch. Law, U. Tenn., 1975; A.S. Graves Meml. scholar, 1974-75. Mem. ABA, Assn. Trial Lawyers Am., Bar Assn. Tenn., Memphis and Shelby County Bar Assn., Tenn. Trial Lawyers Assn., Nat. Assn. Criminal Def. Lawyers, Tenn. Assn. Criminal Def. Lawyers, Nat. Criminal Justice Assn. (charter), Alpha Phi Omega, Delta Theta Phi. Democrat. Jewish. Home: 3303 Spencer Dr Memphis TN 38115 Office: Friedman & Sissman P C Suite 3010 100 N Main St Memphis TN 38103

FRIEDMAN, SHELLIE MILLER, advertising specialist; b. Miami Beach, Fla., Nov. 26, 1951; d. Gershon S. and Jeanette Lee (Tupler) Miller; m. Lynn S. Friedman, July 20, 1979. B.A. in English, Emory U., 1973; M.S. in Advt., Northwestern U., 1977. Research asst. Haymarket Advt. Agy., London, 1972; account exec. Eason Pubs., Atlanta, 1973-76, Cunningham & Walsh, Chgo., 1977-78, Kenyon & Eckhardt, Chgo., 1979; broadcast mgr. Rich's Dept. Store, Federated Stores, Atlanta, 1980-82; account exec. Sta. WZGC, First Media Corp., Atlanta, 1982—. Mem. Chgo. Advt. Club, Am. Women Radio/TV, Atlanta Broadcast Advt. Club. Club: Executive (Chgo.). Home: 795 Mabry Rd Atlanta GA 30328 Office: WZGC 603 W Peachtree St Atlanta GA 30379

FRIEDMAN, STANFORD JOSEPH, real estate executive; b. Cleve., June 27, 1927; s. Sol. H. and Cele (Akers) F.; m. Louise Glatt, July 19, 1949; children—Steven J., Jonathan R., Sally D. B.S., M.E., I.E., U. Mich., 1949. Pres. Danstan Realty Corp., North Miami Beach, Fla., U-Lease Corp., North Miami Beach, 1961—, Solar Steel Corp., 1961-82, Solar Mid-Con, Inc., North Miami Beach, 1961-82, Solar Group, Inc., North Miami Beach, 1982—; dir. Universal Container Corp., N.Y.C., Phillips Syrup Corp., Cleve., Roberts Steel Corp., Cleve., Solar Found., Cleve. Mem. ASME, Soc. Automotive Engrs., Am. Iron and Steel Inst. Clubs: Westview Country (Miami); Jockey, Turnberry Yacht and Racquet (North Miami Beach). Office: The Solar Group Inc 21000 NE 28th Ave Suite 207 Miami FL 33180

FRIEDMAN, SYLVIA, librarian; b. Cape Town, South Africa, Jan. 17, 1940; came to U.S., 1977; d. Benjamin and Minna (Kahn) Daniels; m. Basil Asher Friedman, Jan. 19, 1964; children—Michelle, Alan. Assoc., Trinity Coll., London; student Maas Drama Sch., 1958-62. Librarian, Hebrew Youth Acad. Sch., West Caldwell, N.J., 1977-81, Adath Yeshurun Temple, North Miami Beach, Fla., 1983—. Mem. adv. council Judaic studies Barry U. Mem. Assn. Jewish Libraries (v.p. 1983—, pres. South Fla. chpt. 1985—), ALA. Democrat. Jewish. Home: 17201 NE 11th Ct North Miami Beach FL 33162 Office: Adath Yeshurun Temple 1025 NE 183rd St North Miami Beach FL 33179

FRIEDRICH, GORDON WILLIAM, retired insurance executive; b. San Antonio, May 28, 1909; s. Theodore Wesley and Camille (Gordon) F.; m. Ruth Caruthers, Sept. 10, 1938. B.S., Hampden-Sydney Coll., 1930; M.S. in Bus., Columbia U., 1931. With George C. Eichlitz & Co., San Antonio, 1931-33; ptnr. Sawtelle, McAllister & Friedrich, San Antonio, 1933-81; ret., 1981; instr. ins. course St. Mary's U., San Antonio, 1951-53. Served with USAAF, 1942-46. Mem. Ind. Ins. Agts. Tex. (past pres.), Ind. Ins. Agts. San Antonio (past pres.), Phi Gamma Delta. Club: San Antonio Country, Exchange. Home: 340 Morningside Dr San Antonio TX 78209

FRIEND, WILLIAM B., bishop; b. Miami, Fla., Oct. 22, 1931; student St. Mary's Coll., Ky., Mt. St. Mary Sem., Emmitsburg, Md., Cath. U. Am., Washington, Notre Dame U., Ind. Ordained priest Roman Catholic Ch., 1959; consecrated titular bishop of Pomaria and aux. bishop of Alexandria-Shreveport, La., 1979, bishop of Alexandria-Shreveport, 1982—. Office: Diocese of Alexandria-Shreveport PO Box 7417 Alexandria LA 71306*

FRIES, HELEN SERGEANT HAYNES, civic leader; b. Atlanta; d. Harwood Syme and Alice (Hobson) Haynes; student Coll. William and Mary, 1935-38; m. Stuart G. Fries, May 5, 1938. Bd. mem. Community Ballet Assn., Huntsville, Ala., 1968—; mem. nat. nurses aid com. ARC, 1958-59; dir. ARC Aero Club, Eng., 1943-44; supr. ARC Clubmobile, Europe, 1944-46; mem. women's com. Nat. Symphony Orch., Washington, 1959—, chmn. residential fund drive for apts., 1959; bd. dirs. Madison County Republican Club, 1969-70; mem. nat. council Women's Nat. Rep. Club N.Y., 1963—, chmn. hospitality com., 1963-65; bd. mem. League Rep. Women, 1952-61; patron mem., vol. docent Huntsville Mus. Art; vol. docent Weeden House, Twickenham Hist. Preservation Dist. Assn., Inc., Huntsville. Recipient cert. of merit 84th Div., U.S. Army, 1945. Mem. Nat. Soc. Colonial Dames Am., DAR, Nat. Trust Hist. Preservation, Va., Nat., Valley Forge (Pa.), Eastern Shore Va., Huntsville-Madison County hist. socs., Assn. Preservation Va. Antiquities, Greensboro Soc. Preservation, Tenn. Valley Geneal. Soc., Friends of Ala. Archives, AIM, Nat. Soc. Lit. and Arts, English Speaking Union, Turkish-Am. Assn. Clubs: Army-Navy, Washington, Capitol Hill, Army-Navy Country (Washington); Garden (Redstone Arsenal), Redstone (Ala.) Yacht; Huntsville Country, Heritage (Huntsville, Ala.). Home: 409 Zandale Dr Huntsville AL 35801

FRIESE, HARRISON LEONARD, city official; b. L.I., N.Y., July 17, 1904; s. Herman A. and Marie Louise (Elcholtz) F.; A.B. in Econs. and Banking, Colgate U., 1927; m. Grace M. Fellows, May 6, 1933 (dec. Oct. 1966); children—Harrison Leonard, John Frank; m. 2d, Bette H. Hinsdale, June 29, 1968. With Fellows Engring. & Constrn., Hollis, N.Y., 1934-37; v.p. Fellows and Friese Constrn., 1938-42; planning Grumman Aircraft, Bethpage, L.I., 1942-47; owner, operator Sunrise Nursery, architect, landscape constrn. and design, Fort Lauderdale, Fla., 1948-68; vice mayor Fort Lauderdale, 1967-69, city commr., 1963-71. Vice chmn. Fort Lauderdale Planning and Zoning Bd., 1961-63; mem. Fort Lauderdale-Hollywood Internat. Airport Zoning Bd., 1965-67; mem. area planning bd. Community Shelter Com. Broward County, 1969-71; mem. Broward County Erosion Prevention Bd., 1967-71; mem. Ft. Lauderdale Little Yankee Stadium Com.; Republican precinct committeeman, Fort Lauderdale, 1961-63; bd. dirs. Fort Lauderdale Mus. Arts, 1967-71, Fort Lauderdale Symphony Orch., 1967-71; bd. dirs. Fla. Dist. 5 Mental Health Bd., 1973-77, sec., mem. exec. com., 1975, treas., 1976; bd. dirs., v.p. Fla. Dist. 3 Mental Health Bd., 1977-84; mem. Fla. Planning Council on Alcohol, Drug Abuse and Mental Health, 1985—; trustee Fort Lauderdale Parker Play House, 1967-69. Recipient V.I.P. award Little League Baseball League, 1970. Mem. Fla. League Municipalities (legis. com. 1967-69), Taxpayers League Broward County (v.p. 1960), Fla. Nurserymen and Growers Assn. (charter), Suwannee River Assn. (v.p. at large), Phi Kappa Psi. Methodist. Clubs: Masons, Shriners, Elks, Rotary, Colgate Gold Coast Alumni (pres. 1962), Harbor Beach Surf (pres. 1963-67). Address: Route 3 Box 562 Trenton FL 32693 also 150 NE 15th Ave Fort Lauderdale FL 33308

FRIESEN, WOLFGANG OTTO, biology educator; b. Elbing, Germany, Oct. 31, 1942; s. Helmuth and Trude (Regier) F.; came to U.S., 1950; m. Lynette Campbell, May 2, 1969; children—Laura, Jonathon. B.A., Bethel Coll., 1964; M.A., U. Calif.-Berkeley, 1966; Ph.D., U. Calif.-San Diego, 1974. Research physicist U. Calif.-San Francisco, 1969-70; research assoc. U. Calif.-Berkeley, 1974-77; asst. prof. biology U. Va., Charlottesville, 1977-82, assoc. prof., 1982—. Contbr. articles to profl. jours. Patentee in infant respirator monitor. NIH fellow, 1975-55; grantee NIH, 1978-82, 84—, NSF 1982-85, 85—; U. Va. Sesquicentennial associateship, 1983. Mem. AAAS, Neurosci. Sco., Internat. Soc. Neuroethology. Avocations: Hiking; reading; bird watching. Office: Dept Biology U Va Charlottesville VA 22901

FRIGON, HENRY FREDERICK, diversified company executive; b. Bridgeport, Conn., Nov. 16, 1934; s. Henry Xavier and Veronica Anne (Beloin) F.; m. Anne Marie McCarthy, Sept. 20, 1965; children—Megan, Michele, Henry, Scott, Mark, Stephanie. B.S.C.E., Tufts U., 1957; postgrad., U. Pa., 1958-59; M.B.A., N.Y. U., 1962. With Gen. Foods Corp., 1960-68, various fin. and mktg. positions, 1960-66, chief fin. officer, internat. ops., White Plains, N.Y., 1966-68; v.p. fin., sec., treas. Gen. Housewares Corp., N.Y.C., 1968-70, pres., Stamford, Conn., 1970-74; also dir. parent co.; group v.p. Masco Corp., Taylor, Mich., 1974-81; exec. v.p., chief fin. and adminstrv. officer Batus Inc., Louisville, 1981-83, pres., 1983-85, pres., chief operating officer, 1985, pres., chief exec. officer, 1985—, also dir.; dir. B.A.T. Capital Corp., Appleton Papers Co., Marshall Field & Co., Saks Fifth Ave.; dir. Louisville br. Fed. Res. Bank of St. Louis. Served with USNR, 1957-65. Mem. World Bus. Council, Bretton Woods Com. Home: 4008 Woodstone Way Louisville KY 40222 Office: 2000 Citizens Plaza Louisville KY 40202

FRIHART, BRYANT CLIFFORD, oil company executive; b. Richland Center, Wis., June 14, 1928; s. Bryant and Maude (Farley) F.; B.S. in Petroleum Engring., U. Tulsa, 1951; m. Ruth Helen Siegele, Sept. 1, 1956; children—Bryant Curtis, Matthew Christian, James Eric. Various engring positions Cities Service Co., Okla., Tex., N.Y., 1954-63, v.p. Argentina ops., Buenos Aires, 1963-67, pres., gen. mgr. Argentine ops., Buenos Aires, 1967-74, gen. mgr. Latin Am. ops., Houston, 1974-76, gen. mgr. S. Am./Africa, Houston, 1976-79, dir. Joint Ventures, Tulsa, 1979-81, v.p. govt. and industry affairs, energy resources group, Tulsa, 1981-82, v.p. adminstrn., land and human resources, 1982-83, corp. v.p. govt. affairs, 1983—. Chmn. contbn. com. Cities Service Oil and Gas Corp. Polit. Action Com.; active Tulsa Philharm., Southwestern Art Assn.; bd. dirs. Assistance League of Tulsa; patron Indian Nations council Boy Scouts Am. Served with USMC, 1951-54. Mem. Soc. Petroleum Engrs. of AIME (chmn. N.Y. petroleum sect. 1961-62), Am. Petroleum Inst., Nat. Ocean Industries Assn., Mid-Continent Oil and Gas Assn., Okla.-Kans. Mid-Continent Oil and Gas Assn. (chmn. bd.), Nat. Assn. Mfrs., Okla. C. of C. Republican. Methodist. Club: Petroleum (Tulsa). Lodges: Masons (master, 1973-74), York Rite, Consistory, Shrine. Home: 6627 E 89th Pl Tulsa OK 74133 Office: PO Box 300 Tulsa OK 74102

FRILOT, BERT CLARK, audio recording engineer; b. New Orleans, Apr. 24, 1939; s. Gilbert C. and Rhea (Curry) F.; m. Callie Marie LeBlanc, Dec. 5, 1962 (div. 1971); 1 dau., Lisa. Rec. engr. Cosimo's Rec. Studios, New Orleans, 1961-64, ACA Rec. Studios, Houston, 1964-66; mgr., chief engr. Gilley's Rec. Studios, Pasadena, Tex., 1966—. Served with USN, 1957-61. Recipient Golden Reel award Ampex Tape Corp., 1982, for engring. and miking platinum album by artist Willie Nelson, Somewhere over the Rainbow. Recorded or produced million seller records on artists: Fats Domino, B.J. Thomas, Jimmy Clanton, Pete Fountain, Dr. John, Archie Bell and the Drells, 8 others. Recorded or produced recordings on country artists: Mickey Gilley, Johnny Lee, Charlie Daniels Band, Floyd Tillman. Recorded portion of sound track of Urban Cowboy with John Travolta from movie by Paramount Pictures. Chief recording and miking engr. for Gilley's syndicated radio show Live from Gilley's, aired on 450 stations each week, including overseas. Lodges: Elks, Eagles (Pasadena). Home: 4218 Spencer Hwy Pasadena TX 77504 Office: PO Box 1242 Pasadena TX 77501

FRISELL, WILHELM RICHARD, biochemistry educator; b. Two Harbors, Minn., Apr. 27, 1920; s. Olof Wilhelm and Thyra Magina (Falk) F.; m. Margaret Jane Fleagle, Mar. 6, 1948; children—William Richard, Robert Benjamin. B.A., St. Olaf Coll., Minn., 1942; M.A., Johns Hopkins U., 1943, Ph.D., 1949. Instr. physiol. chemistry Johns Hopkins U. and Sch. Medicine, 1950-51; asst. prof. biochemistry U. Colo. Sch. Medicine, Denver, 1951-58, assoc. prof., 1958-64, prof., 1964-69; prof., chmn. dept. biochemistry N.J. Med. Sch., Newark, 1969-76; acting dean Grad. Sch. Biomed. Sci. Coll. Medicine and Dentistry N.J., Newark, 1971-73; prof. chmn. dept. biochemistry East Carolina U. Sch. Medicine, Greenville, N.C., 1976—, asst. dean grad. affairs, 1976—; mem. fellowships com. Fogarty-Internat. Ctr., NIH, 1962-66, 67-71, 81, chmn. 1968-71, 81, chmn. sr. fellowship com., 1981-83, biomedical scis. study sect., 1983-87. Nat. Def. Research Council, 1943-44, Am. Scandinavian Found. fellow, Uppsala, Sweden, 1949-50. Fellow AAAS; mem. Am. Chem. Soc., Am. Soc. Biol. Chemists, Am. Soc. Microbiology, Soc. Exptl. Biology, Medicine, N.Y. Acad. Scis., Harvey Soc., Phi Beta Kappa, Sigma Xi (pres. Colo. chpt. 1968-69). Author: Acid-Base Chemistry in Medicine, 1968; Human Biochemistry, 1982; also articles and revs. Home: 209 Fairlane Rd Greenville NC 27834

FRISHMAN, FRED, statistics educator, consultant; b. N.Y.C., Aug. 4, 1923; s. Abe and Regina (Eckstein) F.; m. Hilda Ruth Elman, June 20, 1948; children—Susan, Gerald Neil, Ellen, Barry Martin. B.B.A., CCNY, 1947; A.B., George Washington U., 1956, M.A., 1957, Ph.D., 1971. Engr., statistician various facilities U.S. Navy, 1949-60; dir. math. Army Research Office, Durham, N.C. and Washington, 1960-74; chief math. stats. br. IRS, Washington, 1974-79; exec. sec. applied stats. Nat. Acad. Sci., Washington, 1979-83; assoc. prof. Webber Coll., Babson Park, Md., 1983-84; adj. stats. dept. U. Central Fla., Orlando, 1984—; adj. prof. George Washington U., Washington, 1955-83. Author: Introduction to Mathematical Statistics, 1966. Contbr. articles to profl. jours. Served with USAAC, 1942-46. Fellow Am. Statis. Assn.; mem. Internat. Assn. for Stats. in Phys. Scis., Internat. Statis. Inst., Inst. Math. Stats., Math. Assn. Am. Avocations: stamp collecting; tennis. Home: 446 Stanton Pl Longwood FL 32779 Office: U Central Fla Orlando FL 32816

FRISON, PAUL M., health care executive; b. 1937; married. Grad., Occidental Coll., 1958. With Am. Hosp. Supply Corp., 1962-75; with Lifemark Corp., Houston, 1975—, now pres., chief operating officer, dir. Served with USCG, 1959-62. Office: Lifemark Corp 3800 Buffalo Speedway Houston TX 77098*

FRIST, THOMAS FEARN, internist; b. Meridian, Miss., Dec. 15, 1910; m. Dorothy Cate, 1935; children—Thomas Fearn, Robert Armistead, William Harrison, Dorothy Frist Boensch, Mary L. Frist Barfield. B.S., U. Miss., 1929; M.D., Vanderbilt U., 1933. Diplomate Am. Bd. Internal Medicine. Intern U. Iowa, 1933-35; asst. clinician Vanderbilt U., 1935-37; sr. mem. Frist-Scoville Med. Group, Nashville, 1940—; past pres. staff Nashville Gen. Hosp.; past pres., mem. exec. com. St. Thomas Hosp.; co-founder, past pres. Hosp. Corp. Am., 1968-71, now vice chmn. bd., chief med. services; dir. Nashville City Bank & Trust Co.; founder, vice chmn. bd. Am. Retirement Corp.; Past chmn. Pres.'s Com. on Aging, Washington. Founder, past chmn. bd. Park Manor Presbyn. Apts. for Elderly, Cumberland Heights Found. for Rehab. Alcoholics; founder, bd. dirs. Med. Benevolence Found.; bd. dirs. Montgomery Bell Acad., Nashville; hon. trustee Southwestern U., Memphis. Served to maj. USAAF, World War II. Fellow A.C.P.; mem. Southeastern Clin. Club (past pres.), Tenn. Heart Assn. (past pres.), Nashville Soc. Internal Medicine (past pres.), Royal Soc. Internal Medicine (London), Sigma Alpha Epsilon. Clubs: Belle Meade Country (Nashville); Lago Mar Golf Country (Ft. Lauderdale, Fla.). Office: Hosp Corp Am One Park Plaza Med Bldg Nashville TN 37202*

FRITCHIE, GEORGE EDWARD, college administrator; b. Amarillo, Tex., July 12, 1944; s. Charles Clarence and Mary Ellen (Small) F.; m. Dorothy Jo LeFevre, Mar. 5, 1964; 1 child, Mark Preston. A.A.S., Amarillo Coll., 1964; B.S. in Psychology, U. Houston, 1967; M.S. in Pharmacology, U. Tex.-Houston, 1971; Ph.D. in Biophysics, U. Houston, 1974. Research technician TRIMS, Houston, 1968-69, research asst., 1969-76; instr. chemistry Houston Community Coll., 1976-77, chmn. dept., 1977-82, dean, 1982—; coordinator HEMI/HCC, Houston, 1980-83. Editor: Biology—A Laboratory Experiment, 1981. Contbr. chpts. to books, articles to profl. jours. Recipient Eldon Durrett scholarship Amarillo Sch. Dist., 1962. Mem. Tex. Assn. Vocat. Deans and Dirs. Methodist. Avocations: painting; gardening. Office: Houston Community Coll System 22 Waugh Dr Houston TX 77007

FRITH, JAMES BURNESS, construction company executive; b. Henry County, Va., Jan. 29, 1916; s. Jacob Ewell and Sally Ada (Nunn) F.; B.S.C., Nat. Bus. Coll., 1937; m. Mary Kathryn Nininger, Aug. 21, 1947; children—Shelley Anne, Jacob Ewell II, James Burness. Gen. bldg. contractor, 1945—; chmn. bd. Frith Constrn. Co., Inc., Martinsville, Va., 1956—; dir. Frith Equipment Corp., Martinsville, Tultex Corp., Martinsville, Piedmont Trust Bank, Piedmont Bank Group, Martinsville, Henry County Plywood; mem. adv. bd. Hop-In Food Stores, Inc., Roanoke, Va. Bd. dirs. Martinsville-Henry County Econ. Devel. Corp.; trustee Averett Coll., Danville, Va. Served with USAAF, 1942-45. Mem. Asso. Gen. Contractors Am. (state bd. dirs. 1967-72, me. exec. com. 1971-72), Martinsville-Henry County C. of C. (dir. 1973, sec. 1973, v.p. 1974). Clubs: Shenandoah (Roanoke, Va.); Chatmoss Country, Forest Park Country (Martinsville, Va.), Elks, K.P., Kiwanis (pres. 1952, lt. gov. 1955). Home: 1127 Cherokee Trail Martinsville VA 24112 Office: PO Box 5028 Martinsville VA 24112

FRITTS, JOHN RAYMOND, geologist; b. Kansas City, Mo., Sept. 4, 1954; s. Raymond John and Anne (Swaim) F. B.S. in Geology cum laude, Phillips U., 1976; M.S., Okla. State U., 1980. Geologist, Cities Service Co., Jackson, Miss., 1979-82, Jerry Drake, Jackson, 1985—. Mem. Soc. Econ. Paleontologists and Mineralogists, Am. Assn. Petroleum Geologists. Republican. Mem. Christian Ch. Avocations: fencing; canoeing; camping. Home: 107 Pine Knoll Dr Apt 59 Jackson MS 39211 Office: Jerry Drake 1051 Deposit Guarenty Plaza Jackson MS 39201

FRITZ, A. N., natural gas company executive; b. 1921. B.B.A., U. Houston, 1954. Vice pres., treas. Christie, Mitchell & Mitchell Co.; acct. Tower Acceptance 1961; with Southern Natural Gas Co., Birmingham, 1962—, asst. chief acct. and prodn. dir., 1962-64, chief acct. and prodn. dir., 1964-69, asst. treas., 1969-71, comptroller, 1971-74, v.p., comptroller, 1974-80, sr. v.p., comptroller, 1980-82, sr. v.p. fin., 1982-83, exec. v.p., 1983—. Served with USMC, 1945-48. Address: Southern Natural Gas Co 1900 5th Ave N Birmingham AL 35202*

FRITZ, JACK WAYNE, communications and marketing company executive; b. Battle Creek, Mich., Apr. 22, 1927; s. Charles Lewis and Ruth Marie (Lieb) F.; m. Marilyn Joyce Shingleton, Aug. 26, 1950; children—Jack Wayne II, Dain Thomas, Susan Lynne. B.A., U. Mich., 1949. Sales staff Lever Bros., Mich., 1949-51; with sales staff ABC-owned AM and TV stas., Mich. and Ohio, 1951; product mgr. Pepsodent div. Lever Brothers, N.Y.C., 1951-54; salesman, v.p., sales mgr. v.p., gen. mgr. Blair TV div., N.Y.C., 1954-68; with John Blair & Co., N.Y.C., 1954—, dir., 1968—, v.p., gen. mgr. broadcasting, 1968-72; pres., chief exec. officer, 1972—, chief exec. officer, 1972—; mem. adv. bd. Mfrs. Hanover Trust. Hon. sponsor Children of Alcoholics Found. Inc. Served with AUS, 1945-47. Mem. Internat. Radio and TV Soc. (past dir.), Broadcast Pioneers (past dir.). Republican. Episcopalian. Clubs: University (N.Y.C.); Woodway Country (Darien, Conn.). Office: John Blair & Co 1290 Ave of Americas New York NY 10104*

FRITZ, JOSEPH FRANCIS, petroleum geologist; b. Dunlay, Tex., Apr. 3, 1932; s. Ben F. and Josephine M. (Klar) F.; m. Carol Harwell, 1957 (div. 1974); children—Leslie, Beth, Ann-Marie; m. Bebe Jones, Nov. 1, 1975. B.S., Tex. A&M, 1953, M.S., 1954. Petroleum geologist Humble Oil and Refining Col., Gulf Coast region, 1956-61, sole practice, Jackson, Miss., 1962—; founder Fritz Operating Co., Jackson, 1967—, The LBA Co., Jackson, 1973-76; co-founder Britz Systems, Jackson, 1968—, Energy Equipment. Co., Jackson, 1973—. Served to 1st lt. U.S. Army, 1954-56. Mem. Am. Inst. Profl. Geologists (exec. com. 1977-79, chmn. constn. com. 1983-84, chmn. found. 1985—). Republican. Baptist. Club: Petroleum (Jackson). Home: 1211 Monroe St Jackson MS 39202 Office: PO Box 3467 Jackson MS 39207

FRITZ, MICHAEL EDWARD, dean school of dentistry, dentist; b. Boston, Feb. 26, 1938; s. Max and Jean (Meshon) F.; m. Suzanne Wine, Aug. 18, 1960; children—Allyson, Jason, Theron. Student Boston U., 1955-58; D.D.S., U. Pa., 1963, M.S., 1965, Ph.D., 1967. Assoc. prof. and chmn. periodontology, Emory U., Atlanta, 1967-73, prof. and chmn. periodontology, 1973-82, dean Sch. Dentistry, Candler prof., 1982—; cons. VA, Atlanta, 1967—, Ben Massell Dental Clinic, Atlanta, 1982—. Contbr. chpts. to books, articles to publs. Founder Paideia Sch., Atlanta, 1972; officer PTA, Atlanta, 1971-73; Little League coach, 1970-75. Nat. Inst. Dental Research research grantee, 1968-81. Fellow Am. Coll. Dentists, Ga. Dental Assn. (hon.); mem. ADA, Internat. Assn. Dental Research (officer 1973-75), Am. Acad. Periodontology (officer 1978—), Omicron Kappa Upsilon. Republican. Jewish. Avocations: sailing; tennis; reading; jogging. Home: 2057 Renault Ln Atlanta GA 30345 Office: 3316 Piedmont Rd NE Suite 310 Atlanta GA 30305

FRITZ, WILLIAM JON, geologist; b. Vancouver, Wash., Mar. 31, 1953; s. Ernest and Huldah (Petersen) F.; m. Terry Dale McNalty, Apr. 22, 1973; 1 child, Tristan J. B.S., Walla Walla Coll., 1975, M.S., 1977; Ph.D., U. Mont., 1980. Petroleum geologist Amoco Prodn Co., Denver, 1980-81; asst. prof. geology Ga. State U., Atlanta, 1981—. Author: Roadside Geology of the Yellowstone Country, 1985; contbr. articles to profl. jours. Grantee Am. Philos. Soc., 1984. Mem. Soc. Econ. Paleontologists and Mineralogists (tech. program chmn.), Geol. Soc. Am., Am. Assn. Petroleum Geologists (del.), Ga. Geol. Soc. (pres.) Internat. Assn. Sedimentologists, Sigma Xi. Home: 829-4 Twin Oaks Dr Decatur GA 30030 Office: Dept Geology Ga State U Atlanta GA 30303

FRITZE, JULIUS ARNOLD, marriage counselor; b. Albuquerque, Dec. 30, 1918; s. Martin Herman and Mary (Staerkel) F.; student St. Paul's Jr. Coll., 1937-39; diploma Concordia Sem., 1944; B.A., in Edn., U. N.Mex., 1943; M.S., Central Mo. State Coll., 1969; cert. career counselor; m. Marion Caroline Becker, June 4, 1944; children—Christine, Timothy; m. 2d, Anita Carol Dozier, May 18, 1973. Ordained to ministry Lutheran Ch., 1944; pastor in Corpus Christi, Tex., 1944-48, Higginsville, Mo., 1948-57; exec. dir. Marriage and Parenthood Center, Dallas, 1957-59; pvt. practice marriage counseling, Dallas, 1959—; indsl. psychologist N. Am. Mktg., 1975-76; mgmt. cons. Concord Systems, Inc., 1978—. Cons. Mo. Snyod, Luth. Ch., St. Louis, 1961, Tex. dist., 1976—; lectr. to profl. and laymen's insts., 1956—; lectr. Dallas County Jr. Coll. Bd. dirs. Dallas area Am. Lung Assn., 1976—. Lic. profl. counselor, Tex. Mem. Am. Assn. Marriage Counselors, Am. Personnel and Guidance Assn., Nat. Vocat. Guidance Assn., Nat. Council Family Relations, Am., Southwestern, Tex. psychol. assns., Am. Orthopsychiat. Assn., Internat. Platform Assn. Author: The Essence of Marriage, 1969; Mini Manual for Ministers, 1978. Contbr. series of articles to nat. mags. Home: 3118 Royal Gables Dallas TX 75229 Office: 3198 Royal Ln #100 Dallas TX 75229

FRIZZELL, ANN BRONIKOWSKI, life insurance company executive; b. Virginia, Minn., Oct. 15, 1950; d. Leonard J. and Josephine M. (Michaloski) Bronikowski; m. Steven P. Frizzell, Feb. 17, 1973 (div. Sept. 1982). B.A. with honors, U. Fla., 1972. Outside plant engr. So. Bell Tel. & Tel. Co., Jacksonville, Fla., 1972-75; actuarial analyst, actuarial asst., asst. actuary actuarial dept. Gulf Life Ins. Co., Jacksonville, Fla., 1975-82, assoc. actuary, 1982—, sec. bd. dirs. Gulf Life Employees Fed. Credit Union, 1981—. Fellow Soc. Actuaries; mem. Am. Acad. Actuaries, Southeastern Actuaries Club, Phi Beta Kappa. Club: Jacksonville (Fla.) Track.

FRIZZELL, RICHARD WELLINGTON, health care exec.; b. Balt., Oct. 5, 1930; s. Richard Wellington and Dorothy K. (Collins) F.; student public schs., Blacksburg, Va.; children—Rick, Dan, Jill. Owner, Atlas Constrn., Inc., Sarasota, Fla., 1956-67; partner Steel Enterprises Inc., Blacksburg, 1967-73; partner, pres. Health Care Med. Facilities, Blacksburg, 1973—; pres. H.C.M.F. Devel. Corp., Richmond, Va.; dir. First Nat. Bank, Blacksburg. Mem. Va. Gov.'s Bd. for Licensure of Nursing Home Adminstrs., 1979; chmn. United Way campaign, 1979. Mem. Blacksburg C. of C. (pres. 1976-78, Disting. Citizen of Yr. 1979). Clubs: Kiwanis, Blacksburg Country (dir. 1970-74). Office: 701 E Franklin St Suite 1112 Richmond VA 23219

FROCK, CHARLES THOMAS, health care administrator; b. Jacksonville, Fla., Nov. 11, 1948; s. Samuel Edward and Louise Harriet (Hooper) F.; m. Nancy Louise Beetham, Sept. 1, 1973; children—Catherine Edlin, Elizabeth Beetham. B. Indsl. Engring., U. Fla., 1971; M. Health Administrn., Duke U., 1974; cert. Kings Fund Coll., London, 1981, Harvard U., 1981. Mgmt. cons. SunHealth Corp., Charlotte, N.C., 1974-76; dir. Granville Hosp., Oxford, N.C., 1976-78; pres. Lexington Meml. Hosp., 1978-82, Valdese Gen. Hosp., N.C., 1982—; bd. dirs. Hospice Burke County, Morganton, N.C.; lectr. Duke U., Durham, N.C., 1977-79; bd. dirs., chmn. Davidson County Mental Health Bd. Lexington, 1980-82; bd. dirs. N.C. Heart Assn., Davidson County, 1981-82. Bd. dirs. Burke County United Way, Morganton, 1984. Served to capt. U.S. Army, 1971-73. Mem. Am. Coll. Hosp. Administrs., N.C. Hosp. Assn. (dist. vice-chmn. 1984-85), Yadkin Valley Library Consortium (chmn. 1981-82), Lexington Area C. of C. (pres. 1982), Burke County C. of C. (v.p. 1984). Club: Dutch (Lexington) (bd. dirs. 1979-82). Lodge: Rotary. Avocations: photography; hiking; racquet sports. Home: PO Box 148 Campus St Rutherford College NC 28671 Office: Valdese Gen Hosp PO Box 700 Malcolm Blvd Valdese NC 28690

FROE, DREYFUS WALTER, community development executive; b. Bluefield, W.Va., Feb. 18, 1908; s. Lucian Charles and Sallie Ann (Anderson) F.; m. Ethel Cooper, Oct. 29, 1932; children—Dreyfus Lucian, Danna Adolphus. B.S. in Agr., W.Va. State U., 1930; M.S.E., W.Va. U.-Morgantown, 1950. Tchr., prin. Mercer County Sch., Bluefield, W.Va., 1936-59, with community devel., Mercer County, 1967-83; coach Bluefield State Coll., 1938-45; with fgn. community devel. U.S. Dept. State, Africa, S.E. Asia, 1959-69; agr. cons. Flanner House, Indpls., 1959-60. Named Citizen of Yr. Mountain State Bar Assn., 1982; Layman of Yr. W.Va. Annual Conf., 1982; recipient NAACP award Mercer County, 1983. Mem. Sigma Phi. Club: Civitan (pres. 1983). Lodges: Elks, Masons. Office: Box 1560 Princeton WV 24740

FROEHLICH, DAVID JOHN, manufacturer's agent; b. Newburgh, N.Y., Apr. 13, 1922; s. Julius J. and Mary Ellen (Murphy) F.; m. Merry Margaret Adams, Sept. 4, 1948; children—Thomas William, Peter Adams, Anne Mary, Margaret Elizabeth. Student, CCNY, 1939-41; B.A., U. Minn., 1948. Specialist, Remington Rand Co., Mpls., 1948-49, dist. mgr., 1949; dist. mgr. Heinn Co., Dallas, 1950—; mfr.'s agt., 1963—. Sales cons. Lighthouse for the Blind; bd. dirs. Community Fund, 1960-68, United Fund, 1968-75; bd. dirs. St. Vincent DePaul Soc., 1975—, pres., 1979-82. Served with AC, U.S. Army, 1941-46; to maj. USAFR, 1950-65. Decorated D.F.C., Air medal with 3 clusters. Mem. Dallas Mktg. Assn., Dallas Sales and Mktg. Assn., Dallas C. of C., Bus. Profl. Assn. Am. Roman Catholic. Lodge: KC. Home: 7206 Brennans Dr Dallas TX 75214 Office: 6060 N Central Expy Suite 560 Dallas TX 75206

FROID, GARY ROBERT, insurance company executive; b. Burlington, Iowa, Mar. 21, 1937; s. Carl John and Frances Mirian (Hannah) F.; children—Mark, Karen, Lynn, Michael, Katherine, Victoria. A.B., Harvard U.; postgrad. Purdue U. Mktg. Inst., 1960, Am. Coll., 1965. C.L.U.; chartered fin. cons.; cert. fin. planner; registered health underwriter. With Northwestern Mut. Life Ins. Co., 1959—, dist. agt., 1967—; founder, dir. Park Bank of Fla., Fla. Park Banks, Ind. and J.K. Fin., Inc. Mem. Pinellas County Sports Authority (Fla.); charter mem. St. Petersburg Jr. Coll. Devel. Found. (Fla.), 1980; pres. Pinellas County United Way, 1972, gen. campaign chmn., 1971; mem. Eckerd Coll. Pres.' Round Table of Advisors; pres. Community Services Council, St. Petersburg, 1970; bd. dirs. Pinellas Assn. Retarded Children, 1968-69. Recipient Grant Hill award Northwestern Mut. Life Ins. Co., 1976, Top Mgmt. award St. Petersburg Sales and Mktg. Execs., 1980, Disting. Citizens award Pinellas County chpt. Nat. Football Found. and Hall of Fame, 1982; named Man of Yr., 1973. Mem. Million Dollar Round Table, Ten Millions Dollar Forum (bd. dirs.), Assn. for Advanced Life Underwriting, St. Petersburg Assn. of Life Underwriters (chmn. project lifeguard pub. service project, pres. 1968-69, bd. dirs., sr. council, nat. committeeman 1971-73), Am. Soc. C.L.U.s (pres. 1982-83, bd. dirs.), Tampa Bay chpt. C.L.U.s (bd. dirs.), Northwestern Mut. Life Ins. Co. C.L.U. Assn. (pres.), St. Petersburg Area C. of C. (pres. 1974-75), Sigma Alpha Epsilon. Clubs: Harvard West Coast of Fla. (pres. 1965-66), Suncoasters, Inc. of St. Petersburg, St. Petersburg Yacht, Quarterback (bd. dirs.), Squires Inc. of St. Petersburg, Batboys, Lakewood County, Commerce of Pinellas County. Contbr. articles on ins. to profl. jours. Home: Brightwater Blvd NE PO Box 3642 St Petersburg FL 33731 Office: One Plaza Pl NE Suite 1600 St Petersburg FL 33701

FROMHAGEN, CARL, JR., obstetrician-gynecologist; b. Tampa, Fla., 1926; s. Carl Frederick and Minnette Gertrude (Douglass) Von Fromhagen; children—Dana Lynn, Carol Leslie, Carl Scott. B.S., U. Miami, 1950; student U. Utah, 1949; grad. mil. pilot tng. USAF, 1951; M.S., U. Colo., 1952; M.D., Emory U., 1955. Intern, Baylor U., 1955-56, resident in ob-gyn, 1956-59; instr. Sch. Medicine U. Miami, Coral Gables, Fla., 1959-62, asso. prof., 1975—; obstetrician, gynecologist, specialist in aviation medicine, FAA sr. med. examiner, Clearwater, Fla., 1960—; pres. Fromhagen Aviation Inc., 1969—; chmn. bd. Navigate Inc., 1970-73; med. cons. Planned Parenthood, 1963-67. Mem. Fla. State Aviation Council, 1966-67; mem. Com. of 100 Pinellas County, pres. Honduras Relief Soc., 1970; bd. dirs. Am. Cancer Soc., 1962-68; bd. dirs. Interprofl. Family Council, 1967-68. Served to col. USAFR. Named outstanding resident Baylor U. Med. Sch., 1959; recipient award merit Res. Officers Assn., 1964; Silver Wings Frat. award of honor for Winter Frolic, 1981; diplomate Am. Bd. Ob-Gyn. Fellow Am. Coll. Ob-Gyn, ACS, Am. Coll. Abdominal Surgeons; mem. Pan Am. Med. Assn., Fla. Soc. for Preventive Medicine (pres. 1968), Aerospace Med. Assn., Civil Aviation Med. Assn., Flying Physicians (v.p. 1967-68, dir., 1968-74, state pres. 1966-74), Res. Officers Assn. Fla. (Clearwater chpt. pres. 1963-67, state surgeon 1964), N.Y. Acad. Sci., Aviation Maintenance Found., U.S. Power Squadron (fleet surgeon), Iron Arrow, Omicron Delta Kappa, Pi Kappa Alpha, Beta Beta Beta. Clubs: Kiwanis, Carlouel Yacht, Ye Mystic Krewe of Neptune. Home: 1666 Robinhood Ln Clearwater FL 33516 Office: 1745 S Highland Ave Clearwater FL 33516

FROMKIN, AVA LYNDA, investment executive; b. Toronto, Ont., Can., May 3, 1946; d. Joseph and Sara Ann (Hurovitz) F.; came to U.S., 1948, naturalized, 1953; B.S. in Nursing, U. Miami, 1969, cert. adminstrv. scis., 1975, M.B.A., cert. health adminstrn., 1983. Nurse, Mt. Sinai Med. Center, Miami Beach, Fla., 1970-71, 73-76; dir. surg. services Cedars of Lebanon Health Care Center, Miami, 1976-82; adj. prof. intraoperative nursing program Miami-Dade Community Coll., 1982-83; investment coordinator, dir. research M.H. Berkson Assocs., Inc., 1982-84. Mem. S. Fla. Shared Purchasing Assn. (chairperson operating room adv. com. 1976-79), Assn. Operating Room Nurses (dir. Miami chpt. 1979-80). Home: 150 SE 25th Rd Miami FL 33129

FRONABARGER, ALLEN KEM, geochemist; b. Las Vegas, N.Mex., Feb. 2, 1948; s. Ray Edward and Nell Elizabeth (McRae) F.; m. Chantal Rousselin, July 27, 1974; children—Saskia, Derek. B.Sc., Mo. Sch. Mines and Metallurgy, 1972; M.S., U. Tenn., 1980, Ph.D., 1984. Geologist, Peace Corps, Upper Volta, West Africa, 1972-74, FPC, Washington, 1974-76; geochemist Union Carbide Nuclear Div., Oak Ridge Nat. Lab., 1976-77, research fellow Environ. Sci. Div., 1981—; cons. geologist Sci. Applications, Inc., Oak Ridge, 1977-79; teaching asst. geology U. Tenn., Knoxville, 1979-81; asst. prof. geology Coll. of Charleston, S.C., 1984—. Grantee, Geol. Soc. Am., Sigma Xi, 1979. Mem. Soc. Econ. Geologists, Mineral. Soc. Am., Geochem. Soc., Sigma Xi, Sigma Gamma Epsilon. Contbr. articles to profl. jours. Home: 1065 Oakcrest Dr Charleston SC 29412 Office: Dept Geology Coll of Charleston Charleston SC 29424

FRONK, MICHAEL RUSSELL, clergyman, therapist, conference speaker; b. Miami, Fla., Dec. 6, 1951; s. George Eugene and Agnes Marion (Stewart) F.; m. Margaretha Everdina Henriette Caspers, Aug. 3, 1973; 1 son, George Christopher. Student Miami-Dade Jr. Coll., 1970; B.A., Stetson U., 1974; M.Div., So. Bapt. Theol. Sem., 1979. Ordained to ministry So. Bapt. Ch., 1973; Admissions officer Stetson U., Deland, Fla., 1974-75; program dir. St. Matthew's YMCA, Louisville, 1976-78; pastor Union Bapt. Ch., Greensburg, Ind., 1977-78, 1st Bapt. Ch., Pine Island, Fla., 1978-82, Longwood Hills Bapt. Ch., Longwood, Fla., 1982—; conf. leader Lake Yale Bapt. Assembly, Ridgecrest Bapt. Assembly, various chs. Chaplain, Pine Island-Matlacha Vol. Fire Dept., 1979-82; actor Pine Island Players, 1982; chmn. Pine Island Elem. Sch. Faculty Adv. Com. Recipient Green Circle award Omicron Delta Kappa, 1972, Presdl. gavel Steton U. Jud. Council, 1974, Clyde T. Francisco Preaching award So. Bapt. Theol. Sem., 1977, Disting. Service award United Way Campaign, 1981. Democrat. Address: 157 Morning Glory Dr Lake Mary FL 32746

FRONTERHOUSE, GERALD WAYNE, banker; b. Ada, Okla., May 22, 1936; s. Victor and Austa Fronterhouse; m. Gretchen Anne Gover, Jan. 27, 1959; children—Jennifer Anne, Jeffry Scott. B.S., Okla. U., 1959; M.B.A., Harvard U., 1962. With Republic Bank Dallas, 1962—, v.p., 1967, sr. v.p., 1971, exec. v.p., 1974; pres., chief operating officer, Republic Bank Corp., 1978—; dir. Dallas Market Ctr. Co. Bd. dirs. Tex. State Fair; campaign vice chmn. United Way, 1983; bd. trustees Children's Med. Ctr., Lamplighter Sch., Hockaday Sch. Served with USN, 1959-60. Mem. Assn. Res. City Bankers, Tex. Research League. Club: Preston Trail Golf, Dallas Country. Office: Republic Bank Corp Pacific and Ervay Sts Dallas TX 75222

FROST, DAVID EARL, oral and maxillofacial surgeon, educator; b. Denver, Nov. 19, 1949; s. Don Clark and Marjorie Earline (Harvey) F.; m. Claudia Vernelle Marple, May 22, 1971; children—Ryan Edward, Holly Megan, Kyle Edwin. B.S., Tex. A&M U., 1971; D.D.S., Baylor U., 1974; M.S., U. N.C., 1980. Diplomate Am. Bd. Oral and Maxillofacial Surgery. Gen. dentistry resident USAF, Chanute AFB, Ill., 1974-76, staff dentist, 1976-77; oral surgery resident U. N.C., Chapel Hill, 1977-80, research fellow, 1980-81; sr. registrar Canniesburn Hosp., Bearsden, Scotland, 1980; dir. dentofacial deformaties Wilford Hall Med. Ctr., San Antonio, 1984—; adj. assoc. prof. U. Tex. Health Sci. Ctr., San Antonio; adj. asst. prof. La. State U. Charity Hosp., New Orleans, 1983-85; cons. oral surgery VA Hosp., Biloxi, Miss., 1981-84. Contbr. articles to profl. jours., chpts. to books. Coach Youth Soccer, Ocean Springs, Miss., 1984; cub scout leader Pine Burr Area council Boy Scouts Am., 1983-84, Alamo Area council Boy Scouts Am., 1984-85; sr. youth sponsor St. Paul's Ch., Ocean Springs, 1982-84; leader Young Religious Unitarian Universalists, San Antonio, 1985-86. Served to lt. col. USAF, 1971—. Recipient Disting. Mil. Grad. award Tex. A & U, 1971; Moorehead fellow U. N.C., 1977-80. Fellow Am. Assn. Oral and Maxillofacial Surgeons; mem. ADA, Brit. Assn. Oral Surgeons, Internat. Assn. Oral Surgeons. Unitarian Universalist. Avocations: sports; Hobie cats; children; camping; running. Home: 8915 Melinda Ct San Antonio TX 78240

FROST, JAMES HOWARD, manufacturing company executive, civil engineer; b. Savannah, Ga., Oct. 1, 1937; s. Howard Hugo and Mary Louise (McDowell) F.; m. Joanne McAlister, Apr. 11, 1957; children—Roxanne, Ronnie Allen. B.S.C.E., U. Ark., 1963. Registered profl. engr., Ark., Tenn. Design engr. Varco Steel Co., Pine Bluff, Ark., 1963-67, chief engring., 1967-70, dir. engring., 1970-72; v.p. computer services AMCA Internat. Corp., Memphis, 1973—. Served with U.S. Army, 1957-60. Mem. Nat. Soc. Profl. Engrs. Methodist.

FROST, JONAS MARTIN, congressman; b. Glendale, Calif., Jan. 1, 1942; s. Jack and Doris (Marwil) F.; B.A., U. Mo., 1964, B.J., 1964; J.D., Georgetown U., 1970; m. Valerie Hall, May 9, 1976; children—Alanna Shaw, Mariel Jeanne, Camille Faye. Bar: Tex. 1970. Law clk. U.S. Dist. Ct. judge, 1970-71; individual practice law, Dallas, 1972-79; legal commentator Sta. KERA-TV, Dallas, 1971-72; mem. 96th-98th Congresses from 24th Dist. Tex., mem. rules com., budget com., Dem. whip-at-large. Del., Dem. Nat. Conv., 1976, 84; coordinator N.Tex., Carter-Mondale campaign, 1976; Tex. chmn. Gary Hart for Pres. campaign, 1983. Served with USAR, 1966-72. Address: 1238 Longworth House Office Bldg Washington DC 20515

FROST, THOMAS CLAYBORNE, banker; b. San Antonio, Oct. 29, 1927; s. Thomas Clayborne and Ilse (Herff) F.; B.S. in Commerce summa cum laude, Washington and Lee U., Lexington, Va., 1950; LL.D., Austin Coll.; m. Patricia Holden, June 9, 1951; children—Thomas Clayborne III, William, Donald, Patrick. With Frost Nat. Bank, San Antonio, 1950—, pres., 1962-71, chmn. bd., 1971—; chmn. bd. Cullen/Frost Bankers, Inc., 1971—; dir. Elsinore Cattle Co., La Quinta Motor Inns, Inc., Grupo Steele Mexico City, Southwestern Bell Telephone Co., Tesoro Petroleum Corp., Cullen Center Bank & Trust, Houston, Cullen/Frost Bank, Dallas; past dir. San Antonio br. Fed. Res. Bank; past mem. mem. fed. adv. council FRS; 1st chmn. regional adv. com. to comptroller of currency. Hon. trustee San Antonio Med. Found., S.W. Found. Biomed. Research, S.W. Tex. Meth. Hosp.; trustee Austin Coll., McNay Art Inst., Morrison Trusts; past exec. chmn., bd. trustees Tex. Mil. Inst.; past chmn. Tex. Ind. Coll. Fund; mem. devel. bd. U. Tex. Health Sci. Center; trustee emeritus Washington and Lee U.; trustee Pan Am. Devel. Found., Washington; bd. dirs. State Fair of Tex., bd. dirs., mem. exec. com. Downtown Owners Assn. Served with AUS, 1946-47. Named Outstanding Young Man, San Antonio Jr. C. of C., 1961; Mr. South Tex., Laredo (Tex.) George Washington Birthday Celebration Assn., 1974; First Outstanding Alumnus, Tex. Mil. Inst., 1974; San Antonio Man of Year, Exchange Club, 1974; Brotherhood award NCCJ, 1980; Inst. Human Relations award Am. Jewish Com., 1981; W.T. Bondurant, Sr. Disting. Humanitarian award Tex. Mil. Inst., 1983. Mem. Tex. Bankers Assn. (past pres.), San Antonio Clearing House Assn. (past pres.), Tex. Assn. Bank Holding Cos. (bd. dirs.), Assn. Res. City Bankers (pres. 1977), Philos. Soc. Tex., Tex. Cavaliers, Order Alamo, Phi Beta Kappa, Beta Gamma Sigma, Alpha Kappa Psi, Phi Eta Sigma, Sigma Chi. Clubs: San Antonio Country, San Antonio German, Plaza, Argyle. Home: 234 Rosemary St San Antonio TX 78209 Office: Cullen/Frost Bankers PO Box 1600 San Antonio TX 78296

FRUCCI, RICHARD LAWRENCE, trucking company executive; b. Parris Island, S.C., 1932. B.S., U. N.C., 1956. Sr. v.p. ops. Transcon Lines, 1976-77; with McLean Trucking Co., 1956-76, 77-79, exec. v.p., 1977-79; pres. Lee Way Motor Freight Inc., Oklahoma City, 1979—, also dir. Office: Lee Way Motor Freight Inc 3401 NW 63rd St Oklahoma City OK 73116*

FRUCHTENBAUM, ARNOLD GENEKOVICH, organization executive; b. Tobolsk, Siberia, USSR, Sept. 26, 1943; s. Chaim and Adele (Valentinovna (Suppes) F.; m. Mary Ann Morrow, June 29, 1968. Student, Shelton Coll., 1962-65; B.A., Cedarville Coll., 1966; postgrad. Hebrew U. Jerusalem, 1966-67, Am. Inst. Holy Land Studies, 1966-67; Th.M., Dallas Theol. Sem., 1971; postgrad. NYU, 1975—. Minister, Beth Sar Shalom Hebrew Christian Fellowship, Dallas, 1967-71; editor The Chosen People, N.Y.C., 1973-75; assoc. dir. The Christian Jew Found., San Antonio, 1975-77; pres. Ariel Ministries, San Antonio, 1977—; lectr. in field. Mem. Messianic Jewish Alliance. Mem. Fundamental Chs. of Am. Author: Hebrew Christianity: Its Theology, History and Philosophy, 1974; Jesus Was a Jew, 1975; The Footsteps of the Messiah: A Study of the Sequence of Prophetic Events, 1982; Biblical Lovemaking: A Study of Sex from the Song of Solomon, 1983. Home: 10602 Mt Tipton San Antonio TX 78213 Office: 12134 Colwick St San Antonio TX 78216

FRUST, RICHARD W., college dean, business educator. Chmn. fin. dept. U. S.C., Columbia, dir. Charles E. Daniel Ctr. for Mgmt. Edn., J. Henry Fellers prof. fin.; dean Coll. Bus. and Econs., U. Ky., Lexington, 1981—; dir. Host Communications Inc.; trustee Thoroughbred Group Mut. Fund. Author: The Financial Management of Health Care Institutions; (with others) Forecasted Changes in the Health Care Industry. Contbr. articles to profl. jours. Assoc. editor Fin. Mgmt., Jour. Bus. Research. Mem. Eastern Fin. Assn. (bd. dirs.), So. Fin. Assn. (exec. com.), Fin. Mgmt. Assn., Am. Fin. Assn. Office: Coll Bus U Ky Lexington KY 40506

FRY, BARBARA ANN, government official; b. St. Charles, Ill., Nov. 10, 1937; d. Robert Nicholas and Marianne Eloise (Earhart) Wilford; B.S., U. Ill., 1959; M.B.A., Roosevelt U., 1976; m. Ronnie Darrel Fry, June 15, 1974; children—Kim Buskirk, Gena Buskirk. Budget analyst, then budget officer Navy Electronics Supply Office, Great Lakes, Ill., 1962-73; regional budget officer IRS, Chgo., 1973-75, Atlanta, 1975-76, regional fiscal mgmt. officer, 1976-83, regional mgmt. analysis officer, 1983—; former mem. adv. com. EEO. Past treas. Loch Lomond Property Owners Assn., PTA. Served with USAF, 1959-61. Mem. AAUW (past treas.), Federally Employed Women (past co-chmn. Inter-Agy. Council, past pres. Atlanta chpt., past legis. chmn.), Nat. Assn. Female Execs., Atlanta Assn. Fed. Execs. (treas.), Atlanta Womens Network, Decatur Bus. and Profl. Women. Home: 1511 Montevallo Circle Decatur GA 30033 Office: 275 Peachtree St NE Room 613 Atlanta GA 30043

FRY, DAVID DONALD, civil engineer, consultant; b. Canton, Ohio, Oct. 4, 1924; s. Don David and Mary J. (Petch) F.; student Kans. State Coll., 1943-44; B.S.C.E., Case Inst. Tech., 1949; m. Ann Selden Nicholson, Apr. 25, 1958; 1 child, Constance Louise. Engr., Ohio Dept. Hwys., Ravenna, 1949-53; engr. Peter Kiewit Sons Co., Portsmouth, Ohio, 1953-54; area engr. Arabian Am. Oil Co., Dhahran, S.A., 1954-56; design engr. M. H. Connell & Assoc., Inc., Miami, 1956-60; asst. dir. pub. works City of Coral Gables (Fla.), 1960-67; v.p. charge Fla. office Brighton Engring. Co., 1967-69; project engr. Clarkeson, Kononoff & Smith, Inc., Coral Gables, 1970-71; chief engr., gen. mgr. Pavlo Engring. Co., Inc., Coral Gables, 1971-85; cons., 1986—. Registered profl. engr., Ohio, Fla. Mem. Theta Chi. Presbyterian. Home: 6001 SW 81st St South Miami FL 33143 Office: 2012 Ponce de Leon Blvd Coral Gables FL 33134

FRYE, HENRY E., state judge; b. Ellerbe, N.C., Aug. 1, 1932; s. Walter A. and Pearl A. (Motley) F.; B.S., N.C. A&T State U., 1953, LL.D. (hon.), 1983; J.D., U. N.C., Chapel Hill, 1959; LL.D. (hon.) Shaw U.; m. Shirley Taylor, 1956; children—Henry Eric, Harlan Elbert. Admitted to N.C. bar; ptnr. firm Frye, Barbee & Jervay, Greensboro, 1968-83; prof. N.C. Central U. Law Sch., 1965-67; U.S. dist. atty., 1963-65; organizer, Greensboro Nat. Bank, 1971, pres., 1971-81; mem. N.C. Ho. of Reps., 1969-80, N.C. Senate, 1980-83; assoc. justice N.C. Supreme Ct., 1983—. Del. Democratic Nat. Conv., 1972. Served to 1st lt. USAF, 1953-55; Korea. Recipient Alumni Excellence award N.C. A&T State U., 1973; Uncle Joe Cannon award Greensboro C. of C., 1975. Mem. ABA, Am. Judicature Soc., Nat. Bankers Assn. (R.R. Wright award 1983), Nat. Bar Assn. Office: Supreme Ct Justice Bldg Raleigh NC 27611

FRYE, VIRGINIA HEADRICK, psychologist; b. Sevierville, Tenn., June 20, 1938; d. Luke Burns and Lena Mae (Brewer) Headrick; m. Otha Gene Frye, June 4, 1960; children—Amy Lauren, David Gene. B.S., U. Tenn., 1960, M.S., 1971, Ed.D., 1972. Lic. psychologist, Tenn.; cert. sch. psychologist, Tenn. Adolescent day program dir. Lakeshore Mental Health Inst., Knoxville, Tenn., 1972-73; psychologist U. Tenn. Birth Defects and Human Devel. Ctr., Knoxville, 1973-76, dir. psychol. services, 1976—. Author: Making it Till Friday: A Guide to Successful Classroom Management, 1977, 3d edit., 1985; also articles. Bd. dirs. Blount County Ctr. for Handicapped, Maryville, Tenn., 1975-77. Recipient Outstanding Service award Sertoma Learning Ctr., 1984. Mem. Am. Psychol. Assn., Tenn. Assn. Sch. Psychologists. Lutheran. Avocations: travel; cooking. Office: U Tenn Birth Defects and Human Devel Ctr 1924 Alcoa Hwy Knoxville TN 37920

FRYER, WILLIAM NEAL, psychologist; b. Cin., Mar. 10, 1920; s. Roy Charles and Alice (Carson) F.; B.A., Harding Coll., 1948; M.A., Columbia U., 1953, Ed.D., 1965; m. Dorothy Elizabeth McClain, May 11, 1942; children—Bonnie Jean, Debra Lynn. Aircraft painter Aero. Corp. Am., Cin., 1937-39; salesman Sears, Roebuck & Co., Covington, Ky., 1940-41; minister Bklyn. Ch. of Christ, 1948-56; asst. prof. psychology Abilene (Tex.) Christian Coll., 1956-65, asso. prof., 1965-68, part-time tchr. psychology, 1968-70; chief psychologist Abilene State Sch., 1968-85. Mem. Mayor's Com. on Mental Retardation, Abilene, 1964-65; past mem. exec. com., profl. adviser Abilene Suicide Prevention Service. Bd. dirs., past mem. profl. adv. com. Abilene Assn. Mental Health, pres., 1958-59; past bd. dirs. Tex. Assn. Mental Health. Served to capt. USAAF, 1941-46. Mem. Am., Southwestern, Tex., Abilene (pres. 1978-79) psychol. assns., AAAS, N.Y. Acad. Sci., Am. Assn. Mental Deficiency, Phi Delta Kappa, Kappa Delta Pi. Mem. Ch. of Christ. Club: Kiwanis. Author: (with Orval Filbeck, Max Leach) College, Classroom, Campus, and You, 1959. Home: 833 E North 10th St Abilene TX 79601

FRYREAR, JERRY LEE, psychology educator, clinical psychologist; b. Scotland County, Mo., Apr. 12, 1940; s. Harry Franklin and Loveta Florine (Stice) F.; m. Jo Lyhene, 1963 (div.); m. 2d, Martha Josephine Kennedy, Dec. 1, 1973; 1 son, Benjamin Kennedy. Ph.D., U. Mo., 1971. Lic. psychologist, Tex. Asst. prof. psychology Middle Tenn. State U., 1971-73; asst. prof. psychology Tulane U., New Orleans, 1973-79; assoc. prof. psychology U. Houston, Clear Lake, 1979, now prof. psychology; pvt. practice psychology, Houston, 1971—; co-dir. Inst. Psychosocial Applications of Video and Photography, 1982—. Served with USN, 1960-64. Law Enforcement Assistance Adminstrn. grantee, 1972; NIMH grantee, 1978; U. Houston organized research grantee, 1982-83; NIMH fellow, 1967. Mem. Internat. Phototherapy Assn. (treas.), Am. Psychol. Assn., Internat. Visual Literacy Assn., Psi Chi (cert. outstanding contbns. 1974, 75, 76). Author: (with Fleshman) The Arts in Therapy, 1981; Videotherapy in Mental Health, 1981; (with David Krauss) Phototherapy in Mental Health, 1983; contbr. articles to profl. jours. Home: 1614 Richvale Ln Houston TX 77062 Office: U Houston/Clear Lake 2700 Bay Area Blvd Houston TX 77058

FUCHSMAN, ALVIN ABRAHAM, administration of justice educator; b. Washington, Apr. 17, 1928; s. Albert A. and Florence (Genderson) F.; m. Dorothy Gail Winer, Sept. 30, 1956; children—David Howard, Laura Beth, Michael Brent. B.S., Am. U., 1971; M.S., So. Ill. U., 1975; postgrad. Va. Poly. Inst. and State U. Detective, Arlington County Police, Va., 1954-56, sgt., 1956-63, lt., 1963-68, capt., 1968-78; asst. prof. adminstrn. of justice No. Va. Community Coll., Annandale, 1978-83, assoc. prof., 1984—; adj. lectr. George Mason U., Fairfax County, Va., 1982—; mem. curriculum adv. com. Va. Commonwealth U., Richmond, 1984—; pub. safety communications services subcom., nat. industry adv. com. FCC, Washington, 1970; Del., Dem. State Conv., Virginia Beach, Va., 1980. Recipient Disting. Alumni award Am. U., 1975. Mem. Internat. Assn. Chiefs Police, Va. Assn. Criminal Justice Educators (bd. dirs. 1980—), Acad. Criminal Justice Sci., No. Va. Criminal Justice Acad. (regional oversight com. 1970-75). Jewish. Home: 4011 Thornton St Annandale VA 22003 Office: No Va Community Coll 8333 Little River Turnpike Annandale VA 22003

FUENTE, CLAUDIO JESUS, graphic designer; b. Havana, Cuba, Apr. 16, 1950; came to U.S., 1956, naturalized, 1971; s. Claudio Alberto and Caridad Zenaida (Sanchez) F.; student art and design, Miami (Fla.)-Dade Community Coll., 1970; m. Nancy Mercedes Montaner, Apr. 1980; 1 dau., Natasha Marie. Graphics cons. community service Miami-Dade Community Coll., 1970-71; graphics coordinator community improvement program/community analysis div. Met. Dade County, 1971-75; asst. art dir., graphic technician Met. Dade County Planning Dept., 1975-76, art dir., graphics head, 1976—; coordinator Cycling News, 1978; cons. City of Memphis, 1974; pub. relations coordinator Fla. Cycling Fedn. Mem. employee rev. panel City of Hollywood, 1980. Recipient commendation Met. Dade County Bd. Commrs., 1974; award of excellence Gold Coast chpt. Am. Planners Assn., 1981, Am. Inst. Cert. Planners, 1981. Mem. Omega Tau Delta, Tau Kappa Epsilon. Democrat. Roman Catholic. Home: 6410 W 27th Ln Bldg 19 Apt 104 Hialeah FL 33016 Office: 111 NW 1st St Suite 1220 Miami FL 33128

FUENTES, MARTHA AYERS, playwright; b. Ashland, Ala., Dec. 21, 1923; d. William Henry and Elizabeth (Dye) Ayers; B.A. in English (Ione Lester creative writing award), U. South Fla., 1969; m. Manuel Solomon Fuentes, Apr. 11, 1943. Author plays: The Rebel, 1970; Mama Don't Make Me Go To College, My Head Hurts, 1963; Two Characters in Search of An Agreement, 1970; author fiction: A Cherry Blossom for Miss Chrysanthemum. contbr. articles to local, regional and nat. newspapers, feature articles to nat. mags.; author TV plays and feature articles for children and young adults; lectr., condr. workshops on drama, writing for TV. Recipient George Sergel drama award U. Chgo., 1969. Mem. Authors Guild, Authors League Am., Dramatists Guild, Soc. Children's Book Writers, Southeastern Writers Assn., Am. Theatre Assn., Internat. Women's Writing Guild. Roman Catholic. Club: U. South Fla. Alumni. Home and Office: 102 3d St Belleair Beach FL

FUERTES, RAUL A., psychologist, educator; b. Havana, Cuba, Nov. 4, 1940; came to U.S., 1961; s. Raul and Luisa Elvira (Pichardo) F. B.A., U. Miami, 1967, B.Ed., 1968; M.S., Barry U., 1972; A.A., Miami Dade U., 1977. Acad. dean, dir. admissions Miami Mil. Acad. (Fla.), 1967-74; sch. psychologist, guidance counselor Dade County Pub. Schs., Miami, 1974—; instr. Miami Dade Community Coll., 1980—. Mem. Am. Mental Health Counselors Assn., Am. Assn. Counseling and Devel., Nat. Assn. Sch. Psychologists, Nat. Assn. Soccer Coaches, Guidance Counselors Assn. Fla., Democrat. Roman Catholic. Home: 1705 SW 125th Ct Miami FL 33175 Office: Miami Palmetto Sr High Sch 7460 SW 118th St Miami FL 33156

FUGARO, JOSEPH ANTHONY, JR., training and development company executive; b. Camden, N.J., June 6, 1949; s. Joseph, Sr. and Rose (Bocco) F.; m. Janet Mary Schoellkopf, Apr. 7, 1973; children—Denise, Derek, Dana. B.A. in Psychology, LaSalle U., 1972; Cert. in Spl. Edn., Glassboro U., 1975; M. in Edn., Rutgers U., 1980. Cert. spl. edn. tchr., N.J., cert. prin., N.J., Maine. Probation officer Camden Probation Office, N.J., 1972-73; spl. edn. tchr. Camden Bd. of Edn., 1973-81; vice prin. Bancroft Sch., Haddonfield, N.J., 1981-84, prin., 1984; mgr. tng. and devel. Installation & Dismantle, Stone Mountain, Ga., 1984—. Contbr. articles to profl. jours. Assemblyman aide Camden, 1975; mem. Oaklyn Boro Council, N.J., 1974, Oaklyn Bd. Edn., 1977; baseball coach Oaklyn Little League/Tucker Little League, 1981—. Mem. Am. Soc. Tng. and Devel. (co-editor 1985—), Am. Soc. Schs. and Hosps. Democrat. Roman Catholic. Avocations: sports; reading; woodworking. Office: Installation & Dismantle 1492 Kelton Dr Stone Mountain GA 30084

FUGATE, JOHN LETCHER, educator; b. Richmond, Va., Jan. 11, 1941; s. John Banner and Anna May (Letcher) F.; B.A., U. Richmond, 1963, M.A. (Univ. fellow), 1968; m. Judith Ray Butler, Dec. 26, 1970; 1 son, John Letcher. Tchr., Richmond public schs., Bainbridge Jr. High Sch., 1963-70; instr. Va. Community Coll. System, Lord Fairfax Community Coll., Winchester, 1970-74; asst. prof. English, J. Sargeant Reynolds Community Coll., Richmond, 1974—, also asst. chmn. div. humanities and social scis. Vice-pres. Broad Meadows Civic Assn., 1977-78; pres. R.C. Longan Elem. Sch. Community Council; umpire Amateur Softball Assn. Am., 1971-74, Little League Baseball, 1975-78. Mem. AAUP, Southeastern Conf. Tchrs. English in Two-Year Colls., Va. Assn. Tchrs. English, Tchrs. English in Two-Yr. Coll., Phi Delta Theta. Mem. Ch. of Christ. Club: Spider. Home: 9317 Coleson Rd Glen Allen VA 23060 Office: PO Box 12084 Richmond VA 23241

FUKAI, SHIGEKO NIMIYA, political science educator, researcher, author; b. Tokyo, Feb. 21, 1939; came to U.S., 1964, naturalized, 1977; d. Takeo and Haru (Hongo) Nimiya; m. Junichiro Fukai, Dec. 15, 1964; children—Hiro, James Jiro. LL.B., Chuo U. (Japan), 1961; LL.M., U. Tokyo, 1963; M.A., U. Denver, 1967; Ph.D., U. Tenn., 1977. Instr., Ariz. State U., Tempe, 1972-73; asst. prof. Auburn U., Ala., 1977—; vis. research scholar U. Tokyo, 1982, 83, 84-85, Tsukuba U., Japan, 1983-84. Contbr. articles to profl. jours. Fulbright grantee, 1964; MacLure fellow U. Tenn., 1970; Exxon Corp. research grantee, 1984-85. Mem. Assn. Asian Studies, Am. Polit. Sci. Assn. Home: 711 Sherwood Dr Auburn AL 36830 Office: Dept Polit Sci Auburn U Auburn AL 36849

FULBRIGHT, JAMES, bookstore executive, clergyman; b. McLean, Tex., Sept. 8, 1922; s. Barney E. and Nora B. (McClellan) F.; m. Frances Janet Gibson, Apr. 11, 1948; 1 child, Timothy E. B.S., Abilene Christian U., 1947. Salesman, Sears, Abilene, Tex., 1947-48; acct. Banner Daries, Abilene, 1948-50; minister Ch. of Christ, Abilene, 1952—; mgr. bookstore Abilene Christian U., 1950-85, dir. bookstores, 1985—, also dir. ops. Univ. Press. Sec., treas. Little League, Abilene, 1961-64, Abilene Christian U. Credit Union, 1954—. Served to sgt. U.S. Army, 1942-45, PTO. Named Employee of Year Abilene Christian U. 1977. Mem. Tex. Pubs. Assn., Nat. Assn. Coll. Stores, Southwest Assn. Coll. Stores. Lodge: Kiwanis. Avocations: hunting; collecting Am. Indian artifacts; study southwestern history. Home: 2618 Garfield Abilene TX 79601 Office: Abilene Christian U Bookstore ACU Sta Box 8060 Abilene TX 79699

FULCHER, JAMES VAL, lawyer; b. Teague, Tex., Nov. 28, 1952; s. James Armand and Norma Sue (Coats) F. B.B.A., Sam Houston State U., 1975; J.D., Baylor U., 1978. Bar: Tex. 1978, U.S. Dist. Ct. (we. dist.) Tex. 1981. Sole practice, Teague, 1978-80; ptnr. Keils & Fulcher, Teague, 1980. Bd. dirs. Teague Gen. Hosp. Recipient Service Recognition award Teague Gen. Hosp., 1982. Mem. Tex. State Bar (resolutions com.), ABA, Tex. Trial Lawyers Assn., Phi Delta Phi. Democrat. Baptist. Office: Keils & Fulcher 311 Main St Teague TX 75860

FULKERSON, RAYMOND GERALD, communication educator; b. Owensboro, Ky., Feb. 19, 1941; s. Raymond Riggs and Virginia Lee (Fulkerson) F.; m. Mary Joyce Carter, Aug. 30, 1960; children—Rondel Gregg, Jeffery Todd, Michael Brett. A.A., Freed-Hardeman Coll., 1961; B.A., David Lipscomb Coll., 1963; M.A., U. Ill., 1966, Ph.D., 1971. Instr., Freed-Hardeman Coll., Henderson, Tenn., 1965-70, chmn. dept. communications, 1970—, prof. communications, 1984—; group trainer U. Tenn. Ctr. for Govt. Tng., Jackson, 1980-84. Contbr. articles to profl. jours. Mem. Tenn. Speech Communication Assn. (pres. elect 1984—), So. Speech Communication Assn., Speech Communication Assn., Internat. Soc. for History of Rhetoric, Rhetoric Soc. Am. Democrat. Mem. Ch. of Christ. Avocation: rose growing. Home: Route 1 Box 123 Henderson TN 38340 Office: Freed-Hardeman Coll Henderson TN 38340

FULLER, ANNIE LEE, college laboratory administrator, nurse; b. Travelers Rest, S.C., Jan. 19, 1941; d. Flora Mackey; m. Willie Earl Fuller, Feb. 28, 1961; children—Robert, Roland, Wilynda, Ryan. Cert., Greenville County Sch. Practical Nursing, 1966; Assoc. Applied Sci., Greenville Tech. Coll., 1973. Lic. R.N., S.C. Meat saleslady, cashier Nickle Town Super Market, Greenville, S.C., 1958-61; nurse's aide Dr. Joseph I. Converse, Greenville, 1962-65; lic. practical nurse Greenville Gen. Hosp., 1966-67; staff nurse St. Francis Hosp., Greenville, 1973-77; clin. instr. Greenville Tech. Coll., 1981-83, nursing lab. coordinator, 1983—. Asst., Bible sch. I-85 Ch. of Christ, Greenville, 1974-84, tchr., treas. ch. singers, 1982-83. Republican. Home: 14 Pine Dale Dr Greenville SC 29609 Office: Greenville Tech Coll PO Box 5616 Sta B Greenville SC 29606

FULLER, GERALD RALPH, retired veterinarian; b. Chandler, Ariz., Sept. 8, 1919; s. Horace Ralph and Hortense (McClellan) F.; student Ariz. State U., 1937-39; B.S. in Dairy Husbandry, U. Ariz., 1941; M.S. in Dairy Mfg., Tex. A. and M. U., 1943, D.V.M., 1954; m. Glenda Richardson, June 6, 1941; children—Gerald Ralph, Gilbert R., Barbara Ann (Mrs. Melvin Doyle Shurtz), Glen R., Gordon R., Gene R., Grant R. Instr. agrl. sci. Ariz. State U., Tempe, 1946-50; fed. veterinarian U.S. Dept. Agr., Animal and Plant Health Inspection Service-Meat and Poultry Inspection Program Tex., Ark., Okla., 1953-82. Served to 1st lt. AUS, 1943-46, lt. col. Vet. Corps, Res. Mem. Nat. Assn. Fed. Veterinarians (pres. Okla. chpt. 1974-82), Ariz. Aggie Club (pres. coll. chpt. 1940-41), Ariz. State Future Farmers Am. (pres. 1936-37), Alpha Zeta, Lambda Delta Sigma. Democrat. Mem. Ch. of Jesus Christ of Latter Day Saints. Author: Hoop(e)s Genealogy Book, Vol. 1, 1979, Vols. 2 and 3, 1983. Adamic Lineage, 1968; Ancestors and Descendants of Andrew Lee Allen, 1952. Home: 6612 N Grove Ave Oklahoma City OK 73132 Office: Wilson Co PO Box 24001 Oklahoma City OK 73124

FULLER, THEODORE, JR., educator; b. Hempstead, Tex., Nov. 4, 1937; s. Theodore and Bernice V. (Rutledge) F.; B.S., Prairie View (Tex.) A&M U., 1959, M.Ed., 1980. Tchr. vocat. agr., Richards, Tex., 1960; elem. tchr. Houston Ind. Sch. Dist., 1963—. Served with USAR, 1961-63. Mem. NEA, Nat. Council Tchrs. English, Assn. Childhood Edn., Assn. Supervision and Curriculum Devel., Internat. Reading Assn., Soc. Children's Book Writers, Tex. Tchrs. Assn., Houston Tchrs. Assn., Audubon Soc., Sierra Club, Nature Conservancy. Author feature stories, articles in field. Home: 7709 Claibourne St Houston TX 77016 Office: 10130 Aldine-Westfield St Houston TX 77093

FULLER, THOMAS R., manufacturing company executive; b. Cedar Rapids, Iowa, 1927; B.A., U. Wis.; married. With Thomas Industries Inc., 1950—, v.p. sales residential lighting div., then corp. exec. v.p., 1958-72, pres., 1972—, also chief exec. officer, dir. Mem. Ky. Labor-Mgmt. Adv. Council. Mem. NAM (bd. dirs., regional vice chmn.). Office: Thomas Industries Inc 207 E Broadway Box 35120 Louisville KY 40232

FULLER, TOM ALLEN, business owner, real estate salesman, property manager; b. Oklahoma City, June 18, 1935; s. Guy Edward and Jessie Lorene (Gowin) F. Student U. Okla., 1953-57. Cert. Okla. Bd. Realtors. With Yellow Cab Co. Okla., Inc., Oklahoma City, 1957—, now v.p.; with George Wythe Co. Realtors, Oklahoma City, 1978—, J & T Enterprises, Oklahoma City, 1973—. Bd. dirs. Okla. Symphony Orch.; bd. dirs., v.p. Lyric Theatre; mem. Young Republicans, Okla. Mus. Art, Okla. Hist. Soc. Served with USAF, 1960-62. Mem. Apt. Assn. Okla., Nat. Assn. Taxicab Owners, Jr. C. of C. Methodist. Lodges: Kiwanis Internat., Rotary. Home: 212 NW 18th St Oklahoma City OK 73103 Office: Yellow Cab Co 1414 W Main St Oklahoma City OK 73106

FULLMER, HAROLD MILTON, dental educator; b. Gary, Ind., July 9, 1918; s. Howard and Rachel Eva (Tiedge) F.; m. Marjorie Lucile Engel, Dec. 31, 1942 (dec. May 1983); children—Angela Sue, Pamela Rose; m. Vaneta Rosalyn Truett, Sept. 24, 1983; stepchildren—Vaneta Lynne Windham, Jaimee Truett Windham. B.S., Ind. U., 1942, D.D.S., 1944; D. honoris causa, U. Athens, 1981. Intern, Charity Hosp., New Orleans, 1946-47, resident, 1947-48, vis. dental surgeon, 1948-53; instr. Loyola U., New Orleans, 1948-49, asst. prof., 1949-50, assoc. prof. gen. and oral pathology, 1949-53; cons. pathology VA Hosp.s, Biloxi and Gulfport, Miss., 1950-53; asst. dental surgeon Nat. Inst. Dental Research, NIH, Bethesda, Md., 1953-54, dental surgeon, 1954-56, sr. dental surgeon, 1956-60, dental dir., 1960-70, chief histochemistry Nat. Inst. Dental Research, 1967-70, chief exptl. pathology br., 1969-70, cons. to dir., 1971-72; mem. dental caries program adv. com. HEW, 1975-79, chmn., 1976-79; dir. Inst. Dental Research, 1970; prof. pathology, prof. dentistry, assoc. dean Sch. Dentistry, U. Ala. Med. Ctr., Birmingham, 1970—; sr. scientist cancer research and tng. program Diabetics Research and Tng. Ctr., 1970—, mem. sci. adv. com., 1977—; mem. med. research career devel. com. VA, 1977—; mem. U.S. Congressional Adv. Bd., 1984—. Served to capt. AUS, 1944-46. Recipient Isaac Schour award Internat. Assn. Dental Research, 1973; Fulbright grantee, 1976; Disting. Alumnus of Yr., Ind. U. Sch. Dentistry, 1978; Disting. Alumnus Service award Ind. U., 1981; Nat. Inst. Dental Research grantee, 1970—. Diplomate Am. Bd. Oral Pathology. Fellow Am. Coll. Dentists, Am. Acad. Oral Pathology (v.p. 1984-85, pres. elect 1985-86, pres. 1986-87), AAAS (chmn. sect. 1976-78, sec. sect. 1979—); mem. ADA (cons. Council Dental Research 1973-74), Internat. Assn. Dental Research (v.p. 1974-75, pres. 1976-77), Am. Assn. Dental Research (v.p. 1974-75, pres. 1976-77), Internat. Assn. Pathologists, Internat. Assn. Oral Pathologists (co-founder, 1st pres. 1977-80, editor 1977—), Histochem. Soc., Nat. Soc. Med. Research (dir. 1977-79), Biol. Stain Commn. (trustee 1977—), Commd. Officers Assn. Club: Exchange (pres. New Orleans 1952-53) (Birmingham). Editor: (with R.D. Lillie) Histopathologic Technic and Practical Histochemistry, 1976; cons. editor: Oral Surgery, Oral Medicine, Oral Pathology, 1970; editor, founder Jour. Oral Pathology, 1972—; assoc. editor Jour. Cutaneous Pathology, 1973—; editorial bd. Tissue Reactions, 1976—; cons. editor Gerodontology; contbr. articles to profl. jours. Home: 3514 Bethune Dr Birmingham AL 35223 Office: Med Center Univ Ala Birmingham AL 35294

FULTON, DONALD WILLIAM, JR., bank holding company executive; b. Norfolk, Va., Oct. 22, 1946; s. Donald William and Virginia (Thompson) F.; m. Daniela D. Harlow; children—Jason Andrews, Jonathan Belote. B.S., U. Va., 1968; cert. Va. Sch. Bank Mgmt., 1974, Stonier Grad. Sch. Banking, 1979. Asst. v.p., mgr., Nat. Bank & Trust Co., Lovingston, Va., 1973-79, asst. v.p., Charlottesville, Va., 1971-73, fin. planning officer, 1979-81, sr. fin. planning officer, 1981-82; investor relations officer Jefferson Bankshares, Inc., Charlottesville, 1982-83, v.p. investor relations, 1983—; instr. Am. Inst. Banking, Charlottesville, 1981-83. Mem. Richmond Soc. Fin. Analysts, Securities Assn. Va. Office: Jefferson Bankshares Inc 123 E Main St Charlottesville VA

FULTON, GEORGE HENRY, JR., automobile/truck retail company executive; b. Elkin, N.C., June 24, 1921; s. George Henry and Mamie Clyde (Snow) F.; m. Sally Hart Fishburn, Oct. 17, 1952 (div. Mar. 1981); children—Katherine Nelson, Sally Hart. B.A. magna cum laude, Hampden-Sydney Coll., 1942. Pres., Fulton Motor Co., Fulton Trucks, Inc., Roanoke, Va., 1946—; dir. Colonial Am. Nat. Bank, Roanoke. Bd. dirs. YMCA, Roanoke, 1956-68; trustee Roanoke Meml. Hosps., 1963—. Served to lt. USNR, 1942-46. Recipient Quality Dealer award Chrysler Corp., Roanoke, 1957. Republican. Presbyterian. Clubs: Shenandoah (pres. 1968-69), Hunting Hills Country (bd. dirs. 1970—), Country of N.C. Home: Roanoke VA Office: Fulton Motor Co Inc PO Box 8600 Roanoke VA 24014

FULTON, LYMAN AVARD, financial planner, insurance underwriter; b. Johnson City, Tenn., Dec. 25, 1957; s. Lyman A. and Patricia S. F. A.A., Lee's McRae Coll., 1979; B.B.A., U. Miss., 1982. Underwriter, Equitable Life Assurance Soc. of U.S., Johnson City, 1982—. Mem. Nat. Assn. of Security Dealers, Nat. Assn. of Life Underwriters, Gamma Iota Sigma. Republican. Presbyterian. Home: PO Box 4016 Johnson City TN 37602 Office: 208 Sunset Dr Suite 404 First Am Bank Plaza Johnson City TN 37601

FULTON, RICHARD HARMON, mayor; b. Nashville, Jan. 27, 1927; s. Lyle Houston and Labina (Plummer) F.; student U. Tenn., 1946-47; m. Jewel Simpson, Dec. 23, 1945 (dec.); children—Richard, Michael, Barry (dec.), Donna, Linda; m. 2d, Sandra Fleisher; stepchildren—Cynthia Fleisher, Charles Fleisher. Real estate broker Fulton & Riddle Realty Co., Nashville, mem. Tenn. Senate, 1959-60; mem. 88th-94th Congresses, 5th Tenn. Dist.; mayor City of Nashville, 1977—. Served with USNR, 1945-46. Democrat. Methodist. Clubs: Masons, Shrine. Office: Metropolitan Courthouse Nashville TN 37201*

FUNDERBURG, CRAIG SLATON, psychology educator; b. Phila., Feb. 1, 1952; s. Lonnie William and Mary Elizabeth (Walker) F.; m. B.J. Burch, Dec. 17, 1983. B.S., U. Ala.-University, 1975, M.A., 1975, B.S., 1976, Ph.D., 1980. Grad. asst. U. Ala., 1977-80; asst. prof. Campbellsville Coll., Ky., 1980—; child evaluator city schs., Campbellsville, 1984—, DeKalb County, Ala., 1978-79. Served with Army N.G., 1978—. Mem. Am. Psychol. Assn., Am. Assn. Counseling Devel., Am. Mental Health Counselors, Counseling Psychology. Baptist. Avocations: weight training; hiking; woodworking. Home: 2808A 10th Ct S Birmingham AL 35205

FUNDERBURK, ELEANOR JO, all terrain vehicle company executive, realtor; b. Monroe, La., Mar. 31, 1943; d. Hugh Franklin and Clotea Elizabeth (Mayes) Calhoun; m. Robert Andrew Heacock, Aug. 25, 1961 (dec. July 1963); m. 2d, Shelby Dean Funderburk, Dec. 29, 1964. Grad. Real Estate, Inst. Sales clk. S.H. Kress, Monroe, La., 1958-61; receptionist/sec. Dr. R.E. Harvey, Monroe, 1961-63; sec. Rivers Ford, Monroe, 1963-64; teller, sec. Ouachita Bank, Monroe, 1964-66; inventory control clk., sec. Olinkraft, Inc., West Monroe, 1966-70, sec., 1970-78; sec., treas. Funderburk 3-Wheeler, Monroe, 1980—; realtor Century 21 Roberts Realty, Monroe, 1978—. Patentee tire demounting device. Mem. Monroe West Monroe Bd. Realtors (Saleswoman award 1978, 79, Lister of Month, 1978-79), Monroe C. of C., La. Realtors, Nat. Realtors Assn. Democrat. Baptist. Clubs: Ouachita Tennis (Monroe); U.S. Tennis Assn. (N.Y.C.).

FUNDERBURK, (HENRY) HANLY, JR., botany educator, university president; b. Carrollton, Ala., June 19, 1931; s. Henry Hanly and Mary (Ferguson) F.; B.S. in Agrl. Sci., Auburn (Ala.) U., 1953, M.S. in Botany, 1958; Ph.D. in Plant Physiology, La. State U., 1961; m. Helen Hanson, July 26, 1953; children—Debra Elaine Funderburk Dahl, Kenneth Cliff. Mem. faculty Auburn U., 1961—, prof. botany and plant physiology, 1967—, Alumni prof., 1967—, asst. dean Grad. Sch., 1967-68, v.p., chief adminstrv. officer, then chancellor, Montgomery, 1968-80, pres., Auburn 1980-83, also dir. govt. and community affairs, 1983-84; pres. Eastern Ky. U., Richmond, 1985—; investigator grants and contracts, NIH, Dept. Interior, Dept. Agr. Mem. Auburn C. of C., Sigma Xi, Phi Kappa Phi, Alpha Zeta, Gamma Sigma Delta, Omicron Delta Kappa. Address: Eastern Ky U Coates Box 1-A Richmond KY 40475

FUNDORA, RAQUEL (FERNÁNDEZ, poet, writer; b. Bolondrón, Cuba, May 19, 1924; came to U.S., 1959; d. Gerardo Francisco and Carolina (Fernández) Fundora; m. Roberto Rodríguez de Aragón, Sept. 14, 1951; children—Pepín, Lianne, Raquel Aurora. Grad. in Bus. Adminstrn., Immaculada Sch., Havana, Cuba, 1948. Collections of poems include: Nostalgia Inconsolable, 1973, El Canto del Viento, 1983; contbr. poetry to lit. mags., 1970-84. Recipient Diploma of Honor Lincoln-Marti, HEW, 1973; Juan J. Remos, Cruzada Educativa Cubana, 1975; Cert. of Appreciation City of Miami, 1976, Miami Cuban Lions Club, 1980. Mem. Circulo de Cultura Panamericano (pres. Miami chpt. 1982-85, chmn. cultural congress U. Miami 1983-85), Grupo Artístico Literario Abril, Poets and Writers, Latin C. of C. of U.S.A. (founder, 1st dir. Camacol Library 1980). Roman Catholic. Club: Big Five (Miami, Fla.). Home and Office: 935 SW 24th Rd Miami FL 33129

FUNK, GARY LLOYD, control engineer; b. Fairfax, Okla., Oct. 12, 1945; s. George N. and Maymie Lou (Harrell) F.; B.S., Rose Hulman Inst. Tech., 1966; M.S., Purdue U., 1969; Ph.D., U. Pitts., 1974. Research engr. systems control div. Gulf Research & Devel. Co., Harmarville, Pa., 1969-72, engr. exploration div. on systems and instrumentation, 1972-75; systems and control engr. Applied Automation subs. Phillips Petroleum Co., Bartlesville, Okla., 1975, mem. process tech. div., 1975-77, sr. process control engr. computer systems, 1977-83, prin. engr., 1983—. Precinct chmn. Democratic Com., 1981. Registered profl. engr., Okla. Mem. Okla. Soc. Profl. Engrs. (v.p. 1980-81, 82-83), IEEE, Am. Inst. Chem. Engrs. (pres. chpt. 1983-84), Nat. Soc. Profl. Engrs., Jaycees. Presbyterian. Clubs: Masons, Moose, Elks, Kiwanis. Contbr. articles to profl. jours.; patentee in field. Home: 600 S 6th St Fairfax OK 74637 Office: 225 E & A Bldg Pawhuska Rd Bartlesville OK 74004

FUNK, R. WILLIAM, business executive; b. Uniontown, Pa.; m. Ann Marie. B.A., Calif. State Coll., 1970; M.A. in Govt., Ohio U., 1972; M.S. in Indsl. Relations, Purdue U., 1974. With employee relations, labor relations, marine dept. Exxon Co. U.S.A., Houston, 1974-80; assoc. Heidrick & Struggles, Houston, 1980-82, ptnr., dir., v.p., mgr., 1982—. Office: Heidrick & Struggles 3690 Republic Bank Ctr Houston TX 77002

FUNKHOUSER, A. PAUL, transportation holding company executive; b. Roanoke, Va., Mar. 8, 1923; s. Samuel King and Jane Harwood (Cocke) F.; m. Eleanor Rosalie Gamble, Feb. 4, 1950; children—John Paul, Eleanor K. Funkhouser Doar. B.A., Princeton U., 1945; LL.B., U. Va., 1950. Bar: Va. 1951. Assoc. Hunton, Williams, Anderson, Gay & Moore, Richmond, 1950-52; from solicitor to asst. gen. counsel Norfolk & Western Ry. Co., 1952-63; asst. v.p. coal and ore traffic to sr. v.p. sales and mktg. Pa. R.R., and successor Penn Central Transp. Co., Phila., 1963-75; sr. v.p., exec. v.p., pres. Seaboard Coast Line Industries, Jacksonville, Fla., 1975-80; chief exec. officer Family Lines R.R. System (later Seaboard System R.R.), Jacksonville, Fla., 1980-82, now dir.; pres. CSX Corp., Richmond, Va., 1982—, also dir.; dir. N.Y. Corp., Universal Leaf Tobacco Co.; Served with AUS, 1943-46. Mem. Order of Coif, Phi Beta Kappa, Delta Psi, Phi Delta Phi, Omicron Delta Kappa. Episcopalian. Clubs: Laurel Valley Golf (Ligonier, Pa.); Princeton, Union League (N.Y.C.); Metropolitan (Washington); Ponte Vedra (Fla.); Country of Va., Commonwealth (Richmond). Office: CSX Corp 701 E Byrd St Richmond VA 23219

FUQUA, DON, Congressman; b. Jacksonville, Fla., Aug. 20, 1933; s. J.D. and Lucille (Langford) F.; B.S. in Agrl. Econs., U. Fla., 1957; LL.D. (hon.), U. Notre Dame; D.Sc. (hon.), Fla. Inst. Tech.; children—Laura, John. Mem. Fla. Ho. of Reps. from Calhoun County, 1958-62; mem. 88th-98th Congresses from 2d Dist. Fla., chmn. com. sci. and tech., 1979—. Trustee, Fla. Sheriffs Boys Ranch, Rodeheaver Boys Ranch. Served with AUS. Named one of five outstanding young men in Fla., Fla. Jaycees, 1963; recipient Disting. Alumnus award U. Fla., 1971. Mem. Future Farmers Am. (pres. Fla., 1950-51), Red Cross Constantine, Am. Legion, Fla. Blue Key, Fla. State Gold Key, Alpha Gamma Rho. Presbyterian (elder). Clubs: Elks, Woodmen of World, Masons (32 deg.), Shriners, Jesters, Rotary (sec. Blountstown, Fla.). Office: 2269 Rayburn House Office Bldg Washington DC 20515

FUQUA, JOHN BROOKS, diversified conglomerate executive; b. Prince Edward County, Va., June 26, 1918; s. J.B. Elam and Ruth Fuqua; m. Dorothy Chapman, Feb. 10, 1945; 1 son, J. Rex. Student pub. schs., Va.; LL.D., Hampden-Sydney Coll., 1972, Duke U., 1973; L.H.D. (hon.), Fla. Meml. Coll., 1982. Chmn., chief exec. officer Fuqua Industries, Inc., Atlanta, 1965—; chmn. bd. Triton Group, Ltd., 1983—; mem. adv. bd. Central of Ga. R.R.; dir. Ga. Fed. Bank, Kaneb Services, Inc. Mem. Ga. Ho. of Reps., 1957-62, chmn. banking com., 1959-62; mem. Ga. Senate, 1963-64, chmn. banking and fin. coms., 1963-64; chmn. Democratic Exec. Com. Ga., 1962-66; trustee Duke U., 1974—; Hampden-Sydney Coll., 1976—; past mem., fin. chmn. Augusta Hosp. Authority; past mem. Ga. Sci. and Tech. Commn.; bd. visitors Emory U., 1970-76; mem. Augusta Aviation Commn., 1945-67. Recipient Broadcaster Citizen of Year, Ga. Assn. Broadcasters, 1963; Ga. Pioneer in Broadcasting award, 1979; Horatio Alger award, 1984; award of merit U. Pa. Wharton Entrepreneurial Ctr., 1985; Fuqua Sch. of Bus., Duke U., named in his honor, 1980. Mem. World Bus. Council, Chief Execs. Orgn., Conf. Bd., Atlanta C. of C. (past pres.), Horatio Alger Assn. Disting. Ams. (bd. dirs.). Office: Fuqua Industries Inc 4900 Ga Pacific Ctr Atlanta GA 30303

FUQUA, TESSIE HAND, corporation executive; b. Oakland, Calif., July 25, 1938; d. Clyde Vincent and Johnsey Juanita (Lee) Hand; m. Clyde Olan Watts, July 20, 1958 (div. Apr. 1973); children—Tessie Lauretta, Clyde Olan II, Kelly Elizabeth, Scarlett Juanita, Rachael Abigail; m. James Kenneth Fuqua, Aug. 31, 1984. Student pub. schs., Calif., Ala. Exec. sec. Fort McClennan, Anniston, Ala., 1973-76; co-owner, co-operator Holland Tire & Service, Anniston, 1976-79; sales assoc. Harris-McKay Real Estate, Anniston, 1978-81; dept. head Hudson's Dept. Store, Anniston, 1979-81; sr. clk. material control dept. FMC Corp., Anniston, 1981—. Chmn. North Talladega Cancer Crusade, Ala., 1962; sec. Talladega County Hist. Soc., Ala., 1964-73; pres., 1973-74; pres. Talladega Federated Garden Clubs, 1965; past mem. Ala. Real Estate Commn.; prayer chmn. Women's Missionary Union, Talladega, 1964, circle pres., 1965-67. Recipient Achievement award State of Ala., 1968. Mem. Ala. Hist. Assn. Republican. Baptist. Club: Pilot (sec. 1960-62) (Talladega). Home: 19 Dawvon Terr Anniston AL 36201 Office: FMC Corp 2101 W 10th St Anniston AL 36201

FUREY, JAMES JOSEPH, manufacturing company executive; b. Pitts., Feb. 13, 1938; s. James Joseph and Kathleen (Adams) F.; B.B.A., LaSalle Coll., 1970; m. Andree Chalumeau, Dec. 2, 1958; children—Arleen, James, Renee, Philippe. Indsl. engr. Standard Pressed Steel Co., Jenkintown, Pa., 1959-69; plant supt. Henry Troemner, Inc., Phila., 1969-70; cons. Booz, Allen & Hamilton, Inc., N.Y.C., 1970-72, asso., 1972-74, asso., Dallas, 1974-77, prin., 1977-79; v.p. mfg. Purolater Inc., Rahway, N.J., 1979-80; pres. Purolator Technologies, Inc., Newbury Park, Calif., 1980; pres. James Furey & Assos., Inc., Mgmt. Cons., Dallas, 1981—. Served with USAF, 1955-59. Republican. Roman Catholic. Home: 2800 Quail Ridge Carrollton TX 75006 Office: 17060 Dallas Pkwy Dallas TX 75248

FURGIUELE, MARGERY WOOD, educator; b. Munden, Va., Sept. 28, 1919; d. Thomas Jarvis and Helen Godfrey (Ward) Wood; B.S., Mary Washington Coll., 1941; postgrad. U. Ala., 1967-68, Catholic U. Am., 1974-76, 80; m. Albert William Furgiuele, June 19, 1943; children—Martha Jane Furgiuele MacDonald, Harriet Randolph. Advt. and reservations sec. Hilton's Vacation Hide-A Way, Moodus, Conn., 1940; sec. TVA, Knoxville, 1941-43; adminstrv. asst., ct. reporter Moody AFB, Valdosta, Ga., 1943-44; tchr. bus. Edenton (N.C.) High Sch., 1944-45; tchr. bus., coordinator Culpeper (Va.) County High Sch., 1958-82; ret., 1982; tchr. Piedmont Tech. Edn. Center, 1970—. Co-leader Future Bus. Leaders Am., Culpeper, mem. state bd., 1979-82; state advisor 1978-79, Va. Bus. Edn. Assn. Com. chmn., 1978-79. Certified geneal. record Searcher. Mem. Nat., Va. bus. edn. assns., Am., Va. vocat. assns., Smithsonian Assos. Club: Country (Culpeper). Home: 1630 Stonybrook Ln Culpeper VA 22701

FURMAN, HOWARD, lawyer, federal mediator; b. Newark, Nov. 30, 1938; s. Emanuel and Lilyan (Feldman) F.; m. Elaine Sheitleman, June 12, 1960 (div. 1982); children—Deborah Toby, Naomi N'chama, David Seth; m. 2d Janice Wheeler, Jan. 14, 1984. B.A. in Econs., Rutgers U., 1966; J.D. cum laude, Birmingham Sch. Law, 1985. Designer/draftsman ITT, Nutley, N.J., 1957-61; personnel mgr. Computer Products Inc., Belmar, N.J., 1962-64, Arde Engring. Co., Newark, 1964-66; econs. instr. Rutgers U., New Brunswick, N.J., 1966-74; dir. indsl. relations Harvard Ind. Frequency Engring. Labs. Div., Farmingdale, N.J., 1966-74; commr. Fed. Mediation and Conciliation Service, Birmingham, Ala., 1974—. Pres. Ocean Twp. Police Res. (N.J.), 1968. Recipient ofcl. commendation Fed. Mediation and Conciliation Service, 1979, 81, 82. Mem. Soc. Profls. in Dispute Resolution, Fed. Soc. Labor Relations Profls., Sigma Delta Kappa. Jewish. Lodges: Elks, Masons, B'nai B'rith. Home: 900 Kathryne Circle Birmingham AL 35215 Office: Fed Mediation and Conciliation Service 2015 2d Ave N Suite 102 Birmingham AL 35203

FURNESS, CAROLYN VIRGINIA, nursing administrator; b. Everett, Mass., Jan. 19, 1923; d. Howard Francis Furness and Adeline (Proctor) Furness Wendelstein. A.A., Colby Jr., Coll., 1943; Nursing diploma Mass. Gen. Hosp., Boston, 1946; B.S. in Nursing, U. Iowa, 1957; M.S. in Nursing, Boston U., 1961. Pub. health nurse Vis. Nurses Assn., Pittsfield, Mass., 1957-60; program coordinator United Cerebral Palsy of South Shore of Mass., Quincy, 1961-62; supr. Mass. Vis. Nurse Assn., Springfield, 1962-63, exec. dir., 1963-66; dir. nursing services Combined Pub. Health Nursing Service, East Hartford, Conn., 1966-77; exec. dir. nursing A.G. Holley State Hosp., Lantana, Fla., 1977. Mem. editorial bd. Conn. Nursing News Mag., 1966-72. Served as flight nurse USAF, 1950-54, Korea; lt. col. Res. ret. Mem. Am. Nurses Assn. (cert. of service 1972), Nat. League Nursing, Conn. Nurses Assn. (pub. relations chmn. 1966-72), Western Mass. League for Nursing (treas. 1964-66), Nutmeggar Camera Club (v.p. travel 1975-77). Republican. Unitarian. Lodge: Eastern Star. Home: 339-A-2 Knotty Pine Circle Lake Worth FL 33463 Office: AG Holley State Hosp PO Box 3084 Lantana FL 33465

FURNISS, LEESA DIANNE, medical services company executive; b. Asheville, N.C., May 8, 1956; d. Douglas James and Georgia Lucille (Ledbetter) F. B.S. in Pharmacy, U. N.C., 1979; Pharm.D., U. Mo.-Kansas City, 1980, clin. residency, 1981. Asst. prof. U. S.C., Columbia, 1981-83; coordinator Palmetto Poison Ctr., Columbia, 1981-83; asst. dir. med. services Glaxo, Inc., Research Triangle Park, N.C., 1983—. Author: (with J. Elenbaas) Drugdex, 1980; also articles. Mem. Am. Soc. Hosp. Pharmacists, Rho Chi. Democrat. Baptist. Avocations: piano; organ; photography. Home: 9825 Gralyn Rd Raleigh NC 27612 Office: Glaxo Inc 5 Moore Dr Research Triangle Park NC 27609

FURR, O(LIN) FAYRELL, JR., lawyer; b. Clinton, S.C., Jan. 19, 1943; s. Olin Fayrell and Helen Ella (Osborn) F.; m. Ann Longwell, June 10, 1967 (div.); 1 dau., Sara Shannon; m. Karole Jensen, Apr. 1, 1983. B.S., U.S.C., 1965, J.D., 1968. Bars: S.C. 1968, U.S. Dist. Ct. S.C., 1968, U.S. Ct. Appeals (4th cir.) 1982, (5th cir.) 1977, U.S. Supreme Ct. 1977; cert. Nat. Bd. Trial Advocacy, 1984. Mem. Law Offices of Kermit S. King, Columbia, S.C., 1973-77; ptnr. King & Furr, Columbia, 1977-79; sole practice law, Columbia, 1980—; lectr. various univs. Pres. bd. dirs. Contact Help, 1975-76; bd. dirs. Appelate Pub. Defender Orgn., 1980. Served to capt. JAGC, U.S. Army, 1968-73. Decorated Bronze Star. Mem. S.C. Trial Lawyers Assn. (pres. 1979-80; most valuable mem. 1974), S.C. Bar Assn., Assn. Trail Lawyers Am. (state committeeman 1978-79), Richland County Bar Assn., Horry County Bar Assn. Democrat. Baptist. Editor, S.C. Trial Lawyers Bull., 1974-77; contbr. articles to profl. jours. Address: 8106 Beach Dr Myrtle Beach SC 29577

FURR, RICHARD CARR, electrical engineer; b. Staunton, Va., Oct. 14, 1953; s. Charles E. and Julie (Spitzer) F.; m. Nancy Moore, Aug. 18, 1984. B.S.E.E., Va. Tech., 1980. Computer programmer Va. Tech., 1976-78; asst. lab. supr. Va. Tech., 1978-80, supr. computer engring. lab., 1980-81; project engr. Indsl. Drives Div., Kollmorgen Corp., Radford, Va., 1981—; office automation cons.; math tutor. Deacon, First Presbyn. Ch., Staunton, Va., 1971. Recipient Va. Safe Pilot award, 1982. Mem. IEEE, Internat. Soc. Hybrid Microelectronics. Republican. Club: Hokie Flying (v.p.). Contbr. articles to profl. jours. Home: 708 Southgate Dr Blacksburg VA 24060 Office: 201 Rock Rd Radford VA 24143

FURRH, JAMES BROOKE, JR., oil company executive; b. Marshall, Tex., Apr. 13, 1926; s. James Brooke and Margaret (Hagan) F.; m. Mary Leigh Hendee, July 24, 1954; children—James Brooke III, Roy Hendee, Leigh Hagan. B.A. U. Tex., 1948, B.S., 1950. Geologist Ohio Oil Co., Jackson, Miss., 1954-60; owner, operator ind. oil producing cos., Jackson, Miss., 1960—; co-owner, prin. Energy Drilling Co., Natchez, Miss., 1980—; owner, prin. Centennial Oil & Mineral Co., Jackson, 1970—. Sec. Diners of the South, Jackson, 1978-83; del. Republican Nat. Conv., Dallas, 1984; presdl. elector Miss. Rep. Orgn., 1980, 84, fin. chmn. 1985; chmn. Sabine River Compact Adminstrn. Served to 1st lt. USAF, 1951-53. Mem. Mid-Continent Oil and Gas Assn. (chmn. 1982-84), Ind. Petroleum Assn. Am. (bd. dirs. 1981-84, v.p. 1985), Am. Assn. Petroleum Geologists, Miss. Geol. Soc., Kappa Sigma. Republican. Presbyterian. Clubs: Country of Jackson, Capital City Petroleum (bd. dirs. 1980-83), River Hills (bd. dirs. 1978-80) (Jackson). Avocations: tennis, travel. Home: 4015 Boxwood Circle Jackson MS 39211 Office: 1212 Capital Towers Jackson MS 39201

FURST, ALEX JULIAN, thoracic and cardiovascular surgeon; b. Augusta, Ga., Dec. 21, 1938; m. George Alex and Ann (Segall) F.; student U. Fla., 1963; M.D., U. Miami, 1967; m. Elayne Kobrin, Aug. 11, 1962; children—James Andrew, Jeffrey Michael, Joseph Robert. Intern, U. Miami Hosp., 1967-68, resident, 1968-72, clin. instr. dept. surgery, 1974—; chief resident in thoracic and cardiovascular surgery Emory U. Hosp., Atlanta, 1972-73; sr. surg. registrar of thoracic unit Hosp. for Sick Children, London, 1973-74; practice medicine specializing in thoracic and cardiovascular surgery, Miami, Fla.; chief thoracic surgery, pres. med. staff Mercy Hosp.; mem. staff Bapt. Hosp., South Miami Hosp., Doctor's Hosp. (all Miami), North Ridge Gen. Hosp., Ft. Lauderdale. Served with U.S. Army, 1958-60. Fellow Am. Coll. Cardiology, Am. Coll. Chest Physicians, A.C.S.; mem. Dade County Med. Assn., Fla. Med. Assn., Heart Assn. Greater Miami, Soc. Thoracic Surgeons, So. Thoracic Surg. Assn. Office: 3661 S Miami Ave Suite 609 Miami FL 33133 also 8740 N Kendall Dr Suite 215 Miami FL 33176

FURST, EDWARD JOSEPH, educator; b. Chgo., Dec. 23, 1919; s. Joseph and Elizabeth (Pratscher) F.; m. Helene Mae Rowe, Aug. 26, 1951; children—Linda Ann, Donald Edward, Kenneth Lee. A.B., U. Chgo., 1941, M.A., 1947, Ph.D., 1948. Asst. chief to chief evaluation and exams div. U. Mich., Ann Arbor, 1948-56; assoc. prof. psychology U. Idaho, Moscow, 1956-61; assoc. prof. psychology Ohio State U., Columbus, 1961-66, co-dir. cooperative research project, 1963-66; prof., program coordinator U. Ark., Fayetteville, 1966—; cons. editor Jour. of Experimental Edn., 1967—; research editor Jour. of Staff Program and Orgn. Devel., 1983—. Author: Constructing Evaluation Instruments, 1958. Co-author: Taxonomy of Educational Objectives, 1956, Development of Economics Curricular Materials, 1966. Served to capt. U.S. Army, 1942-46. Fellow Am. Psychol. Assn.; mem. Am. Ednl. Research Assn., Mid-S. Ednl. Research Assn., Evaluation Network, Southwestern Philosophy of Edn. Soc. Avocations: travel; hiking. Home: 1729 Greenvalley Ave Fayetteville AR 72703 Office: U Ark Graduate Education 206 Fayetteville AR 72701

FURST, MARIAN JUDITH, geologist; b. Chgo., Jan. 12, 1950. B.A. in Chemistry, Reed Coll., 1972; S.M. in Inorganic Chemistry, U. Chgo., 1973; Ph.D. in Geochemistry, Calif. Inst. Tech., 1979. Geologist, mem. profl. staff Schlumberger-Doll Research, Ridgefield, Conn., 1979-82; well log analyst Schlumberger Well Services, Houston and Dallas, 1982-84, geologist U.S-.A.-East, Dallas, 1984-85, U.S.A.-Land, 1985—. Contbr. articles to profl. publs. Mem. Am. Assn. Petroleum Geologists, Soc. Profl. Well Log Analysts, Assn. Women Geoscientists, AAAS, Sigma Xi. Office: Schlumberger Well Services 4100 Spring Valley Rd #600 Dallas TX 75244

FUTCH, TOMMY RAY, health service corporation executive, pulmonary physiologist; b. Jacksonville, Fla., Dec. 8, 1951; s. Charleston Harris and Barbara Ann (Whidden) F.; m. Virginia Ann Thweatt, Sept. 11, 1976; children—Bradley Allen, Branden Wesley. B.S., Fla. Tech. U., 1974; M.B.A., Nova U., 1981. Registered respiratory therapist, physician/asst.; lic. lab. technologist. Dir. cardiopulmonary Fla. Med. Ctr., Fort Lauderdale, 1976-77, adminstr. profl. services, 1977-82, Southeastern Med. Ctr., North Miami Beach, Fla., 1982; regional adminstr. Rehab. Hosp. Services, Fort Lauderdale, 1982-85, v.p., 1985—; chmn. bd. Sunrise Hosp., Ft. Lauderdale; dir. Fla. Assn. Rehab. Facilities, Tallahassee; del. Fla. Renal Adminstrs., Tamapa, 1981. Contbr. articles to profl. jours. Trustee Am. Lung Assn., Ft. Lauderdale, 1977-80; mem. adv. council Broward Community Coll., Ft. Lauderdale, 1976-82; mem. Southeast Air Quality Council, Ft. Lauderdale, 1978. Mem. Am. Coll. Hosp. Adminstrs., Am. Health Planning Assn., Am. Hosp. Assn., Internat. Assn. Rehab. Facilities, Nat. Assn. Rehab. Facilities, Broward County C. of C. Democrat. Presbyterian. Office: Rehab Hosp Services Corp 4399 Nob Hill Rd Fort Lauderdale FL 33321

FUTRELL, JOHN WILLIAM, lawyer; b. Alexandria, La., July 6, 1935; s. J.W. and Sarah Ruth (Hitesman) F.; B.A., Tulane U., 1957; Fulbright scholar Free U. Berlin, 1958; LL.B., Columbia U., 1965; m. Iva Macdonald, Aug. 13, 1966; children—Sarah, Daniel. Admitted to La. bar, 1966; atty. firm Lemle & Kelleher, New Orleans, 1966-71; prof. law U. Ala. Law Sch., 1971-74, U. Ga. Law Sch., 1974-80; Woodrow Wilson fellow Smithsonian Instn., 1979-80; pres. Environ. Law Inst., Washington, 1980—; lectr. Dept. State in Japan and India, 1978. Pres., Sierra Club, San Francisco, 1977-78, nat. dir., 1971-81; del. UN Conf. on Water, 1977, White House Conf. Inflation, 1974; bd. dirs. Keystone Ctr., Colo. Served as officer USMC, 1957-62. Mem. ABA, Am. Law Inst., AAAS, Phi Beta Kappa, Order of Coif. Club: Cosmos (Washington). Address: 4600 N 7th St Arlington VA 22203

FUTRELL, PATRICIA SIMMONS, public relations administrator; b. Oklahoma City, Nov. 7, 1955; d. William Donald and Maud (Mims) Simmons; m. Edison Leon Futrell, Mar. 5, 1977; 1 child, Lauren Elizabeth. B.A. magna cum laude in Journalism, Miss. U. for Women; M.Journalism, U. Md., 1978. News reporter Starkville Daily News, Miss., 1976-77; grad. teaching asst. U. Md., College Park, 1977-78; dir. pub. relations So. Tech. Inst., Marietta, Ga., 1979-83, spl. projects coordinator, 1983—. Pre-sch. tchr. First Baptist Ch., Atlanta, 1983—. Mem. Council for Advancement and Support of Edn. Avocations: photography; needlework; bicycling. Home: 1196 Laurel Log Pl Austell GA 30001 Office: 1112 Clay St Marietta GA 30060

FUTRELL, ROBERT FRANK, historian; b. Waterford, Miss., Dec. 15, 1917; s. James Chester and Sarah Olivia (Brooks) F.; B.A. with distinction, U. Miss., 1938, M.A., 1939; Ph.D. in History, Vanderbilt U., 1950; m. Marie Elizabeth Grimes, Oct. 8, 1944; m. 2d, Jo Ann McGowan Ellis, Dec. 15, 1980. Spl. cons. U.S. War Dept., Washington, 1946; historian USAF Hist. Office, Washington, 1946-49; asso. prof. mil. history Air U., Maxwell AFB, Ala., 1950-51, prof., 1951-71, sr. historian, 1971-74, prof. emeritus mil. history, 1974—; professorial lectr. George Washington U., 1963-68; guest lectr. Air U. Squadron Officer Sch., Air Command and Staff Coll., Air War Coll., Army War Coll., 1951—; vis. prof. mil. history Airpower Research Inst., Ctr. for Aerospace Doctrine Research and Edn., Air U., 1982-85, hist. advisor to USAF project Corona Harvest, 1969-74. Served from pvt. to capt. USAAF, 1941-45, lt. col. Res. ret. Recipient Meritorious Civilian Service award Air Force, 1970, Exceptional Civilian Service decoration Sec. Air Force, 1973. Mem. Ala. Hist. Assn., SAR (pres. Montgomery County chpt. 1971-74), So. Hist. Assn., Air Force Hist. Found. (mem. editorial advisors 1969-81, trustee 1985—), Inst. Mil. Affairs, Phi Eta Sigma, Pi Kappa Pi. Methodist. Author: Ideas, Concepts, Doctrine: A History of Basic Thinking in the United States Air Force, 1907-1964, 2 vols., 1971, rev. edit. 2 vols. 1907-84, 1985; The United States Air Force in Korea, 1950-53, 1961; The United States Air Force in Southeast Asia, The Advisory Years to 1965, 1981; (with Wesley Frank Craven, James L. Cate) The Army Air Force in World War II, 1948-58; contbr. chpts. to hist. books, articles to scholarly publs. Address: 1871 Hill Hedge Dr Montgomery AL 36106 also 908 Lynwood Dr Montgomery AL 36111

FYNES, WILLIAM AUSTIN, home building executive; b. Phila., Mar. 3, 1935; s. William Austin and Helen B. Fynes; m. Joan K. Kernan, May 30, 1960; children—Meg, William III, Eugene, Molly, Chris. B.S., LaSalle Coll., 1957; M.B.A., Temple U., 1968. With Johnson & Johnson, 1964-80, dir. tng. and devel., New Brunswick, N.J., 1970-78, SW region mgr., Dallas, 1978-80; dir. tng. Redman Industries, Dallas, 1980-83, dir. mktg., 1983—. Author, producer videotape How To Manuals. Active local homeowners' assns. Served with U.S. Army, 1957-58. Mem. Nat. Soc. Sales Tng. Execs. (chmn. nominations com. 1985), Am. Soc. for Tng. and Devel., Am. Mktg. Assn., Meeting Planners Internat. Republican. Roman Catholic. Club: Canyon Creek Country (Richardson, Tex.). Avocations: tennis; jogging. Home: 234 Shady Hill St Richardson TX 75080 Office: Redman Industries 2550 Walnut Hill Ln Dallas TX 75229

GABEL, GEORGE DESAUSSURE, JR., lawyer; b. Jacksonville, Fla., Feb. 14, 1940; s. George DeSaussure and Juanita (Brittain) G.; m. Judith Kay Adams, July 21, 1962; children—Laura Elizabeth, Meredith Rion. A.B., Davidson Coll., 1961; J.D., U. Fla., 1964. Bar: Fla. 1964, D.C. 1972. Mem. firm Toole, Taylor, Moseley, Gabel & Milton, Jacksonville, 1966-74, Wahl and Gabel, Jacksonville, 1974—; mem. Fla. Jud. Nominating Commn., 4th Circuit, 1982—. Pres. Willing Hands, Inc., 1971-72; chmn. N.E. Fla. March of Dimes, 1974-75; mem. budget com. United Way, 1972-74, chmn. rev. com., 1976; bd. dirs. Central and South brs. YMCA, 1973-79, Camp Immokalee, 1982—; elder Riverside Presbyterian Ch., 1970-77, 80—, clk. session, 1975-76, 86—; pres. Riverside Presbyn. Day Sch., 1977-79; chmn. Nat. Eagle Scout Assn., 1974-75; bd. dirs., v.p. adminstrn, chmn. long range planning com. N. Fla. Boy Scouts Am., 1974—, Silver Beaver award, 1978; mem. Jacksonville Council on Citizen Involvement, 1976-79; trustee Davidson Coll., 1984—. Served to capt. U.S. Army, 1964-66. Fellow Am. Coll. Trial Lawyers, Am. Bar Found.; mem. ABA (chmn. admiralty and maritime law com., tort and ins. practice sect. 1980-81), World Assn. Lawyers, Am. Counsel Assn. (bd. dirs. 1980-82), Assn. Trial Lawyers Am., Am. Judicature Soc., Maritime Law Assn. U.S., Fla. Bar (chmn. grievance com. 1973-75, chmn. admiralty law com. 1978-79), Acad. Fla. Trial Lawyers, Southeastern Admiralty Law Inst. (bd. govs. 1973-75), Duval County Legal Aid Assn. (bd. dirs. 1971-74, 81-84). Democrat. Club: Rotary of Jacksonville (bd. mem. 1982-84, treas. 1985—). Home: 1850 Shadowlawn St Jacksonville FL 32205 Office: Wahl and Gabel PA 920 Barnett Bank Bldg Jacksonville FL 32202

GABERMAN, HARRY, lawyer, economic analyst; b. Springfield, Mass., May 6, 1913; s. Nathan and Elizabeth (Binder) G.; m. Ingeborg Luise Gruda, Sept. 24, 1953; children—Claudia Natalie Gaberman Razzook, Victor Lucius. J.D. George Washington U., 1941; LL.M., Catholic U. Am., 1954. Bar: D.C. 1941. Atty.-investigator, atty.-advisor U.S. Mil. Govt. and U.S. High Commn. for Germany, Berlin, Frankfurt, Bonn, 1945-53; dep. legal advisor and attache Am. embassy, Rome, 1953; sole practice, Washington, 1953-55; intelligence analyst Army Transp. Intelligence Agy., Gravelly Point, Va., 1955-56; supervisory atty.-advisor, atty.-advisor Air Force Systems Command, Andrews AFB, Md., 1956-75; asst., alt. to U.S. mem. Four-power liquidation of German War Potential Com., Berlin, 1946; chief deconcentration br. U.S. High Commn., Frankfurt, 1949; dep. U.S. mem. law com. Allied Kommandatura, Berlin, 1951; U.S. mem. 3-power Film Reorgn. Com., Bonn, 1949-50. Contbr. articles to profl. jours. Recipient Profl. Achievement award George Washington U. Law Alumni, 1983. Mem. Fed. Bar Assn. (chmn. govt. contracts council 1970-75, 78-79, dep. chmn. sect. internat. law, editor internat. law sect. newsletter, numerous Disting. Service awards), D.C. Bar Assn. (chmn. govt. contracts com. 1964-66), Diplomatic and Consular Officers Ret. Avocations: walking; swimming; reading. Address: 5117 Overlook Park Annandale VA 22003

GABINET, PAUL GREGORY, college president; b. Balt., Apr. 7, 1953; s. Gregory and Marjorie (McMahan) G. B.S., Milligan Coll., 1974; M.Ed., East Tenn. State U., 1983. Admissions counselor Washington Coll. Acad., Tenn., 1974-80, pres., 1980—. Tenor, Greater Civic Chorale, Greeneville, Tenn., 1982. Baptist. Club: Washington Coll. Ruritan. Lodges: Rotary (Johnson City, Tenn.), Elks. Home: Washington Coll Acad Washington Coll TN 37681

GABLE, ROBERT ELLEDY, real estate investment company executive; b. N.Y.C., Feb. 20, 1934; s. Gilbert E. and Paulina (Stearns) G.; m. Emily Brinton Thompson, July 5, 1958; children—James, Elizabeth, John. B.S., Stanford U., 1956. John. With The Stearns Co. (formerly Stearns Coal & Lumber Co. Inc.), Lexington, Ky., 1958—, asst. to pres., 1958-60, sec., 1960-70, treas., 1961-62, v.p., 1962-70, chmn. bd., 1970—, pres., 1975-78, also dir.; dir. Hilliard-Lyons Govt. Fund, Inc.; former chmn. bd., dir. Ky. & Tenn. Ry., Stearns; former chmn. bd. Lumber King Inc., Stearns; former dir., mem. audit com. Kuhn's-Big K Stores Corp., Nashville, 1979-81; dir. emeritus Blue Cross and Blue Shield Ky.; former dir. Bank of McCreary County. Commr. Ky. Dept. Parks, 1967-70; mem. pub. lands com. Interstate Oil Compact Commn., 1968-70; mem. adv. com. Ky. Ednl. TV, 1971-75; former mem. Breaks Interstate Park Commn.; past pres., past dir. McCreary County Indsl. Devel. Corp.; former trustee Stearns Recreational Assn., Inc.; mem. S.E. regional adv. com. Nat. Park Service, 1973-78, sec., 1977-78; former bd. dirs. Ky. Mountain Laurel Festival Assn., v.p., 1974-75; mem. McCreary County Air Bd., 1967-81; mem. adv. bd. U. Ky. for Somerset Community Coll., 1965-73. Republican candidate for U.S. Senate from Ky., 1972; Ky. co-chmn. Finance Com. for Re-election of Pres., 1972; mem. Rep. Nat. Finance Com., 1971-76; Rep. state finance chmn., 1973-75; mem. Ky. Rep. Central Com., 1974—; Rep. nominee for gov. Ky., 1975; trustee George Peabody Coll. for Tchrs., Nashville, 1970-79, mem. exec. com., 1976-79, chmn. bd., 1979; former trustee Capital Day Sch., Frankfort, Ky.; bd. dirs., past chmn., past pres., founder Ky. Council on Econ. Edn., Inc.; bd. dirs. Joint Council Econ. Edn., N.Y.C., 1982—; trustee Ky. State U. Found., 1979-82; trustee Vanderbilt U., Nashville, 1979—, mem. budget com., 1979—; past mem. bd. dirs. Ky. Better Roads Council, Inc., vice chmn., 1976-79; mem. missions bd. Episcopal Diocese of Lexington; bd. dirs. Lexington Conv. and Tourist Bur., 1982-85, Ky. Opera Assn., 1982—, Rehab. Found., Inc., Louisville, 1982—, Headley-Whitney Mus., Lexington, 1985—; founding bd.Lexington Fund for the Arts, 1984—. Served to lt. (j.g.) USNR, 1956-58. Named Ky. Col., Mr. Coal of Ky., 1970. Mem. Ky. Coal Assn. (dir. 1972—, exec. com. 1974-78, sec. 1979—), Ky. C. of C. (regional v.p., 1971-72, 76-80, exec. com. 1971-72, 76-80, dir. 1971-80, fin. com. 1978-79), Lexington C. of C. (dir. 1982, 84—), Urban Land Inst., Internat. Council Shopping Centers, Soc. Indsl. Realtors (asso.), Tau Beta Pi, Alpha Kappa Lambda (past chpt. pres.). Clubs: Frankfort (Ky.) Country; Keeneland, Lafayette, Bluegrass Auto (dir.) (Lexington); Pendennis, River Valley (Louisville); Capitol Hill (Washington). Home: 1715 Stonehaven Dr Frankfort KY 40601 Office: care The Stearns Co 410 W Vine St Lexington KY 40507

GABRIEL, EUGENE RICHARD, broadcast engineer, consultant; b. Huntington, W.Va., Dec. 31, 1949; s. Daniel Edmund and Mae Susan (Eskew) G.; m. Cynthia Simms Gardner, Feb. 1, 1981 (div. 1982). Student Emory and Henry Coll., 1966-69. Disc jockey Sta. WSWV, Pennington, Gap, 1965-67, broadcast engr., Lee County, Va., 1967-75; dir. engring. Sta. K92-FM CEBE Investments, Inc., Roanoke, Va., 1975—; founder, pres. Dog Gone Corp., Roanoke, 1984—; cons. in field. Mem. Am. Security Council, 1980—; mem. Republican Presdl. Task Force, 1982—. Served with U.S. Army, 1970-71. Mem. Soc. Broadcast Engrs., MENSA. Methodist. Lodges: Lee Jaycees, Eagles (Pennington Gap, Va.). Home: 2898 Tree Swallow Rd SW Roanoke VA 24018 Office: Dog Gone Corp 2728 Colonial Ave SW Box 1180 Roanoke VA 24006

GABRIELE, VINCENZO, restaurateur; b. Palermo, Sicily, Jan. 17, 1948; s. Carmelo and Rosa Eleonora (Romeo) G.; came to U.S., 1969, naturalized, 1982; student Mcht. Marine Sch. for Capt., 1962-68; m. Patricia Ann Tansey, July 3, 1972; 1 dau., Rosa. Asst. capt., then dining room dir. Tony's Restaurant, St. Louis, 1969-75; with Grisanti Inc., corp. of Casa Grisanti, Mamma Grisanti and Sixth Ave. Restaurant Louisville, 1976—, gen. mgr., 1977-78, exec. v.p., co-owner, 1978—; co-owner Mamma Grisanti Inc., 1983—; cons. Jefferson Community Coll. Bd. dirs. Phoenix Hill Assn., 1978—; mem. spl. com. evaluation dept. modern langs. U. Louisville. Recipient award Jefferson County public schs.; Ivy award, 1980. Mem. Italian-Am. Assn. Roman Catholic. Home: 103 Indian Hills Trail Louisville KY 40207 Office: 1000 E Liberty St Louisville KY 40204

GACHET, THOMAS MCINNIS, lawyer; b. Arlington, Va., Nov. 30, 1943; s. Thomas Morton and Edna Lou (McInnis) G.; m. Patricia Veronica Arnold, May 21, 1976; children—Carolyn Leigh, Catherine Eleanor. B.A., Eckerd Coll., 1966; J.D., Harvard U., 1970; M.A., Vanderbilt U., 1971; LL.M. in Taxation, Georgetown U., 1976. Tax advisor Gulf Oil Co., London, 1971-73, supr. planning and research, Pitts., 1974; tax counsel CACI, Arlington, Va., 1974-75; sr. tax atty. Allied Chem. Co., London, 1976-78; internat. tax atty. Amerada Hess, Woodbridge, N.J., 1978-79; sr. counsel-tax Harris Corp., Melbourne, Fla., 1979—. Home: 1407 S Riverside Dr Indialantic FL 32903 Office: 1025 W NASA Blvd Melbourne FL 32919

GADBURY, JOHN DARRELL, chiropractor; b. Grant County, Ind., June 16, 1930; s. John Harold and Helen Beatrice G.; 1 dau., Cynthia Denice Haydel. Student Ball State Coll., 1949-50, Lincoln Chiropractic Coll., 1955-59, Gulf Coast U., 1970-74. Practice chiropractics and homeopathic medicine, Sarasota, Fla., 1959—; dir. research Sarasota Health Found., 1967-69. Served with USNR, 1951-53; Korea. Fellow Hahnemann Med. Soc. Am.; mem. Fla. Chiropractic Soc., S.W. Fla. Chiropractic Soc., Lincoln Coll. Alumni Assn. Presbyterian. Lodges: Moose, Elks (exalted ruler 1983-84). Patentee twist board for rehab. back muscles; author: Psychographology, 1966; Endocrinology Testing, 1968. Office: 2344 Bee Ridge Rd Sarasota FL 33579

GADDIS, HUGHES DONAVON, JR., dentist; b. Winnsboro, La., Oct. 5, 1946; s. Hughes Donavon and Cecil (Tarver) G.; m. Mary Jacquelyn LeGrande, Aug. 8, 1970; children—Todd Donavon, Amy Melissa. B.S., La. State U., 1968; M.S., N.E. La. State U., 1972; D.D.S., La. State U., 1976. Dentist in pvt. practice, Winnfield, La., 1976—; med. staff Humana Hosp., Winnfield, 1982—. Active Boy Scouts Am., Winnfield, 1980—; v.p. Winn Parish Fair Bd., Winnfield, 1981-83, pres., 1983—. Served to 1st lt. U.S. Army, 1969-72, Vietnam. Named Outstanding Young Man of Yr., Winn Jaycees, 1980, Jaycee of Yr., 1980, 82. Mem. Acad. Gen. Dentistry, 8th Dist. Dental Soc. (bd. dirs.), Winn Parish C. of C. (v.p. 1983; Citizen of Year 1982), Winn Jaycees (pres. 1981). Republican. Baptist. Lodge: Kiwanis (v.p. 1978-80). Avocations:

gardening; woodworking; golf. Home: Route 4 Box 627 Winnfield LA 71483 Office: 1605 W Court St Winnfield LA 71483

GADDIS, ROGER GARY, psychology educator, consultant; b. Gastonia, N.C., Nov. 9, 1946; s. Alonzo Alfred and Minalee (German) G.; m. Susan Avery Woodall, Aug. 13, 1968; children—David Benjamin, Deborah Dawn. B.A., U. N.C.-Charlotte, 1968; M.A., U. Tenn., 1969; Ph.D., U. S.C., 1973. Instr. Winthrop Coll., Rock Hill, S.C., 1969-70; asst. prof. Gaston Coll., Dallas, N.C., 1973-74; prof. psychology Gardner-Webb Coll., Boiling Springs, N.C., 1974—, chmn. dept. psychology, 1980—. Contbr. articles to profl. jours. Mem. Am. Psychol. Assn., Soc. Psychology and Philosophy. Home: 231 Beason St Boiling Springs NC 28017 Office: Gardner-Webb Coll 600 College Ave Boiling Springs NC 28017

GADDY, JAMES LEOMA, chemical engineering educator; b. Jacksonville, Fla., Aug. 16, 1932; s. Leoma Ithama and Mary Elizabeth (Edwards) G.; m. Betty Maricella; children—James Courtney, Teresa Ann. B.S. in Chem. Engring., La. Poly. U., 1955; M.S., U. Ark., 1968; Ph.D., U. Tenn., 1972. Registered profl. engr., Ark. Process engr. Ethyl Corp., Baton Rouge, 1955-60; engring. supr. Arkla Gas, Shreveport, La., 1960-66; from asst. to assoc. prof. dept. chem. engring. U. Mo.-Rolla, 1969-79, prof., 1979-80, dir. Renewable Resources Research Ctr., 1979-80; prof. head dept. chem. engring. U. Ark., Fayetteville, 1980—; pres. Engring. Resources; prin. investigator research contracts; cons. various cos., 1976—; dir. Biosyn Corp. Contbr. 250 articles to profl. jours. Faculty fellow Swiss Fed. Inst. Tech., Zurich, 1978. Mem. Am. Inst. Chem. Engrs. (speakers bur. 1978—), Am. Chem. Soc., Am. Soc. Engring. Edn., AAAS, Tau Beta Pi (Eminent Engr.). Baptist. Home: 964 Arlington Terr Fayetteville AR 72701 Office: U Ark Dept Chem Engring 227 Engring Bldg Fayetteville AR 72701

GADDY, MCKETHAN ROGERS, optometrist; b. Florence, S.C., May 22, 1953; s. James Caldwell and Sarah Covington (Rogers) G.; m. Francis Sherrill Morrell, Dec. 22, 1975. B.S., So. Coll. Optometry, 1977, O.D., 1979. Pvt. practice optometry, Dillon, S.C., 1979—. Mem. Am. Optometric Assn., S.C. Optometric Assn. Pee Dee Optometric Assn., Dillon County C. of C., So. Coll. Optometry Alumni Assn. Methodist. Club: Lions (Dillon). Home: 403 E Monroe St Dillon SC 29536 Office: 102 E Madison St Dillon SC 29536

GADE, MARVIN FRANCIS, paper company executive; b. Clinton, Iowa, Nov. 10, 1924; s. Bernhardt Henry and Anna Mae (Jessen) G.; m. Lorraine F. McDonald, Dec. 2, 1944; children—Michael David, Patricia Ann Gade Conn, Steven Dennis, Laura Jean Gade Walls, Mary Kay Gade McIntyre, Karen Lynn Gade Smith, Jeffrey Scott. Mech. Engr./Chem. Engr., U. Iowa, 1952; M.B.A., UCLA, 1961. Process instrumentation engr. Standard Brands Co., Clinton, Iowa, 1946-50; with Kimberly-Clark Co., various locations, 1952—, sr. v.p., group exec., Neenah, Wis., 1974-77, exec. v.p., 1977-81, dir., 1973; pres. KC Health Care, Paper & Spltys. Cos., Coosa Pines, Ala., 1981-83, sr. exec. v.p. K-C, 1983—, vice chmn. bd., 1983—; adj. prof. U. Ala., 1978—; dir. 1st Bank Childersburg, Ala. Trustee Oglethorpe U., Atlanta, Fulton County Hosp. Authority, Northside Hosp., Atlanta, Wesley Woods Med. Ctr., Atlanta. Served with USNR, 1943-46. Roman Catholic. Clubs: Coosa Pines Country; Inverness County (Birmingham). Home: 3800 Old Alabama Rd Alpharetta GA 30201 Office: Kimberly Clark Corp 1400 Holcomb Bridge Rd Roswell GA 30076

GAETZ, DONALD JAY, health care administrator, marketing executive; b. Rugby, N.D., Jan. 22, 1948; s. Stanley J. and Olive (Knutson) G.; B.A. in Religion and Polit. Sci., Concordia Coll., 1970; L.H.D. (hon.), 1983; m. Victoria Quertermous; children—Matthew Louis II, Erin Victoria. Asst. to U.S. senator Milton R. Young, 1966-67; asst. to U.S. senator Everett M. Dirksen, 1968-69; editor, Cavalier County Republican, Langdon, N.D., 1970-72; exec. dir. Communication Arts, Mpls., 1972-74; gen. sec. Bellin Hosp. Found., Green Bay, Wis., 1974-78; v.p. Methodist Hosp., Jacksonville, Fla., 1978-81; pres. ABC Home Health Services of Fla., Jacksonville, 1978-81; adminstr. Methodist Hospice, Jacksonville, 1980-81; exec. v.p. Hospice Care/Hospice, Inc., 1981—; co-chmn. Nat. Hospice Edn. Project, 1980-82; pres. Nat. Hospice Orgn., 1982-83, chmn. bd., 1983-84; health cons. Cath. Charities, Miami, 1981-83. Author: Thomas Jefferson Lives, 1976; A Trilogy of the Land and Lakes: 1776, 1876, 1976, 1976; Admiral Jimmy Flatley, All American Hero of an All American Town, 1976; A Covenant Until Death, 1978; The Case for Hospice, 1981; The High Cost of Cutting Kindness, 1983; The Impact of Hospice Care on DRG Profits/Losses of Acute Care General Hospitals, 1985—. Producer: (film) That They Might Have Life (Gold medal Internat. Film Festival), 1978; The Least of These His Brothers and Sisters (Silver Medal Film Festival of Americas), 1977. State campaign chmn. N.D. Republican Party, 1968; mem. Pres.'s Commn. on Campus Unrest, 1970; chmn. Fla. Gov.'s Com. on Long Term Health Care, 1980; bd. dirs. Green Bay Area Free Clinic, 1977-78, Wis. Cancer Soc., 1975-78, Family Health Might Have Life (Gold Medal Internat. Film Festival), 1978; The Least of These His Brothers and Sisters (Silver Medal Film Festival of Amercas), 1977. State campaign chmn. N.D. Republican Party, 1968; mem. Pres.'s Commn. on Campus Unrest, 1970; chmn. Fla. Gov.'s Com. on Long Term Health Care, 1980; bd. dirs. Green Bay Area Free Clinic, 1977-78, Wis. Cancer Soc., 1975-78, Family Health Services of Fla., 1981-82. Recipient George Washington Honor medal Nat. Freedoms Found., 1965, Am. Bicentennial Adminstrn. medal, 1976; Citizen of Yr. award N.E. Assn. Aid to Retarded Children, 1971; Presdl. commendation, 1982; Legis. commendation Mich. Ho. of Reps. and Senate, 1983; Hon. Tarheel award Gov. of N.C., 1983; Hans M. Rozendaal award for disting. leadership in hospice care, 1983; Founder's award Nat. Hospice Orgn., 1985; named Outstanding Adminstr., Wis. Hosp. Assn., 1976, Hon. Commodore of City Green Bay, 1976, Presdl. medal of merit, 1983; Merit scholar, 1966. Fellow Am. Acad. Polit. Sci.; mem. So. Gerontol. Soc., Am. Soc. Newspaper Editors, Nat. Press Club, Nat. Hospice Orgn. (dir. 1979-84), Fla. State Hospice Orgn. (chmn. 1979-81), Assn. Politics and Life Scis., Pi Kappa Delta. Republican. Lutheran. Nat. coll. and univ. debating champion, 1967, oratory champion, 1968. Home: 800 NE 98th St Miami Shores FL 33138 also Rosewalk House Seaside FL 32454 Office: Suite 211 2331 N State Rd 7 Lauderhill FL 33311 also 979 NW 1st St Miami FL 33128 also 5720 Oram St Dallas TX 572060

GAFFNEY, LEE MARIE, public relations executive; b. Argyle, Minn., Sept. 11, 1926; d. Phillip G. and Marie Louise (Bergeron) Schweich; B.A., U. Minn., 1945. Registered rep. Can. Stock Exchange, Montreal, Que., 1953-55, Toronto (Ont.), Can. Stock Exchange, 1953-55; public relations officer Alitalia Airlines, Montreal, 1955-57; with Hilton Internat., Montreal, 1957-67; dir. public relations Alo Cosmetics, Ft. Lauderdale, Fla., 1968-71; adminstrv. asst. to Alan B. Connell, Jr., Ft. Worth, 1979-81; dir. communications Resorts Internat., 1981-82; columnist Palm Beach Daily News, 1979-82; Palm Beach Life, 1979-82; cons. public relations Hank Meyer Assos., Miami, Fla., 1972-78; asst. mgr. Surf Club, Miami, 1983—. Recipient Dayan award Govt. of Israel, 1967; Key of Miami award, 1975. Mem. Public Relations Soc. Fla., Advt. and Sales Execs. Can., Women in Communications, Fashion Group Internat., Miami Ballet Soc., Big Bros. and Big Sisters Miami, Viscayans. Republican. Roman Catholic. Address: Surf Club 9011 Collins Ave Bal Harbour FL 33154

GAFFORD, FRANK HALL, ret. educator; b. Afton, Okla., Jan. 11, 1903; s. Benjamin Ford and Elizabeth Newman (Payne) G.; B.A., U. Tex., 1925, M.A., 1927, Ph.D., 1940; m. Anita Marguerite Engerrand, Dec. 28, 1926; children—Eleanor Marguerite (Mrs. Ernest Owen Bransford, Jr.), Frank Hall, Jeanne Engerrand. Instr. history U. Miss., 1927-29, asst. prof., 1929-31; asst. prof. history Coll. of Charleston, S.C., 1931-32, asso. prof., 1932-41, prof., 1941-49; asso. prof. history North Tex. State U., 1949-51, prof., 1951-73, prof. emeritus, 1973—, chmn. dept., 1951-52, dir., 1952-65, dean Coll. Arts and Scis., 1953-73; instr. U. of South, summer 1944, Tulane U., summer 1949. Mem. Am. Hist. Assn., AAUP, Phi Alpha Theta, Pi Sigma Alpha, Pi Kappa Alpha. Home: 2520 Royal Ln Denton TX 76201

GAGE, GEORGE RAYMOND, JR., physician; b. Bklyn., Feb. 13, 1919; s. George R. and Mary A. (Green) G.; B.A., Columbia U., 1938, M.D., 1942; m. 2d, Doris Jean Robbins, Aug. 25, 1972; children—Mary, Joanne, Janice, Kathleen, Margaret, George III, Richard, Ernest Lent, Eric Lent, Robin Lent. Practice obstetrics and gynecology, Coral Gables, Fla., 1950-78; former asst. prof. obstetrics and gynecology U. Miami; former med. dir. Group Health, Inc., Coral Gables. Served lt. M.C. USNR, 1943-47. Diplomate Am. Bd. Obstetrics and Gynecology. Fellow A.C.S., Am. Coll. Obstetricians and Gynecologists, South Atlantic Assn. Obstetrics and Gynecology, Internat. Coll. Surgeons; assoc. Royal Soc. Medicine; mem. DAV. Lodge: K.C. Home: 6887 Carolyncrest Dr Dallas TX 75214

GAGE, MICHAEL HENRY, metal company executive; b. Buffalo, Sept. 20, 1948; s. Jeffrey A. and Rachel Z. Gage; m. Barbara Young, Aug. 9, 1969; children—Amy, Melissa, Jeffrey, Charles. B.S. in Finance, Lehigh U., 1970. C.P.A., Pa. Acct., Price Waterhouse & Co., N.Y.C., 1970-73; v.p. Erisco Industries Inc., Erie, Pa., 1973-82; pres. Gage Carolina Metals Inc., Durham, N.C., 1982—. Mem. Am. Inst. C.P.A.s, Pa. Inst. C.P.A.s. Office: PO Box 3863 Durham NC 27702

GAGLIARDI, GIUSEPPE CLAUDIO, civil engineer; b. Malito, Italy, Aug. 8, 1942; s. Gaetano and Nerina Maria (Cassano) G.; m. Margaret Dudley, Feb. 26, 1973; children—Guyton Joseph, Robert Maurice. A.A., St. Petersburg Jr. Coll., 1960; Dottore in Iugegneria, U. Rome, 1968. Registered profl. engr., Fla., La., Md. With Gagliardi Engring. & Constrn. Co., Cosenza, Italy, 1968-73; v.p. engring. George F. Young, Inc., St. Petersburg, 1973-79; mgr. land devel., v.p. constrn. Western div. Trafalgar Developers Fla., Inc., St. Petersburg, 1979—, mgr. engring. design, 1980—. Recipient Odyssey of Opportunity award Gen. Electric, 1983. Mem. ASCE, Nat. Soc. Profl. Engrs., Fla. Engring. Soc., La. Profl. Engring. Soc. Republican. Episcopalian. Lodge: Rotary. Address: 834 21st Ave N Saint Petersburg FL 33704

GAIENNIE, L(OUIS) RENE, retired business executive, business consultant; b. Kansas City, Mo., Oct. 24, 1912; s. L. Rene Gaiennie and Alice Green; m. Beatrice Clark, Apr. 18, 1941; 1 child, Clark Rene. A.B., Washington U., St. Louis, 1936, Ph.D., 1940; M.A., U. Wis., 1938; M.B.A., U. Chgo., 1952. Vice pres. Fairbanks Morse Co., Chgo., 1948-56; v.p. ACF, N.Y.C., 1956-58; exec. v.p. Robert Morse Co., Montreal, Que., Can., 1958-67; pres. Howe Richardson Scale, Clifton, N.J., 1960-67; sr. v.p. The Singer Co., N.Y.C., 1967-75; pres. Strategic Planning Assocs., Inc., Belleaire, Fla., 1981—; disting. lectr. Grad. Sch. Bus., U. South Fla., Tampa, 1981—. Contbr. articles to profl. and tech. jours. Mem. Northbrook Sch. Bd., Ill., 1952-55; mem. Aheka council Boy Scouts Am., 1963-66. Served to lt. comdr. USNR, 1941-45. Decorated Order Brit. Empire. Fellow Am. Psychol. Assn.; mem. Strategic Mgmt. Assn., Phi Beta Kappa, Sigma Xi. Republican. Episcopalian. Club: Belleaire Biltmore. Home: 400 Palmetto Rd Belleaire FL 33516 Office: U South Florida Fowler Ave Tampa FL 33620

GAILLARD, GEORGE SIDAY, III, architect; b. Miami, Fla., Apr. 24, 1941; s. George Siday and Sarah Margaret (Crawford) G.; m. Charlalee Bailey, 1965 (div. 1969); m. Sylvia Gayle Bridgewater, July 18, 1977; 1 child, Barron Matthew. B.S., Ga. Inst. Tech., 1965; postgrad., Ga. State U. Registered architect Ga., Fla. Sole propr. Fox Magnanimus, Atlanta, Ga., 1971-78, Gaillard & Assocs., Atlanta, 1978-81, 83—; mgr. design dept. Deca Inc., Miami, 1982. Sculpture exhibited in group shows at Piedmont Arts Festival, 1971, 73. Mem. AIA, High Mus. Art, Atlanta, 1984—. Served with USMCR, 1962. Avocations: reading; camping; sailing; photography.

GAILLARD, REBECCA MADELINE, educator, guidance counselor; b. Pineville, S.C., Apr. 22, 1933; d. Relious and Martha Elizabeth (Jefferson) G.; 1 child, Lisa Michelle. B.S. in Elem. Edn., Morris Coll., 1955; M.A. in Early Childhood Edn., Columbia U., 1970. Tchr., Bonneau Elem. Sch., Moncks Corner, S.C., 1955-70; tchr.-librarian Macedonia High Sch., 1970-72; tchr. St. Stephen Elem. Sch., 1972-81; guidance counselor J.K. Gourdin Elem. Sch. and St. Stephen Elem. Sch., S.C., 1981—. Leader Pineville-Russellville council Girl Scouts Am., Pineville, S.C., 1965—; sec. Democratic Precinct, Pineville, 1976—; tchr. Sunday sch. Day Dawn Baptist Ch., Pineville, 1955—, also pres. gospel chorus; v.p. Youth Missionary Ch., Pineville, 1976—. Mem. Tri-County Guidance Assn., S.C. Assn. for Counseling and Devel., Am. Assn. Counseling and Devel. Home: Route 1 Box 47 Pineville SC 29468

GAINER, GLEN BERTRAM, JR., state official; b. Parkersburg, W.Va., July 4, 1927; s. Glen B. Sr. and Nettie E. Gainer; m. Sally Jo Padgett, Oct. 31, 1955; children—Beth Lynn Criss, Glen B. III. A.B., Marietta Coll., 1959; student Glenville State Coll., 1947-48, Muskingum Coll., 1948-49; postgrad. W.Va. U., 1961-63. Tchr., coach, Pub. Schs., Parkersburg, 1960-69; mayor City of Parkersburg, 1969-71; auditor State of W.Va., Charleston, 1976—. Served with USN, 1945-47. Democrat. Office: State Auditor State Capitol Charleston WV 25305

GAINER, RUBY JACKSON (MRS. HERBERT P. GAINER), retired educator, civic leader; b. Buena-Vista, Ga.; d. William B. and Lovie (Jones) Jackson; student Miles Meml. Coll.; B.S., Ala. State Tchrs. Coll.; M.A. in English and Social Studies, Atlanta U.; postgrad. Fla. A&M Coll., Western Wash. State Coll., U. Conn., Okla. State U.; H.H.D. (hon.), Selma U., Daniel Payne Coll., 1971; LL.D., Birmingham Bapt. Coll.; LL.D. (hon.), Faith Coll., Birmingham; L.H.D. (hon.), Bishop Coll., Dallas; m. Herbert P. Gainer; children—Ruby Paulette, James H., Cecil F. Tchr., J. B. Turner High Sch., Milton, Fla., pub. schs., Birmingham, Ala., Washington Jr. High Sch., Pensacola, Fla., prior to 1968; guidance counselor Wedgewood Jr.-Sr. High Sch., Pensacola; English tchr. Woodham High Sch., Pensacola, now ret. Brought 2 successful legal cases against Jefferson (Ala.) County Sch. Bd. for equalization of Negro tchr. salaries, 1946-47, re-instatement Negro tchrs. under Tchr. Tenure Act in 1960's; organized 1st tchrs. union, Birmingham; also organized local high sch. chpt. Future Tchrs. Am., local tchr. aide and teen service groups, local and county assns. edn.; local capt. Heart Fund, Mothers March of Dimes, Cancer Fund; active local P.T.A., chmn. Fla. P.T.A. Workshop; participant Gov. Fla. Conf. Edn., Tallahassee, Nat. conf. Profl. Rights and Responsibilities, Arlington, Tex.; participant chmn. numerous profl. ednl. confs. So. U.S.; mem. Escambia County Guidance Council; mem., past officer Fla. Guidance Council; mem., bd. dirs. Partners for Progress. Bd. dirs. Escambia County Tb Assn. Recipient Tchr. of Year award Dist. 1 Fla. State Tchrs. Assn., also award meritorious service, Disting. Service award, 1966; DuShane Outstanding Service award; DuShane Outstanding Dir. award Escambia County Tchrs. Assn., 1967; Disting. Service award civil, human, profl. rights, 1965; Outstanding Tchr. and Leader award Fla. Edn. Assn.; honor award NEA and Fla. State Tchrs. Assn., 1966; Centennial Service to Mankind award Ala. State U., 1974; also numerous awards for disting. service to youth, community orgns.; cited in newspapers, NAACP; honored as alumnus Ala. State U. with meml. tablet in Academic Mall of Univ., 1975; Club Woman of Yr. award Fla. Assn. Women's Clubs, 1985; Pres. of Yr. award Ladies of Distinction Federated Club, 1985. Mem. Jefferson County (past sec., past pres.), Escambia County (past sec., past pres.), Fla. State (past bd. dirs. dist. 1, past pres. dist. 1, mem. tchr. edn. and profl. standards commn. and evaluation com., bd. advisers dept. classroom tchrs.), Ala. (past chmn. secondary sch. tchrs.), Am. tchrs. assns., AAUW, Jefferson County Tchrs. Union (past pres.), NEA, Assn. Classroom Tchrs. (v.p. 1969), Nat. Council English Tchrs., Nat. Council Social Studies Tchrs., Escambia County League Justice, Future Tchrs. Am. Advisers Council, City-Wide Fedn. Women's Clubs (pres.), Fla. Assn. Women's Clubs (pres. 1984), LWV, Top Ladies Distinction (organizer, 1st pres. Pensacola chpt., Top Lady of Year), Alpha Kappa Alpha (Am. Woman's Service award 1974, service award 1984). Outstanding Community Service award). Baptist (mem., pres. Bd. Ushers). Democrat. Mem. Order Eastern Star. Clubs: Mary M. Bethune (officer); New Idea Art and Study (officer). Composer: God Planted You Here, Talking to the Moon, It Is Better Not to Know, In the Quiet of the Day. Contbr. articles, poems, publs. Address: 1516 W Gadsden St Pensacola FL 32501

GAINES, JAMES PENDLETON, real estate administrator; b. Atlanta, Apr. 8, 1947; s. Reuben and C. Mildred (Clark) G.; m. Lois M. Hoffee, June 17, 1978; children—Mary K., Elizabeth A., Jason R. B.B.A., U. Ga., 1968, M.A., 1971, Ph.D., 1975. Asst. prof. fin. and real estate Kent State U., Ohio, 1974-78; assoc. prof. real estate U. S.C., Columbia, 1978-84; dir. real estate research Rice Ctr., Houston, 1984—. Contbr. articles to profl. jours. Mem. Am. Real Estate and Urban Econs. Assn. (sec.-treas. 1981-83). Office: Rice Ctr 0 Greenway Plaza Suite 1900 Houston TX 77046

GAINES, KATHLYN ANNE, nursing administrator; b. Florence, Colo., Dec. 20, 1934; d. William Cody Gaines and Estelle May (Smith) Rizk. B.S. in Nursing, Syracuse U., 1962; M.Nursing, U. Fla., 1969; D.S. in Nursing, U. Ala., 1981. R.N. Rehab. coordinator Ohio State U., Columbus, 1965-67; asst. prof. Western Carolina U., Cullowhee, 1969-73; clinician Duke U./Highland Hosp., Asheville, N.C., 1973-75; mental health coordinator Vis. Nurses Assn., Cleve., 1980-81; chmn. nursing div. Carson-Newman Coll., Jefferson City, Tenn., 1982—; rehab. nursing cons. Ohio Dept. Health, Columbus, 1965-67, Orthopedic Hosp., Asheville, 1970-72; mental health nursing cons. Smokey Mountains Mental Health Ctr., Cullowhee, 1970-72, Highland Hosp., Asheville, 1970-72; mem. adv. council Your Home Vis. Nurse, Knoxville, 1982—. Mem. Friends of the Library, Jefferson City, 1982—. Mem. Am. Nurses Assn., Assn. Rehab. Nurses, Nat. League for Nurses, Council Psychiat. Mental Health Nurses, AAUW, LWV, Sigma Theta Tau, Omicron Delta Kappa, Beta Sigma Phi. Episcopalian. Clubs: Faculty Women's, Les Amies (Jefferson City). Avocations: crocheting; reading; flower gardening; jigsaw puzzles. Home: #31 806 S Branner Jefferson City TN 37760 Office: Carson-Newman Coll Russell St Jefferson City TN 37760

GAINES, MARION LUCEINE, educator; b. Columbia, S.C., Sept. 21, 1925; d. Marion Little and Eloise (Cave) Gaines; student U. S.C., 1941-43, M.B.A., 1964; B.S., U. N.C. 1945; m. Thomas Clark Firzgerald, Jr., June 7, 1947; children—Thomas Clark, Gaines Marion, Carolyn Sarah; m. 2d, John Thomas Rice, June 19, 1963 (dec. July 1969). Staff accountant Peat Marwick Mitchell Co., Greensboro, N.C., 1943-47, Darmody Todd & Co., Boston, 1947-48; accountant J.P. Stevens & Co., Greensboro, 1948-51; partner Fitzgerald & Co., C.P.A.s, Columbia, 1951-63; controller Cardinal Chem. Co., Columbia, 1964-66; head acctg. dept. Palmer Coll., Columbia, 1966-70, Midlands Tech. Edn. Center, 1970-74; asst. prof. acctg. Winthrop Coll., Rock Hill, S.C., 1975-81; asso. prof. Lander Coll., Greenwood, S.C., 1981—. Chmn. fin. com. Girl Scouts Am., Columbia, 1960-63; bd. dirs. Jr. Achievement. Nominated Young Woman of Year, Jr. C. of C., 1960; C.P.A., S.C., N.C. Mem. Nat. Assn. Accountants (sec., dir.), Nat. Assn. Security Dealers, Am Inst. C.P.A.s, S.C. Assn. C.P.A.s, Inst. Internal Auditors, Phi Beta Kappa, Beta Gamma Sigma, Alpha Kappa Psi. Episcopalian. Club: Zonta (treas. 1965-67, dir. Columbia chpt. 1965-68). Home: 108 Greenway Dr Greenwood SC 29646

GAINES, THOMAS, psychologist, consultant; b. Houston, Mar. 1, 1948; s. Tom and Vivian (Schumann) G.; m. Carole Ann (Eichhorn) Aug. 23, 1969; children—Aimee A., Scott. B.A., U. Tex., 1969; M.B.A., U. Tex.-San Antonio, 1982; Ph.D., U. N.C., 1974. Lic. psychologist, Tex.; diplomate Am. Bd. Profl. Psychology. Clin. assoc. prof. psychiatry U. Tex. Health Sci. Ctr., San Antonio, 1974—; dir. sch. and community consultation Community Guidance Ctr., San Antonio, 1982—. Contbr. articles to profl. jours. Mem. Am. Psychol. Assn., Am. Group Psychotherapy Assn., Tex. Psychol. Assn., Southwestern Group Psychotherapy Assn., San Antonio Family Mediation Assn. (sec. 1984—), Beta Gamma Sigma. Avocations: photography; tennis; golf. Home: 13123 Queens Forest San Antonio TX 78230 Office: Community Guidance Ctr 2135 Babcock Rd San Antonio TX 78229

GAINEY, LILAH LEIGH, librarian; b. Lubbock, Tex., Nov. 15, 1950; d. Will Allison and Bertha Beatrice (Proctor) G. B. Music. Edn., Lubbock Christian Coll., 1974; M.Ed., Tex. Tech. U., 1980; M.L.S., Sam Houston State U., 1982. Tchr. music and math. Crosbyton Elem. Sch. (Tex.), 1974-78; tchr., librarian Cactus Elem. Sch., Levelland, Tex., 1979-80; grad. teaching asst. Sch. Library Sci., Huntsville, Tex., 1981-82; librarian Abilene Christian U., 1982—. Contbr. articles to profl. jours. Mem. ALA (Jr. Mems. Roundtable), publicity chmn. 1985-87, Tex. Library Assn. (dist. 1 sec. 1983-84), Sam Houston Library Sch. Alumni Assn. (v.p. 1982-83, pres. 1983-84) AAUW, Delta Kappa Gamma. Office: Abilene Christian U 1600 Campus Ct PO Box 8101 Abilene TX 79699

GAITHER, ANN HEAFNER, sales company executive; b. Lincolnton, N.C., Feb. 12, 1932; d. James Harlan and Evangeline (Houser) H.; m. Albert Cowles Gaither, July 25, 1953; children—William Harlan, Susan Gaither Jones, Lawson Heafner, Albert Comer. Mus.B., U. N.C.-Greensboro, 1953; postgrad. in bus. adminstrn. Catawba Valley Tech. Coll., 1974-76. Music coordinator city schs., Enterprise, Ala., 1953-54, Davidson, N.C., 1954-55; sales cons. Ridgeview Mills, Inc., Newton, N.C., 1973-74; from v.p. mktg. to sr. v.p. Heafner Tire Co., Inc., Lincolnton, 1974-84; pres. Heafner Data Services, Lincolnton, 1983—; exec. v.p., chief exec. officer J.H. Heafner Co., Inc., Lincolnton, 1984—, also dir.; dir. N.C. Nat. Bank, Lincolnton. Pres. Cultural and Phys. Devel. Ctr. Lincoln County, 1985; bd. dirs. Catawba Valley Tech. Coll. Found., Hickory, N.C., 1985; bd. advisors Gardner-Webb Coll., Boiling Springs, N.C., 1982, chmn., 1983-85; bd. visitors Davidson Coll., N.C., 1985—; bd. dirs. Broyhill Acad. for Free Enterprise, 1980—; pres. Bas Bleu Club service league, Newton, N.C., 1964-65. Mem. Nat. Assn. Tire Dealers, Pvt. Brand Tire Dealers, Lincoln County C. of C. (bd. dirs.), Hickory Choral Soc. Democrat. Presbyterian. Avocations: singing; skiing. Office: J H Heafner Co Inc 814 E Main St Lincolnton NC 28092

GAITHER, ROBERT BARKER, mechanical engineering educator; b. North Bay, Ont., Can., Aug. 12, 1929; s. Edwin Hampton Gaither; m. Renate Konstanze Zielke, Dec. 11, 1954; children—Patricia, Vivienne, Francesca. B.S. in Mech. Engring., Auburn U., 1951; M.S., U. Ill., 1957; Ph.D., 1962. Mem. faculty U. Fla., Gainesville, 1962—, prof., chmn. dept. mech. engring., 1964—; cons. in field. Chmn. bd. Fla. Found. for Future Scientists, 1972—. Served to lt. USN, 1951-54; Korea. Ford Found. fellow, 1959-61. Mem. ASME (pres. 1981-82), Am. Soc. Engring. Edn. Roman Catholic. Contbr. articles to profl. jours. Home: 2100 NW 63d Terr Gainesville FL 32605 Office: 237 MEB U Fla Gainesville FL 32611

GALAN, JUAN ARTURO, JR., management consultant; b. Habana, Cuba, Sept. 5, 1944; s. Juan A. and Josefina Galan; m. Martha Florence Foote, June 10, 1969; children—Marta, Mercedes, Matilde. B.S. Indsl. Engring., U. Fla., 1966; M.S. in Adminstrn.; George Washington U., 1972. Cert. mgmt. cons.; cert. info. systems auditor and systems profl. Systems engr. RCA Corp., Coral Gables, Fla., 1966-68; cons. Deloitte Haskins & Sells, Miami, Fla., 1968-75, mgr., 1975-80, dir., 1980-84, ptnr. in charge Fla. Cons. Group, 1984—. Served to lt. (j.g.) USCG, 1969-71. Mem. Inst. Mgmt. Cons., Inst. Internal Auditors, Fin. Mgrs. Soc., Assn. Systems Mgmt., Miami Rowing. Republican. Roman Catholic. Clubs: Country of Coral Gables; Coral Reef Yacht (Coconut Grove, Fla.), Greater Miami C. of C., Internat. Ctr. (past bd. dirs.). Lodge: Kiwanis (past dir.). Office: One SE 3d Ave #2000 Miami FL 33131

GALANTY, WALTER EDWARD, JR., association administrator; b. Detroit, Aug. 19, 1950; s. Walter Edward and Lucille Ann (Pagano) G.; m. Charlene Schaefer, Mar. 1, 1975; children—Katherine, Phillip. B.A., Va. Mil. Inst., 1972; postgrad. Am. U., 1973-75. Lead coordinator 3M Co., Washington, 1974-77; exec. dir. Nat. Assn. Brick Distbrs., Alexandria, Va., 1977—. Mem. exec. com. Small Bus. Legis. Council, Washington, 1978—, chmn., 1985-86; chmn. adv. com. Sta. WNVT-TV Channel 56, Washington, 1983—. Mem. Nat. Truck Weight Adv. Com. (vice chmn. 1984—), Am. Soc. Assn. Execs., Greater Washington Soc. Assn. Execs., ASTM, Va. Mil. Inst. Alumni Assn. (dir. 1983-87). Home: 2709 Viking Dr Herndon VA 22071 Office: Nat Assn Brick Distbrs 1000 Duke St Alexandria VA 22314

GALARDI, WILLIAM MICHAEL, banker; b. N.Y.C., Aug. 22, 1946; s. William Leonard and Elizabeth (Brannan) G.; m. Barbara Claire Riorden, Aug. 4, 1969 (div. 1975); 1 son, William Christopher; m. 2d, Margaret Karen Mitchell, July 30, 1977; children—Michael Mitchell, Katherine Margaret. B.S., Christian Bros. Coll., 1969. Mktg. coordinator Exxon Corp., Baton Rouge, 1969-70; comml. officer Trust Co. Ga., Atlanta, 1970-76, asst. v.p., 1976-79; sr. v.p. Trust Co. of Columbus (Ga.), 1979-80, exec. v.p., 1980-81; pres. Bank South/Columbus, 1981—, also dir.; v.p. govt. banking Bank South N.A., Atlanta, 1984—. Bd. dirs. Boys Club of Columbus, 1981—; bd. dirs., treas. Am. Cancer Soc., 1983—. Mem. Robert Morris Assocs. Republican. Roman Catholic. Home: 2546 Sharondale Ct NE Atlanta GA 30305 Office: Bank South NA Atlanta GA

GALASKA, MICHAEL FRANCIS, lawyer; b. Omaha, Apr. 25, 1950; s. Stanley Francis and Betty Ann (Garvey) G. B.A., Creighton U., 1972; J.D., 1975. Bar: Nebr. 1975, U.S. Dist. Ct. Nebr. 1975, Okla. 1982. Sole practice, Omaha, 1975-82, Geary, Okla., 1982—. Del. Nebr. White House Conf. on Handicapped Individuals, Lincoln, 1976; treas. Omaha chpt. Nat. Paraplegia Found., 1977. Mem. Nebr. Bar Assn., ABA, Okla. Bar Assn., Okla. Trial Lawyers Assn., Blaine County Bar Assn., Canadian County Bar Assn., Geary C. of C. (2d v.p. 1986). Republican. Roman Catholic. Lodge: Elks. Home and Office: 205 S Galena Route 1 Box 113-C Geary OK 73040

GALASSI, JOHN PAUL, JR., psychologist, educator; b. Stamford, Conn., Jan. 22, 1945; s. John Paul and Anna Marie (Pace) G.; m. Merna Dee Posner, June 6, 1967; children—Jennifer Ann, Karen Elizabeth. A.B., Middlebury Coll., 1966; Ed.M., Harvard U., 1967; Ph.D., U. Calif.-Berkeley, 1971. Clin.-counseling psychologist Student Counseling Service, W.Va. U., 1971-73; prof. psychology Sch. Edn., U. N.C., Chapel Hill, 1973—, coordinator counseling psychology and counseling programs, 1980—. Fellow Am. Psychol. Assn., Behavior Therapy and Research Soc. (clin.); mem. Assn. for Advancement Behavior Therapy, Am. Assn. for Counseling and Devel. Editor Behavioral Counseling Quar., 1978-83; contbr. articles to profl. jours. Home:

421 Thornwood Dr Chapel Hill NC 27514 Office: Peabody Hall 037A U NC Chapel Hill NC 27514

GALBRAITH, DALLAS SHERWOOD, petroleum geologist; b. Abilene, Tex., Sept. 22, 1953; s. George Sherwood and Kathryn Walker (Reid) G. B.S. in Geology, Stephen F. Austin U., 1978, B.A. in Geography, 1978. Pvt. practice as geologist, Abilene, 1978—. Fellow Am. Heart Assn.; mem. Am. Assn. Petroleum Geologists (membership com. 1983—), West Central Tex. Oil Gas Assn. (bd. dirs. 1983—), Abilene Geol. Soc. (program chmn. 1984-85), Jaycees, Abilene Gun Club. Republican. Methodist. Avocations: racquetball; baseball; hunting; fishing. Home: 21 Tamarisk Circle Abilene TX 79606 Office: 104 Wagstaff Bldg Abilene TX 79601

GALBRAITH, RUTH LEGG, university dean; b. Lecompte, La., Nov. 5, 1923; d. Byron S. and Dora Ruth (Lindley) Legg; B.S., Purdue U., 1945, Ph.D., 1950; m. Harry W. Galbraith, June 16, 1950; 1 son, Allan Legg. Chemist, E. I. duPont de Nemours, Waynesboro, Va., 1945-46; textile chemist Gen. Electric Co., Bridgeport, Conn., 1946-47; teaching asst. in chemistry Purdue U., 1947-48, research fellow, 1948-50; prof. textiles U. Tenn., Knoxville, 1950-55; asso. prof. textiles U. Ill., Urbana, 1956-64, prof., 1964-70, chmn. div. textiles and clothing, 1962-70; prof. consumer affairs, head dept. consumer affairs Auburn U., 1970-73, dean Sch. Home Econs. and head home econs. research, 1973-85; mem. task force on quality of living Dept. Agr., 1967-68; mem. Nat. Adv. Com. Flammable Fabrics Act, 1971-73; mem. Carpet and Rug Inst. Consumer Action Panel, 1975; mem. home econs. sub-com. Agrl. Expt. Sta. Com. on Policy, 1975-79, 80-83, sec., 1977-79; mem. Com. of 9, U.S. Dept. Agr., 1980-83, chmn., 1983. Recipient Disting. Alumni award Purdue U., 1970; Leader in Home Econs. award, 1984. Fellow Am. Inst. Chemists; mem. Am. Home Econs. Assn. (chmn. agy. mem. unit 1975-76, chmn. research sect. 1978-80), Ala. Home Econs. Assn. (pres. 1983-84), Am. Assn. Textile Chemists and Colorists, Am. Chem. Soc., ASTM (3d v.p. com. D-13 Textiles 1976-79), Assn. Coll. Profs. Textiles and Clothing, Assn. Adminstrs. Home Econs., AAUW, Sigma Xi, Omicron Nu, Phi Kappa Phi. Contbr. articles on textiles to profl. publs.; editorial bd. Research Jour. Home Econs., 1973-77, chmn. policy bd., 1978-80. Office: Sch Home Econs Auburn U Auburn AL 36849

GALBUT, RUSSELL WILLIAM, lawyer, accountant, construction executive; b. Miami Beach, Fla., Oct. 20, 1952; s. Hyman and Bessie (Dulitz) G.; m. Ronalee Eisenberg, Mar. 26, 1978. B.S., Cornell U., 1974; grad. Allstate Constrn. Coll., 1980; J.D., U. Miami, 1980. C.P.A., Fla.; bar: Fla. 1980, U.S. Ct. Appeals (11th dist.) 1980, U.S. Ct. Appeals (5th dist.) 1980, U.S. Tax Ct. 1981, U.S. Supreme Ct. 1983. Staff cons. Laventhol & Horwath, Coral Gables, Fla., 1974-76; sole practice, Miami Beach, Fla., 1976-78; mng. ptnr. Galbut & Bernstein, Miami Beach, 1978-80; pres., mng. dir. U.S. Builders and Developers Corp., Miami Beach, 1979—; tax ptnr. Galbut, Galbut & Menin, Attys., Miami Beach; mng. ptnr. Galbut, Jotkoff & Rogers, C.P.A.s, Miami Beach; mem. Fla. Bd. Accountancy; dir. Hotel Ezra Cornell. Mem. Miami Beach Zoning Bd. Adjustment; pres. Miami Beach Taxpayers Assn.; past bd. dirs. Miami Beach Homeowners Assn.; hon. recruiter U.S. Navy. Mem. Am. Inst. C.P.A.s, Am. Assn. Atty.-C.P.A.s, Fla. Inst. C.P.A.s, ABA, Am. Arbitration Assn. (arbitrators panel), Miami Beach C. of C. (past bd. dirs.), Miami Beach Jaycees (v.p. community devel.). Democrat. Jewish. Home: 4333 Adams Ave Miami Beach FL 33140

GALE, GENE BROOK, insurance actuary, mathematics educator; b. Portland, Oreg., Nov. 16, 1935; s. Brook Isaac and Lillian Wilma (West) G.; m. Deborah Rose Nelson, Aug. 6, 1960 (div. 1974); children—Tanya Avalyn, Brook Isaac. B.A., Reed Coll., 1957; M.A., U. Oreg., 1962; postgrad. U. Calif.-Berkeley, 1974, Law Sch., U. Ark., 1981-82. Asst. prof. math. Calif. State U.-San Jose, 1965-73; part-time instr. Calif. State U.-Sacramento, U. Calif.-Davis, Chapman Coll. regional edn. centers, 1973-76; mathematician Calif.-Western States Life Ins. Co., Sacramento, 1976-80; asst. actuary Nat. Investors Life Ins. Co., Little Rock, 1980-84; asst. actuary Pan Am. Life Ins. Co., New Orleans, 1984—. Active Oreg. Hist. Soc., Ark. Hist. Soc. Fellow Life Mgmt. Inst.; mem. Am. Acad. Actuaries, Soc. Actuaries (assoc.), Am. Risk and Ins. Assn., Math. Assn. Am., Little Rock Actuaries Club (pres. 1983-84). Office: Pan Am Life Center 601 Poydras St New Orleans LA 70130

GALE, ROBERT JAMES, chemistry educator; b. Swindon, Eng., Apr. 18, 1942; came to U.S., 1972; s. Thomas James and Brigid (Gilsenan) G.; m. Julia Mary Herdman, May 8, 1971; children—Juliet Ellen, Thomas Edward. B.Sc., Imperial Coll., London U., 1963; Ph.D., McGill U., Montreal, Que., Can., 1972. Sr. chemist Wilkinson Sword Ltd., London, 1964-67; engr. grade RCA Victor Ltd., Montreal, 1967-68; postdoctoral researcher Colo. State U., Ft. Collins, 1972-74, vis. asst. prof. 1977-81; Colo. postdoctoral teaching fellow McGill U., 1974-75; research fellow Southampton U., Eng., 1975-77; asst. prof. La. State U., Baton Rouge, 1981—; cons. in field. Editor book series Molten Salt Techniques, 1983—. Contbr. articles to profl. publs. Patentee in field. Mem. Am. Chem. Soc. (abstractor 1968-74), Royal Inst. Chemistry. Electrochem. Soc., Baton Rouge Analytical Instruments Discussion Group (exec. com. 1984). Home: 1839 Peck Dr Baton Rouge LA 70810 Office: Chemistry Dept La State U Baton Rouge LA 70803

GALEA, JOHN HENRY, lawyer; b. Albany, N.Y., Jan. 18, 1924; s. John Fortune and Virginia (Sterling) G.; m. Helen Flynn Conway, Aug. 14, 1948; children—Michelle Galea Jeter, Mark C., Mary Ellen, Monica, Madeleine. A.B., Holy Cross Coll., 1947; LL.B., Harvard Law Sch., 1951. Bar: Ohio 1952, Ky. 1953, Va. 1959. Assoc. Grossman, Schlesinger & Carter, Cleve., 1951-53; with Reynolds Metals Co., Richmond, Va., 1953—, asst. gen. counsel, 1964-72, gen. atty., 1972-76, v.p., gen. counsel, 1976-85, sr. v.p., gen. counsel, 1985—; dir. Eskimo Pie Corp.; mem. legal audit com. Aluminum Assn. Served with USAAF, 1943-45. Decorated D.F.C., Air medal with three oak leaf clusters. Mem. Am. Corp. Counsel Assn., Assn. Gen. Counsel, ABA, Va. Bar Assn., Ky. Bar Assn., Richmond Bar Assn., NAM (legal adv. com.). Republican. Roman Catholic. Clubs: International (Washington); Harvard (Richmond). Office: 6601 W Broad St Richmond VA 23261

GALERSTEIN, CAROLYN LIPSHY, educational administrator, educator, researcher; b. Amarillo, Tex., Aug. 14, 1931; d. Harry and Tillie (Swartz) Lipshy; m. Sylvan Busch, Apr. 13, 1952 (dec. Aug. 1966); children—Susan Gail, Alan Lipshy, Saralynn, Lauren Kay; m. George Galerstein, Oct. 31, 1971. B.A., U. Mo., 1951; M.A., Columbia U., 1957; Ph.D., U. Md., 1965. Exec. dir. Zale Found., Dallas, 1963-67; asst. prof. U. Tex., Arlington, 1968-74, assoc. prof., 1975, dean sch. gen. studies, Richardson, 1975—; vis. exec. U.S. Dept. Housing and Urban Devel., Washington, 1981. Author: (with others) Profile of the Dallas Woman, 1976. Editor: Women Writers of Spain, 1985; Un Noviazgo, 1973. Bd. dirs. Nat. Assembly Social Policy and Devel., N.Y., 1964-66, Tejas Council Girl Scouts Am., 1984—; chairwoman Dallas Commn. Status Women, Dallas, 1975-77. Mem. Assn. Gen. and Liberal Studies (exec. council 1981-83), MLA, AAUW. Democrat. Jewish. Home: 3817 Vinecrest Dallas TX 75229 Office: U Tex PO Box 688 Richardson TX 75083-0688

GALL, STANLEY ADOLPH, physician, immunology researcher; b. Bismarck, N.D., May 31, 1936; s. Adolph and Wilma Thelma (Nickisch) G.; m. Florence Marie Ketterling, Aug. 17, 1958; children—Stanley, Kathryn Louise, Mark Allan, Thomas Andrew. B.A., U. Minn., 1958, M.D., 1962. Diplomate Am. Bd. Ob-Gyn. Intern, U. Oreg. Hosp., Portland, 1962-63; resident in ob-gyn U. Minn. Hosp., Mpls., 1963-66; asst. prof. ob-gyn U. Miami, 1968-73; assoc. prof. ob-gyn Duke U. Med. Center, Durham, N.C., 1973-78, prof., 1978—, dir. div. perinatal medicine; prof. ob-gyn, assoc. head dept. ob-gyn U. Ill. Coll. Medicine, 1985—. Served to capt. U.S. Army Med. Corps, 1966-68. Mem. Am. Coll. Obstetricians and Gynecologists, South Atlantic Assn. Obstetricians and Gynecologists, Soc. Perinatal Obstetricians. Contbr. articles to profl. jours.

GALLAGHER, WILLIAM JOHN, JR., environmental scientist; b. Stuttgart, Ger., Dec. 13, 1953; s. William and Alice Annett (Wiley) G.; 1 child, Mary Frances. B.S. in Environ. Health, E. Tenn. State U., 1975; M.P.H., U. Mich., 1980. Registered profl. environmentalist. Environmentalist, Tenn. Dept. Pub. Health, Jasper, 1975-79; environ. scientist U.S. EPA, Atlanta, 1980—; sec.-treas. Lower Eastern Affiliate, Tenn. Environ. Health Assn., 1979. Recipient Cert. of Merit, Tenn. Environ. Health Assn., 1979. Mem. Jasper Jaycees (external v.p. 1978, Presdl. Aid award, 1976). Avocations: camping; hiking; photography. Home: 896 Greenwood Ave Apt 9 Atlanta GA 30306 Office: US EPA 345 Courtland St Atlanta GA 30365

GALLAND, RICHARD I., oil company executive, lawyer; b. Denver, Oct. 13, 1916; s. Raymond F. and Mabel (Wilson) G.; m. Alice Halstead, July 21, 1941; children—Richard I., Holley, John H. A.B., Yale U., 1937, LL.B., 1940. Bar: N.Y. 1940. Asso. Cravath, deGersdorff, Swaine and Wood, N.Y.C., 1940-43, Cravath, Swaine & Moore, 1946-50; chief counsel Mathieson Chem. Corp., 1950-55; v.p., gen. counsel Colo. Oil and Gas Corp., 1955-58; pres. Am. Petrofina Co. of Tex., 1958-76; pres. Am. Petrofina, Inc., 1969-76, chief exec. officer, 1976-83, chmn. bd., 1976—; dir. Republic of Tex. Corp. Served as lt. (j.g.) USNR, 1943-46. Office: Am Petrofina Co of Tex PO Box 2159 Dallas TX 75221*

GALLANT, JOHN HUGH, commercial contracting company executive; b. Los Banos, Calif., July 18, 1944; s. John H. and Louise J. (Rimola) G.; m. Janice Mary Viera, Apr. 14, 1971 (div. July 1983); children—John V., Michael L. B.S., Calif. State Coll.-Long Beach, 1967; M.P.A., Golden Gate U., 1976. Controller, fin. mgr. Thompson Constrn. Co., 1971-80; pres., chmn. bd. H & G Structures, Inc., Clearwater, Fla., 1980—; chmn. bd. F & R Mech., Inc., Clearwater, 1982—, Heritage Tile, Inc., Clearwater, 1982—; v.p. fin. Heritage Assn., Carmel, Calif.; ptnr. MGM Investments. Mem. Am. Associated Gen. Contractors, Suncoast C. of C. (tourist bus. expansion com. 1981). Republican. Roman Catholic. Office: 314 S Missouri Ave Suite 205 Clearwater FL 33517

GALLANT, SANDRA KIRKHAM, psychologist; b. Dallas, July 15, 1933; d. Eugene Raley and Anita Bernice (Brandenburg) Kirkham; A.B., Hollins Coll., 1954; M.S., Va. Commonwealth U., 1956; m. Wade Miller Gallant, Jr., Sept. 15, 1979. Psychologist aide Lynchburg Tng. Sch. and Hosp., 1954-56, Rehab. Center of Rapides Parrish, 1956; clin. psychologist Bowman Gray Sch. Medicine, Wake Forest U., 1956-64, staff psychologist, acting dir. reading, speech and psychology center, 1962-64; staff psychologist Reading Speech and Psychology Center, part-time 1964-74; sch. psychologist Winston-Salem/Forsyth County Schs., part-time, 1974-75; clin. psychologist Child Guidance Clinic, Winston-Salem, N.C., 1975-82; ptnr. Triad Psychol. Assocs., 1982—; cons. to various community orgns. and agys. Bd. dirs. Family Services, 1964-66; bd. dirs. Little Theatre, 1963-66, pres., 1964-65; trustee to exec. com. Arts Council, 1965-68, v.p., 1967-68; bd. dirs. Mental Health Assn. Forsyth County, 1971-77, 79-85, pres., 1974-75; bd. dirs. Mental Health Assn. N.C., 1975-82, sec., 1977-79, v.p., 1979-81. Named Vol. of Yr., Mental Health Assn. Forsyth County, 1976; co-recipient Forsyth Mental Health Bell award, 1981. Mem. Am. Psychol. Assn., N.C. Psychol. Assn. Episcopalian. Home: 2534 Warwick Rd Winston-Salem NC 27104 Office: Triad Psychol Assocs 840 W 4th St Winston-Salem NC 27101

GALLARDO, ALBERT JOSEPH, data processing executive; b. San Antonio, Feb. 25, 1940; s. Albert V. and Annie R. Gallardo; student public schs.; m. Henrietta Castellanos, Aug. 19, 1965; children—Frank, Luis, Roger, Michelle. Programmer, CSC, Dayton, Ohio, 1965-67; systems rep. RCA, Oklahoma City and Dallas, 1967-71; programmer Action Communications Co., Dallas, 1971-72; with Compass Computer Services Co., 1972—, programming mgr., Dallas, 1974-77, dir. Hotel Property Mgmt. Systems, 1977-83, v.p. Property Mgmt. Systems, 1983—. Served with USAF, 1957-58. Address: Compass Computer Services Co 7701 Stemmons Freeway Dallas TX 75247

GALLE, FRED CHARLES, horticulturist; b. Dayton, Ohio, July 10, 1919; s. Alfred M. and Lucienne M. (Rappsilber) G.; m. Betty A. Nevison, Sept. 12, 1945; children—Phillip Charles, Peggy Ann. B.S., Ohio State U., 1943, M.S., 1945. Asst. prof. U. Tenn., 1947-52, Ohio State U., 1952-53; dir. hort. Callaway Gardens, Pine Mountain, Ga., 1953-80, curator, 1980-83. Served to 1st lt., field arty. U.S. Army, 1943-46. Decorated Purple Heart, Bronze Star; recipient Thomas Roland medal Mass. Hort. Soc., 1967; Silver medal Nat. Council Garden Clubs, 1977; Cert. of Merit, Ga. Garden Club, 1977; Henegar Research award So. Nurserymen Assn., 1978; Gov. award Am. Nurserymen Assn., 1980, Landscape award, 1981; award Ohio Arborists Assn., 1982. Mem. Am. Hort. Soc. (citation 1974, Liberty Hyde Bailey medal 1982; past pres.), Am. Rhododendron Soc. (past pres., Gold medal 1983), Am. Holly Soc., Am. Soc. Hort. Sci., Am. Assn. Bot. Gardens and Arboreta (past pres.). Republican. Methodist. Author: Native Azalea, 1962; Azaleas, 1974; Azaleas and Camellia, 1979; All About Azaleas and Rhododendrons, 1985; Azaleas, 1985; contbr. articles to profl. jours. Home: Box 252 Hamilton GA 31811

GALLERY, J. J., chemical company executive. Exec. v.p. agrl. products Occidental Chem. Corp., Houston. Office: Occidental Chem Corp PO Box 4289 Houston TX 77210*

GALLIEN, THOMAS WALKER, dentist; b. Waynesboro, Tenn., Jan. 13, 1946; s. Glenn Sinclair and Marybelle (Hurst) G.; m. Barbara K. Morris, Mar. 12, 1967 (dec. Jan. 1985); children—Thomas Walker Jr., John Morris, Robert Joseph. B.S., U. Tenn., Martin, 1967; D.D.S., U. Tenn. Ctr. Health Scis., Memphis, 1970. Practice dentistry, Savannah, Tenn., 1970-71, Martin, 1971—. Pres., West Weakley Unit Am. Cancer Soc., 1979-80, West Tenn. crusade chmn., 1982, bd. dirs. Tenn. div., 1982—, vice-chmn. Tenn. div. crusade com., 1986. Paul Harris fellow, 1978; named Outstanding Young Man Am., 1974. Mem. Am. Dental Assn., Tenn. Dental Assn., 7th Dist. Dental Soc., Northwest Tenn. Dental Study Club. Methodist. Lodges: Rotary (pres. 1978-79), Masons. Home: 130 Pine Tree Dr Martin TN 38237 Office: Professional Arts Bldg 145 Kennedy Dr Martin TN 38237

GALLIGAN, MICHAEL DELANEY, lawyer; b. Washington, Nov. 23, 1941; s. George Michael and Glenda Lucille (Long) G.; m. Ann Grier, June 24, 1978; children—Devin, Cassell, Trevor. B.S., Middle Tenn. State U., 1964; J.D., U. Tenn., 1970. Bar: Tenn. 1970, U.S. Dist. Ct. Tenn. Sole practice, McMinnville, Tenn., 1970-74, 77—; ptnr. Galligan & Newman, McMinnville, 1974-77; tchr. Motlow Jr. Coll.; atty. Warren County (Tenn.) Sch. Bd. Bd. dirs. River Park Hosp., McMinnville, Jan Davis Center for Mentally Retarded; chmn. McMinnville Regional Planning Commn., McMinnville Zoning Bd. Appeals. Served to capt. USMC, 1965-68; Decorated Purple Heart, Bronze Star; Vietnamese Cross of Gallentry; recipient Humanitarian award Nat. Youth Camps; spl. Recognition award from Senator Howard Baker, 1980. Mem. ABA, Tenn. Bar Assn., McMinnville Bar Assn. (pres.), Tenn. Trial Lawyers Assn. (bd. govs., asst. editor mag.), VFW, Am. Legion. Republican. Episcopalian.

GALLOWAY, BOB LAWRENCE, oil company executive; b. Elk City, Okla., Oct. 21, 1926; s. James Lawrence and Grace (Holley) G.; m. Sue Moore, Dec. 10, 1945; children—Jolene Galloway Munsey, Lon Dixon, Bobby Lawrence. B.S. in Chem. Enging., Okla. State U., 1950; postgrad. U. Tex.-Austin, 1962. With Cities Service Oil Co., Bartlesville, Okla., 1950-64, mgr. ops div., 1965-72; sr. v.p. Cities Service Gas Co., Oklahoma City, 1972-79; v.p. Cities Service Co., Tulsa, 1979-83; exec. v.p. Cities Service Oil & Gas Corp., Tulsa, 1983—; pres., dir. Coltexo Corp., Tulsa, 1979—, Gas Processors Assocs., Tulsa, 1985; dir. Bank of Commerce, Tulsa, Dixie Pipeline Co., Bartlesville. Bd. dirs. YMCA Met. Bd., Tulsa, 1980—, United Way, Tulsa, 1980-83; mem. Tulsa C. of C. Served with USN, 1943-45. Recipient Cert. of Service, Gas Processors Assn., 1972. Mem. Am. Petroleum Inst., Nat. LP Gas Assn. Republican. Methodist. Clubs: Petroleum, Tulsa Country. Avocations: golf; tennis. Office: Cities Service Oil and Gas Corp 7th and Boulder Tulsa OK 74102

GALLOWAY, DOCK ROSCOE, accountant; b. Transylvania County, N.C., July 12, 1915; s. Samuel Roscoe and Laura (Owen) G.; B.S. in Bus. Adminstrn., U. S.C., 1955; m. Lileree Mary Tanner, Sept. 28, 1949; children—Vera Lynn, Roxanne Elizabeth (dec.). Income tax auditor S.C. Tax Commn., Columbia, 1955-61; field auditor Agrl. Stablzn. and Conservation Service, U.S. Dept. Agr., Atlanta, 1961-62; pub. accountant L.C. Dodge, C.P.A., Spartanburg, S.C., 1962-65; plant accountant Spartan Mill, Spartanburg, 1965-67; forester and farmer, Spartanburg, 1967-69; dept. supr. Butte Knitting Mills, Spartanburg, 1969-80; engaged in forestry and real estate devel., 1980—. Served in U.S. Army, 1939-45. Mem. Nat. Mgmt. Assn. (chpt. cert. of appreciation 1979), U. S.C. Alumni Assn., Delta Sigma Pi. Republican. Methodist. Home: 641 Overhill Dr Spartanburg SC 29303

GALLOWAY, GALE LEE, diversified energy executive; b. Jan. 10, 1930; B.B.A. in Econs. Baylor U., 1952, postgrad. Tex. A&I U. 1953-54, S. Tex. Sch. Law 1958-61; m. Connie Galloway. Mgr. gas contracts Tenneco, Houston, 1954-64; sr. v.p. Coastal States, Corpus Christi and Houston, 1964-73; with Celeron Corp. (formerly Central La. Energy Corp.), Lafayette, La., now pres., chief exec. officer, chmn. bd.; mem. Oil and Gas Adv. Bd.; commr. La. Energy Commn.; commr. Bd. Commerce and Industry State of La.; dir. Rapides Bank & Trust, Alexandria, La. Pres., Evangeline area council Boy Scouts Am.; council trustees Gulf South Research Inst.; mem. Baylor Devel. Council; mem. pres.'s council Tulane U.; mem. hon. bd. visitors Grambling U.; co-chmn. United Givers Fund. Recipient Carnegie medal Carnegie Hero Fund Commn. Mem. Greater Lafayette C. of C. (dir.), La. Assn. Bus. and Industry (dir.), Interstate Oil Compact Commn., Mid Continent Oil and Gas Assn. (dir.), Natural Gas Men Houston, Am. Petroleum Inst., Interstate Natural Gas Assn. Am., La. Assn. Ind. Producers & Royalty Owners (dir.), Natural Gas Men's Assn. New Orleans, Nat. Petroleum Refiners Assn., Baylor U. Alumni Assn. (past pres.). Clubs: City of Lafayette (bd. govs.), Lafayette 100 (dir.), Lafayette Town House, Lafayette Petroleum. Address: 100 Shannon Dr Lafayette LA 70503

GALLOWAY, PATRICIA KAY, systems analyst, ethnohistorian; b. Bloomington, Ind., Sept. 7, 1945; d. Samuel B. and Mary Kay (Miller) Galloway. B.A. with honors in French, Millsaps Coll., 1966; M.A., U. N.C.-Chapel Hill, 1968, Ph.D., 1973. Instr. French, German, U. N.C., Wilmington, 1971-72; archaeol. finds supr. Norway and Eng., 1973-77; humanities programming advisor computer unit Westfield Coll., U. London, 1977-79; editor, adminstrv. asst., spl. projects officer Miss. Dept. Archives and History, Jackson, 1979—. Mem. Choctaw Heritage Council, Miss. Band of Choctaw Indians. Woodrow Wilson fellow, 1966-67; U. N.C.-Chapel Hill career teaching fellow, 1967-68. Mem. MLA, Internat. Arthurian Soc., Assn. for Literary and Linguistic Computing, Assn. for Computational Linguistics, Assn. for Computers and the Humanities, others. Democrat. Methodist. Club: Zeta Tau Alpha. Editor: La Salle and His Legacy, Mississippi Provincial Archives: French Dominion, Vols. IV and V (Chinard prize for French hist. studies 1985). Contbr. numerous articles to profl. jours. Office: PO Box 571 100 S State St Jackson MS 39205

GALORENZO, ROBERT, podiatrist; b. Passaic, N.J., Nov. 18, 1951; s. Carmen and Camille (Paparozzi) G.; m. Lisa Capaci, Oct. 9, 1977; children—Mark, Michael. B.A., Rutgers U., 1973; D.P.M., Pa. Coll. Podiatric Medicine, 1977. Diplomate Am. Bd. Podiatric Surgery. Podiatric surg. resident Memphis Eye and Ear Hosp., 1977-78, dir. residency tng., 1978-80; practice podiatry, Memphis, 1978—; adj. prof. Ohio Coll. Podiatric Medicine. Fellow Am. Coll. Foot Surgeons; mem. Am. Podiatry Assn., Tenn. Podiatry Assn., Memphis Podiatry Assn. (pres. 1980-81). Republican. Roman Catholic. Contbr. articles to profl. jours. Home: 99 Kinderkamack Rd Emerson NJ 07630 Office: 515 N Highland St Memphis TN 38122

GALT, JOHN WILLIAM, actor, writer; b. Jackson, Miss., Apr. 4, 1940; s. William Neal and Lyndel Janes (Fortenberry) G.; m. Anna Marie Kolenovsky, Dec. 14, 1965 (div. 1973); children—Joseph William, Edward Wayne; m. 2d, Diane Renee Wallace, June 6, 1981; 1 son, Christopher Wallace. Student U. Md. at Munich (W.Ger.), 1960-61, Mountain View Coll., 1970-72. Toured as folksinger U.S.A. and Europe, 1960-62; voice talent on numerous radio and TV commls., Dallas, 1965-78, 80—, Los Angeles, 1978-80; looped characters in movie Hardcore, First Family; writer film script Iceman, 1976; contbg. writer For The Love of Benji, 1977; writer screenplay Step Back From Angr, 1986; v.p. Tex. Ind. Feature Prodns., Inc., 1981—. Served with USAF, 1957-60. Recipient Dallas Citizen's Cert. Merit, 1973, Clios (10), Addys (16). Mem. Actor's Equity Assn., Screen Actor's Guild, AFTRA, Writers Guild of Am. Office: Industry Dallas 4314 Oaklawn Dallas TX 75219

GALVAN, ANTHONY, III, mass communications research educator, consultant, photographer; b. El Paso, Tex., June 2, 1946; s. T.A. and Soledad (Alvidrez) G. B.A., Colo. State U., 1973; M.A. in Mass Communications, U. Colo., 1978; Ph.D. in Radio-TV Film, Bowling Green State U., 1983. Photographer, U. Americas, Puebla, Mex., 1972-73; editor photographer Nat. Ctr. for Atmospheric Research, Boulder, Colo., 1973-78; asst. prof. Bowling Green (Ohio) State U., 1978-82; U.S. sales officer network sales TV Ontario, Dallas, 1983—; adj. faculty Tex. Christian U., Ft. Worth, 1983; instr. graphics and photography Fashion & Art Inst. Dallas, 1983; mktg. research cons. Sta. KNBN-TV, Dallas; cons. Owens-Fiberglas, Toledo, 1979, U.S. Dept. Agr., 1980, Dallas Mus. Nat. History, 1983. Served as 1st lt. F.A., U.S. Army, 1966-70. Recipient awards U.S. Army Photo Contest, 1969, Aspen (Colo.) Film Festival, 1977, Indsl. Photo Ann., 1981; NSF sci. tng. grantee, 1980. Mem. Soc. Profl. Journalists, Network Hispanic Communicators. Roman Catholic. Author: Professional Photographers of America, 1977; Photo I/Photo II Manual, 1980. Office: 4825 LBJ Freeway Suite 163 Dallas TX 75234

GALYA, THOMAS ANDREW, geologist; b. New Brunswick, N.J., July 11, 1947; s. Andrew Peter and Geraldine Rose G.; B.S., W.Va. U., 1971; M.S., N.E. La. U., 1975; Ph.D., Miami U., Oxford, Ohio, 1983; m. Lanora Lucille Bucklew, Jan. 8, 1970. Geologist, Sewell Coal Co.-Pittston Co., Nettie, W.Va., 1972; chief geologist, Clinchfield Coal Co.-Pittston Co., Dante, Va., 1978-82; sr. coal geologist, head coal quality group Exxon Coal Resources USA, Inc., Houston, 1982—; teaching asst. Northeast La. U., Monroe, 1973-75; teaching fellow Miami U., Oxford, Ohio, 1975-77, dissertation fellow, 1977-78. Mem. Am. Inst. Profl. Geologists, Am. Assn. Petroleum Geologists, Soc. Econ. Paleontologists and Mineralogists, Geol. Soc. Am., Sigma Xi, Sigma Gamma Epsilon. Democrat. Roman Catholic. Home: 6601 Dunlap Apt 2044 Houston TX 77074 Office: Exxon Coal Resources USA Inc PO Box 2180 Houston TX 77001

GAMBLE, ARLENE MARIE, librarian; b. Houston, Feb. 19, 1947; d. Randolph Bernard, Sr., and Antionette (Navy) Jacobs; B.A.L.S., Univ. Without Walls, Internat. Hispanic U., 1979; m. Casanova Gamble, May 10, 1968; children—Troy L'Keith, K'Lah Treniece. Supr., Res. Reading Facility, Rice U., Houston, 1969-77; mgr. tech. services Am. Productivity Center, Houston, 1977—; now fashion designer, prin. Beautiful U Boutique, Houston. Mem. Spl. Libraries Assn., Houston On-Line Users. Office: Beautiful U Boutique PO Box 25202 Houston TX 77265

GAMBLE, RUTH LENORA VERMILLION, hotel executive; b. San Antonio, Jan. 14, 1933; d. Louis Oliver and Elizabeth M. (Rush) Vermillion; m. Cloy Grant Gamble (div. 1966); children—Richard, Joe Bill, Amy, Cindy. Mgr., Town & Country, Bossier City, La., 1969-72; office mgr. Holiday Inn, Bossier City, 1972-79, restaurant mgr., 1980-82, Regency Hotel, Shreveport, La., 1982-83; hotel mgr. Chateau Charles, Lake Charles, La., 1979; gen. mgr. Village at the Downs, Bossier City, 1983—. Contbr. articles to newspapers and mags. Sec., bookkeeper Sports for Boys, Shreveport, 1972-83; asst. to Northwest dir. So. AAU Boxing Program, Shreveport, 1972-80; asst. Nat. AAU Championship Tournament, La., Miss., Las Vegas, 1975, 78, 79, 80, Nat. Golden Gloves Tournament, Shreveport; sustaining mem. Rep. Nat. Com. Mem. Bossier City C. of C., Shreveport-Bossier Hotel/Motel Assn. Baptist. Avocations: boxing judge, painting, camping, fishing, cooking, gardening, reading. Home: 707 Patton Bossier City LA 71112

GAMBLE, WILLIAM BELSER, JR., physician; b. Andrews, S.C., Apr. 17, 1925; s. William Belser and Anna (Moyd) G.; B.S., U. S.C., 1945; M.D., Med. Coll. S.C., 1948; M.P.H., U. N.C., 1972; m. Margaret Florence DuBose, June 7, 1947 (dec.); children—William Belser III, Richard Ervin, Heather Moyd; m. Bertie Hemingway Bunch, Mar. 1986. Intern, Roper Hosp., Charleston, S.C., 1948-49; resident pediatrics, teaching fellow Med. Coll. S.C., Charleston, 1953-56, assoc. prof. pediatrics; practice medicine sub-specializing in pediatric allergy and immunology, Charleston, 1956—; state epidemiologist State Bd. Health, also dir. div. epidemiology State Dept. Health and Environ. Control, Columbia, S.C., 1972-78, dep. chief bur. disease control, 1978—; chief pediatrics Roper Hosp.; mem. staff Med. Coll., St. Francis hosps., Charleston. Pres., Coastal Carolina Tb. and Health Assn. Dist. dir. S.C. Bd. of Health, 1972. Bd. dirs. Charleston County Mental Health Assn., Charleston County Tb Assn., Charleston. Served with M.C., U.S. Army, 1951-53. Diplomate Am. Bd. Pediatrics, Am. Bd. Allergy and Clin. Immunology, Am. Bd. Epidemiology. Fellow Am. Acad. Allergy, Am. Acad. Pediatrics; mem. AMA, Am. Acad. Pediatrics (infectious disease com., Red Book com.), S.C. Soc. Allergy and Clin. Immunology (charter pres.), Southeastern Allergy Assn., Phi Beta Kappa, Alpha Kappa Kappa, Kappa Sigma, Alpha Omega Alpha, Delta Omega. Presbyterian (elder). Club: Rotary (past pres.). Contbr. articles to profl. jours. Address: 3251 Seabrook Island Rd Johns Island SC 29455

GAMBONE, VICTOR EMMANUEL, JR., physician; b. Phila., Aug. 28, 1949; s. Victor Emmanuel and Eleanor Joyce (Porambo) G.; B.S., Pa. State U., 1971, M.D., 1975. Intern and resident in internal medicine U. S. Fla., Tampa, 1975-78; practice medicine specializing in internal medicine, Dunedin, Fla., 1978—; med. dir. Hospice Care, Inc., Pinellas County, 1982—. Diplomate Am. Bd. Internal Medicine. Mem. AMA, ACP, Am. Soc. Internal Medicine. Author: Post Operative Recall of Intra-Operative Events, 1975 (research award U. Miami Med. Sch.). Office: 1972 Bayshore Blvd Dunedin FL 33528

GAMBRELL, LUCK FLANDERS, executive; b. Augusta, Ga., Jan. 17, 1930; d. William Henry and Mattie Moring (Mitchell) Flanders; m. David Henry Gambrell, Oct. 16, 1953; children—Luck Davidson, David Henry, Alice Kathleen, Mary Latimer. B.A., Duke U., 1950; diplome d'etudes français L'Institut de Touraine, Tours, France, 1951. Chmn. bd. LFG Co., 1960—. Mem. State Bd. Pub. Safety, 1981—; bd. dirs. Atlanta Symphony Orch., 1982—; mem. Chpt. Nat. Cathedral, Washington, 1981—; mem. World Service Council YWCA, 1965; elder Presbyterian Ch.; trustee Student Aid Found., Atlanta, 1975; bd. trustees Tift Coll., 1982—; mem. steering com. Carter Presidential Library, 1983—. Mem. Atlanta Jr. League, Alpha Delta Pi.

GAMBRELL, RICHARD DONALD, JR., reproductive endocrinologist; b. St. George, S.C., Oct. 28, 1931; s. Richard Donald and Nettie Anzo (Ellenburg) G.; B.S., Furman U., 1953; M.D., Med. U. S.C., 1957; m. Mary Caroline Stone, Dec. 22, 1956; children—Deborah Christina, Juliet Denise. Intern, Greenville (S.C.) Gen. Hosp., 1957-58, resident, 1961-64; flight surgeon, Hickam AFB, Hawaii, 1958-61; chief ob-gyn, Tinker AFB, Okla., 1964-66; chmn. dept. ob-gyn, cons. to surgeon gen. USAF Hosp., Wiesbaden, Germany, 1966-69; fellow endocrinology Med. Coll. Ga., Augusta, 1969-71; chief gynecologic endocrinology Wilford Hall USAF Med. Center, Lackland AFB, Tex., 1971-78; mem. staff Westlawn Baptist Mission Med. Clinic, San Antonio, 1972-78; clin. prof. ob-gyn U. Tex. Health Sci. Center, San Antonio, 1971-78; clin. prof. ob-gyn and endocrinology Med. Coll. Ga., Augusta, 1978—; mem. consensus devel. panel on osteoporosis NIH, 1984; internat. lectr. Served to col. M.C., USAF, 1958-78. Recipient Chmn.'s Best Paper in Clin. Research from Teaching Hosp. award Armed Forces Dist. of Am. Coll. Ob-Gyn, 1972, Host award, 1977, Chmn.'s award, 1978, Purdue-Frederick award, 1979; award for outstanding exhibit Am. Fertility Soc., 1983, Am. Coll. Obstetricians and Gynecologists, 1983; thesis award South Atlantic Assn. Ob-Gyn; Chmn.'s award for best paper Pan Am. Conf. on Fertility and Sterility, 1976; diplomate Am. Bd. Ob-Gyn (div. reproductive endocrinology). Fellow Am. Coll. Obstetricians and Gynecologists (subcom. on endocrinology and infertility 1983-86); mem. So. Med. Assn., Am. Fertility Soc., Tex. Assn. Obstetrics and Gynecology, San Antonio Ob-Gyn Soc. (v.p. 1975-76), Chilean Soc. Ob-Gyn (hon.), Internat. Soc. Reproductive Medicine (program chmn. 1980, pres. 1985-87, Wyeth award 1985), Internat. Family Planning Research Assn., Internat. Menopause Soc. (exec. com. 1981-84), Am. Geriatric Soc. (editorial bd. 1981-83), Augusta Ob-Gyn Soc., Ga. Ob-Gyn. Soc., Nat. Geog. Soc., Phi Chi, Am. Philatelic Soc., Alpha Epsilon Delta. Baptist (deacon, Sunday sch. tchr. 1971-78, 80—). Contbr. chpts. to med. books, articles to profl. jours.; author: (with R. Greenblatt) The Menopause: Indications for Estrogen Therapy, 1979; Sex Steroid Hormones and Cancer, 1984; (with Greenblatt and V.B. Mahesh) Unwanted Hair: Its Cause and Treatment, 1985; mem. editorial bd. Jour. Reproductive Medicine, 1982-85, Maturitas, 1982—. Home: 3542 National Ct Augusta GA 30907 Office: 903 15 St Augusta GA 30901

GAMMILL, GEORGE DAVIS, clinical pharmacist, administrator, educator; b. Birmingham, Ala., June 4, 1946; s. Charles Lewis and Virginia Rose (Campbell) G.; m. Cynthia Kaye Durham, Feb. 1, 1969; children—Gregory Glen, Virginia Kaye. B.S. in Pharmacy, Samford U., 1969; M.B.A., Rollins Coll., 1976; Pharm.D. in Clin. Pharmacy, U. Fla., 1979. Lic. pharmacist, Ala., Fla., Miss., Va. Pharmacy intern C.K. Gammill Drug Co., Inc., Birmingham, 1969, pharmacist, 1969-70; dir. of pharmacy Brookwood Med. Ctr., Birmingham, 1979—; asst. clin. prof. Samford U., Birmingham, 1979—; asst. prof. Birmingham So. Coll., 1982-84; cons. in field. Contbr. articles to profl. jours. Chmn. Community Health Fair Vestavia Hills, Birmingham, 1983. Served to lt. comdr. USN, 1970-77. Doster Pharmacy Scholar, 1968; John W. Dargavel Found. grantee, 1967-69; recipient Pitman-Moore award Samford U., 1969; Citation for Disting. Service Jefferson County Pharm. Assn., 1969. Mem. Am. Soc. Hosp. Pharmacists, Ala. Soc. Hosp. Pharmacists, Am. Pharm. Assn., Acad. Gen. Practice, Rho Chi Pharm. Honor Soc. Republican. So. Baptist. Lodge: Rotary (bd. dirs. Vestavia Hills chpt. 1984-85, treas. 1985—). Avocations: woodworking; camping; scuba diving. Home: 1764 Shades View Ln Birmingham AL 35216 Office: Brookwood Med Ctr 2010 Medical Ctr Dr Birmingham AL 35209

GAMMON, JAMES EDWIN, clergyman; b. San Diego, Jan. 23, 1944; s. Jack Albert and Thalia Gammon; B.A., Tex. Christian U., 1970, postgrad., 1970-72; m. Sharon Elaine Head, June 27, 1965; children—John Paul, James Edwin, Jeffrey David. Ordained to ministry Ch. of Christ, 1966; minister Carter Park Ch., Ft. Worth, 1966-69, Scotland Hills Ch., Ft. Worth, 1969-70, Northside Ch., Dallas, 1970-73, Central Ave Ch., Valdosta, Ga., 1973-78; debate coach Christian Coll. S.W., Dallas, 1971-73; pres. So. Bible Inst., Valdosta, 1977-78; minister Trinity Oaks Ch. of Christ, Dallas., 1978-80, Parkview Ch. of Christ, Sherman, Tex., 1980-85; pres. Texoma Bible Inst., 1980-85; minister Eisenhower Ch. of Christ, Odessa, Tex., 1985—. Author: Notes on I, II, Thessalonians; Notes on James; Notes on Romans. Served with U.S. Army, 1963-66. Republican. Home: 1707 Laurel Odessa TX 79716 Office: 807 E 21st St Odessa TX 79761

GAMPONIA, HERMINIO LAFRADES, surgeon; b. Badoc, Philippines; s. Andres Bautista Gamponia and Julia Reyes Lafrades; m. Phoebe Tovera Jose, Apr. 4, 1961; children—Jessica-Ann, Melissa, Edgar, Deborah, Julie, Vanessa. A.A., U. Philippines, Quezon City, 1952; B.A., Manila Central U., 1953, M.D., 1958. Gen. rotating intern Mt. St. Mary's Hosp., Niagara Falls, N.Y., 1961-62; resident in gen. surgery Booth Meml. Med. Ctr., Flushing, N.Y., 1962-65, resident in thoracic and cardiovascular surgery L.I. Jewish Hosp. and Queens Hosp. Ctr. (N.Y.), 1966-67, chief resident in thoracic and cardiovascular surgery, 1967-68; fellow in gen. surgery Robert Parker Hosp., Sayre, Pa., 1965-66; practice medicine specializing in surgery, Spencer, W.Va.; mem. staff Roane Gen. Hosp.; med. dir. Gordon Health Care Facility, Spencer. Patentee by-pass catheter for vascular surgery. Bd. dirs. United Methodist Ch., Spencer, 1983-84. Fellow Soc. Abdominal Surgeons Am.; mem. Western Med. Soc. W.Va. (pres. 1983), W.Va. State Med. Soc., Soc. Philippine Surgeons in Am., Contemporary Medicine and Surgery, Spencer C. of C. Lodges: Masons, Shriners (Charleston). Home: 413 Green Acres Circle Spencer WV Office: 300 Hospital Dr Spencer WV 25276

GANN, JEFFERY SCOTT, mortgage company executive, mortgage broker; b. Atlanta, Oct. 1, 1957; s. Ray Garrett and Rose Marie (Terranova) G. Student Central Fla. Community Coll., 1976-77. Lic. ins. agt., Fla.; lic. mortgage broker, Fla. Salesman, Rainbow Mobile Home Sales, Ocala, Fla., 1975-76; v.p. Lendors Indemnity Assocs. Inc., Ocala, 1976-78; v.p. United Cos. Mortgage & Investment of Fla. Inc., Ocala, also Baton Rouge, La., 1978-79; pres. Heritage Fin. Systems, Inc., Gainesville, Fla., 1978—; fin. cons., 1978—. Mem. Fla. adv. bd. Reagan for Pres. Com., 1980. Mem. Fla. Assn. Mortgage Bankers (pres. dist. VII chpt.), Nat. Assn. Mortgage Brokers, Fla. C. of C., Florida Jaycees, Gainesville C. of C. Democrat. Roman Catholic.

GANT, BOBBY LEE, clinical psychologist and neuropsychologist; b. Dallas, Jan. 2, 1951; s. George and Nellie Jane (Sypert) G.; m. Deborah Ann Drom, Aug. 13, 1972; children—Christopher, Hillary. B.J., U. Tex., 1972; M.S., Tex. Christian U., 1974; M.A., U. Mo., 1975, Ph.D., 1977. Diplomate Am. Bd. Profl. Neuropsychology, Am. Acad. Behavioral Medicine. Staff psychologist Child Guidance Clinic, Lincoln, Nebr., 1977-79; asst. prof. U. Nebr., Lincoln, 1979-80; chief rehab. psychology Baylor U. Med. Ctr., Dallas, 1980-83; pvt. practice as psychologist and neuropsychologist Dallas Neurobehavioral Inst., 1984—. Contbr. chpts. to books, articles to profl. jours. Chmn. bd. dirs. Youth Adv. Com., Lincoln, 1980, Assn. for Retarded Citizens, Dallas, 1985. Mem. Am. Psychol. Assn., Tex. Psychol. Assn. (pres. 1984-85). Democrat. Baptist. Club: Sertoma. Avocations: scuba diving; karate. Home: 10114 Chesterton Dallas TX 75238 Office: 7515 Greenville 806 Dallas TX 75231

GANT, WILLIAM MILTON, justice; b. Owensboro, Ky., Nov. 25, 1919; s. Archibald Stuart and Mattie Ellis (Sloane) G.; m. Mary Ellen Price, Dec. 27, 1952; children—Stuart Price, Walter Sloane. A.B., Transylvania U., 1940; LL.B., U. Ky., 1947. Bar: Ky. 1947, fed. cts. 1947, U.S. Supreme Ct. 1966. Commonwealth atty. 6th Jud. Dist., Owensboro, 1962-76; judge Ky. Ct. Appeals, Frankfort, 1976-83; justice Supreme Ct. Ky., Frankfort, 1983—. Curator Transylvania U., Lexington, Ky., 1968—. Served to 1st lt. USAAF, 1942-45. Recipient Disting. Service award Ky. Med. Assn., 1972, Ky. Council on Crime and Delinquency, 1973. Mem. ABA, Am. Judicature Soc., Ky. Bar Assn., U. Ky. Alumni Assn. (nat. pres. 1958-59, 64-65, Disting. Service award 1969). Democrat. Mem. Christian Ch. Home: 1643 Sherwood Dr Owensboro KY 42301 Office: Supreme Ct Ky State Capitol Frankfort KY 40601

GANTER, BERNARD J., bishop; b. Galveston, Tex., July 17, 1928; s. Bernard J. and Marie L. (Bozka) G. Grad., Tex. A&M Coll., St. Mary's Sem., LaPorte, Tex., Catholic U. Am., Washington. Adminstr., Sacred Heart Parish, Conroe, Tex., 1955-56; ordained priest Roman Catholic Ch.; sec. to Bishop W.J. Nold; asst. pastor Sacred Heart Co-Cathedral, Houston, 1956-58, rector, 1969-73; officialis Diocesan Matrimonial Tribunal, 1958-64; chancellor Diocese of Houston, 1964-69, elevated to rev. monsignor, 1969; bishop Diocese of Tulsa, 1973-77, Diocese of Beaumont, Tex., 1977—; organizer Diocesan PreCana Confs.; moderator Post Cana Club Houston; chmn. Diocesan Senate Priests. Office: Chancery Office PO Box 3948 Beaumont TX 77704*

GANTNER, BRUCE ALAN, environmental engineer, industrial hygienist; b. Dayton, Ohio, Sept. 29, 1950; s. Clayton Houston and Naomi Marjene (Sheidler) G.; m. Joyce Ann Wikes (div. 1983); 1 child, Chris; m. Marilyn Rose Byrd, May 5, 1984; 1 child, Randal. B.M.E., Gen. Motors Inst., 1973; M.S. in Environ. Engring., U. N.C., 1975. Cert. indsl. hygienist Am. Bd. Indst. Hygiene; registered profl. engr., Tex., N.C. Indsl. hygienist N.C. Dept. Human Resources, Raleigh, 1976-78; staff indsl. hygienist N.C. Dept. Labor, Raleigh, 1978-79; sr. indsl. hygienist Cameron Iron Works, Houston, 1979-81, mgr. environ. services, 1981-82, mgr. health, safety and environ. services, 1981-85, supr. plant engring., 1985—. Coach Pee Wee football, Dayton, 1979-75, T-Ball, Friendswood, Tex., 1985—. Gen. Motors Corp. fellow, 1974. Mem. Am. Indsl. Hygiene Assn. (pres.-elect Gulf Coast sect. 1985—). Am. Soc. Safety Engrs., Am. Acad. Indsl. Hygiene, Am. Welding Soc. (assoc.). Methodist. Avocations: camping, boating, carpentry. Home: 109 Cherry Tree Ln Friendswood TX 77546 Office: Cameron Iron Works Inc 13013 NW Freeway Houston TX 77251

GANTT, HARVEY B., mayor of Charlotte, North Carolina; b. Charleston, S.C., Jan. 14, 1943. Student Iowa State U., 1960-62; B.Arch., Clemson U., 1965; M., MIT, 1970. Lectr., U. N.C., Chapel Hill, 1970-72; vis. critic Clemson U., S.C., 1972-73; mem. Charlotte City Council, 1975-79; mayor pro tem City of Charlotte, 1981-83, mayor, 1983—. Named Citizen of Yr., Charlotte chpt. NAACP, 1975, 84. Mem. AIA, Am. Planning Assn., N.C. Design Found. Office: Mayors Office 600 E Trade St Charlotte NC 28202*

GANTT, KAREN MARGARET, dietitian, consultant, writer; b. Sarasota, Fla., Oct. 6, 1941; d. Philip Augustus and Bobbie Marie (Yarborough) Edwards; m. Reid Ronald Gantt, Jan. 16, 1960; children—Veronica Lynn Gantt Hill, Robert Reid. B.S., Fla. Internat. U., 1973; M.Ed., Boston U., 1978. Clin. dietitian U.S. Army Hosp., Augsburg, Germany, 1975-78, VA Med. Ctr., Fayetteville, N.C., 1979-84; pvt. practice nutrition cons. Village Therapy Ctr., Fayetteville, 1984—. Chmn. VA Med. Ctr. Combined Fed. Campaign, 1983. Recipient Civil Service Outstanding Performance award, 1978; Leadership award N.C. Agr. Extension Service, 1981. Mem. Am. Dietetic Assn. (registered dietitian), N.C. Dietetic Assn. (voting dir. 1982), Fayetteville Dist. Dietetic Assn. (v.P. 1981, pres. 1982). Cons. Nutritionists Splty. Group, Am. Soc. Parenteral and Enteral Nutrition, Cumberland County Nutrition Council., Am. Rose Soc. (Fayetteville chpt.), Fayettville Mus. Art. Methodist. Contbg. editor The Voice, monthly N.C. Sr. Citizens Assn. newspaper, 1980—. Home: 6866 Towbridge Rd Fayetteville NC 28306 Office: 1750 Metro Medical Dr Fayetteville NC 28304

GARB, FORREST ALLAN, petroleum engineer; b. San Antonio, Dec. 15, 1929; s. Julius and Sada K. Garb; m. Janelda Duke, Feb. 7, 1959; children—David, Kara Lee. B.S. in Petroleum Engring., Tex. A&M U., 1951, M.S., 1963. Petroleum engr. Magnolia Petroleum Co., Tex., La., Kans., 1951-52; engr. Socony Mobil of Venezuela, 1955-57; reservoir engr. H.J. Gruy and Assocs., Inc., Irving, Tex., 1957-59, v.p., 1959-63, exec. v.p., 1963-73, pres., 1973—. Chmn. nat. com. Nat. Council for U.S.-China Trade, 1980; dist. chmn. Boy Scouts Am. Served to 1st lt. USAF, 1952-53. Recipient Silver Beaver award Boy Scouts Am., 1981. Mem. Soc. Petroleum Engrs., Assn. Computing Machinery, Petroleum Engrs. Club of Dallas, Soc. Petroleum Engrs. of AIME, Dallas Geol. Soc., Am. Assn. Petroleum Geologists. Jewish. Clubs: Los Colinas Country, Dallas Corinthian Yacht (past commodore). Contbr. articles to profl. jours. Home: 2973 Sunbeck Circle Farmers Branch TX 75234 Office: 150 W John Carpenter Freeway Irving TX 75062

GARBER, MARILYNN KAREN, registered nurse; b. North Kingston, R.I., Dec. 20, 1953; d. Cazimiro and Esther Mae (Coffey) Farria; m. William Edward Garber, Dec. 23, 1973; 1 dau., Kathryn Esther. A.S. in Nursing, Shenandoah Coll., 1974. Cert. ob/gyn nurse. Sec./bookkeeper Holly Acres Recreational Vehicle Storage, Woodbridge, Va., 1974-75; staff nurse Alexandria Hosp., (Va.), 1975—, Potomac Hosp., Woodbridge, 1975—, also mem. nursing audit com.; office nurse Dr. M. Garvez, Woodbridge, 1976-82; emergency med. technician Prince William County, Woodbridge; mem. Potomac Hosp. Corp. Mem. Nurse's Assn. of Am. Coll. Obstetricians and Gynecologists (cert.), Prince William County C. of C. Baptist.

GARBER, SALLY SEELBACH, mathematics educator; b. Cleve., July 29, 1943; d. Charles Frederick and Jane (Geckler) Seelbach; m. John Cline Garber; children—Margaret Katherine, John Cline, Jr. B.A., Hollins Coll., 1964; Ed.M., U. Va., 1966. Math. tchr. Lord Botetourt High Sch., Daleville, Va., 1964-65, 66-67; math. instr. U. Va., Roanoke, 1972, 73; math. instr., asst. prof. Hollins Coll., Roanoke, 1969, 70, 73—. Mem. Jr. League Roanoke Valley, 1966—; bd. dirs. ARC Roanoke Valley Chpt., 1985—, Botetourt County Heart Assn., Va., 1985—. Mem. Blue Ridge Council Tchrs. Math. (pres. 1984-85), Va. Council Tchrs. Math. (bd. dirs. 1984—), Nat. Council Tchrs. Math., Math. Assn. Am. (sect. regional exam. coordinator), Assn. for Women in Math., Sigma Xi, Delta Kappa Gamma. Unitarian. Home: Route 11 Box 417 Roanoke VA 24019 Office: Hollins Coll Box 9587 Hollins College VA 24020

GARBER, WALTER, JR., safety engineer, insurance company executive, consultant; b. Wilkes-Barre, Pa., Sept. 13, 1935; s. Walter Sr. and Eva (Voytoyvich) G.; m. Dolores Ann Walsh, Aug. 24, 1963; children—Deirdre, Justin. B.S., Temple U., 1959. Auditor, Employers Group, N.Y.C., 1964-67; loss control technician Firemans Fund Ins. Co., Boston, 1967-72, Albuquerque, 1972-77; regional dir. Allendale Ins. Co., Atlanta, 1977-78; mgr. Alexander & Alexander Inc, Atlanta, 1978-85; loss control rep. Zurich-Am. Ins. Co., Atlanta, 1985—; cons. Alexsis, Inc. Atlanta, 1978-85. Contbr. articles to profl. jours. Mem. Am. Soc. Safety Engrs. (cert.; pres. New Mex. chpt. 1974-75). Republican. Club: Albuquerque Amateur Radio. Avocations: amateur radio-extra class license; tennis. Office: Zurich-American Ins Co 3265 Piedmont Rd NE Atlanta GA 30363

GARBIN, ALBENO PATRICK, sociology educator; b. Girard, Ill., June 20, 1932; s. Cipriano and Angelina (Sommavillia) G.; m. Carol Townsend Nichols, Sept. 3, 1969; children—Angela Marie, Tina Ann, A. Patrick, Carol Anne. A.B., Blackburn Coll., 1956; M.A., La. State U., 1959, Ph.D., 1963. Instr., asst. prof. sociology U. Omaha, 1961-64; asst. prof. Fla. State U., Tallahassee, 1964-66; assoc. prof., specialist occupation edn. Ohio State U., Columbus, 1966-68; prof. sociology U. Ga., Athens, 1968—, chmn. dept., 1982—. Contbr. articles to profl. jours., chpts. to books. Served with U.S. Army, 1954-56. Recipient Research award Am. Personnel and Guidance Assn., 1977, Excellence in Undergrad. Teaching award U. Ga., 1978. Mem. Am. Sociol. Assn., So. Sociol. Soc., Ga. Sociol. Assn. (v.p. 1984-85, pres.-elect 1985-86, pres. 1986-87). Democrat. Roman Catholic. Avocations: gardening; photography. Home: 175 Sunnybrook Dr Athens GA 30605 Office: Dept Sociology U Ga Athens GA 30602

GARCIA, DAVID EDDY, petroleum geologist; b. El Paso, Tex., June 1, 1956; s. David S. and Stella (Eddy) G.; m. Linda Diaz, June 23, 1979; 1 child, Brandi Marie. B.S., U. Tex.-El Paso, 1978. Cert. welder, Tex. Geologist Amoco Production Co., Houston, 1979-80, petroleum geologist, 1980-82, petroleum geologist sr. grade, 1982-84; cons. pvt. practice, Houston, 1984—. Mem. Am. Assn. Petroleum Geologists, Houston Geol. Soc. Democrat. Roman Catholic. Avocations: boating; fishing; hunting; golf; baseball. Home: 6707 Liberty Valley Dr Katy TX 77449

GARCIA, DEBORRAH ANN DALGLISH, geophysicist, explorationist; b. San Antonio, May 18, 1955; d. Robert Lawrence and Alicia (Bolado) Dalglish; m. Ernesto Martinez Garcia, June 5, 1976. Student, San Antonio Coll., 1973-75, U. Tex.-San Antonio, 1975-76; B.S. in Geol. Scis., U. Tex., 1976-79. Research scientist assoc. Bur. Econ. Geology, Austin, Tex., 1979-81; staff geophysicist Mobil Exploration and Prodn., Dallas, 1981—. Mem. Soc. Exploration Geophysicists, Am. Assn. Petroleum Geologists, Dallas Geophys. Soc. Avocations: tennis; programming. Home: Route 1 #13 Hickory Hollow Dr Roanoke TX 76262 Office: Mobil Exploration and Prodn Services Inc PO Box 900 Dallas TX 75221

GARCÍA, HENRY, JR., publisher; b. El Paso, Tex., May 30, 1949; s. Enrique and Rosenda (Montoya) G.; student U. Tex.-El Paso; m. Carmen Ruth Luna, May 17, 1980. Owner, Henry's Printing, Clint; Tex., 1978; editor The Luminario, Clint, 1979; pres., owner Island Merc., Fabens, Tex., 1982—, Sand Sun Pub. Enterprises, Inc., Clint, 1982—; chmn. bd. El Paso Graphics Group; editor The Valley Ind., Amigos. Chmn., La Isla Devel. Bd., 1980-82. Named Jr. C. of C. of Yr., Tex. Jr. C. of C., 1980-81, Outstanding Young Man of Yr., 1981, Outstanding Local Pres., 1982, Top Fund Raiser award, Top Recruiter award, Outstanding Chmn. in Tex. award; recipient Carlos Porras award, Melvin B. Evans award, George O. Wilson award. Mem. Fabens Jr. C. of C. (chmn. bd., pres.), Tri-State Associated Grocers. Republican. Roman Catholic. Club: El Paso Printing. Home: 1607 Opossum Circle El Paso TX 79927 Office: 2000 Wyoming El Paso TX 79927

GARCIA, HIPOLITO, judge; b. San Antonio, Dec. 4, 1925; s. Hipolito and Francisca G.; LL.B., St. Mary's U., San Antonio, 1951. Bar: Tex. 1952. With Dist. Atty's Office, San Antonio, 1952; judge County Ct. at Law, 1964-74; judge Tex. Dist. Ct. Dist. 144, 1975-79, judge U.S. Dist. Ct. Western Dist., San Antonio, 1980—. Recipient cert. of Merit, Am. Legion. Mem. San Antonio Bar Assn., ABA, Delta Theta Phi. Democrat. Office: US Dist Ct Hemisfair Plaza 655 E Durango Blvd San Antonio TX 78206

GARCIA, JOE JUNIOR, insurance company executive; b. Clarksburg, W.Va., Oct. 8, 1947; s. Jose and Delfina Garcia; B.S. in Bus. Adminstrn., W.Va. U., 1970; m. Linda Celia, Dec. 18, 1971; 1 dau., Christen. Agt. life ins. Horaceman Ins. Co., Ft. Lauderdale, Fla., 1971-73; fin. planner, employee benefits specialist Randall/Dade Underwriters, Miami, Fla., 1973-75; pres. inst., estate planning and fin. planning Boca Del Mar Ins., Inc., Boca Raton, Fla., 1975-85; dist. agt. Northwestern Mut. Life Ins. Co., 1985—; now pres. Joe Garcia & Assocs., Boca Raton. Treas. Dade County Assn. Retarded Citizens, 1974; chmn. March of Dimes Walkathon, recipient award for contbns. secured. Registered rep. SEC, Nat. Assn. Securities Dealers; registered real estate agt. Mem. Million Dollar Round Table (life), Nat. Assn. Life Underwriters, Broward County Assn. Life Underwriters (dir., chmn. ethics com.), W.Va. Alumni Assn. (founding pres. Ft. Lauderdale-Boca Raton chpt.), Kappa Alpha Order Alumni Assn. Democrat. Roman Catholic. Club: Kiwanis (dir. West Boca Raton 1981—). Home: 6837 Calle Del Paz S Boca Raton FL 33433 Office: 1421 E Oakland Park Blvd Suite 202 Fort Lauderdale FL 33334 also 250 NW 4th Diagonal Boca Raton FL 33432

GARCIA, JUAN OLIVO, school administrator; b. Donna, Tex., Dec. 11, 1949; s. Filiberto Ramírez García and Amalia (Olivo) G.; m. Ida Martínez; children—Olegario, Juan Miguel, Amalia Viané. B.A. in Inter-Am. Affairs, Pan Am. U., 1973, M.Ed. in Adminstrn., 1977. Career edn. tchr. Weslaco Ind. Sch. Dist., Tex., 1975-78, vocat. counselor, 1978-80; asst. prin. Donna Ind. Sch. Dist., 1980-82, vocat. counselor, 1983-85, prin., 1985—; sales rep. Met. Life Ins. Co., N.Y.C., 1982-83; mem. scholarship com. South Tex. Vocat. Tech. Inst., Weslaco, 1985. Active Donna Jr. C. of C., Donna City Planning and Zoning Bd.; officer League United Latin Am. Citizens, 1980-84; v.p. Lions Internat. Mem. Tex. Elem. Sch. Prins. Assn., Tex. Vocat. Guidance Assn., Tex. Secondary Sch. Prins. Assn. Democrat. Roman Catholic. Avocations: reading; fishing; soccer; traveling. Home: 208 S 21st Donna TX 78537 Office: Donna Ind Sch Dist 116 N 10th St Donna TX 78537

GARCIA, JULIET VILLARREAL, college dean; b. Brownsville, Tex., May 18, 1949; d. Romeo Yzaguirre and Pauline (Lozano) Villarreal; m. Oscar Enrique Garcia, Jan. 24, 1969; children—Oscar David, Paulita Clemencia. B.A., U. Houston, 1970, M.A., 1972; Ph.D., U. Tex., 1976. Instr. speech and linguistics Tex. Southmost Coll., Brownsville, 1972-79, dir. self-study, 1979-81, dean arts and scis., 1981—; founder Young Scholars Honors Program, Coll. Summer Program for Youth, 1983—; grant writer Hispanic Immigrant Women Conf., 1984; dir. Tex. Commerce Bank. Chmn. bd. dirs. United Way, Brownsville, 1984; drive chmn. Am. Heart Assn., 1977-78; bd. dirs. Gladys Porter Zoo, Brownsville, 1978—, Econ. Devel. Found., Brownsville, 1983—. Grantee U. Tex., 1979-80, Nat. Inst. Edn., 1977-78; Ford Found. fellow, 1974-76. Mem. Profl. Women Speak (co-founder, chmn. bd. dirs. 1980—), Commn. on Colls. for So. Assn. of Colls. (vis. com. 1981—, chmn. com. visits, 1983—, chmn. standards and reports com. 1985), Phi Kappa Phi, Delta Kappa Gamma. Democrat. Roman Catholic. Lodge: Zonta Internat. (exec. bd. 1983-84). Avocations: reading; gardening. Home: 146 Sally Ln Brownsville TX 78521 Office: Tex Southmost Coll 80 Fort Brown Brownsville TX 78520

GARCIA, LUIS CESAREO, lawyer; b. Hato Rey, P.R., Apr. 19, 1949; came to U.S., 1965; s. Elena and John B. Amos (foster parents); s. Evelina Maura; m. Kathy Jo Mims, Dec. 4, 1970; children—Joseph Amos, Evelyn Kathleen. Student Columbus Coll., 1967-70; J.D., John Marshall Law U., Atlanta, 1973; postgrad. Harvard U., 1978, 84. Bar: Ga. 1974, U.S. Dist. Ct. (mid. dist.) Ga. 1974, U.S. Ct. Appeals (11th cir.) 1983, U.S. Supreme Ct. 1977. Assoc. Keil, Riley & Fort, Columbus, Ga., 1974-75; sole practice, Columbus, 1975-76; sr. ptnr. Garcia & Hirsch, P.C., Columbus, 1976-79; regional mgr. Am. Family Life Assurance Co., Columbus, 1979-82, exec. v.p., chief counsel, Am. Family Laws Life Assurance Co., 1982—, also v.p. Latin affairs; legal counsel LMI, Inc., 1979-82; mem. legis. com. Am. Prepaid Legal Inst., Chgo., 1983—. Bd. dirs. Better Bus. Bur. of W. Ga.-E. Ala.; mem. bd. adv. council CETA, 1979-83; adv. bd. Ga. Pub. TV, 1979-82. Mem. Fed. Bar Assn., ABA, Ga. Bar Assn., Columbus Lawyers Club, Younger Lawyers Club, Sigma Delta Kappa. Episcopalian. Clubs: Toastmasters, Country of Columbus. Office: Am Family Life Assurance Co 1932 Wynnton Rd Columbus GA 31999

GARCIA-ALLEN, EDUARDO AGUSTIN, construction company executive; b. Cuba, Sept. 8, 1942; came to U.S., 1960; s. Eduardo and America (Sanchez Borroto) G.; m. Karin Torp-Madsen, Sept. 9, 1972; children—Yvette, Michelle. B.S.C.E., U. Miami, 1965; postgrad. structural designs U. P.R., 1965. Cert. gen. and engring. contractor Fla. Project supt. constrn. Bank Nova Scotia, Old San Juan, P.R., 1965-66; founder, co-prin. Garcia-Allen Corp., Fajardo, P.R., 1966-68; subcontractor for AMECO, Honduras, 1968-70; pres. Garcia Allen Constrn Co., Inc., Miami, Fla., 1970—, Garcia Allen Internat. Corp. Galtech Inc., Garcia Allen Realty Inc., K.Y.M. Investment Inc. Mem. Latin Builders Assn. (v.p., dir., named contractor of yr. 1983, 1977), Engring. Contractor Assn., Assocs. Builders, Contractors Inc. Republican. Roman Catholic. Club: Ocean Reef (Key Largo, Fla.) Office: PO Box 876 Tamiami Sta Miami FL 33144

GARCIA-BURIA, CARLOS, educational administrator; b. Havana, Cuba, June 5, 1950; came to U.S., 1961; s. Carlos Garcia-Rodriguez and Lucrecia Buria; m. Myriam Jean Bonano, Mar. 4, 1978; children—Lanie Ann, Monica Zoraida. B.A. in Internat. Studies, Am. U., 1972, M.A., 1975. Acct. exec. Trade Fair of the Americas, Miami, Fla., 1980-82; dir. economic services and vocat. tng., U. Miami, 1982-84, dir. office of profl. devel., 1984—; ednl. cons., Miami, 1980—. Chmn. Dem. Hispanic Caucus, Dade County, Fla., 1984—; sec. Cuban-Am. Dem., Miami, 1983—; mem. state affirmative action com. Fla. Dem. Party, Tallahassee, 1984—. Ford Found. fellow 1975-76; recipient Spl. Opportunity Scholarship, Am. Univ., 1972-74, Washington Internat. Semester Scholarship, 1972, Hispanic Leadership Program, United Way, 1984—. Mem. Am. Soc. Tng. and Devel., Econ. Soc. South Fla., Nat. Univ. Continuing Edn. Assn., Coral Gables C. of C. (instl.). Club: Manatee Bay (Miami) (founding mem.). Office: U Miami PO Box 248005 Coral Gables FL 33124

GARCIADIEGO, ALEJANDRO RICARDO, history and philosophy of mathematics educator, researcher; b. Mexico City, Mex., May 3, 1953; s. Javier and Ana Maria (Dantan) Garciadiego; m. Maria Guadalupe Del Rio, June 25, 1977. B.A. in Math., Mexican Nat. U., 1977; M.A., U. Toronto, 1979, Ph.D., 1983. Asst. prof. Mexican Nat. U., 1975-77, U. Toronto, Ont., 1982-83; prof. history and philosophy of math. Mexican Nat. U., 1983—. Contbr. articles to profl. jours. Nat. investigator Conacyt, Mexico City, 1984. Mem. History of Sci. Assn., Philosophy of Sci. Assn., Am. Math. Assn., Brit. Soc. for History of Sci., Brit. Soc. for Philosophy of Sci. Roman Catholic. Avocations: photography; movies. Home: Jose M Velasco 71 Mexico City DF Mexico 03900 Office: Dept Math Facultad de Ciencias Nat U Mexico Mexico City DF Mexico 04510

GARCIA-MELY, RAFAEL, educator; b. N.Y.C., Dec. 28, 1921; s. Rafael and Vivan (Mely) G.; m. Christine Martin, Mar. 2, 1951 (div. Dec. 1968). B.S. in Social Sci., CCNY, 1946; B.D., Yale U., 1949; M.A., NYU, 1951, Ph.D., 1959;

L.H.D. (hon.), World U. (P.R.), 1975. Ordained to ministry United Ch. of Christ U.S.A., 1949. Youth minister First Reformed Ch., Schenectady, 1954-56; prof. edn. Inter-Am. U., San German, P.R., 1957-65; dep. gen. sec. World Council Christian Edn., Geneva, 1966-68; dean of acad. affairs World U., San Juan, P.R., 1969-78; dean grad. program Internat. Inst. Am. San Juan, 1978-83; prof. edn. InterAm. U., San Juan, 1984—. Editor Jour. World Christian Edn., 1966-68. Sec., bd. gov. World Univs., San Juan, 1968-83; v.p., treas. Latin Am. Evang. Council Christian Edn., Lima, Peru, 1968-81; bd. dirs., co-founder World Univs., Inc., San Juan, 1965-83; bd. dirs. govs. World Council Edn., Geneva, 1968-71; regional sec. Scholarship Commn. World Council of Chs., Geneva, 1971—; co-founder Fomento de la Opera, San Juan, 1977. Mem. Am. Assn. Higher Edn., Am. Sociol. Assn., Religious Edn. Assn., Adult Edn. Assn., Phi Epsilon Chi, Phi Delta Kappa. Avocations: music, educational activities.

GARCIA-PAGES, LUCILLE PATRICIA, nurse; b. Bklyn., Jan. 5, 1953; d. Dominick and Anna Rosa (Santoro) Illuzzi; m. Sergio Garcia-Pages, July 13, 1975; 1 son, Francis Illuzzi. B.S., Bklyn. Coll., 1975; B.S. in Nursing, U. Pa., 1980. Hosp. sec. Hosp. U. Pa., Phila., 1976-78; R.N. Bascom Palmer Eye Inst., Anne Bates Leach Eye Hosp., Miami, Fla., 1981—, lectr., 1983, CPR instr., 1983—. Mem. Am. Soc. Ophthalmic R.N.s (treas. Fla. br. 1983—, research com. 1983—), Am. Nurses Assn., Fla. Nurses Assn. Presbyterian. Office: Bascom Palmer Eye Inst Anne Bates Leach Eye Hosp 900 NW 17th St Miami FL 33125

GARCIA-PRATS, JOSEPH ARTHUR, physician, neonatologist; b. El Paso, Tex., Dec. 11, 1944; s. Jose Samuel Garcia and Louisa Prats; m. Catherine Ellen Musco, May 23, 1973; children—Anthony, David, Christopher, Joseph, Matthew, Mark. B.S. in Biology, Loyola U., New Orleans, 1967; postgrad. La. State U., 1967; M.D., Tulane U., 1972. Lic. physician, La., Tex.; diplomate Am. Bd. Pediatrics, Am. Bd. Neonatal and Perinatal Medicine. Intern, Baylor Affiliated Hosps., Houston, 1972-73, resident, 1973-75, neonatal-perinatal tng. fellow, 1975-77; staff neonatologist, asst. prof. pediatrics Baylor Coll. Medicine, 1977-82, assoc. prof. clin. pediatrics, 1983—; med. dir. neonatal ICU, Jefferson Davis Hosp., Houston, 1981—. Mem. So. Soc. Pediatric Research, Tex. Perinatal Assn., Harris County Med. Soc., Alpha Omega Alpha. Roman Catholic.

GARDES, ARTHUR ALBERT, JR., architect; b. New Orleans, July 22, 1950; s. Arthur Albert and Joyce (Mole) G.; B.A. in Bus. Adminstrn., Loyola U. of South, 1972; B.Arch., Tulane U., 1979; m. Christy Gómez, Oct. 16, 1976; 1 son, Jonathan Hutchins. Loan officer, asst. mgr. Nat. Bank of Commerce, Jefferson, La., 1972-76; architect Ehlinger & Assocs., Inc., 1979-80; project mgr., architect Lauricella Land Co., Harahan, La., 1980-83, sr. project mgr. Poydras Services, Inc., 1983—; sales cons. Lauricella Bros. Realty. Mem. New Orleans Mus. Art, Friends of Audubon Zoo; active Goodwill Industries Am. Lic. real estate salesman, La. Mem. Jefferson Bd. Realtors, Nat. Assn. Realtors. Democrat. Roman Catholic. Clubs: Metairie Country, Semreh, Beau Chene Country. Home: 4844 Purdue Dr Metairie LA 70003 Office: 2222 Canal St New Orleans LA 70119

GARDINE, JUANITA CONSTANTIA FORBES (MRS. CYPRIAN A. GARDINE), educator; b. St. Croix, V.I., Aug. 6, 1912; d. Alphonso Sebastian and Petrina (Actien) Forbes; B.A., Hunter Coll., 1934; M.A., Columbia U., 1940; postgrad. U. Chgo., 1949, NYU, 1960-66, Cheyney Coll., 1967; M.Ed., U. Ill.-Chgo., 1985; m. Cyprian A. Gardine, Apr. 23, 1942; children—Cyprian A., Vicki Maria Camilla, Letitia Theresa, Richard Whittington. Tchr. elementary schs., 1934-35; tchr. math. high sch., 1935-41, 48-49; acting asst. high sch. prin., 1941; jr. high sch. prin., 1941-47; substitute tchr. English, math., physics, Montclair, N.J., 1947-48; asst. supt. edn., 1949-55; assoc. dean Community Colls., 1955-57; high sch. prin., 1957-58; supr. ednl. stats., 1958-62; social worker Dept. Welfare, 1962-63; prin. Christiansted (St. Croix) Pub. Grammar Sch., 1963-74; tchr. math. evening session extension classes Cath. U. P.R., 1960-61; part-time instr. math. Coll. V.I., 1974-75, 80-81. Past sec. bd. dirs. St. Croix Fed. chpt. ARC; mem. bd., chmn. supervisory com. St. Croix Fed. Credit Union; past sec. St. Croix Sch. Health Com.; past mem. and pres. St. Croix (V.I.) Mental Health Assn. Pres., Tchrs. Assn., 1940, Municipal Employees Assn., 1942. Sch. named in her honor, 1974; honoree P.R. Friendship Day Com., 1979, St. John's Ch., 1981. Mem. Am. Statis. Assn., NAESP, V.I. Fedn. Bus. and Profl. Women's Clubs (past sec.), Episcopal Ch. Women of V.I. (past chmn. world affairs com.), Christiansted Bus. and Profl. Women's Club (past pres.; Woman of Year 1966), Daus. King (sec.), Christiansted Bus. and Profl. Club (past parliamentarian). Episcopalian (past pres. women's group). Home: 142 Whim Estate Frederiksted St Croix VI 00840 Mailing address: Box 1505 Christiansted St Croix VI 00820

GARDNER, DONALD ANGUS, architect; b. Portchester, N.Y., June 2, 1944; s. Angus John and Mary (Shaw) G.; B.Arch., Clemson U., 1968; m. Gloria Orr, Dec. 27, 1966; children—Angela Renee, Donald Angus, Sonia Dale. Draftsman, J.B. Lindsay, Clemson, S.C., 1970-74; project architect Vickery Allen Bashor, Greenville, S.C., 1974-75; partner Gardner, Edelblut & Assos., Seneca, S.C., 1975-76; project architect Daniel Internat./Daniel Engrs., Greenville, S.C., 1976-79, Lockwood Greene Engrs., Inc., Spartanburg, S.C., 1979-82, project mgr. Enwright Assos., Inc., Greenville, S.C., 1982-84; pres., Donald A. Gardner, Architect, Inc., Greenville, 1978—, also dir. Served to 1st lt. C.E., U.S. Army, 1968-70. Decorated Army Commendation medal. Mem. AIA, Nat. Assn. Home Builders. Methodist (trustee). Home: 104 Westover Pl Greenville SC 29615 Office: PO Box 16045 Station B Greenville SC 29606

GARDNER, GARY VAN, equipment manufacturing company official; b. Fort Wayne, Ind., Jan. 29, 1946; s. Van Watt and Margaret Joann (Little) G.; m. Barbara Rose Lapadot, Sept. 16, 1967; children—Monica Lynn, Gregory Ryan. B.A., St. Francis Coll., 1968, M.S., 1973. Sales coordinator Mobil Aerial Towers, Inc., Fort Wayne, Ind., 1969-75; ops. mgr. Internat. Trade Services, Fort Wayne, 1975-77; internat. bus. cons. Free Trade Resources, Orlando, Fla., 1977-79; mgr. internat. mktg. adminstrn. Altec Industries, Inc., Birmingham, Ala., 1979—; cons. Africa, Europe Free Trade Resources, Orlando, 1977-79. Del., Nat. Catholic Congress. Mem. Jaycees, Orlando C. of C., Ala. World Trade Assn., Sigma Lambda. Club: Letterman's (Ft. Wayne). Home: 5199 Redfern Way Birmingham AL 35243 Office: ALTEC Industries Inc 210 Inverness Center Dr Birmingham AL 35243

GARDNER, GRAHAM A(LLEN), real estate developer; b. Dallas, May 29, 1957; s. Harry Allen and Carolyn Terry (Smith) G. A.B., Harvard U., 1979, M.B.A., 1981. Leasing rep. Paragon Group, Dallas, 1981-82; ptnr. Nova Devel. Co., Dallas, 1982—. Mem. Dallas Symphony Orch. Guild, Dallas Mus. Art. Mem. Urban Land Inst., Nat. Assn. Indsl. and Office Parks, Greater Dallas Bd. Realtors. Methodist. Home: 4317 Larchmont Ave Dallas TX 75205 Office: Nova Devel Co 850 E Central Pkwy Suite 200 Plano TX 75074

GARDNER, HAROLD STEPHEN, economics educator, researcher; b. Dallas, May 17, 1951; s. Clarence Eugene and Nora Evelyn (Stephenson) G.; m. Kathy Susan Stokes, July 2, 1971; children—Daniel Eugene, Jessica Emily. B.A., U. Tex., 1973; Ph.D., U. Calif.-Berkeley, 1978. Instr., Grinnell Coll, Iowa, 1977-78; assoc. prof. Baylor U., Waco, Tex., 1978—. Author: Soviet Foreign Trade, 1983. Research fellow Am. Council of Learned Socs., 1980. Mem. Am. Econ. Assn., Assn. Slavic Studies, Assn. Comparative Econs. Baptist. Avocations: piano. Office: Dept Econs Baylor Univ Waco TX 76798

GARDNER, JOSEPH TATE, food distribution company executive; b. Decatur, Ill., Sept. 24, 1917; s. Harvey Adolph and Mildred (Tate) G.; m. Elizabeth Mitchell, Jan. 25, 1945; children—Elizabeth, Joseph Tate, Louise, Anne. A.B., Duke U., 1940. Co-owner Gardners Super-Markets, Miami, Fla., 1957—, chmn. emeritus, 1984—. Bd. dirs. Dade County Water/Sewer Authority, Miami, 1968-78. Served to capt. USNR, 1941-47; PTO. Decorated D.F.C. Mem. Assoc. Grocers Fla. (chmn. bd. 1970-84), So. Ocean Racing Conf. (bd. govs. 1972-83, chmn. 1975-78, named Councillor of Honor 1984), Fla. Sailing Assn. (commodore). Democrat. Episcopalian. Clubs: Coral Reef Yacht (commodore Miami 1967-68); Ocean Reef (Key Largo, Fla.). Office: Gardners Super Markets 7301 S W 57th Ave Miami FL 33143

GARDNER, LANCE DAVID, stock broker; b. Witchita, Kans., July 28, 1927; s. Bill and Patricia Charlene (Bailey) G.; children—Vicki Jean, Alex Maren. M. in Bus., Kans. State U., 1946, M. in Mgmt., 1955. Vice pres., mgr., supr. Tulsa br. A.G. Edwards & Sons, Inc., Tulsa. Chmn. Tulsa Philharmonic Assn. Served to capt. USAF, 1943. Decorated Purple Heart. Recipient Salesman of Yr. award A. G. Edwards & Sons Inc., 1968, 71, 72, 76, 80, 81, 82. Mem. Rosicrucians. Republican. Episcopalian. Club: So. Hills Country (Tulsa). Lodges: Rotary (chmn. bd. dirs.), Lions (v.p.).

GARDNER, LELA MARSHALL, speech pathologist; b. Wymore, Nebr., June 2, 1908; d. Virgil Ralph and Jeanie Mae (Warriner) Marshall; B.S. in Edn., U. Nebr., 1930; M.S. in Public Adminstrn., Washington U., St. Louis, 1932; postgrad. Columbia U., 1958-59, 60-61; m. John Hall Gardner, June 7, 1932; 1 dau., Marvel Jean. Speech pathologist Toledo Hearing League, 1959-60; grad. asst. Bowling Green (Ohio) State U., 1959-60; speech pathologist Bd. Edn., Newark, 1960-63, Johnstone Tng. Sch., Bordentown, N.J., 1963-66, Bd. Edn., Frederick County, Md., 1966-76, Western Md. Center, Hagerstown, 1976-77; free lance writer weekly Letters on nat. and internat. affairs, 1976—; cons. speech pathology State Home for Boys, Jamesburg, N.J., 1964-67. Mem. nat. adv. bd. Am. Security Council, 1973; life mem. Am. Conservation Union, 1973, John Birch Soc., 1973; founder Center for Internat. Securities Studies, 1977; sponsor Am. Council for World Freedom, 1972; pres. W.Va. Panhandle chpt. Eagle Forum, 1977; mem. Nat. Conservative Polit. Action Com.; U.S. Justice Found., Com. for a Free Afghanistan; mem. Heritage Found.; active Coalition for Peace Through Strength; bd. dirs. Com. to Restore the Constn., 1982; active Found. of Law and Soc., 1978; bd. dirs. Northampton County (Pa.) Soc. for Crippled Children and Adults, 1951-55, dir. pub. relations, 1953-55; coordinator for 2d Congl. dist. Conservative Caucus, 1983; nat. sr. adv. bd. Coll. Republicans; corr. sec. Women's Rep. Club, 1981-83; pub. relations Staff Make Today Count, 1982—; mem. Nat. Conservative Action Com.; 1982—; sponsor Young Ams. for Freedom, 1982—. Recipient tchrs. cert., N.J., 1960, life cert., 1965, Advanced Profl. cert. in speech and hearing, Md., 1969. Mem. Am. Speech and Hearing Assn. (life mem., cert. clin. competence), AAUW (arts chmn. Easton, Pa. br., dir.), Internat. Platform Assn., Internat. Soc. Philos. Enquiry, Gun Owners Am., Second Amendment Found., Ch. League Am. Intertel, Triple Nine Soc., Mensa, Citizen's Fire Company (hon.), Council InterAm. Security (sustaining mem.), Moral Majority, Black Silent Majority (hon. sustaining mem.), Citizens for Republic, Center for Free Enterprise, Pi Lambda Theta. Clubs: Nat. Congl. (sponsor 1982—), Women's (music chmn. Easton). Home: Route 1 Box 240 Jefferson Terr Charles Town WV 25414

GARDNER, PETER CARTER, radio executive; b. Bloomington, Ill., Oct. 28, 1947; s. James Richard and Dorothy (Carter) G.; m. Nancy Jo Purkey, July 19, 1966; children—Kimberly Jo, Peter James, Richard Christopher. News dir. KAYQ Radio, Kansas City, Mo., 1972-74, KLAK Radio, Denver, 1975-76, KITE Radio, San Antonio, 1976-77; writer, Fort Worth bur. chief KRLD Radio, Dallas, 1977-79; news and ops. mgr. KWMS Radio, Salt Lake City, 1979-81; news dir. WOAI Radio, San Antonio, 1981-84, KRLD Newsradio, Dallas, 1984—. Recipient award for best spot news coverage Sigma Delta Chi, 1980, best overall news coverage AP, 1981, best pub. service programming Tex. Assn. Broadcasters, 1983, best pub. service programming UPI, 1982. Mem. Radio-TV News Dirs. Assn., UP Internat. Broadcasters Assn. Tex. (adv. bd.). Office: KRLD Newsradio 1080 7901 Carpenter Freeway Dallas TX 75247

GARDNER, ROBERT GRANVILLE, clergyman, educator; b. Lima, Ohio, Apr. 26, 1924; s. Ernest Granville and Gertrude Marie (Roberts) G.; m. Anne Fargason, Dec. 18, 1947; children—Susan, David. A.B., Mercer U., 1949; B.D., Duke U., 1952, Ph.D., 1957. Minister, Reynolds Bapt. Ch., Ga., 1952-54; prof. religion, head dept. religion and philosophy Shorter Coll., Rome, Ga., 1957—. Author: On the Hill: The Story of Shorter College, 1972; Baptists of Early America: A Statistical History, 1983; First Baptist Church, Rome, Georgia, 1835-1985, 3 vols. Editor Viewpoints: Georgia Baptist History, 1972—. Contbr. revs. and essays to profl. jours. Served with USAF, 1943-46. Mem. Am. Soc. Ch. History, So. Bapt. Hist. Soc. (pres. 1982-83), Ga. Bapt. Hist. Soc. (pres. 1972-74, 75-77), Ga. Bapt. Conv. Com. on Bapt. History. Democrat. Office: Shorter Coll Box 297 Shorter Ave Rome GA 30161

GARDNER, ROBIN PIERCE, nuclear engineering educator; b. Charlotte, N.C., Aug. 17, 1934; s. Robin Brem and Margaret (Pierce) G.; m. Martha Miller, May 31, 1958 (div. 1976); m. Linda Gardner, Oct. 21, 1976; stepchildren—Scott Charles Deuel, Christopher Robert Deuel. B.Ch.E., N.C. State U., 1956, M.S., 1958; Ph.D. in Fuel Tech., Pa. State U., 1961. Registered profl. engr., Tenn. Scientist-in-charge short courses for engrs. on radioisotope applications Oak Ridge Inst. Nuclear Studies, 1961-63; chem. engr., assoc. dir. Measurements and Controls Lab., Research Triangle Inst., Research Triangle Park, N.C., 1963-67; prof. nuclear and chem. engring. N.C. State U., Raleigh, 1967—, dir. Ctr. for Engring. Applications of Radioisotopes. Served to 1st lt., U.S. Army, 1956. Mem. Am. Nuclear Soc. (Radiation Industry award Isotopes and Radiation Div. 1984), Am. Inst. Chem. Engrs., Fine Particle Soc., AIME, Sigma Xi, Phi Kappa Phi, Phi Lambda Upsilon. Club: Raleigh Racquet. Author: Radioisotope Measurement Applications in Engineering, 1967; contbr. articles to profl. jours. Office: PO Box 5636 NC State Univ Raleigh NC 27650

GARDNER, RUSSELL MENESE, lawyer; b. High Point, N.C., July 14, 1920; s. Joseph Hayes and Clara (Flynn) G.; m. Joyce Thresher, Mar. 7, 1946; children—Winthrop Gillet, Page Stansbury, June Thresher. A.B., Duke U., 1942, LL.B., 1948. Bar: Fla. 1948. Assoc., McCune, Hiaasen, Crum, Ferris & Gardner, and predecessors, 1948-50, ptnr., 1950—; dir. Thellian Co., Inc.; dir., sec. Aulhier Investment Co. Mem. Charter Revision Com. Fort Lauderdale, 1957; mem., chmn. info. and edn. subcom. Fort Lauderdale Citizens Adv. Com.; mem. adv. bd. Nova U., also bd. govs. Law Sch.; pres., chmn. bd. Jack & Jill Nursery, Inc.; bd. dirs. United Fund Broward County; trustee Ft. Lauderdale Mus. Arts, pres. bd., 1964-67; bd. dirs. Boys' Clubs Broward County, Cultural Council Greater Ft. Lauderdale, Inc.; bd. dirs. Stranahan House, Inc., pres., 1983-85; founding dir., sec. Broward Performing Arts Found., Inc., 1985—; trustee Broward County Heart Assn. Served from ensign to lt. Supply Corps, USNR, 1942-46. Fellow Am. Coll. Probate Counsel; mem. Fla. Bar (grievance com., probate and guardianship rules com., probate law com.), ABA, Broward County Bar Assn. (chmn. cts. com.), Am. Judicature Soc., Ft. Lauderdale Hist. Soc. (trustee, pres. 1975-85), U.S. Navy League (dir. Ft. Lauderdale council), Phi Delta Phi, Omicron Delta Kappa. Democrat. Presbyterian (trustee, deacon, elder). Clubs: Drummer; Coral Ridge Country; Lauderdale Yacht (dir., rear commodore 1976, vice commodore 1977, commodore 1978-79), Tower. Office: Penthouse Barnett Bank Plaza Bldg One E Broward Blvd Fort Lauderdale FL 33301

GARDNER, SUSANNE, ophthalmology educator, researcher; b. Hofheim, Fed. Republic Germany, Aug. 21, 1946; naturalized, 1968; m. George O. Waring, III, Apr. 27, 1984. B.S., Wayne State U., 1968; D.Pharmacy, U. Mich., 1978. Registered pharmacist, N.Y., Calif., Colo., Ga. Instr., pharmacist U. Mich. Hosp., Ann Arbor, 1971-76; drug info. specialist UCLA, 1978-80, ophthalmology clin. specialist, 1980-83; asst. clin. prof. ophthalmology Emory U., Atlanta, 1983—. Contbr. chpt. to book, ocular therapy and pharmacology newsletter, articles to profl. jours. Wayne State U. scholar, 1967. Mem. Assn. for Research in Vision and Ophthalmology, AAAS, Am. Soc. Hosp. Pharmacists. Avocations: piano; skiing; art and design. Office: Emory Clinic Ophthalmology 1327 Clifton Rd NE Atlanta GA 30322

GARDNER, VERNON EVERETT, consultant engineer; b. Alkabo, N.D., Dec. 7, 1913; s. Timothy William and Julia Olgina (Hillestad) G.; m. Elizabeth Ann Hunt, Mar. 25, 1950. Student N.D. Sch. Forestry, 1934-36; B.S. in Elec. Engring. U. N.D., 1938; postgrad. U. Pitts., 1940. Registered profl. engr., D.C., Calif. Elec. engr. Continental Motors Corp., Muskegon, Mich., 1938-39; instr. elec. engring. U. N.D., 1939; elec. engr. Westinghouse Electric Corp., East Pitts., 1940; elec. electrochem. and reliability engr. Dept. Navy, Washington, 1941-74; reliability engr. Tensor Industries, Inc., Arlington, Va., 1975-78, Columbia Research Corp., Arlington, 1978-79. Mem. joint bd. on sci. and engring. edn. contact mem. for St. James Sch., Falls Church, Va., 1970-82, St. Anthony's Sch., Falls Church, 1983-85. Recipient Superior Performance award Dept. Navy, 1963. Mem. Electrochem. Soc., AAAS, Assn. Scientists and Engrs. Dept. Navy (Outstanding Service award 1972), IEEE (Centennial medal 1984; life sr.; chmn. reliability group Washington sect. 1970-71, chmn. no. Va. sect. Control Systems Soc. 1980-81, chmn. sects. Soc. Social Implications of Tech. 1985-86, chmn. No. Va. sect. 1978-79, chmn. southeastern area region 2, 1981-82, chmn. region 2 bylaws com. 1983-84), Sigma Xi, Tau Beta Pi, Phi Theta Kappa. Unitarian. Clubs: Arts of Washington, Washington Figure Skating. Lodge: Elks. Home: 6624 Kirby Ct Falls Church VA 22043

GARDNER, WALTER DEAN, petroleum company executive; b. Chatfield, Minn., Mar. 27, 1934; s. Donavan Dean and Helen Katherine (Walsh) G.; m. Elizabeth Jean Guidry, Aug. 13, 1956; children—Dean, Mary Helen, Lawrence, Elizabeth. B.S., U. Southwestern La., 1957. Geologist, Ark. Fuel Oil Corp., Lafayette, La., 1957-60; devel. geologist Cities Service, Houston, 1960-61, exploration geologist, Colombia, 1961-69, staff geologist, Tulsa, N.Y.C., 1969-72, exploration mgr., Peru, 1972-76, regional mgr. Latin Am./Middle East, Houston, 1976-80, v.p. Citco Internat., mgr. exploration, 1980-83, Southeast mgr. exploration, 1983—. Harris grantee, 1953-57. Mem. Am. Assn. Petroleum Geologists, Geol. Soc. Am., Houston Geol. Soc., Miss. Geol. Soc., Mid. Continent Oil and Gas Assn., Brazilian Geol. Soc., Geol. and Geophys. Soc. Colombia (past pres.), Sigma Gamma Epsilon. Clubs: Colonial Country, Capitol City Petroleum, Walden Golf. Home: 11 Avery Circle Jackson MS 39211 Office: PO Box 12026 Jackson MS 39211

GARDNER, WILL CLYDE, hospital educator, consultant; b. Dike, Tex., Aug. 27, 1936; s. Will Clyde and F. Mae (Horton) G.; m. Peggy Ann Fernald, Mar. 3, 1957; children—Eva Lyn Gardner Bell, Jane Ann. B.S., Fla. State U., 1958. Asst. mgr. Ritter Fin., Tampa, Fla., 1958-59; cons. Sci. & Tech. Assocs., Montgomery, Ala., 1980; realtor J. Inscoe Agy., Montgomery, 1980-82; stock broker Southeast Brokerage Service, Montgomery, 1982-83; dir. staff devel. St. Margaret's Hosp., Montgomery, 1983—. Contbr. articles to USAF profl. jours., 1965-70. Bd. dirs. Am. Cancer Soc., Montgomery, 1978-84, pres., 1982-84; mem. Jasmine Hill Arts Council, Montgomery, 1980—, Mus. Fine Arts, Montgomery, 1980—, Landmarks Found., Montgomery, 1982—, Montgomery Civic Ballet, 1982—. Served to lt. col. USAF, 1959-80. Decorated Bronze Star, Vietnam Honor medal and others; recipient Vol. award Am. Cancer Soc., 1984, State Vol. of Year award, 1985. Mem. ASTD (mem. Montgomery chpt., treas. 1985—), Ala. Soc. Health and Edn. Tng., Ala. Hosp. Assn., Health Educator's Consortium, Mem. Ch. of Christ. Club: Officers (Maxwell AFB). Lodge: Rotary (sgt. at arms 1981-82). Avocations: collecting cut glass; athletics; fishing; golf. Home: 1748 Croom Dr Montgomery AL 36106 Office: St Margarets Hosp Ripley and Adams Ave Montgomery AL 36195-4701

GARIBALDI, ANTOINE MICHAEL, education educator, researcher; b. New Orleans, Sept. 26, 1950; s. Augustin and Marie Victress (Brule) G. B.A., Howard U., 1973; Ph.D., U. Minn., 1976. Tchr., Holy Comforter Sch., Washington, 1972-73; prin. St. Paul St. Acad., St. Paul, 1975-77; research assoc. Nat. Inst. Edn. U.S. Dept. Edn., Washington, 1977-82; lectr. Howard U., 1981; assoc. prof., chmn. dept. edn. Xavier U., New Orleans, 1982—; mem. Army Sci. Bd., Washington, 1979-83. Author: Educational Psychology, 1979. Editor: In-School Alternatives to Suspension, 1979; Black Colleges and Universities: Challenges for the Future, 1984. Assoc. editor Am. Ednl. Research Jour., 1981-83. Contbr. articles to profl. jours. Bd. dirs. New Orleans Library Bd., 1984—, St. Augustine's High Sch. Adv. Bd., New Orleans, 1984—, Archdiocese of Mpls., St. Paul, 1975, Nat. Catholic Conf. for Interracial Justice, Washington, 1980—. So. Ednl. Found. grantee, 1984—. Mem. Am. Ednl. Research Assn., Am. Psychol. Assn., Assn. Black Psychologists, Black Student Psychol. Assn. Democrat. Avocations: recreational activities, reading, music. Office: Xavier U La 7325 Palmetto St New Orleans LA 70125

GARIEPY, PAUL THOMAS, JR., financial services executive, consultant; b. Detroit, Sept. 16, 1953; s. Paul Thomas and Maryanne (O'Hara) G.; m. Beverly Alice Baker, May 26, 1979. B.A., Tulane U., 1975; M.S., U. New Orleans, 1978. C.P.A. With Peat, Marwick, Mitchell & Co., C.P.A.s, New Orleans, 1978-82, mgr. tax dept., 1982; fin. cons. Nat. Com. for Monetary Reform, Metairie, La., 1982—; exec. v.p., chief fin. officer James U. Blanchard & Co. Inc., Metairie, 1982—; dir. Gladiator Mining Corp., Alpha Omicron Corp. Loaned exec. United Way of Greater New Orleans, 1978, chmn. acctg. com., 1979-83, mem. exec. com., 1981—. Recipient Univ. award., chpt. Balfour award Sigma Chi, 1975, Price Waterhouse Outstanding Grad. Student award U. New Orleans Dept. Acctg., 1978. Mem. Am. Inst. C.P.A.s, La. Soc. C.P.A.s. Contbr. articles to profl. publs. Office: James U Blanchard & Co Inc 4425 W Napoleon Ave Metairie LA 70001

GARLAND, JAMES BOYCE, lawyer; b. Gastonia, N.C., June 16, 1920; s. Peter Woods and Kathleen (Boyce) G.; m. Elizabeth Matthews, Nov. 9, 1951; children—Elizabeth Garland Sarn, Woods Garland Potts, James Boyce, Rebecca Middleton. B.S., U. N.C., 1941, LL.B., 1946. Bar: N.C. 1946. Ptnr. Garland & Garland, Gastonia, 1946-59, Garland & Eck, Gastonia, 1961-62, Garland & Alala, Gastonia, 1962—; mem. N.C. Ho. of Reps., 1949-51. Chmn. bd. trustees Lees McRae Coll.; trustee Gaston Coll.; bd. visitors U. N.C., Chapel Hill; mem. N.C. Local Govt. Commn., 1970-75; pres. Schiele Mus. Natural History and Planetarium, 1984-85. Served to capt. USNG, 1942-45. Decorated Brozne Star. Mem. ABA, N.C. Bar Assn. (chmn. edn. law com., v.p. 1984-85), Gaston County Bar Assn. (pres.), N.C. State Bar, Gaston County Bar Assn. (pres.), Gaston County C. of C. (pres. 1980-81), Jaycees (Disting. Service award 1955; v.p. N.C. 1956), Phi Delta Phi. Democrat. Presbyterian. Club: Gaston Country. Lodge: Rotary (dist. gov. 1966-67). Office: 192 South St Gastonia NC 28052

GARLAND, LARETTA MATTHEWS, educational psychologist, nurse-educator; b. Jacksonville, Fla.; d. Wilburn L. and Clyde-Marian (Chamberlin) Matthews; diploma Fla. State Sch. Nursing, 1942; B.S.N., Emory U., 1950, M.Ed., 1953; B.A. in Edn., U. Fla., 1951; cert. cardiologist nurse specialty Tex. Med. Center, 1965; Ed.D., U. Ga., 1975; postgrad. in counseling and guidance Ga. State U., 1969, grad. cert. in gerontology, 1981; m. John B. Garland, Mar. 2, 1946; children—John Barnard, Brien Freeling, Amy-Gwin. Office and staff nurse, Lakeland, Fla., 1942, 45; nurse ARC, Buffalo, 1956; asst. prof. nursing Med. Coll. Ga., 1965-67; instr. Emory U., 1952-54, assoc. prof., 1967-71, prof., 1972—, ednl. psychologist, dir. gerontol. nurse practitioner program, 1978-80, asst. dean, 1983—. Served with Nurse Corps, U.S. Army, 1942-45. Decorated Bronze Star; recipient Outstanding Teaching award Emory U. Sch. Nursing Grad. Srs., 1977; HEW fellow, 1967-68. Mem. Am. Psychol. Assn., Am. Personnel and Guidance Assn., Am. Nurses Assn., Nat. League Nursing, Bus. and Profl. Women's Club, Alpha Chi Omega, Sigma Theta Tau, Kappa Delta Pi, Alpha Kappa Delta. Methodist. Author: (with Carol Bush) Coping Behavior and Nursing, 1982; contbr. articles to profl. jours. Office: Nell Hodgson Woodruff Sch Nursing Emory U Atlanta GA 30322

GARLAND, MICHAEL MCKEE, physicist, educator; b. Clarksville, Tenn., Jan. 12, 1939; s. Charles Richard and Frances (Wolf) G.; m. Rebecca Lynn Aslinger, June 4, 1979. B.A., Austin Peay State U., 1961; Ph.D., Clemson U., 1965. Mem. faculty Memphis State U., 1965—, prof. physics, 1970—. Recipient Disting. Teaching award Memphis State U., 1978. Mem. Am. Assn. Physics Tchrs., Am. Phys. Soc., Nat. Metric Assn., Sigma Xi, Sigma Pi Sigma. Office: Dept Physics Memphis State U Memphis TN 38152

GARLAND, SHARON ELIZABETH, china company executive; b. Tulsa, Aug. 11, 1948; d. Elmer James and Wilda Phyllis (Studebaker) Chandley. With audience response dept. Radio & TV Commn., Ft. Worth, 1969-72; assoc. dir. devel. Okla. Bapt. U., Shawnee, 1972-76; dir. resources Planned Parenthood Ctr., Houston, 1978-79; v.p. adminstrn. Viletta Party Plants & Skin Care, Houston, 1978-79; v.p. Viletta China Co., Houston, 1980—. Mem. career mktg. bd. Mademoiselle, 1980-84. Mem. Nat. Soc. Fund Raising Execs. Republican. Baptist. Office: 8000 Harwin St Suite 150 Houston TX 77036

GARLAND, T. BEN, JR., telecommunications company official; b. Bluefield, W.Va., June 18, 1932; s. Tanner B. and Violette Mae (Steele) G.; m. Dorothy Constance Barrett, Jan. 8, 1955 (div. Aug. 1975); m. Sylvia Kaye Ranson, Jan. 15, 1976; children—Tanner Ben III, Christopher B., Philip W., Clara Susan. B.S., VA. Tech. U., 1959. Clk. payroll dept. Hercules Powder Co., 1951-57; mgmt. asst. C & P Telephone Co., Parkersburg, W.Va., 1957-60, staff supr., 1960-65, traffic mgr., 1965-68, dist. traffic mgr., 1968-73, dist. mgr. customer services, 1973-81, dist. mgr. maintenance N.W. W.Va., 1981—; v.p. Local Devel. Corp., 1982-83. City councilman, 1978-81. Served with USAF, 1952-55. Mem. Greater Parkersburg C. of C. (chmn. bd., past pres.), W.Va. State C. of C. (chmn. indsl. devel.), Alpha Kappa Psi. Republican. Episcopalian. Home: 3514 Broad St Parkersburg WV 26104 Office: 921 Market St Parkersburg WV 26101

GARLICK, DENISE HARRISON, entreprenuer, restauranteur, advertising executive, art dealer, investor; b. Oklahoma City, Apr. 21, 1959; d. Jackie Olen and Vickey Lee (McCormack) Harrison; m. Harold Curtis Garlick, Jr., Jan. 17, 1981. B.A. magna cum laude in French and Art, Okla. City U., 1980. Advt. mgr. Combined Creative Groups, Inc., Oklahoma City, 1980-81; pres., owner Denise Designs, Ltd., Oklahoma City, 1981—; chief exec. officer G&W Restaurant Ops., Oklahoma City, 1983-85; v.p. Rebel Aviation, Oklahoma City, 1982-83; v.p. Dehege Aviation, Oklahoma City, 1984—; pres. DHG Investments, 1986—; cons. restaurant ops. and fin. packages. Cons. author Finance, Mgmt. and Promotion, 1983. Bd. dirs. Oklahoma City Republican

Women Club, 1984-86, del. conv., 1985, new founders chmn., 1986; active Okla. Mus. Art, Nat. Cowboy Hall of Fame, Meadows Ctr. for Opportunity Aux., Oklahoma City, 1984-85, United Methodist Dist. Women, Oklahoma City, 1984-86, spiritual life worship and communication coms. Chapel Hill United Meth. Ch., Republican Eagles; mem. adv. bd. Oklahoma City U. Sch. Arts and Scis., 1986. Mem. Nat. Assn. Female Execs., Okla. City Advt. Club, Bus. Profls. Mktg. Assn., Nat. Restaurant Assn., Okla. Aircraft Dealers Assn., Gamma Phi Beta (v.p., rush advisor, pres. 1985-86). Avocations: snow skiing; traveling; yachting; cooking. Home: 13054 Twisted Oak Rd Oklahoma City OK 73120 Office: Garlick Bldg 1313 SE 25th St Oklahoma City OK 73109

GARLINGER, BARBARA ELAINE, educator, coach; b. East Meadow, N.Y., Apr. 30, 1950; d. John Henry and Myrtle Irene (Hennings) G. B.S., Winthrop Coll., 1972. Tchr. phys. edn. Aiken High Sch., S.C., 1973—, varsity basketball coach, 1977—, varsity volleyball coach, 1979—, athletic dir., 1984—, student council advisor, 1976-83; sec.-treas. Conf. V-AAA Athletics, S.C., 1985—; state student council advisor S.C. Assn. Student Councils, 1982-83. Named All-County Basketball Coach, Aiken Standard Newspaper, 1983, All-Region Basketball Coach, Region III-AAA S.C., 1982. Mem. NEA, S.C. Edn. Assn., Nat. Assn. Secondary Sch. Advisors, S.C. Assn. Women's Sports, S.C. Basketball Coaches Assn. Democrat. Roman Catholic. Office: Aiken High Sch 211 Rutland Dr Aiken SC 29801

GARLOCK, JOHN ALAN, child psychologist, consultant; b. Bklyn., Dec. 16, 1946; s. Leon Mantis and Catherine (Belden) G. A.A., Eastfield Coll., 1972; B.S., U. Tex.-Dallas, 1973; M.S., East Tex. State U., 1975, 77, Ed.D., 1980; Ph.D., U. So. Miss., 1984. Cert. assoc. psychologist, counselor, sch. psychologist, devel. examiner. Acct. J.W. Bateson Co., Dallas, 1967-70; work study coordinator East Tex. State U., Commerce, 1974-77; asst. dir. student services/fin. aid U. Houston, 1978-81; psychologist intern Hattiesburg Pub. Schs., Miss., 1981-82; psychologist Jefferson Parish Schs., Metairie, La., 1982-84, Associated Counseling, Harker Heights, Tex., 1984—; pvt. practice psychology, Metairie, 1982-84, Hattiesburg, 1981-82; pvt. practice ednl. cons., Houston, 1978-81. Author articles. Active polit. campaign, Dallas, 1979. Served with USAR, 1966-72. Recipient Outstanding Service award Nat. Assn. Student Fin. Aid Adminstrs., 1980; Eddie Estes scholar, 1977. Mem. Am. Psychol. Assn., Am. Assn. Counseling Devel., Nat. Assn. Sch. Psychologists, La. Sch. Psychologist Assn., La. Psychol. Assn., Kappa Delta Pi, Phi Delta Kappa. Republican. Baptist. Club: Apple Computer. Avocations: computers; fishing; sailing. Home: 910-B Saratoga Temple TX 76501 Office: Associated Counseling Services 455 E Central Expressway Suite 103 Harker Heights TX 76547

GARMAN, PHYLLIS METROLIS, hydrogeologist; b. Rockville, Md., Sept. 10, 1939; d. George Joseph and Mildred Evelyn (Woods) Metrolis; m. Roy Keith Garman, Sept. 2, 1961 (div. Feb. 1975); children—K. Michael, Karen L., Mark A. B.S. in Geology, Fla. State U., 1962; M.S. in Environ. Scis., U. Va., 1981. Cert. profl. geologist, profl. environmentalist, Tenn. Geologist, Tenn. Div. Geology, Nashville, 1970-72, geologic editor, 1972-76; hydrogeologist Tenn. Dept. Health and Environ., Nashville, 1976-84; co-chmn. Tenn. Environ. Council Tech. Com.; chmn. Tenn. Groundwater Protection Task Force, 1981-82; cons. Joelton, Tenn., 1984—. Mem. Geol. Soc. Am. (sec.-treas. hydrogeology div. 1983—), Am. Inst. Profl. Geologists (v.p., mem. screening bd. Tenn. 1983, chmn. nat. membership com. 1985), Nat. Water Well Assn. (groundwater tech. div.), Sigma Xi (assoc.). Home and Office: 7570 Bidwell Rd Joelton TN 37080

GARNER, BILLY JACK, optometrist; b. Bryan, Tex., Mar. 20, 1940; m. Laura Sanders, June 8, 1962; children—Julie Ann, Jennifer Kay. B.S. in Pharmacy, U. Tex., 1964; B.S. in Optometry, U. Houston, 1973, O.D., 1975. Registered pharmacist, registered optometrist, Tex. Practice optometry, Houston, 1976—. Trustee Pasadena Ind. Sch. Dist., Tex., 1981—, now also pres. Mem. Am. Optometric Assn., Tex. Optometric Assn., Harris County Optometric Soc. (bd. dirs., treas.). Baptist. Lodge: Optimists (bd. dirs. local club), Gideons Internat. Office: 11408 Hughes Rd Houston TX 77089

GARNER, EARL ALONZO, utility company official; b. Cullman, Ala., Nov. 29, 1927; s. Walter A. and Maude L. (Woods) G.; m. Bula Mae Edwards, Dec. 28, 1948; 1 child, Eny Lea. Student, U. Ala., Birmingham, 1956-58. With Cosby Hodges Milling Co., 1953-64; with Sears Roebuck Co., Vestavia Hills, Ala., 1964-65; with Ala. Power Co., Birmingham, 1965—, resident claims agt., 1971-72, asst. to mgr. claims, 1972, acting mgr. claims, 1972-73, mgr. claims, 1973—. Served with USAF, 1947. Mem. Southeastern Claims Assn., Ala. Claims Assn., Southeastern Electric Exchange (claims com.), Edison Electric Inst. (claims com.). Presbyterian. Lodges: Masons, Shriners. Home: 317 Donna Dr Gardendale AL 35071 Office: 600 N 18th St Birmingham AL 35203

GARNER, HAROLD JOSEPH, art dealer, retail book company executive, investor; b. Tuscaloosa, Ala., June 5, 1930; s. Henry Calvin and Flora Hester (Winter) G.; m. Judith Beatriz Leon Smith, Sept. 1, 1953 (div. July 1972); children—Paul Marvin, David Leon. B.A., U. Ala.-Tuscaloosa, 1952, M.A., 1954; postdoctoral studies U. Tex., 1954-55, 57-58, 60-61. Teaching asst. in Spanish, U. Ala., Tuscaloosa, 1952-54, U. Tex., Austin, 1954-55, 57-58; instr. Spanish, U. Okla., Norman, 1955-58; dir. Centro Columbo-Americano, U.S. State Dept., Manizales, Colombia, S.Am., 1958-60, prof. catedratico U. Caldas, Manizales, 1959; spl. instr. English phonetics and methods of research U. Tex., Austin, 1961-62; ptnr. Garner & Smith Bookstores, Austin, 1962—; dir., ptnr. Garner & Smith Art Gallery, Austin, 1969—. Trustee Sta. KMFA-FM, Austin, 1975—. Mem. Am. Booksellers Assn. Democrat. Avocations: gardening; classical music; books, art, antiques collector. Home: 3208 Gilbert St Austin TX 78703 Office: Garner & Smith Art Gallery 509 W 12th St Austin TX 78701

GARNER, HELEN JUANITA, nurse; b. Blue Springs, Miss., Feb. 11, 1938; d. Wesley Earl and Nancy Emmaline (Wages) Hutcheson; m. Charles Edward Garner, Apr. 21, 1956; children—Emily Ann, Edward Wesley, James Emory. L.P.N., Itwamba Tech. Jr. Coll., 1968, R.N. (Asso. Nursing), 1981. Nurses aide North Miss. Med. Ctr., Tupelo, 1965-68, lic. practical nurse, 1968-69, lic. practical nurse, staff, 1971-74; 74-81, registered staff nurse, 1981—; lic. practical nurse, Tupelo, 1969-71, Okolona (Miss.) Community Hosp., 1974. Democrat. Methodist. Clubs: Tri-County Citizen Band Radio (sec./treas. Nettleton, Miss. 1972-75); North Mississippi Med Ctr Secret Pal (pres. 1982-83). Home: 7 Michael St Tupelo MS 38801 Office: North Mississippi Med Ctr 8305 Gloster St Tupelo MS 38801

GARNER, JERRY NOLAN, architect; b. Poteau, Okla., Feb. 11, 1948; s. Zelmon M. and Dartha C. Garner; B.Arch., Okla. State U., 1973. Architect, Caudill, Rowlett & Scott, 1973-75, Wotkyns Design Assocs., 1975-77, Skidmore, Owings & Merrill, 1977-78; pres. Jerry N. & Garner Assocs., Inc., Architects, Houston, 1978—, Jerry N. Garner Interest Inc., Developers; works include office bldgs., religious bldgs., schools, high density housing, shopping centers, residences. Mem. Houston/Galveston Meth. Bd. Missions, mem. research and devel. com. Lic. architect, Tex. Mem. AIA (com. on design, com. on housing), Houston C. of C. (research com.). Republican. Methodist. Home and Office: 1112 Nantucket C Houston TX 77057

GARNER, JOHN CLAIBORNE, JR., architectural restorationist, consultant; b. Port Lavaca, Tex., Mar. 1, 1939; s. John Claiborne and Lois Merle (Awbrey) G.; m. Shirley Jane Price, June 20, 1975. B.Arch., U. Tex.-Austin, 1963, postgrad. in historic preservation, 1963-65. Field dir. Tex. Architecture Survey, U. Tex.-Amon Carter Mus. Western Art, Austin and Fort Worth, 1964-65; dir. Galveston Hist. Architecture Research Project, Galveston Hist. Found., Inc., Tex., 1966-67, exec. dir. preservation program, 1969; dir. Bexar County Hist. Architecture Research Project, San Antonio Conservation Soc., 1967-69, exec. dir. Miami Purchase Assn., Cin., 1970-72; hist. preservation cons., Ohio and Tex., 1972-73; regional hist. architect southeast regional office U.S. Dept. Interior, Nat. Park Service, 1973-83; pres. Restoration Mgmt. Corp., Yankeetown, Fla., 1983—; assoc. prof. architecture U. Fla., 1983-84; lectr. in field. Major restoration projects include: Castillo de San Juan de Ulua, Veracruz, Mex., 1985; Pres. Andrew Johnson home, Greenville, Tenn., 1982; Fort Barrancas and Advanced Redoubt, Pensacola, Fla., 1976-78. Author: Guidelines for Rehabilitation of the Findlay Market Historic District, 1972; (technical studies) Enhancement of Cultural Sites (Nassau, Bahamas), 1984; Preservation of Fort Pike, 1985, other tech. studies. Recipient Spl. Achievement award U.S. Nat. Park Service, Atlanta, 1976, 81; Roy E. Appleman-Henry A. Judd award, U.S. Nat. Park Service, Washington, 1980. Mem. Internat. Council Monuments and Sites, Nat. Trust Hist. Preservation, Assn. Preservation Technology, Am. Inst. Archaeology, Fla. Trust Hist. Preservation. Presbyterian. Home: 5209 Riverside Dr Yankeetown FL 32698 Office: Restoration Mgmt Corp PO Box 279 Yankeetown FL 32698

GARNER, KENDALL LAYTON, computer company official; b. Temple, Tex., July 29, 1944; s. Layton and Variel (Starr) G.; m. Bettie Cook; children—Tiffany, Paige, Jay. B.B.A., N. Tex. State U., 1966. Mgr. fin. systems Bell Helicopter, Tehran, Iran, 1976-78; mgr. fin. services Moore Bus. Systems, Denton, Tex., 1979-80, assoc. dir. adminstrn., 1980-83, asst. comptroller, 1983—. Baptist. Home: 2133 Pembrooke Denton TX 76205 Office: Moore Bus Systems PO Box 2761 Denton TX 76201

GARNER, ROBERT EDWARD LEE, lawyer; b. Bowling Green, Ky., Sept. 26, 1946; s. Alto Luther and Katie Mae (Sanders) G.; m. Suzanne Marie Searles, Aug. 22, 1981; 1 child, Jessica Marie. B.A., U. Ala.-Tuscaloosa, 1968; J.D., Harvard U., 1971. Bar: Ga. 1971, Ala. 1982, U.S. Dist. Ct. (no. dist.) Ga. 1974, U.S. Ct. Appeals (5th cir.) 1974, U.S. Ct. Appeals (11th cir.) 1981. Assoc., Gambrell, Russell & Forbes, Atlanta, 1972-76, ptnr., 1976-80; ptnr. Haskell, Slaughter, Young & Lewis, Birmingham, Ala., 1981—; sec., gen. counsel, dir. Builders Transport, Inc. Served to 1st lt. JAGC, USAF, 1971-72. Mem. ABA, Ga. Bar Assn., Ala. State Bar, Birmingham Bar Assn., U. Ala. Alumni Assn., Harvard U. Alumni Assn., Phi Alpha Theta, Pi Sigma Alpha. Republican. Baptist. Clubs: Relay House, Cahaba Valley Lions (charter). Home: 5204 Meadow Brook Rd Birmingham AL 35243 Office: Haskell Slaughter Young & Lewis Suite 800 1st Nat Southern Natural Bldg Birmingham AL 35203

GARNER, THOMAS WILLIAM, photographer; b. Monticello, Ark., Feb. 3, 1945; s. William Eli and Mildred Martha (Owen) G.; m. Clara Marie Steele, Apr. 1, 1967 (div. 1972); children—Suzanne Marie, Jeffrey Thomas. B.S., U. N.Mex., 1966. Dist. mgr. K-Mart, Seattle, 1968-70; asst. mgr. Woolco, San Diego, 1971-74; salesman Hanimex, San Diego, 1974-78; regional mgr. Osawa & Co., Houston, 1978—; dir. Trevino's Photo, McAllen, Tex., 1980—. Photographer, U. N.Mex., 1964. Served to capt. USAF, 1966-68; Vietnam. Named Salesman of Yr., Hanimex, 1976, Osawa & Co., 1980, Regional Mgr. of Yr., 1982. Mem. Profl. Photographers Am. Home: 23311 Low Ridge Spring TX 77373

GARNES, RONALD VINCENT, financial broker, consultant; b. Washington, Mar. 7, 1947; s. Ernest W. Love and Vauda Hall Love G.; student U. Dayton, 1965-68; B.S., U. Md., 1975; postgrad. Am. U., 1980. Adminstrv. mgr. Western Union Electronic Mail, Inc., McLean, Va., 1976; dir. mktg. Communications Cons., Inc., Silver Spring, Md., 1977; partner CAC, Washington, 1977; account mgr. PRC Computer Center, Inc., McLean, Va., 1978-79, sr. account mgr., 1979—; mktg. exec. Dun and Bradstreet Corp.; prin. Ronald V. Garnes Assos. Cons. Mem. Fairfax County Republican Com. Mem. Am. Entrepreneurs Assn., Nat. Assn. Self-Employed, Internat. Assn. Bus. and Fin. Cons., Mortgage Banker Assn., Nat. Council Tech. Service Industries, Nat. Assn. Market Developers, Greater Washington Bd. Trade, Rand Group, Delta Group, Fairfax County C. of C. Republican. Roman Catholic. Clubs: Lincoln; U.S. Senatorial. Office: PO Box PP McLean VA 22101

GARNET, ROBERT IRA, podiatrist; b. Jersey City, Sept. 10, 1944; s. Morris Louis and Perle (Ruberman) G.; m. Avis Lorraine Polikoff, Aug. 3, 1974; children—Jenna, Michael, Jonathan. Student Bucknell U., 1962-65; D.P.M., N.Y. Coll. Podiatric Medicine, 1969. Externship, Beth Israel Hosp., N.Y.C., 1968-69; practice podiatry, Cutler Ridge, Fla., 1970—; cons. podiatrist Fusion Dance Co., Miami, Super Stars-ABC Sports, Dade County Jail and Stockade, and others; mem. staff Westchester Gen. Hosp., Miami, Jackson Meml. Hosp., Miami, Larkin Gen. Hosp., South Miami, South Dade Community Health Center, Goulds, Fla., Ambulatory Ctr., Miami, Coral Reef Gen. Hop., Miami, Bapt. Hosp., Miami, Am. Hosp., Miami; clin. assoc. prof. dept. family medicine U. Miami Med. Sch., 1972—; co-dir. Miami Runner-Road Runners Club Am., Miami, 1978—. Fellow Am. Coll. Foot Surgeons, Acad. Podiatric Sports Medicine, Acad. Ambulatory Foot Surgeons; mem. Dade County Podiatry Assn. (pres. 1976-77), Am. Podiatry Assn., Fla. Podiatry Assn., Am. Public Health Assn., Fla. Public Health Assn., Dade-Monroe Profl. Standard Rev. Orgn. Diplomate Am. Bd. Podiatric Surgery. Home: 10620 SW 127th St Miami FL 33176 Office: 18430 S Dixie Hwy Miami FL 33157

GARNETT, E.N., food products company executive. Dir. Flav-O-Rich, Inc., Louisville. Office: Flav-O-Rich Inc 10140 Linn Station Rd Louisville KY 40223*

GARRETT, DAVID CLYDE, JR., airline executive; b. Norris, S.C., July, 1922; s. David Clyde and Mary H. G.; m. Lu Thomasson, Sept. 11, 1947; children—David, Virginia, Charles. B.A., Furman U., 1942; M.S., Ga. Inst. Tech., 1955. With Delta Air Lines, Inc., Atlanta, 1946—, pres., 1971—, chief exec. officer, 1978—, also dir.; dir. Travelers Corp., U.S. Steel, Nat. Service Ind. Served with USAAF, 1943-46. Office: Delta Air Lines Hartsfield Internat Airport Atlanta GA 30320

GARRETT, FRANKLIN MILLER, historian; b. Milw., Sept. 25, 1906; s. Clarence Robert and Ada (Kirkwood) G.; LL.B., Woodrow Wilson Coll. Law, 1941; L.H.D., Oglethorpe Coll., 1970; m. Frances Steele, 1978; children by previous marriage—Patricia Abbott, Franklin Miller. Br. mgr. Western Union Telegraph Co., Atlanta, 1934-38; salesman Ward Wight & Co., Atlanta, 1939-40; mem. exec. staff pub. relations, historian Coca-Cola Co., Atlanta, 1940-68. Chmn., Fulton County (Ga.) Civil Service Bd., 1955-72; ofcl. historian City of Atlanta, 1973—, Fulton County, 1975—. Bd. dirs. Children's Center Met. Atlanta, 1958-70. Served with AUS, 1942-45. Named a City Shaper, Atlanta mag., 1976; recipient Meritorious Pub. Service medal Nat. Assn. Secs. of State, 1985; mainline diesel locomotive Ga. R.R. named in his honor, 1980. Mem. Nat. Ry., Va., Ga., Atlanta (chmn. bd. trustees 1967-68, dir. 1968-74, historian 1974—, trustee 1932—), DeKalb County hist. socs., Newcomen Soc. N.Am., Atlanta Art Assn., Atlanta Civil War Round Table, Grand Jurors Assn. Fulton County, Ga. Geneal. Soc. Presbyterian. Clubs: Rotary, Commerce, Piedmont Driving. Author: Atlanta and Environs I-III, 1954, rev. edit., 1969; Yesterday's Atlanta, a picture history, 1974. Home: 3650 Randall Mill Rd NW Atlanta GA 30327 Office: 3101 Andrews Dr NW Atlanta GA 30305

GARRETT, HELEN MARIE, state senator; b. Paducah, Ky.; d. John Frank and Helen Eunice (Bean) Rickman; m. John Thomas Garrett, 1952 (dec.); children—Tom, Carol. Mem. Ky. Senate, majority whip. Democrat. Office: Ky Senate State Capitol Frankfurt KY 40601*

GARRETT, JAMES BENJAMIN, JR., psychologist, educator; b. Charleston, W.Va., Oct. 20, 1943; s. James Benjamin and Lucy (Bennett) G.; m. Kathleen Laurie Cramer, Dec. 31, 1984. B.S., Hampden-Sydney Coll., 1965; M.A., Ohio State U., 1967, Ph.D., 1970. Asst. prof. psychology Western Ill. U., Macomb, 1970-75, assoc. prof., 1975-78; psychologist Central Va. Tng. Center, Madison Heights, Va., 1979—; prof. psychology Central Va. Community Coll., Lynchburg, 1982—; dir. Transformational Dynamics, 1983; cons. Lynchburg Hospice Program, 1983. Editorial reviewer Human Relations, Tavistock Inst., London. Western Ill. U. Research Council research grantee, 1971, 75. Mem. Soc. Clin. and Exptl. Hypnosis, Am. Psychol. Assn., Va. Counselors Assn., Sigma Xi. Democrat. Presbyterian. Home: 838 Rivermont Ave Lynchburg VA 24504 Office: Central Va Tng Center PO Box 1098 Madison Heights VA 24505

GARRETT, JAMES LEO, JR., theological educator, seminary dean; b. Waco, Tex., Nov. 25, 1925; s. James Leo and Grace Hasseltine (Jenkins) G.; m. Myrta Ann Latimer, Aug. 31, 1948; children—James Leo III, Robert Thomas, Paul Latimer. B.A., Baylor U., 1945; B.D., Southwestern Bapt. Theol. Sem., 1948, Th.D., 1954; Th.M., Princeton Theol. Sem., 1949; Ph.D., Harvard U., 1966; postgrad. Oxford U., 1968-69, St. John's U., 1977. Ordained to ministry Baptist Ch., 1945. Pastor, Bapt. chs. in Tex., 1946-48, 50-51; instr., asst. prof., assoc. prof., prof. theology Southwestern Bapt. Theol. Sem., Fort Worth, 1949-59, 79—, assoc. dean for Ph.D. degree, 1981-84; prof. Christian theology So. Bapt. Theol. Sem., Louisville, 1959-73; dir. J. M.Dawson Studies in Ch.-State, prof. religion Baylor U., Waco, Tex., 1973-79, Simon M. and Ethel Bunn prof. Ch.-State Studies, 1975-79; interim pastor Bapt. chs. in Tex., D.C., Ind. and Ky.; coordinator 1st Conf. on Concept of Believers' Ch., 1967; chmn. Study Commn. on Coop. Christianity, Bapt. World Alliance, 1968-75; sec. Study Commn. on Human Rights, 1980-85; theol. lectr. Wake Forest, N.C., Torreon, Mex., Cali, Colombia, Recife, Brazil, London, Queluz-Lisbon, Portugal, Montevideo, Uruguay. Mem. Am. Soc. Ch. History, Am. Acad. Religion, So. Bapt. Hist. Soc., Conf. on Faith and History. Democrat. Author: The Nature of the Church According to the Radical Continental Reformation, 1957; Baptist Church Discipline, 1962; Evangelism for Discipleship, 1964; Baptists and Roman Catholicism, 1965; Reinhold Niebuhr on Roman Catholicism, 1972; Living Stones: The Centennial History of Broadway Baptist Church, Fort Worth, Texas, 1882-1982, 2 vols., 1984-85; co-author: Are Southern Baptists Evangelicals?, 1983; co-editor: The Teacher's Yoke: Studies in Memory of Henry Trantham, 1964; editor: The Concept of the Believers' Church, 1970; Baptist Relations with Other Christians, 1974; Calvin and the Reformed Tradition, 1980; editor Jour. of Ch. and State, 1973-79. Home: 5525 Full Moon Dr Fort Worth TX 76132 Office: PO Box 22117 Fort Worth TX 76122

GARRETT, LINDA KAY, geophysicist; b. Dallas, Dec. 8, 1957; d. Charles and Edith Pauline (Moore) G. B.S. in Geology, U. Tex.-Arlington, 1980. Geophys. trainee Supron Energy, Dallas, 1980-81; geophysicist Sulpetro Resources, Dallas- 1981-82; sr. geophysicist Placid Oil Co., San Antonio, 1982-83; geophysicist II, Gulf Energy Prodn., San Antonio, 1983-84; sr. geophysicist Placid Oil Co., Dallas, 1984—. Mem. Soc. Exploration Geophysicists, Am. Assn. Petroleum Geologists, San Antonio Geophys. Soc. (pres. 1984), South Tex. Geol. Soc., Alpha Chi, Sigma Gamma Epsilon, Phi Eta Sigma. Republican. Avocations: photography; guitar. Home: 536 E Arawe Circle Irving TX 75060 Office: Placid Oil Co 3900 Thanksgiving St Dallas TX 75201

GARRETT, MARIE MURPHY, English educator; b. Halifax County, Va., July 24, 1942; d. Ernest Claytor and Eva (Wilbourne) Murphy; m. James W. Garrett, June 6, 1964. B.A., Longwood Coll., 1964, M.A., 1968; postgrad. Va. Poly. Inst., 1971-79. Sr. English tchr. Halifax County High Sch., South Boston, Va., 1964-66; asst. prof. English, Ferrum Coll., Va., 1967-68; assoc. prof. Patrick Henry Community Coll., Martinsville, Va., 1968—, acting dean of instrn., 1978-79, chmn. humanities and social scis div., 1976-84. Chmn. bd. dirs. Christian Edn. Bd., Ch. of God. Martinsville, 1981-84. Mem. NEA, Va. Edn. Assn., Va. English Tchrs. Assn., Southeastern Conf. Tchrs. of English in Two-Yr. Colls., Avocations: reading; sr. citizens' aide. Home: 933 Glade St Martinsville VA 24112 Office: Patrick Henry Community Coll PO Box 5311 Martinsville VA 24115

GARRETT, PAT, hospital pharmacy administrator; b. Santa Monica, Calif., Oct. 14, 1945; s. Harrell B. and Mae (Free) G.; m. Carol Evelyn Kelley, May 31, 1968; children—Aimee Kelley, John Patrick. B.S. in Pharmacy, U. Tex., 1969. Pharmacist Dougherty's Pharmacy, Dallas, 1969-70; dir. pharmacy Dallas Meml. Hosp. 1970-77, Meml. Hosp., Nacogdoches, Tex., 1977—; bd. dirs. Greater East Tex. Health Systems. Mem. N.E. Tex. Soc. Hosp. Pharmacists (pres. 1982-83), Tex. Soc. Hosp. Pharmacists (treas. 1984-87), Tex. Pharm. Assn., Am. Soc. Hosp. Pharmacists, Am. Pharm. Assn. Republican. Methodist. Lodge: Kiwanis (bd. dirs. chpt. 1978-81). Avocations: fishing; hunting birds; photography. Home: 3506 Piping Rock Nacogdoches TX 75961 Office: Meml Hosp 1204 Mound St Nacogdoches TX 75961

GARRETT, SIDNEY ASHTON, accountant; b. Kansas City, Mo., July 12, 1946; d. Scott Cornell and Nancy (Newlin) Ashton; m. Gary Ray Garrett, Dec. 23, 1969. Student U. Calif.-Santa Barbara, 1964-65; B.A., U. Kans., 1968, B.S., 1970; postgrad. U. Houston, 1978-79. C.P.A., Tex. Tchr., Eudora High Sch. (Kans.), 1970-73; jr. acct. Crown Zellerbach Corp., Kansas City, Mo., 1973-75; acct., bookkeeper Geospace Corp., Houston, 1975; controller Charter Fin. Group, Inc., Houston, 1976-83; sr. acct. Michael B. Bell & Co., Houston, 1984; assoc. G. William Reiff & Assocs., Inc., Houston, 1985—. Mem. Am. Inst. C.P.A.s, Tex. Soc. C.P.A.s. Clubs: Sugar Creek Country (Sugar Land). Office 5151 San Felipe Suite 890 Houston TX 77056

GARRETT, STEVEN HUGHES, electrical engineer; b. Slater, S.C., Jan. 17, 1942; s. Ira Wister and Dorothey Elizabeth (Fortner) G.; B.S.E., U. N.C., Charlotte, 1972; M.B.A., Queens Coll., Charlotte, 1984; m. Betty Jo McDowell, June 19, 1966; 1 son, Brian Scott. Maintenance engr. Deering Milliken Co., Gaffney, S.C., 1972-73; utility and instrumentation engr. Deering Excelsior plant, Pendleton, S.C., 1973-75; maintenance elec. engr. Westinghouse Electric Corp., Charlotte, N.C., 1975-82, supr.-engr. Power House, 1982-85, telecommunications mgr., 1985—. Founder, pres. bd. Westinghouse Credit Assn., 1979-81. Served with USAF, 1964-68. Mem. IEEE (sr.). Republican. Presbyterian. Patentee in field. Home: 4321 Kuykendall Rd Matthews NC 28105 Office: PO Box 7002 Westinghouse Blvd Charlotte NC 28217

GARRETT, TERRY GLEN, SR., biomedical electronics technician; b. Stonewall, Okla., Sept. 10, 1954; s. William Ernest and Nora Viola (Methvin) G.; m. Patricia Sue Nance, June 1, 1973; children—Aubrey Dawn, Terry Glen, Jr. Cert. in Aerospace Equipment, USAF, 1973, Biomed. Tech., 1977; student East Central U., 1984. Enlisted USAF, 1972; aerospace equipment technician USAF, Altus, Okla., 1973-76, biomed. equipment technician, Phoenix, 1977-80; dir. biomed. engring. Valley View Hosp., Ada, Okla., 1980—; owner, operator Ada Biomed. Services, Ada, 1981—, cons. in field. Served with USAF, 1972-80. Mem. Am. Soc. Hosp. Engring., Okla. Assn. Hosp. Engrs. Democrat. Baptist. Lodges: Masons, Shriners. Avocations: fishing; hunting. Home: Route 1 Box 74 Roff OK 74865 Office: Valley View Hosp 1300 E 6th St Ada OK 74820

GARRETT, WILMA IDA, temporary employment agency executive; b. Santurce, P.R., June 9, 1938; d. Angel Luis and Verania (Morales) Lopez; B.A. in Psychology, U. P.R., 1959; m. Carlos Garrett; children—Rene Luis Aviles, Angel Luis Aviles. Sales mgr. Empresas Diaz, Rio Piedras, P.R., 1964-67; real estate broker Mackle Bros., Daytona, Fla., 1967-70; record mgr. San Juan (P.R.) City Hall, 1970-73; mgr. P.R., Kelly Services, Inc., Hato Rey, 1973—. Mem. Am. Soc. Personnel Adminstrs., P.R. C. of C., P.R. Mfrs. Assn., Sales and Mktg. Execs. Assn., Am. Bus. Women Assn., Zonta Internat. Republican. Roman Catholic. Office: Kelly Services Inc Scotiabank Plaza Suite 701 Hato Rey PR 00917

GARRIS, MARION RHOAD, broadcasting executive; b. Branchville, S.C., Jan. 18, 1947; s. Marion and Margaret (Rhoad) G.; m. Jody Lynn Inabinet, Aug. 30, 1970; 1 dau., Meredith Marie. B.S., U. S.C., 1971. Inst. cons. Met. Life Ins. Co., Orangeburg, S.C., 1971-72; sr. prodn. planner Utica Tool Co., Orangeburg, 1972-75; gen. mgr. Radio Orangeburg, Inc., 1975—; cons. broadcast groups; producer, dir., chmn. Ofcl. Miss Am. Pageant, preliminary, 1978-80. Bd. dirs. Orangeburg Heart Assn., 1978-81, Orangeburg Salvation Army, 1983-84. Recipient Outstanding State Pageant award 1978-80; named Disting. Citizen of S.C., S.C. Researchers Assn., 1983. Mem. S.C. Broadcasters Assn., Nat. Assn. Broadcasters, Greater Orangeburg C. of C. (pres. 1982, dir. 1980-83). Methodist. Club: Country of Orangeburg. Lodge: Orangeburg Rotary (chmn. 1982-83). Home: 1565 Dunes St NW Orangeburg SC 29115 Office: 2580 North Rd Orangeburg SC 29115

GARRISON, ARTHUR WAYNE, chemist; b. Greenville, S.C., Sept. 9, 1934; s. Preston Maxwell and Lois Lillian (Walker) G.; m. Frances Elaine Mullins, Nov. 13, 1978; 1 child, Christian Kaye; children by previous marriage—Authur Wayne, Bonnie Leigh. B.S. in Chemistry, The Citadel, 1956; M.S., Clemson U., 1958; Ph.D., Emory U., 1966. Analytical chemist Div. Water Supply and Pollution Control, USPHS, Atlanta, 1961-65; research chemist Environ. Research Lab., U.S. EPA, Athens, Ga., 1965-73, sect. chief, 1973-83, br. chief analytical chemistry br., 1983-85, chemistry br., 1985—; cons. WHO, The Hague, Netherlands, 1976. Contbr. articles to profl. jours., chpts. to books. Patentee in field. Served to 1st lt. U.S. Army, 1958-60. Recipient Silver medal. Mem. Am. Chem. Soc., Sigma Xi. Methodist. Home: Box 644 Bostwick GA 30623 Office: Environ Research Lab US EPA College Station Rd Athens GA 30613

GARRISON, BRUCE GEORGE, security analyst; b. Freeport, Tex., Aug. 23, 1945; s. Robert Edward and Berniece Agnes (Hammar) G. A.A., Lon Morris Coll., 1965; B.B.A., U. Tex., 1967, M.B.A., 1972. Cert. fin. analyst. Analyst, Morgan Guaranty Trust, N.Y.C., 1972-75, Alexander Brown & Sons, Balt., 1975-76, Underwood Neuhaus & Co., Houston, 1976-83, Lovett, Mitchell, Webb & Garrison, Houston, 1983—; dir. Gulf Tex. Capital Corp., Houston. Contbr. articles to bus. mags. Served with U.S. Army, 1968-71, Vietnam. Mem. Houston Soc. Security Analysts. Republican. Methodist. Home: 6225 Inwood Dr Houston TX 77210 Office: Lovett Mitchell Webb & Garrison Inc 700 Rusk St PO Box 4348 Houston TX 77210

GARRISON, CHARLES HERBERT, III, advertising company executive; b. New Albany, Ind., Nov. 23, 1948; s. Charles Herbert Jr. and Wilma Jean (Heagie) G.; m. Donna Dooley, Mar. 6, 1971; 1 child, David Scott. B.S.B.A., Ind. U., 1971. Sales rep. Moore Bus. Forms, Louisville, 1971; sales mgr., Bruce Fox Co., Inc., New Albany, 1971-78; ptnr., v.p. L.L. Fischer Co., Inc., 1978-81; ptnr., v.p. Motivational Enterprises Inc., Louisville, 1981—, also dir. Contbr. articles to profl. jours. Elder, St. Marks United Ch. of Christ, New Albany, 1985. Mem. Specialty Advt. Assn. Internat. (awards of merit 1984, Golden Pyramid award 1983), Louisville Direct Mktg. Assn., Am. Soc. Safety Engrs. Clubs: Ind. Univ. Alumni, Advt. Louisville. Lodge: Rotary. Avocations: distance running; tennis. Home: 35 Tanglewood Dr Floyds Knobs IN 47119 Office: Motivational Enterprises Inc 922 Franklin St Louisville KY 40206

GARRISON, GEORGE WALKER, JR., mechanical and industrial engineering educator; b. Statesville, N.C., May 21, 1939; s. George Walker and Gladys Mary (Bell) G.; B.S.M.E., N.C. State U., 1961, M.S., 1963; Ph.D., 1966; M.B.A., Vanderbilt U., 1980; m. Nancy Carole Mayfield, June 10, 1961; children—Jennifer Renee, George W. Research and teaching asst. N.C. State U., 1964-66; research engr. Sverdrup/ARO, Inc., Arnold Air Force Sta., Tenn., 1966-70, sr. lead engr., 1970-75, sect. supr., 1975-78, br. mgr., 1978-80, dir. energy systems Sverdrup Tech. Inc., Tullahoma, Tenn., 1980—. Prof. mech. engrng. U. Tenn., Tullahoma, 1980-83. Recipient Col. John W. Harrelson Scholarship award, 1957; NDEA fellow, 1961. Mem. Nat. Mgmt. Assn., ASME, AIAA, Sigma Xi. Mem. Christian Ch. (Disciples of Christ) (deacon-elder 1967-77). Contbr. articles to sci., tech. jours. Home: 203 Kaywood Ave Tullahoma TN 37388 Office: U Tenn Space Inst Tullahoma TN 37388

GARRISON, JACKIE LANE, textile company executive, carding technologist; b. Seneca, S.C., Apr. 23, 1947; s. Paul Jack and Nellie Fay (Black) G.; divorced; children—Johnny Lane, Therese Michelle; m. Bette Jane Farrer, Apr. 13, 1979; children—Kelly Ann, Robert Paul. B.S., Limestone Coll., 1985. Supr. New Holland (Milliken), Gainesville, Ga., 1970-76; shift mgr. Tuscarora Yarn Mill, Mt. Pleasant, N.C., 1976-77; supt. Service Ctr., Taylors, S.C., 1977-85; dept. mgr. J.P. Stevens (Scotland Plant), Laurinburg, N.C., 1985—, cert. chem. control officer, Greenville, S.C., 1984-85, cert. safety adminstr., Greenville, 1984-85. Editor: Card Wire Maintenance, 1983. Cert. lay speaker United Methodist Ch., Greer, S.C., 1984. Mem. Am. Metal Soc., Am. Soc. Safety Engrs. Lodge: Rotary (bd. dirs. 1985—). Avocations: collecting books, fishing. Home: Route 5 Box S-28 McLeod Rd Laurinburg NC 28352 Office: JP Stevens & Co Inc Wagram NC 28396

GARRISON, JOSEPH MARION, JR., British and American literature educator, consultant; b. Columbia, Mo., July 25, 1934; s. Joseph Marion and Evelyn (Hawkins) G.; m. Virginia Bumgardner, July 18, 1958 (div. 1979); children—Alan Fletcher, Kathryn Paige; m. Ann Dexter Herron, Aug. 27, 1980. B.A., Davidson Coll., 1956; M.A., Duke U., 1957, Ph.D., 1961. Instr. English, Coll. William and Mary, Williamsburg, Va., 1960-62; assoc. prof. English, St. Andrews Presbyn. Coll., Laurinburg, N.C., 1962-65; assoc. prof. English, Mary Baldwin Coll., Staunton, Va., 1965-70, prof., 1970—, chmn. dept., 1982—; cons. Va. Poets-in-Pre-Schs., 1975—, Va. Secondary Schs., 1978—, Va. Pvt. Schs., 1978—. Contbr. poems and articles to profl. jours. Project dir. Va. Found. for Humanities and Pub. Policy, 1982—. Recipient Louise McNeill Peace prize Morris Harvey Publs., 1972. Mem. Poets and Writers. Democrat. Presbyterian. Avocations: classical guitar; woodworking. Home: 265 Thornrose Ave Staunton VA 24401 Office: Mary Baldwin Coll Frederick St Staunton VA 24401

GARRISON, MICHAEL LYNN, architect, educator; b. Lansing, Mich., Dec. 2, 1945; s. Vernon Wayne and Edith (Larie) G.; m. Harriet Lee Hughen, Aug. 17, 1968 (div. 1972); 1 child, Kristen Lee; m. Nancy Anne Steele, Mar. 21, 1980. B.Arch., La. State U., 1970; M.Arch., Rice U., 1971. Lic. architect, Tex. Designer T.M. Heesch AIA, Houston, 1972-73; designer Irving Phillips AIA, Houston, 1973-74; architect Page Southerland and Page FAIA, Austin, Tex., 1974-75; pvt. practice as architect, Austin, 1976—; assoc. prof. architecture U. Tex., Austin, 1975—; mem. faculty Laguna Gloria Art Sch., Austin, 1979-84; tech. cons. Tex. Gov.'s Office Energy Resources, Austin, 1979. Author: Living On Borrowed Time, 1976; Passive Solar Test Structure, 1980; Passive Solar Homes For Texas, 1982; also books revs. Mem. Resource Mgmt. Com., City of Austin. Grantee Univ. Research Inst., 1979, Tex. Energy Adv. Council, 1980, HUD, 1980, Tex. Energy and Natural Resources, 1982. Mem. Internat. Solar Energy Soc., Tex. Solar Energy Soc., Assn. Collegiate Schs. Architecture, AIA, Tex. Soc. Architects, Save Austin Neighborhoods and Environment, Austin Solar Energy Soc. (founding), Houston Urban Bunch (founding), Sierra Club, Kappa Sigma. Democrat. Methodist. Avocations: wine collecting; backpacking; mountain hiking. Office: Michael Garrison Architect 1607 W 6th St Austin TX 78713

GARRISON, RONALD CLARK, commerical art school executive; b. Ft. Worth, Sept. 3, 1948; s. Alvin Clark and Emma Juanite (Vaughn) G.; m. Judith E. Dees, Dec. 13, 1968 (div. 1976); 1 son, Robin; m. Sandra L. Croft, Feb. 29, 1980. Student U. Tex.-Austin, 1966-68, Tex. Christian U., Ft. Worth, 1966, 69. Mgr., Radio Shack, Tandy Corp., Ft. Worth, 1968-75; prin., v.p. Action Plus Inc., Akron, Ohio, 1976-78; pres., dir. Ala. Coll. Tech., Birmingham, 1978-81; dir. Tex. Nat. Edn. Corp., San Antonio, 1981-83; pres. Edn. Mgmt. Corp., Art Inst. Houston, 1984—. Served with U.S. Army, 1969-75. Mem. Tex. Assn. Pvt. Schs. (dir. 1981—), Nat. Assn. Trades and Tech. Schs., Bexar County Assn. Pvt. Schs. (pres. 1983), Data Processing Mgmt. Assn. (dir., chmn. edn. 1980-84), Jaycees. Baptist. Lodges: Rotary (Universal City, Tex.); Masons. Home: 3530 Green Springs Dr San Antonio TX 78247 Office: Art Inst Houston 3600 Yoakum St Houston TX 77006

GARRISON, THOMAS ED(MOND), farmer, state senator; b. Anderson, S.C., Jan. 21, 1922; s. Thomas Edmond and Nettie C. (McPhail) G.; m. Juanita Bartlett, May 10, 1955; children—Carol Gaye, Thomas Edmond III, James Bartlett, Anita Lee, Catherine Ann, Elizabeth Reid. B.S. with honors, Clemson Coll., 1942. Farmer, Anderson; mem. S.C. Ho. of Reps., 1959-66, S.C. Senate, 1967—. Bd. dirs. Anderson County Fair Assn., 1957, treas., 1958; pres. Anderson County Farm Bur., 1957. Served with USAF, 1942-45, PTO. Decorated Air medal with five oak Leaf clusters. Recipient numerous awards from civic, ednl. and agrl. orgns. Mem. S.C. Assn. Soil Conservation Suprs. (pres. 1960), Pendleton Farmers Soc. (pres. 1973-74), Am. Dairy Assn. (bd. dirs. S.C. sect. 1962), Phi Kappa Phi, Gamma Sigma Delta. Democrat. Baptist. *

GARRISON, WANDA BROWN, paper manufacturing company employee; b. Madison County, N.C., Sept. 16, 1936; d. Roy Lee Brown and Zella Arizona (Miller) Brown Hannah; m. Charles Mitchell Garrison, July 9, 1955; children—Roy Lee, Marsha Joan; 1 step-son, Charles Mitchell, Jr. Student air-line hostess Weaver Airlines, St. Louis, 1954-55; student Haywood Tech. Coll., Clyde, N.C., 1967-68; student IBM, Asheville, N.C., 1977; student in data processing Agy. Record Control, Atlanta, 1978. Operator Day Co., Waynesville, N.C., 1954-57; driver Haywood County Schs., Waynesville, 1970-71; operator Am. Enka, N.C., 1972-75; bookkeeper L. N. Davis Ins. Co., Waynesville, 1975-80; stock preparation Champion Internat., Canton, N.C., 1980—. Sec./treas. James Chapel Baptist Ch., Haywood County, N.C., 1965-77; pres. Fire Dept. Aux., Crabtree, N.C., 1973—; pres. Women Mission Union, Crabtree Bapt. Ch., Haywood County, 1977-80; v.p. Gideon Aux., Haywood County, 1982-84, pres., 1984—; state aux. follow-up rep., 1984. Recipient Life Saving plaque Lion's Club, Waynesville, 1972. Mem. AFL-CIO. Democrat. Home: Hwy 209 Route 1 Box 230A Clyde NC 28721

GARTLAN, JOSEPH V., JR., state senator, lawyer; b. Glen Head, N.Y., Sept. 21, 1925; m. Fredona Marie Manderfield. B.S.S., Georgetown U., J.D. Mem. Va. Senate, 1972—; mem. Va. Citizens Consumer Council Inc.; mem. Va. Adv. Legis. Council; chmn. Chesapeake Bay Commn., 1981. Served as ensign USNR, 1943-46. Mem. Assn. Trial Lawyers Am., Vernon-Lee C. of C. Democrat. Roman Catholic. Lodge: KC. Office: Va Senate Gen Assembly Bldg 9th and Braod Sts Richmond VA 23219*

GARTLAND, EUGENE CHARLES, JR., mathematics educator; b. St. Louis, June 26, 1950; s. Eugene Charles and Mary Alice (Wolff) G.; m. Karen Loretta Fireman, Jan. 3, 1976 (div. 1983). B.S. in Engring. Sci., Purdue U., 1972, M.S. in Math., 1976, Ph.D. in Math., 1980. Grad. teaching asst. Purdue U., West Lafayette, Ind., 1974-80; asst. prof. math. So. Meth. U., Dallas, 1980—. Contbr. articles to profl. jours. Served with U.S. Army, 1972-74. Mem. Am. Math. Soc., Soc. Indsl. and Applied Math. Avocations: Sports, music. Home: 4119 A Herschel Ave Dallas TX 75219 Office: Math Dept So Meth U Dallas TX 75275

GARVIN, BARNEY WILLARD, oil co. exec.; b. New Holland, S.C., Aug. 15, 1904; s. Ernest Luther and Annabel (Courtney) G.; student Clemson (S.C.) U., 1924-25; B.S., N.C. State U., Raleigh, 1927. Dist. mgr. S.C. Electric & Gas Co., Florence, 1935-42; engr. S.C. Public Service Authority, Columbia, 1943; cotton broker, Aiken, S.C., 1944-45; farmer Wagener, S.C., 1932-82; owner, operator Garvin Oil Co., Inc., Wagener, 1958—. Bd. dirs. Shriners' Children's Hosp., Greenville, S.C. Mem. Sigma Chi. Democrat. Baptist. Clubs: Palmetto (Columbia); Houndslake Country (Aiken); Masons, Shriners (pres. Florence 1937-39), Jesters, Rotary (pres. Florence 1939-40). Home and Office: Route 1 Box 352 Wagener SC 29164

GARWICK, ROBERT WIATT, petroleum geologist; b. St. Louis, May 17, 1921; s. Walter Cleveland and Ruth Beryl (Witt) G.; m. Catherine Augusta Okeefe, Aug. 15, 1942; children—Erin, Kenneth, Lydia, Lorin, Carrie, Gael, Guy, Matthew. B.A., Dartmouth Coll., 1942; M.A., Columbia U., 1947. Geologist, Nfld. Geol. Survey, 1946; stratigrapher Sinclair Ethiopia, 1947; geologist Gen. Crude Oil Co., 1948-53; ind. cons., Houston, 1953-64; cons. geologist Butler, Miller & Lents, Houston, 1964-70; pres. Kaygar Corp., Houston, 1970—. Served with USAF, 1942-45. Decorated Air medal with twelve oak leaf clusters. Mem. Am. Assn. Petroleum Geologists. Home: 66 Patti Lynn Houston TX 77024

GARWOOD, WILLIAM LOCKHART, U.S. judge; b. Houston, Oct. 29, 1931; s. Wilmer St. John and Ellen Burdine (Clayton) G.; m. Merle Castlyn Haffler, Aug. 12, 1955; children—William Lockhart, Mary Elliott. B.A., Princeton U., 1952; LL.B. with honors, U. Tex., 1955. Bar: Tex. 1955, U.S. Supreme Ct. 1959. Law clk. to judge U.S. Ct. Appeals for 5th Circuit, Austin, Tex., 1955-56, judge, 1981—; mem. firm Graves, Dougherty, Hearon, Moody & Garwood, and predecessor firms, Austin, 1959-79, 81, ptnr., 1961-67, 81; assoc. justice Supreme Ct. Tex., Austin, 1979-80; dir. Anderson, Clayton & Co., 1976-79, mem. exec. com., 1977-79. Pres. Child and Family Service of Austin, 1970-71, St. Andrew's Episcopal Sch., Austin, 1972; bd. dirs. Community Council Austin and Travis County, 1968-72, Human Opportunities Corp. Austin and Travis County, 1966-70, Mental Health and Mental Retardation Ctr. Austin and Travis County, 1966-69, United Fund Austin and Travis County, 1971-73; mem. adv. bd. Salvation Army, Austin, 1972—. Served with U.S. Army, 1956-59. Fellow Am. Bar Found.; mem. ABA, Am. Law Inst., Tex. Bar Found. (life mem.), Am. Judicature Soc., Order of Coif, Chancellors. Episcopalian. Office: US Courthouse 200 W 8th St Austin TX 78701

GARY, JOHN, singer; b. Watertown, N.Y., Nov. 29, 1932; s. Harold Strader and Merle (Dawson) G.; m. Shirley Dale Wilson, Oct. 18, 1971; children—John Jr., John Andrew, Matthew, Jason. Spl. student of music Cathedral St. John the Divine, N.Y.C., 1942-44; student Colo. U., 1955. Singer Ken Murray's Blackouts, Los Angeles, 1947-48; rec. artist RCA, 1965-70; summer replacement for Danny Kaye, 1966; host The John Gary Show, 1967-68; ofcl. spokesman Nat. Archery Assn., 1984. Served with USMC, 1949. Recipient awards Nat. Assn. Record Merchandisers, Nat. Assn. Rec. Arts and Scis.; Sullivan-Considine award Fraternal Order of Eagles, 1970. Mem. AFTRA, Am. Guild Variety Artists, Musicians Union New Orleans, ASCAP, Actor's Equity. Episcopalian. Club: Brookhaven Country. Author: A Fragment of Time, 1972. Inventor underwater hand-held transp. device, circular spherical floatation chamber. Home: 7 Briarwood Circle Richardson TX 75080

GARY, SHARON DELIGHT, psychological examiner; b. Decatur, Tex., June 14, 1951; d. Dorthea (Somerville) Gary; B.S. with honors in Psychology, State Coll. Ark. (name changed to U. Central Ark.), 1973; M.S. in Clin. Psychology, Memphis State U., 1975, postgrad. in clin. psychology, 1975-76. Liaison worker Foster Home and Group Home programs N.E. Community Mental Health Center, Memphis, 1975-76; psychol. examiner, asst. dir. Hutt Psychol. Group, Memphis, 1976-79; cons. psychol. examiner Sequoyah Center, Tenn. Psychiat. Hosp. and Inst., Memphis, 1976-77; coordinator, instr. foster care program Center for Govt. Tng., U. Tenn., Memphis, 1978—; owner, psychol. examiner Psychol. Services of Memphis, 1979—; cons. St. Peter Home for Children, 1982-84, Holston's Meth. Children's Home, 1983—; active workshops, seminars on learning disabilities child devel.; mem. Women's Resource Center, 1977-82, Multidisciplinary Child Abuse Rev. Team, 1979—, active NOW march for ERA; mem. Tenn. Juvenile Justice Commn., 1985—; participant in lobbying for Ark. Assn. Children with Learning Disabilities; head panel on psychol. effects of being in foster care Juvenile Ct. Judges Ann. Conf., Tenn., 1980; resource person for adoptive families. Recipient Ark. Traveler cert., 1978, cert. of appreciation Tenn. Foster Care Assn., 1979. Mem. Am. Psychol. Assn., Tenn. Psychol. Assn., Memphis Psychol. Assn., Nat. Rehab. Assn., Assn. for Children with Learning Disabilities, Council on Adoptable Children, Psi Chi. Mem. Unity Christ Ch. Clubs: Exec. Women Memphis (charter mem., sec. 1978-81), Zonta (pres. 1985-86) (Memphis). Author: Parenting Happy Children: Coping with Destructive Behavior, 1985. Contbr. chpt. to Juvenile Court Review Board Manual. Home: 3163 Highmeadow Dr Memphis TN 38128 also 1835 Union Ave Suite 215 Memphis TN 38104

GARY, SHERON ANNE, commodity broker; b. Atlanta, Aug. 25, 1949; d. Stanley Ernest and Doris (Garner) Boak; m. Marion Lamb, Sept. 7, 1968 (div. June 1971); m. William Gary, Sept. 2, 1971; 1 dau., Lené Anne. Sec., trading asst. to commodity brokers E.F. Hutton & Co., Dallas, 1970-71; registered trading asst. Barnes Brokerage Co., 1971-75; commodity broker Ray E. Friedman & Co., Oklahoma City, 1975-78, E.F. Hutton & Co., Houston, 1978-83, Shearson-Lehman Bros. Houston, 1983-85; sec.-treas. Commodity Info. Systems, Inc., Houston, 1971—, v.p., futures cons. to livestock brokers, 1985—. Rebublican. Methodist. Home: 11903 Oakcroft St Houston TX 77070 Office: PO Box 690652 Houston TX 77269-0652

GARY, STUART HUNTER, lawyer; b. Richmond, Va., Nov. 22, 1946; s. Morton Nathan and Blanche (Rudy) G.; m. Donna Joy Rothman, Aug. 19, 1967; children—Kenneth Asher, Robin Leigh. B.A. in Econs., U. Va., 1968; J.D., Washington Coll. Law, 1972. Bar: Va. 1972, D.C. 1973. Law clk. to judge D.C. Ct. Appeals, 1972-73; atty. anti-trust div. FTC, 1973-74; ptnr. Swift and Gary, Washington, 1974, Falcone and Gary Ltd., Fairfax, Va., 1975-81; pres. Stuart H. Gary and Assocs., McLean, Va., 1981—; arbitrator Am. Arbitration Assn.; adv. bd. Guaranty Bank and Trust Co., Fairfax. Chmn. No. Va. Heart Fund Drive, 1976; bd. dirs. No. Va. Jewish Community Ctr. Served with USAR, 1968-74. Mem. ABA, Va. Bar Assn., State Bar Va., D.C. Bar Assn., Fairfax County Bar Assn., Phi Alpha Delta. Club: Westwood Country (Vienna, Va.). Home: 1704 Burlwood Ct Vienna VA 22180 Office: Hadid Investment Group Inc Penthouse 1655 N Fort Meyers Dr Rosslyn VA 22209

GARZA, GENE GARY, mathematics and computer science educator; b. Wedowee, Ala., June 8, 1947; s. Antonio E. Garza and Mavis (Holloway) Hand; m. Rebecca Suzanne Norrell, May 27, 1971; children—Gene Gary, Michael Alexander. B.S. in Math., U. Montevallo, 1972; Ph.D. in Math., U. Ga., 1978. Asst. prof. math. Wingate Coll., N.C., 1978-79; instr. La. State U., Baton Rouge, 1979-82; asst. prof. math., dir. computer sci., U. Montevallo, Ala., 1982—. Contbr. articles to profl. jours. Chmn. Montevallo Acad. Boosters Club, 1984—. Served as staff sgt. USAF, 1965-69. Mem. Math. Assn. Am., Am. Math. Soc., London Math. Soc., Assn. Computing Machinery. Republican. Avocation: camping. Office: Math Dept Univ Montevallo Montevallo AL 35115

GARZA, MARTIN HENRY, health agency administrator; b. San Antonio, Oct. 21, 1940; s. Efrain C. and Emma Vasquez G.; B.A., St. Mary's U., 1966; M.S.W., Our Lady of the Lake U., 1969; m. Evangelina Lopez, Dec. 30, 1966; children—Martin H., Edward. Youth services group worker House of Neighborly Service, San Antonio, 1963-65; project coordinator San Antonio Neighborhood Youth Orgn., 1966-67; manpower devel. specialist U.S. Dept. Labor, San Antonio, 1967; chief social services, community organizer House of Neighborly Service, San Antonio, 1969-71; caseworker Bexar County Mental Health Mental Retardation Drug Dependence Program, San Antonio, 1971, dir. outpatient service, 1972-76, program dir., 1976-79, substance abuse program dir., 1979—; assoc. field practicum prof. Worden Sch. Social Services, 1976—; trustee, sec.-treas. Drug Abuse Central, 1976-79; vice-chmn. Drug Abuse adv. com. Alamo Area Council of Govt., 1977-78; mem. Gov's. Drug Abuse Adv. Council, 1979—. Active, Woodlawn Hills Pop Warner Football Assn., PTA; sec.-treas. Texans for the Funding of McAllister Drug Treatment Act, Inc., 1982—. Cert. social worker, Tex. Recipient award Drug Awareness Ctr., 1983; grad. studies stipend Nat. Child Welfare Bur., 1968. Roman Catholic. Home: 1915 W Magnolia St San Antonio TX 78201 Office: 122 E Durango San Antonio TX 78204

GARZA, RAUL, educational administrator; b. Mercedes, Tex., May 5, 1934; s. Jose T. and Antonia (Briseno) G.; m. Alma Garza, Dec. 30, 1961; children—Raul, Rene R., Yvonne A. B.A., Pan Am. Coll., 1960; M.Ed., Antioch Coll., 1974. Cert. mid-mgmt. adminstr., Tex. Tchr. Hidalgo Elem. Sch., Tex., 1961-79, asst. prin., 1980-81; asst. prin. Hidalgo High Sch., 1982-83; prin. Diaz Jr. High Sch., Hidalgo, 1983—. Served to sgt. USMC, 1953-56. Mem. Hidalgo Edn. Assn. (pres. 1979), Tex. Secondary Sch. Prin. Assn., Rio Grande Valley Prin. Assn. Democrat. Roman Catholic. Lodges: Lions (local pres. 1967-68), Leo's (local bd. dirs. 1967-68). Home: 1124 N 28th St McAllen TX 78501 Office: Diaz Jr High Sch PO Drawer D Hidalgo TX 78557

GARZA, ROBERTO, earth sciences educator, consultant; b. Kingsville, Tex., Dec. 24, 1942; s. Gebardo and Alicia (Perez) G.; m. Rosa Maria Torres, Dec. 27, 1969 (div. 1985); 1 child, Roberto. A.A., Yuba Jr. Coll., 1966; B.A., Tex. A&I U., 1969; M.A., Ind. State U., 1971; Ph.D., U. Colo., 1980. Adminstrv. asst. to dean of extended services San Antonio Coll., 1978-81, assoc. prof. earth scis., 1980-85, prof., 1985—, acting asst. dean extended services, 1981-82, asst. dean extended services, 1982-83, acting dean extended services, 1983, earth scis. coordinator, 1983—, dir. summer sci. enrichment program, 1984—. Tchr. San Antonio Literacy Council, 1980-81; invited speaker on geology to pub. schs. Served with USAF, 1962-66, N.Africa. U. fellow U. Colo., 1974-75, teaching honorarium, 1974; John Hay Whitney Found. opportunity fellow Ind. State U., 1969-70. Mem. Nat. Assn. Geology Tchrs., Nat. Council Geog. Edn., Tex. Jr. Coll. Tchrs. Assn., Tex. Assn. Chicanos in Higher Edn. Democrat. Roman Catholic. Avocations: Travel; camping; rock and fossil collecting; photography; naturalist. Home: 4711 Brierbrook San Antonio TX 78238 Office: San Antonio Coll 1300 San Pedro San Antonio TX 78284

GARZON, MAXIMILIANO, mathematician; b. Bogota, Colombia, Oct. 1, 1953; came to U.S., 1978; s. Maximiliano and Carmen (Hernandez) G.; children—Catalina, Ana Maria. Lic., Nat. U. Colombia, 1975; M.S., U. Ill., 1980, Ph.D., 1983. Instr. Nat. U. Colombia, 1975-78, asst. prof., 1982; teaching asst. U. Ill., Urbana, 1978-81, research asst., 1983-84; asst. prof. dept. math. sci. Memphis State U., 1984—. Mem. Am. Math. Soc., Assn. Symbolic Logic, Sigma Xi, Phi Kappa Phi. Avocations: swimming; hiking; jogging. Office: Memphis State U MMath Dept Memphis TN 38152

GASBARRO, LOUIS DONALD, hospital safety director; b. Tampa, Fla., Nov. 23, 1937; s. Ernest A. and Rose M. (Iasa) G.; m. Ann Nee Dickerson, May 7, 1960; children—Mark, Glenn, David, Donald. B.S., U. Nebr., 1970; A.Sc., Hillsborough Community Coll., 1983; M.S. in Crim. Justice, Nova U., 1981. Commd. airman U.S. Air Force, 1956, advanced through grades to capt., 1980; spl. agt. Office Spl. Investigation, Dept. of Air Force, 1970-80; sch. tchr. Hillsborough County Sch. System, Tampa, Fla., 1980-81; coordinator safety and security County Hosp. Authority, Tampa, 1981-83, dir. safety and security, 1983—; also lectr. Contbr. articles to profl. jours. Soccer coach Tampa County Soccer League, 1977; pres., bd. dirs. Community Swim and Tennis Club, 1981-83. Decorated U.S. Air Force Commendation medal, Vietnam Honor medal. Mem. Internat. Assn. Hospt. Security (pres. Bay Area chpt. 1984—), Fla. Hosp. Assn. (pres.), Soc. Health Care Security Profls. (v.p. 1984—), Am. Soc. Safety Engrs. (program dir. West Fla. chpt. 1984—), Am. Indsl. Hugiene Assn., Nat. Fire Protection Assn., Tampa Area Safety Council. Roman Catholic. Avocations: scuba diving; golfing; tennis; writing. Home: 7343 Brookview Circle Tampa FL 33606 Office: Tampa Gen Hosp Hillsborough County Hosp Authority Davis Island Tampa FL 33606

GASPERONI, ELLEN JEAN LIAS (MRS. EMIL GASPERONI), clubwoman; b. Rural Valley, Pa.; d. Dale S. and Ruth (Harris) Lias; student Youngstown U., 1952-54, John Carrol U., 1953-54, Westminster Coll., 1951-52; grad. Am. Inst. Banking; m. Emil Gasperoni, May 28, 1955; children—Sam, Emil, Jean Ellen. Mem. Coeurde Coeur Heart Assn., Orlando Opera Guild, Orlando Symphony Guild. Mem. Jr. Bus. Women's Club (dir. 1962-64). Presbyterian. Clubs: Sweetwater Country (Orlando, Fla.); Sweetwater Women's Sweetwater Garden (Longwood, Fla.); Lake Toxaway (N.C.) Golf and Country. Home: 1126 Brownshine Ct Longwood FL 32779

GASPERONI, EMIL, real estate executive; b. Hillsville, Pa., Nov. 13, 1926; s. Attico and Rose Mary (Sarnicola) G.; diploma real estate, U. Pitts., 1957; m. Ellen Jean Lias, May 28, 1955; children—Samuel Dale, Emil Attico, Jean Ellen. Owner, pres., chmn. bd. Gasperoni Real Estate Inc., New Castle, Pa., 1956-63, Ft. Lauderdale, Fla.; founder, chmn. bd. Fill-R-Up Auto Wash Systems Inc., Ft. Lauderdale, 1967-70; pres. Investment Property Adv. Corp., Ft. Lauderdale, 1975—. Served with U.S. Army, 1945-46; ETO. Mem. Nat. Inst. Real Estate Brokers, Internat. Real Estate Fedn., Nat. Soc. Fee Appraisers, Fla. Assn. Mortgage Brokers. Clubs: Lake Toxaway (N.C.) Country; Sweetwater Country (Longwood, Fla.). Home: 1126 Brownshire Blvd Sweetwater Club Longwood FL 32779 Office: 2501 E Commercial Blvd Fort Lauderdale FL 33308

GASQUE, (ALLARD) HARRISON, radio announcer, entertainer; b. Richmond, Va., Oct. 10, 1958; s. Thomas Nelson and Susan (Folline) G. Student U. S.C., 1978-81, Columbia Sch. Broadcasting, Hollywood, Calif., 1981-83. Announcer, disc jockey Sta. WKDK, Newberry, S.C., 1983-84, Sta. WEEL, Washington, 1984—; night-club entertainer, Washington, 1985—. Mem. floor com. Nat. Debutante Cotillion. Mem. U. S.C. Alumni, Columbia Sch. Broadcasting Alumni, Country Music Soc. Am. (charter), Ducks Unlimited, Sierra Club, Nat. Trust Hist. Preservation (Capital assoc.), Phi Kappa Psi. Republican. Episcopalian. Club: Fort Myers Officers (Arlington, Va.). Avocations: singing; coin collecting; stamp collecting; record collecting. Home: 7353 Eldorado Ct Hallcrest Heights McLean VA 22102

GASSLER, ROBERT SCOTT, economics educator; b. Akron, Ohio, July 7, 1948; s. Robert Karl and Lois (Conard) G.; m. Vicki Jane Roberts, Jan. 3, 1983; 1 child, Gregory Charles Roberts-Gassler; stepchildren—Travis Frame, Vandi Frame. A.B., Oberlin Coll., 1970; M.S., Columbia U., 1974; M.A., U. Wash., 1976; Ph.D., U. Colo., 1982. Instr. econs. U. Colo., Boulder, 1977; instr. econs. U. Colo., Denver, 1978, Colby Coll., Waterville, Maine, 1979-80; instr. econs. Guilford Coll., Greensboro, N.C., 1980-82, asst. prof., 1982—, acting chmn. dept. econs., 1982-83. Co-author: Handbook of Information About Libraries, 1978; Bibliography on World Conflict and Peace, 1979; author: The Economics of Nonprofit Enterprise, 1985. Contbr. articles to various jours. Mem. Am. Econs. Assn., ALA, Assn. for Comparative Econ. Studies, Assn. for Social Economics, Soc. for Gen. Systems Research. Unitarian Universalist. Avocation: science fiction. Office: Dept Econs Guilford Coll Greensboro NC 27410

GAST, CYNTHIA MARIE, data processing analyst, dancer; b. Frankfurt, Ger., Mar. 13, 1956; came to U.S., 1957; d. L.L. Gast and Helen Jean (Dilley) Barsalou. Student Sch. Am. Ballet, N.Y.C., 1971-72, Am. Ballet Theatre Sch., N.Y.C., 1973; A.S. in Bus. Adminstrn., No. Va. Community Coll., Annandale, 1984; B.A.S. in Computer Info. System, Fla. Atlantic U., 1985. Dancer, Ballet Repertory Co., N.Y.C., 1973-76, Am. Ballet Theatre, N.Y.C., 1976-79; receptionist System Devel. Corp., McLean, Va., 1979-80, data processing technician, 1980-81, data processing specialist, 1981-83, proposal support analyst, 1983-84. Roman Catholic. Club: Ski (Washington). Office: System Devel Corp 7929 Westpark Dr McLean VA 22102

GASTON, VIRGINIA MAXINE, pharmacist; b. Marion, Ohio, Mar. 31, 1911; d. Clarence Earl and Lillian (Bosley) Wood; m. Gail Adams Gaston, July 16, 1939 (dec. 1951); children—Lawrence Gail, David Alan, Susan Virginia. B.S. in Pharmacy, W.Va. U., 1956. Pharmacist, co-owner Gaston's Pharmacy, Belington, W.Va., 1951-62; chief pharmacist Myers Clinic, Phillipi, W.Va., 1957-62, Broaddus Hosp., Phillipi, 1957-62; staff pharmacist W.Va. U. Hosp., Morgantown, 1962-66, asst. chief pharmacist, 1966-73; relief pharmacist various retail pharmacies W.Va., 1973-81. Vol. aid to mil. families ARC, Morgantown, 1973-81; vol. Friends of Univ. Hosp., Morgantown, 1984-85; pres. Federated Women's Club of Belington, 1956-57; mem. Monongalia Hist. Soc. (mem. various coms.). Mem. W.Va. Pharmacists Assn., W.Va. Sch. Pharmacy Alumni Assn. (Outstanding Alumna award 1971), Rho Chi (treas. 1955-56), Theta Sigma Phi (Hub and Spoke award 1956). Republican. Methodist. Home: 501 Van Voorhis Rd #53 Morgantown WV 26505

GASTON, WILLIAM W., agricultural products company executive; b. Fayetteville, N.C., 1926; married. B.S., Clemson U., 1949. With Gold Kist Inc.,

Atlanta, 1950—, sr. v.p., mem. mgmt. exec. com., 1972-77, exec. v.p., mem. mgmt. exec. com., 1977-78, pres., chmn. mgmt. exec. com., 1978—, chief exec. officer, dir. Central Bank Coops., Ga. No. Ry. Co., Cotton States Life and Health Ins. Co., Cotton States Mut. Ins. Co., Nat. Council Farmer Coops., So. Bell Te. & Tel. Co., Trust Co. Ga. Office: Gold Kist Inc 244 Perimeter Center Pkwy NE Box 2210 Atlanta GA 30301*

GATCHELL, JOHN HAMILTON, exploration geologist; b. Sanford, N.C., Aug. 15, 1925; s. Oliver Wickerham and Margaret (Hamilton) G.; children by previous marriage—John Hamilton, Steven A., Margaret A. A.B., U. Mo., 1946, M.A., 1948. Instr. geology U. Mo., Columbia, 1946-48, Atlantic Refining Co., Tulsa, 1948-52; dist. geologist Lion Oil div. Monsanto Co., Oklahoma City, 1952-64; chief geologist Kingwood Oil Co., Oklahoma City, 1964-68; self-employed geologist, Oklahoma City, 1968-80; exec. v.p. Hensen Energy Corp., Oklahoma City, 1980-83; sr. geologist Ray Holifield and Assocs., Oklahoma City, 1983—. Mem., chmn. Okla. City Planning Commn., 1979—. Named to Mystical Seven, U. Mo., 1948. Mem. Am. Assn. Petroleum Geologists (cert.), Am. Inst. Profl. Geologists (cert.), Oklahoma City Geol. Soc. (chmn. continuing edn. 1968-72), Sigma Xi. Republican. Unitarian. Avocations: golf, running. Home: 8408 Surrey Pl Oklahoma City OK 73120 Office: Ray Holifield & Assocs 619 Park Harvey Ctr Oklahoma City OK 73102

GATES, GEORGE E., utilities executive. Chmn. Memphis Light, Gas & Water Div. Office: Memphis Light Gas & Water Div 220 S Main St Memphis TN 38101*

GATES, GEORGIANA CAROL, systems analyst; b. Chgo., Apr. 12, 1945; d. Harry Lion and Charlotte Pearl (Levinson) Boren; m. Michael Jack Gates, Aug. 1965 (div. Aug. 1972); 1 dau., Tabatha Diane. B.S. in Elec. Engring., Rice U., 1966; M.S. in Indsl. Engring., U. Houston, 1970; M.B.A., Houston Bapt. U., 1985. Registered profl. engr., Calif., Tex. Engr., Shell Oil Co., Houston, 1967-73; sr. engring. programmer Bechtel Engring. Co., San Francisco, 1973-78; cons. programmer Gibson Cons., Houston, 1978-80, Brown & Root Engring., Houston, 1980-82; sr. systems analyst Union Tex. Petroleum Co., Houston, 1982—. Mem. City Commn. on Status of Women, San Francisco, 1976. Mem. Soc. Women Engrs. (chpt. sec.), Assn. Computing Machinery, Am. Contract Bridge League. Home: 8313 La Roche St Houston TX 77036 Office: PO Box 2120 Houston TX 77001

GATES, LLOYD EDWARD, book company executive, food company owner; b. Trinity, Tex., Oct. 18, 1926; s. Oscar Lee and Lucindy Elizabeth (Loftin) G.; m. Alice Adams, May 6, 1961; children—William, Ricky, Michael, Martin, Jerry, John, Troy, Lynn, Donna, Beverly, Mary, Woody. B.S., Sam Houston State U., 1949. Chief test pilot Navion Aircraft Co., Galveston, Tex., 1959-61; quality control mgr. Am. Electric Co., Los Angeles, 1961-64, Dixel Industries, Houston, 1964-70; sr. sales rep. N.L. Baroid Co., Houston, 1971-84; pres. Gates Books, Livingston, Lufkin, Houston, Onalaska, Tex., 1974—. Clubs: Pecan Groves (Sugarland, Tex.); The Woodlands (Tex.). Lodge: V.F.W. Avocations: golfing; hunting; fishing; boating; flying. Home: 1601 N Washington Blvd Livingston TX 77351 Office: 1601 N Washington Blvd Livingston TX 77351

GATEWOOD, WILLARD BADGETT, JR., historian, educator; b. Pelham, N.C., Feb. 23, 1931; s. Willard Badgett and Bessie Lee (Pryor) G.; B.A., Duke U., 1953, M.A., 1954, Ph.D., 1957; m. Mary Lu Brown, Aug. 9, 1958; children—Willard Badgett, III, Elizabeth Ellis. Asst. prof. history East Tenn. State U., 1957-58, East Carolina U., 1958-60; asso. prof. N.C. Wesleyan Coll., 1960-64; prof. U. Ga., 1964-70; Alumni Distinguished prof. history U. Ark., 1970—. Recipient Parks Excellence in Teaching award; Michael Research award, 1967; Omicron Delta Kappa Tchr. of Yr., 1978-79; Alumni Research award, 1980. Truman Library fellow, 1963; Acad. Arts, Scis. grantee, 1962. Mem. Am., So., Ark. hist. assns., Orgn. Am. Historians, Assn. Study Afro-Am. Life and History, Phi Beta Kappa. Presbyterian. Author books including: Theodore Roosevelt and the Art of Controversy, 1970; Smoked Yankees, 1971; Black Americans and the White Man's Burden, 1975; Slave and Free Man, 1980; bd. editors Ga. Rev., 1968-70, Jour. Negro History, 1972-74. Home: 1651 Cleveland St Fayetteville AR 72701 Office: Ozark Hall U Ark Fayetteville AR 72701

GATLIFF, BEN FRANKLIN, physician; b. Macon, Ga., Jan. 19, 1922; s. Benjamin and Mellie (Corley) G.; B.S., U. Ga., 1948; M.D., Med. Coll. Ga., 1952; m. Marion Hays, Aug. 19, 1950; children—Gary Edwin, Eda Marie, Laural Francis. Intern, Orange Meml. Hosp., Orlando, Fla., 1952-53; pvt. practice medicine specializing in gen. practice, Plant City, Fla., 1953—; staff mem. South Fl. Bapt. Hosp., Plant City, chief of staff, 1959-60. Mem. dean's council (fine arts) U. South Fla., also life mem. pres.'s council. Served from pvt. to T/5, AUS, 1943-45. Mem. AMA, Fla. Med. Assn., Theta Kappa Psi. Episcopalian. Named Ky. col. Home: 716 Pinedale Dr Plant City FL 33566 Office: 402 Dort St Plant City FL 33566

GATLIN, EUGENE S., JR., English educator; b. Columbia, S.C., Aug. 30, 1935; s. Eugene S. and Alma (Lee) G.; m. Carolyn Maier, Feb. 14, 1972; children—David Ryan, Elizabeth Lee. A.B., Furman U., 1957; M.Ed., U.Sc., 1967, M.A., 1970, Ph.D., 1974. Tchr., dept. head Columbia Pub. Schs., 1961-69; instr. U. S.C., Columbia, 1967-70; prof. English, Midlands Tech. Coll., Columbia, 1969—, head dept., 1973-78, chmn. faculty senate, 1979, 82; speech and bus. communications cons., 1971—; guest prof. U. Wyo., Laramie, summer 1974, Coker Coll., Fort Jackson, S.C., 1983-84. Author: Language of Community College Freshmen, 1974. Mem. editorial bd. Bus. Writing - Concepts and Applications, 1984-85. Contbr. articles to profl. jours. Mem. Midlands Tech. Edn. Found., Columbia, 1979-82; mem. adv. bd. Midlands Tech. Aux. Services, 1981-82. Named Faculty Mem. of Yr., A.C. Flora High Sch., 1969, Midlands Tech. Coll., 1972, 81; U.S. Com. on Humanities grantee, 1965, 79. Mem. NEA, Coll. English Assn., Southeastern Conf. on English in Two-Yr. Colls., S.C. Speech Communication Assn. (evaluator 1979, 81, 83), S.C. Tech. Edn. Assn. Republican. Methodist. Club: Toastmasters (cons. 1981-82) (Columbia). Avocations: theatre; boating; reading; singing; chess. Home: 4533 Ivy Hall Dr Columbia SC 29206 Office: Midlands Tech Coll PO Box 2408 Columbia SC 29205

GATTIS, ELVIS FRANKLIN, sheet metal contractor; b. Jacksonville, Tex., Aug. 21, 1932; s. Arnett M. and Bertha A. (Yancy) G.; student U. Houston, 1972-73; m. Annie Joyce Ermel, June 20, 1953; children—Elvera, Gary, Lera, Jerry. With Straus-Frank Co., Houston, 1951-53, 1954-58, A & M Sheet Metal, Houston, 1958-59; owner E.F. Gattis Sheet Metal, Houston, 1959-66; pres., chief exec. officer Gattis Inc., Houston, 1966—. Mem. Houston Sheet Metal Contractors Assn. (dir. 1969-70, 78-79, pres. 1981, labor chmn. 1983-84), ASHRAE, Nat. Assn. Sheet Metal and Air-Conditioning Contractors (safety com. 1982—, supervisory tng. com. 1984—, nominating com. 1986—), S.W. Conf. Sheet Metal Contractors (pres. 1985), Tex. Environ. Balancing Bur., Gideons Internat., Internat. Biog. Centre (Eng.) Baptist (deacon). Club: Woodmen of World. Home: 746 Sue Barnett Houston TX 77018 Office: 1615 Keene Houston TX 77009

GATTON, DEBORAH JAN, bank examiner; b. Statesville, N.C., Aug. 26, 1953; d. Frank Delano and Nancy Joanne (Wilson) G.; B.A., N.C. State U., 1975. Asst. mgr. S.S. Kresge Co., Raleigh, N.C., 1975; asst. nat. bank examiner Comptroller of Currency, U.S. Dept. Treasury, Charlotte, N.C., 1975-76, Winston-Salem, N.C., 1976-80, Charleston, W.Va., 1980-81, nat. bank examiner, 1981-83; nat. bank examiner, Midland, Tex., 1983-84, Dallas, 1984—. Mem. Am. Mgmt. Assns., N.C. State U. Alumni Assn. Democrat. Presbyterian. Club: Wolfpack. Home: Box 50847 Dallas TX 75250

GATTY, JOHN, petroleum company executive; b. 1920. B.B.A., St. Mary's U., 1951. Asst. prof. mktg. St. Mary's U., Tex., 1944-61; councilman City of San Antonio, 1961-73; mayor City of San Antonio, 1969; with Rauscher Pierce Security Corp., 1973-74; pres. Telecom Corp., 1974-80, exec. v.p., 1980; pres., dir. Sabre Energy Inc., Houston, 1980—. Served with USAF, 1951-54. Address: Saber Energy Inc 1700 Smith St Houston TX 77002*

GAUBERT, LLOYD FRANCIS, shipboard and industrial cable company executive; b. Thibodaux, La., Jan. 6, 1921; s. Camille J. and Leonise (Henry) G.; student Southwestern La. Inst., 1941, U. So. Calif., 1942-43, Tex. Christian U., 1946-47; children—Lloyd Francis, Leonise, Bruce, Blane, Gwen, Greg. Tool engr. Consol.-Vultee Aircraft Corp., San Diego, 1941-45; tool project engr. Ft. Worth plant Convair, 1946-47; founder, owner, pres. L.F. Gaubert & Co., Inc., New Orleans, 1947—; pres. Michoud Indsl. Complex, Inc., Marine Indsl. Cable Corp., Carmel Devel. Corp.; dir. First Nat. Bank Commerce, New Orleans. Chmn. regional planning commn. New Orleans Mayor's Coordinating Com. for NASA, 1961-63, chmn. mfrs. com., 1961-63; bd. dirs. Better Bus. Bur., New Orleans, Met. New Orleans Safety Council, New Orleans Public Belt R.R., New Orleans Port Com., New Orleans Traffic and Transp. Bur., New Orleans Opera House Assn., Christian Bros., New Orleans; trustee Sta.-WYES-TV, New Orleans; founder, chmn. Greatest Bands in Dixie; bd. dirs. U.S. Coast Guard Acad., La Maritime Mus. Served with USAAF, 1942-45. Mem. Am. Soc. Tooling and Mfg. Engrs. (pres. 1948-49), Soc. Naval Architects and Marine Engrs., Am. Soc. Naval Engrs., La. Engring. Soc., Navy League Council New Orleans (pres.), Am. Legion. Democrat. Roman Catholic. Clubs: Optomists (pres. club 1957-58, lt. gov. club 1959-70), Propeller (dir.), Plimsoll, Bd. of Trade, Internat House, KC. Home: 5668 Bancroft Dr New Orleans LA 70122 Office: 700 S Broad St New Orleans LA 70119

GAUL, RUTH JESSAMINE, librarian; b. Chapel Hill, N.C. Jan. 22, 1954; d. Rufus Wharton and Ruth Jessamine (Whalen) Gaul. B.A., Stephens Coll., 1977; M.L.S., U. S.C., 1981. Publicity, membership asst. Mint Mus. Art, Charlotte, N.C., 1977-80; researcher U. S.C. Bur. Govtl. Research and Service, Columbia, 1982; asst. librarian Hilton Head Library (S.C.), 1982—; cons. Bluffton Library (S.C.), 1983. Asst. editor: Understanding United States Information Policy (F. Woody Horton), 1982. Mem. ALA, Freedom to Read Found. Episcopalian. Home: 30 The Oaks Hilton Head SC 29928 Office: Hilton Head Library 539 Hwy 278 Hilton Head SC 29928

GAULD, JOHN DAVID, clothing company official; b. Ft. Riley, Kans., June 27, 1952; s. John D. and Beatrice Emma (Barchey) G.; m. Pamela Jean Gallo, Oct. 24, 1980. A.B., Ind. U.-Indpls., 1974; M.B.A., Ind. U.-Bloomington, 1978. Tchr. lang. arts Carmel (Ind.)-Clay Schs., 1974-77; product mgr. Stokely-Van Camp, Indpls., 1978-80; mktg. mgr. Union Underwear Co., Bowling Green, Ky., 1981—; instr. advt. Western Ky. U., 1982—.

GAULTNEY, JOHN ORTON, life insurance agent, consultant; b. Pulaski, Tenn., Nov. 7, 1915; s. Bert Hood and Grace (Orton) G.; student Am. Inst. Banking, 1936; diploma Life Ins. Agy. Mgmt. Assn., 1948, Little Rock Jr. Coll., 1950; Mgmt. C.L.U. Diploma, 1952; grad. sales mgmt. and mktg. Rutgers U., 1957; m. Elizabethine Mullette, Mar. 30, 1941; children—Elizabethine (Mrs. Donald H. McClure), John Mullette, Walker Orton, Harlow Denny. With N.Y. Life Ins. Co., 1935—, mgr., Little Rock, 1945-55, regional v.p. Atlanta, 1956-64, v.p., N.Y.C., 1964-67, v.p. charge group sales, 1967-68, v.p. mktg., 1969-80, cons., 1981—; v.p. N.Y. Life Variable Contracts Corp., 1970-80; hon. dir. Bank of Frankewing (Tenn.), 1984—. Chmn., Downtown YMCA, Atlanta, 1963-65, bd. dirs. Vanderbilt YMCA, 1966-76, chmn. Vanderbilt, 1974-76; bd. dirs. Greater N.Y. YMCA, 1975-80, mem. public relations com. nat. council, 1965-70, mem. internat. YMCA com., 1967-80, mem. Nashville YMCA, 1981—; mem. Bronxville (N.Y.) Zoning Appeals Bd., 1973-80. Served to capt. inf. AUS, 1942-45; MTO. Decorated Silver Star, Bronze Star with 3 clusters, Purple Heart with 2 clusters; recipient Devereux C. Josephs award N.Y. Life Ins. Co., 1954; named Ark. Traveler, 1955, hon. citizen Tenn., 1956, Ky. col., 1963, Tenn. Ambassador, 1981. C.L.U. Mem. Am., Tenn. socs. C.L.U.s, Nat., Tenn. assns. life underwriters, Tenn. Tenn. Soc. in N.Y. (pres. 1971-74), Am. Risk and Ins. Assn., Newcomen Soc. Am., N.Y. So. Soc. (trustee 1965-80), St. Nicholas Soc. N.Y., Giles County Hist. Soc., Heritage Found. Franklin and Williamson County, Williamson County Hist. Soc. (pres. 1983-85), Carnton Assn. Inc. (bd. dirs. 1985—), Soc. Colonial Wars, SAR (dir. N.Y. 1970-80), 361st Inf. Assn. (pres. 1967-71), Assn. Preservation of Tenn. Antiquities (endowment trustee 1985—). Presbyterian (elder). Clubs: Capital City (Atlanta); Md. Farms Racquet and Country; Brentwood (Tenn.) Country; Rotary (Franklin, Tenn.); Siwanoy (Bronxville, N.Y.), Nashville City, Sojourners. Lodges: Masons, Shriners. Home: 6109 Johnson Chapel Rd Brentwood TN 37027 Office: One Nashville Pl Suite 1610 Nashville TN 37219

GAUMOND, GEORGE RAYMOND, librarian; b. Watertown, N.Y., May 4, 1946; s. Francis George and Hazel Mae (Ellis) G.; m. Arlene Mae Lynch, June 7, 1969; 1 son, Gregory Wade. B.A., U. S.C., 1969; M.S., U. Ill., 1975. Librarian, U. N.C.-Wilmington, 1975-78; dir. library Shepherd Coll., Shepherdstown, W.Va., 1981—. Mem. employee adv. council W.Va. Bd. Regents, Charleston, 1983—. Served to lt. USN, 1969-74. Mem. ALA, Internat. Assn. Marine Sci. Libraries and Info. Ctrs., Southeastern Library Assn., W.Va. Library Assn., Beta Phi Mu. Democrat. Methodist. Lodges: Masons, Kiwanis (dir. 1983-84). Home: PO Box 1327 Shepherdstown WV 25443 Office: Ruth Scarborough Library Shepherd Coll Shepherdstown WV 25443

GAUSE, NORMA NEAL, religion educator; b. St. Joseph, Mo., Sept. 21, 1920; d. Chester Abraham and Theresa Ann (Mull) Dolginoff; m. Robert Pritchard Gause, Feb. 16, 1941; children—Robert Donovan, Shannon Neal, Rebekah Mary, Garrett Bryan. Oral Hygienist magna cum laude, Northwestern U., 1940; B.A. with honors, U. South Fla., 1964, M.A. with honors, 1967; Th.D., Internat. Bible Inst. and Sem., 1983; Litt.D. (hon.), Beacon Coll., 1977. Lic. oral hygienist, Fla. Hygienist, Van Brunt Dental, Clearwater, Fla., 1941-60; instr. U. S. Fla., Tampa, 1967-73; prof. religion Fla. Beacon Coll., Largo, 1973—; pres., lectr. Soncoat Bible Class, Inc., Tarpon Springs, Fla., 1970; pres. Norma Neal Ministries, Inc., Tarpon Springs, 1982—; v.p. Project Look Up Internat., Largo, 1982—. Author: Right Dividing Word, 1982. Author, lectr. cassette tapes: Books of the Bible, 1981; TV series: Spotlight on Israel, 1982; radio programs: Choose Life, 1982—. Mem. adv. bd. Am. Christian Trust, Washington, 1983—; mem. exec. bd. Living Ctr. Bibl. and Archeol. Studies, 1984—. Mem. Am. Assn. Univ. Profs., Mortar Bd. Republican. Methodist. Club: Hadassah (Clearwater). Avocations: travel; reading; writing.

GAUTHIER, WENDELL HAYNES, lawyer; b. Iota, La., Apr. 14, 1943; s. Cylvert Joseph and Florence (Breaux) G.; m. Anne Barrios Gauthier, Aug. 28, 1965; children—Cherie Anne, Michelle Anne, Celeste Anne. B.A., U. Southwestern La., 1966; J.D., Loyola U., New Orleans, 1970. Bar: U.S. Dist. Ct. (ea. dist.) La. 1971, U.S. Ct. Appeals (5th cir.) 1977, U.S. Supreme Ct. 1977. Assoc., John B. Hattier and Louis Heyd, Jr., New Orleans, 1970-71; sole practice, 1971-74; ptnr. Gauthier, Murphy, Sherman, McCabe & Chehardy and predecessors, 1974—; pres., sr. ptnr. Gauthier & Murphy P.L.C.; lectr. Loyola U., New Orleans. Served with USMCR, 1961-62. Mem. Jefferson Bar Assn., La. Bar Assn., ABA, Am. Trial Lawyers Assn., La. Trial Lawyers Assn. Democrat. Roman Catholic. Club: Lions. Home: 10025 Hyde Pl River Ridge LA 70123 Office: Gauthier Murphy et al 3500 N Hullen St Metairie LA 70002

GAUVEY, DAVID HOWARD, computer company executive, educator; b. Dayton, Ohio, May 30, 1938; s. Ralph Abraham and Irene (Howard) G.; m. Mary Bird, Jan. 10, 1961 (div. 1974); children—David, Steven, Julie Lynn. A.S. in Acctg., Tarrant County Jr. Coll., 1974; B.B.A. in Mgmt., Tex. Wesleyan Coll., 1976; M.A. in Pub. Mgmt., U. Houston, 1981; M.B.A., Amber U. Regional mgr. Fact, Inc., St. Louis, 1960-67; exec. v.p. spl. promotions div. Intersystems, Jackson, Miss., 1967-70; pres. Gauvey & Assocs., Arlington, Tex., 1970-73, Compunet, Inc., Dallas, 1982—; dir. edn. Miss Wade's Coll. Fashion Merchandising, Dallas, 1985—; cons. mgmt. mktg; tchr. market salesmanship Tarrant County Jr. Coll., Ft. Worth. Served with U.S. Army, 1957-60. Mem. N.G. Assn. Tex., Am. Soc. Pub. Adminstrs., Acad. Polit. Sci. Republican.

GAVER, JAMES MOLLOY, federal executive; b. Augusta, Ga., Mar. 22, 1943; s. John Milton and Mary (Huston) Molloy. Grad. Groton Sch.; B.A., Princeton U., 1964. Reporter NBC News, Washington, 1969-75; dir. Office of External Affairs, Savannah River Ops. Office, U.S. Dept. Energy, Aiken, S.C., 1976—. Served to lt. USNR, 1965-69. Recipient Sec. of Energy Meritorious Service award, 1964. Clubs: City Tavern (Washington); Idle Hour (Lexington, Ky.); Green Boundary (Aiken). Office: US Dept Energy PO Box A Aiken SC 29802

GAWALT, GERARD W(ILFRED), historian, writer, researcher; b. Boston, Feb. 10, 1943; s. John R. and Regina M. (Chaloux) G.; m. Jane F. Cavanaugh, Aug. 6, 1966; children—Susan, Ann, Ellen. B.A., Northeastern U., 1965; M.A., Clark U., 1968, Ph.D., 1969. Reporter Milford (Mass.) Daily News, 1961-63, Worcester (Mass.) Telegram, 1963-65; instr. Assumption Coll., 1967-68, Clark U., 1968-69; hist. specialist Library of Congress, Washington, 1969—, specialist in legal history, 1969—; adj. prof. George Mason U., 1972, Catholic U. Am., 1981; guest lectr. George Washington U., Smithsonian Instn. Alumni scholar, 1960-61; NDEA fellow, 1965-68; Am. Council Learned Socs. fellow, 1979-80. Mem. Am. Soc. Legal History, Orgn. Am. Historians, Inst. Early Am. History, Assn. Documentary Editors, Library of Congress Profl. Guild (treas. 1977-78, pres. 1978-79). Democrat. Roman Catholic. Author: Manuscript Sources in the Library of Congress for Research on the American Revolution, 1975; The Promise of Power: The Emergence of the Massachusetts Legal Profession 1760-1840 (Choice Outstanding Acad. Book of 1980), 1979; author papers in legal history; editor: Journal of Gideon Olmsted; Adventures of a Revolutionary War Sea Captain, 1978; John Paul Jones' Memoir of the American Revolution, 1979; The New High Priests: Lawyers in Modern Industrial America, 1984; assoc. editor Letters of Dels. to Congress, 1774-1789, 12 vols., 1976—. Home: 6808 Quebec Ct Springfield VA 22152

GAY, DAVID EDWARD RYAN, economist; b. Bryan, Tex., Sept. 19, 1945; s. John Gordon and Emma Louise (Ryan) G.; B.A., Tex. A&M U., 1968; Ph.D. (NDEA fellow), 1973; postdoctoral Kans. U., 1974, U. Chgo., 1979, U. Miami, 1980. Asst. prof. econs. U. Ark., Fayetteville, 1973-77, assoc. prof., 1977-83, prof., 1983—; vis. scholar U. Glasgow (Scotland), 1975, Hoover Instn. Stanford U., 1975; vis. assoc. prof. U. Colo., 1980, Tex. A&M U., 1980-81; vis. prof. Brigham Young U., 1983-84; mem. adv. bd. Nat. Ctr. for Policy Analysis, 1982—. Bd. dirs. N.W. Ark. Community Concerts, 1975-76, Tex. A&M Opera and Performing Arts Soc., 1972-73; bd. govs. Ark. Union, 1977-79, Tex. A&M Commn. on Visual Arts, 1982—. Named Outstanding Faculty Mem., U. Ark., 1979; recipient research award U. Ark. Coll. Bus., 1985, Outstanding Tchr. award econs. dept., 1986. Mem. Am. Econ. Assn., Am. Fin. Assn. (life), Eastern Econ. Assn. (founding, life), Public Choice Soc., Royal Econ. Soc. (life), So. Econ. Assn. (life), Southwestern Econs. Assn. (pres. 1981-82), Southwestern Soc. Economists (v.p. 1986-87), Southwestern Social Sci. Assn. (exec. council 1981-83, sec. 1985-86, v.p. 1986-87), Western Econ. Assn. (life), Western Social Sci. Assn. (exec. council, pres. 1983-84, appreciation award 1985), Mid-South Acad. Econs. and Fin. (exec. council, pres. 1986-87), Missouri Valley Econ. Assn. (dir., exec. com. 1984—), Western Social Sci. Econ. Assn. (exec. dir. 1984—), Beta Gamma Sigma (chpt. sec. 1985—), Alpha Kappa Psi (adviser 1977-79), Phi Kappa Phi, Omicron Delta Epsilon. Republican. Methodist. Editorial bd. Ark. Bus. and Econ. Rev., 1976—mem. editorial bd., Bus. and Econ. Perspectives, 1984—; Social Sci. Quar., 1982-84, dep. editor, 1984—, Midsouth Jour. Econs. and Fin., 1984—; contbr. articles to profl. jours. Office: Dept Econs U Ark Fayetteville AR 72701

GAY, DON DOUGLAS, plant physiologist, researcher, scientist, inventor; b. Oklahoma City, Jan. 17, 1944; s. Virgil Eugene and Ruth Arlene (Nelson) G.; m. Mary Jo Forslund, Sept. 2, 1966; children—Matthew Eric, Meghan Ruth, Nathan Douglas-Eugene. B.A. in Biology and Chemistry, Augustana Coll., 1966; M.S. in Botany, U. Iowa, 1971, Ph.D. in Plant Physiology, 1975. Prin. investigator Pollutant Pathways br. U.S. EPA, Las Vegas, Nev., 1974-78; postdoctoral fellow assoc. in epidemiology and environ. chemistry, U. Iowa, Iowa City, 1978-79; scientist, research plant physiologist DuPont, Savannah River Lab., Aiken, S.C., 1979-86; dir. research and devel., mktg. mgr. Sci. Systems, Inc., State Coll., Pa., 1986—; vis. asst. prof. biology U. Nev., Las Vegas, 1976-78. Treas. Aiken Elem. Sch. PTO, 1978-80; soccer coach, dist. chief Indian Guides, YMCA; active Lutheran Marriage Encounter. Served to lt. Signal Corps U.S. Army, 1966-69; Vietnam. Coll. scholarships, First Luth. Ch., Ottumwa, Iowa, Rotary Club of Ottumwa; tuition scholar U. Iowa, 1971-74. Mem. Sigma Xi. Republican. Lutheran. Contbr. articles to profl. pubs.; patentee analytical instruments, sub-micron particle collector, recycling radioactive waste, new shipment and delivery system for radioactive gases. Home: 1233 Woodbine Rd Aiken SC 29801 Office: Sci Systems Inc 1120 W College Ave State College PA 16801

GAY, JOHN MARION, federal agency administrator, organization-personnel analyst; b. Houston, Sept. 23, 1936; s. John Henry and LolaBell (Collins) G.; children—John Marion II, Dierdre, Michael, Michelle (dec.), Steven, Christina. B.A., Tex. So. U., 1956; B.S., Fla. Meml. Coll., 1976. Cert. tchr., Fla. Compensation analyst SE Banks, N.A., Miami, Fla., 1976-78; personnel job analyst Kaiser Transit Group, Miami, 1978-80; tribal adminstr. Miccosukee Indians, Everglades Nat. Park, Fla., 1980-81; tchr. Broward County Schs., Fort Lauderdale, Fla., 1981-83, Dade County Schs., Miami, 1983-84; postal employee U.S. Postal Service, North Miami Beach, Fla., 1984—, consumer affairs officer, 1985—. Corp. coordinator United Negro Coll. Fund, Dade County, 1977. Served with USAF, 1956-59. Max Fleischmann scholar United Negro Coll. Fund, 1975; recipient mems. award of honor Alpha Kappa Mu, 1974; award Fla. Meml. Coll. Alumni Assn., 1978. Fellow NEA; mem. Nat. Assn. Letter Carriers. Democrat. Avocations: tennis; bowling; writing. Home: 2780 NW 34th Terr Lauderdale Lakes FL 33311

GAY, STEFFEN, physician, educator; b. Geyersdorf, German Dem. Republic, Mar. 22, 1948, came to U.S., 1976, permanent resident, 1978; s. Peter and Ilse (Weller) G.; m. Renate Erika Dorner, Jan. 6, 1973; children—Ann-Britt, Annietta, Max Hans-Peter. Abitur summa cum laude, EOS, German Dem. Republic, 1966; M.D. summa cum laude, Univ. Med. Sch., Leipzig, German Dem. Republic, 1972. Research fellow Max-Planck Inst., Munich, Fed. Republic Ger., 1973-76; research scientist biochemistry Rutgers U., Piscataway, N.J., 1976; assoc. prof. medicine U. Ala., Birmingham, 1978-84, assoc. prof. dermatology, 1978—, prof. medicine, 1984—, dir. WHO Ctr., 1984—; dir. U. Ala. IDR-EM-LM Unit, 1983—; dir., v.p. Mega, Inc., Birmingham, 1980—. Author: Collagen in the Physiology and Pathology of Connective Tissue, 1978 (Carol Nachman prize for Rheumatology 1979). Founder, editor: Jour. Collagen and Related Research, 1980—. Recipient Lessing Gold medal German Dem. Republic Dept. Edn., 1966, Alexander Schmidt prize German Soc. Thrombosis Research, 1975. Mem. Am. Assn. Pathologists, Am. Rheumatism Assn., AAAS, N.Y. Acad. Sci., Am. Assn. Cell Biology. Home: 1100 Beacon Pkwy E Birmingham AL 35209 Office: WHO Ctr U Ala University Station THT/433 Birmingham AL 35294

GAYLES, JOSEPH NATHAN, JR., scientist, college official, consultant; b. Birmingham, Ala., Aug. 7, 1937; s. Joseph Nathan and Earnestine (Williams) G.; m. Gloria Wade, Aug. 20, 1967; children—Jonathan Ifeanyi-Chukw, Monica Saleyeka. A.B. summa cum laude, Dillard U., 1958, L.L.D. (hon.), 1983; Ph.D., Brown U., 1963. Asst. prof. chemistry Morehouse Coll., Atlanta, 1963-66, prof., dir. med. edn. project, 1969-77; staff scientist/project dir. IBM Research, San Jose, Calif., 1966-69; pres., prof. Talladega Coll. (Ala.), 1977-83; v.p. Morehouse Sch. Medicine, Atlanta, 1983—; cons. NSF, NIH; dir. Woodrow Wilson Found., North Ga. Health Systems Agy. Bd. dirs. ARC, YMCA, Donoho Sch., Council Internat. Exchange of Scholars, United Negro Coll. Fund. Recipient Powers Travel award, 1975; named Alumnus of Yr., Dillard U., 1977; Camille and Henry Dreyfus tchr.-scholar. Mem. Am. Phys. Soc., Am. Chem. Soc., Am. Assn. Polit. and Social Scientists, Phi Beta Kappa, Sigma Xi, Beta Kappa Chi, Alpha Phi Alpha, Sigma Pi Phi. Lodge: Kiwanis. Contbr. articles to profl. jours. Home: 1515 Austin Rd Atlanta GA 30331 Office: Morehouse Sch Medicine 720 Westview Dr SW Atlanta GA 30310

GAYLIS, NORMAN BRIAN, rheumatologist, internist, lecturer; b. Johannesburg, South Africa, May 31, 1950; came to U.S., 1976; s. Bernard Gaylis and Jesse Gaylis Berelowitz; m. Natalie Dagnin, June 6, 1976; children, Brett-Ari, Jarrod Michael. M.B.Ch.B. U. Witwatersrand, Johannesburg, South Africa, 1973. Diplomate Am. Bd. Internal Medicine. Intern Mt. Sinai Med. Ctr., Miami, 1976, resident, 1977-78, chief resident in medicine, 1978-79; clin. research fellow U. Miami, 1979-81; practice medicine specializing in rheumatology and internal medicine, North Miami, Fla. 1981—; mem. staff Parkway Med. Ctr., North Miami Gen. Hosp., North Shore Hosp., Biscayne Med. Ctr.; clin. asst. prof. U. Miami, 1982—. Editor: Problems in Rheumatology, 1981, 82 (award Arthritis and Rheumatology Assn. Bd. dirs., adviser Lupus Found. South Fla., 1981-83; bd. dirs., mem. council edn. Arthritis Found. South Fla., 1982-83. Mem. ACP, Am. Rheumatism Assn. (S.E. 1st prize for case presentation 1981), South African Med. Assn., Brit. Med. Assn., AMA. Jewish. Home: 520 N Parkway Golden Beach FL 33160 Office: 909 N Miami Beach Blvd North Miami FL 33162

GAYLORD, EDWARD LEWIS, publishing company executive; b. Denver, May 28, 1919; s. Edward King and Inez (Kinney) G.; m. Thelma Feragen, Aug. 30, 1950; children—Christine Elizabeth, Mary Inez, Edward King II, Thelma Louise. A.B., Stanford U., 1941; LL.D., Oklahoma City U., Okla. Christian Coll., Pepperdine U. Chmn., pres., dir. Gaylord Broadcasting Co., WKY, Oklahoma City, WTVT, Tampa-St. Petersburg, KTVT, Dallas-Ft. Worth, KHTV, Houston, WVTV, Milw., KSTW-TV, Seattle-Tacoma, WVUE-TV, New Orleans, WUAB-TV, Cleve.-Lorain; chmn. bd., dir. Mistletoe Express Service; pres., gen. mgr., dir. Okla. Pub. Co.; editor, pub. Daily Oklahoman, Oklahoma City Times, Sunday Oklahoman; Pubs. Petroleum, Okla. Graphics; pres. Colorado Springs Sun, Sun Resources, Inc., Greenland (Colo.) Ranch,

OPUBCO Resources, Inc., OPUBCO Devel. Co.; chmn. bd. Gayno, Inc., Denver, Farmer-Stockman, Dallas, Gaylord Prodn. Co. Calif.; partner Cimarron Coal Co., Denver, Lazy E Ranch, Saint Jo, Tex., Westwind Ranch, San Saba, Tex. Chmn., trustee Okla. Industries Authority; chmn. bd. govs. Okla. Christian Coll.; bd. dirs. Okla. State Fair, pres., 1961-71; bd. dirs., pres. Nat. Cowboy Hall of Fame and Western Heritage Center; bd. dirs. Okla. Eye Found.; vice chmn. bd. govs. Am. Citizenship Ctr.; trustee S.W. Research Inst., San Antonio; past trustee Casady Sch., Oklahoma City U. Served with AUS, 1942-46. Recipient Brotherhood award NCCJ, Spirit of Am. award U.S. Olympic Com., 1984; named to Okla. Hall of Fame, 1974. Mem. Oklahoma City C. of C. (dir., past pres.), So. Newspaper Pubs. Assn. (past pres.). Conglist. Home: 1506 Dorchester Dr Oklahoma City OK 73120 Office: Gaylord Broadcasting Co PO Box 25125 Oklahoma City OK 73125

GAYLORD, THOMAS KEITH, electrical engineering educator; b. Casper, Wyo., Sept. 22, 1943; s. Earl F. and Vesta J. (Kinsley) G.; m. Janice L. Smith, June 5, 1966; 1 dau., Grace M. B.S. in Physics, U. Mo.-Rolla, 1965, M.S.E.E., 1967; Ph.D. in Elec. Engring., Rice U., 1970. Adj. asst. prof. Rice U., Houston, 1970-72; asst. prof. elec. engring Ga. Inst. Tech., Atlanta, 1972-76, assoc. prof., 1976-80, prof., 1980-85, Regents prof., 1985—, Julius Brown chair, 1985—; cons. in field. Named Outstanding Young Engr. of Yr., Ga. Soc. Profl. Engrs., 1977; Outstanding Tchr. award Ga. Inst. Tech., 1984. Fellow Optical Soc. Am., IEEE (Centennial medal 1984); mem. AAAS, AAUP, Am. Soc. Engring. Edn. (Curtis W. McGraw research award 1979), Soc. Photo-optical Engrs., Sigma Xi (research awards), Omicron Delta Kappa. Contbr. articles to tech. jours. Home: 3180 Verdun Dr NW Atlanta GA 30305 Office: Sch Elec Engring Ga Inst Tech Atlanta GA 30332

GAYNOR, LEAH, radio public relations writer, broadcaster; b. Irvington, N.J.; d. Jack and Sophia Kamish; A.A., Miami Dade Community Coll., 1970; B.A., Fla. Internat. U., 1975, postgrad., 1975—; m. Robert Merrill, Mar. 27, 1954 (div.); children—Michael David, Lisa Heidi, Tracy Lynn. Owner, operator Lee Gaynor Assos., pub. relations, Miami, Fla., 1970-72; exec. dir. Ft. Lauderdale (Fla.) Jaycees, 1970-71; host interview program Sta. WGMA, Hollywood, Fla., 1971-73, stas. WWOK and WIGL-FM, Fla., 1973-79; occupational specialist Lindsey Hopkins Edn. Center Dade County Pub. Schs., publicity-pub. relations, Miami, 1971—, broadcaster talk show Mem. Northeast WEDR-FM. Citizens Adv. Com. Career and Vocat. Edn., 1973—; mem. adv. com. North Miami Beach High Sch., 1977-79; communications com. Council Continuing Edn. Women Miami, 1972-79; mem. publicity Com. Center Fine Arts, Mus. Sci. Mem. Women in Communications, Am. Women in Radio and TV (dir. publicity Goldcoast chpt. 1974-76), Internat. Assn. Bus. Communicators, Pub. Relations Soc. Am., Alliance Career Edn. (publicity chmn.), Nat. Schs. Pub. Relations Assn., Women's C. of C. So. Fla. Republican. Home: 1255 NE 171 Terr North Miami Beach FL 33162 Office: 750 NW 20th St Miami Fl 33127

GEARON, JOHN MICHAEL, professional basketball executive; b. Englewood, N.J., May 6, 1934; s. C.P. and Elizabeth (Asburg) G.; m. Patricia Smith, Jan. 1, 1960; children—Tierney, Michael, Tim. Pres., gov. Atlanta Hawks Profl. Basketball, 1983—; owner Gearon & Co., Atlanta, 1983—. Home: 368 Camden Rd NE Atlanta GA 30309 Office: Atlanta Hawks 100 Teachwood Dr NW Atlanta GA 30303*

GEARY, DAVID LESLIE, air force officer, educator; b. Connellsville, Pa., Sept. 30, 1947; s. Harry and Edith Marie (Halterman) G.; B.A., Otterbein Coll., 1969; M.S.J., W.Va. U., 1971; postgrad. U. Denver, 1974-75. Admissions counselor Otterbein Coll., 1968-69; instr. English, staff counselor Office of Student Ednl. Services, W.Va. U., Morgantown, 1969-71; commd. 2d lt. U.S. Air Force, 1969, advanced through grades to maj., 1982; dir. info. Luke AFB, Ariz., 1971-72; course dir. English and communications U.S. Air Force Acad., Colo., 1972-76; dir. public affairs Loring AFB, Maine, 1976-79, U.S. Air Force Engring. and Services Center, Tyndall AFB, Fla., 1980-84, U.S. Air Forces, Korea, 1984-85; asst. prof. aerospace studies U. Ala., 1985—; guest lectr. U. Maine, 1976-79, U.S. Air Force Inst. Tech., 1981-82, Fla. State U., 1982-83, U. Md., 1984-85, U. So. Calif., 1984-85. Decorated Meritorious Service medal, Air Force commendation medal, others; Reader's Digest Found. grantee, 1970; recipient Pres.'s Extraordinary Service award Otterbein Coll., 1969. Mem. Nat. Acad. TV Arts and Scis., Am. Assn. Public Opinion Research, Public Relations Soc. Am., Internat. Assn. Bus. Communicators. Republican. Episcopalian. Home: 4C Springhill Lake Tuscaloosa AL 35405 Office: Dept Air Force Studies Univ Ala PO Box 1988 University AL 35486

GEARY, JAMES JEWEL, public relations consultant; b. Pitts., May 14, 1914; s. James Madison and Iva Llewellen (Jewel) G.; m. Celia Ward Lavinder, Sept. 6, 1941 (div. 1962); children—Anne, Ellen, Martha, Laetitia; m. Karen Leyonmark, Mar. 6, 1965 (div. 1982); 1 child, Leslie; m. Patricia Ann Little, Oct. 25, 1982. B.S. in Natural Sci., U. Va., 1938; B.A. in Philosophy, James Madison U., 1985. Reporter World News, Roanoke, Va., 1938-46; info. specialist VA, Richmond, Va., 1946-47; newsman AP, Richmond, 1947-58; exec. dir. VA Civil War Ctr., Richmond, 1958-66; dir. New Market Battlefield, Va., 1966-82; pub. relations cons., 1982—. Served to lt. comdr. USNR, 1942-46; PTO. Recipient several writing awards Va. Press Assn. Mem. Va. Travel Council (bd. dirs., Achievement award 1967), Shenandoah Valley Travel Assn. (exec. com. 1966-80, pres. 1978-79, Golden Horseshoe award 1976, Shenandoah Bowl 1980). Republican. Avocations: philosophy; travel; golf. Home: 1183 Nelson Dr Harrisonburg VA 22801 Office: New Market Battlefield Park PO Box 1864 New Market VA 22844

GEDDIE, THOMAS EDWIN, feed and seed company executive; b. Athens, Tex., Oct. 7, 1930; s. Nolen Dawson and Fannie (Troublefield) G.; B.S. in Agr., Okla. State U., 1951; postgrad. Tex. A&M U., 1951; m. Minnie Maxine Smith, Feb. 18, 1968; children—Susan, Tommy, Sherry. Owner, operator Thomas E. Geddie Assocs., Athens, 1955—. Served with U.S. Army, 1952-54. Republican. Presbyterian. Club: Masons (32 deg.), Shriners. Home: 901 Clifford St Athens TX 75751 Office: 200 W Tyler St Athens TX 75751

GEDGAUDAS-MCCLEES, RITA KRISTINA, diagnostic radiologist, educator; b. Winnipeg, Man., Can., Mar. 4, 1950; came to U.S. 1963; d. Eugene Gedgaudas and Vilhelmina (Radzevicius) Gedgaudas; m. Eric Carr McClees, June 26, 1982. B.A. cum laude, Barat Coll., Lake Forest, Ill., 1971; M.D., U. Minn., 1975. Diplomate Am. Bd. Radiology. Intern U. Calif.-San Francisco, 1975-76, resident in radiology, 1976-79, fellow in abdominal imaging, 1979; asst. prof. Duke U. Med. Ctr., Durham, N.C., 1979-82; asst. prof. Emory U. Hosp., Atlanta, 1982—; asst. prof., chief gastro intestinal radiology sect. VA Med. Ctr., Atlanta, 1982—; assoc. prof. Emory U. Hosp., 1984—; vis. prof. dept. radiology U. Calif.-San Francisco, 1980, Georgetown U. Hosp., Washington, 1981, U. Minn. Hosps., Mpls., 1982, Montefiore Hosp., Albert Einstein Sch. Medicine, N.Y., 1984; presentations at edn. instns., profl. meetings. Reviewer, Jour. Clin. Ultrasound; contbr. articles to profl. publs. Mem. Am. Coll Radiology, Atlanta Radiol. Soc., Radiol. Soc. N.Am., Am. Roentgen Ray Soc., Soc. Gastrointestinal Radiologists, Assn. Univ. Radiologists, Ga. Gastroent. Soc. Home: 77 E Andrews Dr NW Apt 386 Atlanta GA 30305 Office: Emory U Hosp 1365 Clifton Rd NE Atlanta GA 30322

GEE, ELWOOD GORDON, university president; b. Vernal, Utah, Feb. 2, 1944; B.A., U. Utah, 1968; J.D., Columbia U., 1971, Ed.D., 1972. Assoc., Lord, Day & Lord, N.Y.C., 1971; law clk. to chief judge U.S. 10th Circuit, Salt Lake City, 1972-73; asst. dean U. Utah Coll. Law, Salt Lake City, 1973-74; jud. fellow U.S. Supreme Ct., Washington, 1974-75; assoc. dean, prof. law J. Reuben Clark Law Sch., Brigham Young U., Provo, Utah, 1975-79; dean Sch. Law W.Va. U., Morgantown, 1979-81, pres. univ., 1981—; mem. Com. to Consider Standards for Admission to Practice in Fed. Cts., 1976—; Aspen Inst. Humanistic Studies fellow, 1977-78; mem. Utah Health Planning Council, 1978—. Mem. ABA, Nat. Orgn. Legal Problems In Edn., Law and Soc. Assn. Author: Bread and Butter: Electives in American Legal Education, 1976; Bridging the Gap: Legal Education and the Lawyer Competency, 1978; Education Law and the Public Schools: A Compendiumm, 1978. Office: Office of President WVa U Morgantown WV 26506

GEE, THOMAS GIBBS, judge; b. Jacksonville, Fla., Dec. 9, 1925; s. James Gilliam and Cecile (Gibbs) G.; student The Citadel, 1942-43; B.S., U.S. Mil. Acad., 1946; LL.B., U. Tex., 1953; 1979; children—Jennifer Gee Updegraf, John Christopher, Mary Cecile, Thomas Gibbs. Bar: Tex. 1953. Assoc., Baker & Botts, Houston, 1953-54; asso. firm Graves, Dougherty, Gee, Hearon, Moody & Garwood, and predecessors, Austin, Tex., 1954, partner, 1955-73; judge U.S. Ct. Appeals, 5th Circuit, Austin, 1973-85, Houston, 1985—. Served with USAAF, 1946-47, USAF, 1947-50. Mem. Am. Law Inst., Am. Bar Assn., Am. Judicature Soc., Tex. Bar Found., Order of Coif. Contbr. articles to profl. jours., publs.; editor-in-chief Tex. Law Rev., 1952-53. Home: 1121 Post Oak Park Dr No E Houston TX 77027 Office: US Courthouse 515 Rusk St Room 11009 Houston TX 77002

GEER, JAMES FOOSHE, accountant, consultant; b. Augusta, Ga., Sept. 8, 1959; s. Harry Calvin and Anita (Taylor) G. B.B.A., Ga. So. Coll., 1981. C.P.A., 1984. Staff acct. Davis, Crittonden, Richter and Fletcher, C.P.A.s, Thomasville, Ga., 1981-82; sr. auditor Anderson, Hunt & Co. P.C., C.P.A.s, Atlanta, 1982—. Troop leader Ga. Carolina Boy Scouts Am., Augusta, 1975-81, editor booklet Where to Go Camping, 1974; mem. hand bell choir 1st Baptist Ch., Augusta, 1974-76; res. dep. sheriff Cobb County. Mem. Am. Inst. C.P.A.s, Nat. Assn. Accts., Ga. Soc. C.P.A.s (assoc.), Acctg. Assn. Ga. So. Coll. (pres. 1980-81), Honor Acctg. Soc. Ga. So. Coll. (founder, pres. 1979-80), Delta Sigma Pi (scholarship chmn. 1980-81, life mem. Epsilon Chi chpt.), Beta Alpha Psi (exec. v.p. 1980-81, outstanding service award 1981). Lodge: Order of Arrow (Arrowman of Yr. Bob White Lodge 1978). Office: Anderson Hung & Co PC CPAs 1950 N Park Pl Suite 600 Atlanta GA 30339

GEFFEN, THEODORE MORTON, petroleum production consultant; b. Calgary, Alta., Can., Feb. 22, 1922; d. Morres and Anne (Rootman) G.; m. Shirley Louise Levin, Sept. 5, 1943 (dec. 1979); children—William, Maureen, Howard; m. Doris K. Altman, Dec. 29, 1985. B.S. in Petroleum Engring., U. Okla., 1944. Field engr. Alta. Petroleum & Natural Gas Conservation Bd., 1943-45, Calif. Standard Co., Alta., 1945-46; research mgr. Amoco Prodn. Co., Tulsa, 1946-81; ind. petroleum cons., Tulsa, 1981—. Recipient John Franklin Carll award Soc. Petroleum Engrs., 1974; Service award, Mid Continent sect. AIME, 1970; named enhanced oil recovery pioneer Joint Symposium Soc. Petroleum Engrs. and Dept. of Energy, 1984. Mem. Soc. Petroleum Engrs. of AIME (Disting. mem.), Am. Assn. Petroleum Geologists. Contbr. articles to profl. jours. Home: 7221 S Gary Pl Tulsa OK 74136 Office: 3500 First Tower Tulsa OK 74103

GEHLE, ROBERT WAYNE, media services specialist, education media supervisor; b. Chgo., Feb. 12, 1949; s. Fred Charles and Clara Helen (Moltzan) G.; m. Janice Marie Jaeger, June 18, 1972. B.S. in English, U. Wis.-Stevens Point, 1971; M.A. in Library Media, U. South Fla., 1981. English tchr. Bayshore High Sch., Bradenton, 1974-78, media specialist, 1978-83; coordinator media services Manatee Community Coll., Bradenton, 1983-85; TV supr. ednl. media Manatee County Sch. Bd., 1985—; chmn. TV adv. com. Manatee County (Fla.) Bd. County Commrs., 1983-86. Recipient award of Recognition, Manatee County Sch. Bd., 1982. Mem. ALA, Fla. Assn. Media in Edn., Am. Assn. Sch. Librarians, Manatee Assn. Media in Edn., Phi Delta Kappa (Educator of Yr. Bradenton 1982). Office: Manatee County Sch Bd 215 Manatee Ave West Bradenton FL 33505

GEIGER, JAMES NORMAN, lawyer; b. Mansfield, Ohio, Apr. 5, 1932; s. Ernest R. and Margaret L. (Bauman) G.; m. Paula Hunt, May 11, 1957; children—Nancy G., John W. Student Wabash Coll., Crawfordsville, Ind., 1950-51; B.A., Ohio Wesleyan U., 1954; J.D., Emory U., 1962. Bar: Ga. 1961, U.S. dist. ct. (mid. dist.) Ga. 1966, U.S. Dist Ct. (so. dist.) Ga. 1983, U.S. Ct. Appeals (5th and 11th cirs.) 1980. Assoc., Henderson, Kaley, Geiger and Thurmond, Marietta, Ga., 1962-64; ptnr. Nunn, Geiger and Pierce and predecessors, Perry, Ga., 1964—, sr. ptnr., 1971—. Trustee Westfield (Ga.) Schs., 1970-74; mem. civilian adv. bd. Warner Robins AFB, 1976; chmn. council ministries Perry United Meth. Ch., 1970-71, mem. adminstrv. bd., 1968—. Served to capt. USAF, 1954-57. Mem. ABA, Ga. Bar Assn., Houston County Bar Assn., Perry C. of C. (pres. 1976), Phi Delta Phi, Pi Sigma Alpha. Methodist. Clubs: Perry Kiwanis (pres. 1968, Man of Yr. 1968), Perry (council 1967). Home: 821 Forrest Hill Rd Perry GA 31069 Office: PO Drawer T Perry GA 31069

GEIS, CLARENCE PAUL, health care services executive; b. Canton, Ohio, June 26, 1938; s. Clarence Lowell and Lucina A. (Gulling) G.; m. Mary Jane D'Agostino, Aug. 18, 1962; children—Lori Ann, Kristine Ann. Student Bowling Green State U., 1957-58, Kent State U., 1958-61. Asst. city mgr. Gateway Sporting Goods Co., Cleve., 1963-67; co-founder, exec. v.p. Med. Records Corp., Cleve., 1967-79; founder, pres., dir. M.L.K. Corp, Boca Raton, Fla., 1979—, Med. Records Corp., Boca Raton, 1979—; v.p. Med. Records Corp. Md.; cons. word processing of health care field. Adviser Jr. Achievement Co., Boca Raton. Served with U.S. Army, 1961-63. Mem. Am. Med. Record Assn., U.S. C. of C. Roman Catholic. Club: Rebounders (Cleve.). Lodge: KC. Office: 3200 N Federal Hwy Boca Raton FL 33431

GEIST, ROBERT MILLER, III, computer scientist, educator; b. Panama City, Fla., Apr. 23, 1948; s. Robert Miller and Vera Helen (Damlos) G.; m. Janice Lynn Robinson, June 6, 1970; children—Robert Miller, Jason Wyatt. B.A., Duke U., 1970, M.A., 1980; M.S., Notre Dame U., 1973, Ph.D., 1974. Asst. prof. math. Pembroke (N.C.) State U., 1974-77; vis. asst. prof. math. U. N.C.-Chapel Hill, 1977; assoc. prof. math. Pembroke State U., 1977-80; research assoc. in computer sci. Duke U., Durham, N.C., 1980, asst. prof. computer sci., 1981-83, assoc. prof. computer sci., 1983; assoc. prof. computer sci. Clemson (S.C.) U., 1984—; cons. to industry. Recipient Julia Dale prize, 1970; NSF trainee, 1970-74; NASA grantee, 1981-85. Mem. Am. Math. Soc., Math. Assn. Am., Assn. Computing Machinery, IEEE Computer Soc. Author research papers, articles in profl. publs. Office: Clemson U Clemson SC 29631

GEITHNER, PAUL HERMAN, JR., bank holding company executive; b. Phila., June 7, 1930; s. Paul Herman and Henriette Antonine (Schuck) G.; m. Irmgard Hagedorn, Sept. 6, 1956; children—Christina, Amy, Paul. B.A. cum laude, Amherst Coll., 1952; M.B.A. with distinction, U. Pa., 1957. Sec.-treas. Ellicott Machine Co., Balt., 1957-68; successively v.p., sr. v.p., exec. asst. First Va. Banks, Inc., Falls Church, 1968-85, chmn., pres., chief adminstrv. officer, 1985—; pres., dir. First Va. Life Ins. Co., 1974—; dir. Arlington Mortgage Co. Served to lt. USNR, 1952-55. Home: 5406 Colchester Meadow Ln Fairfax VA 22030 Office: 6400 Arlington Blvd Falls Church VA 22046

GELB, GEORGE EDWARD, lawyer; b. Miami, Fla., June 23, 1946; s. Monroe and Violet (Abelson) G.; m. Kathryn Mary Peterson, Dec. 21, 1973; children—Christine Mary, Joseph Edward. B.A., U. Miami, 1968; J.D., U. Del., 1975; LL.M., NYU, 1978. Bar: Fla. 1977, N.J. 1977, Pa. 1977, U.S. Dist. Ct. (so. dist.) Fla. 1977, U.S. Ct. Appeals (5th cir.) 1977, U.S. Ct. Appeals (11th cir.) 1981, U.S. Supreme Ct. 1983. Asst. atty. gen. Del. Atty. Gen.'s Office, Wilmington, 1975-76; pres., atty. George E. Gelb, P.A., Miami, Fla., 1978—. Chmn., Wilmington Young Republicans, atty. City of Wilmington Rep. Com., asst. counsel Del. Rep. State Com., 1975-76. Roman Catholic. Club: Coral Gables Country. Office: George E Gelb P A Suite 1116 19 W Flagler St Miami FL 33130

GELINAS, PAUL JOSEPH, psychologist, author; b. Woonosket, R.I., July 17, 1914; s. Edmund J. and Marianne (Desaultnier) G.; m. Eva J. MacFarlane, 1935; 1 child, Robert P. B.A., Acadia U., 1933; M.A., Columbia U., 1954; M.S., CCNY, 1953; Ed.D., NYU, 1955. Supt. schs., Setauket, N.Y., 1950-70; cons., Halifax, N.S., 1967-70; pvt. practice psychology, Setauket, N.Y., 1970—; cons. Tax Action Group, Setauket, 1970-74. Author: History for Young Readers, 1967 (Book of the Month bonus selection), So You Want to Be a Teacher, 1967, Teenagers Can Get Good Jobs, 1970, 71, Coping With Anger, 1972, Coping With Fears, 1972, Coping With Loneliness, 1980, Coping With Emotions, 1981. Receiver taxes Town of Brookhaven, County of Suffolk, 1978-82; v.p. Setauket Civic Assn., 1970-72; mem. bd. edn., Setauket, 1982-84; bd. dirs. Coram Mediation, N.Y., 1982—. Served with USNG, 1930. Recipient Citations, C. of C., Setauket, 1966, 67. Mem. Am. Psychol. Assn., Am. Assn. Marriage and Family Therapists, N.Y. State Psychol. Assn., Suffolk County Psychol. Assn. Presbyterian. Lodge: Lions (pres. 1960-62). Avocation: business writing. Home: 5095 Bay St NE Apt 109 Saint Petersburg FL 33703

GELLINEK, CHRISTIAN JOHANN GEORG, German literature educator, lay theologian; b. Potsdam, Germany, May 11, 1930; came to U.S., 1961, naturalized, 1966; s. Christian Johann Michael Gellinek and Margaretha Christiane Lorenzen; m. Janis Virginia Little, 1962 (div. 1972); m. Josepha Eugénie Schellekens, June 27, 1975; children—Else M., Saskia K., Torsten C. M., Jens. P.C. Cert. Latin and history tchr. Ont. Coll. Edn., Toronto, 1961; M.A., Yale U., 1963, Ph.D., 1964; D.Philosophy Habilitation, U. Basel, Switzerland, 1975. Instr., asst., assoc. prof. Yale Univ., New Haven, 1963-70; prof. German lit. Univ. Fla., Gainesville, 1971—; vis. prof. Basel Univ., Switzerland, 1974-75, U. Utah, Salt Lake City, 1977, Poznan U., Poland, 1976, UCLA, 1984. Author 10 sci. books, 1 volume of poetry. Contbr. articles to profl. jours. Fulbright fellow Münster, W. Ger., 1980-81; Morse fellow Yale Univ., 1964-65. Corr. mem. Grotiana, Den Haag, Netherlands. Mem. Calvinist Ch. Avocation: reading. Office: 261 ASB Dept German Univ Fla Gainesville FL 32611

GELSHENEN, ROSEMARY ROBINSON, marketing executive; b. Queens, N.Y., Feb. 24, 1950; d. John Joseph and Ann (Doyle) Gelshenen; m. Dennis Berkholtz, Oct. 27, 1973 (div. 1980). B.A., Marquette U., 1972. Receptionist Atlanta Conv. Bur., 1974; sales mgr. Rodeway Inns, Atlanta, 1974; pub. relations dir. McDonald's Corp., Atlanta, 1975, McDonald & Little, Atlanta, 1976; dir. mktg. Ga. World Congress Center, Atlanta, 1976—. Banquet chmn. Beastly Feast, Zool. Soc., Atlanta, 1983, 84. Mem. Sales & Mktg. Execs. (dir.), Nat. Assn. Exposition Mgrs., Hotel Sales Mgmt. Assn., Profl. Conv. Mgmt. Assn., Meeting Planners Internat. Roman Catholic. Home: 23110 Plantation Dr Atlanta GA 30324 Office: Ga World Congress Center 285 International St Atlanta GA 30313

GEMMER, H. ROBERT, civic worker, clergyman; b. Indpls., Apr. 4, 1923; s. Hiram Conrad and Edith May (Miller) G.; B.S., Ind. U., 1944; cert. Yale Sch. Alcohol Studies, 1945; B.D., Chgo. Theol. Sem., also U. Chgo., 1947; postgrad. Christian Theol. Sem., 1950; M.A., Western Res. U., 1960; m. Myrna Jean Flory, June 11, 1949; children—David Robert, Jean Annalee (Mrs. Larry J. McCutchan). Ordained to ministry Christian Ch. (Disciples of Christ), 1947; asst. minister, dir. youth activities First Friends Ch., Indpls., 1948-49; pastor First Ch. of Brethren, Cleve., 1951-55, interim co-pastor, 1978-79; asst. to dir. student activities and guidance Fenn Coll. (now Cleve. State U.), 1955-56, acting dir. student activities, 1956-57; dir. social welfare dept. Cleve. Area Ch. Fedn., 1957-63; rep. local councils of chs. in U.S. at World Migration Conf. of World Council of Chs., Leysin, Switzerland, 1960; exec. dir. Council Chs. Mohawk Valley Area, Utica, N.Y., 1963-67, Council Chs. Greater St. Petersburg (Fla.), 1967-70; sales rep. Wholesale Tours Internat. N.Y., 1972—, Ednl. Opportunities, Inc., 1977—; dir. Dean Mohr Plaza Apts., Inc., St. Petersburg, 1976—, sec., 1979—; dean Bapt. Disciples Brethren Sch. Christian Living, Cleve., 1954, 55; mem. adv. com. Sta. WLCY-TV, 1968-74, commentator, 1967-70, corr. at World Council Chs. Assembly, Nairobi, 1975. Mem. nat. council Fellowship of Reconciliation, 1955-65; mem. bd. social welfare and dept. ednl. devel. Nat. Council Chs., 1961-67; sec. Downtown Neighborhood Center, Goodrich House Bd., Cleve., 1962-63; chmn. Adirondack-Mohawk Regional Planning Commn., 1965-67, Utica Area Interreligious Commn. on Religion and Race, 1964-66; pres. Council Human Relations of Greater St. Petersburg, 1968-80, 85—, chmn. edn., 1980—; sec. Religions United in Action for Community, 1968-69, mem. exec. com., 1969-70, observor Pinellas County (Fla.) Sch. Bd., 1971-76; mem. minority relations goals com. City of St. Petersburg, 1970-73 mem. community relations goals com., 1983-84; mem. adv. com. Pinellas County Charter Commn., 1971-72; chmn. Public Health Council, Utica, 1966-67; treas. Suncoast Progress, 1968, Pinellas Opportunity Council, 1969; v.p. Lakewood Property Owners (now Lakewood Civic) Assn., 1972, pres., 1974, 75, 81-84, bd. dirs., 1976—, sec., 1979; mem. Nat. Ch. Commn. on Scouting, 1963-70; pres. H.C. Gemmer Family Christian Found., Indpls., 1956—; edn. chmn., bd. dirs. St. Petersburg br. NAACP, 1969—, treas., 1974-76, 2d v.p., 1976-83, 1st v.p. 1983—, edn. chmn. Fla. state conf., 1976-78; mem. Shalom Task Force, Dist. of Fla. and P.R., Ch. of Brethren, 1977-83, chmn., 1977-78; mem. UN Day Com., St. Petersburg, 1969—; bd. dirs. Tampa Bay chpt. UN Assn. U.S.A., 1969—, 1st v.p., 1980-82, pres., 1982-86; active numerous other orgns.; Republican candidate Pinellas Sch. Bd., 1968, chmn. bi-racial adv. com., 1969-70, sec.-treas., 1970-71, alt., 1971-75, voting mem., 1975-82, vice-chmn., 1977-80, chmn., 1980-82, chmn. zoning com., 1976-82, 85—, mem., 1982—, vice chmn. Sch. Facilities Task Force, 1977-78; non-partisan candidate St. Petersburg City Council, 1970; bd. dirs. Found. Religious Studies Indpls., 1973—, N.Y. Council Chs., 1963-67, Suncoast Goodwill Industries, 1969-72, Nat. Neighbors, Washington, 1978-80, Pinellas Habitat for Humanity, 1984—; bd. dirs. Urban Devel. Corp., St. Petersburg, 1976—, sec., 1979—; internat. bd. dirs. Habitat for Humanity, Inc., 1976—, program devel. and evaluation com. 1976—, 1st v.p. and chmn. program devel. and evaluation com., 1980—; mem. Immokalee bd. dirs. for Habitat for Humanity, 1980—, chmn. site com., 1984—, chmn. fin. com., 1985—; mem. Nat. Farm Workers Support Com., 1969—; del. World Religious Leaders Conf. on Gen. and Nuclear Disarmament, Tokyo, 1981; exec. bd. Pinellas Suncoast Urban League, 1976-84, sec., 1977-78; Democratic precinct committeeman, 1982—; candidate for Pinellas County Sch. Bd., 1982, 86; chaplain Pinellas County Dem. Com., 1982—; bd. dirs. Latchkey Services to Children, St. Petersburg, 1983-85. Recipient citation U.S. Sec. HEW, 1962, numerous other awards. Mem. Acacia. Contbg. editor Peace Action, 1955-68. Contbr. articles to mags. Address: 1863 Lakewood Dr S St Petersburg FL 33712

GENETTI, MARIANNE ELIZABETH, real estate broker; b. Hazleton, Pa., Dec. 9, 1937; d. August H. and Della (Fox) Genetti; B.S., Pa. State U., 1959; postgrad. Am. U., 1967-68, Rollins Coll., 1971-72. Contract adminstr. Dept. Def. Personnel Support Agy., Phila., 1960-63; asst. mgr. Gus Genetti Hotels, Wilkes-Barre and Hazleton, Pa., 1963-65; project specialist Econ. Devel. Adminstrn., Dept. Commerce, Washington, 1965-69; comptroller Gus Genetti Hotel, Hazleton, 1969-71; contracts specialist Sprint missile Martin-Marietta Corp., Orlando, Fla., 1971-73; broker-salesman Borgon Realty Corp., Orlando, Fla., 1973-83; pres. Penn Properties, Inc., Orlando, 1983—; dir. Best Western Genetti, Hazleton; instr. Valencia Community Coll. Open Campus, Orlando, 1982. Grad. Realtors Inst.; recipient Superior Performance award Dept. Commerce, 1969. Mem. Orlando Winter Park Bd. Realtors, Fla. Assn. Realtors, Central Fla. Investors, Fla. Real Estate Exchange, Mensa. Home: 1401 E Church St Orlando FL 32801 Office: PO Box 6298 Orlando FL 32853

GENKINGER, LAUREN BETTIE, advertising executive; b. New Castle, Pa., June 4, 1949; s. Robert S. and Bettie D. Genkinger. B.S., U. Fla., 1971. Research asst. Campbell-Mithun, Inc., Mpls., 1972, research account exec., 1973, research account supr., 1975-78; assoc. research dir. McDonald & Little, Atlanta, 1978, v.p., research dir., 1979-81, sr. v.p., mgmt. supr., research dir., 1981-84; sr. v.p. strategic planning and research Burton-Campbell, Inc., 1984—; ptnr. T.G. Madison, Inc., 1986—. Mem. Am. Mktg. Assn., U. Fla. Advt. Adv. Council. Home: 110 Verlaine Pl NW Atlanta GA 30327 Office: TG Madison Inc 3210 Peachtree Rd NE Atlanta GA 30305

GENTLE, JAMES EDWARD, computer software designer, educator, consultant; b. Statesville, N.C., May 31, 1943; s. Wint Farley and Vertie Mae (Pardue) G.; m. Joyce Ellen Lodge, June 2, 1939. B.S., U. N.C., 1966; M.A., La. State U., 1969; M.C.S., Tex. A&M U., 1973, Ph.D., 1974. Assoc. prof. Iowa State U., 1974-79; mgr. research and design IMSL, Inc., Houston, 1979—; adj. prof. Rice U. Recipient H.O. Hartley award Tex. A&M U., 1981. Fellow Am. Statis. Assn. (dir.), Royal Statis. Soc.; mem. Assn. Computing Machinery, Internat. Assn. Statis. Computing. Author: (with others) Statistical Computing, 1980; editor Procs. 15th Symposium on the Interface, 1983; editor Current Index to Statistics, 1980—; contbr. articles to profl. jours. Home: 8843 Sharpview St Houston TX 77036 Office: IMSL Inc 7500 Bellaire St Houston TX 77036

GENTRY, ANN DENISE, entertainer, clerical worker; b. Oklahoma City, Mar. 13, 1948; d. William Robert and Ann Denise (Andruss) Burchardt; m. Rytti Kattov, Jan. 20, 1968 (dec. 1972); m. William Byron Gentry, May 6, 1979; children—J.J., William Byron. Student Okla. U., 1966-67, UCLA, 1970, Central State U., Okla., 1971-73, Oklahoma City U., 1979-80; practitioner tng. Ch. Religious Sci., 1977-79. Receptionist, bookkeeper Gentry Clinic, Oklahoma City, 1978—. Singer, dancer various Oklahoma City engagements including Christopher's Restaurant, Occasionally Downstairs, Waterford Vista Hotel, Newport Restaurant, Petroleum Club; ballet instr. Robert Bell Sch. Ballet, 1985—. Actress stage plays including Man of La Mancha. Co-wrote song Daddy Long Legs, 1981. Author poetry. Vocal music tchr. Timberridge Sch., 1983-84; mem. publicity com. Ballet Okla. Co., 1983-84; mem. women's com. Okla. Symphony Orch., 1982-83; judge Okla. Kids talent competition, 1985; v.p. Grand Blvd. Dance Co., 1985—. Finalist in talent competition Doc Severinson's, 1984; Miss Okla. Pagaent scholar, 1967; Ind. U. scholar, 1966; named Miss Midwest City, 1966. Democrat. Avocations: interior decorating; gardening; collecting old sheet music; collecting swans; sailing. Office: Gentry Clinic 3616 NW 58th St Oklahoma City OK 73112

GENTRY, GLENN ADEN, microbiology educator; b. Athens, Ga., June 25, 1931; s. Glenn and Helen (Townsend) G.; m. Betty Ruth McInnis, Dec. 27, 1958; children—Susan Swayze Gentry Saidian, Linda Helen. B.A., Maryville Coll., 1953; M.S., Vanderbilt U., 1956; Ph.D., U. Miss. Med. Ctr., 1960. Postdoctoral fellow U. Wis., 1960-63; asst. prof. microbiology U. Miss. Med.

Ctr., Jackson, 1963-65, assoc. prof., 1965-68, prof., 1968—, dir. viral diagnostic lab., 1972—; vis. scientist Glascow U. (Scotland), 1971-72. Elder Fondren Presbyn. Ch., 1977. NIH postdoctoral fellow, 1960-63; NIH grantee, 1963-84; Am. Cancer Soc. grantee, 1979-82, Am. Heart Assn. grantee, 1983-84; recipient NIH Research Career Devel. award, 1963-73. Mem. Am. Soc. Microbiology, Am. Soc. Virology, Am. Soc. Exptl. Pathology; AAAS, Am. Assn. Cancer Research, Am. Guild Organists, Sigma Xi. Patentee filtration apparatus, 1983; contbr. articles to profl. jours. Office: Dept Microbiology U Miss Med Ctr Jackson MS 39216

GENTRY, GRANT CLAYBOURNE, food retail co. exec.; b. Chgo., June 5, 1924; s. Grant Clayborune and Helen C. (Cooley) G.; J.D., DePaul U., 1949; m. Doris L. Helsten, Sept. 8, 1943; children—Grant, Scott. Admitted to Ill. bar, 1949; asso. firm McKnight, McLaughton & Dunn, 1949-53; tax atty. Internat. Harvester Co., 1953-57; exec. v.p., Jewel Cos., Chgo., 1957-75, also dir.; pres., chief adminstrn. officer Great Atlantic & Pacific Tea Co., Montvale, N.J., 1975-78, also dir.; partner Adamy, Foley & Gentry, Chgo., 1978-79; chmn., chief exec. officer Pantry Pride, Inc., Ft. Lauderdale, Fla., 1979—; dir. Borman's Inc. Bd. dirs. Loyola U., Chgo. Served with AUS, 1943-46. Mem. Internat. Assn. Chain Stores (chmn.), Nat. Assn. Food Chains (past chmn.), Am. Bar Assn. Clubs: Blindbrook Country, Park Ridge Country. Home: 4545 N Ocean Dr Boca Raton FL 33431 Office: 6500 N Andrews Ave Ft Lauderdale FL 33309

GENTRY, ROBERT CECIL, research scientist, meteorological consultant; b. Paducah, Ky., Nov. 29, 1916; s. Clarence Houston and Ora (Holt) G.; m. Laura M. Hartness, May 24, 1948; children—Jane O., Judith L., Laura S., Robert L. B.S., Murray State U., 1937; Ph.D., Fla. State U., 1963. Cert. cons. meteorologist Am. Meteorol. Soc. Tchr., Bandana High Sch., Ballard County, Ky., 1937-40; weather observer, technician and researcher, 1941-47, weather forecaster, 1947-55; asst. dir. Nat. Hurricane Research Project, U.S. Weather Bur., West Palm Beach and Miami, Fla., 1955-59; acting dir. Nat. Hurricane Research Lab., Miami, 1959-61, dir., 1961-74; dir. Project Stormfury, Depts. Commerce and Def., Miami, 1966-74; chief research meteorologist Gen. Electric Co., Beltsville, Md., 1975-78; cons. World Meteorol. Orgn., Geneva, 1960-75; research scientist Clemson (S.C.) U., 1976—. Recipient Gold medal award U.S. Dept. Commerce, 1970. Named Outstanding Fed. Employee of Yr., Greater Miami Exec. Bd., 1970; Outstanding Alumnus, Murray State U., 1974. Fellow Am. Meteorol. Soc. (chmn. confs.); mem. Am. Geophys. Union, AAAS, Sigma Xi. Democrat. Lodge: Lions (pres. 1982-84; zone chmn. 1983-84, dep. dist. gov. 1984-85). Contbr. articles to numerous profl. jours. Home: Route 1 Box 632 Salem SC 29676 Office: Dept of Physics and Astronomy Clemson U Clemson SC 29631

GENTRY, WILLIAM NORTON, safety consultant; b. Greenwood, Ark., May 29, 1908; s. William Fred and Lola (Caudle) G.; B.S. in Bus. Adminstrn., U. Ark., 1929, B.A. in History, 1984; m. Margaret Sue Whaley, May 25, 1938 (dec.); children—Susan Margaret, William David. Wire chief SW Bell Telephone Co., Hope, Ark., 1932-34, constrn. foreman, 1935-40, exchange engr., 1940-42, 46-50, plant tng. supr., 1950-57, plant personnel and tng. supr., 1958-67, plant tng. and employment supr., 1967-73; safety cons. Little Rock Mcpl. Water Works, 1974-85, Hiway Safety Corp., Ft. Smith, Ark., 1986—. Div. leader Community Chest, Little Rock, 1949-52; pres., del. from Ark., Pres.'s Conf. on Occupational Safety, 1958; organizing pres. United Cerebral Palsy of Central Ark., 1959-60; chmn. Little Rock Safety Commn., 1970-71, mem., 1966—, vol instr., 1985—; registered instr. Nat. Safety Council Driver Improvement Program; bd. dirs. Little Rock Central YMCA, 1972-74; worker, mem. organizing bd. Contact Inc., Crisis Prevention Center, Little Rock, 1968-76; mem. Gov.'s Com. on Employment of Handicapped, Ark., 1973-80; del. to Pres.'s Conf. on Employment of Handicapped, Washington, 1977; chmn. work area on evangelism First United Meth. Ch., Little Rock, 1980, lay speaker, 1980-81, del. to Internat. Conf. of Christian Heritage in Govt., London, 1981. Served with Signal Corps, U.S. Army 1942-46. Recipient W.H. Sadler trophy Community Chest of Little Rock, 1950, 51; Service award United Cerebral Palsy of Central Ark., 1969; Safety award of commendation Ark. Dept. Labor, 1973. Mem. Am. Soc. Safety Engrs. (charter mem. Ark. chpt., sec. 1974-80, vice chmn. 1959-60, gen. chmn. 1960-61, chmn. ann. safety inst. 1972-76), So. Safety Conf. (pres. 1968-69, exec. dir. 1969-72, dir. 1962-83), United Investment Club (pres. 1983), Pi Alpha Theta (chpt. historian 1983—). Democrat. Lodge: Kiwanis (pres. Hilltop club 1975-76, program chmn., v.p. 1980-81, chmn. major emphasis com. Golden K club 1985—; only hearing mem. of Kiwanis Club for the deaf). Address: 12524 Colleen Dr Little Rock AR 72212

GENZER, FRANK, JR., architect; b. Pasadena, Tex., Oct. 24, 1943; s. Ike F. and Joyce Cecile (Briethaupt) G.; B.S., U. Tex., 1966, B.Arch., 1968; M.S. in Environ. Design, U. Notre Dame, 1971. Asst. prof. architecture La. State U., 1971-72; dir. design devel. Sea Pines, Co., Hilton Head Island, S.C., 1972-73; dir. devel. Laver-Ford Tennis Ventures, Houston, 1973-74; v.p. Portfolio Mgmt. Tex., Houston, 1974-79; v.p. Equity Mgmt. Corp., Gulfport, Miss., 1980-83; v.p. Equity Investments of Miss., Inc., Gulfport, 1983—; trustee, treas. Environic Found. Internat., Inc.; bd. advisors LeRoy Troyer & Assos., Architects. White House Commn. on Arts and Humanities fellow, 1967; Office of CD fellow, 1969-71; registered profl. architect S.C., Tex., Miss. Mem. AIA, Miss. Soc. Architects. Republican. Methodist. Home: 1702 West Beach Dr Biloxi MS 39530 Office: Equity Investments of Miss Inc PO Box 29 Gulfport MS 39502

GEOFFRAY, ALICE RANDAZZA, educational administrator; b. New Orleans, Nov. 18, 1924; d. Peter Charles and Alice Mary Gertrude (Renaud) Randazza; B.A., St. Mary's Dominican Coll., 1944; M.Ed. in Ednl. Adminstrn., Tulane U., 1970; Ed.D., U. New Orleans, 1978; s. Rudolph C. Geoffray, Sept. 8, 1944; children—Andrea, Stephen, Charlotte, Dolores, Paul, Jeanne, Gerald. Tchr. bus. edn. and English, Orleans and Iberville Parishes, 1951-65; supervising dir. Adult Edn. Center, New Orleans, 1965-72; state coordinator career edn. State Dept. Edn., 1972-74; coordinator Job Placement Center, New Orleans Pub. Schs., 1974-79, dir. career/continuing edn. and counseling, 1979-81, dir. spl. programs, 1981-82, dir. program devel./electives, 1982-83, dir. sr. high schs., 1983—; asst. prof. La. State U.; mem. com. Michoud Project; cons., lectr. in field. Mem. adv. council Orleans Regional Inst. Industry Council, Youth Adv. Planning Council. Recipient classroom tchr. award Valley Forge Freedom's Found., 1965; Outstanding Service award La. Assn. Secondary Suprs. Vocat. Edn., 1982; Outstanding La. Vocat. Edn. Educator award, 1983; Tchr.-of-Year award Delta Kappa Phi, 1983; Outstanding Woman of Leader of Community award Sigma Gamma Rho, 1984; featured in Sta. WWL-TV Salute to Quiet Heroes, 1983. Mem. La. Assn. Secondary Suprs. Vocat. Edn., La. Assn. Sch. Execs., So. Regional Assembly of Coll. Bd. (La. rep.), Am. Vocat. Assn., La. Personnel and Guidance Assn., Phi Delta Kappa, Phi Kappa Phi, Delta Epsilon Sigma, Kappa Delta Pi. Democrat. Roman Catholic. Author: Communication Skills for Succeeding in the World of Work, 1977; co-author: Pounding the Pavement, 1979; A Crash Course in College Cash, 1980. invited witness U.S. Senate Subcom. on Devel. Human Resources, 1968. Office: 1815 St Claude Ave New Orleans LA 70116

GEORGAS, PAUL JOHN, JR., training specialist, chemical engineer; b. Fort Leonard Wood, Mo., Mar. 27, 1955; s. Paul John and Mary Catherine (Grant) G.; m. Elaine Maria Lewicki, June 4, 1977; 1 child, Adam Grant. B.S. in Chem. Engring., Rose-Hulman Inst. Tech., 1977. Assoc. engr. B.F. Goodrich Chem., Henry, Ill., 1977-79; engr. II Monsanto Co., Nitro, W.Va., 1979-82; training and mgmt. devel. supr. Degussa Corp., Theodore, Ala., 1982—; task force mem. Ala. Dept. Postsecondary Edn., Montgomery, 1984—; cons. Mobile Jr. Achievement, 1983—. Mem. Am. Soc. Tng. and Devel. (program chmn. 1982-84), Phi Gamma Delta. Avocations: reading history; hunting; fishing; refinishing furniture. Home: 412 Stirrup Ct Mobile AL 36608 Office: Degussa Corp Ala Group Theodore Industrial Park Theodore AL 36590

GEORGE, DAVID WEBSTER, architect; b. Tulsa, Dec. 26, 1922; s. Calvin Webster and Ollie (McReynolds) G.; m. Xena Ruth Gill, Nov. 25, 1950; 1 dau., Molly Evelyn; m. Elizabeth Howard, Dec. 30, 1984. Student U. Okla., 1940-43, 46, 47-48; B.Arch., N.C. State U., 1949. Assoc., Frank Lloyd Wright, Taliesin Assoc. Architects, Scottsdale, Ariz., 1947-48; assoc. Harwell Hamilton Harris, Ft. Worth, Tex., 1954-56; founding ptnr. The Architects Partnership, and predecessor firm, Dallas, 1959—. Bd. dirs. Dallas Theater Ctr. Served to capt. AUS, 1942-46, 51-52. Fellow AIA; mem. Tex. Soc. Architects, Nat. Council Archtl. Registration Bds. Methodist. Club: Horseshoe Bay Country. Home: 4050 Cochran Chapel Rd Dallas TX 75209 Office: 2919 Welborn St Dallas TX 75219

GEORGE, JOHN CLAY, mathematics educator; b. Mesa, Ariz., Sept. 7, 1959; s. Clay Edwin and Mary Elizabeth (Cook) G. B.A., Tex. Tech U., 1981; M.S., U. Ill., 1984. Teaching asst. dept. math. Tex. Tech U., Lubbock, 1985—. Recipient Eagle Scout award Boy Scouts Am., 1975; Nat. Merit scholar, 1977. Mem. Am. Math. Soc., Math. Assn. Am. Avocations: collecting; reading. Office: Dept Math Tex Tech U Lubbock TX 79408

GEORGE, KALANKAMARY PILY, engineering educator, consultant; b. Kadayiruppu, June, 13, 1933; s. Kalankamary V. Pily and Sara Varkey Pily; m. Mary M. George; children—Sara, Anil. B.S. in Engring., Nat. Inst., 1956; M.S., Iowa State U., 1961, Ph.D., 1963. Prof. engring. U. Miss., University, 1968—; cons. and researcher hwys., pavements, geotech. engring. Mem. ASCE, Transp. Research Bd. Contbr. articles to profl. jours. Home: 108 Stone Rd Oxford MS 38655

GEORGE, ROBERT EUGENE, accountant; b. Graham, Tex., Mar. 29, 1950; s. Robert Austin and Billie Faye (Webb) G.; m. Cynthia Kay Warrick, Dec. 26, 1971; children—Gregory Scott, Angela Kay. B.B.A. cum laude, North Tex. State U., 1971; student Kilgore Jr. Coll., 1968. C.P.A., Tex. Acct., Coopers & Lybrand, Fort Worth, 1972-77, Dallas, 1977-83, El Paso, 1983—, ptnr., 1983—. Bd. dirs. Dallas County unit Am. Heart Assn., 1983, recipient Merit award, 1983; bd. dirs. El Paso unit Am. Heart Assn., 1983—, Bridges Sch. for Pyslexic Children; mem. El Paso Sports Hall of Fame Com. Mem. Am. Inst. C.P.A.s, Tex. Soc. C.P.A.s (savs. and loan com. 1982, 86), N. Mex. Soc. C.P.A.s, Nat. Assn. Accts., Tex. Savs. and Loan League, N.Mex. League Insured Instns., Fin. Mgrs. Soc. Thrift Instns., North Tex. State Alumni Assn. Presbyterian. Clubs: Mean Green Eagle; Arlington Runners; Coronado Country (El Paso). Home: 5708 Oakcliff El Paso TX 79912 Office: 4487 N Mesa St 201 El Paso TX 79902

GEORGE, TED MASON, physics educator; b. Lynneville, Tenn., Sept. 22, 1922; s. William Cullen and Myrtle (Mooney) G.; m. Jean Frances Fisher, July 30, 1960. B.A., Vanderbilt U., 1949, M.A., 1958, Ph.D., 1964. Chief engr. sta. WMAK, Nashville, 1953-55; asst. prof. Murray State Coll., Ky., 1956-59, Furman U., Greenville, S.C., 1963-64; chmn., prof. Eastern Ky. U., Richmond, Ky., 1964—. Recipient Sci. Tchr. award NSF, 1961. Mem. Am. Assn. Physics Tchrs., Ky. Acad. Sci. (pres. 1981-82, Outstanding Service award 1982), Ky. Assn. Progress in Sci. (Outstanding Service award 1976), Ky. Assn. Physics Tchrs. (pres. 1967-68), Phi Beta Kappa, Sigma Xi. Club: Torch (pres. 1979-80). Home: 125 Allen Douglas Dr Richmond KY 40475 Office: Eastern Ky U Richmond KY 40475

GEORGE, VICKIE LYNN, psychotherapist; b. Naples, Italy, Mar. 4, 1959; came to U.S., 1961; d. Charles Durwood and Berta Marie (Payne) G. B.A., Taylor U., 1981; M.Ed. in Community Counseling, Ga. State U., 1983; cert. Psychol. Studies Inst., Atlanta, 1983. Interviewing counselor Ga. Dept. Labor, Marietta, 1981; interviewer Compass Mktg. Research Co., Norcross, Ga., 1981-82; counselor Mt. Paran Ch., Atlanta, 1982-83; mental health specialist Peachford Psychiat. Hosp., Atlanta, 1982—; head counselor, adminstr. Assn. Counseling Ctr., Atlanta and Conyers, Ga., 1984—; cons. Home Mission Bd., So. Bapt. Conv., Atlanta, 1985—; presenter seminars. Contbr. articles to religious publs. Mem. Ga. Psychol. Assn., Am. Assn. Pastoral Counselors, Atlanta Adlerian Soc., Am. Assn. Counseling and Devel. Republican. Avocations: travel; skiing; music; dance; theater. Home: 1606 Cumberland Ct Smyrna GA 30080 Office: Assn Counseling Ctr Suite 100 1340 Spring St NW Atlanta GA 30309

GEORGE, VICTOR FRANK, retired landscape architect; b. N.Y.C., May 6, 1904; s. Daniel and Pauline (Salvia) G.; student ed. pub. schs.; m. Lucille May Fisher, July 21, 1934; 1 dau., Marilyn (Mrs. Salvatore Pinzone). Draftsman Westchester County Park Commn., Bronxville, N.Y., 1924-32; landscape architect N.Y.C. Parks Dept., 1934, Shreve, Lamb & Harmon, Architects, N.Y.C., 1934-35, Madigan & Hyland, Cons. Engrs., N.Y.C., 1935-40, Clarke & Rapuano, Cons. Engrs. and Landscape Architects, N.Y.C., 1940-82. Mem. Am. Soc. Landscape Architecture, Am. Security Council. Home: 12461 SW 106th Terr Miami FL 33186

GEORGES, RICHARD MARTIN, lawyer, educator; b. St. Louis, Nov. 17, 1947; s. Martin Mahlon Georges and Josephine (Cipolla) Rice. A.B. cum laude, Loyola U., New Orleans, 1969; J.D. cum laude, Stetson Coll. Law, 1972. Bar: 1972, U.S. Dist. Ct. (mid. dist.) Fla. 1973, U.S. Ct. Appeals (11th cir.) 1981, U.S. Supreme Ct. 1982. Ptnr., Kieffer & Georges, St. Petersburg, Fla., 1973-80, Kieffer, Georges & Rahter, St. Petersburg, 1980-85; sole practice St. Petersburg, 1985—; adj. prof. Fla. Inst. Tech., Melbourne, 1977—, Stetson Coll. Law, 1985—. Contbg. author: Florida Law of Trusts, 1983. Arbitrator, United Steelworkers Union, Continental Can Co., 1975—; hearing examiner City of St. Petersburg, 1982—; exec. committeeman Pinellas County Republican Party, Clearwater, Fla., 1981-82. Served to 1st lt. U.S. Army, 1972. Recipient Rafael Steinhardt award Stetson Coll. Law, 1972, Clint Green award, 1972. Mem. ABA, Fla. Bar, St. Petersburg Bar Assn. (chmn. legal check-up course), Pinellas County Trial Lawyers Assn., Fla. Camera Club Council (pres. 1985), Phi Alpha Delta. Roman Catholic. Clubs: Feather Sound Country, Suncoast Camera (v.p. 1982-84; pres. elect 1984) (Clearwater). Office: 3656 First Ave N St Petersburg FL 33713

GERALDS, GLENN GORDON, pediatric psychologist; b. Detroit, Sept. 1, 1943; s. Jerry and Edna Kathleen (Barber) G.; m. Lois Ruth Toelke, Jan. 24, 1965; children—Glenn Gordon II, Eric Christian. Student Northwestern U., 1961-63; B.A., Culver-Stockton Coll., Canton, Mo., 1965; M.A., U. Tenn., 1967, Ph.D., 1970. Lic. psychologist, cert. sch. psychologist, Tenn. Psychologist, Memphis City Schs., 1970-76; dir. psychol. ednl. services Team Eval. Ctr., Chattanooga, 1976—; mem. Tenn. Bd. Examiners in Psychology, 1976-81. Mem. Am. Psychol. Assn., Tenn. Psychol. Assn., Tenn. Assn. Sch. Psychologists (pres. 1974-75), Chattanooga Area Psychology Assn. (pres. 1985). Lutheran. Avocations: tennis, fishing, boating. Home: 7017 Fairington Circle Hixson TN 37343 Office: Team Evaluation Ctr 960 E 3d St Chattanooga TN 37403

GERBER, ABRAHAM, economic consultant, executive; b. N.Y.C., Dec. 19, 1925; s. Morris and Rose (Levy) G.; m. Beverly Kulkin, Dec. 23, 1948 (dec. 1966); children—Douglas K., Judith E.; m. Ilene Pomerantz, Sept. 28, 1967; children—Barbara J. Nakazawa, Gary L. A.B., Columbia Coll., 1948; M.A., Columbia U., 1950; postgrad. New Sch. for Social Research, 1950-51. Economist U.S. Dept Commerce, Washington, 1951, U.S. Dept. Interior, Washington, 1951-53; economist, asst. to pres., sec. system devel. com. Am. Electric Power Service Corp., N.Y.C., 1953-67; sr. v.p. Nat. Econ. Research Assoc., White Plains, N.Y., Palm Beach, Fla., 1967—; cons. Pres.'s Cabinet Commn. Energy, Washington, 1953; mem. adv. commn. U.S. Dept. Interior Office Coal Research, Washington, 1961-69; chmn. com. Energy Econ. Growth, Nat. Acad. Engring. Com. on Power Plant Siting, Washington, 1971-72. Contbr. articles to profl. jours. Bd. dir. Pub. Utility Research Ctr. Fla., Gainesville, 1982—; panel mem. Nuclear Regulatory Commn. State Regulatory Activity, Washington, 1977. Served with USAAF, 1943-45. Mem. IEEE (sr.), Am. Econ. Assn., AAAS, Am. Nuclear Soc. Internat. Conf. Large High Voltage Electric Systems. Jewish. Club: Governors. Avocations: tennis; swimming; theater; opera. Office: Nat Econ Research Assocs 350 Royal Palm Way Palm Beach FL 33480

GERBER, MYRON DANE, retail executive; b. Balt., 1922. Ed. U. Fla. With Drug Fair Inc., 1938—, chmn. bd., chief operating officer, dir., 1970—. Address: Drug Fair Inc 6295 Edsall Rd Alexandria VA 22314*

GERBER, WILLIAM ROBERT, petroleum geologist; b. Cheltenham, Pa., Jan. 11, 1957; s. William and Margaret Viola (Salvitty) G.; m. Linda Ann Wisnewski, Apr. 28, 1979; children—William Brian, Daniel Thomas. B.S., Pa. State U., 1978. Field engr. Dresser Atlas, Woodward, Okla. and Victoria, Tex., 1978-79; petroleum geologist Barby Energy Corp., Woodward, 1979—; v.p. Latigo Oil & Gas Inc., Woodward, 1983—. Mem. Am. Assn. Petroleum Geologists, Oklahoma City Geol. Soc., Mineral. Assn. of Can., Woodward C. of C. Republican. Roman Catholic. Lodges: Lion (lion tamer 1984-85, tailtwister 1985-86), K.C. (sec.-recorder 1984-85, fin. sec. 1985—). Avocations: rock collecting; soccer; swimming; weight training. Home: 403 Shady Creek Woodward OK 73801 Office: Barby Energy Corp 1000 15th St Woodward OK 73801

GERDES, HERMAN HENRY, III, optometrist; b. Waco, Tex., Nov. 22, 1950; s. Herman Henry and Clare Patton (Whitehead) G.; m. Delmare C. Harris, May 22, 1971; children—Jennie Colleen, Herman Henry IV. O.D., So. Coll. Optometry, 1977. Optometrist, Waco, Tex., 1977—. Mem. Am. Optometric Assn., Tex. Optometric Assn. Republican. Episcopalian. Lodges: Kiwanis, Lions. Office: 1018 Washington Ave Waco TX 76701

GEREN, JACK W., physician; b. East Liverpool, Ohio, Sept. 16, 1946; s. John R. and Deloris J. (Marquette) G.; m. Marilyn Taraszewski, Aug. 28, 1971; children—Jenna, Amanda. B.Engring., Youngstown State U., 1972; D.O., Coll. Osteo. Medicine and Surgery, 1975. Diplomate Am. Bd. Emergency Medicine. Intern, Warren Gen. Hosp., Ohio, 1975-76, emergency physician, 1976-81; resident emergency medicine U. Ky. Med. Ctr., Lexington, 1981-83; emergency physician St. Joseph Hosp., Lexington, 1983—. Served with USN, 1964-67. Mem. Am. Coll. Emergency Physicians, Am. Osteo. Assn., AMA, Ky. Osteo. Med. Assn., Ky. Med. Assn. Republican. Club: Bluegrass Sportsman. Avocations: fishing, hunting, camping. Home: 604 Merrimac Dr Lexington KY 40503 Office: One St Joseph Dr Lexington KY 40504

GERHARD, JACOB ESTERLY, palynologist, consultant; b. McAdoo, Pa., May 17, 1926; s. Peter and Ella M. (Key) G.; m. Lorraine Marie Matter, Nov. 17, 1951; children—Joyce Marie, James Edward, David Peter. B.S., Pa. State U., 1955, M.S., 1958. Research geologist Mobil Research and Devel. Corp., Dallas, 1958-72; sr. paleontological cons. Mobil Exploration and Prodn. Inc., Dallas, 1972-84; palynological cons., Dallas, 1985—. Served to sgt. U.S. Army, 1944-46. Mem. Am. Assn. Petroleum Geologists, Dallas Geol. Soc., Paleonotanical Soc. Am., Brit. Micropaleontological Soc. Lutheran. Avocations: outdoor sports. Home and office: 3423 Willow Crest Ln Dallas TX 75233

GERLACH, GARY G., botanical garden director; b. Louisville, Apr. 28, 1945; s. Henry Elmer and Lorraine (Curry) G.; m. Kathryn Lynn Arnold, Feb. 8, 1969; children—Lynnette, Christopher. B.S. in Hort., U. Ky., 1967; M.S. in Hort., U. Del., 1969. Dir. Birmingham Bot. Gardens, Ala. Home: 3607 E Lakeside Dr Birmingham AL 35243 Office: Birmingham Botanical Garden 2612 Lane Park Rd Birmingham AL 35223

GERLIN, WILLIAM LANCE, lawyer; b. Columbus, Ohio, Jan. 25, 1945; s. Jack Alfred and Jane Graham (Boyle) G.; m. Pamela Jean Gates, Sept. 21, 1974; children—William Sean, Matthew Graham. B.S., U. Fla., 1968, J.D., 1973. Bar: Fla. 1973, U.S. Supreme Ct. 1978, U.S. Dist. Ct. (so. dist.) Fla. 1974, U.S. Tax Ct. 1977, U.S. Ct. Appeals (5th cir. and 11th cir.). Sr. ptnr., dir. Stinson, Lyons & Schuette, Miami, Fla., 1973—; lectr. Acad. Fla. Trial Lawyers, Munich, Germany, Kitzbuehl, Germany, 1982, Davos, Switzerland, also Paris, 1984. Served as capt. U.S. Army, 1968-70. Mem. ABA, Dade County Bar Assn. Republican. Presbyterian. Clubs: University (Miami); Riviera Country (Coral Gables, Fla.); Ocean Reef (North Key Largo); Snowmass (Colo.). Home: 6490 SW 100th St Miami FL 33156 Office: Stinson Lyons & Schuette 1401 Brickell Ave Miami FL 33131

GERMAIN, WILLIAM LEON, metals company executive; b. Winooski, Vt., Sept. 22, 1940; s. Leon William and Doris Kathleen (Merrill) G.; m. Ann Marie Decarreau, Sept. 8, 1962; children—Lori Ann, Susan Lynn. B.S.M.E., U. Vt., 1963. Engr., Monsanto Co., various locations, 1963-71; plant engr. M & T Chems. Inc., South San Francisco, 1971-74; plant mgr. Vulcan Materials Co., Metal Div., Gary, Ind., 1974-77, dir. mktg. services, Sandusky, Ohio, 1977-79, v.p. steel and tin, Birmingham, Ala., 1979-82, exec. v.p., 1982—; dir. Vulcan Materials Co. U.K., Metal Recovery Industries, Steel Can Recycling Assn., Pitts. Avocations: model railroading; painting; reading; travel. Office: Vulcan Materials Co Metal Div PO Box 7588 Birmingham AL 35253

GERRITSEN, JEROEN, aquatic ecologist; b. Leiden, Netherlands, Nov. 6, 1951; s. Alexander Nicolaas and Jacqueline (Koolhaas) G.; m. Jine-i Kou, July 7, 1979. B.S., Antioch Coll., 1974; M.A., Johns Hopkins U., 1976, Ph.D., 1978. Postdoctoral research assoc. dept. zoology U. Ga., Athens, 1978-81, mgr. Okefenokee ecosystem research Inst. Ecology, 1981-84, asst. research scientist, 1982—; dir. flow cytometry facility U. Ga., 1985—. Balt. Gas & Electric Co. fellow, 1976; Franklin Coll., U. Ga. fellow, 1978-80. Mem. AAAS, Am. Soc. Limnology and Oceanography, Ecol. Soc. Am., Sigma Xi. Contbr. articles to profl. jours. Office: Inst Ecology U Ga Athens GA 30602

GERRY, ROBERT, educator, consultant; b. Paterson, N.J., May 11, 1921; s. Samuel and Lane Hannah (Cohen) G.; m. Catherine Hasson, Dec. 21, 1947; children—Patricia, Michael, Matthew. B.S. in Chemistry, UCLA, 1950; M.S. in Edn. and Math., U. So. Calif., 1951; Ph.D. in Ednl. Psychology, U. Tex., 1967. Cert. psychologist, D.C. Commd. 2d lt. USAAF, 1942-45, commd. U.S. Air Force, 1950, advanced through grades to lt. col. 1955, served as navigator, navigator instr., ednl. and tng. staff officer, personnel mgmt. psychologist, dir. instructional services; ret. 1972; prof. edn. U. Tex. Permian Basin, Odessa, 1972—; office mgr. budget Exec. USA, Washington, 1971; chmn. leadership devel. cabinet Dist. 7 B'nai B'rith, Dallas, 1973—. Author: Instructional Systems Design, 1975; Mathematics Methods, 1982; co-author: A Creativity Workshop, 1956; contbr. articles in field to publs. Pres. Temple Beth El, Odessa, 1974, 78. Decorated Legion of Merit, 1972. Mem. AAAS, Am. Psychol. Assn., Am. Ednl. Research Assn., Assn. Supervision and Curriculum Devel., Phi Delta Kappa (Longevity award 1985), Psi Chi. Lodge: B'nai B'rith (pres. Lodge 2409 1975, 76). Avocations: Travel; reading; music. Home: 55 Royal Place Circle Odessa TX 79762 Office: Univ Tex Permian Basin University Blvd Odessa TX 79762-8301

GERSHMAN, ANDREW PAUL, psychologist; b. Cleve., Feb. 23, 1924; s. Meyer James and Jeanette (Jay) G.; B.A., U. Tex., 1961; M.A., N. Tex. State U., 1963; Ph.D. in Psychiatry, U. Sheffield (Eng.), 1970. Clin. psychologist Rusk (Tex.) State Hosp., 1962-64; sr. clin. psychologist Danemore (N.Y.) State Hosp., 1965-66; psychologist NW Psychiat. Clinic, Eau Claire, Wis., 1971-74; pvt. practice Psychiat. Assos., Parkersburg, W.Va., 1974-77; pvt. practice psychology, Parkersburg, 1977—. Bd. dirs. Wood County Heart Assn., 1979-81. Recipient Outstanding Contbn. award, Western Guidance Clinic, 1979-80. Mem. Am. Psychol. Assn., W.Va. Psychol. Assn., Internat. Assn. Suicide Prevention, Am. Assn. Clin. Hypnosis, Internat. Soc. Clin. Hypnosis. Episcopalian. Club: Greenmont Racquet. Office: 1136 1/2 Market St Parkersburg WV 26101

GERSHON, EDWIN MARTIN, consumer products company sales executive; b. Cornwall on Hudson, N.Y., Oct. 8, 1940; s. Charles and Ann (Rothman) G.; m. Gail Dornfest, June 7, 1964; 1 dau., Kimberly Ann. M.S., LIU, 1962; M.B.A., NYU, 1964. Buyer, Abraham & Straus, Bklyn., 1962-64; sales mgr. Westwood Industries, Paterson, N.J., 1964-71; v.p. sales and mktg. Schiller Corday, Hackensack, N.J., 1971-79; v.p. sales Select Industries, N.Y.C. and Atlanta, 1979—; cons. Lamp & Shade Assn. U.S., 1971-79; v.p. 230 Fifth Ave Assn., 1973-79. Mem. Democratic County Com., Allegheny County Pa., 1970-71, Bergen County, N.J., 1978-81; mem. planning com. North Buckhead Civic Assn., Fulton County, Ga., 1983—. Fellow Soc. Advancement Mgmt. (v.p. 1961-62). Jewish. Office: Select Industries 3723 Mayfair Rd NE Atlanta GA 30342

GERSTEN, JOSEPH MORRIS, state senator, lawyer; b. Dade County, Fla., July 19, 1947; s. Joseph J. and Kathryn (Morris) G.; married. B.S., NYU, 1970; postgrad. Sophia U., Japan, 1969; M.A., U. Md., 1972; J.D., U. Miami, 1975. Mem. Fla. Ho. of Reps., 1974-81; mem. Fla. Senate, 1981—; lawyer. Mem. Tropical Audubon Soc., LWV. Democrat. Office: 2303 Ponce de Leon Blvd Coral Gables FL 33134

GERTH, ELMER FRANCIS, high school principal; b. Sentinel, Okla., June 5, 1931; s. William Elmer and Jewell Frances (Smith) G.; m. Betty June Bettis, July 29, 1954; children—Cary, Sharon, Joni. B.S., East Central U., 1956, M.Teaching, 1959. Tchr., elem. prin. Union Pub. Sch., Broken Arrow, Okla., 1956-60; elem. prin. Hickory Elem. Sch., Okla., 1960-65; high sch. prin., instr. driver edn. Latta Pub. Sch., Ada, Okla., 1965—; coach Union Pub. Sch., 1956-60, instr. driver edn., 1956-60; coach Hickory Elem. Sch., 1960-65. Served to SK2 USN, 1950-54. Democrat. Mem. Church of Christ. Avocations: hunting, fishing. Home: Route 1 Box 526 Ada OK 74820 Office: Latta Sch Route 1 Box 811 Ada OK 74820

GESSELL, JOHN MAURICE, clergyman, educator; b. St. Paul, June 17, 1920; s. Leo Lancien and Mabel Aseneth (Wing) G.; B.A., Yale U., 1942, B.D., 1949, Ph.D., 1960. Ordained priest Episcopal Ch., 1951; rector Emmanuel

Episcopal Ch., Nottoway Parish, Southampton County, Va., 1951-53; assoc. rector Grace Ch., Salem, Mass., 1953-61; mem. faculty Sch. Theology, U. of South, Sewanee, Tenn., 1961—, prof. Christian edn., 1961-63, asst. prof. pastoral theology, 1963-74, prof. Christian ethics, 1974-84, prof. emeritus, 1984—, now editor St. Luke's Jour. Theology; priest-in-charge Otey Meml. Ch., Sewanee, 1977-78; mem. nat. exec. com. Episcopal Pace Fellowship; bd. dirs. Absalom Jones Theol. Inst., Atlanta, Mid-South Career Devel. Center, Nashville. Bd. dirs., pres. Multi-County Comprehensive Mental Health Center, Tullahoma, Tenn., 1972-74, Sewanee Civic Assn. and Community Chest, 1967-68. Dwight fellow Yale U., 1949-50; Coll. of Preachers fellow, Washington, 1953. Mem. Am. Soc. Christian Ethics, AAUP, Am. Assn. Theol. Schs. (faculty fellow 1967-68), Phi Beta Kappa. Contbr. articles to theol. books and jours. Home: Carruthers Rd Sewanee TN 37375 Office: Univ of South Sewanee TN 37375

GESUND, HANS, structural engineering educator, consultant; b. Vienna, Austria, Sept. 18, 1928; s. Carl and Else (Sternberg) G.; m. Irmgard Orth, Jan. 28, 1951; children—Peter J., Ann M. B. Eng. with honors, Yale U., 1950, M. Eng., 1953, D. Eng., 1958. Regis. profl. engr., Conn., Ky. Instr. dept. civil engring. Yale U., 1954-58; asst. prof. structural engring. U. Ky., Lexington, 1958-59, assoc. prof., 1959-65, prof. structural engring., 1965—; cons. in field. Served to maj. USAR, 1948-68. Past pres. bd. trustees Ohavay Zion Congregation. Recipient citation for significant contbn. to sci. of bldg. Bldg. Research Inst., 1965; regional prize Design Idea Competition Concrete Reinforcing Steel Inst., 1979. Fellow ASCE, Am. Concrete Inst.; mem. Internat. Assn. Bridge and Structural Engring., ASTM, Am. Soc. Engring. Edn. Jewish. Lodge: B'nai Brith. Contbr. chpts. to books, articles to profl. jours. Home: 844 Celia Ln Lexington KY 40504 Office: Dept Civil Engring U Ky Lexington KY 40506

GETS, LISPBETH ELLA, educational administrator; b. Jhelum, Pakistan, Mar. 18, 1931; came to U.S., 1952, naturalized, 1955; d. Henry Ellis and Constance Selina (Bodell) Glenn; m. Terence Mathew Gets, Jan. 19, 1952; children—Erik Charles, Alison Beth Sanders, Hugh Malcolm, Adrienne Lea. A.A., Santa Fe Community Coll., 1973-74; B.A. with high honors U. Fla., 1976, postgrad., 1977—. Cert. adminstr., supr., Fla. Editorial asst. John Trundell Pub., London, 1950-52; exec. secretarial positions, various cos., Chgo., Ft. Smith, Ark. and Jamestown, N.Y., 1952-58; tchr. spl. edn. Buchholz High Sch., Gainesville, Fla., 1976-81; asst. prin. Sidney Lanier Sch., Gainesville, 1981-83; prin. Monarch Ctr. for Exceptional Students, Gainesville, 1983—. Named Tchr. of Yr. Gatorland chpt. Council for Exceptional Children, 1981. Mem. Council Exceptional Children (chpt. pres. 1983—), Fla. Assn. Sch. Adminstrs., Assn. Severely Handicapped, Phi Delta Kappa, Kappa Delta Pi. Democrat. Episcopalian. Home: 4601 NW 13th Ave Gainesville FL 32605 Office: PO Box 1150 Gainesville FL 32602

GETTEL, MYRTLE ALLEN (MUFF), nursing administrator; b. Baton Rouge, June 9, 1934; d. Leslie Wallace Allen and Mary (Haynes) Nason; m. Kenneth Eugene Gettel, June 30, 1954; children—Steven, Michael. Diploma in nursing, Northwestern U., Natchitoches, La., 1955; B.A. in Social Work, Oral Roberts U., 1975; M.S. in Nursing, U. Okla., 1985. R.N., Okla. Nursing service edn. coordinator St. Francis Hosp., Tulsa, 1968-72; dir. Sweetwater County Drug-Alcohol Abuse Prevention Program, Rock Springs, Wyo., 1973-76; dir. nursing Children's Med. Ctr., Tulsa, 1977—; coordinator Mental Health Nurse Group, Tulsa, 1979—. Mem. Am. Nurse Assn. (sec., bd. dirs. Okla. Nursing Service Adminstrs. 1985), Nat. League Nursing, Am. Orgn. Nurse Execs. Republican. Methodist. Home: 5870 S 76th East Ave Tulsa OK 74145 Office: Children's Med Ctr 5300 E Skeely Dr Tulsa OK 74135

GETTIG, CARL WILLIAM, optometrist; b. Cleve., June 15 1928; s. Edmund Elmer and Arlie (Williams) G.; O.D., No. Ill. Coll. Optometry, 1949; student U. Ala., 1952-53, Spring Hill Coll., 1957; A.B., Oberlin Coll., 1962, B.M., 1962; attended Mozarteum, Salzburg, Austria, 1959-60. Individual practice optometry, Norwalk, Ohio, 1949-50, Mobile, Ala., 1952-58, Foley, Ala., 1963—; part-time music tchr., Foley and Robertsdale, Ala., 1955—. Co-founder Performing Arts Assn., Foley, 1967, pres,, 1968-69, 72-73. Organist, choirmaster Christ Episcopal Ch., Mobile, 1972-84, St. James Episcopal Ch., Fairhope, Ala., 1984—; bd. dirs. Ala. Diabetes Assn., 1983—, v.p., 1985-86, pres. chpt., 1985-86. Served with U.S. Army, 1950-52. Mem. Am. Optometric Assn., Am. Optometric Found., Coll. Optometrists in Vision Devel., Am. Pub. Health Assn., Am. Guild Organists, ALA, Am. Forestry Assn. Composer piano sonata, 1961. Home: 1608 N Alston St Foley AL 36535 Office: 1605 N McKenzie St Foley AL 36535

GETTLE, MICHAEL JAMES, training researcher; b. Ancon, Canal Zone, May 17, 1955; s. Jesse Richard and Olga (Maransky) G.; m. Catherine A. Gettle, Aug. 11, 1979; 1 child, Jennifer. B.S. in Edn., Millersville State Coll., 1977; M.Ed., Ga. State U., 1986. Tng. analyst Ala. Power Co., Birmingham, 1978-80; project engr. Inst. Nuclear Power Ops., Atlanta, 1981-84, sr. project engr., 1984—. Mem. Am. Soc. Tng. and Devel., Nat. Soc. Performance and Instruction. Baptist. Contbr. articles to profl. jours. Office: 1100 Circle 75 Pkwy Suite 1500 Atlanta GA 30339

GETZ, LOWELL VERNON, financial management consultant; b. Schenectady, Feb. 28, 1932; s. Leon and Harriet Esther (Friedman) G.; B.S. in Econs., U. Pa., 1953; M.B.A., Harvard U., 1955; m. Judith Ruth Schwartz, Oct. 14, 1956; children—Marshall, Andrew. Treas., R. Dixon Speas Assos., Inc., Manhasset, N.Y., 1969-72, Coverdale & Colpitts, Inc., N.Y.C., 1972-74; fin. mgr. Bovay Engrs., Inc., Houston, 1974-79; sec., treas. Rice Center, Houston, 1979-81; guest lectr. U. Houston, 1980-81, Harvard Grad. Sch. Design, 1985-86; cons. in fin. mgmt. to architects, engring. firms., 1981—; condr. seminars in field. Served as lt. USNR, 1955-58. Mem. Profl. Services Mgmt. Assn. (dir. 1979-82, treas. 1981-82), Tex. Soc. C.P.A.s (chmn. mgmt. adv. services com. Houston chpt. 1982-83), Am. Inst. C.P.A.s (mem. tech. and industry practices sub com. 1985-86), Fin. Execs. Inst., Assn. Corp. Growth. Author: (with others) Financial Management for the Design Professional, 1984; Financial Management and Project Control for Consulting Engineers, 1983; contbr. articles to profl. publs. Home: 11701 Spriggs Way Houston TX 77024 Office 3815 Richmond Suite 111 Houston TX 77027

GETZ, MALCOLM, economist, educator, library administrator; b. Somerville, N.J., Nov. 1, 1945; s. Harold Edward and Catherine (Minnick) G.; m. Ruthann Lorenzo, Feb. 10, 1968; children—Wystan, Kiesa. B.A., Williams Coll., 1967; Ph.D., Yale U., 1973. Asst. prof. econs. Vanderbilt U., Nashville, 1973-79, assoc. prof., 1979—, dir. library, 1984—. Author: Economics of Urban Fire Department, 1979; Public Libraries, 1980, Price Theory and Its Uses, 1982. Mem. Am. Econs. Assn., So. Econs. Assn., Western Econs. Assn., ALA. Home: 6542 Cornwall Dr Nashville TN 37205 Office: Vanderbilt U Library Box 155 Peabody Nashville TN 37203

GETZ, RODGER RUSSELL, agricultural meteorologist; b. Woodbury, N.J., Oct. 4, 1952; s. Raymond Russell and Florence Jane (Grant) G.; m. Marilyn Low Warner, June 15, 1974; children—Elizabeth, Russell. B.S., Rutgers U., 1974, M.S., 1975. Agrl. meteorologist NOAA Nat. Weather Service, S.E. Agrl. Weather Service Ctr., Auburn U. (Ala.), 1975—. Recipient Nat. Weather Service letter commendation, 1977, cash award, 1978, Outstanding Performance award, 1979, 81, 83. Mem. Council Agrl. Sci. and Tech., Am. Meteorol. Soc., Chi Epsilon Pi. Presbyterian. Contbr. articles to profl. jours. Home: 210 Timberdale Ct Auburn AL 36830 Office: Fisheries Annex Bldg Wire Rd Auburn U Auburn AL 36849

GEVIRTZ, JOEL LEO, geologist, geochemist, researcher; b. N.Y.C., Aug. 26, 1941; s. Morris Harry and Rose (Olsher) G.; m. Linda Coleman, Sept. 1, 1963 (div. 1984); children—Molly, Jesse. B.S., CUNY, 1963; M.S. Renselaer Poly. Inst., 1965, Ph.D., 1969. Asst. prof. SUNY-New Paltz, 1969-71; postdoctoral fellow Rice U., Houston, 1972-74, adj. prof. geology, 1973-78; ind. cons., Houston, 1974-77; sr. exploration geologist Tenneco Oil Co., Houston, 1977—. Contbr. articles to profl. jours. Mem. Am. Assn. for Petroleum Geology, AAAS, Internat. Assn. Math. Geologists, Sigma Xi. Avocations: music; musical instrument repair. Office: Tenneco Oil Co E&P PO Box 2511 Houston TX 77001

GEWIRTZMAN, GARRY BRUCE, dermatologist; b. Albany, N.Y., Mar. 26, 1947; s. Benjamin Joseph and Mary (Leibowitz) G.; m. Sheila Ellen Cuba, July 4, 1971; children—Beth Lauren, Aron Jeffrey. B.A., Rutgers U., 1969; M.D., Albany Med. Coll., 1973. Diplomate Am. Bd. Dermatology. Intern, U. Miami (Fla.), 1973-74; resident in dermatology SUNY-Buffalo, 1974-77; practice medicine specializing in dermatology; mem. staffs Humana Hosp., Plantation Gen. Hosp. Fellow Am. Acad. Dermatology; mem. AMA, Fla. Med. Assn., Broward County Med. Assn., Fla. Soc. Dermatology, Soc. Dermatol. Genetics, Broward Bus. and Profl. Assn. (pres.), Broward County Dermatol. Soc. Contbr. articles to profl. jours. Office: Bennett Med Park 201 NW 82nd Ave Plantation FL 33324

GEYER, RICHARD ADAM, JR., philanthropic consultant, communications consultant; b. Houston, Mar. 24, 1949; s. Richard Adam and Anna M. (Thomson) G.; m. Ginger Sue Henry, June 11, 1977. B.A., Vanderbilt U., 1970. Producer pub. affairs programs Sta. KUT-FM, Austin, Tex., 1970-72; chief fin. officer, dir. alumni and devel. St. Mark's Sch. of Tex., Dallas, 1972-78; exec. dir. devel. and univ. relations U. Tex.-Dallas, 1978-82, v.p. univ. affairs, 1982-83, spl. devel. cons., 1983-84; spl. devel. cons. Dallas Mus. of Art, 1983—; pres. Geyer Communications; mng. gen. ptnr. Video Periodicals. Trustee St. Mark's Sch. of Tex., 1982—, Ctr. for Visual Communications, Inc., 1983—, Pub. Communication Found. for North Tex., 1979-82; elder Preston Hollow Presbyn. Ch., 1984—. Geyer award for interpretive reporting established at Vanderbilt U., 1970. Mem. Council for Advancement and Support of Edn., Vanderbilt U. Alumni Assn. Home: 5606 Boca Raton Dallas TX 75230 Office: PO Box 688 MS AD11 Richardson TX 75080

GHANNADIAN, FARHAD, economics educator; b. Tehran, Iran, May 8, 1958; came to U.S., 1965; s. Moussa and Mahin (Jalilzadeh) G.; m. Joni Jones, Nov. 6, 1982. B.S.B.A., U. Tenn., 1980; M.B.A., Queens Coll., 1981; postgrad. Ga. State U. Mgr. F.W. Woolworth, Palo Alto, Calif., 1981-82; research asst. Ga. State U., Atlanta, 1982-83, instr., 1983—. Fellow Soc. Internat. Devel.; mem. Am. Econ. Assn., So. Econ. Assn., Omicron Delta Epsilon. Avocations: tennis; soccer; swimming; chess. Home: 21 Powers Ferry Manor Marietta GA 30067

GHATE, VIJAY RAMKRISHNA, physician, educator, consultant; b. Nasik, India, Oct. 14, 1937; s. Ramkrishna V. and Manorama R. (Moghe) G.; m. Sunanda V. Patankar, June 5, 1966; children—Sujata, Jayashiri. M.B., B.J. Med. Coll., U. Poona, 1960; M.S. in Otolaryngology, U. Bombay Grant Med. Coll., 1964; postgrad. Coll. Physicians and Surgeons, Bombay, 1964. Intern, Sassoon Hosp., Poona, India, 1960-61, resident, 1961-62; resident MGM Hosp., Bombay, 1962-65, D.Dix Hosp., Raleigh, N.C., 1971-74; ear, nose, throat surgeon M.G.M. Hosp., Bombay, India, 1965-67; staff physician Central State Hosp., Petersburg, Va., 1967-69, D. Dix Hosp., Raleigh, N.C., 1969-71; clin. dir. Wilson Green Mental Health Ctr., Wilson, N.C., 1974—; chmn. dept. psychiatry Wilson Meml. Hosp. (N.C.); pvt. practice medicine specializing in psychiatry, Wilson, 1974—; clin. asst. prof. psychiatry East Carolina U., Greenville, 1977—; cons. disability div. State of N.C., Raleigh, 1982—. Recipient Shankarseth prize, Urankan prize U. Poona, 1960. Diplomate Am. Bd. Psychiatry and Neurology. Mem. N.C. Neuropsychiat. Assn., Am. Psychiat. Assn. (cert. in adminstrv. psychiatry). Club: Optimist Evening. Office: Farris Bldg 100 Douglas St Box 3891 Wilson NC 27893

GHEE, KENNETH LEE, social psychologist; b. N.Y.C., Jan. 23, 1956; s. Sharpie L. and Rosa (Crowder) G. B.A., Boston U., 1978; M.A. U. Houston, 1981, Ph.D., 1983. Project coordinator Lipid Research Clinic, Baylor Coll. of Medicine, Houston, 1979-81; predoctoral fellowship U. Houston, Tex., 1979-82; research asst., 1982-83, postdoctoral fellowship, 1983—; program evaluator Tex. Dept. of Health, Austin, 1980-82; cons. Nat. Cancer Inst., Bethesda, Md., 1984, Family Health Project, Galveston, Tex., 1984. Contbr. articles to profl. jours. Recipient Citizenship award Boys Clubs of Am., Trenton, N.J., 1973; Nat. Heart, Lung and Blood Inst. Nat. Service award, U. Houston, 1979, 83; Acad. scholar Boston U., 1974-78. Mem. Am. Psychol. Assn., Soc. for Personality and Social Psychology, Am. Heart Assn., Assn. Black Psychologists, Kappa Alpha Psi (recipient achievement award 1977). Baptist. Home: 3120 S Macgregor Houston TX 77021 Office: Univ of Houston Dept of Psychology 4800 Calhoun St Houston TX 77004

GHINGOLD, NEIL, business executive; b. Barnwell, S.C., Aug. 20, 1932; s. Abe and Anita (Berstein) G.; m. Stephanie Thompson, Apr. 14, 1984; children—Richard, Jeffrey. B.B.A., U. Ga., 1954. Owner Universal Co., Augusta, Ga., 1956—. Served with USNR, 1948-56. Mem. Augusta Numismatic Soc. (past pres.), Jewish War Vets, Tau Epsilon Phi. Lodges: Rotary, Elks. Office: 1230 Broad St Augusta GA 30902

GHIRARDELLI, ROBERT GEORGE, chemist, educator; b. San Francisco, Nov. 12, 1930; s. George Joseph and Eva Marie (Dondero) G.; m. Mary Virginia Holder, Oct. 26, 1957; children—Mark, Linda, Alice, Thomas, David. B.S., U. San Francisco, 1952; Ph.D., Calif. inst. Tech., 1956. Asst. prof. chemistry Robert Coll., Istanbul, Turkey, 1958-60; chief organic chemistry U.S. Army Research Office, Research Triangle Park, N.C., 1960-68, assoc. dir. chem. and biol. scis. div., 1968-77, dir. chem. and biol. scis. div., 1977—; adj. assoc. prof. Duke U., Durham, N.C., 1972-81, adj. prof., 1982—. Contbr. articles to profl. jours. Mem. Durham City Bd. Edn., 1979, vice chmn., 1980-83, chmn., 1983—. Mem. AAAS, Am. Chem. Soc. (chmn. N.C. sect. 1970). Democrat. Roman Catholic. Office: US Army Research Office PO Box 12211 Research Triangle Park NC 27709

GHOLSON, DONALD PATRICK, data processing executive; b. Washington, July 7, 1943; s. Rex Lowell and Laura Jane (Allen) G.; m. Sandra Kay Hanks, July 27, 1963; children—Elizabeth Anne, Stephen Patrick. B.S. in Aero. Engring., Va. Poly. Inst. and State U., 1966; M.B.A., U. Tenn.-Knoxville, 1975. Engr., Teledyne-Brown Engring., Huntsville, Ala., 1965-68, Avco Aerostructures, Nashville, 1968-71; dir. computer center Knoxville Coll., 1971-72; programmer/analyst SSB-SBC, Nashville, 1972-73; dir. computer ctr. Walters State Community Coll., Morristown, Tenn., 1973-78; dir. computer services George Mason U., Fairfax, Va., 1978-84; sr. scientist REHAB Group, Falls Church, Va., 1984—; cons. in field. Contbr. articles to profl. jours. Vice chmn. Band & Orch. Parents Orgn., Fairfax, 1982. Mem. Assn. Ednl. Data Systems, Adv. Council for Ednl. Computing (chmn. 1981-83). Methodist. Home: 10705 Colton St Fairfax VA 22032 Office: REHAB Group Inc 5203 Leesburg Pike Falls Church VA 22041

GHOUSE, MIKE M., fire equipment executive, accountant; b. Bangalore, India, Jan. 1, 1952; s. Abdul Rahman and Khairun Nisa Hussain; m. Ella Louise Brownell, Oct. 11, 1982. M.Commerce, Bangalore U., 1976. Accounts mgr. Sunder Chems., Bangalore, India, 1971-73; acctg.-adminstr., Food Craft Inst., Bangalore, 1973-77; chief acct. Fluor Corp., Dhahran, Saudi Arabia, 1977-81; gen. mgr./treas. ALewis Fire Equipment Inc., Dallas, 1981—; cons. systems analysis; v.p. Pearl Internat. Corp., Dallas. Fellow Adminstrv. Acctg. Inst. (London). Home: 5723 Caruth Haven Apt 111 Dallas TX 75206 Office: 731 First Ave Dallas TX 75226

GIACONA, CORRADO ANTHONY, container company executive; b. New Orleans, Dec. 14, 1942; s. Louis Joseph and Claire (LaRocca) G.; m. Patricia Ellen Nunez, July 25, 1964; children—Gina Lisa, Corrado Anthony II, Louis. B.A., U. New Orleans, 1965. Plant mgr. Amos C. Harris Can Co., New Orleans, 1962-64; ter. mgr. Ross Labs., New Orleans, 1964-72; pres. Giacona Container, New Orleans, 1972—. Bd. dirs. La. Maritime Mus., Sci. Ctr. Mem. Phi Kappa Theta. Republican. Roman Catholic. Club: Timberlane Country. Home: 704 Fairfield Ave Gretna LA 70053 Office: Giacona Container 121 Industrial Ave New Orleans LA 70121

GIBBONS, CELIA VICTORIA TOWNSEND, editor, publisher; b. Fargo, N.D. d. Harry Alton and Helen (Haag) Townsend; student U. Minn., 1930-33; m. John Sheldon Gibbons, May 1, 1935; children—Mary Vee, John Townsend. Advt. mgr. Hotel Nicollet, Mpls., 1933-37; contbg. editor children's mags., 1935—; partner Youth Assos. Co., Mpls., 1942-65; pub., art dir. Mines and Escholier mags., 1954-65; founder Bull. Bd. Pictures, Inc., Mpls., 1954, pres., 1954—; founder pres. Periodical Litho Art Co., Mpls., 1962-65. Republican chairwoman Golden Valley, Minn., 1950; alternate del. Hennepin County Rep. Conv., 1962. Mem. Mpls. Inst. Arts, Ft. Lauderdale Mus. Arts, Art Guild of Boca Raton, Delta Zeta. Clubs: Woman's, Minikahda. Home: 1416 Alpine Pass Tyrol Hills Minneapolis MN 55416 Office: 1057 Hillsboro Mile Hillsboro Beach FL 33062

GIBBONS, JULIA SMITH, U.S. district judge; b. Pulaski, Tenn., Dec. 23, 1950; d. John Floyd and Julia (Abernathy) Smith; m. William Lockhart Gibbons, Aug. 11, 1973; 1 child, Rebecca Carey. B.A., Vanderbilt U., 1972; J.D., U. Va., 1975. Bar: Tenn. 1975. Law clk. Judge William E. Miller, U.S. Ct. Appeals, 1975-76; mem. firm Farris, Hancock, Gilman, Branan, Lanier & Hellen, Memphis, 1976-79; legal advisor Gov. Lamar Alexander, Nashville, 1979-81; circuit ct. judge 15th Judicial Circuit, Memphis, 1981-83; U.S. dist. judge Western Dist. Tenn., Memphis, 1983—. Mem. ABA, Tenn. Bar Assn., Memphis and Shelby County Bar Assn., Nat. Assn. Women Judges, Am. Judicature Soc., Order of the Coif, Phi Beta Kappa. Presbyterian. Office: US Dist Ct 1157 Federal Bldg Memphis TN 38103

GIBBONS, SAM MELVILLE, congressman; b. Tampa, Fla., Jan. 20, 1920; s. Gunby and Jessie Kirk (Cralle) G.; m. Martha Hanley, Sept. 14, 1946; children—Clifford, Mark, Timothy. J.D., U. Fla., 1947. Bar: Fla. bar 1947. Mem. Fla. Ho. of Reps. from, Hillsborough County, 1952-58, Fla. Senate, 1958-62, 88th-98th Congresses, 7th Dist. Fla., 1962—, mem. ways and means com. Founder, 1st pres. U.S. Fla. Found., 1958. Served to maj. AUS, 1941-45; ETO. Decorated Bronze Star; named Outstanding Young Man Tampa Jr. C. of C., 1954; recipient President's award Tampa C. of C., 1955. Mem. Tampa Bar Assn. (dir.), Hillsborough Bar Assn., (dir.), Greater Tampa C. of C. (dir.). Democrat. Presbyn. (deacon). Office: 2204 Rayburn House Office Bldg Washington DC 20515

GIBBONS, THOMAS MICHAEL, communications executive; b. Springfield, Mass., Nov. 11, 1925; s. Michael D. and Elizabeth A. (McCarthy) G.; m. Rita M. Nicholas, Jan. 14, 1950; children—Michael, Timothy, Gregory, Kathleen, Thomas, Mary Patricia, Brian, David. B.S., John Carroll U., 1949. With Chesapeake & Potomac Telephone Cos., 1956-73; dir. mktg. AT&T, N.Y.C., 1973-75; v.p. C&P Telephone Co. Md., Balt., 1975-79; exec. v.p., chief operating officer C&P Telephone Cos., Washington, 1979-82, pres., chief exec. officer, 1983—; dir. Arundel Corp., Towson, Md., Am. Security Bank, Washington. Washington trustee Fed. City Council; bd. dirs. Nat. Capital area council Boy Scouts Am., Bethesda, Md., Washington/Balt. Regional Assn. Served with USN, 1944-46. Roman Catholic. Office: C&P Telephone Co of Va 703 E Grace St Richmond VA 23219*

GIBBS, BARBARA MANNING, sociology educator; b. Dallas, Nov. 17, 1929; d. Leslie Paul and Gladys (Barton) Manning; B.A., U. Tex., 1951, M.A., 1953, Ph.D. in Sociology, 1972; m. Samuel Moore, June 2, 1950; children—Ellen, Carol. Instr. sociology Southwestern U., Georgetown, Tex., 1963-65, 66-68; teaching asst. U. Tex., Austin, 1968-70; asst. prof. Southwestern U., 1970-72; asst. prof. Tex. Lutheran Coll., 1972-75, assoc. prof., 1975-83, prof., 1983—. Mem. Southwest Sociol. Assn., Southwest Social Sci. Assn., Am. Sociol. Assn., Soc. Study of Social Problems, Phi Beta Kappa, Phi Kappa Phi, Alpha Kappa Delta, Pi Gamma Mu. Democrat. Methodist. Home: 1052 E College St Seguin TX 78155 Office: PO Box 3190 Texas Lutheran College Seguin TX 78155

GIBBS, DENISE PRESKITT, speech-language pathology educator; b. Birmingham, Ala., Jan. 1, 1952; s. William Oscar and Betty Scalco P.; m. Steven Douglas Gibbs, Aug. 5, 1972; children—Jeremy, Billy, Beth. B.S., U. Montevallo, 1974, M.S., 1975; Ed.D., U. Ala., 1985. Learning disabilities tchr. U. Montevallo (Ala.), 1975-77, asst. prof. speech-lang. pathology, 1977-82; coordinator presch. speech-lang.-hearing unit U. Ala., Tuscaloosa, 1982-84; asst. prof. U. Montevallo, Ala., 1984-86; cons. in field. Recipient Vivian I. Roe award, 1975. Mem. Am. Speech-Lang. Hearing Assn. (cert. clin. competence), Council for Exceptional Children, Speech and Hearing Assn. Ala., Alpha Gamma Delta. Republican. Baptist. Home: 72 Shoshone Dr Montevallo AL 35115 Office: Dept Communication Sci & Disorders U Montevallo Montevallo AL 35115

GIBBS, JAMES ALANSON, geologist; b. Wichita Falls, Tex., June 18, 1935; s. James Ford and Clovis (Robinson) G.; B.S., U. Okla., 1957, M.S., 1962; m. Judith Walker, June 18, 1966; children—Ford W., John A. Geologist, Calif. Co., New Orleans, 1961-63, Lafayette, La., 1963-64; cons. geologist, oil producer, Dallas, 1964—. Served with USNR, 1957-59. Mem. Dallas Geol. Soc. (past pres.), Am. Assn. Petroleum Geologists (cert. petroleum geologist; sec. 1983-85), Am. Inst. Profl. Geologists (cert. profl. geologist), Dallas Geophys. Soc., Geol. Info. Library of Dallas (v.p.), Soc. Ind. Profl. Earth Scientists (past chmn. Dallas chpt.), Geol. Soc. Am., Sigma Xi, Sigma Gamma Epsilon, Phi Delta Theta, Petroleum Engrs. Club: Dallas Petroleum. Republican. Methodist. Home: 3514 Caruth Blvd Dallas TX 75225 Office: 1106 One Energy Sq Dallas TX 75206

GIBBY, MABEL ENID KUNCE, psychologist; b. St. Louis, Mar. 30, 1926; d. Ralph Waldo and Mabel Enid (Warren) Kunce; student Washington U., St. Louis, 1943-44, postgrad., 1955-56; B.A., Park Coll., 1945; M.A., McCormick Theol. Sem., 1947; postgrad. Columbia U., 1948, U. Kansas City, 1949, George Washington U., 1953; M.Ed., U. Mo., 1951, Ed.D., 1952; m. John Francis Gibby, Aug. 27, 1948; children—Janet Marie (Mrs. Kim Williams), Harold Steven, Helen Elizabeth, Diane Louise (Mrs. Gregory Mappin), John Andrew, Keith Sherridan, Daniel Jay. Dir. religious edn. Westport Presbyn. Ch. Kansas City, Mo., 1947-49; tchr. elementary schs., Kansas City, 1949-50; high sch. counselor Arlington (Va.) Pub. Schs., 1952-54; counselor adult counseling services Washington U., 1955-56; counseling psychologist Coral Gables (Fla.) VA Hosp., 1956—, Miami (Fla.) VA Hosp., 1956—, chief counseling psychology sect. Miami VA Hosp., 1982—. Sec. bd. dirs. Fla. Vocat. Rehab. Found. Recipient Meritorious Service citation Fla. C. of C., 1965, President's Com. on Employment of Handicapped, 1965; commendation for meritorious service Com. on Employment of Physically Handicapped Dade County, 1965, 81, named outstanding rehab. profl., 1966, 81; named Profl. Fed. Employee of Year, Greater Miami Fed. Exec. Council, 1966; Outstanding Fed. Service award Greater Miami Fed. Exec. Council, 1966; Fed. Woman's award U.S. Civil Service Commn., 1968, Community Headliner award Theta Sigma Phi, 1968, Outstanding Alumni award Park Coll., 1968; certificate of appreciation Bur. Customs, U.S. Treasury Dept., 1969, Fla. Dept. Health and Rehab. Services, 1970. Mem. Am., Dade County (past sec.) psychol. assns., Nat., Fla. (past dir. Dade County chpt.) rehab. assns., Nat. Rehab. Counseling Assn. (past sec.). Patentee. Home: 10260 SW 56th St Miami FL 33165 Office: 1201 NW 16th St Miami FL 33125

GIBLIN, PATRICK DAVID, banker; b. St. Louis, July 24, 1932; s. Patrick Joseph and Ann Jane (Gill) G.; children—Mary Clare, Christopher, Gregory. B.B.A., Manhattan Coll., 1954; M.B.A., St. John's U., Jamaica, N.Y., 1965. Staff auditor Peat, Marwick, Mitchell & Co., N.Y.C., 1956-59; chief plant acct. div. Am. Machine & Foundry, Bklyn., 1959-63; with CBS, N.Y.C., 1963-73, controller electronic video rec. div., 1968-73, dir. corp. acctg., 1967-68; exec. v.p. fin. United Va. Bankshares, Inc., Richmond, 1973—. Served with U.S. Army, 1954-56. Mem. Delta Mu Delta. Roman Catholic. Home: 13 Dahlgren Rd Richmond VA 23233 Office: United Va Bankshares Inc 900 E Main St Richmond VA 23219*

GIBSON, CONNIE JEAN, oil company executive; b. Tulsa, Oct. 19, 1955; d. Leon Vester and Wanda Jean (DeFries) Cowell; m. Gary Dale Gibson, Sept. 7, 1974; children—Kristie Marie, Stacie Dawn. Student Tulsa Jr. Coll., 1973-75; B.S. in Acctg., Okla. State U., 1977. C.P.A., Okla. Adminstrv. trainee Cities Service Co., Tulsa, 1977-78, acct., 1978; DOE acct., 1978-79, task force leader, 1979; supr. crude oil compliance, 1979-80, lease acctg. mgr., 1980-82, royalty and govt. adminstrn. mgr., 1982-83; mgr. crude oil acctg. Cities Service Oil & Gas Corp., Tulsa, 1983-84, mgr. revenue spl. duties, 1984-85, supr. fin. consol., 1985—. Mem. Am. Mgmt. Assn., Petroleum Accts. Soc. Okla., Nat. Assn. Female Execs. Democrat. Methodist. Home: 13407 S 125th E Pl Broken Arrow OK 74011 Office: Box 300 2625 CSB Tulsa OK 74102

GIBSON, GLORIA KAY, librarian; b. Perryton, Tex., Oct. 9, 1953; d. Kenneth and Christine (Jarrett) Gibson; m. Steven Karl Branham, May 17, 1975. A.S., Amarillo Coll., 1974; B.A., West Tex. State U., 1975; M.L.S., Tex. Woman's U., 1977. Library tech. asst. Amarillo Coll. (Tex.), 1975-76; jr. librarian West Tex. State U. Library, Canyon, 1976-77, asst. reference librarian, 1977-80; librarian Southwestern Pub. Service, Amarillo, 1980—. Editor chpt. in Bibliography - Texas Reference Sources, 1978. Librarian First Presbyn. Ch., Amarillo, 1978—; mem. Big Bros./Big Sisters of Amarillo, 1985—. Mem. ALA, Spl. Libraries Assn., Tex. Library Assn. (dist. 2 treas. 1981-82, councilor 1984—), Amarillo C. of C., Beta Phi Mu. Office: Southwestern Pub Service Co 6th at Tyler St Amarillo TX 79170

GIBSON, GORDON LEE MATTHEWS, physician; b. Chgo., Apr. 17, 1932; s. Boyce E. and Esther L. (Matthews) G.; m. Jean H. T.; children—Kathryn Ann, Karen, Karyl. B.A., U. Fla., 1961; M.D., Emory U., 1965; M.P.H., Johns Hopkins U., 1968. Diplomate Am. Coll. Preventive Medicine. Intern, Emory

U. VA Hosps., Atlanta, 1965-66; resident in aerospace medicine Johns Hopkins U., Balt., 1969, Brooks AFB, Tex., 1970, Langley AFB, Tex., 1971; staff Eglin AFB, Ft. Walton Beach, Fla., 1966-68; control bd. human factors specialist, Wright-Patterson AFB, Dayton, Ohio, 1971-72; clinic comdr. McClellan AFB, Calif., 1973-74; hosp. comdr. USAF Hosp., Udorn, Thailand, 1971-72; chief aeromed. function Sch. Aerospace Medicine, Brooks AFB, 1975-77; flight surgeon 301 Tactical Hosp. Carswell AFB, Tex., 1977—; pvt. practice aviation medicine, Lewisville, Tex., 1977—. Named Flight Surgeon of Yr., Systems Command, 1968. Mem. Soc. USAF Flight Surgeons, Air Force Res. Assn., Mil. Surgeons U.S., Civil Aviation Med. Assn., Am. Pub. Health Assn., Air Medics Assn., Am. Heart Assn., Aerospace Med. Assn., AMA, Tex. Med. Assn., Denton County Med. Assn., Dallas Med. Assn. Contbr. articles to profl. jours. Office: 1502 W Main St Suite 105 Lewisville TX 75028

GIBSON, HUGH, federal judge; b. Cameron, Tex., Nov. 8, 1918; s. Hugh and Rene Louise (Blankenship) G.; m. Evalyn Grace Dunlop, Sept. 15, 1954. B.A., Rice U., 1940; LL.B., Baylor U., 1949. Bar: Tex. Judge Probate Ct., Galveston, Tex., 1954-68, State Dist. Ct., Galveston, 1968-79, U.S. Dist. Ct., Galveston, 1979—; asst. dist. atty. State of Tex., Galveston, 1949-54. Served with U.S. Army, 1942-45, PTO. Democrat. Office: Suite 611 US Post Office Galveston TX 77550

GIBSON, JERRY THOMAS, real estate broker; b. Sevier County, Tenn., June 2, 1935; s. Doyle L. and Dee G.; m. Joann Matthews, Aug. 1, 1955; children—Jerry Thomas II, Joel W., Jan E. Student U. Tenn., 1967-69, Tenn. Tech. Inst., 1979-80, Walters State Community Coll.; grad. Realtors Inst. Asst. mgr. Hotel Charles, Shelby, N.C., 1955; agt. Life & Casualty Ins., Sevierville, Tenn., 1956-57; mgr., supr. Thompson Stores, Maryville, Sevierville and Newport, Tenn., 1957-70; owner, mgr. Jerry Gibsons Dry Goods & Shoes, Jerry G. Men's Shop, East Tenn. Delivery Service, New Smokies Restaurant, Lamon's Cafe, Cedar Street Warehouse, Sevierville, 1957-72; broker, mgr. Century 21 Four Seasons Realty, Gatlinburg, Tenn., 1974—; appraiser, auctioneer. Mem. Republican Presdl. Task Force. Recipient Billy Wolfe Meml. award Tenn. Jaycees, 1967. Mem. Sevier County Bd. Realtors, Tenn. Assn. Realtors, Nat. Assn. Realtors, Am. Fraternity Real Estate Appraisers (sr.), Tenn. Auctioneers Assn., Jaycees (life; state dir. past, past state fin. officer). Methodist. Lodge: Elks. Home: Box 11 Cherokee Hills Sevierville TN 37862 Office: 1105 Parkway Gatlinburg TN 37738

GIBSON, ROBERT STANSILL, librarian; b. Rockingham, N.C., Aug. 1, 1925; s. Luke and Edna Lou (Marks) G.; m. Janie Belle Edwards, Aug. 21, 1955 (dec. Oct. 1977). B.A., Duke U., 1949, M.Div., 1953; M.A., Fla. State U., 1961, Advanced M.A., 1970. Cert. profl. librarian, Va. Instr. Spartanburg (S.C.) Jr. Coll., 1949-50; minister N.C. United Meth. Conf., 1952-58; dir. Appalachian Wesley Found., Boone, N.C., 1958-60; asst. social sci. librarian U. Ga., Athens, 1961-63; assoc. librarian Louisburg (N.C.) Coll., 1963-64; pub. service librarian, asst. prof. library sci. Radford (Va.) U., 1964-69, coordinator library sci. program, 1970—. Served with USNR, 1944-46. Mem. ALA, Southeastern Library Assn., Va. Library Assn., Va. Ednl. Media Assn., Beta Phi Mu. Democrat. Home: 108 Hammett Ave Radford VA 24141 Office: Radford U Box 5820 Radford VA 24142

GIBSON, THOMAS RICAUD, chemical company manager; b. Georgetown, S.C., Mar. 27, 1943; s. John Milby Gibson and Elizabeth Page Ricaud; m. Susan Dianne Miller, 1972; 1 child, Caroline Page. Student Mofford Coll. Plant mgr. Emerson Elec. Co., Bennettsville, S.C., 1968-72, Allied Chems., Waynesboro, Va., 1972—; pres. S.C. Real Estate Devel., Bennettesville, 1968-70; owner, mgr. Gibson's Gifts and Crafts, North Myrtle Beach, S.C., 1971. Republican. Methodist. Lodge: Kiwanis.

GIBSON, WILLIAM ANDREW, oral pathology educator; b. Middletown, Ohio, Apr. 22, 1929; s. William Andrew and Blanche Ethel (Bevis) G.; divorced; children—David Hamilton, Donna Lynn, Wayne Bradley. B.A., Ohio State U., 1951, M.A., 1952, D.D.S., 1956; M.D.S., Tufts U., 1961; Ph.D., Georgetown U., 1972. Ind. investigator Nat. Inst. Dental Research, NIH, Bethesda, Md., 1964-70, chief exptl. pathology lab., 1970-74, chief contract rev. staff, 1974-76; dir. research, prof. oral pathology La. State U. Sch. Dentistry, New Orleans, 1976—, also chmn. Instl. rev. bd. Med. Ctr. Author: Elementary Biostatistics for Dental Health Professionals, 1978; also numerous articles. Served to maj. USAF, 1956-64. Mem. ADA (chmn. research council 1983-84), Internat. Assn. Dental Research, Am. Assn. Dental Research (bd. dirs. 1978-80, councilor 1978—), Am. Acad. Perodontology, Biol. Stain Commn., Fedn. Am. Socs. Exptl. Biology, Am. Assn. Pathologists, Am. Acad. Oral Pathology, AAAS, Am. Soc. Cell Biology, Histochem. Soc. (chmn. local arrangement com. 1980—), Am. Coll. Dentists, Sigma Xi, Omicron Kappa Upsilon. Avocations: flying; scuba diving; traveling. Home: 2200 38th St Kenner LA 70065 Office: La State U Sch Dentistry 1100 Florida Ave New Orleans LA 70119

GIBSON, WILLIAM EDWARD, banker; b. Farragut, Idaho, Apr. 11, 1944; s. William Edward and Lucille Elizabeth (Dickehut) G.; m. Judith TenBrock, July 19, 1980; children—William Edward, Christopher Daniel. A.B., U. Chgo., 1964, M.A., 1965, Ph.D. in Econs., 1967. Sr. staff economist Pres. Council of Econ. Advisers, Washington, 1971-73; 1st v.p. Smith Barney Harris Upham & Co., Inc., N.Y.C., 1976-80; v.p. Chase Manhattan Bank, N.Y.C., 1974-76; sr. v.p. McGraw-Hill, Inc., N.Y.C., 1980-81; sr. v.p. econs. and mktg. Republic Bank Corp., Dallas, 1981—; chmn. bd. First Fed. Savs. and Loan Assn. Rochester, N.Y.; dir. First Fed. Savs. Bank P.R., San Juan, V'Soske Carpet Corp., Vega Baja, P.R. Trustee Howe Mil. Acad. (Ind.); vice chmn. Tex. affiliate Am. Diabetes Assn., 1985—; bd. dirs. Dallas Theater Ctr. Mem. Am. Econ. Assn., Am. Fin. Assn., Dallas Economists Club, Fin. Analysts Fedn., N.Y. Soc. Securities Analysts. Clubs: Univ. (N.Y.C.); Cosmos; Royal Oaks Country, Tower (Dallas). Author: Monetary Economics, 1972; assoc. editor Jour. of Money, Credit and Banking, 1976—; contbr. articles to profl. jours. Home: 3612 Harvard Ave Dallas TX 75205 Office: Pacific St at Ervay St Dallas TX 75222

GIBSON, WILLIAM EDWIN, mining engineer; b. Weeksbury, Ky., Sept. 16, 1930; s. Edwin Joseph and Irene (Depew) G.; B.S. in Mining Engring., Va. Poly. Inst., 1955; m. Gwenda Jean Wicker, Dec. 15, 1954; children—James Edwin, Barbara Ann, Deborah Irene. Indsl. engr. U.S. Steel Co., Lynch, Ky., 1956-62; mining engr. Evans Elkhorn Coal Corp., Wayland, Ky., 1964-66; indsl. engr. Eastern Coal Corp., Stone, Ky., 1962-64, mining engr., 1966-70; mining engr. Ky. Carbon Corp., Phelps, 1970-74, Beth Elkhorn Corp., Jenkins, Ky., 1974-77, Va. Iron, Coal & Coke Co., Coeburn, 1978-83, Branham & Baker Coal Co., Prestonsburg, Ky., William E. Gibson & Assocs., Jenkins, Ky., 1983—. Registered profl. engr. Mem. Nat., Ky., Va., W.Va. socs. profl. engrs., AIME. Club: Masons. Home: 596 Mudtown PO Box 179 Jenkins KY 41537 Office: 596 Midtown PO Box 179 Jenkins KY 41537

GIDDENS, MARY ELIZABETH, social services administrator, educator; b. Miami, Fla., Sept. 9, 1948; d. William Ellis and Lettie Josephine (Roberts) G. A.A., South Ga. Coll., 1968; B.S. in Edn., Ga. So. Coll., 1970. Tchr. pub. schs., Ga., 1970-72; supr. info. and referral service, supr. transp. system Polk County (Fla.) Dept. Social Services, 1972-78; dir. student traffic safety program Polk County Ct., Lakeland, 1978-80; asst. dir. Fellowship Dining, Cath. Social Services, Inc., Lakeland, 1980—. Bd. dirs. Polk County Legal Aid, 1975—, pres., 1981-82; bd. dirs. Coalition for Children and Youth, 1978-80; bd. dirs. Rape Crisis Ctr. Polk County, pres., 1978-80; bd. dirs. Polk County Community Services Council, 1982-83, pres., 1978; bd. dirs. Spouse Abuse of Polk County, 1975-77; chmn. Polk County Health-O-Rama, 1977, Fla. Citrus Festival's Sr. Citizens Day, 1977-78; mem. youth adv. council Heartland Employment and Tng. Adminstrn., 1978-80; mem. adv. bd. West Area Adult Sch., 1983—. Named Young Career Woman, Fla. Bus. and Profl. Women, 1976; recipient Disting. Service award Polk County Services Council, 1980. Mem. Fla. Bus. and Profl. Women (state legis. chmn. 1979-81, state lobbyist 1979-81). Democrat. Club: Pionette (pres. 1983—). Home: 4108 Wellington Dr Lakeland FL 33803 Office: Fellowship Dining 807 E Palmetto St Lakeland FL 33801

GIDDENS, TANYA CROCKETT, corporation controller; b. Ft. Worth, Mar. 15, 1955; d. Donald Ray Crockett and C. Lee Holt; m. Gregory Wesley Giddens, Nov. 19, 1983. Student in bus. adminstrn. U. Tex.-Arlington, 1975-77. Bunny, Playboy Internat., Dallas, 1977-79; sec. MCI Prodns., Dallas, 1979-81; controller Dunne Creative, Dallas, 1981-82; controller, corp. sec. G.A. Services Co., G.A. Sales Co., G.A. Constrn. Co. and G.A. Exec. Computing, all divs. Ga.-Am. Cos., Norcross, Ga., 1982—. Office: GA Services Co 6855 Jimmy Carter Blvd Bldg P Suite 1850 Norcross GA 30071

GIDDERS, DENNIS MICHAEL, microfilm company executive; b. Warren, Pa., June 15, 1945; s. John Michael and Delena Catherine (Scalise) G.; m. Nancy Catherine Williams, June 28, 1975; 1 dau., Catherine. B.S., Kent State U., 1967. Programmer, analyst Computing and Software So., Alexandria, Va., 1970-72; regional analyst DatagraphiX, Bethesda, Md., 1972-74; br. mgr. Zytron, Washington, 1974-78; pres. AmeriCOM of Washington, Alexandria, 1978—. Contbr. atricles to profl. jours. Served with U.S. Army, 1967-69. Mem. Assn. Info. and Image Mgmt. (v.p. 1982, pres. 1982-83). Roman Catholic. Home: 3211 Barbara Ln Fairfax VA 22031 Office: AmeriCOM of Washington Inc 3700 Mount Vernon Ave Alexandria VA 22305

GIDDINGS, JEFFREY MAXWELL, ecologist; b. Willimantic, Conn., Oct. 24, 1950; s. Merton Dale and Ruth Lee (Asness) G.; m. Elizabeth Janet Dorschug, Aug. 29, 1970; children—Sarah Kate, Anne Rachel, Dale Patrick. A.B., Cornell U., 1971, Ph.D., 1975. Research staff mem. environ. sci. div. Oak Ridge Nat. Lab., 1975—. Mem. ASTM, Am. Soc. Limnology and Oceanography, Soc. Environ. Toxicology and Chemistry, Sigma Xi. Contbr. articles to profl. jours. Office: PO Box X Oak Ridge TN 37831

GIDEON, LEE BURTON, producer radio and television commercials and shows, entertainer, writer; b. Tulsa, May 18, 1938; s. Russell Arthur and Helen (Belt) G.; m. Carolyn Joyce Kirkpatrick, Sept. 30, 1978. B.A. in English, U. Tulsa, 1960, postgrad., 1964-65. Owner Pickles Restaurant, Tulsa, 1968-73; founder, co-owner Pants Am. Stores, Tulsa and Denver, 1970-75; founder, pres. Lee Gideon Creative Prodns., Tulsa, 1975—. Bd. dirs. March of Dimes, Boy Scouts Am. Served with U.S. Army, 1960-63. Recipient 27 Addy awards for radio and TV commls. Mem. Tulsa Ad Club. Republican. Unitarian. Club: Indian Springs Country. Wrote, voiced and produced 5000 radio and TV commls. Home: 6403 S Kingston St Tulsa OK 74136 Office: 4815 S Sheridan Suite 106 Tulsa OK 74145

GIESE, WARREN KENNETH, health and physical education educator, state senator; b. Milw., July 14, 1924; s. Herbert Elbert and Lydia (Wegehaupt) G.; m. Phyllis Phillips; children—Ann Allison, Mary Melanie, Warren Blair, King Alexander. A.B., B.A. cum laude Wis. State U., Okla. State U., Central Mich. U., 1948; M.Ed., U. Md., 1950; Ph.D., Fla. State U., 1965. Phys. edn. instr., asst. football coach U. Md., 1948-56; head football coach U.S.C., Columbia, 1956-60, athletic dir., 1959-61, assoc. prof. to prof. dept. head of health and phys. edn., 1959-73, prof. and dean Coll. Health and Phys. Edn., 1974-78, prof., 1979-83, disting. prof. emeritus, 1984—; mem. Pres.'s Council on Phys. Fitness and Sports, Washington, 1971-78, 82—; mem. NCAA Nat. Youth Sports Program Com.; U.S. Bd. Vis.; state senator S.C. Senate, Columbia, 1984—. Contbr. articles to profl. jours. Chmn. Richland County Council, Columbia, 1974-76, mem., 1972-76, 1978-82. Served to lt. (j.g.) USNR, 1943-46. Recipient numerous grants including Nat. Heart, Lung and Blood Inst., 1974-82, Nat. Youth Sports Program, Nigerian Sports Project, Summer Feeding Program USDA, Nat. Hwy. Safety Program, S.C. Regional Med. Program and others; recipient Outstanding Faculty award U.S.C., 1968, 75th Anniversary award Central Mich. U., 1968, Phys. Fitness Leadership award State S.C., 1964. Mem. Internat. Fed. Univ. Sports (v.p. 1983—), Phi Kappa Phi, Phi Epsilon Kappa. Republican. Lutheran. Avocations: jogging; swimming; travel. Office: South Carolina Senate Suite 602 Gressette Bldg Columbia SC 29202

GIESELER, RICHARD CONRAD, SR., electrical engineer, consultant; b. New Orleans, Feb. 16, 1929; s. William and Catherine (Leightman) G.; m. Ella Caroline Knight, June 2, 1950; children—Susan Kay Gieseler Smith, Richard Conrad. B.S. in E.E., La. State U., 1951. Registered profl. engr., La. With comml. sales dept. New Orleans Pub. Service, 1952-54; sales engr. Walker Electric Co., Atlanta, 1954-56; magnetic products div. sales engr. 3M Co., St. Paul, 1956-66; sales engr. LuMac, Inc., Baton Rouge, 1966—; pres. Southeast Cruising Cons., Inc., Metairie, La., 1978—. Mem. Conservative Caucus, Inc. Served to 1st lt. U.S. Army, 1950-52. Mem. Instrument Soc. Am., U.S. Power Squadron. Republican. Presbyterian. Club: New Orleans Yacht. Lodge: Masons.

GIESMANN, DONALD JOHN, clergyman; b. Pitts., Apr. 15, 1949; s. John Weber and Harriet Elizabeth (Collingwood) G.; m. Sara Longfellow Mosher, June 2, 1974; children—Carrie Elizabeth, Alison Sara. B.S., Indiana U. of Pa., 1971; M.R.E., Gordon-Conwell Sem., South Hamilton, Mass., 1974; Ed.D., Columbia Pacific U., 1980. Ordained to ministry Presbyn. Ch. in Am., 1975. Chaplain students Gordon-Conwell Sem., 1973-74; assoc. pastor Westminster Presbyn. Ch., Rock Hill, S.C., 1974-76; pastor Heritage Congl. Ch., Middletown, Conn., 1976-77; assoc. pastor discipleship South Park Ch., Park Ridge, Ill., 1977-81; pastor Community Ch., Bristol, Tenn., 1981—; mem. nat. Christian edn. com. Evangelical Presbyn. Ch., 1983—; del. Ill./White House Conf. on Families, 1980; nat. adv. council Pioneer Ministries of Wheaton, Ill. Apptd. Ill. Selective Service System Bd. Recipient Recognition award Pa. State Student Edn. Assn., 1971; Four Way Test award Christian Workers Found., 1974. Mem. Presbyn. Hist. Soc., Bristol Ministerial Assn., So. Hist. Assn., Freedom House (N.Y.C.). Office: 6320 Old Jonesboro Rd Bristol TN 37620

GIEVERS, KAREN A., lawyer; b. Culver City, Calif., Apr. 27, 1949; d. Ernest Conrad and Josephine Theresa (Passolt) Prevost; m. Joseph R. Gievers, Nov. 16, 1968; children—Daniel Steven, Donna Ann. A.A., Miami Dade Community Coll., 1974; B.A., Fla. Internat. U., 1975; J.D. cum laude, U. Miami, 1978. Bar: Fla. 1978, U.S. Dist. Ct. (so. dist.) Fla. 1978, U.S. Dist. Ct. (mid. and no. dist.) Fla. 1979, U.S. Ct. Appeals (5th cir.) 1979, U.S. Ct. Claims 1980, U.S. Ct. Appeals (11th cir.) 1981, U.S. Suprem Ct. 1982. Assoc. Sams, Anderson, Gerstein & Ward, P.A., Miami, Fla., 1978; assoc. Anderson, Moss, Russo & Gievers, P.A., Miami, 1979-83, ptnr. 1983—. Bd. editors So. Dist. Digest, 1981-85. Lectr. FACT, Miami, 1984. Mem. Fla. Bar Assn. (editor trial lawyers sect. 1984, vice-chmn. evidence com. 1985-86), ABA, Acad. Fla. Trial Lawyers (chmn. pub. com. 1984—), Am. Trial Lawyers Assn., Dade County Bar Assn. (bd. dirs. 1981-84, 85—), Dade County Trial Lawyers Assn. (sec. 1984-85, treas. 1985—), Fed. Bar Assn., Fla. Assn. Women Lawyers, Zool. Soc. Fla., Fla. Consumer Fedn. Democrat. Club: City (Miami). Office: Anderson Moss Russo Gievers & Cohen PA 100 N Biscayne Blvd Suite 2300 Miami FL 33132

GIGLIO, PETER M., JR., sales executive; b. Tampa, Fla., July 31, 1944; s. Peter L. and Rose M. G.; B.S., Fla. State U., 1963; m. Elisabeth Fink, Sept. 25, 1975. Sales rep. Gen. Foods Corp., Montgomery, Ala., 1968-70; account mgr., Miami, 1970-72; dist. mgr. Anderson Clayton Foods, Miami, 1972-73; regional sales mgr. H. P. Hood, Inc., Dunedin, Fla., 1974-75; pres. Nat. Food Brokers, Tampa, 1975-77, regional sales dir. foodservice div., 1977—. Recipient Golden Fellowship award, 1983; Regional Sales Dir. of Yr. award H. P. Hood, Inc., 1985. Mem. Valrico Commerce Assn. (pres. 1984). Office: H P Hood Inc 427 San Christopher Dr Dunedin FL 33528

GIGNILLIAT, WILLIAM ROBERT, III, lawyer; b. Sebring, Fla., Mar. 22, 1943; s. William Robert and Ann Josephine (Harris) G.; m. Rosemary Rebecca Bersch, May 29, 1971 (div. July 1979); 1 dau., Meigan Rebecca; m. Laura Crowell Lieberman Mar. 20, 1984; 1 child, William Robert, IV. B.A., U. South, 1965; J.D., Emory U., 1968. Bar: Ga. 1968, U.S. Dist. Ct. (no. dist.) Ga. 1970, U.S. Ct. Apls. (5th cir.) 1970, U.S. Supreme Ct. 1972, U.S. Ct. Apls. (11th cir.) 1982. Atty., Emory Neighborhood Law Office, Atlanta, 1967-71; ptnr. Mantegna, Gignilliat & Wiggins, Atlanta, 1974-75, Gignilliat, Manchel, Johnson & Wiggins, 1977-83; sole practice, Atlanta, 1983—. Pres., chmn. bd. Words of Art, Inc., Atlanta, 1982—. Author: Contracts for Artists, 1983. Bd. sponsors Center for Puppetry Arts, Atlanta, 1979—. Served with AUS, 1968-70. Mem. Ga. Vol. Lawyers for the Arts, ABA, Ga. Criminal Def. Lawyers Assn. Democrat. Office: 918 Ponce de Leon Ave Atlanta GA 30306

GILBERT, BARRY KEITH, librarian, lawyer; b. Paducah, Ky., Sept. 16, 1952; s. James Bailey and Ila Elizabeth (Allison) Gilbert; m. Janice Gerbaz, Jan. 3, 1976. Student Oberlin (Ohio) Coll., 1970-71; B.A., U. Tex., 1973, J.D., 1976, M.L.S., 1979. Bar: Tex. 1976, U.S. Dist. Ct. (we. dist.) Tex. 1979, U.S. Ct. Appeals (5th cir.) 1982, U.S. Supreme Ct. 1982. VISTA atty. Legal Aid, Defender Soc., Austin, 1976-77; assoc. librarian U. Houston Law Library, 1979-84; instr. legal research U. Houston-Clear Lake, 1982-84, 85; law librarian Marathon Oil Co., Houston, 1985—. Mem. Citizens Animal Protection, People for Ethical Treatment of Animals, Animal Legal Def. Fund, Tex. Humane Info. Network, Good Bears of World. Mem. State Bar Tex., Spl. Libraries Assn., Houston Online Users Group, Am. Assn. Law Libraries, S.W. Assn. Law Libraries, Houston Area Law Librarians (exec. com. 1983—), ALA, Phi Kappa Phi, Beta Phi Mu. Office: Marathon Oil Co PO Box 3128 Houston TX 77253

GILBERT, JAMES CUMMINS, JR., shipbuilding company executive; b. Columbia, Miss., Sept. 28, 1942; s. James Cummins and Annie Claire (Barnes) G.; m. Carol Dianne Bryant, Nov. 18, 1978; 1 dau., Ashley Dianne. Draftsman Ingalls Shipbuilding, Pascagoula, Miss., 1964-71, project engr. submarine overhaul, 1971-73, asst. program mgr. submarine overhaul, 1973-75, mgr. prodn. control submarine overhaul, 1975-77, mgr. prodn. planning submarine overhauls, 1977-81, mgr. prodn. planning new constrn., 1981—. Served with U.S. Army, 1968-74. Mem. Ingalls Mgmt. Assn. Democrat. Methodist. Office: Ingalls Shipbuilding Corp PO Box 149 MS/7010-11 Pascagoula MS 39567

GILBERT, JERRY LON, petroleum geologist, consultant; b. Fort Worth, Feb. 14, 1947; s. Joe Pershing and Josephine Elizabeth (Bunch) G.; m. Katherine Anne Snyder, Aug. 30, 1969; children—Jennifer Christine, Julie Anna, John Bryan. B.S., West Tex. State U., 1970, M.S., 1975. Geologist, Sohio Petroleum, Oklahoma City, 1975-76; geologist, Petroleum Inc., Oklahoma City, 1976-79; geologist Search Drilling Co., Amarillo, Tex., 1979-81; v.p. geol. Spur Petroleum, Amarillo, 1981-83; sr. geologist Santa Fe Minerals, Tulsa, 1983-84; consulting petroleum geologist Strat Land Exploration, Tulsa, 1984—. Served to 1st lt. CE U.S. Army, 1971-73. Mem. Panhandle Geol. Soc. (sec. 1980-81, v.p. 1981-82, pres. 1982-83). Am. Assn. Petroleum Geologist (cert. 1983), Tulsa Geol. Soc., Simga Gamma Epsilon. Republican. Methodist. Clubs: Philcrest Hill Tennis (Tulsa), Angel Fire Country (N.Mex.). Avocations: golf; rock collecting. Home: 9810 S Granite St Tulsa OK 74137 Office: Strat Land Exploration Co 9 E 4th St Suite 800 Tulsa OK 74103

GILBERT, JOHN JORDAN, lawyer; b. Americus, Ga., Nov. 18, 1907; s. Osceola Pinckney and Talulah Zuleme (Jordan) G.; m. Dorothy Adams, Apr. 2, 1932; children—Emily, Randall. LL.B., Mercer U., 1929. Bar, Brunswick-Glynn County, 1929; with Gilbert, Whittle, Harrell, Scarlett, & Skelton, and predecessor firms, Brunswick, Ga., 1929—; dir. Sea Island Co. (Ga.); dir. Am. Nat. Bank Brunswick, 1955-78, chmn. bd., 1972-78. Rep., Ga. Ho. of Reps., 1942-46; mem. Brunswick Port Authority, 1946-51, chmn., 1948-51; mem. pres.'s adv. council Med. Coll. Ga., 1978—; trustee Brunswick Coll. Found., 1968-84; mem. Glynn-Brunswick Meml. Hosp. Authority, 1970-82, chmn., 1979-82. Recipient Alfred W. Jones award Brunswick C. of C., 1981. Fellow Am. Bar Found.; mem. Ga. Bar Assn., ABA, Brunswick-Glynn County Bar Assn., Alpha Tau Omega, Delta Theta Phi. Baptist. Lodge: Rotary (pres.). Home: 2502 Frederica Rd St Simons Island GA 31522 Office: 200 First Fed Plaza 777 Gloucester St Brunswick GA 31521

GILBERT, LINDA PHILLIPS, mathematics educator; b. Springfield, Ill., May 17, 1948; d. Rudd George and Georgia H. (Davidson) Phillips; m. Jimmie D. Gilbert, Dec. 20, 1974; children—Rebecca Sue, Jimmie Matthew. B.S., La. Tech U., Ruston, 1970, M.S., 1972, Ph.D., 1977. Computer programmer Continental Can Co., Hodge, La., 1973-75; instr. math. La. Tech U., Ruston, 1977-80, asst. prof., 1980-84, assoc. prof., 1984—. Author: College Algebra, 1981, 2d edit., 1986; Intermediate Algebra, 1983; Elements of Modern Algebra, 1984; College Trigonometry, 1985; College Algebra and Trigonometry, 1986. Recipient Outstanding Achievement award La. Tech U., 1984. Mem. Am. Math. Soc., Math. Assn. Am., Phi Kappa Phi, Pi Mu Epsilon. Methodist. Home: PO Box 25 Quitman LA 71268 Office: La Tech U Math Dept Ruston LA 71272

GILBERT, LUCIA ALBINO, psychology educator; b. Bklyn., July 27, 1941; d. William Veto and Carmelina (Cutro) Albino; m. John Carl Gilbert, Dec. 18, 1965; 1 child, Melissa Carlotta. B.A., Wells Coll., 1963; M.S., Yale U., 1964; Ph.D., U. Tex., Austin, 1974. Lic. psychologist, Tex. Supr. research info. G.S. Gilmore Research Lab., New Haven, 1964-67; tchr. St. Stephen Sch., Austin, Tex., 1967-69; asst. prof. Iowa State U., Ames, 1974-76, U. Tex., Austin, 1976-81, assoc. prof., 1981—. Author: Men in Dual Career Families, 1985. Editor (spl. issue jour.) Parenting. Recipient Excellence in Teaching award U. Tex., 1981; Am. Psychol. Assn. fellow, 1982, 84. Fellow Am. Psychol. Assn. (rep. council 1980-83); mem. Tex. Psychol. Assn., Assn. Women in Psychology. Avocations: swimming; progressive country music; ecology. Home: 4402 Balcones Dr Austin TX 78731 Office: U Texas Dept Ednl Psychology Austin TX 78712

GILBERT, PHILIP HENRY, medical association executive; b. Walpole, N.H., Sept. 15, 1939; s. Bernard Simmons and Ada (Brown) Smalley (guardians); B.S. in Social Welfare, Fla. State U., 1965, postgrad. in Vocat. Rehab., 1966-68; postgrad. in Vocat. Rehab., So. Ill. U., 1967; hon. degree So. Coll. Bus., Orlando, Fla., 1969; m. Carole Frances Roberts, Nov. 26, 1971 (div. 1978); 1 son, Kevin Austin. Counselor vocat. rehab. Bur. Blind Services, State of Fla., Jacksonville, 1966-67, state placement specialist, 1967-68, state supr. social security trust fund program, 1968-71, dist. dir., 1971-72; dir. rehab. Gateway Hope Center, Inc., Jacksonville, 1971; exec. dir. Fla. Council on Aging, Jacksonville, 1972-73; chief Bur. Grants Devel. and Monitoring, Fla. Div. of Aging, Tallahassee, 1973-74; dir. med. edn. and services dept. Fla. Med. Assn., Jacksonville, 1974-75; assoc. dir. Fla. Med. Found., Jacksonville, also dir. found. dept., 1975-77; exec. dir. Fla. Med. Polit. Action Com., Tallahassee, 1977-78, dir. govt. program dept., 1979-80; dir. med. econs. dept., exec. dir. Fla. Med. Found., 1981—; exec. v.p. Duval County Med. Soc., Jacksonville, Fla., 1984—. Mem. steering com. First Internat. Conf. on The Blind in Computer Programming, 1968; mem. Pres.'s Com. on Employment of Handicapped, 1969—; mem. Fla. Gov.'s Com. on Employment of Handicapped, 1969—; bd. govs. Gateway Hope Center, Inc., 1972-74; cons. first blind computer programmer tng. project So. Coll. Bus., 1968-69; cons. placing the blind in competitive employment So. Ill. U., 1968; cons. employment of handicapped Disney World, 1972; mem. Republican Presdl. Task Force. Recipient Outstanding Service award Fla. Council on Aging, 1973. Mem. Am. Assn. Workers for the Blind (dir. 1968), Nat., Fla. rehab. assns. Home: 4446 Coleman St Jacksonville FL 32223 Office: PO Box 2411 760 Riverside Ave Jacksonville FL 32203

GILBERT, THOMAS MARTIN, former government official, consultant; b. Elkmont, Ala., May 7, 1927; s. Van Buren and Mary Daly (McWilliams) G. A.B., Athens State Coll., 1949. Mem. staff Senator Lister Hill, Washington, 1949-53; adminstrv. asst. Rep. Armistead Selden, Washington, 1953-69, Rep. George W. Andrews, 1969-71, Rep. Elizabeth Andrews, 1972-73, Rep. Marjorie Holt, 1973 (all Washington); cons. Grocery Mfrs. Am., Inc., Washington, part time 1973—. Served with USN, 1945-46. Episcopalian. Avocation: theater memorabilia, books and programs collector. Home: PO Box 126 Elkmont AL 35620

GILCHRIST, WILLIAM RISQUE, JR., economist; b. Lexington, Ky., July 16, 1944; s. William Risque and Susan (McLemore) G.; B.B.A., U. Miami, 1966, M.B.A., 1970; postgrad. Northwestern U., 1973—; m. Peggy Linder Gardner, Mar. 20, 1968; children—William Risque, Shannon Linder, Heather Susan. Asso. dir. conf. services div. continuing edn. U. Miami, Coral Gables, Fla., 1966-71; asst. dir. edn. and tng. Mortgage Bankers Assn. Am., Washington, 1971-73; pres. Ventura Fin. Corp., Ft. Lauderdale, Fla., 1973-76; pres. Gilchrist and Assos., Pompano Beach, Fla., London, Basel, Switzerland and Santiago, Chile, 1976—; pres., dir. Intervault, Inc.; cons. in field. Mem. Republican Senatorial Inner Circle, 1985—. Recipient Cert. of Achievement, Savs. and Loan Execs. Seminar, 1971. Mem. Miami-Dade County (Fla.) C. of C., NAB, Econ. Soc. South Fla., Mortgage Bankers Assn., Nat. Assn. Pvt. Security Vaults (dir. 1983—). Republican. Episcopalian. Clubs: Kiwanis. Marina Bay, Mutiny. Author: International Monetary Systems—Alternatives, 1969; Eurodollar Outlook-OPEC and the LDC's, 1978. Home: 1341 SE 9th Ave Pompano Beach FL 33060

GILES, JAMES RAYMOND, educational administrator; b. Gaffney, S.C., Feb. 14, 1932; s. James Alexander and Thelma (Kennedy) G.; m. Linda Kumazawa Rittenhouse, Apr. 30, 1972 (div. 1981). B.S., Samford U., 1959; M.Ed., U. of S.C., 1978; ednl. specialist, U. So. Miss., 1981; Ph.D., Columbia Pacific U., 1983. Cert. secondary tchr., Ga., Tenn., S.C. Tchr. Manchester High Sch., Ga., 1960-61, Powell High Sch., Knoxville, Tenn., 1962-63, Gaffney High Sch., S.C., 1963-65, St. Johns High Sch., Darlington, S.C., 1965-68, Hillcrest High Sch., Sumter, S.C., 1971-73; asst. prin. Wren High Sch., Piedmont, S.C., 1974—; cons. Office of Ednl. TV, S.C. State Dept. Edn., Columbia, 1973-74. Contbr. articles to state jour. Served with USAF, 1950-54. Freedoms Found. scholar, 1968, 83, 84. Mem. Nat. Assn. Secondary Sch. Prins., S.C. Assn. Sch. Adminstrs., Assn. Classroom Tchrs., (v.p. 1968), S.C. Edn. Assn., Nat. Ret. Tchrs. Assn. (asst. dir. nat. activities 1968-71), Phi Delta Kappa. Baptist.

Home: B 2 Country Pl Easley SC 29640 Office: Wren High Sch Route 1 Piedmont SC 29673

GILES, MARTIN LOUIS, fire sprinkler company executive; b. Danville, Va., Dec. 20, 1944; s. Roland Carter and Louise (Towler) G.; certificate, Richmond Profl. Inst., 1965; m. Patricia Kaye Hoffler, July 19, 1979; children—Matthew Jason, Jeffrey Martin. Engr., Va. Sprinkler Co., Ashland, 1965-66, v.p., 1968-71, pres., 1971—, also dir.; dir. Va. Pipe & Supply Co., Ashland. Served with U.S. Army, 1966-68. Mem. Am. Fire Sprinkler Assn., Nat. Fire Protection Assn., Soc. Fire Protection Engrs., Va. Fire Prevention Assn., Nat. Fire Sprinkler Assn., Nat. Inst. Cert. in Engring. Tech. (cert. engring. technician). Home: 1708 Cloister Dr Richmond VA 23233 Office: PO Box 986 Atlee Elmont Exit 195 Ashland VA 23005

GILKEY, HERBERT TALBOT, trade assn. exec.; b. Boulder, Colo., Nov. 27, 1924; s. Herbert James and Mildred Virginia (Talbot) G.; B.S. in Mech. Engring., Iowa State U., 1947, M.S., 1949; postgrad. U. Ill., 1950-53; m. Romona Marie Olsen, June 28, 1946 (dec. 1970); children—Virginia Anne, Herbert David, Edele Christine, Arthur Talbot, Martha Olive; m. 2d, Mary Louise Tucker Brown, Apr. 26, 1974. Research asso. in mech. engring. U. Ill., Urbana, 1949-55; dir. tech. services Nat. Warm Air Heating and Air Conditioning Assn., Cleve., 1955-67; research dir. Waterloo Register div. Dynamics Corp. of Am., Cedar Falls, Iowa, 1967-70; dir. of govt. and consumer affairs Air Conditioning and Refrigeration Inst., Arlington, Va., 1971-77, exec. dir. pub. affairs, 1977-80; dir. codes and govt. liaison Sheet Metal and Air Conditioning Contractors Nat. Assn., Vienna, Va., 1980—. Scoutmaster, Greater Cleve. council Boy Scouts Am., 1964-67, commr. Wapsipinicon and Nat. Capital Area councils, 1967—; mem. Bd. Zoning Appeals, Cedar Falls, 1969-70; mem. Energy Conservation Task Force, Fairfax County, Va., 1977-78; elder Presbyn. Ch., Cleveland Heights, Ohio, 1960-62, Cedar Falls, 1968-70. Served with C.E., U.S. Army, 1943-45. Recipient Award of Merit, Boy Scouts Am., 1974; registered profl. engr., Va., Md., D.C., Ohio, Iowa. Fellow ASHRAE (Disting. Service award 1970, chmn. research and tech. com. 1971-72, chmn. govt. affairs com. 1975-76, chmn. energy conservation com. 1976-77); mem. ASME, Nat. Fire Protection Assn. (air conditioning com. 1960-67), Uniform Boiler and Pressure Vessel Laws Soc. (council 1973-79). Contbr. articles on heating and air conditioning engring. to profl. jours.; editor various air conditioning design and installation manuals, 1955-67. Home: 2606 E Meredith Dr Vienna VA 22180 Office: Sheet Metal and Air Conditioning Contractors Nat Assn 8224 Old Courthouse Rd Vienna VA 22180

GILKEY, SUSAN NICODEMUS, educator; b. Winchester, Va., Mar. 30, 1950; d. Arthur Warren and Suzanna Lucille (Nicodemus) G. A.B. in Modern Langs., Coll. William and Mary, 1974. Tchr. math. John Handley High Sch., Winchester, 1976—. Mem. Winchester Meml. Hosp. Aux., 1978—; vol. Shenandoah Valley Apple Blossom, 1978—. Mem. NEA, Va. Edn. Assn., Nat. Council Tchrs. Math., Va. Council Tchrs. Math., Va. Valley Council Tchrs. of Math., Winchester Edn. Assn. Presbyterian. Home: 314 W Leicester St Winchester VA 22601 Office: PO Box 910 Handley Blvd Winchester VA 22601

GILL, BEN GILMER, fund raising co. exec.; b. Blytheville, Ark., Aug. 13, 1939; s. William Braxton and Bertha Velera Gill; B.A., Baylor U., Waco, Tex., 1962; B.D., Southwestern Sem., Ft. Worth, 1965. Ordained to ministry Baptist Ch., 1959; pastor First Bapt. Ch., La Grange, Tex., 1965-69; dir. endowment capital giving So. Bapt. Conv., 1969-73; founder, 1973, since pres. Resource Services, Inc., Dallas; cons. High Flight Found. Mem. Nat. Soc. Fund Raising Execs. Republican. Club: Lions. Author: Building for Today's Challenge, 1972. Office: 10300 N Central Expressway Suite 295-I Dallas TX 75231 Home: 6514 Covecreek Dallas TX 75240

GILL, GEORGE NORMAN, newspaper executive; b. Indpls., Aug. 11, 1934; s. George E. and Urith (Dailey) G.; A.B. Ind. U., 1957; m. Kay Baldwin, Dec. 28, 1957; children—Norman A., George B. Reporter, Richmond (Va.) News Leader, 1957-60; copy editor, reporter, acting Sunday editor, city editor, mng. editor Courier-Jour., Louisville, 1960-74, v.p. gen. mgr. Courier-Jour. and Louisville Times Co., 1974-79, sr. v.p. corp. affairs, 1979-80, pres., chief exec. officer, 1981—, chief exec. officer affiliates Standard Gravure Corp., WHAS Inc., 1981—. Served with USNR, 1954-56. Recipient Picture Editors award Nat. Press Photographers Assn., 1965. Mem. Am. Soc. Newspaper Editors, Asso. Press Mng. Editors, Louisville Com. on Fgn. Relations, Alpha Tau Omega, Sigma Delta Chi. Mason. Home: 308 Rebel Dr Pewee Valley KY 40056 Office: 525 W Broadway Louisville KY 40202

GILL, GERALD LAWSON, librarian; b. Montgomery, Ala., Nov. 13, 1947; s. George Ernest and Marjorie (Hackett) G.; m. Nancy Argroves, Mar. 5, 1977 (div. 1982). A.B., U. Ga., 1971; M.A., U. Wis., 1973. Cataloger, James Madison U., Harrisonburg, Va., 1974-76, reference librarian, asst. prof., 1976—. Mem. Am. Soc. for Info. Sci., Assoc. Info. Mgrs., Va. Library Assn., Spl. Libraries Assn. (treas. Va. chpt. 1983-85, pres. elect 1985-86), ALA (chmn. bus. reference services com. 1984-86; sec. law and polit. sci. sect. 1982-85), Harrisonburg C. of C. Democrat. Home: 1379 Devon Ln Harrisonburg VA 22801 Office: James Madison U Harrisonburg VA 22807

GILLASPIE, LEON WILLIAM, college administrator, minister; b. Worcester, N.Y., Nov. 10, 1923; s. William Arthur and Ruth Mae (Whiteman) G.; m. Genevieve Langston, Aug. 9, 1948; children—Norman, Patricia, Paul. Diploma, Barrington Coll., R.I., 1944; A.B., Wheaton Coll., 1947; M.A., U. Ala., 1968. Ordained to ministry, Am. Baptist Conv., 1948. Instr., Southeastern Bible Coll., Birmingham, Ala., 1947-54, registrar, 1954-55, acad. dean, 1955-67, acting pres., 1958-60, v.p., 1967—; lab. instr. U. Ala., Tuscaloosa, 1962-63; lectr. on creation-evolution seminars; preacher at numerous chs. Author publs. in field. Violinist Magic City Community Orchestra. Mem. Am. Assn. Coll. Registrars and Admissions Officers (pres. Ala. chpt. 1965-66), So. Anthrop. Assn., Am. Anthrop. Assn., Ala. Acad. Sci. Home: 905 Pine Circle Leeds AL 35094 Office: Southeastern Bible College 2901 Pawnee Ave Birmingham AL 35256

GILLEN, ALBERT J., communications executive; b. 1919. B.S., Syracuse U. Gen. sales mgr. Louisville Courier Jour., 1952-57; v.p. sales Newhouse Broadcasting Co., 1957-60; gen. sales mgr. Capital Cities Communications, Inc., 1960-64; pres. Poole Broadcasting Co., 1964-78; sr. v.p. Knight-Ridder Newspapers, Inc., 1978—; pres. Knight-Ridder Broadcasting, Inc., 1978—; sr. v.p. Viewdata Corp. Am., Inc., 1979—. Served with USCG, 1942-45. Address: Knight-Ridder Newspapers Inc 1 Herald Plaza Miami FL 33101

GILLEN, GEORGE EDWARD, business educator; b. Pine Bluff, Ark., Oct. 7, 1934; s. James Albert and Lois Olga (Howey) G. B.S. in Bus., U. Tulsa, 1957, M.B.A. in Mgmt., 1962, Ed.D. in Adminstrn., 1972; postdoctoral studies Cambridge U., Eng., 1973. Instr. bus. adminstrn. Southwestern Coll., Winfield, Kans., 1960-64, Okla. State U., Stillwater, 1964-65; prof., chmn. bus. dept. Oral Roberts U., Tulsa, 1965—; economist Army Corp. of Eng., Tulsa, 1976, Social Econ. Impact research report, 1976. Cons. editor: Economics, 1984. Elder, Lutheran Ch. of Good Shepherd, Tulsa, 1975; soloist Grace Luth. Ch., Tulsa, 1978; annual speaker Southeast Rotary, Tulsa, 1979. Served to 1st lt. USAF, 1957-60. Named Outstanding Prof., Oral Roberts U. Regents, 1978. Mem. Adminstrv. Mgmt. Soc., Pi Gamma Mu, Delta Sigma Pi, Alpha Phi Omega. Democrat. Avocations: tennis; gardening. Home: 7814 S Florence Ave Tulsa OK 74136 Office: Oral Roberts U 7777 S Lewis Tulsa OK 74171

GILLESPIE, DAVID MARSTON, librarian; b. Webster Springs, W.Va., Aug. 19, 1938; s. Clarence Ward and Bertha Mae (Baughman) W.; m. Yvonne Row, Aug. 23, 1964; 1 dau., Erica Sue. A.B., Glenville State U., 1964; M.L.S., Ind. U., 1968; A.M.L.S., Fla. State U., 1976, Ph.D., 1980. Librarian, Hampshire County Schs., Romney, W.Va., 1964-65, St. Michaels High Sch. (Md.), 1965-66; library dir. Glenville State Coll. (W.Va.), 1968—; cons. Gilmer Pub. Library, 1974—. Editor: Obituaries 1935-1980, 4 vols., 1980; WV Hillbilly: Index, 1979; author: Prison Libraries: Bibliography, 1979. Mayor, City of Glenville, 1973-75, 82—; sec. Glenville State Coll. Fed. Credit Union, 1978—; v.p. W.Va. State Folk Festival Inc., 1979. Recipient Alumni Service award Glenville State Coll. Alumni Assn., 1984. Mem. ALA, W.Va. Library Assn. (service award 1982), Glenville State Coll. Alumni Found., Southeastern Library Assn., Beta Phi Mu. Democrat. Presbyterian. Club: Rotary (pres. 1972-73, Service Above Self award 1983).

GILLESPIE, EDWARD MALCOLM, hospital administrator; b. Mpls., Oct. 19, 1935; s. Harold Livingston and Alice May (Thompson) G.; B.S., U. Minn., 1957, M.P.A., 1959, M.H.A., 1962; m. Magda Armeanu, Mar. 12, 1960; children—Karin, Timothy, Kenneth. Engaged in refugee adminstrn., Linz, Austria, 1958-60; asst. adminstr. Lutheran Med. Center, Denver, 1962-66; asst. gen. sec. Methodist Bd. Health and Welfare Ministries, Evanston, Ill., 1966-69; adminstr. Meth. Hosp., Rochester, Minn., 1969-74, Univ. Hosp., Augusta, Ga., 1974—; bd. dirs. Augusta Area Mental Health, Augusta Speech and Hearing Center, St. John's Towers, CSRA Blood Assurance; chmn. hosp. div. certification council Meth. Health and Welfare. Bd. dirs. local United Way. Boy Scouts Am. Fellow Am. Coll. Hosp. Adminstrs.; mem. Am., Ga. hosp. assns. Methodist. Club: Augusta Rotary (dir.). Home: 705 Gary St Augusta GA 30904 Office: 1350 Walton Way Augusta GA 30910

GILLESPIE, GEORGE CLIFFORD, JR., educational administrator, consultant; b. Nashville, June 2, 1948; s. George Clifford and Anne Carlotte (Watson) G.; m. Gayle Lyons, July 21, 1971; children—Matthew Mead, Lauren Katherine, Michael Clifford. B.S., Middle Tenn. State U., 1970, M. Ed., 1971; Ph.D., Peabody Coll. of Vanderbilt U., 1976. Asst. dir. records Middle Tenn. State U., Murfreesboro, 1970-73, dir. records, 1973-76, dean, admissions, records and info. systems, 1976—; cons. Wayne State U., Detroit, 1985, Bethel Coll., McKenzie, Tenn., 1985. Editor: Management of Student Aid, 1978. Mem. Peabody Coll. Alumni (pres. elect 1985—), So. Assn. Collegiate Registrars and Admissions Officers (local arrangements chmn. 1980-81, Disting. Service award 1981), Tenn. Assn. Collegiate Registrars and Admissions Officers (pres. 1980-81), Am. Assn. Collegiate Registrars and Admissions Officers (sec., treas. 1983—). Democrat. Roman Catholic. Lodge: Rotary. Avocations: gardening; horse show announcing. Home: 721 N Tennessee Blvd Murfreesboro TN 37130-4011 Office: 210 Cope Bldg Middle Tenn State U Murfreesboro TN 37132-0001

GILLESPIE, JOHN DAVID, political science educator; b. Oxford, N.C., Sept. 22, 1944; s. Arthur Samuel and Pauline Montague (Pittard) G.; m. Judi Kathleen Flowers, June 11, 1966. B.A., Wake Forest U., 1966, M.A., 1967; Ph.D., Kent State U., 1973. Instr., history and polit. sci. Davidson Community Coll., Lexington, N.C., 1967-70; asst. prof. polit. sci. Samford U., Birmingham, Ala., 1973-79; assoc. prof. polit. sci. Presbyterian Coll., Clinton, S.C., 1979—, chmn. dept. polit. sci., 1985—. Author: (with others) Employment and Labor Relations Policy, 1980. Contbr. articles to profl. jours. County coordinator Mondale-Ferraro Campaign, Laurens County, S.C., 1984; mem., platform and resolutions com. S.C. Democratic Conv., Columbia, 1984. NDEA Title IV fellow, 1970-73; grantee NEH 1978, Samford U., Presbyterian Coll. Mem. Am. Polit. Sci. Assn., So. Polit. Sci. Assn., S.C. Polit. Sci. Assn. (v.p. 1984-85, pres. 1985-86), Pi Gamma Mu (guest lectr. Samford U. 1984). United Methodist. Lodge: Kiwanis. Avocations: music, travel, golf, short-wave radio. Home: 103 Pinehurst Dr Clinton SC 29325 Office: Presbyterian Coll Dept Polit Sci Clinton SC 29325

GILLESPIE, VIRGIL GRIFFITH, lawyer; b. Meridian, Mis., Aug. 12, 1940; s. Robert Gill and Margaret (Griffith) G.; m. Helen Denny Jackson, Dec. 28, 1963; children—Margaret Amanda, Amy Elizabeth. B.S., U. So. Miss., 1963; J.D., U. Miss., 1965. Bar: Miss. 1965, U.S. Dist. Ct. (so. dist.) Miss. 1965, U.S. Ct. Appeals (5th cir.) 1982. Assoc., Mize, Thompson & Mize, 1965-66; ptnr. Hewes, Gillespie & Lenoir, 1967-70; ptnr. Gillespie & Lenoir, 1970-76; sole practice, Gulport, Miss., 1976—; adj. prof. law Miss. Coll. Law, 1979. Fellow Miss. Bar Found.; mem. Harrison County Bar Assn. (sec. 1967-71), Harrison County Law Library Commn. (sec. 1967-82), Miss. State Bar Assn. Democrat. Presbyterian. Home: 262 Southern Circle Gulfport MS 39501 Office: 1911 23d Ave Gulfport MS 39501

GILLESPIE, WAYNE THOMAS, hospital official; b. Shreveport, La., July 27, 1945; s. Oscar Nolte and Eunice Mildred (Spinks) G.; Med. Technician, Mid-State Coll. Med. Arts, 1965; m. Sandra Jeanne Read, Sept. 13, 1964; children—Andrea Michelle, Carla Renee. Staff technologist Doctors Hosp. and Research Found., Shreveport, La., 1964-66, Bedford County Gen. Hosp., Shelbyville, Tenn., 1966-69, staff and chief technologist, 1969-71; chief technologist Choctaw County Hosp., Ackerman, Miss., 1969; charge technologist mobile component lab. ARC, Nashville, 1971-73; lab. sales rep. Gen. Med., Nashville, 1973; asst. lab. supr. Goodall Clinic and Hosp., Smyrna, Tenn., 1973-74; dir. ancillary services Tipton County Meml. Hosp., Covington, Tenn., 1974-83; mgr. Aware: Indsl. Screening Program, Bapt. Meml. Hosp., Memphis, 1984—. Instl. rep. Big Hatchie council Boy Scouts Am., 1975-76, med. adv. Med. Explorer Post 262, 1978-80; mem. steering com. Tipton County Blood Program, ARC; pres. Holmes Sch. PTA, Covington, 1979; coach, umpire Dixie Youth Baseball and Softball League. Served with USAF, 1966. Recipient gov.'s Outstanding Tennessean award, 1979; cert. clin. lab. technologist HEW; cert. lab. supr., Tenn. Mem. Am. Soc. Med. Technologists (cert., nat. com. public relations 1978-79, Disting. Achievement award 1975), Tenn. Hosp. Assn., Tenn. Soc. Hosp. Public Relations Coordinators, Tenn. Soc. Med. Technologists, Tenn. State Soc. of Am. Med. Technologists (awards of merit 1972, 76, dir. 1973-78, mem. and chmn. coms.). Presbyterian. Club: Covington Exchange (pres. 1978-79). Contbr. articles to publs. in field. Home: 938 Vandergrift Dr Covington TN 38019 Office: 899 Madison Ave Memphis TN 38146

GILLETT, VICTOR WILLIAM, JR., insurance executive; b. El Paso, Tex., Feb. 4, 1932; s. Victor William and Alice Cecelia (Kemper) G.; m. Anita Johanne Dexter, Mar. 1, 1975; children—Victor William III, Blake Andrew. B.B.A., Tex. A&M U., 1953. Vice pres., dist. mgr. Stewart Title Guaranty Co., Corpus Christi, Tex., 1955-61; pres., chief exec. officer Stewart Title & Trust Co., Phoenix, 1961-77, dir., 1965-77; sr. v.p., nat. mktg. dir. Stewart Title Guaranty Co., Houston, 1977—; dir. Stewart Title Co. Tex., 1955-65; dir. Stewart Title Guaranty Co., Stewart Info. Services Corp. Bd. dirs. Ariz. Heart Assn., 1970-73; bd. dirs., sec. Phoenix Civic Improvement Corp., 1974-76. Served with AUS, 1953-55. Mem. Am. Land Title Assn. (gov. 1969-71), Tex. Land Title Assn., Nat. Assn. Corp. Real Estate Execs., Mortgage Bankers Assn., Am. Nat. Assn. Indsl. and Office Parks, Internat. Council Shopping Ctrs., Nat. Assn. Real Estate Investment Trusts, Assn. U.S. Army (pres., dir. Phoenix chpt. 1968), Navy League, Newcomen Soc. N.Am., Former Students Assn. Tex. A&M U. Episcopalian. Clubs: Houstonian; Aggie (Tex. A&M U.). Home: 2803 Fairway Dr Sugar Land TX 77478 Office: 2200 W Loop S Houston TX 77027

GILLETTE, JAMES THOMAS, III, real estate development company executive, residential home builder; b. Utica, N.Y., Dec. 16, 1944; s. James Thomas and Margurite (Adams) G.; m. Michele Tucker, Jan. 11, 1975. B.S. in Civil Engring., Va. Mil. Inst., 1970. Sales exec. C. Heath & Assocs., Richmond, Va., 1971-75; pres. Gillette & Co., Richmond, 1976-82; v.p. sales and mktg. Argyle Forest, Inc., Jacksonville, Fla., 1982-84, pres. Argyle, Div. Gulfstream Land and Devel. Corp., 1984—; ptnr. G & L Assocs., Richmond, 1980—. Served to 1st lt. U.S. Army, 1967-69; Vietnam. Mem. Urban Land Inst., Nat. Assn. Home Builders, Nat. Assn. Realtors, Va. Assn. Realtors (dir. 1978-81), Jacksonville C. of C. Republican. Methodist. Home: 10340 Sequoya Dr Jacksonville FL 32217 Office: Argyle Forest Inc 8351 Westport Rd Jacksonville FL 32244

GILLEY, JERRY WAYNE, marketing educator; b. Beech Grove, Ind., Oct. 26, 1951; s. Bert B. and Lottie (Stallard) G.; m. M. Gail Alderman, Feb. 4, 1976; children—Andrea, Melissa, Shannon, Michael. A.A.S., Vincennes U., 1971; B.S. magna cum laude, Mankato State U., 1974; M.S., Baptist Christian U., 1982; M.A., La. Tech. U., 1983; Ed.D., Okla. State U., 1985. Coordinator, Ind. Dept. Pub. Instrn., Indpls., 1971-72; mdse. and ops. mgr. Team Electronic, Iowa and Ill., 1979-81; prin. Grace Christian Sch., Marion, Iowa, 1979-81, Bapt. Christian Acad., Shreveport, La., 1981-83; teaching assoc. Okla. State U., Stillwater, 1983-85; asst. prof. U. Central Ark., Conway, 1985—. Contbr. articles to profl. jours. Mem. Am. Assn. Adult and Continuing Edn. (research program chair 1985 conf.), Am. Soc. Tng. and Devel., Am. Vocat. Assn., Mktg. and Distributive Edn. Assn., Phi Kappa Phi, Distributive Edn. Clubs Am. (nat. v.p. 1971-72). Republican. Baptist. Avocation: classical and jazz music. Home: UCA PO Box 955 Conway AR 72032 Office: Univ Central Arkansas Coll Bus Adminstrn Conway AR 72032

GILLIAM, M(ELVIN) RANDOLPH, urologist; b. Elliott County, Ky., Jan. 5, 1921; s. Adolphus and Grace (Thornsberry) G.; m. Sara Dee Rainey, May 15, 1948; children—Elizabeth Neal, Virginia Dee, Bryan Randolph, Frank Stuart, Grace Carroll. Student Centre Coll. of Ky., 1938-41; M.D., U. Louisville, 1944. Diplomate Am. Bd. Urology. Intern, Norfolk (Va.) Marine Hosp., 1944-45; resident in urology Nichols VA Hosp., Louisville, 1947-50; practice medicine specializing in urology, Lexington, Ky., 1950—; pres. Gilliam, Ray, Hellebusch & Blackburn, P.S.C., Lexington, 1971—; assoc. clin. prof. urology, U. Ky. Med. Sch., 1964—; chief of urology Good Samaritan Hosp.; mem. staff Central Baptist Hosp., St. Joseph's Hosp. Served to capt. U.S. Army, 1945-47. Mem. AMA, Ky. Med. Assn., Fayette County Med. Soc. (past pres.), Am. Urology Assn. Republican. Methodist. Home: 1244 Summit Dr Lexington KY 40502 Office: 2101 Nicholasville Rd Lexington KY 40503

GILLIKIN, LYNN SCHULZ, psychologist; b. Camden, N.J., Dec. 10, 1945; d. Charles Leighton and Beulah (Eckard) Skerrett; m. Joseph J. Schulz, Aug. 10, 1968 (div. 1980); children—David, Sarah, Robert; m. Dennis O'Neill Gillikin, Apr. 30, 1983; 1 child, Christopher. A.B., Coll. William and Mary, 1967; M.A., U. Va., 1969, Ph.D., 1970. Lic. psychologist, Va. Asst. prof. U. Del., Newark, 1970-73; assoc. dean students, asst. prof. Coll. William and Mary, Williamsburg, Va., 1973-75; pvt. practice Counseling Services, Va., 1975—. Contbr. articles to profl. jours. Bd. dirs. Am. Cancer Soc., Newport News, Va., 1979-85. Mem. Am. Psychol. Assn., Southeastern Psychol. Assn., Va. Psychol. Assn., Phi Beta Kappa, Sigma Xi, Phi Sigma, Psi Chi. Roman Catholic. Avocation: bicycling. Home: 111 Tipton Rd Newport News VA 23666 Office: Hampton Counseling Services 2112 A Exec Dr Hampton VA 23666

GILLILAN, WILLIAM J., III, constrn. co. exec.; b. Pitts., June 20, 1946; s. William J., II and Sara Parker (Wynn) G.; B.S. in Indsl. Engring. with honors, Purdue U., 1968; M.B.A., Harvard U., 1970; m. Susan Woodyard, June 20, 1970; children—William J., Mary, John C., Mark. With Centex Homes, Inc., 1974—, exec. v.p. ops. Centex Homes Midwest, Inc., Palatine, Ill., 1978, pres., 1978-83; v.p. Centex Homes Corp., 1980-83, exec. v.p., 1983-84, chief operating officer, 1984—. Served to lt. USNR, 1970-74. Mem. Delta Tau Delta. Republican. Presbyterian. Clubs: Brookhaven Country (Dallas); Westmoreland Country (Wilmette, Ill.). Home: 6115 Shadycliff Dr Dallas TX 75240 Office: Republic Nat Bank Tower Dallas TX

GILLILAND, MICHAEL BURTON, employee relations executive; b. Lynchburg, Va., Feb. 3, 1953; s. William Carroll and Edith (Burton) G. B.A., Lynchburg Coll., 1975. Cert. secondary tchr., Va. Tchr., Campbell County Schs., Rustburg, Va., 1975-79; personnel mgr. Winebarger Corp., Lynchburg, Va., 1979-81; supr. employee relations Manville Corp., Cleburne, Tex., 1981-83, mgr. employee relations, 1983—. Fellow Am. Soc. Personnel Adminstrn., Greater Athens Personnel Assn. Republican. Baptist. Avocations: tennis; swimming. Home: Route Box 908 Cleveland TN 37311 Office: Manville Corp Route 411 N Etowah TN 37331

GILLIS, ESTEN JOHNSON, nurse artist; b. Duplin County, N.C., June 20, 1923; d. John Perry and Alice (Rouse) Johnson; m. Rudolph F. Hasty, Jan. 8, 1955 (div. 1968); m. 2d, William Arthur Gillis, May 26, 1972 (dec. 1980). R.N. diploma James Walker Hosp., Wilmington, N.C., 1944. R.N., Tex., N.C.; cert. in ob-gyn. Supr. Margaret Hague Hosp., Jersey City, 1945; staff nurse labor, delivery Binghamton City Hosp. (N.Y.), 1945-47; obstet. nurse Wesley Long Hosp., Greensboro, N.C., 1947-48, Seaside Hosp., Long Beach, Calif., 1948-50; night supr. Sampson County Meml. Hosp., Clinton, N.C., 1950-54; head obstet. nurse St. Luke Hosp., Jacksonville, Fla., 1955—; staff nurse, med.-surg. Garrison Hosp., Gastonia, N.C., 1956—; pvt. duty nurse, El Paso, Tex., 1957-63; asst. dir. Nursing SW Hosp., El Paso, 1963-68; nurse ICU, Marin Gen. Hosp., San Rafael, Calif., 1968-69; staff nurse VA Hosp., Charleston, S.C., 1969-75, Dosher Meml. Hosp., Southport, N.C., 1982-83; painter multi-media landscape, 1966—; potter, 1976—; pottery exhibited Franklin Sq. Gallery, Southport, N.C. Mem. Tex. Nurses Assn. (pres. dist. 1 1968), Associated Artists Southport (sec. 1982, 83), Brunswick Arts Council, Democrat. Methodist. Home: 614 Caswell Beach Rd Southport NC 28461

GILLIS, PETER PAUL, engineering educator; b. Newport, R.I., Dec. 23, 1930; s. James Aloysious and Agnes Ursula (Beattie) G.; m. Donna Jean Mason, May 10, 1980; children—Paul, Andrew, James, Mary, Douglas, Eric. Sc.B. in Engring., Brown U., 1953, Sc.M. in Engring., 1961, Ph.D., 1964. Registered profl. engr., Ky. Prodn. engr. Fram Corp., East Providence, R.I., 1956-57; devel. engr. Leesona Corp., Cranston, R.I., 1957-58; instr. R.I. Sch. Design, Providence, 1958-59; research asst. Brown U., Providence, 1959-64; prof. engring. U. Ky., Lexington, 1964—, chmn. dept. metall. engring. and materials sci., 1982—; cons. Spindletop Research, Inc., Lexington, 1964-66, Lawrence Livermore Lab., Calif., 1965-73, Los Alamos Sci. Lab., 1967-79, AEC Directorate Regulatory Ops., Washington, 1970-73. Contbg. author: Metals Handbook, 9th edit., Handbook Physical and Mechanical Testing Paper and Paperboard. Contbr. articles to profl. jours. Served as lt. (j.g.) USN, 1953-56; Atlantic. Fulbright research fellow U.S.-N.Z. Ednl. Found., Wellington, N.Z., 1970-71. Fellow Am. Soc. for Metals; mem. AIME, ASME, Fedn. Am. Scientists, Vols. for Internat. Tech. Assistance, Nat. Rifle Assn., Ky. State Rifle and Pistol Assn., Bluegrass Sportsmen's League. Avocations: duplicate bridge; target shooting. Home: 209 Southpoint Dr Lexington KY 40503 Office: Dept Metall Engring U of Ky Lexington KY 40506

GILLMANN, MARY KATHERINE, architect, artist; b. San Antonio, Dec. 23, 1956; d. Robert W. and Dolores (Hay) G. B.S., Ga. Inst. Tech., 1981, M.Arch., 1984; M.S. in Indsl. Mgmt., 1984. Technical draftsman Henry Howard Smith & Assocs., Atlanta, 1979-80; resident hall dir. Ga. Inst. Tech., Atlanta, 1980-84; asst. project mgr. Atcan Bldg. Corp., Atlanta, 1984-85; architect Bank Bldg. Corp., Atlanta, 1985—; cons. in field. Tour cons. Atlanta Preservation Ctr., Atlanta, 1984-85; mem. Ga. Trust for Hist. Preservation, Atlanta, 1985. Mem. High Mus. Art, AIA (treas. student chpt. 1980), Atlanta Preservation Ctr. Republican. Episcopalian. Club: Young Careers. Avocations: raquetball; tennis; swimming. Office: Bank Bldg Corp 2635 Century Pkwy Atlanta GA 30345

GILLULY, C(HRISTOPHER) W(ILLIAM), computer systems company executive, consultant, former naval officer; b. London, Dec. 18, 1945; came to U.S., 1946; s. John William and Carol Miriam (Carroll) G. B.S.M.E., Marquette U., 1967; M.A. in Adminstrn., Chapman Coll., 1974; Ed.D. in Ednl. Adminstrn., Catholic U. Am., 1982; grad. Naval War Coll., 1976. Commd. ensign U.S. Navy, 1967, advanced through grades to lt. comdr., 1976; naval aviator Vietnam, 1980-81; resigned, 1981; co-founder, pres. chmn. bd. Micro Research, Inc., Falls Church, Va. Pres. Cyrandall Valley Homeowners Assn., 1982-83; campaign mgr. Steve Armstrong for Providence Dist. Supr., Falls Church, 1983. Decorated Air Medal (12). Mem. D.C. Bd. Trade, Greater Washington Soc. Assn. Execs. Republican. Roman Catholic. Office: 7202 Arlington Blvd Falls Church VA 22042

GILMAN, SHELDON G., lawyer; b. Cleve., July 20, 1943. B.B.A., Ohio U., 1965; J.D., Case Western Res. U., 1967. Bar: Ohio 1967, Ky. 1971, Ind. 1982, Fla. 1984, D.C. 1985, Tenn. 1985. Mem. staff accts. tax dept. Arthur Andersen & Co., Cleve., 1967-68; assoc. Handmaker, Weber & Meyer, Louisville, 1971-74, ptnr., 1974-84; ptnr. Barnett & Alagia, Louisville, 1984—; gen. counsel Louisville Assn. Life Underwriters, 1977, 78. Bd. dirs., chmn. Louisville Minority Bus. Resource Ctr., 1975—; bd. dirs. Louisville Orch., 1982—, v.p., sec., 1983-84; pres., bd. dirs. Congregation Adath Jeshurun; bd. dirs. City of Devondale (Ky.), 1976. Served with JAGC, AUS, 1968-71. Mem. Ky. Bar Assn. (ethics com. 1982—), Louisville Employee Benefit Council (pres. 1980). Office: 444 S 5th St Louisville KY 40202

GILMER, ERNEST VERNON, JR., electronics engineer, physicist; b. Birmingham, Ala., Nov. 29, 1949; s. Ernest Vernon and Betty Jean (Tate) G.; m. Linder Cecile Smith, Mar. 9, 1974; children—Marcus Daniel, Cynthia Leia. B.S. with honors, Samford U., 1971; M.S. in Physics, U. Ala.-Huntsville, 1985. Commd. officer U.S. Navy, 1971, advanced through grades to lt., 1981; ret., 1981; sr. engr. Wyle Labs., Huntsville, Ala., 1981-82; specialist engr. Boeing Mil. Airplane Co., Huntsville, 1982-84, Boeing Aerospace Co., Huntsville, 1984—. Sec. Huntsville Ala. L5 Soc., 1983-85. Mem. Am. Phys. Soc., Math. Assn. Am. Baptist. Club: Huntsville Amateur Radio. Avocations: amateur radio; literature; classical music. Home: 718 Graycroft Dr SW Huntsville AL 35802

GILMER, PENNY JANE, biochemistry educator; b. Hackensack, N.J., Aug. 19, 1943; d. Peter E. and Barbara D. (Joynt) G.; m. Sanford A. Safron, Sept. 9, 1980; children—Helena M., Nathaniel S. B.A. in Chemistry, Douglass Coll., 1965; M.A. in Organic Chemistry, Bryn Mawr Coll., 1967; Ph.D. in Biochemistry, U. Calif.-Berkeley, 1972. Bank Am.-Giannini postdoctoral fellow Stanford U. (Calif.), 1973-75, USPHS and NIH postdoctoral fellow, 1975-77, acting asst. prof. human biology, 1976-77; from asst. prof. to assoc. prof. biochemistry, Fla. State U., Tallahassee, 1977-84; lectr. in field. Recipient faculty research award Fla. State U., 1978, 84; grantee NIH, 1979-81, Research

Corp., 1979—, Am. Cancer Soc., 1981-83. Mem. Fedn. Biol. Chemists, Am. Chem. Soc., AAAS, Sierra Club, Audubon Soc., Southeastern Immunology Conf. (dir. 1979—, pres. 1982—), Assn. Women in Sci., Sigma Xi. Democrat. Contbr. numerous articles to profl. jours. Office: Dept Chemistry Fla State U Tallahassee FL 32306

GILMER, ROBERT, mathematics educator; b. Pontotoc, Miss., July 3, 1938; s. Robert William and Lucy Marie (Jernigan) G.; m. Rachel Grace Colson, Aug. 24, 1963; children—David Patrick, Stephen Douglas. Student Itawamba Jr. Coll., 1955-56; B.S., Miss. State U., 1958; M.S., La. State U., 1960, Ph.D., 1961. Instr. Miss. State U., Starkville, 1959; research instr. La. State U., Baton Rouge, 1961-62; vis. prof. Miss. State U., Starkville, 1962; vis. lectr. U. Wis., Madison, 1962-63; asst. prof. Fla. State U., Tallahassee, 1963-65, assoc. prof., 1965-68, prof., 1968-81, Robert O. Lawton Disting. prof., 1981—; vis. prof. Latrobe U., Bundoora, Victoria, Australia, 1974, U. Tex., Austin, 1976-77; vis. research prof. U. Conn., Storrs, 1982. Office of Naval Research fellow, 1962-63; Alfred P. Sloan Found. fellow, 1965-67; NSF grantee, 1965—; Fulbright sr. research scholar, Australia, 1974. Mem. Am. Math. Soc., Math. Assn. Am. Baptist. Author: Multiplicative Ideal Theory, 1967; Multiplicative Ideal Theory, 1972; Commutative Semigroup Rings, 1984; assoc. editor Am. Math. Monthly, 1971-73; mem. editorial bd. Jour. Communications in Algebra, 1974. Office: Fla State U Math Dept Tallahassee FL 32306

GILMORE, ARTIS, professional basketball player; b. Chipley, Fla., Sept. 21, 1949. Grad., Jacksonville U., 1971. Center Ky. Cols., Louisville, 1971-76; with Chgo. Bulls, 1976-82, San Antonio Spurs, 1982—; mem. Am. Basketball Assn. All-Star team, 1972-76, Nat. Basketball Assn. All-Star Team, 1978. Named Rookie of the Year Am. Basketball Assn., 1972, Player of the Year, 1972. Address: care San Antonio Spurs HemisFair Arena PO Box 530 San Antonio TX 78292*

GILMORE, HUGH REDLAND, lawyer, ret. govt. ofcl.; b. Bristol, Vt., Aug. 13, 1916; s. John R. and Rubie (Rathbun) G.; Ph.B. magna cum laude, U. Vt., 1937; J.D., Columbia U., 1941; m. Marjorie V. Havens, May 8, 1942; children—Douglas H., Anne C., Joan L. Admitted to Vt. bar, 1946, N.Y. State bar, 1948; asso. firm Sylvester & Ready, St. Albans, Vt., 1946-47; atty.-adviser Office Gen. Counsel Air Force, Office Sec. Air Force, Washington, 1949-54, asst. gen. counsel Air Force for personnel and adminstrn., 1954-74, asst. gen. counsel for personnel and fiscal matters, 1974-75; ret., 1975. Served to maj. AUS, 1942-46, 47-49; col. Air Force Res. Decorated Asiatic-Pacific ribbon with 3 bronze stars, Phillippine Liberation ribbon with 1 bronze star; recipient Exceptional Civilian Service award U.S. Air Force, 1965; cert. of spl. recognition Sec. Air Force, 1969. Mem. Phi Beta Kappa, Pi Gamma Mu. Mason. Clubs: Overlee Community Assn., Arlington Forest (past dir.). Home: 3020 N Nottingham St Arlington VA 22207

GILMORE, LLOYD MARSHALL, printing company executive; b. Petrolia, Tex., Mar. 22, 1925; s. Ralph E. and Lucille (Price) G.; m. Nancy Bliss Hunter, Nov. 27, 1948; children—Martha Catherine Weigel, Carol Ann Markham. B.B.A., So. Meth. U., 1949. Salesman display advt. Dallas Morning News, 1949-50; supr. stores 7-Eleven div. Southland Corp., Houston, 1950-53; sales rep. William S. Henson Printing Co., Dallas, 1953-57, pres., 1957-61; chmn. bd. The Riverside Press, Inc., 1961—. Pres., Southwest Sch. Printing Mgmt. Found., 1960-63; pres. Camp Fire Girls Dallas County, 1965. Served with USNR, 1942-45. Mem. Printing Industries Am., Nat. Assn. Printers and Lithographers (chmn.), Graphic Arts Tech. Found. Methodist. Clubs: Northwood, Tower (Dallas). Home: 11355 Royalshire Dr Dallas TX 75230 Office: 4901 Woodall St Dallas TX 75247

GILMORE, PAUL WILLIAM, dentist; b. Michigan City, Ind., Dec. 14, 1927; s. Wallace Lewis and Jessie Margaret (Barnett) G.; m. Melva Lee Martin, Feb. 20, 1948; children—Gail Senn, Martin Paul. A.B. in Chemistry, Franklin Coll., 1953; D.D.S., Ind. U., 1957. Practice gen. dentistry, Charleston, S.C., 1957—. Served to sgt. USMC, 1946-50. Mem. Charleston Dental Soc. (pres. 1968-69), Coastal Dist. Dental Soc. (pres. 1961-62), S.C. Dental Soc., ADA, Omni Investment Club (sec.). Episcopalian (past sr. warden). Clubs: Charleston Country, Exchange. Avocations: Golf; fishing. Home: 30 Broughton Rd Charleston SC 29407 Office: 1243 Savannah Hwy Charleston SC 29407

GILMORE, ROBERT BEATTIE, petroleum engineer; b. Tulsa, July 26, 1913; s. Charles R. and Davida (Smith) G.; m. Kathleen Jesse Kirk, Dec. 25, 1940; children—Elizabeth G., Judy, Charlotte Patricia, Sally Kirk. B.S. in Petroleum Engring., U. Tulsa, 1939. Engr., Shell Oil Co., Tulsa, 1934-41; v.p., dir. DeGolyer & MacNaughton, 1949-62, pres., 1962, chmn. bd., 1967, sr. chmn., 1972, vice chmn. exec. com., 1978—; dir. Whitehall Corp., Dallas, Valero Energy Corp., San Antonio. Mem. Bd. Edn., Dallas Ind. Sch. Dist., 1955-64, pres. 1964; mem. Tex. Dept. Water Resources, 1965-78, vice chmn., 1972-78; trustee Children's Med. Ctr., 1955—. Named Disting. Alumnus, U. Tulsa Alumni Assn., 1972. Mem. Soc. Petroleum Engrs. of AIME (DeGolyer Disting. Service medal 1975), Interstate Oil Compact Commn., Am. Assn. Petroleum Geologists. Democrat. Methodist. Clubs: Northwood, Engrs., Lancers (Dallas.). Contbr. articles to profl. jours. Home: 6246 Prestonshire Lane Dallas TX 75225 Office: One Energy Sq Suite 400 Dallas TX 75206

GILSTRAP, JOE JACKSON, insurance executive; b. Pickens, S.C., Apr. 21, 1923; s. Luther Hubbard and Ethel Bulah (Massey) G.; B.A., Furman U., Greenville, S.C., 1948; m. Esterlene Burroughs, Dec. 22, 1945; children—Carol, Donald. Asst. treas. Liberty Life Ins. Co., Greenville, 1948—; v.p. Hampton Ins. Agency, 1969; ins. mgr. Liberty Corp., Greenville, 1970-75, asst. v.p., risk mgr., 1975—; chmn. ins. com. City of Greenville, 1983—. Served with USNR, 1943-46. Fellow Life Office Mgmt. Assn., Risk and Ins. Mgmt. Soc. (nat. bd. dirs., former sec., treas., v.p., pres. Western Carolinas chpt., v.p. Carolina chpt.). Methodist (chmn. coms., tchr., trustee, vice chmn. adminstrv. bd.). Mason (Shriner). Home: 34 Lockwood Ave Greenville SC 29607 Office: PO Box 789 Greenville SC 29602

GINDY, BENJAMIN LEE, insurance executive; b. Detroit, July 23, 1929; s. Roy E. and Anne M. Gindy; B.S., U. Fla., 1951; cert. Disability Ins. Tng. Council; m. Judith Youngerman, Dec. 20, 1953; children—Deborah, Daniel, David. Field rep. Penn Mut. Ins. Co., 1957-59; brokerage mgr. Mass. Indemnity Co., Miami, Fla., 1959-68; gen. agt. Guardian Life Ins. Co. Am., Miami, 1968—; pres. Internat. Risk Cons. Inc.; partner Party Magic; instr. Life Underwriter Tng. Council, C.L.U. diploma course U. Miami; past columnist Miami Rev.; guest speaker Fla. State U., Notre Dame U., various ins. meetings. Recipient Nat. Health Ins. award Guardian Life Ins. Co. Am., 1977. C.L.U. Mem. Am. Soc. C.L.U.'s (past pres. Miami chpt.), S. Fla. Inter-Profl. Council (past pres.), Gen. Agts. and Mgrs. Assn. (past pres.), Miami Assn. Life Underwriters (past pres., Man of Year award), Internat. Assn. Fin. Planning. Home: 1018 Aduana Ave Coral Gables FL 33146 Office: 7615 SW 62d Ave South Miami FL 33143

GINGRICH, NEWTON LEROY, congressman; b. Harrisburg, Pa., June 17, 1943; s. Robert Bruce and Kathleen (Daugherty) G.; m. Jacqueline Battley, June 19, 1962 (div. 1981); children—Linda Kathleen, Jacqueline Sue; m. Marianne Ginther, Aug. 1981. B.A., Emory U., 1965; M.A., Tulane U., 1968, Ph.D., 1971. Faculty West Ga. Coll., Carrollton, 1970-78, prof. history, to 1978; mem. 96th-99th congresses from 6th Dist. Ga. Mem. AAAS, World Futurist Soc., Ga. Conservancy. Republican. Baptist. Clubs: Kiwanis, Moose. Office: 417 Cannon House Office Bldg Washington DC 20515*

GINN, RICHARD VAN NESS, army officer, health care executive; b. Miami, Fla., Mar. 23, 1943; s. Philander Jerome and Alida Loring (Van Ness) G.; m. Angelica Suarez, June 29, 1968; children—Angie Ann, Richard Van Ness. B.A., Stetson U., 1965; M.H.A., Baylor U., 1978; M.A., Duke U., 1980; grad. with honors U.S. Army Command and Gen. Staff Coll., 1981. Commd. 2d lt. U.S. Army, 1965, advanced through grades to lt. col.; chief force devel. and exec. sec. U.S. Army Med. Research and Devel. Adv. Panel, Washington, 1975-76; adminstrv. resident Asst. Sec. Def. for Health Affairs, Washington, 1977-78; profl. services adminstr. Brooke Army Med. Ctr., San Antonio, 1978-80; personnel policy officer Office of Army Surgeon Gen., Washington, 1981-83; spl. asst. chief Med. Service Corps, U.S. Army, Washington, 1983—; also served in Panama, Vietnam. Named Young Fed. Health Care Adminstr., Assn. Mil. Surgeons U.S., 1982, Disting. Hon. Grad. U.S. Army.-Baylor U. Program in Health Care Adminstrn., 1977; recipient Sir Henry Wellcome Medal and Prize, 1977, George Washington Honor medal Freedoms Found., 1978. Mem. Am. Coll. Healthcare Execs., Assn. of Health Care Adminstrs. of Nat. Capital Area (prizes scholarly competition 1982, 84), Fed. Health Care Execs. Inst. Alumni Assn. (v.p. 1985—), Am. Assn. for History of Medicine, Omicron Delta Kappa (chpt. pres. 1964-65), Sigma Tau Delta, Pi Kappa Phi. Club: Soc. of 173d Airborne Brigade. Home: 6825 Spring Beauty Ct Springfield VA 22152 Office: Hdqrs Dept of Army DASG-MS 5111 Leesburg Pike Falls Church VA 22041-3258

GINN, RONN, architect, urban planner, general contractor; b. Jacksonville, Fla., Apr. 17, 1933; s. Angus Theodore and Joan Adelaide (Bailey) G.; A.A., U. Fla., 1957, B.Arch., 1960, B.Landscape Architecture, 1961; m. Valerie Jeanne Broderson, Mar. 15, 1969; children—Sharon Lee, John Norman. Supervising architect, urban designer Roswell (N.Mex.) central bus. dist. redesign, 1964, Tucumcari (N.Mex.) central bus. dist. redesign, 1967, Treasure Island (Fla.) civic center design, 1971; architect, urban designer, prin. Atrium One, Albuquerque, 1965-67; urban design specialist Model Cities Adminstrn., HUD, Washington, 1967-68; practice architecture, constrn., urban planning, landscape architecture, St. Petersburg, Fla., 1968—; pres. ARG Constrn. Corp., 1975-76, ARG/Corp., 1977—, Ginn Corp., 1967-70, Atrium Corp., 1965-72; urban design lectr. U. N.Mex., 1967; planning cons. State Dept., 1967-68; design cons. Am. Revolution Bicentennial Commn., 1967-69; vis. design critic Rice U., 1974. Mem. Albuquerque Fine Arts Commn., 1965-67, St. Petersburg Design Goals Com., 1971-73; moderator radio program Design in Our Community, WPKM, Tampa, Fla., 1971-72; founder, bd. dirs. Pinellas County Red Flag Charrette, 1972—, Catalyst, St. Petersburg; bd. dirs. Fla. Council Clean Air, Fla. Red Flag Charrette; mem. Pinellas County Planning Council, 1972-73. Mayoral candidate City of Treasure Island, Fla., 1973; bldg. dir. City of Seminole, 1975-78; mem. Leadership St. Petersburg, 1978—. Recipient numerous archtl., landscape architecture, urban design awards. Mem. AIA (nat. com. on regional devel. 1969-76, vice chmn., commr. public affairs Fla. chpt.), Am. Inst. Planners, Constrn. Specifications Inst., Am. Inst. Landscape Architects, So. Bldg. Code Congress, Fla. Planning and Zoning Assn. Republican. Presbyterian. Contbg. editor Urban Affairs Symposia, 1965-73; guest columnist St. Petersburg Evening Independent, 1974. Important works include Albuquerque central bus. dist. redesign (nat. AIA award 1966), new town Fla. Center (nat. Am. Soc. Landscape Architects award 1970), Brown residence (AIA Merit award 1975); Penguin Restaurant, Treasure Island, Fla., 1973; Cross residence, 1974; Sheridan Gallery, 1974; Madeira Beach C. of C., 1975; Greenpepper Restaurant, 1975; Mixon Bldg., Ruskin, Fla., 1976; Congregation Beth Chai Synagogue, Seminole, Fla., 1979, Villa Dos Santos Master Plan, St. Petersburg Beach, Fla., 1979, Congregation Kol Ami, Tampa, 1981, Markham Residence, St. Petersburg, 1981, Moorings, Tierra Verde, Fla., 1981, Ginn Residence, St. Petersburg, 1981, Congregation B'nai Israel Synagogue, Clearwater, 1981, Suncoast Seabird Sanctuary, St. Petersburg, 1982, Lilly Residence, Treasure Island, 1983, 1600 Pasadena Office Bldg., South Pasadena, 1983. Home: 735 79 Circle S Saint Petersburg FL 33707 Office: Floor 14 One Plaza Pl Saint Petersburg FL 33701

GINORY, ANA CECILIA, computer programmer; b. Havana, Cuba, Dec. 6, 1956; came to U.S., 1961, naturalized, 1970; d. Roberto Loreto and Ana Luisa (Castellanos) G.; m. William Juan Nodal, June 6, 1981. B.S., Fla. Internat. U., 1979; A.A., Miami-Dade Community Coll., 1976. Student trainee NOAA-/AOML, Miami, Fla., 1978-80; computer programmer IV, Miami-Dade Community Coll., 1980—. Dept. coordinator Miami United Way, 1983. Roman Catholic. Home: 4914 SW 148th Pl Miami FL 33185 Office: Miami Dade Community Coll 11011 SW 104th St Miami FL 33176

GINSBERG, BERNARD LAWRENCE, medical marketing and management company executive; b. Albany, N.Y., May 9, 1946; s. Nathan David and Sylvia Dorothy (Schwartz) G. B.S., Southern Ill. U., 1970; M.A., Wayne State U., 1974; M.P.A., U. So. Calif., Los Angeles, 1981. Pres., Speech, Hearing Ctr., Hollywood, Fla., 1974-79; dir. audiology Centinela Hosp. Med. Ctr., Inglewood, Calif., 1979-80; chief exec. officer Norwalk Community Hosp., Calif., 1982-83, Chalmette Gen. Hosp., New Orleans, 1984-85; assoc. exec. dir. Doctors Hosp. Santa Ana, Calif., 1983-84; pres., owner M3 Med. Mktg. & Mgmt. Co., Los Angeles, 1985—. Cons. Health Adv. Com., 1982-83; bd. govs. Fedn. Am. Hosp. Adv., 1984—. Mem. Am. Coll. Hosp. Adminstrs., Am. Speech and Hearing Assn., U. So. Calif. Alumni Assn. Republican. Lodges: Lions, Kiwanis, B'Nai B'Rith. Avocations: piano; jogging; baseball; racquetball; coin and stamp collecting.

GINSBERG, LEON HERMAN, chancellor; b. San Antonio, Jan. 15, 1936; s. San and Lillian (Gindler) G.; m. Elaine Myrna Kaner, July 29, 1956 (div. 1983); children—Robert, Michael, Meryl Sue; m. Connie Mooney, June 2, 1983; stepchildren—Gretchen, Kathleen Mooney. B.A., Trinity U., 1957; M.S.W., Tulane U., 1959; Ph.D., U. Okla., 1966. Dist. dir. B'nai Brith Youth Orgn., New Orleans, 1958-61; dir. community activities Jewish Community Council, Tulsa, 1961-63; assoc. prof. Sch. Social Work U. Okla., Norman, 1963-68; prof., dir. Sch. Social Work W.Va. U., Morgantown, 1968-71, prof., dean, 1971-77; commr. human services State of W.Va., Charleston, 1977-84; chancellor W.Va. Bd. Regents for Higher Edn., 1984—; Fulbright prof. U. Pontifica Bolivariana, Medellin, Colombia, fall 1974; cons. tng. programs Peace Corps, Head Start, Community Action, Bur. Indian Affairs, pub. welfare depts. Okla. and Pa., Wis., W.Va. Co-author: Human Services for Older Adults, 1979; author: Social Work Practice in Public Welfare, 1983; editor: Social Work in Rural Communities, 1976; co-editor: Life-Span Developmental Psychology, 1975; contbr. articles to profl. jours. Served to lt. AUS, 1957-58. Recipient Disting. Service award W.Va. Welfare Conf., 1970; named W.Va. Social Worker of Yr., 1978; Disting. West Virginian, 1984. Mem. Council Social Work Edn., Nat. Assn. Social Workers, Am. Pub. Welfare Assn. (past pres.), Internat. Conf. on Social Welfare, Child Welfare League of Am. Lodge: B'nai Brith. Home: 3828 Virginia Ave Charleston WV 25304 Office: W Va Bd Regents 950 Kanawha Blvd E Charleston WV 25301

GINSBURG, MARK BARRY, sociology of education educator; b. Los Angeles, Dec. 9, 1949; s. Norman Leslie and Blanche Dorothy (Burg) G.; m. Barbara Iris Chasin, Sept. 5, 1971; children—Jolie Richele, Kevin Eran, Stephanie Alyse. A.B. in Sociology magna cum laude, Dartmouth Coll., 1972; M.A. in Sociology, UCLA, 1974, Ph.D. in Edn., 1976. Lectr. U. Aston, Eng., 1976-78; asst. prof. U. Houston, 1979-82, assoc. prof. sociology of edn., 1982—. Contbr. articles to profl. jours. Mem. steering com. Tex. Mobilization for Peace, Jobs and Justice, Houston, 1985—; mem. health and phys. edn. com. Jewish Community Ctr., Houston, 1982—. Rufus Choate scholar Dartmouth Coll., 1972. Mem. Comparative and Internat. Edn. Soc., Am. Ednl. Research Assn., British Sociol. Assn., Council on Anthropology and Edn. (co-chmn. transnat. issues com.), Phi Delta Kappa (research rep. 1983—). Avocation: Bicycle touring. Home: 4034 Leeshire Dr Houston TX 77025 Office: U Houston ELCS Coll Edn Houston TX 77004

GINTAUTAS, JONAS, neuroscientist, research adminstr., educator; b. Justinava, Lithuania, Oct. 3, 1939; s. Jonas and Elena (Zaveckaite) Sinsinas; came to U.S., 1967, naturalized, 1970; M.D., Moscow Med. Inst., 1967; Ph.D., Northwestern U., 1975; m. Kristina Zebrauskaite, June 13, 1970; children—Pasaka, Vadas. Physician in pediatric neurology Cook County Hosp., Chgo., 1968-1969; asso. prof. speech pathology and psychology, 1975-1977, dir. research grants, 1975-1977, research asso. Brain Research Labs., Health Scis. Center, 1977-1978; dir. research, asso. prof. anesthesiology Health Scis. Ctr., Lubbock, Tex., 1979—; cons. in field. NIH fellow, 1968-1970; Inst. Biomed. Research grantee. Mem. Am. Heart Assn., Internat. Anesthesia Research Soc., Soc. Neurosci., AAAS, Soc. for Research Adminstrs. Methodist. Contbr. articles to profl. jours. Research in higher cortical function disorders, neuropathologies of neuromuscular functioning and neurophysiology of brain-stem-spinal cord. Home: PO Box 911 El Paso TX 79982 Office: Tex Tech U Health Sci Center Sch Medicine Lubbock TX 79430

GIORDANO, JOHN READ, conductor; b. Dunkirk, N.Y., Dec. 31, 1937; s. John C. and Mildred G.; m. Sept. 3, 1960; children—Anne, Ellen, John. B.M., Tex. Christian U., 1960, M.M., 1962; grad.; Fulbright scholar, Royal Conservatory, Brussels, 1965. Mem. music faculty North Tex. State U., 1965-72; mem. faculty, condr. univ. symphony Tex. Christian U., 1972—; chmn. jury Van Cliburn Internat. Piano Competition, 1973, permanent jury chmn., 1974—; founder, condr. Tex. Little Symphony, 1976—. Appeared as saxophone soloist and with orchs., throughout Europe and U.S., 1965-72; music dir. youth Orch., Greater Ft. Worth, 1969—; guest condr., Ft. Worth Symphony, 1971; music dir. and condr., 1972—; guest condr. with various orchs., including, Nat. Symphony of Belgium, Nat. Symphony of El Salvador, Amsterdam Philharm., Brazilian Nat. Symphony, Belgian Nat. Radio Orch., Nat. Symphony of Portugal, English Chamber Orch.; Composer: Composition for Jazz Ensemble and Symphony Orchestra, 1974; subject of: feature film Symphony, 1978. Served with USAR, 1960-68. Recipient Premiere Prix with distinction Royal Conservatory, Brussels, 1965. Mem. Phi Mu Alpha Sinfonia, Phi Kappa Lambda, Kappa Kappa Psi.

GIRARDEAU, ARNETT E., state senator; b. Jacksonville, Fla., July 15, 1929; m. Matilda Carolyn Lee, 1966; children—Arnett, Arnetta C. D.D.S., Howard U. Former mem. Fla. Ho. of Reps.; now mem. Fla. Senate. Served with U.S. Army, 1952-54. Mem. Fla. Med., Dental and Pharm. Assn. (pres. 1967). Democrat. Methodist. Office: Fla Senate Senate Office Bldg Tallahassee FL 32304*

GIRDEN, ELLEN ROBINSON, psychology educator; b. Bklyn., May 14, 1936; d. Robert and Sarah (Bellinoff) Robinson; m. Edward Girden, Sept. 8, 1977. B.A., Bklyn. Coll., 1956, M.A., 1958; Ph.D., Northwestern U., 1962. Instr. psychology Northwestern U., Evanston, Ill., 1960-61; instr., asst. prof. Hobart and William Smith Coll., Geneva, N.Y., 1961-63; asst. prof., assoc. prof. Yeshiva U., N.Y.C., 1963-78; assoc. prof. Sch. of Profl. Psychology, Miami, Fla., 1978-81; assoc. prof. Nova U., Ft. Lauderdale, Fla., 1981-84, prof., 1984—, supr. dissertations, 1981—; research cons. Yeshiva U. Med. Sch., 1967-68. Contbr. articles to profl. jours. NIH grantee, 1963-64, 1966-67. Mem. Am. Psychol. Assn., AAAS, Eastern Psychol. Assn., Southeastern Psychol. Assn. Democrat. Jewish. Avocations: cooking; tennis; swimming; theatre attendance; travel. Home: 2851 NE 183d St Apt 1204 North Miami Beach FL 33160 Office: Nova U 3301 College Ave Fort Lauderdale FL 33314

GIRDNER, MARJORIE JO, association executive; b. St. Petersburg, Fla., Aug. 26, 1926; d. William Edward and Josephine Coe (Plate) Wilson; student U. Ariz., 1945-48; m. Alwin James Girdner, Sept. 1, 1946; children—Allen James, Sharon Lynn Girdner Magee, Kennan Eugene, Mari Jo Girdner Honeycutt. Dist. advisor Chaparrel council Girl Scouts U.S., Albuquerque, 1970-72, resident camp dir. Rancho del Chaparrel, 1970-72; 1st v.p., chmn. personnel com. Moccasin Bend council Girl Scouts U.S., 1980-82, pres., 1982—, bd. dirs., 1974—, chmn. tng. com., 1974-80, trainer, 1973—, del. nat. council, 1975, 81, 83. Pres., Ariz. Dist. Meth. Youth Fellowship, 1945-47; v.p. Woman's Soc. Christian Service, sec. missionary edn. Central Meth. Ch., Albuquerque; pres. United Meth. Women, First Centenary United Meth. Ch., Chattanooga, 1978-79, coordinator Christian Global Concern, 1974-76, yearbook chmn., 1980-83, mem. First Centenary Inner City Com., 1978-83, mem. adminstrv. bd., 1974-79; mem. United Way Allocations Panel, 1983. Recipient Women's Soc. Christian Service spl. membership award, 1957; Thanks Badge, Girl Scouts U.S.A., 1975; Trefoil award Moccasin Bend council, 1983. Mem. Internat. Platform Assn. Republican. Methodist. Club: Phrateres. Home: 7829 Parkshore Circle Chattanooga TN 37343

GIROD, JUDY, interior design firm executive; b. Alexandria, La., Aug. 24, 1948; d. John James and Lily (McKnight) Capdevielle; B.F.A. in Interior Design, La. State U., 1971; m. Jerold S. Girod, Aug. 22, 1970. Interior designer Bowles Inc., 1970-72; interior designer, mgr. dept. Clyde W. Smith Co., 1972-75; interior designer Blitch Architects, 1975-79; owner, pres. Judy Girod Interior Design Inc. (now The Girod Hailey Design Group), New Orleans, 1979—. Bd. dirs. Coliseum Sq. Assn., 1980—, sec., 1985; bd. dirs. St. Charles Ave. Bus. Assn., 1982; co-pres. Magazine St. Bus. Assn., 1984. Mem. La. State U. Alumni Assn. (dir. Greater New Orleans Met. chpt. 1979-80), Am. Soc. Interior Designers (pres. La. dist. chpt. 1982-83, nat. dir. 1985), Inst. Bus. Designers, Fashion Group, Delta Zeta. Republican. Roman Catholic. Clubs: Spring Fiesta Assn., La. Landmarks. Contbr. series on interior design to Gambit Mag. Home: 1402 Magazine St New Orleans LA 70130 Office: 1943 Magazine St New Orleans LA 70130

GIROU, MICHAEL L(LOYD), computer systems company executive; b. St. Louis, July 2, 1947; s. Jack J. and Patricia S. (Sittner) G.; m. Lynn R. Fessler, Apr. 16, 1965 (div. 1974); 1 child, Beverly; m. Theodora L. Dygert, Dec. 13, 1974. B.A. in Math., U. Mo.-Columbia, 1969, Ph.D. in Math., 1985. Tech. analyst McDonnell Aircraft, St. Louis, 1965-67; sr. systems programmer U. Mo.-Columbia, 1967-69; prin. systems analyst Honeywell, Mpls., 1969-73; pres. SSM, Inc., Mpls., 1973-79; M.F.D., Inc., Mo. and Minn., 1979-84; v.p. Presearch, Inc., Aiken, S.C., 1984—; dir. Omni 360, Mpls. Designer computer system, 1971 (ISO award for Outstanding Tech. Achievement, 1971). Bd. dirs. Amicus, Mpls., 1978. Curators scholar U. Mo., 1964. Mem. Soc. Indsl. and Applied Math., Am. Math. Soc., IEEE, Assn. Computing Machinery Pi Mu Epsilon. Republican. Club: Houndslake Country (Aiken). Avocation: bridge. Home: 722 Winged Foot Dr Aiken SC 29801 Office: Presearch Inc 918 Houndslake Dr Aiken SC 29801

GISE, WILLIS LYNN, JR., banker; b. Phila., July 31, 1947; s. Willis Lynn and Ethel (Godsall) G.; m. Pamela Jane Wilbert, July 5, 1969 (div. 1974); m. Dawn Robin Hoette, Oct. 20, 1979; children—Dawn Marie, Willis Lynn III. B.A. in Econ., U. Md., 1969. Buyer, Filnes, Boston, 1971-73; dist. sales mgr. Hit or Miss, Avon, Mass., 1973-76, The Limited, Phila., 1976-78; regional dir. sales Outlet Co., Pawtucket, R.I., 1978-79; v.p., dir. store ops. LaVogue Stores, Richmond, Va., 1979-82; v.p., nat. sales mgr. Bank Va., Richmond, 1982—. Mem. Young Republicans Montgomery County, Md., 1964; swim team coach Daleview Swim Club, Montgomery County, 1963-65. Named Sales Mgr. of Yr., Hotel Corp. Am., 1970, Swim Coach of Yr., Md. Recreation Dept., 1963. Mem. Am. Bankers Assn., Nat. Retail Mchts. Assn., Am. Athletic Union, Hotel Sales Mgmt. Assn. Episcopalian. Club: Izak Walton. Avocations: swimming; tennis; writing. Home: 9503 Catesby Ln Richmond VA 23233

GISTARO, EDWARD PETER, computer company executive; b. Bklyn., May 31, 1935; s. Peter and Eugenia (Esposito) G.; m. Martina Hanke, Nov. 11, 1961; children—Edward Martin, Jean Marie. B.S.E.E., U. Notre Dame, 1957. Dir. product mktg. Honeywell Corp., 1968-72; dir. computer ops. Harris Corp., 1972-73; v.p. mktg. Datapoint Corp., San Antonio, 1973-80, exec. v.p. corp. devel. and fin., 1980-82, pres., chief operating officer, 1982—, also dir. Served to lt. USN, 1957-60. Mem. San Antonio C. of C. (dir.). Roman Catholic. Office: 9725 Datapoint Dr San Antonio TX 78284

GITTESS, RONALD MARVIN, dentist; b. Nyack, N.Y., Nov. 10, 1937; s. David and Mildred (Levin) G.; B.S., Columbia, 1959, D.D.S., 1963; postgrad. U. Pa., 1964-66; m. Carol May Block, Apr. 6, 1963; children—Robert Andrew, Leslie Ellen. Intern, Mt. Sinai Hosp., Miami, Fla., 1963-64, now attending dental surgeon; pvt. practice dentistry specializing in endodontics, Miami, 1966—; mem. staff Variety Children's Hosp., VA Hosp., Miami, Mt. Sinai Hosp.; cons. Dade County Dental Research Clinic; ann. guest lectr. dental div. Pan Am. Med. Conf., 1983—. Asst. coordinator dental div. United Fund Campaign, 1968. Recipient certificate of recognition Jarvie Honor Soc., 1961. USPHS fellow, 1962-63. Diplomate Am. Bd. Endodontics. Mem. ADA, Am. Assn. Endodontics, AAAS, Fedn. Dentaire Internationale, Fla., Miami, Miami Beach, South Dade, East Coast dental socs., So. Endodontic Study Group, Alpha Omega. Home: 14520 SW 84th Ave Miami FL 33158 Office: 7400 N Kendall Dr Miami FL 33156

GIUSEPPE, JESSE IGNACIO, purchasing consultant, electronics engineer; b. Carupano, Venezuela, Jan. 1, 1942; came to U.S., 1975; s. Ignacio J. and Bertha M. (Verdi) G.; m. Anna L. Cova, Aug. 4, 1960 (div.); m. 2d, Raquel R. Rodriguez, Mar. 4, 1963; children—Sandra R., Nancy X., Betty J. B.S. Elec. Engring., Telecommunications Coll., Caracas, Venezuela, 1963. Elec. engr. Tele-Trece, Caracas, 1963-65, Orinoco Mining Co., Ordaz, Venezuela, 1965-67; pres. Broadcast Services, Caracas, 1965-75; export mgr. Electronica Internat., Miami, Fla., 1975-76; pres. Asben Co., Inc., Miami, 1976—mktg. dir. Raymond Mouldings, Miami, 1982—; dir. Inemco Corp., Miami, G.I. Electronics, Miami. Inventor electric water closet deodorizer, 1978, remote control of power meters, 1978, electronic baby sitter, 1980; author: How to Stop Power Meters without Tampering with Them, 1980. Sustaining mem. Republican Party, Miami, 1979; active Republican Presdl. Task. Force, Washington, 1981; bd. dirs. Bent Tree Community Assn., Miami, 1982. Mem. IEEE Colegio de Ingenieros de Venezuela. Roman Catholic. Home: 4381 SW 137th Ct Miami FL 33175

GIVAUDAN, BEN TRESTED, III, television creative director; b. N.Y.C., Oct. 5, 1936; s. Ben Trested Jr. and Winifred (Brown) G.; m. Nancy I. Bartol, May 22, 1956 (div.); children—Scott J., Raymond L.; m. 2d, Trina L. Ferrell, Aug. 26, 1971. B.A. in Radio-TV Prodn., Ariz. State U., 1959. Engr. Stas. KTAR and KVAR Radio-TV, Phoenix, 1954-59; announcer, chief engr. Sta. WOPI-AM, Bristol, Tenn., 1959-60; announcer, chief engr. Sta. WKIN-AM,

Kingsport, Tenn., 1960-61; staff engr. Sta. WDBJ-TV., Roanoke, Va., 1961-65; producer-dir., 1965-80, creative dir., 1980—; vol. examiner amateur radio examining program FCC, 1984—; broadcast engring. cons. to archtl. firms. Active Mill Mountain Theater, March of Dimes, Gourmet Gala Adv. Bd., local community theater. Named Jaycee of Yr., Cave Spring Jaycees, 1968. Mem. Am. Advt. Fedn. (bd. dirs. Roanoke chpt.), Alpha Delta Sigma. Office: Sta WDBJ-TV PO Box 7 Roanoke VA 24022

GIVENS, AARON, psychologist; b. St. Louis, Jan. 17, 1935; s. Aaron and Lillie (Carey) G.; 1 child, Corey A.; m. M. Dean Adams, June 30, 1957. A.B., UCLA, 1960; M.Ed., Loyola U., Chgo., 1970; Ph.D., N.C. U., 1984. Lt. col. U.S. Army, 1960-80, ret., 1980; consulting psychologist Hardees Food Service, Rocky Mount, N.C., 1982-84; staff psychologist VA, Jacksonville, Fla., 1984—. Contbr. articles to profl. jours. Decorated Bronze Star, 1967, 71, Purple Heart, 1971, Meritorious Service award, 1980; N.C. Chancellors scholar, 1983. Mem. Am. Psychol. Assn., Am. Personnel Guidance; Retired Officers Assn., Jacksonville Mental Health Assn. (leader seminar 1984—, bd. dirs. 1984—), Assn. Black Psychologists (pres. 1984—), Grad. Assn. Students Psychology (pres. 1981-83), Nat. Assn. Black Vets (founder), New Life Ctr. Homeless Vets (founder), Minority Inclusion Com. Jacksonville (seminar leader 1984), Psi Chi, Omega Psi Phi. Democrat. Methodist. Lodges: Mason, DAV. Avocations: swimming; bowling; softball; basketball; karate. Home: 2053 Sussex Dr S Jacksonville FL 32073 Office: Veterans Readjustment Ctr 255 Liberty St Jacksonville FL

GLADDEN, DOUGLAS AUSTIN, safety professional, grain company executive; b. Jefferson City, Mo., Nov. 16, 1955; s. Ralph A. and Gladys M. (Heinrich) G.; m. Karen L. Sutton, June 25, 1983; children—Jennifer, William. B.S. in Safety, Central Mo. State U., 1978. Safety adminstr. Bunge Corp., West Memphis, Ark., 1979-80, safety supr., Logansport, Ind., 1980-81, safety and tng. adminstr., Bradley, Ill., 1981-85, sr. safety adminstr., West Memphis, 1985—. Vice pres. Kankakee Area Safety Council, 1983-84, pres., 1984—. Mem. Am. Soc. Safety Engrs. Methodist. Avocations: automobile restoration; boating; water skiing; carpentry; lawn and garden care. Home: 6019 Bartley Ridge Bartlett TN 38134 Office: Bunge Corp PO Box 1987 West Memphis AR 72301

GLADDING, CAROLYN ANNE, nursing administrator; b. Providence, June 20, 1942; d. William Joseph and Louise (Orabona) Dionne; m. Samuel Wesley Gladding, Jr., June 19, 1971. B.S. in Nursing, Salve Regina Coll., 1966; M.S. in Adminstrv. Sci., Hartford Grad. Ctr., 1979. Staff nurse Inst. of Living, Hartford, Conn., 1966-67, nursing supr., 1967-68; psychiat. clin. specialist Hartford Hosp., 1968-71, asst. dir. nursing, 1971-80; assoc. adminstr. nursing Halifax Hosp. Med. Ctr., Daytona Beach, Fla., 1980-85, adminstr. nursing, 1985—. Mem. Am. Soc. for Nursing Service Adminstrs., Fla. Soc. for Hosp. Nursing Service Adminstrs. Democrat. Roman Catholic.

GLADDING, EVERETT BUSHNELL, writer; b. New Haven, June 27, 1917; s. Daniel Henry and Grace A. (Brown) G.; B.A., Wesleyan U., 1938; M.A., Johns Hopkins U., 1946; m. Harriet Allen Clark, June 7, 1941; children—Nicholas Clark, Brenda Bushnell (Mrs. Scott Alexander). Commd. ensign USN, 1941, advanced through grades to capt., 1960; staff SACLANT, 1956-59; chief Nat. Security Agy., Pacific, 1960-63; comdg. officer Naval Communications Sta., Adak, Alaska, 1963-64; chief staff officer Naval Security Group, 1964-66, dir. Naval Security Group, Pacific, 1966-68; ret., 1968; planning specialist LTV Electrosystems, Inc., Greenville, Tex., 1968-70; mgmt. analyst Conn. State Welfare Dept., 1970-72; pub. relations asst. Air Kaman, Inc., 1971-75; editor Flight Line Times, 1974-75; pres. Majors Aviation Service, Inc., 1975-81. Mem. city council, mayor pro tem, Greenville, Tex., 1983—; mem. human devel. policy com. and steering com. Small Cities Council, Nat. League Cities; mem. Commn. Devel. Regional Rev. Com. North Central Tex.; mem. criminal justice policy devel. com., mem. exec. bd. North Central Tex. Council Govts.; regional rep., trustee Dallas Symphony Assn.; vestryman St. Paul's Episcopal Ch., 1976-79, 82-85; judge dog obedience trials, 1957-74. Mem. IEEE (sr.), Quarter Century Wireless Assn., Dallas Amateur Radio Club, Sabine Valley Amateur Radio Assn., Aviation/Space Writers Assn., Am. Radio Relay League, Aircraft Owners and Pilots Assn., various dog clubs. Episcopalian. Clubs: Quinnipiack (New Haven); Army and Navy (Washington). Lodges: Rotary (pres. 1983-84), Masons. Home: 24 Mullaney Rd Greenville TX 75401 Office: Box 911 Greenville TX 75401

GLADDING, WALTER ST. GEORGE, banker; b. Greenwich, Conn., May 2, 1936; s. Walter Marenus and Jane Bell Dabney (Grinnan) G.; m. Ellen Ann Silver, Aug. 21, 1977; children—Jeffrey Taylor, Jennifer Howard, Andrew St. George. B.A., U. Va., 1958; diploma Stonier Grad. Sch. Banking, 1972. Asst. cashier United Va. Bank, Richmond, 1958-65; sr. v.p. Dominion Nat. Bank, Richmond, 1965-70; sr. v.p. Bank of Asheville (now NCNB Nat. Bank), 1970-81, sr. v.p., city exec., Asheville, 1981—. Chmn. bd. dirs. U. N.C.-Asheville Found.; vice chmn. bd. dirs. United Way of Asheville and Buncombe County, Meml. Mission Found.; chmn. Jr. Achievement of Western N.C. Mem. Asheville Area C. of C. (dir.). Episcopalian. Clubs: Country of Asheville, Asheville Downtown City. Home: 11 Sareva Pl Asheville NC 28804 Office: 68 Patton Ave Asheville NC 28801

GLADFELTER, JOHN HENRY, psychotherapist, educator; b. Tomahawk, Wis., Oct. 17, 1926; s. Elmer Sylvester and Dora (Marten) G.; m. Rose Ellen Wilhelm, Oct. 26, 1946. B.S., U. Houston, 1951, M.A., 1953, Ph.D., 1957. Lic. psychologist, Tex. Clin. assoc. prof. Southwest Med. Sch., Dallas, 1955-78; coordinator Fielding Inst., Dallas, 1974—; faculty mem. Southwest Law Enforcement Inst., Dallas, 1968—. Contbg. author chpt. in book. Fellow Am. Group Psychotherapy Assn.; mem. Southwestern Group Psychotherapy Soc. (pres. 1965-66), Dallas Group Psychotherapy Soc. (pres. 1965-74), Am. Psychol. Assn., Internat. Transactional Analysis Assn., Tex. Assn. Magicians (pres. 1965-66). Avocations: magician; photograpy; computer programming. Office: 3300 West Mockingbird St #530 Dallas TX 75235

GLADWIN, WILLIAM JOSEPH, JR., lawyer; b. Tallahassee, Dec. 18, 1946; s. William Joseph and Clara Copeland (Durrance) G. B.A., Fla. State U., 1969, M.S., 1973; J.D., Southwestern U., Los Angeles, 1977. Bar: Fla. 1978, U.S. Supreme Ct. 1983, U.S. Dist. Ct. (no., mid. and so. dists.) Fla., U.S. Ct. Appeals (4th, 5th, 7th, 9th and 10th cirs.). Law clk. W.K. Whitfield, Tallahassee, 1976, 77-78, assoc., 1978-81; asst. gen. counsel Fla. Dept. State Corps., Tallahassee, 1979-81; sole practice, 1981—. Served to lt. (j.g.) USN, 1969-72, Vietnam; lt. comdr. res. Recipient Am. Jurisprudence award, 1975. Mem. Am. Judicature Soc., Tallahassee Bar Assn., Tallahassee Jaycees, Fla. Trust Hist. Preservation, Nat. Trust Hist. Preservation, Vietnam Vets (bd. dirs, 1st v.p. chpt. 1984—), SAR (historian 1981—), Sons of Confederate Vets, Descendants of Washington's Army at Valley Forge, Blue and Gold Officers U.S. Naval Acad. Democrat. Home: 1988 Portland Ave Tallahassee FL 32303 Office: PO Box 1058 Tallahassee FL 32302

GLANCY, WALTER JOHN, lawyer; b. Los Angeles, Mar. 8, 1942; s. Walter Perry and Elva Thomasin (Douglass) G.; m. Sharon Marie Owens, Nov. 24, 1973; children—Jill Marie, Gregory Owens. A.B. summa cum laude, Princeton U., 1964; B.A. with first class honors, Oxford U., 1966; LL.B. cum laude, Yale U., 1969. Bar: Tex. 1971. Law clk. to justice Byron R. White, U.S. Supreme Ct., 1969-70; staff asst. NSC, Washington, 1970-71; staff asst. to Peter M. Flanigan, The White House, 1971; assoc., ptnr. Jackson, Walker, Winstead, Cantwell & Miller, Dallas, 1972-76; ptnr. Hughes & Luce and predecessors, Dallas, 1976-85; ptnr. Baker & Botts, Dallas, 1985—; dir. Holly Corp. Mem. bd. mgmt. Dallas YMCA Urban Services, 1975-84; bd. dirs. Dallas Family Guidance Center, 1982—, pres. bd. dirs., 1985—; mem adminstrv. bd. Lovers Lane Meth. Ch., Dallas, 1984—. Recipient Oxford U. prize, 1966. Mem. ABA, State Bar Tex. (chmn. taxation sect. 1985-86), Dallas Bar Assn. (chmn. legal ethics com. 1980-81), Am. Law Inst., Order of Coif, Phi Beta Kappa. Republican. Methodist. Club: Dallas. Home: 4515 Kelsey Rd Dallas TX 75229 Office: 800 LTV Center 2001 Ross Ave Dallas TX 75201

GLASER, THOMAS WILLIAM, firearms manufacturing company executive; b. Chgo., May 2, 1952; s. Thomas Harry and Cecelia Martha (Hirsch) G.; m. Nancy Lee Poole, Mar. 16, 1983. B.A., Tex. Christian U., 1974; m. Internat. Mgmt., Am. Grad. Sch. Internat. Mgmt., 1975; postgrad. Tex. State U., 1980. Gun dept. mgr. Zales Corp., Cullum & Boren Sporting Goods, Ft. Worth, 1971-75; family security analyst Met. Life Ins. Co., Arlington, Tex., 1975-76; telephone sales coordinator Stocksill Shooters Supply, Grapevine, Tex., 1976-79; coordinator customer service/cost control Greif Bros. Co., Ft. Worth, 1979-82; v.p. mktg. Holloway Arms Co., Ft. Worth, 1982—. Served as maj. Tex. State Guard Mem. Nat. Rifle Assn. (life), Internat. Mil. Arms Soc., Nat. Guard Assn. Tex. (life), Tex. State Rifle Assn. (life.), Civil War Round Table Tex. (treas. 1979-81), Am. Def. Preparedness Assn. (life), Tex. State Guard Assn. (life), Dallas Arms Collectors Assn. (life), So. Hist. Assn., Soc. Historians of Early Am. Republic, Orgn. Am. Historians, Res. Officers Assn., Assn. U.S. Army, Am. Mgmt. Assn., Mensa (nat. coordinator Civil War spl. interest group 1976-80, sec. Ft. Worth 1976-80), Am. Hist. Assn., U.S. Naval Inst., Société Internationale des Officers, Alpha Phi Omega, Phi Alpha Theta (pres. Alpha Lambda chpt. 1983-84). Home: 3132 Meadow Oaks Haltom City TX 76117

GLASGOW, DAVID RAY, school psychologist, educator; b. Paris, Tenn., June 20, 1948; s. Raymond Theodore and Mary B. (Prince) G.; m. Nancee Ann Kerr, June 11, 1971; children—April Lea, Allison Winters. B.A., David Lipscomb Coll., 1970; M.A. in Psychology, U. Tenn., 1973; postgrad. various univs. Lic. psychol. examiner; cert. sch. psychologist; cert. tchr. math., English, Psychology. Substitute tchr. Knoxville City Schs., Tenn., 1972-73; instr. in psychology David Lipscomb Coll., Nashville, 1973-74, Austin Peay State U., Clarksville, Tenn., 1975-77; psychol. intern Montgomery County Schs., Clarksville, 1977-78; sch. psychologist Humphreys County Schs., Waverly, Tenn., 1978-84; tchr. Houston County High Sch., Erin, Tenn., 1984-85; Columbia Acad., Tenn., 1985—; part time pvt. practice psychol. examiner, Waverly, 1979—. Author articles, poem. Adv. bd. Humphreys County Child Protective Services, Waverly, 1979-84; mem. rev. bd. Humphreys County Foster Care Rev. Com., Waverly, 1982-84, adv. bd. Humphreys County Mental Health Ctr., Waverly, 1982—. U.S. Office Edn. trainee, 1974; NSF trainee, 1971. Mem. Am. Psychol. Assn. (assoc.), NEA, Am. Council on Rural Spl. Edn., Phi Kappa Phi. Mem. Ch. of Christ. Avocations: Photography; writing. Home: Route 1 Box 76 Twin Creek Rd Charlotte TN 37036 Office: Columbia Academy Columbia TN 38401

GLASGOW, ROBERT (BOB) J., state senator, lawyer; b. Feb. 28, 1942. B.A., Tarleton State U.; J.D., U. Tex. Mem. Tex. Senate, Austin, 1981—, mem. fin. and jurisprudence coms., vice chmn. econ. devel. com., chmn. subcom. criminal matters. Democrat. Office: Tex Senate PO Box 12068 Austin TX 78711*

GLASS, FRED STEPHEN, lawyer; b. Asheboro, N.C., Oct. 17, 1940; s. Emmett Frederick and Colene F. (Foust) G.; m. Gloria A. Grant, June 12, 1964; 1 dau., Elizabeth Foust; m. Martha G. Daughtry, June 9, 1982. B.A., Wake Forest U., 1963, J.D., 1966. Bar: N.C. 1966, U.S. Dist. Ct. (ea. dist.) N.C. 1966, U.S. Ct. Appeals (4th cir.) 1984, U.S. Supreme Ct. 1984. Research asst. presiding justice N.C. Supreme Ct., 1966-67; ptnr. Miller, Beck, O'Briant and Glass, Asheboro, N.C., 1971-77; exec. dir. and legal counsel N.C. Democratic Party, 1977-78; dep. commr. N.C. Indsl. Commn., 1978; spl. Congl. asst. 4th Congl. Dist. N.C., 1979; ptnr. Harris, Cheshire, Leager and Southern, Raleigh, N.C., 1979—; prof. law and govt. Asheboro Jr. Coll. Bus., 1973-76. Basketball coach and fitness instr. Randolph County YMCA; pub. chmn., United Appeal; bd. dirs. Randolph County Emergency Med. Technician Bd.; active Dem. campaigns, Gen. Greene, Old Hickory, Narragansett, San Diego County and Occoneechee councils Boy Scouts Am., council commr. for Roundtables, 1980—, asst. dist. commr. 1979—, asst. scoutmaster, dist. newsletter editor, council ex. bd., chancellor, council commrs. Coll., 1980—. Served with JAGC USN, 1967-71, capt. Res. Recipient Scouters tng. award Boy Scouts Am., Scouters Key, Den Leaders Tng. award, Dist. award of Merit, Silver Beaver; Young Man of the Year award City of Asheboro. Mem. Randolph County Bar Assn. (pres. 1973-74), 19th Jud. Dist. Bar Assn. (pres. 1974-75), N.C. Bar Assn. (chmn. young lawyer sect. Randolph County), Dist. Criminal Law Symposium (chmn. 1976). Democrat. Methodist. Contbr. articles to profl. jours. Home: 1003 Cindy St Cary NC 27511 Office: PO Drawer 2417 Raleigh NC 27602

GLASS, JOHN D., JR., lawyer, independent oil and gas producer, rancher; b. Oklahoma City, Aug. 17, 1931; s. John D. and Gertrude (Coumbe) G.; m. Joanne Miller, June 7, 1958; children—John Duel, III, Kenneth Neen, Sharah Coumbe, Joel Murphy. B.B.A., U. Tex.-Austin, 1952, J.D., 1955. Bar: Tex. 1955, U.S. Dist. Ct. (ea. dist.) Tex. Ptnr., Glass & Glass, Tyler, Tex., 1955-75; sole practice, Tyler, 1975—; pvt. practice ranching. Served with U.S. Army, 1955-57. Mem. State Bar Tex., Smith County Bar Assn., Tex. and Southwestern Cattle Raisers Assn., Tex. Ind. Producers and Royalty Owners Assn. Republican. Episcopalian. Office: 917 Interfirst Plaza Bldg Tyler TX 75702

GLASS, ROY LEONARD, lawyer; b. Littleton, N.H., Jan. 27, 1947; s. Jack Irving and Noreen (Leuithwait) Kline; m. Suzanne Schmidt Goldstein, May 20, 1967 (div. Oct. 1978); 1 child, Shannon Renee; m. Patricia Lee Wimbish, Dec. 9, 1978; 1 child, Ashley Leigh. A.A. with honors, St. Petersburg Jr. Coll., Fla., 1971; B.A., U. South. Fla., 1972; J.D., Fla. State U., 1975. Bar: Fla. 1976, U.S. Dist. Ct. (mid. dist.) Fla. 1977, U.S. Dist Ct. (no. dist.) Fla. 1978, U.S. Supreme Ct. 1979, U.S. Ct. Appeals (11th cir.) 1983. Assoc., Meyers, Mooney & Adler, Orlando, Fla., 1976-78; assoc. Barrett, Boyd & Bajoczky, Tallahassee, Fla., 1978-79; sole practice, Tallahassee, 1979-81; ptnr. Deserio & Glass, St. Petersburg, Fla., 1981-82; assoc. Battaglia, Ross, Hastings, Dicus & Andrews, St. Petersburg, 1982-85, sole practice, St. Petersburg, 1985—; lectr., Floridians Against Constl. Tampering, Fla., 1984. Served to capt. U.S. Army, 1966-70, Vietnam. Mem. ABA, Am. Trial Lawyers Assn., Am. Arbitration Assn., Am. Soc. Law & Medicine, Acad. Fla. Trial Lawyers (speakers bur.), Fla. Bar (trial lawyers and adminstrv. and govt. law sects., health law com. 1984—), St. Petersburg Bar Assn. (legis. com. 1983-85, liaison with med. soc. 1985-86), Tallahassee Bar Assn., St. Petersburg C. of C. (urban solutions task force 1983—), Phi Kappa Phi, Beta Gamma Sigma. Clubs: Suncoast Tiger Bay (St. Petersburg, Fang & Claw award 1983), Breakfast Sertoma (Cert. of Appreciation 1984). Home: 255 Capri Circle North 11 Treasure Island FL 33706 Office: Law Offices 3000 66th St N Suite B Saint Petersburg FL 33710

GLASSCO, BOBBIE MCCRELESS, sociology educator and administrator; b. Marshall County, Ala., July 14, 1933; d. Walter Emmet and Mary Belle (Ballew) McCreless; m. Truman Edris Glassco, Mar. 15, 1952. Student Snead Jr. Coll., 1958-59; B.S., Jacksonville State U., 1961; M.S., Auburn U., 1964, Ed.D., 1982. Mem. faculty Snead State Jr. Coll., Boaz, Ala., 1961—, instr. home econs., English and sociology, 1961-82, instr. sociology, part-time dir. social sci. div., 1982—, dir. alumni affairs, 1981—, supr. coll. cafeteria, 1970-75. Chmn. Marshall County Heart Fund, 1972, Cancer Drive, 1980. Mem. NEA, Ala. Edn. Assn., Nat. Council Social Studies, Ala.-Miss. Sociol. Assn., Mid South Sociol. Assn., Phi Beta Kappa, Phi Theta Kappa, Alpha Delta Kappa. Republican. Baptist. Office: Snead State Jr Coll Boaz AL 35957

GLASSCOCK, GARY M., health care administrator; b. Birmingham, Ala., Jan. 18, 1951; s. James A. and Kate (Kelly) G.; m. Linda Earl Golson, June 29, 1974. B.A., U. Ala.-Birmingham, 1972, M.S., 1974. Clinic adminstr. Sch. of Optometry, U. Ala.-Birmingham, 1974-76; asst. adminstr. Bapt. Med. Ctr., Birmingham, 1976-81; regional adminstr., 1981-83; adminstr. Lloyd Noland Hosp., Birmingham, 1983—, sec., treas., trustee, 1983—; sec., treas., trustee Home Health, Inc., Birmingham, 1981—; Ala. Licensure Bd., Montgomery, 1983—; bd. dirs. Birmingham Regional Hosp. Council. Mem. Am. Coll. Hosp. Adminstrs., Am. Hosp. Assn., Ala. Hosp. Assn. (trustee, various coms. and chairmanships), Birmingham Regional Hosp. Assn. (bd. chmn. 1985), Nat. Fire Protection Assn. Lodge: Lions. Avocations: scuba diving, traveling, reading, hunting. Home: 431 Shadeswood Dr Birmingham AL 35226 Office: Lloyd Noland Hosp 701 Ridgeway Rd Birmingham AL 35064

GLASSER, JULIAN, chemist, metallurgist; b. Chgo., May 23, 1912; s. Jacob and Sarah (Permut) G.; m. Mildred Demmel, June 27, 1942 (dec. 1976); children—William J., James E.; m. Dorothea Justice, Nov. 6, 1983. B.S. with high honors, U. Ill., 1933, M.S., 1935; Ph.D. in Phys. Chemistry, Pa. State U., 1938. Research chemist Gen. Electric Co., Schenectady, N.Y., 1937; research engr. Battelle Meml. Inst., Columbus, Ohio, 1938-42; chief chemist, chief metallurgist Aluminum div. Olin Industries, Inc., Tacoma, 1942-45; dir. research Gen. Abrasive Co., Niagara Falls, N.Y., 1945-47; supr. Armour Research Found., Chgo., 1947-53; cons. to head metallurgy br. Office Naval Research, Navy Dept., Washington, 1952-53; staff metallurgist, cons. materials adv. bd. Nat. Research Council, Washington, 1951-53; tech. dir. Cramet Inc., Chattanooga; 1953-58; prof. chemistry Vanderbilt U., Nashville, 1958-59; cons. Julian Glasser, Chattanooga, 1958-60; pres. Chem. and Metall. Research, Inc., Chattanooga, 1960—. Contbr. articles to profl. publs. Patentee in field. Mem. Am. Chem. Soc. (chmn. Chattanooga sect. 1973-74), Am. Soc. Metals (chmn. Chattanooga chpt. 1956-57), AIME (mem. publs. com. extractive metallurgy div. 1949-50, chmn. 1951-53), Electrochem. Soc. (chmn. electrothermics div. 1949-51, treas. Chgo. chpt. 1948-49), Am. Soc. Nondestructive Testing (chmn. Chattanooga sect. 1969-70), Am. Ceramic Soc., Am. Powder Metallurgy Inst., Sigma Xi, Sigma Pi Sigma, Phi Lambda Upsilon, Pi Mu Epsilon. Avocations: golf, walking. Home: 3400 Glendon Dr Chattanooga TN 37411 Office: Chem and Metallurgical Research Inc PO Box 80156 Chattanooga TN 37411

GLASSER, KAY ELBAUM, civic worker; b. Lawrence, Mass., July 24, 1918; d. Samuel and Anna Karass; B.A. magna cum laude, Radcliffe Coll., 1940; M.S.W., Simmons Coll., 1956; Ph.D., Brandeis U., 1967; m. Joshua B. Glasser, Nov. 22, 1972 (dec.). Mental health educator Mass. Dept. Mental Health, 1956-62; asso. prof. social work U. Denver, 1967-73; mem. Sarasota County (Fla.) Sch. Bd., 1978—, chmn., 1982-83; past mentor Eckerd Coll. Program Experienced Learners; citizens adv. bd. St. Armand's Banking Center, S.E. 1st Nat. Bank of Sarasota. Chmn. planning com., pres. bd. dirs. United Way of Sarasota; trustee, sec. New Coll. Found.; bd. dirs. Taxpayers Assn. Sarasota County, Sarasota County Civic League, 1977-78, United Way Found., 1980—; mem. Fla. Social Studies K-8 Instrl. Materials Council; former mem. Newton (Mass.) Bd. Public Welfare; former vice chmn. Newton Rep. City Com.; mem. LWV, former v.p. Newton; bd. dirs. Community Coalition for Families, Sarasota County Informed Parents, L.I.F.E., Asolo Theatre Festival Assn., Players; mem. dist. 8 adv. council Health and Rehab. Services; past mem. Property Adjustment Appraisal Bd.; mem. Fla. Adv. Council on Global Edn., Sarasota County Task Force on Mothers Against Drunk Driving; mem. task force on global edn. Nat. Sch. Bds. Assn. Mem. Acad. Cert. Social Workers, Nat. Assn. Social Workers, Council on Social Work Edn., Fla. Women's Network, AAUW, AAUP, Phi Beta Kappa Assocs. Clubs: Bird Key Yacht, Sarasota Women's Rep., Sarasota Bay Women's Rep. Home: 888 Blvd of Arts Apt 807 Sarasota FL 33577 Office: 2418 Hatton St Sarasota FL 33577

GLASSER, WOLFGANG GERHARD, forest products and chemical engineering educator; b. Zwickau, Ger., Oct. 9, 1941; came to U.S., 1969; s. Joachim and Charlotte (Syjatz) G.; m. Heidemarie Reinecke, Mar. 18, 1969; children—Christine M., Stephan A. Diploma in Wood Tech., U. Hamburg (W.Ger.), 1966, Ph.D. in Wood Chemistry, 1969. Research assoc. U. Wash., Seattle, 1969-70, research asst. prof., 1970-71; asst. prof. Va. Poly. Inst. and State U., Blacksburg, 1972-75, assoc. prof., 1975-80, prof. wood chemistry and mem. polymer materials interfaces lab., 1980—; dir. Pulp and Paper Research Inst., Sao Paulo, Brazil, 1976; chmn. panel Nat. Acad. Scis., 1974-76; mem. adv. group Holzforschung, Braunschweig, Ger., 1984—. Patentee; contbr. articles to profl. jours., chpts. to books. Coach, coordinator, v.p. S.W. Va. Soccer Assn., 1980-84. Co-recipient George Olmsted award Am. Paper Inst., 1974. Mem. Am. Chem. Soc. (alt. councilor 1983—), Forest Products Soc., AAAS, Sigma Xi, TAPPI. Lutheran. Office: Va Tech Dept Forest Products Blacksburg VA 24061

GLASSMAN, ARMAND BARRY, physician, educator; b. Paterson, N.J., Sept. 9, 1938; s. Paul and Rosa (Ackerman) G.; B.A., Rutgers U., 1960; M.D. magna cum laude (Johnson Found. scholar), Georgetown U., 1964; m. Alberta C. Macri, Aug. 30, 1958; children—Armand P., Steven B., Brian A. Intern, Georgetown U. Hosp., Washington, 1964-65; resident Yale-New Haven Hosp., West Haven VA Hosp., 1965-69; asst. prof. pathology U. Fla. Coll. Medicine, Gainesville VA Hosp.; practice lab. and nuclear medicine, 1969-71; dir. clin. labs. Med. Coll. Ga., Augusta, 1971-76; cons. physician in pathology VA Hosp., Augusta, 1973-76; cons. physician in nuclear medicine U. Hosp., Augusta, Ga., 1973-76; med. dir. clin. labs. Med. U. Hosp., Med. U. S.C., Charleston, 1976—, attending physician in lab. and nuclear medicine, 1976—; med. dir. clin. labs. Charleston Meml. (S.C.) Hosp., 1976-82, 84—; cons. VA Hosp., Charleston, 1976—; prof., chmn. dept. lab. medicine Med. U. S.C., 1976—, acting chmn. dept. microbiology and immunology, 1985—, assoc. dean Coll. Medicine, 1979-85; assoc. med. dir. Med. U. Hosp., 1984—. Mem. dean's com. Charleston VA Hosp., 1978—; mem. exec. council Charleston Higher Edn. Consortium Grad. Program for Marine Biology, 1980-86; adv. com. Trident Tech. Coll., Charleston, 1977—. Served with USMC, 1956-64. Diplomate Am. Bd. Pathology, Am. Bd. Nuclear Medicine. Fellow ACP, Coll. Am. Pathologists, Assn. Clin. Scientists, Am. Soc. Clin. Pathology, Am. Coll. Nuclear Medicine; mem. Internat. Acad. Pathology, Am. Assn. Pathologists, Soc. Nuclear Medicine (acad. council 1979—), Soc. Nuclear Medicine (chmn. membership com. Southeastern chpt. 1972-74, chmn. edn. com. 1973-77), Ga. Radiol. Soc., AMA (Physician's Recognition award 1970-73, 73-76, 76-79, 79-85), So. Med. Assn., Am. Geriatric Soc. (founding fellow so. div.), Am. Soc. Microbiology, Ga. Heart Assn., Am. Assn. Blood Banks (chmn. cryobiology com. 1974—, edn. com. 1979—, Com. Edn. 1979—, Sci. Council 1981— sci. program com. 1982—, bd. dirs. 1985—), S.E. Area Blood Bankers (exec. bd. 1979-82, pres. 1980-81), Assn. Schs. Allied Health Professions (editorial bd. Jour. Allied Health 1979-82), Soc. Cryobiology (exec. com. 1981-83, bd. govs. 1981-83, treas. 1981-83), AAAS, N.Y. Acad. Scis., Acad. Clin. Lab. Physician and Scientists (exec. council 1978—, pres. 1982-83, rep. to Internat. Soc. Pathology), Palmetto B.B. Assn. (exec. bd. 1982-85), Sigma Xi (program chmn., pres.-elect Med. Coll. Ga. chpt. 1975-76), Alpha Eta, Alpha Omega Alpha. Club: Charleston Tennis. Contbr. articles to profl. jours. Office: Dept of Lab Med Med Univ of South Carolina 171 Ashley Ave Charleston SC 29425

GLASSMAN, EDWARD, biochemistry educator, consultant; b. N.Y.C., Mar. 18, 1929; s. Jacob S. and Riesa B. (Bronfman) G.; children—Lyn Judith, Susan Fiona, Ellen Ruth, Marjorie Riesa. B.A., NYU, 1949, M.A., 1951; Ph.D., Johns Hopkins U., 1955. Mem. staff City of Hope Med. Ctr., Duarte, Calif., 1959-60; vis. prof. Stanford U., 1968-69, U. Calif.-Irvine, 1978; mem. faculty biochemistry dept. U. N.C. Med. Sch., 1960—, prof., 1967—; mem. grants rev. study sect. NIMH, 1966-69; vis. fellow Ctr. Creative Leadership, Greensboro, N.C., 1983. Adam T. Bruce fellow, 1954-55, Am. Cancer Soc. fellow, 1955-57; NIH fellow, 1958-59; Guggenheim fellow, 1968-69; recipient Career Devel. award NIH, 1961-71. Fellow AAAS, Royal Soc. Edinburgh; mem. Soc. Neurosci. (pres. N.C. chpt. 1974-75), Elisha Mitchell Soc. (v.p. 1965-66), Am. Soc. Biol. Chemistry. Author: Molecular Approaches to Neurobiology, 1967; editorial bd. Behavior Genetics, 1970-71, Behavioral Biology, 1971-78, Pharmacology, Biochemistry and Behavior, 1973-78, Neurochem. Research, 1975-78; contbr. articles to profl. jours. Home: 112 Kenan St Chapel Hill NC 27514 Office: Biochemistry Dept U NC Chapel Hill NC 27514

GLATZER, RONALD, ophthalmologist; b. Fairfield, Conn., Aug. 9, 1943; s. Irving and Sally (Silverman) G.; m. Kathy Friedman, Apr. 4, 1976; children—Adam, Emily. B.S., U. Vt., 1964; M.D., N.Y. Med. Coll., 1968. Resident N.Y. Eye and Ear Infirmary, N.Y.C., 1972-75, dir. resident tng., 1975-76; practice medicine specializing in ophthalmology, Fort Lauderdale, Fla., 1976—; vis. surgeon Surgical Eye Expeditions, Campeche, Mex., 1984. Served to capt. M.C., U.S. Army, 1969-71. Mem. Vitreous Soc., AMA, Am. Acad. Ophthalmology. Avocation: aviation. Office: 5601 N Dixie Hwy Fort Lauderdale FL 33334

GLAZE, DIANA LISOWSKI, school principal; b. South Milwaukee, Wis., June 29, 1939; d. Roman John and Apollonia Josephine (Skowronski) Lisowski; B.S., U. Wis., 1960; M.A., Calif. State U., 1965; Ed.S., U. Ark., 1978, Ed.D., 1981; m. John Glaze, Aug. 2, 1968. Tchr., Ont. (Calif.) Sch. Dist., 1960-65; prin. Dept. of Def. Schs., Taegu, Korea, 1965-69; tchr. Little Rock public schs., 1970-76, prin. Oakhurst, Meadowcliff, Garland Meadowcliff Sch., 1976—. Mem. exec. bd. Panel of Am. Women, 1978—. Kappa Kappa Iota nat. scholar, 1979-80. Mem. AAUW (Ark. div. pres. 1979-81), Prins. Roundtable (sec. 1978-79), Primary Prin. Chair, Am. Women's Polit. Caucus, Internat. Reading Assn., Assn. for Supervision and Curriculum Devel., Ark. Assn. Elem. Sch. Prins., Kappa Kappa Iota (pres. 1977-79, exec. bd. 1979—). Democrat. Roman Catholic. Office: 18th and Maple Sts Little Rock AR 77208

GLAZENER, EDWARD WALKER, university administrator; b. Raleigh, N.C., Feb. 3, 1922; s. Julian Austin and Margaret Ruth (Strayhorn) G.; m. Eunice Margaret Williams, June 21, 1947; children—Laurence Williams, Lynette Claire Glazener Spencer. B.S. with highest honors, N.C. State U., 1943; M.S., U. Md., 1945, Ph.D., 1949. Asst. county agt., Pittsboro, N.C., 1944; asst. prof. physiology U. Md., College Park, 1945-46; assoc. prof. N.C. State U., Raleigh, 1946-49, prof. poultry sci., 1949-52, prof. genetics, 1952-55, head dept. poultry sci., 1955-60, dir. resident instrn., Sch. Agr. and Life Scis., 1960-73, assoc. dean and dir. acad. affairs, 1973—; vis. scholar U. Mich., Ann Arbor, 1964; guest scholar Pa. State U., 1972; chmn. nat. higher edn. com U.S. Dept. Agr.; rev. participant U. Fla., U. Tenn., U. Ky., U. Md., others; policy com. contract programs med. scis., also policy bd. inst. nutrition U. N.C. System; cons. various projects U.S. Dept. Agr., Resources for the Future; bd. dirs. program com. Friends of the Coll., 1983—. Mem. bus. bd. Pullen Meml. Ch., 1983. Fellow AAAS; mem. Nat. Assn. State Univs. and Land Grant Colls. (instructional sect.), Am. Assn. Higher Edn., Am. Genetic Assn. (bd. dirs.), Poultry Sci. Assn., Am. Inst. Biol. Scis. Baptist. Clubs: Raleigh Execs., Faculty.

Contbr. articles to profl. jours. Home: 3424 Lewis Farm Rd Raleigh NC 27607 Office: Sch of Agr and Life Scis NC State U PO Box 7601 Raleigh NC 27695-7601

GLAZER, FREDERIC JAY, librarian; b. Portsmouth, Va., Feb. 20, 1937; s. Moses Herman and Charlotte Esther (Blachman) G.; B.A., Columbia U., 1954, M.S., 1964; m. Sylvia Katherine Lerner, Aug. 18, 1963; children—Hoyt Eric, Hilary Alison. Librarian, Kirn Meml. Library, Norfolk, Va., 1964-67; dir. Chesapeake (Va.) Pub. Library, 1967-72; exec. sec.-dir. W.Va. Library Commn., Charleston, 1972—; cons. in field. Vice pres. Tidwater Lit. Council, 1970-71; exec. dir. Va. Nat. Library Week, 1970, 71. Served with AUS, 1960-62. Recipient Presdl. certificate appreciation, 1968; spl. recognition Grolier Nat. Library Week, 1970; Gold award 15th Internat. TV and Film Festival, 1972; Region III Outstanding Citizen's award HEW, 1977; Dora R. Parks award W.Va. Library Assn., 1979. Mem. ALA (gen. chmn. membership com. 1974-77, councilor 1975-80). Creator library six pack, library book bucks, instant carousel library, outpost library; contbr. articles to profl. jours., commd. by ALA to write, produce and dir. media presentation commemorating 25th anniversary of fed. library services and constrn. act legislation. Home: 114 Sheridan Circle Charleston WV 25314 Office: Library Commn Science and Cultural Center Charleston WV 25305

GLEASON, DENNIS MICHAEL, petroleum engineer; b. Fort Collins, Colo., Sept. 23, 1951; s. Thomas Michael and Rose Amelia (Reznicek) G.; m. Virginia Lynne Arzinger, Aug. 16, 1975; children—Kelsey Jean, Brendan Michael. B.S. in Geology, Wichita State U., 1974; M.S. in Geol. Engring., U. Mo.-Rolla, 1976, M.S. in Petroleum Engring., 1977. Registered profl. engr., Tex. Petroleum engr. Tex. Pacific Oil Co., Abilene, 1977-81; pres. D.G.&T. Cons., Abilene, 1981-83; mgr. engrs. Russell Engrs., Abilene, 1983—. Mem. United Way, Abilene, 1983, Am. Heart Assn., 1983. Recipient 100 Heart Club award Am. Heart Assn., 1983. Mem. Soc. Petroleum Engrs. (sec., treas. 1983-85, pres. 1985-86), Soc. Profl. Well Log Analysts, Am. Assn. Petroleum Geologists, Tex. Midcontinent Oil and Gas Assn. (chmn. public affairs 1983—), Abilene C. of C. (petroleum council 1983—). Republican. Roman Catholic. Lodges: Rotary, K.C. Avocations: racquetball; hunting; carpentry; gardening. Home: 5601 Southmoor St Abilene TX 79606 Office: Russell Engrs PO Box 2618 Abilene TX 79604

GLEASON, WALLACE ANSELM, JR., medical educator and researcher; b. Fargo, N.D., July 26, 1944; s. Wallace Anselm and Elizabeth Madeline (Powers) G.; m. Mary Jo-Ann Hofer, Nov. 25, 1972; children—Michael Andrew, Dennis Patrick. Student Creighton U., 1962-65; B.S., U. Minn., 1967, M.D., 1969. Diplomate Am. Bd. Pediatrics. Intern, St. Louis Children's Hosp., 1969-70, resident, 1970-72; asst. in pediatrics Washington U., St. Louis, 1969-73, instr., 1973-74; instr. pediatrics St. Louis U., 1974-75, asst. prof., 1975-77; asst. prof. U. Tex. Health Sci. Ctr., San Antonio, 1977-82, assoc. prof., 1982-84; assoc. prof., chief div. pediatric gastroenterology U. Tex. Med. Sch., Houston, 1984—. Contbr. articles to profl. jours. Fellow Am. Acad. Pediatrics; mem. Am. Gastroenterol. Assn., N.Am. Soc. Pediatric Gastroenterology, So. Soc. Pediatric Research, Soc. Pediatric Research, San Antonio Pediatric Soc. (sec.-treas. 1982-83, pres. 1984). Roman Catholic. Office: Univ Tex Med Sch 6431 Fannin Houston TX 77030

GLEGHORN, LINDA LIPE, lawyer; b. Clarksdale, Miss., Jan. 10, 1948; s. William Ray and Gwendolyn (Strickland) Lipe; m. Larry L. Gleghorn, Feb. 15, 1983. B.B.A. in Accountancy, U. Miss., 1970, J.D., 1971. Bar: Miss. 1971, U.S. Dist. Ct. (no. dist.) Miss. 1971, Ark. 1976, U.S. Dist. Ct. (ea. dist.) Ark. 1976, U.S. Ct. Appeals (8th cir.) 1985. Sr. tax acct. Arthur Young & Co., San Jose, Calif., 1971-74; sr. tax acct. A.M. Pullen & Co., Knoxville, Tenn., 1975; legal counsel to gov. State of Ark., Little Rock, 1975-79; dep. pros. atty. 6th Jud. Dist. Ark., Little Rock, 1979-80; chief counsel Ark. Public Service Commn., Little Rock, 1980-83; asst. U.S. atty. Eastern Dist. Ark., Dept. Justice, Little Rock, 1983—. Mem. ABA, Miss. State Bar, Ark. State Bar Assn. Episcopalian. Office: US Attorney's Office 600 West Capitol PO Box 1229 Little Rock AR 72203

GLEIBER, ROBERT MARTIN, dentist; b. N.Y.C., Feb. 9, 1945; s. Ira and Anita (Ander) G.; m. Renae Janice Levine, June 16, 1968; children—Suzanne, Jennifer, Michael. B.A., N.Y.U., 1966; D.M.D., U. Pitts., 1970. Practice dentistry, West Palm Beach, Fla., 1972—. Served to capt. U.S. Army, 1970-72. Decorated U.S. Army-Dental Corps Achievement award. Fellow Acad. Gen. Dentistry; mem. Am. Dental Assn., Atlantic Coast Dist. Dental Soc., Palm Beach County Dental Assn., Omicron Kappa Upsilon. Club: Palm Beach Tennis. Avocations: numismatics; tennis; basketball; boating. Home: 6 Carnoustie Circle West Palm Beach FL 33401 Office: 4100 Profl Bldg 4100 S Dixie Hwy West Palm Beach FL 33405

GLEIMER, ANITA, marketing and advertising consultant; b. N.Y.C., Jan. 27, 1947; d. Bernard and Evelyn (Richman) G. Student Queens Coll., 1964-66; B.A., Fla. Atlantic U., 1971. Gen. mgr. Galerie Jean Tiroche, Palm Beach, Fla., 1969-74; chmn. bd. Impressions Unltd., Inc., Palm Beach, 1975-83; exec. v.p. Stuart, Gleimer & Assocs., Palm Beach, 1980-83; dir. sales and mktg. A & B Trading Co., North Palm Beach, Fla., 1983-84; exec. Colee & Co., 1984-85. Founding bd. mem., chmn. by-laws com. City of West Palm Beach Community Theatre, 1981; co-founder, founder bd. dirs. Palm Beach Players Community Theatre, 1978, Theatre Arts Co., 1981. Recipient appreciation award Muscular Dystrophy Assn., 1972-81, Spl. Olympics, 1975-81, Big Bros./Big Sisters of Palm Beach County, 1976; Golden Plate award Northwood Inst., 1982. Mem. Am. Mktg. Assn., Palm Beach Gardens C. of C. (founding mem.), Palm Beach County C. of C., Fla. Atlantic U. Alumni Assn. Democrat. Jewish. Clubs: Poinciana, Breakers Beach (Palm Beach); Eastlakes Country (Palm Beach Gardens, Fla.). Home: 3601 College Ave Apt 516 D Fort Lauderdale FL 33314

GLENDENNING, GEORGE WALTER, marketing executive; b. Enid, Okla., Oct. 8, 1943; s. George W. and Carriell (Jacoby) G.; m. Pamela Emogene Plaginos, July 8, 1967; children—Mary Carolyn, George William. Student Ga. Inst. Tech., 1961-63; B. Aviation Mgmt., Auburn U., 1965. Sales rep. various firms Ga., Fla., Ariz., 1966-72; gen. mgr. Lease-A-Plane, Tucson, 1973; bus. devel. mgr. Cooper Aerial Survey Co., Tucson, 1973-80; pres. Glendenning Mktg. Planning Inc., Tucson, 1980-81; v.p. mktg. Dooley-Jones & Assocs., Inc., Tucson, 1981-82; v.p., gen. mgr. Cooper Aerial Survey Tex., Inc., San Antonio, 1982; dir. mktg. UAM, Inc., San Antonio, 1982—. Bd. dirs. So. Ariz. div. Am. Heart Assn., 1980-82, treas., 1981-82; mem. San Antonio Sesquicentennial Com. Mem. Sales and Mktg. Execs. Internat. (internat. dir. 1981-84), Am. Mktg. Assn., Soc. Mktg. Profl. Services, Sales and Mktg. Execs. Tucson (dir. 1977-81, pres. 1978-79), Sales and Mktg. Execs. San Antonio (dir. 1984—). Republican. Roman Catholic. Clubs: San Antonio Gun, Rotary (San Antonio). Home: 7507 Shady Hollow Ln San Antonio TX 78255 Office: 5411 Jackwood Dr San Antonio TX 78238

GLENN, JOHN MORTON, JR., training executive; b. Burlington, N.C., Sept. 23, 1944; s. John Moton and Laura (Morton) G.; m. Mary Leigh Copeland, Oct. 9, 1971; children—Ann Kristian, John Christopher. A.A., Durham Tech. Coll., 1973; B.A., Elon Coll., 1977; M.A., N.C. A&T U., 1978. Tng. dir. Burlington (N.C.) Police Dept., 1968—; mem. N.C. Criminal Justice Commn., 1983—. Served with USN, 1966-68. Recipient Cross of Honor, Order of Demolay, 1979; Order of Long Leaf Pine, Gov. N.C., 1980; Outstanding Service to Law Enforcement award N.C. Atty. Gen., 1982; T.D. Cooper award as law enforcement officer of yr., 1983. Mem. Nat. Assn. Police Planners, N.C. Law Enforcement Planners, N.C. Law Enforcement Tng. Officers (pres. 1983-84), N.C. Police Execs. Assn., N.C. Tng. Officers Assn. (pres. 1983—), Burlington Police Club (pres. 1978, 83). Democrat. Lodges: Masons, Shriners. Home: 1540 W Davis St Burlington NC 27215 Office: Burlington Police Dept PO Box 1358 Burlington NC 27215

GLENN, ROBERT WILSON, JR., power company executive, electrical engineer; b. Burlington, N.C., Oct. 15, 1957; s. Robert Wilson Sr. and Frankie Ann (Strader) G.; m. Mary Annette Turnage, July 21, 1979 (div. 1984); m. Sherry Lynn Jones, May 3, 1985. B.S.E.E., N.C. State U., 1979; postgrad. Lynchburg Coll., 1981. Elec. engr. Appalachian Power Co., Roanoke, Va., 1979-81, adminstrv. asst., 1981-83, energy services engr., 1983-84; power engr., 1984-85, supr. energy services, 1985—. Bd. dirs. Va. Transp. Mus., Roanoke, 1984—, Jr. Achievement Roanoke, 1984-85, Camp Va. Jaycee, Montvale, 1984-85; mem. budget com. United Way Roanoke, 1980-85; pres. Plantation Village Homeowners Assn., Roanoke, 1980-82; asst. scoutmaster Blue Ridge council Boy Scouts Am. Troop 51, Salem, Va., 1980-82. Recipient Outstanding Young Man Am. award, 1983, 84, 85. Mem. Roanoke Jaycees (pres. 1984-85). Republican. Lutheran. Home: 1878 Arlington Rd SW Roanoke VA 24015 Office: Appalachian Power Co PO Box 2021 Roanoke VA 24022

GLENN, WILLIAM ALLEN, former educator, research historian; b. Logan, Ala., Mar. 28, 1925; s. Columbus Grady and Arletta Gertrude (Entrekin) G.; m. Ruth Evangeline McClendon, Sept. 10, 1949; children—Phyllis Ann, Bryan Cleveland. A.B., U. Ala., 1951, M.A., 1965; postgrad. Am. U., summer, 1967, Samford U., summer, 1976. Ordained to ministry So. Bapt. Ch. Civilian research analyst U.S. Air Force and U.S. Army, 1952-58; tchr., prin. Morgan County Schs., Decatur, Ala., 1959-64; tchr., counselor, prin., dir. fed. aid projects Jefferson County Schs., Birmingham, Ala., 1965-77, ret., 1977; researcher Abraham Lincoln family Bible, Nat. Park Service, 1977—; researcher geneal. background of Ala. governors Ala. Hist. Commn., 1977—; part-time minister So. Bapt. Ch. Chaplain Ala. Republican Inaugural Ceremonies for Pres. Nixon, 1969; mem. Ala. Commn. in Intergovtl. Cooperation, 1972-74; adviser Ala. Reagan for Pres. Com., 1980; mem. Rep. Presdl. Task Force, 1981-85; research dir. Senator Jeremiah Denton Forum, 1981-82; cons. Cullman County Mus., 1978-79; deacon Cold Springs So. Bapt. Ch. Served with USN, 1943-46. Recipient awards Freedoms Found., Valley Forge, Pa., Schoolmen medal, 1967, awards, 1969, 70. Mem. Ala. Edn. Assn., Ala. Ret. Tchrs. Assn., Nat. Ret. Tchrs. Assn., Birmingham Jefferson Hist. Assn., Nat. Hist. Soc., North Jefferson Hist. Soc. (v.p. 1979-80), Internat. Platform Assn., Alpha Kappa Delta, Phi Delta Kappa, Kappa Phi Kappa. Republican. Club: Lions. Author biog. sketches for radio broadcast Freedoms Found., 1968-70; co-author History of the Jefferson County Schs. (Ala.), 1967-68; author history of U.S. marshals in Ala. for state constl. bicentennial, 1986—; editor script for filmstrip series History of South Carolina, 1968-69; contbr. articles to profl. jours. and newspapers; writer speeches for govs. and U.S. senators; scholar Shroud of Turin. Home: 1319 Columbia Ave Gardendale AL 35071

GLEYZAL, ANDRE, retired mathematics educator; b. Lake Charles, La., Nov. 23, 1908; s. Noel Eugene and Virginia (Espitalier) G.; m. V. Gene, July 21, 1962. B.A., Ohio State U., 1931, M.A., 1933; Ph.D., Princeton U., 1936. Prof. physics Boston Coll., 1937-38; prof. math. St. Michael's Coll. Burlington, Vt., 1938-41; mathematician U.S. Navy Dept., Washington, 1941-51, Bur. Standards, Washington, 1951-53, U.S. Naval Surface Weapons Lab., Washington, 1953-72; ret., 1972. Contbr. articles to profl. jours. Mem. Am. Math. Soc., Phi Beta Kappa. Avocations: riding motorcycles; writing mathematical and physics papers. Home: 300 NE 44th St Boca Raton FL 33431

GLICK, BRIAN JAY, lawyer, contract advisor; b. Bklyn., Nov. 22, 1954; s. Merton and Vivian (Schwartz) G.; m. Susan Fern Sorgenstein, Aug. 22, 1981; 1 child, Justin Joshua. B.A. in History and English, Fordham U., 1977; J.D., Southwestern U., 1981. Bar: Fla. 1981, U.S. Dist. Ct. (so. dist.) Fla. 1982, U.S. Supreme Ct. 1984, U.S. Tex Ct. 1982. Supr. Credit Exchange, Inc., N.Y.C., 1973-77; sales rep. Hollingsworth, Co., Pottstown, Pa., 1977-78; pres. Legal Researchers, Los Angeles, 1978-81; sole practice, West Palm Beach, Fla., 1981-82, Boca Raton, Fla., 1982—; contract advisor Nat. Football League Players Assn., Washington, 1984. Author short stories, poetry. Advisor West Boca Community Council, 1983; bd. dirs. Estada Homeowners Assn., Boca Raton, 1984. Office: 900 N Federal Hwy Suite 340 Boca Raton FL 33432

GLICK, JACOB EZRA, association executive; b. Burlington, Iowa, Feb. 12, 1920; s. Russell Clyde and Clara Alice (Deptuy) G.; m. Marjorie L. Gardner, Dec. 7, 1951; children—Jeffrey, Susan, Thomas. B.S. Engring., U.S. Naval Acad., 1941; M.S., 1949; M.B.A., George Washington U., 1965; grad. Nat. War Coll., 1965. Registered profl. engr., D.C. Commd. 2d lt. U.S. Marine Corps, 1941, advanced through grades to brig. gen., 1967; unit comdr. World War II, Korea, Vietnam; dep. chief research and devel. Hdqrs., 1962-64; ops. directorate Office Joint Chiefs of Staff, Washington, 1968-71; ret., 1971; nat. sec. Ret. Officers Assn., Alexandria, Va., 1971-85; guest lectr. Nat. War Coll., service schs., 1956-71; instr., head dept. Marine Corps Schs., 1956-59. Commr., Boy Scouts Am. Decorated D.S.M., Legion Merit (3), Bronze Star; Vietnamese Cross Gallantry with palm, Vietnamese Honor medal. Mem. Marine Corps Assn. (past bd. dirs.), Naval Acad. Alumni Assn., 12th Def. Bn. Assn., Ret. Officers Assn., Marine Corps League, Marine Exec. Assn. (chmn. bd. 1984-85). Methodist. Club: Army Navy. Lodge: Optimist (bd. dirs., pres. 1984-85). Home: 407 Skyhill Rd Alexandria VA 22314 Office: 201 N Washington St TROA Alexandria VA 22314

GLICK, RICHARD STEPHEN, physician; b. Pitts., May 18, 1947; s. William and Ruthe (Scher) G. B.A. cum laude, U. Pa., 1969, M.D., 1973. Diplomate Am. Bd. Internal Medicine (also subsplty. bd. rheumatology). Intern, U. Mich. Hosp., Ann Arbor, 1973-74, resident, 1974-77; fellow in rheumatology U. Pa., 1977-78, Albany Med. Coll. Hosp., 1978-79; practice medicine specializing in rheumatology and internal medicine, Ft. Lauderdale, Fla., 1979—. Mem. AMA, Fla. Med. Assn., Am. Rheumatism Assn., Fla. Soc. Rheumatology. Contbr. articles to profl. jours. Office: 4701 N Federal Hwy Suite C-2 Fort Lauderdale FL 33308

GLINN, FRANKLYN BARRY, lawyer; b. Newark, Oct. 22, 1943; s. Dave and Gertrude (Weinstein) G.; m. Sandra Lee Scales, Nov. 3, 1943; children—MacAdam Jordan, Dara Elisabeth, B.A.E., U. Fla., 1965, J.D., 1968. Bar: Fla. 1969, U.S. Ct. Appeals (5th cir.) 1969, U.S. Dist. Ct. (so. dist.) Fla. 1970. Assoc. firm Ser, Greenspahn & Keyfetz, Miami, Fla., 1969-70. Ser & Keyfetz, Miami, 1970-72, Rabin, Sassoon, & Ratiner, Miami, 1972-74; ptnr. firm Ratiner & Glinn, Miami, 1974—. Mem. ABA, Am. Judicature Soc., Assn. Trial Lawyers Am., Acad. Fla. Trial Lawyers, Am. Arbitration Assn. Democrat. Jewish. Office: Ratiner & Glinn 60 SW 13th St Miami FL 33130

GLOVER, CLIFFORD CLARKE, construction company executive; b. Newnan, Ga., May 15, 1913; s. Howard Clarke and Fannie Virginia (Jones) G.; m. Louise Liles, Jan. 16, 1937; children—Edmund Cook, Nancy Liles Glover Kennedy, Virginia Johnston Glover Lee, Laura Clarke. B.C.E., U. N.C., 1934. With Batson-Cook Co., West Point, Ga., 1934—, now chmn.; chief engrs. Contractors, Jacksonville, Fla., 1940-43; dir. First Nat. Bank West Point, Ga.-Ala. Supply Co. Mem. West Point Sch. Bd., 1951-69, chmn., 1964-68; chmn. West Point Planning Bd., 1964—; trustee LaGrange Coll.; pres. George H. Lanier council Boy Scouts Am., 1977-78. Served with USNR, 1945-46. Recipient Silver Beaver award Boy Scouts Am. Mem. Assoc. Gen. Contractors (pres. Ga. br.). Methodist (ofcl. bd.). Clubs: Commerce, Capital City (Atlanta); Riverside (West Point). Lodge: Rotary. Home: 103 Hillcrest Rd West Point GA 31833 Office: Batson-Cook Co 116 4th Ave West Point GA 31833*

GLOVER, DORTHA LOU, county official; b. Red Oak, Okla., Oct. 30, 1924; d. Charles L. and Georgia (Briggs) Dennis; grad. Texarkana Bus. Coll., 1946; m. Bobby Ray Glover, Feb. 25, 1972 (dec. Mar. 1984); stepchildren—Mary Ellen Livingston, Shirley Ann Green, Judy Arlene Chappel, Mollie Virginia Jack, Kathy Louise Brock. Bookkeeper, McAlester (Okla.) Tobacco & Candy Co., 1946-47, Taylor Mfg. Co., Tulsa, 1947-48; auditor John A. Brown Co., Oklahoma City, 1948; legal sec., legal asst. John B. Baument, Atty., McAlester, 1949-74; ct. clerk Pittsburg County (Okla.), 1975—. Mem. County Officers Assn. Okla., Okla. Ct. Clks. Assn., Bus. and Profl. Women's Club, Pittsburg County Legal Secs. Assn., Okla. Assn. Legal Secs., Nat. Assn. Legal Secs., Nat. Assn. Legal Assts. Democrat. Baptist. Home: 804 S 9th St McAlester OK 74501 Office: PO Box 460 McAlester OK 74501

GLOVER, EDWIN EUGENE, university administrator; b. Stillwater, Okla., Mar. 29, 1922; s. William Earl and Grace Althea (Andrews) G.; B.S., Okla. State U., 1947; m. Mary L. Hall, Jan. 18, 1941; children—Linda Glover Mahar, Thomas E. Acct., Okla. State U., 1947-50, asst. chief acct., 1950-58, internal auditor, instl. rep. for grants and contracts, 1958-65, asst. bus. mgr., internal auditor, instl. rep. for grants and contracts, 1965-69, dir. internal audits, instl. rep. for grants and contracts, 1969-78, dir. internal audit, 1978—. Sec., treas. Scabbard and Blade Endowment and Resources, Inc., 1965-75; chmn. Assn. Coll. and Univs. Midyear Seminars. Served with AUS, 1943-46. Decorated Purple Heart, Bronze Star; recipient citations Inst. Internal Auditors, 1972, Oklahoma City chpt. Inst. Internal Auditors, 1975. Cert. internal auditor. Mem. Inst. Internal Auditors (past pres. Oklahoma City chpt. 1965-71, 75—, gov.; Disting. Service award Oklahoma City chpt. 1982), Assn. Coll. and Univ. Auditors (nat. pres. 1976, Stanley C. Smith award 1979, Disting. Service award 1982-83), Okla. State U. Alumni Assn. (life), Ret. Officers Assn., Am. Ex-P.O.W.s (state adj. treas.), Am. Legion, Scabbard and Blade (past nat. comdr.). Democrat. Lion (past pres. Stillwater). Club: Red Red Rose. Home: 1111 W Knapp St Stillwater OK 74074 Office: Oklahoma State U Stillwater OK 74078

GLOVER, NATHANIEL BANKS, JR., management consultant; b. West Point, N.Y., Mar. 12, 1947; s. Nathaniel Banks and Margaret (Wilson) G.; B.S. in Bus. Adminstrn., The Citadel, 1969; M.B.A. in Mgmt., Ga. State U., 1975. Plant mgr. Lunsford Wilson Co., Atlanta, 1969-72; asst. plant mgr. Kaufman & Broad Home Systems, LaGrange, Ga., 1972-73; staff Alexander Proudfoot Co., Chgo., 1975-77; mgr. installations A.T. Oxford, Inc., Coral Gables, Fla., 1977-80; v.p. Am. Mgmt. Systems Co., Washington, 1980-82; pres. Corporate Technology, Inc., Dallas, 1982—. Republican. Baptist.

GLOVER, RICHARD ELTON, mortgage banker; b. Weatherford, Tex., Jan. 8, 1939; s. Elton William and Mattie Carmen (Shaw) G.; m. Eva Jo Addison, June 25, 1958; children—Jana Kay, Richard Elton, Jeffrey Brian. B.B.A. in Acctg., Tex. Christian U., 1964; D.B.A., Western States U. Lic. real estate broker, Tex.; life ins. broker; cert. property appraiser. Draftsman, Tex. Hwy. Dept., Fort Worth, 1959-64; comptroller Reid & Co., Fort Worth, 1964-66; exec. v.p. So. Mortgage Corp., Fort Worth, 1966-68; real estate appraiser HUD, Fort Worth, 1979-82; owner R.E.G. Realty, Fort Worth, 1968—, Glover Ins. Agy., Fort Worth, 1968—; sec.-treas. Security Bankers Investment Co., Fort Worth, 1978—; pres., chmn. bd. Citizens Nat. Mortgage Corp., Fort Worth, 1968—. Mem. Pres. Reagan's Task Force, 1982—; mem. Fort Worth Community Devel. Council, 1973-75; sec. City of Aledo, 1964-69. Served with Air N.G., 1962-70. Mem. Fort Worth Mortgage Bankers (pres. 1975-76), Tex. Mortgage Bankers Assn., Greater Fort Worth Bd. Realtors, Tex. Assn. Realtors, Nat. Assn. Realtors, Tex. Ind. Producers and Royalty Owners, Assn. Govt. Appraisers, Internat. Orgn. Real Estate Appraisers, Nat. Assn. Cert. Real Property. Baptist. Clubs: Colonial Country, Petroleum, Century II (Fort Worth). Home: 3813 Lawndale Ave Fort Worth TX 76133 Office: 5049B Old Granbury Rd PO Box 16339 Fort Worth TX 76133

GLOWCZWSKI, ROBERT VINCENT, manufacturing company official; b. St. Louis, June 18, 1931; s. Lawrence Wellington and Gladys (Tucker) G.; B.S. in Aero. Engring., St. Louis U., 1955, M.S., 1963; children—David, John, Alan, Susan, Melinda. Design engr. McDonnell Aircraft Co., St. Louis, 1955-56, aerodynamist, 1956-58, tech. integration engr., 1958-64; systems engr. McDonnell Douglas Astronautics Co., St. Louis, 1965-66, dynamics engr., 1966-68, program mgr., 1969-72, mgr. tech. integration, 1973-74; mgr. new bus. devel. McDonnell Douglas Tech. Service Co., Houston, 1975-79, mgr. program control and adminstrn., 1980; mission office lead engr., space transp. system Martin Marietta Corp., Houston, 1981-82, chief space sta., 1984—. Pres., Walker Elem. Sch. PTA, 1961-62; deacon, elder Florissant Presbyn. Ch., 1964-68; chief Indian Guides, Bay Area YMCA, 1970, bd. dirs., 1969-72. 74-75, mgr. bd. dirs., 1976. Served with USMCR, 1950-52; Korea. Fellow AIAA (assoc.; treas. Houston sect. 1978-79, Nat. Membership Chmn. of Yr. award 1977, Sect. Service award Houston sect. 1978, dep. dir. region IV membership 1980-83, chmn.-elect Houston sect. 1983-84, chmn. 1984-85); mem. Am. Mgmt. Assn., Nat. Contract Mgmt. Assn., Parks Coll. Alumni Assn. (pres. 1960). Democrat. Club: Seabrook Sailing. Home: 322 Knoll Forest League City TX 77573 Office: 1740 NASA Rd 1 Suite 100 Houston TX 77058

GLOYNA, EARNEST FREDERICK, university dean, educator, researcher; b. Vernon, Tex., June 30, 1921; s. Herman Ernst and Johanna Bertha (Reithmayer) G.; m. Agnes Mary Lehman, Feb. 17, 1946; children—David Frederick, Lisa Ann Gloyna Grosskopf. B.S.C.E., Tex. Tech U., 1946; M.S.C.E., U. Tex., 1949; Dr.Engring., Johns Hopkins U., 1952. Registered profl. engr., Tex. Engr., Tex. Hwy. Dept., 1945-46; office engr. Magnolia Petroleum Co., 1946-47; instr. civil engring. U. Tex., Austin, 1947-49, asst. prof., 1949-53, assoc. prof., 1953-59, prof., 1959—, Joe J. King prof. engring., 1970-82, Bettie Margaret Smith chair environ. health engring., 1982—, dir. Environ. Health Engring. Labs., 1953-70, dir. Ctr. Research in Water Resources, 1963-73, dir. Bur. Engring. Research, 1970—, dean Coll. Engring., 1970—; cons. water and wastewater treatment and water resources for industry and govts., 1947—; mem. U.S. Senate Select Com. on Water Resources, AEC, NIH, USPHS, EPA, NRC. Served to lt. col. C.E., AUS, 1942-46; ETO. Recipient Water Resources Div. award Am. Water Works Assn., 1959; named Disting. Engring. Grad., Tex. Tech. U., 1971, Disting. Alumnus, 1973; named Disting. Engring. Grad., U. Tex., 1982; recipient Nat. Environ. Devel. Assn. award, 1983, Gordon Maskew Fair award Am. Acad. Environ. Engrs., 1982, J.J. King Profl. Engring. Achievement award, 1982, Regional Environ. Educator award EPA, 1977; Order Henri Pittier, Nat. Conservation medal (Republic Venezuela), 1983. Fellow ASCE; mem. Nat. Acad. Engring. U.S. (governing council), Nat. Acad. Scis. Venezuela, Nat. Acad. Engring. Mex. (corr.), Assn. Environ. Engring. Profs. (past pres.), Am. Acad. Environ. Engrs. (past pres., diplomate), Water Pollution Control Fedn. (past pres.; Harrison Prescott Eddy medal 1959, Gordon Maskew Fair medal 1979; hon. mem. award 1980), Tex. Soc. Profl. Engrs. (nat. dir.; pres. elect), Nat. Soc. Profl. Engrs. (bd. dirs.), Am. Soc. Higher Edn., Am. Water Works Assn., Am. Inst. Chem. Engrs., Sci. Adv. Bd. EPA (past chmn.). Lutheran. Clubs: Headliners, Faculty Ctr. (Austin); Cosmos (Washington). Lodge: Rotary. Author: Waste Stabilization Ponds, 1971; (with Joe Ledbetter) Principles of Radiological Health, 1969; editor: (with W.W. Eckenfelder, Jr.) Advances in Water Quality Improvement, 1968; Water Quality Improvement by Physical and Chemical Processes, 1970; (with W.S. Butcher) Conflicts in Water Resources Planning, 1972; (with Woodson & Drew) Water Management by Electric Power Industry, 1975; (with Malina and Davis) Ponds as a Wastewater Treatment Alternative, 1976; contbr. 180 articles to profl. jours. Home: 3317 River Rd Austin TX 78703 Office: ECJ 10 310 University of Texas Austin TX 78712

GLYNN, WILLIAM GEORGE, JR., financial consultant; b. N.Y.C., Aug. 27, 1928; s. William George and Mary Elizabeth (Mooney) G.; student schs. Mineola, N.Y.; m. Jeri Lynn, Sept. 13, 1975; children—William George III, Robert Anthony, Susan Amy, Diane Marie. Mfrs. rep. Kroehler Mfg. Co., Naperville, Ill., 1958-67; pres. Columbia Contract Interiors, N.Y.C., 1967-69, Atlantic Fisherman's Wharf, Pompano Beach, Fla., 1969-77, Glynn Mktg. Corp., Ft. Lauderdale, Fla., 1975-77, Global Resources, Inc., Pompano Beach, 1978-80, Bill Glynn Realty Corp., Ft. Lauderdale, 1980—; cons. Payne Webber, Inc., 1981-83, Pub. Fin. div. Prudential-Bache Securities Inc., 1983—. Active, Republican Orgn., Nassau County, N.Y., 1960-68; trustee, acting mayor, commr. police and public safety, vice mayor, commr. transp. Westbury, N.Y., 1962-68; active polit. campaigns Broward County, Fla., 1972—; pres. Pompano Beach Rep. Club, 1974-82; coordinator all Rep. campaigns Broward County, 1980; Rep. state committeeman Broward County, 1976-80, precinct committeeman, exec. com., 1972—, chmn., exec. com., 1980—; chmn. Fla. Rep. County Chairmen's Assn., 1980—; chmn. Fla. Rep. State Outreach Com., 1981—; del. Rep. Nat. Conv., 1980; active Little League and amateur baseball, Nassau County, 1960-68; life mem. Westbury (N.Y.) Amateur Baseball Assn.; dir. War Meml. Bd., L.I., N.Y., 1962-68; mem. Bishop's Com. of the Laity, Diocese of Rockville Center (N.Y.), 1965-68; hon. life mem. Pompano Beach Profl. Firefighter's Assn.; del. White House Conf. Aging, 1981; dir. United Way Broward County, 1980—. Recipient awards Am. Legion, Pompano Beach, 1975; Edgar Lamkin Meml. award City of Pompano Beach, 1976-81; U.S. Presdl. Bi-centennial award, 1976; pres.'s award Pompano Beach Rep. Club, 1976-78, 80-82; award Fraternal Order Police, Ft. Lauderdale, 1980; Broward Forum award, Hollywood, Fla., 1980; award Kiwanis, Ft. Lauderdale, 1980; Sunrise Jewish Center award, 1980; Broward County Rep. of Yr. award, 1981; Citizenship award Alliance for Responsible Growth, 1981; Interfaith award B'nai B'rith of Broward County, 1981. Home: 1617 N Atlantic Blvd Fort Lauderdale FL 33305 Office: 828 N Federal Hwy Fort Lauderdale FL 33304

GOATES, DONALD RAY, minister; b. Corpus Christi, Tex., Jan. 14, 1943; s. Joe Elbert Goates and Bobbie (Cochran) Goates Hammett; m. Patsy LaNetta Owens, June 7, 1963; children—Gretchen Gwyndolyn, Sunnae Millicent, Donald Ray II. B.A. in Music Edn., East Tex. State U., 1965; M.Div., Southwestern Baptist Theol. Sem., 1975, D.Min., 1979. Ordained to ministry Baptist Ch., 1972. Asst. mgr. G.F. Wacker's, Commerce, Tex., 1964-65; commd. 2d lt. U.S. Army, 1965, advanced through grades to capt., 1972, served in Vietnam; pastor Water St. Bapt. Ch., Waxahachie, Tex., 1972-76, First Bapt. Ch. of Forest Hill, Fort Worth, 1976-80, First Bapt. Ch., Sweetwater, Tex., 1980—; associational moderator Sweetwater Bapt. Assn., 1983-84; pres. Sweetwater Ministerial Alliance, 1985. Contbr. articles to profl. jours. Decorated Silver Star, Bronze Star, Hon. medal 1st class and Cross of Gallantry (Republic of Vietnam). Lodges: Rotary (bd. dirs. 1985), Masons, Shriners. Avocations: hunting; fishing; construction. Office: PO Box 1258 Sweetwater TX 79556

GOBBEL, LINDELL J. HENDERSON CUNNINGHAM, nursing administrator; b. Scott County, Va., Oct. 4, 1940; d. James Patton, Sr., and Irma (Wininger) Henderson; B.S. in Nursing, E.Tenn. State Coll. (Univ.), 1961; m.

George Thomas Cunningham, June 15, 1962 (dec. Dec. 1981); 1 son, George Thomas; m. Henry Donald Gobbel, July 9, 1983. Staff nurse LeBonheur and Tobey Children's Hosps., Memphis; house supr. E.Tenn. Bapt. Hosp., Knoxville, Pitt County Meml. Hosp., Greenville, N.C.; occupational health nurse Texfi-K, Rocky Mount, N.C.; occupational health nurse, personnel mgr. Samsons Mfg. Co., Wilson, N.C.; head nurse pediatrics Charlotte (N.C.) Meml. Hosp.; pediatric nurse, unit mgr. Nash Gen. Hosp., Rocky Mount; dir. nursing services St. Eugene Community Hosp., Dillon, S.C., to 1983; asst. dir. nursing Sampson County Meml. Hosp., Clinton, N.C., 1983—. Red Cross nurse, mem. Blood Mobile com. nat. ARC. Mem. Am. Assn. Indsl. Nurses (corr. sec. 1980-81), Beta Sigma Phi (pres. Alpha Epsilon chpt. 1977-78, city council 1981—, program award 1981). Democrat. Episcopalian. Home: 303 Cooper Dr Clinton NC 28328 Office: 607 Beamon St Clinton NC 28328

GOBLE, ROSS LEE, engineering research administrator, mechanical engineer; b. Richmond, Ind., Mar. 27, 1931; s. Samuel M. and Rose (Ross) G.; B.S. in Mech. Engring., Clemson U., 1959; M.S., N.Y. U., 1964; Ph.D., Va. Poly. Inst. and State U., 1970; m. Mabel Fimple, Feb. 26, 1954; children—Deborah Lee, Pamela Gail, Gregory Ross. Mem. tech. staff Bell Telephone Labs., Whippany, N.J., 1959-60; sr. exptl. engr. Pratt and Whitney Aircraft Co., West Palm Beach, Fla., 1960-63; head systems analysis sect. NASA-Langley Research Center, Hampton, Va., 1963-70, head design and structural integration sect., 1970, structures mgr., advanced transport tech. office, 1970-72, head research facilities planning office, 1972-73, chief research facilities engring. div., 1973-78; v.p. Advex Corp., 1978-80, pres., chief exec. officer, 1980-82; pres. Technology Cons. Internat., 1982-84, pres., co-founder, dir. Engring. Devel. Lab., Inc., 1984—; instr. engring. Hampton Inst., 1971; instr. public adminstrn. Golden Gate U., 1973—. Pres., PTA, Riverside Elem. Sch., Newport News, Va., 1971; pres. James River Civic League, 1970-71, treas., 1971-72; chmn. scout com. Newport News council Boy Scouts Am., 1972-73; program chmn. Peninsula Beautification/Ecology Council, Va., 1975-76; civic adviser Jr. League of Hampton Roads, 1975—; vice chmn. Newport News City Planning Commn., 1975-78, chmn., 1978-80; bd. dirs. Council for Environ. Quality, 1970-74, pres., 1970-71; trustee Peninsula Nature Sci. Center, 1971-75, 1st v.p. finance, 1972-73. Served with USN, 1951-55; Korea. Recipient Lunar Orbiter Project Group Achievement award NASA, 1968, Apollo Achievement award, 1969. Fellow AIAA (asso.); mem. ASME, Am. Soc. Planning Ofcls., Engrs. Club Va. Peninsula (pres. 1975-76), Explorers Club. Contbr. articles to profl. publs. Home: 37 Meade Dr Newport News VA 23602 Office: 704 Gum Rock Ct Suite 400 Newport News VA 23606

GODARD, JOHN ELLINGTON, ophthalomologist; b. Moultrie, Ga., Nov. 23, 1942; s. Johnnie G. and Frances B. (Baker) G. A.B., Emory U., 1964; M.D., Med. Coll. Ga., 1968. Diplomate Am. Bd. Ophthalmology. Intern Med. Coll. Ga., Augusta, 1968-69, resident, 1973-76; practice ophthalmology Carrollton Eye Clinic, Ga., 1976—. Served to maj. USAF. Fellow Am. Acad. Ophthalmology; mem. Ga. Soc. Ophthalmology, AMA, So. Med. Assn., Med. Assn. Ga., Outpatient Ophthalmic Surgery Soc., Am. Intraocular Implant Soc. Episcopalian. Lodges: Rotary, Lions. Avocation: horticulture. Office: 160 Clinic Ave Carrollton GA 30117

GODARD, RANDY EUGENE, lawyer, business advisor; b. Cedar City, Utah, Dec. 16, 1952; s. Gerald Eugene and Fern (Jones) G.; m. Linda Anne Fulks, May 9, 1975; children—Joanne Marie, Jacob Eugene, Benjamin James, Daniel Kinsey. B.A., Brigham Young U., 1977, M.B.A., 1980, J.D., 1980. Bar: Tex. 1981. Assoc. Gray, Cary, et al., San Diego, 1981; legal counsel Tex. State Senate, 1982; corp. counsel Rapada Corp., Houston, 1982; corp. atty. Allied-Signal Corp., Houston, 1983—; cons. in field. Coordinator Houston Area Blood Dr.; mem. Aldine Ind. Sch. dist. PTA, 1982—. Mem. ABA, Nat. Bus. Adv. Council, Phi Delta Phi. Mormon. Editor: Brigham Young U. Jour. Legal Studies, 1980; contbr. articles to profl. jours.

GODBOLD, JAKE MAURICE, mayor of Jacksonville; b. Jacksonville, Fla., Mar. 14, 1934; s. Charles B. and Irene Noegel (Whitfield) G.; m. Jean Jenkins, Feb. 16, 1957; 1 child, Ben. Student pub. schs., Jacksonville. Agt., then supt. nat. hdqrs. Ind. life Ins. Co., until 1969; founder, owner, operator Gateway Chem. Co.; mem. Jacksonville City Council, 1967-79, pres., 1971, 78; mayor City of Jacksonville, 1979—. Bd. dirs. Gator Bowl Assn., Boys Club of Jacksonville, Muscular Dystrophy Assn.; pres. bd. dirs. Big Bros., Jacksonville. Served with U.S. Army, 1951-53; Korea. Recipient Disting. Service award Jacksonville Area C. of C., 1968. Mem. Fla. League of Cities, Nat. League of Cities, U.S. Conf. Mayors. Democrat. Methodist. Clubs: Rotary, Northside Businessmen's, Springfield Businessmen's. Office: Office of Mayor 220 E Bay St Jacksonville FL 32202*

GODBOLD, JOHN COOPER, judge; b. Coy, Ala., Mar. 24, 1920; s. Edwin Condie and Elsie (Williamson) G.; B.S., Auburn U., 1940; J.D., Harvard, 1948; LL.D. (hon.), Samford U., 1981; m. Elizabeth Showalter, July 18, 1942; children—Susan, Richard, John C., Cornelia, Sally. Admitted to Ala. bar, 1948; with firm Richard T. Rives, Montgomery, 1948-49; partner firm Godbold, Hobbs & Copeland, and predecessors, 1949-66; U.S. circuit judge Ct. Appeals 5th Circuit, 1966-81, chief judge, 1981; chief judge Ct. Appeals 11th Circuit, 1981—. Bd. dirs. Fed. Jud. Center, 1976-81. Served with F.A., AUS, 1941-46. Mem. Am. Fed., Ala., Montgomery County bar assns., Alpha Tau Omega, Omicron Delta Kappa, Phi Kappa Phi. Episcopalian. Club: Montgomery Country. Office: Federal Courthouse Montgomery AL 36102 also US Ct of Appeals Courthouse Atlanta GA 30303

GODDARD, EDWARD MCCOY, SR., funeral home executive, consultant; b. Reynold, Ga., Feb. 7, 1918; s. George Henry and Lucy (McCoy) G.; m. Evelyn Naia Gonzalez, Apr. 17, 1941; children—Edward McCoy, Jr., Naia Elizabeth, George C., Robert Bruce. B.A., Emory U., 1939; B.A., Cornell U., 1943. Salesman Ga. Power Co., Macon, 1939; owner G. H. Goddard & Sons operators funeral homes and merchandising cos., Reynolds, Ga., 1946-83, cons., 1941—; dir. Citizen State Bank, Reynolds, owner Chmn. Reynolds Housing Authority; chmn. Taylor County chpt. ARC; bd. dirs. Reynolds Indsl. Devel. Corp.; lt. col. gov.'s staff State of Ga., 1983. Served to lt. USNR, 1943-46. Mem. Nat. Funeral Dirs. Assn., Ga. Funeral Dirs. Assn., Res. Officers Assn. Democrat. Methodist. Clubs: Kiwanis (past lt. gov. Ga. dist.); Reynolds Golf (pres.); Masons. Home: 506 Macon St PO Box 127 Reynolds GA 31076 Office: 500 Collins St Reynolds GA 31076

GODFREY, JOHN MUNRO, bank economist; b. San Antonio, Tex., Mar. 20, 1941; s. George Phillips and Frieda (Allen) G.; m. Nancy Porter, June 4, 1966 (div. 1976); 1 son, John Munro, Jr.; A.A., Armstrong State Coll., 1964; B.B.A., U. Ga., 1964, Ph.D., 1976. Research officer, sr. fin. economist Fed. Res. Bank, Atlanta, 1969-81; sr. v.p., chief economist Barnett Banks of Fla., Inc., Jacksonville, 1981—; mem. Gov.'s Econ. Adv. Com.; mem. econ. adv. com. Am. Bankers Assn. Mem. econ. adv. com. U.S. C. of C.; bd. dirs. Fla. Ballet at Jacksonville. Mem. Econ. Roundtable of Jacksonville (pres. 1982—), Nat. Assn. Bus. Economists (dir.), Am. Econ. Assn., So. Econ. Assn., U. Ga. Coll. Bus. Alumni Assn. (bd. dirs.). Episcopalian. Clubs: Ponte Vedra, Fla. Yacht, Meninak of Jacksonville. Author: Monetary Expansion in the Confederacy, 1977. Home: 3406 Pine St Jacksonville FL 32205 Office: 100 Laura St Jacksonville FL 32231

GODKINS, THOMAS REGIS, university administrator; b. Pitts., Jan. 5, 1944; s. Regis and Ellen K. Godkins; m. Lois Weihiemer, Dec. 26, 1968; children—T. Scott, Heather O'Shea. Student, Youngstown (Ohio) State U., 1965-66; cert. in physicians assistance program Duke U., 1967-69; B.S., U. Okla., 1974, M.P.H., 1983. Physician's asst. dept. internal medicine and cardiology Mayo Clinic, 1969-72; assoc. dir. physician's assoc. program U. Okla., Oklahoma City Health Scis. Ctr., 1972-81, asst. prof. Coll. Medicine, 1974-77, assoc. prof., 1977—, asst. to provost for adminstrv. affairs, 1981—, dir., capital planning, 1986—; staff physician's asst. VA Med. Ctr., Oklahoma City, 1972—. Contbr. chpt. to book, articles to profl. jours.; manuscript reviewer Med. Care, 1978-84, mem. editorial bd., 1980-84. Served with USN, 1961-65. Mem. Am. Pub. Health Assn. Home: 2720 NW 112th St Oklahoma City OK 73120 Office: 1000 Stanton L Young Blvd Oklahoma City OK 73190

GODSEY, WILLIAM COLE, physician; b. Memphis, Dec. 11, 1933; s. Monroe Dowe and Margaret Pauline (Cole) G.; B.S., Southwestern U., 1955; M.D., U. Tenn., 1958; m. Norma Jean Wilkinson, June 18, 1958; children—William Cole, John Edward, Robert Dowe. Intern, John Gaston Hosp., Memphis, 1958-59; resident in psychiatry Gailor Meml. Hosp., Memphis, 1960-63; practice medicine specializing in psychiatry and neurology; mem. staffs Bapt. Meml. Hosp., Mid-South Hosp., Lakeside Hosp., St. Joseph Hosp.; asst. supt. Memphis Mental Health Inst., 1965-74; supt. Central State Hosp., Nashville, 1974-75; med. dir. Whitehaven Mental Health Center, Memphis, 1975-84, St. Joseph Hosp. Life Ctr., 1984—; asst. prof. U. Tenn. Coll. Medicine, 1965-74, Coll. Pharmacy, 1972-75; chief of staff Lakeside Hosp., Memphis, 1976-77; Songwriter, pub.; pres. Memphis Country Music, Inc. Diplomate Am. Bd. Psychiatry and Neurology. Fellow Am. Psychiatric Assn. (past pres. West Tenn. chpt.); mem. Tenn. Psychiat. Assn. (exec. council), AMA, Tenn. Med. Assn., Memphis and Shelby County Med. Soc., Nat. Rifle Assn. Methodist. Club: Moose. Office: 210 Jackson Ave Suite 401 Memphis TN 38105

GODWIN, BENJAMIN BRAXTON, financial executive; b. Daytona Beach, Fla., Oct. 23, 1951; s. Braxton Olie and Ann (Bass) G.; m. Phyllis Hitchcock, Sept. 5, 1970; children—Allison Meredith, Lauren Elizabeth. B.B.A., Ga. State U., 1973. Asst. adminstr. Win Corp., Atlanta, 1971-73; adminstrv. officer First Atlanta Corp., 1973-78; v.p. Sun Bank-Suncoast, St. Petersburg, Fla., 1978-81, NCNB Nat. Bank, St. Petersburg, 1981-84, Home Fed. Bank, St. Petersburg, 1984-85, fin. Aanco Underwriters, Inc., St. Petersburg, 1985—, also dir.; pres./cons. Halifax Fin. Services, Inc., 1985—. Bd. dirs. Fla. Orch., St. Petersburg, 1983—, St. Petersburg Neighborhood Housing Services, 1983—; grad. Leadership St. Petersburg, 1983. Paul Harris fellow, 1985. Mem. Com. of 100. Republican. Episcopalian. Lodge: Rotary (pres. 1984-85). Office: Aanco Underwriters Inc 1901 9th St N Saint Petersburg FL 33704

GODWIN, NANCY GAIL, health and physical education educator; b. Cuthbert, Ga., June 27, 1945; d. Charles Edwin and Floriede (Manry) G. Assoc. in Nursing, Ga. Southwestern Coll., 1966, B.S. in Edn., 1976, M.S. in Edn., 1976. R.N., Ga.; cert. in edn., Ga. Operating room staff nurse St. Francis Hosp., Columbus, Ga., 1966-67; pvt. surg. asst. Dr. R.H. Vaughan, Columbus, 1967-73; tchr. health and phys. edn. Muscogee County Sch. Dist., Columbus, 1976—, head basketball coach Baker High Sch., 1976-81, head softball coach, 1976-83. Named Softball Coach of Yr., Ledger-Enquirer, Columbus, 1982. Mem. AAHPERD, Phi Theta Kappa, Phi Delta Kappa. Democrat. Baptist. Home: 4333 Yates Dr Columbus GA 31907 Office: Baker High Sch 1544 Benning Dr Columbus GA 31903

GODWIN, PAUL MILTON, musician; b. Hot Springs, Ark., June 18, 1942; s. Walter Franklin and Mamie Viola (Meek) G.; B.A., Ark. Tech. U., 1964; M.A., Ohio State U., 1969, Ph.D., 1972; m. Mary Mae Wolfe, July 22, 1967; children—Katherine Elizabeth, Kimberly Ann, Jeremy Wolfe. Band dir. Lewisville (Ark.) Sch., 1966-67, Lee Sr. High Sch., Marianna, Ark., 1972-73; teaching asso. Ohio State U., 1970-71; mem. faculty Belmont Coll., Nashville, 1973—, asso. prof. music, 1975-80, prof., 1980—, coordinator music theory, 1973—, band dir., 1973-79, chmn. dept. acad. studies, 1983—; choir dir. Crievewood United Methodist Ch., Nashville, 1973-74; dir. Middle Tenn. Jr. High Clinic Honors Band, 1979. Served with USAR, 1964-66. Mem. Soc. Music Theory, Coll. Music Soc., Middle Tenn. Sch. Band and Orch. Assn., Music Educators Nat. Conf., Tenn. Music Educators Assn., Phi Mu Alpha Sinfonia. Methodist. Club: Elks. Home: 15459 Old Hickory Blvd Nashville TN 37211 Office: Sch Music Belmont Coll Nashville TN 37203

GODWIN, ROGER THOMAS, architect; b. Atlanta, July 6, 1954; s. James Bryan and Mary Elizabeth (Murrell) G.; m. Nancy Jane Knight, Apr. 27, 1973; children—Katherine Kelly, Michael Drew. B.F.A., Auburn U., 1976, B.F.A. in Environ. Design, 1977, B.F.A. in Architecture, 1978. Registered architect, Ga. Project designer Thompson, Ventulett, Stainback & Assocs., Atlanta, 1978-80; project mgr. Jova, Daniels, Busby, Atlanta, 1980-81; owner, architect Godwin & Assocs., Atlanta, 1981—, ptnr., 1982—. Community spokesman for erosion damage to local lakes, 1983; trustee Faith Meth. Ch., 1980-82; active United Way, 1982-83. Recipient Faculty Sr. Design award Auburn U. Sch. Architecture, 1976. Mem. AIA. Republican. Methodist. Club: Cherokee Town. Office: 3475 Lenox Rd Suite 115 Atlanta GA 30326

GODWIN, RONALD S., association executive; b. Pensacola, Fla., May 6, 1937; s. J.M. Godwin; m. Alice Bradley, June 10, 1959; children—Paul Arlin, Sarah Ronna. B.A., Bob Jones U., 1961; M.S., Old Dominion U., 1969; Ph.D., Fla. State U., 1974. Tchr. Christian schs., Pensacola, Fla.; prin. Panama City Christian Sch., Fla.; dean Pensacola Christian Coll., 1973-78; asst. to pres. Clearwater Christian Coll., Fla., 1978-79, Liberty U., Lynchburg, Va., 1979-80; exec. v.p. Moral Majority Inc., Lynchburg, 1980—; mem. exec. com. Lynchburg Christian Acad., asst. to pres. Liberty Baptist Coll., 1979—; lectr. in field; polit. cons. Bd. dirs. Council for Nat. Policy, Internat. Policy Forum, Anti-Pornography Coalition, People United to Protect Life, The Fairness Com. Against Tax-Funded Politics, Am. Forum for Jewish-Christian Coop., Am. Coalition for Traditional Values. Avocations: tennis; fishing. Office: Moral Majority Inc 305 6th St Lynchburg VA 24504

GOEBEL, PAUL ROBERT, real estate investor, educator; b. Bad Axe, Mich., Jan. 21, 1951; s. Clarence William and Ileen Marie (Stiebe) G.; m. Katherine Archer Harrison, Dec. 3, 1974. B.B.A., Augusta Coll., 1975; M.B.A. in Managerial Fin., U. Ga., 1976, Ph.D. in Real Estate, 1980. Research asst. dept. real estate U. Ga., Athens, 1978-79; asst. prof. fin. Tex. Tech U., Lubbock, 1980-82, now adj. prof.; investment analyst Stribling Co., Lubbock, 1982—. Author: Mortgage Mathematics and Financial Tables, 1981; The Buyer, Seller and Broker's Guide to Creative Home Finance, 1983. Contbr. articles to jours. in field. Active Lubbock Econs. Council, Lubbock C. of C. Served with U.S. Army, 1972-74. Mem. Am. Real Estate Assn., Urban Econs. Assn., Fin. Mgmt. Assn., Tex. Real Estate Tchrs., Assn. Episcopalian. Office: Stribling Co 2345 50th St Lubbock TX 79412

GOEGLEIN, RICHARD JOHN, casino/hotel executive; b. Los Angeles, Aug. 23, 1934; s. Myrwil Louis and Pauline Yvette (Rizer) G.; children—Eric John, William Scott. B.S., U. Wyo., 1957; M.B.A., Stanford U., 1960. Dist. sales rep. Continental Oil Co., Houston, 1960-63; div. v.p. Interstate United Corp., Mountain View, Calif., 1963-70; pres., chief exec. officer Uniworld Foods, Inc., Culver City, Calif., 1970-72; chmn., pres., chief exec. officer Hungry Tiger, Inc., Van Nuys, Calif., 1972-74; v.p. W.R. Grace & Co., N.Y.C., 1974-78; exec. v.p., dir. Holiday Inns, Memphis, 1978—; also pres., chief exec. officer, dir. Harrah's, Inc., Reno. Trustee Culinary Inst. Am. Served with USN, 1957. Mem. Stanford Bus. Sch. Assn., Stanford Alumni Assn., Reno-Sparks C. of C. (dir.). Republican. Home: 3353 Skyline Blvd Reno NV 89509 Office: Holiday Inns Inc 3742 Lamar Ave Memphis TN 38195*

GOETTEE, JAMES HENRY, ret. ednl. adminstr.; b. Carmona, Tex., July 18, 1907; s. Francis Marion and L. Catherine (Welch) G.; B.S., Sam Houston U., 1933; M.Ed., U. Tex., 1937; Ed.D., U. Houston, 1959; m. Edna Mae Survant, Aug. 23, 1933; 1 son, James Lee. Teaching prin. county schs., Trinity County, Tex., 1927-30; teaching prin. Field's Store Sch., Waller, Tex., 1930-33; supt. Spring (Tex.) Ind. Sch. Dist., 1933-38; tchr. Oates Jr. High Sch., Houston, 1938-42, acting prin., 1942-44; asst. prin. Stephen F. Austin Sr. High Sch., Houston, 1944-49, prin., 1949-66; dir. secondary edn. Houston Ind. Sch. Dist., 1966-68, asst. supt., 1968-72. Mem. Tex. Tchrs. Assn. (past v.p.), Houston Council Edn. (past pres.), Houston Assn. Sch. Adminstrs. (past pres.), So. Assn. Coll. and Schs. (Tex. com.), Nat. (life), Tex. (life) congresses parents and tchrs., Nat. Assn. Drs. in U.S., SAR, San Houston State Coll. Ex-Students Assn. (past pres.), Nat. Assn. Secondary Sch. Prins., Phi Delta Kappa, Delta Kappa Pi. Democrat. Baptist. Clubs: Masons (33 deg.), Shriners, Order Eastern Star (past grand patron Tex.), Knife and Fork (Houston), Southeastern Houston Kiwanis (past pres.). Contbr. to profl. publs. Home: 8106 Beverly Hill Ln Houston TX 77063

GOFFMAN, IRVING JAY, economic consultant; b. Montreal, Que., Can., Apr. 21, 1933; came to U.S., 1959; s. William and Ethel (Dumansky) G.; m. Judith Barbara Kasler, June 5, 1956; children—Susan, Sandra. B.A. with honors, McGill U., Montreal, 1954; M.A. in Econs., Duke U., 1957, Ph.D. in Econs., 1959. Instr. econs. N.C. State Coll., 1955; research economist Govt. Can. Dept. Trade and Commerce, Ottawa, Can., 1958-59; vis. faculty scholar Duke U., 1962; vis. research assoc. prof. Queen's U., Kingston, Can., 1963-64; vis. prof. U. Amsterdam, The Netherlands, 1974; vis. prof. Uppsala U., Sweden, 1974, 75; head U.S. delegation to OECD Working Party in Incomes Policy, Paris, 1975-76; dep. asst. sec. for income security policy HEW, Washington, 1975-77; asst. prof. econs. U. Fla., Gainesville, 1959-63, assoc. prof., 1963-68, prof., 1968-79, mem. grad. faculty, 1961-79; adj. prof. ednl. adminstrn., 1972-79, chmn. dept. econs., 1970-75; pres. Cons. in Forensic Econs., Inc., Miami, Fla., 1979—; adj. prof. econs. Fla. Internat. U., 1984; cons. So. Assn. Colls. and Schs., Atlanta, 1971—; spl. master Pub. Employee Relations Commn. State Fla., 1975—; nat. labor arbitrator Am. Arbitration Assn., 1974—; econ. cons. and expert various types of litigation, 1974—. Bd. editors So. Econ. Jour., 1969-72, Eastern Econs. Jour., 1973-76; editor Pub. Fin. Quarterly, 1971-81. Author: Erosion of the Personal Income Tax Base in Canada and the United States, 1960, Some Fiscal Aspects of Public Welfare in Canada, 1965; co-author: The Concept of Education as an Instrument, 1972. Editor: Federal Taxation as an Instrument of Social and Economic Policy, 1972; co-editor: (with J. R. Allan) Restructuring the Tax Structure - Selected Studies, 1966; (with R. L. Johns) Economic Factors Affecting the Financing of Education, 1971. Contbr. articles to profl. jours., chpts. to books. Bd. advisors Nat. Orgn. for Reform of Marijuana Laws, Washington, 1973-81; mem. Taxation with Representation, Washington, 1974-75; mem. policy adv. council Community Action Orgn., Gainesville, 1966-67; liaison U. Fla.-Alachua County Sch. Bd., 1971-72; U. Fla. rep. North Central Fla. Health Planning Council, 1970-71; pres. B'nai Israel Congregation, Gainesville, Fla., 1974-75; campaign chmn. Gainesville United Jewish Appeal, 1972, 73; mem. nat. univ. faculty council United Jewish Appeal, 1974—. Duke U. Commonwealth fellow in econs., 1957, U. Fla. Grad. Sch. fellow, 1967, U. Fla. Bus. Assocs. grantee, 1969, Danforth Found. assoc. grantee, 1968-71, Econ. Effects of Exec. Impoundments grantee, 1973; recipient Outstanding Faculty Advisor award U. Fla., 1963, Disting. Faculty award U. Fla. Blue Key, 1965, Student award for instr. excellence Coll. Bus. Adminstrn. U. Fla., 1967-68, 68-69, 69-70, 71-72, Good Teaching award U. Fla., 1969, Faculty Lectr. award U. Fla., 1972; named Outstanding Faculty/scholar Presdl. Medallion, U. Fla., 1968, Outstanding Tchr. U. Fla., Standard Oil Ind., 1969. Mem. Am. Econ. Assn. (vis. faculty scholar 1955), Nat. Tax. Assn. (fed. taxation and fin. com. 1971-74), Assn. Social Econs. (exec. bd. 1975-77), Eastern Econ. Assn. (exec. bd. 1973-76), Omicron Delta Epsilon, Nat. Assn. Bus. Economists. Democrat. Jewish. Office: Cons in Forensic Econs 111 NW 183d St Suite 106 Miami FL 33269

GOGGANS, THOMAS MARTELE, lawyer; b. Montgomery, Ala., Aug. 4, 1955; m. Kay Clanton, Sept. 19, 1981. B.A., Auburn U., 1977; J.D., Cumberland Sch. Law, 1980. Bar: Ala., U.S. Dist. Ct. (mid. dist.) Ala., U.S. Ct. Appeal (5th and 11th cirs.), U.S. Supreme Ct. Law clk. to judge U.S. Dist. Ct., Montgomery, 1980-81; founding ptnr. Goggans & McInnish, Montgomery. Deacon Westminster Presbyn. Ch., Montgomery, 1982—. Mem. ABA, Ala. Bar Assn., Montgomery County Bar Assn., Ala. Criminal Def. Lawyers Assn. (bd. dirs. 1984—, exec. dir. 1984—), Nat. Assn. Criminal Def. Lawyers, Am. Trial Lawyers Assn. Democrat. Office: Goggans & McInnish 770 S McDonough St Suite 209 Montgomery AL 36104

GOGLIA, GENNARO LOUIS, engineering educator, consultant, researcher; b. Hoboken, N.J., Jan. 15, 1921; s. Frederick A. and Rose (Coppola) G.; m. Lieselotte Else Pause, Oct. 4, 1942; children—Diann Lieselotte, Linda Rose. B.S. in Mech. Engring., U. Ill., 1942; M.S. in Mech. Engring., Ohio State U., 1950; Ph.D. in Mech. Engring., U. Mich., 1959. Registered profl. engr., Mich., Ohio. Instr. mech. engring. Ohio State U., 1947-51; asst. prof. mech. engring. U. Detroit, 1951-59; assoc. prof. N.C. State U., 1959-62; prof., head mech. engring. dept. U. Maine, 1962-64; prof. Old Dominion U., Norfolk, Va., eminent prof., 1979-85, prof. emeritus, 1985—, chmn. dept. mech. engring. and mechanics, 1974-84; cons. in field. Served With U.S. Army. Recipient Disting. Faculty award Old Dominion U., 1983. Fellow ASME; mem. Am. Soc. Engring. Edn. (co-dir. NASA), Sigma Xi, Pi Tau Sigma, Tau Beta Pi, Phi Kappa Phi. Roman Catholic. Lodge: KC (Norfolk). Contbr. tech. reports to profl. lit. Home: 7416 Gardner Dr Norfolk VA 23518 Office: Old Dominion U Rm 222 Duckworth Hall Norfolk VA 23508

GOIDELL, LEWIS CHARLES, environmental scientist; b. Bklyn., Apr. 19, 1950; s. Eugene Frank and Anna (Merer) G.; B.S. in Biology, L.I. U., 1972; M. Environ. Sci., U. Okla., 1974; m. Pamela Joyce Davis, May 24, 1974; children—Adam Joshua, Andrew Davis. Environ. program specialist Air Quality Service Dept. Health, State of Okla., 1974-76; environ. scientist Savannah River Ops., U.S. Dept. Energy, Aiken, S.C., 1977-83, sr. environ. engr., 1983—. Recipient Outstanding Performance award Dept. Energy, 1983, 84, 85, Cash award, 1985. Mem. Air Pollution Control Assn. (chmn. energy and environ. interactions com. 1982-85, vice chmn. 1985—), Carolinas Air Pollution Control Assn. Home: 830 Boardman Aiken SC 29801 Office: US Department of Energy PO Box A Aiken SC 29802

GOIZUETA, ROBERTO CRISPULO, food company executive; b. Havana, Cuba, Nov. 18, 1931; came to U.S., 1961; s. Crispulo D. and Aida (Cantera) G.; B.S., B.Engring. in Chem. Engring., Yale, 1953; m. Olga T. Casteleiro, June 14, 1953; children—Roberto S., Olga M., Javier C. Process engr. Indsl. Corp. Tropics, Havana, 1953-54; tech. dept. Coca-Cola Co., Havana, 1954-60, asst. to sr. v.p., Nassau, Bahamas, 1960-64, asst. to v.p. research and devel., Atlanta, 1964-66, v.p. engring., 1966-74, sr. v.p., 1974-75, exec. v.p., 1975-79, vice chmn., 1979-80, pres., chief operating officer, dir., 1980, chmn. bd., chief exec. officer, 1981—; dir. Trust Co. of Ga., Trust Co. Bank, Atlanta, Sonat, Inc., Birmingham, Ford Motor Co. Trustee Emory U., Atlanta Arts Alliance, Atlanta Symphony Orch. League, Am. Assembly, Atlanta U. Center, Boys Clubs Am., Lauder Inst.; bd. dirs. Central Atlanta Progress; nat. bd. govs. United Way of Am.; hon. trustee U.S.-Asia Inst. Mem. Bus. Council, Trilateral Commn., The Conf. Bd., Am. Soc. Corp. Execs., Council Fgn. Relations, U.S.-USSR Trade Council, Japan Soc. (dir.), Bus. Roundtable, Inst. Food Technologists, Soc. Soft Drink Technologists, Am. Film Inst., Clubs: Capital City, Piedmont Driving (Atlanta); Commerce (dir.), Internat. of Washington, Inc., Peachtree Golf, Variety Internat. Office: Coca-Cola Co 310 North Ave NW Atlanta GA 30313

GOKEE, DONALD LEROY, clergyman; b. Lansing, Mich., Aug. 8, 1933; s. Richard Alden and June Elizabeth (Colenso) G.; B.A., Mich. State U. and Temple U., Chattanooga, 1958; postgrad. (A. Morehouse and William Walker scholar), George Washington U., 1960-64; postgrad. Va. Theol. Sem., 1964-65, Columbia Theol. Sem., 1968, New Coll., U. Edinburgh (Scotland), 1975, Frankfurt U. (Germany), 1977, U. Athens (Greece), 1978; M.A. cum laude, Ph.D. magna cum laude, Columbia Pacific U.; m. Maxine Pawlik Adkins, Apr. 21, 1974; children—Douglas Richard, Charles Jeffrey, Mary Beth, Jessica Lynn. Ordained to ministry Presbyn. Ch., 1965; dir. Christian edn. Central Presbyn. Ch., Chattanooga, 1958-59, Fairlington Presbyn. Ch., Alexandria, Va., 1959-66; asso. pastor Pine Shores Presbyn. Ch., Sarasota, Fla., 1966-69; pastor Conway Presbyn. Ch., Orlando, Fla., 1969—; frequent conf. speaker at high schs. and colls.; chaplain Orange County Juvenile Ct., 1969-73; mem. council Synod of Fla., 1972-75; mem. ecumenical coordinating team as rep. Presbyn. Ch. U.S., 1977-81; 1st ann. Gingerich meml. lectr. Goshen (Ind.) Coll.; vis. prof. So. Coll. Mem. Nat. Task Force on Criminal Justice and Prison Reform, 1976-82. Author: It's a Love-Haunted World. Recipient certificate of merit for distinguished service to Christ, ch. and community, 1970; In-God-We-Trust award Family Found. of Am., 1980; Key to City, Orlando, 1981. Mem. Ministerial Assn. (past pres.). Home: 3026 Carmia Dr Orlando FL 32806 Office: 4300 Lake Margaret Dr Orlando FL 32806

GOKEL, GEORGE WILLIAM, chemistry educator, consultant; b. N.Y.C., June 27, 1946; s. George William and Ruth Mildred (O'Kelly) G.; m. Kathryn Smiegocki, June 2, 1978. B.S., Tulane U., 1968; Ph.D., U. So. Calif., 1971; postdoctoral studies UCLA, 1972-74. Chemist, DuPont Co., Wilmington, Del., summer 1974; asst. prof. Pa. State U., University Park, 1974-78; assoc. prof. U. Md., College Park, 1978-82, prof. chemistry, 1982-84; prof. chemistry U. Miami, Coral Gables, Fla. 1985—; vis. prof. U. Md. Med. Sch., Balt., 1981-82; cons. W.R. Grace & Co., 1978—, Petroleum Research Fund, 1980-81. Author: Phase Transfer Catalysis, 1977; Experimental Organic Chemistry, 1980; Macrocyclic Polyether Syntheses, 1982. Patentee in lariat ethers. NIH grantee, 1978—; named Outstanding Young Scientist in Md., Md. Acad. Scis., 1979; Frontiers of Chemistry lectr. Case Western Res. U., 1980; recipient Leo Schubert award Washington Acad. Scis., 1981. Mem. Am. Chem. Soc., AAAS, Royal Soc. Chemistry (Eng.). Home: 15560 S W 54th St Miami FL 33185 Office: Dept Chemistry U Miami Coral Gables FL 33124

GOLD, ALLAN HAROLD, architect, structural engineer; educator; b. Chgo., Jan. 12, 1942; s. Melvin King and Estelle M. (Zucker) G.; B. Arch., U. Ill., Urbana, 1966, M.S., 1967; m. Barbara Gail Edelstein, June 20, 1967; children—Grant, Ross, Susan. Architect, project engr. various archtl., engring. cos., Chgo. area, 1963-68; project structural engr. Perkins & Will Architects, Inc., Chgo., 1968-70; structural engr. Chgo. Dept. Bldgs., 1970-73; owner, operator Allan H. Gold & Assocs., Architects/Cons. Structural Engrs., Hazel Crest, Ill., 1973-81; project mgr./sr. structural engr. HKS/Structural, Dallas, 1981-84; dir. architecture and structural engring. dept. URS Engrs., Dallas, 1984; owner, operator Allan H. Gold, Architect/Structural Engr., Dallas,

1985—; asst. prof. archtl. tech., dept. constrn. tech. Purdue U., Hammond, Ind., 1976-80; assoc. prof. architecture U. Okla., Norman, 1980-81; guest lectr. U. Wis. Extension, 1981; adj. assoc. prof. architecture U. Tex., Arlington, 1983-85. Mem. Village of Hazel Crest Plan Commn., 1979-81. Registered architect, Ill., Ind., La., Mich., Okla., Tex.; registered structural engr., Ill.; registered profl. engr., Ind., Okla., Tex., La.; cert. Nat. Council Archtl. Registration Bds. (juror 1985). Mem. AIA, Tex. Soc. Architects, Structural Engrs. Assn. Ill., Structural Engrs. Assn. Tex., ASCE (tall bldgs. com. 1983-86), Am. Arbitration Assn. Jewish. Lodges: Masons, Scottish Rite, Shriners (master lodge Skokie, Ill. 1979). Structural engr. Century Shopping Center, Chgo., 1973, Phoenix Tower, Houston, 1983, Xerox II, Irving, Tex., 1984. Home and Office: 6415 McCallum Blvd Dallas TX 75252

GOLD, DONALD DAVIS, JR., psychiatrist, educator, consultant; b. Atlanta, Dec. 2, 1946; s. Donald Davis and Wilna (Woods) G.; m. Eva-Maria Anttila, Dec. 21, 1976; children—Donald Davis, III, Temujin Anttila, Bourtai Kandahar. B.S.Ed., U. Fla., 1969; M.D., Emory U., 1974. Resident psychiatry U. Tenn., 1974-77; dir. med. student tng. psychiatry VA Med. Ctr., Memphis, 1977-78; med. dir. unit 5 Ga. Mental Health Inst., Atlanta, 1978-80; chief psychiat. cons. service City of Memphis Hosp., 1980—; asst. prof. dept. psychiatry U. Tenn. Sch. Medicine, 1980—; cons. psychopharmacology Western Mental Health Inst., Bolivar, Tenn., 1980—, Fed. Correctional Facility, Memphis, 1983-84; asst. clin. prof. Emory U. Sch. Medicine, 1978-80. Diplomate Am. Bd. Psychiatry and Neurology. Editorial reviewer Hosp. and Community Psychiatry, 1982—; contbr. articles to profl. jours. Office: 42 N Dunlap St Suite 441 Memphis TN 38103

GOLD, I. RANDALL, lawyer; b. Chgo., Nov. 2, 1951; s. Albert Samuel and Lois (Rodrick) G.; m. Marcey Dale Miller, Nov. 18, 1978; children—Eric Matthew, Brian David. B.S. with high honors, U. Ill., 1973, J.D., 1976. Bar: Ill. 1976, U.S. Dist. Ct. (no. dist.) Ill. 1976, Fla. 1979, U.S. Dist. Ct. (so. dist.) Fla. 1979, U.S. Ct. Appeals (5th and 7th cirs.) 1979, U.S. Tax Ct. 1979, U.S. Ct. Appeals (11th cir.) 1981, U.S. Supreme Ct. 1982; C.P.A., Ill., Fla. Tax staff Ernst & Ernst, Chgo., 1976-77; asst. state atty. Cook County, Ill., 1977-78, Dade County, Miami, Fla., 1978-82; spl. atty. Miami Strike Force, U.S. Dept. Justice, Fla., 1982—; lectr. Roosevelt U., Chgo., 1976-77. Adviser Jr. Achievement, Chgo., 1976-78, Miami, 1982-84; coach, judge Nat. Trial Competition, U. Miami Law Sch., 1983—. Mem. Fla. Bar (fed. practice com.), ABA (govt. litigation counsel com.), Ill. State Bar Assn., Chgo. Bar Assn., Dade County Bar Assn., Decalogue Soc. Lawyers, Fed. Bar Assn., Assn. Trial Lawyers Am., Am. Inst. C.P.A.s, Ill. Soc. C.P.A.s, Fla. Inst. C.P.A.s (com. on relations with Fla. Bar), Am. Assn. Atty.-C.P.A.s, Delta Sigma Pi. Jewish. Club: Tiger Bay. Office: Miami Strike Force US Dept Justice 77 SE 5th St Suite 401 Miami FL 33131

GOLDBACH, RICHARD ALBERT, shipyard co. exec.; b. East Orange, N.J., Aug. 17, 1936; s. Frank Picker and Charlotte (Horn) G.; B.S., Webb Inst. Naval Architecture and Marine Engring., 1958; m. Janet Olcott Clinton, July 23, 1960. Various positions Gen. Dynamics, Electric Boat Div., Groton, Conn., 1958-65; gen. installation supt. Gen. Dynamics, Quincy, Mass., 1965-68; dir. planning Ingalls Shipbuilding, Pascagoula, Miss., 1968-77; pres. Metro Machine Corp., Norfolk, Va., 1977—, also dir.; dir. Metro Inc., Norfolk, Mid-Atlantic Steel and Boat Works, Inc., Norfolk. Pres. Tidewater Maritime Tng. Inst., 1979-81; chmn. scout show Tidewater Council Boy Scouts Am., 1980-81; exec. adv. Jr. Achievement Tidewater, 1981—. Mem. Soc. Naval Architects and Marine Engrs., Am. Soc. Naval Engrs., Soc. Am. Magicians, Internat. Brotherhood Magicians. Methodist. Home: 2123 Hollybriar Point Norfolk VA 23518 Office: Box 1860 Foot of Chestnut St Norfolk VA 23501

GOLDBERG, ALAN JOEL, lawyer, commercial real estate developer; b. Bklyn, Jan. 22, 1943; s. Ralph and Dorothy (Rolnick) G.; 1 son, Cary Adam. B.A., U. Miami, 1965, J.D., 1968. Bar: Fla. 1968, U.S. Supreme Ct., U.S. Ct. Appeals (4th cir.). Ptnr. Goldberg, Young, Goldberg & Borkson, P.A., Ft. Lauderdale, Fla., 1968-82; atty. City of Margate (Fla.), 1969-70, City of Tamarac (Fla.), 1970-71; sole practice, Ft. Lauderdale, 1982—; pres. Proprty Systems, Inc.; chmn. bd. CulCon Systems, Inc. Mem. Citizen's Task Force on Transp., State of Fla; mem. Broward County Planning Council, 1985—. Mem. ABA, Fla. Bar Assn. Republican. Office: 5100 N Federal Hwy Suite 412 Fort Lauderdale FL 33308

GOLDBERG, JEROME HAROLD, utility company executive; b. Phila., Mar. 1, 1931; B.S., U.S. Mcht. Marine Acad., 1953; M.S., M.I.T., 1960; m. Eleanor M. Andrews, Nov. 29, 1953; children—Steven, Susan. Engr., Bethlehem Steel Co., Quincy, Mass., 1955-64; mgr. Gen. Dynamics Corp., Quincy, 1964-71; v.p. Stone & Webster Engring. Corp., Boston, 1971-80; v.p. Houston Lighting & Power Co., 1980—. Mem. Republican Presdl. Task Force, 1982—. Served with USNR, 1953-55. Registered profl. engr., Calif., Mass., R.I., N.Y., Pa., Tex., Va. Mem. Am. Nuclear Soc. Republican. Office: PO Box 1700 Houston TX 77001

GOLDBERG, LEE DRESDEN, endocrinologist, medical educator; b. Point Pleasant, N.J., July 29, 1937; s. Milton J. and Maude (Dresden) G.; m. Lana Ditchek, July 23, 1967; children—Marissa Julie, Sara Amy, Rachel Sherry. B.S. summa cum laude, Yale U., 1959, M.D., 1963. Diplomate Nat. Bd. Med. Examiners, Am. Bd. Internal Medicine, Am. Bd. Endocrinology. Rotating intern Mount Sinai Hosp., N.Y.C., 1963-64; resident internal medicine Montefiore Hosp., Bronx, N.Y., 1964, 66-68; clin. research fellow endocrinology Albert Einstein Coll. Medicine, Bronx, N.Y., 1968-69; fellow endocrinology Bellevue Hosp.-NYU Med. Ctr., N.Y.C., 1969-70; co-chief endocrinology Mount Sinai Hosp., Miami Beach, Fla., 1974—; teaching asst. NYU Sch. Medicine, 1969-70; clin. instr. medicine U. Miami Sch. Medicine, 1970-71, clin. asst. prof., 1971-80, clin. assoc. prof., 1980—; chief internal medicine South Shore Hosp., Miami Beach, 1975-79; assoc. chmn. med. services St. Francis Hosp., Miami Beach, 1977-78. Bd. dirs. Hebrew Acad. Greater Miami, 1975—. Served to lt. M.C., USNR, 1964-66. Mem. Endocrine Soc., Am. Diabetes Assn. (past dir. Miami chpt.), Dade County Med. Assn., Am. Fedn. Clin. Research, Phi Beta Kappa, Sigma Xi. Jewish. Club: Yale (Miami). Lodge: B'nai B'rith. Contbr. articles on endocrinology to med. jours. Office: 1680 Meridian Ave Suite 204 Miami Beach FL 33139

GOLDBERG, RICHARD MYRON, property management executive; b. Richmond, N.Y., Mar. 4, 1935; s. Mac and Ruth G.; m. Susann Stone, May 27, 1961; children—William, Janet, Andrea. B.S. in Bus. Adminstrn., U. Fla., 1956. Cert. property mgr. Constrn. supr. Taylor Constrn. Co., Miami, Fla., 1956; real estate appraiser U. Fla., Gainesville, 1959-60; stockbroker, analyst Hirsch & Co., Miami Beach, Fla., 1960-71; with IRE Fin. Corp., Miami, 1976—, v.p., 1979-83, sr. v.p., dir. property mgmt., 1983—; cons. in field. Served with U.S. Army, 1957-59. Mem. Nat. Assn. Realtors, Miami Bd. Realtors, Internat. Council Shopping Ctrs., Inst. Real Estate Mgmt. (gov., mem. governing council, pres. South Fla. chpt. 19 1983—, Mgr. of Yr. 1983), Econ. Soc. South Fla. Jewish. Home: 20605 NE 19th Ct North Miami Beach FL 33179 Office: 1320 S Dixie Hwy Coral Gables FL 33146

GOLDEN, EDWARD IRA, lawyer; b. N.Y.C., Dec. 1, 1945; s. Louis and Ann Jean (Kaplan) G.; m. Eve Jacqueline Sohmer, July 27, 1969; 1 child, Jill Alyson. B.A., U. Miami, 1966, M.Edn., 1969, J.D., 1977. Bar: Fla. 1978, U.S. Dist. Ct. (so. dist.) Fla. 1978, U.S. Ct. Appeals (5th cir.) 1978, U.S. Ct. Appeals (11th cir.) 1981. Assoc. Gautier and Ezell, Miami, Fla., 1977-79; assoc. Law Offices Wm. Gautier, Miami, 1979-80; ptnr. Freeman & Golden, P.A., Miami, 1980-82; sr. ptnr. Edward I. Golden, P.A., Miami, 1982—; vice-chmn. Dade County Probate and Guardians Com., Miami, 1981-84. Chmn. Dade County Jr. Miss Program, Miami, 1979—; bd. dirs. U. Miami Athletic Fedn., Coral Gables, 1980—, Coral Gables Youth Boxing Found., Coral Gables, 1981—; v.p. U. Miami Sports Hall of Fame, 1986. HEW fellow, 1967-69. Mem. Dade County Bar Assn. (vice-chmn. 1983-84, Disting. Service award 1983, Cert. of Merit 1983-85), Fla. Bar Assn., ABA (probate law com., guardianship law com. 1981—, life with dignity com. 1984), U. Miami Alumni Assn. (dir. 1982—), U. Miami Hurricane Club (dir. 1980—). Jewish.

GOLDEN, GERALD THOMAS, plastic surgeon, consultant; b. Miami, Fla., June 18, 1942; s. James Quillian and Willie Mae (Glover) G.; m. Sandra Jean Ann Haungs, Jan. 18, 1980; children—Nathan Thomas, Mary Peyton, Sarah Catherine. B.S., Carson Newman U., 1964; M.D., Wake Forest U., 1967. Diplomate Am. Bd. Surgery, Am. Bd. Plastic Surgery. Intern U. Va., Charlottesville, 1967-68; resident, 1970-1976; practice medicine specializing in plastic surgery, Martinsburg, W.Va., 1976—; pres. Shenandoah Surg. Group, Martinsburg, 1980—; vis. plastic surgeon U. Va., Charlottesville, 1976—; chief surgery City Hosp., Martinsburg, 1977-79, 82-84, v.p. med. staff, 1979-82. Contbr. articles to profl. jours. Served as lt. M.C., USNR, 1968-70. Am. Cancer Soc. fellow 1973-74. Fellow ACS, Internat. Coll. Surgeons, Southeastern Surg. Congress, N.Y. Acad. Scis. Republican. Baptist. Clubs: Sons Am. Revolution, Sons Confederate Vets. Avocations: civil war history; civil war reenactment; civil war memorabilia; curator. Home: 1125 W King St Martinsburg WV 25401 Office: 202 Foxcroft Ave Martinsburg WV 25401

GOLDEN, ROLLAND HARVE, artist; b. New Orleans, Nov. 8, 1931; s. John Ferdinand and Ione (Rolland) G.; m. Stella Anne Doussan, Aug. 31, 1957; children—Carrie Marie Golden Ricaud, Mark Damian, Lucille Marie. Student, John McCrady Art Sch., 1955-57. Author: Vieux Carre Courier-Golden Show Tours USSR, 1976-77; one man shows include Moscow, Leningrad, Kiev, Odessa, 1976-77, Miss. Mus. Art, 1979, touring retrospective, 1985; exhibited in group shows at Mo. Bicentennial, 1976. Bd. dirs. Vieux Carre Property Owners, New Orleans, 1970—, Folsom, La., 1982—. Served with USN, 1951-55. Mem. Am. Watercolor Soc., Nat. Watercolor Soc., Watercolor U.S.A., Midwest Watercolor Soc., Nat. Soc. Painters in Casein and Acrylic, Nat. Arts Club, Rocky Mountain Nat. Watermedia, Allied Artists Am. Democrat. Roman Catholic. Club: Artists Fellowship (N.Y.). Home: Route 1 Box 293 G Folsom LA 70437 Office: Studio Route 1 Box 293 Folsom LA 70437

GOLDEN, STANFORD BROWN, JR., automotive company manager; b. Selma, Ala., Apr. 12, 1943; s. Stanford Brown and Annie Lois (Hardy) G.; m. Elane Lee Lamberth, June 10, 1967; children—Lane Davis, Catherine McRae. B.S., U. Ala., 1965; M.A., U. Tenn., 1968, Ph.D., 1969. Lic. psychologist, Tenn. Asst. prof., then assoc. prof. psychology Middle Tenn. State U., Murfreesboro, 1969-82; tng. specialist Nissan Motor Mfg. Corp., U.S.A., 1982, sect. mgr. organization devel., 1983—; cons. State of Tenn., Nashville, 1971-74, pvt. industries, Murfreesboro and Nashville, 1971-82, Metro, Nashville, 1976-78. Contbr. articles to profl. publs. Bd. dirs. Rutherford County Guidance Ctr., Murfreesboro, 1978-83, State Bd. of Examiners in Psychology, Tenn., 1979-82; pres. Campus Sch. PTA, Murfreesboro, 1980-81; sec. Central Middle Sch. PTC, Murfreesboro, 1983-84; sustaining mem. Republican Nat. Com., 1984—; sec. Middle Tenn. State U. Faculty Senate, 1973, pres., 1976. Mem. Am. Psychol. Assn., Southeastern Psychol. Assn., Tenn. Psychol. Assn., Human Resource Planning Soc., Am. Soc. Tng. and Devel. Republican. Episcopalian. Home: 310 Falcon Dr Murfreesboro TN 37130 Office: Nissan Motor Mfg Corp USA Nissan Dr Smyrna TN 37167

GOLDEN, THOMAS FULLER, lawyer; b. New Orleans, May 24, 1942; s. Albert Courter and Thelma Loyce (Fuller) G.; m. Beverly Bost, Feb. 15, 1944; children—Dathel Elizabeth, Laura LeAnne, Julianne Candice. B.A. in Econs., Okla. State U., 1965; J.D., Tulsa U., 1968. Bar: Okla. 1968, U.S. Sup. Ct. 1972. Ptnr., Hall, Estill, Handwick, Gable, Callingsworth & Nelson, Tulsa, 1971—; gen. counsel Williams Bros. Overseas Co. Ltd., Toronto, Ont., Can., 1971-75; gen. counsel Williams Realty Corp., Tulsa, 1973—; gen. counsel Arctic Constructors, Fairbanks, Alaska, 1974-79; mem. U.S. Jud. Nominating Commn., Okla., 1980—. Pres., Tulsa Boys Home, 1980-82; bd. dirs. United Way, Tulsa, 1980-82. Recipient Okla. Gov. award, 1982. Republican. Methodist. Clubs: Pensacola Country (Fla.); Tulsa, Golf of Okla. (Tulsa). Mng. editor: Tulsa Law Jour., 1967-68. Home: 2826 E 48th St Tulsa OK 74105 Office: 4100 Bank of Oklahoma Tower Tulsa OK 74172

GOLDFARB, ALAN KEITH, financial planning adviser; b. N.Y.C., Aug. 24, 1941; s. Walter I. and Adele S. (Lenke) G.; B.S. in Indsl. Engring., Fairleigh Dickinson U., 1966; M.B.A. in Mgmt. Econs., N. Tex. State U., 1970; cert. Coll. for Fin. Planning, 1978; m. Terry L. Schweitzer, July 4, 1966; 1 dau., Diana Lynn. Dist. dir. Fin. Service Corp., Dallas, 1971-75; pres. Fin. Strategies Corp., Dallas, 1975-81; pres., chief exec. officer Fin. Strategies Group, Dallas, 1981—; adj. faculty Dallas County Community Coll. Dist. Former dir., co.-chmn. planned and deferred gifts com. Am. Heart Assn., Silver and Golden Heart awards Tex. affiliate; rec. sec. Temple Emanu-el Brotherhood. Cert. fin. planner Mem. Internat. Assn. Fin. Planning, (nat. dir., dir., past pres. N. Tex. chpt.), Inst. Cert. Fin. Planners. Columnist Dallas/Ft. Worth Bus., Dallas Morning News.

GOLDIN, EDWIN, physics educator; b. Phila., Oct. 12, 1933; s. Max and Clara (Goldenberg) G.; m. Marjorie M. Bernardi, June 21, 1975; children—Philip R., Martin, Lauren Q., Amanda R., Julia D. A.A., Cooper Union, 1964; B.A., Temple U., 1955; M.S., Poly. Inst. N.Y., 1957, Ph.D., 1973. Instr. physics, dir. Univ. of Air, Queens Coll., CUNY, N.Y.C., 1957-70; asst. prof. Fordham U., N.Y.C., 1970-76; asst. prof. physics Ramapo Coll., Mahwah, N.J., 1976-81; prof., head dept. physics, dir. acad. computing Bethany Coll., W.Va., 1981—. Author: Waves and Photons: An Introduction to Quantum Optics, 1982. Writer-producer films: Swinging Quantum, 1973, Packet of Uncertain Gaussian, 1969. Recipient Alumni award Cooper Union Alumni Assn., 1964; diploma of Honor, Internat. Sci. Film Assn., Cairo, 1978; grantee U.S. Steel Found., 1985, Westinghouse Found., 1985. Mem. Am. Assn. Physics Tchrs. (chmn. com. on physics in higher edn. 1985—), Am. Phys. Soc., AAAS. Office: Bethany Coll Bethany WV 26032

GOLDMAN, ALLENE TOWNSEND, marriage-family-child therapist, consultant; b. Roswell, N.Mex., Feb. 19, 1937; d. Thomas T. Mann and Allene (Ballard) M.; children—Emily, Justin. B.S., Colo. State U., 1959; M.S., Oreg. State U., 1965. Clin. trainee, tchr./therapist emotionally disturbed children Observation Clinic for Children, Los Angeles, 1960-63; tutor/therapist for emotionally disturbed and brain damaged children, Roswell, N.Mex., 1963-65; spl. edn. tchr., Roswell, 1964-65; dir., tchr., parent coordinator Midtown Sch., Los Angeles, 1965-66; dir. children's programs Ctr. for Early Edn., Los Angeles, 1966-69, instr., 1966-73; instr. Los Angeles Valley Coll., 1969-74; marriage and family therapist, Los Angeles and Dallas, 1970—; instr. Calif. State U.-Los Angeles, 1972, Santa Monica Coll., 1973-76; co-founder and pres. bd. Richstone Ctr., Los Angeles, 1974, dir., 1974-76; dir. Eastfield Parent/-Child Study Ctr., Eastfield Coll., Mesquite, Tex., 1976-80; exec. dir. Parents Anonymous, Dallas, 1981—; cons. The Family Place, Dallas; community speaker. Interview com. Big Sisters, Van Nuys, Calif., 1974-76. Mem. Nat. Assn. Edn. Young Children, So. Assn. Edn. Young Children, Tex. Assn. Edn. Young Children, Tex. Jr. Colls. Tchrs. Assn., Am. Assn. Marriage-Family Therapists, Tex. Assn. Marriage-Family Therapists, Dallas Assn. Edn. Young Children, Mental Health Assn. Dallas County (chmn. child and adolescent com., ann. parent conf. com., ann. child abuse conf. com.). Contbr. articles to profl. jours. Office: 5747 Morningside Dr Dallas TX 75206

GOLDMAN, HARVEY A., lawyer; b. N.Y.C., Sept. 25, 1945; S. Myron and Pearl (Jacobs) G.; m. Hazel R. Goldman, June 16, 1968; children—Bradley, Evan. Grad. with distinction, U. Va., 1967, J.D., 1971. Bar: N.Y., Fla. Assoc. Davis, Polk & Wardwell, N.Y.C., 1971-74; asst. gen. counsel Ryder System, Inc., Miami, Fla., 1974-76; mem. Greeberg, Traurig, Askew, Hoffman, et al, Miami, 1976—; adj. prof. U. Miami, 1982—. Bd. dirs. WPBT-Channel 2, Miami, 1981—; trustee Coconut Grove Playhouse, Miami, 1982—. Mem. Fla. Bar Assn., ABA. Office: Greenberg Traurig Askew Hoffman et al 1401 Brickell Ave Miami FL 33131

GOLDMAN, JACQUELIN, clinical psychology educator; b. Ocala, Fla., Apr. 26, 1934; d. Leon H. and Mildred Goldman. B.A., U. Fla., 1956; M.A., U. Ill., 1959, Ph.D., 1962. Lic. psychologist, Fla. Asst. prof. U. Fla., Gainesville, 1961-68, assoc. prof., 1969-76, prof., 1976—; chair Fla. State Bd. of Examiners, 1977-79, Southeastern Regional Bd. Am. Bd. of Profl. Psychology, 1983—; trustee Am. Bd. Profl. Psychology, 1984—. Author: Becoming A Psychotherapist, 1976; Psychological Methods of Child Assessment, 1983. Contbr. articles to profl. jours. Mem. Altrusa, Gainesville. Recipient Audrey Schumacher Faculty award dept. clin. psychology U. Fla., 1977. Mem. Am. Psychol. Assn., Southeastern Psychol. Assn., Fla. Psychol. Assn., Phi Beta Kappa, Sigma Xi. Democrat. Jewish. Office: Dept of Clin Psychology Box J 165 JHMHC Gainesville FL 32610

GOLDMAN, JOHN ABNER, rheumatologist, immunologist, educator; b. Cin., June 9, 1940; s. Leon and Belle (Hurwitz) G.; m. Cheryl P. Page, Sept. 12, 1981; children—Joey, Beth, Joseph, Kyle. B.S., U. Wis., 1962; M.D., U. Cin., 1966. Diplomate Am. Bd. Internal Medicine, subspecialty in rheumatology, allergy-immunology. Intern, U. Oreg. Med. Sch., Portland, 1966-67; resident U. Cin. Med. Center, 1967-69, postdoctoral fellow in rheumatology and immunology, 1969-71 assoc. prof. medicine Emory U. Sch. Medicine, Atlanta, 1973-82. Contbr. numerous articles to sci. jours. Bd. dirs. Atlanta Arthritis Found.; med. div. council Lupus Erythematosus Found. Inc. Served to maj. AUS, 1971-73. Fellow ACP, Am. Soc. Lasers in Medicine and Surgery (bd. dirs.); mem. Am. Rheumatism Assn., Ga. Rheumatism Soc. (pres. 1974-75), Med. Assn. Atlanta, Med. Assn. Ga. (interspecialty council). Office: Med Quarters 5555 Peachtree Dunwoody Rd Suite 293 Atlanta GA 30342

GOLDMAN, M. F., athletic wear company executive. Chmn., chief exec. officer Armel Inc., Ft. Lauderdale. Office: Armel Inc 1840 NW 65th Ave Fort Lauderdale FL 33313*

GOLDMAN, MICHAEL STUART, psychologist; b. Mpls., Sept. 17, 1937; s. Hy and Theresa (Weinstein) G.; m. Carole Lee Freedland, July 26, 1959 (div. 1971); children—Thomas, McLissa, Tony; m. Frances Helen Curtis, June 1, 1971; children—Jennifer, Jessica. B.A., U. Minn., 1960, M.A., 1965; Ph.D., U. Wis., 1968. Lic. psychologist, Va. Asst. prof. psychology W.Va. U., Morgantown, 1968-71; dir. psychol. and social services Graydon Manor, Leesburg, Va., 1971—. Mem. Loudoun County Mental Health and Mental Retardation Services Bd., Leesburg, 1973—. Vocat. Rehab. fellow Rehab. Services Adminstrn., 1960-61, 66-67. Mem. Am. Psychol. Assn., Va. Psychol. Assn. Jewish. Avocations: jogging, tennis, reading, music. Home: PO Box 303 Round Hill VA 22141 Office: Graydon Manor 301 Childrens Center Rd Leesburg VA 22075

GOLDMANN, THEODORE BECKWITH, chemical distributor; b. Dallas, Oct. 5, 1923; s. Clarence Rudolph and Wilma Winslett (Beckwith) G.; m. Helen Martin, Apr. 24, 1956; 1 dau., Ann Martin. B.S., Tex. A. and M. U., 1948. Salesman, mgr. Dow Corning Corp., 1948-73; dir. Dow Corning do Brasil, Sao Paulo, 1960-63; mng. dir. Dow Corning S.A.R.L., Paris, 1967-72; dir. internat. mktg. Maremont Corp., Chgo., 1973-76; v.p., co-owner Southwest Silicone Co., Grand Prairie, Tex., 1977—. Bd. govs. 101st Airborne Div. Assn., 1983. Served with AUS, 1942-45. Decorated Purple Heart with oak leaf cluster. Mem. Am. Inst. Chem. Engrs., Am. Chem. Soc.'s So. Rubber Group, AIME, Soc. Petroleum Engrs. Presbyterian. Contbr. articles to profl. jours. Office: 1111 W North Carrier Pkwy Suite 150 Grand Prairie TX 75050

GOLDSMITH, CLAIR WOODROW, mathematics, computer science and systems design educator, consultant; b. Mercedes, Tex., June 30, 1942; d. Lloyd Woodrow and Jeannette (MacKenzie) Goldsmith. B.S.E.E. with honors, So. Meth. U., 1965, M.S.E.E., 1968, Ph.D., 1972. Mem. tech. staff Tex. Instruments, Inc., Dallas, 1966-69; instr. elec. engring., computer sci., So. Meth. U., Dallas, 1965-69, 70-71; mem. tech. staff Telpar, Inc., Dallas, 1969-70; instr. biophysics U. Tex. Southwestern Med. Sch., Dallas, 1971-72; acting dir. Univ. Tex. North Tex. Regional Computer Ctr., Dallas, 1973; dir. computer services Palyn Assocs., Inc., San Jose, Calif., 1973-76; asst. prof. bioengring. U. Tex. Health Sci. Ctr., San Antonio, 1976-78, dir. computing resources, 1976—; adj. assoc. prof. math., computer sci. and systems design U. Tex.-San Antonio, 1983—; cons. Morisaenz, South Am., Quito, Ecuador, 1976-78, Fla.-Ga. Tractor, Inc., Miami, 1979, U. Md. Sch. Medicine, Baltimore, 1981, U. Tenn. Ctr. for Health Scis., Memphis, 1981, Moses Cone Meml. Hosp., Chapel Hill., N.C., 1982, Compix, Inc., Portland, Oreg., 1983; lectr. in field. Mem. Assn. for Computing Machinery, IEEE, Tex. Assn. State Supported Computer Ctrs. (bd. dirs.), U. Tex. System Data Processing Council, Digital Equipment Computer Users Soc. (chmn. publs. com. 1981-82, pres. 1982—), Eta Kappa Nu, Sigma Tau. Home: 7502 Tondre San Antonio TX 78209 Office: Univ Tex Health Sci Ctr 7703 Floyd Curl Dr San Antonio TX 78284

GOLDSMITH, HARRY LOUIS, lawyer; b. Memphis, Sept. 4, 1951; s. Robert Tobias and Elvis (Ginsberg) G. Student Washington and Lee U., 1969-71; B.B.A. magna cum laude, U. Tex., 1973; J.D., Memphis State U., 1977. Bar: Tenn. 1977. Ptnr. Goodman, Glazer, Greener, Schneider & McQuiston, Memphis, 1977-82, Brown, Reese & Goldsmith, Memphis, 1984—; atty. Fed. Express Corp., Memphis, 1982-84; pres. BTG Inc., Memphis, 1980—. Trustee Goldsmith Found., 1984—; bd. dirs. Am. Cancer Soc., Memphis Jewish Community Ctr., Mid-South Fair. Mem. ABA, Tenn. Bar Assn., Shelby County Bar Assn., Beta Alpha Psi, Beta Gamma Sigma. Club: Racquet (Memphis). Home: 6986 Round Hill Cove Germantown TN 38138 Office: 6750 Poplar Ave Suite 210 Memphis TN 38138

GOLDSMITH, WILLIAM ALEE, health physicist, researcher, engineer; b. Memphis, Nov. 5, 1941; s. Jack Gene and Louise Elizabeth (Alston) G.; m. LaVance G. Davis, June 1, 1965; children—Jack Gregory, William Vance, Lara Ellen. B.S., Miss. State U., 1964, M.S., 1966; Ph.D., U. Fla., 1968. Tchr., research asst. Miss. State U., 1964-65; USPHS trainee U. Fla., Gainesville, 1966-68; radiation protection officer William Beaumont Gen. Hosp., El Paso, Tex., 1969-71; sanitary engr. EPA, Dallas, 1971-73; asst. prof. environ. sci. U. So. Miss., Hattiesburg, 1973-74; mem. staff Los Alamos (N.Mex.) Nat. Lab., 1974-75; mem. research staff Oak Ridge Nat. Lab., 1975-81; mgr. remedial action survey and certification activities program, 1981-82; tng. supr. Bechtel Nat. Inc., Oak Ridge, 1982-84, health physics and environ. safety group mgr., 1984-85, sr. engring. specialist, 1985—; vis. lectr. U. Tex.-El Paso, 1969. Treas. Covenant Presbyterian Ch., Oak Ridge, 1978; chmn. stewardship commn. First United Meth. Ch., Oak Ridge, 1981-83. Mem. Am. Chem. Soc., Am. Nuclear Soc., AAAS, Health Physics Soc., N.Y. Acad. Scis., Scabbard and Blade, Sigma Xi, Tau Beta Pi, Phi Kappa Phi, Pi Kappa Alpha. Contbr. articles to profl. jours. Office: Bechtel Nat Inc PO Box 350 Oak Ridge TN 37830

GOLDSTEIN, AILEEN, financial consultant; b. Rosenberg, Tex., June 26, 1914; d. Cecil and Raye (Levine) Robinowitz; B.B.A., U. Tex., 1934; postgrad. in econs. Trinity U., San Antonio, 1959-61; m. Eli Goldstein, Jan. 27, 1935; 1 son, Gerald H. Cotton buyer R.B. Stores, Ft. Bend and Wharton Counties, Tex., 1934; legal sec., 1935-38; sec. Spl. Services, U.S. Air Force, Santa Maria, Calif., 1943; account exec. Dempsey-Tegler, San Antonio, 1961-66, E.F. Hutton, San Antonio, 1966-78; investment exec. Shearson/Am. Express, San Antonio, 1978—; lectr., condr. seminars. Mem. investment com. Temple Beth El, 1979—; pres. San Antonio sect. Nat. Council Jewish Women, 1940-42; 1st pres. San Antonio chpt. Brandeis U. Women's Com., 1949-50, nat. bd. dirs., 1950-51; an organizer Vis. Nurse Service San Antonio, 1952, Sr. Citizens Center, 1958-62; mem. San Antonio Parks and Recreation Bd., 1960-64; charter mem. for San Antonio and Bexar County, Alamo Area Council Govts., 1968; mem. crusade com. Am. Cancer Soc. Mem. Friends of McNay Art Inst., Friends of San Antonio Library, San Antonio Mus. Assn., Smithsonian Assos., S.W. Research Found. Forum, Women's Aux. San Antonio Bar Assn. (charter), ACLU, Jewish Community Center, Am. Jewish Com., San Antonio Zool. Soc. Democrat. Clubs: San Antonio, Giraud. Home: 6803-B West Ave San Antonio TX 78213 Office: 110 E Crockett St San Antonio TX 78298

GOLDSTEIN, DONALD JAY, psychologist, educator, administrator; b. Morristown, N.J., Aug. 11, 1948; s. David and Hilda Irene (Gilbert) G. B.A., Fairleigh Dickinson U., 1970; M.A., East Carolina U., 1973; Ph.D., SUNY-Albany, 1978. Lic. psychologist, N.C. Sr. psychologist, dir. psychol. services Devel. Evaluation Clinic, E. Carolina U. Sch. Medicine dept. pediatrics, Greenville, N.C., 1978-84; clin. asst. prof. dept. pediatrics Bowman Gray Sch. Medicine, Wake Forest U., Winston-Salem, N.C., 1984—, dir. Developmental Evaluation Ctr., 1986—; cons. The Nelson Clinic, Medi Pavilion, Greenville. N.Y. State Research fellow, 1975-78; recipient Phi Omega Epsilon award, 1971. Mem. Am. Psychol. Assn., Assn. Eastern N.C. Psychologists, Am. Ednl. Research Assn., N.C. Psychol. Assn., Southeastern Psychol. Assn., Council Exceptional Children, N.C. Pub. Health Assn. Contbr. articles to profl. jours.; collaborator on infant health research project. Office: DEC/Amos Cottage Rehab Hosp 3325 Silas Creek Pkwy Winston-Salem NC 27103

GOLDSTEIN, HELEN HAFT, writer, sociologist; b. Albany, N.Y., Dec. 7, 1921; d. Harry and Clara (Duchen) Haft; m. Irving S. Goldstein, Dec. 16, 1945; children—Ardath Goldstein Weaver, Darra Goldstein Crawford, Jared Haft. A.B., Rutgers U., 1943; M.S.W., Boston U., 1948; M.Ed., U. Pitts., 1962. Chief psychiat. social worker Brazos County Counseling Service, Bryan, Tex., 1968-71; social work program dir. W.H. Trentman Mental Health Ctr., Raleigh, N.C., 1972-77; dir. social work extension program dept. sociology, N.C. State U., Raleigh, 1977-80; columnist Family Forum, Cary (N.C.) News, 1974—; columnist Kids' Cuisine, Raleigh Times, 1981—; free lance writer. Author: Kids' Cuisine, 1983; Recipes from Rufus, 1983. Bd. dirs. N.C. Conf. for Social Service, 1981-83; mem. N.C. Legis. Commn. on Med. Cost Containment, 1983-85; bd. dirs. YWCA of Wake County (N.C.), 1982-83; adv. bd. Wake County Council on Aging. Served with USNR, 1944-46. Named N.C. Mother of Yr., 1982. Fellow Am. Orthopsychiat. Assn.; mem. Nat. Assn. Social Workers (pres. N.C. chpt. 1981-83), Am. Pub. Health Assn. Democrat. Jewish. Clubs: N.C. State U. Women's (v.p.); Cary Women's (sec. 1982-84). Address: 209 Glasgow Rd Cary NC 27511

GOLDSTEIN, JOSEPH LEONARD, physician, genetics educator; b. Sumter, S.C., Apr. 18, 1940; s. Isadore E. and Fannie A. G. B.S., Washington and Lee U., Lexington, Va., 1962; M.D., U. Tex., Dallas, 1966; D.Sc. (hon.), U. Chgo., 1982, Rensselaer Poly. Inst., 1982. Intern, then resident in medicine Mass. Gen. Hosp., Boston, 1966-68; clin. assoc. NIH, 1968-70; postdoctoral fellow U. Wash., Seattle, 1970-72; mem. faculty U. Tex. Health Scis. Center, Dallas, 1972—, Paul J. Thomas prof. medicine, chmn. dept. molecular genetics, 1977—; Harvey Soc. lectr., 1977; mem. sci. rev. bd. Howard Hughes Med. Inst., 1978—; non-resident fellow The Salk Inst., 1983—. Co-author: The Metabolic Basis of Inherited Disease, 5th edit., 1983; editorial bd.: Jour. Biol. Chemistry, 1980—, Cell, 1983—, Jour. Clin. Investigation, 1977-82, Ann. Rev. Genetics, 1980—, Arteriosclerosis, 1981—. Recipient Heinrich-Wieland prize, 1974, Pfizer award in enzyme chemistry Am. Chem. Soc., 1976; Passano award Johns Hopkins U., 1978; Gairdner Found. award, 1981; award in biol. and med. scis. N.Y. Acad. Scis., 1981; Lita Annenberg Hazen award, 1982. Mem. Nat. Acad. Scis. (Lounsbery award 1979), Assn. Am. Physicians, Am. Soc. Clin. Investigation (pres. 1985-86), Am. Soc. Human Genetics, Am. Soc. Biol. Chemists, A.C.P., Am. Fedn. Clin. Research, Phi Beta Kappa, Alpha Omega Alpha. Home: 3730 Holland Ave Apt H Dallas TX 75219 Office: 5323 Harry Hines Blvd Dallas TX 75235

GOLDSTEIN, STUART BRUCE, geologist, oil company executive; b. N.Y.C., Jan. 12, 1956; s. Stanley David and Rita Lillian (Feinberg) G. B.S., Emory U., 1977; M.S., U. Ga., 1980. Sr. geologist Amoco Prodn. Co., New Orleans, 1980—. Mem. Am. Assn. Petroleum Geologists, New Orleans Geol. Soc. Lodge: B'nai B'rith (New Orleans). Avocations: swimming; tennis; softball; volleyball; photography. Home: 2300 Edenborn Ave Apt 378-III Metairie LA 70001 Office: Amoco Production Co PO Box 50879 New Orleans LA 70150

GOLDTHORPE, JOHN CLIFFORD, hospital administrator; b. Chgo., Feb. 21, 1931; s. Clifford Victor and May Adeline (Fisher) G.; m. Marilee Joan Benedict, Aug. 22, 1957; children—Jeffrey, Micki, Clifford. B.S.E., Western Ill. U., 1956; M.P.A., U. So. Calif., 1970. Asst. adminstr. Nebr. Meth. Hosp., Omaha, 1963-66; materials mgr. Cedars-Sinai Med. Center, Los Angeles, 1966-68; assoc. adminstr. St. Joseph Med. Center, Burbank, Calif., 1968-76; exec. v.p. St. Joseph Hosp., Orange, Calif., 1976-83; pres., chief exec. officer Hillcrest Med. Center, Tulsa, 1983—; advisor U. So. Calif. program in health adminstrn., Los Angeles, 1983; dir. Orange County Health Planning Council, Tustin, Calif., 1978-82. Served to cpl. U.S. Army, 1953-54. Recipient Outstanding Achievement award Health Care Execs. S.C., 1978. Mem. Am. Coll. Hosp. Adminstrs., Calif. Assn. Cath. Hosps. (dir. 1978-83), Okla. Hosp. Assn. (dir.). Republican. Methodist. Office: Hillcrest Med Center Utica on the Park Tulsa OK 74104

GOLDWORN, WILLIAM JAY, aviation sales company executive, lawyer; b. N.Y.C., Aug. 22, 1924; s. Solomon and Beatrice (Berliner) G.; m. Maxine Lois Feinberg, Nov. 9, 1958; children—Jeffrey Scot, Jill Susanne, Stacy Ann. B.S., NYU, 1948; JD., U. Miami, 1956, LL.M. in Taxation, 1963. Bar: Fla. 1956, D.C. 1970. Ptnr. Courshon, Fink & Goldworn, Miami Beach, 1956-60; sole practice, Miami, 1960-66; sr. ptnr. W.J. Goldworn & Assocs., Coral Gables, Fla., 1966-82; dir. contract adminstrn. Aviation Sales Co. div. Ryder System Inc., Miami, 1982-84, v.p. contracts, 1984—; sr. adj. prof. U. Miami Law Sch., Coral Gables, 1963-74; dir. Rose Auto Stores, Miami. Adminstr., coach Khoury League Softball, Miami, 1980-82; mem. com. LPGA Tournament Am. Cancer Soc., Miami, 1980-82. Served to lt. col. AUS, 1968-70. Recipient Disting. Service award Civitans of Miami, 1975. Mem. Fla. Bar Assn., Washington Bar Assn., Coral Gables Bar Assn. (pres. 1975-76), Republican. Hebrew. Lodges: Shriners, Hibiscus, Knights of Pythias. (comdr. 1960-62). Contbr. articles to legal jours. Home: 13605 SW 73d Ave Miami FL 33158 Office: Aviation Sales Co 7840 NW 67th St Miami FL 33166

GOLEMBIEWSKI, ROBERT THOMAS, management educator, consultant; b. Lawrenceville, N.J., July 2, 1932; s. John and Pauline (Pelka) G.; m. Margaret Hughes, Sept. 1, 1957; children—Alison, Hope, Geoffrey. A.B., Princeton U., 1954; M.A., Yale U., 1956, Ph.D., 1958. Registered orgn. devel. practitioner. Instr. dept. politics Princeton U., 1958-60; research asst. prof. Sch. Mgmt. U. Ill., 1960-63; vis. lectr. indsl. adminstrn. Yale U., 1963-64; research prof. pub. mgmt. U. Ga., 1964—; disting. vis. scholar U. Calgary, 1979—; cons. to Kmith Kline Beckman, AT&T, Menley and James, Allergan, Canterra, Calgary Stampede and others. Recipient Hamilton Book award 1967; McGregor award for Excellence in Application of Behavioral Scis., 1976; grantee Lilly Found., Ford Found., NIMH and others. Mem. Am. Soc. Pub. Adminstrn., Orgn. Devel. Inst., Cert. Cons. Internat. (cert.). Club: Princeton (N.Y.C.). Author 15 books including: The Small Group, 1962, Approaches to Planned Change, 1979, Humanizing Public Organizations, 1984; Stress in Organizations, 1986; editor 30 books including Public Administration; 1966, 72, 76, 83; Sensitivity Training and the Laboratory Approach, 1970, 73, 77; Cases in Public Management, 1973, 76, 80, 83; contbr. numerous articles in field to profl. jours. Home: 145 Highland Dr Athens GA 30606 Office: Baldwin Hall Univ Ga Athens GA 30602

GOLLAND, STANLEY, business consultant; b. Phila., Sept. 6, 1935; s. Samuel and Frances (Saffren) G.; m. Elizabeth Jane Waldman, Dec. 25, 1956; children—Jonathan, Debra, Susan. B.S. in Bus. Adminstrn., Temple U., 1957; cert. med. technician, Franklin Sch., 1960. Vice pres. Lawndale Lab., Phila., 1961-65, pres., 1965-68; regional dir. mktg. Damon Labs., Phila., 1968-70; exec. v.p. Beeman Devel. Corp., Miami, Fla., 1970-74; pres. Sandra Lee Products, Miami, 1974-79, Aloe Creme Labs., Ft. Lauderdale, Fla., 1979-81, Janeway Distbr., Ft. Lauderdale, 1980-83; mng. dir. Baird Bus. Assocs., Ft. Lauderdale, 1983—. Bd. dirs. Cheltenham, Pa. Rotary, 1965-68, Ind. Med. Technologists, Phila., 1967; instr., lt. U.S. Power Squadron, Miami, 1975-83. Mem. Am. Mgmt. Assn. (pres. chpt. 1966). Republican. Jewish. Clubs: Ocean Reef (Key Largo, Fla.); Cricket (Miami). 12000 N Bayshore Dr North Miami FL 33181 Office: Baird Bus Assocs 4000 N State Rd 7 Ft Lauderdale FL 33319

GOLOMB, HERBERT STANLEY, dermatologist; b. N.Y.C., Sept. 6, 1933; s. Morris and Ida (Schwartz) G.; A.B., U. Pa., 1955; M.D., State U. N.Y., Bklyn., 1960; m. Suzanne Nazer, Dec. 20, 1964; children—Meredith, Valerie. Intern, Ohio State U. Hosp., Columbus, 1960-61; resident in dermatology State U. N.Y.-Kings County Med. Center, 1961-62, N.Y. U. Skin and Cancer Unit and Bellevue Hosp., N.Y.C., 1962-64; pres. Falls Church Med. Ctr., 1963-64; practice medicine specializing in dermatology, Falls Church, Va., 1964-66, 68—; mem. staff George Washington U., S.E. Community, Fairfax (Va.), Arlington hosps.; instr., then clin. asst. prof. dermatology George Washington U. Sch. Medicine, 1964—; cons. USPHS Dermatology Clinic, 1964-66; chmn. Atlantic Dermatol. Conf., 1978. Pres. Dermatology Found. No. Va., 1962-64, bd. dirs., 1978-79. Served with USPHS, 1966-68. Diplomate Am. Bd. Dermatology. Fellow Am. Acad. Dermatology; mem. AMA, Soc. Investigative Dermatology, Internat. Soc. Tropical Dermatology, Med. Soc. Va., D.C., Fairfax County med. socs., D.C. (pres. 1977-78), Va. dermatol. socs. Clubs: McLean Indoor Tennis, Tuckahoe Swim and Tennis. Home: 1910 Woodgate Ln McLean VA 22101 Office: 6060 Arlington Blvd Falls Church VA 22044

GOLSON, HODGES LLOYD, JR., consulting management psychology firm executive; b. Swannanoa, N.C., Dec. 24, 1944; s. Hodges Lloyd and Josephine (Wilson) G.; B.S. in Indsl. Mgmt., Ga. Inst. Tech., 1967; M.S. in Psychology, Ga. State U., 1974, Ph.D. in Psychology, 1976; m. Mary Donna Hammock, Apr. 13, 1974; children—Holly, Katie, Kelly. Mktg. rep. data processing div. IBM, Atlanta, 1967-71; research, testing and electronic data processing technician Ga. State U., 1973-76; psychologist, v.p. devel. Bleke & Boyd, P.C., Atlanta, 1976-86; pres. Mgmt. Psychology Group, P.C., Atlanta, 1986—. Author: Executive Development: The Three Dimensions. Served to 1st lt. U.S. Army, 1968-70; Korea. Mem. Am. Psychol. Assn. (div. 14), Southeastern Psychol. Assn., Ga. Psychol. Assn. Home: 3030 Towerview Dr Atlanta GA 30324 Office: 3400 Peachtree Rd Atlanta GA 30326

GOMES, JOSEPH LEROY, insurance company executive; b. Honolulu, Jan. 1, 1943; s. William and Marie (Candido) Jordan; m. Patricia Kaye Buerth, June 26, 1966; children—Brian, Stacey. A.Sc. in Tech. Illustration, Daytona Jr. Coll., 1969; B.S. in Indsl. Tech., U. W. Fla., 1971. Cert. safety profl., indsl. hygiene technologist, Okla. Loss control trainee Hartford Ins. Group, Orlando, Fla., 1972-73, loss control rep., 1973-77, loss control cons., 1977-79, loss control tech. cons., 1979-84, loss control mgr., Oklahoma City, Okla., 1984—. Bd. dirs., treas. Orlando Lutheran Towers, 1981-84; pres., council mem. St. Pauls Evangelical Luth. Ch., 1983-84. Served with USAF, 1964-67; Vietnam. Mem. Soc. Safety Engr. Am. (Central Fla. chpt. pres. 1978-79), Am. Soc. Indsl. Security. Republican. Avocations: golfing; sports. Home: 9105 Dena Dr Oklahoma City OK 73132 Office: Hartford Ins Group 3520 NW 58th St Oklahoma City OK 73112

GOMES, NORMAN VINCENT, industrial engineer, broker; b. New Bedford, Mass., Nov. 7, 1914; s. John Vincent and Georgianna (Sylvia) G.; m. Carolyn Moore, June 6, 1942 (dec. Apr. 1983). Grad. U.S. Army Command and Gen. Staff Coll., 1944; B.S. in Indsl. Engring. and Mgmt., Okla. State U., 1950; M.B.A. in Mgmt., Xavier U., 1955. Asst. chief engr. Leschen div. H.K. Porter Co., St. Louis, 1950-52; staff mfg. cons. Gen. Electric Co., Cin., 1952-57: lectr. indsl. mgmt. U. Cin., 1955-56; vis. lectr. indsl. mgmt. Xavier U. Grad. Sch., 1956-57; staff indsl. engr. Gen. Dynamics, Ft. Worth, 1957-60; chief ops. analysis Ryan Electronics, San Diego, 1960-64; sr. engr., jet propulsion lab. Calif. Inst. Tech., Pasadena, 1964-67, mem. tech. staff, 1967, mgr. mgmt. systems, 1967-71; industry rep. and cons. U.S. Commn. on Govt. Procurement, Washington, 1970-72; adminstrv. officer GSA, Washington, 1973-78, program dir., 1979; now bus. broker; vis. lectr. mgmt. San Antonio Coll., 1982-85. Served as 2d lt. to maj. C.E., AUS, 1941-46; engring. adviser to War Manpower Bd., 1945. Decorated Army Commendation medal; recipient Apollo Achievement award, 1969, Outstanding Performance award GSA, 1974, 75, 77, 79. Registered profl. engr., Calif., Tex.; lic. real estate broker, Tex. Mem. Am. Inst. Indsl. Engrs. (nat. chmn. prodn. control research com., 1951-57; pres. Cin. chpt. 1956-57, bd. dirs. Cin., Fort Worth, San Diego, Los Angeles chpts. 1954-71, pres. Los Angeles 1970-71, nat. dir. community services 1969-73), Ret. Officers Assn. U.S. (chpt. pres. 1968-69, recipient Nat. Pres. certificate Merit 1969), Mil. Order World Wars, Freedoms Found. at Valley Forge, Nat. Security Indsl. Assn. (mgmt. systems subcom. 1967-69). Republican. Roman Catholic. Club: K.C. (4 deg.). Address: 2719 Knoll Tree San Antonio TX 78247 Office: 6921 Blanco Rd San Antonio TX 78216

GOMEZ, ESTELLA URIBE, bookstore manager; b. San Antonio, June 25, 1931; d. Santiago Uribe and Hortense (Cavazos) Davila; m. Phillip Rojo, Sept. 4, 1954 (dec. Mar. 1983); children—Steven Richard, Janina Teres. Grad. high sch. San Antonio, 1949. Gen. office clk. Atlantic Credit Co., San Antonio, 1951-54; auto title clk. Tax Assessor Collector, San Antonio, 1954-56; bookkeeper Whitehill Bookkeeping Co., San Antonio, 1968-74; mortgage recorder Accurate Record Service, San Antonio, 1968-74; mgr. bookstore Our Lady of the Lake U. Bookstore, San Antonio, 1974—. Mem. Affiliates of Mary, 1975, King William Assn., 1982; monitor Ctr. for Women in Ch. and Soc., 1984; supr. of students Summer Youth Employment Program, 1980, 81. Mem. Nat. Assn. of Coll. Stores, Our Lady of the Lake U. Staff Orgn. (treas. 1979-81, pres. 1981-83). Avocations: sewing; sketching; singing; playing piano; dancing. Office: Our Lady of the Lake U Bookstore 411 SW 24th St San Antonio TX 78285

GOMEZ, GUILLERMO, dairy executive; b. Havana, Cuba, Jan. 19, 1928; came to U.S., 1945, naturalized, 1950; m. Angelina Sanz; children—William, Charles. Grad. in dairy, U. Miami, 1963. Plant mgmt. and production Foremost Dairy, Miami, Fla., 1947-63, McArthur Dairy, Ft. Lauderdale, Fla., 1976—. Recipient Fed. Agr. Inspection Dept. award, 1985, Bd. Health award, Jacksonville, Fla., 1970, Bd. Health award, Broward County, Fla., 1984, Dean Food award Chgo., 1983.

GOMEZ, HECTOR, social worker; b. Laredo, Tex., Oct. 11, 1943; s. Lorenzo and Conseulo G.; m. Laura H. Gomez. A.A., Tex. A&I U., Laredo, 1969, B.S., Kingsville, 1971; M.S.W. (NIMH grantee), Our Lady of Lake U., 1974. Social worker, The Patrician Movement, San Antonio, 1971-74; dir. Laredo Mental Health Center, 1974-79; probation officer 49th Dist. Ct., Laredo, 1974—, now asst. chief probation officer; cons. The Mitre Corp.; mem. faculty Laredo Jr. Coll., 1979. Counselor, vol. Crisis Hot Line; mem. Webb County Welfare Bd., 1974—, South Tex. Health Agy. Bd., 1974—, Migrant Council Welfare Bd., 1974—, S. Tex. Devel. Council, 1974—; mem. Pres. Carters 1st Com. on Community, 1974; bd. dirs. Mother Cabrini Ch. Food Bank. Mem. Nat. Assn. Social Workers, Tex. Adult Probation Assn. Lodge: K.C. (3 deg.). Home: 2915 Mier St Laredo TX 78040

GOMEZ, JESSE ANTHONY, city official; b. San Antonio, Jan. 22, 1954; s. Jesus Delgado and Maria Consuelo (Lopez) G. B.B.A., St. Mary's U., 1976, M.B.A., 1984. Library aide San Antonio City Library, 1972-77, adminstrv. asst., 1977-78; fin. acct. City of San Antonio, 1978-79, compensation analyst for personnel, 1979-84, mgmt. asst. Office of City Mgmt., 1984—. Named Employee of Month, City of San Antonio Personnel Dept., 1982. Mem. Nat. Assn. Legal Assts., Internat. City Mgmt. Assn., Am. Soc. Notaries, Urban Mgmt. Assts. South Tex., St. Mary's U. Alumni Assn., San Antonio Jaycees, Lambda Chi Alpha. Roman Catholic. Home: 625 Drake St San Antonio TX 78204 Office: City of San Antonio PO Box 9066 San Antonio TX 78285

GOMEZ, RUDOLPH, university administrator; b. Rawlins, Wyo., July 17, 1930; s. Jose Jesus and Guadalupe (Navarro) G.; m. Polly Petty, Nov. 11, 1956; children—Robert Moorman, Clay Petty. B.S., Utah State U., 1959; M.A., Stanford U., 1960; Ph.D., U. Colo., 1963. Asst. prof. Colo. Coll., Colorado Springs, 1962-68; assoc. prof. polit. sci. U. Denver, 1968-70, Memphis State U., 1970-72; prof. polit. sci. U. Tex., El Paso, 1972-74, dept. chmn., 1973-74, grad. dean, dir. research, 1974-80; v.p. adminstrn. U. Tex., San Antonio, 1980—; Fulbright prof. Catholic U., Lima, Peru, 1967; cons. NIMH, Washington, 1978-80, Tex. Coordinating Bd., Austin, 1977—. Active Tex. Grad. Edn. Task Force, Austin, 1983—, Goals San Antonio, 1984—, Goals El Paso, 1974-76; cons. Govs. Task Force Handicapped, Austin, 1982—. Served to s/sgt. USAF, 1950-54. Woodrow Wilson Fellow 1959-60. Mem. Assn. Higher Edn., Polit. Sci. Assn., Nat. Council Univ. Research Adminstrs., Fulbright Alumni Assn., Delta Tau Kappa, Phi Kappa Phi, Pi Sigma Alpha, Omicron Delta Epsilon. Democrat. Roman Catholic. Home: 12506 King Elm San Antonio TX 78230 Office: U Tex Adminstrn Office San Antonio TX 78285-0604

GONGRE, CHARLES EDWARD, university administrator, English educator; b. Orange, Tex., Dec. 19, 1945; s. Louis Joseph and Blanche (Barnes) G.; m. Carolyn Sue Bates, Sept. 2, 1967. B.A., Lamar U., 1967; M.A., Stephen F. Austin State U., 1969; Ph.D., N. Tex. State U., 1980. Grad. asst. dept. English, Stephen F. Austin State U., Nacogdoches, Tex., 1968-69, N. Tex. State U., Denton, 1969-73; instr. English, Lamar U., Beaumont, Tex., 1973-76, asst. prof. English, Port Arthur, Tex., 1977-84, assoc. prof. English, 1984—, dean acad. programs, 1980—. Pres. Kiwanis Club of Port Arthur, 1983-84, named Disting. Pres., 1983-84. Mem. MLA, S. Central Modern Lang. Assn., Melville Soc., Am. Studies Assn. Tex. Roman Catholic. Avocations: salt-water fishing; scuba diving; snow skiing; travel. Office: Lamar U at Port Arthur 1500 Procter Port Arthur TX 77640

GONSHAK, ISABELLE LEE, nurse; b. Newark, Apr. 4, 1932; d. Robert John and Clara Kate (Cooperman) McClelland; m. David M. Gonshak, Aug. 8, 1953; children—Evan J., Brett A., Kathryn Gonshak Ponce, Ricardo Juan Ponce. R.N., Newark City Hosp., 1953. Tchr. Ideal Sch. for Nurse's Aides, Miami, Fla., 1972-74; vocal soloist numerous TV and social affairs. Bd. dirs. Miami Beach Symphony, 1971—, pres. 1978-79; bd. dirs. South Fla. Symphony; mem. Opera Guild Soc. Ft. Lauderdale. Mem. Fla. Nurses Assn., Greater Miami Opera Assn., Hadassah. Jewish. Home: 1700 SW 72d Ave Plantation FL 33317

GONTKO, TONY JOSEPH, banker; b. Waynesburg, Pa., June 18, 1947; s. Tony John and Mary G.; m. Cynthia Carroll, Aug. 30, 1970; children—Scott, Kelley. Grad. Ala. Christian U., 1976, La. State U., 1980, student Auburn U.; grad. Nat. Real Estate Sch. Vice-pres. First Ala. Bank, Montgomery, 1972—. Mem. Am. Bankers Assn., Robert Morris and Assocs., Soc. Real Estate Appraisers. Republican. Methodist. Clubs: Nat. Exchange, FAB (sr. advisor 1981—) (Montgomery). Lodge: Masons. Home: 1501 Merriweather Circle Montgomery AL 36116 Office: First Ala Bank Montgomery NA 8 Commerce St Montgomery AL 36101

GONZÁLEZ, DOREEN ETHEL, insurance agent; b. Phila., May 5, 1948; d. Junius Elbert and Doreen Mary May Davis; B.A. in Spanish, U. Houston, 1971, B.A. in Speech Pathology and Audiology, 1972, M.A., 1974; m. José J. González, Aug. 24, 1974; 1 dau., Amanda Doreen. Speech pathology trainee VA Hosp., Houston, 1972-74; speech pathologist Channelview (Tex.) Ind. Sch. Dist., 1974-75; clin. instr. div. audiology and speech pathology, dept. otorhinolaryngology Baylor Coll. Medicine, Houston, 1975-77; speech pathologist Klein Ind. Sch. Dist., Spring, Tex., 1977-80; staff speech pathologist Meth. and Jefferson Davis hosps., 1975-77; speech and hearing clinic supr., vis. lectr. Sam Houston State U., summer 1979; pres. Nat. Student Speech and Hearing Assn., U. Houston chpt., 1973-74; ins. agt., 1981—. Recipient Winfred E. Garrison award in Latin, U. Houston, 1971. Mem. Am. Speech and Hearing Assn. (cert.; chmn. directory com. conv. 1976), Tex. Speech and Hearing Assn., Phi Kappa Phi. Contbr. articles to profl. publs. Office: 9208 FM 1960 W Houston TX 77070

GONZALEZ, HENRY B., U.S. congressman; b. San Antonio, May 3, 1916; s. Leonides and Genevieve (Barbosa) G.; m. Bertha Cuellar, 1940; children—Henry B., Rosemary, Charles, Bertha, Stephen, Genevieve, Francis, Anna Marie. Grad. San Antonio Jr. Coll., U. Tex., Austin; J.D., St. Mary's U. Sch. Law; postgrad. U. Tex. Formerly with father's translating co., pub. relations counselor for ins. co., San Antonio; chief probation officer Bexar County, 1946; exec. sec. Jr. Deps. of Am. (formerly Pan Am. Progressive Assn.); mem. San Antonio City Council, 1953-56, mayor pro-tem, 1955-56; mem. Tex. State Senate, 1956-61; mem. 87th-99th U.S. Congress from 20th dist. Tex., 1961—, chmn. sub-com. on housing and community devel. 87th-96th Congresses. Mem. banking, fin. and urban affairs com., small bus. com., zone whip Tex.; Democratic Ho. majority whip orgn., 1973—. Civilian cable and radio censor Mil. and Naval Intelligence Dept., World War II. Office: US House of Reps 2413 Rayburn House Office Bldg Washington DC 20515

GONZÁLEZ, JOAQUÍN ANTONIO, tire distributing company executive; b. San José de las Lajas, Cuba, Aug. 16, 1943; s. Antonio and Georgina González (Pérez) G.; came to U.S., 1962, naturalized, 1975; B.A., Inst. Luz Caballero, San José de las Lajas, Cuba, 1957, postgrad., 1960; m. María A. Carmona, Mar. 19, 1966; children—Antonio Rafael, Georgina Armelia, Joaquín Antonio. Pres., TCM Internat., Inc., Miami, Fla., 1970—, TCM Tire Center, Miami, 1978—, Toca Inc., Miami, 1972—, Giant Mart, Miami, 1976—, TMF Investment, Miami, 1976—, Wide World Import & Export, Miami, 1978—; dir. Alliance Nat. Bank, Miami. Pres., Comité Por Rincon a San Lazaro. Mem. Nat. Tire Dealers Retreaders Assn., Fla. Tire Retreaders Assn., Asociación Interamericana de Hombres de Empresa, Camacol. Club: Kiwanis. Office: 2890 NW 35th St Miami FL 33142

GONZALEZ, JOE MANUEL, lawyer; b. N.Y.C., Aug. 18, 1950; s. Reinaldo Fabregas and Mary Louise (Cermeno) G.; m. Ruia Jane Whiteside, Dec. 30, 1977; children—Matthew Ray, Jane Marie, Jeffrey Joseph. B.A., U. South Fla., 1972; J.D., U. Gonzaga, 1980; LL.M. in Taxation, Georgetown U., 1981. Bar: Fla. 1981, U.S. Tax Ct. 1983, U.S. Dist. Ct. (mid. dist.) Fla. 1984, U.S. Ct. Appeals (11th cir.) 1984, U.S. Supreme Ct. 1985. Atty., Gonzaga U. Legal Services, Spokane, Wash., 1980; mng. ptnr. Cotterill, Gonzalez & Hayes, Lutz, Fla., 1981—; atty. Hispanic Def. League, Tampa, Fla., 1982—. Assoc. editor Gonzaga Spl. Report: Pub. Sector Labor Law, 1980. Mem. Sheriff's Hispanic Adv. Council, Tampa, 1982—, Mayor's Hispanic Task Force, Tampa, 1983—. Mem. ABA, Hillsborough County Bar Assn., Assn. Trial Lawyers Am., Nat. Inst. for Trial Advocacy, Phi Delta Phi. Democrat. Presbyterian. Lodge: Rotary. Home: 1708 Richardson Pl Tampa FL 33606 Office: Cotterill Gonzalez & Hayes 126 Flagship Dr Lutz FL 33549

GONZALEZ, JOSE ALEJANDRO, JR., judge; b. Tampa, Fla., Nov. 26, 1931; s. Jose A. and Luisa Secundina (Collia) G.; B.A., U. Fla., 1952, J.D., 1957; m. Frances Frierson, Aug. 22, 1956 (dec. Aug. 1981); children—Margaret Ann, Mary Frances; m. Mary Sue Copeland, Sept. 24, 1983. Bar: Fla. 1958. Practice in Ft. Lauderdale, 1958-64; claim rep. State Farm Mutual, Lakeland, Fla., 1957-58; asso. Watson, Hubert and Sousley, attys., 1958-61, partner, 1961-64; asst. state atty. 15th Circuit Fla., 1961-64; circuit judge 17th Circuit Ft. Lauderdale, 1964-78, chief judge, 1970-71; asso. judge 4th Dist. Ct. Appeals, W. Palm Beach; judge U.S. Dist. Ct. So. Dist. Fla., 1978—; Bd. dirs. Arthritis Found., 1962-72; bd. dirs. Henderson Clinic Broward County, 1964-68, v.p., 1967-68. Served to 1st lt. AUS, 1952-54. Named Broward Legal Exec. of Yr., 1978. Mem. Fla. Bar, Am. Bar Assn., Broward County Bar, Ft. Lauderdale Jaycees (dir. 1960-61), Fla. Blue Key, Sigma Chi, Phi Alpha Delta. Democrat. Kiwanian (pres. 1971-72). Home: 316 SE 17th Ave Fort Lauderdale FL 33301 Office: 205D US Courthouse 299 E Broward Blvd Fort Lauderdale FL 33301

GONZALEZ, JUAN H., hosp. lab. dir.; b. Corpus Christi, Tex., Jan. 27, 1935; s. Antonio and Vencelada (Herrera) G.; B.A., Pan Am. U., 1964, M.S., 1978; m. Matiana Moran, Oct. 17, 1965; children—John, Paul, Monica; 1 adopted son, Alfredo. Med. technologist various hosps., 1960-66; analytical chemist Tex. Health Dept., San Benito, 1966-74; med. technologist Valley Bapt. Med. Center, Harlingen, Tex., 1974-75; lab. dir. Valley Community Hosp., Brownsville, Tex., 1975—; cons. to physicians. Served with AUS, 1958-59. Mem. Am. Soc. Med. Tech., Am. Assn. Clin. Chemistry, Am. Soc. Microbiology, Am. Soc. Clin. Pathologists. Democrat. Roman Catholic. Club: K.C. Home: 13 N Tupelo St Brownsville TX 78520 Office: 1 Ted Hunt St Blvd Brownsville TX 78520

GONZALEZ, MANUEL ENRIQUE, architect; b. Utuado, P.R., Jan. 19, 1919; s. Enrique Gonzalez and Emilia Torres; student CUNY, 1948; B.S. in Archtl. Engring., Ohio U., Athens, 1951; postgrad. Newark Coll. Engring., 1955; m. Ada E. Gonzalez, Feb. 14, 1948; children—Eric M., Wanda E. Pvt. practice architecture, San Juan, P.R., 1957-69; dir., organizer archtl. and constrn. div. Dept. Social Service, Commonwealth of P.R., 1969-73; dir. sch. planning and constrn. Orange County Schs., Orlando, Fla., 1973-76; now owner, pres. Design-Build Team Inc., design and constrn. schs., chs., instnl. bldgs., Altamonte Springs, Fla. Elder, Presbyterian. Ch., Sunday Sch. tchr., 1965-72, organizer Spanish bible study group in Orlando, 1975; pres. Bicentennial Com., Bayamon, P.R., 1971. Served with U.S. Army, 1940-45; ETO. Decorated Silver Star; lic. architect, Fla., Ga., Ala., N.C., Va., Md., N.J., Tex., P.R., Conn., V.I. Fellow Soc. Am. Registered Architects; mem. AIA. Club: Rotary (past pres.). Lodges: Masons (past master), Shriners, Order Eastern Star. Contbr. articles to mags. Home: 431 N Maitland Ave Altamonte Springs FL 32701

GONZALEZ, RAUL FROILAN, communications company sales manager; b. Havana, Cuba, Oct. 5, 1952; came to U.S., 1964; s. Raoul G. and Mirta L. (Viera) G. A.A., Miami-Dade Coll., 1976; B.S., Mercer U., 1983; Cert. Columbia U., 1984, U. Mich., 1985. Coin telephone rep. Ill. Bell, Chgo., 1973-74; service cons. So. Bell, Miami, Fla., 1974-78, account exec., 1979, sales mgr., 1980-81, tng. mgr., Atlanta, 1981-83; regional sales mgr. AT&T Communications Co., Ft. Lauderdale, Fla., 1983—; dir. G&G Service Corp., Miami; pres., chief exec. officer Argos Systems, Miami, 1978—. Chmn. subcom. Dade County Employ Handicapped, Miami, 1976-79; advisor to bd. dirs. United Way Dade County, Miami, 1979; sustaining mem. Republican Nat. Com., Washington, 1981—. Recipient I Dare You Leadership award Clement W. Stone Found., 1972; Ill. State scholar, 1971. Fellow Am. Motel Hotel Assn.; mem. Southeast Airport Mgrs. Assn., Airport Operators Council Internat., Ft. Lauderdale-Broward C. of C. Roman Catholic. Avocations: boating; fishing; reading; spectator sports. Home: 4490 W 19th Ct Apt B-115 Hialeah FL 33012 Office: US Telecom Exec Ctr at Datran 9100 S Dadeland Blvd Suite 1107 Miami FL 33156

GONZALEZ, SANTANA, JR., oil company representative, lawyer; b. Elsa, Tex., June 10, 1953; s. Santana and Azucena (Saenz) G.; m. Nellie Mae Garcia, May 17, 1975; children—Amber Michelle, Lisa Marie. B.A., Pan Am. U., 1976; J.D., U. Houston, 1999. Sole practice, Houston, 1979; registered rep. Gulf Oil Co., Houston, 1979—. Mem. League United Latin Am. Citizens, 1983, Am. G.I. Forum, 1982, Nat. Assn. Latino Elected and Appointed Officials, 1979; mem. adv. council Latino Learning Ctr., 1981; bd. dirs. Assn. Advancement Mexican-Americans, 1983; trustee Hispanic Internat. U., 1981; v.p. Hispanic Energy Forum, 1982, pres. 1981; v.p. IMAGE of Houston, 1979; adv. bd. Harris County Minorities and Law Enforcement Coalition, 1979; corp. mem. Nat. Assn. Latino Elected and Apptd. Ofcls., Houston. Recipient President's award Nat. Council of La Raza, 1983, Am. G.I. Forum Corp. Rep. award, 1983; SER-Jobs for Progress, Inc. Community Service award, 1981, George I. Sanchez Community Service award, 1980. Mem. State Bar Tex. Democrat. Church of Christ. Office: Gulf Oil Co 1301 McKinney St Houston TX 77751

GONZALEZ-RAMOS, PEDRO, university administrator; b. Mayaguez, P.R., July 14, 1935; s. Pedro Gonzalez-Valcarcel and Betty Ramos; m. Nelky Perez, July 16, 1960; children—Pedro Antonio, Eduardo, Nelky Esther. B.A., U. P.R., 1957, M.S., 1959; Ph.D. in Biology, Fordham U., 1961. Prof., dir. Humacao Univ. Coll., U. P.R., 1960-72; pres. U. Sacred Heart, Santurce, P.R., 1972—. P.R. del. 2d Iberoam. Congress Ministers Edn.; pres. Commn. Edn. Reform, 1974-77. Named P.R. Jaycees Outstanding Young Man of Yr., 1973; recipient Sales Mktg. Assn. Top Mgmt. award, 1974. Mem. Angel Ramos

Found., P.R. Mfrs. Assn., P.R. C. of C., Assn. P.R. Univ. Pres., P.R. Humanities Found., P.R. Sci. and Art Acad., Assn. Caribbean Univs., Internat. Fedn. Cath. Univs. Clubs: Caparra Country. Lodge: Villa Caparra Rotary. Office: PO Box 12383 Loiza Sta Santurce PR 00914

GONZALEZ-VALES, LUIS ERNESTO, historian, educational administrator; b. Rio Piedras, P.R., May 11, 1930; s. Ernesto and Carmen (Vales) G.; B.A. with honors, U. P.R., 1952; M.A., Columbia U., 1957; m. Hilda González, July 16, 1952; children—Carmen L., Luis E., Antonio S., Maria G., Rosa Maria, Gerardo, Rosario, Hildita. Instr. humanities U. P.R., Rió Piedras, 1955-58, asst. prof. humanities, 1958-64, asso. prof. humanities, 1964-67, asso. prof. history, 1967, asst. dean faculty gen. studies, 1960-65, asso. dean faculty gen. studies, 1965-67, exec. sec. Council on Higher Edn., 1967-83; exec. sec. Commonwealth Post Secondary Commn., 1973-83. Chancellor P.R. Jr. Coll., 1985—. Served to 2d. lt. inf. U.S. Army, 1952-55; adj. gen. P.R. N.G., 1983-85. Mem. Am. Hist. Assn., Acad. Polit. Scis., P.R. Acad. History, Am. Acad. Polit. and Social Scis., Latin Am. Studies Assn., Assn. U.S. Army, N.G. Assn., Mil. Order World Wars, Res. Officers Assn., Phi Alpha Theta (pres. 1962-63). Roman Catholic. Author: Alejandro Ramirez: La Vida de un Intendente Liberal, 1972; contbg. author: Puerto Rico: A Political and Cultural History, 1983; contbr. articles on Puerto Rican history (in Spanish) to hist. jours.; editorial bd. Revista Historia, 1960-67. Office: Chancellor PR Jr Coll Ana G Mendel Ednl Found Box 21373 Rio Piedras PR 00928

GOOCH, ELWIN GENE, educational administrator, income tax consultant; b. Plainview, Tex., Feb. 21, 1953; s. Elwin Blake and Exia Ruth (Swim) G.; m. Susan Denny, June 7, 1975; children—Richard Ryan, Meredith Denny. B. in Bus., N. Tex. State U., 19. Staff acct. Saville, Dodgen & Co., Dallas, 1973-75, Johnston & King, CPA, Vernon, Tex., 1975-78; dean bus. services Vernon Jr. Coll., Tex., 1978—. Vice pres., dir. Vernon Meals on Wheels, 1978-82; trustee First United Methodist Ch., Vernon, 1980—, asst. treas., 1980—. Recipient Troop Leadership award NW Tex. council Boy Scouts of Am., 1976, Outstanding Service to Youth award, 1977. Mem. Nat. Council Community Coll. Bus. Officials (v.p. 1982—, founding bd. mem. 1982), Nat. Assn. Coll. and U. Bus. Officers, Tex. Jr. Coll. Bus. Officers Assn., Vernon Jaycees (recipient Pres. Honor award 1977, Cert. of Merit 1978). Republican. Avocations: tennis; golf; drawing; painting. Home: 4130 Cottonwood Vernon TX 76384 Office: Vernon Regional Jr Coll 4400 College Dr Vernon TX 76384

GOOCH, JAMES OLIVER, physician; b. Indian Gap, Tex., Nov. 27, 1913; s. James Walter and Ora Ellen (Oliver) G.; m. Feb. 5, 1935; children—Jon David, Joel Phillips. Student So. Meth. U., 1931-33, U. Tex., 1934-35; M.D., Tulane U., 1939; M.Sc. in Otorhinolaryngology, U. Minn., 1949. Diplomate Am. Bd. Otolaryngology. Intern, Shreveport (La.) Charity Hosp., 1939-40; fellow Mayor Found., Rochester, Minn., 1946-49; asst. prof. otolaryngology Baylor Med. Sch., 1949-51; practice otolaryngology and allergy, Midland, Tex., 1951—; mem. staff Midland Meml. Hosp. Served to col. M.C., U.S. Army, 1940-46. Decorated Purple Heart. Mem. Am. Acad. Ophthalmology and Otolaryngology, AMA, Tex. Med. Assn., Allergy Soc., Am. Acad. Otolaryngic Allergy, Quiet Birdman. Republican. Clubs: Austin Country, Midland Country, Horseshoe Bay Country. Lodge: Masons. Home: 1600 W Golf Course Rd Midland TX 79701 Office: 401 N Garfield St Midland TX 79704

GOOCH, NANCY JANE, real estate broker; b. Ann Arbor, Mich., Dec. 19, 1941; d. Donald Burnett and Marjorie (Gilchrist) G. B.A. in Liberal Arts, Western Mich. U., 1963; cert. Eastern Mich. U., 1965. Mich. Tchr. Manchester Pub. Schs., Mich., 1965-68, Broward County Pub. Schs., Fort Lauderdale, Fla., 1968-73; v.p. Chinelly Real Estate, Inc., Miramar, Fla., 1973-82; closing exec. Cenvill Devel., Pembroke Pines, Fla., 1983-85; broker Prestige Realty ERA, Pembroke Pines, 1985—; cons. in field. Editor-designer mag. The Bridle Path, 1983— (hon. award 1983, 84, 85). Treas. Miramar Homeowners Assn., 1971, Miramar Republican Club, 1973; mem. Bass Campaign, Fort Lauderdale, 1975; mem. Branca for Mayor Com., Miramar, 1980. Mem. Hollywood South Broward Bd. Realtors, Fla. Assn. Realtors. Club: S. Fla. Trail Riders (Davie). Home: 1633 Leaird St Ann Arbor MI 48105 Office: Prestige Realty Inc 7766 Plantation Blvd Miramar FL 33023

GOOCH, PATRICIA CAROLYN, cytogeneticist; b. Michie, Tenn., Mar. 28, 1935; d. James Lide and Mary Frances (Hyneman) G.; B.S., U. Tenn., Knoxville, 1957. Tchr. sci. Knoxville (Tenn.) City Sch. System, 1957-58; biologist, biology div. Oak Ridge Nat. Lab., 1958-70, 73—; research assoc. Grad. Sch. Biomed. Sci., U. Tex., Houston, 1970; sr. research analyst Northrop Corp., NASA-Johnson Space Center, Houston, 1970-72; organizing com. sci. confs. Named Outstanding Tenn. Woman, U. Tenn. Pan-Hellenic Assn., 1974. Mem. AAAS, Am. Genetic Assn., Genetics Soc. Am., Environ. Mutagen Soc., U. Tenn. Alumni Assn. (chpt. treas. 1980-81, chpt. sec. 1981-82, chpt. v.p. 1982-83, chpt. pres. 1983-84, nat. bd. govs. 1984—), Oak Ridge Pan-Hellenic Assn. (benefit chmn. 1961), Delta Gamma Alumni Assn. (pres. Knoxville Area 1959-61, 67-69), Sigma Xi (chpt. admissions com. 1977-79). Democrat. Mem. Chs. of Christ. Club: Big Orange (sec. 1978-80, 82-84). Contbr. articles to profl. jours. Home: 226 Tusculum Dr Oak Ridge TN 37830 Office: Biology Div Oak Ridge Nat Lab PO Box Y Oak Ridge TN 37830

GOOCH, WILLIAM KEVIN, financial analyst; b. Silverton, Oreg., Dec. 10, 1954; s. William Treadwell and Betty Lou (Presho) G. B.A., Southwestern at Memphis, 1976; M.B.A., Miami U., Oxford, Ohio, 1977. Instr. Miami U., 1978-79; auditor Winters Nat. Corp., Dayton, Ohio, 1979-80; fin. analyst Morgan, Keegan & Co., Memphis, 1980—. Mem. Memphis Soc. Fin. Analysts. United Methodist. Avocations: cooking; travel; art. Office: Morgan Keegan & Co Inc Morgan Keegan Tower 50 Front St Memphis TN 38103

GOODE, CLEMENT TYSON, educator; b. Richmond, Va., July 10, 1929; s. Clement Tyson and Bessie Mae (Trimble) G.; A.B., Hendrix Coll., 1951; M.A. (teaching fellow), Vanderbilt U., 1953, Ph.D. (teaching fellow, So. Fellowship Fund grantee), 1959; m. Elizabeth Jane Anderson, Aug. 19, 1952; children—Sara Elizabeth, Robert Clement. Instr. English, Vanderbilt U., Nashville, 1954-56; instr. English, Baylor U., Waco, Tex., 1957-58, asst. prof., 1958-60, asso. prof., 1960-63, prof., 1963—, dir. freshman English, 1961-64, grad. dir. English dept., 1968—; exchange prof. Seinan Gakuin U., Fukuoka, Japan, 1972-73. Adv. bd. Salvation Army Waco, 1968-69; deacon 1st Baptist Ch. Waco, 1970—. Mem. MLA, S. Central MLA, Nat. Council Tchrs. English, Coll. Conf. Tchrs. English, Byron Soc., Shelley Soc. Democrat. Author: (with Oscar Santucho) A Comprehensive Bibliography of Secondary Materials in English: George Gordon, Lord Byron with a Review of Research, 1976. Contbr. articles, revs. to profl. publs. Home: 2720 Braemar St Waco TX 76710

GOODE, MARK G., state official; b. Quinlan, Tex., Aug. 12, 1921; s. Mark G. and Nora W. G.; B.S. in Civil Engring., Tex. A&M U., 1947; m. Lucille A. McDermott, June 27, 1942; children—Mark, Scott. With Tex. Dept. Hwys. and Public Transp., 1947—, asst. engr., Austin, 1973-80, engr. dir., 1980—. Served with CE, U.S. Army, 1942-46. Mem. Am. Assn. State Hwys and Transp. Ofcls., Transp. Research Bd., ASCE, Tex. Soc. Profl. Engrs. Presbyterian. Home: 5802 Trailridge Circle Austin TX 78731 Office: 11th St and Brazos St Austin TX 78701

GOODE, PATRICIA WEAVER, import company executive; b. Washington, July 23, 1940; d. Narvin Blake and Elizabeth (Robertson) Weaver; m. Thomas Orden Goode, Dec. 23, 1961 (div. 1981); children—Walter Robert, Catherine Elizabeth. Student Coll. William and Mary, 1958-59, Washington Sch. for Secs., 1959-60. Legal sec. Odin & Feldman, Fairfax, Va., 1965-77; adminstrv. dir. Charles J. Givens Found., Washington, 1977-81; v.p. JCR Imports/Exports, Mt. Vernon, Va., 1982—; cons. Charles J. Givens Fedn., Orlando, Fla., 1981—. Presbyterian. Club: Bus. and Profl. Women's. Office: PO Box 108 Mount Vernon VA 22121

GOODEY, PAUL RONALD, mathematics educator; b. Hull, Eng., Oct. 16, 1946; came to U.S., 1983; s. Ronald and Alison (Swain) G.; m. Patricia Anne Leggett, Sept. 20, 1970; children—Joanna, Adrian. B.S., London U., Eng., 1968, Ph.D., 1970. Lectr. London U., 1970-83; assoc. prof. math. Okla. U., Norman, 1983—; vis. prof. Okla. U., 1979-80; vis. prof. Siegen U., Fed. Republic Germany, 1981-82. Contbr. articles to profl. jours. Mem. Am. Math. Soc., London Math. Soc. (sec. 1981-83). Avocations: wildlife; astronomy. Home: 1712 Homeland St Norman OK 73069 Office: U Okla Dept Math Norman OK 73019

GOODGER, JAMES MILLER, geologist, consultant; b. Electra, Tex., Dec. 25, 1925; s. William Herman and Sarah Esther (Miller) G.; m. Lura Love Parnell, June 26, 1954; children—Robert Gordon, Luann. B.S., U. Okla., 1949. Registered profl. geologist. Area geologist The Pure Oil Co., Oklahoma City, 1953-64; v.p. Southland Royalty Co., Fort Worth, 1964-77; mgr. exploration Burnett Oil Co., Fort Worth, 1977-82; v.p. Penaco Inc., Fort Worth, 1982-84, cons., 1984—. Pres., North Fort Worth Boys Club Endowment Fund, 1983-84. Mem. Am. Assn. Petroleum Geologists (chmn. ho. of dels. 1979, sec., treas. div. profl. affairs 1982-83), Ind. Petroleum Assn. of Am., Am. Inst. Profl. Geologists (pres. Tex. sect. 1982-83). Avocations: gardening; golf. Home: 601 High Woods Trail Fort Worth TX 76112 Office: Penaco Inc Suite 890 Continental Plaza 777 Main St Fort Worth TX 76102

GOODHEER, WILMER CHARLES, clergyman, missionary educator; b. Martinsville, N.J., May 2, 1932; s. Frederick and Dorothy (Wilde) G.; m. Barbara Lee Albright, July 2, 1955; children—Thomas Clark, Jesse Philip, Janet Marye. Student Harding U., 1952-55; B.A., David Lipscomb Coll., 1958; postgrad. Dutch Ref. Sem. of Missions, Leiden, Netherlands, 1967-68; M.A. in Religion, Eastern Bapt. Theol. Sem., Phila., 1974; D.Missiology, Trinity Evang. Div. Sch. Ordained to ministry Ch. of Christ, 1955. Minister of deaf Avalon Heights Ch. of Christ, Washington, 1955-57; missionary-tchr., The Hague, Netherlands, 1958-70; minister Ch. of Christ, West Chester, Pa., 1970-77, King of Prussia (Pa.) Ch. of Christ, 1977-81; assoc. prof. Bible and Missions Abilene (Tex.) Christian U., 1981—; asst. to pres., sec. to bd. trustees European Christian Coll., Vienna, Austria, 1981—; founder, dir. children's camp, Solwaster, Belgium, 1964-70; dir./tchr. Camp Manatawny (Pa.), 1971-76; tchr. Belgium Bible Coll., Verviers, 1967-68; dir./evangelist internat. campaigns, Sweden, Ger., Eng., Belgium, Netherlands, Austria, Portugal, 1961—; dir. Valley Forge Family Encampment, 1977, 78, 79, 80, 81, 82, 83, 84, Valley Forge Evangelism Conf., 1978, 79, 80, Blue Danube Lectureship, Vienna, 1984—; adj. faculty Northeastern Christian Jr. Coll., Villanova, Pa., 1973-81; corp. life mem. Shiloh, Inc., 1972—, trustee, 1978—, pres. corp., 1979—, 4-H Leader, 1976, 77, 78; prison chaplain Chester County Farm, 1974—, Delaware County Prison, 1976—. Named Ark. Traveler, Gov. Winthrop Rockefeller, 1969; Ring of Freedom award Northeastern Christian Jr. Coll., 1977. Mem. Assn. Christian Prison Workers, Am. Camping Assn. Republican. Clubs: Optimists Internat. (dir., community service chmn.), Rotary. Author: The Man of the Messianic Reign, 1980; editor/pub. Het Levende Woord, 1960-70; contbr. to mags. Home: Route 1 Box 364 Abilene TX 79601 Office: Abilene Christian U ACU Sta Box 7939 Abilene TX 79699

GOODING, GLENN J., JR., quality assurance coodinator; b. Feb. 25, 1942; s. Glenn J. and Caroline F. (Campbell) G.; m. Christina A. DeMante; children—Michael, Shawn. Electronic Tech. degree, Columbia Tech. Inst., 1966; A.A., George Washington U., 1974, B.S.A., 1977, M.A.E. in Human Resource Devel., 1980. Customer engr. IBM Corp., Washington, 1961-68, mgr., 1968-81, faculty loan program prof. of bus. Hampton Inst., 1981-83, customer service and admin. mgr., Norfolk, Va., 1983, mgmt. devel. staff, Boca Raton, Fla., 1983-85, quality assurance coordinator entry systems, 1985—; mgmt. cons. Guest speaker at various functions, community and bus. orgns. Contbr. articles to profl. jours. Pres. PTA; bd. dirs., dir. tng. Contact Peninsula; group leader in crisis counseling training. Recipient Excellence Plus Quality awards, IBM Mgrs. Informal awards; named Mgr. of Yr. IBM. Mem. Am. Soc. for Training and Devel. Avocations: tennis, running, fishing, camping, writing. Home: 2415 SW 35th Ave Delray Beach FL 33445 Office: IBM Corp PO Box 1328 Dept 16G/5010 Boca Raton FL 33432

GOODKIN, LEWIS MICHAEL, real estate market analytical company executive; b. Passaic, N.J., Sept. 13, 1935; s. Robert Rubin and Lillian (Ellman) G.; A.B., Temple U., 1956; m. Joanne Myers, Jan. 1, 1980; children—Valarie, Sherrie, Andria. Pres., founder Goodkin Research Corp., Ft. Lauderdale, Fla., 1975—; lectr. in field. Served with U.S. Army, 1958-60, USAR, 1960-64. Mem. Fla. Atlantic Builders Assn. (dir. 1978-80), Inst. Resdl. Mktg., Urban Land Inst. Republican. Jewish. Clubs: Coral Ridge Country, Ocean Reef. Author: When Real Estate and Home Building Become Big Business, 1974; contbr. in field. Office: 275 Commercial Blvd Fort Lauderdale by the Sea FL 33308

GOODLOE, ROBERT KENNETH, osteopathic physician; b. Kurthwood, La., Oct. 4, 1937; s. Rufus Kemp and Avis (Martin) G.; m. Dianna Kay Scott, Nov. 7, 1964; children—Jeffrey Michael, Mark Alan. B.S. in Pharmacy, Southwestern Okla. U., 1959; D.O., Kans. City Coll. Health Scis., 1964. Intern, Hillcrest Hosp., Oklahoma City, 1964-65, chmn. dept. gen. practice, 1969-71; gen. practice osteo. medicine, Mustang, Okla., 1964—. Republican. Office: Mustang Med Ctr 500 Park Ave Mustang OK 73064

GOODMAN, BARRY MICHAEL, lawyer; b. Los Angeles, Nov. 22, 1946; s. Ralph Arthur and Natalie Bell (Hamburger) G.; B.A. in History, Calif. State U., 1967; J.D., U. So. Calif., 1970; m. Susan Lynn Reigrod, June 18, 1969; children—Gregory, Alison. Bar: Calif. 1971, D.C. 1972. Sr. atty. Office of Chief Counsel, Urban Mass Transp. Adminstrn., Washington, 1971-74; dir. Office of Public Transp., City of Houston, 1974-78; exec. dir. Met. Transit Authority, Houston, 1978-79; pres. Barry M. Goodman & Assocs., Houston, 1979—. Mem. Am., Calif., Washington bar assns., Urban Land Inst., Transp. Research Bd. Jewish. Home: 2702 Valley Manor Kingwood TX 77339 Office: CitiCorp Ctr 1200 Smith Suite 3530 Houston TX 77002

GOODMAN, EMERY DAVID, exploration geologist; b. N.Y.C., May 27, 1956; s. Robert Merrill and Sonia Helene (Bjelinki) G.; m. Anne Vallot, May 11, 1985. B.S., SUNY-Stony Brook, 1978; M.S., U. S.C., 1980. Exploration geologist Shell Western E & P, New Orleans, 1980—. Mem. Am. Assn. Petroleum Geologists, New Orleans Geol. Soc. Avocations: long-distance running, hiking. Home: 6815 Colbert St New Orleans LA 70124 Office: Shell Western E & P PO Box 60775 New Orleans LA 70160

GOODMAN, ENOCH ALVIN, building materials company executive; b. Salisbury, N.C., July 30, 1915; s. Enoch Arthur and Frances Jane (Park) G.; m. Dorothy Burl Hedrick, Apr. 22, 1939; children—Michael Alvin, Jeffrey Vance, Dorothy Gail. A.B., Catawba Coll., 1938, D. Humanitarian Service, 1968. Mng. ptnr. lessees of B.V. Hedrick Gravel & Sand Co., Salisbury, from 1945; chmn. bd. So. Concrete Materials, Asheville, N.C., 1982—, pres., 1958-81; chmn. bd. Buncombe Constrn. Co., Asheville, 1982—; gen. ptnr. Caroline Stalite Co., Salisbury, 1949—; dir. Security Bank & Trust, Salisbury. Trustee Meth. Home, Charlotte, N.C., Rowan Meml. Hosp., Salisbury Catawba Coll., Salisbury. Served to lt. USN, 1943-46. Republican. Methodist. Clubs: Rotary, Salisbury Country; Hound Ears (Blowing Rock, N.C.). Home: 214 Confederate Ave Salisbury NC 28144 Office: Box 1044 Salisbury NC 28144

GOODMAN, JERRY DONALD, demographic consultant; b. Denver, May 22, 1947; s. Herman and Dorothy Eva (Berger) G.; m. Rhonda Kushner, Aug. 15, 1982; 1 child, Robert. B.S. in Engring., UCLA, 1969; B.A. in Sociology, U. Tex., 1973, M.A., 1976, Ph.D., 1983. Statistical computer programming cons. U. Tex., 1974-77, research assoc., 1977-79, instr., 1979-80; sr. researcher, demographic analyst Indian Nations Council of Govts., Tulsa, Okla., 1980-84; cons. demographics, Tulsa, 1984—. Contbr. articles to profl. jours. Nat. Inst. Children's Health and Human Devel. fellow, 1977-78. Mem. Am. Sociol. Assn., Population Assn. Am., S.W. Social Sci. Assn., So. Regional Demographics Group. Club: Tulsa Econs. Avocations: running; swimming; bicycling.

GOODMAN, JERRY LYNN, merchandising distribution company executive, lawyer; b. Mangum, Okla., Apr. 17, 1939; s. A.O. and Viola Louise (Bogart) G.; m. Donna L. Rudy, Dec. 16, 1962; children—Courtney L., Polly K., Mallory E., Benjamin R. B.A., U. Tulsa 1961; LL.B., Georgetown U., 1964. Bar: Okla. 1964. Law clk. antitrust div. Dept. Justice, 1962-63; legis. asst. to U.S. Senator J. Howard Edmondson, 1963-64; assoc. Thornton & Stamper, Tulsa, 1964-65; asst. city atty. City of Tulsa, 1965-68; ptnr. Owens & Goodman, Tulsa, 1968-70; gen. counsel OTASCO, Inc., Tulsa, 1970-74, v.p., gen. counsel, 1974, trustee, 1975—; dir. and mem. exec. com., 1976—, pres., 1981—, pres., chief operating officer, 1982, pres., chief exec. officer, 1983—; dir., mem. exec. com. OASCO Credit Corp., 1976—; dir. MICO, Inc., Ryben Distbg. Co., Donlrudy, Inc., Okla.; Bank organizer, dir., corp. sec. Am. State Bank of Tulsa; judge Temporary Ct. Appeals, Okla. Supreme Ct. Bd. dirs. St. John Med. Ctr.; adv. bd. dirs. U. Ctr. at Tula; commr. Consumer Credit Commn. of Okla.; bd. dirs. United Way, 1984; past mem. Utility Bd. of City of Tulsa; past vice chmn. Tulsa Crime Commn.; past bd. dirs., mem. exec. com. Met. YMCA. Served to lt. USNR, 1964-70. Democrat. Presbyterian. Home: 2616 E 33d St Tulsa OK 74105 Office: OTASCO Inc PO Box 885 11333 E Pine St Tulsa OK 74102

GOODMAN, TERRI WOOLRIDGE, public relations and marketing specialist; b. Oklahoma City, Jan. 23, 1955; d. Perry B. and Mayselle (Tidwell) Woolridge; m. Richard Stewart Goodman, May 29, 1981 (dec.). B.S., Okla. State U., 1977. Newspaper editor, 1977-79; dir. community relations South Community Hosp., Oklahoma City, 1979-83; community liaison dir. Healthcare Services of Am./The Bethany Pavilion, 1985—; pub. relations cons. Okla. Cancer Info. Line, 1983. Bd. deacons Presbyterian Ch., 1983-85. Mem. Am. Soc. Hosp. Pub. Relations (dir. region VII), Okla. Hosp. Assn. Pub. Relations Soc. (S.W. dist. dir.), Greater Oklahoma City Hosp. Pub. Relations Council (pres. 1982), Am. Soc. Suicidology, Am. Mkgt. Assn. Office: 7600 NW 23d Bethany OK 73008

GOODNIGHT, CHARLES RAY, tax consultant; b. Waco, Tex., Nov. 10, 1941; s. John Henry and Lois Mary (Poston) G.; student Durham Bus. Coll., 1961, Baylor U., 1964-65; m. Iris Marlene Patrick, Sept. 17, 1970; children—Kristy Michelle, Jennifer Leigh. Asst. grand sec. Grand Lodge of Tex. Masons, 1964-80; fed. tax cons. fraternal orgns. U.S. Mem. Bellmead (Tex.) City Council, 1968-72, mayor, 1970. Served with USNR, 1962-64. Mem. Am. Legion, VFW, Nat. Assn. Enrolled Agts., Tex. Enrolled Agts. Soc., Tex. Assn. Pub. Accts. Republican. Methodist. Lodges: Masons (32 deg., past high priest, past illustrious master council royal and select masters, past dist. dep. grand master), K.T., Shriners. Home: 732 Ivy Ann Waco TX 76710 Office: 900 Austin St Suite 1103 Waco TX 76701

GOODNIGHT, MELVIN MAURICE, real estate broker; b. LaFayette, Ind., July 8, 1910; s. Earl Everett and Carrie Mae (Moore) G.; m. Thelma Ione Abel, July 5, 1932; children—Carole, Earle, Janet. B.S., Purdue U., 1931. Nat. sales mgr. Royal Drug Co., Chgo., 1936-38; pres. Ind. Pharm. Assn., Indpls., 1948; vice chmn. Man. County Tourist Devel. Council, Bradenton, Fla., 1980-85. Councilman LaFayette City Council, 1954-58; mem. Ind. State Legislature, Indpls., 1961-65; Republican. Methodist. Lodge: Kiwanis (state gov. 1958). Avocation: golf. Home: 4109 18th Ave Dr W Bradenton FL 33505 Office: M M Bo Goodnight Realty 3511 US 301 E Ellenton FL 33532

GOODRICH, HENRY CALVIN, investment company executive, retired natural resource and energy company executive; b. Fayetteville, Tenn., Apr. 24, 1920; s. Charles Landess and Maude (Baxter) G.; student Erskine Coll., 1938-39; B.S., U. Tenn., 1943; LL.D. (hon.), Butler U., 1976; D.B.A. (hon.), Marion Coll., 1978; m. Billie Grace Walker, Sept. 10, 1943; children—Thomas Michael, William Walker, Sydney Lee Goodrich Green. Engr., project engr., project mgr. to sr. v.p., dir. Rust Engring. Co., Birmingham, Ala. and Pitts., 1946-67; exec. v.p., dir. Inland Container Corp., Indpls., 1968-69, chmn., pres., chief exec. officer, 1970-79; chmn. Ga. Kraft Co., Rome, Ga., 1974-79; pres., chief operating officer SONAT, Inc., Birmingham, Ala., 1980, chmn., pres., chief exec. officer, 1980-84, chmn., 1984-85; dir. Time, Inc., Protective Life Ins. Co., Ball Corp., Muncie, Ind., Sonat Offshore Co., Sonat Exploration Co., Houston, BE&K, Inc., Birmingham, Ala., Temple-Inland, Diboll, Tex., Sonat Marine, Phila. Bd. dirs. St. Vincents Hosp. Found., Birmingham, 1980—; mem. devel. council U. Tenn.; mem. adv. council U. Ala., Birmingham. Served to lt., C.E., USNR, 1943-46. Fellow ASCE; mem. Am. Paper Inst. (dir.), TAPPI, Newcomen Soc., Kappa Alpha, Tau Beta Pi, Omicron Delta Kappa, Beta Gamma Sigma. Presbyterian. Clubs: Rotary; Blind Brook (N.Y.); Mountain Brook, Shoal Creek (Birmingham); Lyford Cay (Bahamas). Home: 2608 Caldwell Mill Ln Birmingham AL 35243 Office: 2160 Highland Ave Birmingham AL 35205

GOODRUM, DANIEL SHEPARD, banker; b. Leslie, Ga., July 11, 1926; s. John Warren and Inez (Culp) G.; m. Margaret Emily Swanson, June 8, 1949; children—John Daniel, William James. B.S.B.A., U. Fla., 1949. Trainee to store supt. B.F. Goodrich Co., Jacksonville, Fla., 1949-57; v.p. Fla. Nat. Bank, Jacksonville, 1957-62; sr. v.p. 1st Nat. Bank, Ft. Lauderdale, Fla., 1962-66; v.p. 1st Marine Banks Inc., Riviera Beach, Fla., 1966-73; pres., chief exec. officer Century Banks Inc., Ft. Lauderdale, 1973-82; sr. exec., v.p. Sun Banks of Fla., Ft. Lauderdale, 1982—; dir. Fed. Res. Bank, Miami br. Bd. dirs. Broward Community Coll. Found. Trustees, Ft. Lauderdale, 1975—. Served to sgt. USAF, 1950-51. Mem. Fla. Bankers Assn. (pres. 1972-73), Am. Bankers Assn. (exec. council 1977-79). Republican. Episcopalian. Clubs: Sail Fish (Palm Beach, Fla.); Coral Ridge Country (Ft. Lauderdale). Home: 900 Virginia Dr Winter Park FL 32789 Office: Sun Banks Inc Sun Bank NA Bldg Orlando FL 32802*

GOODSELL, DAVID RAY, school administrator; b. Los Angeles, Aug. 4, 1939; s. Harlan J. and Alta Mae (Robbins) G.; m. Jann Wherry, Dec. 18, 1964; children—Crickett, Matthew. B.S., Harvey Mudd Coll., 1962; M.A. in Teaching, Harvard U., 1963; Ed.D., U. Ga., 1972. Asst. dean admissions Claremont Colls., Calif., 1964-68; coll. counselor, tchr. Ft. Worth Country Day Sch., 1968-70; assoc. prof. Valdosta State Coll., Ga., 1972-77; assoc. headmaster Lakehill Prep. Sch., Dallas, 1977-78; headmaster Heritage Hall Sch., Oklahoma City, 1978—. Editor jour. MUM, 1976—. Mem. exec. com. Okla. Mus. Art., Oklahoma City, 1978-84; counselor Ch. of Jesus Christ of Latter Day Saints, Edmond, Okla., 1983—. Kerr Found. fellow, 1981. Mem. Nat. Assn. Ind. Schs., Ind. Schs. Assocs. of S.W. (exec. com. 1984—, standards com. 1982-84, research com. 1980-82), Phi Kappa Phi. Club: Soc. Am. Magicians (editor 1976—, nat. 1st v.p. 1984—). Avocations: writing; magic (conjuring). Home: 11605 Victoria Dr Oklahoma City OK 73120 Office: Heritage Hall 1401 NW 115th St Oklahoma City OK 73114

GOODSON, CAROLE EDITH MCKISSOCK, technology educator; b. Des Moines, Dec. 31, 1946; d. William Thompson and Edith (Johnson) McKissock; m. Robert Peterson, July, 1978; 1 child, David Shelby. B.S., U. Houston, 1968, M.Ed., 1971, Ed.D., 1975. Tchr. Spring Branch Ind. Sch. Dist., Houston, 1968-69; assoc. prof., coll. counselor, coordinator tech. math. U. Houston, 1972-82, assoc. prof., assoc. dean Coll. Tech., 1982—. Co-author: Technical Mathematics with Applications, 1983; Technical Mathematics with Calculus, 1985; Technical Algebra with Applications, 1985; Technical Trigonometry with Applications, 1985. Contbr. articles to profl. publs. Mem. Am. Soc. Engring. Edn. (bd. dirs. ERM div. 1981-82, sec.-treas. 1982-84, pres. Gulf-Southwest sect. 1983, Dow Outstanding Young Faculty award 1982), Math. Assn. Am., Nat. Council Tchrs. Math. Presbyterian. Office: U Houston Coll Tech 361 T2 Houston TX 77004

GOODWIN, ALAN SCOTT, designer; b. El Paso, Tex., Dec. 31, 1952; s. Maurice D. and Mabel J. (Beil) G.; m. Lynda Lee Jones, Oct. 17, 1975. Student U. Colo., 1970, Colo. Mountain Coll., Glenwood Springs, Colo., 1971-72, Anderson Ranch Fine Arts, Snowmass, Colo., 1972. Asst. art dir. Sanders Advt., El Paso, Tex., 1972; free-lance artist/designer, 1973-75; founder Paragon Designs (company name changed to The Goodwin Co. 1981), El Paso, 1976, now pres., chief exec. officer. Public relations chmn. United Way of El Paso, 1983; adviser El Paso Lighthouse for the Blind; bd. dirs. El Paso Youth Found. and Info. and Referral. Recipient awards El Paso C. of C., El Paso Advt. Fedn., dist. 12 Am. Advt. Fedn. Mem. Nat. Fedn. Ind. Businessmen (action council), El Paso C. of C. (vice-chmn. publ. com.), El Paso Advt. Fedn. (past dir.), Graphic Arts Soc. (founding mem. bd., pres.), Am. Inst. Graphic Artists (bd. dirs. Tex. chpt.). Office: 7598 N Mesa St Suite 200 El Paso TX 79912

GOODWIN, BENNIE EUGENE, II, educator, clergyman; b. Chgo., Aug. 27, 1933; s. Bennie Earl and Dessie B. (Christopher) G.; m. Mary Ellen Sawyer, Aug. 17, 1957; children—Bennie Eugene, Mary Ellen, Constance Marie. B.A., Barrington Coll., 1956; M.A., Pitts. Theol. Sem., 1973; Ph.D., U. Pitts., 1974; M.R.E., Gordon-Conwell Theol. Sem., 1965; postgrad. Eastern Nazarene Coll., 1957-58, Mass. Tchrs. Coll., 1959, Temple U., 1969, Atlanta U., 1976, Ga. State U., 1981. Ordained to ministry Ch. of God in Christ, 1955. Founder, dir. Inst. Christian Edn., Boston, 1956-66; chmn. music dept. Christian High Sch., Cambridge, Mass., 1957-64; pastor Faith Mission Ch. of God in Christ, Portsmouth, N.H., 1964-66; pres. State Youth Dept., Chs. of God in Christ, N.H. Diocese, 1965-66; dir. Bishop O.T. Jones Sch. Christian Edn., Phila., 1966-69; advisor to youth Holy Temple Ch. of God in Christ, Phila., 1968-69; chmn. Internat. Teen Conf., 1968-73; admissions counselor Pitts. Theol. Sem., 1970-74; registrar, dir. admissions Interdenominational Theol. Ctr., Atlanta, 1975-77; v.p. Nat. Black Evang. Assn., Atlanta, 1976-78; dean Soul Winners' Inst., Atlanta, 1981—; minister West End Presbyn. Ch., Atlanta, 1982-84; minister of edn. Cathedral of Faith Ch. of God in Christ, Atlanta, 1985—; dir. Friends for Missions, Inc., 1968—; chmn. Internat. Teen Conf., Southeastern Area, 1974—; state dir. Christian Edn., Ch. of God in Christ, No. Ga. Jurisdiction, 1978—; adj. prof. Morris Brown Coll., Atlanta, Beulah Heights Bible Coll., Atlanta; assoc. prof. Christian Edn., Interdominational Theol. Ctr., Atlanta, 1974—; vis. prof. Simpson Coll., San Francisco, summer 1982, 79;

guest lectr. Bapt. Bible Inst., Pitts., 1971-74, others. Named Christian Educator of Yr., Midwest Christian Edn. Conf., 1981. Mem. NAACP, Nat. Urban League, So. Christian Leadership Conf., Religious Research Assn. Contbr. articles to profl. jours.; author: Play the Piano — By Ear —, 1982; The Effective Leader, 1981; Fourteen Great Thinkers, 1980; Reflections on Education, 1978; Dr. Martin Luther King, Jr.: God's Messenger of Love, Justice and Hope, 1976; Pray and Grow Rich, 1974; The Emergence of Black Colleges, 1974; Beside Still Waters, 1973; Speak Up Black Man, 1972; editor: Steps to Successful Writing, 1979; An Introduction to Six Major Religions, 1978; Steps to Dynamic Teaching, 1978; The New Testament Story, 1977. Office: 1137 Avon Ave Atlanta GA 30310

GOODWIN, EARL, state senator, businessman; b. Adger, Ala.; m. Geraldine Hubbard; children—Patricia Dale Goodwin Sexton, Sharon Kay Goodwin Alsobrook, Eva Elizabeth Goodwin Davis, Beverly Ann Goodwin Sousoulas. Student Howard Coll. (now Samford U.), U. Ala. With fed. govt., 1940-42; former pres. Bush Hog, Inc.; dir. J & G Realty Co.; mem. Ala. Senate, 1976—. Del. Democratic Conv., 1964, 68, 76, 80, chmn. del., 1972; mem. Dem. Exec. Com., State Dem. Exec. Com.; past indsl. chmn. local ARC, United Appeal; active Ind. Protestant Ch., mem. bd. stewards; past pres. Morgan Bible class; state chmn. fund drive, Am. Cancer Soc., 1964; chmn. Gov.'s Com. on Hiring the Handicapped, 1964-65. Served as pilot AC, U.S. Army, 1942-45. Recipient Samford U. Athletic Alumni award, 1971; Congress of Freedom award, 1968-69. Mem. Assoc. Industries Ala. (past pres.), Samford U. Alumni Assn. (past pres.), Selma and Dallas County C. of C. (past pres.), Farm Equipment Mfrs. Assn. (past mem. bd. dirs.). Clubs: Selma Country, Civitan (past internat. dir. of membership, Honor Key). Lodges: Masons, Shriners, Elks. Office: Office of State Senate Montgomery AL 36130*

GOODWIN, GEORGE EVANS, public relations executive; b. Atlanta, June 20, 1917; s. George E. and Carrie (Clark) G.; m. Lois Milstead, Nov. 2, 1940; children—Clark, Allen. A.B. with cert. in journalism, Washington and Lee U., 1939. Reporter, feature writer Atlanta Georgian, 1939, News and Courier, Charleston, N.C., 1940, Times-Herald, Washington, 1940-41, Miami Daily News, 1941-42, Atlanta Jour., 1945-52; exec. dir. Central Atlanta Improvement Assn., 1952-54; v.p. advt., pub. relations 1st Nat. Bank Atlanta, 1954-64; exec. v.p. Bell & Stanton, Inc. (nat. pub. relations counseling firm), Atlanta, 1965-76, pres., chmn. Manning, Selvage & Lee, Atlanta, 1976-85, sr. cons., 1985—. Bd. dirs. Ga. chpt. NCCJ; trustee Literacy Action, Inc.; trustee emeritus Oglethorpe U.; former pres. Atlanta Traffic, Safety Council; pres., chmn. Theatre Atlanta; trustee Atlanta Arts Festival, Community Council Atlanta, founder, elder Trinity Presbyn. Ch. others. Served to lt. USNR, 1942-45. Decorated Purple Heart, Philippines Liberation Ribbon with 1 star, Asiatic-Pacific Theater Ribon with 3 stars, Navy Unit Commendation, Recipient AP Ga. award for reporting, 1948, Pulitzer Prize for local reporting, 1949 (both for Telefair County (Ga.) vote frauds story; Pall Mall Big Story Award, 1949. Mem. Pub. Relations Soc. Am., Delta Tau Delta, Sigma Delta Chi (nat. reporting award 1948). Lodge: Rotary. Home: 3302 Ivanhoe Dr NW Atlanta GA 30327

GOODWIN, LEFTRIDGE LAYNE, mfg. co. exec.; b. Charleston, W.Va., Oct. 24, 1933; s. Clifford and Mabel (Brown) B.S. in Mech. Engring., Va. Poly. Inst., 1964; cert. Lynchburg Coll., 1970; m. Mary Lou Johnson, Sept. 15, 1955; children—Leftridge, Deborah Anne, Jonathan Brian, Stephanie Lynn. Sales mgr. Aerofin Corp., Syracuse N.Y. and Lynchburg, Va., 1964-73; pres. Goodwin Refrigeration Co., Huntington, W.Va., 1973—; v.p. Energy Flow Inc., Lynchburg, 1976-83; pres. Goodwin & Assocs., 1983—. Pres., Lynchburg Area Assn. for Retarded Citizens, 1973-74, sr. v.p., 1979-80; pres. Cabel Assn. for Retarded Citizens, 1976-77; treas. Assn. Retarded Citizens Central Va., 1981-82; chmn. bd. Central Va. Mental Health Services, 1972-74, 80-82; vice chmn. CVCSB, 1985. Served with USMC, 1955-58. Mem. ASME, Central Va. Industries Inc., Am. Legion, Sigma Alpha Epsilon. Club: Sertoma (pres. Lynchburg Area chpt. 1972-73). Home: 5813 Rhonda Rd Lynchburg VA 24502 Office: PO Box 10394 Lynchburg VA 24506

GOODWIN, MARK ALLEN, music educator, composer; b. Flagstaff, Ariz., Feb. 22, 1948; s. John Joseph and Norma (Morrison) G.; m. Barbara Sue Redburn, Jan. 24, 1970; children—Scott, Timothy. B.S. cum laude in Edn., U. Mo., 1970, M.Ed., 1972; postgrad. U. South Fla., 1982—. Certified tchr.; licensed specialized ministries, Assemblies of God. Instr. Evangel Coll., Springfield, Mo., 1972-73, Central Mo. State U., Warrensburg, 1973-75; assoc. prof., dir. music interns Southeastern Coll., Lakeland, Fla., 1975—; guest clinician Southwest Mo. Mass Band, 1972; minister music Skyview Assembly of God, Lakeland, Fla., 1976-81; asst. minister music Southside Assembly of God, Lakeland, 1982—; piano tuner, 1975—; speaker in field.. Composer choral anthems, brass ensembles, band music. Univ. scholar U. Mo., Columbia, 1967-70. Mem. Music Educators Nat. Conf., Phi Mu Alpha Sinfonia, Phi Eta Sigma, Sigma Rho Sigma. Republican. Avocations: music; tennis; basketball; golf; running. Home: 5879 Crest Ln Lakeland FL 33803 Office: Southeastern Coll Assemblies of God 1000 Longfellow Blvd Lakeland FL 33801

GOORLEY, JOHN THEODORE, consulting chemist; b. Galion, Ohio, Mar. 12, 1907; s. William H. and Emma (Ness) G.; B.S., Ohio State U., 1930; M.S., Purdue U., 1932, Ph.D., 1934; m. Ethel L. Coleman, Nov. 27, 1935; children—John, Alice (Mrs. Harold A. Breard, Jr.), Robert, Richard. Chief control chemist Burroughs Wellcome & Co., Tuckahoe, N.Y., 1933-38; research dir. Labs. Lex, Havana, Cuba, 1939-42, Ben Venue Labs., Bedford, Ohio, 1946-48, Johnson & Johnson de Argentina, Buenos Aires, 1948-50; owner, dir. Labs. Goorley, Buenos Aires, 1950-55; prof. pharm. chemistry Ohio No. U., Ada, 1956-57; v.p., gen. mgr. Inland Alkaloid Co., Tipton, Ind., 1957-58; prof. pharm. chemistry N.E. La. U., Monroe, 1958-68, prof. pharmacognosy, 1968-72; chemist Laboratorios Finlay, S.A., San Pedro Sula, Honduras, 1974-76; prof. chemistry and pharmacy U. Nacional Autonoma de Honduras, Tegucigalpa, 1976; Fulbright prof. U. Honduras, 1966-67, cons. chemist, 1967—; exec. v.p. Enviro-Med Labs., Ruston, La., 1978-82; vis. prof. U. El Salvador, 1968; cons. pharm. industries. Active Little Theater, Monroe. Served to capt. AUS, 1942-46. Col. staff govs. Ky., La. Mem. Am. Pharm. Assn., Am. Chem. Soc., AAAS, Sigma Xi, Rho Chi, Phi Delta Chi, Tau Kappa Epsilon. Research in pharm. chemistry and biochemistry. Contbr. articles to profl. jours. Patentee in field. Home: 4709 Fairview Austin TX 78731

GOPLEN, DONNELLE, counselor; b. Loco, Okla., Nov. 5, 1936; d. Allen R. and Dorothy R. (Carmichael) Bean; B.A. with honors, U. N.Mex., 1974, M.A., 1977; postgrad. Family Therapy Inst., 1981-82; m. Bruce C. Goplen, Sept. 26, 1969; children—Stephen Harvey, Donald Harvey. State welfare worker State Welfare Agy., N.Mex., 1975-77; counseling intern Presbyn. Hosp., Albuquerque, 1977; social worker State of N.Mex., 1977-78; vol. mental health aide Prince William County (Va.) Community Mental Health Center, 1978-79, coordinator Social Activity Center, after 1979, now family therapist, also mental health counselor, cons. Mem. Am. Personnel and Guidance Assn., AAUW. Home: 18414 Cedar Dr Triangle VA 22172 Office: Prince William Mental Health Center 8807 Sudley Dr Manassas VA 22110

GORAKHPURWALLA, HOMI DHUNJISHAW, electrical engineer, educator; b. Hyderabad, India, Aug. 5, 1937; came to U.S., 1957, naturalized, 1971; s. Dhunjishaw H. and Katy D. (Dinshaw) G.; B.S. with honors, Bombay U. (India), 1957; B.S. in Elec. Engring., Purdue U., 1957, M.S., 1961; m. Anita M. Fuegener, Dec. 2, 1963; children—Catherine Anita, Ashley Homi. Instr. elec. engring. Purdue U., 1959-61, U. Toronto (Ont., Can.), 1961-66; asst. prof. elec. engring. S.D. State U., 1966-69; v.p., engr. DorRan Electronics, Sioux Falls, S.D., 1969-70; prof. elec. engring. Tex. A&I U., Kingsville, 1970—, chmn. dept. elec. engring., 1977-79, 81-82, acting dean Coll. Engring., 1983-84; dir. Task Force on Sci. Edn., 1975-76; sr. research engr. Southwest Research Inst., 1982-83; cons. to TRW, Inc., 1970-71, Entonic, Inc., 1977-79; proposal reviewer NSF edn. programs, 1977-81. U.S. Dept. Agr. grantee, 1971-76; NSF grantee, 1974-77; NASA/ASEE research fellow, 1979; recipient IR-100 Research award, 1984, registered profl. engr., Tex. Mem. IEEE (sr.; chmn. Corpus Christi sect. 1979, Centennial medal 1984), Am. Soc. Engring. Edn., Internat. Microwave Power Inst., India Students Assn., Sigma Xi, Tau Beta Pi, Eta Kappa Nu. Zorastrian. Club: Kiwanis. Contbr. articles on engring. edn. and microwave applications to elec. engring.; patentee in field. Home: 1918 John St Kingsville TX 78363 Office: Coll Engring Texas A&I U Kingsville TX 78363

GORBET, DANIEL WAYNE, agronomist, geneticist, researcher; b. Corpus Christi, Tex., Oct. 16, 1942; s. Daniel Ewell and Edna Lee (Brandt) G.; m. Mary Francis Smith Gurka, Sept. 4, 1962; children—Daniel Karl, Mitchel Wayne. B.S., Tex. A&I U., 1965; M.S., Okla. State U., 1968, Ph.D., 1971. Grad. research asst. Okla. State U., Stillwater, 1965-70; from asst. prof. to prof. agronomy U. Fla. Agr. Research Ctr., Marianna, 1970—. Contbr. articles to profl. jours. Mem. Am. Soc. Agronomy, Crop Sci. Soc. Am., Am. Peanut Research Edn. Soc., Fla. Soil Crop Sci. Soc. Am. Genetic Assn. Democrat. Lutheran. Lodges: Elks, Lions. Avocations: raising cattle; fishing. Home: PO Box 58 Marianna FL 32446 Office: Agr Research Ctr Route 3 Box 493 Marianna FL 32446

GORDEN, GERALD NICCOLA, accountant; b. New Orleans, Nov. 13, 1950; s. Niccola and Helen Elaine (Dabney) G.; m. Sylvia Fontenot, May 19, 1973 (div. 1980); children—Kendall, Keann. B.A., Dillard U., 1974; M.B.A., Tulane U., 1976. C.P.A., La. Asst. accountant Peat, Marwick, Mitchell Co., Chgo., 1974-76; accountant II, Mobil Oil Co., New Orleans, 1976-79; dir. human resource City of New Orleans, 1979-80; accounting mgr. William Bros. Engring., 1980-81; controller Mega Mgmt. Co., 1980-83; mng. ptnr. Buggs & Gorden, Houston, 1983—. Active Big Bros. Greater Houston, Council for Better Pub. Edn., New Orleans. Mem. Nat. Assn. Black Accountants, Internat. Trade Mart, Am. Inst. C.P.A.s. Democrat. Methodist. Home: 3605 NC King Blvd #C New Orleans LA 70125 Office: 801 Congress St Suite 275 Houston TX 77002

GORDON, ARON SAMUEL, jewelry company executive; b. Houston, 1911; married. Student U. Tex., 1928-30. With Gordon Jewelry Corp., Houston, 1930—, pres., chief exec. officer, now co-chmn., also dir. Office: Gordon Jewelry Corp 820 Fannin Houston TX 77002*

GORDON, BARON JACK, stockbroker; s. George M. and Rose (Salsbury) G.; midshipman U.S. Naval Acad., 1946; B.S., Lynchburg Coll., 1953; m. Ellin Bachrach, Aug. 20, 1954; children—Jonathan Ross, Rose Patricia, Alison. Vice pres. Consol. Ins. Agy., Norfolk, 1948-55; asst. treas. Henry Montor Assos., Inc., N.Y.C., 1956; v.p., sec. Propp & Co., Inc., N.Y.C., 1957-58; partner Koerner, Gordon & Co., N.Y.C., 1959-62; sr. partner Gordon, Kulman Perry (and predecessor firm), N.Y.C., 1962-71, pres., chmn. bd., 1971-74; pres., chmn. bd. Palison, Inc., mems. N.Y. Stock Exchange, N.Y.C., 1974—; chmn. bd. Rojon, Inc., real estate and investments, Williamsburg, Va., 1978—. Mem. Harrison (N.Y.) Archtl. Rev. Bd., 1970-72, Harrison Planning Bd., 1975-77. Served to lt. USNR, in U.S.S. Midway, 1953-55. Mem. U.S. Naval Acad. Alumni Assn. (life). Clubs: N.Y. Stock Exchange Luncheon; Poinciana (Palm Beach, Fla.); Town Point (Norfolk, Va.). Home: 113 Elizabeth Meriwether Williamsburg VA 23185 Office: 7 Corporate Park Dr White Plains NY 10604

GORDON, BARTON JENNINGS, U.S. congressman from Tenn.; b. Murfreesboro, Tenn., Jan. 24, 1949. B.S., Middle Tenn. State U., 1971; J.D., U. Tenn., 1973. Individual practice law, 1974-83; exec. dir. Tenn. Democratic party, 1979-83; mem. 99th U.S. Congress from 6th Dist. Tenn., 1985—. Office: US House of Reps Office of House Members Washington DC 20515*

GORDON, DANIEL PAUL, jewelry company executive; b. Houston, 1942; married. B.S., Wharton Sch. Bus., U. Pa., 1963. With Gordon Jewelry Corp., Houston, 1963—, v.p., 1969-77, sr. v.p. ops., from 1977, now pres., chief exec. officer, also dir. Office: Gordon Jewelry Corp 820 Fannin Houston TX 77002*

GORDON, DONALD JOSEPH, physician, retired army officer; b. Washington, May 4, 1942; s. Frank and Frances (Fox) G.; m. Judith Lee Coker, June 9, 1963; children—Martin Douglas, Mathew Charles. B.S. in Chemistry, Howard U., 1964; Ph.D. in Phys. Chemistry, 1971; M.D., U. Md., 1977. Commd. 2d lt. U.S. Army, 1964, advanced through grades to lt. col., 1979; assoc. prof. chemistry U.S. Mil. Acad., 1971-73; intern in surgery Brooke Army Med. Ctr., San Antonio, 1977-78, resident in emergency medicine, 1978-80, chief acute minor illness clinic, 1980-81, chief emergency medicine service, 1981-83, asst. dir. med. edn., 1983-84, ret., 1984; physician-in-charge Meth. Plaza Health Ctr., Southwest Med. Group, San Antonio, 1984—; instr. family medicine U. Okla., 1983-84; mem. Bexar County Emergency Med. Systems Coordinating Council, San Antonio, 1980—. Contbr. articles to profl. jours. Mem. AMA (Physicians Recognition award 1984—), Am. Coll. Emergency Physicians, Tex. Coll. Emergency Physicians, Tex. Med. Soc., Bexar County Med. Soc., Sigma Xi, Phi Beta Kappa. Democrat. Jewish. Avocations: fishing; computer science; music. Office: Southwest Med Group 4499 Medical Dr San Antonio TX 78229

GORDON, HARRY B., jewelry company executive. Student U. Tex., Columbia U. With Gordon Jewelry Corp., Houston, 1930—, chmn. bd., 1977—. Address: Gordon Jewelry Corp 821 Fannin St Houston TX 77002*

GORDON, HARRY EDWARD, safety engineer; b. Moca, Dominican Republic, Nov. 2, 1924; came to U.S., 1934; naturalized, 1943; s. Charles and Grace (Pichardo) G.; m. Patricia A. Moyers, Nov. 19, 1977; children—Bruce, Nancy. B.S. in Indsl. Engring., NYU, 1951. Cert. safety profl. Supervising safety engr. Zurich Ins. Co., N.Y.C., 1948-65, Gt. Am. Ins. Co., San Juan, P.R., 1965; supt. safety engr. Aerospace div. Pan Am, Cape Kennedy, Fla., 1965-66; cons. Risk Control, Inc., N.Y.C., 1966-72; v.p. Group VII Services, Miami, 1972-84; mgr. loss control Johnson and Higgins, Miami, 1984—. Mem. Orange Bowl, Staging Com., Miami, 1974—. Served to sgt. U.S. Army, 1943-45, ETO. Mem. Am. Soc. Safety Engrs. (cert., profl., cons., sec. risk mgmt. ins. div.). Lodges: Park, Masons. Avocations: boating; golfing. Office: Johnson and Higgins 9800 S Dadeland Blvd Miami FL 33156

GORDON, JACK DAVID, institute administrator, state senator; b. Detroit, June 3, 1922; s. A. Louis and Henrietta (Rodgers) G.; B.A., U. Mich., 1942; children—Andrew Louis, Deborah Mary, Jonathan Henry. Engaged in real estate and ins. businesses, Miami Beach, Fla., 1946-52; founding dir., pres., chief mng. officer Washington Savs. & Loan Assn., Miami Beach, 1952-80, vice chmn. bd., 1980-81; founding dir. Jefferson Nat. Bank of Miami Beach, 1962-77, past chmn. exec. com.; mem. Fla. Senate, 1972—; housing fin. cons. Dept. State and expert cons. UN Tech. Assistance Program in Costa Rica, Nicaragua, Panama, Ethiopia, Somali Republic, 1959-63; cons. to ROCAP, 1962-64, Eastern Nigerian Housing Corp., 1963; contract supr. AID Housing Guaranty Program in Latin Am., 1966-69; dir. Inst. Pub. Policy and Citizenship Studies, Fla. Internat. U. Chmn., Miami Beach Housing Authority, 1947-56; mem. Dade County Bd. Public Instrn., 1961-68. Served with AUS, 1943-46. Mem. Am. Jewish Congress, Am. Friends of Hebrew U., ACLU. Democrat. Author: (with others) A Survey of New Home Financing Institutions in Latin America, 1969. Home: 48 Palm Island Miami Beach FL 33139 Office: 420 Lincoln Rd Suite 256 Miami Beach FL 33139

GORDON, JAMES FLEMING, retired judge; b. Madisonville, Ky., May 18, 1918; s. John F. and Ruby (James) G.; LL.B., U. Ky., 1941; m. Jola Young, Sept. 1, 1942; children—Maurice K. II, James Fleming, Marianna. Bar: Ky. 1941; practice in Madisonville, 1941-65; judge U.S. Dist. Ct., Western Dist. Ky., Owensboro 1965-74, chief judge, 1968-75, sr. judge, 1975-84. Chmn. Ky. Pub. Service Commn., 1955-59. Speakers chmn. Ky. Democratic Party, 1955, campaign chmn., 1962. Bd. dirs. Clinic Found., Madisonville. Served to 1st lt., Judge Adv. Gen. Dept., AUS, 1941-46; PTO. Mem. Am. Coll. Trial Lawyers, Am. Legion, V.F.W., Phi Delta Phi. Home: 422 Sprite Rd #5 Louisville KY 40207

GORDON, M. MICHAEL, judge; b. San Francisco, Dec. 21, 1911; s. Rudolph and Sarah (Mesinger) G.; B.A., St. Ignatius Coll., 1931; LL.B., U. San Francisco, 1935. Admitted to Tex. bar, 1935, since practiced in Houston; now mem. firm M. Michael Gordon; judge Houston Municipal Ct., 1962—. Founder, Teenage Jury System, 1964, judge, 1964—. Pres. Juvenile Delinquency and Crime Commn., Houston, 1958-59; mem. Houston Bd. Pub. Welfare, 1948-56; bd. dirs. Am. Acad. Jud. Edn., 1970—, Nat. Center for State Cts., 1971—. Served to capt. USAAF, 1942-46. Recipient Disneyland trophy for achievement in reducing juvenile delinquency in U.S. and Can., Nat. Assn. Municipal Judges, 1965. Mem. Am. Judges Assn. (gov. 1965—, treas. 1965-66, pres. 1969-70, award merit 1976), Am., Houston bar assns., State Bar Tex., Am. Judicature Soc. (dir. 1969-70, Centennial jud. award 1972), Am. Acad. Jud. Edn. (pres. 1972-74). Mason (Shriner). Home: 2014 Southgate Houston TX 77025 Office: 5015 Fannin St Houston TX 77004

GORDON, MICHAEL HERBERT, rheumatologist; b. N.Y.C., Oct. 4, 1941; s. Robert J. and Charlotte J. (Goldstein) G.; m. Beth W. Aisley, June 19, 1966; children—Jill, Stephanie, Craig. B.A., Boston U., 1963; M.D., Chgo. Med. Sch., 1967. Diplomate Am. Bd. Internal Medicine, Am. Bd. Rheumatology. Intern, Cedars-Sinai Hosp., 1967-68; resident Jackson Meml., Miami, 1968-69, 71-72; fellow Albert Einstein No., Phila., 1972-74; practice medicine specializing in rheumatology, Ft. Lauderdale, Fla., 1974—. Served to capt. USAF, 1969-71. Mem. Am. Rheumatism Assn., ACP, AMA, Fla. Med. Assn., Fla. Rheumatology Soc., Broward County Med. Soc. Jewish. Office: 2001 NE 48th Ct Fort Lauderdale FL 33308

GORDON, MICHAEL WALLACE, legal educator; b. Middletown, Conn., May 4, 1935; s. Seery Clarence and Anne Catharine (Gregory) G.; m. Elsbeth Leimomi Kunzig, Mar. 15, 1958; children—Huntly Milne, Elsbeth Wallace. B.S. U. Conn., 1957, J.D., 1963; M.A., Trinity Coll., 1967; Dipl. de Droit Compare, U. Strasbourg, France, 1973; Maestro en Derecho, U. Mex., 1982; student, L'Academie de Droit de la Haye, 1973, 82. Bar: Conn. 1963. Assoc., Shipman & Goodwin, Hartford, Conn., 1963-66, asst. dean U. Conn. Sch. of Law, Hartford, 1966-68; prof. law U. Fla., Gainesville, 1968—; vis. prof. Nat. U. Costa Rica, 1970, Duke U., 1984; Lyle T. Alverson vis. prof. George Washington U., 1986—; Fulbright prof. U. Mex., U. Guatemala, U. Frankfurt; vis. lectr. U. Bombay, U. Brasilia, U. Nairobi, Zagreb U., U. Nicaragua, U. Regensburg; external examiner U. Khartoum; of counsel Ogarrio y Diaz, Mexico City, 1976—; cons. govt. agys. in Nigeria, Brazil, Paraguay, Panama, Oman, Sudan. Contbg. editor Lawyer of the Americas; mem. adv. bd. Syracuse Jour. Internat. Law and Commerce; mem. editorial bd. Fla. Jour. Internat. Trade Law; mem. adv. bd. UCLA Pacific Basin Jour.; lectr. Council Fgn. Relations, Brit. Inst. Internat. and Comparative Law. Served to lt. j.g. USNR, 1957-60. Presdl. scholar, U. Fla., 1977. Mem. Am. Soc. Internat. Law, Am. Fgn. Law Assn., Brit. Inst. Internat. and Comparative Law, Am. Assn. for Comparative Study of Law (dir.). Republican. Episcopalian. Author: Florida Corporation Law Manual, 5 vols., 1975; The Cuban Nationalizations—The Demise of Foreign Private Property, 1976; Multinational Corporations Law-Mexico, Central America, Panama and the CACM (2 vols.) 1978; The Civil Code of Mexico, 1978; (with Glendon & Osakwe) Comparative Legal Traditions, 1982; Commercial, Business and Trade Laws of Mexico, 1983; (with Folsom & Spanogle) International Business Transactions, 1985. Office: College of Law U of Fla Gainesville FL 32611

GORDON, NELLIE REA, retired educator; b. Roanoke, Ala., May 18, 1914; d. John Shirley and Lula (Redmond) Sledge; m. Andrew Dudley Gordon, Mar. 21, 1937 (dec. 1959). Mus.B., Henderson State Coll., 1936, M.S. in Edn., 1957. Cert. tchr. secondary edn., Ark. Tchr. Kirby High Sch., Ark., 1936-37, Knight-Enloe Sch., Roanoke, Ala., 1943-45, Prescott High Sch., Ark., 1955-79; ret., 1979. Registrar Nevada County Hist. Mus., Prescott, 1980—; pres. Nevada County Friends of Library, Prescott, 1981-83, De Ann Cemetery Assn., 1983-85; mem. Nevada County Democratic Central Com., Prescott, 1979—. Recipient Tchr. of Yr. award Nevada County C. of C., 1979. Mem. Ark. Edn. Assn., NEA (life), Ark. Ret. Tchrs. Assn. (life), Nat. Ret. Tchrs. Assn. (life), Nevada County Ret. Tchrs. Assn., DAR (life), Am. Legion Aux., Delta Kappa Gamma (pres. Ark. 1985—). Methodist. Avocations: music; books; bridge. Home: 311 E Main Prescott AR 71857

GORDON, ROBERT JOSEPH, marine company executive, leasing company executive, consultant; b. Cambridge, Mass., Sept. 25, 1940; s. Jack Allen and Rita Jeanne (Murphy) G.; m. Jane Elizabeth Endres, June 3, 1967; children—Julie Elizabeth and Jeanne Haviland (twins). A.A., Cape Cod Community Coll., 1964; B.A., Western Ky. U., 1967. Sales rep. P. Lorillard Tobacco Co., Miami, Fla., 1967-71; owner, pres. R.J. Gordon Trucking Co., Ft. Lauderdale, Fla., 1971-75, Amtek Marine Corp., Palm Beach, Fla., 1975—; pres. Cert. Leasing Corp., Skokie, Ill., 1981—; cons. in marine design and fin. planning fields. Served to 2d lt. Green Berets, U.S. Army, 1959-63. Decorated Purple Heart (2), Bronze Star (2), Vietnamese Expeditionary Force medal, Laotian Medal of Valor, Combat Infantry badge. Mem. Pompano Beach (Fla.) C. of C. Republican. Roman Catholic. Clubs: Royal Palm Polo (Boca Raton, Fla.), Antique Auto Am. (Ft. Lauderdale). Office: Amtek Marine Corp 549 Walker Ave Palm Beach FL 33463

GORDON, WILLIAM KNOX, III, psychologist; b. Fort Worth, Aug. 16, 1943; s. William Knox and Anna Melissa (Hogsett) G.; m. Marcy Kay Molloy (div. 1971); 1 child, Joel Anthony. B.B.A., So. Methodist U., 1965, M.B.A., 1968; M.S., N. Tex. State U., 1974, Ph.D., 1982. Lic. psychologist, Tex. Psychology intern La. State U. Med. Ctr., New Orleans, 1977-78; v.p. Dudley Goodson, Inc., Dallas, 1981—; sr. v.p., dir. psychol. services Behavioral Sci. Research Press, Dallas, 1981—; staff psychologist Fairhill Sch., Dallas, 1983—; practice psychology, Dallas, 1982—; dir. Fairhill Sch., Dallas. Editorial bd. profl. jours. Served with U.S. Army, 1966-68; Vietnam. Grantee N. Tex. State U., 1975, 76, 77, La. State Med. Ctr., 1977. Mem. Am. Psychol. Assn., Dallas Psychol. Assn. Republican. Avocations: tennis; scuba; herpetology; motorsports.

GORDY, ALLEN CRAIG, tire company executive; b. Miles City, Mont., Jan. 10, 1947; s. Ross Franklin and Russem Wanda (Esslinger) G.; m. Jacqueline Pace, Aug. 29, 1969; children—Kyle Pace, Kami Nicole. B.S. in Bus. Adminstrn., U. So. Miss., 1971. Credit sales mgr. Goodyear Tire and Rubber Co., Jackson, Miss., 1971-72; gen. mgr. Service Center div. Pace Oil Co., Inc., Magee, Miss., 1972—; rep. dealer council Goodyear Tire and Rubber Co., 1983—. Alderman, City of Magee, 1977-81; pres. Magee PTA, 1978-79; chmn. adminstrv. bd. 1st United Methodist Ch., Magee, 1979-80; lt. Magee Vol. Fire Dept., 1973—; mem. Simpson County Extension Adv. Council, 1983—; bd. dirs. Andrew Jackson council Boy Scouts Am., 1983; bd. dirs. Miss. affiliate Nat. Soc. for Prevention of Blindness, 1983—. Mem. Miss. Ind. Tire Dealers Assn., Nat. Tire Dealers and Retreaders Assn., Magee Jaycees (pres. 1974-75, Past Pres. award 1975). Democrat. Club: Magee Touchdown (pres. 1982-83). Lodge: Lions (pres. 1981-82) (Magee). Home: 329 3d Ave NW PO Box 656 Magee MS 39111 Office: Service Center div Pace Oil Co Inc 106 N Jackson Dr Magee MS 39111

GORDY, WALTER, physicist, educator; b. Miss., Apr. 20, 1909; s. Walter Kalin and Gertrude (Jones) G.; m. Vida Brown Miller, June 19, 1935; children—Eileen, Walter Terrell. A.B., Miss. Coll., 1932, LL.D. (hon.), 1959; M.A., U. N.C., 1933, Ph.D., 1935; D. honoris causa, U. Lille (France), 1955; D.Sc. (hon.), Emory U., 1983. Assoc. prof. math. and physics Mary Hardin-Baylor Coll., 1935-41; NRC fellow Calif. Inst. Tech., 1941-42; mem. staff radiation lab. MIT, 1942-46; assoc. prof. physics Duke U., Durham, N.C., 1946-48, prof., 1948—, James B. Duke prof., 1958-79, James B. Duke prof. emeritus, 1979—; vis. prof. U. Tex., 1958. NRC fellow 1954-57, 68-74; recipient Oak Ridge Inst. Nuclear Studies Sci. Research award, 1949, Miss. Acad. Scis. 50th Anniversary award, 1980; Disting. Alumnus award U. N.C., 1976; award for sci. State of N.C., 1979. Fellow Am. Phys. Soc. (chmn. S.E. sect. 1953-54, mem. council 1967-71, 73-77; Jesse W. Beams award 1974, Earle K. Plyler prize 1980), AAAS (council 1955); mem. Radiation Research Soc. (council 1961-64), Nat. Acad. Scis., Sigma Xi. Author: (with W.V. Smith, R.F. Trambarulo) Microwave Spectroscopy, 1953; (with Robert L. Cook) Microwave Molecular Spectra, 1970, 3d edit., 1984; Theory and Applications of Electron Spin Resonance, 1980; assoc. editor Jour. Chem. Physics, 1953-58; Spectrochimia Acta, 1957-60; editorial bd. Radiation Research 1969-72. Home: 2521 Perkins Rd Durham NC 27706

GORE, ALBERT, JR., U.S. senator; b. Mar. 31, 1948; s. Albert and Pauline (Lafon) G.; B.A. cum laude, Harvard U., 1969; m. Mary Elizabeth Aitcheson, 1970; children—Karenna, Kristin, Sarah, Albert III. Postgrad. Vanderbilt Sch. Religion, 1971-72, Vanderbilt Sch. Law, 1974-76. Investigative reporter, editorial writer The Tennessean, Nashville, 1971-76; home builder, Carthage, Tenn., 1971-76; owner livestock farm, Carthage, 1973—; mem. 95th-98th congresses from 6th Tenn. Dist., 1977-85, mem. exec. com. Congressional Clearinghouse on the Future; U.S. senator from Tenn., 1985—. Served with U.S. Army, 1969-71; Vietnam. Mem. Smith County Jaycees, Am. Legion, VFW, Farm Bur. Democrat. Baptist. Office: Office of Senate Members US Senate Washington DC 20510*

GORE, HENRY ANTHONY, mathematics educator; b. Atlanta, Feb. 11, 1948; s. Billy Lanier Burney and Bernice Elizabeth Gore. B.A., Morehouse Coll., 1969; M.A., U. Mich., 1970, Ph.D., 1973. Teaching fellow dept. math. U. Mich., Ann Arbor, 1969-72, faculty counselor Coll. Lit., Sci. and Arts, 1970-72; prof. math. Morehouse Coll., Atlanta, 1972—, dept. chmn., 1977—; part time prof. math. Atlanta U., 1973—; Atlanta regional coordinator Blacks and Math., 1981—; math. instr. CETA, Math. and Sci. Enrichment programs for high sch. students, 1977—; judge sci. and engring. falr U. Ga., 1976—. Foreman Fulton County Grand Jury, 1978; dir. Cascade United Methodist Ch. Choir; pianist Ralph Freeman Ministry and Atlanta Chpt. Full Gospel Bus.

Men's Fellowship Internat. Recipient book prize Tchrs.' Coll. Columbia U., 1968, Prof. of Yr. award Morehouse Coll., 1977, Alpha Phi Alpha, 1978. Mem. Am. Math. Soc., Math. Assn. Am., Nat. Council Tchrs. of Math., Phi Beta Kappa, Pi Mu Epsilon, Beta Kappa Chi. Baptist. Office: Morehouse Coll Dept Math Atlanta GA 30314

GORGES, HEINZ AUGUST, research engr.; b. Stettin, Germany, July, 22, 1913; s. Gustav and Marga (Benda) G.; M.E., Tech. U. Dresden (Germany), 1938; Ph.D., Tech. U. Hannover, Germany, 1946; m. Sapienza Teresa Coco, Sept. 2, 1957. Came to U.S., 1959. Group leader LFA Aero Research Establishment, Braunschweig, Germany, 1940-45; with Royal Aircraft Establishment, Farnborough, Eng. 1946-49; prin. sci. officer Weapons Research Establishment, Adelaide, South Australia, 1949-59; sci. asst. George C. Marshall Space Flight Center, NASA, Huntsville, Ala., 1959-61; dir. advanced projects Cook Technol Center, Morton Grove, Ill., 1961-62; scientific adviser Ill. Inst. Tech. Research Inst., Chgo., 1962-66; prin. scientist, dir. research Tracor, Inc., Austin, Tex., 1966—, asst. v.p. Environmental and Phys. Scis. div., 1970-72, v.p. Tracor-Jitco, Rockville, Md., 1972-75; pres. Vineta Inc., sci. consultants, 1975—. Prof. Redstone extension U. Ala., 1960. Registered profl. engr., D.C. Fellow AIIA (asso.); mem. ASME, N.Y. Acad. Scis., Acoustical Soc. Am. Club: Cosmos. Research on thermodynamics, energy systems, resource mgmt., conceptual design and econ. analysis. Home: 3705 Sleepy Hollow Rd Falls Church VA 22041

GORING, ARTHUR WILLIAM, mining engineer; b. Hamilton, Ont., Can., Mar. 6, 1915; came to U.S., 1918, derivative citizenship; s. George Henry and Hilda (Seller) G.; m. Lucile Margaret Sullivan, Aug. 30, 1939 (div. 1960); 1 dau., Margaret Ann; m. 2d, Natalie Thomas Stewart; children—Dale, Thomas (stepsons), Arthur W. B.S., U. Wash., 1941, M.S., 1947. Mining engr., devel. engr. Kennecott Copper Corp., Ruth, Nev., 1947-53; geologist, chief engr. Union Carbide Nuclear Co., Uravan, Colo., 1953-55; supt. New Idria Mining and Chem. Co., Gateway, Colo., 1956-57, div. mgr., Grand Junction, Colo., 1957-58, sec.-treas., Idria, Calif., 1958-60, sec., v.p., Graham, Tex., 1960-63; engr. James A. Lewis Engring. Co., Dallas, 1963-66, Res. Oil and Gas Co., Dallas, 1966-70; sr. mining engr. Canadian Res. Oil and Gas Ltd., Calgary, Alta., 1970-76, Res. Oil and Gas Co., Denver, 1977-80, Getty Oil Co., Denver, 1980; cons., 1980—. Chmn. Community League, Ruth, 1947-52; Republican precinct committeeman, Ruth, 1948-52. Served to maj. USAF, 1941-46. Decorated D.F.C., Air medal; registered profl. engr., Colo., Nev., Alta. Mem. AIME, Air Force Assn., Alta. United Services Inst., Am. Bowling Congress, Canadian Legion, Canadian Inst. Mining and Metallurgy, U. Wash. Alumni Assn. (life). Republican. Methodist. Lodges: Masons (32 deg.), Shriners. Inventor atometer for calculating price uranium and vanadium. Co-author U.S. Bur. Mines publ. Home and office: 3020 Westforest Dr Dallas TX 75229

GORLEY, MARGARET ELIZABETH, course specialist, mathematics educator, consultant; b. Eatonton, Ga., Nov. 12, 1950; d. Frank Griffith and Edith Roy (Beall) G. B.S. in Math., U. Ga., 1972; M.Ed., Ga. State U., 1977, Ed.S., 1982, now postgrad.; postgrad. Woodrow Wilson Coll. of Law, 1977-78. Cert. secondary tchr., Ga. Tchr. DeKalb Co. Bd. Edn., Decatur, Ga., 1972-83; chmn. dept. math. Columbia High Sch., Decatur, 1978-83; with product devel. Chalkboard Co., Atlanta, 1983-84; math instr. Ga. State U., Atlanta, 1983—; pres. ELISE, Clarkston, Ga., 1983—; course specialist Ga. Pacific Co., Atlanta, 1984—; research assoc. SUNY-Stony Brook, 1976; modeling instr. Barbizon Modeling Sch., Atlanta, 1977-81; instr. Ga. State Coll. for Kids, 1984-85; test taking cons. Communication Workers of Am., Atlanta, 1985. Author: (software user manual) Micro Maestro, 1983, Music Math, 1984. Mem. editorial bd. CPA Computer Report, Atlanta, 1984-85. Active DeKalb LWV, 1980, Atlanta Preservation Soc., 1985; tchr. St. Phillips Ch. Sch., Atlanta, 1981-85; vol. Joel Chandler Harris Assn., Atlanta, 1984-85. Named STAR Tchr. DeKalb County Bd. Edn., 1979, 80, 81, Most Outstanding Tchr., Barbizon Schs. of Modeling, 1980. Mem. Nat. Council Tchrs. Math., Ga. Council Tchrs. Math., Am. Soc. Tng. and Devel. Greater Atlanta, Atlanta Women's Network, DeKalb Personal Computer Instr. Assn. (pres. 1984). Democrat. Episcopalian. Club: Atlanta Track. Avocations: piano; creative crafts; aerobics; jogging; fashion modeling. Home: 5300 W Kingston Ct Atlanta GA 30342 Office: Ga Pacific 133 Peachtree St NE Atlanta GA 30303

GORMAN, DAVID EDWARD, pharmacist; b. Dayton, Ohio, Aug. 9, 1942; s. John Thomas and Beatrice Dorothy (Hannahs) G.; m. Peggietta Happel, Sept. 5, 1964; children—Andrea, Sean, Allen. B.S. in Pharmacy, Butler U., 1966. Registered pharmacist, Ind., Fla. Pharmacist staff Parkview Hosp., Ft. Wayne, Ind., 1966-73; mgr. Hook Drugs, Seymour, Ind., 1973-75; pharmacist, mgr. Eckerd Drugs, Orlando, Fla., 1975—; pharmacist, mgr. Jennings Community Hosp., North Vernon, Ind., 1973-75. Recipient Outstanding Store award Hooks Drug, 1975. Mem. Phi Delta Chi. Republican. Presbyterian. Clubs: Orlando Runners, Fla. Freewheelers (Orlando). Avocations: marathons, triathalons; Ironman Finisher 1983. Home: 2924 Summerfield Rd Winter Park FL 32792 Office: Eckerd Drug 908 Lee Rd Orlando FL 32810

GORMAN, JEREMIAH DESMOND, wholesale distributing company executive; b. Lynchburg, Va., Feb. 26, 1937; s. Joseph Vincent and Mary Jane (Desmond) G.; m. Virginia Dare Hawkins, Oct. 12, 1961; 1 son, Jeremiah Desmond; stepchildren—Beth, Sandra. Student U.S. Mcht. Marine Acad., 1956-59. Salesman, Central Lithographic Corp., 1959-63; div. sales mgr. Miller & Rhoads, 1963-67; salesman S.E. Massengill Co., Beecham Labs., 1967-71, Lincoln Nat. Life, 1971-73; v.p. sales Daniel Bell Rental and Sales, Richmond, Va., 1973-77; pres. Charity Games, Inc., Richmond, 1973—. Ward chmn. Republican City Com., Lynchburg, 1965-66; past pres. PTA. Mem. Navy League, Confederate Air Force, U.S. C. of C., Va. C. of C., Richmond C. of C., Am. Legion, Fraternal Order of Police. Republican. Roman Catholic. Club: Pigs (Richmond). Lodges: K.C., Moose, Ancient Order Hibernians. Office: PO Drawer 29268 Richmond VA 23229

GORMAN, LAWRENCE JAMES, banker; b. Albany, N.Y., Mar. 22, 1948; s. Lawrence Edward and Olive Gertrude (MacDowell) G.; grad. Nat. Grad. Trust Sch., 1980; B.S., Syracuse U., 1970; J.D., Albany Law Sch. Union U., 1973; m. Barbara J. Pisarek, Aug. 4, 1973; children—Ryan Patrick, Michael Patrick. Admitted to N.Y. bar, 1976; assoc. Grasso, Rivizzigno & Woronov, Syracuse, 1973-76; asst. v.p. Trust and Investment div. Lincoln 1st Bank N.A., Syracuse, 1976-79; v.p. Trust and Investment div. Bank of N.Y., Syracuse, 1979-83; v.p. 1st Va. Banks, Inc., 1983—; adj. prof. Onondaga County Community Coll.; faculty N.Y. State Bar, 1980-81. Mem. investment com. Am. Cancer Soc. N.Y. State chpt., 1981-83; dir. Fredericksburg Main Street Revitalization Program, 1985-88; trustee N.Y.C. chpt. Leukemia Soc. Am., 1982-83. Mem. ABA, N.Y. State Bar Assn., Onondaga County Bar Assn. (chmn. bank liaison com. 1980-82), Estate Planning Council Fredericksburg (pres.). Clubs: Rotary, Fredericksburg Country. Home: 3 Russell Rd Fredericksburg VA 22405 Office: 1001 Princess Anne St Fredericksburg VA 22401

GORMAN, LYNN RAY, truck rental company executive; b. Des Moines, Iowa, Feb. 13, 1942; s. Raymond Vernon and Virginia (Foote) G.; m. Judy Kay Howard; children—Shannon L., Shelly K. B.B.A., North Tex. State U., 1964. With Ryder Truck Rental, Inc., Dallas, 1957-64, maintenance trainee, Miami, Fla., 1968, dir. warranty, 1973-82, group dir. maintenance, 1982-83, v.p. maintenance, 1983—; sales mgr. Internat. Harvester, Dallas, 1964-68. Recipient Nat. Spirit Honor award USAF, 1964. Served with USAF, 1964-71. Mem. Am. Mgmt. Assn., Am. Truck Assn. (truck maintenance council), Sigma Phi Epsilon. Republican. Baptist. Home: 15831 SW 99th Pl Miami FL 33157 Office: Ryder Truck Rental Inc 3600 NW 82nd Ave Miami FL 33166

GORMAN, MARCIE SOTHERN, franchise executive; b. N.Y.C., Feb. 25, 1949; d. Jerry R. and Carole Edith (Frendel) Sothern; A.A., U. Fla.; B.S., Memphis State U., 1970; divorced; children—Michael Stephen, Mark Jason. Tchr., Memphis City Sch. System, 1970-73; tng. dir. Weight Watchers of Palm Beach County and Weight Watchers So. Ala., Inc., West Palm Beach, Fla., 1973—, area dir., then pres., 1977—; pres. Markel Ads, Inc. Cubmaster pack Boy Scouts Am., 1983-84. Hon. lt. col. aide-de-camp, Ala. Militia. Mem. Womens Am. Orgn. Rehab. Tng. (program chmn. 1975), Weight Watchers Franchise Assn. (advt. com. 1982—), Am. Bus. Womens Assn., NOW, Nat. Assn. Female Execs., Exec. Women Palm Beaches. Home: 3253 Hoy Lake Rd Lake Worth FL 33467 Office: 7597 Lake Worth Rd Lake Worth FL 33467

GORR, LOUIS FREDERICK, museum director; b. North Platte, Nebr., Aug. 1, 1941; s. Ernest Frederick and Eileen Bethel (Green) G.; m. Madeleine Zangla, Dec. 12, 1967; 1 child, Michaela. B.A., U. Nebr., 1963, M.A., 1967; Ph.D., U. Md., 1972; M.B.A., U. Dallas, 1981; mgmt. and real estate courses, So. Meth. U. Spl. asst. to dir. Nat. Mus. History and Tech., Smithsonian Instn., Washington, 1969-73; dir. div. museums and historic preservation Fairfax (Va.) County Govt., 1973-77; dir. Dallas County (Tex.) Heritage Soc., 1977-79, Dallas Mus. Natural History, 1979—, Dallas Aquarium; ptnr. East End Devel. Corp.; cons., lectr. in field, 1970—; adj. prof. mus. studies U. Okla.; mem. bd. commerce Dallas Nat. Bank, 1980—; chmn. bd. commerce Republic Bank Dallas East. Author numerous articles, revs. in field. Pres. Fairfax Symphony Orch., 1976-77; bd. dirs. Met. Washington Cultural Alliance, 1976, Prince George's County (Md.) Arts Council, 1973, Fairfax County Assn. Civic Orgns., 1976-77; mem. arts and culture adv. com. Dallas Ind. Sch. Dist.; leadership devel. trainer United Way. Served with USAF, 1963-64. Research fellow Smithsonian Instn., 1971, Naval Inst. Mem. Am. Assn. Mus. (dir.), Tex. Assn. Mus. (pres. 1981-83, dir.), Am. Mgmt. Assn., Nat. Recreation and Parks Assn., Internat. Council Mus., Assn. Sci. Mus. Dirs. (v.p.), Dallas Bus. League, Am. Soc. Pub. Adminstrn., Council Advancement and Support of Edn., Dallas C. of C., East Dallas C. of C., Leadership Dallas Alumni Assn., Sigma Iota Epsilon, Lambda Chi Alpha. Republican. Clubs: Dallas Commerce, Dallas Lancers, Dallas County Rep. Men's. Lodges: Rotary, Masons (32 deg.). Home: 1606 Yale Blvd Richardson TX 75081 Office: Dallas Mus Natural History PO Box 26193 Fair Park Station Dallas TX 75226*

GORRELL, LORRAINE, music educator; b. Balt.; d. Senator Wilson and Clara Elsie (Horstman) Gorrell; m. Wilburn Wendell Newcomb, May 24, 1969; 1 child, Rachel Claire. B.A. cum laude, Hood Coll.; Mus.M., M.A., Yale U. Instr. music Pa. State U., State College, 1966-69; tchr. Victoria (B.C., Can.) Conservatory of Music, 1970-73; assoc. prof. Winthrop Coll., Rock Hill, S.C., 1973—; recitalist, soloist in the U.S. and Can. Woodrow Wilson fellow, 1963. Mem. Nat. Assn. Tchrs. Singing, Mortar Bd. Contbr. articles fo profl. jours. Home: RR 1 Box 4B Edgemoor SC 29712 Office: Winthrop Coll Sch Music Rock Hill SC 29733

GORRELL, NITA ROSENDAHL, lawyer; b. Fargo, N.D., Sept. 12, 1947; d. Glenn J. and Ardith M. (Johnson) Rosendahl; m. Douglas R. Bell, Feb., 1970; (div. 1975); m. 2d, John Jeffrey Gorrell, Oct. 25, 1975. B.A., U. Wash., 1969; postgrad. U. Fla., 1972-74, Nova U., 1974-75; J.D., Tulane U., 1978. Bar: La. 1978, U.S. Dist. Ct. (ea. dist.) La. 1980, U.S. Dist. Ct. (mid. dist.) La. 1980. Tchr., Duval County Sch. Bd., Jacksonville, Fla., 1970-74; ptnr. Morrison & Gorrell, Hammond, La., 1978-81, Mentz & Gorrell, Hammond, 1981-82, Tillery & Gorrell, Hammond, 1982-84; sole practice, Hammond, 1984—. Chmn. bd. Youth Service Bur., Hammond, 1978-82; sec.-treas., dir. Tangipahoa Council on Aging, Amite, La., 1981-82; vol. Crisis Phone, 1981; v.p. Mayor's Commn. Needs of Women, 1981-82; bd. dirs. Southeastern La. U. Devel. Found., 1983—, S.E. La. Legal Services, Inc., 1985—. Tulane U. scholar, 1977. Mem. La. Bar Assn., La. Trial Lawyers Assn., 21st Jud. Dist. Bar Assn., ABA. Club: Hammond Bus. and Profl. Women. Home: 704 W Robert St Hammond LA 70401 Office: Nita R Gorrell PLC 112 W Morris St PO Box 1537 Hammond LA 70404

GOSS, KAY GENTRY COLLETT, state official; b. Fayetteville, Ark., Aug. 7; d. Kirby and Susan Elizabeth (Sutton) Collett; m. Oscar Eugene Goss, Apr. 25, 1975; 1 child, Susan Laura; 1 stepchild, Iris Elaine. B.A. in Polit. Sci., U. Ark.-Fayetteville, 1963, M.A. in Polit. Sci., 1966; secondary teaching cert. in social scis. N.W. Mo. State U., 1964; postgrad. W.Va. U., 1968-69. Instr. social sci. Westark Community Coll., 1966-68; asst. prof. polit. sci. U. Ark., Fayetteville, 1969-73; legis. asst. Congressman Ray Thornton, 1973-74; adminstrv. asst. Congresswomen Patricia Schroeder, 1974-75; project coordinator, spl. sch. fin. study Ark. Legislature, 1977-78; research dir. Constitutional Conv., Little Rock, 1978-79; project dir. Assn. Ark. Counties, Little Rock, 1979-81; chief dep., state auditor's office State of Ark., Little Rock, 1981-82; intergovtl. relations asst. to gov. State of Ark., Little Rock, 1983—. Editorial bd. Ark. Polit. Sci. Jour., 1983—. Bd. dirs., chmn. personnel com. Ark. Community Found., 1978-85; bd. dirs., sec. Fire Tng. Acad. Bd., So. Ark. U. Tech Br., 1983-85; mem. exec. com. Pulaski County Democratic Central Com., 1982-84; sec.-treas. Community Theater of Little Rock Guild, 1985-86. Mem. Ark. Polit. Sci. Assn. (pres. 1985-86). Methodist. Home: 1806 S Gaines St Little Rock AR 72206 Office: Gov's Office State Capitol Little Rock AR 72201

GOSS, MARK ALAN, exploration geologist; b. Dallas, Oct. 8, 1956; s. Gene Alan and Dorotha Carolyn (Procter) G.; m. Susan Rhea Whittet, July 15, 1973; 1 child, Sara Melissa. B.S., U. Okla., 1983. Cons., Gene A. Goss/Wessely Energy Co., Oklahoma City, 1979-84; pres., chmn. bd. Goss Exploration Inc., Oklahoma City, 1984—. Mem. Am. Assn. Petroleum Geologists, Ardmore Geol. Soc., Oklahoma City Geol. Soc. (Spl. Service award 1982). Republican. Methodist. Avocations: tennis; flying. Home: 2000 Faircloud Dr Edmond OK 73034 Office: Goss Exploration Inc 400 First City Pl Oklahoma City OK 73102

GOSSELIN, MARY ELSIE NOWELL, accountant; b. Belzoni, Miss., July 11, 1934; d. William Henry and Marguerite Helen (Bain) Chatoney; A.A., Hinds Jr. Coll., Raymond, Miss., 1955; B.A., La. Salle U., Chgo., 1972; acctg. cert. Sowela Tech., Lake Charles, 1966; m. Audrey R. Nowell, May 1, 1960 (dec. Dec. 1979); children—Franklin Russell, Margaret Grace Nowell Scott, Denis, Julie, Robert, Marc, Angielynn, Bobby Lee, Audrey Russell; m. Fred C. Gosselin, June 27, 1981. Various clerical and office positions, 1957-71; office mgr. J.C. Penney Supermarket, Lake Charles, La., 1971-76; practice pub. acctg., Lake Charles, 1973-86. Mem. Republican Presdl. Task Force, 1982-86, Nat. Senatorial Com., 1982-86. C.P.A., La. Mem. Am. Inst. C.P.A.s, La. Soc. C.P.A.s, Mayan Soc. Order. Democrat. Methodist. Address: 3563 Monroe St Lake Charles LA 70605

GOSSEN, RONALD HOWARD, public relations executive; b. Corpus Christi, Tex., Mar. 3, 1949; s. Charles and Rosalie (Bentch) G.; m. Eva Lynn McCalla, Feb. 14, 1976; 1 dau., Stephanie Leigh. B.J., U. Tex.-Austin, 1971; postgrad. U. Tex.-San Antonio, 1975. Advt. mgr. Sta. KTFM, San Antonio, 1972-74; advt. exec. Scripps League Newspapers, Truckee, Calif., 1974; dir. pub. info. Tex. Dept. Human Resources, San Antonio, 1975-80; dir. pub. relations services Atkins & Assocs. Advt., San Antonio, 1980-83; pres. Southwest Mktg. Communications Group, Inc., affiliate of Hill & Knowlton, Inc. 1984—; pres. East Kings Devel. Corp., 1984—, chmn. council communications com., 1985-86. Chmn. pub. info., dist. cons., bd. dirs. San Antonio chpt. Am. Heart Assn., 1983; bd. dirs. San Antonio Vol. Ctr., 1980; mem. allocations panel United Way San Antonio, 1981, 82; trustee Pub. Relations Found. Tex., Tau Delta Phi Found., 1985-86; elected commr. Fiesta San Antonio Commn. 1985—. Recipient Silver Spur award Tex. Pub. Relations Assn., 1979, Best of Tex. award, 1981; Bronze Quill award Internat. Assn. Bus. Communicators, 1982, 84; Best of the S.W. U.S. award Adweek mag., 1979; Service award United Way San Antonio, 1977, 78; Addy award San Antonio Advt. Fedn., 1984, 85. Mem. Tex. Pub. Relations Assn. (pres. 1985-86, chmn. Pres.'s Council 1986-87), Pub. Relations Soc. Am. (accredited; dir. San Antonio chpt.), Pub. Relations Found. Tex. (charter life), Tex. State Hist. Soc., San Antonio Conservation Soc. (assoc.). Jewish. Lodge: Rotary (San Antonio). Home: 3423 Trailway San Antonio TX 78247 Office: 1400 One Riverwalk Pl San Antonio TX 78205

GOSSETT, JACK T., engineering company executive; b. 1925. With Goodyear Tire & Rubber Co., 1945-48; pipefitter Fish Engrs., Inc., 1949-50; with Brown & Root, Inc., 1948-49, 51—, pipefitter, 1948, sr. v.p., 1974-78, group v.p., 1978, now exec. v.p. Served with USN, 1943-45. Address: Brown & Root Inc 4100 Clinton Dr Houston TX 77020*

GOSSMAN, FRANCIS JOSEPH, bishop; b. Balt., Apr. 1, 1930; s. Frank M. and Mary Genevieve (Steadman) G. B.A., St. Mary Sem., Balt., 1952; S.T.L., N. Am. Coll., in Rome, 1955; J.C.D., Cath. U. of Am., 1959. Ordained priest Roman Cath. Ch., 1955; asst. pastor Basilica of Assumption, Balt., 1959-68; asst. chancellor Archdiocese of Balt., 1959-65, vice chancellor, 1965-68; pro-synodal judge Balt. Tribunal, 1961; vice officialis Tribunal of Archdiocese of Balt., 1962-65, officialis, 1965-68; made papal chamberlain with title very rev. monsignor, 1965; elected to Senate of Priests of Archdiocese, 1967-68; adminstr. Cathedral of Mary Our Queen, 1968-70; named aux. bishop of Balt. and titular bishop of Aguntum, 1968, apptd. vicar gen., 1968; apptd. to bd. consultors, 1969; urban vicar Archdiocese of Balt., 1970-75; bishop of Raleigh, N.C., 1975—. Mem. Balt. Community Relations Commn., 1969-75; mem. exec. com. Md. Food Com., Inc., 1969-75; bd. dirs. United Fund Central Md., 1974-75. Mem. Canon Law Soc. Am., Nat. Conf. Cath. Bishops, U.S. Cath. Conf. Office: Roman Catholic Ch 300 Cardinal Gibbons Dr Raleigh NC 27606*

GOTAUTAS, VITO ADOLPH, geologist, consultant; b. Chgo., Dec. 6, 1928; s. John Dominic and Anele (Markevich) G.; A.B., Miami U., 1950; M.S., 1951; postgrad. Yale U., 1955-56; m. Mary Jane Dean, Oct. 4, 1952; children—Jane, Patricia, Anita. Exploration geologist Atlantic Refining Co., Lake Charles and Lafayette La., 1956-62; v.p., exploration mgr. Century Mineral Corp., 1962-63; ind. cons. geologist, 1964-80, 82—; v.p., exploration mgr. Intercontinental Petroleum-South La., 1980-82. Served with USNR, 1951-55. ETO. Cert. profl. geologist. Mem. Am. Assn. Petroleum Geologists, AIME, Soc. Exploration Geophysicists, Am. Inst. Profl. Geologists (nat. membership chmn. 1969-71, pres. La. sect. 1965, nat. sec.-treas. 1973), Soc. Econ. Mineralogists and Paleontologists, Am. Assn. Profl. Well Log Analysts, Lafayette Geol. Soc. (past sec.), Houston Geol. Soc., Lafayette Geophys. Soc., Sigma Xi, Sigma Gamma Epsilon. Clubs: Toastmasters (pres. 1971), Civitan of Lafayette (charter pres. 1958-59, gov. La. dist. 1963-64), Lafayette Chess (pres. 1967), Lafayette Petroleum; Oakbourne Country. Contbr. articles to profl. jours. Home: 133 Maurice Lafayette LA 70506 Office: PO Box 51788 OCS Lafayette LA 70505

GOTCHER, (PAUL) WARREN, lawyer; b. Muskogee, Okla., July 19, 1947; s. Paul Warren and Rebecca Jean (Bond) G.; m. Jill Newkirk, Sept. 27, 1946; 1 child, Mills. B.A., U. Okla., 1968, J.D., 1971. Bar: Okla. 1971, U.S. Dist. Ct. (ea. dist.) Okla. 1971, U.S. Ct. Appeals (10th cir.) 1974, U.S. Dist. Ct. (we. dist.) Okla. 1975, U.S. Supreme Ct. 1975, U.S. Dist. Ct. (no. dist.) Okla. 1982. Assoc. Gotcher & Gotcher, McAlester, Okla., 1971-73; ptnr. Gotcher, Gotcher & Gotcher, McAlester, 1973-78; ptnr. Gotcher, Gotcher & Taylor, McAlester, 1978-83, Gotcher, Brown & Bland, Mc Alester, 1983—. Bd. dirs. Tiak council Girl Scouts U.S.A., 1978-80; mem. Carl Albert Mental Health Bd. Advisors, 1975-79, Pittsburg County Mental Health Adv. Bd., 1976-78; active Pittsburg County Democratic Club. Mem. ABA, Okla. Bar Assn., Pittsburg County Bar Assn., Assn. Trial Lawyers Am., Okla. Trial Lawyers Assn., Am. Judicature Soc., Okla. Criminal Def. Lawyers Assn., Nat. Assn. Criminal Def. Lawyers, Phi Alpha Delta. Baptist. Clubs: McAlester Country, Sertoma, Elks. Home: PO Box 1502 McAlester OK 74502 Office: Box 160 321 S 3d Suite 1 McAlester OK 74502

GOTHARD, HEATHER MCCLOUD, educator; b. Birmingham, Eng., Feb. 4, 1947; came to U.S., 1947; d. Frank James and Barbara (Bax) McCloud; B.S., U. Tenn., Chattanooga, 1972, M.Ed., 1974; m. Terry Joseph Gothard, Aug. 31, 1967. Tchr. Daisy Child Devel. Center, Chattanooga, 1968-72; lead tchr. Summit Child Devel. Center, Chattanooga, 1972-73, Bakewell Child Devel. Center, Chattanooga, 1973-75; ednl. coordinator, career devel. coordinator Hamilton County Child Devel. Program, Chattanooga, 1975-82; chpt. 1 coordinator Hamilton County Schs., 1982-86; pres. Teather Corp., 1986—; adj. prof. U. Tenn.-Chattanooga, 1983—; extension tchr. Western Ky. U., Chattanooga State Tech. Community Coll.; adv. com. Child Care Center, Chattanooga State Tech. Community Coll.; mem. craft com. child care program Sequoyah Vocat. Sch.; leader workshops, speaker, lectr. in field. Mem. planning com. Chattanooga Nature Center, 1978, chmn. pre-sch. sect., 1978. Cert. child devel. asso. Mem. Nat. Assn. Edn. Young Children, So. Assn. Edn. Young Children, Tenn. Assn. Young Children (exhibits chmn., 1979), Chattanooga Assn. Young Children (workshop chmn. 1980, 1st v.p. 1982-84, mem. conf. com. 1983, week of Young child com. 1982-84), Internat. Reading Assn., Tenn. Assn. Supervision and Curriculum Devel., Nature Ctr., Am. Contract Bridge League, Ranger Rick Nature Club, Smithsonian Instn., Phi Delta Kappa, Alpha Delta Kappa. Democrat. Methodist. Home: 5 Shingle Rd Chattanooga TN 37409 Office: 201 Broad St Chattanooga TN 37402

GOTTFRIED, ROBERT RICHARD, economics educator, researcher; b. Mexico City, Mex., June 11, 1948; s. Richard Mario and Alice (Davis) G.; came to U.S., 1949; m. Yolande McCurdy; Nov. 22, 1975; children—Alicia Anne, Jeremy Richard. A.B. cum laude, Davidson Coll., 1970; Ph.D. in Econs., U. N.C., 1980. Instr. econs. St. John's U., Collegeville, Minn., 1975-78; Fulbright lectr. U. Rafael Landivar, Guatemala City, Guatemala, 1979; vis. asst. prof., U. N.C., Chapel Hill, summer 1981, Greensboro, 1981-82; MacArthur asst. prof. U. of the South, Sewanee, Tenn., 1982-85; faculty research participant Oak Ridge Assoc. Univs., Ctr. for Energy and Environment Research, San Juan, P.R., 1983. Author: Potential Economic and Environmental Costs to the Puerto Rican Government from Energy Cane Technology, 1984. Contbr. articles to Am. Economist, Social and Econ. Studies, Estudios Sociales, Cultura de Guatemala. Dist. and chpt. coordinator Bread for the World, Sewanee, Tenn., 1982—; mem. Community Action Council, Sewanee, 1985—; mem. exec. com. Sewanee Catholic Community, 1983—; bd. dirs. Appalachian Community Devel. NDEA fellow, 1970; Oak Ridge Assn. Univs. grantee, 1984—. Mem. Am. Econ. Assn., N.Am. Econ. and Fin. Assn., Assn. Environ. and Resource Economists, Save Our Cumberland Mountains (treas. chpt.). Roman Catholic. Avocations: classical, Appalachian and Latin American music performance; baking; hiking. Office: Univ of the South Dept of Econs Sewanee TN 37375

GOTTLIEB, EILEEN BOMSTEIN, marriage and family therapist, consultant; b. Washington, Apr. 23, 1947; d. Solomon Bomstein and Esther (Blankman) Bomstein Baskin; children—Rory Johanna, Noah David; m. David George Gottlieb, Oct. 3, 1980. B.A. cum laude, U. Md., 1969; M.Ed., Northeastern U., 1975; postgrad. Georgetown Med. Sch., Washington, 1980-83. Lic. marriage and family therapist, Fla. Tchr. secondary schs., Md. and Mass., 1969-74; sch. counselor Wilmington Pub. Schs., Mass., 1974-75; chmn. counseling services dept. Windfields Secondary Sch., Toronto, Ont., Can., 1975-77; dir., family therapist Family Ctr., Delray, Fla., 1979—; cons. Bnai Torah Synagogue, Boca Raton, Fla., 1984—, South County Neighborhood Ctr., Boca Raton, 1978-80, Ctr. Group Counseling, Boca Raton, 1978-80, Women's Ctr., Palm Beach Jr. Coll., Lake Worth, Fla., 1979—; South County Mental Health Ctr., Delray, 1983—; lectr. in field. Mem. Judaic edn. com. Bnai Torah Synagogue, 1984—. Recipient Award of Excellence, Palm Beach Mental Health Soc., 1984. Mem. Am. Assn. Counseling and Devel., Am. Mental Health Counselors Assn., Fla. Assn. Marriage and Family Therapists, Am. Assn. Marriage and Family Therapists, Fla. Assn. Profl. Family Mediations, South Fla. Family Therapy Seminar Assn., Palm Beach Profl. Mediation Assn. (pres. 1982-83), Palm Beach Profl. Women's Network (spl. projects chmn. 1982-85), Women's Network Edn. Seminar, Nat. Council Jewish Women (program chmn. 1978-79), Phi Alpha Theta. Democrat. Avocations: long-distance running; aerobic dance; music appreciation; art appreciation; dance appreciation. Office: Family Ctr 2905 S Federal Hwy Delray Beach FL 33444

GOTTLIEB, GILBERT, psychobiologist, educator; b. N.Y.C., Oct. 22, 1929; s. Leo and Sylvia Gottlieb; m. Nora Lee Willis, Feb. 28, 1961; children—Jonathan Brian, David Herschel, Aaron Lee, Marc Sherman. A.B., U. Miami, Fla., 1955, M.S., 1956; Ph.D., Duke U., 1960. Clin. psychologist Dorothea Dix Hosp., Raleigh, N.C., 1959-61; research scientist N.C. Div. Mental Health, Raleigh, 1961-82; Excellence Found. prof., head psychology dept. U.N.C.-Greensboro, 1982-86, prof., 1982—; advisor German NSF, 1977; U.S. del. Internat. Ethological Congress com., 1977-83. Author: Development of Species Identification in Birds, 1971; Behavioral Embryology, 1973; Aspects of Neurogenesis, 1974; Neural and Behavioral Specificity, 1976, Early Influences, 1978; editor: Measurement or Audition and Vision in the First Year of Postnatal Life, 1985. assoc. editor Jour. Comparative and Physiol. Psychology, 1974-80; editorial cons. various sci. jours. and pub. houses. NSF grantee, 1963, 85—; Nat. Inst. Child Health grantee, 1963-85. Fellow Am. Psychol. Assn., Animal Behavior Soc., AAAS. Home: Route 25 Box 234-F Raleigh NC 27604 Office: Psychology Department UNC Greensboro NC 27412 27604

GOTTLIEB, MARISE SUSS, medical educator; b. N.Y.C., July 16, 1938; d. Lester J. and Fannie (Freeman) Suss; m. A. Arthur Gottlieb, July 8, 1958; children—Mindy Cheryl, Joanne Meredith. A.B., Barnard Coll., 1958; M.D., N.Y.U., 1962; M.P.H., Harvard U., 1966. Intern, Mass. Meml. Hosp., 1962-63; resident dept. epidemiology Harvard U., 1965-68, instr. dept. medicine, H.M., Boston, 1969-70, also resident, asst. in Medicine Peter Bent Brigham Hosp.; dir. chronic disease control N.J. Dept. Health, Trenton, 1970-75; asst. prof. Rutgers Med. Sch., Piscataway N.J., 1972-75; assoc. prof. Tulane U. Sch. Medicine, New Orleans, 1975—; assoc. prof. Sch. Pub. Health, 1975-80; chief chronic disease control, La. Dept. Health and Human Resources, New Orleans, 1975—. NIH traineeship, 1965-66, spl research fellow Nat. Inst. Arthritis, Metabolism and Digestive Diseases, 1966-68. Diplomate Am. Bd. Preventive Medicine. Fellow Am. Coll. Preventive Medicine, Am. Coll. Epidemiology; mem. Am. Diabetes Assn. (epidemiological council program com.), Soc. Epidemiological Research, Am. Fedn. Clin. Research, Am. Pub. Health Assn., Contbr. articles to profl jours. Office: Dept Medicine 1430 Tulane Ave Box D 55 Tulane U New Orleans LA 70112

GOTTSCHALK, MARY THERESE, hospital administrator; b. Doellwang, W.Ger., June 21, 1931, came to U.S., 1953; d. John and Sabina (Dietz) G. B.S. in Pharmacy, Creighton U., 1960; M.S. in Hosp. Adminstrn., St. Louis U., 1970. Joined Sisters of the Sorrowful Mother, 1952; dir. pharmacy St. Mary's Hosp., Roswell, N.Mex., 1960-68; asst. adminstr. St. John's Med. Ctr., Tulsa, 1970-72, chief exec. officer, pres., 1974—; chief exec. officer St. Mary's Hosp., Roswell, 1972-74. Fellow Am. Coll. Hosp. Adminstrs.; mem. Okla. Hosp. Assn. (pres. 1984), Tulsa Hosp. Council (pres. 1983), Conf. Cath. Hosps. (past pres. Okla.), Tulsa C. of C., Okla. Health Systems Agy., AMA, ARC, United Way (past med. chmn.), Am. Pharmacy Assn. Roman Catholic. Office: Saint John Medical Center 1923 S Utica St Tulsa OK 74104

GOTTWALD, BRUCE COBB, chemical company executive; b. Richmond, Va., Sept. 28, 1933; s. Floyd Dewey and Anne Ruth (Cobb) G.; B.S., Va. Mil. Inst., 1954; postgrad. U. Va., Inst. Paper Chemistry, Appleton, Wis.; m. Nancy Hays, Dec. 22, 1956; children—Bruce Cobb, Mark Hays, Thomas Edward. With Albemarle Paper Mfg. Co. (became Ethyl Corp. 1962), 1956—, pres., 1970—; dir. Dominion Resources, Inc., Reco Industries, Inc., James Corp. Pres. Va. Museum; bd. govs. Council Econ. Edn.; Mem. Va. Mfrs. Assn. (dir.). Presbyterian. Home: 4203 Sulgrave Rd Richmond VA 23221 Office: 330 S 4th St PO Box 2189 Richmond VA 23217

GOTTWALD, FLOYD DEWEY, JR., chemical company executive; b. Richmond, Va., July 29, 1922; s. Floyd Dewey and Ann (Cobb) G.; B.S., Va. Mil. Inst., Lexington, 1943; M.S., U. Richmond, 1951; m. Elisabeth Morris Shelton, Mar. 22, 1947; children—William M., James T., John D. With Albemarle Paper Co., Richmond, 1943-68, sec., 1956-57, v.p., sec., 1957-62, pres., 1962-68, also dir.; exec. v.p. Ethyl Corp., 1962-64, vice chmn. bd., 1964-68, chmn. bd., 1968—, chief exec. officer, 1970—, also chmn. exec. com.; dir. Reid-Rowell, Inc., Fed. Res. Bank of Richmond, CSX Corp. Trustee, Va. Mil. Inst. Found., U. Richmond, Served to 1st lt. USAR, 1943-46. Decorated Bronze Star, Purple Heart. Mem. Am. Petroleum Inst. (dir.), Chem. Mfrs. Assn. (past dir.), NAM (past dir.). Club: Alfalfa. Home: 300 Herndon Rd Richmond VA 23229 Office: 330 S 4th St Richmond VA 23219

GOUGH, CAROLYN HARLEY, library director; b. Paterson, N.J., Sept. 23, 1922; d. Frank Ellsworth and Mabel (Harrison) Harley; m. George Harrison Gough, Sept. 21, 1944; children—Deborah Ann Gough Bornholdt, Douglas Alan. B.A., Coll. William and Mary, 1943; M.L.S., Drexel U., 1966. Research asst. Young and Rubicam, Inc., N.Y.C., 1943-44; library dir., asst. prof. Cabrini Coll., Radnor, Pa., 1966-81; chmn. Palm Beach County Library Bd., 1984—. Mem. resources study com. Tredyffrin Twp. Library, 1964-65; docent Henry Morrison Flagler Mus., 1982—. Mem. Tri-State Coll. Library Coop. (v.p. 1973-74, pres. 1974-75), Assn. Coll. and Research Libraries (dir. 1978-81), AAUP, DAR, Beta Phi Mu, Kappa Delta. Republican. Episcopalian. Clubs: Questers, Inc. (1st nat. v.p. 1964-66), Atlantis Golf, Atlantis Women's (co-pres. 1982-83). Home: 458 S Country Club Dr Atlantis FL 33462

GOUGH, JESSIE POST (MRS. HERBERT FREDERICK GOUGH), educator; b. Nakon Sri Tamaraj, Thailand, Jan. 26, 1907 (parents Am. citizens); d. Richard Walter and Mame (Stebbins) Post; B.A., Maryville Coll., 1927; M.A. in English, U. Chgo., 1928; Ed.D., U. Ga., 1965; m. Herbert Frederick Gough, June 30, 1934; children—Joan Acland Gough Reed, Herbert Frederick. Tchr. English, Linden Hall, Lititz, Pa., 1930-32; tchr. Fairyland Sch., Lookout Mountain, Tenn., 1955-64; research asst. English curriculum studies center U. Ga., 1964-65; prof. elem. edn. LaGrange (Ga.) Coll., 1965-75; prof. N.W. Ga. Area Tchr. Edn. Services, 1969-71. Mem. Walker County (Ga.) Curriculum Council, 1959-61, Walker County Ednl. Planning Bd., 1958-60. Mem. Am. Ednl. Research Assn., East Tenn. Hist. Soc., Nat., Ga. edn. assns., Delta Kappa Gamma. Home: Savannah Hills Dr Ooltewah TN 37363

GOUGH, STEPHEN BRADFORD, computer scientist, researcher, consultant; b. New Castle, Ind., Sept. 13, 1950; s. Clifford Lea and Grace Elizabeth (Phillips) G.; m. Cynthia Lee Jordan, Dec. 20, 1971; children—Christopher Michael, Jennifer Ann, Lisa Marie. B.S. magna cum laude, Carroll Coll., 1972; Ph.D., U. Wis., 1976. Research fellow dept. botany U. Wis., Madison, 1972-75, teaching asst., 1975-76; research assoc. environ. scis. div. Oak Ridge Nat. Lab., 1976-82; pres., chief exec. officer Gough Enterprises, Inc., Oak Ridge, Tenn. and Fredericksburg, Va., 1979—; computer systems specialist, project leader System Devel. Corp., Fredericksburg, 1982-86; sr. software engr. Internat. Computer Equipment, Inc./A TRW Co., Fredericksburg, 1986—; cons. microbiology, water quality, computer scis., instrumentation; expert witness for Congress and govt. agys. NSF research grantee, 1971-72; U. Wis. fellow, 1972-76. Mem. Phycological Soc. Am., Water Pollution Control Fedn., Am. Soc. Limnology and Oceanography, Inc., AAAS, Ecol. Soc. Am., Sigma Xi, Delta Sigma Nu. Presbyterian. Author: (with Cushman, Moran and Craig). Sourcebook of Hydrologic and Ecological Features, 1980; contbr. articles to sci. jours. Home: 8 Norman Ct Fredericksburg VA 22401 Office: 420 Hudgins Rd Fredericksburg VA 22401

GOULD, CYNTHIA IRENE, county official; b. Phila., Aug. 23, 1948; d. Charlie and Robbye Rogers Martin; 1 dau., Robbye Michele. A.A., Daytona Beach Community Coll., 1979; B.S., U. Central Fla., 1983. Ops. supr. Bankers Trust Credit Corp., N.Y.C., 1967-71; employee benefits specialist Hertz Corp., N.Y.C., 1971-72, Dobbs-life Savers, Inc., N.Y.C., 1972-73; adminstrv. asst. JO-JE Enterprises, Inc., New Rochelle, N.Y., 1973-76; student devel. technician, career planning instr. Daytona Beach Community Coll., 1976-79, adminstrv. specialist Center for Placement and Profl. Practices, 1979-82; asst. coordinator Small Bus. Support Center, Lake Sumter Community Coll., Leesburg, Fla., 1983-84; affirmative action officer Volusia County, DeLand, Fla., 1984—. Vol., Sugar n' Spice Day Care Ctr. Mem. Am. Assn. Women in Community and Jr. Colls., Fla. Assn. Community Colls. (exec. bd. Career Service Commn.; dir., program chmn., 2d v.p.). Democrat. Baptist. Office: Volusia County Govt 135 W New York Ave PO Box 429 DeLand FL 32720

GOULD, KENNETH LAWRENCE, database publishing executive; b. Miami, Fla., Jan. 31, 1925; s. Kenneth Leroy and Mary (Wilson) G.; B.A., Coll. William and Mary, 1947; m. Helen Marilynn Brand, Aug. 12, 1950; children—Alison DeLong, Lawrence Brand, Meredith Wanner. Reporter, Richmond (Va.) News Leader, 1947-50, 52-54, asst. city editor, 1954-58; city editor Roanoke (Va.) Times, 1958-59; asst. city editor Richmond News Leader, 1959-63, city editor, 1963-69, mng. editor, 1969-72; v.p., gen. mgr. Media Gen. Financial Services, Inc., 1972—; exec. editor M/G Financial Weekly, 1970—, pres. M/G Fin. Services, 1979—. Served with USNR, 1943-46, 50-52. Mem. Info. Industry Assn., A.P. Mng. Editors Assn., Sigma Delta Chi. Episcopalian. Home: 10409 Medina Rd Richmond VA 23235 Office: 119 N 3d St Richmond VA 23219

GOULD, LEWIS LUDLOW, history educator; b. N.Y.C., Sept. 21, 1939; s. John Ludlow and Carmen L. (Lewis) G.; A.B., Brown U., 1961; M.A., Yale U., 1962, Ph.D., 1966; m. Karen D. Keel, Oct. 24, 1970. Instr. history Yale U., 1965-66, asst. prof., 1966-67; asst. prof. history U. Tex., Austin, 1967-71, assoc. prof., 1971-76, prof., 1976—, chmn., 1980-84, Eugene C. Barker Centennial prof. Am. history, 1983—. Recipient Carr P. Collins award Tex. Inst. Letters, 1973; Nat. Endowment for Humanities Younger Humanist fellow, 1974-75. Mem. Am., So., Tex. hist. assns., Phi Beta Kappa. Democrat. Author: Wyoming: A Political History, 1868-1896, 1968, Progressives and Prohibitionists: Texas Democrats in the Wilson Era, 1973; (with Richard Greffe) Photojournalist: The Career of Jimmy Hare, 1977; Reform and Regulation: American Politics, 1900-1916, 1978, 2d edit., 1986; The Presidency of William McKinley, 1980; the Spanish-American War and President McKinley, 1982. Editor: (with James C. Curtis) The Black Experience in America, 1970; The Progressive Era, 1974. Home: 2602 La Ronde St Austin TX 78731

GOULD, MARK ALLEN, physician, medical administrator; b. Kenova, W.Va., Dec. 1, 1930; s. Stanley Ackley and Helen (Miller) G.; m. Gloria Norma Charney, May 2, 1933; children—Mark A., Jr., Thomas P. B.S., Bates Coll., 1952; M.D., Tufts U., 1956. Intern Henry Ford Hosp., Detroit, 1956-57; resident Georgetown U.-D.C. Gen. Hosp., 1958, Washington U. and VA Hosp., St. Louis, 1961-63; asst. med. dir. Brawner Hosp., Smyrna, Ga., 1965-69; med. dir. Brawner Psychiat. Inst., Smyrna, 1969—, pres., dir., 1978—; staff psychiatrist Ctr. for Interpersonal Studies, Smyrna, 1970—; pres., dir. Psychiat. Inst. Atlanta, 1979—; dir. Health Facilities Ins. Corp., Hamilton, Bermuda; chmn. accreditation council for psychiat. facilities Joint Commn. on Accreditation of Hosps., Chgo., 1978-79, chmn. psychiat. profl. tech. adv. com., 1979-80; pres. Nat. Assn. Pvt. Psychiat. Hosps., Washington, 1982. Contbr. articles to profl. jours. Served as capt. USAF, 1958-60. Recipient Med. Dir. Leadership award Psychiat. Inst. Am., 1985. Fellow Am. Psychiat. Assn. (pres. Ga. dist. br. 1969, Ga. Man of Yr. 1970), So. Psychiat. Assn.; mem. AMA, Atlanta Clin. Soc. Episcopalian. Home: 550 Riverside Pkwy Atlanta GA 30328 Office: Brawner Psychiat Inst 3180 Atlanta St Smyrna GA 30080

GOULD, RICHARD HENRY, industrial engineer, university administrator, consultant; b. Binghamton, N.Y., Sept. 5, 1930; s. Henry Williams and Kathryn (Grady) G.; m. Jean Norment, May 30, 1953; children—Jeffrey Richard, James Fowler. B.S. in Engring. Adminstrn., U. Miss., 1952, M.S. in Indsl. Engring., 1955; D. Edn., U. Tenn., 1973. Registered profl. engr. Mfg. trainee Gen. Electric, Louisville, 1956-59; unit mgr., Murfreesboro, Tenn., 1959-62, quality mgr., 1962-66; faculty mem. Middle Tenn. State U., Murfreesboro, 1966-79, dept. chmn. indsl. arts, 1979—; cons. Perfect Equipment, Murfreesboro, 1974-77, Nissan Corp., Smyrna, Tenn., 1981—; mem. indsl. adv. bd. First Nat. Bank of Rutherford County, Smyrna, 1984—. Author: Tennessee's First Six Community Colleges, 1973. Served as lt. j.g. USN, 1953-56. Mem. Am. Soc. Quality Control (sr. mem., chmn. 1974-75, recipient Vince Barry Quality award 1980), Am. Inst. Indsl. Engrs., Soc. Mfg. Engrs. Methodist.

GOULD, RONALD JAMES, mathematics and computer science educator; b. Dunkirk, N.Y., Apr. 15, 1950; s. Harry and Margaret Virginia (Novelli) G.; m. Madelyn Gail Teall, Aug. 23, 1980. B.S. in Math., SUNY-Fredonia, 1972; M.S. in Computer Sci., Western Mich. U., 1978, Ph.D. in Math, 1979. Lctr. San Jose State U., Calif., 1978-79; asst. prof. Emory U., Atlanta, 1979-85, assoc. prof., 1985—. Editor (newsletter) Graph Theory, 1977-78. Contbr. articles to profl. jours. Mem. Am. Math. Soc., Math. Assn. Am., Assn. Computing Machinery. Avocations: sports; chess; music. Home: 474 Tallwood Dr Stone Mountain GA 30083 Office: Dept Math Computer Sci Emory U Atlanta GA 30322

GOULD, SYD S., publisher; b. Boston, Dec. 16, 1912; s. Charles M. and Cecelia (Duke) G.; student Coll. William and Mary, 1934; m. Grace Leich, May 22, 1938; 1 dau., Nancy Hamilton Gould Gex. Radio bus., Buenos Aires, Argentina, 1934, 36; advt. dept. Call-Chronicle Newspapers, Allentown, Pa., 1936-42; v.p., adv. dir. Baytown (Tex.) Sun, 1943-55; pub.-owner Cleveland (Tenn.) Daily Banner, 1955—; pres. Cleveland Newspapers, Inc., 1956-67; exec. v.p. So. Newspapers, Inc., 1963-69; pres. Syd S. Gould Assos., 1966—, Bolivar Newspapers, Inc., 1967—, Ironton Tribune Corp. (Ohio), Franklin Newspapers, Inc. (La.), Comet-Press Newspapers, Thibodaux, La., Milton Newspapers, Inc. (Fla.). Mem. Regional Small Bus. Adv. Council; sec. Bradley County (Tenn.) Indsl. Devel. Bd., 1961—; pres. Bradley County Heart Assn., 1960-61; mem. adv. bd. Providence Hosp.; bd. dirs. Mobile Pub. Library, Bayside Acad., Nat. Eagle Scout Assn. Served with USNR, World War II. Recipient Disting. Eagle Scout award. Mem. Newspaper Advt. Execs. Assn., Tenn. Press. Assn., Bur. Advt., Am. Newspaper Pubs. Assn., USCG Aux., U.S. Power Squadron, Navy League U.S. (nat. bd. dirs.), Sigma Delta Chi. Episcopalian. Clubs: Bayou Country, Mobile Big Game Fishing, Isle Dauphine Country, Capitol Hill, Yachting of Am., Internat. Trade, Bienville, Athelstan. Home: 138 Bay Pt Panama City FL 32407 Office: 2111 Thomas Dr Panama City FL 32407

GOULD, THOMAS STANTON, industrial designer, architect; b. Bklyn., July 19, 1940; s. Thomas and Loreta Elizabeth (Bonomo) G.; m. Janet Blair Page, Feb. 9, 1978; children—Natasha, Elizabeth. B.S., N.Y. U., 1962; B. Indsl. Design, Parsons Sch. Design, 1961. Partner, Conn. Design Collaborative, Newtown, 1965-76; ptnr. Architects and Designers, N.Y.C., 1976-83; prof. emeritus design, curriculum dir. Parsons Sch. Design, N.Y.C.; prin. Gould Design, Atlanta, 1983—; design editor Haas Pub./So. Homes Mag., Atlanta, 1983—; pres., vice chmn. Integrated Devels., Inc., Atlanta, 1983—; ptnr. Bernstein, Gould Constrn. Mgmt., Atlanta; cons. Nat. Steel Corp., Parsippany, N.J., 1978-80, Tech. Adv. Service Attys., Phila., 1979—; designer, inventor TV program Office Future, Citicorp N.A., 1979. Commr., Lake Lillinonah Authority, 1969-76; mem. Planning Bd. #5, N.Y.C., 1976-78. Served to capt. U.S. Army, 1963-69. Recipient 1st prize furniture design Nat. Cotton Batting Inst., 1960; Award of Merit/Design in Steel, Nat. Steel Inst., 1974. Mem. Indsl. Designers Soc. Am., Constrn. Specifications Inst., Nat. Council Interior Design Qualifications. Republican. Episcopalian. Office: Gould Design Suite 1106 3390 Peachtree Rd NE Atlanta GA 30326

GOURLEY, JAMES LELAND, editor, publisher; b. Mounds, Okla., Jan. 29, 1925; s. Samuel O. and Lodema (Scott) G.; B.L.S., U. Okla., 1963; m. Vicki Graham Clark, Nov. 24, 1976; children—James Leland II, Janna Lynn, Kelly, Brandon. Pres., pub., editor Daily Free-Lance, Henryetta, Okla., 1955-73, Friday newspaper, Oklahoma City, 1973—; pres. Hugo (Okla.) Daily News, 1953-63; chief staff to Gov. Okla., 1959-63; chmn., pres. State Capitol Bank Oklahoma City, 1962-69; pres. KHEN-AM-FM, Henryetta, 1950-71; v.p. KJEM-AM-FM, Oklahoma City, 1962-67, KXOJ-AM, Sapulpa, Okla., 1973-75. Democratic candidate gov. Okla., 1966; vice chmn. U. Okla. Master Plan, 1967; mem. nat. council State Govts., 1960-63; bd. dirs. So. Regional Edn. Bd., 1959-67; dist. chmn. Boy Scouts Am., 1962-64; exec. dir. Gov.'s Commn. on Higher Edn., 1960-61, Okla. crusade chmn. Am. Cancer Soc., 1964; chmn. Okla. Lake Redevel. Authority, 1960-63. Bd. dirs., Okla. Symphony Soc., 1976—, Oklahoma City Crimestoppers, 1984—; Salvation Army, 1986—; mem. Gov.'s Reform Commn., 1984. Served to maj. AUS, 1942-46. Recipient Best Newspaper Advt. award Suburban Newspapers Am., 1976, 82, 84; Best Weekly Newspaper award Okla. Press Assn., 1977, 78, 79, 80, 83, 84,85; Best Small City daily award, 13 times; named to Okla. Journalism Hall of Fame, 1980; Okla. Heritage Edit. award, 1972. Mem. Oklahoma City C. of C. (dir. 1963—), Okla. State C. of C. (dir. 1983—), UPI Editors Okla. (pres. 1958-59), Suburban Newspapers Am. (dir. 1978—), Okla. Press Assn. (dir. 1981—), Sigma Delta Chi. Mem. Christian Ch. Disciples of Christ (pres. Okla. 1964-65). Clubs: Rotary (dir. 1980—), Oklahoma City Golf and Country, Oklahoma City Econs., Oklahoma City Men's Dinner. Home: 1605 W Wilshire Oklahoma City OK 73116 Office: Box 20340 Oklahoma City OK 73156

GOVE, DOROTHY BERYL, civic worker; b. Haverhill, Mass., Apr. 14, 1905; d. Maurice Leslie and Minnie Evelyn (Tilton) McDaniel; m. William Lionel Gove; children—Inez Beryl Gove Riley, Barbara Evelyn, William Lionel, Donna Ilene Gove Matthews. Student Hall Hosp. Nurses Tng.; grad. Lincoln Inst. Practical Nursing, 1952. Lic. practical nurse, Mass. Treas., sec., founder Pioneer Nursing Assn., Malden, Mass., 1950-60; treas., founder WWI Vets., Woburn, Mass., 1944-60; vol. ARC, Mass., 1952-59; girl scout leader Boston council Girl Scouts U.S.A., 1942-54; leader, founder 4-H, Woburn, 1942-55; mem. Mayor's Democratic race, Woburn, 1943; vol. health and rehab. services Hillsborough County, Tampa, Fla., 1979—; vol. James A. Haley Vets. Hosp., Tampa, 1979—; officer D.A.V. organs., Brandon, Fla.; nat. aux. commdr. Wm. L. Gove Sr. Veterans Inc., Valrico, Fla., 1979—. Mem. D.A.V., Aux. (life), Marine Corps League in Fla. (hon.), Wm. L. Gove Sr. Vets. Aux. (life, founder), Brandon C. of C. Lodges: Women of Moose (founder aux.); Order Eastern Star. Office: Wm L Gove Sr Veterans PO Box 369 Valrico FL 33594

GOYTISOLO, AGUSTIN DE, lawyer; b. Havana, Cuba, Nov. 28, 1924; s. Agustin Alejo and Dolores (Recio) de G.; m. Josefina Gelats de Leon, Sept. 14, 1957; children—Agustin G., Josie, Maria G., Dolores G. J.D., Havana U., 1947; M. Comparative Law, Georgetown U., 1968. Bar: Fla. 1977. Ptnr. firm Salaya & Casteleiro, Havana, 1947-60; prin. Dogwood Developers, Inc., McLean, Va., 1961-73; assoc. firm Helliwell Merlrose & DeWolf, Miami, Fla., 1974-78; ptnr. firm Mahoney Hadlow & Adams, Miami, 1977-80; of counsel Trenan Simmons Kemker Scharff Barkin Frye & O'Neill, Miami, 1984—; dir., counsel Cuban Nat. Planning Council, Miami, 1976—. Bd. dirs. Jesuit Fathers Province of Antilles, Miami, 1976—, Agrupacion Catolica, U. Miami, 1978—. Mem. ABA, Fla. Bar, Interam. Bar Assn. Roman Catholic. Clubs: Miami, American. Home: 4810 Alhambra Circle Coral Gables FL 33146 Office: 1000 Alfred I duPont Bldg Miami FL 33131

GRABOSKI, THOMAS WALTER, designer, artist; b. Chgo., Oct. 20, 1947; s. Walter and Marie (Wruble) G.; m. Gina Goodin, Dec. 29, 1984. B.A. in Fine Arts, Arts Ctr. Coll. Design, 1971; M.S. in Urban Design, U. Miami, 1977. Free lance design cons. Miami, 1976-80; owner, pres. Tom Graboski Assoc., Inc., Miami, 1980—; dir. Miami Art Community Helpers, 1984—. One man shows include Medici Berenson Gallery, 1980. Represented inpermanent collections Miami gallery 99, Virginia Miller Artspace, Gallery West, Cornblatt Gallery. Mem. Soc. Environ. Graphic Designers, Indsl. Design Soc. Am., Inst. Bus. Designers, Am. Inst. Architects (affiliate). Avocation: collecting antique toys. Office: Tom Graboski Assoc Inc 3300 Rice St No 8 Coconut Grove FL 33133

GRABOWSKI, GEORGE JOSEPH, JR., oil company geologist; b. Huntington, N.Y., June 21, 1952; s. George Joseph and Elsa (Larsen) G.; m. Deborah Elizabeth Scott, May 26, 1974. B.S. in Geology, Bucknell U., 1974; M.A. in Geology, Johns Hopkins U., 1976; Ph.D. in Geology, Rice U., 1981. Geologist, Ky. Geol. Survey., U. Ky., Lexington, 1976-78; research specialist, project leader Exxon Prodn. Research Co., Houston, 1981—. Co-author: Geol. map of Ky., 1981; author article on Ph.D. dissertation (Best Paper 1981), 1981. Gulf Oil Found. fellow, 1981; recipient Grad. Merit award for Research and Edn. Rice U.-Tex. Med. Ctr. chpt. Sigma Xi, 1981; named Outstanding Student Houston Geol. Soc., 1981. Mem. Am. Assn. Petroleum Geologists, Soc. Econ. Paleontologists and Mineralogists, Internat. Assn. Sedimentologists. Avocations: camping; sailing. Office: Exxon Production Research Co PO Box 2189 Houston TX 77001

GRACE, JAMES MARTIN, insurance company executive; b. Youngstown, Ohio, Aug. 12, 1943; s. Philip Murray and Jean Anita (Raupple) G.; m. Letitia Jean Stively, Apr. 16, 1966; children—James M., Karin L., Susan M., Kimberly J., Gregory J. B.B.A., U. Notre Dame, 1965. C.P.A., Ohio, Tex. Staff acct. Peat, Marwick & Mitchell, 1969-70; controller Colamco, Inc., 1970-71; v.p., sec.-treas. Fin. Industries Corp., Austin, Tex., 1971—, v.p., controller, treas., 1971—, also dir. subs. Knickerbocker Life Ins. Co.; v.p., treas., dir. Inter Continental Life Corp., pres. Inter Continental Life Ins. Co., both subs. Fin. Industries Corp. Active local ch. lay leadership. Served to 1st lt. U.S. Army, 1965-67. Mem. Fin. Execs. Inst., Am. Inst. C.P.A.s, Ohio Inst. C.P.A.s. Office: 1900 InterFirst Tower 515 Congress Ave Austin TX 78701

GRACE, KENNETH MAYNARD, mental health cons.; b. Superior, Wis., May 24, 1924; s. George Washington and Lenora (Jensen) G.; B.A., U. N.D., 1949; M.S.W., U. Denver, 1953; m. Olive C. Krefting; children—Keith, Barbara, David, Cathryn. Child welfare worker Benson County (N.D.) Welfare Bd., 1950-52, 53-55; psychiat. social worker Cass County Children's Social Service Center, Fargo, N.D., 1955-60, Western Mental Health Center, Marshall, Minn., 1960-64; exec. dir. Eastside Community Mental Health Center, Bellevue, Wash., 1964-73; dir. mental health Dallas County Mental Health and Mental Retardation Center, 1973-75; mental health cons., Plano, Tex., 1975-77; chmn. bd., pres. Am. Interlocked Mental Services, Seattle, 1975—; mental health cons. HEW/USPHS Alcohol, Drug Abuse and Mental Health Region VI, Dallas, 1977-82, HHS/USPHS Health Resources Devel. Region VI, Dallas, 1982—. Served with AUS, 1943-46; ETO. Recipient award VFW of U.S., Grand Forks, 1949; Adminstr.'s Spl. citation Health Resources and Services Adminstrn., USPHS, 1983. Mem. Puget Council Mental Health Programs (pres. 1971-73), Nat. Council Community Mental Health Centers (dir. 1971-73). Home: 3812 Yosemite St Plano TX 75023 Office: 18th Floor 1200 Main Tower Dallas TX 75202

GRACIDA, RENE HENRY, bishop; b. New Orleans, June 9, 1923; s. Henry J. and Mathilde (Derbes) G. Student Rice U., 1942-43; B.S. in Architecture, U. Houston, 1950; postgrad. U. Fribourg, Switzerland, 1950, St. Vincent Coll., Latrobe, Pa., 1951-53, St. Vincent Major Sem., 1953-60. Faculty U. Houston Sch. Architecture, 1948-51; practice architecture with Donald Bartheline & Assos., Houston, 1949-51; ordained deacon Roman Catholic Ch., 1958, priest, 1959, bishop, 1971; asst. pastor Holy Family Parish, North Miami, Fla., 1961-62, St. Coleman Parish, Pompano Beach, Fla., 1962-63, St. Matthew Parish, Hallandale, Fla., 1963-64; adminstr. St. Ambrose Parish, Deerfield Beach, Fla., 1964; asst. pastor Visitation Parish, North Dade, Fla., 1964-65; adminstr. St. Ann Parish, Naples, Fla., 1966-67; pastor Nativity Parish, Hollywood, Fla., 1967-69; rector St. Mary Cathedral, Miami, Fla., 1969-71, St. Patrick Parish, Miami Beach, Fla., 1971-72; pastor St. Kiernan Parish, Miami, 1973-75; 1st bishop Diocese of Pensacola-Tallahassee, 1975-83; apptd. 5th bishop Diocese of Corpus Christi (Tex.), 1983—; mem. Archdiocesan Bldg. Commn., Archdiocese of Miami, 1961-75, sec., 1962-65, chmn., 1967-73, West Coast Deanery, Human Relations Bd., 1966-67; senator Priests Senate, 1967-69, archdiocesan consultor, 1967-75; chmn. Broward Deanery, Human Relations Bd., 1967-69, chancellor, 1968-72, treas., 1969-72, vicar gen., 1969-75; steering com. Biennial Congress Worship, 1966-72; aux. bishop Archdiocese Miami, 1971-75, supt. edn., 1973-75; chmn. com. on migration and tourism Nat. Conf. Cath. Bishops, 1975-81; nat. episcopal promoter of Apostleship of the Sea in U.S., 1975—; Important archtl. works include: remodelling St. Vincent Archabbey Basilica, Latrobe, Ch. of the Nativity, Hollywood, St. Ambrose Ch., Deerfield Beach. Pres. Community Action Fund; bd. dirs. Community Act Fund, 1966-72; mem. bishop's com. liturgy Nat. Conf. Cath. Bishops, 1972-77, chmn., Address: Chancery Office 620 Lipan St Corpus Christi TX 78401

GRADDICK, CHARLES ALLEN, state attorney general; b. Mobile, Ala., Dec. 10, 1944; s. Julian and Elvera (Smith) G.; m. Corinne Whiting, Aug. 19, 1966; children—Charles Allen, Herndon Whiting, Corinne. J.D., U. Ala., 1970. Bar: Ala. 1970. Clk., Ala. Supreme Ct., 1970; asst. dist. atty. Mobile County, Ala., 1971-75, dist. atty., 1975-79; atty. gen. State of Ala., Montgomery, 1979—. Served with N.G., 1969-75. Named Outstanding Young Man of Mobile, Mobile Jr. C. of C., 1976; recipient Appreciation cert. Ala. Peace Officers, 1978, Appreciation award Optimists, 1978. Mem. Nat. Assn. Attys. Gen., Am. Trial Lawyers Assn., ABA, Ala. Bar Assn., Ala. Dist. Attys. Assn., Nat. Dist. Attys. Assn. Democrat. Episcopalian. Office: Office of Atty Gen 64 N Union St Montgomery AL 36130*

GRADY, FRANK JOSEPH, ophthalmologist; b. Bklyn., Aug. 14, 1941; s. Richard Patrick and Mildred (Thau) G.; m. Donna Ruth Holt, July 10, 1976; children—Jonathan, Brent. B.S., Columbia U., 1961; M.D., Yale U., 1965; Ph.D., CUNY, 1970. Diplomate Am. Bd. Ophthalmology. Intern Hosp. of U. Pa., 1965-66; chief resident Columbia Presbyterian Hosp., N.Y.C., 1970; chief ophthalmology USPHS Hosp., Glaveston, Tex., 1970-73; pres. Brazosport Eye Clinic, Lake Jackson, Tex., 1973—; clin. asst. prof. U. Tex., Houston, 1973—. Served to comdr. USPHS, 1970-73. Fellow ACS, Am. Acad. Ophthalmology; mem. Keratorefractive Soc., Am. Intraocular Implant Soc., Tex. Ophthalmology Soc., Phi Beta Kappa, Alpha Omega Alpha. Lodge: Rotary. Office: Brazosport Eye Facility 103 Parking Way Lake Jackson TX 77566

GRADY, JOHN EDWARD, JR., publisher, entrepreneur; b. Boston, June 15, 1935; s. John Edward and Catherine Agnes (Connolly) G.; A.B., Harvard U., 1956, M.B.A., 1965; children—John Edward, Robert Emmet McDonnell, Douglas Anderson. Account exec. Merrill Lynch, Pierce, Fenner & Smith, N.Y.C., 1960-63; sr. asso. Cresap, McCormick and Paget, N.Y.C., 1965-69; v.p., Investment Mgmt. and Research, Inc., St. Petersburg, Fla., 1969-70; v.p. fin., treas. Suncoast Highland Corp., Largo, Fla., 1970-74, v.p. fin. and ops., sec.-treas., 1974-76, dir., 1970-76; v.p. corporate fin. Raymond, James & Assos., Inc., St. Petersburg, Fla., 1976-82; pub. Art Product News, 1982—; pres. Grady Pub. Co., 1982—, pres. In-Art Pub Co., 1982—. Regional chmn. Harvard Bus. Sch. Fund, 1971-74; mem. pres. roundtable Eckerd Coll., 1971-81; mem. Tampa Bay Area Com. Fgn. Relations, 1979—. Trustee Canterbury Sch. Fla., 1973-79, treas. bd. trustees, 1974-75, chmn., 1975-76; mem. com. social service allocations, City of St. Petersburg, 1978; trustee Fla. Orch., St. Petersburg-Tampa, 1979—, St. Petersburg Boychoir, 1980-82; asso. Harvard U. Alumni (Cambridge) (com. on schs. and scholarships, 1980—, com. on Harvard Clubs, 1980—); mem. com. of 100, 1984—. Served to lt. (j.g.) USNR, 1956-60. Clubs: Harvard West Coast (pres. 1975-78, schs. and scholarships chmn. 1978—), Rotary, St. Petersburg (Fla.) Yacht; Suncoast Tiger Bay, Harvard Bus. Sch. Fla. West Coast (dir. 1976—, pres. 1983— (St. Petersburg-Tampa). Home: 5910 Bayou Grande Blvd NE Saint Petersburg FL 33703 Office: 300 3d Ave N Saint Petersburg FL 33701

GRADY, M. G., clergyman. Bishop, Church of God in Christ, Southwest Tex., San Antonio. Office: Ch of God in Christ 325 Terrell Rd San Antonio TX 78209*

GRADY, THOMAS J., bishop; b. Chgo., Oct. 9, 1914; s. Michael and Rose (Buckley) G. S.T.L., St. Mary of Lake Sem., Mundelein, Ill., 1938; student Gregorian U., Rome, 1938-39; M.A. in English, Loyola U., Chgo., 1944. Ordained priest Roman Catholic Ch., 1938; prof. Quigley Prep. Sem., Chgo., 1939-45; procurator St. Mary of Lake Sem., 1945-56; dir. Nat. Shrine Immaculate Conception, Washington, 1956-67; titular bishop Vamalla, aux. bishop Chgo., 1967-74; pastor St. Hilary Ch., Chgo., 1968-74, St. Joseph Ch., Libertyville, Ill., 1974; bishop of Orlando, Fla., 1974—; Chgo. Archdiocesan dir. seminaries and post-ordination priestly tng., 1967-74; chmn. Chgo. Archdiocesan Liturgical Commn., 1968-74; dir. program Permanent Diaconate, Chgo., 1969-74; cons. Bishops' Com. on Priestly Formation, 1967—, chmn., 1969-72; mem. Ad Hoc Com. on Priestly Life and Ministry, 1971-73;

chmn. Bishops' Com. on Priestly Life and Ministry, 1973—. Home: Roman Catholic Ch PO Box 458 Orlando FL 32819*

GRADY-MCDONNELL, SHERRY ANN, engineer; b. Alexandria, Va., May 2, 1953; d. John David and Dorothy Howard G.; student U. N.C., Greensboro, 1971-73; grad. N.C. State U., 1977; m. Peter Daniel McDonnell, Mar. 27, 1982; 1 son, Peter Daniel; 1 stepdau., Melissa Margaret Ann. With Contractors & Engrs. Services, Goldsboro, N.C., 1976—, engr. in charge of chem. lab., also found. and indsl. engring., 1977—, also corp. sec.; corp. sec.-treas. EasyLease Corp.; mem. 1981 Chem. Week Mgmt. Adv. Panel. Mem. Nat. Soc. Profls. Engrs., Soc. Women Engrs. (co-founder N.C. State U. chpt., 1st v.p. pre-charter club 1974-75), Soc. Am. Mil. Engrs. (nominating com.), Profl. Engrs. of N.C. (asso.). Republican. Methodist. Office: PO Box 762 1304 N William St Goldsboro NC 27530

GRAF, JOSEPH CHARLES, foundation executive; b. Jersey City, Sept. 10, 1928; s. John Bernard and Margaret Cecilia (Toomey) G.; B.S., Seton Hall U., 1949; M.B.A., U. Pa., 1954; m. Joleen Schovee, Jan. 22, 1983; children—Claire, Joseph Charles, Michelle, Mary Ellen, Thomas, Richard; stepchildren —Thomas R. Schovee, Stephen W. Schovee, Kathryn L. Schovee. Trainee, Prudential Ins. Co., Newark, 1954-55, systems analyst, 1955-56, asst. research analyst, 1956-58, research analyst, 1958-61, investment analyst, 1961-63, sr. investment analyst, 1963-64, Houston, 1964-67; v.p. So. Nat. Bank, Houston, 1967-69; fin. advisor Quintana Petroleum Corp., Houston, 1969-79, investment mgr., 1979-83; dir. USAlamo, Inc., Triten Corp., Internat. Bank Fin., Cayman Islands; mem. investment com. trust dept. Cullen Bank & Trust. Cons. research com. Houston C. of C., 1966-71; exec. sec. Cullen Found., 1974—; bd. govs., v.p. Center for Retarded Inc., Houston; bd. dirs. Alley Theatre, 1981-83; bd. advisers Wharton Club of Houston. Served with AUS, 1951-53. Mem. Houston Fin. Analysts (pres. 1973-74, dir. 1974-77). Clubs: Houston, Houstonian. Home: 6205 Pickens St Houston TX 77007

GRAFF, GARY WENDELL, history educator, college administrator; b. Mineola, N.Y., June 28, 1944; s. George Ernest and Edna Kathryn (Sauerwein) G.; m. Sharon Joan Sacks, Jan. 10, 1969; 1 son, Jason. A.B., U. Rochester, 1966; M.A., U. Wis., 1969, Ph.D., 1973. Instr. history W.Va. State Coll., Institute, 1971-73, asst. prof., 1973-75, assoc. prof., 1975-84, dir. planning and mgmt., 1975-79, dir. instl. research and planning, 1979-84; dir. instl. research No. Ky. U., 1984—; symposium collaborator Cambridge U., 1986. Cub master Cub Scouts, 1980-83, explorer post adviser, 1984. bd. dirs. Multi-County Action Against Proverty, 1976-78. Fulbright Hayes fellow, 1969-70. Mem. Assn. Instl. Research, Soc. Coll. and Univ. Planning, Latin Am. Studies Assn., U. Wis. Alumni Assn. (bd. dirs. 1986). Lodge: Kiwanis (past pres. 1979). Office: Adminstrv Center No Ky U Highland Heights KY 41076

GRAFT, ROSEMARY NICHOLSON, government program administrator; b. Meridian, Miss., Feb. 10, 1941; d. Roosevelt Ted and Mary Adeline (Burt) Thomas; student Ga. State U., Atlanta, Edison Community Coll., Ft. Myers, Fla.; m. Bobby Lee Nicholson, Aug. 9, 1958; children—Keith Wade, Sheila Kay, Glenn Alan; m. Donald R. Graft, Aug. 10th, 1985. With Social Security Adminstrn., 1965—, asst. dist. mgr., Lakeland, Fla., 1979-80, dist. mgr., Ft. Myers Fla., 1980—. Bd. dirs. Community Coordinating Council Lee County, 1982-83, 85-86, rec. sec., 1983-84; mem. advocacy com. of Mental Health Assn. of Lee County, 1983-84; mem. citizens adv. com. Lee County's Small Cities Program. Recipient various HEW awards. Mem. Am. Bus. Women's Assn. (chpt. pres. 1977, 79, v.p. 1981-82; chpt. Women of Yr. award 1978), Fla. Assn. Health and Social Services (v.p. S.E. chpt. 1981-84, state v.p. 1983-84, state bd. dirs. 1985-87), Nat. Assn. Female Execs., Am. Soc. Profl. and Exec. Women, Social Security Mgmt. Assn. (Atlanta regional rep. to mgmt. com., nat. council), Atlanta Regional Mgmt. Assn., Ft. Myers Network. Democrat. Baptist. Club: Zonta Internat. (corr. sec.) (Ft. Myers). Office: 3090 Evans Ave PO Box 06259 Fort Myers FL 33906

GRAHAM, ARDIS, computer company executive, consultant; b. Marshall, Tex., Mar. 15, 1947; s. Willie and Sally Pearl (Broadnax) G.; m. LaVivian Jones, May 31, 1969; children—Erika, Traci. A.S. in Math., EL Centro Coll., Dallas, 1972; B.A. in Math., U. Tex.-Arlington, 1974. Cert. info systems auditor. Acct., Viking Internat. Travel, Dallas, 1972-73; computer programmer Anderson Clayton Foods, Dallas, 1973-74; computer auditor Arthur Young & Co., Dallas, 1974-79; pres., chief exec. officer Computer Controls, Inc., Dallas, 1979—; mem. U.S. Congress Adv. Bd., 1982—. Bd. dirs. Deaf Action Ctr., Dallas, 1982—; mem. Mayor's Task Force on So. Dallas, 1983. Served to E-5 USN, 1967-74; Vietnam. Ellen B. Demar Scholar, Dallas, 1965. Mem. EDP Auditor Assn. (treas. 1976), Assn. for Systems Mgmt., Nat. Assn. Accts., U. Tex. Acctg. Alumni Assn. (Arlington chpt.), Beta Alpha Psi. Baptist. Avocation: computer research. Office: Computer Controls Inc 1430 Empire Central #130 Dallas TX 75247

GRAHAM, CARL FRANCIS, consultant, former chemical products company executive; b. Limon, Colo., Jan. 2, 1915; s. Karl and Edith (Nesselrode) G.; m. Marjorie Ruth Killebrew, Apr. 27, 1941; children—David Carl, Nancy Lou Graham Flink, Carol Ann. B.S., Baker U., 1938; postgrad. U. Kansas City, 1938-39. Head of lab. Procter and Gamble Mfg. Co., Kansas City, Kans., 1938-41; sec. head research dept. J.B. Ford Co., Wyandotte, Mich., 1941-43; supr. analytical research Wyandotte Chems. Corp. (Mich), 1943-56, mgr. analytical research, 1956-57; dir. research and devel. Turco Products Inc., Wilmington, Calif., 1957-65; adminstrv. asst. to v.p. chem. research Purex Corp., Ltd., Wilmington, 1964-65; mgr. research and devel. Amway Corp., Ada, Mich., 1967-70, mgr. industry and govt. tech. relations, 1970-72, sr. adviser legis. and regulatory standards, 1970-76, mgr. govt. affairs, 1976-81; cons., Royal Palm Beach, Fla., 1981—; cons. Chem. Corps., U.S. Army, 1952-62, Chem-Biol.-Radio Agy., Edgewood Arsenal (Md.), 1962-63. Fellow Am. Inst. Chemists; mem. Am. Chem. Soc. (com. nat. def. 1963-70), ASTM (councilor Detroit dist. 1955-57, councilor So. Calif. Dist. 1962-66), Soap and Detergent Assn. (legal com. tech. and materials div. 1970-74, mem. legis. subcom. 1974-81; chmn. eutrophication task force 1980-81), Cosmetic, Toiletry and Fragrance Assn. (govt. relations com. 1972-80), Chem. Splty. Mfrs. Assn. (chmn. div. legis. standards 1971-77, bd. govs. 1976-78, 81, chmn. state pub. affairs com. 1979-81, vice chmn. detergents and cleaning compounds div. 1979-80, div. chmn. 1981), Am. Def. Preparedness Assn. (tech. com. on surface preservation 1958-66), Chemists Club N.Y. Home and Office: 85 Wood Rose Ct Royal Palm Beach FL 33411

GRAHAM, CHARLES GEORGE, real estate developer; b. Daytona Beach, Fla., Sept. 8, 1946; s. Charles Mayerhoff and Della Stansfield G.; m. Carol Anne Bissmeyer, Aug. 16, 1969; children—Katherine, Brittany, Kristan, Lauren. B.Arch. magna cum laude, U. Notre Dame, 1969; M.B.A., Harvard U., 1972. Registered architect, Ohio. Designer, Skidmore, Owings & Merrill Architects, Chgo., 1969-70; div. mgr. Towne Properties Ltd., Cin., 1972-78; v.p. Chelsea Moore Devel. Corp., Cin., 1978-81; v.p. mktg., John Crosland Co., Charlotte, N.C., 1981—. Active Cin. Inst., Ptnrs. in Edn. Mem. AIA (housing com.; Sch. medal), Nat. Assn. Home Builders (design com., v.p. nat. sales and mktg. council), Inst. Residential Mktg. (trustee), Tau Beta Pi, Tau Sigma Delta. Republican. Roman Catholic. Home: 245 Medearis Dr Charlotte NC 28211 Office: PO Box 11231 Charlotte NC 28220

GRAHAM, CHARLES WESLEY, architect; b. Kerrville, Tex., June 13, 1951; s. Lee Roy and Helen Louise (Garner) G.; m. Bess M'Liss Shipman, July 12, 1974; children—D'Nae Nichole, M'Rhea Leoma. B.Arch., Tex. Tech U., 1974; M.A., U. Tex.-San Antonio, 1978; postgrad Tex. A&M U., 1982—. Registered architect, Tex. Lectr., Tex. A&M U., 1982—; prin. Charles W. Graham & Assocs., San Antonio, 1978-82; instr. San Antonio Acad. Real Estate, 1978-80; research engr. U. Tex., San Antonio, 1978-79; research assoc. Tex. A&M U., College Station, 1984—. Author: Housing Issues, 1985. Grantee Tex. Manufactured Housing Assn., 1984, 85, U.S. Dept. Transp., 1979, Nat. Endowment Arts, 1979. Mem. AIA (treas. Brazos chpt. 1984, bd. dirs. San Antonio 1980-82), Tex. Soc. Architects (chmn. profl. devel. com. 1983), Am. Planning Assn., Urban Land Inst., Tau Sigma Delta. Avocations: Hunting; fishing; art; welding; woodworking. Home: 632 San Mario Ct College Station TX 77840 Office: PO Box 2738 College Station TX 77841

GRAHAM, COLE BLEASE, JR., political science educator; b. White Rock, S.C., Aug. 22, 1942; s. Cole Blease and Bonnie Wylene (Sites) G.; m. Elizabeth Camille Griffin, Dec. 30, 1964 (div. Dec. 1974); children—Cole Blease III, Camelia Macfarlane. B.A., Wofford Coll., 1963; M.A., Northwestern La. U., 1964; M.Govt. Adminstrn., U. Pa., 1965; Ph.D., U. S.C., 1971. Adminstrv. asst. Port Authority N.Y. and N.J., 1965-66; research asst. U. S.C., Columbia, 1966-68; asst. prof., 1971-76, assoc. prof., 1976—; planning dir. Richland Meml. Hosp., Columbia, 1968-71; field assoc. Brookings Instn., Washington, 1973-81. Editor: (with others) Local Government in South Carolina, 1984. Bd. dirs. S.C. affiliate Am. Heart Assn., Columbia, 1977-80; polit. analyst WIS-TV, Columbia, 1980-82; candidate Congl. Primary Campaign, 2d Dist., S.C., 1974; Recipient Bronze award S.C. Heart Assn. 1972. Mem. Am. Polit. Sci. Assn., Am. Soc. Pub. Adminstrn., So. Polit. Sci. Assn., Phi Beta Kappa (pres. Alpha chpt. 1978-79). Democrat. Lutheran. Avocations: tennis, philately. Office: Dept Govt U SC Gambrell Hall Columbia SC 29208

GRAHAM, D. ROBERT (BOB), governor of Florida; b. Coral Gables, Fla., Nov. 9, 1936; m. Adele Khoury; children—Gwendolyn Patricia, Glynn Adele, Arva Suzanne, Kendall Elizabeth. B.A., U. Fla., 1959; LL.B., Harvard U., 1962. Atty.; cattle and dairy farmer; real estate developer; mem. Fla. Ho. of Reps., 1966-70; mem. Fla. Senate, 1971-78; gov. State of Fla., Tallahassee, 1979—; chmn. Edn. Commn. of the States, Caribbean/C. Am. Action, U.S. intergovtl. adv. council on edn., So. Growth Policies Bd.; chmn. elect So. Govs.' Assn.; chmn. com. trade and fgn. affairs Nat. Govs.' Assn. Active 4-H Youth Found., Nat. Commn. on Reform Secondary Edn., Nat. Found. Improvement Edn., Nat. Com. for Citizens in Edn., Sr. Centers of Dade County, Fla.; chmn. So. Regional Edn. Bd.; candidate for U.S. Senate from Fla., 1986. Named one of 5 Most Outstanding Young Men in Fla., Fla. Jaycees, 1971; recipient Allen Morris award for outstanding 1st term mem. senate, 1972, Allen Morris award for most valuable mem. of Senate, 1973, Allen Morris award for 2d most effective senator, 1976. Mem. Fla. Bar. Democrat. Mem. United Ch. of Christ. Office: Office of Gov The Capitol Tallahassee FL 32301*

GRAHAM, JAMES BUTLER, JR., communications company executive; b. Aberdeen, Md., May 2, 1953 (dec. 1985). s. James Butler and Louise (Nystrom) G.; m. Deborah Ann Wood, Sept. 6, 1975. B.S. in Fin., Va. Poly. Inst., 1975, M.B.A., 1980. Mgr. adminstrn. Electronic Mail, Inc., McLean, Va., 1976-79; dir. fin. Carnegie Endowment, Washington, 1979-82; div. dir. Western Union GSD, McLean, 1982-83; exec. product mgr. Western Union Corp., Upper Saddle River, N.J., 1983-84; pres., chief exec. officer Cellular Radio Corp., Vienna, Va., 1984—, also dir. Contbr. articles to profl. jours. Del. Va. Republican Conv., Richmond, 1976, 80. Mem. Am. Mgmt. Assn., Am. Mktg. Assn., Armed Forces Electronics and Communications Assn. Clubs: Dunes (Narragansette, R.I.); Sporting (McLean); Tournament Players (Avenel, Md.). Avocations: golf; tennis. Home: 6553 Dearborn Dr Falls Church VA 22044

GRAHAM, JOHN BORDEN, medical educator; b. Goldsboro, N.C., Jan. 26, 1918; s. Ernest Heap and Mary (Borden) G.; B.S., Davidson Coll., 1938, D.Sc., 1984; C.Med., U. N.C., 1940; M.D., Cornell U., 1942; m. Ruby Barrett, Mar. 23, 1943; children—Charles Barrett, Virginia Borden, Thomas Wentworth. Asst. Cornell U., 1943-44; mem. faculty U. N.C., Chapel Hill, 1946—, Alumni Disting. prof. pathology, 1966—, chmn. genetics curriculum, 1963—, assoc. dean medicine for basic scis., 1968-70, coordinator interdisciplinary grad. programs in biology, 1968—, dir. hemostasis program, 1974—; vis. prof. haematology St. Thomas's Hosp. Med. Sch., London, 1972; vis. prof. Teikyo U. Med. Sch., Tokyo, 1976; mem. selection com. NIH research career awards, 1959-62; genetics tng. com. USPHS, 1962-66, chmn., 1967-71; mem. genetic basis of disease com. Nat. Inst. Gen. Med. Scis., 1977-78; mem. pathology test com. Nat. Bd. Med. Examiners, 1963-67; mem. research adv. com. U. Colo. Inst. for Behavioral Genetics, 1967-71; mem. Internat. Com. Haemostasis and Thrombosis, 1963-67; chmn. bd. U. N.C. Population Program, 1964-67; sec. policy bd. Carolina Population Center, 1972-78; cons. Environ. Health Center, USPHS, WHO; mem. med. and sci. adv. council Nat. Hemophilia Found., 1972-80; hon. cons. in genetics Margaret Pyke Centre, London, 1972—. Served as capt. M.C., AUS, 1944-46. Decorated Combat Med. badge, Presdl. Unit citation; Markle scholar in med. sci., 1949-54. Recipient O. Max Gardner award U. N.C., 1968. Mem. AMA, AAAS, Elisha Mitchell Sci. Soc. (pres. 1963), AAUP, Soc. Exptl. Biology and Medicine, Am. Soc. Exptl. Pathology, Assn. U. Pathologists, Am. Assn. Pathologists and Bacteriologists, Am. Soc. Human Genetics (sec. 1964-67, pres. 1972), Genetics Soc. Am., Internat. Soc. Hematology, Am. Inst. Biol. Sci., Royal Soc. Medicine (London), Med. Soc. N.C., Mayflower Soc., Sigma Xi. Democrat. Presbyn. Club: Cosmos (Washington). Mem. editorial bd. N.C. Med. Jour., 1949-66, Am. Jour. Human Genetics, 1958-61, Soc. Exptl. Biology and Medicine, 1959-62, Human Genetics Abstracts, 1962—, Christian Scholar, 1958-60. Publs. on blood clotting, inherited diseases in humans, human population dynamics; co-discoverer blood coagulant Factor X (Stuart factor). Home: 108 Glendale Dr Chapel Hill NC 27514 Office: Dept Pathology Sch Medicine U NC Chapel Hill NC 27514

GRAHAM, JOHN STUART, air force non-commissioned officer; b. Charlotte, N.C., Sept. 27, 1948; s. Archie Cunningham and Margaret Evelyn (Wilson) G.; m. Helen Louise Bauer, Apr. 5, 1969; children—Lesley Ann, John-Bauer. A.A., U. Md., 1980, B.S., 1981; postgrad. Vt. Coll. of Norwich U., 1985—. Enlisted U.S. Air Force, 1969, advanced through grades to master sgt.; communications ops. mgr. 74 TCF, Pope Air Force Base, N.C., 1974-76; command post communications mgr. 1964 Communications Group, Ramstein, Fed. Republic Germany, 1976-79; leased voice systems mgr. HQ TAC, Langley Air Force Base, Va., 1979-83; air force adviser DET 2 1816 RAS, Gadsden, Ala., 1983—. Vice pres. Etowah Soccer Assn., Gadsden, 1984—; dir. tng. The Shelter, Inc., Gadsden, 1984-85, chmn. bd., 1985—. Decorated Gallentry Cross (Republic of Vietnam). Mem. Am. Assn. Counseling and Devel., Am. Mental Health Counselors Assn., Air Force Assn., Mil. Educators and Counselors Assn. Democrat. Roman Catholic. Club: Meadowood Community Assn. (pres. 1984—) (Southside, Ala.). Avocations: golf; soccer; boating. Home: Route 1 Box 432 Gadsden AL 35901 Office: DET 2 1816 RAS Martin ANGS Gadsden AL 35901

GRAHAM, KERRY BENNETT, advertising copywriter, actor; b. Portsmouth, Va., Dec. 6, 1957; s. Walter Waverly, III, and Ann Elizabeth (Bennett) G.; m. Linda Kathryn Mockler, Nov. 21, 1981; 1 child, Lindsay Bennett. B.A. in English and Drama, Vanderbilt U., 1979; student Univ. Coll., Oxford (Eng.) U., 1977. Profl. actor radio and TV commls.; TV pilot: Breaking Away; tech. writer, creative cons. Tech. Analysis Corp., Atlanta, 1980-82; from copywriter to sr. copywriter Green & Ptnrs. Advt., Atlanta, 1982-83; copywriter Burton-Campbell Advt., Atlanta, 1983-85; sr. copywriter J. Walter Thompson Advt., Atlanta, 1985—. Charter mem. Atlanta High Mus. Art. Recipient 1st place Addy award Am. Advt. Fedn., 3d place Addy award, 1983; Best Actor award, Vanderbilt U., 1977; AD-Q award for outstanding advt. reader response, 1983; Mktg. Campaign of Yr. award Am. Mktg. Assn., 1985; 1st place Gold Atlanta Addy award, 1984. Mem. AFTRA, Screen Actors Guild, Vanderbilt Alumni Assn., Sigma Chi. Republican. Home: 2354 Virginia Pl NE Atlanta GA 30305 Office: 2828 Tower Pl Atlanta GA 30026

GRAHAM, OSCAR DAVID, research electronics engineer; b. Alpine, Tex., May 25, 1935; s. Joe Stanley and Annie Lorean (Loftin) G.; B.S., Tex. A&M U., 1958, M.S., 1959, Ph.D., 1972; m. Juanita Bricker, Nov. 25, 1955; children—Charles D., Michael W., Donna E., Brenda K., Karen S., Lori R., Ronald R., Gary F., Stephen C., Susan D. Commd. 2d lt. USAF, 1959, advanced through grades to lt. col., 1975; instr. pilot Webb AFB, 1960-65, F-4 aircraft comdr. 497th Tactical Fighter Squadron, Ubon RTAB, 1968-69, tech. mgr., electronic warfare engr. Wright-Patterson AFB, Ohio, Electronic Warfare Div., AFAL, 1969-73, radio frequency lab. dir., asso. prof. elec. engring. dept. U.S. Air Force Acad., Colorado Springs, Colo., 1973-77, communications-electronics officers br. chief Keesler AFB, Miss., 1977-79, ret., 1979; asst. mgr. research, dept. research and devel. S.W. Research Inst., San Antonio, 1979-81, mgr. NDE research, 1981—. Troop scoutmaster Boy Scouts Am., 1979-81; bishop Kettering ward, Dayton, Ohio Ch. Jesus Christ of Latter-Day Saints, 1969-71, bishop Beavercreek ward, Dayton, 1971-73. Decorated D.F.C., Air medal with 9 oak leaf clusters; registered profl. engr., Colo. Mem. IEEE, Am. Soc. Nondestructive Testing, Air Force Assn. Home: Route 5 Box 5708 Boerne TX 78006 Office: Southwest Research Inst PO Drawer 28510 San Antonio TX 78284

GRAHAM, SEP, stockbroker, lawyer; b. Jackson, Miss., June 28, 1954; s. Maxwell O. and Margie (Gerety) G. B.S., U.S. Mil. Acad., 1975; M.B.A., Tex. Tech., 1981, J.D., 1981. Bar: Tex. 1981. Lawyer, Freeman, P.C., Lubbock, Tex., 1981; asst. br. office mgr. E.F. Hutton, Lubbock, 1981—. Bd. dirs. Internat. Sunday Sch. Lesson, Inc., Lubbock, Tex., 1981—; chmn. March of Dimes, West Tex., 1984. Served to capt. U.S. Army, 1975-79. Mem. ABA, Am. Econ. Assn., Econ. History Assn. Republican. Baptist. Avocations: hunting; fishing. Office: E F Hutton 1655 Main St Lubbock TX 79401

GRAHAM, SHELLEY ANN, law office administrator; ballet director and choreographer; b. Tyler, Tex., Mar. 23, 1950; d. Thomas William Graham and Ruth (Duncan) Thyng; m. Jimmie Harold Gattis, Nov. 21, 1981; 1 child, Lindsay Logan. B.A. in English and Dance, So. Methodist U., 1971. Instr. dance U. Tex.-Austin, 1972-74; instr. ballet Austin Ballet Theatre, 1972-82; legal sec. Coffee & Goldston, Austin, 1976-77; exec. sec. Tex. Surplus Lines Assn., Austin, 1977-78; adminstr. John Lock & Assocs., Austin, 1978-82, 84—; dir. Ballet Theatre of Northwest Fla., Panama City, 1982-84; dir. jr. co. Austin Ballet Theatre, 1973-76. Choreographer (musicals) Once Upon a Mattress, Austin, 1979, Chicago, Austin, 1981; dir. (ballet) Nutcracker, Panama City, Fla., 1983; dir., choreographer (ballet) Beauty and the Beast, Panama City, 1984. Mem., mentor Tex. Sch. for Blind Gifted Student Program, Austin, 1985. Mem. Panama City C. of C., Assn. Legal Adminstrs., ABA, Nat. Assn. Female Execs., Delta Gamma. Roman Catholic. Avocations: dancing; music; interior design. Home: 9301 Quail Meadow Austin TX 78758 Office: John Lock & Assocs 221 W 6th St Suite 1140 Austin TX 78701

GRAHAM, WALTER WILLIAM, JR., engineer, business owner; b. DeQueen, Ark., Mar. 13, 1925; s. Walter William and Grace Abigail (Chapman) G.; m. M. Bobbie Bradley, Sept. 2, 1949; children—Gail Leslie, Walter William III, Robert Bradley. BSCE, U. Ark., 1949, M.S.E., 1974. Engr.-in-tng. U.S. Corps Civil Engrs., Little Rock dist., 1949; insp., designer-in-charge Mehlburger Engrs., Little Rock, 1949-64; pres. W. William Graham, Jr., Inc., Cons. Engrs., Little Rock, 1964—; v.p. Am. Cons. Engrs. Council, 1975-77. Served with USN, 1943-46. Named Engr. of Year 1980, Ark. Assoc. Gen. Contractors. Fellow Am. Cons. Engrs. Council (Past Pres.'s award 1985); mem. Water Pollution Control Fedn., Am. Water Works Assn., ASCE, Am. Arbitration Assn. Presbyterian. Clubs: Rotary-West (Little Rock), Shriners. Home: 8520 Linda Ln Little Rock AR 72207 Office: 100 N Rodney Parham Rd Little Rock AR 72205

GRAHAM, WILLIAM EDGAR, JR., utility company executive, lawyer; b. Jackson Springs, N.C., Dec. 31, 1929; s. William E. and Minnie A. G.; A.B. in Econs., U. N.C., 1952, J.D. with honors, 1956; m. Jean Dixon McLaurin, Nov. 24, 1962; children—William McLaurin, John McMillan, Sally Faircloth. Admitted to N.C. bar, 1956; law clk. to Chief Judge John J. Parker, U.S. Ct. Appeals, 1956-57; practiced law, Charlotte, N.C., 1957-69; judge N.C. Ct. Appeals, 1969-73; v.p., sr. counsel Carolina Power & Light Co., Raleigh, N.C., 1973-76, sr. v.p., gen. counsel, 1976-81, exec. v.p., 1981-85, vice chmn., 1985—. Served with USAF, 1952-54. Mem. ABA, N.C. State Bar, N.C. Bar Assn., Wake County Bar Assn., Am. Judicature Soc. Presbyterian. Office: PO Box 1551 Raleigh NC 27602

GRAHMANN, CHARLES V., bishop; b. Halletsville, Tex., July 15, 1931. Student Assumption-St. John's Sem., Tex. Ordained priest Roman Catholic Ch., 1956. Ordained titular bishop Equilium and aux., San Antonio, 1981—, 1st bishop, Victoria, Tex., 1982—. Office: Roman Catholic Ch Chancery Office PO Box 4708 Victoria TX 77903*

GRAMM, PHIL, U.S. senator; b. Ft. Benning, Ga., July 8, 1942; B.B.A. in Econs., U. Ga., 1964, Ph.D. in Econs., 1967; m. Wendy Lee, 1970; children—Marshall Kenneth, Jefferson Philip. Prof. econs. Tex. A&M U., 1967-78; partner Gramm & Assos., 1971-78; mem. 96th-98th congresses from 6th Congl. Dist. Tex.; mem. U.S. Senate from Tex., 1985—. Named Outstanding Young Man of Yr., Brazos County Jaycees, 1976, One of 5 Outstanding Young Texans, Tex. Jaycees, 1977. Author several books and monographs; contbr. articles to Am. Econ. Rev., Jour. Money, Credit and Banking, Jour. Econ. History. Office: Room 370 Russell Senate Office Bldg Washington DC 20510

GRAMMER, FRANK CLIFTON, oral surgeon, researcher; b. El Dorado, Ark., Aug. 12, 1943; s. Norman Alexander and Lillie Mae (Martin) G.; m. Ann Marie Beller, Feb. 8, 1964 (div. Feb. 1980); children—William Cody, Tamara Ann; m. Sandra Lanier Boyd, July 5, 1980; 1 child, Jeremy Boyd. B.S., Washington U., St. Louis, 1966, D.D.S. summa cum laude, 1968; M.S.D., U. Minn., 1972, Ph.D., 1973. Diplomate Am. Bd. Oral and Maxillofacial Surgery. Research fellow U. Minn., Mpls., 1968-73; practice dentistry specializing in oral surgery, Fayetteville, Ark., 1973—; cons. Cambridge Hosp., Minn., 1972-73; instr. U. Ark., Fayetteville, 1978-79; asst. prof. U. Tenn., Memphis, 1979-80; mem. adv. com. Am. Bd. Oral and Maxillofacial Surgery, Chgo., 1979-85; bd. govs. Antaeus Research Inst., Fayetteville, 1979-85. Contbr. articles to profl. jours., 1968—. Recipient Research award Am. Soc. Oral Surgeons, 1973. Fellow Am. Coll. Oral and Maxillofacial Surgeons, Am. Dental Soc. of Anesthesiologists, Internat. Coll. Dentists, Am. Coll. Dentists; mem. Ark. Soc. Oral and Maxillofacial Surgeons (pres. 1982-84), N.W. Dist. Dental Soc. (pres. 1983-84). Republican. Presbyterian. Club: Fayetteville Country (pres. 1980-81). Avocations: golf; tennis; hunting. Home: 1973 Greenview Fayetteville AR 72701 Office: PO Box 1807 Fayetteville AR 72701

GRANACHER, ROBERT PHILLIP, JR., psychiatrist; b. Peoria, Ill., July 29, 1941; s. Robert Phillip and Mildred Eileen (Spires) G.; B.A., U. Louisville, 1969; M.D., U. Ky., 1972; m. Myra Linda Farmer, July 6, 1968; 1 son, Phillip Garner. Resident, chief resident psychiatry, U. Ky. Med. Sch., Lexington, 1972-74; fellow Harvard Med. Sch./Mass. Gen. Hosp., Boston, 1974-75; asst. prof. psychiatry U. Ky. Med. Sch., Lexington, 1975-77, asso. clin. prof. psychiatry, 1977-82, clin. prof., 1982—; practice medicine, specializing in gen., forensic and neuro-psychiatry, Lexington, 1978—; med. dir. Sleep Disorders Ctr., St. Joseph Hosp., Lexington, 1983—; cons. in psychopharmacology U.S. Dept. Justice, Washington, 1977—. Served with U.S. Army, 1961-62. Diplomate Am. Bd. Psychiatry and Neurology, Am. Bd. Forensic Psychiatry; accredited clin. polysomnographer. Mem. Am. Acad. Psychiatry and the Law, Am. Psychiat. Assn., N.Y. Acad. Sci., AAAS. Author: (with A. Mason) Clinical Handbook of Antipsychotic Drug Therapy, 1980; contbr. articles to profl. jours. Office: St Joseph Office Park 1401 Harrodsburg Rd Lexington KY 40504

GRANADE, KAREN LEE, advertising production manager, designer, illustrator; b. Dumas, Tex., Apr. 19, 1952; d. Monte Lee and Myrna Jewell (Tryon) Thomas; m. Charles T. Granade, July 7, 1973; children—Cynthia Allison, Kyle Terry, Meredith Lee. B.S. in Advt. Design, Tex. Woman's U., 1977; postgrad. Wiesbaden Sch. Art, 1977. Facility supr. Lee Barracks Multi Craft Shop, U.S. Army Recreation Services, Mainz, W. Ger., 1975-77; fashion illustrator Selber Bros. Inc., Shreveport, La., 1977-79; designer/prodn. artist Cathey Graphics Group, Dallas, 1979-81; prodn. mgr. Graphic Response, Dallas, 1981-82; account service Brownlee & Assocs. Advt., Dallas, 1982; prodn. mgr. DBG&H Unltd., Inc., Dallas, 1982—. Active United Cerebral Palsy Parents Group. Recipient Mainz Community Service award Mainz Mil. Community, 1977. Mem. Irving Network of Career Women. Home: 8729 Irongate St Fort Worth TX 76180 Office: DBG&H Unlimited 1430 Empire Central Suite 3000 Dallas TX 75247

GRANAHAN, THOMAS FRANCIS, lawyer; b. Elmhurst, N.Y., Apr. 29, 1926; s. Thomas Francis and Eileen (Barry) G.; m. Jennie, June 15, 1952; children—Jennie Maarie, Eileen. A.B., Fla. State U., 1950; postgrad. in Polit. Sci., 1950-51; J.D., Stetson U., 1962. Bar: Fla. 1963. Diplomate Law Sci. Acad. Am., Ct. Practice Inst. cert. criminal trial specialist, civil trial specialist Nat. Bd. Trial Advocacy. Ptnr. Granahan & Honig, Tampa, Fla., 1964-70; sole practice, Tampa, 1970—; asst. states atty. Hillsborough County (Fla.), 1966-69; rotating substitute city judge Tampa, 1969-72. Served to lt. inf. U.S. Army, 1944-46; ETO. Fla. State U. fellow, 1950-51. Fellow Am. Acad. Criminal Lawyers; mem. Nat. Bd. Trial Advocacy, ABA, Fla. Bar, Assn. Trial Lawyers Am., Am. Judicature Soc., Nat. Coll. Criminal def. Lawyers, Tex. Trial Lawyers, Calif. Trial Lawyers, N.Y. Acad. Scis., N.Y. Trial Lawyers, Internat. Acad. Law and Sci. Lodge: Shriners (Tampa). Home: 5017 Longfellow Ave Tampa FL 33609 Office: 403 Madison St Suite 405 Tampa FL 33602

GRANBERRY, EDWIN PHILLIPS, JR., safety engineer, consultant; b. Orange, N.J., Aug. 20, 1926; s. Edwin Phillips and Mabel (Leflar) G.; B.S., Rollins Coll., 1950; M.B.A., Embry Riddle Aero. U., 1985; cert. profl. chemist; children—Melissa, Edwin Phillips III, James, Jennifer. Weapons system engr. Martin Co., Orlando, Fla., 1958-62; supt. indsl. safety Guided Missiles Range div. Pan Am. World Airways, Cape Canaveral, Fla., 1962-72; mgr. safety engring. and indsl. hygiene Pratt & Whitney Aircraft Group, West Palm Beach, Fla., 1972—; mem. Fla. State Toxic Substances Adv. Council, 1984-88. Scoutmaster, Boy Scouts Am., 1946-74, dist. chmn. Wekiwa dist. Central Fla. council, 1946-74, also council commr., recipient Silver Beaver award, 1960. Served with USNR, 1944-46; CBI, PTO. Fellow Am. Inst. Chemists; mem.

Rollins Coll. Alumni Assn. (dir. 1958-61), Associated Industries Fla., Am. Chem. Soc., Am. Soc. Safety Engrs. (chmn. Gold Coast chpt. 1979-80, pres. 1981-84; regional v.p. 1984—, nat. dir. 1984—), Safety Council Palm Beach County (pres. 1981-82, chmn. bd. 1983, treas. 1984), Am. Nat. Standards Inst., Am. Indsl. Hygiene Assn. Office: PO Box 2691 West Palm Beach FL 33402

GRANDY, CYRUS WILEY, V, trust banker; b. Norfolk, Va., June 12, 1946; s. Cyrus Wiley and Ann (Sterrett) G.; m. Mary Pearson, Dec. 18, 1971 (div. 1983); 1 dau., Catherine Sterrett; m. 2d Edith Graham, Nov. 19, 1983. B.A., Rollins Coll., 1969; grad. Nat. Grad. Trust Sch., Northwestern U., 1981. Fiduciary adminstr. Mfrs. Hanover Trust Co., N.Y.C., 1970-72; asst. trust officer Sovran Bank, N.A. (formerly Va. Nat. Bank), Norfolk, 1972-74, trust officer, 1974-79, v.p., trust officer, 1979-84, 1st v.p., 1984—; dir. Green Spring Corp., Wythe Corp. Author: The Practical Use of Disclaimers, 1982. Team capt. Four Cities United Way Campaign, 1974; chmn. film festival, bd. dirs. Tidewater Arts Council, 1975-77; bd. dirs. Children's Art Ctr., 1976-77, Va. Opera Assn., 1974-79, Friends of Norfolk Pub. Library, 1974-81; mem. race com. Norfolk Harborfest, 1979—; bd. dirs., pres., sec.-treas. The Norfolk Assembly, 1976—; trustee Westminster-Canterbury of Hampton Roads, Norfolk Acad.; bd. dirs. Armed Services YMCA, Mary Ballentine Home for Aged; mem. adv. council Norfolk Acad. Headmasters, others. Served with USNR, 1969-70. Mem. Richmond Soc. Fin. Analysts, Fin. Analysts Fedn., Tidewater Estate Planning Council. Episcopalian. Clubs: Harbor, Norfolk Assembly, Norfolk German, Norfolk Yacht and Country, Squires Club East, Cruising of Va., Hampton Yacht, Chesapeake Bay Yacht Racing Assn. Home: 606 W Mowbray Ct Norfolk VA 23507 Office: 1 Commercial Pl Norfolk VA 23510

GRANITZ, ADRIENNE DIANA, librarian; b. Sewickley, Pa., Nov. 10, 1946; d. Paul and Mary Ann Delores (Catizone) Hoko; m. Ronald George Granitz, Aug. 31, 1968; 1 child, Ronald George. B.S., Edinboro State U., 1968; M.S.L.S., Cath. U. Am., 1983. Librarian, Reynolds Elem. Sch. Dist., Greenville, Pa., 1968-72; circulation librarian Piedmont Va. Community Coll., Charlottesville, 1974—. Mem. ALA, Va. Library Assn., Va. Govtl. Employees Assn., Va. Community Coll. Assn. Lutheran. Home: 1116 Holmes Ave Charlottesville VA 22901 Office: Piedmont Va Community Coll Route 6 Box 1A Charlottesville VA 22901

GRANROSE, JOHN THOMAS, philosophy and religion educator; b. Miami, Fla., Nov. 5, 1939; s. Sylvester and Kathryn Irwin (Bradfield) G.; children—Karen, Kathleen, Jonathan; stepchildren—Robert Wood, Elizabeth Wood. Student Fla. So. Coll., 1957; B.A., U. Miami, 1961; postgrad. U. Heidelberg (Germany), 1961-62; M.A., U. Mich., 1963, Ph.D., 1966. Instr., U.Mich., 1964-66; asst. prof. U. Ga., 1966-71, assoc. prof., 1971-82, prof. philosophy, 1982—; pres. Western Conf. on Teaching Philosophy, 1976-78; bd. dirs. Ga. Endowment for Humanities, 1982-85. Vestryman Emmanuel Episcopal Ch., 1980-82. Recipient various awards for teaching; Nat. Woodrow Wilson fellow, Danforth Found. assoc., Fulbright grantee. Mem. Am. Philos. Assn., C.J. Jung Soc. of Atlanta, AAUP (pres. U. Ga. chpt. 1971-72), Soc. Values in Higher Edn., Iron Arrow, Blue Key, Phi Kappa Phi, Omicron Delta Kappa. Democrat. Contbr. articles, revs. to profl. jours.; editor books; editor Newsletter on Teaching Philosophy, 1976-79. Home: 215 Georgetown Dr Athens GA 30605 Office: Dept Philosophy U Ga Athens GA 30602

GRANT, DAVID, physician; b. Dallas, Jan. 8, 1949; s. Harold and June (Myers) G.; m. Rhea Levitt, Oct. 25, 1984; 1 child, Adam. A.B. magna cum laude, Harvard U., 1970; M.D., Yale U., 1974. Diplomate Am. Bd. Internal Medicine, sub-bd. cardiovascular disease. Intern, Bexar County Hosp., San Antonio, 1974-75; resident in internal medicine Bexar County Hosp., 1975-77, fellow in cardiology, 1977-79; practice medicine specializing in cardiology, San Antonio, 1979—; attending physician Santa Rosa Med. Ctr., San Antonio, 1979—. Fellow Am. Coll. Cardiology, Am. Heart Assn. Council on Clin. Cardiology; mem. Bexar County Med. Soc., Tex. Med. Assn., ACP. Office: 602 W French Pl San Antonio TX 78212

GRANT, DAVID ALAN, plastic surgeon; b. Mart, Tex., Nov. 28, 1926; s. Walter Lee and Emma (Reichert) G.; student Tex. Christian U., 1944-45; B.A., U. Tex., 1947, M.D., 1951; m. Alice Louise Inskeep, Dec. 23, 1949; children—Cynthia Lynn, Karen Ann. Intern, Emory U., 1951-52; resident U. Tex. Med. Br., 1954-60; practice medicine specializing in aesthetic and reconstructive plastic surgery, Ft. Worth, 1960—; mem. staffs St. Joseph's, All Saints Episcopal. Ft. Worth Children's, W.I. Cook Childrens' hosps.; mem. staff Med. Plaza Hosp., chmn. bd. trustees, 1978-84; chief div. surgery Harris Hosp., 1971-73, surgeon-in-chief, 1975-78; chief div. plastic surgery John Peter Smith Hosp., 1969-74; Pres. bd. dirs. Tarrant County Easter Seal Soc. for Crippled Children and Adults, 1971-72. Served to lt. (j.g.) M.C., USNR, 1952-54. Diplomate Am. Bd. Surgery, Am. Bd. Plastic Surgery. Fellow A.C.S.; mem. AMA, Tex., So. med. assns., Tarrant County Med. Soc., Southwestern Surg. Congress, Ft. Worth Acad. Medicine, Tex., Ft. Worth (v.p. 1977, pres. 1978), Singleton (1st v.p. 1965, 77, pres. 1979) surg. socs., Am. Burn Assn., Tex. Soc. Plastic Surgery (v.p. 1969-70, pres. 1971), Ft. Worth Soc. Plastic Surgeons (pres. 1982), Am. Soc. Plastic and Reconstructive Surgery (parliamentarian 1984), Am. Assn. for Hand Surgery, Am. Assn. Plastic Surgery, Am. Assn. Physicians and Surgeons, Sigma Xi, Phi Beta Pi, Alpha Epsilon Delta, Alpha Phi Omega. Rotarian (dir. 1964-66). Home: 2736 Colonial Pkwy Fort Worth TX 76109 Office: 800 8th Ave Fort Worth TX 76104

GRANT, GAIL GROVER, real estate broker; b. Painesville, Ohio, Nov. 9, 1921; s. Gail Grover and Gladys Felton (Beadle) Grant Gilliland; m. Dinah Tilling, Dec. 31, 1951 (div. Apr. 1960); children—Gail Grover III, Lorna Melanie; m. Elizabeth Clarke Browne, May 17, 1973. B.A., Dartmouth Coll., 1942, M.B.A., Tuck Sch., 1943. Pres. Gail G. Grant Co., Painesville, 1937-58; sales mgr. Service Awning Co., Miami, Fla., 1958-60; salesman Allen Morris Co., Miami, 1960-63; island sales mgr. McPherson & Brown, Freeport, Bahamas, 1963-71; pres. Ocean One Realty Inc., Boca Raton, Fla., 1978—, Royal Palm Properties Corp., Boca Raton, 1971—. Trustee Concord Twp., Ohio, 1953-58. Served as lt. USNR, 1943-45, ETO, PTO. Mem. Nat. Assn. Realtors (cert. comml. investment mem.), Nat. Assn. Realtors, Internat. Real Estate Fedn., Theta Delta Chi. Republican. Methodist. Club: Boca Raton Hotel and Country. Lodge: Elks. Avocations: hunting, fishing, sailing, swimming. Office: Ocean One Realty 1 N Ocean Blvd Boca Raton FL 33432

GRANT, JOSEPH MOORMAN, banker; b. San Antonio, Oct. 30, 1938; s. George William and Mary Christian (Moorman) G.; m. Sheila Peterson, Aug. 26, 1961; children—Mary Elizabeth, Steven Clay. B.B.A., So. Meth. U., 1960; M.B.A., U. Tex.-Austin, 1961, Ph.D., 1970. Comml. banking officer Citibank, N.Y.C., 1961-65; sr. v.p., economist Tex. Commerce Bank, Nat. Assn. and Tex. Commerce Bancshares, Houston, 1970-73; pres. Tex. Commerce Bank, Austin, 1974-75; exec. v.p. Tex. Am. Bank, Ft. Worth, 1975-76, pres., 1976-83, bd. chmn., chief exec. officer, 1984—, also dir.; vice chmn. Tex. Am. Bancshares, 1984-86, chmn., dir., 1986—; dir., past chmn. North Tex. Commn.; dir. Snyder Oil Co., Tex. Am. Bancshares, Inc. Trustee All Saints' Episcopal Hosp., So. Meth. U.; adv. council Coll. of Bus. Adminstrn. Found., U. Tex., Austin; bd. dirs. Pub. Communication Found. for North Tex. Recipient Disting. Alumnus award U. Tex. Coll. Bus. Adminstrn., 1982. Mem. Young Pres's. Orgn. (bd. dirs., pres.-elect YPO Internat., mem. exec. com.), Assn. Res. City Bankers, Am. Bankers Assn., Tex. Bankers Assn. (dir.), Nat. Assn. Bus. Economists (past pres. Houston chpt., 1973), Ft. Worth C. of C. (chmn.), Sigma Alpha Epsilon, Blue Key. Episcopalian. Author: (with Dr. Lawrence L. Crum) The Development of State-Chartered Banking in Texas, 1978. Home: 1408 Shady Oaks Lane Fort Worth TX 76107 Office: 500 Throckmorton Fort Worth TX 76102

GRANT, LA RUE TUCKER, media specialist; b. Winnsboro, La., May 13, 1930; d. Charles Owen and Alma Ethel (Lambert) Tucker; m. Sidney Allen Grant, Dec. 31, 1953; 1 son, Sidney Tucker. B.S., B.A. (summa cum laude), La. Tech. U., 1951; M. Secondary Edn., U. Houston, 1956; M.L.S., Sam Houston U., 1978; D. Edn., U. Houston, 1979. Cert. tchr. all levels, librarian, adminstr., Tex. Auditor Price Waterhouse, Houston, 1951-52; cost acct. Triangle Refineries, Houston, 1952-55; adminstr., tchr. Channelview Ind. Sch. Dist., Tex., 1956-57; lectr. career edn. U. Houston, Univ. Park, 1977-80, lectr., supr. interns in library sci., Clear Lake, 1981-83; media specialist Deer Park Ind. Sch. Dist. (Tex.), 1957-59, 61, 67-83; writer Deer Park Progress, 1979—, Bayshore Sun, LaPorte, Tex., 1979—, LaPorte Broadcaster, 1982—. Vol. Friends of Library; mem. Lomax Citizens Com., LaPorte, Tex., 1960; mem. Tex. Educator's Polit. Action Com., Deer Park, 1983; mem. Aggie Club Tex. A & M U., College Station, 1983; econs. rep. student council La. Tech. U., Ruston, 1950-51. Mem. Tex. Press Assn., Earthwatch, La. Archeol. Soc., Deer Park Educators, Tex. State Tchr. Assn., NEA, Tex. Bus. Educators Assn., Mountain Plains Bus. Educators Assn., Nat. Bus. Educators Assn., Internat. Bus. Educator's Assn., Tex. Library Assn., ALA, Sigma Tau Delta, Phi Kappa Phi, Phi Kappa Delta. Democrat. Methodist. Clubs: Tech. Tchr's., Am. Bus. Women's Assn. (scrapbook chmn. 1980-83). Office: Deer Park Ind Sch Dist 203 Ivy Deer Park TX 77536

GRANT, LYNNE CORNEY, industrial psychologist; b. Rockville Ctr., N.Y., May 20, 1958; d. Blair Shipman and Joanne Lois (Seitz) Corney; m. Robert Thomas Grant, June 7, 1980. B.S. in Psychology, Okla. State U., 1980; M.S. in Indsl. Psychology, North Tex. State U., 1982. Personnel technician Frito-Lay, Dallas, 1980-81; personnel intern Western Co. North Am., Fort Worth, 1981-82; career cons. Mgmt. Personnel, Fort Worth, 1982-83; personnel specialist City of Arlington, Tex., 1983—. Mem. Am. Psychol. Assn. (assoc.), Fort Worth Personnel Assn. Home: 6913 Penhurst Dr Fort Worth TX 76133 Office: City of Arlington PO Box 231/101 W Abram St Arlington TX 76010

GRANT, MYLES NELSON, insurance executive, tax service consultant; b. Darien, Ga., Mar. 6, 1950; s. William A. and Sarah A. McDonald; m. Murlin Priscilla Colbourne, Sept. 13, 1971; children—Myles, Myrne. B.A., Savannah State Coll. (Ga.), Sales rep. Met. Life Ins., Savannah, 1974-76; gen. agt. Myles Grant, Inc., Savannah, 1977—, pres. and owner, 1977—; cons. in field. Served with U.S. Army, 1970-73. Mem. Nat. Assn. Life Underwriters, Internat. Assn. Fin. Planners. Democrat. Baptist. Lodge: Masons (32nd degree, com. chmn.).

GRANT, SIDNEY CAROL, office manager; b. Houston, Sept. 1, 1941; m. Jerry Leonard Grant, Feb. 6, 1960; children—James Madison, Diana Lynne. Student U. Houston, 1958-59, Herman Hosp. Sch. Nursing, 1958-59. Receptionist, asst. Santos Med. Lab., Houston, 1959; collection clk. to asst. collection mgr. Dryer's Furniture Co., San Diego, Calif., 1964-66; data processing operator IRS, Austin, Tex., 1972-74; receptionist, sales sec. Advanced Custom Molders, Inc., Austin, 1977-78, adminstrv. asst., 1978-80, exec. asst., personnel dir., 1980-83, adminstrv. office mgr. and personnel dir., 1983—, also safety dir., ins. coordinator, employee benefits chmn. Vol. Pub. TV; pres. St. Elmo Sch. PTA, Austin, 1973-74. Mem. Austin Personnel Assn., Austin Profl. Sec. Assn. Republican. Baptist. Office: 9204 Brown Ln Austin TX 78754

GRANTHAM, CHARLES EDWARD, broadcast engineer; b. Andalusia, Ala., Mar. 15, 1950; s. J.C. and Geraldine (Brooks) G.; student Enterprise State Jr. Coll., 1968-69; A.A., Lurleen B. Wallace Coll., 1979; m. Sandra J. Mosley, Mar. 9, 1973; 1 son, Christopher Charles. Sales engr., draftsman S.E. Ala. Gas Co., Andalusia, 1968-70; asst. mgr., engr. Sta. WAAO, Andalusia, 1972-78; engr. Ala. Public TV, WDIQ-TV, Dozier, Ala., also chief engr. Sta. WAAO, Andalusia, 1978—; South Ala. microwave engr. APTV, 1980—; owner Grantham & Grantham Cons. Bd. dirs. Carolina Vol. Fire Dept., 1983—; pres. Andalusia Men's Ch. Softball, 1985-86. Notary public, Ala. Served with inf. U.S. Army, 1970-72. Named Civitan Outstanding Young Am., 1967. Mem. Country Music Assn., Nat. Assn. Bus. and Ednl. Radio, Am. Film Inst., Internat. Soc. Cert. Electronic Technicians, Nat. Assn. Radio and TV Engrs., Ala. State Employees Assn. (bd. dirs. Covington County chpt. 1980—), Nat. Rifle Assn. Country Music Disc Jockey Assn., Phi Theta Kappa. Mem. Ch. of Christ. Home: Route 5 Box 177A Andalusia AL 36420 Office: WDIQ TV Route 2 Dozier AL 36028

GRANTHAM, JOHN CARLTON, geologist; b. Freer, Tex., Dec. 1, 1952; s. John Calvin and Winnie Ruth (Payne) G.; B.S. in Pharmacy, U. Houston, 1979; B.S. in Geology, Tex. A&I U., 1983. Pharmacist, Eckerd Drugs, Lake Jackson, Tex., 1980, K-Mart, Portland, Tex., 1980-82; geologist Tex. Oil and Gas, Corpus Christi, Tex., 1984—. Served to specialist 4th U.S. Army, 1972-74. Mem. Am. Assn. Petroleum Geologists, Soc. of Econ. Palentol. Mineralogists. Methodist. Home: 4530 Shea Pkwy Corpus Christi TX 78413 Office: Texas Oil and Gas 500 N Shoreline Corpus Christi TX 78401

GRASSER, ROBERT E., executive director state planning commission. Exec. dir., Central Ala. Regional Planning & Devel. Commn., Montgomery. Office: 2911 Zelda Rd Suite A Montgomery AL 36106

GRASSIE, JOSEPH ROBERTS, bus. exec.; b. Buenos Aires, Argentina, Oct. 3, 1933 (parents Am. citizens); s. Joseph Flagg and Vida Clarisa (Roberts) G.; B.A., U. Chgo., 1958, M.A., 1960; m. Josette Krespi, Mar. 23, 1958; children—Yvonne, Scott. Staff cons. Public Adminstrn. Service, Chgo., 1960-65, supervising cons., 1965-68; dep. city mgr. City of Grand Rapids (Mich.), 1968-69, city mgr., 1970-76; city mgr. City of Miami (Fla.), 1976-80; pres. Worsham Bros. Co., Inc., Miami, 1980—; lectr. public service Grand Valley State Colls., Mich. Mem. adv. council Western Mich. U., U. Miami; trustee Public Adminstrn. Service, Washington, Govtl. Affairs Inst., Washington, Grand Rapids Arts Council. Mem. Internat. City Mgmt. Assn., Am. Soc. Public Adminstrn. Home: 2880 SW 33d Ct Miami FL 33133 Office: 100 N Biscayne Blvd Miami FL 33132

GRATES, FREDERICK RYAN, hospital administrator, health care consultant; b. Herkimer, N.Y., Sept. 11, 1942; s. Joseph James and Florence (Ryan) G.; m. Carolyne Frances DiCecco, Aug. 19, 1967; children—Theresa Lynne, Frederick Jr. B.S. in Mil. Sci. and Engring., U.S. Mil. Acad., 1965; M.B.A., Ind. U., 1971; M.S. in Hosp. Adminstrn., Trinity U., 1976. Commd. officer U.S. Army, 1965, advanced through ranks to maj., 1975; aide de camp to commanding gen. U.S. Army Health Command, Fort Sam Houston, Tex., 1973-75; asst. exec. officer Brooke Army Med. Ctr., Fort Sam Houston, 1975-76; resigned, 1976; asst. adminstr. San Antonio Community Hosp., 1976-77; exec. dir. Sharpstown Gen. Hosp., Houston, 1977-79; pres. Promed Serviced Inc., Stafford, Tex., 1979-82; exec. dir. Fort Bend Hosp., Missouri City, Tex., 1982—; dir. 1st Nat. Bank, Missouri City. Chmn. Missouri City Rd. Referendum Com., 1984; v.p., bd. dirs. Tex. War on Drugs, Fort Bend County, 1984; chmn. Missouri City Econ. Devel. Com., 1985; v.p., pres.-elect Fort Bend C. of C., 1985. Decorated Silver Star medal, Purple Heart medal, Bronze Star medal, 25 Air medals. Mem. Am. Coll. Hosp. Adminstrs., Tex. Hosp. Assn., Am. Hosp. Assn. Republican. Roman Catholic. Clubs: Oyster Creek Rotary (bd. dirs. 1982), VFW. Avocations: jogging; golf; hunting; sports. Home: 3902 E Creek Club Missouri City TX 77459 Office: Fort Bend Hosp 3803 FM 1092 Hwy 6 Missouri City TX 77459

GRATTON, PATRICK JOHN FRANCIS, geologist, oil company executive; b. Denver, Aug. 28, 1933; s. Patrick Henry and Lorene Jean (Johnson) G.; m. Jean Marie McKinney, June 10, 1955; children—Sara, Vivian, Patrick, Lizabeth. B.S. in Geology, U. N.Mex., 1955, M.S. in Geology, 1958. Mining engr. Utah Internat., Denver, 1956; geologist Westvaco Mineral Devel. Corp., Grants, N.Mex., 1955, Shell Oil Co., Roswell, N.Mex., Tyler, Tex., 1957-62; adminstrv. asst. Delhi-Taylor Oil Corp., Dallas, 1962-64; exploration mgr. Eugene E. Nearburg, Dallas, 1965-70; pres. Patrick J.F. Gratton, Inc., Dallas, 1970—; dir. Endevco, Inc., Dallas. Contbr. articles to profl. jours. Served with USCG, 1951-53, U.S. Army, 1956-57. Mem. Dallas Geol. Soc. (Pub. Service award), Soc. Ind. Profl. Earth Scientists (pres. 1977-78), Am. Assn. Petroleum Geologists (v.p. southwest sect. 1976-77, del. 1978-81), Tex. Ind. Producers and Royalty Owners (exec. com.), Petroleum Club, Explorers Club. Republican Roman Catholic. Office: Patrick JF Gratton Inc 2403 Thomas Ave Dallas TX 75201

GRAVES, BEN L., architect, investment company executive; b. Denison, Tex., Feb. 15, 1945; s. Ben E. and Margie G. (Myers) G.; m. Sandrea Lynn Stover, Jan. 28, 1966; children—Darren Lynn, Matthew Shea. B.Arch., U. Okla., 1969. Registered architect, Okla. Designer, Fritzler, Knobock, Architects, Oklahoma City, 1968-69; assoc. Bishop & Quinn Architects, Midwest City, Okla., 1971-74; chmn. Graves, Williams & Assocs., Norman, Okla., 1974—; pres. Ben Graves Investments, Norman, 1978—; bd. advisers Realty Mortgage Co., Oklahoma City, 1980-82; dir. Heritage Ins. Co., Norman, Aspen Properties, Norman, H.T.G. Devel. Corp., Norman, Havenbrook Corp., Norman. Prin. works include Office Bldg and Internat. Summit Office. Mem. Norman C. of C. (Top 20 Salesman of Yr. 1983, Small Bus. Person of Yr. 1985), AIA, Nat. Assn. Homebuilders, Norman Devels. Council, Norman Assn. Homebuilders, U. Okla. Assocs. (charter). Democrat. Baptist. Clubs: Trails Golf, O.U. Chip-In (bd. dirs.) (Norman). Avocations: golf; snow skiing; reading; landscape design. Office: Ben Graves Investments Inc 900 36th Ave NW Norman OK 73069

GRAVES, GERALD ROBERT, industrial engineer, educator; b. Nashville, Ark., Aug. 6, 1950; s. Louis Francis and Wilton Frances (Clements) G.; m. Sarah Herring, Jan. 2, 1982. B.S. in Indsl. Engring., U. Ark., 1973, M.S. in Indsl. Engring., 1980; Ph.D., Okla. State U., 1983. Grad. asst. U. Ark., Fayetteville, 1978-80, asst. prof., 1983-84; research assoc. Okla. State U., Stillwater, 1980-83; asst. prof. indsl. engring. La. State U., Baton Rouge, 1984—, dir. indsl. engring. microcomputer lab, 1984-85; dir. Graves Pub. Co.; cons. to various cos. Contbr. articles to tech. jours., proceedings. Coach, Pony League Baseball, Stillwater, 1982. Served to lt. USNR, 1973-78. Named to Nat. Dean's List, 1982-83; recipient Halliburton Edn. Found. award excellence, 1985. Mem. Soc. Mfg. Engrs. (sr. mem., grantee 1984-85), Inst. Indsl. Engrs., Soc. for Computer Simulation, Am. Prodn. and Inventory Control Soc. (v.p. edn. chpt. 1984). Roman Catholic. Avocations: fishing; photography; music; jogging. Home: 643 Polytech Baton Rouge LA 70808 Office: Louisiana State U Dept Indsl Engring CEBA 3128 Baton Rouge LA 70803

GRAVES, JACK PIERCE, army officer; b. Shepard AFB, Tex., Sept. 9, 1954; s. Walter Pierce and Betty Anne (Ralston) G., Jr.; m. Ora Virginia Estelle Puckett, June 28, 1975; 1 son, Jack Pierce. Student U. Md. (overseas div.), 1978-80; Assoc. in Bus. Adminstrn., Northwestern State U. La., 1984; B.S. in Bus. Adminstrn., U. Md., 1986. Enlisted U.S. Army, 1974, advanced through grades to sgt., 1st class, 1985; automotive parts mgr., Ft. Bragg, N.C., 1974-77, Ft. Knox, Ky., 1977-78; commissary store mgr., Hanau, W.Ger., 1978-80; statis. analyst, commodity mgr., Ft. Polk, La., 1980-85, Kaiserslautern W. Ger., 1985—. Decorated Meritorious Service medal. Republican. Baptist. Club: Toastmasters Internat. (area gov. 1982-84, ednl. v.p. 1985—, Competent Toastmaster award 1983). Home: 304 Ridge Rd Colonial Heights VA 23834

GRAVES, JOHN WILLIAM, history educator; b. Little Rock, June 25, 1942; s. William A. and Mabel (Morehart) G. B.A. in History, U. Ark., 1964, M.A., 1967; Ph.D. in History, U. Va., 1978. Instr. history U. S.W. La., LaFayette, 1966-67; research asst. U. Va., Charlottesville, 1971-72; instr. history S.W. Tex. State U., San Marcos, 1972-77; coll. assistance migrant program, freshman studies coordinator, basic skills specialist, lectr. St. Edward's U., Austin, Tex., 1979-85; assoc. prof. history Henderson State U., Arkadelphia, Ark., 1985—. Philip Francis DuPont fellow U. Va., 1969-72. Mem. Am. Hist. Assn., So. Hist. Assn., Ark. Hist. Assn., Audubon Soc. (pres. Bastrop County 1985), Defenders of Wildlife, Environ. Def. Fund, Ark. Nature Conservancy, Hist. Preservation Alliance Ark., Quapaw Quarter Assn. Contbr. articles to profl. jours. Home: 824 Faculty Pl Arkadelphia AR 71923 Office: Dept History Henderson State U Arkadelphia AR 71923

GRAVES, KENNETH MARTIN, architect; b. Beaumont, Tex., July 6, 1943; s. Ernest Leroy and Margaret Louise (Hillyer) G.; m. Patricia Ann Edwards, Aug. 28, 1965 (div. 1978). B. Arch., Okla. State U., 1967. Lic. architect, Tex., Okla. Architect, designer Ford, Powell & Carson, San Antonio, 1969-73; architect, ptnr. Tuggle & Graves, San Antonio, 1973—. Restoration architect: Alamo Plaza, 1976, Reuter Bldg., 1980, The Commerce Bldg., 1982, Staacke-Stevens, 1983-84, Charles Ct., 1983-85. Bd. dirs. San Antonio Soc. Performing Arts, 1982-84, Friends of McNay, San Antonio, 1983—, Gallery of McNay, San Antonio, 1984—. Served to 1st lt. U.S. Army, 1967-69. Mem. AIA. Republican. Episcopalian. Avocations: oil painting; collecting primitive antiques; travel. Home: 303 Caladium Dr San Antonio TX 78213 Office: Tuggle & Graves Inc 215 Broadway San Antonio TX 78205

GRAVES, LAWRENCE LESTER, historian, educator; b. Perry, N.Y., Nov. 17, 1917; s. Leonard Stanley and Anna Maud (Lalor) G.; B.A., U. Mo., 1942; M.A., U. Rochester, 1947; Ph.D., U. Wis., 1954; m. Mary Rita Ralph (dec.); m. 2d, Opal Louise Oden, Nov. 23, 1966. Instr. history Woman's Coll., U. N.C., 1950-51, 52-55; asst. prof. to prof. history Tex. Tech. Coll., Lubbock, 1955-67, asso. dean grad. sch., 1967-68, interim dean, 1968-70; prof. history, dean Arts and Scis. Tex. Tech. U., Lubbock, 1970-83, interim univ. pres., 1979-80. Served with U.S. Army, 1942-46, 51-52. Mem. Am. Hist. Assn., AAUP (pres. Woman's Coll. chpt. 1953-54, Tex. Tech. U. chpt. 1964-66), Orgn. Am. Historians, So. History Assn., Western History Assn., Tex. State Hist. Assn., Council Colls. Arts and Scis. (dir. 1973-75, 78, pres. 1976-77), Nat. Summer Conf. Acad. Deans (chmn. 1977), Nat. Assn. State Univs. and Land Grand Colls. (commn. on arts and scis. 1977-80), Am. Assn. Colls. (dir. 1978-81), SW Social Sci. Assn. (pres. 1981-82), Phi Kappa Phi. Lodge: Masons. Editor, contbr.: A History of Lubbock, 1962; sr. assoc. editor The Handbook of Texas, 1983—; contbr. articles to profl. jours. Office: PO Box 4203 Tex Tech U Lubbock TX 79409

GRAVES, WILLIAM T., insurance company executive; b. 1934. Student, U. Tenn., U. Mich. Sr. v.p. Liberty National Life Ins. Co., Inc., Birmingham, 1957—; sr. v.p. Torchmark Corp., 1979—. Address: Torchmark Corp PO Box 2612 Birmingham AL 35202*

GRAVLEE, LELAND CLARK, JR., physician; b. Fayette, Ala., Apr. 10, 1928; s. Leland C. and Mary (Wright) G.; B.S., Auburn U., 1951; M.D., U. Ala., 1955; m. Catherine Shook; children—Jan, Luanne, Leland Clark. Intern U. Hosp., Birmingham, Ala., 1955-56, resident in obstetrics and gynecology, 1956-59; practice medicine specializing in obstetrics and gynecology, Birmingham, 1959—; mem. courtesy staff Bapt. Med. Center, Brookwood Hosp.; mem. active staff U. Hosp., Bapt. Med. Center; cons. staff Carraway Meth. Hosp., East End Meml. Hosp.; pres. elect med. staff South Highlands Hosp., 1976-77; asst. clin. prof. medicine U. Ala. Sch. Medicine, Birmingham, 1974-77, clin. prof. obstetrics and gynecology, 1975-77; pres. Cancer Research and Edn. Found., 1974-77; guest lectr. Russian govt. Health Fair and Tumor Inst., 1974, Philippines, 1976, Oxford (Eng.) U., 1974, Grenoble, France, 1974, Republic of China, 1978, Tokyo U., 1978, Hong Kong, 1980, others. mem. cancer coordinating council Ala. State Health Dept., 1968—; mem. Ala. State Health Planning and Devel. Agy. Bd., 1983—. Served with USN, 1946-48. Diplomate Am. Bd. Obstetrics and Gynecology. Fellow Am. Coll. Obstetrics and Gynecology; mem. Med. Assn. of State Ala., Am. Soc. for Study of Sterility, Ala., S. Central, Birmingham obstetrical gynecol. socs., AMA, Birmingham Acad. Medicine, Alpha Omega Alpha, Med. Coll. of Ala. Alumni Assn. (pres. 1964-65). Baptist. Clubs: Rotary, Country Club of Birmingham. Editor: Endometrum, 1976, Endometrum, 1977. Contbr. numerous articles in field to profl. jours.; inventor of uterine cancer detecting device and automatic umbilical cord tying device. Office: 1222 S 14th Ave Suite 112 Birmingham AL 35205

GRAY, BETTY MARIE, state official; b. Martinez, Ga., Sept. 28, 1951; d. Marvin W. and Geneva (Shealy) G. B.A., Augusta Coll., 1973. Edn./prevention specialist Aiken County Commn. Alcohol and Drug Abuse, Aiken, S.C., 1974-75, asst. dir., 1975-76; substance abuse counselor North Central Mental Health, Decatur, Ala., 1977-79; spl. projects coordinator Ala. Dept. Mental Health, Montgomery, 1979-81, state manpower coordinator, 1981-84, adminstrv. asst., 1984—; rep. Nat. Tng. Network, 1984-85. Author: On the Edge, 1981; Consider Your Actions ..., 1983. Recipient cert. of Appreciation, Ala. Dept. Pub. Safety, 1984. Mem. Am. Soc. Tng. and Devel., Ala. Mental Health Resource Pool (trainer). Home: Rt 4 Box 489-N Prattville AL 36067 Office: Ala Dept Mental Health PO Box 3710 Montgomery AL 36193

GRAY, C. G., university administrator, educator; b. Melbourne, Ark., Feb. 10, 1927; s. Hubert S. and Bertha E. (Kidwell) G.; m. Barbara J. Morlan, June 30, 1951; children—John R., David A., Cary G. B.S. in Edn., Tex. Tech. U., 1950, M.Ed., 1952, Ed.D., 1965. Dir. guidance Lubbock Pub. Schs., Tex., 1950-60; dir. sales Sci. Research Assocs., Chgo., 1960-74; assoc. dir. Edn. Service Ctr., Richardson, Tex., 1974-78; exec. planner Dallas Pub. Schs., 1978-81; v.p. Abilene Christian U., Tex., 1981—; cons. reading and microcomputers. Active Rotary Internat., Richardson and Abilene. Served with U.S. Army, 1945-47. Mem. Internat. Reading Assn., Am. Assn. Sch. Adminstrs., Tex. Assn. Sch. Adminstrs., Phi Delta Kappa (chpt. pres. 1960-61, 25 Yr. pin 1983). Republican. Avocations: golf; gardening. Home: 302 Washington Blvd Abilene TX 79601 Office: Abilene Christian U 1600 Campus Ct Abilene TX 79699

GRAY, CLARENCE JONES, educator, dean; b. Red Bank, N.J., June 21, 1908; s. Clarence J. Sr. and Elsie (Megill) G.; m. Jane Love Little, Aug. 25, 1934; children—Frances Gray Adams, Kenneth Stewart. B.A., U. Richmond, 1933, LL.D., 1979; M.A., Columbia U., 1934; postgrad. Centro de Estudios Historicos, Madrid, summer 1935; Ed.D., U. Va., 1962. Underwriter Aetna Life Ins. Co., 1925-30; instr. Spanish, Columbia U., 1934-38; gen. sec., mem. exec. council Instituto de las Espanas en los Estados Unidos, 1934-39; instr., sec. dept. Romance langs. Queens Coll., N.Y.C., 1938-46 (on mil. leave 1943-46); dean students U. Richmond (Va.), 1946-68, asso. prof. modern langs., 1946-62, prof., 1962-79, emeritus, 1979—, dean administrv. services, 1968-73, dean adminstrn., 1973-79, emeritus, 1979—, spl. cons. to pres., 1979—, editor bull., 1968-74, moderator U. Richmond-WRNL Radio Scholarship Quiz Program, mem. bd. Univ. Assos. Cons., Commn. on Colls., So. Assn. Colls. and Schs. Contbr. to profl. jours. Trustee' Inst. Mediterranean Studies. Served from lt. to lt. comdr., USNR, 1943-46. Recipient Nat. Alumni Council award U. Richmond. Mem. Modern Lang. Assn., NEA, Am. Assn. Tchrs. Spanish, Am. Assn. for Higher Edn., Newcomen Soc. N.Am., Inst. Internat. Edn. (cert. meritorius service), Phi Beta Kappa (sec. emeritus), Phi Delta Kappa, Kappa Delta Pi, Omicron Delta Kappa (nat. sec. gen. council 1966-72, Distinguished Service key 1968, nat. chmn. scholarship awards 1972-78), Alpha Psi Omega, Phi Gamma Delta (Disting. and Exceptional Service award), Alpha Phi Omega. Baptist. Mem. Legion of Honor, Order of De Molay. Clubs: Country of Va., Colonnade, Masons, Rotary. Home: 2956 Hathaway Rd #611 Richmond VA 23225

GRAY, DONNA LEA, bookstore and gift shop owner; b. Snyder, Tex., Sept. 5, 1937; d. Dee Roy Chapman and Esther Chapman Weaver; m. C. D. Gray, Jr., Dec. 27, 1953; children—Donna Faye Gray Rosson, Cassandra Louise. Student pub. schs., Ira, Tex. Asst. postmaster, Dunn, Tex., 1955-58; clk. J.C. Penney, Snyder, 1958-59, Fabric Mart, Snyder, 1959-60; owner, opr. Donna's Beauty Shop, Snyder, 1963-65; owner, mgr. La Charme' Health Spa, Snyder, 1968-75, Snyder Bookstore and Gift Shop, 1978—. Active United Way, Heart Assn., Am. Cancer Soc., Snyder; dist. chmn. March of Dimes, Snyder; bd. dirs. Scurry County Fair Assn., Scurry County Hist. Commn., Mem. Christian Booksellers Assn., Am. Booksellers Assn., Am. Bus. Women's Assn., Snyder Retail Mchts. Com., Snyder C. of C. Office: Snyder Bookstore and Gift Shop 2517 College Ave Snyder TX 79549

GRAY, DORA EVELYN, accountant; b. Smith County, Tex., Mar. 26, 1924; d. H. Esten and Mattie E. (Payne) Clyburn; grad. Fed. Inst., 1944; m. Harvie A. Gray, Dec. 22, 1945 (dec.); children—Dennis H., Ladell L. Gray Green. Treas., asst. mgr. Wagner Office Equipment, 1948-61; asst. treas. Pool. Co., San Angelo, Tex., 1962-72; loan officer, acting mgr. Concho Educators Fed. Credit Union, San Angelo, 1972-75; warehouse accountant M System Food Stores, Inc., San Angelo, 1976—. Precinct del. county convs., 1976—; active various community drives; active in legislation regarding ERA, 1959—. Mem. Bus. and Profl. Women's Club (local pres., dist. chmn. for personal devel., mem. found. com., legis. chmn., state dir.), Internat. Platform Assn. Democrat. Mem. Ch. of Christ. Home: 915 N Adams St San Angelo TX 76901

GRAY, DORIS WILLIAMS, marriage and family counselor; b. Dodge County, Ga., Nov. 7, 1936; s. Harry Melton and Evelyn Louise (NeSmith) Williams; m. Robert Floyd Gray, June 14, 1959; children—Pamela, John, Karen. B.S., Ga. Coll., 1958; M.Ed., U. Ga., 1975. Tchr. home econs., Quincy, Fla., 1958-61; extension home economist DeKalb County, Mo., 1963-65; tchr. adult edn. Milledgeville, Ga., 1970-73; psychologist Peachbelt Mental Health Center, Warner Robins, Ga., 1975-79; marriage and family counselor, Warner Robins, 1975—. Mem. Ga. Assn. Marriage and Family Therapists (pres. Middle Ga. chpt. 1983), Ga. Addiction Counselors Assn. (bd. dirs., v.p. 1984, pres. 1985-86), Nat. Fedn. Parents for Drug-Free Youth, Am. Assn. Marriage and Family Therapy, Nat. Assn. Alcohol and Drug Addiction Counselors. Democrat. Baptist. Office: 1764 Watson Blvd Suite 204 Warner Robins GA 31093

GRAY, DUNCAN MONTGOMERY, JR., bishop; b. Canton, Miss., Sept. 21, 1926; s. Duncan Montgomery and Isabel (McCrady) G.; B.E.E., Tulane U., 1948; M.Div., U. of South, 1953, D.D. (hon.), 1972; m. Ruth Miller Spivey, Feb. 9, 1948; children—Duncan Montgomery, Anne Gray Finley, Lloyd Spivey, Catherine Gilmer. Ordained priest Episcopal Ch., 1953, consecrated bishop, 1974; priest-in-charge Calvary Ch., Cleveland, Miss. and Grace Ch., Rosedale, Miss., 1953-57, Holy Innocents Ch., Como, Miss., 1957-60; rector St. Peter's Ch., Oxford, Miss., 1957-65, St. Paul's Ch., Meridian, Miss., 1965-74; bishop coadjutor Diocese of Miss., Jackson, 1974, bishop, 1974—, chmn. House of Bishops Com. Canons, 1975—, chmn. standing com. on constns. and canons Gen. Conv. of Episcopal Ch., 1977-83; pres. Province IV; mem. Council of Advice to Pres. Bishop; pres. Assn. Christian Tng. and Service; chmn. Miss. Religious Leadership Conf., 1977-78. Chmn. bd. trustees All Saints Episc. Sch., Vicksburg, Miss., 1975-77; trustee U. of South, 1974—, bd. regents, 1981—; bd. dirs. Miss. Council on Human Relations, 1962—, pres., 1963-67; mem. Miss. Advisory Com. to U.S. Commn. on Civil Rights, 1975—; bd. dirs. Miss. Mental Health Assn., 1968-73. Named Nat. Speaker of Yr., Tau Kappa Alpha, 1962. Contbr. articles to religious publs. Home: 3775 Old Canton Rd Jackson MS 39216 Office: PO Box 1636 Jackson MS 39215

GRAY, ELMON TAYLOR, state senator; b. Suffolk, Va., May 1, 1925; m. Pamela Spencer Burnside. B.A., Va. Mil. Inst. Mem. Va. Senate, 1972—. Bd. vistors Va. Mil. Inst., 1958-66, pres., 1964-66; mem. Sch. Bd. Sussex County (Va.), 1963—, local bd. John Tyler Community Coll., 1965-72; trustee U. Richmond, 1969-73; pres. Va. Forest, 1969-71; mem. Reforestation Adv. Com., 1971; vestryman Episcopal Ch.; mem. bd. Welfare and Instns., 1968-74. Served with USNR, 1944-46. Democrat. Club: Ruritan. Lodge: Masons. Office: Va Senate Gen Assembly Bldg 9th and Broad Sts Richmond VA 23219*

GRAY, ENID MAURINE, city official, librarian; b. Galveston, Tex., Sept. 2, 1943; d. Willis James and Enid (Childress) G. B.A., N.E. La. State U., 1966; M.L.S., North Tex. State U., 1969. Sch. librarian Caddo Parish Sch. Bd., Shreveport, La., 1966; dir. libraries City of Beaumont, Tex., 1966-84, sr. dir. community services, 1984—; prof. Sch. Library Sci., Sam Houston State U., Huntsville, Tex., 1976; chmn. Library Systems Act adv. bd. Tex. State Library, Austin, 1976-79. Author: History of Medicine in Beaumont, Texas, 1969; Beaumont Libraries, Then and Now, 1976. Pres. Beaumont Civic Opera, 1976-77, Jefferson Theatre Preservation Soc., 1984; arbitrator Beaumont Better Bus. Bur., 1981—. Recipient Disting. Alumnus award Sch. Library and Info. Service, North Tex. State U., 1980. Mem. Tex. Library Assn. (life; pres. 1974-75), ALA, Tex. Mcpl. Library Dirs. Assn. (pres. 1971-72), Beaumont Jr. League. Club: Altrusa (pres. Beaumont 1981-83, Community Service award 1981). Methodist. Office: City of Beaumont PO Box 3827 Beaumont TX 77704

GRAY, FESTUS GAIL, electrical engineering educator, consultant, researcher; b. Moundsville, W. Va., Aug. 16, 1943; s. Festus Porter and Elsie Virginia (Rine) G.; m. Caryl Evelyn Anderson, Aug. 24, 1978; children—David, Andrew, Daniel. B.S. in Elec. Engring., W.Va. U., 1965, M.S. in Elec. Engring., 1967; Ph.D., U. Mich., 1971. Instr. W.Va. U., Morgantown, 1966-67; research asst. Argonne (Ill.) Labs., summer 1967; teaching fellow U. Mich., Ann Arbor, 1967-70; NASA faculty fellow Langley Research Ctr., Hampton, Va., summer 1975; asst. prof. elec. engring. Va. Poly. Inst. and State U., Blacksburg, 1971-77, assoc. prof. elec. engring., 1977-83, prof. elec. engring., 1983—; Sabbatical Ctr. Digital Systems Research, Research Triangle Inst., Research Triangle Park, N.C., 1984-85; chmn. publs. Internat. Symposium on Fault Tolerant Computing, Ann Arbor, Mich.; cons. BDM Corp., McLean, Va. Coach Youth League Soccer, 1979-86; deacon Northside Presbyn. Ch. NSF fellow, 1971, 75, 77; recipient Rome Air Devel. Ctr. award, 1980; NASA award, 1981; Naval Surface Weapons Ctr. award, 1982; Army Research Office award, 1982. Mem. IEEE (chpt. chmn. 1979-80, sect. exec. com. 1980-82), Assn. Computing Machinery, Sigma Xi, Tau Beta Pi, Eta Kappa Nu. Author tech. papers; contbr. articles to profl. jours., chpts. to books. Home: 304 Fincastle Dr Blacksburg VA 24060 Office: Dept Elec Engring Va Poly Inst and State U Blacksburg VA 24061

GRAY, GIBSON HENDRIX, political science educator; b. Lufkin, Tex., Oct. 26, 1922; s. Lee Hendrix and Frances Jeta (Gibson) G.; m. Mary Anna Wells, Nov. 21, 1973. B.B.A., U. Tex., 1947; M.A., Columbia U., 1950, Ph.D., 1967. Asst. chief clk. Gov. of Pa., 1961-63; adminstr. officer Pa. State Planning Bd., 1963-66; asst. prof. govt. North Tex. State U., Denton, 1967-69; asst. prof. polit. sci. Okla. Central State U., Edmund, 1969-71; assoc. prof. polit. sci. Pembroke (N.C.) State U., 1971-77, prof., 1978—, chmn. dept. polit. sci., 1983—. Mem. senatorial com. Robeson County Democratic Exec. Com., 1976-78. Served to cpl. M.C., U.S. Army, 1943-46; CBI N.C. Plan for Fiscal Yr. 1973 grantee. Mem. AAUP, Am. Polit. Sci. Assn. Methodist. Lodges: Masons, Kiwanis (pres. Pembroke club 1979-80). Author: (with Mark Heyman and William Shellabear) The Population of Pennsylvania, 1966; The Lobbying Game, 1970; Your Local Government at Work, 1975. Home: 3630 Kale Dr Lumberton NC 28358 Office: Pembroke State U Pembroke NC 28372

GRAY, HENRY CROCKETT, state govt. ofcl.; b. N. Little Rock, Ark., June 18, 1923; s. Henry Crockett and Celeste Lillian (Bush) G.; B.S. in Wildlife Conservation, U. Wyo., 1950; m. Mary Beth Tanner, Dec. 18, 1950; children—Michael, James, Kathy, Ann. Former mem. staff Wyo. Game and Fish Commn.; Served successively as biologist, asst. fed. aid coordinator, chief game div., chief lands div. Ark. Game and Fish Commn., until 1962; with Ark. Hwy. Depy., 1962—, asst. dir. adminstr. and realty, 1968-70, asst. dir. hwys., 1970-73, dir., 1973—; ex-officio mem. Ark. Public Rds. Needs Study Commn. Past bd. dirs. Ark. Wildlife Fedn., Pulaski County Wildlife Fedn. Mem. Am. Assn. State Hwy. and Transp. Ofcls. (past pres. public affairs subcom.), Soc. Am. Mil. Engrs. Club: Little Rock Engrs. Office: PO Box 2261 Little Rock AR 72203

GRAY, JACK ODELL, real estate, construction and manufacturing company executive; b. Snyder, Tex., Jan. 10, 1932; s. Earl Vivin and Grace Pauline (Prince) G.; m. Margie Lorena Brantley, Jan. 24, 1953; children—Lisa, Jackie, Woody Earl. Student Weatherford Coll., 1953, 54. Traffic mgr. United Cold Storage, Ft. Worth, 1953-55; with WBH, Inc., Houston, 1955—, sr. v.p., 1976—; archtl. hardware cons. Block capt. Fonn Villas Civic Assn., 1968-77. Served with USNR, 1950-53. Mem. Door and Hardware Inst. Am., Assoc. Gen. Contractors Am., Weatherford C. of C. Methodist. Clubs: Waterwood National, University. Office: 2927 Westhollow Dr Houston TX 77082

GRAY, JOHN RICHMOND, hosp. adminstr.; b. Joggins, N.S., Can., May 29, 1922; came to U.S., 1930, naturalized, 1943; s. William and Martha (Orr) G.; grad. Robert Morris Coll. Bus. and Acctg., 1942-45; student acctg. U. Pitts., 1946; m. Patricia Zorn, Nov. 24, 1960; children—Joel W., David Z., Philip J., Mary Ellen. Office mgr. Burkett Tire & Supply Co., Pitts., 1947-58; controller Braddock (Pa.) Gen. Hosp., 1958-61; dir. adminstrn. Morton F. Plant Hosp., Clearwater, Fla., 1961—. Past pres. St. Cecelia's Sch. Bd.; mem. religious community services com. Clearwater Catholic High Sch.; mem., cons. Post Com., Explorer Scouts. Served as 1st lt. U.S. Army, 1943-46, 50-52. Mem. Hosp. Fin. Mgmt. Assn., Fla. Hosp. Assn. (fin. com.), Suncoast C. of C. (chmn.). Club: Kiwanis. Home: 1361 Byron Dr Clearwater FL 33516 Office: 323 Jeffords St Clearwater FL 33516

GRAY, JUDITH MONROE, librarian; b. Big Spring, Tex., Dec. 26, 1940; d. Wilson Adams and Katharine (Hanson) Monroe; m. James Isiah Gray Jr., Nov. 3, 1967 (div.). A.A., Bakersfield Coll., 1960; B.A. in German, UCLA, 1964; M.L.S., U. So. Calif.-Los Angeles, 1967. Librarian reference Kern County Library, Bakersfield, Calif., 1966-67; children's librarian Santa Monica Pub. Library (Calif.), 1967-68; librarian Los Angeles County Library, Montebello, Calif., 1968-69; regional children's librarian Los Angeles County Library, Rosemead, Calif., 1969-71; librarian de Grummond Coll. U. So. Miss. Library, Hattiesburg, 1971-72; sch. librarian Pascagoula Sch. Dist. (Miss.), 1973-78; dir. Howard County Library, Big Spring, Tex., 1980—; resource person Region 18 Edn. Service Ctr., Midland, Tex., 1983—; mem. Future Program Planning Com. West Tex. Library System, Lubbock, 1983—, mem. Automation Rev. Commn., 1983, mem. collection devel. com., 1982, 86, mem. continuing edn. com., 1980-83. Mem. exec. com. Caprock Chpt. March of Dimes, Big Spring, 1982-84. Mem. ALA., Tex. Library Assn. (chmn. dist. 1983-84, councilor 1985—), Big Spring Area C. of C. (Citation 1983, pub. relations com., sec. 1984, chmn. 1985-86, sec. exec. com. 1985-86, women's div.), AAUW (3d v.p. 1982-83, 1st v.p. 1984-85). Presbyterian. Office: Howard County Library 312 Scurry St Big Spring TX 79720

GRAY, KAREN LORETTA, physical education educator; b. New Albany, Miss., Dec. 10, 1956; d. Lee Russell and Ella Pearl (Thompson) G. B.S., U. Miss., 1978, M.Ed., 1979. Cert. instr. 1st Aid, CPR. Asst. instr. phys. edn. U. Miss., University, 1978-79; instr. phys. edn. Northwest Miss. Jr. Coll., Senatobia, 1979—, also dir. phys. edn., asst. tennis coach. ARC vol. tchr. 1st aid, CPR courses, since 19—. Mem. AAHPER, Miss. Assn. Health, Phys. Edn. and Recreation. Baptist.

GRAY, LAMAN A., JR., thoracic surgeon, educator; b. Louisville, May 28, 1940; m. Julie Gray; children—Juliet, Alice, Virginia. B.A. with distinction in Chemistry, Wesleyan U., Middletown, Conn., 1963; M.D., Johns Hopkins U., 1967. Diplomate Am. Bd. Surgery, Am. Bd. Thoracic Surgery. Intern U. Mich. Hosp., Ann Arbor, 1967-68; resident in gen. surgery, 1968-72, resident in thoracic and cardiovascular surgery, 1972-74; practice medicine specializing in thoracic and cardiovascular surgery, Louisville, 1974—; asst. prof. surgery, div. thoracic and cardiovascular surgery U. Louisville, 1974-78, assoc. prof., 1978-84, prof., 1984—, dir. thoracic and cardiovascular surgery, 1976—; mem. staff Univ. Hosp., Audubon Hosp., Norton's Children's Hosp., Ky. Bapt. Hosps., Meth. Hosp., Jewish Hosp., VA Hosp., Suburban Hosp.; presenter at profl. confs. Pioneer in heart transplant and use of ventricular assist devices in Ky. Contbr. numerous articles, abstracts to profl. publs., chpts. to books. Grantee Humana Inc., 1984-87. Mem. Am. Assn. Thoracic Surgery, Am. Coll. Cardiology, Am. Coll. Chest Physicians (com. on cardiovascular surgery, pres. Ky. chpt. 1978-79), ACS, Am. Thoracic Soc., Innominate Soc. Med. History, Jefferson County Med. Soc., John Alexander Soc. (exec. com.), Ky. Surg. Soc., Ky. Thoracic Soc., Louisville Heart Assn. (pres. 1983-85), Louisville Medico-Chirurgical Soc., Louisville Surg. Soc., Med. Forum (v.p. 1976-77), Societe Internationale de Chirurgie, Soc. Thoracic Surgeons, So. Surg. Assn., So. Thoracic Surg. Assn. (exec. council 1983-84, chmn. membership com. 1983-84), Ky. Heart Assn. (research rev. com. 1975-79), Sigma Xi. Office: Dept Surgery U Louisville Louisville KY 40292*

GRAY, MARTIN GROVER, wholesale company executive; b. Chireno, Tex., Nov. 8, 1938; s. Shannon Martin and Selma Joyce (Halbert) G.; m. Ann Phillips, Dec. 21, 1963; children—Mark, Jeffrey. B.S., Stephen F. Austin U., 1961. Acct., Continental Carbon Co., Houston, 1961-63; sales v.p. Houston Supply Co., 1963-72; pres. S. Coast Supply Co., Houston, 1972—. Republican. Mem. Ch. of Christ. Office: South Coast Supply Co Box 55649 1325 Silber Rd Houston TX 77255

GRAY, MARY TAYLOR, bowling center executive; b. Waxahachie, Tex., Jan. 12, 1928; d. Frank Camillus and Christine Elizabeth (Rader) Taylor; B.B.A., So. Methodist U., 1950; m. John Preston Gray, June 30, 1950; children—Sharon Elizabeth, Carol Ann, Mary Jo. Various secretarial positions, 1950-52; corp. sec.-treas., bookkeeper Gray's Lanes, Texas City, Tex., 1955-84, v.p., 1984-85, sec.-treas., 1986—; v.p. C&T Interests, Inc., Texas City, 1970-85, sec.-treas., 1986—; sec.-treas. S.W. Bowling Props.' Conv., 1971-76. Republican. Baptist. Home: 1921 15th Ave N Texas City TX 77590 Office: 2404 Palmer Hwy PO Box 2007 Texas City TX 77590

GRAY, RODNEY PAUL, financial consultant, executive; b. Eunice, N. Mex., Feb. 27, 1947; s. Paul N. and Alice R. Gray; m. Michele Diane Giese, June 22, 1972 (div.); 1 son, Paul Brandon. B.B.A., in Fin., Tex. Tech. U., 1970; postgrad. Tex. Credit Union League, 1972, N.Y. Inst. Fin., 1973. Sr. loan officer, membership services officer, pub. relations officer, Webb AFB Fed. Credit Union, 1972-73; asst. v.p. Kidder, Peabody & Co., Inc., Amarillo, Tex., 1973-81; v.p. Shearson/Am. Express, Amarillo, 1981—, mem. pres.'s council, 1981, 83, mem. chmn.'s council, 1982. Sustaining mem. Republican Nat. Com.; active YMCA. Recipient Kidder, Peabody Outstanding Sales award, 1979. Mem. N.Y. State Stock Exchange, Internat. Assn. Fin. Planning, Nat. Assn. Securities Dealers, Chgo. Bd. Trade, Commodity Futures Trading Corp., Chgo. Mercantile Exchange, Am. Stock Exchange, Tex. State Bd. Ins., others. Club: Tascosa Country (Amarillo). Home: 7400 Baughman Ave Amarillo TX 79121 Office: Tex Am Bank Bldg Suite 1000 Amarillo TX 79101

GRAY, SAMUEL HUTCHISON, geophysicist, researcher; b. WestChester, Pa., Oct. 7, 1948; s. Samuel Hutchison and Frances Borgia (Connelly) G.; m. Julia Ann Wetz, June 12, 1976; 1 child, Christopher. B.S., Georgetown U., 1970; M.A., U. Denver, 1973, Ph.D., 1978. Research mathematician Naval Research Lab., Washington, 1978-79; asst. prof. math. Gen. Motors Inst., Flint, Mich., 1979-82; sr. research scientist Amoco Prodn. Co., Tulsa, 1982—. Contbr. articles to profl. jours. Mem. Am. Math. Soc., Soc. Indsl. & Applied Math., Soc. Exploration Geophysicists (editor tech. program com. ann. meeting 1984), Sigma Xi. Democrat. Roman Catholic. Avocations: astronomy; running. Home: 3463 S Zunis Ave Tulsa OK 74105 Office: Amoco Production Co PO Box 3385 Tulsa OK 74102

GRAY, THOMAS EDWARD, beverage company executive; b. Logansport, Ind., Nov. 26, 1946; s. John Francis and Mary Jane (Powers) G.; m. Peggy Anne Glover, Dec. 28, 1974; children—Matthew Glover, Andrew Thomas. B.A. in Speech and Communications, Ind. U., 1973; M.A. in Journalism, Ball State U., 1977. News anchor/assignment editor Sta. WISH-TV, Indpls., 1974-78; pub. relations dir. Pabst Brewing Co., Milw., 1978-82; media relations mgr. Coca-Cola Co., Atlanta, after 1982, now mgr. internat. Media and Communications; instr. speech Ind. U., Indpls., 1977-78. Recipient Casper Community Service award Indpls. Community Service Council, 1975, 77; Clio Prodn. award Milw. Advt. Club, 1982; named AP Ind. Feature TV Reporter of Yr., 1976. Mem. Pub. Relations Soc. Am. Club: Atlanta Press. Home: 3955 Loch Highland Pass Roswell GA 30075 Office: PO Drawer 1734 NAT-9 Atlanta GA 30301

GRAY, VERNON STELL, JR., banker; b. Opelika, Ala., Sept. 24, 1946; s. Vernon Stell and Leila Belle (Betts) G.; m. Laura Kaye Hancock, June 13, 1970; 1 child, Brian Stell. A.A., Gordon Mil. Coll., 1966; B.B.A., W. Ga. Coll., 1968; M. in Trust New Bus., Northwestern U., 1973; J.D., Woodrow Wilson Coll. Law, 1978; grad. La. State U. Sch. Banking of South, 1981; grad. U. Okla. Nat. Comml. Lending Sch., 1982. Cost acct. Fairfax Mill div. West Point-Pepperell, Inc., 1969-70; asst. v.p., trust officer Peoples Bank, Carrollton, Ga., 1970-74; exec. v.p., trust officer Bank of Griffin (Ga.), 1974-83; v.p. First Bank of Conyers (Ga.), 1983—; instr. in bank compliance and trust Gordon Jr. Coll. Past v.p. Am. Bus. Club, Am. Cancer Soc., Jr. Achievement Inc.; past pres. Griffin Touchdown Club; past chmn., bd. dirs. McIntosh Trail Area Planning and Devel. Commn.; bd. dirs. Flint River council Boy Scouts Am.; Griffin Credit Bur., Jr. Achievement, Inc., Griffin; chmn. adv. bd. Sch. Bus., W. Ga. Coll., Carrollton; trustee Griffin-Spalding County Hosp. Authority; fund drives United Fund, Am. Cancer Soc., Boy Scouts Am. Project Fund. Mem. Ind. Bankers Assn. Am. (pres. young bankers sect.), Ind. Bankers Assn. Ga., Am. Bankers Assn., Ga. Bankers Assn., Griffin C. of C. (Bicentennial Com. award 1976; past chmn. edn. com., dir.). Baptist. Club: Rotary (Conyers, Ga.). Home: 2804-A Briar Hill Ln Conyers GA 30208 Office: First Bank of Conyers 1540 Hwy 138 Conyers GA 30207

GRAY, WILLIAM EWART, III, energy company official; b. Lexington, Ky., Feb. 22, 1932; s. William E. and Amelia Lee G.; m. Bonalyn Simpson, Dec. 19, 1970; children—Ami, Gena. B.S., Wake Forest U., 1955. Midwest mgr. PPG Industries, Chgo., 1958-78; mgr. corp. accounts Diamond Shamrock Corp., Houston, 1978—. Served with USAF, 1958. Mem. Am. Petroleum Inst., Nat. Petroleum Refiners Assn., Nat. Account Mktg. Assn. Republican. Clubs: Lochinvar Golf, Houston Racquet, Univ. (Houston); Ocean Reef (Key Largo, Fla.); Bimini Big Game Fish (Bahamas).

GRAYBEAL, BARBARA, writer, editor; b. Mountain City, Tenn., Sept. 21, 1935; d. Claude Harold and Ruby Lucille (Hodge) G.; m. Lewis N. Kremer, June 7, 1958 (div.); m. Charles L. Ring, May 8, 1982. B.A. magna cum laude, Marietta Coll., 1957. With New Yorker mag., N.Y.C., 1957-58; assoc. editor Saturday Evening Post, Phila., 1958-62, Episcopalian mag., Phila., 1962-69; asst. editor Lutheran mag., Phila., 1971-72; instr. journalism Temple U., Phila., 1972-81; founding editor CGA World mag., 1980-82, sr. editor, 1982—. Mem. com. interpretation and promotion, dept. overseas missions Nat. Council Chs., 1966-68; mem. Phila. Democratic Com., 1968; bd. dirs., sec. Friends of Free Library Phila.; bd. dirs. N.C. Sch. Arts. Mem. Women in Communications (v.p. chpt.), Marietta Coll. Alumni Assn., AAUW (pres. br.), Internat. Platform Assn., Phi Beta Kappa, Sigma Delta Chi, Alpha Xi Delta. Episcopalian (lay reader). Editor/writer: Good and Easy Recipes from Grandmother's House, 1984; editorial cons. Good Ideas for Decorating; contbr. articles, photographs and poetry to various publs. Address: 4201 Sunnydell Dr Winston-Salem NC 27106

GRAY-LITTLE, BERNADETTE, psychologist; b. Washington, N.C., Oct. 21, 1944; d. James and Rosalie (Lanier) Gray; m. Shade Keys Little, Nov. 21, 1971; children—Maura, Mark. Asst. prof. psychology, U. N.C.-Chapel Hill, 1971-76, assoc. prof., 1976-82, prof., 1982—. NIMH fellow, 1967-68; Fulbright fellow, 1970-71; NRC fellow, 1982-83. Mem. Am. Psychol. Assn., Phi Beta Kappa. Office: Psychology Dept U NC Chapel Hill NC 27514

GRAYSON, MARION LOU, art historian; b. English, Ind.; d. Raymond Francis and Ida Mae (Land) Spears; divorced; children—Jon Michael, Craig Martin. B.S., Columbia U., 1968, M.A., 1970, M.Ph., 1979, Ph.D., 1979. Lectr., cons. Mus. Fine Arts, St. Petersburg, Fla., 1979, curator, 1980-82; freelance lectr.-writer, 1982-83; asst. prof. art history, dir. Sewall Art Gallery, Rice U., Houston, 1983—. Mem. Coll. Art Assn., Historians Netherlandish Art, Phi Beta Kappa. Author: (exhbn. catalogues) Paris in the Belle Epoque: People and Places, 1980, Fragonard and His Friends, 1982; contbr. articles to profl. jours. Office: Dept Art and Art History Rice U PO Box 1892 Houston TX 77251

GRAYSON, PHILLIP SIMON, theater designer, educator, consultant; b. Newark, Aug. 25, 1947; s. Matthew and Ruth Mildred (Swartzbach) G.; m. Joann Ressler Hess, Aug. 10, 1969; 1 dau., Kristine. B.A., Gettysburg Coll., 1969; M.A., Ill. State U., 1971; M.F.A., Va. Commonwealth U., 1981. Master properties Repertory Theatre St. Louis, 1971; technician Los Angeles Network TV and movie studios, 1972-74; tech. dir. Illusion Corp., St. Louis, 1974-76; asst. prof. communication arts dept., dir. tech. prodn. James Madison U., Harrisonburg, Va., 1977—; theatre cons. Davis and Assocs. (now Mc Clintock and Assocs.), AIA, 1982—; mem. theatre adv. bd. Children's Theatre of Richmond, 1981—; del. Prague Quadrennial Scenography Congress in Czech, 1983. Alcone Drama Fund grantee, 1980. Mem. U.S. Inst. Theatre Tech., Am. Theatre Assn., Assn. Brit. Theatre Tech., Internat. Alliance Theatre Stage Employees. Contbr. articles to theatre jours. Home: Rural Route 1 Box 188-9 Linville VA 22834 Office: James Madison U Harrisonburg VA 22807

GRAYSON, RICHARD, humanities educator, author; b. Bklyn., June 4, 1951; s. Daniel and Marilyn (Sarrett) G. B.A., Bklyn. Coll., 1973, M.F.A., 1976; M.A., Coll. of S.I., 1975; M.Ed., Fla. Atlantic U., 1985. Lectr. L.I. U., Bklyn., 1975-78, CUNY, N.Y.C., 1978-81; instr. Sch. Visual Arts, 1979-80, Touro Coll., 1979-80; prof. English, Broward Community Coll., Fort Lauderdale, Fla., 1981-84, dir. computer learning systems, 1984—. Cons. New Orleans Ctr. for Creative Arts, 1981—; field rep. Antioch Internat. (Ohio), 1983—; chmn. Floridians for Interstate Banking Polit. Action Com., 1984—. Author: With Hitler in New York, 1979; Lincoln's Doctor's Dog, 1982; Eating At Arby's, 1982; I Brake for Delmore Schwartz, 1983. Treas. Com. for Immediate Nuclear War, Davie, Fla., 1983—. Nat. Arts Club fellow, 1977, MacDowell Colony fellow, 1980, 84, Va. Ctr. for Creative Arts fellow, 1981-82, Fla. Arts Council fellow, 1981. Mem. Authors Guild, PEN, Nat. Council Tchrs. English, Bklyn. Coll. Alumni Assn. Home: 2732 S University Dr Davie FL 33328

GRAYSON, WALTON GEORGE, III, lawyer, business executive; b. Shreveport, La., Aug. 18, 1928; s. Walton George, Jr. and Mary Alice (Lowery) G.; A.B., Princeton U., 1949; LL.B., Harvard U., 1952; m. Bennetta McEwen Purse, May 20, 1955; children—Walton Grayson IV, Mark C., Bennett P., Dwight P. Bar: Tex. 1952. Practiced in Dallas, 1952—. Asst. counsel Gt. Nat. Life Ins. Co., Dallas, 1954-69; v.p., gen. counsel Southland Corp., Dallas, 1965-72; exec. v.p., 1972—, also dir.; partner firm Atwell, Grayson & Atwell, 1961-69, Grayson & Simon, 1969-73; of counsel firm Simon & Twombly, 1973—. Served with USN, 1952-54. Mem. Tex. Bar Assn., Dallas Bar Assn., ABA. Club: Masons. Home: 10525 Strait Ln Dallas TX 75229 Office: 2828 N Haskell Ave Dallas TX 75204

GREACEN, JOHN MORLEY, court administrator; lawyer; b. Washington, Aug. 12, 1942; s. Thomas Edmund and Wynfred Vultee (Fox) G.; m. Virginia Hearn, Jan. 4, 1964; children—Robert Scott, William Stevenson, Grace Elizabeth. A.B., Princeton U., 1965; J.D., U. Ariz., 1968. Bar: Ariz., D.C. Law clk. Judge Oscar H. Davis, U.S. Ct. Claims, Washington, 1968-69; assoc. Kirkland & Ellis, Washington, 1969-71; reporter Ariz. Rules of Criminal Procedure, Tucson, 1971-72; asst. dean, asst. prof. U. Ariz. Coll. Law, Tucson, 1972-73; dep. dir. Nat. Inst. Law Enforcement and Criminal Justice, Dept. Justice, Washington, 1973-74; acting dir. Nat. Inst. Juvenile Justice and Delinquency Prevention, Dept. Justice, Washington, 1974-75; program dir. Police Found., Washington, 1975-78; vis. prof., acting dir. Inst. Advanced Studies in Justice, Washington Coll. Law, Am. U., 1978; dep. dir. programs Nat. Ctr. State Cts., Williamsburg, Va., 1979-84; clk. U.S. Ct. Appeals 4th Cir., Richmond, Va., 1984—. mem. Criminal Justice Working Group, Community Support System Task Panel, Pres.'s Commn. on Mental Health, 1977. Mem. stewardship council United Ch. of Christ, 1972-78, chmn., 1976-78; moderator First Congl. United Ch. of Christ, Washington, 1971. Recipient Ralph W. Aigler award U. Ariz. Coll. Law, 1968; Atty. Gen.'s Spl. Achievement award, 1975. Mem. ABA (mem. exec. com. lawyers conf. judicial adminstrn. div. 1982-86, vice chmn. criminal justice sect. 1985-86, mem. council criminal justice sect. 1982-85), Nat. Assn. Ct. Mgmt., Nat. Conf. Appellate Ct. Clks., Fed. Ct. Clks. Assn. Nat. Center State Cts. (assoc.), Am. Judicature Soc.,

Democrat. Mem. United Ch. of Christ. Office: US Courthouse 10th and Main Sts Richmond VA 23219

GREAR, EFFIE CARTER, educational administrator; b. Huntington, W.Va., Aug. 15, 1927; d. Harold Jones and Margaret (Tinsley) Carter; Mus.B., W.Va. State Coll., 1948; M.A., Ohio State U., 1955; Ed.D., Nova U., 1976; m. William Alexander Grear, May 16, 1952; children—Rhonda Kaye, William Alexander. Band dir. Fla. A&M High Sch., Tallahassee, 1948-51, Smith-Brown High Sch., Arcadia, Fla., 1951-56; band dir. Lake Shore High Sch., Belle Glade, Fla., 1956-60, dean of girls, 1960-66, asst. prin., 1966-70; asst. prin. Glades Central High Sch., Belle Glade, Fla., 1970-76, prin., 1976—. Mem. Nat. Assn. Secondary Sch. Prins., Nat. Community Sch. Edn. Conf., Nat. Sch. Public Relations Assn., Assn. Supervision and Curriculum Devel., Fla. Assn. Secondary Sch. Prins., Palm Beach County Sch. Adminstrs. Assn., Phi Delta Kappa, Alpha Kappa Alpha. Clubs: Elite Community, Women's Civic. Office: Glades Central High School 425 W Canal St N Belle Glade FL 33430

GREAR, SAMUEL CHENEY, medical center pharmaceutical official; b. Anna, Ill., Feb. 8, 1949; s. Samuel Judson and Constance Carolyn (Grabow) G.; m. Mary Roberta Rickelman, May 23, 1970; children—Emily Ann, Sarah Jo. B.S. in Pharmacy, St. Louis Coll. Pharmacy, 1973; postgrad. U. Okla. Univ. Ctr. at Tulsa. Staff pharmacist BVP, Inc., Peoria, Ill., 1973-74, Bill Maher Drug, Washington, Ill., 1974-76, SuperX Drug, Lincoln, Ill., 1976-79, Schnucks Walgreen, Cape Girardeau, Mo., 1979-80, S.E. Mo. Hosp., Cape Girardeau, 1980-83; pharmacy dir. ancillary services Claremore Regional Med. Ctr., Okla., 1983—; adj. tchr. Rogers County Health Dept., Claremore, 1983—. Recipient Meritorious Service Before Self award Central Ill. Pharm. Assn., 1978. Mem. Am. Soc. Hosp. Pharmacists, Am. Coll. Health Adminstrs., Okla. Soc. Hosp. Pharmacists (chmn. Eastern dist. 1984-85), Young Health Adminstrs. N.E. Okla., Lambda Kappa Sigma, Delta Sigma Theta (alumni). Avocations: white water rafting; canoeing; golf; racquetball. Home: 1209 N Miller Dr Claremore OK 74017

GREASON, MURRAY CROSSLEY, JR., lawyer; b. Wake Forest, N.C., Dec. 12, 1936; s. Murray Crossley and Evelyn Elizabeth (Hackney) G.; B.S. magna cum laude, Wake Forest U., 1959, J.D. magna cum laude, 1962; m. Joan Millicent Wilder, June 25, 1960; children—Murray Crossley III, Millicent Wilder, Elizabeth Hillary. Admitted to N.C. bar, 1962, since practiced in Winston-Salem; assoc. firm Womble Carlyle Sandridge & Rice, 1965-70, mem. firm, 1970—; dir. 1st Home Fed. Savs. & Loan Assn. Vis. lectr. Wake Forest U., 1972-74. Pres. Winston-Salem Estate Planning Council, 1973; trustee Denmark Loan Fund, scholarships to Wake Forest U.; bd. visitors Wake Forest Law Sch., 1983—; chmn. N.W. N.C. chpt. ARC, 1986; mem. Commn. on Ministry Episcopalian Diocese of N.C. Served to capt., JAG, AUS, 1962-65. Fellow Am. Coll. Tax Counsel; mem. Forsyth County, Wake Forest U. Alumni Assn. (pres. 1973), ABA, N.C. Bar Assn., Forsyth County Bar Assn. (pres. 1986—), Phi Beta Kappa, Omicron Delta Kappa. Episcopalian (vestryman, sr. warden). Club: Forsyth Country. Home: 745 Arbor Rd Winston-Salem NC 27104 Office: PO Drawer 84 Winston-Salem NC 27102

GREAVER, JOANNE HUTCHINS, mathematics educator, lecturer, author; b. Louisville, Aug. 9, 1939; d. Alphonso Victor and Mary Louise (Sage) Hutchins; m. James William Greaver, Dec. 17, 1977; 1 child, Mary Elizabeth. B.S. in Chemistry, U. Louisville, 1961, M.Ed., 1971; M.A.T. in Math., Purdue U., 1973. Cert. tchr. secondary edn. Math tchr., dept. chmn. J.M. Atherton High Sch., Jefferson County Pub. Schs., Louisville, 1962—; part time faculty Bellarmine Coll., Louisville, 1982—; project reviewer NSF, 1983—; advisor Council on Higher Edn., Frankfort, Ky., 1983—. Author workbook: Down Algebra Alley, 1984; co-author curriculum guides. Charter mem. Commonwealth Tchrs. Inst., 1984—; mem. Nat. Forum for Excellence in Edn., Indpls., 1983; metric edn. leader Fed. Metric Project, Louisville, 1979-82. Recipient Presdl. award for excellence in math. teaching, 1983; awardee NSF, 1983, Louisville Found., 1984; mem. Hon. Order Ky. Cols.; named Outstanding Citizen, SAR, 1984. Mem. Greater Louisville Council Tchrs. of Math. (pres. 1977-78), Nat. Council Tchrs. of Math. (reviewer 1981—), Ky. Council Tchrs. of Math., Math. Assn. Am., Kappa Delta Pi, Zeta Tau Alpha. Republican. Presbyterian. Club: Atherton Faculty. Avocations: tropical fish; gardening; handicrafts; travel; tennis. Home: 11513 Tazwell Dr Louisville KY 40222 Office: J M Atherton High Sch 3000 Dundee Rd Louisville KY 40205

GREAVES, RICHARD LEE, history educator; b. Glendale, Calif., Sept. 11, 1938; m. 1959; 2 daus. B.A. summa cum laude, Bethel Coll., 1960; M.A. magna cum laude, Berkeley Bapt. Div. Sch., 1962; Ph.D., U. London, 1964; postgrad. U. Mo., 1965. Assoc. prof. history Fla. Meml. Coll., 1964-65; asst. prof. William Woods Coll., 1965-66, Eastern Wash. State Coll., 1966-69; asst. to assoc. prof. humanities Mich. State U., East Lansing, 1969-72; assoc. prof. Fla. State U., Tallahassee, 1972-75, prof., 1975—, courtesy prof. religion, 1985—; vis. scholar Clark Library, UCLA, 1977. Merriam Park scholar, 1959-60; K.T. scholar, 1961-62; U. Mo. Regents' grantee, 1965; NEH fellow, 1967, grantee, 1980; Am. Council Learned Socs. fellow, 1975-76, 83; Mellon Found. fellow, 1977; Fla. State U. Found. fellow, 1979; Henry E. Huntington Library fellow, 1981. Fellow Royal Hist. Soc.; mem. Am. Hist. Assn., Am. Soc. Ch. History (council 1981-84), Historians of Early Modern Europe, Bapt. Hist. Soc. Britain, Conf. Brit. Studies, 16th Century Studies. Author: John Bunyan, 1969; The Puritan Revolution and Educational Thought: Background for Reform (Walter D. Love Meml. prize Conf. Brit. Studies 1970); Theology and Revolution in the Scottish Reformation: Studies in the Thought of John Knox, 1980; (with James Forrest) Society and Religion in Elizabethan England, 1981; John Bunyan: A Reference Guide, 1981; (with Robert Zaller) Biographical Dictionary of British Radicals in the Seventeenth Century, 3 vols., 1982-84; Saints and Rebels-Seven Nonconformists in Stuart England, 1985; Triumph over Silence: Women in Protestant History, 1985; Deliver Us from Evil: The Radical Underground in Britain, 1660-1663, 1986. Contbr. articles to profl. jours. Home: 910 Shadowlawn Dr Tallahassee FL 32312 Office: Dept History Fla State U Tallahassee FL 32306

GREEHEY, WILLIAM EUGENE, energy company executive; b. Ft. Dodge, Iowa, 1936; married. B.B.A., St. Mary's U., 1960. Auditor Price Waterhouse & Co., 1960-61; sr. auditor Humble Oil & Refining Co., 1961-63; sr. v.p. fin. The Coastal Corp. and predecessor, 1963-74; with Valero Energy Corp. (formerly Coastal States Gas Producing Co.), 1974—, pres., chief exec. officer LoVaca Gathering Co. (name changed to Valero Transmission Co. subs.), 1974-80, pres., chief exec. officer Valero Energy Corp., San Antonio, 1980—, chmn. bd., 1983—, also dir. Served with USAF, 1954-58. Office: Valero Energy Corp 530 McCullough San Antonio TX 78292*

GREEN, DAVID TRELLIS, insurance and financial services executive; b. Austin, Tex., Aug. 13, 1946; s. Elvin T. and Evelyn (Klotz) G.; m. Ellen Jane Johnson, July 24, 1976; children—David T., Daniel Patrick. B.A., Tex. Tech U., 1969, postgrad., 1969-71. C.L.U.; registered rep. Nat. Assn. Security Dealers. Sales and service rep. S.W. Alloy Supply Co., Houston, 1971-73; profl. ins. practice, 1973—. Lector, minister of Eucharist, Roman Catholic Ch.; nat. officer U.S. Jaycees, 1972-76. Mem. Nat. Assn. Life Underwriters, Million Dollar Round Table, Tex. Leaders Round Table. Club: Tex. Tech Century. Home: 6255 Briar Rose Dr Houston TX 77057 Office: 2121 Sage Rd Suite 100 Houston TX 77056

GREEN, EDWARD THOMAS, JR., educator; b. Oxford, N.J., Apr. 19, 1921; s. Edward Thomas and Euphemia (Lanterman) G.; B.S. cum laude, Ithaca Coll., 1942; M.S., Syracuse U., 1947, Ed.D., 1965; m. Margaret Evelyn Tuttle, Jan. 30, 1944; children—Marsha, Margaret, Barbara. Music instr. high sch., Palmyra, N.Y., 1942-50, dir. guidance, vice-prin., 1946-50; prin. Palmyra-Macedon Central Sch., 1950-54; supervising prin. New Berlin (N.Y.) Central Sch., 1954-58, Rondout Valley Central Sch., Accord, N.Y., also supt. schs., 1958-66; supt. schs., Oneida, N.Y., 1966-77; assoc. prof. edn. Ga. So. Coll., Statesboro, 1977—. Pres., Mid-Hudson Sch. Study Council, New Paltz, N.Y., 1960; vice chmn. CHE-MAD-HER-ON, Inc.; area sec. Central Sch. Study; mem. exec. com. Catskill Study on Small Sch. Design; v.p. N.Y. State Tchrs. Retirement Bd. Vice-pres. Rip Van Winkle council Boy Scouts Am., 1964-66, v.p., then pres. Madison County council, chmn. Madison Dist., pres. Iroquois council; pres. Palmyra Betterment Club 1952; mem. Ulster County Community Action Program; past pres. Ithaca Coll. Alumni Council. Served with AUS, 1942 46; ETO. Mem. N.Y. State Sch. Dist. Adminstrs. (pres.), Am. Assn. Sch. Adminstrs., Assn. for Supervision and Curriculum Devel., Nat. Sch. Pub. Relations Assn., Nat. Orgn. for Legal Problems in Edn., Phi Delta Kappa (chpt. pres., area coordinator), Phi Mu Alpha. Republican. Presbyterian. Clubs: Masons, Shriners. Home: 409 Cardinal Dr Statesboro GA 30458 Office: Landrum 8143 Ga So Coll Statesboro GA 30460

GREEN, HERSCHEL VICTOR, builder; b. Detroit, Oct. 10, 1922; s. Reuben and Eva (Dutchovsky) Greenberg; m. Nancy Joan Flayderman, Nov. 15, 1952; children—Elizabeth Ann, Carolyn Sue, Robert Brian, Susan Dale, Florence Beth. Student, U. Mich., 1942-43; B.B.A., U. Tex., 1947. Chmn. bd. Green Cos., Miami, Fla., 1948—; dir. United Nat. Bank Miami; trustee Bldg. Industry Advancement Program; mem. Dade County Housing Task Force; chmn. bd. Greater Miami Free Trade Zone, Inc. Assoc., found. mem. South Miami Hosp.; bd. dirs. United Way; mem. Combined Jewish Appeal; mem. citizens bd. U. Miami Athletic Fedn.; mem. Dade County Planning Council, South Fla. Coordinating Council. Served to lt. (j.g.) USNR, 1943-46. Recipient Builder of Yr. award Bldrs Assn. South Fla., 1973; Builder of Yr. award Fla. Home Bldrs. Assn., 1974. Mem. Bldrs. Assn. South Fla. (past pres.), Fla. Home Bldrs. Assn. (past pres.), Nat. Assn. Home Bldrs. (life dir., mem. exec. com.), Greater Miami C. of C. (past pres.), South Miami C. of C. (past pres.). Home: 9485 Old Cutler Lane Coral Gables FL 33156 Office: 9100 South Dadeland Blvd PH II Miami FL 33156

GREEN, HUBERT GORDON, health service officer, educator; b. Dallas, Oct. 31, 1938; s. Hubert Gordon and Mary Belle (Gillespie) G.; m. Jean Ann Hunter, June 7, 1969; children—Nancy Elaine, David Gordon, Whitney Anne, Emily Erin. B.A., Rice U., 1962; M.D., U. Tex.-Southwestern at Dallas, 1968; M.P.H., U. Calif., 1972. Diplomate Am. Bd. Pediatrics. Intern, Children's Med. Center, Dallas, 1968-69; resident U. Wash., Seattle, 1969-71; assoc. prof. pediatrics and biometry U. Ark. for Med. Scis., Little Rock, 1972-77; assoc. med. dir. Ark. Children and Youth Project, Little Rock, 1972-73; med. dir. Ark. Children's Hosp., Little Rock, 1973-77; dir. Handicapped Children's Center and Child Devel. Clinic, Ark. Dept. Health, Little Rock, 1975-77; dep. dir. Div. Health Services Delivery, USPHS, Dallas, 1977-83; dir. Dallas County Health Dept., 1983—; mem. med. staff Children's Med. Ctr., Dallas. Served with USN, 1962-64. Mem. Am. Pub. Health Assn., Am. Acad. Pediatrics, Tex. Pediatric Soc., Alpha Omega Alpha. Contbr. articles to profl. jours.; mem. editorial bd. Perinatal Press, 1982—. Office: Dallas County Health Dept 1936 Amelia Ct Dallas TX 75235

GREEN, INA LYNCH, psychologist, educator; b. Ennis, Tex., Mar. 13, 1930; d. Bertie Wayne and Barbara Gertrude (Brock) Lynch; m. William Brent Green, May 29, 1949; children—William Brent, Jr., Heather D'Wayne Green Campbell. B.S., Abilene Christian U., 1963; M.A., Ohio State U., 1965; Ph.D., 1969. Bookkeeper, United Gas Co., Houston, 1949-51; statis. typist Tex. Dept. Pub. Safety, Austin, 1951; key punch operator Exxon, Houston, 1953; prof. psychology Abilene Christian U., 1966—; cons. Abilene Mental Health Assn., Tex. Dept. Human Resources, W.Tex. Rehab. Ctr., Abilene State Sch. Bd. dirs. Abilene Rape Crisis Center, 1979-81. HEW fellow, 1964-66. Mem. Am. Assn. Mental Deficiency, Am. Psychol. Assn., Tex. Psychol. Assn., Abilene Psychol. Assn. (pres. 1971). Mem. Ch. of Christ. Home: 618 EN 19th St Abilene TX 79601 Office: PO Box 6786 Abilene Christian University Station Abilene TX 79699

GREEN, JAMES COLLINS, former lieutenant governor North Carolina; b. Halifax County, Va., Feb. 24, 1921; s. John Collins and Frances Sue (Oliver) G.; student Washington and Lee U.; m. Alice McAulay Clark, 1943; children—Sarah Frances, Susan Clark, James Collins. Mem. Bladen County (N.C.) Bd. Edn., 1955-61; mem. N.C. Ho. of Reps., 1961-65, 69-73, speaker, 1975-76, mem. N.C. State Senate, 1967; lt. gov. N.C., 1977-85; farmer, tobacco warehouse operator. Served with USMC. Lodges: Masons (32 deg.), Shriners. Presbyterian. Office: Office of Gov Adminstrn Bldg Raleigh NC 27611

GREEN, JESSE LEE, clinical psychologist; b. Ft. Worth, Oct. 12, 1932; s. Jesse Hayden and Mary Lee (Elliott) G.; B.A., U. Tex., 1958; M.A., Tex. Christian U., 1961; Ph.D., Okla. State U., 1970; m. Juanita Estelle Webb, June 23, 1957; children—Allan F., Gail A., Roger M., Jesse Lee. Commd. officer USAF, advanced through grades to maj., 1950-54, 61-79; clin. psychologist CIA, 1979-81, Dept. Def., 1981-83; chief clin. psychologist Ft. Worth Police Dept., 1984—. Cert., lic. psychologist, Tex. Mem. Aerospace Med. Assn., Am. Psychol. Assn., Tex. Psychol. Assn., USAF Soc. Clin. Psychologists. Home: 4314 Birchman Ave Fort Worth TX 76107

GREEN, JOHN FRANCIS, nature science center administrator, science educator; b. Berwyn, Ill., Jan 21, 1949; s. Francis John and Margaret Estelle (Novotny) G.; m. Marilyn Kay Miley, Sept. 13, 1971. B.S., Ohio U., 1971; postgrad. Ohio State U., 1973; cert. Audubon Ecology Camps, 1971. Naturalist, Nature and Sci. Ctr., Winston-Salem, N.C., 1974-75, Mus. of Hist. and Sci., Kansas City, Mo., 1975-76; seasonal naturalist Union Coll. Environmental Edn. Ctr., Middlesboro, Ky., 1976; curator Brooklyn Children Mus., N.Y., 1977-79; dir. Nature-Sci. Ctr., Spartanburg, S.C., 1979—; floor mgr. Brooklyn Children Mus., N.Y., 1978-79; sci. cons. Wofford Coll., Spartanburg, 1981—; sci. fair judge Spartanburg Pub. Schs., 1980—; research activities Nature-Sci Ctr., Spartanburg, 1982—. Contbr. articles to sci. jours.; science writer: newspaper column, 1985—. Com. mem. Mary H. Wright Park Com., Spartanburg, 1981-82; lectr. Garden Clubs and Civic Orgns., Spartanburg, 1980—; tour guide Shepards Ctr. Sr. Citizens Group, Spartanburg, 1983-84. Grantee Sci. Equipment Spartanburg County Found., 1983, Friends of the Arts, 1984, Edn. Programming Spartanburg County Found., 1984, Mus. Assessment Inst. of Mus. Services, 1984, Spartanburg County Med. Aux. recipient Certificate of Pub. Achievement Westview and Jesse Bobo Schs., 1985. Mem. Am. Assn. of Mus., S.C. Acad. of Scis., S.C. Assn. of Mus., Natural Scis. for Youth Orgn. Clubs: Sierra (Spartanburg) (outings chmn., 1982-84) Audubon (Spartanburg). Avocations: hiking; reading. Office: Nature-Sci Ctr 385 S Spring St Spartanburg SC 29301

GREEN, JOHN RANDOLPH, college administrator; b. Tarboro, N.C., Apr. 5, 1934; s. John Henry and Mildred (Holloway) G.; m. Mollie Ann Tedder, Apr. 14, 1957; children—Nancy Minton, John Randolph. B.S. in Indsl. Arts Edn., N.C. State U., 1957, M.Ed., 1967. Instr. indsl. arts Raleigh Public Schs., N.C., 1957-66; chmn. elec. dept. Wake Tech. Coll., Raleigh, 1966-77, dean vocat. edn., 1977—. Served to sgt. U.S. Army, 1957. Mem. N.C. Instructional Adminstrs. Assn., Western Film Preservation Soc. Baptist. Avocations: woodworking; reading; western films. Home: 4921 Cindy Dr Raleigh NC 27603 Office: Wake Tech Coll 9101 Fayetteville Rd Raleigh NC 27603

GREEN, MARTIN BARRY, chiropractor; b. N.Y.C., Aug. 1, 1948; s. Morris Joseph and Sally (Zegler) G.; m. Carolyn Meg Bloom, Aug. 16, 1979; 1 child, Sasha Richard. D.C., N.Y. Chiropractic Coll., 1977; B.S., CW. Post Coll., 1970. Diplomate Nat. Bd. Chiropractic Examiners; cert. Meridian Therapy/Acupuncture. With mktg. research staff Ford Motor Co., Falls Church, Va., 1971-73; Brit. Leyland Co., Leonia, N.J., 1973-74; sole practice chiropractic Green Chiropractic Ctr., Tamarac, Fla., 1977—. dir., 1985—. Mem. Social Service Bd., Tamarac, 1985; police surgeon Tamarac Police Dept., 1979. Recipient Community Service award Eastern Airline/W107 FM, Tamarac, 1980. Mem. Fla. Chiropractic Assn., Broward County Chiropractic Soc., Parker Chiropractic Research Found., Tamarac C. of C., Broward Bus. Club (co-founder). Jewish. Office: 8333 W McNab Rd Tamarac FL 33321

GREEN, MARY JUANITA, sales and training manager; b. Lakeland, Fla., June 9, 1927; d. William Harold and Helen Mary (Schmid) Rhoda; m. Glenn William Green, Dec. 18, 1947; children—Lawrence William, Deborah Lynn, Mary Maureen. Clk., typist Polk County Voter Registrar Office, Bartow, Fla., 1945-46; property abstractor Lakeland Abstract, Fla., 1946-52; tupperware dealer Pyramid Party Sales, Tampa, Fla., 1968-70, mgr. bd., 1970-75; mgr. bd. Orange Blossom Parties, Lakeland, 1975-83, Bellringer Sales, Lakeland, 1983—. Sec. community campaign Childrens Home, Lakeland, 1946; bd. dirs. PTA Limestreet Sch., Lakeland, 1955-57; leader Campfire, Inc., Lakeland, 1962-68. Mem. Am. Bus. Women's Assn. (ways and means coordinator 1983-84, program chmn. 1984). Republican. Christian Scientist. Club: Sorosis (pub. affairs chmn. 1963-64). Avocations: cooking; interior decorating; music; travel. Home: 4910 Hidden Hills Dr Lakeland FL 33803

GREEN, MORTON, publisher; b. Boston, Aug. 19, 1933; s. Samuel and Eva Green; m. Shirley Betterman, Mar. 21, 1953; children—Sus, Pamela, Andrew. B.S. in Bus., Bentley Coll., 1957; M.S. in Mktg., Boston U., 1959. Vice pres. sales and mktg. Credit Inc., Boston, 1957 73; pres. United Service Bur., Ft. Lauderdale, Fla., 1973-79; advt. dir. Guide Publs., Pompano, Fla., 1979-81; pub. South Fla. Living mag., Baker Publs., Deerfield Beach, Fla., 1981—. Served as staff sgt. USAF, 1953-57. Recipient Alexander M. Moening award for Sales and mktg. achievement; Baker Publs. award for best designed mag., 1981; spl. award for best mktg. of a mag. Baker Publs., 1983. Silver Medallion award Nat. Orgn. Credit Mgrs. Mem. Nat. Boaters' Assn., Fla. Atlantic Builders Assn., Nat. Assn. Home Builders, Builders Assn. South Fla., South Fla. Mfrs. Assn., Treasure Coast Builders Assn., Mus. Heritage Soc., Broward's Friends of Chamber Music, Nat. Assn. Mag. Pubs. Contbr. articles on mktg. to jours.

GREEN, NANCY NUNN, communicative disorders center executive, clinical audiologist; b. Jacksonville, Fla., May 5, 1957; d. George Lee and Eileen Claire (Colby) Nunn; m. Whitney Curry Green, Feb. 19, 1983. A.A. with highest honors, Fla. Jr. Coll., 1976; B.A. cum laude, Fla. State U., 1980, M.A., 1981. Lic. audiology, Fla.; cert. clinical competence in audiology. Mgr. trainee Leed's Catalog Showrooms, Jacksonville, 1975-81; instr. German, Fla. State U., Tallahassee, 1979-81; clin. fellow Savannah Speech & Hearing, Ga., 1981; dir., chief audiologist Communicative Disorders Ctr., Jacksonville, 1982—; intern supr. Fla. State U., Jacksonville, 1983; course dir. Council on Accreditation in Occupational Hearing Conservation, Haddon Heights, N.J., 1983—. Builder Visual Reinforcement Audiometry System, 1982. Vol. Easter Seals Soc., Jacksonville, 1983; Jacksonville Area Disabled Persons Council, 1984; consumer mem. Nat. Assn. for Hearing and Speech Action, Rockville, Md., 1983—; expert testimony Jacksonville City Council, subcom. on noise, 1984. Fellow Acad. Dispensing Audiologists; mem. Am. Speech, Lang., Hearing Assn., Am. Soc. Safety Engrs. (sec. 1984-85), Am. Acad. Otolaryngology-Head and Neck Surgery, Fla. Speech, Language, Hearing Assn., So. Audiological Soc., Am. Auditory Soc., Nat. Safety Council, The Centurian Club of Deafness Research Found., Fla. Assn. Health and Social Services, Nat. Hearing Conservation Assn., Fla. Hearing Aid Soc., Am. Speech and Hearing Assn. (Continuing Edn. award 1984), Phi Theta Kappa. Avocations: oil painting; science fiction novels; racquetball; needlepoint. Office: Jacksonville Hearing and Noise Control Inc dba Communicative Disorders Ctr 1731 University Blvd South Jacksonville FL 32216

GREEN, PETER MORRIS, literature educator, historian, writer, translator; b. London, Dec., 22, 1924; came to U.S., 1971; s. Arthur and Olive E. (Slaughter) G.; m. Lalage Isobel Pulvertaft, June 28, 1951 (div.); children—Timothy Michael, Nicholas Paul, Sarah Francesca; m. 2d Carin Margreta Christensen, July 18, 1975. B.A. with 1st class honors in Classics, Trinity Coll., Cambridge U., 1950, M.A., 1954, Ph.D., 1954. Dir. studies, classics Selwyn Coll., Cambridge, Eng., 1952-53; freelance writer, translator, London, 1953-63, lit. advisor Bodley Head, 1957-58, fiction critic London Daily Telegraph newspaper, 1953-63, cons. editor Hodder and Stoughton Co., 1960-63, TV critic The Listener, 1961-63, film critic John O' London's Weekly, 1959-62; lectr. Greek history, lit. Coll. Year in Athens, 1966-71; vis. prof. classics U. Tex., Austin, 1971-72, prof. classics, 1972—, James R. Dougherty prof. classics, 1982—; vis. prof. UCLA, 1976; Mellon prof. humanities Tulane U., 1986; translator Penguin Classics series, Juvenal, Ovid. Served with RAFVR, 1943-47. Recipient Heinemann Found. award lit. for novel The Sword of Pleasure, 1957; grantee U. Tex.-Austin Research Inst., 1980, 83, 85; sr. fellow NEH, 1983-84. Fellow Royal Soc. Lit. (council mem. 1959-63), Classics Assn., Hellenic Soc., Am. Philol. Assn., Archeol. Inst. Am. Liberal (U.K.). Club: Savile (London). Author numerous books, including: Armada from Athens, 1971; The Year of Salamis, 480-79 BC, 1971; A Concise History of Greece to the Close of the Classical Era, 1973; Alexander of Macedon, 356-323 B.C., a Historical Biography, 1974; Ovid: Erotic Poems, 1982; numerous translations from French, Italian; contbr. numerous articles to profl. jours. and newspapers including N.Y. Rev. of Books, Times Lit. Supplement. Home: 1505 Sunny Vale St Apt 219 Austin TX 78741 Office: Dept of Classics Waggener Hall Rm 9 U of Tex Austin TX 78712

GREEN, RICHARD JAMES, recruiting company executive; b. Waterbury, Conn., Mar. 21, 1933; s. John Joseph and Anna Pearl (Vestro) G.; m. Sylvia Irene Crawford, Oct. 9, 1953; children—Richard James, David Crawford, Mary Kathleen. B.S., U. Conn., 1959; postgrad U. Wis. Banking Sch., 1966-69. C.P.A., Tex.; cert. personnel cons. Sr. acct. Payne Harrison & Co., C.P.A.s, Dallas, 1959-62; asst. controller Tex. Commerce Bank, Houston, 1962-65; sr. v.p. Capital Nat. Bank, Houston, 1965-73; sr. v.p., sec. treas. Federated Capital Bank Corp., Houston, 1973-76; exec. v.p., dir. Hibbard & O'Connor Govt. Securities, and Hibbard & O'Connor Mcpl. Securities, Inc., Houston, 1976-79 chmn. bd. The Personnel Connection, Inc., Dallas, 1979—. Served as sgt. USAF, 1951-55. Mem. Bank Adminstrn. Inst. (pres. Gulf Coast chpt. 1969-70), Am. Inst. C.P.A.s, Tex. Soc. C.P.A.s, Nat. Assn. Personnel Cons. Roman Catholic. Club: University.

GREEN, ROBERT HAMILTON, engineering company executive; b. Bridgeport, Conn., July 3, 1935; s. Albert Arthur and Mary Elizabeth (Hansen) G.; m. Paula Hathaway Anderson, Sept. 6, 1958; children—Lydia Anne, Edith Hathaway, Elizabeth Anderson, Cecilia Hamilton. B.S. in Engring, U. Fla., 1958, B. Indsl. Engring, 1959; postgrad. Ga. Inst. Tech., 1963. Registered profl. engr., Ga., Fla., Va., N.C., Tenn., S.C., Ala. Flight test engr. Mercury Program, Gen. Dynamics Co., Cape Canaveral, Fla., 1958-61; project engr. LIPCO, Atlanta, 1961-68; scientist assoc. structural and materials lab. Lockheed Ga. Co., Marietta, 1968-70. Mem. Sandy Springs Planning Commn., Atlanta, 1967—, trustee, 1977. Mem. Nat., Ga. (state dir. 1977-79) socs. profl. engrs., ASTM, Am. Arbitration Assn. (arbitrator), Am. Concrete Inst., Ga. Cons. Engrs. Council, Engrs. Joint Council (Engr. of Distinction), Profl. Engrs. in Pvt. Practice. (Ga. state chmn. 1979-80), ASCE Structural Research Council, Tau Beta Pi, Lambda Chi Alpha. Episcopalian. Clubs: Atlanta Yacht (past fleet capt.), Phoenix Soc. (Atlanta); U. Fla. Alumni (Gainesville). Contbr. articles to profl. jours. Patentee in field. Home: 550 High Point Ln NE Atlanta GA 30342 Office: RH Green Engring Co Inc Atlanta GA 30342

GREEN, STANLEY BRUCE, educational administrator; b. Waldo, Ark., Aug. 24, 1937; s. Elliott Hilton and Minnie Earline (Crank) G.; m. Betty Joyce Gray, June 6, 1958; children—Gregory Allen, Todd Bryan, Stacy Lynn. B.S.E., U. Houston, 1959. Tchr. pub. schs., Pasadena, Tex., 1959-61; adv. artist, Houston, 1961-63; art dir. Ozzie Sons & Assocs., Houston, 1963-66; dir. comml. art Harding U., Searcy, Ark., 1966-68, instr. art, 1966—, dir. spl. events and sports info., 1968-71, dir. pub. relations, 1971—; design cons. Universal Software Assocs., Little Rock, 1983-85, Louise, Inc., 1984; freelance designer, 1970—. Mem., chmn. Springtime Searcy, 1982—. Recipient Disting. Service award Harding U., 1979, Disting. Pres. award Kiwanis, 1982, Merit award Nat. Assn. Intercollegiate Athletics, 1976, Clarence Pearson award, 1979, also design awards. Mem. Council Advancement and Support Edn., Nat. Assn. Intercollegiate Athletics (nat. pres. 1974-76), Ark. Intercollegiate Conf. Sports Info. Dirs. (pres. 1972-74, 79-80), Coll. Sports Info. Dirs. Am. (com. chmn. 1979-83), Football Writers Am., U.S. Basketball Writers Assn., U.S. Collegiate Baseball Writers Assn., Alpha Phi Gamma, Kappa Delta Phi, Kappa Pi. Mem. Ch. Christ. Lodge: Kiwanis (pres. 1980-81). Home: 1000 N Hayes St Searcy AR 72143 Office: Harding U Station A Box 759 Searcy AR 72143

GREEN, STEPHANIE, lawyer; b. Coral Gables, Fla., Oct. 6, 1950; d. Thomas Robert and Nilda (Lopez) Green; m. Gerald McBride, Dec. 2, 1978 (div. 1980). B.A., U. Fla., 1973; J.D., U. Miami, 1978. Bar: Fla. 1980. Atty. firm Paige & Catlin, Miami, Fla., 1978-80; adminstrv. mgr. internat. div. Aeromexico, Miami, 1980-82, legal counsel internat. div., 1982—; dir. Corp. Counsel Assn. South Fla., 1980—. Active Am. Cancer Soc., 1983. Mem. ABA, Fla. Bar Assn., Dade County Bar Assn. Republican. Roman Catholic. Clubs: Bath, Surf, Aviation Exec. (dir.). Home: 600 Biltmore Way Apt 713 Coral Gables FL 33134 Office: Aeromexico 8390 NW 53 St Miami FL 33166

GREEN, WALTER LUTHER, university administrator, engineering consultant; b. Roanoke Rapids, N.C., Mar. 13, 1934; s. Luther Clarence Green and Irene (Taylor) Green Walker; m. Jessie Sue Hutcheson, June 16, 1956; children—Michael, Leeda, David. B.S. in Elec. Engring., Auburn U., 1958, M.S. in Elec. Engring., 1961; Ph.D. in Elec. Engring., Tex. A&M U., 1965. Registered profl. engr., Tex. Staff engr. Sandia Corp., Albuquerque, 1961-62; instr. Tex. A&M U., College Station, 1962-65; advisor engr. IBM, Huntsville, Ala., 1965-68; research adj. Union Carbide/Martin Marietta, Oak Ridge, 1968—; prof., head elec. engring. U. Tenn., Knoxville, 1968—; cons. IBM, Boca Raton, Fla., 1978-83, Arnold Engring. Devel., Tullahoma, Tenn., 1977-82. Author: Introduction to CSMP, 1976; also articles; patentee (3) control systems, 1982. Pres. Gulf Park Recreation Assn., Knoxville, 1975, Knoxville Swimming Assn., 1978-79. Served with U.S. Army, 1954-55. Recipient Faculty Achievement award U. Tenn., 1977, Outstanding Service award, 1980, Outstanding Teaching award, 1982, Weston Prof. chair award, 1982. Sr. mem. Instrument Soc. Am. (dir. Automatic Controls System div.

1981-82); mem. IEEE, Am. Soc. Engring. Edn., Sigma Xi. Presbyterian. Club: Fox Den Country. Avocations: golf; hiking; landscaping. Office: U Tenn Elec Engring Dept Knoxville TN 37996

GREEN, WARREN, state senator, automobile dealer; b. Mannford, Okla., Dec. 23, 1921; s. Clarence and Millie Priscilla (Shoumake) G.; m. Betty J. Foster, July 13, 1941; children—Sharon Kay Green Childers, Priscilla Ann Green Davidson, Roberta Susan Green Rogers, Marilyn Louise Green Trout. Brad., Draughon's Bus. Coll., Tulsa, 1941. Pres., Brookside Renault. Mem. Okla. Ho. of Reps., Minority floorleader, 1967-69; mem. Okla. Senate, 1977—. Named Disting. Lay Member of Legislature Okla. Bar Assn., 1976. Mem. Oil Capital C. of C. (Tulsa). Republican. Mem. Disciples of Christ (Christian Ch.). Lodges: Lions, Mason, Shriners. Office: Brookside Renault 4206 S Peoria Tulsa OK 74105

GREEN, WILLIAM LOHR, mathematics educator; b. Harrisonburg, Va., May 1, 1945; s. William Lorenzo Green and Ruth (Ritchie) Hopkins; m. Antoinette Judith Earley, June 9, 1984. B.A., Yale U., 1967; M.A., U. Pa., 1970, Ph.D., 1973. Vis. lectr. U. Oslo, Norway, 1972-74; asst. prof. Williams Coll., Williamstown, Mass., 1975-77; asst. prof. Ga. Inst. Tech., Atlanta, 1974-75, 77-82, assoc. prof. math., 1982—; vis. assoc. prof. Tulane U., New Orleans, 1981. Contbr. articles to profl. jours. Mem. Am. Math. Soc., Math. Assn. Am. Office: Sch Math Ga Inst Tech Atlanta GA 30332

GREEN, WILLIAM WELLS, civil engr.; b. Sioux City, Iowa, Nov. 26, 1911; s. Thomas William and Jessie Eadie (Wells) G.; B.S., U. Notre Dame, 1934; m. Patricia Cecille Gregory, Jan. 10, 1944; children—William Joseph, Mary Teresa. Asst. engr. Iowa Hwy. Commn., Cherokee, 1935-40; asst. engr. City Corpus Christi, Tex., 1940-44; asst. office county surveyor, Nueces County Tex., 1944-54, county surveyor, 1955—. Past mem. Tex. Bd. Registration Pub. Surveyors. Past bd. dirs. Carmelite Day Nursery; regional bd. dirs. Lay Carmelites. Life mem. ASCE; mem. Am. Congress Surveying Mapping, Tex. Surveyors Assn. (bd. dirs.). Democrat. Roman Catholic. K.C. Home: 3149 Topeka St Corpus Christi TX 78404 Office: Room 102 County Courthouse 901 Leopard St Corpus Christi TX 78401

GREENAWALT, JACK ORMAND, engineering executive; b. Princeton, Kans., Oct. 10, 1924; s. Frank Ralph and Ola Marie (McCall) G.; m. Phyllis Marie Fine, May 29, 1949; children—Larry Neal, Kirk Douglas, Scott Curtis, Todd Murray. B.S. in Elec. Engring., B.S. in Bus. Adminstrn., Kans. State U., 1950. Spl. agt. Aetna Ins. Co., Chgo., Des Moines and Columbus, Ohio, 1950-55; cathodic protection engr. Phillips Petroleum Co., Bartlesville, Okla., 1955-72; owner Greenawalt Engring. Co., Bartlesville, 1972-73; pres. Greenawalt-Armstrong Inc., Bartlesville, 1973—. Chmn. adv. bd. Demolay; dist. adminstr. Little League Baseball; Republican Precinct chmn. Served with AUS, 1943-46. Mem. Okla. Soc. Profl. Engrs., Nat. Assn. Corrosion Engrs., Nat. Soc. Profl. Engrs., Okla. Land Surveyers, Am. Congress Surveying and Mapping. Presbyterian. Mason. Home: 307 Ridgecrest Ct Bartlesville OK 74006 Office: 3111 E Frank Phillips Blvd Bartlesville OK 74006

GREENBERG, FRANK S., textile company executive; b. 1929; Ph.B., U. Chgo., 1949. Asst. to pres. Charm Tred Mills, 1949, v.p., 1953, pres., 1953-59; v.p. Charm Tred Mills div. Burlington Industries, Inc., 1959-61, pres., 1961-62, pres. Monticello Carpet Mill div., 1962-70, group v.p., mem. mgmt. com. parent co. Monticello Carpet Mill div., Greensboro, N.C., 1970-72, exec. v.p. Monticello Carpet Mill div., 1972-78, pres. Monticello Carpet Mill div., 1978—. Served with AUS, 1951-53. Address: Burlington Industries Inc 3330 W Friendly Ave Greensboro NC 27410*

GREENBERG, GEORGE, mill company executive; b. 1922; married. With Seaberg, Inc. (acquired by Guilford Mills Inc.), to 1967; v.p. mktg. Guilford Mills, Inc., Greensboro, N.C., 1967-70, exec. v.p., 1970-76, pres., chief operating officer, 1976—, also dir. Office: Guilford Mills Inc 4925 W Market St Greensboro NC 27402*

GREENBERG, NEIL, zoology educator, ethology researcher; b. Newark, Oct. 30, 1941; s. Henry and Norma (Wexelman) G.; m. Alicia Carolyn Berry, June 29, 1969; 1 dau., Haley Jessica Elise. B.A., Drew U., 1963; Ph.D., Rutgers U., 1973. Research ethologist NIMH, Bethesda, Md., 1973-78; research assoc. Mus. Comparative Zoology, Harvard U.; assoc. prof. dept. zoology U. Tenn., Knoxville, 1978—; cons. and lectr. in field. NIMH-Grant Found. research fellow, 1973-75; First Tenn. Bank scholar, 1981; Stokely Inst. lectr., 1983. Mem. AAAS, Animal Behavior Soc., Soc. Neurosci., Internat. Soc. Neuroethology, Sigma Xi. Editor: Appalachian Zool. Soc.; contbr. writings to profl. publs. Office: Dept Zoology U Tenn Knoxville TN 37996

GREENBERG, RONALD, hospital administrator, educator; b. Bklyn., Apr. 3, 1946; s. Aaron H. and Emily Greenberg; m. Ruth Barbara Marx, Jan. 17, 1969; children—Jennifer, Craig. B.A., Queens Coll., 1967; M.A., Columbia U., 1971. Sr. ptnr. and v.p. Greenberg and Greenberg, N.Y.C., 1968-77; dir. personnel L.I. U., Greenvale, N.Y., 1977-80; v.p. Jewish Hosp., Louisville, 1980—; adj. assoc. prof. C.W. Post Coll. Grad. and Undergrad. Schs. Bus., Greenvale, 1977-80; adj. faculty Cornell Sch. Indsl. and Labor Relations, L.I., 1979, U. Louisville Sch. Bus., 1983. Bd. dirs. Kenneseth Israel Congregation; chmn. bd. overseers PBS, 1984. Mem. Am. Coll. Hosp. Adminstrs., Am. Soc. Personnel Adminstrs., Am. Soc. Hosp. Personnel Adminstrn., Louisville Personnel Assn., Ky. Soc. Hosp. Personnel Adminstrn., Ky. Hosp. Assn., Psi Chi, Zeta Beta Tau. Home: 7201 Iron Gate Ct Louisville KY 40222 Office: 217 E Chestnut St Louisville KY 40202

GREENBLATT, EDWARD LANDE, lawyer; b. Augusta, Ga., Mar. 16, 1939; s. Robert B. and Gwendolyn (Lande) G.; m. Sherry Agoos, June 1, 1967; 1 dau., Susan. Student Duke U.; B.A., Birmingham So. Coll., 1961; LL.B., Emory U., 1964; LL.M., NYU, 1965. Bar: Ga. 1963, D.C. 1966, U.S. Supreme Ct. 1971. Atty., U.S. Dept. Treasury, Washington, 1965-66; assoc. Lipshutz, Frankel, Greenblatt, King and Cohen, and predecessors, Atlanta, 1967-71, ptnr., 1971—. Bd. dirs. Atlanta Legal Aid Soc., Atlanta Community Ctr., Paces Battle Assn.; bd. dirs., chmn. Atlanta B'nai B'rith Youth Orgn.; pres. temple, 1985—. Mem. ABA, State Bar Ga., Atlanta Bar Assn., Lawyers Club Atlanta, Am. Judicature Soc. Jewish. Home: 4417 Paces Battle NW Atlanta GA 30327 Office: 2300 Harris Tower Peachtree Center 233 Peachtree St NE Atlanta GA 30043

GREEN-CARR, ETNA ARMISTEAD, educational administrator; b. Richmond, Va., July 31, 1949; d. William Arthur and Etna (Armistead) Green; student Shimer Coll., 1967-68, Fisk U., 1968-70; B.S., Va. Commonwealth U., 1973, M.Ed., 1978; m. Teleceno C. Carr, Jr., Mar. 19, 1972; children—Etna J'moke, Imani Conner. Personnel counselor Eastern Mgmt., Richmond, Va., 1971-72; ednl. therapist Commonwealth Psychiat. Center, Richmond, 1973-77; ednl. therapist/cons., Richmond, 1974—; curriculum coordinator Commonwealth Psychiat. Center, Richmond, 1977-80; dir. ednl. services Psychiat. Inst. Richmond, 1980-83; mgmt. cons. Comprehensive Eval. Services, Ltd. trustee Soweto Stage Co., Richmond; lit. cons., prodn. cons. Creative Artforms, Richmond, 1976-78; guest lectr. adj. faculty Va. Commonwealth U., Richmond, Va. State U. Mem. Council Exceptional Children, Assn. Supervision and Curriculum Devel., Nat. Assn. Female Execs., Assn. Children with Learning Disabilities.

GREENE, CECIL PERCIVAL, medical company executive, hospital administrator; b. Georgetown, Guyana, Sept. 25, 1927; came to U.S., 1963, naturalized, 1985; s. James and Agnes (Patterson) G.; m. Nicole Ileanee Fenty, May 28, 1949; children—Cecil, Jr., Colin A., Michael-Ann. Nat. cert., Brixton Poly., London, 1958; Assoc. degree in Med. Electronics, Norwood Poly., London, 1963; postgrad. in Med. Engring., George Washington U., 1970-72. Doctor's asst., Georgetown, Guyana, 1945-47; test engr. New Electronics Products, London, 1953-63; dir. biomed. Fairfax Hosp., Va., 1970-78; clin. engr. Arlington Hosp., Va., 1979—; pres. Biomed. Clinitronics, Stafford, Va., 1979—; cons. WHO, Washington, 1979—; consumer rep. FDA, Washington, 1972-76; adviser George Washington U., Washington, 1971-77; lectr. in field. Ruling elder First United Presbyterian Ch., Dale City, Va., 1973—; yoga tchr. Brahma Kumar World Spiritual U., N.Y. Mem. Assn. Advancement Med. Instrumentation, Instrument Soc. Am., N.Y. Acad. Scis. Democrat. Avocations: tennis; outdoor camping; singing. Home: 12 Knightsbridge Way Stafford VA 22554 Office: Arlington Hosp 1701 G Mason Dr Arlington VA 22205

GREENE, CHARLES MICHAEL, lawyer; b. N.Y.C., June 28, 1956; s. Myron J. and Ursula W. (Wertheim) G.; 1 son, Michael Andrew. B.A. in Polit. Sci. cum laude, Union Coll., 1978; J.D., Nova U., 1981. Bar: Fla. 1983, U.S. Dist. Ct. (so. dist.) Fla. 1983, U.S. Dist. Ct. (mid. dist.) Fla. 1983, U.S. Ct. Appeals (11th cir.) 1984. Asst. mgr. credit/new accounts Burdines of Fla., Miami, 1978-79; prosecutor State Atty.'s Office 20th Jud. Cir., Ft. Myers, Fla., 1982-83, asst. state atty. 17th Jud. Cir., Ft. Lauderdale, 1983—. Alumni fundraiser Union Coll. Mem. Fla. Bar Assn., ABA, Nat. Dist. Attys. Assn., Fla. Pros. Attys. Assn., Broward County Bar Assn., Nova U. Law Ctr. Alumni Assn., Phi Alpha Delta, Zeta Beta Tau. Jewish. Lodge: B'nai B'rith. Home: 318 Holiday Dr Hallandale FL 33009 Office: State Attys Office 17th Judicial Cir 201 SE 6th St Suite 600 Fort Lauderdale FL 33301

GREENE, DALLAS WHORTON, JR., fire chief; b. Shreveport, La., June 29, 1923; s. Dallas Whorton and Eunice (Lester) G.; student Centenary Coll., 1941; m. Alice Whittington, Oct. 4, 1947; 1 dau., Valerie (Mrs. David Randall Rockett). With La. Fire Dept., Shreveport, 1942—, fire chief, 1965—. Mem. State Fire Marshal's Fire Safety Rev. Bd.; past advisory mem. U.S. Senate Veterans Affairs com. Past bd. dirs. Sports for Boys; mem. Gov.'s Com. on Emergencies, 1978—. Served with C.E., AUS, 1943-45. Recipient Friendship award Fraternal Order Police; Dictograph Salutes award Internat. Assn. Fire Chiefs, 1973. Mem. Internat. Assn. Fire Chiefs (pres. Southwestern div. 1971-72, dir. 1972-78), La. State Fire Chiefs Assn. (dir.), La. Firemens Assn. (life), Fraternal Order Fire Fighters (hon.), 40 and 8, Nat. Fire Protection Assn., La. Emergency Preparedness Assn. (dir.), Am. Legion (past comdr.), VFW, Am. Ordnance Assn. Mem. Christian Ch. Lion. Home: 8826 Stonelake Pl Shreveport LA 71108 Office: PO Box 1143 Shreveport LA 71163

GREENE, GARY MAYNARD, SR., business educator; b. Gastonia, N.C., Apr. 28, 1948; s. Bobby Maynard And Willowdean (Moss) G.; m. Elizabeth Nan Withers, July 10, 1970; children—Mary, Gary Maynard, Jr. A.A., Gaston Coll., 1974; B.A. magna cum laude, Belmont Abbey Coll., 1975; M.B.A., The Citadel, 1982; postgrad. U. S.C., 1985. Social work assoc. VA, Charleston, S.C., 1976-83; instr. Rutledge Coll., Charleston, 1982-83; adj. instr. Gaston Coll., Dallas, N.C., 1984; adj. prof. Limestone Coll., Gaffney, S.C., 1983—; asst. prof., acting chmn. dept. mgmt. Sacred Heart Coll., Belmont, N.C., 1983-84; instr. Spartanburg Meth. Coll., S.C., 1984—; chmn. bd. VA Employees Assn., Charleston, 1980. Served to sgt. USAF, 1967-71. Mem. Am. Acctg. Assn., Am. Econ. Assn., Acad. Mgmt., Assn. M.B.A. Execs., Nat. Council Econ. Edn., Inst. Mgmt. Acctg., Pi Gamma Mu, Delta Epsilon Sigma. Avocations: numismatics, hiking, fishing. Office: Spartanburg Meth Coll Powell Mill Rd Spartanburg SC 29301

GREENE, GAYLE LUCKY, hospital administrator, nursing educator; b. Miami, Fla., July 2, 1938; d. Danny and Ann (Campbell) G.; m. Homer E. Bales, Nov. 3, 1978. Diploma in Nursing, Jackson Meml. Hosp. Sch. of Nursing, 1959; B.S. in Nursing, Fla. State U., 1962; M.A. in Nursing, Columbia U., 1965. Operating room staff nurse Hialeah Hosp., Fla., 1959-60; charge nurse intensive care unit Tallahassee Meml. Hosp., Fla., 1960-63; dir. Sch. Nursing St. Francis Xavier Hosp., Charleston, S.C., 1963-64; dir. nursing program Cameron State U., Lawton, Okla., 1965-70; chmn. dept. nursing Linn-Benton Community Coll., Albany, Oreg., 1970-75; dir. nursing Jupiter Hosp. and Med. Ctr., Fla., 1978—. Asst. dir. play Jupiter Theatre, 1984. Dir. radio talk show WJNO-AM, 1977-78. Charter mem. Friends of the Sr. Citizens, Palm Beach County, Fla., 1985; mem. Lighthouse Gallery, Tequesta, Fla., 1985. Mem. Am. Nurses Assn., Nat. League for Nursing, Am. Soc. Nursing Service Adminstrs., MADD, Kappa Delta Pi, Pi Lambda Theta. Republican. Baptist. Avocations: directing live theater; writing. Home: 8445 Damascus Dr Lake Park FL 33410 Office: Jupiter Hosp Med Ctr Inc 2010 S Dixie Hwy Jupiter FL 33458

GREENE, HOWARD BREEDLOVE, electronic engineer; b. Cocoa, Fla., Feb. 17, 1952; s. Howard Alphonso and Emmie Evon (Hunter) G.; m. Michelle Calhoun Miller, Sept. 22, 1984. B.E.E., Worcester Poly. Inst., 1974; postgrad. Western Electric Edn. Ctr., 1974, Va. Poly. Inst. and State U., summer 1976, Ohio State U., summer 1975; M.E.E., Columbia U., 1979. Sr. tech. aide Bell Labs., Holmdel, N.J., 1973; test engr. transmission products div. Western Electric, Reading, Pa., 1974-75; product engr. component product div., 1975; resident vis. engr., Bell Labs., Holmdel, 1975-77, tech. staff mem. microprocessor/microsystems dept., 1977-79, phys. testing coordinator, 1979-82; sr. assoc. engr. IBM, Manassas, Va., 1982-85; prin. engr. COMSAT Telesystems, Fairfax, Va., 1985—. Home: 10204 Bushman Dr Oakton VA 22124

GREENE, JAMES ALLEN, physician, real estate executive; b. Sneedville, Tenn., Mar. 15, 1939; s. A. Kyle and Argelene (Surgenor) G.; m. Rebecca Rita O'Connor, Sept. 18, 1970; children—John Robert, Rebecca Allen. M.D., U. Tenn.-Memphis, 1963. Diplomate Am. Bd. Family Practice. Intern, U. Tenn., Knoxville, 1963-64; assoc. dir. Oak Ridge Mental Health Clinic, 1969-70; assoc. Psychiatry Assocs., Birmingham, Ala., 1970-79; chief geriatrics James Healy Hosp., Tampa, Fla., 1980-81; med. dir. Gerontology Ctr., Knoxville, 1981—; pres. Health and Creative Aging Clinic, Knoxville, 1980—, Health and Creative Aging Devel. Corp.; med. dir. East Tenn. Bapt. Hosp. Gerontology Ctr., Knoxville, 1982-83; asst. med. dir. Pain Ctr., Knoxville, 1983-84; cons. med. dir. Nat. Health Corp., 1984—; also real estate exec. Columnist: Successful Aging, Knoxville Jour., 1982-83, Geriatric Medicine, Tenn. Med. Jour., 1983—; author: Eight Day Week, 1976. Bd. dirs. Council on Aging, Knoxville, 1983, Alzheimer's Support Group, Knoxville, 1983-84. Served to capt. USAF, 1968-69. Fellow Am. Psychiat. Assn., So. Psychiat. Assn.; mem. Tenn. Med. Assn. (asst. chmn. long term care 1982-83). Methodist. Club: LeConte (Knoxville). Home: 4047 Alta Vista Way Knoxville TN 57919 Office: 310 Blount Profl Bldg Knoxville TN 37920

GREENE, JOHN BOSTRIDGE, air traffic facility manager, auto parts store executive; b. Simpsonville, S.C., Jan. 26, 1941; s. John Bostridge and Florence Allison Green; m. Donna Elaine Ford, Aug. 5, 1966; 1 son, Jeffrey Ford. Student Clemson U., 1959-61, 64-65. Ins. salesman Liberty Life Ins. Co., 1966; air traffic control specialist FAA, Savannah, Ga., 1967-70, Atlanta, 1970-71, air traffic supr., Charleston, S.C., 1971-72, air traffic mgr., Rocky Mount, N.C., 1972-73, Crossville, Tenn., 1973-76, dep. mgr., Atlanta, 1976-77, with FAA Hdqrs., Washington, 1977-78, air traffic mgr., London, Ky., 1978-79, Birmingham (Ala.) Flight Service Sta., 1979—; owner, operator Auto Parts Specialist, 1982—; pvt. pilot. Served with U.S. Army, 1961-64. Mem. Better Bus. Bur., Aircraft Owners and Pilots Assn., U.S. C. of C. Republican. Baptist. Home: 5830 Mockingbird Ln Pinson AL 35126 Office: Birmingham Flight Service Sta 6500 43d Ave N Birmingham AL 35206

GREENE, JOHN CHARLES, educational administrator; b. Fort Gibson, Okla., Jan. 19, 1938; s. Clarence E. and Willie (Reid) G.; m. Loretta Hawkins, Oct. 25, 1962; 1 child, Charlesetta Marie. B.S., Langston U., 1961; M. Ed., Southwestern Okla. State U., 1969. Tchr., coach Grayson High Sch., Henryetta, Okla., 1961-63, Okla. City Schs., 1963-71; dir. human relations Crooked Oak Sch., Oklahoma City, 1971-72; asst. prin. Millwood High Sch., Oklahoma City, 1972-77; guidance counselor Okla. State Dept. Edn., Oklahoma City, 1977-84, human relations adminstr., 1984—; dir After Sch. Program, Oklahoma City, 1964-65; workshop facilitator U. Okla., Norman, 1970-75; panel lectr. Avery Chapel A.M.E. Ch., Oklahoma City, 1976; counselor Classen High Sch., Oklahoma City, 1970-71; driver edn. tchr. John Marshall High Sch., Oklahoma City, 1968-70; coll. basketball official Okla. Collegiate Athletic Conf, Okla. Intercollegiate Conf., Sooner Athletic Conf., Okla. Jr. Coll. Conf., Big 8 Conf., Mo. Valley Conf., 1968—; high sch. basketball official, 1961-80. Mem. Assn. Supervision and Curriculum Devel., Nat. Assn. Secondary Sch. Prins., NEA, Okla. Edn. Assn., YMCA, Okla. Officials Assn., Okla. Collegiate Officials Assn., Big 8 Basketball Officials Assn., Urban League, Okla. Personnel and Guidance Assn., Am. Personnel and Guidance Assn., Phi Delta Kappa. Home: 1309 Northeast 53d St Oklahoma City OK 73111 Office: Okla State Dept Edn 2500 N Lincoln Blvd Oklahoma City OK 73105

GREENE, JOHN JOSEPH, lawyer; b. Marshall, Tex., Jan. 19, 1946; William Henry and Camille Anne (Riley) G.; B.A., U. Houston, 1969, M.A., 1974; postgrad. Oxford (Eng.) U., 1976, U. Okla., 1976; J.D., South Tex. Coll., 1978. Bar: Tex. 1978, U.S. Supreme Ct. 1982. Asst. atty. City of Amarillo, Tex., 1978-79; asst. atty. Harris County, Tex., 1979-83; sole practice, 1983—; city atty. Conroe (Tex.), 1983—. Served to capt. USAR, 1969-76. Decorated Bronze Star, Air Medal. Mem. ABA, Houston Bar Assn., Res. Officers Assn., Assn. for Computing Machinery. Democrat. Roman Catholic. Office: PO Box 3066 Conroe TX 77301

GREENE, JOHN WELLINGTON, judge; b. Ft. Worth, Nov. 16, 1939; s. Edgar H. and Hilda (Andrews) G.; m. Judy Lynn Harris, Aug. 28, 1965; children—Whitney Andrews, Jon Harris, Garrett Wellington. B.S., La. State U., 1962, J.D., 1966. Bar: La. 1966, U.S. Dist. Ct. (ea. dist.) La. 1966. Research asst. La. Water Resources Inst., Baton Rouge, 1965-66, 1st Cir. Ct. Appeals, Baton Rouge, 1966-68; ptnr. firm Burns, Greene & Farmer, Covington, La., 1968-76; dist. judge 22d jud. dist. State of La., St. Tammany and Washington Parishes, Covington, 1976—, chief judge, 1978-79; apptd. judge 1st cir. Ct. Appeals, Baton Rouge, 1981; lectr.; mem. Jud. Planning Com., New Orleans, mem. long-range planning subcom., 1977-81, financing and facilities subcom., 1979-82, appellate ct. delay-ct. reporting subcom., 1982-84; mem. Dept. Health and Human Liaison Com., 1983—, La. Driving While Intoxicated Rev. Bd., 1983. Bd. dirs. Istrouma Area council Boy Scouts Am., 1967-78, dist. chmn. Boy Scouts in St. Tammany Parish, 1969-74; bd. dirs. 1st United Methodist Ch., Covington, 1973-81; chmn. juvenile com., bd. dirs. Youth Service Bur. St. Tammany Parish, Covington, 1981—, pres., 1984. Recipient Silver Beaver award Boy Scouts Am., 1974. Mem. ABA, Am. Judicature Soc., La. Council Juvenile Ct. Judges, La. Bar Assn., Covington Bar Assn., St. Tammany Bar Assn., Am. Judges Assn., La. Trial Lawyers Soc., La. Def. Counsel Soc., La. Dist. Judges Assn. (exec. com. 1984), Covington C. of C. (pres. 1975-76). Democrat. Methodist. Home: Menetre Dr Covington LA 70433 Office: PO Box 997 Covington LA 70434

GREENE, KEVIN THOMAS, minister; b. Lenoir, N.C., Apr. 26, 1954; s. John Stanley and Helen Mamie (Hartley) G.; m. Diana Lynn Barbour, Aug. 22, 1976. B.A., Campbell Coll., 1976; M.Div., Southeastern Baptist Theol. Sem., 1980, Th.M., 1983; postgrad. Regent's Park Coll., Oxford U. Assoc. pastor Princeton (N.C.) Bapt. Ch., 1979-80; minister of edn. and youth Madison Ave. Bapt. Ch., Goldsboro, N.C., 1980-82, interim minister, 1981-82, sr. minister, 1982—; tchr. accredited sem. ext. Bd. dirs. Protestant Kindergarten Sch.; adv. bd. Golden Yrs. Day Care Village. Republican. Author: Communion and Community: A Recovery of the Nurturing Aspect of the Lord's Supper in Baptist Worship, 1983. Home: 400 S Claiborne St Goldsboro NC 27530 Office: 1703 E Laurel St Goldsboro NC 27530

GREENE, RANDALL FREDERICK, real estate co. exec.; b. Palatka, Fla., Apr. 17, 1949; s. Vernon F. and Betty E. (Bould) G.; A.A., U. Fla., 1972; B.A., Eckerd Coll., 1986; m. Debra Marie Holder, Dec. 11, 1976; 1 child, Meredith Anne. Regional mgr. Realty Resource Inc., 1972-75; dir. property mgmt. Bos & Assocs., Jacksonville, Fla., 1976; v.p. Charter Mortgage Co., Jacksonville, 1976-77; chmn. bd., pres., dir. Coastland Corp. Fla., Tampa, Cutler-Fed. Inc., Lakeland, Fla.; pres. Greene Realty Inc., 1976—; pres. Beggins/Greene, Inc., 1984—. Dir., CSI Electronics, Inc., Boca Raton, Marlo Ricklas Cosmetics, Inc., Tampa; tchr. various real estate courses. Bd. dirs. Fla. Apt. Assn., 1974-75; pres. Gainesville (Fla.) Apt. Assn., 1975; bd. dirs., pres. Big Bros. Lee County (Fla.), 1980; bd. dirs. Lee County YMCA, 1980-81, Jr. Achievement Hillsborough County, 1983—; mem. Leadership Tampa, 1983. Mem. Am. Land Devel. Assn., Inst. Real Estate Mgmt., Ft. Myers Bd. Realtors, Fla. Assn. Realtors, Nat. Assn. Realtors, Fla. Jaycees, Fla. Blue Key, Young Pres. Orgn., Mensa, Tampa C. of C., Omicron Delta Kappa, Phi Kappa Tau (pres. chpt. 1972-73). Republican. Home: 344 Blanca Ave Tampa FL 33606 Office: 3102 N Habana Ave Suite 300 Tampa FL 33607

GREENE, RAY JOSEPH, advertising executive; b. Twin Falls, Idaho, Feb. 4, 1933; s. Charles Estus and Anna Marie (Pfieufauf) G.; ed. Sacred Heart Acad., Salem, Oreg., 1948-51; m. Carol Marie Meier, July 12, 1952; children—Tom, Tim, Terry, Cheryl, Kevin, Kerry, Kris, Jenny, James, John, Jeff, Darrin, Heather. Copy boy, retail sales, mgr. classified advt. Oreg. Statesman, Salem, 1951-53, Statesman and Jour., 1953-66; mgr. classified and real estate advt. Balt. News-Am., 1966-73; v.p. Newspaper Advt. Bur., N.Y.C., 1973-76; pres., chief exec. officer Classified Internat. Advt. Services Inc., Hialeah, Fla., 1976—, chmn. bd., 1981—; pres. Greene House of Printing, Hialeah, 1977—. Active Boy Scouts Am., 1956-66; bd. dirs. Exec. Search Program. Mem. Assn. Newspaper Classified Advt. Mgrs. (hon. life mem.; pres. 1970, Disting. Service award 1963), Pacific N.W. Classified Advt. Mgrs. (pres. 1954), Internat. Newspaper Advt. Execs., Western Classified Advt. Mgrs. Assn. (dir. 1954-59), So. Classified Advt. Mgrs. Assn., Northeastern Classified Advt. Mgrs. Assn. (dir. 1968—). Democrat. Roman Catholic. Club: K.C. (grand knight 1961-63). Author: How To Double The Payoff of Your Real Estate Advertising, 1974; New Instant Treasury of Ads That Send Real Estate Sales Soaring, 1982; How to Sell Real Estate in Today's Market with Result-Getting Classified, 1984; author real estate manuals Oreg., Md. Home: 4701 Monroe St Hollywood FL 33021 Office: Classified Internat Advt Services Inc 3211 N 74 Ave Hollywood FL 33024

GREENE, RICHARD EDWARD, consulting company executive; b. Charlotte, N.C., Aug. 22, 1955; s. Edward Franklin and Sara Frances (Curlee) G. Student Wake Forest U., 1973-74; B.A. in Econs. and Bus. Adminstrn., Catawba Coll., 1977. Salesman Lowe's Cos., North Wilkesboro, N.C., 1977, mgr. plumbing heating and elec. dept., 1978, improver mgr., 1978, sales mgr., 1978, merchandising buyer, 1979-83; pres. Reg Corp., North Wilkesboro, 1983—; cons. merchandising, mktg. Bd. dirs., cons. ARC; active Boy Scouts Am. Mem. Am. Mgmt. Assn., Carolina Art Assn., Nat. Assn. Investors, Am. Assn. Microcomputer Investors, U.S. Jaycees. Republican. Methodist. Clubs: Oakwoods Country (Wilkesboro, N.C.); Lodge: Elks (exalted ruler 1981) North Wilkesboro). Office: PO Box 369 North Wilkesboro NC 28659

GREENE, TIMOTHY JAMES, industrial engineering educator, consultant, researcher; b. Lafayette, Ind., Oct. 18, 1952; s. James H. and Barbara H. (Holt) G.; m. Rosemary S. Tafoya, B.S.A.E., Purdue U., 1975, M.S. in Indsl. Engring., 1977, Ph.D., 1980. Co-op engr. Eaton Corp., Detroit, 1972-74; research technician Purdue U., West Lafayette, Ind., 1974-75, grad. research asst., 1975-78, instr., 1978-79; asst. prof. Va. Poly. Tech. Inst., 1980-85, assoc. prof., 1985—. Gen. Electric Found. fellow, 1979; David-Ross fellow, 1979. Mem. Inst. Indsl. Engring., Am. Soc. Engring. Edn., Am. Prodn. and Inventory Control Soc., Soc. Mech. Engrs., Soc. Computer Simulation, Alpha Pi Mu. Contbr. articles to profl. jours. Home: 308 Mulberry Dr Blacksburg VA 24060 Office: 148 Whittemore Hall VaPoly Inst Blacksburg VA 24061

GREENE, WAYNE ALTON, architectural designer, consultant; b. St. Petersburg, Fla., Feb. 2, 1952; s. Clyde and Aletha (Sims) G.; children—Michelle, Wayne Alton, Ricardo. A.A., Stillman Coll., 1970. Cert. archtl. designer. Prin., WAG Designers, St. Petersburg, Fla., since 1976—. Fellow Sickle Cell Anemia Found. (supportive award). Listed Tampa Bay Most Influential Blacks, 1983. Mem. SCLC (assoc.), Fla. Residential Designers Assn., Nat. Trust Hist. Preservation, St. Petersburg C. of C. Democrat. Baptist. Lodge: Mason. Avocations: pro football; swimming; travel; baseball. Home and Office: WAG Designs 2515 15th Ave S Saint Petersburg FL 33712

GREENE, WILLIAM EDWIN, educational administrator, historian; b. East Orange, N.J., May 28, 1946; s. Charles Lyman and Myrtle Agnes (Hubers) G.; m. Karen Ann Fruits, Dec. 28, 1968; 1 dau., Allison. B.A., Fla. Atlantic U., 1968, M.A., 1970, Ed.S., 1977, Ed.D., 1980. Tchr. Sunrise Middle Sch., Ft. Lauderdale, Fla., 1968-70; faculty history dept. Broward Community Coll., Ft. Lauderdale, 1970-77, dir. internat. edn., 1977—; mem. Fla. Adv. Council Global Edn., Tallahassee, 1981-82. Editor: (with S. Fersh) The Community College and International Education, 1984. Contbr. articles to publs. Hon. fellow Inst. for Am. Univs., Aix-en-Provence, France, 1984. Mem. Fla. Assn. Community Colls., Fla. Collegiate Consortium Internat. Edn. (exec. dir. 1977—), Coll. Consortium Internat. Studies N.Y. (exec. com.), Phi Alpha Theta. Republican. Presbyterian. Office: Broward Community Coll Internat Edn Inst 1000 Coconut Creek Blvd Coconut Creek FL 33066

GREENFIELD, MELVIN C., psychologist; b. Spring Lake, N.J., July 24, 1928; s. Joseph and Gussie (Bassin) G.; m. Nancy Lee, Mar. 8, 1958; children—Gloria, Jacqueline, Johnathan, Elizabeth. B.S., Rutgers U., 1960; M.S., Barry Coll., 1970; Ph.D., Century U., 1980. D.H.L., Evang. Soc., Miami, 1971. Marriage and family counselor, Miami, 1960—; dir. family therapy Miami Children's Hosp., 1970-80. Served as sgt. AUS, 1946-49. Mem. Ortho-psychiat. Soc., Nat. Assn. Family Life, Dade County Mental Health Assn., Counsel for Exceptional Children, Masters and Johnson Assn., South Miami C. of C., Dade County Med. Assn. Aux. (dir., chmn. impaired physicians com.). Republican. Club: Tiger Bay. Office: 8500 SW 92d St Miami FL 33156

GREENFIELD, NANCY LEE, psychiatrist; b. Newark, Oct. 10, 1936; d. Hubert Joseph and Ethel (Haskin) Reis; m. Melvin C. Greenfield, Mar. 8, 1958;

children—Gloria, Jacqueline, Johnathan, Elizabeth. A.B., Barnard Coll., 1958; M.D., SUNY-Downstate Med. Ctr., 1962. Intern, U. Miami, 1962-63; resident in pediatrics Jackson Meml. Hosp., Miami, Fla., 1963-65, resident in psychiatry, 1965-68; chief of psychiatry Miami Children's Hosp., 1968-80; practice medicine specializing in psychiatry, Miami, 1968—; clin. instr. psychiatry and pediatrics U. Miami, 1968—; cons. in field. Mem. Am. Physicians Polit. Action Com., 1980. Mem. South Miami C. of C., Dade County Med. Assn., Fla. Med. Assn., AMA, Am. Women's Med. Assn., Am. Psychiat. Assn., South Fla. Psychiat. Soc., Greater Miami Pediatric Soc., Am. Soc. Adolescent Psychiatry, Alpha Omega Alpha. Office: 8500 SW 92d St Miami FL 33156

GREENHILL, ELIZABETH DIANNE, nursing educator; b. Tupelo, Miss., May 6, 1940; d. William I. and Emma Lee (Belk) G. B.SN., U. Tenn.-Memphis, 1962; M.S., U. N.C., 1965; Ed.S., U. Tenn., 1973; Ed.D., Memphis State U., 1976. Faculty mem. U. Tenn. Coll. Nursing, Memphis, 1965-71; dir. nursing Memphis and Shelby County Health Dept., 1971-74; assoc. prof. U. Tenn. Coll. Nursing, Memphis, 1976-78, prof. community health nursing, 1978—, dept. chmn., 1976-81, interim dean coll., 1981-82, assoc. dean, 1983—. Bd. dirs. Josephine Lewis Sr. Citizens Ctr., 1980-82; mem. Early Childhood Devel. Health Adv. Com., 1974—; project dir. for grant on primary care of aged in nursing curriculum USPHS, 1980-83. Served to col. Nurse Corps, U.S. Army Res., 1978—. Recipient Golden Apple Teaching award U. Tenn., 1978. Mem. Am. Nurses Assn., Tenn. Nurses Assn. (treas. 1980-84), Nat. League for Nursing, Am. Pub. Health Assn., Assn. Mil. Surgeons U.S., Res. Officers Assn., U. Tenn. Nat. Alumni Assn. (dir. 1982-84), Phi Kappa Phi, Sigma Theta Tau, Kappa Delta Pi. Baptist. Office: Coll Nursing U Tenn 800 Madison Ave Memphis TN 38163

GREENHOUSE, BARRY DAVID, historic and archeological consulting firm executive; b. Bklyn., Feb. 16, 1946; s. Morton Melvyn and Harriet (Bokor) G.; B.A., CCNY, 1969; M.S. in Planning, Pratt Inst., 1972; m. Meryl Lynn Jurgrau, Aug. 2, 1969; children—Matthew Myles, Marshall Neal, Melissa Beth. Sci. tchr., West Hempstead, N.Y., 1969-72; dir. planning McIntosh Trail Area Planning & Devel. Com., Griffin, Ga., 1972-74; regional dir. Murray-McCormick, Inc., Atlanta, 1974-75; pres. Soil Systems, Inc., Atlanta, 1975-83; founder, pres. Greenhouse Cons., Inc., Atlanta and N.Y.C.; dir. R & D, Inc., Atlanta; instr. Gordon Jr. Coll., W. Ga. Coll., 1973-74; advisor local mun. and county planning commns.; cons. pvt. industry and govt. agys.; archeol. cons. excavation of 17th-18th century sites including earliest Dutch site, N.Y.C. Mem. Am. Planning Assn. (charter), Am. Clean Water Assn. (dir.), High Mus. Art (charter), Am. Inst. Cert. Planners (charter), Am. Def. Preparedness Assn., Nat. Trust Hist. Preservation, Internat. Platform Assn., Council Northeastern Historic Archeology. Republican. Jewish. Clubs: Pipeliners, De Lorean Motor. Contbr. publs. on planning to Nat. Tech. Info. Service, Springfield, Va. Home: 205 Brandon P NW Atlanta GA 30328 also 3 Hanover Sq New York NY 10004 Office: 205 Brandon Pl Atlanta GA 30328 also 50 Trinity Pl New York NY 10006

GREENSTEIN, JOEL SANDOR, industrial engineering educator; b. Chgo., May 7, 1952; s. Benjamin and Muriel (Kazel) G.; m. Katherine Marie Lodenkamp, Sept. 1, 1982. B.S., U. Ill., 1973, Ph.D., 1979; M.S., Stanford U., 1974. Asst. prof. indsl. engring. and ops. research Va. Poly. Inst. & State U., Blacksburg, 1979-85; assoc. prof. indsl. engring. Clemson U., S.C., 1985—. Mem. Am. Soc. Engring. Edn., Assn. for Computing Machinery, Computer and Automated Systems Assn. of Soc. Mfg. Engrs., Human Factors Soc., IEEE, Inst. Indsl. Engrs. Contbr. articles in field to profl. jours. Office: Clemson U Dept Indsl Engring Clemson SC 29634

GREENSTONE, JAMES LYNN, psychotherapist, mediator, consultant, author; b. Dallas, Mar. 30, 1943; s. Carl Bunk and Fifi (Horn) G.; children—Cynthia Beth, Pamela Celeste, David Carl. B.A. in Psychology, U. Okla., 1965; M.S. in Clin. Psychology, N. Tex. State U., 1966, Ed.D. in Edn. and Psychology, 1974. Lic. marriage and family therapist, profl. counselor. Psychologist, Beverly Hills Hosp., Dallas, 1966-67; pvt. practice, 1966—; therapist Family Guidance Service, Dallas, 1967-68; instr. Dallas County Community Coll. Dist., 1967-72, 78-79; asst. prof. Tex. Women's U., 1979; tng. faculty Am. Acad. Crisis Interveners, Louisville, 1972-78; tng. dir. Southwestern Acad. Crisis Interveners, Dallas, 1977—; police instr. Dallas Sheriff's Acad., 1979-86; hostage negotiator, trainer Lancaster Police Dept., Tex.; cons. Dallas County Jails, 1979-86; dir. res. tng. Dallas Sheriff's Res., 1983-84; panel arbitrators Am. Arbitration Assn.; author books, articles, tape series. Trustee Southeastern U., New Orleans; bd. dirs. Jewish Community Ctr., Jewish Family Service, Temple Shalom, Congregation Shearith Israel, 1975-80; active Dallas Sheriff's Res., 1978-86; v.p. Jewish Nat. Fund Dallas; adv. bd. Parents without Ptnrs.; founder Carl B. Greenstone Meml. Library; past dir. Carrollton Rotary Club, Nat. Jewish Com. Scouting, Circle 10 Council Boy Scouts Am. Served with USNR, 1961-65; USMCR, 1965-67; USAR, 1967-69. Recipient Disting. Service award Southeastern Acad. Crisis Interveners, 1981; Disting. Service award Res. Law Officers Assn. Am., 1982; Mem. Am. Assn. Marriage and Family Therapy, Soc. Profls. in Dispute Resolution, Acad. Family Mediators, Nat. Acad. Conciliators, Nat. Panel Consumer Arbitrators, Tex. Family Mediation Assn., Am. Bd. Examiners in Crisis Intervention (diplomate), Am. Acad. Crisis Intervention, Southwestern Acad. Crisis Interveners, Acad. Criminal Justice Scis., Am. Acad. Psychotherapists, Am. Assn. Profl. Hypnotherapists, Assn. Mil. Surgeons U.S., Dallas Assn. Marriage and Family Therapists. Democrat. Lodges: Mason, Scottish Rite. Author: Crisis Intervener's Handbook, Vol. I, 1980; Crisis Intervener's Handbook, Vol. II, 1982; Hotline: Crisis Intervention Directory, 1981; Crisis Intervention: Handbook for Interveners, 1983; Winning Through Accommodation; Handbook for Mediators, 1984; cassette tapes: Crisis Management and Intervener Survival, 1981; Stress Reduction: Personal Energy Management, 1982; Training the Trainer, 1983; contbr. chpts. to books, articles to profl. jours.; sr. editor: Crisis Intervener's Newsletter; editor-in-chief Emotional First Aid: A Jour. of Crisis Intervention; and others. Office: PO Box 670292 Dallas 75367

GREENSTREET, WILLIAM LAVON, mechanical engineer; b. Cora, Mo., Feb. 22, 1925; s. Carl J. and Opal (Abernathey) G.; m. Elizabeth Louise Chedsey, Oct. 21, 1950; children—Timothy, Cynthia, Teresa, Carl. B.S.M.E., Colo. State U., 1950; M.S.M.E., U. Tenn.-Knoxville, 1958; Ph.D. in Engring. and Applied Sci., Yale U., 1968. Design and weights engr. Boeing Co., Seattle, 1950-51; engr. Oak Ridge Nat. Lab., 1951-58, engring. supr., 1958-75, dir. research programs, 1975—. Served with U.S. Navy, 1944-46. Fellow ASME; mem. Welding Research Council, Southeastern Conf. Theoretical and Applied Mechanics (policy bd.), Sigma Xi. Presbyterian. Editorial bd. Nuclear Engring. and Design, 1979—; patentee in field. Office: PO Box Y Oak Ridge TN 37830

GREENWALD, NEVA ELIZABETH FARBIZO, physical therapy educator and administrator; b. New Philadelphia, Ohio, May 24, 1938; d. Clarence A. and Mina A. (Marburger) Farbizo; m. Edward Kenneth Greenwald, Dec. 27, 1959. B.A., B.S., Ohio State U., 1960; M.S.P.H., U. Mo.-Columbia, 1971. Phys. therapist United Cerebral Palsy, Columbus, Ohio, 1960-63; asst. dir. phys. therapy dept. Grant Hosp., Columbus, 1963-67; sr. staff mem., asst. dir. Phys. Therapy Service, Duke U., Durham, N.C., 1967-68; coordinator clin. edn., instr. phys. therapy U. Mo.-Columbia, 1969-73; pvt. practice phys. therapy, New Philadelphia, Ohio, 1973-74; asst. prof., coordinator phys. therapy U. Miss.-Jackson, 1976-79, assoc. prof., chmn. phys. therapy Sch. Health Related Professions, 1979—; dir. phys. therapy Univ. Hosp. U. Miss. Med. Ctr., 1980—; cons. Mo. State Penitentary, 1972-73, Jackson Ballet Co., 1979—, Internat. Ballet Competition, 1979, 82, Miss. Hosp. Assn. Mem. editorial bd. Topics in Geriatric Rehab. Pres. LWV, Jackson, 1980-83, LWV Miss., 1983-85; bd. dirs. Hinds County Human Resources Agy., 1980-86; mem. Gov.'s Task Force on Edn., Dept. Children and Youth, 1984-86. Recipient Outstanding Service award Hinds County Human Resources Agy., 1986. Mem. Am. Phys. Therapy Assn. (vice chmn. sect. on geriatrics 1983—), Miss. Assn. Women in Higher Edn. (council 1982—, sec. 1983-84, pres. 1984-85; Outstanding Woman of Achievement 1985-86), Miss. Alliance Health Related Assns. (chmn. 1979-81), Miss. Women's Polit. Caucus, Career Forum, Miss. Women's Network, AAUW. Clubs: Soroptimist Internat. (v.p. Jackson 1986—), Metro Women's Polit. Caucus (sec. 1985-86). Home: PO Box 4823 Jackson MS 39216 Office: U Miss Med Ctr SHRP 2500 N State St Jackson MS 39216

GREENWOOD, A(LVIN) WILTSHIRE, JR., computer company executive; b. Richmond, Va., Sept. 6, 1940; s. Alvin Wiltshire and Rachel Cother (Chenault) G.; m. Ann Jeanette Holiga Brummer, Oct. 10, 1959 (div. 1969); children—Stephen Kenneth, Tracy Ann Koontz; m. 2d, Barbara Beach White, Feb. 13, 1970. Student Va. Poly. Inst., 1957-59; B.S. in Info. Systems, Va. Commonwealth U., 1982. With data processing Med. Coll. Va., Richmond, 1965-72; div. mgr. The Computer Co., Richmond, 1972-74, 78-81, asst. v.p., 1981-83, v.p., 1983—; data processing mgr. Wards Co., Inc., Richmond, 1974-78. Mem. Assn. Systems Mgmt. (treas. 1979-80). Club: Va-Motor Sport (pres. 1968). Home: 1006 Sharon Ln Richmond VA 23229 Office: Computer Co 1905 Westmoreland St Richmond VA 23230

GREENWOOD, JOHN LINZIE, transportation company executive; b. Seguin, Tex., Mar. 2, 1944; s. Isaac Clerence and Lorine (Ashby) Greenwood Holden; m. Frankie Lee. Student public schs. Yard foreman Structural Metals Co., Seguin, 1963-66; transport driver Chem. Express Co., Dallas, 1969-74; transport driver Enterprize Transp., Houston, 1974-83; owner, pres. Greenwood Co., San Felipe, Tex., 1981—. Author: Look Up, 1980. Mem. Am. Trucking Assn., Am. Mus. Natural History, Splty. Merchandise Corp., Am. Assn. Individual Investors. Home: 1470 College St San Felipe TX 77473 Office: Greenwood Co 1466 College St San Felipe TX 77473

GREER, ALAN GRAHAM, lawyer; b. El Dorado, Ark., May 31, 1939; s. Arthur W. and Marie (Ross) G.; m. Patricia A. Seitz, Aug. 14, 1981. B.S., U.S. Naval Acad., 1961; J.D., U. Fla., 1969. Mem., Floyd Pearson Stewart Richman Greer Weil & Zack, Miami, Fla., 1969—; dir. Trade Nat. Bank of Miami. Chmn. Dade County Council Arts and Scis.; mem. Fla. State Task Force on Water Issues. Served with USN, 1957-61. Mem. ABA, Fla. Bar Assn., Assn. Trial Lawyers Am. Home: 224 Ridgewood Rd Coral Gables FL 33133 Office: 1 Biscayne Tower 25th Floor Miami FL 33131

GREER, ARTHUR ELLIS, psychotherapist, consultant; b. Detroit, June 10, 1929; s. Arthur E. and Edna Anna (Bornefeld) G.; m. Barbara Wahl, June 6, 1954 (div. 1978); m. Rilla Askew, June 17, 1979; children—Daniel, Julia. B.A., Elmhurst Coll., 1951; M.Div., Eden Theol. Sem., 1955; M.Ed., U. Houston, 1972. Lic. clin. psychotherapist, Tex. Ordained to ministry United Ch. of Christ, 1955. Campus minister U. Houston, 1969-72; pvt. practice psychotherapy and mgmt. cons., Houston, 1972—; treatment supr. SLIC Yellow Rose, Dallas, 1985—; mem. faculty Houston Community Coll., 1984—. Sec. bd. S. Central Conf., United Ch. Christ, 1983-84; nat. cons. Palmer Drug Abuse Program, 1978-80; sr. cons. Nat. Fedn. Chem. Dependency Programs, 1986—. Served to maj. USAF, 1956-66. Mem. Am. Assn. Marriage and Family Therapy, Internat. Transactional Analysis Assn. Author: No Grown-Ups in Heaven, 1975; The Sacred Cows are Dying, 1978. Office: 1101 Post Oak Blvd Suite 106 Houston TX 77056

GREER, CARL THOMAS, oil and gas exploration service company executive; b. Kirbyville, Tex., Sept. 5, 1928; s. James Iva and Ruby Vivian (Rigsby) G.; m. Billie Sue Boyd, May 1, 1949; children—Janice Susan Greer Schlotzhauer, Teresa Ann Greer Alford, Thomas Daniel. Student, Arlington State U., 1945-47. Engr. to dist. supt. Hycalog, Inc., Shreveport, La., 1948-52; ptnr. Precision Well Logging, Houston, 1953-56, owner, 1957-77, pres., 1977—. Mem. Am. Assn. Petroleum Geologists, Soc. of Profl. Well Log Analysts (committeeman 1980-83), Houston Geol. Soc. Republican. Mem. Ch. of Christ. Avocations: reading; fishing; hunting. Home: 995 Curtin Houston TX 77018 Office: Precision Well Logging Inc 924 Wakefield Houston TX 77018

GREER, KENNETH GORDON, banker; b. Tulsa, Oct. 28, 1936; s. H. K. and Afton (Goodman) G.; m. Nancy Lang, Nov. 22, 1958; children—Keith G., Scott A. B.S. in Banking and Fin., Okla. State U., 1958; student Grad. Sch. Banking, Madison, Wis., 1964-67. Pres. Liberty Nat. Bank, Oklahoma City, 1958-84; pres., chief exec. officer designate First Nat. Bank and Trust Co. of Tulsa, 1984—. Served with Air Nat. Guard, 1958-64. Named to Hall of Fame, Okla. State U. Bus. Adminstrn. Sch., Stillwater, 1984. Mem. Assn. Res. City Bankers, Am. Bankers Assn. (banking leadership conf.), Okla. Bankers Assn. (pres. 1983-84). Democrat. Methodist. Clubs: So. Hills Country, Tulsa. Avocation: golf. Office: First Nat Bank and Trust Co of Tulsa PO Box 1 Tulsa OK 74193

GREER, KNOX EVANS, retired sewage treatment technician; b. Pikeville, Tenn., Oct. 19, 1917; s. Alton C. and Flora Mae (Thomas) G.; student U. Tenn., Knoxville, 1942-46; m. Anna Lois Stout, June 4, 1939; children—Stephen Arthur, Camilla Ann. Leader, CCC, Franklinton, N.C., 1935-38; engring. aide, SCS, 1939-40, TVA, Chattanooga, 1941; chief acct. Bond-Woolf and and Co., Alcoa, Tenn., 1941-53; ins. salesman N.Y. Life, Chattanooga, 1954-61; with City of Chattanooga, 1962-83, mgr. sewage treatment plants, 1963-75, tech. adminstrv. asst., 1975-77, adminstrv. coordinator, 1977-83. Pres. Blount County (Tenn.) Music Assn., 1953; 1st pres. Optimist Club of Maryville, Tenn., 1952, North River Chattanooga, 1959. Mem. Inst. Water Pollution Control (England), Ky.-Tenn. Water Pollution Control Fedn., Tenn. Water and Wastewater Assn. (hon.). Republican. Club: Chattanooga Engrs. Mem. Ch. of Christ. Home: 1229 Duane Rd Chattanooga TN 37405

GREER, LINDA LISA, interior designer; b. London, Ky., Jan. 9, 1960; d. Garth Rex and Peggy Louise (Hamm) G. B.A. in Housing and Interior Design, U. Ky., 1984. With personnel dept. G&G Coal and Energy Corp., Inc., London, 1976-82; sales rep. Sentinel Echo, London, 1983; interior designer Ryser's Inc., East Bernstadt, Ky., 1984—; design cons. Elmo Greer & Sons., Inc., London, 1983—. Sunday sch. tchr. New Salem Baptist Ch., Pittsburg, Ky., 1982—; asst. dir. Jr. Miss Pageant, London, 1984; chmn. bd. dirs. Miss Laurel U.S.A. Pageant, London, 1985—; youth dir. Bible Sch., New Salem Bapt. Ch., 1985. Mem. Am. Soc. Interior Designers (assoc.). Republican. Avocations: photography; reading; swimming; music; dance. Home: Route 5 Box 396 London KY 40741 Office: Ryser's Inc Route 1 Box 7 East Bernstadt KY 40729

GREER, LOWELL DELBERT, reading service executive; b. Round Mountain, Ala., Nov. 8, 1926; s. William Fitzhugh and Buena Vista (Collier) G.; m. Peggy Joyce Dorman, May 21, 1947; children—Lowell Alan, Thomas R., Jeanne, Anne Marie. Grad. high sch., Rome, Ga., 1942. Branch mgr. Am. News Co., Chattanooga, Tenn., 1947-57; div. mgr. The Hearst Corp., N.Y.C., 1957-72; owner, operator Family Reading Service, Albany, Ga., 1972—; pres., chief exec. officer Family Reading Service, Inc., Greer Entertainment Ctr., Lowell's Entertainment Ctr., Lowell's Video Ctr., Albany, Ga., 1974—. Mem. Atlantic Coast Ind. Distbrs. Assn. (v.p.), Periodical Distbrs. Assn. (bd. dirs. council), Ga. Wholesalers Assn., 25 Yr. Club. Republican. Baptist. Home: 2416 E Doublegate Dr Albany GA 31707 Office: Lowell's 1601 N Slappy Blvd Albany GA 31701

GREER, MARGARET KIRVEN, psychologist; b. Jacksonville, Fla., Oct. 23, 1954. B.A., U. Ga., 1975, M.Ed., 1979, Ph.D., 1982. Cert. psychologist. Clin. counselor Dept. Mental Retardation, Clinton, S.C., 1975-78; coordinator psychol. services Child and Family Guidance Ctr., Athens, Ga., 1980-81; facilitator Navy Alcohol Safety, Sasebo, Japan, 1981-82; psychologist Vince Moseley Clinic, Charleston, S.C., 1982—; designated examiner Probate Ct., Charleston, 1983—. Mem. Am. Psychol. Assn., Nat. Assn. Sch. Psychologists, Am. Assn. Sex Educators, Counselors and Therapists. Club: Jr. League (Charleston). Home: 1130 Morning Glory Ct Mount Pleasant SC 29464 Office: Vince Moseley Clinic 41 Bee St Charleston SC 29403

GREER, ROBERT STEPHENSON, insurance company executive; b. Baton Rouge, Apr. 2, 1920; s. Fred Jones and Nannie (Stephenson) G.; m. Patricia Pettry, Oct. 1, 1944, children—Robert S., John P. B.S., La. State U., 1941. Ins. agt., Union Nat. Life Ins. Co., Baton Rouge, 1941-42, dist. mgr., 1945-48, v.p., 1948-56, exec. v.p., 1956-70, pres. and chief exec. officer, 1970-85, chmn. bd., chief exec. officer, 1985—; pres. and chief exec. officer Union Nat. Fire Ins. Co., Baton Rouge, 1970-85, chmn. bd., chief exec. officer, 1985—; dir. La. Nat. Bank, Baton Rouge Savings & Loan, Union Nat. Life Ins. Co., Union Nat. Fire Ins. Co. Am Campaign chmn. United Way, 1977, pres., 1980-81; bd. dirs. Salvation Army; bd. dirs. Woman's Hosp., Baton Rouge, 1976-80; chmn. bd. trustees First United Methodist Ch., 1970—; bd. dirs. Baton Rouge Area Found., 1978-82. Served to lt. USN, World War II. Mem. Baton Rouge C. of C. (past pres.), Better Bus. Bur. Baton Rouge (past pres.), La. State U. Coll. Bus. Alumni (past pres.), La. State U. Alumni Fedn. (past pres.), Life Insurers Conf. (past chmn.), La. Insurers Conf., Council for a Better La. (past pres.), Kappa Sigma, Beta Gamma Sigma. Clubs: Country (past pres.), City (bd. dirs. 1968-70) (Baton Rouge); Lodge: Rotary (past pres.). Home: 3075 Gilbert Dr Baton Rouge LA 70809 Office: 8282 Goodwood St Baton Rouge LA 70806

GREER, SEDLEY JOSEPH, JR., geologist, research scientist; b. Brookhaven, Miss., Feb. 14, 1930; s. Sedley Joseph and Annie Ruth (Junkin) G.; m. Betty Ann Griffith, July 31, 1964; children—Sherry Angell, Johnny Rand Wilson. B.A., Miss. State U., 1958. Geologist USDA, Ark., P.R., 1958-70; realtor, appraisor, Natchez, Miss., 1970-78; land appraisor Ark. Pub. Service Commn., Little Rock, 1978-80; geologist, research scientist, owner Trace Corp., North Little Rock, Ark., 1980—. Author (with others) A Magnetohydrodynamic Electricity Generator Using Solar Power and Self-Induced Ion Flow, 1980. Patentee MHD Motion Sensor. Served to sgt. U.S. Army, 1952-55. Mem. Soc. Mining Engrs. Home: 1917 Osage Dr North Little Rock AR 72116 Office: TRACE Corp 2500 McCain Pl Suite 121 North Little Rock AR 72116

GREGERSON, PETER VALJEAN, JR., advertising agency executive; b. Davenport, Iowa, Aug. 1, 1952; s. Peter Valjean and Janet Emelyn (Dyke) G.; student public schs., Gadsden, Ala.; m. Susan Ann Warren, Apr. 1, 1972; children—Jennifer Gay, Michelle Kay, Nicole Sue, Erin Janette. Gen. mdse. mgr. Warehouse Groceries Mgmt. Inc., Gadsden, Ala., 1970-76, dir. advt., 1976-79; pres. Mediacom Mktg., Gadsden, 1979—; dir. Coosa Warehouse Groceries, Inc., Carrollton Warehouse Market Inc. Mem. Super Market Inst., Am. Mgmt. Assn., Internat. Entrepreneurs Assn., Nat. Free Lance Photographers Assn., Cousteau Soc., Nature Conservancy, Greenpeace, others. Home: Box 31P Country Club Dr Centre AL 35960 Office: PO Box 2128 Gadsden AL 35999

GREGG, PAUL CHARLES, occupational health medical officer; b. N.Y.C., Mar. 8, 1925; s. Benjamin Paul and Catherine Jane (Fales) G.; m. Ann Taylor Garner, June 11, 1949 (dec. Sept. 1982); children—Paul Charles, Patricia Ann Florek, Janice Taylor Wilkins, Michael Benjamin, Elizabeth Lucette; m. 2d, Mildred Louise Hatcher, Apr. 6, 1983. B.S., Union Coll., 1947; M.D., Johns Hopkins U., 1951, M.P.H., 1967. Diplomate Am. Bd. Preventive Medicine. Joined U.S. Navy, 1943; served in Pacific, 1943-44; commd. lt (j.g.), 1951, served active duty, 1951-53, 62-80, advanced through grades to capt., 1968; intern U.S. Naval Hosp., St. Albans, N.Y., 1951-52; practice gen. medicine, Levittown, Pa., 1953-62; sr. med. officer USS Essex, 1962-64; asst. dir. tng. Naval Aerospace Med. Inst., Pensacola, Fla., 1964-66, resident aerospace medicine, 1967-69; sr. med. officer Naval Air Sta., Corpus Christi, Tex., also med. officer Chief Naval Aviation Advanced Tng., 1969-71; comdg. officer Naval Hosp., med. officer 2d Marine Air Wing, med. officer Marine Air Bases, East Cherry Point, N.C., 1971-73; dep. comdg. officer Naval Aerospace and Regional Med. Ctr., Pensacola, 1974-76; comdg. officer Naval Regional Med. Ctr., New Orleans, 1976-78, U.S. Naval Hosp., P.R., 1978-80; ret., 1980; occupational health med. officer Naval Air Sta., Pensacola, 1981—; assoc. clin. prof. Tulane U., 1976-78, U. P.R., 1978-80. Fellow Am. Coll. Preventive Medicine, Aerospace Med. Assn. (assoc.); mem. AMA, Bucks County (Pa.) Med. Soc., Assn. Mil. Surgeons, Johns Hopkins Med. Surg. Assn., Phi Delta Theta, Phi Chi. Home: 12143 Longwood Dr Pensacola FL 32507 Office: Br Clinic Naval Air Sta Pensacola FL 32508

GREGG, ROSALIE MANN, social service agency administrator; b. Hayden, N.Mex., Sept. 17, 1920; d. John Patterson and Lona Estella (Butler) Mann; grad. Decatur Baptist Jr. Coll., 1942; m. Robert Nolen Gregg, Dec. 16, 1945; children—Sherry Lynn Gregg Harris, Marsha Jill Gregg Eder, Robbie Zane Gregg Weaver, Dana Rene. Sec., Tex. Dept. Pub. Welfare, 1945-57, Govt. of Wise County, 1957-65; ins. clk. Allied Ins. Agy., Decatur, Tex., 1965-68; sec. Decatur C. of C., 1968-75; adminstrv. asst. Wise County Council on Alcoholism, Decatur, 1976-84; adoption investigator Wise County, 1982—. Chmn., Wise County Hist. Commn., 1964—; exec. dir. Wise County Hist. Soc., 1970—; sec.-treas. Pleasant Grove Cemetery Assn.; mem. Wise County Little Theater Guild; chmn. family living dept. Pioneer Dist. Women's Clubs. Mem. Tex. Assn. Mus., Tex. Hist. Found., Am. Legion Aux. (sec.-treas.), DAV Aux. Club: Decatur Woman's (past pres.). Democrat. Methodist. Editor: Do You Know About...Wise County, 1965; History of Wise County...A Link with the Past, vol. I, 1975, vol. II, 1982; also monthly hist. newsletter (awards). Home: 1602 S College Decatur TX 76234 Office: 1602 S College Decatur TX 76234

GREGORCZYK, EVELYN FOJTIK, counselor; b. Beeville, Tex., July 30, 1948; d. Edward Felix and Lela Mae (O'Neal) Fojtik; m. Gilbert Andrew Gregorczyk, June 3, 1967; children—Shane, Sheri. A.S., Bee County Coll., Beeville, Tex., 1978; B.A. in Psychology, Corpus Christi State U., 1980; M.A. in Psychology, 1981. Cert. psychol. assoc., Tex. lic. profl. counselor, Tex. Switchboard operator Southwestern Bell Telephone Co., Sinton, Tex., 1966-67; head teller Sinton Savs. Assn., Tex., 1968-75; practicum Ada Wilson Children's Hosp., Corpus Christi, Tex., 1980, Physicians and Surgeons Gen. Hosp., Corpus Christi, 1981; psychol. testing, evaluations, report writing Alan T. Fisher, Ph.D., Corpus Christi, part-time 1983; psychol. testing, evaluations, report writing Gridley, Fisher & Assocs., Corpus Christi, 1982-83; relocation counselor, H.E.B. Relocation Ctr., Corpus Christi, 1983—, supr., Corpus Christi, San Antonio, 1983-86, human resources devel. specialist HEB Corp. Hdqrs., 1986—; cons. TRW, Corpus Christi, 1982-83. Coordinator Meml. Med. Ctr., Corpus Christi, 1983. Mem. Am. Psychol. Assn., Am. Personnel and Guidance Assn., Tex. Psychol. Assn., Tex. Personnel and Guidance Assn., Nueces County Psychol. Assn. (coordinator 1983, chairperson membership com. 1983, sec. 1984), Assn. Specialists in Group Work, Tex. Mental Health Counselors Assn., Bexar County Psychol. Assn., AAUW, Nat. Assn. Female Execs., Corpus Christi State U. Alumni Assn., Phi Theta Kappa. Roman Catholic. Club: Parent Teacher (pres.). Avocations: tennis; shooting skeet; gardening; involvment with children's activities. Home: Route 1 Box 194 A Sinton TX 78387 Office: H E B Corp Headquarters PO Box 9999 Human Resources Devel San Antonio TX 78204-0999

GREGORIO, PETER ANTHONY, retail grocer, artist; b. Chgo., July 29, 1916; s. Frank and Teresa (Marotta) G.; grad. pub. schs., Chgo., 1942; m. Marie Blanton, Mar. 17, 1945; children—Frank Allen, Carole Teresa. Owner, operator Davis Island Supermarket, Tampa, Fla. 1949—; dir. Ellis Nat. Bank of Davis Island, Tampa 1977-78; dir. Consignment Arts Ctr., Tampa; exhibited in one man show Islands Gallery, 1976-77; group shows Am. Bicentennial, Paris, 1976, Rochester (N.Y.) Religious Art Festival, 1972, Tampa Bay Art Center, 1979, Hillsborough Art Festival, 1976, 77, 78, (award of merit) 79, (3d pl. and honorable mention) 81, (3d pl.) 82, Tampa Realistic Art Assn., 1981, Artist Alliance Guild, Tampa, 1981, Tampa Mus., 1982, Le Salon des Nations a Paris, 1984; represented in permanent collection Vatican Library, Rome, also numerous pvt. collections. Vice pres., Nat. Animal Rights, Inc., nat. hdqrs. Tampa, 1983—. Served to capt. USAF, 1941-46. Decorated Air medal with 6 clusters; recipient award of excellence Hillsborough County Art Fair, Tampa, 1984. Mem. Am., Internat. socs. artists, Graphic Soc. Roman Catholic. Home: 149 Bosphorus Ave Tampa FL 33606 Office: 304 E Davis Blvd Tampa FL 33606

GREGORY, ANN YOUNG, newspaper editor-publisher; b. Lexington, Ky., Apr. 28, 1935; d. David M. and Pauline A. Young; m. Allen Gregory, Jan. 29, 1957; children—David Young, Mary Peyton. B.A. with high distinction, U. Ky., 1956. Traffic mgr. Sta. WVLK, Lexington, 1956-61; tchr. adult basic edn. Wise County (Va.) Sch. Bd., St. Paul, Va., 1967-73; adminstrv. asst. Appalachian Field Services of Children's TV Workshop, St. Paul, 1971-74; editor-pub. Clinich Valley Times, St. Paul, 1974—. Tchr. journalism for high sch. students S.W. Va. Community Coll., 1976. Editor, textwriter Flood of '77, 1977; editor privately printed cookbook. Mem. Wise County Sch. Bd., 1975—, vice-chmn., 1981-86; mem. Va. adv. com. Block Grants for Edn., 1982-86; mem. exec. com. Va. High Sch. League; trustee Lonesome Pine Regional Library, 1972-80, chmn., 1978-80; chmn., organized establishment St. Paul Pub. Library, 1975; chmn. St. Paul Bicentennial Com., 1976, St. Paul Cancer Drive, 1966-73; pres. St. Paul Band Boosters, 1974-78; adv. bd. Wise County YMCA, 1976—; pres. Wise County Humane Soc., Inc.; mem. exec. com. Va. High Sch. League, 1984—. Ky. Broadcaster Assn. scholar, 1955; named Clubwoman of Year, St. Paul Jr. Woman's Club, 1964, 66; S.W. Va. Citizen of Yr., Va. Fedn. Women's Clubs, 1968; recipient art awards for oils; hon. Ky. col. Mem. Women in Communications, Va. Press Assn. (1st place editorial writing 1976), Nat. Newspaper Assn. (asso.), Nat. Press Women, Va. Press Women, Va. Sch. Bds. Assn. (dir., pres.-elect 1984-85, pres. 1985—), Nat. Sch. Bds. Assn., U. Ky. Alumni Assn., Wise County C. of C., St. Paul C. of C., Mortar Bd., Phi Beta Kappa, Alpha Delta Pi, Alpha Lambda Delta, Theta Sigma Phi, Delta Kappa Gamma (hon.), Chi Delta Phi, Alpha Epsilon Rho, Delta Kappa Gamma (hon.). Democrat. Methodist. Club: Saintly Squares Sq. Dance (pres.). Home: Longview Dr PO Box 303 Saint Paul VA 24283 Office: PO Box 817 Russell St Saint Paul VA 24283

GREGORY, EDWARD MEEKS, clergyman; b. Richmond, Va., Sept. 30, 1922; s. George Craghead and Constance (Heath) G. A.B., U. Va., 1947; M.Div., Episcopal Theol. Sch., Cambridge, Mass., 1954; postgrad. George

Washington U., 1949, Va. Commonwealth U., 1980, Harvard U., 1981; D.Min., U. of South, 1977. Ordained deacon Episcopal Ch., 1954, priest, 1955. Instr. Staunton (Va.) Mil. Acad., 1947-48; master Episc. High Sch., Alexandria, Va., 1948-51; curate St. Mark's Episc. Ch., Richmond, 1954-69; vicar St. Peter's Episc. Ch., Richmond, 1969-79; chaplain Christchurch Sch., 1980—; dean East Richmond, 1974-78; diocesan youth dir., 1956-60; diocesan del. Va. Council Chs., 1967-73; spiritual adviser Dignity-Integrity/Richmond, 1976-79; mem. Diocesan Dept. Social Relations, 1970-72, Diocesan Lit. Commn., 1973—; pres. Religious Edn. Council, Richmond, 1961-62, Richmond Episc. Clericus, 1972-73. Bd. dirs. Vol. Service Bur., Richmond, 1960-63, Ednl. Therapy Center, 1964-79, Multiple Sclerosis, 1961-66, Va. Community Devel. Orgn., 1968-75, Va. chpt. ACLU, 1970-71, 76-77, Internat. Council; bd. dirs. Va. Council Human Relations, 1965-70, treas., 1972-73; bd. dirs. Richmond Planned Parenthood, 1969-74, Richmond chpt. ARC, 1973-79, Richmond United Neighborhoods, 1977-79, Met. Area Resources Clearing House, 1977-79, Ch. Hill Revitalization Team, 1979; bd. govs. Christchurch Sch., Va., 1978-79; pres. Richmond Council Human Relations, 1960-62; pres. Friends' Assn. for Children, 1967-70, bd. dirs., 1975-79; mem. adv. bd. Richmond Model Neighborhood, 1971-73; bd. dirs. Richmond Community Sr. Center, 1975-78, Daily Planet, 1974-79, Alcohol and Drug Abuse Prevention and Tng. Services, 1978—, Richmond Health Center, 1981—; vice chmn. Richmond Health Occupations, 1979. Served with Med. Dept., AUS, 1942-46. Mem. Richmond Clergy Assn., Jamestown Soc. (gov. 1951-55), Mayflower Soc. (elder Va. co. 1963-82), Va. Hist. Soc., Braintree (Mass.) Hist. Soc., Episcopal Soc. Cultural and Racial Unity (chmn. Richmond 1964-66), Assn. Preservation Va. Antiquities, Valentine Mus., Va. Mus. Fine Arts, Chi Phi. Clubs: James River Catfish, 2300. Home and Office: Christchurch Sch Christchurch VA 23031

GREGORY, GEORGE TILLMAN, JR., justice S.C. Supreme Court; b. McConnellsville, S.C., Dec. 13, 1921; s. George T. and Inez Anderson G.; m. Willie Mae Elliott, Dec. 27, 1951; children—George Tillman III, William Elliott. A.B., U. S.C., 1943, LL.B., 1944. Bar: S.C. 1944. U.S. commr., 1945-46, city recorder, Chester, 1946-50; judge S.C. Circuit Ct., 6th Jud. Circuit, 1956-78; assoc. justice S.C. Supreme Ct., 1975—. Mem. S.C. Ho. of Reps., 1951-52, 55-56; trustee Furman U., 1968-72. Mem. ABA, Law Fedn. and Euphradian Library Soc. (pres.). Office: Supreme Ct SC Columbia SC 29211*

GREGORY, HARDY, JR., state supreme court justice; b. Vienna, Ga., Aug. 11, 1936; s. Hardy and Mary Wood (Gaither) G.; m. Carolyn Burton, June 14, 1959; children—Hardy, Elizabeth Marywood. B.S., U.S. Naval Acad., 1959; LL.B., Mercer U., 1967. Bar: Ga. 1966. Ptnr., Adams & O'Neal, Macon, Ga., 1966-71, Davis & Gregory, Vienna, Ga., 1971-76; judge Cordele Jud. Circuit, Ga., 1976-81; justice Ga. Supreme Ct., Atlanta, 1981—. Served with USN, 1954-55, USAAF, 1959-64. Democrat. Methodist. Home: 6140 Rivershore Pkwy NW Atlanta GA 30328 Office: 536 State Judicial Bldg Atlanta GA 30334

GREGORY, JAMES DOUGLAS, forestry educator; b. Angier, N.C., May 1, 1943; s. Ben Evis and Gladys (Pollard) G.; m. Janice Raye Jones, Aug. 29, 1964; children—Michele Janeen, Erin Leigh. B.S., N.C. State U., 1965, M.S., 1968, Ph.D., 1975. Cert. profl. soil scientist, Am. Registry of Profls. in Agronomy, Crops and Soils. Asst. prof. forestry Va. Poly. Inst. and State U., Blacksburg, Va., 1975-78; asst. prof. forestry N.C. State U., Raleigh, 1978-81, assoc. prof. forestry, 1981—, coordinator undergrad. forestry program, 1985—. Served to capt. U.S. Army, 1968-72. Decorated Bronze Star, Air medal, Army Commendation medal. Grantee U.S. Office Coastal Mgmt., 1980, Water Resources Research Inst., U. N.C., 1982. Mem. Soc. Am. Foresters, Soil Sci. Soc. Am., Am. Water Resources Assn., Soil Conservation Soc. Am., N.C. Acad. Sci. (v.p. 1983-84), So. Forest Hydrology Group (chmn. 1984-85), Assn. Univ. Watershed Scientists, Sigma Xi. Democrat. Contbr. articles to profl. jours. Home: 1500 Lake Dam Rd Raleigh NC 27600 Office: Dept Forestry NC State U Box 8002 Raleigh NC 27695

GREGORY, PEGGY ELLEN, art investment firm executive, writer, lecturer, art consultant; b. Chgo., Mar. 13, 1950; d. Warren Frank and Wanda Francis (Karas) G.; m. William Jerome Hare, Apr. 1, 1981. Student So. Meth. U., 1968; B.S.B.A in Mktg., U. Ark.-Fayetteville, 1971; student in lang. Mercer U., 1981. Cert. Internat. Soc. Artists; bus. voted Best in Atlanta, Atlanta Mag. Pres. Greggie Fine Art, Atlanta, 1971—. Author: Pension World, 1981; contbr. articles to Robb Report, 1978-81. Art instr., Atlanta, 1983. Mem. Women's Bus. Orgn., New Mus. (founding), High Mus. Art, Direct Mail Council.

GREGORY, ROBERT A., banker. Exec. v.p. comml. banking Liberty Nat. Bank & Trust Co. Oklahoma City. Office: Liberty Nat Bank & Trust Co 100 Broadway Oklahoma City OK 73102*

GREGORY, STEVEN MICHAEL, psychologist, communications company executive; b. Joliet, Ill., Apr. 14, 1951; s. Steven Bruce and Betty Lou (Satterfield) G. B.A., N. Tex. State U., 1976; M.S., U. Tex.-Dallas, 1980. Cons. psychologist, Dallas, 1980—; v.p., sec. Decision Models, Inc., Dallas, 1981-84; chief exec. officer Innovative Strategies Co., Dallas, 1984-85; pres. Tyrell Communications, Ltd., Dallas, 1984—; cons. Med. City Hosp., Dallas, 1982-84, Anatole Hotels, Dallas, 1983-84, SW Airlines, Dallas, 1981-82; dir. Behavioral Resources, Dallas. Author: Rational Behavior Therapy for Cigarette Smokers, 1979; Self-Hypnosis and the Structure of Experience, 1982. Mem. Am. Biofeedback Assn., Am. Assn. Profl. Hypnotherapists, 500 Club. Republican. Office: Suite 218 12810 Hillcrest Rd Dallas TX 75230

GREGSON, JOHN RANDOLPH, II, real estate development company executive; b. New Orleans, Sept. 10, 1952; s. James Randolph and Mary Isabel (Gannaway) G.; m. Charlotte Lee Thompson, Oct. 23, 1981; 1 son, John Randolph III. Student Princeton U., 1970-72; B.A., Tulane U., 1975. Urban policy specialist Office Mayor, New Orleans, 1973-76; project coordinator Skid Row, Downtown Devel. Dist., New Orleans, 1976-77; dep. dir. property mgmt. City of New Orleans, 1977-78; exec. asst. to pres. Joseph C. Canizaro Interests, New Orleans, 1978-79; sales and devel. asst. Plantation Bus. Campus, Destrehan, 1979-80; asst. project mgr., program exec. Canal Place 2000, New Orleans, 1980-85. Bd. dirs. Preservation Resource Ctr. New Orleans, 1976, Neighborhood Improvement Assn. Irish Channel, 1977-79; bd. commrs. Community Improvement Agy., 1977-79; bd. dirs. Contemporary Arts Ctr., 1979; trustee La. chpt. Nat. Hemophilia Found., 1977-81, pres. La. chpt., 1979-81, nat. bd. dirs., 1979-80; chmn. Am. Hemophilia Youth, 1980-81. Democrat. Episcopalian. Avocation: Tennis.

GREIG, JEROME KEITH, data processing executive; b. Lafayette, La., Apr. 4, 1951; s. Harry Denis and Jessie Amelia (LeBlanc) G.; m. Nancy Iles Hawkins, Aug. 4, 1973; children—Jerome K., Jr., Kelly Denise. B.S. cum laude in Math., U. Southwestern La., 1973; M.S. in Math., Clemson U., 1975; postgrad. in computer sci. U. Tex., 1975-78; cert. in data processing Inst. for Cert. Computer Profls. Systems devel. analyst Sun Co., Dallas, 1975-78; systems analyst So. Structures, Inc., Lafayette, La., 1978-80; dir. data processing Petroleum Helicopters, Inc., Lafayette, La., 1980-84; mgr. application devel. Tenngasco Corp., Lafayette, 1984—. Mem. Assn. Computer Machinery, Data Processing Mgmt. Assn. (pres.), Univac Users Group. Democrat. Roman Catholic. Home: 400 Corona Dr Lafayette LA 70503 Office: PO Box 90908 Lafayette LA 70509

GREINER, KENNETH DONALD, JR., nursing home company executive; b. Cushing, Okla., Aug. 19, 1938; s. Kenneth Donald Greiner and Billie Alene (Williams) Greiner/Kannady; m. Leitner Louise Jarrell, Sept. 2, 1961; children—Katherine Louise, Kenneth Donald III, Jennifer Lee, Cheryl Sue. B.S. in Econs., Okla. State U., 1960; M.B.A., Harvard U., 1962; B.S. in Health Care Adminstrn., Okla. Bapt. U., 1977. Adminstrv. asst. Doric Corp., Oklahoma City, 1962-64; asst. to treas. Skelly Oil Co., Tulsa, 1964-66; loan officer AID, Lahore, Karachi, Pakistan, 1966-69; ptnr. Resource Analysis & Mgmt. Group, Oklahoma City, 1969-74; v.p., dir. Texal Internat. Co., Oklahoma City, 1974-76; pres. Amity Care Corp., Oklahoma City, 1976—; asst. trustee in bankruptcy Four Seasons Nursing Ctrs. Am., Oklahoma City, 1972-73; dir. Community Bank-Warr Acres, Oklahoma City, 1972-82, Will Rogers Bank, Oklahoma City; trustee in bankruptcy Gulf South Corp., Oklahoma City, 1974. Chmn., Cath. Social Ministries, Archdiocese of Oklahoma City, 1977-81; treas., bd. dirs. Neighborhood Services Orgn., Oklahoma City Met. Area, 1978-83; chmn. bd. New World Sch., Oklahoma City, 1973-74. Mem. Okla. State U. CBA Assocs. (assoc.), Phi Delta Theta Alumni (pres. Oklahoma City 1969-71). Democrat. Roman Catholic. Clubs: Harvard Business School Alumni (pres. Oklahoma City 1970-71), Business Boosters (pres. 1985), Oklahoma City Dinner, Quail Creek Golf and Country. Home: 6224 Commodore Ln Oklahoma City OK 73132 Office: Amity Care Corp 4415 Highline Blvd Box 23017 Oklahoma City OK 73123

GRENINGER, EDWIN THOMAS, educator; b. Montoursville, Pa., Apr. 12, 1918; s. Fred R. and Martha (Cutler) G.; student Susquehanna U., 1936-38; A.B., Gettysburg Coll., 1941; M.A., Temple U., 1947; Ph.D., U. Pa., 1958; m. Jane Torbert, June 26, 1948 (dec. Mar. 1963); m. 2d, Gem Kate Taylor, Oct. 26, 1968. Instr. history Valparaiso U., 1948-49, Pa. State U., Ogontz, 1950, 52-53, Wilkes Coll., 1951-52; asst. prof. history E. Tenn. State U., Johnson City, 1958-61, asso. prof. 1961-64, prof. history, 1964—. Writer ann. travelogue, 1963—. Mem. com. on higher edn. Synod Va., United Luth. Ch. Am., 1959-63, Southeastern Synod, 1963-77; mem. human studies sub com. Mountain Home VA Ctr. Served with AUS, 1942-46. Mem. Luth. Hist. Conf., So. Hist. Assn. (European sect.), Internat. Council for Edn. of Tchrs., Lexington Group, AAUP (chpt. v.p. 1969-70, pres. 1970-72), Phi Delta Kappa, Pi Kappa Alpha, Pi Gamma Mu (treas. local chpt. 1961—, gov. Tenn. province 1975—). Author: Fifteen Days in Russia, 1966. Book rev. editor: Social Science, 1961-62. Home: 2210 Wyndale Rd Johnson City TN 37601

GRESHAM, ANN ELIZABETH, retailer, horticulturist executive; b. Richmond, Va., Oct. 11, 1933; d. Allwin Stagg and Ruby Scott (Faber) Gresham. Student, Peace Coll., Raleigh, N.C., 1950-52, East Carolina U., 1952-53, Penland Sch., N.C., 1953-54, Va. Commonwealth U., 1960-64. Owner, prin. Ann Gresham's Gift Shop, Richmond, 1953-56; pres., treas. Gresham's Garden Ctr., Inc., Richmond, 1955-79; v.p. Gresham's Nursery, Inc., Richmond, 1959-73, pres., treas., 1973—; pres., treas. Gresham's Country Store, Richmond, 1964—; tchr., 1982—. Bd. dirs. Bainbridge Community Ministry, 1979, Handworkshop, 1984—; class agent Peace Coll., Raleigh, 1979, mem. alumnae council, 1983; Focus Group mem. Hand Workshop, Richmond, 1983. Mem. Midlothian Antique Dealers (treas. 1975-79), Richmond Quilt Guild (chpt. v.p. 1983-84), Nat. Needlework Assn., Quilt Inst., Am. Hort. Soc. Episcopalian. Clubs: Chesmond Women's (v.p. 1979-80), James River Woman's (Richmond). Home: 2324 Logan St Bon Air VA 23235 Office: Gresham's Inc 6725 Midlothian Pike Richmond VA 23225

GRESHAM, DEBORAH BRAMLETT, registered nurse; b. Greenville, S.C., Jan. 18, 1958; d. Joe Douglas and Doris Irene (Green) Bramlett; m. Timothy William Gresham, June 4, 1977. B.S.N. cum laude, Clemson U., 1980. Registered nurse, S.C. Nursing asst. Greenville Meml. Hosp. (S.C.), 1977-80, staff nurse, 1980-82, head nurse gen. surgery, 1982—, co-chmn. head nurse com., 1984—, sec., 1982-83, sec. physician nurse com., 1983—, mem. quality assurance com., 1982—. Mem. Sigma Theta Tau. Democrat. Baptist. Office: Greenville Meml Hosp 701 Grove Rd Greenville SC 29602

GRESHAM, JOHN KENNETH, state senator; b. Drew, Miss., May 12, 1930; student U. Miss., U. So. Miss.; m. Betty Jo Overstreet. Mem. Miss. Senate; ins. agt.; real estate broker; health care exec. Bd. dirs. Trinity Meth. Ch.; bd. dirs. S. Washington County Hosp. Mem. Farm Bur., Delta Council, Am. Legion, VFW, Greenville C. of C. Democrat. Office: Miss State Senate Jackson MS 39205*

GRESHAM, THOMAS ANDREW, counselor; b. Tuscaloosa, Ala., Sept. 20, 1953; s. Richard Andrew and Martha (Yow) G. B.S., U. Ala., 1983, M.A., 1985. Cert. alcoholism counselor Ala. Program dir. Nova Clinics Inc., Tuscaloosa, 1984-85; therapist Central Va. Community Services Bd., Lynchburg, 1985—. Pres., Handicapped Students Orgn., 1983-85; mem. Mayors Com. on Handicapped and Elderly, Tuscaloosa, 1983. Served with USN, 1972-80; Vietnam. Mem. Am. Assn. Counseling and Devel., Am. Rehab. Counselors Assn., Am. Mental Health Counselors Assn., Nat. Rehab. Counselors Assn., Nat. Rehab. Adminstrs. Assn. Baha'i. Avocations: photography; motorcycling; reading. Office: Arise Residential Ctr PO Box 60 Forest VA 24551

GRESS, GARNETTA MARGARET, management analyst; b. Balt., May 10, 1943; d. Harold James and Garnetta Margaret (Ramsay) Potee; student East Carolina U., 1967-71, Pitt Community Coll., 1969-70, Coastal Carolina Community Coll., 1973-74, Pepperdine U., 1975, Syracuse U., 1977—; grad. cert. Antioch Sch. Law, 1982, M.A., 1985; m. James A. Gress, Mar. 11, 1978; children—William Potee Klages, Jenifer Raye Klages. Fed. Women's program mgr. U.S. Marine Corps, Camp Lejeune, N.C., 1979-83; mgmt. analyst USMC, Camp Lejeune, N.C., 1983-84; vol. programs coordinator MAG-26, New River, N.C., 1984—. Mem. Onslow County Council on Status of Women, 1979—, past vice-chmn.; mem. USO Council for Jacksonville, 1975—; bd. dirs. Balt. Regional chpt. ARC, 1960-61, hon. chmn., New River, 1984—. Named Woman of Yr. chpt. Beta Sigma Phi, 1975-76, chpt. Am. Bus. Women's Assn., 1974. Mem. N.C. Assn. EEO Personnel, Am. Soc. Mil. Comptrollers, Am. Bus. Women's Assn., Federally Employed Women, Inc., NOW, Beta Sigma Phi.

GRESSETT, CHARLES LARRY, coach, educator, broadcaster; b. Clark County, Miss., Apr. 16, 1949; s. Lewis Edwin and Margaret Jewel (Cook) G.; m. Ruth Mabry, Aug. 16, 1968; children—Bradley, Daniel, Erin. B.S., Miss. Coll., 1971, M.Ed., 1975. Cert. tchr., Miss. Tchr., coach Holly Bluff Sch., Miss., 1971-72, Lake High Sch., Miss., 1972-74; instr., dean of students Clarke Coll., Newton, Miss., 1974-80, instr., phys. edn., 1983—; sports announcer Sta. WQST-AM, Forest, Miss., 1975—, asst. mgr., 1980-83. Alderman City of Lake, 1977. Named to Outstanding Young Men Am., U.S. Jaycees, 1974. Mem. Miss. Assn. Coaches, Lake Jaycees (pres. 1972-73), Kappa Delta Pi. Lodges: Rotary, Masons (master). Avocations: music; sports; poetry. Home: PO Box 222 Lake MS 39092 Office: Clarke Coll PO Box 440 Newton MS 39345

GRESSMAN, EUGENE, legal educator, consultant; b. Lansing, Mich., Apr. 18, 1917; s. William Albert and Bess Beulah (Nagle) G.; m. Nan Alice Kirby, Aug. 6, 1944; children—William, Margot and Nancy (twins), Eric. A.B., U. Mich., 1938, J.D., 1940. Bar: Mich. 1940, D.C. 1948, Md. 1959, U.S. Supreme Ct. 1945. Atty., SEC, Washington, 1940-43; law clk. to Justice Frank Murphy, U.S. Supreme Ct., 1943-48; ptnr. Van Arkel, Kaiser, Gressman, Rosenberg & Driesen, Washington, 1948-77; William Rand Kenan, Jr. prof. law U. N.C. Sch. Law, Chapel Hill, 1977—; of counsel Bredhoff & Kaiser, Washington, 1981-84, Brand & Lowell, Washington, 1984—; disting. vis. prof. Sch. Law, Fordham U., 1982-83; vis. prof. law Ohio State U. Law Sch., 1967, U. Mich. Law Sch., 1969, Law Sch., George Washington U., 1971-77, Sch. Law, Ind. U., Indpls., 1976, Sch. Law, Cath. U. Am., 1977; spl. counsel U.S. Ho. of Reps., 1976—; judge Appeal Tax Ct. Montgomery County (Md.), 1959-62; chmn. rules com. U.S. Ct. Appeals for 4th circuit. Mem. ABA, Fed. Bar Assn., Am. Law Inst., Am. Judicature Soc., D.C. Bar, Order of Barristers, Order of Coif, Phi Beta Kappa. Author: (with Robert L. Stern and Stephen M. Shapiro) Supreme Court Practice, 6th edit., 1986; (with Charles A. Wright and others) Federal Practice and Procedure, Vol. 16, 1977; contbr. articles and book revs. to legal jours. Home: 325 Glendale Dr Chapel Hill NC 27514 Office: Sch Law Univ NC Chapel Hill NC 27514

GRETHER, J(AN) WICHERT (WICK), insurance broker; b. Houston, Mar. 27, 1944; s. James Wichert and Adrienne (Brown) G.; m. Susan Fox, Oct. 21, 1972; 1 dau., Taylor Fox. B.B.A., U. Houston, 1971. Salesman, John S. Dunn & Co., Houston, 1969-72; pres. Grether & Assocs., Houston, 1972-81; pres. Grether/King, Houston, 1981—; pres. Ins. Placement Bd., Houston, 1980. Served with USN, 1965-69. Mem. Young Ins. Agts. Soc. (founding pres. 1975-77), Ind. Ins. Agts. Houston (pres. 1980, bd. dirs. 1976-80). Home: 315 Glenwood Dr Houston TX 77007 Office: Grether/King & Assocs Inc 6699 Portwest Dr Houston TX 77024

GREVELLE, JAMES VERNON, lawyer; b. Waco, Tex., Sept. 2, 1938; s. James Ennis and Jimmie Elna (Lee) G.; m. Garnett Dowell Brown, Sept. 15, 1971; children—Garnett Anne, Caroline Elizabeth. B.A., U. Tex., 1961, LL.B., 1963. Bar: Tex., 1963, Calif. 1968. Assoc. firm Baker & Botts, Houston, 1963-67; corp. counsel Teledyne, Inc., Los Angeles, 1967-72; ptnr. Shank, Irwin, Conant, Williamson & Grevelle, Dallas, 1972-81; chmn. Grevelle & Assocs. Inc., and predecessors, Dallas, 1981—. Mem. Dallas Bar Assn., Tex. Bar Assn., Calif. Bar Assn., French-Am. C. of C. (bd. dirs., sec.), Phi Beta Kappa, Beta Theta Pi. Club: Park City. Office: Suite 800 8300 Douglas Ave Dr Dallas TX 75225

GRIDLEY, GREGORY CHARLES, psychologist, executive search consultant; b. Milw., Dec. 11, 1948; s. James Gregory and Priscilla Jones G.; A.B., Colgate U., 1971; Ph.D. (NIMH fellow), U. Tex., Austin, 1975; m. Jane Elizabeth Bryan, July 23, 1977; children—Blythe Lea, Andrew James. Chief psychologist Corpus Christi (Tex.) Ind. Sch. Dist., 1975-78; pres. Gregory Gridley Assos., Inc., Corpus Christi, 1978—. Chmn. vol. services council Corpus Christi State Sch., 1979-80; pres. bd. dirs. Corpus Christi Drug Abuse Council, 1977-78; bd. dirs. Coastal Bend Assn. Mental Health, 1976-79, Family Counseling Service, 1977-79, Big Bros./Big Sisters, 1975-78, Driscoll Hosp., 1977, Friends of Library, 1980—. Mem. Am. Psychol. Assn., Nueces County Psychol. Assn. (pres. 1984), Corpus Christi C. of C., Phi Kappa Phi. Republican. Episcopalian. Club: Rotary. Office: 3817 Alameda St St Corpus Christi TX 78411

GRIDLEY, JOHN WILLIS, JR., electronics company executive; b. Rochester, Minn., May 10, 1939; s. John Willis and Dorothy Janet (Root) G.; B.A., Hamline U., 1960; postgrad. Princeton U., 1961-62, Harvard U., 1973; m. Elizabeth Linda Lohn, Sept. 8, 1962 (div. Feb. 1976); children—James, Janet, Richard; m. Jean Ruth Johnson, June 30, 1984. Securities analyst Value Line Investment Survey, N.Y.C., 1962-64; mgr. profit analysis Ford Motor Co., Dearborn, Mich., 1964-74; asst. controller Xerox Info. Systems, El Segundo, Calif., 1974-76; controller TRW Energy Systems, Redondo Beach, Calif., 1976-79; v.p., controller McQuay, Inc., Mpls., 1979-82; v.p., controller First Bank System, Inc., Mpls., 1982-83; fin. v.p., chief fin. officer, treas., asst. sec. Intergraph Corp., Huntsville, Ala., 1983—; dir. Intergraph Systems Ltd. (Can.). Budget and taxation commr. City of Redondo Beach, 1976-80. Served with AUS, 1959. Mem. Fin. Execs. Inst. Republican. Episcopalian. Club: King Harbor Yacht. Lodges: Mason, Shriners. Home: 2522 Garth Rd SE Huntsville AL 35801 Office: One Madison Indsl Park Huntsville AL 35807

GRIER, BARBARA G. (GENE DAMON), editor, lectr., author; b. Cin., Nov. 4, 1933; d. Phillip Strang and Dorothy Vernon (Black) Grier; grad. high sch. Author: The Lesbian in Literature, 1967, (with others) 2d edit., 1975, 3d edit., 1981; The Least of These (in Sisterhood is Powerful), 1970; The Index, 1974; Lesbiana, 1976; The Lesbian Home Jour., 1976; The Lavender Herring, 1976; Lesbian Lives, 1976; pub. The Ladder mag., 1970-72, fiction and poetry editor, 1966-67, editor, 1968-72; dir. promotion Naiad Press, Reno, Nev., 1973—, treas., 1976—, v.p., gen. mgr., Tallahassee, Fla., 1980—. Democrat. Home: Route 1 Box 3319 Havana FL 32333 Office: Naiad Press Inc PO Box 10543 Tallahassee FL 32302

GRIER, WILLIAM BOYD, engineering company official; b. Shelby, N.C., Apr. 2, 1943; s. George W. and Mozell (Scism) G.; m. Betty Carol Wheless, July 27, 1942; children—Mark William, Crystal Elizabeth; B.S. in Vocat. and Indsl. Edn., N.C. State U., 1969; M.B.A., Pepperdine U., 1977. Wage practices specialist Western Electric Co., Greensboro, N.C., 1969-73; area tng. mgr. Daniel Constrn. Co., Greenville, S.C., 1973-75; corp. tng. mgr. R.M. Parsons Co., Pasadena, Calif. 1975-77; region tng. mgr. Weyerhaeuser Co., Longview, Wash., 1977-78, human resources devel. mgr., 1980-83; planning engr. Saudi Arabian Parsons, Yanbu, 1978-79, mgr. human resources devel., 1983—; cons. engr. pulp and paper mfg. Planner, designer vocat. tech. edn. ctr. and complex for indsl. complex Saudi Arabia. Vol. personnel bd. Am. Cancer Soc., 1976-77; mem. adv. council Pasadena City Coll., 1976-77; personnel advisor Guilford County EEO Council, 1972-73. Served with U.S. Army, 1962-65. Mem. Am. Soc. Tng. and Devel., Am. Soc. Personnel Adminstrs., Epsilon Pi Tau, Kappa Phi Kappa. Baptist. Club: Toastmasters.

GRIESE, NOEL LEE, oil company public relations executive, economist; b. Appleton, Wis., Dec. 19, 1937; s. Orville Carl and Thelma (Derus) G.; m. Heather Hamacher, Mar. 27, 1962 (div. 1982); children—Noel N., Mary E.; m. 2d, Kathleen Holdampf Splinter, Sept. 25, 1982; stepchildren—Dawn C., Shannon S., Laura L. B.S., U. Wis., 1960, M.S. in English, 1967, M.S. in Journalism, 1978. Editor, Batavia (Ill.) Herald, 1960-62; pub. relations exec. Ill. Bell Telephone Co., Chgo., 1964-69; teaching asst. to vis. asst. prof. journalism U. Wis., Madison, 1969-73; asst. prof. pub. relations U. Ga., Athens, 1973-80; dir. corp. communications Colonial Pipeline Co., Atlanta, 1980—; cons. in field. Bd. dirs. Am. Lung Assn. Ga., Ga. chpt. Nat. Multiple Sclerosis Soc. Served to capt. U.S. Army, 1962-64. Mem. Internat. Assn. Energy Economists, Transp. Research Forum, Pub. Relations Soc. Am., Soc. Profl. Journalists, Phi Beta Kappa, Phi Kappa Phi, Phi Eta Sigma. Republican. Contbr. articles to profl. jours. Home: 3852 Allsborough Dr Tucker GA 30084 Office: 3390 Peachtree Rd NE Atlanta GA 30326 also Box 18855 Atlanta GA 30326

GRIFFEE, CAROL MADGE, journalist, editorial services company executive; b. Washington, Dec. 30, 1937; d. John Franklin and Leda Mae (Woodruff) G.; B.A. with honors, U. Tulsa, 1959, M.A., 1966. Reporter. Ft. Smith (Ark.) Times-Record, 1955, Tulsa Daily World, 1958-60; news editor Annandale (Va.) Free Press, 1961-62; staff writer Washington Eve. Star, 1963-66; city editor No. Va. Sun, Arlington, Va., 1967-69, exec. editor, 1969-72; capitol reporter Walter E. Hussman Co., Camden, Ark., 1973; reporter Ark. Gazette, Little Rock, 1973-85; pres. Editorial Services, Inc., 1982—. Past pres. George Mason Republican Women's Club; past dir. research Fairfax County Rep. Com.; past bd. dirs. Arlington chpt. ARC; past bd. visitors George Mason U., Fairfax, Va.; mem. membership com. Fairfax County Cultural Assn.; mem. nat. fire com. Filene Ctr. Performing Arts, Wolf Trap Farm Park, Vienna, Va., 1970. Recipient Very Spl. Lady award Advt. Club Met. Washington, 1967, Spl. award Ark. Sanitarians Assn., 1977; Disting. Service awards dept. journalism U. Ark., Little Rock, 1979, 83; also awards Nat. Fedn. Press Women, Ark. Press Women, 1977; named Conservationist of Yr., Ark. Wildlife Fedn., 1985. Mem. Nat. Fedn. Press Women (dir. 1977-78, legislature-resolutions dir. 1979-80, nat. conv. chmn. 1988), Ark Press Women (pres. 1977-78), Ark. Polit. Sci. Assn., Ark. Hist. Assn., Mortar Bd., Phi Delta Epsilon, Phi Gamma Kappa, Phi Delta Theta, Pi Gamma Mu, Phi Mu, Soc. Profl. Journalists-Sigma Delta Chi (chpt. v.p. 1979-80, chmn. freedom of info. com. 1981-83, regional mem. nat. freedom of info. com. 1984). Project dir. Horizons: 100 Arkansas Women of Achievement, 1980; author: Aging in Arkansas, 1981; Images and Realities of Arkansas, 1982; Toxicology: Today's Target for Tomorrow, 1983; Capital: The Missing Link, 1984. Home: 2610 N Taylor St Little Rock AR 72207

GRIFFIN, BILLY L., electric utility company executive; b. 1930. B.S., Clemson U., 1952. With Fla. Power Corp., St. Petersburg, 1954—, dir. div. ops., 1970-71, asst. v.p. div. ops., 1971-72, asst. v.p. constrn. maintenance ops., 1972-73, v.p. systems ops., 1973-77, sr. v.p. engring. constrn., 1977-83, exec. v.p., 1983—. Served to 1st lt. U.S. Army, 1952-54. Address: Florida Power Corp 3201 34th St S Saint Petersburg FL 33733

GRIFFIN, ERVIN VEROME, college administrator, consultant, researcher; b. Coalwood, W.Va., May 15, 1949; s. Roy and Martha Griffin; divorced; 1 child, Ervin V. Griffin, Jr. B.S., Bluefield State Coll., 1971; M.S. Western Ill. U., 1974; Cert. Advanced Grad. Study in Edn., Va. Tech. Inst., 1979, Ed.D., 1980. Cert. counselor, Va. Dir. student aid S.W. Va. Community Coll., Richlands, 1974-78; counselor upward bound Va. Tech. Inst., Blacksburg, 1978-79; coordinator co-curricular activities S.W. Va. Community Coll., Richlands, 1979-84; coordinator student devel. Patrick Henry Community Coll., Martinsville, Va., 1984—; cons. various colls., 1984. Vol. FOCUS, Martinsville, 1984; mem. Martinsville Henry County Men's Roundtable, 1984—. Named Outstanding Young Man Am. Jaycees, 1978. Mem. Am. Coll. Personnel Assn. (bd. dirs. commn. XI 1984-87), Am. Assn. Counseling Devel., Assn. Non-white Concerns, Tazewell County Helpline (dir. 1984-86), NAACP, Crusaders Ruritan Club. Avocations: tennis; writing. Home: 621 Lee Terr Martinsville VA 24112 Office: Patrick Henry Community Coll PO Drawer 5311 Martinsville VA 24112

GRIFFIN, HAROLD CARTER, special education administrator; b. Norfolk, Va., June 13, 1945; s. Harold Thomas and Sallie (Carter) G.; children—Andrew, Sarah, James; m. 2d, Julia Hall, Dec. 18, 1982. B.A., Wake Forest U., 1967; M.A., U. Iowa, 1970; Ph.D., U. Tex., 1979. Cert. tchr., Md., Va., N.C. Tchr., Fairfax City pub. schs. (Va.), 1967-69, Prince George's pub. schs., Upper Marlboro, Md., 1970-71; cons. N.C. Dept. Pub. Instrn., Raleigh, 1971-77; asst. prof. U. New Orleans, 1979-82; chief quality assurance O'Berry Ctr., Goldsboro, N.C., 1982—. Contbr. chpts. to books, articles to profl. jours. Fellow Am. Acad. Cerebral Palsy; mem. Am. Assn. Mental Deficiency, Council for Exceptional Children, Assn. for Severely Handicapped. Office: O'Berry Ctr PO Box 247 Goldsboro NC 27830

GRIFFIN, JAMES BROOKS, physician; b. St. Louis, Mar. 1, 1953; s. James Curtis and Elizabeth (Brooks) G.; m. Catherine Jayne Calloway, May 27, 1975;

children—Jayne, Lacey, James. B.S., Miss. Coll., 1974; M.D., U. Miss., 1978. Instr. dept. obstetrics and gynecology U. Miss. Med. Ctr., Jackson, 1982—. Fellow Am. Coll. Obstetrics and Gynecology; mem. AMA, Miss. Med. Assn., Miss. Ob-Gyn Soc., Jackson Gynesic Soc. (sec. treas. 1984-85, pres. 1985—), Bapt. Med.-Dental Fellowship. Clubs: Ducks Unlimited, Am. Wildlife Fedn., Conservation 82. Avocations: hunting; fishing. Home: 1111 Lyncrest Ave Jackson MS 39202 Office: The Woman's Clinic 953 North St Jackson MS 39202

GRIFFIN, JAMES CRAIG, developmental disabilities researcher, psychologist; b. Lubbock, Tex., Sept. 4, 1948; s. J.C. and Mary Louise (Cunningham) G.; m. Hilda Kaye Henderson, Aug. 9, 1980; 1 dau., Erica Keely. B.A., Tex. Tech. U., 1972, Ph.D., 1978. Conf. coordinator Research and Tng. Center in Mental Retardation, 1972-75; sr. psychologist Western Carolina Ctr., Morgantown, 1975-77; clin. psychologist Gulf Coast Mental Health and Mental Retardation Center, Galveston, Tex., 1977-78; lectr. U. Houston, 1978-79, pvt. practice psychology, Houston, 1978-79; dir. edn. and tng. Richmond (Tex.) State Sch., 1979-83; project dir. Tex. Devel. Disabilities Program, 1982-83; dir. spl. programs Tex. Dept. Mental Health and Mental Retardation, Richmond, 1983—. Grantee Tex. Devel. Disabilities Program, 1982—, Dept. Health and Human Services, 1983—. Mem. AAAS, Am. Assn. on Mental Deficiency, Am. Psychol. Assn., Council for Exceptional Children. Author: Manipulation of Potential Punishment Parameters in the Treatment of Self-Injury, 1975; Maintenance of Self-Help Training Programs for Non-Professional Staff, 1976; Toward Behavioral Architecture: Effects of Crowding on the Behavior of the Retarded, 1978; Self-Injurious Behavior: A State-Wide Prevalence Survey of Extent and Circumstances, 1983. Office: 2100 Preston St Richmond TX 77469

GRIFFIN, JAMES WILLIAM, heavy construction corporation executive, building firm executive; b. Moultrie, Ga., July 10, 1953; s. Orris Stanton and Hilda Allene (Bell) G.; m. Jenny Lynn McWilliams, June 9, 1979 (div. Dec. 1981). B.Engring.Tech., Ga. So. Coll., 1977. Engr., Batson-Cook, Inc., Atlanta, 1977-78; supt. G.C. Bailey Co. Inc., Atlanta, 1978-79; mgr., engr. DSI, USA, Inc., Marietta, Ga., 1980—; pres. Asgard Constrn. Co., Inc., Atlanta, 1983—. Mem. Cobb County C. of C., ASCE, Cobb County Young Council Realtors. Republican. Home: 5306 Treelodge Pkwy Dunwoody GA 30338 Office: DSI USA Inc Suite C-10 1240 Johnson Ferry Pl Marietta GA 30067

GRIFFIN, JOHN DUNCAN, lawyer; b. Houston, Aug. 24, 1954; s. Bill Fuller and Lyndell (Hairgrove) G. B.A., U. Tex.-Austin, 1975; J.D., South Tex. Coll. Law, 1979. Bar: Tex. 1979, U.S. Dist Ct. (ea. dist.) Tex. 1980. Assoc. Bill F. Griffin Jr., Center, Tex., 1979—. Active Pres.'s Assocs. U. Tex.-Austin, 1979-84; pres. Shelby County Tex. Ex-Students, 1980-84; youth coordinator First Methodist Ch., 1984; chmn. Deep East Tex. Mental Health-Mental Retardation, 1984. Mem. ABA, Assn. Trial Lawyers Am. (treas. student div. 1978-79), Shelby County Bar Assn. (v.p. 1981), Tex. State Bar Assn. Methodist. Office: Bill F Griffin Jr 131 Tenaha St Center TX 75935

GRIFFIN, LEIGH SPRAGENS, insurance underwriter, agent; b. Lexington, Ky., Dec. 16, 1955; d. Gerald Robin and Elizabeth Lee (Spragens) Griffin; m. Danny Lynn Barbour, Nov. 9, 1974 (div. 1981). Cert. in gen. ins. Ins. Inst. Am.; cert. profl. ins. woman. Clk. Miller Griffin & Marks, Attys., Lexington, 1972-75; property underwriter Buckley & Co., Inc., Lexington, 1975-77; comml. underwriter Wombwell Ins. Agy. Inc., Lexington, 1977-80; comml. underwriter, agt. Progressive Ins. Agy. Inc., Lexington, 1980-84, property and casualty mgr., 1984—. Vol. Fire Prevention Week, Lexington Fire Dept., 1981-83. Mem. Blue Grass Assn. Ins. Women (exec. bd. 1980-81, 2d v.p. 1982-83, sponsor Make It Click Program Drunk Driving Booths 1981-83, vol. Ky. state police Lock Your Car campaign 1980-83, Rookie of Yr. award 1982), Ind. Ins. Agts. Ky., Nat. Assn. Ins. Women Internat. (Rookie of Yr. award 1982, Ky. state chmn. project invest 1982-85), Jr. League Lexington (provisional mem.). Democrat. Presbyterian. Home: 2091 Spring Grove Ave Lexington KY 40503 Office: Progressive Ins Agy Inc 351 Burley Ave PO Box 4065 Lexington KY 40544

GRIFFIN, MARY FRANCES, library media consultant; b. Cross Hill, Laurens County, S.C., Aug. 24, 1925; d. James and Rosa Lee (Carter) G.; A.B., Benedict Coll., 1947; M.S.L.S., Ind. U., 1957; student S.C. State Coll., summers 1948-51, Atlanta U., 1953, Va. State Coll., 1961. Tchr.-librarian Johnston (S.C.) Tng. Sch., Edgefield County Sch. Dist., 1947-51; librarian Lee County Sch. Dist., Dennis High, Bishopville, S.C., 1951-52, Greenville County (S.C.) Sch. Dist., 1952-66; library cons. S.C. Dept. Edn., Columbia, 1966—; vis. tchr. U. S.C., 1977. Recipient Cert. of Living the Legacy award Nat. Council Negro Women, 1980. Mem. ALA, Assn. Ednl. Communications and Tech. S.C., Assn. Curriculum Devel., AAUW (pres. Columbia br. 1978-80), Southeastern Library Assn. (sec. 1979-80), S.C. Library Assn. (sec. 1979), S.C. Assn. Sch. Librarians. Baptist. Home: PO Box 1652 Columbia SC 29202 also 1100 Skyland Dr Columbia SC 29210

GRIFFIN, MATHEW MCCRARY, II, pharmacist; b. Konawa, Okla., Nov. 5, 1937; s. Mathew McCrary and Waymon Wilma (Archer) G.; m. JoAnn Bowd Griffin, July 25, 1964; children—Mathew, Melinda Marie. B.S., Okla. U., 1960. Registered pharmacist. Pharmacist, Pierce Pharmacy, Muskogee, Okla., 1962-65; dir. pharmacy Sparks Regional Med Ctr., Fort Smith, Ark., 1965-80, dir. pharmacy and central supply, 1980—. Bd. dirs., adv. Area Agy. Aging, Fort Smith, 1984—. Served as col. USAR, 1960-81. Mem. Am. Pharm. Assn., Am. Soc. Hosp. Pharmacists, Ark. Pharm. Assn., Ark. Assn. Hosp. Pharmacists (leadership award 1970, pres. 1969-70). Republican. Mem. Ch. of Christ. Lodge: Optomist. Avocations: woodworking; gardening. Home: 3320 S 66th St Fort Smith AR 72903 Office: Sparks Regional Med Ctr 1311 South I St Fort Smith AR 72902

GRIFFIN, NELL, English educator; b. Gadsden, Ala., Oct. 12, 1930; d. Ben Barton and Mary Delana (Sewell) G.; B.S., U. Ala., 1952, M.A., 1954; Ph.D., Vanderbilt U., 1971. Instr., Auburn U., 1954-59; asst. prof. Murray State U., 1959-65; asst. prof. English, Jacksonville State U., 1965-66; instr. U. Tenn. Nashville, 1968-69; assoc. prof. English, Jacksonville State U., 1969-83, prof., 1983—; cons. humanities. Del., Ala. Gov.'s Conf. on Library and Info. Services, 1978-79; mem. Anniston Mus. League, Ala. Shakespeare Festival Assn., Friends of the Library; bd. dirs. Gadsden Cultural Arts Found., 1984—. Mem. Ala. Council English Tchrs. Assn. (mem. curriculum com. 1975-78), South Atlantic Modern Lang. Assn., Ala. Edn. Assn., AAUW (v.p. Gadsden chpt. 1978, edn. chmn. 1979). Baptist. Club: Altrusa Internat. (chmn. Decorators' Show House 1982, corr. sec. 1984, bd. dirs. 1985-87). Author script At the Foot of These Mountains, outdoor pageant, 1981. Home: 1129 Christopher Ave Gadsden AL 35901 Office: Jacksonville State U Jacksonville AL 36265

GRIFFIN, PERRY DONALD, pharmacist; b. Waycross, Ga., Nov. 5, 1946; s. Pury Donald and Doris (Lane) G.; m. Deborah Orr, July 30, 1971; children—Stacey Michelle, Lori Donelle. B.S. in Pharmacy, U. Ga., 1971. Pharmacist, Brownings, Waycross, 1971-73; chief pharmacist Prescription Shop, Waycross, 1973-79, pres., 1979-80; pres. Griffin's Prescription Shop, Waycross, 1980—. Vice-pres. Ware County Bd. Edn., 1982—; pres. Okefenokee Regional Library, Ware County, 1985-87, Waycross Pub. Library, 1985-87. Mem. Waycross Pharm. Assn. (pres. 1973—), 8th Dist. Pharm. Assn. (v.p. 1984—), Jaycees (Waycross pres. 1977-78), Ga. Jaycees (dist. pres. 1978-79). Democrat. Baptist. Avocations: horses; fishing; skiing; racquetball. Home: 3055 Warrior Rd Waycross GA 31501 Office: Griffins Prescription Shop PO Box 455 Waycross GA 31501

GRIFFIN, TIM DALE, music educator; b. Midland, Mich., Sept. 26, 1952; s. Alvin D. and Shelley June (Yoder) G.; m. Susan M. Drow, Mar. 26, 1977. B.Mus., Western Mich. U., 1975, M.A., 1982. Assoc. dir. bands Hartford pub. schs., Mich., 1976-79; dir. bands Lawton Community Schs., Mich., 1979-81; fin. aid auditor Kalamazoo Coll., 1981; adminstrv. asst. Western Mich. U., Kalamazoo, 1982; adj. faculty U. Ala., Huntsville, 1982—, asst. to v.p. student affairs, 1982—; dir. U. Ala. Huntsville Jazz Ensemble and Pep Band, 1982—; adjudicator Ala. Music Educators Conf., 1982—. Musical dir. Paw Paw Civic Players (Mich.), 1976-82; co-dir. Huntsville Horn Club. Mem. Am. Assn. Counseling and Devel., Nat. Assn. Student Personnel Adminstrs., Am. Coll. Personnel Assn., ACLU, Sierra Club, Phi Mu Alpha. Home: 333 Jack Coleman Dr Huntsville AL 35805 Office: Office Student Affairs U Ala Huntsville AL 35899

GRIFFIN, WILLIAM ALBERT, educator, college administrator, minister; b. Washington, N.C., Oct. 29, 1939; s. Norfleet Edward and Julia Lucille (Dunbar) G.; m. Patricia Swindell, June 9, 1962; children—Mark Alan, Carol Lynne. A.B., Roanoke Bible Coll., 1962, Milligan Coll., 1963; M.A., E. Carolina U., 1970; M.A., Cin. Christian Sem., 1979; cert. Coll. William and Mary, 1981. Prof. Roanoke Bible Coll., Elizabeth City, N.C., 1963—, dean students, 1975—; minister Fairfield Christian Ch., N.C., 1980—. Author: Ante-Bellum Elizabeth City, 1970; RBC-The First 25 Years, 1981. Pres. Pasquotank County Hist. Soc., Elizabeth City, 1967-70. Mem. Delta Epsilon Chi. Home: 715 First St Elizabeth City NC 27909 Office: Roanoke Bible Coll PO Box 387 Elizabeth City NC 27909

GRIFFING, CLAYTON A., financial executive; b. Pine Bluff, Ark., Oct. 20, 1940; s. Hugh M. and Vernon C. G.; m. Jean Lack; children—Clayton Lance, Kimberly. B.Ceramic Engring., Ga. Inst. Tech., 1963; M.B.A., Emory U., 1965. Fin. analyst Atlantic Steel Co., Atlanta, 1965-69, asst. treas. corp. fin., 1969-71, treas., chief fin. officer, 1971-78, v.p. fin., chief fin. officer, 1978-80; sr. v.p. fin., chief fin. officer Lowe's Cos., Inc., North Wilkesboro, N.C., 1980—. Vice-chmn. bd. trustees Fernbank Sci. Ctr., Atlanta, 1973-80; pres., founder Ga. Sci. and Natural History League, 1973-80; active Leadership Atlanta, Leadership Ga. Mem. Am. Assn. Mus. Trustees, Emory Bus. Sch. Alumni Assn. (pres. 1976), Emory U. Alumni Assn. (v.p. bus. sch. 1976), Ga. Tech. Alumni Assn.

GRIFFIS, HUGH CLINTON, III, businessman; b. Jackson, Miss., Sept. 14, 1955; d. Hugh Clinton, Jr. and Louise Sible (Coleman) G.; B.A. in History and Polit. Sci. with high honors, Emory U., 1977, M.A., 1978. Mem. staff Office Lt. Gov. Ga., 1978-79; with computer ops. dept. Trust Co. Bank, Atlanta, 1979-80; ind. polit. and legal cons., East Point, Ga., 1980-84; Southeastern rep. Welsh Industries, DeKalb, Ill., 1984-85; pres. Fish'n Camp Marine and Outdoor Ctr., Newnan, Ga., 1985—. Mem. Fulton County Republican Com., 1980—; vice chmn. Atlanta area Nat. Eagle Scout Assn., 1977—. Recipient various awards Boy Scouts Am. Mem. Am. Polit. Sci. Assn., So. Hist. Assn., Tenn. Squire Assn., Nat. Rifle Assn., Bass Angler's Sportsman Soc., U.S. Bass Assn., Newnan-Coweta C. of C., Marine Trade Assn., Nature Conservancy, Pi Sigma Alpha, Phi Alpha Theta. Republican. Baptist. Home: 2364 Ridgeway Ave College Park GA 30337 Office: 35 Amlajack Blvd Newnan GA 30265

GRIFFITH, DOROTHY AUBINOE, interior designer; b. Washington, Feb. 19, 1927; d. Alvin Love and Dorothy (Barron) Aubinoe; A.B., Rollins Coll., 1948; grad. teaching cert. U. Md., 1949; diploma Internat. Inst. Interior Design, 1958; children—June, Paul, Tod, Holly. Owner, interior designer Griffith Assos., Inc., Bethesda, Md., 1958-78; owner, dir. Griffith Gallery, Coral Gables, Fla., 1978—. Mem. alumni council Rollins Coll., 1982—, trustee, 1983-86; nat. chmn. Rollins Fund, 1985-86. Mem. Am. Soc. Interior Designers. Club: Coral Gables Country. Home: 440 Giralda Ave Coral Gables FL 33134 also Islamorada FL

GRIFFITH, JACK WILLIAM, medical librarian; b. Rockwell City, Iowa, Dec. 19, 1929; s. William J. and Nell J. Griffith; B.A., U. Md., 1966; M.S. in Geography, U. Nebr., 1969, B.S., 1972; M.A. in Library Media, U. S.D., 1975; m. Lydia Griffith; children—Mary A., Anna B. Served with U.S. Air Force, 1950-70; tchr., Lewis Central High Sch., Council Bluffs, Iowa, 1970-72, librarian, 1972-75; librarian Def. Systems Mgmt. Sch., Ft. Belvoir, Va., 1975; med. librarian Archbishop Bergan Mercy Hosp., Omaha, 1976-78; now med. librarian VA Med. Center, North Little Rock, Ark. Cert. dir. library services, tchr., librarian, Iowa; tchr., ednl. media specialist, Nebr. Mem. ALA, Am. Assn. Sch. Librarians. Clubs: Masons, Elks. Contbr. articles to profl. jours. Home: 5713 N Cedar North Little Rock AR 72116 Office: Med Library VA Med Center Little Rock AR 72114

GRIFFITH, JANE ELIZABETH, museum administrator; b. Edgefield, S.C., Sept. 19, 1939; d. William Arthur and Elizabeth (Pritchard) Byrd; B.A., Winthrop Coll., 1961; M.A.T., U. N.C., 1965; postgrad. Duke U., 1962, Tex. A.&M. U., 1970-80; m. George Wayne Griffith, 1966 (dec. 1972); m. 2d James W. Wilson, Sept. 25, 1982. Tchr., Columbia (S.C.) Public Sch. System, 1961-63; biologist Nat. Marine Fisheries Lab., Oxford, Md., 1963-64; tchr. Texas City (Tex.) Ind. Sch. Dist., 1965-67, Galveston (Tex.) Coll., 1967-71; research asst. U. Tex. Med. Br., Galveston, 1972-73; spl. projects analyst Amoco Chem. Co., Alvin, Tex., 1974-82; pres. Griffith Enterprises, Hitchcock, Tex., 1981—; dir. edn. BTA Mus., 1982—; owner, chmn. bd. Savory Farm. George W. Griffith Scholarship Program dir., 1972—; bd. dirs. Hitchcock Library, 1973-74; mem. City of Galveston Anti-litter Com., 1971-72. Mem. AAUW (state bd. 1972-74). Home: Route 2 Box 753 Donalds SC 29638 Office: PO Box 305 Donald SC 29638

GRIFFITH, JOSEPH PARKWOOD, real estate developer; b. Charleston, S.C., May 15, 1929; s. George Louis and Alice Helen (Schrage) G.; m. Elizabeth Smith, Sept. 10, 1955; children—Joseph, Helena, Louis, Stephen, Elizabeth. B.A., St. Bernard's Coll., 1955. Owner, pres. Joe Griffith, Inc., Charleston, 1959—; chmn. bd. dirs. First Trident Savs. & Loan, Charleston. Chmn. Council of Govts., Charleston, 1968-78. Served with U.S. Army, 1953-55. Named adm. S.C. Navy, 1983. Mem. Charleston Real Estate Bd., Charleston Trident C. of C. (pres. 1984), Hibernian Soc. (v.p.). Democrat. Roman Catholic. Club: Exchange (pres. 1967) (Charleston). Lodges: K.C., Knights of Malta. Avocations: reading; golf. Home: 117 Broad St Charleston SC 29401 Office: Joe Griffith Inc 180 E Bay St Charleston SC 29401

GRIFFITH, LYNN JOAN, lawyer; b. Newark, Apr. 19, 1949; d. Lambert Charles and Joan Marie (Schilling) Stadtman; m. Allan Thomas Griffith, Jan. 25, 1974; children—Charles Arthur, Valerie Lynn. B.A., Fla. So. Coll., 1971; J.D., Stetson U., 1974. Bar: Fla. 1974. Assoc. law firm Friedman & Britton, Orlando, Fla., 1974-76; sole practice law Lynn J. Griffith, Ft. Myers Beach, Fla., 1976-79; mng. ptnr. Griffith & Griffith, P.A., Ft. Myers, Fla., 1979—. Commr., Ft. Myers Beach Library Tax Dist., 1977-79; bd. dirs., Fla. Children's Home Soc., 1975, 76. Mem. ABA, Fla. Bar Assn., Comml. Law League Am. Office: 12875 Cleveland Ave S Suite 1 Fort Myers FL 33907

GRIFFITH, MELVIN EUGENE, retired government official; b. Lawrence, Kans., Mar. 24, 1912; s. George Thomas and Estella (Shaw) G.; A.B., U. Kans., 1934, A.M., 1935, Ph.D. (fellow in entomology), 1938; postgrad. U. Mich., summers 1937-40; m. Pauline Sophia Bogart, June 23, 1941. Instr. zoology N.D. Agrl. Coll., Fargo, 1938-39, asst. prof., 1939-41, asso. prof., 1941-42; commd. lt. USPHS, 1943, advanced through grades to capt., 1954, malaria control entomologist USPHS, La., 1942-43, Okla. 1943-46; communicable disease center entomologist, 1946-51; chief malariologist ICA, Thailand, 1951-60; asso. dir. Malaria Eradication Tng. Center, Jamaica, 1960; regional malaria adviser S.E. Asia, Agy. Internat. Devel., New Delhi, India, 1960-62, Near East and So. Asia, 1962-64, dep. chief malaria eradication br., Washington, 1964-67, chief, 1967-71, ret., 1971; cons. Office of Health, AID, Washington, 1971-75. Asso. prof. zool. scis. U. Okla., Norman, 1946-52, prof., 1952-56. Recipient citation for disting. service U. Kans., 1962. Mem. AAAS, Am. Pub. Health Assn., Am. Soc. Tropical Medicine and Hygiene, Am. Soc. Limnology and Oceanography, Entomol. Soc. Am., USPHS Commd. Officers Assn., Siam Soc., Explorers Club, Phi Beta Kappa, Sigma Xi. Contbr. articles and monographs on entomology, malaria control, pub. health. Address: PO Box DG Williamsburg VA 23187

GRIFFITH, ROBERT CHARLES, allergist; b. Shreveport, La., Jan. 9, 1939; s. Charles Parsons and Madelon (Jenkins) G.; m. Loretta Dean Secrist, July 15, 1969; children—Charles Randall, Cameron Stuart, Ann Marie. B.S., Centenary Coll., 1961; M.D., La. State U., 1965. Intern, Confederate Meml. Med. Ctr., Shreveport, 1965-66, resident in internal medicine, 1966-68; fellow in allergy and chest disease, instr. Va. Med. Sch. Hosp., Charlottesville, 1968-70; practice medicine specializing in allergies, Alexandria, La., 1970-72, The Allergy Clinic, Shreveport, 1972; pres. Griffith Allergy Clinic, Shreveport, 1973—; faculty internal medicine La. State U., 1972—. Bd. dirs. Caddo-Bossier Assn. Retarded Citizens, 1977—, Access (fomerly Child Devel. Ctr.), Shreveport, 1979—; mem. med. adv. com., spl. edn. adv. com. Caddo Parish Sch. Bd., 1977—, mem. commission on missions and social concerns First Methodist Ch., 1981-84, mem. adminstrv. bd., 1981-84. Served to maj. M.C., U.S. Army, 1965-71. Recipient Physician of the Yr. award Shreveport-Bossier Med. Assts., 1984; mem. Am. Acad. Allergy Am. Coll. Allergy, Am. Assn. Allergy and Clin. Immunology, Am. Coll. Chest Physicians, Am. Thoracic Soc., AMA, So. Med. Assn., La. Med. Soc., Shreveport Med. Soc. (allergy spokesman 1984-84), La. Allergy Soc. (charter; past pres.), U. Va. Alumni Assn., La. State U. Alumni Assn., SCV, Mil. Order Stars and Bars, Shreveport C. of C. Methodist. Lodges: Masons, Jesters. Clubs: Shreveport Country, Ambassadors, Cotillion, Royal, Plantation. Home: 7112 E Ridge Dr Shreveport LA 71106 Office: 2751 Virginia Ave Shreveport LA 71103

GRIFFITH, STEVEN FRANKLIN, lawyer, real estate title insurance agent; b. New Orleans, July 14, 1948; s. Hugh Franklin and Rose Marie (Teutone) G.; m. Mary Elizabeth McMillan Frank, Dec. 9, 1972; children—Steven Franklin, Jason Franklin. B.B.A., Loyola U. of the South, 1970, J.D., 1972. Admitted to La. bar, 1972, U.S. Dist. Ct. (ea. dist.) La. 1975, U.S. Ct. Appeals (5th cir.) 1975, U.S. Supreme Ct. bar 1976. Law offices Senator George T. Oubre, Norco, La., 1971-75; sole practice, Destrehan, La., 1975—. Served to 1st lt. U.S. Army, 1970-72. Mem. ABA, La. State Bar Assn., La. Trial Lawyers Assn., New Orleans Trial Lawyers Assn., Fed. Bar Assn. Democrat. Club: Lions. Office: 9001 River Rd Destrehan LA 70047

GRIFFITH, WAYLAND COLEMAN, mechanical engineering educator; b. Champaign, Ill., June 26, 1925; s. Coleman Roberts and Mary Louise (Coleman) G.; m. Sylvia Brigitte Kuhn, May 25, 1961; children—Susan Jane, Rachel Diane. A.B., Harvard U., 1945, M.S. in M.E., 1946, Ph.D. in Engring. Sci., 1949. With Pratt and Whitney Aircraft Co., summers 1945-48; instr. physics Princeton U., 1950-51, asst. prof., 1951-57; mgr. Flight Scis. div. Lockheed Missiles and Space Co., Sunnyvale, Calif., 1957-58, acting tech. dir. polaris missiles system, 1960-61, asst. dir. research, 1959-62, dir. research, 1962-66, v.p., asst. gen. mgr. research and tech., 1966-73, R.J. Reynolds prof. mech. and aerospace engring. N.C. State U., Raleigh, 1973—; cons. in field to industry, state and fed. govt. AEC fellow, 1949-50; NSF fellow, 1955-56; named 1 of 5 Outstanding Young Men in Calif., Calif. Jr. C. of C., 1958; recipient N.C. Gov.'s award, 1978. Fellow Am. Phys. Soc., Royal Aero. Soc., AAAS, AIAA. Democrat. Methodist. Club: Cosmos (Washington). Contbr. articles to profl. jours.; assoc. editor Jour. Fluid Mechanics, 1956—. Home: 809 Rosemont Ave Raleigh NC 27607 Office: NC State U 3217A Broughton Hall Raleigh NC 27695-7910

GRIFFITHS, LEWIS GENE, JR., manufacturing executive; b. Orange, N.J., Feb. 21, 1940; s. Lewis G. (dec.) and Dorothy Helene (Quinn) G.; m. Georgia Glen Gregory, Aug. 24, 1963; children—Harriet, Charlotte, John, Margaret. B.A. in Polit. Sci., Roanoke Coll., 1962; LL.B., Washington and Lee U., 1965; diploma, Def. Lang. Inst., 1967. Bar: Va. 1965. Spl. agt. FBI, Miami, N.Y.C., 1965-70; asst. mgr. Gregory Mfg. Co., Jackson, Miss., 1970-73, mgr., 1973-74, pres., chief exec. officer, 1974—; mem. adv. council Fed. Res. Bank Atlanta, 1985—; del. White House Conf. on Small Bus., 1986. Co-founder, pres. Childbirth Edn. Assn. Miss.; del. White House Conf. on Small Bus., 1986; bd. dirs. United Way of Capitol Area. Mem. Soc. Former Spl. Agts. FBI (chmn. Miss. chpt. 1978), Va. State Bar Assn., Miss. Mfrs. Assn. (bd. dirs.), Nat. Hardwood Lumber Assn., Marking Device Assn. (bd. dirs. 1979-85), Nat. Small Bus. Assn. (trustee), Met. Mfrs. Council (chmn. 1983-84), Jackson C. of C. Roman Catholic. Clubs: Rotary (bd. dirs.), Hanging Moss, Swim and Tennis (Jackson). Home: 451 NE Madison Dr Ridgeland MS 39157 Office: Gregory Manufacturing Co Inc 110 Capers Ave Jackson MS 39203

GRIGAR, LOUIS ALBERT, state agency administrator; b. Taylor, Tex., Aug. 24, 1936; s. Louis Joseph and Ann Marie (Kasper) Grigar Fojtek; m. Judy Caroline Berry, Nov. 4, 1957 (div. 1973); children—James, Teresa, Julie; m. Andra Sue Jones, Sept. 14, 1973; children—Michael, Bryan. B.A., U. Tex., 1961; M.Ed., Southwest Tex. State U., 1967. Tchr., Victoria Ind. Sch. Dist., Tex., 1961-66; cons. edn. Tex. Edn. Agy., Austin, 1966-75, dir. social studies, 1975—; review panelist NSF, 1977-80; advisor Tex. Sesquicentenniel Oral History Workshop, 1983-84. Contbr. articles to profl. jours. Sec., treas. Young Democrats Club, 1964. Mem. Nat. Council for Social Studies (adv. com. 1980-83, others), Austin Council for Social Studies, Tex. Council for Social Studies (various coms.), Council State Social Studies Specialists, Social Studies Suprs. Assn., Tex. State Hist. Assn., Assn. Supervision and Curriculum Devel., Phi Delta Kappa. Roman Catholic. Avocations: tennis; reading; bowling; camping. Home: 2306 Rogge Austin TX 78723 Office: Tex Dept Edn 1701 N Congress Austin TX 78701

GRIGG, WILLIAM HUMPHREY, utility executive; b. Shelby, N.C., Nov. 5, 1932; s. Claud and Margy (Humphrey) G.; m. Margaret Anne Ford, Aug. 11, 1956; children—Anne Ford, John Humphrey, Mary Lynne. A.B., Duke U., 1954, LL.B., 1958. Bar: N.C. 1958. Gen. practice, Charlotte, 1958-63; with Duke Power Co., 1963—, v.p. fin., 1970-71, v.p., gen. counsel, 1971-75, sr. v.p. legal and fin., Charlotte, 1975-82, exec. v.p. fin. and adminstrn., 1982—, also dir.; dir. Hatteras Income Fund, Inc. Editor-in-chief Duke Law Jour, 1957-58; Contbr. articles to profl. jours. Trustee Charlotte Latin Sch., Methodist Home Aged, Eugene M. Cole Found.; bd. dirs. Charlotte-Mecklenburg YMCA. Served to capt. USMCR, 1954-56. Mem. ABA, N.C. bar assn. Methodist. Club: Charlotte Country. Home: 2301 Hopedale Ave Charlotte NC 28207 Office: Duke Power Co 422 S Church St Charlotte NC 28242*

GRIGGS, DAWN FITZGERALD, commerical leasing executive; b. Alexandria, Va., Dec. 27, 1955; d. James Lloyd and Ellen (White) Fitzgerald; m. Steve Allen Griggs, May 17, 1980. B.S., William and Mary, 1978, postgrad., 1979-82. Lic. real estate, Va. Juvenile Probation counsel Va. State Cts., Williamsburg, 1978-81, family counselor, 1981-82; mktg. rep. Eastern Internat., Newport News, Va., 1982-83; real estate leasing spl. Read Comml. Properties, Inc., Hampton, 1983—. Bd. dirs. Task Force for Battered Women, Williamsburg, 1983—. Recipient Disting. Sales and Mktg. award Peninsula Sales and Mktg., 1985. Mem. Deal Makers, Tidewater Women's Network, Va. Small Bus. Advanced Tech. Assn. (program com. 1984-85), Kappa Kappa Gamma (personnel advisor 1983-85). Baptist. Club: Jr. Women's. Avocations: tennis; skiing; sewing; biking; piano.

GRIGGS, RICHARD ALLEN, psychology educator, researcher; b. Peoria, Ill., Nov. 14, 1942; s. Jessie P.K. and Hattie Isabel G.; m. Neta Mary Cowan, Aug. 5, 1967; 1 dau., Jennifer Diane. B.S. in Psychology, Bradley U., 1970; Ph.D. in Exptl. Psychology, Ind. U., 1974. Asst. prof. psychology, U. Fla., Gainesville, 1974-79, assoc. prof. psychology, 1979-85, prof., 1985—; editorial cons., textbook reviewer pub. cos. including McGraw-Hill, Holt, Rinehart & Winston, Allyn & Bacon, Prentice-Hall, Inc., Harcourt Brace Jovanovich, Brooks/Cole Pub. Co., W.H. Freeman and Co., Scott, Foresman and Co. Served with U.S. Army, 1965-67. Research grantee Behavioral Social Scis. Council U. Fla., 1976, NSF, 1977-78; NIMH math. psychology tng. fellow, 1970-71; Nat. Def. Title IV predoctoral fellow, 1971-73; nominee U. Fla. Tchr.-Scholar award, 1979. Mem. Am. Psychol. Assn., Midwestern Psychol. Assn., Southeastern Psychol. Assn., Psychonomic Soc., Cognitive Sci. Soc., Soc. Math. Psychology, Sigma Xi, Phi Eta Sigma, Phi Kappa Phi. Contbr. articles to profl. jours. Home: 2601 NW 23d Blvd Apt 170 Gainesville FL 32605 Office: Dept Psychology Univ Fla Gainesville FL 32611

GRIGGY, KENNETH JOSEPH, food company executive; b. Suffield, Ohio, Mar. 7, 1934; s. Edward F. and Margaret M. (Rothermel) G.; B.A., Athenaeum of Ohio, 1956; M.Ed., Xavier U., 1961; m. Janice Marie Doetzel, July 30, 1960; children—Jill, Matthew, Mark, Jennifer. With Am. Heart Assn., Cin., 1960-61, Mead Johnson & Co., Evansville, Ind., 1962-64; v.p., dir. consumer product group Ralston Purina Co., St. Louis, 1964-73; pres., dir. domestic ops. Riviana Foods, Inc., Houston, 1973-75; chmn. bd., pres., chief exec. officer Wilson Foods Corp., Oklahoma City, 1975—. Bd. dirs. State Fair Okla. Served with U.S. Army, 1959-60. Mem. Am. Meat Inst., Okla. C. of C. (dir.), Young Pres.'s Orgn. Clubs: Oklahoma City Golf and Country, Oak Tree Golf, Whitehall. Home: 1708 Kingsbury Ln Oklahoma City OK 73116 Office: 4545 Lincoln Blvd Oklahoma City OK 73105

GRIGSBY, CHESTER POOLE, JR., oil and investments company executive; b. Ruston, La., Mar. 4, 1929; s. Chester Poole and Vera Aura (Lamkin) G.; B.S., La. Tech. U., 1951; postgrad. U. Ariz., 1953-54; m. Audrey Jane Tombrink, Mar. 27, 1954; children—Jayne, Chester Poole III, Julia, Diana. Accountant, Hudson Gas & Oil Corp., 1955-61; gen. acctg. supr. San Jacinto

Gas Processing Corp., 1961-63; v.p., treas., dir. Kinsey Corps., Shreveport, La., 1964—, Kinsey Interests, Inc., Enkay Corp., Alliance Prodn. Co., Norman Corp. Caddo, Inc.; ptnr. Freestate Warehouse Co., 1972—, Freestate Circle Ltd. Served with USAF, 1951-55. C.P.A., La. Mem. Am. Inst. C.P.A.s, Soc. La. C.P.A.s, U.S. Power Squadron, Am. Legion. Home: 5721 River Rd Shreveport LA 71105 Office: 1805 Louisiana Tower Shreveport LA 71101

GRIGSBY, DONALD LEROY, education educator; b. Warrensburg, Mo., Sept. 5, 1934; s. Lewis Towsend and Grace Ethel (DeShurley) G.; m. Cordelia Houston, Mar. 20, 1965; children—Karin, Carol. B.S., Central Mo. State U., 1956; M.A., UCLA, 1965; Ph.D., U. So. Calif., 1971. Tchr., Adrian (Mo.) High Sch., 1956-57, Los Angeles City Schs., 1959-62; physicist Hughes Aircraft Co., Culver City, Calif., 1962-71; asst. prof. edn. U. Ala., Birmingham, 1971-73, assoc. prof., 1973—. Served with U.S. Army, 1957-59. Mem. Am. Phys. Soc., Am. Sci. Affiliation. Republican. Baptist. Author: Niobium Alloys and Compounds, 1966; editor: Electronic Properties of Materials: A Guide to the Literature, 1967. Office: Sch Edn Univ Ala Birmingham AL 35294

GRIGSBY, ORIN ADAM, JR., publishing company administrator, retired air force officer; b. Los Angeles, Apr. 14, 1930; s. Orin Adam and Estella Grace (Gerber) G.; m. Jacqueline Vanni, May 26, 1954 (div. Jan. 1968); children—Brian Allen, Brett Sherman, Jocelyn Kay, Ivy Erin; m. Linda Lucille Sartain, Dec. 24, 1968. B.A., Park Coll., 1974. Lic. comml. pilot. Commd. 2d lt. U.S. Air Force, 1954, advanced through grades to lt. col., 1969; served as pilot, comptroller technician, ops. staff officer, maintenance staff officer, orgn. comdr.; ret., 1981; gen. mgr. Morning Publs., Inc., Ft. Worth, 1981—. Bd. dirs. 1st Ch. of Christ, Scientist, Ft. Worth, 1979-82, chmn. bd., 1981-82, 1st reader; mem. Christian Sci. Ch. Speakers Bur., State of Tex. Decorated Air medal, Joint Service Commendation medal, Bronze Star, Meritorious Service medal with 2 oak leaf clusters, Vietnam Service medal with 2 silver stars, numerous others. Mem. Ret. Officers Assn. Republican. Lodge: Masons (Riverside, Calif.). Contbr.: Researched Bible Guide, 1981-82. Office: Morning Publs Inc 6000 Camp Bowie Blvd Suite 388 Fort Worth TX 76116

GRILLS, GEORGE BENJAMIN, broadcast engineer; b. Kingsport, Tenn., May 10, 1940; s. George Benjamin and Helen Rose (Kinkead) G.; m. Barbara Lamar Whittle, Aug. 10, 1974; 1 son, Bennett Hamilton. B.S.E.E., Duke U., 1962; M.A.C., U. N.C.-Chapel Hill, 1969. Registered profl. engr., N.C. Studio engr., transmitter engr. Sta. WUNC-TV, Chapel Hill, N.C., 1962-63; assoc. dir. ops. dept. radio, TV and motion pictures U. N.C., Chapel Hill, 1964-70, dir. ops., 1970-78; dir. engring. Village Companies, Chapel Hill, 1978-80; dir. engring. Jefferson-Pilot Communications Co., Charlotte, N.C., 1980-81, v.p. engring. and facilities, 1982—; instr. U. N.C., Chapel Hill, 1964-79. Mem. Westerly Hills/Ashley Park Small Area Planning Group for Charlotte-Mecklenburg Planning Commn., 1982-83; mem. elec./electronics engring. tech. adv. com. Central Piedmont Community Coll., 1982-83. Mem. Soc. Motion Picture and TV Engrs., Soc. Cable TV Engrs., Broadcast Edn. Assn., Nat. Soc. Profl. Engrs., Profl. Engrs. N.C., Charlotte Engrs. Club, IEEE (sr.), Soc. Broadcast Engrs. Home: 10043 Four Mile Creek Rd Matthews NC 28105 Office: One Julian Price Pl Charlotte NC 28208

GRIM, WILLIAM EDWARD, JR., musicology educator; b. Columbus, Ohio, Aug. 29, 1955; s. William Edward and Rosemary (Jones) G.; m. Deborah Jo Binkley, May 26, 1979. Mus.B. cum laude, Ohio Wesleyan U., 1977; Mus.M., U. Akron, 1979; Ph.D., Kent State U., 1985. Prof. music St. Andrews Coll., Laurinburg, N.C., 1982—. Editor The St. Andrews Rev., 1984—; contbr. articles to profl. jours. Chmn., Harris Blake for Congress, Scotland County, 1984; bd. dirs. Scotland County Republican Com., 1985. Mem. Internat. Musicol. Soc., Internat. Clarinet Soc., Coll. Music Soc. (bd. dirs. 1985—), Am. Musicol. Soc., Soc. Music Theory. Avocations: reading; short-wave radio. Home: 2009 Lake Dr Laurinburg NC 28352 Office: St Andrews Coll S Main St Laurinburg NC 28352

GRIMBALL, BERKELEY, school administrator; b. Charleston, S.C., Nov. 25, 1922; s. Berkeley Grimball and Anne Carson (Strohecker) Elliott; m. Emily Lawton Kirkland, June 25, 1949; children—Berkeley, Lawton, Meta. B.A., U. of the South, 1943, D.C.L. (hon.), 1969, M.A., Duke U., 1951. Headmaster Gaud Sch., Charleston, 1948-64, Porter-Gaud Sch., Charleston, 1964—. Served to pfc inf. U.S. Army, 1943-45, ETO. Mem. Palmetto Assn. of Independent Schs. (pres. 1979), Greater Charleston Assn. of Independent Schs. (pres. 1980). Episcopalian. Club: Carolina Yacht. Lodge: Rotary (bd. dirs. 1973-74). Avocations: reading; music. Home: 205 Albemarle Rd Charleston SC 29407 Office: Porter-Gaud Sch Albemarl Rd Charleston SC 29407

GRIMBALL, CAROLINE GORDON, ladies retail store merchandise manager, buyer; b. Columbia, S.C., Dec. 21, 1946; d. John and Caroline Grimball. B.A. in Polit. Sci., Converse Coll., 1968; postgrad., S.C. Law Sch., 1968-69. Asst. buyer, buyer Rich's Inc., Atlanta, 1971-78, spl. events fashion coordinator, Columbia, S.C., 1978-83; gen. mdse. mgr. Rackes, Inc., Columbia, 1983-84, Parasol Boutique, Columbia, 1984—. Bd. dirs. Palmetto State Orch. Assn., Columbia, 1979—, Women's Symphony Assn., Columbia, 1985; com. chmn. Columbia Action Council, 1984-85. Named one of Outstanding Young Women Am., 1979, 80; recipient Community Service award Rich's, Inc., 1981. Mem. Nat. So. Colonial Dames Am., Columbia Jr. League. Democrat. Episcopalian. Clubs: Colonial, Columbia Drama. Avocations: bridge; reading; needlepoint; tennis. Home: 1825 Saint Julian Pl #8C Columbia SC 29204 Office: Parasol Boutique Inc 2324 Devine St Columbia SC 29205

GRIMBALL, WILLIAM HEYWARD, lawyer; b. Charleston, S.C., Feb. 6, 1917; s. William Heyward and Panchita (Heyward) G.; m. Frances Lucas Ellerbe, Aug. 9, 1944; children—William Heyward, Henry E., Arthur, Francis E. A.B., Coll. Charleston, 1938; LL.B., U. Va., 1941. Bar: S.C. 1941. Assoc. Mitchell & Horlbeck, Charleston, 1941-50; sole practice, Charleston, 1950-59, 63-64; mem. Figg, Gibbs & Grimball, 1959-63; ptnr. Grimball, Cabaniss Vaughan & Robinson, 1964-84, Grimball & Cabaniss, 1984—. Pres. Preservation Soc., Charleston, 1974-75; mem. S.C. Legislature, 1952-58, chmn. Charleston County del., 1965-68; alderman City of Charleston, 1960-72, mayor pro tem, 1969. Served with USNR, 1942-46, to lt. comdr., 1962. Fellow Am. Coll. Trial Lawyers, Am. Bar Found.; mem. Am. Law Inst., ABA, S.C. Bar Assn., S.C. Bar Found. (bd. dirs. 1983—), Maritime Law Assn., Charleston County Bar Assn. (past pres.), Alumni Assn. Coll. Charleston (pres. 1953), Soc. of Cin., S.C. Soc., St. Andrews Soc., St. Cecilia Soc. Republican. Episcopalian. Clubs: Carolina Yacht. Lodges: Masons (past grand master S.C.); Shriners. Home: 107 Chadwick Dr Charleston SC 29407 Office: 151 Meeting St Charleston SC 29402

GRIMES, EDWARD WILLIAM, endodontist; b. Barnsdall, Okla., May 3, 1934; s. Daniel Lyons and Clella Faye (Davis) G.; m. Jo Ann Vermillion, June 14, 1955 (div. July 1978); children—Daniel Joseph, Marc Edward; m. Joyce Marie Smith, Jan. 27, 1979; 1 child, Kristina Marie. Student Tulsa U., 1951-54; D.D.S. cum laude, Washington U., St. Louis, 1958. Diplomate Am. Bd. Endodontists. Gen. practice dentistry, Tulsa, 1960-71; practice dentistry specializing in endodontics (1st in Okla.), Tulsa, 1971—; mem. faculty for gen. practice residencies Hastings Indian Hosp., Tahlequah, Okla., 1984—. Mem. Hosanna Contemporary Christian Singing Group, Tulsa, 1980—. Served to lt. USNR, 1958-60. Mem. ADA, Am. Assn. Endodontists, Southwest Soc. Endodontists, Ozark Endodontic Soc. (pres. 1972), Tulsa County Dental Soc. (pres. 1971), MENSA, Omicron Kappa Upsilon. Republican. Methodist. Avocations: music—instrumental (clarinet and saxophone) and singing (bass); racquetball; skiing; hunting; fishing. Office: 6112 E 61st St Tulsa OK 74136

GRIMES, ROBERT GERALD, state official; b. Oklahoma City, Jan. 29, 1941; s. Robert Weldon and Lucille (Bivens) G.; m. Linda Moore, Sept. 25, 1973; 1 dau., Amy. B.B.A., Central State U., 1965. With Hartford Ins. Co., 1965-70; adminstrv. asst., dir. claims and agts. licensing State of Okla., Oklahoma City, 1970-73, dep. commr., 1973-75, ins. commr., 1975—; pres. State Bd. Property and Casualty Rates; Campaign chmn. Leukemia Soc., 1975; bd. dirs. Jane Brooks Sch. for Deaf, 1975—; state dir. Firemen's Relief and Pension Fund; state dir. and sec. Police Pension and Retirement Fund; state dir. Okla. Automobile Assigned Risk Plan; mem. State Burial Bd., Employees Group Health, Life and Dental Ins. Bd., Okla. Employees Retirement System, Employment of Handicapped. Mem. Soc. Fin. Examiners, Nat. Assn. Ins. Commrs. Democrat. Baptist. Contbr. articles to profl. jours. Office: 408 Will Rogers Bldg Oklahoma City OK 73105

GRIMLAND, JOHN MARTIN, JR., accountant, organization official; b. Clifton, Tex., May 11, 1917; s. John Martin and Mayme (Gollihar) G.; B.S. in Commerce, Tex. Christian U., 1939, LL.D. (hon.), 1979; m. Phyllis Montgomery, Nov. 1, 1947; children—Diane, Donna Jean, Norma Gayle. With Universal C.I.T. Corp., 1940-42, IRS, 1946-47; pub. accountant, Midland, Tex., 1947-51, C.P.A., 1951—; partner Main Hurdman, 1968-83, cons., 1983—. Mem. Optimist Internat., 1949—, gov. Dist. 7, 1957-58, internat. v.p., 1958-59, chmn. internat. pub. relations com., 1959-62, internat. pres., 1962-63, chmn. internat. community service com., 1966-69; treas. Midland Symphony Assn., 1960-62, pres. 1963-65; pres. Midland United Fund, 1969, Indsl. Found. of Midland, 1971-74. Trustee, Tex. Christian U., 1972—, Midland Meml. Hosp., 1977-81; pres. Midland YMCA, 1980-82, mem. exec. com., 1979-83. Served to lt. USNR, World War II. C.P.A., Tex. Mem. Am. Inst. C.P.A.s, Tex. Christian U. Alumni Assn. (pres. 1965-66), Midland C. of C. (pres. 1970). Methodist (chmn. bd. 1961-62, chmn. bd. trustees 1974, 83-84). Club: Midland Country (dir. 1982-85, pres. 1984). Home: 1605 Country Club Dr Midland TX 79701 Office: HBF Bldg Midland TX 79702

GRIMSLEY, JAMES ALEXANDER, JR., university president, former army officer; b. Florence, S.C., Nov. 14, 1921; s. James Alexander and Anne (Darby) G.; B.S., The Citadel, 1942; M.A., George Washington U., 1964; m. Jessie Lawson, Dec. 8, 1945; children—James Alexander III, Anne, William. Mgr., Peoples Gas Co., Florence, 1946-48; commd. 2d lt. U.S. Army, 1942, advanced through grades to maj. gen., 1974; ret., 1975; v.p. adminstrn. and finance The Citadel, Charleston, S.C., 1975-80, pres., 1980—. Decorated Silver Star medal, D.S.M., Legion of Merit, Bronze Star medal, Purple Heart, Combat Inf. badge. Mem. Assn. U.S. Army Episcopalian. Address: The Citadel Charleston SC 29409

GRISEUK, GAIL GENTRY, financial consultant; b. Providence, Jan. 24, 1948; d. Marvin Houghton and Gertrude Emma (Feather) Gentry; student (Fla. Power Corp. scholar), Fla. State U., 1966-70; m. Steven Paul Griseuk, Oct. 20, 1979; 1 dau., Christina Deborah. Asst. div. controller Mobile Home Industries, Tallahassee, 1968-70; owner, mgr. BDI Services, Tallahassee and Lake Charles, La., 1970-78; fin. cons. Aylesworth Fin., Inc., Clearwater, Fla., 1978-82; chmn. bd., chief exec. officer Griseuk Assocs. Inc., 1982—; instr., dir. vet. outreach Angelina Coll., Lufkin, Tex., 1975-76. Vol., Sunland Tng. Center, 1970-72, George Criswell House, 1969-73. Admitted to practice Registry Fin. Planning Practitioners; cert. fin. ops. prin.; cert. gen. securities prin.; registered investment advisor. Mem. Inst. Cert. Fin. Planners, Internat. Platform Assn., Internat. Assn. Fin. Planners. Am. Kennel Club. Methodist. Contbr. short stories to Redbook, McCall's, Christian Home. Home: 1024 Woodcrest Ave Clearwater FL 33516 Office: 6462 Central Ave Saint Petersburg FL 33707

GRISH, SEVERIN CYRILL, real estate company executive; b. Zurich, Switzerland, July 12, 1939; came to U.S., 1956; s. Albert Jacob and Marie (Jungi) G.; m. Carolyn Ann Crist, Dec. 28, 1978; children—Eric Severin, Christopher Jonathan. Vice pres. Holland & Lyons, Washington, 1976-79; ptnr. Internat. Funding of Washington, 1982-85, Strategic Properties, McLean, Va., 1985—; past dir. Elan Air Corp., Hartford, Conn. Fund raiser Republican Party, Washington, 1985. Served to capt. USMC, 1962-68. Episcopalian. Avocations: flying; skiing. Home: 3618 S Place Alexandria VA 22309

GRISSOM, EUGENE EDWARD, art educator, consultant, researcher, musician; b. Melvern, Kans., May 15, 1922; s. Edward Hobart and Elizabeth Elma (Sattler) G.; m. Marjorie Jean Fanestil, Aug. 14, 1949 (div.); children—Jon F., Joni F.; m. 2d, Nancy Lorraine Day, Dec. 9, 1961. B.S. in Music, Kans. State Tchrs. Coll.-Emporia, 1948; postgrad. U. Philippines, Manila, 1945; M.F.A. in Art History and Printmaking, State U. Iowa, 1951. Instr. Kans. State Tchrs. Coll.-Emporia, summer 1951, U. Ky., Lexington, 1951-53; asst. prof. drawing and art history U. Fla., Gainesville, 1953-60, acting chmn., 1961, chmn., 1963-78, now prof. art; mem. Gainesville Community Jazz Ensemble; pres. Gainesville Friends of Jazz, 1985-86. Served with USAAF, 1943-46. Decorated Philippine Liberation ribbon with 1 Bronze Star. Mem. Internat. Trombone Assn., Coll. Art Assn. Am., Internat. Assn. Jazz Record Collectors, Drawing Soc., Pratt Inst. Graphics Center, Internat. Preview Soc., Am. Fedn. Jazz Socs. (bd. dirs.). Represented in pvt. collections prints/engravings. Home: 4607 Clear Lake Dr Gainesville FL 32607 Office: Dept Art FAD 211 U Fla Gainesville FL 32604

GRISSOM, ROBERT JESSE, criminal justice educator; b. Little Rock, June 4, 1927; s. Robert Clarence and Eva Snowden (Downs) G.; m. Mildred Louise Cossey, Aug. 29, 1966; children—Robert Jesse, Eva Dawn, Syble Louise. B.S., U. Central Ark., 1951; M.A., Harding U., 1958; Ed.S., Pittsburg State U., 1972; Ed.D., U. Fla., 1977. Tchr. pub. schs., Ark., 1951-52, 56-60, Calif., 1962-68; vocat. rehab. counselor Mo. Dept. Edn., Farmington, 1968-71; tng. officer Fla. Div. Youth Services, Ocala, 1972-73; supr. research and planning Ark. Dept. Corrections, Pine Bluff, 1978-79; dir. corrections data Ala. Dept. Corrections, Montgomery, 1979-80; prof. criminal justice Central Fla. Community Coll., Ocala, 1980—. Bd. dirs. Arnette House, 1982—. Served with USN, 1952-56. Recipient Nat. Jaycee award, 1980; Ark. Traveler award, 1986. Mem. Nat. Council on Crime and Delinquency, Nat. Orgn. Am. States, Assn. for Supervision and Curriculum Devel., So. States Correctional Assn., Internat. Platform Assn., Alpha Kappa Delta, Alpha Psi Omega, Kappa Delta Pi, Phi Kappa Phi. Home: 720 NE 45th St Ocala FL 32670 Office: Central Fla Community Coll Dept Criminal Justice PO Box 1388 Ocala FL 32670

GRISWOLD, ALINDA LOUISE, human resource development consultant, counselor; b. LaCrosse, Wis., Jan. 5, 1952; d. Clinton Richmond and Wilma Louise (Goedecke) G. B.A., U. Okla., 1974, M.Ed., 1975. Counselor Okla. Natural Gas, Tulsa, 1976-77, tng. and devel. specialist, 1977-80, human resource devel. specialist, 1980—; instr. psychology Tulsa Jr. Coll., 1977. Contbr. articles on biofeedback and psychology to profl. jours., 1974-75. Mem. Indsl. Relations Assn. (pres. 1981-82), Am. Soc. Tng. and Devel., Am. Petroleum Inst., So. Gas Assn., Tulsa Personnel Assn., Internat. Transactional Analysis Assn. (cert.), Women in Energy, U. Okla. Alumni Assn., Tulsa Assn. (mem. exec. com. alumni U. Okla.), Profl. Assn. Diving Instrs., Am. Paint Horse Assn. Republican. Presbyterian. Club: Horizons Unlimited (Tulsa). Avocations: equestrian; scuba diving; golf; travel. Office: Okla Natural Gas Co 100 W Fifth St Tulsa OK 74102-0871

GRIZZLE, JAMES ENNIS, statistics educator; b. Coeburn, Va., Apr. 20, 1930; s. Joseph Jackson and Jeanette Ellen (Bise) G.; m. Barbara Ann Huntsman, Aug. 18, 1951; children—William Joseph, Linda Jean, Thomas Bruce. B.S., Berea Coll., 1951; M.S., Va. Poly. Inst., 1954; Ph.D., N.C. State U.-Raleigh, 1960. Asst. prof. biostats. U. N.C., Chapel Hill, 1960-64, assoc. prof., 1964-69, prof., chmn. dept. biostats., 1969—; cons. to NIH and several pharm. firms. Served with U.S. Army, 1956-57. Recipient several research grants and contracts NIH-Ciba-Giegy. Fellow Am. Statis. Assn., AAAS, Am. Heart Assn. (epidemiology sect.); mem. Am. Pub. Health Assn., Biometric Soc., Soc. Clin. Trials, Sigma Xi. Club: Ruritan. Contbr. numerous articles to sci. publs. Home: Route 2 Box 310 Graham NC 27253 Office: Dept Biostats Sch Pub Health Univ NC Chapel Hill NC 27514

GRIZZLE, MARY R., state senator; b. Ohio, Aug. 19, 1921; m. Ben F. Grizzle (dec.); six children; m. Charles H. Pearson, Dec. 31, 1982. Student Portsmouth Inst. Bus. Coll., Ohio. Pres., Sand Dollar Restaurant, Inc.; v.p. Martin Luther Found. Town commr., 1960-62; chmn. Pinellas Legislative Delegation, 1964-66; mem. Fla. Ho. of Reps., 1963-78, minority leader pro-tempore 1974-78; mem. Fla. Senate, mem. appropriations com., select com. on aging, 1978—. Mem. Pinellas County Planning Council, High Speed Rail Task Force; mem. Pinellas Nat. Safety Council; pres. Anona Parents Tchrs. Assn., 1960-61; chmn. Fla. Commn. on Status of Women, 1968-70; pres. Fla. Fedn. of Republican Women, 1965-69. Recipient award Fla. Rehab. Assn., 1970; named Fla. League of Hosps. Outstanding Legislator, 1983; recipient Legislative award for Service to Children, 1976; recipient many other awards and honors. Mem. Largo Bus. and Profl. Women, LWV, Arts and Letters (Clearwater chpt.), Nat. Order of Women Legislators. Republican. Episcopalian. Clubs: Altrusa, Women's (Clearwater, Fla.); Belleair Women's. Office: Florida Senate Dist 20 2601 Jewel Rd Suite C Belleair Bluffs FL 33540

GROBMYER, MARK WOOTTEN, lawyer; b. Little Rock, Dec. 13, 1950; s. John R. and Jessie Wootten (Mallory) G.; m. Libby Darwin, Dec. 29, 1972; children—John Darwin, Andrew Mallory, Mark Draper. B.A., Washington and Lee U., 1972; J.D., U. Ark., 1975; postgrad. Harvard U., Exeter (Eng.) U. Bar: Ark. 1975. Spl. chmn. Ark. State Claims Commn., 1981; spl. justice Ark. Supreme Ct., 1981; ptnr. Davidson, Horne, Hollingsworth, Arnold & Grobmyer, Little Rock, 1977—. Chmn. Ark. State Merit Bd., 1981—. Mem. ABA, Ark. Bar Assn. (liaison to ABA securities law com.), Pulaski County Bar Assn. (dir.), Little Rock Com. on Fgn. Relations. Episcopalian. Clubs: Little Rock Country, Little Rock. Lodge: Rotary. Mng. editor Ark. Law Review; contbr. articles to profl. jours. Office: First Fed Savings Plaza 5th Floor Little Rock AR 72203

GROESBECK, ELISE DE BRANGES DE BOURCIA, artist; b. Versailles, France, Jan. 31, 1936 (parents Am. citizens); d. Viscount Louis de Branges de Bourcia II and Diane (McDonald) de Branges de Bourcia; student Phila. Coll. Art, 1954-55; m. James Richard Groesbeck, Oct. 3, 1958 (div. June 1969); children—Gretchen Atlee, Genevieve de Branges. One-man shows: The Agnes Irwin Sch., Rosemont, Pa., 1973, Phila. Cricket Club, Chestnut Hill, Pa., 1973. Recipient prize Rehoboth Beach Art League, 1944; Agnes Allen Art prize Agnes Irwin Sch., 1954. Republican. Episcopalian. Home: 3204 Leigh Rd Pompano Beach FL 33062 Office: Box 58 Pompano Beach FL 33061

GROGAN, TIMOTHY KEVIN, financial executive; b. Louisville, Jan. 6, 1954; s. Thomas Joseph and Bernadine May (Wire) G.; m. Jan Lee Kuhn, Aug. 28, 1976; children—Shane Grant, Chelsea Lynn. B.A. in Psychology cum laude, U. Okla., 1976; M.B.A. in Fin., Harvard U., 1981. Mgmt. intern Dept. Justice, Washington, 1976; fin. analyst GAO, Washington, 1976-79; corp. planner Gulf Oil Corp., Pitts., 1980; asst. to fin. v.p. Helmerich & Payne, Inc., Tulsa, 1981-83, asst. to pres., 1983—, mem. exec. com., 1981—. Trustee Preservation Inc., Tulsa, 1981—; bd. dirs. Family Action Ctr. Recipient Community Service award Big Bros., 1976; Rockwell Internat. fellow, 1979-81; Ewing Congl. fellow, Washington, 1974. Mem. Nat. Trust Hist. Preservation, Harvard Bus. Sch. Club, Leadership Tulsa. Episcopalian. Home: 5839 E 22d Pl Tulsa OK 74114 Office: Helmerich & Payne Inc Utica at 21st St Tulsa OK 74114

GROGG, DONALD LOUIS, industrial pump distributing company executive; b. Houston, July 3, 1949; s. John L. and Bernice (Ellison) G.; m. Donna Carolyn Good, May 17, 1969; children—Susan, Mark. Sales engr. Houston Welding Supply, 1967-69; field engr. Crane Co., Houston, 1969-71; pres. Tex. Process Equipment, Houston, 1971—; dir. Mchts. Park Bank, Houston. Bd. dirs. Cypress Community Assn. (Tex.), 1983. Mem. Am. Welding Soc., Nat. Assn. Corrosion Engrs., Houston Engring. and Sci. Soc., Am. Red Brangus Assn. Republican. Lutheran.

GROLL, ELKAN WILEY, architect, landscape architect, city planner; b. Mpls., Feb. 15, 1914; s. Sirach and Rachel (Cohn) G.; B.S. in Architecture, U. Minn., 1936; M.L.A., Harvard U., 1939; C.E. in City Planning, George Washington U., 1942; m. Jessie A. Jacobson, Oct. 22, 1939; children—Sharon Lynn, Gail Allison, Gary Steven. Architect, Resettlement Adminstrn., 1936-37; architect, site planner Office Chief of Engrs., U.S. Dept. Army, Washington, 1939-43; chief architect Atomic Bomb Project, Hanford, Wash., 1943-45; urban devel. specialist Nat. Housing Agy., Washington, 1945-47; prin. Elkan W. Groll & Assos., Silver Spring, Md., 1947-73; cons. architect, city planner, 1973—; cons. architect Dept. Army, 1948-58; spl. project coordinator Broward County (Fla.); mem. Planning Bd., Pompano Beach, Fla. designer numerous army, navy and air force installations, also internat. airports in Iceland, Azores, Bermuda and Hawaii. Recipient Civilian Service award War Dept., 1943, Sec. War Service award, 1945. Mem. AIA (emeritus), Am. Soc. Landscape Architects, Am. Inst. Cert. Planners, Am. Soc. Planning Ofcls. Author publs. on zoning, sub-div. regulations, site planning, airfield planning, recreation. Home and office: 3100 N Course Ln Pompano Beach FL 33069

GRONO, WALTER JOSEPH, hospital administrator; b. Yonkers, N.Y., June 18, 1949; s. Walter Joseph and Cecelia (Drozdowski) G.; m. Cheryl Weigand, Aug. 14, 1971; children—Kenneth Allan, Jeffry Adam. B.S., SUNY-Cortland, 1971; Ed.M., Syracuse U., 1973. Spl. edn. tchr. Elmcrest Child Ctr., Syracuse, N.Y., 1971-74, assoc. exec. dir., 1975-77; ter. mgr. Econs. Labs., Syracuse and Rochester, N.Y., 1978-79; asst. supt. Columbus Devel. Ctr., Ohio, 1979-82; hosp. adminstr. Hosp. Corp. Am., Houston and Wichita Falls, Tex., 1982-19, Petersburg, Va., 1984—; mem. faculty Ctr. on Health Studies, Nashville, 1984—. Bd. dirs. Wichita Falls chpt. ARC, 1983-84, Big Bros./Sisters, Wichita Falls, 1983-84; sect. chmn. Wichita Falls United Way, 1983-84; active Citizens Com. on Mental Health, Houston, 1983. Mem. Am. Assn. Mental Health Adminstrs., Petersburg C. of C. (bd. dirs.). Episcopalian. Avocations: midget soccer; woodworking and carpentry; racketball. Home: 1032 Northampton Rd Petersburg VA 23805 Office: Poplar Springs Hosp 350 Wagner Rd Petersburg VA

GRONOUSKI, JOHN AUSTIN, university dean, educator; b. Dunbar, Wis., Oct. 26, 1919; m. Mary Metz, Jan. 24, 1948; 2 children. Ph.D. in Econs., U. Wis., 1955; D.H.L. (hon.), Alliance Coll., 1964; LL.D., Fairleigh Dickinson U., 1967, St. Edward's U., 1970, Babson Coll., 1973. Prof. econs. U. Maine, Orono, 1948-50, Wayne State U., Detroit, 1957-59; commr. taxation State of Wis., 1960-63; postmaster gen. U.S. Cabinet of Pres. Kennedy and Pres. Johnson, 1963-65; spl. master U.S. Dist. Ct. Eastern Dist. Wis., 1976-77; ambassador to Poland and U.S. Rep. between U.S. and China, 1965-68; dean Lyndon G. Johnson Sch. Pub. Affairs, U. Tex., Austin, 1969-74, prof. pub. affairs and econs., 1974—. Trustee Nat. Urban League, 1968-73, Austin Area Urban League, 1977-82, pres., 1982-83; chmn. bd. Internat. Broadcasting, 1977-81; active Presdl. Study Commn. Internat. Radio Broadcasting, 1972-73; contbr. Mich. Tax Study, 1957-58; mem. Austin Area Pvt. Industry Council, 1985—; chmn. Joint Commn. on Met. Govt., Austin and Travis County, 1985—. Served as 1st lt. USAAF, 1942-45. Mem. Nat. Acad. Pub. Adminstrn., Polish Inst. Arts and Scis. Am., Inc. (pres.), Am. Econ. Assn., Nat. Tax Assn. Office: U Tex-Austin Lyndon B Johnson Sch Pub Affairs Austin TX 78712

GROOM, DENISE DORIS, nurse, artist; b. Lowell, Mass., Apr. 24, 1953; d. Charles Emile and Theresa Alice (Gregoire) Loiselle; m. Craig Charles Groom, Aug. 5, 1972; children—Brett Thomas, Nathan Charles. A.A. in Nursing, Skagit Valley Coll., 1981. Jr. sec. Millpore Corp., Bedford, Mass., 1972-74; personnel clerk Kadena AFB, Okinawa, Japan, 1976; dictating machine transcriber U.S. Naval Regional Med. Ctr., Okinawa, 1976-77; med. records clerk Whidbey Island Naval Hosp. (Wash.), 1978-81; nurse perioperative W. Fla. Hosp., Pensacola, 1982-83, New Eng. Med. Ctr., Boston, 1983—. Author poetry: Today's OR Nurse, 1983; artist/designer med. alert logo, 1982, nursing student orientation to O.R. booklet, 1982. Mem. Assn. Operating Room Nurses (ways and means com. 1982-83, advt. and promotion com. 1982-83). Republican. Roman Catholic.

GROOVER, RALPH EDWIN, college administrator, educator; b. Winston-Salem, N.C., Aug. 5, 1945; s. Charles W. and Ruth (Miller) G.; m. Belinda Jean Lee, June 7, 1974; children—Gregory Edwin, Michael Richard. B.A., Atlanta Christian Coll., 1967; M.Div., Emmanuel Sch. Religion, 1972; Ph.D., Emory U., 1982. Assoc. minister West Hills Christian Ch., Bristol, Tenn., 1967-70; prof. history Atlanta Christian Coll., East Point, Ga., 1970—, acad. dean, 1980—. Contbr. articles to profl. jours. Mem. Disciples of Christ Hist. Soc., Southeastern 19th-Century Studies Assn., Delta Epsilon Chi. Home: 2504 Dodson Dr East Point GA 30344 Office: Atlanta Christian Coll 2605 Ben Hill Rd East Point GA 30344

GROSCH, DANIEL S., genetics educator; b. Bethlehem, Pa., Oct. 25, 1918; s. E. Samuel and Laura F. (Hoodmaker) G.; m. Edith Taft, Mar. 27, 1944; children—Laura, Barbara T., Douglas T., Robert L., Gustav. B.S., Moravian Coll., 1939; M.S., Lehigh U., 1940; Ph.D. in Zoology-Genetics, U. Pa., 1944. Instr. zoology U. Pa., Phila., 1941-44; asst. prof. zoology N.C. State U., Raleigh, 1946-51, assoc. prof. genetics, 1951-57, prof., 1957-85, emeritus, 1985—; investigator Marine Biol. Lab., Woods Hole, Mass., 1947—; co-investigator U.S. Biosatellite Program; lectr. to biology clubs various instns., 1960—. Served with U.S. Army, 1944-46. Recipient Comenius Alumni award Moravian Coll.; Research grantee NIH, 1964—, NASA, 1964-72, U.S. AEC, 1951-64. Fellow AAAS; mem. Am. Soc. Naturalists, Entomol. Soc. Am., Genetics Soc. Am., Radiation Research Soc. Author: Biological Effects of Radiations, 1955, 2d edit., 1979; contbr. articles to profl. jours.

GRÖSCHEL, DIETER HANS MAX, physician, educator; b. Würzburg, Germany, May 13, 1931; came to U.S., 1963, naturalized, 1969; s. Friedrich Wilhelm and Anne (Burger) G.; m. A. Margarete Pusteny, June 9, 1958; children—Anne, Henrike. Med. grad. U. Würzburg, Erlangen and Cologne, 1957; Dr.med., U. Cologne, 1958. Intern, U. Cologne, 1957-59, resident, 1959-60, assoc. instr. Inst. Hygiene, 1960-63; assoc. Wistar Inst., Phila., 1963-65; assoc. prof. microbiology Temple U., 1965-68; dir. microbiology and infectious diseases Baystate Med. Center, Springfield Mass., 1968-71; prof.

pathology U. Tex. M.D. Anderson Hosp. and Tumor Inst., Houston, 1971-79; assoc. prof. medicine and pathology U. Tex. Med. Sch., Houston, 1973-79; mem. staff Hermann Hosp., Houston, 1973-79; prof. pathology and medicine U. Va. Med. Center, Charlottesville, 1979—. Served with Deutscher Volkssturm, 1945. Fulbright scholar U. Colo., 1954-55. Fellow Am. Acad. Microbiology, Infectious Diseases Soc. Am.; mem. German Soc. Hygiene and Microbiology, Austrian Soc. Hygiene, Microbiology and Preventive Medicine, Am. Soc. Microbiology, Fedn. Am. Scientists, Sigma Xi. Home: 150 Terrell Rd E Charlottesville VA 22901 Office: Box 168 U Va Med Center Charlottesville VA 22908

GROSS, JOHN C(HARLES), broker, industrialist; b. N.Y.C., Apr. 2, 1904; s. Edward H. and Anna Catharine (Muelhaus) G.; student pub. schs., N.Y.C.; m. Helen Victoria Newman, Sept. 26, 1926 (dec. 1979); 1 dau., Jean Anne; m. 2d, Catherine T. Donohue, Apr. 23, 1983. Pres., treas., dir. John C. Gross, Inc., Yacht Club Island Corp., Yacht Club Island Apts., Yacht Club Island Estates; treas., dir. Gen. Automation Fla., Metrodynamics Corp.; pres., treas. Ponce de Leon Realty Corp., Artifacts Recovery Corp.; chmn. bd. Mdse. Distributors Corp.; pres., dir. New Smyrna Subcontractors Corp. Mem. Com. of 100 of New Smyrna Beach; mem. Edgewater (Fla.) Planning Bd.; chmn. Southeast Volusia Area Devel. Council; pres. Edgewater Civic Assn.; mem. Edgewater Indsl. Bd. Mem. Nat. Assn. Security Dealers, New Smyrna Beach C. of C. Lutheran (council). Clubs: Halifax Yacht, Fairgreen Country, Halifax, Rotary. Home: 404 N Riverside Dr Edgewater FL 32032 Office: 404 N Riverside Dr Edgewater FL 32032

GROSS, MARTIN PETER, international agricultural/trade and computer consultant; b. Newark, Nov. 30, 1945; s. Wilbur Julius and Katherine Elizabeth (Mayer) G.; B.S. in Biology, Boston Coll., 1967; Marine Biology Engr., U. Mass., Gloucester, 1972; postgrad., Boston Coll., 1972-74; grad. cum laude, Control Data Inst., 1983. Foreman, Gelineau Constrn., Boston, 1971-74; 1st mate and bus. agt. Internat. Bulk Carriers, Ltd., George Town, Grand Cayman, 1974-76, ship master, pres., 1976-80, trade cons., Miami, Fla., 1980—; agrl. cons. Jojoba Project, Belmopan, Belize, 1980—, Ghana Jojoba Project, Accra, 1981—, Senegalese Jojoba Project, Dakar, 1981—, Baluchistan Jojoba Project, Karachi, Pakistan, 1981—. Served with U.S. Army, 1967-70. Mem. Jojoba World Trade Assn., Internat. Airline Passengers Assn., Nat. Space Inst., Internat. Photog. Soc., Nat. Parks & Conservation Assn., Cousteau Soc., Am. Rottweiler Club.

GROSS, RUTH BRILL, clinical psychologist; b. Moorefield, W. Va., Feb. 9, 1934; d. Ronald Woodrow and Mabel Fern (Hess) Brill; m. Stanley B. Gross; children—Cheryl and Caren (twins), Gregory. B.S., W. Va. U., 1957, M.S., 1958, Ph.D., 1965. Lic. clin. psychologist, Va.; on Nat. Register of Health Service Providers. Clin. counselor Ohio State U. Counseling Ctr., 1965-67; Faculty dept. psychiatry and psychology U. of Cin., 1967-74, Xavier U., Cin., 1974-75, George Mason U., Fairfax, Va., 1976-79; psychologist Washington VA Med. Center, 1981-85; clin. dir. outpatient services Graydon Manor Hosp., Leesburg, Va., 1985—; pvt. practice psychology, Leesburg, Va. Mem. Am. Psychol. Assn., Va. Acad. Clin. Psychologists. Designed Gross Geometric Forms Creativity Test; contbr. articles in field to profl. jours. Home: Route 1 Box 137 Ashburn VA 22011 Office: Graydon Manor Leesburg VA 22075

GROSSEL-ROSSI, MARION NICHOLAS, lawyer, business executive; b. New Orleans, June 22, 1931; s. Arthur and Helen G. (Troyanovich) Grossel-R.; B.S., Tulane U., 1955, LL.B., 1962, J.D., 1977. Geologist, Forest Oil Corp., Lafayette, La., 1955-59; admitted to La. bar, 1962; with firm Jackson & Hess, New Orleans, 1962-63; partner firm Leach & Grossel-Rossi, New Orleans, 1963-68, Leach, Grossel-Rossi & Paysse, 1968-77; of counsel firm Leach, Paysse & Baldwin, 1977-80; exec. v.p. Tex. Sch. Book Depository, Inc., Dallas, 1977-81; partner firm Drury & Grossel-Rossi, New Orleans, 1981-83; pres. M.N. Grossel-Rossi, P.C., 1981—. Bd. govs. Southeastern Admiralty Law Inst. Mem. Fed., Am., La. bar assns., Maritime Law Assn. U.S., Am. Judicature Soc., La. Hist. Soc., Upper Audubon Assn. (pres. 1971-72), Audubon Soc., Nat. Rifle Assn. (life), Internat. Oceanographic Found., Friends of Cabildo, Am. Arbitration Assn. (panel arbitrators), Defense Research Inst. (panel arbitrators), La. Assn. Def. Counsel. Clubs: Essex, Sports Car of America (pres. Delta region 1965). Home: 7115 Camp St New Orleans LA 70118 Office: Suite 901 225 Baronne St New Orleans LA 70130

GROTHAUS, EDWARD BERNARD, surgeon; b. Chgo., Aug. 10, 1925; s. Edward Bernard and Anna A. (Wallish) G.; m. Darlene Mae Maust, Sept. 22, 1951; children—Linda, Maureen, Sandra, Edward, Lis, Michael, Robin, Mark. M.D., U. Tex., 1950. Diplomate Am. Bd. Surgery. Intern, Sacramento County Hosp., 1950-51; resident Baylor U. Coll. Medicine Affiliated Hosps., Houston, 1953-57; practice medicine specializing in surgery, Visalia, Calif. and Sierra Vista, Ariz., 1959-75; surgeon outpatient clinic VA Hosp., Kerrville, Tex., 1976—. Served to lt. M.C., USN, 1951-53. Fellow ACS; mem. AMA. Republican. Roman Catholic. Home: Box 571 FF Harper Star Route Kerrville TX 78028 Office: HCR 5 Box 571 FF Kerrville TX 78028

GROVE, EDWARD RYNEAL, artist, sculptor; b. Martinsburg, W.Va., Aug. 14, 1912; s. Harry Muth and Bertha Mae (Sigler) G.; m. Jean Virginia Donner, June 24, 1936; children—David Donner, Eric Donner. Art studies Nat. Sch. Art, Washington, 1933-34, Corcoran Sch. Art, Washington, 1934-37, 40-45, Robert Brackman, 1946. Die sinker, 1936-40; vignette and portrait engraver Bur. Engraving and Printing, Washington, 1940-47, Security-Columbian Banknote Co., Phila., 1947-62; sculptor-engraver U.S. Mint, Phila., 1962-65; freelance artist, West Palm Beach, Fla., 1965—; one-man shows: Nat. Philatelic Mus., Phila., 1954, Phila. Art Alliance, 1960, Norton Gallery Art, West Palm Beach, 1971; group shows: Cayuga Mus. History and Art, Auburn, N.Y., 1964, Episcopal Acad. Gallery, Phila., 1966, nat. and regional ann. exhibits; represented in permanent collections: Met. Mus. Art, Carnegie Inst., Corcoran Art Gallery, U. Pa. Div. Grad. Medicine, Pangborn Corp., Hagerstown, Md., Pa. Hist. Soc., Phila., Am. Bag & Paper Corp., Phila., U.S. Dept. Navy, Smithsonian Instn., Rehab. Inst. Chgo., The Citadel, Charleston, S.C., Washington Cathedral, Ch. of Bethesda-by-the-Sea, Palm Beach, Fla., Coventry (Eng.) Cathedral, Imperial Palace, Tokyo, Miami Heart Inst., Mus. Medallic Art, Breslau, Poland, U.S. Capitol Hist. Soc., Portsmouth (Eng.) Royal Naval Mus.; instr. drawing and portraiture Flagler Art Center, West Palm Beach, 1972-73; works include Congressional gold medal for Bob Hope, 1963, World War II medal series, 1966-70, mural Ch. of Holy Comforter, Drexel Hill, Pa., 1952-58, four coin set for Knights of Malta, 1965, alphabet medal Soc. Medalists, 1973, Magnuson Meml. plaque Rehab. Inst. Chgo., 1974, Imperial Japanese visit medal, 1975, Am. Legion armed forces bicentennial medal series, 1975, Soyuz-Apollo medal, 1975, bronze Bicentennial monument, Palm Beach, Fla., 1976, E. Sterling Nichol Meml. plaque, Miami, 1977, John Paul Jones Nat. medal, 1979, 2d prize Brookgreen Gardens Soc. Medalists sculpture competition, 1979, medal of honor Norton Gallery of Art, 1980, A N A Boston Conv. medal, 1982; Am. Express Goldpiece, 1982. Contnbr. articles to profl. jours., chpts. to books. Pres., Animal Rescue League Palm Beaches, Inc., 1979-80, 82-83. Recipient bronze medals Washington Landscape Club, 1945, 53, Grumbacher watercolor award Cumberland Valley Art Exhibit, Hagerstown, 1965, Lindsey Morris meml. prize Nat. Sculpture Soc., 1967, Bennett meml. prize, 1971, gold medal Am. Numis. Assn., 1969. Fellow Nat. Sculpture Soc.; asso. NAD; mem. Artists Equity Assn. (nat. v.p. 1965-67), Engravers Guild, Steel and Copper Plate Engravers League Phila. (pres. 1957-59), Phila. Sketch Club, Am. Numis. Assn. (Heath Lit. cert. 1979), Token and Medal Soc., Fedn. Internat. de Medaille (U.S. del.), Am. Medallic Sculpture Assn., Art Mus. Palm Beaches, Soc. Four Arts, Mensa, Knights of Malta (chevalier), English-Speaking Union. Republican. Episcopalian. Home and studio: Sea Lake Studio 3215 S Flagler Dr West Palm Beach FL 33405

GROVE, RUSSELL SINCLAIR, JR., lawyer; b. Marietta, Ga., Dec. 25, 1939; s. Russell Sinclair and Miriam (Smith) G.; m. Charlotte Mariam Glascock, Jan. 9, 1965; children—Farion Smith Whitman, Arthur Owen Sinclair. B.S., Ga. Inst. Tech., 1962; LL.B. with distinction, Emory U., 1964; postgrad. U. Melbourne (Australia) Faculty Law, 1965. Bar: Ga. 1965, U.S. Supreme Ct. 1971, U.S. Ct. Appeals (11th cir.) 1983. Assoc. Smith, Currie & Hancock, Atlanta, 1966-67; assoc. Hansell & Post, Atlanta, 1968-72, ptnr., 1972—; mem. adv. com. Ctr. for Legal Studies; Active Central Atlanta Progress, Inc.; bd. dirs. Caribbean Mission Bd., Inc. Served with USMCR, 1960-65. Fellow Am. Coll. Real Estate Lawyers, Am. Scotch Highland Breeders Assn., Canadian Highland Cattle Soc., Highland Cattle Soc. (U.K.); mem. ABA, Ga. Bar Assn., State Bar of Ga. (exec. com. real property law sect.), Atlanta Bar Assn., Bryan Soc., U.S. Marine Corps Assn. Ga. Lawyers, Eastern Mineral Law Found., Am. Coll. Mortgage Attys., Ga. Cattlemen's Assn., Phi Delta Phi, Omicron Delta Kappa. Episcopalian. Clubs: Dunwoody County, Ashford, Commerce, Lawyers of Atlanta. Author: Word Processing and Automatic Data Processing in the Modern Law Office, 1978; Legal Considerations of Joint Ventures, 1981; Structuring Endorsements and Affirmative Insurance, 1981; Management's Perspective on Automation, 1982; Mineral Law: Current Developments and Future Issues, 1983; co-author: The Integrated Data and Word Processing System, 1981; Georgia Partnership Law: Current Issues and Problems, 1982; editor-in-chief Jour. Pub. Law, 1963-64. Office: 56 Perimeter Ctr E NE Suite 500 Atlanta GA 30346

GROVER, NORMAN RALPH, ophthalmologist; b. Boston, Aug. 18, 1939; s. Milton and Rose (Katz) G.; m. Wilma Stephanie Swett, June 30, 1963; children—Michael James, Steven Frederick. A.B., Harvard U., 1961; M.D., NYU, 1965. Diplomate Am. Bd. Ophthalmology. Intern Downstate Med. Ctr., Bklyn., 1965-66; resident NYU Med. Ctr., 1966-70; chief dept. ophthalmology R.W. Bliss Army Hosp., Ft. Huachuca, Ariz., 1970-72, Meml. Hosp., Hollywood, Fla., 1983-84; instr. ophthalmology U. Miami Sch. Medicine, Fla., 1984—. Served to maj. U.S. Army, 1970-72. Fellow ACS. Jewish. Club: Harvard (pres. 1983-84). Office: 4420 Sheridan St Hollywood FL 33021

GROVER, ROSALIND REDFERN, oil and gas company executive; b. Midland, Tex., Sept. 5, 1941; d. John Joseph and Rosalind (Kapps) Redfern; m. Arden Roy Grover, Apr. 10, 1982; 1 dau., Rosson. B.A. in Edn. magna cum laude, U. Ariz., 1966, M.A. in History, 1982; postgrad. So. Meth. U. Law Sch. Librarian, Gahr High Sch., Cerritos, Calif., 1969; ptnr. Hanaho Ltd., Midland, 1970—; pres. The Redfern Found., Midland, 1982—; dir. Flag-Redfern Oil Co., Midland, 1980—. Mem., past pres. women's aux. Midland Community Theatre, 1970; sec. Park and Recreation Commn. Midland, 1969-71; 1st v.p. Midland Symphony Assn., 1975; chmn. Midland Charity Horse Show, 1975-76; mem. Midland Am. Revolution Bicentennial Commn., 1976; trustee Mus. S.W., 1977-80, pres. bd., 1979-80; publicity chmn. Jr. League Midland, Inc., 1972, edn. chmn., 1976, corr. sec., 1978; Midland co-chmn. Gov. Clements Fin. Com., 1978; trustee Midland Meml. Hosp., 1978-80, Midland Community Theatre, 1983—; del. Objectives for Midland Convocation, City of Midland, 1980; chmn. challenge grant Midland Community Theatre Bldg. Fund, 1980; chmn. Tex. Yucca Hist. Landmark Renovation Project, Midland Community Theatre, 1983, HamHock award, 1978. Mem. Ind. Petroleum Assn. Am., Tex. Ind. Producers and Royalty Owners Assn. (dir.), Phi Kappa Phi, Pi Lambda Theta. Republican. Clubs: Petroleum, Racquet (Midland); Tower (Dallas). Home: 1906 Crescent Pl Midland TX 79705 Office: PO Box 2280 Midland TX 79702

GROVES, DAVID UPDEGRAFF, trade association executive, public relations consultant; b. Lexington, Mo., Nov. 10, 1926; s. William Lester and Adelaide Rebecca (Updegraff) G.; m. Nancy Jane Bustamante, June 23, 1951; children—Nancy Alice, Patricia Rebecca. B.A., U. Md., 1950; M.A., Johns Hopkins U., 1951. Cartoonist, Stars & Stripes, 1946, Washington Post, 1947-48; artist, researcher syndicated newspaper feature Spotlight on Bus., 1949-51; cons. mgmt., pub. relations and indsl. relations, Washington, 1951-54, Guatemala City, 1954-58, Havana, Cuba, 1958-60; gen. mgr. pub. and indsl. relations Relaciones Publicas Interamericanas S.A., Mexico City, 1960-72; Midwest regional dir. Internat. Mgmt. Ctr., Cleve., 1973-78; pres. David U. Groves and Assocs., Cleve., 1977-79, Bethesda, Md., 1979-83, Casselberry, Fla., 1983—; sr. cons. Silver Inst., Gold Inst., Washington, 1978—; pub. Stamp Research Report, 1980-83; exec. dir. Precious Metals Industry Assn., N.Y.C., Washington, Casselbury, 1983—. Bd. dirs. Mexican Devel. Found., 1969-72, Fomento Ednl. Found., 1971-72, Precious Metals Industry Assn, 1983—. Served with AUS, 1944-46. Mem. Pub. Relations Soc. Am. (chmn. univ. students activities com. 1980-81), Am. Counselors Acad., Internat. Assn. Bus. Communicators, Am. Philatelic Soc., Newsletter Assn. Am., Am. Soc. Assn. Execs., Phi Theta Kappa. Roman Catholic. Clubs: University (Mexico City); Nat. Press (Washington). Home: 649 Tuskawilla Point Ln Casselberry FL 32707 Office: PO Box 3550 Winter Springs FL 32708

GROVES, STEVEN FREDERICK, veterinarian; b. Indpls., Aug. 16, 1948; s. Robert and Kathleen (Evans) G.; m. Patricia Ann Fleming, Aug. 24, 1968; children—Jon-Paul, Stephanie Leann. Student Western Ky. U., 1966-68; D.V.M., Auburn U., 1972. Veterinarian, Shivley Animal Clinic, Louisville, 1972-73; owner Scottsville (Ky.) Animal Clinic, 1973—. Mem. AVMA, Am. Assn. Bovine Practitioners, Ky. Vet. Med. Assn., Tenn. Vet. Med. Assn., Southeast Ky. Vet. Med. Assn., Alpha Psi. Baptist. Lodge: Rotary (pres. 1979-80). Home: 1590 Gallatin Rd Scottsville KY 42164 Office: 160 Woodbriar Dr Scottsville KY 42164

GROWCOCK, FREDERICK BRUCE, chemist; b. Monterrey, Mex., May 1, 1948; s. Fred Bruer and Carolyn (Lumpp) G.; m. Lou Ann Wright, Dec. 26, 1971; 1 child, Erick Keith. B.A., U. Tex., 1969, B.S., 1969; M.S., N.Mex. State U., 1971, Ph.D., 1974. Teaching and research asst. N.Mex. State U., University Park, 1970-74; research assoc. Brookhaven Nat. Lab., Upton, L.I., N.Y., 1974-76, asst. scientist, 1976-79, assoc. scientist, 1979-82; sr. research chemist, project leader Dowell div. Dow Chem., Tulsa, 1982-84, research scientist, 1984—. Contbr. articles to profl. jours. Inventor corrosion inhibitors. Mem. Nat. Assn. Corrosion Engrs., Soc. Petroleum Engrs., Am. Chem. Soc. Am. Carbon Soc. Republican. Methodist. Lodge: Lions (pres. 1984—). Avocations: soccer; choir and guitar music. Home: 8308 S 5th St Broken Arrow OK 74011 Office: Dowell Schlumberger 5051 S 129th E Ave Tulsa OK 74134

GRUBAUGH, TONY RAND, accountant; b. Jefferson, Tex., May 15, 1948; s. Henry Nathan and Elsie Rebecca (Greeney) G.; B.B.A., Tex. Christian U., 1970; m. Patty Jeanne McIlhaney, June 7, 1969; children—Tony Rand, Missy Elaine. With Ft. Worth C.P.A. firms, 1970-79; partner Williams-Grubaugh & Co., C.P.A.s, Ft. Worth, 1980, owner Tony R. Grubaugh, C.P.A., Burleson, Tex., 1980—. Treas., South Burleson Baptist Ch. C.P.A., Tex. Mem. Am. Inst. C.P.A.s, Tex. Soc. C.P.A.s, Burleson C. of C. Home: 701 Lynnewood St Burleson TX 76028 Office: 228 NE Wilshire St Suite E Burleson TX 76028

GRUBB, KITTY GOLDSMITH, lawyer; b. Bennettsville, S.C., July 29, 1952; d. Harry Simon and Carolyn (Davis) Goldsmith; m. Lawrence Logan Grubb, Aug. 6, 1972. A.B., U. Ala.-Tuscaloosa, 1974; J.D. cum laude, Cumberland Sch. Law, 1977; LL.M. in Taxation, NYU, 1981. Bar: Ala. 1977, U.S. Ct. Appeals (5th cir.) 1979, Tenn. 1981, U.S. Ct. Claims 1981, U.S. Tax Ct. 1981, U.S. Ct. Appeals (4th cir.) 1980, U.S. Dist. Ct. (ea. dist.) Tenn. 1982, U.S. Ct. Appeals (6th and Fed. cirs.) 1984, U.S. Ct. Mil. Appeals 1984. Staff atty. TVA, Knoxville, 1977-79; assoc. Lockridge & Becker, P.C., Knoxville, 1981-82; ptnr. Dunaway, Harrell, Grubb, Van Hook & Cotton, LaFollette, Tenn., 1982-85; assoc. Wagner & Myers, P.C., Knoxville, 1985-86; ptnr. McGehee, Grubb & Currier, P.C., 1986—; lectr. St. Mary's Hosp., Knoxville, Knoxville Women's Ctr., Small Bus. Assn., U. Ala., various other orgns.; mem. So. Pension Conf., Atlanta, 1981-82, Am. Pension Conf., N.Y.C., 1981-82. Assoc. editor Cumberland Law Rev., 1975-77. Chmn. fund drive, eastern Tenn. region Cumberland Sch. Law, 1979-80. Recipient Curia Honoris award Cumberland Sch. Law, 1978, cert. merit Cumberland Sch. Law chpt. Phi Delta Phi, 1977, cert. appreciation Knoxville Women's Ctr., 1983, Annie P. Selwyn award, 1986. Mem. Knoxville Bar Assn. (continuing legal edn. 1982—), ABA (Tenn. membership chmn. Young Lawyer's Conf. div. 1983—), Ala. Bar Assn., Tenn. Bar Assn., Assn. Trial Lawyers Am., Cumberland Law Sch. Alumni Assn., NYU Law Sch. Alumni Assn., U. Ala. Alumni (v.p. eastern Tenn. chpt. 1983, pres. chpt. 1984, merit awards eastern Tenn. chpt. 1982, 83, 84, nat. award 1984), AAUW, Knoxville Assn. Women Execs. (v.p. 1986), Nat. Assn. Women Execs., Knoxville Zool. Soc., Polit. Button Collectors (Dixie chpt., Am. chpt.), Century Club of U. Ala. Alumni (eastern Tenn. chpt.), Omicron Delta Epsilon, Pi Sigma Alpha. Democrat. Methodist. Office: McGehee Grubb & Currier PC 1634 Plaza Tower Knoxville TN 37929

GRUBB, ROBERT LYNN, computer scientist; b. Knoxville, Tenn., Nov. 23, 1927; s. William Henry and DoLores Alfisi (Pierucci) Hollinshead; B.S., Central State Coll., Edmond, Okla., 1972; m. Donna Jean Chicado, May 28, 1973; children—Barbara, Robert Lynn, Paul, Werner, Luke. Air traffic controller FAA, Ft. Worth, 1955-62; engr. Philco-Ford Corp., Oklahoma City, 1962-65; service co. exec. Lear-Siegler Inc., Oklahoma City, 1965-67; computer specialist U.S. Navy, Corpus Christi, Tex., 1967-71, U.S. Army, Petersburg, Va., 1971-77, U.S. CSC, Washington, 1977-79, U.S. Dept. Justice, San Antonio, 1979-80; pres. Tex. Office Systems Co., San Antonio, 1980—; cons. Durham Bus. Coll., Corpus Christi; cons. Corpus Christi Pub. Sch. Bd. Committeeman Boy Scouts Am., 1963-64; bd. dirs., athletic coach Southside Youth League, 1970. Served in USNR, 1945-46; PTO. Mem. Western Writers Am., Am. Hist. Soc. (charter). Author: Conversion and Implementation of CS3 Computer System, 1973; Economic Analysis of Automated System-TOPS, 1977. Contbr. articles and stories on Western history to various periodicals. Home and Office: Route 1 Box 1068 Wetmore TX 78163

GRUBBS, FRANK LESLIE, JR., history educator; b. Lynchburg, Va., June 21, 1931; s. Frank Leslie and Grace Louise (Smith) G.; m. Carolyn Barrington, July 31, 1965; children—Thomas Ashby, Robert Barrington. B.A. in English, Lynchburg Coll., 1959; M.A. in History, U. Va., 1960, Ph.D. in History, 1963. Mem. quality control staff Mead Paper Products, Lynchburg, 1949-59; asst. instr. Grad. Sch., U. Va., Charlottesville, 1961-62, instr., 1962-63; prof. history Meredith Coll., Raleigh, N.C., 1963—. Author: Struggle for Labor Loyalty, 1968 (Choice award 1970); Protecting Labor's Standards, 1982. Contbr. articles to profl. jours. Lectr. Episcopal Ch., Raleigh and Cary, N.C., 1965—; instr. Occaneechi council Boy Scouts Am., 1975—; mem. dept. records and history N.C. Diocese Episcopal Ch., Raleigh, 1984—; mem. Commn. on Ch., Episcopal Ch., Raleigh, 1985—. Served to sgt. U.S. Army, 1952-54; Korea. Nat. Humanities grantee, 1968; named outstanding Tchr., Meredity Coll., 1975; recipient Perry award in research Meredith Coll., 1985. Mem. Smithsonian Assocs., So. Hist. Assn., Torch Internat. (pres. Raleigh chpt. 1970-80), Phi Alpha Theta. Avocations: painting; historical travel. Home: 1706 Baker Rd Raleigh NC 27607 Office: Meredith Coll Box X109 Hillsborough NC 27607

GRUEN, FRANK XAVIER, JR., accountant; b. San Antonio, July 31, 1943; s. Frank Xavier and Mary Katherine (Schliesing) G.; m. Shireley Jean Neugebauer, Sept. 8, 1965 (div. 1983); children—Sheryl Robin, Scott Xavier. B.B.A., Tex. A&M U., 1965; M.S., U. Houston, 1973. Accountant, Armco Steel Corp., Houston, 1965-68; staff accountant Weinstein & Spira, Houston, 1968-69; staff accountant Seidman & Seidman, Houston, 1969-73, mgr., 1973-75, prin., 1975-76, ptnr., 1976—, dir. audit and mktg., 1977—, chmn. personnel and recruiting com., 1980-83. Bd. trustees Ft. Bend Ind. Sch. Dist., 1981-82, pres., 1983-85; bd. dirs. Sugar Creek Homes Assn., 1978-81; treas. Dullas Elem. PTO; mem. audit com. United Way Harris County, 1977-81; mem. budget panel, 1973-81, mem. allocations com., 1977, vice chmn. adult services panel, 1977, chmn. adult services panel, 1978. Mem. Am. Inst. C.P.A.s, Tex. Soc. C.P.A.s, Tex. Soc. Adlarian Psychology (treas. 1975-79), Assn. Corp. Growth. Republican. Lutheran. Club: Houston City. Home: 1115 Heron Ct Sugar Land TX 77478 Office: 500 Citicorp Ctr 1200 Smith St Houston TX 77002

GRUM, CLIFFORD J., business executive; b. Davenport, Iowa, Dec. 12, 1934; s. Allen F. and Nathalie (Cate) G.; m. Dona Janelle Lewis, May 1, 1965; 1 son, Christopher J. B.A., Austin Coll., 1956; M.B.A., U. Pa., 1958. Vice-pres., Republic Nat. Bank, Dallas, 1958-65; v.p. Temple Industries, N.Y.C., 1965-68; v.p. fin., 1968-73; with Time Inc. (acquired Temple Industries 1973), N.Y.C., 1973-83, treas., 1973-75 v.p., 1975-80, exec. v.p., 1980-83, pub. Fortune mag., 1975-79; pres., chief exec. officer Temple-Inland Inc., Diboll, Tex., 1983—; dir. Time Inc., Cooper Industries, Inc., 3 Beall Bros. 3 Inc. Trustee, Austin Coll. Home: PO Box 368 Diboll TX 75941 Office: PO Drawer N Diboll TX 75941

GRUND, CLARENCE B., JR., utility executive; b. Portland, Oreg., July 31, 1925; s. Clarence B. and Frances (Eckert) G.; B.E.E., Ala. Poly. Inst., 1951, M.E.E., 1952; m. Marilyn Grace Hornsby, May 2, 1948. Engr. system planning Ala. Power Co., Birmingham, 1953-58; engr. rate dept. So. Services, Inc., Birmingham, 1958-63; supr. research rate dept., 1964-67, asst. mgr. rate dept., 1967-69, mgr. rate dept., 1969-72, asst. v.p., 1972-85, sr. cons. engr. rates and regulation, 1986—; instr. Ala. Poly. Inst., 1951-52, extension center U. Ala., 1952. Pres., Rocky Ridge Vol. Fire Dept., 1957-58, bd. dirs., 1956-62. Served with USAAF, World War II. Registered profl. engr., Ala., Miss. Mem. IEEE, Nat. Soc. Profl. Engrs., Assn. Energy Engrs., Birmingham Soc. Engrs., Newcomen Soc. N.Am., Internat. Platform Assn., Am. Legion, Phi Kappa Phi, Tau Beta Pi, Eta Kappa Nu. Contbr. articles to profl. jours. Home: 3421 Cruzan Dr Birmingham AL 35243 Office: So Co Services Inc PO Box 2625 Birmingham AL 35202

GRUNFELD, STEVEN MICHAEL, podiatrist; b. Buffalo, Nov. 23, 1950; s. Sy Philip and Julia (Portincasa) G. B.A. in Chemistry, SUNY-Buffalo, 1973; D. Podiatric Medicine, Ohio Coll. Podiatric Medicine, 1978. Practice podiatric medicine, Birmingham and Cullman, Ala., 1980—; mem. staff Cullman Med. Ctr. N.Y. Regents scholar, 1969; recipient Judges award Red Mountain Mus. Photography Contest, 1982; 4th place Hasselblad Photography Contest, 1983, various photog. award Jewish Community Ctr., 1983, 86, Birmingham Downtown Action Com., Ala. State Fair, 1984, 85. Mem. Am. Podiatry Assn., Acad. Ambulatory Foot Surgery (assoc.), Ala. Podiatry Assn. (chmn. peer rev. com.), Am. Soc. Podiatric Dermatology (assoc.), Cullman C. of C., Friends Photography. Home: 5529 13th Ave S Birmingham AL 35205 Office: 2012 8th Ct S Birmingham AL 35205 also 203 2d Ave NE Cullman AL 35055

GRYSKIEWICZ, NUR DOKUR, industrial psychologist, educator; b. Turkey, Mar. 15, 1951; came to U.S. 1978; d. Huseyin Rasim and Sevim (Yalciner) Dokur; m. Stanley Steven Gryskiewicz, July 7, 1978; 1 son, Steven Kent. Higher lic. Hacettepe U., Turkey, 1973; Ph.D. in Occupational Psychology, U. London, 1979. Mktg. research analyst Kayser-Roth Corp., Greensboro, N.C., 1979-81, cons. consumer, mgmt. research, 1981-82; asst. prof. psychology N.C. A&T State U., Greensboro, 1982-83; career devel. cons., Greensboro, 1983—; lectr. dept. mgmt. U. N.C., Greensboro, 1986—. Mem. Brit. Psychol. Assn., Am. Psychol. Assn., Am. Mktg. Assn., AAUW. Home: 208 Mayflower Dr Greensboro NC 27403 Office: 1030 W Market St Suite 315 Greensboro NC 27403

GRYTING, HAROLD JULIAN, chemist; b. Belview, Minn., Dec. 31, 1919; s. Reier Elling and Julia Mathilda (Olsen) G.; B.A. cum laude, St. Olaf Coll., 1941; student N.D. State U., 1941-42; Ph.D. (Alrose Chem. Co. fellow, Air Force fellow, Mallinckrodt fellow, Westinghouse fellow), Purdue U., 1947; m. Barbara Jean Ruggles, June 25, 1954; children—Corrine Suzanne, Paul Julian. Grad. asst. chemistry N.D. State U., 1941-42; chemist E. I. du Pont de Nemours & Co., Inc., Joliet, Ill., 1942-43; chemist Naval Weapons Center, China Lake, Calif., 1947-52, head explosives research br., 1952-65, tech. asst. for explosives, 1965-72, asso. head Applied Research and Processing div., 1972-74, safety and tech. coordinator, 1974-75, sr. research chemist, 1975-80; cons. dept. energetic systems Southwest Research Inst., San Antonio, 1980—; chmn. Joint Army, NASA, Air Force, Navy Safety and Environ. Working Group, 1973-77; mem. steering com. 1973-80; chmn. initiators com. Joint Tech. Coordinating Group Air Launched Nonnuclear Ordnance Working Party for Fuzes, 1975-80, chmn. qualification com. working party for explosives, 1971-80. Scoutmaster, Boy Scouts Am., 1977-80, scouting coordinator Post 341, San Antonio, 1981—. Fellow AAAS, Am. Inst. Chemists; mem. Am. Chem. Soc. (chmn. Mohave Desert sect. 1959, 74), Research Soc. Am., Am. Defense Preparedness Assn., N.Y. Acad. Sci., Sigma Xi, Phi Lambda Upsilon. Republican. Lutheran. Contbr. articles to profl. jours.; patentee temperature-resistant explosives and dispersion methods for ordnance materials. Home: 1324 Klondike St San Antonio TX 78245 Office: Div 06 Dept Energetic Systems Southwest Research Inst San Antonio TX 78284

GUDE, ALBERTO, JR., energy company executive; b. Cuba, Sept. 28, 1939; came to U.S., 1961, naturalized, 1971; s. Domingo Alberto and Rosa Benita (Barrios) G.; m. Nancy Carlson, June 30, 1973. B.S. in Acctg., Profl. Sch. Commerce, Camaguey, Cuba, 1959; M.B.A., U. Houston, 1986. Dir. mgmt. info. system Meth. Hosp., Louisville, 1962-70; v.p. ops. and systems Space Age Computer, Washington, 1970-75, also founder, dir.; v.p. Fla. Software Services, Altamonte Springs, Fla., 1975-76; v.p. info. systems HNG/Internorth, 1977—. Mem. Hosp. Fin. Mgmt. Assn., Mgmt. Info. Systems Assn., Data Processing Mgmt. Assn. Republican. Methodist. Club: Heritage. Home: 1101 River Reach Dr Fort Lauderdale FL 33315 Office: PO Box 1088 Houston TX 77001

GUDE, NANCY CARLSON, communications company executive; b. Kane, Pa., Aug. 5, 1948; d. Edward Walter and Theo Alberta (Herzog) Carlson; m. Alberto Gude, Jr., June 30, 1973. B.A. in History, Pa. State U., 1969; M.S. in Computer Sci., U. Central Fla., 1981. Programmer Group Hospitalization, Inc., Washington, 1969-70; programmer analyst Space Age Computer Systems, Washington, 1970-73; programmer analyst Ky. Fried Chicken, Louisville, 1973-75; systems analyst Sentinel Star Co., Orlando, Fla., 1975-77, programming supr., 1977-78, systems and programming mgr., 1978-80, asst. dir. data processing, 1980, mgr. staff devel., 1981-82; adj. instr. U. Central Fla., Orlando, 1981-82; mgmt. info. services mgr. News and Sun-Sentinel Co., Ft. Lauderdale, Fla., 1982-83, v.p., dir. info. systems, 1983—. Mem. Am. Mgmt. Assn., Data Processing Mgmt. Assn., Assn. Systems Mgmt., Soc. Mgmt. Information

Systems. Methodist. Home: 1101 River Reach Dr 216 Fort Lauderdale FL 33315 Office: 101 N New River Dr East Fort Lauderdale FL 33302

GUE, WILLIAM PAUL, apparel industry executive; b. Grove City, Ohio, Sept. 13, 1938; s. William Harold and Mabel Pauline (Sheets) G.; m. Carol Kuenning, Apr. 16, 1966; children—William Randall, Robert Scott. B.S. in Bus. Adminstrn., Ohio State U., 1963. Div. mdse. mgr. F&R Lazarus & Co., Columbus, Ohio, 1963-71; v.p. J. Riggings, Atlanta, 1972-74; pres. Elan Internat., Atlanta, 1974-83; Southeastern regional mgr. Sasson Jeans L.A., Inc., Atlanta, 1983-84; pres. Elan Internat., Ltd., Atlanta, 1984—. Fund dr. capt. United Appeal, Columbus, 1969. Served with USMC, 1958-61; Pacific. Home: 7585 Chaparral Dr Atlanta GA 30338

GUENTER, HAL, investment company executive; b. San Antonio, Mar. 4, 1953; s. Harold L. and Jessie (West) Guentert. B.S. in Engring. Tech., Am. Tech. U., 1976; M.B.A., U. Tex.-San Antonio, 1981. Registered investment advisor, SEC, Tex. With S.W. Research Inst., San Antonio, 1976-81; pvt. investor, 1981-82; pres., dir. River City Investor Services, Inc., San Antonio, 1982—; sec.-treas. Micro/mation, Inc., 1984-85. Office: PO Box 100987 San Antonio TX 78201

GUERRERO, SUSAN JANE, marketing director; b. Newport, R.I., Feb. 7, 1952; d. John Guzman and Jean Gladys Guerrero; B.F.A., Old Dominion U., 1975. Front office supr. Omni Internat. Hotel, Atlanta, 1976-77, front office asst. mgr., 1977-78, reservation promotion mgr., 1978-80, sales mgr., 1980-85; dir. mktg. Peachtree Ctr. Mgmt., Atlanta, 1981—, v.p., 1985—; pres. In-Town, Inc., 1983-84. Bd. dirs. Travelers Aid, 1982—; chmn. downtown promotion Egelston Festival of Trees, 1982-83; pub. relations com. Atlanta Conv. and Visitors Bur., 1982—; promotion com. Atlanta C. of C., 1983—. Recipient Support award ARC, 1984. Mem. Nat. Retail Mchts. Assn., Internat. Council Shopping Ctrs., Pub. Relations Soc. Am., Ga. Hospitality and Travel Assn., Atlanta Conv. and Visitors Bur. Office: Peachtree Ctr Mgmt 225 Peachtree St Suite 610 Tower Atlanta GA 30303

GUERRIERE, MICHAEL, social services administrator; b. L.I., N.Y., Sept. 11, 1950; s. Anthony Michael and Jean Marie (Scarpati) G.; m. Alice Marie McGuinness, Mar. 24, 1975. B.S., SUNY-Stony Brook, 1973; M.S.W., Barry U., 1981; postgrad. Cath. U. Am. Asst. dir. ARC, Parris Island, S.C., 1975-77, dir., Boblingen, Fed. Republic Germany, 1977-79, program cons. nat. hdqrs., Washington, 1981-84, chief disaster family assistance eastern ops. hdqrs., Alexandria, Va., 1984—. Author: A Network of Service, 1983; The Aftermath of a Tornado: The Social Casework Process in the Amish Community of Atlantic, Pa., 1985. Treas. Polit. Action for Candidate Election, Washington, 1984—. Mem. Nat. Assn. Social Workers. Democrat. Roman Catholic. Home: 4300 Cedar Lake Ct Alexandria VA 22309 Office: ARC Eastern Ops Hdqrs 615 N Saint Asaph St Alexandria VA 22314

GUESS, FRANCIS SCOTT, state official; b. Nashville, June 14, 1946. B.S. in Polit. Sci., Tenn. State U., 1972; M.B.A., Vanderbilt U., 1974; postgrad. Harvard U., 1980. Chief info. services Tenn. Housing Devel. Agy., Nashville, 1974-78; instr., practice mgr. dept. family medicine Meharry Med. Coll., Nashville, 1978-79; asst. commr. Dept. Personnel State Tenn., Nashville, 1979-80; commr. Tenn. Dept. Gen. Services, 1980-83, commr., 1983—. Sec.-treas. exec. bd. Nat. Assn. Govt. Labor Ofcls.; mem. U.S. Civil Rights Commn., 1983—; mem. exec. com., pres. Nashville-Middle Tenn. Muscular Dystrophy Assn.; pres. Nashville Ripson Soc.; mem., vice-chmn. Tenn. Human Rights Commn.; vice-chmn. Middle Tenn. Regional Minority Purchasing Council; mem. Tenn. adv. com. SBA; mem. exec. com. Tenn. Vietnam Vets. Leadership Program; mem. adv. bd. Citizens Savs. Bank and Trust Co.; bd. dirs. Valley Devel. Corp., Leadership Nashville Alumni Assn.; mem. The Davidson Group. Served with U.S. Army, 1968-70. Mem. Am. Legion, Nashville Urban League, NAACP. Office: 501 Union Bldg 2d Floor Nashville TN 37219

GUESS, JOSEPH FRED, canned juices company executive; b. 1924. Co-operator Bordo Citrus Products, 1969—; chmn. bd. Citrus Central Inc., Orlando, Fla., 1983—. Address: Citrus Central Inc PO Box 17774 Orlando FL 32860*

GUEST, RITA CARSON, interior designer; b. Atlanta, Aug. 17, 1950; d. Walter Harold and Doris Rebecca (Reeves) Carson; m. John Franklin Guest, Jr., Jan. 20, 1979. B.V.A., Ga. State U., 1973. Designer, Alan L. Ferry Designers, Inc., Atlanta, 1973-80; v.p. Ferry Hayes Designers, Inc., Atlanta, 1980-84; pres., head designer Carson Guest, Inc., Atlanta, 1984—; lectr. in field. Recipient Presdl. citation Am. Soc. Interior Designers, Ga. chpt., 1984, Comml. Design Project award, 1983. Mem. Am. Soc. Interior Designers (dir. 1984, treas. 1985-86). Presbyterian. Clubs: High Mus. of Art, Atlanta Preservation Center, Shallowford Canoe. Avocation: painting. Office: Carson Guest Inc 1720 Peachtree St NW Suite 1001 Atlanta GA 30309

GUFFIN, RAYMOND LONNIE, JR., college administrator, art educator, artist; b. Marietta, Ga., Jan. 11, 1935; s. Raymond Lonnie and Mary Lou (Stephens) G.; m. Mary Robinson, Aug. 1, 1971; children—Rosemary Robinson, Ramona Elizabeth, Andrew Royall George. B.A., Mercer U., 1958; M.F.A., U. Ga., 1964. Instr. Art Samford U., Birmingham, Ala., 1964-65, U. North Ala., Florence, 1965-66; from asst. prof. to prof. art Stillman Coll., Tuscaloosa, Ala., 1966-83, prof., 1984—, chmn. div. humanities, 1980—. Author: A Glossary of Art and Music Terms, 1978; also family histories. Exhibited in one-man shows: U. Ga., 1964, Samford U., 1964; group shows include Stillman Coll., 1968, Birmingham Mus., 1969, W.Va. State U., 1970, U. Ala., 1972; represented in permanent collections: Mercer U., U. Ga., Jemison Collection, Birmingham. Recipient numerous awards for paintings, drawings and sculpture, 1958—; Danforth Found. grantee, 1978; Mellon Found. travel grantee, Italy, 1984. Mem. Ala. Conf. Deans, Tuscaloosa Geneal. Soc. (founder 1975, pres. 1975-82, 84). Democrat. Baptist. Avocations: genealogy; photography. Home: 1439 49th Ave E Tuscaloosa AL 35404 Office: Stillman Coll Div Humanities PO Box 1430 Tuscaloosa AL 35403

GUHA, TRIDIB KUMAR, geologist; b. Malda, India, May 20, 1943; came to U.S., 1968, naturalized, 1974; s. Bibhuti Bhusan and Bani (Roy Chowdhury) G.; m. Mita Nandi, July 28, 1974; children—Neela, Joyashree. B.S., Calcutta U., India, 1963; M.S., Ranchi U., India, 1963-65; M.A., Bklyn. Coll., 1972; grad. studies U. Kans., 1973-74. Geophysicist, Aero Service, Houston, 1974-76; geophysicist, geologist C.H. Burt, Inc., 1977; geologist Subsurface, Inc., Bellaire, Tex., 1977-80, Conoco Inc., Houston, 1980—. Contbr. sci. articles to profl. jours. Grantee Sigma Xi, 1973, T.N. Das Found., 1974. Mem. Houston Geol. Soc. (chmn. field trip com. 1983—), Am. Assn. Petroleum Geologists, Soc. Exploration Geophysicists, Houston Geol. Soc., Geophys. Soc. Houston. Avocations: soccer; gardening; duplicate bridge. Home: 9303 Tooley St Houston TX 77031

GUICE, STEPHEN LEE, urologist, administrator; b. New Orleans, Apr. 18, 1946; s. Stephen Lee and Edna Florence (Kuhn) G.; m. Jocelyn Windsor Stebbins, Aug. 12, 1978; children by previous marriage—Elizabeth Terry; children by present marriage—Huntington Lee, Cameron Charles. B.A., Emory U., 1968; M.D., La. State U., 1972. Diplomate Am. Bd. Urology. Intern, Ochsner, New Orleans, 1972-73; resident in surgery, Ochsner, 1973-74; resident in urology Duke U., Durham, N.C., 1975-78, instr. urology 1977-78; fellow in pediatric urology Mass. Gen. Hosp., Boston, 1978—, Johns Hopkins Hosp., Balt., 1978; attending staff Ochsner Clinic and Ochsner Found. Hosp., New Orleans, 1979—; bd. mgmt. Ochsner Clinic, 1984—, now asst. med. dir.; med. dir. Ochsner HMO, 1984—; bd. govs. Orleans Parish Med. Soc., 1982—. Contbr. articles to profl. jours. Pres. La. chpt. Stepfamily Assn. Am., 1983—. Mem. Am. Urol. Assn., La. Urol. Assn. (sec.-treas. 1982-85), New Orleans Urol. Assn., Soc. Pediatric Urology, Omicron Delta Kappa. Democrat. Presbyterian. Club: Stratford. Avocations: sailing; photography; gardening. Office: Ochsner Clinic 1514 Jefferson Hwy New Orleans LA 70121

GUICE, VANESSA, computer programmer; b. Houston, Dec. 22, 1957; d. Clarence Damies and Fannie Mae (Phillips) Davis; m. Ray Anthony Guice, July 31, 1982. B.S. in Computer Sci., Sam Houston State U., 1980. Computer progammer assoc. Lockheed Engring. & Mgmt. Services Co., Inc., Houston, 1981-82; systems analyst Compucon, Inc., Dallas, 1982-83; contract programmer MTEK Services, Inc., Houston, 1983—. Mem. Assn. Computing Machinery, Alpha Kappa Psi (life). Democrat. Baptist. Office: MTEK Services Inc 3317 Creston St Houston TX 77026

GUIDROZ-GREEN, FAY THRASHER, psychologist; b. Wyhne, Ark., Dec. 17, 1935; d. Andrew Justin and Joy Maud (Charles) Thrasher; B.S., Miss. State U., 1958; M.Ed., McNeese State U., 1963; M.A., La. State U., 1968, Ph.D., 1970; m. Richard E. Green, Feb. 1978; children—Jeffrey Kane, Sidney Joseph. Chief psychologist Lake Charles (La.) Mental Health Center, 1970-73; clin. psychologist VA Hosp., Salisbury, N.C., 1973-76; chief psychology service VA Outpatient Clinic, San Antonio, 1976-77; chief psychology service, Alvin C. York Med. Ctr., Murfreesboro, Tenn., 1977—; regional trainer Tng. in Ind. and Group Effectiveness, 1974-76. Mem. Am. Psychol. Assn., Menninger Found., Nat. Register Health Care Providers, Assn. VA Chief Psychologists, AMA Aux. Home: 210 S College St Woodbury TN 37190 Office: VA Med Center Lebanon Rd Murfreesboro TN 37130

GUIDRY, WAYNE EDWARD, transportation company executive; b. Baton Rouge, Aug. 17, 1947; s. Leo and Bernice (LeBlanc) G.; m. Suzanne M. Hurst, Apr. 16, 1971. Student pub. schs., Baton Rouge. With Gulf States Utilities Co., 1970, La. Welfare Dept., 1970-71, City of Atlanta, 1971-72; systems programmer Electronic Data Systems, 1976-77; sr. programmer Pan Am. Life Ins. Co., New Orleans, 1977; mgr. communication and systems programming Central Gulf Lines, Inc., New Orleans, 1977-79; mgr. systems programming and computer ops. Central Freight Lines, Waco, Tex., 1979—. Served with USAF, 1966-70. Mem. Am. Legion, VFW. Democrat. Roman Catholic. Clubs: Forest Hills Civic, Richland Hills Homeowners Assn., Optimists. Home: 236 Lindenwood E Hewitt TX 76643 Office: PO Box 2638 Waco TX 76702

GUILARTE, PEDRO MANUEL, utility company executive; b. Cuba, May 19, 1952; s. Miguel G. and Emma G.; B.S. in Indsl. Engring. (scholar), Northwestern U., 1975; M.B.A., Washington U., St. Louis, 1977; cert. systems dynamics MIT, 1978; m. Zulima Piedra, May 26, 1979. Market analyst Cummins Engine Co., Columbus, Ind., 1976; performance analysis supr. Fla. Power & Light Co., Miami, 1977—. Consortium for Grad. Study in Bus. fellow, 1975-77. Mem. Northwestern U. Alumni Admission Council (dir. S. Fla. region 1979—), Planning Execs. Inst. Republican. Methodist. Home: 13232 SW 12th Ln Miami FL 33184 Office: PO Box 529100 Miami FL 33152

GUILBEAU, ROBERT WALTER, restaurateur; b. Lafayette, La., Aug. 14, 1948; s. Joseph Albert and Eva Delle (Prejean) G.; m. Cheryll Lucile Williams, Jan. 26, 1985; children—Amie Christine, Eric Tyson. B.A., U. Southwestern La., 1972. Warehouse mgr. Internat. Chems., Lafayette, La., 1970-72; sales and engring. staff Dresser Magcobar, Cloverdale, Calif., 1972-73, Milchem Inc., Lafayette, 1973-74; v.p., ptnr. Profl. Drilling Fluid Services Inc., Ventura, Calif., 1974-78; owner, pres. Prejean's Restaurant Inc., Lafayette, 1978—. Mem. Greater Lafayette C. of C., La. Crawfish Farmers Assn., La. Travel Promotion Assn., Gulf Coast Conservation Assn., U.S. C. of C. Democrat. Roman Catholic. Clubs: Hobie Fleet 93, Cajun Ski (Lafayette). Home: 104 White Oak Dr Lafayette LA 70506 Office: Prejean's Restaurant Inc 3480 U S Hwy 167 N Lafayette LA 70507

GUILD, THOMAS EUGENE, political science educator, lawyer; b. Wichita, Kans., Apr. 14, 1954; s. Carl Holmes and Freda Mae (Meyer) G. B.A., Okla. U., 1976; J.D., So. Meth. U., 1979. Bar: Okla. 1979. Intern, Dist. Attys. Office, Bartlesville, Okla., 1979; asst. prof. polit. sci. Central State U., Edmond, Okla., 1979—; practiced in, Oklahoma City, 1979—. Mem. Okla. del. Republican Nat. Conv., 1976; sargeant-at-arms Okla. Rep. State Conv., 1983. Bass scholar Okla. U., 1974-75, 75-76; So. Meth. U. Sch. Law scholar, 1976-79. Mem. Okla. Polit. Sci. Assn., Okla. Bar Assn. Republican. Baptist. Lodge: Masons. Author: Constitutional Criminal Procedure, 1983. Home: Box 21038 Oklahoma City OK 73156

GUILLOT, ROBERT MILLER, university president; b. Headland, Ala., Jan. 2, 1922; s. Clarence Miller and Ruth (Lindsay) G.; B.S. Auburn (Ala.) U., 1943; J.D., U. Ala., 1948; m. Patty Shirley, Sept. 1, 1947; children—Patricia Ann, Shirley Lynne, Robert Miller. Admitted to Ala. bar, 1948; practice in Dothan, 1948-51; sr. v.p., sec. Vulcan Life & Accident Ins. Co., Birmingham, 1952-66; chmn. bd. Am. Educators Life Ins. Co., Birmingham, 1966-72; pres. U. North Ala., 1972—. Pres. Ala. League Municipalities, 1971-72, Assn. Ala. Life Ins. Cos., 1970-71. Mayor, Vestavia Hills, Ala., 1960-72. Trustee Troy (Ala.) State U., 1964-72. Served with USAF, 1951-52. C.L.U. Baptist. Lodges: Masons, Shriners, Rotary. Address: U North Ala Florence AL 35632

GUILMETTE, RONALD MAURICE, data processing executive; b. New Britain, Conn., Jan. 17, 1951; s. Maurice J. and Yvette (Thibault) G.; m. Carol Jean O'Malley, Sept. 15, 1973; children—Thomas Andrew, Cynthia Jean. Student, Embry Riddle Aero. U., 1972-73, Computer Processing Inst., 1976. Proofreader Daytona Beach (Fla.) News Jour., 1973-74; ins. agt. John Hancock Life Ins., Rocky Hill, Conn., 1974-75; computer operator Sun Bank, Daytona Beach, Fla., 1976-77; data processing mgr. Aluma Shield Ind., Inc., Daytona Beach, 1977—. Served with U.S. Army, 1969-72. Mem. Data Processing Mgmt. Assn. Home: 5 Sycamore Circle Ormond Beach FL 32074 Office: 405 Fentress Blvd Daytona Beach FL 32014

GUILORY, RAPHAEL, micropaleontologist, palynologist; b. Mamou, La., Oct. 12, 1931; s. Adam and Ada (Guillory) G.; m. Dorothy Jean Campbell, June 25, 1955; children—Ronald Ray, Rebecca Jeanne. B.S. in Geology, La. State U., 1958. Micropaleontologist, Amoco Prodn. Co., Houston and New Orleans, 1958-68, research scientist, Tulsa, 1968-69, palynologist, Houston, 1969-82, regional paleontologist, Houston, 1982—. Cubmaster, Houston Area council Boy Scouts Am., 1969-71; bd. dirs. Amoco Houston Credit Union, 1980-84. Served with USAF, 1950-54. Mem. Am. Assn. Petroleum Geologists, Am. Assn. Stratigraphic Palynolgists, Gulf Coast Soc. Econ. Paleontologists and Mineralogists. Republican. Roman Catholic. Avocations: Photography; swimming; water skiing; gardening. Home: 5431 Spanish Oak Houston TX 77066 Office: PO Box 3092 501 Westlake Park Blvd Houston TX 77253

GUIN, JUNIUS FOY, JR., federal judge; b. Russellville, Ala., Feb. 2, 1924; s. Junius Foy and Ruby (Pace) G.; m. Dorace Jean Caldwell, July 18, 1945; children—Janet Elizabeth Smith, Judith Ann Mullican, Junius Foy III, David Jonathan. Student Ga. Inst. Tech., 1940-41; A.B. magna cum laude, J.D., U. Ala., 1947; LL.D., Magic Valley Christian Coll., 1963. Bar: Ala. 1948. Practiced in Russellville; sr. ptnr. Guin, Guin, Bouldin & Porch, 1948-73; fed. dist. judge, Birmingham, Ala., 1973—; commr. Ala. Bar, 1965-73, 2d v.p., 1969-70; pres. Abstract Trust Co., Inc., 1958-73; sec. Iuka TV Cable Co., Inc., Haleyville TV Cable Co., Inc., 1963-73; former dir., gen counsel First Nat. Bank of Russellville, Franklin Fed. Savs. & Loan Assn. of Russellville.; lectr. Cumberland-Samford Sch. Law, 1974—, U. Ala. Sch. Law, 1977—; mem. adv. com. on rules of civil procedure Ala. Supreme Ct., 1971-73; mem. adv. com. on standards of conduct U.S. Jud. Conf., 1980—. Chmn. Russellville City Planning Com., 1954-57; 1st chmn. Jud. Commn. Ala., 1972-73; Republican county chmn., 1954-58, 71-72, Rep. state fin. chmn., 1972-73; candidate for U.S. Senator from, Ala., 1954; Ala. Lawyers' Finance chmn. Com. to Re-elect Pres., 1972; trustee Ala. Christian Coll. Served to 1st lt., inf. AUS, 1943-46. Named Russellville Citizen of Yr., 1973; recipient Dean's award U. Ala. Law Sch., 1977. Mem. Am. Radio Relay League, ABA (mem. spl. com. on residential real estate transactions 1972-73), Ala. Bar Assn. (com. chmn. 1965-73, award of Merit 1973), Jefferson County Bar Assn., Fed. Bar Assn., Am. Law Inst., Ala. Law Inst. (dir. 1969-73, 76—), Am. Judicature Soc., World Peace Through Law Ctr., Farrah Law Soc., Farrah Order Jurisprudence, Quarter Century Wireless Assn., Phi Beta Kappa, Delta Chi. Mem. Ch. of Christ (elder). Lodge: Rotary. Home: 3400 Stoneridge Dr Birmingham AL 35243 Office: 106 Federal Courthouse Birmingham AL 35203*

GUINN, DAVID CRITTENDEN, petroleum engineer, drilling and exploration company executive; b. Port Arthur, Tex., Nov. 29, 1926; s. Leland Lee and Corrie Andrews (Avery) G.; A.A., Lamar Inst. Tech., 1948; B.S. in Petroleum Engring., U. Tex., Austin, 1951; m. Marguerite V. Guinn, Oct. 7, 1966; children—Susan, David, Jay, Jeffrey. Engr. trainee Dowell, Inc., Alice, Tex., 1949; petroleum engr. Calif. Co., Lafayette, La., 1951-52, area prodn. and drilling engr., Venice, La., 1953-54, evaluation engr., New Orleans, 1954-55; dist. engr. Republic Natural Gas Co., 1955-56, div. drilling engr., 1956-57; div. engr. Shaffer Tool Works, Inc., 1957-63, sales mgr., Midcontinent div., Beaumont, 1963-65; div. mgr. Mid-Continent-Gulf Coast div., 1965-67; pvt. practice as cons. petroleum engr., New Orleans, 1957, Houston, 1967—; owner Guinn and Assos., Engrs., Guinn Resources Co.; founder Internat. Mission Drilling and Exploration Corp., Tropic Drilling and Exploration Co.; pres. Consol. Offshore Corp., 1978, mining div. Guinn Resources Co., Henderson, Nev., Lakeway Nat. Bank, Austin. Life mem. Pres. Assos., U. Tex.; mem. Tejas Found. Served from pvt. to cadet USAAF, 1943-46. Registered profl. engr., La., Tex. Mem. Nat., Tex. socs. profl. engrs., ASME, AIME, Soc. Petroleum Engrs., Internat. Assn. Drilling Contractors, Houston Engring. and Sci. Soc., Am. Soc. Oceanology, Nomads, Internat. Oceanographic Found., Explorers Club, U. Tex. Ex-Students Assn. (life), SAR, U.S. C. of C., Houston C. of C. Clubs: West Lake, Houston (Houston); Lakeway Country (Austin, Tex.). Contbr. articles to profl. jours.; pioneer, patentee in domestic and fgn. offshore and floating vessel drilling, offshore petroleum subsea prodn. systems. Home: 40 Sugarberry Circle Houston TX 77024 also 927 Electra-Lakeway Austin TX 78734 Office: 19 Brair Hollow Ln Suite 150 Houston TX 77027

GULDE, ROBERT EMMETT, cardiologist; b. Amarillo, Tex., May 10, 1934; s. John Fidelis and Philippina Marie (Lutz) G.; B.S., U. Notre Dame, 1956; M.D., St. Louis U., 1960; children—Lauri, Marjorie, Robert, Michele, Michael, Jonathan. Intern, St. Joseph's Hosp., Denver, 1960-61, resident, 1961-62; resident Hermann Hosp., Houston, 1962-64, Tex. Children's Hosp.-St. Luke's Hosp., Houston, 1963-64; spl. fellow in cardiovascular disease Cleve. Clinic, 1964-66; research fellow Naval Med. Research Inst., Bethesda, 1966-68; instr. dept. cardiology Naval Med. Sch., Bethesda, Md., 1966-68; staff cardiologist Nat. Naval Med. Center, 1966-68; staff cardiologist St. Anthony's Hosp., Amarillo, 1968—, chief cardiopulmonary lab., 1968-72; staff cardiologist High Plains Baptist Hosp., Amarillo, 1968—; staff cardiologist Northwest Tex. Hosp., Amarillo, 1968—; cons. cardiologist VA Hosp., Amarillo, 1972-77, chief cardiology, 1977, 78, 82; cons. cardiologist Palo Duro Hosp., 1984, Family Hosp. Ctr., 1984; assoc. clin. prof. U. Tex., Lubbock, 1972—; founder, dir. The Heart Inst. for CARE, Amarillo, 1975—; internat. lectr., China and USSR. Served as lt. comdr. USNR, 1966-68. Diplomate Am. Bd. Internal Medicine. Fellow Am. Coll. Chest Physicians, Clin. Council Cardiology, Soc. Cardiac Angiography; mem. AMA, Tex. Med. Assn., Potter-Randall County Med. Soc., ACP, Tex. Soc. Internal Medicine, Amarillo Soc. Internal Medicine. Roman Catholic. Club: Rotary. Contbr. articles to profl. jours. Home: 1601 Rusk St Amarillo TX 79102 Office: 1901 Medi-Park St Suite 1010 Amarillo TX 79106

GULISANO, GEORGE ALBERT, accountant; b. Miami, Sept. 13, 1961; s. Luis Albert and Josefa Isabel (Tarrado) G. B.B.A., U. Miami, 1982. Jr. acct. Arthur Andersen, Miami, 1978-81; broadcaster Music Man, Surfside, Fla., 1979-82, Festival Prodn., North Miami, Fla., 1982-83, pub. acct. Laventol & Horwath, Coral Gables, Fla., 1983—. Treas., Campaign for Vice-Mayor Mr. James Slaughter, West Miami, Fla., 1980. Mem. Internat. Hospitality Accts., Beta Alpha Psi. Democrat. Roman Catholic. Home: 926 SW 65th Ave Miami FL 33144 Office: Laventol & Horwath 201 Alhambra Circle Coral Gables FL 33134

GULKA, JOHN MATTHEW, computer consulting company executive; b. Schuylkill Twp., Pa., Dec. 8, 1953; s. John and Mary Ann (Litto) G.; m. Nina Maria Mandzy, Feb. 16, 1980. B.S., George Mason U., 1976. Jr. systems analyst COV VEC, Richmond, Va., 1978-79; sr. systems analyst Commonwealth of Va., Richmond, 1979-80; cons. CGA Computer Inc., Washington, 1980-82, account mgr., cons., 1982-84, tech. dir., Falls Church, Va., 1984-86; tech. dir. CAP Gemini Am., Vienna, Va., 1986—; ptnr. NVP Gems, Alexandria, Va., 1975—. Mem. Data Processing Mgmt. Assn., Am. Soc. Pub. Adminstrn. (pres. Interuniv. Student Assn. 1974-76, pres. local chpt. 1975-76). Republican. Roman Catholic. Avocations: conchology; gemology; music; photography; enophile and collector. Home: 4607 Kling Dr Alexandria VA 22312 Office: CAP Gemini Am 8381 Old Courthouse Rd Suite 300 Vienna VA 22180

GULLETTE, IRENE D., librarian, educator; b. Morley, Mo., Feb. 25, 1906; d. Charles A. and Minnie (Simpson) Daughtrey. A.B., Western Ky. U., 1929; M.S., U. Ky., 1959; postgrad. U. Chgo., 1960. Cert. librarian, supr. Young people's librarian Gary Pub. Library (Ind.), 1944-47, head children's work, 1957-59, head popular library dept., 1959-62; editor young people's books ALA Booklist, Chgo., 1948-53; coordinator Ky. Bookmobile Project, Frankfort, 1953-54; supr. sch. libraries Ky. Dept. Edn., Frankfort, 1954-57; librarian elem. sch., Pompano Beach, Fla., 1962-65; asst. supr. instructional materials, Fort Lauderdale, Fla., 1965-74. Author nat. library skills test (Dutton-Macrae award), 1966; contbr. articles to profl. jours.; editor: Many Happy Returns, 1976. Asst. state dir. Nat. Ret. Tchrs., 1979, 80. Name Ky. Col. Mem. ALA (life), Fla. Library Assn. (chmn. CLA 1967-68), Fla. Assn. Sch. Libraries (life; pres. 1969-70, mem. coms.), Beta Phi Mu, Delta Kappa Gamma. Lodge: Zonta (pres. Pompano Beach 1968-69). Home: 9309 S Orange Blossom Trail Orlando FL 32821

GULLEY, JACK HAYGOOD, lawyer; b. Uvalde County, Tex., Dec. 29, 1935; s. David and Elizabeth (Haygood) G. B.S., Trinity U., San Antonio, 1958; J.D., U. Tex.-Austin, 1962. Bar: Tex., U.S. Dist. Ct. (we. and so. dists.) Tex., U.S. Ct. Appeals (5th cir.), U.S. Supreme Ct. Assoc., Suttle & Kesser, Uvalde, Tex., 1964-65, George Red, Houston, 1965-66; ptnr. Doran, Gulley & Etzel, Del Rio, Tex., 1966—. Mem. ABA, Tex. Bar Assn., Val Verde County Bar Assn. Democrat. Clubs: Rotary (Del Rio); Mason (Uvalde). Address: PO Box 42048 Del Rio TX 78842

GULLICKSON, JOHN CHARLES, manufacturing executive; b. Chattanooga, Oct. 5, 1940; s. Charles Henry and Florence Virginia (Higgins) G.; B.S., Ga. Inst. Tech., 1963; J.D., Emory U., 1966; m. Nancy Ann Bowen, June 25, 1966; children—Jay Weldon, Christine Lee. Indsl. engr. Sweetheart Plastics, Conyers, Ga., 1970-72; adminstrv. asst. to exec. v.p., corp. counsel Owen of Ga., Inc., Lawrenceville, 1972-80; exec. asst. to exec. v.p. So. Engring. Co. of Ga., Inc., 1980-82, cons., 1982-85; chief exec. GRI, 1985—; arbitrator nat. panel Am. Arbitration Assn. Chmn. adv. com. Gwinnett County (Ga.) United Way; bd. dirs. Atlanta Met. United Way, 1976-78, mem. area devel. com.; v.p., bd. dirs. Mental Health Assn. Met. Atlanta; also mem. planning, allocations and community services coms. United Way; mem. child service and family counseling adv. com. DeKalb, Gwinnett, Newton and Rockdale counties. Served with U.S. Navy, 1966-69. Decorated Bronze Star; recipient NASA Apollo Achievement award, 1969; Atlanta Met. United Way Appreciation award, 1978. Roman Catholic.

GULLION, SALLIE ROGERS, medical administrator; b. Houston, Sept. 29, 1935; d. Murray Maurice and Mary Henrietta (Parkins) Rogers; B.S. in Biology, Rice U., 1957; m. Jerry Campbell Gullion, Dec. 22, 1955; children—Guy Rogers, Laura Michelle, Gregg Campbell (dec.). Intern in med. tech. Parkland Meml. Hosp., Dallas, 1957-58; chief technologist spl. hemotology Wadley Research Center, Dallas, 1958-59; clin. lab. technologist Garland (Tex.) Meml. Hosp., 1959, 60; pathology lab. technologist Drs. Grossman and Smith, Dallas, 1960-63, nuclear medicine technologist Dr. M.H. Mitchell and Assos., Lubbock, Tex., 1965-66; clinic adminstr. Marshall (Tex.) Internal Medicine Assos., 1968—; pres. J&S Rentals, Inc., Marshall, Pres. LWV Marshall/Harrison County, 1978-79; mem. Meml. Hosp. Aux., Harrison County Med. Soc., Aux.; sec.-treas. E. Tex. Pastoral Counseling Center; mem. City of Marshall Citizen Adv. Com.; chmn. bldg. com. Marshall Public Library; chmn. Marshall Planning and Zoning Commn.; mem. Pvt. Industry Council, Jobs Tng. Partnership Act; chmn. Harrison County Com. on Subdiv. Regulations. Named Woman of Yr., City of Marshall, 1983. Cert. med. technologist Am. Assn. Clin. Pathologists; cert. med. asst. Mem. Med. Group Mgmt. Assn., Marshall C. of C. (chmn. med. com. 1969-82, mem. water ways com.). Home: 2800 Waubun Dr Marshall TX 75670 Office: 1900 S Washington St Marshall TX 75670

GUMMELT, SAM, artist; b. Waco, Tex., Aug. 28, 1944; s. Harry Lee and Ivy Mary (Fike) G.; m. Mary Melville Ennis, Jan. 6, 1977. B.A., North Tex. State U., 1968; M.F.A., So. Meth. U., Dallas, 1971. One man shows: So. Meth. U., Dallas, 1971, Contract Graphics Assocs., Houston, 1972, Janie C. Lee Gallery, Dallas, 1973, 74, Houston, 1977, 79, 82, North Tex. State U., Denton, 1978, Mus. South Tex., Corpus Christi, 1978, Ft. Worth Art Mus., 1979, Carol Taylor, Art, Dallas, 1983; group shows include: El Paso Mus. Art (Tex.), 1970, Laguna Gloria Mus., Austin, Tex., 1970, Ft. Worth Art Ctr. Mus., 1970, 71, 73, 75, 77, Okla. Art Mus., 1970, So. Ill. U., 1971, Dallas Mus. Fine Arts, 1971, 72, 73, 75, Janie C. Lee Gallery, Dallas, 1972, Houston, 1977, Contemporary Art Mus., Houston, 1972, 79, McNay Art Inst., San Antonio, 1972, Tyler (Tex.) Mus. Art, 1972, 80, David Gallery, Houston, 1972, Walker Art Ctr., Mpls., 1973, Phyllis Kind Gallery, Chgo., 1973, Lobby Gallery, Chgo., 1975, So. Meth. U., 1975, Art Mus. South Tex., Corpus Christi, 1975, Delahunty Gallery, Dallas, 1975, San Francisco Mus. Art, 1976, D.W. Co-op Gallery, Dallas, 1976, 77, Elmira (N.Y.) Coll., 1977, Madison (Wis.) Art Ctr., 1977, U. Chgo., 1978, Beaumont (Tex.) Art Mus., 1978, Vice-Pres.'s House, Washington, 1978, Kristan Murchison, Dallas, 1978, 79, John Michael Kohler Art Ctr.,

Sheboygan, Wis., 1978, U. Tex.-Austin, 1979, Contemporary Art. Ctr., New Orleans, 1979, Bklyn. Mus., 1980, Two Houston Ctr., 1981, Charles Cowles, N.Y.C., 1981, Simone Stern Gallery, New Orleans, 1982, U. Tex.-Dallas, 1983, Janie C. Lee Gallery, Houston, 1984; represented in pub. collections: Ft. Worth Art Mus., Dallas Mus. Art, Beaumont Art Mus., Ark. Art Ctr. Recipient various awards juried exhibitions; Nat. Endowment for the Arts fellow, 1982. Address: 5909 Palo Pinto Dallas TX 75206

GUMNICK, JAMES LOUIS, university official; b. Balt., Oct. 5, 1930; s. Michael and Mary Rose (Schap) G.; m. Jean Kathleen Lawler, Oct. 30, 1959; children—John, Anne, Edward, Mary, Jane, Elizabeth. B.S., Loyola Coll., Md., 1953; Ph.D., U. Notre Dame, 1958. Prof. physics Martin-Loyola Coll., Balt., 1957-64; exec. dir. Nat. Council Energy Co., Phila., 1973-76; chmn. govt. program com. Pa. Gov's. Energy Council, Phila., 1973-74; dir. research devel. U. Houston, 1976-80; gen. mgr. Gulf Univs. Research Co., Houston, 1980-82, pres., 1982-84; univ. relations dir. Oak Ridge Assoc. Univs., 1984—. Contbr. articles to profl. jours.; inventor multiple reflection photocathode; discoverer cyclic migration of CS on refractory metals. Danforth Found. fellow, 1953; hon. mention Outstanding Young Scientist in Md., Md. Acad. Sci., 1959. Mem. Am. Physics Soc., Nat. Council Univ. Adminstrs., AAAS, Soc. Research Adminstrs., Sigma Xi, Alpha Sigma Nu. Democrat. Roman Catholic. Lodge: Rotary. Avocations: fishing; gardening; canoeing. Home: 933 W Outer Dr Oak Ridge TN 37830 Office: Oak Ridge Associated Univs 200 Badger Ave Oak Ridge TN 37830

GUNBY, WILLIAM RICHARDSON, JR., developer, construction educator; b. Tampa, Fla., Feb. 20, 1931; s. William Richardson and Violet (Eversole) G.; children—Robert, Richard, Greer, Adrienne. Student Centre Coll., 1950; B.Bldg. Constrn., U. Fla., 1953; M.B.A., Stetson U., 1972; Archtl. engr., Atlanta, 1957-59; archtl. engr., Jacksonville, Fla., 1960-69, constrn. mgr., 1970-71, constrn. cons., 1971-75; pres. Fla. North Central Co., Inc., Gainesville, 1979-83; v.p. Black Forest Builders, Inc., Gainesville, 1978—; partner Gunby-Halperin Properties, Gainesville, 1977—; prof. sch. bldg. constrn. U. Fla., Gainesville, 1973—. Served to 1st lt. USAF, 1953-55; capt. Res. ret. Named Tchr. of Yr., Coll. Architecture, U. Fla., 1978. Mem. Am. Inst. Constructors, Assoc. Schs. Constrn. (pres. 1982-83), Soc. of Cincinnati, Kappa Alpha Order. Episcopalian. Clubs: Heritage (Gainesville); Ponte Vedra. Home: 2313 Costa Verde Blvd Jacksonville Beach FL 32250 Office: Sch Bldg Constrn U Fla Gainesville FL 32611

GUNN, ALBERT EDWARD, physician, lawyer, hospital and university administrator; b. Port Washington, N.Y., Oct. 31, 1933; s. Albert Edward and Esther Frances (Williams) G.; B.S., Fordham Coll. 1955, LL.B., 1958; M.B., B.Ch., B.A.O., Nat. U. Ireland, Galway, 1967; m. Joan Marie Jacoby; children—Albert Edward III, Emily Williams, Andrew Robert, Clare Margaret, Catherine Ann, Philip David. Bar: N.Y. 1958, D.C. 1972. Intern Montefiore Hosp., N.Y.C., 1967-68; med. resident Roosevelt Hosp., N.Y.C., 1968-70; USPHS trainee in neurology U. Rochester, 1970-72; asst. dir. govtl. relations AMA, Washington, 1972-74; med. dir. Geriatric Services Suffolk County (N.Y.), Hauppauge, 1974-75; med. dir. Rehab. Ctr., U. Tex./M.D. Anderson Hosp. and Tumor Inst., Houston, 1975—; asst. prof. medicine U. Tex. Med. Sch. at Houston, 1976-80, assoc. prof., 1980—, now also assoc. dean for admissions; del.-at-large White House Conf. on Handicapped Individuals, 1977. Mem. nat. adv. health council HEW, 1974-75; mem. adv. com. Nat. Inst. Law Enforcement and Criminal Justice, Law Enforcement Assistance Adminstrn., U.S. Dept. Justice, 1974-76; chmn. bd. regents Nat. Library of Medicine, NIH, 1986-87. Served with USAF, 1958-61. Diplomate Am. Bd. Internal Medicine. Mem. Harris County (Tex.) Med. Soc. (exec. bd.), AMA, Tex. Med. Assn., Royal Coll. Physicians (London) (licentiate), Royal Coll. Surgeons (Eng.), Houston Acad. Medicine, Houston Bar Assn., D.C. Bar. Roman Catholic. Clubs: Doctors (Houston); Lawyers (Washington). Co-author: Rehabilitation of the Cancer Patient, 1976; editor, contbg. author: Cancer Rehabilitation, 1984; editorial bd. Cancer Bull., Gerontology and Geriatrics Edn., Yearbook on Cancer; mem. editorial bd. Cancer Bull., Gerontology, Geriatrics Edn., Yearbook of Cancer; contbr. articles to profl. jours. Home: 2329 Watts Rd Houston TX 77030 Office: 6723 Bertner Ave Houston TX 77030

GUNN, JEANETTE WALTON, interior designer; b. Leary, Ga., Dec. 8, 1923; d. Elmo William and Macy (Rooks) Walton; m. Otis Benton Gunn, Dec. 26, 1946; children—Daniel Franklin, Otis Walton. Student Shorter Coll., 1945-46, Wesleyan Coll., Macon, Ga., 1954, Ga.-Ala. Bus. Sch., Macon, Ga., 1944, N.Y. Sch. Interior Design, 1952-56. Owner, operator Gunn's, Warner Robins, Ga., 1954-71, J. Gunn Ltd., Hilton Head Island, SC, 1978—. Mem. Art League, Hist. Savannah Found. Methodist. Club: Yacht (Hilton Head Island). Home: 17 Live Oak Rd Hilton Head Island SC 29928 also 1106 Swift St Kenwood Court Townhouse Perry GA 31069 Office: 1100 Plantation Center Hilton Head Island SC 29928

GUNN, M. D., fire department official. Fire chief, Jacksonville, Fla. Office: City Hall 220 El Bay Jacksonville FL 32202*

GUNN, ROBERT GIBSON, investment banking executive; b. Pitts., Dec. 2, 1916; s. Robert Gibson and Lydia Lincoln (Goodnough) G.; B.A., Union Coll., Schenectady, 1939; student Gen. Motors Inst., 1947-48; m. Carrie G. Newton, June 5, 1948; 1 son, Robert Gibson, III. Vice pres. Gunn Pontiac Inc., Pitts., 1946-59; v.p., dir. Russ & Co., Inc., San Antonio, 1960-73; v.p., Rotan Mosle, Inc., San Antonio, 1973-79; pres., dir. Robert G. Gunn Corp., San Antonio, 1961—; pres., dir. Gunn Capital, Inc., San Antonio, 1979—; chmn. Gunn & Co. Inc., San Antonio, 1980—; dir. Sewanee Drilling Corp., San Antonio. Bd. dirs. Salvation Army of San Antonio, 1966—, chmn. bd., 1968-69; bd. dirs. St. Luke's Episcopal Sch., San Antonio, 1964-75, chmn., 1972-75; bd. dirs. Easter Seals Soc. for Crippled Children and Adults, San Antonio, 1976-81; chmn. Friends of St. Luke's Sch., 1970—; active campaigns ARC, 1961-62, United Way San Antonio, 1961-70, Boy Scouts Am. Bexar County, 1969-70. Served with AUS, 1942-46. Mem. Nat. Assn. Securities Dealers, Tex. Stock and Bond Dealers Assn. Clubs: Duquesne (Pitts.); Rolling Rock (Ligonier, Pa.); Argyle, San Antonio Country; Birnam Wood Golf, Valley of Montecito (Santa Barbara, Calif.); Masons, Shriners. Home: 225 Westover Rd San Antonio TX 78209 Office: Robert G Gunn Corp 711 Navarro St Suite 406 San Antonio TX 78205

GUNNING, CAROLYN SUE, nursing educator; b. Ft. Smith, Ark., Dec. 16, 1943; d. Laurence George and Flora Irene (Garner) G. B.S., Tex. Woman's U., 1965; M.S., U. Colo., 1973; Ph.D., U. Tex.-Austin, 1981. Registered nurse, Tex. Clinician III, Bexar County Hosp., San Antonio, 1968-71; instr. U. Tex. Sch. Nursing, San Antonio, 1973-74, asst. prof., 1974-83, asst. to dean, 1977-79, assoc. prof., asst. dean undergrad. programs, 1983-84, assoc. dean, 1984—; accreditation site visitor Nat. League for Nursing, 1982—. Active Leadership San Antonio, 1978-79. Served to capt. Nurse Corps, U.S. Army, 1965-68; to maj. Army N.G., 1980—. Decorated Army Commendation medal. Mem. Am. Nurses Assn., Nat. League for Nursing, Am. Edni. Research Assn., Sigma Theta Tau, Kappa Delta Pi. Contbr. articles to profl. jours. Office: 7703 Floyd Curl Dr San Antonio TX 78284

GUNTER, ANNIE LAURIE, Alabama state treasurer; b. N.C., June 23, 1919; d. Samuel Franklin and Daisy (Callahan) Cain; student public schs., Lake Wales, Fla.; m. William A. Gunter, Oct. 14, 1946; 1 son, William A., IV. Sec., Lake Wales Public Sch. System, then exec. sec. citrus and real estate devel. co. until 1946; coordinator Ala. Office Hwy. and Traffic Safety, Montgomery, 1971-72; dir. Ala. Office Consumer Protection, 1972-78; treas. State of Ala., Montgomery, 1978—. Mem. platform com. Nat. Democratic Conv., 1972, 76; mem. Ala. Dem. Exec. Com., 1974—; mem. Montgomery County Dem. Exec. Com. Mem. Women in Communications, Nat. Assn. Consumer Affairs Adminstrs., DAR, Daus. Am. Colonists, Eagle Forum. Presbyterian. Club: Soroptomists. Office: Treasury Room 111 State Capitol Montgomery AL 36130

GUNTER, MARJORIE MOORE, accounting educator; b. Birmingham, Ala., Jan. 28, 1934; d. Marvin Edward and Ada Mae (McLaughlin) Moore; m. Edward Calvin Gunter, Sept. 26, 1958; children—Edward Craig, Robert Gregory, Leslie Michelle. B.S., Samford U., 1970, M.B.A., 1971. C.P.A., Fla. Auditor, Arthur Young & Co., Birmingham, 1971-73, Miami, Fla., 1973-74; asst. prof. acctg. Miami Dade Community Coll., 1974-78; asst. prof. acctg. Birmingham-So. Coll. 1978-80, chmn. div. econs. and bus. adminstrn., 1980—, assoc. prof., 1981—; instr. practice sect. Person Wolinsky C.P.A. Rev., 1982-83. Kellog grantee, 1980, Acctg. Systems for Small Bus. Title III grantee, 1983. Mem. Am. Soc. Women Accts., Am. Acctg. Assn., Ala. Assn. Acctg. Educators. Democrat. Baptist. Author: Accounting Can Be Fun and Easy, 1980; Series of 30 vido tapes on intermediate acctg., 1983. Home: 2416 6th Pl NW Birmingham AL 35215 Office: Dept Acctg Box A-23 Birmingham-Southern Coll Birmingham AL 35254

GUNTER, WILLIAM DAWSON, JR., state official; b. Jacksonville, Fla., July 16, 1934; s. William Dawson and Ruth Tillie (Senterfitt) G.; B.S.A., U. Fla., 1956; m. Teresa Arbaugh Gunter, June 26, 1971; children—Bartlett D., Joel S., Rachel D., Rebecca M. Mem. Fla. Senate, 1966-72; mem. 92d Congress from 5th Fla. Dist., 1973-74; pres. Southland Capital Investors, Inc., Orlando, Fla., 1975-76; sr. v.p. Southland Equity Corp., Orlando, 1975-76; treas., ins. commr. State of Fla., Tallahassee, 1976—. Tchr., Sunday Sch., deacon First Baptist Ch., Tallahassee. Served with U.S. Army, 1956-58. Recipient Fla. Jaycee Good Govt. award for outstanding public service, 1972. Mem. Nat. Assn. State Treas. (pres. 1981-82), Nat. Assn. Ins. Commrs. (pres. 1983-84, chmn. task force on state and fed. health ins. legis. policy, mem. exec. com.), Jaycees, Orlando Area C. of C. Democrat. Clubs: Kiwanis, Masons. Home: 3802 Leane Dr Tallahassee FL 32308 Office: Plaza Level The Capitol Tallahassee FL 32301

GUPTA, MAHESH, research consultant, educator; b. Moradabad, India, Jan. 1, 1942; came to U.S., 1978; s. Dwarka Prasad and Shanti (Devi) G.; m. Suversha Malhotra, June 15, 1982; children—Sumati, Arun. B.S. in Physics, Agra U., India, 1960; M.A. in Psychology, Delhi U., 1963; M.S. in Math., Meerut U., 1968; Ph.D. in Social Psychology, Indian Inst. Tech., 1976. Lectr. psychology, Rajasthan U., India, 1976-77, Makerere U., Uganda, 1976-78; research fellow U. Vienna, Austria, 1978-79; research assoc. UCLA, 1981-83; contract faculty Calif. State U., Northridge, 1982-83; research cons. Talladega Coll., Ala., 1983—; vis. scholar U. Mich., Ann Arbor, 1983-84; asst. prof. Lincoln U., Pa., 1985—. Contbr. articles to profl. jours. Mem. Am. Psychol. Assn., Internat. Council Psychologists, S.E. Psychol. Assn., So. Soc. Philosophy and Psychology. Office: PO Box 156 Talladega Coll Talladega AL 35160

GURWITCH, HARRY, financial corporation executive; b. Mobile, Ala., Oct. 2, 1934; s. Isaac and Rebecca (Ripps) G.; m. Shirley Masiel, June 9, 1957; children—Lisa Diane, Annabelle. B.A., Vanderbilt U., 1955; postgrad. Sch. Law, U. Ala.-Tuscaloosa, 1955-56. Registered mortgage underwriter, cert. rev. appraiser. Asst. v.p. Ro-Gur Mortgage & Devel. Corp., Mobile, 1956-58; gen. agt., underwriter Travelers Ins. Co. and U.S. Life, Mobile, 1958-64; v.p. Nat. Properties & Mining Corp., Mobile, 1962-67; from v.p. to exec. v.p. Belmont Nat. Corp. and investment banking affiliates, Wilmington, Del., 1968-73; pres., chief exec. officer Equity Mortgage Corp., Miami, Fla., 1973-78; founding ptnr. Union Center Venture Ptnrs., Miami, 1974-79; chmn. bd., chief exec. officer Motion Picture Investment Corp., Miami, 1976-81; pres., chief exec. officer Bedford Fin. Corp. and subs., Miami, 1981—; cons. on rehab., renovation, restoration Nat. Hist. Landmark. Active Miami Design Preservation League, Nat. Trust for Hist. Preservation, Miami Met. Mus., Bass Mus., Assn. for Corp. Growth. Served with USAR, 1958-64. Mem. Nat. Assn. Rev. Appraiser and Mortgage Underwriters Mortgage Bankers Assn. Am., Jewish. Club: Jockey. Purchased Union Sta., St. Louis, now designated Nat. Hist. Landmark. Home: 2525 Sunset Dr Miami Beach FL 33140 Office: 444 Brickell Ave Suite 415 Miami FL 33131

GUSTAFSON, DWIGHT LEONARD, educational administrator, conductor; b. Seattle, Apr. 20, 1930; s. Carl Leonard and Rachel Doris (Johnson) G.; m. Gwendolyn Anne Adams, May 28, 1952; children—Dianne, David, Donna Gale. B.A., Bob Jones U., 1952, M.A., 1954; D. Mus., Fla. State U., 1967; LL.D., Tenn. Temple U., 1960. Grad. asst. Bob Jones U., Greenville, S.C., 1952-54, acting dean Sch. Fine Arts, 1954-56, dean Sch. Fine Arts, 1956—, condr. orch., 1955—, condr. chorale, 1984—. Composer choral and instrumental works, film scores, one act operas. Mem. Am. Choral Dirs. Assn. (pres. state chpt. 1978), Music Educators Nat. Conf., Southeastern Composers League, Pi Kappa Lambda. Office: Bob Jones U Wade Hampton Blvd Greenville SC 29614

GUSTE, ROY FRANCIS, lawyer, banker, planter, restaurateur; b. New Orleans, Nov. 28, 1923; s. William Joseph and Marie Louise (Alciatore) G.; B.A., Loyola U. at New Orleans, 1943, LL.B., 1948; m. Beverly Taylor, July 1, 1948; children—Roy Francis, Taylor, Colette, Robert, Beatrice, Michael. Admitted to La. bar, 1948, since practiced in New Orleans; asso. firm now Guste, Barnett & Shushan and predecessor firm, New Orleans, 1948-56, mem. firm, 1956—; owner, dir. Antoine's Restaurant, New Orleans, 1972—, Guste Island Plantation, Madisonville, La.; v.p., dir. Continental Savs. & Loan Assn., New Orleans, 1966-83. Pres. Young Men's Bus. Club, New Orleans, 1955-56, Pres's. Council Loyola U., 1973-77. Mem. adv. bd. Delgado Trade Sch., New Orleans, 1955-56; bd. dirs. Internat. House, New Orleans, 1955-56, Nat. Cath. Conf. for Interracial Justice, 1974—; trustee Loyola U., 1980—. Served with USNR, 1943-46. Decorated knight comdr. of Holy Sepulchre. Mem. New Orleans, La. State, Am. bar assns., Am. Judicature Soc., St. Thomas More Law Club, Alpha Delta Gamma, Delta Theta Phi. Democrat. Roman Catholic (pres. archdiocese human relations com., 1971-73). K.C. (4 deg.). Order of St. Louis. Home: 2603 St Charles Ave New Orleans LA 70130 Office: 1624 Nat Bank of Commerce Bldg New Orleans LA 70112

GUSTE, WILLIAM JOSEPH, JR., attorney general Louisiana; b. New Orleans, May 26, 1922; s. William Joseph and Marie Louise (Alciatore) G.; A.B., Loyola U., New Orleans, 1942, LL.B., 1943, LL.D., 1974; m. Dorothy Schutten, Apr. 17, 1947; children—William Joseph III, Bernard Randolph, Marie Louise, Melanie Ann, Valerie Eve, Althea Maria, Elizabeth Therese, James Patrick, Anne Duchesne, John Jude (dec.). Bar: La. 1943. Practiced in New Orleans, 1943-72; mem. firm Guste, Barnett & Colomb, 1970-73; atty. gen. La., 1972—; chief counsel New Orleans Housing Authority, 1957-71; pres. New Orleans Met. Crime Commn., 1956-57; chmn. Juvenile Ct. Adv. Com. Orleans Parish, 1961-63; mem. New Orleans St. Paving Study Commn., 1965-66; mem. exec. working group U.S. Dept. Justice; mem. Pres.'s Commn. on Organized Crime, 1983—; co-owner, Antoine's Restaurant, New Orleans, 1944—. Pres. New Orleans Cancer Assn., 1960-62, United Cancer Council, 1965-67, Asso. Catholic Charities New Orleans, 1960-62, La. Housing Council, 1965-66; chmn. Nat. Housing Conf., 1963-64; sec. United Fund Greater New Orleans. Mem. La. Senate from 21st Dist., 1968-72. Trustee Xavier U., New Orleans, 1967—, chmn. bd. lay regents, 1956. Served with AUS, 1942-46. Named Outstanding Young Man U.S. Jaycees, 1955; recipient John F. Kennedy Leadership award Young Democrats La. State U., 1973; Gautrelet award Springhill Coll., Mobile, Ala., 1977; Nat. Penology award State of La., 1979, award Anti-Defamation League, B'nai B'rith, 1980; named Housing Man of Yr., Nat. Housing Conf., 1976. Mem. New Orleans Bar Assn., St. Thomas More Cath. Lawyers Assn., Am. Assn. Small Bus. (dir.), Nat. Assn. Housing and Redevel. Ofcls. (dir., Man of Year 1976), Nat. Conf. Dem. State-wide Elected Ofcls. (chmn.), Am. Judicature Soc., Legal Aid Bur., Blue Key, Knights of Malta, Order St. Lazarus, Sigma Alpha Kappa. Democrat. Clubs: K.C. (state dep. 1965-66); Internat. House, Pickwick, Bienville (New Orleans). Office: PO Box 44005 Baton Rouge LA 70804

GUSTIN, ANN WINIFRED, psychologist; b. Winchester, Mass., Oct. 21, 1941; d. Bertram Pettingill and Ruth Lillian (Weller) G.; B.A. with honors in Psychology, U. Mass., 1963; M.S. (USPHS fellow), Syracuse U., 1966, Ph.D., 1969; m. Carl George Beal, Sept. 17, 1966 (div.); m. Thomas Licardi, Jan. 26, 1985. Research asst., psychology trainee U. Mass., Tufts U., Harvard U., Syracuse U., 1961-66; psychology intern VA, Canandaigua, N.Y., 1967-68; asst. prof. psychology U. Regina (Sask., Can.), 1969-74, asso. prof. psychology, dir. counseling services, head clin. tng., 1974-78; pvt. practice psychology, Atlanta and Carrollton, Ga., 1978—; staff tng. cons. Frobisher Bay Dept. Social Services, N.W. Territories, Can., 1979-80; cons. staff Tanner Hosp.; staff West Paces Ferry Hosp., Atlanta; psychiat. cons. disability adjudication sect. Social Security Adminstrn.; dir. The Incommunicado Group. Membership chmn. Carroll County Mental Health Assn., 1979-81. Registered psychologist, Sask.; lic. psychologist, Ga. Mem. Am. Psychol. Assn., Can. Psychol. Assn., Ga. Psychol. Assn., Sask. Psychol. Assn. (mem. exec. council 1971-72, registrar 1972-73), Nat. Assn. Disability Examiners. Office: 107 College St Carrollton GA 30117 also 105 Beaumont Ave Decatur GA 30031

GUTENBERG, RHONDA LYNN, industrial psychologist; b. Detroit, July 28, 1957; d. Harold and Arlene Dorothy G. B.A. with honors, U. Calif.-Berkeley, 1978; M.A., U. Houston, 1980, Ph.D., 1982. Mgmt. cons. Jeanneret & Assocs., Inc., Houston, 1980—. Mem. Am. Psychol. Assn., Acad. Mgmt., Australian Am. Bus. Group of Houston, Houston Area Indsl./Organizational Psychologists, Houston Bus. Forum. Office: 3223 Smith St Suite 212 Houston TX 77006

GUTERMUTH, CLINTON RAYMOND, conservationist, naturalist; b. Fort Wayne, Ind., Aug. 16, 1900; s. Henry Christian and Alice Virtue (Zion) G.; student U. Notre Dame, 1918-19; grad. Am. Inst. Banking, 1927, postgrad., 1927-28; D.Sc. (hon.), U. Idaho, 1972; m. Ila Bessie Horm, Mar. 4, 1922 (dec. Dec. 3, 1975); m. Marian Schutt Happer, Mar. 21, 1977. Asst. cashier St. Joseph Valley Bank, Elkhart, Ind., 1922-34; dir. div. edn. Ind. Dept. Conservation, Indpls., 1934-40, dir. div. fish and game, 1940-42; Ind. rent dir. OPA, Indpls., 1942-45; exec. sec. Am. Wildlife Inst., Washington, 1945-46; v.p. Wildlife Mgmt. Inst., 1946-71. Chmn. Natural Resources Council Am., 1959-61, hon. mem., 1971; pres., dir. Wildfowl Found. Inc., 1956—; nat. adv. council Pub. Land Law Rev. Commn., 1964-70; trustee, sec. N.Am. Wildlife Found., Inc., 1945-74; trustee, pres. Stronghold (Sugarloaf Mountain) Inc., 1947—; bd. dirs., pres. World Wildlife Fund (U.S.), 1961-73, hon. pres., 1973—; internat. trustee, exec. com. World Wildlife Fund (Internat.), 1971-75; bd. dirs., pres. Nat. Inst. Urban Wildlife, 1976—. Recipient Leopold medal Wildlife Soc., 1957; named to Fishing Hall of Fame, Sportsman's Club Am. 1958; Disting. Service award Nat. Assn. Soil Conservation Dists., 1958; Meritorious Service award Nat. Watershed Congress, 1963; Nat. Service award Keep Am. Beautiful, 1965; Nat. Conservation award Mich. United Conservation Clubs, 1967; Disting. Service award Nat. Wildlife Fedn., 1969; Horace M. Albright medal Am. Scenic and Hist. Preservation Soc., 1970; Order of Golden Ark Prince Netherlands, 1972; named to Hunting Hall of Fame, 1975; Gold medal Camp Fire Club Am., 1977. Fellow AAAS; mem. Am. Com. Internat. Wildlife Protection (hon.), Nat. Rifle Assn. life; mem.; dir. 1963—, pres. 1973-75, life mem. exec. council 1975—), African Safari Club (Conservation award 1977), Izaak Walton League Am. (life), Outdoor Writers Assn. Am., The Wildlife Soc. (hon. mem., trustee 1951—), Nat. Audubon Soc. (Audubon medal 1982), Wilderness Soc. (life), Am. Fisheries Soc., Internat. Assn. Game, Fish and Conservation Commrs. (hon.), Am. Forestry Assn. (hon.; Citizen of Yr. 1971), Am. Soc. Range Mgmt., Conservation Edn. Assn., Nat. Parks Assn., The 1001-Nature Trust, World Wildlife Fund, Polar Inst. N.Am., Soil Conservation Soc. Am. (hon.), Arctic Inst. N. Am., Safari Club Internat., Zool. Soc. (N.Y.), Explorers Club. Clubs: Cosmos, Nat. Press, University (Washington); Boone and Crockett (hon.); Camp Fire N.Y.C.; Booneville (Ind.) Press (hon.); Elkhart (Ind.) Conservation (hon.); Miami (Fla.) Sailfish; Tanana Valley (Alaska) Sportsmen's (hon.); Outdoor Boating Am. (hon.). Lodges: Masons (32 deg.), KT. Author: Where to Go in Indiana, Official Lake Guide, 1938; Quips and Queries page on natural history, Outdoor Indiana, 1934-42; W.M.I. bi-weekly Outdoor New Bull., 1947-50. Co-author: The Fisherman's Encyclopedia, 1950; The Standard Book of Fishing, 1950. Program chmn. ann. N. Am. Wildlife Conf., 1946-71. Numerous articles and lectures on various phases of natural resource conservation. Home: 2111 Jefferson Davis Hwy Apt 605 S Arlington VA 22202

GUTHRIE, DAN CALVIN, JR., lawyer; b. San Antonio, Nov. 19, 1948; s. Dan Calvin and Nova Jean (Sheppard) G.; m. Sherrill Reagan, Dec. 28, 1979; children—Reagan Jessica, Tiffany Amber, Chase Alexander. B.A., Rice U., 1971; J.D., U. Tex., 1974. Bar: Tex. 1974, U.S. Ct. Appeals (5th cir.) 1978, U.S. Ct. Appeals (11th cir.) 1981, U.S. Supreme Ct. 1979. Asst. dist. atty. Dallas County (Tex.), 1975-78; asst. U.S. atty. No. Dist. Tex., 1978-80; ptnr. Burleson, Pate & Gibson, Dallas, 1981—. Mem. Nat. Assn. Criminal Def. Lawyers, Fed. Bar Assn., Assn. Trial Lawyers Am., ABA, State Bar Tex. (mem. penal code, code criminal procedure com.), Tex. Criminal Def. Lawyers Assn., Tex. Trial Lawyers Assn., Dallas Bar Assn. Recipient Dean Hugh Scott Cameron Service award Rice U., 1971. Methodist. Office: 2414 N Akard St 7th Floor Dallas TX 75201

GUTHRIE, JOHN ROBERT, physician, medical clinic executive; b. Spartanburg, S.C., Mar. 8, 1942; s. Clarence Luther and Rosa (Thackston) G.; m. Kathryn Jean Bottorff, Oct. 19, 1984; children—Jennifer Carolyn, Jenny Erin, Christopher, Jason, Elizabeth, John Luther. B.S., Mercer U., 1969; M.A., Duke U., 1971; D.O., Chgo. Coll. Osteo. Medicine, 1979. Diplomate Nat. Bd. Exam. Osteo. Medicine and Surgery. Prof. sci. Fayetteville Tech. Inst., N.C., 1971-75; intern Doctors Hosp., Tucker, Ga., 1979-81; practice family osteo. medicine, Spartanburg, 1980-82; owner Guthrie Family Practice Clinic, Spartanburg, 1982—; bd. dirs. Spartanburg Teen Ctr., 1984—. Contbr. articles to profl. jours. Mem. Children's Com. Spartanburg First Bapt. Ch. Mem. AMA, Am. Osteo. Assn., S.C. Med. Assn., S.C. Osteo. Med. Assn., Spartanburg County Med. Assn., Spartanburg C. of C., Spartanburg Meth. Coll. Alumni (bd. dirs.), Kappa Delta Phi, Sigma Sigma Phi. Club: Carolina Country. Avocations: flying; shooting. Home: 216 Beechwood Dr Spartanburg SC 29302 Office: Guthrie Clinic 870 N Church St Spartanburg SC 29303

GUTIERREZ, JAIME RAUL INCHAUSTI, architect, planner, educator; b. La Paz, Bolivia, Dec. 19, 1939; came to U.S., 1966, naturalized, 1971; s. Jose Carlos Bernal Gutierrez and Carmen (Lopez) Inchausti; m. Nancy C. Marinovic, Mar. 19, 1964 (div. 1976); children—S. Carolina M.; m. Marcia Lisbela Paredes Zepeda, Nov. 27, 1981. B.S. in Architecture, San Andres Mayor U., Bolivia, 1963, M.S., 1964. Prin., Otapic, La Paz, 1964-66; assoc. Thomas Gilbert Architect, Metairie, La., 1966-72; prin. Jaime R. Gutierrez I. AIA, Architect Planner, Metairie, 1972—; prof. Delgado Coll., New Orleans, part-time 1983—. Mem. Vets. Beautification Bd., Metairie, 1976; bd. dirs. Latin World, New Orleans, 1984; mem. La. State Gov.'s Hispanic-Am. Commn., 1985. Mem. AIA, La. Architects. Republican. Roman Catholic. Lodge: Gallilleo Mazzini (32 deg.). Avocations: painting; music. Home: 3409 Purdue Dr Metairie LA 70003 Office: PO Box 7564 Metairie LA 70010

GUTMAN, D. MILTON, advertising agency executive; b. Wheeling, W.Va., Feb. 21, 1933; s. D. Milton and Elizabeth (Henderson) G.; m. Katrine Rempe, Sept. 10, 1955; 1 son, J. Milton. B.S. cum laude, W. Va. U., 1955. TV and creative dir. Gutman Advt. Agy., Wheeling, W.Va., 1957-62, pres., 1963—; dir. Security Nat. Bank & Trust Co., 1969—, exec. com., 1974—. Bd. dirs., exec. com. Wheeling Soc. Crippled Children, 1960—; pres. Oglebay Inst., 1972-75, devel. chmn., 1980—; trustee Linsly Inst., 1968—, v.p., 1975—; trustees Wheeling AAA, 1972—; trustee Ohio Valley Gen. Hosp., 1970—, pres., 1977-80; sec. Ohio Valley Health Services and Edn. System, 1983—; bd. visitors Bethany Coll., 1972—; pres. Youth Found. Greater Wheeling, Chem. People Task Force. Served with U.S. Army, 1955-57. Recipient Silver award Advt. Fedn. Am. and Printers' Ink, 1962; Helen Gaynor Billboard award, 1968-73; Outstanding Shriner award Osiris Temple, 1978; Disting. Service award W.Va. Soc. Crippled Children and Adults, 1976; named Paul Harris fellow Wheeling Rotary, 1981. Mem. Wheeling Area C. of C. (dir. 1967-70). Clubs: Wheeling Rotary (dir., v.p., pres. 1967-68); Blue Pencil (exec. com.). Office: Board of Trade Bldg Wheeling WV 26003

GUTTERMAN-REINFELD, DEBRA ELLEN, physician, consultant; b. N.Y.C., Nov. 13, 1948; d. George and Nettie (Liss) Gutterman; m. Stuart Glenn Reinfeld, June 20, 1982; children—Alan Jeffrey, Naomi Rebecca. B.S., R.N. magna cum laude, SUNY Downstate Med. Ctr., 1972; postgrad. U. Auton, Guadalajara Sch. Medicine (Mex.), 1973-75; M.D., Coll. Medicine and Dentistry N.J., 1977. Intern, Boston City Hosp., 1977-78; resident in medicine Maimonides Med. Ctr., Bklyn., 1978-79, 79-80, Mt. Sinai Med. Ctr., Miami Beach, Fla., 1982-83; fellow Jackson Meml. Hosp., Miami, Fla., 1980-82; internist, cons. infectious diseases, chief dept. internal medicine Health Am., Ft. Lauderdale, Fla., 1983—. Fellow ACP. Democrat. Jewish. Home: Coral Springs FL

GUTZMAN, RICHARD DEAN, pharmacist; b. Leona, Kans., Apr. 2, 1932; s. Leo Calvin and Alice May (Cluck) G.; m. Mary Louise Wright McGill, May 23, 1959; children—Kenneth McGill, Richard Dean, Jr., Gretchen Holly Gutzman Philmon. B.S., U. Houston, 1959; cert. in hosp. adminstrn. Herman Hosp., Houston, 1959. Cert. pharmacist. With Richlou Pharmacy, West Columbia, Tex.; pres. Central Emergency Med. Service, 1985—. Precinct chmn., West Columbia, 1970—; state del. Democratic Conv., 1968-82; pres. bd. trustees West Columbia Damon Hosp. Dist. 1974—. Served with USN, 1950-54. Mem. Am. Pharm. Assn., Acad. Gen. Practice, Brazoria County Pharm. Soc. (pres. 1968-69), VFW, Am. Legion. Lutheran. Lodge: Rotary (bd. dirs. West Columbia). Avocations: sailing; horseback riding and training; tennis. Home: 1004 Loggins Dr West Columbia TX 77486 Office: Richlou Pharmacy 301 E Brazos West Columbia TX 77486

GUY, EDWARD LEE, inventory services company executive; b. Garland, N.C., Oct. 28, 1937; s. Lee Livingston and Mary Susan (Johnson) G.; B.A., Catawba Coll., 1969; m. Olivia Gail Hartsell, Sept. 7, 1972 (div.); 1 child, Stacy

Lee. Adminstrv. asst. Cons. Services, Inc., Salisbury, N.C., 1969-71; owner, mgr. Inventory Services Co., Tampa, Fla., 1971-72; pres. Multi-Chek Systems, Inc., Tampa, 1972-77, Super Chek Systems, Inc., Tampa, 1977—. Served with U.S. Army, 1960-62. Recipient F. M. Knetsche award, 1967. Mem. Intertel, Mensa. Office: 8438 Boxwood Dr Tampa FL 33615

GUY, ROXANNE JOSEPHINE, physician; b. Galesburg, Ill., Aug. 15, 1952; d. Robert Edward and Gertrude Josephine (Hoegg) Bowman; B.S., Ill. State U., 1974; postgrad. Salzburg Coll., 1973; M.D., So. Ill. U., 1977; m. Curtis Eugene Guy, May 17, 1980. Diplomate Am. Bd. Surgery. Resident So. Ill. U. Sch. Medicine Affiliated Hosps., Springfield, 1977-81, chief resident gen. surgery, 1981-82, resident in plastic surgery, 1982-83, chief resident in plastic surgery, 1983-84. Mem. AMA, Am. Med. Women's Assn., Fla. State Med. Soc., Broward County Med. Soc., So. Ill. U. Sch. Medicine Alumni Soc. Methodist. Contbr. articles to profl. jours. Home: 255 E Paradise Blvd #16 Indialantic FL 32903 Office: 1355 S Hickory #103 Melbourne FL 32901

GUYETTE, WAYNE CHARLES, hotel administration educator; b. Providence, Aug. 31, 1942; s. Irvin and Laura Rose (Farley) G.; B.S., U. Nev., 1973; M.S., Fla. Internat. U., 1977; Ph.D., Fla. State U., 1979; m. June M. Silver, Mar. 10, 1970. Dir., hospitality mgmt. programs Clark County Community Coll., Las Vegas, 1972-75; pres. Hospitality Dynamics, Inc., Las Vegas, 1974-76; dir. hotel mgmt. Coll. of Boca Raton (Fla.), 1976-77; state dir. Sch. Food Service Tng. Tallahassee, Fla., 1977-78; assoc. prof. hotel adminstrn. U. New Orleans, 1979-85; chmn. bd. dirs. Guyette Assocs., Inc., Metairie, La., 1979-84; nat. exec. dir. Corp. Food and Beverage Exec. Council; chmn. bd. trustees Les Chefs des Cuisines de la Louisianne, 1980-82; chmn. bd. trustees Culinary Apprenticeship Program of La., 1983-85; cons. in field. Trustee, Am. Culinary Fedn. Ednl. Inst., 1981-83. Served with U.S. Army, 1966-69. Statler Found. fellow, 1965; Nat. Inst. for Food Service Industry fellow, 1977; Club Mgmt. Assn. of Am. grantee, 1978; Am. Hotel and Motel Assn. Grantee, 1978. Mem. Food Service Execs. Assn. (v.p. 1974-75), Am. Hotel and Motel Assn., New Orleans Chefs Assn. (dir. 1980-85), Council on Hotel, Restaurant and Instl. Edn., Nat. Restaurant Assn., Am. Soc. for Tng. and Devel., Culinary Inst. of Am. Alumni Assn. Author: Property-Level Food and Labor Cost Reduction, 1983, also 4 other books; contbr. articles to profl. jours. Office: Sch of Hotel Restaurant and Tourism Adminstrn Univ of New Orleans New Orleans LA 70122

GUZMAN, LORENZO GILBERTO, physician; b. P.R., Sept. 18, 1924; s. Felipe and Maria (Quinones) G.; m. Lucrecia Flores, Sept. 9, 1948; 2 children. A.B., L.L. U., 1950; M.A., NYU, 1951; postgrad. Webb Inst. Engring., 1951-53; M.D., U. P.R., 1957. Diplomate Am. Bd. Family Practice. Intern, Flushing Gen. Hosp. (N.Y.), 1957-58; resident in medicine Phila. Gen. Hosp., 1958-59; resident in surgery USPHS Hosp., S.I., N.Y., 1961-64; commd. med. officer USPHS, 1959; chief med. officer, S.D., 1959-61; chief surgery, Talihina, Okla., 1964; dep. chief surgery, Galveston, Tex., 1965-67; chief surgery ENT, S.I., N.Y., 1967-69; chief med. officer USPHS Clinic, San Juan, P.R., 1979-81, chief med. officer Ft. Allen, Ponce, P.R., 1981-82. Served with U.S. Army, 1942-45; ETO. Decorated Bronze Star, Silver Star. Mem. AAAS, Nat. History Soc., Royal Soc. Health, Assn. Mil. Surgeons, AMA, VFW, Trudeau Soc., Am. Acad. Family Physicians, Royal Coll. Surgeons, Am. Coll. Emergency Room Physicians, N.Y. Acad. Scis. Address: PO Box 638 Sabana Grande PR 00747

GUZY, KARIN ELIZABETH, advertising executive; b. Milw., Apr. 19, 1948; d. Bernhard H. and Elizabeth Helene (Leven) Verhoeven; m. Larry Thomas Guzy, Dec. 19, 1969. Student Marquette U., 1966-70. Reporter, Milw. Sentinel, 1967-68; asst. print media dir. Mathisson & Assocs., Milw., 1968-69; media dir. McDonald, Davis & Assocs., Milw., 1970; office mgr. Kent Advt., Norfolk, Va., 1972-73; media dir. Scofield/Malone, Atlanta, 1974-76; polit. media buyer Rafshoon Advt., Atlanta, 1976; v.p., mgr. spot broadcast D'Arcy Masius Benton & Bowles, Atlanta, 1977—; lectr. in field. Mem. Atlanta Broadcast Advt. Club (pres. 1980, dir. 1979-81), Atlanta Media Planners Assn. (sec. 1978), Mensa. Office: 400 Colony Sq Suite 1901 Atlanta GA 30361

GYAPONG, SAMUEL KWASI, business educator, researcher; b. Sefwi Bekwai, Western Region, Ghana, June 21, 1936; came to U.S., 1978; s. Dominic Kwadwo and Elizabeth Akuah (Foriwah) G.; m. Mercy Amma Dadzie, Oct. 23, 1965; children—David, Jonathan, Samuel Kwasi. B.S., Embry-Riddle Aero. U., Daytona Beach, Fla., 1980, M.B.A. with distinction, 1981; Ph.D., Pa. State U., 1985. Cert. in bus. adminstrn., bus. logistics. Aviation weather forecaster Ghana Civil Service, 1964-66; electronic maintenance officer Ghana Air Force, 1966-77; grad. teaching asst. Pa. State U., University Park, 1983-85; asst. prof. Sch. Bus., Ky. State U., Frankfort, 1985—. Roger Girling Meml. scholar Transp. Clubs Internat., 1984; L.L. Waters scholar, 1985. Episcopalian. Avocations: sports; music; gardening; vol. high school soccer coach. Office: School of Business Kentucky State Univ Frankfort KY 40601

GYURKO, MICHAEL G., banker; b. Toledo, Mar. 23, 1947; s. E.P. and Olga G.; m. Christine Siwa, June 30, 1968; children—Kristin, Angela. Grad., Ohio State U., 1970; M.B.A., U. Toledo, 1972. Divisional comptroller Owen-Corning Fiberglas, 1968-73; treas. Goslin-Envirotech, 1973-74; with AmSouth Bank, N.A., Birmingham, Ala., and predecessor 1st Nat. Bank of Birmingham, 1974—, comptroller, v.p., 1975-77, sr. v.p., from 1977, now exec. v.p. operation/adminstrn. div.; dir. AmSouth Mortgage Co., AmSouth Fin. Corp. Pres. Hoover Homeowners Assn., 1980-81; bd. dirs., chmn. audit com., mem. exec. com., mem. fin. com. ARC; bd. dirs. Ala. Symphony Assn. Mem. Fin. Execs. Inst. (pres. 1983-84), Nat. Assn. Accts., Am. Bankers Assn., Ala. Bankers Assn. Roman Catholic. Clubs: Green Valley Country, Downtown, Riverchase Country. Office: 1900 5th Ave N Birmingham AL 35203

HAACK, DAVID ARNO, geologist; b. St. Louis, Dec. 21, 1931; s. Arno John and Florence (Reppert) H.; A.B., Washington U., St. Louis, 1954, M.A., 1955; m. Katherine Ann Vanston, June 6, 1953; children—William James, Robert David. Teaching asst. Washington U., 1954-55; geologist, dist. devel. supr. Texaco, Inc., Corpus Christi, Tex., 1957-67, div. staff geologist, well log analyst, devel. supr., Houston, 1967-69; dist. geologist Clark Oil Producing Co., Corpus Christi, 1969-71; chief geologist Normandy Oil and Gas Co., Corpus Christi, 1971-72; sr. exploration geologist Mitchell Energy & Devel. Corp., Houston, 1972-75, dist. geologist So. div., 1975-77; exploration geologist Kilroy Co. of Tex. Inc., Houston, 1977-82, chief devel. geologist, 1982-83; exploration mgr. Am. Shoreline, Corpus Christi, 1983—. Served to 1st lt. AUS, 1955-57. Mem. Am. Assn. Petroleum Geologists, Houston, Corpus Christi geol. socs., Sigma Xi, Tau Kappa Epsilon. Clubs: Imperial Point Civic (exec. bd. 1967-69), Alief Band Boosters (v.p. 1968-69) (Houston). Home: 4313 Wood River Dr Corpus Christi TX 78410 Office: Am Shoreline Inc 1250 Texas Commerce Plaza Corpus Christi TX 78470

HAACK, DENNIS GEORGE, consulting firm executive; b. Geneseo, Ill., Jan. 21, 1944; s. William F. and Beatrice B. (Ehlers) H.; m. Geraldine A. Clancy, Jan. 28, 1967; children—Mary Clancy, Daniel Song. B.S. in Edn., Ill. State U., 1966, M.S., 1968; Ph.D., U. Iowa, 1971. Cert. epidemiologist, Am. Coll. Epidemiologists. Researcher, tchr., cons. U. Ky., Lexington, 1971-81; pres. Statis. Cons., Inc., Lexington, 1981—; cons. pharm. firms, mktg. researcher, computer software devel. and sales; lectr. on statis. literacy. Author: Statistical Literacy: a Guide to Interpretation, 1979; contbr. articles to statis. and med. jours. Mem. Am. Statis. Assn., Soc. for Epidemiologic Research, AAAS, Nat. Council Tchrs. English (com. pub. doublespeak), Biometric Soc. Home: 227 Desha Rd Lexington KY 40502 Office: Statistical Consultants Inc 462 E High St Lexington KY 40508

HAAS, GREGORY GEORGE, mechanical engineer; b. Phila., Mar. 3, 1949; s. Joseph J. and Edith (LaBelle) H.; M.E., Temple U., 1973. Prodn. mgr. Bruce Industries, Inc., Phila., 1973-76; supt. woodworking Dunning Industries, Inc., Greensboro, N.C., 1976-80; East Coast sales mgr. Ind. Moulding Co., Lexington, N.C., 1980-82; dir. mfg. Advanced Technology Inc., 1982—; owner Ltd. Prodn., mktg. inventions, Two-Bit Video, operator amusement and vending machines. Recipient letter of commendation Dept. of Navy, 1968. Inventor specialized machinery for lighting, woodworking and picture frame industry. Home: 6306 Roblyn Rd Greensboro NC 27410 Office: PO Box 19303 Greensboro NC 27419

HAAS, HAROLD IRWIN, psychology educator; b. Buffalo, Sept. 26, 1925; s. Elmer John and Gladys Kingdon (Ford) H.; m. Ruth Ann Miller, Sept. 6, 1952; children—Rachel; Peter, Sara, Lois, Elizabeth. Diploma, Concordia Coll., Bronxville, N.Y., 1945; A.B., Concordia Sem., St. Louis, 1946, M.Div., 1949; M.A., Washington U., 1949; Ph.D., U. Buffalo, 1956. Diplomate Am. Bd. Profl. Psychology. Asst. prof. psychology Concordia Sr. Coll. Fort Wayne, Ind., 1957-67, assoc. prof., 1959-67, prof., 1967-77; prof. Valparaiso U., Fort Wayne, 1977-79; prof. Lenoir-Rhyne Coll., Hickory, N.C., 1979—, chmn. dept. sociology and psychology, 1983—. Author: The Christian Encounters: Mental Illness, 1966; Pastoral Counseling with People in Distress, 1970. Mem. Citizens' Adv. Com., Hickory, 1984—. Stipendiate in W.Ger., Lutheran World Fedn., 1969. Mem. Am. Psychol. Assn., N.C. Psychol. Assn. Democrat. Lutheran. Avocations: fishing; hiking. Home: 1759 4th St Pl NE Hickory NC 28603 Office: Lenoir-Rhyne Coll Hickory NC 28603

HAAS, HARRY, JR., architect; b. New Orleans, Jan. 18, 1914; s. Harry and Dora (Van Os) H.; m. Thelma Irene Caplinger, July 1, 1942; children—Steven A., Barbara J. Haas Patton, Nancy G. Haas Brown, Elaine L. Haas Marshall. B.Arch., Tulane U., 1933; postgrad. Cornell U., 1933-34. Registered architect, Miss., La. With Armco Steel Co, New Orleans, 1934-38, A.M. Lockett Jr., New Orleans, 1935, Diboll-Kessels, New Orleans, 1938-41; statistician U.S. Air Force, Dayton, Ohio, 1941-44; owner, mgr. Jones & Haas, Jackson, Miss., 1946—. Served to 1st lt. C.E., U.S. Army, 1944-46. Mem. AIA, Mensa. Baptist. Lodges: Masons, Shriners, Lions. Home: 1414 Brecon Dr Jackson MS 39211 Office: Jones & Haas 2727 Old Canton Rd Jackson MS 39216

HAAS, KENNETH ROBERT, advertising executive; b. Allentown, Pa., Jan. 30, 1950; s. Kenneth Robert and Rose Evelyn (Sullivan) H.; m. Carol Lee Brandmeir, Oct. 26, 1974; children—Adam Kenneth, Jacob Adrian. Cert., Sch. Visual Arts, N.Y.C., 1970. Jr. copywriter, Lennen & Newell, Inc., N.Y.C., 1970-71, Chester Gore Advt., N.Y.C., 1971-72; copywriter Cargill, Wilson & Acree, Charlotte, N.C., 1972-74; copywriter, producer Richardson, Myers & Donofrio, Balt., 1974-76; sr. copywriter, producer Bozell & Jacobs Advt., Atlanta, 1976-82; owner, mgr. Ken Haas Enterprises, Inc., Atlanta, 1982; ptnr. Sullivan and/or Haas, Inc., Atlanta, 1982-83; ptnr. Sullivan Haas Coyle, Inc., Atlanta, 1983—; instr. advt. concept devel. Portfolio Ctr., Atlanta, also bd. advisors. Bd. dirs. Pets Are People Too, Inc.; mem. pub. relations adv. bd. Nat. Kidney Found. Ga. Recipient Pub. Relations award Nat. Kidney Found. Ga., 1983. Mem. Writers Guild Am. Author: How to Get a Job in Advertising, 1980; screenwriter: The Box, 1983. Office: Ivy Pl 3243 Piedmont Rd Atlanta GA 30305

HAAS, ROBERT EDWARD, clinical nutritionist, consultant, reseacher; b. N.Y.C., July 3, 1948; s. Albert and Ann Haas. B.S., Fla. State U., 1970, M.S., 1978; Ph.D., Columbia Pacific U., San Rafael, Clalif., 1980; Ed.D., Nova U., 1984. Pres. Haas Inst., Miami, Fla., 1979—; clin. nutritionist Bonaventure Spa, Ft. Lauderdale, Fla., 1983—; chief exec. officer, pres. Small Planet Systems, Miami, 1983—. Author: Fast Food Nurtition Guide, 1983; Eat To Win, 1983. Recipient Journalism award Dade County Tb Assn., Miami, 1963, 64. Mem. Am. Inst. Sports Nutrition (pres. Miami 1983), Am. Heart Assn., Am. Coll. Sports Medicine, AAAS.

HAAS, STANLEY ALAN, architect; b. Temple, Tex., Nov. 27, 1950; s. Arthur Fred and Pearl Estella (Beerwinkle) H.; m. Nancy Dearing, May 17, 1980 (div. 1984). B.Arch., U. Tex., 1973. Registered architect, Tex. Draftsman, Dan Leary, Architect, Austin, Tex., 1971; lighting and graphic design Evans & Hillman, Inc., N.Y.C., 1974-75; draftsman, designer Youssef Bahri, Architect, Peekskill, N.Y., 1975-76; dir. design Thompson Parkey Assoc., Dallas, 1977-79; dir. design, assoc. Parkey & Ptnrs., Dallas, 1979-82; design ptnr. Good, Haas & Fulton, Dallas, 1982—; asst. adj. prof. U. Tex.-Arlington, 1980-81; mem. staff Dallasights: Anthology of Architecture and Open Spaces tour guide, 1978. Mem. Dallas Mus. Art, 1985. Mem. AIA (v.p. Dallas chpt. 1984), Tex. Soc. Architects (v.p. 1985). Republican. Methodist. Avocations: golf; graphic design. Office: Good Haas & Fulton Architects 300 LVT Ctr 2001 Ross LB132 Dallas TX 75201

HAAS, WILLIAM HENRY, sociology educator; b. Chgo., July 2, 1951; s. William Christian and Martha Clara (Tews) H.; m. Marilyn Louise Younghouse, Sept. 3, 1977; children—William Christian, Kenneth Paul. B.A., Valparaiso U., 1973, M.A., 1976; Ph.D., U. Fla., 1980. Instr. Lake City Community Coll., Fla., 1976-80; grad. asst. U. Fla., Gainesville, 1976-80; asst. prof. sociology U. N.C., Asheville, 1980—, research asst., prof. family medicine Chapel Hill Sch. Medicine, 1983—. Contbr. articles to profl. jours. Pres. Buncombe County Council Aging, 1985; bd. dirs. Western N.C. Health System Agy., Morganton, 1985; mem. adv. com. Buncombe County Nursing Home, 1985. Mem. Am. Sociol. Assn., Gerontol. Soc. Am. Office: U N C 1 University Heights Asheville NC 28804-3299

HABEGER, HAROLD (BUTCH) EDWARD, hospital pharmacy manager; b. Chester, S.D., July 13, 1947; s. Edward William and Helen May (Rhoden) H.; m. Sheryl May Vanaman, June 22, 1972; children—Jason Edward, Sarah May. B.S.Pharmacy, S.D. State U., 1970; M.B.A., U. Puget Sound, 1981. Outpatient pharmacy supr. VA Med. Ctr., Tacoma, 1979-81; asst. pharmacy dir. High Plains Baptist Hosp., Amarillo, Tex., 1981-82, pharmacy dir., 1982—. Contbr. articles to profl. jours. Coach Kid's Inc. Summer T-Ball Kindergarten, Amarillo, 1983; head usher Beautiful Savior Lutheran Ch., Amarillo, 1985. Served to capt. U.S. Army, 1970-77. Decorated Commendation medal. Mem. Am. Soc. Hosp. Pharmacists, West Tex. Pharm. Assn., Am. Pharm. Assn., S.D. Pharm. Assn., Wash. Pharm. Assn., Tex. Soc. Hosp. Pharmacists (chmn. council pub. affairs 1985, chmn. canvassing com. 1984, bd. dirs. 1984-86), Panhandle Soc. Hosp. Pharmacists (pres. 1984, Pres.'s award 1985). Club: Nuernberg Internat. Ski (W. Ger.) (treas. 1976-77). Avocations: golf; alpine skiing; camping; family activities. Home: 4429 Kingston Rd Amarillo TX 79109 Office: High Plains Baptist Hosp 1600 Wallace Blvd Amarillo TX 79106

HABER, MICHAEL JORAM, statistics educator; b. Ramat-Gan, Israel, Oct. 3, 1943; came to U.S., 1980. B.Sc., Hebrew U., Jerusalem, 1965, M.Sc., 1968, Ph.D., 1976. Lectr., U. Haifa, 1975-79; vis. asst. prof. U. Waterloo, 1979-80; assoc. prof. Memphis State U., 1980-83; assoc. prof. Emory U., Atlanta, 1983—. Contbr. articles to profl. jours. Mem. Am. Statis. Assn., Biometric Soc., Internat. Assn. Statis. Computing. Office: Dept Biometry Emory U Atlanta GA 30322

HABERFELD, JOSEPH LAWRENCE, geologist; b. Queens, N.Y., Nov. 20, 1953; s. Norman Harold and Gloria Edna (Rosenberg) H.; m. Maureen Brigid Reilly, May 15, 1981; 1 child, Alissa Katherine. B.S. in Geology, SUNY-Fredonia, 1975; M.S. in Geology, So. Ill. U., 1977. Geologist, Lake Erie Environ. Studies Program, Fredonia, 1975; teaching asst. So. Ill. U., Carbondale, 1975-77; sr. project geologist Gulf Oil Corp., Houston, 1977—. Author: Late Pleistocene Sands of Southwestern Illinois, 1977. Mem. Am. Assn. Petroleum Geologists, Houston Geol. Soc. Jewish. Club: Gulf Employees. Avocations: sports, traveling, hiking, stamps, cooking. Home: 3418 Pecan Point Dr Sugar Land TX 77478 Office: Gulf Oil Corp PO Box 1635 Houston TX 77251

HABERMAN, MICHAEL ALLEN, psychiatrist, educator; b. N.Y.C., Oct. 31, 1947; s. Harvey Hyman and Sylvia (Blecker) H.; B.S. with distinction, U. Wis., 1969; M.D., SUNY, Buffalo, 1973; m. Judith Lynn Sajowitz, June 22, 1969; children—Alison Melanie, Erica Sharon. Intern, resident in psychiatry SUNY, Buffalo, 1973-74; resident Emory U., Atlanta, 1974-76; staff physician Fulton County Alcoholism Treatment Center, Atlanta, 1975-77; clin. asst. prof. psychiatry Emory U. Sch. Medicine, Atlanta, 1976—; staff psychiatrist Grady Meml. Hosp., Atlanta, 1976-79; practice medicine specializing in psychiatry, Atlanta, 1976—; cons. Disability Adjudication Sect., State of Ga., Dept. Human Resources, 1979; med. dir. dept. psychiatry West Paces Ferry Hosp., 1979—, sec. dept. psychiatry, 1978, chief of staff, 1986—; mem. psychiatry specialty panel Met. Atlanta Found. for Med. Care, Inc., 1977—. VA fellow, 1970; Am. Cancer Soc. summer fellow, 1971. Diplomate Am. Bd. Psychiatry and Neurology. Fellow Am. Psychiat. Assn.; mem. AMA, Atlanta Hypnosis Soc. (treas. 1978—, pres. 1981-82), James A. Gibson Anatomical Soc., Ga. Psychiat. Assn., Med. Assn. Ga., Med. Assn. Atlanta (chmn. alcohol and drug abuse com. 1986), Am. Soc. Clin. Hypnosis (chmn. edn. com. 1985-86), Am. Med. Soc. on Alcoholism, Internat. Soc. Hypnosis, Atlanta Hypnosis Soc., Am. Assn. Psychiat. Adminstrs. (pres. Ga. chpt. 1986—). Contbr. articles to profl. jours. Office: 3280 Howell Mill Rd NW Suite 230 Atlanta GA 30327

HABICHT, FRANK HENRY, industrial company executive; b. Chgo., Sept. 4, 1920; s. George and Gertrude H. (Tronc) H.; m. Jeanne Patrick, Mar. 9, 1943; children—Pamela, Patrica, Frank Henry. B.S.M.E., Purdue U., 1942; postgrad. Cornell U., Am. U. From sales engr. to pres. Marshall & Huschart Machinery Co., 1946-70; vice chmn. Cone-Blanchard Machine Co.; chmn., pres. United Tech. Corp.; now v.p., dir. Steego Corp.; now pres. Steego Tech. Corp.; dir. UNISIG Corp., Am. SIP Corp., BotempCorp., King & Gavaris Cons. Engrs., Inc., Marshall & Huschart Machinery Co.; mem. def. indsl. plant equipment com. Dept. Def. Served to lt. comdr. USN, 1942-46. Mem. Am. Machine Tool Distbrs. Assn. (dir., past pres.), Fabricating Mfrs. Assn. (dir., past pres.), ASME, Conf. Bd. (exec. council). Clubs: Oakbrook Polo, Palm Beach, Beach, Palm Beach Yacht. Lodge: Masons. Author: Modern Machine Tools, 1963. Office: 319 Clematis St Suite 900 West Palm Beach FL 33401

HACK, PAULA RUTH, public relations executive; b. Phila., June 2, 1925; d. Davis H. and Bertha (Schafritz) Shapiro; m. Morris J. Hack, Feb. 14, 1961 (dec. 1973); children—Daniel, Jonathan. B.A., U. Wis., 1947. Creative copywriter BBDO Co., N.Y.C., 1954-60; freelance writer and newspaper feature columnist, Milw., 1961-73; advt. mgr. Miami (Fla.) Computer Mktg. Div., 1975-76; mktg. asst. Sun Bank Miami, 1979-81; pub. relations coordinator Fin. Fed. Savs. and Loan, Miami, 1981—. Mem. Pub. Relations Soc. Am., Common Cause. Jewish. Office: 6625 Miami Lake Dr Miami FL 33114

HACKER, GARY LEE, lawyer; b. Denver, Nov. 28, 1939; s. Andrew Aris and Lena May (Brandt) H.; m. Aleta Szemcsak, Nov. 14, 1975; 1 child, Andrew John. B.A., U. Colo., 1963; M.A., U. Denver, 1971; J.D., Baylor U., 1976. Bar: Tex. 1977, Fla. 1978. Commd. 2d lt. U.S. Army, 1963, advanced through grades to maj.; asst. dist. atty., Abilene, Tex., 1977; asst. dist. atty. Taylor County, Abilene, 1978; ptnr. Whitten, Haag, et al, Abilene, 1978—; dir. Steamboat Mountain Water Corp., Tuscola, Tex., 1984—, Centennial Title Abilene, 1982—. Mem. ABA, Am. Trial Lawyers Assn., Abilene Bar Assn. Democrat. Lutheran. Avocation: golf. Office: Whitten Haag Hacker Hagin & Cuttbirth PO Box 208 500 Chestnut St Suite 1402 Abilene TX 79604

HACKERMAN, NORMAN, university president emeritus, chemist; b. Balt., Mar. 2, 1912; s. Jacob and Anne (Raffel) H.; A.B., Johns Hopkins U., 1932, Ph.D., 1935; m. Gene Allison Coulbourn, Aug. 25, 1940; children—Patricia Gale, Stephen Miles, Sally Griffith, Katherine Elizabeth. Asst. prof. Loyola Coll., Balt., 1935-39; research chemist Colloid Corp., 1936-40; chemist USCG, S.I., 1939-41; asst. prof. Va. Poly. Inst., Blacksburg, 1941-43; research chemist Kellex Corp., 1944; asst. prof. chemistry U. Tex., 1945-46, assoc. prof., 1946-50, prof., 1950-70, chmn. dept., 1952-61, dir. corrosion research lab., 1948-61, dean research and sponsored programs, 1960-61, v.p., provost, 1961-63, vice chancellor acad. affairs, 1963-67, pres., 1967-70; prof. chemistry Rice U., Houston, 1970—, pres., 1970-85; chmn. Gordon Corrosion Research Conf., 1950; cons. in corrosion, 1946—; chmn. Inter Soc. Corrosion Com., 1956-58, Gordon Research Conf. on Chemistry, 1959; mem. nat. sci. bd. NSF, 1968-80, chmn., 1974-80; mem. Def. Sci. Bd., 1978-85; chmn. sci. adv. bd. Welch Found., 1982—; mem. Nat. Bd. Grad. Edn., 1971-75; chmn. bd. energy studies Nat. Acad. Scis./NRC Commn. Natural Resources, 1974-77; mem. Energy Research Adv. Bd., 1980—; mem. Tex. Gov.'s Task Force on Higher Edn., 1981-82; trustee MITRE Corp., 1980—. Recipient Whitney award Nat. Assn. Corrosion Engrs., 1956; Joseph J. Mattiello Meml. lectr. Fedn. Socs. Paint Tech., 1964; Gold medal Am. Inst. Chemists, 1978; Mirabeau B. Lamar award Assn. Tex. Colls. and Univs., 1981; Disting. Alumnus award Johns Hopkins U., 1982; Alumni Gold medal for disting. service to Rice U., 1984. Fellow AAAS, Am. Acad. Arts and Scis., N.Y. Acad. Scis.; mem. Am. Chem. Soc. (bd. editors 1956-62, exec. com. colloid div. 1955-58, chmn. chemistry and public affairs com. 1982—; 1965 S.W. Regional award), Electrochem. Soc. (pres. 1957-58, Palladium medal 1965, Edward Goodrich Acheson award 1984), Faraday Soc., Nat. Corrosion Engrs. (dir. 1952-55, chmn. com. edn. Corrosion Research Council 1957-60), Argonne Univs. Assn. (chmn. bd. trustees 1969-73), Nat. Acad. Scis., Am. Philos. Soc., Sigma Xi, Phi Lambda Upsilon, Alpha Chi Sigma, Phi Kappa Phi. Editor Jour. Electrochem. Soc., 1969—; mem. editorial bd., mem. adv. edn. bd. Corrosion Sci., 1969-73; mem. editorial bd. Catalysis Rev. Home: 12 Pecos Sq 3421 Pecos Austin TX 78703 Office: Dept Chemistry President's House Rice Univ PO Box 1892 Houston TX 77251

HACKETT, CHARLES WILSON, JR., educator; b. Austin, Tex., Oct. 26, 1921; s. Charles Wilson and Jean (Hunter) H.; B.A., U. Tex., 1942, M.B.A., 1948; Ph.D., U. Wash., 1955; m. Ruby E. Bloomquist, July 25, 1953; children—Jean Elizabeth, Ruth Christina. Instr., Air Activities Tex., Corsicana, 1942-44, Schreiner Inst., Kerrville, Tex., 1946; mgmt. engr. Gulf Oil Corp., Port Arthur, Tex., 1948-50; instr., research bus. adminstr. U. Wash., Seattle, 1950-55; asst. prof. bus. orgn. Ohio State U., Columbus, 1955-56; industry fin. analyst, credit rep. U.S. Steel Corp., Pitts., 1956-64; asst. dist. credit mgr., Houston, 1964-66; asst. prof. fin. U. Tex. at Austin, 1966-69, asso. prof., 1969—. Served with USAAF, 1944-46. Recipient Exec. award Dartmouth Coll. Grad. Sch. Credit and Fin. Mgmt., 1964. Mem. Am., Southwest (pres. 1975-76) fin. assns., Fin. Mgmt. Assn., Phi Beta Kappa, Beta Gamma Sigma, Phi Kappa Sigma, Alpha Kappa Psi, Sigma Iota Epsilon, Pi Sigma Alpha, Sigma Delta Pi, Phi Eta Sigma. Episcopalian. Author: A Techno-Fundamental Portfolio Management Simulation with Computer Applications, 1967. Home: 102 W 33d St Austin TX 78705 Office: Dept Fin U Tex Austin TX 78712

HACKETT, RICHARD CECIL, mayor; b. Memphis, July 21, 1949; s. William E. and Rosemary (Benedict) H.; m. Kathleen O'Brien, Feb. 14, 1981; children—Michael Jason, Mary Shea. Student Memphis State U.; D.H.L. (hon.), So. Coll. Optometry, 1984. Dir. Mayor's Action Ctr., City Govt., Memphis, 1972-78; county clk. Shelby County Govt., Memphis, 1978-82; mayor City of Memphis, 1982—; v.p. Tenn. Mcpl. League, Nashville, 1984-85; mem. resolutions com. Nat. League Cities, Washington, 1984-85, mem. community and econ. devel. com., transp. and communication com., fin., adminstrn. and intergovtl. relations policy com., 1984-85. Named Outstanding Young Man of Yr., Memphis Jaycees, 1977, 79, Tenn. Jaycees, 1979; Vol. of Yr., Vols. in Action, 1979; recipient Western Tenn. Service to Mankind award Sertoma Internat., 1979. Mem. U.S. Conf. Mayors. Lodge: Rotary. Office: City of Memphis 125 N Main St Suite 200 Memphis TN 38103

HACKLER, RUTH NADINE, home economics educator, extension clothing specialist; b. Cloud Chief, Okla., Oct. 16, 1935; d. B.L. and Essie M. (Richey) Hackler. B.S. in Home Econs. Edn., Okla. A&M Coll., 1957; M.S. in Clothing, Textiles, Merchandising, Okla. State U., 1962. Vocat. home econs. tchr. pub. schs., Alva, Okla., 1957-61; instr. clothing and textiles Fla. State U., Tallahassee, 1962-69; asst. prof. U. Fla., Gainesville, 1969-74, assoc. prof., 1974-82, prof., 1982—. Recipient Past Pres.'s plaque Gamma Sigma Delta, 1981; Gen. Foods Fund fellow, 1961-62. Mem. Am. Home Econs. Assn., Fla. Home Econs. Assn., Assn. Coll. Profs. Textiles and Clothing, The Fashion Group, Am. Assn. Textile Colorists and Chemists, Am. Assn. Textile Technologists, Nat. Assn. 4-H Extension Agts., Internat. Fedn. Home Econs., Okla. State U. Alumni Assn., Okla. State Home Econs. Alumni Assn., Epsilon Sigma Phi (cert. meritorious service 1980), Phi Kappa Phi, Gamma Kappa Omicron, Omicron Nu, Phi Upsilon Omicron, Delta Kappa Gamma. Contbr. numerous extension publs. on clothing and textiles. Office: U Fla 3002 McCarty Hall Gainesville FL 32611

HACKNEY, DAVID ALAN, food industry executive; b. Greenville, Tex., Mar. 3, 1949; s. George Rankin and Oleta (Cardwell) H.; m. Gayla June Tibbets, Aug. 3, 1974 (div. 1978); m. Mara Sampaio, Aug. 18, 1984. B.S., East Tex. State U., 1971, M.S., 1974. Cert. tchr. secondary schs. High sch. tchr. Elkhart Ind. Schs. (Tex.), 1974-75; quality control supr. Safeway Stores, Inc., Garland, Tex., 1975-77, beverage plant mgr., Denver, 1977-79, quality control mgr., Walnut Creek, Calif., 1979-82, mktg. mgr., Walnut Creek, 1979, plant mgr., Denison, Tex., 1982—. Office: Safeway Stores Inc 1404 W Washington Denison TX 75020

HACKWORTH, HOWARD BING, educator; b. Mangum, Okla., Oct. 26, 1932; s. Howard R. and Ada Lee (Durall) H.; m. Helen Lee Gladstone, Dec. 27, 1973; children—Lori Jean, Scott Raymond, Courtland Brandon Lee, Jordan Ross. B.A., U. Tulsa, 1954; M.S., U. Utah, 1957; Ed.D., U. Tulsa, 1964. Cert. speech pathologist. Faculty speech pathology program dir. U. Tulsa, 1956-68; faculty, dept. chmn. speech pathology SUNY-Cortland, 1968-78; pvt. practice speech pathology, Tulsa, 1978-81; asst. prof. speech pathology coordinator Central State U., Edmond, 1981—; cons. N.Y. State grantee, 1974. Mem. Am. Speech-Lang.-Hearing Assn., Okla. Speech-Lang.-Hearing Assn., N.Y. Speech Assn. Republican. Methodist. Club: Sertoma. Author: Angle Orthodontist, 1965; Southern Speech Journal, 1967; contbr. articles to profl. jours. Home: 1704 Canary Cir Edmond OK 73034 Office: Central State Univ Edmond OK 73034

HADAWAY, CHRISTOPHER KIRK, sociologist, research administrator; b. Nashville, Oct. 6, 1951; s. James Edward and Nelwyn Elsie (Cooke) H.; m.

Pamela Ann Painter, Dec. 28, 1974. B.A. in Anthropology with honors and distinction, Southwestern U. at Memphis, 1973; M.A., Memphis State U., 1975; Ph.D. in Sociology, U. Mass., 1978. Researcher Bapt. Home Mission Bd., Atlanta, 1978-81; research dir. Ctr. for Urban Ch. Studies, Nashville, 1981-85, exec. dir., 1985—. Southwestern U. at Memphis scholar, 1969. Mem. Am. Sociol. Assn., Soc. for Sci. Study Religion, Religious Research Assn., Assn. for Sociology Religion, Phi Beta Kappa. Democrat. Baptist. Author: The Urban Challenge, 1982; An Urban World, 1984; Home Cell Groups and House Churches, 1986. Editor Urban Rev. Contbr. articles to profl. pubis. Office: 127th 9th Ave N Nashville TN 37234

HADDAD, FRED, lawyer; b. Waterbury, Conn., Sept. 14, 1946; s. Fred Melad and Nancy Anne (Crean) H.; m. Julia Hester, Aug. 2, 1980; 1 dau., Allison Hester; children by previous marriage—Tonja, Tristan, Matthew. Student U. Conn., 1964; B.A., U. New Haven, 1971; J.D., U. Miami (Fla.), 1974. Bar: Fla. 1974, U.S. Dist. Cts. (so. and mid. dists.) Fla. 1975, U.S. Cts. Appeals (4th, 5th, 6th, 11th cirs.) 1975, U.S. Supreme Ct. 1977, U.S. Dist. Ct. (we. dist.) Tenn. 1982. Ptnr. Sandstrom & Haddad (changed to Sandstrom & Haddad, Fort Lauderdale, Fla., 1974—. Mem. Fla. Bar (criminal law, reverse sting coms.), Broward County Criminal Def. Attys. Assn., Nat. Assn. Criminal Def. Lawyers. Democrat. Office: Sandstrom & Haddad 429 S Andrews Ave Fort Lauderdale FL 33301

HADDAD, WADI DAHIR, consulting firm executive, medical equipment company executive; b. Aindara, Lebanon, Mar. 14, 1941; came to U.S., 1976; s. Dahir Boutros and Wardy (Khater) H.; m. Houda Nashef, June 27, 1964; children—Sandra, Loubna. B.S., Am. U., Beirut, 1962, M.A., 1964; Ph.D., U. Wis., 1968. Prof., dir. Am. U., Beirut, 1966-72; pres. Ctr. for Ednl. Research and Devel., Beirut, 1972-76; staff mem., div. chief World Bank, Washington, 1972-82; nat. security adviser to Pres. Lebanon, Beirut, 1982-84; vis. sr. fellow Ctr. for Strategic Studies, Washington, 1984-85; pres. Trans Devel. Corp., Vienna, Va., 1985—; chmn. bd. Digital Medicine, Boston, 1985—; cons. Ford Found., Beirut, 1968-71. Author: Physical Science, 1972; Education Sector Policy, 1980; Efficiency of Education Systems, 1982; Lebanon, The Politics of Revolving Doors, 1985. Co-founder Lebanese Assn. for Advancement Sci., Beirut, 1972; pres. Path of Light Philanthropic Soc., Beirut, 1960-66. Ford Found. grantee U. Wis., 1964-66; AID grantee, Beirut, 1959-62; decorated by Pres. Romania. Fellow AAAS; mem. Am. Ednl. Research Assn. Baptist. Avocations: reading; gardening; travel; drawing. Office: Trans Devel Corp 8230 Boone Blvd Vienna VA 22180

HADDAWAY, JAMES DAVID, insurance executive; b. Louisville, July 25, 1933; s. Charles Montgomery and Viola (Sands) H.; B.S.C., U. Louisville, 1961; M.B.A., Xavier U., 1973; m. Myrna Lou Harris, June 5, 1954; children—Peggy Ann, Robert Marshall, Susan Gayle. Ins. cons. Met. Life Ins., Louisville, 1955-59; supt. Byck Bros. & Co., Louisville, 1959-61; dir. purchasing Liberty Nat. Bank, Louisville, 1961-63; v.p., mgr. gen. services adminstrn. Citizens Fed. Bank, Louisville, 1963-79; asst. v.p., mgr. human resources Ky. Farm Bur. Ins. Co., 1979—; nat. chmn. Personnel Conf. Casualty Ins. Cos., 1983. Founder, chmn. emeritus Kentuckiana Expn. of Bus. and Industry, 1973-85; nat. chmn. Personnel Conf. Casualty Ins. Cos., 1983. Served with U.S. Army, 1953-55. Named Boss of Year, Louisville chpt. Nat. Secs. Assn., 1978, 79. Cert. adminstrv. mgr., cert. purchasing mgr., accredited personnel mgr. Mem. Am. Soc. Personnel Adminstrn. (Western Ky. dist. dir. 1984-85, chmn. regional conf. 1984, v.p. region 9 1985-86), Internat. Adminstrv. Mgmt. Soc. (internat. dir. area 7 1979-81), Adminstrv. Mgmt. Soc. Louisville (pres. 1975-76, dir. 1976—), Adminstrv. Mgmt. Soc. Found. (charter mem. 1980), Purchasing Mgmt. Assn. Louisville (pres. 1969-70), Nat. Assn. Purchasing Mgmt. (dir. nat. affairs 1984-85), Louisville Personnel Assn. (pres. 1983-84), Nat. Eagle Scout Assn., Hon. Order Ky. Cols. Baptist. Clubs: Wally Byam Caravan Internat., Good Sam Recreational Vehicle, Bass Anglers Sportsman Soc., Masons, Shriners. Home: 4015 Wimpole Rd Louisville KY 40218 Office: 120 S Hubbard Ln Louisville KY 40207

HADDEN, ROBERT LEE, librarian; b. Clarksville, Tenn., Sept. 4, 1951; s. William James and Margaret Shumate H.; cert. Europaisches Inst., Bonn, Germany, 1972; B.A., U. N.C., 1973; M.L.S., East Carolina U., 1977; B.S., SUNY, 1982. Salesman, School Bookhouse, Inc., Charlottesville Va., 1973-76; restaurateur Die Hooghuis, Doel aan de Schelde, Belgium, 1974; library intern N.C. State Mus. Natural History, Raleigh, 1976-77; plant librarian Burroughs Wellcome Co., Greenville, N.C., 1977-81; med. librarian King Fahad Hosp., Al Baha, Saudi Arabia, 1981-83; med. library cons. King Khaled Eye Specialist Hosp., Riyadh, Saudi Arabia, 1982-83; indexer Pharm. Tech., Pharm. Tech. Pub. Co., Marina Del Rey, Calif., 1979-81; supervisory librarian USAG Camp Page, Chunchon, Korea and USAG Camp Long, Wonju, Korea, 1984-85; med. librarian USAF Regional Med. Ctr., Clark AFB, Philippines, 1985; engring. systems librarian U.S. Army Ballistic Research Lab., Aberdeen Proving Grounds, Md., 1985—. Mem. Spl. Libraries Assn. (reporter Eastern N.C. 1980—), Med. Library Assn., Middle East Library Assn., Am. Soc. Indexers, N.C. Library Assn., U.S. Chess Fedn., N.C. Wildlife Fedn., Mensa, Royal Asiatic Soc., N.C. On-Line Users Group. Episcopalian. Clubs: Unicorn Computer, N.C. Wildlife Fedn., Pitt County Wildlife, Greenville Chess, N.C. Vols. (1st regiment). Home: 1600 E 6th St Greenville NC 27834 Office: STINFO Ballistic Research Lab Aberdeen Proving Grounds MD 21005

HADDOX, JIMMY VERLON, petroleum geologist, consultant; b. Columbia, La., May 28, 1938; s. Ezra Calvin and Leona Chlotile (Fox) H.; m. Ina Faye Owens, Nov. 25, 1959; children—Lori Gayle, Lana Faye. B.S., Northeastern La. U., 1960; M.S., Miss. State U., 1963. Cert. petroleum geologist, profl. geol. scientist. Exploration geologist Texaco, Inc., Wichita Falls, Tex., 1963-67; exploration and exploitation geologist Sun Oil Co., Beaumont, Tex., 1967; dir. men's housing Northeastern La. U., Monroe, 1967-74, prof. geology, 1974-79, vice-chmn. Geology Found., 1981—; petroleum geologist, cons., West Monroe, La., 1968—; petroleum geologist, founder, pres. Haddox Petroleum Co., West Monroe, 1978—. Chaplain Jaycees, Monroe, 1969-71; co-dir. Miss. La. Pageant, Monroe, 1969-72. Served to 1st lt. U.S. Army, 1960-61. Mem. Am. Petroleum Inst. (pres. Monroe chpt. 1977-78), Am. Assn. Petroleum Geologists, Am. Inst. Prof. Geologists, Ind. Petroleum Assn. Am., La. Assn. Ind. Producers and Royalty Owners, Wildcatter, Shreveport Geol. Soc., West Monroe C. of C. Baptist. Clubs: Northeastern La. U. Booster, Bayou De Siard Country, Pine Hills Country (Calhoun, La.), Highland Park Country (West Monroe, La.). Lodge: Elks. Office: Haddox Petroleum Co Inc 715 Trenton St West Monroe LA 71291

HADEN, CHARLES H., II, judge; b. Morgantown, W.Va., Apr. 16, 1937; s. Charles H. and Beatrice L. (Costolo) H.; B.S., W.Va. U., 1958, J.D., 1961; m. Priscilla Ann Miller, June 2, 1956; children—Charles H., Timothy M., Amy Sue. Partner firm Haden & Haden, Morgantown, W.Va., 1961-69; state tax commr. W.Va., 1969-72; justice Supreme Ct. Appeals of W.Va., 1972-75, chief justice, 1975; judge U.S. Dist. Ct. No. and So. Dists. W.Va., Parkersburg, 1975-82, chief judge So. Dist., 1982—; mem. com. adminstrn. of probation system U.S. Jud. Conf.; mem. W.Va. Ho. of Dels., 1963-64; asst. prof. Coll. Law, W.Va. U., 1967-68. Mem. Bd. of Edn., Monongalia County, W.Va., 1967-68. Mem. W.Va. Bar Assn., Monongalia-Kanawha Counties Bar Assn., W.Va. Jud. Assn. Office: PO Box 1139 Parkersburg WV 26101

HADGOPOULOS, SARALYN DE HAVEN POOLE, educator, author; b. Atlanta, Aug. 31, 1931; d. George Grady Poole and Sarah (Wimberly) Shaw; student Vassar Coll., 1949-51, Sorbonne, Paris, 1951, U. Ga., 1952; B.S., Columbia, 1955; M.A., N.Y. U., 1961; Ph.D., Emory U., 1965; m. Kerim Onder, 1953 (div. 1954); m. William E. Campbell III, 1960 (div. 1960); m. George John Hadgopoulos, Nov. 23, 1963 (div. 1978); 1 son, John George de Haven. Promotion asst. TV Programs Am., N.Y.C., 1955-56; asst. to fashion and beauty editor Am. Weekly Mag., N.Y.C., 1956-57; tchr. Miami Edison Sr. High Sch., Fla., 1958-60; asso. prof. English, Slippery Rock (Pa.) State Coll., 1967-69; asso. prof., lectr. George Washington U. Tidewater Center, Hampton and Norfolk, Va., 1972-79, PACE prof., 1973-75. Author: Poems of North Africa, 1973; Poems of Greece, 1975; The Crystal Mandala, 1976; Imagination's Wine, 1977. Home: 2309 Treasure Island Dr Virginia Beach VA 23455

HADLEY, CHARLES DAVID, JR., political science educator, researcher; b. Springfield, Mass., June 5, 1942; s. Charles David and Caroline Marion (Filip) H.; m. Mary Turner, Feb. 7, 1970 (div. 1980); 1 child, Nathaniel. B.A. in Polit. Sci., U. Mass.-Amherst, 1964, M.A. in Polit. Sci., 1967; Ph.D. in Polit. Sci., U. Conn., 1971. Instr., U. New Orleans, 1970-71, asst. prof., 1971-74, assoc. prof., 1974-86, prof., 1986—, asst. to chmn., dept. polit. sci., 1971-75, coordinator grad. studies, dept. polit. sci., 1975-76, asst. dean Coll. Liberal Arts, 1976-79, dir. internship program dept. polit. sci., campus coordinator City Hall internship program, 1982—; asst. prof. polit. sci. Inst. for Social Inquiry, U. Conn., 1973-74; cons. pub. opinion poll, State Rep. Candidate Vinturella, 1983, Title Research Corp., New Orleans, 1983, Ednl. Testing Service, Princeton, N.J., 1971, Commn. on Human Rights and Opportunities, Conn., 1973; co-investigator report Conn. Bank & Trust Co., 1972. Author: Political Parties and Political Issues: Patterns in Differentiation Since the New Deal, 1973; (with Everett C. Ladd, Jr.) Transformations of the American Party System: Political Coalitions from the New Deal to the 1970s, 1975, 2d edit. 1978; contbr. chpts. to books, articles to pubis.; panelist, speaker profl. confs. in field. Bd. dirs. Irish Channel Neighborhood Assn., 1976-78, 80—, pres. 1983, 84, 85; bd. dirs. Children's Community, 1979-81; room parent John Dibert Elem. Sch., 1981-82, sch. site planning com., 1982-83, organizer Friends of Dibert Library, 1983, mgmt. team, 1983—; mem. alumni admissions council U. Mass., Amherst, 1980—; mem. adv. council and reelection steering com. Rep. Mary Landrieu, 1980—; mem. Neighborhood Council Preservation Resource Ctr., 1981-84; mem. credit com. U. New Orleans Fed. Credit Union, 1982-85; participant leadership forum Met. Area Com., 1984, mem. Met. Area Com., 1985—; bd. dirs. Human Services in Cable, 1985—. NEH younger humanist fellow, 1973; faculty research fellow U. Conn., summer 1972; predoctoral research grantee, U. Conn. Research Found., 1969-70, summer fellow, 1970; summer research tng. grantee U. Conn. to Inter-Univ. Consortium for Polit. Research, 1968. Mem. Am. Polit. Sci. Assn., So. Polit. Sci. Assn. (exec. council 1978-81, rec. sec. 1984—, editorial bd. Politics jour. 1977—), Com. for Party Renewal (exec. com. 1984—), Midwest Polit. Sci. Assn., New Eng. Polit. Sci. Assn., Pi Sigma Alpha. Congregationalist. Home: 3117 Constance St New Orleans LA 70115 Office: Dept Polit Sci U New Orleans New Orleans LA 70148

HADLEY, KATE HILL, geologist; b. N.Y.C., Mar. 24, 1950; d. Arthur Twining II Hadley and Mary (Hill) Hadley Randolph. B.S., MIT, 1971, Ph.D., 1975. Various tech. and supervisory positions with Exxon USA and Exxon Prodn. Research Co., 1975-81, project leader Gulf Coast div. Exxon USA, Houston, 1981-82, planning assoc. hdqrs. exploration, Houston, 1982-84, div. ops. geologist eastern div., New Orleans, 1984—; mem. vis. com. dept. earth, ocean and atmospheric scis. MIT, Cambridge, 1984—; mem. bd. earth scis. Nat. Acad. Scis.; chmn. U.S. Nat. Com. Rock Mechanics, 1981-83. Mem. Am. Assn. Petroleum Geologists, Am. Geophys. Union, Soc. Petroleum Engrs., Internat. Soc. Rock Mechanics, Continental Sci. Drilling Com. Office: Exxon Eastern Div 1555 Poydras PO Box 61812 New Orleans LA 70161

HAEBERLE, FREDERICK ROLAND, petroleum geologist, consultant; b. Phila., Oct. 6, 1919; s. Frederick Edward and Faye Vivian (Davis) H.; m. Cynthia Lee Davis, Feb. 24, 1946; children—Cynthia Faye, Frederick Edward II. B.S., Yale U., 1947, M.S., 1948; M.B.A., Columbia U., 1962. Cert. profl. geol. scientist. Geologist, Standard of Calif., Houston, 1948-52; chief geologist J.J. Lynn, Abilene, Tex., 1952-53; div. mgr. Mayfair Minerals, Abilene, 1953-54; cons. geologist, Abilene, 1954-57; chief subsurface geologist Atlantic Richfield, Caracas, Venezuela, 1957-60; geol. specialist Mobile Oil, Dallas, 1962-83; cons. geologist, Dallas, 1983—; asst. prof. U. Houston, 1948-50; prof. McMurray Coll., Abilene, Tex., 1954-57. Contbr. articles to profl. jours. Mem. Rep. Presdl. Task Force, Washington, 1984-85; mem. Nat. Rep. Senatorial Com., Washington, 1984-85. Served to 1st lt. U.S. Army, 1941-46, PTO. Fellow Geol. Soc. Am.; mem. Am. Assn. Petroleum Geologists, Soc. Profl. Well Log Analysts, Assn. Profl. Geol. Scientists, Dallas Geol. Soc. Presbyterian. Clubs: Brook Haven Country, Lancers (Dallas); U.S. Senatorial (Washington). Lodge: Rotary. Home: 4036 Northview Ln Dallas TX 75229 Office: 4036 Northview Ln Dallas TX 75229

HAEBERLE, GLENN FREDERICK, physician; b. Ashland, Ky., Nov. 6, 1949; s. Clarence Irwin and Geraldine Girard (Bible) H.; m. Sally Ann Demling, July 6, 1974; children—Elizabeth Ann, Grant Field. B.S., U. Ky., 1971; M.D., U. Louisville, 1975. Intern, then resident obstetrics and gynecology Meml. Med. Ctr., Savannah, Ga., 1975-79; pvt. practice ob-gyn, Ashland, Ky., 1979—; chief gynecology Our Lady of Bellefonts Hosp., Russell, Ky., 1983—; chief ob-gyn. Kings Daus. Hosp., Ashland, Ky., 1982—. Mem. AMA, Ky. Med. Assn., Boyd County Med. Soc. Democrat. Methodist. Home: 8 Farmers Ln Ashland KY 41101 Office: 3300 13th St Ashland KY 41101

HAEUSSLER, ALFRED HENRICH KARL, engineer; b. Vaihinger-enz, Germany, June 28, 1921; came to U.S., 1953, naturalized, 1958; s. Eduard Sixth and Elise Maria (Haushild) H.; student Gewerbeschule Vaihingen-enz, Stuttgart, Germany, 1936-39; diploma Metal Fabrication Inst., Rockford Coll., 1968; m. Christine Möller, June 24, 1955; children—Theodor, Gerd, Esther, Rebeccah, Deborah, Judith, Thomas. With aircraft engring. div. Ford Motor Co., 1953-56, Vernon All Steel Press Co., 1954, Am. Machining Co., Oak Lawn, Ill., 1956-59, Ingersoll Products div. Borg Warner Corp., Chgo., 1960-69, Lenard Baritz Handy Button Machining Co., Chgo., 1969-77, David S. Varon Crown Metal Mfg. Co., Chgo., 1977-78; chief tool engr. Friedrich Group, San Antonio, 1978-83, chmn. bd. apprenticeship program; engr. Al Zamil Refrigeration Industries, Damman, Saudi Arabia, 1982-83; chief engr. Crown Metal Western Calif., 1983-84; instr. indsl. start-up Tex. Edn. Agy. Served with German Mil. Forces, Africa, 1939-43. Mem. Am. Def. Preparedness Assn. Lutheran. Inventor press and wire feeder; pub. tool engring. ideas. Home and Office: 1821 Crystal Springs Bend New Braunfels TX 78130

HAFELY, MARGARET RUTH, columnist; b. Noranda, Quebec, Can., May 17, 1939; came to U.S., 1977; naturalized, 1982; d. Frederick Ratcliffe and Doris Pearl (Kindree) Archibald; m. Douglas Barney Laffey, Oct. 28, 1967 (dec. 1972); m. Richard Warren Hafely Jan. 3, 1978 (div. 1980); children—Patrick Douglas, Aliza Lynn. Student Royal Conservatory Music, Toronto, Ont., Can., 1952-57, U. Toronto, 1960-62, Edison Coll., 1981-82; honor grad. North Toronto Coll., 1954-59. Florist Eunice Denby Flowers, Toronto, 1960-61; cons. Merle Norman Cosmetics, Naples, Fla., 1980-82; columnist Naples Daily News, Fla., 1982—. Mem. Nat. Rep. Congressional Com., D.C., 1980—, Am. Security Council Found., Washington, 1980—; dir. Naples Council World Affairs, 1984—. Recipient Cert. Recognition award Nat. Rep. Congressional Com., 1981-85. Presbyterian. Club: Naples Womens. Avocations: gardening; swimming; skating; composing music. Office: Naples Daily News 1075 Central Ave Naples FL 33940

HAFF, RODERICK CANAVAN, surgeon; b. Panama, Canal Zone, July 10, 1936; s. Alexander O. and Blanche (Canavan) H.; B.A., Yale U., 1958, M.D., 1962; m. Veronica Ling, June 2, 1962; children—Alexander, Christopher S., William O. Intern Barnes Hosp., St. Louis, 1962, asst. resident in surgery, 1962-69, resident in surgery, 1969-70; practice medicine specializing in surgery, 1970—; commd. capt. U.S. Air Force, 1962, advanced through grades to col., 1977; asst. surgeon USAF Hosp., March AFB, Calif., 1964-66; surgeon USAF Hosp., Clark AFB, Philippines, 1970-72, chief of gen. surgery, 1971-72; comdr. 657th Tactical Hosp., Clark AFB, 1970-72; staff surgeon Wilford Hall USAF Med. Center, Lackland AFB, Tex., 1972-77, asst. chief of gen. surgery service, 1972-77; clin. asst. prof. surgery U. Tex. Health Center, San Antonio, 1972-77. Vestryman St. Thomas Episcopal Ch., San Antonio, 1974-76, 80-81, sr. warden, 1976. Diplomate Am. Bd. Surgery. Fellow A.C.S.; mem. Soc. Surgery of Alimentary Tract, Tex. Surg. Soc., San Antonio Surg. Soc., Southwestern Surg. Congress, Alpha Omega Alpha. Contbr. articles in field to profl. jours. Home: 15060 Cadillac Dr San Antonio TX 78248 Office: 8601 Village Dr San Antonio TX 78217

HAFFNER, GEORGE LESLIE, optometrist; b. Pittsfield, Mass., Oct. 8, 1932; s. Harold Richard and Maude (Barnum) H.; A.A., U. Fla., 1953; B.S., So. Coll. Optometry, 1958, O.D., 1958; m. Marjorie Newsom, Dec. 30, 1956; children—Marjorie Gail Mabry, April Charlene, Kimberlee Anne, George Leslie. Practice optometry, Tampa, Fla., 1959—. Dir. Mineral Resources, Inc. Sec., dir. Vision Care, Inc. of Fla., 1969-75; mem. Fla. Health Manpower Council, 1969-74; mem. profl. staff Easter Seal Soc. Crippled Children, 1967-69; mem. adv. staff optometric assistance course Hillsborough County Sch. System, 1971-76, 82—. Chmn. optometry div. United Fund, 1966, 70—; mem. Pres.'s council Fla. So. Coll. Trustee Hillsborough Vision Care Found., 1964—, Fla. Kiwanis Found., 1974-76; mem. Gallon Club, S.W. Fla. Blood Bank, 1972—. Served to capt. AUS, 1954-56. Recipient Disting. Service award Key Club Internat., 1967, Outstanding Service certificates and awards Greater Tampa Lions Sight Fund, Inc., 1961—. Fellow Am. Acad. Optometry, Coll. Syntonic Optometry (pres. 1980—); mem. Am. (chmn. career guidance com. 1972-74, 75-76, chmn. com. assistance to grads. and undergrads. 1977-80, Outstanding Service pin 1970; manpower and new acad. project team 1979-82, chmn. AOA Trust/OPIC Program 1979-81; Optometric Recognition award 1980-86; regional cons. 1981-83), Fla. (trustee 1971-73, chmn. career guidance 1965-74, sec.-treas. 1973-74, pres. 1976-77, chmn. new acad. facilities com. 1977-84, mem. Profl. Standard Rev. Orgn., 1980-81; Optometrist of Yr., 1980-81) optometric assns., Hillsborough Soc. Optometrists (pres. 1964-66; Optometrist of Yr. 1980-81), So. Council Optometrists (trustee 1976-77), Acad. Corrective Optometry. Democrat. Methodist (dist. lay leader Fla. Conf. 1985—). Lodges: Masons (32 deg., Shriner), Kiwanis (lt. gov. Div. 8 Fla. dist. 1973-74; trustee Fla. dist. Kiwanis Internat. 1973-74). Home: 408 Lakewood Ave Tampa FL 33612 Office: 4515 S Manhattan Ave Tampa FL 33611

HAGAMAN, LEN DOUGHTON, JR., city official; b. Boone, N.C., Aug. 17, 1950; s. Len Doughton and Louise Virginia (Kirkman) H.; m. Ruth Love Klutz, Mar. 25, 1972; children—Len D. III, Daniel Christopher. A.A., Wingate Coll., 1970; B.S., Appalachian State U., 1978, M.A., 1983, Ed.S., 1985. Dir. funeral services Reins Sturdivant Mortuary, Boone, 1973-75; police adminstr. Town of Boone, 1975-82, city mgr., 1982—; instr. criminal justice Appalachian State U., Boone, 1982-84, instr. pub. adminstrn., 1984—. Chmn. Watauga County Comm., Boone, 1983, vice chmn., 1982, commr., 1976-82; bd. dirs. Appalachian Health Dept., Boone, 1979—. Recipient Disting. Service award Jaycees 1984. Mem. Internat. City Mgrs. Assn., N.C. Mcpl. Clks. Assn., Boone C. of C. (bd. dirs.). Democrat. Baptist. Lodge: Masons. Avocations: private pilot; underwater diving. Home: PO Box 1625 Boone NC 28607 Office: Town of Boone Drawer 192 Boone NC 28607

HAGAN, SHIRLEY SMITH, medical technologist; b. Sherman, Tex., Apr. 20, 1936; d. J.B. and Frances Winnifred (Groce) Smith; diploma med. tech., Parkland Meml. Hosp., Dallas, 1961; B.S., Southeastern Okla. State U., 1977; M.S., Tex. Woman's U., 1981; m. George Philip Hagan, Apr. 16, 1954; children—Phillip Ray, Stephen Russell. Med. technologist hosps. in Tex., 1956-75; instr. med. lab. tech. Grayson County Coll., Denison, Tex., 1974—. Mem. Am. Soc. Clin. Pathologists (assoc.), Am. Soc. Med. Technologists, Tex. Soc. Med. Technologists, Tex. Jr. Coll. Tchrs. Assn. Baptist. Home: PO Box 684 Sherman TX 75090 Office: 6101 Grayson Dr Denison TX 75020

HAGAN, WALLACE WOODROW, geologist, consultant; b. Griggsville, Ill., Feb. 3, 1913; s. Warren Lynn and Mabel Rea (Bruner) H.; m. Mary Elizabeth Levan, Nov. 30, 1940; children—Karen Hagan Wade, Elizabeth Annette. B.S., U. Ill., 1935, M.S., 1936, Ph.D., 1942. Cert. profl. geologist, Ind. Asst. geologist J.V. Wicklund Devel. Co., Detroit, 1937-39; cons. geologist Greenville, Ky. and Urbana, Ill., 1939-40; geologist in charge ground water sect. div. geology dept. conservation State of Ind. Indpls., 1942-44; geologist Sohio Petroleum Co., Owensboro, Ky., 1945-48, Felmont Oil Corp., Owensboro, 1948-52; cons. geologist, Owensboro, 1952-58; dir., state geologist Ky. Geol. Survey, U. Ky., Lexington, 1958-78; Ky. state geologist emeritus, 1978; cons. geologist, Lexington, 1978—; mem. Ky. Geol. Survey Adv. Bd., 1952-58, 78—, ex-officio mem., 1958-78, Recipient John Wesley Powell award U.S. Geol. Survey, Dept. Interior, 1972; Disting. Service award Ky. Oil and Gas Assn., 1978; Disting. Scientist award Ky. Acad. Sci., 1977. Fellow Geol. Soc. Am.; mem. Am. Inst. Profl. Geologists (sect. pres. 1982-83), Am. Assn. Petroleum Geologists (del. 1984-86; Pub. Service award 1982), Geol. Soc. Ky. (hon. life), Ind.-Ky. Geol. Soc. (hon. life), Ky. Acad. Sci., Am. Assn. State Geologists (hon.), Phi Beta Kappa, Sigma Xi, Sigma Gamma Epsilon, Phi Kappa Phi. Republican. Methodist. Club: Rotary. Contbr. articles to oil and gas jours. Home: 317 Jesselin Dr Lexington KY 40503

HAGAN, WILLIS COBB, JR., aircraft company executive; b. Birmingham, Ala., Sept. 19, 1925; s. Willis Cobb and Elizabeth (Gueard) H.; student Howard Coll., 1946; LL.B., U. Ala., 1950; m. Jane Jeffers, Apr. 25, 1952; children—Jane Jeffers, Willis Cobb. With Hayes Internat. Corp., Birmingham, Ala., 1951—, corp. sec., 1957-64, v.p. orgn., systems and indsl. relations, 1964-67, v.p. mfg., 1967, exec. v.p., 1967-69, pres., chief exec. officer, 1969—; dir. Guaranty Savs. & Loan Assn., Hayes Internat. Corp. Served with USAAF, 1943-45. Mem. Assoc. Industries Ala., Air Force Assn., U.S. C. of C., Nat. Aerospace Services Assn., Ala. Bar Assn., Birmingham Bar Assn., Ala. Zool. Soc., Ala. C. of C., Birmingham C. of C. Episcopalian. Clubs: Birmingham Country, Downtown, The Club, Relay House, Mountain Brook Country, SAR. Home: 2916 Pump House Rd Birmingham AL 35243 Office: PO Box 2287 Birmingham AL 35201

HAGEMEYER, RICHARD HERMAN, college president; b. Toledo, Dec. 15, 1917; B.S., Bowling Green State U., 1939; M.A., U. Mich., 1951; Ed.D., Wayne State U., 1961; m. Janet Stump, Aug. 10, 1940 (dec. May 1982); children—Richard Herman, Carol Jean; m. Virginia Bates; June 24, 1983; stepchildren: Richard Bates, Beth Bates Root, Robert Bates. Tchr., Waterville (Ohio) High Sch., 1939-41, Fordson High Sch., Dearborn, Mich., 1946-52, Wayne State U., Detroit, 1958-60; coordinator related instrn. div. Henry Ford Community Coll., Dearborn, Mich., 1952-62; asst. supt. Charlotte (N.C.) Mecklenburg Schs., 1962-63; pres. Central Piedmont Community Coll., Charlotte, 1963—; dir. So. Nat. Bank N.C., Charlotte Mem. adv. council N.C. Bd. Edn., 1967—. N.C. Joint Com. Dental Edn., 1969-72; cons. Nat. Apprenticeship Adv. Council, 1951-52; mem. profl. adv. bd. Bus. Council for Effective Literacy, 1984. Bd. dirs. Nat. Lab. Higher Edn., Charlotte Symphony; bd. advisers Johnson C. Smith U.; bd. visitors Community Coll. of the Air Force. Served with USAAF, 1941-46. Recipient Meritorious Service award U.S. Dept. Labor, 1962, Alumni Community award Bowling Green State U., 1975. Danforth Fund grantee, 1972. Mem. Am. Council on Edn. (dir. 1977-80, mem. commn. higher edn. and adult learner 1981—), Am. Assn. Community and Jr. Colls. (commn. curriculum 1968-71, commn. adminstrn. 1970-72, bd. dirs. 1974—, chmn. bd. 1976-77), N.C. (pres. 1966-68), So. (exec. com. 1971-73, pres. 1972-73) assns. jr. colls., League for Innovation in Community Coll. (bd. dirs. 1969—, pres. 1976-77), Charlotte C. of C. (bd. dirs. 1968-71, 74—), Sigma Alpha Epsilon, Phi Delta Kappa. Lodge: Rotary (bd. dirs. Charlotte 1970—). Home: 3201 Landerwood Dr Charlotte NC 28210

HAGEN, ROBERT PETER, management consultant, writer; b. Bismarck, N.D., Jan. 23, 1915; s. Melvin G. and Marguerite A. (Bannerman) H.; m. Jeanne Bonnet Powell, Sept. 14, 1943; children—R. Peter, Jr., Charles M. B.S., N.D. State U., 1936; M.A., U. Va., 1949; cert., Commn. and General State Coll., 1946, Army War Coll., 1954. Lt. U.S. Army, 1936, advanced through grades to col., 1966; mgr. personnel and adminstrn. Koppers Co., Inc., Pitts., 1966-81; ptnr. DFH & Assocs., Pitts., 1968-81; mng. ptnr. Hagen Assocs., Alexandria, Va., 1981—; mem. adv. bd. Robert Morris Coll., Pitts., 1976-78; counsellor SBA, Washington, 1983—. Author: The Place of the Schools in National Defense, 1949; contbr. articles to profl. jours. Com. chmn. European council Boy Scouts of Am., Naples, Italy, 1958-60, Mo. Valley council, 1960-63 group leader Nat. Alliance of Businessman, Pitts., 1966-68. Decorated Silver Star, Legions of Merit (2), Bronze Stars (2); recipient Service award Boy Scouts Am., 1962. Mem. Am. Soc. for Tng. and Devel. (life), Service Corps of Ret. Execs., Ret. Officers Assn. Clubs: Officers, Army Navy Country (Washington). Lodge: Masons. Avocations: gardening; travel; golf; music.

HAGENDOORN, WILLEM JACOB, mechanical engineer; b. Rotterdam, Netherlands, July 13, 1932; s. Jan and Adriana (Boender) H.; came to U.S., 1957, naturalized, 1965; Mech. Engr., U. Delft (Netherlands), 1953; B.A., U. Louisville, 1965, postgrad., 1965-68; m. Barbara Jo Chaddic, Sept. 30, 1972; children—Tanja, Michelle, Lee; stepchildren—Rob and Robin RoBards. Research and devel. engr. Am. Air Filter, Inc., 1957-65; design engr. Gen. Electric Co., Louisville, 1965-68; mgr. engring. and sales Fisher-Klosterman Inc., dust control and pneumatic conveying, Louisville, 1968-79; pres., chmn. bd. Air Action Systems Internat., Inc., Louisville, 1979—; dir. Packaging Services Corp., Inc., Louisville. Served to 1st lt. Dutch Army, 1953-56. Registered profl. engr., Ky., Miss., Ind. Patentee in field. Home: 1219 Constitution Dr Louisville KY 40214 Office: PO Box 34383 Louisville KY 40232

HAGENDORF, STANLEY, lawyer, writer; b. Bklyn., Mar. 1, 1930; s. David and Fanny (Hammer) H.; m. Tilbeth Greene, Nov. 18, 1962; children—Lauren, Wayne, Richard. B.S. in Econs., U. Pa., 1953; M.D. cum laude, Harvard U., 1956; LL.M. in Taxation, NYU, 1961. Bar: N.Y. 1956, Fla. 1975; cert. tax atty., Fla. Assoc., Hellerstein, Rosier & Brudney, N.Y.C., 1957-59; sole practice, N.Y.C., 1960-70; ptnr. Karow & Hagendorf, N.Y.C., 1970-75, Hagendorf & Schlesinger, N.Y.C. and Coral Gables, Fla., 1975-83, Hagendorf, Deason & Frank, N.Y.C. and Tampa, 1984; sole practice, 1985—; assoc. prof. U. Miami Law Sch., Coral Gables, 1975-80; dir.-lectr. Hagendorf-Chaykin Tax Workshop, N.Y.C., 1973—; mem. adv. bd. Fin. and Estate Planning, pub. Commerce Clearing House, Chgo., 1981—. Author: Tax Guide for Buying and Selling a Business, 6th edit., 1985; Tax Manual for Corporate Liquidations, Redemptions and Estate Planning Recapitalizations, 1978; Liquidations, Redemptions and Recapitalizations: Taxation and Planning, 1986; contbr. articles to profl.

jours. and mags. Served with U.S. Army, 1948-51. Recipient Disting. Lectr. award Nat. Soc. Pub. Accts., 1980; cert. of appreciation N.Y. County Lawyers Assn., 1982. Mem. ABA, N.Y. State Bar Assn., Fla. Bar Assn. Office: 1000 Century Park Dr Suite 301 Tampa FL 33607

HAGERMAN, JOHN DAVID, lawyer; b. Houston, Aug. 1, 1941; s. David Angle and Noima (Clay) H.; m. Linda L. Lambright, Aug. 26, 1947; children—Clayton Robert, Holly Elizabeth. B.B.A., So. Meth. U., 1963; J.D., U. Tex., Austin, 1966. Bar: Tex. 1966, U.S. Dist. Ct. (so. dist.) Tex. 1967, U.S. Ct. Appeals (5th cir.) 1967, U.S. Supreme Ct. 1969. Ptnr. firm, Spring, Tex., 1967—; condr. legal econs. seminars. Res. dep. sheriff, Montgomery County, Tex. Mem. ABA, Tex. Bar Assn., Houston Bar Assn., Gulf Coast Family Law Specialists Assn., Gen. Civil Trial Specialists Assn. Club: Petroleum (Houston). Contbr. articles to legal jours. Office: 24800 Interstate 45 Spring TX 77373

HAGERTY, HARVE JOHN, adult corrections consultant, educator; b. New Orleans, Feb. 18, 1934; s. Vaughn Clifton and Wilhelmina (Wettstein) Hagerty Bilbo; m. Elizabeth Anne Garner, Oct. 10, 1959; children—Harve J., Vaughn C., Michael. B.S., U. Southern Miss., 1959; M.A., U. Okla., 1975. Director classification Okla. State Penitentiary, McAlester, 1976-77; project supr. Ex-Offender Placement Service, San Antonio, 1977-80; project dir. Kerper House, San Antonio, 1980-82; instr. Tex. A&M U., San Antonio, 1982—. Bd. dirs. Valley Forge Homeowners Assn., San Antonio, 1981—; adv. bd. Vista, 1985. Served to lt. col. U.S. Army, 1954-76. Decorated Bronze Star. Mem. Am. Correctional Assn., Tex. Correctional Assn., Retired Officer's Assn. Republican. Lodges: Lions, Shriners. Avocations: writing for profl. jours.; public speaking; community affairs.

HAGES, RICHARD JOSEPH, JR., chiropractor; b. Bay City, Mich., Nov. 5, 1954; s. Richard Joseph and Donna Lou (Cripps) H.; m. Cheryl Ann Wahlen, Nov. 20, 1981; 1 dau., Nicole Marie. D.Chiropractic, Palmer Coll., 1975; postgrad. U. New Orleans, 1975-78, Nat. Coll. Chiropractic, 1978-81. Diplomate Nat. Bd. Chiropractic Examiners. Staff doctor Causeway Clinic, Metairie, La., 1975-77, Baker Clinic, Baton Rouge, 1977-78; owner, clinic dir. David Drive Chiropractic Clinic, Metairie, 1978—; chiropractic cons. La. Ins. and Legal Professions, 1978-83. Tng. dir. City of Kenner Civil Def., 1983. Recipient Clin. Excellence award Palmer Coll., 1975. Mem. Am. Chiropractic Assn. (mem. council on sports injuries), Sacrooccipital Soc. Internat., Parker Chiropractic Research Soc., Chiropractic Assn. La. (bd. dirs. 1983-84, appreciation award 1978, 84, sec.-treas. 1985-86), Motion Palpation Inst., Palmer Coll. Alumni Assn. Clubs: New Orleans Scuba Diving; Sierra. Office: 2614 David Dr Metairie LA 70003

HAGGARD, CARL DOUGLAS, lawyer; b. May 13, 1948; m. Charlene Cusimano; children—Stephanie, Peter, Jarrett. B.A., U. Houston, 1970; J.D., South Tex. Coll. Law, 1973. Bar: Tex. 1973, U.S. Dist. Ct. (ea. dist.) Tex. 1985, U.S. Dist. Ct. (we., no. and so. dists.) Tex. 1985, U.S. Ct. Appeals (5th cir.) 1985. Law clk. Nations, Cross & Delhomme, 1972-73; sole practice Brazoria, Ft. Bend, Galveston, Harris Counties, Tex., 1973-76; prosecutor, chief prosecutor Harris County Dist. Atty.'s Office, 1976-84; mem. legal dept. Phillips Petroleum Co., Houston, 1984—; part-time prof. law Abiline Christian Coll., Houston, 1973-75, U. Houston, 1974-75, 79, U. Houston Bates Coll. Law, 1980-82. Named Outstanding Young Man, Jaycee's, 1980. Avocation: scuba diving (instr. and leader of expeditions). Home: 7702 Candlegreen Ln Houston TX 77071 Office: Phillips Petroleum Co Legal Dept PO Box 1967 Houston TX 77001

HAGGART, ROBERT IRA, real estate executive; b. Sulphur, La., Mar. 17, 1930; s. Burns Archie and Allie (Baker) H.; B.A., Centenary Coll. La., 1951; postgrad. So. Meth. U., 1951-52; m. Vivian Janell Spear, July 8, 1951; children—Robert David, Duncan Kent. Vice pres. Holly Corp., Dallas and Azusa, Calif., 1959-62; asst. to pres. Daga Co., Dallas, 1962-65; various positions to sr. v.p. and treas. Centex Corp., Dallas, 1965-79; sr. exec. v.p. Southland Real Estate Resources, Inc., Dallas, 1979—; pres. Southland Investment Properties, Inc., 1982—. Bd. trustees C.C. Young Home, 1975-83, sec. bd., 1980-82; bd. dirs. Dallas Theater Ctr., 1982—, Meth. Retirement Homes Tex., Inc., 1983—. Served with USAF, 1952-59. Republican. Methodist. Home: 4555 Lorraine Ave Dallas TX 75205 Office: 5215 N O'Connor Blvd Suite 1400 Irving TX 75062

HAGLER, JOHN CARROLL, III, metals fabricating company executive; b. Augusta, Ga., Feb. 14, 1923; s. John Carroll and Susan (Barrett) H.; m. Mary Anne Tyler, Oct. 16, 1948; children—Mary Anne, John Carroll, Richard Belton, Katharine Waterman, Elizabeth Tyler. B.S., U. Ga., 1946. Chmn. bd. Ga. Iron Works Co., 1947—; pres., chief exec. officer GIW Engineered Systems; chmn. bd. GIW Industries, Inc., 1965—; pres., treas. Winfield Hills, Inc., Augusta, 1967—; dir. First Columbia Savs. & Loan Assn., FCS Fin. Corp., Thompson Design Group, Inc., Thompson Woodworks, Inc. Pres., Ga. Trust Hist. Preservation; mem. Augusta Aviation Commn., 1962—; trustee Hist. Augusta, Inc., pres., 1971-74, now mem. exec. com.; pres. Richmond County Hist. Soc.; bd. dirs. St. Joseph Hosp., Augusta-Richmond County Mus., Augusta Coll. Found., Med. Coll. Ga. Found., Augusta/Richmond County Cancer Soc.; mem. pres.'s club and pres.'s adv. council Med. Coll. Ga.; bd. dirs. Jr. Achievement Augusta. Served as pilot USAAF, World War II. Named Alumnus of Yr., Augusta Coll., 1982. Mem. Nat. Foundry Assn. (dir.), Am. Foundrymen's Soc., Steel Founders Soc., AIME, ASTM, Am. Soc. Metals, NAM, Aircraft Owners and Pilots Assn., Quiet Birdmen, Sigma Alpha Epsilon. Roman Catholic. Clubs: Silver Wings; Ducks Unltd. (area chmn. 1971), Augusta Country; Pinnacle (Augusta). Home: 999 Highland Ave Augusta GA 30904 Office: PO Box 626 Grovetown GA 30813

HAGLER, MARY ANNE TYLER, physician; b. Nashville, Jan. 30, 1927; d. John Luck and Edythe (Belton) Tyler; B.S., U. Ga., 1947, postgrad. Sch. Medicine, 1947-48; M.D., Med. Coll. Ga., 1975; m. John Carroll Hagler, III, Oct. 16, 1948; children—Mary Anne (Mrs. Peter J. Roberts), John Carroll IV, Richard B., Katharine W. (Mrs. K.H. Burnham), Elizabeth T. Family practice resident Med. Coll. Ga., Augusta, 1975-78; med. dir. St. Joseph Hosp. Home Health Care and Hospice, Augusta, 1978-81; med. staff St. Joseph Hosp., Univ. Hosp., Doctors Hosp. of Augusta. Diplomate Am. Bd. Family Practice. Fellow Am. Acad. Family Physicians; mem. AMA, Med. Assn. Ga., Richmond County Med. Soc., Ga. Acad. Family Physicians, Am. Geriatrics Soc., Historic Augusta, Inc., Ga. Trust for Hist. Preservation, Jr. League of Augusta, Nat. Soc. Colonial Dames Am. in State of Ga. Roman Catholic. Clubs: Augusta Country, Pinnacle. Home: 999 Highland Ave Augusta GA 30904

HAGLER, THOMAS EVANS, school system administrator; b. Buena Vista, Ga., Dec. 19, 1941; s. Edward and Lillie Hagler; m. Judy Roberts; 1 child, Jill. B.A. in Edn., U. Fla., 1968, M.Ed., 1969, Ed.S., 1970, Ph.D., 1975. Supt. Grant County Pub. Schs., Dry Ridge, Ky., Bibb County Pub. Schs., Macon, Ga., 1981—. Served with USMC, 1960-66. Mem. Am. Assn. Sch. Adminstrs., Ga. Assn. Ednl. Leaders, Ga. Assn. Sch. Supts., Macon C. of C., Phi Delta Kappa. Democrat. Methodist. Lodge: Rotary. Office: PO Box 247 Macon GA 31298

HAGOOD, MARK REGENALD, insurance agency owner, consultant, publisher; b. Houston, Mar. 18, 1943; s. Marvin M. and Mary Martha (Fuller) H.; m. Ramona Anne Castille, Dec. 29, 1979; children—Mark S., Timothy M., Ronnie M., Mark A., Crystal D., Christopher M. B.B.A., U. Tex.-Austin, 1968. Cons., gen. agt. Ins. Unltd. of Tex., Austin, 1970—; cons., gen. agt. Ins. Service Bus., 1983—; pres. Mark VI Publishers, Austin, 1979—. Author: The Family Information & Survivor's Handbook, 1980; inventor Hol-E-Board game, 1982. Served with M.P., U.S. Army, 1960-66; Vietnam. Lodges: Shriners, Scottish Rite, Masons. Home: PO Box 26681 Austin TX 78755 Office: 4307 S 1st St Austin TX 78745

HAHN, LOUISE O'CONNOR, psychotherapist; b. Astoria, N.Y., June 26, 1941; d. Daniel Francis and Louise (Kolarik) O'Connor; B.A. in Psychology, Coll. New Rochelle (N.Y.), 1963; M.A. in Counseling, Appalachian State U., Boone, N.C., 1976; m. Robert A. Hahn, July 8, 1967; children—Pamela Patricia, Jennifer Kathleen. Pre-kindergarten tchr. N.Y.C. Bd. Edn., 1967; elem. sch. music tchr. Okaloosa County (Fla.) Bd. Edn., 1970-71; adult basic edn. tchr. Wilkes Community Coll., Wilkesboro, N.C., 1973-75; staff therapist New River Mental Health Center, Wilkesboro, 1976-78; founder, 1978, since dir. Counseling Assos., Wilkesboro; registrar Rutledge Jr. Coll., Greensboro, N.C., 1980-81; dir. Guilford County Alcohol Info. Center, Greensboro, 1981-83; program coordinator Office of Continuing Edn., U. N.C.-Greensboro, 1983-85; asst. dean for spl. programs Rockingham Community Coll., Wentworth, N.C., 1985—. Mem. Am. Assn. Humanistic Edn. and Devel., Am. Assn. Women in Community and Jr. Colls., Am. Assn. Counseling and Devel., AAUW, N.C. Community Coll. Adult Edn. Assn., Club: Toastmasters. Home: 3005-B Patriot Ct Greensboro NC 27408

HAHN, THOMAS MARSHALL, JR., forest products company executive; b. Lexington, Ky., Dec. 2, 1926; s. Thomas Marshall and Mary Elizabeth (Boston) H.; m. Margaret Louise Lee, Dec. 27, 1948; children—Elizabeth Hahn McKelvey, Anne Hahn Clarke. B.S. in Physics, U. Ky., 1945; Ph.D., MIT, 1950; LL.D. (hon.), Seton Hall U., 1976. Physicist, U.S. Naval Ordnance Lab., 1946-47; research asst. MIT, 1947-50; assoc. prof. physics U. Ky., 1950-52, prof., 1952-54; prof., head dept. physics Va. Poly. Inst. and State U., 1954-59, pres. 1962-75; dean arts and scis. Kans. State U., 1959-62; exec. v.p. Ga.-Pacific Corp., 1975-76, pres., 1976-85, chief operating officer, 1982-83, chief exec. officer, 1983—, chmn., 1984—, also dir.; dir. Trust Co. Ga., Norfolk So. Corp.; mem. Nat. Sci. Bd., 1972-78; pres. So. Assn. State Univs. and Land-Grant Colls., 1965-66 mem. exec. com. So. Regional Edn. Bd., 1972-74. Bd. dirs. Keep Am. Beautiful, Inc.; chmn. Va. Met. Areas Study Commn., 1966-68; bd. dirs. Salvation Army, 1972—Atlanta Arts Alliance, Central Atlanta Progress; trustee Emory U.; bd. visitors Air U., 1966-69; chmn. Va. Cancer Crusade, 1972; mem. Nat. Capitol and Va. div. adv. bd. Salvation Army, 1972-74, chmn. capital funds campaign Atlanta Area Services for Blind, 1984; state chmn. U.S. Savs. Bonds Programs, 1985; campaign chmn. Ga. chpt. Am. Diabetes Assn., 1985. Served with USN, 1945-46. Recipient Outstanding Citizen award State of Va., 1966; award for outstanding profl. contbns. Va Citizens Planning Assn., 1970, Corp. Leadership award MIT, 1976. Fellow Am. Phys. Soc.; mem. Am. Paper Inst. (dir., chmn. 1982-83), Chem. Mfrs. Assn. (dir.), Atlanta C. of C. (dir.), Phi Beta Kappa, Sigma Xi, Omicron Delta Kappa, Sigma Pi Sigma, Pi Mu Epsilon. Republican. Methodist. Clubs: Piedmont Driving, Links, Shenandoah, Capital City. Office: Georgia Pacific Corp 133 Peachtree St NE Atlanta GA 30303

HAHN, WILLIAM JEFFREY, manufacturing company executive, real estate agent; b. Amsterdam, N.Y., June 28, 1947; s. William Warner and Shirley Hahn; m. Bonnie Joyce Roberts, Apr. 27, 1985. B.B.A., Moravian Coll., 1970; M.S. in Mgmt., Frostburg State Coll., 1972. Quality control group leader Kelly-Springfield, Cumberland, Md., 1972-75; quality control engr. Union Camp Corp., Savannah, Ga., 1975-76, tng. mgr., 1976-77, wood and yard auto maintenance supt., 1978-81, mech. maintenance supt., 1982-85, mfg. mgr., 1986—. Bd. dirs. Leadership Savannah, 1978-82. Mem. Paper Industry Mgmt. Assn., Tech. Assn. Pulp and Paper Industry. Republican. Methodist. Club: Hamilton Ridge (bd. dirs. 1979-80). Avocations: hunting; fishing; sports; reading. Home: Lady Helen Ct Fayetteville GA 30214 Office: Union Camp Corp 5115 Pinetree St Forest Park GA 30050

HAILEY, EVELYN MOMSEN, former state senator; b. St. Paul, Apr. 12, 1921; m. Robert Hailey. Student George Washington U., U. Hawaii. Mem. Va. Ho. of Dels., 1974-82; mem. Va. Senate, 1982-84. Mem. Va. Congress of PTAs (life), Tidewater YWCA; trustee Chesapeake Bay Found.; mem. adv. com. Citizen's Program for the Chesapeake Bay. Mem. LWV. Democrat. Methodist.

HAIMBAUGH, GEORGE DOW, JR., law educator, lawyer; b. Rochester, Ind., Nov. 21, 1916; s. George Dow and Agnes Elizabeth (Sharp) H.; m. Katharine Louise Draper, Aug. 20, 1960. A.B., DePauw U., 1938; postgrad. Georgetown U., 1938-40; J.D., Northwestern U., 1952; J.S.D., Yale U., 1962. Bar: Ill. 1953; S.C. 1973; U.S. Dist. Ct. (no. dist.) Ohio 1962, U.S. Supreme Ct. 1969. Asst. prof. U. Akron Coll. Law, 1960-63; spl. master U.S. Dist. Ct. (no. dist.) Ohio 1962-63; assoc. prof. law U. S.C., 1963-70, prof., 1970—, David W. Robinson prof. law, 1979—; mem. adv. bd. Nat. Inst. Justice, 1982-85; assoc. U. S.C. Inst. Internat. Studies, 1967—, Belle W. Baruch Inst. for Marine Biology and Coastal Research, 1978—; mem. adv. council Byrnes Internat. Ctr., U. S.C. Mem. Ga.-S.C. Boundary Commn., 1978—; deacon First Presbyterian Ch., Columbia, S.C. Served to maj. USMC, 1940-46. Mem. Am. Law Inst., ABA (chmn. adv. com. to standing com. on law and nat. security 1979-82), S.C. Bar Assn., Richland County Bar Assn., Am. Soc. Internat. Law, Assn. Am. Law Schs. (chmn. sect. constitutional law 1975-77), Phi Delta Phi, Delta Phi Epsilon, Sigma Delta Chi, soc. Profl. Journalists, Phi Gamma Delta. Republican. Club: Mil. Order World Wars. Office: U SC Law Sch Columbia SC 29208

HAIMM, SHARLYNE, retail apparel company executive; b. Lithuania, Jan. 10, 1922; d. Morris and Sarah Sneider; children—Michael, Cindy. Pres., Michael's Discount Women's Apparel, Hallandale, Fla., 1972—. Mem. Broward Forum, Hallandale C. of C. (bd. dirs., pres. 1984). Clubs: Turnberry Yacht and Racquet, Jockey. Home: 3625 N Country Club Dr Penthouse 3 North Miami Beach FL 33180 Office: Michael's 383 NE 2d Ave Hallandale FL 33009

HAINLINE, FORREST ARTHUR, JR., retired automotive company executive, lawyer; b. Rock Island, Ill., Oct. 20, 1918; s. Forrest Arthur and Marian (Pearson) H.; m. Nora Marie Schrot, July 7, 1945; children—Forrest Arthur, Jon, Patricia, Judith, Brian, David, Nora. A.B., Augustana Coll., Rock Island, Ill., 1940; J.D., U. Mich., 1947, LL.M., 1948. Bar: Ill. 1942, Mich. 1943, Fla. 1970, U.S. Supreme Ct. 1946. Mem. firm Cross, Wrock, Miller & Vieson and predecessor, Detroit, 1948-71, ptnr., 1957-71; v.p., gen. counsel Am. Motors Corp., Detroit, 1971-84, sec., 1972-84, ret. Chmn., Wayne County Regional Interagy. Coordinating Com. for Developmental Disabilities, Mich., 1972-76; chmn. grievance com. U.S. Tennis Assn., 1970-85, mem. exec. com., 1972-74, 83—, chmn. constn. and rules, 1983—, v.p. So. region, 1985—; arbitrator Men's Internat. Profl. Tennis Council, 1977-85; pres. Cath. Social Services Oakland County, Mich., 1972-75; mem. exec. com. Western Tennis Assn., 1964—, pres., 1972-73, chmn. constn. and rules com., 1976-84; mem. Men's Internat. Profl. Tennis Council, 1985—; pres. Western Improvement Assn., 1969-75; bd. dirs. Augustana Coll., 1974-82, sec., 1975-82; bd. dirs. Providence Hosp., Southfield, Mich., 1975-84, sec. 1980, vice chmn., 1981, chmn., 1982, chmn. exec. com., 1983-84. Served to 1st lt. AUS, 1942-46. Named (with family) Tennis Family of Yr., U.S. Tennis Assn., 1974; recipient Outstanding Service award Augustana Coll., 1977; named to Rock Island High Sch. Sports Hall of Fame, 1977, Mich. Amateur Sports Hall of Fame, 1978, Augustana Coll. Sports Hall of Fame, 1980. Mem. ABA, Fed. Bar Assn., Mich. Bar. Assn., Ill. Bar Assn., Fla. Bar Assn., Detroit Bar Assn., Am. Judicature Soc., Augustana Coll. Alumni Assn. (pres. bd. dirs. 1973-74), Phi Alpha Delta. Clubs: Suntide Condominiums, Rossmoor Condominiums. Home: 1357 NE Ocean Blvd Apt 104 Stuart FL 33494 also: 450A Roxbury Ln Jamesburg NJ 08831

HAIR, ELIZABETH USSERY, educator; b. Columbia, S.C., July 13, 1954; d. Preston Leroy and Mary (Hallman) Ussery; m. Ronny Horton Hair, Aug. 13, 1977; 1 dau., Kimberly Elizabeth. B.S. in Mental Retardation, Winthrop Coll., 1976. Spl. edn. tchr. Guinyard-Butler Middle Sch., Barnwell, S.C., 1976—; math. tchr. Wade Hampton Acad., Orangeburg, S.C., 1983-84. Mem. S.C. Edn. Assn., NEA, Porche Club Am. Baptist. Home: 104 River Dr Barnwell SC 29812

HAIR, MATTOX STRICKLAND, state senator; b. Coral Gables, Fla., Jan. 18, 1938; s. Henry Horry and Frances Alberta (Strickland) H.; B.S., Fla. State U., 1960; J.D., U. Fla., 1964; m. Elizabeth Winstead. Admitted to Fla. bar, 1964, practice as partner Marks, Gray, Conroy & Gibbs, Jacksonville; asst. atty. gen., Fla., 1964-65; mem. Fla. Ho. of Reps. from 22d Dist., 1972-74, Fla. Senate from 9th Dist., 1974—. Served as 1st lt. U.S. Army, 1962. Mem. ABA. Fla. Bar Assn., Jacksonville Bar Assn. (bd. govs. 1968-72), Nat. Conf. State Legislators, Conf. Ins. Legislators, Jacksonville C. of C., Fellowship Christian Athletes. Democrat. Baptist. Clubs: Rotary, Southside Business Men's. Home: 5357 Oak Bay Dr N Jacksonville FL 32211 Office: 4981 Atlantic Blvd Jacksonville FL 32207

HAIR, WILLIAM BATES, III, librarian; b. Gastonia, N.C., Mar. 16, 1952; s. William Bates and Lou (Holland) H.; m. Mary Elizabeth Timanus, Dec. 9, 1972; children—Melissa Bain, Laura Elizabeth, Megan Holland. B.S., U. Tenn., 1976; M.Div., Mid-Am. Bapt. Theol. Sem., 1980; M.L.S., Vanderbilt U., 1982. Sales rep. Groves Thread Co., Inc., Gastonia, N.C., 1972-73; minister of youth Lexa Bapt. Ch. (Ark.), 1977-78; library asst. Mid-Am. Bapt. Theol. Sem., Memphis, 1978-80, cataloger and tech. services head, 1980-82, dir. library, 1982—. Trustee Memphis and Shelby County Pub. Library and Info. Ctr., 1983—, v.p., 1985. Mem. ALA, Am. Theol. Library Assn., Tenn. Theol. Library Assn. (v.p. 1985), Tenn. Library Assn., Southeastern Library Assn., Beta Phi Mu, Kappa Sigma. Republican. Home: 6173 Stoney Cove Memphis TN 38134 Office: Mid-Am Bapt Theol Sem 1255 Poplar Ave Memphis TN 38104

HAIRE, MARY FRANCIS, nurse, educator; b. Copperhill, Tenn., Apr. 22, 1947; d. Ray Edward and Betty Ann (Gilmore) H.; m. Randall Lee Freese, Dec. 26, 1970 (div. Aug. 1974). B.S.N., Berea Coll., 1969; M.S.N., Vanderbilt U., 1981; postgrad. Ind. U.-Indpls., 1983—. Staff nurse Piedmont Hosp., Atlanta, 1969-70, Bristol Meml. Hosp. (Tenn.), 1970-75; fetal monitor coordinator Vanderbilt U. Med. Sch., Nashville, 1976-77, coordinator obstet. regionalization, 1977—, asst. in obsetrics, 1979-81, assoc. in obsetrics, 1981—; adj. asst. prof. Vanderbilt U. Nursing Sch., 1983—; liaison So. Perinatal Assn./Nat. Perinatal Assn., 1983-84; speaker for civic groups, 1975, 81. Contbr. articles, chpts. to profl. publs. Named an Outstanding Young Woman of Am., U.S. Jaycees, 1982. Mem. Nurses Assn. of Am. Coll. Ob-gyn (co-chmn. dist. program 1983-85), So. Perinatal Assn. (program chmn. 1983-84, v.p./pres.-elect 1984-85, pres. 1985-86), Nat. Perinatal Assn. (program chmn. 1980-82), Tenn. Perinatal Assn. (v.p. 1985), Am. Nurse's Assn., Am. Nursing Found. (mem. Century Club 1983-84), Sigma Theta Tau. Home: 910 Woodmont Blvd Apt H-4 Nashville TN 37204 Office: Vanderbilt U Maternal-Fetal Div C-2213 MCN Nashville TN 37232

HAIRFIELD, MYRL LEWIS, development company executive; b. Roanoke, Va., May 13, 1942; s. Kenneth and Carrie Leon (arthur) H.; m. Alice Graham, Oct. 24, 1970; children—Sandra Lynn, Carol Ann. B.S. in Bus. Mgmt., Va. Commonwealth U., 1968; diploma in acctg. and bus. adminstrn. Smithdeal-Massey Bus. Coll., 1961; postgrad. T.C. Williams Sch. Law, 1978-80. Dividend/ops. clk. Wheat First Securities, Inc., Richmond, Va., 1965-68; registered rep. Davenport & Co. of Va., Inc., Richmond, 1968-73; mgr. gen. sales and mktg. Busch Properties, Inc., Williamsburg, 1973-79; pres. Kingsmill Realty, Inc., Williamsburg, 1973-79; dir. mktg. The Fla. Cos., Jacksonville, Fla., 1981-82; v.p. McMiller Corp., Williamsburg, 1982—; dir. Widmill Properties, Ltd., Fredericksburg, Va., 1983—, Va. Land and Time-Sharing Assn., 1979—. Campaign mgr. Brown for Supr. Com., 1983; bd. dirs. Brevard Symphony Orch., Melbourne, Fla., 1982; pres., bd. dirs. Brevard Arts Arts Council, 1982. Recipient Hon. Citizen award Am. Legion Boys' State, Williamsburg, 1977. Mem. So. Indsl. Devel. Council, Peninsula Housing and Bldg. Assn. (dir. 1976-79), Va. Home Builders Assn. (alternate dir. 1976-79), So. Indsl. Realtors, Nat. Assn. Realtors. Republican. Episcopalian. Club: German (Williamsburg). Home: 108 William Allen Williamsburg VA 23185 Office: McMiller Corp care Williamsburg Landing 161-C John Jefferson Sq Williamsburg VA 23185

HAIRGROVE, GERRY MEANS, investment banker; b. Fort Worth, Dec. 14, 1954; s. Bert Leonard and Lottie Bell (Hester) M.; m. Marvin Ellis Hairgrove, Jr., July 2, 1947. B.B.A., U. Tex., 1977; postgrad. bus. adminstrn. St. Thomas U., 1980-82. Adminstrv. asst. Kanematsu Gosho Inc., Houston, 1977-79; 1st v.p. health care capital markets group Underwood Neuhaus, Houston, 1979—. Mem. Houston Soc. Fin. Analysts (jr.), Fin. Analysts Fedn. (jr.). Club: Mpcl. Bond of Houston. Office: Underwood Neuhaus 724 Travis St Houston TX 77002

HAISLEY, WALDO EMERSON, JR., physicist; b. Taft, Tex., Oct. 6, 1914; s. Waldo Emerson and Arietta Melissa (Mendenhall) H.; A.B., U. Tex., 1936; M.A. in Econs., Columbia U., 1940; Ph.D. in Physics, U. N.C., Chapel Hill, 1952; m. Mary Doris Weaver, July 8, 1939; 1 son, Lindsay Emerson. Asst. prof. Brown U., 1952-54; asst. prof. Lawrence Coll., Appleton, Wis., 1954-56, asso. prof., 1956-60; asso. prof. U. N.C., Chapel Hill, 1960-71, prof., 1971-78, prof. emeritus and lectr., 1978—, mem. adminstrv. bd. library, 1969-71, 72-75. Precinct committeeman Democratic party, 1978-83. Served from ensign to lt. (j.g.) USNR, 1943-45. Endowed Michael Polanyi Vis. Lectureship, U. N.C.-Chapel Hill, 1981. Mem. AAUP, Am. Assn. Physics Tchrs., Am. Phys. Soc., AAAS, History Sci. Soc., Assn. Evolutionary Econs., Phi Beta Kappa, Sigma Xi. Mem. United Ch. of Christ. Club: Faculty (U. N.C.). Contbr. articles to sci. jours. Home: 317 Burlage Circle Chapel Hill NC 27514 Office: Dept Physics and Astronomy U NC Chapel Hill NC 27514

HAITHCOCK, WILLIAM DANA, JR., physician; b. Bennettsville, S.C., Feb. 19, 1946; s. William Dana and Clarice Anna (Skaggs) H.; m. Nancy Lee, Feb. 10, 1973; children—Judson Legare, Walker Calloway. B.S., Wofford Coll., 1968; M.D., Med. U. S.C., 1973. Diplomate Am. Bd. Ob-Gyn. Intern, Wm. Beaumont Army Med. Ctr., El Paso, Tex., 1973-74, resident, 1974-77; practice medicine specializing in ob-gyn Fayetteville (N.C.) Woman's Clinic, 1980—; staff Cape Fear Valley Med. Ctr., Highsmith-Rainey Meml. Hosp. Mem. Cumberland County Mental Health Bd., 1980—. Served to maj. U.S. Army, 1973-80. Decorated Army Commendation medal. Fellow Am. Coll. Obstetricians and Gynecologists; mem. So. Med. Assn., N.C. Med. Soc., Pi Kappa Alpha. Presbyterian.

HALACHMI, ARIE, educator, consultant, policy analyst; b. Jerusalem, July 7, 1944; came to U.S., 1970; s. Israel and Judith (Haimson) H.; m. Miriam Birnbaum, May 26, 1964; children—Shlomit, Alan. B.A., Hebrew U., 1964, M.A., 1970; Ph.D. with distinction, SUNY-Buffalo, 1972. Cert. sr. orgn. and method analyst. Dir. advanced tng. Central Sch. Pub. Adminstrn., Jerusalem, 1967-69; sr. ops. and mgmt. analyst Civil Service Commn., Jerusalem, 1969-70; asst. prof. Tel Aviv U., Israel, 1973-77; project dir. U. Kans., Lawrence, 1977-78; assoc. prof. Tenn. State U., Nashville, 1979-83, prof., 1983—; vis. prof. Inst. for Personnel and Career Devel., Mt. Pleasant, Mich., 1980-84; commentator radio and TV, Nashville, 1979—; cons. state and local agys. U.S. and other countries, 1973—; mng. editor Pub. Productivity Rev., 1985—. Editorial bd. Polit. Sci. Jour., 1979—; contbr. articles to publs. in field. Dir. Energy Edn. Inst., Tenn. State U., 1981-83; dir., coordinator Minority Careers in Energy, Nashville, 1984; speaker adult edn. programs and community groups, 1979-85. Fellow: Internat. Consortium Polit. Sch., Ann Arbor, Mich., 1977, Hudson Inst., Croton-on-Hudson, N.Y., 1971, Ford Found., 1970. Mem. Am. Soc. Pub. Adminstrn. (pres. Tenn. chpt. 1983-84), Evaluation Network, Polit. Sch. Assn., Policy Studies Orgn. Jewish. Home: 52 Vaughns Gap Nashville TN 37205 Office: Nat Ctr Pub Productivity John Jay Coll 445 W 59th St New York NY 10019

HALBERSTEIN, ALEX, industrial engineer, banker; b. Vienna, Austria, Oct. 28, 1933; came to U.S., 1974; s. Isaac Leon and Clara (Weinraub) H.; B.S., U. Colo., Boulder, 1954; m. Elsie Eskenazi, July 31, 1955; children—Eduardo, Daniel, Jennifer, Cecilia, Ariela, Florence, Janeth, Mauricio, Abel, Mark, Deborah, Jaime, Jason, Isaac. Founder tin can mfg. plants, real estate corps., liquor bottling and mfg. plant, Lima, Peru, 1956-74; pres. Pan Amco Fin. Corp., North Miami Beach, Fla., 1974—, Fabrica Nacional de Envases, Lima, Peru, 1957; vice chmn. bd. Capital Bank, Miami; dir. Capital Bank Corp., Miami. Bd. dirs. Greater Miami Jewish Fedn. Active Jewish orgns., sports, philanthropic orgns., Peru and U.S. Office: 145 E Flagler St 3d Floor Miami FL 33131

HALBERSTEIN, FLORENCE, occupational therapist; b. Havana, Cuba, Jan. 29, 1956; d. Jaime and Judith (Cherches) Pozo; m. Daniel Halberstein, Feb. 20, 1982; children—Mark Darren. B.Health Sci., U. Fla., 1978. Occupational therapist Easter Seals Rehab. Ctr., Miami, Fla., 1978—, Home Med. Services, Miami, 1979-81, Biscayne Med. Ctr., 1981-83, Dodge Meml. Hosp., 1979-81. Recipient Ann Ballard award, Occupational Therapy Faculty U. Fla., 1978. Mem. Am. Occupational Therapy Assn., Fla. Occupational Therapy Assn. Jewish.

HALBERT, OUIDA WARE, country club executive; b. Abilene, Tex., Sept. 7, 1930; d. Bennie B. and Lorena M. (Carpenter) Ware; m. William K. Halbert, Aug. 14, 1954. Student Abilene Christian U., 1947-52. Mgr. Fairway Farm Hunt Club, San Augustine, Tex., 1955-60, Hereford Country Club, Tex., 1964—; asst. mgr. Hillcrest Country Club, Lubbock, Tex., 1960-64. Mem. Deaf Smith C. of C. (Bull Chip award 1985), Club Mgrs. Assn. Am. (pres. West Tex. chpt. 1985-86). Republican. Mem. Ch. of Christ. Club: Bayview Study (Hereford). Avocations: reading, antiques. Home: 824 W Park Hereford TX 79045 Office: Hereford Country Club PO Box 587 Hereford TX 79045

HALBOUTY, MANAH ROBERT, retired air force officer; physician; b. Beaumont, Tex., Apr. 28, 1914; s. Tom C. and Sodia (Monolley) H.; M.D., Tulane U., 1937; grad. Sch. Aviation Medicine, 1940, Med-Field Service Sch., 1941, Army Air Staff Command and Gen. Staff Sch., 1944, Sr. Med. Officers Staff Sch., 1944, Atomic Bomb and Chem. and Biol. Warfare Schs., 1947; m. Gracye Collinsworth, Mar. 23, 1940; 1 child, Michel Robert William. Intern, St. Paul's Hosp., Dallas, 1937-38, resident internal medicine, 1938-39; house doctor Mo.-Kans.-Tex. R.R. Hosp., Denison, Tex., 1939-40; commd. 1st lt., M.C., USAAF, 1940, advanced through ranks to col., USAF, 1951; aviation med. examiner, flight surgeon, sr. flight surgeon, chief flight surgeon and med. aircraft observor; research aviation medicine Mayo Clinic, 1941-42; asst. chief med. processing center SAACC, Tex., 1942; hosp. comdr., Ohio and Fla., 1943-44; troop carrier wing surgeon, Italy, Germany, 1944-46, comdr. hosps., wing and base surgeon, N.Y. State, Alaska, Ariz., Tex., 1946-57; div. surgeon 43d Air Div., comdr. 8th Tactical Hosp., also 6160th USAF Hosp., Itazuke AB, Japan, 1957-60; chief flight surgeon, div. surgeon 819th Air Div., dir. base med. services hosp. and 819th Med. Group, Comdr. Dyess AFB, Abilene, Tex., 1960-66, also chief preventive medicine and comdr. USAF Hosp.; mem. phys. evaluation bd. Hdqrs. USAF Mil. Personnel Ctr., 1966-68; USAF surgeon gen.'s staff med. rep. on USAF Phys. Rev. Council, Hdqrs. USAF Mil. Personnel Ctr. and hosp. clinician. Randolph AFB, Tex., 1968-74; ret., 1974; chmn. dept. med. bds. and exams. Wilford Hall USAF Med. Ctr., San Antonio, 1980-82; cons. med. disability USAF/VA, 1983—; practicing med. clinician Randolph AFB Hosp. and Wilford Hall USAF Med. Center, 1974-83; cons. med. disability. Decorated Legion of Merit with oak leaf cluster, Purple Heart. 2 Army and 3 Air Force Commendation medals; Gold Flight Surgeon's Wings with citation from Comdg. Gen. Chinese Nationalist Air Force, others. Mem. Assn. Mil. Surgeon's U.S., Aerospace Med. Assn. U.S., Am. Acad. Family Practice, Japanese-Am. Med. Assn. (founder), Assn. U.S. Flight Surgeons. Contbr. numerous articles to mil. and profl. med. jours. Home and Office: 6002 Wildwind Dr San Antonio TX 78239

HALBOUTY, MICHEL THOMAS, geologist, petroleum engr., ind. producer, operator; b. Beaumont, Tex., June 21, 1909; s. Tom Christian and Sodia (Manolley) H.; B.S., Tex. A&M Coll., 1930, M.S., 1931, Profl. Degree in Geol. Engring., 1956; E.D., Mont. Coll. Mineral Sci. and Tech., 1966;; m. Billye Stevens, Dec. 27, 1981. Geologist, petroleum engr. Yount-Lee Oil Co., Beaumont, Tex., 1931-33, chief geologist, petroleum engr., 1933-35; v.p., gen. mgr., chief geologist and petroleum engr. Glenn H. McCarthy, Inc., Houston, 1935-37; owner firm cons. geologists and petroleum engrs., Houston, 1937-81; chmn., chief exec. officer Michael T. Halbouty Energy Co., Houston, 1981—; discovered numerous oil fields La. and Tex.; pioneer discovery of gas field Alaska; chmn. bd. North Side State Bank, Houston, 1st Nat. Bank, San Angelo, Tex., West Side Nat. Bank, San Angelo, 1st Nat. Bank, Paris, Tex., 1st Nat. Bank, Deport; dir. Allied Bank of Tex., Post Oak Bank, Houston. Served as lt. col. AUS, 1942-45. Mem. numerous tech. and sci. socs. Episcopalian. Clubs: Houston, Petroleum, River Oaks Country (Houston); Eldorado Country (Palm Desert, Calif.); Dallas Petroleum; New Orleans Petroleum; Broadmoor Golf (Colorado Springs, Colo.); Vintage (Indian Wells, Calif.); Cosmos (Washington). Author: Petrographic and Physical Characteristics of Sand from Seven Gulf Coast Producing Horizons, 1937; Salt Domes—Gulf Region, United States and Mexico, 1967, rev. and enlarged edit., 1979; co-author: Spindletop, 1952, The Last Boom, 1972; Grady Barr, 1981; also numerous tech. and sci. papers on geology and petroleum engring. Home: 49 Briar Hollow Houston TX 77027 Office: The Halbouty Center 5100 Westheimer Rd Houston TX 77056

HALBROOK, T.A., geophysicist; b. Potean, Okla., June 9, 1913; s. John T. and Atha Mae (King) H.; m. Katherine Foust; 1 child; John Tower. B.S. in Engring., Okla. State U., 1934. Geophysicist, Calgary, Alta., Can., 1936-59, Tulsa, 1959—. Mem. Soc. Exploration Geophysicists (v.p.), Am. Geol. Soc. Republican. Methodist. Club: Petroleum. Avocation: Opera. Home: 3740 E 47th Pl Tulsa OK 74135

HALCAME, DAVID LAWRENCE, training manager, management consultant; b. Augusta, Ga., Apr. 29, 1935; s. David Elli and Alma (Inglett) H.; m. Shelby Smith, June 21, 1958; children—David Anthony, Christopher Troy, Jennifer Alyssa. Student Am. Inst. of Banking, Augusta, 1960-62; B.A., Columbia Pacific U., 1985; Ph.D., 1985. Asst. br. mgr. Ga. Railroad Bank, Augusta, Ga., 1957-63; mgr. Comml. Credit Corp., Aiken, S.C., 1963-65, Genesco Corp. Augusta, 1966-68; art dir. Southeastern Newspaper, Augusta, 1968-76; owner Graphic Communication Assocs., Augusta, 1976-80; supr. tng. devel. Continental Forest Ind., Augusta, 1980-83; tng. mgr. Club Car, Inc., Augusta, 1983—; owner Instructional Graphics Services, Augusta, 1979—. Contbr. articles to profl. jours. Mem. Indsl. Graphics Internat., Am. Soc. Tng. and Devel., Augusta Jaycees (bd. dirs. 1957-65). Methodist. Club: Exchange (bd. dirs. 1970-74) (Summerville/Augusta). Avocations: golf; fishing; scuba diving; bowling. Home: 115 Holiday Ct Martinez GA 30907 Office: Club Car Inc PO Box 4658 Augusta GA 30907

HALE, ARNOLD WAYNE, retired army officer, educational specialist, clergyman; b. Colome, S.D., Sept. 2, 1934; s. Archiebald William and Alvena Lucille (Williams) H.; B.A., U.S.D., 1959; M.Ed., Our Lady of the Lake U., 1971, M.Ed., 1973; B.S., SUNY-Albany, 1976; A.A., Austin Comm. Coll., 1979; ministerial cert., Gospel Ministry Inst., 1981; D.D. (hon.), Gospel Ministry Inc., 1981; diploma specialized ministries Berean Sch. of Bible, 1982, diploma ministerial studies, 1983; Th.D., Reeves Christian Coll., 1984; m. Mary Alice Mauricio, Nov. 30, 1962; 1 son, Alexander; children by previous marriage—Colleen, Zola; stepchildren—Charles, Marlow. Ordained minister Full Gospel Ch. in Christ, Victory New Testament Fellowship Internat., 1983. Infantryman, U.S. Army, 1953-55, commd. lt., 1959, advanced through grades to maj., 1973, served in various staff and mgmt. positions with Med. Service Corps, 1959-67, med. adviser, Mil. Assistance Command, Vietnam, 1967-68, ednl. tng. officer, U.S. Army Med. Tng. Center, Ft. Sam Houston, Tex., 1968-73, hosp. comdr., Ft. Campbell, Ky., 1973-75, med. adviser, Tex. Army N.G., Austin, 1975-77, ret., 1977; learning resources specialist, Thorndale/Milano Independent Sch. Dists., Milam County, Tex., 1977-78; instr. psychology, Austin Community Coll., 1977-79; librarian-counselor, Austwell-Tivoli Ind. Sch. Dist., Tex., 1979-81; adult probation officer, Travis County (Tex.), 1981-82; founding Biblio pastoral counselor Biblio Edn. Counseling ministry, 1983—; ednl. Chaplain, 1983—. Decorated Bronze Star. Recipient Duke of Paducah award, 1975; Experienced Pastoral Counselor award, Inst. Experienced Pastoral Counselors, 1981. Fellow, Am. Biog. Inst. Research Assn. (life); mem. ALA bibliotherapy discussion group, Am. Personnel and Guidance Assn., Christians United for Israel, PTL Club, NEA, Tex., Milam County, Tex. Jr. Coll. tchrs. assns., CAP (maj., med. advisor, chaplain), Ret. Officers Assn. (life), N.G. Assn. Tex. (life), Mil. Order World Wars, Assn. U.S. Army, U.S. Armor Assn., Pastoral Counsellors Assn. (diplomate), Nat. Chaplains Assn. (maj., life). Democrat. Clubs: Masons (W. Ger.); Lions. Home: 10412 Firethorn Ln Austin TX 78750

HALE, ELMER, JR., food company executive; b. 1919. With Hale-Halsell Co., Tulsa, 1940—, now chmn. bd., also dir. Office: Hale-Halsell Co 9111 E Pine St Tulsa OK 74115*

HALE, JAMES THORNTON, university administrator; b. Jackson, Miss., Aug. 21, 1944; s. James T. and Ruby (Brand) H.; m. Paula L. Zeno, Dec. 17, 1967 (div. Jan. 1978). B.B.A., Sam Houston State U., 1967, M.B.A., 1971. Grad. fellow Sam Houston State U., Huntsville, Tex., 1969-71; bus. mgr. U. Tex.-San Antonio, 1971-73; vice chancellor U. Houston-Clear Lake, 1973—; mem. Upper-Level Formula Com. Coordinating Bd., Austin, Tex., 1973—; adv. dir. Inter-First Bank, Nassau Bay, N.A., 1984—; mem. budget com. Clear Lake Econ. Devel. Found., Houston, 1984—. Treas., vice chmn. bd. mgmt. Bay Area YMCA, Houston, 1975—; bd. dirs. Bay Area Mus., 1985—. Served with U.S. Army, 1967-69. Named Vol. of Yr., Bay Area YMCA, 1980, Outstanding Young Men of Am., 1976, 77, 78. Mem. Assn. Coll. and Univ. Auditors, Nat. Assn. Aux. Services, Nat. Assn. State Sr. Coll. and Univ. Bus. Officers, Tex. Assn. State Sr. Coll. and Univ. Bus. Officers, So. Assn. State Sr. Coll. and Univ. Bus. Officers, U. Houston-Clear Lake Alumni Assn. (ex-officio dir. 1983—). Club: Optimist. Home: 16443 Heatherdale St Houston TX 77059 Office: U Houston-Clear Lake 2700 Bay Area Blvd Houston TX 77058

HALE, LEE LOUIS, lawyer; b. Atlanta, Sept. 17, 1948; s. Jack Lee and Margaret Louise (Deano) H.; m. Josephine Alyce Nichols, June 19, 1971; children—Lee Louis, Lauren Alyce, John Robert. B.A. summa cum laude, Spring Hill Coll., 1970; J.D., Duke U., 1973. Bar: Ala. 1973, U.S. Dist. Ct. Ala. (so. dist.) Ala. 1973, U.S. Supreme Ct. 1977, U.S. Dist. Ct. (mid. dist.) Ala. 1982, U.S. Ct. Appeals (11th cir.) 1982. Assoc. Hamilton, Butler, Mobile, Ala., 1973-74; asst. dist. atty., Mobile, 1974-79; dep. atty. gen. State of Ala., Montgomery, 1979-80, spl. asst. atty. gen., 1981-84; sole practice, Mobile, 1980—; mem. Ala. form indictment com. Ala. Law Inst., Montgomery, 1979-80, mem. drug law rev. com., Mobile, 1980-82; lectr. continuing legal edn. Ala. State Bar, Tuscaloosa, 1980-83. Vice chmn. Graddick for Dist. Atty., Mobile, 1974, campaign mgr., 1978. Mem. Assn. Trial Lawyers Am., Ala. Trial Lawyers, Ala. State Bar, Mobile Bar Assn. Democrat. Roman Catholic. Home: 851 Graymont Dr Mobile AL 36608 Office: PO Box 495 118 N Royal St Mobile AL 36601

HALE, LUCY REAGER, nursing educator; b. Huntly, Va., May 9, 1935; d. Charles Thomas and Viola Virginia (Wines) Reager; m. John Allison Hale, Aug. 3, 1963; 1 dau., Carol Reager. Diploma in nursing Grace Hosp., Richmond, Va., 1961; B.S. in Social Sci., Tift Coll., Mercer U., 1970; B.B.A., Ga. Coll., 1974; M.S. in Nursing, Med. Coll. Ga., 1975. Staff nurse VA Hosp., Richmond, 1961-62, Dublin (Ga.) VA Ctr., 1965-66, Robins AFB, Ga., 1966-68; assoc. prof. nursing San Antonio Coll., 1976—; film reviewer Am. Assn. Med. Colls., 1977-81. Served with USAF, 1962-65. Mem. AAUP, Tex. Jr. Coll. Tchrs. Assn. (state chmn. health occupations group, 1981-82), Tex. Nurses Assn. (govtl. affairs com. dist. 8, 1977-78). Co-author: Pharmacology Math, 1978. Address: 2507 Blue Quail San Antonio TX 78284

HALES, DOROTHY GRAEFE, librarian; b. Balt., Sept. 24, 1912; d. William Bernhardt and Albertine Henrietta (Graefe) Henkel; B.S., Johns Hopkins U., 1933, M.A., 1936; M.A. in L.S., Peabody Coll., 1964; m. Charles Albert Hales, Sept. 1, 1936; children—Charles Albert, Mary Elizabeth. Mem. faculty U. Tenn., 1946-50, Wesleyan Coll., Macon, Ga., 1950-54; library asst. Washington Meml. Library, Mason, Ga., 1954-64; reference librarian Middle Ga. Regional Library, 1965-68, asso. dir., 1968-70; dir. Sequoyah Regional Library, Canton, Ga., 1970—; cons. in field. Mem. ALA, Southeastern Library Assn., Ga. Library Assn., N.Ga. Asso. Libraries, Bus. and Profl. Women's Club. Presbyterian. Home: 306 Hembree Hill Rd Box 1075 Canton GA 30114 Office: 400 E Main St Canton GA 30114

HALES, JACK, JR., accountant; b. Chillecothe, Tex., Nov. 8, 1933; s. Jack and Frances Esto (Burch) H.; B.B.A. in Acctg. and Econs., Pan Am. U., 1957; m. Lula Mae Ivey, Oct. 8, 1954; children—Jack Robert, Pat Lawrence, Lynn Candise, Richard Allen. Staff acct. R.J. Welch, C.P.A., Weslaco, Tex., 1956-60; ptnr. Welch, White & Co., Weslaco, 1961-85, Hales, Bradford & White, Weslaco, 1985—; v.p., dir. Seal Produce Co., Pharr, Tex., 1975-85. Treas., bd. dirs. Mid Valley Elem. Sch., Weslaco, 1979-84; bd. dirs. United Fund, 1963. Served with USAF, 1951-53. Named Boss of Yr., Weslaco Jaycees, 1979. Mem. Weslaco C. of C., Valley C. of C., Aircraft Owners and Pilots Assn., Am. Inst. C.P.A.'s, Tex. Soc. C.P.A.'s, Am. Acctg. Assn., Am. Taxation Assn. Republican. Baptist. Home: 415 Westgate St 15 Weslaco TX 78596 Office: 322 S Missouri Ave PO Box 8458 Weslaco TX 78596

HALEY, BILLY GERALD, financial executive; b. Ft. Worth, Tex., July 29, 1934; s. Willie Andrew and Beulah (Pennington) H.; m. Wanda Sue Burklow, Dec. 24, 1959 (div. 1983); children—Debra Lynn, Michael Don; m. 2d, Donna Ray Barham, July 16, 1983. Student Paris Jr. Coll., 1952-53. With Babcock & Wilcox, Paris, Tex., 1953-54; with Local Loan Co., Abilene, Tex., 1954-55, mgr., 1956-57; mgr. Sweetwater Loan Service, Sweetwater, Tex., 1957-59; sec., gen. mgr. P-A-F Fin. Service, Inc., Sweetwater, 1959-65; owner Flower Fashions & Gifts, Sweetwater, 1965-67; pres. Local Loan & Investment Corp., Sweetwater, 1967—, v.p. Lamesa Pawn Loans, Inc., 1978—; pres. Weatherford Fin. & Pawn Inc., 1974-82. Mem. Tex. Pawn Brokers Assn. (dir. 1980-83), Tex. Fin. Inst. (dir. 1972-83), Tex. C. of C. (dir. 1974-77). Baptist. Club: Kiwanis (pres. 1969-70, 80-81, lt. gov. Tex.-Okla. Dist. 1971-72). Home: 1607 Bristol Dr Sweetwater TX 79556 Office: 607 Lamar St Sweetwater TX 79556

HALEY, WARREN JAY, county educational administrator, consultant; b. Mountain Home, Ark., Jan. 18, 1934; s. Jennings Bryan and Ruby Ethel (Johnson) H.; m. Sara Ann St. John, Jan. 27, 1962 (div. 1963). B.A., Ouachita U., 1960; M.S. in Edn., U. Central Ark., 1969. Lic. profl. counselor, cert. secondary counselor. Tchr., counselor Flippin High Sch., Ark., 1962-69; counselor Ark. Rehab., Little Rock, 1969-70; dir., spl. edn. Ark. State Hosp., Little Rock, 1970-72; supr., adult edn. Ark. Dept. Edn., Little Rock, 1972-77; supr., program evaluation Houston Community Coll., Tex., 1977-80; coordinator adult edn. Harris County Dept. Edn., Houston, 1980—; cons. Ark. Hosp. Assn., Little Rock, 1974-75, Ark. Library Commn., Little Rock, 1975-76, U. Kans. Research Inst., Lawrence, 1978-80. Served with U.S. Army, 1956-58. Spl. project grantee, Tex. Edn. Agy., Houston, 1983-84, statewide, 1984-85; recipient Outstanding Service award Future Farmers Am., 1968. Mem. Am. Assn. Adult and Continuing Edn. (v.p. 1983-85, Membership award 1984, Meritorious Service award 1984), Tex. Assn. Adult Edn. (sec. 1978-79, bd. dirs. 1983-84), South Central Assn. for Lifelong Learning (pres. 1979-80), Mountain Home Jaycees (v.p. 1964), Phi Delta Kappa, Phi Mu Alpha (sec. 1958-59). Episcopalian. Avocations: bicycling; swimming; dancing. Home: 2504 Yorktown St Houston TX 77056 Office: Harris County Dept Edn 6208 Irvington Blvd Houston TX 77022

HALFF, ALBERT HENRY, civil engineer; b. Midland, Tex. Aug. 20, 1915; s. Henry M. and Rosa Wechesler (Barnet) H.; m. Lee Benson, Aug. 24, 1940; children—Henry Mayer, Albert Lee. B.S. in Civil Engring., So. Meth. U., 1937; M.S. in Civil Engring., Ill. Inst. Tech., 1942; D. Eng., Johns Hopkins U., 1950. Design engr. Koch & Fowler, Dallas, 1937-39; asst. prof. dept. engring. Tex. A&I U., Kingsville, 1939-41; design engr. DeLeuw, Cather & Co., Stroud, Okla., 1942, Brown & Bellows, Contractors, McAlester, Okla., 1943; asst. prof. So. Meth. U., Dallas, 1946; owner Albert H. Halff, San., Engr., Dallas, 1950-53, Hundly & Halff, Cons. Engrs., Dallas, 1953-60; owner Albert H. Halff Assoc., Dallas, 1960-70, pres., 1970-83, chmn. bd., 1983—. Mem. Dallas County Hist. Com., Dallas Heritage Soc., Dallas Mus. Fine Arts, Greater Dallas Planning Council, City of Dallas Design of City Com., Goals for Dallas, Dallas Council on World Affairs, Urban Design Task Force, Dallas Area Indsl. Devel. Assn., Dallas Area Rapid Transit Transp. Task Force; bd. dirs., exec. com., chmn. bldg. com. Dallas Theater Ctr. Served to lt. col. U.S. Army, 1943-46. Recipient Outstanding Engr. of Yr. Dallas/Ft. Worth Region, 1979, State of Tex., 1980, 82; Service award for Personal Support and Assistance, Carrollton Flood Control Dist., 1975-82, Spl. recognition award Dallas Mayor and City Council, 1985; Hall of Achievement award U. Tex., Arlington, 1986. Fellow ASCE (recognition award Tex. sect. 1983, award of merit 1984, award of honor 1985); mem. AAAS, N.Y. Acad. Scis., Water Pollution Control Fedn., Am. Water Works Assn., Nat. Soc. Profl. Engrs., Am. Acad. Environ. Engrs., Am. Geophys. Union, Tex. Soc. Profl. Engrs., Soc. Am. Mil. Engrs., Polit. Action Com. Engrs., Tex. Good Rds./Transp. Assn., Sigma Xi, Chi Epsilon, Sigma Tau. Clubs: Dallas Tech., Big D Toastmasters. Numerous patents (13); contbr. articles to profl. jours. Office: Albert H Halff Assocs Inc 8616 NW Plaza Dr Dallas TX 75225

HALFORD, RAYMOND GAINES, lawyer, state official; b. Columbia, S.C., Apr. 10, 1925; s. Richard Eugene and Henrietta (Levy) H.; m. Wilma Eleazer, Dec. 31, 1960; children—Anne Lindsey, Richard Gaines. B.S., U. S.C., 1949, LL.B. cum laude, 1950. Bar: S.C. 1950, U.S. Dist. Ct. S.C. 1971, U.S. Ct. Appeals (4th cir.) 1978. Atty.-advisor U.S. Corps Engrs., Savannah River Project, Aiken, S.C., 1950-52; account exec. Harris Upham & Co., Columbia, 1952-54; mortgage banker and ins. agt., Columbia, 1954-65; asst. atty. gen. Office of Atty. Gen. S.C., Columbia, 1966—; dep. atty. gen., gen. counsel S.C. Dept. Social Services, Columbia, 1983-84, S.C. Health and Human Services Fin. Commn., Columbia, 1984—. Div. chmn. United Fund, Columbia, 1958-59; trustee United Community Services, Columbia, 1966-68. Served with U.S. Army, 1943-46. Recipient Outstanding Mem. award Columbia Jr. C. of C., 1958; Disting. Service award Region IV Nat. Welfare Fraud Assn., 1978. Episcopalian. Home: 1162 Eastminster Dr Columbia SC 29204 Office: SC Health and Human Services Fin Commn Jefferson Sq PO Box 8206 Columbia SC 29202

HALICZER, BONNIE DIKMAN, fashion editor, retailer; b. N.Y.C., Sept. 9, 1942; d. George Henry and Ruth (Hymes) Dikman; B.A. in English Edn., U. South Fla., 1968; children—Shera Lyn, Scott Harris. Feature and fashion writer St. Petersburg (Fla.) Times, 1956-64; writer Congl. Quar., Washington, 1961-62; fashion writer Tampa (Fla.) Tribune, 1977-84; fashion editor On Design mag., 1984-85; fashion reporter WXFL-TV, 1984—; Owner What's New, Inc., women's retail clothing store, 1984—; instr. journalism U. Tampa, 1979; mem. nat. nominating com. Cutty Sark Com. Men's Fashions Awards, 1983—; fashion editor On Design mag., Miami-Tampa Bay monthly mag. Pres. Tampa Hadassah Group, 1974-76; founder Hillel Sch., Jewish Day Sch., Tampa. Recipient Men's Fashion Assn. Am. award 1980, 81, award J.C. Penney, Mo., 1980. Mem. The Fashion Group, Sigma Delta Chi. Club: Palma Ceia Jr. Women's Westcoast editor Fla. Designer's Quar. mag., 1980—. Contbr. articles to profl. jours. Home: 4804 Culbreath Isles Rd Tampa FL 33629 Office: 12924 N Dale Mabry Tampa FL 33618

HALISKY, JAN GREGORY, lawyer; b. Fort Baker, Calif., Mar. 13, 1948; s. John Robert and Doris Marie (Handerhan) H.; m. Mary Jo Dewoody, June 23, 1973; children—Michael A., Alexander B., Scott I., Timothy R., John G., Julia M., Marie E. B.A., U. Fla., 1970; J.D., Emory U., 1974. Bar: Fla. 1974. Ptnr. Griffin, Uber & Halisky, Clearwater, Fla., 1974-79; pres. Jan G. Halisky, P.A., Clearwater, 1979—. Pres. Pinellas County Right to Life Com., Inc., Clearwater, 1976—; pres. Fla. Right to Life, Inc., 1981-85; bd. dirs. Fla. Right to Life Polit. Action Com., 1981—, chmn., 1985—; bd. dirs. Kimberly Home, Inc., Clearwater, 1980—; mem. steering com. 9th Congl. Dist. Action Com., 1976—; mem. adv. bd. Resident Home Assn., Clearwater, 1979—, Diocese of St. Petersburg Natural Family Planning Commn., 1982—; condr. Pinellas Schola Cantualis, Clearwater, 1979—. Recipient commendations Upper Pinellas Assn. for Retarded Children, 1979, Refugee Resettlement Program of Cath. Social Services, St. Petersburg, Fla., 1980, Suncoast Conservative Union, 1980, Women for Responsible Legislation, St. Petersburg, 1981. Mem. Fla. Bar Assn., Clearwater Bar Assn., Acad. Fla. Trial Lawyers. Republican. Roman Catholic. Office: 507 S Prospect Ave Clearwater FL 33516

HALL, ANDREW CLIFFORD, lawyer; b. Warsaw, Poland, Sept. 16, 1944; came to U.S., 1949, naturalized, 1954; s. Edmund and Maria (Hahn) H.; B.A., U. Fla., 1965, J.D. with high honors, 1968; children—Michael Ian, Adam Stuart. Bar: Fla. 1968, Ga. 1971, U.S. Supreme Ct. 1973. Law clk. U.S. Dist. Ct. So. Dist. Fla., 1968-70; assoc. firm Haas, Holland, Levison & Gilbert, Atlanta, 1970-72, firm Frates, Floyd, Pearson & Stewart, Miami, Fla., 1972-75; ptnr. Storace, Hall and Hauser, Miami, 1975-79, Hall & Hauser, Miami, 1979-82, Hall & O'Brien, Miami, 1982-86, Hall, O'Brien & Cohen, P.A., Miami, 1986—. Mem. ABA, Am. Judicature Soc., Acad. Fla. Trial Lawyers (diplomate), Am. Trial Lawyers Assn., Phi Kappa Phi, Phi Alpha Delta, Order of Coif. Democrat. Jewish. Home: 1581 Brickell Ave Miami FL 33129 Office: 1401 Brickell Ave Miami FL 33130

HALL, ANITA B., anatomy and marine biology educator, consultant; b. Selma, Ala., June 3, 1915; d. Sherman Ralph W. and Mary T. (Moore) Smith. A.B., Talladega Coll., 1933; M.A., U. Mich., 1942. Assoc. prof. biology Hampton (Va.) Inst., 1942—; cons. in marine biology; dir. People's Savs. and Loan Co., Hampton; realtor Plymouth Land Co., Newport News, Va. Mem. AAUW (pres. Hampton br.), Sigma Xi. Home: 1219 Old Buckroe Rd Hampton VA 23663 Office: Hampton Inst PO Box 6035 Hampton VA 23368

HALL, BENJAMIN DRAKE, editor; b. Elkton, Ky., May 8, 1930; s. Benjamin Corbett and Zelma Elizabeth (Tunstill) H.; m. Leslie Catherine North, Nov. 9, 1984; children—Benjamin Drake, David Bryan, Daniel Sean. B.S., Murray State Coll., 1954; M.A., U. Louisville, 1961. Dir. Rauch Meml. Planetarium, U. Louisville, 1960-63; curator Burke Baker Planetarium, Houston Mus. Natural Sci., 1963-65; asst. prof. Murray State U., Ky., 1965-75; unit mgr. Olin Mills, Chattanooga, 1979-81; city editor The Messenger, Madisonville, Ky., 1981—. Contbr. articles to profl. jours. Recipient Nat. Hunting and Fishing Day Writer's award Nat. Shooting Sports Found., 1982; Best Sports Column award Ky. Press Assn., 1983, Best Gen. Column award, 1983. Mem. Nat. Rifle Assn., League Ky. Sportsmen (Conservation Communicator of Yr. award 1982, bd. dirs. 1985), Ducks Unltd. Avocations: hunting; fishing; camping. Home: 2908 B Meadowlark Ln Henderson KY 42420 Office: The Messenger 221 S Main Madisonville KY 42420

HALL, CHARLES ALBERT, labor relations educator, arbitrator; b. Miami, Fla., May 7, 1930; s. Charles Albert and Ethel Elizabeth (Moreland) H.; m. Anselma Emerita, Aug. 15, 1959; children—Sharon Marie, Richard Gary, Charles Albert III. B.A. in Labor and Manpower Studies, Fla. Internat. U.; cert. Harvard U. Grad. Sch., 1968. Fire fighter City of Miami, 1952-79; v.p. Internat. Assn. Fire Fighters, Washington, 1968-80; instr. labor relations Fla. Internat. U., Miami, 1979—; mem. Fla. Ho. of Reps., 1980-81; permanent arbitrator South Fla. Marble Polishers, 1982—. Author: (with others) White Paper—Collective Bargaining in Florida, 1967; Techniques of Collective Bargaining, 1969. Mem. Dade County Personnel Adv. Bd.; trustee City of Miami Pension System. Mem. Am. Arbitration Assn. (labor panelist), Indsl. Relations Research Assn., Univ. and Coll. Labor Edn. Assn. Democrat. Home: 7800 SW 131 Ave Miami FL 33183 Office: Fla Internat U Ctr For Labor Research and Studies Tamiami Trail Miami FL 33199

HALL, CLAUDIA HELT, counselor; b. Cuero, Tex., Mar. 5, 1948; d. Chester Richard and Dorothy Marie (Hirsch) Helt; m. William A. Hall, May 24, 1968 (div. Feb. 1985). B.S., Tex. A&M U., 1975, M.S., 1978. Lic. profl. counselor, Tex. Tchr. Jack Yates High Sch., Houston, 1978-79; real estate agt. Bolding Real Estate, Austin, Tex., 1979-83; coordinator women's coops. U. Tex., Austin, 1983-84, acad. counselor, 1984—; therapist Waterloo Counseling Ctr., Austin, 1984—; pvt. therapist, Austin, 1985—; counselor Womenspace, Austin, 1983—; therapist support groups, 1983—. Mem. Am. Assn. for Counseling Devel., Tex. Assn. for Counseling Devel., Am. Coll. Personnel Assn., Tex. Coll. Personnel Assn., Nat. Acad. Advising Assn. Democrat. Roman Catholic. Home: 7205 Hart Ln Apt 2006 Austin TX 78731 Office: U Tex Coll Natural Scis Austin TX 78731

HALL, DENNIS ALLISON, hospital administrator; b. Winchester, Mass., Nov. 1, 1946; s. Victor A. and Julia (Manie) H.; m. Dixie Lynn Logan, June 22, 1965; children—Geoffrey, Bradley. B.S. in Commerce, U. Louisville, 1971; M.S. in Health Care Adminstrn., Washington U.-St. Louis, 1973. Adminstrv. trainee Ky. Bapt. Hosp., Louisville, 1971; adminstrv. resident Central Bapt. Hosp., Lexington, Ky., 1972-73; asst. adminstr. Western Bapt. Hosp., Paducah, Ky., 1973-74; exec. dir. Hardin Meml. Hosp., Elizabethtown, Ky., 1974-76; exec. v.p. Central Bapt. Hosp., Lexington, 1976-80; exec. v.p. Bapt. Med. Ctr.-Montclair, Birmingham, Ala., 1980—. Recipient Outstanding Young Man in Elizabethtown award Jaycees, 1976, Outstanding Young Man of Ky. award, 1977. Mem. Ala. Assn. Hosp. Execs., Ala. Hosp. Assn., Am. Coll. Hosp. Adminstrs., Birmingham Regional Hosp. Council, Bapt. Hosp. Assn. Clubs: Kiwanis, Spring Creek Hunting (pres. 1983-84). Home: 3609 Westchester Circle Mountain Brook AL 35223 Office: Bapt Med Ctr Montclair 800 Montclair Rd Birmingham AL 35213

HALL, DICK, state legislator; b. Vicksburg, Miss., May 12, 1938; s. John E. and Audrey (Lard) H.; B.S., Miss. State U., 1960; m. Lisa Williams, Aug. 20, 1957; children—Robert E., John Christian, Donald Richard. Sales rep. U.S. Pipe & Foundry Co., Birmingham, Ala., 1963-67; successively sales rep., area sales mgr. Price Brothers Co., Jackson, Miss., dist. gen. mgr.; mem. Miss. Ho. Reps., 1976—, chmn. com. on conservation and water resources. Mem. Gov.'s Task Force on Econ. Devel.; bd. dirs. Miss. Soc. Prevention Blindness, Jr. Achievement Jackson; bd. govs. Jackson Symphony Orch.; chmn. Mid-Miss. March of Dimes. Served with AUS. Named Man of Yr., Am. Water Works Assn., Ala.-Miss., 1974; recipient 1st Friend of Edn. award Jackson Assn. Educators, 1979; 1st Hugh L. White Free Enterprise award, 1981. Mem. Miss. Bd. Econ. Devel., Miss. Research and Devel. Council (exec. com.), Miss. Mfrs. Assn. (chmn. bd.), Agrl. and Indsl. Bd. Miss., Am. Water Works Assn., Am. Public Works Assn., Water Pollution Control Assn., Jackson C. of C. (dir.), Delta Sigma Pi, Sigma Chi, Chi Lambda Rho. Office: PO Box 55942 Jackson MS 39216

HALL, FROZENIA, state educator; b. Montgomery, Ala., Oct. 5, 1940; d. James and Elvene (McCall) H. B.S., Ala. State U., 1964, M.Ed., 1973; learning disabilities endorsement Auburn U., 1976. Elem. tchr. Shelby County Bd. Edn., Alabaster, Ala., 1964-65, 71-75, summer tchr., 1972-74; elem. tchr. Lorain City Schs., Ohio, 1965-70; owner, operator, tchr. Day Care Ctr./Kindergarten, Montgomery, 1970-71; learning disabilities tchr. Montgomery County Bd. Edn., Montgomery, 1975-78; edn. specialist Ala. Dept. Edn., Montgomery, 1978—; Headstart tchr. Lorain City Schs., summers 1966-67; supr. Assn. Children with Learning Disabilities, Montgomery, summers 1976-77; resource speaker for local sch. systems, community groups, others. Mem. steering com. Coalition of Concerned Alumni and Friends for Ala. State U. Affairs, Montgomery, 1979-80; sec. Feminiques Civic and Social Club, Montgomery, 1980-83; v.p. Basic Life Instruction and Survival Skills, Inc., Montgomery, 1981—; vice chmn. Support Com. for Fairview Med. Ctr., Montgomery, 1982; pres. Highland Village Civic Assn., Montgomery, 1982—; mem. adv. council Nat. Com. for Sch. Desegregation, 1984; dep. registrar Montgomery County Registrar's Office, Montgomery, 1984—; active Sickle Cell Found. Greater Montgomery, 1984—; active Ala./Montgomery County Democratic Conf., 1982-84. Mem. NEA, Ala. Edn. Assn., Montgomery County Edn. Assn., Ala. State Employees Assn., YMCA, NAACP, Assn. Children and Adults with Learning Disabilities (steering com. 1975—), Ala. Coalition for Women and Girls in Edn., Ala. State U. Alumni Assn. (v.p. Montgomery chpt. 1983—, editor handbook 1982, Miss Ala. State U. Alumni attendant, 1976). Baptist. Lodge: Shaaban Ct. (local marshall 1984—). Avocations: traveling; listening to music. Home: 1051-A Highland Village Dr Montgomery AL 36108 Office: Ala Dept Edn Profl Services Div Tech Assistance Sect 501 Dexter Ave Room 352 Montgomery AL 36130

HALL, HORACE EDWARD, II, psychologist, consultant, school administrator; b. Brewton, Ala., Aug. 4, 1949; s. Horace Edward and Alma Lou (Straughn) H.; m. Betty Jean Gilley, Dec. 26, 1976 (div. 1982). B.A., Southeastern Coll., 1971; Ed.M., Rollins Coll., 1976; Ed.D., Fla. State U., 1982; cert. in psychology U. Northwest Fla., 1979. Cert. tchr., Fla. Guidance counselor Escambia County Sch. Bd., Pensacola, Fla., 1979-80; dir. psychol. services Washington County Sch. Bd., Chipley, Fla., 1980-84; dir. admissions, guidance, psychology Bradford County Sch. Bd., Starke, Fla., 1984—; cons. psychol. Tri-County Sch. System, Starke, 1984—; mem. collective bargaining Bradford County Edn. Assn., Starke, 1984—; mem. com. Tchr. of Yr., Starke, 1985. Nominated Sch. Psychologist of Yr., Fla. Assn. Sch. Psychologists, 1982, 83. Mem. Am. Psychol. Assn., Nat. Assn. Sch. Psychologists, Fla. Assn. Sch. Adminstrs., Fla. Assn. Sch. Psychologists, Council Exceptional Children, Council Adminstrs. Spl. Edn., Collie Club Am., Phi Delta Kappa. Democrat. Baptist, Presbyterian. Avocations: collies; nature; farming. Home: 312 N Adams St Quincy FL 32351 Office: 3838 Trojan Trail Tallahassee FL 32301

HALL, JACK CHARLES, science educator, researcher; b. Grand Rapids, Mich., Oct. 9, 1955; s. Charles Arthur and Thressa Dora (Jannereth) H.; m. Barbara Jean Brown, July 16, 1977; 1 child, Matthew Evan. B.S., Grand Valley State Coll., 1977; M.S., U. N.C., 1981; Ph.D., Ohio State U., 1986. Research asst. U. N.C., Chapel Hill, 1978; assoc. tchr. Ohio State U., Columbus, 1981-83; lectr. U. N.C.-Wilmington, 1979-81, 84—; cons. E.I. DuPont & Co., Aiken, S.C., 1981. Shell doctoral fellow Shell Oil Co., 1983-84; research grantee Appalachian Basin Ind. Assocs., 1983-84, ARCO Research Fund, 1983—, Chevron Fieldwork Fund, 1983—, Friends of Orton Hall Fund, Ohio State U., 1983-84; recipient Edmund M. Spieker Annual award Ohio State U., 1983. Mem. Am. Assn. Petroleum Geologists (research grantee 1983), Carolina Geol. Soc., Pander Soc., Paleontol. Soc., Paleontol. Research Inst., Soc. Econ. Paleontologists and Mineralogists, Internat. Paleontol. Soc., Phi Kappa Phi. Avocations: scuba diving; golf; running; hiking; camping. Office: Dept Earth Scis U NC 601 S Coll Rd Wilmington NC 28403-3297

HALL, JAMES, III, architect, urban planner; b. Chickasha, Okla., May 13, 1934; s. James and Lella Mae (Bogney) H.; B.S., Hampton Inst., 1959; M.S., Ill. Inst. Tech., 1966; M.City Planning, Harvard U., 1974; m. Shirley Maria Sullivan, July 11, 1965; children—Sandra Maria, Marisa Annette, James IV. Designer, draftsman Henry L. Livas & Assos., Hampton, Norfolk, Va., 1957-59; archtl. cons. Ken L. Freeman, Bethesda, Md., 1963; designer, draftsman PACE Assos., Chgo., 1964-66; project architect Tidewater Design Group, Hampton, Va., 1967-70; asst. prof. architecture Hampton Inst., 1966-72, asso. prof., 1974-77, prof., 1977—; prin. staff planner Roxbury Action Program, Inc., Boston, 1972-74. Served with U.S. Army, 1959-63. NSF fellow, 1968. Mem. AIA, Am. Inst. Planners, Alpha Phi Alpha. Office: Dept Arch Hampton Inst Hampton VA 23668

HALL, JAMES MILTON, III, city official; b. Dallas, Oct. 30, 1947; s. James M. and Minnie Mae (Crump) H., Jr.; m. Myong Chu Sin, Dec. 26, 1975; children—James M. IV, Jonathan Michael. Accredited human resources profl. B.A. in Internat. Relations, U. Calif.-Davis, 1969; B.A. in Psychology, U. Tex., 1977; M.S. in Indsl. Psychology, Tex. A&M U., 1979, M.P.A. in Personnel Adminstrn., 1980. Dir. personnel City of Odessa (Tex.), 1980-82, acting asst. city mgr., 1982, dir. adminstrv. services, 1982—. Served to capt. U.S. Army, 1969-76. Decorated Army Commendation medal with 2 oak leaf clusters; U.S. Army ROTC scholar, 1967-69; recipient Eagle Scout and Order of Arrow, Boy Scouts Am. Mem. Internat. Personnel Mgmt. Assn., Tex. City Mgrs. Assn., Permian Basin Personnel Assn., Am. Soc. Pub. Adminstrn., Mensa, Odessa VFW, Pi Alpha Alpha, Phi Kappa Tau, Gamma Sigma (founder, past pres.). Club: Downtown Lions. Home: 213 Pecan Dr Odessa TX 79764 Office: City of Odessa PO Box 4398 Odessa TX 79760

HALL, JAMES WILLIAM, JR., media broker, newspaper publisher; b. Montgomery, Ala., Dec. 23, 1931; s. James William and Hazel (Kemp) H.; student Huntington Coll., 1950; B.A., U. Ala., 1958, M.A., 1968; postgrad. Tulane U., 1964; m. Martha Faye George, Aug. 31, 1958. Gen. assignment reporter Montgomery Advertiser, 1956-57; with So. Bell Telephone Co., New Orleans, 1958-66, directory compilation mgr., 1963-64, public relations mgr., 1965-66; exec. dir. Ala. Press Assn., University, 1966-74; asst. to pres. Troy (Ala.) State U., 1974-79, dean Hall Sch. Journalism, 1977-79; asso. Chancey Cons., 1981—1981-84; Greene County Democrat, Eutaw, Ala., 1981-84; pres. Jim Hall Media Services, Inc., 1984—; lectr. journalism dept. U. Ala., Tuscaloosa, 1966-72; pres. Quest. Inc., Tuscaloosa, 1968-71; v.p. Ala. News Service, Tuscaloosa, 1969-71; pres. Leader Enterprises, 1979—. Mem. Ala. Safety Coordinating Com., 1968-74, Ala. Farm-City Week Com., 1970-74; 2d v.p. New Orleans Floral Trail, 1966; chmn. Nat. Newspaper Week, 1973. Sec. Ala. Press Assn. Journalism Found., 1968-74. Served with USAF, 1951-54. Named Outstanding Indsl. Editor, Greater New Orleans Area United Fund, 1966; Hon. Blind Man Ala. Sch. for Deaf and Blind, 1967; Distinguished Alumnus, U. Ala. Dept. Journalism, 1972. Mem. Troy Council Arts and Humanities (sec.), Jasons, Phi Beta Kappa, Omicron Delta Kappa, Phi Kappa Phi, Phi Eta Sigma, Chi Phi, Sigma Delta Chi (pres. 1970). Presbyterian. Clubs: Masons (32 deg.), Capitol City. Home: The Abattoir Troy AL 36081

HALL, JOHN RANDOLPH, JR., physician, retired army officer; b. Napton, Mo., June 20, 1913; s. John Randolph and Ferda (Roberts) H.; m. Josephine Miles, Aug. 5, 1937; children—John Randolph, Sarah M., Miles Bruce, Rogers Pierpoint. A.B., Central Methodist Coll. (Mo.), 1935; B.S. in Medicine, U. Nebr., 1937; M.D., Washington U., St. Louis, 1939; M.S., U. Chgo., 1949; M.P.H., Johns Hopkins U., 1954; grad. Nat. War Coll., 1959. Diplomate Am. Bd. Preventive Medicine in Pub. Health and Occupational Medicine. Commd. 2d lt. USAR, 1934; commd. 1st lt. M.C., U.S. Army, 1940, advanced through grades to col., 1946; surgeon, chief med. officer 1st cav. div., X Corps, SW Pacific, Philippines and Japan, 1942-46, supr. studies at Nagasaki and Hiroshima; ret., 1964; ptnr. Kelsey-Seybold Clinic, 1964-69; pres. Space Ctr. Med. Assocs., Houston, 1969-79; ret., 1979; part-time examiner Mil. Entrance Processing Sta., San Antonio, 1980—; dean Sch. Pub. Health, U. Tex.-Houston, 1968-69; writer, editor U.S. Mil. Med. and Cav. History, 1970—. Decorated Silver Star, Legion of Merit with oak leaf cluster, 3 Bronze Stars with V. Air medal, Purple Heart; recipient Andreas Vesalius medallion, Stadt Augsburg, W.Ger., 1961. Fellow ACP, Am. Coll. Preventive Medicine, Assn. Mil. Surgeons, Internat. Health Soc.; mem. AMA, Tex. Med. Assn., Bexar County Med. Soc., 1st Cav. Div. Assn. (pres. 1980-82), U.S. Horse Cav. Assn. (dir. 1982—), Nu Sigma Nu, Alpha Epsilon Delta. Episcopalian. Clubs: Randolph AFB Officers, Marines Meml. Lodges: Masons, Shriners, Rotary, KT. Home: 741 Winfield Circle San Antonio TX 78239

HALL, JOHN RICHARD, oil company executive; b. Dallas, Nov. 30, 1932; s. John W. and Agnes (Sanders) H.; m. Donna S. Stauffer, May 10, 1980. B.Chem. Engring., Vanderbilt U., 1955. Chem. engr. Esso Standard Oil Co., Balt., 1956-58, Ashland Oil Co., Ky., 1959-63, coordinator carbon black div., Houston, 1963-65, exec. asst. v.p., 1965-66, v.p., 1966-68, sr. v.p., 1970-71; also dir.; pres. Ashland Chem. Co., 1971-74; exec. v.p. Ashland Oil, Inc., 1974—, group operating officer, 1976—, chief exec. officer petroleum and chems., 1978—, vice chmn., chief operating officer, 1979-81, chmn., chief exec. officer, 1981—. Mem. com. visitors Vanderbilt U. Engring. Sch., Nashville; bd. curators Transylvania U., Lexington, Ky. Served as 2d lt., Chem. Corps AUS, 1955-56. Mem. Mfg. Chemists Assn., Nat. Petroleum Refiners Assn., Am. Petroleum Inst., Ky. Soc. Profl. Engrs., Tau Delta Pi, Sigma Chi, Delta Kappa. Republican. Home: 99 Stoneybrook Dr Ashland KY 41101 Office: PO Box 391 Ashland KY 41114

HALL, JOHNNY LEE, oil company executive; b. Holdenville, Okla., Sept. 29, 1951; s. Emmett Coy and Peggy Louise (Heltcel) H.; m. Janna Jo Sims, Jan. 4, 1975; children—Jonathan Michael, Jason Matthew, Jennifer Lee. B.S., Northeast La. U., 1974, M.S., 1976. Cert. petroleum geologist. Sr. geologist South Tex. div. Exxon, Kingsville, Tex., 1976-79, sr. petroleum geologist Gulf Coast div., Houston, 1979-80, supervisory geologist Southeastern div., New Orleans, 1980-81, dist. prodn. geologist, 1981-82, dist. prodn. geologist Offshore dist., New Orleans, 1982-85, div. geol. mgr., 1985-86, dist. exploration mgr., 1986—. Coach Little League Baseball, Kingsville, Tex., 1976-77. Mem. Am. Assn. Petroleum Geologists, Sigma Gamma Epsilon. Democrat. Baptist. Avocations: hunting, fishing, sports. Home: 829 Kingsway East Gretna LA 70053

HALL, JOSEPH CARTER, JR., mechanical engineer; b. Ft. Towson, Okla., Dec. 4, 1931; s. Joseph Carter and Ruth Allyn (Osburn) H.; B.S.M.E., Okla. State U., 1954; m. Jere Lovell Hogue, Aug. 24, 1954; children—Andrea Elise, James Eric. Test engr. nuclear div. Babcock and Wilcox Co., Lynchburg, Va., 1959-60; process engr., machine tool engr. Nuclear div. Union Carbide Corp., Oak Ridge, 1960-80, supt. plant services, 1980-82, mgr. quality improvement, 1982—. Mem. Roane County Heritage Commn., 1980—. Served to lt. comdr. USNR, 1954-57. Registered profl. engr., Tenn. Fellow Inst. Prodn. Engrs.; mem. Soc. Mfg. Engrs. (pres. 1979-80), Am. Assn. Engring. Socs. (gov. 1979-81, mem. exec. com. 1981-82), Pi Tau Sigma, Sigma Tau, Blue Key, Sigma Phi Epsilon. Republican. Methodist. Lodges: Masons, Lions. Home: Route 5 Box 97 Kingston TN 37763 Office: Union Carbide Corp PO Box P Bldg K-1001 MS 124 Oak Ridge TN 37830

HALL, JOSEPH RICHARD, periodontist; b. Independence, Kans., Feb. 23, 1920; s. John Curtis and Alice Gertrude (Burt) H.; m. Hazel Kathryn Rowley, June 5, 1942; children—Scott Richard, Stephen Curtis. B.S., U. Okla., 1942; D.D.S., Baylor U., 1945, B.S.D., 1957. Internship USPHS, Kirkwood, Mo., 1945-46; practice dentistry, Tulsa, 1946-56; practice dentistry specializing in periodontics, Tulsa, 1957—; clin. prof. U. Okla. Dental Sch., 1974-79. Served to capt. USAF, 1951-52. Mem. Southwest Soc. Periodontists (fellow, pres. 1968), Tulsa County Dental Soc. (pres. 1955), Okla. State Dental Assn., ADA, Am. Acad. Periodontology (exec. council 1975—, Spl. Citation 1984), Okla. Soc. Periodontists (pres. 1974). Republican. Presbyterian. Avocations: tennis; sailing. Home: 3856 S Victor Ave Tulsa OK 74105 Office: 6465 S Yale Ave # 922 Tulsa OK 74136

HALL, JULIA MARIE, cable company executive; b. Dayton, Ohio, Oct. 8, 1962; d. James Alexander and Phyllis Jean (Abels) H. B.A. in Telecommunications, Ind. U., 1983. Corp. tng. coordinator Arlington Cable Partners, Arlington, Va., 1983—; tng. coordinator Suburban Cable Co., Mpls., 1985. Campaign coordinator United Way, Arlington, 1985. Mem. Women in Cable, Nat. Acad. Cable Programming. Republican. Roman Catholic. Avocations: running; biking; reading. Home: 7841 Enola St # 206 McLean VA 22102 Office: Arlington Cable Ptnrs 2707 Wilson Blvd Arlington VA 22201

HALL, KENNETH KELLER, judge; b. Greenview, W.Va., Feb. 24, 1918; s. Jack and Ruby (Greene) H.; m. Gerry Tabor, Apr. 6, 1940; 1 son, Kenneth Keller. J.D., W.Va. U., 1948. Bar: W.Va. 1948. Practiced law, Madison, W.Va., 1948-52; mem. firm Garnett & Hall, 1948-50; judge 25th Jud. Circuit Ct. W.Va., Madison, 1953-69, U.S. Dist. Ct. for So. Dist. W.Va., Charleston, 1971-76, U.S. Ct. Appeals, 4th Circuit, 1976—. Served with USNR, 1942-45. Recipient Silver Beaver award Boy Scouts Am., 1962. Mem. ABA, W.Va. Jud. Assn., W.Va. Bar Assn. Democrat. Baptist. Lodge: Rotary. Home: Charleston WV Office: PO Box 2549 Charleston WV 25329

HALL, LARRY LEE, toxicologist; b. Cleve., Jan. 31, 1937; s. J. Lee and Jane Viva (Barnette) H.; m. Carolyn Knestrick, Oct. 31, 1959; children—Susan G., Elisabeth C., Bruce B., James L. B.A., Hiram Coll., 1961; M.S., U. Rochester, 1968, Ph.D., 1974. Diplomate Am. Bd. Toxicology. Sect. chief inhalation toxicology EPA, Cin., 1971-74; sect. chief acute and chronic studies EPA, RTP, N.C., 1974-78, research toxicologist reproductive toxicology br., 1979—, team leader dermal absorption, 1981—. Contbr. articles to profl. jours. Served with USNR, 1955-67. USPHS fellow in toxicology, 1968-71. Mem. Soc. Toxicology, N.Y. Acad. Scis., Am. Chem. Soc., AAAS, N.C. Acad. Sci., Sigma Xi. Office: US EPA MD-72 Research Triangle Park NC 27711

HALL, MARY OWENS, nursing educator, university administrator; b. East Point, Ga., July 5, 1927; d. Charles D. and Mary (Short) O.; m. Robert T. Hall, Dec. 25, 1948; children—Robert David, William Daniel. B.S.N., Emory U., 1949, M.N., 1962, Ph.D., Inst. Liberal Arts, 1983; M.S. in Urban Life, Ga. State U., 1974. Instr. in nursing Emory U., Atlanta, 1949-50, 62-64, asst. prof. nursing, 1964-67, assoc. prof., 1967—, asst. dean, dir. grad. program Sch. Nursing, 1983—, interim dean, 1984-85; staff nurse Fulton County Health Dept., Atlanta, 1958-61; bd. dirs. Met. Atlanta Vis. Nurse Assn.; mem. health delivery systems task force Atlanta Regional Commn. USPHS trainee Emory U., 1960-61; tuition scholar and merit stipend awardee Emory U., 1980-81. Mem. Am. Nurses' Assn., Nat. League Nursing, Am. Assn. Colls. Nursing, Am. Pub. Health Assn., Ga. League Nursing, Sigma Theta Tau, Omega Delta Kappa. Baptist. Home: 3509 Carriage Way East Point GA 30344 Office: Nell Hodgson Woodruff Sch Nursing Emory U 531 Asbury Circle Atlanta GA 30322

HALL, MILES LEWIS, JR., lawyer; b. Ft. Lauderdale, Fla., Aug. 14, 1924; s. Miles Lewis and Mary Frances (Dawson) H.; A.B., Princeton U., 1947; J.D., Harvard U., 1950; m. Muriel M. Fisher, Nov. 4, 1950; children—Miles Lewis III, Don Thomas. Bar: Fla. 1951, U.S. Supreme Ct. 1959. Practiced in Miami, 1951—; ptnr. firm Hall & Hedrick, 1953—; dir. Gen. Portland, Inc., Dallas, 1974-81. Vice pres. Orange Bowl Com., 1961-63, pres., 1964-65, dir., 1966—, sec.-treas., 1983—; mem. Fla. Council of 100, vice chmn., 1961-62; mem. exec. bd. South Fla. council Boy Scouts Am., 1966-67; vice chmn., bd. dirs. Dade County chpt. ARC, 1961-62, chmn., 1963-64, bd. dirs., 1967-73, nat. fund cons., 1963, 66-68; pres. Dade County Bar Assn. Ednl. Found., 1967-68; mem. adv. bd. Salvation Army, 1968-73; bd. dirs. Coral Gables War Meml. Youth Center, 1967—, v.p., 1968-69, pres., 1969-72; mem. citizens bd. U. Miami, 1961-66; pres. Ransom Sch. Parents Assn., 1966; chmn. South Fla. Gov.'s Scholarship Ball, 1966; mem. nominating com. Dade County Met. Ct., 1968-72; chmn. nominating commn. Dist. Ct. Appeal 3d Dist. Fla., 1972-75; mem. Biltmore Devel. Bd., City of Coral Gables, 1971-73; bd. visitors Coll. Law, Fla. State U., 1974-81; bd. dirs. Am. Found., 1985—. Served to 2d lt. USAAF, 1943-45. Mem. ABA (Fla. co-chmn. membership com., sect. corp. banking and bus. law 1968-72), Dade County Bar Assn. (dir. 1964-65, pres. 1967-68), Fla. Bar, Am. Judicature Soc., Miami-Dade County C. of C., (v.p. 1962-64, dir. 1966-68), Harvard Law Sch. Assn. Fla. (dir. 1964-66), Alpha Tau Omega. Methodist (steward). Clubs: Princeton So. Fla. (past pres., dir.); Harvard of Miami; Cottage; The Miami, City (Miami). Lodge: Kiwanis. Author: Titles, Ejectment and Election of Remedies, Vol. VIII, Fla. Law and Practice, 1958. Home: 2907 Alhambra Circle Coral Gables FL 33134 Office: Peninsula Federal Bldg Suite 1104 200 SE 1st St Miami FL 33131

HALL, MILLARD FRANK, JR., hospital administrator; b. Marion, N.C., June 23, 1945; s. Millard Frank and Eula (Lonon) H.; m. Ruth Ellen Powell, Dec. 5, 1970; 1 child, Ashley Elizabeth (dec.). B.A., Appalachian St. U., 1973, M.A., 1979; Cert. U. N.C. Sch. Bus. Adminstrn. Execs. Inst., 1983. Program developer Dept. Human Resources, Black Mountain, N.C., 1973-74, grants mgr., 1974-76; regional coordinator Div. Mental Health, Black Mountain, 1976-79; dir. Rutherfordton-Polk area Mental Health/Mental Retardation/-Substance Abuse Authority, N.C., 1979-82; adminstr. ARC Specialty Hosp., Black Mountain, 1982-85, John Umstead Hosp., Butner, N.C., 1985—; chmn. Western Region Mgmt. Team, Morganton, N.C., 1983—; chmn. Mental Retardation Com., Morganton, 1980-81; chmn. Regional Substance Abuse Commn., Morganton-Black Mountain, 1974-79; cons. Rutherfordton-Polk Area Authority, Spindale, N.C., 1982-83. Bd. dirs. Rutherford Greater United Way, Forest City, N.C., 1980—, chmn. community div., 1981; chmn. Heart Fund Sunday N.C. Heart Assn., 1982; mem. N.C. Council on Status of Women, Shelby, 1979. Served with USAF, 1965-69. Recipient Community Service award United Way, 1980, Outstanding Leadership award Alcohol Rehab. Ctr. Specialty Hosp., Black Mountain, 1984. Mem. Western Regional Mgmt. Team (chmn. 1979-85, N.C. Plaque 1985), Am. Coll. Hosp. Adminstrs., Assn. Mental Health Adminstrn., N.C. Div. Mental Health Joint Conf. Com., Western N.C. Region Substance Com. (chmn. 1974-79). Democrat. Methodist. Avocations: woodworking; assisting in building pine box derby cars for underprivileged scouts. Home: 182 Pine Cone Dr Oxford NC 27565

HALL, PATRICIA DELAY, accountant; b. Texarkana, Tex., Dec. 24, 1930; d. Byron N. and Esther J. DeLay; B.B.A., Lamar U., Beaumont, Tex., 1982; m. Miles A. Hall, Apr. 16, 1969; children—Kathryn, Andrew. Bookkeeper, Am. Bridge div. U.S. Steel Corp., Orange, Tex., 1948-59; with du Pont Co., Orange, 1959—, acct., 1976-79, acctg. specialist, 1979—. Pres. Orange County Ballet Soc. Mem. AAUW, Phi Kappa Phi, Beta Gamma Sigma. Home: 309 Sandy Dr Bridge City TX 77611 Office: PO Box 1089 Orange TX 77630

HALL, PHOEBE POULTERER, lawyer, judge; b. Watertown, N.Y., Dec. 4, 1941; d. William Taylor, Jr., and Betty (Bennett) Poulterer; m. Franklin P. Hall, July 26, 1969; children—Kimberly Ann, Franklin P. B.A., U. Del.-Wilmington, 1963; J.D., Georgetown U., 1969. Bar: Va. Assoc., Hall & Hall, Richmond, Va., 1969—; substitute judge Gen. Dist. Cts., City of Richmond, 1983—, commr. in chancery, circuit cts., 1981—; founding dir., Cardinal Savs. & Loan Assn., Richmond, 1978—. Bd. trustees, Va. Mus. Fine Arts, 1983—; commr. Human Relations Commn., Richmond, 1972-73; dir. Family and Children's Services, Richmond, 1976-78; mem. worship com. 1st Presbyterian Ch., Richmond, 1983—; mem. state central com. Democratic Party, Va., 1974-80. Recipient Outstanding Citizenship award Urban League, Richmond, 1983; first woman pub. defender, City of Richmond, 1970; designer, instr. first course for paralegals, Va. State Bar, 1974. Mem. ABA, Richmond Bar Assn., Met. Richmond Women's Bar (founding 1971—), Va. Trial Lawyers Assn., Assn. Trial Lawyers Am., Def. Research Inst., Bus. and Profl. Women's Assn., Am. Bus. Women's Assn. Lodge Soroptimists. Home: 9006 Cherokee Rd Richmond VA 23235 Office: Hall and Hall Suite One 700 Bldg Richmond VA 23219

HALL, RALPH MOODY, congressman; b. Tex., May 3, 1923; s. Hugh O. Hall; student U. Tex., Tex. Christian U.; LL.B., So. Meth. U., 1951; LL.D., East Tex. State U.; m. Mary Ellen Murphy, Nov. 14, 1944; children—Hampton, Brett, Blakeley. Bar: Tex. County judge Rockwall County, Tex., 1950-62; mem. Tex. Senate, 1962-72; former pres., chief exec. officer Tex. Aluminum Corp.; former gen. counsel Tex. Extrusion Co., Inc.; organizer, former chmn. bd. dirs. Lakeside Nat. Bank of Rockwall (name now Lakeside Bancshares, Inc.), now dir.; former vice chmn. bd. dirs. Bank of Crowley; former chmn. bd. dirs. Lakeside News, Inc.; pres. North & East Trading Co. Inc.; chmn. bd. Linrock, Inc., v.p Crowley Holding Co.; mem. 97th-98th congresses from Tex. Served to lt. USNR, 1942-45. Mem. Am. Legion, VFW. Methodist. Lodge: Rotary (past pres.). Office: 1728 Longworth House Office Bldg Washington DC 20515

HALL, ROBERT HOWELL, judge; b. Soperton, Ga., Nov. 28, 1921; s. Instant Howell, Jr. and Blanche (Mishoe) H.; B.S. in Commerce, U. Ga., 1941; LL.B., U. Va., 1948; LL.D. (hon.), Emory U., 1973; m. Alice Marie Coberly, June 8, 1946; children—Carolyn C., Patricia A., Howell A.; m. 2d, Janice Wren, July 15, 1982. Bar: Ga. 1948, U.S. Supreme Ct. Prof. law Emory U., 1948-61; asst. atty. gen. Ga., 1953-61, head criminal div. Ga. Law Dept., 1959-61; judge Ga. Ct. Appeals, Atlanta, 1961-74; justice Ga. Supreme Ct., Atlanta, 1974-79; judge U.S. Dist. Ct. for No. Dist. Ga., Atlanta, 1979—. Chmn. Jud. Council Ga., 1973—, Gov.'s Commn. on Jud. Processes, 1971-73. Served with AUS, 1942-46; lt. col. Res., ret. Recipient Leadership award Harvard Law Sch. Assn. Ga., 1971; Golden Citizenship award Fulton Grand Jurors Assn., 1975. Fellow Am. Bar Found.; mem. Am. Bar Assn. (ho. dels. 1971-73, chmn. com. Nat. Inst. Justice 1976), Am. Judicature Soc. (pres. 1971-73, Harley award 1974), Nat. Center State Cts. (adv. council 1971—, dir. 1977—), Inst. Ct. Mgmt. (trustee 1976—), Am. Acad. Jud. Edn. (gov. 1964-71), Atlanta Lawyers Club, State Bar Ga., Delta Tau Delta, Delta Sigma Phi, Phi Delta Phi. Author 3 legal texts, also articles. Home: 2186 Fairhaven Circle NE Atlanta GA 30305 Office: 2188 Russell Bldg 75 Spring St SW Atlanta GA 30303

HALL, ROGER CLIFFORD, JR., design company executive; b. Seattle, Mar. 10, 1948; s. Roger Clifford and Barbara (Berens) H.; m. Patricia Walden, Aug. 8, 1970 (div. 1986); children—Roger Clifford, Whitney Paige. B.S. in Home Econs., Fla. State U., 1970. Cert. Nat. Council on Interior Design Qualifications. Designer Paul T. Ward, Inc., Tampa, Fla., 1970-74; pres. Design Concepts & Assocs., Tampa, 1974—. Past treas. Henry B. Plant Mus. of City of Tampa; mem. curriculum adv. bd. interior design dept. Erwin Vocat. Tech. Sch. Mem. Inst. Bus. Designers (v.p. 1984—), Am. Soc. Interior Designers (2d v.p. 1977), Constrn. Specification Inst., C. of C., Com. of 100. Republican. Roman Catholic. Home: 307 1/2 S Newport Tampa FL 33606 Office: Design Concepts & Assocs Inc 214 S Armenia Tampa FL 33609

HALL, RUSSELL DAVID, lawyer; b. Blytheville, Ark., Feb. 21, 1949; s. Harold Elwood and Lillian Kathryn (Kime) H. B.A., U. Okla., 1973; M. Criminal Justice, Oklahoma City U., 1976, J.D., 1978. Bar: Okla. 1978, U.S. Dist. Ct. (we. and no. dists.) Okla. 1978, U.S. Ct. Appeals (10th cir.) 1978, U.S. Supreme Ct. 1981. Asst. gen. counsel State of Okla. Dept. Human Services, Oklahoma City, 1978—. Mem. Okla. Bar Assn., ABA, Okla. Criminal Justice Assn., Am. Correctional Assn., Phi Delta Phi. Democrat. Baptist. Home: 3110 N Lake Oklahoma City OK 73118 Office: PO Box 25352 Oklahoma City OK 73125

HALL, SAM BLAKELY, JR., U.S. District judge, former congressman; b. Marshall, Tex., Jan. 11, 1924; s. Sam Blakely and Valerie (Curtis) H.; m. Madeleine Segal, Feb. 9, 1946; children—Linda Rebecca Hall Palmer, Amanda Jane Hall Wynn, Sandra Blake. Student Coll. Marshall, 1942; LL.B., Baylor U., 1948. Bar: Tex. 1948. Sole practice, Marshall, 1948-76, formerly with Hall, Huffman & Palmer, Marshall; mem. 94th-98th Congresses, 1st Dist. Tex., 1975-84; U.S. dist. judge, Eastern Dist. Tex., 1985—. Past pres. Marshall Jaycees; past v.p. Tex. Jaycees; past nat. dir. U.S. C. of C.; past bd. dirs. East Tex. area council Boy Scouts Am.; past trustee Wiley Coll., Marshall; past chmn. Marshall Bd. Edn.; past chmn. bd. dirs. Harrison County Hosp. Assn., Marshall; mem. bd. devel. Baylor U. Served with USAAF, 1943-45. Recipient Richard W. Blalock award Marshall Jaycees; Boss of Yr. award Harrison County Legal Secs. Assn., 1965; Outstanding Citizen award Marshall C. of C., 1970. Mem. Am. Bd. Trial Advocates, ABA, Tex. Bar Assn., N.E. Tex. Bar Assn., Harrison County Bar Assn. (past pres.), Marshall C. of C. (past pres.). Democrat. Mem. Ch. of Christ. Club: Kiwanis (past pres. Marshall, past lt. gov.). Address: US Dist Ct PO Box 88 Beaumont TX 77704*

HALL, TIMOTHY ALAN, energy, environmental management company executive; b. Stillwater, Okla., Sept. 3, 1946; s. Forrest L. Hall and Barbara J. (Gallagher) Hall Komarek; m. Kay Smalling, Aug. 13, 1966 (div. 1981); children—Josef T., Nathan S.; m. Helen Lucas, Oct. 6, 1984. B.A. magna cum laude, Bethany Coll., 1969; M.A., U. Okla., 1977, Ph.D., 1978. Research asst. sci. and pub. policy program U. Okla., Norman, 1973-77, research assoc., 1977-78; asst. prof. Ga. Inst. Tech., Atlanta, 1978-79; sr. scientist Radian Corp., Austin, Tex., 1979-80, program mgr., 1980—; cons. U.S. Congress Office Tech. Assessment, Washington, 1976-77; advisor Nat. Conf. State Legis., Denver, 1980-82. Author: (with others) Energy and the Way We Live, 1980 (award Acad. Ednl. Devel. 1980); Energy From the West, 1981. Served with U.S. Army, 1969-72. Mem. AAAS (appointed mem. com. sci., engring., pub. policy, Washington), Policy Studies Orgn., Am. Polit. Sci. Assn., Phi Delta Lambda. Democrat. Presbyterian. Avocations: racketball; softball; jogging. Home: 303 Country Club Rd Chapel Hill NC 27514 Office: Radian Corp PO Box 13000 Research Triangle Park NC 27709

HALL, WILLIAM LLOYD, surgeon; b. Wichita Falls, Tex., Aug. 25, 1925; s. Lloyd Lorenso and Frankie (Hodges) H.; M.D., Southwestern Med. Coll., 1947; student N. Tex. State U., 1942-44; m. Ann Carolyn Short, July 11, 1947 (div. 1976); children—Marc William, Michael Steven, Lisa Merenith, Jay Jonathan. Intern George Washington U. Hosp., 1947-48; resident Gt. Lakes Naval Hosp., 1948-49, Baylor U. Hosp., 1953-56; practice medicine specializing in surgery, Dallas, 1956—; chief staff Oak Cliff Med. and Surg. Hosp., 1986—. Served as lt. M.C., USN, 1948-53. Diplomate Am. Bd. Surgery. Mem. Am., Tex. med. assns., Dallas County Med. Soc. Home: 1419 Yakimo Dr Dallas TX 75208 Office: 122 W Colorado Dallas TX 75208

HALL, WILLIAM STONE, retired psychiatrist, state official; b. Wagener, S.C., May 1, 1915; s. Henry F. and Mary (Gantt) H.; M.D., Med. U. S.C., 1937; student Sch. Mil. Neuropsychiatry, 1944, Columbia, 1947, U. Chgo., 1959; m. Oxena Elizabeth Gunter, June 29, 1940; children—William Stone, Carol Lynn, Richard F. Intern, Columbia (S.C.) Hosp., 1937-38; mem. staff S.C. State Hosp., Columbia, 1938-52, supt., 1952-69; supt. Pineland State Tng. Sch. and Hosp., 1953-66, Palmetto State Hosp., 1952-66; commr. mental health S.C. Dept. Mental Health, 1963-85; clin. prof. psychiatry Med. U. S.C., 1957—; clin. prof. psychiatry U. S.C., 1976—. Mem. Presdl. Task Force on Mentally Handicapped, 1970; chmn. planning com. Surg. Gen.'s Conf. State and Ter. Mental Health Authorities, 1971, 72; mem. S.C. Child Devel. Council, 1971-80; liaison mem. Nat. Adv. Mental Health Council, Nat. Inst. Mental Health, 1972-73; mem. Gov.'s State Health Planning Council, 1973-74, Gov.'s Social Devel. Policy Council, 1973-74; mem. S.C. Methadone Maintenance Council, 1973-80; mem. coordinating council S.C. Commn. on Aging, 1974-85; mem. Adv. Council for Comprehensive Health Planning, 1967-75, 1st vice chmn., 1972, 73; councillor, accreditation council for psychiat. facilities Joint Commn. on Accreditation Hosps., 1973-79; mem. Gov.'s Com. on State Employees and their Employment, 1973-85; mem. S.C. Statewide Health Coordinating Council, 1976-85; mem. S.C. Gov.'s Interagy. Coordinating council on Early

Childhood Devel. and Edn., 1980-85; mem. S.C. Pre-trial Intervention Adv. Com., 1980-85. Trustee United Community Fund, 1968-71; bd. dirs. United Way of Midlands, 1976-80; adv. bd. Remotivation Technique Orgn., 1972-75. Served as maj. M.C., AUS, 1942-46. Recipient disting. service plaque S.C. Mental Health Assn., 1960; center for intensive treatment, research edn., Columbia, named William S. Hall Psychiat. Inst., 1964; recipient Orgnl. award S.C. Vocational Rehab. Assn., 1969, Outstanding Physician of Yr. award, 1985; Ann. Disting. Service award S.C. dept. Am. Legion, 1970; Dist. Service award S.C. Hosp. Assn., 1972; Disting. Alumnus award Med. U. S.C., 1974; named to S.C. Hall of Fame, 1975; named Physician of Yr., Mayor's Com. on Employment of Handicapped; Outstanding Physician of Yr., Gov.'s Com. on Employment of Handicapped, 1986. Diplomate Am. Bd. Neurology and Psychiatry. Fellow Am. Psychiat. Assn. (life, nominating com. 1968, chmn. program com. 12th Mental Hosp. Inst. 1960, com. certification in adminstrv. psychiatry, 1972-80, pres. S.C. dist. br. 1957), Am. Coll. Psychiatrists (charter), Am. Coll. Mental Health Adminstrn.; mem. Am. Hosp. Assn. (chmn. governing council psychiat. hosp. sect. 1971), A.M.A. (com. nursing 1966-73), S.C. Mental Health Assn., Columbia Med. Soc. (pres. 1958), Assn. Med. Supts. Mental Hosps. (pres. 1964, 65, meritorious service award 1971), Nat. Assn. State Mental Health Program Dirs. (v.p. 1968, 69, pres. 1970, 71), S.C. State Employees Assn. (dir. 1968-76), v.p. 1971-73, pres. 1973-75, Outstanding State Employee 1967). Baptist (deacon). Lodge: Rotary. Home: 5314 Lakeshore Dr Columbia SC 29206

HALL, WILLIAM TOMPIE, business executive; b. Fort Worth, Tex., Feb. 16, 1946; s. William Tompie and Jo Ann Hall; children—Tompie, Taylor. B.S., Tex. Wesleyan Coll., 1972. Mgr. contracts adminstrn. Tex. div. Tech. Devel. Calif., Arlington, 1980; mgr. risk assessment and contracts Martin Marietta Corp., Orlando (Fla.) Aerospace, 1980—; chief exec. officer Marlow Hall Inc., 1983—; sr. mgr. Peat, Marwick & Mitchell Co., C.P.A.s, 1985—. Mem. Nat. Contract Mgmt. Assn., Soc. Logistic Engrs., Nat. Mgmt. Assn., Sigma Phi Epsilon. Republican. Am. Baptist. Contbr. articles to profl. jours. Home: 1000 Jarvis Ln Azle TX 76020 Office: Suite 1400 Thanksgiving Tower 1601 Elm St Dallas TX 75201

HALLAN, BRENDA HURLEY, educator; b. Mouthcard, Ky., Dec. 8, 1947; d. James L. and Goldie M. H.; B.S., Concord Coll., 1971; M.S., Radford U., 1976; doctoral candidate W.Va. U., 1980—; m. R. Witter Hallan, May 31, 1980; children—Tina, Brian. Tchr., Mercer Sch., Princeton, W.Va., 1972-77, counselor elem. guidance, 1977-80; research assoc. Appalachia Ednl. Lab., Charleston, W.Va., 1979—; policy analyst, cons. W.Va. Dept. Edn., Charleston, 1982-83. Dir. spiritual life 1st Ch. God, Princeton, 1977-78, dir. missionary edn., 1979-80; bd. dirs. CDC Inc., 1978-80. Mem. Phi Delta Kappa. Home: 1805 Huber Rd Charleston WV 25314

HALLANAN, ELIZABETH V., U.S. district judge; b. Charleston, W.Va., Jan. 10, 1925; s. Walter Simms and Imogene (Burns) H. A.B., U. Charleston, 1946; J.D., W.Va. U., 1951; postgrad. U. Mich., 1964. Atty., Cricton & Hallanan, Charleston, 1952-59; mem. W.Va. State Bd. Edn., Charleston, 1955-57; mem. Ho. of Dels., W.Va. Legislature, Charleston, 1957-58; asst. commr. pub. instns., Charleston, 1958-59; men., chmn. W.Va. Pub. Service Commn., Charleston, 1969-75; atty. Lopinsky, Bland & Hallanan and Deutsch & Hallanan, Charleston, 1975-84; U.S. dist. judge, so. W.Va., 1984—. Mem. White House Conf. on Children and Youth. Mem. ABA, W.Va. Bar Assn. Office:; PO Box 2546 Charleston WV 25329*

HALLE, CLAUS M., beverage company executive; b. 1927; married. With Lemgol Lippe, W.Ger., 1946; with Coca-Cola Export Corp. subs., Atlanta, 1950—, Coca-cola GmbH, Essen, Germany, 1950-56, sales mgr., Germany, 1956-62, mgr., 1962-65, v.p. exprot, area mgr. Central Europe, 1965-70; corp. sr. v.p., pres., chief exec. officer Coca Cola Europe, 1970-73; pres., dir. Coca-Cola Export Corp., 1973; v.p. Coca-Cola Co., 1973-74, sr. v.p., 1974-76, exec. v.p., 1976-79, vice chmn. bd., 1979-80, exec. v.p., 1980-81, sr. exec. v.p., 1981—. Office: Coca Cola Co 310 North Ave NW Atlanta GA 30313*

HALLENBURG, JAMES KING, geophysical logging consultant; b. Chgo., May 21, 1921; s. Roy Edwin and Pearl Eleanor (King) H.; B.A. in Physics, Northwestern U., 1947; m. Jacquelyn Barry, May 22, 1944; children—Karen Jane, Susan Barry, James Chris. Sr. engr. Schlumberger Well Services Co., Houston, 1947-64, Mohole Project, Houston, 1965-66, Western Co. N.Am., Ft. Worth, 1966-67; owner Data Line Logging Co., Casper, Wyo., 1967-70; geophysicist Teton Exploration Co., Casper, 1970-75, Century Geophys. Corp., Casper and Tulsa, 1975-79; pres. D.L. Enterprises, Inc., Tulsa, 1979—, owner Data Line Logging Co., 1967—; pres. Hallenburg and Co., Inc., Tulsa, 1981—; instr. Casper Coll., 1971; condr. seminars on logging, 1979—. Served with USAAF, 1942-45. Registered profl. geologist, Calif. Mem. AAAS, Am. Inst. Profl. Geologists, Soc. Mining Engrs., Soc. Petroleum Engrs., Soc. Exploration Geophysicists, Soc. Profl. Well Log Analysts, Am. Inst. Profl. Geologists, N.W. Mining Assn., Wyo. Geol. Assn. Club: Windycrest Sailing. Author: Exploration for Uranium, 1981; Mineral Logging, 1980; Geophysical Logging for Mineral and Engineering Purposes, 1983; Formation Evaluation Programs for the HP 41C, 1984; also articles. Inventor method for cooling downhole instruments, free piston generator, vessel heave compensator, several logging and measuring devices. Address: 336 29th St Tulsa OK 74114

HALLER, JAMES CONAWAY, hospital administrator dental services; b. Abilene, Tex., June 10, 1934; s. James Carson and Clora (Conaway) H.; m. Barbara Ann Black, Aug. 20, 1960; children—David, Robert. B.S., Abilene Christian U., 1956, M.S., 1959; D.D.S., U. Tex.-Houston, 1964. Diplomate Tex. State Bd. Dental Examiners. Intern USPHS, New Orleans, 1964-65; gen. practice dentistry, Abilene, Tex., 1965-67; assoc. prof. U. Tex. Dental Br., Houston, 1967-82; dir. dental services Big Spring State Hosp., Tex., 1982—; dental cons. Dept. Health and Human Services, Dallas, 1978—. Contbr. articles to profl. jours. Mgr. Little League Baseball, Kingwood, Tex., 1970-79, pres., 1973-74. Mem. ADA, Tex. Dental Assn., Permian Basin Dist. Dental Soc., So. Assn. Instnl. Dentists, Big Spring Dental Study Club, Omicron Kappa Upsilon. Mem. Ch. of Christ. Avocations: snow skiing; farming; picture framing; church work. Home: PO Box 3597 Big Spring TX 79721 Office: Big Spring State Hosp PO Box 231 Big Spring TX 79721

HALLIBURTON, JEAN ELIZABETH, journalist; b. Dallas, Nov. 3; d. Orville Garrett and Lydie Jeanne (Houghton) H.; B.A. in Journalism, Stanford U.; m. G. Arnold Stevens (dec.); children—Arnold Jr., Carole Stevens Jackson, Harley Stevens Tucker. Women's editor West Los Angeles (Calif.) Ind.; asst. fashion editor Los Angeles Herald Examiner; contbg. editor Los Angeles Mag., mem. founding staff, 1960-63; owner JHPR Public Relations Co., Newport Beach, Calif., 1964-77; lifestyle editor Sutton News Group (Newport Ensign, Irvine Today, Costa Mesa News), Corona del Mar, Calif., 1978-81; v.p. Color Me Beautiful, Inc., McLean Va., 1981—. Mem. Women in Communications, Public Relations Soc. Am., Soc. Profl. Journalists, Nat. Press Club. Club: Capitol Hill. Home: 6817 Tennyson Dr McLean VA 22101 also 154 Lexington Ln Costa Mesa CA 92626 Office: Color Me Beautiful Inc 2721-A Merrilee Dr Fairfax VA 22031

HALLIGAN, JAMES EDMUND, university president; b. Moorland, Iowa, June 23, 1936; s. Raymond Anthony and Ann Margaret (Crawford) H.; B.S., Iowa State U., 1962, M.S., 1965, Ph.D. in Chem. Engring., 1967; m. Ann E. Sorenson, June 29, 1957; children—Michael, Patrick, Christopher. Process engr. Humble Oil and Refining Co., 1962-63; postdoctoral fellow Iowa State U., 1967-68; mem. faculty Tex. Tech. U., Lubbock, 1968-76, chmn. dept. chem. engring., 1976-77; dean of engring. U. Mo., Rolla, 1977-79; dean Coll. Engring. U. Ark., Fayetteville, 1979-82, vice chancellor for acad. affairs, 1982-83, interim chancellor, 1983; now pres. N. Mex. State U., Las Cruces; cons. to industry. Mem. Gov. Tex. Energy Adv. Council, 1975-77. Served with USAF, 1954-58. Recipient Disting. Teaching award Tex. Tech. U., 1972, 73, Disting. Research award, 1973, 74; Outstanding Teaching award U. Mo., Rolla, 1977. Mem. Am. Inst. Chem. Engrs., Am. Chem. Soc., Ark. Soc. Profl. Engrs., Tau Beta Pi. Contbr. articles to profl. jours.

HALLMARK, GARNETT CLAUD, automobile parking lot executive; b. Garland County, Ark., Jan. 7, 1930; s. John Thomas and Nellie Pearl (Kinsey) H.; m. Bettie Ruth Hightower, May 10, 1958 (div. June 1966); children—Kevin Claud, Garnetta Ann, Kerwin Bud; m. 2d, Janet Delores Dietrich, Apr. 17, 1984. Student U. Denver, 1952. Parking lot attendent Allright Auto Parks, Dallas, 1956-57, ops. mgr., 1957-66, pres. Birmingham (Ala.) sub., 1967-69, New Orleans sub., 1969-74, regional mgr., 1974-78, sr. v.p., div. mgr., 1978—. Ex-officio bd. dirs. New Orleans Philharm. Symphony, 1981. Served with USN, 1948-52. Named to Condrs. Circle, New Orleans Symphony, 1982. Republican. Club: Athletic (dir. 1980-81) (New Orleans). Home: 442 Canal St 200 Sanlin Bldg New Orleans LA 70130

HALL-SHEEHY, JAMES WILLIAM, data processing educator; b. LaCrosse, Wis., Jan. 26, 1949; s. Thomas James and Betty (Pauline) Sheehy; m. Karen Ann Hall, July 12, 1975; 1 child, Christopher James. B.A. in Govt., N.Mex. State U., 1975, M.A. in Pub. Adminstrn., 1976. Adminstrv. supr. Prudential Ins. Co., Houston, 1977-79, employee devel. cons., 1979-81, assoc. personnel mgr., 1981-83; dir. edn. data processing Am. Gen. Co., Houston, 1983—. Contbr. articles to profl. jours. Dir., chmn. bd. dirs. Kingsridge Municipal Utility Dist., Houston, 1984—. Served with U.S. Army, 1968-71; Vietnam. Decorated Bronze Star, Purple Heart; recipient Most Valuable Staffer award Am. Newspaper Assn., 1967. Mem. Data Tng. Assn. Southeast Tex., Am. Soc. Tng. and Devel., Houston Orgn. Indsl. Psychologists. Democrat. Avocations: reading; running; writing short stories. Home: 8858 Chelsworth Houston TX 77083 Office: Am Gen Data Processing 2727 Allen Pkwy Houston TX 77019

HALPERN, MARTIN, oil company manager; b. Montreal, Que., Can., Dec. 24, 1937; s. Harry and Rachel (Cohen) H.; children—Andrea, Adam. B.S., McGill U. Que., 1959; M.S., U. Wis., 1961, Ph.D., 1963. Research scientist Southwest Ctr. Advanced Studies, Dallas, 1964-70; prof. U. Tex., Dallas, 1970-81; sr. staff geologist Enserch Exploration Inc., Dallas, 1981-82, exploration mgr., Houston, 1982—; cons. Mexican Petroleum Inst., Mexico City, 1978-80; vis. prof. Tel-Aviv U., 1977-78; research fellow U. Leads, Eng., 1971-72; assoc. dean U. Tex., Dallas, 1976-77. Contbr. articles to profl. jours. Grantee NSF, 1962-79, Nat. Acad. Scis., 1970. Recipient Antarctic Service medal U.S. Govt. 1976. Fellow Geol. Soc. Am.; mem. Am. Assn. Petroleum Geologists, Am. Geophys. Union, Houston Geol. Soc. Home: 722 B Country Place Dr Houston TX 77079 Office: Enserch Exploration Inc 10375 Richmond #1102 Houston TX 77042

HALPIN, ROBERT E., JR., elementary school principal, consultant; b. Glen Ridge, N.J., June 3, 1946; s. Robert E. and Catherine (Kirwan) H.; m. Sandra Ann Guthrie, May 19, 1968; children—Jennifer Leigh, Kristy Michelle. B.S. in Edn., Western Carolina U., 1968; m. Ed., Middle Tenn. State U., 1970; Ed.D., Vanderbilt U., 1980. Cert. advanced elem. prin. Spl. edn. tchr. Metro Nashville Pub. Schs., 1968-71, elem. tchr., 1971-73, prin., 1973-84, prin. Pennington Elem. Sch., 1985—; state evaluator Tenn. Dept. Edn., Nashville, 1984-85. Author: Teacher Attitudes toward Mainstreaming, 1980; contbg. author evaluator tng. materials. Bd. dirs. Model Vision Project, Peabody Coll., 1977-78; mem. credentials com. Educators Credit Union, Nashville, 1984-85. Fellow Nat. Assn. Elem. Sch. Prins.; mem. Tenn. Assn. Elem. Sch. Prins. (pres. 1979-80, cons. Nashville 1984), Middle Tenn. Assn. Elem. Sch. Prins. (pres. 1977-78), United Teaching Profession, Metro Nashville Prins. Assn. Presbyterian. Avocations: camping; fishing. Home: 3905 Brick Church Pike Nashville TN 37207 Office: Pennington Elem Sch 2817 Donna Hill Dr Nashville TN 37214

HALSAVER, RICHARD ALLEN, management consultant; b. Meadville, Pa., Mar. 4, 1939; s. Kenneth George and Kathryn Irene (Proper) H.; m. Donna Jean Watson, May 11, 1973; children—Richard Allen, Jr., Jeffrey Craig. B.A., Allegheny Coll., 1960; M.A., Central Mich. U., 1980. Mgr. tng. systems Betac Corp., Arlington, Va., 1982-84; sr. v.p. Mgmt. Logistics Internat., Ltd., Arlington, 1984-85, exec. v.p., 1985—; cons. Dept. State, Washington, 1982-85. Served to lt. col. USAF, 1960-82. Mem. Am. Soc. Tng. and Devel., Am. Def. Prepardness Assn. Republican. Home: 2502 Freetown Dr Reston VA 22091 Office: Mgmt Logistics Internat Ltd 1401 Wilson Blvd Arlington VA 22209

HALSEY, BRENTON SHAW, paper company executive; b. Newport News, Va., 1927. B.S. in Chem. Engring., U. Va.; postgrad. Inst. Paper Chemistry. Vice pres. planning Albermarle Paper Co., 1955-66; pres., gen. mgr. Interstate Bag. Co., 1966-68; co-founder James River Corp. of Va., Richmond, 1969, now chmn., chief exec. officer, dir.; dir. Dominion Bankshares, Dominion Nat. Bank, Westmoreland Coal Co. Office: James River Corp Va PO Box 2218 Richmond VA 23217*

HALSEY, WILLIAM, artist, educator; b. Charleston, S.C., 1915; m. Corrie McCallum. Student U. S.C., 1932-34, Boston Mus. Sch. Fine Arts, 1935-39, U. Mex., 1939-41. Instr. Boston Mus. Fine Arts Sch., Newberry Coll., S.C.; dir. Telfair Acad. Sch., Savannah, Ga., Gibbes Art Gallery Sch., Charleston, S.C.; artist-in-residence Castle Hill Found., Ipswich, Mass., Mus. Sch., Greenville County Mus., S.C.; vis. critic archtl. dept. Clemson U., S.C.; instr. to asst. prof. to artist-in-residence Coll. Charleston, 1965-84. One-man shows include: Bertha Schaefer Gallery, N.Y., Domus Gallery, Mexico City, Bershire Mus., Pittsfield, Mass.; Norton Gallery, West Palm Beach, Fla., Mint Mus. Art, Charlotte, N.C., Greenville County Mus. Art, Greenville, S.C., Columbia Mus. Art., S.C., Spoleto Festival, USA; exhibited in group shows: Met. Mus. N.Y., Boston Mus. Fine Arts, Whitney Mus. Am. Art, Mus. Modern Art, N.Y.C., Bklyn. Mus., Jewish Mus., N.Y., Chgo. Art Inst., Pasadena Art Inst., Birmingham Mus., Ringling Mus., Sarasota, Fla.; represented in permanent collections at Balt. Mus., NAD, Container Corp. of Am., Ford Motor Co., Ind. U., Ga. Mus., Greenville County Mus., Gibbes Art Gallery, Columbia Mus., S.C. State Art Commn., S.C. Nat. Bank, C&S Nat. Bank, First Fed. Savs. & Loan Assn., Spring Mills; executed mural in Berkshire Mus., Pittsfield, Mass., Balt. Hebrew Congl. Temple, Balt., Md., Beth Elohim Synagogue Tabernacle, Charleston; decorations and paintings in Dock St. Theatre, Charleston; portraits in Simons Fine Arts Ctr., Coll. of Charleston, Charleston County Court Room, Dock St. Theatre. Author: (with Corrie McCallum) A Travel Sketchbook, 1971, Maya Jour., 1976. James W. Paige fellow, 1939-41; Pepsi-Cola fellow, 1948; Hughes Found. fellow, 1950-51; grantee S.C. Com. for Humanities, 1982, Coll. of Charleston, 1982; fine arts gallery at Coll. of Charleston named in his honor, 1984.

HALTER, EDMUND JOHN, mechanical engineer; b. Bedford, Ohio, May 10, 1928; s. Edmund Herbert and Martha (Demske) H.; student Akron U., 1946-48; B.S. in Mech. Engring., Case Inst. Tech., Cleve., 1952; M.S. in Mech. Engring., So. Meth. U., 1965; m. Carolyn Amelia Luecke, June 29, 1955; children—John Alan, Amelia Katherine, Dianne Louise, Janet Elaine. Flight test engr., analyst Chance Vought Aircraft, Dallas, 1952-59; chief research and devel. engr. Burgess-Manning Co., Dallas, 1959-68; engring. specialist acoustics Vought div. LTV Aerospace Corp., Dallas, 1968-69; mgr. continuing engring. Maxim Silencer div. AMF Beaird, Inc., Shreveport, La., 1969-72; chief research and devel. engr. Burgess-Manning div. Burgess Industries, Dallas, 1972-79; chief engr. Vibration & Noise Engring. Corp., Dallas, 1979—; cons. Organizer Citizen Noise Awareness Seminar, Irving, 1977. Served with USNR, 1946-49. Registered profl. engr., Tex., Ohio; cert. fallout shelter analyst. Mem. Inst. Environ. Scis. (pres. S.W. chpt. 1977-78), Indsl. Silencer Mfrs. Assn. (chmn. 1975-77), Acoustical Soc. Am., Nat., Tex. socs. profl. engrs., ASME. Inst. Noise Control Engrs. Republican. Lutheran. Contbr. articles to profl. jours. Patentee in field. Home: 200 Hillcrest Ct Irving TX 75062 Office: 2655 Villa Creek Dr Dallas TX 75234

HALTOM, ELBERT BERTRAM, JR., judge; b. Florence, Ala., Dec. 26, 1922; s. Elbert Bertram and Elva Mae (Simpson) H.; student Florence State U., 1940-42; LL.B., U. Ala., 1948; m. Constance Boyd Morris, Aug. 19, 1949; 1 dau., Emily Morris Haltom Olsen. Bar: Ala. 1948. Practiced in Florence, 1948-80; mem. firm Bradshaw, Barnett & Haltom, 1948-58, Haltom & Patterson, 1959-80; judge U.S. Dist. Ct. No. Dist. Ala., 1980—; bar commr. 11th Jud. Circuit Ala., 1976-80. Mem. Ala. Ho. of Reps., 1954-58; mem. Ala. Senate, 1958-62; candidate lt. gov. Ala., 1962; mem. Ala. Democratic Exec. Com., 1966-80. Served with USAAF, 1943-45. Decorated Air medal with four oak leaf clusters. Fellow Internat. Soc. Barristers, Am. Coll. Trial Lawyers; mem. Am. Judicature Soc., Am., Ala. bar assns., Newcomen Soc. N.Am., Am. Legion, VFW, Phi Gamma Delta, Phi Delta Phi. Methodist. Office: US Post Office and Federal Courthouse Room 207 Huntsville AL 35801

HALVATZIS, GREGORY JAMES, petroleum geologist; b. Wilkinsburg, Pa., Aug. 30, 1951; s. James Christ and Shirley Louise (Wilson) H.; m. Marie Lynne Williams, Aug. 28, 1976; children—James, Christina. B.S., Waynesburg Coll., 1973; M.S., U. Fla., 1975; postgrad. U. Ariz., 1975-76; M.B.A., Miss. Coll., 1979. Region geologist Cities Service Co., Jackson, Miss., 1976-81; dist. geologist Whitmar Exploration Co., Jackson, 1981-82; v.p. exploration First Energy Corp., Houston, 1982—; instr. U. So. Miss., Jackson, 1982-83, Hinds Jr. Coll., Raymond, Miss., 1981-83. Contbr. articles to profl. jours. Recipient Able Toastmaster award Toastmasters Internat., 1983. Mem. Am. Assn. Petroleum Geologist (cert.), Soc. Econ. Paleontologists Mineralogists, Am. Inst. Profl. Geologists (cert.). Greek Orthodox. Club: Toastmasters Internat. (Jackson) (lt. gov. 1981-82 div. C dist. 43). Home: 5215 Manor Glen Dr Kingwood TX 77345 Office: First Energy Corp 16701 Greenspoint Park Dr Suite 200 Houston TX 77060

HALVERSON, ROGER MICHAEL, insurance company executive; b. Manitowoc, Wis., May 3, 1940; s. Erwin Joseph and Wilma H.; m. Deanna C. Durben, June 17, 1961; 1 child, Troy. B.S. in Econs., U. Wis., 1964. Supr. checking dept. Allstate Ins. Co., Milw., 1965; supr. steno dept., 1965-66; asst. mgr. customer service Surg. Care Blue Shield, Milw., 1966-67, asst. mgr. Wis. Medicaid, 1967-68, mgr. Wis. Medicaid, 1968-70, mgr. Blue Shield claims, 1970-74, v.p. Blue Shield ops., 1974-77; asst. v.p. instl. benefits adminstr. Blue Cross and Blue Shield of Greater N.Y., 1977-80; v.p. claims and govt. programs Blue Cross of Northwest Ohio, Toledo, 1980-84; regional dir. Hosp. Corp. Am., Richmond, Va., 1984—. Mem. Adminstrv. Mgmt. Soc. Home: 3303 Monument Ave Richmond VA 23221 Office: 5020 Monument Ave Richmond VA 23230

HALVERSTADT, DONALD BRUCE, urologist, educator; b. Cleve., July 6, 1934; s. Lauren Oscar and Lillian Frances (Jones) H.; B.A. magna cum laude, Princeton U., 1952-56; M.D. cum laude, Harvard U., 1960; m. Margaret Ann Marcy, Aug. 4, 1956; children—Donna, Jeffrey, Amy. Intern, Mass. Gen. Hosp., Boston, 1960-61, resident in surgery, 1961-62, resident in urology, 1964-67; practice medicine specializing in urology, Oklahoma City, Okla., 1967—; chief pediatric urology service Oklahoma Children's Meml. Hosp., Oklahoma City, 1967—, chief of staff, 1974-79; clin. prof. urology U. Okla., 1975—, provost Health Scis. Center, 1979-80, clin. prof. pediatrics, 1975—; chief exec. officer State of Okla. Teaching Hosps., 1980-83. Served with USPHS, 1962-64. Fellow A.C.S.; mem. AMA (recipient physician recognition award 1969, 72, 77, 79, 82, 84), Am. Urol. Assn., Inc., Am. Acad. Pediatrics, Soc. Pediatric Urology, Okla. State Med. Assn., Okla. County Med. Soc., So. Med. Assn., Am. Soc. Nephrology, Soc. Univ. Urologists. Presbyterian. Contbr. articles in field to profl. jours. Home: 2932 Lamp Post Ln Oklahoma City OK 73120 Office: 711 Stanton L Young Blvd Oklahoma City OK 73104

HAM, JAMES HENRY, JR., engineering company executive; b. Lexington, Ky., Apr. 6, 1919; s. James Henry and Nannie (Ward) H.; m. Lady Gray, Apr. 18, 1942; children—James Henry, III, Sandra Lynn Howse, John Michael. B.S. in Elec. Engring., U. Ky., 1941. Registered profl. engr., Fla., Ky., Ga., N.C., N.Mex. Jr. elec. engr. TVA, Knoxville, 1941-42; elec. engr. Swift & Co., Chgo., 1946-57; mgr. design engring. Wellman Lord Engring., Inc., Lakeland, Fla., 1957-70; pres. N.Am. Steel Corp., Lakeland, 1970-83, J.H. Ham Engring., Inc., Lakeland, 1974—. Pres., Lakeland Jr. Achievement, 1968; bd. dirs. United Way Lakeland, 1970. Served to 1st lt. U.S. Army, 1942-46. Mem. IEEE, Nat. Soc. Profl. Engrs., Fla. Engring. Soc., Lakeland C. of C. (dir. 1975). Democrat. Baptist. Lodge: Citrus Ctr. Kiwanis (pres. 1965). Home: 311 Pablo Lakeland FL 33803 Office: J H Ham Engring Inc 602 Brannen Rd Lakeland FL 33803

HAM, WILLIAM CHARLES, safety engineer; b. Refugio, Tex., Oct. 23, 1943; s. Howard Cecil, Sr. and Thelma Lee (Curley Coward) H. B.S. in Edn., Southwest Tex. State U., 1971. Dorm adv. Tex. Ednl. Found., San Marcos, 1966-70; tchr., coach Brazosport Sch. Dist., Lake Jackson, Tex., 1970-71, North Forest Sch. Dist., Houston, 1971-73, Houston Sch. Dist., 1973-77; safety engr. Brown and Root, Inc., Houston, 1977-79, Fish Engring. and Constrn., Houston, 1984, H.B. Zachry Co., San Antonio, 1985—; dir. safety and personnel Am. Magnesium Co., Synder, Tex., 1980-81. Sponsor Fellowship Christian Athletes, Wheatley High Sch., Houston, 1973-77. Southwest Tex. State U. scholar, 1961; recipient Grand Champion Steer award Matagorda County Livestock Show, Bay City, Tex., 1960. Mem. Tex. State Tchrs. Assn., Tex. High Sch. Coaches Assn., Am. Soc. Safety Engrs., Houston Tchrs. Assn., Houston Classroom Tchrs. Assn. Republican. Methodist. Club: Bobcat Athletic (bd. dirs. 1982—). Lodge: Masons. Avocations: outdoor sports; dogs; livestock. Home: 1400 N 10th St Box 3 La Porte TX 77571 Office: H B Zachry Co PO Box 21130 San Antonio TX 78285

HAM, WILLIAM TAYLOR, JR., biophysics educator, researcher; b. Norfolk, Va., Sept. 20, 1908; s. William Taylor and Lucy Goode (Coleman) H.; m. Jean Anderson, Oct. 5, 1940; children—Christina Anderson, Elspeth Read. B.S., U. Va., 1931, M.S. in Physics, 1933, Ph.D. in Physics, 1935. Research assoc. U. Va., 1935-36, Manhattan Project, Office Sci. Research and Devel., 1940-43; instr. physics Columbia U., 1936-37; research physicist Kendall Mills Co., 1937-39; pres. W.T. Ham & Co., brokers, 1939-40; div. head physics and electronics Inst. Textile Tech., Charlottesville, Va., 1946-48; assoc. prof. biophysics Med. Coll. Va., Va. Commonwealth U., Richmond, 1948-53, prof., chmn. dept., 1953-76, prof. emeritus, 1976—; mem. fellowship panel NSF, 1955-58; cons. NRC-Nat. Acad. Scis., Bell Telephone Co. Labs., Xerox, Polaroid Co., Gen. Electric Co., Eastman Kodak Co., NCR, Corning Glass Works; mem. radiation adv. bd. Commonwealth of Va., 1964-83. Served to maj. USMCR, 1943-46. Grantee NIH, U.S. Army, USN, others. Fellow Am. Physics Soc.; mem. Biophysics Soc., Am. Soc. Photobiology, Assn. Research in Vision and Ophthalmology, Health Physics Soc. (pres. 1963-64), AAAS, Bioelectromagnetic Soc., Sigma Xi. Episcopalian. Clubs: Farmington Country (Charlottesville); Westwood Racquet (Richmond). Contbr. over 100 articles to profl. jours. Home: 8653 Cherokee Rd Richmond VA 23235 Office: Va Commonwealth U Med Coll Va Sta PO Box 694 Richmond VA 23298

HAMACHER, HORST WILHELM, mathematics educator; b. Buir, Germany, Apr. 21, 1951; came to U.S., 1981, permanent resident, 1983; s. Alois G. and Helene G. (Hanussek) H.; m. Renate K. Kremer, Aug. 22, 1972; children—Elke J., Jens W., Anna J. Pre-diploma Universitaet Koeln, Germany, 1973, diploma Math., 1977, Doctor Rer. Nat., 1980. Asst. prof. U. Koeln, 1977-81; asst. prof. U. Fla., Gainesville, 1981-84, assoc. prof. optimization and combinatorics, 1984—; commencement marshal, 1983-85, dir. Ctr. for Combinatorics and Optimization, 1986—. Author: Flows in Regular Matroids, 1981. Contbr. articles to profl. jours. Grantee NSF, 1983-85, 85, 85-87, Office Naval Research, 1985, NATO, 1985-87. Mem. Math. Programming Soc., Ops. Research Soc. Am., Soc. Indsl. Applied Math., Rudolf Steiner Ednl. Assn. (treas. 1982-83, pres. 1984). Roman Catholic. Avocations: woodworking; reading; music. Home: 5229 NW 26th Pl Gainesville FL 32606 Office: U Fla Dept Indsl Systems Engring 303 Weil Hall Gainesville FL 32611

HAMBLEN, LYONS ALEXANDER, JR., training supervisor; b. Knoxvile, Tenn., May 26, 1956; s. Lyons Alexander and Muriel (Bennett) H. B.A., Carson Newman Coll., 1978; M.S., Clemson U., 1980. Paralegal, Webster, Chamberlain & Bean, Washington, 1980-81; asst. personnel mgr. TRW, Inc., Rogersville, Tenn., 1981-84, tng. supr., 1984—. Chmn. State Vocat. Sch. Adv. Com., 1985. Mem. Am. Soc. Tng. and Devel. (chpt. pres. 1984—). Republican. Baptist. Lodges: Masons (32 deg., master), Shriners. Avocations: golf; basketball. Home: F4 Chasden Rogersville TN 37857 Office: TRW Inc PO Box 558 Rogersville TN 37857

HAMBRICK, MARVIN K., energy company executive; b. Cin., 1922. B.A., U. Okla., 1948. Mgr., Arthur Andersen & Co., Oklahoma City, 1949-57, mng. ptnr., 1957-73; v.p. fin. Kerr-McGee Corp., Oklahoma City, 1973-77, exec. v.p., 1977—, also dir. Office: Kerr-McGee Corp PO Box 25861 Oklahoma City OK 73125

HAMBY, A. GARTH, beverage company executive; b. Oneota, Ala., 1938. B.A. in Journalism, U. Ala., 1959. Reporter Columbus Ledger News, 1959-61; various positions Ga. Power Co., 1961-67; staff rep. pub. reins. dept. Coca-Cola Co., Atlanta, 1967-70, mgr. editorial group pub. reins. dept., 1970-74, asst. to chmn. bd., 1974-78, v.p., sec., dir., corp. external affairs, 1978-79, sr. v.p., sec., dir. corp. external affairs, 1979-80, exec. v.p., sec., 1980-81, exec. v.p., 1981—. Office: Coca Cola Co 310 North Ave NW Atlanta GA 30313*

HAMBY, EDWINA EVONNE HARRIS, educator, administrator; b. Braddock, Pa., Nov. 16, 1946; d. William Henry and Katheryne Mae (Dickey) Harris; m. William Davidson Hamby, June 3, 1968; children—William Davidson, Darius Jerome. B.A., Fisk U., 1968; M.A., U. D.C., 1973; postgrad. U. Md., 1974-76, Cath. U. Am., 1978-79, Vanderbilt U., 1983—. Asst. to bus. mgr. Fisk U., Nashville, 1968-69; tchr. English and reading Chgo. public schs., 1969-71; regional lang. arts coordinator D.C. public schs., Washington, 1971-73; instr., acad. retention program coordinator Bowie (Md.) State Coll., 1973-74, asst. prof., acad. retention program coordinator, 1974-76, asst. prof., asst. to dean for undergrad. studies, 1976-77, asst. prof., dir. freshman-sophomore div., 1977-79; dir. tng. and research, labor recruitment program Internat. Assn. Fire Fighters, Washington, 1979-80; assoc. dir. div. sponsored research Vanderbilt U., Nashville, 1980-81; asst. prof., adminstr. dept. family medicine Sch. Medicine, Meharry Med. Coll., Nashville, 1981-84, dir. area health edn. ctrs. program of Tenn., 1984—; cons. in field to various colls., univs., orgns. Bd. dirs. Minerva Hawkins Found., Nashville. Fisk U. scholar, 1965; Chgo. Bd. Edn.-U. Chgo. fellow, 1969. Mem. Assn. for Supervision and Cirriculum Devel., Soc. Research Adminstrs., Nat. Council Univ. Research Adminstrs., Soc. Tchrs. of Family Medicine, Nat. Council Tchrs. English, Internat. Reading Assn., Fisk U. Gen. Alumni Assn. (nat. sec.), Delta Sigma Theta. Democrat. Roman Catholic. Home: 728 Work Dr Nashville TN 37207 Office: 1005 Dr D B Todd Jr Blvd Nashville TN 37208

HAMDY, MOSTAFA KAMAL, microbiologist, educator; b. Cairo, Egypt, May 27, 1921; s. Hamed Alimobark and Nefisa Mohamed (Sultan) H.; m. Kathryn Ann, May 29, 1954; children—David Hamed, Kathryn Ann. B.S., Cairo U., 1944, M.S., 1949; Ph.D., Ohio State U., 1953. Instr. Alexandria U., 1944-48; instr. Cairo U., 1944-49, lectr., 1948-49; Muelhaupt postdoctoral fellow Ohio State U., 1953-54, postdoctoral fellow biochemistry dept., 1954-58; asst. prof. food sci. U. Ga., Athens, 1958-62, assoc. prof., 1962-65, prof., 1965—; field sci. advisor FDA. Vice pres. Timothy Estate Assn., Athens, 1972-73. Recipient Sears Roebuck Found. award, 1963; Creative Research award, 1982; Disting. Research Faculty award, Coll. Agr., U. Ga., 1968; D.W. Brooks research award, 1984; P.R. Edwards award, 1985. Fellow Acad. Microbiology, Inst Food Technologists (councilor 1975-78), Am. Soc. Microbiology; mem. Soc. Exptl. Biology and Medicine (pres. S.E. br. 1973-75), N.Y. Acad. Scis., So. Assn. Agrl. Scientists (sec. treas. food sci. and tech. sect. 1972-74, prof. scientist award 1974), Sigma Xi (Disting. Research award 1967, 81), Phi Kappa Phi, Phi Sigma, Gamma Sigma Delta (sr. faculty award 1975). Methodist. Clubs: Stamp, Chess (Athens). Contbr. articles to profl. jours.

HAMEL, DAVID CHARLES, health and safety engineer; b. Plattsburgh, N.Y., Feb. 19, 1953; s. Charles Joseph and Helena Mary (Tormey) H.; m. Maxine Frances Gendiellee,, June 3, 1978 (div. 1981). B.S., Fla. Inst. Tech., 1977. Cert. paramedic, Fla. Safety engr. United Space Boosters, Kennedy Space Ctr., Fla., 1977-81; safety and health supr. STC Documation, Inc., Palm Bay, Fla., 1981-82, Martin Marietta Corp., Ocala, Fla., 1983; sr. health and safety engr. Hughes Aircraft Co., Titusville, Fla., 1983—; tchr. Nat. Safety Council, Brevard Safety Council, Cocoa, Fla., 1978-84; cons. Continental Shelf, Inc., Tequesta, Fla., 1976-77. Emergency med. technician Harbor City Vol. Ambulance Squad, Melbourne, Fla., 1974-81, paramedic, 1981—. Recipient Group Achievement award NASA, 1979, Cert. of appreciation, NASA, 1979, 81. Mem. Am. Soc. Safety Engrs. (treas. 1980-81), Am. Indsl. Hygiene Assn. Avocations: scuba diving; skiing; horseback riding; hiking. Home: 2172 Canal Ridge Titusville FL 32780 Office: Hughes Aircraft Co 1520 Chaffee Dr Titusville FL 32780

HAMES, CURTIS GORDON, physician; b. Claxton, Ga., Feb. 19, 1920; children—Curtis Gordon Jr., Richard C. B.S., U. Ga., 1941, M.D., 1944. Rotating intern Univ. Hosp., Augusta, Ga., 1944-45; practice medicine specializing in cardiovascular epidemiology, Claxton, Ga., 1947—, prin. Hames Clinic 1947—; appointee Ga. Commn. on Malnutrition and Hunger, 1972—; clin. prof. dept. medicine Med. Coll. Ga., Augusta, 1980—; vis. clin. prof. dept. medicine Med. U. S.C., Charleston, 1977; clin. prof. dept. epidemiology U. N.C., Chapel Hill, 1983; vis. prof. dept. medicine Mercer Med. Ctr., Macon, Ga., 1985. Served to capt. U.S. Army, 1945-47. Recipient Disting. Achievement award Am. Heart Assn., 1978; Disting. Alumni award Med. Coll. Ga., 1978; John D. MacArthur Found. fellow, 1984—; grantee USPHS, Nat. Heart and Lung Inst., Nat. Inst. Child Health and Human Devel. Fellow Am. Coll. Cardiology; mem. Nat. Acad. Sci. Inst. Medicine, Am. Heart Assn. Council on Epidemiology, Ogeechee River Med. Soc. Office: Hames Clinic 405 E Long St Claxton GA 30417

HAMILTON, CLYDE H., federal judge; b. Edgefield, S.C., Feb. 8, 1934; s. Clyde H. and Edwina (Odom) H.; m. Mary Elizabeth Spillers, July 20, 1957; children—John C., James W. B.S., Wofford Coll., 1956; J.D. with honors, George Washington U., 1961. Bar: S.C. 1961. Assoc. J.R. Folk, Edgefield, 1961-63; assoc., gen. ptnr. Butler, Means, Evins & Browne, Spartanburg, S.C., 1963-81; judge U.S. Dist. Ct. S.C., Columbia, 1981—; reference asst. U.S. Senate Library, Washington, 1958-61; gen. counsel Synalloy Corp., Spartanburg, 1969-80. Mem. editorial staff Cumulative Index of Congl. Com. Hearings, 1955-58; bd. editors George Washington Law Rev., 1959-60. Pres., Spartanburg County Arts Council, 1971-73; pres. Spartanburg Day Sch., 1972-74, sustaining trustee, 1975-81; mem. steering com. undergrad. merit fellowship program and estate planning council, Converse Coll., Spartanburg; trustee Spartanburg Methodist Coll., 1979-84; mem. S.C. Supreme Ct. Bd. Commrs. on Grievances and Discipline, 1980-81; del. Spartanburg County, 4th Congl. Dist. and S.C. Republican Convs., 1976, 80; mem. past chmn. fin. com. and adminstrv. bd. Trinity United Meth. Ch., Spartanburg, trustee, 1980-83. Served to capt. USAR, 1956-58. Mem. ABA, S.C. Bar Assn., Spartanburg County Bar Assn. Club: Piedmont (Spartanburg, bd. govs. 1979-81). Office: US Dist Ct PO Box 867 Columbia SC 29202

HAMILTON, DALTON EARL, civil engineer; b. Dalhart, Tex., Aug. 14, 1930; s. William E. and Verna (Miller) H.; B.S. in Civil Engring., Tex. Tech U., 1951; m. Anita Reynolds, Oct. 20, 1951; children—Cheryl Annette Hamilton Ponath, Mary Anna Hamilton Sulser. Constrn. engr. CAA, Ft. Worth, 1951-52; hwy. engr. U.S. Army Corp Engrs., Tulsa, 1952-55; constrn. engr. City of Abilene (Tex.), 1955-59; v.p., dir. Trinity Engring. Testing Corp., Austin, Tex., 1959—; vis. profl. Tex. A&M U., 1972—. Scoutmaster Boy Scouts Am., 1952-58. Mem. C. of C., Am. Council Ind. Labs., Tex. Soc. Profl. Engrs. (former regional v.p., Engr. of Yr. 1980), Nat. Soc. Profl. Engrs., Tex. Constrn. Council, Am. Welding Soc., Tex. Council Engring. Labs. (past pres.), Am. Concrete Inst. Methodist (past trustee). Home: 12507 Silver Spur St Austin TX 78727 Office: PO Box 572 Austin TX 78767

HAMILTON, EDSEL POSTON, III, electrical engineer, consultant; b. Dallas, Nov. 17, 1949; s. Edsel Poston, Jr. and Roberta Anne (Gray) H.; B.S. magna cum laude, U. So. Calif., 1972, M.S. (Hughes fellow 1972-74), 1974; Ph.D. (univ. fellow 1974-77), U. Tex., Austin, 1977; m. Susan Lynn Galpin, June 23, 1973; 1 child, Edsel Poston IV. Sales rep. Am. Airlines, 1969-74; mem. tech. staff Hughes Research Labs., 1972-74; staff scientist Radian Corp., Austin, 1977-79, sr. engr., group leader, 1979-82; pres. E.P. Hamilton & Assos., Pflugerville, Tex., 1982—; lectr. elec. engring. U. Tex., Austin, U. So. Calif. Chmn. feasibility study com. Central Tex., Tex. Ind. Express Project, Tex. Sesquicentennial Commn., 1982; mem. passenger rail adv. council Tex. Legis. Com. Passenger Rail, 1981—; mem. community adv. com. Sta. KUT-FM, 1981—; mem. community adv. bd. Capital Met. Transit Authority; v.p. Springhill Village Neighborhood Assn. Registered profl. engr., Tex. Mem. IEEE (sr.), ASME, Am. Soc. Engring. Edn., Surface Transp. Systems Inst. (dir.), Austin C. of C. (chmn. Amtrak com. 1979—), Sigma Xi, Phi Kappa Phi, Tau Beta Pi, Eta Kappa Nu, Phi Eta Sigma. Republican. Baptist. Author: (with D.R. Brown) Electromechanical Energy Conversion, 1984. Author papers in field. Home: 15306 Horborne Ln Pflugerville TX 78660 Office: PO Box 10998 426 Austin TX 78766

HAMILTON, JAMES LYNN, crime investigator, international fingerprint expert, consultant; b. Miami, Fla., Nov. 10, 1943; s. William Harold and Jocelyn Rose (Keen) H.; m. Carmen Gibson, May 22, 1965 (div. 1966); 1 child, Susan; m. Susan Ann Frischman, July 25, 1970; children—James L. Jr., Robert Alexander. Student Fla. State U., 1961-63, Miami-Dade Jr. Coll., 1964. Identification technician Hialeah Police Dept., Fla., 1965-70; crime scene investigator Palm Beach County Sheriffs Office, Fla., 1970—, chief latent print examiner; lectr. in field. Contbr. articles to profl. jours. Fellow Fingerprint Soc. U.K.; mem. Internat. Assn. Identification (Fla. div., chmn. fingerprint sci. 1982-84, internat. rep. 1985), Can. Identification Soc. Home: 9792 Mockingbird Trail Jupiter FL 33458 Office: Palm Beach County Sheriffs Office 3228 Gun Club Rd West Palm Beach FL 33406

HAMILTON, JOSEPH HEBERLING, textile company executive; b. Iowa City, Aug. 8, 1920; s. Clair E. and Prudence M. (Heberling) H.; m. Joan Van Gonsic, Oct. 8, 1952; children—Holly Heberling, Joseph Jeffrey. B.A., Harvard U., 1946, M.B.A., 1948. Asst. to chmn. bd. Burlington Industries, Greensboro, N.C., 1948-55; pres. Burlington Throwing Co., High Point, N.C., 1955-60; v.p. Madison Throwing Co., N.C., 1960-63; founder Textured Fibres, Inc. (name changed to Texfi Industries Inc. 1969), Greensboro, 1963, now chmn., chief exec. officer. Served to lt. USNR, 1942-45. Episcopalian. Home: 617 Blair St Greensboro NC 27408 Office: Texfi Industries Inc 1400 Battleground Ave Greensboro NC 27420*

HAMILTON, KENNETH LEROY, international consulting firm executive; retired air force officer, business educator, researcher; b. Macon, Ga., May 22, 1943; s. Clarence Eugene and Lotte Katherine (Young) H.; m. Frances Ellen (Nancy) DuBois Greer, Jan. 27, 1970; children—Kate Louise, Kendra Leslie. B.S. in Chemistry, U. Ga., 1963; M.S. in Quantitative Methods, Ga. Inst. Tech., 1972, Ph.D. in Econs. and Acctg., Mgmt. and Info. Scis., 1979. Commd. 2d lt. U.S. Air Force, 1963, advanced through grades to lt. col., 1984; dir. research applications Air Force Leadership and Mgmt. Devel. Ctr., Maxwell AFB, Ala., 1979-81; Air Force fellow Ctr. for Strategic and Internat. Studies, Georgetown U., Washington, 1981-82; assoc. ptnr. Meridian Corp., Falls Church, Va., 1984—; mem. faculty Nat. Def. U., Ft. McNair, 1982-84, Emory U. Sch. Medicine, Atlanta, 1979-82, Auburn U. Sch. Bus., Montgomery, Ala., 1979-81, George Mason U., Fairfax, Va., 1984—; cons. in field. Contbr. articles to profl. publs. Vestry mem. St. Aidan's Episcopal Ch., Alexandria, Va., 1982-84. Gov.'s fellow State of Ga., 1978-79. Mem. Am. Econ. Assn., Mil. Ops. Research Soc., Inst. Mgmt. Scis., Health Economists Study Group U.K., Am. Inst. Decision Scis., Beta Gamma Sigma. Avocation: kitchen design. Home: 8405 Brewster Dr Alexandria VA 22308 Office: Meridian Corp 5113 Leesburg Pike Suite 700 Falls Church VA 22308

HAMILTON, MARIAN ELOISE, director program services; b. Salt Lake City, Mar. 21, 1931; d. Frederic William and Kathryn Eloise (Core) Wrathall; m. Stanley Keith Hamilton, Feb. 2, 1951 (dec. 1983); children—Edmond Scott, Perri Collette, Deena Kathryn. Student U. Utah, 1949-51, U. Calif.-Santa Barbara, 1951-52, U. Montana, 1952-53. Field exec. Cross Timbers, Denton, Tex., 1972-75; camp dir. Camp Kadohadacho, Pottsboro, Tex., 1972-75; field dir. 1st Tex. Council Campfire, Fort Worth, 1979-81; dir. program services Denton Housing Authority, 1981—; cons. Shared Housing Tex. Agy. Aging, Austin, 1984-85. Apple Inc. grantee 1984—. Mem. Nat. Assn. Housing and Redevel. Officials (Best Newsletter award 1982, 83), Am. Assn. Homes for Aging, Elderly Service Providers Denton County, Nat. Assn. Female Execs. Democrat. Avocations: writing; travel; painting; family. Home: 900 Sierra Dr Denton TX 76201 Office: Heritage Oaks 2501 Bell Ave Denton TX 76201

HAMILTON, MICHAEL R., state agency administrator; b. Montgomery, Ala., Nov. 4, 1950; s. Raymond W. and Inez (Jones) H.; m. Janet Mason, July 9, 1974; 1 child, Michael Wayne. B.A., Auburn Univ., 1973. News editor Ledger-Enquirer, Columbus, GA., 1972-74; political writer The Advertiser, Montgomery, 1974-76; pub. relations dir. Ala. Edn. Assn., Montgomery, 1976-80; asst. to state supt. edn. Ala. Dept. Edn., Montgomery, 1980—; campaign cons. 37 candidates, 1978—. Editor Ala. Sch. Jour., 1976-79 (Outstanding Assn. Newspaper award 1979), The Apple, 1977 (Gold award 1977), Ala. Edn., 1980—(Most Outstanding Dept Newspaper award 1982); author political ads Powell Senate Campaign (Silver award 1978). Mem. Nat. Sch. Pub. Relations Assn., Nat. Assn. State Edn. Depts., Sigma Delta Chi. Democrat. Methodist. Avocations: golf; baseball; writing; gardening. Home: 1206 Lyman Ct Montgomery AL 36109 Office: Ala Dept Edn State Office Bldg Montgomery AL 36130

HAMILTON, MORRIS BEAR, JR., healthcare executive; b. Bay Minette, Ala., Mar. 19, 1934; s. Morris Bear and Lucile (Hall) H.; Student, Spring Hill Coll., 1952-55, 68-69, Fla. State U., 1955; B.A. in English/Music, U. South Ala., 1970, M.A., 1971. Dir. alcohol and drug abuse unit Searcy State Hosp., Mt. Vernon, Ala., 1971-73; dir. therapeutic community Gateway Drug Abuse Ctr., Mobile Mental Health Ctr., Ala., 1973-77; dir. counseling and treatments Brookwood Lodge, Valley Springs, Warrior, Ala., 1977-79, exec. dir., 1979-83; v.p., dir. quality assurance, Brookwood Recovery Ctrs., Inc., Birmingham, Ala., 1983-85; exec. dir. Brookwood Recovery Ctr., 1979—. Mem. Republican Nat. Com., 1982-83. Served with U.S. Army, 1956-59. Mem. Am. Personnel and Guidance Assn., Am. Rehab. Counseling Assn., Am. Mental Health Counselors Assn. Roman Catholic. Home: 321 Crosshill Ln Warrior AL 35180 Office: Brookwood Lodge Valley Springs PO Box 128 End Allbritton Rd Warrior AL 35180

HAMILTON, PETER SCOTT, psychotherapist, business consultant; b. Denton, Tex., Mar. 15, 1945; s. F. Sidney and Lucia Mary (Rushing) H.; m. Carolyn Francis Blake, Apr. 12, 1968; children—Jaina, Blake, Darren. B.S., North Tex. State U., 1967, M.S., 1968, Ph.D., 1982. Lic. counselor, Tex. Psychologist, Denton State Sch., Tex., 1968-69; unit dir. Tex. Dept. Mental Health-Mental Retardation, Denton, 1972-75; gen. mgr. Pierce Contractors, Inc., Dallas, 1976-82; dir. Ctr. for Counseling-Psychotherapy Services, Denton, 1982—; adj. prof. North Tex. State U., 1983; adj. prof. psychology Tex. Woman's U., 1984—; freelance bus. cons., 1978—; speaker in field. Mem. allocation com. Denton United Way, 1983-85; chmn. bd. Dance Theater, Denton, 1980-82. Mem. Am. Assn. Marriage and Family Therapists, Am. Psychol. Assn., Am. Soc. Clin. Hypnosis, Soc. Clin. and Exptl. Hypnosis, Internat. Acad. Profl. Counseling and Psychotherapy, North Tex. Behavioral Sci. Found. Lodge: Kiwanis (bd. dirs. 1983-85, chmn. Children's Clinic 1982). Avocations: pilot; hunting; fishing; boating; computer programming. Home: 2005 Northwood Terr Denton TX 76201 Office: Ctr of Counseling Psychotherapy Services Westgate Med Ctr 4401 A I-35N Suite 390 Denton TX 76201

HAMILTON, REBECCA BECK, educational administrator; b. Dunbar, W.Va., Jan. 4, 1927; d. John Theodore and Ruth Carolyn (Meeks) Beck; m. Earl Robert Hamilton, July 16, 1950; children—William Kent, Edward Robert. B.S., W.Va. State Coll., 1968; M.A., W.Va. U., 1972; Ed.D., Va. Poly. Inst. and State U., 1979. Dept. coordinator W.Va. Coll. Grad. Studies, Institute, 1972-74, staff assoc., 1976-77, dir. Title I, 1976-79, dir. career planning/placement, 1979—; grad. research asst. Va. Tech. Inst. and State U., 1974-75; cons. in field. Swim instr. ARC, Putnam County, W.Va., 1962-74; mem. council City of Nitro, W.Va., 1962-68; charter chmn. Library Commn. of Nitro, 1964; research advisor Episcopal Diocese of W.Va., Charleston, 1978. Mem. Am. Soc. Personnel Adminstrs., Assn. for Specialists in Group Work, Coll. Placement Council, Middle Atlantic Placement Assn., So. Coll. Placement Council, Am. Assn. Counseling and Devel. Avocations: travel; baseball. Home: 1316 W 13th St Nitro WV 25143 Office: West Virginia State Coll 216 Wallace Hall Institute WV 25112

HAMILTON, RUSSELL LEROY, ship building executive; b. Laurel, Miss., Jan. 19, 1942; s. R. L. and Abbie (Stewart) H.; children—Terri R., Tammi J. B.S., U. So. Miss., 1965; A.A., Jones County Jr. Coll., 1963. Asst. controller Glass Container Corp., Jackson, Miss., 1971-73; controller and mgr. Craven & Sons Inc., Laurel, 1973-76; cost acct. No. Electric Co. (NECO), Laurel, 1976-79; cost coordinator NECO de Mexico, Matamoros, Mexico, 1979-82; v.p. fin. Valley Shipbuilding, Brownsville, Tex., 1982—; owner, pres. Cameron Shipbuilding, Brownsville, 1983—. Mem. Nat. Assn. Accts., Nat. Rifle Assn., Ducks Unltd. Methodist. Lodge: Moose. Home: Route 1 PO Box 1125 Ovett MS 39464 Office: Cameron Shipbldg PO Box 5243 Brownsville TX 78520

HAMILTON, SUSAN OWENS, lawyer; b. Birmingham, Ala., Aug. 7, 1951; d. William Lewis Owens and Vonnette (Wilson) O.; m. Raymond Hamilton, June 8, 1974. B.A. in Polit. Sci., Auburn U., 1973; J.D. (Dean's award), Samford U., Cumberland Law Sch., Birmingham, Ala., 1977. Bar: Ala. 1977, Fla. 1982, U.S. Supreme Ct. 1981, U.S. Dist. Ct. (mid. dist.) Fla. 1982. Claim agt. Louisville & Nashville R.R., Birmingham, 1977-78, atty. Louisville, 1978-80, claims atty., 1980-81, asst. gen. atty. (merger Louisville & Nashville, and Seaboard Coast Line R.R.) Seaboard System R.R., Jacksonville, Fla., 1981-83, asst. gen. solicitor, 1983-84, gen. mgr. freight claim services dept., 1984-85; asst. v.p. casualty prevention, adminstrn. Chessie System R.R., 1985—; lectr. in field. Contbr. articles in field to publs. Mem. ABA, Jacksonville Bar Assn., Assn. Am. R.R.s Legal Affairs (chmn. subcom. freight claims 1983-84), Jacksonville Bus., Profl. Women (pres. 1984-85), Fla. Fedn. Bus. and Profl. Women (named outstanding young career woman 1982), Louisville Bus. and Profl. Women (named outstanding young career woman 1980), Ky. Fedn. Bus. and Profl. Women (named outstanding young career woman dist. V 1981). Democrat. United Methodist. Club: Uptown Civitan (dir. 1983—). (Jacksonville). Home: 12154 Hidden Hills Dr Jacksonville FL 32225 Office: Seaboard System RR 500 Water St Jacksonville FL 32202

HAMILTON, WILLIAM T., petroleum company executive. Exec. v.p. exploration and prodn. Coral Petroleum, Inc. Office: Coral Petroleum Inc 980 Town and Country Blvd Houston TX 77024*

HAMILTON-KEMP, THOMAS ROGERS, organic chemist; b. Lebanon, Ky., May 13, 1942; s. Thomas Rogers and Catherine Rose (Hamilton) K.; A.A., St. Catharine Coll., 1962; B.A., U. Ky., 1964, Ph.D. in Chemistry, 1970; m. Lois Ann Groce, Sept. 13, 1980. Mem. faculty U. Ky., Lexington, 1970—, asst. prof. plant chemistry, 1970-75, assoc. prof., 1975-85, prof., 1985—. Mem. Am. Chem. Soc., Am. Soc. Hort. Sci., AAAS, AAUP, Sigma Xi. Contbr. articles to profl. jours. Home: 868 Laurel Hill Rd Lexington KY 40504 Office: Dept Horticulture N-308 Agrl Sci Center-North, U Kentucky Lexington KY 40546

HAMLIN, GARY LEE, fire chief; b. Perry, Ga., May 12, 1956; s. Olin S. and Mary (Bozeman) H.; m. Angela Lara Martin, June 21, 1981; 1 child, Clinton Lee. Cert. firefighter, Ga.; diploma 1st class fire fighters Ga. Fire Acad. Mem. Perry Fire Dept., Ga., 1975—, chief, 1980—. Chmn. adv. bd. Salvation Army, Perry, 1983. Mem. Ga. Firemens Assn., Ga. Assn. Fire Chiefs. Democrat. Baptist. Avocations: Hunting; archery; pyrotechnics. Office: Perry Fire Dept 1207 Washington St Perry GA 31069

HAMLIN, JULIAN ELDRIGE, III, sales representative, realtor; b. Macon, Ga., Dec. 13, 1955; s. Julian E. and Mary Evelyn (Atkinson) H.; m. Melinda Davis, Sept. 13, 1983. B.B.A., U. Ga., 1977. Sales rep. Calcomp, Atlanta, 1977-78, Veisatec div. Xerox Corp., Atlanta, 1978-81, Gerber Systems, Atlanta, 1981—; mem. Macon Bd. Realtors. Mem. Soc. Mfg. Engrs., Sigma Alpha Epsilon (Order of Phoenix 1977, cons.). Methodist. Home: 379 Redland Rd Atlanta GA 30309 Office: Gerber Systems Tech 2960 Brandywine Atlanta GA 30341

HAMLIN, WINBORNE LEIGH, church worker, educator; b. Norfolk, Va., Aug. 12, 1937; d. Southgate and Maud (Winborne) Leigh; m. Jefferson Davis Hamlin, June 27, 1959; children—Jeff, John, Frank. B.A. magna cum laude, Sweet Briar Coll., 1958; M.A.T., John Hopkins U., 1959. English tch., pub. schs., Balt., 1958-59, Lancaster, S.C., 1959-60, 62-63; ch. sch. tchr. Christ Episcopal Ch., Lancaster, 1961-63, St. Michael and All Angels Ch., Dallas, 1974-80; adult Bible study tchr., 1981-84. Leader troop Girl Scouts U.S., Lancaster, 1961-63; tchr., dir. art program High Mus. Art, Atlanta, 1965-67; bd. dirs. St. Michael Sch., 1973-75; pres. University Park Sch. PTA, Dallas, 1978-79; bd. dirs. McCulloch Middle Sch. PTA, 1981-82, Highland Park High Sch. PTA, 1981-83, 85-86; bd. dir. Jr. League of Dallas, 1972-74, 76-78, exec. com., 1977-78; sec. Citizens' Study Com. to Recommend Best Form of Govt. for City of University Park, Tex., 1976-77; rec. sec. Dallas Mus. of Fine Arts League, 1979-80; pres. Women of Ch., St. Michael and All Angels, 1980-81, vestry mem., 1982-85, sec. Ministry with Aging, Inc., 1982-85, pres. parish council, 1983-85; del. Triennial Conv., bd. dirs. Province VII, 1984—; chmn. Central Convocation, Episcopal Ch. Women, Dallas, 1982-85; Episcopal Ch., 1982, 85; leader Camp Fire Girls, Dallas, 1970-73; mem. Dallas Civic Opera. Mem. Sweet Briar Coll. Alumnae Assn. (exec. bd. 1977-83, 85—), Phi Beta Kappa. Dallas TX

HAMM, GEORGE F., university president, psychology educator; b. Rapid City, S.D., June 26, 1931; s. Michael and Mae E. (Howard) H.; m. Jane Sigler, Aug. 29, 1958; children—Jean Marie, Gregory F., Robert Joseph, Daniel G. (dec.). B.A., S.D. State U., 1953; M.A., U. Wyo., 1958, Ph.D., 1961. Lic. prof. counselor, Tex. Counselor, Ariz. State U., Tempe, 1962-63, dean students, 1963-69, v.p. student affairs, 1969-81; pres. U. Tex.-Tyler, 1981—, prof. psychology, 1981—; nat. chmn. Nat. Assn. State Univ. and Land Grant Colls., 1976-78, exec. com. council on student affairs, 1979-81; mem. acad. planning com. Inst. for Advanced Strategic and Policy Planning, Jerusalem, 1985. Bd. dirs. Fiesta Bowl, Tempe, 1978-81, East Tex. Hosp. Found., Tyler, 1982; chmn. internat. bd. Sister Cities Internat., Washington; trustee St. Edwards U., Austin, Tex., 1982—. Named Outstanding Young Man of Yr., Ariz. Jr. C. of C., 1964; recipient Highest Civilian award U.S. Air Force, 1967; Disting. Alumnus award S.D. State U., Brookings, 1983. Mem. Am. Assn. State Colls. and Univs., Am. Assn. for Higher Edn., Tempe C. of C. (bd. dirs. 1980-81), Phi Kappa Phi, Omicron Delta Kappa, Psi Chi. Roman Catholic. Home: 9438 Cherokee Trail Tyler TX 75703 Office: U Tex-Tyler 3900 University Blvd Tyler TX 75701

HAMMACK, CHARLES JOSEPH, thermal engineering executive; b. Alamogorda, N. Mex., June 2, 1923; s. Charles Ross and Margueritte Ruperta (Cavett) H.; m. Gladys Lorene Mann, Sept. 4, 1949; children—Charles Randall, Cynthia Lorain, Kelly Joseph. Student John Tarleton Coll., 1946-47; B.S. Chem. Engring., U. Tex., 1951. Chemist Sheffield Steel Corp., Houston, 1951-54; tech. fieldman Sinclair Refining Co., Houston, 1954-57; heat transfer trainee Engrs. and Fabricators Co., Houston, 1957, v.p. thermal engring., 1958—. Mem. editorial com. GPSA Engineering Data Book, 10th edit.; contbr. articles to profl. pubs. Congregational sec. Zion Lutheran Ch., 1959-61, elder, 1961-66; elder St. Mark Luth. Ch., 1971-75, congregational sec., 1975-81; cert. tchr., trainer Evangelism Explosion III Internat. Served with USN, 1942-45. Mem. Am. Inst. Chem. Engrs., Process Heat Exchanger Soc. Democrat. Home: 8926 Theysen Houston TX 77080 Office: 3501 W 11th Houston TX 77008

HAMMER, DAVID CLARKE, healthcare administrator; b. Wichita, Kans., Dec. 14, 1953; s. Lowell Clarke and Beverly (Wellborn) H.; m. Patricia Clara Pace, June 27, 1981. A.A. with high honors, U.Fla., 1974; postgrad. U. North Fla., Jacksonville, 1983. Cert. mgr. patient accounts. Bus. office support unit supr. Alachula Gen. Hosp., Gainesville, Fla., 1979-81; dir. ambulatory services St. Vincent's Med. Center, Jacksonville, 1981—. First v.p. Fla. Assn. Adolescent Devel., Gainesville, 1982. Recipient Leadership award U. Fla. Coll. of Arts and Scis., 1976. Mem. Healthcare Fin. Mgmt. Assn. Democrat. Methodist. Home: 2144 St Johns Ave Jacksonville FL 32204 Office: St Vincents Med Center 1800 Barrs St Jacksonville FL 32203

HAMMER, EDWIN KING, special educator; b. Big Spring, Tex., Sept. 16, 1933; s. Thomas Marion and Willie Blanche (Adair) H.; m. Frances Lascari, Aug. 16, 1964; children—Mark, Scott. B.A., U. Tex., 1956; M.S., U. Kans., 1966; Ph.D., U. Tex., 1969. Tchr. Holton High Sch., Kans., 1964-66; exec. dir. Austin Cerebral Palsy Ctr., Tex., 1966-69; regional dir. deaf-blind ctr. Callie Ctr., Dallas, 1969-75; assoc. prof. U. Tex., Dallas, 1973—; pres. Found. Developmentally Disabled, Dallas, 1984—; bd. dirs. Assn. Retarded Citizens, Dallas, 1977—, Ctr. Computers for Disabled, Arlington, Tex., 1983—; chmn. adv. bd. Brainworks Sch. for Gifted, Carrollton, Tex., 1978—; dir. Functional Resources Enterprises, Austin. Guest lectr. Nordic Tng. Ctr., Helsinor, Denmakr, 1983, Aalborg, Denmark, 1985, Donninlund, Denmark, 1985, Bergen, Norway, 1985, Oslo, 1985. Adv. Deaf Blind Multihandicapped Assn. Tex., 1975—. Recipient Sammy Rankin award Am. Assn. Workers for the Blind, 1976; Citation award Am. Acad. Pediatrics; Commendation award Mountain Plains Regional Services, 1983. Fellow Am. Orthopsychiatry Assn., Am. Acad. Developmental Medicine and Cerebral Palsy; mem. Am. Psychol. Assn., Council Exceptional Children (founder U. Tex.-Dallas chpt.), Nat. Assn. Deaf-Blind (Merit award 1982). Home: 3528 Mockingbird Ln Dallas TX 75205 Office: U Tex Dallas PO Box 688 Richardson TX 75080

HAMMER, JOHN WILLIAM, JR., dentist; b. Charleston, W.Va., June 1, 1945; s. John William and Mary George (Spangler) H.; D.D.S., W.Va. U., 1969; postgrad. cert. periodontology Temple U.; m. Brenda Kay Subach, May 4, 1983; children—Jennifer Lee, Kristen Lee, Susan Elizabeth, Kassandra Kay, Caroline Ashley. Residency USPHS Hosp., Balt., 1970-71; gen. practice dentistry, Martinsburg, W.Va., to 1979; periodontal resident Temple U., Phila., 1979-81; periodontist USAF, Andrews AFB, Md., 1981-83; practice periodontology, Beckley, Princeton and Huntington, W.Va., 1983—. Served with USPHS, 1969-71. Fellow Acad. Gen. Dentistry; mem. ADA, W.Va. Dental Assn., W.Va. U. Sch. Dentistry Alumni Assn., New River Dental Soc., W.Va. Dental Assn., ADA, Am. Acad. Periodontology. Home: 5311 Stephen Way Cross Lanes WV 25313 Office: 1208 S Walker St Princeton WV also Country Club Profl Bldg 5505 Route 60 E Huntington WV 25705

HAMMER, WADE BURKE, oral surgeon, educator; b. Lakeland, Fla., Apr. 21, 1932; s. Orval Seown and Lilly Pearl (Wade) H.; A.A., U. Fla., 1956; D.D.S., Emory U., 1960; postgrad. U. Pa., 1962; m. Betty Dean Webb, June 22. 1956; children—Robert Burke, Joanna Wade. Practice dentistry, Orange Park, Fla., 1960-61; resident in oral and maxillofacial surgery Grady Hosp., Emory U., Atlanta, 1963-65; active staff Med. Coll. Ga. Hosp., Augusta, Ga., 1966—; cons. Univ. Hosp., Augusta, 1968—, VA Complex, Augusta, 1968—, Ft. Gordon Army Hosp., 1969—; clin. asst. prof. oral surgery Emory U., 1966-68; asst. prof. oral surgery and surgery Med. Coll. Ga., Augusta, 1968-71, assoc. prof. oral surgery, 1971-75, prof., 1975—. Active Boy Scouts Am. Bd. govs. Dental Found. Ga., 1974-77, pres., 1976-77. Served with USN, 1950-54;

col. Dental Corps, USAR. Diplomate Am. Bd. Oral & Maxillofacial Surgery. Fellow Am. Dental Soc. Anesthesiology, Am. Coll. Dentists, Am. Assn. Oral and Maxillofacial Surgeons; mem. ADA, Ga., Mem. Am., Ga., Eastern Dist. dental assns., Augusta Dental Soc., Southeastern (past pres.), Ga. Soc. Oral and Maxillofacial Surgeons (past pres.), Internat. Assn. Dental Research, Am. Assn. Dental Schs., Omicron Kappa Upsilon (past supreme chpt. pres.). Contbr. articles to profl. jours. Home: 3020 Vassar Dr Augusta GA 30909 Office: Med Coll Ga Augusta GA 30912

HAMMERMAN, ROBERT, financial services firm executive; b. N.Y.C., May 16, 1934; s. David S. and Fay (Chaimowitz) H. B.B.A., Pace U., 1957. Pres. Robert Hammerman Assocs. Inc., Alexandria, Va., 1974-81; acct. exec. E.F. Hutton, D.C., 1982-83, Smith Barney, D.C., 1983-85; fin. planner Baker, Watts and Co., McLean, Va., 1985—. 1st vice chmn. Rep. Com. 1979; bd. dirs. Alexandria Symphony, 1980, Performing Arts Assn., 1980; mem. Charter Rev. Commn., 1981. Mem. Internat. Assn. Fin. Planners (treas. nat. capital chpt. 1985-86). Lodge: Rotary (dir. 1981). Avocations: piano; classical music; art. Home: 6434 Rockshire St Alexandria VA 22310 Office: Baker Watts and Co 7926 Jones Br Dr McLean VA 22102

HAMMERSCHMIDT, JOHN PAUL, congressman; b. Harrison, Ark., May 4, 1922; s. Arthur Paul and Junie (Taylor) H.; student The Citadel; U. Ark.; Okla. State U.; m. Virginia Sharp; 1 son, John Arthur. With Hammerschmidt Lumber Co., Harrison, 1946—, pres., 1959—; dir. Harrison Fed. Savs. & Loan Assn.; mem. Harrison City Council, 1948, 60, 62; mem. 90th-98th Congresses, 3d Dist. Ark. Served as pilot USAAF, World War II; CBI. Decorated Air medal with 4 oak leaf clusters, D.F.C. with 3 oak leaf clusters. Mem. Ark. Lumber Dealers Assn. (past pres.), Southwestern Lumbermens Assn. (past pres. Kansas City), Nat. Lumber and Bldg. Material Dealers (dir.), Harrison C. of C. (named Man of Yr. 1965), Am. Legion, V.F.W. Presbyn. (elder) (deacon). Mason (32 deg., Shriner), Elk, Rotarian (past pres. Harrison). Home: PO Box 999 Harrison AR 72601 Office: Rayburn House Office Bldg Washington DC 20515

HAMMETT, BOBBY LYNN, computer installation cons.; b. Sherman, Tex., Mar. 16, 1935; s. William Henry and Leola (Gurley) H.; student various IBM Data Processing Schs., 1960-75; student Lamar U., 1977—; m. Dorene Yvonne Gantt, June 6, 1958; children—Susan Alysia, Deena Marque. With Levingston Shipbuilding Co., Orange, Tex., 1953-77, planner, 1961-65, mgr. data processing, 1965-77; cons. computer installations, 1977—; instr. Lamar U. Councillor, Jr. Achievement, 1967-72; master Three Rivers Council Boy Scouts, Am., 1954-55; res. dep. sheriff, Orange County, Tex. Mem. data processing com. Lamar U., 1971-73. Mem. COMMON, HASU (computer users groups), Am. Numismatic Assn., Data Processing Mgrs. Assn., Citizens Radio Assistance Corp. Home: 3106 Western Ave Orange TX 77630 Office: 3106 Western Ave Orange TX 77630

HAMMETT, R.C., chiropractor; b. Morganton, N.C., Jan. 1, 1951; s. Ralph C. and Ethel (Hill) H.; m. Cindy Moore, June 2, 1973; 1 son, Christopher Kyle. B.A., Furman U., 1973; D. Chiropractic, Palmer Coll., 1978. Supr., Tarr Heel Constrn., Salisbury, N.C. summers 1971-74; regional sales rep. Dale Carnegie Courses, Winston-Salem, N.C., 1974-75; assoc. doctor Furr Clinic, Salisbury, 1978-79; owner, chiropractor Hammett Clinic, Waynesville, N.C., 1979—. Dir. Waynesville Heart Fund (N.C.), 1981. Mem. Am. Chiropractic Assn., N.C. Chiropractic Assn., We. Dist. Assn. (pres. 1981-82), Clinic Mgmt. Corp. (baron 1983). Democrat. Methodist. Lodge: Waynesville Rotary. Office: Hammett Clinic 111 Walnut St Waynesville NC 28786

HAMMOCK, SARAH OWENS, business manager, educator; b. Panama City, Fla., Nov. 4, 1954; d. Durward Lenton and Betty Ann (Gaskin) Owens; m. Alan Morris Hammock, Jan. 28, 1978. A.A., Gulf Coast Community Coll., 1974; B.A., Fla. State U., 1976; B.S. in Mgmt., U. Central Fla., 1984. Reading tchr., CETA supr. and counselor Gulf County Schs., Port St. Joe, Fla., 1976-78; asst. mgr. D&H Landscaping, Longwood, Fla., 1978-79; tchr. Seminole County Schs., Longwood, 1979-80; ops. coordinator Ag. Carriers, Inc., Leesburg, Fla., 1980-82; constrn. coordinator Fla. Pools of Central Fla., Maitland, 1982-84. Mem. Am. Prodn. and Inventory Control Soc., Am. Mgmt. Assn., Kappa Delta Pi, Zeta Tau Alpha. Republican. Baptist. Home and office: 871 Sutter Loop Longwood FL 32750

HAMMOND, GEORGE ROBERT, chiropractor; b. Porterdale, Ga., Sept. 10, 1925; s. George Gibson and Anne Mae (Coley) H.; D.C., Lincoln Coll., Indpls., 1949; P.T., Nat. Coll. Chiropractic, 1958; m. Eleanor Emilie Maurer, Dec. 27, 1947; children—Carol Ann Hammond Reaves, Jody Hammond Bissette, Robin, Allyson Hammond Neville. Practice chiropractic, Wilson, N.C., 1950—. Pres. N.C. Bd. Chiropractic Examiners, 1969-75. Trustee Boys' Home at Lake Macamaw (N.C.), 1957-60, Civitan Found., 1960-64, Nat. Coll. Chiropractic. Served with AUS, 1943-44. Decorated Purple Heart; recipient Sci. Journalism award N.C. Chiropractic Assn. Jour., 1960. Fellow Internat. Coll. Chiropractors; mem. N.C. Chiropractic Assn. (pres. 1962), Wilson Civitan Club (pres. 1957-58), Civitan Internat. (lt. gov. dist. 1960-61), Delta Tau Alpha. Democrat. Episcopalian. Home: 212 Wilshire Blvd Wilson NC 27893 Office: 800 W Hines St Wilson NC 27893

HAMMOND, MICHAEL KENT, optometrist; b. Terre Haute, Ind., Nov. 25, 1946; s. Olen G. and Rose W. (Brown) H.; m. Deanna Angela Lyn, July 5, 1981; 1 child, Matthew Kent. Assoc., So. Ill. U., 1966, B.S., 1970, M.S., 1971; D.Optometry, U. Houston, 1977. Pvt. practice optometry, Grand Prairie, Tex., 1977—; organizer, dir. 1st Continental Nat. Bank, Grand Prairie, 1984-85; land, bldg. developer N & H Joint Venture, Grand Prairie, 1983-85. Bd. dirs. Lions Eye Tissue Bank, Dallas, 1983-84. Served with USAF. Mem. Am. Optometric Assn., North Tex. Optometric Assn. Lodge: Lions (bd. dirs. 1984, Outstanding Lion award 1982). Avocation: amateur radio. Office: 2634 S Carrier St Suite 101 Grand Prairie TX 75051

HAMMOND, NELLIE BLY, educator; b. Beechy, Ky., Feb. 16, 1932; d. Marquis de Lafayette and Nellie (Fossett) Fannin; m. John Frederick Hammond, Nov. 29, 1952; 1 dau., Mary Margaret. B.A. in Polit. Sci., Morehead State U., 1972, M.A. in Edn., 1978. Tchr. Beechy Sch., 1951-52, Sunshine Elem. Sch., Greenup County, Ky., 1957-70, Parker Elem. Sch., Pike County, Ohio, 1970-72, McKell Elem. Sch., South Shore, Ky., 1972—; sec. Coldiron & Warnock, attys., Greenup, Ky., 1952-57; sec. traffic dept. RCA, Hamilton, Ohio, 1954; office corr. Allis Chalmers Co., Cin., 1955; tchr. adult edn. Greenup Elem. Sch., 1980-81. Del., Greenup County Women's Democratic Club, 1980; precinct chmn. South Shore Dem. Com., 1972—. Recipient cert. Scioto County (Ohio) Drug Abuse Council; named Ky. col., 1983. Mem. NEA, Greenup County Edn. Assn. (pres. 1983), NEA, Ky. Edn. Assn., Nat. Geog. Soc., Alpha Delta Kappa. Methodist. Home: PO Box 792 James E Hannah Dr South Shore KY 41175 Office: Box 528 South Shore KY 41175

HAMMOND, RALPH CHARLES, real estate executive; b. Valley Head, Ala., Feb. 1, 1916; s. William Bleve and Alice Corina Jane (Holleman) H.; student Snead Jr. Coll., 1938-39, Berea Coll., 1940-41; A.B., U. Ala., 1945; m. Myra Leak, June 20, 1954; children—James, Ben. Press sec. to gov. Ala., Montgomery, 1946-50, exec. sec., 1955-59; gen. rep. ARC, Greensboro, N.C., 1950-54; mayor of Arab (Ala.), 1963-69; pres. City Center, Inc., Arab, 1959—. Commr. from Ala., U.S. Study Commn. S.E. River Basins, 1958-64; bd. dirs. Ala. Tb Assn., 1956-83, pres., 1972-74; hon. Christmas Seal chmn., Ala., 1974; v.p. Ala. Lung Assn., 1980-83. Served with AUS, 1941-45. Mem. Ky. Hist. Soc., Phillip Hamman Family Assn. Am. (pres. 1972-78), Ala. Poetry Soc. (pres. 1981-84, Ala. Poet of Yr. 1985), Ala. Writers' Conclave (pres. elect 1985-86), Nat. Fedn. State Poetry Socs. (treas. 1985-86). Democrat. Methodist. Lodge: Masons. Author: My GI Aching Back, 1945; Ante Bellum Mansions of Alabama, 1951; Philip Hamman, Man of Valor, 1976; Song of Appalachia, 1982; How High the Stars, 1982; Upon the Wings of the Wind, 1982; One Golden Apple a Day, 1983; Collected Poems, 1983; Wisdom Is, 1984; Edging Through the Grass (Book of Yr. Ala. Poetry Soc.), 1985; contbr. short stories and feature articles to jours., mags.; poems pub. in 40 ed. and poetry jours. Home: 1202 Guntersville Rd Arab AL 35016 Office: Box 486 Arab AL 35016

HAMMOND, RAYMOND WILLIAM, clinical pharmacist; b. Port Arthur, Tex., May 16, 1944; s. Woodrow Wilson and Anna Mary (Brockman) H.; m. Sandra Louise Borel, Feb. 1, 1964; children—Cynthia Lynn, Jeffrey Carl. B.S. in Pharmacy, U. Houston, 1973; Pharm.D., U. Tenn. Ctr. Health Scis., 1981. Lic. pharmacist, Tex., Mo., Ga., Okla. Staff pharmacist USPHS Hosp., S.I., N.Y., 1974-75; dep. chief pharmacist Med. Ctr. Fed. Prisoners, Springfield, Mo., 1975-77; dep. chief pharmacist USPHS Outpatient Clinic, Savannah, Ga., 1977-78, chief, 1978-79, chief pharmacist, Port Arthur, Tex., 1981; pharmacist USPHS Indian Hosp., Whiteriver, Ariz., 1981-83; asst. chief inpatient pharmacy services W.W. Hastings Indian Hosp., Tahlequah, Okla., 1983—; clin. resource speaker SW Okla. State U. Sch. Pharmacy, 1984—. Contbr. articles to profl. jours. Mem. instl. rev. bd. NE State U., Tahlequah, 1985—; bd. dirs. Cherokee County Hospice Assn. Served to comdr. USPHS, 1974—. Mem. Am. Soc. Hosp. Pharmacists, Okla. Soc. Hosp. Pharmacists, Commd. Officers Assn. USPHS, Rho Chi. Democrat. Roman Catholic. Avocations: photography; backpacking; computer science; fishing; beer and winemaking. Home: 903 Francis St Tahlequah OK 74464

HAMMOND, ROBERT LINDEN, aluminum manufacturing company executive; b. Lexington, Ala., Apr. 8, 1930; s. Robert Lee and Mary Alice (Bergin) H.; B.S., U. Ala., 1956; m. Reba Ellen Walker, Nov. 26, 1950; children—Ann Walker, Lee Allen. With Reynolds Metals Co., 1957—, regional tng. mgr., Sheffield, Ala., 1979—. Served with U.S. Army, 1951-53. Mem. Am. Soc. for Tng. and Devel., Alpha Kappa Psi. Mem. Ch. of Christ. Home: Route 15 Box 86 Florence AL 35633 Office: Reynolds Metals Co PO Box 910 E 2d St Sheffield AL 35660

HAMMOND, RONNIE LYNNEL, systems engineer; b. Tyler, Tex., July 17, 1948; s. George Author and Nathell Miller (Beck) H.; student (scholar) St. Phillip's Jr. Coll., 1966-68, (scholar) Huston-Tillotson Coll., 1968-70; B.A. in History, St. Mary's U., 1977. Dietary worker Bapt. Meml. Hosp., 1966-68; with So. Pacific R.R., 1970-72; computer operator St. Mary's U., San Antonio, 1973-74, ops. mgr. Computer Center, 1974-79; systems engr. NCR Corp., 1979—; data processing clk. San Antonio Ind. Sch. Dist., 1974. Mem. Am. Prodn. and Inventory Control Soc., Am. Space Found., Omega Psi Phi, Phi Alpha Theta (historian). Mem. Churches of Christ. Home: 8711 Townpark Dr Apt 2161 Houston TX 77036 Office: NCR Corp 6808 Hornwood Houston TX 77074

HAMMONDS, CLEVELAND, educational administrator. Supt. of schs. Durham, N.C. Office: PO Box 2246 Durham NC 27702*

HAMMONDS, DANNY LEE, coal company executive; b. Hazard, Ky., July 27, 1949; s. James Edgar and Pauline (Dunn) H.; m. Judith Diane Everage, June 13, 1970; children—Kevin Wade, Jennifer Lynn. Student U. Ky., 1967-69, Eastern Ky. U., 1969-70; grad. Ky. State Police Acad., 1971. Cert. emergency med. technician. State trooper, Hazard, 1971-79, detective, 1979-81; safety insp. Golden Oak Mining Co., Ison, Ky., 1981-82; safety dir. Bledsoe Coal Co., Chappell, Ky., 1982-84, supt., 1984-85; supt. Big Elk Creek Coal Co., Chappell, 1985—. Presbyterian. Lodges: Masons, Shriners. Avocations: motorcycle riding; archery. Home: Box 53 Mallie KY 41836 Office: Big Elk Creek Coal Co General Delivery Chappell KY 40816

HAMMONDS, OLIVER WENDELL, lawyer; b. De Queen, Ark., Aug. 4, 1911; s. Oliver Overstreet and Mamie Levonia (Scott) H.; m. Ellen Hewes Floweree, May 22, 1941 (div. 1969); children—Oliver Edmund (dec.), Harry Hewes, Patricia, James Wilson, John Scott. B.A., Okla. U., 1932; LL.B., Harvard U., 1936. Bar: Okla. 1936, U.S. Supreme Ct. 1940, Tex. 1946. Atty., office gen. counsel U.S. Treasury Dept., Washington, 1936-37; spl. asst. to atty. gen. tax div. Dept. of Justice, Washington, 1937-42; ptnr. Ray & Hammonds, Dallas, 1946-60; sole practice, Dallas, 1960—; lectr. Oil and Gas Inst., Southwestern Legal Found., 1954-58, Tax Inst. NYU. Contbr. numerous legal articles to profl. jours.; developed financing for endowment Manley O. Hudson chair in Internat. Law, Harvard Law Sch., 1977. Served to maj. USAAF, 1942-45. Decorated Bronze Star; recipient personal letter of commendation Gen. Hap Arnold, comdg. gen. USAAF, 1945. Mem. Tex. Bar Assn., Dallas Bar Assn. (chmn. com. ethics 1959-60), Dallas Council World Affairs (bd. dirs. 1951—), Phi Delta Phi. Episcopalian. Clubs: Brookhollow Golf (Dallas); Chevy Chase, Metropolitan (Washington). Office: 211 N Ervay Bldg Suite 309 Dallas TX 75201

HAMMONN, ABE, educational administrator. Supt. of schs. Mobile County, Ala. Office: PO Box 1327 Mobile AL 36633*

HAMNER, CANDACE GAIL, information systems educator; b. Cumberland, Md., Jan. 23, 1954; d. Ray Frederick Hamner and Evelyn (Milton) Hamner Kuykendall. B.A. in Math., Carson-Newman Coll., 1976; M.S. in Math., Baylor U., 1978, Ph.D. in Stats., 1983. Statis. cons. Sid Richardson Computation Ctr., Baylor U., Waco, Tex., 1978-80, lectr., asst. prof. info. systems dept. Hankamer Bus. Sch., 1983—; research asst. Methodist Home Children's Guidance Ctr., Waco, 1980-81. Mem. Am. Statis Assn. Democrat. So. Baptist. Avocations: piano; organ; jogging; water and snow skiing; tennis; sewing. Home: 4200 Grim Ave Waco TX 76710

HAMNER, CHARLES EDWARD, JR., medical center executive, research management consultant; b. Schuyler, Va., Mar. 26, 1935; s. Charles Edward and Mattie May (Butler) H.; m. Sharon Kay Boone, June 21, 1961; children—Elizabeth Diana, Clifton Charles. B.S., Va. Poly. Inst., 1956; D.M., U. Ga., 1960, M.S., 1962, Ph.D., 1964. Postdoctoral fellow U. Ga., Athens. 1960-64; asst. prof., div. vivarium U. Va., Charlottesville, 1964-67; assoc. prof., dir. reproductive biology, 1967-74; dir. progress coordination research and devel. A.H. Robins Co., Richmond, 1974-77; asst. to assoc. v.p. health affairs U. Va., Charlottesville, 1977—; cons. NIH, NSF, WHO, Rockefeller Found., Ford Found., 1964—. Editor: Drug Development, 1982. Contbr. articles to profl. jours., chpts. to books. Pres. Camp Albermarg, Inc., Charlottesville, 1981—. Mem. AAAS, Soc. Study of Fertility, Soc. Study of Reproduction, Physiology Soc. Episcopalian. Avocations: gardening; tennis. Home: 111 Reynard Dr Charlottesville VA 22901 Office: U Va Med Ctr Box 179 Charlottesville VA 22908

HAMNER, REGINALD TURNER, legal association executive, lawyer; b. Tuscaloosa, Ala., June 4, 1939; s. Raiford Samuel and Ellie Wells (Turner) H.; m. Anne Ellen Young, Nov. 8, 1969; children—Patrick Turner, William Christian. B.S., U. Ala., 1961, J.D., 1965. Cert. Am. Soc. Assn. Execs. Bar: Ala. 1965. Law clk, Supreme Court Ala., Montgomery, 1965; gen. counsel Med. Assn. Ala., Montgomery, 1968-69; exec. dir. Ala. State Bar Assn., Montgomery, 1969—. Contbr. articles to Ala. Lawyer; editor: Ala. State Bar Found. Bull., 1969-80. Deacon, First Bapt. Ch., Montgomery, Ala., 1977-80; bd. dirs. YMCA, Montgomery, 1979-82; vice chmn. State Child Welfare Com., Montgomery, 1982—. Served to capt. JAGC USAF, 1965-68 (to lt. col. USAFR 1968—). Named Outstanding Res. Officer U.S. Air Force Maxwell AFB, 1977. Fellow Am. Bar Found.; mem. ABA (mem. house of dels. 1972-76, 1985—), Nat. Assn. Bar Execs. (pres. 1978-79, Bolton award 1981), Judicial Conf. U.S. Eleventh Circuit, Am. Judicature Soc., Ala. Council of Assn. Execs. (pres. 1984). Republican. Southern Baptist. Club: Montgomery Country (Ala.). Avocations: tennis; running. Office: Ala State Bar Assn 415 Dexter Ave Montgomery AL 36104

HAMPTON, CHARLES EDWIN, lawyer, mathematician, computer programmer; b. Waco, Tex., Oct. 22, 1948; s. Roy Mizell and Hazel Lucretia (Cooper) H.; m. Cynthia Torrance, Sept. 14, 1968; children—Charles Edwin, Adam Ethan. Student, Baylor U., summer 1967, Rice U., 1967-68; B.A. with highest honors (Moody Found. scholar), U. Tex., Austin, 1971, J.D. with high honors, 1977; M.A. (NSF fellow 1971-74), U. Calif.-Berkeley, 1972, C.P., 1975. Bar: Tex. 1977, U.S. Dist. Ct. (we. dist.) Tex. 1979, U.S. Dist. Ct. (no. dist.) Tex. 1980. Research asst. U. Calif.-Berkeley, 1974-75; briefing atty. to justice Tex. Supreme Ct., 1977-78; asso. Law Offices Don L. Baker, P.C., Austin, 1978-81; legal counsel Office Ct. Adminstrn., Tex. Jud. Council, Austin, 1981; staff atty. Supreme Ct. Tex., 1981-84; assoc. Rinehart & Nugent, Austin, 1984—. Del., Travis County Democratic Conv., 1978, 80, 82, 84, 86. Mem. ABA, State Bar Tex., Travis County Bar Assn., Tex. Young Lawyers Assn. (co-recipient award for best law rev. article in Tex. 1979), Austin Young Lawyers Assn., Chancellors, Order of Coif, Phi Beta Kappa, Phi Kappa Phi, Phi Delta Phi. Mem. Ch. of Christ. Club: West Austin Lions. Office: 1000 MBank Tower Austin TX 78701

HAMPTON, JOHN LEWIS (JIM), newspaper editor; b. Verda, Ky., Jan. 13, 1935; s. John Lewis and Ruby Lillian (Slagle) H.; children—Rachel McCauley, Jessica Morris, Jonathan Hugh. A.B. in Journalism, U. Ky., 1959; M.A. in Communications and Journalism, Stanford U., 1960. Staff writer AP, Lexington, Ky., 1960-61; bur. chief Louisville Courier-Jour., 1961-67; staff writer Nat. Observer, Washington, 1967-71, sr. editor, then asst. mng. editor, 1971-77; mem. editorial bd. Miami (Fla.) Herald, 1977, editor, 1978—. Mem. Commn. on Ct. Costs and Delay, Fla. Bar, 1979-80. Served with AUS, 1953-56. Named to Hall Disting. Alumni, U. Ky.; grad. fellow Stanford U., 1960; recipient Pulitzer prize in editorial writing, 1983. Mem. Am. Soc. Newspaper Editors. Inter-Am. Press Assn., Fla. Soc. Newspaper Editors. Office: Miami Herald 1 Herald Plaza Miami FL 33101

HAMPTON, THOMAS EDWARD, real estate appraiser, consultant; b. Tuscaloosa, Ala., June 24, 1943; s. William Edward and Winnie Rivers (Wallace) H.; m. Susan Judd Linder, July 14, 1979; 1 dau., Virginia Rivers. B.S. in Bus. Adminstrn., U. So. Miss., 1970. Staff appraiser Fla. Dept. Transp., Clearwater, 1971-74; appraiser C.F. Erickson, MAI, Clearwater, 1974-76; v.p. Barnhill & Hampton, Clearwater, 1976-78; ind. fee appraiser Thomas E. Hampton, Clearwater, 1978-80; asst. v.p., chief appraiser First Fedn. Savs. and Loan, Tullahoma, Tenn., 1980-81; owner, appraiser, cons. Hampton Appraisal Services, Tullahoma, 1981—; instr. St. Petersburg Jr. Coll., Clearwater, 1977-79, Motlow State Community Coll., Tullahoma, 1980, 84. Bd. dirs., v.p. Assn. to Revitalize Community Heritage, Tullahoma, 1984—. Served to sgt. Spl. Forces, U.S. Army, 1964-67, Panama Canal Zone. Named Eagle Scout, Nat. Council Boy Scouts Am., Yazoo City, Miss., 1959; Aide de Camp, Gov.'s Staff, State of Tenn., Nashville, 1985. Mem. Soc. Real Estate Appraisers (chmn. pub. relations com. 1976-78, chmn. admissions com. 1984, edn. com. 1980-82, sr. real property appraiser, Am. Inst. Real Estate Appraisers (chmn. roster com. local chpt. 1984, edn. com. local chpt. 1981-83), Internat. Right of Way Assn. (local chpt. newsletter editor 1982, chmn. edn. com. 1983, chmn. membership com. 1984, Pres.'s Sphere award 1983, 84), Coffee County Bd. Realtors (affiliate), Pi Sigma Epsilon (Outstanding Member award-mktg. 1969). Republican. Episcopalian. Club: Lakewood County (Tullahoma). Lodges: Masons, Rotary. Avocations: boating; photography. Home: Route 1 Box 350-D Tullahoma TN 37388 Office: Hampton Appraisal Services 116 W Lauderdale St PO Drawer 1717 Tullahoma TN 37388

HAMRICK, DOVIE MELINDA, social worker; b. Shelby, N.C., Sept. 3, 1947; d. Hugh Ferguson and Dovie Blanton (Logan) H. B.A., U. N.C., 1969. Social worker Moore County Dept. Social Services, Carthage, N.C., 1969-79, supr. family and children's services, 1980-83, dir. social services, 1983—. Mem. Moore County Youth Services Commn., 1975-82, chmn., 1977-79, vice-chmn., 1979-80; mem. Head Start Adv. Com., 1980-82, chmn., 1981-82. Named Social Services Employee of Yr., 1980. Mem. N.C. Social Services Assn. (past dist. chmn., vice-chmn.). Home: 255 E Connecticut Ave Southern Pines NC 28387 Office: PO Box 938 Carthage NC 28327

HANAHAN, JAMES LAKE, insurance executive; b. Burlington, Iowa, Aug. 27, 1932; s. Thomas J. and Clarice P. (Lorey) H.; B.S., Drake U., 1955; postgrad. George Williams Coll., 1956; m. Marilyn R. Lowe, Dec. 27, 1952; children—Bridget Sue Bahlke, Erin Rose Hoff. Phys. dir. Monmouth (Ill.) YMCA, 1955-56; mem. community relations staff Caterpillar Tractor Co., Peoria, Ill., 1956-57; rep. Conn. Gen. Life Ins. Co., Des Moines, 1957-59, asst. mgr., 1959-63, mgr. group ins. ops., Tampa, Fla., 1963-80; pres. Wittner Hanahan & Peck, Inc., 1980—; dir. Williamsburg Reins. Co. Ltd.; ptnr. City Ctr. St. Petersburg, 1983—; instr. C.P.C.U. courses; seminar leader C.L.U. workshop; cons. ins. seminar Fla. State U. Bd. dirs. Jr. Achievement, Hillsborough County Health Council, 1983—, W. Coast Employee Benefit Council; bd. dirs. Pinellas Emergency Med. Service Inc. Recipient Double D award Drake U., 1978. Mem. Sales and Mktg. Execs. Tampa (dir., past pres.; Sales and Mktg. Exec. of Yr. 1982), Tampa Commerce Club, Soc. Profl. Benefit Adminstrs., Nat. Assn. Life Underwriters, Self Ins. Inst. Am., Greater Tampa C. of C. (gov.), St. Petersburg C. of C., Sun Coast C. of C. (adv. council), Minerat Soc. U. Tampa, Tampa Sports and Recreation Council (dir.), Com. of 100. Democrat. Roman Catholic. Clubs: 7th Inning (chmn.), Nat. D (Drake U.) (v.p., dir.); Innisbrook Golf Resort; President's (St. Petersburg). Home: 8012 W Hiawatha St Tampa FL 33615 Office: PO Box 24450 Tampa FL 33623

HANCOCK, BARRY WOOD, criminal justice educator; b. Guymon, Okla., July 10, 1954; s. John Walden and Vera (Jensen) H. B.S. in Psychology, Okla. State U., 1977, M.S. in Corrections, 1980, Ph.D. in Sociology, 1982. Instr., Okla. State U., Stillwater, 1978-80; prof. criminal justice Albany State Coll., Ga., 1981—; guest lectr. U. Stockholm, 1973-75; cons. Youth Devel. Ctr., Albany, State Diversion Ctrs., Albany, Office Juvenile Justice, Dept. Justice, Washington. Author: Doc N Stu, 1977. Contbr. articles to profl. jours. Sr. staff mem. Sheltered Workshop for Mentally Handicapped, Stillwater, 1977; bd. dirs. Albany Girl's Club, 1982—. Recipient Disting. Service award Albany State Coll., 1983, 84. Mem. So. Sociol. Soc., Am. Criminol. Soc., Soc. for Study Social Problems, Acad. Criminal Justice Scis., Phi Kappa Phi. Office: Dept Criminal Justice Albany State Coll Albany GA 31705

HANCOCK, JAMES EDWARD, radiation therapist; b. Ripley, Tenn., Mar. 7, 1927; s. William Christopher and Mary Isabel (Gilmore) H.; B.S., U. Tenn., 1952, M.D., 1961. Intern, Methodist Hosp., Memphis, 1961-62, resident, 1964-66; resident Oak Ridge Inst. Nuclear Studies, 1963; radiation therapist St. Jude Childrens Research Hosp., Memphis, 1968, Bapt. Meml. Hosp., Memphis, 1968-75; med. dir., radiotherapist Mary Bird Perkins Radiation Center, Baton Rouge, 1975—; mem. cons. staff Woman's Hosp., Drs. Meml. Hosp., Baton Rouge Gen. Hosp., Our Lady of the Lake Hosp., Earl K. Long Meml. Hosp. (all Baton Rouge); asst. clin. prof. Coll. Medicine U. Tenn., Memphis, 1968-75; mem. faculty La. State U. Med. Sch., Baton Rouge, 1975—. Bd. dirs. Am. Cancer Soc., 1971-75. Served with USNR, 1945-46. Fellow, U. Tex. M.D. Anderson Hosp., 1967-68. Diplomate Am. Bd. Therapeutic Radiology. Mem. AMA, Am. Coll. Radiology, Mid South Med. Soc., Tenn. Radiologic Soc., Sports Car Club Am. Home: 12814 Pecos St Greenwell Springs LA 70739 Office: 9042 Airline Hwy Baton Rouge LA 70815

HANCOCK, JAMES HUGHES, U.S. district judge; b. 1931. B.S., U. Ala., 1953, LL.B., 1957. Ptnr. Balch, Bingham, Baker, Hawthorne, Ward & Williams, Birmingham, 1957-73; U.S. dist. judge, No. Ala., 1973—. Mem. Ala. Bar Assn. Office: 357 Federal Courthouse Birmingham AL 35203*

HANCOCK, ROBERT WADE, chief of police; b. Jacksonville, Fla., Aug. 31, 1948; s. Robert Clyde and Maxine (Noegel) H.; m. Terri Gallo, Nov. 25, 1978; children—David, Antoinette. A.S., Seminole Community Coll., 1972; B.S., Rollins Coll., 1980. Chief of police Oviedo Police Dept., Fla., 1983—; voting mem. Crime Commn., Orlando, Fla., 1983—. Served to 1st lt. U.S. Army N.G., 1967—. Mem. Internat. Assn. Chiefs of Police, Fla. Police Chiefs Assn., Am. Soc. Indsl. Security. Republican. Roman Catholic. Lodges: Rotary, Optimists. Avocations: scuba diving; hunting; competitive shooting. Office: Oviedo Police Dept 42 S Central Oviedo FL 32765

HANCOCK, THOMAS RAY, geologist, geophysicist; b. Wingate, Tex., May 3, 1933; s. Lonnie R. and Julico (Garrett) H.; m. Gigi R. Glasscock, Nov. 16, 1968. B.S. in Geology, Tex. Western U., 1961. Geologist, geophysicist Chevron Co., Ardmore, Okla., Dallas, Corpus Christi, Tex., New Orleans, 1961-72, Louisiana Land Co., New Orleans, 1972—. Served to sgt. USAF, 1953-57. Mem. Am. Assn. Petroleum Geologists, Soc. Exploration Geologists, European Soc. Exploration Geophysicists. Republican. Methodist. Home: 3717 Pin Oak Ave New Orleans LA 70114 Office: Louisiana Land & Exploration Co 225 Baronne St New Orleans LA 70112

HAND, HERBERT HENSLEY, management educator, consultant; b. Hamilton, Ohio, July 11, 1931; s. Herbert Lawrence and Berta Elizabeth (Hensley) H.; m. Katharine Harris Gucker, July 26, 1952; children—Stephen Harris, Herbert Gucker. B.S., Ind. U., 1953; M.B.A., U. Miami, 1966; Ph.D., Pa. State U., 1969. Vice pres. Hand Oil Co., 1955-65; instr. Pa. State U., 1968-69; asst. prof. Ind. U., Bloomington, 1969-73, assoc. prof., 1973-76; prof. mgmt. U. S.C. Coll. Bus. Adminstrn., Columbia, 1976—; state dir. Small Bus. Devel. Ctr. S.C., 1968-69; exec. v.p. Carter-Miot Engrng. Co., Columbia, S.C., 1981; pres. Carolina Consultants, 1973-84; pres. Phronesis, Inc., 1985—; cons. to numerous cos., 1973—. Author: (with H.P. Sims, Jr.) Managerial Decision Making in the Business Firm-A Systems Approach, 1972, The Profit Center Simulation, 1975; (with A.T. Hollingsworth) A Guide to Small Business Management, 1979, Practical Readings in Small Business, 1979; contbr. research articles, papers in field to profl. jours.; mem. editorial bd. Bus. Horizons, 1971-73. Active YMCA, 1956-65, ARC, 1956-65, United Way, 1956-65, Cancer Soc., 1956-65, Camp Campbell Gard, 1956-65. Served to 1st lt. USAF, 1953-55. Recipient Western Electric award for most innovative bus. course, 1971; Small Bus. Inst. Regional award SBA, 1976, 80, 81, Small Bus. Inst. Nat. award, 1980; Office Naval Research grantee, 1976, 77, 78. Mem. Acad. Mgmt. (editorial bd. Rev. Jour. 1975-79), So. Mgmt. Assn., Am. Inst. Decision Scis.,

Internat. Council for Small Bus. Episcopalian. Lodge: Rotary. Office: Dept Bus Mgmt Coll Bus Adminstrn Univ South Carolina Columbia SC 29208

HAND, WILLIAM BREVARD, U.S. district judge; b. Mobile, Ala., Jan. 18, 1924; s. Charles C. and Irma W. H.; B.S. in Commerce and Bus. Adminstrn., U. Ala., 1947, J.D., 1949; m. Allison Denby, June 17, 1948; children—Jane Connor Hand Dukes, Virginia Alan Hand Hollis. Allison Hand Peebles. Admitted to Ala. bar, 1949; mem. firm Hand, Arendall, Bedsole, Greaves & Johnston, Mobile, 1949-71; U.S. dist. chief judge So. Dist. Ala., 1971—, now chief judge. Chmn. Mobile County Republican Exec. Com., 1968-71. Served with U.S. Army, 1943-46. Decorated Bronze Star medal. Mem. Am., Ala., Mobile bar assns. Methodist. Office: PO Box 1964 Mobile AL 36633

HANDEL, RICHARD CRAIG, lawyer; b. Hamilton, Ohio, Aug. 11, 1945; s. Alexander F. and Marguerite (Wilks) H.; m. Katharine Jean Carter, Jan. 10, 1970. A.B., U. Mich., 1967; M.A., Mich. State U., 1968; J.D., Ohio State U., 1974; LL.M. in Taxation, NYU, 1978. Bar: Ohio 1974, U.S. Dist. Ct. (so. dist.) Ohio 1975, U.S. Dist. Ct. S.C. 1979, U.S. Tax Ct. 1977, U.S. Ct. Appeals (4th cir.) 1979, U.S. Supreme Ct. 1979, S.C. 1983. cert. specialist taxation law. Assoc. Smith & Schnacke, Dayton, Ohio, 1974-77; asst. prof. U. S.C. Sch. Law, Columbia, 1978-83; ptnr. Nexsen, Pruett, Jacobs & Pollard, Columbia, 1983—. Served with U.S. Army, 1969-70; Vietnam. Gerald L. Wallace scholar, 1977-78; recipient Outstanding Law Prof. award, 1980-81. Mem. ABA, Richland County Bar Assn., S.C. Bar Assn., Order of Coif. Contbr. articles to legal jours. Office: 1401 Main St Suite 1200 Columbia SC 29202

HANDLER, BARBARA HERSHEY, systems analyst, mathematics and computer science educator; b. Detroit, Sept. 10, 1939; d. William and Irene Ida (Goldstaff) H.; m. Leonard Handler, June 25, 1961; children—Charles Andrew, Amy Elisabeth. B.S., Mich. State U., 1961, M.A., 1964; Ed.D, U. Tenn., 1982. Tchr. Williamston High Sch., Mich., 1961-64, Farragut High Sch., Tenn., 1964-65, Webb Sch., Knoxville, Tenn., 1969-70; instr. U. Tenn., Knoxville, 1969-80, 85, Maryville Coll., Tenn., 1980-83, State Tech. Inst., Knoxville, 1983-84, System Source, Knoxville, 1983-84; system analyst Martin Marietta Co., Oak Ridge, 1985—. Rev. editor Nat. Council of Math., 1981—. Chmn. arts and craft U. Tenn. Faculty Women, Knoxville, 1970—; treas. LWV, Knoxville, 1965-67; bd. dirs. Jewish Community Ctr., Knoxville, 1983-86; v.p. Childrens Internat. Summer Villages, Knoxville, 1984-85. Mem. AAUP, Nat. Council Tchrs. Math., Math. Assn. Am., Phi Kappa Phi, Pi Lambda Theta, Phi Delta Kappa. Democrat. Jewish. Avocations: traveling, cooking, knitting, reading, computer activities. Office: Martin-Marietta PO Box X 4500 N MS-H32 Oak Ridge TN 37831

HANDLEY, HOWARD EDWARD, JR., railroad executive; b. San Antonio, Aug. 30; s. Howard Edward and Gloria (Shepherd) H.; m. JoAnn Wilhelm, Aug. 6, 1960; children—Edie Jo, Terrie Lynn, John Keith. Student San Antonio Coll., 1956-57, Harvard Bus. Coll., 1972. Trainmaster, MP R.R. Co., various locations, 1964-69, supt., 1969-71, asst. gen. mgr., 1971-81; gen. mgr. Port Terminal R.R. Assn., Houston, 1981—, mem. bd. operation, 1983—. Mem. railroad ops. mgmt. transp. research bd. NRC, Washington, 1983—. Mem. Am. Assn. R.R. Supts., Tex. Transp. Inst. Republican. Roman Catholic. Clubs: Houston Center, Ravenaux Country. Home: 9010 Napfield Dr Spring TX 77379 Office: Port Terminal Railroad 501 Crawford St Houston TX 77002

HANDLOGEN, CLARENCE J., management consultant; b. Grand Rapids, Mich., Jan. 3, 1930; s. Benjamin and Wava Belle (Porter) H.; B.S., Detroit Coll. Bus., 1968; M.L.A., So. Methodist U., 1974; m. Faye Elaine Schut, Jan. 16, 1954; children—Gail Dianna, Lynda Kae. Controller, plant personnel mgr. Rospatch Industries, Grand Rapids, 1956-65; controller, treas. Big Dutchman div. U.S. Industries Inc., Zeeland, Mich., 1965-66; exec. v.p. Hope Coll., Holland, Mich., 1966-72; v.p. H.R. Sand Co., also exec. dir. Henry Found., Dallas, 1972-74; v.p., dir. Haworth, Inc., Holland, 1974-77; pres. Handlogen Corp., Dallas, 1977—. Bd. dirs. Highland Acad. Served with AUS, 1951-53. Mem. Assn. Mgmt. Cons. Republican. Presbyterian. Clubs: Commerce (Dallas); U.S. Power Squadron (Meritorious Service citation for rescue operation 1971). Address: 9235 Whitehurst St Dallas TX 75243

HANDMAN, STANLEY EDWARD, mechanical engineer; b. N.Y.C., Jan. 17, 1923; s. William and Jessie (Hantman) H.; m. Emily Amelia Bonvicino, Apr. 16, 1949. B.M.E., Poly. Inst. Bklyn., 1944, M.M.E., 1950. Devel. test engr. Gen. Electric Co., Bloomfield, N.J. and Bridgeport, Conn., 1946-47; instr. mech. engring. Poly. Inst. Bklyn., 1947-51; with M.W. Kellogg Co., Houston, 1951—, mgr. mech. engring. devel. dept., 1964-73, chief mech. engr., 1973-78, chief engr., 1978-81, worldwide chief engr., 1981—. Served with USN, 1944-46. Registered profl. engr., N.Y., N.J. Mem. ASME (mem. bd. safety codes and standards; Centennial medal 1980), Sci. Research Soc. Am., AAAS, N.J. SOc. Profl. Engrs., Nat. Soc. Profl. Engrs., Welding Research Council (exec. com.), Combustion Inst., N.Y. Acad. Sci., Sigma Xi, Pi Tau Sigma, Tau Beta Pi. Patentee in field; contbr. articles to profl. jours. Office: 3 Greenway Plaza E Houston TX 77046

HANES, GORDON, former hosiery manufacturing company executive; b. Winston-Salem, N.C., Mar. 3, 1916; s. James Gordon and Emmie (Drewry) H.; m. Helen Grever Copenhaver, Aug. 30, 1941; children—James Gordon III, Eldridge C., Margaret Drewry. B.A., Yale U., 1937; postgrad. Pace Inst., 1937-39; H.H.D. (hon.), N.C. State U. Acct., Hanes Hosiery Mills Co., Winston-Salem, 1939-41, sec., 1947-48, v.p., 1948-53, exec. v.p., 1954-57, pres., 1958-65; pres., chief exec. officer Hanes Corp., 1967-74, chmn. bd., 1965-79, also dir.; ret. 1979; dir. Hanes Dye & Finishing Co. Mem. N.C. Senate, 1963-65; chmn. bd. trustees N.C. Mus. Art; mem. assocs. exec. com. Smithsonian Instn.; trustee Folger Library; mem. nat. collectors' com. Whitney Mus. Art; mem. collectors' and adv. com. Nat. Gallery Art. Served as adminstrv. officer Ordnance USNR, 1941-45. Address: 480 Shepherd St Winston-Salem NC 27103*

HANES, MICHAEL L., educator, educational administrator, researcher; b. Bremen, Ind., Sept. 27, 1947; s. Charles E. and E. Kathleen (Kirby) H.; m. Madlyn A. Levine, July 22, 1977; children—Cara, Jena, Michael Ross. B.S., Ind. U., 1970, M.S. (univ. fellow), 1972, Ph.D. (univ. fellow), 1973. Asst. prof. Coll. Edn., U. Fla, Gainesville, 1973-76, assoc. prof., 1977, research assoc. Inst. for Devel. of Human Resources, 1973-77; dir. High/Scope Ednl. Research Found., Ypsilanti, Mich., 1977-80; prof., asst. dean adminstrv. and acad. affairs Coll. Edn., U. S.C., Columbia, 1980-84, exec. dir. presdl. commn., 1984—. Recipient Grad. Research awards U. Fla., 1974-75; numerous grants U.S. Dept. Edn., 1977-80; Southeastern Council for Ednl. Improvement grantee, 1981. Mem. Am. Ednl. Research Assn., Am. Assn. Colls. Tchr. Edn. Author: (with N. Anastasiow) Language Patterns of Poverty Children, 1976; (with N. Anastasiow and M. Levine Hanes) Language and Reading Strategies for Poverty Children, 1982; (with I. Flores and J. Rosario) Un Marco Abierto, 1979; Directions for Academic Excellence, 1985; editor: (with I. Gordon and B. Brievogel) Update: The First Ten Years of Life, 1977. Office: Coll Edn Univ South Carolina Columbia SC 29108

HANEY, DONALD LEE, quantitative management educator, electrical engineer, consultant; b. Decaturville, Tenn., Mar. 2, 1944; s. Reuben Lee and Carrie Lou (Powers) H.; m. Mary Bell Trout, Aug. 15, 1967; children—James R., Donald Louis. B.S. in Elec. Engring., MIT, 1966; Ph.D., Clemson U., 1969. Registered profl. engr., Tex. Engr. in tng. MIT Instrumentation Labs., Cambridge, summer 1966; asst. statistician, NSF trainee Clemson (S.C.) U. Computing Ctr., 1969-70; commd. 1st lt. U.S. Air Force, 1970, advanced through grades to maj., 1980; sci. analyst Kirtland AFB, N.Mex., 1970-71, Pease AFB, N.H., 1971-74, Brooks AFB, Tex., 1975-78, Randolph AFB, Tex., 1978-82; separated, 1982; asst. prof. quantitative mgmt. Sch. Bus. and Adminstrn., St. Mary's U., San Antonio, 1982—; cons. in field. Mem. IEEE, Inst. Mgmt. Sci., Am. Statis. Assn. Methodist. Office: One Camino Santa Maria Sch Bus and Adminstrn St Mary's U San Antonio TX 78284

HANEY, MARY BELL, civil engineer; b. Miami, Fla., Nov. 10, 1946; d. James Bell and Suzanna (Allen) Trout; m. Donald Lee Haney, Aug. 15, 1967; children—James Reuben, Donald Louis. B.S.C.E., Clemson U., 1967, M.S. in Environ. Systems Engring. (USPHS trainee), 1968, postgrad. in mgmt., 1968-76; postgrad. in chemistry U. Tex.-San Antonio, 1980-81. Registered profl. engr., Tex. Vis. lectr. and adj. prof. U. N.Mex., 1970-72; v.p. engring. Ruben Rodriguez Land Devel. Inc., Albuquerque, 1970-74; asst. project mgr. Pape-Dawson Cons. Engrs., Inc., San Antonio, 1976-78, project engr., 1978-82, project mgr., 1982—. Mem. properties com. San Antonio area Girl Scouts U.S.A.; mem. Universal City (Tex.) Library Bd., Universal City Planning and Zoning Commn. Mem. Nat. Soc. Profl. Engrs., Tex. Soc. Profl. Engrs. (dir. 1980, treas. 1981, sec. 1982, mem. Speakers Bur. 1979—, Outstanding Young Engr. Yr. award Bexar chpt. 1982, Tex. State Young Engr. Yr. award 1982), Soc. Women Engrs., Assn. Women Engrs., Assn. Women in Sci., Nat. Assn. Female Execs., Am. Statis. Assn., Water Pollution Control Fedn., Planetary Soc., ASCE, San Antonio Council Engring. Edn., NOW, YWCA, Tau Beta Pi (Women's Badge 1965), Phi Kappa Phi, Sigma Tau Epsilon. Methodist. Clubs: Altrusa, Protestant Women of Chapel (pres. 1975-76). Contbr. articles to profl. jours. Home: 318 Amistad Blvd Universal City TX 78148 Office: Pape Dawson Cons Engrs 9310 Broadway San Antonio TX 78217

HANIGAN, JOHN LEONARD, business executive; b. N.Y.C., Aug. 15, 1911; s. John P. and Winifred L. (Brennan) H.; student Stevens Inst. Tech., 1930-33; grad. advanced mgmt. program Harvard U., 1944; children—Joan C., John F. With R.H. Macy & Co., N.Y.C., 1933-35; with Corning Glass Works (N.Y.), 1937-62, v.p., 1953-62; pres. Corning Glass Works Can., Ltd., 1957-62; exec. v.p. Dow Corning Corp., 1962-63; pres., dir. Brunswick Corp., 1963-76, chief exec. officer, 1966-76, chmn. exec. com., dir. 1976-83, ret., 1983; chmn. bd. Genesco Inc., Nashville, 1979-84, ret., 1984; dir. Allis-Chalmers Corp., Nat. Can. Corp. Served as 1st lt. inf. U.S. Army Res., 1935-37. Mem. Sigma Nu. Office: 11760 US Hwy 1 2d Floor North Palm Beach FL 33408

HANKINSON, RISDON WILLIAM, chemical engineer; b. St. Joseph, Mo., Dec. 11, 1938; s. William Augusta and Rose Mary (Thompson) H.; B.S., U. Mo., Rolla, 1960, M.S., 1962; Ph.D. (Am. Oil fellow), Iowa State U., 1972; Hon. degree, Chem. Engr., U. Mo., Rolla, 1982; m. Lyla Pollard, June 4, 1960; children—Kenneth, Michelle, Michael, Mark, Douglass. Instr. chem. engring. U. Mo., Rolla, 1960-62; instr. chem. engring. Iowa State U., 1964-67; engr. Phillips Petroleum Co., Bartlesville, Okla., 1967-69, group leader, 1969-70, cons., 1970-78, prin., thermodynamics, 1978-80, prin. process engr., 1980-82, sr. staff assoc., 1982-85, mgr. engring. scis. br. tech. systems devel., 1985, mgr. tech. systems br. engring. and services, 1985—, adj. prof. math. Okla. State U., 1967-75, Bartlesville Wesleyan Coll., 1969-71. Vice pres. Tech. Careers Adv. Com., 1972-73, pres., 1973-74; v.p. Vol. Okla. Overseas Mission Bd., 1970-71; cub scout leader; tchr. religious edn., minister of Eucharist, lector, Roman Cath. Ch., 1976—; chmn. bd. dirs. Alcohol and Drug Center, Inc., 1984—. Served from 2d lt. to 1st lt. AUS, 1962-63. Recipient Outstanding Alumnus Achievement award Ia. State U., 1971; named Outstanding Young Engr. in Okla., 1970, Outstanding Engr. in Okla., 1984; registered profl. engr., Okla. Mem. Am. Inst. Chem. Engrs. (dir., past pres. Bartlesville sect.), Okla. Soc. Profl. Engrs. (Young Engr. of Year Bartlesville chpt. 1970, 84, Outstanding Engr. in Okla. award 1984), Am. Petroleum Inst. (chmn. phys. properties com. static measurement 1979-82). Clubs: Elks, KC, Kiwanis. Contbr. articles to profl., sci. jours. Home: 701 Sooner Park Dr Bartlesville OK 74006 Office: 11B1 Phillips Bldg Phillips Petroleum Co Bartlesville OK 74004

HANKS, JERALD EDWIN, public relations and advertising agency executive; b. Bethlehem, Pa., Aug. 13, 1931; s. Jerald Smith and S. Louise (McCullough) H.; m. Roberta de Cordova; children—Jerald Robert, Lee Alexandra. B.A., Lehigh U., 1953; M.S., Columbia U., 1957. Cert. pub. relations profl., Fla. Newspaper editor, reporter Allentown (Pa.) Morning Call, 1949-56, Fla. Times-Union, Jacksonville, 1957-59, Jacksonville Jour., 1959-61, Honolulu Star-Bull., 1961-62, Miami (Fla.) Herald, 1962-63; pub. affairs officer Apollo-Saturn V launch facilities, Kennedy Space Center, Fla., 1963-68; dir. info. services Reynolds, Smith & Hills, Architects, Engrs., Planners, Inc., Jacksonville, 1969-72; pres. Hanks-Livingston, Inc., Jacksonville, 1972—; speaker in field. Sec., Jacksonville Health Facilities Authority, 1980—; mem. budget com. Jacksonville United Way, 1971-72; mem. spl. commn. Goals and Priorities for Human Services, Jacksonville, 1973; mem. spl. commn. pub. relations Fla. Engring. Soc., Tallahassee, 1971-74; mem. exec. council Jacksonville U.; mem. pub. relations curriculum adv. council U. Fla. Served with USAF, 1954-56. Mem. Pub. Relations Soc. Am., Fla. Pub. Relations Assn., Cape Canaveral Pub. Relations Assn. (hon.), Democrat. Episcopalian. Lodge: Rotary. Contbr. articles to profl. publs. Home: 1335 Woodward Ave Jacksonville FL 32207 Office: 6034 Chester Ave Suite 200 Jacksonville FL 32217

HANKS, WILLIAM LARRY, municipal official; b. Elkin, N.C., Oct. 13, 1942; s. William Raymond and Celia Plutina (Guyer) H.; B.S., Taylor U., 1966; m. Susan Carol Tatum, June 16, 1978. Engr., United Technologies Essex div., Georgetown, Ky., 1966-75; mgr. Georgetown Mcpl. Water and Sewer Service, 1975—; mem. Ky. Bd. Cert. Wastewater Treatment Plant Operators, 1984—. Lic. water treatment plant operator, wastewater treatment plant operator, water distbn. system operator. Mem. Am. Water Works Assn., Water Pollution Control Fedn., Ky. Water and Wastewater Operators Assn. (pres. 1980-81, 85-86, seminar moderator 1980-86). Lodges: Masons, Shriners. Home: 510 Fountain Ave Georgetown KY 40324 Office: 214 W Main St Georgetown KY 40324

HANLIN, HUGH CAREY, JR., life insurance company executive; b. Chattanooga, Mar. 16, 1925; s. Hugh Carey and Irene (Thompson) H.; student Emory U., 1942-44, 46-47; B.A., U. Mich., 1948; m. Wilma Jean Deal, June 23, 1951; children—Timothy Carey, Chris Allan. With Provident Life & Accident Ins. Co., 1948—, exec. v.p., 1973-77, pres., 1977-79, pres., chief exec. officer, 1979—, dir., 1973—; dir. Am. Nat. Bank & Trust Co., Chattanooga, Third Nat. Corp., Nashville, Munford, Inc., Atlanta, Am. Council Life Ins., Provident Gen. Ins. Co. Bd. dirs. Chattanooga Opera Assn., 1970-79, pres., 1973-74; mem. resource group of opera adv. panel Tenn. Arts Commn., 1974-76; trustee U. Chattanooga Found., 1977—; mem. Urban League Chattanooga, 1981-82; past pres. Chattanooga-Hamilton County Speech and Hearing Center; bd. dirs. Allied Arts Fund of Chattanooga, v.p., 1975-76, pres., 1982-84; pres. Cherokee Area council Boy Scouts Am., 1980-82; bd. dirs. Moccasin Bend council Girl Scouts, 1971-75, Girls' Club Chattanooga, 1976-77, Tenn. Council Econ. Edn., 1978-80, United Way, 1979, Tenn. Ind. Colls. Fund, 1979; bd. visitors Berry (Ga.) Coll., 1981-84; trustee Am. Coll., 1981-83; chmn. River City Co., Chattanooga, 1986—. Served to lt. (j.g.) USNR, 1943-46. Recipient Silver Beaver award Boy Scouts Am., 1983; Liberty Bell award Chattanooga Bar Assn., 1984. Fellow Soc. Actuaries; mem. Am. Council Life Ins. (public relations policy com. 1979-82), Southeastern Actuaries Club (pres. 1956-57), Chattanooga C. of C. (downtown devel. com. 1980—), Phi Beta Kappa, Alpha Tau Omega. Presbyterian. Clubs: Mountain City (bd. govs.), Chattanooga Golf and Country, Rotary (pres. 1984-85). Home: 7472 Preston Circle Chattanooga TN 37421 Office: Provident Life and Accident Ins Co Chattanooga TN 37402

HANN, J. DAVID, telecommunications company executive; b. Kansas City, Mo., July 7, 1931; s. J. Berry and Mary Jane (Sanders) H.; B.E.E., U. Minn., 1954; m. Mary Leigh Allison, June 19, 1954; children—Peter Charles, James Kenneth, Andrew Steven, Jonathan David. With Gen. Electric Co., 1956-64; mktg. mgr. computer control div. Honeywell Inc., 1965-68; program dir. computer div. Honeywell Info. Systems/Gen. Electric Co., 1968-71; v.p. ops. and engring. Courier Terminal Systems, Inc., 1971-73; pres., chief ops. officer Boothe Computer Corp., 1976-78; pres. chief exec. officer Courier Terminal Systems, Inc., 1973-79; exec. v.p., dir. UNC Resources, Inc., Falls Church, Va., 1979-80; pres., chief exec. officer GTE Telenet, 1980—; dir. Boothe Fin. Corp., Tesdata Corp. Served with USN, 1954-56. Home: 10201 Cedar Pond Dr Vienna VA 22180 Office: 8229 Boone Blvd Vienna VA 22180*

HANNA, ANA IDRIS, personnel specialist; b. Havana, Cuba, Jan. 27, 1951; d. Jose Jesus and Dolores (Rubinstein) Perez; m. Sylvester Lawrence Hanna, Nov. 9, 1983. A.A., Miami Dade Jr. Coll., 1971; B.A., U. Miami, 1973. Adminstrv. asst. Better Bus. Bur., Houston, 1974; counselor Neighborhood Ctrs., Pasadena, Tex., 1975-78; social worker III Harris County Child Welfare, Houston, 1978-79; sr. personnel specialist City of Houston, 1979-85; plant personnel mgr. Coca Cola Foods, Houston, 1985—. Recipient Cert. of Appreciation Mayor of South Houston, Tex., 1978. Mem. Am. Soc. Tng. and Devel. Democrat. Office: Coca Cola Foods Div 7105 Katy Rd PO Box 2079 Houston TX 77024

HANNA, JAMES RAY, music educator, composer; b. Siloam Springs, Ark., Oct. 15, 1922; s. Arthur Ray and Achsah Westland (Ford) H.; m. Margie Ola Owen, Dec. 17, 1949; children—James Ford, Elizabeth Owen. B.Mus., Northwestern U., 1948, M.Mus., 1949. Prof. music U. Southwestern La., Lafayette, 1949-83. Composer: Song of the Redwood Tree, 1954, Woodwind Trio, 1957, Elegy, 1957, Fugue and Chorale, 1961. Contbr. articles to profl. jours. Violist Lake Charles Symphony, La., 1958-66, Baton Rouge Symphony, La., 1980-83. Served with U.S. Army, 1943-46. Symphony Number 2 grantee La. Council of Music and Performing Arts, Shreveport, 1968; recipient Composition award La. Fedn. of Music Clubs, 1954, 56, 58, 64. Mem. Am. Musicological Soc., Am. Fedn. of Musicians. Am. Viola Soc., Southeastern Composers' League (sec. 1956-58), Music Tchrs. Nat. Assn., Pi Kappa Lambda. Methodist. Avocations: genealogy; philatelics; model railroading; photography; travel. Home: 523 W Taft St Lafayette LA 70503

HANNA, SAMIA RIZK, physician; b. Cairo, Aug. 25, 1946; came to U.S. 1978, naturalized, 1983; d. Quirguis R. and Soad A. (Boctor) Rizk; m. Wahid T. Hanna, Dec. 19, 1970; 1 child, Michael W. M.B., B.Ch., Einshams U., Egypt, 1969; postgrad. diploma tropical medicine and hygiene, Liverpool U., Eng., 1977. Intern, Ein-Shams U. Hosps., Cairo, 1969-70; sr. house officer in pathology Chatterbridge Hosp., Bebington, Merseyside, Eng., 1970-72, registrar in pathology, 1972-76; resident in pathology U. Tenn. Meml. Hosp., Knoxville, 1978-82; practice medicine specializing in pathology, Knoxville, 1982—; pathologist Bapt. Hosp., Knoxville, 1982—. Mem. Am. Soc. Clin. Pathology, Am. Lung Assn. Tenn., Am. Heart Assn. Coptic Orthodox. Home: 7009 Sheffield Dr Knoxville TN 37919 Office: Dept Pathology East Tenn Bapt Hosp Box 1788 Knoxville TN 37901

HANNA, SYLVIA TAYLOR, association administrator; b. Columbia, S.C., Apr. 6, 1948; d. Moses and Cynthia (Carroll) Taylor; m. Marion Crosby Hanna, July 19, 1969; 1 child, Michael Crosby. B.A., Allen U., 1969; postgrad. U. S.C. Social worker Columbia Housing Authority, 1970; job counselor Richland Meml. Hosp., Columbia, 1972; basic edn. instr. Midlands Tech. Coll., Columbia, 1972-73; field rep. Columbia Urban League, 1973-78; asst. dir. Greater Columbia Community Relations Council (affiliate Greater Columbia C. of C.), 1978—. Bd. dirs. Rape Crisis Network, sec., 1984—; bd. dirs. Action Council-Mental Health, Killingsworth; adult advisor Christian Youth Orgn., Columbia, 1978-84. Named Outstanding Career Woman, YWCA, Columbia, 1980; recipient recognition of excellence award Careers Employment Experience, Columbia, 1981, Outstanding South Carolina award Nat. Council Negro Women, 1983. Mem. Am. Bus. Women's Assn. (pres. 1981-83, bd. dirs.), Nat. Assn. Female Execs. (bd. dirs.), LWV (bd. dirs.). Democrat. Roman Catholic. Avocations: coin/stamp collecting; swimming; sports. Home: 1861 Cheltenham Ln Columbia SC 29223 Office: Greater Columbia Community Relations Council PO Box 1360 1308 Laurel St Columbia SC 29202

HANNAN, DAVID CARROLL, lawyer; b. Wilmington, Del., Dec. 8, 1945; m. Barbara Lott; children—Leann. Student Emory and Henry Coll., 1964-65; B.A., Auburn U., 1968; J.D., U. Ala.-Tuscaloosa, 1971. Bar: Ala. 1971. Ptnr. Johnstone, Adams, Mobile, Ala., 1971—. Mem. adv. council Mobile Head Start Program, 1972-74; pres. Mobile Track and Field Assn., 1976-77, Mobile Pre-Sch. for Deaf, Inc., 1979-81, Vol. Mobile, Inc., 1982-83; fellow Leadership Mobile Program, 1978; vestry St. Paul's Episcopal Ch., 1976-79; council commr., dist. chmn., dist. fin. chmn. Boy Scouts Am., 1972—, recipient Award of Merit, Silver Beaver; bd. dirs. Leadership Mobile, Inc., 1980—, Boys Clubs of Mobile, 1979—, Am. Cancer Soc., 1983-84, Mobile Pre-Sch. for Deaf, 1977-83, Vol. Mobile, Inc., 1980-83; mem. adv. bd. Parade Against Drugs, 1984—; mem. Sr. Bowl Com., 1974—. Mem. ABA, Ala. Bar Assn., Mobile Bar Assn., Def. Research Inst., Ala. Def. Lawyers Assn., Internat. Assn. Ins. Counsel. Episcopalian. Home: 4124 Woodhill Dr Mobile AL 36608 Office: Johnstone Adams Howard Bailey & Gordon PO Box 1988 Mobile AL 36633

HANNAN, PHILIP MATTHEW, archbishop; b. Washington, May 20, 1913; s. Patrick Francis and Lilian Louise (Keefe) H.; student St. Charles Coll., 1931-33; A.B., Cath. U. Am., 1935, M.A., 1936, J.C.D., 1949; postgrad. North Am. Coll., Rome, 1936-40; S.T.B., S.T.L., Gregorian U., Rome, 1940. Ordained priest Roman Catholic Ch., 1939, consecrated bishop, 1956. Asst., St. Thomas Aquinas Ch., Balt., 1940-42; student Cath. U., 1946-49, vice chancellor, 1948-51, chancellor, 1951-62, vicar gen., 1960—; archbishop of New Orleans, 1965—; adminstr. St. Patrick's Ch., Washington 1951-56, pastor, 1956-65; aux. bishop Archdiocese of Washington, 1956-65; chmn. ad hoc com. Nat. Conf. Cath. Bishops Office Priestly Life and Ministry, 1971—; nat. Chaplain Cath. Daus. Am., 1974—. Mem. White House Conf. on Children and Youth, 1970—; chmn. bd. trustees Cath. U. Am., 1973—; mem. bd. dirs., chmn. interfaith com. United Fund New Orleans, 1970—; bd. dirs. Met. Council Boy Scouts Am., 1975—. Served as chaplain USAAF, 1942-46. Address: 7887 Walmsley Ave New Orleans LA 70125

HANNER, JOHN GEORGE, banker; b. Madison, N.C., Apr. 27, 1926; s. John Goldson and Margaret (Macy) H.; m. Wanda June Simmons, Aug. 2, 1947; children—John Gregory, Gary Steven, Brenda June. Riveter Aeronca, Middletown, Ohio, 1943, assembly foreman, Vandalia, Ohio, 1946; final insp. Nat. Cash Register Co., Dayton, Ohio, 1947-49; service and parts mgr. Hanner Motors, Tarboro, N.C., 1949-51; proof operator, teller, bookkeeper, asst. cashier, Edgecombe Bank, Tarboro, N.C., 1951-58; exec. v.p. Troy Citizens Bank, Troy, Ohio, 1958-69; pres. Lowndes Bank, Clarksburg, W. Va., 1969—, also dir.; dir., cons. Alamco, Inc., 1972—; dir. Aeromech Airlines; dir., treas. United Hosp. Ctr., Inc., 1971—. Advt. council SBA. Served with USAAF, 1943-45. Recipient Jaycees Young Man of Yr. award, 1959, Ky. Col. award, 1972, Hon. W. Va. award, 1974. Mem. W. Va. Bankers Assn., Ohio Bankers Assn. (Miami County), Assn. Indsl. Devel. (bd. dirs., past pres.), Clarksburg Indsl. Devel. Assn. (bd. dirs. 1973—), Eagle Indsl. Devel. Assn. (bd. dirs., v.p. 1973—). Democrat. Methodist. Clubs: Clarksburg Country, Sunny Croft Country (Clarksburg). Lodges: Elks, Shriners, Masons. Home: Route 1 PO Box 198 Lost Creek WV 26385 Office: 1 Lowndes Sq Clarksburg WV 26301

HANNIGAN, JOHN DENNIS, logistics engineer; b. Boston, Apr. 19, 1935; s. John Joseph and Catherine Rita (Donahue) H.; m. Joanne Clark, Aug. 5, 1955 (dec. 1963); children—John Clark, Catherine Mae, David Brian, Debra Jo; m. Jo Ann Hansen, Nov. 13, 1964 (div. 1978); children—David Anthony, Denice Michelle; m. Karen Sue Stanberry, Dec. 2, 1978; children—Stacey Nicole, Bridget Marie. Student Am. U., 1964-66, Ind. U./Purdue U.-Ft. Wayne, 1970-72. Supply cataloger U.S. Govt., Vinthill Farms Sta., Va., 1964-66; mgr. engring. services Wells Industries, Springfield, Va., 1966-68; sr. logistics analyst Magnavox, Ft. Wayne, 1968-76; supr. tech. pubs. ESystems Huntington, Ind., 1976-78; logistics program mgr. Northrop DSD, Rolling Meadows, Ill., 1978-80; mgr. logistics support engring. ESystems, St. Petersburg, Fla., 1980-82; sr. logistics engr. Sperry Gyroscope, Clearwater, Fla., 1982—. Served with U.S. Army, 1953-64. Mem. Soc. Logistics Engrs., Nat. Mgmt. Assn., Electronics Industries Assn., Armed Forces Communications and Electronics Assn., Soc. Old Crows. Republican. Ch. of God. Home: 6100 22d Ave N Saint Petersburg FL 33710 Office: PO Box 4648 Clearwater FL 33518

HANNIGAN, JOSEPH FRANCIS, physicist; b. Ft. Sill, Okla., July 10, 1926; s. Francis Hugh and Ava Lodema (Wilson) H.; B.S., Okla. State U., 1950; M.Teaching Sci., Cath. U. Am., 1971; m. JoAnn Young, Nov. 5, 1955; children—Michael Kevin, Patrick Sean, Mary Kathleen. Physicist, U.S. Army Engr. Research and Devel. Lab., Ft. Belvoir, Va., 1953-60, U.S. Army Engr. Topographic Labs., Ft. Belvoir, 1960-81; instr. George Mason U., Fairfax, Va., 1981—. Served with USAAF, 1944-46, U.S. Army, 1950-52. Recipient Army Sci. Conf. Outstanding Sci. Achievement award, 1978; Army Research and Devel. Achievement award for tech. achievement, 1973; Spl. Act Service award, 1972, 74, 75, 76, 77. Mem. IEEE, Sigma Xi. Roman Catholic. Contbr. articles to profl. jours.; patentee in field. Home: 6018 Meriwether Ln Springfield VA 22150

HANSELMAN, RICHARD WILSON, apparel company executive; b. Cin., Oct. 8, 1927; s. Wendell Forest and Helen E. (Beiderwelle) H.; B.A. in Econs., Dartmouth Coll., 1949; m. Beverly Baker White, Oct. 16, 1954; children—Charles Fielding, II, Jane White. Vice pres. merchandising RCA Sales Corp., Indpls., 1964-66, v.p. product planning, 1966-69, v.p. product mgmt., 1969-70; pres. luggage div. Samsonite Corp., Denver, 1970-73, pres. luggage group, 1973-74, exec. v.p. ops., 1974-75, pres. Samsonite Corp., 1975-77; sr. v.p. Beatrice Foods Co., Chgo., 1976-77, exec. v.p., 1977-80; pres., chief operating officer, dir. Genesco Inc., Nashville, 1980—, chief exec. officer, 1981—; dir. Becton Dickinson & Co., Arvin Industries, Third Nat. Corp. Club: Denver Country. Office: Genesco Inc Genesco Park Nashville TN 37202

HANSEN, DUANE ALAN, dentist, naval officer; b. St. Ansgar, Iowa, Jan. 15, 1933; s. Arthur and Marie Margarete (Denning) H.; m. Nancy Ann Cunningham, Apr. 20, 1968; children—Laurel Elizabeth, Leeann Marie. B.A., St. Olaf Coll., 1955; D.D.S., State U. Iowa, Iowa City, 1959; clin. fellow dental medicine Forsyth Dental Ctr. and Harvard Sch. Dental Medicine, Boston, 1961. Commd. lt. U.S. Navy, 1963; advanced through grades to comdr., 1969;

clinic supr. 22d Dental Co., Camp Lejeane, N.C., 1971-74, head, br. dental clinic Naval Air Sta., Lakehurst, N.J., 1974-77, head dental dept. U.S.S. Gilmore, Sardinia, Italy, 1977-79, head dental annex The Basic Sch., Quantico, Va., 1979-84, dir. br. dental clinic Naval Surface Weapons Command, Dahlgren, Va., 1984—. Mem. ADA, Acad. Gen. Dentistry. Republican. Presbyterian. Avocations: reading; traveling; bicycling; physical fitness.

HANSEN, EVA BUSEMANN, mathematics educator; b. Gottingen, Germany, Jan. 2, 1931; came to U.S., 1948; d. Adolf and Magda (Krage) Busemann; m. Donald Vernon Hansen, Aug. 23, 1958; children—Peter, Norman, Christa. B.A. in Math., Mary Washington Coll., 1952; M.A. in Math. Edn., Tchrs. Coll. Columbia U., 1954. Asst. prof. Fla. Meml. Coll., Miami, 1978—. Mem. Math. Assn. Am. Home: 5900 SW 104th St Miami FL 33156

HANSFORD, WILLIAM CASSON, physician; b. Tuscaloosa, Ala., Nov. 9, 1940; s. William Earl and Grace L. (Casson) H.; m. Gerrie Ann Fowler, May 30, 1970; children—Anne Elizabeth, Amy Lynn, William C., Jr. B.S., Auburn U., 1964; M.D., Med. Coll. Ala., 1969. Lic. physician, Ala.; diplomate Am. Bd. Family Physicians. Intern Lloyd Noland Hosp., Fairfield, Ala., 1969-70, resident, 1972-75; staff Jefferson Health Found, Bessemer, Ala., 1975-76; pvt. practice, Opp, Ala., 1976—; mem. adv. bd. Covington County Health Dept. Home Vis. Service; mem. adv. bd. Phenix Fed. Savs. & Loan Assn. Served to with USPHS, 1970-72. Mem. AMA (Physicians Recognition award 1979-82, 82—); Med. Assn. Ala., Covington County Med. Soc., Am. Assn. Family Physicians, Am. Profl. Practice Assn. Methodist. Club: Rotary. Home: 1206 N Main St Opp AL 36467 Office: Physicians Office Bldg Opp AL 36467

HANSON, RONALD WINDELL, cardiologist; b. Jeffersonville, Ind., Apr. 30, 1947; s. Erwin D. and Bernice (Windell) H. B.S. summa cum laude, Ariz. State U., 1968, M.S., 1969, Ph.D. in Physics, 1972; M.D., U. Ala., 1977. Diplomate Am. Bd. Internal Medicine, Am. Bd. Cardiovascular Diseases. Asst. prof. physics U. Ala., 1972-74; resident in internal medicine and cardiology Good Samaritan Hosp., Phoenix, 1977-82; practice medicine specializing in cardiology, Gadsden, Ala., 1982—. Served to lt. col. CAP. Fellow Am. Coll. Cardiology; mem. ACP. Office: 801 Gaines Ave #305 Gadsden AL 35903

HANSON, VICTOR HENRY, II, newspaper publisher; b. Augusta, Ga., Aug. 17, 1930; s. Clarence Bloodworth, Jr. and Elizabeth (Fletcher) H.; m. Elizabeth Stallworth, Dec. 29, 1953; children—Clarence Bloodworth III, Victor Henry III, Elizabeth Mickel, Mary Fletcher, Robert Stallworth. Grad., Choate Sch., 1949; student, U. Va., 1949-51; B.A., U. Ala., 1954. With Birmingham (Ala.) News & Post Herald, 1946-54, 57—, gen. mgr., 1963—; with advt. and prodn. dept. WAPI-TV, Birmingham, 1954-55; v.p. Birmingham News Co., 1960-79, pres., pub., 1979—; pres. Mercury Express, Inc.; dir. AmSouth Bank, N.A., AmSouth Bancorp. Vice chmn., trustee So. Research Inst., Birmingham. Served to capt. USAAF, 1955-57. Mem. Birmingham C. of C., Kappa Alpha. Presbyn. Clubs: Birmingham Country, Relay House, Mountain Brook, The Club (Birmingham). Lodge: Rotary. Office: 2200 4th Ave N Birmingham AL 35203

HANZEL, MARSHA WEINSTEIN, writer; b. Columbus, Ohio, Oct. 3, 1947; d. Marcus Leroy and Eleanor Frances (Reich) Weinstein; B.J., U. Mo., 1969; postgrad. U. Va., 1970-71; m. Jeffrey Sheldon Hanzel; children—Michael Brian, William Stephen. Staff writer Norfolk (Va.) Virginian-Pilot, 1969-70; editor Norfolk Naval Sta. newspaper, 1972-73; staff writer Hartford (Conn.) Courant, 1973-74; free-lance writer and photographer, 1974—; food editor Richmond Jewish News, 1981—. Mem. Chesterfield County-Colonial Heights Multidiscipline Team on Child Abuse and Neglect; bd. dirs. Va. chpt. Nat. Com. Prevention of Child Abuse, Parents Anonymous of Va.; mem. state subcom. multidisciplinary teams Gov.'s Adv. Com. Child Abuse and Neglect; state bd. dirs. Parents Anonymous. Mem. Women in Communications, Nat. Fedn. Press Women. Club: Bon Air Jr. Woman's. Home: 1613 Robindale Rd Richmond VA 23235

HAPALA, MILAN ERNEST, political science educator; b. Hranice, Czechoslovakia, Sept. 19, 1919; s. Vladimir and Marie (Mloochova) H.; m. Adelaide M. Hamilton, Sept. 6, 1947; children—Milan Ernest, Mary Elizabeth. B.A., Beloit Coll., 1940; M.A., U. Nebr., 1941; Ph.D., Duke U., 1947. Instr. govt. Sweet Briar Coll., 1947-49, asst. prof., 1949-56, assoc. prof., 1956-60, prof. govt., 1960, Carter Glass Prof. govt., 1962—, dept. chmn., 1952-63, 65-68, 72-75, 83—, chmn. Div. Social Studies, 1983—. Chmn. Amherst (Va.) Bicentennial Commn., 1976—. Served with USAAF, 1942-45. Carnegie fellow, U. Mich., 1961-62; Fulbright fellow, India, 1962; postdoctoral fellow NDEA, U. Pa., 1964-65. Mem. Am. Polit. Sci. Assn., Assn. for Asian Studies, Am. Assn. for Advancement of Slavic Studies, Assn. for Internat. Studies, Czechoslovak Soc. for Arts and Sci., Phi Beta Kappa. Democrat. Presbyterian. Clubs: Rotary, Sphex, Thirteen (Lynchburg, Va.). Contbr. articles to profl. jours. Home: Waugh's Ferry Rd Amherst VA 24521 Office: Box X Sweet Briar Coll Sweet Briar VA 24595

HAPP, JOHN WALLER, chemistry educator; b. Dallas, Apr. 26, 1943; s. Howell Chester and Marjorie (Watt) H.; m. Joanne Roulette, Sept. 11, 1966; children—Jennifer, James. B.S. in Chemistry, U. Md., 1965; Ph.D. in Chemistry, U. Ga., 1969. Postdoctoral fellow U. N.C., Chapel Hill, 1970-71; prof. chemistry, chmn. sci. and math div. Shenandoah Coll., Winchester, Va., 1972—, co-dir. grad. summer computer inst., 1983—. Mem. Am. Chem. Soc. Va. sect. exec. com. 1985), Nat. Sci. Tchrs. Assn. (co-dir. software swapshop 1983—), Phi Delta Kappa, Chi Beta Phi. Home: Route 1 Box 215 Clearbrook VA 22624 Office: Sci and Math Div Shenandoah Coll Winchester VA 22601

HAQUE, SYED MEHBOOBUL, geologist; b. Puri, Orissa, India, Jan. 4, 1945; came to U.S., 1973, naturalized, 1981; s. Syed Fazlul and Samsun (Nissa) H.; m. Shirin Taher, Oct. 8, 1976; children—Mansoor, Nadia. B.S., Ravenshaw Coll., 1966, M.S., 1968; B.P.S. in Bus., Pace U., 1975. Geologist, Orissa Industries, Barang, 1969-73; coll. asst. Pace U., N.Y.C., 1974-77; field geologist Imperial Coal Co., Muskogee, Okla., 1978-79; sr. research geologist La. Geol. Survey, Baton Rouge, 1979-84, chief geologist coastal protection, 1985—. Author: Water Level Trends in Florida Parishes, 1982; Ground Water Quality in Lake Charles Area, 1984. Contbr. articles to profl. jours. Sec., Ravenshaw Coll. Social Service Guild, Cuttack, India, 1967; pres. Muslim Youths Cultural Assn., Cuttack, 1969. Mem. Am. Assn. Petroleum Geologists, Baton Rouge Geol. Soc. Avocations: rock and coin collecting. Office: La Geol Survey Box G Univ Sta Baton Rouge LA 70893

HARALSON, MABLE KATHLEEN, state official; b. Abbeville, S.C., May 8, 1935; d. Ralph Quillen and Minnie (Murphy) Haralson. B.S., U. S.C., 1974; M.P.H., U. Tenn., 1976. Adminstrv. asst. community health service S.C. Dept. Health and Environ. Control, 1968-74, health educator, 1974, dist. dir. health edn., 1976-79; state dir. public info. and edn. S.C. Water Resources Commn., Columbia, 1979—; mem. S.C. Gov.'s Beautification and Community Improvement Adv. Bd., 1979-83, State Natural Resources Council, 1983—. Bd. dirs. State Employees Assn., 1980-83. USPHS trainee, 1975-76; cert. Am. Assn. Sex Educators, Counselors and Therapists. Mem. Am. Pub. Health Assn. (Disting. Service award So. br. health edn. sect.), So. Health Assn. (chmn. health edn. sect. 1980), S.C. Public Health Assn. (sec.), S.C. Environ. Edn. Assn. (chmn. 1985). Baptist. Home: PO Box 515 Abbeville SC 29260 Office: 3830 Forest Dr Columbia SC 29250

HARB, MITCHELL ABRAHAM, inventor, craftsman, mechanic; b. Greensboro, N.C., Oct. 15, 1919; s. Fareed J. and Catherine Mae Hannah H.; student U. Wis., 1942-45; m. Marilee Cruse, Oct. 25, 1941; children—Mitchell Joseph, Marille Priscilla. Propr., owner Harb Tire Service, mgr. Foundry, Lexington, N.C., 1949—; patent cons., 1957—; instr. Nat. Rifle Assn., 1957—; designer patterns and molds for plaques and medals, 1949—; created a Silver Jubilee medallion for Queen of Eng., 1977; miniature models of Am. ships and cannons represented in permanent display at Mariners Mus. Monitor and Merrimac, Beauford, N.C., various Davidson County libraries and state mus.; created baby gorilla for N.C. Zool. Park, Ashboro; created world's largest scales of justice, Salisbury, N.C. (Guinness Book of World Records); created cast bronze plaque recognizing Lexington as Barbecue Capital of N.C., placed on site of 1st barbecue tent in city. Served with U.S. Army, 1942-44, USAF, 1944-45. Recipient Presdl. Sports award (Rifle), 1977; nominated to Nat. Inventors Hall of Fame, 1979. Mem. Nat. Rifle Assn. (life), High Rock Lake Assn. Democrat. Baptist. Club: Eagle Coin (charter). Inventor daul tire cutting machine; patentee in field (3). Home: 1 Harb Dr Lexington NC 27292 Office: 8 Conrad St Lexington NC 27292

HARBAUGH, WILLIAM SHELDON, safety engineer; b. Bethesda, Md., Nov. 28, 1952; s. Charles William and Charlotte Ruth (Cooper) H.; m. Livia Diana Venable, Sept. 4, 1981; 1 child, Michelle Diane. B.S. in Indsl. Mgmt., Ga. Tech. U., 1976. Loss prevention cons. Liberty Mutual Ins. Co., Knoxville, Tenn., 1976-83; dir. safety and tng. Skyline Transp., Knoxville, 1983-84; sr. loss control rep. CNA Ins. Co., Knoxville, 1984-85; safety supr. Highway Transport Inc., 1985—. Mem. Am. Safety Engrs., Bd. Cert. Safety Profls. Republican. Avocations: kart racing. Home: 3040 Shropshire Blvd Powell TN 37849

HARBIN, KENNETH WAYNE, railcar leasing company executive; b. Austin, Tex., Nov. 22, 1947; s. Wayne DeWitt and Elinor Victoria (Tolish) H.; m. Carol Ann Morrow, July 8, 1972; children—Meredith Elaine, Matthuews McVey. B.B.A., U. Tex., 1974. Sales rep. N.Am. Car Corp., Houston, 1974-75; asst. v.p. Richmond Tank Car Co., Houston, 1975-81, corporate sec., 1978-82, pres. subs. Richmond Leasing Co., 1981—; dir. Dardanelle & Russellville R.R., Dardanelle, Ark. Served with USN, 1969-72. Office: Richmond Leasing Co 1700 W Loop S Houston TX 77027

HARBISON, WILLIAM JAMES, state supreme court justice; b. Columbia, Tenn., Sept. 11, 1923; s. William Joshua and Eunice Elizabeth (Kinzer) H.; student The Citadel, 1943-44; B.A., Vanderbilt U., 1947, J.D., 1950; m. Mary Elizabeth Coleman, June 14, 1952; children—William Leslie, Mary Alice. Bar: Tenn. 1950. Pvt. practice law, Nashville, 1950-74; spl. justice Tenn. Supreme Ct., Nashville, 1966-67, justice, 1974—, chief justice, 1980-82; adj. prof. law Vanderbilt Law Sch., Nashville, 1950—; chmn. civil rules com. Tenn. Supreme Ct., 1965-74. Mem. Metro Nashville Bd. Edn., 1970-74. Served with AUS, 1943-46. Mem. Am., Tenn., Nashville (pres. 1970-71) bar assns., Order of Coif, Phi Beta Kappa. Democrat. Methodist. Clubs: Cedar Creek, Cumberland, Rotary. Editor-in-chief Vanderbilt Law Review, 1949-50. Home: 1031 Overton Lea Rd Nashville TN 37220 Office: 314 Supreme Ct Bldg Nashville TN 37219

HARDAWAY, EVELYN RENEE, data processing executive; b. Columbus, Muscogee, Ga., Dec. 19, 1948; d. Roscoe and Vesta Mae (Mitchell) H.; student Johnson C. Smith U., Charlotte, N.C., 1967-68, Am. Inst. Banking, Columbus, Ga., 1969-70. Auditing clk. First Nat. Bank, Columbus, Ga., 1969-72; office mgr. Cagle, Inc., Omaha, 1972-74; account exec. Flair Personnel Service, Atlanta, 1974-76; tech. adv. Am. Mgmt. Services, Denver, 1976-80; data processing coordinator Lifemark Corp., Houston, 1981—. Recipient Operations Excellence award Am. Mgmt. Services, 1979. Mem. Nat. Assn. Female Execs., Internat. Platform Assn. Office: PO Box 656 Katy TX 77449

HARDAWAY, GARY LYNN, architect, poet; b. Waco, Tex., Oct. 24, 1950; s. William Fred and Nancy Mary (Phillips) H.; m. Laurie Anne Lewins, May 1, 1976; 1 son, David Christopher. B.S., U. Tex.-Arlington, 1974, postgrad., 1974-80. Registered architect, Tex. Urban planning technician City of Dallas, 1973-74, urban planner, 1974-78; archtl. designer Vantage Properties, Inc., Dallas, 1978-83, design architect, 1983—. Mem. AIA, Tex. Soc. Architects. Democrat. Author: Because I Can't Play Electric Guitar, 25 Poems, 1975; Hors d'oeuvres, Thirty Poems of Ten Lines or Less, 1975; 3 New Poems, 1976; prin. archtl. works include North Dallas C. of C. Bldg., Tex. and Southwestern Cattle Raisers Bldg., Ft. Worth, Northcreek Place, Phases I and II, Dallas, Atrium at Bent Tree, Dallas, Atrium III, Denver Technol. Ctr., Trinity Sq. Plaza, Carrollton, Campus Circle Tech Ctr., Irving. Home: 5807 Northaven Rd Dallas TX 75230 Office: 2777 Stemmons Freeway Suite 357 Dallas TX 75207

HARDEE, BILLIE CHARLENE, nurse; b. Williamson County, Tex., July 26, 1934; d. Robert Newton Gaines and Madge Leola (Fisher) Gaines Neal; student Huston-Tillotson Coll., Austin, 1952-58; L.V.N., Sid Peterson Sch. Vocat. Nurses, 1967; m. Raymond Julius Hardee, Aug. 20, 1958; children—Julius Earl, Todd Ray, Lateesha Charlene. With Sid Peterson Meml. Hosp., Kerrville, Tex., 1962-85, head nurse central service, 1970-85; activity therapist Kerrville State Hosp., 1986—; tchr.'s aide Kerrville Inc. Sch. Dist., 1980. Mem. Alpha Kappa Alpha. Methodist. Club: Home Demonstrators Civic. Home: 320 Pearl St Kerrville TX 78028

HARDEN, DOYLE BENJAMIN, import-export company executive; b. Banks, Ala., Oct. 15, 1935; s. J.C. and Gladis C. (Romine) H.; m. Elvira Harden; children—Janet Denice, Misty Lyn, Dusty Lyn, Wesley Doyle. Student pub. schs. Salesman, Gordon Foods, Atlanta, 1955-64; pres. Kwik Shop Markets, Columbus, Ga., 1964-73, Exportaciones Chico, S.A., Juarez, Mex., 1973-76, Chico Arts, El Paso, Tex., 1976—, Transp. Interoceanica, S.A., Honduras, C.Am., 1975—. Office: 1045 Humble Dr El Paso TX 79915

HARDEN, RICHARD MARTIN, accountant; b. Cordele, Ga., Sept. 12, 1944; s. Delton Henry and Katherine E. (Hinson) H.; m. Mary O'Day Vann, Aug. 27, 1966; children—Katherine, Richard. Student Davidson Coll., 1962-64; B.B.A., Ga. State U., 1966, M.B.A., 1968. Commr. Ga. Dept. Human Resources, Atlanta, 1972-74; spl. asst. to Pres., White House, Washington, 1977-81; cons., Washington, 1981; dir. MAS Connally, Pechter and Co., P.C., Atlanta, 1981-84; mgr. Deloitte, Haskins & Sells, 1984—. Mem. Am. Inst. C.P.A.s, Ga. Soc. C.P.A.s, Cobb C. of C. (v.p.). Democrat. Presbyterian. Club: Gridiron (Athens). Home: 3356 Stovehill Ct Marietta GA 30067 Office: Suite 1600 200 Gallcaia Pkwy Atlanta GA 30339

HARDESTY, ROBERT LOUIS, university president; b. St. Louis, June 4, 1931; s. John Frank and Lucille (Hetzel) H.; m. Mary A. Roberts, May 1, 1954; children—Elizabeth W., Bruce R., John O., Ann H. B.A., George Washington U., 1957; LL.D. (hon.), Huston-Tillotson Coll., Tex., 1983. Assoc. editor Army Times, 1955-57; advt. exec., Washington, 1957-64; spl. asst. to U.S. Postmaster Gen., 1964-65; asst. to Pres. U.S., 1965-69; spl. asst. to former Pres. U.S., 1969-72; press sec. to Gov. Tex., 1973-76; vice chancellor U. Tex. System, 1976-81; pres. Southwest Tex. State U., San Marcos, 1981—; mem. intergovtl. adv. council edn. U.S. Dept. Edn., 1979-81; mem. Edn. Commn. of the States, 1983—. Bd. govs. U.S. Postal Service, 1976-84, chmn., 1981-84; trustee Southwest Research Inst., San Antonio. Served with U.S. Army, 1953-55. Recipient Postmaster Gen's Benjamin Franklin award, Disting. Service award Southwest Journalism Forum, 1976. Mem. Philos. Soc. Tex. Democrat. Clubs: Argyle (San Antonio); Headliners (Austin); University, Metropolitan (Washington). Lodge: Rotary. Office: President's Office Southwest Texas State Univ San Marcos TX 78666

HARDEWAY, GRANT ULYSESS, SR., lawyer; b. Houston, Sept. 15, 1945; s. Arthur R. and Flora Dell (Gaynor) H.; B.B.A., Tex. So. U., 1969, J.D., 1973; m. Verna Mae Boatner, Dec. 17, 1965; children—Grant Ulysess, Gabriel Uyvette, Gretchen Undria. Bar: Tex. 1973, U.S. Supreme Ct. 1976, U.S. Ct. Appeals (5th cir.) 1973, U.S. Tax Ct. 1979, U.S. Dist. Ct. (so. dist.) Tex. 1979. Acct., IBM, Greencastle, Ind., 1966, systems operator, Houston, 1966-67, asso. programer Houston Sci. Project, 1968-72; supr. Houston Data Center, 1972-74; individual practice law, Houston, 1973—. Dir. Tex. So. U. Ex Student Assn.; active Houston Legal Found. Recipient Congressional cert. appreciation, 1964. Mem. Houston Jr., Houston bar assns., Nat., Tex. (dir.), Harris County (chmn.) assns. criminal def. lawyers, Am. Trial Lawyers Assn., Tex. Trial Lawyers Assn. Home: 9630 Highmeadow St Houston TX 77063 Office: 1903 Lexington St Houston TX 77098

HARDGRAVE, ROBERT LEWIS, JR., political science educator, writer, consultant; b. Greensburg, Pa., Feb. 6, 1939; s. Robert L. and Orlene (Pirtle) H.; B.A., U. Texas, 1960; M.A., U. Chgo., 1962, Ph.D., 1966. Asst. prof. Oberlin Coll., 1966-67; prof. U. Tex., Austin, 1967—; cons. U.S. Dept. State, Washington, 1982-83. Author: The Nadars of Tamiland, 1969; India: Government and Politics in a Developing Nation, 4th edit., 1986; India under Pressure, 1984; American Government: The Republic in Action, 1986. Mem. Assn. Asian Studies, Am. Polit. Sci. Assn. Office: U Tex at Austin Dept Govt Burdine Hall 536 Austin TX 78712

HARDIMAN, RICHARD LAWRENCE, former oil co. ofcl.; b. Cheviot, Ohio, May 16, 1912; s. Randolph Lawrence and Bertha Celesta (Henderson) H.; A.A., Ashland Jr. Coll., 1948; B.S., Morehead State U., 1972; m. Ella Louise Stafford, May 18, 1941; children—Jane (Mrs. Charles E. Patterson), Martha (Mrs. George M. Prout). With Ashland Oil, Inc. (Ky.), 1933-77, tech. service engr. product application dept., 1958-77. Served with USNR, World War II; PTO. Mem. Am. Soc. Lubrication Engrs. (chmn. 1974-75), Soc. Automotive Engrs., Greenup County Hist. Soc., Big Sandy Valley Hist. Soc., Ky. Hist. Soc., Eastern Ky. Geneal. Soc. Presbyterian (deacon 1955-57, treas. 1955-57, 69-70, ruling elder 1959-61, 64-66, 74-76, trustee 1965-—). Author geneal. booklets. Home: 108 Bellefonte Dr Ashland KY 41101

HARDIN, BETTY JOAN, dental assisting educator, consultant; b. Lebanon, Ind., Jan. 14, 1943; d. Frank Eugene Estelle and Pearl Adeline (Shoaf) Estelle Haffner; m. John Thomas Hardin, Jr., Sept. 27, 1963 (div. Dec. 1974); 1 child, John Thomas III. A.A.S., James H. Faulkner State Jr. Coll., 1983; postgrad. 1984—. Cert. dental asst. Am. Dental Assts. Assn., 1966. Lic. dental hygienist, Ala. Dental asst., Huntsville, Ala., 1961-74; instr. James H. Faulkner State Jr. Coll., Bay Minette, Ala., 1974-77, dir. dental asst. dept., 1977—; cons. Syntex-Dentalez Corp., 1977—; presentor ednl. clinics; speaker in field. Mem. Ala. Edn. Assn., NEA, Faulkner Ala. Edn. Assn., Ala. Assn. Community and Jr. Colls., Am. Assn. Dental Schs., Ala. Dental Hygienists Assn., Ala. Dental Assts. Assn. (pres. 1974-75, mem. exec. bd. 1975-76, Dental Asst. of Yr. 1972, Pryor Service award 1973, Onzalee Blatzer award 1974), Huntsville Dental Assts. Soc. (pres. 1967-68, Dental Asst. of Yr. 1967). Republican. Home: 918 E Pleasant Ave Bay Minette AL 36507 Office: James H Faulkner State Jr College Hammond Circle Bay Minette AL 36507

HARDIN, ELIZABETH CRAWFORD, commercial display artist, interior designer; b. Lumberton, N.C., Sept. 16, 1942; d. Theodore McLellan and Elizabeth (McAshan) Crawford; m. Edward Reel Hardin, July 1, 1967 (div. Apr. 1985); 1 child, Edward Reel. A.A., Peace Coll., 1962; B.A., U. N.C., 1964; accreditation des etudes artistiques Sorbonne U. Paris, 1965; M.S., U. N.C., 1967. Interior designer The Alderman Co., High Point, N.C., 1967-74; show room designer Singer Furniture Co., Roanoke, Va., 1975-81; freelance designer Elizabeth C. Hardin ASID, High Point, 1981—; cons. showroom displays, photography cons. Pilliod Cabinet Co., Swanton, Ohio, 1982-84, Wesley Allen Co., Los Angeles, 1983—, Webb Furniture Enterprises, Galax, Va., 1984—, Baldwin Furniture, Pompano Beach, Fla., 1985—; photography designer The John Henry Co., Lansing, Mich., Norling Studios, High Point, Tatum, Toomey & Whicker Agy., High Point. Author, editor teaching kit on design. Design lectr. Guilford County Community Coll., High Point, 1974, 85. U. N.C. teaching fellow, 1966-67. Mem. Am. Soc. Interior Designers, Assn. of Jr. League. Methodist. Avocations: tennis; skiing. Home and Office: 1014 N Rotary Dr High Point NC 27262

HARDIN, JAY CHARLES, research scientist, educator; b. Indpls., Oct. 22, 1942; s. Max Carter and Iris Lucille (Grimes) H.; m. Ellen Huey, June 7, 1964; children—Lance, Shane, Brooke. B.S., Purdue U., 1964, M.S., 1965, Ph.D., 1969; postdoctoral U. Southampton, Eng., 1972. Research instr. Purdue U., West Lafayette, Ind., 1964-69; engr. Midwest Applied Sci. Corp., West Lafayette, 1964-69; adj. prof. Old Dominion U., Norfolk, Va., 1983; research scientist NASA Langley Research Ctr., Hampton, Va., 1969—; adj. prof. Christopher Newport Coll., Newport News, Va., 1981—; professorial lectr. George Washington U., 1970—. Author: Introduction to Time Series Analysis, 1985. Contbr. articles to profl. jours. Recipient regional award for personal computing to aid the handicapped IEEE Computer Soc., 1981, Spl. Achievement award NASA, 1984. Mem. Sigma Xi, Tau Beta Pi. Presbyterian. Avocations: sailing; water skiing. Home: 116 Mistletoe Dr Newport News VA 23606 Office: NASA Hampton VA 23665

HARDIN, KENNETH TOLLEY, educational administrator; b. Hampton, Ky., Nov. 19, 1915; s. H. Clyde and Lora J. (Slayden) H.; m. Mary Louise Utx, Dec. 19, 1942; 1 child, Kenneth Michael. B.S. in Sci., Murray State U., 1947; M.Ed., U. Ky., 1962. Elem. sch. tchr. Livingston County Bd. Edn., Ky., 1936-42, secondary sch. tchr., 1942-43; tchr. agr. Livingston County High Sch., Smithland, Ky., 1947-55; prin. Livingston Central High Sch., Smithland, 1955-85. Served with U.S. Army, 1943-46. Mem. Nat. Assn. Secondary Sch. Prins., Ky. Assn. Sch. Adminstrs., NEA, Purchase Area Vocat. Agr. Tchrs. (v.p. 1951-52), Livingston County Edn. Assn. (pres. 1952-54), Livingston County C. of C. (sec. 1957-58). Democrat. Methodist. Lodge: Masons. Avocations: bird hunting; fishing; farming; travel. Home: General Delivery Hampton KY 42047 Office: Livingston Central High Sch PO Box 367 Smithland KY 42081

HARDIN, LARRY GENE, manufacturing engineer; b. Bowling Green, Ky., May 19, 1948; s. William Gentry and Zelpha Lee (Westerfield) H.; student Western Ky. U., Bowling Green; m. Sharon Faye Edmondson, May 4, 1968; children—Jeffrey Allen, Judy Michelle. Indsl. engr. FMC Corp., Bowling Green, 1975-79; prodn. supr. Tube Turns Co., Louisville, 1979; sr. indsl. engr. Clark Equipment Co., Georgetown, Ky., 1979-80; mfg. engring. mgr. Thomas Industries, Inc., Beaver Dam, Ky., 1980-85; plant mgr. Jackson Buff, Conover, N.C., 1985—. Mem. Ohio County Citizens Alcohol and Drug Action Com., adv. Ohio County Jr. Achievement. Served with USAF, 1968-74; mem. Ky. Air NG. Decorated Commendation medal. Mem. Soc. Mfg. Engrs. (officer), Am. Welding Soc., Am. Inst. Indsl. Engrs. (officer), Ohio County C. of C. Democrat. Baptist. qome: Route 6 Box 212 Taylorville NC 28681 Office: PO Box 699 Conover NC 28613

HARDIN, LUTHER, state senator; b. Searcy, Ark., Sept. 16, 1951; s. Luther S. and Chrystal D. (Waldo) H.; m. Mary Margaret Bowen, 1975; 1 son, Luther Scott. Grad. Ark. Tech. U., 1973, U. Ark. Sch. Law, 1976. Mem. Ark. Senate, 1983—. Mem. Kappa Alpha, Phi Alpha Delta. Democrat. Methodist. Office: Ark Senate State Capitol Little Rock AR 72201*

HARDIN, ROBERT ALLEN, audio video executive; b. Miami, Fla., May 3, 1934; s. Florian Armstrong and Pauline (Clark) H.; m. Clara Keyes, Jan. 16, 1971; 1 son, Keyes Christopher. Student U. Miami, 1952-53, U. Fla., 1955-56. Reporter, Miami Herald, 1956-58; writer, asst. city editor San Francisco Chronicle, 1959-64; writer, editor San Francisco Examiner, 1964-65; writer Paramount Studios, Los Angeles, 1965; assoc. editor Tropic, Miami Herald, 1967-68; publs. editor Miami Dolphins, 1969-70; ptnr. Keyes-Hardin Prodns., Miami, 1971—; asst. state atty. Dade County, Fla., 1973-74; pub. Rewrite, South Fla. journalism rev. Co-author: Mountains to Miami, 1983; author films: What's a Cop, 1972 (Cine Golden Eagle 1973); Officer Down, Code 3 (U.S. Film Festival award 1976); Tarnished Badge (Columbus Film Festival award 1977); contbr. articles to Esquire, Sports Illust., Yachting, Miami mag., others. Mem. Dade County Marine Council; adv. bd. Miami Office Profl. Compliance. Served with USMC, 1953-55. Mem. Writers Guild Am. West, Am. Newspaper Guild. Club: Coral Reef Yacht (Miami). Home: 1770 Micanopy Ave Miami FL 33133 Office: 2640 S Bayshore Dr Miami FL 33133

HARDINGE, BYRON CANTINE, engring. co. exec.; b. Albany, N.Y., Feb. 8, 1921; s. Harlowe and Florence Cummings (Donnelly) H.; student U. Pa., 1948-53, U. Mo.-Rolla, 1955-57; m. Therese Thompson, Apr. 1985. Asst. prodn. mgr. York Shipley Inc. (Pa.), 1945-48; devel. engr. Hardinge Co. Inc., York, 1948-55, now dir.; chief metallurgist Dresser Minerals Co., Houston, 1957-61; metall. cons., 1961-64; dept. mgr. engring. Brown & Root Inc., Houston, 1964-80, div. sr. cons. engr., 1980—. Served with USAAF, 1942-45. Registered profl. engr., Calif., N.H., N.B., Can. Mem. N.Y. Acad. Scis., Am. Soc. Safety Engrs., AIME, Am. Inst. Chem. Engrs., Nat., Tex., Calif. socs. profl. engrs., Houston Engring. and Sci. Soc., Theta Xi. Contbr. articles in mineral processing field to profl. publs. Home: 6500 Harbor Town Rd #3409 Houston TX 77036 Office: PO Box 4574 Houston TX 77210

HARDISON, HUGH, state official; b. Crawford County, Ga., Aug. 29, 1929; s. Dudley Hughes and Lydia Pauline (Bryant) H.; 1 dau., Lee Anne. Student N. Ga. Coll., 1953, Ga. Inst. Tech., 1954. From license examiner Ga. State Patrol to commr. Ga. Dept. Pub. Safety, 1955—. Served with USMC; Korea. Baptist. Lodges: Masons, Shriners, Caledonia. Office: 959 E Confederate Ave SE Atlanta GA 30316

HARDISON, JOSEPH HAMMOND, JR., physician, educator; b. Raleigh, N.C., Apr. 25, 1932; s. Joseph Hammond and Katherine Clark (Smith) H.; m. Cynthia Ann Stoltze, Apr. 8, 1962; children—Joseph Hammond III, Sanborn Stoltze, Anna Katherine. M.D., Duke U., 1956. Diplomate Am. Bd. Internal Medicine, 1964. Intern, resident Cornell Med. Ctr., N.Y. Med. Ctr., 1956-58; fellow in internal medicine Mayo Clinic, 1960-62, fellow in gastroenterology, 1962-64; practice internal medicine, Raleigh, N.C. (with Dr. Cynthia Hardison), 1964-68, (with Dr. Paar), 1968-71; sr. ptnr. Raleigh Internal Medicine Assocs., 1971—; asst. prof. medicine U. N.C., Chapel Hill, 1964-76, assoc. prof. medicine, 1976—; mem. med. staff Rex, Wake Meml., Raleigh Community hosps.; chmn. dept. medicine Raleigh Community Hosp., 1978-79; dir. First Union Nat. Bank Raleigh, The Edwards and Broughton Co. Pres. Raleigh Heart Assn., 1967-68. Served to lt. commdr. M.C., USN, 1958-60. Recipient N.C. Heart Assn. Founders award. Mem. Wake County Med. Soc., N.C. Med.

Soc., AMA, Am. Coll. Gastroenterology (bd. govs.), Raleigh Soc. Internal Medicine (pres. 1975-76). Democrat. Episcopalian. Clubs: Carolina Country, Capital City, Sphinx (Raleigh); Coral Bay Beach (Atlantic Beach, N.C.). Home: 2801 Lakeview Dr Raleigh NC 27609 Office: 1212 Cedarhurst Dr Raleigh NC 27609

HARDMAN, JAMES NEIL, police chief; b. Spencer, W.Va., Jan. 8, 1933; s. James F. and Eula M. (Gandee) H.; m. Constance Kesler, 1956 (div. 1969); children—Thomas Neil, Teresa Hardman Kemper; m. Mary Jane McIntosh, Aug. 1982. Student Glenville State Coll., 1951-53, W.Va. U., 1953-55. Spl. agt. U.S. Treasury Dept., Fla., 1959-66; instr. fed. law enforcement Acad. U.S. Treasury, Washington, 1966-69, asst. spl. agt. in charge alcohol, tobacco, firearms, Washington, 1969-74, spl. agt. in charge, Boston, 1976-78; chief of police, Spencer, 1981—; police coordinator Regional Devel. Authority, Charleston, W.Va., 1969-70; lectr. various state police acads., 1964-78. Writer outdoor and nature stories. Served as spl. agt. CIC, U.S. Army, 1955-58, Fed. Republic Germany. Recipient Outstanding Achievement awards U.S. Govt., 1966, 68, 73, U.S. Treasury Dept., 1974; J. Edgar Hoover Meml. award Nat. Police Acad., 1984. Mem. Nat. Assn. Chiefs Police, Internat. Assn. Chiefs Police, Nat. Assn. Narcotic Officers. Baptist. Avocations: hunting, fishing, outdoor sports. Home: 809 Summit St Spencer WV 25276 Office: Police Dept 207 Court St Spencer WV 25276

HARDMAN, JERRY WILLIAM, hospitality industry consultant; b. Chgo., July 20, 1941; s. William John and Carlota D. (Dawney) H.; m. Maria Martha Basso, Feb. 19, 1963 (div. Mar. 1977); children—William John, Eric Leonard. M.A. in Spanish, U. Buenos Aires, Argentina, 1962. Head translator Dodero Travel, Buenos Aires, 1962-63; gen. mgr. Holiday Inn, Crystal City, Va., 1969-75, Springfield, Va., 1975-81; dir. pre-openings Calvert Mgmt. Corp., Woodbridge, Va., 1981—; cons. Econo Lodge, Springfield, Comfort Inns, Woodbridge, Ramada Inn, Annapolis, Md. Republican. Episcopalian. Club: Optimist (Arlington, Va.) (pres. 1973-75). Avocations: soccer; Spanish; H-O gauge trains. Office: 12658 Lake Ridge Dr Woodbridge VA 22192

HARDT, JOHN WESLEY, bishop; b. San Antonio, July 14, 1921; s. Wesley W. and Ida Hardt; m. Martha Carson, Sept. 13, 1943; children—Betty Hardt Lesko, William C., John S., Joe. Student Lon Morris Coll., 1940; B.A., So. Meth. U., 1942; B.D., Perkins Sch. Theology, 1946; postgrad. Vanderbilt U., Nashville and Union Theol. Sem.; D.D. (hon.), Southwestern U., 1965; hon. degree Oklahoma City U., 1980. Pastor, Dekalb Cir., 1941, Alba Cir., 1942, Malakoff, 1943-44, Pleasant Retreat, Tyler, Tex., 1944-50, 1st United Meth. Ch., Atlanta, 1950-55, 1st United Meth. Ch., Marshall, Tex., 1955-59, 1st United Meth. Ch., Beaumont, Tex., 1959-77; dist. supt. Houston E. Dist., 1977-80; bishop Okla. United Meth. Ann. Conf., Okla. Indian Missionary Conf., 1980—. Active C. of C., Rotary Club. Author: Not the Ashes, but the Fire, 1976. Office: 2420 N Blackwelder St Okalahoma City OK 73106

HARDTNER, QUINTIN THEODORE, III, lawyer; b. Shreveport, La., Mar. 5, 1936; s. Quintin Theodore, Jr. and Jane (Owen) H.; m. Susan Mayer, June 30, 1962; children—Susan Owen, Quintin Theodore IV, George Jonathan. B.B.A., Tulane U., 1957, J.D. 1961. Bar: La. 1961. Assoc. Jones, Walker, Waechter, Poitevent, Carrere & Denegre, New Orleans, 1961-62; ptnr. Hargrove, Guyton, Ramey and Barlow, Shreveport, 1962—; dir. First Nat. Bank Shreveport. Adv. bd. Salvation Army; past trustee All Sts. Episcopal Sch., Vicksburg, Miss.; past trustee, past chmn. St. Mark's Day Sch.; past vestrymen St. Mark's Episcopal Ch.; trustee Southfield Sch.; past bd. dirs., v.p. Shreveport Assn. for Blind; past bd. dirs. Family and Children's Services; past co-chmn. Centenary Coll. Fund. Served with USMC, 1957-59. Fellow Am. Coll. Probate Counsel; mem. ABA, La. State Bar Assn., Shreveport Bar Assn. (pres.), Estate Planning Council Shreveport (dir., past pres.). Clubs: Boston (New Orleans); Shreveport. Lodge: Rotary (1st v.p.) (Shreveport). Home: 910 Ockley Dr Shreveport LA 71106 Office: 700 First Fed Plaza 505 Travis St PO Box B Shreveport LA 71161

HARDWICH, GERALD CARLTON, marketing executive, researcher; b. Syracuse, N.Y., Sept. 4, 1943; s. Carlton Stuart and Harriette Mae (Wiltsie) H.; m. Diane Melanie Pearce, Aug. 20, 1966; children—Elizabeth Ann, James Matthew. B.S., U. Md., 1967; M.B.A., U. Cin., 1968. Distbn. analyst Shell Chem. Co., N.Y.C., 1968-69; sr. mktg. planner and analyst Mattel, Inc., South Plainfield, N.J., 1969-72; dir. mktg. research Mohasco Corp., Amsterdam, N.Y., 1972-79; dir. market research Tupperware Home Parties, Orlando, Fla., 1979—. Bd. dirs. Fla. Symphony Orch., Orlando, 1980-82; asst. scoutmaster Citrus council Boy Scouts Am., 1982—; elder, trustee Wekiva Presbyterian Ch., Longwood, Fla., 1983-85. NSF scholar, 1960; U. Cin. fellow, 1967-68. Mem. Am. Mktg. Assn. (v.p.), Quill and Scroll, Alpha Delta Sigma (pres. chpt. 1966-67). Republican. Home: 6 Old Post Rd Longwood FL 32779 Office: Tupperware Home Parties PO Box 2353 Orlando FL 32802

HARDWICK, JAMES CARLTON, JR., business financial planner; b. Atlanta, Sept. 11, 1943; s. James Carlton and Agnes (Kelley) H.; B.A. in Econs., Davidson Coll., 1965; M.B.A. in Fin., Harvard U., 1970; m. Mary Gettys Robinson, Sept. 25, 1965; children—James Carlton, Benjamin Robinson. With R.J. Reynolds Industries, Inc., 1970—, sr. fin. analyst, 1970-73, sr. systems analyst, 1973-75, mgr. corp. acctg. analysis, 1975-78, asst. treas. Aminoil, Houston, 1978-79, budget mgr., Winston-Salem, N.C., 1979—. Served with U.S. Army, 1966-68. Cert. in mgmt. acctg. Mem. Winston-Salem C. of C., Am. Mgmt. Assn., Assn. M.B.A. Execs., Nat. Assn. Accts., Mensa. Democrat. Methodist. Clubs: Forsyth Country, Elks. Home: One Sheffield Pl Winston-Salem NC 27104 Office: 3C-WHQ Reynolds Blvd Winston-Salem NC 27102

HARDWICK, PHILLIP D., real estate educator, consultant; b. Mendenhall, Miss., June 20, 1948; George Clayton Hardwick and Nina P. (Gill) Ward; m. Carol Anne Vickers, May 31, 1980; 1 child, Kemberly Carol. B.S. in Real Estate, Belhaven Coll., 1982; M.B.A., Millsaps Coll., 1984. Cert. real estate investigator. Police officer Fairfax County (Va.), 1970-73; chief investigator Miss. Atty. Gen., Jackson, 1973-74; supr. Munford, Inc., Jackson, 1975-76; exec. dir. Miss. Real Estate Commn., Jackson, 1977-85; dir. Real Estate Inst., Millsaps Coll., 1985—. Author: The Newspaper Column, also real estate brokers manual. Served with U.S. Army, 1968-70. Mem. Nat. Assn. Real Estate License Law Officials (dir. 1984—), Miss. Real Estate Educators Assn. (sec., treas. 1983-84). Episcopalian. Avocation: sailing. Home: 610 Patton Ave Jackson MS 39216 Office: Millsaps Coll Jackson MS 39210

HARDY, ANNE DUNLAP, artist, educator; b. Birmingham, Ala., Jan. 15, 1910; d. James Thompson and Georgia Bailey (Dixon) D.; m. Charles Lambdin Hardy, Nov. 18, 1936; children—Albert Sidney II, Charles Lambdin Jr., Georgia Hardy Luck. A.B., Brenau Coll., Gainesville, Ga., 1931; postgrad. Mus. Modern Art, L.I., N.Y., 1965, North Georgia Coll., 1966, U. Ga., 1970. Supr. art schs., Dawsonville, Ga., 1963-72; pvt. instr. art, Gainesville, 1960—, Dallas, 1961-63. One women shows: Gainesville, 1960, Piedmont Interstate Fair, Spartanburg, S.C., 1977, Lake Lanier Islands Art Show, Ga., 1977; group shows include: Telfair Mus., Savannah, Ga., 1952, Columbus Art Mus., 1960, Motorola Art Show, Chgo., 1962, U. Ga. Cortona, Italy, 1970; represented in numerous pvt. collections. Mem. Hall County Library Bd., 1951-61, Atlanta Symphony Orch. Bd., 1953-58; pres. Yonah council Girl Scouts U.S.A., 1955-57, exec. dir., 1958-61; mem. Gainesville Beautification Com., 1979-81. Mem. Assn. Ga. Artists (v.p. 1952-54), Gainesville Art Assn. Democrat. Episcopalian. Clubs: Garden of Ga. (bd. dirs. 1948-60), Gainesville Garden, Gainesville Book (pres. 1970-71), Chattahoochee Country. Avocations: gardening; cooking. Home: 3165 Tan Yard Branch Rd Gainesville GA 30501

HARE, JOHN, IV, planetarium director; b. Wilmington, Del., July 7, 1940; s. John and Katharine (Bebout) H.; m. Linda Lee Naugle, Oct. 26, 1963; children—Holly Marie, Page. B.A. in Telecommunications, Mich. State U., 1975. Electronics technician Spitz Space Systems, Yorklyn, Del., 1963-65; tech., dir. Abrams Planatarium at Mich. State U., East Lansing, 1965-74; program dir., 1974-79; exec. dir. Bishop Planetarium/South Fla. Mus., Bradenton, 1979—; cons. ASH Enterprises, Richmond, Va., 1979—, J.H. Enterprises, Bradenton, 1983—. Active March of Dimes, Bradenton, 1985—. Mem. Southeastern Planetarium Assn. (pres. 1985—), Internat. Planetarium Soc. Club: South Manatee Sertoma (v.p. 1984—). Avocations: gourmet foods; sailing; tennis. Home: 3602 23d Ave W Bradenton FL 33505 Office: S Fla Mus 201 10th St West Bradenton FL 33505

HARE, ROBERT LEE, JR., evangelist; b. McKinney, Tex., Jan. 12, 1920; B.A., Harding U., Searcy, Ark., 1950, M.A., 1956; m. Ruth Bradley, June 4, 1949; children—Reggy Lynn Hare Hiller, Mary Lee, Linda Jean Glenn. Served Chs. of Christ in Ark., 1946-50; missionary, Munich, W. Ger., 1950-55; 1st missionary to Salzburg (Austria), 1952-55, Vienna, 1956-73, Wiener Neustadt, Austria, 1974-81, Yugoslavia, 1958, Czechoslovakia, 1960, Hungary, 1960, E. Ger., 1961, Poland, 1962, Bulgaria, 1964, Romania, 1964; mem. Com. for Furtherance and Preservation Religious Freedom in Austria, 1973—. Home: 307 S Harding St Breckenridge TX 76024

HARELIK, MARCIA DEAN, hospital community relations official; b. Hico, Tex., May 10, 1954; d. Milton Joseph and Geraldine Lee (Finkelstein) H. B.S., U. Tex.-Austin, 1976. Advt. mgr. Austin (Tex.) Citizen Newspaper, 1975-79; advt. dir. Austin Home and Gardens Mag., Austin, 1979-80; mgr. publicity, promotion and pub. relations Tex. Union, U. Tex., Austin, 1980-83; community relations coordinator Brackenridge Hosp., Austin, 1983—. Club: Faculty Center U. Tex. (Austin). Office: Brackenridge Hosp 601 E 15th St Austin TX 78701

HARGEST, THOMAS SEWELL, III, engineering educator, consultant; b. Phillipsburg, N.J., Jan. 3, 1925; s. William Milton and Edna (Parker) H.; m. Miriam Vermelle MacFarlane, Apr. 20, 1945; children—Judith Ann, Thomas Scott, Margaret Phyllis, William Milton. B.A., Lafayette Coll., 1950; postgrad. U. Mo. Dir. research Metcon div. Chatleff Controls, 1964-65; dir. engring. devel. sect. Shriners Burn Inst., 1964-65; dir. div. clin. engring., prof. dept. surgery Med. U. S.C., Charleston, 1965-85; adj. prof. dept. mech. engring. and biomed. engring. Clemson U., 1970-85; cons. Royal Thai Air Force, Am. Hosp. Supply Corp., Asian Devel. Bank, Hill-Rom Corp., Support Systems Internat. Served with USCG, 1942-45; to lt. AUS, 1946-48; ETO. Recipient honorable mention Am. Urol. Assn., 1969; George Washington Kidd award Lafayette Coll., 1970; JURADE de Saint Emilon, France, 1 1977. Mem. Am. Burn Assn. (continuing edn. awardee, 1978), Am. Soc. Artificial Internal Organs, Assn. Advancement Med. Instrumentation (clin. engr. achievement award 1983). Presbyterian. Contbr. articles to profl. jours.; patentee in field. Home: 330 Concord St Dockside/TH4 Charleston SC 29401 Office: 212 1/2 King St Suite 206 Charleston SC 29401

HARGETT, HERBERT PECKOVER, ophthalmologist; b. Augusta, Ky., Oct. 5, 1918; s. Marmaduke and Susan Oridge (Barnhard) H.; m. Marion Hurlbut, June 9, 1945 (dec.); children—William, Kathryn Hargett Webb, Pamela Hargett Wheeler; m. S. June Cleveland, Aug. 3, 1974. A.B., U. Ky., 1940; M.D., U. Louisville, 1943; postgrad. in ophthalmology NYU, 1947-48. Diplomate Am. Bd. Ophthalmology. Intern, Springfield City Hosp., Ohio, 1943; resident in ophthalmology Nichols VA Hosp., Louisville, 1948-50; practice medicine specializing in ophthalmology, Springfield, 1950-61, Jeffersonville, Ind., 1962-85; head dept. opthalmology Clark County Meml. Hosp., 1962-85; pres. Clark County Optical Service Inc., 1962-85; instr. ophthalmology U. Louisville, 1948-50. Pres., Clark County chpt. Am. Cancer Soc., 1964. Served to capt. M.C., AUS, 1944-46. Mem. Internat. Eye Found., Soc. Eye Surgeons. Lodges: Elks, Lions. Address: 30 Lake Ct Oldsman FL 33557

HARGIS, DAVID MICHAEL, lawyer, writer; b. Warren, Ark., Feb. 10, 1948; s. James Von Hargis and Noma Lee (Anderson) Watkins; m. Carolyn Jane Sangster (div. 1981); children—Michelle Leigh, Michael Bradley; m. Linda Jane Huckelbury, Jan. 8, 1981; 1 child, Christopher Key. B.S.B.A. with honors, U. Ark., 1970, J.D., 1973. Bar: Ark. 1973, U.S. Dist. Ct. (ea. and we. dists.) Ark. 1974. Assoc. Williamson Law Firm, Monticello, Ark., 1973-74; asst. U.S. atty. Eastern Dist. Ark., Little Rock, 1974-75; assoc. House, Holmes & Jewell, Little Rock, 1975-79; ptnr. House, Holmes & Jewell, P.A., Little Rock, 1979-85; ptnr. Wilson, Wood & Hargis, 1985—; atty. Legal Services Corp., Little Rock, 1977; county atty. Pulaski County, Ark., 1980-82; atty. Pulaski County Quorum Ct., 1980-82; spl. circuit judge Pulaski County Circuit Ct., 1982; atty. Office of Spl. Prosecutor, Pulaski County Grand Jury, 1983-84; spl. trial counsel Ark. Ins. Dept., 1983. Editor Ark. Law Rev., 1972-73; guest columnist Ark. Gazette, 1984. Contbr. articles to legal jours. Recipient spl. commendation Legal Services Corp., 1977, Ark. Edn. Assn., 1984. Mem. ABA (legal edn. sect., corp. sect.), Ark. Bar Assn., Omicron Delta Kappa, Beta Gamma Sigma. Methodist. Home: 36 River Ridge Circle Little Rock AR 72212 Office: House Wallace & Jewell PA 1507 Tower Bldg Little Rock AR 72201

HARGRAVE, RUDOLPH, judge Oklahoma Supreme Court; b. Shawnee, Okla., Feb. 15, 1925; s. John Hubert and Daisy (Holmes) H.; m. Madeline Hargrave, May 29, 1949; children—Cindy Lu, John Robert, Jana Sue. LL.B., U. Okla., 1949. Began legal practice at Wewoka, 1949; asst. county atty., Seminole County, 1951-55; judge Seminole County Ct., 1964-67, Seminole County Superior Ct., 1967-69; dist. judge Okla. Dist. Ct., Dist. 22, 1969-79; assoc. justice Okla. Supreme Ct., 1979—; news dir. Sta.-KWSH. Mem. adv. com. Boy Scouts Am. Mem. ABA, Seminole County Bar Assn., Okla. Bar Assn. Democrat. Methodist. Lodges: Lions; Masons. Office: Supreme Ct Okla State Capitol Lincoln Blvd Oklahoma City OK 73105*

HARGRODER, CHARLES MERLIN, journalist; b. Franklin, La., Sept. 5, 1926; student La. State U., 1943-47. Writer, Baton Rouge Morning Advocate, 1947-50, Monroe (La.) Morning World, 1952-53; exec. asst. to gov. La., 1953-56; public relations sec. to Congressman Hale Boggs, 1956-57; regional rep. Inter-Industry Highway Safety Com., 1957-58; writer New Orleans Times-Picayune, 1959—, polit. writer, columnist, 1961—. Served with U.S. Army, 1950-52. Republican. Methodist. Office: PO Box 44122 Capitol Station Baton Rouge LA 70804

HARGROVE, BERNARD L., recreational products retailing executive. Pres. Red River Marine Inc., Heber Springs, Ark. Office: Red River Marine Inc 2001 Hwy 25 N Harbor Springs AR 72543*

HARGROVE, JOHN RUSSELL, lawyer; b. Chgo., Jan. 20, 1947; s. John Francis and Dolly (Arzich) H.; m. Mary Cheryl Fuller, Feb. 12, 1972; children—John Ashby, James Fuller. B.S., Butler U., 1969; J.D. magna cum laude, Ind. U., 1972. Bar: Ind. 1972, Fla. 1974, U.S. Supreme Ct. 1976. Law clk. to judge U.S. Ct. Appeals (8th cir.), 1972-74; ptnr. Finley, Kumble, Wagner, Heine, Underberg, Ft. Lauderdale, Fla.; mem. adv. com. U.S. Dist. Ct. (so. dist.) Fla., 1983—; mem. ct. adv. com. Fla. Dist. Ct. Appeals (4th dist.), 1976—. Editor Ind. Law Rev., 1972. Recipient Faculty award Ind. U. Sch. of Law, 1972. Fellow Fla. Acad. Probate Litigators; mem. Fed. Bar Assn. (pres. 1981-82), Fla. Bar Assn., Ind. Bar Assn. Roman Catholic. Club: Lauderdale Yacht (legal officer 1983—). Avocations: snow skiing; long distance running. Office: 110 E Broward Blvd Fort Lauderdale FL 33301

HARGROVE, ROBERT CLYDE, lawyer; b. Shreveport, La., Dec. 13, 1918; s. Reginald Henry and Hallie (Ward) H.; m. Marjorie Clare Chinski, Sept. 29, 1920; 1 son, Reginald Henry II. B.A., Rice U., 1939; LL.B., Yale U., 1942. Bar: La. 1946, D.C. 1975. Ptnr., Hargrove, Guyton, Van Hook & Hargrove, Shreveport, La., 1946-58; v.p. Bechtel Internat. Corp., San Francisco, 1958-61; sole practice, Shreveport, 1961—; of counsel Casey, Lane & Mittendorf, Washington, 1975-80, Hargrove, Guyton, Ramey & Barlow, Shreveport, 1976-78; ptnr. Hargrove Oil & Gas Co., Shreveport, 1948—. Past trustee U. South, Sewanee, Tenn.; past mem. vestry St. Mark's Episcopal Ch., Shreveport; mem. Met. Opera Nat. Council, N.Y.C.; past pres. Southfield Sch., Shreveport; past officer, bd. dirs. YMCA, Opera Assn.; exec. v.p., dir. Shreveport Opera; pres. Shreveport Bridge Assn. lifetime assoc. Rice U. Served to capt. U.S. Army, 1942-46. Decorated D.S.C., Purple Heart, Combat Infantryman's Badge, others. Named One of Top 20 Energy Practitioners, Nat. Law Jour. Mem. ABA Fed. Energy Bar Assn., La. Bar Assn., D.C. Bar Assn., Shreveport Bar Assn. Democrat. Episcopalian. Clubs: Shreveport Bridge, Cambridge, Shreveport (La.); Metropolitan (Washington); Hawkeye Hunting (Center, Tex.). Office: 1123 Commercial Nat Bank Bldg Shreveport LA 71101

HARGROVE, STEPHEN HAUSMAN, electrical construction company executive; b. Odessa, Tex., Mar. 23, 1951; s. Raymond Leon and Johnnie Mae (Hausman) H.; m. Jennie Kathryn Young, Oct. 15, 1983. B.B.A. in Mktg., Tex. Christian U., 1973. Vice pres. Hargrove Electric Co. Inc., Dallas, 1974-79, pres., 1979—; mem. devel. bd. Allied Bank, Dallas, 1977-80; dir. Grand Banks, Dallas. Sec. Greater Dallas Crime Commn., 1980—; bd. dirs. Dallas Community Chest Trust Found., 1980—; vice chmn. Operation Service Edn. Resources Jobs for Progress, Dallas, 1980-82; chmn. Open, Inc., Dallas, 1981-84; bd. dirs. Leadership Dallas, 1985. Named Outstanding Dir., Dallas Jr. C. of C., 1974. Mem. Dallas Elec. League (bd. dirs. 1982-85), Dallas 40 (bd. dirs. 1978-85), Sigma Alpha Epsilon Alumni Assn. (pres. 1981-82). Republican. Presbyterian. Clubs: Chimeras (pres. 1980-81), Exchange (pres. 1980) (Dallas). Home: 9611 Hillview St Dallas TX 75231 Office: Hargrove Electric Co Inc 1522 Market Center Blvd PO Box 57068 Dallas TX 75207

HARGROVE, THOMAS MARION, investment company executive; b. Shreveport, La., Oct. 24, 1949; s. James Ward and Marion (Smith) H.; m. Elizabeth Ann Greene, Nov. 27, 1971; 1 son, Derek Marion. B.A. in Econs., U. Tex., 1971. With First City Nat. Bank, Houston, 1971-79, asst. v.p., loan officer, 1974-76, asst. v.p. corp. financing, 1976-79; v.p. corp. fin. Underwood, Neuhaus & Co., Houston, 1979-83, 1st v.p. venture capital activities, 1983-85; v.p. corp. fin. Rotan Mosle, Inc., 1985—; dir. Chamberson Corp.; adv. dir. Decor Noel Corp. Mem. Houston C. of C., Phi Delta Theta. Presbyterian. Clubs: Met. Racquet.

HARIG, MICHAEL JOHN, lawyer; b. Auburn, N.Y., Dec. 11, 1954; s. Paul Thomas and Agnes Mary (Carmody) H.; m. Constance Colleen Fowler, June 18, 1977; children—Tracy Kalene, David Michael. A.S., Adirondack Community Coll., 1975; B.A., SUNY-Buffalo, 1977; J.D., Loyola U.-New Orleans, 1980. Bar: N.Y. 1981, La. 1982, U.S. Dist. Ct. (no. dist.) N.Y. 1981, U.S. Dist. Ct. (mid. dist.) La. 1982, U.S. Dist. Ct. (ea. dist.) La. 1983, U.S. Ct. Appeals (5th cir.) 1982, U.S. Supreme Ct. 1984. Assoc. Bascom & Prime, Glens Falls, N.Y., 1980-81; estate adminstr. U.S. Bankruptcy Ct. (mid. dist.) La., Baton Rouge, 1981-83; ptnr. Keogh, Keogh, Cox & Wilson, Baton Rouge, 1983—. Merit badge counselor Istrouma Area council Boy Scouts Am., 1981—. Mem. La. Trial Lawyers Assn., ABA, N.Y. Bar Assn., La. Bar Assn., Assn. Trial Lawyers Am., Phi Alpha Delta. Republican. Roman Catholic. Club: St. Thomas More Soc. Office: Keogh Cox & Wilson Ltd 660 Government St Baton Rouge LA 70801

HARING-HIDORE, MARILYN, educational administrator; b. Jerome, Ariz., Aug. 29, 1941; d. Earl Austin and Genevieve Teresa (DeFilippi) Spitler; m. John J. Hidore. B.A. in Edn., Ariz. State U., 1963, M.A. in Edn., 1966, Ph.D., 1978. Vis. asst. prof. Ariz. State U., Tempe, 1978-80, asst. prof., 1980-84; assoc. dean sch. edn. U. N.C.-Greensboro, 1984—. Co-author texts: Problem Solving in World Geography, 1973; Introduction to Geography as a Social Science, 1975. Contbr. articles to profl. publs. Grantee Ariz. Dept. Edn., 1982-84, Tempe United Way, 1983. Mem. Am. Psychol. Assn., Am. Ednl. Research Assn., Research on Women and Edn. (asst. chmn. 1983-85), Women Educators (treas. 1985—). Home: 6 W Oak Ct Greensboro NC 27407 Office: U NC-Greensboro Sch Edn Greensboro NC 27412

HARITUN, ROSALIE ANN, educator; b. Johnson City, N.Y., May 30, 1938; d. George and Helen (Ternosky) Haritun; B.Mus., Baldwin-Wallace Conservatory, 1960; M.S., U. Ill., 1961; Profl. Diploma, Columbia U. 1966, Ed.D., 1968; Music tchr. Union Free Sch. Dist., Patchogue, N.Y., 1961-63, jr. high sch. instr., 1963-65; teaching fellow Columbia U. Tchrs. Coll., 1966-68; instr. music edn. Temple U. Sch. Music, 1968-71; asst. prof. music edn., clarinet instr. East Carolina U. Sch. Music, from 1972, now asso. prof. music edn., asst. dir. summer string camp, 1976-78; adjudicator Eastern N.C. Instrumental Choral Solo and Ensemble Contests, 1973—; cons. curriculum devel. programs, N.C.; choir dir. Landmark Bapt. Ch., Greenville, N.C., 1975—; mem. Summer Sunday-in-the-Park Concert Band, 1974—; lead clarinetist Albemarle Theater Players, Elizabeth City, N.C., 1981. United Way chmn. faculty/staff E. Carolina U., 1980-81. Mem. N.C. Music Educators Conf., Music Educators Nat. Conf., Coll. Music Soc. (chpt. sec.-treas. 1984-86), Sigma Alpha Iota (pres. chpt., chpt. advisor), Pi Kappa Lambda (pres. E. Carolina U. 1977-83), Delta Kappa Gamma (chmn. world fellowship com. 1980-84, pres. 1984-86). Democrat. Baptist. Contbr. articles to profl. jours. Home: 206 N Oak St Apt 8 Greenville NC 27834 Office: 204 Sch Music East Carolina U 10th St Greenville NC 27834

HARKINS, ELIZABETH BATES, medical sociologist, educator; b. Camden, S.C., June 11, 1946; d. William Wannamaker and Anne Johnson (Clarkson) B.; 1 child, Emily Barrington. B.S.N., U. N.C., 1967; M.A., Duke U., 1972, Ph.D., 1975. Program leader Battelle Human Affairs Research Ctrs., 1978-79, research scientist, Seattle, 1974-79; asst. prof. gerontology Va. Commonwealth U., Richmond, Va., 1979—, asst. prof. health adminstrn. Med. Coll. Va., Richmond, 1982—, program dir., 1983—. Contbr. articles to profl. jours. Bd. dirs. Lower Fan Civic Assn., Richmond, 1983—. Recipient Alzheimer's Disease Research award Commonwealth of Va., 1982. Mem. Am. Sociol. Assn., Gerontol. Soc., Assn. Health Services Research, Am. Pub. Health Assn. Office: Dept of Health Adminstrn Box 203 Med Coll Va Stat Richmond VA 23298

HARKINS, JAMES A., banker. Exec. v.p. Liberty Mortgage Co. div. Liberty Nat. Bank & Trust Co. Oklahoma City. Office: Liberty Nat Bank & Trust Co 100 Broadway Oklahoma City OK 73102*

HARKNESS, DONALD RAY, American studies educator, publishing company executive; b. St. Paul, Sept. 26, 1921; s. Alfred Ray and Gertrude Marie (Swanson) H.; m. Genevieve Mary Ann Olson, Oct. 6, 1946 (div. Aug. 1967); children—Judith Louise Harkness Canning, Kristine Southwick Harkness Bosserman; m. Mary Lou Barker, Sept. 2, 1967. B.A., Hamline U., St. Paul, 1942; M.A., U. Minn., 1947, Ph.D., 1955. Payroll timekeeper The Austin Co., Oak Harbor, Wash., 1942; instr. English, communication U. Minn., Mpls., 1946-50; instr. English, humanities, logic, social sci. U. Fla., Gainesville, 1950-56, asst. prof., 1956-60; assoc. prof. English, Am. studies U. South Fla., Tampa, 1960-74, prof., 1974—; founder, pres., editor in chief Am. Studies Press, Inc., Tampa, 1977—; vis. prof. Am. civilization Bemidji State Coll. (Minn.), 1956-57; coll. rep. Coll. Entrance Examination Bd., Southeastern U.S., Sewanee, Tenn., 1965-66. Author: Crosscurrents: American Anti-Democracy from Jackson to the Civil War, 1828-1860, 1955; editor: Edited Sports in American Culture, 1980, Humanistic Issues in Child Abuse, 1980. Contbr. articles and book revs. to profl. jours. Mem. pres.'s council U. South Fla. Served to 1st lt. AUS, 1943-46, lt. col. USAR, 1946-81. Mem. AAUP (pres. Fla. conf. 1962-63), Am. Studies Assn., United Faculty of Fla., Assn. Gen. and Liberal Studies, UN Assn., Fla. Hist. Assn., Fla. Library Assn., Southeastern Library Assn., Am. Library Assn., Assn. Am. Historians, Inter-Univ. Seminar on Armed Forces & Soc. Democrat. Mem. United Ch. of Christ. Home: 13511 Palmwood Ln Tampa FL 33624 Office: LET 309 Univ South Fla Tampa FL 33620

HARLE, WILEY BASCOM, geologist; b. Port Arthur, Tex., Dec. 1, 1924; s. James Wiley and Mabel (Stark) H.; m. Mary Elizabeth Sander, Apr. 19, 1958; children—Anne Elizabeth (dec.), James Wiley, Bascom Sander. B.S. in Geology, U. Tex., 1950. Cert. petroleum geologist, Tex. Geologist, Union Oil of Calif., New Orleans, 1951-55; div. geologist Midcon Corp., Houston, 1955-82; v.p. exploration Onset Exploration, Houston, 1981-85, ret., 1985; cons. geologist, Houston, 1985—. Trustee, Grace Presbyterian Ch., Houston, 1984-85, Grace Ch. Sch., 1975-85. Served to sgt. USAC, 1943-46. Mem. Houston Geol. Soc., Am. Assn. Petroleum Geologists (ho. of dels. 1979-82), Assn. Profl. Geol. Scientists, S.A.R., S.C., Sons Republic of Tex. Republican. Presbyterian. Avocations: coin collecting; stamp collecting; amateur lapidarist. Home: 9643 Winsome Ln Houston TX 77063

HARLOW, HAROLD EUGENE, newspaper editor; b. Miami, Fla., Nov. 28, 1925; s. Eugene L. and Hattye (Tygrett) H.; student Western Ky. State U., 1946-47; B.S. in Journalism, U. Tenn., 1950; m. Lela Mae Brenan, Sept. 1, 1950; children—Eugene Brenan, Mary Lee, Harold Alan, Carol Ann. Copy editor Knoxville (Tenn.) News-Sentinel, 1949-59, asst. news editor, 1959-67, news editor, 1967-69, mng. editor, 1969-83, assoc. editor, 1983—. Served with USAAF, 1943-46 Mem. Tenn. Press Assn., Asso. Press Mng. Editors Assn., Sigma Delta Chi. Presbyn. (elder). Home: 11545 Nassau Dr Concord TN 37922 Office: 204 W Church Ave Knoxville TN 37901

HARLOW, JAMES GINDLING, JR., utility executive; b. Oklahoma City, May 29, 1934; s. James Gindling and Adalene (Rae) H.; m. Jane Marriott Bienfang, Jan. 30, 1957; children—James Gindling III, David Ralph. B.S., U. Okla., 1957, postgrad., 1959-61. Research analyst Okla. Gas and Electric Co., Oklahoma City, 1961-63, div. auditor, 1963-65, adminstrv. asst., 1965-66, asst. treas., 1966-68, treas., 1968-69, sec.-treas., 1969-70, v.p., treas., 1970-72, exec. v.p., treas., 1972-73, pres., 1973-76, pres., chief exec. officer, 1976-82, chmn. bd., pres., chief exec. officer, 1982—, also dir.; dir. Mass. Mut. Life Ins. Co., Fleming Cos., Inc., Oklahoma City. Pres. Missouri Valley Electric Assn., 1977-78; bd. dirs. Edison Electric Inst., 1983—. Bd. dirs. State Fair of Okla.; adv. bd. St. Anthony Hosp.; trustee Okla. Zool. Soc., Oklahoma City U., U. Okla. Found., Inc.; bd. govs. Okla. Center for Sci. and Arts, Inc.; pres. Allied Arts Found., 1982-84. Served with USNR, 1957-59. Mem. U.S. C. of C. (dir.

1978-84), Okla. C. of C. (dir. 1973—, pres. 1980), Oklahoma City C. of C. (pres. 1976), Okla. Soc. Security Analysts. Clubs: Petroleum, Oklahoma City Golf and Country, Economic of Okla., Men's Dinner, Beacon, Whitehall (Oklahoma City). Home: 1713 Pennington Way Oklahoma City OK 73116 Office: PO Box 321 Oklahoma City OK 73101

HARLOW, JEFFREY WAYNE, food company executive, educator; b. Aberdeen, Miss., Sept. 12, 1954; s. Percy Wayne and Joann Marget (McCary) H.; m. Eunice Naugle Aycock, June 7, 1980; 1 child, Joanna Joyce. A.A. in Edn., Itawamba Jr. Coll., 1975; B.S., Miss. State U., 1977. Counselor, Amory High Sch., Miss., 1977-79; tchr., distributive coordinator West Point High Sch., Miss., 1980-81, safety dir. Bryan Foods, West Point, 1981—. Author: Safety and Supervising Management, 1985. Recipient Hall of Fame award Distributive Edn. Clubs Am., 1981, Rookie Tchr. of Yr. award, 1981; Outstanding Mgmt. award Bryan Foods, 1983. Republican. Avocations: Hunting; fishing; racquetball. Home: Route 3 Box 352 West Point MS 39773 Office: Bryan Foods Churchill Rd West Point MS 39773

HARLOW, VERNON RAY, oil and gas company executive; b. Kerrville, Tex., May 15, 1951; s. Vernon and Josephine (Lee) H.; m. Dianne Lynne Hunnicutt, June 12, 1970; children—Ronald Dwayne, Katherine Anne. B.S. in Geology, Abilene Christian U., 1973. Drilling foreman Arco Oil and Gas Co., Lafayette, La., 1974-77; drilling engr. Amoco Prodn., Houston, 1977-79; drilling mgr. Transcontinental Oil, Shreveport, La., 1979-80; v.p. prodn. Latham Exploration Inc., Shreveport, 1980-82; mng. ptnr. exploration, prodn. Hyde Oil and Gas Co., Shreveport, 1982—. Bd. dirs. Shreveport Christian Sch., 1981-85; pres. bd., mng. dir. Shreveport Country Day Sch., 1985—. Mem. Soc. Petroleum Engrs., Am. Assn. Petroleum Geologists, Ind. Producers Assn. Mem. Am. Ch. of Christ. Avocations: hunting; fishing; snow skiing; golf; flying. Office: A Michael Hyde Oil and Gas Co 500 American Tower Shreveport LA 71101

HARLSON, HOWARD H., JR., natural gas company executive; b. 1934. B.S., Okla. State U., 1957. With Bray Lines, Inc., 1959-73; with Ligon Specialized Haulers, Inc., 1973-78; with B.F. Walker, Inc., 1978-81; v.p. Noble Affiliates, Inc., 1981-84, exec. v.p., Ardmore, Okla., 1984—. Address: Noble Affiliates Inc PO Box 1967 Ardmore OK 73402*

HARMAN, ALEXANDER M(ARRS), state justice; b. War, W.Va., Feb. 7, 1921; s. Alexander M. and Rose Sinclair (Brown) H.; student Concord Coll., Athens, W.Va., 1938-41, LL.D. (hon.), 1970; LL.B., Washington and Lee U., 1944, LL.D. (hon.), 1974; grad. Nat. Coll. State Trial Judges, 1965. Admitted to Va. bar, 1943; practice in Pulaski, 1944-64; partner firm Gilmer, Harman & Sadler, 1952-64; judge 21st Jud. Circuit, 1964-69; justice Supreme Ct. Va., 1969-79, sr. justice, 1980—; town atty., Pulaski, 1944-46; substitute trial justice, 1945-47. Mem. Va. Com. Constl. Revision, 1968. Chmn. Pulaski County Devel. Authority, 1962-64; chmn. bd. zoning appeals, Pulaski, 1958-64; pres. N.R.V. Indsl. Found., 1963-81. Chmn. Battle for Gov. Com. Pulaski County, 1949, Va. Bd. Elections, 1955-64, Pulaski County Democratic Com., 1960-64; mem. finance com. Va. Dem. Central Com., 1956-64; 19th Dist. Dem. Senatorial Com., 1956-64. Home: PO Box 1438 Pulaski VA 24301 Office: Supreme Ct Bldg Richmond VA 23219 also Municipal Bldg Pulaski VA 24301

HARMAN, ROY STEPHEN, bank executive, financial consultant; b. Biloxi, Miss., Aug. 13, 1947; s. Roy Samuel and Ruth Freeman (Baker) H.; m. Carol Ann Wisman, Dec. 21, 1969; children—Ryan, Megan, Derek. B.S. in Bus. and Econs., W.Va. Wesleyan Coll., 1969; M.B.A., W.Va. U., 1976. With Grant County Bank, Petersburg, W.Va., 1972—, v.p., 1978—; dir. Tallheim Resort Village, Inc., Canaan Valley, W.Va., 1984—. Pres. Grant County Bd. Edn., Petersburg, 1984-85. Served with U.S. Army, 1970-71. Mem. Bank Adminstrn. Inst., Am. Bankers Assn., W.Va. Bankers Assn. Republican. Methodist. Lodge: Kiwanis (pres. 1973-74). Avocations: golf; hunting; fishing. Home: 203 Judy St Petersburg WV 26847

HARMON, FREDERICK INGERSOLL, engineering and equipment company executive; b. Waukesha, Wis., Feb. 15, 1923; s. John Neal and Louise (Ingersoll) H.; B.S., U. Tex., 1946; m. Marjorie Elfreda Hanna, Dec. 27, 1944; children—Scott Ingersoll, Keith Hanna, Cynthia Lynn. Process engr. Gasoline Plant Constrn. Corp., Corpus Christi, 1945-46; v.p., chief engr. Gulf Engrs., Houston, 1946-49; founder Southwestern Engring & Equipment Co., Dallas, 1949, v.p., 1949-64, owner, pres., 1964—; v.p. Hanna Devel. Co.; dir. Analytica, Inc. Judge, Sci. Fairs, 1971—; mem. adv. council Engring. Found., U. Tex., Austin; mem. adv. council, sci. div. Skyline Tex. Center, Dallas. Served as 2d lt. USAAF, World War II. Named Disting. Grad. Coll. Engring., U. Tex., 1975. Registered profl. engr., Tex., N.Mex. Asso. fellow AIAA; mem. IEEE, Inst. Environ. Scis., AAAS, Nat. Soc. Profl. Engrs., Tex. Soc. Profl. Engrs., Instrument Soc. Am. Home: 1009 Waterford Dr Dallas TX 75218 Office: 6510 Abrams Suite 560 Dallas TX 75231

HARMON, JOHN LAFAYETTE, oil consultant firm executive; b. Hillsboro, Hill County, Tex., June 24, 1929; s. John Lee and Winnie Kate (Stallings) H.; m. Lucile Gracy, Dec. 23, 1949 (div. 1973); children—John C., David L., Christopher L.; m. 2d, Bettye Sue McKinney, June 21, 1975. B.S. in Geology, U. Tex., 1952; cert. in surf and sub-sea well control U. Southwest La., 1983. Cert. U.S. Geol. Survey, U.S. Minerals Mgmt. Service. With Continental Oil Co., 1951; engr. trainee Midstates Oil Corp., Abilene, Tex., 1952-54; geol. scout Connally Oil Co., Abilene, 1954-63; supt., pres., chief exec. officer J.L. Harmon & Assocs., Abilene, 1963—; cons. on air drilling projects. Mem. Soc. Petroleum Engrs. of AIME. Republican. Episcopalian. Clubs: Petroleum (Fort Worth); de Cordova Bend Country (Acton, Tex.). Author publs. in field. Home: 612 Fairway DCBE Granbury TX 76048 Office: Suite 220 310 N Willis St Abilene TX 79603

HARMON, (LOREN) FOSTER, art dealer; b. Judsonia, Ark., Nov. 5, 1912; s. Alfred Roscoe and Mae (Foster) H.; student Ind. U., 1930-32, Ohio U., 1932-33; B.A., State U. Iowa, 1935, M.F.A., 1936; m. Martha Rowles Foster, July 25, 1943. Dir., Univ. and Exptl. Theatre, Ind. U., Bloomington, 1936-42; pub. relations mgr. WKBN Broadcasting Corp., Youngstown, Ohio, 1943-48; owner, developer, dir. Pine Shores Park, Sarasota, Fla., 1950-54 v.p., dir. Players, Sarasota, 1955-57; pub. relations dir. Ringling Mus. Art, 1958-59; dir. Oehlschlaeger Galleries, Sarasota, 1961-70; v.p. Vandium Tool Co., Athens, Ohio, 1954-64; founder, owner, dir. Harmon Gallery, Naples, Fla., 1964-79; owner, dir. Foster Harmon Galleries Am. Art, Sarasota, 1979—; advisor Ohio U. Collection Am. Art. Mem. Ringling Mus. Mems. Council, 1957—; bd. dirs. Asolo State Theater 1982—, Sarasota Opera Assn., 1983—; advisor Fla. Artists Group Mus./Gallery, 1974—; trustee Ringling Sch. Art, Sarasota, 1981—. Recipient cert. of merit Ohio U., 1970. Mem. Am. Ednl. Theatre Assn. (founder), Am. Fedn. Arts, Sarasota Art Assn. (pres. 1959-60), Fla. League Arts, Smithsonian Inst., Archives Am. Art, Am. Fedn. Arts, St. Armands Assn. (pres. 1957-58), Internat. Platform Assn. Methodist. Clubs: Sarasota Yacht, University, Players (Sarasota). Home: PO Box 6187 Sarasota FL 33578 Office: Foster Harmon Galleries Am Art 1415 Main St Sarasota FL 33577

HARMON, WILLIAM HAYNE, civil engineer; b. Columbia, S.C., Oct. 13, 1937; s. James E. and Ruby (Keel) H.; m. Gloria Seay, May 31, 1959; children—William Hayne, Michael, Karen, Patrick. B.S. in Civil Engring., U. S.C., 1959; M.S. in Mgmt., Naval Postgrad. Sch., 1972. Registered profl. engr., Miss.; lic. comml. pilot with instrument rating. Commd. ensign U.S. Navy, 1959, advanced through grades to capt., 1981—; main propulsion officer USS Ammen, 1959-60, USS Tingey, 1960-61; staff commandant 5th Naval Dist., 1961-62, asst. resident officer in charge constrn., Mayport, Fla., 1962-64, asst. pub. works officer, Charleston, S.C., 1964-66, pub. works officer, Clarksville Base, Tenn., 1966-68, resident officer in charge constrn. Republic of Vietnam, 1968-69, sr. activity civil engr. Pub. Works Ctr., Pensacola, Fla., 1969-71; staff no. div. Navy Facility, Phila., 1972-77; pub. works officer, Charleston, S.C., 1977-79; dir. pub. works Naval Edn. and Tng. Ctr./Naval War Coll., Newport, R.I., 1979-82; comdg. officer Navy Pub. Works Ctr., Pensacola, 1982-84. Decorated Joint Service Commendation medal, Legion of Merit, Navy Commendation medal with combat V and gold star; Vietnamese Cross of Galentry with palm. Mem. Nat. Soc. Profl. Engrs., Ret. Officers . Assn., Soc. Am. Mil. Engrs., Eagle Scout Assn., ASCE, Aircraft Owners and Pilots Assn. Republican. Lutheran. Clubs: Charleston Aero, Charleston Air Force Base. Contbr. articles to profl. jours.

HARMS, LOUISE IVIE, librarian; b. Birmingham, Ala., June 25, 1924; d. Henry J. and Lola Bell (Hicks) Ivie; m. Willard D. Harms, Oct. 17, 1955 (dec.); children—Dennis Leon, Danial Lee (dec.), Willard Daniel. B.S., U. Ala., 1944; B.S. in Library Sci., George Peabody Coll. for Tchrs., 1946. Asst. librarian Coll. of Edn. Library, U. Ala., 1944-45; ref. asst. George Peabody Coll. for Tchrs., 1945-46; cataloguer Allegheny Coll., Meadville, Pa., 1946-47; 1st asst. cataloger U. Ark., Fayetteville, 1947; head cataloger Coll. of Edn., U. Ala., 1948-51; spl. services librarian U.S. Army-Europe, 1951-55, 58-63; tchr. English Sweetwater High Sch. (Tenn.), 1963-64; asst. librarian Tenn. Wesleyan Coll., Athens, 1964-65, head librarian, 1965—; cons. Olin Corp., Charleston, Tenn. Named Tchr. of Yr., U. Ala., 1950. Mem. Am. Library Assn., Southeastern Library Assn., Tenn. Library Assn., VFW Ladies Aux., Kappa Delta Pi, Alpha Beta Alpha. Democrat. Presbyterian. Home: 112 Hickory Ln Sweetwater TN 37874 PO Box 40 Tenn Wesleyan Coll Athens TN 37303

HARNESS, WILLIAM WALTER, lawyer; b. Ottumwa, Iowa, Apr. 14, 1945; s. Walter W. and Mary E. (Bukowski) H.; m. Carolyn Margaret Barnes, Jan 4, 1969; children—Matthew William, Michael Andrew. B.A., U. Iowa, 1967; J.D., Cleve. State U., 1974. Bar: Ohio 1975, U.S. Dist. Ct. (no. dist.) Ohio 1975, D.C. 1976, U.S. Dist. Ct. D.C. 1976, U.S. Ct. Appeals (D.C. cir.) 1976, U.S. Ct. Appeals (5th cir.) 1981, U.S. Dist. Ct. (we. dist.) N.C. 1979, U.S. Ct. Appeals (1st cir.) 1980, U.S. Ct. Appeals (4th cir.) 1981, U.S. Ct. Appeals (11th cir.) 1981. Mem. labor relations staff Monogram Industries, Cleve., 1970-75; asst. counsel Nat. Treasury Employees Union, Washington, 1975-77, nat. counsel, Atlanta, 1977—; lectr. Emory U., Atlanta, 1978—; participant various seminars Ga. State U. Pres. Spring Mill-Kingsborough Ct. Corp., Atlanta. Served to 1st lt. U.S. Army, 1967-70. Mem. ABA (com. on fed. labor-mgmt. 1981-84), D.C. Bar Assn., Soc. Fed. Labor Relations Profls., Indsl. Relations Research Assn. Home: 1133 Kingsborough Ct Atlanta GA 30319 Office: Nat Treasury Employees Union 2801 Buford Hwy Suite 430 Atlanta GA 30329

HARNEY, JEAN PETERS, nurse educator; b. Fredonia, N.Y., Mar. 21, 1922; d. Harry W. and June (Waterhouse) Peters; m. James Harney, Nov. 29, 1947; children—James, John, Janet. R.N., U. Rochester, 1945; B.S.Ed., Edinboro State U., 1955; M.P.H., U. N.C., 1967. Cert. nurse practitioner U. Ark., 1972. Nurse, Saegertown Area Schs. (Pa.), 1952-56, Richmond (Va.) pub. schs., 1959-62; pub. health nurse Va. Health Dept., Chesterfield County, Richmond, 1962-66; project dir. inactive nurse recruitment Va. Nurses Assn., 1967-68; asst. prof. nursing U. Ark., 1969-73; night adminstr. Ark. Childrens Hosp., Little Rock, 1974-75; assoc. prof. nursing U. Central Ark., Conway, 1975—. Recipient Outstanding Tchr. award U. Central Ark., 1976. Mem. Am. Pub. Health Assn., Am. Sch. Health Assn., Ark. Sch. Health Assn. (pres. 1982-83), Sigma Theta Tau. Republican. Episcopalian. Home: 6 Brandywine Ln Little Rock AR 72207 Office: Dept Nursing Univ Central Ark Conway AR 72032

HARNEY, ROBERT CHARLES, laser technologist, researcher, consultant, physics educator; b. Pasadena, Calif., Sept. 28, 1949; s. Ervin Charles and Ethel Josephine (Erickson) H.; m. Jane Withers, June 23, 1972; children—Elizabeth, Catherine, Robert Joseph. B.S. in Chemistry, Harvey Mudd Coll., 1971, B.S. in Physics, 1971; M.S. in Applied Sci., U. Calif.-Davis, 1972, Ph.D. in Applied Sci., 1976. Participating guest physicist Lawrence Livermore (Calif.) Lab., 1971-76; research engr. U. Calif.-Davis, 1976; staff scientist MIT, Lincoln Lab., Lexington, 1976-82; profl. staff Martin Marietta Aerospace, Orlando, Fla., 1982-84, mgr., 1984—; cons. Lawrence Livermore Lab., 1976-81; lectr. applied physics U. Lowell (Mass.), 1980-81. Recipient Dept. Def. Exec. Intern award, 1969; Fannie and John Hertz Found. fellow, 1972-76; 1st prize Laser Inst. Am. Laser Quiz, 1977. Mem. Am. Chem. Soc., Am. Phys. Soc., Optical Soc. Am., Soc. Photo-Optical Instrumentation Engrs. (chmn. conf. 1981, 83), IEEE (sr. mem.), Astron. Soc. Pacific, Am. Assn. Physics Tchrs. Republican. Mem. Ch. of Christ. Editor: Physics and Technology of Coherent Infrared Radar, 1982; Coherent Infrared Radar Systems and Technology II, 1983; patentee: Laser Pulse Shaping Techniques, 1977; Raman Scattering Isotope Ratio Measurement Technique, 1978; Coherent Infrared Radar System, 1981; Quasi-Three-Dimensional Display System, 1982; contbr. articles to profl. jours. Home: 6852 Parson Brown Dr Orlando FL 32819 Office: Martin Marietta Aerospace PO Box 5837 Orlando FL 32855

HARPER, CARL BROWN, JR., accountant; b. Clover, S.C., Nov. 18, 1934; s. Carl Brown and Nannie Lillian (Dickson) H.; student Presbyn. Coll., 1952-53; B.S. in Acctg., U. S.C., 1957; m. Mary Ann Johnson, Apr. 16, 1954; children—Rhonda Ann Harper Mitchell, Jennifer Lynne Harper Earnhardt, David Scott. Jr. acct. S.D. Leidesdorf and Co. (merger with Ernst & Whinney 1978), Greenville, S.C., 1957-62, audit mgr., 1962-65, Spartanburg, S.C., 1965—, partner in charge Spartanburg office, 1967-81, mng. partner Greenville and Spartanburg offices, 1981—; speaker ednl. and civic orgns.; instr. Spartanburg Tech. Coll., 1966, Wofford Coll., 1974, U. S.C., 1969, 75; mem. S.C. Bd. Accountancy, 1979—, sec.-treas., 1983—, chmn., 1985. Deacon, 1st Presbyn. Ch., Spartanburg, 1977-84; elder Westminster Presbyn. Ch., 1984—, chmn. capital needs campaign, 1985; bd. dirs., United Way of Spartanburg, 1973—, treas., 1976—; chmn. program and budget rev., bd. dirs. United Way Greenville County, 1984—; bd. dirs., treas., Arts Council Spartanburg County, 1975—, 1st v.p., 1986; S.C. Legis. Audit Council, 1975—, chmn., 1975-77; mem. adv. council Spartanburg County Commn. Higher Edn., 1976—; bd. dirs. Greenville Art Mus., 1984, treas., 1985—. Served with U.S. Army, 1953-55. Recipient Presdl. award Spartanburg County United Way, 1981; C.P.A., S.C., N.C. Mem. Nat. Assn. Accts. (pres. Western Carolinas chpt. 1970-71, participant tax panel, speaker), Am. Inst. C.P.A.s (practice rev. com. 1973—, chmn. 1976—, S.C. mem. to council 1976—), S.C. Assn. C.P.A.s (pres. 1972-73, Service to Profession award 1979, Disting. Pub. Service award 1982), Estate Planning Council Spartanburg (pres. 1975), Middle Atlantic States Acctg. Conf. (sec., treas. 1975-81), Nat. Assn. State Bds. Accountancy (dir. 1984—). Clubs: Sertoma Internat. (Centurian award 1972, Honor Club pres. 1972, pres. Spartanburg, 1971-72), Spartanburg County. Lodge: Rotary (program chmn. 1986). Home: 911 Parkins Mill Rd Greenville SC 29607 Office: C & S Tower Two Shelter Ctr Greenville SC 29602

HARPER, DIXON LADD, broadcaster; b. Ames, Iowa, Nov. 29, 1922; s. Harlan Howard and Mary Joan (Parsons) H.; student Mich. State U., 1943; B.S., Iowa State U., 1948; m. Shirley Thevenin, Mar. 22, 1947; children—Susan Shirley, Tod Dixon. Vice pres. broadcast Aubrey, Finlay, Marley & Hodgson, Chgo., 1956-63; account supr. Foote, Cone & Belding, Inc., Chgo., 1963-70; v.p. Lennen & Newall, Inc., Chgo., 1970-72; mgmt. supr. Clinton E. Frank, Inc., Chgo., 1972-75; pub. Specialized Agrl. Publs., Raleigh, N.C., 1975-82; dir. agrl. prodns. Capitol Broadcasting Co., 1982—; cons. Nat. Project in Agrl. Communications. Bd. dirs. North Bend Townhouse Homeowners Assn. Served with USAAF, 1943-44. Mem. N.C. Assn. Farm Writers and Broadcasters, Nat. Agrl. Mktg. Assn., Nat. Agrimktg. Conf. (chmn.), Nat. Assn. Farm Broadcasters (v.p., Meritorious Service award 1959), Wake County Agribus. Council (pres.), Sigma Delta Chi. Democrat. Methodist. Office: PO Box 12800 Raleigh NC 27605

HARPER, DOROTHY GLEN, education educator; b. San Antonio, June 25, 1927; d. Jack Wallace and Bess Mae (Hopkins) Douglas; children—Nancy Gail, John Douglas; m. Orville Earl Harper, Apr. 2, 1975. A.A., Cisco Jr. Coll., 1978; Ed.B., Hardin-Simmons U., 1981, Ed.M., 1983. Cert. tchr., Tex. Adj. faculty Hardin Simmons U., Abilene, Tex., 1981—. Vice pres. Taylor-Jones Haskell Counties Med. Aux., Abilene, 1978, treas., 1980, mem. nominating com., 1985; active Abilene Met. Ballet, 1980-83; bd. dirs. Abilene Ballet Theatre. Mem. Alpha Chi, Kappa Delta Pi, Pi Gamma Mu, Phi Delta Kappa. Republican. Methodist. Avocations: horseback riding; swimming. Home: 780 Rivercrest Dr Abilene TX 79605 Office: Hardin-Simmons U Abilene TX 79698

HARPER, EDWIN ADAMS, JR., financial executive; b. Lynchburg, Va., Nov. 2, 1935; s. Edwin Adams and Margaretta Smedley (Howe) H. B.A., Lynchburg Coll., 1961; postgrad. U. Va., 1961-62, Am. Coll., 1979-83. Claims adjustor Markel Services, Inc., 1962-64; jr. acct. Harer & Jones, 1965, Manning, Perkinson & Floyd, 1966; staff acct. Ernst & Ernst, 1967-69; controller Computer Electronics Corp., Richmond, Va., 1969; acct. and fin. cons., Va., 1969—; treas., owner Stafford Meml. Park, Inc. (Va.), 1973—. Chmn. bd. Econ. Devel. Corp., Richmond. Mem. Internat. Assn. Fin. Planning (pres. chpt.), Soc. Advancement Mgmt. (past internat. v.p.). Club: Kiwanis. Home: 2205 Link Rd Lynchburg VA 24503

HARPER, ESTON LEON, food company executive; b. Oakwood, Okla., Mar. 21, 1935; s. James Alexander and Mattie Ethel (Mosley) H.; m. Diana Avalon Davie; children—Robert A., Scott R., Craig R. Student, Tex. Christian Coll., Oklahoma City U. Purchasing clk. Anchon San. Co., Pitts., 1957-58; supr. Retail Credit Corp., Fort Worth, 1959-62; sales rep. Gen. Foods Corp., Oklahoma City, 1962-65, key account mgr., Toledo, 1965-67, ter. sales mgr., Okla., 1979—. Pres. Coweta Bd. Edn., Okla., 1977; bishop Ch. of Jesus Christ of Latter-day Saints, Broken Arrow, Okla., 1977-83, region welfare agt. Tulsa-Springfield region 1984—. Served with U.S. Army, 1954-57. Republican. Avocations: jogging; weight lifting; coin collecting. Home: Route 1 Box 45-A Coweta OK 74429

HARPER, JEWEL BENTON, pharmacist; b. Springfield, Tenn., Nov. 14, 1925; s. William Henry and Violet Irene (Benton) H.; m. Josephine Cook, Feb. 12, 1953; children—Pamela Jewel, Karen Jo. B.S., Austin Peay State U., 1948, B.S., Samford U., 1950. Pharmacist Battlefield Pharmacy, Nashville, 1950-52; hosp. pharmacist VA Hosp., Nashville, 1952-63, Lexington, Ky., 1963-67, Durham, N.C., 1967-76, Manchester, N.H., 1976-82, Vanderbilt U., Nashville, 1982—. Served to col. Med. Service, USAR, 1944-79. Recipient Hosp. Adminstrn. Diploma, Acad. Health Scis., 1970, Nat. Security Mgmt. Diploma, Indsl. Coll. Armed Forces, 1973, Logistics Exec. Devel. Diploma U.S. Army Logistics Mgmt. Ctr., 1977. Fellow Am. Coll. Apothecaries; mem. Assn. Mil. Surgeons U.S., Am. Pharm. Assn., Am. Soc. Hosp. Pharmacists, Nat. Inst. History Pharmacy, Res. Officers Assn. U.S. (pres. chpt. 1962-63, sec. 1970-73, dept. surgeon 1977-82), The Guideons Internat., Lambda Chi Alpha, Kappsi Psi. Republican. Baptist. Avocations: country music; deep sea fishing. Home: 503 Cuniff Ct Goodlettsville TN 37072 Office: Vanderbilt U Med Ctr 1211-22 Ave South Nashville TN 37203

HARPER, PATRICK WILLIAM, JR., corporation executive, retirement plan consultant; b. New Orleans, Apr. 8, 1947; s. Patrick William and Dorothy (Prevost) H.; m. Cynthia Rita Ketchum, Dec. 18, 1976; 1 dau., Heather Marie; stepchildren—Roxanna, Juan, Cheryl, Joseph, Stephen, Guadaloupe, Rita. B.A., U. New Orleans, 1970, postgrad., 1971-72; postgrad. Sch. Law Loyola U.-New Orleans, 1975-76. Claims rep. Social Security Adminstrn., Beaumont, Tex., Gretna, New Orleans, Covington, La., 1974-81; owner Harper Brokerage, Slidell, La., 1981—; asst. mgr. Eckerd Drugs Inc., Slidell and New Orleans, 1982-83; mgr., v.p. Eyecare Profls. Inc., Slidell, 1983—, cons., 1983; regional personnel officer U.S. Dept. Def., Def. Investigative Service, 1985—. Author short story. Pres., Broadmoor Homeowners' Assn., Slidell, 1981-82; mem. Young Democrats, New Orleans, v.p., 1968-69, treas., 1968. Grad. fellow EPDA, 1971; alumni senate rep. U. New Orleans, 1981. Mem. Am. Fedn. Govt. Employees (shop steward 1981-83), Internat. Personnel Mgmt. Assn., U. New Orleans Alumni Assn. (pres. 1973-74, dir. 1973-74, 81-82, cert. achievement 1974). Roman Catholic. Home: 1535 Broadmoor Dr Slidell LA 70458

HARPER, ROBERT JEROME, educator; b. Birmingham, Ala., Jan. 15, 1940; s. Homer J. and Edith (Stagner) H. children—Gerri Ann, Stephanie Lee. B.S., U. Ala., Tuscaloosa, 1961, M.A., 1962; Ed.S., Fla. Atlantic U., 1981, Ed.D., 1982. Tchr., athletic dir. Orange County Sch. Bd., Orlando, Fla., 1964-73, adminstrv. dean, 1973-81; asst. dean So. Coll., Orlando, 1981-83, dean, 1983-85; with Osceola Sch. Dist., 1985—; pres. Ednl. Software Cons., Orlando, 1981—; mem. rev. team Fla. State Dept. Edn., 1982; mem. eval. team So. Assn. Secondary Schs., Ormond Beach, Fla., 1981; cons. Mgmt. Assessment Exec., Atlanta, 1983. Named Tchr. of Year, Winter Park Jr. High Sch., 1973-74; Coach of the Year, Orange County, 1973, 74, 75. Mem. Fla. Assn. Pvt. Schs., Fla. Assn. Curriculum Devel., Orlando C. of C., Phi Delta Kappa, Kappa Delta Phi. Democrat. Methodist. Address: 4183 Fallwood Cir Orlando FL 32806

HARPER, SPENCER EARL, JR., lawyer; b. Little Rock, Oct. 17, 1933; s. Spencer Earl and Eleanor (Rieder) H.; B.A., U. Louisville, 1955, J.D. cum laude, 1957; m. Clarice Carol Sharpe, July 1, 1955; children—Spencer Earl III, Grafton Sharpe. Admitted to Ky. bar, 1958; practiced in Louisville, 1961—; partner firm Grafton, Ferguson, Fleischer & Harper, 1961-76, Harper, Ferguson & Davis, 1977—; Trustee, Louisville Law Alumni Found.; mem. exec. com. Louisville Central Area, Inc. Served to capt. Judge Adv. Gen. Corps, USAF, 1958-61. Mem. Am., Fed., Ky., Louisville (mem. exec. com.) bar assns., Am. Judicature Soc., Arnold Air Soc., Phi Kappa Phi, Pi Kappa Phi, Delta Theta Phi, Omicron Delta Kappa. Democrat. Presbyterian. Clubs: Pendennis, Tavern, Jefferson, Harmony Landing Country, Fincastle Beagles. Contbr. articles to profl. jours. Home: 3309 Green Hill Ln Mockingbird Valley Rd Louisville KY 40207 Office: 310 W Liberty St Louisville KY 40202

HARPOLE, JERRY LEE, agri-business executive; b. Calhoun City, Miss., Feb. 29, 1928; s. Ben Ward and Cora Lynn (Jackson) H.; m. Ina Gail Sims, Mar. 23, 1968; children—Jennifer, Pamela, Jerry Jr., Susan. B.S. in Acctg., Miss. State U., 1951. Bookkeeper, F.C. Wagner Plantation, Leland, Miss., 1951-53; pres. MFC Services (AAL), Madison, Miss., 1953; dir. Miss. Chem. Corp., Deposit Guaranty Corp., Miss. Council of Farm Coops., Agrl. Coop. Devel. Internat., Washington; trustee Am. Inst. Coop., Washington, 1983—; chmn. Red Panther Chem. Corp., 1979—; pres. Lamar Refining Co., Cloverleaf Coop. Bd. dirs. Miss. Econ. Council, Jackson, 1983—. Served with USMC, 1946-47. Named Businessman of Yr. Madison County C. of C., 1977. Republican. Baptist. Avocations: golf; hunting. Office: MFC Services (AAL) PO Box 500 Hwy 51 North Madison MS 39110

HARPSTER, JAMES ERVING, lawyer; b. Milw., Dec. 24, 1923; s. Philo E. and Pauline (Daanen) H.; Ph.B., Marquette U., 1950, LL.B., 1952. Bar: Wis. 1952, Tenn. 1953; dir. info. services Nat. Cotton Council Am., Memphis, 1952-55; dir. public relations Christian Bros. Coll., 1956; mgr. govt. affairs dept. Memphis C. of C., 1956-62; exec. v.p. Rep. Assn. Memphis and Shelby County, 1962-64; individual practice law, Memphis, 1965; ptnr. Rickey, Shankman, Blanchard, Agee & Harpster, and predecessor firm, Memphis, 1966-80, Harpster & Baird, 1980-83; pvt. practice, 1984—. Mem. Shelby County Tax Assessor's Adv. Com., 1960-61; editor, asst. counsel Memphis and Shelby County Charter Com., 1962; mem. Shelby County Election Commn., 1968-70; mem. Tenn. State Bd. Elections, 1970-72, sec., 1972; mem. Tenn. State Election Commn., 1973-83, chmn., 1974, sec., 1975-83; a founder Lions Inst. for Visually Handicapped Children, 1954, chmn. E. H. Crump Meml. Football Game for Blind, 1956; pres. Siena Student Aid Found., 1960; bd. dirs. Memphis Public Affairs Forum; mem. Civic Research Com., Inc., Citizens Assn. Memphis and Shelby County; Republican candidate Tenn. Gen. Assembly, 1964; v.p. Nat. Council Rep. Workshops, 1967-69; pres. Rep. Workshop Shelby County, 1967, 71, 77, 78, Rep. Assn. Memphis and Shelby County, 1966-67; chmn. St. Michael the Defender chpt. Catholics United for the Faith, 1973, 75. Served as sgt. USAAF, 1942-46. Mem. Am., Tenn., Wis. bar assns., Navy League U.S., Am. Conservative Union, Conservative Caucus, Cardinal Mindszenty Found., Am. Security Council, Am. Cause, Am. Legion, Latin Liturgy Assn. Roman Catholic. Home: 3032 E Glengarry Rd Memphis TN 38128 Office: Suite 3217 100 North Main Bldg Memphis TN 38103

HARRELL, CECIL STANFORD, pharmacy management services company executive; b. Thomaston, Ala., Apr. 12, 1934; s. William Bedwell and Gertrude (Golden) H.; m. Frances Garner; children—Christopher Gaines, Whitney Elizabeth. B.S., Auburn U., 1958; postgrad., U. South Fla., 1963. Pharmacist Wallgreens, Fla., 1958-59, Rexall Drug Co., Fla., 1954-60; salesman Eli Lilly Co., Indpls., 1960-63; chief exec. officer, pres. Pharmacy Mgmt. Services Co., Tampa, Fla., 1965—. Served with U.S. Army, 1953-55. Republican. Baptist. Clubs: Tampa Yacht, Palma Ceia Golf and Country, Merry Makers. Home: 910 S Himes Tampa FL 33629 Office: Pharmacy Mgmt Services Inc PO Box 32178 Tampa FL 33679

HARRELL, DAVID LYNN, utility executive; b. Sandersville, Ga., May 7, 1953; s. Ivey Duane and Shirley Frances (Page) H.; A.A., Hillsboro Community Coll., 1973; B.S. in Mech. Engring., U. South Fla., 1978; m. Carmen Valentin, Apr., 1973; children—Chyrisse Lynnette, David Alexander. Sec., inventory clk. Bay Sportswear, Tampa, Fla., 1971-73; inventory clk. Spartan Slacks, Tampa, 1973-74; balance clk. 1st Nat. Bank Data Processing Center, Tampa, 1974-74; tech. engring. asst. Westinghouse Electric Corp., Tampa, 1974-75, quality control technician, 1975-78; asso. piping engr. Pullman Kellogg, Houston, 1978-79; sr. engr. power plant engring. Houston Light & Power, 1979—; ptnr., dir. Haloco Mech. Engring. Inc., Houston, 1982—. Registered profl. engr., Tex. Mem. ASME, ASHRAE. Republican. Baptist. Home: 12220 Sapling Way Apt 1904 Houston TX 77031 Office: Houston Light & Power PO Box 1700 Houston TX 77001

HARRELL, HENRY HOWZE, tobacco company executive; b. Richmond, Va., Sept. 18, 1939; s. Theron Rice and Susan Howze (Haskell) H.; m. Jean Covington Camp, Feb. 7, 1970; children—Susan Hampton, Shelby Madison. A.B., Washington and Lee U. Vice pres. Universal Leaf Tobacco Co., Richmond, 1974-81, sr. v.p., 1981-82, exec. v.p., 1982—; dir. Jefferson Bankshares, Inc., Charlottesville, Va., Lawyers Title Ins. Co., Richmond, Universal Leaf Tobacco Co., Richmond. Bd. dirs. Richmond Soc. for

Prevention Cruelty to Animals. Served to lt. USNR, 1962-66. Mem. Phi Beta Kappa, Omicron Delta Kappa. Republican. Episcopalian. Clubs: Country of Va., Deep Run Hunt, Forum. Avocations: fishing; gardening.

HARRELL, RHETT DAVIS, JR., public accountant; b. Miami, Fla., Nov. 25, 1947; s. Rhett Davis and Daphne Arlene (Waldron) H.; m. Susan Edna Whaley, June 28, 1969; children—Kathryn Scarlett, Rhett Davis III. B.S., Fla. State U., 1969; postgrad. U. Central Fla., 1977-78, George Washington U., 1980. C.P.A., Fla., Ga. Supr., Tornwall, Lang & Lee, C.P.A.s, St. Petersburg/Orlando, Fla., 1969-74; supr. Lovelace, Roby & Co., C.P.A.s, Orlando, 1974-75; dir. fin. City of Kissimmee (Fla.), 1975-79; asst. dir. Mcpl. Fin. Officers Assn., Washington, 1979-81; mgr. May Zima & Co., C.P.A.s, Tallahassee, 1981-84; mgr. Touche Ross & Co., C.P.A.s, Atlanta, 1984—; mem. Nat. Council Govtl. Acctg., 1979-80; instr. Fla. State U. Econ. Devel. Ctr., 1982-83. Served with U.S. Army, 1969-70. Mem. Am. Inst. C.P.A.s, Am. Acctg. Assn., Govt. Fin. Officers Assn., Ga. Soc. C.P.A.s, Nat. Corp. Cash Mgrs. Assn., Sigma Iota Epsilon. Republican. Methodist. Club: Rotary (pres.-elect 1979, Outstanding Rotarian of Yr., Kissimmee 1978). Author: Money Market Management for Governmental Units, 1981; Developing a Financial Management Information System for Local Governments, 1981; Banking Relations-A Guide for Local Government, 1982, 2d edit., 1986. Contbr. articles to profl. publs. Home: 2580 N Arbor Trail Marietta GA 30066 Office: 225 Peachtree St NE Suite 1400 Atlanta GA 30043-6901

HARRELL, STANLEY MAXIE, city government official; b. Murfreesboro, N.C., Oct. 30, 1933; s. Emmett Maxie and Merlie (Harrell) H.; m. Olia Elizabeth Harrell, Oct. 30, 1956; children—Stanley Maxie, Keith Marshall. B.S., U. Southern Miss., 1975, M.B.A., 1975. C.P.A., Va. Enlisted U.S. Air Force, 1951; computer technician, Pentagon, 1964-71; instr. computer maintenance Keesler AFB, Miss., 1971-75; ret., 1975; tax technician IRS, Greenville, N.C., 1975-76; staff acct. Frank Edward Sheffer, CPA, Suffolk, Va., 1976-79; prin. acct. City of Norfolk (Va.), 1979-81, controller spl. projects, 1981—. Decorated Air Force commendation medal (2). Mem. Am. Inst. C.P.A.s, Va. Soc. C.P.A.s. Baptist. Lodges: Masons, Tidewater Toastmasters (Norfolk). Home: 228 Coliss Ave Virginia Beach VA 23462

HARRER, ANTHONY JONATHON, law educator, lawyer; b. Washington, Sept. 24, 1945; s. Anthony Franklin and Polly Anna (Goertz) H.; m. Linda Lee Drechsler, Apr. 28, 1979; 1 dau., Audrey Ann. B.A., Georgetown U., 1968; J.D., St. John's U., 1971; LL.M. in Taxation, Georgetown U., 1974. Bar: N.Y. 1972, Va. 1980 U.S. Dist. Ct. D.C. 1971. Atty. VA, 1971-72; sole practice, Washington, 1972-79, Woodstock, Va., 1980—; asst. prof. law James Madison U., Harrisonburg, Va., 1979—. Served to capt. USAR, 1968-76. Mem. ABA, D.C. Bar Assn., Va. Bar Assn., Phi Alpha Delta. Republican. Episcopalian. Home: 409 N Main St Woodstock VA 22664 Office: James Madison U Harrisburg VA 22807

HARRES, BURTON HENRY, JR., college administrator; b. Granite City, Ill., June 29, 1952; s. Burton H. Harres Sr. and Grace (Greer) Hoermann; m. Louise Nurse, Aug. 4, 1979. B.S., SE Mo. State U., 1974; M.S., Ind. U., 1976; postgrad. U. South Fla.; Ph.D., U. Fla., 1982. Resident instr. U. South Fla., Tampa, 1976-78, area adminstr., 1978-80; asst. to pres. Hillsborough Community Coll., Tampa, 1981—. Author: Need Fulfillment, Satisfaction, and Importance for Chief Business, Instructional, and Student Affairs Administrators in Florida's Community College System, 1982. Contbr. articles to profl. jours. Vol. Spl. Olympics Fla. State Games, Tampa, 1979—; bd. dirs. Lake Forest Homeowners Assn., Lutz, Fla., 1985. Mem. Am. Soc. Tng. and Devel., Fla. Assn. Community Colls. (legis. coordinator 1985—), Fla. Assn. Staff Program Devel. (bd. dirs. 1985—), Nat. Inst. for Staff Orgnl. Devel. Avocations: jogging; tennis; reading. Home: 14834 Oak Vine Dr Lutz FL 33549 Office: Hillsborough Community Coll PO Box 22127 Tampa FL 33630

HARRINGTON, BRUCE MICHAEL, lawyer; b. Houston, Mar. 12, 1933; s. George Haymond and Doris (Gladden) H.; m. Anne Lawhon. Oct. 18, 1937; children—Julia Griffith, Martha Gladden, Susan McIver. B.A., U. Tex.-Austin, 1960, J.D., 1961. Bar: Tex. 1961, U.S. Dist. Ct. (so. dist.) Tex. 1962, U.S. Ct. Appeals (5th cir.) 1962, U.S. Supreme Ct. 1973. Assoc. Andrews, Kurth, Campbell & Jones (now Andrews & Kurth, Houston, 1961-73, ptnr., 1973—; dir. Offenhauser Co. and Allied Metals Inc. Trustee St. John's Sch., 1981—; bd. mgrs. YMCA; bd. dirs. Houston Legal Found., St. Luke's Episcopal Hosp., Tex. Med. Ctr. Mem. ABA (fed. regulation of securities com.), Tex. Bar Assn. (com. on continuing edn., arts), Houston Bar Assn. (com. lawyer referrals, continuing edn.), Episcopalian. Clubs: Houston Country, Petroleum (Houston), Houston. Office: 4200 Tex Commerce Tower Houston TX 77002

HARRINGTON, RALPH LAMAR, JR., publishing company executive; b. Pasadena, Tex., Sept. 24, 1952; s. Ralph Lamar and Helen Virginia (Alsup) H.; m. Vivian Marie Reeves, Mar. 8, 1980. B.B.A. cum laude in Mktg., U. Houston, 1975. Research analyst Houston Chronicle, 1975-77, chief analyst, 1977-80, mktg. research mgr., 1980-85, dir. consumer mktg., 1985—; tchr. mktg. research U. Houston. Mem. Am. Mktg. Assn. (pres., bd. dirs.), Tex. Econ. and Demographic Assn. (founding bd. dirs.), Research Roundtable, Newspaper Research Council, Houston C. of C. (mem. econ. newsletter panel, census statis. areas com.). Home: 3214 Grove Terrace Dr Kingwood TX 77339 Office: Houston Chronicle 801 Texas Ave Suite 845 Houston TX 77002

HARRINGTON, TERRY LORENZO, physics educator; b. Ft. Benning, Ga., June 6, 1953; s. Walter Lee and Hester Lucille (Macon) H.; m. Shirley Mae Carter, 1971 (div. 1975); children—Alfonte, Terrel. B.S., Clark Coll., 1978; postgrad. Kent State U., 1980-81; M.S. in Physics, Atlanta U., 1984. Environmentalist EPA, Atlanta, 1973-75; research asst. Clark Coll., Atlanta, 1975-76, instr. in physics, 1978—, researcher, 1983—. Mem. Soc. Physics Students, Nat. Inst. Sci., Am. Assn. Physics Tchrs. Methodist. Club: Clark Coll. Physics (v.p. 1973-74). Home: 794 Tift Ave Atlanta GA 30310

HARRIS, ALAN JAY, counseling and forensic psychologist, counseling psychologist; b. Roanoke, Va., Mar. 9, 1950; s. Morton Jacob and Rose Gussie (Malsky) H. Student U. Fla., 1968-70; B.A., LaGrange Coll., 1972; M.A., Stephen F. Austin State U., 1975; Ph.D., U. So. Miss., 1981. Lic. psychologist, Fla.; diplomate Am. Acad. Behavioral Medicine. Staff psychologist Terrell State Hosp., Paris, Tex., 1975-76; psychology intern M. Bliss Mental Health Ctr., St. Louis, 1978-79; staff psychologist E. Ark. Mental Health Ctr., West Memphis, Ark., 1980-82; postdoctoral fellow Wilmington Inst., Dallas, 1982-84; pvt. practice psychology, Jacksonville, Fla., 1984—; founder, dir. Phobia Treatment Ctr. of N. Fla., Jacksonville, 1984—; chief psychology Pain Mgmt. Ctr., Jacksonville, 1985—; cons. psychologist Care Unit Hosp., Jacksonville Beach, Fla., 1984—. Author: Improving Sports Performance, 1981; author psychol. test: Mental Health Check-Up, 1985, Professional Satisfaction Survey, 1983. Editor audio tape: The Psychological Report, 1984. Vol. Mental Health Assn., Jacksonville, Fla., 1984—; bd. dirs. Vol. Board Bank, Jacksonville, 1985—, Jewish Family and Community Services, Jacksonville, 1986—. Postdoctoral fellow Wilmington Inst., Dallas, 1982-84. Mem. Am. Psychol. Assn., Phobia Soc. Am., Fla. Psychol. Assn., Fla. Council Alcoholism and Drug Abuse, Fla. Sheriff's Assn. (hon.). Democrat. Jewish. Clubs: New Trends, Gator (Jacksonville). Avocations: weight lifting; swimming; skydiving; camping; white water rafting. Home: 5800 Barnes Rd Apt 63 Jacksonville FL 32216 Office: 3716 University Blvd S Suite 6-B Jacksonville FL 32216

HARRIS, ALICE CARMICHAEL, linguist; b. Columbus, Ga., Nov. 23, 1947; d. Joseph Clarence and Georgia (Walker) H.; m. James Vaughan Staros, Aug. 7, 1976; children—Joseph Vaughan, Alice Carmichael. B.A., Randolph-Macon Woman's Coll., 1969; M.A., U. Essex (Eng.), 1972; Ph.D., Harvard U., 1976. Teaching fellow linguistics Harvard U., Cambridge, Mass., 1972-74, 75-76, lectr. linguistics, 1976-77, research fellow linguistics, 1977-79; research asst. prof. linguistics Vanderbilt U., Nashville, 1979-84, assoc. prof. linguistics, 1985—; assoc. research U. Tbilisi, USSR, 1974-75; tutor linguistics Dunster House, Harvard U., Cambridge, 1975-77. Author: Georgian Syntax, 1981; Diachronic Syntax, 1985. Contbr. articles to profl. jours. Sinclair Kennedy fellow Harvard U. 1974-75; grantee Internat. Research and Exchange Bd., 1977, Linguistic Soc. Am., 1981, NSF 1980-83, 81-83, 83-85, 85-87; scholar Harvard U. 1972-73, Georgetown U., 1973; recipient Mellon Found. Regional Faculty Devel. award 1981. Mem. Internat. Soc. Hist. Linguistics, Linguistic Soc. Am., Southeastern Conf. Linguistics. Office: Vanderbilt U Program in Linguistics Box 37 Station B Nashville TN 37235

HARRIS, ARTHUR HORNE, biology educator; b. Middleborough, Mass., May 18, 1931; s. Frank Arthur and Winifred Stevens (Deane) H.; div.; children—Tina Melissa, Rebecca Ann, Megan Aneen. B.A., U. N.Mex., 1958, M.S., 1959, Ph.D., 1965; postgrad. U. Ariz., 1959-60. Asst. prof. Ft. Hays Kans. State Coll., 1962-65; from asst. prof. to prof. U. Tex.-El Paso, 1965—, curator vertebrate paleobiology, 1967—, co-dir. resource collections lab. environ. biology, 1980—, curator higher vertebrates, 1983—. Co-author: The Mammals of New Mexico, 1975, The Faunal Remains from Arroyo Hondo Pueblo, 1984; author: Late Pleistocene Vertebrate Paleocology of the West, 1985. Served with U.S. Army, 1951-53. NSF grantee, 1967-70; Nat. Geog. Soc. grantee, 1971-73, 84-86; recipient Faculty Research award U. Tex.-El Paso, 1976. Mem. Am. Soc. Mammalogists, Soc. Vertebrate Paleontology, Southwestern Assn. Naturalists (editor 1978-82), Soc. Systematic Zoology, Am. Quaternary Assn. Democrat. Home: 665 Stedham El Paso TX 79927 Office: U Tex Lab Environ Biology El Paso TX 79968

HARRIS, BILL J., utilities executive; b. Mill Creek, Okla., Oct. 17, 1924; s. John M. and Irene W. (Penner) H.; B.S. in Biol. Sci. and Physics, East Central State Coll., 1947; M.S. in Secondary Edn., Okla. State U., 1952; m. Margarett Maxine Howard, July 25, 1947; children—Deborah, Gerald. With Pub. Service Co. of Okla., 1955-76, area mgr., McAlester, 1962-72, v.p. adminstrn., Tulsa, 1972-75, v.p. fuel, 1975-76; pres. Transok Pipe Line Co., 1975-76; pres., dir., chief operating officer Central & Southwest Corp., Dallas, 1976—. Served with USAAF, 1943-45. Mem. Edison Electric Inst. (dir., com. on research). Democrat. Methodist. Clubs: Masons (32 deg.); Bent Tree Country. City (Dallas). Office: 2121 San Jacinto Suite 2500 Dallas TX 75266

HARRIS, BRUCE ALEXANDER, JR., obstetrics-gynecology educator; b. Ann Arbor, Mich., May 15, 1919; s. Bruce Alexander and Clara Alfreda (Lindquist) H.; m. Joan Leigh Maddy, Feb. 21, 1944; children—William Bruce, Glenn Ferguson, Joan Elizabeth. A.B., Harvard U., 1939, M.D., 1943. Diplomate Am. Bd. Ob-Gyn. Intern, Boston City Hosp., 1943-44, ob-gyn intern Vanderbilt U. Hosp., 1946-47, Johns Hopkins Hosp., Balt., 1947-48, resident, 1948-50, 50, Detroit Receiving Hosp., 1950, Kings County Hosp., Bklyn., 1951; asst. in obstetrics Johns Hopkins U., 1948-50, instr., 1950; clin. instr. ob-gyn SUNY, 1952-53, asst. clin. prof. ob-gyn, 1953-59; assoc. prof. ob-gyn U. Ala., Birmingham, 1974-76, clin. assoc. prof., 1974-76, clin. prof., 1976-78, 78—; prof. ob-gyn U. Ala.-Tuscaloosa, 1976; prof. and chmn. ob-gyn U. Ala. in Huntsville, 1976-78; various hosp. appts. including cons. in gynecology House of St. Giles The Cripple, Bklyn., 1965-74; mem. ob-gyn staff Druid City Hosp., Tuscaloosa, 1974-76, Hale Meml. Hosp., Tuscaloosa, 1976, Huntsville Hosp., 1976-78, University Hosp., Birmingham, 1978—, Cooper Green Hosp., Birmingham, 1978—; mem. courtesy ob-gyn staff Med. Center Hosp., Huntsville, 1977-78; con. in field. Mem. Ala. State Perinatal Adv. Com., 1976—, dist. III com., 1980—; mem. med. adv. bd. HELP Line, Madison County, Ala., 1976-78, v.p., 1977-78; mem. med. adv. com. Well-Child Clinic, Madison County, 1977; mem. MCQ3 Nat. Bd. Med. Examiners, 1983—. Contbr. numerous articles to med. jours.; editor Women's Care Quar., 1979-82, Ala. Perinatal Bulletin, 1981—. Med. dir. N. Suffolk Planned Parenthood, N.Y., 1957-64; Tuscaloosa County Planned Parenthood, 1975-76. Served to capt. AUS, 1944-46. Recipient U. Ala. in Huntsville Student award, 1978; U. Ala. in Birmingham Caduceus Club award, 1979, Chief Residents Dept. Ob-Gyn award, 1979, Superlative award, 1980. Fellow ACS (com. on candidates L.I. eastern dist. 1969-74), Am. Coll. Ob-Gyn; mem. AMA, Am. Fertility Soc., Med. Assn. State of Ala., Ala. Assn. Ob-Gyn (pres. 1978-79), So. Perinatal Assn. (bd. dirs. southeastern regional adv. bd. 1976—, chmn. 1978-79), Jefferson County Med. Soc. (ob-gyn assurance panel 1983—), Charles E. Flowers Jr. Soc., Assn. Profs. Ob-Gyn, Birmingham Ob-Gyn Soc., Soc. Perinatal Obstetricians. Republican. Episcopalian. Clubs: Inverness Country, Relay House (Birmingham). Home: 3000 Dundee Ln Birmingham AL 35243 Office: Div Maternal and Fetal Medicine Dept Ob-Gyn U Ala in Birmingham Birmingham AL 35294

HARRIS, CALVIN D., educator; b. Clearwater, Fla., Aug. 27, 1941; s. Augustus and Alberta Beatrice (Brooks) H.; m. Ruth H. Harris, Dec. 19, 1964; children—Randall, Cassandra, Eric. B.A., U. South Fla., 1966; M.A., N.E. Mo. State U., 1970; Ed.D., Nova U., 1975. Instr., Gibbs High Sch., St. Petersburg, Fla., 1966-68, Seminole High Sch., Fla., 1968-70; dir. community service St. Petersburg Jr. Coll., 1970-75, dir. programs spl. students, 1975-79, provost open campus, 1979—; mem. Fla. EA/EO Com., 1981—, Fla. Standing Com. Continuing Edn., 1979—, State Employment Tng. Council, 1980-82, Spl. Curriculum Com., Pinellas County, Fla., 1981—. Sec., Juvenile Welfare Bd., Pinellas County, Fla., 1982—; mem. instl. rev. com. Morton Plant Hosp., Clearwater, Fla., 1980—; mem. ARC Service Adv. Com., 1983; v.p. Suncoast Sound Drum & Bugle Corps, 1983—; mem. sch. adv. com. Largo Middle Sch., Fla., 1982—. Mem. Phi Alpha Theta. Democrat. Baptist. Home: 1621 Young Ave Clearwater FL 33516 Office: St Petersburg Jr Coll Box 13489 Saint Petersburg FL 33733

HARRIS, CATHLEEN, marketing consultant, financial services company executive; b. McAllen, Tex., Apr. 9, 1960; d. Phillip Maurice Harris and Barbara JoAnne (Allen) Daxton. B.F.A. in Communication, Baylor U., 1983. Advt. cons. Hills, Reynolds & Elliot, Waco, Tex., 1979-82; account rep. Carich Reprographics, Dallas, 1983-84; mktg. coordinator Gulf-Tex, Irving, Tex., 1984-85; freelance artist, model, 1976—; mktg. coordinator Highland Corp., Burleson, Tex., 1985—; dist. mgr. Williams, Little & Assocs., Hurst, Tex., 1984—. Mem. Young Republicans, Dallas, 1982—. Recipient Hon. Mention award Miss Nat. Teen, 1976, 1st runner-up Miss Waco, 1980. Mem. Am. Mktg. Assn., Assoc. Builders and Contractors (pub. relations com. N. Tex. chpt.), Kappa Pi, Alpha Delta Pi. Baptist. Avocations: skiing; motorcycling; equestrian; hunting; scuba diving. Home: 1217 Nicole #1809 Fort Worth TX 76112 Office: Williams Little & Assocs 500 Grapevine Hwy #118 Hurst TX 76054 also Highland Corps 321 NW Hillery Burleson TX 76028

HARRIS, CHARLES EDGAR, bank director, former wholesale distbg. co. exec.; b. Englewood, Tenn., Nov. 6, 1915; s. Charles Leonard and Minnie (Borin) H.; m. Dorothy Wilson, Aug. 20, 1938; children—Charles Edgar, William John. With H.T. Hackney Co., Knoxville, Tenn., 1948-82, dir., 1962-82, pres., treas., chief adminstrv. officer, 1971-72, pres., chmn., chief exec. officer, 1972-82; former chmn. bd., dir. Hackney Carolina Co., Murphy, N.C., Hackney Jellico Co., Harlan, Ky., Haywood Wholesale Grocery Co., Waynesville, N.C., Dale San. Supply Co., Knoxville, Jellico Wholesale Grocery Co., Oneida and Elizabethton, Tenn., Corbin and Somerset, Ky., Tri-State Wholesale Co., Middlesboro, Ky., Brink's, Inc., Knoxville, Park Oil Co., Alcoa, Tenn., Knoxoil Co., Knoxville, Valley Oil Co., Athens, Tenn., Testoil Co., Harlan, Carolina Oil & Gas Co., Bryson City, N.C., Pride Markets, Inc., Knoxville, Foodser. Distbrs., Inc., Knoxville, Central Oil Co., Mid-State Investment Corp., McMinnville, Tenn., Appalachian Realty Corp.; dir. Park Nat. Bank, 1966-83, First Am. Nat. Bank Knoxville, 1983—. Treas., Knox County Baptist Assn., 1964-67, chmn. fin. com., mem. exec. bd., 1973-77; deacon, trustee Central Bapt. Ch.; mem. exec. bd. Tenn. Bapt. Conv., 1976-82; asso. chmn. Laymens Nat. Bible Com., Inc., 1977; bd. dirs. Met. YMCA of Knoxville, 1971-77, 82-83, mem. exec. com., 1971-76, treas., 1975; dir. exec. bd. Gt. Smoky Mountain council Boy Scouts Am., 1956-57, 82-83; bd. dirs. Downtown Knoxville Assn., v.p., 1979-83; bd. dirs. Tenn. Taxpayers Assn., 1976-84; bd. dirs. U.S. Indsl. Council, 1975-81, mem. exec. com., 1977-81; bd. dirs. Vols. of Am., 1981-83; mem. budget com. United Way Greater Knoxville, 1974-79, chmn. fin. com., bd. dirs., 1979; mem. budget rev. com. 1982 World's Fair, Knoxville, 1980-82; trustee Carson-Newman Coll., Jefferson City, Tenn., 1983—. Recipient Outstanding Community Leadership award Religious Heritage Am., 1978, YMCA Red Triangle award, 1979. Mem. Greater Knoxville C. of C. (dir. 1973-76, v.p. 1975-76; Outstanding Corporate Citizen award 1982), Knoxville Wholesale Credit Assn. (pres. 1956-57), Nat. Assn. Wholesalers-Distbrs. (trustee 1977-82). Club: Rotary of Knoxville (dir. 1973-76, v.p. 1975-77). Home: 7914 Gleason Rd Unit 1071 Knoxville TN 37919 Office: Fidelity Bldg Gay St PO Box 238 Knoxville TN 37901

HARRIS, DAN L., architect; b. Oklahoma City, Dec. 13, 1937; s. Paul A. and Nan. S. (McFall) H.; m. Colleen Allison, Aug. 30, 1959; children—Allison, Gregory, Kyle. B.Arch., Okla., State U., Stillwater, 1961. Registered architect, Okla. Archtl. apprentice Sorey, Hill & Sorey Architects, 1961, W. Dow Gumerson, Architect, Oklahoma City, 1961-62, C. Neal Carpenter, Architect, Greeley, Colo., 1962-64, T.M. Rogers, Enid, Okla., 1964-66; architect Day & Davies, Enid, 1968-71; prin. Dan L. Harris, Architect, Enid, 1966-68, 71—. Major works include Okla. Natural Gas Co., Enid, 1972; Christ United Methodist Ch. Enid, 1985; Edmond Trinity Christian Ch., Edmond, Okla., 1985. Pres., organizer Enid Community Theatre, 1966, Greater Enid Arts and Humanities Council, 1968, Enid Symphony Assn., 1970, Assembly Community Arts Councils Okla., 1971, Railroad Mus. of Okla., Enid, 1977. Mem. AIA, Constrn. Specifications Inst. Republican. Mem. Christian Ch. (Disciples of Christ). Club: Ambucs (Enid). Avocations: model railroads, railroad history, photography. Office: 723 W Randolph St Suite 4 Enid OK 73701

HARRIS, DAVID ALLEN, physician; b. Stillwater, Okla., July 22, 1950; s. Jack Allen and Betty Ann (Fry) H.; m. Dana Lalene Wood, July 18, 1970; children—Amanda Ruth, Justin Marcus. B.S., Okla. State U., 1972; D.O., Okla. Coll. Osteo. Medicine, 1977. Intern Okla. Osteo. Hosp., 1977-78, now med. dir. chem. dependency unit; resident U. N.Mex., Albuquerque, 1978-81; practice osteo. medicine specializing in neurology, Tulsa, 1981—; asst. prof. medicine Okla. Coll. Osteo. Medicine, 1983-84; co-dir. Headache Clinic Eastern Okla., 1984—. Bd. dirs. Green County chpt. Multiple Sclerosis Soc. Am., 1985—. Mem. Am. Osteo. Assn., Am. Acad. Neurology, Am. Electroencephalogy Soc., Am. Soc. Neuroimaging. Republican. Avocations: photography; fishing. Office: 4415 S Harvard Suite 206 Tulsa OK 74135

HARRIS, DAVID JEFFREY, lawyer; b. Columbia, La., Oct. 10, 1951; s. Cecil L. and Barbara (Ramsey) H. B.S., La. State U., 1973; J.D., Memphis State U., 1976. Bar: Tenn. 1976. Law clk. Shelby County Chancery Ct., Memphis, 1976; mem. firm Robinson, Fisher, Avery & Douglas, Memphis, 1976-81, Burch, Porter & Johnson, Memphis, 1982—. Bd. dirs. Boys Club, 1983—, Commitment Memphis, 1983—, Shelby County Commn. on Missing and Exploited Children, Phoenix Club, 1979-86; vol. adv. bd. Memphis in May Internat. Festival. Mem. Young Lawyers (dir., sec., pres.), Memphis and Shelby County Bar Assn. (dir.), Tenn. Bar Assn., ABA (dist. rep. young lawyers sect.). Methodist. Home: 4541 Shady Grove Rd Memphis TN 38117 Office: 130 N Court Ave Memphis TN 38103

HARRIS, DAVID MICHAEL, accountant; b. Houston, Mar. 14, 1947; s. Edwin Fleener and Mary Gayle (McKinney) H.; B.B.A., U. Tex., Austin, 1970; M.S. Accountancy, U. Houston, 1971; m. Rachel Anne Williams, June 6, 1970 (div. 1983); 1 son, Matthew Edwin. Mem. audit staff and tax staffs Arthur Andersen & Co., Houston, 1971-73; mem. Exxon Co. U.S.A. controllers dept. at Friendswood Devel. Co., Houston, 1973-75, at Exxon Minerals Co. U.S.A., Houston, 1976-79; mem. market research staff Friendswood Devel. Co., Houston, 1975-76; staff fin. analyst supply controllers Exxon Co. U.S.A., Houston, 1979; v.p., controller Eden Corp. subs. Gen. Homes Consol. Cos., Houston, 1979-82; v.p., chief fin. officer The Johnson Corp., Houston, 1981—; pvt. practice acctg., 1971—; vol. cons. Am. Cancer Soc., So. Bible Coll. Vol. worker U. Houston Excellence Campaign Fund, 1975-79, mem. exec. council Ann. Fund, 1981—. C.P.A., Tex. Mem. Am. Inst. C.P.A.s. Republican. Methodist. Clubs: Kingwood Runners (founder, team capt.), Houston City. Home: 5220 Weslayan C-309 Houston TX 77005 Office: 1300 Post Oak Blvd Suite 1800 Houston TX 77056

HARRIS, DIANA KOFFMAN, sociologist; b. Memphis, Aug. 11, 1929; d. David Nathan and Helen Ethel (Rotter) Koffman; student U. Miami, 1947-48; B.S., U. Wis., 1951; postgrad. Tulane U., 1951-52; M.A., U. Tenn., 1967; postgrad. Oxford (Eng.) U., 1968-69; m. Lawrence Alvin Harris, June 24, 1951; children—Marla, Jennifer. Advt., sales promotion mgr. Wallace Johnston Distbg. Co., 1952-54; welfare worker Tenn. Dept. Public Welfare, Knoxville, 1954-56; instr. sociology Maryville (Tenn.) Coll., 1972-75, Ft. Sanders Sch. Nursing, Knoxville, 1971-78; instr. U. Tenn., 1967—, chmn. Council Aging, 1979—. Organizer, Knoxville Gray Panthers, 1978; mem. Tenn. Gov.'s Task Force Pre-retirement Programs for State Employees, 1973; mem. White House Conf. Aging, 1981; bd. dirs. Knoxville-Knox County Council Aging, 1976, Sr. Citizens Info. and Referral, 1979—. Sr. Citizens Home-Aide Service, 1977—; del. East Tenn. Council Aging, 1977. Recipient award Nat. Univ. Continuing Edn. Assn., 1982. Mem. Am. Sociol. Assn., AAAS, Gerontol. Soc., Popular Culture Assn., So. Sociol. Soc., So. Gerontol. Soc. N. Central Sociol. Soc. Author: Readings in Social Gerontology, 1975; (with Cole) The Elderly in America, 1977; The Sociology of Aging, 1980; co-author: Sociology, 1984; The Sociology of Aging: An Annotated Bibliography and Sourcebook, 1985; contbr. articles to profl. jours. Home: 4505 Landon Dr Knoxville TN 37921 Office: U Tenn Dept Sociology Knoxville TN

HARRIS, DONALD LEE, geological design draftsman; b. Medford, Okla., Oct. 23, 1928; s. Otto Lee and Mardie Faye H.; A.S., No. Okla. Jr. Coll., 1948; m. Patricia McIntire Veros, Dec. 14, 1974; children by previous marriage—Terry, Robert. Gen. mgr. Early Hardware, Medford, 1949-56; jr. draftsman Sunray D-X, Oklahoma City, 1956-58; chief corp. drafting design div. exploration Kerr-McGee Corp., Oklahoma City, 1958—; instr. geol. drafting Okla. State U. Extension, 1976-83, drafting adviser, 1967—; condr. slide symposiums, speaker, slide adviser Am. Assn. Profl. Geologists, slide short courses ann. nat. conv., 1981-84. Active Last Frontier council Boy Scouts Am., 1959-73, Girl Scouts U.S.A., 1981—. Recipient Slide Service award Nat. Am. Assn. Profl. Geologists, 1968, 78, cert. for design of display Okla. Dept. Energy, 1976-78. Mem. Kerr-McGee Golf Assn., Oklahoma City Jaycees. Democrat. Methodist. Club: Westbury Country. Author: Geological Map Drafting, 1977, 2d rev. edit., 1982; designer geol. model of Gulf of Mexico, 1973; research on color slide artwork and materials effects, 1964—. Home: 2021 Norwich Pl Yukon OK 73099 Office: PO Box 25861 Oklahoma City OK 73125

HARRIS, DOROTHY DEANE, accountant, educator; b. New Canton, Va., Apr. 4 1915; d. Myrtle Emmett and Lillian Eleanor (Johnson) Deane; m. Julian Newton Harris, Aug. 6, 1938. B.S. in Bus. Adminstrn., U. Richmond, 1974; M.S. in Acctg., Va. Commonwealth U., 1981. C.P.A., Va. Asst. cashier, trust officer Planters Bank, Chatham, Va., 1940-47; bursar Chatham Hall, Chatham, 1947-53; acct. Greater Richmond C. of C., 1973-74; staff acct. Manning Perkinson & Floyd, Richmond, 1974-76; pvt. practice acctg., Chatham, 1976—; asst. prof. J. Sargeant Reynolds Community Coll., Richmond, Va., 1976—. Mem. Am. Inst. C.P.A.s, Am. Soc. Women Accts. (past pres. Richmond chpt.), Va. Soc. C.P.A.s, Garden Club Va. Democrat. Episcopalian. Club: Garden (Chatham). Contbr. articles to profl. publ. Home and office: RFD 2 Box 30P Chatham VA 24531

HARRIS, DOUGLAS CLAY, newspaper executive; b. Owensboro, Ky., Oct. 9, 1939; s. Marvin Dudley and Elizabeth (Adelman) H.; B.S., Murray State U., 1961; M.S., Ind. U., 1964, Ed.D., 1968. Counselor, asst. to dean of students Ind. U., Bloomington, 1965-68; mgmt. appraisal specialist United Air Lines, Elk Grove Village, Ill., 1968-69; dir. manpower div. Computer Age Industries, Washington, 1969; area personnel dir. Peat Marwick Mitchell & Co., N.Y.C., 1969-72; v.p. personnel Knight-Ridder Newspapers, Inc., Miami, Fla., 1972-85, v.p., sec., 1986. Served to capt. U.S. Army, 1961-62. Mem. Am. Psychol. Assn., Fla. Psychol. Assn., Southeastern Psychol. Assn., Am. Soc. Personnel Adminstrs., Newspaper Personnel Relations Assn., Am. Compensation Assn. Democrat. Home: 1408 S Bayshore Dr Apt 1211 Miami FL 33131 Office: 1 Herald Plaza Miami FL 33101

HARRIS, DWIGHT, archivist; b. Jackson, Miss., Nov. 3, 1952; s. Cliff and Susie Harris. B.A. in History and Polit. Sci., Belhaven Coll., 1974. Pvt. manuscripts curator dept. archives and history State of Miss., Jackson, 1974-77, historian, 1977-81, chief archivist, 1981—; cons. to univ. archives. Mem. Miss. Archivist Soc., Assn. Records Mgrs. and Adminstrs. Author: Reconstruction in Mississippi, 1979. Office: 100 S State St Jackson MS 39205

HARRIS, EARL DOUGLAS, lawyer; b. Athens, Ga., Apr. 9, 1947; s. Roland Russell and Martha Sue (Davis) H.; m. Jean Wright, Dec. 26, 1975; children—Jeannette, Stephanie. B.S.A.E., U. Ga., 1970, M.B.A., J.D., 1973. Bar: Ga. 1973, U.S. Dist. Ct. (mid. dist.) Ga. 1973, U.S. Ct. Appeals (5th cir.) 1973, U.S. Ct. Claims 1977, U.S. Tax Ct. 1977, U.S. Patent Office 1977, U.S. Customs Ct. 1977, U.S. Supreme Ct. 1977, U.S. Ct. Customs and Patent Appeals 1980, U.S. Ct. Internat. Trade 1981, U.S. Ct. Appeals (11th cir.) 1981. Sole practice, Watkinsville, Ga., 1973-76, 85—; city atty. Town of Bogart, Ga., 1974-75, 85—; sr. ptnr. Harris & Rice, Watkinsville, 1977-78; mem. Harris, Rice & Alford, P.A., Watkinsville, 1978-80; ptnr., pres. Harris & Alford, P.A., Watkinsville, 1980-85; pres. Fed. Title Corp., 1978—; county atty. Oconee County, Ga., 1978-80; corp. sec. Lawlog Corp., 1980—. Bd. dirs. Clarke County unit Am. Cancer Soc., 1970-72; mem. Oconee County Democratic Exec. Com., 1976—, treas., 1976-82; active Red Cross of Constantine. Served with USCMR, 1965-68; with USAF, 1968. Mem. Ga. Trial Lawyers Assn., ABA, State Bar Ga., Western Cir. Bar Assn., Gridiron Secret Soc., U. Ga. Agrl. Alumni Assn. (pres. young alumni div. 1975-76), Oconee County C. of C. (dir., sec. 1976-78), Blue Key, Sphinx, Omicron Delta Kappa, Sigma Iota Epsilon, Alpha Zeta. Presbyterian (ruling elder). Clubs: Tall Cedars of

Lebanon, Royal Order of Scotland. Lodges: Masons (sr. grand deacon 1984, jr. grand warden Ga. 1985), Order of Eastern Star, Shriners. Home: 8700 Macon Rd Athens GA 30606 Office: PO Box 498 Main St Watkinsville GA 30677

HARRIS, EDWARD FREDERICK, orthodontics educator, physical anthropologist; b. San Jose, Calif., Oct. 2, 1947; s. Roy Hayward and Bonnie (Keeble) H.; m. Karen J. Morse, May 29, 1970 (div. July 1983); children—Jeremy T., Emily J.; m. Barbara K. Steppe, June 22, 1985. B.A., San Jose State U., 1969; M.A., Ariz. State U., 1972, Ph.D., 1977. Asst. prof. orthodontics U. Conn., Farmington, 1978-80; asst. prof. orthodontics Coll. Dentistry, U. Tenn. Center for Health Scis., Memphis, 1980—. NIH fellow, 1973-80. Mem. Am. Assn. Phys. Anthropologists, Internat. Assn. Dental Research, Sigma Xi. Democrat. Methodist. Contbr. articles to profl. jours. Office: 875 Union Ave S301 Memphis TN 38163

HARRIS, ELMER BESELER, electric utility executive; b. Chilton County, Ala., Apr. 8, 1939; s. Alton Curtis and Lero (Mitchell) H.; m. Glenda Steele, Sept. 15, 1962; children—Lera Lorraine, Thomas Alton. B.E. in Elec. Engring., Auburn U., 1962, M.S., 1968, M.B.A., 1970; student U.S. Air Force Flight Sch., Tex., 1964, Air Command and Staff Coll., Maxwell AFB, Montgomery, Ala., 1970. With Ala. Power Co., Birmingham, Ala., 1975—, asst. v.p., 1975, asst. v.p., asst. treas., 1975-76, v.p. corp. fin. and planning, 1976, sr. v.p., 1978, exec. v.p., chief fin. officer, 1979, dir., 1980—; dir. So. Electric Gen. Co., Birmingham. Fund solicitor Boy Scouts Am., Birmingham; funds solicitor Am. Heart Assn., Birmingham. Served to capt. USAF, 1964-65. Mem. Nat. Mgmt. Assn., Edison Elec. Inst. (corp. planning com.), Fin. Execs. Inst. Lodge: Kiwanis. Home: 3115 Club Dr Birmingham AL 35226 Office: Ala Power Co 600 N 18th St Birmingham AL 35291*

HARRIS, EWING JACKSON, lawyer; b. Sylvia, Tenn., Mar. 17, 1901; s. John Chastain and Sarah Frances (Walker) H.; ed. pub. schs. Tenn. and Detroit; LL.B., Cumberland U., 1928; m. Lena Sue Hartman, Mar. 28, 1931; children—Frances Ann Harris (Mrs. Frank Avent), Marjorie Sue Harris (Mrs. Dean Lucht), Ewlene Harris. Admitted to Tenn. bar, 1928 and practiced in Bolivar, 1932—; city atty., Bolivar, 1942—; county atty. Hardeman County, 1942-70; dir. Bank of Bolivar. Pres. State Bd. of Elections, 1949-53, Tenn. Democratic Exec. Com. 1949-51, 1953-55; mem. Tenn. State Senate, 1937-39; del. Tenn. Constl. Conv., 1965. Fellow Am. Coll. Probate Counsel; mem. Am., Tenn. (bd. govs. 1959-62, mem. Ho. Dels. 1973-75, mem. spl. joint com. on ct. modernization), Hardeman County bar assns., Am. Judicature Soc., C. of C. (pres.1958), Phi Beta Gamma. Methodist (trustee). Clubs: Masons, Elks, Rotary (Paul Harris fellow). Home: 608 S Union St Bolivar TN 38008 Office: Bank of Bolivar Bldg Box 148 Bolivar TN 38008

HARRIS, GLENN WILLIAM, government official; b. Los Angeles, Jan. 24, 1947; s. Frank Stanley and Thelma Eliza (Montgomery) H. B.M.E., East Carolina U., 1974. Supply systems analyst Dept. Navy, Washington, 1976-84; insp. gen. rep. Dept. Def., Washington, 1984—. Contbr. articles to profl. jours. Mem. Aurora Highlands Civic Assn., Arlington, Va. Served with USAF, 1969-73. Recipient Commandant's award Army Logistics Mgmt. Ctr., 1976. Mem. Am. Fedn. Musicians, Wedding Photographers Internat., East Carolina U. Alumni Assn. Clubs: Washington Apple Pi (Bethesda, Md.); Internat. Apple Core (Santa Clara, Calif.). Avocations: Travel photography; reading. Home: 637 S 22d St Arlington VA 22202 Office: Dept of Def Inspector Gen 1300 Wilson Blvd Room 106 Arlington VA 22209

HARRIS, HARRIET KAYE, bank executive; b. Hanau, W.Ger., Mar. 16, 1949; d. Harry Lee and Junita (Stevens) Willingham; m. Robert Samuel Harris, Dec. 27, 1968; children—Robert Lee, Heather Dawn. Student, U. Ga., 1967-68. Teller, Bank of Fulton County, Atlanta, 1970-71, Pacific Nat. Bank, Tacoma, 1974-75; note teller, ops. officer North Pacific Bank, Tacoma, 1975-79; asst. v.p. ops., loans Comml. Bank of Kendall, Miami, Fla., 1979-80; ops. officer, chief data processing Pan Am. Bank, Miami, 1980-83; sr. v.p., controller Eastern Nat. Bank, Miami, 1983—; cons. banking practices, Miami, 1982—; advisor ethical bank practices Banking Practices Com., 1982—. Author various manuals, pamphlets. Asst. leader local Brownie troop Girl Scouts U.S.A., Miami, 1980-82, advisor local scout troop, 1983. Mem. Profl. Bankers of Fla. Republican. Methodist. Office: Eastern Nat Bank 1550 W 84th St Miami FL 33014

HARRIS, HENRY RAY, oil company supervisor, drafting consultant; b. Utica, Miss., Mar. 19, 1951; s. Joseph E. and Willie B. (Bythers) H.; m. Rosa M. Dural, Dec. 29, 1973; children—Henry R. Jr., Jonathan J. A.S., Utica Jr. Coll., 1972. Draftsman, Skelly Oil Co., Lafayette, La., 1972-74, Tex. Pacific Oil, Lafayette, 1974-76; drafting coordinator Mobil Oil Corp., Lafayette, 1976-85, drafting supr., 1985—; cons. drafting, Lafayette, 1976—. Mem. Am. Inst. Design and Drafting (sec. 1982-83, recipient plaque 1983). Democrat. Baptist. Avocations: basketball; football; travel. Home: 119 Woodrow St Lafayette LA 70506 Office: Mobil Oil Corp PO Box 51108 Lafayette LA 70505

HARRIS, J. ROBIN, savings and loan executive; b. 1926. Pres., chief exec. officer, dir. Decatur Fed. Savs. & Loan, Ga. Office: Decatur Fed Savs & Loan 250 Ponce De Leon Ave Decatur GA 30030*

HARRIS, JACK HOWARD, II, consulting firm executive; b. Chgo., Mar. 22, 1945; s. Jack Howard and Myrtice Geneva (Dickson) H.; A.B., U. Chgo., 1966; M. Ph., George Washington U., 1984; m. Barbara Jeanne Beck, Jan. 1, 1983; children—Jack, William, T. Patrick; stepchildren—Joseph C. Czika, Brad D. Czika. Chief China desk Air Force Intelligence, U.S. Air Force, Washington, 1971-74; dir. policy studies BDM Corp., Washington, 1974-78; sr. assoc. Booz-Allen and Hamilton, Washington, 1979; corp. v.p., govt. ops. Sci. Applications, Inc., Washington, 1980-85; exec. vp. The Harris Group, Inc., Washington, 1985—. Served with USAF, 1967-71. Mem. Air Force Assn., Assn. U.S. Army, Am. Legion, D.A.V., V.F.W. Home: 911 Challedon Rd Great Falls VA 22066 Office: 1761 Business Center Dr Suite 200 Reston VA 22090

HARRIS, JAN LEE, state education department administrator; b. Richmond, Va., July 5; d. William Henry and Dorothy (Willard) H. B.S., Madison Coll., 1958; M.S., Old Dominion U., 1968; advanced cert. in counseling, Coll. William and Mary, 1971, Ed.D., 1973. Registered profl. counselor, Va. Tchr., Henrico County Pub. Schs., Richmond, Va., 1958-64, Norfolk Pub. Schs. (Va.), 1964-67; asst. dir. counseling Old Dominion U., Norfolk, 1968-70; counselor Virginia Beach Pub. Schs. (Va.), 1970-73; assoc. dean students Longwood Coll., Farmville, Va., 1973-78, assoc. prof. student personnel, 1973-78; supr. data utilization and reporting Va. Dept. Edn., Richmond, 1979-84, supr. guidance, 1984—. Mem. gen. stats. task force subcom. council of Chief State Sch. Officers, Washington, 1979-84. Mem. Am. Psychol. Assn., Am. Assn. Counseling and Devel., Am. Sch. Counselor Assn., Am. Coll. Personnel Assn., Assn. for Specialists in Group Work, Assn. for Counselor Edn. and Supervision, Nat. Vocat. Guidance Assn., Kappa Delta Pi. Lodge: Soroptimist. Office: Va Dept Edn PO Box 6Q Richmond VA 23216

HARRIS, JESSE GRAHAM, psychologist, educator; b. Jacksonville, Fla., Jan. 5, 1926; s. Jesse Grahamm and Mona Marx (Woods) H.; m. Julia Patricia McNamee, Sept. 5, 1953; children—Julia Kathleen Harris Miller, Cecilia Anne. B.A., Harvard U., 1946; Ph.D., Duke U., 1955. Diplomate Am. Bd. Profl. Psychology; lic. psychologist, Ky. Asst. prof. dept. psychology U. Conn., Storrs, 1958-60; assoc. prof. and dir. psychology, dept. of psychology U. Ky. Med. Ctr., Lexington, 1960-63; prof. dept. of psychology U. Ky., Lexington, 1963—, dept. chmn., 1963-67, 80—, dir. clin. tng., 1963-67, 69-75; chmn. Ky. Bd. Psychology, 1970-75, bd. dirs., 1966-75; chmn. Ky. Mental Health Manpower Commn., 1971-74; chmn. Ky. Manpower Devel., Inc., Louisville, 1974-78; field selection officer and research cons. U.S. Peace Corps, 1968-71. Contbr. chpts. to books, articles to profl. publs. in field; adv. editor: Jour. Cons. and Clin. Psychology, 1970—. Served with USN, 1955-58, to capt. USNR, 1944-85. Sr. fellow Culture Learning Inst., East-West Ctr., Honolulu, 1975; research contract U.S. Peace Corps, 1971. Fellow Am. Psychol. Assn.; mem. Ky. Psychol. Assn. (pres. 1980, Disting. Service award 1983), Southeastern Psychol. Assn., Phi Beta Kappa, Sigma Xi. Presbyterian. Avocations: pianist; gardening; hiking. Office: Dept Psychology Univ Kentucky Lexington KY 40506

HARRIS, JESSIE G. (MRS. HUBERT LAMAR HARRIS), ret. ednl. adminstr.; b. Athens, Ga., May 12, 1909; d. Wiley Jackson and Dora (Hilley) Ginn; B.B.A., U. Ga., 1956; A.B., Ga. State Coll., 1960; m. Hubert Lamar Harris, Nov. 25, 1930; children—Mary Ann Harris (Mrs. William Wallace Holley), Hubert Lamar, Dorothy Elizabeth (Mrs. Ronald Zazworsky), Martha Susan (Mrs. R.R. McCue, Jr.). Various secretarial positions, ins. and law offices, 1923-30; sec. div. of gen. extension U. Ga., 1930-35, asst. dir. div. gen. extension, 1935-47; asst. compilation survey Univ. System, Ga., 1949-50, adminstrv. asst. to regents, 1951-63, asst. exec. sec., 1963-67, asso. exec. sec., 1967-73, asst. vice chancellor personnel, 1973-74, asst. exec. dir. and asst. vice chancellor emeritus, 1974—; ret., 1974. Asst. exec. dir. State Scholarship Commn., 1965-66; bd. dirs. Ednl. Info. and Referral Service, Inc. Mem. AAUW (chmn. study group 1964-66, treas. 1972-74), Crimson Key Honor Soc., Mortar Board, So. Hist. Assn., Atlanta Hist. Soc., Sandy Springs Arts and Heritage Soc., Phi Chi Theta, Delta Mu Delta, Psi Chi. Club: Atlanta Writers. Home: Rosemont Route 4 Box 274 Monroe GA 30655

HARRIS, JOE FRANK, governor of Georgia; b. Cartersville, Ga., Feb. 16, 1936; s. Grover Franklin and Frances (Morrow) H.; B.B.A., U. Ga., 1958; m. Elizabeth Carlock, June 25, 1961; 1 son, Joe Frank, Jr. LL.D. (hon.), Asbury Coll., 1983, Woodrow Wilson Coll. Law, 1981, Morris Brown Coll., 1983. Sec., treas. Harris Cement Products, Inc., Cartersville, Ga., 1958-79; pres. Harris Georgia Corp., Cartersville, 1979-83; gov. of Ga., Atlanta, 1983—. Mem. Ga. Gen. Assembly, 1965-83. Served with U.S. Army, 1958. Democrat. Methodist. Home: 391 W Paces Ferry Rd Atlanta GA 30305 Office: State Capitol Atlanta GA 30334

HARRIS, JOHN FLOYD, geologist, consultant; b. Turley, Okla., May 16, 1926; s. Robert A. and Gladys L. (Mills) H.; m. Patricia Carmack, June 3, 1948; 1 dau., Rebecca Anne Harris Gilmore. B.S., U. Tulsa, 1948, M.S., 1959. Surface geologist Stanolind Co., 1945; geologist Stanolind-PanAm., Casper, Wyo., Salt Lake City and Tulsa, 1948-59; pvt. practice geology cons., Tulsa, 1959—, worldwide lectr. Lay reader, vestry St. Luke's Episcopal Ch., Tulsa. Recipient Best Paper award Gulf Coast Geol. Soc., 1970. Mem. Am. Assn. Petroleum Geologists (cert.), Am. Inst. Profl. Geologists (cert.), Tulsa Geol. Soc., Mich. Basin Soc., Oklahoma City Geol. Soc., Wyo. Geol. Soc. Republican. Contbr. numerous articles to profl. jours.

HARRIS, JOHN WOODS, banker; b. Galveston, Tex., Sept. 23, 1893; s. John Woods and Minnie (Hutchings) H.; LL.B., U. Va., 1920; m. Eugenia Davis, June 14, 1917; children—Eugenia (Mrs. Archibald Rowland Campbell, Jr.), Anne (Mrs. Donald C. Miller), Joan (Mrs. Alvin N. Kelso), Florence (Mrs. Marshall McDonald, Jr.) (dec.). Admitted to Tex. bar, 1920; practiced as atty., mng. agt. oil, farm, ranch properties in Tex., 1922—; dir. Hutchings Sealy Nat. Bank, 1930-58; chmn. exec. com., chmn. bd. 1st Hutchings Sealy Nat. Bank (now by merger InterFirst Bank Galveston N.A.), 1960—; pres. Hutchings Joint Stock Assn., 1936—; dir. Galveston Corp., Cotton Concentration Co., Gulf Transfer Co., Tex. Fibreglas Products, Inc., Galveston; mem. U.S. Congl. Adv. Bd., 1981—. Sr. v.p., chmn. land com. The Sealy and Smith Found. for John Sealy Hosp.; pres. Galveston Found. Inc.; v.p. Ball Charity Found.; pres. bd. Rosenberg Library, Galveston Orphans Home; trustee Galveston Ind. Sch. Dist., 1927-30. Served as aviator USN, 1918. Named Man of Yr., Galveston br. Boys Clubs Am., 1980; recipient Rabbi Henry Cohen humanitarian award, 1981. Mem. Sons Republic of Tex., Am. Legion, Early and Pioneer Naval Aviators Assn., Nat. Frat. Mil. Pilots, Order Daedalians, Delta Kappa Epsilon. Episcopalian. Clubs: Galveston Artillery; Farmington Country (Charlottesville, Va.); Bob Smith Yacht. Home: 2603 Ave O Galveston TX 77550 Office: 801 Interfirst Bank Bldg Galveston TX 77550

HARRIS, M. MARVIN, English educator; b. Eagle Pass, Tex., Dec. 28, 1931; s. Ross Enoch and Willie Bea (Woodward) H.; m. Sandra Elaine Dickson, Dec. 28, 1956; children—Angela Beth Harris Robberts, Mark Steven, Cynthia DeAnne. B.A., Baylor U., 1952, M.A., 1963; B.D., Southwestern Bapt. Theol. Sem., 1957; M.A., U. Tex., 1969, Ph.D., 1972. Cert. tchr., Tex. Lang. arts tchr. Geneva Pub. Schs., Ohio, 1956-57, Smiley Ind. Sch. Dist., Tex., 1957-58, Temple Ind. Sch. Dist., Tex., 1958-65; instr. English, E. Tex. Bapt. U., Marshall, 1965-67, 69—, dept. chmn., 1972—. Editor Jour. Am. Studies Assn. Tex., 1978—. Contbr. articles to profl. jours. Pastor Belfalls Bapt. Ch., Temple, Tex., 1959-62, Acad. Bapt. Ch., 1962-65. W. Tex. State U. grantee, 1965. Mem. Nat. Council Tchrs. English, E. Tex. Council Tchrs. English, Tex. Joint Council Tchrs. English (exec. sec.), Am. Studies Assn. Tex., Sigma Tau Delta, Phi Delta Kappa. Democrat. Avocations: reading; fishing; touring. Lodge: Lions (past bd. dirs.). Home: 4300 Pine Burr Terr Marshall TX 75670 Office: E Tex Bapt U 1209 N Grove St Marshall TX 75670

HARRIS, MASON, marketing specialist; b. N.Y.C., July 10, 1956; s. Eugene and Irene (Pollack) Herskovitz. B.A., Queens Coll., 1978; M.B.A., SUNY-Buffalo, 1980. Instr., researcher SUNY-Buffalo, 1978-80; mktg. assoc. GTE Service Corp., Stamford, Conn., 1980-82; mgr. mktg. nat. accounts GTE Telenet, Vienna, Va., 1982-83, account exec., 1983-84, sr. account exec., 1985, regional mgr., 1986—. Home: 1889 Cold Creek Ct Vienna VA 22180 Office: GTE Telenet Communications Corp 12490 Sunrise Valley Dr Reston VA 22076

HARRIS, MAX ADDISON, title and mortgage services company executive; b. Muleshoe, Tex., Nov. 18, 1951; s. Marion F. and Maxine O. H.; m. Sandra F. Oparenovich, Sept. 9, 1972 (div. Nov. 1980). Student Tex. Tech. U., 1971. Vice-pres. mktg. Glendale Ins. Agy., Inc., Houston, 1974-78; owner Max A Harris Ins. Agy., Houston, 1978-80; chmn. bd., pres. Dual H Enterprises, Inc., Houston, 1979—; chmn. bd., pres. Comprehensive Mortgage and Title Services, Inc., Houston, 1980—; chmn. bd. Tidal Enterprises, Inc., Galveston, 1984—. Club: Masons. Office: 4001 N Shepherd St Suite 108 Houston TX 77018

HARRIS, MICHAEL ODELLE, international accounting firm executive; b. Amarillo, Tex., Dec. 11, 1953; s. John Thomas and Nancy Ann (Hubbard) H.; m. Jo Ellen Sigler, Mar. 8, 1980; 1 child, Patricia Lynn. B.B.A. with honors, Tex. Tech U., 1976. C.P.A., Tex. With Peat, Marwick, Mitchell & Co., Amarillo, 1976—, supr., 1981-82, mgr., 1982-83, sr. audit mgr., 1983—; statis. audit specialist, 1983—, microcomputer audit coordinator Amarillo office, 1984—. Mem. Inst. C.P.A.s, Tex. Soc. C.P.A.s (chmn. Panhandle chpt., com. for communications with banks and bank regulatory authories 1984-85, mem. subcom. for communications with Office of Comptroller of Currency 1984-85), Nat. Assn. Accts., Tex. Cattle Feeders, Amarillo C. of C. (leadership program 1983-84), Aircraft Owners and Pilots Assn., Beta Alpha Psi, Beta Gamma Sigma, Phi Kappa Phi, Phi Eta Sigma. Republican. Baptist. Home: 3723 Rutson Dr Amarillo TX 79109 Office: Peat Marwick Mitchell & Co Suite 600 First National Pl II Amarillo TX 79105

HARRIS, MICHAEL PRINCE, petroleum corporation executive, geological consultant; b. Greenville, S.C., May 17, 1949; s. Benjamin Samuel Hampton and Lillian (Prince) H.; m. Rebecca Turner, Aug. 12, 1972; 1 child, Benjamin Samuel Hampton, IV. B.S. in Geology, Clemson U., 1972; postgrad. La. State U., 1973-75. Geologist, Mobil Oil Corp., New Orleans, 1975-78, Lynal, Inc., Lafayette, La., 1978-84; pres. Prince Petroleum, Lafayette, 1981—; geol. cons. Southport Exploration, Lafayette, 1985. Advisor, Explorer Scouts, Boy Scouts Am., Lafayette, 1981; mem. fin. com. Republican Party, Lafayette, 1982. Mem. Am. Assn. Petroleum Geologists, Lafayette Geol. Soc. Episcopalian. Club: Lafayette Townhouse, Red Lerilles Health (Lafayette). Avocations: swimming; running; camping; racing; skiing. Home: 111 Gussie Dr Lafayette LA 70508 Office: Prince Petroleum Corp 109 Jomela St Lafayette LA 70503

HARRIS, OLLIE, state senator; b. Anderson, S.C., Sept. 2, 1913; s. John Frank and Jessie Mae (Hambright) H.; grad. Gupton-Jones Coll. Embalming, Nashville, 1935; m. Abbie Wall, May 4, 1934; children—Ollie, Jane Wall. With Lutz-Austell Funeral Home, Shelby, N.C., 1928-47; pres., treas. Harris Funeral Home, Kings Mountain, N.C., 1947—; dir. First Union Nat. Bank, Kings Mountain; past pres. N.C. Bd. Embalmers; coroner Cleveland County, 1946-70; mem. N.C. Senate, 1971—. Served with AUS, 1943-45. Decorated Bronze Star; recipient Valand award N.C. Assn. Mentally Ill and Mentally Retarded, 1979; Disting. Service award N.C. Public Health Assn., 1979. Mem. N.C. Funeral Dirs. and Embalmers Assn. (past pres.). Democrat. Baptist. Clubs: Lions, Shriners. Home: 921 Sharon Dr Kings Mountain NC 28086 Office: 108 S Piedmont St Kings Mountain NC 28086

HARRIS, ORVILLE R., physical scientist; b. Sedalia, Mo., Oct. 19, 1909; s. Thomas Lester and Lula Jane (Thomas) H.; m. Doris M. Shockley, Dec. 13, 1933 (dec. 1969); children—Linda Michael, Thomas Arthur; m. Helen Duncan Barron, Aug. 8, 1970. B.S.M.E., Washington U., 1932; M.E.E., U. Va., 1952; Ph.D. in Physics, 1954; E.E. (hon.), Washington U., 1932. Registered profl. engr. Va. Instr. AAF Tech. Sch., Rantoul, Ill., 1940-42; aeronautical engr. NASA, Langley Field, Va., 1946-51; prof. physics U. Va., Charlottesville, 1948-75; phys. scientist U.S. Army Charlottesville, 1975—; cons. Philip-Morris Research Ctr., Richmond, Va., 1948-75, Old Dominion Mfg. Co., Culpeper, Va., 1969-82. Patentee in field. Mem. Presdl. Task Force, Washington, 1985. Served to maj. U.S. Army, 1942-46. Mem. IEEE (chmn. central Va. sect. 1968), Sigma Xi. Avocation: personal computers.

HARRIS, PATRICK BRADLEY, real estate broker, state legislator; b. Mount Carmel, S.C., Apr. 19, 1911; s. Calhoun and Frances (Morrah) H.; m. Elizabeth Orr, July 30, 1936; 1 child, Patrick Bradley. Student Presbyterian Coll. Real estate broker, v.p. Real Estate div. Exec. Services and Planning, Inc.; owner, pres. Harris Beltane Gas Co., 1948-63; mem. S.C. Ho. of Reps., 1969—, chmn. joint appropriations rev. com., ethics com. Mem. Anderson City Council, 1964-66; chmn. S.C. Appalachian Council Govts.; chmn. local bd. SSS, 1960-68; pres. Am. Cancer Soc., 1965; chmn. ARC; chmn. govt. div. United Fund; mem. exec. com. Anderson County Democratic Com. Mem. S.C. Liquified Petroleum Gas Assn. (former v.p.), Anderson Bd. Realtors (chmn. annexation com. 1963). Lodge: Elks. Office: Box 655 Anderson SC 29621*

HARRIS, PAULETTE PROCTOR, educator; b. Augusta, Ga., Oct. 5, 1949; d. Paul Eugene and Ilma Hankinson Proctor; B.A., Augusta Coll., 1971, M.Ed., 1974; Ed.D., U. S.C., 1983; m. Kenneth Harris, Dec. 22, 1968. Elem. tchr. pub. schs., Augusta, 1971-73, remedial reading instr., 1973-76, instructional lead tchr., 1976-78; mem. faculty Sch. Edn., Augusta Coll., 1978—. Vol., Multiple Schlerosis Soc., Am. Cancer Soc., Leukemia Soc. Am. Named Elem. Tchr. of Yr., Houghton Elem. Sch., 1974. Mem. Internat. Reading Assn., Assn. Supervision and Curriculum Devel., AAUW, Nat. Council Tchrs. English, Assn. Childhood Edn. Internat., Am. Ednl. Research Assn., Augusta Coll. Alumni Assn., U. S.C. Alumni Assn., CSRA Reading Council (pres. 1985), Delta Kappa Gamma, Phi Delta Kappa (area research award 1984). Home: 3033 Park Ave Augusta GA 30909 Office: Sch Edn Augusta Coll 2500 Walton Way Augusta GA 30910

HARRIS, RACHEL JOAN, psychotherapist, psychological researcher; b. Camden, N.J., Dec. 2, 1946; d. David Paul and Rita S. (Schiff) H.; m. Brian T. Logan, Sept. 15, 1979; 1 child, Ashley Harris. B.A., Boston U., 1968; M.S.W., Barry U., 1975; Ph.D., Union Grad. Sch., 1977. Lic. psychologist, Fla. Psychol. researcher VA Med. Ctr., Miami, Fla., 1975-82; adj. asst. prof. psychiatry U. Miami Sch. Medicine, 1978—; pvt. practice as psychotherapist, Miami, 1975—; cons. Eckerd Coll., Miami, 1983—; leader profl. tng. workshops, 1970—. Editor Dance Therapy - Theory, Research, Practice Jour., 1979-81. Contbr. chpts. to books, articles to profl. jours. Recipient New Investigator's award NIH, 1979-82; Esalen Inst. fellow, 1968-69. Mem. Am. Psychol. Assn., Am. Dance Therapy Assn., Soc. for Psychotherapy Research, Am. Soc. for Psychosomatic Obstetrics Gynecology, Assn. for Humanistic Psychology, Mental Health Assn., Zool. Soc., Mus. Sci., Youth Mus. Art. Democrat. Club: Grove Isle. Avocations: sailing; reading. Home: 327 SW 29th Rd Miami FL 33129 Office: 1550 S Dixie Hwy Suite 214 Coral Gables FL 33146

HARRIS, R(ANSOM) BAINE, philosophy educator, association executive; b. Hudson, N.C., June 5, 1927; s. Ransom Z. and Hettie L. (Crouch) H.; m. Ettie Jeanne Johnson, June 8, 1958; 2 children. A.A., Mars Hill Coll., 1946; B.A., U. Richmond, 1948, M.A., 1954; B.D., So. Baptist Theol. Sem., 1951; M.A., Emory U., 1960; Ph.D., Temple U., 1971. Instr. philosophy U. Richmond (Va.) 1953-54; instr. philosophy and social scis. Ga. Inst. Tech., 1956-60; prof. philosophy, chmn. Frederick Coll., 1960-65; asst. prof. Clemson U., 1965-70; prof., chmn. Eastern Ky. U., 1970-73; prof. Old Dominion U., Norfolk, Va., 1973—, chmn., 1973-79, eminent prof., 1981—; organizer, dir. nat. and internat. confs.; dir., host TV series. Grantee Eli Lilly Found., 1971, Dept. State, 1974-75. Mem. Am. Philos. Assn., Va. Philos. Assn., Hellenic Soc. Philos. Studies, Indian Philos. Soc., Metaphys. Soc. Am., Internat. Soc. for Neoplatonic Studies (founder, exec. dir. 1973—), So. Soc. Philosophy and Psychology, Soc. Philosophy of Religion, Soc. Study History of Philosophy. Democrat. Editor: Authority: A Philosophical Analysis, 1976; The Significance of Neoplatonism, 1976; Neoplatonism and Indian Thought, 1981, The Structure of Being: A Neoplatonic Approach, 1981; gen. editor: (series) Studies in Neoplatonism: Ancient and Modern; contbr. articles to profl. jours. Home: 4037 Windymille Dr Portsmouth VA 23703 Office: Dept Philosphy Old Dominion Univ Norfolk VA 23508

HARRIS, RICHARD FOSTER, JR., insurance company executive; b. Athens, Ga., Feb. 8, 1918; s. Richard Foster and Mai Audli (Chandler) H.; B.C.S., U. Ga., 1939; m. Virginia McCurdy, Aug. 21, 1937 (div.); children—Richard Foster, Gaye Karyl Harris Law; m. Kari Melandso, Dec. 29, 1962. C.L.U. Bookkeeper, salesman 1st Nat. Bank, Atlanta, 1936-40; agt. Vol. State Life Ins. Co., Atlanta, 1940-41; asst. mgr. N.Y. Life Ins. Co., Atlanta and Charlotte, N.C., 1941-44; mgr., agt. Pilot Life Ins. Co., Charlotte and Houston, 1944-63; mgr., agt., bus. planning div.; city agy. Am. Gen. Life Ins. Co., Houston, 1963—; dir. Fidelity Bank & Trust Co., Houston, 1965-66. Contbr. articles to profl. jours. Chmn. fund drive Am. Heart Assn., Charlotte, Mecklenburg County, 1958-59, chmn. bd., 1959-61; gen. chmn. Shrine Bowl Promotion, Charlotte Shriners, 1955; v.p., dir. Myers Park Meth. Ch. Men's Class, 1956-59, bd. stewards, Charlotte, 1959-61; charter mem. Republican Presdl. Task Force; bd. dirs. Houpac; co-chmn. fundraising, bd. dirs. Christian Community Service Ctr., Houston. Recipient Pres.'s Cabinet award Am. Gen. Life Ins. Co., 1964-67, 69, 71, 77, 78, 79, 80, 81, Disting. Salesman award Charlotte Sales Exec. Club, 1955, 57-59, Bronze Medallion award Am. Heart Assn., 1959, Nat. Quality award Life Ins. Agency Mgmt. Assn. and Nat. Assn. Life Underwriters, 1976-85. Mem. Assn. Advanced Life Underwriters, Am. Soc. C.L.U.s, Nat. Assn. Life Underwriters, SAR (sec. chpt. 5, Tex. Soc. 1974—, v.p., dir.), Sertoma Internat. (life, v.p., dir. Charlotte chpt.), Life Underwriters Polit. Action Com., Ky. Cols., Houston Estate and Fin. Forum, English Speaking Union, Mensa Internat., Houston Assn. Life Underwriters, Lone Star Leaders Club, Tex. Leader's Round Table (life), Million Dollar Round Table, Tex. Assn. Life Underwriters, Am. Security Council (nat. adv. bd. 1979—), Tex. Crime Prevention Assn., Nat. Platform Assn., Com. of 300, Pi Kappa Phi. Republican. Episcopalian. Clubs: Warwick, Napoleon, 100, Kiwanis (dir. 1979—), Houston Knife and Fork, Masons (32 deg.), Heritage (charter), Circle R of Tex., Congressional, Shriners, Royal Order of Jesters. Home: 2701 Westheimer Rd Houston TX 77098 also Dunbar Ln Sea Island GA 31561 Office: Am Gen Bldg 2727 Allen Parkway Suite 500 Houston TX 77019

HARRIS, RICHARD JOHN, sociology educator; b. Belgrade, Minn., Apr. 5, 1948; s. John Lee and Marjorie Lorraine (Meyers) H.; m. Carolyn Anne Besser, June 26, 1970; children—Karl Besser, Mark Besser. B.A., Macalester Coll., 1971; M.A., Cornell U., 1974, Ph.D., 1976. Asst. prof. sociology U. Tex., San Antonio, 1976-80; asst. prof., 1982-84, assoc. prof., 1984—; post-doctoral fellow, lectr. sociology U. So. Calif., Los Angeles, 1980-82; researcher in field. Served with USAFR, 1970-73. Nat. Inst. Child Health and Human Devel. trainee, 1973-75. Mem. Am. Sociol. Assn., Population Assn. Am., So. Sociology Assn., S.W. Sociology Assn. Co-editor: The Politics of San Antonio: Community Progress and Power, 1983; contbr. articles to profl. jours. Home: 701 State Rock San Antonio TX 78232 Office: Div Social and Policy Scis U Tex San Antonio TX 78285

HARRIS, RICHARD MICHAEL, electronic systems engineer; b. Balt., Nov. 22, 1941; s. Richard Elmer and Alice Alden (Hartline) H.; B.S.E.E., MIT, 1963, S.M.E.E. in Ops. Research, 1965; Ph.D. in Engring.-Econ. Systems, Stanford U., 1972; m. Carole Stallings, Dec. 28, 1963; children—Michael, David, Susan, Catherine, Paul. Instr., M.I.T., 1963-65; cons. celestial nav. Jet Propulsion Lab., Calif. Inst. Tech., Pasadena, 1963-65; tech. staff air transp. systems The MITRE Corp., McLean, Va., 1968-71, group leader advanced airport systems, 1972-74, asso. dept. head systems planning, 1975-78, dept. head advanced systems, 1979-81, dept. head advanced air traffic control automation systems engring., 1981-82, assoc. tech. dir. naval systems engring., 1983-84, tech. dir., 1984—; seminar lectr. Served to lt. USNR, 1965-67. Ford Found. fellow, 1967-68; MITRE fellow, 1969-71. Assoc. fellow AIAA; mem. Planetary Soc., Armed Forces Communications Electronics Assn., Navy League, Sigma Xi, Tau Beta Pi, Eta Kappa Nu, Beta Theta Pi. Contbr. articles to profl. jours. Home: 2038 Freedom Ln Falls Church VA 22043 Office: 1820 Dolley Madison Blvd McLean VA 22102

HARRIS, ROBERT L., welding engineer; b. Plattsburgh, N.Y., May 1, 1927; s. Platt John and Nora Mary (Trombley) H.; m. Nannette Ellen Hollister, Sept.

26, 1948; children—Nancy Elaine, Alan Robert, David Paul. Student, Rutgers U.; grad. Modern Welding Sch., Schenectady, N.Y., 1948. Welder, Alco Products Inc., Schenectady, 1948-52, Hi-Grade Welding, Amsterdam, N.Y., 1952-53; welding technician Gen. Electric Co., Schenectady, 1953-57, metallurgy specialist, 1962-64, welding devel. engr. Alco Products Inc., Schenectady, 1957-62; welding engr. Electric Boat div. Gen. Dynamics, Groton, Conn., 1964-65; supr. Combustion Engring. Inc., Chattanooga, Tenn., 1965-69; mgr. welding dept. Badenhausen Corp. div. Riley Stoker Corp., Cornwells Heights, Pa., 1969-70; staff materials engr. TVA, Knoxville, 1970-75, supr. welding engring. staff, 1975-81; mgr. nuclear quality assurance Bristol Steel & Iron Works, Va., 1975; lead welding engr. Butler Services Group Inc., Midland, Mich., 1982-83; welding quality engr. Piping Design Services, Moscow, Ohio, 1983-84; lead welding engr. So. Calif. Edison Co., San Onofre Nuclear Generating Sta., 1984—. Served to cpl. U.S. Army, 1945-46. Recipient numerous awards for profl. excellence. Mem. ASME, Am. Welding Soc. (cert. welding inspector, Dist. Meritorious award 1982), Am. Soc. Metals. Republican. Presbyterian. Club: Deane Hill Country (Knoxville). Avocations: golf; bowling. Home: 2914 B Camino Capistrano San Clemente CA 92672 Office: RL Harris Assoc Inc 708 Walker Springs Rd Knoxville TN 37923

HARRIS, RONALD BLYTHE, ophthalmologist; b. Toronto, Ont., Can., Apr. 2, 1930; s. William Wallace and Hazel Jean (Pollard) H.; m. Eileen Jennings, June 6, 1953; children—David C., Rhonda L., Andrew J. M.D., U. Toronto, 1953. Diplomate Am. Bd. Ophthalmology. Intern, Huron Rd. Hosp., East Cleveland, Ohio, 1953-54; resident in ophthalmology, Gill Meml. Hosp., Roanoke, Va., 1955-59, now sr. ophthalmologist; surg. dir. Eye Bank of Va., Roanoke. Bd. dirs. Mill Mountain Playhouse, Roanoke, 1974—. Fellow ACS; mem. AMA, Va. Med. Soc., Roanoke Acad. Medicine, Eye Bank Assn. Am. (pres. 1973). Clubs: Lions, Hunting Hills Country, Jefferson. Home: 3419 Winterberry Ln Roanoke VA 24014 Office: Gill Meml EENT Clinic 707 S Jefferson Roanoke VA 24018

HARRIS, RYLAND MICHAEL, clergyman; b. Durham, N.C., Mar. 14, 1952; s. Ryland Pett and Emogene (Gravett) H.; m. Wanda Bagbey, Aug. 15, 1971; children—Bryan Allen, Heather Lynn. B.A., Campbell Coll., 1974; M.Religious Edn., Southeastern Bapt. Theol. Sem., 1977. Ordained to ministry, Bapt. Ch., 1976. Assoc. pastor Tabernacle Bapt. Ch., Raleigh, 1985—; minister of edn. and youth First Bapt. Ch., Aberdeen, N.C., 1976-79; minister of edn. Emmanuel Bapt. Ch., Raleigh, 1980-85; Sun. sch. ch. cons. So. Bapt. Conv., Nashville, 1985—, Bapt. State Conv., Raleigh, 1976—; sr. adult cons., 1985—. Author: Depth Study of New Hope Baptist Church, Raleigh, 1974. Democrat. Lodge: Optimist (newsletter editor 1985—, chaplain 1984), Masons. Home: 3413 Cheyenne Rd Raleigh NC 27609 Office: Tabernacle Baptist Ch 118 S Person St Raleigh NC 27601

HARRIS, SIDNEY LEWIS, clergyman, sociology educator; b. Miles, Tex., Feb. 6, 1927; s. Samuel Lee and Bertha Jewell (Johnson) H.; m. Fleta Nell Lindley, June 22, 1948; children—Emily Ann, Donna Carol, Paula Karen. B.A., Howard Payne Coll., 1948; B.D., Southwest Bapt. Theol. Sem., 1952; M.A., Sam Houston State Tchrs. Coll., 1961; D.Arts, Western Colo. U., 1976. Ordained to ministry Baptist Ch., 1945. Pastor, Joshua and Austin, Tex., 1945-53; student dir., Bible tchr. Sam Houston State U., Huntsville, 1953-59; Tex. Tech. U., Lubbock, 1959-65; dean of students, instr. sociology Wayland Coll., Plainview, Tex., 1965-67; adminstrn. cons. Bapt. Sunday Sch. Bd., Nashville, 1967-68; counselor, assoc. prof. Tarrant County Jr. Coll., Fort Worth, 1968-77; pres. Clarke Coll., Newton, Miss., 1977-79; v.p. student affairs Howard Payne U., Brownwood, Tex., 1979-80, dean sch. social scis., 1980-84; assoc. pastor, counselor First Baptist Ch., Brownwood, 1984—; trustee Western Colo. U., Grand Junction, 1977-78, adv. bd., 1977-84; dir. Fort Worth Literacy Council, 1971-73. Author: Leadership Unlimited, 1969; Leadership Improvement Plan, 1968. Contbr. articles to profl. jours., chpts. to books. Mem. Mayor's Adv. Com. on Youth, Hurst, Tex., 1970-71; active in ch. and civic groups. Mem. Tex. Council on Family Relations, So. Bapt. Assn. Ministries with the Aging, Southwest Social Sci. Assn., Southwest Sociol. Assn., Tex. Bapt. Family Life Ministers Assn. Democrat. Avocation: travel.

HARRIS, STEVEN MICHAEL, lawyer, accountant; b. Miami, Fla., Feb. 27, 1952; s. Joseph Herbert and Mollye (Rinzler) H. B.B.A., U. Ga., 1973, M.Acctg., 1974; J.D., U. Miami, 1979. Bar: Fla. 1979, U.S. Dist. Ct. (so. dist.) Fla. 1979, U.S. Claims Ct. 1979, U.S. Tax Ct. 1979, U.S. Ct. Appeals (11th cir.) 1982; C.P.A., Fla. Adj. lectr. tax course Fla. Internat. U., 1976; adj. lectr. U. Miami Grad. Sch. Bus., 1978-83; assoc. Law Office of Philip T. Weinstein, Miami, 1980. Mem. ABA (com. prosecutiion and def. of criminal tax cases, criminal justice sect. 1979—; civil and criminal tax penalties, sect. taxation 1977—). Republican. Contbr. numerous articles to profl. jours. Office: PO Box 248202 Miami FL 33124

HARRIS, THOMAS MUNSON, chemistry educator, researcher; b. Niagara Falls, N.Y., May 29, 1934; s. Charles Roberts and Elizabeth Lynn (Munson) H.; m. Constance McKnight Malmar, June 7, 1958; children—Mary Elizabeth, Jennifer Lynn. B.S., U. Rochester, 1955; Ph.D., Duke U., 1959. Research chemist Union Carbide Corp., South Charleston, W.Va., 1958-61; research associate Duke U., Durham, N.C., 1961-64; asst. prof. chemistry Vanderbilt U., Nashville, 1964-67, assoc. prof., 1967-70, prof., 1970-84, Centennial prof. chemistry, 1984—, mem. Ctr. in Environ. Toxicology, 1980—, assoc. dir. Ctr. in Molecular Toxicology, 1984—; cons. Abbott Labs., North Chicago, Ill., 1981-84; vis. prof. Cambridge U., Eng., 1969-70. Contbr. articles to profl. jours. Fellow Alfred P. Sloan Found., Vanderbilt U., 1967-69, NSF, Duke U., 1956-58, USPHS spl. postdoctoral Duke U., 1963-64; recipient USPHS Research Career Devel. award, 1967-72. Mem. Am. Chem. Soc., Phi Beta Kappa, Sigma Xi. Office: Dept Chemistry Vanderbilt U Box B-1715 Nashville TN 37235

HARRIS, VINCENT MADELEY, retired bishop; b. Conroe, Tex., Oct. 14, 1913; s. George Malcolm and Margaret (Madeley) H. Student, St. Mary's Sem., La Porte, Tex., 1934; S.T.B., N.Am. Coll., Rome, 1936, J.C.B., 1939; J.C.L., Cath. U. Am., 1940; L.H.D., St. Edward's U., Austin, Tex., 1982. Ordained priest Roman Catholic Ch., 1938; prof. St. Mary's Sem., 1940-51; chancellor Diocese Galveston-Houston, 1948-66, diocesan consultor, 1951-66; domestic prelate, 1956, bishop of Beaumont (Tex.), 1966-71, coadjutor bishop of Austin (Tex.), 1971-86, bishop, 1971. Decorated knight grand cross Equestrian Order Holy Sepulchre Jerusalem. Mem. Sons Republic of Tex. Club: K.C. (chaplain Tex. 1967-69). Address: 8900 Glencrest 7307 Houston TX 77061

HARRIS, WALKER HALL, JR., insurance company executive; b. Rutherfordton, N.C., Sept. 17, 1921; s. Walker H. and Ann M. (Walker) H.; m. Bernice Juanita Dorsey, Apr. 17, 1949; 1 son, Walker H., III. B.S. in Commerce, U. N.C., 1947. Buyer Sears, Roebuck & Co., Greensboro, N.C., 1947-49; with G. B. Harrill Agy., Forest City, N.C., 1949—, sec., treas., 1954-67, sr. v.p., 1967-75, pres., 1975—, also dir.; asst. v.p. Iowa Mut. Ins. Co., Dewitt, 1975—. Served with U.S. Army, 1943-46; ETO. Mem. Carolina Assn. Profl. Ins. Agts., Ind. Ins. Agts. N.C. Democrat. Methodist (bd. stewards, treas.). Home: 208 Knollwood Dr Forest City NC 28043 Office: Allendale Dr Forest City NC 28043

HARRIS, WILLIAM BURLEIGH, geologist, educator; b. Norfolk, Va., July 2, 1943; s. Roy Solomon and Emily (Kasey) H.; B.S. in Geology, Campbell U., 1966; M.S. in Geology, W.Va. U., 1968; Ph.D. in Geology, U. N.C., Chapel Hill, 1975; m. Sharon Jones, Aug. 25, 1965; children—Daniel Wyatt, Timothy Roy. Petroleum geologist Texaco, Inc., Tulsa, 1968-70; econ. geologist Va. Div. Mineral Resources, Charlottesville, 1970-72; asst. prof. geology U. N.C., Wilmington, 1976-81, assoc. prof., 1981-82; research specialist Exxon Prodn. Research Co., Houston, 1982-83; prof. geology U. N.C., Wilmington, 1984—; cons. DuPont-Savannah River Lab., 1978, 79, ARCO Resources Tech., 1985. N.C. Bd. Sci. and Tech. grantee, 1976-77. Mem. Am. Assn. Petroleum Geologists, Carolina Geol. Soc., Geol. Soc. Am., Soc. Econ. Paleontologists and Mineralogists, Sigma Xi, Sigma Gamma Epsilon. Presbyterian. Contbr. articles to profl. jours. Home: 330 Tanbridge Rd Wilmington NC 28405

HARRIS, WILLIAM M., planning educator, consultant; b. Richmond, Va., Oct. 29, 1941; s. Rosa M. (Minor) H.; m. Catherine Elizabeth Branch; children—Rolisa C., Dana D., William M. B.S., Howard U. 1964; M. Urban Planning, U. Wash., Seattle, 1972, Ph.D., 1974. Physicist AEC, Richland, Wash., 1968-70; research fellow Battelle Seattle, 1970-73; asst. prof. Western Wash. State U., Bellingham, 1973-74, Portland State U., Oreg., 1974-76; assoc. prof. urban planning U. Va., Charlottesville, 1976—; tech. advisor Mennonite Econ. Devel. Project, Chgo., 1982-85; chmn. Indsl. Devel. Authority, Charlottesville, 1983-85. Narrator: (movie) Blacks in Oregon, 1975. Author: Black Community Development, 1976. Site reviewer Planning Adv. Bd., Washington, 1985; bd. dirs. Charlottesville Mediation Ctr., 1985. Recipient Community Service award Albina Lions Club, 1975; vis. scholar Cornell U., 1985. Mem. Am. Inst. Cert. Planners, Am. Planning Assn. (editorial bd. jour. 1985), Assn. Study Afro-Am. Life and History, Community Devel. Soc. (pres. Va. chpt. 1983-84), Assn. Voluntary Action Scholars. Episcopalian. Club: Charlottesville Anglers (bd. dirs. 1984). Lodge: Masons. Avocations: handball; reading. Office: U Va Campbell Hall Charlottesville VA 22903

HARRIS, WILLIE GRAY, JR., religious educator; b. Carthage, N.C., May 25, 1945; s. Willie Gray and Fonnie Ann (Blake) H.; m. Joyce Louise Shipley, Mar. 24, 1948; 1 dau., Heather. B.A., High Point Coll., 1967; M.Div., Southeastern Bapt. Theol. Seminary, 1967-70, Th.M., 1972. Mem. faculty Sandhills Community Coll., Carthage, N.C., 1972—, prof. religion, 1975—; asst. area supr. Tel Batash Archael. Excavation, Israel, 1978, 79, 83. Recipient Hays-Fulbright award U.S. Dept. Edn., 1980; Nat. Endowment Humanities Summer Seminar award Rutgers U., 1982. Mem. Soc. Bibl. Lit., Am. Acad. Religion, Community Coll. Humanities Assn., Bibl. Archeology Soc., N.C. Family Life Council. Republican. Baptist. Home: Route 2 Box 48 West End NC 27376 Office: Route 3 Box 182-C (TC-5) Carthage NC 28327

HARRIS-OFFUTT, ROSALYN MARIE, counselor, therapist, nurse, anesthetist; b. Memphis; d. Roscoe Henry and Irene Elnora (Blake) Harris; 1 child, Christopher Joseph. R.N., St. Joseph Catholic Sch. Nursing, Flint, Mich., 1965; cert. in anesthesia Hurley Med. Ctr., Flint, 1969; B.S. in Wholistic Health Scis., Columbia-Pacific U., 1984, postgrad., 1985—. Nat. cert. counselor. Staff nurse anesthetist, clin. instr. Cleve. Clinic Found., 1981-82; pvt. practice psychiat. nursing and counseling; Assoc. Counselor in Human Services, Shaker Heights, Ohio, 1982-84; ind. contractor anesthesia Paul Scott & Assocs., Cleve., 1984, Via Triad Anesthesia Assocs., Thomasville, N.C., 1984—; sec. Cons., Psychology and Counseling, P.A., pvt. practice psychiat. nursing and counseling, Greensboro, N.C., 1984—. Co-sponsor adolescent group Jack and Jills of Am., Inc., Bloomfield Hills, Mich., 1975; co-sponsor Youth of Unity Ctr., Cleveland Heights, Ohio, 1982-84; vol. chmn. hospitality Old Greensboro Preservation Soc., 1985; bd. dirs. Urban League, Pontiac, Mich., 1972. Columbia-Pacific U. scholar, 1983. Fellow Soc. Preventitive Nutritionists; mem. Am. Assn. Profl. Hypnotherapists (registered profl. hypnotherapists, adv. bd.), Am. Assn. Nurse Anesthetists (cert.), Am. Assn. Counseling and Devel., Am. Assn. Clin. Hypnotists, Am. Assn. Wholistic Practitioners, Negro Bus. and Profl. Women Inc. (v.p., parliamentarian 1961-83), Oakland County Council Black Nurses (v.p. 1970-74). Mem. Unity Ch. Avocations: music; nature; reading; Egyptian history; metaphysics. Office: Cons Psychology & Counseling P A 1007 N Elm Suite D Greensboro NC 27401

HARRISON, AIX BARNARD, physiology of exercise educator; b. Zearing, Iowa, Feb. 14, 1925; s. J. Rollin and Anna (Barnard) H.; m. Gwen Adair Laufer, Jan. 7, 1950; children—George Andrew, Nancy Ann. B.S., U. Ill., 1949, M.S., 1950; Ph.D., Mich. State U., 1959. Tchr. phys. edn., coach Community Schs., Galva, Ill., 1949-50; asst. prof. Okla. A&M Coll., Stillwater, 1950-58; assoc. prof. Okla. State U., Stillwater, 1959-68; prof., program dir. Health and Fitness Ctr., Okla. State U., 1968—. Contbr. articles to profl. jours. Served to 2d lt. USAF, 1942-45, PTO. Recipient Cert. of Meritorous Service, ARC, 1968, Honor award Okla. Assn. Health, Phys. Edn., Recreation, Dance, 1971. Fellow Am. Coll. Sports Medicine (program dir.) (life); mem. AAHPER and Dance (life), Am. Coll. Sports Medicine (pres. Central States chpt. 1975-76), Sigma Xi (life, sec. chpt. 1977-79). Republican. Methodist. Lodges: Masons (master 1970-71, grand high priest 1970). Home: 2135 W University St Stillwater OK 74074 Office: Okla State U PEC 103 Stillwater OK 74078

HARRISON, BETTY CAROLYN COOK, vocational teacher educator and administrator; b. Cale, Ark., Jan. 11, 1939; d. Denver G. and Minnie (Haddox) Cook; m. David B. Harrison, Dec. 31, 1956; children—Jerry David, Phyllis Lynley. B.S.E., Henderson State Tchrs. Coll., Arkadelphia, Ark., 1959; M.S., U. Ark., 1971; Ph.D., Tex. A&M U., 1975. Tchr. secondary schs., McCrory, Ark., 1962-64, Taylor, Ark., 1964-69, Shongaloo, La., 1969-73, Minden, La., 1974-76, 77-80; cooperating tchr., supr. student tchrs. Grambling State U. (La.), 1974-76, La. Tech. U., Ruston, La., 1974-76, 78-80; asst. prof. vocat. edn. Va. Poly. Inst. and State U., Blacksburg, 1976-77; asst. prof. vocat. edn. Coll. Agr., La. State U., Baton Rouge, 1980—, head dept. home econs. edn. and bus. edn. Sch. Vocat. Edn. and Tech. HEW fellow, 1973; grantee: Future Homemakers Am., 1956, Coll. Academics, 1956, Ark. Edn. Assn., 1956-69, Internat. Paper Co., 1966-68, La. Dept. Edn., 1972. Mem. Am. Home Econs. Assn., La. Home Econs. Assn. (bd. dirs., pres.-elect), La. Vocat. Assn. (bd. dirs.), La. Assn. Vocat. Home Econs. Tchrs. (pres.), Nat. Assn. Vocat. Home Econs. Tchrs., Nat. Assn. Vocat. Home Econs. Tchr. Educators, Home Econs. Edn. Assn. (regional dir., nat. v.p.), NEA (nat. assembly del.), Family Relations Council La. (edn. chmn. officer), Phi Delta Kappa, Delta Kappa Gamma, Gamma Sigma Delta. Contbr. articles to profl. jours. Democrat. Baptist. Home: 2100 College Dr #157 Baton Rouge LA 70808 Office: Sch Vocat Edn and Technology La State U Baton Rouge LA 70803

HARRISON, CHRISTOPHER GEORGE ALICK, geophysicist, educator; b. Oxford, Eng., Dec. 29, 1936; s. Alick Robin Walsham and Margaret Edith (Ross) H.; m. Martha Helen Raitt, Mar. 21, 1964; children—Ewen Jeremy, Susannah Ariel. B.A., Cambridge U., 1960, M.A., 1964, Ph.D., 1966. Postgrad. research geophysicist Scripps Instn. Oceanography, U. Calif., 1961-67; asst. prof. Rosenstiel Sch. Marine and Atmospheric Sci., U. Miami, 1967-68, assoc. prof., 1968-74, prof., 1974—, chmn. div. marine geology and geophysics, 1976-83; scientist, chief scientist Sci. Research Cruises in Atlantic, Pacific and Indian Oceans, 1961. Served to lt., Corps Royal Engrs., Brit. Army, 1955-57. Marlborough Coll. sr. scholar, 1953-55; scholar Peterhouse, Cambridge U., 1957-60. Fellow Royal Astron. Soc.; mem. Am. Geophys. Union (chmn. publs. com. 1978-80, chmn. budget and fin. com. 1980-84). Editor various books; editor Earth and Planetary Sci. Letters, 1978—. Home: 3851 Braganza Ave Miami FL 33133 Office: Rosenstiel Sch Marine and Atmospheric Sci 4600 Rickenbacker Causeway Miami FL 33149

HARRISON, CLARENCE BUFORD, JR., oil co. exec., lawyer; b. Dallas, Sept. 27, 1944; s. Clarence Buford and Clara Janie (Jones); m. Kate Butler, July 19, 1969; children—Amy Elizabeth, Patrick Buford, Amanda Mae. B.B.A. in Fin., U. Tex.-Austin, 1967; J.D., U. Tex., 1970. Bar: Tex. 1970. Tax staff Touche Ross & Co., Dallas, 1970-71; assoc. Diamond Goodner Winkle, Wells & Harrison, Dallas, 1971-72; gen. counsel, gen. mgr., dir. Scoggins Petroleum Corp., Dallas, 1972-75; pres. Interam. Oil & Minerals Inc., successor corp., 1981—; ptnr. firm Harrison Vernon & Clark, Dallas, 1975—; speaker profl. seminars including Tri State Oil & Gas, Ind., Ill., Ky., Ind. Oil Producers. Roman Catholic. Club: Dallas Petroleum, University, Canyon Creek Country (Dallas). Home: 1138 Wilderness Trail Richardson TX 75080 Office: 6606 Lyndon B Johnson Freeway Suite 5135 Dallas TX 75240

HARRISON, DOROTHY GORDY, data processing executive; b. Jan. 1, 1939; m. Frank R. Harrison, III, Sept. 10, 1966. B.A. in Chemistry, U. N.C.-Greensboro, 1960; Cert. Info. Sci., Ga. Inst. Tech., 1962, M.S. in Info./Computer Sci., 1965; Cert. Physics, Math., Wake Forest U., 1964; M.Ln. in Info. Systems Adminstrn., Emory U., 1973. Tech. writer, dir. Tech. Library and Info. Services Cone Mills Research and Devel., Greensboro, N.C., 1960-63; chmn. physics dept. Pittsfield High Sch., Mass., 1964; research asst. Price Gilbert Meml. Library Ga. Inst. Tech., Atlanta, 1964-66, research asst. Engring. Expt. Sta., 1965-66; research assoc. Sch. Info. and Computer Sci., 1967; info. scientist, projects dir. Office Computing Activities U. Ga., Athens, 1971-73; cons. computer sci., info. systems and adminstrn., 1962—; dir. Computer Ctr., Clarke County Bd. Commns., 1983—. NSF scholar, 1965-66, fellow 1964-65, grantee summer 1964; recipient Univ. stipend 1973, assistantship 1968-69, Recording for the Blind citation, 1968, 69, 70, Young Info./Computer Scientist award, 1969; Outstanding Tchr. award, 1964; named Young Woman Engr. Yr., 1964. Mem. Beta Phi Mu, active mem. in various local, state, regional and nat. orgns. of computer users and data processing mgrs. Office: PO Box 448 Courthouse Athens GA 30603

HARRISON, EDWARD MATTHEW, industrial educator; b. Baton Rouge, La., Mar. 19, 1943; s. Nicholas Samuel and Sadie (Kelly) H.; m. Natalie Marie Ricard, Aug. 7, 1976. B.S., So. U., 1965, M.Ed., 1970; Ph.D., Kans. State U., 1977; postgrad. Harvard U., 1984. Tchr., Houston Sch. System, 1965, Buena Vista Sch. Dist., Saginaw, Mich., 1965-72; asst. prof. indsl. edn. So. U., Baton Rouge, 1972-80; assoc. prof., head dept. indsl. tech., Grambling State U., La., 1980—, dir. vocat. edn. and indsl. arts, 1980—, dir. Title III activity IV, 1982—. Mem. Am. Vocat. Assn., Am. Indsl. Arts Assn., Nat. Assn. Indsl. Tech., Am. Council on Indsl. Arts Tchr. Edn., Phi Delta Kappa., Phi Beta Sigma. Democrat. Baptist. Lodge: Lions (treas. 1982-84). Avocations: sports cars; fishing; reading; wood and plastic crafts. Home: PO Box 228 Grambling LA 71245 Office: Grambling State U Dept Indsl Tech PO Box 34 Grambling LA 71245

HARRISON, FRANK, retired university president; b. Dallas, Nov. 21, 1913; s. Frank and Ruby (Davison) H.; m. Elsie Claire Redfearn, June 26, 1946; children—Frank, Susan Claire, James Redfearn. B.S., So. Methodist U., 1935; M.S., Northwestern U., 1936, Ph.D., 1938; M.D., U. Tex. Southwestern Med. Sch., 1956. Mem. faculty U. Tenn. med. units, Memphis, 1938-51, prof., 1946-51, chief div. anatomy, 1946-51; prof. anatomy U. Tex. Southwestern Med. Sch., Dallas, 1952-68, asso. dean, 1956-68; asso. dean grad. studies U. Tex. at Arlington, 1965-68, acting pres., 1968-69, pres., 1969-72, Health Sci. Center, San Antonio, 1972-85, dir. Inst. of Bacteriology, 1985. Named Distinguished Alumnus So. Meth. U., 1971. Mem. Am. Assn. Anatomists, Am. Physiol. Soc., Tex. Philos. Soc., Biophys. Soc., IEEE, Soc. Exptl. Biology and Medicine, Phi Beta Kappa, Alpha Omega Alpha, Kappa Sigma, Alpha Kappa Kappa. Home: 4168 Valley Ridge Dallas TX 75220

HARRISON, FRANK RUSSELL, III, educator; b. Jacksonville, Fla., Mar. 11, 1935; s. Frank Russell, Jr. and Annye Mae (Blackwelder) H.; B.A. in Philosophy with honors and optime merens, U. of South, Sewanee, Tenn., 1957; M.A., U. Va., 1959, Ph.D., 1961; m. Dorothy Louise Gordy, Sept. 10, 1966. Grad. asst. U. Va., 1958-61; instr. philosophy Roanoke Coll., Salem, Va., 1961-62; mem. faculty U. Ga., Athens, 1962—, prof. philosophy, 1972—, Sandy Beaver disting. prof., 1985—; vis. prof. U. N.C., Chapel Hill, summer 1963, Emory U., summer 1965, Sch. Info. and Computer Sci., Ga. Inst. Tech., 1965-66, U. Keele, Eng., 1984. Mem. nat. bd. examining chaplains Episcopal Ch., 1974-78. Mem. Ga., Am. philos. assns., Soc. Philosophy Religion (pres. 1984-85), So. Soc. Philosophy and Psychology (chmn. program com. 1973, sect. chmn. 1965, 74, 75, 76, 78, council 1973-75), Metaphys. Soc. Am., Am. Guild Scholars (pres. 1968-69), Soc. Christian Philosophers (chmn. planning com. Eastern div. 1985—), AAAS, Gridiron Secret Soc., Phi Kappa Phi, Phi Sigma Tau. Lodges: Rotary, Torch. Author: Deductive Logic and Descriptive Language, 1969; also monographs, articles, chpts. in books; mng. editor Internat. Jour. Philosophy Religion, 1972—. Office: Dept Philosophy Univ Ga Athens GA 30602

HARRISON, GAYLE DELOACH, civic worker, counselor, elementary educator; b. Madison Co., Tenn., Jan. 22, 1940; d. William R. and Maxine (Simmons) DeLoach; m. Nelson C. Harrison, Jr., Dec. 27, 1964; children—Nelson C. III, Paul Hunter, Edward Hayden. B.S., Lambuth Coll., 1962; M.S. magna cum laude, Memphis State U., 1985. Cert. elem. tchr., Tenn. Tchr. Memphis City Schs., 1962-69. Chmn. West Tenn. Strawberry Festival Judges Luncheon, Humboldt, Tenn., 1973-78, West Tenn. Strawberry Festival Territorial Queens, 1979-84; sec. Humboldt Planning Commn., 1979-81; mem. Humboldt City Sch. Bd., 1981-84. Recipient PTO Courageous Devotion award Humboldt Elem. Sch. PTO, 1985; mem. Tenn.'s Outstanding Sch. Bd. of Yr., Tenn. Sch. Bd. Assn., 1983. Mem. Am. Assn. Counseling Devel., Phi Delta Kappa. Republican. Methodist. Avocations: interior design; golf; bridge. Home: 2400 LaLatta Ln Humboldt TN 38343

HARRISON, JANET ELAYNE, nurse; b. Pensacola, Fla., Aug. 29, 1954; d. Palmer Luzon and Betty Mae (Mimms) Singletary; m. Byron Lee Harrison, May 1, 1982. Diploma, Ida V. Moffett Sch. Nursing, 1974. R.N., Ala., S.C., Fla. Staff nurse surg. floor Bapt. Med. Ctr.-Princeton, Birmingham, Ala., 1974-77; staff nurse pediatric unit West Fla. Hosp., Pensacola, 1977; staff nurse renal dialysis unit U. Ala., Birmingham, 1977-79, Bapt. Med. Ctr., Birmingham, 1979-80; staff nurse med. ICU, Bapt. Med. Ctr., Birmingham, 1980, 82; head nurse Low Country Dialysis Facility, Beaufort, S.C., 1980-81; health profl. affiliate Drs. Renneker and McCutchen, P.C., Birmingham, 1982-83. Methodist.

HARRISON, JOHN EDWARDS, lawyer, real estate executive; b. Arlington, Va., Aug. 15, 1946; s. Hunter Creycroft and Margaret (Edwards) H.; m. Sally Hart Jones, July 23, 1969; children—Lucy Love, Sally Hart. Student U. N.C., 1964-66; B.S. in Fgn. Service, Georgetown U., 1971; J.D., George Washington U., 1977. Bar: Va. 1977, U.S. Ct. Appeals (4th cir.) 1977, D.C. 1980, U.S. Ct. Appeals (D.C. cir.). Assoc. Tolbert, Smith Fitzgerald & Ramsey, Arlington, 1977-79, Melrod, Redman & Gartlan, Washington, 1979-81; ptnr. Light & Harrison, P.C., McLean, Va., 1981—; chmn. bd. George H. Rucker Realty, Arlington, 1981—, McLean Fin. Corp., 1981—; dir. McLean Savs. and Loan. Served to Capt. U.S. Army, 1966-69, Vietnam. Decorated Silver Star, Bronze Star with V and cluster, Purple Heart. Mem. ABA, Va. Bar Assn., Nat. Assn. Trial Lawyers, D.C. Bar Assn., Nat. Assn. Realtors. Episcopalian. Clubs: Army Navy (Washington); Farmington Country (Charlottesville, Va.). Home: 6341 Georgetown Pike McLean VA 22101 Office: Light & Harrison PC 6849 Old Dominion Dr McLean VA 22101

HARRISON, JOSEPH ROBERT, JR., private investor; b. Chgo., June 20, 1918; s. Joseph Robert and Catherine Marie (Kohl) H.; m. Jane Anne Lucke, Sept. 22, 1962 (div. Sept. 1963); 1 son, Joseph Robert, III; m. 2d, Patricia Corinne Fuller, Oct. 12, 1968; children—James Fuller, Catherine Merle. B.A., Wabash Coll., Crawfordsville, Ind., 1940; postgrad. U. Chgo., 1940-42. Dir. Applied Dynamics, Inc., Ann Arbor, Mich., 1961-68, Trion Instruments, Inc., Ann Arbor, 1961-62, Coconut Grove Bank, Miami, 1970-75, Perceptics, Inc., Knoxville, Tenn., 1983—. Bd. editors U. Chgo. Law Rev., 1942. Trustee Met. Mus. and Art Ctr., Miami, 1970—, pres., 1974-77, chmn., 1976-79; bd. dirs. Dade Heritage Trust, Miami, 1972-75; bd. dirs. Fla. Philharm., Miami, 1976, Vizcayans, Miami, 1974-77; councillor Dade County Council of Arts and Scis., Miami, 1976-78. bd. patrons Greater Miami Opera, 1977—; mem. Com. of 100, Miami Beach, Fla. Served with USN, 1942-45. Mem. Am. Assn. Mus. Trustees, Phi Delta Phi, Phi Beta Kappa. Republican. Clubs: Bath (gov. 1974-77, 80-82); Miami, Coral Reef Yacht, Riviera Country (Miami); University (Chgo.). Home: 3120 Munroe Dr Miami FL 33133

HARRISON, LARRY RAY, allied health educator, consultant; b. Elkhart, Ind., Aug. 18, 1944; s. John Edward and Ruth Romaine (Mann) H.; m. Nellanne Williams, May 16, 1970; children—Michael Scott, Bethanne. B.S.N., Ind. U., 1973. R.N., cert. emergency nurse. Paramedic program coordinator Aultman Hosp., Canton, Ohio, 1976-79; dir. EMT-Paramedic programs Marshall U., Huntington, W.Va., 1979-82; dir. emergency med. tech. programs Jackson (Tenn.) State Community Coll., 1982—; cons. EMS. Served with U.S. Army, 1964-67; served to 1st lt. USAF, 1974-75. Mem. Nat. Assn. Emergency Med. Technicians, Emergency Dept. Nurses Assn. Office: Jackson State Community Coll 2046 N Parkway Jackson TN 38301

HARRISON, RICHARD, diversified company executive; b. Salt Lake City, 1923. Grad., Stanford U., 1946, U. Mich., 1949. Mgr. Okla. div. Fleming Cos. Inc., Oklahoma City, 1953-57, v.p., 1957-64, prof., 1964-66, chief exec. officer, 1966-82, chmn. bd., chief exec. officer, 1982—, also dir.; dir. The Quaker Oats Co., The Coleman Co. Inc., First Nat. Bank. Office: Fleming Cos Inc 6601 N Broadway St Oklahoma City OK 73126*

HARRISON, WILLIAM EARL, petroleum geochemist; b. Galveston, Tex., Apr. 7, 1942; s. Thomas Otto and Macie Beatrice (Clark) H.; children—William Scott, Joy Nicole. B.S. in Geology, Lamar U., 1966; M.S., U. Okla., 1968; Ph.D., La. State U., 1976. Exploration geologist Shell Oil, Houston, 1968-71; sr. research geologist Atlantic Richfield, Dallas, 1974-76; petroleum geologist, geochemist U. Okla., Norman, 1976-84; research dir. Atlantic Richfield, Plano, Tex., 1984—; Klapzuba prof. U. Okla., Norman, 1982-83; cons. in field. Contbr. articles to profl. jours. Recipient numerous grants. Mem. Am. Assn. Petroleum Geologists, Am. Inst. Profl. Geologists (pres. 1983), Geochem. Soc., Soc. Econ. Paleontologists and Mineralogists. Avocations: antiques, art, tennis. Home: 804 Thoreau Ln Allen TX 75002 Office: Arco Exploration & Tech 2300 W Plano Pkwy Plano TX 75075

HARRISON, WILLIAM GRADY, retail executive; b. Thomasville, Ala., Apr. 22, 1946; s. Grady Byrd and Elizabeth (Palmer) H.; m. Miriam Wilkinson, Sept. 24, 1971; children—Shawn Grady, Wendy Alish. B.S., U. Ala., 1968. With Bedsole Dry Goods, Thomasville, 1968—, v.p., 1976-79, pres., 1979—, dir., 1976—; dir. Bank Thomasville, United Security Bankshares, United Security Bank, 1st Nat. Bank of Butler. Served with N.G., 1969-74. Mem. Nat. Retail Mchts. Assn., Ala. Retail Mchts. Assn., Thomasville C. of C. Baptist. Home: 712 Morningview Dr Thomasville AL 36784

HARROLD, GORDON COLESON, environmental consultant; b. Mount Jewett, Pa., July 5, 1906; s. John Joseph and Clarissa H. (Coleson) H.; m. Florence W. Bristow, Oct. 7, 1927 (dec. 1984); children—Dianne Collier, Lynn Batte, Susan Schmidt. B.S., Antioch Coll., 1930; M.S., U. Cin., 1932, Ph.D., 1934. Indsl. hygiene engr. Indsl. Health Conservacy Lab., Detroit, 1934-35; chief indsl. hygienist Chrysler Corp., Detroit, 1935-45; dir. Indsl. Health Hygiene and Safety Service, Detroit, 1945—; gen. co-chmn. First Midwest Conf. Occupational Diseases, Detroit, 1937, Am. Conf. on Indsl. Diseases, Cleve., 1939; cons. Noise Abatement Com., Detroit Bd. Commerce; cons. to various cos. Mem. Am. Chem. Soc. (emeritus), Am. Soc. Heating and Ventilating Engrs., Am. Inst. Chemistry (fellow emeritus), Am. Pub. Health Assn. (emeritus fellow), Am. Indsl. Hygiene Assn. (co-organizer, 1st sec.-treas. 1939-42, Cummings Meml. award 1960,Gordon C. Harrold Loan fund established in his honor 1982; recipient Borden award 1980, hon. emeritus), Engring. Soc. Detroit. Republican. Methodist. Avocations: travel, gardening. Home and Office: PO Box 1116 423 NE 3d St Boca Raton FL 33432

HARRY, WILLIAM MICHAEL, veterinarian; b. Fayetteville, Tenn., June 21, 1951; s. Jerry Albert and Martha Maybelle (Reese) H.; m. Violet Ruth Hopkins, Aug. 30, 1970; 1 son, Stephen Reese. Student U. Tenn., 1969-72; D.V.M., Auburn U., 1976. Preceptorship, Central Ky. Vet. Center, Georgetown, 1976; pvt. vet. practice Upper Cumberland Vet. Clinic, Crossville, Tenn., 1976, Central Ky. Animal Clinic, Bardstown, Ky., 1976-79, Rocky Hill Vet. Clinic, Knoxville, Tenn., 1979-80, Fayetteville Animal Clinic P.C. (Tenn.), 1980—. Mem. AVMA, Tenn. Vet. Med. Assn., Middle Tenn. Vet. Med. Assn., Soc. Theriogenology, Order Ky. Cols., Phi Eta Sigma, Alpha Zeta, Omega Tau Sigma. Presbyterian. Club: Block and Bridle. Home: 602 E Scenic Dr Fayetteville TN 37334 Office: Fayetteville Animal Clinic 1920 Wilson Pkwy Fayetteville TN 37334

HARSH, EMILY HUDSON, university athletic director, educator; b. Nashville, Sept. 16, 1938; d. Marcellus George and Dorothy Ann (Hamilton) H. B.S., Belmont Coll., Nashville, 1967. Tchr., coach Harpeth Hall Sch. for Girls, Nashville, 1967-69; instr. Vanderbilt U., Nashville, 1969—, dir. women's phys. edn., 1971-74, women's tennis coach, 1971-76, assoc. dir. club sports, intramurals and phys. edn., 1974-82, women's athletic dir., 1977—; treas. women's athletic council Southeastern Conf., 1980—. Water safety instr. ARC, 1969—. Mem. U.S. Tennis Assn., Tenn. Assn. Health, Phys. Edn. and Recreation, Belmont Coll. Alumni Assn. (exec. bd. 1971-77), Assn. Intercollegiate Athletics for Women (nat. track com. 1979-81), Nat. Collegiate Athletic Assn. (nat. swimming com. 1981), Tenn. Coll. Women's Sports Fedn. (bd. dirs. 1980-83). Republican. Baptist. Club: Md. Farms Racquet and Country (Brentwood, Tenn.). Home: 2011 Richard Jones Rd Apt TH 305 Nashville TN 37215 Office: McGugin Center Vanderbilt University Jess Neely Dr Nashville TN 37212

HART, DOROTHY, actress, international affairs speaker; b. Cleve.; d. Walter C. and Mabel (Keister) H.; B.A. with honors, Flora Stone Mather Coll., Case-Western Res. U., 1948; 1 son, Douglas Hart. Starred in 24 movies including The Naked City, 1949, Gunfighters, 1949, Take One False Step, 1949, The Story of Molly X, 1950, Loan Shark, Down to Earth, I Was a Communist for the FBI, Outside the Wall, Raton Pass, Second Dawn, 1953; also many TV dramas including Omnibus, Suspense, Playhouse 90, Medallion Theatre (opposite Ronald Reagan) Studio One, Robert Montgomery Presents, Kraft Theater, Four Star Playhouse (opposite Charles Boyer); TV panel shows include Pantomine Quiz, Stump the Stars, 1954-64, I've Got a Secret, Take a Guess, To Tell the Truth, Girl Talk, 1969; portrait artist; apptd. U.S. observer UN Conf., Geneva; speaker Motion Picture Producers Assn., Zonta Internat., UN 10th anniversary, Am. Assn. UN; ofcl. hostess reception com. N.Y.C. Mayor's Gracie Mansion, 1958-64; active USO, United Theatrical War Activities Com., ARC, Vis. Nurses Assn., work for retarded children. Recipient Golden Key award for outstanding actress Screenplay Motion Pictures Arts and Scis. Mem. Kappa Alpha Theta. Author poetry and prose. Home: 43 Martindale Rd Asheville NC 28804

HART, JAMES RONALD, association executive; b. Nashville, Nov. 15, 1946; s. Joseph Edwin and Elizabeth (Ashburn) H.; m. Paulette Corbitt, Dec. 10, 1965; children—Clinton Dwayne, Angela Chae. Student U. Tenn., 1965-69. Restaurant mgr. Minit Burger Corp., Nashville, 1969-71, purchasing agt., 1971-73, owner, 1973-78; v.p. Laro Corp., Nashville, 1973-78; exec. v.p. Tenn. Restaurant Assn., 1978—. Mem. Tenn. Filmtape and Music Commn. Mem. AUS N.G. Mem. Internat. Soc. Restaurant Assn. Execs. (pres. 1981-82), Tenn. Soc. Assn. Execs. Republican. Baptist. Club: Optimist (Franklin, Tenn.) (dir.). Home: 119 Gilbert Dr Franklin TN 37064 Office: Tennessee Restaurant Association 229 Court Sq Franklin TN 37064

HART, RICHARD LOUIS, architect; b. El Paso, Tex., July 7, 1948; s. David Marion and Margaret Celestine (Daven) H.; B.Arch., Washington U., 1972; m. Carol Ann Howe, Aug. 28, 1971; 1 dau., Alexa Catherine. Pres., Richard L. Hart & Assocs., El Paso, Tex., 1974-77; dir. design group Trigon Corp., El Paso, 1976-77; prin. Richard L. Hart, Architect, El Paso, Tex., from 1977; now prin. Wayne, Hart & Klink, Inc.; pres. Richard L. Hart, Architect, Inc.; instr. constrn. mgmt. El Paso Community Coll., 1975-76; lectr. planning Universidad Autónoma de Ciudad Juarez, 1981. Bd. dirs. Tex. Hist. Found., 1979—; original in corporator Texans for Quality Edn.; mem. com. for establishment resource ctrs. for tchrs. Tex. history Tex. Heritage Assn.; bd. dirs. Tex. Lyceum Assn., also chmn. conf. com.; mem. bus. and profl. com. Tex. Commn. on Arts. Named A Rising Star of Texas, Tex. Bus. mag., 1980. Mem. Tex. Soc. Architects, AIA, El Paso County Hist. Commn. (past chmn.). Roman Catholic. Clubs: Kiwanis, Sunturians (dir.). Office: 1330 E Yandell El Paso TX 79902

HART, ROBERT CARMON, manufacturing company executive; b. Elizabethton, Tenn., Oct. 29, 1926; s. Samuel R. and Virginia E. (Snodgrass) H.; m. Hazel Campbell, Dec. 30, 1948; children—John Philip, Janet Hart Collins, James Robert, Joel Bruce, Julie Ellen. Student, Milligan Coll., 1944-45; B.M.E., U. Louisville, 1947; postgrad., U. Tenn., 1949-50. With Ky. Insp. Bur., 1947-48, N. Am. Rayon Corp., 1948-49; with Tenn. Eastman Co., Kingsport, 1950—, pres., 1979—; dir. First Tenn. Bank N.A., Kingsport/Bristol. Bd. dirs. Holston Valley Health Care Found., Retirement Living, Inc., Tenn. Tech. Found., Knoxville; pres. Rocky Mount Hist. Assn.; mem. exec. bd. Sequoyah council Boy Scouts Am., also mem. exec. bd. S.E. Region. Served with USNR, 1944-46. Fellow ASME; mem. Am. Inst. Chem. Engrs., Am. Assn. Textile Tech., Nat. Soc. Profl. Engrs., Soc. Chem. Industry, Rocky Mount Hist. Assn., Kingsport C. of C., Tau Beta Pi. Republican. Presbyterian. Office: PO Box 511 Kingsport TN 37662

HART, ROBERT FREDRIC, import company executive; b. N.Y.C., Sept. 22, 1932; s. Lester I. and Blanche K. Hart; m. Valerie Gail Oppenheim, Mar. 29, 1959; children—Alexandra Caryn Hart Bosshardt, Gregory Steven, Katherine Ann. B.B.A. in Mktg., Sch. Bus., U. Miami, 1950-54. Account analyst Richard J. Bucks & Co., 1959-63, pres. Imports For The Trade, Miami, Fla., 1962—, Import Mktg. Corp., 1974—; chmn. bd. Valhart Real Estate Co. Club: Bankers (Miami); Surf (Miami Beach, Fla.). Home: 60 La Gorce Circle La Gorce Island Miami Beach FL 33141 Office: Imports For The Trade 26 NE 27 St Miami FL 33137

HART, ROBERT PAUL, psychologist, educator; b. Balt., Mar. 17, 1954; s. Robert Harold and Mary Lou (Kruto) Woodtke; m. Janet Mary Eddy, May 13, 1978. B.A., No. Ill. U., 1975, M.A., 1977, Ph.D., 1980. Lic. psychologist, Va. Clin. psychology intern Rush Presbyterian St. Lukes Hosp., Chgo., 1979-80; post-doctorate fellow U. Okla., Oklahoma City, 1980-81; asst. prof. psychiatry, neurology, neurosurgery Med. Coll. Va., Richmond, 1981—, dir. research, 1983—, dir. psychol. services, 1983—, dir. neuropsychology research lab., 1984—. Contbr. articles to profl. jours., also chpts. to books. Sponsor Am. Refugee Com., Chgo., 1979-80; English tchr. Refugee Resettlement Com., Richmond, 1982; mem. Va. Head Injury Found., Richmond, 1983—, Amnesty Internat., 1985. Principal investigator U. Okla., 1981, Va. Commonwealth U., 1984, NIMH, 1984—; NSF fellow, 1982. Mem. Internat. Neuropsychol. Soc. (task force), Am. Psychol. Assn., Southeastern Psychol. Assn., Va. Psychol. Assn. Club: Courts Royal (Richmond); Nautilus. Avocations: backpacking; softball. Home: 1520 Avondale Ave Richmond VA 23227 Office: Med Coll Va Box 268 Richmond VA 23298

HART, THOMAS HUGHSON, III, lawyer; b. Montgomery, Ala., Aug. 19, 1955; s. Thomas H. and Nora A. (McDonald) H.; m. Jane Elizabeth Morgan, Aug. 4, 1979; children—Morgan Elizabeth, Katherine McDonald, Mary MacQuarrie. B.A. in Polit. Sci., Furman U., 1977; J.D., U. S.C., 1980. Bar: S.C. 1980, U.S. Dist. Ct. S.C. 1981, U.S. Ct. Appeals (4th cir.) 1981, U.S. Ct. Appeals (5th & 11th cir.) 1982, U.S. Ct. Appeals (10th cir.) 1985. Assoc. Blatt and Fales, Barnwell, S.C., 1980-83, ptnr., 1983—. Editor S.C. Law Rev., 1978-80. Nat. Merit Scholar, Baruch scholar Furman U., Greenville, S.C., 1973-77; James Vesnen scholar U. S.C. Law Sch., 1978, Paul Cooper scholar, 1979. Mem. S.C. Trial Lawyers Assn. (bd. govs.), Assn. Trial Lawyers Am., ABA. Roman Catholic. Home: 1906 Main St Barnwell SC 29812 Office: Blatt and Fales 1611 Allen St Barnwell SC 29812

HART, WILLIAM BRANTLEY, banker; b. Anderson, S.C., Nov. 19, 1935; s. Francis Montague and Frances Janet (Hamilton) H.; B.S., Presbyn. Coll., 1957; postgrad. Grad. Sch. Banking, La. State U., 1966; LL.B., Atlanta Law Sch., 1969, LL.M., 1972; m. Salena Watson Clark, June 4, 1957; 1 child, William Brantley. With First Nat. Bank of Atlanta, 1958—, mgr. bus. devel., 1959-67, mgr. adminstrv. services, 1967-72, mgr. property mgmt., 1972-76, mgr. personnel adminstrn., 1976—, group v.p., 1971—; dir. Presbyn. Pub. House, Inc. Trustee, Presbyn. Coll., 1978—, chmn. hon. degrees program, 1983—; trustee Thornwell Home for Children, 1978—, vice chmn. bd., 1986—; chmn. Atlanta Presbytery Council, 1976, mem. council, 1972-76, 81—, chmn. property mgmt. div., 1982-84, moderator, 1983-84. Served with U.S. Army, 1957-58. Named Atlanta Neighbor of Month, June 1974; recipient alumni service award Presbyn. Coll., 1972. Mem. Presbyn. Coll. Alumni Assn. (pres., 1971). Republican. Presbyterian. Office: PO Box 4148 Atlanta GA 30302

HARTDEGEN, FRED WILLIAM, III, sales executive; b. New Orleans, May 20, 1935; s. Fred. W. and Estelle Mary (Cain) H.; m. June Stella Clements, Jan. 8, 1961 (div. 1979); children—Lauren Ann, Lana Elaine, Fred W.; m. 2d Barbara Anne Braun, Dec. 8, 1979; 1 dau., Lara Lee. B.S.E.E., La. State U., 1958. Registered profl. engr. Field engr. gen. Schlumberger, Morgan City, La., 1959-67; pres. Underwater Service Assocs., 1967-81; regional sales mgr. Geosource 1981-82; exec. liaison officer Petroleum Assocs. of Layfayette, (La.), 1982-83; pres. Double Bar A Corp., Houston, 1983—; sr. sales mgr. Vector/Schlumberger, Houston, 1984—; internat. expert in field underwater TV; cons. in field. Chmn. Morgan City Planning and Zoning Bd., 1976-79, chmn. com. on ocean engring. and devel., 1972-75. Served to 1st lt. U.S. Army, 1958-65. Mem. Nat. Soc. Profl. Engrs., Soc. Profl. Well Log Analysts, Marine Tech. Soc., Tau Kappa Epsilon. Roman Catholic. Club: Krewe of Argus. Contbr. articles to profl. jours. Pioneer video tape recs. from submarines. Home: 4523 Treasure Trail Sugar Land TX 77479 Office: 10910 W Bellfort St Suite 703 Houston TX 77099

HARTE, EDWARD HOLMEAD, newspaper publisher; b. Pilot Grove, Mo., Dec. 5, 1922; s. Houston and Isabel (McCutcheon) H.; m. Janet Frey, Feb. 8, 1947; children—Christopher, Elizabeth, William, Julia. B.A., Dartmouth Coll., 1947. With Kansas City Star, 1948-50; editor, co-owner Synder Daily News, Tex., 1950-52; pres. San Angelo Standard-Times, Tex., 1952-56; v.p. Corpus Christi Caller Times, Tex., 1956-62, pub., 1962—. Home: 222 Ohio St Corpus Christi TX 78404 Office: 820 Lower Broadway Corpus Christi TX 78401*

HARTE, HOUSTON H., communications company executive; b. 1927; married. B.A., Washington and Lee U., 1950. Editor Snyder Daily News, 1950-54; with promotion dept. Des Moines Register & Tribune, 1954-56; pres. San Angelo Standard Times, 1956-62, San Antonio Express & News, 1962-73; v.p. Harte-Hanks Communications Inc. (formerly Harte-Hanks Newspapers Inc.), San Antonio, 1956-71, chmn. bd., 1971—, also dir. Served with USN, 1945-46. Office: Harte-Hanks Communications Inc 40 NE Loop 410 San Antonio TX 78216*

HARTGROVE, BILLY RAY, manufacturing executive; b. Beaumont, Tex., Sept. 10, 1931; s. L.B. and Virginia (Ledenham) H.; student McNeese State Coll., Lake Charles, La., 1949-52, U. Houston, 1959-60; m. Evelyn Summers, Mar. 31, 1955; children—Billy Ray, Brian Lee. Vice pres. Great Midwest Life Ins. Co., Oklahoma City, 1962-64; v.p., sec. Security Brokers Investment Corp., Oklahoma City, 1964-66, Great Midwest Life Ins., 1967-69; v.p., sec. United Investors, Inc., 1969-73, pres., 1974-81; v.p., sec. Mid-American Investors Life Ins. Co., Oklahoma City, 1969-71, pres., 1971-72 (merged into Investors Life), pres. Investors Life, 1973-75, Liberty Investors of Okla., 1975-82, Liberty Investors Life of Ariz., 1981-82; chmn. bd. Town and Country Ins. Co., 1982-85; exec. v.p. Southwest Mfg. Co., 1985—. Served to lt. (j.g.) USNR, 1952-57. Home: #11 6204 Waterford Blvd Oklahoma City OK 73118 Office: 1432 W Main Oklahoma City OK 73106

HARTGROVE, BRUCE NORMAN, clergyman, musician; b. Greensboro, N.C., July 21, 1949; s. Leroy and Doris (Johnson) H.; m. Sara Charlcie White, June 28, 1974; 1 child, Joshua Bruce. B.Mus. Edn., Mars Hill Coll., 1971; M.Ch. Music, So. Baptist Theol. Sem., 1974. Ordained to ministry Baptist Ch., 1971. Minister of music and youth Trinity Bapt. Ch., Moultrie, Ga., 1974-76, Locust Grove Bapt. Ch., Smyrna, Ga., 1976-81; minister of music First Bapt. Ch., High Point, N.C., 1981—; v.p. Ga. Bapt. Ch. Music Conf., 1978-79; pres. Sons of Jubal, Ga., 1979-81; bd. dirs., judge choral festivals Ga. Bapt. Conv., 1981-85. Mem. So. Bapt. Ch. Music Conf., N.C. Bapt. Ch. Music Conf. (regional bd. dirs. 1985—), Am. Guild English Handbell Ringers, Choristers Guild, Singing Churchmen N.C. Avocations: model railroads; picture framing; photography. Home: 206 W Parkway Ave High Point NC 27262 Office: First Bapt Ch 405 N Main St High Point NC 27260

HARTIGAN, GREGORY FRANCIS, health care systems executive, computer consultant; b. Chgo., July 7, 1946; s. Cyril Gregory and Lucille Mary (Roche) H.; divorced; children—Lisa Ann, Diane Michelle. A.S., McHenry County Coll., 1976; B.A., Northeastern Ill. U., 1978. Dep. sheriff McHenry County Sheriff's Dept., Woodstock, Ill., 1972-75; programmer, analyst Mgmt. Data, Rosemont, Ill., 1980-81, INA Healthplan, Inc., Los Angeles, 1981—; systems programmer CIGNA Healthplan, Inc., Dallas, 1981—, mgr. tech. support, 1981—. Served with USN, 1965-70. Recipient Citation of Bravery, McHenry County Dept. Sheriff's Assn., 1973. Mem. Data Processing Mgmt. Assn. Republican. Roman Catholic. Avocations: community theater; golf; trivia pursuit. Home: 3637 Trinity Mills Rd #811 Dallas TX 75252 Office: CIGNA Systems 4115 Keller Springs Rd #200 Dallas TX 75234

HARTLEY, JOHN T., corporate executive; b. 1930; B.S. in Elec. Engring., B.S. in Chemistry, Auburn U., 1955; married. With Harris Corp., 1956—, v.p., gen. mgr., 1968-71, corp. v.p., group gen. exec., 1971-76, exec. v.p., dir., 1976-78, pres., chief operating officer, 1978—. Office: Harris Corp Corporate Hdqrs Melbourne FL 32919

HARTLEY, LOU ANN, nursing educator, consultant; b. Charleston, W.Va., Oct. 16, 1954; d. Thomas Howard and Glenna Jane (Shamblin) Bailey; m. Steven Michael Hartley, May 15, 1982. A.D.N., U. Charleston, 1974; B.S.N., W.Va. U., 1980, postgrad., 1985—. Head nurse Charleston Area Med. Ctr., 1977-78, coordinator staff devel., 1980-82, asst. dir. nursing, 1982-85; paramedic coordinator W.Va. State Coll., Institute, 1978-80; nursing instr. U. Charleston, 1985—. Sec.-treas. Charleston Heart Assn., 1982-84, bd. dirs., 1982-83. Mem. Am. Nurses Assn., W.Va. Nurses Assn., Sigma Theta Tau. Lodge: Order Eastern Star. Avocations: hiking; camping; swimming. Home: 27 First St Saint Albans WV 25177 Office: U Charleston Sch Nursing 2300 MacCorckle Ave SE Charleston WV 25304

HARTLEY, ROBERT REED, day care company executive; b. Birmingham, Ala., July 14, 1948; s. John C. and Imogene (Lewis) H.; m. Judy Ann Junkins, June 6, 1973; children—Robert Austin, Casey Marie. B.S., U. Ala., Tuscaloosa, 1971. Founder, pres. Pedro Food Systems, 1974-81; v.p. mktg. Kinder-Care, Inc., Montgomery, Ala., 1981—. Deacon, Evangel Temple, Montgomery, Ala., 1983—; state chmn. Yr. of the Bible, 1983; active Jefferson County council Boy Scouts Am., Birmingham, 1961—. Served with USMC, 1969-72. Recipient MVP award Nat. Restaurant Assn., 1978-79; ECHO award DMA of N.Y., 1984. Republican. Office: Kinder-Care Learning Centers Inc 2400 Presidents Dr Montgomery AL 36116

HARTMAN, DONALD LEVOID, credit executive; b. Thomasville, N.C., June 25, 1946; s. Robert James and Ethel (Gardner) H.; m. Deborah Carol Kilgore, Sept. 6, 1975; children—Michelle, Noel, Brandi, Nichole. B.B.A., Notre Dame U., 1968; M.B.A., LaSalle Coll., 1971. Credit supr. Am. Nat. Stores, St. Louis, 1971-75; credit mgr. Marietta Tobacco (Ga.), 1975-77; br. mgr. Aaron Sales & Rents, Atlanta, 1977-79; regional credit mgr. NCR, Atlanta, 1979-80; regional credit mgr. Nixdorf Computer, Atlanta, 1980-82; corp. credit mgr. Transus, Atlanta, 1982—; council mem. Nat. Trucker's Credit, Washington, 1983—. Mem. Republican Nat. Com., 1982, 83. Republican. Baptist.

HARTMAN, FREDERICK COOPER, biochemist; b. Memphis, Aug. 17, 1939; s. Fred Francis and Raymie Constance (Cooper) H.; m. Patricia Jean Ballard, Sept. 7, 1961; children—Patricia Suzanne, Sheila Katherine. B.S. in Chemistry, Memphis State U., 1960; M.S. in Biochemistry, U. Tenn., 1962, Ph.D. in Biochemistry, 1964; postgrad. U. Ill., 1964-66. Research assoc. U. Ill.-Champaign, 1964-66; sr. research biochemist Oak Ridge Nat. Lab., 1966—, acting dir. biology div., 1976, sect. head molecular and cellular scis., 1975—, group leader protein chemistry, 1972—; prof. biomed. scis. U. Tenn.-Knoxville, part-time 1969—. Contbr. numerous articles to profl. jours.; editorial bd. Jour. Biol. Chemistry, BioSci., Jour. Protein Chemistry. Grantee Dept. Agr., 1978—, NSF, 1980—; fellow USPHS, 1962-64, NIH, 1963, 65. Fellow AAAS; mem. Am. Chem. Soc. (Pfizer award 1979, nominating com. 1982), Am. Soc. Biol. Chemists (nominating com. 1979, 81), N.Y. Acad. Scis., Am. Inst. Biol. Scis., Sigma Xi.

HARTMAN, JAMES PAUL, mech. engr.; b. Hannibal, Mo., June 21, 1937; s. Bert Emerson and Alta Lucille (Agnew) H.; B.S., U. Mo., Rolla, 1959, M.S., 1963; postgrad. N.C. State U., 1964-66; postgrad. Calif. State U., 1967-73; grad. Command and Gen. Staff Coll., 1977; postgrad. E. Tenn. State U., 1978, U. So. Miss., 1979; m. Ingrid Winfriede Stenzenberger; children—Susan, Nancy, Peter, Andrea. Engr., Lockheed Calif. Co., Burbank, 1962-63, Space Gen. Corp., El Monte, Calif., 1963-64; instr. N.C. State U., Raleigh, 1964-66; mech. engr. Aerojet Nuclear Co., Sacramento, 1966-74, TVA, Chattanooga, 1974—; partner Systems Engring., Knoxville, 1975—; adj. instr. U.S. Command and Gen. Staff Coll. Served with AUS, 1959-62. Recipient Curators award U. Mo.; registered profl. engr., Tenn. Mem. ASME, Nat. Rifle Assn. (life), Appalachian Zool. Soc., U. Mo. Alumni Assn., Assn. U.S. Army, Res. Officers Assn., 101st AB Div. Assn., Order of Eagles, Sigma Phi Epsilon. Republican. Home: 1217 Glencliff Rd Kingsport TN 37663 Office: PO Box 938 Kingsport TN 37662

HARTMAN, JOHN WALTER, advertising agency executive; b. Oklahoma City, June 18, 1943; s. Theodore Joseph and Zella Hester (Hulsey) H.; m. Barbara Ann Taylor, Aug. 31, 1974 (div. Jan. 1976); m. 2d, Carolotta Kitchens Brandon, Sept. 4, 1979 (div. Jan. 1985). B.S. in Mktg., Central State U., 1965; postgrad. U. Tulsa, 1975, 80. With Fidelity Union Life, Edmond, Okla., 1965-66, Internat. Harvester, Oklahoma City, 1966-67, Kerr-McGee Corp., Oklahoma City, 1967-69; bus. relations mgr. Better Bus. Bur. Central Okla., Oklahoma City, 1969-71; pub. relations dir. U.S. Jaycees, Tulsa, 1971-74; asst. communications mgr. The Williams Cos., Tulsa, 1974-78, mgr. advt. and pub. relations Edgcomb Metals Co. div., Tulsa, 1978-81; pres. Hartman Communications, Inc., Tulsa, 1982—; v.p., sec., dir. TypeHouse, Inc., Tulsa, Bd. dirs. Tulsa chpt. Am. Heart Assn., 1981-83, Central State U. Alumni Assn., 1982—; adv. dir. Community Interaction Early Edn. Program, U. Tulsa, 1982-84. Served to staff sgt. Air N.G., 1965-71. Named Disting. Alumnus, Sch. Bus., Central State U., 1981; recipient numerous advt., writing and editing awards. Mem. Pub. Relations Soc. Am. (accredited; membership chmn. 1983, mem. Counselors Acad.), Internat. Assn. Bus. Communicators (accredited, pres. Tulsa chpt. 1975, 80), Am. Advt. Fedn., Nat. Investor Relations Inst., Okla. Wildlife Fedn., Thomas Gilcrease Mus., Tulsa Press Club, Acacia, Order of Pythagoras (past nat. editor). Republican. Contbr. articles to profl. jours. Office: Hartman Communications Inc 1723 South Boston Tulsa OK 74119

HARTMAN, TIMOTHY PATWILL, financial executive; b. Ft. Wayne, Ind., Mar. 1, 1939; s. Harold Albert and Mary Margaret (Sheehan) H.; m. Antoinette Marie Hart, Aug. 20, 1960; children—Melanie, Jeanne-Marie, Andrea. A.B. in Acctg., Xavier U., 1961; cert. Advanced Mgmt. Program, Harvard U., 1973. Acctg. trainee PXat, Marwick, Mitchell & Co., Cin., 1959-62, sr. acctg., 1962-66; chief internal auditor Baldwin-United Corp., Cin., 1966-68, asst. controller, 1968-69, controller, 1969-74, v.p., controller, 1974-82; exec. v.p. NCNB Corp., Charlotte, N.C., 1982—. Mem. pres.'s council Xavier U. Mem. Fin. Execs. Inst. Roman Catholic. Clubs: Charlotte City, Charlotte Athletic, Quail Hollow Country. Home: 2600 Beretania Circle Charlotte NC 28211 Office: One NCNB Plaza Charlotte NC 28255

HARTNETT, RICHARD ANDREW, university departmental administrator, researcher; b. N.Y.C., Nov. 11, 1942; s. Richard H.; m. Koula Svokos, Oct. 3, 1968; children—Marc, Christopher. B.A. in English, W.Va. U., 1966, M.A. in English, 1968, Ed.D. in Ednl. Adminstrn., 1975. Assoc. dean Kirkland Hall Coll., Easton, Md., 1969-72; mem. faculty dept. ednl. adminstrn. W.Va. U., Morgantown, 1975—, asst. prof., 1980-85, assoc. prof., 1985—, chmn. dept. ednl. adminstrn., 1983—; cons. to colls., 1979-82; editor OECD, Paris, 1980—; program chmn. S.W. Philosophy Edn. Soc., Norman, Okla., 1981-83. Chmn. Bd. Homeowners, Baker's Ridge, W.Va., 1975-77. Postdoctoral fellow U. Calif.-Berkeley, 1979. Mem. Assn. Instl. Research, European Assn. Instl. Research. Roman Catholic. Avocations: music; reading. Office: W Va U 606 Allen Hall Morgantown WV 26506

HARTNETT, RICHARD ARTHUR, elec. engr.; b. Springfield, Mo., June 25, 1944; s. Charles Richard and Mary Margaret (Starnes) H.; B.S. in Elec. Engring., La. State U., 1970; m. Elaine Marie Burgad, July 23, 1966; 1 dau., Monica Rose Margaret. Sr. field engr. Stone & Webster Engring. Corp., Fort Churchill #2 Power Sta., Nev., 1970-71, Surry Nuclear Power Sta. 1 and 2, Williamsburg, Va., 1971-72, Beaver Valley Nuclear Power Sta. #1, Beaver Valley, Pa., 1972-73; site quality assurance engr. Ebasco Services, Inc., Saint Lucie #1 Nuclear Power Sta., Fla., 1973-75; quality assurance site supr. Ebasco Services, Inc., Waterford #3 Nuclear Power Sta., La., New Orleans, 1975—; tchr. elec. tng. courses U.S. Nuclear Regulatory Commn., Korean Constrn. Co., 1979-80. Poll commr., 1979. Served with USAF, 1962-66. Registered profl. engr., La., Calif. Mem. IEEE, ASME, Am. Soc. Quality Control, La. Nuclear Soc. Republican. Methodist. Author: Electrical Quality Control Inspection Textbook, 1980. Home: 2220 Litchwood Ln Harvey LA 70058 Office: PO Box 70 Killona LA 70066

HARTNETT, THOMAS FORBES, congressman; b. Charleston, S.C., Aug. 7, 1941; s. Thomas C. and Catherine (Forbes) H.; m. Bonnie Lee Kennerly, 1965; children—Thomas Forbes, Lee Anne. Student, Coll. Charleston, 1960-62, U. S.C., 1978; cert. real estate appraisal U. Ga., 1978. Sr. cert. appraiser Am. Assn. Cert. Appraisers; pres. Hartnett Realty Co.; mem. S.C. Ho. of Reps., 1965-73, S.C. Senate, 1973-80, 97th-99th Congresses from 1st Dist. S.C. Served with USAF, 1963. Mem. S.C. Realtors Assn., Greater Charleston Bd. Realtors, Nat. Assn. Realtors, Hibernian Soc. Charleston. Republican. Roman Catholic. Lodges: K.C., Elks. Office: Room 228 Cannon House Office Bldg Washington DC 20515*

HARTSTEIN, HAROLD HERMAN, psychology educator, consultant; b. N.Y.C., Jan. 9, 1921; s. Samuel and Margaret Amanda (Wussow) H.; m. Marion Elizabeth Shea, Apr. 11, 1953; children—Marion Farnham Collins, Margaret Ann. B.G.S., U. Nebr.-Omaha, 1971; M.A., U. South Fla., 1972; Ed.D., Nova U., 1978. Enlisted U.S. Army, 1942, commd. 2d lt., 1948, advanced through grades to lt. col., 1967; served in ETO, 1944-45, Japan, 1949-50, Korea, 1950-51, W. Ger., 1955-57, Vietnam, 1960-61; with 3d Inf. Honor Guard, Washington, 1951-54; comdg. officer Signal Battalion, Korat, Thailand, 1967-68; gen. staff officer Hdqrs., U.S. Army Strategic Communications Command, Ft. Huachua, Ariz., 1968-70; ret., 1970; prof. psychology Hillsborough Community Coll., Tampa, Fla., 1973—; cons. textbook pubs. Decorated Legion of Merit, Bronze Star medal, Army Commendation medal. Mem. NEA, Ret. Officers Assn., Am. Assn. Ret. Persons, Am. Legion, Common Cause, U. Nebr. at Omaha Alumni Assn., U. South Fla. Alumni Assn., Nova U. Alumni Assn. Democrat. Mem. United Ch. of Christ. Club: Krewe Theatre U. South Fla. (Tampa). Office: Hillsborough Community Coll PO Box 30030 Tampa FL 33630

HARTT, BARBARA H., psychologist; b. Pontiac, Mich.; Dec. 16, 1937; d. James McCallum and Angeline A. (Sontag) Hartt; m. Roger Allan Gallion, Aug. 30, 1957; children—Kirk A. Gallion, Ashley H. Gallion. B.A. summa cum laude, U. S.C., 1974; Ph.D. in Clin. Community Psychology, 1983. Psychology intern William S. Hall Psychiat. Inst., Columbia, S.C., 1978-79; psychologist S.C. Dept. Mental Health, Columbia, 1980—. Co-chmn. Irish Children's Summer Program, 1984; mem. peacemaking com. Congaree Presbytery. NIMH fellow, 1975-76. Mem. Embroiderers' Guild Am. (v.p. Columbia chpt. 1983, pres. 1984). Presbyterian. Contbr. articles to publs. Home: 319 Valcour Rd Columbia SC 29210 Office: 220 Faison Dr Columbia SC 29203

HARTWIG, CHARLES WALTER, political science educator, university administrator; b. St. Charles, Mo., Dec. 15, 1941; s. Hellmut Arthur Albin and Anna Beata (Erickson) H.; m. Mary Elizabeth Steen, Dec. 29, 1967; children—Karin Beata, Markus Daniel. B.A., So. Ill. U., 1964; exchange student U. Hamburg, W. Ger., 1963-64; postgrad. U. Minn., 1964-65; M.A., U. Ky., 1968, Ph.D., 1975. Cert. secondary tchr., Ill. Teaching asst. polit. sci. U. Minn.-Mpls., 1964-65; vol. Peace Corps, Monrovia, Liberia, 1965-67; hosp. administr. Presbyterian Ch. Hosp., Tumutumu, Kenya, 1969-70; asst. prof. polit. sci. Slippery Rock State Coll., Pa., 1971-73; asst. assoc. prof. Ark. State U., Jonesboro, 1973—, dept. chmn. polit. sci., 1982—, assoc. dir. Taft Inst. Govt., 1979, area coordinator Great Decision Program, 1979-82; Fulbright lectr. Cuttington U. Coll., Liberia, 1985-86. Contbr. articles to profl. jours. Dist. coordinator Ark. Common Cause, congl. dist. 1, 1978—; bd., dirs., state-wide, 1983—; mem. Peace/Justice Task Force No. Ark. U. Methodist Conf., 1983—. Mem. African Studies Assn., Am. Polit. Sci. Assn., Ark. Polit. Sci. Assn. (pres. 1979-80, editor Newsletter 1981-85), Internat. Studies Assn., So. Polit. Sci. Assn., Pi Gamma Mu (gov. 1976—). Avocations: travel; music; tennis. Home: PO Box 309 State University AR 72467 Office: Ark State U Polit Sci Dept State University AR 72467-1890

HARTZLER, STANLEY JAMES, mathematics and science educator, consultant, lecturer, editor; b. Peoria, Ill., June 12, 1947; s. Robert James and Agnes Evelyn (Nafziger) H.; m. Sheila Diane Ullrich, Mar. 9, 1980; children—Beth, Amy, Michael, Robert, Molly. B.S., Western Ill. U., 1969; Ph.D., U. Tex., 1982. Cert. tchr., Okla., Ill. Camp dir. Chgo. YMCA, 1969-75; tchr. Prairie State Coll., Chicago Heights, Ill., 1970-76; tchr., coach Sch. Dist. 201-U, Crete, Ill., 1970-79; instr. U. Tex., Austin, 1979-82; program leader math., sci. Oklahoma City Pub. Schs., 1982—; bd. dirs. Okla. State Sci. Fair, Oklahoma City, 1982—; head judge Okla. State Mathcounts, Oklahoma City, 1983—; pres. Stan Hartzler and Assocs., Inc.; dir. Okla. Engring. Tech. Guidance Council, Oklahoma City, 1983—. Author: Bibliography of 900+ American Algebra Textbooks 1806-1982, 1983; Algebra Textbooks in the United States 1806-1982, 1982; also articles. Recipient Best Instr. Math. award Exxon Oil Corp., 1981, Best Math. Tchr. award Coll. Natural Scis, 1981. Mem. Nat. Council Tchrs. Math. (life), Nat. Geog. Soc. (life), Sch. Sci. Math. Assn. (life), Nat. Audubon Soc. (life), Nat. Wildlife Fedn. (life), Am. Math. Soc., Math. Assn. Am., Okla. Council Tchrs. Math. (bd. dirs. 1982—), South Inter-Conf. Assn. Coaches Bd. Control (chmn., vice chmn. 1972-79), Kappa Delta Pi. Republican. Baptist. Avocations: running; gardening; music. Home: 2200 Rambling Rd Edmond OK 73034 Office: Oklahoma City Pub Schs 900 N Klein Oklahoma City OK 73106

HARTZMAN, EDWIN, mechanical engineer; b. Kiowa, Kans., Jan. 1, 1913; s. Carl Thedore and Fannie Warder (Dunn) H.; m. Juanita Claire Creech, Oct. 1, 1938; 1 son, Carl Davis. B.S. in Mech. Engring., U. Minn., 1935. Marine engine salesman Fairbanks Morse & Co., 1935-41; marine engr. Avondale Shipyards, New Orleans, 1941-51, mgr. foundry div., 1951-61, v.p. engring., 1961-72, pres., 1972-78; cons., 1978-83. Bd. dirs. So. Bapt. Hosp. Mem. Soc. Naval Architects and Marine Engrs., Navy League U.S. (pres. New Orleans chpt. 1978, 79), New Orleans C. of C. Baptist. Home: 1138 Washington Ave New Orleans LA 70130

HARVATH, LEE W., JR., lawyer; b. Cleve., June 28, 1945; s. Lee W. and Patricia B. (Baker) H.; m. Paula Davis, Dec. 22, 1969; children—Hunter, Trey. B.A., Vanderbilt U., 1967; J.D., U. Ky., 1970. Assoc., English, McCaughan & O'Bryan, Ft. Lauderdale, Fla., 1970-73, ptnr., 1973—. Bd. dirs. Kiwanis Youth Found.; pres., past vice chmn. bd. trustees First Ch. of Christ Scientist, Ft. Lauderdale; chmn. bd. dirs. Daystar, Inc. Mem. ABA, Ky. Bar Assn., Broward County Bar Assn., Fla. Bar, Order of Coif. Clubs: Tower, Touchdown, Coral Ridge Country, Kiwanis. Mem. editorial staff Ky. Law Jour. Home: 4310 NE 23d Ave Fort Lauderdale FL 33308 Office: 100 NE 3d Ave Fort Lauderdale FL 33301

HARVEY, EDWIN MALCOLM, manufacturing company executive; b. Hattiesburg, Miss., July 23, 1928; s. Clarence C. and Ezilda (Pegues) H.; m. Charlotte Trewolla, July 7, 1951; children—Sylvia Jane, Sharon Ann, Rebecca Lynn. B.S. in Chem. Engring. La. State U., 1950. With Ethyl Corp., Richmond, Va., 1950-66, mgr. econ. research, dir. econ. evaluation, 1963-66; pres., treas. William L. Bonnell Co., Inc. subs. Ethyl Corp., Newnan, Ga., 1966—; also dir.; v.p. Aluminum div. Ethyl Corp., 1975—; pres. Capitol Products Corp. subs., 1975—; dir. First Nat. Bank, Newnan. Bd. dirs. Newnan Hosp., Bus. Council Ga. Mem. Ga. C. of C., Newnan-Coweta C. of C., Aluminum Assn. (dir.). Episcopalian. Club: Newnan Country. Home: 246 Jackson St Newnan GA 30264 Office: 25 Bonnell St Newnan GA 30264

HARVEY, FRANK W., retail company executive; b. Knoxville, Tenn., Apr. 13, 1931; s. Frank R. and Mildred (Noe) H.; m. Patricia Johnson, Mar. 3, 1963; children—Heather Lea, Frank Whitney. B.S. in Econs., Vanderbilt U., 1957. With Cain Sloan Co., 1958, 66-76, sr. v.p., gen. mdse. mgr., Nashville, 1966-70, pres., 1970-76; divisional mdse. mgr. The Fashion, Columbus, Ohio, pres., mng. dir., 1965-66, Maas Bros. of Fla., Tampa, 1976—; dir. Exchange Nat. Bank, Tampa. Bd. dirs. U. South Fla. Found.; trustee chmn. bd. fellows U. Tampa. Served with USMC, 1950-52. Mem. Greater Tampa C. of C. (sec.-treas.). Methodist. Clubs: Palma Geia Golf and Country, Tampa Yacht, University. Home: 4901 New Providence St Tampa FL 33609 Office: Maas Bros PO Box 311 Tampa FL 33601*

HARVEY, GEORGE WILKINS, JR., broadcasting executive; b. Chgo., Dec. 10, 1941; s. George Wilkins and Elizabeth (Drake) H. B.A. in Psychology, Washington and Lee U., 1963. Prodn. assoc. sta. WFGA-TV (now WTLV), Jacksonville, Fla., 1963-64; media trainee, media buyer, sr. media buyer Young and Rubicam Advt., N.Y.C., 1964-66, sr. media buyer, media supr., San Francisco, 1966-69; account exec. sta. WFLA-TV (now WXFL-TV), Tampa, Fla., 1969-82; local/regional sales mgr. sta. WFTS-TV, Family TV Corp., Tampa, 1982—. Pres. Easter Seal Soc. Hillsborough County, 1973, bd. dirs., past chmn. Easter Seal Telethon; chmn. Hillsborough County Salvation Army Adv. Bd., 1980-82; mem. adv. bd., exec. com., bd. fellows U. Tampa; Steward St. Andrew's Soc. Fla.; chmn. bd. counselors U. Tampa, 1978-79; past vice chmn. advance gifts div. Tampa United Fund; past bd. dirs. Greater Tampa Citizens' Safety Council, Jr. Achievement, Tampa chpt. ARC; past v.p. Hillsborough County Humane Soc. Served with USAR, 1964-70. Mem. Tampa Advt. Fedn., Com. 100, Greater Tampa C. of C., Mchts. Assn. Greater Tampa (dir.), Sigma Nu. Republican. Presbyterian. Clubs: Tampa Yacht and Country, Ye Mystic Krewe of Gasparilla, University (Tampa), Tower, Exchange, Merrymakers. Lodges: Masons, Scottish Rite, Shriners. Home: 3008 Villa Rosa Park Tampa FL 33611 Office: 4501 E Columbus Dr Tampa FL 33605

HARVEY, JAMES CARDWELL, political science educator; consultant; b. Italy, Tex., July 15, 1925; s. Fred N. and Ola Victoria (Whitt) H.; 1 dau., Nancy; m. 2d, Lillian Smith, July 11, 1974; 1 dau., Nakis. B.A., So. Meth. U., 1949; M.A., U. Tex.-Austin, 1952, Ph.D., 1955; M.A., U. Ariz., 1969. Asst. prof. Pan Am. U., U. Tex., El Paso, 1957-64; assoc. prof. Ft. Lewis Coll., 1964-65; assoc. prof., chmn. dept. Western N. Mex. U., 1965-68; prof. Coll. Artesia, 1969-70, Jackson State U., 1970-74; HUD fellow, 1974-75; prof. Jackson State U., 1975—; cons. HUD, 1976, Hinds City Bd. Suprs. Mem. resources bd. Jackson Community Housing; bd. dirs. Jackson Urban League, 1981-82. Served with USNR, 1942-46; PTO. Fulbright scholar to France, 1952-53; HUD fellow, 1974-75. Mem. Am. Soc. Pub. Adminstrn., Internat. Democrat. Episcopalian. Author: Civil Rights during the Kennedy Administration, 1971; Black Civil Rights during the Johnson Administration, 1973; contbr. articles to profl. jours.

HARVEY, JAMES LESLIE, JR., state official; b. Ridgeland, S.C., July 11, 1947; s. James Leslie and Verna (Wall) H.; m. Charlotte Ann Rickenbaker, Nov. 17, 1968; children—Ann Margaret, James Leslie III. A.A., North Greenville Coll., 1967; B.A., U. S.C., 1970, M. Criminal Justice, 1978. Correctional officer S.C. Dept. Corrections, Columbia, 1968-70, adminstrv. asst., 1970-72, dep. warden, 1972-74, warden, 1974-79, regional adminstr., 1979—; tchr. Lake City Jr. High Sch. (S.C.), 1970. Mem. adv. bd. S.C. State Jail Resource Ctr., Lexington, 1982-83. Mem. Am. Correctional Assn., So. States Correctional Assn., N.Am. Wardens Assn., S.C. Correctional Assn. (pres. 1982-83), S.C. Employees Assn., S.C. Law Enforcement Officers Assn. Club: Toastmasters. Office: SC Dept Corrections 4444 Broad River Rd Columbia SC 29221

HARVEY, LEONARD A., chemical company executive; b. St. Catharines, Ont., Can., Aug. 20, 1925; came to U.S., 1952, naturalized, 1960; m. Shirley Williams, Oct. 7, 1950; children—Brian, Bruce, Christopher. B.Sc. with honors, Queens U., 1950. With Borg Warner Chems. Inc., 1952—, pres., Parkersburg, W.Va., 1976-86; exec. v.p. Borg-Warner Corp., Chgo., 1986—; dir. McGean Chem. Co., Parkersburg Nat. Bank. Served with RCAF, World War II. Mem. Soc. Plastics Industry, Chem. Mfrs. Assn., Parkersburg C. of C. (pres. 1981-82).

HARVEY, MARSHALL, JR., podiatrist; b. Lubbock, Tex., Nov. 12, 1941; s. Marshall and Betty (Compton) H.; B.S., Tex. Tech. U., 1962; grad. Ill. Coll. Podiatric Medicine, 1966; m. Sue Kadane, Feb. 1, 1981; children by previous marriage—Jason, Jacob; stepchildren—Chris Robertson, Jill Robertson, Brent Robertson. Intern, Community Hosp., Lubbock, Tex., 1966-67; practice podiatry specializing in foot surgery, Wichita Falls, Tex., 1967—. Active rebuilding Quail Creek sect., Wichita Falls following tornado, 1979. Mem. Am. Podiatry Assn., Tex. Podiatry Assn. (dir. 1975—, pres.; service award 1978), Am. Coll. Foot Surgeons (asso.). Republican. Office: 1612 10th St Wichita Falls TX 76301

HARVEY, NORRIS ORVILLE, mathematics educator; b. Fayetteville, N.C., June 4, 1958; s. Lonnie Lovelace and Janie Otelia (Hart) H. B.S., Fayetteville State U., 1980; M.S., Jackson State U., 1981. Instr. math Fayetteville State U., 1981-82; phys. scientist Dept. Army, Texarkana, Tex., summer 1982; instr. math. Pembroke State U., N.C., 1982—. Mem. Nat. Council Tchrs. Math., Math. Assn. Am., Am. Math. Soc., Beta Kappa Chi (pres. 1979-80). Democrat. Mem. Disciples Christ Ch. Club: Math. (pres. 1979-80) (Fayetteville). Avocations: Bowling; basketball; summer math. computer camps. Home: 315 Tucson Dr Fayetteville NC 28303 Office: Pembroke State U Dept Math Pembroke NC 28372

HARVIN, CHARLES ALEXANDER, III, lawyer, state legislator; b. Sumter, S.C., Feb. 7, 1950; s. Charles Alexander Harvin, Jr. Grad. in history and polit. sci. Baptist Coll., Charleston, S.C., 1972, Augusta Law Sch., 1976; hon. degree Sherman Chiropractic Coll., Spartanburg, S.C., 1979. Mem. S.C. Ho. of Reps., 1976—, asst. majority leader, majority whip, 1978-82, majority leader, 1982—, mem. ways and means com., vice chmn. rules com. Pres. Bapt. Coll. Young Democrats, 1970-72; officer Charleston County Young Dems., 1971-72; chmn. 6th Congl. Dist. Young Dems., 1975-76; life mem. S.C. Young Dems.; chmn. Clarendon County Dem. Com.; vice chmn. S.C. Dem. Com., 1976-78, also mem. exec. com.; del. Dem. Nat. Conv., 1984; mem. S.C. Gov.'s Agr. Study Com.; U.S. Constn. Bicentennial Commn., 1985—; trustee S.C. Hall of Fame; vice chmn. alumni bd. Bapt. Coll., 1975-76; bd. visitors Clemson U., 1977-78. Recipient Outstanding Service award Charleston County Young Dems., 1972, S.C. Young Dems., 1977; Disting. Service award S.C. Dem. Com., 1981; appreciation award S.C. Tech. Edn. Colls., 1981; Legislator of Yr. award S.C. Young Dems., 1982, S.C. Student Legislature, 1981, S.C. State Library Bd., 1982, S.C. Assn. for Deaf, 1985; award S.C. Council for Exceptional Children, 1982, S.C. Agrl. Community, 1982; Outstanding Legislator Service award United Parcel Service, 1984; Disting. Service award Bapt. Coll. of Charleston Alumni Assn., 1984, also numerous other awards and commendations. Mem. ABA, Am. Judicature Soc., S.C. Trial Lawyers Assn., Clarendon County Farm Bur., Clarendon County Hist. Soc. (v.p. 1983-84, pres. 1985-86), S.C. State Employees Assn., NAACP, Alpha Phi Omega (life). Lodges: Masons, Shriners. Office: SC Ho of Reps Columbia SC 29211

HARVIN, L. H., III, department store company executive; b. 1938. B.A., U. N.C., 1961; LL.B., Duke U., 1963. Atty., Wilcox Cooke Savage & Lawrence, 1963-64; asst. mgr. real estate dept. Roses Stores Inc., Henderson, N.C., 1964-66, mgr. real estate dept., 1966-67, asst. treas., 1967-69, treas., 1969-72, v.p. expansion, 1972-75, sr. v.p., chief operating officer, 1975-80, chief operating officer, dir., 1980—. Office: Roses Stores Inc 218-22 S Garnett St Henderson NC 27536

HARWELL, BARBARA ANN, advertising agency executive; b. San Angelo, Tex., June 9, 1933; d. George German and Mary Irene (Holland) Harwell. Student, Tex. Woman's U., 1950-52; B.S., U. Ark., 1954. Copywriter, A. Harris & Co., 1954-55; advt. mgr. Volk Bros. Co., 1955-63; copywriter Tracy-Locke, Inc., 1963-67; v.p., creative dir. Rominger Advt., Inc., 1967-76; copy chief Norsworth Mercer Kerss, 1976; v.p., assoc. creative dir. KCBN, Dallas, 1977-78, exec. v.p., creative dir., 1978-81; chmn. bd., exec. creative dir. Arnold Harwell McClain & Assocs., Inc., Dallas, 1982-85, Austin & Harwell, Inc., 1985—. Recipient Addy gold medals (36); Clio awards (6); awards of excellence N.Y. Art Dirs. Club, 1978-81, Houston Art Dirs. Club, 1976, 77. Mem. Southwestern Assn. Advt. Agys., Dallas Soc. Visual Communications (past bd. dirs., 11 medals), Dallas Advt. League (bd. dirs., Most Valuable Mem. 1985). Republican. Presbyterian. Clubs: Cimarron, Cotillion (Dallas).

HARWELL, DAVID WALKER, state supreme ct. justice; b. Florence, S.C., Jan. 8, 1932; s. Baxter Hicks and Lacy (Rankin) H.; J.D., U. S.C., 1958; children—Robert Bryan, William Baxter. Admitted to S.C. bar, 1958; partner firm Harwell & Harwell, Florence, S.C., 1958—; mem. S.C. Ho. of Reps., 1962-73; circuit judge 12th Judicial Circuit Ct., 1973-80; justice S.C. Supreme Ct., 1980—. Served with USN, 1952-54. Mem. Am. Bar Assn., Am. Trial Lawyers Assn., S.C. Bar Assn., S.C. Trial Lawyers Assn. Presbyterian. Office: South Carolina Supreme Court Drawer X City-County Complex Florence SC 29501

HARWOOD-NUSS, ANN LATIMER, physician; b. Sigourny, Iowa, July 22, 1948; d. Arthur Manning and Nyta Pauline (Latimer) Harwood; m. Gary Larsen, June 22, 1974 (div. 1976); m. Robert C. Nuss, Sept. 21, 1984. B.S., U. Iowa, Iowa City, 1969, M.D., 1973. Resident in gen. surgery and urology Mich State U.-Grand Rapids, 1973-76, residency dir. in emergency medicine Mich. State U., Grand Rapids, 1976-80; resident dir. U. Chgo., 1980-81; chmn. emergency medicine University Hosp., Jacksonville, Fla., 1981-85; div. chief U. Fla., 1981-85, assoc. prof., 1984—; mem. Nat. Adv. Council Grad. Med. Edn.; Cons. Am. Heart Assn., Dallas, 1981, Smith-Kline-French, Los Angeles, 1982, cost containment Am. Coll. Emergency Physicians, 1983. Author: Cardio-pulmonary Resucitation, 1982; Textbook of Emergency Medicine: Urologic Emergencies, 1983; series editor Churchill Livingstone Pubs., 1986—; mem. editorial bd. Jour. Emergency Medicine, 1983, sect. editor, 1984—. Mem. affiliate faculty Am. Heart Assn., Dallas, 1979-84. Mem. Am. Coll. Emergency Physicians (chmn. comprehensive rev. emergency medicine 1980-82, pres. future workshop Chgo. 1979, bd. dirs. Fla. chpt. 1981-84), Soc. Tchrs. Emergency Medicine (bd. dirs. 1979-81, orators award Atlanta 1979), Fla. Med. Found. Emergency Med. Service, Duval County Med. Soc. (emergency medicine service), Univ. Assn. Emergency Medicine (moderator 1982) ACS (trauma com. 1982-84, symposium speaker 1986), So. Med. Assn. (chmn. sect. on emergency medicine 1985-86). Office: University Hosp 655 W 8th St Jacksonville FL 32209

HASAN, SAIYID ZAFAR, social work educator, college dean; b. Allahabad, India, July 5, 1930; came to U.S., 1971, naturalized, 1979; s. Saiyid Akhtar and Alia (Khatoon) H.; m. Nuzhat Ara, Nov. 3, 1961; children—Shirin, Simin, Akbar, Jafar. B.A. with honors, U. Lucknow, India, 1948, M.A., 1949, LL.B., 1949, diploma in social service, 1950, M.S. in Social Work, 1955; D.Social Work, Columbia U., 1958. Cert. social worker, Ky. Research asst. U. Lucknow, 1950-51, lectr. in social work, 1951-57, reader in social work, 1957-65, prof., head dept. social work, 1965-71; prof. social work U. Ky., Lexington, 1971—, dean Coll. Social Work, 1979—; mem. Council Social Work Edn., Washington, 1971—; mem. adv. council Multidisciplinary Ctr. on Gerontology and Human Devel., Lexington, 1981—. Author: Federal Grants and Public Assistance, 1963; Research in Sociology and Social Work, 1971; Mental Health Professionals Perceive Knowledge and Skill Needs, 1981—; Mental Health-Rural Aging Multidisciplinary Curriculums, 1982. Contbr. articles to profl. pubs. Active civic and social orgns. India; pres. Tenant Services and Assistance, Inc., Lexington, 1980-82; active United Way of Bluegrass, Lexington, 1983—. UN Social Welfare scholar, 1954-56; Rose Morgan Vis. Prof., U. Kans., 1974. Mem. Indian Assn. Trained Social Workers, Council Social Work Edn., AAUP. Democrat. Islam. Home: 735 Brook Hill Dr Lexington KY 40502 Office: Coll Social Work U Ky Lexington KY 40506

HASEY, MARTIN JAMES, lawyer; b. Detroit, Jan. 7, 1955; s. William Joseph and Regina (Boucher) H.; m. Catherine Pagano, June 23, 1979; children—William J., Michael P., Patrick M., Ryan M. B.S.B.A., U. Fla., 1976, J.D., 1979. Bar: Fla. 1980. Assoc. Hatch Fenster & Faerber, Plantation, Fla., 1979-82; ptnr. Hatch & Hasey, Fort Lauderdale, Fla., 1982-85, Hasey and Beraha, Ft. Lauderdale, 1985—; dir. Banyan Bank. Bd. dirs., sec., Hasey Found., Fort Lauderdale, 1979—. Mem. Boca Raton C. of C., Broward County Bar Assn. Roman Catholic. Clubs: Pinetree Golf (Boynton, Fla.); Boca Raton Country. Office: Martin J Hasey 6400 N Andrews Ave Suite 402 Fort Lauderdale FL 33309

HASMAN, GLENN RAYMOND, manufacturing company executive; b. Cleve., June 6, 1954; s. Raymond Joseph and Martha Aurelia (Klimo) H.; m. Petrina Marie Kaye, Aug. 28, 1981; 1 stepson, Christopher. B.S. in Acctg., Miami U., Oxford, Ohio, 1976. C.P.A., Ohio. Staff acct. Ciulla Stephens & Co., Cleve., 1976-78, sr. acct., 1978-79; dir. internal auditing RPM, Inc., Medina, Ohio, 1979-82; treas., chief fin. officer Proko Industries, Inc., Mesquite, Tex., 1982-85, v.p.-treas., chief fin. officer, 1985—. Treas. Chaunticlair Phase IIIA Condo Assn., North Royalton, Ohio, 1981, pres. 1982. Mem. Am. Inst. C.P.A.s, Ohio Soc. C.P.A.s. Roman Catholic. Club: Oakridge Country (Garland, Tex.). Home: 3226 Laurel Oaks Ct Garland TX 75042 Office: Proko Industries Inc 18601 LBJ Freeway Suite 400 Mesquite TX 75150

HASSELBRING, MICHAEL EDWARD, restaurant executive; b. Cin., Mar. 9, 1953; s. Paul Edward and Helen I. (Parsons) H.; m. Kathryn M. Ells, July 18, 1981. B.S., Manchester Coll., 1975. Trainee, Lebanon Citizens Nat. Bank (Ohio), 1975-76; tennis professional Peter Burwash Internat. Ltd., Honolulu, 1976-78; night auditor and mgr., food and beverage controller, safety and security chmn. Sheraton Hotels Hawaii, Volcano Nat. Park, 1978-81; v.p., gen. mgr. Julius Fred Enterprises, Inc., Sarasota, Fla., 1981—. Recipient Eagle Scout award Boy Scouts Am., 1968. Mem. Nat. Eagle Scout Assn. Home and office: 4613 Longwater Chase Sarasota FL 33580

HASSELLE, MARY CAROLYN, poet, artist; b. Memphis, May 21, 1943; d. Mary Frances (Sledge) H. Cert. European Studies, U. Aix Marseilles, France, 1964; B.A., Rhodes Coll., 1966. Author: Soul Poetry, 1982; (poem) Angel Sunset, 1982. Charter mem. Nat. Mus. of Women in the Arts, Washington, 1986; mem. Nat. Resourse Def. Council, Washington, 1985. Recipient Most Talented Art award Lausanne European Seminar, Lausanne Sch., 1961. Mem. Nat. Assn. for Female Execs., Nat. Writers Club, Am. Acad. Poets, PEO., Brooks Art Gallery League. Avocations: diving; synchronized swimming.

HASSIN, GUIDO, physicist, electrical engineer, biophysicist; b. Lucera, Italy, Jan. 23, 1945; s. Woodrow Wilson and Luigina Carmella (Vinditi) H. B.S., Ark. State U., 1967; M.S., U. Calif.-Santa Barbara, 1970; Ph.D., U. Minn., 1977; postdoctoral fellow SUNY-Stony Brook, 1977-79. Physicist, Naval Ship Weapon Systems Engring. Sta., Port Hueneme, Calif., 1968-73; faculty SUNY-Stony Brook, 1979; research assoc. Lockheed, 1979-80; prin. scientist BDM, Huntsville, Ala., 1980-81; laser div. GRC, Huntsville, 1981-82; dep. mgr. directed energy div. SPARTA, Huntsville, 1982—; adj. asst. prof. biophysics U. Ala., Huntsville, 1983—. Acad. scholar, 1963; recipient Chemistry Achievement award, 1964, Chi Sigma Scholarship award, 1965; runner-up Sparta Innovator of Yr., 1985; Naval Grad. fellow, 1969; recipient Sustained Superior Performance award, 1973; spl. dissertation grantee, U. Minn., 1976; ARVO travel fellow, 1975. Mem. Naval Ship Weapon Systems Engring. Sta. Profl. Assn. (past pres.), Sigma Xi, Phi Eta Sigma. Contbr. chpt. to book, articles to sci. jours. Address: 1010 Monte Sano Blvd Huntsville AL 35801

HASSON, JAMES KEITH, JR., lawyer; b. Knoxville, Tenn., Mar. 3, 1946; s. James Keith and Elaine (Biggers) H.; B.A. with distinction in Econs., Duke U., 1967, J.D. with distinction, 1970; m. Loretta Jayne Young, July 27, 1968; 1 child, Keith Samuel. Admitted to Ga. bar, 1971; assoc. firm Sutherland, Asbill & Brennan, Atlanta, 1970-76, partner, 1976—; dir. House-Hasson Hardware Co., Knoxville; adj. prof. law Emory U., Atlanta, 1973—. Chmn., trustee, Met. Atlanta Crime Commn., 1978—; mem. Atlanta Civilian Rev. Bd.; trustee Am. Cancer Soc. (Atlanta unit), 1981-83; participant Leadership Atlanta, 1981-82; pres. Habersham-Andrews Hist. Preservation Soc., Inc., 1983—. Served to 1st lt. USAR. Mem. ABA, State Bar Ga., Atlanta Bar Assn. (gen. counsel 1976-80, Pres.'s Disting. Service award 1980), Nat. Health Lawyers Assn., Nat. Assn. Coll. and Univ. Attys. Presbyterian. Club: Lawyers (Atlanta). Home: 3185 Chatham Rd NW Atlanta GA 30305 Office: 3100 1st Atlanta Tower Atlanta GA 30383

HASTINGS, ALCEE LAMAR, federal judge; b. Altamonte Springs, Fla., Sept. 5, 1936; s. Julius Caesar and Mildred Louvenia (Merritt) H.; m. Delores Henry, (div. 1973); 1 son, Alcee Lamar II. B.A., Fisk U., 1958; postgrad. Howard U. Law Sch., 1958-60; J.D., Fla. A&M U., 1963. Bar: Fla. Ptnr. Allen & Hastings, Ft. Lauderdale, Fla., 1964-67; sole practice, Ft. Lauderdale, 1967-77; judge Broward County Cir. Ct., Ft. Lauderdale, 1977-79; judge U.S. Dist. Ct. Fla., Miami, 1979—. Trustee Bethune Cookman Coll., Daytona Beach, Fla.; hon. trustee Broward Community Coll., Ft. Lauderdale; bd. dirs. Broward County chpt. NCCJ, Ft. Lauderdale; mem./lectr. So. Regional Council on Black Am. Affairs; bd. dirs. Urban League Broward County. Recipient Outstanding Leadership award North Miss. Rural Legal Services, 1983, Humanitarian award Nat. Assn. of Blacks in Criminal Justice, 1983; honoree resolution of Cleve. Mcpl. Ct., 1983. Mem. Nat. Assn. Black Narcotics Officers, ABA, Nat. Bar Assn., Fla. Bar Assn., Assn. Trial Lawyers Am., Kappa Alpha Psi. Mem. African Methodist-Episcopal Ch. Lodge: Elks. Office: US Dist Ct 301 N Miami Ave 5th Floor Miami FL 33128

HASTINGS, EDMUND STUART, petroleum geologist, retired naval officer; b. New Orleans, Jan. 2, 1924; s. James Stuart and Winnie Dorothy (Miller) H.; student U.S. Naval R.O.T.C., U. Tex., 1943, Command Staff Course Naval War Coll., 1959, Gen. Staff Coll., 1969; B.S., U. So. Calif. 1950; m. Elizabeth Theresa Dean, June 21, 1947; children—Theresa Christine (Mrs. Aaron R. Folse), Margaret Elizabeth, James Stuart. Commd. ensign USN, 1943, advanced through grades to comdr., 1971; with weapons tng. unit NAS, Dallas; with Naval Ammunition Depot, Pusan, Korea; ret.; spl. projects geologist Phillips Petroleum Co., Lafayette, La., 1956-59, dist. div. geologist, 1959-62, regional staff geologist, Bartlesville, Okla., 1962-64, petroleum geologist, Houston, 1964-70, 1973-85, Lafayette, 1970-73; chmn., chief exec. officer Pet Cons & Assocs., Houston, 1985—; expert witness petroleum exploration, devel., drilling prodn. opns., onshore offshore; v.p., then chief exec. officer Hastings Properties, Gautier, Miss., 1967-75; ship's master Oceans Unltd.; dir. First Nat. Bank. Recipient commendations U.S. Dept. Def., 1962, 68, 69. Mem. Explorers Club, Am. Inst. Profl. Geologists (state v.p. 1973), Soc. Profl. Well Log Analysts (state v.p. 1972-73), Am. Assn. Petroleum Geologists (del., foreman, silver cert. for 25 yrs.), Naval Res. Assn., Soc. Exploration Geophysicists (silver cert. for 25 yrs.), SAR, Phi Kappa Tau. Club: Phillips (bd. dirs.). Lodges: Elks, Optimists. Home: 8414 Braes Meadow Dr Houston TX 77071 Office: PO Box 741619 Houston TX 77274

HASTINGS, JACK BYRON, artist; b. Kennett, Mo., Nov. 16, 1925; m. Arlyn Ende; m. Dorothy Furlong (div.); 1 child, Dorian Hastings. Student La. State U., 1947-49, Escuela de Pintura y Escultura, Mexico City, 1949. One man shows Barone Gallery, N.Y.C., 1960; Fine Arts Ctr., Cheekwood, Nashville, 1974; Delgado Mus. Art., New Orleans, 1958; exhibited in group shows Orleans Gallery, New Orleans, 1957-59, also founding mem.; Georg Jensen, N.Y.C., 1962; Signature Shop and Galleries, Atlanta, 1979; executed sculpture An Environmental Garden, Welcome Ctr., Chattanooga, 1983, sunscreen sculpture exterior Free Med. U. West Berlin, 1960, bronze sculpture 4 pub. schs. N.Y.C., 1961-63, carved cemnt fountain El Presidio Civic plaza Tucson, 1970; fountain Vol. State Community Coll., Gallatin, Tenn., 1982; atrium moblie sculpture TVA, 1986. Mem. Tenn. Artist Craftsmen's Assn.

HASTINGS, ROBERT CLYDE, research physician, pharmacologist; b. Tipton County, Tenn., Apr. 23, 1938; s. Robert Simpson and Margaret Marie (Peterson) H.; student Vanderbilt U., 1956-59; M.D., U. Tenn., 1962; Ph.D., Tulane U., 1971; children—Cynthia Margaret, Robert Clyde, Jeffrey Scott. Med. intern City of Memphis Hosps., 1963-64; commd. sr. asst. surgeon USPHS, 1964, advanced through grades to med. dir., 1976; staff physician and dep. chief clin. br. USPHS Hosp., Carville, La., 1964-68, staff physician, 1971—, chief pharmacology research dept., 1971—, chief lab. research br., 1983—. Instr. dept. medicine La State U., New Orleans, 1966—; adj. instr. dept. pharmacology Tulane U. Sch. Medicine, New Orleans, 1970-71, asst. prof., 1971-74, asso. prof., 1974-83, prof., 1983—, clin. asso. prof. dept. medicine, 1976-83, clin. prof., 1983—; asso. med. staff Tulane Med. Center Hosp., New Orleans, 1977—, chmn. com. for use of humans in med. research, 1977—; mem. U.S. Leprosy Panel, U.S.-Japan Coop. Med. Sci. Program, NIAID, NIH, 1977—, chmn., 1981—. Recipient Physicians Recognition award AMA, 1972, 76, 80, 82; Kellersberger Meml. Lecture, Addis Ababa, Ethiopia, 1979. Fellow Am. Coll. Clin. Pharmacology; mem. USPHS Commd. Officers Assn., Internat. Leprosy Assn., Am. Soc. Tropical Medicine and

Hygiene, AAAS, Reticuloendothelial Soc., Am. Chem. Soc., Am. Fedn. Clin. Research, Am. Soc. Pharmacology and Exptl. Therapeutics, Soc. Exptl. Biology and Medicine, N.Y. Acad. Sci., Am. Soc. Microbiology, Am. Soc. Clin. Pharmacology and Therapeutics, Sigma Xi. Democrat. Methodist. Contbr. articles to profl. jours.; editor Internat. Jour. Leprosy, 1978—. Office: USPHS Hosp Carville LA 70721

HASTY, FREDERICK EMERSON, III, laywer; b. Coral Gables, Fla., Oct. 21, 1950; s. Frederick and Rose (Irwin) H.; m. Deborah Thornton, Oct. 20, 1979; 1 son, Frederick Emerson, IV. B.A., U. Fla., 1973; J.D., Mercer U., 1976. Bar: Fla., Ga. Legal advisor City Macon, Ga., 1976-79; asst. state atty. 11th Jud. Circuit, Miami, Fla., 1979; assoc. Thornton & Herndon, Miami, 1979-83; ptnr. Schwartz & Hasty, Miami, 1983-85, Wicker, Smith Blomquist, Tutan, O'Hara, McCay, Graham & Lane, 1985—. Bd. dirs. Admirals of Fleet Fla., Miami, 1983. Democrat. Roman Catholic. Home: 1502 El Rado St Coral Gables FL 33134 Office: 19 W Flagler St Miami FL 33130

HASTY, GERALD RICHARD, political science educator, retired army officer; b. Pekin, Ill., Apr. 12, 1926; s. Leslie Parke and Bernice Arthene (Brown) H.; B.S., Bradley U., 1952; M.B.A., 1954; postgrad. Harvard, 1961; M.A., Am. U., 1962; Ph.D., Northwestern U., 1963; LL.B., Blackstone Sch. Law, 1968; postgrad. summers U. Toledo, 1958, U. Maine, 1963, State U. N.Y. at Buffalo, 1963, Armed Forces Staff Coll., 1968, Air War Coll., 1965, Harvard Law Sch., 1976; D.D. (hon.), Am. Fellowship Ch., 1977; m. Betty Anne Osmundson, June 23, 1951; children—Grant Rutledge, Mark Osmund, Deborah Anne. Commd. 2d lt. U.S. Army, 1954, advanced through grades to lt. col., 1966; chief Q.M. Supply div. 7th Logistical Command, Korea, 1961-62; comdg. officer 34th Supply and Service Bn., Vietnam, 1966, also dir. adminstrn. 58th Field Depot; exec. asst. joint logistics rev. bd. Office Sec. Def., Washington, 1969-70; comdg. officer Charleston (S.C.) Army Depot, 1970-72; joint logistics plans officer on staff comdr.-in-chief UN Command, 1972-73; logistics staff officer Joint and Strategic Forces Directorate, Army Concepts Analysis Agy., Bethesda, Md., 1973-74, ret.; asst. prof. pub. adminstrn. George Washington U., Washington, 1964-65, 67, assoc. prof., 1968-69, 73; vis. prof. polit. sci. Bapt. Coll., Charleston, 1970-72, now prof.; tchr., lectr., various colls., U.S. Korea, Vietnam; vis. prof. Central Mich. U., 1974—. Counselor, Boy Scouts Am., 1968—; mem. citizen's adv. and action council to gov. Coastal Carolina Community Pre-release Center, S.C. Dept. Corrections; bd. dirs. Charleston Safety Council; apptd. spl. envoy by gov. for Commonwealth of Pa., 1970; del. S.C. Republican Conv., 1978, 80, 82, 84, 86; pres. 20th Rep. Precinct, S.C., 1978-86. Served AUS, 1944-50. Decorated Legion of Merit with oak leaf cluster, Purple Heart with oak leaf cluster; recipient Presdl. Achievement award Pres. Ronald Reagan, 1982; Nat. Endowment for Humanities fellow U. Ga., summer 1978; Freedoms Found. at Valley Forge fellow, summers 1984-86. Mem. Charleston Trident C. of C., La Societe Francaise deBienfaisance de Charleston, Navy League, Mil. Order Purple Heart, Fed. Exec. Assn. (com. on govt.-wide policy areas), Armed Forces Mgmt. Assn., S.C. Law Enforcement Officers Assn., Nat. Def. Transp. Assn., Am. Bar Assn., S.C. Polit. Sci. Assn. (exec. council, pres.), Mensa, Pi Sigma Alpha, Tau Kappa Epsilon, Pi Gamma Mu. Lutheran. Mason (32 deg., Shriner), Kiwanian. Address: Sandhurst-on-the-Ashley 1282 Winchester Dr Charleston SC 29407

HATCHER, CHARLES, congressman; b. Doerun, Ga., July 1, 1939; student Ga. So. Coll., U. Ga. Sch. Law. Admitted to Ga. bar, 1969; practice law, Albany, Ga.; mem. Ga. Ho. of Reps., 1973, asst. adminstrn. floor leader for Gov. George Busbee; mem. 97th-99th congresses from 2d Ga. Dist.; mem. com. agrl., com. small bus.; chmn. subcom. antitrust and restraint of trade activities affecting small bus. Served with USAF. Office: Room 405 Cannon House Office Bldg Washington DC 20515

HATCHER, CHARLES ROSS, JR., medical center executive, cardiothoracic surgeon; b. Bainbridge, Ga., June 28, 1930; s. Charles Ross and Vivian Elizabeth (Miller) H.; m. Celeste Barnett, Aug. 15, 1953 (div. Jan. 1978; children—Marian Barnett, Charles. B.S. magna cum laude, U. Ga.; M.D. cum laude, Med. Coll. Ga., 1954. Intern, Johns Hopkins Hosp., Balt., 1954-55; resident in surgery, 1955-62; prof. surgery, chief cardiothoracic surgery Emory U. Sch. Medicine, Atlanta, 1971—, dir. Emory Clinic, 1976-84; dir. Woodruff Med. Ctr., Atlanta, 1984—. Served to capt. U.S. Army, 1956-58. Mem. ACS, Am. Coll. Cardiology, Am. Coll. Chest Physicians, Am. Surg. Assn., So. Surg. Assn., Am. Assn. Thoracic Surgery, Soc. Thoracic Surgery, Phi Beta Kappa, Sigma Xi, Alpha Omega Alpha. Methodist. Clubs: Capital City, Piedmont Driving. Lodge: Rotary. Contbg. author profl. publs. Home: 1105 Lullwater Rd NE Atlanta GA 30307 Office: 1440 Clifton Rd NE Atlanta GA 30322

HATCHER, LUCIA CORSIGLIA, dance instructor, choreographer; b. Miami, Feb. 13, 1956; d. Albert Anthony and Lucia Grace (Ferrara) Corsiglia; m. John Southall, Mar. 20, 1978; 1 child, Helen Grace. Student Nat. Acad. of Arts, 1973-74, U. So. Fla., 1975-78, Am. Ballet Theatre Sch., 1974-75, Dance Notation Bur., 1980. Instr., Avery Sch. of Dance, Miami, 1971-73, Cuca Martinez Sch. of Ballet, Miami, 1972-75; dir., instr. Conchita Espinosa Acad., Miami, 1974-75, Joe Mooney Sch. of Mus. and Dance, Tampa, 1976-78, Firethorn Sch. of Dance, Tampa, 1979—; dancer Miami Ballet Co., 1973-74; guest artist Fla. West Ballet Co., Clearwater, 1981-82. Choreographer, dancer (video production) Celebrity Video Productions, N.Y.C., 1981; artistic dir., choreographer (modern dance) Firethorn Modern Dance Co., Tampa, 1977—. Author, illus.: My First Ballet Book, 1983; choreographer (ballet) Dance Masters video, N.Y.C., 1981. Instr., dancer Hillsborough Community Mental Health Ctr., Fla., 1978-79; choreographer Fla. Orange Bowl Com., 1973. Nat. Acad. Arts scholar, 1974; Plant City Arts Council grantee, 1978; Mainsail Performing Arts Competition cash award, 1980. Mem. Dance Masters Am., State Dance Assn., Dance Notation Bur. Baha'i Faith. Home: 10606 Altman St Tampa FL 33612 Office: Firethorn Sch of Dance 10630 N 56th St Temple Terrace FL 33617

HATCHER, MARTHA OLIVIA TAYLOR (MRS. FRANK PRIDGEN HATCHER, SR.), educator; b. Birmingham, Ala., Feb. 17, 1920; d. Sanford Allia and Mary (McCullough) Taylor; B.S., Howard Coll., 1936-40; M.Ed. in Sci. Edn., U. Ga., 1966, Ed.D., 1973; tchrs. certificate Breanu Coll., 1964; m. Frank Pridgen Hatcher, Sr., Nov. 7, 1941; children—Frank Pridgen, Martha Elizabeth, Nancy Louise. Chief bacteriologist vet. div. Ga. Dept. Agr., Atlanta, 1943-45; supr. surg. pathology lab. Jefferson Hillman Hosp., Med. Coll. Ala., Birmingham, 1945-46, research asst. in pathology, 1945-46; mgr. offices Fran Mar Farms, Inc., Gainesville, Ga., 1957-66; instr. biology Gainesville Jr. Coll., 1966-67, asso. prof. biology, 1967, chmn. div. natural scis. and maths., 1968-82, prof. biology; accompanist music dept. Brenau Coll., Gainsville, 1959-61, prof. biology, adminstrv. asst., 1982—. Chmn. Gray Ladies Vol. Services, Gainesville chpt. A.R.C., 1957-62; sec. Yohah council Girl Scouts U.S.A., 1959-61; bd. dirs. Community Concert Assn. Gainesville, 1968-70. NSF sci. faculty fellow in microbiology, 1970-71. Mem. AAUP, AAAS, Am. Guild Organists, Am. Inst. Biol. Scis., Nat. Assn. Biology Tchrs., Assn. S.E. Biologists, Nat. Assn. Research Sci. Teaching, Ga. Acad. Sci. Nat. Sci. Tchrs. Assn., Am. Legion Aux. (pres. 1948-50), Am. Soc. Zoologists, UDC (chpt. pres. 1949-51), Am. Soc. Microbiology, AAUW, Kappa Delta Pi, Alpha Epsilon Delta, Delta Kappa Gamma, Phi Delta Kappa, Delta Zeta. Clubs: Music (pres. 1950-52), Federated Music (sec. Gainesville 1957-58, state historian Ga.), Pilot Internat. (pres. Gainesville chpt. 1983-84), Phoenix Soc. Home: 840 Memorial Dr NE Gainesville GA 30501 Office: PO Box 1358 Gainesville Jr Coll Gainesville GA 30501

HATCHETT, EDWARD EARL, aerospace manufacturing company executive; b. Amarillo, Tex., Aug. 18, 1923; s. Edward Lockett and Cora (Graham) H.; m. Kathryn Farwell, Apr. 27, 1943; 1 dau., Diane Hatchett Sanford. B.S. in Mgmt. Engring., Tex. A&M U., 1947; cert. exec. program, Stanford U., 1968. Registered profl. engr., Tex. Timestudy engr. Montgomery Ward & Co., Ft. Worth, 1947-49; with Ft. Worth div. Gen. Dynamics Corp., 1949—, v.p. fin., 1970—. Div. sec., chmn. Ft. Worth United Way, 1974-80; bd. dirs., mem. adv. council Ft. Worth Salvation Army, 1978-83; bd. dirs. Casa Manana Musicals, 1980—; mem. exec. bd. Longhorn council Boy Scouts Am., 1981—; mem. N. Tex. Commn. Strategic Issues Adv. Council; chmn. Ft. Worth Area Com. for Employer Support of Guard and Res. Served to maj. USAAF, 1943-46, 51-53; lt. col. USAFR, ret. Recipient Presdl. citation Am. Soc. Value Engrs., 1974; Exec. of Yr. award Exec. Women Internat., 1976, Outstanding Leadership award local chptr. Am. Def. Preparedness Assn. Mem. Fin. Execs. Inst., Air Force Assn., Gen. Dynamics Mgmt. Assn., Am. Def. Preparedness Assn. (pres. local chptr. 1976-78, dir. 1979—), Ft. Worth Air Power Council, Ft. Worth C. of C. (dir. 1976, 81-82). Methodist. Club: Ridglea Country. Office: General Dynamics Corp PO Box 748 MZ 1230 Fort Worth TX 76101

HATCHETT, JOSEPH WOODROW, judge; b. Clearwater, Fla., Sept. 17, 1932; s. John Arthur and Lula Gertrude (Thomas) H.; A.B., Fla. A. and M. U., 1954; J.D., Howard U., 1959; cert. mil. judge course U.S. Naval Justice Sch., Newport, R.I., 1973; m. Betty Lue Davis, Aug. 20, 1956; children—Cheryl Nadine, Brenda Audrey. Bar: Fla. 1959; practice in Daytona Beach, 1959-66; asst. U.S. atty. Dept. Justice, Jacksonville, Fla., 1966-70; U.S. magistrate U.S. Cts., Jacksonville, 1971-75; justice Supreme Ct. Fla., Tallahassee, 1975-79; judge U.S. Ct. Appeals, 5th Cir., 1979-81, U.S. Ct. Appeals, 11th Cir., 1981—. Cooperating atty. NAACP Legal Def. Fund, 1960-66; gen. counsel Masons of Fla., 1963-66; cons., mem. staff dept. urban renewal, Daytona Beach, 1963-66; spl. asst. to city atty., Daytona Beach, 1964. Mem. com. selection for Jacksonville Naval Res. Officer Tng. Corps, 1971; mem. John T. Stocking Meml. Trust, med. sch. scholarships, 1961-66. Co-chmn. United Negro Coll. Fund of Volusia County (Fla.), 1962; bd. dirs. Jacksonville Opportunities Industrialization Center, 1972-75. Served to 1st lt. AUS, 1954-56; Germany. Recipient Mary McCloud Bethune medallion for community service Bethune-Cookman Coll., 1965, medallion for human relations, 1975. Mem. Am., Nat., Fla., Jacksonville, D. W. Perkins, Fed. bar assns., Am. Judicature Soc., Nat. Council Fed. Magistrates, V.F.W., Omega Psi Phi. Baptist (trustee). Club: Fla-Jax (Man of Year 1974) (Jacksonville). Contbr. articles to profl. jours. Home: PO Box 981 Tallahassee FL 32302 Office: Suite 810 Lewis State Bank Bldg PO Box 10429 Tallahassee FL 32302

HATFIELD, BRUCE PATRICK, health care consultant; b. Canton, Ohio, Apr. 24, 1948; s. William Ray and Dolores Mary (Ledger) Hatfield; m. Anne Marie Findlay, Apr. 15, 1972 (div. Dec. 1975); m. Barbra Dianne Campbell, May 22, 1982. B.S. in Biology and Chemistry, Ohio State U., 1970; B.S. in Pharmacy, U.Tex., 1975; M.S. in Mgmt., Troy State U., 1980; diploma in Health Care Adminstrn., Acad. Health Scis., Ft. Sam Houston, Tex., 1986; grad. Command and Gen. Staff Coll., 1986. Pharmacy officer Martin Army Hosp., Columbus, Ga., 1976-79; dir. pharmacy Phys. and Surg. Hosp., Atlanta, 1979-80; pres. Hosp. Mgmt. Resources, Atlanta, 1980-85; devel. cons. Universal Health Services, King of Prussia, Pa., 1985—. Producer, host Jobwatch show Cable TV, Atlanta, 1983; producer On the Job campaign WSB-TV, 1983. Contbr. articles to profl. jours. Served with U.S. Army, 1971-73, 76-79. Mem. Am. Soc. Hosp. Pharmacists, Am. Hosp. Assn., Assn. Mil. Surgeons. Republican. Presbyterian. Clubs: Eufuala Sailing, Eufuala Boat (Ala.). Avocations: Sailing; canoeing; skiing; backpacking. Home: PO Box 3101 Kennesaw GA 30144 Office: Universal Health Services 367 Gulph St King of Prussia PA 19406

HATFIELD, DAVID MARTIN, industrial education educator; b. Westminster, Eng., Oct. 1, 1944; came to U.S., 1946; s. James Martin and Brenda (Skidamore) H.; m. Faye Helen Walraven, Nov. 27, 1965. B.S., Austin Peay State U., 1969; M.A., Tenn. State U., 1975; Ed.D. candidate U. Tenn. Tchr., Christian County Schs., Hopkinsville, Ky., 1969-71; tchr., chmn. dept. Clarksville-Montgomery County Schs., Clarksville, Tenn., 1971-76; tech. coordinator Austin Peay State U., Clarksville, 1979-80; dir. coop. edn. Middle Tenn. State U., Murfreesboro, 1981—. Active Big Bro./Big Sister Program, 1977-82; mem. ch. vestry, jr. warden Episcopal Ch., 1980, 82; cons. Montgomery County Sch. System, 1979—. Recipient Outstanding Middle Tenn. Indsl. Arts Tchr. award Middle Tenn. Indsl. Arts Assn., 1976. Trane Co. scholar, 1968; Marvin-Haynes scholar, 1967. Mem. Am. Indsl. Arts Assn., NEA, Tenn. Coop. Edn. Assn., Tenn. Indsl. Arts Assn., Epsilon Pi Tau, Omicron Tau Theta. Democrat. Office: Middle Tenn State U PO Box 153 Murfreesboro TN 37132

HATFIELD, GARY DAN, quality engineer; b. Tulsa, Aug. 23, 1954; m. Melita Jane Wyatt, June 24, 1977; children—Rebecca, Meghan. B.S. in Math., Okla. State U., 1976, M.S. in Stats., 1978. Statis. cons. Phillips Petroleum Co., Bartlesville, Okla., 1978-81; quality engr. Phillips Chem. Co., Borger, Tex., 1981—. Mem. Am. Soc. Quality Control (cert. quality engr.), Am. Statis. Assn. Methodist. Avocations: photography; reading. Home: 106 Brierwood Apt 95 PO Box 3243 Borger TX 79008 Office: Phillips Chem Co Philblack Plant PO Box 1526 Borger TX 79008

HATFIELD, STEVEN KIM, oil company executive, petroleum engineering consultant; b. Royal Oaks, Mich., June 23, 1952; s. R.J. and Mary Ruth (Pennington) H.; m. Suzette Baggerly, Aug. 6, 1976; children—Colleen Janell, Kathleen Marie. B.S., in Petroleum Engring., U. Okla., 1974, M.S. in Petroleum Engring., 1979. Engr. Atlantic Richfield Co., Houston, 1974-76; course moderator U. Okla. Blowout Prevention Sch., Norman, 1976-79; chief engr. Nelson Oil & Gas Co., Shreveport, La., 1979-80; v.p. Crawley Petroleum Corp., Oklahoma City, 1980-85, pres., 1985—; dir. P.D.I., Inc., Oklahoma City, 1983—, Empire Oil of N.J., Oklahoma City, 1982—; lectr., cons. Petroleum Tng. & Tech. Services, Norman, 1979—. Author: Well Control: An Evaluation of Current Techniques, 1978. Mem. Soc. Petroleum Engrs., Am. Assn. Petroleum Geologists (jr.). Republican. Mem. Ch. of Christ. Avocations: squash; beekeeping. Office: Crawley Petroleum Corp 515 Hightower Bldg Oklahoma City OK 73102

HATHAWAY, AMOS TOWNSEND, naval officer, educator; b. Pueblo, Colo., Dec. 5, 1913; s. James Amos and Nina (North) H.; B.S., U.S. Naval Acad., 1935; postgrad. U.S. Naval War Coll., 1947-48; M.A. in Teaching, Duke U., 1965-66; m. Marianne Langdon Train, June 10, 1937 (dec. Dec. 1972); children—Joan Langdon, Marianne Train, Melinda North (dec.), Barbara Spencer, Sarah Townsend; m. 2d, Gay Johnson Blair, Jan. 2, 1979. Commd. ensign U.S. Navy, 1935, advanced through grades to capt., 1954; exec. officer, navigator destroyer minesweeper Zane, Guadalcanal, 1942; command destroyer Heermann, Battle off Samar, 1944; mem. faculty U.S. Naval Acad., 1945-47, U.S. Naval War Coll., 1951-53; mem. war staff Gen. MacArthur, Korea, 1948-50, writer theater logistic plan Inchon Landing, 1950; exec. officer cruiser St. Paul, 1950-51; command Destroyer Div. 92, 1953-54, command attack transport Okanogan, 1958-59; command cruiser Rochester, 1959-60; mem. joint staff Joint Chiefs of Staff, 1961-63, dir. logistic plans Office Chief of Naval Operations, 1963-65, ret., 1965; asst. prof. math. The Citadel, Charleston, S.C., 1966-79. Decorated Navy Cross, Legion of Merit (2), Bronze Star (2). Mem. Math. Assn. Am., U.S. Naval Acad. Alumni Assn., U.S. Naval Acad. Athletic Assn. (dir. 1945-47), U.S. Naval Inst., Kappa Delta Pi. Club: Army Navy (Washington). Home: 11 Sayle Rd Charleston SC 29407 also PO Box 5463 Charlottesville VA 22905

HATHAWAY, ARTHUR JUSTIN, printing and graphics executive; b. Dallas, Jan. 11, 1953; s. Herbert Hoover and Dawn (Leggett) H.; student S.W. Tex. State U., 1976-77; m. Delia Sanchez, Mar. 31, 1977; 1 son, Brian Patrick. Print shop mgr. BBA Advt., San Antonio, 1969-72; prodn. mgr. Pacesetter Pub. Co., San Antonio, 1972-73; print shop mgr. Sherwood Van Lines, San Antonio, 1973-75; vocat. printing instr., supr. Gary Job Corps., San Marcos, Tex., 1975-78; prodn. mgr. Bennett Printing Co., Dallas, 1978-80; v.p., gen. mgr. Multicopy Printing Co., San Antonio, 1980-82; dir. graphics div. Sherwood Van Lines, San Antonio, 1982—; coordinator graphic communications Woodcreek Resort, Wimberly, Tex., 1977-78. Bd. dirs. Miss. Black San Antonio Beauty Pagent, 1976-77. Recipient cert. of Achievement, Eastman Kodak Co., 1979, 82, Dallas Sch. Printing Papers, 1979. Mem. Internat. Graphic Arts Edn. Assn. (Disting. service award 1982), Plant Printing Mgmt. Assn., Internat. Club Printing Craftsman, San Antonio Litho Club, Dallas Litho Club, Council Reprographics Execs., Graphic Arts Tech. Found., Am. Printing History Assn. Democrat. Baptist. Club: Dallas Litho. Home: 1115 Thorain Blvd San Antonio TX 78201 Office: 3507 Copeland St San Antonio TX 78219

HATHAWAY, WALTER MURPHY, museum director; b. Norfolk, Va., Feb. 25, 1939; s. Alvin Earl and Minneta Seybolt (Kerton) H.; m. Anna Elizabeth Burton, Nov. 26, 1960; children—Anna Elizabeth, Michael Burton, John Carter. B.F.A., Va. Commonwealth U., 1961; M.S., Fla. State U., 1964. Tchr. art Norfolk Pub. Schs., 1961-63; instr. Lake City Jr. Coll., 1964-67; asst. prof. art Longwood Coll., 1967-70; cons. in art N.C. Dept. Public Instrn., Raleigh, 1970-72; dir. Roanoke (Va.) Fine Arts Center, 1972-77, Columbia Mus. Art and Sci., S.C., 1977—. Mem. Am. Assn. Mus., Assn. Art Mus. Dirs., Southeastern Mus. Conf., S.C. Fedn. Mus. Roman Catholic. Lodge: Rotary. Office: Columbia Museum 1112 Bull St Columbia SC 29201*

HATHORN, GARY (LARUE), architect, civil engineer, real estate broker; b. Jefferson Davis County, Miss., Mar. 7, 1936; s. John Alford and Ollie Mae (Burge) H.; m. Sue Gaddy, Aug. 16, 1959; 1 dau., Jacquelyn. B.S. in Civil Engring., Miss. State U., 1962. Registered engr., Miss.; registered architect, Miss., Tex., Colo., Ky.; lic. real estate broker, Miss. Ptnr. John L. Turner & Assocs., Jackson, Miss., 1971-76, The Turner Partnership, Jackson, 1976-78; prin. Hathorn Assocs., Jackson, 1978-80; ptnr. Architects Plus (renamed architects Plus The Hathorn Tyson Warrington Group Ltd. 1981), Jackson, 1980-81, pres., 1981— (renamed Architects Plus A Profl. Assn. 1985). Prin. works include U.S. Naval Home, Naval Oceanography Bldg., Arthur Casagrande Geotech. Lab., VA Clin. Bldg., Capitol Towers Office Bldg., Choctaw Indian Hosp., Naval Tech. Tng. Command Adminstrn. Bldg., Primary Computer Ctr. Addition. Mem. Miss. Econ. Council, Miss. Indsl. Devel. Council. Served to engineman 2d class USCG, 1954-58. Mem. AIA, (Miss. chpt. sec.-treas. 1981-82), Nat. Soc. Profl. Engrs., Miss. Engring. Soc., Jackson C. of C., Nat. Rifle Assn. (life), Safari Club Internat., Miss. Bowhunter's Assn., Magnolia Rifle and Pistol Club, Buzzard Roost Hunting Club, Miss. Geneal. Soc., Sons Confederate Vets., Mil. Order Stars and Bars. Republican. Baptist. Lodge: Lions. Avocations: hunting; fishing; photography; genealogy; travel. Home: 3805 Crane Blvd Jackson MS 39216 Office: Architects Plus A Profl Assn 3780 I-55 Frontage Rd Jackson MS 39211

HAUGEN, ALYS JOY, psychologist; b. Shelby County, Iowa, Jan. 8, 1940; d. Harry Albert Wetzel and Helen Myrtle (Wendt) Wetzel; m. Arthur Dennis Haugen, Aug. 3, 1958; children—Debra Suzan Haugen-Davis, Lisa Michelle, Jill Danene. Student Minn. Bible Coll., 1957-61, Marshalltown Community Coll., 1974, Eastfield Community Coll., 1975-76; B.A., U. Tex.-Dallas, 1977, Ph.D., 1981. Lic. psychologist, Tex.; registered health service provider in psychology. Staff psychologist Salesmanship Club Youth and Family Ctrs., Dallas, 1981-84; pvt. practice clin. psychology, Granbury, Tex., 1985—; clin. supr. U. Tex. Health Sci. Ctr., Dallas, 1983—. Mem. LWV, Marshalltown, Iowa, 1973-74. Mem. Am. Psychol. Assn. (div. psychology of women, div. psychoanalysis). Democrat. Mem. Christian Ch. Club: Granbury Bus. and Profl. Women's. Avocations: singing, sailing, snow skiing, hiking, horseback riding. Office: Granbury Med Clinic and Profl Bldg 1312 Paluxy Hwy Granbury TX 76048

HAUGHT, WILLIAM DIXON, lawyer; b. Kansas City, Kans., June 12, 1939; s. Walter Dixon and Florence Louise (Rhoads) H.; B.S., U. Kans., 1961, LL.B., 1964; LL.M., Georgetown U., 1968; m. Julia Jane Headstream, July 22, 1967; 1 dau., Stephanie Jane. Admitted to Kans. bar, 1964, Ark. bar, 1971; asso. firm Stanley, Schroeder, Weeks, Thomas & Lysaught, Kansas City, Kans., 1968-70; partner firm Wright, Lindsey & Jennings, Little Rock, 1970—. Served to capt. USAR, 1964-68; Korea and Washington. Decorated Army Commendation medal with oak leaf cluster. Mem. Am. Bar Assn. (council, co-chmn. coms.), Am. Coll. Probate Counsel (regent, editor studies program), Internat. Acad. Estate and Trust Law, Am. Agrl. Law Assn., Ark. Bar Assn. (chmn. probate law sect. 1981-82, chmn. econs. and law practice com. 1982-84), Central Ark. Estate Council, Pulaski County Bar Assn. Presbyterian. Clubs: Country of Little Rock, Capital, Little Rock. Author: Arkansas Probate System, 1977, 2d edit., 1979, 3d edit., 1981; co-author: Arkansas Probate, 1984; other publs. Office: 2200 Worthen Bank Bldg Little Rock AR 72201

HAURAND, RUTH ANN, insurance executive; b. Norwich, Conn., July 29, 1943; d. Adam and Ann Maria (Strenkowski) Jacobik; m. George Leonard Haurand, Jr., Jan. 14, 1967 (dec.); children—Deborah, Florence, Susan, Theresa, Christine. Personal service rep. Noblit Ins. Agy., Inc., Tarpon Springs, Fla., 1973-79, personal lines sales mgr., 1979-81, personal lines mgr., after 1981, dir., corporate sec., 1985—. Mem. Ind. Ins. Agts. Tarpon Springs (sec. 1984, v.p. 1985, pres. 1986), Ins. Women West Pasco (pres. 1979, 80). Republican. Roman Catholic. Home: 2706 Cypress Circle E New Port Richey FL 33552 Office: Noblit Ins Agy Inc 701 E Tarpon Ave Tarpon Springs FL 33589

HAUSEN, JUTTA, mathematician; b. Berlin, Germany, Jan. 6, 1943; came to U.S., 1967, naturalized, 1983; d. Harald Walter and Martha (Duente) Hausen; m. Nicholas C. Chriss, May 23, 1984. Dip. in Math., U. Frankfurt, W. Ger., 1967, Ph.D., 1967. Postdoctoral fellow N. Mex. State U., Las Cruces, 1967-68; from asst. prof. to assoc. prof. U. Houston, 1968-77, prof., 1977—. Assoc. mng. editor Houston Jour. Math., 1974-80; editor, 1980—. Contbr. articles to profl. jour. U. Houston Research grantee, 1969, 76, 77, 80, 82, 84, 86; NSF Research grantee, 1971-73. Mem. Am. Math. Soc., Deutsche Math. Vereinigung, Tex. Assn. Coll. Tchrs. (treas. 1983—). Office: U Houston-Univ Park 4800 Calhoun Houston TX 77004

HAUSER, ALAN JON, Biblical scholar, educator; b. Chgo., Oct. 15, 1945; s. Edward Frederick and Esther Caroline (Lindblade) H.; m. Rhoda Edith Gutzwiller, Aug. 5, 1967 (dec.); children—Deborah Esther, Mary Elizabeth. B.A., Concordia Tchrs. Coll., 1967; M.A. in Religion, Concordia Sem., 1968; Ph.D., U. Iowa, 1972. Asst. prof. dept. philosophy and religion Applachian State U., Boone, N.C., 1972-77, assoc. prof., 1977-82, prof. dept. philosophy and religion, 1982—, chmn. dept., 1982—, chmn. faculty senate, 1979-81; chmn. faculty assembly U. N.C. system, 1981-84. Mem. Soc. Biblical Lit. (chmn. rhetorical criticism sect. 1979—). Lutheran. Editor: Art and Meaning: Rhetoric in Biblical Literature, 1982; contbr. articles to profl. jours. Office: Dept Philosophy and Religion Appalachian State U Boone NC 28608

HAUSER, STANLEY FILLMORE, bishop; b. Laredo, Tex., Aug. 7, 1922; s. Stanley Fillmore and Elizabeth Mary (Merriman) H.; m. Madelyn May Horner, June 5, 1947; children—Mary Madelyn, Christine, Stanley, John, Mark. B.A., U. of the South, 1943, D.D. (hon.), 1985; M.Div., Va. Theol. Sem., 1946, D.D., 1980. Ordained priest Episcopal Ch., 1946. Rector Calvary Episcopal Ch., Menard, Tex., 1946-47; priest-in-charge St. James' Episcopal Ch., Fort McKavett, Tex., 1946-47; rector St. John's Episcopal Ch., Sonora, Tex., priest-in-charge Trinity Episcopal Ch., Junction, Tex., 1947-51; rector Zion Episcopal Ch., Charlestown, W.Va., 1951-60, St. Mark's Episcopal Ch., Houston, 1960-68, St. Mark's Episcopal Ch., San Antonio, 1968-79; bishop suffragan Episcopal Diocese W. Tex., San Antonio, 1979—; pres. Community of Chs., San Antonio, 1976-77. Trustee Va. Theol. Sem., Alexandria, 1958-60; bd. trustees U. of the South, Sewanee, Tenn., 1979—; bd. dirs. Amigos de las Americas, Houston, 1975-79. Office: Episcopal Diocese W Tex PO Box 6885 San Antonio TX 78209

HAVARD, FRANK DUBOIS, transportation executive; b. Mobile, Ala., Oct. 10, 1956; s. Ralph Wesley and Ellen Patterson (DuBois) H.; m. Lyn Crowell Havard, Aug. 1984. B.A., U. N.C., 1980. Dir. communications Nat. Hdqrs. Pi Kappa Phi, Charlotte, N.C., 1978-80; dir. personnel Searail Industries, Inc., Mobile, 1980—, sec.-treas., 1983—. Named Greek Man of Yr., U. South Ala., 1978; recipient Outstanding Alumni award Pi Kappa Phi, 1981. Mem. Mobile Personnel Assn. (pres.), Am. Soc. Personnel Adminstrs., U. South Ala. Alumni Assn. (pres.-elect), Gulf Coast Alumni Assn. (pres.), Pi Kappa Phi. Presbyterian. Club: Internat. Trade (Mobile). Lodge: Knights of Revelry. Home: 212 S Fulton St Mobile AL 36606 Office: PO Box 909 Mobile AL 36601

HAVASI, GEORGE, anesthesiologist; b. Venscello, Hungary, Nov. 23, 1941; s. Gyorgy and Anna (Frank) Hengsperger; M.D., Budapesti Orvostudomanyi Egyetem, Hungary, 1966; m. Ilona Tar, June 29, 1974. Asso. anesthesiologist Mississauga (Ont., Can.) Hosp., 1976-77, Regina (Sask., Can.) Gen. Hosp., 1978; asst. anesthesiologist, lectr. Toronto (Ont.) Gen. Hosp. and U. Toronto, 1978; asst. prof. anesthesiology Tex. Tech. U. Health Sci. Center, Lubbock, 1979-82; asst. clin. prof. anesthesiology Tex. Tech. U., Amarillo, 1982—; assoc. anesthesiologist High Plains Bapt. Hosp., Amarillo, 1982—. Adv. Am. Security Council. Recipient certs. Internat. Anesthesia Research Soc., N.Y. State Soc. Anesthesiologists. Mem. AMA, Am. Soc. Anesthesiology, Tex. Med. Assn., Tex. Soc. Anesthesiologists, Soc. Cardiovascular Anesthesiologists, Internat. Anesthesia Research Soc., Western Pharmacology Soc., Acad. Polit. Sci., Internat. Platform Assn. Roman Catholic. Home: 3524 Sleepy Hollow Blvd Amarillo TX 79121 Office: 6103 Amarillo Blvd W Amarillo TX 79106 also PO Box 10190 Amarillo TX 79106

HAVELOS, SAM GEORGE, ret. restaurant exec.; b. Pavlpoulon, Greece, Dec. 4, 1915; s. George D. and Spyridoula G. (Kanavos) H.; student Distributive Edn., Wytheville, Va., 1955-60, Parkwood Bus. Coll., Marion, Va., 1961, Statesville (N.C.) Coll., 1963, Zanerian Coll. Penmanship, Columbus, Ohio, 1964; m. Dina K. Karageorge, Sept. 12, 1953. Owner, Presto Restaurant, Winston-Salem, N.C., 1932-34; mgr. Central Restaurant, Fayetteville, N.C., 1934-38, owner, 1940-52; mgr. San. Restaurant, Winston-Salem, 1938-40; owner Washington Restaurant, Wytheville, Va., 1952-61, Reynolda Manor Cafeteria, Winston-Salem, 1962-64; mgr. Sam's Gourmet, Winston-Salem, 1965-69, Greeks Cellar, Blacksburg, Va., 1969-82; treas. Wytheville Twins baseball team, 1960. Active ARC. Recipient cert. meritorious service Nat. Soc. SAR, 1973. Mem. Restaurant Assn. Cumberland and Robinson Counties (pres.), N.C. Restaurant Assn. (dir.), Am. Numis. Assn., Nat. Geog. Soc.,

Evrytanian Assn., Statue of Liberty Ellis Island Found., Am. Helenic Edn. Progressive Assn., F.M. Philatelic Assn., Smithsonian Inst., C. of C., Three Hundred Knights of Thermophylae (responsible for financing constrn. meml. monument 1951), Patriots of Am. Bicentennial, Nat. Wild Life Fedn., Nat. Flag Found. Greek Orthodox. Clubs: KP, Dram Order Knights of Korassan, Quarterback, Execs. Am., Moose. Calligraphist; designed suggested new U.S. flag at Hawaii statehood, 1959. Address: Drawer E Blacksburg VA 24060

HAVERTY, RAWSON, retail executive; b. Atlanta, Nov. 26, 1920; s. Clarence and Elizabeth (Rawson) H.; B.A., U. Ga., 1941; m. Margaret Middleton Munnerlyn, Aug. 25, 1951; children—Margaret Elizabeth Haverty Glover, Jane Middleton Langford, James Rawson, Jr., Mary Elizabeth, Ben Munnerlyn. With Haverty Furniture Co., 1941-42, Haverty Furniture Cos., Inc., Atlanta, 1946—, pres., 1955—, chmn. bd., chief exec. officer, 1984—, also dir.; instr. credit and collection So. Retail Furniture Assn. Sch. for Execs., U. N.C., 1950, instr. credits, collections, market analyses, 1951; instr. br. stores Nat. Retail Furniture Sch. for Execs., U. Chgo., 1957—; chmn. bd., dir. Bank South Corp.; dir. Piedmont Aviation, Inc., Winston-Salem, N.C., Central Atlanta Progress. Former chmn. Met. Atlanta Rapid Transit Authority; former chmn. bd. trustees St. Joseph's Hosp.; pres. U. Ga. Alumni Soc., 1973-75, mem. exec. com., 1975—, chmn. loyalty fund, 1969-70, 70-71; past pres. bd. trustees St. Joseph's Village; trustee Atlanta Arts Alliance, Westminster Sch., Atlanta, U. Ga. Found.; past pres. bd. sponsors Atlanta Art Sch.; bd. sponsors High Mus. Art; former mem. Fulton Indsl. Authority. Served as maj. AUS, 1942-46. Decorated Bronze Star medal; Order of Leopold, Croix de Guerre with palms (Belgium); named All Am. Mcht. in retail furniture industry, 1958. Mem. Atlanta Retail Mchts. Assn. (past pres., dir.), Nat. Home Furnishings Assn. (past v.p., dir., Retailer of Year 1979-80), Am. Retail Fedn., Atlanta Jr. C. of C. (hon. life), Assn. U.S. Army (past pres., adv. bd.), Atlanta C. of C. (dir., past pres.), Sigma Alpha Epsilon. Roman Catholic. Clubs: Piedmont Driving, Capital City (Atlanta); Ponte Vedra (Fla.). Lodge: Kiwanis. Office: 866 W Peachtree St NW Atlanta GA 30308

HAVICK, JOHN J., political science educator; b. Omaha, Apr. 29, 1940; s. J.C. and Alice M. (Anderson) H.; m. Barbara Wagner, June 26, 1965; children—Ann, Steve. B.A., Coe Coll., 1962; M.A., U. Ia., 1966, Ph.D., 1975. Instr., Luther Coll., Decorah, Ia., 1968-70; vis. instr. Ia. State U., Ames, 1974; from asst. to assoc. prof. Ga. Inst. Tech., Atlanta, 1975—; govt. programs cons. Job Tng., Rome, Ga., 1984-85. Editor and contbr.: Communications Policy and the Political Process, 1983. Contbr. articles to profl. jours. Fellow NIMH, 1977, NEH, 1981. Mem. Am. Polit. Sci. Assn., Midwest Polit. Sci. Assn. Home: 5251 Rockborough Trail Stone Mountain GA

HAVRILESKY, THOMAS MICHAEL, economics educator; b. Johnstown, Pa., Mar. 18, 1939; s. Michael and Pauline (Duranko) H.; m. Susan Newberry, Sept. 25, 1964 (div. 1979); children—Thomas Eric, Laura Jean, Heather Paula. B.S., Pa. State U., 1960, M.A., 1963; Ph.D., U. Ill., 1966. Fellow Fed. Res. Bank Chgo., 1966; asst. prof. econs. U. Md.-College Park, 1966-69, Rice U., Houston, 1970-71; prof. Duke U., Durham, N.C., 1971—; vis. prof. various univs., Can., Australia, Netherlands, Mexico; cons. in field, 1974—. Author: Contemporary Developments in Financial Markets, 1983; Introduction to Modern Macroeconomics, 1984; Modern Concepts in Macroeconomics, 1985; Dynamics of Banking, 1985. Bd. dirs. Five Oaks Recreation Assn., Durham, 1983—; chmn. Hickory Downs Owners Assn., Durham, 1985—. Mem. Am. Econ. Assn., Phi Kappa Phi, Omicron Delta Epsilon. Roman Catholic. Avocations: tennis, swimming, competitive running. Home: 4101 Five Oaks Dr #13 Durham NC 27707 Office: Dept Econs Duke U Durham NC 27706

HAWK, ROBERT DOOLEY, wholesale grocery company executive; b. Hominy, Okla., Aug. 27, 1940; s. Henry Dooley and Loretta Elizabeth (Rutherford) H.; m. Sandra Lynn Winters, Dec. 30, 1963; 1 son, Robert Dooley. B.B.A., U. Okla., 1963; M.B.A., U. Tulsa, 1969. Buyer, Hale Halsell Co., Tulsa, 1963-68, purchasing dir., 1968-72, asst. sec., treas., 1972-78, v.p. fin., sec., treas., 1978—, also dir.; dir. Git-N-Go, Inc., Foodland, Inc., Foodtown, Inc., Ark. Valley Distbn. Co., Inc., Sipes Food Markets Inc., Texoma Drug Sales Co. Inc., United Supermarkets, Inc., Fadler, Inc., Guaranty Nat. Bank, Tulsa. Mem. Nat. Am. Wholesale Grocery Assn., Tulsa Better Bus. Bur. Club: Cedar Ridge Country, Shadow Mountain Tennis. Lodges: Masons.

HAWKINS, ADOLPHUS WISE, JR., international business consultant, investment banker; b. Culpeper, Va., Mar. 4, 1922; s. Adolphus W. and Clara (Taylor) H.; m. Bette Worsham; children—John Thomas Worsham, David Telford, Lisabeth Jill. B.A. in Econs., U. Va., 1948; postgrad. U. Paris, 1949, Balliol Coll., Oxford (Eng.) U., 1950; D.C.S., London Inst. Applied Research, 1972. Owner A.W. Hawkins, Inc., Culpeper, 1951-59, Ashley Transfer & Storage Co., Charleston, S.C., 1954-56, Hawkins Moving and Storage Co., Fayetteville, N.C., 1954-58; assoc. Elam & Funsten, Richmond, Va., 1960-64; specialist corp. mergers and acquisitions Merrill Lynch, Pierce, Fenner and Smith, Inc., 1966-69; v.p. Anderson & Strudwick Inc., 1969-79, Scott & Stringfellow Inc., Richmond, 1979-83; dir. Doughtie's Foods, Inc.; mem. N.Y. Stock Exchange; pres. Mediterranean Foods S.P.A. Former mem. Richmond Democratic Com.; past mem. bd. dirs. Multiple Sclerosis Soc. Served with USN, 1942-46; PTO. Mem. Va. Squash Racquets Assn. (founder, life), U. Va. Alumni Assn., U.S. Squash Racquets Assn., ETA Ednl. Found., Phi Kappa Sigma. Clubs: Westwood Racquet (dir.), Farmington Country. Home: 3808 Dover Rd Windsor Farms Richmond VA 23221

HAWKINS, ARMIS EUGENE, judge; b. Natchez, Miss., Nov. 11, 1920; s. Charles Mayfield and Lela (Hill) H.; m. Patricia Burrow, Aug. 20, 1948; children—Janice Hawkins Shrewsbury, Jean Ann, James Charles. Student Wood Jr. Coll., 1938-39, Millsaps Coll., 1943; LL.B., U. Miss., 1947. Bar: Miss. Sole practice law, Houston, Miss., 1947; dist. atty. 3d Circuit Ct. Dist. Miss., 1951-59; assoc. justice Miss. Supreme Ct., 1980—. Served with USMC, 1942-46, PTO. Mem. ABA, Am. Judicature Soc., Miss. Trial Lawyers Assn., Miss. State Bar. Baptist. Office: Office Supreme Ct Miss Jackson MS 39205*

HAWKINS, CAROLYN SIVLEY, sales executive; b. Ft. Smith, Ark., Feb. 8, 1952; d. Robert Edward and Edith Emily (Sivley) H.; m. James Jones Pryor; 1 son, Benjamin Robert. B.S., U. Ark., Little Rock, 1974; Med. Technologist, VA Sch. Med. Tech., 1974; student (Ark. Jr. Miss. scholar), Ouachita Bapt. U., 1970-72. Med. technologist Bapt. Med. Center, Little Rock, 1974-75; tech. dir. United Blood Services, Ft. Smith, 1975-79; sales engr. Hawkins Co., Inc., Ft. Smith, 1980-81, ter. mgr., 1982—. Mem. Gov.'s Youth Council, 1970. Mem. Am. Soc. Clin. Pathologists (registered med. technologist), Am. Assn. Blood Banks, S. Central Assn. Blood Banks (publs. com. 1976-77), Am. Soc. Med. Tech., Ark. Soc. Med. Tech. (dir. 1977-79, chmn. public relations com. 1978-79, nominations com. 1979-80), Jr. League (dir., chmn. Niteliners), Pi Beta Phi Alumnae. Methodist. Office: 222 Towson Ave Fort Smith AR 72901

HAWKINS, DORISULA WOOTEN, business educator, administrator; b. Mt. Pleasant, Tex., Nov. 15, 1941; d. Wilber F. and Artesia (Ellis) W.; m. Howard Hawkins, Dec. 22, 1963; children—Darrell Eugene, Derek Dyon. B.S., Jarvis Christian Coll., 1962; M.S., Prairie View A&M U., 1967; Ed.D., U. Houston, 1975. Sec. Jarvis Christian Coll., Hawkins, Tex., 1962-63; instr. Roxton Ind. Sch. Dist., Tex., 1963-66; instr., then assoc. prof. Prairie View A&M U., Tex., 1966-76, interim dean, 1983-84, dept. head, 1976—; mem. adv. bd. Milady Pub. Co., N.Y., 1978-79; cons. Prairie View City Council, Tex., 1982. Vice pres. Prairie Hills Civic Assn., 1980. Recipient Disting. Alumnus award Jarvis Christian Coll., 1982, Merit cert. Prairie View A&M U., 1979-82, Outstanding Achievement in Edn. award Prairie View A&M U., 1975, Disting. Alumni citation Nat. Assn. Equal Opportunity in Higher Edn., 1986. Mem. Tex. Bus. Educators (dist. rep. 1981), Tex. Bus. Tchrs. Edn. Council (pres. 1985—), Nat. Bus. Edn. Assn., Phi Delta Kappa, Alpha Kappa Alpha. Democrat. Baptist. Club: Jack and Jill of Am. Home: PO Box 2448 Prairie View TX 77446 Office: Prairie View A&M U Prairie View TX 77446

HAWKINS, EDWARD STANLEY, city official; b. Collinsville, Okla., June 23, 1921; s. Harvey Hamilton and Nannie Lou (Bean) H.; student Okla. Sch. Bus. and Accountancy, Tulsa, 1946-47; m. Cleda C. Francis, 1971; 1 son, Dennis L. (dec.). Iron worker, Tulsa, 1940-42; operator clk. Empire Pipe Line Co., Tulsa, 1945-46; bookkeeper County of Tulsa, 1946-48; with Fire Dept. City of Tulsa, 1948—, fire prevention insp., 1952-62, fire marshal, 1962-64, fire chief, 1964—; chmn. Okla. State Firefighter Legis. Com.; appointed by Pres. Nixon to Nat. Commn. on Fire Prevention and Control. Served with U.S. Navy, 1942-45. Mem. Internat. Assn. Fire Chiefs (dir. 1977-79, 2d v.p. 1979-80, 1st v.p. 1980-81, pres. 1981—), Tulsa Fire Chiefs Assn., Okla. State Firefighters Mus. Bd. (trustee mus. 1960—), Okla. State Fire Chiefs Assn., Okla. State Fire Marshals Commn., Nat. Fire Protection Assn., Am. Soc. Safety Engrs., Am. Legion, VFW. Baptist. Clubs: Mason, Shriner, Rotary. Home: 6914 E 50th Pl Tulsa OK 74145 Office: 411 S Frankfort St Tulsa OK 74120

HAWKINS, ELINOR DIXON (MRS. CARROLL WOODARD HAWKINS), librarian; b. Masontown, W.Va., Sept. 25, 1927; d. Thomas Fitchie and Susan (Reed) Dixon; A.B., Fairmont State Coll., 1949; B.S. in L.S., U. N.C., 1950; m. Carroll Woodard Hawkins, June 24, 1951; 1 son, John Carroll. Children's librarian Enoch Pratt Free Library, Balt., 1950-51; head circulation dept. Greensboro (N.C.) Pub. Library, 1951-56; librarian Craven-Pamlico Library Service, New Bern, N.C., 1958-62; dir. Craven-Pamlico-Carteret Regional Library, 1962—; storyteller children's TV program Tele-Story Time, 1952-58, 63—; mem. adv. bd. First Am. Savs. Bank. Mem. New Bern Hist. Soc., 1973—, Tryon Palace Commn., 1974—; mem. adv. bd. Salvation Army. Mem. N.C. Assn. Retarded Children, N.C. Library Assn., Salvation Army Advisory Bd. Baptist. Club: Pilot (pres. 1957-58, v.p. 1962-63). Home: PO Box 57 Cove City NC 28523 Office: 400 Johnson St New Bern NC 28560

HAWKINS, ELMER JOHN, physician; b. Jayton, Tex., July 8, 1922; s. Elmer and Arlis (Cunningham) H.; B.S., McMurry Coll., 1942; M.D., Baylor U., 1945; m. Gabie Smallwood, June 19, 1943; children—Lou Ann, James Earl, Sharon Kay, Jonathan Lewis. Intern, Meth. Hosp., Madison, Wis., 1945-46. practice gen. medicine, Roby, Tex., 1948-49, Hamlin (Tex.) Hosp. & Clinic, 1949-72, Elmer J. Hawkins Clinic, Stamford, Tex., 1972-83, Fisher County Clinic, 1983—. Served to capt. AUS, 1946-48. Mem. AMA, Tex. Med. Assn., Am., Tex. acads. family physicians, Taylor-Jones County Med. Soc. Methodist. Club: Petroleum (Abilene). Home: Rotan TX 79546

HAWKINS, FALCON BLACK, judge; b. Charleston, S.C., Mar. 16, 1927; s. Falcon Black and Mae Elizabeth (Infinger) H.; B.S., The Citadel, 1958; LL.B., U. S.C., 1963, J.D., 1970; m. Jean Elizabeth Timmerman, May 28, 1949; children—Richard Keith, Daryl Gene, Mary Elizabeth Hawkins Eddy. Steely Odell II. Bar: S.C. 1963. Leadingman electronics Charleston (S.C.) Naval Shipyard, 1948-60; salesman ACH Brokers, Columbia, S.C., 1960-63; assoc. to sr. partner firm Hollings & Hawkins and successor firms, Charleston, 1963-79; U.S. dist. judge Dist. of S.C., Charleston, 1979—. Served with Mcht. Marines, 1944-45, AUS, 1945-46. Mem. Jud. Conf. 4th Jud. Circuit, ABA, S.C. Bar Assn., Charleston County Bar Assn., Am. Trial Lawyers Assn., S.C. Trial Lawyers Assn. Democrat. Methodist. Clubs: Hibernian Soc. Charleston, Masons. Office: US Courthouse Charleston SC 29402

HAWKINS, FRANCES EARLINE, nurse; b. Memphis, Apr. 9, 1952; d. Charles Jack Hawkins and Frances Juanita (Frayser) Hawkins Shelnut. Student Blue Mountain Coll., 1971-72; R.N., St. Joseph Hosp. Sch. Nursing, 1974. Charge nurse, in-patient supr. St. Jude Children's Hosp., Memphis, 1974-80; sec., counsellor Reach Out Inc., Chattanooga, 1980-82; staff nurse Meml. Hosp., Chattanooga, 1982-83; chemotherapy/oncology nurse Med. Oncology Assocs., Chattanooga, 1983—. Presbyterian. Home: 501 E 5th St Apt 210 Chattanooga TN 37403 Office: Medical Oncology Assocs 975 E 3d St Box 144 Chattanooga TN 37403

HAWKINS, FRANK NELSON, JR., media company executive, writer; b. Macon, Ga., Sept. 2, 1940; s. Frank N. and Lottie (Norton) H.; m. Inge Lehmitz, Apr. 22, 1967; children—Liv Marion, Daphne Virginia. B.A., Cornell U., 1962. Corr., AP, New Delhi, 1969-70, Jakarta, Indonesia, 1970-71, chief bur., Manila, 1971-73, chief Middle East services, Beirut, 1973-75; bus. mgr., adminstrv. dir. AP-Dow Jones, London, 1975-80; dir. corp. relations Knight-Ridder Newspapers, Inc., Miami, Fla., 1980-83, v.p. planning and corp. relations, 1983—. Author: Ritter's Gold, 1980; others. Vol. Miami United Way, 1983-85; bd. dirs. Bus. Assistance Ctr., Found. for Excellence in Pub. Edn. in Dade County. Served to capt. U.S. Army, 1963-67. Mem. Assn. Former Intelligence Officers, Miami Bankers Club. Office: Knight-Ridder Newspapers Inc One Herald Plaza Miami FL 33101

HAWKINS, GARY DALE, systems analyst; b. Tulsa, Apr. 27, 1946; s. Dero Blitson and Mary Elizabeth (Sawrey) H.; B.A. in Math., U. Tulsa, 1969; m. Patricia Louise Lemons, Nov. 23, 1968; children—Sheila Catherine, Kevin Todd. Programmer, DX/Sun Oil Co., Tulsa, 1968-71; sr. programmer, analyst McDonnell Douglas Automation Co., St. Louis, 1971-73; programmer, analyst U.S. Jaycees, Tulsa, 1973-74; cons. McDonnell Douglas Automation Co., Houston, 1974-76, Tulsa, 1976-79; systems analyst Williams Cos., Tulsa, 1979—; pres. Spectrum Data Services Co., Houston, 1976-77. Served with USAR, 1968. Mem. Assn. Systems Mgmt. Republican. Lutheran. Home: 1221 N Ironwood Pl Broken Arrow OK 74012 Office: 1 Williams Center 32-8 Tulsa OK 74172

HAWKINS, IDA FAYE, educator; b. Fort Worth, Dec. 28, 1928; d. Christopher Columbus and Nannie Idella (Hughes) Hall; student Midwestern U., 1946-48; B.S. in Elem. Edn., North Tex. State U., 1951; postgrad. Lamar U., summers 1968-70; M.S. in Applied Psychology, McNeese State U., 1970; m. Gene Hamilton Hawkins, Dec. 22, 1952; children—Gene Agner, Jane Hall. Tchr., Dequeen Elem. Sch., Port Arthur, Tex., 1950-54, Tyrrell Elem. Sch., 1955-56, Roy Hatton Elem. Sch., Bridge City, Tex., 1967-68, Oak Forest Elem. Sch., Vidor, Tex., 1968—. Second v.p. Travis Elem. Sch. PTA, 1965-66, 1st v.p., 1966-67; corr. sec. Port Arthur City Council PTA, 1966-67; tchr. Sunday Sch., Presbyn. Ch., 1951-53, 60-66. Mem. NEA (life), Tex. State Tchrs. Assn. (life), Classroom Tchrs. Assn., Am. Psychol. Assn. (asso.), Am. Platform Assn. Home: 4075 Laurel Apt 73 Beaumont TX 77707 Office: 2400 Hwy 12 Vidor TX 77662

HAWKINS, JERALD DALE, sport studies educator, exercise physiologist, athletic trainer, consultant, researcher; b. Jefferson City, Tenn., Mar. 4, 1946; s. William J. and Margaret G. (Wyatt) H.; m. Linda Ann Randles, Aug. 21, 1966; children—Lisa Michelle, Jennifer Erin. B.S., Carson-Newman Coll., 1967; M.Ed., Memphis State U., 1971; Ed.D., U. Ga., 1975. Cert. trainer Nat. Athletic Trainers Assn. Tchr., coach various schs., Fla., La., 1967-69, 1971-73; grad. asst. Memphis State U., U. Ga., 1970-71, 1973-75; asst. prof. Lander Coll., Greenwood, S.C., 1975-77, Liberty Bapt. Coll., Lynchburg, Va., 1977-78; assoc. prof., coordinator phys. edn. U. S.C., Aiken, S.C., 1978-81; assoc. prof., chmn. dept. sport studies Guilford Coll., Greensboro, N.C., 1981—; nat. faculty U.S. Sports Acad., Mobile, Ala., 1985—, Ctr. Study Sport in Soc., Boston, 1984—; adv. bd. Youthsports Edn. Found., Greensboro, 1985—, Sport Studies Found., Greensboro, 1985—. Author: (with others) Successful Sport Management, 1985; Successful Sport Management, 1985; Sports and the Child, 1986. Editor and author (with others): Sports Medicine: A Guide for Youth Sports, 1984. Contbr. articles to profl. jours. Deacon, soloist, tchr. Friendly Ave. Bapt. Ch., Greensboro, 1981—. Named Outstanding Tchr. of Year U. S.C.-Aiken, 1979-80. Mem. Am. Alliance for Health, Phys. Edn., Recreation and Dance, Am. Coll. Sports Medicine, Nat. Athletic Trainers Assn., N.C. Alliance for Health, Phys. Edn., Recreation and Dance, Kappa Delta Pi, Phi Kappa Phi. Democrat. Avocations: music; fitness; sports. Home: 5701 Wildberry Dr Greensboro NC 27409 Office: Guilford Coll Dept Sport Studies 5800 W Friendly Ave Greensboro NC 27410

HAWKINS, OSIE PENMAN, JR., opera and concert singer; b. Phenix City, Ala., Aug. 16, 1913; s. Osie Penman and Eula Myrtle (Brown) H.; pvt. vocal studies with Margaret Hecht, Frederich Schorr, Renato Cellini, Samuel Margolis. Choir soloist First Presbyn. Ch., also Temple Israel, Columbus, Ga., 1930-42; Wagnerian bartione Met. Opera Co., N.Y.C., 1941—, debut as Donner in Das Rheingold, Jan. 1942, exec. stage mgr., 1963-78, spl. cons., 1978—; leading baritone appearing roles Central City (Colo.) Opera House Assn., singer with Cin. Zoo Summer Opera; concert, radio, TV and oratorio singer; European tour, summer and fall 1954. Appearances on Ed Sullivan Show, Omnibus and 1st closed circuit theater TV-Carmen. Opera recs. RCA Victor, Met. Opera Book-of-the-Month Recs. Recipient Verdi Meml. award for Achievement, Met. Opera Nat. Council, 1978; Met. Opera scholar. Mem. Am. Guild Mus. Artists (gov.), AFTRA, Ala. (hon.), Ga. (hon.) fedns. music clubs, Phenix City Jaycees. Baptist. Club: Orpheus (Columbus). Home: 904 19th St Phenix City AL 36867 also 500 E 77th St New York NY 10162

HAWKINS, PAULA (MRS. WALTER E. HAWKINS), U.S. senator, Republican nat. committeewoman; b. Salt Lake City; d. Paul B. and Leoan (Staley) Fickes; student Utah State U., 1944-47; m. Walter Eugene Hawkins, Sept. 5, 1947; children—Genean, Kevin Brent, Kelley Ann. Mem. Fla. Pub. Service Commn., Tallahassee, 1972-74, chmn., 1977-79; mem. U.S. Senate from Fla., 1980—; dir. S.E. 1st Nat. Bank, Maitland, Fla., 1963-74, Rural Telephone Bank Bd., Washington Rep. precinct committeewoman Orange County, Fla., 1965-74; speakers chmn. Rep. Exec. Com. Fla., 1967; mem. Fla. Rep. Nat. Conv., 1968, 72, mem. rules com., 1972; mem. Nat. Fedn. Rep. Women, 1965—; bd. dirs. Fla. Fedn. Rep. Women, 1968—; mem. Rep. Nat. Com. for Fla., 1968—, mem. rule 29 com., 1973-75. Mem. Maitland Civic Center, 1965—; charter mem. bd. dirs. Fla. Americans Constl. Action Com. of 100, 1966-68, sec.-treas., 1966-68; mem. Central Fla. Museum Speakers Bur., 1967-68; mem. Fla. Gov.'s Commn. Status Women, 1968-71; co-chmn. March of Dimes of Orange County, 1970. Vice chmn. Fla. State Awards Com., 1974-80; mem. consumer affairs/spl. impact com. FEA, 1974-76; mem. Pres.'s Commn. White House Fellowships, 1975. Recipient citation for service Fla. Rep. Party, 1966-67; Above and Beyond award as outstanding woman in Fla. politics, 1968; nominated Orange County Woman of Yr., Maitland Womans Club, 1969; named Woman of Yr., KC award, 1973. Mem. Maitland C. of C. (chmn. congl. action com. 1967), Alpha Kappa Psi (hon.). Mem. Ch. of Jesus Christ of Latter-day Saints (pres. Relief Soc., Orlando Stake 1964-64, Sunday sch. tchr. 1964-81). Clubs: Winter Park (Fla.) Racquet; Maitland Woman's; Capitol Hill (Washington). Office: Room 313 Hart Senate Office Bldg Washington DC 20510

HAWKINS, PHILLIP LEE, travel consultant; b. Oklahoma City, Feb. 16, 1926; s. Charles Bartow and Norma Gladys (Thompson) H.; m. Cora May Nickell, May 29, 1965; children—Valerye Kirsten, Allyson Kelly, Phillip Lee. With various oil cos., Tulsa, 1949-62; asst. supr. travel Cities Service, Tulsa, 1962-68; mgr. corp. travel, meetings coordination Conoco, Inc., Houston, 1968-85; cons. Hawkins and Assocs., Houston, 1985—; cons. Harper Travel Internat., Houston, 1985—, Internat. Tours., Inc., Tulsa, 1985—. Active Assn. Retarded Citizens, 1979—. Mem. Tex. Passenger Traffic Assn. (life), Nat. Passenger Traffic Assn. (hon.), Nat. Passenger Traffic Assn. (bd. dirs. 1979-83), Conn. Westchester Passenger Traffic Assn. (pres., chmn. 1974-77), Del. Inst. Travel Mgrs., Internat. Bus. Travel Assn., Soc. Co. Meeting Planners. Christian Scientist. Home and Office: 14751 Kellywood Ln Houston TX 77079

HAWKINS, ROBERT A., college administrator; b. Anabelle, W.Va., Aug. 21, 1924; s. Lawrence R. Hawkins and Grace O. (Lauer) Glover Hawkins; B.A., Abilene Christian Coll., 1948, M.A., 1967; Ed.D., Tex. Tech U., 1974; m. Nina Jo Milton, June 6, 1943; children—Paul C., Sheila Ann. Adminstr. youth camps, 1949-64; tchr., adminstr. Denver schs., 1953-56; instr. Abilene (Tex.) Christian Coll., 1965-68; instr., registrar Lubbock (Tex.) Christian Coll., 1968-74; dir. guidance Midland (Tex.) Coll., 1974-83, dir. testing, 1982—, instr. behavioral and social sci. depts., 1974—. Recipient Outstanding Tchr. award Lubbock Christian Coll., 1971. Mem. Am., Tex., Permian Basin personnel and guidance assns., Jr. Coll. Student Personnel Assn. Tex., Tex. Jr. Coll. Tchrs. Assn., Phi Kappa Phi, Alpha Chi. Author, translator: Bible Student's New Testament; Spiritual Awareness; contbr. articles to profl. jours. Home: 3305 Providence Dr Midland TX 79707 Office: 3600 N Garfield St Midland TX 79705

HAWKINS, TERRY RAY, occupational therapy educator, consultant; b. St. Joseph, Mo., Jan. 5, 1946; s. James C. and Mabel E. (Manifold) H.; m. Linda Jane Wilkerson, May 30, 1970; children—Joshua Adam, Noah Andrew. B.S., U. Kans., 1972; M.P.H., U. Okla., 1982. Registered occupational therapist, 1972. Occupational therapist Mid-Mo. Mental Health Ctr., Columbia, 1972-74, Harry S. Truman Vets. Med. Ctr., Columbia, 1974-79; asst. prof. occupational therapy U. Okla. Health Sci. Ctr., Oklahoma City, 1979—; cons. Okla. Christian Home, Edmond, 1982—, Willow View Hosp., Spencer, Okla., 1981—. Served with USAF, 1965-68. Am. Occupational Therapy Found. grantee, 1981. Mem. Am. Occupational Therapy Assn., World Fedn. Occupational Therapists, Okla. Occupational Therapy Assn., Gerontology Soc. Mem. Christian Ch. (Disciples of Christ). Home: 9805 Chesterton Pl Oklahoma City OK 73120 Office: 801 NE 13th St PO Box 26901 Oklahoma City OK 73190

HAWKINS, TOM GILLIAM, geography educator; b. Portland, Tenn., June 2, 1921; s. Calvin Carl and Ivy (Sloan) H.; m. Juanita Ralph, Feb. 14, 1944; 1 child, Annelle Ralph. B.S., Austin Peay State Coll., 1943; M.A., George Peabody Coll., 1947, postgrad., 1952-54. Cert. elem. and secondary tchr. Faculty, Paducah Jr. Coll., Ky., 1947-52; tchr. Hillsboro High Sch., Nashville, 1954-56; asst. prof. geography Miss. State Coll. for Women, Columbus, 1956-62; asst. prof., head dept. geography Central State U., Edmond, Okla., 1962—; past mem. summer or part-time faculty George Peabody Coll., Fla. State U., Tallahassee, Belmont Coll., Nashville, West Tex. State U., Canyon, Troy State U., Ala. Contbr. articles to profl. jours., encys. Served to sgt. U.S. Army, 1943-46; PTO. Mem. NEA, Okla. Edn. Assn., Okla. Acad. Sci. Democrat. Baptist. Avocations: birdwatching; conservation of birds and other wildlife.

HAWKSHEAD, RICHARD MATHER, savings and loan executive; b. Mobile, Ala., July 31, 1948; s. Ernest Mather and Vivian Nell (Kennedy) H.; B.S., U. W.Fla., 1970; m. Francine Judy Berman, May 11, 1974; children—Sean, Chad. Auditor, U.S. Army, 1970-72; supervising sr. acct. Peat, Marwick, Mitchell & Co., Miami, Fla., 1972-76; v.p., tax mgr. Housing Investment Corp. Fla., Miami, 1976-78; chief fin. officer, treas. Heaton Companies, Ft. Lauderdale, Fla., 1978-82; controller, chief fin. officer Heritage Fin. Corp., Ft. Lauderdale, 1982-83; sr. v.p. Citizens Fed. Savs. & Loan Assn., Ft. Lauderdale, 1983—. Served with AUS, 1970-72; Vietnam. C.P.A., Fla. Mem. Am. Inst. C.P.A.s, Fla. Inst. C.P.A.s, Am. Mgmt. Assn. Democrat. Clubs: Sportsrooms, Racquet Ball of Plantation, Sea Gardens Tennis. Office: 1100 W McNab Rd Fort Lauderdale FL 33309

HAWLEY, AMOS HENRY, sociologist, educator; b. St. Louis, Dec. 5, 1910; s. Amos Henry and Margaret Belle (Heltzclaw) H.; m. Gretchen Haller, Sept. 5, 1937; children—Steven Amos, Margie Lynn, Susan Esther, Patrice Ann. A.B., U. Cin., 1936; M.A., U. Mich., 1938, Ph.D., 1941; D.Litt. (hon.), U. Cin., 1978. From instr. to prof. U. Mich., 1941-66; prof. sociology U. N.C., Chapel Hill, 1966-76, Kenan prof., 1971-76, prof. emeritus, 1976—; adviser in field. Author: Human Ecology, 1950; Urban Society, 1971; contbr. articles to profl. jours. and chpts. to books. Fellow Am. Acad. Arts and Scis., AAAS; mem. Am. Sociology Assn. (pres. 1978), Population Assn. Am. (pres. 1971), Delta Kappa Epsilon. Club: Chapel Hill Country. Home: 407 Brookside Dr Chapel Hill NC 27514 Office: Sociology Dept U NC Chapel Hill NC 27514

HAWLEY, PHILLIP EUGENE, investment banker; b. Tecumseh, Mich., Dec. 9, 1940; s. Paul P. and Vadah Arlene (Lawhead) H.; m. Linda Darlene Miller, Feb. 14, 1957; children—Pierre Lee, Paul Marvin, Danny Parke, David Eugene, Martin Edward. Student Yale U., 1959-63; B.S., Northwestern Coll., Tulsa, 1980. Pvt. investigator, Fla. With Credit Bur. Fort Myers, Inc. (Fla.), 1956—, chmn. bd., 1979—; founder, pres. Gold Coast Devel. Corp., Ft. Myers, 1975—; v.p. Transworld Investigators, Inc., Ft. Myers, 1970—; pres. Phillip Hawley, Investment Banking, Ft. Myers, 1976—; dir. Caribbean Industries Internat. Corp., Future Investment Corp.; pres. Diversifield Investment Security Fund. Chaplain, sec. treas., v.p. Gideons Internat.; cofounder, dir. Collier Lee Wrestling Assn., 1974—; mem. Lee County Republican Com., 1972; bd. dirs. Lee County Republican Club, 1974. Mem. Fla. Collectors Assn., Assoc. Credit Burs. Fla., Am. Collectors Assn., Assoc. Credit Burs. Am., Med.-Dental Hosp. Burs. Am., Fla. Assn. Mortgage Brokers, Fla. Assn. Pvt. Investigators, Blue Book Detectives, Comml. Law League, Internat. Consumer Credit Assn., Am. Numis. Assn. Republican. Mem. Ch. Nazarene. Author: The Happiest Man in the World, 1970; The Best Buys in Fort Myers, 1982. Home: 6435 Winkler Rd Fort Myers FL 33907 Office: 2079 Cleveland Ave Fort Myers FL 33901

HAY, EDWARD CRAIG, clergyman; b. Chester, S.C., Oct. 25, 1921; s. John Richards and Sara (Craig) H.; m. Mary Thomas Stockton, Nov. 28, 1947; children—Edward Craig, Robert Stockton, Thomas Douglas, Mary Sara Hay-Gwynn. A.B. cum laude, Davidson Coll., 1942; B.D., Louisville Presbyterian Sem., 1949, Th.M., 1952; D.D. (hon.), Rhodes Coll., 1966. Ordained to ministry Presbyterian Ch. U.S.A., 1949. Pastor, Nicholasville Presbyn. Ch., Ky., 1949-52, First Presbyn. Ch., Franklin, Tenn., 1952-56, St. Johns Presbyn. Ch., Jacksonville, Fla., 1956-64, First Presbyn. Ch., Birmingham, Ala., 1965-73, First Presbyn. Ch., Wilmington, N.C., 1973-84; interim exec. Presbyter, Wilmington, Presbytery, 1985—; mem. bd. Christian Edn. Presbyn. Ch. U.S., 1960-69. Contbr. sermons to publs. Bd. mem. St. John's Mus. of Art, Wilmington, 1985—; trustee St. Andrews Presbyn. Coll., Laurinburg, N.C., 1974-82, Davidson Coll., 1985—. Served to maj. U.S. Army, 1942-46, PTO, Japan. Democrat. Clubs: Civitan (internat. chaplain 1969-70), Cape Fear

Country. Avocations: watercolor painting; golf. Home: 1422 Country Club Rd Wilmington NC 28403

HAY, GEORGE NORMAN, pastoral counseling executive; b. Tuscumbia, Ala., Jan. 1, 1928; s. Idus Linwood and Lettie Missouri (Clark) H.; m. Cecily Jack, June 10, 1950; 1 dau., Laura Katheleen. B.A., Stetson U., 1955; postgrad. So. Bapt. Theol. Sem., 1955-57; M.Div., New Orleans Bapt. Theol. Sem., 1962; D.Ministry, Drew U., 1981. Ordained to ministry Southern Baptist Ch., 1954; diplomate Internat. Acad. Profl. Counseling and Psychotherapy. Pastor First Bapt. Ch., Palm Bay, Fla., 1954-55; assoc. pastor, Tuscumbia, Ala., 1957-61; pastor, Grand Isle, La., 1961-64; pastor Port Sulphur Bapt. Ch. (La.), 1964-68; founding exec. dir. Gulf S. Yokefellow Ctr., New Orleans, 1968-72; ins. agt. Prudential Ins. Co., 1969-70; instr. Trinity Christian Tng. Inst., 1972-76; dir. Westbank Bible Inst., 1974-78; supr. counseling, dept. family medicine La. State U., 1980-81; founding exec. dir. George Hay Ministries, Inc., Gretna, La., 1972—; pres. Life Enhancers, Inc., 1985—; adj. faculty social sci. dept. Holy Cross Coll., New Orleans, 1984—, cons., mem. adv. com. Greenbrier Psychiat. Hosp., Covington, La., 1985—. Mem. World's Fair Chaplaincy Com., 1983—; chmn. supervision and tng. sub.-com. Greater New Orleans Fedn. Chs., 1983—; mem. exec. com. Terrytown Chem. Dependency Task Force, 1983—; mem. adv. bd. Young Life New Orleans, New Orleans Family Life Ctr.; cons. Teen Challenge La. Served with USAAC, 1946-47. Fellow Am. Assn. Pastoral Counselors; mem. Am. Assn. Marriage and Family Therapy (approved supr.), Am. Acad. Psychotherapists, N.Y. Acad. Scis., Internat. Platform Assn., D.A.V. Republican. Club: Rotary. Home: 653 Fielding St Gretna LA 70053 Office: 564 Terry Pkwy Gretna LA 70053

HAY, JESS THOMAS, financial company executive; b. Forney, Tex., Jan. 22, 1931; s. George and Myrtle H.; m. Betty Jo Peacock, 1951; children—Deborah Hay Werner, Patricia Hay Mauro. B.B.A., So. Meth. U., 1953, J.D. magna cum laude, 1955. Bar: Tex. Assoc. Locke, Purnell, Boren, Laney & Neely, 1955-61, ptnr., 1961-65; pres., chief exec. officer Lomas & Nettleton Fin. Corp., Dallas, 1965-69, chmn. bd., chief exec. officer, 1969—, also dir.; chmn. bd., chief exec. officer Lomas & Nettleton Mortgage Investors, 1969—, also dir.; chmn. bd., chief exec. officer, dir. Lomas & Nettleton Co., L & N Housing Corp.; dir. Trinity Industries, Inc., Merc. Tex. Corp., Verex Corp., Republic Fin. Services, Inc., Allied Fin. Co., Exxon Corp., Greyhound Corp. Former mem. Democratic Nat. Com.; former nat. fin. chmn. Dem. Nat. Com.; trustee bd. govs. So. Meth. U.; bd. regents U. Tex. System; mem. Dallas Citizens Council; former mem. Dallas Assembly; mem. Dallas Council on World Affairs; mem. governing bd. Tex. Arts Alliance; treas. Greater Dallas Planning Council; mem. adv. council Dallas Community Chest Fund, 1981—; bd. dirs. Tex. Research League. Mem. ABA, Dallas Bar Assn., Tex. Bar Assn., Am. Judicature Soc., Newcomen Soc. N.Am. (vice chmn. Dallas com.). Methodist. Home: 7236 Lupton Circle Dallas TX 75225 Office: Lomas & Nettleton Fin Corp PO Box 225644 Dallas TX 75265*

HAY, RICHARD CARMAN, anesthesiologist; b. Queens, N.Y., June 9, 1921; s. Richard Carman and Frances Pauline (Woodbury) H.; B.S., U. Vt., 1944, M.D., 1946; m. Martha Fambrough, Mar. 2, 1957; children—Richard C., William W., Anne H., Sandra L., Bradford T., Holly K. Practice medicine, specializing in anesthesiology, Houston. Served with M.C., U.S. Army, 1948-50. Mem. AMA, Tex. Med. Soc., Harris County Med. Soc., Am. Soc. Anesthesiologists, Tex. Soc. Anesthesiologists. Republican. Baptist. Home: 1930 Country Club Dr Sugarland TX 77478 Office: Memorial Profl Bldg Suite C64 Houston TX 77074

HAYAUD DIN, MIAN AHMED, real estate developer; b. Peshawar, Pakistan, Feb. 6, 1947; came to U.S., 1973; s. Mian and Begum Haniya (Rahman) H.-D.; m. Yasmin Salam, Mar. 15, 1973; children—Mian Ahad, Sofia, Mian Amjad. B.C.E., Peshawar U., 1968; D.I.C., Imperial Coll., London, 1970; M.B.A., Harvard U., 1975. Asst. engr. Gammon (Pakistan), Ltd., Islamabad, 1968-69; asst. prof. U. Peshawar, 1970-73; regional mgr. consumer services Citicorp, Southfield, Mich., 1975-78; assoc. McKinsey & Co., Inc., Chgo., 1978-79; fin. mgr. Equity Assocs., Inc., Chgo., 1979-81; project mgr. Gerald D. Hines Interests, Miami, Fla., 1981—. Aga Khan fellow, 1974. Mem. ASCE, Inst. Civil Engrs. London (assoc.), Greater Miami C. of C. (trustee). Republican. Moslem. Clubs: Harvard (N.Y.C.); University (Chgo.); City of Miami. Home: 17843 SW 77th St Miami FL 33157 Office: Gerald D Hines Interests Suite 200S Biscayne Blvd Suite 3250 Miami FL 33131

HAYDEN, MARY ELLEN, neuropsychologist; b. Gorman, Tex., Jan. 23, 1940. B.S. in Psychology, U. Houston, 1972, M.A. in Psychology, 1973, Ph.D. in Psychology, 1976. Lic. psychologist, Tex. Research asst. Parent Child Devel. Ctr., U. Houston, 1972-73, grad. research asst. psychology dept., 1973-76, teaching fellow, 1973-75, tchr., 1979—; postdoctoral tng. U. Tex. Health Sci. Ctr., 1976-79, tchr., 1977-79; pvt. practice neuropsychology, Houston, 1979—; chmn. dept neuropsychology Med. Ctr. Del Oro Hosp., Houston, staff dept. phys. medicine and rehab.; staff dept. medicine Meml. Hosp. Southwest, Houston; founder, dir. Tex. Head Injury Found., Houston, Transitional Learning Community, Galveston, Tex.; mem. adv. bd. Houston Area Assn. for Communication Disorders. Contbr. articles to profl. jours. Mem. Nat. Head Injury Found. (profl. adv. bd.), Am. Psychol. Assn. (Div. 40), Internat. Neuropsychol. Soc. Office: 2624 S Loop W Suite 120 Houston TX 77054

HAYES, CHARLES A., mill company executive; b. Gloversville, Ky., 1935; married. With Lee Dyeing Co., Inc., to 1961; exec. v.p. Guilford Mills, Inc., Greensboro, N.C., 1961-68, pres., chief exec. officer, 1968-76, chmn. bd., 1976—, also dir. Office: Guilford Mills Inc 4925 W Market St Box U-4 Greensboro NC 27402*

HAYES, GLADYS GILL, auditor, real estate broker; b. Pine Bluff, Ark., Jan. 9, 1951; d. Arnett LeRoy and Catherine Jewell Gill; m. Stephen Lamont Hayes, Mar. 22, 1971; children—Phillip, Tatum, Hamilton. B.A., Ark. A. M. & N. Coll., 1972. Acct., Am. Found. Mortgage Co., Little Rock, 1972-74; asst. mgr. Red Carpet Inn, Little Rock, 1974-76; tax rep. IRS, Little Rock, 1976; privilege license auditor City of Little Rock, 1976-77, internal auditor fed. programs, 1977—; owner Arnett Gill Realty Co.; instr. music Ark. Arts Center, Little Rock, 1982-83. Mem. adv. bd. Ark. Symphony; pianist Miles Chapel C.M.E. Ch., Bethel A.M.E. Chapel, Art Porter Singers. bd. dirs. Community Theater Little Rock. Mem. Inst. Internal Auditors, Twin City Real Estate Bd., Alpha Kappa Alpha. Home: 2418 S State St Little Rock AR 72206 Office: Room 306 City of Little Rock 500 W Markham St Little Rock AR 72203

HAYES, JACK DEE, insurance company executive; b. Hutchinson, Kans., June 22, 1940; s. Elmer William and Margaret (Dondlinger) H.; B.A., Wichita U., 1962, M.A., 1964; m. Paula K. Williams, Jan. 2, 1982; children—Terry, Mischelle, Jackie, Dana, Natasha. Football coach Derby (Kans.) High Sch., 1963-64; agt. Fidelity Union Life Ins., Wichita, Kans., 1964-65, gen. agt., Omaha, 1965-66, regional dir., Kansas City, Kans., 1965-66, supt. of agencies, Midwest Region, 1967-68, asst. v.p., Atlanta, 1968-70, v.p. sales, Dallas, 1970-81, exec. v.p., chief mktg. officer, 1981—. Mem. Nat. Assn. Life Underwriters, Tex. Assn. Life Underwriters, Gen. Agts. and Mgrs. Assn. Democrat. Roman Catholic. Home: 1530 Palm Valley St Garland TX 75043 Office: 1511 Bryan St Dallas TX 75221

HAYES, JOHN FLYNN, controller; b. Elmira, N.Y., Nov. 26, 1940; s. Malachi Eugene and Marianna Elizabeth (Flynn) H.; m. Karen Luise Mettler, Nov. 20, 1965; children—Andrew, Jeffrey. B.S. in B.A., Elmira Coll., 1969; M.A. in Mgmt., Webster Coll., 1982. Sr. acct. R.G. Post & Co., C.P.A.'s, Clifton, N.J., 1969-70; sr. fin. analyst Westinghouse Electric Corp., Elmira, N.Y., 1968-69, 70-73; controller Dyna Pak Corp., Elmira, N.Y., 1973-78; controller Anvil Knitwear, Mullins, S.C., 1978—; cons. Mem. adv. council bus. curriculum Florence Darlington Tech. Coll., 1981—. Served with USN, 1958-62. Republican. Home: 28 Manigault Ct Florence SC 29501 Office: Cypress St Mullins SC 29574

HAYES, JOHN PATRICK, manufacturing company executive; b. Manistee, Mich., May 9, 1921; s. John David and Daisy (Davis) H.; m. Margaret Barbara Butler, Apr. 12, 1947; children—John Patrick, Timothy Michael. Student, U. Detroit, 1939-42, 46-47. With Nat. Gypsum Co., 1947—, group v.p., 1970-75, pres., 1975—, chmn. bd., chief exec. officer, 1983—, also dir.; dir. Republic Bank Dallas. Served to 1st lt. AUS, 1942-45. Clubs: Brookhollow Golf, Petroleum (Dallas). Office: 4500 Lincoln Plaza Dallas TX 75201

HAYES, MARTHA BELL, cosmetologist; b. Fayetteville, N.C., Oct. 20, 1943; d. Otha James and Earlean (Williams) Bell; m. Dirk K. Lambert; children by previous marriage—Wilfred, Henry, Gwendolyn, Daniel A.; 9 adopted children. Owner Martha's, Inc., Fayetteville, 1969—, Martha's Discount Beauty Salon, Fayetteville, 1976—, Martha's Beauty Salons 1, 2, and 3, Fayetteville, 1978—; dean Cape Fear Beauty Inst. and Hair Weaving, 1978; mgr. Shade's of Beauty Modeling Club, 1979. Recipient numerous awards and certs. Mem. Nat. Beauty Culturists League, Nat. Hairdressers and Cosmetologists Assn., Internat. Ind. Hairweaving Assn., NAACP, Fayetteville C. of C., Fayetteville Bus. and Profl. League, Beauticians Club (v.p., historian Fayetteville). Baptist. Lodge: Order Eastern Star. Author hairweaving booklet. Address: Cape Fear Beauty Inst PO Box 0844 Fayetteville NC 28302

HAYES, REBECCA THOMASON, rehab. counselor, vocational, disability cons.; b. Rome, Ga., June 13, 1939; d. Oliver Bruce and Sarah Kathryn (Yoder) Thomason; m. Larry B. Hayes, Feb. 7, 1959; children—Laura Alison, Lawrence Bruce. B.A. in Edn., U. Fla., 1961; M.Ed., U. Tex., 1973. Cert. rehab. counselor. Tchr. pub. and pvt. schs., Fla., 1961-68; counselor Tex. Rehab. Commn., San Antonio, 1972-78, Dallas, 1978-81, sr. counselor, Dallas, 1981—; sr. counselor Parkland Meml. Hosp., Dallas, 1981—, Southwestern Med. Sch., Dallas, 1981—; vocat. rehab. cons. Pain Control Program, 1981—; liaison counselor Spinal Pain Clinic, Dallas Rehab. Inst., 1982—; clin. instr. dept. rehab. counselor edn. Sch. Allied Health Scis., U. Tex. Health Sci. Center, Dallas, 1981—; intern, practicum supr. dept. rehab. counselor edn. North Tex. State U., Denton, 1981—. Mem. Nat. Rehab. Assn., Tex. Rehab. Assn. (dir. 1979-80), Nat. Rehab. Counseling Assn. (Tex. Rehab. Counselor of Yr. 1979, S.W. Regional Counselor of Yr. 1979), Tex. Rehab. Counseling Assn., Coalition of Texans with Disabilities, Kappa Delta. Democrat. Methodist. Home: 4309 Purdue Dallas TX 75225

HAYES, STEVEN CHARLES, psychology educator, researcher, therapist; b. Phila., Aug. 12, 1948; s. Charles Aloysius and Ruth Ester (Dryer) H.; m. Angela Fe Butcher (div.); 1 dau., Camille Rose. B.A. cum laude in Psychology, Loyola U., Los Angeles, 1970; postgrad. Calif. State U., San Diego, 1971-72; M.A. in Clin. Psychology, W.Va. U., 1974, Ph.D., 1977. Lic. psychologist, N.C. Intern psychology Brown U. Sch. Medicine, Providence, 1975-76; asst. prof. U. N.C.-Greensboro, 1976-82, assoc. prof., 1982—. W.Va. U. Found. Inc. grantee, 1975; NIMH grantee, 1976-77; U. N.C. grantee, 1976-77, 77-78, 81-82, 82-83. Mem. AAAS, Am. Psychol. Assn. (div. 25 student affairs coordinator, 1977, 78, continuing ed. chmn. 1980-82, program co-chmn. 1980-82, chmn. long-term planning com. 1982, mem.-at-large 1982—), Assn. Behavior Analysis, Assn. Advancement Behavior Therapy (student affairs coordinator 1978, assoc. program chmn. 1979, program chmn. 1980, chmn. task force student involvement 1980-81), Soc. Exptl. Analysis Behavior, Southeastern Psychol. Assn., Sigma Xi. Democrat. Author: The Effects of Monthly Feedback, Rebate Billing and Consumer Directed Feedback on the Residential Consumption of Electricity, 1977; Research Opportunities in Clinical Psychology Internships, 1979; Abnormal Psychology, 1979; (with J.D. Cone) Environmental Problems/Behavioral Solutions, 1980; (with D.H. Barlow and R.O. Nelson) The Scientist Practitioner: Research and Accountability in Clinical and Educational Settings, 1983; contbr. chpts. to books, articles to profl. jours.; assoc. editor Jour. Applied Behavior Analysis, 1982—; editorial bd. Behavioral Assessment, Behavior Modification, Jour. Cons. and Clin. Psychology, The Behavior Analyst, Behaviorism. Home: 1944 Spring Garden St Greensboro NC 27403 Office: Dept Psychology U NC Greensboro NC 27412

HAYES, WALTER HAROLD, civic worker, retired federal agency administrator; b. Balt., July 5, 1907; s. Walter Paschall and Elizabeth (Link) H.; m. Isabella Mallory, Nov. 9, 1935 (dec. July 1984); 1 child, Anne Hayes Hume. B.A., Duke U., 1928, M.A., 1930. Reporter Roanoke Times, Va., 1929-33; reporter, columnist, feature writer Roanoke World-News, 1933-42; N.C. State dir. U.S. Office War Info., 1942; pub. info. officer Richmond br. VA, 1946-49; editor Rural Electrification News, Rural Electrification Adminstrn., Washington, 1949-51; editorial chief U.S. Office Price Stabilization, 1951-53; chief of publs. Office of Info. for the Armed Forces, Dept. Def., 1953-67, ret., 1967. Head St. Johns County br. ARC, Fla., 1976-77. Served to lt. USN, 1942-45. Recipient Outstanding Citizenship award Am. Heritage Found., 1961, Freedoms Found. award, 1967, Meritorious Achievement award Mil. Order of World Wars. Mem. St. Augustine Hist. Soc., Washington Duke U. Club, Phi Kappa Sigma. Home: 70 Willow Dr Saint Augustine FL 32084

HAYES, WAYLAND JACKSON, JR., toxicologist; b. Charlottesville, Va., Apr. 29, 1917; s. Wayland J. and Mary L. (Turner) H.; m. Barnita Donkle, Feb. 1, 1942; children—Marie Hayes Sarneski, Maryetta Hayes Hacskaylo, Lula Hayes McCoy, Wayland, Roche del Hayes Moser. B.S., U. Va., 1938, M.D., 1946; M.A., U. Wis., 1940, Ph.D., 1942. Intern, USPHS Marine Hosp., N.Y.C., 1946-47; individual practice as toxicologist, Savannah, Ga., 1949-60, Atlanta, 1960-68, Nashville, 1968—; chief Vector Transmission Investigations Br., USPHS, Savannah, 1947-48; chief toxicology sect., Savannah, 1949-60, Atlanta, 1960-67, chief toxicologist, 1967-68; prof. biochemistry Vanderbilt U. Sch. Medicine, Nashville, 1968—; cons. WHO, 1950—, NRC, 1964—, various govt. agys. and profl. orgns., 1953—. Author: Clinical Handbook on Economic Poisons, 1963; Toxicology of Pesticides, 1975; Pesticides Studied in Man, 1982. Contbr. articles to sci. jours. Mem. editorial bd. jour. Pharmacology and Exptl. Therapeutics, 1962-64, Archives of Environ. Health, 1965-72, 76—, Food and Cosmetics Toxicology, 1967-78. Served with U.S. Army, 1943-46. Recipient Meritorious Service medal USPHS, 1964. Mem. Am. Soc. Pharmacology and Exptl. Therapeutics, Am. Soc. Tropical Medicine and Hygiene, Soc. Toxicology (pres. 1971-72, Ambassador of Toxicology award 1985). Club: Univ. Home: 2317 Golf Club Ln Nashville TN 37215 Office: Vanderbilt U Nashville TN 37232

HAYMAN, CAROL BESSENT, poet, author; b. Southport, N.C., June 9, 1927; d. George Howard and Minnie May (Guthrie) Bessent; A.A., Louisburg (N.C.) Jr. Coll., 1945; student East Carolina U., 1945, 65; m. Louis De Maro Hayman, Aug. 30, 1945; children—Richard Louis, Susan Carol Hayman Lynch. Columnist, Onslow Herald, Jacksonville, 1974-76; works include: Keepsake, 1962, These Lovely Days, 1971-72, 76, 81, Collection of Writings Published in North Carolina Christian Advocate, 1972, What is Christmas?, Tidings, 1974, Advent material, 1975-78; contbr. articles and poems to numerous mags. including Vista, Listen, Marriage and Mature Living, The Upper Room, Pathways to God and Ideals, Hallmark, Inc.; guest instr. Coastal Carolina Community Coll., 1978-82; lectr., poetry contest judge. Trustee Louisburg Coll., 1965-72, recipient Distinguished Alumnus award, 1978, poet in residence, 1982. Recipient numerous awards poetry confs. N.C., Ga., Fla., Calif. Named Goodwill Ambassador by Mayor, City of Jacksonville, 1973. Mem. Nat. League Am. Pen Women (Southeastern regional editor Pen Woman 1972-74, mem. exec. bd. 1974-75), Southeastern Writers Assn., (charter), World Poetry Soc., Carteret Writers (organizer, pres.), N.C. Poetry Soc., N.C. Writers Network (trustee, chmn. fin. com.), DAR, Carteret County Friends of the Library, Beaufort Hist. Soc., N.C. Symphony. Methodist. Club: N.C. Congl. Home and Office: 618 Ann St Beaufort NC 28516

HAYMAN, THOMAS JULIAN, contractor; b. Cold Springs, Tex., Dec. 31, 1914; s. Thomas Norman and Harriet (Moffett) H.; m. Alyne Beazley, Sept. 4, 1937; 1 son, Charles Herman. Student, Sam Houston State U., 1934-36. With Boettcher Lumber Co., Huntsville, Tex., part-time 1934-37; with Humble Oil & Refining Co., Houston, 1937-39; ptnr. H & G Beazley Lumber Co., Grapeland, Tex., 1939-45; civilian engr., 1941-45; pres. Inge-Hayman Constrn. Co., 1945-60, Thomas J. Hayman, Inc., 1960-64, Hayman Bryant Andres, 1964-70, Hayman-Andres, 1970-77; pres. Hayman Co., 1977-81, chmn. bd., 1982; with Hayman Co. (joint venture ptnrs. with Sogetexas Constrn.) SGE Société Générale d'Entre prises, Paris, 1978—, Hayman Co. (joint venture ptnrs. with Delphinance), U.S.A. Internat. Devel. and Constrn. Co., Athens, Greece, 1981—; dir. Met. Savs. & Loan Dallas, 1962-83, chmn. bd., 1983—; dir. Fidelity Life Ins. Co., Dallas and Munich, First City Bank, Dallas. Bd. dirs. Dallas Council World Affairs, Dallas Are A Crime Stoppers, 1980—, Dallas C. of C., 1969—, Bapt. Found. Tex., 1963—; bd. advisors, investment com. Bapt. Found. Tex., 1960—; trustee Annuity Bd. So. Bapt. Conv., 1962-68; mem. adv. council Community Found. Tex., 1980—, Dallas Citizens Council, 1975—; mem. adv. bd. Windham Sch. System Tex. Dept. Corrections, 1984—. Named Man of Yr., Brotherhood citation of Constrn. Industry, Dallas chpt. NCCJ, 1973; Rotary Club Found. fellow, 1972; Disting. Service award Bapt. Found. Tex., 1963-72; Service award Annuity Bd. So. Bapt. Conv., 1962-68. Mem. Associated Gen. Contractors Am. (pres. 1951-52). Republican. Baptist. Clubs: Rotary (pres. 1961), Petroleum, Dallas Country, Salesmanship, Dallas Knife and Fork Dinner (dir. 1959—).

HAYNES, CHARLES THOMAS, security executive; b. Atlanta, May 30, 1920; s. James Loyd and Ruth (Barrett) H.; m. Marguerite Shingler, Oct. 31, 1942; 1 dau., Laura. B.B.A., U. Ga., 1942. Spl. agt. FBI, 1947-77; pres. Haynes Security/Cons. Investigations, Inc., Atlanta, 1978—; corp. security dir. John H. Harland Co., Atlanta, 1980—; v.p. Atlanta Metropole, Inc., 1982—. Mem. Atlanta Crime Commn., 1983—. Mem. Soc. Former Spl. Agts. of FBI (chpt. pres.), Ga. Assn. Security Personnel (pres.), Am. Soc. Indsl. Security (chmn. law enforcement liaison). Club: Atlanta City. Home: 142 Laurel Forest Cir Atlanta GA 30342 Office: John H Harland Co PO Box 105250 Atlanta GA 30348

HAYNES, DONALD, librarian; b. Fieldale, Va., Oct. 8, 1934; s. Thomas Bernard and Laura Jeannette (Richardson) H. B.A., U. Va., 1960; M.L.S., U. N.C., 1966. Tchr. Va. pub. schs., 1960-62; manuscripts and reference asst. U. Va. Library, Charlottesville, 1963-65; librarian, asst. prof. Eastern Shore br., U. Va., Wallops Island, 1966-69; dir. library services Va. State Library, Richmond, 1969-72, state librarian, 1972-86; dir. Va. Hist. Soc., Richmond, 1986—. Editor: Virginiana in the Printed Book Collections of the Virginia State Library, 1975. Mem. Va. Historic Landmarks Commn., 1973—; chmn. Va. Hist. Records Adv. Bd., 1976—, Va. State Rev. Bd. for Landmarks, 1980—; Statewide coordinator Va. United Way, 1976; bd. dirs. Central Va. Ednl. TV, 1972—; mem. exec. bd. Edgar Allan Poe Found., 1982—. Served with AUS, 1954-56. Mem. Am., Southeastern, Va. library assns., Am. Hist. Assn., So. Hist. Assn., Assn. for Documentary Editing, Assn. for Preservation of Va. Antiquities, Hist. Richmond Found., Soc. Am. Archivists, Beta Phi Mu. Home: 300 W Franklin St Richmond VA 23220 Office: Virginia Hist Soc Boulevard at Kensington Ave Richmond VA 23221

HAYNES, EMERSON PAUL, Episcopal bishop; b. Marshfield, Ind., May 10, 1918; s. Ora Wilbur and Lydia Pearl (Walsh) H.; m. Helen Charlene Elledge, Nov. 15, 1935; children—Rosaline Elledge Haynes Triano, Emerson Paul II, Roland Lewis (dec.). A.B., Ind. Central U., 1942, LH.D., 1976; M.Div., United Theol. Sem., 1946; D.D., U. of South, 1975. Ordained as deacon Episcopal Ch., 1948, priest, 1949, bishop, 1974. Rector Holy Trinity Parish, Cin., 1948-53, All Saints Parish, Portsmouth, Ohio, 1953-57, Calvary Parish, Cin., 1957-59; canon chancellor St. Luke's Cathedral, Orlando, Fla., 1959-64; rector St. Luke's Parish, Ft. Myers, Fla., 1964-74; bishop coadjutor Diocese of S.W. Fla., St. Petersburg, 1974—, mem. standing com., 1969-74, del. to provincial synod, 1969-74, dep. to Episcopal Gen. Conv., 1970, 73, chmn. Christian edn. of diocese, 1969-74. Mem. Ft. Myers City Planning Bd., 1968-73; trustee U. of South, Suncoast Manor, Bishop Gray Inn. Mem. County Ministerial Assn. (pres. 1956, 73). Address: 219 4th St PO Box 491 Saint Petersburg FL 33731*

HAYNES, J. NEAUELL, clergyman. Bishop, Church of God in Christ for Northeast Tex., Dallas. Office: Ch of God in Christ 6743 Talbot Pkwy Dallas TX 75203*

HAYNES, JAMES FRANKLIN, economics educator; b. Jackson, Miss., Nov. 19, 1939; s. Robert Raymond and Gladys (Vaughn) H.; m. Jonita Sharp, Dec. 22, 1962; 1 dau., R. Jeneane. B.A., Millsaps Coll., 1962; M.S., Ala. A&M U., 1973; Ph.D., Vanderbilt U., 1981. Credit mgr. Atlas Fin. Co., 1963-64; claims adjuster Continental Ins. Cos., Birmingham, Ala., 1964-67, claims mgr., 1968-70; instr. Huntsville (Ala.) City Schs., 1970-80; prof. econs. Athens (Ala.) State Coll., 1980—, dir. Small Bus. Devel. Ctr., 1982—, also dir. Ctr. for Econ. Edn., chmn. div. bus. adminstrn.; cons. Webb Sch., Bellbuckle, Tenn., Huntsville C. of C.; adj. prof. U. Ala., Huntsville. Contbr. articles to profl. jours. Mem. Southeastern Small Bus. Council. Mem. Joint Council Econ. Edn., Ala. Council on Econ. Edn. (bd. dirs.), Nat. Assn. Econ. Educators, Am. Econ. Assn., Ala. Acad. Sci., Athens/Limestone County C. of C., Delta Mu Delta, Lambda Chi Alpha, Omicron Delta Epsilon. Democrat. Episcopalian. Home: 7713 Logan Dr Huntsville AL 35802 Office: PO Box 213 Athens State Coll Athens AL 35611

HAYNES, JIM, university administrator, communication consultant; b. Grand Saline, Tex., Dec. 26, 1937; s. James Milton and Clause Indiana (Winn) H.; m. Nelda B. Boenig, Jan. 13, 1962; children—Amy C., Bert W., Evan G. B.J., U. Tex., 1959; postgrad. U. Houston, 1962-63. Dir. pub. info. Tex. Rehab. Ctr., Gonzales, 1959-62; pub. relations supr. Tex. Eastern Corp., Houston, 1962-68; dir. pub. relations Tracor, Inc., Austin, 1968-73; dir. pub. relations Media Communications, Inc., Austin, 1973-75; pres. LaMancha Group, Inc., Austin, 1975-77; owner Jim Haynes Pub. Relations, 1975-77; exec. v.p. KCBN Advt. and Pub. Relations, Inc., Dallas, 1977-80; communications cons. Hay Mgmt. Cons., Dallas, 1980-82; asst. dean profl. programs Coll. Communication, U. Tex., Austin, 1983—; tchr. pub. relations U. Tex., Austin, 1972-77, 83—, So. Meth. U., Dallas, 1981, Tex. Christian U., Fort Worth, 1979. Bd. dirs. Goodwill Industries, Austin, Dallas, 1975-80; mem. pub. relations com. ARC, Austin, 1975-77. Recipient Nat. Pub. Relations Achievement award Ball State U., 1981. Mem. Internat. Assn. Bus. Communicators (Communicator of Yr. 1979), Pub. Relations Soc. Am. (dir. Austin chpt. 1983-85, pres. N. Tex. chpt. 1982, outstanding Tex. Ex award U. Tex. Alan Scott chpt. 1981), Tex. Pub. Relations Assn. (pres. 1975), Pub. Relations Found. Tex. (founder, trustee). Lutheran. Contbr. articles to profl. jours. Office: Office of the Dean Coll Communication U Tex Austin TX 78712

HAYNES, KAREN SUE, social work educator, university dean; b. Jersey City, July 6, 1946; d. Edward J. and Adelaide M. (Hineson) Czarnecki; children—Kingsley Eliot, Kimberly Elizabeth. A.B., Goucher Coll., 1968; M.S.W., McGill U., 1970; Ph.D., U. Tex., 1977. Dir. Social Work dept. Mary Hardin-Baylor Coll., Belton, Tex., 1971-72; asst. prof. S.W. Tex. State U., San Marcos, 1972-74; research assoc. U. Tex.-Austin, 1975; cons. Inst. Nat. Planning, Cairo, 1977-78; asst. prof. Ind. U., Indpls., 1978-81, assoc. prof., 1981-85; prof. social work U. Houston, 1985—, dean, 1985—; pres. Ind. Coalition Human Services, Indpls., 1984-85. Author: Sage Publications, 1984; Longman, 1986, also articles. Mem. Nat. Assn. Social Workers, Council Social Work Edn., Internat. Assn. Schs. Social Work, Nat. Alliance Info. and Referral (pres. 1983—). Avocation: sailing. Office: Grad Sch Social Work U Houston 4800 Calhoun Houston TX 77004

HAYNES, LINDA FAYE, physical education educator, coach; b. Opelousas, La., Sept. 24, 1955; d. Willie Clint and Lillie Mae (Watkins) H. B.S., Grambling State U., 1977. Tchr., Brame Jr. High Sch., Alexandria, La., 1977-78; tchr./coach Holy Rosary Inst., Lafayette, La., 1978-79, Melville High Sch. (La.), 1979—; shipping clk. Garan Industries, Simmesport, La., summers 1981, 83. Recipient plaques Holy Rosary Inst., 1978-79, Melville High Sch., 1982-83. Mem. NEA, La. Assn. Educators, La. High Sch. Coaches Assn., La. Assn. Health, Phys. Edn., Recreation and Dance. Democrat. Baptist. Lodge: Order Eastern Star. Home: PO Box 157 Melville LA 71353 Office: Melville High Sch Box 466 Melville LA 71353

HAYNES, MACK WILLIAM, oil company executive; b. Lafayette, La., Mar. 29, 1948; s. Mack W. and Violet E. (Henry) H.; m. Gretchen Hoffer, Nov. 29, 1977. B.S., Northwestern State U., 1973. Sr. research technician Exxon Prodn. Research Ctr., Houston, 1975-79, applications programmer, 1980-81, systems and applications programmer, 1981; sr. programmer, analyst Tenneco Oil Co., Houston, 1981-82, system mgr., 1982—. Mem. Assn. for Computing Machinery, Soc. Exploration Geophysicists, Houston Geophys. Soc., IEEE, IEEE Computer Soc., Digital Equipment Users Group, Intergraph Users Group. Republican. Home: 11523 Ensbrook Houston TX 77099 Office: Tenneco Oil Co PO Box 2511 Mail Stop IFP 2954 Houston TX 77001

HAYNES, MICHAEL RODDY, SR., financial executive; b. Ft. Worth, Mar. 27, 1951; s. Floyd Morris and Doris (Roddy) H.; m. Cathy Lynn Chadwick, Apr. 14, 1973; children—Michael Roddy, Jr. B.S. in Mech. Engring., So. Meth. U., 1973, M.B.A., 1976. Cert. fin. planner, Colo. Mech. engr. Texaco Co., Port Arthur, Tex., 1973-74; pres. Heritage Capital Corp., Dallas, 1974—, dir., 1980-86. Nat. Kidney Found. Tex., 1982—, TACA, Dallas, 1981—. Mem. Internat. Assn. Fin. Planners, Industry Council for Tangible Assets, Pi Tau Sigma, Phi Delta Theta. Club: Royal Oaks Country. Office: Heritage Bldg 311 Market St Dallas TX 75202

HAYNIE, JAMES ALLAN, computer company executive; b. Anniston, Ala., July 9, 1941; s. Joseph S. and Virginia (Davis) H.; m. Sandra Gail Butler, Nov. 22, 1961; children—Tara Lynn, Tracy Leigh, Tammy Lanee. B.S., U. Ala., 1963. Mfg. engr. Gen. Electric Co., various locations, 1963-69; dir. materials Singer Co., San Leandro, Calif., 1969-73; plant mgr. GTE Info. Systems, Mt. Laurel, N.J., 1973-77; v.p. ops. Mgmt. Assistance, Inc., Houston, 1977-81; exec. v.p., gen. mgr. Comspec Inc., Houston, 1981—. Mem. Houston Jr. C. of

C. Republican. Presbyterian. Home: 2302 Colonial Ct Missouri City TX 77459 Office: 10000 Old Katy Rd Suite 275 Houston TX 77055

HAYS, LARRY WELDON, lawyer; b. Houston, Feb. 8, 1936; s. Weldon Edgar and Clara Elizabeth (Carney) H. B.A., U. Tex., 1958; J.D., U. Houston, 1968. Bar: Tex. 1968. Asst. county atty. Harris County (Tex.), 1969-81, 83—; counsel Stewart Title Co., Houston, 1981—. Mem. Harris County Hist. Commn. Served to capt. U.S. Army, to 1972. Mem. Houston Bar Assn., Tex. State Hist. Assn., Sons Republic of Tex., SAR, SCV, English Speaking Union, Navy League, Phi Alpha Delta. Office: 1001 Preston Room 634 Houston TX 77002

HAYS, (MARION) STEELE, state supreme court justice; b. Little Rock, Mar. 25, 1925; s. Lawrence Brooks and Marion (Prather) H.; m. Sarah Lee Brown, Nov. 1, 1952 (div. June 1980); children—Andrew Steele, Melissa Hays Licon, Sarah Anne; m. 2d, Miriam Wall, July 12, 1980. B.A., U. Ark., 1948; J.D., George Washington U., 1951. Bar: Ark. 1951. Ptnr., Spitzberg, Mitchell & Hays, Little Rock, 1953-79; judge Ark. Ct. Appeals, 1969-70; justice Ark. Supreme Ct., Little Rock, 1980—. Served with USCG, 1943-44. Mem. Inst. Judicial Adminstrn., Ark. Bar Assn., Sigma Chi. Episcopalian. Office: Justice Bldg Little Rock AR 72201

HAYS, SANDY MILLER, editor; b. Ft. Smith, Ark., June 25, 1955; d. Joe Warren and Nell Rae (Inklebarger) Miller; m. Mark Wayne Hays, Apr. 17, 1976. Student Ark. State U., 1973-74; B.A. magna cum laude, U. Ark., 1979. Entertainment writer Ark. Democrat, Little Rock, 1979-81, farm editor, 1981—, bus. editor, 1984—; regional v.p. Newspaper Farm Editors Am., 1983-84. Sec., mem. bd. dirs. Ark. Cystic Fibrosis Found., Little Rock, 1981—. Recipient Agrl. Promotion award Ark. Press. Assn., 1983, 85; spl. award U.S. Dept. Agrl. Soil Conservation Service; Media Pub. Interest Reporting award WEHCO Media, Little Rock, 1983, 84; selected participant European Econ. Community Vis.'s Programme, 1985. Mem. Council Agrl. Sci. and Tech., Newspaper Farm Editors Am. (regional v.p. 1983-84), Investigative Reporters and Editors, Sigma Delta Chi, Phi Kappa Phi, Kappa Tau Alpha. Home: 4015 W 10th St Little Rock AR 72204 Office: Arkansas Democrat PO Box 2221 Little Rock AR 72203

HAYS, STEELE, judge; b. Little Rock, Mar. 25, 1925; s. L. Brooks and Marion (Prather) H.; m. Peggy Wall, July 12, 1980; children of previous marriage—Andrew Steele, Melissa Louise, Sarah Anne. B.A., U. Ark., 1948; J.D., George Washington U., 1951. Bar: Ark. 1951. Adminstrv. asst. to Congressman Brooks Hays, 1951-53; practice in, Little Rock, 1953-79; mem. firm Spitzberg, Mitchell & Hays, 1954-70, 71-79; circuit judge 6th Jud. Circuit Ark., Little Rock, 1969-70; judge Ark. Ct. Appeals, 1979-81; assoc. justice Ark. Supreme Ct., 1981—; chmn. bd. Law Examiners, 1968-70. Mem. Ark. com. U.S. Civil Rights Commn.; Del. Presbyn. Ch. Consultation on Ch. Union, 1968-70; Trustee Presbyn. Found. Mem. ABA, Ark. Bar Assn. (past sec.-treas.), Sigma Chi, Delta Theta Phi. Home: 3515 Hill Rd #4 Little Rock AR 72205 Office: Justice Bldg Little Rock AR 72201

HAYS, WILLIAM GRADY, JR., financial consultant; b. Covington, Ga., July 9, 1927; s. William Grady and Ella Maude (Wofford) H.; m. Emily Ann Holcombe, Aug. 1, 1954; children—Woodfrin Grady, Steven Gregory, William Danfield. B.S., U. Ga., 1949; M.Litt., U. Pitts., 1950. Pres. First So. Corp., Atlanta, 1955-57; v.p. Comml. Trust Co., 1957-59; pres., chief exec. officer Comml. Acceptance Corp., 1959-74; fin. cons. William G. Hays & Assocs., Inc., 1974—; cons., chief exec. officer N.Am. Acceptance Corp., 1974—; cons. Kaleidoscope, Inc., 1979—, Speir Ins. Agy., Inc., 1982—; chief exec. officer United Am. Fin. Corp., Knoxville, Tenn., 1983—. Contbr. articles to profl. jours. Mem. Kappa Delta Pi. Republican. Presbyterian. Clubs: Cherokee Town and Country, Univ. Yacht. Home: 2755 Normandy Dr NW Atlanta GA 30305 Office: William G Hays & Assocs Inc 1720 Peachtree Rd NW Suite 1024 Atlanta GA 30309

HAYS, WILMA RUBY, health agency executive; b. Pleasant Hill, Mo., Apr. 25, 1923; d. Floyd George and Ruby Margaret (Overton) Shurtleff; student Okla. State U. Tech., 1978-80; m. Thomas Richard McCullagh, Dec. 29, 1943; children—Patricia Ann McCullagh, Claudia Kay McCullagh; m. Thomas Marshall Hays, Oct. 29, 1954; children—Mary Margaret, Cecilia Marie. Exec. sec. Armed Forces Induction Sta., Tulsa, 1941-43; sec. Guaranty Abstract Co., Tulsa, 1943-49, Earlougher Engring. Co., Tulsa, 1949-51, Bethlehem Supply Co., Tulsa, 1951-54; exec. dir. Kidney Found. of Okla., Oklahoma City, 1969—; treas. Nat. Health Agys., Okla., state chmn., 1981-83. Mem. Profl. Staff Assn. of Nat. Kidney Found., Okla. Soc. Assn. Execs., Am. Mgmt. Assn., Nat. Assn. Female Execs., LaPetite Seur Book Rev. Club, LWV. Republican. Roman Catholic. Clubs: Bus. and Profl. Women's (rec. sec. 1978, pres. 1980) (Oklahoma City); Zonta Internat., Christian Women's of Okla. Home: 4040 NW 61st St Oklahoma City OK 73112 Office: 3313 NW Classen Oklahoma City OK 73118

HAYWARD, OLGA LORETTA HINES,, librarian; b. Alexandria, La.; d. Samuel James and Lillie (George) Hines; A.B., Dillard U., 1941; B.S. in L.S., Atlanta U., 1944; M.A., U. Mich., 1959; M.A. in History, La. State U., 1977; m. Samuel E. Hayward, July 12, 1945; children—Anne Elizabeth, Olga Patricia (Mrs. William Ryer). Tchr., Marksville (La.) High Schs., 1941-42; head librarian Grambling (La.) Coll., 1944-46; br. librarian br. nine New Orleans Pub. Library System, 1947-48; reference librarian So. U., Baton Rouge, 1948-73, prof. library sci., social scis. librarian, 1973-84, dir. collection devel., 1984—. Bd. dirs. La. Diocese Episcopal Community Services, 1972-78. Mem. ALA, La. Library Assn. (pres.-elect subject specialists div. 1985—), Spl. Libraries Assn. (pres. La. chpt. 1978-79). Episcopalian. Author: Graduate Theses of Southern University 1959-71; A Bibliography of Literature By and About Whitney Moore Young, Jr., 1929-71, 1972; The Influence of Humanism on Sixteenth Century English Courtesy Texts, 1977; also other bibliographies. Contbr. articles to profl. jours. Home: 1632 Harding Blvd Baton Rouge LA 70807

HAYWARD, VIRGINIA D., career counselor, nurse, educator; b. Egypt, Tex., Oct. 24, 1940; d. Harry and Willie (Anderson) Davis; m. Abbie Dean, Aug. 23, 1963; children—Orlando, Anthony. B.S. in Nursing, Prairie View A&M U., 1963, M.Ed., 1974; postgrad., London, Eng. R.N.; cert. counselor, supervision, CPR, critical nursing, health occupations. Charge nurse St Elizabeth Hosp., Houston, 1963-66, VA Hosp., Houston, 1966-69; pvt. duty nurse, Houston, 1969-70; tchr. nursing Houston Tech. Sch., 1970-79; tchr. High Sch. Health Professions, Houston, 1979-83, career counselor, 1983—; nursing cons. Nursing Program, Houston, 1983-85; judge Health Occupations, Houston, 1980-85; home health cons. Diversified Nursing, Houston, 1984-85; nursing cons. Creston Baptist Ch., Houston, 1970-85. Musician, Creston Bapt. Ch., 1970-85, choir dir., 1975; active blood pressure program Houston Ind. Sch. Dist., 1975-83; chaperone French Club, 1982; mem. health occupations adv. com. United Negro Coll. Fund, active campaign Democratic Party, Houston, 1979. Recipient Ten Yr. Service Pin Houston Ind. Sch. Dist., 1980, Outstanding award Health Occupations, 1974, award Outward Bound, Denver, 1984, service trophy nursing class, Houston, 1983. Mem. Am. Assn. Counseling, Smithsonian Assocs., Am. Heart Assn., Tex. Vocat. Tech. Assn., Am. Vocat. Assn., NEA, Am. Cancer Soc., Tex. Tchrs. Assn., Houston Assn. Counseling and Devel., Houston Sch. Counselor Assn., Phi Delta Kappa. Baptist. Club: World Wide. Avocations: Sewing; playing piano; bicycling; gardening; elderly nursing care; traveling. Home: 5418 Candletree Houston TX 77091 Office; Houston Ind Sch Dist 3100 Shenandoah St Houston TX 77021

HAYWOOD, LESLIE WRIGHT, writer, photographer; b. N.Y.C., Apr. 28, 1938; d. Charles Leslie and Margaret (MacArthur) Wright; 1 child, John M. Haywood, Jr. A.A., Colby-Sawyer Coll., 1957; diploma Katherine Gibbs Sch., 1958. Prodn. asst. Time, Inc., N.Y.C., 1958-60; exec. asst. Jefferson Standard Broadcasting Co., Charlotte, N.C., 1960-67, G.B. Wilkins, Inc., Charlotte, 1981-83; pres. Wright Communications, Charlotte, 1983—; pub. relations dir. Am. Soc. Interior Designers, Carolinas chpt., 1984—. Mem. Am. Soc. Interior Designers, Profl. Photographers of N.C., Am. Bus. Women's Assn. Republican. Episcopalian. Address: Wright Communications 4620 Town and Country Dr Charlotte NC 28226

HAZEL, JAMES WELLINGTON, geologist; b. Owensboro, Ky., Apr. 10, 1941; s. Guy Wellington, Jr. and Helen (Bamberger) H.; m. Joyce Hagan, June 15, 1963 (div. 1982); children—James Wellington, Joelle M.; m. Linda Borum, Nov. 26, 1985. B.S., U. Dayton, 1963; M.S., U. Ky., 1973. Geologist, Exxon Co. U.S.A., Hattiesburg, Miss., 1965-67, Harvey, La., 1967-70, New Orleans, 1970-75, Houston, 1975-76, hdgrs. geologist, Houston, 1976-78, sr. supr. geologist, New Orleans, 1978-80, Harahan, La., 1981-82, div. ops. geologist, New Orleans, 1980-81, dist. prodn. geologist, Lafayette, La., 1982; geologist Hercules Petroleum Co., Owensboro, Ky., 1982—. Mem. Am. Assn. Petroleum Geologists. Democrat. Roman Catholic. Lodge: Lions. Avocations: hunting; fishing.

HAZELRIG, JANE B., biomathematics educator, researcher; b. Chattanooga, May 29, 1937; d. William Russell and Elizabeth Cecil (Marquet) Brownlee; m. Cooper Green Hazelrig, Aug. 31, 1958; children—William Russell, Susan Jane. B.S., U. Ala.-Tuscaloosa, 1958; M.S., U. Minn., 1965; Ph.D., U. Ala.-Birmingham, 1976. Assoc. physicist, So. Research Inst., Birmingham, Ala., 1958-62; math. instr. U. Ala., Birmingham, 1959-62, instr. biomath., 1967-77, asst. prof., 1977-80, assoc. prof., 1980-82, assoc. prof. biostats. and biomath., 1982—; biophysics technician Mayo Clinic, Rochester, Minn., 1962-67; mem. biotech. resources rev. com. Div. Research Resources, Washington, 1985—. Contbr. articles to sci. publs. Site visitor NIH. Mem. Soc. for Math. Biology (bd. dirs. 1980-84), AAAS, Soc. Indsl. and Applied Math., Mortar Bd., Sigma Xi, Phi Beta Kappa, Pi Mu Epsilon, Sigma Pi Sigma. Office: Dept Biostatistics and Biomath Univ Ala Birmingham University Station 1801 University Blvd Birmingham AL 35294

HAZEN, CHARLES MELVILLE, mathematics educator; b. N. Girard, Pa., May 25, 1941; s. Charles Edward and Gladys Estelle (Miller) H. B.S., Edinboro State Coll., 1962; M.A.T., Jacksonville U., 1973. Tchr. Kenton City Schs., Ohio, 1963-67; tchr. math. Episc. High Sch., Jacksonville, 1967—, chmn. dept. math., 1973—, sr. master, 1985—. Designer computer programs for acad. office. Layreader Episc. Ch. various locations, 1962—, mem., clk. vestry Ch. of the Good Shepard, Jacksonville, 1981-84; mem. Cummer Gallery Art, Jacksonville Art Mus., Riverside Avondale Preservation Assn. Recipient Chaplains award Jacksonville High Sch., 1976. Mem. Nat. Council Tchrs. Math., Math. Assn. Am., Kenton Edn. Assn. (sec. 1964-65, pres. 1965-67), Nat. Assn. Railroad Passengers, Nat. Ry. Hist. Soc., Nat. Model Railroad Assn. (life), Gateway Model Railroad Club (past sec., treas., pres.), Jacksonville Episc. High Sch. Alumni Assn. (hon.) Democrat. Avocations: model railroading; photography; singing; travelling. Home: 474 Laurina St Jacksonville FL 32216 Office: Episcopal High Sch Jacksonville 4455 Atlantic Rd Jacksonville FL 32207

HAZEN, TERRY CLYDE, microbial ecologist, educator; b. Pontiac, Mich., Feb. 7, 1951; s. Leo Robert and Phyllis Virginia (Hawley) H.; m. Gayle Kanne Reinecke, June 12, 1972; children—Tracy Heather, Brooks Trevor. B.S. with honors, Mich. State U., 1973, M.S., 1974; Ph.D., Wake Forest U., 1978. Research assoc. Wake Forest U., Winston-Salem, N.C., 1978-79; asst. prof. biology U. P.R., Rio Piedras, 1979-82, assoc. prof., 1982-85, prof., 1985—, acting chmn. dept., 1984-85, chmn. grad. studies, 80-84; cons. micro-computer applications in lab.; tchr., cons. in water quality. Head coach Pee Wee Football of P.R., 1983. Winner 1st prize Sci. Writing, Puerto Rican Culture Soc., 1983. Mem. Am. Soc. Microbiology, AAAS, Sigma Xi (research award 1977). Republican. Contbr. articles to profl. jours. Home: K-15 Calle 5 Hillside Rio Piedras PR 00926 Office: Dept Biology Univ Puerto Rico Rio Piedras PR 00931

HAZOURI, LOUIS ABRAHAM, JR., business executive; b. Memphis, Dec. 19, 1948; s. Louis Abraham and Katherine Minnie (Palmer) H.; m. Michele Susan Manseau, June 10, 1978; children—Emily Rose, Christina Lydia. A.B., Mercer U., 1972; M.A., Emory U., 1975, Ph.D., 1983. Asst. instr. sociology Ga. State U., Atlanta, 1977-78; sr. ops. analyst Ga. Dept. Human Resources, Atlanta, 1978-79; ops. analyst Am. Family Life, Columbus, Ga., 1979-80, asst. v.p. ops. research, 1980-81, corp. sec., 1981—; dir. Am. Family Corp., Columbus, Am. Family Life Assurance Co. N.Y., Poughkeepsie. Trustee Hist. Columbus Found., 1983. NIMH fellow, 1973. Mem. Am. Mgmt. Assn., Am. Mktg. Assn., Am. Sociol. Assn., Mktg. Research Soc., Ops. Research Soc. Am., Planning Execs. Inst. Lutheran. Club: Big Eddy (Columbus). Lodge: Kiwanis. Avocations: horseback riding; writing; piano; guitar; gardening. Home: PO Box 37 Pine Mountain Valley GA Office: Am Family Corp 1932 Wynnton Rd Columbus GA 31999

HEACOCK, DONALD DEE, social worker, priest; b. Anthony, Kans., Feb. 21, 1934; s. C.W. and Thelma Olive (Hilton) H.; m. Margaret Newberry, Sept. 4, 1953; children—Teresa Ellen, Mark Dee. A.B., Washburn U., 1956; B.D. cum laude, United Sem., 1959; M.S.W., Barry Coll., 1971. Ordained priest Episcopal Ch., 1965; parish minister St. John's Ch., Clinton, Mich., 1961-66; chaplain, Margarita, Canal Zone, 1966-69; tchr. Christ Ch. Acad. Secondary Sch., Colon, Panama, 1966-69; counselor South Fla. Neighborhood Youth Corp., Miami, 1969-70; chief social service, instr. pediatric comprehensive health care program U. Miami, 1971-72; asst. dir. Alpha House, Dade County, Fla. and field supr. Barry Coll., 1972-73; marriage and family therapist Psychiatric Assocs., Shreveport, La., 1973-75; pvt. practice social work, Shreveport, 1975—; lectr. sociology Centenary Coll., 1981—. Served with USAF, 1959-61. Mem. Am. Assn. Marriage and Family Therapy, Nat. Assn. Social Workers, Acad. Cert. Social Work, Phi Kappa Mu, Phi Gamma Mu. Lodge: Masons. Home: 748 Thora Blvd Shreveport LA 71106 Office: 929 Olive St Shreveport LA 71104

HEACOCK, GEORGE THOMAS, industrial-government consultant; b. Sylacauga, Ala., June 21, 1920; s. John Warren and Mexie (McDowell) H.; student U. Ala., 1939-40; B.C.S., Benjamin Franklin U., 1963; m. Marie Terese Baltes, Oct. 23, 1948; children—Thomas Michael, Mark Alan, David Andrew. Intelligence officer, specialist CIA, various locations, 1947-69; prin. firm Heacock Govt. Mktg. Agy., Falls Church, Va., 1969-84. Asst. scoutmaster, mem. exec. com. Nat. Capital Area council Boy Scouts Am., 1962-72, chmn. fund drive, 1972; bd. dirs. Sleepy Hollow Recreation Assn., 1971-72. Served with M.I., USNR, 1942-46. Recipient letter of merit Dir. CIA, 1953. Mason. Address: 5696 Montilla Dr Fort Myers FL 33907

HEAD, HAYDEN W., JR., U.S. district judge; b. 1944. Student, Washington and Lee U., 1962-64; B.A., U. Tex., 1966, LL.B., 1968. Atty., Head & Kendrick, 1968-69, 72-76, ptnr. Head, Kendrick & Head, 1981; U.S. dist. judge So. Tex., Corpus Christi, 1981—. Mem. ABA, Tex. State Bar. Office: PO Box 2567 521 Starr St Corpus Christi TX 78401*

HEAD, HOLMAN, association executive; b. Mineola, N.Y., Jan. 13, 1926; s. Middleton Edward and Fannie Marie (Holman) H.; m. Harriet Fuller, Nov. 7, 1953; children—Hallie Head Rawls, Robert Holman, Martin Edward. Student Dartmouth Coll.; A.B., U. Ala., 1947, M.B.A., 1955. Asst. dir. U. Ala. Montgomery Ctr., 1950-53, dir., 1953-58; asst. dir. Mobile Ctr., 1950-53; dir. personnel and adminstrn. Blount Bros. Corp., Montgomery, 1958-68, exec. asst. to pres., 1968-69, v.p. adminstrn., 1969; exec. asst. to Postmaster Gen. U.S. Postal Service, Washington, 1969-71; exec. v.p. Birmingham Area C. of C., 1971-74; v.p. adminstrn. Blount, Inc., Montgomery, 1974-79; exec. v.p. Ala. C. of C., 1980—. Bd. dirs. Montgomery Area United Way, campaign chmn., 1976, pres., 1979; bd. dirs. Met. YMCA, Birmingham, 1972-74, Birmingham Festival of Arts Assn., 1972-74, Ala. Council Econ. Edn., 1960-65, S.E. Ala. Regional Sci. Fair, 1959-64, Montgomery Mental Health Assn., 1956-60, Montgomery Spastic Sch., 1955-58; founding trustee Montgomery Acad.; mem. Art Inc. Com., Montgomery Mus. Fine Arts. Served with USNR, 1943-46. Mem. Ala. Assn. Ind. Colls. and Univs. (bd. govs.), Assoc. Industries Ala. (dir.), Montgomery Area C. of C. (dir.), U.S. C. of C., U. Ala. Nat. Alumni Assn. (past v.p.), U. Ala. Alumni Assn., Montgomery County (past pres.). Republican. Episcopalian. Clubs: Mountain Brook, Montgomery Country, Capital City (bd. govs.). Home: 2442 Midfield Dr Montgomery AL 36111 Office: Ala C of C 468 S Perry St Montgomery AL 36195*

HEAD, RICHARD RAY, computer research scientist; b. El Dorado, Ark., Dec. 25, 1947; s. Richard Theron and Sarah Eunice (Mayes) H.; m. Cynthia Leigh Orr, May 28, 1972. B.A. in Math., Hendrix Coll., 1969; M.S. in Math., U. Ark., 1971, Ph.D. in Math., 1977. Systems programmer U. Ark., Fayetteville, 1972-77; project leader Middle S. Services, New Orleans, 1977-81; group leader AMOCO Prodn. Co., New Orleans, 1981-85, research scientist, Tulsa, 1985—. Block capt. Neighborhood Watch, New Orleans, 1983-85. Fellow NSF, NASA, 1969-74. Mem. Assn. for Computing Machinery, Am. Math. Soc., Math. Assn. Am. Avocations: jogging, basketball; mathematics and physics research. Home: 2655 E 33d Pl Tulsa OK 74105 Office: AMOCO Prodn Co Research Ctr Tulsa OK 74102

HEAD, WILLIAM IVERSON, SR., retired chemical company executive; b. Tallapposa, Ga., Apr. 4, 1925; s. Iverson and Ruth Britain (Hubbard) H.; B.S. in Textile Engring. with honors, Ga. Inst. Tech., 1950; hon. doctorate in textile engring. World U., 1983; m. Mary Helen Ware, June 12, 1947; children—William Iverson, Connie Suzanne, Alan David. Research and devel. engr. Tenn. Eastman Co., Kingsport, 1949-56, quality control-mfg. sr. engr., 1957-67, dept. supt., 1968-74; supt. acetate yarn dept. Chems. div. Eastman Kodak Co., Kingsport, 1975-85. Info. officer U.S. Naval Acad., 1983—. Served with USN, 1943-46; capt. Res. Decorated Navy commendation medal and Meritorious Service award, 1980. Mem. Am. Chem. Soc., Am. Assn. Textile Tech., Internat. Soc. Philos. Enquiry (sr. research fellow and internat. pres. 1980—, personnel cons. 1978-79), Internat. Platform Assn., Prometheus Soc., Naval Res. Assn., Mil. Order World Wars, Res. Officers Assn. (Tenn. pres. 1981-82), VFW, Internat. League of Intelligence, Mensa (pres. Upper East Tenn. 1976-79). Republican/Libertarian. Unitarian. Clubs: Kiwanis, Elks, Eagles. Patentee textured yarns tech. in U.S., Gt. Britain, Ger., Japan and France. Home: 4035 Lakewood Dr Kingsport TN 37663

HEALEY, MICHAEL PATRICK, pediatric dentistry educator; b. Providence, May 31, 1950; s. John F. and Claire L. (Gavin) H. B.A., U. Conn., 1972; D.D.S., Case Western Res. U., 1976. Resident U. Conn., Farmington, 1981; asst. prof. Emory U., Atlanta, 1982—. Served to capt. U.S. Army, 1976-79. Mem. Am. Acad. Pediatric Dentistry, Sandy Springs C. of C. Roman Catholic. Home: 1001 Riverbend Club Dr Atlanta GA 30338 Office: 8613 Roswell Rd NE Atlanta GA 30338

HEAP, WILLIAM OTTO, geophysicist, researcher; b. Joliet, Ill., Sept. 25, 1923; s. Otto Dewey and Ruth Maud (Jones) H.; m. Shirley Jean Jahn, Mar. 2, 1946 (dec. Dec. 1982); children—James Ellis, Kathleen Rae. B.E.E., U. Ill., 1944; postgrad. U. Tulsa, 1958. Registered profl. engr., Okla., profl. geophysicist, Calif. Field engr. Schlumberger Well Surveying, Houston and Colombia, South Am., 1944-46; chief party Seismograph Service Corp., Tulsa, 1946-53, sr. supr., mgr. data processing, 1953-59, engr. sr. research., seismic research, 1959-64, area supr., Midland, Tex., 1971-73, supr. staff, eastern hemisphere mgr., Tulsa, 1975-76, mgr. tech. devel. fgn. div., 1976-77, mgr. mid-continent area, 1977-80, mgr. research sect., 1980—, mgr. gen. Colombian Geophys. Corp. div. Seismograph Service Corp., Cairo, Egypt, 1964-71, Mex. div. Seismograph Service Corp., Mexico City, 1973-75. Mem. Am. Assn. Petroleum Geologists (assoc.) Soc. Exploration Geophysicists, Geophys. Soc. Tulsa. Republican. Presbyterian. Avocations: chess; golf; woodworking. Home: 7208 S 90 E #1032 Tulsa OK 74133 Office: Seismograph Service Corp PO Box 1590 6200 East 41st St Tulsa OK 74102

HEARIN, WILLIAM JEFFERSON, publishing company executive; b. Mobile, Ala., Aug. 27, 1909; s. William Jefferson and Mary Lou (Ludington) H.; m. Emily Staples Van Antwerp, July 2, 1981; 1 child, Ann Bartlett. Classified and retail advt. solicitor Mobile News-Item, 1927-32; retail advt., solicitor, retail advt. mgr., nat. advt. mgr., circulation mgr., advt. dir., bus. mgr. Mobile Press Register, 1932-44, gen. mgr., exec. v.p., 1944-65, co-pub., 1965-70, pub., pres., 1970—, also dir.; pub., pres. Miss. Press Register, Pascagoula; dir. Mobile Gas Service Corp., First Nat. Bank Mobile. Bd. dirs. United Fund, YMCA; mem. nat. adv. bd. Salvation Army, Jr. Achievement; regent Spring Hill Coll. Named hon. col. Salvation Army, 1974, Lion of Yr., 1975, Mobilian of Yr., 1977. Mem. Am. Newspaper Pubs. Assn., So. Pubs. Assn., Ala. Press Assn., Mobile C. of C. (pres.), Sigma Delta Chi. Office: Mobile Register 304 Government St Mobile AL 36630*

HEARN, GLORIA WILLIAMS, educator; b. Greenwood, La., Apr. 22, 1934; d. James Chambers and Mary Thelma (Robertson) Williams; B.A., La. Tech. U., 1956; M.Ed., La. State U., 1974; postgrad. Tulane U., U. Southwestern La.; m. George Earl Hearn, June 22, 1956; children—Patricia Gail, George Eugene. Tchr., Caddo Parish Schs., Shreveport, La., 1956-61; tchr. public schs., Waco, Tex., 1961-64; tchr. England Air Force Base Elem. Sch., 1965-66; organizer, 1st dir., mem. staff First Baptist Day Sch., 1st Bapt. Ch., Pineville, La., 1968-73; tchr. gifted students public schs., Alexandria, La., 1974—; organizer gifted students program for secondary schs., Rapides Parish. Ednl. chmn. Cenla Hist. Soc.; state chmn. 1979 Yr. of Child Commn. Contbg. author: The Pebble Book, 1977. Mem. La. State Supt.'s Tchr. Adv. Com., 1984—. Mem. Central La. Presch. Assn. (organizer, 1st pres.), Assn. Childhood Edn. Internat. (exec. bd. internat.), NEA, La. Assn. Edn., Polit. Action Com. (state com.), Rapides Assn. Educators, Internat. Reading Assn., AAUW (br. and state pres.), Delta Kappa Gamma (state officer, pres. chpt.). Democrat. Clubs: Matinee Musical, Community Concert Assn., Faculty Women's of La. Coll. (past pres.). Home: 111 Myrtlewood Dr Pineville LA 71360 Office: PO Box 8275 Alexandria LA 71301

HEARN, JOYCE CAMP, educator, state legislator; b. Cedartown, Ga., d. J.C. and Carolyn (Carter) Camp; m. Thomas Harry Hearn (dec.); children—Theresa Hearn Potts, Kimberly Ann, Lee Becker. Student U. Ga.; B.A., Ohio State U., 1957; postgrad U. S.C. Former high sch. tchr.; dist. mgr. U.S. Census, 2d Congl. Dist., 1970; mem. S.C. Ho. of Reps., 1975—, asst. minority leader, 1976-78. Mem. Richland County Planning Commn.; bd. dirs. Meml. Youth Ctr. and Stage South; chmn. Nat. Adv. Com. on Occupational Safety and Health, 1982-84; chmn. Sexual Assault Awareness Week; vice chmn. Dist. Republican Com., 1968; chmn. 2d Congl. Dist., 1969, Richland County Rep. Com., 1972; del., platform com. Rep. Nat. Conv., 1980, 84; moderator Kathwood Bapt. Ch., 1979-80, former asst. Sunday Sch. tchr.; bd. dirs. Columbia Coll., Columbia Urban League, Fedn. of Blind. Club: S.C. Womens.

HEARST, GLADYS WHITLEY HENDERSON, writer; b. Wolfe City, Tex.; d. William Henry and Helen (Butler) Whitley; student Trinity U., 1924-26; B.A., U. Tex., 1928, M. Journalism, 1928, postgrad., 1938-40; m. Robert David Henderson, May 17, 1933 (dec. 1941); m. 2d, Charles Joseph Hearst, Oct. 30, 1943 (dec. Nov. 1980). Editor, Future Farmer News, Austin, Tex., 1930-33; dir. Service Bur., Tex. Congress Parents and Tchrs., Austin, 1933-36; dir. Student Union, U. Tex., 1939-42; free lance writer, 1945—; instr. U. No. Iowa, 1946-47. Instr. writing Waterloo YWCA, 1966-69. Vice chmn. Black Hawk County Democratic party, 1945-57; mem. County Extension Program Planning Com., 1965-68; past deaconess United Ch. of Christ, chmn. long-range planning com., 1975-79; sec. Residents Assn. of Westminster Manor Retirement Ctr., 1984; pres. Elleen Begg class Univ. Presbyn. Ch., 1984 Served to lt. WAVES, USN, 1942-45. Mem. AAUW (life, Iowa chmn. Status of Women 1954-56, past pres. Cedar Falls br.), Women in Communications (nat. pres., Disting. Service award 1962, 73, nat. chmn. by laws 1969-74, nat. citation 1969, Task Force Long Range Planning Com. 1973-74; charter mem., v.p. NE Iowa chpt. 1978), U. Tex. Ret. Faculty and Staff Assn. PEO, Zeta Tau Alpha, Kappa Tau Delta, Sigma Delta Chi (scholarship award). Club: Capital Gains Investment (past pres., treas. 1970-73) (Cedar Falls). A writer Cedar Falls Centennial Pageant, 1952; writer, editor hist. book Cedar Falls Naval Station 1942-45, Anthology Family Histories Northeast Iowa (Iowa Arts Council grant), 1978; editor pictorial directory United Church of Christ, 1982. Address: 4100 Jackson St Apt 230 A Austin TX 78731

HEATH, CHARLES CHASTAIN, management consultant; b. Sapulpa, Okla., Sept. 7, 1921; s. Connie Clifton and Karen (Boyd) H.; m. Doris Roe. B.A., Eastern Ill. U.; children—Janice Heath Chuk, Brian Neal, Eric Scott. Mgr., Shelby Gas, Inc., Shelbyville, Ill., 1946-49; supt. gas Ill. Power Co., Decatur, Ill., 1950-54, City of Shelby (N.C.), 1954-59; pres. Heath & Asso., Shelby, 1959—; chmn. bd. Regency Prodns., Inc.; pres. Heath Motion Pictures, Inc.; officer, dir. N.C. R.R. Co., 1960-62. Charter mem. N.C. Indsl. Devel. Found., 1960-62; bd. dirs. N.C. Conservative Union, 1978-79, The Conservative Caucus, 1976. Served with USMC, 1942-46. Recipient Distng. Service award Jaycees, 1957. Mem. Am. Gas Assn., Southeastern Gas Assn. Republican. Baptist. Club: N.C. Congressional. Author: You Can Save America, 1972; The Golden Egg, the Goose and Us, 1976; Look Up of Look Out, 1980. Home: 97-3 Edgemont Ave Shelby NC 28150 Office: 7 N LaFayette St Shelby NC 28150

HEATH, FRANK BRADFORD, dentist; b. Houston, Dec. 11, 1938; s. Robert Bradford and Maudie H. (Sweeney) H.; m. Heide J.M. Schmidt, Aug. 20, 1965; children—Dirk Alan, Shannon Erika, Kent Bradford. B.A., Sam Houston State U., 1961; D.D.S., U. Tex.-Houston, 1965. Pvt. practice dentistry, Houston, 1967—. Served as capt. U.S. Army, 1965-67. Fellow Acad. Gen. Dentistry, Acad. Dentistry Internat.; mem. Houston Dist. Dental Soc., Tex. Dental Assn., ADA, Delta Tau Delta, Xi Psi Phi. Republican. Methodist. Home: 12904 W Shadowlake St Cypress TX 77429 Office: 12315 Jones Rd Houston TX 77070

HEATHINGTON, KENNETH WAYNE, university official, educator, consultant;. A.S., Tarleton State Coll., 1957; B.S., U. Tex.-Austin, 1961, M.S. in Civil Engring., 1966; Ph.D. in C.E., Northwestern U., 1969. Registered profl. engr., Ill., Ind., Tenn. With Continental Oil Co., 1961-63; mem. staff research sect. design div. Dept. Hwy. State of Tex., 1963-66; traffic research engr. Ill. Div. Hwys., 1967-69; assoc. prof. civil engring. Purdue U., 1969-72; prof. civil engring. U. Tenn., Knoxville, 1972—, dir. Transp. Ctr., 1972-83, assoc. v.p. research, 1983—, mem. staff of v.p. for acad. affairs and research, 1983—, exec. dir. UT Research Corp., 1983—; pres. Applied Research Assocs., Inc., Knoxville, 1979—, also dir.; formerly chmn. group 1 council Transp. Research Bd., chmn. Double Trailer Truck Monitoring Study; U. Tenn. rep. to White House Conf. on Domestic and Econ. Affairs, Knoxville; cons., speaker in field. Served with U.S. Army, 1961-62. Mem. Inst. Traffic Engrs. (pres. U. Tex. chpt.), Airport Ground Transp. Assn. (exec. dir.), Tennesseans for Better Transp. (dir.), Transp. Research Bd. (chmn. sect. E, group 1 council), Nat. Safety Council, Council of Univ. Transp. Ctrs. (sec. treas., v.p., pres.), Inst. for Safety in Transp., ASCE, Inst. Transp. Engrs., Nat. Soc. Profl. Engrs., Am. Soc. Engring. Edn., Soc. Research Adminstrs., Sigma Xi, Chi Epsilon, Tau Beta Pi. Contbr. numerous articles to profl. jours. Office: 713 Andy Holt Tower U Tenn Knoxville TN 37996

HÉBERT, GLORIA ANN, research biologist; b. Monroe, La., Dec. 25, 1935; d. Jerome Harry and Margie Ann (Tarver) Hébert. B.S., La. State U., 1959; cert. med. technologist Grady Meml. Hosp., 1960. Med. technologist Grady Meml. Hosp., Atlanta, 1960-61, Linden Assocs., Atlanta, 1961-62; with Center for Disease Control, USPHS, Atlanta, 1962—, research biologist, 1977—. Bd. dirs. DeKalb Humane Soc., Inc., Decatur, Ga., 1970—. Mem. Am. Soc. Microbiology, Am. Soc. Med. Technologists, Atlanta Zool. Soc., LWV, DAR, Sigma Xi. Democrat. Baptist. Contbr. articles to profl. publs. Home: 3199 Wynn Dr Avondale Estates GA 30002 Office: USPHS Centers Disease Control Bldg 5 Room 210 1600 Clifton Rd NE Atlanta GA 30333

HEBERT, JOHN EDWARD, aviation company executive, engineer; b. Shreveport, La., Nov. 30, 1943; s. Earl Thomas and Novalene Mildred (Campbell) H.; m. Sharon LeClair, Jan. 18, 1969; children—Marni Lynn, Autumn Noel. B.S.M.E., La. Tech. U., 1966, postgrad., 1972-74; postgrad. So. Ill. U., 1976-78. Commd. 2d lt. U.S. Marine Corps, 1966, advanced through grades to capt., 1978; naval aviator with marine reconnaissance squadrons, 1966-78; ret., 1978; mfg. engr. Tex. Instruments, Inc., Dallas, 1978-79; aircraft salesman, flight instr. Miller-Wills Aviation, Inc., Jackson, Miss., 1979-82, gen. mgr., 1980-82; corp. pilot W.E. Walker Stores, Inc., Jackson, 1982-83; aircraft salesman, ptnr. AVCON, Brandon, Miss., 1982—. Decorated D.F.C., Air medal with 8 gold stars. Office: PO Box 194 Brandon MS 39042

HEBERT, MARY MARGARET, business educator; b. Port Arthur, Tex., Sept. 30, 1933; d. Francis Joseph and Marie (Melancon) Hebert. B.A., Dominican Coll., 1960; M. Edn., U. Houston, 1968, Ed.D., 1973. Instr. Dominican Coll., Houston, 1968-72; asst. prof. U. Houston, 1973-74, assoc. prof., 1977—; assoc. prof. Pan Am. U., Edinburg, Tex., 1974-77. Mem. sch. bd. St. Pius High Sch., Houston, 1984—. Mem. Tex. Bus. Edn. Assn. (dist. rep. 1979-80), Nat. Bus. Edn. Assn. (various coms.), Am. Bus. Women's Assn. (com. 1983-84), Assn. Bus. Communication, Office Services Research Assn., Delta Pi Epsilon (pres., sec. Alpha Gamma chpt.). Republican. Roman Catholic. Avocations: backpacking; camping; fishing. Home: 7700 Creekbend Apt 2 Houston TX 77071 Office: U Houston Downtown 1 Main St Houston TX 77002

HEBERT, ROBERT FRANCIS, economics educator; b. Donaldsonville, La., Apr. 2, 1943; s. Robert Marie and Shirley Louise (Harp) H.; m. Diane Elizabeth Dupont, Dec. 28, 1965; children—Corie Gail, Charles Andre. B.S., La. State U., 1965, M.S., 1966, Ph.D., 1970. Asst. prof. Clemson U., S.C., 1970-74; assoc. prof. Auburn U., Ala., 1974-80, prof. econs., head econs. dept., 1980—. Author: (with R.B. Ekelund, Jr.) History of Economic Theory and Method, 1975, 2d edit., 1983; (with A.N. Link) The Entrepreneur, 1982. Contbr. articles and revs. to profl. jours. Mem. Am. Econ. Assn., So. Econ. Assn., History of Econs. Soc., Auburn C. of C. (bd. dirs. 1984—), Phi Kappa Phi, Beta Gamma Sigma, Omicron Delta Epsilon. Roman Catholic. Avocations: tennis; carpentry. Home: 107 Carter St Auburn AL 36830 Office: Econs Dept Auburn U Auburn AL 36849

HEBERT, SIMON JOSEPH, mental health counselor; b. Keene, N.H., Feb. 5, 1942; s. Bruno Joseph and Simone Elizabeth (Mercure) H. Theology degree, ordination, Sacred Heart Sem., 1965; B.A., St. Michael's Coll., 1969; M.S., Nova U., 1984. Nat. cert. counselor. Tchr., adminstr. Brothers of the Sacred Heart, Woonsocket, R.I., 1960-80; mental health counselor, Tampa, Fla., 1984—; asst. prin. St. Lawrence Sch., Tampa, 1978-79; prin. St. Joseph Sch., Pascoag, R.I., 1977-78, St. Lawrence Sch. Religious Edn., Tampa, 1978-79; special asst. to supt. schs., Woonsocket, 1973-74. Recipient Service award Dignity Tampa Bay, 1982-86. Mem. Am. Assn. Counseling and Devel., Am. Assn. for Specialists in Group Work, Am. Mental Health Counselors Assn., Fla. Assn. Counseling and Devel., Fla. Assn. Specialists in Group Work, Fla. Mental Health Counselors Assn. Club: Dignity (Tampa Bay) (sec. 1978-80, pres. 1980-82, treas. 1983-84, bd. dirs.). Democrat. Avocations: piano; organ; tennis; racquetball. Home: 209 Columbia Dr #9 Tampa FL 33606 Office: Tampa Med Services Counselor 3903 S Westshore Blvd Tampa FL 33611

HECETA, ESTHERBELLE AGUILAR, anesthesiologist; b. Cebu City, Philippines, Jan. 1, 1935; came to U.S., 1962, naturalized, 1981; d. Serafin Vasquez and Elsie (Nichols) Aguilar; m. Wilner G., Heceta, Apr. 5, 1962; children—W. Cristina, W. Elgine, Wuela E. B.S. Chemistry cum laude, Silliman U., Dumaguete City, Philippines, 1955, B.S. cum laude, 1956; M.D. cum laude, U. East Ramon Magsaysay Meml. Med. Center, Quezon City, Philippines, 1961. Diplomate Am. Bd. Anesthesiology, Philippine Bd. Anesthesiology. Intern, Youngstown (Ohio) Hosp. Assocs., 1962-63, resident in anesthesiology, 1963-66; anesthesiologist Salem (Ohio) City Hosp., 1967, St. Joseph's Hosp., Manapla, Philippines, 1967-72; instr. dept. anesthesiology U. Tenn., Memphis, 1972-74; staff anesthesiologist Wheeling (W.Va.) Hosp., 1974-76, Ohio Valley Med. Ctr., Wheeling, 1974—, Bellaire (Ohio) City Hosp., 1975—; vol. med.-surg. mission to Philippines, 1982. Fellow Am. Coll. Anesthesiology; mem. Am. Soc. Anesthesiologists, Philippine Soc. Anesthesiologists in Am., W.Va. Soc. Anesthesiologists, Internat. Anesthesia Research Soc., AMA, Am. Med. Women's Assn. (organizer, pres. 1983), W.Va. Med. Soc., Ohio County Med. Soc., Nat. Assn. Female Execs., Assn. Women in Sci. Presbyterian. Home: 15 Holly Rd Wheeling WV 26003 Office: Dept Anesthesiology Ohio Valley Med Ctr 2000 Eoff St Wheeling WV 26003

HECHLER, KEN, former congressman, political science educator, author; b. Roslyn, N.Y., Sept. 20, 1914; s. Charles Henry and Catherine Elizabeth (Hauhart) H. A.B., Swarthmore Coll., 1935; A.M., Columbia U., 1936, Ph.D., 1940. Lectr. govt. Barnard Coll., Columbia Coll., N.Y.C., 1937-41; research asst. to Judge Samuel I. Rosenman, 1939-50; research asst. on Pres. Roosevelt's pub. papers, 1939-50; sect. chief Bur. Census, 1940; personnel technician Office Emergency Mgmt., 1941; adminstrv. analyst Bur. of Budget, 1941-42, 46-47; spl. asst. to pres. Harry S Truman, 1949-53; research dir. Stevenson-Kefauver campaign, 1956; adminstrv. aide Senator Carroll of Colo., 1957; mem. 86th to 94th Congresses from 4th W.Va. Dist.; mem. Sci. and Tech. Com. 86th to 94th Congresses from 4th W.Va. Dist.; chmn. Energy (Fossil Fuels) Subcom.; mem. Joint Com. on Orgn. of Congress, 1965-66, NASA Oversight Subcom. (U.S. Congress); asst. prof. politics Princeton U., 1947-49; prof. polit. sci. Marshall U., Huntington, W.Va., 1957, 82-84; sci. cons. U.S. House Com. on Sci. and Tech., 1978-80; radio, TV commentator Sta. WHTN, Huntington, 1957-58, Sta. WWHY, 1978; adj. prof. polit. sci. U. Charleston, W.Va., 1981; Sec. of State, W.Va., 1985—. Author: Insurgency: Personalities and Politics of the Taft Era, 1940, The Bridge at Remagen, 1957, West Virginia Memories of President Kennedy, 1965, Toward the Endless Frontier, 1980, The Endless Space Frontier, 1982, Working with Truman, 1982. Bd. dirs. W.Va. Humanities Found., 1982—; del. Democratic Nat. Conv., 1964, 68, 72, 80. Served to maj. U.S. Army, 1942-46; served to col. Res. Decorated Bronze Star. Mem. Am. Polit. Sci. Assn. (assoc. dir. 1953-56), Civitan, Am. Legion, V.F.W., D.A.V. Democrat. Episcopalian. Lodge: Elks. Home: 917 5th Ave Huntington WV 25701

HECHT, SIDNEY M., research company executive, educator; b. N.Y.C., July 27, 1944; A.B. in Chemistry, U. Rochester, 1966; Ph.D. in Chemistry, U. Ill., 1970. Research assoc. Lab. Molecular Biology, U. Wis., Madison, 1969-71; asst. prof. chemistry MIT, Cambridge, 1971-75, assoc. prof., 1975-79; John W. Mallet prof. chemistry, prof. biology U. Va., Charlottesville, 1978—; v.p. chem. research and devel. Smith Kline & French Labs., 1981—. NIH fellow, 1967-70, 70-71; Alfred P. Sloan research fellow, 1975-79; John Simon Guggenheim fellow, 1977-78; recipient NIH Career Devel. award, 1975-80. Mem. Am. Chem. Soc., The Chem. Soc., Am. Soc. Biol. Chemists, AAAS, Phi Lambda Upsilon, Sigma Xi. Office: U Va Chemistry Dept Charlottesville VA 22901

HECK, FREEMAN JAMES, III, college administrator; b. New Orleans, Feb. 20, 1950; s. Freeman James Jr. and Dorothy Ann (Paul) H.; m. Sherry Lynn Dickson, Aug. 29, 1970; 1 child, Jeremy Bradford. A.S. in Radiol. Tech., Midwestern State U., 1973, B.S. in Radiol. Tech., 1974; Ed.M., Stephen F. Austin U., 1980. Registered radiographer. Instr., staff technologist U.S. Air Force, Sheppard AFB, Tex., 1969-77; assoc. dir. health careers div. Angelina Coll., Lufkin, Tex., 1977—. Mem. Am. Registry Radiol. Technologists, Am. Soc. Radiol. Technologists, Tex. Soc. Radiol. Technologists. Republican. Methodists. Lodge: Lions. Home: 309 Echo Ln Lufkin TX 75901 Office: Angelina Coll PO Box 1768 Lufkin TX 75901

HECK, WALTER WEBB, research plant physiologist; b. Columbus, Ohio, May 28, 1926; s. Arch Oliver and Frances Margaret (Agnew) H.; m. Corinne Ruth Schiller, Dec. 23, 1959; children—Carolyn R., Ninon, Frederick R., Lee A., Frances E. B.S. in Edn., Ohio State U., 1947; M.S., U. Tenn., 1950; Ph.D., U. Ill., 1954, postgrad. in radiocarbon techniques, 1954-55; asst. prof. biology Ferris State Coll., Big Rapids, Mich., 1955-58, assoc. prof., 1959; assoc. prof. plant physiology Tex. A&M U., 1959-63; research plant physiologist U.S. Dept. Agr., Cin., 1963-69, supervisory plant physiologist, Raleigh, N.C., 1969—; prof. dept. botany N.C. State U., Raleigh, 1969—; research leader Air Quality Effects on Agr.; cons. Recipient Frank A. Chambers award, 1981; grantee EPA, NASA, Dept. Energy. Mem. Air Pollution Control Assn., Am. Soc. Plant Physiologists, Bot. Soc. Am., AAAS, Am. Inst. Biol. Scis., Soil Conservation Soc. Am. Contbr. articles to profl. jours.

HEDGECOCK, JOHN PHILLIP, chemical engineer, government agency official; b. North Little Rock, Ark., Nov. 6, 1933; s. Charles Arthur and Bessie Louise (Stevens) H.; B.S. in Chem. Engring., U. Ark., 1960; m. Ila Trene Kelley, Jan. 24, 1959; children—Kelley Leigh, John Keith, Cathryn Anne, Eric Andrew. Chem. engr. Stauffer Chem. Co., Houston, 1960-64; chem. engr. Pine Bluff (Ark.) Arsenal, 1965-72; chem. engr. Nat. Center Toxicological Research, Jefferson, Ark., 1972—. Served with USN, 1953-55. Recipient Exemplary Civilian Service award U.S. Army, 1972; Commendable Service award FDA, 1981. Registered profl. engr., Ark., Tex. Mem. U.S. Judo Assn. (life). Club: River City Rugby (pres. 1978-79), Twin City Rugby (pres. 1980). Contbr. articles to sports mags. Home: 105 Coronado Pl North Little Rock AR 72116 Office: Nat Center Toxicological Research Jefferson AR 72079

HEDRICK, JOHN CHARLES, JR., minister; b. West Milford, W.Va., Apr. 7, 1940; s. John C. and Christine L. (Jones) H.; m. Carrie Faye Stears, June 1, 1963; children—Cindy Carole and Charles Allan (twins), Rebecca Ann. Student Ky. Bus. Coll., 1958-61; B.A., Campbellsville Coll., 1965; Th.M., New Orleans Baptist Sem., 1967, Am. Div. Sch., 1968; D.Min., Luther Rice Sem., 1975. Ordained to ministry So. Baptist Conv., 1962; pastor Rockbridge Bapt. Ch., Tompkinsville, Ky., 1962-63, Raikes Hill Mission, Campbellsville, Ky., 1963-65, Concrod Bapt. Ch., Hartford, Ky., 1966-68, Pleasant Hill Bapt. Ch., Hopkinsville, Ky., 1968-70, First Bapt. Ch., Napolean, Ohio, 1970-73, Central Bapt. Ch., Maysville, Ky., 1973-81, First Bapt. Ch., Mt. Vernon, 1981—; dir. missions Rockcastle Assoc., Mt. Vernon, 1984. Bd. dirs., treas. YMCA, Maysville, Ky., 1975-77; mem. Drug and Alcohol Abuse Com., Maysville, 1975-77. Mem. Maysville/Mt. Vernon Ministerial Assn. (pres. 1976-77). Republican. Avocations: golf; sports activities. Home: PO Box 639 Mount Vernon KY 40456 Office: First Bapt Ch PO Box 639 Main St at Craig St Mount Vernon KY 40456

HEEBE, FREDERICK JACOB REGAN, U.S. district judge; b. Gretna, La., Aug. 25, 1922; s. Bernhardt and Marguerite (Reagan) H.; m. Betty Mae Rowden, Dec. 25, 1976; children—Frederick Riley, Adrea Dee. B.A., Tulane U., 1943, LL.B., 1949. Bar: La. 1949. Practice in Gretna, 1949-60; dist. judge div. B, 24th Jud. Dist. Ct., Jefferson Parish, La., 1961-66; U.S. dist. judge Eastern Dist. La., 1966—, now chief judge. Charter mem. Community Welfare Council Jefferson Parish, 1957—; chmn. Jefferson Parish Bd. Pub. Welfare, 1953-55; Mem. Jefferson Parish Council, 1958-60, vice chmn., 1958-60; bd. dirs. Social Welfare Planning Council New Orleans, New Orleans Regional Mental Center and Clinic, W. Bank Assn. for Retarded. Served to capt., inf. AUS, World War II. Decorated Purple Heart, Bronze Star. Mem. ABA, La., New Orleans, Fed. bar assns., Am. Judicature Soc., Phi Beta Kappa. Office: Chambers C-525 US Courthouse 500 Camp St New Orleans LA 70130*

HEEMANN, (PAUL) WARREN, college administrator; b. Balt., July 27, 1933; s. Paul A. and Loretta M. (Lange) H.; m. Mary Ellen Placht, Aug. 14, 1958; children—Eve Anne, Lori Barbara, Paul Joseph. A.B. in English, U. N.C., 1956, M.A. in English, 1959. Exec. trainee Van San Dugdale Advt. & Relations, Balt., 1956-57; instr. Coll. William and Mary, Williamsburg, Va., 1962-65, asst. prof. English, 1965-73, assoc. prof., 1973-79, coordinator research, 1965-67, dir. instl. resources, 1967-69, asst. v.p. for sponsored programs, 1969-71, dir. Va. Assoc. Research Campus, 1969-71, v.p. for devel., 1971-79; v.p. for communications and devel. Ga. Inst. Tech., Atlanta, 1979—, sec. nat. adv. bd., 1980—; exec. dir. Centennial Campaign, 1983—, v.p. Found., 1979—; sec. Alexander-Tharpe Fund, Inc., 1980—. Prin. author: Management Reporting Standards for Educational Institutions, 1982. Editor: Analyzing the Cost-Effectiveness of Fund Raising, 1979. Chmn. Regional Com. for Pub. Kindergartens Now, 1968-69; mem. corp. bd. Williamsburg Community Hosp., 1979; bd. dirs. Peninsula Assn. Retarded Children, 1965-72, Williamsburg Pre-Sch for Spl. Children, 1970-72, Peninsula Indsl. Devel. Com., 1971-72. Mem. Council for Advancement and Support Edn. (trustee 1980-83, Frank Ashmore award 1985), Nat. Soc. Fund Raising Execs., Pub. Relations Soc. Am., Ga. Inst. Tech. Alumni Assn. (v.p. 1983—). Lutheran. Club: Capital City (Atlanta). Office: Ga Inst Tech 205 Alumni-Faculty House 190 North Ave NW Atlanta GA 30332

HEFFINGTON, JACK GRISHAM, lawyer, bank executive, insurance company executive, horse breeder; b. Lawrenceburg, Tenn., Mar. 8, 1944; s. Charles Alexander and Kathlyn (Grisham) H.; m. Nancy Caroline Heffington, Sept. 29, 1979; 1 dau., Jacquelyn Elliott. B.S., Memphis State U., 1967; J.D., U. Ark., 1971. Bar: Tenn. 1971, Ala., 1972. Ptnr., Heffington & Thomas, Murfreesboro, Tenn., 1972—; pres., chmn. Middle Tenn. Mortgage Co., Murfreesboro, 1973—; pres., chmn. Keg Life Ins. Co. of S.C., Columbia, 1977—; owner Tan Oak Farms, Murfreesboro; dir. 1st Nat. Bank of Rutherford County. Murfreesboro. Mem. ABA, Ala. Bar Assn., Tenn. Bar Assn., Sigma Delta Chi. Mem. Ch. of Christ. Home: 634 E Main St Murfreesboro TN 37130 Office: 209 N Spring St Murfreesboro TN 37130

HEFLIN, HOWELL THOMAS, U.S. senator, former chief justice Supreme Ct. Ala.; b. Poulan, Ga., June 19, 1921; s. Marvin Rutledge and Louise D. (Strudwick) H.; A.B., Birmingham So. Coll., 1942; J.D., U. Ala., 1948; 9 hon. degrees; m. Elizabeth Ann Carmichael, Feb. 23, 1952; 1 son, Howell Thomas. Bar: Ala. 1948. Practiced in Tuscumbia; mem. firm Heflin, Rosser and Munsey; chief justice Supreme Ct. Ala., 1971-77; chmn. Nat. Conf. Chief Justices, 1976-77; U.S. senator from Ala., 1979—; lectr. U. Ala., 1946-48, Florence State Tchrs. Coll., 1949-52; Tazewell Taylor vis. prof. law Coll. William and Mary, 1977. Mem. Ala. Edn. Commn., 1957-58; chmn. Colbert County ARC, 1950; Ala. field dir. Crusade for Children, 1948; pres. Ala. Com. Better Schs., 1958-59; chmn. Tuscumbia Bd. Edn., 1954-64, Ala. Tenure Commn., 1959-64; pres. U. Ala. Law Sch. Found., 1964-66; co-chmn. Tri-Cities area NCCJ, chmn. Brotherhood Week; bd. dirs., v.p. Nat. Center State Cts.; hon. pres. Troy State U.; bd. dirs. Meth. Pub. House, 1952-64. Served to maj. USMCR, 1942-46. Decorated Silver Star, Purple Heart; recipient Ala. Citizen of Yr. award Ala. Cable TV Assn., 1973, 83; Outstanding Alumnus award U. Ala. and Birmingham So. Coll., 1973; Herbert Lincoln Harley award Am. Judicature Soc.; Ala. Citizen of Year award Ala. Broadcasters Assn., 1975; mem. Ala. Acad. Honor; named Outstanding Appellate Judge in U.S., Assn. Trial Lawyers Am., 1976; recipient Highest award Am. Judges Assn., 1975; Disting. Service award Ala. Farm Bur., 1981, Ga. Peanut Commn., 1981. Fellow Internat. Acad. of Law and Scis., Internat. Acad. Trial Lawyers, Internat. Soc. Barristers, Am. Coll. Trial Lawyers; mem. Ala. Law Inst. (v.p.), Am., Ala. (pres. 1965-66), Colbert County (past pres.) bar assns., Ala. Bar Found. (past pres.), Am. Judicature Soc. (v.p.), Ala. Law Sch. Alumni Assn. (past pres.), Ala. Plaintiff Lawyers Assn. (past pres.), VFW, Am. Legion, 40 and 8, DAV, Third Marine Div. Assn., C. of C., Omicron Delta Kappa, Phi Delta Phi, Tau Kappa Alpha, Lambda Chi Alpha. Methodist. Office: 728 Hart Senate Office Bldg Washington DC 20510

HEFNER, W. G. (BILL HEFNER), congressman; b. Elora, Tenn., Apr. 11, 1930; s. Emory James and Icie Jewel (Holderfield) H.; m. Nancy Louise Hill, Mar. 23, 1952; children—Stacye Hugh, Shelly Gay. Grad. high sch. Mem. 94th-99th Congresses from 8th N.C. Dist., mem. Dem. steering and policy com., appropriations com., budget com. Former profl. entertainer with Harvesters Quartet; former performer weekly gospel show, WXII-TV, Winston-Salem, N.C.; also appeared on WBTV, Charlotte, N.C., WRAL-TV, Raleigh, N.C., WGHP-TV, High Point, N.C., WBTW-TV, Florence, S.C. Bd. dirs. Piedmont Residential Redevel. Center, Concord, N.C. Democrat. Home: Concord NC Office: 2161 Rayburn House Office Bldg Washington DC 20515*

HEGER, HERBERT KRUEGER, educator; b. Cin., June 15, 1937; s. J. Herbert and Leona (Krueger) H.; m. Julia E. Wilson, June 27, 1970; children—William, Charlene. A.S., Ohio Mechanics Inst., 1956; B.S., Miami U., 1962; M.Ed., 1965; Ph.D., Ohio State U., 1969. Tchr., Marshall Jr. High Sch., Pomona, Calif., 1962-63; tchr. math. Mt. Healthy High Sch. (Ohio), 1963-66; grad. asst., grad. assoc. Miami U., Ohio State U., 1966-69; dir. Environ. Studies Center, Central State U., Wilerforce, Ohio, 1968-69; asst. prof. U. Ky., 1969-75, assoc. dir. Louisville Urban Edn. Center, 1971-75; vis. prof. Sch. Profl. Studies, Pepperdine U., 1975-78; dir. student teaching U. Tex., San Antonio, 1975-77, coordinator curriculum and instrn., 1977-78; prof. edn. Whitworth Coll., Spokane, Wash., 1978-82, chmn. dept., 1978-79, dean Grad. Sch., 1979-82; prof. edn., chmn. dept. curriculum and instrn. U. Tex.-El Paso, 1982—; cons. in field. Contbr. articles in field to profl. jours. Mem. Nat. Urban Edn. Assn. (past pres.), Am. Ednl. Research Assn., Am. Assn. Univ. Adminstrs., Nat. Soc. Study Edn., Phi Delta Kappa. Republican. Presbyterian. Home: PO Box 1221 Santa Teresa NM 88008 Office: Dept Curriculum and Instrn U Tex El Paso TX 79968

HEGGIE, ROBERT, research chemist, consultant; b. Glasgow, Scotland, Jan. 19, 1909; came to U.S., 1920; s. Robert Heron and Agnes Russell (Lawrie) H.; m. Florence Theresa Sokovich, Nov. 25, 1939; children—Patricia Robin, Frances Jean. S.B., MIT, 1933, Ph.D., 1936. Research assoc. MIT, Cambridge, 1936-39; with Am. Chicle Co., Long Island City, N.Y., 1939-62, exec. v.p., 1961; v.p. applied scis. Warner-Lambert Co., Morris Plains, N.J., 1962-68, v.p. tech. devel. and control, 1968-71. Contbr. papers to profl. and tech. jours. Patentee chemistry, food products, vitamins, sensory perception. Vice mayor Town of South Palm Beach, Fla., 1974-76, chmn. budget and fin. com., 1976—. Fellow Am. Inst. Chemists, AAAS, N.Y. Acad. Scis.; mem. Soc. Chemical Industry (Am. sect., hon. comptroller 1948-71), Am. Chem. Soc. (councillor 1946-47, auditor N.Y. sect. 1949-70). Republican. Presbyterian. Clubs: Chemists (N.Y.C.); Palm Beach Nat. Home: 3570 S Ocean Blvd Palm Beach FL 33480

HEGSTROM, WILLIAM JEAN, educator; b. Macomb, Ill., Oct. 21, 1923; s. Carl William and Thelma (Canavit) H.; student Western Ill. U., 1941-42; B.Sc., Rutgers U., 1949, Ed.M. 1952; M.A. in Teaching, Purdue U., 1964; postgrad. U. Fla., 1961, Fla. Atlantic U., 1965-68; Ed.D., U. Miami, 1971; m. Grace Ann Paladino, May 3, 1944; children—Elizabeth Louise (Mrs. Edward Cook), William Jean II, Jean. Tchr. jr. high sch., South Plainfield, N.J., 1949-52, high sch., Bernardsville, N.J. 1952-54, Oak St. Sch., Bernard's Twp., N.J., 1954-55, high sch., Summit, N.J., 1955-58, jr. high sch., Delray Beach, Fla, 1958-65; chmn. math. dept. John I. Leonard High Sch., Lake Worth, Fla., 1965-68, dir. Palm Beach County research project, 1966-68; adj. prof. Fla. Atlantic U., 1965-69, assoc. prof., 1969-70; counselor coordinator John Leonard Adult Center, Lake Worth, 1965-68; supr. research and evaluation Palm Beach County Sch. Bd., West Palm Beach, Fla., 1970-74; adj. prof. Palm Beach Jr. Coll., 1981—, Palm Beach Atlantic Coll., 1984—; cons. math. prof. Palm Beach County Sch. Bd., 1985—. Served with USAAF, 1942-46. Mem. NEA, Nat. Council Tchrs. Math., Am. Assn. Individual Investors, Phi Delta Kappa. Contbr. articles to profl. jours. Home: 225 NE 22d St Delray Beach FL 33444

HEIDBRINK, VIRGIL EUGENE, paper company executive; b. Ireton, Iowa, Dec. 4, 1925; s. Edward H. and Luella (Dittmer) H.; A.B., U. S.D., 1949; B.F.T., Am. Inst. Fgn. Trade, 1950; postgrad. Hunter Coll., 1952-53, CCNY, 1953-54, N.Y. U. Grad. Sch. Bus., 1954-56. Export asst. fgn. trade, various firms, N.Y.C., 1951-56; with Hammermill Paper Co., Erie, Pa., 1956, Chgo., 1956-57, dist. sales mgr. Southwest ter., Dallas, 1958—. Del., Tex. Republican State Conv., 1964, 70, 72, 74, 82, 84, precinct chmn. Served with Med. Dept., AUS, 1944-46, 50-51. Decorated Bronze Star. Mem. Dallas Advt. League, Dallas Council World Affairs, Alianza Cultural de Artes y Letras de Mexico, Internat. Good Neighbor Council, Tex. Internat. Bus. Assn. Dallas, Dallas Fgn. Visitors Bur., Phi Beta Kappa. Lutheran. Clubs: Toastmasters (pres. 1965, dist. gov. 1968-69), Dallas Litho. Lodge: Brookhollow Rotary (v.p. 1981-82, pres. 1982-83). Home: 2623 Hudnall St Dallas TX 75235 Office: 1545 W Mockingbird Ln Suite 5038 Dallas TX 75235

HEIDT, GARY ALLEN, biology educator; b. South Bend, Ind., May 20, 1942; s. Vernice W. and Doris B. H.; student Rose Poly. Inst., 1960-61; B.S., Manchester Coll., 1964; M.S., Mich. State U., 1968, Ph.D., 1969; m. Marcia Lynn Rogers, May 12, 1983; children—Deborah, Scott, Nora; stepchildren—Wendy, Jackson Rogers. Asst. prof. Mich. State U., 1969-70; asst. prof. biology U. Ark., Little Rock, 1970-74, assoc. prof., 1974-79, prof., 1979—, dir. basic animal service unit, 1974—; adj. prof. biology Memphis State U., 1983—; cons. in field. Trustee Little Rock Mus. Sci. and History, 1973-79, pres., 1974-75, v.p., 1976-77; bd. dirs. Friends of Zoo, 1975-77; mem. Ark. Endangered Species Tech. Com., 1976—; mem. sci. adv. com. Ark. Sci. and Tech. Authority, 1986. Mem. Am. Soc. Mammalogists, Southwestern Assn. Naturalists, Wildlife Soc., Ecol. Soc. Am., Am. Assn. Lab. Animal Sci. (pres. Ark. chpt. 1978-79), Ark. Acad. Sci. (editor 1977-81, v.p. 1983-84, pres.-elect 1984-85, pres. 1985-86), Wildlife Disease Assn.). Methodist. Home: 12106 Teton Forest St Little Rock AR 72212 Office: Dept Biology U Ark at Little Rock 33d and University Sts Little Rock AR 72204

HEIN, SALLY LEE, hospital administrator; b. Cin., May 8, 1851; d. David Edward and Virginia (Herzog) H. B.S., U. Cin., 1973; M.A., Vanderbilt U., 1974; Ph.D., Memphis State U., 1980. Cert. speech pathologist, Tex. Clin. speech pathologist U. Ala. Med. Ctr., Birmingham, 1975-77; asst. prof. N. Tex. State U., Denton, 1980-84; dir. ednl. services Parkland Meml. Hosp., Dallas, 1984—. Vol. Am. Heart Assn., Dallas, 1984—. Recipient Outstanding award for research of handicapped U.S.A. Mil. Order of Purple Heart, 1981. Mem. Am. Speech, Lang., Hearing Assn., N.Y. Acad. Scis., Am. Soc. Tng. and Devel., Am. Hosp. Assn., Tex. Hosp. Assn. Jewish. Avocation: volunteer work. Home: 8215 Meadow Rd Apt 2116 Dallas TX 75231 Office: Parkland Meml Hosp 5201 Harry Hines Blvd Dallas TX 75235

HEIN, VIRGINIA HERZOG, history educator; b. Atlanta, May 17, 1926; s. Ralph and Callie (Blum) Herzog; m. David Edward Hein, June 22, 1947; children—Sally Lee, Merideth Hein Northcutt; B.A., Skidmore Coll., 1947; M.A., Ga. State U., 1971, Ph.D., 1978. Grad. asst., teaching asst., Ga. State U., Atlanta, 1971-78; lectr. history So. Tech. Inst., Marietta, Ga., 1978-80, asst. prof., 1980—. Bd. dirs. Pub. Broadcasting Assn. Greater Atlanta, 1981—, treas., 1983—, exec. com., 1983—; bd. dirs. Atlanta Arts Festival, 1953-69, pres., 1962, 63, YWCA, 1964, 65, Am. Jewish Com., 1971-83. Mem. Grand Jurors' Assn. Fulton County. High Mus. Art. Selected for Am. Jewish Com.'s Academicians' seminar in Israel, 1978. Mem. Am. Hist. Assn., So. Hist. Assn., Ga. Assn. Historians (exec. council 1981—, editor newsletter 1981—) Atlanta Hist. Soc., Humanities, Tech. Assn., Assn. Bibliography History, Phi Alpha Theta, Mu Tau (pres. Ga. State U. chpt. 1974-75). Club: English Speaking Union (London). Contbr. articles to publs. Home: 125 Blackland Rd NW Atlanta GA 30342 Office: So Tech Inst Dept English and History Marietta GA 30060

HEINLEIN, WILLIAM EDWARD, school psychologist, consultant; b. Erie, Pa., Aug. 11, 1951; s. William Peter and Rita G. (Berchtold) H. B.A., Gannon U., 1973; Ed.M., Edinboro U., 1974, Ed.S., 1975; Ed.D., Va. Poly. Inst., 1985—. Lic. sch. psychologist, profl. counselor, Va., Ohio, Pa. Project dir. Exceptional Children's Ctr., Erie, Pa., 1975-77; program coordinator Learning Disability Ctr., Erie, 1977-81; sch. psychologist Elyria City Schs., Cleve., 1981-83; research asst. Va. Tech. U., Blacksburg, 1983-85; pvt. practice psychology, Blacksburg, 1985—; cons. Lorain County Juvenile Ct., Ohio, 1982-83, Comprehensive Family Services, 1984—, Lee County Sch., Jonesville, Va., 1985—, Dickenson County, Clintwood, Va., 1985—. Mem. adv. council Mental Health/Mental Retardation Task Force, Erie, 1979-81; cons. Elyria

Lorain Coop. Program for Severe Behavior Disorders, Cleve., 1982-83; bd. dirs. Youth Services Coordinating Council, Erie, 1978-81. Mem. Am. Edn. Research Assn., Am. Assn. Counseling Devel., Nat. Assn. Sch. Psychologists, Am. Psychol. Assn., Soc. for Indsl. Organizational Psychology. Home:Office: Va Poly Inst Blacksburg VA 24061

HEISCHOBER, HAROLD, mayor. Mayor of Virginia Beach, Va. Office: Municipal Ctr Virginia Beach VA 23456*

HEISER, ROLLAND VALENTINE, retired army officer, foundation executive; b. Columbus, Ohio, Apr. 25, 1925; s. Rudolph and Helen Cecile H.; B.S., U.S. Mil. Acad., 1947; M.S. in Internat. Affairs, George Washington U., 1965; m. Gwenne Kathleen Duquemin, Feb. 26, 1949; children—Helen Heiser Sanford, Charlene Heiser Geiger. Commd. 2d lt. U.S. Army, 1947, advanced through grades to lt. gen., 1978; served in Europe, Korea, Vietnam; army planner, Washington, 1973-74; comdr. 1st Armored div., Ger., 1974-75; chief of staff U.S. Army Europe, 1975-76; chief staff U.S. European Command, 1976-78; pres. New Coll. Found., Sarasota, Fla., 1979—; dir. Coast Fed. Savs. and Loan Assn., Sarasota. Mem. Sarasota Com. 100; gen. chmn. 1986 Suncoast Offshore Grand Prix, 1986, also dir. Decorated D.S.M. (2), Def. Disting. Service medal, Legion of Merit (3), Bronze Star, others. Mem. Ret. Officers Assn. Ret. Officers Club Sarasota (dir.), Sarasota C. of C. (bd. dirs.), Republican. Episcopalian. Clubs: Bird Key Yacht, Univ. of Sarasota. Lodge: Masons. Home: 988 Blvd of the Arts Sarasota FL 33577 Office: 5700 N Tamiami Trail Sarasota FL 33580

HEITZMAN, HARRY BRADLEY, physician; b. Biloxi, Miss., Oct. 26, 1943; s. Harry McMillan and Shirley Ann (Redding) H.; A.S., Miss. Gulf Coast Jr. Coll., 1963; B.S., U. Miss., 1965, M.D., 1969; m. Vivian Ann McNair, Dec. 23, 1965 (div.); children—Brandy Alesia, Hunter McMillan; m. Melinda Owen, Oct. 22, 1983. Intern, Roanoke (Va.) Meml. Hosp., 1969-70; resident U. Hosp. Jackson, Miss., 1973; internist Coastal Med. Center, Biloxi, Miss., 1973-75; internist, chmn. bd. Gulf Coast Surg. and Diagnostic Center, Ocean Springs, Miss., 1975—, also dir.; sec.-treas med. staff Ocean Springs Hosp., 1982-83, Chief-of-staff, 1984—. Named King Krewe of Neptune, Biloxi Mardi Gras, 1984. Mem. Miss. Thoracic Soc., Ocean Springs Art Assn. Republican. Episcopalian (vestryman 1974-77). Clubs: Ocean Springs Yacht, Krewe of Les Badineurs, Krewe of Neptune. Home: 9532 Red Bluff Ocean Springs MS 39564 Office: Medical Plaza Van Cleave Rd Ocean Springs MS 34564

HEIVILIN, THOMAS STUART, air force officer, engineer; b. Klemme, Iowa, May 21, 1937; s. Edward Stuart and Irene Annabelle (Johnson) H.; m. Carol Jeanette Passailaigue, Dec. 24, 1969; 1 child, Rexford Thomas. B.S. in Math., State U. Iowa, 1963; M.B.A., Pepperdine U., 1978. Commd. 2d lt. U.S. Air Force, 1963, advanced through grades to col., 1982; electronics officer, various locations, 1964-70, systems engr., San Antonio, 1971-75, comdr., 1976-78, electronics dir., 1978-84, ret., 1984; sr. engr. Nat. Air Space div. Aero. Radio Inc., Washington, 1984—. Designer electronics system for Air Force aircraft, 1981-83 (Meritorious Service award 1983). Recipient Resource Mgr. Yr. award Dept. Defense, 1976, Presdl. Mgmt. award White House, 1977. Mem. Armed Forces Communication Electronics Assn. (pres. Pacific Area 1976-78). Republican. Methodist. Club: Rod and Gun (Collinsville, Ill.) (pres. 1982-84). Avocations: sky diving; water skiing; tennis. Office: ARINC Research Inc 3240 Norman Berry Dr Suite 524 Hopeville GA 30354

HEIZER, PATRICIA HUDSON, insurance company official; b. Dallas, July 31, 1927; d. Daryl Jack and Mary Lila (Hale) Hudson; m. E.C. Webb, Sept. 8, 1950 (div. 1952); m. Bobby V. Heizer, July 29, 1966; 1 dau., Mary Patricia. B.A., So. Meth. U., 1948. Gen. clk. Travelers Ins. Co., Dallas, 1948-51; tchr. Dallas Pub. Schs., 1952-56; clk. thru underwriter U.S.-Ins. Group, Dallas, 1956-76, trainer, 1976—, sr. tng. assoc. of underwriting, 1976—. Mem. Ins. Women Dallas (dir., chmn., pres.), Am. Soc. Tng. and Devel., Nat. Assn. Ins. Women (cert.; Ins. Woman of Yr. 1981; dir. Dallas). Methodist. Lodge: Eastern Star. Home: 1110 Lakeview Rd Grand Prairie TX 75051 Office: US Ins Group Crum & Foster 4040 N Central Expressway Box 2639 Dallas TX 75221

HEJTMANCIK, KELLY ERWIN, medical microbiologist, immunologist, educator, researcher, consultant; b. Galveston, Tex., Sept. 10, 1948; s. Milton Rudolph and Myrtle Lou (Erwin) H.; m. Sharron Gaye Myers, Jan. 8, 1969; children—Ann Marie, Kelly Erwin Jr. B.S., Southwest Tex. State U., 1970; M.S., Trinity U., 1972; Ph.D., U. Tex. Med.-Galveston, 1978. Lab. instr. Trinity U., San Antonio, 1970-71; sci. tchr. biology and phys. sci. Luther Burbank High Sch., San Antonio, 1971-72; research assoc. U. Tex.-Galveston, 1972-74, McLaughlin fellow, 1974-78, sr. research assoc., postdoctoral fellow, 1978-79, chmn. dept. biol. scis., 1979—; cons., reviewer W.B. Saunders Pub. Co., N.Y.C., 1978—, Holt. Reinhard, Winston Pub. Co., N.Y.C., 1979—, C.V. Mosby Pub. Co., St. Louis, 1979—. Contbr. articles to profl. jours. Active Galveston Jaycees, 1972-75; sci. fair judge Galveston High Sch., 1984, Citywide and Dist. schs., Galveston, 1984, 85, Univ. Interscholastic League, 1984, 85. Mem. AAAS, Am. Soc. Microbiology, Sigma Xi, Phi Kappa Psi. Republican. Methodist. Avocations: boating; motorcycling; stamp collecting. Home: 15 Back Bay Circle E Galveston TX 77551 Office: Galveston Coll 4015 Ave Q Galveston TX 77550

HEJTMANCIK, MILTON RUDOLPH, physician, educator; b. Caldwell, Tex., Sept. 27, 1919; s. Rudolph Joseph and Millie (Jurcak) H.; m. Myrtle Lou Erwin, Aug. 21, 1943 (dec. June 1975); children—Kelly Erwin, Milton Rudolph, Peggy Lou; m. Myrtle M. Granberry, Nov. 27, 1976. B.A., U. Tex., 1939, M.D., 1943. Resident internal medicine U. Tex., 1946-49, instr. internal medicine, 1949-51, asst. prof. internal medicine, 1951-54, assoc. prof. internal medicine, 1954-65, prof. internal medicine, 1965-80, dir. heart clinic, 1949-80, dir. heart station, 1965-80; chief staff John Sealy Hosp., 1957-58; chief staff U. Tex. Med. Br. Hosps., 1977-79; prof. medicine Tex. A&M Coll. Medicine and cardiologist Olin E. Teague VA Hosp., Temple, Tex., 1981-82; cardiologist Beaumont VA Clinic, Tex., 1982-86. Served from 1st lt. to capt. M.C., AUS, 1944-46, ETO. Diplomate in cardiovascular diseases Am. Bd. Internal Medicine. Fellow ACP, Am. College Chest Physicians, Am. Coll. Cardiology; mem. Am. (fellow council clin. cardiology), Tex. (chmn. med. and sci. com. 1976-78, pres. 1979-80), Galveston Dist. (pres. 1956) heart assns., AMA (Billings Gold medal 1973), Am. Fedn. Clin. Research, AAAS, Tex. Acad. Internal Medicine (gov. 1971-73, pres. 1976), Tex. Club Cardiology (pres. 1972-73), Tex. (del. 1972-79), Galveston County (pres. 1971) med. assns., N.Y. Acad. Sci., AAUP, Phi Beta Kappa, Sigma Xi, Alpha Omega Alpha, Phi Eta Sigma, Mu Delta. Contbr. numerous papers on cardiovascular disease to profl. jours. Home: Port Bolivar TX 77850

HEKMAN, SUSAN JEAN, political science educator; b. Grand Rapids, Mich., Feb. 28, 1949; d. Edward John and Florence Guisina (Stuart) Hekman; m. Evan Marcus Anders, Feb. 15, 1985. B.A., Carleton Coll., 1971; M.A., U. Wash., 1973, Ph.D., 1976. Vis. prof. Lewis and Clark Coll., Portland, Oreg., 1976-77; asst. prof. U. Tex.-Arlington, 1977-83, assoc. prof. polit. sci., 1983—; dir. honors program, 1982—. Author: Weber, The Ideal Type and Contemporary Social Theory, 1983. Contbr. articles to profl. jours. U.S. Steel Corp. fellow 1975; grantee NEH 1981, U. Tex. 1980, 84. German Acad. Exchange Service scholar 1975. Mem. Am. Polit. Sci. Assn. Democrat. Avocation: horseback riding. Home: 2047 Fleur de Lis Arlington TX 76012 Office: U Tex Dept Polit Sci Arlington TX 76012

HELD, PHILIP, painter, photographer; b. N.Y.C., June 2, 1920; s. Conrad Christopher and Charlotte Virginia (Ditchett) H.; m. Isobel Ann Caine, Sept. 12, 1950; 1 son, Andrew Christopher. Student Art Students League N.Y., 1938-42, 46, Sch. Art Studies, 1947-48, Tchrs. Coll., Columbia U., 1949. One-man shows: Ward Eggleston Gallery, N.Y.C., 1948, Berkshire Mus., Pittsfield, Mass., 1949, 67, Camino Gallery, N.Y.C., 1960, 62, Winthrop Coll., S.C., 1963, Gladstone Gllaery Gallery, Woodstock, N.Y., 1965, Phoenix Gallery, N.Y.C., 1965, 67, Fontana Gallery, Narberth, Pa., 1965, 72, Polari Gallery, Woodstock, N.Y., 1970, Ringling Mus., Fla., 1972, Brevard Coll., Cocoa, Fla., 1973, Lighthouse Gallery, Tequesta, Fla., 1980, St. Petersburg (Fla.) Library, 1982; group shows include: Internat. Print Club, N.Y.C., 1953, Phila. Print Club, 1957, Audubon Artists, N.Y.C., 1957, Mus. Modern Art, N.Y.C., 1957, Riverside Mus., N.Y.C., 1959, 60, Albany (N.Y.) Inst. Art and History, 1960, 63, L.I. U., 1960, Pa. Acad. Fine Arts Ann., Phila., 1962, Brown U., Providence, 1963, St. Paul Art Ctr., 1963, Fairleigh Dickinson U., N.J., 1964, Drew U., N.J., 1966, U. Mass., Amherst, 1966, Gallery Contemporary Art, Winston-Salem, N.C., 1972, St. Petersburg (Fla.) Arts Ctr., 1974, Pleiades Gallery, N.Y.C., 1978, Shirley Shire Gallery, Sarasota, Fla., 1979, Harmon Gallery, Sarasota, 1980, 83, Fla. Artists Group Ann., 1980, 83; represented in permanent collections: U. Mass., Berkshire Mus., Art Students League N.Y., also pvt. collections. Kleinert Found. grantee. Mem. Art Students League N.Y. (life), Sarasota Art Assn., Art League Manatee County (Fla.), Am. Fedn. Musicians, Fla. Artists Group. Address: 3035 Wood St Sarasota FL 33577

HELGUERA, J. LÓN, history educator, lecturer, consultant; b. N.Y.C., Oct. 29, 1926; s. José Agustín Helguera y Aranda and Antoinette Celestine (Seis) H.; m. Charlotte Byrd Stone, Sept. 10, 1950; children—Joseph Hamilton Castle, Eugenia Byrd, Lón Arcadio Eduard. B.A., Mexico City Coll., 1948; M.A. in History, U. N.C., 1951, Ph.D. in History, 1958. From instr. to assoc. prof. N.C. State U., 1957-63; assoc. prof. history Vanderbilt U., Nashville, 1963-68, prof., 1968—; vis. sr. fellow St. Anthony's Coll., Oxford, 1972; cons. Hispanic Found., Library of Congress, 1958-71. Served with U.S. Army, 1944-46; USAR, 1950-54. Recipient Disting. Classroom 107 award N.C. State U., 1961-62; Order of Andrés Bello by Venezuelan Govt., 1970; Waddell fellow U. N.C., 1953-54; Doherty travelling fellow S.A., 1953-54; OAS fellow, 1962, 66; Am. Philos. Soc. Penrose Fund grantee, 1974. Mem. Academia of History Colombia (corr.), Ecuador (corr.), Panama (corr.), Venezuela (corr.), Centro de Estudios Montañeses of Santander (Spain) (corr.). Club: Popayán, Colombia. Author: Bibliografía de la Guerra de los Supremos: 1839-1842, 1978; Indigenismo in Columbia: A Facet of the National Identity Search, 1821-1973, 1974; The Problem of Liberalism Versus Conservatism in Colombia: 1849-1885, 1969; editor: (with Robert H. Davis) Archivo Epistolar del General Mosquera, 4 vols., 1966-78. Home: 2309 Sterling Rd Nashville TN 37215 Office: PO Box 1606 Sta B Vanderbilt U Nashville TN 37235

HELLER, ESTHER BURT, counselor; b. Phila., Nov. 18; d. Philip Jay and Anna (Kagel) Amsterdam; m. Samuel Matthew Burt, Apr. 29 (dec. June 1975); children—Robert, Jeffrey, Carolyn; m. Milton Leonard Heller, July 16, 1978. B.S. in Edn., Temple U.; M.A. in Conseling, U. Md., 1964. Lic. counselor. Tchr., Wheaton High Sch., Montgomery County, Md., 1953-60; sch. counselor Eastern Jr. High Sch., Montgomery County, 1960-70, Parkland Jr. High Sch., Montgomery County, 1970-78; pvt. practice career counseling, North Miami Beach, Fla., 1979—. Mem. NEA, Montgomery County Edn. Assn., Md. State Edn. Assn., Assn. Jewish Communal Service Workers, Assn. Jewish Vocat. Profls. Clubs: Brandeis Univ. Women (facilitator study group), Nat. Council Jewish Women, Hadassah Ctr. Fine Arts. Avocations: crafts; exercise classes; music; theatre; travel. Home and Office: 3731 N Country Club Dr 1728 Miami Beach FL 33180

HELLER, GEORGE LOUIS, chem. engr.; b. Albany, N.Y., Dec. 5, 1908; s. Frederick Louis and Christine Catherine (Dorn) H.; Ch.E., Rensselaer Poly. Inst., 1931, M.Ch.E., 1933; m. Marguerite Rose Hoffman, Oct. 12, 1935; children—Richard L., Robert G., Frederick L., George E., Thomas P. Asst. bridge engr. D&H R.R., 1929-30; air conditioning and heating engr. M.W. Co., 1931-32; dir. research Gen. Atlas Carbon Co., Pampa, Tex., 1933-41; dir. devel. Cities Service Co., Monroe, La., 1941-74, ret., 1974; cons. engring. to carbon black industry, Monroe, La., 1974—. Mem. bishop's adv. com. Roman Catholic Diocese of Alexandria, 1948-52; chmn. bldg. com. Our Lady of Fatima Parish, Monroe, 1951-77; mem. Presdl. Task Force; precinct capt.; hon. col. La. Gov.'s Staff; mem. vol. involvement program, tutor in math. Ouachita High Sch. System. Recipient Tech. Achievement award State of La., 1974, Outstanding Creativity award Cities Service Co., 1973. Mem. Am. Chem. Soc. (life; chmn. 1935-39, charter mem. So. Rubber Group), Am. Inst. Chem. Engrs. (life; chmn. 1952-54), Nat. Soc. Profl. Engrs., La. Engring. Soc. (life; chmn. 1970-71, chmn. engring. edn. com.), Sigma Xi (life). Club: K.C. (Order of Merit 1977), Knights of St. Gregory. Contbr. articles to profl. jours., bulls.; U.S. fgn. patentee in field. Home and Office: 4710 Bon Aire Dr Monroe LA 71203

HELLMUTH, WILLIAM FREDERICK, JR., economics educator; b. Washington, Jan. 8, 1920; s. William Frederick and Sybel May (Grant) H.; m. Jean Adele Dieffenbach, Feb. 14, 1943; children—James M. (dec.), Suzanne, William L., Peter G. B.A., Yale U., 1940, Ph.D. in Econs., 1948. Instr. in econs. Yale U., New Haven, 1945-48; asst. prof. to prof. Oberlin Coll., Ohio, 1948-68, dean, 1960-67; prof. econs. Va. Commonwealth U., Richmond, 1973—; dep. asst. sec. for tax policy U.S. Treasury Dept., Washington, 1968-69; v.p. arts McMaster U., Hamilton, Ont., Can., 1969-73; chief economist Cleve Met. Services Commn., 1957-59; mem. field staff Rockefeller Found., Dar es Salaam, Tanzania, 1965, 66; fiscal economist mission to east Africa, IMF, Washington, 1972; chief of staff Capital City Govt. Commn., Richmond, Va., 1980-81. Co-author: Financing Government in a Metropolitan Area, 1961. Co-editor: Tax Policy and Tax Reform, 1961-68, 1973. Contbr. chpt. to book: Homeowner Tax Preferences, 1977. Recipient Outstanding Service award Sch. Bus. Va. Commonwealth U., 1985. Mem. Am. Econ. Assn., Nat. Tax Assn., So. Econ. Assn., Nat. Econs. Club, Va. Assn. Economists (pres. 1978-79), Phi Beta Kappa. Democrat. Unitarian. Clubs: Richmond First, Torch. Avocations: baseball, travel, military history of World War II. Home: 3117 Bute Ln Richmond VA 23221 Office: Va Commonwealth U Dept Econs 1015 Floyd Ave Richmond VA 23284

HELM, BOYD EDWARD, cardiologist; b. New Orleans, Jan. 28, 1942; s. James Boyd and Helen (Friloux) H.; B.S., Loyola U. of South, 1964; M.D., La. State U., 1967; m. Barbara Mahoney, July 2, 1966; children—Shannon, Boyd, Eric, Brendan, Mollie. Intern, Charity Hosp. La., New Orleans, 1967-68, resident in internal medicine, 1968-71: NIH fellow in cardiology U. Tenn., 1973-75; cons. cardiologist, invasive cardiologist Cardilogy Clinic, Baton Rouge, 1975—; practice medicine specializing in cardiology, Baton Rouge, 1975—; mem. med. staff Baton Rouge Hosp., Gen. Hosp., Our Lady of Lake Hosp., Med. Ctr. Baton Rouge, mem. teaching staff U. Tenn., 1973-75, E.K. Long Hosp., 1975. Tchr., advisor Mended Heart Assn., 1977—; bd. dirs. Am. Heart Assn. La. Served to lt. comdr. USN, 1971-73. Cancer Assn. grantee, 1962-63; Am. Heart Assn. grantee, 1964. Fellow Am. Heart Assn., Am. Coll. Cardiology, Am. Coll. Chest Physicians; mem. AMA, La. Med. Assn., East Baton Rouge Parish Med. Soc., So. Med. Soc. Republican. Roman Catholic. Club: K.C. Office: 5231 Brittany Dr Baton Rouge LA 70809

HELM, HUGH BARNETT, retired judge; b. Bowling Green, Ky., Dec. 27, 1914; s. Hugh Barnett and Ermine (Cox) H.; B.A., Vanderbilt U., 1935, postgrad. law sch., 1936-37, 52-53, Stanford U., 1953-56, Nat. Coll. Judiciary, 1976; m. Vivian Loreen Downing, June 5, 1943; children—Beverly, Hugh B. III, Nathaniel Henry. Admitted to Ky. bar, 1938, Tenn. bar, 1938, U.S. Supreme Ct. bar, 1942; atty. Trade Practice Conf., FTC, Washington, 1938-42; asso. counsel U.S. Internat. Prosecution Sect. Gen. Hdqrs., SCAP, Tokyo, 1946; practiced in Nashville, 1946-53; bond specialist Swett & Crawford, San Francisco, 1956-57; resident mgr. Totten & Co., San Francisco, 1958, v.p. gen. mgr., 1959-60; sr. trial atty. Bur. Restraint of Trade, FTC, Washington, 1961-66, chief div. of adv. opinions, 1966-70, acting dir. Bur. Industry Guidance, 1969-70, atty. adviser FTC Bur. Consumer Claims, until 1971; adminstrv. law judge Bur. Hearing and Appeals, Social Security Adminstrn., HEW, Chattanooga, 1971-73, adminstrv. law judge charge Western Ky. and So. Ill., Paducah, Ky., 1973-76, Louisville, 1976-78; adminstrv. law judge in charge Miami (Fla.) Office Hearings and Appeals, 1979-81, adminstrv. law judge, Louisville, 1981-82; mem. regional jud. council Social Security Adminstrn. Pres. Surety Claims Assn. No. Calif., 1957-58. Mem. Tenn. Ho. of Reps., 1949-50. Served with inf. USAAF, 1941-45; served to capt. U.S. Army, 1950-52. Decorated Bronze Star, Combat Infantry Badge; recipient Founders medal for oratory Vanderbilt U., 1935, Disting. Service Commendation FTC, 1969. Mem. Am. (com. on civil service law), Ky., Tenn. bar assns., Nat. Lawyers Club, Pi Sigma Alpha, Tau Kappa Alpha. Presbyterian (deacon). Home: 23301 Lago Mar Circle Boca Raton FL 33433

HELM, ROBERT MEREDITH, philosophy educator; b. Winston-Salem, N.C., Feb. 19, 1917; s. Robert Meredith and Mary Alma (Jones) H. B.A., Wake Forest Coll., 1939; M.A., Duke U., 1940, Ph.D., 1950. Mem. faculty Wake Forest U. (N.C.), 1940—, prof. philosophy, 1962—, Worrell prof. philosophy, 1983—; assoc. prof. Salem Coll., 1958-60; mem. faculty N.C. Sch. Arts, 1967-69. Bd. dirs., pres. James W. Denmark Loan Fund. Served to maj. AUS, 1941-46, ETO. Decorated Army Commendation medal; recipient Patriotic Civilian Service citation Dept. Army, 1979. Mem. Am. Philos. Assn., Am. Acad. Religion, AAUP, N.C. Philos. Soc., Internat. Soc. Neoplatonic Studies, Phi Beta Kappa, Omicron Delta Kappa, Delta Sigma Rho, Tau Kappa Alpha, Sigma Pi. Democrat. Moravian. Author: The Gloomy Dean: The Thought of William Ralph Inge, 1962; co-editor, contbr. Studies in Nietzsche and the Classical Tradition, 1976; co-author: Meaning and Value in Western Thought, vol. 1: The Ancient Foundations, 1981. Co-editor, translator Studies in Nietzsche and The Judaeo-Christian Tradition, 1985. Home: PO Box 7243 Reynolda Sta Winston-Salem NC 27109

HELME, DONALD WADE, banker; b. Knoxville, Tenn., Feb. 18, 1939; s. Wade Hampton and Edith Belle (Watkins) H.; student U. Tenn., 1957-60; J.D., Woodrow Wilson Coll. Law, 1964; LL.M., John Marshall U., 1965; cert. grad. Northwestern U. Sch. Mortgage Banking, 1968; m. Karen Durisch, Aug. 6, 1961; children—Karen E., Courtney L., Donald Wade. Vice pres. Phipps-Harrington Corp., Atlanta, 1964-71; pres. Helme Homes Inc., Atlanta, 1971-73; v.p. Commonwealth Mortgage Corp., Richmond, Va., 1973-75; v.p. Am. Century Advs., Inc., Jacksonville, Fla., 1976-78, pres., chief operating officer, 1980-83; also dir.; sr. v.p., dir. Am. Century Corp., San Antonio; dir., v.p., vice chmn. Am. Century Trust; v.p. Atlantic Nat. Bank Fla., Jacksonville, 1983—. Served with U.S. Army, 1960-63; lic. in real estate, lic. mortgage broker, Fla. Mem. Fla. Mortgage Brokers Assn., Mortgage Bankers Assn. Am., Fla. Home Builders Assn., Kappa Sigma, Sigma Delta Kappa. Republican. Presbyterian. Clubs: Sawgrass (Ponte Vedra Beach, Fla.); River, Univ. (Jacksonville. Office: Atlantic Nat Bank of Fla 200 W Forsyth St 5-T Jacksonville FL 32202

HELME, JAMES BUCKELEW, physician; b. Port Chester, N.Y., Apr. 27, 1924; s. James Buckelew and Mary DeHaven (Van Deren) H.; grad. Choate Sch., 1942; A.B., Princeton U., 1947; M.D., U. Wash., 1952; m. Josephine Coleman Douglas, May 22, 1953 (div. Sept. 1974); children—Susan Van Deren, Catherine Douglas, Martha Buckelew, John Franklin. Intern, Kings County Hosp., Bklyn., 1952-53; intern Johns Hopkins Hosp., 1953-54, resident, 1954-55; resident Vanderbilt U. Hosp., Nashville, 1955-56; practice medicine, specializing in pediatrics, Nashville, 1956-68; instr. pediatrics and community health Meharry Med. Coll., 1968-71; pediatrician Davidson County Health Dept., 1971-72; med. dir. Nashville Drug Treatment Center, 1972-78, Tenn. State Prison and Hosp., 1978-81; mental health cons., 1981—; chief pediatrics service Nashville Gen. Hosp., 1956-60. Cons., Tenn. Fine Arts Commn., 1968-70. Pres. Nashville Arts Council, 1963-65; bd. dirs. Tenn. Fine Arts Mus., 1963-65, Theatre Nashville Mgmt., 1973-74. Served to 1st lt. USMCR, 1943-45. Mem. Nashville Acad. Medicine, Tenn. Med. Assn., Tenn., Davidson County pediatric socs., Am. Philatelic Soc. (expert com. and writers unit), Middle Tenn. Princeton Alumni Assn. (pres. 1962-65). Clubs: Princeton, Collectors (N.Y.C.); Colonial (Princeton). Contbr. to The Yucatan Affair, 1974, Collectors Club Jour., 1986. Home: 3704 Estes Rd Nashville TN 37215 Office: 1918 Church St Nashville TN 37203

HELMERICH, WALTER HUGO, III, oil company executive; b. Tulsa, Jan. 12, 1923; s. Walter Hugo, Jr. and Cadijah (Colcord) H.; B.A., U. Okla., 1948; M.B.A., Harvard, 1950; m. Peggy Varnadow, Nov. 24, 1951; children—Walter Hugo IV, Dow Zachary, Matthew Galloway, Hans Christian, Jonathan David. With Helmerich & Payne, Inc., Tulsa, 1950—, pres., 1960—, also dir.; dir. Natural Gas Odorizing, Inc., Rikwell Co., Atwood Oceanics, Inc., First Tulsa Bancorp., Inc., 1st Nat. Bank & Trust Co. Tulsa, I.C. Industries; trustee Northwestern Mut. Life Ins. Co. Chmn. Okla. World's Fair Commn., 1964-65; bd. dirs. Salvation Army, Okla. Acad. for State Goals, Okla. Health Scis. Found., Okla. Med. Research Found., Holland Hall Sch., 1962-71; trustee Tulsa Psychiat. Center, Inc., Retina Research Found. (Houston), Hillcrest Med. Center. Mem. Ind. Petroleum Assn. Am. (dir.), Chief Execs. Forum, World Bus Council, Tulsa C. of C. (dir.), Sigma Nu. Methodist (bd. stewards, chmn. 1967-70). Home: 3003 S Rockford Rd Tulsa OK 74114 Office: Utica at 21st Tulsa OK 74114*

HELMINIAK, DANIEL ALBERT, theologian, priest; b. Pitts., Nov. 20, 1942; s. Albert and Cecelia (Ziolkowski) H. B.A., St. Vincent Coll., 1964; S.T.B., S.T.L., Gregorian U., Rome, 1966, 68; M.A. in Psychology, Boston U., 1983; Ph.D. in Theology, Boston Coll. and Andover Theol. Sch., 1979; postgrad. in ednl. psychology U. Tex.-Austin, 1985—. Ordained priest Roman Catholic Ch., 1967. Assoc. pastor Sts. Simon & Jude Ch., Pitts., 1968-72; instr. St. Mary Sem., Balt., 1972-73; spl. asst. Sacred Heart Ch./St. John Evangelist Ch., Newton, 1973-81; coordinator Paulist Leadership & Renewal Project, Boston, 1978-80; asst. prof. Oblate Sch. Theology, San Antonio, 1981-85; chaplain Dignity/San Antonio, 1982-85. Author: The Same Jesus: A Contemporary Christology. Contbr. articles to profl. jours. Mem. Am. Acad. Religion, Am. Assn. Pastoral Counselors, Am. Psychol. Assn., Cath. Theol. Soc. Am. Psi of San Antonio. Democrat. Club: Community Cath. Counselors. Address: PO Box 13527 Austin TX 78711

HELMS, ERIC COURTLAND, business executive, author, numismatist; b. Florence, S.C., Oct. 26, 1947; s. James Ralph and Evelyn Louise (Liles) H.; m. Trudy Katherine Cochran, July 5, 1969; children—Andrew, Katherine. B.Indsl. Engring., Ga. Inst. Tech., 1970; M.B.A., U. Tenn., 1976. Registered rep. Equity Funding Securities, Knoxville, Tenn., 1972-73; indsl. engr. Alcoa, 1970-72; sr. mfg. planning engr., div. mgr. Kingsport Press (Tenn.), 1973-77; asst. plant mgr. Consol. Aluminum, Murphysboro, Ill., 1977-79; asst. to mgr. Greenville plants, Cooper Industries (Miss.), 1979-82; plant mgr. Cooper Steel, Greenville, 1982; mfg. mgr. Nicholson Saw, Greenville, 1982—; owner Silver Numismatics. Bd. dirs. Royal Ambassadors, ARC. Mem. Inst. Indsl. Engrs. (sr.), Assn. M.B.A. Execs., Am. Numismatic Assn., Internat. Numismatic Soc., Miss. Numismatic Assn. (life). Republican. Baptist. Club: Greenville Golf & Country. Lodge: Lions (pres.). Author: Coinshooting with a Metal Detector, 1982. Office: Silver Numismatics PO Box 4761 Greenville MS 38701

HELMS, JESSE, U.S. senator; b. Monroe, N.C., Oct. 18, 1921; s. Jesse A. and Ethel Mae (Helms) H.; student Wingate Jr. Coll., 1936-37, Wake Forest Coll., 1937-40; LL.D., Bob Jones U., Greenville, S.C.; m. Dorothy Jane Coble, Oct. 31, 1942; children—Jane (Mrs. Charles R. Knox), Nancy (Mrs. John C. Stuart), Charles. City editor Raleigh (N.C.) Times, 1945-46; adminstrv. asst. to N.C. senators Smith and Lennon, Washington, 1951-53; exec. dir. N.C. Bankers Assn., Raleigh, 1953-60; exec. v.p., vice chmn. bd., asst. chief exec. officer Sta. WRAL-TV, Sta. WRAL-FM and Tobacco Radio Network, Raleigh, 1960-72; U.S. senator from N.C., 1973—, asst. minority whip, mem. Fgn. Relations com., rules com., ethics com., chmn. com. on agr., forestry and nutrition. Mem. Raleigh City Council, 1957-61, chmn. law and finance com., 1957-61. Bd. dirs. N.C. Cerebral Palsy Hosp., United Cerebral Palsy N.C., Wake County Cerebral Palsy and Rehab. Center, Raleigh; founder, bd. dirs. Camp Willow Run, Littleton, N.C.; trustee Meredith Coll., John F. Kennedy Coll., Campbell Coll., Wingate Coll. Recipient Freedoms Found. award, 1962, 73; So. Bapt. Nat. Award, 1972; awards V.F.W., 1970, Am. Legion, 1971, Raleigh Exchange Club, 1971; Golden Gavel award, 1973, 74; Man of the Year award Women for Const/Govt., 1978. Baptist (deacon, Sunday sch. tchr.). Clubs: Rotary (past pres.), Raleigh Execs. (past pres.), Masons. Editor, Tarheel Banker, 1953-60; author newspaper, radio, TV editorials, 1960-72. Office: Dirksen Office Bldg Washington DC 20510

HELMS, THOMAS JOSEPH, entomology educator; b. St. Louis, Dec. 20, 1939; s. Warren Joseph and Frances Viola (Hubbard) H.; m. Margaret Wideman, Nov. 14, 1981; children—Timothy, Jean, John, Kathryn. B.S., Ark. State U., 1961; M.S., 1963; Ph.D., Iowa State U., 1967. Asst. prof. U. Nebr., Lincoln, 1967-70, assoc. prof., 1970-78, asst. dean. Coll. Agr., 1973-78; product devel. mgr. Monsanto Agrl. Products Co., St. Louis, 1978-80; head, prof. entomology Mississippi State U. (Miss.), 1981—; cons. agrl. entomology. Pres., East Campus Neighborhood Community Orgn., Lincoln, 1975-76. Served with Ark. N.G., 1957-63. Mem. Entomol. Soc. Am., AAAS, Am. Registry Profl. Entomologists, Miss. Entomol. Assn. Methodist. Club: Rotary (Starkville, Miss.). Office: Drawer EM Mississippi State MS 39762

HELSINGER, MARC HOWARD, geologist; b. N.Y.C., May 21, 1948; s. Philip and Dorothy (Schlesinger) H.; m. Irene Susan Cahn, July 1, 1973; children—Adam Philip, Scott David. B.S., CCNY, 1970; M.S., Rensselaer Poly Inst., 1973, Ph.D., 1975. Research assoc. NOAA, Albany, N.Y., 1973-75; exploration geologist Amoco Prodn. Co., Houston, 1975-78, Anadarko, Houston, 1978-79; sr. exploration geologist Samson Resources, Houston, 1979-85, La. Land and Exploration Co., 1985—. Fellow NDEA, 1970-73, NSF, 1971; recipient Penrose award Geol. Soc. Am., 1973, 74, Research award Sigma Xi, 1973-74. Mem. Soc. Exploration Paleontologists and Mineralogists, Am. Assn. Petroleum Geologists (cert. geologist; assoc. editor), Houston Producers Forum, Soc. Profl. Well Log Analysts, East Tex. Geol. Soc. Office: La Land and Exploration 2950 North Loop West Suite 1200 Houston TX 77092

HELTON, MARY VIRGINIA, civil engineer; b. Collin County, Tex., Feb. 4, 1919; d. Walter Ennis and Laurine Lavinia (Neighbors) Williams; B.A. in Math., McMurry Coll., Abilene, Tex., 1940; m. Beryl Thomas Helton, Dec. 22, 1945 (div.); 1 dau., Virginia Beryl. Tchr. math. Stamford Sr. High Sch., 1940-43; head math. dept. Ranger Jr. Coll., 1943-45; with Tex. Dept. Hwys. and Public Transp., Dallas, 1945-80, sr. design engr. dist. 18, 1973-75; tech. cons. Albert

H. Halff Assocs., 1982—. Dir., Mesquite (Tex.) Social Services, 1971-73; mem. Mesquite Coordination Council, 1976-79; ruling elder Emmanuel Presbyn. Ch., Mesquite, 1970-73, clk. session, 1970-73, 83—; ruling elder St. Mark Presbyn. Ch., Dallas, 1974-77, del. to Presbytery, 1970-77. Recipient appreciation award Am. Gen. Contractor's, 1980. Mem. Am. Soc. Profl. and Exec. Women, Tex. Public Employees Assn., Tex. State Employees Assn. (dir. 1977-79). Democrat. Presbyterian. Clubs: Bus. and Profl. Women's, Altrusa (pres. 1977-79, 81-82) (Mesquite). Home: 3526 Bonito Vista Circle Mesquite TX 75150

HEMBREE, HUGH LAWSON, III, holding company executive; b. Ft. Smith, Ark., Nov. 16, 1931; s. Raymond N. and Gladys (Newman) H.; B.S. in Bus. Adminstrn., U. Ark., 1953, LL.B., 1958; m. Sara Janelle Young, Sept. 1, 1956; children—Hugh Lawson IV, Raymond Scott. In middle mgmt. Ark.-Best Freight System, Inc., Ft. Smith, 1958-61, dir. fin., 1961-65, v.p., 1965-67; pres., dir. Ark.-Best Corp., Ft. Smith, 1967-73, dir., 1973—; chmn. bd. CEO, 1973—; pres. Sugar Hill Farms, Inc., Ft. Smith, 1962—; dir. Riverside Furniture Corp., Mid-Am. Industries, Mchts. Nat. Bank (all Ft. Smith), Scheduled Skyways Airlines, Fayetteville, Ark., Murco Drilling Co., Shreveport, La., Fed. Res. Bank, St. Louis; nat. adv. bd. Comml. Nat. Bank of Little Rock. Pres., Westark Area council Boy Scouts Am., 1966-67, mem. nat. council, mem. regional exec. bd., 1967—, chmn. regional sustaining membership com., 1974-75, U.S. staff mem. World Boy Scout Jamboree, Norway, 1975; treas. Endowment Trust Fund, U. Ark., bd. dirs., mem. dean's adv. com. Sch. Bus., 1969-73; chmn. bd. devel. St. Edward Mercy Med. Center, 1972-78; sec. Ft. Smith-Sebastian County Joint Planning Commn., 1959-72; mem. Ark. Legis. Tax Study Commn., 1969; pres. Sebastian County Mental Health Assn., 1964; justice of peace Sebastian County, 1959-76; past mem. Ark. Democratic Central Com.; bd. dirs. Jr. Achievement of Ft. Smith, Coalition for Rural Am., 1971, Ark. Council Econ. Edn., 1964—; chmn. Ark.-Okla. Edn. and Livestock Found., 1974—; sec.-treas. Sunbelt Water Dist., 1981; trustee John Brown U., Hendrix Coll.; chmn. bd. trustees St. Edwards Mercy Med. Center, 1970-78; mem. Ark. Bd. Higher Edn., 1975—. Served to 1st lt. USAF, 1953-55. Recipient Silver Beaver, Silver Antelope awards Boy Scouts Am., Disting. Service award Ft. Smith Jr. C. of C., 1965, Leadership award State of Ark., 1970, Disting. Alumni award U. Ark., 1977; named Ark. Outstanding Young Man of Year, 1967. Mem. Nat. Assn. Devel. Orgns. (chmn. adv. com.), Ark. (v.p. 1969-73, pres. 1973-75, chmn. bd. 1975-77), Ft. Smith (pres., dir. 1970-73) chambers commerce, Young Pres.'s Orgn., U. Ark. Alumni Assn. (dir., bldg. com.), Am. Trucking Assn. (nat. acctg. and fin. council), NAM (nat. dir. 1971-78), Ark. Arts Center, Delta Theta Phi, Sigma Alpha Epsilon. Episcopalian (vestryman, co-chmn. ch. fin. com.). Clubs: Masons (32 deg.); Garden of the Gods (Colorado Springs); Town, Fianna Hills Country, Ft. Smith Hardscrabble Country (Ft. Smith); Capital (Little Rock). Home: 3220 Park Ave Fort Smith AR 72901 Office: 1000 S 21st St Fort Smith AR 72901

HEMBREE, JOY EDWARDS, civic worker; m. Charles R. Hembree; 1 child, Joy Hembree Maclin. Student East Tenn. State U., U. Tenn.; B.S. in Elem. Edn., U. Louisville. Chmn. leadership program Lexington C. of C., 1982-83; chmn., steering com., community rep. to regional com. Kellogg Found.-United Way Leadership Devel. Program; bd. dirs. United Way of Bluegrass, 1980-84; pres. Ky. State Lawyers Aux., 1976-77, mem. law-focused edn. com., to present; mem. Gov.'s Commn. on Higher Edn. in Ky.'s Future, 1980—; vice-chmn. Teens Who Care, Ky. Manpower Devel., Inc., Louisville, to present; mem. Gov.'s Vol. Adv. Council, Bur. Social Ins., to present; mem. adv. council, mem. coms. Univ. Hosp. Council of Suprs., U. Ky., 1980—; mem. Midway Coll. Women's Study Commn.; bd. dirs. Lexington Philharm. Soc., 1976—; mem. Lexington Arts Council; chmn. membership and nominating coms.; mem. Town and Country Garden Club; bd. dirs. Wilderness Rd. council Girl Scouts U.S.A., Lexington YWCA, Voluntary Action Ctr., Lexington; bd. dirs., treas. Manchester Ctr., Lexington; mem. Lexington Woman's Club, 1965—, pres., 1972-74; mem. Ky. Fedn. Women's Clubs, 1965—, chmn. community improvement program, 1974-76, chmn. edn. dept., 1976-78, chmn. home life dept., 1978-80; mem. Women's Missionary Soc., Immanuel Baptist Ch. Named Lexington's Outstanding Woman of 1975, Beta Sigma Phi; recipient Community Cornerstone award C. of C., 1978, Citizen of Yr. award Kelly Services, 1979, Optimist Cup, Optimist Club, 1981. Mem. Kappa Delta Pi. Avocations: reading; needlework; bridge; gardening. Home: 620 Raintree Rd Lexington KY 40502

HEMINGWAY, RICHARD W., law educator; b. Detroit, Nov. 24, 1927; s. William Oswald and Iva Catherine (Wildfang) H.; m. Vera Cecilia Eck, Sept. 12, 1947; children—Margaret, Carol, Richard. B.S., U. Colo., 1950; J.D., So. Meth. U., 1955; LL.M., U. Mich., 1968. Bar: Tex. 1955, Okla. 1981. Assoc. law firm Fulbright, Crooker, Freeman, Bates and Jaworski, Houston, 1955-60; assoc. prof. Baylor Law Sch., 1960-65; assoc. prof. So. Meth. U. Sch. Law, 1965-68; Cook fellow U. Mich., 1968-69; Horn prof. Tex. Tech. U., 1969-80, acting dean, 1974-75, dean ad interim, 1979-80; Eugene Kuntz prof. oil, gas and natural resources law U. Okla. Sch. Law, Norman, 1980—; of counsel McAfee & Taft, Oklahoma City. Served with USAAF, 1945-47. Mem. ABA, Okla. Bar Assn., Tex. Bar Assn. Lutheran. Author: Law of Oil and Gas, 2d edit., 1983, Lawyers' edit., 1983; West's Texas Forms, Minerals and Mines, 1979; Cases and Materials on Oil and Gas Taxation, 1982. Home: 1411 Greenbriar Dr Norman OK 73069 Office: U Okla Sch Law 300 Timberdale Norman OK 73019

HEMNESS, RAY LESLIE, hospital administrator; b. Milltown, Wis., Oct. 28, 1926; s. Louis H. and Maria (Ruud) H.; B.C.S., Strayer Coll., 1948; m. Peggy Ann Sims, Feb. 14, 1947; 1 dau., Deborah Kay. Treas., Standard Engrng. Co., Washington, 1956-61; asst. adminstr. No. Va. Doctors Hosp., Arlington, 1961-62, adminstr., dir., 1962—, sec., 1970—, exec. v.p., 1977—; sec. Va. Doctors Properties, Arlington, 1969-83; dir. Seven Corners Med. Bldgs., Inc., Falls Church, Va., 1962-71. Chpt. chmn. ARC, Arlington, 1967-70, now bd. dirs.; bd. dirs. No. Va. Heart Assn. Mem. Va. Hosp. Assn. (dir. 1980-81), Internat. Underwater Explorers Soc., C. of C. Arlington (v.p. 1980-82, pres. 1983, dir.). Mason (32 deg.), Rotarian (pres. Arlington 1976-77). Home: 3027 Hazelton St Falls Church VA 22044 Office: 601 S Carlyn Springs Rd Arlington VA 22204

HEMPHILL, JEAN HARGETT, college dean; b. Pollocksville, N.C., Aug. 21, 1936; d. Robert Franklin and Frances (Hill) Hargett; m. Raymond Arthur Hemphill, Feb. 28, 1964; 1 child, Gerald Franklin. B.S., East Carolina U., 1958; M.Ed., U. Nev.-Las Vegas, 1968. Exec. sec. Edward Lumley & Sons Ltd., Melbourne, Australia, 1959; tchr. Mad River Twp. Sch. Dist., Ohio, 1961-62; exec. sec. Voorhies-Trindle & Co., Inc., Las Vegas, 1962-64; tchr. Clark County Sch. Dist., Nev., 1964-66; sec.-treas. Five Points Milling Co., Inc., New Bern, N.C., 1968-77; instr. Craven Community Coll., New Bern, 1973-80, dean service techs., 1980—; sec., mem. New Bern-Craven County Vocat. Edn. Adv. and Support Council, 1982—; mem. New Bern-Craven County Career Devel. Adv. Com., 1984—; mem. Elderly Action Adv. Com., New Bern, 1984—. Scholarship chmn. continuing edn. div. Woman's Club, New Bern, 1981—. Mem. N.C. Assn. Community Coll. Instructional Adminstrs., New Bern C. of C. (co-chmn. agrl.-bus. com. 1984-85), Phi Kappa Phi. Democrat. Mem. Christian Ch. (Disciples of Christ). Office: Craven Community Coll PO Box 885 Glenburnie Rd at College Ct New Bern NC 28560

HEMPHILL, MARLENA LOIS, consulting engineer firm supervisor, administrative services specialist; b. Oakland, Calif., Mar. 12, 1945; d. Gordon Walter Brokopp and Shirley Mae (Borchardt) Slack; m. Kenneth Ray McKenzie, June 22, 1974 (div. 1982); children—Ronald Joseph, Shane Little-Sun; m. Paul Thomas Hemphill, June 5, 1982. Student Foothill Jr. Coll., 1963-64. Acct. rep. Credit Bur. of Santa Clara Valley, San Jose, Calif., 1963-66; patient acct. rep. Stanford U. Hosp., Palo Alto, Calif., 1966-71; with respiratory therapy personnel O'Connor Hosp., San Jose, 1974-80; adminstrv. asst. Deer Island Corp., Biloxi, Miss., 1981-82; adminstrv. services specialist CH2M Hill Engrs., Ocean Springs, Miss., 1982—. Editor: (booklet) Medicare Funny Antics, 1971. Contbg. editor several newsletters. Manpower mem. Miss Universe Pageant, Biloxi, 1981. Named Preliminary Finalist Miss Universe Pageant, San Jose, 1964. Mem. Ocean Springs Art Assn., Ocean Springs C. of C. (rep. 1984—). Baptist. Lodge: Elks (chmn. Miss. Firefighters Meml. Burn Ctr. 1984, Oceans Springs Nursing Home, 1984, v.p. 1983-84, pres. 1984-85). Avocations: snowskiing; dancing; music; Mardi Gras Krewe's modeling. Home: 8712 Neptune Ave Ocean Springs MS 39564 Office: CH2M Hill Engrs 3002-C Bienville Blvd Ocean Springs MS 39564

HEMPHILL, ROBERT DONALD, farm management specialist; b. Tryon, Okla., Feb. 26, 1922; s. Leroy E. and Daisy O. Hemphill; m. Betty Jo Ferguson, Jan. 10, 1946; children—Joyce Lynn Hemphill Poitevent, Ronald D. B.S. in Agrl. Econs., Okla. State U.-Stillwater, 1948, M.S. in Rural Adult Edn., 1962, M.S. in Agrl. Econs., 1968. Instr., Vets. Agrl. Tng. Program, Hulbert, Okla., 1948-52; asst. county extension agt. Okla. State U., Tahlequah and Jay, 1952-67, area specialist farm mgmt., Okmulgee, 1967—; cons. in field; fieldman for Northeast Farm, Inc. (Okla.). Served with AUS, 1942-45; ETO. Mem. Nat. Assn. Country Agrl. Agts. (Disting. Service award 1976), Okla. Assn. Farm Mgrs. Democrat. Methodist. Clubs: Lions, Okmulgee Circle Square Dance, Elks. Office: Route 1 PO Box 94F Okmulgee OK 74447

HENBEST, JACQUELINE LEE, business executive; b. Elmira, N.Y., Dec. 1, 1953; d. Robert Leroy and Grace (Rowley) H. B.A., Cedar Crest Coll., 1975. Word processing sales rep. Lanier Bus. Products, Atlanta, 1979-80; account exec. Genigraphics, Atlanta, 1980-81, sales mgr., 1981-82, br. mgr., 1982-84, ctr. mgr., 1984—. Office: Genigraphics-Atlanta Bldg 9 Suite 100 3495 Piedmont Rd NE Atlanta GA 30305

HENDERSHOT, KENNETH CHARLES, mechanical engineer; b. Highland Park, Mich., Mar. 17, 1930; s. George F. and Edith (Golden) H.; m. Connie M. Bates, Nov. 10, 1962; children—Julie, Marci, Carlye, Craig. B.S., U. Mich., 1952, M.S., 1953. Registered profl. engr., Calif. engr., Gen. Dynamics-Convair, San Diego, 1953-62; sect. head Bell Aerospace Corp., Niagara Falls, N.Y., 1962-63; prin. engr. Calspan Corp., Buffalo, 1963-78, head transp. research dept., 1978-80; dir. Von Karman facility Arnold Engring. Devel. Ctr. Div., Arnold Air Force Sta., Tenn., 1981—. Mem. AIAA (Aerospace Pioneer award 1980, Disting. lectr. 1982), Nat. Mgmt. Assn. Contbr. articles to tech. jours. Office: Von Karman Facility Arnold Engring Devel Ctr Arnold Air Force Station TN 37389

HENDERSHOTT, CHARLES HENRY, JR., educator; b. Marked Tree, Ark., Oct. 13, 1923; s. Charles Henry and Bertya Mae (Cooper) H.; B.S.A., U. Ark., Fayetteville, 1951, M.S., 1952; Ph.D., N.C. State U., 1959; m. Ollie Virginia Layne, May 5, 1944 (div. Feb. 1960); children—Charles Larry, David Lynn, Carol Ann Hendershott Hallack, Ronald Wayne, Barbara Kay Hendershott Neal; m. 2d, Mary Edith Young, June 24, 1960. Asst. prof. agr. U. Ark., 1952-57; asst. prof. Fla. Citrus Commn., Lake Alfred, 1959-63, asso. prof. 1963-64; asso. prof. U. Fla., 1964-67, prof., 1967—; head dept. horticulture U. Ga., Athens, 1967-75, prof. horticulture, 1975—, chmn. div. horticulture, 1975-79; cons., research adv. Agrl. Expt. Sta., Aguadulce, Panama, 1954-57. Served with AUS, 1942-46; MTO, ETO, PTO. AID grantee, 1969-70, 70-71, 71-72. Fellow Am. Soc. Hort. Sci. (Gourley award for Outstanding Paper 1955); mem. Am. Soc. Plant Physiologists, Am. Inst. Biol. Sci., Sigma Xi, Gamma Sigma Delta, Alpha Zeta. Contbr. articles to profl. jours.

HENDERSON, ALBERT JOHN, judge; b. Canton, Ga., Dec. 12, 1920 s. Albert Jefferson and Cliffie Mae (Cook) H.; LL.B., Mercer U., 1947; m. Jenny Lee Medford, Feb. 24, 1951; children—Michael John, Jenny Lee. Bar: Ga. 1947; practiced law, Marietta, Ga., 1948-60; judge Juvenile Ct. Cobb County (Ga.), 1953-60. Superior Ct. Cobb County, 1961-68, U.S. Dist. Ct. No. Dist. Ga., Atlanta, 1968-76, chief judge, 1976-79; judge U.S. Circuit Ct. Appeals 5th Circuit, 1979—; asst. solicitor gen. Blue Ridge Jud. Circuit, 1948-52. Chmn. Cobb dist. Atlanta council Boy Scouts Am., 1964. Served with AUS, 1943-46. Fellow Am. Bar Found.; mem. State Bar Ga., Am., Atlanta. Cobb Jud. bar assns., Lawyers Club Atlanta, Am. Judicature Soc. Office: US Ct Appeals PO Box 1638 Atlanta GA 30301

HENDERSON, BERNARD LEVIE, JR., state official; b. Richmond, Va., Aug. 9, 1950; s. Bernard Levie and Thelma May (Johnson) H.; m. Olga Marie Jimenez, June 15, 1974; children—Carrie Ruth, Angela Lee. B.A., Old Dominion U., 1972. Legis. asst. to state del. Junie Bradshaw, Richmond, Va., 1967-71; asst. tally clk. U.S. Ho. of Reps., Washington, 1971-72; adminstrv. asst. to state Senator William Parkerson, Richmond, 1972; adminstr. Va. Bur. of Ins., Richmond, 1972-74; asst. to commrs. Va. State Corp. Commn., Richmond, 1974-82; dir. commerce Commonwealth of Va., Richmond, 1982-86; dir. Va. Dept. Health Regulatory Bds., 1986—; chmn. Gov.'s Regulatory Reform Task Force, 1984-86; sec.-treas. Southeastern Assn. of Regulatory Utility Commns., 1976-82; exec. dir. Conf. on Econ. Regulation U. Va., 1977-78; exec. mgr. Great Lakes Conf. of Pub. Utility Commrs., 1980-82. Mem. Henrico County (Va.) Democratic Com., 1970—, sec., 1980-82; mem. Va. 3d Dist. Dem. Com., 1976-85, sec., 1976-85; mem. Va. Dem. Central Com., 1976-85. Recipient Gov. Pub. Service certificate, 1977. Baptist. Contbr. in field. Office: 517 W Grace St Richmond VA 23230

HENDERSON, CLAUDINE LESTER, charitable organization executive; b. Cape Girardeau, Mo., Jan. 21, 1926; d. Claude Limon and Lillian I. (Hickerson) Lester; B.S., U. Mo., 1947; m. Harold Dale Henderson, Dec. 22, 1946; children—Jeffrey Scott, Susan Kay, Sandra Jean. Congressional sec., Washington, 1944-45; co-founder, sec.-treas. Dale Henderson, Inc., Houston, 1965-83; exec. Houston Regional Council on Alcoholism (United Way), 1983—. Active PTA, 1955-65; den mother Cub Scouts Am., 1958-60; participant fund drives Heart Assn., Cancer Soc., Multiple Sclerosis Assn., United Way. Mem. Public Relations Soc. Am. (exam. coms. for accreditation 1978, Silver Anvil award 1973, Silver Spur awards 1977, 79), Alpha Phi. Presbyterian.

HENDERSON, DONALD BLANTON, lawyer, state senator; b. Houston, Aug. 25, 1949; s. Donald Veitch and Marjorie Nell (Blanton) H.; m. Marjorie Frances Butcher, Sept. 2, 1977; 1 child, Donald Lee. Student Tulane U., 1967-68; B.A., U. Houston, 1971; postgrad. South Tex. Coll. Law, 1975-77. Bar: Tex. 1978. Mem. Adams, Adams & Blackburn, Houston, 1978-81, Blackburn, Gamble, Henderson & Grubb, Houston, 1981—; v.p. Central Iron Works, Houston, 1971—; dir. Charter Bank-Colonial, Houston, GHR Energy Corp., Houston; mem. Tex. Ho. of Reps., 1973-83; chmn. com. transp., 1979-83; mem. Tex. Senate, 1983—. Del. Constl. Conv., 1974; bd. dirs. Performing Arts Ctr., Houston, 1982—; mem. adv. bd. Houston N.W. Med. Ctr., 1977—. Recipient Community Service award Houston N.W. C. of C., 1981, 84, Spl. Service award Tex. Mcpl. Cts. Assn., 1979. Mem. State Bar Tex., Houston Bar Assn., Kappa Alpha. Republican. Episcopalian. Club: Exchange. Avocations: golf; jogging; reading. Home: 139 Old Bridge Lake Houston TX 77069 Office: Senate District Office 7915 FM 1960 W Suite 202 Houston TX 77070

HENDERSON, EDWARD NEIL, gas company executive; b. Andalusia, Ala., Dec. 10, 1920; s. J. V. and Maude (McNair) H.; m. Virginia Estelle Whatley, Apr. 3, 1948; children—Robert E., Bruce C. B.S. in Mech. Engring., Auburn U., 1943, 1947. Jr. engr. Ark. La. Gas Co., Shreveport, 1947-48, engr. gen. engring. dept., 1948-52, asst. supt. natural gas div., 1952-53, spl. assignment ops., 1953, acting chief engr., 1953-57, v.p., chief engr., from 1957; now exec. v.p.; v.p., dir. Arla Air Conditioning, 1957—; pres., dir. Ark. Cement Corp., 1958—; dir. Ark. Exploration Co., Ark. La. Fin. Corp., Arkla Chem. Corp., Arkla Industries Inc. Pres., bd. mem. English Speaking Union; co-chmn. United Fund campaign; chmn. indsl. div. United Fund; mem. City Charter Study Task Force, Task Force on Planning and Zoning; bd. dirs. Lyric Ball, Parents League, Shreveport Opera; mem.; Met. Planning Commn. Mayor's Adv. Fiscal Policy Com.; bd. dirs., exec. v.p. Shreveport Symphony; pres. Shreveport Opera. Served with C.E. U.S. Army, World War II. Mem. Am. Gas Assn., Ind. Petroleum Assn. Am., Air Force Assn., Am. Legion, Mid-Continent Oil and Gas Assn., So. Gas Assn. C. of C. (govt. affairs com.). Republican. Presbyterian. Clubs: Shreveport Country (dir., treas.), Shreveport, Cotillion (dir., pres.), Ambassadors (dir.), Pierremont Oaks Tennis, Racket. Lodge: Rotary. Office: Arkla Inc PO Box 21734 Shreveport LA 71151*

HENDERSON, GWENDOLYN WITHERSPOON, teacher educator; b. Charleston, S.C., Sept. 11, 1931; d. James William and Myrtle Louise (Ruff) Witherspoon; A.B., Fisk U., Nashville, 1951; M.S., Oreg. State U., 1974, Ph.D., 1976; divorced; children—Valton D., Alan C. Researcher, Sloan-Kettering Inst., N.Y.C., 1951--53; tchr. sci., chmn. dept. W.A. Perry Jr. High Sch., Columbia, S.C., 1956-62; tchr. math. and chemistry, div. chmn. Tolleston High Sch., Gary, Ind., 1962-68; tchr. phys. scis., chemistry, chmn. sci. dept. Lower Richland High Sch., Columbia, 1968-73; instr. sci. edn. Oreg. State U., 1973-76, EOP dir., acad. coordinator 1974-79; asso. dir. govt. contract leadership/mgmt. tng. Atlanta U., 1979-80; asso. prof., coordinator math. and sci. dept. edn. U. N.C., Asheville, 1980—; past pres. Richland County Edn. Assn. Exec. bd., exec. com., chmn. budget com. United Way Benton County (Oreg.), 1974-79; exec. bd., exec. com. Consumer Credit Counseling Service, Asheville, 1980-84; pres. Corvallis NAACP, 1976-79; mem. exec. bd. LWV, Columbia, 1968-73; mem. Oreg. Gov.'s Commn., 1976-78; exec. bd. YWCA, Asheville, 1982—. Recipient award S.C. Edn. Assn.; grantee Carnegie Corp., 1954-55, NSF, 1957, 59-60, 71-73, Oreg. State U. Found., 1973, 75, 77; N.C. State Dept. Public Instrn. grantee; F. Smith Reynolds grantee. Mem. Nat. Sci. Tchrs. Assn., Nat. Assn. Women Deans, Adminstrs. and Counselors, Assn. Edn. Tchrs. of Sci. (bd. dirs. 1984—), Am. Chem. Soc., N.C. Sci. Tchrs. Assn. (award 1985), N.C. Assn. Colls. Tchrs. Edn., Urban League (exec. bd. Columbia 1970-73), Phi Delta Kappa, Delta Sigma Theta (chpt. community relations com. chmn. 1949, service cert. 1981). Methodist. Club: Altrusa (v.p., chmn. internat. relations com. Corvallis, Oreg. 1977-79, Asheville, 1980-85). Author articles in field. Home: 24 Pinecroft Ln Fletcher NC 28732 Office: PO Box 8467 University Heights Asheville NC 28814

HENDERSON, HARRIET, librarian; b. Pampa, Tex., Nov. 19, 1949; d. Ervin Leon and Hannah Elizabeth (Yoe) H. A.B., Baker U., 1971; M.L.S., U. Tex., 1973. Sch. librarian Pub. Sch. System, Pampa, Tex., 1971-72; city librarian City of Tyler, Tex., 1973-80, City of Newport News, Va., 1980-84; dir. libraries and info. services City of Newport News, 1984—; bd. mem. Tex. Library Systems Act Adv. Bd., 1979-80. Reviewer, contbr. Pub. Library Quarterly, 1981—. Budget panel chmn. Peninsula United Way, Hampton, Va., 1984-85; mem. bd. Peninsula council Boy Scouts Am., 1982-84, Peninsula Womens Network, Newport News, 1983-85; diaconate Hidenwood Presbyterian Ch., Newport News, 1983-85. Recipient Tribute to Women in Bus. and Industry, Peninsula YWCA, Newport News, 1984. Mem. ALA, Internat. City Mgmt. Assn., Data Processing Mgmt. Assn., Va. Library Assn. (chmn. legis. com. 1981-84, v.p. 1985). Office: City of Newport News/Libraries 2400 Washington Ave Newport News VA 23607

HENDERSON, HUGH COLLINS, lawyer; b. Atlanta, July 8, 1953; s. Hugh Tarpley and Norma H. (Zollars) H.; m. Mary Elizabeth Jones, Jan. 6, 1977 (div. 1979); m. Julia Milton Power, Mar. 6, 1982. B.A., Auburn U., 1975; J.D., Samford U., 1978. Bar: Ala. 1978, U.S. Dist. Ct. (no. dist.) Ala. 1978, U.S. Supreme Ct. 1985. Sole practice, Birmingham, Ala., 1978-84; ptnr. Burttram and Henderson, Birmingham, 1984—. Active Downtown Democrat Club, Birmingham, 1982-84; deacon First Christian Ch., Birmingham, 1982—. Mem. Birmingham Bar Assn. (criminal justice com. 1980-81, 82-83, 83-84), Ala. State Bar Assn. (young lawyers rep. to indigent def. com. 1984-85), Ala. Trial Lawyers Assn., Am. Trial Lawyers Assn., Ala. Criminal Def. Lawyers Assn. (membership chmn. 1980-81). Home: 3145 Woodhaven Dr Birmingham AL 35243 Office: Burttram and Henderson 2100 11th Ave N Lindley Bldg Birmingham AL 35234

HENDERSON, JACK CARL, marine corps officer; b. Gorman, Tex., Mar. 11, 1947; s. Carl Elbert and Mary Jane (Hudman) H.; m. Jamie Jackson, July 2, 1972; children—James, Jacquelyn. A.S., Pensacola Jr. Coll., 1972; B.S. in Indsl. Mgmt., Ga. Inst. Tech., 1979; postgrad. Advanced Communication Officers Sch., 1981. Enlisted U.S. Marine Corps, 1965, commd. 2d lt., 1973, advanced through grades to maj., 1983; served with 1st Marine Div., Vietnam, 1966-68; bn. communication officer 1st Marine Div., Camp Pendleton, Calif., 1974-75; adj. and co. comdr. Marine Corps Recruit Depot, Parris Island, S.C., 1976-78; regtl. communication officer 3d Marine Div., Okinawa, Japan, 1981-82; communication-electronics ops. officer Hdqrs. Communications-Electronics Office, Fleet Marine Forces Atlantic, Norfolk, Va., 1982—. Decorated Navy Commendation, Navy Achievement; named Marine Corps Recruiter of Yr.-Tex., 8th Marine Corps Dist. Hdqrs., 1970. Mem. Armed Forces Communication-Electronics Assn., Gamma Beta Phi (pres. chpt. 1977, state sec. 1978, state dir. Ga. 1979-80, Disting. Service award Nat. Hdqrs. 1980). Baptist. Home: 839 Chimney Hill Pkwy Virginia Beach VA 23462 Office: HQ FMFLANT CEO Norfolk VA 23515

HENDERSON, JOHN WALTON, educator; b. Paris, Tenn., Aug. 30, 1925; s. Willie B. and Lillian (Claxton) H.; B.S., U. Louisville, 1950; M.P.A., Syracuse U., 1973; m. Irene Hasch, May 9, 1947; children—Pamela Henderson Lyttle Brown, Leah Denise Henderson Arcuragi. Dist. dir. IRS, Atlanta, 1972-80; sr. and mng. partner Henderson & Lewis, Tax Cons., 1980-81; asso. prof. taxation Ga. State U., 1981—; disting. practitioner lectr. U. Ga. Bd. dirs. United Way. Served with AUS, 1943-46. Recipient Ednl. award Syracuse U., 1968. Mem. Nat. Assn. Accts., Nat. Exec. Inst., Ga. Soc. C.P.A.s (life). Methodist. Club: Kiwanis. Home: 5290 Manhasset Cove Dunwoody GA 30338 Office: Room 234 Title Bldg University Plaza Georgia State U Atlanta GA 30338

HENDERSON, KAYE NEIL, civil engineer, business executive; b. Birmingham, Ala., June 10, 1933; s. Ernest Martin and Mary (Head) H.; B.S., Va. Mil. Inst., 1954; B.A. with honors, U. South Fla., 1967; m. Betty Jane Belanus, June 26, 1954; children—David Scott, Alan Douglas, Helen Kaye. Mgmt. trainee Gen. Electric Co., Schenectady, 1954; sales engr. Fla. Prestressed Concrete, Tampa, 1956-57; field engr. Portland Cement Assn., Tampa, 1957-63; gen. mgr. residential and comml. sales Tampa Electric Co., 1963-66; v.p. Watson & Co., architects and engrs., Tampa, 1966-69; v.p. Reynolds, Smith & Hills, architects, engrs. and planners, Jacksonville, Fla., 1969-78, sr. v.p., 1978—, dir., 1976—; dir. Environ. Sci. and Engring., Gainesville, Fla., RSH Internat., RS&H of N.C. Vice chmn. Temple Terrace Planning and Zoning Bd., 1962-67; pres. Guidance Center Hillsborough County, 1969; mem. adv. bd. Multi-State Transp. System, 1976-82; mem. Duval County Republican Exec. Com., 1970-72; bd. dirs. Salvation Army Home and Hosp. Council, 1964-69. Mem. found U. South Fla. Served to 1st lt. USAF, 1954-56. Recipient Service awards Greater Tampa C. of C., 1964-66; named Outstanding Young Man of Tampa Jr. C. of C., 1965; Outstanding Young Man of Am., U.S. Jr. C. of C., 1967; Boss of Year award Am. Bus. Women's Assn., 1978; registered profl. engr., Fla., N.C. Mem. Fla. Engring. Soc., Navy League U.S., Tau Beta Pi, Phi Kappa Phi. Republican. Episcopalian. Clubs: Ye Mystic Revellers, Timuquana Country, River, St. Johns Dinner, University, Rotary (dir. 1984—) (Jacksonville). Home: 4606 Yacht Club Rd Jacksonville FL 32210 Office: 6737 Southpoint Blvd S Jacksonville FL 32216

HENDERSON, MARJORIE CALVERT, computer company executive; b. Houston, Apr. 19, 1924; d. Cecil Howard and Mineola (Prothro) C.; m. William McCoy Henderson, Apr. 18, 1980. B.B.A., St. Mary's Coll., 1944. Licensed real estate broker. Gen. mgr. and dir. Kallison Properties, San Antonio, Tex., 1945-68; asst. to chmn. bd. H.B. Pat Zachry, Sr., San Antonio, 1968-75; v.p., dir. mktg. Micro Mode, Inc., San Antonio, 1978—. Author: America Sings, 1955, Our World's Most Beloved Poems, 1984. Mem. Assn. Computer Users, Profl. Services Mgmt. Assn., Profl. Services Mktg. Assn., Bus. and Profl. Women's Club (chmn. publicity and TV 1953-54). Lodge: Soroptimist (co-founder Girlsville 1953).

HENDERSON, MYRTICE WINSLETT, music educator; b. Wilkinson County, Ga., Dec. 21, 1928; d. William Thomas and Bertha Lucile (Butler) Winslett; B.S. in Edn., Georgia Coll., 1950, M.Ed., 1973; D. Arts candidate, Carnegie-Mellon U.; m. Howard James Henderson, July 31, 1950 (dec.); children—Howard James, William Winslett. English tchr., choral music dir. Manor (Ga.) High Sch., 1950-57, Twiggs County (Ga.) High Sch. 1957-64, Cochran (Ga.) High Sch., 1964-73; voice instr. Middle Ga. Coll., 1965-70, asst. prof. English, music, 1973—; music dir. 1st Methodist Church Cochran, 1970—; organizer, dir. Cochran Jr. Women's Club Vocal Ensemble; soprano soloist, choral dir. coll. theater prodns. Recipient Spl. Music award Ga. C. of C., 1975; Service award Ga. 4-H Club, 1976; Fred Waring Choral Music Workshop grantee, 1975. Mem. NEA, Ga. Assn. Edn., D.A.R., Internat. Platform Assn., Southeastern Conf. Teaching of English in Two-Year Coll., Delta Kappa Gamma (Ga. state scholar 1978). Clubs: Cochran Woman's (co-chmn. fine arts com.), Ga. Federated Women's, Cochran Pilot (charter). Home: Box 86 Cochran GA 31014 Office: Middle Ga Coll Cochran GA 31014

HENDERSON, RICHARD CLEVELAND (RICK), III, manufacturing company executive; b. Greenville, S.C., Oct. 21, 1948; s. Richard Cleveland and Dorothy Edna (Rowe) H.; m. Jeanne Rice, Oct. 9, 1971; children—Jeanna Rice, Richard Cleveland IV. B.S., Clemson U., 1970; assoc. degree in apparel mfg. So. Tech. Inst., Marietta, Ga., 1972. Mgmt. trainee J.C. Penney Co., Anderson, S.C., 1970-71; v.p. Rice Mills Inc., Belton, S.C., 1971—. Troop leader Blue Ridge council Boy Scouts Am., 1973-74; vice chmn. United Way Campaign, Belton, 1982; chmn. personnel com. 1st Baptist Ch., Belton, 1982, 83; vocalist Christian Connection Group, 1977—. Hon. guest World's Fair Christian Connection, Bapt. Pavillion World's Fair, Knoxville, Tenn., 1982. Mem. S.C. Needle Trades Assn., Am. Apparel Mfrs. Assn., Clemson U. Alumni Assn. (area chmn. 1977), Belton-Honea Path Area Personnel Group. Republican. Club: Belton Cotillion (pres.). Lodge: Lions Internat. Home: Wildwood Dr Route 1 Belton SC 29627 Office: Rice Mills Inc 110 Rice Rd Belton SC 29627

HENDERSON, SANDRA RUSSELL, economics educator; b. N.Y.C., Apr. 1, 1936; d. Charles B. and Agnes (Brown) Russell; m. W. Elliott Henderson, Sept. 6, 1958 (div. 1975); children—Allison, Kevin R. B.B.A., U. Pitts., 1958, M.A., 1960. Instr., Waynesburg Coll., Pa., 1960-64, W.Va. U., Morgantown, 1964-67; asst. prof. W.Va. Inst. Tech., Montgomery, 1967-68; assoc. prof., chmn. div. bus. econs. W.Va. State Coll., Institute, 1968—; cons. Henderson, Russell & Brown, Charleston, W.Va., 1984—. Mem. Am. Econ. Assn., Am. Soc. Pub. Adminstrn., Omicron Delta Epsilon, Beta Gamma Sigma. Avocation: gardening. Home: 1034 Valley Rd Charleston WV 25302 Office: WVa State Coll Institute WV 25112

HENDERSON, WALTER G., utility executive; b. Edgemont, S.D., Dec. 19, 1930; s. Andrew M. and Agnes (Galbraith) H.; B.A. in Bus., U. Nebr., 1953; LL.B., U. Colo., 1957; m. Pamela J. Naeve, Oct. 26, 1974; children—Kevin, Jennifer. With El Paso (Tex.) Natural Gas Co., 1957—, asst. v.p., 1974-77, v.p., 1977-79, sr. v.p., 1979-80, exec. v.p., 1980—; dir. various subsidiaries and affiliates of El Paso Natural Gas Co. Served with USMC, 1953-55. Mem. Pacific Coast Gas Assn., So. Gas Assn. Episcopalian. Office: PO Box 1492 El Paso TX 79978

HENDERSON, WILLIAM DONALD, antiquarian, consultant; b. Bluefield, W.Va., June 20, 1914; s. Thomas Ewell and Cordie Ethel (Nelson) H.; B.S.E.E., Va. Poly. Inst., 1936, postgrad. in Mech. Engring., 1938-39; postgrad. in Bus. Adminstrn., U. Pa., 1937, in Edn., U. Md., 1939-40; m. Edythe May Edwards, 1957. Docent, Am. Automobile Assn., Washington; jr. engr. Washington Inst. Tech., College Park, Md., 1940-41; civilian electronics engr. Airborne Communications and Nav., Design Br., Bur. Ships, Navy Dept., Washington, 1941-46; pvt. practice real estate mgmt., Cleveland, Ga., 1946-52, 54—; field service rep. nav. electronic guidance and control of Matador, Glenn L. Martin Co., Essex, Md., 1953; surveyor White County, Ga., 1961—. Lic. pvt. pilot. Mem. AAAS, Am. Def. Preparedness Assn., U.S. Naval Inst. (life), History of Sci. Soc. Developer surveying techniques; inventor entrance lock and deadbolt, doorknocker. Office: PO Box 164 Cleveland GA 30528

HENDLEY, DAN LUNSFORD, banker; b. Nashville, Apr. 26, 1938; s. Frank E. and Mattie Lunsford H. m. Patricia Fariss, June 18, 1960; children—Dan Lunsford, Laura Kathleen. B.A., Vanderbilt U., 1960; grad. Stonier Grad Sch. Banking, Rutgers U., 1969; student Program Mgmt. Devel., Harvard U., 1972. With Fed. Reserve Bank, Atlanta, 1962-73, v.p. Birmingham, Ala., br., 1969-73; v.p., exec. v.p. AmSouth Bancorp., Birmingham, 1973-77; exec. v.p. 1st Nat. Bank Birmingham, 1976-77, pres., 1977-79, chmn. bd., chief exec. officer, 1979-83; vice chmn bd., dir. AmSouth Bancorp., pres. chief operating officer, chmn. AmSouth Bank N.A.; dir. AmSouth Mortgage Co. Pres., chmn. Hall of Fame Bowl; trustee Children's Hosp., Samford U.; mem. U. Ala.-Birmingham Pres.'s Council; 1st v.p. fin. Boy Scouts Am. Served with Tenn Air N.G., 1961-67. Mem. Fin. Execs. Inst., Am. Inst. Banking. Baptist. Clubs: Kiwanis, Mountain Brook, Vestavia Country, Riverchase Country, Shoal Creek, The Club (bd. govs.). Home: 3258 Dell Rd Birmingham AL 35223 Office: PO Box 11007 Birmingham AL 35288

HENDLEY, ROBERT LOYD, ophthalmologist; b. Atlanta, Oct. 8, 1944; s. Jack Dewitt and Margaret Aileen (Still) H.; m. Pamela Ann Cargal, June 10, 1978; children—Robert Loyd Jr., David Scott. B.S. in Applied Biology, Ga. Inst. Tech., 1966; M.D., Vanderbilt U., 1970. Diplomate Am. Bd. Ophthamology. Intern U.S. Navy, Portsmouth, Va., 1970-71; resident Emory U. Med. Sch., Atlanta, 1975-78, clin. instr. in ophthalmology, 1983—; practice medicine specializing in ophthalmology, Roswell, Ga., 1978—; cons. So. Bell, Atlanta, 1978—; chmn. med. adv. com. Ga. Soc. to Prevent Blindness, Atlanta, 1984—. Mem. adminstrv. bd. Roswell United Methodist Ch., 1981—. Served with USN, 1970-74. Fellow Am. Acad. Ophthalmology; mem. Ga. Soc. Ophthalmology. Atlanta Ophthal. Soc. (pres. 1986), Fulton County Med. Soc., Med. Assn. Ga., Med. Assn. Atlanta. Republican. Avocations: Biblical prophecy; sports cars; model railroading. Office: Suite 107 11050 Crabapple Rd Roswell GA 30075

HENDON, DONALD W., marketing educator, consultant; B.B.A., Ph.D., U. Tex.; M.B.A., U. Calif.-Berkeley. Formerly with sales and product mgmt. Armour-Dial and Nabisco Brands; mgmt. cons., 1970—; pres. Bus. Cons. Internat.; prof. mktg. Ark. State U., Jonesboro, 1984—; cons. numerous firms including McDonald's Corp., Celanese Chem. Corp., Kmart Corp., Time Mag., Nat. Assn. Broadcasters, numerous clients in Asia, Australia; lectr., seminar leader in mgmt. devel., mktg., sales mgmt., productivity, time mgmt., profit improvement, negotiation. Author monographs; contbr. articles to profl. jours. Mem. Acad. Internat. Bus., Sales and Mktg. Execs. Internat., Am. Acad. Advertising, Am. Mktg. Assn., Am. Psychol. Assn., Assn. for Consumer Research, Am. Soc. Tng. and Devel., Acad. of Mgmt., Mensa. Home: PO Box 264 Jonesboro AR 72403 Office: Ark State U Dept Mktg-Mgmt Coll of Bus Box 59 Jonesboro AR 72467

HENDON, WILLIAM, U.S. congressman; b. Asheville, N.C., Nov. 9, 1944; s. J. William and Mary Adams (Ward) H.; m. Robbie Peters, 1968; children—Carrie, Jennie. B.S., U. Tenn., 1966; M.S. in Bus., 1968. Mem. faculty U. Tenn., Knoxville, 1968-70, Western Carolina U., 1971-72; mgr. H. Putsch & Co., Asheville, N.C., 1980; mem. 97th-99th Congresses from 11th Dist. N.C. Founder, 1st pres. Asheville Boy's Club; bd. dirs. Mission Hosp. Mem. Asheville Area C. of C. Address: Ho of Reps Office of House Mems Washington DC 20515*

HENDRICK, KINGSLEY MONROE, safety and occupational health program educator; b. Canandaigua, N.Y., Sept. 5, 1935; s. Warren Monroe and Alita Ruth (Lawrence) H.; m. Christine Grace Andrews, Jan. 10, 1959 (div. Apr. 1962); 1 child, Mark Wayne. A.B., Syracuse U., 1957; M.A., U. Rochester, 1962; M.A., U. Ala., 1966; Ph.D., U. Wash., 1978. Cert. hazard control mgr. Commd. ensign U.S. Coast Guard, 1959, advanced through grades to capt., 1979; ret., 1979; instr. English, SUNY-Oswego, 1959-61, Onondaga Community Coll., Syracuse, N.Y., 1962-65; pub.'s rep. Charles Scribner's Sons, N.Y.C., 1965-68; instr. Highline Community Coll., Des Moines, Wash., 1968-72; sr. personnel analyst City of Seattle, 1972-74; dir. residence edn. ctr. Chapman Coll., Oak Harbor, Wash., 1974-76; chief standards and performance staff U.S. Coast Guard, Washington, 1979-85; mgr. Coast Guard/Army safety div. Transp. Safety Inst., Oklahoma City, 1985—. Mem. safety and occupational health program adv. com. dept. agr., Washington, 1982—; presenter in field. Author: Improving Performance for Safety and Occupational Health, 1982; (with Ludwig Benner, Jr.) Small Scale Accident Investigation, 1986. Mem. Nat. Safety Council (traffic edn. and tng. com.), Joint Services Safety Conf. (chmn. edn. and tng. com. 1979-84), Res. Officers-Assn., Alpha Sigma Phi, Roman Catholic. Lodge: Elks. Home: 1505 SW 70th St Oklahoma City OK 73159 Office: Transp Safety Inst Coast Guard/Army Safety Div 6500 S MacArthur Blvd Oklahoma City OK 73125

HENDRICK, RANDALL, linguist; b. Chico, Calif., Apr. 29, 1951; s. Walter Frank and Joan Lillian (Lamoreaux) H.; m. Gretel Meta Gleitsman, Aug. 25, 1973 (div. 1979). B.A., U. Calif.-Irvine, 1973; M.A., U. Toronto, Can., 1974; Ph.D., U. Calif.-Los Angeles, 1979. Vis. asst. prof. U. of N.C., Chapel Hill, 1979-81, asst. prof. linguistics, 1981—. Recipient Fulbright award, 1983. Mem. Linguistic Soc. Am., Southeast Conf. Linguistics. Home: 47 Polks Landing Sta Chapel Hill NC 27514 Office: U of NC 329 Greenlaw Bldg 066A Chapel Hill NC 27514

HENDRICKS, CHARLES LEIGHTON, safety director, instructor; b. Savannah, Ga., Jan. 28, 1948; s. Merida Cuyler and Gloria Ann (Hagins) H.; m. Deborah Holton, Aug 4, 1977 (div. Nov. 6, 1981); children—Tiffany, Leighton; m. Sarah Sue Dupay, July 21, 1983. Student Armstrong State Coll., 1966-68; B.A., Mo. Southern U., 1972. Assoc. safety profl. Firefighter, emergency med. technician City of Savannah, 1972-80; safety dir. Meml. Med. Ctr., Savannah, 1980—. Author Policy and Procedure Emergency Ops. Plan, 1984. Mem. Chatham County Rep. Party, Savannah, 1975—; bd. dirs. March of Dimes Found., Savannah, 1980—, telethon chmn., 1982-83. Mem. Am. Soc. Safety Engrs., Nat. Saftey Council, Nat. Fire Protection Assn. (mem. health care com. 1980—), Am. Assn. for Hosp. Security, Internat. Mgmt. Council. Methodist. Lodges: Sertoma, Jaycees, Masons (trustee 1982—), Elks (hon. life mem., state v.p. Ga. 1984-85, state Tiler Ga., 1985, pres. 1983-84). Avocations: golf; fishing; working with area children's homes and other charitable groups. Home: 132 Holland Park Circle Savannah GA 31419 Office: Meml Med Ctr PO Box 23089 Savannah GA 31419

HENDRICKS, J(AMES) EDWIN, historian, educator, consultant, author; b. Pickens, S.C., Oct. 19, 1935; s. J.E. and Cassie (Looper) H.; m. Sue James, June 28, 1958; children—James, Christopher, Lee. B.A., Furman U., 1957; M.A., U. Va., 1959, Ph.D., 1961. Vis. prof. history U. Va., summer 1961; asst. prof. history Wake Forest U., Winston-Salem, N.C., 1961-66, assoc. prof., 1966-75, prof., 1975—, dir. Hist. Preservation Program, 1973—; vis. prof. history U. Tex.-El Paso, summer 1965; preservation cons.; vis. dir. Mus. Albermarle, Elizabeth City, N.C., summer 1975; dir. Preservation Field Sch., summer 1983-85. Trustee Hist. Bethabara; pres. Hist. Winston, 1979; chmn. Winston-Salem/Forsyth County Hist. Dists. Commn., 1978-79; pres. Wachovia Hist. Soc., 1983-85. Served with U.S. Army, 1958-59. Am. Philos. Soc. research grantee, 1969, 70; recipient R.J. Reynolds research leave, 1973. Mem. N.C. Lit. and Hist. Soc., Hist. Soc. N.C., Hist. Preservation Soc. N.C., Soc. Historians Early Am. Republic, Nat. Trust Hist. Preservation, others. Democrat. Baptist. Clubs: Kiwanis, Torch. Co-author: Liquor and Anti-Liquor in Virginia, 1619-1919, 1967; editor, contbr. Forsyth, the History of a County on the March, 1976; author: Charles Thomson and the Making of a Nation, 1729-1824, 1979. Office: Dept History Wake Forest U PO Box 7806 Winston-Salem NC 27109

HENDRICKS, JAMES OREN, petroleum geologist; b. Beaver, Okla., Nov. 15, 1948; s. James Lee and Ozella May (Pearson) H.; m. Lynda Susan Pauwels, Dec. 31, 1970; children—Andrea Lyn, James Adam. B.S. in Geology, West Tex. State U., 1976. Wellsite logging engr. Universal Well Logging, Inc., Elk City, Okla., 1976-78; staff geologist Alpar Resources, Inc., Perryton, Tex., 1978-79, Falcon Petroleum Co., Perryton, 1979-81, Tierra Petroleum Corp., Oklahoma City, 1981-82; ptnr. J&D Exploration, Inc., Oklahoma City, 1982-84; ind. geologist, Oklahoma City, 1984—. Served with USAF, 1971-75. Mem. Am. Assn. Petroleum Geologists, Panhandle Geol. Soc., Oklahoma City Geol. Soc. Republican. Methodist. Avocations: golf; bowling; rock collecting; photography; arts. Home and Office: 1318 Aries Rd Edmond OK 73034

HENDRICKS, NATHAN VANMETER, III, lawyer; b. Decatur, Ga., Dec. 16, 1943; s. Nathan VanMeter and Ella L. (Ward) H.; B.A., Washington and Lee U., 1966, LL.B., 1969; m. Kathryn A. Barnes, Aug. 19, 1972; children—Nathan VanMeter, Seaton Grantland. Bar: Ga. 1970. Practiced in Atlanta, 1969—; assoc. firm Swift, Currie, McGhee and Hiers, 1969-70, Henning, Chambers and Mabry, 1970-71; asso. firm Redfern, Butler and Morgan, 1971-73, partner, 1973-77; partner firm Cobb, Hyre & Hendricks, Atlanta, 1978—. Chmn. Younger Lawyers Com., Campaign for mayor, Atlanta, 1972. Mem. High Mus. of Art, group leader ann. fund-raising campaign, 1973-75, chmn. young careers group, 1972-73, sec. young men's round table, 1974-75; active ann. fund raising campaign Atlanta Symphony Orch. Assn., 1977-78, Atlanta Arts Alliance, 1977-79; bd. dirs. Atlanta Hunter-Jumper Classic, 1978-79, pres., 1979; bd. dirs. Save America's Vital Environment, sec., 1971-74; bd. dirs. Merrie-Woode Found., v.p., 1978-79, chmn., pres., 1981—. Mem. Am., Atlanta (mem. real estate sect. 1972—, com. 1978) bar assns., State Bar of Ga. (mem. real estate sect. 1972—), Lawyers Club Atlanta, Washington and Lee U. Alumni Assn. (dir. 1972—, pres. Atlanta chpt. 1973-75), Beta Theta Pi, Phi Delta Phi. Episcopalian. Clubs: Ansley Golf, Piedmont Driving, Wildcat Cliffs Country, The Nine O'Clocks. Home: 230 The Prado Atlanta GA 30309 Office: Suite 200 6085 Lake Forrest Dr Atlanta GA 30328

HENDRICKS, PAIGE KELLY, public relations executive; b. New Orleans, Aug. 23, 1949; d. Gordon Brooks and Joan (Perkins) Kelly; m. G. David Hendricks, Jr., Feb. 13, 1971; children—Jeffrey Kyle, Erin Elizabeth. Student Mount Vernon Coll., 1967-68; B.A., Tex. Christian U., 1970; postgrad. in English, N. Tex. State U., 1977-80. Student pub. relations dir. Tex. Christian U., 1970; advt. designer, layout, copywriter, salesman Selma Times Jour. (Ala.), 1971-72; advt. designer, layout, copywriter Clinton Courier, Courier County News, Rome (N.Y.) Daily Sentinel, 1973; pub. relations dir. Utica Community Trust Fund (N.Y.), 1974; theatre producer, upstate N.Y., 1973-76; theatrical set designer, producer Kids & Co., Inc., Dallas, 1978-79; communications specialist, Dallas, 1979—; owner Paige Hendricks Pub. Relations, Dallas/Ft. Worth, 1980—; freelance writer, drama coach. Vice-pres. The Assemblage; mem. Jr. League; chmn. bd. Kids & Co., Inc. Grantee Women in Communications, Inc., Kappa Kappa Gamma, 1979-80. Mem. Pub. Relations Soc. Am., Women in Communications, Inc., KERA, Kappa Kappa Gamma Alumni Assn. Episcopalian. Office: PO Box 470960 Fort Worth TX 76147

HENDRICKSON, ELLWOOD ROBERT, engineering corporation executive; b. York, Pa., Nov. 4, 1921; s. Elwood Harkins and Myrtle (Hollinger) H.; m. Cecelia Marie Berry, June 25, 1946; 1 dau., Lynda Hendrickson James. B.S., Pa. State U., 1942; M.S., U. Wis., 1948, Ph.D., 1950. Diplomate Am. Bd. Indsl. Hygiene, Am. Acad. Environ. Engrs.; registered profl. engr., Fla. San. engr. Officina Tecnica Stubbins, Caracas, Venezuela, 1946-47; instr. U. Wis., 1949-50; assoc. prof. U. Fla., Gainesville, 1950-58, prof., 1958-66, dir. research, 1964-66, adj. prof., 1966—; v.p. Resources Research, Inc., Falls Church, Va., 1966-68; pres. Environ. Engring., Inc., Gainesville, 1968-73; chmn. bd. Environ. Sci. & Engring., Inc., Gainesville, 1973—; spl. cons. USPHS, 1954—. Chmn., Fla. Air Pollution Control Commn., 1958-66, Gordon Research Conf., 1967. Author: (with H.D. Townsend) Register of Air Pollution Analysis, 1958, also others; contbr. articles to profl. jours. Served from 2d lt. to capt. C.E., AUS, 1942-46. Mem. ASCE (sect. pres. 1953-54), Nat. Soc. Profl. Engrs. (bd. dirs. 1964-68), Fla. Engring. Soc. (pres. 1962-63, Disting. Service award 1968), Air Pollution Control Assn. (pres. 1964-65, Frank A. Chambers award 1975), ASTM, Am. Indsl. Hygiene Assn., TAPPI. Clubs: Gainesville Golf and Country; Tampa (Fla.) Yacht and Country. Home: 2044 NW 7th Pl Gainesville FL 32603 Office: PO Box ESE Gainesville FL 32602

HENDRICKSON, JAMES LYNN, air force officer; b. Springfield, Ohio, Apr. 11, 1942; s. William Richard and Floryne Leona (Thompson) H.; B.S. in Mktg., Ohio State U., 1965; M.Mil.Scis., U.S. Army Command and Gen. Staff Coll., 1978; m. Maria Gloria Albanes, Mar. 25, 1978. Commd. 2d lt. U.S. Air Force, 1965, advanced through grades to col., 1984; supply officer Bergstrom AFB, Tex., 1965-67; navigator trainee, electronic warfare trainee Mather AFB, Calif., 1967-68; combat tour in S.E. Asia, Takhli AB, Thailand and Danang AB, 1969-70; wing electronic warfare officer, Danang and Homestead AFB, Fla., 1970-74; Tactical Air Command staff, Langley AFB, Va., 1974-77; adv. to Imperial Iranian Air Force, 1978-79; tactical fighter wing chief of weapons and readiness, ops. officer George AFB, Victorville, Calif., 1979-81, dep. comdr. Cadets Composite Squadron 120, wing adviser CAP, 1979-81. Decorated Silver Star, D.F.C. (2), Air medal (15), Air Force Commendation medal, Meritorious Service medal, Joint Services Commendation medal; recipient Res. Officer's Assn. award, 1965. Mem. Air Force Assn., Soc. Wild Weasels, Assn. Old Crows. Contbr. articles to profl. jours. Home: 19 Nordberg Circle Valparaiso FL 32580 Office: USAFTAWC/EW Eglin AFB FL 32542

HENDRIX, BETTY DUNN, banker; b. Dozier, Ala., Sept. 19, 1938; d. William Cubert and Mary Orell (Moore) Dunn; m. Charles Edgar Hendrix, Aug. 23, 1958; children—Michael Ray, Christine Renee. Student Springhill Coll., 1976, 82; basic cert. Am. Inst. Banking. Bookkeeper, Mchts. Nat. Bank, Mobile, Ala., 1957-61; with Am. Nat. Bank-Am. South, Mobile, 1963—, now v.p., mgr.; instr. Am. Inst. Banking, Credit Women's Internat. Recipient Woman of Yr. award Am. Bus. Women's Assn., 1975, Boss of Yr. award, 1984; Outstanding Career award Gayfers Career Club, 1981; Ala. State Legislature Recognition award, 1985. Mem. Nat. Assn. Bank Women, Am. Inst. Banking, Bank Adminstrn. Inst., Ala. Bankers Assn., Internat. Mgmt. Council (v.p. 1982, service award 1980, 83), Mobile Area C. of C. Republican. Baptist. Club: Pilot (sec. 1983). Home: 2251 Brandeis Dr Mobile AL 36618 Office: 5301 Moffat Rd Mobile AL 36618

HENDRIX, DENNIS RALPH, energy industry, engineering and construction executive; b. Selmer, Tenn., Jan. 8, 1940; s. Forrest Ralph and Mary Lee (Tull) H.; B.S., U. Tenn., 1962; M.B.A., Ga. State U., 1965; m. Jennie L. Moore, Dec. 28, 1960; children—Alisa Lee, Natalie Moore, Amy Louise. Staff acct. Arthur Andersen & Co., Atlanta, 1962-65; faculty Ga. Inst. Tech., 1965-67; sr. cons. Touche, Ross & Co., Memphis, 1967-68; pres. United Foods, Inc., Memphis, 1968-73; asst. to pres. Tex. Gas Resources Corp., Owensboro, Ky., 1973-75, pres., 1976-78, pres., chief exec. officer, 1978-83; vice chmn. CSX Corp., 1983-84; exec. v.p., dir. Halliburton Co., Dallas, 1984—; dir. First City Bancorp., Pan Handle Eastern Corp., Houston. Bd. dirs. Nat. Jr. Achievement, U. Tenn. Devel. Council; trustee Brescia Coll., Owensboro. C.P.A. Mem. NAM (dir.). Presbyterian. Clubs: Owensboro Country; River Oaks Country, Ramada (Houston). Home: 28 Stonecourt Dallas TX 75225 Office: 2600 Southland Ctr 400 N Olive LB 263 Dallas TX 75201

HENDRIX, HAROLD VICTOR (HAL), retired correspondent and corporation executive; b. Kansas City, Mo., Feb. 14, 1922; s. Clarence Virgil and Grace Frances (Lee) H.; m. Mary Frances Sheehan, May 25, 1944; 1 dau., Kathleen Ann Hendrix Gorishek. Reporter, assignment editor, Latin Am. corr. Kansas City Star, 1944-57; Latin Am. corr. Miami News/Cox Newspapers, 1957-63, Scripps-Howard Newspaper Alliance, 1963-67; dir. corp. relations Latin Am., ITT, 1967-73; dir. devel. Latin Am., IHC/Pan Am., 1973-76; v.p. corp. relations Wackenhut Corp., 1978-85. Recipient Pulitzer prize for internat. reporting, 1963. Mem. Sigma Delta Chi. Clubs: Riviera Country (Coral Gables, Fla.); Jockey (Buenos Aires). Home: 2400 S Ocean Dr Seascape I Apt 4362 Fort Pierce FL 33449

HENDRIX, JAMES ROBERT, investment banker; b. Birmingham, Ala., May 5, 1905; s. William Robert and Sarah Amanda (Coburn) H.; m. Sarah Palmer Nesbit, Apr. 27, 1940 (dec.); children—James Coburn, Virginia Nesbit Hendrix Scruggs; m. Marion Calhoun Cardwell, Apr. 27, 1973. B.S. in Commerce, Washington and Lee U., 1926. Investment officer Birmingham Trust Nat. Bank (Ala.), 1930-35; br. mgr. King Mohr & Co., 1935-38; ptnr. King Mohr & Hendrix, 1938-42; v.p. Hendrix & Mayes, Inc., 1942-48, pres., chmn., 1948—; pres., chmn., chief exec. officer Hendrix, Mohr & Yardley, Inc., Birmingham, 1960-78, chmn., chief exec. officer, 1978—. Chmn. adv. commn. State of Ala. Retirement Systems, 1976-77; mem. Ala. Indsl. Devel. Securities Commn., 1974-78; chmn. Mountain Brook Bd. Edn. (Ala.), 1959-70. Served to lt. comdr. USNR, 1942-45. Mem. Nat. Assn. Securities Dealers, Security Investor Protective Corp., Ala. Securities Dealers Assn. Republican. Episcopalian. Clubs: Mountain Brook Country, Redstone, Downtown, The Club; Linville Country (N.C.).

HENDRIX, ROBERT MILTON, financial executive; b. Dyersburg, Tenn., Feb. 1, 1925; s. Daniel Forrest and Helon Elizabeth (Towery) H.; m. Patricia Daws, Feb. 21, 1947 (dec. 1975); children—Robert M., Patricia Jane; m. 2d Jackie Clymer, Aug. 25, 1982. Student pub. schs., Dyersburg, Tenn. Farmer, rancher, Dyersburg, 1940-83; chmn. bd. Dyersburg Prodn. Credit Assn., 1976—; chmn. nat. com. Prodn. Credit Assn. Nat. Com., 1970-72. Trustee sec. Parkview Hosp., 1960-76; mem. Dyer County Farm Bur., Dyer-Farmer Co-op. Served with U.S. Army, 1944-46. Named Outstanding Farmer of Am., 1971, Parent of Yr., Parents without Partners, 1980-81. Mem. Tenn. Fedn. Prodn. Credit Assns., Tenn. Livestock Assn., Am. Angus Assn., Tenn. Farmers Mktg. Co-op, others. Baptist. Lodges: Masons (32 deg.), Shriners. Office: Dyersburg Prodn Credit Assn Hwy 51 S Dyersburg TN 38024

HENDRY, JAMES E., lawyer, retired automobile club executive; b. Perry, Fla., Nov. 7, 1912; s. Wesley Alonzo and Mae (Weaver) H.; student St. Petersburg Jr. Coll., 1930-32; J.D., U. Fla., 1935; m. Frances Swope, June 25, 1948; children—James E., Jayne L., Thomas S., John W., David F. Vice pres. Hendry Lumber Co., 1935-42, sec., treas., 1946-60; ptnr. mgr. Hendry Bldg. Co., 1946-60; practice law as James E. Hendry, atty., 1961—; pres. Gulf Housing Corp., 1946; sec.-mgr. St. Petersburg AAA Motor Club, 1962-67, exec. v.p., gen. mgr., 1967-81, pres., 1981-85; pres. Club Ins. Agy., Inc., 1982-85; dir. Guardian Bank, 1975-85, chmn., 1975-76; adv. bd. First Union Bank, 1985—. Mem. City Planning and Zoning Bd., 1948-57, Pinellas County Sch. Bd., 1957-66; mem. Pinellas Co. Airport Com., 1952; mem. St. Petersburg Planning Commn., 1974-75. Mem. citizens adv. com. St. Petersburg Jr. Coll., 1948-68, bd. govs., 1938-48, chmn. dist. bd. trustees, 1968-75; pres. bd. dirs. YMCA, 1951; mem. Mound Park Hosp. Bd., 1951-52; cancer drive Am. Cancer Soc., 1962; pres. Fla. Sch. Bd. Assn., 1964; sec.-treas. Southeastern Conf. AAA Motor Clubs, 1964, v.p., 1965, pres., 1966, treas. Eastern Conf. AAA Motor Clubs, 1970-71, vice chmn., 1972-75, chmn., 1975-77; exec. com. Continuing Ednl. Council Fla., 1964; mem. Nat. Com. Support Pub. Schs., 1964; mem. Pinellas Com. of 100, State Community Coll. Council, 1970-75; v.p. St. Petersburg Jr. Coll. Devel. Found., 1980-83, exec. com., 1984-85; former mem. Pinellas Tourist Devel. Council. Lt. comdr. USCG Res. Mem. Am., St. Petersburg bar assns., Fla. Bar, Am. Judicature Soc., Fla. C. of C. of C. U.S., St. Petersburg C. of C. (bd. govs. 1979-82); Community Betterment award 1982), Nat. Assn. Home Builders (past dir.), Contractors and Builders Assn. of Pinellas County (pres. 1953), Fla. Home Builders Assn. (v.p. 1955), Soc. Preservation and Encouragement of Barber Shop Quartet Singing in Am. (Harmony award 1983), Phi Delta Theta, Phi Alpha Delta. Democrat. Methodist. Clubs: Circumnavigators, St. Petersburg Yacht, St. Petersburg Quarterback, Pres.'s Skal, Feathersound Country. Home: 409 Snell Isle Blvd Saint Petersburg FL 33704

HENDRY, ROBERT RYON, lawyer; b. Jacksonville, Fla., Apr. 23, 1936; s. Warren Candler and Evalyn Marguerite (Ryon) H.; m. Lee Comstock, June 21, 1956; children—Lorraine Evalyn, Lynette Comstock, Krista Ryon. B.A., in Polit. Sci., U. Fla., 1958, J.D., 1963. Bar: Fla. 1963. Assoc. Harrell, Caro, Middlebrooks & Wiltshire, Pensacola, Fla., 1963-66; assoc. Helliwell, Melrose & DeWolf, Orlando, Fla., 1966-67, ptnr., 1967-69; ptnr., pres. Hoffman, Hendry, Parker & Smith and predecessor Hoffman, Hendry & Parker, Orlando, 1969-77, Hoffman, Hendry & Stoner and predecessor, Orlando, 1977-82, Hendry, Stoner, Sims & Sawicki, Orlando, 1982—. Mem. Dist. Export Council, 1977—, vice chmn., 1981; bd. dirs. World Trade Ctr. and predecessor, Orlando, 1979—, pres., 1980-82, 84; chmn. Fla. Gov.'s Conf. on World Trade, 1983; mem. internat. fin. and mktg. adv. bd. U. Miami Sch. Bus. Author: U.S. Real Estate and the Foreign Investor, 1983; contbr. to profl. pubs. Served to 1st lt. U.S. Army, 1958-60, to capt. Army N.G., 1960-70. Mem. Fla. Council Internat. Devel. (dir. 1972-85, chmn. 1977-79, adv. bd. 1985), Fla. Bar (vice chmn. internat. law com. 1974-75, chmn. com. 1976-77, mem. exec. council internat. law sect. 1982—), Orange County Bar Assn. (treas. 1971-74), Brit.-Am. C. of C. (dir., sec. 1984—). Club: University (Orlando). Office: 215 E Central Blvd Orlando FL 32801

HENEGAR, MARTHA LUCILE, educational administrator; b. McMinnville, Tenn., July 9, 1937; d. Ulric Shaw and Lucile (Angel) H. B.A., George Peabody Coll., 1959, M.A., 1960. Tchr. Metro Pub. Schs., Nashville, 1959-68; promotion dir. Sta. WMCV-TV, Nashville, 1968-70; dir. pub. relations Nashville State Tech. Inst., 1970-84, head pub. affairs and devel., 1984—. Editor mag. Print-Out, 1970—. Contbr. articles to profl. publs., mags. Recipient Pub. Relations Program of Yr. award Tenn. Tech. Edn. Council, 1984. Mem. Internat. Assn. Bus. Communicators (pres. local chpt. 1976), Pub. Relations Soc. Am. (pres. local chpt. 1980). Office: Nashville State Tech Inst 120 White Bridge Rd Nashville TN 37209

HENGELS, CHARLES FRANCIS, research and development executive, educator; b. Oak Park, Ill., Sept. 4, 1948; s. Charles Leo and Vivian Marguerite (Brust) H. B.S. in Econs., Purdue U., 1970, B.A. in Political Sci., 1970, M.S. in Edn., 1976, M.S. in Sociology, 1978. Cert. secondary tchr. Staff resident, teaching asst. Purdue U., West Lafayette, Ind., 1975-78; dir. Am. Med. Buildings, Milw., 1978-80; exec. dir. System Planning Corp., Arlington, Va., 1980—; cons. Ind. Council for Econ. Edn., West Lafayette, 1976-77. Author: (poetry) America, 1971 (Freedom Found. award 1971). Regional dir. Com. for Responsible Health Care, Washington, 1978-80, Virginians for Zumwalt U.S. Senate campaign, Richmond, 1976. Served to lt. Spl. Duty (Intelligence), USN, 1970-74. Decorated Navy Achievement medal with Combat V (2), Combat Action ribbon; recipient Pres.'s Acad. award Purdue U., 1970, Gen. Dynamics award Gen. Dynamics Corp., 1970, Chgo. Tribune award, 1970; named Disting. Naval Grad., 1970. Mem. Purdue Alumni Assn. (life), Mensa, Kappa Delta Pi, Alpha Kappa Delta, Pi Sigma Alpha, Phi Kappa Phi, Delta Rho Kappa, Phi Eta Sigma. Republican. Roman Catholic. Avocations: athletics; writing; teaching. Home: 5917 Larpin Lane Alexandria VA 22310 Office: System Planning Corp 1500 Wilson Blvd Arlington VA 22209

HENICAN, CASWELL ELLIS, lawyer; b. New Orleans, Feb. 10, 1905; s. Joseph Patrick and Alice (Boning) H.; LL.B., Tulane U., 1926; m. Elizabeth Cleveland, June 18, 1930; children—Alice (Mrs. Claude V. Perrier, Jr.), Caswell

Ellis Jr., Margaret (Mrs. F. Gordon Wilson, Jr.), Dorothy (Mrs. Charles E. Heidingsfelder), Joseph Patrick III. Admitted to La. bar, 1926, since practiced in New Orleans; asso. firm Lemle, Moreno & Lemle, 1926-33; sr. partner firm Henican, Carriere & Cleveland, 1933-40, Henican, James & Cleveland, 1940—. Chmn. La. Bd. Pub. Welfare, 1940-47; pres. New Orleans Community Chest, 1940, Council Social Agys., 1939, Asso. Catholic Charities New Orleans, 1938, Archidiocesian Vocation Devel. Commn. Chmn. adv. bd. Mercy Hosp., Retreat House of Cenacle for Women; bd. dirs., trustee, pres. Magnolia Sch. Decorated Knight of St. Gregory, Order of St. Louis King of France; recipient medal as most outstanding young man New Orleans Jr. C. of C., 1940, F. Edward Hebert award as most outstanding alumnus of Jesuit High Sch., 1960. Mem. Am., La., New Orleans (pres. 1958) bar assns., Soc. Hosp. Attys. (charter), Nat. Health Lawyers Assn., Tulane U. Hall of Fame, Greater New Orleans Hall of Fame. Club: Serra (chpt. pres. 1960). Home: 1831 Octavia St New Orleans LA 70115 Office: 1200 Heritage Plaza 111 Veterans Blvd PO Box 19300 New Orleans LA 70179

HENINGER, SIMEON KAHN, JR., English language educator; b. Monroe, La., Oct. 27, 1922; s. Simeon Kahn and Elsye (Lieber) H.; m. Irene Callen, July 16, 1957; children—Dale Callen, Kathryn Leigh, Philip Ward, Polly Elizabeth, Simeon Kahn III; m. 2d, Dorothy Cooper Langston, May 30, 1971. B.S., Tulane U., 1944, B.A., 1947, M.A., 1949; B.Litt. (Fulbright scholar), Oxford, 1952; Ph.D., Johns Hopkins U., 1955. Instr., Duke U., Durham, N.C., 1955-57, asst. prof., 1957-62, assoc. prof., 1962-65, prof., 1965-67; prof. English, U. Wis.-Madison, 1967-71, chmn. dept., 1968-70; prof. English U. B.C., Vancouver, 1971-82; distg. prof. English, U. N.C.-Chapel Hill, 1982—. Exec. sec.-treas. Southeastern Renaissance Conf., 1958-67; mem. Nat. Shakespeare Anniversary Com., 1963-64; mem. central exec. com. Folger Inst. Renaissance and Eighteenth-Century Studies, 1982—. Served to capt. USAAF, 1943-46. Folger Library fellow, 1961; Guggenheim fellow, 1962-63; Southeastern Inst. Medieval and Renaissance Studies fellow, 1967; Huntington Library fellow, 1970-71, 81; Killam Sr. fellow, 1975-76. Mem. MLA, Am., Renaissance Soc. Am. (mem. adv. council, 1958-68, 75-80, Spenser Soc. (adv. council 1977-80), Milton Soc. (adv. council 1980-83), Medieval Acad. Am., ACLU, Phi Beta Kappa. Author: A Handbook of Renaissance Meteorology, 1960, Touches of Sweet Harmony, 1974; The Cosmographical Glass, 1977. Editor: Thomas Watson, The Hekatompathia, 1964; Edmund Spenser, Poetry, 1970; Edmund Spenser, Shepheardes Calender, 1979; Kalendar of Sheepehards, 1979. Asst. editor Modern Language Notes, 1953-55; editorial bd. Studies in English Literature, 1978—, Spenser Studies, 1977—; Duquesne Studies in Language and Literature, 1976—; Renaissance and Reformation, 1976—; John Donne Journal, 1982—, Huntington Library Quar., 1982—; contbr. articles to profl. jours. Home: 505 Lakeshore Ln Chapel Hill NC 27514 Office: Dept English U NC Chapel Hill NC 27514

HENINGTON, DAVID MEAD, city library official; b. El Dorado, Ark., Aug. 16, 1929; s. Bud Henry and Lucile Check (Scranton) H.; m. Barbara Jean Gibson, June 2, 1956; children—Mark David, Gibson Mead, Paul Billins. B.A., U. Houston, 1951; M.S. in L.S., Columbia U., 1956. Young adult librarian Bklyn. Public Library, 1956-58; head lit. and history dept. Dallas Public Library, 1958, asst. dir., 1962-67; dir. Waco (Tex.) Public Library, 1958-62, Houston Public Library, 1967—; pres. HBW Assos. (Library Planners & Cons.), Houston, 1979—. Served with USAF, 1951-55. Council on Library Resources fellow, 1970-71; recipient Liberty Bell award Houston Bar Assn., 1976. Mem. ALA, Southwestern Library Assn., Tex. Library Assn. (Librarian of Year 1976), Am. Mgmt. Assn., Tex. Mcpl. Librarian Assn. Methodist. Club: Rotary. Home: 6225 San Felipe Rd Houston TX 77057 Office: Houston Public Library 500 McKinney Ave Houston TX 77002

HENKEL, DONALD DALE, leisure service professional, association administrator; b. Oak Park, Ill., June 26, 1929; s. George Fred and Gertrude (Bradshaw) H.; m. Marilyn Ruth Bartle, Oct. 2, 1953; children—Scott, Donna, William. B.A., Ind. U., 1951; M.S., George Williams Coll., 1955; Ph.D., U. Ill.-Urbana, 1967. Dir. recreation City of Loveland, Colo., 1955-60; dir. parks and recreation City of Villa Park, Ill., 1960-65; dir. profl. services Nat. Recreation and Park Assn., Alexandria, Va., 1967—, also prin. staff person responsible for nat. accreditation and cert. Served to 1st lt. USAF, 1951-53. Recipient Disting. Fellow award Soc. Park and Recreation Educators, 1984; Charles Brightbill award U. Ill., 1984; award Congress Program Com., 1984. Fellow Am. Acad. Park and Recreation Adminstrs. (award 1982); mem. Nat. Recreation and Park Assn. Home: 6912 N 30th St Arlington VA 22213 Office: Nat Recreation and Park Assn 3101 Pk Ctr Dr Alexandria VA 22302

HENKEL, JOHN HARMON, educator; b. Kentwood, La., Aug. 14, 1924; s. William Hatton and Margaret Gwendolyn (Watson) H.; student Southeastern La. Coll., 1941-43; B.S., Tulane U., 1947, M.S., 1948; Ph.D., Brown U., 1954; m. Sara Ernestine Saucier, Apr. 23, 1948; children—Wendolyn Elizabeth, Sally Lee (Mrs. Howard Barry Bone Jr.) (dec.), Jenny Saucier, Margaret Loraine, Pamela Ann (dec.). Jr. research technologist Magnolia Petroleum Co., Dallas, 1948-51, sr. research technologist, 1954-55; research asst. Brown U., Providence, 1951-54; asst. prof. U. Ga., Athens, 1955, assoc. prof., 1958-64, prof. physics, 1964—, acting head dept. physics and astronomy, 1975-77. Dir. 19th Ann. Ga. State Sci. Fair, 1967; adviser Ga. chpt. Circle K Internat., 1966-72. Co-pres. Barrow Sch. PTA, Athens, 1964-66; area chmn. Tulane Alumni Found., 1970-76; bd. dirs. Wesley Found., Athens, Ga., 1966-72, pres., 1971-72. Served with USNR, 1943-46. NSF fellow, 1959-60; NSF grantee, 1962-69; NRC sr. research asso., 1973-74. Fellow AAAS; mem. Am. Phys. Soc., Ga. Acad. Sci. (fellow editorial bd. 1964-77, council mem. 1964-67, pres. 1968), Sigma Xi, Sigma Chi. Methodist. Clubs: Green Hills Country (pres. bd. dirs. Athens 1967-71, 84-86), Kiwanis (pres. 1985-86). Home: 395 Hampton Ct Athens GA 30605

HENLEY, EDGAR FLOYD, JR., pharmacist, consultant; b. Corpus Christi, Tex., Feb. 11, 1940; s. Edgar Floyd and Marzelle (Smalling) H.; 1 son, Michael Paul; m. Sylvia Nesbit, Dec. 26, 1981. B.S. in Pharmacy, U. Ark. Coll. Pharmacy, 1964; D.Pharmacy (hon.), 1983; Ph.D., Kensington U., 1985. Registered pharmacist; lic. cons. pharmacist. Intern, Pine Bluff, Ark., 1964-65; pres. Bruce Drugs, Inc., Smackover, Ark., 1967—; cons. pharmacy Smackover Nursing Home, 1975—. Pres. Smackover Band Parents, 1974-76, Smackover Retail Credit Assn., 1973-76; chmn. Union County Democratic Com., 1974-76, Union County Election Com., 1974-76; troop leader Girl Scouts U.S.A.; packmaster Cub Scouts Am., 1971-74; bd. dirs. Union County chpt. ARC, 1975-79, Smackover Devel. Corp., 1970—, Smackover Indsl. Devel. Corp., 1970—; mem. Ark. Drug Abuse Authority, 1975; mem. alumni adv. council U. Ark. for Med. Scis., 1984—, chmn.-elect, 1985—; alderman Smackover City Council, 1983—. Served with USAF, 1958-61. Recipient Bowl of Hygeia award A.H. Robins, Inc., 1974; named Key Man, Jr. C. of C., 1968. Fellow Am. Soc. Cons. Pharmacists; mem. Smackover Jr. C. of C. (pres.), Ark. Pharm. Assn. (v.p., dir. Ark. Pharm. Community Service award 74), Nat. Assn. Retail Druggists, Frat. Order Police, Nat. Rifle Assn., Smackover C. of C. (pres. 1974, dir. 1975-80, treas. 1980—, Outstanding Citizen award 1974), Acacia. Democrat. Methodist. Club: Pine Hills Country (past pres.). Lodges: Masons (master), Shriners, K.T. Home: 1101 Cedar St Smackover AR 71762 Office: 711 Broadway Smackover AR 71762

HENLEY, GORDON B., JR., zoo dir.; b. McAlester, Okla., Oct. 30, 1946; s. Gordon B. and Aline (Robbins) H.; student U. Okla., 1964-67; B.S., Central State U. Okla., 1973; M.S., Stephen F. Austin State U., 1981; m. Charlotte Jean Kerr, Aug. 8, 1975; children—Charlotte Jennifer, Gordon Brian. Zookeeper, Oklahoma City Zoo, 1970-72; supr. birds and reptiles Tulsa Zool. Park, 1973-76; zoo dir. Ellen Trout Zoo, Lufkin, Tex., 1976—. Past pres. Angelina County Humane Soc. Served with AUS, 1968-69. Decorated Bronze Star, Air medal. Fellow Am. Assn. Zool. Parks and Aquariums (profl.); mem. Am. Soc. Ichthyologists and Herpetologists, Herpetologists League, Soc. for Study Amphibians and Reptiles, Nat. Wildlife Fedn., Audubon Soc., Am. Mus. Natural History, Lufkin Hist. and Creative Arts Center. Methodist. Address: PO Drawer 190 Lufkin TX 75902-0190

HENLEY, SALLIE HAMLET, artist, deaf interpreter; b. Norfolk, Va., Sept. 29, 1933; d. Charles McDowell and Sarah Speight (White) Hamlet; student pub. schs., Norfolk; m. William Franklin Henley, Jr., July 21, 1951; children—William Franklin III, Robert Matthew. Pub. speaker, Milw., 1968-71, Houston, 1971—; book dramatist, Milw., 1969-71, Houston, 1971-72; interpreter for deaf, Milw., 1969-71, Houston, 1971—; free-lance artist, Atlanta, 1963-65, Houston, 1975—; exhibited Sportsmans Gallery, The Galleria, Houston. Interpreter to deaf Elmbrook Ch., Brookfield, Wis., 1969-70; vol. tchr. deaf retardate Fairview North Elementary Sch., Brookfield, 1970; narrator, interpreter Deaf Olympics, 1969; sec. Quail Valley Civic Assn., 1974-75; bd. dirs. Ephphatha, Inc., Milw., 1969-70. Mem. Registry Interpreters for Deaf. Republican. Home: 2806 E Pebble Beach Dr Missouri City TX 77459

HENLEY, SYLVIA N., counselor; b. El Dorado, Ark., Feb. 5, 1940. B.A., Ouachita Bapt. U., Arkadelphia, Ark., 1961; M.A., La. Tech. U., 1975. Cert. tchr., counselor, Ark. Tchr., El Dorado pub. schs., 1962-80; counselor Camden Pub. Schs., Ark., 1980—. Pres. Northwest Elem. Sch. PTA, El Dorado, 1969-70; sec. El Dorado Boys Club Aux., 1968-70, pres., 1970-71; sec. El Dorado City Council PTA, 1969-70, 79-80; bd. dirs. El Dorado Teen-Age Club, 1973-80, El Dorado Racquet Club, 1976-79, El Dorado Camp Fire Girls Council, 1979-81; mem. adminstrv. bd. Smackover First United Methodist Ch., Ark., 1982—. Mem. Am. Assn. Counseling and Devel., Am. Sch. Counselor Assn., Ark. Assn. Counseling, Guidance and Devel. (dir 1980-83), Ark. Sch. Counselors Assn. (pres. 1982-83), S.W. Ark. Sch. Counselors Assn. (sec. 1981, pres. 1982), La. Tech. U. Alumni Bd., Delta Kappa Gamma, Phi Delta Kappa. Home: 1101 Cedar St Smackover AR 71762 Office: Camden High Sch 647 Jefferson Dr NW Camden AR 71701

HENN, SHIRLEY EMILY, librarian; b. Cleve., May 26, 1919; d. Albert Edwin and Florence Ely (Miller) H.; A.B., Hollins Coll., 1941; M.S., U. N.C., 1966; m. John Van Bruggen, July 14, 1944 (div. May 1947); 1 son, Peter Albert (dec.). Library asst. Hollins (Va.) Coll., 1943-44, 61-64, reference librarian, 1965-84, emeritus, 1984—; advt. mgr. R.M. Kellogg Co., Three Rivers, Mich., 1946-47; exec. sec. Hollins Coll. Alumnae Assn., 1947-55; real Intern, estate salesman Fowlkes & Kefauver, Roanoke, Va., 1955-61. Pres. Soc. for Prevention Cruelty to Animals, 1959-61, 69-72, bd. dirs., 1972-81. Mem. Am. Alumni Council (dir. 1952-54, dir. women's activities 1952-54), ALA, Va. Library Assn. (membership chmn. coll. and univ. sect. 1969—), Pub. Documents Forum Va., DAR (chpt. regent 1984—), Collie Club Am., Roanoke Bird Club, Roanoke Kennel Club. Club: Quota (chpt. pres. 1958-60) (Roanoke). Author and illustrator: Adventures of Hooty Owl and His Friends, 1955; editor: Hollins Alumnae Bull., 1947-56. Home: 6915 Tinkerdale Hollins VA 24019

HENNECY, BOBBIE BOBO, educator; b. Tignall, Ga., Aug. 11, 1922; d. John Ebb and Lois Helen (Gulledge) Bobo; A.B. summa cum laude, Mercer U., Macon, Ga., 1950; postgrad. Oxford (Eng.) U., 1961; M.A. (NDEA fellow), Emory U., 1962; m. James Howell Hennecy, Dec. 28, 1963; 1 dau., Erin. Adminstrv. asst. to pres., instr. Mercer U., 1950-61, instr. English, 1961-76, asst. prof., 1976—; a founder Tattnall Sq. Acad., Macon, 1968, sec., 1968-73, dir., 1968-78. Mem. President's Club, Mercer U. Mem. AAUW (chpt. pres. 1965), MLA, South Atlantic MLA, So. Comparative Lit. Assn., Nat. Assn. Tchrs. English, Ga. Assn. Tchrs. English, English Speaking Union, Nat. Soc. Dames Magna Charta, U.D.C., DAR (registrar 1980-82), Daus. of 1812, Daus. of Colonial Clergy, Daus. of Am. Colonists, Colonial Dames XVII Century, Jamestowne Soc., Mid. Ga. Hist. Soc., Cardinal Key, Sigma Tau Delta, Phi Kappa Phi, Sigma Mu (past pres.), Alpha Psi Omega, Chi Omega (alumnae advisor 30 yrs.). Baptist. Home: 1347-B Adams St Macon GA 31201 Office: Mercer Univ Macon GA 31207

HENNECY, JAMES HOWELL, procurement analyst; b. Marion, S.C., Mar. 10, 1913; s. Gabriel Marion and Annie Laurie (Boatwright) H.; student Mercer U., 1948-51; J.D., Walter F. George Sch. Law, 1953; m. Bobbie Helen Bobo, Dec. 28, 1963; 1 dau., Ardith Erin. Plant cashier Bordens Milk Co., Macon, Ga., 1953-55; contract specialist Dept. Air Force, Robins AFB, 1955-58, contract negotiator, 1964-74, contracting officer, 1975-86, procurement analyst, 1986—; law librarian, instr. in law Walter F. George Sch. Law, Mercer U., Macon, 1958-63. Active Boy Scouts Am.; spokesman Macon Citizens for Better Hwy. Planning, 1959-62. Adviser, Young Democrats Club, 1960-63. Served with AUS, 1942-45; ETO, MTO. Decorated Bronze Star medal; recipient Cross of Mil. Service, Sidney Lanier chpt. UDC, 1981. Mem. VFW, Young Americans for Freedom (asso.), Marion (S.C.) Jr. C. of C. (charter), Am. Ordnance Assn., Am. Legion, Air Force Assn., Internat. Platform Assn., SCV, Alpha Tau Omega, Delta Theta Phi, Alpha Psi Omega. Baptist (deacon). Clubs: Toastmasters (local pres. 1965, dist. edn. chmn. 1959-60), Lions; President's (Mercer U.). Home: 1347-B Adams St Macon GA 31201 Office: Directorate Contracting and Manufacturing WRALC Robins AFB GA 31098

HENNEKE, EDMUND GEORGE, II, engineering educator; b. Balt., May 30, 1941; s. Edmund George and Marguerite (Herrmann) H.; m. Gloria Johnson, Sept. 7, 1963; children—Christian E., Samantha M. B.E.S., Johns Hopkins U., 1963, M.S.E., 1966, Ph.D., 1968. Asst. prof. Fla. State U., Tallahassee, 1968-71; asst. prof. engring. sci. and mechanics Va. Poly. Inst. and State U., Blacksburg, 1971-73, assoc. prof., 1973-78, prof., 1978—. Asst. scoutmaster, roundtable commr. Blue Ridge Mountains council Boy Scouts Am. Mem. Am. Soc. for Nondestructive Testing, ASTM, Acoustics Soc. Am. Club: Civitan (Mr. Civitan, Appalachian dist. 1982). Assoc. tech. editor Materials Evaluation, 1981—. Contbr. numerous articles to profl. jours. Co-developer nondestructive testing technique, vibrothermography.

HENNESSEY, WILLIAM JOHN, museum director; b. Summit, N.J., July 15, 1948; m. Leslie Griffin, June 10, 1978. B.A., Wesleyan U., 1970; M.A., Columbia U., 1971, Ph.D., 1978. Ford Found. fellow Worcester Art Mus., 1971-73; research assoc. Solomon R. Guggenheim Mus., N.Y.C., 1973-74; curator Spencer Art Mus., U. Kans., Lawrence, 1975-79; dir. Vassar Coll. Art Gallery, Poughkeepsie, N.Y., 1979-82; dir. U. Ky. Art Mus., Lexington, 1982—; asst. prof. U. Kans., Vassar Coll., Bklyn. Coll. Trustee Intermus. Conservation Assn. Mem. Am. Assn. Mus., Coll. Art. Assn., Soc. Archtl. Historians, Assn. Art Mus. Dirs. Contbr. articles to profl. jours. Office: U Ky Art Mus Lexington KY 40506

HENNESY, GERALD CRAFT, artist; b. Washington, June 11, 1921; s. Gerald Craft and Frances Lee (Moore) H.; m. Elizabeth Ann Lovering, Mar. 4, 1950; children—Kathleen, Paul, Brian, Shawn, Hugh, Craig. Student Corcoran Sch. of Art, 1939; George Washington U., 1940; B.S., U. Md., 1948. Artist advt. dept. Times Herald Newspaper, Washington, 1941-42; enlisted U.S. Navy, 1942; advanced through grades to comdr., 1956; mgmt. analyst U.S. Air Force Hdqtrs., Pentagon, Washington, 1948-52, 54-56; asst. dir. for orgn. and mgmt. AEC., 1956-72; artist, dir. Studio of Hennesy, Clifton, Va., 1972—; exhbns. include: Corcoran Gallery Art, Washington, 1957, 59, 67, Smithsonian Inst., Washington, 1962, 64, Allied Artists of Am., N.Y.C., 1975, 76; one man shows include: PLA Gallery, McLean, Va., 1967, Gallery Kormendy, Alexandria, Va., 1979, Tolley Galleries, Washington, 1983; represented in permanent collections: U.S. House of Reps., Washington, Md. State Exec. Mansion, Annapolis, Md., Nat. Hdqtrs. Am. Legion, Washington; Nat. Hdqtrs. DAR, Washington; Hdqrs. Fed. Deposit Ins. Corp., Washington, and others. Decorated Air Medal with one star. Mem. Artists Equity Assn., Fairfax County Council of Arts, Landscape Artists of Washington. Republican. Office: 6811 White Rock Rd Clifton VA 22024

HENNING, CHARLES PAUL, acquisition management analyst; b. Ft. Worth, Sept. 2, 1956; s. William Vernon and Nancy Virginia (Levi) H. B.A., Tex. U.-Austin, 1980; M.A. Pub. Policy, U. Chgo., 1982. Research asst. U. Chgo., 1981-82; research cons. No. Trust Co., Chgo., 1981; econ. strategic planning analyst Gen. Dynamics, Ft. Worth, 1983-85; acquisition management analyst Analytic Scis. Corp., Arlington, Va., 1985—; mem. Def. Task Force/Dem. Bus. Council, Washington, 1983—. Arts and Scis. Found. scholar, 1975, 80; U. Chgo. scholar, 1980-82. Mem. Am. Econ. Assn., Assn. for Pub. Policy Analysis and Mgmt. Democrat. Christian Ch. Office: Analytic Scis Corp 1700 N Moore St Suite 1220 Arlington VA 22204

HENNING, DAN, professional football coach; b. Bronx, N.Y., June 21, 1942. Student, William and Mary Coll.; m. Sandy Henning; children—Mary, Patty, Terry, Donny, Mike. Player, San Diego Chargers, AFL, 1964-67; asst. coach Homer L. Ferguson High Sch., Newport News, Va., 1967; asst. coach Fla. State U., Tallahassee, 1968-70, 74; asst. coach Va. Tech. U., 1971, 73; asst. coach Houston Oilers, NFL, 1972; asst. coach N.Y. Jets, NFL, 1976-78; asst. coach Miami Dolphins, NFL, 1979-80; asst. coach Washington Redskins, NFL, 1981-82; head coach Atlanta Falcons, NFL, 1983—. Office: care Atlanta Falcons I 85 & Suwanee Rd Suwanee GA 30174

HENNING, EMILIE ANNE, college dean, nursing educator; b. Scotrun, Pa., Dec. 4, 1930; d. Lester Dimmick and Ada (Warner) Detrick. Diploma Methodist Hosp., N.Y.C., 1951; B.S. in Nursing, Seton Hall U., 1962; M.Ed. in Nursing Edn., Columbia U., 1965, Ed.D. in Nursing Edn., 1974. Cons. Newark Maternal/Infant Care Project, 1965-66; from instr. to asst. prof. Rutgers U., Newark, 1966-71, chmn., assoc. prof., 1973-76; dean and prof. Fla. State U., Tallahassee, 1976-82, East Carolina U., Greenville, N.C., 1982—; curriculum cons. univ. schs. of nursing, 1971—. Contbr. chpt. to book, articles to profl. jours. Chmn. Capitol Adv. Council, Fla. Panhandle Health Systems Agy., 1981-82; active in polit. campaigns. Recipient honor cords Sigma Theta Tau, 1985. Mem. N.C. Nurses Assn. (chmn. forum 1983-85), Nat. League for Nursing (bd. rev. 1980—), N.C. League for Nursing, N.C. Deans and Dirs. (sec.-treas. 1983—), N.J. State Nurses Assn. (bd. dirs. 1975-76), Nat. Assn. Women Deans, Adminstrs. and Counselors. Avocation: travel. Home: 76 Quail Ridge Rd Greenville NC 27834 Office: Sch Nursing East Carolina Univ Greenville NC 27834

HENRICH, CAMILLE MARTHA, nurse; b. New Orleans, Feb. 8, 1947; d. William Gregory and Lois Mae (Erickson) H.; m. Leroy Gene Stadler, Sept. 17, 1966 (div. Oct. 1979); children—Andrea, Christopher, Dean, Bethany. R.N., Charity Hosp., R.N., La., Alaska, Wis.; Cert. in urology; diplomate Am. Urology Assn. Allied. Staff nurse Touro Infirmary, New Orleans, 1969-72; clin. nurse Tulane Med. Sch., New Orleans, 1972-73, pediatric urology nurse Univ. Hosp., 1981—; staff nurse Charity Hosp., New Orleans, 1973-74, night supr., 1980-81; staff nurse Holy Cross Hosp., Merrill, Wis., 1975-77; charge nurse Wausau Hosp. (Wis.), 1977-78; emergency nurse Fairbanks Meml. Hosp. (Alaska), 1978, East Jefferson Gen. Hosp., 1978-80. Author articles for profl. jours. Democrat. Roman Catholic. Office: Tulane Medical Center 1415 Tulane Ave New Orleans LA 70112

HENRION, ROSEMARY, nurse; b. Greenville, Miss., Oct. 2, 1930; d. Vincent and Camille (Portera) Provenza; R.N., St. Mary's Sch. Nursing, Galveston, Tex., 1951; B.S. in Nursing, U. Tex. Med. Br., Galveston, 1963; M.S.N. (NIMH fellow 1971), Vanderbilt U., 1972; M.Secondary Edn., U. So. Miss., 1974; cert. logotherapist (diplomate); m. Albert Joseph Henrion, Sept. 8, 1956 (dec.); 1 son, Albert Joseph. Staff nurse St. Mary's Hosp., Galveston, 1951-52; office nurse and pvt. duty surg. nurse, Galveston, 1952-53; head nurse Ob and med.-surg. nursing, Greenville (Miss.) Gen. Hosp., 1953-54, supr. obstetrical nursing, 1954-56; nursing instr. Providence Hosp. Sch. Nursing, Waco, Tex., 1957-59; dir. inservice edn. Meml. Hosp., Gulfport, Miss., 1966-67, asst. dir. nursing service, 1966-67, dir. nursing service, 1967-68; psychiat. clin. nurse specialist Biloxi (Miss.) VA Med. Center, 1972—, in-house cons., 1975—; participant research projects So. Region Edn. Bd., 1973-75; asst. clin. prof. psychiat.-mental health nursing Grad. Sch. Nursing, La. State U., New Orleans, 1975-77; mem. Miss. Bd. of Nursing, 1975-79, pres., 1976-78. Mem. Pass Christian Carnival Assn., 1975-78; ednl. council local chpt. Am. Cancer Soc., 1977. Recipient service award Biloxi VA Center, 1970, 79; Menninger Found. fellow, 1978—. Mem. Am. Nurses Assn., Dist. Nurses Assn. (membership com., 1964-66, chmn., 1966-67), Miss. Nurses Assn. (vice chmn., program chmn. spl. interest group 1972-75), Council Advanced Practitioners Psychiat.-Mental Health Nursing, U. Tex. Alumni Assn., Vanderbilt U. Alumni Assn., U. So. Miss. Alumni Assn., Am. Bus. Women's Assn., Sigma Theta Tau. Roman Catholic. Club: Officers. Researcher, speaker, panelist profl. confs., contbr. articles in field to pubis. Home: 19 Wenmar Ave Pass Christian MS 39571 Office: VA Med Center Biloxi MS 39571

HENRY, ALAN, mayor. Mayor of Lubbock, Tex. Office: PO Box 2000 Lubbock TX 79457*

HENRY, CHARLES EDWIN, chem. co. exec.; b. Cleve., Sept. 20, 1932; s. Ewald C. and Hanna E. (Lang) H.; B.S. in Chem. Engring., Case Inst. Tech., 1954; m. Georgia June Eichner, Jan. 30, 1953; children—Susan Elaine, David Charles. Staff tech. devel. B.F. Goodrich, 1954-58; tech. sales Tenn. Products & Chems., 1958-60; tech. sales Diamond Shamrock Corp., 1960-63, tech. mktg. and sales mgmt., 1963-69, v.p. mktg. and sales, 1969-75; v.p. mktg. Va. Chems., Inc., 1975—; v.p., gen. mgr. UCB Chem. Corp., Joint Venture UCB S.A. Del. Republican State Conv., 1981; active United Fund; sustaining mem. Chrysler Mus., 1977-82. Mem. Am. Inst. Chem. Engrs., Am. Chem. Soc., TAPPI, PIMA, SOCMA, Sigma Alpha Epsilon, Alpha Phi Omega. Lutheran. Club: Chemists (N.Y.C.); Cavalier Golf and Yacht. Home: 908 Oriole Dr Virginia Beach VA 23451 Office: 3340 W Norfolk Rd Portsmouth VA 23703

HENRY, DAN BOYD, dentist; b. Texarkana, Tex., Aug. 19, 1946; s. Edward Maxwell and Helen Louise (Adams) H.; m. Melinda Mavourneen Conn, June 11, 1969; children—Matthew Jackson, Kelly Aileen. Assoc. Sci., Pensacola Jr. Coll., 1967; B.S., Fla. State U., 1970, M.S. in Genetics, 1972; D.D.S., U. Md., 1975. Pvt. practice dentistry, Pensacola, Fla., 1979—. Served to capt. USAF, 1975-78. Mem. ADA, Fla. State Dental Assn., Escambia Santa Rosa Dental Soc., Gamma Phi Delta. Democrat. Methodist. Avocations: advanced woodworking; boating. Office: 4731 N Davis Hwy Pensacola FL 32503

HENRY, DAVID HOWE, II, former diplomat, internat. orgn. ofcl.; b. Geneva, N.Y., May 19, 1918; s. David Max and Dorothy (Buley) H.; student Hobart Coll., 1935-37, Sorbonne, 1937-38; A.B., Columbia U., 1939, student Russian Inst., 1948-49; student Harvard U., 1944-45, Nat. War Coll., 1957-58; m. Margaret Beard, Nov. 16, 1946; children— David Beard, Peter York, Michael Max, Susan. Ins. agt., 1939-41; mem. fgn. service Dept. State, 1941-71, assigned Montreal, 1941-42, Beirut, 1942-44, Washington, 1944-45, 48-52, 57-66, 70, Moscow, 1945-48, 52-54, Vladivostok, 1945-46, Berlin, 1955-57; acting dir. Office Research and Intelligence Sino-Soviet bloc, 1958-59; faculty Nat. War Coll., 1959-61; dep. dir. Office Soviet Affairs, 1961-64; dir. Office Soviet Affairs, 1964-65, Policy Planning Council, 1965-66; dep. chief of mission Am. embassy, Reykjavik, Iceland, 1966-69; info. systems specialist, 1970; polit. and security council affairs UN, N.Y.C., 1971-78. Mem. Kappa Alpha. Presbyterian. Club: Rotary. Home: Seaside Apt 20 3541 NE Ocean Blvd Jensen Beach FL 33457

HENRY, DAVID RAY, communications executive; b. Henryetta, Okla., Oct. 1, 1953; s. Raymond Paul Henry and Joan Claudia (Watzke) Maetzold; m. Yvonne McReynolds, July 3, 1976. B.B.A., U. Okla., 1975, M.B.A., 1979. Account exec. AT&T Long Lines, Dallas, 1979-81, account exec. II, 1982—, also cert. industry cons. Mem. Dallas Mus. Fine Arts; supporting mem. Dallas council Boy Scouts Am. Mem. Assn. M.B.A. Execs., Internat. Teleconferencing Assn. Republican. Episcopalian. Home: 9010 Bryson Dr Dallas TX 75238 Office: AT&T Communications 717 N Harwood Suite 2320 Dallas TX 75201

HENRY, GORDON CHARLES, journalism educator, college administrator; b. Sioux City, Iowa, July 29, 1931; s. H. John and Edith (Briggs) H.; m. Audrey Fae Roorda, Aug. 8, 1957; children—Laura Jayne, Karl Steven. B.A. in Speech, Iowa State Tchrs. Coll., 1953; M.A. in Journalism, U. Iowa, 1960. Tchr. Iowa Pub. Schs., 1955-59; with Western Electric Co., Cicero and Aurora, Ill., 1960-67; dir. news service Ft. Hays Kans. State Coll., Hays, 1967-69; dir. coll. relations Newberry Coll., S.C., 1969—. Bd. dirs. United Way Midlands, Newberry and Columbia, S.C., 1970-86. Served with USN, 1953-55. Mem. Council for Advancement Support Edn., Nat. Council Coll. Publs. Advisors, Carolina News Service Orgn., S.C. Press Assn., Sigma Delta Chi. Republican. Methodist. Lodge: Rotary. Avocations: photography; traveling; reading mysteries; attending theatre. Home: 1609 Circle Dr Newberry SC 29108 Office: Newberry Coll Newberry SC 29108

HENRY, JACK HOPKINS, orthopedic surgeon; b. Lubbock, Tex., Apr. 20, 1937; s. Wells Blackburn and Mattie Allene (Hopkins) H.; B.A. in Chemistry, Tex. Tech U., 1960; M.D., U. Tex., 1964; m. Jane Hopkins Underwood, June 10, 1965; children—David Blackburn, Robert Underwood. Intern, Ben Taub Hosp., Houston, 1964-65; resident in gen. surgery U. Pa. Hosp., 1965-66; resident in orthopedic surgery Columbia-Presbyn. Med. Center, N.Y.C., 1966-69, sr. Annie C. Kane fellow in hip surgery, 1971-72; practice medicine specializing in orthopedic surgery, San Antonio, 1972—; mem. staff Meth., Bapt., Santa Rosa, Nix Meml., N.E. Bapt., Met. Gen., San Antonio Community hosps.; nat. v.p. student AMA, 1963-64. Served to maj. USAF, 1969-71. Carl Berg traveling fellow, 1972. Diplomate Am. Bd. Orthopedic Surgery. Mem. Am. Acad. Orthosurgeons, Phi Gamma Delta, Nu Sigma Nu. Presbyn. Address: 8042 Wurzbach Rd Suite 540 San Antonio TX 78229

HENRY, JAMES HERBERT, defense analyst; b. Toronto, Can., Oct. 29, 1922; came to U.S., 1946; naturalized, 1951; s. James and Christiana Munro (Sneath) H.; m. Marion Dare Wetmore, May 4, 1949; children—James Watson, Nan Paterson, John Badger. B.A.Sc., U. Toronto, 1943; S.M., MIT, 1948. Registered profl. engr., D.C., Ont., Can. Research asst., instr. MIT, Cambridge, 1946-48; chief air def. div. Ops. Research Office, Johns Hopkins U., Chevy Chase, Md., 1948-62; sr. staff mem. Inst. Def. Analyses, Alexandria, Va., 1962—. Contbr. articles to profl. jours. Served to lt. Royal Can. Vol. Res.,

1943-46. Fellow Ops. Research Soc. Am., 1955. Mem. Ops. Research Soc. Am., Washington Ops. Research Mgmt. Sci. Council. Episcopalian. Avocations: oenology; viticulture. Home: 9 Primrose St Chevy Chase MD 20815 Office: Inst Def Analyses 1801 N Beauregard St Alexandria VA 22311

HENRY, JANE COVINGTON, medical technologist; b. Mayfield, Ky., Apr. 10, 1917; d. George Jenkins and Bessie (Key) Covington; m. Earl O'Dell Henry, Oct. 20, 1941; 1 son, Earl O'Dell. A.B., Western Ky. State Tchrs. Coll., 1938; postgrad. Murray (Ky.) State Coll., 1952; M.T., VA Sch. Med. Tech., 1953. Cert. med. technologist, histotechnologist Am. Soc. Clin. Pathologists. Tchr. art Clinton (Tenn.) Grammar Sch., 1938-39; tchr. art and English, Christenberry Jr. High Sch., Knoxville, Tenn., 1939-41; supr. histotech. VA Med. Ctr., Nashville, 1959-76, supr. diagnostic morphology, 1976—; tchr. VA Hosp. Sch. Med. Tech., 1959-76, Aquinas Coll., 1980—. Mem. Soc. Med. Technologists, Nat. Soc. Histotech. (charter), Tenn. Soc. Histotech. (founder). Methodist. Clubs: Altrusa, Hillwood Country (Nashville). Home: 436 Westview Ave Nashville TN 37205 Office: VA Medical Center 1310 24th Ave S Nashville TN 37203

HENRY, JOAN CAROL, college dean; b. Detroit, Nov. 18, 1944; d. John Wilson and Helen (Morrison) Farris; m. James H. Henry, Aug. 4, 1962 (div. 1983); children—James H., Jr., Andrea Leigh. B.A. in Social Studies and English magna cum laude, Marshall U., 1966, M.A. in History, 1973; postgrad., W.Va. U., 1984. Social worker Dept. Welfare, Logan, W.Va., 1966; pub. sch. tchr. Logan County Bd. Edn., Logan, 1966-73; instr. So. W.Va. Community Coll., Logan, 1979-82, chmn. humanities, 1982-84, assoc. dean instrn., 1984—, chmn. basic skills com., 1980-81, coordinator music seminars, 1983, chmn. fin. and adminstrn. self-study com., 1982-83, supr. track 12 programs, 1983-84, coordinator off-campus classes, 1984—; state ad hoc liberal arts com. W.Va. Bd. Regents, Charleston, 1984—. Editor: The Little Messenger, 1983-84. Sec. bd. Justice Christian Ch., Justice Addition, 1982-84, youth dir., 1982-84, dir. vacation Bible sch., 1982-84; supr. Community Helpers, Justice Addition, 1982-84; pres. homeroom mothers Justice Grade Sch., 1984—. Mem. W.Va. Community Coll. Assn., W.Va. Assn. Acad. Deans, W.Va. Reading Assn., W.Va. Coll. Council, Internat. Reading Assn. Chi Rho (dist. rep., 1982-84). Lodge: Order Eastern Star (Esther 1981, 82). Avocations: local history; traveling; reading. Home: 460 Palmer Ave Logan WV 25601 Office: So WVa Community Coll Dempsey Branch Rd Logan WV 25601

HENRY, JOHN JAMES, physicist; b. White Pine, Tenn., Feb. 12, 1929; s. Herbert Holloway and Clara (Spurgeon) H.; student U. Fla., 1946-48; B.S., Lincoln Meml. U., 1954; m. Audrey Duffield, Sept. 14, 1954: children—Mark Stephen, Claudia Alexandra, John James. Instrument technician Carbide & Carbon Chem. Co., Oak Ridge, 1954-56; asso. physicist Union Carbide Corp., Oak Ridge, 1956-61, physicist nuclear div., 1961-74, devel. specialist, 1974-76, devel. staff I, 1976-84; devel. staff I, Martin Marietta Energy Systems, Oak Ridge, 1984—. Instr. transistor circuit theory Oak Ridge Adult Edn. Program, 1962-65. Scoutmaster, Boy Scouts Am., Oak Ridge, 1960-62; tympanist Oak Ridge Symphony Orch., 1965-73, publicity chmn., 1966-67, v.p., 1968-69. Served with USMC, 1949-52. Recipient IR-100 award Industrial Research Mag., 1979. Mem. Instrument Soc. Am. (sr.), AAAS, IEEE. Episcopalian (vestryman 1974-76, 84—, chmn. music and worship com. 1974-75, chmn. outreach com. 1976). Clubs: Atomic City Stamp (editor 1978, v.p. 1981-83); Commodore Users (pres. 1984) (Oak Ridge). Patentee in field. Home: 639 Pennsylvania Ave Oak Ridge TN 37830 Office: K-25 Plant Oak Ridge TN 37830

HENRY, KATHERINE SAVAGE, physician; b. Marietta, Ga., Aug. 30, 1944; d. James Ernest and Audrey Louise (Armstrong) Savage; B.A., Birmingham-So. Coll., 1966; M.D., Emory U., 1971. Intern, resident in internal medicine Ga. Bapt. Hosp., Atlanta, 1971-73; emergency room physician Baylor Med. Center, Dallas, 1973-74; family physician The Family Clinic, Garland, Tex., 1974; family practice medicine, Richardson, Tex., 1974—; chmn. dept. family practice Richardson Gen. Hosp., 1975; exec. com. Richardson Med. Ctr., 1975-78, chmn. dept. family practice, 1983—; clin. asst. prof. family practice and community medicine U. Tex. Health Scis. Ctr.-Dallas; cons. health care Richardson YWCA; first physician, designer health service U. Tex., Dallas, 1974-76. Chmn. Med. com. Dallas Hospice, Inc., 1984:13 . Diplomate Am. Bd. Family Practice. Fellow Am. Acad. Family Physicians, Am. Coll. Cryosurgery; mem. AMA (physicians recognition award), Am., Tex. acads. family practice, Dallas County Med. Soc., Tex. Med. Assn., Am. Med. Women's Assn. (charter pres. Dallas chpt. 1980). Home: 16007 Ranchita Dr Dallas TX 75248 Office: 721 W Arapaho Suite 2 Richardson TX 75080

HENRY, MARK SIMPSON, telecommunications executive, researcher; b. Norfolk, Va., July 10, 1954; s. Frank Rowe and Florence Marie (Sawyer) H.; m. Susan Diane Gilley, Jan. 20, 1979; children—Danica Lynne, Mark Simpson, Jr. B.A., U. Richmond, 1976; M.S. Va. Poly. Inst. and State U., 1978. Research asst. Va. Poly. Inst. and State U., Blacksburg, 1976-78; market analyst C & P Telephone Co., Washington, 1978-81, econ. analyst, 1981-84; fin. analyst Bell Atlantic Corp., Arlington, Va., 1984—. Contbr. articles to profl. publs. Dir., Royal Ambassador Youth Orgn., Alexandria, Va., 1979-81; dir., treas. Homeowners Assn., Fredericksburg, Va., 1982-84; co-chmn. Fredericksburg Jaycees, 1983-84. Mem. Am. Sociol. Assn., So. Sociol. Soc., D.C. Sociol. Soc., Christian Sociologists. Republican. Baptist. Avocation: boating. Home: 14704 Braddock Rd Centreville VA 22020 Office: Bell Atlantic Corp 1310 N Courthouse Rd Arlington VA

HENRY, THORNTON MONTAGU, lawyer; b. Bermuda, May 8, 1943; s. Otis R. and Barbara M. Henry; m. Ann Portlock, Aug. 28, 1971; children—Ruth Montagu, Thornton Bradshaw, John Gordon. B.A., Washington and Lee U., 1966, LL.B., 1969; LL.M., Georgetown U. Bar: Fla. 1972, U.S. Tax Ct., U.S. Ct. Claims, U.S. Dist. Ct. (so. dist.) Fla., U.S. Ct. Appeals (11th cir.). Cert. in taxation, Fla. Tax law specialist IRS, Washington, 1972-74; tax law dept. Jones & Foster, P.A., West Palm Beach, Fla., 1974—; prof. Am. Coll. Mem. endowment com. United Way; mem. deferred giving com. Palm Beach Jr. Coll. Found.; ruling elder Meml. Presbyterian Ch.; bd. dirs., chmn. long-range planning com. Rehab. Ctr. Children & Adults, Inc., Palm Beach; mem. Planned Giving Council Palm Beach County. Served to capt. C.E., U.S. Army, 1970-72. Mem. ABA (tax com.), Fla. Bar Assn., Fla. Bar (exec. council tax sect.; chmn. com. profl. corps.), Palm Beach County Bar Assn. (probate and guardianship com.), East Coast Estate Planning Council, Indian River Estate Planning Council, Martin County Estate Planning Council, Palm Beach Tax Inst. Lodge: Kiwanis (dir., pres.-elect). Office: PO Drawer E West Palm Beach FL 33402

HENSARLING, WILLIAM A., JR., savs. and loan exec.; b. Jourdanton, Tex., July 25, 1921; s. William A. and Mary Ella (Winn) H.; student U. Tex., 1938-42; m. Bobbie Melba Pytel, Feb. 16, 1943; children—James L., Gary A., Robert G. Pres. dir. Garner Abstract & Land Co., Uvalde, Tex., 1946—; owner Hensarling Ins. Agy., Uvalde, 1948—; chmn. bd., sr. v.p. chief exec. officer First Savs & Loan Assn. div. Home Savs. & Loan Assn., Uvalde, 1949—. Mem. Planning Bd., City of Uvalde, 1948-50; past pres. Uvalde Area Devel. Found.; bd. dirs. Uvalde Meml. Hosp., 1956-62, chmn., 1962. Served to lt. col. USAF, 1942-46. Mem. U.S. League Savs. Assns., Tex. Savs. and Loan League (past dir.), Uvalde C. of C. (past dir.). Democrat. Baptist. Clubs: Rotary, Masons. Home: 900 Cherry St Uvalde TX 78801 Office: 400 N Getty St Uvalde TX 78801

HENSEL, ROBIN ANN MORGAN, mathematician; b. Buffalo, Dec. 1, 1960; d. Robert R. and Vivian J. (Kline) Morgan; m. John Peter Max Hensel, Aug. 27, 1983. B.S. in Math., Wheaton Coll., 1981; M.A., SUNY-Buffalo, 1983; postgrad. in Math. Higher Edn., W.Va. U., 1984—. Mathematician, Morgantown Energy Tech. Ctr., U.S. Dept. Energy, W.Va., 1983—. Violinist Morgantown Community Arts Orch., 1984—, Amherst Symphony, N.Y., 1981-83; instr. ARC, 1982. N.Y. State Regents scholar, 1978. Mem. Am. Math. Soc., Cum Laude Soc., Assn. Women in Math. Republican. Mem. Christian and Missionary Alliance. Avocations: swimming; tennis; bowling; music; camping. Home: 69 Estate Dr Morgantown WV 26505 Office: US Dept Energy PO Box 880 Morgantown WV 26505

HENSHAW, SIGRID MARGUERITE, lawyer, accountant; b. Des Moines, Aug. 19, 1932; d. Hadar Oscar and Marguerite (Gonda) Ortman; m. Harold W. Henshaw, Apr. 2, 1977. B.B.A. with distinction, Northwestern U., 1963; J.D., South Tex. Coll. Law, 1978. Bar: Okla. 1978; C.P.A., Ill., Tex., Okla. Managerial positions with C.P.A. firms and various corps., Phoenix, Chgo. and Los Angeles, 1955-71; asst. sec., dir. corporate tax Cordura, Inc., Los Angeles, 1971-73, Geosource, Ind., Houston, 1973-76; C.P.A. in individual practice, Tulsa, 1977—; sole practice law, Tulsa, 1978-80; mng. atty. Henshaw & Leblang, Tulsa, 1980—. Mem. ABA (tax sect.), Okla. Bar Assn., Tulsa County Bar Assn., Assn. Am. Trial Lawyers (sustaining), Okla. Soc. C.P.A.s Tex. Soc. C.P.A.s, Phi Alpha Delta. Office: Henshaw & Leblang 7661 E 61st St Suite 251 Tulsa OK 74133

HENTON, WILLIS RYAN, bishop; b. McCook, Nebr., July 5, 1925; s. Burr Milton and Clara Vaire (Godown) H.; B.A., Kearney State Coll., 1949; S.T.B., Gen. Theol. Sem., N.Y., 1952, S.T.D., 1972; D.D., U. of South, 1972; m. Martha Somerville Bishop, June 7, 1952; 1 son, David. Ordained priest Episcopal Ch., 1953, consecrated bishop, 1971; missionary, Mountain Province, Philippines, 1952-57; asst. pastor, N.Y.C., 1957-58; rector ch., Mansfield, La., 1958-61, Baton Rouge, 1961-64; archdeacon of La., 1964-71; bishop coadjutor of N.W. Tex., 1971-72, bishop, 1972-80, bishop of Western La., 1980—. Trustee, regent U. of South; trustee Sem. of Southwest. Home: PO Box 4046 Alexandria LA 71301

HENTSCHEL, DAVID A., diversified energy company executive; b. Kansas City, Kans., 1934. B.S., La. State U., 1957, Okla. State U., 1957. Reservoir engr. Ark. Fuel Corp., 1957-61; with Cities Services Corp., Tulsa, 1961—, prodn. engr., 1961-64, gas ops. engr., 1964-65, buyer purchasing div., 1965-68, auto services mgr., 1968-70, gen. mgr. purchasing, 1970-74, gen. mgr. so. region, 1974-77, v.p. western internat. area, 1979-80, exec. v.p. planning, 1980-82, exec. v.p., 1982-85, chmn., chief exec. officer, 1985—. Address: Cities Services Corp Cities Service Bldg Tulsa OK 74102*

HERBAN, NANCY LYNN, nursing educator, clinical nurse specialist; b. Kansas City, Mo., Feb. 16, 1934; d. E. Frank and Sara Jane (Gass) Barnes; m. James F. Herban, Aug. 9, 1958 (div. 1977); 1 son, David Andre. Diploma, St. Luke's Hosp. Sch. Nursing, Kansas City, Mo., 1955; B.S.N., Mo. Valley Coll., 1956; M.S. in Hygiene, Tulane U., 1967; M.S.N., U. Ala., 1982, D.S.N., U. Ala. at Birmingham, 1986. R.N., Miss., Ala. Mem. staff St. Luke's Hosp., Kansas City, 1955-56, Kennewick (Wash.) Gen. Hosp., 1956-57; with Vis. Nurses Assn., New Orleans, 1960; mem. staff Touro Infirmary, New Orleans, 1960-62, Charity Hosp., New Orleans, 1962-64; with div. tropical medicine Tulane U. Sch. Medicine, 1964-67; with dept. pharmacology La. State U. Sch. Medicine, 1967-69; instr. pediatrics Meharry Med. Coll., Nashville, 1969-71, Vanderbilt U. Sch. Nursing, Nashville, 1971-72, Tenn. State U. dept. nursing, Nashville, 1972; with Delta Community Hosp. Health Ctr., Mound Bayou, Miss., 1973; asst. prof. Ind. U. Sch. Nursing, Indpls., 1973-75; asst. prof. and dir. grad. program in nursing Miss. U. for Women, Columbus, 1975-81, asst. prof., 1981—; clin. nurse specialist The Pines Alcoholic Rehab. Ctr., Columbus, 1982—; cons. Emory U. Sch. Nursing, 1981-82, Birmingham-Jefferson County Women's Ctr., 1982. Served with Nurse Corps, USAF, 1957-60. Recipient Golden Poet award, 1985; HEW grantee, 1974, 75, W.K. Kellogg grantee, 1978. Mem. Am. Nurses Assn., So. Health Assn. (Hall of Fame of pub. health nursing 1982), Miss. Nurses Assn., DAR, Sigma Theta Tau. Baptist. Author: (with C. Braden) Community Health: A Systems Approach, 1976; mem. editorial bd. Jour. So. Health, 1982—; contbr. articles to profl. jours. Home: 2811 Forrest Glen Rd Columbus MS 39701 Office: Miss U for Women Sch Nursing Columbus MS 39701

HERBEIN, DONALD BRUCE, data processing education administrator; b. Baden, Pa., Aug. 5, 1932; s. Earl High and Elsie Mae (Fields) H.; m. Sally Roberts, Nov. 29, 1958; children—William, Susan, Elizabeth. B.A., Pa. State U.-University Park, 1954. Mktg. rep. IBM Corp., South Bend, Ind. and Detroit, 1959-68, mktg. instr., Detroit, 1968-69, mktg. mgr., 1970-71, systems engring. mgr., 1972-73, regional edn. mgr., 1974-76, nat. program adminstr., Atlanta, 1977—. Bd. dirs. Lady Tara Classic, Atlanta, 1983-84; chmn. bd. Ga. Spl. Olympics, Atlanta, 1985-86. Served to capt. USAF, 1954-57. Recipient numerous co. awards. Episcopalian. Lodge: Rotary (pres. Sandy Springs 1982-83, pres. Atlanta).

HERBERT, DAVID CHARLES, emergency physician; b. Port Arthur, Tex., Nov. 2, 1949; s. James Francis and Leah Celestine (Crespo) H.; m. Brenda Kay Yates, Sept. 20, 1975; children—Jacqueline Kay, Mark David. Student Amarillo Coll., 1967-70; B.S. in Math., West Tex. State U., 1972; M.D. Tex. Tech U., 1975. Diplomate Am. Bd. Emergency Medicine. Resident in surgery Wilford Hall U.S. Air Force Med. Ctr., Lackland AFB, Tex., 1975-76; chief Aerospace Medicine Clinic, Reese AFB, Tex., 1976-78; emergency physician Meth. Hosp., Lubbock, Tex., 1978-84; dir. emergency services Angelo Community Hosp., San Angelo, Tex., 1983—. Served as capt. USAF, 1975-78. Recipient Odessie Cleavenger award West Tex. State U., 1972; Physiology award Tex. Tech Sch. Medicine, 1973; Lange Pubs. award, 1974. Mem. Am. Coll. Emergency Physicians, Tex. Med. Assn., AMA, So. Med. Assn. Republican. Baptist.

HERBERT, GEORGE RICHARD, research executive; b. Grand Rapids, Mich., Oct. 3, 1922. Student Mich. State U., 1942, 47-48; B.S.E.E., U.S. Naval Acad., 1945; D.Sc. (hon.), N.C. State U., 1967; LL.D., Duke U., 1978, U. N.C., 1984. Instr. Mich. State U., East Lansing, 1947-48; asst. to dir. Stanford Research Inst., Menlo Park, Calif., 1948-51, mgr. bus. ops., 1951-55, exec. assoc. dir., 1955-56; treas. Am. and Fgn. Power Co., N.Y.C., 1956-58; pres. Research Triangle Inst., Research Triangle Park, N.C., 1958—; mem. bd. sci. and tech. for internat. devel. Nat. Acad. Scis., 1978-81; mem., sec. N.C. Sci. and Tech. Com., 1963-79; vice-chair bd. trustee N.C. Sch. Sci. and Math., 1978-80; mem. tech. adv. bd. U.S. Dept. Commerce, 1964-69, chair panel high speed ground transp., 1966-67; U.S. del. Conf. Sino-Am. Sci. Cooperation, 1968; chair bd. dirs. Microelectronics Ctr. N.C., 1980—; mem. Transp. Research and Edn. Council, U. N.C., 1976—, N.C. Atomic Energy Adv. Com., 1964-71; dir. Central Carolina Bank, Duke Power Co. Contbr. articles to profl. jours. Trustee Triangle Univs. Ctr. Advanced Studies, 1976—, Found. for Internat. Progress in Mgmt., 1957-58, Duke U., 1985—; bd. visitors Sch. Engring., Duke U., 1967-79, chair, 1973-76; bd. dirs. N.C. Engring. Found., Inc., 1977-81; bd. dirs. Oak Ridge Associated Univs., 1971-73, 78-80, 81-83, 84-85, v.p., 1979-85. Served as ensign USN, 1945-47. Office: Research Triangle Inst Research Triangle Park NC 27709

HERBERT, IRA C., food processing company executive; b. Chgo., Oct. 5, 1927; s. Solomon David and Helen (Burstyn) Chizever; m. Lila Faye Eilman, Jan. 6, 1951; children—Carrie Jo, Jeffrey, Fred. B.A., Mich. State U., 1950. Account exec. McFarland Aveyard, Chgo., 1951-56; account supr. Edward H. Weiss, Chgo., 1956-63; v.p. McCann Erickson, Los Angeles and Atlanta, 1963-65; sr. v.p. Coca-Cola U.S.A., 1965-74; exec. v.p. Coca-Cola Co., pres. food div., from 1975, exec. v.p., 1979—; dir. Pabst Brewing Co., Tex. Commerce Bank. Served with USAAF, 1945-47; with U.S. Army, 1951-52. Mem. Advt. Council (dir.). Jewish. Clubs: Westwood Country, Univ. (Houston); Standard, Commerce (Atlanta). Office: Coca-Cola Co 310 North Ave NW Atlanta GA 30313*

HERD, JOHN KENNETH, educator; b. New Brunswick, N.J., Jan. 12, 1929; s. Edmund John Moffat and Edith Marion (Venn) H.; m. Kathryn Estelle Mitchell, Mar 3, 1956; children—Jeffrey Brian, Daniel Gordon, Barbara Allison. B.S., Rutgers U., 1950; M.D., Cornell U., 1954. Pediatric intern U. Rochester, N.Y., 1954-55, asst. resident pediatrics, 1955-56; asst. resident pathology in pediatrics Babies Hosp., N.Y.C., asst. pathologist Columbia U. Coll. Physicians and Surgeons, N.Y.C., 1956-57; assoc. resident pediatrics U. Rochester, 1959-60, postdoctoral fellow, 1960-63; asst. prof. pediatrics, Buswell fellow SUNY-Buffalo, 1963-67, research asst. prof. pediatrics, 1969-72; spl. NIH fellow pediatrics U. Chgo., 1967-69, assoc. prof. pediatrics Creighton U., Omaha, 1972-76, prof. pediatrics, 1976-78; prof. pediatrics East Tenn. State U., Johnson City, 1978—; cons. in field. Contbr. articles to profl. jours. Chmn. med. adv. com. Nebr. chpt. Arthritis Found., 1974-76, mem. governing bd., N.Y.C., 1975-76. Served to capt. M.C., U.S. Army, 1957-59. Recipient Bausch & Lomb Sci. award, 1946; Rutgers U. Oakley Van der Poel prize, 1950; Arthritis and Rheumatism Found. postdoctoral fellow, 1960-63; NIH spl. fellow, 1967-69; NIAMD grantee, 1972-75, others. Fellow Am. Acad. Pediatrics; mem. Am. Rheumatism Assn., AAUP, AAAS, Midwest Soc. Pediatric Research, Soc. Complex Carbohydrates, Tissue Culture Assn., Omaha Midwest Clin. Soc., Fedn. Am. Scientists, Soc. for Exptl. Biology and Medicine, N.Y. Acad. Sci., Sigma Xi. Democrat. Home: 715 Judith Dr Johnson City TN 37601 Office: PO Box 19840A Pediatrics East Tenn State Univ Johnson City TN 37614

HEREFORD, FRANK LOUCKS, JR., retired university president; b. Lake Charles, La., July 18, 1923; s. Frank L. and Marguerite (Roussel) H.; m. Ann Lane, Jan. 3, 1948; children—Frank, Sarah, Robert. B.A., U. Va., 1943, Ph.D. in Physics, 1947; D.Sc., Fla. Inst. Tech., 1974; LL.D., Hampden-Sydney Coll., 1974. Physicist Bartol Research Found., Swarthmore, Pa., 1947-49; mem. faculty U. Va., 1949—, prof. physics, 1952—, dean, 1962-66, Robert C. Taylor prof. physics, 1966—, provost, v.p., 1966-71, pres., 1974-85; Fulbright scholar U. Birmingham, Eng., 1957-58; vis. prof. U. St. Andrews, Scotland, 1971-72; dir. Gould, Inc., Rolling Meadows, Ill. Contbr. profl. jours. Bd. govs. Belfield Sch., Charlottesville, 1959-62, 63-65, chmn. bd., 1962; bd. dirs. St. Anne's Sch., Charlottesville, 1966-70; trustee Woodberry Forest Sch., 1968-74, Mariner's Mus., Newport News, Va., 1975-85. Recipient Devel. award U.S. Navy Ordnance Dept., 1945; Horsley Research prize Va. Acad. Sci., 1953. Fellow Am. Phys. Soc. (chmn. Southeastern sect. 1961-62), Phi Beta Kappa, Sigma Xi, Omicron Delta Kappa, Alpha Tau Omega. Home: Carr's Hill Charlottesville VA 22901

HERGE, HENRY CURTIS, SR., retired educator; b. Bklyn., June 29, 1905; s. Henry John and Theresa (Maaz) H.; B.S., N.Y. U., 1929, M.A., 1933, Ed.D., 1942; M.A. (hon.), Wesleyan U., 1946; Ph.D., Yale U., 1956; m. Josephine E. Breen, July 2, 1931 (dec. 1975); children—Joel Curtis, Henry Curtis; m. Alice V. Wolfram, 1976. Tchr. English high sch., Port Washington, N.Y., 1928-38; dist. prin., Bayville, N.Y., 1938-41, Bellmore, N.Y., 1941-45; asst. dir. study on Armed Services edn. programs Am. Council Edn., Washington, 1945-46; dir. higher edn. and tchr. certification Conn. Dept. Edn., 1946-53; dean, prof. edn. Rutgers U., 1953-64, prof., 1964-75, prof. emeritus, 1975—, program asso. Rutgers Internat. Center, 1968-75; vis. prof. edn. U. So. Calif., summer 1964, N.Y. U., 1964-65. Del. White House Conf. Edn., 1957; dir. nationwide survey edn. Ministry Edn., Asuncion, Paraguay, 1961; team leader Rutgers-U.S. AID field survey, Zambia and Malawi, 1961-62; chief edn. devel. officer AID mission to Jamaica, 1966-68; rapporteur Italian U. Rectors Ednl. Exchange Project, 1969-70; Fulbright scholar Italian Univs., summer 1970. Trustee Shadow Lake Assn. (Vt.), 1975-76, pres., 1976-78, now hon. life mem.; sec. Fedn. Lakes Assn., No. Vt. 1980-84; chmn. bd. trustees Coll. Hilton Head, Inc., 1984—. Served as lt. comdr. USNR, 1942-48. Recipient certs. of recognition NCCJ, 1958, N.J. Congress Parents and Tchrs., N.J. Vo-Tech. Sch. Dirs., N.J. Secondary Sch. Tchrs. Assn. Mem. Naval Res. Assn. (life), Internat. Study Assn., Am. Assn. Higher Edn., N.J. Congress Parents and Tchrs. (hon. life), N.J. Schoolmasters Club, Phi Delta Kappa, Epsilon Pi Tau (laureate trustee), Kappa Delta Pi (compatriot in edn. 1976). Republican. Presbyterian. Author: Wartime College Training Programs of Armed Services, 1948; The College Teacher, 1965; Disarmament in Western World, 1969; Common Concerns in Higher Edn.; An Italian-American Universities Project, 1971. Contbr. articles to profl. publs. Home: 39 Pineland Rd Hilton Head Island SC 29928

HERIA, FERNANDO EDUARDO, lawyer; b. Consolacion del Sur, Cuba, Oct. 13, 1950; came to U.S., 1962, naturalized, 1972; s. Angel Manuel and Adelaida (Alvarez) H. A.A., Miami-Dade Community Coll., 1973; B.A. in Polit. Sci., Fla. Internat. U., 1975, B.A. in History, 1975; J.D., Thomas M. Colley U., 1979. Bar: Mich. 1979, U.S. Dist. Ct. (ea. dist.) Mich. 1979, Fla. 1980, U.S. Ct. Appeals (5th cir.) 1980, U.S. Dist. Ct. (so. dist.) Fla. 1980, U.S. Dist. Ct. (mid. and no. dists.) Fla. 1981, U.S. Ct. Appeals (11th cir.) 1982, U.S. Supreme Ct. 1983. Sr. law clerk Atty. Gen. Office Mich., Lansing, 1978-79; sr. assoc. Irma W. Hernandez, Hialeah, Fla., 1980-81, ptnr., 1981-83; sole practice, Hialeah, 1983—. Active Fla. Democratic Party, 1972—. Served with U.S. Army, 1970-72. Mem. Assn. Immigration and Nationality Lawyers, Nat. Assn. Criminal Def. Lawyers, Mich. Trial Lawyers Assn., ABA, Assn. Trial Lawyers Am., Nat. Def. Lawyers Am. Roman Catholic. Lodge: Kiwanis. Office: 1780 W 49th St Hialeah FL 33012

HERIN, WILLIAM ABNER, judge; b. Macon, Ga., May 14, 1908; s. William Abner and Caroline (Davenport) H.; m. Frances Christian, Aug. 2, 1952. A.B., U. Fla., 1930, J.D. with honors, 1933. Bar: Fla. Adminstrv. asst. to Fla. congressman, Washington, 1936-38; assoc. Hudson & Cason, Miami, Fla., 1933-48; legis. counsel to Dade del., Tallahassee, Fla., 1939-41; sr. circuit judge 11th Jud. Cir., State of Fla., Miami, 1948-84. Contbr. articles to legal jours. Chmn. adminstrv. bd. First United Methodist Ch., 1970; a founder Boys Clubs of Miami, 1940; hon. bd. dirs., life mem. Met. YMCA 1982; sustaining mem. So. Fla. Council Boy Scouts Am. Recipient Tom C. Clark award Nat. Conf. Met. Cts., 1975; Outstanding award Fla. Grand Jury Assn., 1972; Compass award So. Fla. council Boy Scouts Am., 1957; Met. Dade County Proclamation for Leading Opinion in U.S., Am. Law Rev., 1976. Mem. Fla. Bar (chmn. pub. relations com. 1941), Dade County Bar Assn. (life mem., v.p. 1941), Nat. Conf. Met. Cts. (pres. 1969-70), ABA (life), Am. Law Inst. (life), Phi Beta Kappa, Phi Kappa Phi, Phi Delta Phi, Sigma Nu. Democrat. Methodist. Lodges: Kiwanis (Legion of Honor), Jaycees (past pres. 1941, life mem.). Office: 14 SW 2d Ave Miami FL 33130

HERMAN, CHARLES ROBERT, opera association executive; b. Glendale, Calif., Feb. 24, 1925; s. Floyd Caves and Anna (Merriken) H. A.B. summa cum laude in German, U. So. Calif., 1949. Asst. to head opera dept. U. So. Calif., Los Angeles, 1949-53; asst. mgr., artistic adminstr. Met. Opera, N.Y.C., 1953-72; exec. dir. New World Festival of the Arts, Miami, 1979-82; gen. mgr. Greater Miami Opera Assn., 1973-85. Co-author: From Shoestring to Showpiece, 1985. Panel chmn., panelist Nat. Endowment for the Arts Opera-Musical Theater and State Programs, Washington, 1980-85. Served to 1st lt. U.S. Army, 1944-46, ETO; lt. col. Res. (ret.). Decorated Army Commendation Ribbon, Cavaliere, Order of Merit, Republic of Italy, Officers Cross, Order of Merit, Fed. Republic of Germany, Honor Cross for Arts and Scis., Republic of Austria. Mem. OPERA Am. (treas. 1974-83, pres. 1983-85), Cultural Execs. Council (pres.). Avocations: philately, travel. Office: Greater Miami Opera Assn 1200 Coral Way Miami FL 33145

HERMAN, FRED L., lawyer; b. New Orleans, Mar. 25, 1950; s. Harry and Reba (Hoffman) H.; m. Amanda Luria, Mar. 4, 1975. B.A., Tulane U., 1972; J.D., Loyola U.-New Orleans, 1975. Bar: La. 1975, U.S. Dist. Ct. (ea. dist.) La. 1975, U.S. Ct. Appeals (5th cir.) 1978, U.S. Dist. Ct. (we. and mid. dists.) La. 1981, U.S. Ct. Appeals (11th cir.) 1981. Assoc. Herman & Herman, New Orleans, 1975-80; ptnr. Herman, Herman, Katz & Cotlar, New Orleans, 1980—; adj. prof. Tulane U. Sch. Law, 1982—. Commr. New Orleans Pub. Belt R.R. Commn., 1983—; sec., gen. counsel Odyssey House of La., 1985—. Mem. Fed. Bar Assn., Assn. Trial Lawyers Am., La. Trial Lawyers Assn. (bd. govs. 1983—), La. Bar Assn. Office: Herman Herman Katz & Cotlar 820 O'Keefe Ave New Orleans LA 70113

HERMAN, JAMES JAY, allergist; b. Ft. Worth, Nov. 28, 1947; s. Paul F. and Helen (Levy) H.; m. Rowena Ann Fischer, June 28, 1970; children—Hugh Mitchell, Elana Gabrielle. B.S in Pharmacy with honors, U. Tex., 1970, M.D., 1973. Diplomate Nat. Bd. Med. Examiners, Am. Bd. Pediatrics, Am. Bd. Allergy and Immunology. Research asst. pharmacognosy U. Tex. Coll. Pharmacy, Austin, 1969; intern, resident in pediatrics Children's Meml. Hosp., Northwestern U.-McGaw Med. Ctr., Chgo., 1973-76; fellow pediatrics, allergy-clin. immunology Children's Hosp. Med. Ctr., Harvard U. Med. Sch., Boston, 1976-78, instr. pediatrics, allergy-clin. immunology, 1978-79; asst. prof. pediatrics Northwestern U., Chgo., 1979-83; head div. allergy Children's Meml. Hosp., Chgo., 1979-83; med. adv. bd. Children's Research Found., 1979-83, U. Tex. Health Sci. Ctr., Houston; asst. clin. prof. pediatrics Baylor U., Houston, 1983—; staff Tex. Children's Hosp., St. Luke's Hosp., Hermann Hosp., Cypress-Fairbanks Med. Ctr. Hosp., Meth. Hosp. Mem. Nat. Com. Young Democrats; mem. Ill. Dist. 198 Sch. Coucus; mem. Common Cause, Nat. Audubon Soc. Welch fellow U. Tex., 1967-70; NSF Summer Inst. fellow, 1968-69. Fellow Am. Acad. Pediatrics, Am. Acad. Allergy; mem. Am. Coll. Allergy, Am. Assn. Immunology, Chgo. Immunology Assn., Houston Pediatric Soc., Ill. Allergy Soc., Chgo. Allergy Soc., AAAS, Am. Thoracic Soc., Asthma and Allergy Found. Am., Joint Council Allergy and Clin. Immunology, N.Y. Acad. Scis., Midwest Pediatric Soc., AMA, Tex. Med. Assn., Harris County Med. Soc., Tex. Allergy Soc., Houston Allergy Soc., Phi Eta Sigma, Rho Chi. Jewish. Lodge: B'nai B'rith. Contbr. articles profl. jours. Home: 11827 Moorcreek Houston TX 77070 Office: 11302 Fallbrook Dr Suite 303 Houston TX 77065 also 6600 Fannin Suite 1504 Houston TX 77030

HERMAN, RUSS MICHEL, lawyer; b. New Orleans, Apr. 26, 1942; s. Harry and Reba Nell (Hoffman) H.; m. Barbara Ann Kline, July 5, 1965; children—Stephen Jay, Penny Lynn, Elizabeth Rose. B.A., Tulane U., 1963, LL.B., 1966. Bar: La. 1966, U.S. Dist. Ct. (ea. dist.) La. 1966, U.S. Ct. Appeals (5th cir.) 1970, U.S. Supreme Ct., 1972. Law clk. U.S. Ct. Appeals (4th cir.), New Orleans, 1965-66; ptnr. Herman, Herman, Katz & Cotlar (formerly Herman & Herman), New Orleans, 1966—; sec. Citizens for Justice, Inc., 1980; guest lectr. Tulane U. Law Sch., Loyola U. Law Sch., La. State U. Law Sch., Practising Law Inst.; adj. prof. law Tulane U. Law Sch., 1979—; spl. trial counsel New Orleans Aviation Bd., 1974-76; mem. adv. council La. chpt. Am. Arbitration Assn., 1976—; mem. Civil Dist. Ct. Commn. on Local Rules and Forms, 1979, U.S. Dist. Ct. Com. on Disciplinary Rules and Revision Local Rules, 1979-80; mem. disciplinary com. U.S. Dist. Ct. (ea. dist.) La., 1980—. Mem. New Orleans Bd. Zoning Appeals, 1974-80; bd. dirs. Jewish Welfare Fedn., New Orleans; trustee Jewish Family and Children's Services, New Orleans; campaign chmn. for Gov. David C. Treen in Greater Met. area, 1980, 84. Served with U.S. Air N.G., 1959-65. Named Boss of Yr., New Orleans Legal Secs. Assn., 1981-82; life fellow Roscoe Pound Found. Mem. Fed. Bar Assn., Am. Trial Lawyers Assn. (bd. govs. 1984-87), ABA, La. Bar Assn. (ho. of dels. 1980-81, asst. bar examiner 1975-80), La. Bar Found. (trustee 1980—), La. Trial Lawyers Assn. (pres. 1980-81, Pres.'s award 1977, Leadership award 1981-82). Democrat. Jewish. Home: 5346 Chestnut St New Orleans LA 70115 Office: Herman Herman Katz & Cotlar 820 O'Keefe Ave New Orleans LA 70113

HERMAN, STEPHEN GERALD, ophthalmologist; b. Boston, Sept. 23, 1939; m. Bettina Gershinzon, Mar., 1965. B.S., Rensselaer Poly. Inst., 1961; M.D., Chgo. Med. Sch., 1965. Diplomate Am. Bd. Ophthalmology, Am. Acad. Ophthalmology. Intern USPHS, Boston, 1965-66; resident Bronx Eye Infirmary, N.Y.C., resident, 1968-71; practice medicine specializing in ophthalmology, St. Petersburg and Seminole, Fla., 1971—; clin. asst. prof. U. South Fla. Coll. Medicine, Tampa, 1974-77, 84-86. Served with USPHS, 1966-68, Fellow Am. Acad. Ophthalmology; mem. Fla. Med. Assn., Pinellas County Med. Soc. Avocations: gardening; boating; travel; archeology; collecting antiques. Office: 9375 Seminole Blvd Seminole FL 33542

HERN, MICHAEL GARY, communications company executive; b. Youngstown, Ohio, May 1, 1949; s. Michael and Viola Yolanda (Priley) Hryniak; m. Paula Kaarina Kangas, Oct. 12, 1974; children—Kerstin, Erik. B.S.J., Ohio U., 1971, M.Ed., 1974. Athletic sales dir. U. Wash., Seattle, 1977-78; account exec. Paine Webber, Tampa, Fla., 1978-80; trust officer Landmark Bank, St. Petersburg, Fla., 1982-85; athletic bus. mgr. U. S. Fla., Tampa, 1980-82; dir. mktg. JTP Communications, Inc., Tampa, 1985; account exec. Eva-Tone, Inc., Clearwater, Fla., 1985—. Contbr. investment articles to newspapers and mags. Pres. Clearwater for Youth, 1984. Mem. Pinellas County Sports Authority (mem. spl. com.), Clearwater C. of C. (council chmn. 1985), Ohio U. Alumni (pres. Tampa Bay area 1980—). Republican. Roman Catholic. Clubs: Tampa Sports (bd. dirs. 1979-81), Sertoma (bd. dirs. Clearwater chpt. 1984). Avocations: travel; reading; athletics. Home: 2536 Cypress Bend Dr Clearwater FL 33519 Office: Eva-Tone Inc 4801 Ulmerton Rd Clearwater FL 33518

HERNANDEZ, EDUARDO LUIS, food service director; b. Havana, Cuba, July 20, 1932; came to U.S., 1957; s. Eduardo Francisco and Maria Luisa (Mares) H.; m. Maria Magdalena Velasco, July 21, 1962; children—Eduardo Jr., Carlos, Teresa M., Isabel M. Student U. Havana, 1952-54; B.S., T.A. Edison Coll., 1977. Dir. nutrition and food service DeKalb Pub. Hosp. (Ill.), 1973-75; dir. food service N. Aurora Ctr., Aurora, Ill., 1975-76; food service dietar dir. Community Hosp. Palm Beaches, West Palm Beach, Fla., 1976-78; asst. chief dietary food service U. Miami/Jackson Med. Ctr., Miami, Fla., 1979-83; asst. dir. food service Marriott Corp., Miami, 1983—. Editor bilingual newsletter Centro Hispano-Americano, 1968-70. Pres. Spanish Am. Ctr., Aurora, 1969-70; bd. dirs. Aurora Coordinating Council Community Orgns., 1969-70; rep. Ill. Human Relations Commn., 1970. Mem. Nat. Restaurant Assn. (Silver award 1975), Am. Soc. Hosp. Food Service Adminstrs., Am. Hosp. Assn. Democrat. Roman Catholic. Home: 616 Bird Rd Coral Gables FL 33146 Office: Marriott Corp St Francis 250 W 63rd St Miami Beach FL 33141

HERNANDEZ, GRISELLE CLAUDIA, hospital administrator; b. Havana, Cuba, May 18, 1953; d. Sabino and Maria Cecilia (Vigoa) Hernandez. B.P.A. summa cum laude, Biscayne Coll., 1977; postgrad. Fla. Internat. U., 1977-79. Ednl. services rep. Blue Cross of Fla., Miami, 1971-74, profl. relations rep., 1974-79; mgr. patient acctg. services Mt. Sinai Med. Ctr., Miami, 1980-82, asst. dir. patient fin. services, 1982—, asst. dir. mktg., 1983—; cons. in field; guest prof. Hosp. Mil. Central, Bogota, Colombia, 1983. Ford Found. dance scholar, 1968-69. Mem. Hosp. Fin. Mgmt. Assn., Nat. Orgn. Female Execs., Am. Guild Patient Account Mgrs., Fla. Hosp. Assn. Democrat. Home: 1925 Brickell Ave Apt D702 Miami FL 33129 Office: 4300 Alton Rd Miami Beach FL 33140

HERNANDEZ, PEDRO ARMANDO, civil engineer; b. Havana, Cuba, Aug. 6, 1937; came to U.S., 1971; s. Pedro Jose and Maria del Pilar (Franco) H.; m. Virla Jeannette Torres, Apr. 1, 1978; 1 son, Pedro Armando. B.S. in Civil Engring., U. Havana, 1963; postgrad. diploma in Hydrological Engring., Delft Tech. U., The Netherlands, 1970; M.S., U. Idaho, 1972. Registered profl. engr., Fla. Research asst. Coll. Engring., Water Research Inst., U. Idaho, Moscow, 1971-73; hydrologist III water resources div. S.W. Fla. Water Mgmt. Dist., Brooksville, 1973-78; head hydrology dept. Diaz/Seckinger & Assocs., Tampa, Fla., 1978-81; head drainage dept. Hillsborough County, Fla., 1981-82; dist. engr. Fla. Dept. Environ. Regulation, Tampa, 1982-84; head drainage dept. Hillsborough County, Fla., 1984—. Mem. ASCE, Am. Water Resources Assn. Republican. Baptist. Office: Hillsborough County Div Pub Works PO Box 1110 Tampa FL 33610

HERNANDEZ (HEGARTY), ANNE PATRICIA, university counselor; b. Boston, Dec. 9, 1950; d. Patrick Joseph and Anne F. (McCourt) Hegarty; m. Pedro Reinaldo Hernandez Lattuf, July 3, 1976. A.A., Colby-Sawyer Coll., 1971; B.A., U. Mass., 1973; Ed.M., U. Houston, 1976. Asst. prof. Universidad Metropolitana, Caracas, Venezuela, 1976-80; behavioral sci. coordinator Tex. Tech Med. Sch., Amarillo, 1982—. Vol. VISTA Cerebral Palsy Greater Boston, Newton, Mass.; sec. High Plains Perinatal Assn., 1985; vol. Domestic Violence Council, 1982-83, Parenting Services, Amarillo, 1981-82; bd. dirs. Parents Anonymous, Amarillo, 1984-85. Mem. Am. Assn. for Counseling Devel., Am. Mental Health Counselors Assn., Assn. for Counselor Edn. Supervision, Assn. for Humanistic Edn. Devel., Assn. for Measurement Evaluation Counseling Devel., Yorkshire Terrier Club Am. Roman Catholic. Avocations: travel; raising showdogs; horseback riding; cultural, communty endeavors. Office: Tex Tech U Health Scis Ctr Dept Pediatrics 1400 Wallace Blvd Amarillo TX 79106

HERNANDEZ-AVILA, MANUEL LUIS, physical oceanography educator, researcher, administrator, consultant; b. Quebradillas, P.R., Apr. 15, 1935; s. Manuel and Luisa (Avila) H.; m. Evangelina Fradera, Dec. 8, 1956; B.S. in Biology, U. P.R., 1967, M.S. in Marine Scis., 1970; Ph.D. in Marine Scis., La. State U., 1974. Research asst. dept. marine scis. U. P.R., Mayaguez, 1963-67, dir. dept. marine scis., 1978—, prof., 1982—, dir. Sea Grant Program, 1980—; research asst. Coastal Studies Inst., La. State U., Baton Rouge, 1967-70. Mem. Smithsonian Instn., Am. Acad. Arts and Scis., Am. Meteorol. Soc., Am. Geophys. Union, Internat. Oceanographic Found., Marine Tech. Soc., Assn. Island Marine Labs. Caribbean, Coastal Soc., Oceanic Soc., N.Y. Acad. Scis., Sigma Xi, Phi Sigma Alpha. Roman Catholic. Lodge: Lions (San German, P.R.). Contbr. articles to profl. jours. Office: Dept Marine Scis RUM U PR Mayaguez PR 00708

HERNANDEZ-COLON, RAFAEL, governor; b. Ponce, P.R., Oct. 24, 1936; s. Rafael Hernandez Matos and Dorinda Colon; m. Leila Mallorai, 1959; children—Rafael, Jose Alfredo, Daria Mercedes, Juan Eugenie. A.B., Johns Hopkins U., 1956; LL.B., U. P.R. Assoc. commr. pub. service P.R. Pub. Service Commn., 1960-62; atty. gen., P.R., 1965-67; senator, pres. P.R. Senate, 1969-73; gov. P.R., 1972-76, 85—. Mem. pres. com. Popular Democratic Party of P.R., 1968—; Dem. Nat. committeeman, P.R., 1968-78; del. Dem. Nat. Conv., 1972, 76, 80; trustee Johns Hopkins U. Address: Commonwealth Capitol Seante San Juan PR 00904*

HERNDON, CHESLEY COLEMAN, JR., petroleum geologist, consultant; b. Tulsa, Jan. 18, 1927; s. Chesley Coleman and Ethel Alta (Dunn) H.; m. Rose Ann Evans, July 2, 1949; children—Chesley Coleman, Mary Jane, James Noel, Anne Elizabeth. B.S. in Bus. Adminstrn., U. Tulsa, 1948; M.A. in Geology, U. Mich., 1952. Landman, Carter Oil Co., Denver, 1948-50, geologist, Grand Rapids, Mich. and Carmi, Ill., 1952-55; dist. geologist Toklan-Kirby Oil Co., Tulsa, 1955-59; sr. geologist, dist. geologist Skelly Oil Co., Midland, Tex., Tulsa and Oklahoma City, 1959-73; self-employed geologist, Oklahoma City, 1973—; pres. CRAMJAC, Inc., Oklahoma City, 1981—, also chmn. bd.; dir. HAP, Inc.; cons. in field. Co-author: CONTROL-American Petroleum Institute, 1970; author geol. reports. Precinct chmn. Midland County Republican Party, Tex., 1963-65, county chmn., 1967-69; precinct chmn. Tulsa County Rep. Party, 1970-71, Oklahoma County Rep. Party, Oklahoma City, 1972-73. Mem. Am. Assn. Petroleum Geologists, Am. Inst. Profl. Geologists, Soc. Ind. Profl. Earth Scientists, Oklahoma City Geol. Soc., West Tex. Geol. Soc., Nat. Rifle Assn. (life), Beta Theta Pi. Episcopalian. Clubs: Petroleum, Beacon (Oklahoma City). Avocations: photography, travel, history, canoeing. Home: 12300 Blue Sage Rd Oklahoma City OK 73120 Office: CRAMJAC Inc First Nat Ctr Suite 1816 120 N Robinson St Oklahoma City OK 73102

HERNDON, HENRIETTA, personnel executive; b. Shreveport, La., Apr. 9, 1944; d. Louie and Ethelene (Amos) Herndon; B.A., Wiley Coll., 1967. Tchr., employment counselor Caddo Community Action Agy., Shreveport, La., 1969-74; personnel interviewer Interfirst Bank, Dallas, 1974-77; personnel adminstr. Recognition Equipment, Inc., Irving, Tex., 1977-79; supr., personnel adminstrn. Tech. Devel. Calif., Arlington, Tex., 1980; employment supr. ENI Co., Bellevue, Wash., 1980-81; employment services mgr., affirmative action coordinator Comml. Nat. Bank, Shreveport, La., 1981—; lectr. high sch. bus. students on employment and interviewing procedures. Mem. Am. Soc. Personnel Adminstrn., Northwest La. Personnel Assn. (legal corr.), Am. Inst. Banking (chpt. bd. mem.), Nat. Assn. Bank Women, Shreveport Job Service. Office: 329 Texas St Shreveport LA 71101

HERNDON, LANCE HARRISON, data processing consultant, economist; b. N.Y.C., Apr. 4, 1955; s. Russell Harrison and Jackie (Lonesome) H. A.S. in Data Processing, LaGuardia, N.Y.C., 1976; B.S. in Computer Sci., 1978, Cons., Gen. Sci., Inc., N.Y.C., 1972-78; sr. cons. Ins. Systems Am., Atlanta, 1978-80; pres. ACCESS, Inc., Atlanta, 1981—. Author: Systems Design, 1972. Recipient Martin Luther King, Jr. Community Service award, 1983. Mem. Atlanta C. of C. (recognition award for outstanding bus. achievements with Atlanta Bus. Devel. Ctr.), Data Processing Mgmt. Assn., Assn. Computer Machinery, Atlanta Bus. League, NAACP. Home: 4882 Old Mountain Park Rd Roswell GA 30075

HEROLD, RUTH MAE, nurse; b. Butler, Tenn., Nov. 18, 1945; s. Frank Buster Turnmire and Edna Mary (Stansberry) Fritts; m. Norman Wayne Herold, June 23, 1962; children—Cheryl Denise, Norman Duane. Assoc. in Nursing, Caldwell Community Coll., 1979. Cook, baker sch. cafeteria Hudson (N.C.) Elem. Sch., 1975-77; practical nurse Caldwell Meml. Hosp., Lenoir, N.C., 1979-80, staff nurse, 1980-81, charge nurse, 1981-82, nurse, part-time relief patient care supr., 1982—, mem. staff devel. com., 1981, mem. procedure com., 1983-84. Active Girl Scouts U.S.A.; first aider Girl Scout Day Camp, Hudson, 1972-77. Lenoir Lions Club scholar Bowman Gray Sch. Medicine, 1981. Mem. N.C. Nurses Assn., Am. Nurses Assn. Democrat. Baptist. Home: Route 1 Box 340 Hudson NC 28638 Office: Caldwell Meml Hosp 227 S Mulberry St SW Lenoir NC 28645

HEROLD, WILLIAM PAUL, software systems engineer; b. Mt. Vernon, Ohio, Mar. 25, 1950; s. Robert Ralph and Eleanor Ruth (Wolfe) H.; m. Mary Elizabeth Talbot, June 10, 1972; 1 child, Angela Kathleen. B.S. in Computer and Info. Sci. Engring., Ohio State U., 1972. Engr. North Electric, Galion, Ohio, 1972-75; computer programmer Collins Radio Group, Rockwell Internat., Richardson, Tex., 1975-76; mgr. systems engring. ITT, Cape Canaveral, Fla., 1976-80; prin. engr. SCI Systems, Huntsville, Ala., 1980-85, program mgr. F-16 avionics, 1985—. Republican. Lutheran. Club: Am. Contract Bridge League (Huntsville). Avocations: duplicate bridge; fishing; swimming. Home: 13010 Percivale Dr Huntsville AL 35803 Office: SCI Systems 8600 S Memorial Pkwy Suite MS12 Huntsville AL 35802

HERRENTON, W. W., educational administrator. Supt. of schs. Memphis. Office: 2597 Avery Ave Memphis TN 38112*

HERRERA, ALBERTO, management consultant; b. Guatemala, Jan. 11, 1941; came to U.S., 1965; s. Alberto and Rosario (Guzman) H.; m. Beatriz Otero, May 19, 1977; 1 child, Alberto. B.A. in Math. and Computer Scis., NYU, 1970; postgrad. in mgmt. Clayton U. Sr. systems analyst Am. Express Co., N.Y.C., 1965-69; mgmt. cons. Booz Allen & Hamilton, N.Y.C., 1969-72; research and devel. dir. Gamboa & Schlesinger, Venezuela, 1972-74; pres. Kohoutek Inc., N.Y.C., 1974-79, Info. Strategies Corp., Miami and Dallas, 1983—; v.p., fin. dir. Kexar Internat. Corp., N.Y.C., 1977-80; dir. edn. div. Beke, Santos y Asociados, Venezuela, 1980-82; cons. U.S. and abroad. Contbr. articles to profl. jours. Mem. EDP Auditors Assn., Am. Mgmt. Assn., Assn. Computing Machinery. Office: 444 Brickell Ave Suite 650 Miami FL 33131

HERRERA, LOURDES LAVANDERA, school psychologist; b. Havana, Cuba, Jan. 15, 1948, came to U.S., 1967, naturalized, 1973; d. Andres and Margarita (Brana) Lavandera; m. Gaspar Manuel Herrera, July 23, 1982; 1 child, David Daniel. B.A. in Psychology, Calif. State U., 1971; M.S., Barry U., 1979; doctoral candidate Miami Inst. Psychology, 1982—. Tchr. St. Monica Sch., Opa Locka, Fla., 1971-72; supr. intensive care unit Montanari Treatment Ctr., Hialeah, Fla., 1972-74, 76-78; dir. guidance, psychol. services Miccosukee Sch., Miami, Fla., 1979—. Mem. Am. Assn. Counseling and Devel., Am. Psychol. Assn., Nat. Assn. Sch. Psychologists, Barry U. Assn. Counselors, Kappa Delta Pi, Delta Kappa Gamma, Alpha Delta Kappa, Psi Chi. Roman Catholic. Home: 12225 SW 119th Terr Miami FL 33144 Office: Miccosukee Tribe Box 440021 Miami FL 33144

HERRERA DE LA FUENTE, LUIS, conductor, music director; b. Mexico City, Mex.; student piano Bach Acad., Mex., Faculty of Music, U. Mex.; studied composition with Rodolfo Halffter, Mex.; studied conducting with Sergiu Celebidache and Herman Scherchen, Zurich, Switzerland; D. Arts (hon.), Oklahoma City U.; married; 4 children. Music dir., condr. Orquesta de Cámara de Mex., Orquesta Sinfonica Nacional, Mex., Orquesta Sinfónica Nacional, Peru, Orquesta Sinfónica de Chile, Orquesta Sinfónica Xalapa, Mex., Orquesta Filarmónica de las Americas, Mex.; now condr., music dir. Okla. Symphony Orch., Oklahoma City, Mineria Symphony, Mexico City, guest condr. numerous orchs. including: Bonn Philharmonic, London Royal Philharmonic, Orchestra National, Paris, Orch. Nat. Belge, Brussels, Philharmonic Orch., Leningrad, USSR, State Orch. Moscow, Athens Philharmonic, Mpls. Symphony, San Diego Symphony, New Orleans Symphony, Dallas Symphony, Montreal Symphony, Filarmonica de Chile, Filarmonica de Sao Paulo, Berlin Radio Orch., Hamburg Radio Orch., Am. Philharmonic, Filarmonica de la Habana, NBC Symphony, N.Z. Symphony; condr. festivals including Casals' Festival, Montreux Festival, Switzerland, Athens Festival, Aspen (Colo.) Festival; guest of honor Internat. Tchaikovsky Competition, Moscow; mem. jury First Internat. Van Cliburn Competition, Ft. Worth. Decorated knight Order King Leopold (Belgium); recipient gold medal Jewish Group of Peru; diploma Mex. Soc. Theater and Music Critics. Mem. Manuel M. Ponce Chamber Music Soc. (pres.). Office: Okla Symphony Orch 512 Civic Center Music Hall Oklahoma City OK 73102

HERRING, GROVER CLEVELAND, lawyer; b. Nocatee, Fla., Dec. 9, 1925; s. Joseph I. and Martha (Selph) H.; J.D., U. Fla., 1950; m. Dorothy L. Blinn, Apr. 17, 1947; children—Stanley T., Kenneth Lee. Admitted to Fla. bar, 1950; asso. firm Haskins & Bryant, Sebring, 1950-52; practiced in West Palm Beach, Fla., 1952-60, 64—, mem. firm Blakeslee, Herring & Bie, and predecessor firm, 1953-60, Warwick, Paul & Herring, 1964-70, Herring & Evans, 1970, now Arnstein, Gluck, Lehr, Barron & Milligan; atty. City of West Palm Beach, 1960-63, City of Atlantis, 1959-61, Town of Ocean Ridge, 1953-61, 1964-66, Village of Royal Palm Beach, 1964-72, Town of South Palm Beach (Fla.), 1966-72; spl. master-in-chancery 15th Jud. Circuit in and for Palm Beach County, 1953-54; judge ad litem Municipal Ct., West Palm Beach, 1954-55. Field rep. Lawyers Title Guaranty Fund, 1955-60, 64—; dir. Lawyers Title Services, Inc., West Palm Beach. Active PTA, Family Service Agy., Palm Beach County Mental Health Assn.; chmn. profl. sect. A.R.C., 1960; mem. Charter Revision Com. West Palm Beach, 1960-65, Palm Beach County Resources Devel. Bd., 1959—; apptd. mem. Govtl. Study Commn. by Fla. Legislature. Bd. dirs. Community Chest. Mem. Democratic Exec. Com., 1965-70. Served with USNR, 1944-46. Mem. Am., Palm Beach County (treas. 1960), John Marshall bar assns., Fla. Bar, Am. Judicature Soc., Lawyer's Title Guaranty Fund, East Coast Estate Planning Council, Nat. Inst. Municipal Law Officers, Law-Sci. Acad., Am. Trial Lawyers Assn. (asso. editor 1960—), Lawyers Lit. Club, Nat. Municipal League, U. Fla. Law Center Assn., World Peace Through Law Center, Fla. Sheriff's Assn. (hon.), U. Fla. Alumni Assn., VFW, Am. Legion, West Palm Beach C. of C., Civic Music Assn., Palm Beach County Hist. Soc. (pres. 1969-72), New Eng. Hist. Geneal. Soc. Boston. Mason (32 deg.), Elk, Moose. Clubs: West Palm Beach Country (hon.); Airways (N.Y.C.); Eight Oaks River Lodge; History Book (Stamford, Conn.). Contbr. legal articles to profl. revs. Home: 3515 Australian Ave West Palm Beach FL 33407 Office: Forum III Bldg Tower B West Palm Beach FL 33401

HERRING, JACK WILLIAM, English language educator; b. Waco, Tex., Aug. 28, 1925; s. Benjamin Oscar and Bertha K. Elizabeth (Shiplet) H.; A.B., Baylor U., 1947, M.A., 1948; Ph.D., U. Pa., 1958; m. Daphne L. Norred, June 10, 1944; children—Penny Elizabeth, Paul William. Instr. in English, Howard Coll., Birmingham, Ala., 1948-50; assoc. prof., acting chmn. dept. English, Grand Canyon Coll., 1951-55; asst. prof. English, Ariz. State U., 1955-59; prof. English, Baylor U., 1959—; Margaret Root Brown prof. Robert Browning Studies, 1973—, dir. Armstrong Browning Library, 1959—. Served with U.S. Army, 1944-46. Mem. MLA. Baptist. Club: Kiwanis (pres. Waco 1976-77). Author: Old School Fellow (Browning), 1972; editor: Studies In Browning, 1973; Complete Works of Robert Browning (14 Vols.). Home: 200 Guittard Ave Waco TX 76706 Office: Baylor U Dept English Waco TX 76798

HERRING, LEONARD GRAY, marketing company executive; b. nr. Snow Hill, N.C., June 18, 1927; s. Albert Lee and Josie (Sugg) H.; m. Rozelia Sullivan, June 18, 1950; children—Sandra Grey, Albert Lee II. B.S., U. N.C., 1948. With Dun & Bradstreet, Inc., Raleigh, N.C., 1948-49; with H. Weil & Co., Goldsboro, N.C., 1949-55; pres., chief exec. officer Lowe's Cos., Inc., North Wilkesboro, N.C., 1955—; dir. First Union Corp., Charlotte, N.C., Lowe's Cos. Profit Sharing Plan and Trust.; mem. listed co. adv. com. N.Y. Stock Exchange, N.Y.C. Trustee Pfeiffer Coll., Misenheimer, N.C.; mem. adv. bd. Duke U. Hosp., Durham, N.C. Mem. Chi Psi. Democrat. Methodist. Home: 310 Coffey St North Wilkesboro NC 28659 Office: Lowe's Cos Inc Hwy 268 East North Wilkesboro NC 28656

HERRING, SAMUEL DAVID, banker; b. Birmingham, Ala., May 4, 1936; s. Joseph and Ora Caruthers H.; B.S., U. Ala., 1958. Officer mgr. Gen. Fin. Corp., Birmingham, 1964-72; with First Ala. Bank of Birmingham, 1972—, sr. v.p., dir. personnel, 1975—. Chmn., Jefferson County Democratic Exec. Com., 1968—; mem. City Council of Birmingham, 1974—, now pres.; mem. Democratic Exec. Com. of Ala., 1978—, also dir.; founder, pres. Big Bros. of Greater Birmingham, 1978—. Served to lt. QMC, U.S. Army, 1959-61. Mem. Am. Soc. Personnel Adminstrn. Baptist. Home: PO Box 55203 Birmingham AL 35255 Office: 417 N 20th St Birmingham AL 35202

HERRIS, WILLIAM PATRICK, JR., sales manager; b. Cleve., Aug. 26, 1946; s. William Patrick and Katherine Patricia (McNulty) H.; m. Paulette Frances Dvorchak, June 28, 1969; children—Hilary, Paul, Alison. Sales rep. Am. Tobacco, Cleve., 1968-69; sales rep. Minn. Mining and Mfg. Co., Detroit, 1969-72, mktg. mgr., St. Paul, 1972-78, area sales mgr., Atlanta, 1978—. Vice pres. Parish Council Holy Family Catholic Ch., Atlanta, 1983-84, mem., 1978—. Served with U.S. Army, 1965-68; Vietnam. Decorated Bronze Star. Home: 2207 Old Orchard Dr Marietta GA 30067 Office: Minn Mining & Mfg Co 6597 Peachtree Ind Blvd Norcross GA 30092

HERRMANN, RONALD JOSEPH, bowling ball manufacturing company executive; b. San Antonio, Dec. 21, 1934; s. Albert and Helen (Luthy) H.; B.A., St. Mary's U., 1957, J.D., 1959; m. Karen Heizer, Oct. 1, 1977; children—Karin, Carol, Helen, David, Emilie. Admitted to Tex. bar, 1959; individual practice law, 1959—; sr. v.p. Am. Grain Corp., 1962-66; farmer, rancher, Kans. and Tex., 1952—; pres., dir., co-owner Columbia Industries, Inc., San Antonio, 1961—; owner FM Inc., 1969—; dir. Sun Harvest Farms, Inc., others. Trustee, St. Mary's U., San Antonio Bar Found. Served with USAR, 1952-61. Recipient Disting. Law Alumni award St. Mary's U., 1978. Fellow Tex. Bar Found.; mem. San Antonio Bar Assn., Tex. Bar Assn., Tex. Hist. Soc., Tex. and Southwestern Cattle Raisers Assn., Kans. Hist. Soc. (life), World Affairs Council San Antonio (bd. dirs). Democrat. Roman Catholic. Restored two-story rock home in Fredericksburg Tex., originally built in 1850 (Tex. Hist. Soc. Commemorative Plaque 1973). Office: 5005 West Ave San Antonio TX 78213

HERRON, EDWIN HUNTER, JR., energy consultant; b. Shreveport, La., June 7, 1938; s. Edwin Hunter and Helen Virginia (Russell) H.; B.S. in Chem. Engring., Tulane U., 1959, M.S., 1963, Ph.D. (NSF fellow, 1963-64), 1964; m. Frances Irvine Hunter, June 27, 1959; children—Edwin, David, Ashley. Research engr. Exxon Research & Engring. Co., Linden, N.J., 1959-61; sr. research engr. Exxon Production Research Co., Houston, 1964-66; corp. planning advisor Esso Europe, London, Eng., 1966-74; fin. analyst Exxon Corp., N.Y.C., 1974-78; v.p. Gruy Petroleum Tech., Inc., McLean, Va., 1978-84; pres. Petro-Analysis Inc., 1984—. Recipient Levey award, Tulane U., 1970. Mem. Soc. Petroleum Engrs. of AIME, Am. Inst. Chem. Engrs., Sci. Research Soc., Soc. Tulane Engrs., Tau Beta Pi. Contbr. articles to profl. publs. Office: Petro-Analysis Inc 8029 Old Dominion Dr McLean VA 22102

HERRON, JAMES M., lawyer; b. Chgo., May 4, 1934; s. J. Leonard and Sylvia H.; m. Janet Ross, June 12, 1955; children—Kathy Lynn, Tracy Ellen, Andrew Ross. A.B., U. Mo., Columbia, 1955; postgrad., Northwestern U., 1958-59; J.D., Washington U., 1961. Bar: Mo. 1961, Ohio 1971, Fla. 1975. Asst. gen. counsel, asst. sec. May Dept. Stores Co., St. Louis, 1961-70; asso. counsel Federated Dept. Stores, Inc., Cin., 1970-71; v.p., sec., gen. counsel Kenton Corp., N.Y.C., 1971-73; gen. counsel Ryder System, Inc., Miami, Fla., 1973-74, v.p., sec., gen. counsel, 1974-78, sr. v.p., sec., gen. counsel, 1978-79, exec. v.p., gen. counsel, 1979—, sec., 1983—. Trustee, bd. dirs. Greater Miami Opera Assn., 1980-81, chmn. corp. devel. com., 1981-82, sec., bd. dirs., mem. exec. com.; bd. dirs. Am. Cancer Soc.; trustee Ransom Everglades Sch. Served with USMC, 1955-58. Mem. various legal orgns. Club: Royal Palm Tennis (dir.). Home: 5945 SW 113th St Miami FL 33156 Office: 3600 NW 82d Ave Miami FL 33166

HERSCH, JAMES BARRY, geologist; b. Bethlehem, Pa., Apr. 15, 1952; s. William Robert and Hallah Mai (Rodgers) H. B.A., Appalachian Coll., 1974; M.S., U. Tenn., 1978. Assoc. geologist Exxon, Denver, 1977; sr. geologist Exxon Co. U.S.A., Houston, 1978-80; staff exploration geologist Anadarko Prodn. Co., Houston, 1980—. State of N.C. scholar, 1973-74, Fed. Edn. Opportunity Grant scholar, 1970-75. Mem. Am. Assn. Petroleum Geologists, Am. Inst. Profl. Geologists, Houston Geol. Soc., AIME. Republican. Avocations: baseball; fishing; hunting. Home: 3634 El James Spring TX 77379 Office: Anadarko Prodn Co 16801 Greenspoint Pk Dr Houston TX 77060

HERSH, SOLOMON PHILIP, textile engineering educator; b. Winston-Salem, N.C., Jan. 14, 1929; s. Max and Milly Diane H.; m. Rosalie Berta Peskin, Feb. 21, 1954; children—Marla Rene, Camille. B.S., N.C. State U., 1949; M.S., Inst. Textile Tech., 1951; M.A., Princeton U., 1953, Ph.D., 1954. Research chemist Union Carbide Corp., South Charleston, W.Va., 1954-62; sr. research chemist Chemstrand Research Center, Research Triangle Park, N.C., 1962-66; assoc. prof. textile tech. N.C. State U., Raleigh, 1966-70, prof., 1970-85, Charles A. Connon prof. textiles, 1973—, head dept. textile engring. and sci., 1985—. Recipient O. Max Gardner award U. N.C., 1979. Mem. Am. Chem. Soc., Am. Assn. Textile Chemists and Colorists, Fiber Soc., Electrostatics Soc. Am., Air Pollution Control Soc., Internat. Inst. for Conservation of Hist. and Artistic Works, Sigma Xi. Patentee (9); contbr. articles to profl. jours. Home: 2314 Weymouth Ct Raleigh NC 27612 Office: Sch of Textiles NC State U Campus Box 8301 Raleigh NC 27695

HERSH, THEODORE, physician, educator; b. Mexico City, Mexico, May 27, 1933; came to U.S., 1965, naturalized, 1968; s. Bernat and Rosa (Helfand) Herskovic; grad. cum laude Harvard U., 1955; M.D., Columbia U., 1959; postgrad. Mayo Found. Grad. Sch. Medicine, 1963; m. Rebecca Siman, Feb. 25, 1979; children—Mark, Ellen, David, Wendy, Sharon. Fellow in gastroenterology Harvard Med. Sch., 1965; asst. prof. medicine Yale U., 1969; asso. prof. Baylor Coll. Medicine, 1971; prof. medicine Emory U., Atlanta, 1973—, chmn. human investigations com., 1973—; intern Mt. Sinai Hosp., N.Y.C.; resident Mayo Clinic, 1960-63; practice medicine, Mexico City, 1963-65; staff Emory U. Clinic and Hosp., Grady Meml. Hosp.; v.p. Unichem, Inc., 1982—. Treas., Atlanta Assn. Internat. Edn. Recipient Noble Found. award Mayo Found., 1963; teaching awards Baylor Coll. Medicine, 1971. Mem. Am. Gastroent. Assn., Ga. Gastroent. Assn. (v.p. 1982-84, pres. 1984—), Am. Assn. Study Liver Diseases, Am. Coll. Gastroenterology (Ga. gov.), Am. Fedn. Clin. Research, AMA, Sigma Xi. Democrat. Jewish. Co-author: Diarrhea, 1978; Digestive Diseases, 1983; Textbook Medicine, 1983; mem. editorial bd. Jour. Clin. Gastroenterology, 1984—, Am. Jour. Gastroenterology, 1985—; contbr. articles to profl. jours. Home: 2273 Briarwood Trail Decatur GA 30033 Office: 1365 Clifton Rd Atlanta GA 30322

HERSHNER, ROBERT FRANKLIN, JR., bankruptcy judge; b. Sumter, S.C., Jan. 21, 1944; s. Robert Franklin and Druie (Goodmen) H.; m. Sylvia Lanette Hatton, June 11, 1966; (div. June 1985); children—Bryan Douglas,

Andrew Landis. A.B., Mercer U., 1966; J.D., 1969. Bar: Ga. 1971. Mem. staff Ga. Legal Services Corp., 1972; assoc. Adams, O'Neal, Hemingway & Kaplan, Macon, Ga., 1972-76; ptnr. Kaplan & Hershner, Macon, 1976-80; bankruptcy judge U.S. Bankruptcy Ct. middle dist., Ga., 1980—; adj. prof. law Walter F. George Sch. Law, Mercer U., Macon, 1982—. Co-author (with Kaplan): Post-Judgment Procedures in Georgia in Ga. Lawyers Basic Practice Handbook, 2d edit. 1979; contbg. editor Norton Bankruptcy Law Advisor; contbr. articles to Ann. Survey Bankruptcy. Bd. dirs., v.p. Macon Heritage Found., 1977-78. Served to capt. U.S. Army, 1970-75. Mem. Ga. Bar Assn., Macon Bar Assn., Comml. Law League Am. Methodist. Avocations: golf; fishing. Office: US Bankruptcy Ct US Courthouse 475 Mulberry St PO Box 86 Macon GA 31202

HERST, HERMAN, JR., writer, philatelic appraiser, consultant; b. N.Y.C., Mar. 17, 1909; s. Herman Sr. and Lillian (Myers) H.; m. Ingeborg Adam (dec. Sept. 1954); children—Patricia June, Kenneth Reed; m. Ida Busch, June 26, 1957; stepchildren—Gary Kenneth Busch, Gail Carol Busch. B.A., Reed Coll., 1931; M.A., U. Oreg., 1932; LL.D., William Penn Coll., 1982. Statistician, Lebenthal & Co., N.Y.C., 1933-35; profl. philatelist Herman Herst Jr. Inc., N.Y.C., Shrub Oak, N.Y., 1935-73. Author: Nassau Street, 1960 (Gold medal 1962); Fun and Profit in Stamp Collecting, 1964 (Gold medal 1966, 70), More Stories to Collect Stamps By, 1968 (Gold medal 1968), The Compleat Philatelist, 1976 (2 Gold medals 1979). Bd. dirs. Boca Atlantic Home Owners Assn., 1981-85; vol. Boca Raton Police Dept., 1983, 84, Gumbo Limb Nature Ctr., 1984, 85. Recipient John A. Luff award Am. Philatelic Soc. 1962, Mayflower award Am. Stamp Soc., New Haven Merit award New Haven Philatelic Soc., Irregular Shilling award Baker Street Irregulars 1968, Writers' Hall Fame award Am. Philatelic Soc. 1974. Mem. Soc. Philatelic Ams. (v.p. 1946-68), Am. Stamp Dealers Assn. (dir. 1982—), Philatelic Traders Soc. (council mem. London, 1968-72), Springfield Philatelic Soc. (hon.), Okla. Philatelic Soc. (hon.), Trans-Miss. Philatelic Soc. (hon.), Edmonton Philatelic Soc. (hon.), Fla. Fedn. Stamp Clubs (hon.), Oreg. Stamp Soc. (hon.). Democrat. Jewish. Clubs: Boca Raton, Boca Pointe. Lodges: Kiwanis, Masons, Shriners. Avocations: philately; autographs. Home: 1098 Spanish River Rd Boca Raton FL 33432

HERTZ, ELLEN SHAPIRO, mathematical statistician; b. N.Y.C., Apr. 5, 1937; d. Max and Rose (Sandlow) Shapiro; m. Rene Daniel Hertz, July 3, 1963; children—Joseph Robert, Julia Ann. B.S. CCNY, 1958; M.A., Columbia U., 1960, Ph.D., 1970. Lectr. math. CCNY, 1968-70; asst. prof. math. Bronx Community Coll., N.Y.C., 1972-74; statistician U.S. Army, Ft. Monmouth, N.J. and Falls Church, Va., 1979—. Contbr. articles to profl. jours. Woodrow Wilson fellow, 1958; Carnegie Found. teaching intern, 1961. Mem. Math. Assn. Am., Sigma Xi, Phi Beta Kappa. Home: 2260 Wheelwright Ct Reston VA 22091

HERZEG, LADD KEITH, football club executive; b. Jan. 31, 1946; s. Steve Herczeg and Agnes (Stolz) H.; m. Kathleen M. Vinson, Aug. 31, 1968. Student U. Hawaii, 1964-65; B.S., Ohio State U., 1968. Audit mgr. Arthur Andersen & Co., Cleve., 1968-76; v.p. fin. Houston Oilers, Inc., 1976-79, sr. v.p., 1979-81, exec. v.p., gen. mgr., 1981—; mem. pension com. Nat. Football League; dir. KSA Industries, Adams Resources. Served with U.S. Army, 1969-70. Office: Houston Oilers PO Box 1516 Houston TX 77001*

HERZOG, RICHARD B., insurance company executive; b. Cin., May 21, 1937; s. Arthur E. and Bessie Lois (Berger) H.; cert. Hamilton County (Ohio) Police Acad., 1969; cert. Mktg. Devel. Inst., Purdue U., 1979; m. Gloria; children—Cindy Sue, Shelly Lynn, Matthew Barrett; step-children—Valerie Dell Feltham, Robin Kristi Mastley, Charlie E. Feltham. Draftsman, Avco, Cin., 1955-56, Kettcorp., Cin., 1956-57, Trailmobile, Inc., Cin., 1957-62; prin. Allied Film Agy., Cin., 1962-63; enrollment rep. Blue Cross of S.W. Ohio, Cin., 1963-68, mgr. mktg., 1968-72; mgr. regional mktg. Blue Cross Assn., Atlanta, 1972-77, dir. mktg., 1977-78; sr. dir. mktg. S.E. region Blue Cross and Blue Shield Assns., Atlanta, 1978-83, v.p. mktg. Textile-Apparel div., 1983—. Bd. dirs. Jr. Achievement, Cin., 1965-66, Cin. chpt. Cystic Fibrosis Research Found., 1963-64; bd. dirs. Carriage Cluster Civic Assn., 1975-76, pres., 1979-82; minister Dekalb Christian Ch., Atlanta, 1974-78; co-chmn. Aronoff campaign for state senate, 1966-72. Recipient various awards Jaycees. Office: Blue Cross and Blue Shield Assns 4488 N Shallowford Rd Atlanta GA 30338

HESS, GEORGE FRANKLIN, II, lawyer; b. Oak Park, Ill., May 13, 1939; s. Franklin Edward and Carol (Hackman) H.; m. Diane Ricci, Aug. 9, 1974; 1 son, Franklin Edward. B.S. in Bus., Colo. State U., 1962; J.D., Suffolk U., 1970; LL.M., Boston U., 1973. Bar: Pa. 1971, Fla. 1973, U.S. Tax Ct. 1974, U.S. Dist. Ct. (so. dist.) Fla. 1975. Assoc. firm Hart, Childs, Hepburn, Ross & Putnam, Phila., 1970-72; instr. Suffolk U. Law Sch., Boston, 1973-74; ptnr. firm Henry, Hess & Hoines, Ft. Lauderdale, Fla., 1974-79; sole practice George F. Hess, II, P.A., (merged with Mousaw, Vigdor, Reeves, Heilbronner & Kroll., Rochester, N.Y., 1981, name now Mousaw, Vigdor, Reeves & Hess), Ft. Lauderdale, 1979—, now ptnr. Served to lt. USNR, 1963-66. Mem. ABA, Fla. Bar Assn., Broward County Bar Assn., U.S. Navy League, SAR, Phi Alpha Delta. Episcopalian. Clubs: Tower, Logo Mar (Ft. Lauderdale). Home: 2524 Castilla Isle Fort Lauderdale FL 33301 Office: 1410 One Financial Plaza Fort Lauderdale FL 33394

HESS, JANET LINDLEY, geologist; b. Houston, Jan. 23, 1956; d. Gene Ray and Sally (Hackney) Lindley; m. D. Edward Hess, Nov. 17, 1979; 1 child, Sarah Marie. B.S. in Geology, U. Tex.-Austin, 1978. Geologist, Union of Calif., Lafayette, La., 1978-81, Aminoil, U.S.A., Lafayette, La., 1981-82, Union Tex. Petroleum, Houston, 1982—. Mem. choir Chapelwood Methodist Ch., Houston, 1983—; student mem. Inst. for Children's Lit., 1985—. Mem. Am. Assn. Petroleum Geologists, Houston Geol. Soc., Phi Beta Kappa. Avocations: camping; reading; music. Home: 2806 Quincannon Ln Houston TX 77043 Office: Union Tex Petroleum Co 1330 Post Oak Blvd PO Box 2120 Houston TX 77252

HESSELTINE, WILLIAM HENRY, JR., financial executive; b. Bloomfield, Mo., Sept. 14, 1932; s. William Henry and Leona Belle (Eaton) H.; m. Mary Ann Griffin, Aug. 29, 1953; children—Joanna Marie Harger, Linda Sue Feldman, William Henry III. B.S., U. Mo., 1954; M.B.A., U. Pa., 1960. Commd. USAF, 1965, advanced through grades to lt. col., 1971; advisor to Gen. Weyland, MACV, Saigon, Vietnam, 1970-71; dept. head, prof. Air U., Montgomery, Ala., 1971-75; in constrn., Dadeville, Ala., 1975-76; systems analyst West Point Pepperell, West Point, Ga., 1977-78, fin. analyst, 1978-79; v.p. fin. Conpack South, Inc., Marion, Ala., 1980—. Mem. Republican Presdl. Task Force. Served to lt. col. USAF, 1955-75. Named Ideal Boss, Mo. U. Bus. Sch., 1954. Mem. Air Force Assn., Res. Officers Assn., Wharton MBA Alumni Assn., Sigma Alpha Epsilon, Alpha Kappa Psi. Republican. Methodist. Lodge: Masons. Author: Budgetary Control Techniques, 1960; Management Analysis-Past, Present and Future, 1965. Home: 210 Crestwood Dr Marion AL 36756 Office: Conpack South Inc S Washington St Marion AL 36756-3499

HESSON, PAUL ANTHONY, architect; b. Luck, Wis., Sept. 4, 1923; s. Lynn James and Clara Ann (Paulson) H.; m. Margaret June Lovaas, Apr. 6, 1942; children—Kathi Lyn Hesson Curtis, Paula Diane Hesson Dove. B.Arch., U. Minn., 1949. Registered architect, Tex., La., Okla. Intern architect Perry Crosier Assoc., Mpls., 1950-51, Hal Fridlund Assoc., 1951-52; architect Cerf Ross Assoc., San Antonio, 1952-53; ptnr. Hesson & May Assoc., 1953-83; pres. Hesson/Andrew/Sotomayor, San Antonio, 1983—; dir. Comml. Nat. Bank. Bd. dirs. North San Antonio C. of C., 1981—. Served to cpl. USAAF, 1942-45. Mem. Greater San Antonio C. of C., AIA (pres. San Antonio chpt. 1967-76), Nat. Council Archtl. Registration Bds. (pres. So. conf. 1985-86), Tex. Bd. Archtl. Examiners. Republican. Clubs: San Antonio Country, Petroleum. Lodge: Kiwanis. Avocations: flying; traveling; golfing. Home: 250 Rio Dr New Braunfels TX 78130 Office: Hesson Andrews Sotomayor 9901 Broadway Suite 115 San Antonio TX 78217

HESTER, GARY WAYNE, trucking company executive; b. N.Y.C., Apr. 8, 1949; s. Robert Charles and Gladys (Riley) McGinnis. B.A. in English, U. Md., 1976, B.Sc. in Polit. Sci., 1977; M.Sc. in Internat. Relations, Troy State U., 1977; postgrad. U. Capetown (South Africa), 1979—. Lectr. African history U. Md. Europe, W.Ger., 1977-80; founder, pres., treas. Computer Moving Co., Alexandria, Va., 1981—; dir. A.C.T. Ltd. Active Va. Republican Com. Served with U.S. Army, 1972-76; mem. Res. N.Y. Regents scholar, 1967-69; Edwin Gould scholar, 1967-70. Mem. Am. Def. Preparedness Assn., So. African Research Assn. Mem. Ch. Jesus Christ of Latter-day Saints. Book reviewer Nat. Def. mag., 1979-82, So. Africa Rev., 1979-82.

HESTER, HORTENSE, physical education educator; b. Montgomery, Ala., Oct. 16, 1931; d. Roland Arthur, Jr. and Josie Lee (Almon) H. A.B., Judson Coll., 1954; M.S., U. Ala., 1959; D. Phys. Edn., Ind. U., 1972. Cert. secondary tchr., Ala. Phys. edn. tchr. Andalusia High Sch., Ala., 1954-56; math. tchr. Capitol Heights Jr. High Sch., Montgomery, Ala., 1957-58; grad. asst. U. Ala., Tuscaloosa, 1958-59, Ind. U., Bloomington, 1964-66; phys. edn. instr. James Madison U., Harrisonburg, Va., 1959-64; prof., chmn. dept. phys. edn. Livingston U., Ala., 1966—. Sec. Presbyterian Women of the Ch., Livingston, 1967—; area coordinator Ala. Spl. Olympics, Livingston, 1972—; chmn. City Recreation Bd., Livingston, 1972-82. Mem. Ind. U. Alumni Found., AAHPERD, Nat. Assn. Phys. Edn. in Higher Edn. (charter mem.), Judson Coll. Alumnae Assn. (bd. dirs. 1981—), Ala. State Assn. Health, Phys. Edn. and Recreation (co-adviser student sect. 1972-73), Delta Kappa Gamma. Home: PO Box 88 Shady Heights Circle Livingston AL 35470 Office: Livingston U Station Room 11 Livingston AL 35470

HESTER, JAMES ARTHUR, educational administrator, educator; b. Little Rock, Sept. 25, 1946; s. James Lynn and Katherine Janet (Green) H.; m. Sharon Louise Hensley, June 25, 1983. B.S., Ark. Tech. U., 1968; M.S., U. Miss., 1972. Instr. art Hughes Elem. Sch., Ark., 1968-71, prin., 1978-81; instr. art Hughes High Sch., 1971-74, curriculum supr., 1974-78; ednl. adminstrv. supr. Ark. Dept. Edn., Little Rock, 1981—, chmn. media ctr. com., chmn. Charlie May Simon reading com., 1978-81. Artist pen and ink drawings; contbr. articles to profl. jours. Mem. exec. bd. Sylvan Hills United Methodist Ch., North Little Rock, Ark., 1982—. Sr. fellow in art Ark. Tech. U., 1967-68; Ark. Edn. Assn. scholar, 1971; named Ambassador of Goodwill, Gov. Ark., 1981. Mem. Assn. for Childhood Edn. Internat. (dir. 1982—, service award 1975), Ark. Assn. Ednl. Adminstrs., Ark. Assn. Elem. Sch. Prins., Ark. PTA (bd. mgrs., service award 1982-85, chmn. reflections 1985—, v.p. edn. 1985—), Ark. Assn. Sch. Curriculum Devel., Ark. Assn. for Childhood Edn. Internat. (meritorious award 1979). Democrat. Avocations: pottery; needlepoint; pen and ink; gardening; golf. Home: 10213 Sylvan Hills Rd North Little Rock AR 72116 Office: Ark Dept Edn 4 Capitol Mall Little Rock AR 72201

HESTER, JAMES CONNARD, supply company executive, retired army officer; b. Dacusville, S.C., Apr. 28, 1933; s. Jim Conway and Rachel Elmeda (Hamet) H.; m. Caroline Bradberry (dec. Nov. 1981); children—Karen Michele, Michael James; m. Betty Jean Raby, Jan. 1, 1984. Student, U. Colo., 1958-59, Cameron State Agr. Coll., 1960-62, U. Md., 1963-64. Enlisted U.S. Army, 1949, advanced through grades to maj., ret., 1970; office mgr. Binswanger Glass Co., Greenville, S.C., 1970-72; yard clk. So. Ry., Greenville, 1972-73; letter carrier U.S. Postal Service, Anderson, S.C., 1973-83; plant mgr. Plastex Supply Co., Inc., Greer, S.C., 1983—. Mem. Nat. Republican Election Com., Washington, 1983-84. Decorated Bronze Star with oak leaf. Mem. Ret. Officers Assn. (life). Republican. Methodist. Club: Ft. Hill Flying (Clemson). Home: 224 Clark Stream Dr Anderson SC 29621

HESTER, PATRICIA LANE O'QUINN, educational administrator, educator; b. Sanford, N.C., Jan. 20, 1942; d. Elbridge Brice and Ruth (Holland) O'Quinn; m. Clyde Ray Hester, Dec. 15, 1973. B.A., Campbell U., 1964; M.A., E. Carolina U., 1984. Tchr. Raleigh/Wake County Schs., N.C., 1964-69, Ravenscroft Sch., Raleigh, N.C., 1969-73; cons. Universal Learning and Literacy, Emporia, Va., 1973-75; tchr. Pinecrest/Moore County Schs., Southern Pines, N.C., 1975-76; tchr., adminstrv. council Wayne County Schs., Goldsboro, N.C., 1976-79; instructional specialist, supr., cons., 1976—; cons. in field. Author poetry; contbr. articles to ednl. publs. Judge, dir. scholarship pageants, Wayne County, N.C., 1976—. Alpha Delta Kappa scholar, 1985. Mem. Assn. Supervision and Curriculum Devel., Nat. Council Tchrs. English, NEA, N.C. Edn. Assn. Republican. Baptist. Club: Walnut Creek County. Avocations: art; reading; crafts; tennis; writing. Office: Wayne County Schs 301 N Herman St Goldsboro NC 27530

HETHERLY, JUDITH ANN, state administrator vocational home economics education; b. Lampasas, Tex., July 11, 1942; d. Clearence William and Valla Jean (Freeman) H. B.S., S.W. Tex. State U., 1963; M.S., Tex. Woman's U., 1969. Home econs. tchr., Bay City Sch. Dist., Tex., 1963-65; teaching fellow Tex. Woman's U., Denton, 1965-66; home econs. tchr. N.E. Sch. Dist., San Antonio, 1966-71; home econs. cons. Tex. Edn. Agy., Houston, 1971-79, asst. dir., Austin, 1981-83, dir. home econs. program, 1983—; home econs. instr. U. Tex., Austin, 1980-81; buyer Good Friends Clothing, Austin, 1965-66; instr. Wood Reading Dynamics, Austin, 1980-81; cons. Poult Pak Inc., Houston, 1979-80. Contbr. articles to profl. publs.; dir. research project. Active Harris County Fair Assn., Houston, 1977-85; mem. Pvt. Industry Council, Lampasas, 1979. Recipient State Staff award, Vocat. Home Econs. Assn., 1973, Disting. Service award, 1984. Mem. Am. Vocat. Assn., Am. Home Econs. Assn., Vocat. Home Econs. Tchrs. Assn. (pres. 1970-71), State Suprs. for Vocat. Home Econs., Future Homemakers Am. (hon.), Phi Delta Kappa, Alpha Delta Phi. Avocation: reading. Office: Tex Edn Agy 1701 N Congress Austin TX 78701

HETRICK, ETHEL WIEST, psychologist; b. Canon City, Colo., Nov. 4, 1943; d. Joseph Emory and Ethel May (Hyatt) Means; m. Robert Hugh Hetrick, Feb. 14, 1970; children—John Emory, Samuel Logan. B.S., U. Tex., 1965, M.A., 1966; Ph.D., Tex. Woman's U., 1976. Lic. psychologist, Tex., Ariz., La. Tchr. Clear Creek Sch., League City, Tex., 1967-71; spl. edn. counselor, Irving Sch., Tex., 1971-74; psychologist Northwestern State U., Natchitoches, La., 1976-78, dir. dept. spl. edn., 1978-81; sch. psychologist Tangue Verde Schs., Tucson, 1981-84, Longview Schs., Tex., 1984—; supervising psychologist various Parish Schs., Natchitoches, La., 1978-81; adj. prof. McPherson Coll., Tucson, 1982-84. Contbr. articles to profl. jours. Grantee Bur. Edn. Handicapped, 1978-80, La. Dept. Edn., 1978-81; fellow Tex. Women's U., 1974-75. Mem. Am. Psychol. Assn., Council Exceptional Children, Nat. Assn. Sch. Psychologists, NEA, Tex. State Tchrs. Assn. Democrat. Methodist. Home: PO Box 4049 1700 McCord Longview TX 75606 Office: Longview Ind Sch Dist PO Box 3268 Longview TX 75606

HETZENDORFER, DENNIS RAYMOND, audio engineer, producer; b. Buffalo, Apr. 2, 1953; s. Frederick Anthony and Geraldine Anne (Stuby) H. A.A., St. Petersburg Jr. Coll., 1973; B.Music, U. Miami, 1976; grad. Rec. Inst. Am., 1975. Staff engr. Criteria Recording Studios, North Miami, Fla., 1976-81, sr. engr., 1981-83; self-employed ind. engr.-producer, North Miami, 1983—. Mem. Nat. Acad. Rec. Arts and Sci. Roman Catholic. Avocations: traveling; swimming; skiing. Home: 2450 NE 135th St Apt 606 North Miami FL 33181 Office: Criteria Recording Studios 1755 NE 149th St Miami FL 33181

HEUER, MARTIN, temporary help services company executive; b. Algoma, Wis., Oct. 16, 1934; s. Orland Fred and Gertrude Mamie (Zimmerman) H. A.A., SUNY, 1973, Assoc. Sci., 1975; m. Rita Mae Prokash, Oct. 27, 1954; children—Martin Joseph, Ronald James. Commd. 2d lt. C.E., U.S. Army, 1954, advanced through grades to lt. col., 1968; flight comdr., adminstrv. and maintenance officer 1st Aviation Co., Fort Riley, 1958-61; with 937th Engr. Aviation Co., Panama, Lima, Peru, 1961-65; maintenance officer 174th Aviation Co., Vietnam, 1966; adj. 14th Combat Aviation Bn., 1966-67; dir. systems, curriculum and spl. projects div. Army Primary Helicopter Sch., Fort Wolters, Tex., 1967-69; aviation advisor Wis. Army N.G., West Bend, 1969-70; airfield comdr. Cu Chi Army Airfield, Vietnam, 1970; adj. 165th Combat Aviation Group, Vietnam, 1970-71; engr. advisor Wis. N.G., Eau Claire, 1971-73; mgr., area mgr. Manpower Temp. Services, 1973-76; exec. v.p. Aide Services, Inc. and KARI Services, Inc., Tampa, Fla., 1976-80, pres., chmn., 1980—; pres., chmn. Capitol Services, Inc., Tallahassee, 1982—; pres. bd. dirs. Fort Wolters Fed. Credit Union, 1967-69; chmn. bd. Digital Control Corp., Seminole, Fla., 1981—. Pres., Seminole High Sch. Band Boosters, 1974-79, Pinellas County Band Boosters, 1977-78; bd. dirs. Seminole High Sch. Booster Assn., 1975-79, pres., 1978-79. Decorated Legion of Merit with 1 oak leaf cluster, Bronze star medal with 3 oak leaf clusters, Air medal with 3 oak leaf clusters; recipient First Band Booster Pres. award Seminole High Sch., 1979; Service to Mankind award Sertoma, 1980. Mem. Assn. Manpower Franchise Owners (dir. 1980-82, 83—, treas. 1981-82, chmn. 1984-86), Assn. U.S. Army (chmn. bd. govs. 1981-82, asst. state v.p. Suncoast chpt. and Fla. 1981-82, state v.p. 1982-84, chmn. chpt. communications com. nat. adv. bd. 1982—), Army Aviation Assn. Am., Air Force Assn., Soc. Am. Mil. Engrs., Res. Officers Assn., Retired Officers Assn. Republican. Club: Runaway Bay (Tex.) Country. Office: 5402 Beaumont Center Blvd Suite 102 Tampa FL 33614

HEUSI, JOE DUANE, insurance company executive; b. Defiance, Ohio, June 12, 1942; s. Oscar Joseph and Ernestine (Penrod) H.; m. Frances Jean Hyland, Aug. 15, 1964; children—Richard Duane, Michael David. B.Music, Baldwin Wallace Coll., 1964, B.Music Edn., 1965; M.S., Columbia U., 1979. Tchr. Bedford (Ohio) Pub. Schs., 1965-66, Berea (Ohio) Pub. Schs., 1966-69; career account rep. Variable Annuity Mktg. Co., Cleve., 1968-71, v.p., regional mgr., Cranford, N.J., 1971-80, v.p. mktg. services, 1980-81, sr. v.p. mktg., Houston, 1981-83, pres., 1983—, dir., 1981—; chmn. Variable Annuity Life Ins. Co.; dir., pres. Timed Opportunity Fund, Valic Capital Accumulation Fund, Houston, 1983—, Separate Accounts One and Two, 1983—. Chmn., dir. Concert Chorale of Houston, 1983—. Mem. Am. Mgmt. Assn., Phi Mu Alpha, Sinfonia, Sigma Phi Epsilon. Home: 650 W Forest Dr Houston TX 77079 Office: Variable Annuity Life Ins Co 2929 Allen Pkwy Houston TX 77019

HEWETT, WENDELL CLARK, business administration educator; b. Stamford, Tex., July 26, 1935; s. Eddie Alton and Lula Belle (Goodwin) H.; m. Mary Edith Ralston, June 9, 1961; children—Dean, Chris, Pam, Mike. B.B.A., Tex. Tech U., 1960, M.B.A., 1961, D.Bus. Adminstrn., 1969. Instr. mktg. Tex. Tech U., Lubbock, 1963-68; assoc. prof. mktg. Northeast La. U., Monroe, 1968-69, U. Ala., Tuscaloosa, 1970-76; dean sch. bus. adminstrn. U. Tex.-Tyler, 1981-84, prof. bus. adminstrn., 1976—. Contbr. articles to profl. jours. Served with U.S. Army, 1955-57. Recipient George W. and Robert S. Pirtle Disting. Professorship of Free Enterprise, U. Tex.-Tyler, 1985. Mem. Am. Mktg. Assn., Acad. Mktg. Sci., So. Mktg. Assn. (treas. 1975-76), Southwestern Mktg. Assn., Sales and Mktg. Execs. Internat., Beta Gamma Sigma. Baptist. Avocations: boating; swimming; water skiing. Home: Route 3 Box 182 Flint TX 75762 Office: U Tex-Tyler 3900 University Blvd Tyler TX 75701

HEWITT, GERALD NEAL, hospital administrator; b. Maiden, N.C., Oct. 21, 1931; s. Artis Clifton and Ella Colene (Tuttle) H.; m. Phyllis Marion Beattie, Apr. 16, 1952; children—Timothy Neal, Scott Beattie, Angela Denise. B.A., Wake Forest U., 1958; M.Div., Southeastern Bapt. Theol. Sem., 1962; M.A., Appalachian State U., 1976; Ed.D., U. N.C.-Greensboro, 1983. Ordained to ministry So. Bapt. Ch., 1957; pastor First Bapt. Ch., Welcome, N.C., 1962-65; bus. mgr. N.C. Bapt. Hosp., Winston-Salem, 1965-71, controller, 1971-73, v.p. patient fin. services, 1973—; lectr. hosp. adminstrn. Bowman Gray Med. Sch., 1975—; bivocat. pastor South Fork Bapt. Ch., Winston-Salem, 1980-84; adj. prof. Broyhill Sch. Bus., Gardner-Webb Coll., Boiling Springs, N.C., 1984—. Mem. Forsyth Adv. Com. on Nursing Homes; chmn. Bapt. State Conv. Com. on Aging, 1976-80; pres. Southwest Forsyth Community Assn., 1979—; pres. Griffith PTA, 1969, Anderson High Sch. PTA, 1971; trustee N.C. Bapt. Homes, 1978-79; mem. Winston-Salem/Forsyth County Bd. Edn., 1984—; bd. dirs. Forsyth County Council for Older Adults, 1984—; co-chmn. Forsyth Medicine/Bus. Coalition. Served with USAF, 1951-55. Recipient Muncie award, 1982. Mem. Healthcare Fin. Mgmt. Assn. (advance mem. Follmer award 1974, Reeves award 1978), pres. N.C. chpt. 1977-78), Am. Coll. Healthcare Execs. Mem. editorial adv. bd. Healthcare Fin. Mgmt. 1982-84. Home: 3060 Brookhill Dr Winston Salem NC 27107 Office: 300 S Hawthorne Rd Winston Salem NC 27103

HEWITT, RUTH PRICE, educator, librarian; b. Washington, May 17, 1948; d. Irby Lee Price and June Helen (Garrison) Price Kurze; m. Stephen Allen Hewitt, Oct. 17, 1981. B.A. in Elem. Edn., Newberry Coll., 1970; postgrad. U. S.C., Clemson U., LaVerne Coll., Furman U. Cert. elem. tchr., S.C. Elem. tchr. Laurel Creek Sch., Mauldin, S.C., 1970-71, Sue Cleveland Sch., Piedmont, S.C., 1971, Alexander Sch., Greenville, S.C., 1971-73, Haynsworth Pvt. Sch., Greenville, 1974-77; substitute tchr. Prince Georges County schs., Upper Marlboro, Md., 1973-74, Greenville County pub. schs., Trinity Luth. Sch., 1977-80; librarian, media specialist Ambler Elem. Sch., Pickens, S.C., 1980-83. Chmn. tenant adv. com. Breckinridge Apts., 1976; sec. sch. bd. Our Saviour Luth. Ch., Greenville. Newberry Coll. Pres. scholar, 1967-68. Mem. Assn. Classroom Tchrs. (sch. rep. 1972-73), ALA, Kappa Delta (chaplain 1968-69). Republican.

HEWLETT, GLADYS FAYE, banker; b. Raceland, Ky., Dec. 24, 1924; d. Joseph and Belva (Mowery) McClanahan; student Am. Inst. Banking, Ashland, Ky., 1957-62; m. Wayne B. Hewlett, May 11, 1946; children—William Wayne, Joetta Dean. Treas., Raceland Bd. Edn., 1943-47; with 1st and Peoples Bank, Russell, Ky., 1957—, asst. cashier, 1975—. Mem. Working Women Cleve. Democrat. Methodist. Club: Eastern Star, Shriners. Home: 816 Raceland Ave Raceland KY 41169

HEYCK, GERTRUDE PAINE DALY (MRS. THEODORE R. HEYCK), club woman; b. Houston, Nov. 30, 1910; d. David and Gertrude (Paine) Daly; student Wellesley Coll., 1929, Pembroke Coll., 1931-34; B.A., Brown U., 1934; m. Theodore R. Heyck, May 1, 1935; children—Jane Peel (Mrs. Donald H. Gaucher), Theodore Daly. Dir., Union Stock Yards, San Antonio, 1961-64. Sustaining mem. Jr. League, Houston. Clubs: Brown-Pembroke, Brown U. Faculty. Home: 1907 Bolsover St Houston TX 77005 also 400 Bellevue Ave Newport RI 02840

HEYER, ANNA HARRIET, retired music librarian; b. Little Rock, Aug. 30, 1909; d. Arthur Wesley R. and Harriet Anna (Gage) H. A.B., B.Mus., Tex. Christian U., 1930; B.S. in L.S., U. Ill., 1933; M.S. in L.S., Columbia U., 1939; M.Mus. in Musicology, U. Mich., 1943. Elem. sch. music tchr. Ft. Worth Pub. Schs., 1931-32; high sch. librarian, 1934-38; cataloguer library, U. Tex.-Austin, 1939-40; music librarian, asst. prof. L.S., N. Tex. State U., Denton, 1940-65, librarian emeritus, 1976; cons. music library materials Tex. Christian U., Ft. Worth, 1965-79; ret., 1979. Author: A Check-List of Publications of Music, 1944; A Bibliography of Contemporary Music in the Music Library, North Texas State College, 1955; Historical Sets, Collected Editions and Monuments of Music: A Guide to Their Contents, 1957, 2d edit., 1969, 3d rev. edit., 1980; contbr. articles to profl. publs. Recipient citations for contbn. to music librarianship Music Library Assn., 1980, to music librarianship in Tex., 1983. Mem. ALA, Tex. Library Assn., Music Library Assn., AAUW, DAR. Mem. Disciples of Christ Ch. Clubs: Altrusa, Woman's Club Ft. Worth, Colonial Country. Home: 2538 Greene Ave Fort Worth TX 76109

HEYMAN, JOSEPH SAUL, administrator, physicist; b. New Bedford, Mass., Nov. 4, 1943; s. Sam and Leah (Schwartz) H.; m. Berna Judith Levine, Nov. 23, 1968; 1 dau., Laura Dawn. Student in English, Cornell U., 1961-63; B.A. in Physics with honors, Northeastern U., 1968; M.A. in Physics, Washington U., St. Louis, 1971, Ph.D., 1975. Physicist radiation damage in materials NASA Langley Research Center, 1966-68, research physicist Solar Wind Apollo Expt., 1968-69, staff physicist Phonon-Electron Interactions, Hampton, Va., 1970-75; head Lab. for Ultrasonics, Hampton, 1975-81; adj. prof. physics Coll. William and Mary, Williamsburg, Va., 1979—; head Materials Characterization Instrumentation sect., 1981—; mgr. NASA-NDE Research program, Hampton, Va., 1983—. Mem. Hampton Roads Sanitation Dist. Commn., 1985—. Recipient Indsl. Research Devel. IR-100 awards, 1974, 76, 78, 81; Arthur S. Fleming award for outstanding fed. employees, 1981; NASA Exceptional Service award, 1979; NASA Inventor of Yr. award, 1982. Mem. Am. Phys. Soc., IEEE, AAAS, Soc. Exptl. Stress Analysis, Sigma Xi. Patentee 15 primarily in field of applied ultrasonics and nondestructive evaluation of materials; contbr. articles to profl. jours. Home: 130 Indian Springs Rd Williamsburg VA 23185 Office: NASA-Langley Research Ctr Mail Stop 231 Hampton VA 23665

HEYWARD, CONSTANCE HOLLER, librarian; b. Columbia, S.C., Jan. 3, 1932; d. Arthur William and Miriam (Hearon) Holler; children—Halcott Green, Constance Reid, Cary Carrington, William Barnwell. A.B., U. S.C., 1953; M.L.S., Emory U., 1975. Librarian, Dunwoody Sch., Ga., 1964-67, Wheeler High Sch., Marietta, Ga., 1969—. Mem. ALA, Assn. Am. Sch. Librarians, Met. Atlanta Library Assn., Cobb County Assn. Media Specialists, Atlanta Hist. Soc. Democrat. Episcopalian. Avocations: horses. Home: 902 E Lake Dr Marietta GA 30062 Office: Wheeler High Sch 375 Holt Rd Marietta GA 30067

HIBBARD, WALTER ROLLO, JR., engineering educator; b. Bridgeport, Ct., Jan. 20, 1918; s. Walter R. and Helen S. (Kenworthy) H.; m. Charlotte H. Tracy, Mar. 21, 1942 (dec. 1970); children—Douglas, Lawrence, Diana; m. 2d, Louise A. Brembeck, Jan. 29, 1972. A.B., Wesleyan U., 1939; D.Engring., Yale U., 1942; D.Laws, Mich. Tech. U., 1968; D.Engring. (hon.), Montana Coll. Mineral Scis. and Tech., 1970. Registered profl. engr., Conn., Ohio, Va. Asst., then assoc. prof. Yale U., 1946-51; mgr. metallurgy and ceramics General Electric Research Lab., Schenectady, 1951-65; dir. U.S. Bur. Mines, Washington, 1965-68; v.p. Owens Corning Fiberglas Corp., 1968-74; prof. engring. Va. Poly. Inst., Blacksburg, 1974—; dir. Va. Center for Coal and Energy Research. Blacksburg, 1977—; dir. Norton Co., Worcester, Mass. Served to lt. comdr. USNR, 1942-46. Recipient Yale U. Engring. Alumni award, 1955; Wesleyan U. Disting. Alumnus award, 1979. Mem. Nat. Acad. Engring., Am. Acad. Arts and Scis., AIME (R.W. Raymond award 1950, J. Douglas medal 1969, Mineral Econs. award 1983), Am. Soc. Metals, Am. Ceramic Soc. Club: Cosmos (Washington). Contbr. numerous articles to profl. publs. Home: 1403 Highland Circle Blacksburg VA 24060 Office: 617 N Main St Blacksburg VA 24060

HIBBERT, WILLIAM ANDREW, JR., surgeon; b. Pensacola, Fla., June 15, 1932; s. William Andrew and Blanche Marie (Blair) H.; B.S., U. of South, 1953; M.D., Emory U., 1957; children—Andy III, Blair, Reb Stuart. Diplomate Am. Bd. Surgery, also recert., Am. Bd. Colon and Rectal Surgery. Intern, Duval Med. Center, U. Fla., Jacksonville, 1957-58; resident in gen. surgery Grady Meml. Hosp., Emory U., Atlanta, 1958-62; fellow in colon-rectal surgery Ochsner Found. Hosp., New Orleans, 1962-63, Baylor U. Med. Center, Dallas, 1964-65; practice medicine specializing in colon-rectal surgery, Austin, Tex., 1965—; mem. staff St. David, Seton, Brackenridge, Holy Cross hosps.; instr. Tulane U. Med. Sch., New Orleans, 1962-64; cons. U. Tex. Student Health Center. Bd. govs. Shrine Burn Hosp., Galveston, Tex.; bd. dirs. St. David Hosp. Found., Austin. Served with USPHS, 1963-64. Fellow ACS, Am. Soc. Colon and Rectal Surgeons; mem. Pan Am. (past chmn. colon-rectal sect.), So. Med. Assn. (past sect. chmn.), Tex. Med. Assn. Tex. Colon-Rectal Soc. (past pres.), Pan Pacific Surg. Soc., Royal Soc. Medicine (hon.), Internat. Soc. Univ. Colon and Rectal Surgeons. Club: Austin Downtown. Lodges: Masons, Shriners (potentate 1985; past dir. gen. Shrine Circus), Royal Order of Jesters, Rotary. Assoc. editor So. Med. Jour., 1973-75. Contbr. articles to med. jours. Office: 4210 Medical Pkwy Austin TX 78756

HIBBS, LEON, university president; b. Balko, Okla., Oct. 15, 1930; s. Paschal Otho and Luella (Smith) H.; m. Maxine Parker, Sept. 6, 1950; children—Max, Gaye, Craig, LeAn. B.S., Northwestern Okla. State U., 1952; Ed.M., U. Okla., 1956; M.S., Okla. State U., 1957, Ed.D., 1959. Successively tchr., prin., supt. Greenough schs., Beaver County, Okla., 1952-56; dir. instructional TV Okla. Dept. Edn., 1957-60; dir. course devel., coordinator spl. projects Purdue Research Found., 1960-62; dean edn. Oklahoma City U., 1962-67; pres. Southeastern Okla. State U., 1967—; cons. infield, 1960—. Author: Using the Stereomicroscope, 1964, A Programmed Textbook in Mathematics for Elementary School Teachers, 1966, Living Science, 1966. Chmn. Goals for Durant, 1969—; Chmn. bd. dirs. Southeastern Found., 1967—. Recipient Favorite Faculty award Oklahoma City U., 1965; Student Edn. Assn. award, 1966; fellow NSF, 1956. Mem. Nat., Okla. edn. assns., Durant C. of C. (dir. 1967—). Lodges: Masons, Rotary (dir. Durant 1967—). Office: Station A Durant OK 74701

HIBEL, JANET, psychologist; b. Boston, Oct. 22, 1954; d. William Richard and Doris Ethyl (Rostler) H. B.A., Brandeis U., 1976; M.A., Fla. Atlantic U., 1978; Ph.D., U. Mo., 1983. Lic. psychologist, Tex. Dir. human sexuality edn. program U. Mo., Columbia, 1980-82; sr. staff psychologist U. Iowa, Iowa City, 1982-83; counseling psychologist Tex. Woman's U., Houston, 1983—. Contbr. articles to profl. jours. Mem. Am. Psychol. Assn., Am. Counseling Personnel Assn., Am. Counselor Devel. Assn., Houston Psychol. Assn. Democrat. Jewish. Club: Kenada Farms Fox Hunt (Waller). Office: Tex Woman Univ Counseling Ctr Houston TX 77030 also West Houston Psychol Assocs 1011 Hwy 6-South Houston TX

HICKAM, DOROTHY (MOLLY), librarian; b. Miami, Fla., Feb. 6, 1926; d. George Worthington and Edris (Lauritzen) Butler; m. Charles Edwin Hickam, Feb. 15, 1952 (div. Oct. 1955); 1 son, Ross Butler. B.A., U. Miami, 1948; M.A., Columbia U. Tchrs. Coll., 1959; M.L.S., Fla. State U., 1985. Cert. elem. edn., Calif.; cert. librarianship, Fla. Tchr. Cortez Elem. Sch., Covina, Calif., 1954-55, C.Z. Schs., Balboa, 1956-58; librarian Tchrs. profl. Library, Miami, 1959-68, Sonora High Sch., La Habra, Calif., 1968-70, Miami Heights Elem. Sch., Miami, 1970-81; head librarian Profl. Resource Ctr., Miami, 1982—; union steward United Tchrs. Dade, Miami, 1980-81. Mem. ALA, Fla. Assn. Media in Edn., Dade County Media Specialists Assn., Mensa. Democrat. Unitarian. Home: 11345 SW 154 Terr Miami FL 33157 Office: Profl Resource Ctr 1080 Labaron Dr Miami Springs FL 33166

HICKEY, HAZEL SEBREN, banker; b. Belmont, La., Aug. 25, 1929; d. Lucien H. and Nettie Hampton (Skinner) Sebren; student public schs., also various specialized banking courses; m. J.J. Hickey, Mar. 14, 1959; children—Kenneth Webb, David Webb, Michael Webb, Rick Webb. Teller, First Nat. Bank, Shreveport, 1953-63, 63-66; savs. and comml. teller Mechanics Nat. Bank Burlington County, Burlington, N.J., 1963; loan teller Longview Nat. Bank (Tex.), 1967; with Longview Bank & Trust Co., 1968—, sr. v.p., dir. mktg. and personnel, 1981—; adv. bd., dir. La. Bankers Sch. Supervisory Tng.; coordinator fin. seminars; dir. Fireman's Pension Bd., 1982-83. Treas., Longview Symphony Guild, 1978-80; bd. dirs. Longview Symphony League, Longview unit Am. Heart Assn.; chmn. Gregg County Heart Fund, 1979, pres. Heart Assn., 1982—; bd. dirs., v.p. Voluntary Action Ctr., 1983; past dir. Longview Civic Chorale; mem. adv. bd. LaTourneau Coll., 1981. Citizenship scholar, 1947. Mem. Sales and Mktg. Execs. (charter, past dir.), Am. Inst. Banking, Nat. Assn. Bank Women, Bank Mktg. Assn., Longview C. of C., Fedn. Women's Clubs (1st v.p.). Baptist. Clubs: Oak Forest Country, Summit (Longview); E. Tex. Knife and Fork (dir., past pres.). Home: NF 40 Lake Cherokee Longview TX 75603 Office: 300 W Whaley St Longview TX 75601

HICKEY, NORMAN WILBUR, county official; b. Belleville, N.J., Aug. 31, 1927; s. John E. and Jeannette (Gebhard) H.; B.A., Pa. State U., 1954; M.Govtl. Adminstrn. (Fels scholar, fellow) U. Pa., 1957; m. Dolores F. Jacobs, Oct. 17, 1956; 1 son, Christopher N. Mem. staff office of city mgr. City of Windsor (Conn.), 1955; asst. city mgr. City of Ft. Lauderdale (Fla.), 1956-58, 61-62; city mgr. City of Titusville (Fla.), 1958-62, City of Daytona Beach (Fla.), 1962-66; city sr. adviser, dir. devel. ops., chief field ops. land reform, Vietnam, Saigon, 1967-70; chief mission HUD/AID to Colombia, Bogota, 1970-72; dep. city mgr., cons. City of Hollywood (Fla.), also exec. dir. Daytona Beach (Fla.) Downtown Devel. Authority, 1972-73; city mgr. City of Titusville (Fla.), 1973-80; county adminstr. Hillsborough County (Fla.), 1981—. Vice-pres. Fla. United Fund, 1960—, chmn., 1964—. Served with USMC, 1945-49, 50-51. Recipient Good Govt. award Jaycees Titusville, 1960, 76, Daytona Beach, 1965; State of Fla. Good Govt. and Outstanding Contbn. awardee, 1965; Meritorious Honor award AID/Dept. State, 1969; Sertoma Service to Mankind award, 1979; Roy Wilkins Humanitarian award. Mem. Internat. (v.p.), Fla. (pres.) city and county mgrs. assns., Fla. League Cities (state dir.), Am. Public Works Assn. Episcopalian. Clubs: Civitan, Optimist, Rotary. Office: PO Box 1110 Tampa FL 33601

HICKEY, ROBERT CORNELIUS, surgeon, educator; b. Hallstead, Pa., Dec. 9, 1917; s. Cornelius E. and Jennie (Murphy) H.; m. Rose Van Vranken, June 11, 1942; children—Kathryn Ann (Mrs. Geoffrey White), Robert C., Stephen P., Dennis V., Sarah E. B.S., Cornell U., 1938, M.D., 1942; postgrad., State U. Iowa, U.S. Naval Hosp., San Diego, Meml. Hosp. Cancer and Allied Diseases, N.Y.C. Diplomate: Am. Bd. Surgery. Staff U. Hosp. and State U. Iowa, 1951-62, successively asso. surgery, clin. asst. prof., asso. prof., 1951-57, prof. surgery, 1957-62, asso. dean research in medicine, 1955-62; asso. dir. research U. Tex. M.D. Anderson Hosp. and Tumor Inst., 1962-63, dir., 1969—, exec. v.p., 1976—; prof. surgery U. Tex., 1962-63, 68—; prof., chmn. dept. surgery U. Wis. Med. Sch., Madison, 1963-68; cons. surgeon gen. USPHS, 1959-68. Dir. Iowa div. Am. Cancer Soc., 1954-62; pres. Iowa div., 1959-60; dir.-at-large Tex. div., 1968—; mem. U.S. nat. com. Internat., Union Against Cancer, 1977—; mem. nat. cancer adv. com. USPHS, 1980—. Served to lt. M.C. USNR, 1943-46. Fellow A.C.S. (gov. 1968-71, vice chmn. bd. govs. 1971-73, chmn. bd. 1973-74, pres. So. Tex. chpt.); mem. Houston Surg. Soc., Am. Soc. Clin. Oncology, AAAS, AAUP, Am. Radium Soc. (v.p. 1964-65), Central Surg. Assn., AMA, N.Y. Acad. Scis., James Ewing Soc. (v.p. 1964-65), Western Surg. Assn. (v.p. 1973-74), Iowa Acad. Surgery (pres. 1962), Am. Surg. Assn., Soc. Surgery Alimentary Tract (v.p. 1977—), Tex. Surg. Soc., Sigma Xi. Home: 435 Tallowood Dr Houston TX 77024

HICKMAN, DARRELL DAVID, state justice; b. Searcy, Ark., Feb. 6, 1935; s. James Paul and Mildred Margaret (Jackson) H.; student Harding Coll., Searcy, 1952-55; LL.B., U. Ark., 1958; m. Kerry Lee Hardcastle, Oct. 16, 1971; children—Dana, David, Torrie. Bar: Ark. 1958. Pvt. practice, Searcy, 1964-70; dep. pros. atty. White and Woodruff counties, 1965; chancery judge 1st Chancery Circuit, 1972-76; asso. justice Ark. Supreme Ct., 1977—. Served with USN, 1958-64. Mem. Ark. Bar Assn. Mem. Ch. of Christ. Office: Justice Bldg Little AR 72201

HICKMAN, HOYT LEON, clergyman; b. Pitts., May 22, 1927; s. Leon Edward and Mayme (Hoyt) H.; B.A. magna cum laude, Haverford Coll., 1950; M.Div. cum laude, Yale U., 1953; S.T.M., Union Theol. Sem., 1954; D.D. (hon.), Morningside Coll., 1978; m. Martha Jean Whitmore, Dec. 16, 1950; children—Peter, John, Stephen, Mary. Ordained to ministry Meth. Ch., 1953; pastor 1st Meth. Ch., Windber, Pa., 1954-57, Claysville and Stony Point Meth. Chs., Claysville, Pa., 1957-59, Coll. Hill Meth. Ch., Beaver Falls, Pa., 1959-64, Cascade United Meth. Ch., Erie, Pa., 1964-72; dir. office local ch. worship, gen. bd. discipleship United Meth. Ch., Nashville, 1972-78, asst. gen. sec. gen. bd. discipleship, 1978-85, dir. resource devel., gen. bd. discipleship, 1985—; exec. sec. Gen. Commn. on Worship, United Meth. Ch., 1968-72; mem. Commn. on Worship, World Meth. Council, 1971-81; mem. nat. program com. Christian Family Movement, 1969-73; pres. Erie County Council Chs., 1970-71. Bd. dirs. Liturgical Conf., 1973-80. Served with USN, 1945-46. Mem. Phi Beta Kappa. Democrat. Author: Strengthening Our Congregation's Worship, 1981; At the Lord's Table, 1981; United Methodist Altars, 1984; A Primer for Church Worship, 1984; The Acolyte's Book, 1985; (with others) Handbook of the Christian Year, 1986. Contbr. numerous articles to mags. Home: 2034 Castleman Dr Nashville TN 37215 Office: PO Box 840 Nashville TN 37202

HICKS, BETH BOATRIGHT, nurse, state administrator; b. Elkins, Ark., Jan. 11, 1935; d. William Freeman and Elsie Irene (Benson) Boatright; m. Charles Ernest Hicks, July 4, 1958; children—Karen Sue Hicks Withers, Charles Kevin, James Keith. Student U. Ark.-Fayetteville, 1954-56; B.S. in Nursing, U. Ark.-Little Rock Med. Ctr., 1958. Staff nurse VA Hosp., Little Rock, 1958-61; coronary care nurse Drew Meml. Hosp., Monticello, Ark., 1975-77, supr. nursing staff, 1976-79; inservice dir. McGehee-Desha County Hosp., McGehee, Ark., 1979-80; dir. nursing S.E. Ark. Human Devel. Ctr., Warren, 1980-81; home health case mgr. Ark. Dept. Health, Hamburg, 1981—; chmn. hearing and vision testing, elem. sch., Monticello, 1973-74. County chmn. Am. Heart Assn., Ashley County, Ark., 1963-64; den mother Cub Scouts, DeSoto Area council Boy Scouts Am., 1978-79; Tchr. Sunday Sch., pianist, mem. handbell choir Bapt. Ch. Mem. Pub. Health Assn. Ark., Ark Pub. Health Nurses Assn., Ark. State Employees Assn. Club: Monticello Jr. Aux. (chmn. publicity 1975, chmn. scholarship com. 1976). Lodge: DAR. Home: 514 E Parker Hamburg AR 71640 Office: Ashley County Health Dept Court House Annex Hamburg AR 71646

HICKS, BYRON ADNA, banker; b. Moneta, Va., Aug. 30, 1916; s. Wesley Peters and Sally Walthal (Holland) H.; student Roanoke Coll., 1934-35; B.S. in Econs., U. Va., 1938; postgrad. Stonier Grad. Sch. Banking, Rutgers U., 1950-52; m. Agnes Rose Cunningham, Apr. 20, 1940; children—Martha Holland, Celia Parry. With Univ. Credit Co., Raleigh, N.C., 1939-42, Hercules Powder Co., Radford, Va., 1942-43; with First Nat. Exchange Bank of Va., Roanoke, 1946—, chmn. bd., chief exec. officer, 1977—, also dir., mem. exec. com., mem. trust com.; with Dominion Bankshares Corp., Roanoke, 1967—, pres., chief adminstrv. officer, 1973-77, pres., chief exec. officer, 1977-81; chmn., 1981—, also dir., mem. exec. com. Bd. dirs., chmn. finance com. Community Hosp. of Roanoke Valley; trustee, vice-chmn. bd. Baptist Children's Home, Salem, Va.; vice chmn. bd. trustee, chmn. mem. exec. com. Roanoke Coll. Served to lt. USNR, 1943-46. Baptist. Home: 2726 Cornwallis Ave SE Roanoke VA 24014 Office: PO Box 13327 Roanoke VA 24040

HICKS, CHERYL SUSAN, physician; b. Spartanburg, S.C., Sept. 19, 1950; d. Roy Lee and Lois Rachel (Johnson) Hicks; m. Robert Duren Johnson, Jr., Sept. 22, 1973 (div. 1981); m. 2d, Charles Maurice Davis, June 26, 1982. B.S., Duke U., 1972; M.D., Med. U. S.C., 1976. Diplomate Am. Bd. Nuclear Medicine, Am. Bd. Radiology. Diagnostic radiology resident Med. U. S.C., Charleston, 1976-80, nuclear medicine fellow, 1980-81; asst. prof. U. S.C. Sch. Medicine, Columbia, 1981-82; pres., physician Breast Diagnostic Center, Inc., Columbia, 1982—; diagnostic radiologist Richland Meml. Hosp., Columbia, 1982—; pres. Breast Diagnostic Center, Inc., Columbia, S.C., 1982—; mem. staff Dorn VA Hosp., Columbia. Mem. Nat. Network Female Execs. Mem. Soc. Nuclear Medicine, Am. Coll. Radiology, Am. Assn. Women Radiologists, Am. Med. Women's Assn., Columbia Med. Soc., S.C. Med. Assn., S.C. Capitol chpt. Am. Med. Womens Assn. (treas. 1982-83). Home: Route 2 Box 396 Irmo SC 29063 Office: Breast Diagnostic Center Inc Suite 1 4600 Forest Dr Columbia SC 29206

HICKS, GRETA PATTERSON, accountant; b. Aspermont, Tex., Oct. 14, 1940; d. Herman Johnson and Zina O'Zella (Daniels) Patterson; children—Ted Aaron, Tina Marie. B.B.A., U. Tulsa, 1972. C.P.A., Okla., Tex. With IRS, various locations, 1973-80, group mgr., Houston, 1979, resident lead instr., Dallas region, 1979, dist. tng. and recruitment coordinator, Houston, Tex., 1979-80; tax mgr. Arthur Young & Co., Houston, 1980-81; sole practice Greta P. Hicks C.P.A., Houston, 1981—. Coordinator, panelist Ann. Income Tax Forum, KTRK-TV, Houston, 1977-85; mem. career devel. adv. com. Houston Ind. Sch. Dist., 1980-81, 85, 86. Am. Soc. Women Accts. scholar, 1972. Mem. Am. Inst. C.P.A.s, Tex. Soc. C.P.A.s, Am. Soc. Women's Accts. (pres. 1981-82), Am. Women's Soc. C.P.A.s, Bus. and Profl. Women's Club, Phi Gamma Sigma, Beta Gamma Sigma. Contbg. author Fax Return, Matrix mag., Tex. Woman, Singles Scene, Downtown News, Houston Woman. Office: 2855 Mangum Suite 303 Houston TX 77092

HICKS, ROGER F., insurance company executive; b. Detroit, Mar. 26, 1941; s. Earl Edward and Marie Olive (Nowacki) H.; m. Jill K. Hicks, Nov. 24, 1967 (div. 1983); children—Laurie, Karen, Steven. B.S., Eastern Mich. U., 1977; M.P.A., U. Okla., 1984. Sr. mgmt. market, govt. programs Blue Cross/Blue Shield Mich., Detroit, 1966-78; sr. mgr. mktg. Blue Cross/Blue Shield Okla., Oklahoma City, 1978-81; dir. mktg. Delta Dental Plan Okla., Oklahoma City, 1981, exec. dir., 1982-84; pres. Hicks & Assocs. Group Ins., Oklahoma City. Mem. Nat. Assn. Life Underwriters, Nat. Assn. Health Underwriters, Gen. Mgrs. and Agts. Council Greater Okla., Oklahoma City Assn. Health Underwriters (pres. 1985-86). Club.: Green's Country (Oklahoma City). Lodge: Kiwanis (chmn. com.). Home: 2209 Woodford Way Edmond OK 73034 Office: Hicks & Assocs Group Ins 4801 N Classen Blvd Suite 253 PO Box 18227 Oklahoma City OK 73154

HICKSON, SHIRLEY ANN, historian, educator; b. Grove Hill, Ala., Apr. 19, 1944; d. Furman Fuller and Eleanor (Harrison) H.; B.A. (UDC scholar), Judson Coll., 1966; M.A., U. Ala., 1971; Ph.D., U. S.C., 1985. Preceptor, Judson Coll., Marion, Ala., 1966-68; social studies tchr. Hudson High Sch., Selma, Ala., 1969-70; instr. history North Greenville Coll., Tigerville, S.C., 1971-76, asst. prof., 1976-82, assoc. prof., 1982—, adviser coll. newspaper staff, 1971-76, social scis. div. chmn., 1972-76; teaching asst. dept. history U. S.C., Columbia, 1978-80. Nat. Endowment of Humanities grantee, summer 1976, N. Greenville Coll. grantee, 1981. Mem. AAUP (pres. chpt. 1973-75), So. Hist. Assn., S.C. Hist. Assn., S.C. Hist. Soc., S.C. Bapt. Hist. Soc., Clarke County Hist. Soc., Nat. Trust Historic Preservation, S.C. Com. for Humanities (scholars' forum 1983—), Phi Alpha Theta. Author chpts. in Dictionary Lit. Biography. Office: North Greenville Coll Tigerville SC 29688

HICKSTEIN, ROBERT JOHN, real estate sales manager; b. Milw., Feb. 20, 1936; s. Frederick Robert and Dorothy Barbara (Ignera) H.; m. Kathy Ann Wilkey, Aug. 3, 1968 (div. 1985); 1 child, Patricia Lynn; m. Rosetta Bernadette Sbrocco, June 14, 1985. Cert. real estate brokerage mgr. Sales assoc., gen. sales mgr. Crisp Co. Realtors, St. Petersburg, Fla., 1972-80; br. mgr. Merrill Lynch Realty, Clearwater, Fla., 1980-84, dist. mgr., 1984-85, gen. mgr., 1985—. Mem. Sales and Mktg. Execs. (dir. 1985—), Mensa, Com. of 100. Republican. Roman Catholic. Clubs: Tiger Bay, Presidents (founding mem. St. Petersburg). Avocations: Music; fishing; golf; gourmet dining and wines. Home: 1700 Brightwaters Blvd NE Saint Petersburg FL 33704

HIDALGO, CHESTER PAUL, design engineer; b. Opelousas, La., Dec. 19, 1926; s. Archange Leo and Mary Lilla (Briley) H.; student La. State U., 1944; B.S. in Agrl. Engring., U. S.W. La., 1951; student Tex. Christian U., 1963-66; m. Mary Louise Childress, July 18, 1953; children—LeRoy, Casey, Michael, Paula, Melody, James. Engr., Halliburton Co., Lafayette, La., 1953-55; farmer, rancher, Lockney, Tex., 1955-62; design engr. Gen. Dynamics, Ft. Worth, 1962-73; owner, mgr. Granbury Stone and Nursery, Granbury, Tex., 1970-75; pres. ADAL Corp., Granbury, 1975—; sr. design engr. Gen. Dynamics, Ft. Worth, 1975-83; chief engr. Wilson Machine Co., Ft. Worth, 1983—. Mem. Sch. Bd. S. Plains, Tex., 1958-62; del. Democratic Party, Floyd County, Tex., 1960; v.p. Granbury C. of C., 1974-76; mem. Met. Hwys. Com. Hood County (Tex.), 1973-76; mem. Parks Bd. Granbury City, 1975-80; mem. Planning Bd. Hood County, 1976-80, bicentennial bd., 1976-84. Served with USN, 1944-46, as 1st lt. with USAF, 1951-53. Recipient Hood County Bicentennial Civic award, 1978. Registered landscape irrigation specialist, Tex. Mem. Am. Mgmt. Assn., Am. Nurserymen Assn., Tex. Assn. Nurserymen, Internat. Platform Assn. Republican. Roman Catholic. Clubs: Optimists, Lions, KC. Home: 1106 Gifford St Granbury TX 76048

HIDAY, LANNY L., lawyer; b. Indpls., May 28, 1944; s. Wilford T. and Dorothy M. (Snyder) H.; m. A. Virginia Marie Aldigé, Sept. 5, 1970; 1 son, Jeffrey L. Student Duke U., 1962-64; A.B., U. N.C.-Chapel Hill, 1971, postgrad., 1971-72; J.D., U. Colo., 1975. Bar: N.C. 1975. Law practice, Durham, N.C., 1975-76; asst. prof. law N.C. Central U., Durham, 1976-80; vis. prof. law U. N.C.-Chapel Hill, 1978; law practice, Chapel Hill, 1980—; gen. counsel Wheeler Airlines; cons. N.C. Bar Assn. Bar Rev., 1981. Mem. ABA (forum com. air and space law), Fed. Bar Assn., N.C. State Bar, N.C. Bar Assn., Nat. Transp. Safety Bd. Bar Assn. Democrat. Episcopalian. Home: 1424 Arboretum Dr Chapel Hill NC 27514 Office: Suite 206 University Sq E 123 W Franklin St Chapel Hill NC 27514

HIDDEN, GREGORY RICHARD, investment company executive; b. Fresno, Calif., Mar. 25, 1947; s. Morton Earl and Jannette Marshall (Bridger) H.; m. Sharon Lee Krejcu, Dec. 16, 1973; 1 child, Jennifer Michelle. B.S., Tex. Christian U., 1976. Account exec. Prudential Ins. Co., Fort Worth, 1973-76; mgr. Great So. Ins. Co., Dallas, 1976; account exec. E.F. Hutton & Co., Inc., N.Y.C., 1976-80; regional v.p. Anchor Nat. Fin. Services, Phoenix, 1980-81, Putnam Funds Distbn. Co., Boston, 1981-82; sr. v.p. Equitec Securities Co., Oakland, Calif., 1982—, Fort Worth, 1966—. Mem. Inst. Cert. Fin. Planners, Internat. Assn. Fin. Planners. Republican. Methodist. Club: Sertoma. Lodges: Kiwanis.

HIETT, JOE HARICE, education educator, administrator; b. Benton, Ky., July 30, 1935; s. Hoy Herbert and Hilda (Aaron) H.; m. Sally Parker, June 30, 1962; children—Katherine, Kearns. B.A., Lambuth Coll., 1957; B.D., Vanderbilt U., 1960; Ph.D., Fla. State U., 1971. Ordained to ministry Methodist Ch., 1960; asst. minister 1st Meth. Ch., Memphis, 1960-63; minister Pleasant Valley Meth. Ch., Union City, Tenn., 1963-68; asst. to pres. Fla. State U., Tallahassee, 1970-72, provost, v.p., 1972-77, assoc. prof. higher edn., 1977—; dir. Area Ednl. Consortium; cons. Sloan Commn. on Higher Edn. Chmn. Memphis Mayor's Com. to Resettle Cuban Refugees, 1961; mem. Tenn. Commn. to Hire the Handicapped, 1965, White House Edn. Mission to Vietnam, 1969; chmn. Gov.'s Conf. on Higher Edn. Fla., 1981. Merrill fellow Harvard U., 1967. Mem. Phi Delta Kappa, Kappa Delta Phi. Democrat. Episcopalian. Author: Florida State-Wide Governing Board for Higher Education, 1905-1969, 1971; Changing Role of Government and Higher Education in Florida, 1978; contbr. articles to profl. jours. Home: 419 Vinnedge Ride Tallahassee FL 32303 Office: 207 Stone Bldg Fla State U Tallahassee FL 32306

HIGBY, EDWARD JULIAN, safety engineer; b. Milw., June 9, 1939; s. Richard L. Higby and Julie Ann (Bruins) O'Kelly: m. Frances Ann Knoodle, 1959 (div. 1962); 1 child, Melinda Ann Mozader; m. Sandra Yvonne Fasano, June 1, 1976. B.S. in Criminal Justice, Southwestern U., Tucson, 1984. Tactical officer Miami Police Dept., Fla., 1967-68; intelligence officer Fla. Div. Beverages, 1968-72; licensing coordinator Lums Restaurant Corp., Miami, 1972-73; legal asst. Walt Disney World, Lake Buena Vista, Fla., 1973-78; loss control cons. R.P. Hewitt & Assocs., Orlando, Fla., 1978-79; safety coordinator City of Lakeland, Fla., 1979—. Author: Safety Guide for Health Care, 1979. Bd. dirs. Tampa Area Safety Council, 1983—, Imperial Traffic Safety Council, Lakeland, 1983—; mem. Bay Lake City Council, 1974-76, mayor, 1975-76; bd. dirs. Greater Lakeland chpt. ARC, 1980—, chmn. health services, 1980—; mem. budget com. United Way Central Fla., 1983—; mem. Fla. League Cities, 1974-76, Tri-County League Cities, 1974-76, Orange County Criminal Justice Council, 1974-78, Central Fla. Safety Council, 1978-79. Served with U.S. Army, 1963-64. Named Vol. of Yr., Greater Lakeland chpt. ARC, 1983, 84. Mem. Fla. Sheriffs Assn. (hon. life), Internat. Assn. Identification, Polk County Phamacists Assn., Fla. Fedn. Safety, Risk and Ins. Mgmt. Soc., Am. Soc. Safety Engrs. (chpt. pres. 1984-85, Safety Profl. of Yr. 1984-85), Heartland Safety Soc. (pres. 1983), Fla. Citrus Safety Assn. (pres. 1981-83), Nat. Fire Protection Assn., Am. Indsl. Hygiene Assn. Republican. Avocations: hunting; fishing. Home: PO Drawer 120 Kathleen FL 33849 Office: 1108 E Parker St Lakeland FL 33801

HIGDON, DEBORAH WEST, educator; b. Bowling Green, Ky., Dec. 17, 1957; d. Charles Preston and Betty Jane (Sweeney) West; m. Steven Leslie Higdon, June 25, 1983. B.S., Samford U., 1979; M.Ed. in Spl. Edn. candidate Middle Tenn. State U. Educator, St. Paul Acad., Nashville, 1980-82; educator 2d grade Franklin Rd. Acad., Nashville, 1982—. Mem. Hypatia, Alpha Delta Pi Alumni Assn. (corr. sec. 1980-81), Kappa Delta Pi, Kappa Delta Epsilon, Omicron Delta Kappa, Pi Gamma Mu. Baptist. Office: Franklin Rd Acad 4800 Franklin Rd Nashville TN 37220

HIGGINBOTHAM, HENRY KESLER, II, dentist; b. Bluefield, W.Va., Mar. 16, 1949; s. Upshur and Catherine (Crockett) H.; m. Victoria Lee Warren, June 5, 1971. B.S., Marshall U., 1971; D.D.S., W.Va. U., 1976. Gen. practice dentistry, Pulaski, Va., 1976—; advisor to dental assts. Wytheville Community Coll., Va., 1977—. Mem. Southwest Va. Dental Assn., Va. Dental Assn., ADA. Presbyterian. Avocations: hiking; fishing; hunting; bicycling; basketball. Home: Route 2 Box 149 Pulaski VA 24301 Office: 73 3d St NW Pulaski VA 24301

HIGGINBOTHAM, HUGH OLIVER, JR., educator; b. Memphis, Jan. 19, 1937; s. Hugh Oliver and Mary Kathryn (Sullender) H. Student, St. Bernard Sem., 1955-58; B.S., Memphis State U., 1967, M.Ed., 1969, postgrad., 1980—; postgrad. Vanderbilt U., 1972 L.H.D. (hon.), Cambridge U. Tchr., St. Michael Sch., Memphis, 1963-68; tchr., counselor Christian Bros. High Sch., Memphis, 1968-76; prin., counselor St. Anne Sch., Memphis, 1976-79; prof. Latin, religious studies, ethics Christian Bros. High Sch., Memphis, 1979—; asst. prof. Legal-Med. Inst. of Memphis. Served with U.S. Army, 1960-62. Recipient Service awards St. Peters Home for Children, 1966, Cath. Diocese of Memphis, 1984. NSF grantee, 1972. Mem. Am. Classical League, Nat. Catholic Edn. Assn., Nat. Assn. Secondary Sch. Prins., Tenn. Fgn. Lang. Tchrs. Assn., Elem. Sch. Prins., Tenn. Assn. for Counseling and Devel., Tenn. Sch. Counselors Assn. (pres. 1972-74), Tenn. Assn. Supervision and Curriculum Devel. Clubs: Memphis Petroleum, Moose. Home: 638 Watson Memphis TN 38111 Office: 5900 Walnut Grove Rd TN 38119 also 1217 Getwell Memphis TN 38111

HIGGINBOTHAM, PATRICK ERROL, judge; b. Ala.; student Arlington State Coll., 1956-57, N. Tex. State U., 1958, U. Tex., 1958; B.A., U. Ala., 1960, LL.B., 1961. Bar: Ala. 1961. Tex. 1962, U.S. Supreme Ct. Ptnr., Coke & Coke, Dallas, 1964-75; judge U.S. Dist. Ct. No. Dist. Tex., Dallas, 1976-82, U.S. Ct. Appeals 5th Cir., 1982—; lectr. on Constl. law, fed. complex litigation So. Meth. U. Law Sch., 1971—, lectr. constl. law, 1981—; mem. faculty Am. Inst. Banking Fed. Jud. Center, Washington, Columbia U. Trial Seminar, Nat. Inst. Trial Advocacy; lectr. in field; conferee Am. Assembly, 1975, Pound Conf., 1976. Chmn. bd. First United Methodist Ch., Richardson, Tex.; trustee Southwestern Legal Found. Named Outstanding Alumnus, U. Tex., Arlington, 1978. One of Nation's 100 Most Powerful Persons for the 80's, Next Mag. Fellow Am. Bar Found.; mem. Am. Bar Assn. (chmn. com. to compile fed. jury charges antitrust sect., mem. council antitrust sect.), Dallas Bar Assn. (dir., chmn. coms. legal aid, civic affairs), Dallas Bar Found. (dir.), Continuing Legal Edn. (chmn. subcom. civil litigation), Am. Law Inst., S.W. Legal Found., Am. Judicature Soc. (dir.). Farrah Law Soc. Bench and Bar, Order of Coif, Omicron Delta Kappa. Contbr. articles, revs. to profl. publs.; note editor Ala. Law Rev., 1960-61; adv. Southwestern Law Jour.; editorial bd. Am. Bar Jour.; narrator Law in Changing Soc., one-hour video tape, 1977. Office: 1100 Commerce St Dallas TX 75242

HIGGINBOTHAM, PRIEUR JAY, city official, writer; b. Pascagoula, Miss., July 16, 1937; s. Prieur Jay and Vivian Inez (Perez) H.; m. Alice Louisa Martin, June 27, 1970; children—Jeanne-Felicie, Denis Prieur, Robert Findlay. B.A., U. Miss.; postgrad. Am. U., CCNY. Asst. clk. Miss. Ho. of Reps., Jackson, 1955-58; tchr. Mobile County Pub. Schs., Ala., 1962-73; head local history Mobile Pub. Library, 1973-83; dir. Mobile Mcpl. Archives, 1983—. Author: Old Mobile, 1977 (ALA prize 1978); Fast Train Russia, 1983; 11 other books, articles; contbg. editor The Citizen Diplomat, Gainesville, Fla., 1985—; editorial dir. Gulf Coast Hist. Rev., 1984—; book reviewer Library Jour., N.Y.C., 1985—; bd. dirs. Ala. Records Commn., 1984—. Pres. Mobile Soc. for Soviet-Am. Understanding, 1982—; chmn. Mobile Com. on Fine Arts, 1985—; exec. bd. Mobile Internat. Festival, 1984-86, Neighborhood Improvement Council, 1974-79. Served with USAR, 1956-62. Recipient Gen. L. Kemper Williams award La. Hist. Assn., 1977, award of Merit, Miss. Hist. Soc., 1979, Gilbert Chinard prize, Franco-Am. Soc., Duke U., 1979, Elisabeth Gould award Mobile Hist. Devel. Commn., 1981. Mem. Soc. Am. Archivists, Smithsonian Soc., Nat. Geog. Soc., Authors League, Am. Com. on East-West Accord. Democrat. Methodist. Avocations: tennis; painting; music. Office: Mobile Mcpl Archives 111 S Royal St Mobile AL 36633

HIGGINS, ALAN MILLS, real estate executive; b. Cin., Jan. 10, 1945; s. Jack and Agnes (Mills) H.; m. Elaine Marie Benes, May 11, 1968; children—Scott, Jason. B.S., Miami U., Oxford, Ohio, 1967. Site developer Standard Oil Co. Ohio, 1967-72; corp. real estate rep. Gen. Tire Realty Co., Gen. Tire and Rubber Co., 1972-74, mgr. corp. real estate, v.p., 1974-76, pres., dir., 1976-83; sr. v.p. Vantage Cos., Dallas, 1983—; chmn. bd., pres. Am. Realty Acquisition Cons., 1978—; mem. bus. devel. council 1st Union Nat. Bank N.C.; vice chmn. Am. Inst. Asset Mgmt.; staff schs. continuing edn. U. Okla., 1977-79, U. Wis., 1979; staff U. N.C., Charlotte, 1980. Mem. Brecksville (Ohio) Charter Rev. Com., 1973. Served with AUS, 1967-69. Mem. Nat. Assn. Corp. Real Estate Execs. (chmn. bd. dirs.), Soc. Indsl. Realtors, Indsl. Devel. Research Council, Soc. Real Estate Appraisers, Am. Inst. Corp. Asset Mgmt. (founder). Contbr. articles to profl. jours., chpts. to tech. books; mem. editorial adv. bd. Corp. Design mag. Home: 405 Guadalajara Circle Irving TX 75062 Office: 2525 Stemmons Freeway Dallas TX 75207

HIGGINS, KENNETH RAYMOND, landscape architect; b. Holyoke, Mass., Nov. 2, 1915; s. Alfred and Lillie (Ritter) H.; student R.I. State Coll., 1934; B.S. Mass. State Coll., 1937, B.Landscape Architecture, 1939; m. Mary Douthat Smith, Sept. 5, 1942; children—Kenneth Hewlett, Ralph Barton, Janie Lyle. Landscape architect, site planner Richmond (Va.) Field Office Pub. Housing Adminstrn., 1948-51; pvt. practice landscape architecture, Richmond, 1951-76; prin. Higgins Assos., 1976—. Instr., Richmond Profl. Inst., evenings 1956; cons. in field. Chmn., Richmond Beautification Com., 1954-64; treas. River Rd Citizens Assn., 1956, bd. dirs., 1983—; bd. dirs. Lewis Ginter Bot. Garden; chmn. Monument Av. Commn., 1969-85. Bd. dirs. Berkeley Thanksgiving Fest. Served to capt. USAAF, 1942-46. Recipient Landscape award Am. Assn. Nurserymen, 1969; Richmond Urban Design award, 1970; Masonry Contractors Assn. Va. award, 1977. Mem. Am. Soc. Landscape Architects (past Va. chmn., Pres.'s award Potomac chpt. 1968), Landscape Architects Va., U. Mass. Landscape Archtl. Assn., Va. Hist. Soc., Soc. Archtl. Historians, Nat. Trust for Historic Preservation, Eastern Nat. Park and Monument Assn., Assn. for Preservation Va. Antiquities (life), Am. Arbitration Assn. Lambda Chi Alpha. Episcopalian (former vestryman). Club: Country of Virginia. Address: 908 S Gaskins Rd Richmond VA 23233 Office: 908 S Gaskins Rd Richmond VA 23233 also 8501 Patterson Ave Richmond VA 23229

HIGGINS, LEE, geologist; b. Fort Knox, Ky., May 9, 1952; s. Gordon Clair and Julia Stella (Krason) H.; m. Tonda Jean Privette, Feb. 1, 1975; children—Allison K., Jacob Lee, Chelsea Bree. Student Jefferson Community Coll., 1978-81; B.S. in Geology, U. Louisville, 1981-83; M.S. in Geology, U. Ky., 1986. Owner, pres. Higgins Drafting Service, Louisville, 1972-81, Higgins Co., Louisville, 1981—; v.p. John Lawson Realty Co., 1976-79; pres. Higgins Homes Inc., 1978-81; chief geologist Nall Oil & Gas Co., Owensboro, Ky., 1982-84. Designer custom single family homes. Scholar Edmonds Found., 1982-83. Mem. Willow Creek Assn. (v.p. 1980-81), Am. Assn. Petroleum Geologists (jr. mem.), Nat. Assn. Home Builders (assoc.), Ind. Geol. Soc., Ky. Geol. Soc., Soc. Econ. Paleontologists and Mineralogists. Avocations: soccer; softball; racquetball; scuba diving; photography. Home and Office: 11208 DeHam Dr Louisville KY 40222

HIGGINS, PAUL CLIFFORD, business executive; b. Plymouth, Mass., Sept. 22, 1945; s. Albert Clifford and Madeline (Liddell) H.; student U. Miami, 1964, U. Fla., 1965, Chesapeake Coll., 1970; m. Anne Edgcomb, Feb. 17, 1975; children—Allison Bond, Peter Andrew Edgcomb, Elizabeth Liddell. Vice pres. Nat. First Mortgage Corp., Anaheim, Calif., 1969-71; pres. Nat. Funding Corp., Washington, 1972-80, Allison Group, Easton, Md., 1980-83, Fair Wind Travels, Easton, 1981-83, Coastal Shipping Corp., Ltd., Grand Turk, Turks and Caicos Islands, 1981—; pres. Consol. Foods, Inc., Gainesville, Fla., 1983-85; pres., chief exec. officer Salt Cay Trust, Salt Cay, Turks and Caicos Islands, 1981—; dir. Longmead Bay Corp., Ltd., Anguilla, W.I., Atlas Publ. and Mktg., London, Haamsa, S.A., Port-au-Prince, Haiti; pub. Haiti-Lumie, Lantana, 1985. Sr. advanceman Office of Vice Pres., 1968-69, Humphrey for Pres., 1972; bd. dirs. Historic Easton, 1982-83, Historic Gainesville, 1983-84. Mem. Am. Philatelic Soc., Brit. Caribbean Philatelic Study Group, Am. Pilots Assn., Roses Philatelic Group, Palm Beach Hist. Soc. Democrat. Episcopalian. Club: Ocean (Salt Cay, Turks and Caicos Islands). Home: 811 8th Ln Palm Beach Gardens FL 33418

HIGH, BELVA HOWLE, psychologist, educator, consultant; b. Hartsville, S.C.; d. Woodrow Byrd Howle and Jessie Elizabeth (Gainey) Rucker; 1 dau., Heather Dawn. B.A., U. S.C., 1963, Ph.D., 1970; M.Ed., U. Ga., 1966. Nat. bd. cert. counselor; cert. sch. psychologist, S.C. Tchr., counselor Richland Sch. Dist., Columbia, S.C., 1963-65, 66-67; counsel Charlotte-Mecklenburg Sch. Dist., N.C., 1968-70; adj. faculty N.C. State U., Ft. Bragg, 1972, East Carolina U., Sanford, N.C., 1972; sch. psychologist Florence Sch. Dist. 1, S.C., 1973-74; assoc. prof. edn. Francis Marion Coll., Florence, 1975—; cons. Ft. Bragg, Fayetteville, N.C., 1972, Coker Coll., Hartsville, S.C., 1973, Gen. Electric Co., Florence, 1984-85, Sonoco Products Co., Hartsville, 1983-85, Daniel Mgmt. Ctr. of U. S.C., Columbia, 1984. Mem. Florence Dist. 1 Sch. Bd., 1977-83, chairperson, 1980-83. R.J. Reynolds fellow U. N.C., 1964. Mem. Nat. Sch. Bd. Assn., Am. Psychol. Assn., Am. Assn. Counseling and Devel., LWV, AAUW, Phi Beta Kappa, Phi Kappa Phi, Delta Kappa Gamma. Avocation: travel. Home: 533 Arbor Dr Florence SC 29501 Office: Francis Marion Coll PO Box 7500 Florence SC 29501

HIGH, KATHERINE NOEL, university administrator, consultant; b. Ottawa, Ohio, Nov. 29, 1948; d. Byron Roll and Mary Catherine (Hackett) Huggins; m. Robert Louis Bertelsen, Apr. 26, 1974 (div. Dec. 1981); 1 child, Matthew Albert; m. Reginald Morris High, Dec. 23, 1984. A.B., Miami U., Oxford, Ohio, 1970, M.A.T., 1971; Ed.D., U. Tenn., 1983. Cert. elem. tchr., Tenn. Tchr. Collinsville Elem. Sch., Ohio, 1970-71; asst. to v.p. for bus. Western Coll., Oxford, Ohio, 1971-74; tchr. Knoxville schs., Tenn., 1974-76, Clinton City schs., Tenn., 1976-80; dir. human resources devel. U. Tenn., Knoxville, 1980-84, exec. asst. to v.p., 1985—; cons. Knoxville City Govt., 1984-85, Kingsport City Govt., Tenn., 1983-85, Johnson City, Tenn., 1984-85. Named Outstanding Grad. Student, U. Tenn., 1982. Mem. Mid-South Ednl. Research Assn., Am. Ednl. Research Assn., Am. Soc. Tng. and Devel. Republican. Roman Catholic. Club: Commission for Women (Knoxville). Avocations: restoring older homes; photography; gardening; writing poetry; reading. Home: 5613 Lake Shore Dr Knoxville TN 37920 Office: 727 Andy Holt Tower U Tenn Knoxville TN 37996-0175

HIGHFILL, C(ARLYLE) PAGE, architect, computer programmer, consultant; b. Richmond, Va., Jan. 29, 1937; s. John Henry and Mary Elizabeth (Mullins) H.; m. Kate Innis Byrd, June 18, 1960; children—Bryan Scott, Marc Austin, Ann Page, Katherine Lynn. B.Arch., Va. Poly. Inst., 1960. Cert. architect. Archtl. designer Frederick T. Hyland, 1960-63; project architect Edward F. Sinnott & Son, Richmond, 1963-65; ptnr. Hyland & Highfill, Richmond, 1965-67; faculty mem. Va. Commonwealth U., Richmond, 1964-73; pres. Highfill Assocs. Inc., mng. ptnr. EMA Assocs., Richmond, 1971-75; pres. Highfill-Smith Assocs., Inc., Richmond, 1971—, EMA Mgmt. Assocs., Inc., Richmond, 1981—; seminar leader, 1981—. Recipient 1st prize Future Ideas in Design/Reprographics, 1984. Mem. AIA (Design Excellence Honor award Nat. Conf. on Religious Architecture 1974, Va. chpt. 1974). Baptist. Contbr. material to profl. lit.; creator numerous computer programs.

HIGHLAND, JAMES LEE, educator; b. Clarksburg, W.Va., Apr. 21, 1940; s. Howard and Aline Vera (King) H.; m. Anna Lee Terneus, May 20, 1960; children—Dorothea, Kathy Deborah. B.S.J., W.Va. U., 1965, M.S.J., 1966. Reporter, Clarksburg (W.Va.) Exponent, 1959-62, Morgantown (W.Va.) Post, 1962-66; press sec. State of W.Va., 1962-68; fed. govt. reporting specialist Charleston (W.Va.) Daily Mail, 1968; instr. Okla. State U., 1969, asst. prof., 1970-73; investigative reporter Stillwater (Okla.) News-Press, 1969-73; asst. prof. Western Ky. U., Bowling Green, 1973-75, assoc. prof., 1975-83, prof., 1983—, head dept. journalism, 1984—; investigative reporter, editorial columnist Bowling Green Daily News, 1973—; coordinator Western Ky. U. Contbg. editor Western Alumnus, 1975—; pub. The Fourth Estate Newsletter, 1975—. Recipient Investigative Reporting award Ky. Press Assn., 1981, 80; Disting. Campus Chpt. Adviser award Sigma Delta Chi, 1979. Mem. Ky. Press Assn., Western Ky. Press Assn., Ky. Weekly Newspaper Assn., Assn. for Edn. in Journalism, Kappa Tau Alpha, Phi Eta Sigma, Omicron Delta Kappa, Sigma Delta Chi (dep. regional dir. 1977—, mem. nat. freedom of info. com. 1981—). Democrat. Roman Catholic. Contbr. articles to profl. jours. Home: 1948 Nashville Rd Bowling Green KY 42101 Office: 323 Academic Complex Dept Journalism Western Ky Univ Bowling Green KY 42101

HIGHSMITH, LOUIS EDWARD, insurance company consultant; b. Morehead City, N.C., Sept. 22, 1948; s. Roma Earl and Sally Marie (Hancock) H.; m. Linda Ann Robinson, Nov. 8, 1980; children—Natalie, Blake, James. Grad. in marine engring. Newport News Apprentice Sch., Va., 1971; B.B.A., N.C. State U., 1978. Supt. nuclear shipfitters quality assurance Newport News Shipbuilding, Va., 1971-74; police officer Raleigh Police Dept., N.C., 1975-78; loss control specialist, safety engr. USF & G Ins., Raleigh, 1978—; pres. Raleigh Police Acad., 1975; cons. to civic orgns.; speaker in field. Author manual in field. Named Best Lineman, West Carteret Football, Morehead City, N.C., 1966; All Conf., Northeastern Conf., 1966; recipient Gold Athletic award Newport News Apprentice Sch., 1971. Mem. Am. Soc. Safety Engrs., Mid-State Safety Council. Republican. Episcopalian. Avocations: tennis; golf; jogging; home-made video movies. Home: 8709 Colesbury Dr Raleigh NC 27609 Office: USF & G Ins Co 3801 Old Wake Forest Rd Raleigh NC

HIGHSMITH, WILLIAM EDWARD, university chancellor; b. Eastland, Tex., Mar. 21, 1920; s. Robert A. and Dollie (Marshall) H.; A.B., Southeastern Coll., 1942; M.A., La. State U., 1947, Ph.D., 1953; m. Allene Sugg, Aug. 15, 1953; children—William Edward, John Marshall. Julius Rosenwald research fellow, 1948-49; instr. history U. Ark., 1949-50, La. State U., 1950-51; dir. Caribbean program La. State U., 1951-54; dir. Gadsden Center U. Ala., 1954-57; prof. Jacksonville U., 1957, dean, 1957-62; pres. Asheville-Biltmore Coll., 1962-69; chancellor U. N.C., Asheville, 1969—. Dir. Duval Safety Council, Jacksonville; chmn. Opportunity Corp. Asheville-Buncombe County. Mem. bd. advisers St. Luke's Hosp. Sch. Nursing; bd. dirs. Greater Asheville Council, United Fund, Asheville Symphony Soc., Asheville Community Concert Assn.; chmn. Mountain Area Health Edn. Center; trustee St. Mary's Coll., Asheville Country Day Sch.; bd. dirs. Art Mus.; bd. dirs., pres. Meml. Mission Hosp.; gen. chmn. Venture in Mission, Diocese of Western N.C.; mem. governing body Western N.C. Health Systems Agy. Served to cpl. USAAF, 1942-46. Mem. So., Miss. Valley hist. assns., Asheville C. of C. (dir.), N.C. Assn. Colls. and Univs. (pres.), Conf. Acad. Deans So. States (sec.-treas. 1961-62), Blue Key, Phi Kappa Phi, Theta Xi (nat. pub. relations com.). Democrat. Episcopalian (vestryman). Clubs: Pen and Plate (pres.), Rotary (pres., dir.). Author articles, reviews. Office: Office of Chancellor U NC-Asheville University Heights Asheville NC 28801

HIGHTOWER, JIM ALLEN, state commissioner; b. Denison, Tex., Jan. 11, 1943; s. William F. and Lillie (Johnson) H.; B.A. in Govt., North Tex. State U., 1965; postgrad. Columbia U., 1966-67. Legis. aide U.S. Senator Ralph Yarborough, 1967-69; dir. Agribusiness Accountability Project, Washington, 1970-75; nat. campaign dir. Fred Harris for Pres., 1975-76; editor The Tex. Observer, Austin, 1976-79; pres. Tex. Consumer Assn., Austin, 1980-81; commr. Dept. Agr. State of Tex., Austin, 1981—. Named Journalist of Yr., Tex. Farmers Union, 1979; Man of the Yr., Tex. Women's Polit. Caucus, 1980. Mem. Tex. Farmers Union, Tex. State Employees Union. Democrat. Author: Hard Tomatoes, Hard Times, 1972; Eat Your Heart Out, 1975. Office: PO Box 12847 Austin TX 78711

HILDEBRANDT, ALVIN FRANK, physicist, educator, research administrator; b. Spring, Tex., Dec. 31, 1925; s. Ludwig Otto and Anna Arina (Weindorff) H.; m. Cornelia Nelle Margaret Nohle, Dec. 23, 1950; children—George Flavius, William Jon Edward. B.S., U. Houston, 1949; Ph.D., Tex. A&M U., 1956. Research group supr. Quantum Physics Group and Low Temperature Physics Group, Jet Propulsion Lab., Pasadena, Calif., 1956-60; sr. research fellow chemistry div., Calif. Inst. Tech., Pasadena, 1960-63, physics dept., 1963-64; assoc. prof. physics U. Houston, 1965-69, prof., dept. chmn., 1969-75, prof., dir. solar energy lab., 1975-77, prof., dir. energy lab., 1977—. Pres. Energy Found. Tex., Houston, 1975-80; mem. com on energy and environment. Nat. Assn. State Univs. and Land Grant Colls. Served with USNR, 1945-46. Recipient Outstanding Contbn. award solar thermal div. Dept. Energy, 1982; Outstanding Contbn. award Am. Solar Energy Soc., 1982. Mem. AAAS, Am. Phys. Soc., Internat. Solar Energy Soc., Houston C. of C. (future studies com.), Sigma Xi, Phi Kappa Phi. Clubs: Cosmos (Washington); Explorers (N.Y.C.). Patentee on superconducting magnetic flux pumps, prodn. of pure He4 by superfluid flow; originator of solar tower energy collector concept; contbr. to numerous profl. jours., confs. in field. Home: 3029 Underwood St Houston TX 77025 Office: Energy Lab U Houston 4800 Calhoun St Houston TX 77004

HILDER, JACK REGINALD, JR., oil tools company executive, engineer; b. Burkburnett, Tex., Oct. 15, 1925; s. Jack Reginald and Myrtle Mae (Dodson) H.; m. Mary Katherine Schramm, Nov. 15, 1945 (div. June 1963); children—Jack Reginald, Robert A., Henry W., Guy M.; m. 2d, Gloria Marjorie Fuggetta, Aug. 19, 1967; children—Gloria L., Pamela R. A.S., U. Tex.-Arlington, 1945, B.S., Austin, 1948, B.B.A., 1948. With IDECO div. Dresser Industries, Dallas, 1948-62, v.p. sales, 1957-62; chmn., chief exec. officer TEC-Prodns., Inc., Huntsville, Ala., 1962-65; chief exec. officer Am. Marine & Machinery Corp., New Orleans, 1965-71; pres., chief exec. officer Gulf Marine div. Marathon Mfg. Co., Houston, 1971-74; group pres. Internat. Systems & Controls, Houston, 1974-78; pres., chief exec. officer Baker ProLift, Inc., Houston, 1978-83; pres., chief exec. officer, dir. Houston Systems Mfg. Co., 1983—; dir. Reed Tool Co., Reed Am. Products Co., Baker ProLift Inc. Bd. dirs. Mercy Hosp., Brownsville, Tex. Served to lt. comdr. U.S. Navy, 1943-46. Named Man of Yr., Propeller Club Brownsville 1973. Mem. Soc. Naval Architects and Marine Engrs., Am. Petroleum Inst., Petroleum Equipment Suppliers Assn., Chaine des Rotisseurs, Houston Livestock and Rodeo Com. Republican. Episcopalian. Clubs: Houston Petroleum, Warwick, Raveneaux Country, NOMADS. Contbr. articles to profl. jours.; patentee in field. Office: 6022 Cullen Blvd PO Box 14551 Houston TX 77221

HILER, MONICA JEAN, reading and sociology educator; b. Dallas, Sept. 3, 1929; d. James Absalom and Monica Constance (Farrar) Longino; m. Robert Joseph Hiler, Nov. 1, 1952; children—Robert, Deborah, Michael, Douglas, Frederick. B.A., Agnes Scott Coll., Decatur, Ga., 1951; M.Ed., U. Ga., Athens, 1968, Ed.S., 1972, Ed.D., 1974. Social worker Atlanta Family and Children's Services, 1962-63; tchr. Hall County pub. schs., Ga., 1965-67; mem. faculty Gainesville Jr. Coll., Ga., 1968—, prof. reading and sociology 1975—, chmn. devel. studies program, 1973-85; cons. So. Regional Edn. Bd., 1975-83. Mem. Internat. Reading Assn., Ga. Sociol. Assn., Assn. Supervision and Curriculum Devel., Gainesville Music Club, Phi Beta Kappa, Phi Delta Kappa, Phi Kappa Phi. Avocations: piano, painting, sewing.

HILL, BILL JOE, banker; b. Little Rock, July 30, 1941; s. Ralph Edward and Hazel Dolois (Shepherd) H.; m. Janice Cheryl Miller, Mar. 11, 1966; 1 dau., Shawnna Rochelle. B.S. in Acctg., Abilene Christian U., 1963; J.D., Baylor U., 1970; postgrad. Southwestern Grad. Sch. Banking, So. Meth. U., 1972-74. Bar: Tex. 1970. Credit rep. Internat. Harvester Corp., Amarillo, Tex., 1964-65; sales rep. Hallmark Cards, Amarillo, 1965-68; exec. v.p., mgr. trust div. Republic Bank First Nat., Midland, Tex., 1970—. Assoc. editor Baylor Law Rev., 1969-70. Trustee Midland Christian Sch., 1976-78, Medina Childrens Home, 1981—; mem. Big Bros./Big Sisters of Midland, 1976-77, pres., 1976; mem. Family Services of Midland, 1976-79, pres., 1979; bd. dirs. Am. Diabetes Assn., 1978-82, Am. Cancer Soc., 1978-82; mem. adv. bd. Salvation Army, 1984—. Served with USAR, 1966-70. Mem. Am. Bankers Assn. (personal trust com.), Tex. Bankers Assn. (legis. com.), Tex. Bar Assn., Midland County Bar Assn. (sec.-treas.), Midland Bus. and Estate Council, Midland Jaycees (dir. 1972-73, chaplain 1973-75, fin. v.p. 1976). Republican. Mem. Ch. of Christ (deacon). Club: Midland Country. Home: 2308 Metz Pl Midland TX 79705 Office: 303 West Wall Midland TX 79701

HILL, BILLY JOSEPH, educator; b. Taylorville, Ill., July 6, 1928; s. Theodore Augustine and Anna Irene (Morris) H.; m. Sadie Marie Giordano, Oct. 28, 1950; children—Cecilia Ann, Claudia Adele, Constance Antoinette. A.A., Coastal Carolina Community Coll., 1972; B.A., U. N.C.-Wilmington, 1974. Enlisted in U.S. Marine Corps, 1945, advanced through grades to maj., 1962, ret., 1969; tchr. Northwoods Park Jr. High Sch., Jacksonville, N.C., 1974-76; tchr. history, chmn. social studies dept. Southwest High Sch., Jacksonville, 1976—. Mem. policy com. Onslow County Bd. Edn., 1979—. Decorated Bronze Star, Joint Service Commendation medal. Mem. NEA, N.C. Assn. Educator, Onslow County Assn. Educators, Nat. Geog. Soc., Smithsonian Assocs., Fleet Res. Assn., Ret. Officers Assn. Democrat. Roman Catholic. Home: 806 Mitchell Rd Jacksonville NC 28540 Office: 500 Burgaw Hwy Jacksonville NC 28540

HILL, BOBBY WAYNE, physician; b. La Grange, Ga., May 16, 1948; s. David Leon and Leola (Barber) H.; m. Barbara Susan Bickford, Sept. 28, 1966; children—Robert Avery, Jacob Adrain. B.A., LaGrange Coll., 1966; D.O., U. Health Scis., 1977. Intern, Drs. Hosp., Tucker, Ga.; gen. practice osteo. medicine, Powder Springs, Ga., 1978—. Ga. Med. Bd. scholar 1973. Mem. Am. Osteo. Assn., Ga. Osteo. Med. Assn., Am. Coll. Gen. Practitioners. Democrat. Methodist. Lodge: Lions (pres. 1983). Avocations: computers, flying, scuba diving, sailing. Office: Powder Springs Med Clinic 4045 Lindley Circle Powder Springs GA 30073

HILL, BRYCE DALE, school administrator; b. Seminole, Okla., Mar. 5, 1930; s. Charles Daniel and Ollie (Nichols) H.; B.S., East Central State Coll., 1952, M.Teaching, 1957; postgrad. U. Okla., 1959-70; profl. adminstrs. certificate, 1969; m. Wilma Dean Carter, Aug. 16, 1956; children—Bryce Anthony, Brent Dale. Tchr. pub. schs., New Lima, Okla., 1952-56, supt. pub. schs., 1956—; owner New Lima Gas Co., 1958-82. Chmn. bd. dirs. Seminole County chpt. ARC, 1969—; v.p. bd. dirs. Redland Community Action Program, 1968-71; mem. Seminole County Bd. Health, 1985—; mem. Seminole County Rural Devel. Council. Chmn. Seminole County Democratic Central Com., 1962-64, 70—. Mem. NEA, Okla. Edn. Assn., Am. Assn. Sch. Adminstrs., Okla. Assn. Sch. Adminstrs. (exec. com. 1976-78, 79-81, Adminstr. of Yr. 1983), Seminole County Tchrs. Assn. (pres. 1964-65, 71-72, 79-80), Seminole County Sch. Adminstrs. Assn. (chmn. 1969-70), Seminole County Schoolmasters Club (pres. 1963-64, 69-70, 77-78), Seminole Hist. Soc. (v.p. 1971-73, 74-76). Baptist. Home: Route 1 Box 96 Wewoka OK 74884

HILL, CAROLYN LEE, graphic artist; b. Vallejo, Calif., Aug. 26, 1943; d. Mitchell Lewis and Corinne Libby (McGinnis) Mariscal; m. David Coleman Hill, July 10, 1964 (div. July 1979); children—Marla Jean, Stacy Lynn. Student Columbus Coll., 1975-80. Freelance graphic artist, 1965—; publicity dir. Saber Newspaper, Columbus (Ga.) Coll., 1979-80; graphic arts prodn. specialist Blue Cross and Blue Shield, Columbus, 1981—; cons. in field; art dir. various firms and orgns. Publicity dir. Georgetown Elem. PTA, Columbus, 1972-73, pres., 1974-75. Served with WAC, 1962-64. Recipient Community Club award, 1980; 4th place art award Historic Soc., Columbus, 1978. Home: 1613 15th Ave Columbus GA 31901 Office: 2357 Warm Springs Rd Columbus GA 31908

HILL, CLARENCE WARREN, industrial education educator; b. Mobile, Ala., Feb. 7, 1948; s. Robert and Lauretta (Ladner) H.; m. Doris Walton, Aug. 5, 1969; children—Shana D., Robert L. B.S., Jackson State U., 1970; M.Ed., S.C. State Coll., 1979. Tchr. indsl. arts Richland Dist. One, Columbia, S.C., 1974-81; project mgr. Archizign, Architects, Columbia, 1980-85; dir. bus. devel., 1982-85; co-founder, project mgr. Gus Roberts and Assocs., Architects/Planners, Columbia, 1985—; instr. indsl. edn. S.C. State Coll. Orangeburg, 1981—; sec., treas. Archizign, Inc., 1979-85; Vol. United Way, Columbia, 1978-83; pres. P.T.O. Greenview Elementary Sch., Columbia, 1984-85; mem. adv. council Cope Vocat. Ctr., Bamberg, S.C., 1982-85, Greenview Elementary Sch., Columbia, 1983-84; mem. adv. com. engring. graphics Denmark Tech. Coll., S.C., 1985—. Served with U.S. Army, 1970-73. Recipient Vol. award United Way, Columbia, 1981, Achievements in Bus. award Columbia Urban League, 1982; named Outstanding Young Man of Am., U.S. Jaycees, 1981, 83, Tchr. of Yr., S.C. State Coll., Orangeburg, 1984. Mem. AIA (assoc.), Columbia Council Architects, Houston Engrs. Soc. (outstanding service award 1982), Greater Columbia Bus. League (v.p. 1983-85), Phi Delta Kappa, Omega Psi Phi (v.basileus 1985-86). Republican. Baptist. Avocations: golf; leathercraft. Home: 221 Glenshire Dr Columbia SC 29204 Office: Gus Roberts and Assocs 7430 Fairfield Rd Columbia SC 29203

HILL, DENNY EUGENE, sociology educator; b. Logan, W.Va., Apr. 24, 1939; s. Edgar Patton and Ida Etta (Browning) H.; m. M. Jane Seymour, Sept. 10, 1977; children—Gary Wayne, Marshall Joseph, Gaynell Denise, Joshua Redman. B.A. in Sociology with honors, 1971, M.A., 1973. With Sears, Roebuck and Co., 1957-67; instr. sociology Ga. So. Coll., Statesboro, 1973-79, asst. prof., 1979—, dir. applied sociology program, 1978—. Bd. adminstrs. Pittman Park United Methodist Ch., 1981-83; mem. mission team to Choctow Indians, Philadelphia, Miss., summer 1981; bd. dirs. Wesley Found., 1981—. Ford Found. fellow, 1969-71; NSF fellow, 1971-73. Mem. Ga. Sociol. Assn. (sec.-treas. 1980-82, exec. com. 1983-84), So. Sociol. Soc., Nat. Acad. Advising Assn., Am. Sociol. Assn., Am. Heart Assn. (sci. mem.), Phi Beta Kappa. Co-author: Encounters with Death Dying and Bereavement. Contbr. articles to profl. jours. Home: 107 Springdale Rd Statesboro GA 30458 Office: GA So Coll Statesboro GA 30460

HILL, DONALD M., mathematician; b. Knoxville, Iowa, Oct. 28, 1942; s. D. Merle and Virginia June (Lindly) H.; B.S., Iowa Wesleyan Coll., 1962; M.A., Dartmouth Coll., 1964; French cert., Ecole d'Administration de Bruxelles (Belgium), 1965; Ph.D., Fla. State U., 1972; m. Kandace Marguerite Carpenter, May 26, 1968; children—Rebecca Marguerite, D. Matthew. Prof. math. Ecole de Wembo Nyama (Congo), also adj. prof. U. Libre du Congo, 1965-67; prof. math. Fla. A&M U., Tallahassee, 1972—, asst. dean Coll. Sci. and Tech., 1974-76; internat. cons., Zaire, 1973, Senegal, 1974, Indonesia, 1978, Senegal, 1982; mem. commn. on math. instrn. Nat. Acad. Scis./NRC, 1981-85, chmn., 1983-85. Vice pres. Fla. A&M U. High Sch. PTA, 1974; mem. steering com. Leon County Sch. Vols., 1974-76; mem. dist. adv. com. Leon County Sch. Bd., 1976-78; bd. dirs. Camping Opportunities for Children, 1975. Nat. Acad. Sci. travel grantee, 1976. Mem. Nat. Council Tchr. of Math. (liaison internat. math. edn. 1983-87), Math. Assn. Am. (gov. 1983-86), Fla. Council Tchrs. of Math. Democrat. Methodist. Home: 3017 Godfrey Pl Tallahassee FL 32308 Office: Math Dept Fla A&M U Tallahassee FL 32307

HILL, DOUGLAS WHITTIER, clergyman, administrator; b. Dayton, Ohio, Apr. 11, 1927; s. Eric Leslie and Helen Elizabeth (Metz) H.; m. Helen G. Kleinhenz, June 14, 1952; children—Linda E. Hill Hickok, David D., Peter D. B.S. in Edn., Miami (Ohio) U., 1949; M.Div., Colgate Rochester Div. Sch., 1952; D.D. (hon.), Alderson-Broaddus Coll., 1978. Ordained to ministry Baptist Ch., 1952. Minister Christian edn. Delaware Ave. Bapt. Ch., Buffalo, 1952-57; organizing pastor South Hills Bapt. Ch., Pitts., 1957-62; assoc. pastor Fifth Ave. Bapt. Ch., Huntington, W.Va., 1962-67; area minister, minister campus ministry W.Va. Bapt. Conv., Parkersburg, 1967-77, exec. minister, 1978—; founding dir. W.Va. Bapt. Found. for Campus Ministry, 1967-75; mem. gen. staff Am. Bapt. Ch. U.S.A., 1978—. Trustee, Alderson-Broaddus Coll., 1978—; bd. dirs. East Central region Boy Scouts Am., 1985—. Recipient Good Shepherd award Assn. Bapts. for Scouting. Mem. Regional Exec. Ministers Council (sec./treas. 1982-85). Editor W.Va. Bapt., 1978—. Office: PO Box 1019 Parkersburg WV 26102

HILL, EDWINA WOODARD, school administrator; b. Cartersville, Ga., May 5, 1933; d. Archie and Annie Laura (Johnson) Woodard; m. Charles Webster Hill, Dec. 18, 1956 (div.); 1 dau., Charla Winnetta. A.B. in Biology, Morris Brown Coll., 1953; M.S. in Biology, Atlanta U., 1962, Ed.S. in Adminstrn., 1977, predoctoral in adminstrn. and policy studies. Tchr. Summer Hill High Sch., Cartersville, Ga., 1953-56, Howard High Sch., Atlanta, 1956-70, chairperson schedule com., 1970-73; resource tchr. Area IV and Area I, Atlanta, 1973-75; acting prin. Peeples St. Elem. Sch., Atlanta, 1975; prin. Oglethorpe Elem. Sch., Atlanta, 1975—; sci. cons. and reviewer Scott Foresman Pubs., 1982-83. Active Voter Registration Com., Atlanta, 1983; student tchr. supr. U.S. Peace Corps., 1968; interview team Gov.'s Honor Program, 1976; bd. dirs. Planned Parenthood Atlanta, 1979-82, Phyllis Wheatley br. YWCA, Atlanta, 1982—; block leader Harwell Heights Community Club, Atlanta, 1976—. Woodrow Wilson fellow, 1959; recipient Tchr. of Yr. award Howard High Sch., 1971; Boss of Yr. award Atlanta Bus. Women's Assn., 1979. Mem. Ga. Assn. Elem. Sch. Prins., Assn. Curriculum and Supervision Devel., Atlanta Assn. Elem. Sch. Prins. (sec. 1979-81), Nat. Assn. Elem. Sch. Prins., Phi Delta Kappa. Methodist. Home: 2115 Jones Rd NW Atlanta GA 30318 Office: Oglethorpe Elem Sch 601 Beckwith St SW Atlanta GA 30314

HILL, GREGORY ALAN, sanitary supply company executive; b. Louisville, Jan. 6, 1950; s. Edwin G. and Katie B. (Harris) H.; m. Bethany Rogers, June 26, 1971; children—Ryan G., Matthew A. B.S., U. Ky., 1971. Chief acct. Dura Corp., Paris, Ky., 1971-73; budget analyst Kuhlman Electric, Versailles, Ky., 1973-74; treas. Thompsons Sanitary, Lexington, Ky., 1975—; fin. adviser Carpet Genie Systems, Boone, N.C., 1978—, Beards Art Needlework, Lexington, 1980—, Derby Decorators, Lexington, 1981—, Applied Mgmt.

Systems, Boone, N.C., 1983—. Mem. Republican. Nat. Com., 1981—; mem. Lexington Cath. 21st Century Preservation Group; active Cub Scouts Am. Mem. Nat. Acctg. Assn., Ky. Assn. Woodworkers. Home: 107 Irvine Rd Lexington KY 40502 Office: Thompsons Sanitary Supply 761 E 75th St Lexington KY 40505

HILL, HAROLD NELSON, JR., state supreme court justice; b. Houston, Apr. 26, 1930; s. Harold N. and Emolyn Eloise (Geeslin) H.; B.S. in Commerce, Washington and Lee U., 1952; LL.B., Emory U., 1957; m. Betty Jane Fell, Aug. 16, 1952; children—Ward, Douglas, Nancy. Admitted to Ga. bar; assoc., then ptnr. Gambrell, Harlan, Russell, Moye and Richardson, Ga., 1957-66; asst. atty. gen. Law Dept., State of Ga., 1966-68, exec. asst. atty. gen., 1968-72; ptnr. Jones, Bird and Howell, Ga., 1972-74; assoc. justice Supreme Ct. Ga., 1975-80, presiding justice, 1980-83, chief justice, 1983—; adj. prof. Emory U. Law Sch. Served with Ordnance Corps, U.S. Army, 1952-54. Fellow Am. Bar Found.; mem. Am. Law Inst., State Bar Ga., Atlanta Bar Assn., Lawyers Club Atlanta, Old War Horse Lawyers Club. Methodist. Office: 533 State Judicial Bldg Atlanta GA 30334

HILL, HARVARD H., JR., investment company executive; b. Phoenix, Oct. 16, 1936; s. Harvard H. and Louvenia E. (Norton) H.; m. Janet L. Jones, June 5, 1958; children—Scott, James, Kelli. B.S. in Bus. Adminstrn., U. Ariz., 1958; M.B.A., Pepperdine U., 1973. Cert. fin. planner Coll. Fin. Planning. Vice pres. So. Calif. region Dean Witter & Co., 1962-76; pres., chief operating officer Rotan Mosle, Inc., Houston, 1976-82; mng. dir. Criterion Group, pres. Criterion Investments, ptnr. Criterion Venture Ptnrs. subs. Criterion Group, Houston, 1982-85; mgn. ptnr. Houston Ptnrs., 1985—; dir. R. J. Fin. Corp. Founding bd. dirs. Am. Leadership Forum. Served to 1st lt. arty. U.S. Army, 1958-62. Mem. Internat. Assn. Fin. Planners, Houston Soc. Fin. Analysts, Houston Venture Capital Assn. (pres.), Tex. Club, Alpha Kappa Psi, Phi Gamma Delta. Baptist. Clubs: Houstonian (bd. govs.), Houston Racquet. Office: Capitol Ctr 401 Louisiana Houston TX 77002

HILL, HOWARD DARNELL, teacher educator; b. Texarkana, Ark., May 4, 1942; s. Howard, Jr. and Della Mae (Williams) H.; m. Clemmie Faye Coulter, Dec. 24, 1963; children—Ray Darnell, Edith Renee. B.A. in Social Studies, Philander Smith Coll., 1964; M.S. in Secondary Sch. Adminstrn., Ark. State U., 1968; Ph.D. in Curriculum and Instrn., Kans. State U., 1973; postdoctoral in ednl. adminstrn. U. S.C., 1983-85. Secondary tchr. Jonesboro Pub. Schs., Ark., 1964-66; supr. instrn. Marion Schs., Ark., 1966-69; asst. prin. West Memphis Schs., Ark., 1969-70; secondary tchr. Tunica Pub. Sch., Miss., 1970-71; asst. prof. edn. U. Houston, 1973-77; assoc. prof. Miss. Valley State U., Itta Bena, 1977-78; prof., chmn. dept. edn. S.C. State Coll., Orangeburg, 1978—; dir. Assocs. in Edn., Orangeburg. Contbr. articles to profl. jours. Named Tchr. of Yr., S.C. State Coll. Sch. Edn., 1983. Mem. Southeastern Regional Assn. Tchr. Educators (pres. 1986), S.C. Soc. for Social, Hist. and Philos. Study Edn. (pres. 1985), S.C. Assn. Tchr. Educators (pres. 1983-84), Phi Delta Kappa (chpt. pres. 1982-85). Office: SC State Coll Dept Edn Box 1716 Orangeburg SC 29117

HILL, JACQUELINE VAN VLIET, broadcasting co. exec.; b. Sioux City, Iowa, Dec. 10, 1943; d. John Huff and Miriam (Samelson) Van Vliet; B.A., Hastings Coll., 1965; postgrad. U. Iowa, 1968-69. Tchr. pub. schs., Omaha, 1965-66, Houston, 1966-67, Iowa City, 1967-71; with communications dept., chmn. bd. Sta. WMFE-TV, Orlando, Fla., 1979—. Vice pres. Human Services Planning Council, 1973-80; mem. Orange County Pollution Control Bd., 1979-80; commr. Environ. Regulation Commn., State of Fla., 1981-85. Mem. LWV, Pub. Broadcasting Service, Sierra Club, Nat. Audubon Soc. Republican. Episcopalian. Home: PO Box 18 Windermere FL 32786

HILL, JAMES CLINKSCALES, judge; b. Darlington, S.C., Jan. 8, 1924; s. Albert Michael and Alberta (Clinkscales) H.; B.S. in Commerce, U. S.C., 1948; J.D., Emory U., 1948; m. Mary Cornelia Black, June 7, 1946; children—James Clinkscales, Albert Michael. Bar: Ga. 1948, U.S. Supreme Ct 1969. Assoc., Gambrell, Russell, Killorin & Forbes, Atlanta, 1948-55, partner, 1955-63; partner Hurt, Hill & Richardson, Atlanta, 1963-74; U.S. dist. judge, No. Dist. Ga., 1974-76; judge U.S. Ct. Appeals 5th Circuit, Atlanta, 1976-81, 11th Circuit, Atlanta, 1981—. Mem. bd. visitors Emory U. Served with USAAF, 1943-45. Fellow Am. Coll. Trial Lawyers, Am. Bar Found.; mem. ABA, Am. Law Inst., World Assn. Judges, State Bar Ga., Atlanta Bar Assn., Am. Judicature Soc. Republican. Baptist. Clubs: Lawyers of Atlanta, Old War Horse Lawyers. Office: US Courthouse Room 246 56 Forsyth St NW Atlanta GA 30303

HILL, JEFFREY ALLEN, nursing administrator; b. Hackensack, N.J., Nov. 5, 1947; s. Allen Robert and Wathina Denora (Smith) H. B.S. in Nursing, Cornell U., 1970; M. in Nursing, Emory U., 1975. Instr. Ga. Baptist Hosp. Sch. Nursing, Atlanta, 1972-73; nurse clinician West Paces Ferry Hosp., Atlanta, 1974-76; asst. adminstr. Am. Hosp. Tehran, Iran, 1976; owner, mgr. antique store, Atlanta, 1977-81; dir. nursing Psychiatric Inst. Atlanta, 1981-85, Charter Lake Hosp., Macon, Ga., 1985—. Served to lt. USN, 1970-72. Recipient Alumni award Cornell U., 1970. Mem. Ga. Nurses Assn., Am. Nurses Assn., Am. Nurses Found., Am. Orgn. Nurse Execs. Home: 4150 Arkwright Rd Apt 23 Macon GA 31210 Office: Charter Lake Hosp 3500 Riverside Dr PO Box 7067 Macon GA 31209

HILL, JOHN ALLEN, state senator; b. Miami, Fla., May 20, 1931; s. Eugene Prentice and Frances (Allen) H.; student Miami-Dade Jr. Coll., 1968-69; m. Vivian Carlson; children—John Alfed, Richard Allen, Kathy Ann. Pres. IBEW 359, Miami, 1961-62; asst. bus. mgr. U-4, 1963-64; mem. Fla. Ho. of Reps., 1974-78, former majority leader; mem. Fla. Senate, 1979—, majority leader, 1983-84, also chmn. exec. bus. com. Mem. bd. Nova U. Served with USMC, 1950-63. Recipient George Groome Found. award, 1975; also various ins. sales awards. Mem. Nat. Assn. Life Underwriters, Hialeah-Miami Springs C. of C. Presbyterian. Clubs: Masons, Order Eastern Star, Hialeah Spotlite (dir.), Rotary (pres.). Office: Room 216 Senate Office Bldg Tallahassee FL 32301

HILL, JOSEPH JOHN, financial consulting company executive; b. N.Y.C., Feb. 3, 1944; s. Carl and Agnes (Hazel) H.; m. Marilyn Boll, June 1969 (div. 1973); m. 2d, Ann Marie Wilson, May 5, 1976; children—Justin Joseph, Stephen Joseph, Andrew John. B.B.A., St. Francis Coll., Bklyn., 1968; Grad. Sch. cert., Dartmouth Coll., 1979. With Irving Trust Co., N.Y.C., 1966-67; v.p. Franklin Nat. Bank, N.Y.C., 1967-74, Barnett Bank of Jacksonville (Fla.), 1974-75; v.p. Bankers Trust Co., N.Y.C., 1975-77, 78-82; v.p., sr. comml. officer Barnett Bank of Broward County, Ft. Lauderdale, Fla., 1977-78; exec. v.p., dir. Schramm Bus. Opportunities, Inc., Falls Church, Va., 1982-84; exec. v.p. Global/Fidelity Inc., Vienna, Va., 1984—; sr. v.p. Bank of Va., McLean, 1982-83; pres., dir. Arlington Capital Resources, Inc., Falls Church, 1982—; pres. Faratron Oil Corp., Ocean Ridge, Fla., 1984—; dir. Solitron Devices, Inc., Riviera Beach, Fla.; adv. bd., dir. Nat. Energy Capital Corp., Armonk, N.Y., 1983—. Served with USMCR, 1964-70. Assoc. mem. Robert Morris Assocs. also Faratron Oil Corp 5101 N Ocean Blvd Ocean Ridge FL 33435

HILL, KAREN KATHLEEN DRINKARD, insurance company official; b. Ft. Worth, Oct. 14, 1946; d. Curtis Allen and Anita Margarita (Skelton) Drinkard; m. David Alan Hill, Dec. 14, 1965. B.S. in Psychology, North Tex. State U., Denton, 1967. Assoc. engr. Ling-Temco-Vought, Grand Prairie, Tex., 1967-70; systems engr. Electronic Data Systems, Dallas, 1970-80; lead systems engr. Southwestern Life Ins. Co., Dallas, 1980-81, dir. product services systems-EDP, 1981—. Block capt. and mem. city task force for historic ordinance compliances. Fellow Life Mgmt. Inst.; mem. Hist. Preservation League, Dallas Hist. Soc., Munger Pl. Homeowners Assn., Dallas Mus. Fine Arts. Republican. Mem. Disciples of Christ Ch. Club: Capitol. Home: 5109 Reiger Ave Dallas TX 75214 Office: Southwestern Life Ins Co 1807 Ross Ave PO Box 2699 Dallas TX 75221

HILL, MAX LLOYD, JR., realtor; b. Belleville, Ill., Aug. 15, 1927; s. Max L. and Leora (Jacobs) H.; student Purdue U., 1944-47; B.S., U.S. Naval Acad., 1951; postgrad. Harvard Law Sch., 1955-56; m. Jane Olivia Evatt, June 23, 1951; children—Larkin Payne, Max Lloyd III, Naomi Evatt. Sales engr. indsl. equipment Indsl. Welding Supplies, Inc., 1957-59; real estate salesman Simmons Realty Co., Inc., Charleston, S.C., 1959-63; pres. Max L. Hill Co., Inc., realtors, Charleston, 1964—; Charleston dir. Citizens & So. Nat. Bank S.C.; lectr. S.C. Realtor's Inst., 1967-73, U. S.C. Sch. Gen. Studies and Extension, 1962-64. Pres. Greater Charleston YMCA, 1965-67; mem. Charleston Planning and Zoning Commn., 1969-74; mem. Charleston Zoning Bd. Adjustment, 1971-74; sec. Charleston County Bd. Assessment Control, 1972-75; bd. dirs. Edn. Found., 1966-74, Charleston Symphony Orch., 1980—; bd. dirs. Carolina Art Assn., 1979-83, pres., 1985-86. Served with AUS, 1945-46, USNR, 1946; to 1st lt. USAF, 1951-55. Mem. Nat. Assn. Realtors (dir. 1976-84, v.p. coms. 1981, regional v.p. 1982), S.C. Assn. Realtors (dir. 1966—, pres. 1976), Greater Charleston Bd. Realtors (pres. 1970), Charleston Trident C. of C. (dir. 1981-85), St. Andrews Soc., Phi Gamma Delta. Methodist (ofcl. bd. 1964-76). Mason. Clubs: Carolina Yacht, Charleston, Seabrook Island. Home: 109 Tradd St Charleston SC 29401 Office: 33 Broad St Charleston SC 29401

HILL, PAUL DRENNAN, banker; b. Bklyn., Jan. 8, 1941; s. John Drennan and Margaret Henrietta (Gens) H.; B.A., Williams Coll., 1962; J.D., Columbia U., 1966; m. Ann Kilbourne Patch, June 6, 1964; children—Hal Chase, John Andrew. Bar: Ga. 1966. Mgmt. asso. Time Inc., 1962-63; ptnr. Gambrell, Russell & Forbes, Atlanta, 1970-75; sr. v.p., gen. counsel First Atlanta Corp., 1975-78, exec. v.p., chief fin. officer, 1978—, also dir.; dir. 1st Nat. Bank Atlanta; adj. prof. Emory U. Law Sch. Trustee Met. Atlanta Crime Commn., 1980-82; v.p., trustee Atlanta Bot. Garden, 1979—. Served with USAR, 1963. Mem. ABA, Am. Inst. Banking, Conf. Board (exec. conf.), Ga. Bar Assn. (chmn. corp. and banking law sect. 1974), Atlanta Bar Assn. (chmn. continuing legal edn. com. 1981-82). Congregationalist. Club: Brookwood Hills Community. Office: 2 Peachtree St PO Box 4148 Atlanta GA 30302

HILL, RICHARD H., insurance company executive; b. Kansas City, Mo., Dec. 19, 1921; s. Jule Hudson Hill and Frances Elizabeth (Humble) Foster; m. Marie Louise Power, Apr. 21, 1948; children—Richard H., Jr., Malcolm Scott, Stephen Power. B.S. in History and Econs. North Tex. State U., 1947. C.L.U.; Life Underwriter Tng. Council Fellow. Special agt. Prudential Ins. Co., Wichita Falls, Tex., 1947-50, div. mgr., Ft. Worth, 1950-56, assoc. mgr., 1956-57, agy. mgr., Waco, Tex., 1957-82, mgr. emeritus (agt.), Waco, 1982—. Contbr. articles to profl. jours. Chmn. letter writing campaign on behalf of POW's and MIA's, Central Tex., 1971, mem. delegation of 12 to Paris, 1972; chmn. steering com. Freedom Found., Red Cross Chpt. and Blood Ctr., Waco, 1971-73; v.p. Heart of Tex. council Boy Scouts Am., 1960-65. Served to lt. (j.g.) USN, 1943-46; PTO. Recipient Huebner Sponsorship award Am. Soc. CLU's, 1964, Clara Barton Service award Heart O Tex. chpt. ARC, 1979. Fellow Nat. Assn. Life Underwriters (tchr. 1984, designated Admiral Tex. Navy 1984), mem. Waco-Temple Gen. Agts. and Mgrs. Assocs. (pres. 1959-60, Louis I. Dublin Pub. Service award 1962-63), Waco Assn. Life Underwriters (pres. 1962-63), Charter Life Underwriters (pres. Waco Chpt. 1967-68), Tex. Gen. Agts. and Mgrs. Assn. (pres. 1979-80, special award 1981), Tex. Life Underwriters Polit. Action Com. (chmn. 1972-77, hon. vice-chmn. 1979), Nat. Life Underwriters Polit. Action Com. (vice chmn. 1976-83), Tex. Assn. Life Underwriters (pres. 1983-84, hon. mayor 1984). Republican. Methodist. Clubs: Downtown, Inc. (bd. dirs. 1983—), City (v.p. 1978-80), Methodist Mem's (Waco) (pres. 1969-70). Lodges: Rotary (com. chmn. 1983—), Masons (Master 1956). Office: Richard H Hill Agy 7209 Sanger St Waco TX 76710

HILL, RICHARD MICHAEL, energy company executive; b. Conroe, Tex., Aug. 6, 1942; s. Richard E. and Aline (McMichael) H.; m. Bonnie Louise McDougal, June 7, 1980; children from previous marriage—Bradley, Paul. B.B.A. in Fin., So. Methodist U., 1964. C.P.A., Tex. Ptnr. in charge Fox & Co., Houston, 1975-80; sole practice fin. cons., Houston, 1980; sr. v.p., chief fin. officer Sparkman Energy Corp., Corpus Christi, Tex., 1980; dir. Esperanza Transmission Co., Yale E. Key Inc. Mem. Am. Inst. C.P.A.'s, Tex. State Soc. C.P.A.'s. Office: 710 N Mesquite Corpus Christi TX 78401

HILL, ROSANNA, laboratory official; b. Macon, Ga., July 1, 1949; d. Henry and Julia (Chambliss) Hill; B.S., Clark Coll., 1971; postgrad. Howard U., 1971-72. Med. technologist Ga. Bapt. Med. Center, Atlanta, 1972-77, lab. supr., 1977—; v.p. Acculabs, Inc., Atlanta, 1981—. Mem. Am. Public Health Assn., Clin. Lab. Mgmt. Assn., Nat. Assn. Female Execs. Mem. African Methodist Episcopal Ch. Home: 3110 Godby Rd Apt 21C College Park GA 30349 Office: 730 Peachtree St Suite 1020 Atlanta GA 30308

HILL, SAMUEL RICHARDSON, JR., university president, medical educator; b. Greensboro, N.C., May 19, 1923; s. Samuel Richardson and Nona (Sink) H.; m. Janet Redman, Oct. 28, 1950; children—Susan Dustin, Samuel Richardson III, Elizabeth, Margaret Hanes. B.A., Duke U., 1943; M.D., Bowman Gray Sch. Medicine, 1946; D.Sc. (hon.), U. Ala., 1975, Wake Forest U., 1979. Intern medicine Peter Bent Brigham Hosp., Boston, 1947-48, asst. resident medicine, 1948-49, asst. medicine, 1949-50; teaching fellow medicine Harvard Med. Sch., 1948-49, research fellow medicine, also Dazian Med. Found. research fellow, 1949-50; chief resident medicine N.C. Bapt. Hosp., also instr. medicine Bowman Gray Sch. Medicine, 1950-51; asst. medicine Harvard Med. Sch., also Peter Bent Brigham Hosp., 1953-54; asst. prof. medicine, dir. metabolic and endocrine div. Med. Coll. Ala., also chief metabolic div. VA Hosp., Birmingham, 1954-57; assoc. prof. medicine, dir. metabolic and endocrine div. U. Ala. Med. Center and VA Hosp., Birmingham, 1957-62; prof. medicine, dean U. Ala. Med. Coll., 1962-68, prof. medicine, 1968—; v.p. for health affairs, dir. Med. Center, 1968-77; pres. U. Ala. at Birmingham, 1977—; dir. med. edn. program U. Ala. System, 1972-79; dir. Birmingham br. Fed. Res. Bank of Atlanta, 1981-83, chmn. Birmingham br., 1983; dir. Vulcan Materials Co., 1981—. Contbr. articles to med. jours. Bd. regents Nat. Library Medicine, 1978-80, chmn. bd. regents, 1979-80. Served to maj. M.C. USAF, 1951-53. Fellow A.C.P. (Willard O. Thompson Meml. traveling scholar 1960), AAAS, Royal Soc. Medicine; mem. Soc. Exptl. Biology and Medicine, Am. Fedn. Clin. Research (pres. 1961-62), Endocrine Soc., Am., Ala. diabetes socs., N.Y. Acad. Scis., Mass., Jefferson County med. socs., Am. Thyroid Soc., AMA, Inst. Medicine of Nat. Acad. Scis., So. Soc. Clin. Investigation, Med. Assn. State Ala. (councillor), Assn. Am. Med. Colls., Assn. for Acad. Health Centers (pres. 1972), Sigma Xi, Alpha Omega Alpha. Episcopalian. Home: 4101 Altamont Rd Birmingham AL 35213 Office: Office of Pres U Ala at Birmingham Univ Sta Birmingham AL 35294

HILL, SANDRA STROPE, newspaper editor; b. Sayre, Pa., June 21, 1938; d. Mahlon Brewster and Margaret Mary (Jones) Strope; B.A. magna cum laude, Pfeiffer Coll., 1960; m. William Ross Hill, Dec. 31, 1960; 1 dau., Heather Margaret. Reporter, Charlotte (N.C.) News, 1960-73, asst. city editor, 1973-78, day city editor, 1978, mag. editor, 1979-80, features editor, 1980-83; dep. graphics editor/features Charlotte Observer & News, 1983—, entertainment editor, 1985—; instr. journalism U. N.C. Charlotte, part-time 1978-80. Bd. dirs., pub. relations Hornets Nest council Girl Scouts U.S.A., 1977; v.p., program chmn. Mecklenburg Registry of Interpreters for the Deaf, 1983—; reader CPCC Radio for Blind. Recipient Service award Mecklenburg Assn. for Blind, 1971-72. Mem. Women in Communications (treas. 1976-77, chmn. freedom of press 1979—, sec. 1980—), Women Execs., Mensa, U.S. Figure Skating Assn., Ice Skating Inst. Am. Republican. Methodist. Office: Charlotte Observer PO Box 32188 Charlotte NC 28232

HILL, SARA LYNN, architectural company executive, artist, architectural delineator; b. Montclair, N.J., May 25, 1951; d. Lawrence and Mary (Allanson) H.; m. William James Van Cleve., Jr. B.Arch. cum laude, Tulane U., 1974; B.F.A. magna cum laude, Newcomb Coll., 1974. Lic. architect, contractor, La. Archtl. designer J. Buchanan Blitch & Assocs., Architects, New Orleans, La., 1975-76; archtl. cons. F. Monroe Labouisse, Jr., Architect, New Orleans, 1976-79; staff architect, plans examiner Vieux Carre Commn., New Orleans, 1979; ptnr. V.C. Builders, Gen. Contractors, New Orleans, 1980—; sole propr. Hill Co., Architects, New Orleans, 1979—; v.p. Robin Riley & Assocs., Architects, New Orleans, 1981—; founding mem., sec. Art-Op Coop., New Orleans, 1975; agt. Tulane U. Alumni Assn., New Orleans, 1975—. Illustrator: New Orleans Home Care Handbook, 1978; Great Louisiana Recipes, 1977; Razing the Roofs, 1978. Co-editor, founder Marsharch Jour., 1973-74. Mem. Preservation Resource Ctr., New Orleans, Friends of the Cabildo, New Orleans, 1978—, Contemporary Arts Ctr., New Orleans, 1977—. John W. Lawrence fellow Tulane U., 1973, Dorothy Lubbe Dunkerley fellow Tulane U., 1972; recipient 2d place award Reynolds Aluminum Corp., 1973, 1914 prize in Art Newcomb Coll., 1974. Mem. AIA (medal, cert. 1974), Nat. Trust for Historic Preservation, Constrn. Specifications Inst., Urban Land Inst., Internat. Platform Assn., Tulane U. Alumni Assn. (bd. dirs. 1977-82). Methodist. Clubs: So. Yacht, Corinthian Sail (New Orleans). Office: S Stewart Farnet AIA and Assocs Architects Inc 2331 St Claude Ave New Orleans LA 70117

HILL, THOMAS GLENN, III, dermatologist; b. Atlanta, Dec. 15, 1942; s. Thomas Glenn, Jr. and Wilella (Burns) H.; B.A. in History, Emory U., 1964; M.D., Med. Coll. Ga., Augusta, 1968; children—Elizabeth Burns, Jennifer Michelle, Thomas Glenn IV. Diplomate Am. Bd. Dermatology Intern, USAF Med. Center, Keesler AFB, 1968-69; resident in dermatology Med. Coll. Va., 1972-75; practice medicine specializing in dermatology and cutaneous surgery, Decatur, Ga., 1975—; mem. staff DeKalb Gen., Grady Meml., Rockdale County, Newton County hosps.; pres. Physician's Skin Care Services, Inc. clin. asst. prof. dermatology Emory U. Med. Sch., 1975—. Mem. Ga. Gov.'s Medicaid Adv. Panel, 1978-79. Served as officer M.C., USAF, 1967-72. Decorated Disting. Service award, Presdl. Unit citation. Fellow Am. Acad. Cosmetic Surgeons, Internat. Assn. Cosmetic Surgeons; mem. AMA (Physician Recognition award 1975), Am. Acad. Dermatology, Am. Soc. Dermatologic Surgery, Internat. Soc. Dermatologic Surgery, Am. Dermatologic Soc. Allergy and Immunology, So. Med. Assn., Ga. Soc. Dermatologists, Ga. Soc. Dermatologic Surgeons (sec.-treas. 1986, bd. dirs. 1985-88), Atlanta Dermatologic Assn. Republican. Clubs: Sea Pines, Moss Creek Golf, Druid Hills Golf, Snapfinger Woods Country, Bent Tree Country. Author numerous papers in field. Office: 5071 Snapfinger Woods Dr Decatur GA 30035

HILL, TOMMIE ANN, mathematics educator; b. Clearwater, Fla., Nov. 23, 1948; d. Willie James and Bernice Lee (Walker) H.; B.A. in Math., Emory U., 1969; M.S. in Math., Northwestern U., 1970; Ed.D. in Curriculum and Instrn. (Univ. fellow), U. Houston, 1976. Instr. math. Spelman Coll., 1970-71, W.Va. State Coll., 1971-74; asst. prof. math., dir. freshman studies Prairie View A&M U., 1976—; summer instr. Tufts U., 1972; instr. math. North Harris County Coll. 1975—; summer fellow Hampton Inst.-NASAS Research Program, 1979. Parliamentarian M.E. Rickmeyer Missionary Soc., Wesley Chapel AME Ch., Houston, 1979, 81-82, publicity chmn., 1980, treas., 1982—. Mem. Math. Assn. Am., Nat. Council Tchrs. Math., S.W. Ednl. Research Assn., Am. Ednl. Research Assn., Research Assn. Minority Profs. (pres. 1986—), Phi Beta Kappa, Kappa Delta Epsilon, Kappa Delta Pi, Phi Delta Kappa. Democrat. Mem. African Methodist Episcopal Ch. Author: (with Frank Hawkins) Trigonometry: A Laboratory Manual, 1979. Home: 1106 Carlton St Clearwater FL 33515 Office: PO Box 2845 Prairie View TX 77446

HILL, W. BERNARD, securities trader. Treas., UMIC Securities Corp., Memphis, chmn., sec. subs. UMIC Inc. Office: UMIC Inc 959 Ridgeway Loop Rd Memphis TN 38119*

HILLAR, MARIAN, biology educator; b. Bromberg, Poland, Mar. 22, 1938; came to U.S., 1969; s. Henry and Elisabeth (Lassmann) H.; m. Janett Faundez, Aug. 24, 1970; children—Anne Margueritte, Christopher Jacques. M.D., U. Med. Sch. Danzig (Poland), 1962, Ph.D., 1966. Instr. to asst. prof. dept. biochemistry U. Med. Sch., Danzig, Poland, 1958-69; sr. research assoc. dept. cell biophysics Baylor Coll. Medicine, Houston, 1969-70; adj. asst. prof. div. cell biophysics Baylor Coll. Medicine, 1970-78; asst. prof. dept. biology Tex. So. U., Houston, 1971-75, assoc. prof., 1975-81, prof., 1981—. Author: Biochemical Energetics, 1977; contbr. articles to profl. jours. Pres., Copernicus Soc., Houston, 1975-78. Recipient research award Polish Acad. Scis., 1965; award U. Med. Sch. Danzig, 1967; Fulbright award Italy, 1980; Research grantee Faculty Research Fund, Tex. So. U., 1971-72, NIH, 1972-77, Faculty Research Fund, Tex. So. U., 1975-76, NIH, 1976-77, Faculty Research Fund, Tex. So. U., 1976-77, NIH, 1977-80, Nat. Cancer Inst., 1980-83, U. Genetics, 1982-83, Nat. Cancer Inst., 1983-84. Mem. Biophys. Soc., Biochem. Soc. (London), AAAS. Office: Dept Biology Molecular Biology and Biochemistry Lab Tex So U Houston TX 77004

HILLER, E. A. STURGIS, JR., education consultant; b. Foxboro, Mass., Jan. 20, 1928; s. Edward Abbott Sturgis and Ruth Helen Hiller; cert. FAA, 1958, 59, U.S. Dept. Agr. Grad. Sch., 1959, 60, 70, Office CD, 1962; children—Wyatt T.M., Christine M. LaGarde, Susan R. Buchanan, James R. With FAA, 1958-64; office mgr. Martinsburg Veneer Corp., 1964; owner Martinsburg Bus. Services, 1965-66; spl. project officer FAA, 1965; dir., mgr. telecommunications, mail processing, micrographics, printing mgmt., distbn. programs FDA, 1965-78; founder, pres. People & Orgns., Inc., Merritt Island, Fla., 1978. Served with USCG, 1945-57. Recipient Outstanding Performance awards FAA, 1959, FDA, 1966. Mem. Adminstrv. Mgmt. Soc., Am. Soc. Public Adminstrn., Am. Soc. Tng. and Devel., Am. Mgmt. Assn., Soc. Advancement Mgmt., Nat. Small Bus. Assn. Republican. Clubs: Lions, Fraternal Order Policemen. Author: Leadership Skills for Office Supervisors, 1977; Managing the Administrative Services Function, 1978; Effective Management of Mail, 1979; Personnel Management for Supervisors/Managers, 1979; Women—You Can Be the Success You Want To Be, 1981; Total Managerial Success—The Whole Person Approach, 1982. Home: 300 S Banana River Blvd Apt 306 Cocoa Beach FL 32931 Office: PO Box 1948 Merritt Island FL 32952

HILL-GONZALES, CAROL, communications specialist; b. El Paso, Tex., Aug. 23, 1957; d. Jack F. and Shirley (Silveus) H. B.A., Austin Coll., 1979; student U. Tex.-Austin, 1976, N.Tex. State U., 1977. Internist, Sherman Democrat (Tex.), 1978-79; promotional mgr. San Lorenzo of Tex., Dallas, 1979-82; mktg. editor, writer Mary Kay Cosmetics, Inc., Dallas, 1982—; cons. freelance promotional writing, mktg. communications. Mem. Women in Communications Inc., Internat. Assn. Bus. Communicators. Democrat. Episcopalian. Office: 8787 Stemmons Freeway Dallas TX 75247

HILLIARD, EARL FREDERICK, lawyer, state senator; b. Birmingham, Ala., Apr. 9, 1942; s. Iola H.; B.A., Morehouse Coll., 1964; J.D., Howard U., 1967; M.B.A., Atlanta U., 1970; m. Mary Franklin, June 9, 1967; children—Alesia, Earl F. Research asst. Howard U., 1965-67; instr. Miles Coll., 1967-68; asst. to pres. Ala. State U., 1968-70; v.p. Met. Bus. Assn., Birmingham, 1973-74; partner firm Hilliard, Jackson, Little & Stansel, Birmingham, 1974-78; individual practice law, Birmingham; pres. Am. Trust Life Ins. Co.; mem. Ala. Ho. of Reps., 1974-80, chmn. Black legis. caucus, 1975; mem. Ala. Senate, 1980—. Reginald Herber Smith Community Lawyer fellow, 1970-71. Mem. Nat. Bar Assn. (life), Ala. Black Lawyers Assn., Pratt Civic League, NAACP (life), Ala. Civil Liberties Union, Morehouse Coll. Alumni Assn. (life), Alpha Phi Alpha. Baptist. Club: KP. Author: Victim of Circumstance, 1970. Home: 1625 Castleberry Way Birmingham AL 35214 Office: 1605 8th Ave North Birmingham AL 35203

HILLIARD, SAM BOWERS, geography educator; b. Bowersville, Ga., Dec. 21, 1930; s. Asa Faris and Flora Elizabeth (Bowers) H.; m. Mildred Joyce Collier, June 4, 1955; children—Steven Glen, Anita Joy. A.B., U. Ga., 1960, M.A., 1962; M.S., U. Wis., 1963, Ph.D., 1966. Electrician, DuPont Co., 1954-59; instr. U. Wis., Milw., 1965-67; asst. prof. So. Ill. U., Carbondale, 1967-71; assoc. prof. La. State U., Baton Rouge, 1971-75, prof. geography, 1975-82, alumni prof., 1982—, chmn. dept. geography and anthropology, 1975-78, 85—, dir. Sch. Geosci., 1976-77. Served with USN, 1950-54. Recipient Summer award Am. Philos. Soc.; Nat. Endowment for Humanities travel grantee. Mem. Assn. Am. Geographers, Nat. Geog. Soc., Am. Geog. Soc., Agrl. History Soc., Orgn. Am. Historians, So. History Assn. Author: Hog Meat and Hoecake; Atlas of Antebellum Southern Agriculture; contbr. articles to profl. jours. Home: 739 N Coventry Dr Baton Rouge LA 70808 Office: Dept Geography and Anthropology La State U Baton Rouge LA 70803

HILLIER, GEORGE THOMAS, computer software company executive; b. San Francisco, June 19, 1930; s. George Robert and Thelma Laura (Lowery) H.; student Coll. William and Mary Extension, 1949-51; m. Etta Louise Stender, Aug. 19, 1955; children—Bruce Thomas, Paul Thomas. With Norfolk (Va.) Broadcasting Corp., 1958-64; chief engr. Peninsula Broadcasting Corp., Hampton, Va., 1964-82; pres. BSI, Norfolk, 1982—; course cons. Norfolk Tech. Vocat. Sch., 1973—. Served with USAF, 1950-53. Decorated Purple Heart. Mem. Soc. Broadcast Engrs., Soc. Motion Picture and TV Engrs., Exptl. Aircraft Assn., Aircraft Owners and Pilots Assn. Baptist. Home: 1064 W Ocean View Ave Norfolk VA 23503 Office: PO Box 8545 Norfolk VA 23503

HILLIN, LONNIE RAY, chemical engineer; b. Santa Anna, Tex., Jan. 25, 1946; s. Lonnie Cleve and Evelyn Marie (Clendenon) H.; stepson Glenn C. Roy; B.S., W. Tex. State U., 1968, M.S., 1972; m. Ronni Sue Oliphant, June 11, 1968; children—Brent Taylor, Christopher Todd. Ops. engr. Texaco Inc., Amarillo, 1971-73; cons., sales engr. Nalco Chem. Co., Beaumont, 1973-78, dist. mgr., 1978—. Served with AUS, 1969-70; Vietnam. Decorated Bronze Star. Mem. Am. Inst. Chem. Engrs., ASME, Instrument Soc. Am., TAPPI, Phi Delta Theta. Republican. Methodist. Clubs: Rotary, Lions.

HILLMAN, HARRY RANDALL, hospital administrator; b. Monroe, La., Oct. 13, 1951; s. Harry J. and Kay (Mayfield) H.; m. Susan Gardner, Jan. 18, 1975; 1 child, Alison Riann. Dir. central service Good Shepard Med. Ctr., Longview, Tex., 1978-80; asst. instr. Tarrant County Jr. Coll., Fort Worth, 1981; dir. central service Fort Worth Osteo. Med. Ctr., 1980—. Recipient Eagle Scout award Boy Scouts Am., 1968, Vigil award Order of Arrow, 1969. Mem.

Internat. Assn. Hosp. Central Service Personnel, Am. Hosp. Assn. (div. central service personnel), Assn. Advancement Med. Instrumentation, Tex. Hosp. Assn., Tex. Soc. Central Service Personnel (bd. dirs. 1981—). Office: Fort Worth Osteo Med Ctr 1000 Montgomery St Fort Worth TX 76107

HILLMAN, JACQUELYN FAITH GIVENS, nurse; b. Mobile, Ala., July 24, 1958; d. James Floyd and Barbara Legay (Burkett) Givens; m. Benjamin Gillentine Hillman, Nov. 21, 1981. B.S. in Nursing, U. S. Ala., 1980. R.N., Ala., Miss., La. Staff nurse pediatrics U. South Ala. Med. Ctr., Mobile, 1980-81; staff nurse neurol. ICU, Singing River Hosp., Pascagoula, Miss., 1981-82, 84-85; charge nurse Valley Springs Meml. Hosp., Defuniak Springs, Fla., 1982-83; staff nurse Madison County Meml. Hosp., Madison, Fla., 1983; critical care supr. Suwanee County Hosp., Live Oak, Fla., 1983; staff nurse George County Hosp., Lucedale, Miss., 1983-84; instr. diversified health occupations George County Occupational Tng. Ctr., 1984—; staff nurse DeQuincy Meml. Hosp., La., 1985; outpatient coordinator/emergency room supr. Sabine Med. Ctr., Many, La., 1985—. Mem. Am. Assn. Critical Care Nurses. Republican. Methodist. Home: Route 1 Box 587 Many LA 71449

HILSENBECK, NANA ELAINE, educator; b. Black Mountain, N.C., Oct. 12, 1939; d. J. Caldwell and Mae (Miller) Owenby; B.A., Wake Forest U., 1968; M.Ed., Stetson U., 1979; m. David H. Hilsenbeck, July 5, 1959; children—Elaina Lee, Anita Joy, Angela Renée. Mem. faculty DeLand (Fla.) High Sch., 1977—, dean of curriculum 1979-81; lang. arts supr. Volusia County Schs., 1981—. Mem. Fla. Teaching Profession, So. Speech Assn., Fla. Staff Devel. Assn., Fla. Council Tchrs. English (v.p. 1985-86, pres. 1986-87), Volusia County Council Tchrs. English, Assn. for Supervision and Curriculum Devel., Fla. Assn. Suprs. and Adminstrs. Democrat. Baptist. Office: Ednl Devel Ctr 729 Loomis Ave Daytona Beach FL 32015

HIMEL, CHESTER MORA, entomologist, educator; b. Des Plaines, Ill., Mar. 10, 1916; s. Charles Maurice and Mary Eleanor (Mora) H.; m. Ann Walter, June 21, 1943; children—Barbara Holly Pietrowski, Shelley Jeane Scharnberg. B.S. in Chemistry, U. Chgo., 1938; Ph.D. in Organic Chemistry, U. Ill., 1942. Research chemist E.I. du Pont de Nemours & Co., Wilmington, Del., 1942-43, Allied Chem. Co., N.Y.C., 1943-44; research group leader Phillips Petroleum Co., Bartlesville, Okla., 1944-49; sr. organic chemist, dir. organic research div. Stanford (Calif.) Research Inst., 1949-65; research prof. entomology U. Ga., Athens, 1965—; indsl. cons., chmn. bd. Environ. Chem. Co. Inc. Intra-sci. Research Found. fellow; grantee NIH, Office Naval Research, Dept. Agr., EPA, Army Med. Research and Devel. Command. Mem. Entomol. Soc. Am., Am. Chem. Soc., AAAS, Ga. Entomol. Soc., Sigma Xi, Gamma Sigma Delta. Episcopalian. Contbr. articles to sci. jours., chpts. in books. Holder 43 U.S. patents. Office: Dept Entomology U Georgia Athens GA 30602

HIMES, JOSEPH SANDY, sociology educator emeritus; b. Jefferson City, Mo., Apr. 4, 1908; s. Joseph Sandy and Estelle Carlotta (Bomar); m. Estelle Jones, Dec. 22, 1941; A.B., Oberlin Coll., 1931, A.M., 1932; Ph.D., Ohio State U., 1938, D.Sc. (hon.), 1974. Research dir. Urban League, Columbus, Ohio, 1936-43; editorial writer Ohio State News, Columbus, 1943-46; prof. sociology N.C. Central U., Durham, 1946-69; Fulbright lectureships U.S. Govt., Helsinki, Madras, 1961-62, 66-67; disting. prof. sociology U. N.C., Greensboro, 1969-80; cons. Nat. Acad. of Scis., Washington, 1979-81, Nat. Urban League, Washington, 1971-73, Consortium on Research Tng., Greensboro, 1973-81, Am. Friends Service Com.-Quakers, Phila., 1981-84. Author: The Study of Sociology, 1968; Racial Conflict in American Society, 1973; Racial and Ethnic Relations, 1974; Conflict and Conflict Management, 1980. Bd. dirs. Greensboro Symphony Orch., 1978-83, Mental Health Assn., 1979-81; mem. adv. com. Am. Friends Service Com.-Quaker, Greensboro, 1981—; mem. edn. com. Ad hoc Council, Greensboro, 1982-84. Recipient Centennial Achievement Ohio State U., 1970; NSF grantee, 1976. Mem. Internat. Sociol. Assn., Am. Sociol. Assn. (com. chairs, DuBois-Johnson-Frazier award, 1980), So. Sociol. Soc. (pres. 1965-66, honor roll, 1984), N.C. Sociol. Assn. (pres. 1970-71). Democrat. Presbyterian. Avocations: travel, reading, gardening. Home: 1110 Moody St Greensboro NC 27401 Office: Dept of Sociology Univ NC Greensboro NC 27412

HINCKLEY, HARRY GLENN, JR., judge; b. Miami, Fla., Jan. 14, 1928; s. Harry Glenn and Gladys O. (Tucker) H.; children—William Pelham, Erin Lee, Harry Glenn, III. A.B., John B. Stetson U., 1950; LL.B., U. Miami, 1955. Ptnr., Wicker, Smith, Blomquist, Hinckley and Davent, Miami, Fla., 1955-65; ptnr. Fischer and Hinckley, Ft. Lauderdale, Fla., 1965-72; ptnr. Hinckley Shores and Hill, 1973-81; judge criminal felony div. 17th Jud. Circuit, Ft. Lauderdale, 1980—. Pres., Rio Vista Propery Owners Assn., 1965-66; bd. dirs. Fed. Little League, 1965-68. Served with USN, 1946, U.S. Army, 1951-52. Mem. ABA, Fla. Bar Assn., Broward County Bar Assn., Internat. Assn. Ins. Counsel, Pi Kappa Alpha, Phi Alpha Delta. Republican. Roman Catholic. Clubs: University, Lauderdale Yacht. Office: Broward County Courthouse 201 SE 6th St Fort Lauderdale FL 33301

HINCKLEY, JOSEPH (JOE) PATRICK, construction executive; b. Muncie, Ind., Mar. 25, 1947; s. George Terence and Mary Ann (Weisse) H.; m. Angelika C. Hammacher, July 24, 1971 (div. Sept. 1978); 1 dau., Elke Dyana. B.S.C. in Econs., Spring Hill Coll., 1969; M.B.A., U. Balt., 1973. Controller, Plantation Patterns div. Gen. Housewares Corp., Birmingham, Ala., 1971-72; div. cost mgr. ITT Grinnell, Princeton, Ky., 1972-75, ITT North Electric, Deerfield Beach, Fla., 1975-77, div. controller ITT Thermotech, St. Petersburg, Fla., 1977; v.p., controller, dir. So. Utility Constrn. Inc., Birmingham, Ala., 1978—; small bus. cons. Mem. Republican Presdl. Task Force. Served to capt. U.S. Army, 1969-73; Vietnam. Decorated. Mem. Nat. Assn. Accts., Am. Mgmt. Assn. Roman Catholic. Clubs: Altadena Country, Downtown (Birmingham). Home: 4801 Riverwood Dr Birmingham AL 35243 Office: PO Box 20727 Birmingham AL 35216

HINDS, ARTIS ANN, counselor; b. Oklahoma City, Sept. 16, 1939; d. Meade and Helen Elizabeth (Hepner) Corley; m. Gary Arlis Hinds, Mar. 20, 1957 (dec. Feb., 1980); children—Nathan Ward, David Meade, Arlis Ann. B.A., Sul Ross U., 1960, M.A., 1970, postgrad.; postgrad. Southwest Tex. State U., East Tex. State U., Tex. Tech. U. Cert. tchr., lic. cert. counselor, Tex. Tchr. Roswell Ind. Sch. Dist., N.Mex., 1961-65, Monahans Ind. Sch. Dist., Tex., 1965-70, Midland Ind. Sch. Dist., Tex., 1970-75; tchr., counselor Junction Ind. Sch. Dist., Tex., 1975-84; counselor Denver City Ind. Sch. Dist., Tex., 1984—. Phillips Petroleum scholar, 1960; NDEA grantee, 1964; Named one of Outstanding Young Women Am., 1970. Mem. Am. Assn. Counseling and Devel., Tex. Assn. Counseling and Devel., U.S. Nat. Merit Leadership Awards Orgn. (advisor 1983—), Phi Delta Kappa, Kappa Delta Pi, Sigma Tau Delta, Delta Kappa Gamma, Alpha Chi. Presbyterian (elder). Avocation: writing. Home: 303 Duvall St Denver City TX 79323 Office: Denver City Intermediate Sch 1003 N Ave F Denver City TX 79323

HINDS, INEZ LETITIA, education educator, consultant; b. N.Y.C., Sept. 13, 1918; d. Jerome DuBois and Mary Letitia (Harris) Jones; m. Henry Lee Hinds, Sr., Oct. 25, 1948 (div. Jan. 1970); children—Henry Lee, Christopher Jerome; m. Albert Edward Hinds; 1 stepdau., Mryna Hinds Anderson. B.S., Morgan State U., 1945; M.A., Columbia U., 1955; Ph.D., Walden U., 1978; postgrad. U. Vt., 1973, U. Ala., Birmingham, 1983. Instr. home econs. Del. State Coll., Dover, 1957-59; family life educator Assocs. Family Living, Chgo., 1959-61; spl. edn. tchr., Shelyville, Del., 1961-62; jr. high home econs. tchr., Trenton, N.J., 1962-65; pre-kindergarten supr. Phila. Sch. System, 1965-69; instr. early childhood Trenton State Coll., 1969-79; early childhood cons., adj. prof. U. Ala., Tuscaloosa, 1978—; assoc. prof. edn., coordinator early childhood edn. Talladega (Ala.) Coll., 1979—; cons. Head Start, Clay, Calhoun, Talladega, St. Clair and Randolph counties; mem. CDA Review Bd., Head Start, Ala. Mem. Women in Global Issues, Southeastern region, 1982-84. Named Outstanding Woman, Phi Beta Sigma, 1981. Mem. Am. Home Econs. Assn., AAUW, Nat. Assn. Bus. and Profl. Women, Nat. Assn. Coll. Women, NEA, Assn. Supervision and Curriculum Devel., Nat. Assn. Edn. Young Children, Council Exceptional Children, Alpha Kappa Alpha. Democrat. Episcopalian. Author: Handbook for Parents, 1968; Handbook for Training Paraprofessional for CDA, 1972. Office: Talladega Coll Talladega AL 35160

HINDS, JACKSON CEIVERS, utility company executive; b. Brownsville, Tex., Aug. 28, 1921; s. Jackson Ceivers and Tallulah G. (Raffo) H.; m. Artie Lee Page, June 18, 1946; children—Stephen Randolph, Page Aline, Denise Jacqueline. B.B.A., U. Tex., 1942, LL.B., 1948; postgrad. indsl. adminstrn., Harvard U., 1943, M.B.A., 1947. Bar: Tex. 1948. Practiced in Houston, 1948; with Fulbright, Crooker, Freeman, Bates & Jaworski, 1948-56; gen. counsel Houston Natural Gas Corp. and subs., 1956-69, sr. v.p., dir., 1962-67, exec. v.p., dir., 1967-69; pres. United Gas Distbn. Co., Houston, 1969—; now chmn. bd., chief exec. officer Entex, Inc., Houston; Univ. Savs. & Loan Assn., Houston, Bank of S.W., Kroger Stores, Inc., Cin. Pres. Houston Housing Devel. Corp., 1968—; chmn. Houston Mayor's Adv. Com. on Housing, 1967—; bd. dirs. Meml. Hosp., Houston. Served to lt. USNR, 1942-46. Decorated Bronze Star. Mem. Am., Tex., Houston, Fed. Power Communications bar assns., Am., So. gas assns. Office: Entex Inc 1200 Milam St Houston TX 77001*

HINE, ALBERT CASE, III, science educator; b. Hartford, Conn., June 4, 1945; s. Albert Case and Onalea (Stamp) H.; m. Jane Louise Templeton, June 22, 1968; children—Tristan, Charles. A.B., Dartmouth Coll., 1967; M.S., U. Mass., 1972; Ph.D., U. S.C., 1975. Research assoc. U. N.C., Chapel Hill, 1975-77, asst. prof., 1977-79; asst. prof. U. South Fla., St. Petersburg, 1979-83, assoc. prof., 1983—. Contbr. articles to profl. jours. Served to lt. USAF, 1969-72. Mem. Soc. Econ. Palentol./Minerologists, Am. Assn. Petroleum Geologists, Geol. Soc. Am. Office: U South Fla Dept Marine Sci 140 7th Ave S Saint Petersburg FL 33701

HINE, EDWARD, JR., state senator; b. Rome, Ga., Dec. 26, 1952; s. Edward W. and Barbara (Brown) H.; m. Casey Nickoloric, 1981; 1 son, Edward Taylor. B.A., Emory U., 1973, J.D., 1976. Sec.-treas. Hine & Carroll, P.C., 1980—; mem. Ga. Senate, 1983—. Mem. ABA, Ga. Bar Assn., Chi Phi. Democrat. Episcopalian. Office: Ga Senate State Capitol Atlanta GA 30334*

HINER, WILBER LEE, personnel administrator. B.B.A. in Mgmt. Personnel, U. Miami, 1972; M.S. in Mgmt., Fla. Internat. U., 1974. Asst. personnel dir., mgr. employee relations dept. Jackson Meml. Hosp., Miami, Fla., 1967-79; dir. personnel Palmetto Gen. Hosp., Hialeah, Fla., 1979-82; asst. adminstr./personnel Miami Gen. Hosp., 1982-84; dir. human resources Imperial Point Med. Ctr., Ft. Lauderdale, Fla., 1984—. Mem. adv. com. Fla. Sch. System. Served with USAF, 1954-59. Mem. South Fla. Hosp. Personnel Dirs. Assn. (pres., membership chmn.), Am. Soc. Personnel Adminstrn., Personnel Adminstrn. Council Fla. Hosp. Assn., Personnel Assn. Greater Miami, Nurse Recruiters, Am. Soc. Pub. Adminstrn., Aircraft Owners and Pilots Assn., Internat. Personnel Mgmt. Assn. Republican. Baptist. Home: 1063 SW 78th Pl Miami FL 33144 Office: 6401 N Federal Hwy Fort Lauderdale FL 33308

HINES, ANDREW HAMPTON, JR., industry executive; b. Lake City, Fla., Jan. 28, 1923; s. Andrew Hampton and Louise (Howland) H.; m. Ann Groover, June 28, 1947; children—Hampton, Elizabeth, Brad, Daniel. B.M.E. with high honors, U. Fla., 1947. Registered profl. engr., Fla. Research and devel. Gen. Electric Corp., 1947-51; Chmn. bd., pres. Fla. Progress Corp., St. Petersburg, 1982—; also chmn. bd., chief exec. officer subs. Fla. Power Corp., 1951—; chmn. bd. Landmark Union Trust Bank; dir. Landmark Banking Corp. of Fla., Advanced Reactor Corp.; former chmn. N.Am. Electric Reliability Council; bd. dirs., past pres. Southeastern Electric Exchange.; mem. com. on utilities Com. of U.S., World Energy Conf. Bd. overseers Stetson U. Coll. Law; trustee Asbury Theol. Sem.; bd. dirs. Fla. Council on Econ. Edn. trustee, mem. exec. com. Rollins Coll.; bd. dirs. U. Fla. Found. Served as 2d lt. USAAF, 1944-45; maj. Res. (ret.). Decorated Air medal. Fellow ASME; mem. NAM (bd. dirs.), Fla. Council of 100, Presidents Assn., Fla. Blue Key, Sigma Tau, Phi Kappa Phi, Tau Beta Pi, Beta Gamma Sigma. Methodist (Sunday sch. tchr.). Clubs: Presidents, St. Petersburg Yacht, Lakewood Country (St. Petersburg); Citrus (Orlando, Fla.). Office: Fla Progress Corp PO Box 33042 Saint Petersburg FL 33733

HINES, ANGUS IRVING, JR., oil jobber; b. Suffolk, Va., Aug. 7, 1923; s. Angus Irving and Lois E. (Howell) H.; m. Genevieve Hopkins McCollum, Nov. 24, 1949 (div. 1977); children—Ann Russell Hines Taylor, Marilyn N., A. McCollum, Angus Irving III. Student, Ga. Inst. Tech., 1942. Pres., Angus I. Hines, Inc., Suffolk, 1945—. Served with U.S. Maritime Service, 1943-45; ETO. Mem. Nat. Oil Jobbers Council, Va. Petroleum Jobbers Assn. (past pres.). Methodist. Home: 810 Riverview Dr Suffolk VA 23434 Office: PO Box 1080 Suffolk VA 23434

HINES, DAVID LOWELL, technical librarian; b. Chehalis, Wash., July 22, 1939; s. Wayne Lowell and Dorothy Elizabeth (Allison) H. B.A., U. Wash., 1961, M.A., 1966; postgrad. U. Calif.-Berkeley, 1964-67. Lic. tchr., Wash. Asst. librarian West High Sch., Bremerton, Wash., 1962-63, Olympic Coll., Bremerton, 1963-64; teaching asst. U. Calif.-Berkeley, 1964-67; librarian IBM, Rochester, Minn., 1967-72, sr. librarian, 1972-79, tech. librarian, 1979, Irving, Tex., 1980-84, devel. analyst, 1984—; cons. in field. Mem. Rochester (Minn.) Civic Symphony Chorale, 1978-80. Co-recipient (with A.A. Pastuszak) IBM Dir.'s Award for developing TECLIB, 1982. Mem. Spl. Libraries Assn., Assn. Computing Machinery, Phi Delta Kappa, Delta Phi Alpha, Beta Phi Mu. Club: Greater No. Tex. Orchid Soc. Lodge: Elks. Contbr. articles to profl. jours. Address: IBM Library and Learning Center PO Box 2750 Irving TX 75062

HINES, DONALD CRAIG, educator, dean, consultant; b. Riley, Miss., Nov. 26, 1944; s. Bryant Craig and Dollie Mae (Doyle) H.; m. Linda Outlaw, June 1, 1980. B.S., Miss. State U., 1968, M.S., 1970; Ph.D., Kans. State U., 1973. Research asst. Kans. State U., Manhattan, 1970-73; asst. prof. Troy State U., Ala., 1973-76, asst. dean, 1976-81; dean Livingston U., Ala., 1981—; bd. dirs. Tenn.-Cumberland Waterways Council, Decatur, Ala., 1984—, Ala. Small Bus. Devel. Consortium, Birmingham, 1981—. Editor: Ala. Bus. and Econs. Jour., 1982—; author publs. in field. Bd. dirs. Livingston Indsl. Bd., 1985, Livingston Utilities Bd., 1985. Named Most Outstanding Tchr., Sch. Bus. Troy State U., 1980, Coll. Bus. Livingston U., 1984; recipient Outstanding Achievement award Am. Acad. Higher Edn., 1984. Mem. S.E. Small Bus. Council, Ala. Assn. Higher Edn. in Bus., Tenn-Tombigbee Devel. Council. Republican. Presbyterian. Club: Exchange (pres. Troy 1978). Avocations: collecting antique coins and guns. Home: PO Box 795 Livingston AL 35470 Office: Coll Bus Livingston U Livingston AL 35470

HINES, WILEY EARL, dentist; b. Greenville, N.C., Apr. 29, 1942; s. Wiley and Lelia Bell (Langley) H.; m. Gloria Dean Moore, June 26, 1965; children—Wandria, Wiley Earl, Derrick. B.S., Knoxville Coll., 1963; D.D.S., Meharry Med. Coll., 1971. Biologist, Oak Ridge Nat. Lab., 1963-64, Melpar, Springfield, Va., 1964-67; pub. health dentist N.C. Bd. Health, Elizabeth City, 1971-73; pvt. practice dentistry, Ahoskie, N.C., 1973-77, Greenville, N.C., 1977—. Commr., Planning and Zoning Commn., Greenville, 1981—. Mem. Mental Health Assn., Nat. Dental Assn., Old North State Dental Assn., ADA, N.C. Dental Soc., 5th Dist. Dental Soc., Alpha Phi Alpha. Democrat. Baptist. Club: 20th Century (Greenville). Lodge: Masons. Avocations: sports; reading. Home: 406 Sedgefield Dr Greenville NC 27834 Office: 608 E Tenth St Greenville NC 27834

HINKLE, ARTHUR LLOYD, JR., manufacturing company executive; b. Houston, July 15, 1950; s. Arthur L. and Roberta Rose (Norman) H. B.S. in Aerospace Engring., Tex. A&M U., 1972. With Chgo. Bridge & Iron Co., 1972—, engr., Houston, 1972-76, Oak Brook, Ill., 1976-77, Houston, 1978-83, plant supt., 1983; material control mgr. DAS Island Project, United Arab Emirates, 1984—; assoc. Am. Productivity Center, Houston, 1977-78. Home: 3323 Oakdale St Houston TX 77004 Office: PO Box 40066 Houston TX 77040

HINOJOSA, RICARDO H., federal judge. Judge U.S. Dist. Ct. So. Dist. Tex. Office: 428 US Courthouse PO Box 2066 Brownsville TX 78520*

HINSON, JEAN MARIE, nurse; b. Bartlesville, Okla., Oct. 22, 1927; d. Phillip Frederick and Thelma Marie (Charles) Magerkurth; m. Oscar John Hinson, Feb. 18, 1947; children—Cecelia, John, Helen, Carole, Joseph, James. Student, Oklahoma City Sch. Practical Nursing, 1964-66. Lic. practical nurse. Staff nurse Midwest City Meml. Hosp., Okla., 1966-69, head nurse central supply, 1970—; office nurse Dr. Franklin Barnett, Midwest City, 1969; treas. Okla. Central Service Assn., 1984—; bd. dirs. Midwest City Employees Credit Union, 1984—. Mem. Am. Soc. Hosp. Central Service Personnel, Am. Hosp. Assn. Roman Catholic. Club: Ladies Alter Soc. Avocations: travel; crocheting; reading. Home: 15201 S Dobbs Rd Newalla OK 74857 Office: Midwest City Meml Hosp 2825 Parklawn Dr Midwest City OK 73110

HINTZ, ROBERT LOUIS, railroad executive; b. Chgo., May 25, 1930; s. Louis A. and Gertrude V. (Herman) H.; m. Gloria Mae Safbom, Nov. 12, 1955; children—Cary, Leslie, David, Erin. B.S. in Bus. Adminstrn. magna cum laude, Northwestern U., 1960, M.B.A., 1965. With Chessie System Inc., 1963—; internal audit officer C. & O. Ry., Cleve., 1963-65; staff asst. to v.p. C. & O. Ry.-B. & O. R.R., Cleve., 1965-68, asst. to v.p., 1968-70, comptroller, Balt., 1970-72, asst. to pres. parent co., Cleve., 1972-74, v.p. corporate services, 1974-76, v.p. fin., 1976-78, sr. v.p. fin., 1978-80; exec. v.p. CSX Corp., Richmond, Va., 1980—; pres., chief exec. officer Tex. Gas Resources Corp.; dir. Chesapeake Corp.; Aviation Enterprises, Chesapeake and Ohio R.R., Robertshaw Control Co., Balt. and Ohio R.R., Third Nat. Bank Corp., Western Md. R.R., Nat. Mine Services, Seaboard Coast Line R.R., Louisville and Nashville R.R. Co. Trustee St. Joseph's Villa; bus. adv. council Va. Poly. Inst., Va. Commonwealth U., U. Richmond. Served with USAF, 1950-54. Mem. Am. Mgmt. Assn. (fin. council), Fin. Execs. Inst. Roman Catholic. Clubs: Lakewood Country, Hermitage Country, Commonwealth., Country of Va. Home: 10002 Walsham Ct Richmond VA 23233 Office: One James Center Richmond VA 23261

HIPP, BOYD CALHOUN, II, real estate developer; b. Greenville, S.C., Aug. 18, 1951; s. Boyd Calhoun and Jean (Jones) H.; m. Susan Goodridge Barber, June 4, 1977; children—Susan Reeve, Elizabeth Moffett, Boyd Calhoun III. B.A., Wofford Coll., 1974; M.B.A., U. S.C., 1976. Account exec. WIS-TV, Columbia, S.C., 1976-79; pres. Laurel Properties, Inc., Columbia, S.C., 1979—; dir. Cosmos Broadcasting Corp., Greenville. Trustee, Historic Cola Found., Columbia, 1980—; vice chmn. Township Ctr., 1981—; co-chmn. Am. Cancer Soc. 500 Club, 1980; co-chmn. edn. program, Riverbanks Zool. Park, 1981. Named Outstanding Young Man of Yr., U.S. Jaycees, 1980, Young Alumnus of Yr., Wofford Coll., 1982. Mem. Wofford Coll. Alumni Assn. (nat. v.p., pres.-elect, bd. dirs. 1983-84). Episcopalian. Club: Summit (bd. govs. 1982—); Midlands Bus. Home: 1117 Glenwood Ct Columbia SC 29204 Office: Laurel Properties PO Box 50123 Columbia SC 29250

HIPP, FRANCIS MOFFETT, insurance executive; b. Newberry, S.C., Mar. 3, 1911; s. William Frank and Eunice Jane (Halfacre) H.; m. Mary M. Looper, Nov. 10, 1935 (dec. 1962); children—Mary Elizabeth (dec.), William, John, Mary Jane; m. Shirley A. Mattoon, May 11, 1964. Student, The Citadel, 1929-31; A.B., Furman U., 1933, LL.D., 1968; LL.D., U. S.C., 1964, The Citadel, 1968, Clemson U., 1980, Benedict Coll., 1983, Newberry Coll., 1985. With Liberty Life Ins. Co., 1933—, asst. treas., 1936-41, v.p., 1942, pres., chmn. bd., 1943—; chmn. bd. Liberty Corp., 1977—, pres., chmn. bd., Greenville, S.C., 1976-77; chmn. exec. com., dir. Cosmos Broadcasting Corp., Greenville; dir. S.C. Nat. Corp., Columbia; dir. emeritus S.C. Electric & Gas Co., Columbia.; Mem. S.C. Devel. Bd., 1955—, chmn., 1959-63; state v.p. Am. Life Conv., 1947-57, mem. exec. com., 1957-63, Life Insurors Conf., 1961-64. Trustee S.C. Found. Ind. Colls., Queens Coll., N.C., The Citadel Devel. Found.; nat. adv. council Bus. Partnership Found. of U. S.C.; nat. bd. govs. Inst. Living, Hartford; chmn. Palmetto Found., Columbia, Palmetto Bus. Forum. Recipient Businessman of Yr. award S.C. C. of C., 1980. Mem. Newcomen Soc., Kappa Alpha, Beta Gamma Sigma. Presbyn. Clubs: Greenville Country, Poinsett, Green Valley Country, Commerce (Greenville, S.C.); Augusta (Ga.); Nat. Golf; Summit (Columbia). Home: 33 W Avondale Dr Greenville SC 29609 Office: Wade Hampton Blvd Greenville SC 29602

HIPP, WILLIAM HAYNE, insurance and broadcasting executive; b. Greenville, S.C., Mar. 11, 1940; s. Francis Moffett and Mary Matilda (Looper) H.; B.A., Washington and Lee U., 1962; M.B.A., Wharton Sch., U. Pa., 1965; grad. program mgmt. devel., Harvard U., 1971; m. Anna Kate Reid, June 14, 1963; children—Mary Henigan, Francis Reid, Anna Hayne. With Met. Life Ins. Co., 1965-69; with mktg. and investments dept. Liberty Life Ins. Co., Greenville, S.C., 1969-79, chmn. bd., 1979—; pres., chief exec. officer Liberty Corp., 1979—; dir. Cosmos Broadcasting Co., Greenville, S.C. Nat. Corp., Columbia, Dan River, Inc., Danville, Va., Textile Hall, Greenville, SCANA Corp., Columbia Trustee, vice chmn. Nat. Urban League, 1977—; trustee Episcopal High Sch., Alexandria, Va., 1982—, Washington and Lee U., Lexington, Va., 1984—; mem. S.C. Devel. Bd., 1980—; trustee Greenville County Found., 1978-82, Greenville County Sch. System, 1975-77; pres. Greenville Met. YMCA, 1979-81. C.L.U. Mem. Am. Council Life Ins. (dir. 1979-83), Greenville C. of C. (chmn. 1985). Office: PO Box 789 Greenville SC 29602

HIPPS, F(LOYD) JUDSON, petroleum geologist, consultant; b. Asheville, N.C., Mar. 8, 1929; s. Floyd R. and Gladys Anne (Lindsey) H.; m. Dorothy Sorrells, Aug. 30, 1950; children—Victoria Lynn, Alan Hosea, Melissa Leigh. B.S. in Geology, U. N.C., 1951. Regional geologist Cities Service Oil Co., Bartlesville, Okla., 1953-67; geologist Pickrell Drilling Co., Wichita, Kans., 1967-73, Thunderbird Drilling Co., Wichita, 1973-74, Beren Corp., Wichita, 1974-76; exploration mgr. A. Scott Ritchie, Wichita, 1976-82; cons. geology, Brevard, N.C., 1982—. Mem. Am. Assn. Petroleum Geologists, Kans. Geol. Soc. Avocations: outdoor sports; stained glass. Home and Office: Route 1 Box 202D Brevard NC 28712

HIRL, J. R., chemical company executive. Pres., chief operating officer Occidental Chem. Corp., Houston. Office: Occidental Chem Corp PO Box 4289 Houston TX 77210*

HIRSCH, ERIC DONALD, English educator; b. Memphis, Mar. 22, 1928; m. Mary Pope; children—John, Frederick, Elizabeth. B.A., Cornell U., 1950; student U. Paris, 1948-49; M.A., Yale U., 1955, Ph.D., 1957; postgrad. U. Bonn, 1955-56. Instr. English, Yale U., 1957-61, asst. prof., 1961-64, assoc. prof., 1964-66; prof. English, U. Va., Charlottesville, 1966—, dept. chmn., 1968-71, 81-83, dir. composition, 1971-80, William R. Kenan prof. English, 1973—; mem. N.Y. State Bd. Regents Adv. Bd. for Competency Tests in Writing, 1979—; mem. Coll. Bd.-ETS Adv. Panel for Advanced Placement Tests in English, 1982—; cons. Nat. Council on Ednl. Research, 1983, U.S. Dept. Edn., Office of Research, 1985; mem. adv. com. Conf. on Theory in Humanistic Studies, Am. Acad. Arts and Scis., 1968-69. Fulbright predoctoral fellow, U. Bonn., 1955-56; Morse fellow, Yale U., 1962-63; NEH sr. fellow, 1971-72, 80-81; fellow Center for Humanities, Wesleyan U., 1973, 74; fellow Center for Advanced Study in Behavioral Scis., 1980-81; short-term fellow Council of the Humanities, Princeton U., 1976; Bateson lectr. Oxford U., 1983. Mem. Am. Acad. Arts and Scis., MLA (officer, bd. dirs.), Am. Council Learned Socs. (officer, bd. dirs.), NEH. Mem. adv. bd.; Blake Studies, Critical Inquiry, Genre, Literature and Performance, New Literary History, PTL; author: Wordsworth and Schelling: A Typological Study of Romanticism, 1960; Innocence and Experience: An Introduction to Blake, 1964, 2d edit., 1975 (The Explicator award 1964); Validity in Interpretation, 1967, German transl., 1972, Italian transl., 1973; The Aims of Interpretation, 1976, paperback, 1978, Italian transl., 1979; The Philosophy of Composition, 1977, paperback, 1978; contbr. articles to publs. in field. Address: 2006 Pine Top Rd Charlottesville VA 22903

HIRSCH, SAMUEL, JR., newspaper consultant; b. N.Y.C., July 12, 1928; s. Samuel and Emmaline (Pike) H.; m. Mary Frances Banks, May 27, 1950; children—Samuel III, Jeffrey Robert, Laurie Frances. B.B.A., 1950. Pres. Hirsam Realty, N.Y.C., 1950-64; pub., owner Broward Times, Fort Lauderdale, Fla., 1964-73; surburban dir. Knight-Ridder Newspapers, Miami, 1973-75; pres. Hirsch & Assocs., Daytona Beach, Fla., 1976—; nat. dir. Nat. Assn. Advt. Pubs., Chgo., 1966-68, Suburban Newspapers Am., Washington, 1973-75. Pres. Plantation City Commn., Fla., 1959-64; founder Drs. Hosp., Plantation, 1964. Served with U.S. Army, 1945-47, PTO. Recipient Honors Achievement award Freedoms Found. at Valley Forge, 1974; also many profl. assn. awards for newspaper pub. Republican.

HIRSHBERG, EDGAR WALTER, English educator; b. Detroit, Aug. 21, 1915; s. David Walter and Alice (Lilienthal) H.; m. Ann Berry, Apr. 26, 1947; children—Carolyn, Lucy, Jane. B.A., Harvard U., 1938; M.A., Cambridge U., Eng., 1951; Ph.D., Yale U., 1951. Instr. English, Ind. U., 1948-49, N.C. State U., 1950-51, Ohio U., 1951-52; asst. prof., then assoc. prof. East Caroline U., 1953-60; assoc. prof., then prof. U. South Fla., 1960—. Author: Biography of George Henry Lewes, 1970; Biography of John D. MacDonald, 1985. Bd. dirs. Hillsborough County Friends Library, Asolo Theater Festival Assn.; exec. com. Hillsborough County Democratic Party, 1970-75. Served with USAF, 1942-46. Recipient various fellowships and grants Fla. Endowment Humanities and Fla. Arts Council, 1974—. Mem. Fla. Coll. English Assn. (pres., dir.), South Atlantic Modern Lang. Assn., Popular Culture Assn., Popular Culture in South (dir.), Fla. Suncoast Writers' Conf. dir.). Home: 3304 Nakora Dr Tampa FL 33618 Office: U South Florida Dept English Tampa FL 33620

HISAM, HORST GUENTHER, business consultant, investment co. exec.; b. Berlin, May 2, 1921; came to U.S., 1976, naturalized, 1977; s. Theodor

Friedrich Wilhelm and Helene Amalie Rosalie (Meyer) H.; J.D., U. Tuebingen, 1945; m. Ursula M. Domdey, May 25, 1965; children—Thorsten G., Nicole. Bus. cons., Germany, 1946-76; prof. mgmt. U. Bad Harzburg, 1957-73; pres. various investment cos., Germany, 1958-76; bus. cons., U.S., 1976—; pres. Swiss and German Investments, Inc., Ft. Lauderdale, Fla., 1976—, Investment and Holding Co. of Fla., Inc., Ft. Lauderdale, 1976—, Gulf Tarra, Inc., Marco Island, Fla., 1976—, German Am. Devel. Corp. Mayor, City of List auf Sylt (Germany), 1969-73. Club: Lions (Lauderdale by the Sea.). Author: Die Satzungsgewalt der Gemeinde, 1945; Der Handel in der industriellen Gesellschaft, 1963. Home and Office: 2218 NE 17th Ct Fort Lauderdale FL 33305

HITCHCOCK, JAMES GUY, JR., architectural engineer; b. Hiram, Ga., Feb. 12, 1927; s. James Guy and Mary Victoria (Denton) H.; m. Ann Sinclair, May 7, 1949; children—Vicki, Jim; m. Joyce McMillan, May 13, 1961; 1 dau., Jocelyn; m. Roberta Orcutt Siefkin, Sept. 23, 1982. Student Davidson Coll., 1944-45, Ga. Inst. Tech., 1968, 74. Cert. occupational safety Nat. Safety Council. Freelance designer, 1948-50; draftsman Frank Manning Architect, 1950-53; bank designer Tomberlin-Sheetz Architects, 1953-55, Harold Norris Architect, 1955-57; materials handling designer Stevens & Wilkinson Architect, Atlanta, 1957-59; interior design, constrn. supr. Rich's, Atlanta, 1959-62; architl. engr. Fed. Res. Bank Atlanta, 1962—; design cons., 1968—. Served with AUS, 1945-46. Designer Monetary Mus. Fed. Res. Bank Atlanta, 1970-72. Home: 673 Sunnybrook Dr Decatur GA 30033 Office: 104 Marietta St Atlanta GA 30303

HITCHINGS, GEORGE HERBERT, pharmacologist, educator; b. Hoquiam, Wash., Apr. 18, 1905; m. Beverly Reimer, 1933; 2 children. B.S. cum laude, U. Wash., 1927, M.S., 1928; Ph.D. in Biochemistry, Harvard U., 1933; D.Sc. (hon.), U. Mich., 1971, Strathclyde U., Scotland, 1977, N.Y. Med. Coll., 1981, Emory U., 1981, Duke U., 1982, U. N.C., Chapel Hill, 1982, Mt. Sinai Sch. Medicine, N.Y.C., 1983. Teaching fellow U. Wash., Seattle, 1926-28, Harvard U., Boston, 1928-34, instr., tutor, 1932-36, research fellow, 1934-36, assoc., 1936-39; sr. instr. Western Res. U., Cleve., 1939-42; biochemist Burroughs Wellcome Co., Tuckahoe, N.Y., 1942-46, chief biochemist, 1946-55, assoc. research dir., 1955-63, research dir. chemotherapy div., 1963-67, v.p. in charge research, 1967-75, dir., 1968-84, scientist emeritus and cons., 1975—; prof. pharmacology Brown U., Providence, 1968-80; adj. prof. pharmacology and exptl. medicine Duke U., Durham, N.C., 1970—; adj. prof. pharmacology U. N.C.-Chapel Hill, 1972—; pres. The Burroughs Wellcome Fund, 1971—, dir., 1968—; vis. prof. clin. pharmacology Chuang-Ang U., Seoul, Korea, 1974-77; vis. lectr., Pakistan and Iran, 1976, Japan and India, 1980, South Africa, 1981; staff Roger Williams Gen. Hosp., Brown U., 1980; mem. com. on growth NRC, 1952-53; mem. chemistry panel Cancer Chemotherapy Nat. Service Ctr., 1955-57; cons. USPHS, 1956-60; mem. drug devel. com. Nat. Cancer Inst., 1975-78; dir. Westchester Sci. Adv. Council, 1959-61; mem. nat. med. and sci. adv. com. Leukemia Soc. Am., 1969-73, trustee, 1969-73; mem. research and evaluation adv. com. N.C. State Dept. Corrections, 1974-76; mem. N.C. State Sci. and Tech. Com., 1975-79; mem. external adv. com. Duke Comprhensive Cancer Ctr., 1978—; Clowes lectr., 1968; Charles E. Dohme lectr. Johns Hopkins U., 1969; Walter H. Hartung Meml. lectr. U. N.C., 1972; Michael Cross Meml. lectr. Cambridge U., 1974; Pfizer lectr. SUNY-Stonybrook, 1981; Burroughs Wellcome Disting. lectr. Phila. Coll. Pharmacy, 1981. Numerous patents in field. Contbr. numerous articles to profl. jours. Mem. editorial bd. Research Communications in Chem. Pathology and Pharmacology, 1969—, Molecular Pharmacology, 1967—, Biochem. Pharmacology, 1967—, Life Scis., 1978. Bd. dirs. United Fund Durham and Durham County, 1971-75, v.p. agy. affairs, 1976-78; bd. dirs. chpt. ARC, 1972-77, 78—; bd. dirs. Found. for Better Health of Durham, 1978—, pres., 1982-83; bd. dirs. chpt. Am. Cancer Soc., 1972-75; pres. Greater Durham Community Found., 1983—; bd. dirs. Med. Found. N.C., Inc., 1984—. Recipient Gregor Mendel medal Czechoslovak Acad. Sci., 1968; Gairdner award Gairdner Found., Toronto, 1968; Passano award laureat, 1969; Robert de Villier Sci. award Leukemia Soc. Am., 1969; medal Purkinje Med. Soc., Czechoslovakia, 1971; award Am. Chem. Soc., 1972; Cameron prize U. Edinburgh, 1972; Disting. Achievement award Modern Medicine mag., 1973, Durham C. of C., 1973; award Bertner Found., 1974; Papanicolaou award for sci. achievement, 1978; N.C. award in Sci., 1980; C. Chester Stock medal Sloan Kettering Inst., 1981; Disting. Service award U. N.C., 1982, Alfred Burger award in medicinal chemistry, 1984. Fellow Royal Soc. Medicine (hon.; Mullard award 1976), AAAS, Am. Chem. Soc., Chem. Soc. (London), Am. Soc. Biol. Chemists, Soc. Exptl. Biol. Medicine, Am. Assn. Cancer Research (Cain award 1984), Internat. Transplantation Soc., Royal Soc. Chemistry (hon.); mem. Am. Soc. Clin. Pharmacology (Oscar B. Hunter award 1984), U.S. Nat. Acad. Scis., Am. Soc. Toxicology (hon.), Phi Beta Kappa, Sigma Xi, Phi Lambda Upsilon. Home: 4022 Bristol Rd Durham NC 27707 Office: 3030 Cornwallis Rd Research Triangle Park NC 27709

HITCHINGS, OWEN LYMAN, city official, jewelry executive; b. Corvallis, Oreg., July 19, 1937; s. Edward Leroy and Dorothy Frances (Owen) H.; m. Clemmie Baham, Aug. 15, 1958; children—Monica Rene, Kim Louise, Terri Lynne, Lisa Marie. B.B.A., Columbia Coll., Mo., 1975. Commd. officer U.S. Air Force, 1961, advanced through ranks to maj., 1971; comdr. detachment 409 U.S. Air Force Recruiting Office, Oklahoma City, 1974-76, 552 CAMS Squadron, Tinker AFB, Okla., 1976-77; command pilot, 1977; ret., 1977; salesman Bob Moore Cadillac, Oklahoma City, 1977-78; mgr., appraiser Midwest Jewelers, Oklahoma City, 1978-83; utility services supr. City of Midwest City, Okla., 1983—; advisor Black and Black Investment, Oklahoma City, 1978—, Mcpl. Electric Systems of Okla., Midwest City, 1985, Post Office Adv. Bd., Oklahoma City, 1985. Contbr. articles to profl. jours. Donor mem. Okla. Symphony Orch., 1985, Smithsonian Instn., 1985, Okla. Aviation and Space Mus., 1985. Decorated 14 awards for valor. Mem. Air Force Assn., Ret. Officers Assn., Gemological Inst. Am., Order of Daedalians (flight capt. 1985—, service award 1979, recruiting award 1978). Republican. Roman Catholic. Club: Vietnam Vets. Lodge: Rotary. Avocations: public speaking; golf; bowling; flying; collecting art. Home: 5025 Federal Ct Oklahoma City OK 73135 Office: City of Midwest City 100 N Midwest Blvd Midwest City OK 73140

HITE, DONALD BLANDING, otolaryngologist, resort executive, former air force officer; b. Pelion, S.C., May 13, 1935; s. William Hoyt and Beatrice (Garvin) H.; m. Laure Bailie, Aug. 22, 1958 (div. 1966); children—Cynthia Lynn, Mark Wayne. B.S., The Citadel, 1957; M.D., Med. Coll. Ga., 1961. Diplomate Am. Acad. Otolaryngology and Head and Neck Surgery. Commd. 2d lt. U.S. Air Force, 1961, advanced through grades to lt. col., 1971, intern, Tacoma, Wash., 1961-62, flight surgeon, San Antonio, 1962, Sumter, S.C., 1962-63, Vietnam, 1964-65, resident in otolaryngology, San Antonio, 1965-69, chief orolaryngology, Dayton, Ohio, 1969-74, resigned, 1974; practice medicine specializing in otolaryngology, Greenville, S.C., 1974—; owner Carolina Shores Golf Club, North Myrtle Beach, S.C., 1979—. Contbr. med. articles to pubs. Mem. Senate-Bus. Adv. Bd., Washington, Republican Senatorial Adv. Bd. Mem. Am. Acad. Otolaryngology and Head and Neck Surgery, AMA, S.C. Med. Assn., Greenville County Med. Soc. (state del. 1979). Baptist. Clubs: Greenville Country, Commerce.

HITT, H. H., educational administrator. Supt. of schs. San Antonio. Office: 141 Lavaca St San Antonio TX 78210*

HITTNER, STEVEN BRYAN, publisher; b. Bronx, N.Y., Feb. 13, 1942; s. Sol H. and Elsie (Selig) H.; m. Carol Brenner, July 6, 1963; children—Elyse Dawn, Stacy Lynn. B.B.A. in Mktg., Adelphi U., 1963; M.B.A., Harvard U., 1965. Asst. to pres. Remco Industries, Harrison, N.J., 1963-71; v.p. mktg. Esther Miller Co., Long Island City, N.Y., 1971-74; pres. Hardware Distbrs. Co., Secaucus, N.J., 1974-80; pub. Golden Years Mag., Melbourne, Fla., 1980—. U.S. presdl. appointee as chmn. Selective Service Bd., Brevard County, Fla., 1982; Fla. bd. dirs. Sr. Olympic Com.; mem. Brevard County Planning Bd. Mem. Am. Mgmt. Assn., Fla. Mag. Assn., Internat. Exec. Service Corps. Jewish. Club: Presidents. Lodge: B'nai B'rith.

HOAR, THOMAS FRANCIS XAVIER, clergyman, college official; b. Boston, Aug. 18, 1951; s. James Francis and Geralding Elizabeth (Congdon) H. B.A., St. Michael's Coll., Winooski, Vt., 1974; M.Div., St. Michael's U., Toronto, Ont., Can., 1977; M.A., Fordham U., 1978; Ph.D., Mich. State U., 1985. Ordained priest Roman Catholic Ch., 1978. Dir. spl. events St. Michael's Coll., Winooski, 1978-80, resident dir., 1978-80, dir. campus ministry, 1980-82, now trustee; adj. instr. Coll. Edn., Mich. State U., East Lansing, 1983-85; v.p. student affairs Christian Bros. Coll., Memphis, 1985—. Chaplain, Vt. Fire Fighters Assn., 1978-82. Mem. Catholic Campus Ministers Assn., Nat. Assn. Student Personnel Adminstrs., Assn. Coll. Student Personnel, Am. Assn. for Counseling and Devel., Soc. St. Edmund. Lodge: K.C. (4th degree). Avocation: French cooking. Address: Christian Bros Coll 650 East Pkwy S Memphis TN 38104

HOATSON, ROBERT JOSEPH, geologist; b. Sutherland, Nebr., Dec. 5, 1949; s. Earl William and Mildred Ruth (Fairhead) H.; m. Diane Bognar, May 17, 1975; 1 child, Matthew Earl. B.S. in Geology, Central Mo. State U., 1975. Field log engr. Dresser Atlas, Houston, 1975-76, instr. log analysis, 1976-79; exploration geologist Border Exploration, Houston, 1979-82; staff geologist Coastal Oil & Gas Corp., Houston, 1982—; environ. analyst cons. Environ. Sci. & Engring., Inc., St. Louis, 1976; geol. cons. Rockwell Internat., St. Louis, 1976. Mem. Am. Assn. Petroleum Geologists, Soc. Profl. Well Log Analysts, Houston Geol. Soc., W. Tex. Geol. Soc., Corpus Christi Geol. Soc. Methodist. Republican. Home: 306 Fry Rd Katy TX 77450 Office: Coastal Oil & Gas Corp 9 Greenway Plaza Houston TX 77046

HOBACK, JOHN HOLLAND, chemistry educator; b. Huntington, W.Va., Sept. 6, 1920; s. Jesse Lawrence and Myriam Melvina (Holland) H.; A.B., Marshall U., 1941, M.S., 1942; Ph.D., W.Va. U., 1957; m. Florence Elizabeth Kunst, Oct. 27, 1945; children—Mary Holland, Conaway Kunst. Instr. chemistry Marshall U., Huntington, W.Va., 1945-47, asst. prof., 1947-54, assoc. prof., 1954-63, prof., 1963—. Mem. Am. Chem. Soc. (chmn. Central Ohio Valley sect. 1967), Am. Inst. Chemistry, W.Va. Acad. Sci., Sigma Xi, Phi Lambda Upsilon. Methodist. Contbr. articles to profl. jours. Home: 2658 3d Ave Huntington WV 25702 Office: Chemistry Dept Marshall U Huntington WV 25701

HOBACK, KARL FRANKLIN, patent agt.; b. Huntington, W.Va., Jan. 5, 1929; s. Jesse Lawrence and Myriam Melvina (Holland) H.; B.S., Marshall U., 1950, M.S., 1951; Ph.D., W.Va. U., 1956. Asst. prof. chemistry Va. Mil. Inst., Lexington, 1956-58; patent agt. Beale & Jones, Washington, 1958-72; patent agt. Lubrizol Corp., Cleve., 1972-75, patent agt., Cleve., 1975-79; patent agt. Sherman & Shalloway, Alexandria, Va., 1979—. Fellow Am. Inst. Chemists; mem. Am. Chem. Soc., Sigma Xi, Phi Lambda Upsilon. Home: PO Box 702 Alexandria VA 22313 Office: 413 N Washington St Alexandria VA 22314

HOBBS, CLAUDE MACK, pharmacist; b. Citronelle, Ala., Jan. 16, 1943; s. George Burgsbee and Gladys Estelle Hobbs (Jones) Bethea H.; m. Shirley Faye Evans, June 4, 1965; children—Burgsbee Lee, Forrest Trent, Creighton Aubrey. B.S., Auburn U., 1965. Lic. pharmacist, Ala., Tenn., Miss. Staff pharmacist Mobile Infirmary, Ala., 1965-66, Central Inc., Prichard, Ala., 1966-69, Delchamps Inc., Mobile, 1969-71; staff pharmacist, owner, mgr. Burnham, Inc., Escatawpa, Miss., 1971-76; staff pharmacist, sole proprietor, mgr. Escatawpa Pharmacy, Miss., 1976—. Mem. exec. com. Republican party, Jackson County, Miss., 1980-88; deacon, mem. fin. com. Escatawpa Bapt., Miss., 1975—; mem. Miss. Small Bus. Assn., Jackson, 1976—; bd. dirs. Exodus House, Pasc-Moss Point, Miss., 1974-75; mem. Escatawpa Civic Com., 1984—. Named Employer of Yr., Moss Point High Sch. Diversified Edn. Clubs Am., 1984. Mem. Nat. Assn. Retail Druggists, Miss. Pharm. Assn., Tenn. Pharm. Assn., Pas Point C. of C., Auburn U. Alumni Assn., Auburn Pharmacy Alumni. Republican. Baptist. Club: Jaycees (Escatawpa, Miss.). Avocations: pilot; hunting; gardening. Home: PO Box 504 Escatawpa MS 39552 Office: Escatawpa Pharmacy PO Drawer 580 Escatawpa MS 39552

HOBBS, DONALD EDWARD, sheriff; b. Maryville, Tenn., Mar. 3, 1936; s. Charles Arthur and Alma Bell (Bowerman) H.; m. La Wanda Burchfield, Mar. 30, 1939; children—Daniel Leon, Robin, Rhonda, Ronny, Randy. A. in Police Sci., Walter State Coll., 1975. Police officer CoCoa Police Dept., Fla., 1958-71; dep. sheriff Blount County Sheriff Dept., Maryville, Tenn., 1971-72; police officer Maryville Police Dept., Tenn., 1972-82; sheriff Blount County Sheriff Dept., Maryville, 1982—. Served with USNG, 1955-57. Recipient Cert. Appreciation VFW, 1983. Mem. Tenn. Sheriff's Assn., Republican Women's Club. Republican. Baptist. Club: Pine Lakes Golf. Lodges: Masons. Avocations: wood working; golf; fishing. Home: Route 5 Box 27 Maryville TN 37801 Office: Blount County Sheriff's Dept 301 Court St Maryville TN 37801

HOBBS, JOAN MCLEAN, real estate executive; b. Detroit, Oct. 12, 1943; d. William Hector and Ruth Ellen McLean; student Albion Coll., 1961-63; B.A., Mich. State U., 1964. Exec. asst. to bd. Fed. Res. Bd., Washington, 1965-79; pvt. practice mgmt. cons., Houston, 1979—; dir. mgmt. Interfin Corp., Houston, 1980-82, v.p., gen. mgr. sales and mktg. and property mgmt., 1982—. Recipient spl. achievement award for profl. performance Fed. Res. Bd., 1978. Mem. Nat. Assn. Exec. Women. Methodist. Home and Office: 5100 San Felipe Houston TX 77056

HOBBS, MARGIE JOHNSON, mathematics educator; b. Eudora, Ark., June 13, 1943; d. Robert S. and Edrie C. (Smith) J.; m. Allen Hobbs, Dec. 28, 1963; 1 child, Holly Margaret. B.S., Memphis State U., 1965, M.S.T., 1970; postgrad. U. Miss., 1982—. Tchr., Memphis City Schs., 1965-75; assoc. prof. State Tech. Inst. at Memphis, 1975—. Author: Mathematics of the Business World, 1979; Basic Mathematics for Trades and Technologies, 1983. Mem. planning commn. City of Piperton, 1983. Mem. Am. Math. Assn. (conv. chmn. 1985, chmn. membership com. 1982-85, v.p. 1985—), Nat. Council Tchrs. Math. (editor jour. sect. new projects), Tenn. Math. Assn. (two-year coll. pres. 1982-84, sec.-treas. 1984-85), Phi Delta Kappa, Phi Kappa Phi. Baptist. Avocations: reading, traveling, sports. Home: 812 N Chulahoma St Collierville TN 38017 Office: State Tech Inst Memphis 5983 Macon Cove Memphis TN 38134

HOBBS, MICHAEL AUBREY ALLAN, aerospace engineering executive; b. Ponteland, Northumberland, Eng., Sept. 6, 1930; came to U.S., 1980; s. Raymond Holmstead and Iris St. Clare (White) H.; student Durham U., 1951; m. Patricia Eileen Streeter, Jan. 25, 1958; children—Belinda Clare, Christine Anne, Pamela Denise. Mgmt. apprentice Vickers Armstrong Naval Yard, Walker, Newcastle-on-Tyne, 1948-52; commd. pilot RAF, 1952, advanced through grades to squadron leader, 1966; mem. Air Staff, 1971-74; ret., 1974; tech., gen. sales mgr. Martin Baker Aircraft Co., Buckinghamshire, Eng., 1974-79; pres. Stencel Aero. Engring. Co., Asheville, N.C., 1980-85; v.p., gen. ptnr. United Emission Catalyst, Arden, N.C., 1986—. Mem. S.A.F.E. Episcopalian. Clubs: Biltmore Forest Country; RAF (London). Lodge: Rotary (Arden). Home: 86 Braddock Way Asheville NC 28803 Office: PO Box 889 Arden NC 28704

HOBBY, WILLIAM MATTHEWS, III, lawyer, photographer, educator; b. Millen, Ga., Aug. 5, 1935; s. Wensley Henry and Nell (Weeks) H.; m. Gretchen Clark, Apr. 22, 1939; children—Amy Louise Livingston, William Matthews IV. Student Tulane U., 1953-55; B.M.E., U. Fla., 1959; postgrad. Western Electric Grad. Engring. Sch., 1959-60, U. N.C., 1960-61; J.D., George Washington U., 1963; postgrad. Pat. Off. Acad., 1964-65; Bar: Fla. 1967, U.S. Pat. Off., 1966, U.S. dist. ct. D.C. 1963, U.S. Sup. Ct. 1968. Engr., Western Electric, 1959-60, U.S. Naval Research Labs., 1961-63; pat. examiner U.S. Pat. Office, 1963-65; asst. pat. csl. Martin Marietta Corp., Orlando, Fla., 1965-67; ptnr. Duckworth, Hobby, Allen, Dyer & Pettis, P.A., Orlando, 1967-81; sole practice, Orlando, 1981—; tchr. photography Maitland (Fla.) Art Ctr., 1977—, curator photog. exhibit, 1982; photographer Orange County Bar Assn., The Briefs. Bd. dirs. Fla. Conservation Found., 1976—; bd. dirs. Central Fla. Civic Theatre, 1979—, 1st v.p., 1981-85, pres., 1985—. Served with U.S. N.G., 1957-61. Recipient Spl. award Mus. Store Assn., 1975, numerous awards in fine art photography, 1977-82. Mem. ABA, Fla. Bar Assn. (chmn. Pat. trademark and copyright 1973-74, 80-81), Orange County Bar Assn. (asst. editor The Briefs, 1978-82), Am. Pat. Law Assn., SAR, Phi Delta Phi, Sigma Alpha Epsilon. Republican. Clubs: Winter Park (Fla.) Racquet, U. Orlando. Office: 1327 N Mills Ave Orlando FL 32803

HOBBY, WILLIAM PETTUS, lieutenant governor Texas, newspaper and broadcast executive; b. Houston, Jan. 19, 1932; s. William Pettus and Oveta (Culp) H.; B.A., Rice U., 1953; m. Diana Poteat Stallings, Sept. 11, 1954; children—Laura Poteat (Mrs. John Beckworth), Paul William, Andrew Purefoy, Katherine Pettus. Ownership and mgmt. Houston Post Co., 1957-83; vice chmn. Channel Two TV Co., KPRC Radio Co., 1970-83, chmn. bd., 1983—; chmn. bd. Channel Five Co., Nashville, 1975—, Channel Four TV Co., Tucson; pres. H&C Communications, 1979-83, chmn. bd., 1983—; chmn. bd. Hobby-Catto Interests, Inc., 1983—, KCCI-TV Broadcasting, Inc., Des Moines, 1985—, WESH-TV Broadcasting, Inc., Daytona Beach, Fla., 1985—. Parliamentarian, Tex. Senate, 1959; lt. gov. State of Tex., 1973—; chmn. Nat. Conf. Lt. Govs., 1976-77. Bd. dirs. Child Guidance Center Houston, 1957-63, pres., 1960-62. Served to lt. (j.g.) USNR, 1953-57. Mem. Am. Soc. Newspaper Editors, Tex. Hunter and Jumper Assn. (dir. 1953—, pres. 1959-61), U.S. Equestrian Team (v.p. 1959-60). Office: PO Box 326 Houston TX 77001 also State Capitol Capitol Sta Austin TX 78711

HOBSON, ANNE GLEN, pharmacist; b. Lawrence, Mass., Apr. 11, 1925; d. William Harvey and Ina (Brown) Sparks; student Radcliffe Coll., 1942-43; B.A., Stanford U., 1946, M.A., 1947; postgrad. U. Houston, 1969-70; Ph.D., U. Tex., 1972, B.S. in Pharmacy, 1974; m. William C. Hobson, Jan. 9, 1960; children—Floyd, Bruce, Scott, William. Research asst. in preventive medicine U. Calif., San Francisco, 1947; research asso. in pharmacology Stanford Med. Sch., San Francisco, 1948; tchr. U.S. Army Dependents Sch., Manila, Philippines, 1949-51, Miss Harker's Sch., Palo Alto, Calif., 1951-53; med. lab. technician Palo Alto Clinic, 1953-54; tchr. Anglo-Am. Sch., Kifissia, Athens, Greece, 1954-56; chief lab. technician Dale County Hosp., Ozark, Ala., 1956-57; tchr. Bloomfield (N.J.) High Sch., 1957-58, Clark (N.J.) High Sch., 1958-59; asst. prof. Hellenika Anglaise Collegion, Athens, Greece, 1959-60; tchr. Molesworth AFB, Eng., 1960-61; asst. prof. Ashton Community Coll., Ashton-under-Lyne, Eng., 1961-62; tchr. Hartshead Sec. Sch., Ashton-under-Lyne, 1962-63, Droylsden (Eng.) Secondary Sch. for Girls, 1963-64; asst. coordinator Trenton Jr. 5 Exptl. Sch. program, for Disadvantaged, 1964-65; tchr. Trenton High Sch., 1965-66; research asso. Princeton (N.J.) U., 1966-67; tchr. Sam Rayburn High Sch., Pasadena, Tex., 1967-70; chief adult councilor Juvenile Drug Addiction, Pasadena, 1970-72; NSF grantee U. Tex., Austin, 1970-74; pharmacist, asst. mgr., mgr. Sommers Drug Stores, Austin, 1974-76; owner, pharmacist Hobson Pharmacy, Pflugerville, Tex., 1976—. Recipient Outstanding Alumna award U. Tex., 1977; registered pharmacist, Tex. Fellow Am. Coll. Apothecaries; mem. Am. Soc. Hosp. Pharmacists, Am. Pharm. Assn., Tex. Pharm. Assn., Capital Area Pharm. Assn., Am. Inst. History of Pharmacy (cert. of recognition 1973), Am. Tchrs. Assn., Tex. Tchrs. Assn., AAUW, Bus. and Profl. Women, Better Bus. Bur., Kappa Epsilon. Republican. Episcopalian. Clubs: Rainbow Girls, Am. Luth. Ch. Women's Assn. Contbr. articles to profl. jours.; researcher in RH blood factor and leukemia, possible relationship with epilepsy, and mongolism, possible causal relationship between jaundice and hepatitis, others. Home: 18 Rowe Loop Pflugerville TX 78660 Office: 100 E Main St Pflugerville TX 78660

HOBSON, FRED COLBY, JR., English educator, author; b. Winston-Salem, N.C., Apr. 23, 1943; s. Fred Colby and Miriam Brevard (Tuttle) H.; m. Linda V. Whitney, June 17, 1967 (div. 1977); 1 child, Jane Gregory; m. Cynthia L. Graff, Mar. 7, 1981. A.B., U.N.C., 1965, Ph.D., 1972; M.A., Duke U., 1967. Editorial writer Winston-Salem Jour. and Sentinel, 1969-70; asst. prof. English U. Ala., Tuscaloosa, 1972-75, assoc. prof., 1975-79, prof., 1980—; vis. prof. Am. studies U. Hull (Eng.), 1982; cons. NEH, 1979-83. Co-recipient Pulitzer Prize in Journalism, 1970; NEH fellow, 1976-77. Mem. Modern Lang., Assn., Soc. for Study So. Lit., So. Hist. Assn., Mencken Soc. Democrat. Presbyterian. Author: Serpent in Eden: H.L. Mencken and the South, 1974; Tell About The South: The Southern Rage to Explain (Jules F. Landry award), 1983; editor: South-Watching: Selected Essays of Gerald W. Johnson (Lillian Smith award), 1983; co-editor Literature at the Barricades: The American Writer of the 1930's, 1982; mem. editorial bd. S. Atlantic Rev.; contbr. essays to lit. jours. Home: 12111 Northwood Lake Northport AL 35476 Office: U Alabama Dept English University AL 35486

HOCHSTRASSER, DONALD LEE, cultural anthropologist, community health and public administration educator; b. Taylorsville, Ky., June 10, 1927; s. Emil John and Mary E. (Schad) H.; m. Marie Emlen, Apr. 9, 1960; 1 child, Letitia Cope; stepchildren—Eloise Q. Hatch, Laura A. Hatch. B.A., U. Ky., 1952, M.A., 1955; postgrad. (univ. fellow) Northwestern U., 1955-56; Ph.D. in Anthropology, U. Oreg., 1963; M.P.H., U. Calif.-Berkeley, 1969. Research asst. dept. rural sociology U. Ky., Lexington, 1954-55, instr. dept. anthropology, 1956-57, 1959-60, instr. dept. community medicine, 1961-63, asst. prof., 1963-66, assoc. prof., 1966-73, prof., 1973-80, assoc. dir. Ctr. Developmental Change, 1970-73, prof. community health Coll. Allied Health and prof. pub. adminstrn. Grad. Ctr. Pub. Adminstrn., 1980—; teaching fellow dept. anthropology U. Oreg., Eugene, 1957-58, instr., 1958-59, NSF research fellow, 1960-61; USPHS spl. research fellow Sch. Pub. Health, U. Calif.-Berkeley, 1968-69; chmn. state family planning rev. com. Ky. State Comprehensive Health Planning Council, 1972-74; mem. state family planning task force Council Health Services, Ky. State Dept. Human Resources, 1974-78; cons., adv. numerous orgns.; vis. scholar dept. adminstrv. and social health scis. Sch. Pub. Health, U. Calif.-Berkeley, 1979; dir. Bluegrass Regional Birth Planning Council, Inc., Lexington, 1978-81, Lexington Planned Parenthood, Inc., 1982—. Mem. Union of Concerned Scientists, Am. Farmland Trust, Friends of the Earth. Served with USN, 1946-47. Grantee pub. health, family planning, sickle cell anemia, Tb control and occupational health-risk factors. Fellow Am. Anthrop. Assn., Soc. Applied Anthropology; mem. Soc. Med. Anthropology (founding), Am. Pub. Health Assn. (founding mem. population sect.), Assn. Tchrs. Preventive Medicine, AAAS, AAUP, Phi Beta Kappa, Sigma Xi, Alpha Kappa Delta, Delta Omega. Democrat. Clubs: Univ. Faculty, Alumni. Contbr. numerous articles to profl. pubs. Home: 953 Holly Springs Dr Lexington KY 40504 Office: 208A Annex 2 Univ Ky Med Ctr Univ Ky Lexington KY 40536

HOCKETT, SHERI LYNN, radiologist; b. Cleburne, Tex., Apr. 20, 1953; d. Dale and Rosamond (Prater) Hockett; B.A., So. Meth. U., 1974; M.D., Southwestern Med. Sch., 1978; m. David Alexander Campbell, Apr. 22, 1978; children—Courtney Michelle, Jonathan David. Resident diagnostic radiology St. Paul Hosp., Dallas, 1978-81, chief resident, 1980-81; fellow, 198-82; staff radiologist Meml. Hosp. of Garland (Tex.), and Garland Community Hosp. Diplomate Am. Bd. Radiology. Mem. Am. Assn. Women Radiologists, Am. Coll. Radiology, Radiol. Soc. N.Am., Tex. Radiol. Soc., AMA, Dalls-Ft. Worth Radiol. Soc. Office: 2300 Marie Curie Dr Garland TX 75042

HOCKMAN, CHARLES HENRY, neuroscience educator; b. Montreal, Que., Can., Mar. 15, 1923; came to U.S., 1958; s. Charles and Blanche (Lajeunesse) H.; m. Mildred Adele Jardin, Aug. 16, 1952; children—Kenneth Charles, Gail Andrea, Laurie Anne. B.A., Queen's U., Kingston, Can., 1958; M.Sc., Brown U., 1960, Ph.D., 1963. Asst. prof. neurol. sci. and psychiatry Med. Coll. Va., Richmond, 1962-66; assoc. prof. pharmacology U. Toronto, Can., 1966-72; assoc. prof. basic med. sci. and physiology U. Ill., Urbana, 1972-82, chmn. med. physiology program, 1975-77; prof. neurosci. Mercer U. Sch. Medicine, Macon, Ga., 1982—. Editor: Chemical Transmission in the Mammalian Central Nervous System, 1976; Limbic System Mechanisms and Autonomic Function, 1972. Served with Can. Mcht. Navy, 1943-45. Can. Council fellow, 1959-61; grantee NIH, USPHS, Med. Research Council Can., Can. Dept. Health and Welfare, Ill. Dept. Mental Health. Mem. Am. Physiol. Soc., Can. Physiol. Soc., Soc. Neurosci., Sigma Xi. Roman Catholic. Lodge: K.C. Home: 1088 Magnolia St Macon GA 31201 Office: Mercer U Sch Med 1400 Coleman Ave Macon GA 31207

HOCOTT, JOE BILL, chem. engr., educator; b. nr. Big Flat, Ark., Sept. 19, 1921; s. Jeiks Edmonds and Frances Clara (Berry) H.; B.S., U. Ark., 1945; M.S., Okla. State U., 1951. Insp. Maumelle Ordnance Works, U.S. Army Ordnance Dept., Little Rock, 1942-43; head sci. dept. Joe T. Robinson High Sch., Little Rock, 1945-46; instr. chemistry U. Tulsa, 1946-47; teaching fellow Okla. A. and M. Coll., Stillwater, 1947-49; research chem. engr. Deep Rock Petroleum Corp., Cushing, Okla., 1950, Kerr-McGee Oil Corp., Stillwater, 1951; chem. engr. cons. Joe Bill Hocott, Little Rock, 1952-55, 63—; med. technician U. Ark. Med. Center, Little Rock, 1955-56, research asso., 1956-57, instr. internal medicine, 1957-62; head chemistry dept. Little Rock Central High Sch., 1963-66; head sci. dept. Met. Vocat.-Tech. High Sch., Little Rock, 1967-73. Asst. scoutmaster Boy Scouts Am., 1945-46, troop committeeman, 1945-46, 57-58, neighborhood commr., 1969-70. Bd. dirs. Ark. Jr. Sci. and Humanities Symposium, 1965-75, asst. dir., 1972. Mem. Am. Inst. Chem. Engrs., Nat. Soc. Profl. Engrs., Ark. Jr. (dist. dir. 1966-70) acads. sci., Sigma Xi, Phi Lambda Upsilon, Unitarian. Home: 1010 Rice St Little Rock AR 72202

HODGE, GAMEEL BYRON, surgeon; b. Spartanburg, S.C., Sept. 16, 1917; s. Charles B. and Mary (Bargot) H.; m. Katie Adams, Sept. 22, 1943; children—Susan, Byron, John Adams. B.S., Wofford Coll., 1938; M.D., Vanderbilt U., 1942. Diplomate Am. Bd. Surgery. Intern, Duke U. Med. Sch. and Hosp., Durham, N.C., 1942-43, asst. resident, 1943-47, chief resident surgeon, 1947-48; practice medicine specializing in gen., thoracic and cardiovascular surgery, Spartanburg, 1948—; attending surgeon Spartanburg Gen. Hosp.; cons. surgeon St. Luke's Hosp., Tryon, N.C., 1948-58, Cherokee County (S.C.) Meml. Hosp., 1948-74; thoracic surgeon Spartanburg County Tb Hosp.,

1948-69; chief of surgery Mary Black Meml. Hosp., 1969-72; asso. clin. prof. surgery Med. U. S.C., Spartanburg, 1970—. Chmn. Spartanburg County Comm. for Higher Edn., 1967—; trustee Spartanburg Day Sch., 1958—. Contbr. articles on surgery and gen. medicine to profl. jours. Served to 1st lt. M.C., U.S. Army Res., 1942-53. Fellow Am. Coll. Chest Physicians, Internat. Acad. Proctology, N.Y. Acad. Sci., Am. Fedn. Clin. Research, Indsl. Medicine Assn.; mem. Am. Heart Assn., S.C. Med. Assn. (past chmn., com.mem.), S.C. Surg. Soc., S.C. Vascular Surg. Soc., AMA, Spartanburg Med. Soc., Am. Geriatrics Soc., Deryl Hart Surg. Soc., Spartanburg Area C. of C. (past pres.), Duke U. Med. Alumni Assn. (past pres.), Order of Palmetto, Phi Beta Kappa, Phi Beta Pi. Episcopalian. Clubs: Spartanburg Country, Kiwanis (Citizenship of Year award 1969), Piedmont. Home: 2500 Old Knox Rd Spartanburg SC 29302 Office: 3 Catawba St Spartanburg SC 29303

HODGES, ALLEN, psychologist; b. Greenville, S.C., Feb. 16, 1925; s. William L. and Estelle (Smith) H.; B.A., U. Minn., 1947; M.A., U. Tenn., 1948, Ph.D., 1953; m. Elizabeth Swanson, June 27, 1944; children—Nancy Elizabeth, Susan Kathleen Hodges McDonnell, Sara Louise Hodges Juarez, Jane Ellen Hodges Carona. Sch. psychologist, dir. guidance Oak Ridge Public Schs., 1948-53; clin. psychologist, dir. So. Minn. Mental Health Center, Albert Lea, 1953-57; cons. psychologist, acting dir. community mental health Minn. Dept. Public Welfare, St. Paul, 1957-59; asst. prof., dir. sch. psychology tng. program U. Minn., 1959-61; mental health cons. clin. psychology NIMH, USPHS, HEW, 1961-63, program dir. mental health services, 1964-67, asso. regional health dir., 1967-70, asst. regional dir. planning and evaluation, 1970-78, dir. service delivery assessment, 1978-79; asst. clin. prof. dept. psychiatry U. Colo. Sch. Medicine, 1965-79; lectr. Regis Coll., 1962-79; HEW fellow on loan to Ga. Dept. Human Resources, 1979-82; pvt. practice psychology, 1982—; sec. Minn. Bd. Exam. Psychologists, 1957-61. Served to lt. (j.g.) USNR, 1943-46; PTO. Fellow Am. Psychol. Assn., Am. Public Health Assn. Office: 218 Fraser Dr Hinesville GA 31313

HODGES, CAROLYN VIRGINIA, college official; b. Forest, Va., May 14, 1942; d. Clarence Marvin and Bedie Elizabeth (Wingfield) H. B.S., Lynchburg Coll., 1964; M.S. in Phys. Edn., U. N.C.-Greensboro, 1968, D.Ed., 1983. Mem. faculty Lynchburg (Va.) Coll., 1964-72, field hockey coach, 1966-67, basketball coach, 1967-72, lacrosse coach, 1966-72; mem. faculty, women's athletic dir. Longwood Coll., Farmville, Va., 1972-81, field hockey coach, 1972-75, basketball coach, 1975-80; athletic dir. men's and women's programs, 1981—; Tidewater I field hockey coach U.S. Field Hockey Assn., 1974. First aid instr. ARC, Lynchburg, 1960-72, Farmville, 1972-80; CPR instr. Am. Heart Assn., Farmville, 1974-79. Recipient service award ARC, 1975, Chi commendation Longwood Coll., 1976, Disting. Service award, 1975; named to Sports Hall of Fame, Lynchburg Coll., 1979. Mem. Va. Women's Lacrosse Assn. (treas. 1972-75), Va. Assn. for Girls and Women in Sport (pres. 1974-76), Va. Assn. for Intercollegiate Athletics for Women (pres. 1982-84). Baptist. Office: Dept Athletics Longwood Coll Farmville VA 23901

HODGES, JOHN WILLIS, police chief; b. Eden, N.C., Jan. 3, 1935; s. Charlie Fields and Essie (Ellington) H.; m. Virginia Gayle Dyson, Feb. 16, 1963; children—Charles Leonard, Stephen Timothy. Grad. high sch., Eden, N.C. Cert. police officer, N.C. Police officer Mayodan Police Dept., N.C., 1956-58, Spray Police Dept., N.C., 1958-59; spl. agt. U.S. Army Criminal Investigation Div., 1960-79; capt. Police Dept., Hope-Mills, N.C., 1979-82; chief Police Dept., Mt. Olive, N.C., 1982—. Adv. Police Explorer, Mt. Olive, 1983—. Mem. N.C. Chief Police Assn. (bd. dirs. 1983—), N.C. Law Enforcement Assn., Execs. Assn. Democrat. Baptist. Avocations: softball; racquet ball; golf; official for N.C. High Sch. Athletic Assn. Home: 530 N Center St Mount Olive NC 28365 Office: Police Dept Hdqrs Mount Olive NC 28365

HODGES, JOT HOLIVER, JR., lawyer, financial consultant; b. Archer City, Tex., Nov. 16, 1932; s. Jot Holiver and Lola Mae (Hurd) H.; B.S., Sam Houston State U., 1954, B.B.A., 1954; J.D., U. Tex., 1957; m. Virginia Pardue, June 11, 1955; children—Deborah Lee, Jot Holiver III, Darlene Dee. Bar: Tex. 1958. Asst. atty. gen. State of Tex., 1958-62; founder, sr. partner firm Hodges & Grant, Houston; dir. Presidio Devel. Co., Heritage Trust Co. First Nat. Bank-Missouri City. Served to capt. AUS, 1957-58. Mem. Am., Tex., Houston, Ft. Bend bar assns., Assn. Trial Lawyers Am., Delta Tau Delta, Delta Theta Phi. Club: Houston. Contbr. articles to profl. jours. Home: 3527 Thunderbird St Missouri City TX 77459 Office: 3660 Hampton Dr Suite 200 Missouri City TX 77459

HODGES, RICHARD EDWARD, advertising and public relations executive; b. Pikeville, Ky., Feb. 9, 1928; s. Richard Edward and Marian Elizabeth (McQueen) H.; m. Barbara Ann Burke, Sept. 27, 1952; children—Richard E. III, Burke Vincent. Student Washington and Lee U., 1946-48; A.B., Emory U., 1950. Reporter, Ashland (Ky.) Daily Ind., 1944-48, Atlanta Constn., 1950-51; mem. staff pub. relations dept. Liller, Neal Battle & Lindsey, Inc., Atlanta, 1951-54, account exec., 1951-56, pub. relations dir., 1956-67, v.p., 1960-67, exec. v.p., 1968-75, pres., 1975-78; chmn. bd. Liller, Neal, Weltin, Inc., 1978-82; chmn. bd. Liller Neal, Inc., 1982—, chief exec. officer, 1983—; pres. Cert. Audit of Circulation, 1973-76. Mem. mem's adv. com. Atlanta Music Club, 1965-72; chmn. spl. pub. relations adv. com. Atlanta Community Chest-United Appeal, 1966-67, v.p., 1968-72; v.p. United Way Met. Atlanta, 1975; mem. Atlanta Bd. Edn., 1973; bd. dirs. Atlanta area Camp Fire Girls, 1958-60; bd. govs. Pub. Broadcasting Service, 1974-76, bd. dirs., 1977-80; pres. Pub. Broadcasting Council Atlanta and Fulton County Pub. Schs., 1977-79; pres. Pub. Broadcasting Assn. of Greater Atlanta, Inc., 1979-81; bd. dirs. North Central Ga. Health System Agy., 1976-83, Atlanta Consumer Credit Counseling Service, 1980—; bd. dirs., exec. com., chmn. pub. relations com. Met. Atlanta chpt. ARC, 1982-86; trustee Ga. State U. Found., 1978—; bd. dirs. Spl. Audiences, Inc., 1982-85; bd. visitors Emory U., 1984—. Mem. Pub. Relations Soc. Am. (accredited mem., Paul M. Lund Pub. Service award 1979), So. Indsl. Editors Assn. (pres. Atlanta 1953), Atlanta Advt. Club (pres. 1962-63), Am. Assn. Advt. Agys. (mem. com. for work with students and educators 1965-68, client services com. 1983-84, chmn. S.E. council 1968-69), Atlanta C. of C. (dir. 1973, chmn. edn. task force 1974-75), Leadership Atlanta Alumni Assn., Ga. Motor Club (vice chmn. 1984—), Inquiry Club, Fulton County Grand Jurors Assn., Sigma Delta Chi, Kappa Alpha, Omicron Delta Kappa. Episcopalian. Clubs: Capital City, Georgian. Lodge: Rotary. Home: 4615 Brook Hollow Rd Atlanta GA 30327 Office: 2700 Cumberland Pkwy Suite 200 Atlanta GA 30339

HODGES, WILLIAM TERRELL, judge; b. Lake Wales, Fla., Apr. 28, 1934; s. Haywood and Clara Lucy (Murphy) H.; B.S.B.A., U. Fla., 1956, LL.B., 1958, J.D., 1967; m. Peggy Jean Woods, June 8, 1958; children—Judson, Daniel, Clay. Admitted to Fla. bar, 1959; mem. firm Macfarlane, Ferguson, Allison & Kelly, Tampa, 1958-71; instr. bus. law U. South Fla., Tampa, 1961-66; judge U.S. Middle Dist. of Fla., Tampa, 1971—, now chief judge. Mem. Am. Tampa-Hillsborough County bar assns., Fla. Bar (chmn. grievance com. 1967-70, chmn. uniform comml. code com. 1970-71), Am. Judicature Soc. Exec. editor U. Fla. Law Rev., 1957-58. Office: PO Box 2908 Tampa FL 33601

HODGETTS, RICHARD MICHAEL, business management educator; b. Bronx, N.Y., Mar. 10, 1942; s. Harold Thomas and Regina Gertrude (McDermott) H.; m. Sara Josefina Fontana, Aug. 1, 1970; children—Steven Michael, Jennifer Anne. B.S., NYU, 1963; M.B.A., Ind. U., 1964; Ph.D., U. Okla., 1968. Faculty, U. Nebr., Lincoln, 1966-76, prof. mgmt., 1966-76; prof. mgmt. Fla. Internat. U., Miami, 1976—. Author: Management, 1985; Organized Behavior, 1985; Organizational Communication, 1986; Effective Small Business Management, 1986. Recipient Outstanding Tchr. award U. Nebr. Coll. Bus., 1973, 75, Outstanding Univ. Tchr.-Ryder award Fla. Internat. U., 1984. Fellow Acad. Mgmt.; mem. Acad. Internat. Mgmt., So. Mgmt. Assn. Democrat. Roman Catholic. Avocations: jogging; racquetball. Home: 3930 Durango Coral Gables FL 33134 Office: Coll Bus Adminstrn Fla Internat U Tamiami Trail Miami FL 33199

HODGIN, KATHARINE WYATT, mathematics educator, consultant; b. Dublin, Ga., Dec. 7, 1926; d. William Garner and Zelma Lee (Fincher) Wyatt; widowed; children—Robert Edwin, Thomas Elbridge. B.A., Meredith Coll., Raleigh, N.C., 1948; M.A., U. Ala.-Tuscaloosa, 1961, Ed.D., 1966. Jr. high sch. tchr. Wayne County Pub. Schs., Goldsboro, N.C., 1948-50, 54-55, 56-58; math. tchr. Tuscaloosa Pub. Sch., Ala., 1958-63; asst. prof. math. E. Carolina U., Greenville, N.C., 1966-71, assoc. prof., 1971-85, coordinator math. edn., 1979—, assoc. dir., sci. Math. Edn. Ctr., 1984—, prof., 1985—; vis. prof. U. Montevallo, Ala., summer 1976, U. Ala., Gadsden, summer 1978, Furman U., Greenville, 1982, 83, 84. Author: (with others) Hands-On Mathematics, 1979, Experiencing Mathematics, 1981. Contbr. articles to profl. publs. Trustee Meredith Coll., Raleigh, N.C., 1979-83. Mem. N.C. Council Tchrs. of Math. (treas. 1974-76, pres. 1981-83, W.W. Rankin award for excellence in math. edn.), Nat. Council Tchrs. of Math., Assn. Supervision and Curriculum Devel., Research Council Diagnostic and Prescriptive Math., E. Carolina Univ. Fedn. Tchrs., Delta Kappa Gamma (Beta Alpha chpt. treas. 1978-81). Home: 1411 N Overlook Dr Greenville NC 27834 Office: E Carolina Univ Math Dept Greenville NC 27834

HODGIN, LONNIE WAYNE, farmer; b. Haskell, Tex., Sept. 8, 1950; s. James Fredricks and Winnie (Best) H.; m. Sara Lee Yeary, Aug. 14, 1971; children—Wayne, James C., John Mark. Student Cisco Jr. Coll., 1969-71, West Tex. State U., 1971-74. Clk. Busters Grocery, Haskell, 1968-69; bookkeeper Rhoad Way Inn, Amarillo, Tex., 1971; supr. data processing Levi Strauss, Amarillo, 1971-75; v.p. Hodgin Farms, Inc., Haskell, 1976—; dir. Haskell County Farm Bur. Mem. Tex. Milo Producers, Rolling Plains Prodn. Credit, Producers Grain Corp., Rule Coop. Gin and Elevator. Democrat. Baptist. Lodge: Lions. Avocations: trap shooting; golf; hunting; fishing. Home and Office: 902 N 5th St Haskell TX 79521

HODGIN, NANCY GRAY, former concrete pipe company financial executive; b. Winston-Salem, N.C., May 13, 1932; d. Fred Burton and Margaret Jean (Roddick) Gray; m. John Nolan Hodgin, July 21, 1956; 1 dau., Jean Gray. A.B. in Bus. Adminstrn., Duke U., 1954. C.P.A., N.C. Asst. to internal auditor Duke U., Durham, N.C., 1954-55; controller/cost acct. Gray concrete Pipe Co., Inc., Thomasville, N.C., 1955-63, dir., 1955-85, treas., 1978-85; staff acct. Donald R. Cox, C.P.A., Thomasville, 1975. Mem. N.C. Assn. C.P.A.s, Nat. Assn. Accts., Phi Beta Kappa, Kappa Delta. Presbyterian. Home: 411 Maisons-sur-Mer Myrtle Beach SC 29577

HODGKINSON, KENNETH ALLRED, geologist, oil company paleontologist; b. Vernal, Utah, Sept. 3, 1930; s. Lowell Hodgkinson and Zelda (Allred) Heatherly; m. Erlene Schreiber, Dec. 23, 1963; children—Heather, Kenneth David. Paleontologist, Exxon Co., Houston, 1965-74, Imperial Oil Co., Calgary, Alta., Can., 1974-77, Exxon Co., New Orleans, 1977—. Author books on fossil mollusks. Mem. exec. bd. New Orleans Area Council Boy Scouts Am., 1980—. Served with U.S. Marines, 1951-53, Korea. Mem. Am. Assn. Petroleum Geologists, Soc. Econ. Paleontologists, Mineralogists, Soc. Econ. Paleontologists Mineralogists (treas. Gulf Coast sect. 1978-79, v.p. 1981-82). Mormon. Home: 5201 Elmwood Pkwy Metairie LA 70003 Office: Exxon Co 1550 Poydras New Orleans LA 70161

HODGSON, ANGUS MACMILLAN, insurance company executive, arson investigator; b. Newton Highlands, Mass., Aug. 18, 1952; s. Robert James and Shirley (MacMillan) H.; m. Gaye Lynn Wilson, Aug. 29, 1981; 1 child, Ian MacMillian. B.S., Norwich U., 1975. Cert. fire fighter, N.H.; cert. peace officer, field safety rep., Tex. Firefighter Concord Fire Dept., N.H. 1977-78; loss prevention rep. Mchts. Ins. Co., Rochester, N.Y., 1978-79; loss control rep. Md. Casualty Co., Cin., 1979-83, Reliance Ins. Co., San Antonio, 1983—; arson team leader Bexar County Fire Marshall, San Antonio, 1984—. Mem. Nat. Fire Protection Assn., Am. Soc. Safety Engrs. Home: 3431 Oakdale St #2803 San Antonio TX 78229 Office: Reliance Ins Co 4100 Piedras Dr E San Antonio TX 78228

HODSON, RANDY DALE, sociology educator; b. Lawrence, Kans., Oct. 25, 1952; s. Warren Gayler and Erma Louise (Paxson) H.; m. Susan Gay Rogers, June 6, 1976. B.A., U. Wyo., 1975; M.S., U. Wis., 1977, Ph.D., 1980. Asst. prof. U. Tex., Austin, 1980-84, assoc. prof., 1985—, research assoc. population research ctr., 1984—; cons. Abbott Labs., 1982; faculty fellow Blanton Hall U. Tex., 1983-84. Author: Workers' Earnings and Corporate Economic Structure, 1983, Readings in Sociology, 1983. Contbr. articles to profl. jours. Reviewer various publs. Richardson Family Trust Fund scholar, 1970; Wis. Alumni Research Found. fellow, 1975-76, 78-79; grantee U.S. Dept. Labor, 1979-80, U. Tex., 1982, NSF, 1984-86. Mem. Am. Sociol. Assn., Soc. Study Social Problems, Southwestern Social Sci. Assn., So. Sociol. Soc., Alpha Kappa Delta. Home: 3002-B Windsor Rd Austin TX 78703 Office: Dept Sociology Burdine Hall U Tex Austin TX 78712

HODZIC, ARIF H.SEIN, architect; b. Belgrade, Yugoslavia, Oct. 22, 1942, came to U.S., 1969, naturalized, 1975; s. Husein and Piroska (Saz) H.; m. Vukosava C. Perisic, July 23, 1966; children—Arif A., Branko A. B. Arch., U. Belgrade, 1966. Registered architect, Va., D.C., Md., Ohio. Ptnr. Callmer & Millstead, Washington, 1970-73; assoc. SC&A Architects, Alexandria, Va., 1973-77, Leo A. Daly Co., Washington, 1977-78; owner, Hodzic Architects, Annandale, Va., 1978-84; ptnr. Hodzic, Brown & Novcic Architects, Annandale, 1984—. Mem. AIA (charter mem. No. Va. chpt.). Avocations: sailing; tennis; scuba; skiing. Home: 4948 Chowan Ave Alexandria VA 22312 Office: Hodzic Brown & Novcic Architects 4300 Evergreen Ln Annandale VA 22003

HOEFER, MARGARET J., librarian; b. Bklyn., July 28, 1909; d. Thomas A. and Margaret Emma (Skillin) Ford; B.S., Kans. State Coll., 1932; M.A., Colo. State Coll., 1939; B.L.S., U. Denver, 1943. Tchr., Smith Ctr. High Sch., Kans., 1934-38; head English dept. Iola (Kans.) Sr. High Sch., 1939-43; head circulation dept. Topeka (Kans.) Pub. Library, 1943-44; librarian Pueblo (Colo.) Jr. Coll., 1944-46; bookmobile librarian U.S. Army, Nurnberg, Germany, 1946-48; dir. SCAP Civil Info. and Edn. Library, Osaka, Japan, 1948-50; comd. librarian PHILCOM & 13th Air Force, Clark AFB, Manila, 1950-51; staff librarian Cen. Air Def. Force, Kansas City, Mo., 1951-53; county librarian, Carroll County, Md., Westminster, 1958-62; head librarian Woodlawn Jr. High Sch., Balt., 1962-63; head reference services Smithtown (N.Y.) Library, 1963-65; dir. Emma S. Clark Meml. Library, Setauket, N.Y., 1965-67; reference librarian Nassau Community Coll., Garden City, N.Y., 1967-69; asst. prof. library sci. Suffolk County Community Coll., Selden, N.Y., 1969-72; librarian Golden Hills Acad., Ocala, Fla., 1972-74; reference librarian Melbourne (Fla.) Pub. Library, part-time, 1975-78; corp. librarian Harris Corp., Melbourne, Fla., 1980-85. Mem. Palm Bay Community Assn., 1976—; v.p., membership com. Brevard Assn. for Advancement of Blind, 1975—; archivist Sebastian Inlet Dist., Melbourne, Fla., 1977—; mem. Brevard County Library Bd., 1977-81, pres., 1979; mem. Friends of the Palm Bay (Fla.) Library, 1980—, pres., 1981-82; cert. tutor Literacy Council South Brevard; cons. libraries Brevard Art Ctr. and Mus., South Brevard Women's Ctr. Mem. ALA, Am. Library Trustee Assn. (edn. and legis. coms.), Fla. Library Assn., Southeastern Library Assn., Library Assn. Brevard County. Republican. Home: 3251 Edgewood Dr NE Palm Bay FL 32905

HOEKSTRA, HAROLD DERK, aeronautical engineer; b. Chgo., Aug. 18, 1902; s. Dirk Jans and Grietje (Zandt) H.; m. Laura Marie Barker, Nov. 25, 1931; children—Elizabeth Hoekstra, Thomas Barker, Ann Wehr Hoekstra Geis, Dirk Macy. Student Mich. State U., 1922-26; B.S. in Aero. Engring., U. Mich., 1929. Registered profl. engr., Washington. Chief engr. Crosley Aircraft Co., Cin., 1929-31; aero. engr. Ford Motor Co., Dearborn, Mich., 1931-32, Curtiss Aeroplane & Motor Co., Buffalo, 1932-33; designer flight test engr. Stinson Aircraft Co., Wayne, Mich., 1933-37; with FAA, 1937-70, chief project officer Flight Standards Service, 1945-61, chief engr. and safety div. Aircraft Devel. Service, 1961-70; v.p. engring. Flight Safety Found., Arlington, Va., 1970-72; U.S. tech. advisor Miles-Phoenix, LTD, U.K., 1976-84; lectr. Am. U., Washington, 1952-57, U. Md., College Park, 1970-71; advisor USAF, Dayton, Ohio, 1963-65; com. mem. NACA, Washington, 1944-55, 1960-68. Author: Safety in General Aviation, 1971; A Letter to Sarah, 1983. Donovan Scholar U. Mich., 1928; Disting. Alumnus fellow Royal Aero. Soc., U.K., 1953, AIAA, Soc. Automotive Engrs.; recipient tech. writing award Air Traffic Control Assn., Inc., 1984. Methodist. Clubs: Nat. Aviation (Arlington, Va.); Army and Navy (Washington). Avocations: piloting; airplanes; world history. Home and Office: 253 N Columbus St Arlington VA 22203

HOEL, DAVID GERHARD, federal administrator, statistician, scientist; b. Los Angeles, Nov. 18, 1939; s. Paul Gerhard and Hazel Bessie (Helvig) H.; m. Nancy Carolyn Keller, Sept. 3, 1961; children—Erik Gerhard, Brian David, Christian Paul. A.B., U. Calif.-Berkeley, 1961; Ph.D., U. N.C., 1966. Postdoctoral fellow Stanford U., Calif., 1966-67; sr. mathematician Westinghouse Research Labs., Pitts., 1967-68; statistician Oak Ridge Nat. Lab., 1968-70; math. statistician Nat. Inst. Environ. Health Scis., Research Triangle Park, N.C., 1970-73, chief biometry br., 1973-81, acting sci. dir., 1977-79, program dir. biometry and risk assessment program, 1981—; adj. prof. dept. biostats. U. N.C., Chapel Hill, 1970—; vis. scientist Radiation Effects Research Found., Hiroshima, Japan, 1979-80, dir., 1984-86; mem. Nat. Acad. Sci. Bd. on Toxicity and Environ. Health Hazards, Washington, 1982-85; mem. sci. adv. bd. Nat. Ctr. for Toxicological Research, 1977-80. Contbr., co-contbr. articles to profl. publs. Co-editor workshop, conf. proceedings. Recipient NIH Dir. award, 1977; Mortimer Spiegelman Gold medal award Am. Pub. Health Assn., 1977; Pub. Health Service Supr. Service award USPHS, 1980; sr. Exec. Service Bonus Nat. Inst. Environ. Health Scis., 1983. Fellow Am. Statis. Assn. (sec. biometrics sect. 1979); mem. Internat. Statis. Inst., Inst. Math. Stats., Royal Statis. Soc., Biometric Soc., Soc. for Risk Analysis council mem. 1982-85). Home: 324 Glendale Dr Chapel Hill NC 27514 Office: Nat Inst of Environ Health Scis PO Box 12233 Research Triangle Park NC 27709

HOEN, SHEILA ELIZABETH FLEETWOOD, lawyer, oil and gas company executive; b. Victoria, B.C., Can., Sept. 8, 1935; came to U.S., 1969, naturalized, 1983; d. William Leslie and Winnifred M. (Thomas) Hardie; m. Ernst Leon Wilhelm B. Hoen, Sept. 14, 1957; children—Liza, Margot, Zarah. B.A., U. B.C., 1957; M.B.A., Calif. State U., 1975; J.D., Okla. City U., 1981. Bar: Okla. 1981, U.S. Dist. (we. dist.) Okla., 1981. Biomed. librarian U. B.C., Vancouver, 1957-58 Royal Victoria Hosp., Montreal, Que., Can., 1959-60; tchr. South Peace High Sch., Dawson Creek, B.C., 1958-59, Brit. Sch., Tripoli, Libya, 1962-66; asst. to exploration mgr., scout Occidental Pet-Corp., Tripoli, 1968-69, econ. asst., sr. petroleum economist, Bakersfield, Calif., 1970-73, 1974-75; fin. analyst, mgr. gas contracts Grace Petroleum Corp., Oklahoma City, 1975-78; law clk. oil and gas atty. Andrews, Davis et al, Oklahoma City, 1979-83; v.p. land, gen. counsel Hoen Exploration Co., Oklahoma City, 1983—; commr. Edmond Arts and Humanities Council, 1985—; pres. Concerned Citizens for Captiva, Inc., Captiva Island, Fla., 1985—. Mem. Okla. Zool. Soc., Oklahoma City, 1983—. Mem. Women's Com. for Symphony, Oklahoma City, 1983—. Recipient Am. Jurisprudence award, Bancroft-Whitney, Lawyer's Coop. Pub. Co., 1979; Equal Rights Amendment award, AAUW, 1981. Mem. Edmond C. of C., Women's Polit. Caucus (past legislative chmn.), AAUW (past legis. chmn.), ABA, Okla. Bar Assn., Internat. Bar Assn., Am. Assn. Petroleum Landmen, Natural Gas Assn. Okla., Internat. Assn. Energy Economists. Episcopalian. Club: The Greens (Oklahoma City). Home: 504 Clegern Dr Edmond OK 73034 Office: Hoen Exploration Co 1800 S Canyon Park Circle Suite 101 Edmond OK 73013 also Concerned Citizens for Captiva Inc Box 335 Captiva Island FL 33924

HOERTER, SAM SPALDING, airport director; b. Montgomery, Ala., Jan. 12, 1955; s. George Joseph and May LaMotte (Smith) H.; m. Nancy Sue Shaffer, July 12, 1980; 1 child, Joseph Adam. B.S. in Aviation Mgmt., Auburn U., 1978; M.B.A., U. Ala.-Birmingham, 1983. Accredited airport exec. Adminstrv. asst. Birmingham Mcpl. Airport (Ala.), 1975-77, airport ops. mgr., 1978-83; exec. dir. Gulfport-Biloxi Regional Airport (Miss.), 1983-86; dir. airports Charleston County Aviation Authority, Charleston, S.C., 1986—; instr. airport mgmt. and mktg. Embry-Riddle Aero. U. Bd. dirs. Gulfport-Biloxi Fgn. Trade Zone, Inc. Mem. Am. Assn. Airport Execs. (sec. S.E. chpt.), Southeastern Airport Mgrs. Assn., Miss. Airports Assn. (v.p.), Gulfport C. of C. (dir.). Roman Catholic. Contbr. articles to publ. in field. Office: Charleston County Aviation Authority Charleston Internat Airport PO Box 10308 Charleston SC 29411

HOETKER, WILLIAM JAMES, educator; b. St. Louis, July 23, 1932; s. Carl Henry and Mary (O'Neill) H.; m. Barbara Hoetker Ash; children—William, Glenn, Morna. B.S., S.E. Mo. State U., 1953; M.A., Washington U., St. Louis, 1960, Ed.D., 1967. Tchr. English Clayton High Sch., Mo., 1960-65; dir. theater research Cemrel, Inc., St. Louis, 1967-70; assoc. prof. English U. Ill.-Urbana, 1970-73; prof. English edn. Fla. State U., Tallahassee, 1973—, prof. curriculum and instrn. Coll. Edn., 1978—, head curriculum and instrn., 1984—; vis. prof. U. B.C., 1975, Nakamura Aakeun U., Japan, 1982. Assoc. editor: Research in Teaching of English, 1973-77; contbr. articles to profl. jours. Mem. Nat. Council Tchrs. English Assn. Supervision and Curriculum Devel. Democrat. Home: 1802 Ivan Dr Tallahassee FL 32303 Office: Fla State U 205 Stone Bldg Tallahassee FL 32306

HOEVELER, WILLIAM M., judge; b. Aug. 23, 1922; student Temple U., 1941-42; B.A., Bucknell U., 1947; LL.B., Harvard U., 1950; m. Mary Griffin Smith, 1950; 4 children. Bar: Fla. 1951. Practice law, Miami, Fla., 1951—; judge U.S. Dist. Ct. for Fla. So. Dist., 1977—; mem. U.S. Dist. Ct. Com. for Rev. Local Rules; lectr. in field. Incorporator, bd. dirs. Youth Industries, Inc.; mem. vestry St. Stephens Episcopal Ch., 1973-75, chancellor, 1973—. Served to lt. USMC, 1942-46. Mem. Am. Judicature Soc., Fla. Bar (personal injury and wrongful death adv. com. 1976), Phila. Bar Assn., Dade County (Fla.) Bar Assn. (chmn. charity drives com. 1966). ABA (chmn. com. on products, profl. and gen. liability law 1972-73, program chmn. sec. ins., negligence and compensation law 1975, mem. sect. governing council 1975-78, mem. governing com. of forum com. on constrn. industry). Omicron Delta Kappa. Office: PO Box 013660 Flagler Sta Miami FL 33101*

HOFER, CHARLES WARREN, strategic management educator; b. Phoenixville, Pa., Nov. 11, 1940; s. Charles Emil and Alice May (Howard) H.; m. Judith Racella Millner, Oct. 22, 1980. B.S. in Engring. Physics summa cum laude, Lehigh U., 1962; M.S. in Applied Math., Harvard U., 1966, M.B.A. in Mktg. with distinction, 1965, D.B.A. in Bus. Policy, 1969. Research asst. Harvard Bus. Sch., Boston, 1965-66; asst. prof. Northeastern U., Boston, 1968-69; vis. lectr. Singapore Inst. of Mgmt., 1969-70; asst. prof. Northwestern U., Evanston, Ill., 1970-75, assoc. prof., 1975-76; vis. assoc. prof. Stanford U. (Calif.), 1976-77, Columbia U., N.Y.C., 1978, NYU, 1978-80; vis. prof. U. Calif.-Riverside, 1980; prof. strategic mgmt. U. Ga., Athens, 1980—; cons. in field; lectr. Chgo. C. of C., 1976-78. Campaign cons. Congressman Donald W. Riegle, Mich., 1968, 72. NSF fellow, 1962-63; Baker scholar, 1965; Ford Found. fellow, 1966-67. Mem. Acad. Mgmt., Inst. Mgmt. Sci., Decision Scis. Inst., Soc. for Entrpreneurial Research, Am. Econ. Assn., Phi Eta Sigma, Pi Mu Epsilon, Tau Beta Pi, Phi Beta Kappa, Sigma Iota Epsilon, Beta Gamma Sigma. Republican. Lutheran. Clubs: Harvard Bus. Sch. Atlanta, Harvard of Ga., Econs. (Atlanta). Author: Strategy Formulation: Analytical Concepts, 1978; Strategic Management: A New View of Business Policy and Planning, 1979; Strategic Management: A Casebook in Business Policy and Planning, 1980, 84; Strategic Management of Not-for-Profit Organizations, 1986. Home: 4445 Stonington Circle Dunwoody GA 30338 Office: Dept Mgmt U Ga Athens GA 30302

HOFF, TIMOTHY, law educator, priest; b. Freeport, Ill., Feb. 27, 1941; s. Howard Vincent and Zillah (Morgan) H. A.B., Tulane U., 1963, J.D., 1966; student U. London, 1961-62; LL.M., Harvard U., 1970. Bar: Fla. 1967, Ala. 1973, U.S. Dist. Ct. (mid. dist.) Fla. 1967. Assoc., Williams, Parker, Harrison, Dietz & Getzen, Sarasota, Fla., 1966-69; asst. legal editor The Fla. Bar, 1969; asst. prof. U. Ala., 1970-73, assoc. prof., 1973-75, prof. law, 1975—; cons. Ala. Law Inst.; reporter Ala. Adminstrv. Procedure Act, 1977—; ordained priest Episcopal Ch. Vice-pres., founding dir. Hospice of West Ala.; priest assoc. Canterbury Chapel, U. Ala., 1985—; interim rector Ch. of Holy Comforter, Montgomery, Ala., 1984-85; founding dir. Community Soup Bowl, Inc. Recipient Hist. Preservation Service award, 1976. Mem. ACLU, Maritime Law Assn. U.S., AAUP, Council on Religion and Law, Episc. Soc. for Ministry in Higher Edn., Phi Beta Kappa, Order of Coif, Omicron Delta Kappa, Eta Sigma Phi. Democrat. Club: Aquatic Booster's of Ala. (pres. 1982-83). Author: Alabama Limitations of Actions, 1984. Contbr. articles to profl. jours. Home: 615 11th St Tuscaloosa AL 35401 Office: U Ala Law Sch Box 1435 University AL 35486

HOFFMAN, DENNIS ROBERT, biochemist; b. LaMoure, N.D., Sept. 7, 1951; s. Harold Ben and Ethel Marian (Styles) H.; m. Beth Ann Betzer, Aug. 15, 1972; 1 child, Sara Beth. B.S., Jamestown Coll., 1973; Ph.D., U. N.D., 1979. Fellow dept. biochemistry U. N.D., Grand Forks, 1979-80; Nat. Cancer Inst. trainee biology div. Oak Ridge Nat. Lab. and U. Tenn., 1980-83; research assoc. med. div. Oak Ridge Assoc. Univs., 1983-84; Chiton fellow in ob-gyn and biochemistry U. Tex. Health Sci. Ctr., Dallas, 1984—. Mem. AAAS, Sigma Xi. Presbyterian. Contbr. articles to profl. jours. Office: Dept Biochemistry U Tex Health Sci Ctr Dallas TX 75235

HOFFMAN, GARY MICHAEL, lawyer; b. Phila., Feb. 25, 1946; s. Joseph and Bessie (Weiner) H.; m. Ileene J. Hoffman, Jan. 25, 1969; children—Jordonna, Rachel. B.S. in Elec. Engring., U. Pa., 1967; J.D., George Washington U., 1971. Bar: Va. 1971, D.C. 1972. Patent examiner, law clk. U.S. Patent Office, 1967-72; assoc. Spencer & Kaye, Washington, 1972-74, Watson, Cole, Grindle & Watson, Washington, 1974-78; ptnr. LeBlanch & Shur, Washington, 1978-79, LeBlanc, Nolan, Shur & Nies, Arlington, Va., 1979-84; now ptnr. Odin, Feldman & Pittleman, Fairfax, Va. Bd. dirs. Upper Occoquan Sewage Authority, 1980-84; program chmn. Fairfax County Com. 100, 1980-82; v.p., edn. chmn. Fairfax County Council of PTAs, 1982-84, pres., 1984—; mem. Presdl. Inaugural Com., 1981; pres. Fairfax County. Fedn. Citizens Assns., 1979-80; mem. seminar com. Fairfax County Chamber, 1985—. Mem. Am. Pat. Law Assn. (chmn. subcom. young lawyers com. 1980-81, chmn. subcom. on fed. rules civil procedure 1981—), Va. State Bar (bd. govs. Pat. trademark and copyright com. 1980—, sec. 1983-84, vice chmn. 1984-85, chmn. elect 1985—). Republican. Jewish. Contbr. articles on high tech. law to legal jour. Home: 5017 King David Blvd Annandale VA 22003 Office: 10505 Judicial Dr Fairfax VA 22030

HOFFMAN, GERALD MILES, physician; b. Chgo., July 3, 1934; s. Benjamin and Eleanore Anna (Nudelman) H.; m. Diane Michael Skubin, May 3, 1973; children—Jody, Jeffrey. B.S., U. Miami, 1956; D.O., Kirksville Coll., 1960. Am. Osteo. Bd. Internal Medicine. Intern, Glandview Hosp., Dayton, Ohio, 1960-61; resident in internal medicine Mt. Clemens Hosp., Mich., 1961-64, chief nuclear medicine, 1964-69; chief dept. medicine Community Hosp., Hollywood, Fla., 1971-78; gen. practice osteo. medicine, Hollywood, 1978—. Contbr. articles to profl. jours. Fellow Am. Coll. Osteo. Internists (chmn. 1974); mem. Am. Osteo. Assn., Soc. Nuclear Medicine, Fla. Osteo. Med. Assn., Broward County Osteo. Med. Assn. Democrat. Jewish. Avocations: fine arts, antiques, skiing, sailing. Office: 2647 Hollywood Blvd Hollywood FL 33020

HOFFMAN, GILBERT EARL BOOHER, architect, printing executive; b. Stillwater, Okla. Nov. 19, 1939; s. Gilbert Earl and Pauline (Booher) H.; m. Carol Louise Lutz, May 11, 1958 (div. 1975); children—Susan Lynn, Patricia Alison; m. Mei-ing Liu, Aug. 29, 1982; 1 child, Kristan Liu. B.Arch., Carnegie Inst. Tech., 1962; M.Arch., U. Pa., 1963. Registered architect, Pa., Conn., Tex. Architect, V.G. Kling & Assocs., Phila. 1963-64, Eero Saarinen & Assocs., Hamden, Conn., 1964-65, Roche-Dinkeloo & Assocs., Hamden, 1965-67, Charles Moore & Assocs., New Haven, 1967-69; instr. architecture Yale U., 1967-69; sr. design architect 3D/Internat., Houston, 1978-85; dir. archtl. design White, Budd Van Ness Partnership, 1985—; redevel., planning cons. Redevel. Authority, New Castle, Pa., 1973-78; design cons. Kingdom of Qatar, 1981, Transit Authority, City of New Castle, Pa., 1974; lectr. Contbr. articles to profl. jours. Bd. dirs. pub. Hoyt Inst. Fine Arts, New Castle, 1971-78; pres. Community Playhouse, New Castle, 1974-75; mem. Arts Council, New Castle and Youngstown, Ohio, 1975-78; v.p. Hist. Soc., Lawrence County, Pa., 1977-78. Recipient Mona Design award Retail Ad Club, 1976. Mem. AIA, Rice Design Alliance, New Castle Jaycees. Avocation: model railroading. Home: 6458 Burgoyne Rd Houston TX 77057 Office: White Budd Van Ness 2900 Weslayan St Suite 300 Houston TX 77027

HOFFMAN, HARMON F., truck rental company executive; b. 1932. B.S., Bklyn. Poly. Inst., 1954; M.B.A., Drexel Inst. Tech., 1960. With Mobil Oil Corp., 1954-74, 78-80, v.p., gen. mgr. mktg., 1978; pres. Mobile Shipping and Transp. Co., 1974-78; sr. v.p. Energy Resources div. Ryder Systems, Inc., Miami, Fla., 1980-83, chief operating officer, exec. v.p. transp. group, 1983-85, sr. exec. v.p., chief operating officer, 1985—; pres. Ryder Truck Rental. Address: Ryder System Inc 3600 NW 82d Ave Miami FL 33166

HOFFMAN, IVAN BRUCE, psychiatrist, educator; b. Newport News, Va., Oct. 13, 1949; s. Joe and Sarah (Goldberg) H.; B.A., U. Va., 1971, M.D., 1975; m. Carol Dianne Scholem, Dec. 18, 1976; children—Adria Rachel, Stephanie Meira. Intern, Spartanburg (S.C.) Gen. Hosp., 1975-76, resident dept. family practice, 1975-78; resident in psychiatry U. Va., Charlottesville, 1978-79, Med. Coll. Va., Richmond, 1979-81; pvt. practice medicine specializing in psychiatry and psychotherapy, Richmond, 1981—; clin. instr. dept. psychiatry Med. Coll. Va. Diplomate Am. Bd. Psychiatry and Neurology, Am. Bd. Family Practice. Mem. Am. Psychiat. Assn., Richmond Psychiat. Soc., Va. Neuropsychiat. Soc., AMA, Med. Soc. Va., Richmond Acad. Medicine, Am. Acad. Family Physicians, Sigma Xi. Jewish. Home: 2602 Pleasant Run Dr Richmond VA 23233 Office: Suite 113 2010 Bremo Rd Richmond VA 23226

HOFFMAN, JOHN EDWARD, JR., electrical engineer; b. Ft. Sill, Okla., Apr. 29, 1946; s. John Edward and Margaret Joy (Smith) H.; B.S. in Math., Okla. State U., 1973, M.S. in Elec. Engring. (NSF grantee), 1974; m. Dovie Kay McClendon, Apr. 27, 1967; children—Christopher Scott, David Michael, Brenda Suzanne, Becky Lynn. Sr. software engr. Tex. Instruments, Dallas, 1974-79; computer engring. specialist E-Systems, Garland, Tex., 1979-83; pres. Integrated Concepts Corp., Plano, Tex., 1983—. Served with USAF, 1965-69; Vietnam. Mem. Am. Mgmt. Assn., IEEE, Old Crows, Eta Kappa Nu. Mem. Ch. of Christ. Home and Office: 1712 Cherokee Trail Plano TX 75023

HOFFMAN, KARLA LEIGH, mathematician; b. Paterson, N.J., Feb. 14, 1948; d. Abe and Bertha (Guthaim) Rakoff; m. Allan S. Hoffman, Dec. 26, 1971; 1 child, Matthew Douglas. B.A., Rutgers U., 1969; M.B.A., George Washington U., 1971, D.Sc., 1975. NSF-Nat. Acad. Scis. postdoctoral research fellow NSF, Nat. Bur. Standards, 1975-76; adj. prof. George Washington U., Washington, 1977-84; mathematician Nat. Bur. Standards, Gaithersberg, Md., 1976—; assoc. prof. George Mason U., systems engring. dept. Fairfax, Va., 1985—; cons. FAA, Dept. of Energy, Dept. of Transp., IRS, Washington, 1976—. Co-editor: Mathematical Programming Study on Computational Mathematical Programming, 1985; Impact of Microcomputers and Operations Research. Contbr. articles to profl. jours. Mem. Clifton Betterment Assn., Va., 1982—, Clifton Horse Soc., 1979—. Recipient Silver medal Commerce Dept., Washington, 1984, Applied Research award Nat. Bur. Standards, Gaithersburg, Md., 1984. Mem. Ops. Research Soc. Am. (mem. council 1985-88, chmn. tech. sects. com. 1983—, Math. Program Soc. (chmn. com. on algorithms 1982-85, editor newsletter 1979-82, council 1985-88), Ops. Research Soc. Am. (chmn. computer sci. tech. sect. 1983). Home: 6921 Clifton Rd Clifton VA 22024 Office: George Mason U System Engring Dept 4400 University Dr Fairfax VA 22030

HOFFMAN, RICHARD ALLEN, clinical psychologist; b. N.Y.C., Mar. 2, 1948; s. A. Charles and Helen (Gloria) H.; m. Bonnie Lyn Dreier, May 25, 1975; 1 child, Haylie Ilena. B.S., Union Coll., Schenectady, 1969; M.A., Bradley U., 1972; Ph.D., Ga. State U., 1978. Intern, VA Hosp.-Duke Med. Ctr., Durham, N.C., 1976-77; pvt. practice clin. psychology, Tampa, Fla., 1978—; supervising psychologist Tampa Heights Hosp., 1981-83. Pres., Courtyard Sq. Med. Ctr. Condo Assn., Tampa, 1983—. Mem. Am. Psychol. Assn., Fla. Psychol. Assn. (pres. Bay region 1983-84, mem. pub. and legis. affairs com. 1982—), Fla. Soc. Clin. Hypnosis. Democrat. Jewish. Club: Carrollwood Village Tennis. Avocations: tennis; jogging; weight lifting. Home: 3626 Berger Rd Lutz FL 33549 Office: 13701 N 30th St Suite 111 Tampa FL 33613

HOFFMAN, WILLIAM WALTER, surgeon; b. Evanston, Ill., July 20, 1928; s. William and Stella (Krygiel) H.; student Loyola U., Chgo., 1945-47; B.S., Northwestern U., 1949, M.D., 1951; m. Doris Rosemary McNamara, Aug. 4, 1956; children—Jo Ann, Virginia, William Walter III. Intern Cook County Hosp., Chgo., 1951-52; resident Northwestern U., Wesley Meml. Hosp., Chgo., 1954-57; staff urologist Chgo. VA Research Hosp., 1957-58; staff urologist Dallas Med. and Surg. Clinic, 1958—, mem. exec. com., 1969—, chmn. bd. dirs., 1977—; dir. Dallas Med. and Surg. Clinic Investment Co., 1969—, chmn. bd. dirs., 1977—; clin. asst. prof. urology U. Tex. Southwestern Med. Sch., Dallas, 1958-79, assoc. clin. prof. urology, 1979—; vice chief urology Baylor U. Med. Center, Dallas, 1975-76, chief urology, 1976—, chmn. med. bd. and its exec. com., 1980-81; mem. staffs Children's Med. Center, Dallas, Parkland Meml. Hosp., Dallas, Presbyn. Hosp., Bristol Hosp., Gaston Episcopal Hosp.; cons. ambulatory health care accreditation program Joint Commn. on Accreditation of Hosps., 1972—. Served to capt. USAF, 1952-54. Diplomate Am. Bd. Urology, Am. Bd. Med. Examiners. Fellow ACS, Internat. Coll. Surgeons, Am. Acad. Pediatrics; mem. AMA (Physicians Recognition award 1971), Tex. Med. Assn., Dallas County Med. Soc. (treas. 1976-78, del. 1981—), Soc. Pediatric Urology, Am. Urol. Assn., Intercity Urol. Soc. (pres. 1970-71), Am. Group Practice Assn. (trustee 1976-79, 84—, pres. South Central sect. 1974-76), Am. Assn. Med. Clinics (commr. accreditation 1970-73, 76-78, chmn. editorial adv. com. 1979-84, trustee liaison editorial adv. com. 1984-87). Contbr. articles and chpts. to profl. jours. and books. Home: 6727 Meadow Lake Ave Dallas TX 75214 Office: 4105 Live Oak St Dallas TX 75221

HOFFMANN, MANFRED WALTER, oil company executive; b. Bklyn., Apr. 21, 1938; s. Hermann Karl and Emilie Talmon H.; B.S., Cornell U., 1960; M.Ed., Temple U., 1972, Ph.D., 1977; m. Barbara Ann Kenvin, Aug. 5, 1961; children—Lisa Joy, Lauren Kimberly, Kurt William. Mktg. rep. H. T. Heinz Co., N.Y.C., 1960-61; regional mgr. Swift & Co., Curtis Bay, Md. and Reading, Pa., 1961-63; salesman Sun Oil Co., Syracuse, N.Y., 1963-67, personnel mgr., 1967-71, mgr. mktg. devel., Rosemont, Pa., 1971-72, mgr. tng., 1973-77, dir. orgn. and mgmt. devel., 1977-79; dir. human resources and adminstrn. Sun Prodn. Co., Dallas, 1979-83; dir. human resources Sun Exploration & Prodn. Co., 1983—; lectr. Grad. Sch., U. Tex., Dallas, 1979—. Pres., PTA, bd. mem. Beechwood Sch., 1975-77; cons. exec. com. Orgns. Industrialization Congress Am., 1975-79; bd. dirs. Job Opportunity for Youth, 1980-81. Served with USMCR, 1956-62. Mem. Am. Soc. Tng. and Devel. (mgr. petroleum industry spl. interest group 1977-78, cert. of Appreciation 1977), Am. Soc. Personnel Adminstrn. (cert. of Appreciation 1977, 78), Am. Psychol. Assn. Republican. Episcopalian. Club: Chaparral. Home: 7020 Mumford St Dallas TX 75252 Office: PO Box 2880 Dallas TX 75221

HOFMANN, PAUL BERNARD, hospital administrator; b. Portland, Oreg., July 6, 1941; s. Max and Consuelo Theresa (Bley) H.; m. Lois Bernstein, June 28, 1969; children—Julie, Jason. B.S., U. Calif., Berkeley, 1963, M.P.H., 1965. Research asso. in hosp. adminstrn. Lab. of Computer Sci., Mass. Gen. Hosp., Boston, 1966-68, asst. dir., 1968-69; asst. adminstr. San Antonio Community Hosp., Upland, Calif., 1969-70, asso. adminstr., 1970-72; dep. dir. Stanford (Calif.) U. Hosp., 1972-74, dir., 1974-77; exec. dir. Emory U. Hosp., Atlanta, 1978—; instr. computer applications Harvard U., 1968-69; lectr. hosp. adminstrn. UCLA, 1970-72, Stanford U. Med. Sch., 1972-77; asso. prof. Emory U. Sch. Medicine, Atlanta, 1978—. Contbr. articles to profl. jours. Served with U.S. Army, 1959. Fellow Am. Coll. Hosp. Adminstrs. (recipient Robert S. Hudgens meml. award 1976); mem. Am. Hosp. Assn., Assn. Univ. Programs in Health Adminstrn., U. Calif. Alumni Assn. Home: 2767 Briarlake Woods Way Atlanta GA 30345 Office: Emory U Hosp 1364 Clifton Rd NE Atlanta GA 30322

HOFMANN, ROBERT PAUL, consulting petroleum company engineer, engineering company executive; b. Scottsbluff, Nebr., Nov. 17, 1948; s. Cecil Sylvestor and Frances Melvina (Moore) H.; m. Mallory Jane Hartman, Dec. 24, 1975; children—Paul Wesley, Carissa Ruth, Rachel Chevonne, Robert John Patrick. B.S. in Petroleum Engring., Colo. Sch. Mines, 1970; M.B.A., Oklahoma City U., 1975; M.S. in Petroleum Engring., U. Okla., 1983. Registered profl. engr., Okla. Dist. reservoir and prodn. engr. Sun Oil Co., Pampa, Tex., Tulsa, and Oklahoma City, 1970-75; staff reservoir engr. Mitchell Energy & Devel. Co., Houston, 1975-77; petroleum loan officer, v.p. Fidelity Bank, Oklahoma City, 1977-79; v.p., reservoir engring. mgr., mng. ptnr. Long, Benton & Assocs. Engring. Co., Oklahoma City, 1979-83; pres. Centurion Energy Corp., Oklahoma City, 1980— Hofmann & Assocs. Engring. Co., Inc., 1983—; sec./treas. LBA Operating Co., Oklahoma City, 1981—; investment counsel, gen. ptnr. to drilling funds; advisor to regional banks; expert witness Okla. Corp. community and dist. cts. Bd. dirs. Lakeview Acad., Oklahoma City; active Cerebral Palsy drive. Mem. Okla. Hist. Soc., Okla. Heritage Soc. (exec. com.), Nat. Soc. Profl. Engrs., Okla. Soc. Profl. Engrs., Econs. Club, Okla. Geol. Soc., Soc. Petroleum Engrs., Am. Inst. Mining Engrs., Am. Soc. Log Analysts, Am. Mgmt. Assn. Republican. Mem. Assembly of God Ch. Home: 3900 NE 143d St Edmond OK Office: 701 NW 63d St Suite 404 Oklahoma City OK 73102

HOFMANN, ROSS ELWOOD, cons. health care and energy recovery; b. Mpls., June 9, 1917; s. Charles Elwood and Jessica Alberta (Ross) H.; honor matriculation Upper Can. Coll., Toronto, Ont., 1935; M.A. cum laude in Econs. and Polit. Sci., U. Toronto, 1939; postgrad. Harvard Bus. Sch., 1941; m. Louisa Anne Simpson, June 10, 1963; children—Gale Elizabeth, Carol Lynette Hofmann Lafitte, Anne Bernadette Hofmann Craddock, Robert M., Susan Eleanor Hofmann Wilcox. Asst. to exec. v.p. McGraw-Hill Pub. Co., N.Y.C., 1939-41; pres. So. Cross Trading Co. & Carbosand Corp., Washington, 1946-52, So. Cross Mfg. Corp., Chambersburg, Pa., 1953—, Ross Hofmann Assos., Coral Gables, Fla., 1954—; v.p. Lightval Mines, Toronto, 1951—, Teddy Bear Mines, Toronto, 1954—; chmn., panelist, lectr. health care and energy prodn. seminars, panels, meetings; cons. in field. Served with USNR, 1941-46. Mem. Am. Hosp. Assn., Hosp. Mgmt. Systems Soc., Am. Public Health Assn., Am. Acad. Cons., Internat. Materials Mgmt. Soc., ASME (solid waste com.), Am. Inst. Biol. Scis., AAAS, Am. Soc. Microbiology, Inst. Indsl. Engrs., Nat. Environ. Health Assn., Theta Delta Chi. Republican. Anglican. Author: (textbook) Automation of Hospital Sterile Processing, 1968. Inventor, developer numerous equipment items, systems in health care delivery, mgmt. and energy prodn., steam and electricity from solid waste. Home: 1104 Malaga Ave Coral Gables FL 33134 Office: 2903 Salzedo Ave Coral Gables FL 33134

HOFSTEAD, JAMES WARNER, telephone company executive; b. Jackson, Tenn., Feb. 3, 1913; s. Harry Oliver and Agnes Lucile (Blackard) H.; m. Ellen Frances Bowers, Dec. 27, 1940; 1 dau., Eda Lucile. A.B., Vanderbilt U., 1935, LL.B., 1938. Bar: Tenn. Sole practice law; v.p., dir. United Telephone Co., 1969—; pres., dir. Wishy Washy, Inc., Nashville, 1946—; pres., dir. Wishy Sales Inc., 1959—. Served to capt. USMC, 1942-45. Mem. SAR (pres. Nashville, state v.p.), So. Srs. Golf Assn., Soc. of the Cincinnati, English Speaking Union (pres. Nashville br.), Soc. Colonial Wars, Sigma Chi, Methodist. Clubs: Belle Meade, Cumberland, Exchange (Nashville); Eccentric (London). Home: 215 Deer Park Circle Nashville TN 37205 Office: 3729 Charlotte Ave Nashville TN 37209

HOGAN, BEN MILES, gen. contractor; b. Helena, Ark., July 11, 1928; s. Ben Miles and Alyne (Russell) H.; B.S.C.E., Stanford U., 1950; m. Brenda Hamm, Jan. 24, 1976; children by previous marriage—Ben Miles III, Magdalene Ingram, Dan Phillips. With Ben M. Hogan Co., Inc., Little Rock, 1950—, pres., 1964—; dir. 1st Nat. Bank of Little Rock, Capital Savs. & Loan Assn. Past pres. Quapaw Area council Boy Scouts Am.; bd. dirs. Ark. Orch. Soc.; del. Constn. of 1970; fin. chmn. Ark. for the Constn.; chmn. Ark. Game and Fish Commn.; chmn. Ark. Hwy. Com. Mem. Asso. Gen. Contractors (nat. pres. 1976, pres., exec. com. Ark. chpt.), Nat. Asphalt Pavement Assn. (regional dir.), Ark. Bankers Assn. Democrat. Methodist. Office: 1100 Fairpoint St Little Rock AR 72203

HOGAN, CHRISTOPHER AMOS, interior design firm executive; b. Atlanta, Jan. 18, 1954; s. Robert Elbert and Barbara (Busbin) H. Student pub. schs. Foreman, Lamar White Drywall, 1972-74; v.p., estimator Midsouth Acoustical Co., Albany, Ga., 1974-78; owner, operator Chris Hogan Specialty Contracting, Albany, 1978-80; owner, operator H & W Interiors, Albany, 1980—. Republican. Baptist. Lodge: Moose (Albany). Home: Lot 44 Kinchafoonee Leesburg GA 31763 Office: 612 Roosevelt Ave Albany GA 31702

HOGAN, EUGENE ERNEST, environmental engineer; b. Niagara Falls, N.Y., July 19, 1933; s. Charles Lewis and Catherine Rachael (Dunham) H.; student Erie County Tech. Inst.; A.A., State U. N.Y., 1954; m. Lois Ann Pickens, Nov. 29, 1968; children—Lynn, Mary, Sarah, Robert, Charles. Estimator, Bilmac Iron Works, Buffalo, 1954; welding mgr. Mid Atlantic Industries, Niagara Falls, N.Y., 1955; staff environ. engr. metals div. Union Carbide Corp., Niagara Falls, 1956, Alloy, W.Va., 1956—; adj. prof. environ. engring. U. W.Va.; cons. Mesch Asso., Lockport, N.Y. Mem. Republican Com., Niagara County, 1960, sec. Rep. Party, 1962; chmn. Zoning Commn. City of N. Tonawanda (N.Y.), 1960, alderman, 1966; publicity chmn. Congressman H. Smith, 1964; asst. dir. CD, 1965; elder, fin. sec. United Methodist Ch., 1971; mem. Area Mgrs. Pollution Adv. Com.; chmn. Kanawha Valley Electrostatic Precipitator Seminar. Recipient Union Carbide Corp. Special Merit award, 1966, 1976. Lodge: Masons. Research in design, application of environ. equipment to process, power houses. Home: PO Box 516 Persimmon Rd Gauley Bridge WV 25085 Office: Elkem Metals Co Alloy WV 25002

HOGAN, JOHN DONALD, insurance company executive; b. Binghamton, N.Y., July 16, 1927; s. John D. and Edith J. (Hennessy) H.; m. Anna Maynard Craig, Nov. 26, 1976. children—Thomas P., James E. A.B., Syracuse U., 1949, M.A., 1950, Ph.D., 1952. Prof. econs., chmn. dept. Bates Coll., Lewiston, Maine, 1953-60; dir. edn. fin. research State of N.Y., 1959, chief of mcpl. fin., 1960; staff economist, dir. research Northwestern Mut. Life, Milw., 1960-68; v.p. Nationwide Ins. Cos., Columbus, Ohio, 1968-76; dean Sch. Bus. Adminstrn. Central Mich. U., Mt. Pleasant, 1976-79; v.p. Am. Productivity Ctr., Houston, 1979-80; pres., chief exec. officer Variable Annuity Life Ins. Co., Houston, 1980-83; sr. v.p. investment Am. Gen. Corp., Houston, 1983-85, asst. to chmn., sr. v.p., 1985—; chmn., chief exec. officer Variable Annuity Life Ins. Co., Houston, 1983-85, also dir.; Bd. dirs. Goodwill Industries, Columbus, Ohio, 1972-76, chmn. capital fund drive, 1974-75; mem. Houston Com. on Fgn. Relations, 1980—. Served to capt. U.S. Army, 1944-46; ETO; ret. USAR. Maxwell fellow, 1950-52, Maxwell Centenial lectr., 1970. Mem. Acad. Mgmt., Am. Econ. Assn., Inst. Mgmt. Sci., Nat. Assn. Bus. Economists, Nat. Tax Assn. (dir. Tax Inst. Am. 1981-85), Inst. for Research on Econs. of Taxation (dir.). Clubs: Heritage, Texas (Houston). Author: American Social Legislation, 1956, 73; Fiscal Capacity of the State of Maine, 1958; School Revenue Studies, 1959; U.S. Balance of Payments and Capital Flows, 1967; editor: Dimensions of Productivity Research, 2 vols., 1981. Office: American Gen Corp 2929 Allen Pkwy Houston TX 77019

HOGGE, PAUL WAVERLY, government contractor; b. Hampton, Va., June 3, 1943; s. George Raymond and Annie Roberta (Briggs) H.; m. Sandra Lee Smith, July 12, 1969; 1 son, Bryan Mitchell. A.A., Christopher Newport Coll., 1964; B.A., Coll. William and Mary, 1966. C.P.A., Va. Audit sr. Arthur Andrsen & Co., Washington, 1966-73; controller Earth Satellite Corp., Washington, 1973-75; sr. v.p. VSE Corp., Alexandria, Va., 1975—; pres., dir. Starr Mgmt. Corp., Alexandria, 1977-85, now dir.; chmn. bd., pres. PS&B Enterprises Ltd., Vienna, Va., 1984—. Coach, Vienna Little League, 1982. Mem. Am. Inst. C.P.A.s, D.C. Inst. C.P.A.s (chmn. C.P.A.s in industry com. 1984-85). Presbyterian. Clubs: Leesburg Golf, Cardinal Hill Swim. Home: 1858 Abbotsford Dr Vienna VA 22180 Office: VSE Corp 2550 Huntington Ave Alexandria VA 22303

HOGLUND, FORREST EUGENE, petroleum executive; b. Lawrence, Kans., July 1, 1933; s. Roy A. and Edna M. (McMichael) H.; B.S. in Mech. Engring., U. Kans., 1956; m. Sally Sue Roney, June 19, 1956; children—Kelly M., Shelly L., Kristan K. With Exxon Corp., 1957—, mgr. E. Tex. div., 1970-73, v.p. ops. Middle East, 1973-76, v.p. gas, 1976-77, pres. Tex. Oil and Gas, 1977—, chief exec. officer, 1982—. Served with C.E., U.S. Army, 1957-58. Mem. Am. Petroleum Inst., AIME, Tau Beta Pi, Pi Tau Sigma, Sigma Tau, Omicron Delta Kappa. Presbyterian. Clubs: Darien Country (bd. govs. 1977—); Petroleum, Dallas Country (Dallas). Home: 4330 Armstrong Pkwy Dallas TX 75205 Office: First City Center 1700 Pacific Ave LB10 Dallas TX 75201

HOHENBERGER, ARTHUR LEE, hospital administrator; b. Sherman, Tex., Apr. 28, 1948; s. Troy Willie and Theresa May (McBurnett) H.; m. Judith Ann Beaulieu, Feb. 22, 1969; 1 child, Brad Wayne. B.A. in Psychology, North Tex. State U., 1974; M.S. in Health Care Adminstrn., Tex. Woman's U., 1984. Operating room technician Physicians and Surgeons Hosp., Irving, Tex., 1970-74; adminstrv. asst. Pioneer Park Med. Ctr., Irving, 1974-76, asst. adminstr. 1976-81; exec. dir., chief exec. officer Grapevine Med. Ctr., Tex., 1981—. Contbr. articles to profl. jours. Pres. bd. devel. First Nat. Bank, Grapevine, Tex., 1982—; bd. dirs. Community Continuing Edn. Adv. Bd., Grapevine, 1984—; deacon First Baptist Ch., Grapevine, 1985—. Mem. Am. Coll. Hosp. Adminstrs. Republican. Baptist. Lodge: Rotary (bd. dirs. 1985—). Avocations: Golf; family. Home: 3021 Creekview Dr North Grapevine TX 76051 Office: Grapevine Med Ctr 1650 W College St Grapevine TX 76051

HOHENWARTER, MARK WILLIAM, clinical pharmacist, drug research executive; b. Lancaster, Pa., Oct. 28, 1955; s. William Frances and Lucille (Stork) H.; m. Susan Barbara Menendez, Nov. 27, 1982. B.S. in Pharmacy, U. N.C., 1978; Pharm. D., Med. U. S.C., 1981. Lic. pharmacist, Ala., N.C., S.C. Clin. asst. prof. Med. U. S.C., 1982-84; pharmacy clin. coordinator Roper Hosp., Charleston, S.C., 1982-84; clin. pharmacist Mobile Infirmary Med. Ctr., Ala., 1984-85, pharmacy clin. coordinator, 1985—; exec. v.p. Serotonin Industries, Inc., Charleston, 1984—; cons. in field. Contbr. articles to profl. jours. and chpt. to book. Recipient Burroughs Wellcome Hosp. Pharmacy Research award N.C. Soc. Hosp. Pharmacists. Greensboro Drug Club Aux. scholar, 1975; Am. Soc. Hosp. Pharmacists fellow, 1981. Mem. Ala. Pharmacy Assn., Am. Soc. Hosp. Pharmacists, Am. Soc. Parenteral and Enteral Nutrition, Pharmacy Assn. Mobile County, N.Y. Acad. Scis., S.C. Soc. Hosp. Pharmacists, Rho Chi. Roman Catholic. Club: YMCA. Avocations: sailing; scuba diving; skiing. Home: 2100 Ryegate Ct Mobile AL 36609 Office: Mobile Infirmary Med Ctr End of Louiselle St Mobile AL 36601

HOHLOCH, FAITH JEFFERSON, nurse educator; b. Bklyn., Sept. 26, 1933; d. Fred and Helen (Jefferson) H. B.S.N., Cornell U., 1956; M.A., Columbia U., 1962; Ed.D., Ind. U., 1974. Lic. nurse, S.C. Faculty, Med. Coll. Va.-Va. Commonwealth U., 1962-72, assoc. prof. nursing, 1969-72; faculty Emory U., 1974-79, prof., dir. grad. program and research, 1974-79; acting dean, prof. nursing Coll. Nursing, Med. U. S.C., Charleston, 1979—. Mem. Am. Nurses Assn., Nat. League Nursing, S.C. League Nursing, S.C. Nurses Assn., Pi Lambda Theta, Sigma Theta Tau. Office: Coll Nursing Med Univ SC 171 Ashley Ave Charleston SC 29425

HOHOLICK, JOHN DANIEL, petroleum geologist; b. Midvalley, Pa., July 24, 1956; s. Basil and Dorothy (Franchak) H. B.A., U. Pa., Millersville, 1978; M.S., U. Cin., 1980. Geologist, Exxon Co. U.S.A., Midland, Tex., 1980-81, sr. geologist, 1981-84, sr. petroleum geologist, 1984—. Contbr. articles to profl. jours. Adviser, Jr. Achievement Midland, 1982-84; group leader United Way Midland, 1984-85. Mem. Am. Assn. Petroleum Geologists, W.Tex. Geol. Soc., Soc. Econ. Mineralogists and Paleontologists, Rocky Mountain Assn. Petroleum Geologists. Avocations: coin collecting, antique collecting; meteors. Office: Exxon Co PO Box 1600 Midland TX 79702

HOLADAY, FRANK LEWIS, acct.; b. Dallas, Nov. 4, 1954; s. Robert Louis and Jessie Ruth (Tucker) H.; B.B.A. cum laude, U. Tex. at Austin, 1977; M.B.A., N. Tex. State U., 1978. Staff acct. Summers Assos., Inc., Dallas, 1977-78; tax supr. Peat Marwick Mitchel & Co., Dallas, 1979-82; v.p. fin. Three M Oil Co., Dallas, 1982—. Active Junius Heights Homeowners Assn., Young Republicans, C.P.A., Tex. Mem. Am. Inst. C.P.A.s, Tex. Soc. C.P.A.s, Methodist. Clubs: Dervish, U. Tex. Ex-Students, 100, Lakewood Country (Dallas). Lodges: Masons, Shriners, Scottish Rite. Contbg. author: Federal Income Taxation of Natural Resources, 1981. Home: 723 Parkmont Dallas TX 75214 Office: 400 One Energy Sq Dallas TX 75206

HOLBEIN, THOMAS JAMES, marketing research company executive; b. Laredo, Tex., July 16, 1941; s. Alfred Ray and Emily Armond (Chitwood) H.; m. Mary Jacqueline Trussell, Jan. 29, 1962 (div. Dec. 1979); children—Lisa Marie, Thomas James, Matthew Robert; m. Susan Joy Hoverstadt, Jan. 1985. B.A., Tex. A&M U., 1962; M.A., U. Iowa, 1963, Copy editor Dallas Morning News, 1967-68; research assoc. Belden Assocs., Dallas, 1968-71, v.p., 1971-79, sr. v.p., 1979-81, exec. v.p., 1981—; mem. faculty Editor's Research Workships, Am. Soc. Newspaper Editors; vis. lectr. Am. Press Inst., Reston, Va.; instr. research methods Tulsa U., So. Methodist U., Fla. Internat. U.; cons. to Pub. Broadcasting System. Served to capt. Signal Corps, U.S. Army, 1962-67. Decorated Bronze Star. Mem. Am. Mktg. Assn., Am. Assn. for Pub. Opinion Research, World Assn. Pub. Opinion Research, Council Survey Research Orgns., Internat. Newspaper Promotion Assn., Tex. A&M Ex-Students' Assn., U. Iowa Alumni Assn. Methodist. Author: (with Joe Belden) A New Front Page, 1974; (with Deanne L. Termini) The 'New' Front Page: Looking Back at 1974, 1982; contbr. serveral white papers to newspaper industry publs.

HOLBROOK, EDWARD LIONEL, pneumatic control consultant; b. Bristol, Eng., Oct. 27, 1911; s. Frederick Lionel and Eliza Lott (Slade) H.; came to U.S., 1920, naturalized, 1936; student U. Pitts., 1930-34, Carnegie Inst. Tech., 1934-38, Pa. State U., 1938-41, Milw. Sch. Art (correspondence), 1937-38, Alexander Hamilton Inst. Mgmt., 1956-57; m. Annie Lou Gann, Mar. 1, 1941 (dec.); children—Cynthia Holbrook Wynn, Elizabeth Holbrook Shelton, Edward Lionel. Tester, test engr. Westinghouse Air Brake Co., Wilmerding, Pa., 1929-40, dist. mgr. Southeastern ty., Washington, 1940-45, mgr. govt. sales indsl. products div., 1945-54, dir. European ops., Geneva, 1954-56, gen. sales mgr. indsl. products div., Wilmerding, 1956-59; mgr. eastern div., mgr. govt. sales, mgr. fng. sales and licensing Modernair Corp., Cleve., 1959-61; v.p. Barker Air & Hydraulics, Greenville, S.C., 1961-63; dir. research Numatics Co., Highland, Mich., 1963-64; v.p., gen. mgr. Clippard Instrument Lab., Cin., 1964-67; v.p., gen. mgr., dir. Pneucon, Inc., Richmond, Calif., 1967-77; pneumatic control cons., Taylor, S.C., 1977—. Named to Exec. and Profl. Hall of Fame; registered profl. engr., D.C., Ga. Mem. AIM, Naval Architects and Marine Engrs., Nat. Soc. Profl. Engrs., Soc. Am. Mil. Engrs., European Pneumatic Assn., Am. Soc. Tool and Mfg. Engrs., Fluid Power Soc. (Fluid Power Design award 1970), Wash. Soc. Engrs. Author book on pneumatic logic design, 1984; contbr. articles to profl. jours. Patentee in field. Address: Route 2 Manley St Taylor SC 29687

HOLBROOK, TARYL ANN, psychological consultant; b. Columbus, Ohio, Mar. 28, 1954; d. Argus and Mildred Arlene (Schiller) H. B.S. in Spanish, B.A. in Psychology, Ohio State U., 1976, M.A., 1978, Ph.D., 1983. Acad. advisor Univ. Coll., Columbus, 1977-81, 82-83; psychology intern Counseling Ctr. for

Human Devel. U. South Fla., Tampa, 1981-82; counselor Counseling and Consultation Services, Ohio State U., Columbus, 1982-83; psychol. cons. Juvenile Ct. Pinellas County, Clearwater, Fla., 1983—; mem. Health and Rehab. Services, Case Rev. Com. for Severely Emotionally Disturbed Children and Adolescents, Clearwater, Fla., 1984—. Mem. Am. Psychol. Assn., Ohio State U. Alumni Assn., Phi Delta Kappa. Republican. Baptist. Avocations: jogging; dancing. Home: 374 115th Ave N Apt 4 Saint Petersburg FL 33702 Office: Pinellas County Juvenile Ct 14500 49th St N Clearwater FL 33620

HOLCOMB, DOROTHY TURNER, publicist; b. Roanoke, Va., June 15, 1924; d. Wiley Bryant and Lena Mae (Gray) Turner; m. Joseph E. Baxter, Aug. 1, 1944 (dec. Nov. 1944); m. 2d, G. William Holcomb, May 8, 1948 (div. 1962). Student Coronet Bus. Sch., Roanoke, 1943; interior decorator certificate N.Y. Sch. Interior Design, 1953; student U. Miami, 1962-63. Exec. sec. Am.'s Jr. Miss Pageant, Mobile, Ala., 1962; exec. asst. to pres. Gilbert Mktg. Group, Inc., N.Y.C., 1963-65; br. dirs. Heart Assn., Miami, Fla., 1965-66; publicist in charge on-air promotion Screen Gems, Hollywood, Calif., 1966-68; publicity dir. Mus. of Sci./Planetarium, Miami, 1968-71, Bryna Cosmetics, Inc., Miami, 1973-74; freelance publicist, 1971-73, 76—; pub. relations/communications ECKANKAR, Menlo Park, Calif., 1974-75. Mem. Publicists Guild, Internat. Alliance Theatrical Stage Employees, Moving Picture Machine Operators, Women in Communications. Home: 3727 Parliament Rd SW Apt 11 Roanoke VA 24014

HOLCOMB, JAMES REED, religious school executive; b. Panhandle, Tex., July 31, 1932; s. James Leon and Estelle (Simms) H.; B.A. in Bus. Adminstrn., Wayland U., 1957; M.R.E., Southwestern Bapt. Theol. Sem., 1978; m. Tula Faye Rose, Mar. 5, 1953; children—Roseann, Cheryl, James. Graphic arts engr. So. Bapt. Radio-TV Commn., Ft. Worth, 1957-61, dir. printing and mail expdns., 1961-65, dir. bldgs. and services, 1965-68, mktg. dir., 1968-72, v.p. support services, 1972-78; community services mgr. United Way Am., Ft. Worth, 1979-81; dir. Vision/85, Southwestern Bapt. Theol. Sem., Ft. Worth, 1981-83, dir. devel., 1984—. Mem. Forum Ft. Worth, 1974—; mem. Ft. Worth Sesquecentemial Comm.; mem. exec. bd. Longhorn council Boy Scouts Am., 1982—; bd. dirs. Tarrant County chpt. ARC, 1982—; v.p., mem. exec. com., bd. dirs. Tex. Soc. to Prevent Blindness, 1980—. Served with U.S. Army, 1952-54. Mem. Nat. Soc. Fund Raising Execs. (v.p., Profl. Fund Raiser of Yr. 1985), Am. Soc. Tng. Dirs., Ft. Worth C. of C. (dir. 1978—). Baptist. Club: 2001 (Dallas). Lodge: Lions. Home: 3733 Ashford St Fort Worth TX 76133 Office: Southwestern Baptist Theological Seminary PO Box 22000 Fort Worth TX 76122 also 2001 Bryan Room 1520 Dallas TX 75201

HOLCOMB, LYLE DONALD, JR., lawyer; b. Miami, Fla., Feb. 3, 1929; s. Lyle Donald and Hazel Irene (Watson) H.; m. Barbara Jean Roth, July 12, 1952; children—Susan Holcomb Davis, Douglas J., Mark E. B.A., U. Mich., 1951; J.D., U. Fla., 1954. Bar: Fla. 1955, U.S. Supreme Ct. 1966, U.S. Ct. Appeals (5th and 11th cirs.) 1981. Ptnr. Holcomb & Holcomb, Miami, 1955-72; assoc. Copeland, Therrel, Baisden & Peterson, Miami Beach, Fla., 1972-75; ptnr. Therrel, Baisden, Stanton, Wood & Setlin, Miami Beach, 1976-85, Therrel Baisden & Meyer Weiss, Miami Beach, 1985—. Author: The Watson Family in Barry County, Michigan, 1966. Contbr. to Florida Law & Practice, legal ency. Mem. organizing bd. Econ. Opportunities Legal Services Program (now Legal Services Greater Miami) 1965-75; pres. South Fla. Migrant Legal Services Program (now Fla. Rural Legal Services), 1966-68; mem. exec. bd. S. Fla. council Boy Scouts Am., 1958—; organizer, pres. Cutler Ridge Civic Assn., 1955-66; mem. S.E. Fla. Religious Task Force Planning Com., 1968-69; pres. Inter-Faith Agy. for Social Justice, Inc., 1968-69; mem. Dade County Mayor's Ad Hoc Com. on Adminstrn. Justice under Emergency Conditions, 1968-69; bd. dirs. Community Relations Bd., 1971-74. Served with USNR, 1945-52. Recipient Silver Beaver award Boy Scouts Am. Mem. ABA, Am. Judicature Soc., Estate Planning Council Greater Miami, Am. Coll. Probate Counsel, Acad. Fla. Probate and Trust Litigation Attys. Inc., Fla. Bar, Miami Beach Bar Assn. (pres. 1980), Dade County Bar Assn. (sec. 1963-71), John Marshall Bar Assn. (pres. 1953), Soc. Mayflower Descendants (pres. Miami 1968-70), Huguenot Soc. Fla. (pres. Miami 1980-83), Nat. Rifle Assn. (life), Hist. Assn. S. Fla., Antique Bottle Collectors Assn. Fla. (past dir.), SAR (pres. Miami chpt. 1960-62), Beta Theta Pi, Phi Delta Phi. Republican. Mem. United Ch. Christ. Club: Univ. Yacht (treas. Coral Gables 1958-60). Home: 700 Malaga Ave Coral Gables FL 33134 Office: Therrel Baisden & Meyer Weiss 1111 Lincoln Rd Mall Suite 600 Miami Beach FL 33139

HOLDER, HOWARD RANDOLPH, broadcasting executive; b. Moline, Ill., Nov. 14, 1916; s. James William and Charlotte (Brega) H.; B.A. Augustana Coll., 1939; m. Clementi Lacey-Baker, Feb. 21, 1942; children—Janice Clementi Holder Collins, Susan Charlotte Holder Mason, Marjory Estelle, Howard Randolph. With Sta. WHBF, Rock Island, Ill., 1939-41, Sta. WOC, Davenport, Iowa, 1945-47, Sta. WINN, Louisville, 1947, Sta. Athens, Ga., 1948-56, Sta. WGAU-WNGC, Athens, 1956—; pres. Clarke Broadcasting Corp., Athens, 1973; dir. Citizens & So. Nat. Bank Athens. Mem. adv. bd. Salvation Army, chmn., 1962, 63; chmn. Athens Parks and Recreation Bd., 1952-62; mem. adv. bd. Athens-Clarke County chpt. ARC, 1950-70, Clarke County Juvenile Ct., 1960-72; chmn. region IV Am. Cancer Soc., 1968; chmn. Cherokee dist. Boy Scouts Am., 1966, 67, mem. adv. bd. N.E. Ga. Area council, 1968—; mem. adv. bd. Henry W. Grady Sch. Journalism and Mass Media, U. Ga., 1973-78; bd. dirs. Athens Crime Prevention Com., 1960-70, Augustana Coll. Alumni Assn., 1974-77, Rec. for Blind, 1977-80, Athens Symphony, 1981-85, AP Broadcasting Bd., 1982—; mem. Model Cities Policy Bd., 1970-71, Georgians for Safer Hwys., 1970, Ga. Productivity Bd., 1984-86; trustee Ga. Rotary Student Fund, 1973—; mem. Ga. Productivity Bd., 1984-86; mem. adv. bd. Ga. Mus. Art, 1984—; co-pres. Friends Ga. Mus. Art, 1974-75, Friend of Mass Communications, U. Ga.; bd. advisors Ga. State Mus. Art, 1983—; mem. Nat. AP Broadcasting Bd., 1983—. Served with AUS, 1941-46; ETO. Recipient Silver Beaver award Boy Scouts Am., 1973; Outstanding Achievement award Augustana Coll. Alumni Assn., 1973, Robert Stolz medaille, 1973; cert. of merit UDC, 1983; named Boss of Year, Athens Jaycees, 1959; Broadcaster-Citizen of Year, Ga. Assn. Broadcasters, 1962; Employer of Yr., Athens Bus. and Profl. Women, 1969; Ky. col., 1961; Athens Citizen of Year, Athens Woman's Club, 1971; Liberty Bell award Athens Bar Assn., 1977; Paul Harris fellow, 1978; Will Watt fellow, 1984; Advocacy award N.E. Ga. Planning and Devel. Commn., 1979; nat. medal of honor DAR, 1983; cert. of merit UDC; Arch award Friends of U. Ga., 1986. Mem. Res. Officers Assn. (pres. Athens 1962), Ga. Assn. Broadcasters (pres. 1961), Ga. AP Broadcasters Assn. (pres. 1963), Internat. Platform Assn., Athens Area C. of C. (pres. 1970), Golden Quill, Sigma Delta Chi, Alpha Delta Sigma, Alpha Psi Omega, Phi Omega Phi, Di Gamma Kappa (Ga. Pioneer Broadcaster of Year award 1971). Clubs: Rotary (pres. Athens club 1957-58, dist. gov. 1969-70, Citizen of Yr. award 1971), Athens Country, Gridiron, Touchdown (pres. Athens 1963-64). Home: 383 Westview Dr Athens GA 30606 Office: 850 Bobbin Mill Rd Athens GA 30610

HOLDERMAN, JAMES BOWKER, university president; b. Morris, Ill., Jan. 29, 1936; s. Samuel James and Helen Boynton (Bowker) H.; m. Carolyn Meadors, Aug. 16, 1959; children—Elizabeth, Nancy, Jamie. B.A. with Honors, Denison U., 1958; Ph.D., Northwestern U., 1961; also hon. degrees. Asst. prof. govt. U. Ill., Urbana, 1961-63, asst. prof. polit. sci., 1965-67, assoc. prof., 1967-69; asst. supt. public instrn. State of Ill., 1963-65; vice-chancellor U. Ill.-Chgo., 1968-69; exec. dir. Bd. of Higher Edn. State of Ill., Chgo., 1969-73; v.p. for edn. Lilly Endowment, Inc., Indpls., 1973-76; sr. v.p., dir. public policy div. Acad. for Edn. Devel., 1976-77; pres. Inst. for Public Policy Devel., Indpls., 1977; pres. U. S.C., 1977—; dir. So. Bell. Contbr. articles to profl. jours. Mem. task force on Financing of Higher Edn. Nat. Council of Ind. Colls., 1972—; mem. task force on statewide planning Edn. Commn. of the States, 1969-70; mem. task force on coordinating governance and structure of postsecondary edn., 1972—; mem. Gov.'s Task Force on Health Planning, Ill., 1970-73; gov. mem. Ill. Council on Econ. Edn., 1969-73; mem. Elmhurst (Ill.) Bd. Edn., 1968-73, pres., 1971-73; mem. edni. adv. com. Inst. Internat. Edn., 1978—, Am. Council on Edn. panel on women 1978—; chmn. U.S. Nat. Commn. for UNESCO, 1982—; trustee North Central Coll., Naperville, Ill., 1974, Denison U., Granville, Ohio, 1973-74, Aerospace Edn. Found., 1978—, 70001 Devel. Found., Wilmington, Del., Fairleigh Dickinson U. bd. dirs. Friends of Our Little Bros., Cuernavaca, Mex., 1976—, United Way of Midlands, Columbia, S.C., 1978—; head U.S. del. ICRC Quadrennial Conf., Manila, 1981. Citizenship Clearing House fellow in state govt., 1960; Ford Found. fellow, 1973; named Chicagoan of the Year in Govt. and Polit. Sci. Chgo. Jr. Assn. Commerce and Industry, 1967, South Carolinian of Yr., Sta. WIS-TV, 1984, Ambassador of Yr. Greater Columbia C. of C., 1984; decorated comdr.'s Cross, Order of Merit (W.Ger.); comdr. Order of Merit of Duarte, Sánchez and Mella. Mem. Am., Midwest Polit. Sci. Assns., Ill. Agrl. Assn., Assn. of State Higher Edn. Exec. Officers, Delta Upsilon, Omicron Delta Kappa, Blue Key, Mortar Board, Phi Beta Kappa, Phi Sigma Alpha, Phi Alpha Theta. Clubs: Tavern (Chgo.); Univ. (Chgo., N.Y.); Summit. Home: Pres' House Univ SC Columbia SC 29208 Office: Office of Pres Univ SC Columbia SC 29208

HOLDERNESS, RICHARD THURSTON, trust company executive; b. Greensboro, N.C., Feb. 25, 1946; s. Howard and Adelaide Lucinda (Fortune) H.; m. Maureen Hassenfelt, July 25, 1971 (div. Aug. 1977); children—Richard Thurston, Howard Austen; m. Julie Anderson, Oct. 14, 1978; children—Hilary McRee Vance, Anne McRee Vance, Julie Fortune. B.A., U. N.C.-Chapel Hill, 1968, M.B.A., 1973. Chartered fin. analyst. Asst. v.p. Durham Life, Raleigh, N.C., 1974, v.p. securities, 1974-83; pres. Holderness Investments, Raleigh, 1983-84; pres., chief fin. officer N.C. Trust Co., Greensboro, 1984—, also dir. Bd. dirs. Holderness Med. Scholarship Found., Chapel Hill, 1982-85, N.C. Mus. Natural History, Raleigh, 1985; bd. visitors Peace Coll., Raleigh, 1982-85, vice chmn., 1984. Fellow Life Mgmt. Inst., 1976. Mem. N.C. Soc. Fin. Analysts (v.p., dir. 1984-85), Phi Beta Kappa. Republican. Presbyterian. Avocations: tennis; skiing; running; reading; gardening. Home: 405 Kimberly Dr Greensboro NC 27408 Office: NC Trust Co 125 S Elm St Greensboro NC 27402

HOLINDE, MELANIE THOMAS, educator; b. Bellefonte, Pa., Aug. 3, 1943; d. Robert Kenneth and Ruth Evelyn (Mulbarger) Thomas; B.S., Lock Haven State Coll., 1965; M.A., Western Ky. U., 1974. Tchr., Elmira Heights (N.Y.) Sch. Dist., Thomas Edison High Sch., 1965-66, White Pines Sch. Dist., Ely, Nev., 1966-67, Poway (Calif.) Sch. Dist., 1967-69; tchr. English dept. Daviess County Sch. Dist., Owensboro, Ky., 1969—; chmn. gifted com. Apollo High Sch., Owensboro, Ky., 1969—; mem. steering com. Mid-Am. Conf. on Composition, 1980—. Mem. Daviess County Republican Exec. Com., 1979—; chair Daviess County Reps., 1980—; sponsor Nat. Rep. Congl. Com., 1980—; mem. Ky. Rep. Com., Rep. Presdl. Task Force, Rep. Nat. Com., Am. Legis. Exchange Council. Mem. Nat. Council Tchrs. English, AAUW, Assn. Supervision and Curriculum Devel., Ky. Council Tchrs. English, Alpha Delta Kappa. Republican. Presbyterian. Club: Pilot. Home: Rural Route 4 Box 103 Owensboro KY 42301 Office: Apollo High Sch Tamarack Rd Owensboro KY 42301

HOLLADAY, J. MAC, association executive. Pres., Charleston C. of C., S.C. Office: Charleston C of C 17 Lockwood Dr PO Box 975 Charleston SC 29402*

HOLLADAY, RONALD BELL, cattle rancher, farmer; b. Selma, Ala., Jan. 1, 1947; s. Fred Wells and Winnie (Bell) H.; m. Mitzi Cecile Lane, Aug. 5, 1967; children—Sandra Lynn, Cecil Lane, Richard Bell. B.S., Auburn U., 1969. Cattle rancher and farmer, Tyler, Ala., 1969—; owner, operator cotton gin, Tyler, 1970—; dir. Selma Oil Mill. Dist. supr. Lowndes County Soil and Water Conservation Dist., 1978—; sec.-treas. Lowndes County Pvt. Sch. Found., Lowndesboro, Ala., 1981—; bd. dirs. Ala. Fellowship Christian Athletes, 1982—; deacon Benton Baptist Ch., 1969—. Mem. Southeastern Livestock Expn., Ala. Cattlemen's Assn. (1st v.p. 1986—; Pres.'s award 1983), Lowndes County Cattlemen's Assn. (past pres., bd. dirs.), Lowndes County Farm Bur. (bd. dirs.), Nat. Cattlemen's Assn. Home: Route 1 Box 141 Tyler AL 36785 Office: Holladay Gin Co Tyler AL 36785

HOLLAND, DONALD REGINALD, store owner, author, promoter, scientist; b. Abbott, Tex., Sept. 16, 1940; s. Oather Clifford and Dorothy (Murphy) H.; m. Janet Marie Welk, Aug. 20, 1961; children—Donald R., Jr., Diana Renee, Dorothy Ruth, Deborah Rae. B.S., Naval Postgrad. Sch., 1972; M.B.A., Tarleton State U., 1980. Enlisted in U.S. Navy, 1957, advanced through grades to lt.; served in various locations, ret., 1977; student, farmer, Abbott, Tex., 1978-80; retail store owner Abbott Trading Post, Willie Nelson Souvenirs, Abbott, 1981—. Decorated Navy Achievement medal, Combat Action ribbon, 1968, Good Conduct medal with Bronze Star, Nat. Def. Service medal, Vietnam Service medal with 4 bronze stars, Vietnam Armed Forces Meritorious Unit commendation with Palm and Gold Frame; recipient Appreciation award Lions Club, Carmel Valley, Calif., 1970-72; Cert. of Appreciation as Asst. Webelos Leader, 1973. Mem. Nat. Rifle Assn., Tex. State Rifle Assn., Am. Legion, VFW, Navy Supply Corps Assn., Ret. Officers Assn. U.S., Naval Res. Assn., Res. Officers Assn. U.S., Am. Def. Preparedness Assn. Home: PO Box 59 Abbott TX 76621 Office: Willie Nelson Souvenirs-N-Stuff PO Box 59 Abbott TX 76621

HOLLAND, GENE GRIGSBY (SCOTTY), artist; b. Hazard, Ky., June 30, 1928; d. Edward and Virginia Lee (Watson) Grigsby; B.A., U. S. Fla., 1968; pupil of Ruth Allison, Talequah, Okla., 1947-48, Ralph Smith, Washington, 1977, Clint Carter, Atlanta, 1977, R. Jordan, Winter Park, Fla., 1979, Cedric Baldwin Egeli, Edgewater, Md., 1984; m. George William Holland, Sept. 22, 1950; 3 children. Various clerical and secretarial positions, 1948-52; news reporter, photographer Bryan (Tex.) Daily News, 1952; clk. Fogarty Bros. Moving and Transfer, Tampa and Miami, Fla., 1954-57; tchr. elem. Schs., Hillsborough County, Fla., 1968-72; owner, pres. Holland Originals. Numerous group shows of paintings including: Tampa Woman's Clubhouse, 1973, Cor Jesu, Tampa, 1973, bank, Monks Corner, S.C., 1977, Summerville Artists Guild, 1977, 78, Apopka (Fla.) Art and Foliage Festival, 1980, 81, 82, Fla. Fedn. Women's Clubs, 1980, 81, 82; Island Gifts, Tampa, 1980-82, Brandon (Fla.) Station, 1980-81, Holland Originals, Orlando, Fla.; represented in permanent collections including Combank, Apopka, also pvt. collections. Vol., ARC, Tampa, 1965-69, United Fund Campaign, 1975-76; pres. Mango (Fla.) Elem. Sch. PTA, 1966-67; sec. Tampa Civic Assn., 1975-76; vol. Easter Seal Fund Campaign, 1962-63. Recipient numerous art awards, 1978-82. Mem. Internat. Soc. of Artists, Council of Arts and Scis. for Central Fla., Fedn. of Women's Clubs (pres. Hillsborough County 1974-75, v.p. Tampa 1974-75), Meth. Women's Soc. (sec. 1976-77), Nat. Trust for Historic Preservation, Nat. Hist. Soc., Central Fla. Geneal. and Hist. Soc., Am. Guild Flower Arrangers. Clubs: Friday Morning Musicale (1st v.p. bd. incorporators Tampa 1974-75), Apopka Woman's (pres. 1981-82, exec. dir. 1983-84), Apopka Garden, Internat. Innerwheel (dist. pres. 1973, pres. Tampa 1972). Home: 1080 Errol Pkwy Apopka FL 32703 Office: 1225 1/2 N Orange Ave Orlando FL 32804

HOLLAND, HERBERT, advertising executive; b. Houston, Oct. 1, 1952; s. Joseph Jacob and Rita (Serchuk) H.; m. Gervaise Marie Dumas, Dec. 3, 1977. Student U. Tex.-Austin, 1970-74. Sportswriter, Houston Chronicle, 1974-76; pub. Houston Sports Rev., 1976; reporter Houston Chronicle, 1977-78; writer, producer Sta. KUHT-TV, Houston, 1977-80, sportscaster Sta. KILT Radio, Houston, 1978-80; pres. The Holland Group, Inc., Houston, 1978-81; writer-producer Gray, O'Rourke, Sussman Advt., Houston, 1981; assoc. creative dir. Gulf State Advt. Agy., Houston, 1981—; prodn. cons. TM Cos., Dallas, Billboard mag., N.Y.C., 1979—. Pres., Texoma region B'nai B'rith Youth Orgn., 1969-70. Served with AUS, 1971-72. Recipient Gabriel award for Woodstock, Ten Years Later, 1980. Jewish. Office: 8300 Bissonnet St Suite 500 Houston TX 77074

HOLLAND, HILLMAN RANDALL, interior designer, art dealer; b. Athens, Ala., Apr. 17, 1950; s. Hillman Hoyt and Bessie (White) H. B.A., Auburn U., 1973; B.S., Ga. State U., 1975; J.D., Atlanta Law Sch., 1976; certs. Parsons in Paris, 1980, Attingham Summer Sch., London, 1982, Winterthur Mus., Wilmington, Del., 1983, Harvard U., 1984. Conf. coordinator Ga. State U., Atlanta, 1975-77; owner Hillman Holland Designs, Atlanta, 1977—. Dep. registrar Fulton County Voter Registration, Atlanta, 1976-80; v.p. Soc. for Olmsted Parks, Atlanta, 1983-85; mem. nat. steering com. Assn. for Olmsted Parks, N.Y.C., 1982-84; vol. Ga. Trust for Hist. Preservation, Atlanta, 1981-83; trustee Decorative Arts Acquisition Trust, High Mus., Atlanta, 1983—; trustee, sec. Nexus Contemporary Art Ctr., Atlanta, 1982-85; trustee Friends of Decorative Arts, High Mus., Atlanta, 1981-83, Atlanta Coll. Art, 1985—. Named Outstanding Student in Nation, Delta Theta Phi, Worthington, Ohio, 1976. Mem. Internat. Soc. Interior Designers (pres. Ga. chpt. 1985—), Beta Theta Pi (sec.-treas. Auburn alumni assn. 1974-76). Republican. Episcopalian. Clubs: St. James's (London); West Paces Racquet (Atlanta). Home: 2575 Peachtree Rd Penthouse C Atlanta GA 30305 Office: 2575 Peachtree Rd Lobby Atlanta GA 30305

HOLLAND, LAWRENCE ROZIER, research physicist, educator; b. Phila., Aug. 11, 1930; s. Leicester Bodine and Louise E. W. (Adams) H.; m. Anesia Costa Araujo, June 9, 1969. B.A., Harvard Coll., 1952; M.A., Bryn Mawr Coll., 1957, Ph.D., 1962. With Lehigh U., Bethlehem, Pa., 1960-66, Colo. Sch. Mines, Golden, 1969-71, Instituto Tecnologico de Aeronautica, Brazil, 1966-69, 71-77, Universities' Space Research Assn., NASA, 1977-81; research physicist U. Ala.-Huntsville, 1982-84; prof. physics Ala. A & M U., Normal, 1984—; cons. engring. physics. Bd. dirs. Huntsville Community Chorus, 1979-83. Served with USMC, 1953-55. Mem. Am. Assn. Physics Tchrs., Am. Inst. Physics, Sigma Xi. Club: Harvard (Phila.). Contbr. articles to publs. including Jour. Applied Physics, Rev. Scientific Instruments, Jour. Crystal Growth, Jour. of the Vacuum Soc., Ciencia e Cultura, others; patentee. Home: 4605 Wilshire Cove Huntsville AL 35816 Office: Dept Physics Ala A & M U Normal AL 35762

HOLLAND, RICHARD JOYNER, state senator, banker; b. Suffolk, Va., Aug. 12, 1925; m. Jean Marks Culpepper. Student Harvard U.; B.S., U. Va.; grad. Stonier Grad. Sch. Banking, Rutgers U. Mem. Va. Senate, Richmond, 1980—. Trustee Elon Coll.; mem. Wight County Dem. Com.; mem. Windsor Town Council, 1953-74; former mem. Bd. of Visitors, Radford Coll. Served to lt. (j.g.) USN, World War II. Mem. Va. Bankers Assn. (past pres.). Democrat. Congregationalist. Club: Ruritan. Lodge: Masons. Office: Va Senate Gen Assembly Bldg 9th and Broad Sts Richmond VA 23219*

HOLLAND, TAYLOR GRIFFITH, JR., utility executive; b. Phila., Sept. 13, 1928; s. Taylor Griffith and Anne (Miles) H.; B.E., Vanderbilt U., 1950; m. Cornelia Murray Goodloe, Feb. 3, 1951; children—Delia Adair, Cornelia Goodloe, Katherine, Taylor III. With Nashville Gas Co., 1950-73, v.p. mktg., 1968-71, sr. v.p., 1971-73; exec. v.p. Mississippi Valley Gas Co., Jackson, Miss., 1973-74, pres., chief exec. officer, 1974-76; chmn. bd., pres., chief exec. officer, 1976—; pres., dir. J.I.D. Corp.; dir. Trustmark Nat. Bank. Vice pres. United Way of Capitol Area, Jackson, 1975-76, pres., 1977-78; bd. dirs., pres. Jackson Symphony, 1976; pres. Jr. Achievement; vice chmn. Miss. Arts Center-Planetarium Commn., Jackson, 1977-81, chmn., 1981—. Mem. Am. Gas Assn. (bd. dirs.), So. Gas Assn. (chmn. 1984-85), Tenn. Gas. Assn., ASME, Jackson C. of C. (pres. 1985-86). Republican. Episcopalian. Clubs: Jackson Country, Colonial Country, River Hills, Univ., Capital City Petroleum, Masons; Shriners (Nashville). Home: 2560 Lake Circle Jackson MS 39211 Office: 711 W Capitol St Jackson MS 39207

HOLLEN, DONALD EDWARD, utility company executive; b. Buckhannon, W.Va., July 19, 1922; s. Cecil Edwin and Leona Dove (Cutright) H.; m. Betty Lee Baumgartner, Aug. 23, 1947; children—Donald Edward, II, Terri Lee. B.S. in Forestry, W.Va. U., 1949; grad. Advanced Mgmt. Program, Harvard U., 1968. Asst. extension forester W.Va. U., 1949-51; buyer, forester Kimball-Tyler Cooperage Co., Buckhannon, 1951-53; with Monongahela Power Co., Fairmont, W.Va., 1953—, now pres.; dir. City Nat. Bank, Fairmont. Campaign chmn. United Way, 1967, pres., 1977; bd. dirs. Found. Ind. Colls.; trustee Alderson-Broaddus Coll. Served with inf. U.S. Army, 1940-45. Decorated Silver Star, Purple Heart. Mem. Soc. Am. Foresters, Pub. Utilities Assn. of Virginias (exec. com., pres. 1977), W.Va. Research League, Edison Electric Inst., Ohio Electric Utility Inst., W.Va. C. of C. (dir.). Baptist. Lodge: Kiwanis (pres. club 1967-68). Office: Monongahela Power Co Monongahela Power Bldg Fairmont WV 26554*

HOLLERS, HARDY, lawyer; b. Clarendon, Tex., May 20, 1901; s. James Lemuel and Mattie (Mays) H.; student Southwestern U., 1918-19; LL.B., U. Tex., 1927, J.D., 1927; m. Mildred Bernice Calk, Apr. 18, 1921; children—Hardy Warren, Richard Van, James Carlyle. Admitted to Tex. bar, 1927, since practiced in Austin; asst. county atty., Travis County, 1928-29; asst. dist. atty., Travis County, 1933-34; spl. dist. judge, Travis County, 1935-36. Trial counsel maj. war criminals, Nuremberg, Germany, 1945. Gen. chmn. Greater Austin Assn., 1968-72. Served from maj. to col. AUS, 1941-46; ETO. Decorated Legion of Merit (U.S.); Croix de Guerre with palm (France). Fellow Tex. Bar Found. (life); mem. Nat. Res. Officers Assn. (life), Am. Legion (past post comdr.), Tex. (past dir.), Travis County bar assns. Methodist. Mason (Shriner). Club: Headliners. Home: 2710 Townes Lane Austin TX 78703 Office: Am Bank Tower Austin TX 78701

HOLLEY, BYRON EDWARD, ophthalmologist, educator; b. Tampa, Fla., Dec. 13, 1940; s. Albert and Miriam H.; m. Sondra Dobbs; children—Chuck, John, Allison. B.S., U. Tampa, 1963; M.D., U. Miami, 1967. Diplomate Am. Bd. Ophthalmology. Intern, Bapt. Meml. Hosp., Memphis, 1968; resident Tulane U., 1971-74; practice ophthalmology, Tampa, 1975—; pres. Cataract Surgery Facility, Tampa, 1984—; clin. prof. U. South Fla. Sch. Medicine, 1979—. Served as capt. U.S. Army, 1968-69, Vietnam. Decorated Bronze Star with 2 oak leaf clusters, Army Commendation medal, Air medal. Mem. Hillsborough County Med. Assn., Outpatient Ophthalmic Surgery Soc., AMA, Fla. Med. Assn., Am. Intra-ocular Implant Soc. Republican. Baptist. Home: 1011 Cherwood Ln Brandon FL 33511 Office: Cataract Surgery Facility 4710 N Habana Ave Suite 100 Tampa FL 33614

HOLLEY, HORACE PRESTON, JR., physician; b. Durham, N.C., Oct. 11, 1947; s. Horace Preston and Patsy Willis (Baker) H.; m. Judith Anne Depro, Aug. 17, 1969; children—Christopher Lee, Heather Linn. Student Wake Forest U., 1965-67; B.S., U. Md., 1969, M.D., 1973. Diplomate Am. Bd. Internal Medicine and Infectious Disease. Intern, U. Ala. Hosps., Birmingham, 1973-74, resident in internal medicine, 1974-76; fellow in infectious diseases U. Md., Balt., 1976-78; asst. prof. medicine Med. U. S.C., Charleston, 1978—, cons. Charleston Vets. Hosp., Treas. Boy Scouts Am., Troop 11 Boy Scouts. Mem. ACP, Infectious Diseases Soc. Am., Am. Soc. Microbiology, Am. Heart Assn., Charleston County Med. Assn., Sigma Xi, Alpha Omega Alpha. Methodist. Office: 171 Ashley Ave Charleston SC 29425

HOLLEY, JAMES W., III, dentist, mayor; m. Mary Walker Holley; children—Robin, James W. IV. B.S., W.Va. State Coll., 1949; D.D.S., Howard U. Practice dentistry specializing in dental surgery, Portsmouth, Va.; mem. Portsmouth City Council, 1968-80, 82-84; vice-mayor City of Portsmouth, 1978-80, mayor, 1984—; lectr. dental orgns.; chmn. subcom. on pub. transp. Commonwealth of Va. Dir. fin. com. ARC, Portsmouth; past chmn. Gosport Dist. Boy Scouts Am., mem. exec. bd. Tidewater Council; past pres. Portsmouth Central Civic Forum; bd. dirs. Child and Family Service, Maryview Hosp., W.Va. State Coll. Found.; past treas. Miller Day Nursery; mem. adv. com. Neighborhood Facility Study, Portsmouth; mem. adv. com. dept. nursing Norfolk State U.; trustee Obici House Hist. Restoration Com.; mem. budget com. Portsmouth United Way. Served with U.S. Army, World War II. Recipient Silver Beaver award Boy Scouts Am.; Medallion award Brighton Rocke AME Zion Ch., 1984; Appreciation award Cavalier Manor Police, 1984; Alumni award Howard U., 1985; Recognition award Mcpl. Fin. Commn., 1985; Salute to Black Mayors award Nat. Black Caucus State Legislators, 1984, numerous service awards from civic orgns. Mem. Am. Coll. Dentists, Acad. Gen. Dentistry, Am. Dental Assn., Black Conf. Mayors, Chgo. Dental Soc., John L. McGriff Dental Soc., Nat. Dental Assn. (recipient awards), Old Dominion Dental Soc., Pierre Fauchard Acad., Portsmouth Dental Soc., Tidewater Dental Assn., U.S. Conf. Mayors, Va. Dental Assn., Am. Soc. Planning Officials, NAACP (life), Nat. Naval Officers Assn., Negro Heritage Library, Smithsonian Assocs., Urban League Tidewater, Va. Citizens Planning Assn., Portsmouth C. of C. (dir.), Chi Delta Mu, Omega Psi Phi, Sigma Pi Phi, Am. Legion.

HOLLIDAY, CHARLES EDWARD, property management executive; b. Fayetteville, N.C., Oct. 12, 1942; s. Jasper Talbert and Louise (Price) H.; B.S., Va. Commonwealth U., 1975; m. Judith H., Apr. 10, 1971; children—Charles E., Danielle Nicole. Airline agt. United Airlines, So. Airways, Washington, 1967-70; asst. credit mgr. Washington Hilton Hotel, 1975; front office mgr. John Marshall Hotel, Richmond, Va., 1975; gen. mgr. Boar's Head Inn, Charlottesville, Va., 1975-79; v.p., dir. hotel ops. Hotel Mgmt. Corp., Sheraton Salisbury Inn (Md.) and Sheraton Potomac Inn, Rockville, Md., 1979-81; dist. dir. ops. Victor Mgmt. Co., Newport News, Va., 1982-86; dir. hotels Leadership Lodging Corp., Rockville, Md., 1986—. Mem. Albemarle County Sign Commn. Served with USAF, 1961-65. Mem. Va. Motel Assn. (dir.), Charlottesville-Albemarle Lodging Assn. (pres.), Charlottesville-Albemarle Tourism Com. Baptist. Home: 525 N 5th St Arlington VA 22203 Office: 6101 Montrose Rd Rockville MD 20852

HOLLIDAY, JACKSON RILEY, architect; b. Macon, Ga., Dec. 4, 1922; s. Peter O. and Martha Elizabeth (Riley) H.; m. Cordelia Dessau, Nov. 25, 1949; children—Martha Francis, Riley Dessau. B.S., Ga. Inst. Tech., 1948; B.Arch., 1949. Registered architect, Ga. Draftsman Dennis & Dennis Architects, Macon, 1949-53; prin. J.R. Holliday Architect, Macon, 1953-63, Matthews, Holliday, Couch & Hollis, Macon, 1964-76, Holliday, Couch, Hollis & Jelks, Macon, 1976—; dir. First Atlanta Bank, Macon. Mem. Macon Urban Devel. Authority, 1979—. Served to 1st lt., Signal Corps, U.S. Army, 1943-46. Mem.

AIA (pres. local chpt. 1960). Republican. Methodist. Lodge: Elks (com.) Avocations: boating; photography. Home: 373 Vista Circle Macon GA 31204 Office: Holliday Couch Hollis & Jelks 577 Mulberry St Macon GA 31202

HOLLIDAY, ROBERT KELVIN, newspaper executive, state senator; b. Logan, W.Va., Feb. 11, 1933; s. James Kelvin and Helen Kathleen H.; B.A., W.Va. Tech. U., 1954; M.A., Marshall U., 1955; children—Kelvin Edward, Kathleen Bressler, Stephen Kerr, Robert L. Co-owner, editor Montgomery (W.Va.) Herald, 1955—, Fayette Tribune, Oak Hill, W.Va., 1955—, Meadow River Post, Rainelle, W.Va., 1966—; mem. W.Va. Ho. of Dels., 1963-68, W.Va. Senate, 1968-72, 80—. Mem. W.Va. State Democratic Exec. Com., 1978-80. Served with U.S. Army. Presbyterian. Clubs: Fayette Needy Assn., Masons. AUthor: Test of Faith, About Montgomery, Our Chat, A Portrait of Fayette, Politics in Fayette County. Office: PO Box 137 Oak Hill WV 25901

HOLLIDAY, WILLIAM STEPHEN, petroleum geologist; b. San Antonio, Sept. 24, 1949; s. Frederick Joseph and Mildred Catherine (Schlosser) H.; m. Mary Virginia Essary, Dec. 23, 1972; children—Catherine, Sara. B.S., West Tex. State U., 1973. Geologist Coastal States Gas Corp., Amarillo, Tex., 1973-77; exploration geologist El Paso Natural Gas, Amarillo, 1977-79; sr. geologist Tex. Oil and Gas Corp., Corpus Christi, Tex., 1979—. Discoverer Oakville 9700 Sand, Live Oak County, Tex., 1980. Mem. Am. Assn. Petroleum Geologists, Am. Inst. Profl. Geologists, Corpus Christi Geol. Soc., Coastal Bend Geophys. Soc., Panhandle Geol. Soc. (treas. 1978-79). Avocations: wildlife photography; hunting and fishing; cutting precious gems; astronomy. Office: Tex Oil and Gas Corp 600 M Bank North Corpus Christi TX 78471

HOLLINGS, ERNEST FREDERICK, U.S. senator; b. Charleston, S.C., Jan. 1, 1922; s. Adolph G. and Wilhelmine D. (Meyer) H.; B.A., The Citadel, 1942; LL.B., U. S.C., 1947; m. Martha Patricia Salley, Mar. 30, 1946; children—Michael Milhous, Helen Hayne, Patricia Salley, Ernest Frederick III; m. Rita Liddy, Aug. 21, 1971. Bar: S.C. 1947; mem. S.C. Ho. of Reps., 1948-54, speaker pro tem, 1950-54; lt. gov. of S.C., 1955-59; gov. of S.C., 1959-63; practiced in Charleston, 1963-66; U.S. senator State of S.C., 1966—. Mem. Hoover Comm. on Intelligence Activities, 1954-55; mem. President's Adv. Comm. on Intergovtl. Relations, 1959-63; mem. exec. council Lutheran Ch. Am. Trustee Newberry Coll. Named one of Ten Outstanding Young Men, U.S. Jr. C. of C., 1954. Mem. Assn. Citadel Men, Hibernian Soc., Phi Delta Phi. Democrat. Lutheran. Club: Sertoma (Charleston). Office: Room 125 Russell Office Bldg Washington DC 20510

HOLLINGSWORTH, BOBBY J., mathematician; b. Sunset, Tex. Aug. 17, 1927; s. Ralph E. and Georgia (Davis) H.; B.S. in Civil Engring., La. Poly. Inst., 1949; M.S., Okla. A. and M. Coll., 1951; Ph.D., Kan. U., 1955; m. Bettie Rea Fox, June 8, 1953; children—Rebecca Rea, Lee Ann. With United Gas Corp., Shreveport, La., 1955-68, research mathematician, 1955-61, operations research asso., 1961-63, corporate planning asso., 1963-65, corporate devel. analyst, 1966-68, exec. asst. corporate finance, 1968-71; mgr. fin. analysis Pennzoil Co., Inc., Houston, 1971-78, v.p. mgmt. controls, 1978—; instr. math. evening div. Centenary Coll., 1959-65, La. Poly. at Barksdale AFB, 1965-68. Served with USNR, 1945-46. Mem. Am. Gas Assn. (research com. on transient flow 1962—), Am. Math. Soc., Soc. Indsl. and Applied Math., Canadian Math. Congress, Lambda Chi Alpha, Phi Kappa Phi. Democrat. Methodist. Home: 5339 Tilbury Houston TX 77056 Office: Pennzoil Pl PO Box 2967 Houston TX 77002

HOLLINS, PAMELA YOLONDA, physician; b. Baton Rouge, La., Aug. 26, 1952; d. Henry Huddleston and Ivory Mae (Yates) H. B.A., Dillard U., 1974; M.D., Meharry Med. Coll., 1978; postgrad. Tulane U. Med. Sch., 1978-81. Intern Tulane U. Affiliated Hosps., New Orleans, 1978-79, resident, 1979-81; staff physician Bayou Comprehensive Med. Ctr., Lake Charles, La., 1981—, med. dir., 1983—; Bd. dirs. Southwest La. Hospice Agy.; adv. bd. Big Bros./Big Sisters of Southwest La., Calcasieu Parish Heart Unit, Am. Heart Assn. Mem. La. State Med. Soc., Calcasieu Parish Med. Soc., Am. Soc. Internists, Delta Sigma Theta. Baptist. Office: 1733 Moeling St Lake Charles LA 70601

HOLLIS, CHARLES EUGENE, JR., savings and loan executive; b. Daytona Beach, Fla., Sept. 14, 1948; s. Charles Eugene and Betty Lou (Beech) H.; m. Carol Repass Hollis, Mar. 20, 1971; children—Stephanie Dyane, Charles Preston, Robin Jene. A.A., Dayton Beach Jr. Coll., 1968; B.A., U. South Fla., 1972. C.P.A., Fla. Asst., Deloitte Haskins & Sells, Tampa, Fla., 1972-73, sr. asst., 1973-75, sr., 1975-78, mgr., 1978-82; audit mgr. Jack Eckerd Corp., Clearwater, Fla., 1982-85; v.p. fin., controller Freedoms Savs. and Loan Assn., Tampa, 1985—. City councilman City of Temple Terrace, Fla., 1976—, vice mayor, 1981-82; chmn. fin. and taxation com. Fla. League Cities, Tallahassee, 1979-81; mem. fin. com. Nat. League Cities, Washington, 1980—; treas. Christ Our Redeemer Luth. Ch., 1984—. Recipient award Disting. Service, U. South Fla. Coll. Bus., 1972; Outstanding Alumnus award Beta Alpha Psi, 1983. Mem. Am. Inst. C.P.A.s, Fla. Soc. C.P.A.s, Nat. Assn. Accts., Municipal Fin. Officers Assn., Beta Alpha Psi. Democrat. Home: 809 Bannockburn Ave Temple Terrace FL 33617 Office: Freedom Savs and Loan Assn One N Dale Mabry Hwy Tampa FL 33630

HOLLIS, HARRIS WHITTON, state official, retired army officer; b. Richburg, S.C., June 25, 1919; s. William Gill and Gertha (Henderson) H.; B.S., Clemson U., 1942; postgrad. Inf. Sch., 1943, 49, Command and Gen. Staff Coll., 1953, Armed Forces Staff Coll., 1958, U.S. Naval War Coll., 1962; J.D., U. S.C., 1980; m. Anna Airheart, June 25, 1946; children—Harris Whitton, William Alexander. Commd. 2d lt. U.S. Army, 1942, advanced through grades to lt. gen., 1971; dep. comdr. 1st Field Force, comdr. 9th and 25th Inf. Divs., S. Vietnam, 1968-70; dep. chief of staff for personnel U.S. Army Europe and 7th Army, also chief Office of Res. Components, Dept. of Army, Washington, 1971-73; U.S. rep. Permanent Mil. Deps. Group, also chief U.S. element Central Treaty Orgn., 1973—; dir. S.C. Commn. on Continuing Lawyer Competence, 1980-86. Pres., Protestant Men of Chapel in Europe, 1970-71; mem. exec. bd. Transatlantic council Boy Scouts Am., 1970, chmn. Crusader dist., 1974; bd. mgrs. Army Emergency Relief, 1971-73; sr. warden St. Michael's Ch., Columbia, S.C., 1978, 83; mem. Columbia council USO. Decorated D.S.M. with two oak leaf clusters, Legion of Merit, D.F.C., Bronze Star medal, Air medal with 12 oak leaf clusters; recipient Disting. Alumni award Clemson U., 1973, George Washington Honor medal Freedoms Found., 1973. Mem. Assn. U.S. Army (pres. European dept. 1970, pres. Greater Columbia chpt. 1976), 25th Inf. Div., 9th Inf. Div. Octofoil Assn., Mil. Order World Wars. Episcopalian. Club: Rotary. Office: 3703 Overcreek Rd Columbia SC 29206

HOLLIS, MARY FERN CAUDILL, nurse, concert singer, author; b. Augusta, Ga., Mar. 13, 1942; d. Robert Paul and Ethel Fern (Alderton) Caudill; student Okla. Bapt. U., 1960-61, Memphis State U., 1961-62; B.Music Edn., U. Louisville, 1964; postgrad. George Peabody Coll. Tchrs., 1970-74, U. Tenn., Nashville, 1975-80; A.S. in Nursing, Tenn. State U., 1980; m. Harry Newcombe Hollis, Jr., Dec. 25, 1962; children—Harry III (dec.), Mary Melissa, Newcombe IV. Tchr. music, piano and vocal studies, 1962-75; profl. soloist, Louisville, 1962-69; concert soloist, Mid-South area, 1969—; mem., soloist Nashville Symphony Chorus and Orch., 1972-75; counselor Alive Hospice, Nashville, 1978—; registered nurse St. Thomas Hosp., Nashville, 1981-82; hospice nurse Alive Hospice, Nashville, 1982—, dir. pediatric program, 1984—; dir. nursing Home and Health Services of Nashville, 1985—. Mem. Nat. Oncology Nursing Soc., Middle Tenn. Oncology Nursing Soc. (historian 1981—), Nashville Bonsai Soc., Sigma Alpha Iota, Gamma Phi Beta. Baptist. Author: My Hedges Were Down, 1982; Out of My Suffering: Reflections of a Hospice Nurse, 1983; contbr. articles to profl. jours. Home: Nashville TN

HOLLIS, RHONDA KATRINA, nurse; b. Columbus, Ga., Apr. 13, 1950; d. Ernest J. and Ponjola DaMon (Brinson) H. B.S. in Nursing, Tuskegee Inst., 1972; M.S. in Nursing, Med. Coll. Ga., 1976. Staff nurse Crawford Long Hosp., Atlanta, 1972-73; charge nurse Ga. Mental Health Inst., Atlanta, 1973-76; pub. health nurse supr. Fulton County (Ga.) Health Dept., 1976—; instrn. specialist ARC. Recipient Vol. Community Service award ARC, 1980. Mem. Am. Pub. Health Assn., Nat. Black Nurses Assn. Baptist. Home: 3200 Stone Rd Apt D 13 Atlanta GA 30331 Office: Fulton County Health Dept 626 Parkway Dr Atlanta GA 30308

HOLLIS, WALTER JESSE, physician; b. Bossier City, La., Mar. 17, 1921; s. Charles Basil and Evie (Barber) H.; M.D., La. State U., 1945; m. Hazel Loree West, Dec. 22, 1945; children—Walter Jesse, Clara Jean, Mary Evelyn. Intern Charity Hosp. La., Shreveport, 1945-46, asst. resident, 1946-47, asso. resident, 1947-48, vis. physician, 1948-51; asst. in medicine Sch. Medicine, La. State U., New Orleans, 1948, mem. faculty, 1953—, prof. medicine, 1965-80, prof. emeritus, 1980—, dir. Student Health Service, 1955-77; practice gen. medicine, Bossier City and Shreveport, 1948-51; cardiologist Charity Hosp. La., New Orleans, 1956-64, sr. vis. physician, 1963—; med. examiner, cons. La. Dept. Pub. Welfare, New Orleans, 1960-71; cons. S.E. La. Hosp., Mandeville, 1953-59, electrocardiogram heart sta. Hotel Dieu Hosp., New Orleans, 1971-74; med. cons. Pike-Faller Meml. Clinic and Hosp., Kentwood, La., 1968-71; electrocardiographer La. State U. Pvt. Med. and Surg. Clinic, 1976-80. Served to capt. M.C., USAF, 1951-53. Diplomate Am. Bd. Internal Medicine. Fellow ACP; mem. La. Med. Soc., Orleans Parish, La. med. socs., Phi Chi, Alpha Omega Alpha. Baptist. Contbr. articles to profl. jours. Home: 761 Glouster Pl Gretna LA 70053

HOLLMAN, KENNETH WAYNE, insurance educator, researcher, consultant; b. Loretto, Tenn., Aug. 25, 1941; s. Willie S. and Ethel N. (Quillen) H. B.S., Middle Tenn. State U., 1965; M.B.A., U. Ala., 1966, Ph.D., 1970. C.L.U. Dir. Bur. Bus. Research, prof. econs. U. Miss., Oxford, 1970-82; Martin chair ins. Middle Tenn. State U., Murfreesboro, 1982—; cons. risk mgmt. Rutherford County Exec. Com., Murfreesboro, 1984—. Contbr. articles to profl. jours. Pres. Exchange Club Oxford, Miss., 1979. Served to sgt. U.S. Army, 1960-63. Named Outstanding Young Man, Am. Jaycees, 1978; recipient Research Excellence award Merritt Co., 1984; NDEA fellow, 1966-69. Mem. Am. Econ. Assn., Am. Risk Ins. Assn., Nat. Assn. Life Underwriters. Democrat. Avocation: numismatics. Home: 915 E Northfield Murfreesboro TN 37130 Office: Box 165 Middle Tenn State U Murfreesboro TN 37132

HOLLOMAN, HASKELL ANDREW, ret. judge, rancher; b. Frederick, Okla., Nov. 12, 1907; s. Andrew Harvey and Dora (Prophit) H.; student Okla. State U., 1926-27, U. Okla. Coll. Law., 1935-38; m. Cornelia Louise Lewis, May 23, 1940. Admitted to Okla. bar, 1938; county atty., Frederick, Okla., 1939-41; atty. for state examiner and insp., Oklahoma City, 1941-42; asst. atty. gen. Okla., 1946; county atty. Frederick, 1946-47, county judge, 1947-49, 52-69; spl. dist. judge Southwestern Okla. Dist., 1969-71. Dir. Tex.-Okla. Fair Assn., Tillman County Mental Health Assn.; dir., past pres. Tillman County Farmers Union Assn. Served from lt. (j.g.) to lt. comdr. USN, 1942-46. Mem. Okla. Assn. County Judges (past pres.), Am. Judicature Soc., Am. Legion, Okla., Caddo County, Tillman County (past pres.) bar assns., Okla. Jud. Conf., Okla.-Texas (director), Okla. (dir.) polled hereford assns., Tex.-Okla. (dir.), Red River Valley (past pres.), Big Pasture (dir.), Shortgrass (dir.) hereford assns., Southwestern Okla. Cattlemen's Assn. (dir.), Tillman County League of Young Democrats (past pres.), V.F.W. Democrat. Methodist. Kiwanian. Club: Frederick Golf and Country. Home: 1501 N 14th St Frederick OK 73542

HOLLOWAY, CARL CLAYTON, JR., petroleum engineer; b. Richland, Nebr., Aug. 6, 1939; s. Carl Clayton and Helen May (Turner) H.; m. Glenda Nell Westmoreland, Dec. 19, 1964; children—Jennie Lee, Carl Clayton. B.S., Okla. State U., 1962, M.S., 1963; Ph.D., U. Houston, 1968. Registered profl. engr., Okla. Design engr. Texaco, Inc., Port Arthur, Tex., 1963-64; reservoir engr. research and devel. Phillips Petroleum Co., Bartlesville, Okla., 1968-74, reservoir engr. computing dept., 1974-78, sr. reservoir engr. exploration and prodn. dept., 1978—. Mem. Soc. Petroleum Engrs., AIME. Republican. Baptist. Home: 1320 Grandview Bartlesville OK 74006 Office: Phillips Petroleum Co 342 FPB Bartlesville OK 74004

HOLLOWAY, DIANE ELAINE, psychotherapist; b. Tulsa, Oct. 19, 1937; d. Lawrence Lynn and Helen May (Six) Hatcher; B.S., Tex. Woman's U., 1972, M.A., 1974, Ph.D., 1979; m. B.W. Cheney, 1980; children—Brian, Kathleen. British rep. Study Abroad, Inc., London, 1957-59; psychologist Presbyn. Hosp., Dallas, 1970-75, dir. psychol. services and asso. dir. continuing edn. in psychiatry, 1976-78; mental health/mental retardation cons. Drug Rehab. and Law Enforcement Offices, Dallas County, 1975-77; psychotherapist in pvt. practice, Dallas, 1978—; asso. Pain Therapy Assn., Dallas, 1979—; pres. Security & Mgmt. Systems, Dallas, 1979-81; v.p. Mental Health Profl. Group, 1980—. Hogg Found. grantee, Southwestern Med. Sch., 1972-73; lic. psychotherapist, Tex.; registered criminologist, Tex. Mem. Am. Med. Writers Assn., Tex. Psychol. Assn., Am. Psychol. Assn., Tex. Police Assn., Internat. Assn. Chiefs of Police, Archaeol. Inst. Am., Soc. Police and Criminal Psychology, Mensa. Contbr. articles to profl. jours. Home: 11130 Cactus St Dallas TX 75238 Office: Suite 619 8210 Walnut Hill Dallas TX 75231

HOLLOWAY, ERNEST LEON, univ. pres.; b. Boley, Okla., Sept. 12, 1930; B.S., Langston U., 1952; M.S., Okla. State U., 1955; Ed.D., U. Okla., 1970; m. Jan. 19, 1957; children—Ernest L., Reginald, Norman. Tchr., prin. Boley High Sch., 1952-62; with Langston U., 1963—, prof. sci. higher edn., 1978—, v.p. adminstrn., 1975-77, acting pres., 1977-78, pres., 1979—; cons. in field. Mem. Okla. Higher Edn. Alumni Council, Nat. Assn. State Univs. and Land-Grant Colls., Nat. Assn. Equal Opportunity in Higher Edn., Langston U. Alumni Assn., Alpha Phi Alpha, Phi Delta Kappa. Clubs: Lions, Shriners. Home: PO Box 666 Langston OK 73050 Office: PO Box 907 Langston U Langston OK 73050

HOLLOWAY, GERALDINE BUFORD, librarian, educator; b. Chgo., Jan. 2, 1929; d. Samuel and Emma L. (Walker) Buford; m. Clarence W. Holloway, Nov. 3, 1951; children—Emma, Clarissa, Clarence W., Lynne, Lynda, Sheila, Gerald, Patrick. B.S. in L.S., Ala. State U., 1951; M.S. in L.S., Our Lady of Lake, 1974. Librarian, Baldwin County High Sch., Daphne, Ala., 1951-52, Ala. State Coll. br., 1952-57; acquisitions librarian St. Philip's Coll., San Antonio, 1973—. Mem. ALA, Tex. Library Assn., Tex. Jr. and Community Coll. Assn., Bexar Library Assn. (pres. 1979). Democrat. Roman Catholic. Club: San Antonio. Home: 7623 Stagecoach St San Antonio TX 78227 Office: 2111 Nevada St San Antonio TX 78203

HOLLOWAY, HELEN JEANNETTE, accountant, real estate developer; b. Chilton, Tex., June 11, 1927; d. J.B. and Della Mae (Stuessel) Roberts; m. Howard E. Holloway, May 27, 1950. B.B.A., U. Corpus Christi, 1954. C.P.A., Tex. Tax adviser ind. oil ops., Corpus Christi, Tex., 1955-60; dealer John Deere Indsl. Equipment, Corpus Christi, 1960-64; owner Dryden & Holloway Co., C.P.A.s, Corpus Christi, 1964—. Bd. dirs. Coastal Bend Youth City, Driscoll, Tex., 1972—; adv. dir. Children's Heart Inst. Tex., Corpus Christi, 1980—, YMCA Bd, 1985. Recipient Profl. Woman of Yr. award YWCA, Corpus Christi, 1981. Mem. Tex. Soc. C.P.A.s, Corpus Christi Soc. C.P.A.s, Am. Inst. S.P.A.s, Estate Planning Council, Exec. Women Internat. Methodist. Home: 4018 Lowman St Corpus Christi TX 78411 Office: Dryden & Holloway Co CPAs 700 Everhart Terr Corpus Christi TX 78411

HOLLOWAY, LEONARD L(EVENE), association executive, clergyman; b. Ada, Okla., Mar. 23, 1923; s. Leonard L. and Mamie B. H.; m. Betty Gould, May 20, 1944; children—Shalia Kay, Jamie Lynn. B.A., Okla. Baptist U., 1948; M.A., U. Okla., 1949, M.S., 1962, D.D. (hon.), 1958. Ordained to ministry Baptist Church, 1951; cert. pub. relations cons. Dir. pub. relations Bapt. Gen. Conv. Tex., 1953-59; v.p., mem. faculty So. Bapt. Theol. Sem., Louisville, 1960-63; v.p., mem. faculty New Orleans Bapt. Theol. Sem., 1963-65; pres. Mary Hardin-Baylor Coll., 1965-68; pres. U. Corpus Christi (Tex.), 1968-70; exec. staff H. E. Butt Found., Kerrville, Tex., 1970-84; exec. v.p. Kerrville C. of C.; dir. Nat. Bank of Commerce, Kerrville; cons. in field; speaker. Chmn. bd. devel. Tex. Bapt. Children's Home, Tex. Republicans' Com.; pres. Hill Country Music Found., Elderly Housing Found., bd. dirs. Hill Country Arts and Crafts Found.; mem. research council Kerrville State Hosp. Served with USAAF, 1941-45; served to lt. col. USAF, 1951-53. Decorated D.F.C., Air medal with oak leaf clusters. Mem. Assn. Humanistic Psychology, Nat. Semantics Soc. Author: Model Program of Church Public Relations, 1951; Encounter with God, 1972; editor Newsbriefs, 1973; contbr. articles to publs. Home: 803 Bow Ln Kerrville TX 78028 Office: PO Box 670 Kerrville TX 78028

HOLLOWAY, MARVIN LAWRENCE, automobile club executive; b. Gordon, Ga., May 27, 1911; s. Percy Thomas and Lillie Mae (Bozeman) H.; m. Elizabeth Kirkland, Feb. 14, 1948. B.A., Wofford Coll., 1933. Sec., mgr. Peninsula Motor Club, Tampa, Fla., 1938-53, pres., 1953-76, chmn. bd., 1976-80, chmn. bd., chief exec. officer, 1980—; bd. dirs. Am. Automobile Assn., 1974—; chmn. eastern conf. AAA Motor Clubs, 1960-62, Southeastern Conf., 1974. Recipient Achievement award U. Tampa, 1955, Top Mgmt. award Sales and Mktg. Execs. of Tampa, 1983, Dynamic Leadership award Southeastern Conf. AAA Clubs, 1983, Disting. Service award Wofford Coll., 1983, Disting. Service award Fla. Sheriffs' Assn., 1984; named Mr. Motorist, AAA Clubs Fla., 1982. Mem. Blue Key, Scabbard and Blade, Sr. Order Gnomes, Pi Kappa Phi. Republican. Home: 49 Whippoorwill Ln Wesley Chapel FL 34249 Office: 1515 N Westshore Blvd Tampa FL 33607

HOLLOWAY, STRICKLAND, JR., insurance company executive; lawyer; b. Statesboro, Ga., June 25, 1951; s. Strickland and Nanilou (Tucker) H.; m. Pamela Morris, Dec. 18, 1971; children—Strickland III, Whitney Lauren, Morris Ashton. B.B.A., U. Ga., 1973, J.D., 1976. Bar: Ga. 1976, U.S. Dist. Ct. (so. dist.) Ga. 1976; lic. real estate broker, Ga. Ptnr. Neville, Neville & Holloway, Statesboro, 1976-78; sr. ptnr. Holloway, Quick & Boren, Statesboro, 1978-81; pres. Legaline, Inc., Atlanta, 1981—; pres., v.p., dir. Pizza Inn of Dublin, Inc. (Ga.), 1979—; v.p., dir. Pizza of Albany, Inc. (Ga.), 1983—, Rocheser's, Original Recipes, Inc., Dublin, 1983—. Recipient Merit award U. Ga., 1969. Mem. State Bar Assn. Ga., Ga. Assn. Criminal Def. Lawyers, High Mus. Art, Sigma Nu. Baptist. Club: U. Ga. Alumni Found. Pres.'s. Home: 3395 Mathieson Dr Atlanta GA 30305 Office: Legaline Inc 7 Piedmont Ctr Suite 414 Atlanta GA 30305

HOLLOWAY, WARREN ARVLE, III, publishing company executive; b. New Orleans, July 13, 1955; s. Warren Arvle and Delores Philamene (Duplex) H. B.A., La. State U., 1978. News editor St. Tammany Guide, 1978-80; copywriter Swigart, 1980-81, account exec., 1981-82; account mgr. Peter A. Mayer Advt., New Orleans, 1982-83; gen. mgr. Newswheel's Pub. Corp., Jefferson, La., 1983—. Campaign chmn. United Way, New Orleans region, 1983. Mem. Am. Advt. Fedn., Advt. Club New Orleans (Addy award 1981). Democrat. Methodist. Club: La. State Auto Boosters. Editor Banklines, 1981, St. Tammary Guide, 1978-80. Office: 300 Jefferson Hwy Jefferson LA 70121

HOLLOWAY, WILLIAM, JR., judge U.S. Ct. Appeals 10th Circuit. Oklahoma City. Office: US Ct of Appeals 10th Circuit PO Box 1767 Oklahoma City OK 73101*

HOLM, GARY LUNDE, army officer; b. Rugby, N.D., Oct. 31, 1947; s. Albert Christopher and Bertina (Lunde) H.; m. Kiyoko Kong, June 14, 1969; children—Mijiko, Christopher, Sonja, Tina. B.S. in Edn., U. N.D., 1974; Ed.M., Boston U., 1978; student Minot State Coll., 1965-66, U. Minn., 1967-68. Commd. 2d lt., U.S. Army, 1967, advanced through grades to capt., 1979; asst. comptroller U.S. Army Air Def. Command, Europe, 1976-78; dep. fin. officer Ft. Dix, N.J., 1978-79; asst. fed. aid coordinator of N.D., Bismarck, 1979-81; dep. fin. officer U.S. Army, Japan, Tokyo, 1981-85; budget officer U.S. Army Operational Evaluation Agy., Washington, 1985—; cons. Dept. Pub. Inst., State of N.D., 1985—. Mem. Gov.'s Re-election Com., State of N.D., 1980; chmn. Carter-Mondale Re-election campaign, Mandan, N.D., 1980; active various Dem. campaigns; chmn. Hoffner for Congress com., N.D., 1966. Recipient Internat. Peace Gardner award, State of N.D., 1981; Medal of Appreciation, Japan Armed Forces Assn., 1985; Cert. of Appreciation, Republic of Korea Nat. Assembly, 1973. Mem. Assn. of Govt. Accts., Am. Soc. Mil. Comptrollers (pres. 1983-84), NEA, Assn. U.S. Army, Mil. Retirees Assn. Japan, V.F.W. Lodges: Toastmasters, Sons of Norway. Home: 6718 Capstan Dr Annandale VA 22003 Office: US Army OTEA 5600 Columbia Pike Falls Church VA 22041

HOLMAN, ROBERT CHARLES, mathematical statistician; b. St. Petersburg, Fla., Dec. 27, 1950; s. Robert Cecil and Maria Ann (Panzarino) H.; m. Roberta Katherine Portaro, Dec. 15, 1973; children—Ryan Robert, Brandon Robert. B.A., U. South Fla., 1972; M.S., Ga. State U., 1980. Stock forecaster Western Electric Co., Norcross, Ga., 1973-76; statistician Ctr. for Disease Control Bur. Epidemiology, Viral Diseases div., Atlanta, 1976-81, math. statistician Ctr. for Prevention Services, Diabetes Control Div., 1981-83, Ctr. for Infectious Diseases, div. Host Factors, 1983—. Contbr. articles to profl. jours. Mem. Am. Statis. Assn., Sigma Xi, Alpha Tau Omega (sec.). Club: River Oak Village (Lawrenceville, Ga.). Avocations: tennis; photography. Home: 705 Westbrook Pl Lawrenceville GA 30245 Office: Ctrs for Disease Control 1600 Clifton Rd Atlanta GA 30333

HOLMBERG, ALBERT WILLIAM, JR., publishing executive; b. Orange, N.J., Sept. 18, 1923; s. Albert William and Margaret (Flanagan) H.; B.S. in Bus. Adminstrn., Lehigh U., 1947; m. Dorothy McCollum, Oct. 27, 1945 (div. Apr. 1972); children—Jeanne (Mrs. Fletcher J. Johnson) Margaret D. (Mrs. Roy D. Duckworth III), Ellen T., m. 2d, Ruth Sulzberger Golden, May 26, 1972. With N.Y. Times, 1947-70, circulation mgr., 1964-70; pres., gen. mgr. Chattanooga Times, 1970—; pres., dir. Times Pub. Co. Served to 1st lt. USAAF, World War II. Clubs: Rotary, Mountain City (Chattanooga). Home: 1108 Cumberland Rd Chattanooga TN 37419 Office: 117 E 10th St Chattanooga TN 37401

HOLMES, ANNA-MARIE, ballerina, ballet mistress; b. Mission City, B.C., Can., Apr. 17, 1946; came to U.S., 1981; d. George Henery and Maxine Marie (Botterill) Ellerbeck; m. David Holmes, 1962; 1 dau., Lian-Marie. Student U. B.C.; diploma Royal Conservatory of Music. Appeared in Swan Lake, Cinderella, Romeo and Juliet, Sleeping Beauty, Bayadere, Laurencia, Paquita, Graduation Ball, Les Sylphides, Prince Igor, Giselle, Nutcracker, Firebird, Raymonda; guest appearances at numerous theatres including: Berlin Staarts Opera, Royal Albert Hall, London, Roy Alex, Toronto, Ont., Royal Festival Hall, London, Teatro Colon, Buenos Aires, Covent Garden, London; danced with Kirov Ballet, Leningrad, 1963; featured ballerina in dance films including Tour En L'Air, Ballet Adagio, Don Juan, Chinese Nightengale; numerous appearances on European and North Am. TV; artistic dir., prin. choreographer Tenn. Festival Ballet, Oak Ridge, 1981—; mng. dir. Peforming Arts/Dance Ctr., Oak Ridge, 1982—; co-dir. ballet co. Massimo Opera Theate, Palermo, Italy, 1982-83; guest tchr. Nervi Festival, Genoa, Italy; lectr. in field. Producer film documentation of Kirov Vagonova Teaching system. Office: Tenn Festival Ballet 140 Mitchell Rd Oak Ridge TN 37830

HOLMES, DARRELL E., state senator; b. Kanawha County, W.Va., Oct. 19, 1934; s. Russell J. and Macel F. (Carpenter) H.; m. Nell Jean Kiser, Jan. 17, 1950; children—David E., Gregory A., Eric J. Millright. Student Morris Harvey Coll., W.Va. State Coll. Mem. W.Va. Ho. of Dels., 1974-82, W.Va. Senate, 1983—, chmn. labor com. Served with USAF. Mem. Internat. Assn. Machinists. Democrat. Baptist. Lodge: Masons. Office: W Va Senate Charleston WV 25305*

HOLMES, GARY LEE, naval officer; b. Hamilton, Ohio, May 29, 1954; s. Roger Lee and Judith (Daughters) H. B.A. with high distinction in math., U. Va., 1976; postgrad. U.S. Navy Nuclear Power Sch., 1976-77, Submarine Sch., 1977-78. Commd. ensign U.S. Navy, 1976, advanced through grades to lt., 1980—, elec. officer new constrn. fast attack submarine USS Birmingham, 1978-79, damage control asst., 1979-80, weapons officer, 1980-81, electronics officer, 1981-82; detached from Birmingham, 1982, assigned as asst. nuclear propulsion program coordinator NROTC hdqrs., Pensacola, Fla., 1982—. Decorated Naval Achievement medal. Methodist. Office: CNET Code N535 NAS Pensacola FL 32508

HOLMES, JACK DAVID LAZARUS, forensic historian; b. Long Branch, N.J., July 4, 1930; s. John Daniel Lazarus and Waltrude Helen (Hendrickson) H.; B.A. cum laude, Fla. State U., 1952; M.A., U. Fla., 1953; postgrad. Universidad Nacional Autonoma de Mexico, 1954; Ph.D., U. Tex. at Austin, 1959; m. Anne Elizabeth Anthony, Sept. 6, 1952 (div. Dec. 1965); children—David H., Jack Forrest, Ann M.; m. Martha Rachel Austin, Feb. 11, 1966 (div. June 1967); m. Gayle Jeanette Pannell, July 1967 (div. 1970); 1 child, Daniel; m. Stephanie Pasneker, Apr. 10, 1971, 1 child, Sean Burkett. Instr. history Memphis State U., 1956-58; asst. prof. McNeese State U., Lake Charles, La., 1959-61; lectr. U. Md. at Constantina, Spain, 1962; assoc. prof. U. Ala. in Birmingham, 1963-68, prof., 1968-79. Reading clk. Fla. Ho. of Reps., 1955; reporter-photographer Memphis Press-Scimitar, 1957-58; hist. cons., 1962—; cons. U.S. Parks Service, 1962, Pensacola (Fla.) Hist. Commn., 1969-70, New Orleans Cabildo Museum, 1968-73, Nat. Endowment Humanities, 1972-83, Miss. Dept. Archives-History, 1978—, Boundary of Mississippi Sound: U.S., Ala. and Miss., 1980-85, Granadero de Galvez Hidalgo of San Antonio, 1981, State of La., 1983—, Mowa Indians, 1983—; dispatcher off-shore oil drilling rig, Gulf of Mexico, 1982. Served with inf. AUS, 1951. Created knight, cruz de caballero Royal Order Isabel La Catolica (Spain), 1979; Charles W. Hackett fellow, 1959; Am. Philos. Soc. fellow, 1961, 66; Fulbright fellow, 1961-62; Assn. State and Local History grantee, 1966, award of merit, 1978; U. Ala. grantee, 1964, 66, 68, 72, 74-79; Mexican Govt. grantee, 1954. Mem. Tenn. Squires, So. (life mem.), La. (dir. 1977-78) hist. assns., Miss., Fla. hist. socs., Soc. History of Discoveries, Am. Assn. Geographers, Phi Beta Kappa, Phi Kappa Phi, Sigma Delta Pi, Phi Alpha Theta, Pi Kappa Phi. Author: Documentos ineditos para la historia de la Luisiana, 1963; Gayoso, 1965; Honor and Fidelity, 1965; Jose de Evia, 1968; Francis Baily's Journal, 1969; New Orleans: Facts and Legends, 1970; Luis de Onis Memoria, 1969; Guide to Spanish Louisiana, 1970; New Orleans Drinks and How to Mix Them, 1973; History of the University of Alabama Hospitals and Clinics, 1974; The 1779 Marcha de Galvez: Louisiana's Giant Step Forward in the American Revolution, 1974; Gálvez 1981; Stephen Minor, 1983; editor, dir. La. Collection Series, 1965—; contbr.: French in Mississippi Valley, 1965; Frenchmen and French Ways in Mississippi Valley, 1969; Spanish in Mississippi Valley, 1974; Handbook of Texas, Vol. 3, 1978; Cardinales de dos Independencias, 1978; Readings in Louisiana History, 1978; Ency. So. History, 1979, Acad. Am. Ency., 1980, LaSalle and his Legacy, 1982; Anglo-Spanish Confrontation on the Gulf Coast, 1982; Louisiana's Legal Heritage, 1983. also numerous articles to U.S. and fgn. hist. jours. Home: 520 S 22d Ave Birmingham AL 35205

HOLMES, JAMES STEVENS, JR., utility company executive; b. Jackson, Miss., May 21, 1926; s. James Stevens and Frances Glynn (Tyler) H.; m. Dorothy Miriam Singletary, June 11, 1951; children—James Stevens III, Benjamin Ford III. B.S., Millsaps Coll., 1948; B.S., Ga. Inst. Tech., 1950, M.S., 1950. With So. Bell Tel. & Tel. Co., 1957—, gen. mgr., Atlanta, 1966-71, dir. labor relations, 1971-82, sec., 1982—. Bd. dirs. United Way, Atlanta, 1968, Jr. Achievement, Atlanta, 1979; scoutmaster Atlanta Area council Boy Scouts Am., 1970-76; trustee Gerontology Ctr., Ga. State U., 1983—. Served to comdr. USN, 1944-47, ETO. Decorated comdr. Mil. Order Stars and Bars. Fellow Alpha Epsilon Delta; mem. SAR, Sons of Confederate Vets. Republican. Mem. Christian and Missionary Alliance Ch. Lodge: Lions (pres. Louisville 1951-54). Home: 2216 Springwood Dr Decatur GA 30033 Office: So Bell Tel & Tel Co 675 W Peachtree NE Room 42P75 Atlanta GA 30374

HOLMES, LEONARD GEORGE, psychologist, educational administrator, researcher; b. Roanoke, Va., May 31, 1954; s. George Washington and Mary Maxine (Templeton) H.; m. Susan Rose Tankersley, June 19, 1976; children—Allison Gayle, Mary Kathleen. B.A. in Psychology and Religious Studies with high distinction, U. Va., 1976; M.S. in Clin. Psychology, Fla. State U., 1979, Ph.D., 1981. Lic. clin. psychologist, Va. Psychology intern William S. Hall Psychiat. Inst., Columbia, S.C., 1980-81; lectr., clin. psychologist Ctr. for Psychol. Services, Coll. of William and Mary, Williamsburg, Va., 1981—, asst. dir., 1984—; practice clin. psychology, Williamsburg, 1984—; cons. Westinghouse Health Systems. Univ. fellow Fla. State U., 1977-78, 79-80. Mem. Am. Psychol. Assn., Southeastern Psychol. Assn., Phi Kappa Phi. Avocations: gardening, computers, camping, hiking. Home: 104 Viking Rd Williamsburg VA 23185 Office: Ctr Psychol Services Coll of William and Mary Williamsburg VA 23185

HOLMES, MALCOLM HERBERT, telecommunications company executive; b. London, Nov. 11, 1934; U.S., 1975; s. Harold and Gladys H.; m. Veronica Menezes, June 26, 1982. Grad., Scotland, 1956. Pres. Jamaica Telephone, Kingston, 1970-75; v.p. eastern region Continental Telephone, Washington, 1975-79, v.p. fin., Atlanta, 1979-82; exec. v.p. fin. Continental Telecom. Inc., Atlanta, 1982-83, exec. v.p. ops., 1983-85, exec. v.p., chief fin. officer, 1985—. Mem. Fin. Execs. Inst., Brit. Inst. Mgmt., Inst. Chartered Accts. Scotland. Home: 120 Laurel Dr Atlanta GA 30342 Office: Continental Telecom Inc 245 Perimeter Center Pkwy Atlanta GA 30346

HOLMES, MARTHA HAYDEN KENDALL, social worker; b. Sayre, Okla., Aug. 5, 1945; d. James Milton and Mary Marie (Hayden) Kendall; B.Music, U. Okla., 1970, M.S.W., 1976; m. Fred William Holmes, Sept. 11, 1965 (dec. 1967). Sec., asso. Dist. Atty., Beckham County, Sayre, 1965-67; social worker Beckham County Welfare Dept., 1970-72; supr. child abuse unit Oklahoma County Child Welfare, Oklahoma City, 1974-75, social worker, 1973-74, 76; social worker neonatal ICU, Okla. Children's Meml. Hosp., Oklahoma City, 1977—; mem. adv. council Passageway Shelter for Battered Women, 1982-83; mem. adv. bd. Parent to Parent. Mem. affirmative action com. The Meadows. Mem. Acad. Cert. Social Workers, Nat. Assn. Social Workers (program chmn. Oklahoma City unit 1977-78), Nat. Assn. Perinatal Social Workers (dir., nat. sec. 1980-83), Forum for Death Edn. and Counseling, Okla. Group Process Soc., UN Assn., Oklahoma City Women's Polit. Caucus (membership chmn. 1981-82), Women in Community Service, AAUW, OK-ERA Coalition, Sigma Alpha Iota. Club: Zonta (dir. v.p. 1981-83, pres. 1983-85). Home: 3319 N Youngs Blvd Oklahoma City OK 73112 Office: 940 NE 13th St Oklahoma City OK 73104

HOLMES, MARY JIM, nurse; b. Winfield, Ala., May 10, 1931; d. Elisha Jefferson and Desmer Louise (Young) Hawkins; m. James Russell Holmes, May 15, 1954; 1 child, Jimmie Carol. R.N., Bapt. Meml. Sch. Nursing, 1953. Staff nurse Ivy Meml. Hosp., West Point, Miss., 1953-55, supr., asst. dir. nurses, then dir. of nurses, 1960-68, operating room supr., 1969-76; office nurse Flowers-McCharen Clinic, West Point, 1955-60; staff-head nurse Columbus Hosp., Miss., 1968-69; operating room supr., central service mgr. Golden Triangle Regional Med. Ctr., Columbus, 1976—. Mem. Assn. Operating Room Nurses (northeast chpt. pres. 1975-76, 79-80), Am. Soc. Hosp. Central Service Personnel, Internat. Assn. Hosp. Central Services Mgrs. Baptist. Avocations: cooking; sewing; travel; reading. Home: 252 N City Limit Rd West Point MS 39773 Office: Golden Triangle Regional Med Ctr 2520 5th St N Columbus MS 38701

HOLMES, NICHOLAS HANSON, III, architect; b. Mobile, Ala., Sept. 21, 1952; s. Nicholas Hanson Jr. and Nancy Ann (Neiswender) H.; m. Lucille Strother Little, Dec. 30, 1978; children—Kate Garrett, Clara Little. B. Forestry, Auburn U., 1976, B. Environ. Design, 1978, B. Arch., 1978. Technician HABS, Talequah, Okla., Summer 1975—; draughtsman Arch Winter, Planner, Mobile, summer 1977; N.H. Holmes Architect, Mobile, 1978-83; ptnr. Holmes & Holmes Architects, Mobile, 1983—. Mem. AIA (treas. local chpt. 1983-84), chmn. hist. resources com. Ala. council 1985—). Episcopalian. Lodge: Rotary. Avocations: art; hunting; fishing. Office: Holmes & Holmes Architects 257 N Conception St Mobile AL 36603

HOLMES, PAUL HERMON, government official; b. Nashville, Mar. 30, 1939; s. Dennis Hawkins and Fransena (Cooper) H.; m. Bonnie Marie McIntyre, Sept. 5, 1965; 1 child, Alison Cooper. B.S., U. Tenn., 1965, M.A., 1971. Tchr. polit. sci. U. Tenn., Knoxville, 1968-70; editor, writer TVA, Knoxville, 1971-74, asst. Washington rep., Washington, 1974-78, asst. chief Citizen Action Office, Knoxville, 1978-84, chief mgmt. services, land and econ. resources. 1984—. Contbr. articles to newspapers and mags. Served to SP-4 U.S. Army, 1957-60, Korea, Japan. Ford Found. grantee, 1968-70. Mem. Sons of Am. Revolution, Sons of Confederacy, Nat. Geneal. Soc., Tenn. Hist. Soc., East Tenn. Hist. Soc., West Tenn. Hist. Soc., Nat. Press Club, Sigma Delta Chi, Phi Kappa Phi, Delta Gamma Sigma. Avocations: writing; genealogy; reading; fishing; gardening. Home: Route 2 Box 1025 Stage Coach Rd Friendsville TN 37737 Office: TVA Div Land and Econ Resources 2F73 Old City Hall Knoxville TN 37902

HOLMES, PRESLEY DIXON, public broadcasting executive; b. Chgo., Apr. 11, 1929; s. Presley D. and Mildred R. (Rufsvold) H.; m. Cynthia J. Waites, Dec. 1, 1956; children—Karen, Margret, Kristin, Neil, Reid. B.A., U. Mich., 1950, M.A., 1951; cert. Sorbonne U., Paris, 1954; Ph.D., Wayne State U., 1959. Adminstrv. asst., asst. prof. Wayne State U., Detroit, 1957-62; assoc. dean, prof. Ohio U., Athens, 1962-70; dir. broadcasting Sta. WOUB-AM-FM-TV, 1964-70; dir., v.p. Nat. Assn. Ednl. Broadcasters, Pub. Broadcasting Service, Nat. Pub. Radio, Washington, 1970-77; pres. Chgo. Met. Higher Edn. Council, 1977-82; exec. dir. W.Va. Edn. Broadcasting Authority, Charleston, W.Va., 1982—; mem. vis. prof. com. U. Charleston, W.Va., 1984—; mem. curriculum com. W.Va. State U., Institute, 1984—; cons. AID, PBS, Washington. Producer TV programs, 1959-64. Mem. Olympia Fields Planning Council, Ill., 1981-82; pres. Carlmar Place Owners Assn., Charleston, W.Va., 1983—; bd. dirs. Edn. Network for Older Adults, Chgo., 1978-80, WBEZ Adv. Com., Chgo., 1978-80; mem. Martin Luther King, Jr. Holiday Commn., 1985—. Served with U.S. Army, 1951-53. Recipient Service award NAEB-ETS, Washington, 1973, Key award W.Va. U. Broadcast Ctr., Morgantown, 1983. Mem. So. Ednl. Communications Assn., Internat. Inst. Communication, Sigma Delta Chi. Avocations: filmmaking; remodeling. Office: 1900 Washington St E Suite B-424 Charleston WV 25305

HOLMES, ROSCETTE YVONNE, ednl. adminstr., consultant; b. Portland, Oreg., Dec. 1, 1944; d. Roscoe Warfield and Burnadine (Langston) Lewis; B.S., Tex. So. U., 1965, M.S., 1970, now postgrad.; cert. in adminstrn. and supervision U. Houston, 1979; m. Johnny Mason Holmes, Jr., July 28, 1971; children—Roderick Earl, Andriette Yvonne. With Houston Ind. Sch. Dist., 1965—, sch. tchr. E.O. Smith Jr. High Sch., 1965-69, tchr. biology, coordinator sch. sci. fair, sponsor student council Madison Sr. High Sch., 1970-74, sci. content team mem. Emergency Sch. Aid Act, 1974-76, staff devel. specialist for tchr. tng. in sci., English, math, and social studies, 1976-78, instructional specialist for sci. Area I, 1978-81; asst. prin. Hogg Middle Sch., 1981—; owner, operator Roscette's Diversified Services, cons. for devel. needs; cons. Prairie View, Tchr. Corp, Peace Corps, 1976-78; cons. Ednl. Leadership Inst., Prescription Learning Inc. NSF ednl. grantee, 1968-70. Mem. Nat. Sci. Tchrs. Assn., Tex. Assn. Sci. Tchrs., Met. Assn. Tchrs. of Sci., Met. Chemistry Tchrs. Assn., Assn. for Supervision and Curriculum Devel., Houston Profl. Adminstrs. (exec. bd.), Expt. in Internat. Living, Coalition of 100 Black Women, Delta Sigma Theta (voter registration, Sch. after Sch. Project, hypertension screening, v.p., dean of probates, 1967, v.p., 1980-81, com. chmn., pres. suburban Houston-Ft. Bend Alumnae chpt. 1981-83, voting del. to nat. conv. 1981, del. regional conv. 1982), Beta Beta Beta, Beta Kappa Chi, Phi Delta Kappa. Democrat. Episcopalian. Home: 7607 Fawn Terrace Dr Houston TX 77071 Office: 1100 Merrill St Houston TX 77009

HOLOWAY, THEODORE RODNEY, elec. engr.; b. Springfield, Mass., Oct. 11, 1949; s. Clayton Frank and Irene (Siemaszko) H.; B.S. in E.E. with honors, U. Tenn., 1972, postgrad., 1979-81; postgrad. Middle Tenn. State U., 1981—. Elec. maintenance engr. Scottish Inns of Am., Knoxville, 1973-77; with Sverdrup Tech./ARO, Inc., Tullahoma, Tenn., 1977—, project lead elec. engr.-indsl. computer automation, 1980—. Mem. IEEE, Middle Tenn. Soc. Profl. Engrs. (Young Engr. of Yr. award 1981). Methodist. Clubs: Kiwanis, Toastmasters, Masons, Shriners. Home: 506 Reavis St PO Box 1111 Tullahoma TN 37388 Office: Sverdrup Tech Inc Engine Test Facility Arnold Engring Devel Center Tullahoma TN 37389

HOLSINGER, JAMES WILSON, JR., physician; b. Kansas City, Kans., May 11, 1939; s. James Wilson and Ruth Leona (Reitz) H.; student Duke U., 1957-60, M.D., 1964, Ph.D., 1968; M.S., U. S.C., 1981; m. Barbara Jenn Craig, Dec. 28, 1963; children—Anna Elizabeth, Martha Ruth, Sarah Frances, Rachel Catherine. Intern, Duke Hosp., Durham, N.C., 1964, resident in surgery, 1965, fellow in thoracic surgery, 1966; fellow in anatomy Duke U., Durham, 1966-68; resident in surgery U. Fla., Gainesville, 1968-70, fellow in cardiology, 1970-72; with VA, 1969—, chief of staff VA Med. Center, Augusta, Ga., 1978-81, dir. Hunter Holmes McGuire VA Med. Center, Richmond, Va., 1981—; prof. medicine and anatomy Med. Coll. Ga., Augusta, 1978-81; prof. medicine and health adminstrn. Med. Coll. Va., Richmond, 1981—, asst. v.p. for health scis., 1985—. Mem. com. evangelism N. Ga. conf. United Meth. Ch., 1980-81; bd. discipleship Va. Conf. United Meth. Ch., 1982—; mem. com. 80, World Meth. Council, 1981—; bd. laity Va. Conf., United Meth. Ch., 1985—; mem. World Meth. Council, 1986—. Served to col. M.C. USAR, 1983—. Fellow Am. Coll. Cardiology, ACP; mem. Am. Coll. Hosp. Adminstrs., Am. Assn. Anatomists, Am. Heart Assn. (fellow clin. council), Soc. Am. Magicians, Internat. Brotherhood Magicians. Republican. Author/editor med. books; contbr. articles to med. and religious publs. Home: 8915 Tresco Rd Richmond VA 23229 Office: Hunter Holmes McGuire VA Ctr 1201 Broad Rock Blvd VA Med Center Richmond VA 23249

HOLT, BERTHA MERRILL, state legislator; b. Eufaula, Ala., Aug. 16, 1916; d. William Hoadley and Bertha Harden (Moore) Merrill; A.B., Agnes Scott Coll., 1938; LL.B., U. Ala., 1941; m. Winfield Clary Holt, Mar. 14, 1942; children—Harriet Wharton Holt Whitley, William Merrill, Winfield Jefferson. Bar: Ala. 1941. With Treasury Dept., Washington, 1941-42, Dept. Interior, Washington, 1942-43; mem. N.C. Ho. of Reps., 1975—, chmn. legis. ethics com., 1980, chmn. constl. amendment com., 1983, mem. Joint Commn. Govtl. Ops., 1982—. Pres., Democratic Women of Alamance, 1962, chmn. hdqrs., 1964, 68; mem. N.C. Dem. Exec. Com., 1964-75; pres. Episcopal Ch. Women, 1968; sr. warden vestry Ch. of Holy Comforter, 1974; mem. council N.C. Episc. Diocese, 1972-74, 83-86, chmn. fin. dept., 1973-75, parish grant com., 1973-80, mem. standing com., 1975-78, chmn. budget com., 1986; chmn. Alamance County Social Services Bd., 1970; mem. N.C. Bd. Sci. and Tech., 1979-82. Recipient Outstanding Alumna award Agnes Scott Coll., 1978; legis. award N.C. Nurses Assn., 1979, Family Group Homes, 1981, Hospice of N.C., 1983, Health Educators Assn., 1985. Mem. Women's Forum N.C., Law Alumni Assn. U. N.C. Chapel Hill (dir.), N.C. Bar Assn., NOW, English Speaking Union, N.C. Hist. Soc., Les Amis du Vin, Pi Beta Phi. Club: Century Book. Office: PO Box 111 Burlington NC 27215

HOLT, CHARLES ASBURY, economics educator; b. Richmond, Va., Oct. 2, 1948; s. Charles Asbury and Josephene (Hannah) H.; m. Mary Zanne Macdonald, Jan. 31, 1971; children—Abbi Anne, Sarah Holliday. B.A., Washington and Lee U., 1970; M.S., Carnegie-Mellon U., 1974, Ph.D., 1977. Asst. prof. econs. U. Minn.-Mpls., 1976-82, assoc. prof., 1982-83; assoc. prof. U. Va., Charlottesville, 1983—, dir. undergrad. studies in econs., 1984—; cons. FTC, Washington, 1982—. Assoc. editor Atlantic Econ. Jour., 1982-85. Contbr. articles to profl. jours., chpt. to book. Served to E4 USNR, 1971-73. Recipient Savage Dissertation award NBER-NSF, 1977, Henderson Dissertation award Carnegie-Mellon U., 1977. Mem. Econometric Soc., Am. Econ. Assn., Atlantic Econ. Assn., So. Econ. Assn., Western Econ. Assn. Home: 1641 Oxford Rd Charlottesville VA 22903 Office: Dept Econ Rouss Hall U Va 114 Charlottesville VA 22901

HOLT, CHERYL ADAMS, archaeologist; b. Neodesha, Kans., Jan. 5, 1947; d. John Elvin and Pennie (Cobb) Adams; m. Herbert Allen Holt, July 15, 1967. B.A., George Washington U., 1976; M.A., Case Western Res. U., 1978; postgrad. Brandeis U., 1981. Lab. asst. Alexandria (Va.) Archaeology Lab., 1974-76; survey archaeologist Mus. Natural History, Cleve., 1976-77, field archaeologist, lab. asst., 1977, survey archaeologist, 1977; field archaeologist Western Ill. U., Macomb, 1978, Iroquois Research Inst., Fairfax, Va., 1979; sr. archaeologist Soil Systems, Inc., Alexandria, 1982—; reviewer Nat. Endowment for Humanities, 1979—. George Washington U. bd. trustees scholar, 1976; Brandeis U. anthropology scholar, 1979-81; Tannenbaum fellow, 1979-81. Mem. Am. Anthropol. Assn., Soc. Am. Archaeology. Contbr. articles to profl. jours. Home: 909 Cameron St Alexandria VA 22314 Office: 711 Pendleton St Alexandria VA 22314

HOLT, DAVID EARL, librarian; b. Magna, Utah, May, 17, 1928; s. William Renold and Jenny (Kerr) H.; m. Mary Elizabeth Black, Apr. 30, 1955; children—Helen Lorraine, Jane Elizabeth, David Renold (dec.), Steven Earl. Student, U. Utah, 1946-47, 52-54, 58-59; B.A., Brigham Young U., 1957, M.A., 1958; M.S., Emory U., 1963. Library dir. Hayner Pub. Library, Alton, Ill., 1963-65; dir. libraries Waco-McLennan County Library, Waco, Tex., 1965-67; dir. Austin (Tex.) Pub. Library, 1967—; book editor Austin Am.-Statesman, 1967-69; staff Library/U.S.A. Exhibit, Fed. Pavilion, New York Worlds Fair, 1965; tchr. library adminstrn. Baylor U., 1966; columnist Waco Herald-Tribune, 1967. Trombonist, Sonny Dunham Orch., Tony Pastor Orch., Glenn Gray Orch., Gene Krupa Orch., Tex Beneke Orch., 1947-52; trombonist, arranger, Tommy Dorsey Orch., 1954-55; Editor: Waco Rotary Club Bull, 1966-67; Contbr. articles profl. jours. Mem. ALA, Tex. Library Assn., S.W. Library Assn. Mormon. Lodge: Rotary. Address: 1802 Forest Trail Austin TX 78703

HOLT, JOHN B, theologian; b. Abilene, Tex., June 15, 1915; s. Holland and Emma Cleora (Morriset) H.; B.S., McMurray Coll., 1937, D.D. (hon.), 1954; postgrad. U. Tex., 1938-39, U. Chgo., 1958; M.Th., So. Meth. U., 1945; D.D. (hon.), Paul Quinn Coll., 1962; m. Margaret Ann Buster, Feb. 14, 1940; children—John Michael, Stephen Lee, Paul Holland. Youth dir. Central Tex. Conf., United Meth. Ch., 1941-43; ordained to ministry United Meth. Ch., 1944; exec. sec. Bd. Edn., 1944-46; asso. pastor Austin Ave. Meth. Ch., Waco, Tex., 1946-48; pastor Knox Ch., Manila, 1948-58; asso. dean Perkins Sch. Theology, So. Meth. U., Dallas, 1958—; sec. Gen. Conf. United Meth. Ch., 1973—. Trustee, Mary Johnston Hosp., Union Theol. Sem., Am. Bible Soc., Philippine Christian Coll. Clubs: Kiwanis, Masons. Author: Our Methodist Heritage, 1952; A Study Guide for the Book of Acts, 1956; Financial Aid for Seminarians, 1966. Editor Perkins Perspective, 1958-72. Contbr. articles to mags. and jours. Home: 3420 Centenary Dr Dallas TX 75225 Office: Perkins Sch Theology So Meth U Dallas TX 75275

HOLT, JOHN D., law enforcement official. Chief of police, Memphis. Office: City Hall 125 N Mid America Mall Memphis TN 38103*

HOLT, MILDRED FRANCES, educator; b. Lorain, Ohio, July 30, 1932; d. William Henry and Rachel (Pierce) Daniels; B.S., U. Md., 1962, M.Ed., 1967, Ph.D., 1977; m. Maurice Lee Holt, Sept. 11, 1949 (dec.); children—Claudia, Frances, William, Rudi. Tchr. spl. edn. St. Mary's (Md.) County Public Schs., 1962-64, coordinator Felix Johnson Spl. Edn. Center, 1964-66; demonstration tchr. spl. edn. U. Md., College Park, summer 1970, instr. spl. edn. dept. Coll. Edn., 1969-73; supr. spl. edn. Calvert and St. Mary's (Md.) Counties, 1968-69; asso. prof. spl. edn. West Liberty (W.Va.) State Coll., 1973-75; asst. prof. Eastern Ill. U., Charleston, 1975-77; supr. spl. edn. Warren County Public Schs., Front Royal, Va., 1977-85; educator Dallas Ind. Sch. Dist., 1985—. Mem. NEA, Warren County Edn. Assn., Council Exceptional Children, Assn. for Gifted, Assn. Supervision and Curriculum Devel., Va. Edn. Assn., Va. Council Exceptional Children, Blue Ridge Orgn. Gifted and Talented, Assn. Children with Learning Disabilities, Nat. Assn. Gifted Children, Phi Theta Kappa, Kappa Delta Pi. Contbr. articles to profl. jours.; author: Reach Guidebook, 1979. Office: Dallas Ind Sch Dist Dallas TX

HOLT, SMITH LEWIS, university administrator; b. Ponca City, Okla., Dec. 8, 1938; s. Smith Lewis and Esther (Doepel) H.; m. Elizabeth Manners, Aug. 24, 1963; children—Alexandra, Smith III. B.Sc., Northwestern U., 1961; Ph.D., Brown U., 1965. Asst. prof. chemistry Poly. Inst. Bklyn., 1966-69; from assoc. prof. to prof. chemistry U. Wyo., Laramie, 1969-78; head chemistry dept., prof. chemistry U. Ga., Athens, 1978-80; prof. chemistry, dean arts and scis. Okla. State U., Stillwater, 1980—; mem. corp. Inorganic Syntheses, 1975—; mem. profl. standards bd. Okla. Bd. Edn., 1983—; trustee Okla. Middle Level Edn. Assn., 1983—. Editor: Solid State Chemistry, a Contemporary Overview, 1980; Inorganic Reactions in Organized Media, 1982; Inorganic Syntheses, Vol. 22, 1983. Contbr. articles to profl jours. Trustee Okla. Found. for Humanities, 1983—. Recipient Paul Simon award Central States Fgn. Lang. Assn., 1984; Advanced Placement Spl. Recognition award Coll. Bd. S.W. Region, 1985. Mem. Am. Chem. Soc., Am. Assn. for Higher Edn., AAAS, Sigma Xi. Home: 2807 Fox Ledge Ln Stillwater OK 74074 Office: Okla State U 201 LSE Stillwater OK 74078

HOLT, THOMAS CARLYLE, geophysical consultant; b. Kopperl, Tex., Nov. 18, 1919; s. Thomas A.C. and Mason Agusta (Gardner) H.; m. Ruth V. Hiatt, Sept. 27, 1942; children—Nancy Joan, Lucianne, Nathan C., Jessie Marie. B.A., U. Colo., 1945. Various positions The Superior Oil Co., various locations, 1946-72, v.p. geophysics, Houston, 1972-79; dir. Conquest Exploration Co., Houston, Anders Energy Corp, Conroe, Tex. Served to 1st lt., USAF, 1943-45. Mem. Soc. Exploration Geophysicist, Am. Assn. Petroleum Geologist. Republican. Club: Lakewood Yacht (Seabrook). Avocation: sailing. Home: Route 1 Box 875 Dickinson TX 77539

HOLTON, WILLIAM COFFEEN, electrical engineering corporation executive; b. Washington, July 24, 1930; s. William B. and Esther (Coffeen) H.; m. Mary Schaeffer, Aug. 5, 1953; children—Elizabeth, William, Sarah Anne. B.S. in Physics, U. N.C., 1952; Ph.D. in Physics, U. Ill., 1960. With Tex. Instruments Inc., 1960-84, mem. tech. staff solid state physics, Corp. Research Labs., 1960-65, mgr. quantum electronics, 1965-72, dir. advanced components lab., 1972-78, dir. research, devel. and engring., Semicondr. Group, Dallas, 1978-84; dir. Microstructure Scis. Semicondr. Research Corp., Research Triangle Park, N.C., 1984—; researcher in field. Served to lt. j.g. USN, 1952-54. Recipient J. Daniels award, 1952, Best Paper award, Soc. for Info. Display, 1978; Union Carbide fellow, 1959. Fellow IEEE, Am. Phys. Soc. (div. solid state physics); mem. Phi Beta Kappa, Phi Eta Sigma. Presbyterian. Contbr. writings to publs., patentee in field. Home: 601 Brookview Dr Chapel Hill NC 27514 Office: Semiconductor Research Corp PO Box 12053 Research Triangle Park NC 27709

HOLTZ, NOEL, neurologist; b. N.Y.C., Sept. 13, 1943; s. Irving and Lillian H.; B.A., NYU, 1965; M.D., U. Cin., 1969; m. Carol Sue Smith, June 9, 1968; children—Pamela Wendy, Aaron David, Daniel Judah. Intern, Cin. Gen. Hosp., 1969-70; resident in internal medicine and neurology Emory U., Atlanta, 1970-71, 73-76; practice medicine specializing in neurology, Marietta, Ga., 1977—; mem. faculty Emory U. Coll. Medicine, Atlanta, 1977—, asst. prof. dept. neurology, 1977—; mem. staffs Kennestone Hosp., Grady Meml. Hosp. Co-author: Conceptual Human Physiology, 1985. Served with USN, 1971-73. Diplomate Am. Bd. Psychiatry and Neurology. Mem. Am. Acad. Neurology, Ga. Neurol. Soc., Alpha Omega Alpha. Office: 522 North Ave Marietta GA 30060

HOLTZCLAW, DEBORAH KAY, commercial artist; b. Monroe, La., May 16, 1956; d. Robert Pervis and Carolyn Jean (Gunter) H. B.F.A., N.E. La. U., 1978. Owner graphic arts studio and printing firm, Dallas, 1979—. Mem. Monroe Advt. League, Farmers Br. Bus. C. of C. (coms.), Graphic Artists Guild, Printing Industries Am., Nat. Composition Assn., Am. Quick Printers Am., Quick Printers Tex., Alpha Omicron Pi, Theta Xi, Chi Omega, Kappa Pi. Republican. Mem. Christian Ch.

HOLTZMAN, ABRAHAM, political science educator; b. Detroit, Nov. 3, 1921; s. Morris and Rebecca H.; m. Sylvia Hochfield, Dec. 16, 1947; children—Joshua Peter, Adam Paul, Seth Matthew. B.A., UCLA, 1943, M.A., 1947; M.A., Harvard U., 1950, Ph.D., 1952. Teaching asst. UCLA, 1945-47; teaching fellow Harvard U., 1950-52; instr. Dartmouth Coll., 1952-53; asst. to chmn. Democratic Nat. Com., Washington, 1954; prof. polit. sci. N.C. State U., Raleigh, 1955—. Author: Interest Groups and Lobbying, 1966; Legislative Liaison: Executive Leadership in Congress, 1970; American Government; Ideals and Reality, 1980, 84. Contbr. articles to profl. jours. Mem. N.C. Gov.'s Coordinating Com. on Aging, 1960, Labor Force Devel. Council, 1978-79, Pvt. Industry Council, 1979-80, Conf. on Aging, 1981; grant co-dir. The Constitution: Continuity and Conflict, NEH, 1983-87. Named Disting. Classroom Tchr. N.C. State U., Raleigh, 1959-60, 64-65, Outstanding Tchr., 1965-66, 71-72, Alumni Disting. Prof., 1974-77. Mem. AAUP, Am. Polit. Sci. Assn., N.C. Polit. Sci. Assn., So. Polit. Sci. Assn. (mem. exec. council 1980-83), Am. Profs. for Peace in Middle East, Nat. Com. for an Effective Congress. Home: 3606 Alamance St Raleigh NC 27609 Office: NC State U Dept Polit Sci Box 8102 Raleigh NC 27695

HOLTZMAN, GARY YALE, company executive; b. N.Y.C., Aug. 7, 1936; s. Abram and Pearl (Kashetsky) H.; m. Alice A. Lang, Sept. 5, 1958; children—Bruce, Sheri, Michele. B.B.A., CCNY, 1958. Exec. v.p. control and ops. Jordan Marsh Co., Miami, 1980—. Bd. dirs. Dade County Safety Council, Miami, 1978—, South Fla. Jewish Community Ctr., Miami, 1983—, Fla. Bus. Roundtable, Miami, 1975-80; bd. advisers Opportunities Industrialization Ctr., Miami, 1982—; v.p. Michael-Ann Russell Jewish Community Ctr., Miami, 1982—, Temple Adath Yeshurun, Miami; active Fla. Jewish Fedn., United Way of Dade County. Served to lt. U.S. Army, 1958-59; capt. USAR, 1958-65. Recipient Americanism award Anti-Defamation League, 1983; Adath Yeshurun Man of Yr. award, 1978. Mem. Greater Miami C. of C., Fla. Retail Fedn. Democrat. Office: Jordan Marsh Co 1501 Biscayne Blvd Miami FL 33132

HOLYER, ROBERT KENT, theologian, educator; b. Sioux Falls, S.D., Mar. 31, 1946; m. Karen Elizabeth Steinbinder, Sept. 5, 1970; children—Christiana Elizabeth, James Bentley Bringhurst, John Michael Milford, Margaret Alexandra. B.A. summa cum laude, Bethel Coll., 1968; postgrad. Westminster Theol. Seminary, 1968-69; B.D., Yale U., 1971; Ph.D., U. Cambridge (Eng.), 1978. Asst. prof. religion dept. religious studies U. Va., Charlottesville, 1976-79; asst. prof. dept. religion Converse Coll., Spartanburg, S.C., 1979—, chmn. spl. events and lectures com.; freshman advisor, honors com., founder, chmn. Converse Film Soc., pre-law adv. com., chmn. humanities div. com. on curriculum revision, 1982-83, chmn. dept. religion. Bethel Coll. Honors scholar, 1966-68; Cambridge U. (Eng.) Pembroke Coll. Bethune-Baker fellow, 1974-75; U. Va. Dean's List of Disting. Tchrs., 1979. Mem. Am. Acad. Religion, Soc. Christian Philosophers, Soc. Philosophy Religion. Democrat. Lutheran. Contbr. to theol. publs. Home: 437 N Park Dr Spartanburg SC 29302 Office: Converse College Dept Religion Spartanburg SC 29301

HOLZWORTH, MONTA LAVERN, nuclear power company executive; b. Barberton, Ohio, June 21, 1923; s. Monta Dean and Ruth Elizabeth (Wardell) H.; m. Frances Marie Fager, June 18, 1949; children—Donald Alan, Marie-Laverne, Peter Dale, Monta Raymond, Clara Frances. B.S., U. Notre Dame, 1947, M.S., 1949; Ph.D., Ohio State U., 1952. Metallurgist, Battelle Meml. Inst., 1948-50; research assoc. Ohio State U., 1950-52; research supr. Du Pont Corp., Aiken, S.C., 1952-62, staff metallurgist, 1962-78, sr. editor Savannah River plant, Aiken, S.C., 1978—; instr. metallurgy U. S.C.-Aiken. Active Boy Scouts Am., 1955-80. Served with USMC, 1943-45. Mem. Sigma Xi. Presbyterian. Lodge: Masons. Contbr. articles to profl. jours. Home: 816 Woodlawn Ave North Augusta SC 29841 Office: Savannah River Plant Aiken SC 29801

HOMEWOOD, GEORGE MORGAN, JR., management consultant; b. Annapolis, Md., Aug. 3, 1924; s. George Morgan and Ellen Sharpless (Marlin) H.; m. Katrina Margaret Stolp, Apr. 21, 1956; 1 son, George Morgan III. Chem.E., U. Del., 1949; B.S. in Mktg., Syracuse U., 1950. Market analyst Atlas Powder Co., Wilmington, Del., 1950-55; mktg. research mgr. J.T. Baker Chem. Co., Phillipsburg, N.J., 1955-62, Va.-Carolina Chem. Co., Richmond, Va., 1962-65; pres. Morwood Assocs., Richmond, 1965—; owner Gen. Bus. Services, Richmond, 1973—; instr. small bus. mgmt. Henrico Mgmt. Ctr., 1973-76; mem. dist. adv. council SBA, 1975-82, vice-chmn., 1978-79, Va. legis. coordinator, 1975-80. Dist. chmn. Boy Scouts Am., Richmond, 1965-67, 73-75, chmn. various coms. 1976—, exec. com. U.S. Power Squadron, Wilmington, 1953-55; sailing chmn. Wilmington YMCA, 1953-55; chmn. water transp. Del. Civil Def., 1954-55; v.p. Hoguenot Little League, Richmond, 1969-72; mem. parents adv. com. Richmond Pub. Schs., 1973-75; mem. Pub. TV Auction Com., Richmond, 1977—; adv. bd. Jobs for Va. Grads., 1982—. Served with USNR, 1943-46. Recipient award of merit Boy Scouts Am., 1973, Silver Beaver award 1979. Mem. Am. Mktg. Assn. (chpt. v.p. 1959-61), Am. Chem. Soc., Comml. Devel. Assn. (exec. com. 1963-64), Chem. Mktg. Research Assn. (exec. com. 1964-65), Nat. Soc. Pub. Accts. Mem. Moravian Ch. (trustee, 1957-62, elder 1981—). Clubs: Masons, Shriners. Author: Auto Parts Distribution-Profit Opportunities, 1973; Outdoor Recreation Business-Profit Opportunities, 1974; Small Business Tax Newsletter, 1978—. Office: 9613 Northridge Ct Richmond VA 23235

HOMMES, FRITS AUKUSTINUS, educator; b. Bellingwolde, Netherlands, May 28, 1934; came to U.S., 1979; s. Aukustinus and Anje (Wester) H.; M.Sc. in Chemistry, U. Groningen (Netherlands), 1951-58; Ph.D., U. Nijmegen (Netherlands), 1961; m. Grietje Renes, June 14, 1958; children—Peter, Anneliek. Research asst. dept. biochemistry U. Nijmegen, 1959-61; postdoctoral fellow dept. biochemistry and biophysics U. Pa., Phila., 1961-63; instr. dept. biochemistry U. Nijmegen, 1963-66; head lab. dept. pediatrics U. Groningen, 1966-72, asso. prof., 1972-79; prof. dept. cell and molecular biology Med. Coll. Ga., Augusta, 1979—, dir. biochem. genetics lab., 1980—; cons. genetic diseases Dutch Health Council, 1974-79; chmn. Dutch Bioenergetics Study Group, 1975-77. Chmn.. Groningen chpt. Round Table, 1970-71, No. Dist., Netherlands, 1973-75, mem. nat. bd., 1974-75. Fulbright fellow, 1961-63; ASBC lectr., 1965. Mem. European Soc. Pediatric Research, Soc. Study of Inborn Errors of Metabolism, Am. Soc. Biol. Chemists, Soc. Inherited Metabolic Disease, Am. Soc. Human Genetics, AAAS, N.Y. Acad. Sci. Roman Catholic. Lodge: Rotary. Author: Inborn Errors of Metabolism, 1973; Normal and Pathological Development of Energy Metabolism, 1975; Models for the Study of Inborn Errors of Metabolism, 1979; editorial bd. Nutrition & Metabolism, 1975—; contbr. articles to profl. jours. Patentee. Home: 793 Brookfield Pkwy Augusta GA 30907 Office: Dept Cell and Molecular Biology Med Coll Ga Augusta GA 30912

HON, RALPH CLIFFORD, arbitrator; b. Jonesboro, Ark., Jan. 29, 1903; s. Earl Augustus and Mary Oma (Little) H.; m. Hazel McLain, July 14, 1930. Student Central Methodist U., 1920-23; A.B., U. Ill., 1924; M.A., Harvard U., 1926; Ph.D., U. N.C., 1930; postgrad. Am. U., 1928-29. Prof. econs. and bus. adminstrn. Nebr. Wesleyan U., Lincoln, 1929-31, Southwestern at Memphis, 1931-73; vis. prof. Duke U., Durhan, N.C., 1941-43; fin. analyst SEC, Phila., 1943-46; prof. emeritus Rhodes Coll., Memphis, 1973—. Mem. Nat. Acad. Arbitrators, So. Econ. Assn. (past pres. 1941-42). Home: 1760 Jackson Ave Memphis TN 38107 Office: Rhodes Coll 2000 N Parkway Memphis TN 38112

HONABLUE, VALRIE (MAE) BIGGS, pathologist; consultant; b. Bocas Del Toro, Panama, Apr. 16, 1951; came to U.S., 1969; d. Abraham Lincoln and Tharzabell (McKenzie) Biggs; m. Richard Roderick Honablue, July 19, 1973; children—Richard, Xavier, Michael. B.S., Oakwood Coll., 1973; M.S., M.D., Meharry Med. Coll., 1977. Resident in pathology Eastern Va. Grad. Sch. Medicine, Norfolk, 1977-81; pathologist, dir. lab. services Whittaker Meml. Hosp., Newport News, Va., 1981—; cons. obesity clinic. Bd. dirs. Child Devel. Resources, Williamsburg, Va., 1983—; chairperson Civic League of Concerned Citizens, Williamsburg, 1984—. Mem. Assn. Practitioners in Infection Control, Peninsula Med. Soc., Alpha Kappa Alpha. Seventh-day Adventist. Club: Yokettes (Williamsburg). Home: 22 Bray Wood Williamsburg VA 23185

HONIG, ORIE CHARLES, retired energy company executive; b. Dallas, Sept. 24, 1918; s. Orie Charles and Bennie May (Pendley) H.; m. Jean Davis, Feb. 5, 1944; children—Lawrence Edward, Philip Charles, Susan Randolph. B.B.A., U. Tex., 1940; M.B.A., Harvard U., 1943. Co-founder, exec. v.p., dir. Alaska Interstate Co. (now Enstar Corp.), Houston, 1966-70, pres., 1970-74, chief exec. officer, 1974, chmn. bd., 1975-84. Served with U.S. Army, 1943-46. Republican. Presbyterian. Clubs: Harvard, River Oaks Country, University. Home: 10 S Briar Hollow Ln No 65 Houston TX 77027

HOOD, CHARLES HURLBURT, advertising agency executive; b. Cedar Rapids, Iowa, June 23, 1938; s. Charles Manrose and Pauline B. (Hurlburt) H.; B.J., U. Mo., 1960; m. Judy Drew Frost, Apr. 2, 1977; children by previous marriage—Cindy, Cary, Cathy. Advt. copywriter Sears Roebuck & Co., Chgo., 1960-61; copywriter, account exec. Wilson Advt. Agency, Tulsa, 1962-63; account exec. Whitney Advt. Agency, Tulsa, 1963-66; dir. advt. and pub. relations Unit Rig & Equipment Co., Tulsa, 1967; account supr., account exec. Ackerman Advt. Agency, Tulsa, 1968-69; chmn. bd. Hood-Hope & Assos., Inc., Tulsa, 1970—. Recipient Am. Advt. Fedn. Silver Addy award. Mem. Am. Assn. Advt. Agys. (chmn. Okla. council). Republican. Presbyterian. Clubs: Cedar Ridge Country, Tulsa Petroleum, Tulsa So. Tennis. Office: 8023 E 63d Pl Tulsa OK 74153

HOOD, DARDEN GWALTNEY, geologist, research company executive; b. Norfolk, Va., Mar. 12, 1958; s. Donald Eugene and Margaret Darden (Gwaltney) H.; m. Teresa Ann Nunenkamp, Aug. 1, 1981. B.S., U. Miami, 19-. Technician Beta Analytic, Miami, 1980-82; sr. geochronologist Alpha Analytic, Miami, 1982-83; pres. Hood Research Inc., Miami, 1983—; sr. geochronologist Alpha/Beta Analytic, Miami, 1983—. Clubs: Jacksonville Univ. Water Skiers (v.p. 1977-78); Geodessy (v.p. 1979-80) (U. Miami). Home: 7621 SW 138 Court Miami FL 33183 Office: Hood Research Inc PO Box 248519 Coral Gables FL 33124

HOOD, DOROTHY, artist; b. Bryan, Tex., Aug. 22, 1919; d. Frank and Earl and Georgianna B. (Simpkins) H.; B.A., R.I. Sch. Design, 1940; student Art Students League N.Y., 1940. Tchr., Houston Mus. Sch. Mus. Fine Art, 1961-79; artist-in-residence across U.S., 1974—; one-man exhibits McNay Art Inst., San Antonio, 1978, Phila. Art Alliance, 1961, Witte Meml. Mus., San Antonio, 1965, Contemporary Arts Mus., Houston, 1970, Rice U., Houston, 1971, Everson Mus., Syracuse, N.Y., 1972, 74, 76, Mus. Fine Arts, Houston, 1963, 74, Tibor de Nagy Gallery, N.Y.C., 1974, Internat. Kunstmesse, Basel, Switzerland, 1974, Michener Galleries, U. Tex., Austin, 1975, Mus. S. Tex., 1976, retrospective U. Houston, 1978, Meredith Long Contemporaries, N.Y.C., 1978, 80, Kunstverein, Berlin, 1983-84, Salzburg Kuntsverein, 1983, Palazzio Lichenstein, Vienna, 1983, others; group shows include: Am. Acad. Arts and Letters, N.Y.C., 1975, Kunsthalle, Dusseldorf, W. Ger., McNay Art Inst., 1976, Meredith Long Contemporaries, N.Y.C., Everson Mus., 1976, 78, Edmonton Art Gallery, 1977, Tamarind Inst., Albuquerque, 1979; setting for ballet Allen's Landing, Bicentennial Celebration Houston Ballet, 1975, settings for Toronto Truck Theater's Gold for the Golds celebration, Royal Ont. Mus., 1976; represented in permanent collections including: Mus. Modern Art, N.Y.C., Phila. Mus. Art, San Francisco Mus. Modern Art, Santa Barbara (Calif.) Mus. Art, Whitney Mus. Am. Art, N.Y.C., Worcester (Mass.) Art Mus., LaJolla (Calif.) Mus., Meml. Found., Houston, other instl. collections in Switzerland, Mexico City, U.S. Recipient Childe Hassam award Am. Acad. Arts and Letters, 1973; Mayor's award Houston, 1983.

HOOD, DOROTHY HUSTON, accountant; b. Louisville, May 17, 1924; d. Elijah Northcutt and Vida Fern (Carpenter) Huston; B.S.B.A., U. Louisville, 1981; m. James Clifton Hood, Jan. 4, 1940; children—Gloria Hood Costanzo, Barbara Hood Kidd, James Clifton. Mgr. classification, control and research IRS, Louisville, 1951-61, conferee, 1961-66, tax auditor, 1966-73, internal revenue agt., 1973—; exec. v.p., nat. treas. Employee Union chpt. 25, Louisville, 1981. Sec.-treas. Louisville and Jefferson County Youth Orch., 1958-61. Recipient Superior Performance awards IRS, 1965, 80, Spl. Service award, 1974. Mem. Am. Soc. Women Accts. Methodist. Home: PO Box 907 Louisville KY 40201 Office: PO Box 1146 Louisville KY 40201

HOOD, EMILY JANE, dental hygiene educator; b. Peebles, Ohio, Oct. 22, 1945; d. Glenn Leroy and Alma (Day) Hook; m. Paul H. Carr, Jr., Aug. 31, 1968 (div. 1974); m. C. Wayne Hood, Dec. 8, 1984; 1 stepchild, Christopher. B.S., Ohio State U., 1967; M.Edn., U. Cin., 1972. Lic. dental hygienist, Ohio, Ind., Colo.; cert. dental asst. Instr., asst. prof. U. Cin., 1968-75; asst. prof., program supr. Ind. U. N.W., Gary, 1975-77; asst. prof. U. Colo., Denver, 1977-83; program chmn. dental hygiene St. Petersburg Jr. Coll., Fla., 1983—. Manuscript rev. bd. Dental Hygiene, 1983—; contbr. articles to dental hygiene jours. Mem. Am. Dental Hygiene Assn., Am. Assn. Dental Schs., Met. Denver Dental Hygienists' Soc. (pres. 1980-81), Kappa Delta Pi. Presbyterian.

HOOD, MARY BRYAN, museum director, painter; b. Central City, Ky., July 5, 1938; d. Irving B. and Mary Louise (Anderson) Cayce; m. Ronnie L. Hood, Oct. 16, 1960. Student Ky. Wesleyan Coll., 1956-59, 68-73. Exec. dir. Owensboro Arts Commn., Ky., 1974-76; founding dir. Owensboro Mus. Fine Art, 1976—. Author/editor exhbn. catalogues. Mem. exec. com. Ky. Citizens for Arts, 1980—, Owensboro Arts Commn., 1977—; mem. Ky. Arts Commn., 1974-76; bd. dirs. Owensboro Symphony, 1975-76, Owensboro Area Mus., 1970-72, Theatre Workshop Owensboro, 1968-70; chair Owensboro Mayor's Arts Com., 1970-75. Mary Bryan Hood Day named in her honor, Owensboro, 1974. Mem. Southeastern Mus. Conf., Am. Assn. Mus., Ky. Assn. Mus. (pres. 1980-82). Office: Owensboro Mus Fine Art 901 Frederica St Owensboro KY 42301

HOOD, WILLIAM DOUGLAS, financial executive; b. Frankfort, Fed. Republic Germany, Mar. 19, 1959 (parents Am. citizens); s. William Robert and Mattielene (Abercrombie) H.; m. Leslie Marilea Spivey, June 15, 1979. B.B.A., North Ga. Coll., 1981. Bank officer Bank South, Forest Park, Ga., 1981-83; loan officer Atlantic Bank, Orlando, Fla., 1983-84; S.E. rep. ITT Small Bus. Fin. Corp., Atlanta, 1984—; speaker, cons. SBA, Orlando and Atlanta, 1984—. Exec. dir. Jr. Achievement, 1982; bd. dirs. Am. Cancer Soc., 1983, United Way, 1983. Recipient Ga. gov.'s citation for work with Jr. Achievement, 1983. Mem. Ga. Indsl. Developers Assn., Sigma Chi, Theta Epsilon. Democrat. Baptist. Avocations: refinishing antiques; fishing. Home: 2659 J Delk Rd Marietta GA 30067 Office: ITT Small Bus Finance Corp 100 Galleria Pkwy Tower 1 Suite 400 Atlanta GA 30339

HOOD, WILLIAM WAYNE, JR., lawyer; b. Tulsa, July 22, 1941; s. William Wayne and Alys (Charles) H.; children—W. Wayne III, Kristina L. B.A., U. Okla., 1963; LL.B., U. Tulsa, 1966. Bar: Okla. 1966, U.S. Dist. Ct. (no. dist.) Okla. 1966. Sole practice, Tulsa, 1966-70; pub. defender Tulsa County, 1966-68; ptnr. firm Hood & Lindsey, Tulsa, 1970—. Served to maj. JAGC, USAR, 1966—. Fellow Am. Acad. Matrimonial Lawyers (v.p. 1986—); mem. ABA, Okla. Bar Assn. (dir. continuing legal edn.-family law 1980-84, chmn. family law sect. 1975-77, 80-82), Tulsa County Bar Assn. (exec. com. 1979), Okla., Trial Lawyers Assn. (family law editor The Adv. 1979—1979-84). Republican. Roman Catholic. Office: Hood & Lindsey 1914 S Boston Tulsa OK 74119

HOODENPYLE, RICHARD LEE, peridontist; b. Gainesville, Ga., Aug. 16, 1946; s. Hugh Charles and Colleen (Hughes) H.; m. Miriam Dianne Pinnell, June 7, 1970; children—Leigh Anne, Lauren Emily. B.A., Emory U., 1969; D.M.D., Med. Coll. Ga., 1973; cert. in periodontics, Columbia U., 1975. Staff Luth. Med. Ctr. Dental Clinic, Bklyn., 1973-75, staff periodontist, 1975-76; pvt. practice, Nyack and White Plains, N.Y., 1975-76, High Point, N.C., 1976—; med. staff dental sect. High Point Meml. Hosp., 1977-83, chief dental sect., 1979-82, med. staff exec. com., 1979-82, mem. profl. quality assurance com., 1982-83; clin. instr. periodontics Columbia U., 1975-76; clin. asst. prof. Sch. Dentistry, U. N.C., Chapel Hill, 1980-81, 81-82, 82-83; guest lectr. periodontics Guilford Tech. Inst., Jamestown, N.C., 1977-81. Contbr. articles to profl. jours. Mem. adminstrv. bd. Wesley Meml. United Methodist Ch., High Point, 1979-82; mem. N.C. Urban Transp. Policy Task Force; bd. dirs. High Point Rescue Squad, 1979-81, chmn. bd. dirs., 1980-81; mem. nominating com. High Point Mental Health Assn., 1985; chmn. dental adv. com. Guilford Tech. Inst., 1980-81; chmn. Area Health Edn. Com., 1980-83. Mem. ADA, N.C. Dental Soc. (legis. com. 3d dist. 1981-83), High Point Dental Soc. (pres. 1979-80, exec. com. 1980-81), Guilford County Dental Soc., Assn. Piedmont Periodontists, Am. Acad. Periodontology, N.C. Soc. Periodontists, So. Acad. Periodontology, Northeastern Soc. Periodontists, High Point C. of C. (bd. dirs. 1983—, chmn. transp. com. 1983-85). Democrat. Methodist. Avocations: travel; tennis; family. Home: 802 Kingston Ct High Point NC 27260 Office: 100 Westwood Ave High Point NC 27262

HOOFMAN, CLIFF, state senator; b. June 23, 1943; m. Carole Denice Merritt; 1 child, Ragan. B.A., U. Central Ark.; J.D., U. Ark. Bar: Ark., U.S. Supreme Ct. Mem. Ark. Ho. of Reps., 1974-82; mem. Ark. Senate, 1983—; ptnr. Hoofman & Bingham. Mem. Big Bros. Assn., Area Agy. on Aging. Recipient Oustanding Young Man award Ark. Jaycees, 1978; Outstanding Young Man of North Little Rock, Rose City Jaycees. Mem. North Pulaski County Bar Assn. Democrat. Office: Ark Senate State Capitol Little Rock AR 72201*

HOOGERWERF, FRANK WILLIAM, music educator, administrator, researcher; b. Rotterdam, Netherlands, June 24, 1946; came to U.S., 1956, naturalized, 1961; s. Frank and Wilhelmina (Mulder) H.; m. Sharon Ruth Scripps, May 27, 1969; children—Brett Ian, Justin Clay. B.A., Calvin Coll., 1969; Mus.M., U. Mich., 1970; Ph.D., 1974. Asst. prof. music Emory U., Atlanta, 1974-79, assoc. prof. music, 1980—, chmn. dept. music, 1980—. Author, editor monographs. Contbr. articles to profl. jours. Grantee Ford Found. 1970-71, 73-74, U. Mich. 1973, Ga. Endowment for Humanities 1978-79, Emory Faculty Research 1976-78, 78-80; Nat. Endowment Humanities fellow 1981. Mem. Am. Musicol. Soc., Coll. Music Soc., Sonneck Soc. Am. Music. Avocation: jogging. Home: 1270 Oakdale Rd NE Atlanta GA 30307 Office: Dept Music Emory U Atlanta GA 30322

HOOK, HAROLD SWANSON, insurance company executive; b. Kansas City, Mo., Oct. 10, 1931; s. Ralph C. and Ruby (Swanson) H.; m. Joanne T. Hunt, Feb. 19, 1955; children—Karen Anne, Thomas W., Randall T. B.B.A., U. Mo., 1953, M.A., 1954; grad., So. Meth. U. Inst. Ins. Marketing, 1957; postgrad., N.Y. U., 1967-70; LL.D. (hon.), U. Mo., 1983, Westminster Coll., 1983. C.L.U. Faculty U. Mo. Sch. Bus., 1953-54; asst. to pres. Nat. Fidelity Life Ins. Co., Kansas City, Mo., 1957-60, dir., 1959-66, adminstrv. v.p., 1960-61, exec. v.p., investment com., 1961-62, pres., exec. com., 1962-66; sr. v.p. U.S. Life Ins. Co., N.Y.C., 1966-67, dir., 1967-70, exec. v.p., mem. exec. com., 1967-68, pres., 1968-70; pres., mem. bd., exec. com. Calif.-Western States Life Ins. Co., Sacramento, 1970-75, chmn., 1975-79, sr. chmn., 1979—; pres. Am. Gen. Corp., Houston, 1975-81, chmn., chief exec. officer, 1978—, mem. exec. com., 1975—, dir., 1972—; founder, pres. Main Event Mgmt. Corp., Sacramento, 1970—; dir. Panhandle Eastern Corp., Houston, Continental Airlines Corp., Tex. Commerce Bancshares, Inc., United Telecommunications, Inc., Kansas City, Mo. Trustee, chmn. fin. com. Baylor Coll. Medicine, Houston; mem. council of overseers Jesse H. Jones Grad. Sch. Adminstrn., Rice U., Houston; bd. dirs. Tex. Research League, Houston Symphony, Soc. for Performing Arts, Houston., Business Arts Fund, Houston Area Research Ctr. Served to lt. USNR, 1954-57. Recipient Citation of Merit, U. Mo. alumni award, 1965; Faculty-Alumni award U. Mo., 1978; Silver Beaver award Boy Scouts Am., 1974; Distinguished Eagle Scout award, 1976; named Man of Year Delta Sigma Pi, 1969, Chief Exec. Officer award Fin. World Mag., 1979, 82, 84, 86; honored by Wall St. Transcript, 1981, 82, 83, 84, 85. Mem. Philos. Soc. Tex., Houston C. of C. (chmn. 1983-84), Beta Gamma Sigma Dirs. Table (nat. honoree 1984). Presbyterian. Clubs: Forum (bd. govs.), University, River Oaks Country, Petroleum, Ramada, Heritage (Houston); Economic (N.Y.C.); Morris County Golf (Morristown, N.J.); Mission Hills Country (Kansas City); Eldorado Country (Indian Wells, Calif.), Rotary. Home: 2204 Troon Rd Houston TX 77019 Office: 2929 Allen Pkwy Houston TX 77019

HOOKER, JOHN PATRICK, neurological surgeon; b. Frost, Tex., Sept. 5, 1926; s. Rea Ferdinand and Ada (Walker) H.; B.A., U. Tex., 1950; M.D., U. Tex. at Galveston, 1954; m. Mariam Shearin Squires (dec.); m. Mary Katherine Donahue. Intern, Jackson Meml. Hosp., Miami, Fla., 1954-55, resident gen. surgery, 1955-56; fellow neurol. surgery Mayo Found., Rochester, Minn., 1956-58, Ochsner Found., New Orleans, 1958-61; practice medicine, specializing in neurol. surgery, Midland, Tex., 1961-71, Augusta, Maine, 1971-73, Lumberton, N.C., 1973-78, McAllen Gen. Hosp., 1977-81, St. Joseph's Hosp., 1980—. Bd. dirs. Midland chpt. ARC, 1965-71. Served with U.S. Army, 1944-46. Diplomate Am. Bd. Neurol. Surgery. Fellow ACS, Internat. Coll. Surgeons, Internat. Coll. Angiology, Am. Geriatric Assn., Royal Soc. Health (U.K.); mem. Am. Assn. Neurol. Surgeons, Congress Neurol. Surgeons, So. Neurosurg. Soc., Pan-Pacific Surg. Assn., Pan Am. Med. Assn., Brazos-Robertson County Med. Soc., AMA, Tex. Med. Assn., Nat. Aero. Assn., Aircraft Owners and Pilots Assn., European Acad. Arts, Sci. and Humanities, Royal Soc. Medicine (U.K.), Order of Quiet Birdmen, Airline Transport Pilots Assn. Republican. Episcopalian. Club: Ft. Worth. Lodge: Rotary. Home: 504 S Dexter St College Station TX 77840

HOOKS, EUGENE JAMES, educator, theatre specialist; b. St. Louis, Jan. 1, 1938; s. Eugene Russell and Dorothy Mae (Petway) H.; B.S. in Edn., U. Mo., 1969, M.A., 1970, Ph.D. in Theatre, 1973; m. Marianne Jolly, Jan. 1, 1960; children—James David, Michael Lewis, Jeffrey Quarles, Hugh David. Instr. theatre U. Mo., Columbia, 1970-71, asst. tech. dir., 1970-71, instr., tech. dir., 1971-73; instr. Stephens Coll., Columbia, Mo., 1971; dir. theatre U. Fla., Gainesville, 1973-75, asst. prof., advisor, scene designer, 1973-75, interim chmn. dept. theatre, asst. prof., advisor, scene designer, 1975-76, chmn. dept., assoc. prof., advisor, dir., 1976-84, prof. theatre, 1981—; actor, dir.; dir. Fla. state play Cross and Sword, 1980. Served with USMC, 1956-57. Recipient Gold Medallion award Am. Coll. Theater Festival, 1981. Grantee Fla. Arts Council, 1975-79, So. Fedn. State Arts Agys., 1977, Panama City (Fla.) Civic Music Assn., 1975-76. Mem. Fla. (univ. and coll. rep. 1977), Southeastern (fin. com. 1977-79) theatre confs., Am. Theatre Assn. (conv. planning com. 1977-79), Speech Communication Assn. Am. (chmn. theatre div. 1977-79); Univ. Research Theatre Assn. (dir. 1982), Screen Actors Guild, Soc. Stage Dirs. and Choreographers. Contbr. numerous profl. scene designs, publs. and programs; co-author: (with S. Smiley) Theatre: The Human Art, 1980; adapter, editor: The Country Wife (William Wycherly). Home: 478 NE 22nd St Gainesville FL 32603 Office: 494 Winston Little Hall U Fla Gainesville FL 32611

HOOKS, KAREN LEAH, accounting educator; b. Lakeland, Fla., Dec. 27, 1955; d. Wilbur Ocie and Frankie Emily (Grimes) H.; m. Stephen Srygley Walker, July 23, 1983. A.A., Polk Community Coll., 1974; B.A., U. S. Fla., 1976; Ph.D., Ga. State U., 1981. C.P.A., Fla. Asst. prof. acctg. U. South Fla., Tampa, 1979-85, assoc. prof. acctg., 1985—; staff acct. Touche Ross & Co., Tampa, 1976-77. Mem. Am. Woman's Soc. C.P.A. (v.p. nat. 1983-85, nat. dir. 1982-83), Nat. Assn. Accts. (dir. 1981-83), Fla. Inst. C.P.A.s, Am. Inst. C.P.A.s, Am. Acctg. Assn. Contbr. articles to profl. jours. Methodist. Office: Dept Acctg Coll Bus Univ South Fla Tampa FL 33620

HOOPER, GLENN SCOBLE, pathologist; b. Bay Minette, Ala., June 28, 1929; s. Leonard John and Lalla Camella (Northcutt) H.; B.S., Auburn U., 1950; M.D., Med. Coll. Ala., 1960; m. Carole Elizabeth King, June 8, 1957; children—James Glenn, John David, Joel Thomas. Process engr. Union Carbide Corp., Oak Ridge and Paducah, Ky., 1951-55; intern St. Vincent Hosp., Birmingham, Ala., 1960-61; resident in pathology Carraway Methodist Hosp., Birmingham, 1961-64, Med. Coll. Va., 1964-65; asst. pathologist St. Joseph Hosp., Lexington, Ky., 1965-66; pathologist Tampa (Fla.) Gen. Hosp., 1966—; asso. pathologist Meml. Hosp. Tampa, 1970—, Women's Hosp. Tampa, 1974; pathologist, dir. labs. Univ. Community Hosp., Tampa, 1968—; asso. clin. prof. pathology U. So. Fla. Coll. Medicine, 1973—. Mem. AMA, Fla. Med. Assn., Hillsborough County Med. Assn. (pres. 1984-85), Am. (dir. 1978-82), Fla. (pres. 1978-79) assns. blood banks, Fla. Soc. Pathologists (pres. 1983-86), Am. Soc. Clin. Pathologists, Coll. Am. Pathologists, Fla. West Coast Assn. Pathologists (pres. 1976-77). Democrat. Methodist. Club: Midtown Kiwanis (treas. 1974-75, v.p. 1975-76, pres. 1977-78). Home: 2408 S Dundee Tampa FL 33629 Office: 3100 E Fletcher Ave Tampa FL 33629

HOOPER, JERRY LEE, industrial appraiser; b. Milan, Ind., Mar. 3, 1944; s. James Thomas and Winifred Loretta (Bowling) H.; m. Marky Corum, Dec. 22, 1965; children—Jerry Lee, Jeffrey Lee, Jennifer Leigh. B.A., U. Evansville, 1968. County assessor County of Dearborn, Lawrenceburg, Ind., 1970-76; sr. tax cons., indsl. appraiser Thomas Y. Pickett & Co., Inc., Corpus Christi, Tex., 1976—; owner, operator Andy's Strips, Inc., 1983—. Served to capt. USAF, 1968-70. Mem. Tex. Assn. Assessing Ofcls. Home: 3332 Bali Dr Corpus Christi TX 78418

HOOPER, WALTER JOSEPH, electronic diagnostic medical equipment manufacturing company executive; b. New Orleans, Jan. 30, 1950; s. Marion Joseph and Iris Rita (Shexnayder) H.; m. Judith Cathryn Haney, July 5, 1975; 1 dau., Christie Michelle. B.S. in Indsl. Engring., B.A. in Internat. Relations, La. State U., 1973; M.S., U. Tex., Dallas, 1980. Staff engr. Unitog Co., Kansas City, Mo., 1973-75, sr. staff engr., 1975-77; plant engr. Fox & Jacobs, Inc., Carrollton, Tex., 1977-78, engring. mgr., 1978-80; plant mgr. RMax, Inc., Dallas, 1980-82, v.p. mfg., 1982-84; pres. Medmax, Inc., Dallas, 1984—; cons. Constrn. Students Assn., Plano, Tex., 1982; lectr. Inter-city High Sch. Vis. Lectures Plano, Tex., 1981—. Advisor, Jr. Achievement, Dallas, 1980-81; assoc. Inter-Campus Exchange, La. State U., 1972-73; mem. judges council Tex. High Sch. Speech Competition, Dallas, 1981-83; vice chmn. Citizens Com., Plano, 1982—. Served with USAF, 1969-75. Recipient 2d Degree Black Belt, Am. Karate Assn., 1980; Mem. Am. Mgmt. Assn., Nat. Assn. Home Builders (council 1983). Roman Catholic. Club: Toastmaster's (v.p. edn. 1979-81, Able Toastmaster 1981). Home: 3200 Winchester Dr Plano TX 75075 Office: Medmax Inc Two Turtle Creek Village Suite 1600 Dallas TX 75219

HOOPER, WILLIAM EDWARD JAMES, dentist; b. Bay Minette, Ala., Feb. 24, 1927; s. Leonard John and Lallah Camella (Northcutt) H.; m. Qwendolyn Areta Riley, May 29, 1955; children—Qwendolyn Dawn, William Edward James Jr., Shelley Blythe, Benjamin Talbot. B.S., U. Ala., 1950; D.D.S., U. Ala. Sch. Dentistry, 1954. Practice dentistry, Bay Minette, 1954—; mem. adv. com. Dental Assisting Sch. Faulkner State Jr. Coll., Bay Minette, 1970-83; mem. subcom. Ala. Health Study Commn, Montgomery, 1971. Served with USN, 1945-46. Mem. Ala. Dental Assn. (pres. 1984-85, Most Excellent Fellow award 1984), ADA (alt. del. 1982-85), 1st Dist. Dental Assn. (pres. 1971-72), Acad. Gen. Dentistry, Pierre Fauchard Acad. Republican. Methodist. Avocations: fishing; tennis; dancing. Office: 112 W 3rd St Bay Minette AL 36507

HOOTEN, NORMAN HOWELL, county sheriff; b. Lampasas, Tex., Mar. 16, 1941; s. Claude W. and Marcella V. (Clark) H.; m. Joyce Lee Sowell, June 18, 1977; children—Norman Glenn, Shannon Sue, Stacy Lynn, Ginger Renee. Grad. high sch., Garland, Tex. Cert. in law enforcement. Game warden Tex. Parks and Wildlife Dept., Ozona, 1963-66, Seabrook, 1966-67; dep. sheriff Dallas County Sheriff's Dept., 1966; constable Brackettville, Tex., 1976-80; chief of police City of Brackettville, 1980-82; sheriff Kinney County, 1982—, tax assessor-collector, 1982—; mem. adv. bd. dirs. Middle Rio Grande Law Enforcement Acad., Uvalde, Tex., 1980—. Served with USN, 1958. Recipient Friends of 4-H award Crockett County 4-H Club, Ozona, 1965, Man of Yr. award Brackettville C. of C., 1981, Outstanding Service award Brackettville Police Dept., 1982. Mem. Uvalde Peace Officers Assn., Tex. Sheriffs Assn. Home: 403 4th St Box 925 Brackettville TX 78832 Office: Kinney County Sheriff's Dept 109 North St Box 1200 Brackettville TX 78832

HOOTMAN, HARRY EDWARD, nuclear engr.; b. Oak Park, Ill., June 5, 1933; s. Merle Albert and Rachel Edith (Atkinson) H.; B.S., Mich. Technol. U., 1959, M.S., 1961; LL.B., LaSalle Extension U., 1971; m. Linda Pearl Smith, Nov. 23, 1963; children—David Ernest, Holly Jean, John Christian. Research asso. Argonne (Ill.) Nat. Lab., 1960-62; reactor engr. Savannah River plant E.I. du Pont de Neumours & Co., Inc., Aiken, S.C., 1962-65, sr. design engr., reactor engring. div., 1965-68, research physicist, theoretical physics div., 1968-74, research staff engr. environ. effects div. Savannah River lab., 1974-80, isotope separations div., 1980-85, research assoc. nuclear engring. div., 1985—. Dir. Central Savannah River Area Sci. and Engring. Fair, Inc.; troop committeeman Boy Scouts Am., Aiken. Served in USAF, 1953-57. Dow Chem. scholar, 1958; registered profl. engr., S.C. Mem. Am. Nuclear Soc., Nat., S.C. socs. profl. engrs., Am. Acad. Environ. Engrs., Am. Phys. Soc., Augusta Opera Assn., Sigma Xi, Phi Lambda Upsilon. Baptist. Home: 820 Brandy Rd Aiken SC 29801 Office: Savannah River Lab Aiken SC 29801

HOOTON, EDWARD JEFFREY, dentist; b. Elizabeth, N.J., July 16, 1948; s. Edward and Charlotte Delaney (Sieratowicz) H.; m. Belinda Gail Robinson, June 20, 1982; children—Jennica Babbette, Christina Sage. B.A., Northeast La. U., 1975, B.S. (hon.), 1981; D.D.S., La. State U., 1984. Dir., mgr. Rodeway Inns of La. Inc., Monroe, 1975-80; gen. practice dentistry, Monroe, 1984—. Served to sgt. U.S. Army, 1969-72, Vietnam. Named Mgr. of Yr. Rodeway Inns of La. Inc., 1978, 79, 80; recipient Cert. Appreciation La. State U. Dental Sch., 1984. Mem. ADA, La. Dental Assn., Fifth Dist. Dental Assn., Am. Soc. Dentistry for Children, Acad. Gen. Dentists. Democrat. Roman Catholic.

Club: Park Ave. Am. Assn. (Monroe). Home: 26 Kathy Ln Monroe LA 71203 Office: Monroe Dental Arts Bldg 2816 Armand Monroe LA 71201

HOOVER, DIANNA LYNN, librarian; b. Owensboro, Ky., Jan. 28, 1956; d. William D. and Juanita Gertrude (Curry) H. B.A., Ky. Wesleyan Coll., 1978; M.A., Western Ky. U., 1980; postgrad. Ind. U., 1982—. Cert. tchr., Ky. Cataloger Owensboro Area Mus. (Ky.), 1978-79; substitute tchr. McLean County Schs., Calhoun, Ky., 1979; tchr. Ohio County Schs., Hartford, Ky., 1979-80, librarian, 1980—; career coordinator, computer instr. Centertown Sch. (Ky.). Bd. dirs. tchr. Pleasant Hill United Methodist Ch., Livermore, Ky. Mem. Am. Assn. Sch. Librarians, ALA. Democrat.

HOOVER, HERBERT CHARLES MARSH, banker; b. Newburgh, N.Y., Mar. 16, 1934; s. Charles Webster and Viola Marion (Marsh) H.; m. Betty Bruce Howard, Sept. 3, 1961; children—David Andrew, Howard Webster, Lorraine VanSiclen. B.A. in Acctg., Mich. State U., 1956; postgrad. Nat. Trust Grad. Sch., ABA, 1965-67; J.D., Wake Forest U., 1961; postgrad. Exec. Program, U. N.C., 1969-70. Bar: N.C. 1961, Fla. 1977. Exec. v.p., chief exec. officer Citizens Bank & Trust Co., Henderson, N.C., 1964-73; sr. v.p., sr. trust officer NCNB of Fla. (formerly Exchange Bancorp., Inc.) Tampa, 1974-84, trust counsel, 1984—. Bd. dirs., chmn. fin. adv. com. The Home Assn.; bd. dirs. Greater Tampa Red Cross. Served with U.S. Army, 1957-59. Mem. Hillsborough County Bar Assn., Fla. Bar, N.C. Bar, Fla. Bankers Assn. (vice chmn. trust div.), Tampa Bay Estate Planning Council (pres.), Nat. Assn. Estate Planning Councils (state chmn.), Greater Tampa C. of C. (chmn. energy task force). Republican. Episcopalian. Clubs: Berkeley Preparatory Sch. Dad's Club (dir., pres., v.p., treas.), Suncoast Midshipmen Parents (v.p.). Lodge: Masons.

HOOVER, JIMMIE HARTMAN, librarian; b. Board Camp, Ark., Nov. 5, 1930; s. James Thomas and Alice Victoria (Peters) H.; student Coll. Ozarks, 1948-49; B.A., Ark. Poly. Coll., 1952; M.S., La. State U., 1958; m. Lillian Elaine Fitzgerald, Jan. 2, 1959. With La. State U. Library, Baton Rouge and New Orleans, 1958-84, head order dept., Baton Rouge, 1965-67, head bus. adminstrn. and govt. documents dept., 1968-84, mem. faculty Sch. Library Sci., 1972-73, affiliate faculty Grad. Sch. Library Sci., 1974-81; head reference East Baton Rouge Parish Library, 1984—. Served with Security Service, USAF, 1952-56. Mem. La. (bus. mgr. bull. 1964-65), Southwestern library assns., ALA, Spl. Libraries Assn. (nat. govt. info. service com. 1969-71), Am. Legion. Author: (with J. Norman Heard) Bookman's Guide to Americana, 6th edit., 1970, 7th edit., 1977; editor Spl. Libraries Assn. Ark., Miss. and La. chpt. Bull., 1970, La. Library Assn. Coll. Sect. Bull., 1968-80; govt. documents reviewer Reference Service Rev., 1973-81; feature writer Lost Treasure, 1983—. Home: 1815 Myrtledale Ave Baton Rouge LA 70808

HOOVER, RICHARD LEE, chem. co. exec.; b. South Bend, Ind., Aug. 16, 1949; s. George W. and Mercea M. (Baer) H.; B.S. in Aero. and Mech. Engring., Tri-State U., Angola, Ind., 1971; m. Lee Ann Bryar, Aug. 19, 1972; children—Stacey, Kristin. Sales engr. Trane Co., Pitts., 1971-72; dist. sales mgr. Nalco Chem. Co., Oak Brook, Ill., 1972—; sales and cons. in water treatment, fuel treatment, energy conservation. Membership dir. YMCA Indian Guide and Princess. Named Top Dist. Salesman, Nalco Chem. Co., 1976, Top Dist. Mgr., 1984. Mem. Am. Water Works Assn., Assn. Iron and Steel Engrs., Water Pollution Control Fedn., Louisville Area Jaycees. Methodist. Club: Masons. Address: 803 Sandness Ct Louisville KY 40243

HOOVER, ZANDRA BURT, rehabilitation center administrator; b. Adel, Ga., Nov. 25, 1952; s. Earl Parks and Eleanor Estelle (Wright) Burt; m. Michael Richard Hoover, Sept. 7, 1975 (div. 1979); 1 dau., Erin Michelle. B.S. in Occupational Therapy, U. Fla., 1975; postgrad. U. North Fla., 1981. Registered occupational therapist, Fla. Dir. occupational therapy North Fla. Evaluation and Treatment Ctr. Gainesville, 1977-78; chief occupational therapist, dir. crisis line Winter Haven (Fla.) Hosp., 1979-80; individual practice occupational therapy Winter Haven, 1980-82; owner, adminstr. Polk Rehab. and Devel. Ctr., Inc., Winter Haven, 1982—. Bd. dirs. Am. Heart Assn., Polk County, Fla., 1983-84; mem. med. adv. bd. Multiple Sclerosis Assn., Polk County, 1983—; mem. steering com. Easter Seals, Polk County, 1983-84. Mem. Am. Occupational Therapy Assn. (Sustaining Mem. award 1981), Fla. Occupational Therapy Assn., Nat. Rehab. Assn., Am. Soc. Hand Therapists, Arthritis Found. (med. adv. com. Fla. chpt. 1982-83, instr. 1982-83), Winter Haven C. of C. Unitarian. Club: Bus. and Profl. Women's (Winter Haven). Home: 5850 Cypress Gardens Blvd Apt 607 Winter Haven FL 33880 Office: 332 Ave B SW Winter Haven FL 33880

HOPE, MARGARET LAUTEN, civic worker; b. N.Y.C., Dec. 17; privately educated; m. Paul C. Debry, Jr., Nov. 9, 1943; m. 2d, Fred H. Hope, Jr., Mar. 30, 1959; 1 son, Frederick H., III. Bd. dirs. Nat. Leukemia Soc., 1974—; co-chmn. gift com. Heart Ball, Palm Beach, Fla., 1967; mem. ball coms. various charity fund raising events. Clubs: Jr. League, Women's Nat. Republican (N.Y.C.); Everglades, Sailfish (Palm Beach). Address: 236 Dunbar Rd Box 601 Palm Beach FL 33480

HOPE, PAUL ANTHONY, oil company executive; b. Dallas, Apr. 9, 1926; s. James Lemarcus and Sue Ella (Mitchell) H.; m. Veronica McKinnon, Sept. 5, 1959; children—Elizabeth Ann, Joan Catherine, Joseph Anthony. B.B.A., U. Tex.-Austin, 1950; M.B.A., So. Meth. U., 1957. C.P.A., Tex. Staff acct. Haskins & Sells, Dallas, 1950-60; with Hunt Energy Corp. (and Hunt Oil Corp. previously), Dallas, 1960—, mgr. internal audit, 1960-71, mgr. HLH Products, 1971-75, controller, 1975—, sec., 1983—; part time instr. So. Meth. U., Dallas, 1960-64; trustee W.H. Hunt Trust Estate, Lyda Hunt-Bunker, Herbert, and Lamar Trusts; v.p., dir. Hunt Internat. Petroleum Corp.; dir. Hunt Properties, Inc., Prosper Energy Corp., Petro-Hunt Corp.; mgr. Portal Boat Co. Served with USAF, 1944-46. Mem. Tex. Soc. C.P.A.s, Denton Area Soc. C.P.A.s, Petroleum Accts. Soc. Dallas, Ind. Petroleum Assn. Am. (principles and fin. reporting com.). Republican. Roman Catholic. Lodge: K.C. Home: 2408 Northwood Terr Denton TX 76201 Office: 2400 Thanksgiving Tower Dallas TX 75201

HOPEN, GARY ROBERT, ophthalmologist; b. Phila., Dec. 11, 1954; s. Joseph Martin and Selma Rochelle (Goodman) H. B.S., Pa. State U., 1973; M.D., Jefferson U., 1977. Intern, U. Oreg., Portland, 1977-78; postdoctoral fellow Baylor U., Houston, 1978-79; resident in ophthalmology U. Pitts., 1979-82; neuro-ophthalmology fellow Bascom Palmer Eye Inst., Miami, Fla., 1982-83; practice medicine specializing in ophthalmology, Hollywood, Fla., 1983—. Contbr. articles to profl. jours. Fellow Am. Acad. Ophthalmology; mem. AMA, Broward County Med. Assn., Miami Ophthal. Soc., Fla. Ophthal. Soc. Avocations: scuba diving; horseback riding; tennis; skiing. Home: 2808 N 46th Ave #E-351 Hollywood FL 33021 Office: Hopen & Lane MD PA 3419 Johnson St Hollywood FL 33021

HOPEWELL, CLIFFORD ALAN, clinical psychologist; b. Dallas, Oct. 13, 1948; s. Clifford Henry Hopewell and Mary Penelope (Van Buskirk); m. Trena Catherine Davies, Aug. 11, 1973; children—Clay Alan, Joseph Clark. B.S., Tex. A&M U., 1971; M.A., North Tex. State U., Denton, 1973, Ph.D., 1978. Diplomate Am. Bd. Clin. Neuropsychology. Psychology intern Dallas Police Dept., 1975; psychology resident U. Tex. Med. Br., Galveston, 1976; dir. psychology Baylor Inst. for Rehab., Dallas, 1982—; staff mem. Green Oaks Hosp., Dallas, 1984—. Contbr. articles to profl. jours. Served to maj. USAR, 1976-82. Mem. Am. Psychol. Assn., Internat. Neuropsychol. Soc., Tex. Psychol. Assn., Tex. Head Injury Found. (adv. bd., chmn. legis. com. 1984—). Methodist. Avocations: photography; snow skiing; classical and medieval history. Office: Baylor Inst for Rehab 3504 Swiss Ave Dallas TX 75204

HOPKINS, ANTHONY DUANE, retail exec.; b. Los Angeles, Aug. 29, 1956; s. Walter H. and Annie (Lee) H.; A.S., Dallas Fashion Mdse. Coll., 1976; student Dallas Bapt. Coll., 1976—. Salesman, Neiman Marcus, Dallas, 1973-75; asst. mgr. Kinney Shoe Corp., Dallas, 1975-77; owner, dealership Natural World Candy Co., Dallas, 1977—; pres. Hopco Co., Dallas, 1977—; A.D. Hopkins Investments; part owner New World Industries, Inc. Chmn. precinct 3326, Dallas Republican Com.; Rep. Presidential Task Force (vice-chmn. com. 100). Mem. Inst. Logopedics, Nat. Forensic League, Mail Order Assn., Am. Assn. Commodity Buyers, Bradford Exchange, Am. Inst. Banking, Treins Exchange, Unity Buying Service. Republican. Baptist. Clubs: Commonwealth, Original Print Collectors Group, Nat. Health. Home: 3215 South Blvd Dallas TX 75210

HOPKINS, DAVID LEE, JR., land surveyor; b. Chattanooga, Mar. 23, 1934; s. David Lee and Sarah M. (Seward) H.; m. Barbara Ann Bell, Dec. 3, 1960; children—Mark D., Tracy E. B.S. in Indsl. Mgmt., U. Chattanooga, 1958. Registered land surveyor, Tenn. With Hopkins Morton Engring. Co., Inc., Chattanooga, 1960—, active design and devel. of land, 1983—. Bd. dirs. Skymont Camp, Cherokee council Boy Scouts Am.; bd. dirs. Chattanooga Symphony, Friends of the Festival; vice chmn. profl. div. Allied Arts Fund Drive; alumni trustee U. Chattanooga. Served with USNR, 1960. Named Ky. Col., 1980; apptd. Col. Tenn. Camp de Aide, 1982; recipient Youth Service award, YMCA, 1965, 79. Fellow Am. Congress Surveying and Mapping; mem. Tenn. Assn. Profl. Surveyors (pres. 1978-79, chmn. State Bd. Examiners for Land Surveyors), Nat. Soc. Profl. Engrs., Nat. Council Engr. Examiners, U. Tenn. Nat. Alumni Assn. (pres.-elect), U. Tenn.-Chattanooga Alumni Assn. (pres. 1980). Methodist. Clubs: Ga. Balloon Assn., Hot Air Balloon Pilot. Office: 415 Georgia Ave Chattanooga TN 37402

HOPKINS, GEORGE MATHEWS MARKS, patent lawyer; b. Houston, June 9, 1923; s. C. Allen and Agnes Cary (Marks) H.; student Ga. Sch. Tech., 1943-44; B.S. in Chem. Engring., Ala. Poly. Inst., 1944; LL.B., U. Ala., 1949, J.D., 1969; postgrad. George Washington U., 1949-50; m. Betty Miller McLean, Aug. 21, 1954; children—Laura McLean, Edith Cary. Admitted to Ala. bar, 1949, Ga. bar, 1954; instr. math. U. Ala., 1947-49; asso. atty. A. Yates Dowell, 1949-50, Edw. T. Newton, 1950-62; asst. dir. research, legal counsel Auburn Research Found., 1954-55; partner firm Newton, Hopkins and Jones, 1962-68, Newton, Hopkins and Ormsby, 1968—; spl. asst. atty. gen. State of Ga., 1980, 82; sec.-treas. Tufted Patterns, Inc., 1959-62; exec. v.p., sec., treas. Fabulous Fabrics, Inc., 1960-62; chmn. bd. Southeastern Carpet Mills, Inc., Chatsworth, Ga., 1962-78; pres. Entertainment Investments, Inc., 1967-69, GNG Corp., Montgomery, Ala., 1971-72; dir. Xepol Inc.; chmn. bd. Thomas Daniels & Assos., Inc. Served as lt. submarine service USNR, 1944-46, 50-51. Registered profl. engr., Ga.; registered patent atty., U.S., Can. Mem. Am., Ga. (chmn. patent sect. 1970-71), Atlanta bar assns., Am. Patent Law Assn., Am. Soc. Profl. Engrs., Submarine Vets. of World War II (pres. Ga. chpt. 1977-78, vice comdr. 1976-77, 78-79), Phi Delta Phi, Sigma Alpha Epsilon. Episcopalian. Clubs: Nat. Lawyers (Washington); Cherokee Town and Country; Atlanta City, Atlanta Lawyers; Univ. Yacht. Home: 1765 Old Post Rd NW Atlanta GA 30328 Office: Equitable Bldg Atlanta Ga 30303

HOPKINS, H. E., police official. Police chief City of Fort Worth. Office: City Hall 1000 Throckmorton Fort Worth TX 76102*

HOPKINS, LARRY J., congressman; b. Detroit, Oct. 25, 1933; m. Carolyn Pennebaker; children—Shae, Tara, Joshua. Student, Murray State U., 1951-53. Stockbroker J.J.B. Hilliard and W.L. Lyons, Lexington, Ky., 1978; clk., Fayette (Ky.) County, 1969; mem. Ky. Ho. of Reps., 1972-78, Ky. Senate, 1978, 96th-99th congresses from 6th Ky. Dist. chmn. Spl. Olympics, 1973. Served with USMC, 1954-56. Named Legislator of Yr., 1974, 76, 78. Mem. Am. Legion. Republican. Methodist. Lodges: Kiwanis, Masons, Pyramid, Shriners. Office: 331 Cannon House Office Bldg Washington DC 20515*

HOPKINS, LINDA ANN, school psychologist; b. Bristol, Va., Aug. 23, 1937; d. James Robert and Trula Mae (Mink) Broce; A.B., King Coll., 1959; M.A., East Tenn. State U., 1977, postgrad., 1977-79; postgrad. Radford U., 1978-79; lic. psychol. examiner, Tenn.; lic. sch. psychologist, Va.; m. James Edwin Hopkins, Oct. 8, 1960; children—James Edwin, David Lawrence. Social worker Washington County Welfare Dept., Abingdon, Va., 1959-61; social worker Bristol (Va.) Welfare Dept., 1963-65, Washington County Welfare Dept., 1965-68, Bristol Meml. Hosp., 1968-72; psychologist Washington County Public Schs., Abingdon, 1978—; lectr. Va. Highlands Community Coll., Abingdon, 1981—. Mem. Nat. Assn. Sch. Psychologists, Va. Psychol. Assn., Va. Assn. Sch. Psychologists, Phi Kappa Phi. Methodist. Home: 436 Brookwood Dr Bristol TN 37620 Office: Washington County Public Schs PO Box 1388 Abingdon VA 24210

HOPKINS, MEGAN VICTORIA, medical administrator; b. St. Petersburg, Fla., Mar. 24, 1954; d. John Francis and Megan Wanda-Ruth (Morris) Scott. Cert. U. History and Tech., Bath, Eng., 1971; student Mary Washington Coll., 1972-74; student hosp. adminstrn. Va. Commonwealth U., 1974—. Adminstrv. asst. dept. ob-gyn Med. Coll. Va., Richmond, 1975-77; office mgr. Bernard Suher, Gross & Binder, Richmond, 1977; adminstr. Richmond Fertility and Reproductive Medicine Ltd., 1977-80; adminstrv. med. sec., cardio-thoracic surgery Med. Coll. Va., Richmond, 1981—. Lay therapist Crisis Center, Family and Children's Service of Richmond, 1980—. Named Vol. of Month, Oct. 1980. Mem. Nat. Assn. Exec. Females (exec., dir. Va. network), Am. Assn. Med. Assts., Va. Group Med. Mgmt. Assn., Med. Group Mgmt. Assn., Internat. Platform Assn. Democrat. Episcopalian. Contbr. articles to profl. jours. Home: 2421-A Park Ave Richmond VA 23220 Office: 707 E Main St Richmond VA 23219

HOPKINS, ROBERT E., state senator, real estate and insurance broker; b. Tulsa, Feb. 2, 1929; s. Harry L. and Mildred I. (Kitchen) H.; m. Frances L. Yandell, 1967; children—Marvin, Michael L. With Tex. Oil Co., Tulsa; real estate and ins. broker; mem. Okla. Ho. of Reps., 1959-63, 65-82, Okla. Senate, 1983—. Mem. Southwest Tulsan's and Tulsa County Democratic party; mem. AFL-CIO. Served with USMC; PTO. Lodge: Masons. Office: Okla Senate Room 517 Oklahoma City OK 73105*

HOPKINS, ROY VANVERT, business services company executive; b. Sneedville, Tenn., July 11, 1928; s. James and Cora H.; grad. in acctg. Morristown (Tenn.) Sch. Bus., 1960; m., Sept. 6, 1952; children—Wanda, Yvonne, Angela. Part-owner, operator Little Dutch Restaurant, Jefferson City, Tenn., 1949-50; meat cutter A & P Co., Morristown, 1954-59; owner, operator Hopkins Meat Market, Morristown, 1961-76; pres. Hopkins Diversified Bus. Services, Morristown, 1976—, Hopkins Ins. and Fin. Services, Inc., 1980—; cons. in field; pres. Add-O-Cycle Corp., Morristown, 1977—. Mem. exec. com. Democratic party Hamblen County (Tenn.), 1975-80. Served with USAF, 1950-54. Mem. Nat. Assn. Life Underwriters, Nat. Fedn. Ind. Bus., Gideons Internat. Baptist. Club: Sertoma (pres. 1967-68). Inventor in field. Home: 404 Spruce St Morristown TN 37814 Office: Hopkins Diversified Bus Services 166 W Main St Sneedville TN 37814

HOPPER, WILLIAM WALTER, art director, consultant, illustrator; b. Cin., Aug. 29, 1939; s. William Calvin and Lena Irene (McDaniel) H.; student Cin. Art Mus., Art Acad. Cin., 1959; B.S., Miami U., 1964; M.S., Xavier U., 1972; m. Shirley Fugate, Nov. 19, 1971; children—Noel R., Erin B., Megan I., Ian Michael; children by previous marriage—William David, Daniel. Artist, Palm Bros Decalomania, 1960; with Kroger Co., 1961-65, advt. mgr., 1965-73; advt. dir. Eastern div. Nat. Bldg. Centers, Miami, Fla., 1973—; owner, pres. Advt. Diversified Services, Ft. Lauderdale, Fla., 1976—; exhibited in group shows, Cin. Mem. Advt. Fedn. Ft. Lauderdale, Fine Arts Soc., Soc. Am. Magicians, Internat. Brotherhood Magicians. Democrat. Mormon. Cartoons pub. in nat. mags.; designer city logo for bicentennial yr. of Sunrise, Fla. Home: 6131 NW 12th St Sunrise FL 33313 Office: PO Box 9664 Fort Lauderdale FL 33310

HOPPING, JANET MELINDA, educational adminstrator; b. Washington, Dec. 27, 1943; d. Russell Leroy and Janet Louise (Cloud) H. B.S. in Elem. Edn., Tex. Christian U., 1965; M.Ed. in Adminstrn., Ga. State U., 1977. Tchr. 6th Centennial Elem. Sch., Littleton, Colo., 1965-67, 7th-8th Goddard Middle Sch., Littleton, 1967-68, 7th Central Park Elem., East Point, Ga., 1969, 6th, 7th Riley Elem. Sch., Atlanta, 1969-75, 8th Sandy Springs Middle Sch., Atlanta, 1975-78; Title IVC coordinator Fulton County Schs., Atlanta, 1978-81; middle sch. project coordinator, 1981-82; asst. prin. West Middle Sch., East Point, Ga., 1982-83; prin. Holcomb Bridge Middle Sch., Alpharetta, Ga., 1983—; mem. Com. to Develop Middle Sch. Core Curriculum, Littleton, 1966-67, Com. to Develop Interdisciplinary Curriculum, Atlanta, 1975-78, Com. to Develop Olympic Interdisciplinary Curriculum, Atlanta, 1976; chmn. Com. to Develop Minicourse Program, Atlanta, 1975-78; cons., trainer Atlanta City Schs., Berrien County Schs., Nashville, Ga., Bleckley County Schs., Cochran, Ga., 1978, Camden County Schs., Kingsland, Ga., 1981, Chatham County Schs., Savannah, Ga., 1979, Cherokee County Schs., Woodstock, Ga., Cook County Schs., Adel, Ga., Douglas County Schs., Douglasville, Ga., 1978, Early County Schs., Blakely, Ga., 1980, Effingham County Schs., Springfield, Ga., 1980, McDuffie County Schs., Thomson, Ga., Pulaski County Schs., Hawkinsville, Ga., 1978, Putnam County Schs., Eatonton, Ga., Rockdale County Schs., Conyers, Ga., 1979, Vidalia City Schs., Ga., 1979-80, Lake City Schs., Fla., 1978, Walker County Schs., Lafayette, Ga., 1980, Waycross City Schs., Ga., Pender County Schs., N.C., 1981; instr. Fulton County Staff Devel. Course, Atlanta, 1982. Mem. Atlanta Hist. Soc., 1977-79. Mem. adv. bd. Principal's Inst.; mem. State Ga. ad hoc com. Middle Sch. Planning and Devel. Mem. Assn. Supervision and Curriculum Devel., Nat. Middle Sch. Assn., Ga. League Middle Grade Educators (pres. 1984-85), Delta Kappa Gamma. Republican. Roman Catholic. Avocations: golf; tennis. Home: 720 Spring Creek Ln Dunwoody GA 30338 Office: Holcomb Bridge Middle Sch 2700 Holcomb Bridge Rd Alpharetta GA 30201

HORA, STEPHEN C., business educator, consultant; b. Pasadena, Calif., Nov. 30, 1942; s. John Joseph and Josephine Louise (Hare) H.; m. Judith Ann Twardowski, Sept. 9, 1967; children—Erika Lynn, Gregory John. B.S., U. So. Calif., 1964, D.B.A., 1973. Asst. prof. Ariz. State U., Tempe, 1972-76; assoc. prof. U. Oreg., Eugene, 1976-77; assoc. prof. Tex. Tech U., Lubbock, 1977—, assoc. dean, 1978-81; cons. specializing in risk analysis, Sandia Nat. Labs., Albuquerque, 1983—. Author statis. articles. Served to lt. USNR, 1964, S.E. Asia. Mem. Am. Statis. Assn., Am. Inst. for Decision Scis., Beta Gamma Sigma, Phi Kappa Phi. Home: 3508 78th Dr Lubbock TX 79423 Office: Tex Tech U Box 4320 Lubbock TX 79409

HORADAM, VICTOR WILLIAM, physician; b. Victoria, Tex., May 20, 1950; s. Gilbert Frederick Adolph and Lillian Bertha (Thamm) H.; student Tex. A&M U., 1968-69; B.A., U. Tex., Austin, 1972; M.D., U. Tex. Southwestern Med. Sch., Dallas, 1976. Intern, St. Paul Hosp., Dallas, 1976-77, resident, 1977-79; infectious disease fellow, 1979-80; hematology/oncology fellow U. Tex. Health Sci. Center, San Antonio, 1980-82, Nat. Cancer Soc. research fellow, 1981-82. Bd. dirs. Dallas Central unit Tex. div. Am. Cancer Soc.; chmn. Youth Against Cancer. Diplomate Am. Bd. Internal Medicine. Mem. ACP, Tex. Med. Assn., Dallas County Med. Soc. Lutheran. Contbr. articles to profl. jours. Office: 8220 Walnut Hill Ln Suite 500 Dallas TX 75231

HORAN, CHRISTINE PATRICIA, health care agency administrator, nurse practitioner; b. Jamaica, N.Y., Apr. 1, 1941; d. Joseph Peter Serrano and Mae (Grace) Serrano O'Neill; m. Robert Nelson Horan, May 5, 1962; children—Karen M. Victoria, Sheila. R.N. diploma Mary Immaculate Hosp. Sch. Nursing, Jamaica, 1961; family nurse practitioner Cornell U.-N.Y. Hosp., N.Y.C., 1975; B.S.N., Ga. Southwestern Coll., 1983—. R.N., Ga. Head nurse New Paltz Nursing Home (N.Y.), 1971-75; joint practice H.M. Weinman M.D., New Paltz, 1975-79; adminstr. Plains Primary Health Care, Inc., (Ga.), 1979—; mem. health adv. bd. Head Start Program, Americus, Ga., 1982—; mem. rural health adv. bd. Ga. Dept. Med. Assistance, Atlanta, 1983—. Contbr. to Emergency Care Dynamics, 1984. Mem. Plains City Council, 1982—. Recipient Superior Service award USPHS, 1979; Ga. Southwestern Nursing scholar, 1985. Mem. Ga. Nurses Assn. (pres. Dist. 12 1980—, Dist. honoree 1980, 84, sec. 1985), Ga. Assn. Primary Care (v.p. 1980), Am. Nurses Assn. (congl. dist. coordinator 1982—). Democrat. Roman Catholic. Office: Plains Primary Health Care Inc PO Box 100 Plains GA 31780

HORAN, THOMAS ROGER, computer system consultant; b. McGehee, Ark., May 11, 1944; s. Roger M. and Mabel Ruth (Howell) H.; m. Katherine Gale Corley, Jan. 18, 1969; children—Clinton, John T., Joseph L. B.A. in History, La. Tech. U., 1972; M.L.S., La. State U., 1976. Programming asst. Houston Aerospace div. Lockheed Electronics Co., 1967-70; warehousing mgr. Horan Welding Supply and Warehouse, McGehee, Ark., 1972-74; adminstrv. asst. Rapides Parish Library, 1974-75; community services librarian Chattahoochee Valley Regional Library, Columbus, Ga., 1976-77; asst. dir. Rapides Parish Library, Alexandria, La., 1978-80, dir., 1980-83; co-owner ByteMasters Computer Services, Alexandria, 1984—. Active Rapides Parish Arts and Humanities Council, 1980, Rapides Parish Community Concert Assn., Assn. Parents of Gifted Children; Royal Ambassador councilor, deacon Pineville Park Baptist Ch. Mem. La. Library Assn., S.W. Library Assn., S.E. Library Assn. Club: Pineville Kiwanis. Home: Rt 2 Box 404 Deville LA 71328 Office: PO Box 687 Alexandria LA 71309

HORCHOW, S(AMUEL) ROGER, mail order executive; b. Cin., July 3, 1928; s. Reuben and Beatrice (Schwartz) H.; B.A., Yale U., 1950; m. Carolyn Pfeifer, Dec. 29, 1960; children—Regen, Elizabeth, Sally. Buyer, Foley's, Houston, 1953-60; v.p. Neiman-Marcus, Dallas, 1960-68, 69-71; pres. Design Research, Cambridge, Mass., 1968-69, Kenton Collection, Dallas, 1971-73; chmn. Georg Jensen, Inc., N.Y.C., 1971-73; pres. Horchow Collection, Dallas, 1973—. Bd. dirs. Am. Inst. Public Service, Hockaday Sch. Nat. Trust Hist. Preservation, World Wildlife Fund, Asthma and Allergy Found., Circle 10 Boy Scouts Am., Better Bus. Bur., Dallas; v.p. Dallas Mus. Fine Arts; mem. nat. com. Whitney Mus., N.Y.C. Served to 1st lt., security U.S. Army, 1950-53. Clubs: Yale of N.Y.C., Nantucket Yacht. Home: 5722 Chatham Rd Dallas TX 75225 Office: 4435 Simonton Rd Dallas TX 75240

HORD, RICHARD ANDERSON, engineering mathematician; b. Lexington, Ky., Aug. 12, 1922; s. Richard Anderson and Lillian Virginia (Downing) H.; m. Margaret C. Johnston, Mar. 24, 1951 (div. 1974); children—Caroline Johnston, Richard Anderson. A.B. cum laude, Princeton U., 1943; M.S. U. Ky., 1949; D.Sc., U. Va., 1969; profl. cert. in Meteorology, UCLA, 1944. Registered profl. aero. engr., Ky. Aero. research scientist NACA, Langley Field, Va., 1954-58; aerospace technologist NASA, Langley Field, 1958-72; math. researcher, Williamsburg, Va., 1978—; instr. in engring. math., U. Va. Extension, Va. Poly. Inst. Extension, Langley Research Ctr., Langley Field, 1955-71. Author numerous govt. publs. on aerospace engring. sci. and math. Served to lt. USNR, 1943-46, PTO. Recipient Apollo Achievement award NASA, 1970. Assoc. fellow AIAA; mem. Math. Assn. Am. (life), Navy League of U.S. (life; v.p. 1979-85, dir. 1985—), Aircraft Owners and Pilots Assn., Exptl. Aircraft Assn., Tidewater Flying Club (dir. Newport News, Va.), Sigma Xi. Episcopalian. Avocations: skiing; light airplane flying; fishing; sailing; swimming.

HORKEY, WILLIAM RICHARD, diversified oil company executive; b. Tulsa, Apr. 22, 1925; s. William Edward and Clara Doris (Rice) H.; m. Barbara Jeanne Williamson, Oct. 18, 1952; children—Elaine Gail, Edward Richard, Ellen Beth. B.A., State U. Iowa, 1947; LL.B., U. Okla., 1950; grad., Advanced Mgmt. Program, Harvard U., 1962. Bar: Okla., 1950. With Gulf Oil Corp., 1950-51, Skelly Oil Co., 1951-55, Helmerich & Payne, Inc., Tulsa, 1955—, sec., legal counsel, 1957-64, v.p., 1960-64, exec. v.p., 1964—, also dir.; v.p., dir. Helmerich & Payne Internat. Drilling Co., Helmerich & Payne Coal Co.; dir. Energy Fuels Devel. Corp., Atwood Oceanics, Inc. Vice chmn. of oil div. of Tulsa Community Chest, 1964-69; chmn. met. div. Tulsa United Way, 1975-78, bd. dirs., 1978—; mem. bd. mgmt. S.E. Tulsa YMCA, 1963—, vice chmn., 1969-70, chmn., 1970-72; bd. mgmt. Met. Tulsa YMCA, 1970—, pres., 1972-73; bd. dirs. Tulsa chpt. ARC, North Tulsa Ambulatory Health Care, Inc., 1976—; trustee Tulsa Med. Edn. Found., Tulsa Emergency Med. Authority, 1977—; chmn. Tulsa Emergency Med. Authority, 1981; mem. med. adv. com. on indigent care Okla. Dept. Human Services. Served to 2d lt. USAAF, 1943-45. Mem. Am., Okla., Tulsa County bar assns., Am. Judicature Soc., Order of Coif, Phi Delta Phi, Phi Delta Theta. Presbyn. (deacon and elder). Clubs: Tulsa, So. Hills Country, Mid-Continent Harvard AMP (Tulsa) (pres. 1969-75). Home: 5686 S Evanston St Tulsa OK 74105 Office: 1579 E 21st St Tulsa OK 74114

HORN, ANDREW WARREN, lawyer; b. Cin., Apr. 19, 1946; s. George H. and Belle (Collin) H.; m. Melinda Fink; children—Lee Shawn, Ruth Belle. B.B.A. in Acctg., U. Miami, 1968, J.D., 1971. Bar: Fla. 1971, U.S. Dist. Ct. (so. dist.) Fla. 1972, U.S. Tax Ct. 1974. Ptnr. Giliman & Horn P.A., Miami, Fla., 1973-74; sole practice, Miami, 1974—. Bd. dirs. Young Democrats of Dade County. Recipient Am. Jurisprudence award Lawyers Coop. Pub. Co., 1970. Mem. ABA, Fla. Bar. Club: Tiger Bay. Office: 111 SW 3d St 6th Floor Miami FL 33130

HORN, ANTHONY WILLIAM, computer graphics company executive, consultant; b. Birmingham, Ala., Jan. 13, 1947; s. Raymond Johnathan and Glenera (Thornton) H.; m. Elmatha Cranford, June 18, 1968 (div. 1980). B.S. in Engring., U. Ala.-Birmingham, 1970; B. Arch., U. Houston, 1978. Owner, mgr. Horn Ctr., Houston, 1968—. Contbr. chpt. to book. Served with U.S. Army, 1968-74. Mem. IEEE, Third Coast Computer Graphics Soc., Soc. Computer Aided Engring., Phi Kappa Phi. Office: Horn Ctr 4815 Gulf Freeway Houston TX 77023

HORN, DORIS CROW GRIFFIN, nursing administrator, nurse; b. Lincoln, Ala., Mar. 11, 1930; d. John Tillman and Sarah Florence (Bunn) Crow: m. Vance Alton Griffin, Sr., Sept. 18, 1949 (dec. 1974); children—Vance, Jr., Terry Wayne, Jerry Blayne, Nancy Darlene, Merry Angela; m. Wallace Allen Horn,

Feb. 23, 1985. Student, Sylacauga Hosp. Sch. Nursing, 1964-67, U. Ala., 1965; diploma in nursing, Ala. Bd. Nursing, 1967. R.N. Staff nurse Clay County Hosp., Ashland, Ala., 1967-68, operating room supr., 1968-81, nurse adminstr., 1981—. Mem. Ala. State Nurses' Assn. (named nurse of Yr. 1969-70, pres. dist. 4 1975-77), Ala. Soc. for Nurse Adminstrn., DAR (regent Colonel John Hull chpt. 1984—), Clay-Talladega Soc. Baptist. Avocations: flowers, genealogy. Home: Route Two Box 103 Ashland AL 36251 Office: Clay County Hosp 544 E 1st Ave Ashland AL 36251

HORN, LISTER WAYNE, educator, author; b. Richlands, Va., Sept. 22, 1942; s. Lister and Edith Eccles Horn; m. Juliana Elizabeth Esfakis, Aug. 10, 1971. B.S. in Edn., U. Ariz., 1963, M.Ed., 1965; M.A.S., So. Meth. U., 1973; Ed.D., Fla. State U., 1983. Tchr. Tubac Sch. Dist., Ariz., 1963-69, Pensacola Jr. Coll., Fla., 1969-83, dept. head, 1983—. Author: Beginning Structured Cobol, 1983; Essentials of Flowcharting, 1985; BASIC, 1983; Advanced Structured Cobol, 1985. Mem. Assn. for Computing Machinery, Fla. Assn. for Ednl. Data Systems. Republican. Presbyterian. Avocations: jogging, cooking. Home: 108 Hampshire Contonment FL 32533 Office: Pensacola Jr Coll 1000 College Blvd Pensacola FL 32504

HORN, PAUL LAFLEUR, radiologist, educator, consultant; b. Winston-Salem, N.C., Sept. 22, 1925; s. Paul Lafleur and Lela Maud (Hawks) H.; B.S., Wake Forest U., 1945; M.D., Bowman Gray Sch. Medicine, 1947. Diplomate Am. Bd. Radiology. Intern Charity Hosp., New Orleans, 1948-49, resident, 1955-57; resident So. Bapt. Hosp., New Orleans, 1954-57; gen. practice medicine, Reserve, La., 1950-53; assoc. radiologist So. Bapt. Hosp., New Orleans, 1957-58, Our Lady Lake Hosp., 1973-75; chief dept. radiology Howard Meml. Hosp. Biloxi, Miss., 1958-72, Oteen VA Hosp., N.C., 1972-73; assoc. dir. dept. radiology Our Lady Lake Med. Ctr., 1975-78; assoc. prof. La. State U. Med. Ctr., New Orleans, 1978; chief dept. radiology Union County Gen. Hosp., New Albany, Miss., 1979-85, retired; cons. in radiology Biloxi VA Hosp., Miss., 1959-71, Keesley AFB Hosp., Biloxi, 1959-71, Vets. Hosp., New Orleans, 1973-79, La. Corrections Dept., Angola, 1978-79; sec. med. staff Howard Meml. Hosp., Biloxi, 1959-71, Union County Gen. Hosp., New Albany, Miss., 1979-81; mem. exec. com. Howard Meml. Hosp., Biloxi, 1960-71; sr. vis. staff physician dept. radiology Charity Hosp. La., New Orleans, 1973-78; clin. instr. Univ. Med. Ctr., Jackson, Miss., 1969-72; clin. asst. prof. Tulane U. Sch. Medicine, New Orleans, 1973-74; clin. assoc. prof. La. State U. Sch. Medicine, New Orleans, 1973-78, 79—, assoc. prof., 1978-79, Pres., bd. dirs. Tallahatchie Arts Council, New Albany, 1983-84. Served with USN, 1943-60. Mem. Am. Coll. Radiology, Radiol. Soc. N.Am., So. Radiol. Soc., Soc. Nuclear Medicine, Am. Coll. Nuclear Physicians, Miss. State Med. Soc., Miss. State Radiol. Soc., Miss. State Soc. Nuclear Medicine, N.E. Miss. Med. Soc., So. Med. Assn., AMA, Am. Inst. Ultrasound in Medicine. Democrat. Methodist. Club: Plimsoll (New Orleans). Lodges: Masons, Shriners. Home: 4590 W Beach Blvd Biloxi MS 39535-4416

HORN, THOMAS D., educator; b. Iowa City, Iowa, June 26, 1918; s. Ernest and Madeline (Darrough) H.; B.A., State U. Iowa, 1940, M.A., 1946, Ph.D., 1947; student Cambridge U., Eng., 1945; m. Grace Ellen Adams, Aug. 2, 1941; 1 dau., Diane. Tchr., public schs., Denver, 1940-42, River Forest, Ill., 1942-43; asst. prof. U. No. Iowa, 1947-51; vis. lectr. U. Pitts., summer 1949, Harvard, summer 1959, U. Mich., 1963; asso. prof. curriculum and instrn. Coll. Edn., U. Tex., Austin, 1951-59, prof., 1959—, chmn., 1962-73; dir. USOE Project, 1964-65, Bi-Cultural Sect., Coll. Edn. Research and Devel. Center, 1965-67, San Antonio Lang. Research Project, 1967-68, Lang. Research Project, 1968; Tex. commn. Services to Children and Youth, 1972-83, chmn., 1973-75, vice chmn., 1978-79. Served with U.S. Army, 1943-46; capt. USAFR, 1950-55. Named to Reading Instrn. Hall of Fame, 1984. Mem. Am. Ednl. Research Assn., Assn. Student Teaching (exec. bd. 1953-59, pres. 1957-58), Tex. Assn. for Student Teaching (pres. 1952-53), Internat. Reading Assn. (Spl. Service Award 1979), Nat. Conf. on Research in English (exec. bd. 1957-60, nat. pres. 1958-59), Nat. Council Tchrs. English (dir. elem. sect. 1965-68), Nat. Edn. Assn., Nat. Soc. Study Edn., Phi Delta Kappa, Phi Kappa Phi, Phi Gamma Delta. Contbr. articles to profl. jours. Co-author, cons. spelling and reading textbooks, instrnl. films. Editor research monographs, book. Home: 5302 Ridge Oak Dr Austin TX 78731 Office: Dept Curriculum and Instrn U Tex Austin TX 78712

HORNBERGER, MARJORIE ELLEN, accountant; b. Ft. Smith, Ark., Feb. 19, 1951; d. Evans Zacharias and Nancy Cravens (Eads) H. B.A., Emory U., 1973; M.B.A., So. Meth. U., 1978. C.P.A., Mass., Tex. Staff acct. Coopers & Lybrand, Boston; gen. practice ptnr. Coopers & Lybrand, Dallas, 1985—; instr. Sch. Mgmt. and Adminstrv. Scis., U. Tex., Dallas, 1980-81. Bd. dirs. Shakespeare Festival Dallas, 1983-86, Leadership Dallas, 1985-86; mem. Jr. League, The 500, Inc.; workshop leader, vol. Community Bd. Inst.; cons. Ctr. for Non Profit Mgmt. Mem. Am. Inst. C.P.A.s, Mass. Soc. C.P.A.s, Tex. Soc. C.P.A.s, So. Meth. U. M.B.A. Alumni Assn., Kappa Kappa Gamma, Alpha Iota Delta, Beta Gamma Sigma. Presbyterian. Home: 8401 Linwood St Dallas TX 75209 Office: 1999 Bryan St Suite 3000 Dallas TX 75201

HORNE, ALAN MITCHELL, architect; b. Jackson, Tenn., Nov. 22, 1953; s. Paul Jones and Ann Elizabeth (Mitchell) H.; m. Nora Ruiz, Apr. 8, 1978; 1 child, Alan Mitchell. Student U. Tenn.-Martin, 1971-74; B.Arch., U. Tenn., Knoxville, 1977. Registered architect, S.C. Draftsman Wiseman, Bland, Foster, & O'Brien, Memphis, 1976, Lockwood-Greene Engrs. Inc., Spartanburg, S.C., 1978; designer Ard-Wood Architects Inc., Greenville, S.C., 1978-79, MBTB Architects-Engrs. Inc., Greenville, 1979-81; architect Townsend Archtl. Planning Group, Greenville, 1981—. Mem. Greenville Council Architects, AIA, AIA (S.C. chpt.), Constrn. Specifications Inst. (Greenville chpt.) (profl. dir. 1982-85, tech. chmn. 1983, program chmn. 1984, chmn. membership 1985). Republican. Methodist. Avocations: photography; electronics; fishing; hunting; gardening. Home: 20 Richwood Dr Greenville SC 29607 Office: Townsend Archtl Planning Group PO Box 3917 18 W McBee Ave Greenville SC 29608

HORNE, CHARLES BANARD, insurance agent; b. Shreveport, La., May 21, 1954; s. Charles Lucien and Dorothy Jean (Frazier) H. B.S., Centenary Coll., 1976, postgrad., 1977-78. Agt., State Farm Ins. Co., Shreveport, La., 1978—. Pres., N.W. La. Basketball Assn. Mem. Nat. Life Assn. Republican. Roman Catholic. Clubs: Pierremont Oaks Tennis; Univ. (Shreveport); East Ridge Country.

HORNER, SALLY MELVIN, university administrator; b. Fayetteville, N.C., Nov. 17, 1932; d. John Stephen and Lila Williams (Chestnutt) Melvin; m. William Wesley Horner, June 9, 1950 (div. Mar. 1982); children—Stephanie McKay Horner Toney, John Wesley. Student, Meredith Coll., 1949-51, U. Colo.-Denver, 1951-54; B.S., U. N.C., 1957, Ph.D., 1961. Research assoc. chemistry, instr. chemistry U. N.C., Chapel Hill, 1961-67; physics cons. Research Triangle Inst., N.C., 1967; vis. sr. research assoc. chemistry Duke U., Durham, N.C., 1972; prof. chemistry, dept. chmn., dir. instl. research Meredith Coll., Raleigh, N.C., 1967-78; dean Coll. Arts and Scis., univ. provost U. Charleston (W.Va.), 1978-81, v.p. adminstrn. and fin., 1981-83, sr. v.p., chief operating officer, 1984; vice-chancellor W.Va. Bd. Regents, 1983-85; vice-chancellor adminstrv. services and fiscal affairs U.S.C.-Coastal Carolina Coll., 1984-85; v.p. planning and instl. advancement W.Va. State Coll., 1985—; bd. bd. dirs. N.C. Acad. Sci., 1976-79; cons. curriculum planning N.C. pvt. colls., 1976-78; nat. forum participant Women Adminstrs. in Higher Edn., 1980. Bd. trustees Kanawha Players, Charleston, W.Va., 1983; bd. dirs., treas. capital campaign YWCA, Charleston, 1983-84; mem. W.Va. Gov.'s State Adv. Group on Juvenile Justice and Delinquency Prevention Act, 1980-83. Recipient Alpha Chi Sigma chemistry award U. N.C., 1956; NSF predoctoral fellow, 1957-60. Mem. UDC, Colonial Dames 17th Century (chpt. pres. 1977-79), Am. Chem. Soc. (chmn. elect N.C. sect. 1978, exec. com. 1975-78), N.C. Assn. Instl. Research (exec. com. 1977-79), W.Va. Council Women Adminstrs. in Higher Edn., Order of the Valkries, Phi Beta Kappa, Sigma Xi. Contbr. articles in field to chem. jours. Office: W Va State Coll Institute WV 25112

HORNICK, FREDERIC RICHARD, medical technologist; b. Asmara, Ethiopia, June 25, 1950; s. Richard Lester and Alice Marie (Gould) H.; m. Joanna Cooke, Nov. 2, 1972; children—John, Joseph; 1 stepson, Jacob. B.S. in Biology, U. S.C., 1978, B.A. in Anthropology, 1978; M.S., 1983. Med. Technologist Moncrief Army Hosp., Fort Jackson, Columbia, S.C., 1971—; instr. parasitology U. S.C., 1982-84; parasitology cons. Riverbank Zoo. Served with U.S. Army, 1968-71. Mem. Am. Soc. Biologists, Southeastern Soc. Parasitologists, Am. Soc. Parasitology, Am. Soc. Clin. Pathologists, Sigma Xi. Republican. Roman Catholic. Office: Box 494 Moncrief Army Hospital Fort Jackson SC 29209

HORNSBY, JAMES RUSSELL, lawyer; b. Manchester, Ky., July 3, 1924; m. Peggy E., Feb. 11, 1982; children—Lawrence, Russell, Kevin Lee, Tonya Lisa, Brandon, Richard Earl, Tara Regan. Student Center Coll., 1946-47; LL.B., John B. Stetson U., 1950. Bar: Fla. 1950, U.S. Supreme Ct. 1959. Sole practice, Orlando, Fla., 1950—. Mem. Orange County Bar Assn., ABA, Fla. Bar Assn., Acad. Fla. Trial Lawyers, Internat. Acad. Law and Sci.

HOROWITZ, HARRY I., podiatrist; b. Astoria, N.Y., Nov. 8, 1915; s. Jacob and Fannie (Singer) H.; student CCNY, 1932-34; Pod.G, First Inst. Podiatry, N.Y.C., 1937; D.Podiatry, L.I. U., 1946; D.P.M., N.Y. Coll. Podiatric Medicine, 1967 L.H.D. (hon.), 1982; m. Sylvia Glaser, Feb. 11, 1940; children—Marc, Susan. Diplomate Am. Bd. Ambulatory Foot Surgery (hon.). Pvt. practice podiatry, Astoria, N.Y., 1937, 76, Belleair, Fla., 1976—; mem. podiatry practice com. Workmen's Compensation Bd. N.Y. State, 1953-66, chmn. com., 1966-76; chief podiatry dept. Queens Hosp. Center-L.I. Jewish Hosp., Jamaica, L.I., 1958-76; dir. Foot Clinics of N.Y., 1970-71; chmn. bd. Suncoast Orthotic Labs., Clearwater, Fla., 1978-83; podiatry panel Dept. Welfare N.Y.C.; arbitrator between Am. Bd. Foot Surgery and Am. Bd. Ambulatory Foot Surgery, 1982. Mem. citizens com. Union Free Sch. Dist. 29, Merrick, N.Y., 1957; mem. library com. dist. 29, 1964; founder Fund for Advancement Podiatry Edn., 1958; hon. pres. Fund for Podiatry Edn. and Research, 1963—, sec., 1963-66; chmn. Task Force on Podiatry, Health and Hosp. Corp., N.Y.C., 1976-78; trustee N.Y. Coll. Podiatric Medicine, 1973-74, cons., 1981—; chmn. Commn. to Study and Evaluate Foot Clinics of N.Y., 1980-81. Recipient award Jour. Podiatry, 1948; Podiatrist of Year Queens County Podiatry Soc., 1956, 71, Podiatry Soc. State N.Y., 1957, 61, testimonial N.Y. Coll. Podiatric Medicine, 1971. Mem. Am. Podiatry Assn. (exec. council, trustee 1955-62, award 1963, Disting. Service award 1982, Spl. Service award 1983), Am. Assn. Hosp. Podiatrists, Am. Public Health Assn., Fla. Public Health Assn. (chmn. podiatric sect. 1983-85), Acad. Podiatry. Clubs: Masons, B'nai B'rith, K.P. Home: 100 Oakmont Ln Belleair FL 33516

HOROWITZ, ROSALIND, educator, researcher; b. St. Paul, Aug. 24, 1946; d. Cantor Louis and Fannie (Hartman) H. B.S., U. Minn., 1968, M.A., 1973, Ph.D., 1982; postgrad. Harvard U., 1968. Hebrew U., Jerusalem, 1971. Tchr. English, Marshall-Univ. High Sch., Mpls., 1969-70; instr. edn. U. Minn., Mpls., 1970-75, supr. of student tchrs., 1973-75, adminstrv. fellow for assoc. dean Coll. Edn., 1975-81, research coordinator edn. planning and devel. office, U. Minn., 1975-81, affiliate mem. Ctr. for Research in Human Learning, 1979-81; prin. Hebrew and Judaic studies program, Adath Jeshurun Religious Sch., Mpls., 1974-76; asst. prof. reading, edn. Coll. of Social and Behavioral Scis., U. Tex., San Antonio, 1981—; lectr. in field; researcher text processing, text linguistics, discourse analysis; cons. in field. Mpls. Council PTA Scholar, 1964; U. Minn. Nicholson Bookstore Scholar, 1965; HEW-U. Minn. grantee 1966, 67; Harvard U. Scholar, 1968; Wesley E. Peik scholar, U. Minn., 1979; Doctoral Dissertation Spl. grantee, 1979; U. Tex. research grantee, 1984; Spencer fellow Nat. Acad. Edn., 1985-88. Mem. Am. Ednl. Research Assn., Am. Assn. for Higher Edn., Internat. Reading Assn. (Outstanding Dissertation award 1983), Nat. Council of Tchrs. of English (Promising Research 1983), Nat. Reading Conf. Contbr. chpts. to books, articles to profl. jours. Co-editor: Comprehending Oral and Written Language, 1987; reviewer: Applied Psycholinguistics, Jour. Ednl. Psychology, Reading Research Quar., Jour. Reading Behavior, 1979—; editorial adv. bd. Nat. Reading Conf. Yearbook, 1984-86; acquisition editor Reading and Literacy. Office: Coll Social and Behavioral Sciences Div Edn U Tex San Antonio San Antonio TX 78285

HORRIGAN, EDWARD A., JR., tobacco co. exec.; b. N.Y.C., Sept. 23, 1929; s. Edward A. and Margaret V. (Kells) H.; B.S. in Bus. Adminstrn., U. Conn., 1950; grad. Advanced Mgmt. Program, Harvard, 1965; m. Elizabeth R. Herperger, June 27, 1953; children—Ellen, Christopher, Gordon, Brian. Sales mgr. Procter & Gamble Co., N.Y.C., 1954-58; gen. mgr. Ebonite Co., Boston, 1958-61; div. v.p. T.J. Lipton Inc., 1961-73; chmn. bd., pres. Buckingham Corp., N.Y.C., 1973-78; chmn. bd., chief exec. officer R.J. Reynolds Tobacco Internat., Inc., Winston-Salem, N.C., 1978-80; chmn. bd., pres., chief exec. officer R. J. Reynolds Tobacco Co., Winston-Salem, 1980—, exec. v.p. R.J. Reynolds Industries, Inc., 1981—. Served as officer, inf., U.S. Army, 1950-54. Decorated Silver Star, Purple Heart, Combat Inf. badge, Parachute badge. Mem. Mil. Order World Wars. Clubs: Old Town Country; Vintage. Home: 2815 Bartram Rd Winston-Salem NC 27106 Office: Reynolds Bldg 401 N Main St Winston-Salem NC 27102

HORST, WILLIAM HENRY, computer systems company executive; b. Cumberland, Va., Apr. 3, 1946; s. Willi and Lucy (Morrison) H.; m. Linda Warne, June 25, 1968 (div. 1978); 1 child, Amy. B.A. in English, Va. Poly. Inst., 1968; M.A. in English, U. Ky., 1970; Ed.D. in English Edn., 1986. Instr. English, East Carolina U., Greenville, N.C., 1970-71; chmn. English dept. Moody Middle Sch., Henrico County Pub. Schs., Richmond, Va., 1971-81; tchr. Fairfax County Schs., Reston, Va., 1982-84; mgr. ednl. services Tesdata Systems Corp., McLean, Va., 1984—; cons. in field. Author: Sentence Combining, 1983. Dept. editor English Jour., 1976-79. Contbr. articles to profl. jours. Fellow Nat. Council Tchrs. English (secondary sect. com. 1979-83, instr. tech. com. 1983—); mem. Am. Soc. Tng. and Devel., Va. Assn. Tchrs. English (pres. 1979), Jr. High/Middle Sch. Assembly Nat Council Tchrs. English (chmn. 1976). Avocations: tennis; writing, science fiction; museums. Home: 55 Skyhill Dr #304 Alexandria VA 22314 Office: Tesdata Systems Corp Spring Park Tech Ctr 460 Spring Park Pl Herndon VA 22070

HORTON, BILLY RAY, county sheriff; b. Clovis, N.Mex., Apr. 28, 1932; s. Golden Wesley and Gracie (Pruitt) H.; m. Joa Dawn Berry, Sept. 23, 1950; children—Mike, Danny, Dawna. Ed. pub. schs., Bovina, Tex. Cert. in law enforcement, Tex. Dep. sheriff, Bovina, part-time 1960-62; dep. sheriff Dawson County Sheriffs Dept., Lamesa, Tex., 1962-72, chief dep., 1972-78, sheriff, 1978—. Mem. Sheriffs Assn. Tex., Tex. Narcotics Officers Assn. (bd. dirs. 1980-81, tng. officer 1982-83, sgt. at arms 1983-84). Democrat. Baptist. Office: Dawson County Sheriffs Dept 300 Bloct S 1st St Lamesa TX 79331

HORTON, CARRELL PETERSON, college educator; b. Daytona Beach, Fla., Nov. 28, 1928; d. Preston Steward and Mildred Geneva (Adams) Peterson; m. Richard G. Horton, Apr. 14, 1954 (div. 1958); 1 child, Richard Preston. B.A., Fisk U., 1949; M.A., Cornell U., 1950; Ph.D., U. Chgo., 1972. Instr. and research assoc., Nashville, 1950-55; Statis. analyst and project adminstr. Meharry Med. Coll., Nashville, 1955-66; from instr. to prof., chmn. psychology div. dir. social scis. Fisk U., Nashville, 1966—; dir. Rochell Ctr., Nashville, 1968-72, 1978-85; child care adv. com. Nashville Vocat. & Tech. Sch., 1970-72; cons. Health Service Research Study Sect., Washington, 1977-80. Contbr. articles to profl. jours. Bd. dirs. Wesley Found., Nashville, 1977—; mem. United Meth. Ch. Higher Edn. Commn., 1983; bd. dirs. Belmont Samaritan Pastoral Counseling Ctr., 1983. Mem. Am. Psychol. Assn. Office: Fisk U Nashville TN 37203

HORTON, GRANVILLE EUGENE, physician, retired air force officer; b. Jean, Tex., July 2, 1927; s. James Granville and Etna (Boyle) H.; B.A., Tex. Technol. Coll., 1950; M.D., U. Tex., 1954; m. Mildred Helen Veale, June 13, 1953; children—Robert Herman Newlin, Linda Kay, Kevin Bruce, Carson Scott. Intern, Detroit Receiving Hosp., 1954-55; tng. in radioactive isotope techniques Oak Ridge Inst. Nuclear Studies, 1958; practice medicine, Weslaco, Tex., 1955-56, Outlar-Blair Clinic, Wharton, 1956-72; dir. dept. nuclear medicine Nightingale Hosp., El Campo, Tex., 1973-75; mem. staff Horton Med. Clinic, El Campo, 1972-75; part-time research asso. radioisotope dept. Meth. Hosp., Houston, 1961-66; mem. med. adv. com. and sec. med. staff Caney Valley Meml. Hosp., Wharton, 1956-72; clin. dir. Wharton County Tb Assn., 1957-67; commd. lt. col. U.S. Air Force, 1975; postgrad. U.S. Air Force Sch. Aerospace Medicine, 1975; chief aeromed. services Brooks AFB, Tex., 1976-82. Bd. dirs. Wharton County div. Am. Cancer Soc., pres., 1960-61; dir. 8th dist. Tex., Citizens Com. for Hoover Report, 1957-58. Served with USN, 1946-47. Fellow Am. Coll. Angiology (state gov. 1979), Am. Coll. Nuclear Medicine; mem. Am. Coll. Emergency Physicians, Wharton C. of C. (dir., v.p. 1960-61), Am., Tex. (ho. of dels. 1959-61) med. assns., Soc. Nuclear Medicine, Tex. Assn. Physicians Nuclear Medicine, AAAS, Law Enforcement Officers Tex. (asso.), Am. Nuclear Soc., Tex. Med. Found., El Campo C. of C., Phi Chi. Republican. Episcopalian. Lodge: Elks. Contbr. articles to med. publs. Home: 15102 Oakmere San Antonio TX 78232 Office: Occupational Med Clinic San Antonio 2200 McCullough San Antonio TX 78212

HORTON, JAMES WRIGHT, JR., geologist; b. Anderson, S.C., June 14, 1950; s. James Wright and Eunice Todd (Rice) H.; m. Beverly Field Rose, May 19, 1973; children—James Fontaine, Sarah Rose. B.S., Furman U., Greenville, S.C., 1972; M.S., U. N.C., 1974, Ph.D., 1977. Asst. prof. geology U. So. Maine, 1977-79; NRC postdoctoral assoc. U.S. Geol. Survey, Reston, Va., 1978-80, research geologist, 1980—, asst. br. chief, 1985—; adj. asst. prof. U. N.C., 1978-79; mem. state geologic map com. N.C. Geol. Survey Sect., 1983-85; mem. working group E-4 Geodynamics Continental-Ocean Transects Program, 1982-85. Mem. Vestry St. James Episcopal Ch., Leesburg, Va., 1984-86. . Grantee N.C. Geol. Survey 1973, 74, 78, Geol. Soc. Am. 1975, Sigma Xi, 1975, S.C. Geol. Survey, 1976, NSF, 1979. Mem. Carolina Geol. Soc. (pres. 1981-82), Geol. Soc. Am. (Penrose Conf. com. 1983-85), Am. Geophys. Union, Geol. Soc. Wash. (awards com. 1981), Potomac Geophys. Soc., Geol. Soc. Maine, Ga. Geol. Soc., AAAS, Sigma Xi. Editor: Geological Investigations of the Kings Mountain Belt and Adjacent Areas in the Carolinas, 1981; contbr. articles to profl. jours. Home: 12601 Millbank Way Herndon VA 22070 Office: 928 Nat Ctr US Geol Survey Reston VA 22092

HORTON, JANICE FAYE, state senator; b. Barnesville, Ga., Jan. 23, 1945; d. Grover George and Sara Alice (Zellner) Shiver; A.B., Tift Coll., Ga., 1967; postgrad. Woodrow Wilson Law Sch., Atlanta; m. Charles Douglas Horton, Aug. 26, 1967; children—Amy Elaine, Sara Leigh. Tchr. high sch. English, 1967-72; owner Horton Realty & Investment Co., McDonough, Ga., 1975—; mem. McDonough City Council, 1975-78, Henry County Bd. Commrs., 1976-78; mem. Ga. Senate, 1979—. Bd. dirs. local Am. Cancer Soc.; del. Dem. Nat. Conv., 1980. Mem. Bus. and Profl. Women (chpt. v.p. 1975—). Democrat. Baptist. Home: 430 Burke Circle McDonough GA 30253 Office: Room 122G State Capitol Atlanta GA 30334

HORTON, JOHN LEN, educational administrator, consultant; b. Owensboro, Ky., Aug. 18, 1944; s. Len M. and Wanda Lee (Wilson) H.; 1 child, Carson Chance. Adminstrs. cert. U. Ky., 1976; B.S., Western Ky. U., 1967, M.A., 1972. Tchr., coach Daviess County High Sch., Owensboro, Ky., 1967-72; state supr. Ky. Dept. Edn., Frankfort, 1972-83; dir. curriculum devel. Ky. Dept. Edn., Frankfort, 1983—. Bd. dirs. Ky. Spl. Olympics, Frankfort, 1978-82, chmn. bd. dirs., 1981-82, bd. dirs., 1984—. Tex. Gas Corp. grad. scholar in econs., Owensboro, 1972. Mem. Am. Vocat. Assn., Ky. Vocat. Assn., Ky. Practical Arts Assn. (state pres. 1978), Delta Pi Epsilon, Delta Sigma Pi. Republican. Methodist. Avocations: pilot; realtor. Home: 904 Tierra Linda Dr Frankfort KY 40601 Office: Ky Dept Edn 2024 Capital Plaza Tower Frankfort KY 40601

HORTON, JOSEPH JULIAN, JR., finance economics educator; b. Memphis, Nov. 7, 1936; s. Joseph Julian and Nina Amanda (Williams) H.; m. Linda Anne Langley, May 30, 1964; children—Joseph, Anne, David. B.A., N.Mex. State U., 1958; M.A., So. Meth. U., 1964, Ph.D., 1968. Fin. economist FDIC, Washington, 1967-71; prof., chmn. dept. Slippery Rock U., Pa., 1971-81; dean Sch. Bus. Bellarmine Coll., Louisville, 1981—; vis. fin. economist Fed. Home Loan Bank Bd., 1978-79; postdoctoral research fellow Harvard U., Cambridge, Mass., 1970-71. Contbr. articles to profl. jours., author monographs and papers. Recipient Cokesbury award Meth. Ch., 1966; Bank Adminstrn. Inst. Clarence Lichtfeldt fellow, 1982, Ford Found. fellow, 1967; NSF grantee, 1975-79. Mem. N.Am. Econs. and Fin. Assn. (v.p. 1973—), Eastern Econs. Assn. (v.p. 1982-83), Pa. Econ. Assn. (pres. 1978), Midwest Bus. Econs. Assn. (exec. sec. 1985—). Methodist. Avocations: history; chess; science fiction. Home: 234 Maevi Dr New Albany IN 47150 Office: Bellarmine Coll Rubel Sch Bus Newburg Rd Louisville KY 40205

HORTON, ODELL, federal judge; b. Bolivar, Tenn., May 13, 1929; s. Odell and Rosa H.; A.B., Morehouse Coll., 1951; cert. U.S. Navy Sch. Journalism, 1952; J.D., Howard U., 1956; H.H.D. (hon.), Mass. Indsl. Coll., 1969; m. Evie L. Randolph, Sept. 13, 1953; children—Odell, Christopher. Bar: Tex. 1956. Individual practice law, Memphis, 1957-62; asst. U.S. atty. Western Dist. Tenn., Memphis, 1962-67; dir. div. hosp. and health services City of Memphis, 1968; judge Criminal Ct. Shelby County. Memphis, 1969-70; pres. Le-Moyne-Owen Coll., Memphis, 1970-74; commentator Sta. WREC-TV (CBS), Memphis, 1972-74, judge U.S. Dist. Ct. Western Dist. Tenn., 1980—. Bd. mgrs. Methodist Hosp., Memphis, 1969-79; bd. dirs. Family Service of Memphis, United Negro Coll. Fund, N.Y.C., 1970-74; trustee Mt. Pisgah Christian Methodist Episcopal Ch., Memphis, 1957—. Served with USMC, 1951-53. Recipient Disting. Alumni award Howard U., 1969; Bill of Rights award West Tenn. chpt. ACLU, 1970. Disting. Service award Mallory Knights. Charitable Orgn., 1970, Smothers Chapel C.M.E. Ch., 1971; Outstanding Citizen award Frontiers Internat., 1969; Ralph E. Bunche Humanitarian award Boy Scouts Am., 1972; Outstanding Educator and Judge award Salem-Gilfield Bapt. Ch., 1973; Spl. Tribune award A.M.E. Ch., 1974; United Negro Coll. Fund award, 1974; Humanities award Citizens Com. Council of Memphis, 1969; Shelby County Penal Farm award, 1974; Disting. Service award LeMoyne-Owen Coll., 1974, Lane Coll., 1977; Dedicated Community Service award Christian Meth. Episc. Ch., 1979. Mem. Am. Bar Assn., Nat. Bar Assn., NAACP. Home: 2183 S Parkway East Memphis TN 38114 Office: Fed Bldg and US Courthouse 167 N Main St Room 957 Memphis TN 38103*

HORTON, PAUL BRADFIELD, lawyer; b. Dallas, Oct. 19, 1920; s. Frank Barrett and Hazel Lillian (Bradfield) H.; B.A., U. Tex., Austin, 1943, student Law Sch., 1941-43; LL.B., So. Methodist U., 1947; m. Susan Jeanne Diggle, May 19, 1949; children—Bradfield Ragland, Bruce Ragsdale. Admitted to Tex. bar, 1946, since practiced in Dallas; partner firm McCall, Parkhurst & Horton, 1951—; lectr. mcpl. bond law and public fin. S.W. Legal Found. Mem. Tex. Gov.'s Com. Tex. Edn. Code, 1967-69. Served to lt. USNR, 1943-46. Mem. Am. Bar Assn., Dallas Bar Assn., Nat. Water Resources Assn., Tex. Water Conservation Assn., Govt. Fin. Officers Assn., The Barristers, Delta Theta Phi, Beta Theta Pi. Clubs: Dallas Country, Tower, Crescent, City, Chaparral (Dallas); Austin. Home: 5039 Seneca Dr Dallas TX 75209 Office: 900 Diamond Shamrock Tower Dallas TX 75201

HORTON, RONALD LEE, music educator; b. Wytheville, Va., Apr. 8, 1948; s. George Ernest and Margaret Naomi (Proffit) H.; m. Patricia Darlene Brewster, July 7, 1973; children—Edward Lee, Timothy Wayne, Patrick Neal. B.A. in Music Edn., Marshall Coll., Huntington, W.Va., 1970; M.A. in Performance, Radford (Va.) Coll., 1976; Ph.D., Columbia Pacific U., 1983. High sch. band dir., Va., 1974-76; dir. music Hargrave Mil. Acad., Chatham, Va., 1976—; adj. instr. S.W. Va. Community Coll., Richlands, 1973; interim band master 90th Army Band, Va. Nat. Guard, 1978; continuing edn. instr. Danville (Va.) Community Coll., 1984. Author: Music for Worship, 1984. Contbr. articles to profl. publs. Mem. Christian Instrumental Dirs. Assn., Coll. Band Dirs. Nat. Assn., Internat. Horn Soc., Coll. Music Soc., Phi Mu Alpha Sinfonia. Baptist. Office: Hargrave Mil Acad Military Dr Chatham VA 24531

HORTON, WILLIAM LAMAR, music educator; b. Rock Hill, S.C., Aug. 26, 1935; s. Luther Burns and Ruth (Stogner) H.; Mus.B., Furman U., 1956; M.Sacred Music, So. Bapt. Theol. Sem., 1958, D.Mus. Arts, 1970; postdoctoral study U. Mich., 1968, Paris Académie des Arts Musicaux, 1975, U. So. Calif., 1981; m. Peggy Ann Small, June 16, 1956; children—Richard Lamar, Ronald William, Randall Alan, Julie Anne. Minister music First Bapt. Ch., Taylors, S.C., 1954-56, Broadway Bapt. Ch., Louisville, 1956-58, First Bapt. Ch., Douglas, Ga., 1958-59; instr. music U. Ga., 1958-59, So. Bapt. Theol. Sem., Louisville, 1959-62; prof. music, chmn. dept. ch. music Ouachita Bapt. U., Arkadelphia, Ark., 1963-68; prof. music Okla. Bapt. U., Shawnee, 1968—, chmn. dept. ch. music, 1979-81; minister music Univ. Bapt. Ch., Shawnee, 1968-74, 1st Christian Ch., Shawnee, 1977-82; organist-choir master Emmanuel Epis. Ch., Shawnee, 1982—. Clinician, adjudicator music festivals throughout South and S.W.; baritone soloist various musicals, oratorios, other prodns.; pres. Shawnee Band Parents Assn., 1975-76; mem. State Arts Council Okla., 1977—, v.p., 1981-82, exec. com., 1981—, pres., 1982-83; pres. Shawnee Community Concerts Assn., 1977-79, Shawnee Arts Council, 1977-79; trustee B.B. McKinney Music Research Found., 1972-74; bd. dirs. Shawnee Little Theatre, 1981-83. Named Okla. Musician of the Year, 1975; recipient Gov.'s Arts award, 1983. Mem. Music Tchrs. Nat. Assn., Nat. Assn. Tchrs. of Singing (pres. Okla. chpt. 1973-75), Okla. Music Tchrs. Assn. (3d v.p. 1970-74), ASCAP, Okla. Advocates for the Arts (pres. 1983—), Phi Mu Alpha Sinfonia (Okla. province gov. 1968-78). Club: Masons. Author: Introduction to Singing, 1968; Score Reading, 3 vols., 1975. Contbr. critiques, revs. to profl. jours.; art, music and drama critic Shawnee News-Star. Composer: Song of the Lamb, 1958, Salvation to Our God, 1962, How Excellent is Thy Name, 1962, Praise Ye The Lord, 1963, Cindy, 1977. Home: 18 Mojave Dr Shawnee OK 74801

HORVAT, KENNETH JOHN, landscape and maintenance company owner; b. Flushing, N.Y., Jan. 10, 1955; s. Joseph J. and Ruthy J. (Tramposch) H.; m. Kathleen A. McGarry, Dec. 9, 1983. Student City Community Coll., Ohio,

1973-75. Salesman, Senco Products, Westlake, Ohio, 1975-79; mgr. Party Shoppe, Inc., North Olmsted, Ohio, 1979-82; owner The Gardeners, Inc., Atlanta, 1982—. Soccer coach North Olmsted High Sch., 1980; instr. youth orgns., 1976—. Recipient Coach of Yr. award Coaches Assn., 1977. Mem. Nat. Landscape Assn. Roman Catholic. Home: 11900 Old Mountain Park Rd Roswell GA 30075 Office: The Gardeners Inc 2515 NE Expy Suite L-7 Atlanta GA 30345

HORVATH, PAUL SAMUEL, oil company executive; b. Johnstown, Pa., July 9, 1934; s. John and Anna (Boratko) H.; m. Belva Magee, Apr. 22, 1955; children—Jeff, Terre Horvath Patterson. B.S., U. Pitts., 1971. Geophysicist, Gulf Research & Devel. Co., Pitts., 1966-72; sr. geophysicist Thailand Gulf Oil, Asia, 1972-74; geophys. mgr. Singapore Gulf Oil, S. Asia, 1974-75; dist. geosci. mgr. Gulf Oil Exploration & Prodn. Co., New Orleans, 1975-77, area exploration mgr., 1977-80, gen. mgr. exploration, 1980—. Contbr. articles to profl. jours. Mem. New Orleans C. of C., Soc. Exploration Geophysicists, Am. Assn. Petroleum Geologists, New Orleans Geol. Soc., Southeastern Geophys. Soc., Petroleum Landman's Assn. New Orleans, New Orleans Petroleum Club. (fin. com. 1983-84). Avocations: golfing; fishing; hunting. Home: 2651 Hudson Pl New Orleans LA 70114 Office: Gulf Oil Exploration & Prodn Co 1515 Poydras St New Orleans LA 70162

HORVIT, MICHAEL M., music educator, composer; b. Bklyn., June 22, 1932; s. John and Rose Horvit; m. Nancy Joy Harris, June 12, 1957; children—Mark Harris, Adam Daniel. Mus.B., Yale U., 1955, Mus.M., 1956; postgrad. Harvard U., 1957; D.M.A., Boston U., 1959. Bass trombonist New Haven Symphony Orch., 1952-56; assoc. prof. So. Conn. State Coll., New Haven, 1959-66; music critic New Haven Register, 1965-66; prof. U. Houston, 1966—; music dir. Temple Emanuel, Houston, 1967—. NEA grantee 1974; U. Houston research grantee, 1967, 75, 78, 81, 83; M.B. Rockefeller grantee, 1968; recipient ASCAP awards, 1976-83; New Music prize Houston Symphony Orch. and Fridge Trust, 1976. Mem. Am. Music Center, Am. Soc. Univ. Composers, ASCAP, Coll. Mus. Soc., Nat. Opera Assn., Opera for Youth, Central Opera Service. Composer: Concerto for Guitar and Orchestra, 1983; Chamber Concerto for English Horn and String Quartet, 1983; Antiphon V for Viola and Electronic Tape, 1983; The Gardens of Hieronymus, 1976; Adventure in Space-chamber Opera, 1977; Trio for Violin, Cello and Piano, 1982; Dialogues for Harp and Percussion, 1981; Chamber Concerto For English Horn and String Quartet, 1984; Concerto for Percussion and Wind Symphony, 1985. Office: Sch Music U Houston University Park Houston TX 77004

HORVITZ, PAUL MICHAEL, finance educator; b. Providence, R.I., Aug. 6, 1935; s. Abraham and Rose (Gershkoff) H.; m. Carol Broomfield, Nov. 17, 1955; children—Marcia Ellen, Steven Jay. B.A., U. Chgo., 1954; M.B.A., Boston U., 1956; Ph.D. in Econs., MIT, 1958. Fin. economist Fed. Reserve Bank of Boston, 1957-60; asst. prof. Boston U., 1960-62; sr. economist, comptroller of currency, Washington, 1963-66; dir. research FDIC, 1967-77; Judge James A. Elkins prof. banking and finance U. Houston, 1977—; dir. Fed. Home Loan Bank of Dallas, Ameriway Bank-Brookhollow, Houston. Mem. Am. Econ. Assn., Am. Fin. Assn., Fin. Mgmt. Assn., So. Fin. Assn. Club: Tiburon Tennis (Ocean City, Md.). Author: Management of Bank Funds, 1981; Monetary Policy & the Financial System, 5th edit., 1983; mem. editorial bd. Jour. Bank Research, Jour. Fin. Research; contbr. articles to profl. jours. Home: 150 Sugarberry Circle Houston TX 77024 Office: Dept Finance U Houston Houston TX 77004

HORWITZ, SIDNEY HAROLD, pediatric dentist; b. Richmond, Va., June 13, 1940; s. Nat and Ella (Wolf) H.; children—Deborah S., Joel A., Richard N. B.S., U. Richmond, 1960; D.D.S., Med. Coll. Va., 1964, cert. in pediatric dentistry, 1966. Ptnr., owner Shocket, Horwitz, Keeton, Raddin, Ltd., Richmond, Va., 1968—; asst. clin. prof. Sch. Dentistry, Med. Coll. Va., Richmond, 1965-76. Gen. chmn. Jewish Welfare Fund Drive, Richmond, 1981-82; bd. dirs. Council Jewish Fedns., N.Y.C., 1983—, Am. Jewish Joint Distbn. Com., N.Y.C., 1983—; pres. Jewish Community Fedn. Richmond, 1983-84; chmn. honors com. Va. Commonwealth U., Richmond, 1985—. Recipient Maimonides award State of Israel Bonds, Richmond, 1981. Mem. ADA, Va. Dental Assn., Richmond Dental Assn., Southeastern Soc. Pediatric Dentistry, Alpha Omega, Omicron Kappa Upsilon. Avocation: photography. Office: Shocket Horwitz Keeton Raddin Ltd 121 Wyck St Richmond VA 23225

HOSKINS, ROBERT NATHAN, agribusiness consultant; b. Keota, Iowa, Feb. 23, 1917; s. Frank A. and Ora E. (Wayman) H.; student U. Mo., 1934-37; B.S., Iowa State U., 1939; m. Julia L. Jones, July 19, 1946; children—Nancy Carol, Mary Susan, Julia Ann, Robert Nathan. Towerman, Sam A. Baker State Forest, Mo. Conservation Commn., 1939, sr. forester, 1940-41; extension forester Fla. Forest Service, 1941-45; indsl. forester Seaboard Air Line R.R. Co. (name changed to Seaboard Coast Line R.R. Co. 1967), Richmond, Va., 1945-46, gen. forestry agt., 1956-64, gen. indsl. and forestry agt., 1964-65, gen. mgr. indsl. devel., 1965-68, asst. v.p. containerization and spl. projects, 1968-69, asst. v.p. forestry and spl. projects, 1969-79; cons. agribus., 1979—; dir. F.A. Bartlett Tree Expert Co. Mem. core com. Keep Fla. Green, 1946-50, Keep N.C. Green, 1947-49; mem. Gov.'s Adv. Com. on Forestry, Va. Economy, 1950-53; mem. adv. com. on forestry program in agrl. edn. Va., N.C., S.C., Ga., Fla., Ala., 1950-65; mem. adv. com. vocational edn. Va. State Bd. Edn., 1950-60; mem. profl. adv. group indsl. devel. Commonwealth Va., 1967-68; mem. staff of resources Future, 1949-50; adviser on forestry edn. So. Regional Edn. Bd., 1957-58; southeastern regional chmn. sponsoring com. Nat. Future Farmers Am. Found., 1969-74, state chmn., Va., 1975-76; mem. nat. adv. com. to sec. agr. on state and pvt. forestry, 1970-73; mem. Va. Agri-Bus. Council; vice chmn. publicity centennial com. Va. Dept. Agr. and Commerce, 1977. Pres. Parents' Assn. U. Richmond, 1975-76; bd. dirs. Henrico County chpt. ARC, 1981-83; mem. Henrico County Republican Com. Named Norfolk's Outstanding Young Man, Norfolk Jr. C. of C., 1951, recipient certificate of merit, 1952; recipient Distinguished Service award S.C. Agrl. Tchrs., 1953, Alumni Merit award Chgo. Alumni Assn., Iowa State U., 1954, Key to City, Mayor of Cin., 1960, Mayor of Phila., 1961, Merit award Fla. Vocational Agrl. Assn., 1965, Appreciation award Va. Agrl. Tchrs. Assn., 1967, Disting. Service award S.C. Future Farmers Am. Assn., 1968, Spl. award for disting. service to sponsoring com. Nat. Future Farmers Am., 1971, Hon. State Farmer degree Tenn. Assn., 1977; Order Palmetto, 1973. Mem. Am. (Merit award 1954, awards chmn. 1949-54, Disting. Ser. award 1978, Soil Conservation award Va. chpt. 1978), Ga. (liaison and coordinating com. 1955-56), N.C. (reforestation com. 1951-52), Ala., Fla. forestry assns., Va. Forests, Fla. Forest and Park Assn., Soc. Am. Foresters, Ry. Tie Assn. (chmn. conservation com. 1956-58, mem. pub. affairs com. 1977-78), Forest Farmers Assn. (ednl. com. 1957-58), Am. Vocat. Assn. (award merit 1958), U.S. (mem. agribus. and rural affairs com. 1972-75), Soc. of Va. (exec. council 1975—), Fla. State (forestry com. 1952-53), Va. State (indsl. devel. com. 1965-68), Richmond chambers commerce. Methodist (finance com. 1962-63). Clubs: Va. Press (Richmond), Soc. of Va. (dir. 1973-75), Hermitage Country. Author: (with M.D. Mobley) Forestry in the South, 1956. Editor SCL Forestry Bull., 1945-65. Contbr. articles to profl. jours. Home: 7605 Cornwall Rd Richmond VA 23229

HOST, W. JAMES, public relations and advertising executive; b. Kane, Pa. A.B., U. Ky., 1959. Baseball player; sports announcer, Lexington, Ky.; with Procter & Gamble, Cin., to 1964; builder, Realtor, ins. agt., Lexington, 1964-67; commr. Ky. Dept. Pub. Info., Lexington, 1967-70, commr. Dept. Parks, 1970; candidate for lt. gov. Ky.; pres. Host Communications, Inc., Lexington, to present. Chmn. Ky. Arthritis Campaign, 1969; vice-chmn. Fayette County Heart Drive; past bd. dirs. Florence Crittenden Home, United Cerebral Palsy of Ky., Lexington Deaf-Oral Sch.; past pres. Blue Grass council Boy Scouts Am., now mem. adv. bd. dirs.; past mem. U.S. Travel Service Travel Adv. Bd.; past v.p. Lincoln Heritage Trail Found. Mem. Nat. Tour Assn. (exec. v.p.), Travel Industry Assn. Am. (travel policy council, bd. dirs.), Ky. Jaycees, Ky. C. of C. (bd. dirs.), Greater Lexington Area C. of C. (past chmn.), Pub. Relations Soc. Am., Nat. Sportscasters and Sportswriters Assn., Civil War Round Table, Lexington Advt. Club, Fellowship of Christian Athletes, U. Ky. Alumni Assn. (life), Ky. Assn. Mut. Ins. Agts. (past pres.), Delta Tau Delta. Clubs: Nat. Press, Lexington Country, Lafayette, Ky. Athletic. Lodge: Rotary (pres. Lexington 1979-80, chmn. endowment). Office: Host Communications Inc 546 E Main St Lexington KY 40508

HOUCK, CHARLES WESTON, federal judge; b. Florence, S.C., Apr. 16, 1933; s. William Stokes and Charlotte Barnwell (Weston) H. grad. U. N.C., 1954; LL.B., U. S.C., 1956; m. Wana Kaye Hutchinson, Mar. 28, 1980; children—Charles Weston, Charlotte Elizabeth. Bar: S.C. Sole practice, Florence, 1958-79; ptnr. firm Houck, Clarke & Johnson, 1971-79; U.S. dist. judge Dist. S.C., Florence, 1979—. Mem. S.C. Ho. of Reps., 1963-66; chmn. Florence City-County Bldg. Commn., 1968-76. Served with AUS, 1957-58. Mem. ABA, S.C. Bar Assn. Episcopalian. Home: 506 Oleander Dr Florence SC 29501 Office: McMillan Fed Bldg PO Box 2260 W Evans St Florence SC 29503*

HOUCK, LINDA ROBINSON, home economist; b. Wadesboro, N.C., Sept. 30, 1949; d. George Jackson and Mattie Lois (Marsh) Robinson; m. Jacob Albert Houck, May 31, 1970. B.S. in Home Econs., U. N.C.-Greensboro, 1971; M.Ed., Coll. William and Mary, 1978. Cert. tchr., counselor, Va. Extension agt. in home econs. Va. Coop. Extension Service, Hampton, 1971—. Telephone crisis counselor, small group facilitator Contact Peninsula, Newport News, Va., 1978—. Mem. Am. Home Econs. Assn., Peninsula Nutrition Council (chmn. 1984-86), Nat., Assn. Extension Home Economists, Am. Assn. Counseling and Devel., Peninsula Women's Network. Avocation: reading. Home: 3 Redman Ct Hampton VA 23669 Office: Va Coop Extension Service 1320 LaSalle Ave Room 6 Hampton VA 23669

HOUGH, THOMAS BRYANT, minister; b. Anson County, N.C., Nov. 7, 1903; s. Robert Andrew and Janie (Simpson) H.; B.A., Duke U., 1937, postgrad. theology Emory U., 1930-34, U. Iowa, 1950; Th.M., Am. Bible Sch., 1950, Th.D., 1952, D.D., 1952; m. Mary Garnett Martin, June 15, 1928; 1 dau., Mary Jane (Mrs. Thoroughgood Fleetwood Hassell). Ordained to ministry United Methodist Ch., 1929; pastor various chs., N.C., 1929-62; supt. Burlington (N.C.) dist., 1962-67; pastor First Ch., Rockingham, N.C., 1967-71; mem. bd. ministerial tng. United Meth. Ch., 1958-62. Del., Jurisdictional Conf., 1964, World Conf. United Meth., London, 1966. Vol. chaplain Richmond County Meml. Hosp., 1967-71, civilian adviser to 3d Army, 1958-70; dist. commr. Cherokee Council Boy Scouts Am., 1948-49. Bd. trustees N.C. United Meth. Conf., 1960-72, Meth. Retirement Homes, 1962-76. Named Citizen of Yr., Rockingham, 1979. Democrat. Lodge: Kiwanis. Author: Steeple Tones, 1958-62. Contbr. articles to religious jours. and lodge mags. Home and Office: 430 Curtis Dr Rockingham NC 28379

HOUGHTON, E. C. (TED), banker; b. El Paso, Tex., Jan. 25, 1931; s. George W. and Madge A. (McElroy) H.; m. Marietta Bunsen, Sept. 24, 1950; children—Edward Cone, Marcy Houghton Gray, George, Linda, Brian. Successively routeman, dist. mgr., br. mgr. Prices Creameries, Alamogordo and Las Cruces, N.Mex., 1951-69, pres., chief exec. officer, 1969-71; v.p. mktg. and sales Farah Mfg., 1971-74; exec. v.p. mktg. and consumer services div. State Nat. Bank of El Paso, 1974—; dir. State Nat. Bank of Bassett, State Nat. Bank of Franklin, Wilson-Walz Corp.; dir. Dairy Products of Tex.; nat. mktg. dir. Beatrice Foods. Dir. Jr. Achievement El Paso, El Paso Indsl. Devel. Bd.; pres. Sun Bowl Assn., 1979-80; dir. United Way of El Paso, NCCJ, U. Tex.-El Dorado. Named Outstanding Alumnus, N.Mex. Mil. Inst., 1981; recipient Conquistador award City of El Paso, 1981, award Tex. Youth Council, 1981, 82, 83. Mem. Tex. Bankers Assn. (mktg. dir.). Roman Catholic. Clubs: Sertoma, S.W. Roundtable. Lodge: El Paso Rotary. Contbr. numerous research articles on mktg., dairy industry and banking to profl. jours. Home: 644 De Leon St El Paso TX 79912 Office: PO Box 1072 El Paso TX 79958

HOULIHAN, ED, association executive. Pres., Lexington C. of C., Ky. Office: Lexington C of C 21 N Broadway Lexington KY 40508*

HOUSER, JOHN EDWARD, lawyer; b. Richmond, Va., Dec. 24, 1928; s. Aubrey Alphin and Winnifred (Savage) H.; B.S., U. Va., 1959, LL.B., 1959; m. Rives Pollard; children—Allen Rives Cabell Lybrook, Andrew Murray Lybrook II. Admitted to Fla. bar, Fed. bar, 1959, U.S. Supreme Ct. bar, 1970; practiced in Jacksonville, Fla., 1959—; dir. Wm. P. Poythress & Co., Richmond, Neal F. Tyler & Sons, Jacksonville. Served with AUS, 1953-57. Mem. Internat. Assn. Indsl. Accident Bds. and Commns., Maritime Law Assn. U.S., Southeastern Admiralty Law Inst., Jacksonville, Atlanta claimsmen assns., Am., Jacksonville bar assns., Fla. Bar, Fla. Def. Counsel Assn., Am. Judicature Assn., Am. Arbitration Assn., Nat. Trust for Historic Preservation, Fla. Inst. Pub. Affairs, Navy League, Jacksonville Assn. Def. Counsel, Def. Research Inst., Jacksonville U. Council, Jacksonville Symphony Assn., Fla., Jacksonville hist. socs., Cummer Gallery of Art, Jacksonville Art Mus., Jacksonville C. of C., English-Speaking Union (dir. 1970—, pres. 1974-78, nat. regional chmn. 1973-76, nat. dir. 1975-81), Thomasville Landmarks, Thomasville Arts Guild, Thomas County Hist. Soc., Theta Delta Chi, Sigma Nu Phi. Clubs: River, Fla. Yacht; Deerwood, Ponte Vedra River, Exchange, German, Ye Mystic Revellers, University; Princeton of N.Y.; Glen Arven (Thomasville); Commonwealth, 2300 (Richmond). Office: 403 St James Bldg 117 W Duval St Jacksonville FL 32202 Office: 403 St James Bldg 117 W Duval St Jacksonville FL 32202

HOUSER, MARK E., gasoline company executive. Pres., gen. mgr. Texas City Refining Inc., Tex. Office: Texas City Refining Inc Box 1271 Texas City TX 77590*

HOUSEWRIGHT, WILEY LEE, music educator, author, consultant; b. Wylie, Tex., Oct. 7, 1913; s. Jick and Lillie D. (Townsend) H.; m. Lucilla Elizabeth Gumm, Dec. 27, 1939; B.S., No. Tex. State U., 1934; M.A., Columbia U., 1938; Ed.D., NYU, 1943. Music. tchr. pub. schs., Tex. and N.Y., 1934-37, 38-41; lectr. in music NYU, 1942; prof. Fla. State U., Tallahassee, 1947-80, dean Sch. Music, 1966-79, prof. emeritus, 1980—; guest prof. Ind. U., Bloomington, 1955, U. Mich., Ann Arbor, 1960; asst. prof. U. Tex.-Austin, 1946-47; cons. Ednl. Testing Bur., Princeton, N.J., 1978—, Carnegie Found. Academically Talented Program, Washington, 1966—; cons., adjudicator Internat. Music Festivals, Parchment, Mich., 1979—. Author: (with others) Birchard Music Series, 1962, vols. I, II, III, IV, VI. Chmn. editorial bd. Mus. Educators Jour., 1957-66; editorial assoc. Jour. of Research in Mus. Edn., 1953-63; choral rev. editor The Sch. Dir., 1955-57. Mem. U.S. Nat. Commn. for UNESCO, Washington, 1958-61, Mus. adv. panel, U.S. Dept. of State, Cultural Presentations Abroad Dept., 1958-79. Served to 1st lt. U.S. Army, 1943-46, PTO. Fulbright scholar, Kobe Jogakuin and Doshisha U., Japan, 1956-57; Ford Found. grantee, 1966-68, U.S. Dept. of Edn. grantee. Mem. Music Educators Nat. Conf. (pres. 1968-70), Am. Musicol. Soc., Music Library Assn., Sonneck Soc., Coll. Mus. Soc., Pi Kappa Lambda, Omicron Delta Kappa, Phi Mu Alpha, Phi Delta Kappa (Gold Key award), Lambda Chi Alpha. Democrat. Clubs: Gov's., Econs., Capital City Country. Lodge: Rotary (Tallahassee). Avocations: swimming; travelling. Home: 515 S Ride Rd Tallahassee FL 32303 Office: Fla State U Sch of Music Tallahassee FL 32306

HOUSKA, MARY DITTMER, economics educator; b. Amityville, N.Y., Sept. 20, 1932; s. Bradford and Mary Rose (Umhauer) Dittmer; m. Charles Robert Houska, Aug. 15, 1953; children—Catherine, Robert, Susan. B.S. in Econs., Simmons Coll., 1954; Ph.D. in Econs., MIT, 1963. Asst. to div. controller Dewey & Almy Chem. Co. div. W. R. Grace & Co., Cambridge, Mass., 1954-57; asst. prof., chmn. dept. econs. Radford Coll. (Va.), 1964-66; asst. prof. Hollins Coll. (Va.), 1966-72, assoc. prof., 1972—. Mem. Va. Conf. (pres.), AAUP, Am. Econs. Assn., So. Econs. Assn., Indsl. Relations Research Assn. Democrat. Unitarian. Home: 2301 Spring Hollow Ln Blacksburg VA 24060 Office: Hollins Coll Hollins College VA 24020

HOUSTON, JAMES VAN, accountant; b. Oakland, Calif., May 5, 1949; s. Van and Irene A. (Horne) H.; A.A., Tarrant County Jr. Coll., 1975; B.B.A., U. Tex., Arlington, 1976; m. Lyn Struan June 25, 1972. Sr. acct. Am. Mfg. Co. of Tex., Ft. Worth, 1976-78; asst. controller William Rigg Co., Ft. Worth, 1978-81; pres. Struan-Houston, Inc., 1979—; acct. mgr. Internat. Service Ins. Co., Ft. Worth, 1982-84; controller First Am. Title Co., Ft. Worth, 1984-85; exec. v.p. Vacation Time (Tex.), Irving, 1985—; pres. Venture Investment Property, Inc., 1982-85; sec.-treas. WNP Investments, Inc., 1984—. Participant Foster Parent Program-Tex. Youth Council, 1980-82; asst. scoutmaster Boy Scouts Am., 1983—. Served with AUS, 1968-72. Decorated Purple Heart with oak leaf cluster, Army Commendation medal. C.P.A., Tex. Mem. Am. Inst. C.P.A.s, Beta Gamma Sigma, Alpha Ch. Office: 1425 Greenway Dr Irving TX 75038

HOUSTON, JAY M., carpet manufacturing executive. Pres., chief operating officer Coronet Industries, Inc., Dalton, Ga. Office: Coronet Industries Inc Cleveland Rd Dalton GA 30720*

HOVEN, ARD, clergyman; b. Athena, Oreg., Oct. 21, 1906; s. Victor and Leona (Bodine) H.; B.A., Eugene Bible Coll., 1930, B.D., 1931; B.A., U. Oreg., 1933; M.A., Cin. Bible Sem., 1937; D.S.T., Milligan Coll., 1954; D.D., Ky. Christian Coll., 1954; m. Dorothy Lillian Harris, Sept. 30, 1938; children—Ardis Dee, Vicki Lee. Ordained to ministry Christian Ch., 1933; minister, Ceres, Calif., 1933-34, Cin., 1934-51, Broadway Christian Ch., Lexington, Ky., 1951-66, First Christian Ch., Columbus, Ind., 1966-78; head dept. Christian ministry Ky. Christian Coll., Grayson, 1978—. Speaker radio program Christians' Hour, 1943—; pres. N.Am. Christian Conv., 1950, mem. continuation com., 1950—; writer weekly Bible Sch. lesson The Lookout, Standard Pub. Co., Cin., 1958-85, mem. pub. com., 1957—. Republican. Mason, Rotarian. Author: Christ Is All, 1953; Meditations and Prayers for the Lord's Table, 1962. Office: Kentucky Christian College Grayson KY 41143

HOVERATH, JACQUELINE ARENTZ, nursing educator; b. Harrisburg, Pa., Nov. 13, 1938; d. James Kremer and Geraldine Russell (Graeff) Arentz; m. Theodore Perzak, Jan. 2, 1961 (div. 1978); children—Deborah, Theodore J.; m. 2d, August Hoverath, Sept. 26, 1982; stepchildren—Reiner, Ulrica. B.S.N., U. Pitts., 1961; M.A., Furman U., 1979. R.N., Pa. Staff nurse, team leader Vis. Nurse Assn., Pitts., 1961-64; weekend day relief supr. Shadyside Hosp., Pitts., 1965-67; clin. nurse specialist Cystic Fibrosis Found., Greenville, S.C., 1970-73; nurse educator, course team coordinator for nursing process III, Greenville Tech. Coll., 1973—. Deacon Presbyterian Ch., Mauldin, S.C., 1974-77; bd. dirs. Phyllis Wheatley Ctr., 1979. Mem. S.C. Perinatal Assn. Republican. Lodge: Order Eastern Star. Home: 410 Camelot Dr Simpsonville SC 29681 Office: Dept Nursing Greenville Tech Coll Box 5616 Greenville SC 29606

HOVIS, ROBERT HOUSTON, III, lawyer; b. Washington, Apr. 19, 1942; s. Robert Houston and Lera Frances (Robbins) H.; m. Mary Ann Jennings, Dec. 27, 1965. B.S., U. Tenn., 1964, J.D., 1966. Bar: Tenn. 1967, Va. 1967, U.S. Dist. Ct. (ea. dist.) Va. 1973. Asst. commonwealth atty. Fairfax County, Va., 1969-71; pvt. practice law, Fairfax County, 1971—; prin. Hovis & Assocs., Annandale, Va.; commr. in chancery Circuit Ct. Fairfax County, 1969—. Mem. adv. council Salvation Army, Annandale, 1984—; bd. dirs. Annandale C. of C., 1984. Served with U.S. Army, 1967-69, Germany. Mem. Assn. Trial Lawyers Am. (cert. Nat. Coll. Advocacy 1981, Med. Malpractice Advanced Coll. 1983, Trial Advocacy Advanced Coll. 1985), Va. Trial Lawyers Assn., Fairfax County Bar Assn., Va. State Bar. Democrat. Methodist. Lodge: Rotary (pres. 1983-84). Home: 3401 Hickory Hills Dr Oakton VA 22124 Office: Hovis & Assocs 4544 John Marr Dr Annandale VA 22003

HOWARD, BERNARD EUFINGER, mathematics and computer science educator; b. Ludlow, Vt., Sept. 22, 1920; s. Charles Rawson and Ethel (Kearney) H.; m. Ruth Belknap, Mar. 29, 1942. Student Middlebury Coll., 1938-40; B.S., MIT, 1944; M.S., U. Ill., 1947, Ph.D., 1951. Staff mem. Radiation Lab, MIT, Cambridge, 1942-45; asst. math. U. Ill., Champaign-Urbana, 1945-49; sr. mathematician Inst. Air Weapons Research, U. Chgo., 1951, asst. to dir. Inst. for Systems Research, 1951-54, assoc. dir., 1956-60, assoc. dir. Labs. for Applied Sci., 1958-60; dir. Sci. Computing Ctr. U. Miami, Coral Gables, Fla., 1960-64, prof. math. and computer sci., 1960—; exec. sec. Air Force Adv. Bd. Simulation, 1951-54; cons. Systems Research Labs, Inc., Dayton, Ohio, 1963-67, acting dir. math. scis. div., 1965; cons. Variety Children's Research Found., Miami, 1964-66, Fla. Power & Light Co., Miami, 1968, Shaw & Assocs., 1964-75; vis. fellow Dartmouth Coll., Hanover, N.H., 1976; co-investigator Positron Emission Tomography Ctr., U. Miami Dept. Neurology/Mt. Sinai Med. Ctr., 1981-84. Co-creator: Sociocybernetics, 1971, Optimum Curvature, 1964, Torsion, 1974. Chmn. bd. dirs. Blue Lake Assn., Inc., Miami, 1969—. Am. Soc. Engring. Edn.-Office of Naval Research fellow Naval Underwater Systems Ctr., 1981, 82. Mem. Am. Math. Soc., Soc. Indsl. and Applied Math. (treas. S.E. sect. 1964), Am. Phys. Soc., Assn. Computing Machinery (chpt. chmn. 1969-70), IEEE, AAUP (chpt. sec. 1974—), Sigma Xi, Phi Kappa Phi, Pi Mu Epsilon, Alpha Sigma Phi. Home: 7320 Miller Dr Miami FL 33155 Office: U Miami Coral Gables FL 33124

HOWARD, CAROLE CODER, physician; b. Quincy, Ill., Sept. 20, 1952; d. James Aubrey Jr. and Anne Ruth (Gorton) Coder; m. James Lewis Howard, Dec. 20, 1970; children—David, Daniel, Thomas. B.S., Northeast Mo. State U., 1971; D.O., Kirksville Coll., 1976. Am. Osteo. Bd. Medicine. Intern, Suncoast Osteo. Hosp., Largo, Fla., 1976-77; gen. practice osteo. medicine, Broken Arrow, Okla., 1977—. Pres., Green Country Civitans, Broken Arrow, 1982. Mem. Am. Osteo. Assn., Okla. Osteo. Assn., Tulsa Dist. Osteo. Assn. Republican. Baptist. Avocations: golf, gardening. Home: 12505 E 136th St S Broken Arrow OK 74011 Office: Broken Arrow Family Clinic 702 W Oakland Broken Arrow OK 74012

HOWARD, C(LARENCE) EDWARD, geologist, educator, consultant, researcher; b. Roseboro, N.C., May 31, 1929; s. Hubert Royster and Irene (Britt) H.; m. Evelyn Kline Baker, Oct. 22, 1955; 1 dau., Wendy Gail; m. Evelyn Anne Barker, Mar. 28, 1981. B.S. in Geology, Duke U., 1953; M.S. in Geol. Engring., N.C. State U., 1955; Ph.D. in Sedimentary Petrology, La. State U., 1963. Teaching asst. N.C. State U., Raleigh, 1953-55; mining and geol. engr. Tungsten Mining Corp., Henderson, N.C., 1955-57; teaching asst. La. State U., Baton Rouge, 1959-63; asst. prof. geology Campbell U., Buies Creek, N.C., 1963-64, assoc. prof. geology, 1964-76, chmn. dept. geology, 1964-76, prof. geology, 1966-76; prin. geologist Geotech. Engring. Co., Research Triangle Park, N.C., 1976-78, v.p., 1977-78; pres. Carolina Earth Resources Co., Lillington, N.C., 1977—; dir. div. soil and water conservation N.C. Dept Natural Resources and Community Devel., Raleigh, 1981-82; vis. prof. geology N.C. State U., Raleigh, 1982; cons. geologist, 1983; sr. research geologist Research Triangle Inst., Research Triangle Park, N.C., 1984, coordinator earth and mineral scis. programs, 1985—. Fellow Geol. Soc. Am.; mem. Am. Inst. Profl. Geologists, Assn. Engring. Geologists, Soc. Mining Engrs., AIME (past chmn. student relations com.), Carolina Geol. Soc., Sigma Xi, Phi Kappa Phi. Baptist. Contbr. articles to profl. jours. Home: 102 Chisholm Ct Cary NC 27511 Office: Research Triangle Inst PO Box 12194 Research Triangle Park NC 27709

HOWARD, DENNIS R., loss prevention consulting executive; b. Greenville, Ga., Nov. 6, 1946; s. Thomas Edwin and Katherine Lula (Barrett) H.; m. Lynna Diane Odom, Nov. 4, 1972; 1 child, Allison Lindsey. A.A., Central Fla. Jr. Coll., 1966; B.S., Fla. State U., 1968; postgrad. La. State U., 1977. Cert. safety profl. Sr. safety and loss control engr. Aetna Casualty & Surety, Atlanta, 1969-72; corp. dir. safety Bendix Home Systems, Atlanta, 1972-75; safety/protection supr. Kaiser Aluminum & Chem. Corp., Baton Rouge, 1975-79; pres. Safety Mgmt., Inc., Baton Rouge, 1979—, Harvest Communications Corp., Baton Rouge, 1985—; advisor workmen's compensation State La., 1983; cons. Greater Baton Rouge Safety Council, 1982; safety expert Fed. & State Cts., La., 1980—. Author: Safety and Loss Control manuals, 1972, 80, 82-85. Chmn. bd. dirs. Singing Waters Ranch, Baton Rouge, 1982-84; chmn. deacons Chapel on the Campus, Baton Rouge, 1982; chmn. fund drive Boy Scouts Am., 1984. Mem. Am. Soc. Safety Engrs., Marine Safety Soc., Am. Indsl. Hygiene Assn. Republican. Avocation: water and outdoor sports. Office: Safety Mgmt Inc 4664 Jamestown Ave Suite 103 Baton Rouge LA 70808

HOWARD, DENNIS WILLIAM, book store executive, writer; b. Asheville, N.C., Jan. 9, 1950; s. Joe Thomas and Georgia Rhobenia (Ingle) H. Student, U. N.C., Asheville, 1968-70. Owner Super Giant Books, Asheville, 1977—; chmn. SkyCon, Asheville, 1981—, Land Sky Antiquarian Book Fair, Asheville, 1984—, SpartaCon, Spartanburg, S.C., 1984—, Catawba Valley Expo, Hickory, N.C., 1984—. Contbr. articles to profl. jours. Mem. Jules Verne Awards Com. (chmn. 1980—), James Branch Cabell Soc. Avocation: numismatic literature. Office: Super Giant Books 38 Wall St Asheville NC 28801

HOWARD, DEWEY WAYNE, private scholar, author; b. Grenada, Miss., Sept. 7, 1942; s. Charles Vernon and Viola Corinne (Blaylock) H.; B.A., Belhaven Coll., 1964, Mus. B., 1964; Mus. M., Ind. U., 1967; Ph.D., 1975. Teaching assoc. Ind. U., Bloomington, 1967-71; instr. Kent State U., Ohio, 1973-75; asst. prof., 1975-76; pvt. scholar, Winona, Miss., 1976—; vis. lectr. U. Ga., Athens, 1979; regional dir. Ind. Scholars Asia, Winona, 1982-84. Author: Samavedic Chant, 1977; Veda Recitation in Varanasi; The Decipherment of the Samavedic Notation of the Jaiminiyas. Editor: Classical Music of South India: Karnatic Tradition in Western Notation. Contbr. articles and book reviews to profl. jours. Fulbright scholar 1970-71. Mem. Am. Musicological Soc., Assn. Asian Studies. Avocations: cooking; armchair astronomy; piano. Home: 315 Shirley Ave Winona MS 38967

HOWARD, GEORGE, JR., federal judge; b. Pine Bluff, Ark., May 13, 1924. Student, Lincoln U., 1951; B.S., U. Ark., J.D., 1954; LL.D., 1976. Bar: Ark. bar 1953, U.S. Supreme Ct. bar 1959. Pvt. practice law, Pine Bluff, 1953-77; spl. assoc. justice Ark. Supreme Ct., 1976, assoc. justice, 1977-79; assoc. judge

Ark. Ct. Appeals, 1979-80; U.S. dist. judge, Eastern and Western dists., Little Rock, 1980—; Mem. Ark. Claims Commn. 1969-77; chmn. Ark. adv. com. Civil Rights Commn. Named Outstanding Trial Judge, Ark. Trial Lawyers Assn., 1984-85. Mem. Am. Bar Assn., Ark. Bar Assn., Jefferson County Bar Assn. (pres.). Baptist. Office: PO Box 349 Little Rock AR 72203

HOWARD, GROVER LATHAM, III, data processing and management consultant; b. New Brunswick, N.J., Apr. 29, 1945; s. Grover Latham and Joy Elizebeth (Gibson) H.; m. Mary Catherine Jones, Nov. 10, 1966 (div. July 1973); children—Grover Latham IV, Peter W.; m. Ana Cristina Eichman, Feb. 24, 1974; children—Mathew M., Mary Tazewell. Student La. State U., New Orleans, 1963-65. Enlisted U.S. Air Force, 1965, advanced through grades to sgt., 1969; planning research corp. project mgr. World Wide Mil. Command and Control System, Heidelberg, W.Ger., 1972-74; project mgr. USAF Europe Tactical Air Intelligence system architecture design, Ramstein, W.Ger., 1980-81; pres. GCM, Inc., Alexandria, Va., 1981—. Mem. Alexandria Republican City Com. Mem. Am. Security Council, Center for Entrepreneurial Mgmt., Alexandria Crime Solvers, Washington Ind. Computer Cons. Assn., Aircraft Owners and Pilots Assn., Nat. Aviation Club, Nat. Trust for Historic Preservation, Alexandria C. of C. Republican. Methodist. Lodge: Kiwanis. Office: 4601-H Pinecrest Office Park Dr Alexandria VA 22312

HOWARD, INEZ LAWHORN, physical education educator; b. Camden, S.C., Sept. 2, 1935; d. Myles Leroy and Carolyn Beatrice (Canty) Lawhorn; m. Berlyn Franklin Howard, Aug. 24, 1963; 1 son, Berlyn Cedric. B.S., N.C. Central U., Durham, 1957; M.A., Columbia U., 1962. Tchr., Norcom High Sch., Portsmouth, Va., 1957-62; asst. prof. phys. edn. Norfolk (Va.) State U., 1962—, dir. Dance Theatre, 1962—, Band Front, Majorettes, Dancing Girls, 1962—; dance cons. Cultural Experiences Unltd.; dir. Nat. Youth Sports Program; tchr. inservice workshops; dir. Christmas Dance Workshop, Chesapeake, Va., 1982, 83. Mem. adv. bd. Parks and Recreation Chesapeake, 1981—; mem. Fine Arts Commn., Chesapeake, 1983—; dir. cotillion Chesapeake Med. Aux., 1962—. Mem. AAHPERD, Va. Assn. Health, Phys. Edn., Recreation and Dance, Southeastern Va. Art Assn. Clubs: Jack and Jill of Am. Home: 1020 Main Creek Rd Chesapeake VA 23320 Office: Dept Phys Edn and Recreation 2401 Corprew Ave Norfolk State Univ Norfolk VA 23504

HOWARD, JAMES KENTON, university administrator, journalist; b. Ponca City, Okla., June 30, 1943; s. Arthur R. and Dora G. (Utt) H.; B.A., U. Okla., 1965, M.A., 1979; m. Lynn M. Marsh, Sept. 23, 1982; children—Lara L., James M. Asst. to dean students U. Okla., Norman, 1965-67, asst. to pres., 1967-68, asst. to v.p. for univ. relations and devel., 1978; editor Northland Press, Flagstaff, Ariz., 1972-77; cons. Okla. Dept. Public Safety, Oklahoma City, 1977; asst. dean student affairs Northeastern State U., Tahlequah, Okla., 1978-79, dir. univ. services, 1979-82, asst. prof. journalism, 1979—, v.p. adminstrn., 1982—, trustee Ednl. Found., 1981—; mem. Council on Fin. and Budgeting, Okla. State Regents for Higher Edn., 1982—. Bd. dirs. Friends of Mus. No. Ariz., 1974-77; chmn. No. Ariz. March of Dimes campaign, 1973-74; No. Ariz. coordinator candidate for atty. gen. campaign, 1974; trustee Flagstaff-Coconino County Public Library, 1976-77, chmn. bd. trustees, 1976-77; pres. Indian Nations Soccer Council, 1981-82. Served with USAF, 1968-72. Recipient Eason Book Collection award, 1965; Book Design award Rounce and Coffin Club of Los Angeles, 1974, 75. Mem. U. Okla. Assn. (life), Nat. Cowboy Hall of Fame and Western Heritage Center (life), Tahlequah Area C. of C. (bd. dirs. 1985—). Sigma Delta Chi, Kappa Tau Alpha, Mensa Soc., Lambda Chi Alpha. Democrat. Mem. Disciples of Christ Ch. Club: Rotary (pres. 1986—). Author: Ten Years With the Cowboy Artists of America, 1976. Office: Adminstrn Bldg Northeastern State U Tahlequah OK 74464

HOWARD, JOHN WILFRED, artist; b. Corinth, Ky., Aug. 20, 1924; s. John David and Veral (Kemper) H.; m. Leona Belle Thompson, June 22, 1979; children—Bonnie, Connie, Sharon, Terresa, Sandra. Farmer, 1940-45, 1947-72; life and health ins. agt., 1972-79; comml. artist, Corinth, Ky.; works displayed in Artists U.S.A. (internationally distributed art book), 1981-82. Served with AUS, 1945-47. Mem. Nat. Mus. Women in Arts, Creative World. Democrat. Baptist. Home and Office: Rural Route 2 Corinth KY 41010

HOWARD, LARRY ARNOLD, safety supervisor; b. Port Arthur, Tex., Apr. 4, 1948; s. Buford Johnnie and Helen Melissa (Porter) H.; m. Jean Ann Beach, May 8, 1971; children—Laurie Ann, Justin Arnold. B.S. in Edn., Lamar U., 1970. Cert. safety profl., safety assoc.; life teaching cert., Tex. Sci. and speech tchr. Port Neches-Groves Sch. Dist., Port Neches, Tex., 1972-74; chlorine-caustic controlman Jefferson Chem. Co., Port Neches, 1974-76; safety and fire protection specialist Texaco Chem. Co., Port Neches, 1976-82, sr. safety and fire protection specialist, 1982-85; mgr. safety Tenngasco Corp., Houston, 1985—; instr. Fire Sch. Tex., A&M U., 1979—; hazardous materials instr. City of Beaumont Fire Acad., Tex., 1982—, Lamar U. Indsl. Fire Sch., Beaumont, 1983—, planning com. Lamar U. Sunbelt Safety Conf., 1985; tng. cons. USCG Response Team, Port Arthur, 1984—. Asst. in devel. Confined Space Entry Manual, 1983, Hazardous Material Response Team, Texaco Chem. Co., 1976. Bd. dirs. Mid and South Jefferson County Crime Stoppers. Served to capt. USMCR, 1970-76. Recipient U.S. Coast Guard Disting. Pub. Service award, medal, 1985. Mem. Am. Soc. Safety Engrs. (pres. Sabine Neches chpt. 1985-86), Sabine Neches Chiefs Orgn. Baptist. Clubs: Nat. Rifle Assn., Golden Triangle Gun, Goldwing Roadriders (Phoenix). Lodge: Masons. Avocations: hunting; guitar; woodworking; camping. Home: 3004 Uvalde Nederland TX 77627 Office: Tenngasco Corp PO Box 2511 Houston TX 77001

HOWARD, MARCIA ANN, histologic technology educator; b. Muskogee, Okla., Aug. 18, 1953; d. Will Owen and Forrest Irva (Hohimar) Lubbes; m. John Michael Howard, June 6, 1981. Grad. Indian Capitol Vo-Tech Sch., Muskogee, 1971; student Bacone Jr. Coll., Muskogee, 1971-72, U. Okla., 1972-73; B.S., Northeastern Okla. State U., 1975; postgrad. U. Okla., 1977, Central State U., Okla., 1983. Diplomate Am. Soc. Clin. Pathologists. Asst. histology technician Mercy Health Ctr., Oklahoma City, 1975-77; supr. histopathology lab. Okla. Children's Meml. Hosp., Oklahoma City, 1977-80; chief histotechnologist/asst. diener Office of State Chief Med. Examiner Okla., Oklahoma City, 1980-81; instr. Oscar Rose Jr. Coll., Oklahoma City, 1981, edn. coordinator/instr., 1982—. Adj. faculty Okla. Children's Meml. Hosp., 1978-80. Chmn. spl. events Kidney Found. Okla., 1979, bd. dirs., 1979-80. Mem. Okla. Soc. Histotechnologists (charter; state pres. 1978-80, chmn. bd./publs. dir. 1980-82); Ernestine Walton Meml. scholar 1981-82), Nat. Soc. Histotech. (ho. of dels. 1978-79, pub. relations com. 1982—, chmn. legis. com. 1983), Okla. Soc. Electron Microscopists, N. Tex. Soc. Histotechnologists (corr.), Ark. Soc. Histotechnologists (corr.), Bus. and Profl. Women's Club (pres. 1982-83), Okla. Fedn. Bus. and Profl. Women's Clubs (10th dist. sec. 1983-84), Okla. Zool. Soc., Phi Theta Kappa. Republican. Mem. Christian Ch. Contbr. articles to profl. jours. Home: 3518 NW 22d St Oklahoma City OK 73107 Office: 6420 SE 15th St Midwest City OK 73110

HOWARD, PIERCE JOHNSON, personnel consultant; b. Kinston, N.C., Aug. 7, 1941; s. Curtis William and Eleanor (Johnson) H.; m. Jane Mitchell, Feb. 4, 1984; children—Hilary Ren, Allegra Blythe. B.A., Davidson Coll., 1963; M.A., E. Carolina U., 1967; Ph.D., U. N.C., 1972. Dir. sch. services N.C. Advancement Schs., Winston-Salem, 1971-76; staff devel. specialist Charlotte Mecklenburg Schs., Charlotte, 1976-78; vis. prof. U. N.C.-Charlotte, 1978-79; mgr. personnel research LEAD Assocs. Inc., Charlotte, 1979—. Served to sgt. U.S. Army, 1963-66. Mem. Am. Soc. Tng. and Devel., Am. Soc. Personnel Adminstrs., Psychometric Soc. Democrat. Presbyterian. Avocation: chamber music. Home: 719 Romany Rd Charlotte NC 28203 Office: LEAD Assocs Inc PO Box 35409 Charlotte NC 28235

HOWARD, REDEMOUS ALVIN, business consultant; b. Petersburg, Va., Oct. 25, 1947; s. Redemous and Jessie Lee (Cousins) H. B.S.W. in Sociology, Va. State U., 1980. TV film technician Sta. WXEX-TV, Petersburg, 1966-68; TV media specialist Nationwide Communications, Inc., Petersburg, 1972-84; data transcriber Def. Gen. Supply Ctr., Richmond, Va. 1983-84, vehicle lic. examiner, 1984-85, communications equipment operator, Office of Telecommunications and Info. Systems, 1985—; pres. RAH 47 Creative Services, Inc., Petersburg, 1980—. Former mem. Commn. on Community Relations Affairs, Petersburg; mem. Republican Presdl. Task Force, 1982—, U.S. Senatorial Club, 1983—. Served USAF, 1968-72. Recipient Presdl. Medal of Merit. Mem. Va. Council on Social Welfare, Petersburg C. of C., DAV. Home and office: 83 Slagle Ave Petersburg VA 23803

HOWARD, RICHARD TURNER, construction company executive; b. Rock Hill, S.C., Jan. 3, 1935; s. Paul Noble and Pauline (Sugg) H.; children—Richard Turner, James Fowles, George Anderson. B.S., U. S.C., 1957. Vice pres. Howard Constrn. Co., 1957-72; exec. v.p. Paul N. Howard Co., Greensboro, N.C., 1972-77, pres., chief exec. officer, 1977—; mng. dir. Howard Internat., Howard of Saudi Arabia; dir. Geneva Corp. Bd. dirs. Greensboro Devel. Corp., Green Hill Art Gallery.; trustee U. N.C., Greensboro, NCCJ; bd. visitors Guilford Coll. Served with U.S. Army, 1957. Mem. Greensboro C. of C. (bd. dirs. 1972-78). Republican. Episcopalian. Clubs: Greensboro Country, Palm Bay. Home: Route 1 Box 296 High Point NC 27260 Office: 201 N Elm St Greensboro NC 27420

HOWARD, ROBERT A., sculptor, art educator; b. Sapulpa, Okla., Apr. 5, 1922; s. Jacob Walter and Edith (Cross) H.; m. June Louise Mayfield, Sept. 24, 1947; 1 son, David. Student Phillips U., 1942-43; B.A., M.A., U. Tulsa, 1949; postgrad. Ossip Zadkine, Paris, 1949-50. Prof. art U. N.C., Chapel Hill, 1951—; vis. prof. U. So. Calif., Los Angeles, 1972-73. Served with U.S. Army, 1943-46. Decorated Battle Star (5); recipient Purchase awards N.C. Mus., 1957-58, 62; Duke U. Coop. Program in Humanities grantee, 1965; Nat. Endowment Arts grantee, 1972. Democrat. Selected exhbns. include: Pa. Acad. Fine Arts, 1958, Young American Sculpture, N.Y. World's Fair, 1965, contemporary sculpture Whitney Mus., N.Y., 1968, 70, 72, Sculpture of the Sixties, Los Angeles Mus. Art, 1967, Monumental Sculpture, Fed. Bldg., Louisville Project, 1976. Home: 1201 Hillview Rd Chapel Hill NC 27514 Office: 103 Art Lab Bldg U NC Chapel Hill NC 27514

HOWARD, WILLIAM EAGER, III, astronomer, administrator; b. Washington, Aug. 25, 1932; s. William Eager Jr. and Frances (Bacon) H.; m. Miriam Sitler, June 22, 1957; children—William E. IV, Jennifer M. B.S. in Physics, Rensselaer Poly. Inst., 1954; A.M. in Astronomy, Harvard U., 1956, Ph.D. in Astronomy, 1958. Astronomer Harvard Radio Astronomy Sta., Ft. Davis, Tex., summer 1958; research assoc. U. Mich., Ann Arbor, 1959-61, instr., 1959-60, asst. prof., 1960-62, assoc. prof. astronomy, 1962-64; asst. to dir. Nat. Radio Astronomy Obs., Charlottesville, Va. and Green Bank, W. Va., 1964-74, assoc. scientist, 1964-67, scientist, 1967-77, asst. dir. Green Bank Ops., 1974-77; dir. div. astron. scis. NSF, 1977-82; on detail Office Technology Assessment U.S. Congress, Washington, 1982, other fed. agys., 1982-85; tech. dir. Naval Space Command, 1985—. Served with U.S. Army, 1958-59. Rensselaer Poly. Inst. scholar, 1950-54; Agassiz fellow, 1957-58; John G. Thayer scholar, 1957-58; recipient NSF Sustained Superior Performance award, 1979. Mem. Internat. Astron. Union, Am. Astron. Soc. (treas., exec. com. 1975-77), U.S. Naval Inst., Internat. Sci. Radio Union, AAAS, Astron. Soc. Pacific, Sigma Xi. Lutheran. Club: Chesterbrook (McLean, Va.). Contbr. articles to profl. jours.

HOWARD, WILLIAM REED, airline executive; b. Wheatland, Wyo., May 26, 1922; s. Albert Thompkins and Antha Jane (Taylor) H.; m. Lusadel Moore (dec.); children—Thomas Morton, David Patrick, William Reed. A.B., George Washington U., 1952; LL.B., 1956. Assoc. firm Gambrell, Russell & Forbes, Atlanta, 1955-67; v.p. Eastern Airlines, N.Y.C., 1967-71, sr. v.p., Miami, Fla., 1971-78; sr. v.p. and asst. to pres. Piedmont Airlines, Winston-Salem, N.C., 1978-80, exec. v.p., 1980-81, pres., chief operating officer, dir., 1981-83, pres., chief exec. officer, 1983—; chmn. bd. subs. Air Service, Inc., 1983—, Aviation Supply Corp., 1983—; dir. Wachovia Bank & Trust Co. Bd. dirs. United Way Forsyth County, 1979-81. Served to capt. USAAF, 1942-46. Recipient George Washington U. Alumni Achievement award, 1984. Mem. Greater Winston-Salem C. of C. (dir. 1981-82), Air Transp. Assn. Am. (dir. 1983—). Office: Piedmont Airlines Winston-Salem NC 27156

HOWARD, WILLIE ABBAY, planter, former state official; b. Tunica, Miss., June 5, 1891; d. William G. and George Anne Elizabeth (Irwin) Abbay; student U. Miss., summer 1933; m. Thomas Percy Howard, Oct. 12, 1920 (dec.); children—Thomas Percy (dec.), George Anne Irwin (Mrs. Robert Peel Sayle), Elizabeth Irwin (Mrs. Cooper Yerger Robinson). Partner, Howard Plantation, Lake Cormorant, Miss., 1922-55, owner, operator, 1955—. Commr. Yazoo-Miss. Delta Levee Bd., 1955-75; welfare dir. DeSoto County, Miss., 1932-36, DeSoto and Tate counties, 1933-34; organizer, instr. Gulf div. ARC, 1917-18; co-organizer, trustee DeSoto County Library Bd., 1946—, chmn. bd. trustees, 1970-75; co-organizer Citizens Library Movement, DeSoto County, Miss., 1947, first Regional Library Miss., 1950, trustee, 1950-63; pres. Miss. Citizen's Library Movement, 1950-52; del. nat. conv. Nat. Rivers and Harbors Congress, Washington, 1964. Trustee Northwest Jr. Coll., Senatobia, Miss., 1943-77. Recipient citation for flood control work Miss. River Commn., 1974, Outstanding Civilian Service medal, 1976; Meritorious Service award Yazoo-Miss. Delta Levee Bd., 1975; Spl. Alumni Assn. award, 1979; honored by naming of Willie Abbay Howard Coliseum, N.W. Jr. Coll., 1979. Mem. Miss. Fedn. Women's Clubs (state rec. sec. 1920-22), English-Speaking Union, Memphis Execs., Lower Miss. Valley Flood Control Assn. (v.p. 1961, 71), DAR, Colonial Dames 17th Century (Woman of Yr. Miss. 1977). Presbyterian. Clubs: Memphis Country, Memphis Woman's (pres. 1968-69), Tunica County Woman's (founder 1914, pres. 1916, 1921, 28-29, trustee 1915—). Editor: DeSoto County C.L.M. Handbook, 1946. Address: Howard Plantation Lake Cormorant MS 38641

HOWE, LYMAN HAROLD, III, chemist; b. Wilkes-Barre, Pa., Nov. 5, 1938; s. Lyman Harold and Esther Madeline (Smith) H.; B.S., Duke U., 1960; M.S., Emory U., 1961; Ph.D., U. Tenn., 1966; m. Mary Louise Reinhart, June 16, 1962; 1 dau., Jennifer. Research assoc. Emory U., 1960-61; research and teaching assoc. U. Tenn., 1962-66; research chemist div. services and field ops. TVA, Chattanooga, 1966—. Bd. dirs. Greater Chattanooga Pub. TV Corp., Sta. WTCI, 1984—. Mem. ASTM (water com. results advisor 1976—, Max Hecht award 1985), Am. Chem. Soc., Nat. Mgmt. Assn., Presbyterian. Clubs: Torch (1st v.p. chpt. 1981, pres. 1982-83, 2d v.p. 1984-85), The Nost. Co-author publs. in field. Reviewer Environmental Science and Technology, 1981—. Home: 1241 Mountain Brook Circle Signal Mountain TN 37377 Office: 150-401 Chestnut St Circle Chattanooga TN 37401

HOWELL, ALLEN WINDSOR, lawyer; b. Montgomery, Ala., Mar. 10, 1949; s. Elvin and Bennie Merle (Windsor) H.; m. Shirley Ann Darby, Dec. 30, 1972; children—Christopher Darby, Joshua Darby. B.A., Huntington Coll., 1971; LL.B., Jones Law Sch., 1974. Bar: Ala. 1974, U.S. Supreme Ct. 1977, U.S. Ct. Appeals (fed. cir.) 1983, U.S. Ct. Appeals (11th cir.) 1981, U.S. Tax Ct. 1979, U.S. Claims Ct. 1982, U.S. Dist. Ct. (mid. dist.) Ala. 1975, U. Dist. Ct. (so. dist.) Ala. 1978. Archivist, Hist. Research Center, Air U., Maxwell AFB, Ala., 1972-75; sole practice, Montgomery, 1975-82, 83—; asst. atty. gen., chief legal sect. Ala. Medicaid Agy., Montgomery, 1982-83; adj. prof. Jones Law Sch., 1983—, Ala. Christian Coll., 1975— (both Montgomery). Mem. ABA, Assn. Trial Lawyers Am., Montgomery County Bar Assn. (newsletter editorial com. 1984-85). Republican. Mem. Ch. of Christ. Home: 537 Bowling Green Dr Montgomery AL 36117 Office: PO Box 7367 Montgomery AL 36107

HOWELL, BRADLEY SUE, librarian; b. McKinney, Tex., July 15, 1933; d. Jessie Leonard and Carrie Pearl (Nickerson) LaFon; m. Richard Dunn Howell, May 18, 1957; children—Mark Richard, Celeste Ella, Jane Elizabeth. B.S. in Edn., So. Meth. U., 1955; M.S. in L.S., East Tex. State U., 1968. Tchr., J.B. Hood Jr. High Sch., Dallas, 1955-56, Mineral Wells Jr. High Sch. (Tex.), 1957-58; librarian Ascher Silberstein Sch., Dallas, 1963, San Jacinto Sch., Dallas, 1960-62, 65-81, Woodrow Wilson High Sch., Dallas, 1981—. Pres., Tex. United Meth. Hist. Soc., 1980-84; sec. South Central Jurisdiction, Archives and History of United Meth. Ch., 1980—; pres. PTA, Woodrow Wilson High Sch., 1983-84; leader Camp Fire, Inc., 1970—. Recipient Wakan award Camp Fire Girls, 1976, Hiiteni award, 1982; Terrific Tchr. award Texas PTA, 1984. Mem. Dallas Assn. Sch. Librarians (pres. 1975-76), Tex. Assn. Sch. Librarians, Am. Library Services To Children (Newbery com. 1980) Delta Kappa Gamma, Alpha Delta Pi, Phi Delta Kappa, Pi Lambda Theta. Democrat. Home: 722 Ridgeway St Dallas TX 75214 Office: Woodrow Wilson High Sch 100 S Glasgow Dr Dallas TX 75214

HOWELL, DOROTHY COLVIN, home economist; b. Mansfield, La., June 17, 1922; d. Hardwick Joyner and Margeret Mellissa (Pickels) Colvin; B.S., La. State U., 1942; M.S., 1944; postgrad. Tex. Women's U., 1975; m. Sylvanus Thaddeus Howell, Jr., Apr. 10, 1945; children—Sylvanus Thaddeus III, Suzanne Antionette. Research asst. La. Agr. Expt. Sta., Baton Rouge, 1944-45; tchr. home econs. Youree Drive Jr. High Sch., Shreveport, La., 1960-62; assoc. prof. foods and nutrition La. State U., Baton Rouge, 1962-83, asst. to dir. Sch. Home Econs., 1981-83; freelance home economist, 1984—. Mem. Family Relations Council, State of La.; adult Sunday sch. tchr. Univ. Baptist Ch. Recipient Service award La. State U. Alumni, 1975, La. State U. Home Econs. Alumni Assn., 1983. Mem. Coll. and Univ. Tchrs. of Food and Nutrition (pres. Tex., La. Ark. Okla. sect. 1980—), La. Home Econs. Assn. (pres. S. Central dist. 1979—, treas. 1981), Am. Home Econs. Assn., Inst. Food Technologists, Am. Bus. Women's Assn. (Chpt. Woman of Yr. 1981, pres. chpt.), DAR, Gamma Sigma Delta, Delta Kappa Gamma, Phi Upsilon Omicron, Phi Mu. Author: (with others) Louisiana Tiger Bait, 1976. Home: 874 Delgado Dr Baton Rouge LA 70808 Office: Sch Home Econs La State U Baton Rouge LA 70803

HOWELL, FRANK MOBLEY, sociology educator; b. Duluth, Ga., Dec. 23, 1952; s. William Thomas and Sara Ruth (Mobley) H.; m. Mary Elizabeth Robbins, Aug. 3, 1974 (div. Aug. 1983); 1 child, Jonathan Clark. B.A., Ga. Coll., 1975; M.A., Miss. State U., 1977, Ph.D., 1979. News dir. Sta. WXLX, Milledgeville, Ga., 1974-75; asst. prof. Tex. Christian U., Fort Worth, 1981-83; asst. prof., assoc. dir. social sci. research and instructional computing lab. N.C. State U., Raleigh, 1983—; cons. Nat. Inst. Edn., Washington, 1977, Assn. Univ. Programs in Health Adminstrn., Washington, 1982-83; vis. research scientist O'Hara Ctr. for Youth Devel., Dallas, 1985—. Author: Making Life Plans, 1982; contbr. articles to profl. jours.; creator SocNet: internat. computer network for sociologists. Hon. chmn. Ga. Mental Health Assn., Milledgeville, 1975. Grantee Miss. Dept. Edn., 1980, Wadsworth, Inc., 1985; postdoctoral fellow Miss. State U., 1979-80. Mem. Am. Sociol. Assn., Am. Ednl. Research Assn., Rural Sociol. Soc., Sigma Xi. Democrat. Baptist. Avocations: Chess; fishing; shortwave listening; running. Home: 826 W Chatham St Cary NC 27511 Office: Dept Sociology Drawer C Miss State U Mississippi State MS 39762

HOWELL, HOWARD LESTER, orthodontist, retail executive; b. Plant City, Fla., July 15, 1947; s. Lester A. and Oppie (Moseley) H.; m. Robin Elizabaeth Adams, Dec. 16, 1979; 1 child, Jonathan Ryan. B.S. in Zoology, U. Fla., 1970; D.D.S., Med. Coll. Va., 1984. Dental cons. C&Y Clinic, Charlottesville, Va., 1974; researcher U. N.C. Dental Sch., Chapel Hill, 1974-75; practice orthodontics, Hollywood and Plant City, Fla., 1977—, Pembroke Pines, Fla., 1980—, Ft. Lauderdale, Fla., 1978—, Clearwater and New Port Richey, Fla., 1981—; U.S. orthodontic dir. Smile Dental Ctrs. Am., Plantation, 1983—; ptnr., cons. Restaurant Cons., Inc., New Orleans, 1979—, Broward Investments Hotel and Restaurants, Fort Lauderdale, 1978—; ptnr., dir. Kwik Pak Foods, Inc., Fla., 1984—; pres., dir. PCB Ltd., Plant City, 1981—, Robinwood Nurseries, Richmond, Va., 1982—; orthodontic cons. Chubb Group Ins., Atlanta, 1982-85; dental staff Hollywood Meml. Hosp., Fla., 1978-83, South Fla. Bapt. Hosp., Plant City, 1982—. Pres., bd. dirs. Spottis Woode Homeowners Assn., Clearwater, 1984—; mem. Acad. 100, Gainesville, 1981—. Mem. ADA, Fla. Dental Soc., West Coast Dental Soc., Am. Assn. Orthodontists, So. Soc. Orthodontists, Fla. Soc. Orthodontists, Greater Miami Acad. Orthodontists, Am. Soc. Dentistry for Children, Psi Omega, Sigma Zeta. Avocations: sailing; scuba diving; horticulture. Office: 707 Druid Rd E Clearwater FL 33516

HOWELL, HUGH HAWKINS, JR., lawyer; b. Atlanta, Aug. 18, 1920; s. Hugh and Ethleen (Horne) H.; student Riverside Mil. Acad., Boys High Sch., Atlanta, Emory U., A.B., U. Ga., 1942; LL.B., John Marshall Law Sch., 1947, LL.M., 1958, J.D., 1959, LL.D., 1960; m. Dorris Callahan; children—Hugh Howell III, James Finn, Jay. Bar: Ga. Dir. Spring Lakes Apts., Inc., Bolton Apts. Mem. Ga. Vets. Service Bd., chmn., 1963-71. Rear adm. USNR. Mem. Judge Advs. Assn. (nat. pres. 1968), Am. Judicature Soc., Fed. (v.p. 5th U.S. Circuit), Am., Ga., Atlanta bar assns., Atlanta Hist. Soc., DeKalb Hist. Soc. (pres.), Am. Legion (comdr. post 134), Navy League (nat. dir.), Naval Res. Assn. (nat. v.p.), SAR (v.p. dist.), SCV (comdr.), Naval Hist. Found., Old Guard of Gate City Guard (comdt.), Phi Delta Theta, Sigma Delta Kappa. Clubs: Masons (32 deg.), Shrine, Jesters, Kiwanis, Athletic, Ansley Golf, Nat. Lawyers, Old War Horse Lawyers. Home: 2811 Ridgewood Rd NW Atlanta GA 30327 Office: 1505 Rock Springs Circle NE Atlanta GA 30306

HOWELL, JOHN FRANKLIN, JR., ophthalmologist; b. Jackson, Miss., May 5, 1933; s. John Franklin and Mary Louise (Watts) H.; m. JoAnn Smith, June 7, 1955 (div. 1975); children—John Franklin III, Clemons Alfred, Lesley Laurin, Henry Smith; m. Ross Lynn Spradling, June 25, 1977. B.S., Tulane U., 1955, M.D., 1958. Diplomate Am. Bd. Ophthalmology. Intern Henry Ford Hosp., Detroit, 1958-59, resident in ophthalmology, 1959-62. Pvt. practice ophthalmology, Amarillo, Tex., 1964—. Bd. dirs. Lone Star Ballet Bd., Amarillo, 1983—. Served to capt. USAF, 1962-64. Fellow ACS, Am. Acad. Ophthalmology; mem. Potter-Randall County Med. Soc., Tex. Med. Assn., Tex. Ophthal. Assn. (treas. 1975-79), Tex. Soc. Ophthalmology and Otolaryngology. Republican. Episcopalian. Avocations: golf; hunting; skiing. Home: 3206 Lipscomb Amarillo TX 79109 Office: 14 Medical Dr Amarillo TX 79106

HOWELL, JOHN MCDADE, university chancellor, political science educator; b. Five Points, Ala., Jan. 28, 1922; s. John William and Bettie Mae (Lee) H.; m. Gladys Evelyn David, Aug. 9, 1952; children—David Noble, Joseph Lee. A.B., U. Ala. 1948, M.A., 1949; Ph.D., Duke U., 1954. Instr. U. Idaho, 1950; instr. Randolph-Macon Woman's Coll., Lynchburg, Va., 1951-52, Duke U., 1952-53; asst. prof. Sweet Briar Coll., Lynchburg, 1953-54, Memphis State U., 1954-57; assoc. prof. E. Carolina U., Greenville, N.C., 1957-61, prof., 1961—, chmn. polit. sci. dept., 1963-66, dean Coll. Arts and Scis., 1966-69, dean Grad. Sch., 1969-73, provost, 1973-77, vice chancellor for acad. affairs, 1977-79, chancellor, 1982—. Author: (with others) Conflict of International Obligations and State Interests, 1972; Contbr.: chpts. to The International Law Standard and Commonwealth Developments, 1966, De Lege Pactorum, 1970; articles to profl. jours. Served with USAAF, 1942-45. Decorated Bronze Star medal. Mem. Phi Beta Kappa, Phi Kappa Phi, Pi Sigma Alpha. Home: 605 E 5th St Greenville NC 27834

HOWELL, LEONARD RUDOLPH, JR., educator mathematics; b. Valdosta, Ga., May 19, 1925; s. Leonard Rudolph and Lily Irene (Stidham) H.; m. Edna Myrtis Avera, Sept. 2, 1944; children—Leonard Rudolph III, David Alan, Paul Michael, Elizabeth Avera. B.A., Mercer U., 1948; M.S., Emory U., 1951; Ph.D., Fla. State U., 1965. Instr. math. Emory U., Valdosta, Ga., 1948-53; commd. officer U.S. Air Force, 1953, advanced through ranks to lt. col., 1970; ret., 1972; assoc. prof. math. Valdosta State Coll., Ga., 1972-81; tchr. math. Valwood Sch., Valdosta, 1982—. Mem. Math. Assn. Am., Am. Math. Soc. Republican. Baptist. Home: Route 1 Box 279 Quitman GA 31643 Office: Valwood Sch 1903 Gornto Rd Valdosta GA 31602

HOWELL, SARAH SMITH, author, artist; b. Birmingham, Ala., Mar. 18, 1929; d. Willie Lofton and Sarah Berta (Masters) Smith; B.S. in Home Econs., U. Louisville, 1951; M.S., U. Tenn., 1967; postgrad. U. Ala., Samford U., David Lipscomb Coll., Arrowmont Sch. Arts and Crafts, U. Tenn. (Nashville); m. A. Crawford Howell, Mar. 18, 1949; 1 dau., Cynthia Ann Howell Williams. Art therapist, tchr. behavior modification Nashville Evaluation Center, 1968-69; home economist utilities, 1954-56, 63-64; dietitian Nashville Gen. and Ky. Bapt. hosps., 1951-52, 57-59; regular participant in craft feature Noon Show, TV, 1978; author, artist, Franklin, Tenn., 1969—; activities dir. Belmont Plaza Retirement Center, 1980-81; nutritionist Tenn. Dept. Health and Environ., 1983-85, ednl. cons., 1985—; weaving exhibited Tenn. State Mus. Archives. Charter mem. Williamson County Heart Assn.; mem. Williamson County Humane Assn.; adv. bd. Tenn. Com. Arts for Handicapped; active Nashville Nutrition Council. Mem. Nashville Artist Guild (past pres., dir.), Tenn. Artist Craftsmen Assn., Nashville Home Econs. Assn. Republican. Baptist. Clubs: Cheekwood Fine Arts Center, Hist. Belmont Assn. Author: Creative Crafts for Self-Expression, 1978; Home Cooking in a Hurry, More Home Cooking in a Hurry, 1986. Home: Rt 3 Bois d'Arc Rd Franklin TN 37064

HOWELL, SUSAN BROOKS, nurse, oncology clinical coordinator; b. Savannah, Ga., May 31, 1955; d. Louis Baker, Sr., and Frances Elizabeth (Harvey) Harkins; m. James Finn. A.D.N., Armstrong State Coll., Savannah, 1974, B.S. in Nursing, 1977; M.S. in Nursing, Med. Coll. Ga., 1978; postgrad. U. Ga., 1982—. R.N., Ga., 1974. Staff and charge nurse St. Joseph's Hosp., Savannah, 1974-77; med. nurse clinician Meml. Med. Ctr., Savannah, 1978-79, clin. nurse specialist in medicine, 1979-80, in oncology, 1980-82, oncology clin. coordinator Community Hosp. Oncology Program, 1982-85; nursing staff devel. coordinator Candler Gen. Hosp., Savannah, 1985—; CPR instr. Ga. Heart Assn.; adj. faculty Armstrong State Coll., Ga. So. Coll.; cons. Nat. Cancer Inst. Contbr. article to profl. jour. Mem. Oncology Nursing Soc., Sigma Theta Tau. Baptist. Club: 99's.

HOWELL, WILLIAM ASHLEY, III, lawyer; b. Raleigh, N.C., Jan. 2, 1949; s. William Ashley II and Caroline Erskine Greenleaf; m. Esther Holland, Dec. 22, 1973. B.S., Troy State U., 1972; J.D., Birmingham Sch. Law, 1977;

postgrad. U. Ala.-Birmingham. Bar: Ala. 1977, U.S. Dist. Ct. (no. dist.) Ala. 1977, U.S. Ct. Appeals (5th cir.) 1977, U.S. Ct. Appeals (llth cir.) 1982, U.S. Supreme Ct. 1982. Atty. pub. defender div. Legal Aid. Soc. of Birmingham, 1977-78, later civil div.; dist. office atty. SBA, Birmingham, 1980-82, dist. counsel Ala. Dist., 1982—. Bd. dirs. Hoover Homeowners Assn., 1977-81. Recipient spl. achievement award SBA, 1984. Mem. ABA (sect. corp., banking and bus. law), Ala. Bar Assn. (sect. corp., banking and bus. law, sect. bankruptcy and comml. law, com. on future of the profession 1978-81, 83-85), Birmingham Bar Assn., Fed. Bar Assn., Comml. Law League, Sigma Delta Kappa (v.p. Birmingham chpt.). Episcopalian. Home: 1439 Steven Circle Birmingham AL 35226 Office: US Small Bus Adminstrn 2121 8th Ave N Room 200 Birmingham AL 35256

HOWELL-TAYLOE, MARGARET AFFARENE, psychologist; b. Brownfield, Tex., May 31, 1926; d. Kennedy Watson and Laura Exa (Leveritt) Howell; m. William Carr Tayloe, Apr. 8, 1980. B.A., Baylor U., 1947; M.A., U. Rochester, 1949; Ph.D., U. Calif., 1965. Research psychologist USPHS, Washington, 1950-68, HEW, Washington, 1968-72; research epidemiologist Nat. Cancer Inst., Bethesda, Md., 1972-74; free-lance writer, 1974—; cons. NRC, Served mil. duty USPHS, 1950-52. AAUW scholar, 1947-48; USPHS Mental Health Career Devel. fellow, 1962-64. Mem. Am. Psychol. Assn., Ret. Officers Assn., USPHS Commd. Officers Assn. Republican. Contbr. articles to profl. jours. Home: The Riverside Box 31 Tappahannock VA 22560

HOWETT, JOHN, art history educator; b. Kokomo, Ind., Aug. 7, 1926; B.F.A., Herron Art Inst., Indpls., 1953; M.A., U. Chgo., 1962, Ph.D., 1968. Asst. prof. art history dept. Emory U., Atlanta, 1966-69, assoc. prof., 1970-81, prof., 1981—, chmn. 1973-76, 78-79, 80-81, 83-84. Author: Annette Cone-Skeleton, 1982; What Artists Have to Say about Nuclear War, 1983; Carl Andre, 1983; (with Catherine M. Howett) Martin Emanuel: 1980, 1980. Bd. dirs. Atlanta Coll. Art, 1975—, High Mus. Art, Atlanta, 1974—. Served with inf. U.S. Army, 1944-46. Recipient Sr. Class Teaching award Emory U., 1981. Mem. Coll. Art Assn., Soc. Archtl. Historians. Office: Dept Art History Emory U Carlos Hall Atlanta GA 30322

HOWIE, CHARLES LESTER, financial and personnel administrator; b. Fayetteville, N.C., Aug. 21, 1935; s. Samuel Massey and Mabel Claire (Wills) H. Student, Western N.Mex. U., 1951-52, East Carolina U., 1959. Dept. mgr. Security Life & Trust Co., Winston-Salem, N.C., 1959-61; adminstrv. officer Dept. Def., Ft. Bragg, N.C., 1961-66, tng. specialist John F. Kennedy Ctr. and Inst. for Mil. Assistance, Ft. Bragg, N.C., 1966-80, fin. and personnel adminstr. Dept. Def., 1980-83; ROTC liaison officer, Ft. Bragg, 1983—; mgmt. cons. Bd. dirs. Fed. Credit Union. Served with USAF, 1951-55. Mem. Am. Mgmt. Assn., Am. Assn. Antique Dealers and Appraisers. Democrat. Methodist (mem. ofcl. bd.). Home: 2710 Mirror Lake Dr Fayetteville NC 28303 Office: Bldg 3956 Fort Bragg NC 28307

HOWIE, JOHN ROBERT, lawyer; b. Paris, Tex., June 29, 1946; s. Robert H. and Frances (Caldwell) H.; m. Eileen Yates, May 3, 1969; children—John Robert, Ashley Elizabeth. B.B.A., North Tex. State U., 1968; J.D., So. Meth. U., 1976. Bar: Tex. 1976. Trial lawyer, aviation litigation mgr. Windle Turley, P.C., Dallas, 1976—; guest lectr. Dallas County Community Colls., 1980-83. Dallas Summer Musicals guarantor, 1982—. Served to lt. comdr. USN, 1968-78. Mem. ABA, Assn. Trial Lawyers Am. (chmn. aviation sect.), State Bar Tex., Tex. Trial Lawyers Assn. (dir.), Dallas Trial Lawyers Assn. (dir. 1982-84, pres. 1986), Dallas Bar Assn. (law in changing soc. vol. judge 1981-83, pro bono panel 1982—, fee dispute subcom. chmn. 1983, profl. services com. 1984). Democrat. Presbyterian. Home: 4328 Livingston Dallas TX 75205 Office: 6440 N Central Expressway 1000 University Tower Dallas TX 75206

HOWIE, RONALD RAY, planner, safety consultant; b. Terrell, Tex., Nov. 9, 1950; s. Albert VanBuren Howie and Iva Lea (Meador) Davis. Asst. to mgr. So. Sales Co., Terrell, Tex., 1964-69, planner, 1984-85; planner City of Terrell, 1970, Terrell State Hosp., 1976, Varo Semiconductor, Inc., Garland, Tex., 1978-84; chmn. bd. Howie Service Co. Inc., Terrell, 1983—; safety cons. Varo Semiconductor, Inc., Garland, 1980-84, Kaufman County Rolling Oaks Vol. Fire Dept., Tex., 1984—. Author: A Midland Route, 1976. Researcher of book: A Century of Masonary, 1974; contbr. to Kaufman County History, Vol. 2, 1984; author of manual: Safety Specifications, 1984. Mem. Terrell Vol. Fire Dept., 1977-80. Mem. Ry. and Locomotive Hist. Soc., Dallas Geneal. Soc., Nat. Fire Protection Assn., Coll. Mound Cemetery Assn., Terrell Heritage Soc., Inc. (vice pres. 1976). Avocations: genealogy; history; writing; woodworking; restoring antiques. Home: PO Box 841 Terrell TX 75160-0841

HOWORTH, RICHARD CAPEL, bookseller; b. Marks, Miss., Jan. 8, 1951; s. M. Beckett and Mary Hartwell (Bishop) H.; m. Lisa C. Neumann, Dec. 31, 1973; children—Elizabeth Claire, M. Beckett IV. B.A., U. Miss., 1972. Mgr. Savile Bookshop, Washington, 1976-78; proprietor Square Books, Oxford, Miss., 1979—. Mem. Am. Booksellers Assn. Office: Square Books On The Square Oxford MS 38655

HOY, GILBERT R., physics educator; b. Cleve., June 17, 1932; s. George Hansen and Esther (Plum) H.; m. Chobee Agnes Kyle (div.); children—Gilbert Jr., Dyke, Tracy; m. 2d, Gloria Jeannette Viale; 1 dau., Valerie. B.S. in Gen. Engring., Davis and Elkins Coll., 1954; M.S. in Physics, Cornell U., 1958; Ph.D. in Physics, Carnegie Inst. Tech., 1963. Instr. Evening Coll. Rochester Inst. Tech., 1962-63; scientist Xerox Corp., Solid State Research Dept., 1962-63; research assoc. Carnegie Inst. Tech., Pitts., 1963-65; asst. prof. dept. physics Boston U., 1965-69, assoc. prof., 1969-73, prof., 1973-80, acting chmn. dept. physics, 1979-80; scientist Centre d'Etudes Nucleaires de Grenoble (France), 1976-77; chmn. dept. physics Old Dominion U., Norfolk, Va., 1980—. NATO Conf. grantee, 1966; recipient Oak Ridge research participant award, summer 1968; invited lectr. Magnetism Conf., Chania, Crete, Greece, 1969; hon. research assoc. Harvard U., 1972; invited chmn. Mossbauer Frulingsschule, Germany, 1975; invited chmn. Internat. Conf. Mossbauer Spectroscopy, Portoroz, Yugoslavia, 1979; cons. U. Alexandria, Egypt, 1979, NIH, 1979-81, Inst. for Def. Analyses, 1985—. NIH grantee 1982-83; NSF grantee, 73-76, 1977-80; U.S. AEC grantee, 1968-72. Mem. Am. Phys. Soc., Sigma Xi. Contbr. articles to profl. jours.

HOY, WILLIAM IVAN, educator; b. Mt. Meridan, Va., Aug. 21, 1915; s. William Isaac and Ileta (Saufley) H.; B.A., Hampden-Sydney Coll., 1936; B.D., Union Theol. Sem., 1942; S.T.M., Biblical Sem. in N.Y., 1949; Ph.D., U. Edinburgh, 1945; m. Wilma Lambert, Apr. 29, 1945; children—Doris Lambert Hoy Bezanilla, Martha. Ordained to ministry Presbyn. Ch., 1942; asst. prin., athletic dir. Virginia High Sch., 1936-39; asst. prof. Bible, Guilford Coll., 1948-49; asst. prof. religion U. Miami, Fla., 1953-57, asso. prof., 1957-60, chmn. dept. religion, 1958-79, prof., 1960—; moderator Presbytery of Everglades, 1960-61, stated clk., 1968-73, 78-79, mem. council, 1983—; moderator Synod of Fla., 1984-85; mem. bd. Christian edn. Presbyn. Ch. U.S., 1969-73, mem. Gen. Assembly Mission Bd., 1978—; pres. Greater Miami Ministerial Assn., 1964, 80-82; observer, cons. World Council Christian Edn., Venezuela, Peru, 1971; bd. dirs. Met. Fellowship Chs., 1969—, v.p., 1971-73, interim exec. sec., 1974-77; trustee Davidson Coll., 1975—. Commdr. USNR. Mem. Am. Oriental Soc., Soc. of Biblicial Lit., Acad. of Religion, Am. Soc. of Ch. History, Scottish Ch. History Soc., Internat. Sociol. Assn., Religious Research Assn., Studiorum Novi Testamenti Societas, Soc. for the Sci. Study of Religion, Iron Arrow, Phi Kappa Phi, Omicron Delta Kappa, Lambda Chi Alpha, Alpha Psi Omega, Theta Delta (founder), Omega. Clubs: Rotary, Tiger Bay. Contbr. articles and book reviews to religious pubs.; co-author: The History of the Chaplains Corps, 1960; contbr. to Dictionary of Christian Ethics, 1973. Home: 5881 SW 52nd Terr Miami FL 33155 Office: PO Box 248348 University of Miami Coral Gables FL 33124

HOYER, DAVID RALPH, oil company executive; b. Phila., Aug. 12, 1931; s. Ralph W. and Clara Barton (Patterson) H.; children—David, Ann, Richard. B.S., U. Del., 1953. Vice pres. refining Gulf Oil Co., Houston, 1972-75, v.p. supply and transp., 1975; pres. Warren Petroleum Co. div. Gulf Oil Corp., Tulsa, 1976-77, Gulf Oil Co.-Internat., London, 1977-82, Warren Petroleum Co. div. Chevron U.S.A. Inc., Tulsa, 1983—. Methodist.

HOYLE, FRANK LEWIS, III, municipal bond broker; b. Kings Mountain, N.C., June 29, 1943; s. Frank Lewis and Mildred (Moss) H.; Student U. N.C., 1961-63; B.S., East Tenn. State U., 1967. Account rep. Hereth, Orr & Jones, Inc., Atlanta, 1978-84; fin. and ins. cons. ADR Ins. Group, Raleigh, N.C., 1973-75, The Moore Group, Atlanta, 1975-78. Bd. dirs. Ga. Residential Care Assn., Atlanta, 1984. Author: Olio Collected Stories, 1968. Mem. N.C. Assn. Long-Term Care Facilities, Nat. Assn. Residential Care Facilities, Members Guild of High Mus. Presbyterian. Club: Rockhaven Country (Hendersonville). Home: 99 Adrian Pl NW Atlanta GA 30327

HOYLE, JOHN DOUGLAS, hospital administrator; b. Springfield, Ohio, Aug. 27, 1943; s. Paul Vollmer and Elizabeth (Steiner) H.; M.Hosp. Adminstrn., Xavier U., 1967; B.A., Wittenberg U., 1965; m. Janet Lee Weatherspoon, July 24, 1965; children—John D., Christopher, Allison. Pres., chief exec. officer St. Luke Hosp., Ft. Thomas, Ky., 1975—, adminstr., 1972-75, asst. adminstr., 1968-72; evening adminstr. The Christ Hosp., Cin., 1968, adminstrv. asst., 1967; clin. instr. U. Ky., Lexington, 1971-76; instr. Ky. Coroner Basic Tng. Program, 1980—; mem. Ky. Bd. Dentistry, 1976-80. Vice chmn. disaster services Cin. ARC, 1976—; mem. adv. bd. Nat. Disaster Med. System; bd. dirs. Campbell County YMCA, 1975-77; v.p. Ky. Bd. Dentistry and Dental Examiners, 1980—; mem. bd. No. Ky. Emergency Med. Service, 1977-83; chmn. disaster and emergency services com. City of Ft. Thomas, 1976—; treas. Greater Cin. Hosp. Council, 1977, exec. com., 1979—; class rep. Wittenberg U. Alumni Council, 1970-80; scoutmaster Boy Scouts Am., Ft. Thomas, 1978—; chmn. bd. Archival Document Conservation Center, 1984—; pres. Tri-State Community Cancer Orgn., 1984-86; treas. Tri-State Community Clin. Oncology Program, 1983-84; bd. dirs. Delta Dental Plan of Ky., 1981—; exec. com. Greater Cin. Hosp. Council, 1983—; mem. adv. bd. Nat. Disaster Med. System. Recipient Pfizer award of merit, U.S. CD Council, 1977; Citizenship award, SAR, 1960, Am. Legion, 1960; Pro Patria cert. of appreciation Dept. Def., 1985. Mem. Ky. Hosp. Assn. (v.p. 1976-77), Ky. Peer Rev. Orgn. (dir. 1976-77), Am. Hosp. Assn., Am. Coll. Hosp. Adminstrs., Royal Soc. Health, Hosp. Fin. Mgmt. Assn., Am. Trauma Soc., Ky. Hosp. Assn., Phi Kappa Psi. Methodist. Club: Optimist. Contbr. articles to profl. jours. Home: 47 Winston Hill Rd Fort Thomas KY 41075 Office: 85 N Grand Ave Fort Thomas KY 41075

HOYT, DANIEL REXFORD, management educator; b. Joplin, Mo., May 20, 1943; s. Rexford P. and Oletha Bell (Mills) H.; m. Sara Lou Payne, Dec. 16, 1967; children—Judith Danielle, Audrey Elizabeth. A.A., Mo. So. State Coll., 1963; B.A., U. Mo., 1965; M.B.A., Memphis State U., 1969; Ph.D., U. Nebr., 1976. Teaching asst. Memphis State U., Tenn., 1968-69; asst. prof. bus., Mo. Western State U., St. Joseph, 1969-76; prof. mgmt., dir. transp. mgmt. program Ark. State U., Jonesboro, 1976—; dir. Am. Soc. for Personnel Adminstrn. Found., Alexandria, Va., 1985—. Author: (with others) Personnel, HRM, Instructors Manual, 1984. Recipient Outstanding Faculty Mem. award Ark. State U., 1983-84, Faculty Achievement award Ark. State U., 1985. Mem. Am. Soc. for Personnel Adminstrn. (bd. dirs. 1985—, v.p. personnel research 1985—), Acad. Mgmt., Northeast Ark. Transp. Club (pres. 1983), Indsl. Relations Research Assn., Soc. Nonprofit Mgmt., Northeast Ark. Personnel Mgrs. Assn. (pres. 1981). Lodge: Lions. Avocations: reading; travel; fishing. Home: Route 1 Box 181 Jonesboro AR 72401 Office: Ark State U PO Box 115 State University AR 72467

HOYT, GEORGE SAYRE, manufacturing company executive; b. Bainbridge, N.Y., Apr. 17, 1943; s. Richard Wilson and Dorothy Mae (Corcoran) H.; m. Marie Louise Syracuse, Nov. 12, 1966; 1 son, Richard Wilson. B.S. in Indsl. Engring., Purdue U., 1967; M.B.A., U. Chgo., 1975. Quality engr. Sundstrand Corp., Rockford, Ill., 1966-72, materiel systems mgr., 1972-74, mfg. systems mgr., 1974-78, prodn. planning mgr., 1978-79, materiel tng. mgr., 1979-82; materials mgr. Duracell Battery, Lexington, N.C., 1982-83; owner Hoyt Video Prodns., 1981-82; mfg. resource planning mgr. AMP Inc., Winston-Salem, N.C., 1983—; project bus. cons. Mem. adv. bd. No. Ill. U.; mem. curriculum adv. bd. Rock Valley Coll., 1979-82, chmn., 1981-82. Cert. quality engr. Am. Soc. Quality Control, 1972; cert. fellow Am. Prodn. and Inventory Control Soc., 1977, cert. chmn., 1979-82. Mem. Am. Film Inst., Am. Prodn. and Inventory Control Soc., Alpha Pi Mu. Home: 4187 Dimholt Ct Winston-Salem NC 27104 Office: 3700 Reidsville Rd Winston-Salem NC 27101

HREBENAR, ROBERTA LEE, geologist; b. Uniontown, Pa., May 25, 1959; d. Robert E. and Bertha (Krzysiak) H. B.A., U. South Fla., 1981. Assoc. geologist Getty Oil Co., Houston, 1981-82, project geologist, 1982-84; geologist Texaco U.S.A., Houston, 1984—. Mem. Am. Assn. Petroleum Geologists (jr.). Roman Catholic. Avocations: Crochet; shell collecting; music. Office: Texaco 6750 W Loop S Bellaire TX 77401

HRENAK, VALERIE WOOD, computer scientist, graphic artist; b. Honolulu, Sept. 14, 1948; d. Franklin and Beatrice Elizabeth (Wentura) Wood; m. Vincent Joseph Hrenak, Sept. 20, 1980; 1 child, Brian Vincent. A.A., Am. Coll. in Paris, 1968; B.A., George Washington U., 1970; M.B.A., Golden Gate U., 1979. Comptroller, Natural Energy Corp., Washington, 1977; mem. tech. staff Computer Scis. Corp., Falls Church, Va., 1978-80, computer scientist, 1981—; mgmt. analyst Dept. Energy, Washington, 1980-81; cons. SBA Small Bus. Inst., Washington, 1978-79. Recipient 1st Place award Creative Newspaper Advt., Va. Press Assn., 1974, Cert. of Merit, SBA, 1978. Mem. Assn. Inst. for Cert. Computer Profls. Democrat. Club: Mayflower Soc. Avocations: skiing; yoga. Office: Computer Scis Corp 6521 Arlington Blvd Falls Church VA 22042

HREZO, ANDREW PAUL, university counseling director; b. Gary, Ind., June 1, 1940; s. Andrew John and Barbara Theresa Hrezo; m. Harriet C. Cox, Nov. 24, 1962; children—Robert, Paul, Marie, Donna. B.S., Rose Poly. Inst., 1962; M.S., Ind. U., 1968, Ed.D., 1974. Engr. Delco-Remy div. Gen. Motors, Anderson, Ind., 1962-63; coordinator univ. div. counseling Ind. U., Bloomington, 1970-72; mem. faculty, asst. dean Coll. St. Thomas, 1972-79; counselor Oral Roberts U., 1979-81, dir. univ. counseling center, 1981-84; cons. Christian Family Inst., Tulsa, 1979-83; dean of students U. Steubenville (Ohio), 1984-85, dir. counseling, 1985—. Served with U.S. Army, 1963-67. NDEA Title IV fellow, 1968-70; HEW grantee, 1976-79; Control Data Corp. grantee, 1979. Mem. Am. Psychol. Assn., Am. Assn. for Counseling and Devel., Assn. Christian Therapists. Roman Catholic.

HRNA, DANIEL JOSEPH, educator, lawyer, pharmacist; b. Taylor, Tex., March 19, 1940; s. Stephan Peter and Anna Ludmilla (Baran) H.; B.S., U. Houston, 1963, J.D., 1970; m. Velma Isobel Lesson, Sept. 3, 1963; children—Anna Marie, Daniel Steven, Brian Keith. Bar: Tex. 1972. In mgmt., Gunning-Casteel Co., El Paso, Tex., 1963-65; dir. pharmacy services Tex. Inst. Rehab. and Research, Houston, 1966-79; dir. pharmacy Alief Gen. Hosp., Belhaven Hosp., Houston, 1979-85, West Houston Med. Ctr., 1985—; mem. faculty Baylor U. Coll. Medicine, 1977-79; with Houston Continental Enterprises, Tex. Rampage, Inc. Mem. ABA, Am. Pharm. Assn., Tex. Pharmacy Assn., State Bar Tex., Tex. Soc. Hosp. Pharmacists, Am. Soc. Pharmacy Law, Am. Hosp. Assn., Harris County Pharm. Assn., Houston Bar Assn., Galveston-Houston Pharm. Hosp. Assn., Profl. Photographers Guild Houston (hon.), Delta Theta Phi, Kappa Psi, Phi Delta Chi. Roman Catholic. Office: 12141 Richmond Ave Houston TX 77082 also 11920 Beechnut Houston TX 77072

HRUSKA, FRANCIS JOHN, marine surveyor and consultant; b. Trnovec N/V, Czechoslovakia, Jan. 19, 1935, came to U.S., 1977; s. Ferdinand and Julia (Klepanec) H.; m. Ludmila Liptak, Apr. 19, 1958; children—Zuzana, Daniela, Martin. Grad. with honors, Nautical Sch. for Inland Waterways, Czechoslovakia, 1952, State Nautical Sch., Poland, 1955; student Walsey Hall Corr. Coll., Oxford, Eng., 1973-74. Cert. master mariner, 1961, marine pilot, 1969. Ships nautical officer Czechoslovak Ocean Shipping, Prague, 1955-62; exec. nautical engr. State Nautical Authority, Czechoslovakia, 1962-66; master C.S.P.D. Sea Branch, Czechoslovakia, 1966-68; marine pilot Ghana Rys. and Ports, 1968-72, Nat. Port Authority, Liberia, 1972-75; harbour master, chief marine officer, 1975-77; marine surveyor Nautech, Inc., Latham & Assocs., Master Marine Cons., Inc., New Orleans, 1978-82; pres. Plimsoll Marine Surveyors, Inc., Covington, La., 1983—; chmn. exam. bd. for pilots Nat. Port Authority, Monrovia, Liberia, 1975-77; nautical advisor Govt. of Liberia, 1975-77; cons. Comprehensive Study for Devel. of Port of Monrovia, 1975-77, Elbe-Oder-Danube Waterways System, Czechoslovakia, 1963-66. Contbr. articles to profl. jours. Office: Plimsoll Marine Surveyors Inc PO Box 8528 Mandeville LA 70448

HSU, TING CHEN, economist; b. Shanghai, China, Dec. 2, 1921; came to U.S., 1945, naturalized, 1960; s. Tse Chien and Lan Ying (Tsong) H.; m. Sylvia Martin, Nov. 29, 1953. B.S., U. Mo., 1950, M.A., 1953; postgrad. U. Mich., 1954-56. Research asst. Alfred Politz, Inc., N.Y.C., 1957-58; econ. cons. P.R. Planning Bd. Santurce, P.R., 1958-59; research supr. W.R. Simmons & Assocs. Research Inc., N.Y.C., 1959-60; sr. research analyst Girl Scouts U.S.A., N.Y.C., 1960-63; cons. P.R. Treasury Dept., San Juan, 1963-69, exec. dir., 1970, chief economist, 1971-73, dir., 1974-77, acting asst. sec. of treasury, 1978-81, acting dir., 1982, spl. asst. to sec. of treasury, 1983—; lectr. Met. Campus Inter Am. U. of P.R., 1967—. Mem. men's adv. com. Caribe council Girl Scouts U.S., 1967—, chmn., 1971-74. Served to capt. Chinese Nationalist Army, 1943-46. Mem. Am. Econ. Assn., Fin. Mgmt. Assn., Chinese Students' Assn. (pres. Columbia, Mo. 1950-51), Alpha Pi Zeta. Clubs: Cosmopolitan (pres. Columbia, Mo. 1951-52). Office: PO Box 1948 San Juan PR 00903

HUBBA, THOMAS JOHN, hotel executive; b. Newark, Jan. 30, 1948; s. John Jay and Marie (Wilcox) H.; m. Julie Ann Fiddes, July 6, 1974. B.A. in Polit. and Social Sci., Mansfield U., 1969. Restaurant mgr. FRFC-Dayton, St. Mary's, Ohio, 1974-78; night mgr. ARLTEC Hotel Corp., Arlington, Va., 1978-79, front office mgr., 1979-81, resident mgr. Sheraton Nat. Hotel, 1981-84, gen. mgr., 1984—; cons. Lewis Internat. Hotel Sch., Washington, 1978-79. Served with U.S. Army, 1969-71. Recipient cert. St. Mary's Civic Assn., 1978. Mem. Am. Def. Preparedness Assn. Republican. Office: Sheraton Nat Hotel 900 S Orme St Arlington VA 22204

HUBBARD, CARL MASON, finance educator, consultant; b. Abilene, Tex., Sept. 17, 1945; s. Charles Mason and Bennie Katherine (Byram) H.; m. Karen Dorothy Klahn, Jan. 7, 1972; children—Kevin Robert, Jason Kent. B.B.A., McMurry Coll., 1968; M.B.A., Hardin-Simmons U., 1972; Ph.D. in econs., Tex. Tech. U., 1975. Asst. prof. Trinity U., San Antonio, Tex., 1975-80, assoc. prof., 1980—; cons. Security Service Fed. Credit Union, San Antonio, 1978, Trinity Nat. Bank, 1983. Adv. Boysville, Inc., San Antonio, Tex., 1977. Mem. Am. Econs. Assn., Am. Fin. Assn., Fin. Mgmt. Assn., Alpha Chi, Omicron Delta Epsilon. Baptist. Avocations: Trap and skeet shooting; hunting; reading. Home: 2219 Fawn Glen San Antonio TX 78232

HUBBARD, CARROLL, JR., congressman; b. Murray, Ky., July 7, 1937; s. Carroll and Beth (Shelton) H.; B.A., Georgetown Coll., 1959; J.D., U. Louisville, 1962; m. Carol Brown, Feb. 12, 1984; children—Kelly Lynn, Krista Leigh. Admitted to Ky. bar, 1962; practice law, Mayfield, Ky., from 1962; mem. Ky. Senate from 1st Dist. of Ky., 1967-75; mem. 94th-97th Congresses from 1st dist. Ky. Mem., deacon, moderator 1st Baptist Ch., Mayfield. Served with Air N.G., 1962-67, Army N.G., 1968-70. Named 1 of 3 Outstanding Men of Ky., Ky. Jaycees, 1968; Outstanding Young Democratic Legislator, Ky. Young Democrats, 1970. Office: 2182 Rayburn House Office Bldg Washington DC 20515

HUBBARD, JOHN RAST, computer science educator, mathematician; b. Grand Rapids, Mich., Aug. 2, 1943; s. Willard Wright and Sara Eloise (Rast) H.; m. Ellen Brown, July 1, 1967 (div. 1980); children—Sara Elizabeth, John Behrens; m. Anita Huray. Student Cornell U., 1961-64; A.B. in Math., U. Rochester, 1966; A.M. in Math., U. Mich., 1968, Ph.D. in Math., 1973; M.S. in Computer Sci., Pa. State U., 1983. Instr., Allegheny Coll., Meadville, Pa., 1968-70; asst. prof. Columbus Coll., Ga., 1972-75; asst. prof. Lycoming Coll., Williamsport, Pa., 1975-78, chmn. dept., 1978-82, assoc. prof., 1978-83; assoc. prof. computer scis. U. Richmond, Va., 1983—; cons. pvt. lawyers, Williamsport, 1982, Am. Youth Soccer Orgn., Williamsport, 1981; judge Va. Jr. Acad. of Sci., Williamsburg, 1985. Author: A Gentle Introduction to the VAX, 1984; Introduction to Mathematics, 1978. Contbr. articles to profl. jours. Soccer coach Am. Youth Soccer Assn., Williamsport, 1976-81. Mem. Assn. Computing Machinery, Math. Assn. Am., Sigma Xi, Pi Mu Epsilon, Delta Kappa Epsilon (pres. Alumni Assn. 1980-83). Home: 2401 Wadebridge Rd Midlothian VA 23113-3841 Office: Dept Math and Computer Sci U Richmond Richmond VA 23173

HUBBARD, RANDALL DEE, manufacturing company executive; b. Smith Center, Kans., June 13, 1935; s. Miner and Louise H.; m. Joan Dale McLain; children—Derrol, Bret, Shana. B.A., Butler Community Coll., Kans., 1956. Tchr., coach Kans. Jr. High Sch., Towanda, 1956-57; loan mgr. MFC Fin., Wichita, Kans., 1957-59; gen. mgr., v.p. Safelite Industries, Wichita, 1959-68; pres. Safelite Industries, Wichita, 1968-78; chmn. bd. AFG Industries, Inc., Kingsport, Tenn., 1978—. Mem. Tenn. Dist. Export Council, 1980-82, Gov.'s Ambassador Program, 1983. R. Dee Hubbard Hall, Wichita State U., named in his honor. Mem. Internat. Assn. Businessmen and Profls. Found (life; Outstanding Achievement award 1982). Office: AFG Industries Inc PO Box 929 Kingsport TN 37662*

HUBBARD, THOMAS EDWIN, (TIM), lawyer; b. Roseboro, N.C., July 10, 1944; s. Charles Spence and Mary Mercer (Reeves) H.; m. Leslie Howard, July 20, 1985. B.S. in Biomed. Engring., Duke U., 1970, postgrad., 1970-71; J.D., U. N.C., 1973. Bar: N.C. 1973. Regulation writer, med. devices FDA, Washington, 1974-75; asst. dir. clin. affairs Zimmer USA, Warsaw, Ind., 1975, dir. regulatory affairs, 1975-76; house counsel Gen. Med. Corp., Richmond, Va., 1976-79; prin. Tim Hubbard Law Firm, Pittsboro, N.C., 1979—; pres. Chathamborough Research Group, Inc., Pittsboro, 1979—; v.p. Knight & Hubbard, Inc., Chapel Hill, N.C., 1983—, chmn. 1986—; treas./sec. Hubbard-Corey, Inc., Pittsboro, 1985—; pres. Chathamborough Farms, Inc., Sanford, N.C., 1985—; dir. treas. No. State Legal Service, Hillsborough, N.C., 1980—, pres. bd., 1986—. Vice pres. N.C. Young Democrats 4th Congl. Dist., 1970-71, named Outstanding Young N.C. Democrat, 1971, mem. State Dem. Exec. Com., 1972-73. Served to sgt. USMC, 1963-67. Mem. N.C. Bar Assn., ABA, Assn. for Advancement Med. Instrumentation (govt. affairs com. 1976). Democrat. Methodist. Office: Chathamborough Research Group Inc 105 West St Pittsboro NC 27312

HUBBELL, FLOYD GORDON, JR., banker; b. Stroud, Okla., Aug. 7, 1946; s. Floyd Gordon and Esther Joyce (Collins) H.; B.B.A., U. Okla., 1972; M.B.A., Central State U., 1978; grad. Mgmt. Sch. of Bank Mktg., U. Ga., 1980; m. Gail McCann Altman, Mar. 25, 1982; children—Elizabeth Scott, Natalie Gail, Sally Paige. Loan servicing mgr. savs. ops., mortgage loan officer, mktg. officer, asst. v.p. Mut. Fed. Savs. and Loan Assn. of Oklahoma City, 1973-77; v.p. mktg. Central Nat. Bank and Trust Co., Enid, Okla., 1977—, sr. v.p. mktg. dept., 1982—; adj. prof. bus. adminstrn. Phillips U., Enid. Bd. dirs. Garfield County (Okla.) ARC, 1977-79, United Way, 1979, Cherokee Strip council Girl Scouts U.S.A., 1978-79; bd. dirs. Enid Community Speech and Hearing Ctr.; trustee Community Devel. Support Assn. Assn., pres., 1979-80. Served with USAF, 1968-72. Mem. Bank Mktg. Assn. (pres. Okla. chpt.), Am. Mktg. Assn., Am. Inst. Banking (co-founder Enid chpt., pres. 1978-79), Okla. Bankers Assn., Nat. Assn. Bus. Economists. Democrat. Club: Am. Bus. (gov. Enid chpt.). Home: 3533 Chickadee Ln Enid OK 73703 Office: 324 W Broadway Enid OK 73701

HUBEL, RICHARD EVERED, diversified conglomerate executive; b. San Jose, Calif., June 8, 1929; s. Percy Evered and Helen Gertrude (Swisher) H.; m. Alma Genevieve Ladd, July 18, 1959; children—Keith, Allen, Mark, Pamela. B.A., San Jose State Coll., 1954; M.B.A., Stanford U., 1956. Exec., Western Electric Co., San Leandro, Calif., 1956-59, N.Y.C., 1959-64, Anchor Rental Co., Ramsey, N.J., 1964-77, Anchor Med. Aids, Midland Park, N.J., 1972-78, Anchor Keystone Med. Aids, Greenville, S.C., 1974—, Anchor Fire & Safety Equipment, 1974—; exec., chief exec. officer Anchor Industries, Greenville, 1971—; dir. Med. Personnel Pool, Greenville, 1982—. Com. chmn. Small Bus. Council, Greenville, 1982. Served with USAF, 1949-52. Mem. Am. Rental Assn. (council 1981-82), N.J. Rental Assn. (pres. 1966-68), C. of C. (com. chmn. 1981), Commerce Club (pres. 1982-83). Republican. Baptist. Club: Rotary (Greenville, S.C.). Home: Route 7 Red Bud Ln Greenville SC 29609 Office: Anchor Med Aids 207 W Antrim Dr Greenville SC 29607

HUBENY, PHILLIP CHARLES, oil company executive, inventor; b. Chgo., Aug. 18, 1952; s. Charles Raymond and Arlene Francis (Dresden) H. B.A. in Lit., U. Md.-Balt., 1974; postgrad. Nicholls State U., 1980, U. Tex.-Austin, 1983, La. State U., 1983; B.S. in Mech. Engring., Kennedy Western U., 1986. Security cons., Atlanta, 1975-77; operator Texhoma Contractors, Grand Island, La., 1977-79; head maintenance operator Conoco Inc., New Orleans, 1979—; sole propr. Sunset Enterprises, Cottonport, La., 1982—. Inventor pressure sensor, pressure relief valve. Mem. Cottonport Vol. Fire Dept., 1981; adv. bd. Am. Security Council, 1983. Served with U.S. Army, 1971-75. Mem. U.S. Jaycees. Roman Catholic. Home: 823 Coco Ave Cottonport LA 71327 Office: Sunset Enterprises PO Box 247 Cottonport LA 71327

HUBERT, JOSEPH ARTHUR, lawyer; b. Northport, N.Y., Mar. 22, 1930; s. Joseph F. and Adelyn (Condon) H.; A.B., Centre Coll., 1951; LL.D., U. Miami, Coral Gables, Fla., 1956; m. Marianne Picton Rudd, Apr. 26, 1974; children by previous marriage—Nancy, Lisa, James, Robert, Jean Marie. Bar: Fla. 1956; Ptnr. firm Watson, Hubert & Clark, and predecessor, Fort

Lauderdale, Fla., since 1956; now sole practice, Pompano Beach, Fla.; dir. Pan Am. Bank, Southeast Bank of Broward. Pres., Community Service Council, 1965, Econ. Opportunity Coordinating Group Broward County, 1965, United Fund of Broward County, 1967. Served with CIC, AUS, 1951-53; Korea, Japan. Mem. ABA, Broward County Bar Assn. (pres. 1969) Fla. Bar, Execs. Assn. Ft. Lauderdale. Home: 4111 Bayview Dr Fort Lauderdale FL 33308 Office: 201 SE 24th Ave Pompano Beach FL 33062

HUCK, LEWIS FRANCIS, lawyer, real estate consultant and developer; b. Bklyn., Mar. 19, 1912; s. Frank and Jessie (Green) H.; LL.B., St. John's U., 1938, LL.M., 1939; m. Frances M. Love, Jan. 7, 1950; children—Janet Ahearn, L. Frank, William G., Robert L., James J. Admitted to N.Y. bar, 1939, also Tex., Mass. bars; practice law, 1939—; with trust dept. Guaranty Trust Co. N.Y., 1929-41; atty. Gen. Electric Co., Schenectady, 1945-47, chem. counsel, 1947-48, atomic energy counsel, 1948-51, gen. mgr., Richland, Wash., 1951-55; asst. to exec. v.p. Gen. Dynamics Corp., 1955-57; lawyer, real estate cons. and developer, 1957-68; v.p., dir., cons. real estate devel. Eastern Airlines, Inc., 1968—; pres. Huck Enterprises Co. Inc., 1980—. Served maj. AUS, 1941-45. Democrat. Home: 15127 Kimberley Ln Houston TX 77079 Office: Exec Office Eastern Airlines Miami Internat Airport Miami FL 33148 also Huck Enterprises Co Inc 14518 Hempstead Hwy Houston TX 77040

HUCKABY, THOMAS J. (JERRY), congressman; b. Hodge, La., July 19, 1941; s. Thomas Milton and Eva (Toland) H.; B.S. in Elec. Engring., La. State U., 1963; M.B.A., Ga. State U., 1968; m. Suzanna Woodard, Dec. 21, 1962; children—Michelle, Clay. With Western Electric Co., 1963-73; owner-operator farm, Ringgold, La., 1973—; mem. 96th-99th Congresses from 5th La. Dist., mem. Agr. Com., Interior and Insular Affairs Com. Democrat. Methodist. Home: PO Box 544 Ringgold LA 71068 Office: 2421 Rayburn House Office Bldg Washington DC 20515

HUCKSHORN, ROBERT JACK, political science educator, university administrator; b. Houston, Mo., Oct. 7, 1928; s. Wilford Lee and Rosamond John (Protiva) H.; m. Carolyn Stefanides, May 20, 1950; children—Kevin Ann, Kristin Rae, Dana Leigh. B.S. in Edn., Southwest Mo. State U., 1950; M.A., U. Iowa, 1954, Ph.D., 1956. Asst. prof. UCLA, 1956-57, U. Idaho, Moscow, 1957-62; staff asst. Republican Nat. Com., Washington, 1962-63; assoc. dir. Nat. Ctr. for Edn. in Politics, N.Y.C., 1963-64; prof. Fla. Atlantic U., Boca Raton, 1964-85, dean Coll. Social Scis., 1976-85. Author: Party Leadership in States, 1976; Political Parties in America, 1980, 2d edit. 1984; co-author: Politics of Defeat, 1971. Mem. Fla. Election Commn., Tallahassee, 1973—. Served to cpl. U.S. Army, 1951-53. Named Outstanding Tchr., U. Idaho, 1962; NSF grantee, 1970-74, 79-82. Mem. Am. Polit. Sci. Assn., Western Polit. Sci. Assn., So. Polit. Sci. Assn. (pres. 1983-84). Presbyterian. Home: 1221 S W 13th Pl Boca Raton FL 33432 Office: College Social Scis Florida Atlantic U Boca Raton FL 33431

HUDAK, RICHARD G., security consultant; b. Elizabeth, N.J., May 3, 1944; s. George and Agnes Elizabeth (Brush) H.; B.A., Harvard U., 1966; M.A. in Criminal Justice, Interam. U., 1978; m. Georgia Ann Lundin, Apr. 11, 1970 (div., 1981); children—Ned, Caroline, Josie, Paul. Agt., FBI, Ky., Ohio, P.R., N.C., 1970-81; security cons. Ackerman & Palumbo Inc., Miami Beach, Fla., 1981-82; dir. corp. security Merc. Bank, Dallas, 1982-85; pres., owner Hudak and Assoc., Dallas, 1985—. Served to capt. USMC, 1966-69. Mem. Am. Bankers Assn., Bank Adminstrn. Inst., Am. Soc. Indsl. Security, Soc. Former FBI Agts., Dallas Mus. Art, Honorable Order Ky. Cols. Clubs: Harvard (N.Y.C. and Dallas); Harvard Varsity. Home: 1829 Wisteria Grand Prairie TX 75050 Office: PO Box 225415 Dallas TX 75265

HUDDLESTON, ANNE GIBSON, school counselor, educational administrator; b. Cleburne, Tex., Feb. 28, 1928; d. Alonzo Newton and Lota Margaret (Moore) Gibson; m. H. Clyde Huddleston, June 19, 1949 (div. 1958); 1 child, Patrick Neale. B.S., North Tex. State U. 1948; counseling cert. U. Tex., 1961; M.Ed., Sam Houston State U., 1982. Lic. profl. counselor, Tex. Tchr., Austin Ind. Sch. Dist., Tex., 1958-70; mgr. print shop Urban Research Group, Austin, 1975-76; petition verifier Tex. Democratic Com., Austin, 1978; sch. counselor Splendora Ind. Sch. Dist., Tex., 1979-83, dir. guidance, 1983-85, counselor, asst. prin., 1985—. Author, compiler: (curriculum guides) Fine Arts, 1984, Creative Writing, 1984. Charter mem. Splendora Founders Day, 1980; commr. City Vending Commn., Austin, 1974-76; del., sec. County and State Dem. Com., Austin, Splendora, 1970-84. Sam Houston State U. grantee, 1983. Mem. NEA, Tex. Tchrs. Assn. (pres. 1980-83, citation 1983), PTA (hon. life), Spring Creek Assn. for Counseling and Devel. (treas. 1983), Sam Houston Area Reading Council, DAR, LWV, Alpha Chi, Sigma Delta Pi, Alpha Rho Tau, Delta Kappa Gamma, Alpha Delta Kappa, Pi Lambda Theta. Mem. Ch. of Christ. Avocations: painting; writing; sailing. Home: PO Box 773 Splendora TX 77372 Office: Splendora Ind Sch Dist Box 168 Splendora TX 77372

HUDDLESTON, FRANCES EMILY, retired guidance director; b. Pendleton, Ind., Jan. 27, 1900; d. Ulysses Grant and Estella May (Manifold) Taylor; A.B., DePauw U., 1922; A.M., N.Y.U., 1949; postgrad Catholic U. Am., 1934-35, Colo. U., 1936, Ind. U., 1948-50; m. Baron Emanuel Carol Fadda, 1929 (div. 1938); m. 2d, Earl R. Huddleston, June 18, 1938. Tchr., Portland (Ind.) High Sch., 1923-24, Huntington (Ind.) High Sch., 1925-29, Hammond (Ind.) High Sch., 1929, Lew Wallace High Sch., Gary, Ind., 1929-30; guidance dir. William A. Wirt High Sch., Gary, 1930-64; ret.; with Chgo. Travel Bur., 1964—. Mem. travel com. Gary YWCA. Mem. Friends of Library Sebring, Alpha Phi, Delta Kappa Gamma. Club: Sebring (Fla.) Woman's (edn. com.). Home: 207 NE Lakeview Dr Sebring FL 33870

HUDDLESTON, REGINA LEE, advertising artist; b. Roanoke, Va., Aug. 15, 1949; d. Woodrow Wilson and Emma Viola (Walters) H. Student Va. Western Community Coll., 1968-70; A.A.S., Va. Poly. Inst., 1971. Designer, Brand Edmonds Packett Advt., Salem, Va., 1971-73; designer Piedmont Label Co., Bedford, Va., 1973-75; art dir. Groseclose Poindexter Advt., Roanoke, Va., 1975-77; advt. mgr. Atlantis Group, Roanoke, Va., 1977-79; prodn. mgr. Garrett Lewis Johnson, Atlanta, 1979-80; studio owner Regina Huddleston Advt. Art, Atlanta, 1980—. Bd. dirs. Park Place Manor Condominium Assn., Ansley House Condominium Assn. Recipient Addy 1st place, 1980, Ad 2 Pub. Service Advt. award, 1981. Mem. Am. Advt. Fedn., Advt. Fedn. Roanoke Valley, Ad Club 2 (exec. v.p. 1979), Art Dirs. Club of Atlanta. Club: Druid Hills Golf and Country. Office: 1422 W Peachtree St Suite 415 Atlanta GA 30309

HUDDLESTON, WILLIAM ENNIS, physician; b. Batesville, Ark., Aug. 25, 1928; s. William McKinley and Edna Cecil (Ennis) H.; student Ark. Coll., 1946-48, Ark. State Tchrs. Coll., 1948-49; B.S. in Medicine, M.D., U. Ark., 1953; m. Pauline Maxine Coffman, Sept. 7, 1953; children—Thomas Kevin, Linda Marshaun, Kelly Ennis. Intern, Mo. Meth. Hosp., St. Joseph, 1953-54; practice medicine, specializing in family practice, Iowa Park, Tex., 1956-57, Bridgeport, Tex., 1957—; mem. staff Bridgeport Hosp., chief of staff, 1973-84, Bridgeport City Council, 1960-72. Mem. Bridgeport City Council, 1984—. Served with USAF, 1953-56. Diplomate Am. Bd. Family Practice. Fellow Am. Acad. Family Practice (charter), Am. Acad. Family Physicians (charter); mem. Am., Tex. med. assns., Am. Soc. Contemporary Medicine and Surgery, So. Med. Soc. Mason. Methodist (trustee 1962-84). Home: 26 Robinhood Ln Bridgeport TX 76026 Office: 1301 Halsell St Bridgeport TX 76026

HUDGINS, CATHERINE HARDING (MRS. ROBERT SCOTT HUDGINS, IV), business executive; b. Raleigh, N.C., June 25, 1913; d. William Thomas and Mary Alice (Timberlake) Harding; B.S., N.C. State U., 1929-33; grad. tchr. N.C. Sch. for Deaf, 1933-34; m. Robert Scott Hudgins, IV, Aug. 20, 1938; children—Catherine Harding, Deborah Ghiselin, Robert Scott. Tchr., N.C. Sch. for Deaf, Morganton, 1934-36; sec. Dr. A. S. Oliver, Raleigh, 1937; tchr. N.J. Sch. for Deaf, Trenton, 1937-39; sec. Robert S. Hudgins Co., Charlotte, N.C., 1949—, v.p., sec., treas., 1960—, also dir. Mem. Jr. Service League, Easton, Pa., 1939; project chmn. ladies aux. Profl. Engrs. N.C., 1954-55, pres., 1956-57; pres. Christian High Sch. PTA, 1963; program chmn. Charlotte Opera Assn., 1959-61, sec., 1961-63; sec. bd. Hezekiah Alexander House Restoration, 1949-52, Hezekiah Alexander House Found., 1975—; sec. Hezekiah Alexander Aux. 1984, treas., 1983-84, v.p. 1984-85, pres., 1985-86. Mem. N.C. Hist. Assn. English Speaking Union, Mint Mus. Arts (pres. drama guild 1967-69), Daus. Am. Colonists (state chmn. nat. def. 1973—74, 78-80, corr. sec. 1978-80), DAR (chpt. regent 1957-59, N.C. program chmn. 1961-63, state rec. sec. 1977-79, state chmn. nat. def. 1973-76, state rec. sec. 1977-79, state regent 1979-82, hon. state regent, 1982—, mem. state officers club, mem. Nat. Officers Club, Nat. Chairmen's Assn.), Children Am. Revolution (N.C. sr. pres. 1963-66, nat. bd. mgmt. 1963—, hon. sr. state pres. 1968—, nat. DAR vice chmn. Southeastern region, 1965-68, sr. nat. corr. sec. 1966-68, sr. nat. 1st v.p. 1968-70, sr. nat. pres., 1970-72, nat. chmn. for DAR 1970-72; 2d v.p. nat. officers club 1975-77, 1st v.p. 1977-79, now mem.), Internat. Platform Assn. Presbyterian (past chmn. home missions, annuities and relief Women of Ch., past pres. Sunday Sch. class). Clubs: Arts (Washington); Carmel Country Tower, Charlotte City (Charlotte). Home: 1514 Wendover Rd Charlotte NC 28211 Office: PO Box 17217 Charlotte NC 28211

HUDGINS, LESTER LEE, JR., construction corporation executive; b. Richmond, Va., July 5, 1941; s. Lester Lee and Frances (Hatchette) H.; 1 dau., Stephanie Elaine. Pres. Hudgins Constrn. Co., Inc., Newport News, Va., 1971—; dir. Builders and Constrn. Exchange, Norfolk, Va., 1983—, Bank of Va., Newport News, Va., 1983—. Bd. dirs. Va. Choral Soc., Newport News, 1984, Fishburne Mil. Sch., Waynesboro, Va., 1984. Named Most Outstanding Young Man, Young Republican Club, 1971. Mem. Va. Assn. Contractors (pres. 1983-84), Assn. Gen. Contractors (v.p. 1983-84, chmn. polit action com. 1980), Peninsula Builders Exchange (pres. 1974), Peninsula C. of C. Episcopalian. Clubs: James River Country, Hampton Yacht. Lodge: Kiwanis (pres. Warwick chpt. Newport News 1973-74). Home: 220 Mill Point Dr Hampton VA 23669 Office: Hudgins Construction Co Inc 11832 Fishing Point Dr Newport News VA 23606

HUDGINS, MARY DENGLER, writer; b. Hot Springs Nat. Park, Ark., Nov. 24, 1901; d. Jackson Wharton and Ida (Dengler) H.; B.A., U. Ark., 1924; student Rice Sch. of Spoken Word, 1925, U. Chgo., 1940, U. Wis., 1941, Emory U., 1952. Tchr., Waldo (Ark.) High Sch., 1924-25; free-lance writer, 1925-39, 60—; librarian Hot Springs Pub. Library, 1939-43; med. and gen. librarian Army and Navy Gen. Hosp., Hot Springs, 1943-59; writer articles (specializing in Ark. topics) pub. in ency., hist., lit., profl. and popular publs.; dir. Hot Springs Writers' Workshop, 1960-61. Incorporator, dir. Fine Arts Council, Hot Springs, 1960—; local historian YWCA, Hot Springs; active Hot Springs Little Theater, 1928-34. Mem. Ark. Hist. Assn. (dir. 1963-71, v.p. 1972—), Garland County Hist. Soc. (pres. 1962-63), Ark. (sec. spl. libraries div. 1959-60, reporter to S.W. div. ALA 1955), Med. library assns., Ark. Folklore Assn. (1st v.p. 1958-59), AAUW (Ark. 1st v.p. 1929-30, pres. Hot Springs br. 1927, Ark. fellowship chmn. 1959-61), Ark. Geneal. Soc. (dir.), DAR, Altrusa Internat. Presbyterian (historian). Clubs: Hot Springs Music, Fortnightly, Sabina (pres. 1935), Current Book (pres. Hot Springs 1952, 64). Contbr. articles on Ark. music to periodicals; donor Arkansiana to U. Ark., Fayetteville; donor endowments in music and hist. research. Address: 1030 Park Ave Hot Springs National Park AR 71901

HUDGINS, MICHAEL J., dentist; b. Ft. Worth, Aug. 7, 1955; s. Bobby Jack and Rose May (Harris) H.; m. Rhonda Spray Dawn, Jan. 3, 1979 (div. 1983); m. 2d, Sharon Kelly, June 4, 1983. B.S., Tex. Christian U.; D.D.S., Baylor U., 1981. Practice gen. dentistry, Ft. Worth, 1981—; cons. Quest, Inc., Dallas, 1981—. Fellow Acad. Gen. Dentistry; mem. Downtown Ft. Worth Inc., Fort Worth C. of C. Republican. Methodist. Club: Century (Ft. Worth). Home: 2133 Fountain Sq Fort Worth TX 76107 Office: 107 Two Tandy Ctr Fort Worth TX 76102

HUDGINS, WILLIAM HENRY, retired lawyer; b. Chase City, Va., Nov. 19, 1915; s. Edward Wren and Lucy (Morton) H.; B.J., A.B., Washington and Lee U., 1938; J.D., U. Va., 1941; postgrad. Fgn. Service Inst., Washington, 1947. Admitted to Va. bar, 1953; vice consul Am. embassy, Santiago, Chile, 1947-48; atty. Office Judge Adv. Gen. of Navy and White House aide, 1949-50; aide flag lt. to Comdr.-in-Chief Eastern Atlantic and Mediterranean, London, 1950-51; sr. aide to comdr.-in-chief S. Europe, NATO, Naples, Italy, 1951-53; apptd. to spl. assignments as aide to supreme NATO comdr. (Gen. Eisenhower) and to King Paul of Greece, 1952-53; mil. aide de camp to Va. govs. Tuck, Battle, Stanley and Almond; atty., Chase City, Va., 1953-70; co-owner, partner Marine Transport Assos., Inc., N.Y.C., 1971—; owner Reveille Plantation, Mecklenburg County; world traveller and lectr. on fgn. affairs. Trustee Roanoke River Mus.; trustee Prestwould Found., mem. fin. com., 1979-82; chmn. Task Force on Redevel. Downtown Chase City, 1981. Commd. midshipman USNR, 1940, advanced through grades to comdr., 1953. Decorated commendatore de Italia (Italy); commandeur de l'Ordre du Ouissam Alaouite Cherifien (France). Mem. Assn. Preservation Va. Antiquities (dir., pres. Roanoke River br. 1983—), Nat. Trust Historic Preservation, Chase City C. of C. (chmn. civic com., pres. 1982-83), Soc. Colonial Wars, SAR, Soc. Descs. of Original Knights of the Garter, Magna Carta Barons, Roanoke River Art Assn. (pres. 1979-80, chmn. bd. trustees 1982—), Va. Mus., Archaeol. Soc. Va. (pres. Roanoke River br. 1982-83), Va. Hist. Soc., Mecklenburg Hist. Soc., Phi Alpha Delta, Sigma Delta Chi, Omicron Delta Kappa, Beta Theta Pi. Episcopalian (vestryman 1964-65, gen. chmn. bicentennial commemoration 1966). Club: Univ. (Washington). Home: MacCallum More 500 Walker St Chase City VA 23924 Office: 601 Hudgins St Chase City VA 23924

HUDGINS, WILLIAM ROBERT, physician; b. Ft. Worth, Mar. 10, 1939; s. William Douglas and Nina Blanche (Jones) H.; student U. Okla., 1957-69; M.D., U. Miss., 1964; m. Cynthia Anne Kite, Aug. 20, 1960; children—Catherine, David, Anne, Lauren. Intern, Duke U., Durham, N.C., 1964-65; resident in neurosurgery U. Tenn., Memphis, 1965-69; research fellow in cerebrovascular disease Regional Stroke Center, Memphis, 1968-69; practice medicine specializing in neurosurgery, Jackson, Miss., 1971-73; mem. staff Scott and White Clinic, Temple, Tex., 1973-75; neurosurgeon Dallas Neurosurg. Assn., 1975—; mem. staff Presbyn. St. Paul hosps., Dallas, 1975—; clin. instr. Laser Workshops, Dallas, 1981—; mem. stroke council Am. Heart Assn., 1978. Served with USN, 1969-71. Decorated Vietnamese Cross of Gallantry with Bronze star. Diplomate Am. Bd. Neurol. Surgery. Mem. Am. Assn. Neurol. Surgeons, Congress Neurol. Surgeons, So. Neurosurg. Soc., Tex. Med. Assn. (1st pl. sci. exhibit award 1976), Alpha Omega Alpha. Baptist. Assoc. editor: Clinical Neurosurgery, 1974. Mem. editorial bd. jour. Neurosurgery, 1985—. Home: 4208 Edmondson Dallas TX 75205 Office: 8210 Walnut Hill Suite 905 Dallas TX 75231

HUDIBURG, JOHN JUSTUS, JR., utility executive; b. Raleigh, N.C., Jan. 16, 1928; s. John Justus and Lucille (Pearson) H.; m. Joan Helen Adams, Apr. 24, 1954; children—Lee Ann, Carol Joan, John Justus, Mark Adams. B.S., Ga. Inst. Tech., 1951; grad. Advanced Mgmt. Program, Harvard U., 1972. Registered profl. engr., Fla. With Fla. Power & Light Co., Miami, 1951—, dir. mgr., 1969-71, v.p., 1971-72, exec. v.p., 1973-79, pres., 1979—; chmn. Fla. Electric Power Coordinating Group, 1983-84. Mem. Fla. Prison Industries Commn., 1977-79; chmn. West Palm Beach United Fund campaign, 1967; pres. United Fund Palm Beach County, 1968; v.p. Goodwill Industries, West Palm Beach, 1968. Served with USNR, 1946-47. Mem. IEEE (chpt. chmn. 1964), Nat. Soc. Profl. Engrs., Fla. Engring. Soc. Episcopalian. Clubs: Internat. (Washington); Bankers (Miami); Harvard Bus. Sch. So. Fla. (pres. 1976). Office: Fla Power & Light Co PO Box 529100 Miami FL 33152*

HUDNALL, WILLIAM ROOSEVELT, antiquarian bookseller; b. Mammoth, W.Va., June 23, 1933; s. Jesse and Mable (Wilkinson) H.; m. Naomi Gail Connard, June 30, 1956; children—Melanie Jo, Penni Sue, Rebecca Leigh. B.S., Kent State U., 1961; M.A., Monmouth Coll., West Long Branch, N.J., 1972. Commd. 2d lt. U.S. Army, 1961, advanced through grades to lt. col.; signal ops. officer, Vietnam, 1968-69; corps signal adviser, Iran, 1972-73; strategic plans officer Atlantic NATO Command, 1977-79, ret., 1979; antiquarian bookseller, Norfolk, Va., 1977-85, Buckingham, Va., 1985—. Recipient Honor medal Freedoms Found., 1967. Republican. Club: Ruritan (Dillwyn, Va.). Lodge: Masons. Avocation: amateur radio. Home: RFD 1 Box 186 New Canton VA 23123

HUDSON, CHARLES DAUGHERTY, insurance agency executive; b. LaGrange, Ga., Mar. 17, 1927; s. J.D. and Janie (Hill) H.; student Auburn U., 1945-48; LL.D., LaGrange Coll.; m. Ida Cason Callaway, May 1, 1955; children—Jane Alice Hudson Craig, Ellen Pinson, Charles Daugherty, Ida Callaway. Ptnr., Hudson Hardware Co., LaGrange, 1950-57; ptnr. Hammond-Hudson Ins. Agy., LaGrange, 1957-58, owner, 1958-78; pres. Hammond, Hudson & Holder, Inc., 1978—; ptnr. PCH Properties; dir., mem. exec. com. Citizens & So. Bank West Ga., La Grange, 1963—; acting pres. LaGrange Coll., 1979-80; dir., v.p. LaGrange Industries, Inc., 1956—. Mem. exec. com. Camp Viola, Lagrange, 1956—; v.p., trustee Callaway Found., Inc., 1965—, Fuller E. Callaway Found., 1957—; chmn. LaGrange chpt. United Fund, 1964—; mem. LaGrange Bd. Edn., 1967—, chmn., 1971-74, 81-82; chmn. bd. trustees LaGrange Coll., Ga. Baptist Hosp., Atlanta; chmn. West Ga. Med. Center, LaGrange, 1973-81, 83-85, Ocfuskee Hist. Soc., 1975—; trustee Ga. Bapt. Found., 1980-85; trustee, chmn. Florence Hand Home Charitable Trust, 1982—; chmn. endowment com. Ga. Bapt. Conv., 1983-85; sec. Ga. State Bd. Office Rehab., 1983—; bd. dirs., v.p. Ga. Dept. Corrections, 1983—; trustee Ga. Council Econ. Edn., 1985—; chmn., trustee Ga. Hosp. Financing Authority, 1984—. Recipient pres.'s award Colonial Life Ins. Co., 1966, 69, 70, 75, 76, 77, 78, 79, 80, Disting. Alumni award Ga. Mil. Acad., 1971, Respect Law award Optimists Assn., 1967, Public Service award Ga. chpt. AIA, 1977, Leading Producer award Aetna Life & Casualty, 1979, Disting. Service award Ga. Hosp. Assn., 1980. Mem. Ga. Hosp. Assn. (trustee 1982-85), Ga. Assn. Independent Ins. Agts., Ga. Sch. Bd. Assn. (area dir.), S.A.R., Amicale de Groupe Lafayette (hon.), Chattahoochee Valley Art Assn., Ga. Trust Historic Preservation (trustee 1981-84), Beta Gamma Sigma, Sigma Alpha Epsilon. Baptist (deacon 1953—). Mason, (Shriner), Elk, Rotarian (pres. club 1964-65; Paul Harris fellow). Clubs: Highland Country (La Grange); Commerce (Atlanta). Home: 407 Country Club Rd LaGrange GA 30240 Office: 206 W Haralson St LaGrange GA 30240

HUDSON, DORIS WHITLOCK, insurance company executive; b. Fieldale, Va., Apr. 14, 1943; d. James Edgar and Beatrice Marie (Martin) Whitlock; m. James F. Hudson, Sr., Sept. 2, 1958; children—James F., Tina, L. Student pub. schs. Co-founder, owner Hudson Ins. Co., Martinsville, Va., 1978—. dir., 1978—, agt., 1978—, office mgr., 1978—. Den mother Pack 339 Cub Scouts Am., Martinsville, Va., 1972; mem. adv. bd. Henry County Pub. Schs., Collinsville, Va., 1980-81. Mem. Nat. Assn. Ins. Women (v.p. 1979-80), Patrick Henry Assn. Ind. Ins. Agts. Republican. Methodist. Home: Route 1 Box 424 H Fieldale VA 24089 Office: 705 Starling Ave Martinsville VA 24113

HUDSON, HUBERT R., lawyer; b. Oklahoma City, July 31, 1928; s. Hubert R. and Dorothy (Hoffman) H.; grad. Culver Mil. Acad., 1945; B.A. with highest honors, Williams Coll., 1949; LL.B., J.D., U. Tex., 1952; m. Sarah Gibbs Pell, June 25, 1949 (div. Sept. 1955); children—William Parke Custis, Sarah Gibbs; m. 2d, Nancy Paxton Moody, Dec. 4, 1959. Admitted to Tex. bar, 1952; pvt. practice law, Brownsville, Tex.; chmn. bd. Ciero-Smith Lumber Cos.; ltd. ptnr. Braham Engery, Inc.; sr. ptnr. H&H Partnership; pres. Gt. Nat. Corp., Dallas, 1978-79, dir., 1978—; pres. S. Tex. Acceptance Co.; trustee Hudson Estate; pres., trustee Aspern J. Camille Playhouse, Deco-Unicel, Matamoros, Mex.; dir. Brownsville Savs. & Loan, Brownsville Fin. Corp., South Tex. Lumber Co., Seaport Service and Supply, Automatic Insect Control Co., Dalto Electronics (Norwood, N.J.), O.T.C., El Centro Supermarkets, Boca Chica Leasing Co.; dir., mem. exec. com., chmn. trust com., loan and discount com. 1st Nat. Bank, Brownsville; adv. council United Savs. Tex., Houston, dir., mem. exec. compensation com. Southwestern Group Investors, Inc.; dir. Savs. & Loan Holding Co. S.W.; chmn. audit com. Southwest Group Fin., Inc.; prof. history and constl. law Tex. Southmost Coll., also mem. long-range planning com.; former chmn. State of Tex. Investments Com.; mem. fathers com. Foxcroft Sch., Middleburg, Va.; adv. mem. Tex. Council Crime and Delinquency; chmn. bd. dirs. Greater Brownsville Commn., Episcopal Day Sch. Found.; bd. dirs. Citizens Com., 1955-59; trustee United Fund, Brownsville, 1954-56; chmn. founding of Good Neighbor Settlement House, 1953—; dir. Valley council Boy Scouts Am. 1954--58; pres. Charro Days, Brownsville, 1954, 55; chmn. Rio Grande Valley Festival of Music; trustee, fellow L.S.B. Leakey Found.; mem. governing bd. Tex. Art Alliance; commr. City of Brownsville Water Bd., 1956—; mem. Tex. Senate, 1956-63; chmn. fin. com. Tex. Southmost Coll. 1956-58; sr. trustee Hudson Found., 1956-79; mem. chancellor's com. U. Tex.; mem. U. Tex. Com. of 75, 1957-60; mem. U. Tex. Centennial Commn.; mem. com. Selection of Acad. Standards of Books, State of Tex. bd. dirs. U. Tex. Found. Sch. Bus.; trustee Episcopal Day Sch., U. Tex. Sch. Architecture, Tex. Mil. Inst., Little Theatre Brownsville, Rio Grande Valley Zool. Soc., S. Tex. Heritage Found. Recipient Outstanding Community Award Service medal Nat. Jr. C. of C., 1954, 56. Mem. Am., Tex. bar assn., Rio Grande Valley C. of C. (pres. 1960), Brownsville Hist. Soc. (trustee), San Antonio Symphony Soc. (dir.), Phi Beta Kappa, Phi Alpha Delta. Mem. Church of the Advent. Episcopalian (vestryman 1953-55). Clubs: Austin (Tex.); Piping Rock, Racquet and Tennis (N.Y.C.). Author: The Roosevelt Corollary, 1949. Home: Casa Poinciana Paredes Rd Brownsville TX 78520 Office: PO Box 3229 Brownsville TX 78520

HUDSON, JAMES T., food company executive; b. 1924. Regional dir. operations Ralston Purina Co., 1946-72; pres., chief exec. officer Hudson Foods Inc., Rogers, Ark., 1972—, also dir.; dir. First Nat. Bank, Rogers. Office: Hudson Foods Inc 13th St and Hwy 102 Rogers AR 72756*

HUDSON, JANICE MARIE, educator, coach; b. Roscoe, Tex., Dec. 4, 1943; d. Henry Grady and Kittie Mae (Stephens) Hudson. A.A., Howard Coll., 1964; B.S., Lamar U., 1966; M.Ed., Sam Houston State U., 1972. Tchr., coach N.E. Ind. Sch. Dist., Houston, 1966-68, Monahans-Wickett Ind. Sch. Dist., Tex., 1968-75, Deer Park High Sch., Tex., 1985—; instr. phys. edn., coach Tex. Tech U., Lubbock, 1975-85, dir. volleyball camp, 1976-85; clinician El Paso Area Tchrs., 1976-81, Pasadena Area Tchrs., 1978; clinician/dir. Rollo Kans. Volleyball Camp, 1984—. Named S.W. Conf. Coach of Yr., 1985; teams won Tex. High Sch. State Championships, 1969, 70, 74, 75. Mem. AAHPERD, Tex. Assn. Health, Phys. Edn., Recreation and Dance, U.S. Volleyball Assn., Collegiate Volleyball Coaches Assn., Tex. Assn. Coll. Tchrs. Baptist. Home: 4809 13th St Lubbock TX 79416 Office: Deer Park High Sch 710 San Augustine Deer Park TX 77536

HUDSON, JERRY CHARLES, educator; b. Carthage, Tex., July 1, 1941; s. Thomas Newton and Sybil (Barton) H.; B.S., W. Tex. State U., 1971, M.A., 1972; Ph.D., N. Tex. State U., 1980; m. Sue Carol Fowler, Aug. 30, 1968; children—Aleshia Lin, Jerry Charles II. With Sta. KDET, Center, Tex., 1960-62, Sta. KWRD, Henderson, Tex., 1962-63, Sta. KMIN, Grants, N.Mex., 1964-67, Sta. KIXZ, Amarillo, Tex., 1967, Sta. KPUR, Amarillo, 1967-69, Sta. KFDA-TV, Amarillo, 1969-72; dir. mass communications Lamar U., Beaumont, Tex., 1972-78; asso. prof. mass communications Tex. Technol. U., Lubbock, 1978—; pres. Tex. Assn. Ednl. Broadcasters, 1975-76. Recipient AMOCO Teaching Excellence award, 1981. Mem. Internat. Radio/TV Soc., Radio TV News Dirs. Assn., Assn. Edn. Journalism, Kappa Tau Alpha (Disting. Faculty award 1980). Republican. Methodist.

HUDSON, JOSEPH RONALD, wholesale/distributing company executive; b. Aliquippa, Pa., Jan. 21, 1943; s. Deweitt Talmadge and Mattie Rose (Thomas) H.; m. Shirley M. Massenburg, Nov. 11, 1974; children—Gregory, Sabrina. Student Howard U., 1963-64, Am. U., 1965-69, U. Tulsa, 1967; cert. Am. Inst. Banking, 1969, Stanford U., 1978. Cert. adminstrv. mgr. Asst. treas. Am. Security and Trust Co., Washington, 1964-69; exec. dir., v.p. Interracial Council Bus. Opportunity, Atlanta, 1969-77; v.p. adminstrn. Gourmet Services, Inc., Atlanta, 1977-80; spl. asst. to asst. dir. Intergovtl. Personnel Programs, U.S. Office Personnel Mgmt., Washington, 1980-81; pres., chief exec. officer Davis-Hudson & Assocs., Inc., Atlanta, 1981—; mem. adv. council SBA; dir. Gourmet Services, Atlanta; lectr. symposiums, bus. convs., univs. Pres. Atlanta Bus. League, 1981—; chmn. Atlanta Downtown Devel. Authority, 1982—; bd. dirs. Fulton County Family and Children's Services, 1984, Southwest Atlanta Youth Bus. Orgn., 1983—, Ga. Women's Polit. Caucus, 1983—. Internat. Bus. fellow Ga. World Congress Inst., 1982. Fellow Soc. Internat. Bus. Fellows, Presidents Exec. Exchange Assn.; mem. World Trade Club, NAACP. Methodist. Office: Davis-Hudson & Assocs 1465 Westwood Ave SW Atlanta GA 30310

HUDSON, LEONARD LESTER, former school administrator; b. Decatur, Tex., July 23, 1910; s. Harve Hubert and Laura Hilda (Watson) H.; A.S., Decatur Bapt. Coll., NEA, B.S., N. Tex. State U., 1957, M.Ed., 1960; D.D., Kansas City Bible Coll., 1958; Ph.D., Central Christian Coll., 1963; D. Arts-Religion, Internat. U., 1977, Ph.D. 1978; H.D., World U., 1983; m. Reba Fae Porter, Oct. 16, 1928; children—Robert Lester, Frank L. Clk., asst. mgr. Griffin Grocery, Chickasha, Okla., 1928-43; aircraft foreman Douglas Aircraft Mfg., Oklahoma City, 1943-45; owner Hudson Grocery, Chickasha, 1945-53; instr. Decatur (Tex.) Bapt. Coll., 1953-55, North Tex. State U., Denton, 1955-57; prin. Era (Tex.) Consol. Schs., 1957-61; supt. schs., Beeler, Kans., 1961-66, Ingalls-Alta Vista, Kans., 1966-70, Ford, Kans., 1970-73; adminstr. Bill's Mobile Home Park, Oklahoma City, 1973—. Mem. NEA, Assn. Higher Edn., Am. Assn. Higher Edn., Pi Sigma Alpha. Author: Faith, 1948. Inventor in aircraft field. Home: 5945 S Terry Joe Ave Oklahoma City OK 73129 Office: 2145 SE 59th St Oklahoma City OK 73129

HUDSON, LESTER A., JR., fabric company executive; b. Sumter, S.C., 1939. B.A., Furman U., 1961; M.B.A., U.S.C., 1965. Supt. weaving Deering-Milliken Co., 1965-70; asst. div. mgr. Dan River Inc., Greenville, S.C., 1970-72, div.

mgr., 1972-76, v.p., gen. mgr., 1976-77, pres. Danville group, 1977-79, corp. v.p., pres. Grey Mills Danville div., 1979-81, pres., chief operating officer, 1981—; dir. First Nat. Bank, Mchts. Nat. Bank, Danville (Va.) Mfrs. Assn., So. Indsl. Reins. Conf. Office: Dan River Inc 107 Frederick St Greenville SC 29606

HUDSON, MARIAN SUE PARSONS, pharmacist; b. Pinehurst, N.C., Sept. 24, 1951; d. Solomon Lankester and Doris Eva (Bost) Parsons; A.A., Sandhills Community Coll., Southern Pines, N.C., 1971; B.S. in Pharmacy, U. N.C., 1974; 1 son, Stephen Ray. Intern, Duke Med. Center, 1973, Howell Drug Co., Inc., Raeford, N.C., 1974-75; pharmacist Bryan Drug Co., Inc., Aberdeen, N.C., 1975; dir. pharmacy McCain (N.C.) Hosp., 1975-83; pharmacist in Tb control Div. Health Services for N.C., Raleigh, 1983—; instr. in field. Vol. fund dr. Heart Assn., Southern Pines; bd. dirs. N.C. PharmPAC. Mem. N.C. Soc. Hosp. Pharmacists, N.C. State Drug Adv. Com. for Purchasing and Contract, Am. Soc. Hosp. Pharmacists, N.C. Pharm. Assn., N.C. State Employees Assn. Democrat. Presbyterian. Office: NC Div Health Services PO Box 2091 Raleigh NC 27602

HUDSON, PHYLLIS JANECKE, librarian; b. Rock Island, Ill., Aug. 16, 1933; d. Clair Gordon and Helen Marie (Caffery) Janecke; m. Paul Alfred Hudson, Apr. 9, 1955; children—Helen Leora, Nancy Jan, Paula Kay, J. Phillip, Danae Claire. B.S., U. Ill., 1964; M.L.S., 1970. Reference librarian Edn. Library U. Ill., Urbana, 1969-71, asst. librarian, 1971-72; head circulation Library U. Central Fla., Orlando, 1972-73, cataloger, 1973-74, reference librarian, 1974—. Editor: (column) Florida Libraries, 1978; contbr. articles to profl. jours. Mem. Nat. Commn. for Pay Equity, Washington, 1979—. Mem. ALA, Fla. Library Assn., Spl. Library Assn., Fla. Online Users Group, Fla. Assn. Coll. and Research Libraries (pres. 1982-83), United Faculty of Fla. (pres. U. Central Fla. chpt. 1981-83, lobbyist 1981-83, v.p. 1984—, chief negotiator state univ. system 1984-86), NOW (officer Seminole County chpt. 1980-82). Democrat. Office: U Central Fla 203 Library Orlando FL 32816

HUDSON, WILLIAM GERARD, insurance executive, consultant; b. Bklyn., Nov. 7, 1932; s. Randolph A. and Eleanor G. (Gordon) H.; m. Grace M. Wolfe, May 29, 1958; children—William, Iris, Kimberly. B.B.A., St. Francis Coll., 1958; postgrad. Adelphi U., 1972. Claims adjuster Am. Ins. Group, 1957-60, claims supr., 1960; claims mgr. Republic Ins. Co., N.Y.C., 1960-64, sec., 1964-80, asst. v.p., 1980-83, v.p., 1983—; v.p. Republic Fin. Services Inc., Dallas, 1983—. Mem. Internat. Platform Assn. Served with USN, 1951-54. Republican. Club: Chandler's Landing Yacht. Home: 130 Shepherd Glen Rd Rockwall TX 75087 Office: 2757 Turtle Creek Blvd Dallas TX 75222

HUDSPETH, HARRY LEE, judge; b. Dallas, Dec. 28, 1935; s. Harry Ellis and Hattilee (Dudney) H.; B.A., U. Tex., Austin, 1955, J.D., 1958; m. Vicki Kathryn Round, Nov. 27, 1971; children—Melinda, Mary Kathryn. Bar: Tex. 1958. Trial atty. Dept. Justice, Washington, 1959-62; asst. U.S. atty. Western Dist. Tex., El Paso, 1962-69; mem. firm Peticolas, Luscombe & Stephens, El Paso, 1969-77; U.S. magistrate, El Paso, 1977-79; U.S. dist. judge Western Dist. Tex., El Paso, 1979—. Bd. dirs. Sun Carnival Assn., 1976, Met. YMCA El Paso, 1980—. Mem. U. Tex. Ex-students Assn. (exec. council 1980—), Am. Bar Assn., El Paso Bar Assn., Chancellors, Order Coif, Phi Beta Kappa. Democrat. Mem. Christian Ch. (Disciples of Christ.). Club: Kiwanis (pres. 1975). Home: 9337 Turrentine St El Paso TX 79925 Office: 433 US Courthouse El Paso TX 79901

HUERTA, JUAN FRANCISCO TREVINO, educational consulting firm executive, consultant, evaluator; b. Kingsville, Tex., Sept. 9, 1948; s. Candelario F. and Celia (Trevino) H.; m. Minga Rubio, Feb. 18, 1955; children—Victoria Ann, Juan F.T. B.S., Tex. A. & I U., Kingsville, 1971, M.S., 1974, Ed.D., 1981. Cert. tchr., counselor, supr., Tex. Tchr., Alice Ind. Sch. Dist. (Tex.), 1971-74; cons. Edn. Service Center Region II, Corpus Christi, Tex., 1974-75; cons., dir. Tex. A & I U., 1975-81, adj. prof., 1974—, dir. masters program, 1979-81; v.p., cons. Child Advocacy Research Assocs., Inc., Kingsville, 1980—; dir. Inst. Human Advocacy, Inc., Rio Grande Valley Title VII. Named Outstanding Young Men of Am., Jaycees. Mem. Tex. Assn. Bilingual Edn. (constitution chmn. 1982-84), Nat. Assn. Bilingual Edn., Phi Delta Kappa. Roman Catholic. Lodge: K.C. Home: 2005 Shannon St Alice TX 78332 Office: Child Advocacy Research Assocs Inc 307 E Kleberg St Kingsville TX 78363

HUEY, MELISSA JEAN, grain surveyor and broker; b. Quincy, Ill., July 23, 1956; d. Samuel McKelvie and Nancy (Gilbert) H.; m. Scott Frank Stains, Nov. 28, 1981. B.S., U. Fla., 1978. Sect. mgr. Proctor and Gamble, Ft. Lauderdale, Fla., 1978-80; mktg. mgr. Huey, Inc., Cocoa Beach, Fla., 1980-81; pres. Mila Marine Services, River Ridge, La., 1981—. Mem. Nat. Assn. Female Execs., Nat. Grain and Feed Assn. Office: Mila Marine Services 1847 Dock St Suite 206 New Orleans LA 70123

HUFF, HENRY BLAIR, lawyer; b. Louisville, Aug. 30, 1924; s. Joseph B. and Mattie (Ireland) H.; B.S., J.D., Wake Forest Coll., 1949; M.A., U. Louisville, 1958; LL.D. (hon.), Campbellsville Coll., 1982; m. Mary Anderson, May 24, 1969. Bar: N.C. 1949, Ky. 1954. Law practice, Lenoir, N.C., 1949-54, Louisville, 1954—; dir. Zoeller Co. Chmn. bd. trustees City of Brownsboro Village, 1958-65; trustee Clear Creek Bapt. Sch., 1967-73; trustee Campbellsville Coll., 1973—, chmn., 1978—; pres. Ky. Bapt. Conv., 1975-76, mem. exec. bd., 1982—; moderator Long Run Bapt. Assn., 1980-81; trustee So. Bapt. Theol. Sem., 1984—; mem. ch. relations adv. bd. Cumberland Coll.; 2d v.p. So. Bapt. Conv., 1985-86. Served with C.E., AUS, 1943-46. Mem. ABA, Ky., Louisville bar assns. Home: 6003 Glen Hill Rd Louisville KY 40222 Office: 324 Starks Bldg 455 S 4th Ave Louisville KY 40202

HUFF, LINDA SHERYL, physician; b. Tuscaloosa, Ala., Dec. 10, 1951; d. Arthur Morgan and Mattie Ruth (Behel) Wallace; m. Jack Shephard Huff, Dec. 10, 1982. B.S., U. Ala., 1974; M.D., U. South Ala., 1978. Diplomate Am. Bd. Radiology. Intern, U. South Ala. Med. Ctr., Mobile, 1978-79, resident radiology, 1979-82; instr. radiology U. South Ala., Mobile, 1982-83, asst. prof., 1983—. Mem. Agape S. Ala., Mobile, 1983. Mem. Am Roentgen Ray Soc., AMA, Am. Inst. Ultrasound in Medicine, Med. Assn. State Ala., Mobile County Med. Soc. Mem. Ch. of Christ. Home: 2403 Lilac Ave Mobile AL 36606 Office: U South Ala Med Ctr 2451 Fillingim St Mobile AL 36606

HUFF, MARGARET JOAN FARRIS, learning resource center executive; b. Danville, Ky., Oct. 23, 1925; d. Maurice Joseph and Irene Driscoll (Kennedy) Farris; m. Frank Rouse Huff, Nov. 7, 1948; children—Frank Rouse, Thomas Farris, Mary Ann Weathers. A.B., U. N.C., 1947; B.S. in Library Sci., 1948. Asst. librarian VA Hosp., Columbia, S.C., 1948-49; asst. librarian Calhoun County Pub. Sch., St. Matthews, S.C., 1967-68; librarian Orangeburg-Calhoun Tech. Coll., Orangeburg, S.C., 1968-77, dean Learning Resource Ctr., 1977—; del. S.C. Gov.'s Conf. Library, Info. Service, Columbia, 1979. Mem. ALA, Southeastern Library Assn., S.C. Library Assn. (sec. 1977), S.C. Tech. Edn. Assn. (bd. dirs. 1982—), So. Assn. Colls. and Schs. (vis. com. mem.) Democrat. Methodist. Home: 111 Dantzler Ave Saint Matthews SC 29135 Office: Orangeburg-Calhoun Tech Coll 3250 St Matthews Rd NE Orangeburg SC 29115

HUFF, OZZIE, environ. scientist; b. Marion, Ala., Mar. 30, 1944; s. Emmit and Adelle (Jones) H. B.S., Ala. State U., 1965; M.S., Fisk U., 1972; postgrad. U. West Fla., Oak Ridge Associated Univs., UCLA, Tuskee Inst., U. Detroit; m. Vivian Foster, Dec. 31, 1975; children—LaQuedia Machelle, Vanessa Renee, Gary Bernard, Donnie, Arlethia. Instr. chemistry R. B. Hudson High Sch., Selma, Ala., 1965-67; chmn. jr. coll. sci. dept. Selma U., 1967-71, asst. basketball coach, dean of men, 1968-71; analytical chemist TVA, Muscle Shoals, Ala., 1972, project mgr., environ. scientist, 1973—. Named Tchr. of Yr., 1971. NSF grantee, 1967, 68, 69, 70, 1971-72. Mem. Am. Chem. Soc., TVA Engring. Assn., AAAS, Air Pollution Control Assn., Black Ednl. Tutoring Assn., Fed. Assn. Blacks, Blacks in Govt. (v.p. Muscle Shoals area chpt.), NAACP, Nat. Orgn. for Profl. Advancement Black Chemists and Chem. Engrs., Phi Beta Sigma. Democrat. Contbr. articles to profl. jours. Home: 3501 Union St Florence AL 35630 Office: TVA Air Quality Br 440 MPB Muscle Shoals AL 35660

HUFF, RUSSELL JOSEPH, business executive, author; b. Chgo., Feb. 24, 1936; s. Russell Winfield and Virgilist Marie (McMahon) H.; m. Beverly Diane Staschke; 1 child, Michelle Lynn. B.A. in Philosophy cum laude, U. Notre Dame, 1958; S.T.B. in Theology, Cath. U. Santiago, Chile, 1960; M.A. in Communication Arts, U. Notre Dame, 1968. Ordained priest Roman Catholic Ch., 1962. Exec. editor Catholic Boy and Miss, Notre Dame, Ind., 1963-68; mng. editor Nation's Schs., McGraw Hill, Chgo., 1968-70; v.p. pub. affairs Homart Devel. Co., Chgo., 1971-76; dir. pub. relations, internat. ops. Sears, Roebuck Co., Chgo., 1976-82, dir. pub. affairs Sears Roebuck Found. Internat. Projects, 1981-82; v.p. Turbo Internat., 1982-83; exec. dir. War Memorabilia Collectors Soc., 1981-83; realtor assoc., 1983-84; supr. Herbalife Internat., Sarasota, Fla., 1983—; property mgr., real estate salesman, dir. pub. relations Lofino-Poppa Devel. Corp., Sarasota, 1984-85; real estate broker; pres., owner R.J. Huff and Assoc., Inc., 1985—. Author: Come Build My Church, 1966; On Wings of Adventure, 1967; Wings of World War II, 1985. Contbr. articles to family mags. Recipient Outstanding Mag. award Cath. Press Assn., 1965, 67; Ptnrs. of the Ams. award, 1981; named for Best Cover Nation's Schs., 1968; Mem. Pub. Relations Soc. Am. (accredited), Fla. Bd. Realtors, Nat. Bd. Realtors. Home: 4062 Kingston Terr Sarasota FL 33583 Office: Beneva Sq Exec Office Ctr Suite B 7140 Beneva Rd Sarasota FL 33583

HUFF, WILLIAM ACHLEISS, communications educator; b. LaFayette, Ga., Aug. 7, 1956; s. William Riley and Mary Lynn (Morrison) H. A.A. in Journalism, Dalton (Ga.) Jr. Coll., 1977; B.A. in Pub. Relations, U. Ga., 1979, M.A. in Speech Communications, 1982; A.B.D. in Communicatinos, U. So. Miss., 1986. Announcer, Sta. WBLJ-AM, Dalton, Ga., 1979; announcer, sports reporter, WRFC-AM, Athens, Ga., 1980; air talent, pub. relations WAGQ-FM, Athens, 1980-81; freelance pub. relations, promotions, Chattanooga, 1982-83; dir. news, sports, publ. relations Sta. WJTH-AM, Calhoun, Ga., 1983—; instr. journalism, and Mass Communication Ga. So. Coll., Statesboro, 1983-84; instr. journalism and radio, TV and film and speech communication U. So. Miss., Hattiesburg, 1984—; cons. pub. relations The Idealists, Atlanta, NCAA Baseball Ofcls.; adviser Ga. Assn. Broadcasters. Crystal Found. scholar, 1974-78. Mem. Nat. Fedn. Interscholastic Ofcls. Assn. U.S. Golf Assn., Am. Journalism Historians Assn., Assn. Educators in Journalism and Mass Communication, Speech Communication Assn., Ga. High Sch. Assn., Dalton Jr. Coll. Alumni Assn., Miss. High Sch. Activities Assn., U. So. Miss. Communication Grad. Assn. (pres.), U. Ga. Alumni Assn., Zeta Beta Tau. Democrat. United Methodist. Home: Route 5 Box 3045 Chickamauga GA 30707 Office: Sch Communication So Sta Box 5158 U So Miss Hattiesburg MS 39406

HUFF, WILLIAM JENNINGS, lawyer, educator; b. Summerland, Miss., Mar. 3, 1919; s. William Yancey and Hattie Lenora (Robinson) H.; B.S. with honors, Miss. State U., 1956; M.A. (asst. fellow 1956-59), Rice U., 1957, Ph.D. (Tex. Gulf Producing Co. fellow 1960), 1960; LL.B., U. Miss., 1947, J.D., 1968; m. Frances Ellen Rossman, Feb. 26, 1944; 1 son, John Rossman. Bar: Miss. 1947, Tenn. 1948. Closing atty. Commerce Title Guaranty Co., Memphis, 1947-49; atty., adviser FCC, Washington, 1953-54; asso. prof. geology U. So. Miss., Hattiesburg, 1960-65; asst. prof. natural scis. Mich. State U., East Lansing, 1966-68; asso. prof. geology U. South Ala., Mobile, 1968-82; ret., 1982; practice law, 1982—. Pascagoula, Miss. Served with USAF, 1941-45, judge adv., 1949-52; lt. col. USAF ret. Decorated Air medal with ten oak leaf clusters. Named Outstanding Grad. Student in Dept. Geology, Rice U., 1959-60. Mem. Miss. Bar, Tenn. Bar, Am. Assn. Petroleum Geologists, Soc. Econ. Mineralogists and Paleontologists, Paleontol. Research Soc., N.Y. Acad. Sci., Ala. Geol. Soc., Sigma Xi, Phi Delta Phi, Sigma Gamma Epsilon. Lodges: Masons, Shriners. Contbr. articles to various publs. Home: 5917 Montfort Rd S Mobile AL 36608

HUFFINGTON, ROY MICHAEL, petroleum executive; b. Tomball, Tex., Oct. 4, 1917; s. Roy Mackey and Bertha (Michel) H.; m. Phyllis Gough, Oct. 26, 1945; children—R. Michael, Terry Lynn. B.S., So. Meth. U., 1938; M.A. in Geology, Harvard U., 1941, Ph.D., 1942, A.M.P., 1976. Teaching fellow Harvard U., Cambridge, Mass., 1939-42, instr. geology, 1942; field geologist Humble Oil & Refining Co., N.Mex., Tex., 1946, sr. geologist, div. exploration geologist, until 1956; chmn. bd., pres. Roy M. Huffington, Inc., Houston, 1956—; dir. AMF Inc., N.Y.C., First City Bank Corp. Tex., Houston, ENSTAR Corp. Trustee So. Meth. U., Dallas; chmn. The Asia Soc., N.Y.C.; mem. Council Fgn. Relations, N.Y.C., Nat. Petroleum Council, Univ. Cancer Found., Houston; vice-chmn. Interferon Found., Houston; bd. visitors U. Tex.; adv. trustee Houston Ballet Found.; trustee Ctr. for Internat. Bus. Served with USN, 1942-45. Recipient Alumni Achievement award Harvard Bus. Sch., 1982. Fellow AAAS (life), Geol. Soc. Am., Am. Assn. Petroleum Geologists; mem. Ind. Petroleum Assn. Am. (dir.), Tex. Mid-Continent Oil and Gas Assn. (dir.), Am. Petroleum Inst. (dir.), Geochem. Soc., Marine Tech. Soc., Mid-Continent Oil and Gas Assn., Tex. Ind. Producers and Royalty Owners Assn., Houston Geol. Soc. Presbyterian. Clubs: Houston (v.p. 1969-70), Houston Country, Petroleum (v.p. 1980-81) (Houston); Metropolitan (N.Y.C.). Home: 307 Shadywood Rd Houston TX 77057 Office: 5500 InterFirst Plaza 1100 Louisiana St PO Box 4455 Houston TX

HUFFMAN, DALE L., meat science educator; b. Churchville, Va., July 23, 1931; s. Elmer L. and Ina M. Huffman; m. Jo-Ann Johnson, Feb. 4, 1956; children—Sharon, Randy, Emily. Student Bridgewater Coll. (Va.), 1950-52; B.S., Cornell U., 1959; M.S., U. Fla., 1960, Ph.D., 1962. Research scientist Swift Research and Devel. Ctr., Chgo., 1962-63; asst. prof., assoc. prof., prof. meat sci. Auburn (Ala.) U., 1963—; indsl. fellow Armour and Co., 1970-71. Served with USAF, 1952-56. Recipient award of Merit Ala. Cattleman's Assn.; Harrey L. Rudnick educators award Nat. Assn. Meat Purveyors, 1984; sr. research award Ala. Agrl. Expt. Sta., 1984; commendation for outstanding contbns. to Ala. agr. Ala. Legislature, 1984. Mem. Am. Meat Sci. Assn. (pres. 1982, Meat Processing award 1983), Am. Soc. Animal Sci., Inst. Food Technologists, Sigma Xi (pres.), Gamma Sigma Delta (pres.), Alpha Zeta. Contbr. numerous articles on meat sci. to profl. jours. Home: 219 Deer Run Rd Auburn AL 36830 Office: Dept Animal and Dairy Sci Auburn AL 36849

HUFFMAN, ROBERT ALLEN, JR., lawyer; b. Tucson, Dec. 30, 1950; s. Robert Allen and Ruth Jane (Hicks) H.; m. Marjorie Kavanagh Rooney, Dec. 30, 1976; children—Katharine Kavanagh, Elizabeth Rooney, Robert Allen III. B.B.A., U. Okla., 1973, J.D., 1976. Bar: Okla. 1977, U.S. Dist. Ct. (no. dist.) Okla. 1977, U.S. Ct. Appeals (10th cir.) 1978, U.S. Supreme Ct. 1982. Assoc. Huffman, Arrington, Kihle, Gaberino & Dunn, Tulsa, 1977-81, ptnr. 1981—. Mem. ABA, Tulsa County Bar Assn., Fed. Energy Bar Assn. Republican. Roman Catholic. Clubs: Southern Hills Country (Tulsa), Tulsa Club. Home: 5808 S Delaware Tulsa OK 74105 Office: Huffman Arrington Kihle Gaberino & Dunn 1000 ONEOK Plaza Tulsa OK 74103

HUFFMASTER, MICHAEL ARTHUR, chemical engineer; b. Oakland, Calif., Dec. 5, 1947; s. William Arthur and Anna Katherine Huffmaster; m. Robbie N. Sharp, Nov. 6, 1982. B.S., Ga. Inst. Tech., 1967. Process engr. Norco refinery, Shell Oil Co., 1969-75, chem. engr., coastal div. Exploration and Prodn., 1975-79, sr. chem. engr., 1979-81; sr. chem. engr. offshore East div., Shell Offshore Inc., New Orleans, 1982-83; sr. chem. engr. E. and P. head office central engring., Shell Oil Co., Houston, 1983—. Contbr. articles to profl. publs. Served with AUS, 1970; N.G., 1970-81. Mem. Gas Processors Assn., Am. Inst. Chem. Engrs. (chmn. New Orleans chpt. 1978). Clubs: Metairie Power Squadron; Pontchartrain Yacht. Home: 10715 Olympia Dr Houston TX 77042 Office: PO Box 2099 Houston TX 77001

HUGG, CHARLES HAMPTON, school administrator; counselor; b. Amarillo, Tex., Mar. 2, 1947; s. Linley E. and Iris Leone (Rowell) H.; A.S., Amarillo Coll., 1971; B.S., West Tex. State U., 1973; M.S., Abilene Christian U., 1975; m. Saundra M. Hulen, Aug. 20, 1972; 1 dau., Andrea Rhea. Grad. asst. Abilene (Tex.) Christian U., 1974-75; staff psychologist Abilene State Sch., 1975-78, asst. chief, psychol. services, adminstr. tech. programs Abilene State Sch., 1978-84, dir. mgmt. and program eval. div., 1984—. Mem. adv. bd. Abilene Citizens Advocacy for Mentally Retarded Persons, 1978-79. Mem. Tex. Psychol. Assn., Am. Assn. Mental Deficiency, Tex. Assn. Mental Deficiency. Mem. Christian Ch. Club: Greater Abilene Kiwanis (dir.). Home: 1209 Chriswood St Abilene TX 79601 Office: Abilene State School PO Box 451 Abilene TX 79604

HUGHART, JOAN PAULA, nurse; b. S.I., June 8, 1953; d. John Paul and Mary Ann (Kohler) Wincelowicz; m. Keith Allen Hughart, Oct. 18, 1980. B.S.N., Incarnate Word Coll., 1975; M.S.N., Tex. Woman's U., 1978. Charge nurse Meth. Hosp., Houston, 1976-77; staff nurse Meml. S.W. Hosp., Houston, 1977-78; coordinator cardiovascular nursing Lynchburg Gen. Hosp. (Va.), 1978-80; staff nurse Spohn Hosp., Corpus Christi, Tex., 1980; instr. nursing Del Mar Coll., Corpus Christi, 1980-82, paramedic instr., 1981-83; head nurse, clin. nurse specialist Corpus Christi Cardiac Rehab. Ctr., 1982—; instr. Coastal Bend Council Govts., 1983—; CPR instr. Am. Heart Assn., Corpus Christi, 1980—. Mem. Am. Assn. Critical Care Nurses, Am. Nurses Assn., Tex. Nurses Assn., Am. Heart Assn. (cardiovascular nursing task force and cardiac rehab. subcom.), Corpus Christi State U. Nursing Honor Soc. (sec.). Roman Catholic. Home: 4029 Manhattan St Corpus Christi TX 78411 Office: Corpus Christi Cardiac Rehab Center 4628 Weber Suite 1145 Corpus Christi TX 78411

HUGHES, BILLY RAY, educational administrator; b. El Dorado, Ark., Feb. 14, 1932; s. Jesse G. and Bonnie Vay (Middlebrooks) H.; m. Carolyn Ann Lee, Nov. 30, 1957; children—Barry Ray, Lee Ann. B.E., Hendersen State U., Arkadelphia, Ark., 1954, M.Ed., 1957. Dir. spl. edn. Crossett Pub. Schs., Ark., 1960-65; dir. pub. relations Texarkana Community Coll., Tex., 1965-67, dir. continuing edn., 1967-68, dean of students, 1968—. Author: American Handmade Knives, 1971; Modern Handmade Knives, 1982; (with others) Book of Knives, 1971, Book of Folding Knives, 1977. Pres., Texarkana Baseball Assn., 1969-71. Named Outstanding Am. Handgunner, Am. Handgun Found., 1984. Mem. Texarkana Softball Assn. (pres. 1981—), Northwest Tex. Jr. Coll. Baseball Assn. (commr. 1983—), Am. Blacksmiths Soc. (bd. dirs. 1976—), Tex. Assn. Chief Student Affairs Adminstrs., Tex. Jr. Coll. Student Personnel Adminstrs., Southwest Assn. Student Personnel Adminstrs. Presbyterian. Avocation: competitive handgun shooting. Home: 110 Royale Dr Texarkana TX 75501 Office: Texarkana Coll 2500 N Robinson Rd Texarkana TX 75502

HUGHES, BYRON WILLIAM, lawyer, oil exploration company executive; b. Clarksdale, Miss., Nov. 8, 1945; s. Byron B. and Francis C. (Turner) H.; m. Sarah Eileen Goodwin, June 23, 1973; children—Jennifer Eileen, Stephanie Ann. B.A., U. Miss., 1968; J.D., Jackson Sch. Law (name changed to Miss. Coll. Law), 1971. Bar: Miss. 1971, U.S. Supreme Ct. 1975. Atty., Abstractor Miss. Hwy. Dept., 1971-76; atty., ind. landman Byron Hughes Oil Exploration Co., Jackson, Miss., 1976—; tchr. high sch.; real estate broker. Mem. ABA, Miss. Bar Assn., Hinds County Bar Assn., Am. Judicature Soc., Am. Landmen Assn., Miss. Landmen Assn., Ala. Landmen Assn., Black Warrior Basin Landman's Assn., Ole Miss. Alumni Assn., Miss. Coll. Alumni Assn. Methodist. Club: Miss. Art Assn. Home: 101 Spencer Cove Clinton MS 39056 Office: PO Box 1485 Jackson MS 39215

HUGHES, CARL DOUGLAS, lawyer; b. Sapulpa, Okla., Aug. 29, 1946; s. Kenneth Gordon and Louise (Coffield) H.; m. Alice M. Hughes, May 12, 1978; children—Sarah Elizabeth, Kenneth James. B.B.A., U. Okla., 1968, J.D., 1971. Bar: Okla. 1971, U.S. Supreme Ct. 1974. Assoc. Stipe, Gossett, Stipe & Harper, Oklahoma City, 1971-76; ptnr. Hughes & Nelson, and predecessors, Oklahoma City, 1976—. Legal counsel Okla. Democratic Com., 1978—; gen. counsel Spl. Olympics, 1976—, chmn., 1981, 84, 85. Served to capt. USAR, 1968-73. Mem. Assn. Trial Lawyers Am., Okla. Trial Lawyers Assn. (dir. 1971-78, chmn. judiciary com. 1977-78, chmn. criminal law com. 1981), Okla. Bar Assn., Oklahoma County Bar Assn. Episcopalian. Mem. editorial bd., torts editor Advocate mag., 1975-78. Home: 5909 Oak Tree Rd Edmond OK 73034 Office: 5801 N Broadway Extension Suite 302 Oklahoma City OK 73118

HUGHES, D. P., police administrator; b. Ft. Wayne, Ind., Feb. 5, 1947; s. W.O. and Gala (Studebaker) H.; B.S., Ind. U., 1970; J.D., U. Miami, 1978; m. Bobbie Jane Schwaninger, July 18, 1981; children—Michelle, Jon. Investigator, Allen County (Ind.) Adult Probation Dept., Ft. Wayne, 1968-70; dep. sheriff Dade County (Fla.) Public Safety Dept., Miami, 1970-71; staff asst. to chief Miami Shores (Fla.) Police Dept., 1971-78, project dir. Burglary/Robbery Control Project, 1976-78; chief investigations Dade County (Fla.) Med. Examiner's Office, Miami, 1978-80; chief ops. Broward County (Fla.) Med. Examiner's Office, Ft. Lauderdale, 1980—; legal adviser Miami Shores (Fla.) Police Dept., 1981—; instr. Southeast Fla. Inst. Criminal Justice, Miami, Broward County (Fla.) Criminal Justice Inst.; participant Fla. Criminal Justice Standards and Goals Conf., Miami, 1975; admitted to Fla. bar, 1981. Counsel, Fla. Police Chiefs Legis. Com.; mem. Dade Police Chief's Policy Com. Certified instr. Fla. Police Standards Council. Mem. Fla. Bar Assn., ABA, Am. Judicature Soc., Assn. Trial Lawyers Am., Internat. Assn. Chiefs of Police (legal officers sect.), Fla. Police Chiefs Assn., Fla. Assn. Police Attys., Broward County Police Chiefs Assn. Republican. Home: 250 NE 104th St Miami Shores FL 33138 Office: 5301 SW 31st Ave Fort Lauderdale FL 33312

HUGHES, DONALD R., fabric manufacturing company executive; b. 1929. M.B.A., Harvard U., 1957. Research assoc. Harvard Bus. Sch., Boston, 1957-59; with Burlington Industries Inc., Greensboro, N.C., 1959—, mem. controller's staff, 1959-63, mgr. ops. research dept., 1963-66, asst. controller, 1966-70, sr. asst. controller, 1970-73, controller, 1973-75, treas., controller, 1975-76, v.p. fin., controller, 1976—, exec. v.p., chief fin. officer, dir. Served with USN, 1946-50. Office: Burlington Industries Inc 3330 West Friendly Ave PO Box 21207 Greensboro NC 27420

HUGHES, EDWIN LAWSON, technical management consultant; b. Pittsburg, Kans. B.S. in Elec. Engring., U. Mo., 1949; M.S., U. Ill., 1950. Radio operator, engr., announcer Sta. WMBH and WDWS, Joplin, Mo. and Champaign, Ill., 1946-49; research assoc. Digital Computer Lab., U. Ill., Urbana, 1949-52; staff engr. Internat. Telemeter Corp., Los Angeles, 1952-55, 56-57; group leader missile systems div. Lockheed Aircraft Co., Van Nuys, Calif., 1955-56; group leader System Devel. Corp., Santa Monica, Calif., 1957-60; tech. dir. Delco Electronics div. Gen. Motors Corp., Milw., 1960-71; v.p. reprographics tech. group Xerox Corp., Rochester, N.Y., 1971-81; v.p. engring. RC Sanders Tech. Systems, Inc., Amherst, N.H., 1981-82; pres., chief exec. officer Fla. Data Corp., Melbourne, 1982-83; mgmt. cons., 1984—. Served with U.S. Army, 1943-46. Decorated Bronze Star. Mem. IEEE. Office: 447 Pauma Valley Way Melbourne FL 32940

HUGHES, GEORGE FARANT, JR., safety engineer; b. Roanoke, Va., June 22, 1923; s. George Farant and Pattie (Shafer) H.; B.S., Va. Mil. Inst., 1948; m. Frances Miriam Perdue, July 1, 1950. With roadway maintenance dept. N. & W. Ry. Co., Roanoke, 1948, with Liberty Mut. Ins. Co., Roanoke, Balt., 1949-61, asst. div. mgr., Pitts., 1962-63; safety supr. Westinghouse Electric Corp., Balt., 1963-64; supr. safety and accident prevention, Buffalo, 1965-67; safety dir. U.S. Naval Weapons Sta., Yorktown, Va., 1967-73; head occupational safety U.S. Naval Safety Center, Norfolk, Va., 1973—. Served with AUS, 1943-46, 50-52. Decorated Bronze Star with oak leaf cluster, Purple Heart. Registered profl. engr., Va., Calif.; certified safety profl. Mem. Am. Soc. Safety Engrs. (profl. mem.), Western N.Y. Safety Conf. (dir. 1966-67), Nat. Soc. Profl. Engr., Va. Safety Assn. (bd. dirs. 1979—), Nat. Eagle Scout Assn., SAR, Assn. Presevation Va. Antiquities (bd. dirs. 1984—), Vets. Safety. Home: 520 Randolph St Williamsburg VA 23185 Office: Naval Safety Center Norfolk VA 23511

HUGHES, HENRY MERVIN, II, management consultant; b. Atlanta, Jan. 4, 1930; s. Henry Mervin and Uldine (Sullivan) H.; m. Virginia B. Biggart, Dec. 29, 1956; children—Sherrie, Cindy, Henry. A.B., Mercer U., 1952; M.A., U. Houston, 1979; Ph.D., Kensington U., 1983. Sr. mgmt. analyst NASA Johnson Space Center, 1961-83; pres., chief fin. officer CCC Inc. of Tex., 1983—; mgmt. cons., Houston. Author: Productivity and Creativity in the Knowledge Worker, 1984. Served to 1st lt. USAF, 1952-56. Patron Boy Scouts Am.; mem. dedication com. U. Houston, Clear Lake City; chmn. pub. relations com. Houston Fed. Exec. Bd. Mem. AIAA, Am. Soc. for Tng. and Devel., Nat. Contract Mgmt. Assn., Am. Soc. for Pub. Adminstrn. (past v.p.), Am. Mgmt. Assn., Acad. Polit. Sci., Nat. Assn. Self Employed, Clear Lake Personnel Assn., DAV, VFW, Ret. Officers Assn., Friends of Freeman Meml. Library, Air Force Assn. Sigma Iota Epsilon. Lodges: Rotary Internat. (perfect attendance award 1983), Elks: Bay Area Lions. Home: PO Box 58246 Houston TX 77258

HUGHES, JOSEPH KENNETH, beverage company executive; b. Leonard, Tex., 1927; s. Medford F. and Ina M. (Akins) H.; student N. Tex. State Coll.; B.A., So. Meth. U., 1948; m. Betty Penry, Feb. 26, 1949; children—Timothy J., Mark D. Writer, then asst. city editor Dallas Times Herald, 1948-53; mgr. Dallas office Harshe-Rotman, Inc., pub. relations, 1953-55; account exec., v.p., mgr. Dallas office Grant Advt., Inc., 1956-64, exec. v.p., 1964-68; v.p. franchise Dr. Pepper Co., 1968-69, v.p. marketing services, 1969-70, v.p. mktg., 1970-73, exec. v.p., 1973-84, pres., chief operating officer, 1984—, vice chmn., 1985—, also dir.; dir. Dr. Pepper Japan Co., Sherry Ln. Nat. Bank. Bd. dirs. Cotton Bowl Council, Dallas Summer Musicals. Mem. Assn. Broadcast Execs. Tex., Dallas Advt. League, Dallas Sales and Mktg. Execs., Sigma Delta Chi. Clubs: Dallas Press (charter, dir. 1952-53); Lakewood Country. Home: 3420 Wentwood Dr Dallas TX 75225 Office: Dr Pepper Co PO Box 225086 Dallas TX 75265

HUGHES, KENNETH JAMES, petroleum engineer; b. Glencoe, Okla., May 18, 1921; s. James Andrew and Winnie (Wilkerson) H.; B.Ch.E., Okla. State U., 1943; m. Doris Elizabeth Fortson, Oct. 12, 1946; children—Marilyn Hughes Peacock, Janet Susan Hughes Orr. Petroleum pilot plant engr. Bur. Mines, Bartlesville, Okla., 1946-49, sr. combustion engr., 1949-55, chem. engr. Air Pollution studies, 1955-59, supt. Bartlesville Energy Research Center, 1959-74, mgmt. officer, 1974-78, dir. div. ops., 1978-83, mgr. adminstrn. and facilities, 1983-86. Commr., City of Bartlesville, 1971-74, vice-mayor, 1971-72; mem. Bartlesville Utility Com., 1972-73. Served with USNR, 1944-46. Recipient Meritorious award Dept. Interior; named Outstanding Engr., Bartlesville, 1970, Outstanding Engr. in Mgmt., 1978. Mem. Nat. Soc. Profl. Engrs. (chmn. constn. and bylaws com. 1971-73), C. of C. (dir. 1981), Am. Legion (vice comdr. 1969-70), Okla. Soc. Profl. Engrs. (pres. 1970-71), Am. Chem. Soc. (pres. 1957-58). Democrat. Presbyterian (elder 1967-69). Clubs: Elks, Kiwanis (pres. 1973-74). Contbr. articles to profl. jours. Home: 305 SE Rockwood St Bartlesville OK 74003 Office: Cudahy and Virginia Sts Bartlesville OK 74003

HUGHES, LINDA RENATE, lawyer, educator; b. Hanau, Germany, Oct. 25, 1947; came to U.S. 1950; d. J.A. and Ilga (Vankins) Eglite; m. Richard J. Hughes, July 4, 1984. B.A. magna cum laude, U. Minn., 1968; J.D. cum laude, Wayne State U., 1980. Bar: Mich. 1980, Ga. 1982, Fla. 1984. Human resource mgr. Browning Marine Co., St. Charles, Mich., 1973-76; law clk. to fed. judge eastern dist. Mich., 1980-81; assoc. Miller, Cohen, Martens & Sugerman, Detroit, 1982, Thompson, Sizemore & Gonzalez, Tampa, 1984-85; asst. county atty. for litigation Hillsborough County, Fla., 1985—; instr. Valdosta State Coll. (Ga.), 1981; adj. prof. U. Detroit Law Sch., 1982; researcher comparative labor policy, Leigh Creek, Australia, 1983. Editor-in-chief Advocate, Wayne State U. Law Sch., 1979-80, also law rev. Vol. Community Mental Health Crisis Intervention, Saginaw, Mich., 1975-76, Ann Arbor, Mich., 1976-78, Clearwater Fla., 1984; dept. registrar Outreach Voter Registration, Pinellas County, Fla., 1983-84; vol. intake atty. Bay Area Legal Services, 1984-85. Mem. State Bar Mich., Ga. State Bar, Fla. State Bar, Hillsborough County Bar Assn., Fla. Women Lawyers Assn. (bd. dirs.), ABA, AAUW (past sec.). Club: Tampa. Office: Hillsborough County Atty's Office PO Box 1110 Tampa FL 33601

HUGHES, RAY HARRISON, clergyman, theological seminary official; b. Calhoun, Ga., Mar. 7, 1924; s. J.H. and Emma Hughes; m. Euverla Tidwell; children—Janice, Ray H., Donald, Anita. B.A., Tenn. Wesleyan Coll.; M.S., Ed.D., U. Tenn.; Litt. D., Lee Coll., Cleveland, Tenn. Ordained to ministry Ch. of God, 1950. Pastor, Fairfield Ch. of God (Ill.), 1945-46, North Chattanooga Ch. of God, 1948-52; organized churches in Spain, Md., Ill., Tenn., Ga.; pres. Lee Coll., Cleveland, Tenn., 1960-66; Md.-Del.-D.C. overseer Ch. of God, 1956-60, mem. exec. council 1956-60, 62-82, nat. Sunday Sch. and youth dir., 1952-56, exec. dir. gen. bd. edn., 1st asst. gen. overseer, 1970-72, gen. overseer, 1972-74, 78-82, Ga. overseer, 1974-76; speaker for convs., preaching missions, ministers retreats. Chmn. Pentecostal Fellowship of N.Am.; vice chmn. Pentecostal World Conf. Mem. Nat. Assn. Evangelicals (pres.), Pi Delta Omicron, Phi Delta Kappa. Author: Planning for Sunday School Programs, 1960; Order of Future Events, 1962; What is Pentecost?, 1963; The Effect of Lee College on World Missions, 1963, The Transition of Church Related Junior Colleges To Senior Colleges, 1966; Church of God Distinctives, 1968; The Outpouring of the Spirit; Dynamics of Sunday School Growth, 1980; Pentecostal Preaching, 1981; editor the Pilot; contbr. in field. Office: Church of God Sch of Theology PO Box 3330 Cleveland TN 37320-3330

HUGHES, ROBERT KING, engineering educator; b. Memphis, July 8, 1936; s. Charles A. and Mary E. (Robertson) H.; m. Glenna Bennett, Aug. 9, 1973; children—Robert K., Kathryn L., Tonya R. B.S. in C.E., The Citadel, 1958; M.S., Okla. State U., 1963, Ph.D., 1973. Registered profl. engr., Wis. Commd. officer U.S. Army, advanced through grades to col., 1980, combat engr. troop units, 1958-64; area engr., Sondestrom, Greenland, 1964-65; asst. Army attache, Indonesia, 1967; asst. div. engr. 101st Airborne Div., Hue, South Vietnam, 1969-70; dep. dir. Waterways Expt. Sta., Vicksburg, Miss., 1973-76; asst. dir. mil. programs Office Chief Engrs., Washington, 1979-80; dist. engr. U.S. Army C.E., Wilmington, N.C., 1980-83; head Sch. Civil Engring., Okla. State U., Stillwater, 1983—. Bd. dirs. United Way, Wilmington, 1980-83; chmn. Combined Fed. Campaign, Greater Cape Fear area, 1980-83. Served to col., C.E., U.S. Army, 1958-83. Decorated Legion of Merit, Bronze Star medals (3), Air medals (5). Mem. Nat. Soc. Profl. Engrs., ASCE, Soc. Am. Mil. Engrs., Assn. U.S. Army. Presbyterian. Club: Rotary (Wilmington). Home: 703 Lakeshore Dr Stillwater OK 74075 Office: Sch Civil Engring Okla State U Stillwater OK 74078

HUGHES, SUE MARGARET, librarian; b. Cleburne, Tex., Apr. 13; d. Chastain Wesley and Sue Willis (Payne) H.; B.B.A. with highest honors, U. Tex. at Austin, 1949; M.L.S., Tex. Woman's U., 1960, doctoral candidate. Sec.-treas. several privately owned corps., Waco, Tex., 1949-59, asst. in pub. services Baylor U. Moody Library, Waco, 1960-64, acquisitions librarian, 1964-79, librarian, 1980—. Mem. AAUP (chpt. pres. 1979-80), AAUW (pres. Waco br. 1974-76, br. Outstanding Woman of Year 1978, state bylaws chmn. 1977-79), ALA (sec. RTSD Reprinting com., past chmn. duplicates exchange union com.), Tex. (local chmn. dist. 3 meeting 1975) library assns., Library Club (Waco), Tex. Woman's U. Alumnae Assn. (pres. 1979-81), Sigma Delta Pi, Beta Gamma Sigma, Delta Kappa Gamma (rec. sec. 1978-80), Beta Phi Mu. Methodist. Clubs: Baylor Round Table (treas. 1974-75); Altrusa of Waco. Home: 2101 Trinity Dr Waco TX 76710 Office: Box 6307 Waco TX 76706

HUGHES, THOMAS RUSSELL, religious educator; b. Beaumont, Tex., Nov. 8, 1940; s. Charles Samuel and Electra (Phillips) H.; m. Nancy Henderson, Apr. 2, 1966; children—Christopher Alan, Todd Ryan. B.A., Wayland Bapt. U., 1966; M.R.E., Southwestern Bapt. Theol. Sem., 1969. Minister of edn. Calvary Bapt. Ch., Borger, Tex., 1971-73; minister of edn. Maize Rd. Bapt. Ch., Columbus, Ohio, 1973-75; minister of edn. Mt. Carmel Bapt. Ch., Cin., 1975-78, 1st Bapt. Ch., Calvert City, Ky., 1978-80, Central Bapt. Ch., Port Arthur, Tex., 1980-83, Skycrest Bapt. Ch., Clearwater, Fla., 1983—; spl. worker, cons. Fla. Bapt. Conv., Jacksonville, 1983—; growth cons. Ky. Bapt. Conv., Middletown, 1978-80, State Conv. of Baptists in Ohio, Columbus, 1973-78. Asst. coach Little League Baseball, Calvert City, 1977, 78. Recipient Campus Leadership Favorite award Wayland Bapt. U., 1966. Mem. Fla. Bapt. Religious Edn. Assn., Southwestern Bapt. Religious Edn. Assn., So. Bapt. Religious Edn. Assn. Republican. Lodge: Lions. Home: 2101 McKinley St Clearwater FL 33575 Office: Skycrest Baptist Ch 1835 Drew St Clearwater FL 33575

HUGHES, WAUNELL MCDONALD (MRS. DELBERT E. HUGHES), psychiatrist; b. Tyler, Tex., Feb. 6, 1928; d. Conrad Claiborne and Bernice Oletha (Smith) McDonald; B.A., U. Tex. at Austin, 1946; M.D., Baylor U., 1951; m. Delbert Eugene Hughes, Aug. 14, 1948; children—Lark, Mark, Lynn, Michael. Intern VA Hosp., Houston, 1951-52; resident Parkland Hosp., Dallas, 1964-67; practiced gen. medicine in Tyler, Tex., 1952-64; acting chief psychiatry service VA Hosp., Dallas, 1967-68, asst. chief, 1968-73, chief Mental Hygiene Clinic and Day Treatment Center, 1973-82, unit chief acute inpatient psychiatry Med. Center, 1982—; clin. instr. psychiatry Southwestern Med. Sch., U. Tex. Health Sci. Center, Dallas, 1968—. Chmn. pre-sch. vision and hearing program Pilot Club, Tyler, 1960-64. Mem. Am. Med. Women's Assn. (pres. Dallas 1980-81), Am. Psychiat. Assn., Am. Group Psychotherapy Assn., (pres. Dallas chpt. 1984—), Dallas Area Women Psychiatrists (archivist 1985—), Alpha Epsilon Iota (pres. 1950-51). Home: 3428 University Blvd Dallas TX 75205 Office: 4500 Lancaster Rd Dallas TX 75216

HUGHSTON, NANCY JOSEPHINE, needlepoint teacher and designer; b. Dallas, Aug. 23, 1939; d. Richard Lively and Maurice(Harris) Hughston; m. Edwin Eldridge Watts, Sept. 3, 1960; children—David Edwin, Daniel Hughston. Student Randolph Macon Woman's Coll., 1957-59, U. Valencia (Spain), 1959; B.A., U. Tex., 1961. Tchr. needlepoint in Austin, Beeville, Lamesa, Santa Fe, Ruidosa, Albuquerque and Midland, 1971—, also nat. conf. Am. Needlepoint Guild, 1978; designer kneelers St. Nicholas Episcopal Ch., Midland, 1980, St. Ann's Cath. Ch., Midland, 1983; cons. on design and creative stitching; broker, sales asst. Shearson Am. Express. Docent Bayou Bend Mus., Houston, 1968-70; coordinator Ptnrs. in Reading Program, Midland Pub. Schs.-Jr. League of Midland, 1977-78; campaign chmn. Am. Heart Assn., 1977, trustee, 1977-79, mem. regional task force Tex. affiliate, 1977-79; pres. San Jacinto Jr. High Sch. PTA, 1977-80; fund raising chmn. Midland Symphony Guild, 1973; bd. dirs. Midland Jr. Cotillion, 1978-81, pres. bd. dirs., 1980-81. Mem. Am. Needlepoint Guild, Jr. League of Midland, DAR, Pi Beta Phi. Republican. Presbyterian. Home: 1409 Bedford St Midland TX 79701

HUGIN, ADOLPH CHARLES, lawyer, engineer, inventor, educator; b. Washington, Mar. 28, 1907; s. Charles and Eugenie (Vigny) H. B.S. in Elec. Engring., George Washington U., 1928; M.S. in Elec. Engring., MIT, 1930; cert. radio communication Union Coll., 1944; J.D., Georgetown U., 1934; LL.M., Harvard U., 1947; S.J.D., Catholic U. Am., 1949; cert. better bus. mgmt. Gen. Electric Co. Exec. Continuing Edn. Program, 1946; cert. Christian doctrine and teaching methods Conf. Christian Doctrine, 1960; cert. social service and charity Ozanam Sch. Charity, 1972. Bar: Mass., D.C., U.S. Supreme Ct., U.S. Ct. Customs and Patent Appeals, U.S. Ct. Appeals (fed. cir.), U.S. Ct. Claims; registered atty. U.S. Patent and Trademark Office; registered profl. elec. and mech. engr., D.C. Examiner, U.S. Patent Office, 1928; with Gen. Electric Co., 1928-46, engr. research and devel. instrument lab. West Lynn (Mass.) works, 1928, engr.-in-charge charge insulation lab, 1929, engine-electric drive devel. lab., River Works, Lynn, Mass., 1929-30, patent asst., Schenectady, 1930, patent investigator, Washington, 1930-33, patent atty., Washington and Schenectady, 1933-46, engr.-in-charge sect. aeros. and marine engring. div., Schenectady, 1942-45, organizer, instr. patent practice course, 1945-46; practiced law and cons. engring., Cambridge, Mass., 1946-47; vis. prof. law Cath. U. Am., 1949-55; practice law, cons. engr., Washington, 1947—; assoc. Holland, Armstrong, Bower & Carlson, N.Y.C., 1957. Bd. dirs. St. Margaret's Fed. Credit Union, 1963-67, 1st v.p., 1965-67; mem. Schenectady com. Boy Scouts Am., 1940-42; charter mem., 1st bd. mgrs. Schenectady Cath. Youth League, 1935-38, hon. life mem., 1946; chmn. St. Margaret's Bldg. Fund, 1954; lector St. Margaret's (Md.) Parish, 1966-68, lector-commentator St. Michael's (Va.) Parish, 1969-80; mem. St. Margaret's Parish Council, 1969-71; mem. adv. bd. St. Michael's Ch., 1974-77. Recipient Charities Work award St. Margaret's Parish, 1982. Mem. Holy Name Soc. (parish pres. 1950-52, pres. Prince Georges County sect. 1953, pres. Washington archdiocesan union 1953-55), St. Vincent de Paul Soc. (parish conf. v.p. 1949-65, pres. 1965—, pres. particular council Prince George County, Md., 1959-61, rep. Prince George County on Washington Archdiocesan Central Council Soc. 1961-62, 1st pres. Arlington diocesan central council, Va., 1975-77, trustee nat. soc. 1975-77, St. Margaret's Parish Confraternity of Christian Doctrine (pres., instr. 1960-61), Archdiocesan Council Cath. Men (pres. So. Prince Georges County deanery 1956-58, 65-68), Men's Retreat League (exec. bd. Washington, 1954-58, St. Margaret's Retreat Group capt. 1965-68), Nocturnal Adoration Soc., John Carroll Soc., Elfun Soc., Nat., D.C. socs. profl. engrs., ABA (life), Am. Intellectual Property Law Assn. (life, cert. of honor for 50 yr. service), Schenectady C. of C. (legis. com. 1940-46), Delta Theta Phi (emeritus). Club: Cath. Men's First Friday. Author: International Trade Regulatory Arrangements and the Antitrust Laws, 1949; editor-in-chief bull. Am. Patent Law Assn., 1949-54; editor notes and decisions Georgetown Law Jour., 1933-34, staff, 1930-34; contbr. articles on patents, copyrights, antitrust, radio and air law to profl. jours. Patentee dynamoelectric machines, dynamometers, insulation micrometers, ecology and pollution control, mus. instruments, others. Avocations: travel; sketching; photography; horticulture; determing and solving problems. Home: 7602 Boulder St North Springfield VA 22151

HUKILL, WILLIAM VIRGIL, architect, engineer; b. Washington, Sept. 11, 1930; s. William V. and Maybelle Ella (Burt) H.; m. Lina Schommer; children—Craig, Linda, Sue, Molly, Brook, Jill, Eric. B.S. in Archtl. Engring., Iowa State U., 1952. Registered profl. engr. and architect, Iowa, Fla. With Gerald I. Griffith, Architect, Des Moines, 1955-56, N. Clifford Prall, Architect, 1956-59, Kohlmann & Eckman, Architects, Cedar Rapids, Iowa, 1959-60; mem. firm Kohlmann-Eckman-Hukill Architects, 1960-68, Hukill, Pfiffner, Alexander, Duenow, Architects and Engrs., 1969-71; sr. ptnr. Design Assoc. Architects and Engrs., 1971-82; sch. bd. architect, Palm Beach County, Fla., 1982-84; dir. facilities planning, 1984—; vis. lectr. Indian Hills Community Coll., 1978—, Coe Coll., 1979—, Mt. Mercy Coll., 1981; pres., dir. HEK, Ltd., Cedar Rapids; participant Environ. Planning Inst., Palo Alto, Calif., 1969, Seismic Inst., San Diego, Calif., 1982. Author: Winning Bond Elections, 1978; guest editorial writer Cedar Rapids Gazette, 1978—. Mem. Bd. Appeals Cedar Rapids, 1963-69; bd. dirs. Camp Wapsie, Central City, Iowa, 1962-72, Cedar Rapids YMCA, 1972-78. Served with C.E., U.S. Army, 1953-55. Recipient honor award Ch. Archtl. Guild Am., 1964, Nat. Council Schoolhouse Constrn., 1966, award Didacta Internat. Exhibit, Switzerland, 1975. Fla. Mem. AIA (chpt. treas. 1964-67), Nat. Sch. Facilities Council, Am. Assn. Sch. Adminstrs., Assn. Sch. Bus. Ofcls., Constrn. Specifications Inst., Council Ednl. Facilities Planners, Nat. Guild Religious Architecture, Phi Delta Theta, Phi Eta Sigma. Mem. Christian Ch. (deacon 1955-57, elder 1958-59). Club: Optimist (Golden Circle award). Home: 6161 Eagles Nest Dr Jupiter FL 33458 Office: 3323 Belvedere Rd West Palm Beach FL 33402

HULCHER, WENDELL ELLSWORTH, business and economics educator, administrator, consultant; b. Girard, Ill., Nov. 3, 1922; s. Elmer Ellsworth and Vena Mary (Thompson) H.; m. Violet Marie Bell, Nov. 27, 1946; children—Karen Marie Hulcher Standfest, Larry Ellsworth, Randall Kent, Philipp Lynn. Student Ill. Wesleyan U., 1946-47, Harvard Coll., 1947-48; M.B.A., Harvard U., 1950, student Inst. Higher Edn., 1981. Budget examiner, U.S. Dept. State, 1950-52; mgmt. cons. McKinsey & Co., 1952-54; mgr. various mktg. and product planning depts. Lincoln Mercury div. Ford Motor Co., Dearborn, Mich., 1954-69; various positions U.S. govt. including Exec. Office of Pres., Dept. State, HUD, ICC, SBA, Washington, 1969-83; William F. Chatlos prof. bus. adminstrn., chmn. dept. bus. and econs. Fla. So. Coll., Lakeland, 1983—; mgmt. cons. bus. and higher edn. Mayor of Ann Arbor, Mich., 1965-69, mem. City Council and various commns. and bds., 1960-64; mem. World Service and Fin. Commn. Detroit Conf. Methodist Ch., 1964-69; mem. Gov.'s Spl. Commn. on Urban Problems, 1966-69; chmn. U.S. Bicentennial Com. Potomac, Md., 1974-76; chmn. commn. on fin. Meth. Ch., Potomac, 1973-80, Lakeland, Fla., 1980-82; chmn. staff parish relations Meth. Ch., Lakeland, 1983—; mem. Mich. Hist. Soc., 1980—. Served to maj. USAAF, 1941-46; served with USAF, 1950-52. Decorated D.F.C., Air Medal with three oak leaf clusters. Recipient Civic awards Ford Motor Co., 1961-64, All-Am. City award C. of C. Ann Arbor, 1966, Spl. Achievement award SBA, 1977. Mem. Harvard Bus. Sch. Assn., Am. Mgmt. Assn., Omicron Delta Kappa, Phi Chi Theta. Club: Kiwanis. Author Master Plan for Ind. Colls. Mich., 1965; contbr. writings in field to publs. Office: Fla So Coll Lakeland FL 33802

HULL, DAVID FRANKLIN, JR., university administrator; b. Hagerstown, Md., Apr. 20, 1946; s. David Franklin and Doris Louise (Crawford) H.; divorced; children—David Warren, Elizabeth Crawford; m. Laura Inez Weil, July 2, 1977; stepchildren—Camille Katherine, Matthew Raul. B.A., La. State U., 1969; Ph.D., Ind. U., 1983. Asst. dean of men La. State U., Baton Rouge, 1968-69, asst. to vice chancellor, 1973-77, asst. vice chancellor, 1977—; dir. Campus Fed. Credit Union, Baton Rouge, 1974-76. Author chpt. (with others) Understanding Student Affairs Orgns., 1983. Organizer Internat. Spl. Olympics, Baton Rouge, 1983; co-chmn. United Way, La. State U., 1983-85; bd. dirs. Stratford Homeowners Assn., Baton Rouge, 1985. Served to capt. U.S. Army, 1969-73, Vietnam. Rotary Found fellow, 1980. Mem. Am. Coll. Personnel Assn., Nat. Assn. Student Personnel Adminstrs., Am. Ednl. Research Assn., Assn. for Study of Higher Edn., Phi Kappa Psi (officer, bd. dirs. 1976—), Phi Kappa Psi Found. (officer, bd. dirs. 1982—), South La. Rotary Ednl. Found. (officer, bd. dirs. 1984—). Democrat. Club: County Club of La. Lodge: Rotary. Avocations: golf; snow skiing; travel. Home: 6111 Stratford Ave Baton Rouge LA 70808 Office: Vice Chancellor for Student Affairs La State Univ Baton Rouge LA 70803

HULL, DOYLE EDWIN, banker; b. Hawthorne, Calif., May 18, 1933; s. James E.; m. Camilla S. Oestreich, June 9, 1963; children—Patricia Lynn, Doyle E., David B. B.S. in Bus. Adminstrn., N.E. Mo. State U., Kirksville, 1957; grad. Stonier Grad. Sch. Banking, Rutgers U., 1969. Exec. v.p. Va. Nat. Bankshares, Inc., Norfolk, 1980-84, Va. Nat. Bank, 1980-84; sr. exec. v.p. Sovran Fin. Corp. and Sovran Bank, N.A. (consolidation), Norfolk, 1984—; chmn. bd. Allied Internat. Bancorp, Inc. Past chmn. bd. Tidewater Community Coll.; past treas., trustee Norfolk Acad.; past pres. bd. dirs., exec. com. Greater Norfolk Corp.; bd. dirs., exec. com. Downtown Norfolk Devel. Corp.; past chmn. Norfolk Indsl. Devel. Authority; mem. Mayor's Devel. Com.; chmn. commrs. Eastern Va. Med. Authority. Mem. Tidewater Builders Assn. (dir. emeritus). Office: Sovran Financial Corp One Commercial Pl Norfolk VA 23510

HULL, HENRIETTA SUE, elementary school counselor; b. Memphis, July 1, 1953; d. William Henry and Irene Elizabeth (Haddock) H. A.A., Freed-Hardeman Coll., 1973; B.A., Harding U., 1975; M.S. in Edn., Ark. State U., 1979, Ed.S., 1985. Cert. tchr. elem. edn., sch. counselor, sch. adminstr. Tchr. Dixon Middle Sch., Mo., 1975-77, Trumann Middle Sch., Ark., 1977-79; elem. sch. counselor Wynne Intermediate Sch., Ark., 1979—; grad. teaching asst. Ark. State U., Jonesboro, 1981-85; cons. in field; speaker local groups. Chmn. Task Force on Child Abuse and Neglect, Cross County, Ark., 1984-85; tchr. Bible Sch., Ch. of Christ, Wynne, 1979—. Mem. Am. Assn. Counseling and Devel., Am. Sch. Counselors Assn., Ark. Assn. Counseling, Guidance and Devel., Ark. Sch. Counselors Assn. (elem. v.p. 1984—), N.E. Ark. Sch. Counselors Assn. (v.p. 1980-82, pres. 1982-83), Delta Kappa Gamma. Club: Wynne Music. Avocations: singing; needlecrafts. Home: 327 Levesque Wynne AR 72396 Office: Wynne Intermediate Sch PO Box 69 Wynne AR 72396

HULL, MARGARET RUTH, artist, educator, consultant; b. Dallas, Mar. 27, 1921; d. William Haynes and Ora Carroll (Adams) Leatherwood; m. LeRos Ennis Hull, Mar. 29, 1941; children—LeRos Ennis, Jr., James Daniel. B.A., So. Meth. U., 1952, postgrad., 1960-61; M.A., North Tex. State U., 1957. Art instr. W. W. Bushman Sch., Dallas Ind. Sch. Dist., 1952-57, Benjamin Franklin Jr. High Sch., Dallas, 1957-58; art instr. Hillcrest High Sch., Dallas, 1958-61, dean, pupil personnel counselor, 1961-70; tchr. children's painting Dallas Mus. Fine Art, 1956-70; coordinator visual art careers cluster Skyline High Sch., Dallas, 1970-71, Skyline Career Devel. Ctr., Dallas, 1971-76, Booker T. Washington Arts Magnet High Sch., Dallas, 1976-82; artist, ednl. cons., 1982—; ednl. cons., 1982—; mus. reprodns. asst. Dallas Mus. Art, 1984—. Group shows: Dallas Mus. Fine Arts, 1958, Arts Magnet Faculty Shows, 1978, 79, 80, 81, 82, Arts Magnet High Sch., Dallas Art Edn. Assn. Show, 1981, D'Art Membership Show, Dallas, 1982, 83, represented in pvt. collections. Trustee Dallas Mus. Art, 1978-84. Mem. Tex. Designer/Craftsmen, Craft Guild Dallas, Fiber Artists Dallas, Dallas Art Edn. Assn., Tex. Art Edn. Assn., Nat. Art Edn. Assn., Dallas Counselors Assn. (pres. 1968), Delta Delta Delta.

HULL, ROBERT BETTS, landscape architect, land planner; b. Oklahoma City, May 1, 1944; s. Robert Cowles and Edna Louise (Betts) H.; m. Eileen Brown, Dec. 14, 1985; children—Jory Anson, Jeremy Snedecor, Lisa, Gregory, Christine. B.S.L.A., U. Mass., 1968. Registered landscape architect, S.C. With Richard Strong Assocs., Toronto, Ont., Can., 1967-68, Bur. State Parks, Commonwealth of Pa., Harrisburg, 1968-70, Emil Hanslin Assocs., Grantham, N.H., 1970-72, Charles Delk & Assocs., Walnut Creek, Calif., 1972-73, Sea Pines Co. and Kiawah Island Co., Charleston, S.C., 1973-79, EDAW, Inc., Atlanta, 1979-80; pres. Hull-Mozley Assocs., Inc., Atlanta, 1981-85; pres. Robert B. Hull & Assocs., 1985—. Vice pres. Arts Festival Atlanta, 1979-81. Mem. Am. Soc. Landscape Architects (Merit award 1978), Am. Planning Assn., Urban Land Inst. Congregationalist. Developer master plans for Kiawah Island, S.C., Foxfire, N.C., Stratton Mountain, Vt., others. Home: 635 Old Dorris Rd Alpharetta GA 30201 Office: Robert B Hull & Assocs 227 DeKalb-Peachtree Airport Atlanta GA 30341

HULL, THOMAS G., U.S. district judge; b. 1926. Student Tusculum Coll.; J.D., U. Tenn., 1951. Atty., Easterly and Hull, Greeneville, Tenn., 1951-63; mem. Tenn. Ho. of Reps., 1955-65; atty. Thomas G. Hull, 1963-72; chief clk. Tenn. Ho. of Reps., 1969-70; cir. judge 20th Jud. Cir., Greeneville, Morristown, Rogersville, Tenn., 1972-79; legal counsel Tenn. Gov. Lamar Alexander, 1979-81; atty. Hull, Weems, Greery & Terry, Greenville, 1981-82; U.S. dist. judge, Eastern Tenn., 1983—. Mem. Tenn. Bar Assn. Office: PO Box 149 101 Summer St W Greeneville TN 37743*

HULL, WILLIAM MARTIN, JR., ophthalmologist; b. Rock Hill, S.C., June 23, 1937; s. William Martin and Elizabeth (McDowell) H.; m. Anna Transou, Dec. 14, 1963; children—William Martin III, Alice Howard. B.S., Davidson Coll., 1959; M.D., Duke U., 1963. Diplomate Am. Bd. Ophthalmology. Intern in medicine Duke Hosp., Durham, N.C., 1963-64, resident in ophthalmology, 1964-67; practice medicine specializing in ophthalmology, Rock Hill, S.C., 1969—; pres. Rock Hill Eye Clinic; mem. staff Piedmont Med. Ctr., 1969—, chief of staff, 1980; dir. Home Fed. Bldg. & Loan, Rock Hill. Vice chmn. S.C. Med PAC, 1975—; bd. dirs. Rock Hill ARC, 1976-80, The Catawba Sch., Rock Hill, 1976—. Served to maj. M.C., U.S. Army, 1967-69; Vietnam. Fellow Am. Acad. Ophthalmology; mem. S.C. Med. Assn. (trustee 1978—, vice chmn. bd. trustees 1983-84), S.C. Ophthalmology Assn., (exec. com. 1976-81), York County Med. Soc. (v.p., then pres. 1976-80), Rock Hill C. of C. (bd. dirs. 1978-81). Episcopalian. Clubs: Rock Hill Country, Rock Hill Cotillian (pres. 1976-81). Avocations: tennis; skiing; reading; travel. Home: 1520 Granville Rd Rock Hill SC 29730 Office: Rock Hill Eye Clinic 1665 Ebewezen Rd Rock Hill SC 29770

HULME, GEORGE, humane society administrator; b. Hulme, Manchester, Eng., July 1, 1913; s. George and Emily (Cavanagh) H.; m. Ruth M. McRory, Oct. 14, 1944; children—Sheila Miriam, George David. Chartered sec., U. Toronto. Sec.-treas., Art Gallery Toronto (Ont., Can.), 1946-54; sec. to bd. trustees, bus. adminstr. Nat. Gallery Can., Ottawa, 1954-57; engaged in advt., 1958; sec., gen. mgr. Toronto Humane Soc., 1959-72; sec., exec. dir. Animal Rescue League of the Palm Beaches, Inc., West Palm Beach, Fla., 1972—. Sec.-treas., Can. Mus. Assn., 1948-72, Art Inst. Ont., 1948-72, Can. Group Painters, 1966-72, Sculptors Soc. Can., 1966-72. Served to lt. comdr. Royal Can. Navy, 1939-46. Recipient cert. of merit Ont. Humane Soc., 1963; mem. $100,000 Club, Animal Rescue League of the Palm Beaches, 1982. Fellow Inst. Chartered Secs. and Adminstrs. (profl.); mem. Soc. Animal Welfare Adminstrs. (charter 1970—), Naval Officers Assn. Can. Anglican. Club: Arts and Letters (Toronto). Lodges: St. George's Soc. (life); Masons (Ottawa); Shriners (Ottawa Valley). Office: 3200 N Military Trail West Palm Beach FL 33409*

HULS, HARRISON, wholesale and retail grocery company executive; b. 1923; married. With Hale-Halsell Co., Tulsa, 1953—, v.p., 1962-73, pres., 1973—. Office: Hale-Halsell Co Box 41298 Tulsa OK 74151*

HULSEY, BENJAMIN HOY, oil company executive, accountant; b. Marlow, Okla., May 10, 1954; s. B.W. and Peggy S. (Byrd) H.; m. Margaret Eileen McNearney, Nov. 6, 1976; children—Sarah, Natalie. B.S., Okla. State U., 1976. C.P.A., Okla. Dir. internal control Gulf Oil Corp., Houston, 1976-81; asst. controller Drilling Mud, Inc. subs. W.R. Grace & Co., Oklahoma City, 1981—; dir. Midcontinent Fuels Devel. Corp., Oklahoma City, DOXA Corp., Norman, Okla. Commr. Last Frontier Council Boy Scouts Am., Oklahoma City, 1981-83; treas. Gensis project Oklahoma City, 1980. Mem. Am. Inst. C.P.A.s, Soc. Petroleum Engrs., AIME, Okla. Soc. C.P.A.s, Nat. Assn. Credit Mgmt., Houston Bonsai Soc. Republican. Club: Kuvasz Am. Office: 6303 N Portland St Suite 300 Oklahoma City OK 73112

HULSEY, SAM BYRON, bishop, Episcopal Church; b. Ft. Worth, Feb. 14, 1932; s. Simeon Hardin and Ruth (Selby) H.; m. Linda Louise Johnson, Oct. 3, 1959. B.A., Washington and Lee U., 1953; M.Div., Va. Theol. Sem., 1958. Asst., St. John's Ch., Corsicana, Tex., 1958-60; rector, 1960-63; dean So. Deanery, 1961-63; asst. dir. Christian edn. St. Michael and All Angels Ch., Dallas, 1963-66; rector St. Matthew Ch.; headmaster parochial sch. Pampa, Tex.; priest-in-charge All Saints Ch., Perryton, 1966-73; rector St. David Ch., Nashville, 1973-78, Holy Trinity Ch., Midland, Tex., 1978-80; bishop of N.W. Tex., 1980—. Address: PO Box 1067 Lubbock TX 79408*

HUMAK, BARBARA ANNE, resource specialist; b. N.Y.C., Apr. 28, 1954; d. Walter Peter and Anne Harriet (Wasylik) Humat. B.A. in Spanish, Boston Coll., 1976; M.A.T., Fairleigh Dickinson U., 1979; M.B.A., Barry U., Miami, Fla., 1981. Personnel asst. Vornado, Inc., Garfield, N.J., 1976-78; instr. English as a Second Lang., Rutherford Pub. Schs. (N.J.), 1978-79; program dir. ESL, adult edn., Ft. Lauderdale, Fla., 1979—. Mem. Am. Mktg. Assn., Am. Soc. Tng. and Devel., Soc. Advancement Mgmt. Home: 4360 SW 52d Ct 7 Fort Lauderdale FL 33314 Office: 701 S Andrews Ave Fort Lauderdale FL 33315

HUMBURG, JAY MERRILL, veterinarian, educator; b. La Crosse, Kans., Mar. 10, 1933; s. Merrill M. and Dorothy V. (Meyer) H.; m. Margaret McCall, June 22, 1963; children—Merrillee, Kenneth. B.S., Kans. State U., 1957, D.V.M., 1957; M.S., Auburn U., 1962. Diplomate Am. Bd. Vet. Practitioners. Instr. Auburn U. (Ala.), 1958-62; gen. practice vet. medicine, Broken Bow, Nebr., 1962-66, Winter Park, Fla., 1971-72; head dept. surgery and medicine Kans. State Univ. AID project Ahmada Bello U., Zaria, Nigeria, 1966-71; head equine section dept. large animal surgery and medicine Auburn U., 1973—. Mem. AVMA, Am. Assn. Equine Practitioners, Am. Bd. Vet. Practitioners (bd. regents). Republican. Presbyterian. Lodges: Masons, Shriners. Home: Route 5 PO Box 186 G Opelika AL 36801 Office: Large Animal Surgery Auburn U Auburn AL 36849

HUME, ERNEST HARDING, geophysicist; b. Glasgow, Ky., Feb. 25, 1924; s. Archie and Pearl May (Hall) H.; student U. Chgo., 1947-48; B.S. in Geology, U. Okla., 1952; m. Gwendolyn Frances Meffen, Mar. 31, 1945; children—Jennifer Carolyn, Bonita Jean. Sr. geophysicist Humble Oil Co., Corpus Christi and Houston, 1952-60, Esso-Rep, Bordeaux, France, 1960-62; geophysicist supr. Humble Oil, Tyler and Midland, Tex., 1963-67; sr. geophysicist Esso Exploration, Singapore, 1968; chief geophysicist P.T. Stanvac, Indonesia, 1969-74; dir. ARAMCO project Digicon, Inc., London, 1975-76; cons. Seismograph Service Corp., Tulsa, 1977, ARCO, Jakarta, 1978, 80, 81, 84, Exxon, New Orleans, 1979, Esso UK, London, Delta Drilling, Tyler, Tex., 1981; instr. geology U. Corpus Christi (Tex.), 1955-56. Served with U.S. Army, 1943-46, ETO; 1950-51; Japan. Registered geophysicist, Calif. Mem. Assn. Petroleum Geologists (cert.), Soc. Exploration Geophysicists. Republican. Club: Rotary. Home and Office: Hickory Oaks Route 7 Harrison AR 72601

HUMES, ARTHUR MANLEY, JR., educator; b. Miami, Fla., Sept. 23, 1948; s. Arthur Manley and Elnora Frances (Smith) H.; m. Christine Rachel Wright, Dec. 27, 1969 (div.); 1 son, Arthur Manley. B.S., Hampton Inst., 1969; M.S., Barry Coll., 1977; doctoral studies NYU, 1980. Instr. fgn. langs., English and journalism Dade County Pub. Schs., Miami, Fla., 1969—; instr. humanities Miami Dade Community Coll., 1974-80; adj. prof. English edn. Nova U., Ft. Lauderdale, Fla., 1981—, practicum adv., 1983—; pres. Arch, Inc., Miami, 1983—; publs. advisor Miami Northwestern Sr. High Sch., Miami. Mem. Nat. Council Tchrs. English, Am. Assn. Tchrs. Spanish and Portuguese, Nat. Hampton Alumni Assn., Omega Psi Phi. Democrat. Mem. Church of Christ. Office: Arch Inc PO Box 381231 Miami FL 33138

HUMES, CHARLES WARREN, II, counselor educator; b. Cambridge, Mass.; s. Charles W. and Alice E. Humes; m. Marilyn A. Harper, Aug. 7, 1965; children—Rebecca Ellyn, Malinda Maye. B.A., NYU, M.A., NYU, 1952; Ed.M., Springfield Coll., 1956; Ed.D., U. Mass., 1968. Lic. profl. counselor, Va. Sch. psychologist Westfield Pub. Schs. (Mass.), 1955-62; dir. guidance Westfield Pub. Schs. (Mass.), 1962-70; adj. assoc. prof. Springfield Coll. (Mass.), 1968-70; dir. pupil service and spl. edn. Greenwich Pub. Schs. (Conn.), 1970-80; assoc. prof. No. Va Grad. Ctr., Va. Tech. U., Falls Church, 1980—; cons. Am. Assn. Counseling and Devel. Vice pres. Westfield Area Child Guidance Clinic, 1963-65, pres., 1965-66; mem. Greenwich Hosp. Nursing Council, 1970-75. Mem. Am. Psychol. Assn., Conn. Assn. Counselor Edn. and Supervision (pres. 1979-80), Am. Assn. Counseling and Devel., Va. Counselors Assn., InterAm. Soc. Psychology, Phi Delta Kappa (v.p. Va. Tech. 1982-83), Phi Kappa Phi, Author: (with Dean L. Hummel) Pupil Services: Development, Coordination, Administration, 1984. Book rev. edito Sch. Counselor, 1984. Contbr. articles on counseling to profl. jours.

HUMMER, CHARLES WALTER, JR., dredging and marine engineer; b. Ancon, Panama, June 21, 1937; came to U.S., 1979; s. Charles Walter and Kathryn Charlotte (Laurie) H.; m. Greta Navarro, Sept. 1, 1957 (div. June 1983); 1 child, Charles Walter; m. 2d, Sandra Ann Lary, June 6, 1984. B.S. in Chem. Engring., U. Notre Dame, 1959, M.S. in Chem. Engring., 1961. Corrosion, petroleum engr. Naval Research Lab., Panama Canal Zone, 1960-70; chief pollution control officer Dredging Div., Panama Canal Zone, 1970-73; with environ. energy office Office of Gov./Pres., Panama Canal Zone, 1973-74; asst. chief dredging Panama Canal Co., Panama Canal Zone, 1974-79; asst. chief dredging U.S. Army Corps Engrs., Washington, 1979—; chem. engr. rep. Canal Profl. Engr. Panel, Panama Canal Zone, 1976-79; cons. in field. Contbr. articles to profl. jours. Legis. rep. Central Labor Union Metal Trades Council, Panama Canal Zone, 1964-70; personal adv. to gov. Labor & Treaty Affairs, Panama Canal Zone, 1977-79. Recipient Excellence award Panama Canal Co., 1978, 79; Excellence award Corps of Engrs., 1980, 81, 82, 83. Mem. Soc. Am. Mil. Engrs. (pres. 1979), Western Dredging Assn. (pres. 1985, chmn. bd. 1986), World Orgn. of Dredging (bd. dirs. 1986—), Permanent Internat. Assn. Navigation Congresses, Sigma Xi. Lodges: Rotary (pres. 1978-79, 80-82), Elks, K.C. Avocations: computers; photography; gardening; woodworking. Home: 11914 Oakwood Ave Woodbridge VA 22192 Office: Water Resources Support Ctr Casey Bldg Fort Belvoir VA 22060

HUMPHREYS, HOMER ALEXANDER, former educator; b. nr. Waynesboro, Va., Feb. 7, 1902; s. Lewis Greenberry and Annie (Sampson) H.; B.A., Bridgewater Coll., 1928; M.A., U. Va., 1941, research fellow, 1943-44; m. Ruth Elizabeth Gilbert, Sept. 1, 1926; children—Faye (Mrs. Hezekiah Sadler), Joye (Mrs. James Malcolm Hart Harris, Jr.), Anne (Mrs. Richard Edward Talman), Homer Alexander, Jane (dec.), Kaye (Mrs. Ralph Edward Frazier). Instr. Moyock (N.C.) High Sch., 1928-29; prin. Darlington Heights (Va.) High Sch., 1929-33, Green Bay (Va.) High Sch., 1934-44; supervising prin. West Point (Va.) High Sch., 1944-65; gen. supr. instrn. Williamsburg-James City County Schools, 1965-67; dir. aviation edn. Mont. State U., Missoula, also Eastern Coll. Edn., Billings, Mont., summers 1954, 55, U. Va., Charlottesville, summers 1956-71; instr. Coll. William and Mary Extension, 1963-68. Coordinator, Civil Def., King William County and Town of West Point, 1950-61. Served from 2d lt. to lt. col. USAF, CAP, 1945—; dir. aviation edn. Va. Wing, Civil Air Patrol, 1956-65. Mem. N.E.A. (past 1st zone v.p. dept. audio-visual instrn.), Va. High Sch. League (chmn. 1955-57), King William-King and Queen Edn. Assn. (pres. 1956-58), Phi Delta Kappa. Kiwanian (pres. West Point 1949, lt. gov. capital dist. div. four 1956). Author: A History of Education in Prince Edward County, Va., 1941; column Wings Over Va., 1956-62; also numerous articles, reports and surveys. Home: 110 Oxford Circle Williamsburg VA 23187

HUMPHREYS, (JAMES) HERBERT, JR., corporation executive, marine archaeology researcher; b. Memphis, Apr. 3, 1948; s. James Herbert and Wilda (Mathis) H.; m. Nicola Spencer-Barnes, Mar. 9, 1979; 1 son, James Herbert III. Student Rollins Coll., 1966-69, Broward Coll., 1969-70, Navigation Sch., 1982, Sea Sch., 1983. Master U.S. Mcht. Marine; lic. pilot, Gt. Britain, U.S.; lic. air controller, scuba diver, glider flyer. Pres., founder Humphreys (Cayman), Ltd., 1970—; owner, operator Holiday Inn Grand Cayman, 1972—; founder George Garner Travel, 1976; pres. Summit Club, Inc., 1978—, Humphreys Investment Co., Inc., 1978—, Marine Archaeol. Research of Grand Cayman and Haiti, 1983—. Dep. sheriff of Shelby County; mem. Republican. Nat. Com.; lt. CAP. Served with USNR, 1967-75. Decorated chevalier St. John of Jerusalem; named Ky. col., Tenn. col. Mem. Internat. Assn. Holiday Inns. Episcopalian. Memphis Country, Memphis Yacht, Confederate Air Force, Royal Southampton Yacht, Summit. Office: 5100 Poplar Ave Memphis TN 38137

HUMPHREYS, JAMES MACK, JR., hospital administrator; b. Wilmington, N.C., Feb. 10, 1943; s. James Mack and Barbara Urban (Clark) H.; B.A., Baylor U., 1965; M.D., U. Tex., Dallas, 1969; m. Marian Pittman Stephens, 1982; children—Loyd, Robert, Earl, Adrienne, Stephania Stephens, Christopher Stephens. Intern in surgery, then resident in ob-gyn Bexar County Hosp. Dist., 1969-73; practice medicine specializing in ob-gyn Midland (Tex.) Women's Clinic Assocs., 1973-86; v.p. Med. affairs Midland Meml. Hosp., 1986—; dir. Midland City/County Health Dept., 1978—; mem. quality assurance Com. Tex. Med. Found. Trustee Midland Meml. Hosp., 1984-86. Served with USAFR, 1970-76. Decorated AF Commendation medal. Diplomate Am. Bd. Ob-Gyn. Mem. Midland County Med. Soc., Tex. Med. Assn., AMA, Am. Guild Organists. Baptist. Home: 1701 W Kansas Midland TX 79701 Office: 2200 W Illinois St Midland TX 79701

HUMPHREYS, KENNETH KING, association executive, educator; b. Pitts., Jan. 19, 1938; s. Meredith Harold and Olga (Adamitis) H.; B.S., Carnegie Inst. Tech., 1959, postgrad., 1961-62; M.S., W.Va. U., 1967; postgrad. Ill. Inst. Tech., 1960, U. Pitts., 1965; m. Harriet Elizabeth Moss, May 6, 1961; children—Kenneth King, Keith Alan, Kevin James, Karen Elizabeth. Tech. asst. U.S. Steel Corp., Applied Research Lab., Chgo., 1959-60, tech. asso., Monroeville, Pa., 1960-62, asst. technologist, Universal, Pa., 1962-63, assoc. research engr., 1963-65; cost engr. W.Va. U. Coal Research Bur., Morgantown, 1965-67, sr. staff and cost engr., 1967-71, asst. dir., 1971-81; asst. prof. Coll. Mineral and Energy Resources, W.Va. U., Morgantown, 1970-73, assoc. prof., 1973-76, prof., 1976-82, adj. prof., 1982—, asst. to dean, 1971-77, chmn. minerals program, 1978-81, asst. dean acad. affairs, 1979-82; engring. cons. metallurgy and fuel tech., 1963-81; exec. dir. Am. Assn. Cost Engrs., 1971—. Leader, Boy Scouts Am., 1961—, dist. commr., 1969-72, dist. tng. chmn., 1972-74, chmn. council tng., 1975-77, vice-chmn. leadership devel. Area 6, E. Central Region, 1977-79. Recipient Silver Beaver award, award Merit, Woodbadge award Mountaineer Area council Boy Scouts Am., Het Schaap mit vijf Poten award for distinguished service, Royal Netherlands Industries Fair; named Hon. West Virginian, Gov. of W.Va. Registered profl. engr., Pa., W.Va.; cert. cost engr. Fellow Assn. Cost Engrs. (U.K.), Am. Assn. Cost Engrs. (nat. chmn. 1969-72, nat. dir. 1971; pub. Cost Engring. mag.; named Mem. of Moment 1970, award recognition 1979); mem. Sociedad Mexicana de Ingenieria Economica y de Costos (Mex.), Soc. Mining Engrs., AIME, Internat. Cost Engring. Council (sec. 1976-82, 84—, treas. 1982—), Nat., W.Va., (pres. Morgantown 1969-70, dir. Morgantown 1970-76, state dir. 1971-76, state v.p. 1980-81, state pres. 1982-83) socs. profl. engrs., Am. Assn. Engring. Socs. (bd. govs. 1979-83), W.Va. Coal Mining Inst., Sigma Xi, Beta Theta Pi, Alpha Phi Omega. Democrat. Presbyterian (deacon 1968-70, ruling elder 1972-75, pres. congregation 1975-77). Contbr. articles to profl. jours.; author and co-author several books in field. Patentee in field. Home: 305 Lebanon Ave Morgantown WV 26505

HUMPHRIES, FREDERICK S., university president; b. Appalachicola, Fla., Dec. 26, 1935; s. Thornton and Minnie H.; B.S. magna cum laude in Chemistry, Fla. A&M U., 1957; Ph.D. in Phys. Chemistry, U. Pitts., 1964; m. Antoinette McTurner, June 1960; children—Frederick Stephen, Robin Tanya, Laurence Anthony. Pvt. tutor in sci. and math., 1959-64; asst. prof. chemistry U. Minn., Mpls., 1966-67; asso. prof. chemistry Fla. A&M U., Tallahassee, 1964-67, prof. chemistry, 1967-68, dir. thirteen-coll. curriculum program, 1967-68; dir. innovative instl. research consortium Inst. Services to Edn., Washington, 1972-73, dir. interdisciplinary program, 1973-74, dir. Knoxville Coll. study of sci. capability of the Black coll., 1972-74, dir. two-univs. grad. program in sci., 1973-74, v.p. ISE, 1970-74; pres. Tenn. State U., Nashville, 1974—; mem. bd. grad. advocates Meharry Med. Coll., 1976; cons. various colls. and univs., 1978-79. Chmn., Fairfax County Anti-Poverty Commn., 1972-74; mem. bd. ethical conduct Met. Govt. Nashville and Davidson County, 1978—; co-chmn. Reston's Black Focus, 1973; bd. dirs. YMCA, 1975. Served with U.S. Army Security Agy., 1957-59. Recipient Disting. Service award Inst. Services to Edn., 1974; Disting. Edn. and Adminstr. Meritorious award Fla. A&M U., 1975; Human Relations award Met. Human Relations Commn. Nashville, 1978. Mem. Am. Chem. Soc., Am. Council Edn. (dir. 1977-78, sec. bd. 1978-79), Am. Assn. Higher Edn., AAUP, AAAS, NAACP, Nat. Assn. State Univs. and Land-Grant Colls., Nashville Area C. of C. (edn. com. 1975), Fla. A&M Alumni Assn. (Disting. Service award 1976). Roman Catholic. Contbr. articles on edn. in Black colls. to profl. publs.; Frederick S. Humphries Day declared in his honor by City of Indiana. Office: Office of Pres Tenn State Univ 3500 Centennial Blvd Nashville TN 37203

HUMPHRIES, JOAN ROPES, psychologist, educator; b. Bklyn., Oct. 17, 1928; d. Lawrence Gardner and Adele Lydia (Zimmermann) Ropes; B.A., U. Miami, 1950; M.S., Fla. State U., 1955; Ph.D., La. State U., 1963; m. Charles C. Humphries, Apr. 4, 1957; children—Peggy Ann, Charlene Adele. Part-time instr. U. Miami, Coral Gables, Fla., 1964-66; asso. prof. dept. psychology Miami-Dade Community Coll., 1966—. Bd. dirs., v.p. Inst. Evaluation, Diagnosis and Treatment, Miami, 1975—. Mem. AAUP (v.p., sec., mem. exec. bd.), Internat. Platform Assn. (gov.), Am. Psychol. Assn., AAUW (v.p. Tamiami chpt.), Dade County Psychol. Assn., Colonial Dames 17th Century, N.Y. Acad. Scis., Regines in Miami, Soc. Mayflower Descs. (elder William Brewster colony). Democrat. Clubs: Country of Coral Gables, Jockey. Editorial staff, maj. author: The Application of Scientific Behaviorism to Humanistic Phenomena, 1975; researcher in biofeedback and human consciousness. Home: 1311 Alhambra Circle Coral Gables FL 33134 Office: Miami Dade Community Coll North Campus Miami FL 33167

HUNDLEY, FRANK T., financial executive; b. 1932. Grad. Washington & Lee U., 1954; M.B.A., U. Tex., 1958. With Dittmar & Co., Investment Bankers, 1955-56, 58-72; exec. v.p. fin Southland Fin. Corp., Dallas, 1982—. Office: Southland Life Ins Co 409 N Olive St Dallas TX 75201*

HUNG, CHAO-SHUN, economics educator, researcher; b. Taiwan, Republic China, Jan. 20, 1942; came to U.S., 1969, naturalized, 1977; s. Chiang-shu and Yu-mei (Chen) H.; m. Jane Anne Chien, May 14, 1984. B.A., Taiwan Normal U., Taipei, Republic China, 1964; M.B.A., St. Louis U., 1972; Ph.D. in econs., Tex. A&M U., 1982. Research asst. Tex. A&M U., Coll. Sta., 1977-82; asst. prof. econs. Fla. Atlantic U., Boca Raton, 1982—; dir. of Grad. Studies in Econs. Fla. Atlantic U., Boca Raton, 1982—. Served to lt. Chinese Marine Corps., 1964-65, Taiwan. Mem. Am. Econ. Assn., Mo. Valley Econ. Assn. Avocations: fishing; swimming; classical music. Office: Dept Econs Florida Atlantic Univ 500 NW 20th St Boca Raton FL 33432

HUNG, NGUYEN MANH, political science educator, consultant; b. Hanoi, Vietnam, Mar. 8, 1937; s. Nguyen Quan Chinh and Pham Thi Tho; m. Do Kim Ninh, May 6, 1968; children—Nguyen Hung Phi, Nguyen Hung Phong. LL.B., U. Saigon, 1960; M.A. in Internat. Relations, U. Va., 1963, Ph.D., 1965. Prof. internat. politics Nat. Sch. Adminstrn., Saigon, Vietnam, 1965-74; professorial lectr. Sch. Law, U. Saigon and Nat. Def. Coll., 1965-74; vice dean Sch. Econs. and Bus., Minh Duc U., Vietnam, 1970-72; advisor for planning Nat. Econ. Devel. Fund, Vietnam, 1973-74; dep. minister Nat. Planning and Devel., Republic of Vietnam, 1974-75; assoc. prof. govt. and politics George Mason U., Fairfax, Va., 1976—, dir. Indochina Inst.; lectr. Catholic U. Am., 1976-77; grant reviewer div. pub. programs NEH, 1979—. Chmn. subcom. on Reorgn. of Supreme Council of Civil Service and Central Office of Personnel Mgmt., Vietnam, 1967; chmn. Interagy. to Draft New Civil Service Statute for Vietnam, 1968; mem. Postwar Planning Bd., 1968-69; mem. Nat. Sci. Research Council, 1970-75, Vietnam Council on Fgn. Relations, 1971-75; v.p. Vietnam Found., 1975-81; mem. adv. group on Indochinese Refugees to Dep. Dir. ACTION, 1979; mem. nat. adv. com. Asian/Pacific Women's Ednl. Equity Conf., 1979; pres. Nat. Assn. for Vietnamese Am. Edn., 1982-84; governing bd. Woodburn Ctr. for Community Mental Health, 1980-82; bd. advisors Vietnamese Lawyers Assn., 1978-80; v.p. Vietnam Econ. Assn., 1974-75, League Vietnamese Assns. in Washington Met. Area, 1984—; Soc. Sci. Research Council research scholar, 1986; Smith-Mundt-Fulbright scholar, 1960-62; grad. scholar U.S. AID, 1962-64; Woodrow Wilson Dept. Fgn. Affairs fellow, U. Va., 1965. Mem. Internat. Studies Assn., Am. Polit. Sci. Assn., Assn. for Asian Studies, Nat. Capital Area Polit. Sci. Assn. Buddhist. Author: Introduction to International Politics (Vietnamese), 1971; co-author: Peace and Development in the Republic of Vietnam (Vietnamese), 1973; contbr. articles to Vietnamese and Am. jours. Home: 3206 Wynford Dr Fairfax VA 22031 Office: Dept Pub Affairs George Mason U Fairfax VA 22030

HUNLEY, WILLIAM TRAVIS, banker, consultant; b. Dallas, Dec. 11, 1949; s. Raymond Lewis and Margaret Estelle (Cooper) H.; m. Cynthia Louise Nunn, Aug. 7, 1971 (div. 1978); m. 2d, Margaret Elizabeth Milligan, June 21, 1980. B.S., North Tex. State U., 1972, M.B.A., 1974. Sr. systems analyst 1st City Bank Houston, 1974-75; ops. officer, mgr. planning Allied Bank of Tex., Houston, 1975-79; sr. v.p., field ops. mgr. Profit Tech. Corp., Houston, 1979-81; v.p. InterFirst Service Corp., Dallas, 1981; sr. v.p., cashier InterFirst Bank San Antonio, 1981—; voting rep. Bank Adminstrn. Inst., San Antonio, 1982—. Sec. psychology curriculum com. N.Tex. State U., Denton, 1971-72; chmn. fin. com. Boy Scouts Am., San Antonio, 1983. Named Eagle Scout, Kansas City, Kans., 1967. Mem. Am. Mgmt. Assn., Am. Inst. Banking, Bank Adminstrn. Inst., Houston Clearing House Task Force on Point of Sale. Republican. Baptist. Club: Psychology Assn. (sec. Denton 1971-72). Office: InterFirst Bank San Antonio NA InterFirst Plaza 300 Convent St San Antonio TX 78205

HUNSAKER, DONALD BLEVENS, JR., research scientist; b. Chgo., Oct. 11, 1952; s. Donald Blevens and Audrey (Jacobsen) H.; m. Carolyn Marie Thomas. B.S., U. Wis.-Whitewater, 1974; M.S., Wayne State U., 1976; Ph.D., UCLA, 1980. Tech. engr. Tech. Service Corp., Santa Monica, Calif., 1977-78; staff scientist Woodward-Clyde Cons., San Francisco, 1978-79; environ. engr. III Assn. Bay Area Govts., Berkeley, Calif., 1979-81; research assoc. Oak Ridge Nat. Lab., 1981—. Recipient F. W. Ring Phys. and Math. Scis. award Thornton Community Coll., 1972; Wayne State U. fellow, 1974-75; UCLA Regents fellow, 1976-77. Mem. Air Pollution Control Assn., Nat. Assn. Environ. Profls., Am. Chem. Soc. (award 1973), Phi Lambda Upsilon, Phi Kappa Phi, Phi Theta Kappa. Democrat. Mem. Ch. of Christ. Home: Kingston TN Office: PO Box X 4500N MS D-33 Oak Ridge TN 37830

HUNSBERGER, PETER CHRISTIAN, petroleum geologist; b. Aiken, S.C., Apr. 18, 1954; s. Johnson Newton and Shirley Elizabeth (Minker) H.; m. Deborah Susan Shwayka, 1981; 1 child, Katherine Minker. B.A., Middlebury Coll., 1977. Mudlogger, Core Labs., Saudi Arabia, 1977-78; offshore geologist Hunt Oil Co., Dallas, 1978-81, sr. offshore geologist Houston, 1981-83, dist. offshore geologist, 1983—. Mem. Am. Assn. Petroleum Geologists, Houston Geol. Soc., Dallas C. of C., Inwood North Civic Assn. Avocations: Sailing; scuba-diving; photography. Office: Hunt Oil Co 2950 N Loop W #900 Houston TX 77092

HUNSUCKER, ROBERT DEAN, pipeline company executive; b. Winchester, Kans. Formerly chief operating officer, pres. Panhandle Eastern Corp., Houston, pres., chief exec. officer, 1983—; now vice chmn., chief exec. officer Panhandle Eastern Pipe Line Co., Trunkline Gas Co., Houston; dir. Gifford Hill Corp., Anadarko Prodn. Co., Century Refining Co., Dixilyn-Field Drilling Co., Nat. Helium Co. Office: Panhandle Eastern Corp 3000 Bissonnet Ave Box 1642 Houston TX 77251*

HUNT, ALEXANDER CLARK, industrial designer, manufacturing company executive, inventor; b. St. Petersburg, Fla., May 9, 1947; s. William Alexander and Doris Overton H.; m. Gerry Coe, Aug. 20, 1965 (div.); 1 dau., Holly Hunt Coe. B.S., East Tenn. State U., 1971. Founder, owner Huntal Mfg. Co., Santa Monica, Calif., 1978—, Summit Resources, Winter Graden, Fla., 1980—; owner High Reach Helicopter, 1983—; real estate assoc. Fla. Equity Investments, 1984—. Republican. Patentee in field; inventor Wild Bass Bandit, fishing lure. Home: 3511 Pelican Ln Orlando FL 32801 Office: Box 1564 Winter Garden FL 32787

HUNT, EARL GLADSTONE, JR., bishop; b. Johnson City, Tenn., Sept. 14, 1918; s. Earl Gladstone and Tommie Mae (DeVault) H.; B.S., E. Tenn. State U., 1941; M.Div., Emory U., 1946; D.D., Tusculum Coll., 1956, Duke U., 1969, Lambuth Coll., 1978, Fla. So. Coll., 1980, Emory U., 1983; LL.D., U. Chattanooga, 1957; D.C.L. (hon.), Emory and Henry Coll., 1965; D.H.L., Belmont Abbey Coll., 1976; m. Mary Ann Kyker, June 15, 1943; 1 son, Earl Stephen. Ordained to ministry Methodist Ch., 1944; pastor Sardis Meth. Ch., Atlanta, 1942-44; assoc. pastor Broad St. Meth. Ch., Kingsport, Tenn., 1944-45; pastor Wesley Meml. Meth. Ch., Chattanooga, 1945-50, First Meth. Ch., Morristown, Tenn., 1950-56; pres. Emory and Henry Coll., 1956-64; resident bishop Charlotte Area, Meth. Ch., 1964-76, Nashville Area, 1976-80, Fla. area, 1980—; pres. Southeastern Jurisdiction Coll. Bishops, 1973; Willson lectr. S. Central Jurisdiction and Tex. Wesleyan Coll., 1976; Simpson lectr. First United Meth. Ch., Wichita, Kan., 1978; participant Meth. series Protestant Hour, nationwide broadcast, 1956; frequent preacher Chgo. Sunday Evening Club; mem. Meth. Gen. Bd. Edn., 1956-68; del. Meth. Gen. Conf., 1956, 60, 64; del. S.E. Jurisdictional Conf., 1952, 56, 60, 64; chmn. gen. commn. on family life United Meth. Ch., 1968-72, mem. gen. council ministries, 1972-80, pres. Gen. Bd. Higher Edn. and Ministry, 1980-84; exec. com. World Meth. Council, 1976—, chmn. N.Am. sect., 1981—; mem. governing bd. Nat. Council Chs., 1968-84. Bd. fellows Interpreters' House, Inc.; trustee Wesleyan Coll., Emory U., Bethune-Cookman Coll., Fla. So. Coll., Lake Junaluska Meth. Assembly, A Fund for Theol. Edn.; mem. Com. One Hundred, Emory U. Named Young Man of Year, Morristown Jr. C. of C., 1952. Mem. Blue Key, Newcomen Soc., Pi Kappa Delta. Author: I Have Believed: A Bishop Talks about His Faith, 1980; editor: Storms and Starlight; contbr. articles to mags. and profl. jours. Home: 1120 Hunt Ave Lakeland FL 33801 Office: PO Box 1747 Lakeland FL 33802

HUNT, JAMES CALVIN, physician, university chancellor; b. Lexington, N.C., Sept. 11, 1925; s. James Lee and Sarah Della (Frank) H.; m. Irene Kivett, Sept. 17, 1949; children—James Calvin, Michael S., Cynthia Irene. A.B., Catawba Coll., 1949; M.D., Bowman Gray Sch. Medicine, 1953; M.S., U. Minn., 1958. Intern N.C. Bapt. Hosp., Winston-Salem, 1953-54; resident, fellow Mayo Grad Sch. Medicine, Rochester, Minn., 1954-58; practice medicine, specializing in internal medicine (cardiovascular-renal diseases), Rochester, 1958-78; cons., instr. to asst. prof. dept. medicine Mayo Clinic and Mayo Med. Sch., 1958-63, asso. prof., chmn. div. nephrology, 1963-72, prof., chmn. dept. medicine, 1974-78; prof., asso. dean clin. ednl. programs Mayo Med. Sch., 1972-74; prof. medicine U. Tenn., Memphis, 1978—, dean, 1978-81, chancellor, 1981—; mem. Nat. Heart, Lung and Blood Adv. Council, NIH. Contbr. articles to med. jours. Pres. Nat. Kidney Found., 1973-76; bd. dirs. Kidney Found. Upper Midwest; trustee Christian Bros. Coll., 1983. Served with USAAF, 1943-46; ETO. Recipient Disting. Service award Bowman Gray Sch. Medicine, Wake Forest U., 1975; Disting. Alumnus award Catawba Coll., 1974. Fellow A.C.P., Am. Coll. Cardiology, Am. Heart Assn. (council on circulation); mem. Internat., Am. socs. nephrology, Internat. Soc. Hypertension, Soc. Nuclear Medicine, Council for High Blood Pressure Research, Am. Soc. Internal Medicine, AMA, Am. Soc. Clin. Pharmacology and Therapeutics, Sigma Xi, Alpha Omega Alpha, Phi Rho Sigma. Home: 343 S Goodwyn Memphis TN 38111 Office: U Tenn Memphis 62 S Dunlap St Memphis TN 38163

HUNT, JAMES EDWARD, civil engineer; b. Oklahoma City, June 19, 1947; s. Elmer Hal and Juanita Mildred (Tibey) H.; B.S. in Civil Engring., U. Okla., 1970; m. Kathy Jo Krehbiel, Jan. 6, 1979; children—Joseph James, Spencer James. With Tex. Dept. Hwys. and Public Transp., Dallas, 1970—, assoc. resident engr., 1974-78, resident engr., 1978-82, sr. resident engr., 1982-84, sr. R.O.W. engr., 1984-85, supr. resident engr., 1985—. Bd. dirs. THD Credit Union, 1976—, treas., 1977-79, vice chmn., 1979-85, O.U. Club, 1985—. Registered profl. engr., Tex. Mem. U. Okla. Alumni Assn., Nat. Soc. Profl. Engrs., Tex. Soc. Profl. Engrs. Roman Catholic. Club: U. Okla. Home: 8519 Baumgarten Dr Dallas TX 75228 Office: PO Box 3067 Dallas TX 75221

HUNT, J(ULIAN) COURTENAY, artist; b. Jacksonville, Fla., Sept. 17, 1917; s. Julian Schley and Ruth Rosalind (Loftin) H.; student Ringling Sch. Art, 1946-47, Farnsworth Sch. Art, 1948-52. Artist, 1950—; tchr. pvt. classes painting, 1950—; exhibited in one-man shows at Cummer Gallery of Art, Jacksonville, 1963—, Flair Gallery, Palm Beach, Fla., 1970-71; exhibited in group shows at Palm Beach Art Gallery, Soc. Four Arts, Palm Beach, 1968-69, Audubon Artists of Am., N.Y.C., Allied Artists Am., N.Y.C., 1952-56, Atlanta High Mus., 1950-54, St. Augustine (Fla.) Art Assn., 1970-73, Sarasota (Fla.) Art Assn., 1952-56, Fla. Artists Group Show at Norton Art Gallery of the Palm Beaches, 1975; portraits in permanent collections U. Fla., Gainesville, Jacksonville U., City Hall of Jacksonville, Duval County Circuit Ct., Jacksonville, Ind. Life Ins. Co., Jacksonville. Served with USAAF, 1942-46; ETO. Address: 2587 Windwood Ln Orange Park FL 32073

HUNT, RAY L., oil company executive; s. Haroldson Lafayette Hunt; ed. So. Methodist U.; m. Nancy, 5 children. Pres., Hunt Oil Co., Dallas. Office: Hunt Oil Co 2900 InterFirst One Bldg Dallas TX 75202*

HUNT, ROBERT STEPHEN, transportation executive; b. St. Petersburg, Fla., June 8, 1948; s. John Kenneth and Georgia (Davis) H.; m. Ann Lee Francis, May 29, 1976; 1 child, Stephen Andrew. Student U. Ill., 1966-67, Parkland Jr. Coll., 1970-72. Ops. mgr. Stahly Truck City, Champaign, Ill., 1970-78; pres. RH Ford Trucks, Urbana, Ill., 1978-79; corp. fleet maintenance mgr. Super Valu Stores, Inc., Mpls., 1979-85; dir. transp. Grocers Supply Co., Houston, 1985—; bd. dirs. Nat. Automotive Inst. Service Excellence, Washington, 1984—. Contbr. articles on fleet mgmt. to profl. jours. Served with U.S. Army, 1967-69, Vietnam. Decorated Silver Star, Purple Heart with 2 clusters. Mem. Soc. Automotive Engrs., The Maintenance Council (vice chmn. 1981—), Pvt. Truck Council (com. mem. 1982—), VFW. Republican. Methodist. Avocation: golf. Home: 12423 Chadwell St Houston TX 77031 Office: Grocers Supply Co PO Box 14200 Houston TX 77221

HUNT, STEPHEN GARRETT, economic analyst; b. Denver, Dec. 7, 1945; s. Ivy Garrett and Betty Jane (Brown) H.; A.A., Arapahoe Community Coll., 1971; B.A., U. Colo., 1974; m. Gretchen Ann Muller, Dec. 7, 1966; children—Stephen Christopher, William Brice, Andrew Garrett. Budget analyst Public Service Co. Colo., Denver, 1974-80; econ. analyst Delta Drilling Co., Tyler, Tex., 1980-85; pres. Hunt Bus. Cons., 1985—. Precinct committeeman Littleton, Colo., 1974-76. Served with Submarine Service, USN, 1966-70; Vietnam. Mem. Soc. Petroleum Engrs., Am. Petroleum Inst., Am. Mgmt. Assn., Am. Soc. Bus. Economists. Author: Efficient Use of SCR Rig Power, 1981; Drilling Model Forecast, 1984; Fartilolrum, 1986. Office: 814 Gilmer Rd Suite 5 Longview TX 75604

HUNT, SUSANNE CAROL KRAFT, registered nurse; b. Plainfield, N.J., Dec. 25, 1943; d. Rudolph A. and Helen A. (Thomas) Kraft; diploma East Orange Gen. Hosp. Sch. Nursing, 1964; m. Kenneth G. Hunt, Oct. 29, 1965 (div.); children—Kenneth G., Kristen S. Nurse, Overlook Hosp., Summit, N.J., 1965-67; head nurse Woodbine Nursing Home, Alexandria, Va., 1967-68; staff nurse Circle Terrace Hosp., Alexandria, 1969-70; head intensive care Manassas (Va.) Manor Nursing Home, 1976-77, dir. nurses, 1977-79; head nurse Barcroft Inst., Falls Church, Va., 1979, Martin Meml. Hosp., Stuart, Fla., 1979—. Bd. dirs., chmn. pub. edn. com. Am. Cancer Soc. Cert. intravenous therapy technician, chemotherapy nurse. Mem. Va. Nurses Assn., No. Va. Dirs. of

Nursing Assn., United Methodist Women. Home: 1464 NE 24th St Jensen Beach FL 33457 Office: Martin Meml Hosp Hospital Ave Stuart FL 33457

HUNT, VICTORIA SILEK, electric company manager; b. Winchester, Va., Jan. 1, 1950; d. Abraham Frank and Najila Josephine (Haddad) Silek; m. Sam Hunt, Aug. 13, 1977. B.A. in Am. Studies, Mary Wash. Coll., 1972; M.L.S., U. N.C., 1974. Profl. librarian pub. relations Central N.C. Regional Library, Burlington, 1974-75; head librarian May Meml. Library, Burlington, 1975-77; administrv. mgr. Hunt Electric Supply Co., Burlington, 1977—. Trustee, Tech. Coll., Alamance. Mem. N.C. Telecommunications Assns., Nat. Assn. Elec. Distbrs., Triad IBM Users Group. Democrat. Home: 1218 W Davis St Burlington NC 27215 Office: 1213 Maple Ave Burlington NC 27215

HUNTER, ALICE JOAN, construction company official; b. Bellaire, Ohio, Nov. 1, 1961; d. Samuel Joseph and Ilda Cecile (Lindley) H. Student L'Ermitage, France, 1979, Russian Lang. Sch., Vt., 1981; B.A. in Russian Civilization, Smith Coll., Mass., 1983. Tutor, tchr. Russian lang. Smith Coll., Northampton, Mass., 1981-83; field office mgr. Calibre Constrn. Co. of Va., Fairfax, 1983-84, constrn. mgr., 1984—. Republican. Episcopalian. Home: 300 W Columbia St Apt 1 Falls Church VA 22046 Office: Calibre Co of Va Summit Sq Project 3869 Plaza Dr Fairfax VA 22030

HUNTER, BEVERLY CLAIRE, systems analyst, educator; b. Pitts., Apr. 19, 1941; d. Eldon Clare and Ethel Mae (Kamer) Roberts; B.A. cum laude (Nat. Merit scholar), U. Pitts., 1963; m. Harold G. Hunter, Jan. 7, 1966; children—Cynthia Claire, Gregory Shawn. Computer programmer U.S. Navy, 1964-65; systems engr. IBM Corp., 1965-66; dir. instructional programming Human Resources Research Orgn., Alexandria, Va., 1966-68, sr. staff scientist, 1970—; staff scientist Matrix Research, 1969; cons. U.S. Congress, U.S. Office Edn., Bell Labs., Telenet Communications; pres. Targeted Learning Corp.; v.p. Piedmont Research Center, 1979-80; peer reviewer NSF. Bd. dirs. Apple Edn. Found. NSF grantee, 1979-83; faculty assoc. Cath. U. Mem. AAAS, Nat. Sci. Tchrs. Assn., IEEE Computer Soc., Assn. Ednl. Data Systems, Assn. Computing Machinery, Union Concerned Scientists, Wilderness Soc., Nature Conservancy, Friends of the Earth, Rappahannock League Environ. Protection. Co-author: Learning Alternatives in U.S. Education: Where Student and Computer Meet, 1975; Computer Literacy, 1982; My Students Use Computers, 1983; Managing Information with your Personal Computer, 1984; Scholastic Data Bases for U.S. History, Government, Life Science and Physical Science; mem. editorial bd. Computing Internat. Jour.; contbr. articles to publs. Home: Route 1 Box 190 Amissville VA 22002

HUNTER, BOBBY ROY, credit union executive, consultant; b. Sanford, N.C., Sept. 18, 1938; s. Roy Myrover Hunter and Altie Inez (Hunter) Norris; m. Patricia Jean Sheets, June 16, 1961 (div. 1976); children—Blake Roland, Lori Dwan; m. 2d, Andrea Jane Humphrey, Feb. 14, 1977; children—Alan Howard Burt, Timothy Carl Burt. B.S. in Bus. Mgmt., Troy State U., 1978. Enlisted U.S. Air Force, 1957, advanced through grades to master sgt. 1975; programming technician Security Service, Elmendorf AFB, Alaska, 1970-74, Data Systems Design Center, Gunter AFS, Ala., 1974-78, ret., 1978; programmer analyst State of Ala., Montgomery, 1978-79, Union Camp Corp., Montgomery, 1979-80; data processing mgr. Water Works Bd., Montgomery, 1980-81; v.p. data processing Maxwell-Gunter Fed. Credit Union, Montgomery, 1981—; cons. Burroughs Corp., Montgomery, 1981—. Active YMCA. Mem. Data Processing Mgrs. Assn., Ala. Mgrs. Assn., Air Force Sgts. Assn. Democrat. Methodist. Home: 416 Planters Rd Montgomery AL 36109 Office: Maxwell-Gunter Fed Credit Union 400 Eastdale Montgomery AL 36193

HUNTER, BRENDA MCCOY, career development consultant; b. Winston-Salem, N.C., Mar. 11, 1947; d. Birden Dixon and Lovie Josephine (Dalton) McCoy; m. Arlanders Hunter, Jr., Feb. 7, 1969; children—Arleida LaVonne, Nathan Brenard. B.S., N.C. A&T State U., 1969; M.A. in Edn., Tenn. State U., 1976. Tchr., Fayetteville Pub. Schs. (N.C.), 1970-71, Neighborhood Youth Corp., Winston-Salem, N.C., 1971-72, Opportunities Industrialization Ctr., Nashville, 1974-75; adminstrv. analyst Metro Action Commn., Nashville, 1975-77; counselor, Nashville State Tech., 1977-80, TVA, Knoxville, 1981-82; pres., founder Arrival, Inc., career and personal devel. tng. firm; speaker in field. Active Women's Polit. Caucus. Mem. Am. Soc. Tng. and Devel. Clubs: Toastmasters Internat. (bd. dirs.), Cable Club of Nashville (bd. dirs.). Office: PO Box 24612 Nashville TN 37202

HUNTER, EMMETT MARSHALL, JR., oil co. exec.; b. Denver, Aug. 18, 1913; s. Emmett Marshall and Pearl Jo (Hubby) H.; LL.B., So. Methodist U., 1936; m. Marjorie Louise Roth, Nov. 21, 1941; children—Marsha Louise, Marjorie Maddin, Margaret Anne. Bar: Tex. 1936. Practiced law, Dallas, Longview and Houston, 1936-41; with Exxon Co. USA (formerly Humble Oil & Refining Co.), Tyler, Tex., 1945-78, exploration land supr., 1965-78; pres. Internat. Oil Investments, Tyler, 1978—. Bd. dirs. Tex. Rose Festival. Served as lt. USNR, 1942-45. Mem. State Bar Tex., Am. Petroleum Inst., Bus.-Industry Polit. Action Com., E. Tex. C. of C., So. Meth. U. Alumni Assn., Hockaday Dads Club, U.S. Naval Inst., SAR (pres. Tyler chpt., registrar Tex. soc., bd. mgrs.), Lambda Chi Alpha, Pi Upsilon Nu. Author: Adventuring Abroad on a Bicycle and $180, 1938; Marinas: A Boon to Yachting, 1948. Home: 2924 Sunnybrook Dr Tyler TX 75701 Office: PO Box 7402 Tyler TX 75711

HUNTER, LELAND CLAIR, JR., utility executive; b. Phila., Feb. 22, 1925; s. Leland Clair and Lillian Mae (Failor) H.; B.S., Villanova U., 1948; postgrad. Columbia U., 1944-45; M.B.A., Fla. Research Inst., 1971; grad. Advanced Mgmt. Program, Harvard U., 1973; m. Elva Joy Charlton, July 5, 1946; children—Charlton Lee, Steven Kent, Brian Scott, Donna Joy. Test engr. Gen. Electric Co., Phila., 1949-50; with Fla. Power & Light Co., 1950—, v.p. indsl. relations, Miami, 1966-72, v.p. transmission and distbn., 1972-73, group v.p., 1973—, sr. v.p., 1978—; mem. spl. labor com. Sec. of Labor U.S., 1975-76; mem. Labor and Mgmt. Polit. Action Com. for Utility Industry, 1977, Gov.'s Adv. Council Productivity, 1981—. Vice chmn. adv. com. Dade County (Fla.) Sch. Bd., 1966; bd. govs. Gold Coast AAU, 1967-68; bd. dirs. Crime Commn. of Greater Miami, 1974—, Fla. Lawyers Prepaid Legal Services Inc., 1980—; chmn. bd. Victoria Hosp., 1984—; mem. bus. adv. com. Brookings Instn., Washington, 1983; adv. bd. Stetson U., 1982; exec. v.p. Atlantic Gamefish Found., 1982. Served with USN, 1943-46. Recipient Key to City, Toledo and Coral Gables Fla.). Mem. Am. Soc. Tng. Dirs. (pres. local chpt. 1955-56). Clubs: Fla. Athletic (pres. 1962); Coral Gables (Fla.) Country; Univ. (Miami); Univ. (Jacksonville, Fla.). Home: 5577 SW 100 St Miami FL 33156 Office: PO Box 029100 Miami FL 33102

HUNTER, MATTHEW CHARLES, pharmaceutical chemist, consultant; b. Greenville, Ohio, May 8, 1922; s. Matthew Charles and Catherine (Foody) H.; m. Barbara Bell, June 13, 1948; children—Katherine, Elizabeth, Matthew. B.S. La. Coll., Pineville, 1943; M.S., La. State U., 1945; Ph.D. in Microbiology and Biochemistry, Ohio State U., 1949. Sr. research microbiologist Smith, Kline & French Labs., Inc., Phila., 1949-51; research microbiologist, devel. engr. Monsanto Chem. Co., St. Louis, 1951-53; pres. Hunter Labs., Inc., New Orleans, 1953-61; assoc. prof. med. tech., prof. Dental Coll., Grad. Sch., Loyola U. South, New Orleans, 1954-55; head quality control labs., research labs., prodn. dept. Carrtone Labs., Inc., Metairie, La., 1958-61; research assoc., product mgr. pharms., dir. small animal mktg. Diamond Labs., Inc., Des Moines, 1961-66; v.p. corp., pres. labs. Hart-Delta, Inc., Delta Labs., Inc., Baton Rouge, La., 1966-69; owner Chemage Co., Bay St. Louis, Miss., 1969-72; v.p. sci. Medico Industries, Inc., Elwood, Kans., 1972-75; pres. Technel, Inc., Waveland, Miss., 1975—; cons. new product devel. Vice pres. Jefferson Democratic Assn., 1956; pres. Council Civic Orgns. Greater New Orleans, 1955, Bridgedale Civic Assn., 1954-55. La. State U. teaching fellow, 1944-45. Mem. Am. Soc. Microbiology, Am. Pharm. Assn., AAAS, Am. Mgmt. Assn., Am. Pub. Health Assn., Tissue Culture Soc., Sigma Xi, Beta Beta Beta, others. Club: Bay-Waveland Yacht. Lodge: Rotary. Contbr. articles to profl. publs. Home: 436 Waveland Ave Waveland MS 39576

HUNTER, MIRIAM EILEEN, artist, educator; b. Cin., June 6, 1929; d. James R. and Bertha (Oberlin) H. B.S., Ball State U., 1951, M.A. in Art, 1957; M.A. in Christian Edn., Wheaton Coll., 1958; Ed.D., Nova U., 1979. Tchr. art and English, Madison-Marion Consol. Schs., 1951-52; tchr. art Wheaton Coll., Ill., 1952-84, chair art dept., 1969-70, 75-79; asst. prof. art Fine Arts Gallery, Chgo., then assoc. prof., 1971-84; dir. Sch. Edn., Calvin Simmons Coll., Lawrenceville, Ga., 1984—; freelance art cons.; broker First Am. Nat. Securities Corp., 1982—; div. mgr. A.L. Williams Corp., Chgo. and Lilburn, Ga., 1982—. Vol., Cook County Hosp., Chgo., 1955-58; mem. Wheaton Human Relations Orgn., 1965-67. Recipient Ingersol award for painting, 1946, 47; 2d place award DuPage Sesquicentennial, 1968; Outstanding Alumnus award Ball State U., 1975. Mem. Nat. Assn. Securities Dealers, Ill. Art Edn. Assn., Nat. Soc. Lit. and the Arts, Art Inst. Chgo., Delta Phi Delta, Sigma Tau Delta, Kappa Delta Pi. Home: 8725 Lake Dr Lithonia GA 30058

HUNTER, RICHARD EDMUND, plant pathologist; b. Jersey City, Jan. 26, 1923; s. Frederick William and Margaret (Dahlgren) H.; B.S., Rutgers U., 1949; M.S., Okla. State U., 1951, Ph.D., 1968; m. Edith Earline Clark, June 2, 1946; children—Catherine Hunter Hays, Margaret Ann Hunter Adamson, Richard Clark. Asst. in biology N.Mex. State U., State College, 1951-55; instr., research plant pathologist Okla. State U., Stillwater, 1958-68, asst. prof., 1968-71, asso. prof., 1971-72; research plant pathologist Nat. Cotton Pathology Research Lab., College Station, Tex., 1972-75; research plant pathologist Southeast Fruit and Tree Nut Lab., Byron, Ga., 1975-79, research leader Nut Prodn. unit, 1976-79, supervisory research plant pathologist, research leader, location leader W.R. Poage Pecan Field Sta., Brownwood, Tex., 1979—. Served to capt. USAAF, 1943-46. Mem. Am. Phytopath. Soc., Am. Soc. Hort. Scientists, Internat. Soc. Plant Pathologists, Southeast Pecan Growers Assn., No. Nut Growers Assn., Alpha Zeta, Phi Sigma, Sigma Xi. Methodist. Contbr. articles to various jours.; Southeastern regional editor Pecan Quar., 1977-79. Home: 3903 Glenwood Dr Brownwood TX 76801 Office: WR Poage Pecan Field St 701 Woodson Rd Brownwood TX 76801

HUNTER, ROY, JR., medical school administrator, embryologist; b. Birmingham, Ala., Jan. 7, 1930; s. Roy and Pearl (Walker) H.; m. Julie Ann Varner, Nov. 20, 1965; 1 dau., Judith Marlene Hunter Boozer. B.S., Morehouse Coll., 1950; M.S., Atlanta U., 1953; Ph.D., Brown U., 1962; cert. in embryology Marine Biol. Lab., 1958. From asst. prof. to assoc. prof. biology Morehouse Coll., Atlanta, 1961-64; assoc. prof. biology Atlanta U., 1964-68, prof. biology, 1968-70; chmn., prof. biology Morgan State U., Balt., 1970-73; prof. biology Atlanta U., 1973-81, chmn. dept., 1976-79; dir. fellows program Morehouse Sch. Medicine, Atlanta, 1982—, Trustee Atlanta Zool. Soc., 1981-84; v.p. bd. dirs. Atlanta Council Internat. Programs, 1982—. Postdoctoral fellow So. Fellowships Fund, 1981-82; NSF fellow, 1957-58. Mem. Soc. Tech. Communications, Am. Soc. Zoologists, Soc. Devel. Biology, Ga. Acad. Sci., N.Y. Acad. Scis., Assn. Southeastern Biologists, Nat. Inst. Sci., Sigma Xi, Beta Kappa Chi. Democrat. Baptist. Contbr. articles to profl. jours.

HUNTER, SUE PERSONS, law enforcement administrator; b. Hico, Tex., Aug. 21, 1921; d. David Henry and Beulah (Boatwright) Persons; m. Charles Force Hunter; children—Shelley Hunter Richardson, Mary Hunter McCullough, Margaret Hunter Brown. B.A., U. Tex., 1942. Air traffic controller CAA (now FAA), San Antonio and Houston, 1942-52; writer Bissonet Plaza News, 1969-72; coordinator Goals for La., 1971-74; adminstrv. dir. Jeff Publs., Inc.; contbg. editor The Jeffersonian, 1975; communications coordinator Jefferson Parish Dist. Atty., 1974-78, adminstr. child support enforcement div., 1979-85. Pres. United Ch. Women East Jefferson (La.), 1958-59, LWV Jefferson Parish, La., 1961-64; pres. LWV La., 1967-71, bd. dirs., 1962-67; mem. probation services com. Community Services Council, Jefferson, 1966-73, v.p., 1970-72; mem. Library Devel. Com. La., 1967-71, Nat. Com. Support of Pub. Schs., 1967-72; mem. Goals Found. Council Met. New Orleans, 1969-75, sec., 1970, 72; mem. Goals La. Task Force State and Local Govt., 1969-70; pres. MMM Investment Club, 1969-72; bd. mem. New Orleans Area Health Planning Council, 1969-75; adv. council La. State Health Planning, 1971-75, La. Commn. Status of Women, 1971-72, La. Consumer Council, 1971-72; mem. La. Citizens Ednl. Found. Criminal Justice, 1973-76, Council Internat. Visitors, 1962—; title I adv. council La. State Dept. Edn., 1970-72; adv. bd. Muscular Dystrophy Assn. New Orleans, 1975-77; chmn. Jefferson Women's Polit. Caucus, 1979-80; bd. dirs. New Orleans Area/Bayou River Health Systems Agy., 1978-82, pres., 1980-81; bd. dirs. La. Child Support Enforcement Assn., 1980—, pres., 1982, 83; mem. Task Force La. Talent Bank of Women, 1979-81, La. State Health Coordinating Council, 1980-83, Gov.'s Commn. on Child support Enforcement, 1984—; bd. dirs. Nat. Child Support Enforcement Assn., 1983—, legis. chmn., 1984; bd. dirs. Friends of Westminster Tower, 1986—. Recipient Outstanding Citizens award Rotary Club, Metairie, La., 1962; River Ridge award, 1976. Mem. New Orleans Panhellenic Assn. (pres. 1956-57), Am. Assn. Individual investors (pres. New Orleans chpt. 1986—), Alpha Xi Delta. Presbyterian (elder). Home: 210 Stewart Ave River Ridge LA 70123

HUNTLEY, PATRICK ROSS, economic educator, research consultant; b. Newton, Kans., Jan. 7, 1924; s. George Donald and Verna Grace (Daves) H.; m. Margaret Elizabeth Mullis, Dec. 9, 1945; 1 child, Mikel. B.A., Washburn U., 1951; M.A., U. N.C., 1956, Ph.D., 1961. Sr. research economist U.S. Dept. Commerce, Washington, 1961-64; assoc. prof. George Washington U., Washington, 1964-66; div. dir. Ctr. for Naval Analyses, Arlington, Va., 1966-69; prof. quantitative analysis U. Ark., Fayetteville, 1968—; v.p. Attys. Econ. Cons., Little Rock, 1982—; in-house cons. U.S. Treasury, Washington, 1972; prin. sr. cons. U.S. Gen. Service Adminstrn., Washington, 1976-77. Contbr. articles to profl. jours. Fellow U.S. Bur. Census, 1960-61. Mem. Am. Inst. Decision Sci. (v.p. 1969-70), Am. Econ. Assn., Am. Statistics Assn., So. Econ. Assn., Soc. Govtl. Economists, Pi Gamma Mu, Phi Kappa Gamma. Republican. Avocations: sporting activities research. Home: 1219 W Lakeridge Dr Fayetteville AR 72703 Office: U Ark Fayetteville AR 72701

HUPFELD, STANLEY FRANCIS, health care executive; b. Balt., July 18, 1944; s. Stanley Francis and Dorothy (Heibler) H.; m. Suzanne Dunne, July 20, 1968; children—Matthew, Kelly, Kate. B.A., U. Tex., Austin, 1966; M.S., Trinity U., San Antonio, 1972. Asst. adminstr. Providence Meml. Hosp., El Paso, Tex., 1972-73; pres. St. Joseph's Hosp., El Paso, 1973-77; pres. All Saints Hosp., Ft. Worth, 1977—; trustee Tex. Hosp. Assn., 1983-88; chmn. Dallas/Ft. Worth Hosp. Council, 1980-81. Campaign chmn. Tarrant County United Way, Ft. Worth, 1988; dir. Interfirst Bank Univ., Ft. Worth, 1988. Served to 1st lt. U.S. Army, 1968-70. Recipient Dean Duce award Trinity U. Health Care Alumni Assn., 1980-81. Fellow Am. Coll. Hosp. Execs. Lodge: Rotary (dir. 1984-86). Home: 5312 Benbridge Rd Fort Worth TX 76107 Office: All Saints Episcopal Hosp 1400 Eighth Ave Fort Worth TX 76101

HUPP, HAROLD DEAN, animal scientist; b. Akron, June 12, 1948; s. Hubert Denzle and Martha Mae (Ogan) H.; m. Laura Rose Smolenski, Oct. 21, 1978; children—Benjamin, Matthew, Andrea. B.S., Wilmington Coll. (Ohio), 1971; M.S., U. Ky., 1973; Ph.D., Va. Poly. Inst. and State U., 1977. Research animal scientist V.I. Agrl. Expt. Sta., St. Croix, 1977—; extension livestock specialist V.I. Coop. Extension Service, St. Croix, 1979—; asst. dir. Agrl. Expt. Sta., St. Croix, 1980—; coordinator agr. degree Coll. of V.I., 1978-81. Mem. Am. Soc. Animal Sci., Genetics Soc. Am., Am. Genetics Assn., Sigma Xi. Contbr. articles to profl. jours. Home: Rural Route 2 Box 10005 Kingshill St Croix VI 00850

HURLBURT, HARLEY ERNEST, oceanographer; b. Bennington, Vt., Apr. 12, 1943; s. Paul Rhodes and Evelyn Arlene (Lockhart) H.; B.S. in Physics (scholar), Union Coll., Schenectady, 1965; M.S., Fla. State U., 1971, Ph.D. in Meteorology, 1974. NASA trainee Fla. State U., 1970-72; postdoctoral fellow advanced studies program Nat. Center Atmospheric Research, Boulder, Colo., 1974-75; staff scientist JAYCOR, Alexandria, Va., 1975-77; oceanographer Naval Ocean Research and Devel. Activity, Bay St. Louis, Miss., 1977—, br. head, 1983-85. Vice pres. Burgundy Citizens Assn., 1976-77. Recipient Disting. Scientist medal 13th Internat. Colloquium, Liege, Belgium, 1981, publ. award for best basic research paper Naval Ocean Research and Devel. Activity, 1980; Office Naval Research grantee, 1975-77; Dept. Energy grantee, 1975-78; Tex. A&M U. grantee, 1976. Mem. Am. Meteorol. Soc., Sigma Xi, Sigma Tau, Chi Epsilon Pi. Methodist. Contbr. articles to sci. jours. Home: 274 Hermitage Ct Pearl River LA 70452 Office: Naval Ocean Research and Devel Activity Code 323 Bldg 1100 Nat Space Tech Lab MS 39529

HURLBUT, ELVIN MILLARD, JR., petroleum geologist, former technical editor; b. El Campo, Tex., Dec. 4, 1921; s. Elvin Millard and Iva Sarepta Marie (Leech) H.; m. Virginia Lee Andrews, Nov. 21, 1950. B.S. in Geology, U. Tex., 1943; M.A. in Geology, U. Calif.-Berkeley, 1948. Tech. writer, data retrieval specialist Fed. Electric Corp., Houston, 1969-71; tech. writer, data retrieval specialist, tech. editor Service Tech. Corp., Houston, 1971-72; engr., publs. engr. Lockheed Electronics Co., Inc., Houston, 1972-74; tech. editor Kentron Internat., Inc., Houston, 1974-83, Omniplan Corp., Houston, 1983-85. Charter mem. Republican Presdl. Task Force, 1984—; contbr. Nat. Rep. Senatorial Com., 1984—, Nat. Rep. Congl. Com. Recipient Merit medal Rep. Presdl. Task Force, 1984. Mem. Am. Assn. Petroleum Geologists, Soc. Econ. Paleontologists and Mineralogists, Soc. Tech. Communication (sr. mem.), Assn. Earth Sci. Editors, N.Y. Acad. of Scis. Mem. Disciples of Christ Ch. Avocations: music; movies; reading; economics.

HURLBUT, FLOYD WAYNE, wholesale electrical supply company executive; b. Jennings, La., Sept. 21, 1939; s. Virgil Floyd and Nettie (Myers) H.; B.S. in Acctg., La. State U., 1970; M.B.A., So. Ill. U., 1974; m. Nancy Bernhardt, Sept. 4, 1965; children—Nicole, Steven Floyd. Region cost and budget analyst Internat. Paper Co., Georgetown, S.C., 1974-75, sr. fin. analyst, N.Y.C., 1975-76, corp. project mgmt. cons., 1976-77; asst. group controller internat. group Ethyl Corp., Baton Rouge, 1977-79; ptnr. Franklin-Hurlbut, Lafayette, La., 1979-80; v.p. fin., sec.-treas., dir. Aamwell Workover Service, Inc., Lafayette, 1980-82; chmn. bd., v.p. fin. Aalpha Exploration Co., 1981-83; gen. partner BEMLARS Mineral Interests, Ltd., 1981-84; v.p., gen. mgr. Carlberg Supply, Inc., Lafayette and Lake Charles, 1981—; instr. Internat. Paper Co. Bus. Mgmt. Sch. Scoutmaster troup Boy Scouts Am., Lafayette. Served with USMC, 1961-67. Decorated Air medal with oak leaf cluster. Mem. Nat. Assn. Accts. (named Most Valuable Mem. Charleston, S.C. chpt. 1972, founder, past pres. Acadiana chpt.), Jaycees (v.p. Georgetown chpt. 1974). Methodist. Home: PO Box 6888 Lake Charles LA 70606 Office: 206 W 11th St Lake Charles LA 70601

HURLEY, ALFRED FRANCIS, university chancellor, administrator, historian; b. Bklyn., Oct. 16, 1928; s. Patrick Francis and Margaret T. (Coakley) H.; B.A., St. John's U., 1950; M.A., Princeton U., 1958, Ph.D., 1961; m. Joanna H. Leahy, Jan. 24, 1953; children—Alfred Francis, Thomas J., Mark P., Claire T., John K. Enlisted in USAF, 1950, Commd. 2d lt., 1952, advanced through grades to col., ret. as brig. gen., 1980; served in flying, tng. and planning assignments, Tex., N.C., Ger., Washington, 1952-56, 63-66; mem. faculty U.S. Air Force Acad., Colo., 1958-63, 66-80; v.p. adminstrv. affairs, mem. faculty North Tex. State U., Denton, 1980—, chancellor, 1982—; chancellor Tex. Coll. Osteo. Medicine, Ft. Worth, 1982—. Trustee, Am. Mil. Inst., 1973-77, 1980-84; dir. Am. Com., History World War II, 1976—. Decorated Legion of Merit with oak leaf cluster; Guggenheim fellow, 1971-72; Smithsonian fellow, 1976-77. Mem. Am. Hist. Assn., Orgn. Am. Historians, Air Force Assn. Roman Catholic. Author: Billy Mitchell: Crusader for Air Power; editor: (with Robert Ehrhart) Air Power and Warfare: Procs. 8th Air Force Acad. Mil. History Symposium, 1979. Home: 828 Skylark Denton TX 76205 Office: North Tex State Univ Denton TX 76203

HURLEY, FRANK THOMAS, JR., Realtor; b. Washington, Oct. 18, 1924; s. Frank Thomas and Lucille (Trent) H.; A.A., St. Petersburg Jr. Coll., 1948; B.A., U. Fla., 1950. Reporter, St. Petersburg (Fla.) Evening Ind., 1948-53; editor Arcadia (Calif.) Tribune, 1956-57; reporter Los Angeles Herald Express, 1957; v.p. Frank T. Hurley Assos., Inc. Realtors, 1958-64, pres., 1964—; sec., dir. Beau Monde, Inc., 1977-79. Mem. St. Petersburg Beach Bd. Commrs., 1965-69; candidate Fla. Ho. of Reps., 1966; chmn. Pinellas County Traffic Safety Council, 1968-69; pres. Pass-A-Grille Community Assn., 1963, Gulf Beach Bd. Realtors, 1969; mem. St. Petersburg Mus. Fine Arts; mem. governing bd. Palms of Pasadena Hosp., 1979—. Served with USAAF, 1943-46. Recipient Citizen of Yr. award St. Petersburg Beach C. of C., 1983. Mem. Fla. Assn. Realtors (dist. v.p. 1971), Vina del Mar Island Assn., Am. Legion, St. Petersburg Beach C. of C. (pres. 1975-76), Sigma Delta Chi, Sigma Tau Delta. Author: Surf, Sand and Post Card Sunsets, 1977. Home: 2808 Sunset Way Saint Petersburg Beach FL 33706 Office: 2506 Pass-A-Grille Way Saint Petersburg Beach FL 33706

HURLEY, ROBERT JOSEPH, oil executive; b. Chgo., May 21, 1932; s. Michael James and Dorothy Elizabeth (Pries) H.; m. Emily Costello, Sept. 14, 1957; children—Brenda, Nancy, Robert, Christopher, Michael, Matthew. B.S., St. Benedict's Coll., 1953; J.D., Loyola U., 1962. Bar: Ill. 1963, Okla. 66, Tex. 75. Acct. mgr. Shell Oil Co., Chgo., 1958-64, atty., Tulsa, 1965-69, Chgo., 1970-72, Houston, 1972-77; sr. group counsel N L Industries, Houston, 1978-82, v.p., gen. counsel, 1983—; mem. oil and gas adv. bd. Southwestern Legal Found. Served with U.S. Army, 1954-55. Mem. Ill. Bar Assn., Okla. Bar Assn., Tex. Bar Assn., ABA, Am. Corp. Counsel Assn. (dir. Houston chpt.). Club: University (Houston). Office: N L Industries 3000 North Belt E Houston TX 77032

HURST, ERNEST CONNOR, lawyer; b. Lexington, Tex., Sept. 27, 1926; s. Ernest V. and Grace E. (King) H.; m. Barbara Ann Hurst, Oct. 19, 1951; 1 dau., Susan D. Hurst Hensley. Student Sam Houston State U., 1946-48; J.D. with honors, U. Tex.-Austin, 1951. Bar: Tex. 1950, U.S. Dist. Ct. (so. dist.) Tex. 1956, U.S. Ct. Appeals (5th cir.) 1969. Assoc. Liddell, Austin, Dawson & Huggins, Houston, 1951-57; sr. ptnr. Caldwell & Hurst, Houston, 1958—; corp. sec. Adams Resources & Energy, Inc., KSA Industries, Inc. Served with USN, 1944-46. Mem. Houston Bar Assn., Tex. Bar Assn., Am. Judicature Soc., Phi Delta Phi. Republican. Methodist. Student editor Tex. Law Rev., 1950-51.

HURST, JOHN EMORY, JR., airline executive; b. Phoenix, Feb. 9, 1928; s. John Emory and Katherine Ann (Prechtel) H.; B.S., U.S. Mil. Acad., 1950; M.S., U. Ill., 1956; M.A., Columbia U., 1960; m. Sara Bland Waugh; children—Craig Kenton, Susan Marie, John Jeffrey. Commd. 2d lt. U.S. Army, 1950, advanced through grades to col., 1969; served in Korea, France, Vietnam; mem. army staff Pentagon; ret., 1971; v.p. facilities Eastern Airlines, Miami, Fla., 1971-75, v.p. properties and facilities, 1975-76, v.p. tech. support services, 1976-77, sr. v.p., 1977—. Decorated Legion of Merit, Air medal, Bronze Star. Mem. ASCE. Republican. Episcopalian. Clubs: Kiwanis, Masons. Office: Eastern Airlines Miami Internat Airport Miami FL 33148

HURST, MICHAEL EDWARD, restaurant executive, educator; b. Milw., July 8, 1931; s. Leslie Mark and Jean (Devlin) H.; B.A. magna cum laude, Mich. State U., 1953, M.A., 1954; postgrad. Am. U., 1956-59; m. Ann Loraine Bangerter, Feb. 25, 1955; children—Christopher, Catherine, Martha, Eleanor, Andrew. Asst. to 1st v.p. Marriott Corp., Washington, 1956-59; exec. v.p. Win Schuler's, Inc., Marshall, Mich., 1959-69; instr. Sch. Hotel and Restaurant Mgmt., Mich. State U., East Lansing, 1959-69; pres. Don the Beachcomber, Pacific Palisades, Calif., 1970-72; v.p., gen. mgr., founding partner Marina Bay Hotel & Club, Miami, Fla., 1972-79; prof. Sch. Hospitality Mgmt., Fla. Internat. U., Miami, 1972—; owner 15th St. Fisheries Restaurant, Fort Lauderdale, 1980—; dir. Mr. Steak, Inc., Denver, 1972-80; cons., speaker in field; mem. Governor's Council on Tourism, State of Fla., 1977-81. Served with Q.M.C., U.S. Army, 1954-56. Mem. Nat. Restaurant Assn. (dir., chmn. strategic planning coms.), Fla. Restaurant Assn. (dir.), Nat. Inst. Foodservice Industry (dir. 1984—), Fla. Internat. Univ. Faculty. Republican. Roman Catholic. Club: Marina Bay. Contbr. articles in field to profl. jours. Home: 890 Renmar Dr Plantation FL 33317 Office: 1900 SE 15th St Fort Lauderdale FL 33316

HURST, ROBERT EVAN, biochemist, educator; b. Orlando, Fla., May 10, 1944; s. Coy Franklin and Anita Katherine (Davis) H.; m. Jean McKenzie, Sept. 6, 1964; children—Tanya Elaine, Eric Jason. B.S. in Chemistry, Auburn U., 1965; Ph.D. in Biochemistry, Fla. State U., 1969. Asst. chief clin. chemistry, Walter Reed Gen. Hosp., Washington, 1969-72; asst. prof. engring. biophysics and biochemistry U. Ala.-Birmingham, 1972-78, assoc. prof. environ. health scis., biochemistry and chemistry, 1979-83; prof. urology, biochemistry and environ. health, U. Okla., 1983—, dir. div. biol. monitoring Program for Coop. Indsl. Biomed. Research. Active various civic orgns.; mem. exec. bd. Edgewater Neighborhood Assn.; mem. citizens adv. com.; pres. Assn. Responsible Growth. Served to capt. M.S.C., U.S. Army, 1969-72. NIH research grantee, 1974-77, 79-84, 83-87. Mem. AAAS, Am. Chem. Soc., Am. Heart Assn., Am. Pub. Health Assn., Soc. for Complex Carbohydrates, Sigma Xi. Contbr. articles to profl. jours. Office: Dept Urology U Okla Ctr for Health Scis PO Box 26901 Oklahoma City OK 73190

HURT, FRANK BENJAMIN, emeritus educator, banker; b. Ferrum, Va., Oct. 22, 1899; s. John Kempleton and Lelia (Angle) H.; A.B., Washington and Lee U., 1923; M.A., U. Va., 1925; A.M., Princeton U., 1926; postgrad. Johns Hopkins, 1929-30, Harvard, summers 1938-40; H.H.D. (hon.), Ferrum Coll., 1982; m. Mary Ann Wescott, June 3, 1943. Teaching fellow U. N.C., 1926-27; instr. Ferrum Coll., 1927-29; asso. prof. polit. sci. Western Md. Coll., 1930-65, prof. emeritus, 1965—, head div. polit. sci., 1949; head div. social sci. Ferrum Jr. Coll., 1965—, prof. emeritus, 1970—, trustee 1983—; lectr. sch. spl. and continuation studies U. Md., 1950-65; instr. summers Hun Sch., Princeton, 1927-32; dir. First Nat. Bank, Ferrum, v.p., 1977—. Trustee, Longwood Coll. Found., 1976—. Mem. Am. Polit. Sci. Assn., Am. Hist. Assn., Am. Acad. Polit. and Social Sci., Nat. Collegiate Fgn. Lang. Soc., Franklin County Hist. Soc. (pres. 1969-70), AAUP, Pi Gamma Mu, Phi Theta Kappa. Democrat.

Methodist. Lion (pres. Ferrum 1968). Author: History of Ferrum College, 1975; The Heritage of the German Element in Franklin County, Virginia in the Eighteenth Century. Address: Ferrum Coll Ferrum VA 24088

HURT, HARRY, III, editor, author; b. Houston, Nov. 13, 1951; s. Harry and Margaret Regina (Bitting) H. B.A. magna cum laude, Harvard U., 1974. Freelance writer various mags., 1974-77; assoc. editor Tex. Monthly, Houston, 1977-82, sr. editor, 1982—; script writer ABC Byline, 1980. Author: Texas Rich: The Hunt Dynasty From the Early Oil Days Through the Silver Crash, 1981. Contbr. articles to Playboy, Boston Herald Examiner, Oui, New Orleans Mags. Recipient Frank Kelly award Am. Assn. Petroleum Landmen, 1981, Anson Jones award for med. writing, 1982. Mem. Tex. Inst. Letters. Club: Tejas Breakfast, Met. Racquet. Office: 4600 Post Oak Pl Suite 306 Houston TX 77027

HURT, WILLIAM CLARENCE, dental educator; b. Waynesboro, Miss., Oct. 11, 1922; s. Walter Harvey and Rose (Green) H.; m. Elizabeth Cain, Nov. 24, 1943; children—William Rollins, Duane Forrest, John Nesbitt, Stephen Michael. Student U. Miss., 1940-42; D.D.S., Loyola U.-New Orleans, 1944-47. Diplomate Am. Bd. Periodontology, Am. Bd. Oral Medicine. Residency in periodontics Walter Reed Army Hosp., Washington, 1957-58; officer Dental Corps, U.S. Army, advanced through grades to col.; ret., 1969; prof. periodontics U. Tex. Dental Br., Houston, 1969-72; prof., chmn. dept. periodontics Baylor Coll. Dentistry, Dallas, 1972—; cons. U.S. Army, 1970-80. Editor: Periodontics in General Practice, 1976, Jour. Periodontology. Co-editor Current Therapy in Dentistry, 1980. Contbr. articles to profl. Decorated Legion of Merit, Outstanding Civilian Service medal. Fellow Am. Coll. Dentists, Am. Acad. Oral Pathology, Am. Acad. Periodontology; mem. ADA. Republican. Episcopalian. Home: 1616 Park St Greenville TX 75401 Office: Baylor Coll of Dentistry 3302 Gaston Ave Dallas TX 75246

HUSK, G. RONALD, chemist, researcher; b. Waynesburg, Pa., Oct. 19, 1937; s. Woodrow W. and Freda (Wells) H. B.S. summa cum laude, Waynesburg Coll., 1959; M.S. in Chemistry, U. Mich., 1964, Ph.D., 1964. Research assoc. U. Wis.-Madison, 1964-66; asst. prof. Villanova U., Pa., 1966-71; chief organic chemistry br. Army Research Office, Durham, N.C., 1971-73; chief chemistry br. U.S. Army European Research Office, London, U.K., 1973-77; chief organic and polymer chemistry br. Army Research Office, Research Triangle Park, N.C., 1977—; vis. research adj. prof. U. N.C.-Chapel Hill, 1977-84; sec. Army Fellowship, 1984-85; vis. scientist U. Tex.-Austin, 1984-86; adj. prof. Southwest Tex. State U., 1984-86; scientist in residence Durham Sch. System, 1982-83. Mem. Am. Chem. Soc., AAAS, Am. Inst. Chemists, Sigma Xi. Contbg. author scientic publs. Home: 5419 Revere Rd Durham NC 27713 Office: US Army Research Office PO Box 12211 Research Triangle Park NC 27709

HUSSEY, JOHN B., mayor. Mayor of Shreveport, La. Office: PO Box 31109 Shreveport LA 71130*

HUSSEY, ROBERT JONES, cotton factor; b. Memphis, Sept. 25, 1904; s. Clarance Wellington and Neva (Jones) H.; m. Kathleen Conant; children—Robert Jones, Richard Wellington, Edwin Conant. LL.B., U. Ala., 1962. Cotton factor, Memphis; pres. Memphis Cotton Exchange, 1946-65. Trustee Memphis U. Sch. Mfg., 1965; chmn. bd. trustees Presbyterian Day Sch., Memphis, 1955; elder Ind. Presbyn. Ch., Memphis, 1972—. Republican. Clubs: Memphis Country, U. Ala. A. Home: 337 Inkberry Ln Memphis TN 38117

HUSSUNG, MELVIN VERN, JR., company executive; b. Nashville, Apr. 6, 1943; s. Melvin Vern and Elizabeth Anne (Lawrence) H.; m. Raleigh McDonald, Mar. 12, 1963; children—Melvin Vern III, Michael Lawrence, John Mills. B.A., Vanderbilt U., 1965. Vice pres. Winners Corp., Brentwood, Tenn., 1974-76, sr. v.p. 1979-80, pres. chief exec. officer, 1980—, also dir., pres. Wendy's of S.C. subs. Winners, Greenville, 1976-79; dir. Nashville City Bank. Bd. dirs. United Way Nashville. Mem. Nat. Restaurant Assn., Am. Mgmt. Assn., Nat. Assn. Investment Clubs, Nashville Area C. of C., Nat. Fedn. Ind. Business, Chaine de Rotisseurs. Republican. Roman Catholic. Clubs: Richland Country (Nashville); Maryland Farms (Brentwood). Lodge: Rotary. Avocations: golf; boating; racquetball; water skiing. Office: Winners Corp 101 Winners Circle Brentwood TN 37027

HUSTON, DANIEL CLIFF, geophysics researcher; b. Anchorage, June 29, 1955; s. Arthur Cliff and Allie Mae (Ogdon) H. B.S. in Geology and Geophysics, U. Hawaii, 1980; postgrad. U. Tex., 1983—. Surveyor Trans Alaska Pipeline, 1975-78; geologist R & M Cons., Anchorage, 1980; geophysicist U.S. Minerals Mgmt. Service, Anchorage, 1981-83; research asst. U. Tex. Inst. for Geophysics, Austin, 1983-84, Project S.E.E.R., Austin, 1984—; geophys. intern Sohio Petroleum Co., San Francisco, summer 1984; research asst. Miss. Canyon Project, Austin, 1983-84. Presenter: Deconvolution in Practice, 1984. Recipient Marine Option Program cert. U. Hawaii, 1980; Indsl. Assocs. of U. Tex. fellow, 1983; Winner Best Speaker award. Mem. Soc. Exploration Geophysicists (presenter workshop 1984), Am. Assn. Petroleum Geologists. Methodist. Avocations: travel; scuba diving; skiing; lifting weights; reading history.

HUSTON, NANCY ELIZABETH, educator, civic worker; b. N.Y.C., July 13, 1947; d. Cord Henry and Catherine Frances (Nahrwold) Sump; m. Rea Askew Huston, June 22, 1974; 1 child, Mary Catherine. A.B. with honors in Spanish, U. Chattanooga, 1969; M.A., U. Ga., 1971. Cert. tchr., N.C., Tenn. Chmn. fgn. lang. dept. Hixson Jr. High Sch., Tenn., 1970-74, tchr. Spanish, French and music, 1975-78; tchr. Spanish, Charlotte Mecklenburg Schs., N.C., 1975; substitute tchr. Hamilton County Schs., Snow Hill Elem. Sch., Chattanooga, 1983—, chmn. living curriculum conf. fgn. lang. sect., 1971-72. Singer Chattanooga Opera Chorus, 1966-67; chmn. pub. relations and fund drive Cystic Fibrosis Assn., Harrison, Tenn., 1981-82; scrapbook chmn. Hickory Valley Garden Club, Chattanooga, 1982—. Ford Found. fellow U. Ga., 1969-71. Mem. Sigma Delta Pi, Chi Omega. Presbyterian. Avocations: counted cross stitch; piano; hiking; sewing; teaching young peoples' choir. Home: 7637 Morgan Estate Rd Ooltewah TN 37363

HUSZAGH, FREDRICK WICKETT, law educator, information management company executive, lawyer; b. Evanston, Ill., July 20, 1937; s. Rudolph LeRoy and Dorothea (Wickett) H.; m. Sandra McRae, Apr. 4, 1959; children—Floyd McRae, Fredrick Wickett II, Theodore Wickett II. B.A., Northwestern U., 1958; J.D., U. Chgo., 1962, LL.M., 1963, J.S.D., 1964. Bar: Ill. 1962, U.S. Dist. Ct. D.C. 1965, U.S. Supreme Ct. 1966. Market researcher Leo Burnett Co. Chgo., 1958-59; internat. atty. COMSAT, Washington, 1964-67; assoc. Debevoise & Liberman, Washington, 1967-68; asst. prof. law Am. U., Washington, 1968-71; program dir. NSF, Washington, 1971-73; assoc. prof. U. Mont., Missoula, 1973-76, U. Wis.-Madison, 1976-77; exec. dir. Dean Rusk Ctr., U. Ga., Athens, 1977-82; prof. U. Ga., 1977—; chmn. TWH Corp., Athens, 1982—; cons. Pres. Johnson's Telcommunications Task Force, Washington, 1967-68; co-chmn. Nat. Gov.'s Internat. Trade Staff Commn., Washington, 1979- 81. Author: International Decision-Making Process, 1964; Comparative Facts on Canada, Mexico and U.S., 1979; also articles. Editor Rusk Ctr. Briefings, 1981-82. Mem. Econ. Policy Council, N.Y.C., 1981—. NSF grantee, 1974-78. Republican. Presbyterian. Home: 3890 Barnett Shoals Rd Athens GA 30605 Office: U Ga Law Sch Athens GA 30602

HUSZAGH, SANDRA MCRAE, marketing educator; b. Atlanta, Nov. 16, 1937; d. William Floyd and Evelyn Corey (Hamilton) McRae; m. Fredrick Wickett Huszagh, Apr. 4, 1959; children—Floyd McRae, Fredrick Wickett, Theodore Wickett. B.A., Northwestern U., 1959; M.A., Am. U., 1969, Ph.D., 1977; postgrad. Hague Acad. Internat. Law, 1963. Assoc. prof. mktg. U. Ga., Athens, 1977—; co-founder, vice-chmn. TWH Corp.; cons.-reviewer internat. mktg. texts. NSF grantee, 1974-78. Mem. Am. Mktg. Assn., Acad. Internat. Bus., Acad. Mktg. Sci., Phi Sigma Alpha, Phi Gamma Mu, Phi Kappa Phi, Beta Gamma Sigma. Presbyterian. Contbr. chpts. to books, articles to profl. jours. Office: U Ga Brooks Hall Dept Mktg Athens GA 30602

HUTCHENS, EUGENE GARLINGTON, college administrator; b. Birmingham, Ala., Nov. 26, 1929; s. Wallace Luther and Reydonia (Corry) H.; B.A., Samford U., 1952; Th.M., New Orleans Baptist Theol. Sem., 1957; M.S. in Econs., U. Mo.-Columbia, 1972; m. Betty Frances Goode, Aug. 26, 1951; children—Dale Eugene, Wayne Goode, Dennis Wade. Ordained to ministry, 1952; minister N. Brewton Bapt. Ch., Brewton, Ala., 1952-56, 1st Bapt. Ch., Ashland, Ala., 1956-63, Highlands Bapt. Ch., Huntsville, Ala., 1963-67; tchr. public schs., Huntsville, 1967-71; instr. econs. N.W. Ala. State Jr. Coll., 1972-77, acting pres., 1981, dir. Tuscumbia campus N.W. Ala. State Jr. Coll., Tuscumbia, 1977—; mem. Ala. Bapt. State Exec. Bd., 1961-63; v.p. Ala. Bapt. State Pastors Conf., 1966. NSF grantee, 1971-72. Mem. Ala. Edn. Assn., Ala. Jr. and Community Coll. Assn. (exec. com. 1981-84), NEA. Home: 801 E 2d St Tuscumbia AL 35674 Office: 1105 Hwy 72 W Tuscumbia AL 35674

HUTCHENS, JOHN G., food company executive; b. High Point, N.C., Nov. 28, 1928; m. Jane Davis; children—John G., Julie, Jimmy, Cam. B.S., Davidson Coll., 1951; LL.B., U. N.C., 1954, J.D., 1970. Pres. Food World, Inc., Greensboro, N.C., 1974-82, chmn. bd., 1973-74, 82—; sec.-treas., dir. Westwood Devel. Co.; v.p., dir. United Roasters, Inc.; dir. Wachovia Bank & Trust Co. Mem. adv. devel. com. Salvation Army; chmn. orgn. and expansion com. Boy Scouts Am., High Point, 1965-66; mem., past dir. Guilford County Better Bus. Bur.; pres. U.S. Indsl. Council; chmn. Policy Statement Com., High Point Republican party, 1965, 6th Congl. dist., 1970-71; state chmn. Jim Gardner for Gov. Com.; mem. exec. com. Guildford County Rep. Com., 1964-73; mem. state exec. com. and central com. N.C. Rep. Com., 1970-74; dir. N.C. Conservation Union; N.C. fin. chmn. Citizens for Reagan, 1976-80; Southeastern fin. coordinator Regan for Pres., 1980; past deacon, treas., chmn. bd. dirs., elder Forest Hills Presbyn. Ch.; mem. Pres. Adv. Com. on Trade Negotiations, 1982—; civilian aide Sec. of Army, 1982—. Mem. Food Merchandisers Ednl. Council, Super Market Inst., Nat. Assn. Food Chains, ABA, N.C. Bar Assn., High Point Bar Assn., Winston-Salem C. of C., Greenboro C. of C., High Point Mchts. Assn., High Point C. of C. (dir., past chmn. indsl. devel. com.). Office: Food World Inc 200 Distribution Dr Greensboro NC 27410*

HUTCHEON, WALLACE SCHOONMAKER, JR., history educator; b. N.Y.C., June 27, 1933; s. Wallace Schoonmaker and Dorothy Mae (Tate) H.; m. Margaret Marie Crossen, Sept. 29, 1963; children—Dorothy Lee, Hillary Ann. B.S. in Agrl. Econs., Pa. State U., 1954; M.A. in History, George Washington U., 1969, M.Phil. in History, 1971, Ph.D. in History, 1975. Commd. ensign U.S. Naval Res., 1955, advanced through grades to comdr., 1970; communications officer Naval Air Sta., Key West, Fla., 1955-59; edn. officer in USS Kitty Hawk, 1962-64; air intelligence officer CVW-2, 1964-66; intelligence analyst, 1966-70, released to inactive duty, 1970, ret., 1975; lectr. George Mason U., Fairfax, Va., 1970; instr. St. Marys Coll., Md., 1971; asst. prof. history No. Va. Community Coll., Annandale, 1971-75, assoc. prof., 1975-80, prof., 1980—, head dept., 1974—, asst. chmn. div. social scis. and pub. services, 1979—; mgmt. tng. cons. Health Resources Adminstrn., HEW, Hyattsville, Md., 1978; cons. mil. evaluations program Am. Council Edn., Washington, 1980; mem. adv. bd. Annual Editions, Dushkin Pub. Co.; pub. speaker Mariners Mus., D.C. Historians Luncheon, others. Author: Robert Fulton: Pioneer of Undersea Warfare, 1981. Contbr. to manuscripts collection U.S. Navy History Div. Mem. U.S. Naval Inst., Orgn. Am. Historians, No. Va. Assn. Historians, U.S. Capitol Hist. Soc., Delta Chi. Democrat. Episcopalian. Avocations: swimming; reading; music; theatre. Home: 4425 Village Dr Fairfax VA 22030 Office: No Va Community Coll 8333 Little River Turnpike Annandale VA 22003

HUTCHERSON, BARBARA FAYE, office transcription services executive; b. Tyler, Tex., July 4, 1944; d. Alfred and Lorine Isabell Hackett; B.A., U. Nebr., 1966; med. sec. cert. C. E. Sch. Commerce, 1965; IBM keypunch cert. Tyler Comml. Coll., 1968; computer programming cert. Computer Careers Inst., Dallas, 1971. Med. sec. Nebr. Psychiat. Inst., Omaha, 1965-66; stenoclk. No. Natural Gas Co., Omaha, 1965-67, U.S. Atty., Tyler, Tex., 1967-69, VA Hosp., Dallas, 1969-76; grants clk. HEW Office Edn., EEO, 1975-76; fed. women's program mgr./program ops. clk. ACTION, Dallas, 1976-77; legal clk. U.S. Atty., Tyler, Tex., 1977-79; dep. clk. U.S. Dist. Ct., Tyler, Tex., 1979-81, supervising dep. clk., Marshall, Tex., 1981-82; owner, exec. dir. Profl. Office Transcription Services, Dallas, 1982—; instr. Operation LIFT, Dallas, 1975-77. Bd. dirs. East Tex. Opportunities Industrialization Ctr. Mem. Profl. Secs. Internat., Federally Employed Women, Am. Woodmen, State Bar of Tex. Legal Assts., Tyler Legal Secs. Assn., Dallas Downtown Noon Bus. and Profl. Women (sec. 1974-75, Woman of Yr. award 1977, Woman on Move award 1976), Tyler Evening Bus. and Profl. Women (rec. sec. 1981-82, Woman of Yr. award 1981). Baptist. Club: Rosebud Civitan. Home: 1619 N Ross St Tyler TX 75702 Office: PO Box 760921 Dallas TX 75376

HUTCHINSON, ERIC, alternate energy company executive; b. Tacoma, July 21, 1952; s. Harry C. and Yolanda Marie (Espinosa) H.; student bus. adminstrn. (Gibson-Duncan Meml. Trust scholar 1970-73), U. Ark., Little Rock, 1970-73; m. Donna Ruth Gentry, Aug. 15, 1971; children—Amy Carol, Bryan Walter. Mgr., Sears, Roebuck & Co., Little Rock, 1970-75; salesman Dale Carnegie courses, Little Rock, 1975-77; v.p. Lynndale Mfg. Co. Inc., Little Rock, 1977-79; gen. mgr. Lakewood Products, Inc., Little Rock and Toronto, Ont., Can., 1979—; v.p. Catalytic Damper Corp., Conway, Ark., 1982—; instr. Dale Carnegie courses, speaker seminars and workshops. Mem. Ark. N.G., 1971-78. Mem. Sales and Mktg. Execs. Club Little Rock, Wood Energy Inst. Mem. Christian Ch. (Disciples of Christ). Club: Kiwanis.

HUTCHISON, WILLIAM L., oil and gas company executive; b. Dallas, 1932; married. Grad., So. Methodist U., 1955. Practice law, 1955-57; v.p. Tex. Oil & Gas Corp., Dallas, 1957-65, exec. v.p., 1965-70, pres., 1970-76, pres., chief exec. officer, 1976-77, chmn. bd., chief exec. officer, 1977—, also dir. Office: Tex Oil & Gas Corp 1507 Pacific Dallas TX 75201*

HUTH, WILLIAM LESTER, university educator, researcher, consultant, pilot; b. Fostoria, Ohio, Sept. 25, 1950; s. Donald Eugene and Jeanne Marie (Valter) H.; m. Theresa Eileen Miller, Aug. 25, 1973; children—Jennifer Anne, Jonathan Adam. B.S., La. Tech. U., 1974, M.B.A., 1976; Ph.D., U. Ark., 1979. Corporate pilot Ga. Pacific Corp., Crossett, Ark., 1972-73; instr. La. Tech. U., Ruston, La., 1973-76; instr., research assoc. U. Ark.-Fayetteville, 1976-79; asst. prof. Northeastern U., Boston, 1979-84; asst. prof. Northeast La. U., Monroe, 1984—; dir. aviation dept. Haigh-Farr, Inc., Lexington, Mass., 1982-84. Served in U.S. Army, 1970-72. Decorated Bronze Star, U.S. Army, 1972, Commendation medal, 1972, Air medal, 1972, Vietnamese Cross of Galantry, 1972. Mem. Am. Econ. Assn., Eastern Econ. Assn., So. Econ. Assn., Am. Statis. Assn., Univ. Aviation Assn., DECUS. Club: Greater Boston Soaring (Boston) (chief pilot 1982-84). Avocations: soaring; scuba diving; astronomy. Office: Northeast LA Univ 700 University Ave Monroe LA 71209

HUTTENSTINE, MARIAN LOUISE, educator; b. Bloomsburg, Pa., Jan. 26, 1940; d. Ralph Benjamin and Marian Louise (Engler) H.; B.S., Bloomsburg State Coll., 1961, M.Ed., 1966; postgrad. (NDEA fellow, Newspaper Fund fellow), Rutgers U., 1962-63; Ph.D., U. N.C., 1985. High sch. English, journalism tchr., dept. chmn., 1961-66; asst. prof. Lock Haven (Pa.) State Coll., 1966-73, assoc. prof. English, 1973-74; teaching asst., lectr. Sch. Journalism, U. N.C., Chapel Hill, 1974-76; cons., dir. Diener & Assocs., Research Triangle Park, N.C., 1975-77; asst. prof. journalism Sch. Communication, U. Ala.-Tuscaloosa, 1977—; cons. various publs., Ala., 1977—. adult leader, vol. worker Luth. Ch., 1962—. Mem. Assn. Edn. in Journalism, Soc. Profl. Journalists, Am. Advt. Fedn., Am. Acad. Advt., AAUW, Journalism Edn. Assn., ACLU, NOW, Kappa Tau Alpha, Soc. Profl. Journalists-Sigma Delta Chi (dir.). Clubs: Tuscaloosa Advt., Ala. SPJ-SDX. Contbr. papers to profl. lit. Home: K-1 Woodland Trace Tuscaloosa AL 35405 Office: Box 1482 Journalism Dept U Ala University AL 35486

HUTTO, EARL, Congressman; b. Midland City, Ala., May 12, 1926; s. Lemmie and Ellie (Mathis) H.; B.S., Troy State U., 1949; m. Nancy Myers, July 8, 1967; children—Lori, Amy. Tchr. Cottonwood (Ala.) High Sch., 1949-51; sports and program dir. Sta. WDIG, Dothan, Ala., 1951-54; sports dir. Sta. WEAR-TV, Pensacola, Fla., 1954-60; pres. Sta. WPEX-FM, Pensacola, 1960-65; sports dir. Sta. WSFA-TV, Montgomery, Ala., 1961-63; sports dir., state news editor Sta. WJHG-TV, Panama City, Fla., 1963-74; mem. Fla. Ho. of Reps., 1972-78; mem. 96th-98th Congresses from 1st Dist. Fla. Served with USN. Mem. Gideons Internat. (Panama City Camp). Baptist. Club: Civitan (dep. dist. gov. Ala-West Fla. dist. 1967-71). Office: 330 Cannon House Office Bldg Washington DC 20515

HUTTO, RUTH BISHOP, nursing adminstrator; b. Harleyville, S.C., May 14, 1927; d. Sidi Hamet and Harriet Elizabeth (Sillivant) Bishop; m. Julius Otey, Oct. 6, 1968; 1 child, Elizabeth. Grad. Med. Coll. S.C., 1951; B.S. in Nursing, Vanderbilt U., 1956; M.A., Columbia U., 1962. Supr. pediatric nursing Med. U. S.C., Charleston, 1956-60; instr., asst. prof. U. Ky. Coll. Nursing, Lexington, 1962-67; chmn. pediatric nursing Med. U. S.C. Coll. Nursing, Charleston, 1967-72, asst. dean, 1972-80, chmn. pediatric nursing, 1980-81, program nurse dir., 1981—. Mem. Substance Abuse Com., Charleston County, 1978—; mem. Parent-Child Adv. Bd., Dorchester County, 1982—; mem. Palmetto-Low country Health Systems Agy., Charleston, Berkley & Dorchester Counties, 1981—; vol. citizens in need of primary nursing skills, Harleyville, S.C., 1968—. Recipient Cert. of Service, Camp High Hope for Exceptional Children, Charleston, 1971, 72, 73, 74, Resolution, S.C. Ho. of Reps. and Senate, 1980; named Career Woman of Yr., Trident Bus. and Profl. Woman's Club, Greater Charleston, 1977. Mem. Internat. Hyperthermia Clin. Soc. (bd. dirs. 1985—), Clin. Nurse Specialist Group, S.C. League Nursing (bd. dirs. 1984—, editor newsletter 1984—), Med. U. S.C. Alumni Assn. (disting. alumni 1974). Methodist. Clubs: Tuesday Afternoon (Harleyville) (sec. 1968—). Home: Route 2 Box 304 Harleyville SC 29448 Office: Clin Nursing Med U SC Med Ctr 171 Ashley Ave Charleston SC 29425

HUTTON, CONNIE CLIFFORD, thoracic and cardiovascular surgeon; b. Clifton, Tex., Oct. 31, 1944; s. Finis D. and Tinnie Rose (Blacklock) H.; m. Paula Lynne Johnson, July 4, 1964 (div. 1974); 1 dau., Tracey Lea; m. Linette Bailey, July 7, 1975. B.S. with honors, North Tex. State U., 1968; M.D., U. Tex.-Galveston, 1972. Diplomate Am. Bd. Surgery. Resident thoracic and cardiovascular surgery U. Okla., 1979; practice medicine specializing in thoracic and cardiovascular surgery, Odessa, Tex., 1979—; chief surgery Med. Center Hosp., 1984-86. Bd. dirs. Am. Heart Assn., 1980—, United Way of Odessa, 1983-85; mem. U.S. Congl. Adv. Bd., Heritage Found., Republican Presdl. Task Force. Mem. Ector County Med. Soc., Tex. Med. Assn., AMA, ACS, Tex. Med. Polit. Action Com., Southwest Surg. Congress, Tex. Med. Found., World Med. Assn., AAAS, Am. Med. Polit. Action Com., Phi Chi. Office: 419 W 5th St Odessa TX 79761

HUTTON, JERRY BOB, educator, consultant; b. Gorman, Tex., Apr. 28, 1938; s. Alvie C. and Dora Lucille (English) H.; m. Sandra J. Brumlow, July 17, 1959; children—Cynthia, Jerry B., Jr., Blake, Jeffrey, Jennifer. B.A., Howard Payne U., 1960; M.S., North Tex. State U., 1962; Ph.D., U. Houston, 1970. Lic. psychologist. Asst. prof. Dallas Bapt. Coll., 1969-70; psychologist U. Tex. Health Sci. Ctr., Dallas, 1970-71; dir. Fairhill Sch., Dallas, 1971-72; dir. Fedn. North Tex. Area Univs., Dallas, 1980-82; prof. spl. edn. East Tex. State U., Commerce, 1972—, dir. Metroplex Facility, Garland, 1982-85; cons. Grand Prairie pub. schs., Tex., 1983—, DeSoto pub. schs., Tex., 1975—, Lancaster pub. schs., Tex., 1975—. Author: Teacher Checklist of School Behavior, 1981; (with others) Social-Emotional Dimension Scale, 1986. Contbr. articles to profl. jours. Mem. Am. Psychol. Assn., Council Exceptional Children, Am. Ednl. Research Assn., Southwestern Psychol. Assn., Tex. Council for Children with Behavior Disorders (v.p. 1985-86). Democrat. Mem. Disciples of Christ Ch. Avocation: camping. Home: 727 Little Creek Duncanville TX 75116 Office: East Tex State U Metroplex Facility 2625 Anita St Garland TX 75041

HUYSMAN, ARLENE WEISS, psychologist; b. Phila.; d. Max and Anna (Pearlene) Weiss; B.A., Shaw U., 1973; M.A., Goddard Coll., 1974; Ph.D., Union Grad. Sch., 1980; m. Pedro Camacho; children—Pamela Claire, James David. Actress, dir. Dramatic Workshop, N.Y.C., also various theaters in Fla., 1956-68; music and drama critic and columnist Orlando (Fla.) Sentinel Star, 1966-68; psychodramatist Volusia County Guidance Center, Daytona Beach, Fla., 1966-68; pres. C.S. Advt. Inc., Coral Gables, Fla., 1969-72; free-lance journalist, 1968-70; psychodramatist Psychiat. Inst., Jackson Meml. Hosp., Miami, 1972-77, acting dir. Adult Day Treatment Center, 1974-75, dir., 1975-77, dir. Lithium Clinic, 1976-77; psychodramatist South Fla. State Hosp., Hollywood, 1971-72; supr., coordinator clin. neurosci. until St. Francis Hosp., 1984—. asst. prof. Med. Sch., U. Miami, 1976—; psychotherapy supr., neurosci. program coordinator St. Francis Hosp. Mem. adv. panel Fine Arts Council Fla., 1976-77; mem. Fla. Gov.'s Task Force on Marriage and the Family Unit, 1976; vol. Rec. for Blind, 1974—. Recipient Best Dirs. award and Best Actress award Fla. Theatre Festival, 1967. Mem. Am. Psychol. Assn., Mental Health Assn. Dade County, Internat. Assn. Group Psychotherapy, Am. Assn. Group Psychotherapy and Psychodrama, Moreno Acad., Fedn. Partial Hospitalization Study Groups, Fla. Assn. Practicing Psychologists (bd. dirs.). Office: Center for Psychol Growth 3050 Biscayne Blvd Miami FL 33137

HWANG, SHIN JA, linguistics educator; b. Nanam, Ham Kyong, Korea, May 24, 1943; came to U.S., 1966, naturalized, 1979; d. Byung Im and Dong Joo Wol Joo; m. Myung Kyu Hwang, Dec. 16, 1967; children—Harold, Grace, Lisa. B.A., Ewha Women's U., Seoul, Korea, 1961-65; M.L.S., U. Okla., 1968; M.A., U. Tex.-Arlington, 1974, Ph.D., 1981. Librarian, U. So. Calif., Los Angeles, 1968-71; tchr. Summer Inst. Linguistics, Dallas, 1982—; adj. asst. prof. linguistics U. Tex., Arlington, 1984—. Author: Korean Clause Structure, 1975; Discourse Features of Korean Narration, 1986. Contbr. articles to profl. jours. Mem. Linguistic Soc. S.W., Linguistic Soc. Am. Methodist. Home: 210 Genoa Dr Duncanville TX 75116 Office: Summer Inst Linguistics 7500 W Camp Wisdom Dallas TX 75236

HYATT, LEE EDWARD, educator; b. Asheville, N.C., Apr. 21, 1951; s. Carl Battle and Dorothy (Kanipe) H. B.S. in Bus. Adminstrn., Western Carolina U., 1973. Office supr. Carolina Power and Light Co., Wilmington, Asheville and Oxford, N.C., 1973-78, instr., Raleigh, N.C., 1978—. Mem. Am. Soc. Tng. and Devel. Democrat. Methodist. Lodge: Kiwanis (pres. 1982-83, sec. 1983—; Outstanding Lt. Gov. award 1972). Avocations: bowling; dancing. Home: 8305 Wycombe Ln Raleigh NC 27609 Office: Carolina Power and Light Co 411 Fayetteville St Mall Raleigh NC 27609

HYDE, JOSEPH R., III, business executive; b. Memphis, 1942. A.B., U. N.C., 1965. With Malone & Hyde Inc., Memphis, 1965—, pres. Super D Drugs subs., 1966, v.p. parent co., 1967-68, exec. v.p., 1968-69, pres., chief exec. officer, 1969-72, chmn. bd., 1972—, also dir.; dir. 1st Tenn. Corp., Fed. Express Corp., Browning Ferris Inc. Bd. dirs. Memphis U. Sch. Office: Malone & Hyde Inc 3030 Poplar Memphis TN 38111

HYDE, RALPH A., university administrator; b. Ripley, Tenn., Sept. 19, 1927; s. Henry J. and Annie L. (Steelman) H.; m. Donna L. Hare, June 9, 1956; children—Genia L., Greg A., H. Carey. B.S., U. Tenn., 1954, Ed.D., 1969; M.A., Memphis State U., 1963. Adminstrv. asst. U. Tenn., Knoxville, 1954-58, asst. dir., 1958-60, assoc. dir., 1960-68; dir. Memphis State U., 1969-74; assoc. dean U. Tenn., Memphis, 1974-82, interim dean, 1982-84, assoc. dean Coll. Allied Health Professions, U. Tenn. Health Sci. Ctr., 1984—; cons. in field. Contbr. articles to profl. jours. Served to sgt. USAF, 1946-48. Named Commencement Speaker, U. Tenn. Health Scis. Ctr., 1983. Mem. Am. Soc. Allied Health, Tenn. Adult Edn. Assn. (v.p. 1974-75, pres. 1975-76, adv. bd. 1976-78, Appreciation award 1978), Memphis Vocat. Coordinating Com. (chmn. 1979-80), Phi Delta Kappa, Alpha Eta. Democrat. Presbyterian. Lodge: Rotary (Memphis, Explorer award 1982). Avocations: Golf; fishing; gardening; woodworking. Home: 3753 Winderwood Memphis TN 38128 Office: U Tenn Ctr Health Scis 801 Madison Memphis TN 38163

HYDE, WILLIAM FREDERICK, economics and forestry educator, researcher, consultant; b. Rochester, N.Y., Sept. 7, 1942; s. Frederick R. and Ruth (Stetson) H.; m. P. Camille Lambert, Jan. 20, 1966 (div. May 1979). B.A., Am. U., Washington, 1969, M.A., 1970; M.S., U. Mich., 1975, Ph.D., 1977. Asst. prof. U. N.H., Durham, 1973; sr. research assoc. Resources for the Future, Washington, 1973-78; assoc. dir. Pacific Northwest Forest Policy Project, Vancouver, Wash., 1978-79; assoc. prof. econs. and forestry Duke U., Durham, 1979—; pres. Natural Resources Mgmt. Served to lt. U.S. Army, 1964-68. Rockefeller Found. Environ. Quality fellow, 1969-73. Mem. Am. Econ. Assn., Soc. Am. Foresters, Assn. Pub. Policy Analysis and Mgmt., Soc. Risk Analysis, Am. Agrl. Econs. Assn., Sigma Xi, Phi Kappa Phi. Author: Economic Evaluation of Investments in Forestry Research, 1983; Timber Supply, Land Allocation & Economic Efficiency, 1980; contbr. articles to profl. jours., chpts. to books. Home: 2304 Cranford Rd Durham NC 27706 Office: Duke U 102 Biosci Bldg Durham NC 27706

HYLANDER, WALTER RAYMOND, JR., civil engineer; b. Memphis, July 22, 1924; s. Walter Raymond and Mary Howard (Douglass) H.; m. Marjorie Jean Gunter, Mar. 8, 1951; children—Walter Raymond, Joyce Elizabeth. B.S., U.S. Mil. Acad., 1945; M.S. in Civil Engring., MIT, 1950. Registered profl. engr., N.Y., Miss. Commd. 2d lt., U.S. Army, 1945, advanced through grades to col., 1969, ret., 1973; tng. dir. Bechtel Power Corp., Grand Gulf, Miss., 1974-76; tng. and edn. mgr. Saudi-Arabian Bechtel Co., Jubail, 1976-77; tng. dir. St. Regis Paper Co., Montecello, Miss., 1978-79; chief civil engr. Bechtel Power Corp., Grand Gulf, 1979—; chmn. Panel of Experts on Mine Warfare, NATO, London, 1962-65; sr. advisor on engr. tng., Vietnam, 1967-68; mem.

U.S. Army Com. on Mil. History, West Point, N.Y., 1972-73; mem. U.S. ACDA, Washington, 1968-69. Contbr. articles to profl. jours. Fellow ASCE; mem. Soc. Am. Mil. Engrs., Nat. Assn. Model Railroaders, La. Miss. Christmas Tree Assn., Phi Kappa Phi. Methodist. Avocations: growing Christmas trees; model railroading; civil war history. Home: Rosswood Plantation Lorman MS 39096 Office: Bechtel Power Corp Grand Gulf Nuclear Sta Port Gibson MS 39150

HYMAN, ALBERT LEWIS, physician; b. New Orleans, Nov. 10, 1923; s. David and Mary (Newstadt) H.; m. Neil Steiner, March 27, 1964; 1 son, Albert Arthur. B.S., La. State U., 1943; M.D., 1945; postgrad. U. Cin., U. Paris, U. London. Diplomatae Am. Bd. Internal Medicine. Intern, Charity Hosp., 1945-46, resident, 1947-49, sr. vis. physician, 1959-63; resident Cin. Gen. Hosp., 1946-47; instr. medicine La. State U., 1950-56, asst. prof. medicine, 1956-57; asst. prof. medicine Tulane U., 1957-59, assoc. prof., 1959-63; assoc. prof. surgery Tulane Med. Sch., 1963-70, prof. research surgery in cardiology, 1970—, adj. prof. pharmacology, 1974—, also prof. clin. medicine; dir. Cardiac Catheterization Lab., 1957—; sr. vis. physician Touro Hosp., Touro Infirmary, Hotel Dieu; chief cardiology Sara Mayo Hosp.; cons. in cardiology USPHS, New Orleans Crippled Children's Hosp., St. Tammany Parish Hosp., Covington, La. area VA, Hotel Dieu Hosp., Mercy Hosp., East Jefferson Gen. Hosp., St. Charles Gen. Hosp.; electrocardiographer Metairie Hosp., 1959-64, Sara Mayo Hosp., Touro Infirmary, St. Tammany Hosp.; cons. cardiovascular disease New Orleans VA Hosp.; cons. cardiology Baton Rouge Gen. Hosp., Barlow lectr. in medicine U. So. Calif., 1977. Contbr. articles to profl. jours. Fellow ACP, Am. Coll. Chest Physicians, Am. Coll. Cardiology, Am. Fedn. Clin. Research; mem. Am. Heart Assn. (fellow and regional rep. council clin. cardiology, chmn. cardiopulmonary council 1982-84, mem. research com., co-chmn. cardiovascular study sect. D 1985—), La. Heart Assn. (v.p. 1974), Am. Soc. Pharmacology and Exptl. Therapeutics, So. Soc. Clin. Investigation, So. Med. Soc., Am. Physiol. Soc., AAUP, N.Y. Acad. Scis., Alpha Omega Alpha. Research in cardiopulmonary circulation. Home: 5550 Jacquelyn Ct New Orleans LA 70124 Office: 3629 Prytania St New Orleans LA 70115

HYMAN, BARBARA SUSAN, public relations executive; b. Lexington, Miss., May 9, 1953; d. Herbert A. and Henrietta (Baum) Hyman. B.Journalism, U. Tex.-Austin, 1975. Asst. dir. communications Peachtree Center, Atlanta, 1975-76, dir. communications, 1977-80; editor Hosp. Peer Review, Atlanta, 1976-77; account exec. Hopkins & Assocs., Inc., Dallas, 1980-82, v.p., 1982—. Active The 500, Inc., Dallas, 1982—, Dallas Mus. Art, 1980—, Dallas Bus. League; mem. com. on adminstrn. Central br. YWCA; bd. dirs. Arts Festival Atlanta, 1977-80, mem. Art Dist. Friends, 1985—. Recipient Award of Merit, Internat. Assn. Bus. Communicators, 1975. Mem. Women in Communications (v.p. Dallas chpt. 1983-84, pres.-elect 1984-85 pres. 1985-86, nat. vice chmn. programs 1985-87), Pub. Relations Soc. Am., Kappa Tau Alpha, Phi Theta Kappa, Phi Kappa Phi. Jewish. Office: 3206 Southland Center Dallas TX 75201

HYMER, ROBERT CHARLES, college dean; b. Kansas City, Mo., Oct. 4, 1926; s. Herbert Collins and Edna Frances (Bean) H.; m. Eileen Mae O'Donnell, June 19, 1954; children—Charles Donald, Kathleen Susan. B.S., Rockhurst Coll., Kansas City, 1950; M.A., U. Mo.-Kansas City, 1954; Ed.D., U. No. Colo., 1962. Cert. tchr., administr., Mo. Tchr., prin. Pub. Schs., Kansas City, 1950-66, gen. supr., 1966-68; assoc. prof. U. Mo., Columbia, 1968-72; prof., dir. edn. ctr. U. Wyo., Laramie, 1972-81; dean Coll. Edn., Jacksonville State U., Ala., 1982—; dir. Ala. Tchr. Hall of Fame, Jacksonville; profl. cons. U. Wyo., Laramie. Editor Nat. Assn. Lab. Sch. Jour., 1979—. Contbr. articles to profl. publs. Served with U.S. Army, 1945-46. Mem. Nat. Assn. Lab. Schs. (pres. 1975-76), Assn. Supervision and Curriculum Devel., Nat. Assn. Elem. Sch. Prins., NEA, Ala. Edn. Assn., Albany County C. of C. (chmn. govtl. affairs 1980), Kappa Delta Pi (co-founder, counselor U. Mo. 1970-72, Honor Key award 1981), Phi Delta Kappa (pres. chpt. 1985-86). Club: Exchange (pres. Jacksonville 1984-85). Lodges: Masons (32 degree), Kiwanis (pres. Laramie 1979-80). Office: Coll of Edn N Pelham Rd Jacksonville AL 36265

HYNE, NORMAN JOHN, petroleum geology educator, petroleum company executive; b. Berwyn, Ill., Nov. 17, 1939; m. Janet E. Grimm, Sept. 4, 1967; children—Randy, Lisa. B.A., Pomona Coll., 1961; M.S., Fla. State U., 1965; Ph.D., U. So. Calif., 1969. Prof., U. Tulsa, Okla., 1969—; pres. Tulsa Internat. Petroleum Inst., Okla., 1981—; chmn. Geology and Geophysics Dept., U. Tulsa, 1972-80. Author: Geology for Petroleum Exploration, Drilling and Production, 1984; Finding Oil and Gas, 1985. Editor: Pennsylvanian Sandstones of the Mid-Continent, 1979. Limestones of the Mid-Continent, 1984. Commr., Tulsa Met. Area Planning Commn., 1972-78. Fellow Geol. Soc. Am.; mem. Am. Assn. Petroleum Geologists, Soc. Econ. Paleontol. and Mineralogists, Tulsa Geol. Soc. Republican. Home: 4415 E 75th St Tulsa OK 74136 Office: Dept Continuing Edn U Tulsa Tulsa OK 74104

HYNEK, CHARLES EUGENE, petroleum exploration company executive; b. Sabetha, Kans., July 1, 1927; s. Charles and Rena Frances (Hill) H.; m. Nedra Ann Hawks, 1946 (div. 1972); children—Layne Lee, Janis Lynn Hynek Monserrat, Denise Hynek Underwood, Kirk Bradley; m. Geraldine Ann Dwyer, Nov. 17, 1972; children—Anna, Kate. B.S., U. Nebr., 1951; M.Ed., U. Houston, 1966. Project geologist Shell Oil Co., 1953-58, dist. geologist, Tex., 1958-62, researcher, 1963-64; exploration mgr. Assoc. Oil and Gas Co., Tex., La., 1964-66, Kirby Exploration Co., 1975-78; pres. Charles E. Hynek, Inc., Dallas, 1979—; exploration advisor SONATRACH (Algerian State Oil Co.), 1966-68; exploration mgr. Planet Oil Co., Sydney, Australia, 1969-70; mgr. S.E. Asia, Kenneth McMahon & Assocs., Singapore 1970-71; internat. cons., assoc. Keplinger and Assocs., Houston, 1971-72; dir. internat. exploration Lone Star Gas Co., Dallas, 1972-75. Served with USN, 1945-47. Mem. Am. Assn. Petroleum Geologists (cert. geologist), Soc. Exploration Geophysicists, Soc. Ind. Profl. Earth Scientists, Am. Soc. Photogrammetry, Dallas Geol. Soc., Tex. Ind. Producers and Royalty Owners Assn., Dallas C. of C. Republican. Clubs: T-Bar-M Racquet (Dallas); Century II (Fort Worth). Office: 10722 Bushire St Dallas TX 75229

HYNSON, LAWRENCE MCKEE, JR., educator, consultant; b. Thayer, Mo., Mar. 27, 1940; s. Lawrence McKee and Lillian L. (Jacobson) H.; m. Katherine Flo Miller, Aug. 5, 1967; children—Jonathan, Janette, Jennifer, Jason. B.A., Tex. Christian U., 1963, M.A., 1969; Ph.D., U. Tenn., 1972. Dir. Univ. Coop. Edn. Okla. State U., Stillwater, Okla., 1977-78, prof., 1972—; with Oak Ridge Nat. Lab., 1980; cons. mgmt. edn. Served to capt. U.S. Army, 1963-65. Mem. Am. Soc. Tng. and Devel. (asst. div. dir. Internat. Div.), Am. Coop. Edn. Assn., Demographic Group, Alpha Kappa Delta, Pi Kappa Phi, Gamma Upsilon (chpt. advisor), Alpha Phi Omega (chpt. advisor). Author: Spiritual Well Being, 1979; Meaning of the City, 1980; Evaluation Procedures, 1980; Technology in Japan and America, 1984; Organizing with Style: Japanese and American Patterns, 1985. Home: 2210 W Arrowhead Dr Stillwater OK 74074 Office: 034 CLB Oklahoma State U Stillwater OK 74078

IACCINO, PAUL A., ret. labor union ofcl.; b. Chgo., Oct. 14, 1917; s. Anthony C. and Rose (Manzella) I.; student Ill. Bus. Coll., 1936-37; m. Marietta H. Smith, Apr. 26, 1941 (dec. Apr. 1973); children—Richard, Gerald, James, William, Diane; m. 2d, Kathrine B. Durham, May 26, 1974. Former musician, dance band leader; employed Hart, Schaffner & Marx Co., 1936-42, Revere Copper & Brass Co., Inc., 1942-52; rep. CIO (now AFL-CIO) to Welfare Council Met. Chgo., 1952-57; sec., treas. Cook County (Ill.) Indsl. Union Council, CIO, 1957-62, asst. to pres. Chgo. Fedn. Labor and Indsl. Union Council AFL-CIO, 1962-68; asst. dir. labor affairs dept. Blue Cross-Blue Shield, 1968-70, adminstr. labor affairs dept., 1970-72, asst. v.p., 1972-74; dir. AFL-CIO Community Services Dept. Crusade of Mercy, 1974-81; pres. and founder Italian-Am. Labor Council, 1966-68, sec., 1968-74, treas., 1974-76, mem. bd. dirs., 1976—; chmn. community services com. Chgo. AFL-CIO, 1962-68, dir. community services dept., 1962-68. Bd. dirs., vice-chmn. Met. Chgo. Crusade Mercy, 1965, 66, 67; chmn. Chgo. Mayor's Sr. Citizens Employment Com.; mem. blood bank com. Chgo. ARC, planning com. Ill. Inst. Labor, Health, and Rehab., Ill. Com. Fair Credit Practices, Com. to Form a Pre-Paid Dental Plan, Gov. Ill. Commn. Credit Legis., Gov. Ill. coms. Status of Women and Retardation; mem. ad-hoc com. planning welfare services Proviso Twp.; mem. Ill. Child Labor Com., Ill. Com. on Minimum Wage, Ill. Com. Migratory Labor, Jewish Labor Com.; mem. labor com. Nat. Safety Council; co-chmn. Boys' Town Italy, 1st vice-chmn. Ill. Coll. Podiatric Medicine; bd. dirs. Welfare Council Met. Chgo., Blue Cross, Community Fund. Recipient awards Boys' Town Italy, Italian-Am. Labor Council, Sr. Citizen's Met. Chgo.; Civil Rights award Jewish Labor Com. Home: 1672 Point Rd Route 2 Westminster SC 29693

IACOBUCCI, GUILLERMO ARTURO, chemist; b. Buenos Aires, Argentina, May 11, 1927; s. Guillermo Cesar and Blanca Nieves (Brana) I.; M.Sc., U. Buenos Aires, 1949, Ph.D. in Organic Chemistry, 1952; m. Constantina Maria Gullich, Mar. 28, 1952; children—Eduardo Ernesto, William George. Came to U.S., 1962, naturalized, 1972. Research chemist E.R. Squibb Research Labs., Buenos Aires, 1952-57; research fellow in chemistry Harvard U., Cambridge, Mass., 1958-59, prof. phytochemistry U. Buenos Aires, 1960-61; sr. research chemist Squibb Inst. Med. Research, New Brunswick, N.J., 1962-66; head bio-organic chemistry labs. Coca-Cola Co., Atlanta, 1967-74, asst. dir. corp. research and devel., 1974—; adj. prof. chemistry Emory U., 1975—. John Simon Guggenheim Meml. Found. fellow, 1958. Mem. AAAS, Assn. Harvard Chemists, Am. Chem. Soc., N.Y. Acad. Scis., Am. Soc. Pharmacognosy, Assn. Quimica Argentina. Contbr. articles on organic chemistry to sci. jours. Patentee in field. Home: 160 North Mill Rd NW Atlanta GA 30328 Office: Coca Cola Co PO Drawer 1734 Atlanta GA 30301

IACONO, CARMINE UMBERTO, psychology educator; b. Providence, Nov. 24, 1942; s. Pasquale Michael and Rita (Donnatelli) I.; m. Nancy Rose LeClair, Oct. 19, 1969; 1 child, Kelly Jean. B.A., U. R.I., 1967; Ed.M., R.I. Coll., 1969; Ph.D., U. Mo., 1975. Lic. psychologist, R.I., Pa., Tex. Staff psychologist VA Med. Ctr., Marion, Ind., 1975-76; asst. prof. Temple U., 1976-81; asst. prof. Tex. Tech. U., 1981-84; assoc. dir. Pain Ctr., Tex. Tech. U. Health Scis. Ctr., Lubbock, 1985—. Contbr. articles to profl. jours. Recipient Humanitarian award Disabled Am. Veterans, 1980; Ins. Co. N.Am. grantee, 1979. Mem. Am. Psychol. Assn., Internat. Assn. Study of Pain, Biofeedback Soc. Am., Am. Pain Soc. Roman Catholic. Avocations: computer science; radio control modeling; model shipbuilding; electronics. Home: 6 Ridge Rd Ransom Canyon TX 79366 Office: Tex Tech Univ Health Scis Ctr Lubbock TX 79430

IACOVELLA, PASQUALE P., restaurant owner; b. Benevento, Italy, Apr. 17, 1952; s. Joseph and Filomena Mancini, I. B.A., U. So. Conn. Pres., CDB Italian Restaurant Corp., Tampa, Fla., 1975-83, Olde So. Sale Co. Inc., Tampa, 1975-83, So. Oven Co., Inc., Tampa, 1976—. Mem. Fla. Restaurant Assn., Nat. Restaurant Assn., Italian-Am. Golf Assn. Roman Catholic. Office: 11710 N 51st St Tampa FL 33617

IBACH, DOUGLAS THEODORE, clergyman; b. Pottstown, Pa., July 23, 1925; s. Hiram Christian and Esther (Fry) I.; B.S. in Edn., Temple U., 1950, postgrad. Sch. Theology, 1950-52; M.Div., Louisville Presbyn. Theol. Sem., 1954; m. Marion Elizabeth Torok, Sept. 2, 1950; children—Susan Kay, Marilyn Lee, Douglas Theodore, Grace Louise. Ordained to ministry Presbyn. Ch., 1953; pastor, Pewee Valley, Ky., 1952-55, West Nottingham Presbyn. Ch., Colora, Md., 1955-61, Irwin, Pa., 1961-67, Knox Presbyn. Ch., Falls Church, Va., 1967-72, United Christian Parish Reston (Va.), 1972—. Youth ministry cons. Nat. Capital Union Presbytery, 1967—; ecumenical officer Nat. Capital Presbytery, chmn. stewardship com., 1986—; mem. ecumenical relations com. Synod of Virginias, also mem. Ecumenical Conf.; bd. dirs. Reston Inter-Faith, Inc.; dir. Presbyn. Internat. Affairs Seminars. adv. bd. Christmas Internat. House, Served with USNR, 1943-44. Mem. Council Chs. Greater Washington (pres., chmn. instl. ministry commn.), Piedmont Synod U.P. Ch. (dir. youth, camping), Acad. Parish Clergy Assn. Presbyn. Christian Educators, Fairfax County Council Chs. (pres.), Com. 100 Fairfax County. Home: 11709 Riders Ln Reston VA 22091 Office: 2222 Colts Neck Rd Reston VA 22091

ICHINOSE, HERBERT, physician; b. Koloa, Kauai, Hawaii, July 25, 1931; s. Samuro and Katsue (Yamamoto) I.; student U. Hawaii, 1949-51; B.S., Tulane U., 1953, M.D., 1957; m. Beverly Hodges Burlison, Dec. 31, 1982; children—Linda, Lorna, John, Eugene, Jack, Robert. Intern, Charity Hosp. New Orleans, 1957-58, resident, 1958-62; practice medicine, specializing in pathology, New Orleans, 1958—; vis. pathologist Charity Hosp., 1964—; pathologist, dir. lab. services Meth. Hosp., New Orleans, 1972—; mem. faculty dept. pathology Med. Sch., Tulane U., New Orleans, 1958—, assoc. prof., 1967-71, prof., 1971-74, clin. prof., 1974—. Service Club scholar, 1949; USPHS grantee, 1954; recipient John Herr Musser Meml. award Tulane Med. Sch., 1957, Undergrad. Research award Borden Co., 1957. Diplomate Am. Bd. Pathology. Mem. New Orleans Acad. Pathology (pres.), Thoracophilus Soc., Orleans Parish, La. med. socs., AMA, N.Y. Acad. Scis., Am. Soc. Clin. Pathologists. Contbr. articles to profl. jours. Office: 1430 Tulane St New Orleans LA 70112 also Dermatopathology Lab 234 Loyola Ave Suite 603 New Orleans LA 70112

ICHIYE, TAKASHI, oceanographer, educator; b. Kobe, Japan, Oct. 1, 1921; came to U.S., 1957, naturalized, 1972; s. Mankichi and Ume (Yumoto) I.; m. Chiyoko Nagao, Oct. 6, 1952; children—Toshiko, Keiko. B.S., U. Tokyo, 1944, D.Sc., 1953. Oceanographer Kobe Marine Obs., 1945-54; assoc. chief marine sect. Japan Meteorol. Agy., Tokyo, 1954-57; vis. scientist Woods Hole Oceanographic Instn., Mass., 1957-58; asst. prof. Fla. State U., Tallahassee, 1958-63; sr. research scientist Lamont Geol. Obs., Palisades, N.Y., 1963-68; prof. Tex. A&M U., College Station, 1968—; cons. Exxon Research and Devel. Co., Houston, 1979-83, EG&G Co., Waltham, Mass., 1974-78; coordinator JECSS Program, UNESCO-IOC, 1981—. Author: Graphical Oceanography, 1954; editor: Diffusion in Oceans and Fresh Waters, 1965, 1st JECSS Workshop, 1983, Ocean Dynamics of the Japan and East China Seas, 1984. Recipient Disting. Research award Japan Meteorol. Agy., 1952. Mem. Am. Geophys. Union, Am. Meteorol. Soc., Oceanographic Soc. Japan, French Japanese Oceanographic Soc. (overseas editor 1983—). Avocation: photography. Home: Route 5 Box 1357 Timbercrest College Station TX 77840 Office: Tex A&M U Dept Oceanography College Station TX 77843

IDDINS, MILDRED, retired librarian; b. Fountain City, Tenn.; d. Joseph Franklin and Lucy (Chandler) I.; A.B., Carson-Newman Coll., 1936; B.S., George Peabody Coll., 1941. Tchr., Bell House Sch., Knoxville, Tenn., 1936-37; tchr. Roane County High Sch., Kingston, 1937-41; librarian Dandridge (Tenn.) High Sch., 1941-43; Army librarian, Ft. Oglethorpe, Ga., 1943-44; librarian Carson-Newman Coll., Jefferson City, Tenn., 1944-81. Mem. AAUW (br. treas. 1964-66). Baptist. Clubs: Monday Literary, Modern Literary. Home: 403 Russell St Jefferson City TN 37760

ILER, WILLIAM BENNIE, JR., city law enforcement official; b. Winter Haven, Fla., Aug. 17, 1944; s. William Bennie Sr. and Vera (Collins) I.; m. Sandra Joyce Salemi, Sept. 10, 1967; children—Christopher Alan, Tracy Lynn. A.A. in Police Sci., Hillsborough Community Coll., 1972; B.A. in Social and Behavioral Scis., U. of So. Fla., 1974; M.S. in Criminal Justice, Rollins Coll., Winter Park, Fla., 1979. With Tampa (Fla.) Police Dept., 1966—, patrol supr., 1979-81, detective police acad., 1977-79, supr. street anti crime squad, 1981—; instr. Tampa Police Acad., 1973—; instr. Hillsborough Community Coll., U. of Tampa. Block capt. Neighborhood Watch Program. Served with USAR, 1965-71; to chief petty officer USNR, 1979—. Mem. Fraternal Order Police, Tampa Police Dept. Pistol and Rifle Club, U.S. Naval Inst., Sons of Confederate Vets. Republican. Office: City of Tampa Police Dept 1710 Tampa St Tampa FL 33602

ILIFF, RICHARD JAMES, electrical engineer, educator; b. Fayette, Iowa, Nov. 30, 1938; s. George James and Helen Louise (Carler) I. B.S. in Engring. Physics, B.S. in Bus., U. Colo., 1974; M.S., Ga. Coll., 1977, M.B.A., 1982. Registered profl. engr., Ga. Draftsman, Martin Marietta, Denver, 1957-59, designer, engr., 1963-75; with USAF, Robins AFB, Ga., 1975—, GM-13, engring. supr., 1983—; pres., owner Iliff Enterprises, Inc.; part-owner, treas Nat. Electronic Sales Co., 1979—; part-time instr. Fort Valley State Coll., 1976—. Dep. comdr. srs. CAP. Served with USAF, 1959-63. Recipient Outstanding Performance award USAF, 1978, Merit award, 1982, 83, 84, 85; named Engr. of Yr., Ga. Soc. Profl. Engrs., 1981; Supr. of Yr., Warner Robins Air Logistics Ctr., 1983. Mem. Nat. Soc. Profl. Engrs., IEEE, AIAA. Methodist. Clubs: Robins AFB Officers, Aero. Contbr. articles to profl. jours.

ILLE, BERNARD GLENN, insurance company executive; b. Ponca City, Okla., Feb. 8, 1927; s. Frank Louis and Marie (Cornwell) I.; m. Mary Lou Allen, Aug. 23, 1952; children—Meredith, Les, Frank. B.S. in Bus. Adminstrn., U. Okla., 1950. C.L.U. Exec. v.p., agy. dir. United Founders Life, Oklahoma City, 1958-66, pres., 1966—, also dir.; dir. Landmark Land Co., LSB Industries, Founders Bank & Trust, Dixie Fed. Savs. and Loan. Organizing mem. Oklahoma City chpt. Big Bros., 1960-61; pres. Okla. chpt. Nat. Football Found., 1968-80. Served with USCG, 1945-46. Mem. Oklahoma City Assn. C.L.U.s, Oklahoma City Assn. Life Underwriters, Okla. Assn. Life Ins. Cos. (pres. 1975-76, 83-84), Okla. Life and Health Ins. Guaranty Assn. (chmn. 1985), Kappa Alpha (dir.) Roman Catholic. Clubs: Petroleum Quail Creek Golf and Country, Oak Tree Golf, Oak Tree Country, U. Okla. Touchdown (trustee). Office: 5900 Mosteller Dr Oklahoma City OK 73112

IM, SOPHANN, research pharmacist; b. Battambang, Cambodia, Apr. 22, 1940; came to U.S., 1973, naturalized, 1982; s. Phan Im and Sorn Tuot; m. Lean Oan So, May 13, 1966; children—Sitthivedh W., Sitthivong Paul. B.S. in Pharmacy, U. N.Mex., 1963; M.S. in Pharmacy, Ohio State U., 1965; diploma in Indsl. Pharmacy Montpellier Inst. Indsl. Pharmacy, France, 1967; Ph.D. in Pharmacy, U. Montpellier, 1970. Registered pharmacist, Ga., N.J. Assoc. dir. Central Pharm. Labs., Phnom-Penh, Cambodia, 1970-71; tech. dir. Tchenla Pharms., Phnom-Penh, 1971-73; postdoctoral fellow U. Ga., Athens, 1974-75; asst. prof. U. Ky., Lexington, 1975-79; group leader, research and devel. Boehringer Ingelheim, Ltd., Ridgefield, Conn., 1979-81; group leader research and devel. Alcon Labs., Fort Worth, Tex., 1981—. Contbr. articles to profl. jours. Recipient Research Achievement award Hosp. Pharmacy, 1966. Mem. Am. Pharm. Assn., Acad. Pharm. Scis., N.Y. Acad. Scis., Parenteral Drug Assn., AAAS. Mem. Ch. of the Nazarene. Home: 7008 Santa Rita Ct Fort Worth TX 76133

IMHOFF, WALTER JOSEPH, investment holding company executive, consultant; b. Richmond, Ind., Dec. 14, 1940; s. William P. and Carmella J. (Vecera) I.; m. Ann J. Benjamin, Oct. 15, 1960; children—Lisa Ann, William Gregory. B.B.A., Northwestern U., 1968; postgrad. Ind. U., 1958-60. Vice pres. ops. leaf div. W.R. Grace Co., Chgo., 1973-76; group v.p. Allied Food Group div. W.R. Grace, Singapore, 1976-77, v.p. consumer services group, 1976-78; group v.p. Jim Walter Corp., Tampa, Fla., 1978-85; pres. Interlink, Inc., 1985—; cons. internat. bus. Mem. Fla. Dist. Export Council, Fla. Internat. Trade Council, Tampa Bay Internat. Trade Council, Indsl. Research Inst., Fla. Council Internat. Devel. (bd. dirs.). Republican. Roman Catholic. Club: Palma Ceia Golf and Country (Tampa). Office: Interlink Inc Suite 346 Lincoln Ctr 5401 W Kennedy Blvd Tampa FL 33609

IMMEL, FLINT, veterinarian; b. Fredericksburg, Tex., Nov. 21, 1934; s. Thomas August and Wyoma (Evans) I. Student Tex. Lutheran Coll., 1953-56, Southwest Tex. State U., 1971-74; B.S., Tex. A&M U., 1976, D.V.M., 1977. With Milk Producers Assn., San Antonio, 1961-69; assoc. veterinarian Larson (Tex.) Vet. Clinic, 1978, Jacksboro (Tex.) Vet. Clinic, 1978—. Served with U.S. Army, 1957-61. Mem. AVMA, Tex. Vet. Med. Assn., Am. Bovine Practitioners Assn. Republican. Mem. Ch. of God. Lodge: Northside Lions (San Antonio). Home: Pine Manor Apts 37 Jacksboro TX 76056 Office: 263 W Belknap St Jacksboro TX 76056

IMPSON, LOREN CAIL, designer, builder; b. Durant, Okla., Jan. 21, 1951; s. Boytt and Mary June (Curtis) I. Student in speech communications Kans. U., 1982. Prin., Impson Constrn. Co., Denton, Tex., 1970—, Spatial Experiences, earth sheltered housing constrn.,Denton, 1981—; cons. in field. Contbr. articles to profl. jours. Candidate Kans. Ho. of Reps., 1972. Served with USNG, 1971-75. Office: Spatial Experiences 912 Bell Ave Denton TX 76201

INABINET, LAWRENCE REDMON, textile company executive; b. Florence, S.C., Jan. 26, 1939; s. Isaac Horace and Ruth (Brunson) I.; student Clemson U., 1957-58; B.A. in History and Econs., Wofford Coll., 1961; postgrad. U. Ga., 1961-62. Dir. personnel, office mgr. Beaunit Textiles, Fountain Inn, S.C., 1967-68; dir. indsl. relations Alice Mfg. Co., Inc., Easley, S.C., 1968—. Bd. dirs. Pickens United Way, 1972—, pres., 1981, 84, 85, v.p., 1983-84, chmn. ARC, 1972-76; adv. com. Tri-County Tech. Coll., 1976—; mem. S.C. State Pvt. Industry Council; chmn. Pvt. Industry Council Pickens, Anderson, Oconee Counties; mem. Republican Nat. Com. Served with USAF, 1962-67; capt. USAFR. Mem. Pickens Area Personnel Assn. (pres. 1975), Indsl. Hygienist Round Table, S.C. Safety and Health Assn., S.C. Textile Mfg. Assn., Easley C. of C. (dir. 1972-76, pres. 1976), Am. Textile Mfg. Assn. (safety and health com.). Home: 2009 Pelzer Hwy Easley SC 29640 Office: PO Box 369 Easley SC 29641

INBAU, ELIZABETH ANN, arson investigator; b. New Orleans, Oct. 3, 1951; d. William James and Allie Elizabeth (Prestridge) I. A.S., Delgado Coll., 1976. Registered emergency med. technician. Adminstrv. asst. Delgado Coll., New Orleans, 1972-79, safety instr., part-time 1977-82; safety coordinator Ochsner Hosp., New Orleans, 1979-81; fire insp. Jefferson Parish Fire Dept., Metairie, La., 1981-83, arson investigator, coordinator emergency med. services, 1983—; instr. CPR Am. Heart Assn., New Orleans, 1976—; instr. first aid ARC, New Orleans, 1977—. Mem. Am. Soc. Safety Engrs., La. Assn. Nationally Registered Emergency Med. Technicians, Delta Safety Soc. (pres. 1982-83). Avocations: hunting; sewing; gardening. Office: Jefferson Parish Fire Dept 3330 N Causeway Blvd Metairie LA 70002

INCAPRERA, FRANK PHILIP, internist, indsl. physician; b. New Orleans, Aug. 24, 1928; s. Charles and Mamie (Bellipanni) I.; B.S., Loyola U. of South, 1946; M.D., La. State U., 1950; m. Ruth Mary Duhon, Sept. 13, 1952; children—Charles, Cynthia, James, Christopher, Catherine. Intern, Charity Hosp., New Orleans, 1950-51, resident, 1951-52; resident VA Hosp., New Orleans, 1952-54; practice medicine specializing in internal medicine, New Orleans, 1957—; adminstrv. mgr. Internal Medicine Group, New Orleans, 1973—; med. dir. Owens-Ill. Glass Co., New Orleans, 1961-85, Kaiser Aluminum Co., Chalmette, La., 1975-84, Tenneco Oil Co., Chalmette, 1978-84; co-founder Med. Center E. New Orleans, 1975; clin. asso. prof. medicine Tulane U. Sch. Medicine, 1971—; mem. New Orleans Bd. Health, 1966-70. Bd. dirs. Methodist Hosp., 1971—, Lutheran Home New Orleans, 1976-80, Chateau de Notre Dame, 1977-82, New Orleans Opera Assn., 1975—; mem. New Orleans Human Relation Com., 1968-70; bd. dirs. Emergency Med. Services Council, 1977-86, pres., La. southeastern region, 1979-81; bd. dirs. New Orleans East Bus. Assn., 1980—, v.p., 1981-83; mem. pastoral care adv. com. So. Bapt. Hosp., 1982-83. Served to capt. USAF, 1955-57. Diplomate Am. Bd. Internal Medicine. Fellow ACP, Am. Occupational Medicine Assn., Am. Geriatrics Soc.; mem. AMA, La. (v.p. 1975-76, Orleans Parish (sec. 1972-74) med. socs., New Orleans Acad. Internal Medicine (pres. 1969), La. Occupational Medicine Assn. (pres. 1971-72), La. Soc. Internal Medicine (exec. com. 1975—, pres. 1983-85), New Orleans East C. of C. (dir. 1979-85), Order of St. Louis, Blue Key, Delta Epsilon Sigma. Club: Optimists (dir. 1964-69) (New Orleans). Home: 2218 Lake Oaks Pkwy New Orleans LA 70122 Office: 5640 Read Blvd New Orleans LA 70127

INCE, DAVID LEWIS, librarian; b. Gonzales, Tex., Dec. 28, 1941; s. William Richard and Cecile Adel (Finch) I.; m. Cecelia Hope Hackler, Dec. 31, 1966; children—Meredith, David Lewis. B.A., Tex. A&I U., 1964; M.L.S., U. Tex., 1970. Spl. asst. U. Tex., Austin, 1968-72; chief, adminstrv. services U. N.Mex., Albuquerque, 1972-74; asst. library dir. N.Mex., State U., Las Cruces, 1974-77; dir. libraries Valdosta State Coll. (Ga.), 1977—. Cons. Young Harris Coll. (Ga.), 1982—. Editor: Georgia Union List of Serials, 1979, 82; Proc. Ga. Library Assn. CUD, 1981; also articles. Mem. ALA, Ga. Library Assn., Southeastern Library Assn. Episcopalian. Home: 2308 Sherwood Dr Valdosta GA 31602 Office: Valdosta State Coll Library Valdosta GA 31698

INDELICATO, GREGORY JOHN, geophysicist, petroleum explorationist; b. Bklyn., June 11, 1954; s. Gregory and Antoinette (Sonego) I.; m. Laura Ann Pickering, Jan. 3, 1981 (div. 1983); m. Donna Gayle Grimes, Mar. 22, 1985. B.A. in Geology, Queens Coll., 1976; M.S. in Earth and Space Sci., Stonybrook U., 1978; student Colo. Sch. Mines, 1980; M.B.A. in Info. Systems, Oklahoma City U., 1985. Petroleum geologist Texaco, New Orleans, 1975; geologist Bendix Field Engrs., Pitts., 1979-80, geophysics supr., Grand Junction, Colo., 1980-81; geologist, geochemist Golder Assocs., Lakewood, Colo., 1981; petroleum geophysicist Kerr-McGee Corp., Oklahoma City, 1981-84; dist. geophysicist Fina Oil & Chem. Co., Oklahoma City, 1984—; v.p. Computerworld Internat., Golden, 1981. Author numerous papers in field. Captain Bendix-Grand Junction Vol. Fire Team, 1980-81; CPR, first aid instr. ARC, Grand Junction, 1980-81; squadron comdr. U.S. Air Force Aux. CAP, Grand Junction, 1980-81, capt., 1985, dep. comdr. Oklahoma City squadron, 1986. Recipient Geology Honors award Queens Coll., 1976, M.B.A. High Honors award Oklahoma City U., 1985, M.B.A. Faculty award Oklahoma City U., 1985, Data Processing Mgmt. Assn. Outstanding Student award Oklahoma City U., 1985. Mem. AIME, Soc. Exploration Geophysicists, Am. Assn. Petroleum Geologists, Oklahoma City Geol. Soc., Geophys. Soc. Oklahoma City. Republican. Avocation: lacrosse. Office: Fina Oil & Chem Co 1601 NW Expressway Suite 900 Oklahoma City OK 73118

INGELS, JEROME J. C., petroleum consultant; b. Abilene, Tex., May 7, 1929; s. Jerome J. and Alice (Verest) I.; m. Joell Fleming, Feb. 14, 1981. A.S., U. Tex., Arlington, 1953; B.S., So. Meth. U., 1955, M.S., 1957, Ph.D., Northwestern U., 1960; cert. bus., Alexander Hamilton Inst., 1968. Exploration geologist Lone Star Prodn. Co., Dallas, 1955-57; asst. div. geologist Pan

Am. Petroleum Corp., Denver, 1960-69; v.p., gen. mgr. Geosci. div., D.R. McCord & Assocs., Dallas, 1969-73; pres. ERGCO, Corp., Dallas, 1973—; instr. Colo. Sch. Mines and Petroleum Council, U. Wyo. and Oil Industry Com. Served with U.S. Army, 1951-52. Gulf Oil fellow, 1957-59; Northwestern U. scholar, George Pirtle scholar, 1955-56. Mem. Am. Assn. Petroleum Geologists (pres. div. profl. affairs), Soc. Ind. Profl. Earth Scientists (chmn. Dallas chpt., nat. pres. 1981-82), Dallas Geol. Soc., Rocky Mountain Assn. Geologists, Dallas Assn. Petroleum Landmen, Houston Geol. Soc. Editor Dallas Geol. and Geophysics Soc. Bull.; contbr. articles to profl. jours. Office: Meadows Building 5646 Milton Street Suite 334 Dallas TX 75206

INGHAM, RICHARD PAUL, optometrist; b. North Adams, Mass., Dec. 10, 1940; s. Clifford and Helen Ingham; m. Lorraine Bernice Toynbee, May 29, 1965; children—Jennifer, Kimberly. B.A., St. Michael's Coll., 1963; M.A., Fordham U., 1965; O.D., New Eng. Coll. Optometry, 1974. Staff optometrist The Eye Assoc., Tarpon Springs, 1974-80; gen. practice optometry, Palm Harbor, Fla., 1980—. Served with U.S. Army, 1966-68, Vietnam. Mem. Fla. Optometric Assn., Am. Optometric Assn. Democrat. Roman Catholic. Avocations: oil painting; piano; bridge. Home: 805 Maple Ridge Rd Palm Harbor FL 33563 Office: 3302 Buffalo-Sears Bldg Tampa FL 33607

INGRAHAM, JOE MCDONALD, judge; b. Pawnee County, Okla., July 5, 1903; s. Millard F. and Emma (Patton) I.; LL.B., Nat. U., 1927; m. Laura Munson, Oct. 29, 1954. Bar: Okla. and D.C. 1927, Tex. 1928. Practice law, Stroud, Okla., 1927-28, Ft. Worth, 1928-35, Houston, 1935-54; judge U.S. Dist. Ct. So. Dist. Tex., 1954-69; judge U.S. Ct. Appeals for 5th Circuit, 1969-73, sr. judge, 1973—; judge Temporary Emergency Ct. Appeals of U.S., 1976—. Served as officer USAAF, 1942-46. Mem. ABA, Houston Bar Assn., Tex. State Bar, Am. Judicature Soc., S.A.R. (pres. Tex. Soc. 1937-38; Good Citizenship award Tex. Soc. 1958), Am. Legion. Republican. Presbyterian. Home: 4718 Hallmark Apt 203 Houston TX 77056 Office: US Courthouse Houston TX 77002

INGRAM, CHARLES CLARK, JR., energy company executive; b. Henryetta, Okla., Dec. 10, 1916; s. Charles Clark and Winnie (Edwards) I.; B.S., U. Okla., 1940; LL.D., Oral Roberts U., 1983; m. Maxine Waterbury, Jan. 29, 1939; children—James C., Jack R. With Oneok Inc., Tulsa, 1940—, chmn. bd., 1966—, pres., 1966-71, chief exec. officer, 1971-81; dir. Bank of Okla. former chmn. bd. trustees Frontiers of Sci. Found. of Okla., Inc., 1973-74; adv. bd. Downtown Tulsa Unlimited; bd. govs. Am. Citizenship Center, Oklahoma City; mem. pres.'s bd. visitors U. Okla. Served from 2d lt. to maj. AUS, 1941-46. Named to Okla. Hall of Fame, 1982; registered profl. engr., Okla. Mem. Am. Assn. Petroleum Geologists, Am. Gas Assn. (chmn. 1979-80), So. Gas Assn. (past pres.), AIME, Engrs. Soc. Tulsa, Ind. Petroleum Assn. Am., Okla. State C. of C. (pres. 1981), Oklahoma City C. of C., Tulsa C. of C., Okla. Ind. Petroleum Assn., Okla.-Kans. Oil and Gas Assn. (dir.), Okla. Petroleum Council (dir.), Nat. Alliance Businessmen (chmn. Eastern Okla. and Tulsa 1973-74), Sigma Tau, Sigma Gamma Epsilon. Baptist. Clubs: Propeller of U.S., Tulsa, Summit, So. Hills Country (gov., past pres.); Cedar Ridge County (Tulsa). Lodge: Masons. Office: PO Box 871 Tulsa OK 74102

INGRAM, CONLEY, lawyer; b. Dublin, Ga., Sept. 27, 1930; s. George Conley and Nancy Averett (Whitehurst) I.; m. Sylvia Williams, July 26, 1952; children—Sylvia Lark, Nancy Randolph, George Conley. A.B., Emory U., 1949, LL.B., 1951. Bar: Ga. 1952. City atty. Smyrna, Ga., 1958-64, Kennesaw, Ga., 1964; judge Cobb County Juvenile Ct., 1960-64, superior Cobb County Jud. Cir. Ct., 1964-68; assoc. justice Supreme Ct., Ga., 1973-77; ptnr. Alston, Miller & Gaines and successor firm Alston & Bird, Atlanta, 1977—. Vice chmn. bd. trustees Agnes Scott Coll.; past chmn. council Emory U. Law Sch. Served with AUS, 1952-54. Recipient Disting. Service award Kennesaw Mountain Jaycees, 1961, Ga. Jaycees, 1961; Disting. Citizen award City of Marietta (Ga.), 1973; hon. life mem. Ga. PTA. Fellow Am. Bar Found., Internat. Soc. Barristers; mem. ABA, Ga. Bar Assn., Lawyers Club Atlanta, Assn. Trial Lawyers Am., Old War Horse Lawyers Club, Am. Law Inst., Cobb County C. of C. (past pres., pub. service award 1970). Democrat. Methodist. Club: Commerce (Atlanta). Home: 540 Hickory Dr Marietta GA 30064 Office: 1200 C&S Nat Bank Bldg 35 Broad St Atlanta GA 30335

INGRAM, JAMES LARRY, propane gas company official; b. McMinn County, Athens, Tenn., Dec. 25, 1950; s. James Walter and Martha Bernice (Raper) I.; m. Brenda Ruth Green, June 29, 1969; children—Michael Chad, Christopher Bo. Student Cleve. State Coll., 1970. With Pargas, Inc., 1969—, dist. mgr., Opelika, Ala., 1971-72, Pulaski, Tenn., 1972-80, sales mgr. parts, 1981-82, regional mgr., 1983—. Pres. Giles County Little League Assn., 1982. Mem. Miss. Liquid Propane Gas Assn. (dir.), Tenn. Liquid Propane Gas Assn. (pres. 1978-79, dir. 1974-82; T.G. Tackett Meml. award 1982). Republican. Baptist. Club: Exchange (Pulaski). Home: Rt 3 Houston Rd Laurel MS 39440 Office: PO Box 2716 Choctaw Station Laurel MS 39440

INGRAM, LAWRENCE WARREN, editor, publisher; b. Mt. Moriah, Mo., June 19, 1921; s. Earl Russell and Ella Elizabeth I.; A.A., George Washington U., 1947; B.Jour., U. Tex., Austin, 1949; m. Irene Farrell, Oct. 11, 1942. Research asst. Pres.'s Commn. on Higher Edn., Washington, 1946-47; editor Tex. State Parks Bd. mag., 1947-49; city editor, mng. editor, exec. editor Temple (Tex.) Daily Telegram, 1949-56, exec. editor, editor, 1961-72; with Denver Post, 1956-61, asst. city editor, 1958-59, radio-TV editor, 1959-60, editorial writer, 1960-61; pres. Stillhouse Hollow Pubs., Inc., Temple, Tex., 1973—; editor, pub. Belton Jour., 1973-81; editor, bus. mgr. S.W. and Tex. Water Works Jour., Temple, 1977—; pub. Vestnik, Temple, 1981-84. Served with U.S. Army, 1942-45. Mem. Am. Water Works Assn., Temple C. of C., Belton Area C. of C., Slavonic Benevolent Order of State of Tex. Clubs: Temple Rotary, Temple Country, Wildflower Country. Home: 3605 Buffalo Trail Temple TX 76501 Office: 306 E Adams St Temple TX 76501

INGRAM, ROBERT BERNARD, city manager; b. Miami, Fla., Aug. 5, 1936; s. Harold Atlaston and Arimentha Doretha (Womble) I.; A.A. with honors, Miami-Dade Coll., 1974; B.S., Fla. Internat. U., 1974, M.S., 1975; Ph.D., Union Experimenting Colls. and Univs., Cin., 1978; m. Delores Newsome, June 25, 1961; children—Tirzah Chezarena, Tamara Cheri. Officer, Miami (Fla.) Police Dept., from 1959; former chief of police City of Opa Locka, Fla.; now city mgr. City of South Miami, Fla.; instr. Miami-Dade Community Coll., 1975—; adjunct prof. Nova U., Ft. Lauderdale, Fla., 1977—. Bd. dirs. Opa Locka Family Mental Health Center, Biscayne Coll., 1976-77, chmn., 1976—; bd. dirs. Children's Psychiatric Center, Inc. of Dade County, Fla., 1976-77, Mental Health Bd., Miami, 1977—. Served with U.S. Army, 1956-59. Recipient officer of yr. award, Miami Police Dept., 1969, William D. Pawley award, Fraternal Order Police, 1969; named one of eleven outstanding police officers Nat. Internat. Assn. of Police Chiefs and Parade Magazine, 1970; police sci. award nominee, 1976; Disting. Budget award Gen. Fin. Officers Assn. Mem. Community Police Benevolent Assn. (pres. 1967), Fraternal Order of Police, Internat. Assn. of Police Chiefs, Nat. Assn. Blacks in Criminal Justice (founder Fla. chpt., pres.), Fla. Police Assn., Criminal Justice Educators, Applied Social and Behavioral Scientists, Phi Theta Kappa, NAACP, Nat. Orgn. Black Law Enforcement Execs. (chpt. founder, pres.), Kappa Alpha Psi, Sigma Pi Phi, Alpha Rho Boule. Democrat. African Methodist Episcopal. Clubs: Elks, KT, Shriners. Contbr. poem, articles to profl. jours; active in documentary films; selected as 1st Black officer in all white area, to ride motorcycle patrol, and to supervise vice control, internal security, and police tng. unit. Home: 1155 Sharar Ave Opa Locka FL 33054

INGRAM, ROY LEE, geology educator; b. Mamers, N.C., Mar. 12, 1921; s. Byron Perry and Berlena (McLean) I.; m. Jacqueline LaVon Sparks, June 5, 1944; children—Keith Sparks, Karen Ann. B.S., U. N.C., 1941; M.S., U. Okla.-Norman, 1943; Ph.D., U. Wis., 1947. Mem. faculty U. N.C.-Chapel Hill., 1947—, prof. geology, 1957—, chmn. geology dept., 1957-64, 74-79; cons. in field. Served to capt. U.S. Army, 1943-46. Mem. N.C. Earth Resources Council, Geol. Soc. Am. (pres. southeastern sect. 1958), Nat. Assn. Geology Tchrs. (treas. 1965-68), Am. Assn. Petroleum Geologists, Clay Minerals Soc., Internat Assn. Sedimentologists, Internat. Peat Soc., Sigma Xi. Democrat. Contbr. numerous geol. articles to profl. pubs. Home: 601 Oteys Rd Chapel Hill NC 27514 Office: Univ NC Geology Dept 029A Chapel Hill NC 27514

INGRAM, SAM HARRIS, university president; b. Acton, Tenn., Jan. 31, 1928; s. J. Quinn and Lois (Abernathy) I.; B.S. in Social Sci., Bethel Coll., 1951; M.A., Memphis State Coll., 1953; Ed.D., U. Tenn., Knoxville, 1959; children—Sam W., Glenn D. Elementary and high sch. prin., McNairy County, Tenn., 1949-57; supr. curriculum Tenn. Dept. Edn., 1959-62; asst. prof. edn. Memphis State U., 1962; chmn. edn. dept. Middle Tenn. State U., 1962-67, dean Sch. Edn., 1967-69; pres. Motlow State Community Coll., 1969-75; commr. edn. State of Tenn., Nashville, 1975-79; pres. Middle Tenn. State U., Murfreesboro, 1979—. Trustee Bethel Coll. Served with USMCR. Mem. Nat., Tenn. edn. assns., Council Chief State Sch. Officers, Edn. Commn. States, Tenn. Assn. Supervision and Curriculum Devel., Tenn. Curriculum Com. (past pres.), Tenn. Profs. Ednl. Adminstrn. (past pres.). Office: Middle Tenn State U Murfreesboro TN 37132

INGRAM, SHERRY ELIZABETH, elementary guidance counselor; b. Savannah, Ga., Oct. 17, 1950; d. Joseph Lonnie Ingram and Ouida Elizabeth (Wyatt) Franklin; m. Charles Donald MacCormack, Aug. 19, 1972 (div. Apr. 1974). B.A., Vanderbilt U., 1972; M.A., Ga. So. Coll., 1975, Edn. Specialist, 1978. With policyholder's service dept. Lincoln Am. Life, Memphis, 1972-73; property value assessment County Property Assessor, Jackson, Tenn., 1973-74; sch. counselor Portal Sch., Ga., 1975-78; supr. J.H. Wyatt Co., Brooklet, Ga., 1978-79; elem. counselor Juliette Low Sch., Savannah, Ga., 1979-81; guidance counselor Savannah Country Day Lower Sch., 1981—. Mem. adminstrv. bd. Wesley Monumental Ch., Savannah, 1984—. Mem. Am. Assn. Counseling and Devel., Ga. Edn. Assn., NEA, Bulloch County Edn. Assn. (sec. 1976-78), Ga. Sch. Counselors Assn. (exec. bd., fall conf. coordinator 1984, elem. worksetting v.p. 1985), Phi Kappa Phi, Kappa Delta Pi, Delta Kappa Gamma. Democrat. Methodist. Avocations: needlepoint; reading; travel. Office: Savannah Country Day Lower Sch PO Box 14256 Savannah GA 31416

INGRAM, WILLIAM ALLAN, banker; b. Dallas, Sept. 9, 1949; s. Allen Baccus and Willie Fae (Zackery) I.; m. Marilyn Wyrick, Nov. 18, 1978; children—William Preston, Mason Wyrick. B.A., U. Tex., 1972; M.B.A., So. Meth. U., 1981. Banking officer Republic Bank, Garland, Tex., 1972-77, asst. v.p., comml. loan officer, 1977-79, v.p., mgr. comml. loan adminstrn., 1979-81; asst. v.p., credit rev. officer Inter First Bank, Dallas, 1981-83, v.p., div. adminstrv. officer, 1983-85, v.p., corp. lending officer, 1985—. Bd. dirs. Garland br. YMCA, 1980-81; exec. mem. The 500, Inc., 1978-83; mem. capital improvement drive Presbyn. Hosp. of Dallas, 1981. Mem. Robert Morris Assocs., Am. Inst. Banking, Garland C. of C. Presbyterian. Club: Ambassadors. Lodge: Kiwanis (Kiwanian of Yr. 1979, bd. dirs., pres., v.p., treas. 1974-81). Office: PO Box 83000 Dallas TX 75283

INGRAM, WILLIAM THOMAS, III, mathematics educator; b. McKenzie, Tenn., Nov. 26, 1937; s. William Thomas and Virginia (Howell) I.; m. Barbara Lee Gordon, June 6, 1958; children—William Robert, Kathie Ann, Mark Thomas. B.A., Bethel Coll., 1959; M.S., La. State U., 1961; Ph.D., Auburn U., 1964. Instr. Auburn U., Ala., 1961-63; instr. math. U. Houston, 1964-65, asst. prof., 1965-68, assoc. prof., 1968-75, prof., 1975—. Contbr. articles to profl. jours. Mem. Am. Math. Soc. Presbyterian. Avocation: photography. Home: 8210 Braesview Houston TX 77071 Office: Dept Mathematics U Houston 4800 Calhoun Houston TX 77004

INGWERSON, DONALD, educational administrator. Supt. of schs. Jefferson County, La. Office: 3332 Newburg Rd Louisville KY 40218*

INHABER, HERBERT, risk analyst, physicist; b. Montreal, Que., Can., Jan. 25, 1941; s. Samuel and Mollye (Blumenfeld) I.; m. Elizabeth Rose Bowen, Dec. 21, 1964 (div. 1981). B.Sc., McGill U., 1962; M.S., U. Ill., 1964; postgrad. U. Rochester, 1965-67; Ph.D., U. Okla., 1971. Sci. advisor Sci. Council Can., Ottawa, 1971-72; policy analyst Fed. Dept. Environment, Ottawa, 1972-77; vis. lectr. dept. history sci. and medicine Sch. Forestry and Environ., Yale U., New Haven, 1975; sci. advisor Atomic Energy Control Bd., Ottawa, 1977-80; lectr. physics dept. Carleton U., Ottawa, 1976-80; coordinator Office Risk Analysis, Oak Ridge Nat. Lab., 1980-84; prin. Risk Concepts Inc., 1984—. Pres., Oak Ridge Friends of the Library, 1983-84. Served with RCAF, 1957-61. Mem. Am. Nuclear Soc., Soc. Risk Analysis (nat. membership chmn.), AAAS, Mensa, Sigma Xi, Sigma Pi Sigma. Author: Environmental Indices, 1976; Physics of the Environment, 1978; Energy Risk Assessment, 1982; What in the World?, 1984; contbr. articles to profl. jours.; writer weekly column Oak Ridger, 1981—. Home: 28 Montclair Rd Oak Ridge TN 37830 Office: Box 1231 Oak Ridge TN 37830

INLOW, D(AVID) RONALD, university administrator, food service consultant, consumerism lecturer; b. Cheyenne, Wyo., Mar. 18, 1943; s. Gail Maurice and Joanne Francis (Currie) I.; m. Beverly Jean Walden, June 20, 1964; children—Deborah Sue, Robert John, Jennifer Lynn. B.A., No. Ill. U., 1965, M.S., 1972. Food service mgr. No. Ill. U., DeKalb, 1965-72; dir. food service Valparaiso U., Ind., 1972-78; dir. food service U. Richmond, Va., 1978-80, dir. aux. services, 1980—; evaluator profl. standards Nat. Assn. Coll. and Univ. Food Services, East Lansing, Mich., 1984—; cons. Francis Marion Coll., Florence, S.C., 1983—, Dolly Madison Retirement Home, Richmond, 1981. Speaker on the mentally handicapped in the work force, 1985. Sec. Community Involvement Citizens Adv. Group to sch. system, Richmond, 1983—; elder Gayton Kirk Presbyn. Ch., Richmond, 1984—; originator Sanitation Certification Program Richmond, Va., Valparaiso, Ind., 1981, Meals on Wheels Program, Valparaiso, 1973. Recipient Disting. Service award Nat. Inst. for Food Service Industry, 1977. Adminstr./Staff award U. Richmond Student Govt., 1979. Mem. Nat. Assn. Coll. and Univ. Food Services (regional pres. 1976-78), Nat. Restaurant Assn., Am. Personnel and Guidance Assn., Va. Coll. Book Store Assn., Nat. Inst. for Food Service Industry (cert.), DeKalb Jaycees (pres. 1970-71). Club: Octopi Synchronized Swimming (pres. 1981-83) (Richmond). Lodge: Rotary (bd. dirs. 1975-77). Avocations: coaching Little League baseball; administration of synchronized swimming activities at regional level. Home: 11402 Creekside Dr Richmond VA 23233 Office: Univ Richmond Commons Bldg 3d Fl Richmond VA 23173

INMAN, FRANKLIN POPE, biochemist, educator; b. Hamlet, N.C., Aug. 2, 1937; s. Franklin Pope and Aieleen (Shelton) I.; m. Barbara Bullock, Aug. 30, 1959; children—Jody Lin, James Walter. A.B., U.N.C., 1959, Ph.D., 1964. Asst. prof. biochemistry and microbiology U. Ga., Athens, 1966-70, assoc. prof. biochemistry and microbiology 1970-75, prof., 1975-77; prof., chmn. dept. biochemistry East Tenn. State U. Coll. Medicine, 1977—; mem. faculty Med. Coll. Ga., 1970-71; mem. faculty continuing edn. courses Basic and Clin. Immunology, Atlanta, 1978, Basic Sci. Rev. Immunology, 1979, Allergy-Immunology, 1981, Johnson City, Tenn.; vis. lectr. in immunology Harvard U. Med. Sch., 1975-76; dir. So. Immunology Conf. Inc., chmn., 1968, 70, 85; participant in numerous symposia, panels and workshops. U.N.C. John M. Morehead scholar, 1955-59; Am. Cancer Soc. scholar, 1976; sr. McMaster fellow Commonwealth Sci. and Indsl. Research Orgn., Sydney, Australia, 1985-86; recipient U. Ga. M.G. Michael award, 1969. Mem. Am. Assn. Immunologists (travel award to 2d Internat. Congress in Immunology Brighton, Eng. 1974, rep. FASEB pubs. com. 1983-86), Am. Soc. Biol. Chemists, Am. Soc. Microbiology, Am. Chem. Soc., Assn. Med. Sch. Depts. Biochemistry, N.Y. Acad. Scis. Editor, contbr. numerous med. textbooks, also articles for sci. jours. Home: 707 Willmar St Johnson City TN 37601 Office: East Tennessee State U Quillen-Dishner College of Medicine Dept Biochemistry PO Box 19930A Johnson City TN 37614

INNES, RUTH STARRATT, counselor, educational consultant; b. North Adams, Mass., Aug. 6, 1941; d. Howard Manuel and Mabel Annette (Bishop) Starratt; m. John F.K. Innes, May 24, 1965; 1 son, Howard Michael. B.S., North Adams State Coll., 1964; M.A., U. Mass., 1968; M.A., U. South Fla., 1979, Ed.S., 1983. Instr. Colby Sawyer Coll., New London, N.H., 1967-68, Nyack (N.Y.) Coll., 1968-70, Dominican Coll., Blauvelt, N.Y., 1968-70; social worker Mass. Dept. Pub. Welfare, 1970-72; prof. North Adams State Coll., 1972-76; social worker Mass. Children's Protective Services, Pittsfield, Mass., 1977; pvt. practice ednl. counseling, St. Petersburg, Fla., 1979—; dir. guidance and counseling Shorecrest Prep. Sch., St. Petersburg, 1979—; cons. Fla. Council Ind. Schs., Pinellas County (Fla.) Schs.; lectr. in field. Mem. Am. Sociol. Assn., Suncoast Personnel and Guidance Assn., Fla. Personnel and Guidance Assn., Nat. Assn. Coll. Admission Counselors, Am. Personnel and Guidance Assn., So. Assn. Admissions Counselors. Home: 5533 Sycamore St N Saint Petersburg FL 33703 Office: 5101 1st St N Saint Petersburg FL 33703

IODICE, EMILIO FRANCIS, diplomat; b. N.Y.C., Apr. 13, 1946. B.S., Fordham U., 1968; M.B.A., Bernard Baruch U., 1971; D.B.A., George Washington U., 1986. Corp. planning staff Continental Group, N.Y.C., 1971-73; economist, office dir. U.S. Dept. Commerce, Washington, 1973-78; chief economist Customs Service, U.S. Dept. Treasury, Washington, 1978-82; comml. counselor U.S. and Fgn. Comml. Service U.S. Embassy, Brasilia, Brazil, prof. 1982-85, Mexico City, 1985—; George Mason U., 1980-82, N.V.C. Coll., Annadale, Va., 1975-82. Contbr. articles to profl. jours. Recipient Superior Performance award U.S. Dept. Commerce, 1985, Meritorious award, 1984, Silver medal, 1983; Gold medal award for heroism, 1985; Plaque, Va. Coal Assn., 1985. Mem. Am. Econ. Assn., Beta Gamma Sigma. Roman Catholic. Avocations: writer; historian.

IOVACCHINI, ERIC VINCENT, university administrator, educational law consultant; b. Vineland, N.J., Oct. 19, 1947; s. Vincent T. and Evelyn (Brezzo) I.; m. Helen Kincade, Feb. 1, 1970 (div.); children—Dana Anne, Nicholas. B.A., Gettysburg Coll., 1970; J.D., U. Nebr., 1972; Ph.D., U. Wyo., 1978. Bar: Nebr. 1973. Sole practice law, Lincoln, Nebr., 1972-74; asst. dean of students U. Wyo., Laramie, 1974-76, assoc. dean of students, 1976-78; vice chancellor for student affairs U. N.C., Asheville, 1978—; cons. S.C. Bd. for Tech. and Comprehensive Edn., Columbia, 1982, N.C. Dept. Community Colls., Raleigh, 1982, Wyo. Dept. Edn., Cheyenne, 1978. Contbr. articles to profl. jours. Bd. dirs. Asheville-Buncombe County Youth Council, 1980—. Grantee N.C. Dept. Transp., 1981-82, W. K. Kellogg Found., 1982—. Mem. Am. Coll. Personnel Assn., Nat. Assn. Student Personnel Adminstrn., Am. Assn. Counseling and Devel., Nebr. Bar Assn. Democrat. Unitarian. Avocations: gardening; outdoor recreation; reading. Home: 17 Marne Rd Asheville NC 28803 Office: U NC 1 University Heights Asheville NC 28804-3299

IPACH, CHARLOTTE RESS, nurse; b. Cin., Sept. 11, 1958; d. Friedrich and Barbara (Novak) Ress; m. Peter Anton Ipach, June 23, 1984. B.S. in Nursing, U. Cin., 1980. Staff nurse Emerson A. North Hosp., Cin., 1980-81; staff nurse Children's Psychiat. Hosp. No. Ky., Covington, Ky., 1981-83, dir. nursing, 1983—. Mem. Donauschwaben Soc. Avocations: embroidery; German folk dancing.

IRBY, GEORGE HENRY, SR., educational administrator; b. Blackstone, Va., July 7, 1949; s. Harry and Maurice (Copeland) I.; m. Marsha Jeter, June 16, 1973; children—George, Jr., Joi Marshae. B.S. in Health and Phys. Edn., Va. State U., 1971, M.Edn. Adminstrn. and Supervision, 1972, postgrad. in urban services, 1986. Tchr. health and phys. edn. Blackstone Jr. High Sch., Va., 1973; asst. prin. Amelia County Elem. Sch., Va., 1976-78, planning prin. 1978-79; asst. prin. Brookland Middle Sch., Richmond, Va., 1979-80; supr. compensatory edn. Va. Dept. Edn., Richmond, 1980—; dir. migrant edn. State of Va., 1980—; extern personnel adminstr. Richmond Pub. Schs., 1985. Mem. Gov.'s Migrant and Seasonal Farm Workers Commn., Richmond, 1980—; mem. adv. bd. Henrico Edn. Adminstrn., Va., 1983—. Served to capt. U.S. Army, 1973-76. Mem. Nat. Assn. Secondary Prins., Nat. Migrant Edn. Assn. (sec. 1983-84), Va. Middle Sch. Forum, Nat. Middle Sch. Assn., Assn. Supervision and Curriculum Devel., Amelia Jaycees (v.p. 1976-79, Outstanding Jaycee award 1978, Outstanding Young Men in Am. award 1983), Phi Delta Kappa, Alpha Phi Alpha. Roman Catholic. Club: Scabbard and Blade. Lodge: K.C. Avocations: running; tennis; all athletics. Home: 8400 Flinthill Dr Richmond VA 23227

IRELAND, ANDY, congressman; b. Cin., Aug. 23, 1930; s. Ellsworth Frederick and Dorothy Marie (Poysell) I.; m. Nancy Haydock, Sept. 12, 1981; children—Debbie, Mimi, Drew, Dutch. B.A. in Indsl. Adminstrn, Yale Sch. Engring. Chmn. bd. Barnett Bank of Winter Haven, Cypress Gardens, Auburndale, Fla.; treas. Fla. Bankers Assn.; dir. Jacksonville (Fla.) br. Fed. Res. Bank Atlanta; Fla. state v.p. Am. Bankers Assn.; mem. 95th-97th Congresses from 8th Fla. Dist., 98th Congress from 10th Fla. dist.; public rep. UN, 1981. Mem. Winter Haven City Commn., 1966-68. Mem. Winter Haven Area C. of C. (past pres.), Fla. Soc. D.C. (pres.). Episcopalian. Clubs: Masons, Shriners, Jesters, Elks, Kiwanis, Moose. Office: 2416 Rayburn House Office Bldg Washington DC 20515*

IRELAND, TIMOTHY CHARLES, management science educator, economic analyst; b. Enid, Okla., Aug. 16, 1952; s. John Benjamin and Maxine Louise (Dillon) I.; m. Sandra Kay McKinney, May 31, 1975; children—Craig Thomas, Jill Kathleen. B.S. in Math., Phillips U., 1974; M.S. in Econs., Okla. State U., 1976, Ph.D. in Econs., 1978. Faculty research assoc. Coll. Bus. Adminstrn. Okla. State U., Stillwater, 1978-81, asst. prof. mgmt. sci., 1981-85, assoc. prof., 1985—; dir. Okla. State Econometric Model. Mem. So. Econ. Assn., Am. Inst. for Decision Scis. Republican. Mem. Christian Ch. Contbr. articles to profl. jours.; contbr. econ. outlook presentations to media sources. Home: 2801 N Keller Stillwater OK 74075 Office: Coll Bus Adminstrn Okla State U Stillwater OK 74078

IRICK, PAUL EUGENE, retired research project director, statistician; b. Greenville, Ohio, Nov. 4, 1918; s. Simon H. and Mary (Long) I.; m. Ruth Anderson, Feb. 14, 1939 (div. 1956); children—Jo Ann, Gene, David; m. Vanis Jean Deeter, July 5, 1957; children—Christopher Neil, Todd Joel. B.S., Purdue U., 1940, M.S., 1945, Ph.D., 1950. Assoc. prof. stats. Purdue U., Lafayette, Ind., 1950-55; research statistician Hwy. Research Bd. NRC, Washington, 1955-67; asst. dir. spl. projects Transp. Research Bd. NRC, Nat. Acad. Scis., Washington, 1967-82; dir. Engring. Index, Inc., N.Y.C., 1968-76, pres., 1973-76. Mem. Am. Statis. Assn. Methodist. Club: Cosmos. Home: 484 Windmill Point Rd Hampton VA 23664

IRISH, WILLIAM MITCHELL, V, college administrator; b. Houston, Oct. 14, 1954; s. William Mitchell and Anne Houston (Hogan) I. A.A., Blinn Coll., 1974; B.A., U. St. Thomas, 1976. Lic. Realtor, Tex. Adminstrv. asst. Hogan Allnoch Co., Houston, 1975-78; adminstrv. asst. Phila. Life Ins. Co., Houston, 1978-79, acctg. supr., 1979-82; area mgr. Borg Warner Ins. Corp., Houston, 1982-83; realtor Martin Comml. Properties, Houston, 1981-84; dir. community relations Houston Gamblers Football Team, U.S. Football League, 1984-85; athletic bus. mgr. Rice U., 1985—. Precinct judge Democratic Precinct 227 Harris County; del. Dist. Dem. Conv., 1982, State Conv., 1982; chmn. Cystic Fibrosis Walk, 1977; co-chmn. 336 Mile Walk to Dallas, Com. to Combat Huntington's Disease, 1976; chmn. security, escort and transp. and spl. services coms. Bluebonnet Bowl, Greater Houston Bowl Assn., 1981—, bd. dirs., 1983—; vol. Jerry Lewis Telethon for Muscular Dystrophy, 1982; emergency services technician Harris/Montgomery counties ARC, 1983—. Mem. Am. Mgmt. Assn., Life Office Mgmt. Assn. Democrat. Roman Catholic. Lodge: Kiwanis (Disting. Service award 1981). Home: 2233 Welch #3 Houston TX 77019 Office: PO Box 1892 Houston TX 77251

IRONS, E. H., educational administrator. Supt. of schs. Lubbock, Tex. Office: 1628 19th St Lubbock TX 79401*

IRONS, STEPHEN ELDEN, safety engineer; b. Providence, Mar. 26, 1947; s. Elden LeRoy and Alice Marie (Fortes) I.; m. Sandra Jean Crouch, Aug. 2, 1969; 1 child, Jennifer Ruth. B.S. in Biology, Valdosta State Coll., 1974. Sr. sanitarian South Health Dist., Valdosta, 1974-80; safety supr. ITT Rayonier Inc., Jesup, Ga., 1980-85; safety coordinator Container Corp. Am., Brewton, Ala., 1985—. Served as staff sgt. USAF, 1966-70. Mem. Am. Soc. Safety Engrs. Lodges: Masons, Lions. Avocations: photography; woodworking; church activities; softball. Home: 103 Fairway Dr Brewton AL 36427 Office: Container Corp Am Brewton Mill Brewton AL 36427

IRONS, WILLIAM LEE, lawyer; b. Birmingham, Ala., June 9, 1941; s. George Vernon, Sr., and Velma (Wright) I.; m. Karen Phillips, Oct. 30, 1976. B.A., U. Va., 1963; J.D., Samford U., 1966. Bar: Ala. 1966. Ptnr., Speir, Robertson, Jackson & Irons, 1970-72, Speir & Irons, 1972-73; founding and sr. ptnr. William L. Iron Atty. at Law, Birmingham, 1973—. Bd. dirs. Planned Parenthood Assn. Birmingham, 1973—; assoc. deacon Mountain Brook Baptist Ch., 1971-73; mem. Nat. Trust Hist. Preservation, 1977—. Served to capt. JAGC, USAF, 1966-70. Named Outstanding Jr. Officer of USAF, 1969; Dupont regional scholar, 1963. Mem. ABA, Birmingham Trial Lawyers Assn., Ala. Trial Lawyers Assn., Assn. Trial Lawyers Am., Res. Officers Assn., SAR, Fed. Bar Assn., Birmingham Execs. Club (v.p. 1979-81), SR, Descendants of Gen. George Washington's Army at Valley Forge. Club: Downtown. Office: 805 Jefferson Federal Bldg Birmingham AL 35203

IRVIN, LESLIE DAVID, police chief; b. Jasper, Tex., Jan. 24, 1944; s. Walter Raymond Crutchfield (stepfather) and Myrtie Ellen (Smith) Irvin Crutchfield; m. Melba Rae Hollier, Aug. 19, 1966; 1 dau., Leah Denise. B.S. in Criminal Justice, Lamar U., 1976. Cert. in advanced law enforcement, Tex. Patrolmen Port Neches Police Dept., Tex., 1966-68; field investigator Galveston Police Dept., Tex., 1970-72; patrolman, research analyst Beaumont Police Dept., Tex., 1972-78; police chief Crockett Police Dept., Tex., 1978-81, Muleshoe Police Dept., Tex., 1981—. Pres. Bailey County Child Welfare Bd., Tex., 1982-83;

chmn. Muleshoe chpt. Am. Cancer Soc., 1984; active Muleshoe Athletic Boosters, 1984-85, Muleshoe Fine Arts Boosters, 1984-85. Served with USAF, 1962-66. Mem. Internat. Assn. Chiefs of Police, Nat. Assn. Chiefs of Police (state v.p. 1980-83), Tex. Police Chiefs Assn., Tex. Police Assn. Mem. Assembly of God Ch. Lodge: Lions (pres. local lodge 1984-85). Avocations: high school athletics; hunting; skiing; reading; raising tropical fish. Home: PO Box 69 Muleshoe TX 79347 Office: Muleshoe Police Dept 215 E Ave B Muleshoe TX 79347

IRVINE, FREEMAN RAYMOND, JR., education educator, clergyman; b. Madison, Fla., Sept. 12, 1931; s. Freeman Raymond and Susie (Swilley) I.; m. Emma Joseph, Dec. 2, 1954; (div. 1971); children—Rodney L., Charlton A.; m. Carolyn Green, Nov. 21, 1977; children—Pamela R., Fredreka R., Freeman III. B.S., Fla. A&M U., 1958; cert. Okla. State U., 1960; M.S., U. Tenn., 1968, Ed.D., 1972. Assoc. prof. electronics Fla. A&M U., Tallahassee, 1958-61, assoc. prof. edn., 1964—; tchr. electronics Broward County Sch., Ft. Lauderdale, Fla., 1961-63; engring. aide SYSY Engineering Labs., Ft. Lauderdale, 1963-64; pastor Antioch Missionary Baptist Ch., Perry, Fla., 1981—. Author: Teach Handicapped, 1984. Served with U.S. Army, 1951-54. Mem. Am. Vocat. Assn. Am. Indsl. Arts Assn., Fla. Vocat. Assn., Fla. Indsl. Arts Assn., Iota Lambda Sigma, Phi Delta Kappa, Alpha Kappa Mu. Democrat. Baptist. Avocations: fishing; photography; hunting; reading. Home: 618 Brookridge Dr Tallahassee FL 32304 Office: Fla A&M U Coll Of Edn Box 106 Tallahassee FL 32307

IRVINE, JOHN ALEXANDER, lawyer; b. Sault Ste. Marie, Ont., Can., Aug. 10, 1897; came to U.S., 1952; s. Alexander and Ruth Catherine (Woolrich) I.; m. Jacquelyn Louise Church, June 13, 1970 (div. 1980); children—John Alexander, Allison Brooks; m. Lynda Kaye Myska Jenkins, May 24, 1981; 1 child, James Woolrich. B.S., Auburn U., 1969; J.D., Memphis State U., 1972. Bar: Tenn. 1972, Ohio 1982, Tex. 1985. Law clk. to presiding justice U.S. Dist. Ct. for Western Dist. Tenn., Memphis, 1972-73; asst. dist. atty. gen. 15th Jud. Cir. Tenn., Memphis, 1973-78; assoc. Glankler, Brown, Gilliand, Chase, Robertson & Raines, Memphis, 1978-81; asst. gen. counsel Mead Corp., Dayton, Ohio, 1981-84; ptnr., Porter & Clements, Houston, 1984—. Bd. visitors Memphis State Law Sch., 1978-79; bd. dirs. Make-A-Wish Found. of Tex. Gulf Coast, Houston, 1985—. Mem. ABA, Tex. Bar Assn., Tenn. Bar Assn., Ohio Bar Assn., Houston Bar Assn., Memphis Bar Assn., Shelby County Bar Assn., Dayton Bar Assn., Memphis State U. Sch. Law Nat. Alumni Assn. (pres. 1975-76, 78-79), Young Lawyers Assn. (bd. dirs., treas. 1975-77), U.S. C. of C. (council on antitrust policy 1983—). Republican. Presbyterian. Clubs: Briar, Texas, Houston Met. Racquet, Heritage, Forum (Houston); Phoenix (bd. dirs. 1978-80) (Memphis). Home: 2111 Chilton Rd Houston TX 77019 Office: Porter & Clements 3500 Republic Bank Ctr Houston TX 77002

IRVING, HERBERT, food products company executive; b. 1917. B.A., U. Pa., 1938. With Ultima Corp., 1945-48; vice chmn. bd. Sysco Co., Houston. Address: Sysco Corp 1177 W Loop S Houston TX 77027*

IRWIN, DONALD PAULDING, lawyer; b. N.Y.C., Oct. 15, 1944; s. Donald McDonald and Sarah Paulding (Ray) I.; m. Dorothy Porcher Deane, May 10, 1980; children—Louise Porcher Gray, Elizabeth Sinclair. A.B., Princeton U., 1965; J.D., Yale U., 1971, M.A. in Polit. Sci., 1971. Bar: Va. 1971, D.C. 1977. Assoc., Hunton & Williams, Richmond, Va., 1971-78, ptnr., 1978—; vis. prof. law Coll. William and Mary Law Sch., 1979-80, 81-82; speaker nuclear regulatory symposium Am. Law Inst., Washington, 1984-85. Pres. Monument Ave Preservation Soc., Richmond, 1985-86; bd. dirs. Fan Dist. Assn., Richmond, 1983—, Richmond Symphony, 1983—. Served to lt. USNR, 1965-67, Suez, Vietnam. Mem. ABA. Republican. Episcopalian. Clubs: Met. (Washington); Country of Va., Commonwealth (Richmond); Princeton (N.Y.C.). Avocations: white water canoeing, golfing. Home: 2704 Monument Ave Richmond VA 23220 Office: Hunton & Williams 707 E Main St Richmond VA 23219

IRWIN, PETER JOHN, orthopaedic surgeon; b. East St. Louis, Ill., July 7, 1934; s. Peter and Anne (Sokalski) Iwasyszyn; m. Kathryn Swanson, June 15, 1960; children—Kathryn Linda, Mary Elizabeth, Amy Marie, Kenneth John, James Patrick. B.S. in Biology, St. Louis U., 1955, M.D., 1959. Diplomate Am. Bd. Orthopaedic Surgery. Intern, Creighton Meml. St. Joseph Hosp., Omaha, 1959-60; resident orthopaedic surgery U. Ark. Med. Ctr., 1961-65, teaching staff, 1965—; practice medicine specializing in orthopaedic surgery, Fort Smith, Ark., 1965—; mem. staff St. Edward Mercy Med. Ctr., 1965—; mem. staff Sparks Regional Med. Ctr., 1965—, chief of staff, 1979, bd. dirs., 1980—. Served to lt. comdr. M.C., USN, 1966-68. Fellow Am. Acad. Orthopaedic Surgeons (councillor 1983—), ACS; mem. AMA, So. Med. Assn., Sebastian County Med. Soc., Ark. Orthopaedic Assn. (pres. 1976-77), Mid-Am. Orthopaedic Assn. (founding mem.), Mid-Central States Orthopaedic Soc. (pres. 1979-80), So. Orthopaedic Assn., Am. Orthopaedic Soc. for Sports Medicine, Am. Soc. Sports Medicine, Ark. Hand Club. Office: 1500 Dodson Ave Fort Smith AR 72901

ISAACS, DOROTHY ANN, community activist; b. St. Thomas, V.I., Nov. 20, 1948; d. Walter John and Thelma Ruth (Watson) Maguire; m. Mark Aldes Isaacs, Apr. 8, 1972; children—Julie, Elisabeth. B.A., B.S., Castleton State Coll., 1970. Rep., Mt. Vernon Citizens Assn. Edn. Com., Fairfax County, Va., 1983-85, Task Force on Declining Enrollment, Fairfax County, Va., 1984, Mt. Vernon Ednl. Adv. Com., Fairfax County, 1985. Bd. dirs. Belle View PTA, Fairfax County, 1980—, pres., 1981-82; unit co-chair League Women Voters, Fairfax County, 1984-85; bd. dirs. Tauxemont Pre-Sch., Alexandria, 1977-84. Home: 7204 Marlan Dr Alexandria VA 22307

ISAACS, GERALD WILLIAM, agricultural engineer; b. Crawfordsville, Ind., Sept. 3, 1927; s. William Paul and Verna Ethel (Johnson) I.; m. Phyllis Joyce Seaton Aug. 22, 1948; children—David, Donald, Susan, Linda. B.S.E.E., Purdue U., 1947, M.S.E.E., 1949; Ph.D., Mich. State U., 1954. Registered profl. engr., Fla. Instr. agrl. engring. Purdue U., West Lafayette, Ind., 1948-52; grad. research asst. Mich. State U., East Lansing, 1952-54; asst. prof. Purdue U., 1954-57, assoc. prof., 1957-60, prof., 1960-64, head dept. agrl. engring., 1964-81; prof., head dept. agrl. engring. U. Fla., Gainesville, 1981—; cons. various mfrs. of grain drying and storage equipment. Contbr. articles to profl. jours. Served with USN, 1945-46. Recipient Silver medal Max Eyth-Gesellschaft, 1979. Fellow Am. Soc. Agrl. Engrs. (pres. 1981-82); mem. Nat. Soc. Profl. Engrs., Am. Soc. Engring. Edn., Tau Beta Pi, Alpha Zeta. Lutheran. Avocations: photography; camping. Home: 2221 NW 27th Terr Gainesville FL 32608 Office: Agrl Engring Dept Rogers Hall U Fla Gainesville FL 32611

ISAACS, MARK ANDREW, architectural designer, energy consultant; b. Louisville, Jan. 6, 1956; married. B.S.A.D., MIT, 1977, M.Arch., 1980; student Internat. Architecture Lab., Urbino, Italy, 1979. Lady Davis fellow Technion, Haifa, Israel, 1978; prin. Energy Efficient Design, Louisville, Ky., 1981—; chmn. Ky. Solar Coalition, 1984, Urban Shelter Assocs., 1985; vice chmn. Environ. Alternatives, 1983. Mem. Louisville Forum, 1984-85, The Third Century, 1980—. Profl. designer fellow NEA, 1980; recipient Ky. Solar Design award Energy Cabinet, 1984. Mem. AIA (assoc. mem.; program coordinator), Home Builders Assn. Democrat. Avocations: sailing; swimming. Office: Energy Efficient Design 533 Brown & Williamson Tower Louisville KY 40202

ISAACS, RUSSELL L., department store executive; b. 1932. B.S., W.Va. U. Staff acct. Witschey, Harman, & White, 1958-62; with Heck's Inc., Nitro, W.Va., 1962—, comptroller, 1965-73, chief fin. officer, treas., 1973-79, pres., 1979-83, chmn. bd., chief exec. officer, 1983—. Address: Hecks Inc PO Box 158 Nitro WV 25143*

ISAACSON, IRA JAY, anesthesiologist; b. Chgo., Oct. 24, 1951; s. Maurie and Ruth Isaacson. B.S. with distinction in Physiology, U. Ill., 1972; M.D., Chgo. Med. Sch., 1976. Postgrad. med. edn. Northwestern U. Sch. Medicine, Chgo., 1976-79; research fellow Harvard Med. Sch., Boston, 1979-80; postgrad. resident Peter Bent Brigham Hosp., Boston, 1979-80; asst. prof. anesthesiology Emory U. Sch. Medicine, Atlanta, 1980—, instr. in field. Chmn. resident sect. Ill. State Med. Soc., 1978-79. Mem. AMA (nat. governing council resident sect. 1979-80), Ga. Med. Soc., Med. Assn. Atlanta, Am. Soc. Anesthesiologists, Ga. Soc. Anesthesiologists, Soc. Cardiovascular Anesthesiologists. Lectr. profl. confs. Home: 5636 River Oaks Place NW Atlanta GA 30327 Office: 1364 Clifton Rd NE Atlanta GA 30322

ISAACSON, MARVIN GERALD, psychiatrist; b. Bklyn., July 23, 1918; s. Julius and Ida I.; student CCNY, 1937-40; M.D., Coll. Physicians and Surgeons, 1944; cert. psychiatry, neurology and neurosurgery Syracuse U., 1951; m. Illene Juanita Rosenberg, Mar. 25, 1970; children—Ronald, Anita Louise, Dean Marco, Clark, Fern. Intern, Maimonides Hosp., Bklyn., 1943-45; resident Parkway Gen. Hosp. N.Y.C., 1945-49; supervising psychiatrist Willard State Hosp., 1949-52; practice medicine specializing in psychiatry, Miami, Miami Beach, Fla., 1954—; attending psychiatrist Jackson Meml. Hosp., Miami, 1955—; cons. St. Francis Hosp., Miami Beach, Fla., 1969—, VA Hosp., 1955-59, Mt. Sinai Hosp., Miami Beach, 1955-59; exec. dir. P. L. Dodge Meml. Hosp., Miami, 1962-82; instr. U. Miami Med. Sch., 1955-72, asst. clin. prof., 1972—, instr. Nursing Sch., 1975—; cons. in psychiatry Dodge Hosp., Miami, 1982-85; cons., attending in psychiatry Harbor View Hosp., Miami. Pres., P. L. Dodge Found., 1962—, bd. dirs. 1959-82; dir. Jewish Vocat. Service, 1964—; bd. dirs. Dade County Council on Alcoholism, 1971-78, Humane Soc. of Dade County, 1974—; chmn. med.-psychiat. staff Broward County Mental Health Div., Fla., 1984—; bd. dirs. Douglas Gardens Community Mental Health Center, 1981-82. Served with USAF, 1952-54. Recipient Cert. of Appreciation, Dade Community Coll., 1981. Mem. World Med. Assn., AMA, Am. Psychiat. Soc., Nat. Assn. Pvt. Psychiat. Hosps. (mem. legis. com. 1981), Fla. Assn. Pvt. Psychiat. Hosps. (pres. 1975), S. Fla. Psychiat. Soc. (chmn. ins. com. 1971-72), Fla. Med. Assn., Dade County Med. Assn. Democrat. Jewish. Clubs: Jockey, California Country. Office: 1861 NW South River Dr Miami FL 33125

ISAKSON, HANS ROBERT, real estate educator; b. Milw., Apr. 27, 1944; s. Hans Isac and Josephine (Velican) I.; m. Dorothy Jane Riebe, Jan. 23, 1965; children—Timothy, Tameron. B.S. in Econs. with honors, U. Wis.-Milw., 1972, Ph.D. in Urban Econs. and Pub. Fin., 1977. Cert. rev. appraiser; registered mortgage underwriter. Asst. dir. Urban Research Ctr., Milw., 1974-75; asst. prof. U. Ga., Athens, 1975-78, Wash. State U., Pullman, 1978-81; assoc. prof. fin. and real estate U. Tex.-Arlington, 1981—, acting dir. Real Estate Ctr., 1981-82; prin. investigator FEA, 1976-77, U.S. Dept. Energy, 1977-78, 78-79. Contbr. articles and chpts. to profl. jours. and books. Active Boy Scouts Am. Served with USNR, 1966-68. Recipient Arthur A. May Fund award Am. Inst. Real Estate Appraisers, 1979; Manuscript award Lincoln Inst., Cambridge, Mass., 1983; Best Profl. Article award U. Tex.-Arlington Coll. Bus., 1984. Mem. Nat. Assn. Rev. Appraisers and Mortgage Underwriters, Am. Real Estate and Urban Econs. Assn., Am. Econ. Assn., Am. Inst. for Decision Scis., Phi Kappa Phi (Charlotte Walleager award 1973), Omicron Delta Epsilon. Republican. Methodist. Avocation: racquetball. Home: 4308 Three Oaks Dr Arlington TX 76016 Office: U Tex at Arlington Dept Fin and Real Estate Arlington TX 76019

ISBELL, JAMES ALFRED, electronics engineer; b. San Diego, Sept. 3, 1936; s. James Alfred and Barbara (Fox) I.; m. Martha Anne Fincher, Sept. 20, 1958; children—Martha Louanne, Maria Louise. B.A. in Math. and Physics, U. Tex., 1971, M.Ed. in Sci., 1975. Engring. technician Geotech. Corp., Garland, Tex., 1961-67; engr. U. Tex. Radio Astronomy, Austin, 1967-77; engr., scientist Pinson Assocs. Inc., Austin, 1977—; owner Free Lunch Industries, Austin, 1975—, Harvey & James, Austin, 1971-72, Isbell Industries, Austin, 1983—; lectr. in field. Author tape cassettes on sailing, 1982. Chmn. bd. trustees St. Paul Lutheran Ch., Austin, 1971; chmn. Com. to Establish a Luth. High Sch., Austin, 1981. Served with USAF, 1958-61. Mem. Old Crows Assn. Republican. Clubs: Austin Yacht; Rolls Royce Owners. Home: 5252 McCormick Mt Dr Austin TX 78734 Office: Pinson Assocs Inc 10139 Metropolitan Dr Austin TX 78758

ISBELLE, BARRY MICHAEL, computer engineer; b. Chattanooga, June 16, 1953; s. Thomas Jefferson and Virginia (McCauley) I.; E.E., Va. Poly. U., 1976; m. Charlie Sue Hooper, June 19, 1976. Engr., Digital Equipment Corp., 1976-78; sr. engr. Data Card Corp., Richmond, Va., 1978—; sr. partner L. Bell Assos., Richmond, 1977—. Republican. Office: PO Box 29159 W Richmond VA 23229

ISCAN, MEHMET YASAR, anthropologist, educator; b. Maras, Turkey, Feb. 17, 1943; came to U.S., 1968; s. Mustafa and Ayse (Yürürdurmaz) I.; m. Walda Mae Engelbrecht, Feb. 14, 1976; 1 dau., Meryem Ayse. B.A., U. Ankara (Turkey), 1968; M.A., Cornell U., 1973, Ph.D., 1976. Diplomate Am. Bd. Forensic Anthropology. Asst. prof. anthropology Fla. Atlantic U., Boca Raton, 1977-84, assoc. prof., 1984—; assoc. med. examiner Palm Beach County, Fla., 1978—; cons. Broward County Med. Examiner's Office, Ft. Lauderdale, Fla., 1981—; chmn. anthrop. scis. Fla. Acad. Sci., 1981-82. Ales Hrdlicka fellow, 1968-69; NSF grantee Cornell Energy Project, 1973-75, Fla. Atlantic U., 1978—. Mem. Am. Assn. Phys. Anthropologists, Am. Anthrop. Assn., Soc. Med. Anthropology, European Anthrop. Assn., Internat. Congress Anthrop. and Ethnol. Scis., Am. Acad. Forensic Scis., Fla. Acad. Scis., Human Biology Council, Sigma Xi, (pres. Fla. Atlantic Club 1981-82). Assoc. editor The Fla. Anthropologist, 1982-84; author: A Topical Guide to the American Journal of Physical Anthropology, 1983; co-author: The Human Skeleton in Forensic Medicine, 1986; contbr. articles to profl. jours. Office: Dept Anthropology Fla Atlantic U Boca Raton FL 33431

ISENHOWER, NELSON NOLAN, anesthesiologist; b. Newton, N.C., Feb. 9, 1948; s. Homer Hallard and Genevieve Elizabeth (Caldwell) I.; m. Rebecca Sue Wilson, Sept. 18, 1976; children—Lori Suzanne, Matthew Wilson. B.S. cum laude, Wake Forest U., 1970; M.D., Bowman Gray Sch. Medicine, 1974. Diplomate Am. Bd. Anesthesiology. Commd. 2d lt. M.C., U.S. Army, 1970, advanced through grades to lt. col., 1980; intern Walter Reed Army Med. Ctr., Washington, 1974-75, resident in anesthesiology, 1975-78, mem. anesthesiology teaching staff Brooke Army Med. Ctr., Fort Sam Houston, Tex., 1978-79, asst. chief anesthesiology, 1979-80, chief anesthesiology and operative services, dir. anesthesiology residency tng., 1980-83; cons. in anesthesiology U.S. Army Health Services Command, 1980-83; staff anesthesiologist Winchester Med. Ctr. (Va.), 1983—. Fellow Am. Coll. Anesthesiology; mem. AMA, Med. Soc. Va., No. Va. Med. Soc., Am. Soc. Anesthesiology, So. Soc. Anesthesia, Internat. Anesthesia Research Soc., Am. Soc. Regional Anesthesia, Va. Anesthesiology Soc., Soc. Ambulatory Anesthesia. Republican. Baptist. Contbr. articles to profl. lit. Home: 3463 Forest Valley Rd Winchester VA 22601 Office: Winchester Anesthesiologists 1720 Amherst St Winchester VA 22601

ISERN-AMARAL, JESS HERMINIO, anesthesiologist, educator; b. Humacao, Puerto Rico, Apr. 25, 1941; s. Jess Isern and Carmen Amaral Noya; m. Janet Rae Swan, Aug. 11, 1962; children—Maria Teresa, Sandra Isabel, Kevin Antonio, David Lee, Bryan Michael. B.S., U. Puerto Rico, 1961, M.D., 1970. Commd. U.S. Air Force, 1970, advanced through ranks to maj., ret., 1976; intern Wilford Hall Med. Ctr., Lackland AFB, San Antonio, 1970-71, resident in anesthesiology, 1971-73, Wilford Hall cardiovascular anesthesiology fellow, 1973-74, asst. chief dept. anesthesiology, 1975-76; U. Utah Sch. Medicine fellow; Am. Coll. Anesthesiology fellow, 1973-74; Am. Bd. Anesthesiology fellow, 1974; clin. instr. U. Tex. Sch. Medicine, 1973-76, mem. teaching staff Wilford Hall, USAF Med. Ctr., San Antonio, 1974-76; active staff in anesthesia High Plains Bapt. Hosp., Amarillo, Tex., 1974—; courtesy staff N.W. Tex. Hosp., Amarillo; cons. in anesthesia VA Hosp., Amarillo; assoc. prof. anesthesiology Tex. Tech U. Sch. Medicine, Lubbock, 1983—; dir. Med. Devel. Co. Mem. Am. Soc. Anesthesiologists, Internat. Anesthesia Research Soc., Air Force Soc. Anesthesiologists, Potter-Randall Co. Med. Soc., Tex. Soc. Anesthesiologists, Tex. Med. Assn., Am. Assn. Nurse Anesthetists (lectr.), Nu Sigma Beta, Beta Beta Beta, Alpha Omega Alpha (Lederle research award 1970). Republican. Roman Catholic. Contbr. articles to profl. jours. Home: 4301 W 3d St Amarillo TX 79106 Office: 6103-B Amarillo Blvd Amarillo TX 79106

ISHEE, WILLIAM WILLIS, JR., educational administrator; b. Pasadena, Tex.; s. William Willis and Mozelle (Williams) I.; m. Marie Apel, June 1, 1973; 1 child, Jonathan. B.A., U. Houston, 1969; M.Ed., Sam Houston State U., 1972; D.Edn., Tex. A&M U., 1981. Tchr. Spring Br. Schs., Houston, 1969-71, counselor, 1971-74, prin., 1974-75; dir. project Klein Pub. Schs., Tex., 1975-76, dir. personnel, 1976—. Mem. Gulf Coast Personnel Adminstrs. (pres. 1984), Tex. Assn. Sch. Personnel Adminstrs. (regional rep. 1985), Am. Assn. Sch. Personnel Adminstrs. (conf. chmn. 1985-86), Nat. Audubon Soc., Sierra Club, Ctr. Transp. and Commerce, Tex. Hist. Found. Democrat. Baptist. Avocation: horticulture. Home: 8319 Oak Moss Dr Spring TX 77379 Office: Klein Independent Sch Dist 7200 Spring Cypress Rd Klein TX 77379

ISING, JOHN WILLIAM, JR., pharmacist; b. Louisville, June 16, 1947; s. John William and Beverly (Knoop) I.; m. Linda Susan Eskew, Aug. 31, 1968; children—David, Abigail. B.A., U. Louisville, 1969; B.S. in Pharmacy, U. Ky., 1974. Registered pharmacist. Pharmacist Meth. Hosp., Louisville, 1974-75, Murphy & Cloyd Pharmacy, Jeffersonville, Ind., 1974-75; pharmacist, owner Fountain Drugs, Inc., Louisville, 1975—, Fountain Drugs 2, Louisville, 1983—; pharmacist U. Louisville Sports, 1980—, Louisville Redbirds Baseball, 1982—. Coach St. Matthews Little League, Louisville, 1984. Served with U.S. Army, 1970-72, Korea. Mem. Ky. Pharmacist Assn., Jefferson County Acad. Pharmacy, Phi Delta Chi (treas. 1973-74), Am. Legion. Democrat. Roman Catholic. Clubs: Am. Turners (Louisville). Lodge: K.C. Avocations: softball; golf; boating. Office: Fountain Drugs Inc 9306 Blue Lick Rd Louisville KY 40229

ISLEY, R(OBERT) ARNOLD, pediatrician; b. Greensboro, N.C., June 23, 1947; s. William Robert and Annie Rebecca (Isley) I.; m. Loretta Jean Piechocki, Oct. 5, 1974; children—Leanne Jeanette, June Caroline, Rachel Marie. A.B., U. N.C., 1969; M.P.H., 1979; M.D. John Hopkins U., 1973. Diplomate Am. Bd. Pediatrics. Intern, Children's Med. Ctr., Dallas, 1973-74, resident in pediatrics, 1974-76; pediatrician USPHS Nat. Health Service Corps, Guntersville, Ala., 1976-78; med. cons. div. health services HHS, Region IV, Atlanta, 1979-81; practicing medicine specializing in pediatrics, Snellville (Ga.) Pediatrics, 1981—. Mem. Johns Hopkins Med. and Surg. Assn., Am. Acad. Pediatrics, Gwinnett-Forsyth Med. Soc., Med. Assn. Ga., Delta Omega. Office: 2121 Fountain Dr Suite A Snellville GA 30278

ISLEY, SAMUEL LEE, insurance executive, accountant; b. Burlington, N.C., July 23, 1948; s. Charles Worth and Hilda (Love) I.; m. Kathy Kennington, Jan. 19, 1974; children—Samuel L., Jr., Julie Charlene. B.S. in Bus. Adminstr., East Carolina U., 1971; B.A. in acctg., U. N.C., 1974; B.A. in acctg., Elon Coll., 1974. C.P.A., N.C. Pres. Isley Karate Studios, Inc., Burlington, 1969-75; acct. Stephen I. Moore Jr. CPA, Burlington, 1975-77; v.p. Aviation Underwriting Agy., Inc., Greensboro, N.C., 1977—; dir. Vista Reinsurance Co. Bermuda, Ins. Acquisitions, Inc.; v.p., treas. Vista Group, Inc. Trustee Friendship Methodist Ch., 1982—, bd. dirs., 1982. Recipient Black Belt in karate Sakuri Karate Assn., 1972; named No. 8 fighter in the South, Prof. Karate Mag., 1975. Fellow Am. Inst. C.P.A.s, N.C. Assn. C.P.A.s, Sons Confederate Vets., So. Black Belt Alliance. Home: PO Box 16634 Greensboro NC 27406 Office: Greensboro Regional Airport Greensboro NC 27410

ISOM, DOTCY IVERTUS, JR., bishop; b. Detroit, Feb. 18, 1931; s. Dotcy and Laura (Scales) I.; m. Esther L. Jones, Jan. 30, 1955; children—Dotcy, III, Jon Mark, David Carl. B.S., Wayne State U., 1956; grad. Eden Sem., 1967, M.Div., 1968; D.D., Miles Coll., 1982, Balt. Bible Coll., 1976. Ordained to ministry Methodist Ch., 1957. Pastor Allen Temple, Christian Meth. Epis. Ch., Paris, Tenn., 1957-58, St. Luke Christian Meth. Epis. Ch., Saginaw, Mich., 1958-67, Carter Chapel, Gary, Ind., 1961-62, Pilgrim Temple, East St. Louis, Ill., 1962-68, St. Paul Ch., Chgo., 1968-82; bishop Christian Meth. Epis. Ch., Birmingham, Ala., 1982—; dir. Christian Edn., Southeast Mo. and Ill. Conf., 1978-82. Mem. Human Relation Commn., East St. Louis, 1964-68; mem. Mayor's Task Force on Hunger; bd. dirs. Greater Birmingham Ministries; chmn. bd. dirs. Miles Coll., Birmingham. Served with U.S. Army, 1948-52. Mem. NAACP, So. Christian Leadership Conf. (vice chmn. 1976-80), Fla. Council of Chs. Home: 1728 3d Ave North Birmingham AL 35203

ISOM, JOHN WILLIAM, geophysicist; b. Dallas, Oct. 12, 1945; s. James Starke and Bethlee (Watkins) I.; m. Linda Ann Bandsma, Oct. 2, 1970 (dec. 1984); children—Patrick, Christie; m. Pamela Lindley, Feb. 16, 1985; stepchildren—Libby, Matthew. B.A. in Geology, Columbia U., 1968; M.S. in Geology, U. Okla., 1971. Geophysicist Exxon Co. U.S.A., Midland, Tex., 1971-74, Exxon Prodn. Research, Houston, 1974-75; prodn. geologist Exxon Co. U.S.A., Houston, 1975; v.p. geophysics HNG Oil Co., Midland, 1976-82; geophys. mgr. Roden Oil Co., Midland, 1982—. Advisor Jr. Achievement, Midland, 1972; active United Way, Midland, 1973; packmaster, advisor Buffalo Trails Council, Boy Scouts Am., 1976-78. Chevron Standard of Tex. fellow, 1969. Mem. Soc. Exploration Geophysicists, Am. Assn. Petroleum Geologists, Permian Basis Geophys. Soc. (v.p. 1979-80), West Tex. Geol. Soc. Clubs: Green Tree Country, Petroleum (Midland). Avocations: hunting; camping. Home: 1 Chatham Ct Midland TX 79705 Office: Roden Oil Co Box 10909 Midland TX 79702

ISRAEL, GEORGE MATTHEW, III, mayor of Macon (Georgia); b. Macon, Feb. 10, 1948; s. George Matthew and Margaret I.; Asso. B.A., Middle Ga. Coll., 1968; student U. Ga., 1968-69, Am. Coll., Bryn Mawr, Pa., 1974; m. Pamela Witherington, Sept. 11, 1971; 1 dau., Katheryn. Agt., Mass. Mut. Life Ins., 1970—; former alderman City of Macon (Ga.), chmn. appropriations com., 1975-79, chmn. ordinances and resolutions com., 1975-79, trustee Fire and Police Pension Fund, 1975—; mayor City of Macon, 1980—. Active Boy Scouts Am., 1970-76; charter mem. Round Table, 1975—, chmn., 1975-76, 1st v.p., 1975, life mem., 1976—; singing dir. Cen. Ch. of Christ, 1973, sr. adult sch. tchr., 1977—; chmn. Coffee Day, March of Dimes, 1970, chmn. Walk-A-Thon, 1976; bd. dirs. Cen. of Ga. Speech and Hearing Found., 1974, com. chmn., 1975, v.p., 1976; mem. exec. com. Bibb County (Ga.) Republican Party, 1974—, 1st vice chmn., 1975-76, city council candidate, 1975; mem. Cen. Ga. Med. Sch. Coordinating Com., 1976-77. Served with U.S.N.G., 1969-75. Named to Mass. Life Ins. Co. Pres.'s Club, 1972-74, 76-77, 78, Million Dollar Round Table, 1978; recipient Life Underwriters Nat. Quality award, 1975. Office: Office of Mayor PO Box 247 Macon GA 31298*

ISSERMAN, ANDREW MARK, economist, university administrator; b. N.Y.C., June 28, 1947; s. Manfred Alexander and Ellen Sophie (Kann) I.; m. Ellen Lise Jacobsen, July 23, 1977; children—Jacob David, Noah Jacobsen. B.A., Amherst Coll., 1968; M.A. U. Pa., 1970, Ph.D., 1975. Instr. econs. Pa. State U., 1972-73; lectr. U. Ill., 1973-75, asst. prof. planning and econs., 1975-77, assoc. prof., 1977-81; assoc. prof. planning, geography and econs. U. Iowa, Iowa City, 1981-84, prof., 1984-85; dir. Regional Research Inst., prof. econs. and geography W.Va. U., Morgantown, 1984—; vis. assoc. prof. planning U. So. Calif., 1977-78; vis. scholar U. Liverpool, Eng., 1984; cons. in field; mem. United Nations Expert Group on Urbanization, Population, and Environment, 1983. Author: (with Marilyn Brown) Suburbs in Distress, 1985. Editor: Population Change and the Economy, 1986; bd. editors Jour. Am. Planning Assn., 1979-85, Central Ill. Econ.-Bus. Rev., 1979-81, Jour. Planning Edn. and Research, 1981—, Growth and Change, 1984—. Contbr. articles to profl. jours. Am. Statis. Assn. research fellow, 1979-81, NSF trainee, 1970, Mellon fellow, 1975, HUD grantee, 1978-80, Econ. Devel. Adminstrn. grantee, 1984-86. Mem. Am. Econs. Assn., Regional Sci. Assn. (editor Internat. Regional Sci. Rev. 1976—, mem. N.Am. program com. 1979-81), Assn. Am. Geographers, Am. Statis. Assn. (conf. dir. 1982), Am. Planning Assn., Assn. Collegiate Schs. Planning (publ. and membership coms. 1984-86), Population Assn. Am. Office: Regional Research Inst W Va U Morgantown WV 26506

IUSI, MARK DOUGLAS, television journalist; b. Albuquerque, Dec. 8, 1953; s. John Gabriel and Betty Jane (Greer) I. B.S. cum laude in Mass Communications, Fla. State U., 1976; M.A. in Broadcast Journalism, U. Mo., 1980. Radio announcer Sta. WFSU-FM, Tallahassee, 1976-77; prodn. asst. Sta. WECA-TV, Tallahassee, 1977, 78; TV news writer Fla. Pub. Broadcasting Co., 1977, 78; news dir. Sta. WTAI-AM/WLLV-FM, Melbourne, Fla., 1978-79; radio reporter Sta. KFRU-AM, Columbia, Mo., 1980; grad. teaching asst. Sta. KBIA-FM, Columbia, 1980; bur. chief Sta. WBBH-TV, Fort Myers, Fla., 1981, crime reporter, 1981-83; reporter Sta. WTSP-TV, St. Petersburg, Fla., 1983—. Recipient 1st place investigative reporting for small markets in Fla., UPI, 1982. Mem. Investigative Reporters and Editors. Roman Catholic. Office: WTSP-TV PO Box 10000 Saint Petersburg FL 33733

IVENS, MARY SUE, medical microbiologist, medical mycologist; b. Maryville, Tenn., Aug. 23, 1929; d. McPherson Joseph and Sarah Lillie (Hensley) I.; B.S., E. Tenn. State U., 1949; M.S. (NIH research trainee), Tulane U., 1963; Ph.D., La. State U., 1966; postgrad. Oak Ridge Inst. Nuclear Studies. Dir. microbiol. labs. Lewis-Gale Hosp., Roanoke, Va., 1953-56; research mycologist Centers Disease Control, Atlanta, 1957-60; research asso. La. State U. Med. Sch., 1963-66, instr. medicine, 1966-72, clin. prof., 1972—; asso. prof. natural scis. Dillard U., New Orleans, 1972—; assoc. Marine Biol. Lab., Woods Hole, Mass., 1978—; cons. in field; expert witness La. Assn. Def. Counsel, 1985—. Bd. dirs. Girl Scouts Council La., Community Relationships Greater New Orleans, Zoning Bd. River Ridge (La.); mem. exec. bd. River Ridge Civic Assn., 1982—, sec., 1982-84; chmn. personnel bd. Riverside Bapt. Ch., River Ridge, La. Macy fellow, MBL, Woods Hole, Mass., 1978-79; grantee NSF,

NIH; diplomate Am. Bd. Microbiology; recipient Rosicrucian Humanitarian award, 1981. Mem. Internat. Soc. Human and Animal Mycology, Med. Mycological Soc. Am., Am. Soc. Microbiology (nat. com. on membership 1983—), AAAS, Nat. Inst. Sci., Sigma Xi. Author articles in field. Home: 408 Berclair Ave New Orleans LA 70123 Office: Dillard U Div Natural Sci New Orleans LA 70122

IVER, WILLIAM HENRY, dentist; b. Port Chester, N.Y., June 22, 1917; s. Alex R. and Beulah (Levy) E.; student U. Wis., 1936-38; D.D.S. cum laude, Georgetown U., 1942; m. Ruth Levin, Nov. 29, 1981; children—Robert Drew, Randolph, Laurence. Pvt. practice dentistry, Miami Beach, Fla., 1945—; dir. Lincoln Small Bus. Investment Corp., Ka-Line Mfg. div. Sun Engrng. Corp. Served to lt. comdr. USNR, 1942-45. Mem. ADA, Fla., East Coast, Miami Beach dental assns. Clubs: Cricket, Jockey, Carriage. Home: Charter Club Miami FL Office: 605 Lincoln Rd Miami Beach FL 33139

IVERSON, FRANCIS KENNETH, metals company executive; b. Downers Grove, Ill., Sept. 18, 1925; s. Norris Byron and Pearl Irene (Kelsey) I.; m. Martha Virginia Miller, Oct. 24, 1945; children—Claudia (Mrs. Wesley Watts Sturges), Marc Miller. Student, Northwestern U., 1943-44; B.S., Cornell U., 1946; M.S., Purdue U., 1947. Research physicist Internat. Harvester, Chgo., 1947-52; tech. dir. Illium Corp., Freeport, Ill., 1952-54; dir. mktg. Cannon-Muskegon Corp., Mich., 1954-61; exec. v.p. Coast Metals, Little Ferry, N.J., 1961-62; v.p. Nucor Corp. (formerly Nuclear Corp. Am.), Charlotte, N.C., 1962-65, pres., chief exec. officer, dir., 1965—; dir. Southeastern Savs. & Loan Co., C.H. Heist Co., Cato Corp.; bd. mgrs. Wachovia Bank and Trust Co., Charlotte. Contbr. articles to profl. jours. Served to lt. (j.g.) USNR, 1943-46. Named Best Chief Exec. Officer in Steel Industry, Wall St. Transcript, 1980. Mem. NAM (dir.), Steel Joist Inst., Am. Soc. Metals, AIME, Am. Foundrymens Soc. Clubs: Carmel Country, Quail Hollow Country, Charlotte City Old Providence Racket (Charlotte). Office: Nucor Corp 4425 Randolph Rd Charlotte NC 28211*

IVERSON, MAYNARD JAMES, vocational educator, consultant; b. Mohall, N.D., Mar. 15, 1939; s. Marvin John and Alice Theresa (Frank) I.; m. Gayle Marie (Mitzi) Van Sweringen, June 13, 1964; children—Michael James, Melissa Jean. B.S., N.D. State U., 1961; Ed.M., Colo. State U., 1967; Ph.D., Ohio State U., 1971. Tchr. vocat. agr. high sch., Fessenden, N.D., 1961-62; tchr. vocat. agr. Minot High Sch., N.D., 1962-69; asst. prof. U. Ky., Lexington, 1971-77; assoc. prof. Auburn U., Ala., 1977-81; assoc. prof. dept. occupational edn. N.C. State U., Raleigh, 1981—; cons. curriculum devel. and teaching Saudi Tech. Devel. Program, ARAMCO, Dhahran, Saudi Arabia, summers 1983—; chmn. Nat. Agrl. Edn. Research Meeting, Atlanta, 1981; chmn. So. Regional Research Project in Agrl. Edn., 1979. Contbr. articles to profl. jours.; author reports, curriculum programs. Recipient hon. state degrees N.D., Ala. Future Farmers Am. Assn., 1968, 80. Mem. Am. Soc. Tng. and Devel., Am. Vocat. Assn., Am. Assn. Tchr. Educators in Agr., Am. Vocat. Agr. Tchrs. Assn., Am. Vocat. Edn. Research Assn., Alpha Gamma Rho (So. region v.p. 1978-85, cert. merit 1976), Gamma Sigma Delta, Phi Delta Kappa. Democrat. Roman Catholic. Lodge: Elks. Home: 512 Loch Ness Ln Cary NC 27511 Office: Dept Occupational Education North Carolina State U 502 Poe Hall Raleigh NC 27695-7801

IVES, GEORGE ALLEN, JR., real estate and investments executive; b. New Bern, N.C., Aug. 15, 1931; s. George Allen and Dorothy (Gregory) I.; m. Gisela Nora von zur Muehlen, Feb. 21, 1956; children—Caroline, Tanya, Dorothy, Allen. B.A., Princeton U., 1953. Various positions Dept. of State, Washington, 1959-64; sales mgr. Ives Oil Co., New Bern, 1964-71, pres., chief exec. officer, 1971-84; pres., chief exec. officer Ives Transport, Inc., New Bern, 1971-84; pres. Ives Enterprises, Inc., New Bern, 1984—; pres. Carolina Oil Fuel Inst., Raleigh, 1971. Vice chmn. New Bern/Craven County Bicentennial Celebration, 1974; mem. Tryon Palace Commn., New Bern, 1974—; chmn., 1985—. Served to lt. (j.g.) USNR, 1953-55. Mem. N.C. Oil Jobbers Assn. (v.p. 1973; named Fuel Oil Man of Yr. 1971). Republican. Episcopalian. Clubs: New Bern Golf and Country (pres. 1971), Coral Bay (Atlantic Beach, N.C.). Avocations: tennis; sailing; boating.

IVES, JOHN ELWAY, hospital administrator; b. Hartford, Conn., Oct. 21, 1929; s. Louis King and Erma Marcella (Elway) I.; m. Ann Poindexter, June 23, 1951; 1 son, Ralph Edward. A.B., Dartmouth Coll., 1951; M.S., Yale U., 1956. Asst. dir. Yale-New Haven Hosp., 1956-65; asst. to dean Yale U. Sch. Medicine, New Haven, 1963-65; adminstr. Middlesex Meml. Hosp., Middletown, Conn., 1965-66; hosp. dir. U. Conn. Health Ctr., Farmington, 1966-77; exec. dir. Shands Hosp., Gainesville, Fla., 1977-80, exec. v.p., 1980—; commr. Accrediting Commn. on Edn. for Health Services Adminstrn., 1985-88; dir. Am. Bank of Alachua County; cons., reviewer clin. cancer program rev. com. NIH, Washington, 1976-80, gen. clin. research ctrs. com., 1984-85. Mem. editorial bd. Jour. Med. Edn., 1985-88. Bd. dirs. Civitan Regional Blood Ctr., Gainesville, 1977-81, Neighborhood Housing Service, Gainesville, 1984—. Served as 2d lt. AUS, 1951-53. Mem. Consortium for Study U. Teaching Hosps. (pres. 1981-83), Appalachian Council U. Teaching Hosps., Soc. Health Service Adminstrs., Am. Hosp. Assn., Fla. Hosp. Assn. (trustee 1981—). Office: Shands Teaching Hosp and Clinics U Fla Box J-326 JHMHC Gainesville FL 32610

IVES, RONN BRIAN, artist, educator; b. South Bend, Ind., Apr. 12, 1950; d. Bill H. and Shirley J. (Ryker) I. B.F.A., U. Ariz., 1975; M.F.A., U. Ariz., 1978. Freelance artist, Tucson, 1975-79; grad. instr. Intaglio printmaking U. Ariz., Tucson, 1975-77; instr. photography Tucson Mus. Art Sch., 1979—; prof. art Old Dominion U., Norfolk, Va., 1979—; Nat. Endowment Arts grantee, 1982-83. Mem. Nat. Print Council U.S. One-man show: Colo. State U., Ft. Collins, 1970; group shows include: U. Ariz. Mus. Art, Tucson, 1979, Internat. Exhbn., Charleroi, Belgium, 1981, Multicultural Arts Inst., San Diego, 1982, Alpho Gallery, San Francisco, 1982, Internat. Invitational Exhbn., San Giorgio, Italy, 1983, San Francisco Art Inst., 1983, La Galleria Dell'Occhio, N.Y.C., 1983, Soker-Kaseman Gallery, San Francisco, 1983, Amnesty Internat., Lima, Peru, 1983; Franklin Furnace, N.Y.C., 1983; Art Ctr. Coll. Design, Pasadena, Calif., 1983; Va. Mus. Art, Richmond, 1983, 85; represented in permanent collections: Centro de Cultura Altenativa, Rio de Janeiro, Brazil, San Antonio Mus. Art, Internat. Hist. Archive Mail Art, Rome, San Francisco Art Inst., Erie Art Ctr., Pa., San Antonio Mus. Modern Art, U. Wis., Madison, Mus. Modern Art, N.Y.C. Artist Book Collection. Contbr. articles to profl. publs.

IVESTER, MELVIN DOUGLAS, beverage and entertainment company executive; b. New Holland, Ga., Mar. 26, 1947; s. Howard Edward and Ada Mae (Pass) I.; m. Victoria Kay Grindle, Mar. 20, 1969. B.B.A. cum laude, U. Ga., 1969. Acct., Ernst & Ernst, Atlanta, 1969-75; mgr. Ernst & Whinney, Atlanta, 1975-79; asst. controller, dir. corp. auditing Coca-Cola Co., Atlanta, 1979-81, v.p., controller, 1981-83, sr. v.p. fin., 1983-84; sr. v.p., chief fin. officer, 1985—; dir. Tristan Pictures, Inc. Trustee, mem. exec. com. Ga. Council on Econ. Edn.; trustee Morehouse Coll.; chmn. nat. adv. found. Beta Alpha Psi; mng. trustee U. Ga. Found. Served with USAR, 1970-76. Mem. Atlanta C. of C. (bd. dirs.). Home: 5025 Trailridge Way Dunwoody GA 30338 Office: 310 North Ave NW Atlanta GA 30313

IVEY, DENNIS CARL, plastics company executive; b. Huntsville, Ala., Nov. 10, 1941; s. Carl William and Annice C. (McGinness) I.; m. Dianne Crane, June 15, 1963; children—Dennis Carl II, David Glen, Daniel Thomas. Student U. Ala., 1962-64. Supr. passenger service United Airlines, Dulles Airport, Washington, 1964-72; pres., ptnr. P.I. Enterprises, landscaping firm, Washington, 1972-76; regional sales mgr. Universal Plastics, Inc., Roanoke, Va., 1976-80, nat. mktg. dir., Cookeville, Tenn., 1980—. Pres. Cookeville Am. Little League, 1982-83. Mem. Am. Soc. Tng. and Devel. Mem. Ch. of Christ. Creator, writer of manual, audio-visual recruiting program and sales tng. seminar for Universal Plastics. Home: Rural Route 15 Box 223 Cookeville TN 38501 Office: Universal Plastics Inc 33 S Willow Ave Cookeville TN 38501

IVEY, EDWIN HARRY, petrochemical consultant; b. Galveston, Tex., Apr. 19, 1921; s. Edwin Harry and Louise Madeleine (LaCorne) I.; m. Frances H. Randol, Jan. 25, 1943 (dec. Aug. 1983); children—Kitty, Ed, Mary, Elizabeth, Sara Helen; m. Helen M. Hannon Lynch, Nov. 24, 1984. B.S. in Chem. Engring., Tex. A&M U., 1941, M.S. in Chem. Engring., 1947; postgrad. Va. Poly. Inst., 1941-42. Registered profl. engr., Tex. Instr. Tex. A&M U., College Station, 1942-43, 46-57; research and devel. engr. Houdry Process Corp., Marcus Hook, Pa., 1947-50; project mgr., prodn. supt. Dow Chem. Co., Freeport, Tex., 1950-68; gen. mgr., project mgr. P.R. Olefins Co., Ponce, 1968-72; pres., cons. E. H. Ivey & Co., cons. engrs., Houston, 1972—. Patentee in field. Served to capt. USAF, 1943-46. Mem. Am. Inst. Chem. Engrs., Am. Chem. Soc., S.W. Chem. Assn., Tex. A&M Former Students Assn. Republican. Roman Catholic. Lodge: K.C. Avocations: photography; philately; dancing. Home: 14207 Stokesmouth Dr Houston TX 77077 Office: E H Ivey & Co 14207 Stokesmount Dr Houston TX 77077

IVEY, ROBERT CARL, artistic director, educator, choreographer; b. Australia, Aug. 28, 1939; came to U.S., 1951; s. Carl Roy and Virginia (Fulford) I. Student Ga. Southwestern U., 1958-59, Sch. Am. Ballet, 1959, Columbia U., 1959-61, Manhattan Med. Sch., N.Y.C., 1961, Emory U., 1962, Swedish State Theatre Sch., Stockholm, 1968. Soloist Den Norske Opera Ballet, Oslo, Norway, 1964-68, Svenska Riksteatre, Stockholm, Sweden, 1969-75; featured actor Det Norske Theatre, Oslo, 1968-69; choreographer Spoleto Festival USA, Charleston, S.C., 1977-79, choreographer in residence, 1979-83; dir. Robert Ivey Ballet, Charleston, 1979-83; mem. faculty Coll. Charleston, 1979—, choreographer, 1979-83, now prof. dance; asst. dir. Savannah (Ga.) Ballet, 1979-80 choreographer Charleston Opera Co., 1980-83, mem. artistic bd., 1981—. Pres. Charleston Area Arts Council, 1982—; mem. Govs. Task Force Dance, Columbia, S.C., 1983—; mem. Gov.'s steering com. S.C. Arts Commn., 1983—; Recipient choreography award S.C. Arts Commn., 1980. Mem. Actor's Equity Assn., Charleston Area Arts Council, Screen Actor's Guild. Episcopalian. Office: Robert Ivey Ballet 1632 Ashley Hall Rd Charleston SC 29407

IVEY, WILLIAM JAMES, foundation executive; b. Detroit, Sept 6, 1944; s. William James and Grace Christine (Hammes) I.; m. Patricia A. Hall, Mar. 6, 1977 (div. 1982). B.A. in History, U. Mich., 1966; M.A. in Folklore and Ethnomuscicology Ind. U., 1969. Cataloguer Ind. U. Archives Traditional Music, 1969-71; library dir. Country Music Found., Nashville, 1971, dir. found. 1971—; assoc. prof. music Bklyn. Coll., 1979-80; chmn. folk music panel Nat. Endowment Arts, 1976-78; bd. visitors Mid-South humanities project Middle Tenn. State U., 1979-80; bd. dirs. Nashville Songwriters Assn., 1974-75; mem. music industry adv. panel Belmont Coll., 1975-79. Author articles in field, chpts. in books; editor: Jour. Country Music, 1972-75; exec. editor, 1977—; rec./rev. editor: Western Folklore, 1976-78. Recipient Billboard Country Liner Notes of Yr. award, 1974; sr. research fellow Inst. Studies Am. Music, 1979-80. Mem. Nat. Acad. Rec. Arts and Scis. (trustee 1976-80, v.p. 1980-81, 83-84, nat. pres. 1981-83), Am. Folklore Soc., Assn. Rec. Sound Collections, Am. Assn. State and Local History, Internat. Soaring Soc. Am., Nashville Area C. of C. (chmn. music industry liason com. 1978-80). Office: Country Music Hall of Fame and Museum 4 Music Sq E Nashville TN 37203*

IVIE, PAUL EDWARD, JR., civil engineer; b. Atlanta, May 28, 1954; s. Paul Edward and Marjorie (Shirley) I.; m. Gail Spencer Faulkner, Aug. 23, 1980; children—Alexander Scott, Kristin Anne. B.C.E., Ga. Inst. Tech., 1975; M.S., U. Tenn.-Knoxville, 1981, M.B.A., 1983. Registered profl. engr., Tenn. Computer programmer Alliance Bldg. Systems, Atlanta, 1974, Ga. Inst. Tech., 1975; civil engr. TVA, Knoxville, 1975—. Mem. ASCE, Knoxville Jaycees (exec. v.p. 1978), Chi Epsilon. Baptist. Office: TVA 400 W Summit Hill Dr Knoxville TN 37902

IYER, RAGHURAMAN K. S., statistics educator, researcher; b. Madras, India, June 4, 1956; came to U.S., 1982; s. Subramanyam and Saraswathi I. B.S. in Stats., Loyola Coll., U. Madras, 1977; M.B.A. in Mktg., U. Delhi, 1979; M.B.A., U. Houston, 1983, Ph.D. candidate, 1983—; Praveen degree in Hindi Lang. (hon.), Dakshin Bharat Hindi Prachar Sabha, Madras, 1976. Mktg. exec. DCM Data Products, New Delhi, India, 1979-80; account exec. R. K. Swamy Advt. Agy., New Delhi, 1980-82; teaching fellow U. Houston, 1982—. Recipient Dean's award, Coll. Bus. U. Houston, 1984; Heyne fellow, 1985. Mem. Am. Statis. Assn., Ops. Research Soc. Am., Beta Gamma Sigma. Hindu. Clubs: Talkers (organizer Madras 1975-76), Gadwingsa (founder Loyola Coll. 1976-77). Avocations: music; public speaking; reading. Office: QMS Dept M 250 Coll of Bus U Houston Houston TX 77004

IZATT, JERALD RAY, physics educator, researcher, consultant; b. Preston, Idaho, Sept. 22, 1928; s. Angus John and Leora Mae (Christensen) I.; m. Mary Ann Louise Fassler, Oct. 18, 1951; children—Richard Angus, James Arthur, Peggy Jean, Nancy Lynne, Joseph Adam. B.S. in Physics, U. Utah, 1952; Ph.D. in Physics, Johns Hopkins U., 1960. Computer programmer Douglas Aircraft, Long Beach, Calif., 1952-54; systems engr. Westinghouse Co., Balt., 1954-55; research scientist Northrop Space Labs., Hawthorne, Calif., 1960-61; vis. scientist Air Force Cambridge Research Labs., Bedford, Mass., 1967-68; prof. N.Mex. State U., Las Cruces, 1961-70; prof. Université Laval, Que., Can., 1970-81; vis. scientist Max Planck Institut, Stuttgart, W. Ger., 1979-80; prof. dept. physics and astronomy U. Ala., Tuscaloosa, 1981—; cons. indsl. firms and govt. agys. NRC grantee, 1970-83; Max Planck Institut grantee, 1979-80; Dept. Def. grantee, 1963-71; Ministère d'Education de Québec grantee, 1977-79; Def. Research Bd. Can. grantee, 1974-76; ARI grantee, 1984-86. Mem. Optical Soc. Am., Can. Assn. Physicists, N.Y. Acad. Scis., Sigma Xi. Democrat. Mem. Ch. of Jesus Christ of Latter-day Saints. Patentee opto-electronic and laser devices; contbr. articles to profl. jours. Home: 3-N Northwood Lake Northport AL 35476 Office: Dept Physics and Astronomy U Ala University AL 35486

JABLIN, FREDRIC MARK, communication educator; b. N.Y.C., July 23, 1952; s. Irving and Mildred (Joseph) J.; m. Marie A. Giannattasio, Aug. 1974 (div. May 1977); m. Piper A. Rountree, Oct. 14, 1983. B.A., SUNY-Buffalo, 1973; M.A., U. Mich., 1974; Ph.D., Purdue U., 1977. Teaching fellow U. Mich., 1973-74; teaching asst. Purdue U., 1974-77; asst. prof. U. Wis., Milw., 1977-79; asst. prof. U. Tex. at Austin, 1979-83, assoc. prof. organizational communication, 1983—; pvt. cons., 1976—. Contbr. chpts. to books, articles to profl. jours. Mem. editorial bd. Human Communication Research, 1980—, Organizational Communication Abstracts, 1980—, Acad. Mgmt. Jour., 1985—. Recipient AMOCO Found. Outstanding Tchr. award U. Tex., Austin, 1981-82, Coll. Communication Outstanding Faculty Research award, 1983-84. Mem. Internat. Communication Assn. (sec. div. 4, 1983-85, Top 3 Papers awards 1978, 80, 84), Acad. Mgmt., Am. Psychol. Assn., Speech Communication Assn., Am. Bus. Communication Assn. Avocations: sailing, woodworking, running, tennis. Office: U Tex Austin Dept Speech Communication Austin TX 78712

JACINTO, GEORGE ANTHONY, counselor, educator, consultant; b. Gilroy, Calif., Dec. 21, 1949; s. George Peter and Isabelle Agnes (Joseph) J. B.S. in Criminology-Corrections, Calif. State U.-Fresno, 1974; postgrad. Wash. Theol. Union, 1975, U. Wis., 1980, Boise State U., 1981; M.Ed. in Guidance and Counseling-Gen. Personnel Services, Coll. Idaho, 1982. Intern counselor drug and alcohol Mt. Carmel Guild, Paterson, N.J., 1974; dir. recreation program Summer Markham, Toronto, Ont., Can., 1975; pastoral asst. Ch. St. Peter, Toronto, 1975; youth minister Ch. St. Michael, Olympia, Wash., 1976-77; dir. youth ministry St. James Congregation, Franklin, Wis., 1977-80; diocesan youth dir. Cath. Diocese of Boise, Idaho, 1980-83; intern., counselor, grant writer Salvation Army Drug Rehab. Ctr., Boise, 1982; dir. religious edn. St. Andrew Ch., Orlando, Fla., 1983-84; vocat. rehab. counselor HRS, State of Fla., Orlando, 1984—; part-time youth minister Good Shepherd Ch., Orlando, 1985—; founder Am. Life Planning Assocs., Orlando, 1985—; counselor, career and life planning cons., youth programming cons., youth minister. Active diversion program Union St. Ctr., Olympia, Wash.; campaign leader for children's toys Indo-China Refugee Relief, Milw.; mem. adv. community agys. concerned with youth issues; coordinator community service program for young people, Franklin, Wis. Mem. Am. Assn. Counseling and Devel., Am. Rehab. Counselors Assn., World Future Soc., Nat. Fedn. Cath. Youth Ministry, Assn. Transpersonal Psychology, Fellowship of Reconciliation. Democrat. Roman Catholic. Home: PO Box 66154 Orlando FL 32853 Office: Vocat Rehab 2520 N Orange Ave Orlando FL 32804

JACKS, BENJAMIN BAREND, religious educator; b. Cape Town, Republic of South Africa, Oct. 11, 1939; came to U.S., 1972; s. William Charles and Jane (Augustine) J.; m. Olive Marks, Mar. 9, 1968; children—Eleanor Cecilia, John William, Cheryl Roseanne, Paul Barend. Dipl. in Christian Edn., Johannesburg Bible Inst., 1965; B.A., Northeastern Bible Coll., Essex Fells, N.J., 1974; M.R.E., Southwestern Bapt. Theol. Sem., 1976, grad. specialist in Religious Edn., 1980; diploma in Theology, Bapt. Coll. So. Africa, 1977. Preacher, Nashville Bapt. Ch., Gwelo, Zimbabwe, 1968-72; tchr. Fort Worth Ind. Sch. Dist., 1980—; minister of edn. Mt. Olive Missionary Bapt. Ch., Fort Worth, 1983—; mem. com. Fort Worth Social Studies Council, 1983-84; mem. Bldg. Rep., Fort Worth, 1983—. Mem. Cable TV Adv. Bd., Forest Hill, 1985. Mem. NEA, Tex. State Tchrs. Assn., Fort Worth Classroom Tchrs. Assn. (mem. by-laws com.), Phi Alpha Theta. Address: 3229 Centennial Fort Worth TX 76119

JACKS, JAMES HOWARD WELLS, designer; b. Refugio, Tex., June 3, 1939; s. James E. and BeBe (Heard) J.; m. Marla Summerford, Sept. 20, 1939; children—Lydia, Alessandra, Marlita. B.A., Tex. Christian U., 1962; postgrad. U. Florence, 1965-67. Introduction of Jay Jacks of Florence menswear line, (Italy), 1968-75; pres. Jay Jacks Courtier, Dallas, 1976—. Chmn. bd. dirs. Dallas Civic Opera; mem. chancellor's com. Tex. Christian U. Recipient Tex. Designer award, 1982. Mem. Dallas C. of C., Italian Trade Commn., Dallas Hist. Soc., Dallas Mus. Fine Arts, Van Cliburn Found., Sons of Republic Tex., Tex. Arts Alliance, Theater Arts Custom Auction, Internat. Petroleum Assn. Am., Tex. Ind. Petroleum Royalty and Oil Assn., Sigma Chi. Episcopalian. Clubs: Brook Hollow Country; The Argyle (San Antonio); Corpus Christi Town. Office: 2715 Fairmount St Dallas TX 75201

JACKSON, ALTHEA, nun, bookstore executive; b. Taunton, Mass., June 27, 1922; d. Harold Robinson Hall and Jeannette (Cahoon) Tingwall; m. John E. Jackson, June 15, 1945 (dec. Aug. 1974); children—Jean, Paul. B.A., Middlebury Coll., 1944; M.S., Simmons Coll., 1965. Cert. profl. librarian. Librarian, Mass., 1959-74; propr. Agape Bible & Book Store, St. Augustine, Fla., 1982—. Bd. dirs. St. Gerard's House Unwed Mothers, St. Augustine, 1984. Mem. Christian Booksellers Assn., ALA (life). Roman Catholic. Office: Agape Bible & Book Store 173 San Marco Ave Saint Augustine FL 32084

JACKSON, BARBARA ANN GARVEY, music educator; b. Normal, Ill., Sept. 27, 1929; d. Neil Ford and Eva (Burkhart) Garvey; m. Robert Seagrave (div.); m. Kern C. Jackson, Mar. 29, 1970; stepchildren—Kern, Ross, Bruce, Paul. Mus. B., U. Ill., 1950; Mus. M., Eastman Sch. Music, 1952; Ph.D. in Musicology, Stanford U., 1959. Asst. prof. music U. Ark., Fayetteville, 1954-56, prof. music, 1961—; spl. music tchr. Los Angeles Pub. Schs., 1956-57; asst. prof. music Ark. Tech. U., Russsville, 1957-61. Author: (with others) Practical Beginning Theory, 1962; A.S.T.A. Dictionary of String Bowing Terms, 1968. Editor, pub. music compositions. Mem. Am. Musicological Soc., South Central Soc. 18th Century Studies, Viola da Gamba Soc. Am., Am. Soc. 18th Century Studies, Sigma Alpha Iota (hon.), Pi Kappa Lambda, Phi Kappa Phi, Sigma Alpha Iota. Democrat. Episcopalian. Avocations: gardening, wildflower photography, studies of women botanical illustrators. Home: 235 Baxter Ln Fayetteville AR 72701 Office: U Ark Music Dept Fine Arts Annex 201 Fayetteville AR 72701

JACKSON, BLYDEN, educator; b. Paducah, Ky., Oct. 12, 1910; s. George Washington and Julia Estelle (Reid) J.; A.B., Wilberforce U., 1930, D.Hum. (hon.), 1977; A.M., U. Mich., 1938, Ph.D. (Rosenwald fellow 1947-49), 1952; LL.D. (hon.), U. Louisville, 1978, U. N.C., 1985; m. Roberta Bowles, Aug. 2, 1958. Tchr. English, Louisville pub. schs., 1934-45; asst., then asso. prof. English, Fisk U., 1945-54; prof. English, head dept. So. U., 1954-62, dean Grad. Sch., 1962-69; prof. English, U. N.C., Chapel Hill, 1969-81, prof. emeritus, 1981—, asso. dean Grad. Sch., 1973-76; spl. research criticism Negro lit. Mem. Coll. Lang. Assn. (pres. 1957-59), Modern Lang. Assn., Nat. Council Tchrs. English (Distinguished lectr. 1970-71, chmn. coll. sect. 1971—), Coll. English Assn., Speech Assn. Am., La. Edn. Assn., Alpha Phi Alpha. Contbr. articles to profl. jours.; asso. editor CLA Bull., 1959—; mem. editorial adv. bd. So. Lit. Jour. Home: 102 Laurel Hill Rd Chapel Hill NC 27514

JACKSON, C(HARLES) WALLACE, lodge ofcl., retired bus. exec.; b. Bklyn., Jan. 21, 1901; s. Frederick John and Marie Hartwick (Thorpe) J.; student U. Louisville, 1919-20; B.S., Purdue U., 1924; m. Garnett Hope Tonkin, Apr. 4, 1927; 1 dau., Hope Jackson Vernon. Southeastern rep. Nat. Lead Co., Phila., 1927-61; U.S. commr. U.S. Dist. Ct., Fayetteville, N.C., 1961-71; fraternal sec. Masonic York Rite Bodies, Fayetteville, 1963—, chief exec. officer, 1966, Southeastern dept. comdr. Grand Encampment, 1967-70, sec.-treas. Masonic Center Fayetteville, 1971—. Vestryman, St. John's Episcopal Ch., Fayetteville, 1958-60. Mem. Purdue Alumni Assn. Republican. Episcopalian. Clubs: Rotary, Masons, Shriners. Home: 1709 Ft Bragg Rd Fayetteville NC 28303 Office: 2860 Village Dr Fayetteville NC 28304

JACKSON, DAVID LEON, directory publishing company sales executive; b. Ft. Wayne, Ind., Jan. 16, 1949; s. Leon F. and Marjorie J. (Grable) Jackson; m. Sheila Kostik, Apr. 10, 1976; children—Michael, Christopher. B.A. in Pub. Adminstrn., U. Fla., 1971; M.S. in Mgmt., Crummer Sch. Bus., Rollins Coll., 1983. Buyer Ivey's Dept. Stores, Winter Park, Fla., 1974-78; sales exec. Am. Tourister, Inc. div. Hillenbrand Industries, Orlando, Fla., 1978-85; sales exec. Donnelley Directory div. Dun & Bradstreet, Orlando, 1985—. Served with USNR, 1971-77. Mem. Fla. Blue Key. Methodist. Home: 4226 Woodlynne Ln Orlando FL 32806

JACKSON, DELLA ROSETTA HAYDEN, civic worker, educator, author; b. Mill Spring, N.C., Mar. 2, 1905; d. Robert Twitty and Amanda (Petty) Hayden; B.A., Johnson C. Smith U., 1948; M.A., N.C. Coll., 1956; m. G. Franklin Davenport, Sept. 28, 1930 (dec. Jan. 1936); children—Evelyn Frances Davenport Petty, Amanda Elizabeth Davenport Gray, Robert Franklin; m. 2d, Clarence Eugene Jackson, Oct. 30, 1943 (dec. Mar. 1951); children—Mae Carolyn Jackson Williams, Clarence Stinson. Tchr., Stony Knoll Sch., Polk County, N.C., 1927-30, Tryon Sch., 1930-31, Pea Ridge Sch., 1932-39, Union Grove Sch., 1939-48, Edmund Embury Sch., 1949-51, Cobb Elementary Sch., Tryon, N.C., 1951-65; tchr. adult edn. Isothermal Community Coll., Mill Spring, N.C., 1971-77; organizer, librarian Stony Knoll Community Library, 1937—, pres., 1972—, also chmn. bd. trustees; spl. edn. tchr. Polk Central High Sch., Mill Spring, 1966-69; resource person Polk County Community Schs., 1982—. Mem. Central Highlands Health Council, 1968-70; 2d v.p. Polk County Homemakers Council; pres. Polk County Extension Homemakers, 1974-75; sec.-treas. Polk County Community Devel. Council; mem. Polk County Family Life Study Com., 1978-79; mem. Ancillary Manpower Planning Bd., Region C, 1972-82, mem. exec. com., 1976-83; leader 4-H Clubs, 1965-85; v.p. Polk County Child Devel. Council, 1971-75, Eastern Appalachian Children's Council, 1971-73; chmn. Polk County Child Care Com., 1971-73; mem. Polk County Emergency Med. Service Adv. Com., 1973-75, Polk County Commn. on Aging, 1974-81, N.C. Child Care, N.C. Children's 100; bd. dirs. Isothermal Health Council, sec., 1972-76; bd. dirs. Polk County Mental Health Council, 1972-73, St. Luke Hosp. Aux., 1970-77, Regional Health Council Eastern Appalachia, 1970-77, Polk County unit Am. Cancer Soc., 1979-82; bd. govs., mem. exec. com. Western N.C. Health System Agy., 1977-81, mem. resource devel. com., 1978-81; steering com. Gov.'s Regional Conf. on Leadership Devel. for Women, 1978-79; mem. Region C Employment and Tng. Adv. Com., 1978-83, Polk County Interagy. Council, 1978-81, Polk County Family Life Council, 1978; club rep. Polk County Community Resource Council, 1986—. Named Mother of Year, Afro, 1948, Mother of Year, Homemakers Council Polk County and Western Dist. N.C., 1971; recipient cert. service N.C. Recreation Soc., 1962; cert. leadership for service Western N.C. Community Devel. Program Asheville Agrl. Devel. Council, 1962; award for outstanding leadership and service Western N.C. Devel. Assn., 1979, Woman of Year, 1979; cert. of appreciation Western N.C. Health System Agy., 1981; cert. of award Polk County Hist. Assn., 1980; Sunday Sch. Tchr. of Yr., Stony Knoll C.M.E. Ch., 1980. Mem. LWV (dir. 1970—), Stony Knoll Recreation Soc., Polk County Hist. Assn., St. Luke Hosp. Aux. Clubs: Order of Calanthe (worthy counselor), Stony Knoll Community (pres. 1959-62). Author: Special Approaches for Sunday School in Small Churches, 1981; Poems of Experience and Emotion, 1981; Twenty Little Prayers, 1981; Let My People Go, 1982. Home: Box 95 Mill Spring NC 28756

JACKSON, DON G(ENE), recording company executive, concert and recording artist; b. Fulton, Ky., July 19, 1938; s. Elvin C. Jackson and Lola (Pittman) Jackson Turner; m. Stella M. Gay, Jan. 1, 1957; children—Donald Mark, Shannon Blake, Shari Dawn. B.A. in Music Edn., U. Tex.-Arlington, 1960; M.R.E. in Religious Edn., Southwestern Sem., Ft. Worth, 1962; postgrad. Murray U. (Ky.), 1965. Ordained to ministry Baptist Ch., 1971. Minister of music/youth Northside Bapt. Ch., Chattanooga, 1962-63, First Bapt. Ch., Chamblee, Ga., 1963-65, Bethany Bapt. Ch., Dallas, 1966-73; minister of music Southside Bapt. Ch., Spartanburg, S.C., 1973-75, First Bapt. Ch., Duncanville, Tex., 1975-80; pres. Rainbow Sound Inc., Dallas, 1981—; soloist/music dir. Crusade of Ams., B.C., Can., 1969, Northwest Bapt. Evangelism Conf., Portland, Oreg., 1972; music dir. Dallas Bapt. Assn. Chs., 1971-72; rec. artist sacred albums. Songwriter: He's Wonderful, 1958; Peace For Our Restless World, 1967. Named to Outstanding Young Men Am., U.S. Jr. C. of C., 1971; named Ky. col., Gov. Ky., 1976. Home: 211 Naples Dr

Duncanville TX 75116 Office: Rainbow Sound Inc 1316 Inwood Rd Dallas TX 75247

JACKSON, DOROTHY LOUISA GREENLEE, court reporter; b. Hamburg, Iowa, Feb. 19, 1911; d. Henry Oliver and Mattie (Landreth) Greenlee; student public schs.; m. Fred Knox Jackson, Oct. 3, 1944 (dec.). Asst. county ct. reporter, Auburn, Nebr., 1927-29; sec. local atty., 1927-29; sec. Berksons, Kansas City, Mo., 1929-33; corr. A.A.A., Washington, 1933-36, sec. Intelligence Unit, Kansas City, St. Louis, 1936-40; free-lance ct., conv. reporter, St. Louis, 1940-44; freelance ct. reporter, Prattville, Ala., 1948—; contract reporter Ala. Public Service Commn., Montgomery, 1967-80; co-owner, operator Prattville (Ala.) Quick Freeze, 1948-63. Chmn., Autauga County Operation Santa Claus, State Christmas Card, Bryce Mental Hosp., Tuscaloosa, Ala., 1963-70; active Birmingham Opera Guild, 1960-70, Montgomery Symphony League. Mem. Nat. League Am. Pen Women (br. pres. 1964-68, 72-74, 76-78, state pres. 1972-74, state v.p. 1982-84, state pres. 1984—), Ala. Writers Conclave, Montgomery Creative Writers Club, Autauga County Creative Writers Club, Montgomery Press and Authors Club (pres. 1971-72), Ala. Shorthand Reporters Assn., Montgomery Assn. Legal Secs., Nat. Shorthand Reporters Assn., Ala. Poetry Soc., Autauga County Bus. and Profl. Women's Club (County Woman of Achievement 1972), Romance Writers Am., Internat. Platform Assn. Autaugo County Assn. Ret. Persons (legis. chmn. 1981-83), Nat. Assn. Ret. Persons, Autauga County Art Guild. Author: (poetry) Fallen Leaves, 1968; Poody, 1970. Home: 856 Gillespie St Prattville AL 36067

JACKSON, FRANCES KAY, educator; b. San Antonio, Mar. 24, 1950; d. Hallie Franklin and Mary Etna (Johnson) Williams; m. Willie Gene Jackson, Sr., Jan. 9, 1971; children—Willie Gene, Jr., Wendy Janine. B.A., Culver-Stockton, Canton, Mo., 1972; M.A.T.M., U. Ky., 1984. Tchr. math. Copperas Cove High Sch., Tex., 1973-76, 84—; GED specialist Am. Prep. Inst., Fort Wood, Mo., 1979; math. educator Waynesville Jr. High Sch., Mo., 1979-83; grad. asst. U. Ky., Lexington, 1983-84; math. coordinator Univ. Interscholastic League, Copperas Cove, 1984—. Pres. Jr. Womens Aux., Bibleway Ch., Copperas Cove, Tex., 1984-85. Mem. Am. Math. Soc. Democrat. Baptist. Avocation: mystery reader. Home: Route 3 Box 829 Kempner TX 76539 Office: Copperas Cove High Sch Sunny and Ridge Copperas Cove TX 76522

JACKSON, FRED CAPERS, JR., insurance company executive; b. Selma, Ala., June 4, 1933; s. Fred C. and Mildred A.J.; m. Carla Jane Kelso, Aug. 24, 1957; children—Patricia Jane, Fred Capers, Philip K. B.S., Miami U., Oxford, Ohio, 1955. C.L.U.; chartered fin. cons. Field mgr. Conn. Gen., Jacksonville, Fla., 1955-69; gen. agt. ins. mktg. Gulf Life Ins. Co., Jacksonville, 1967—; pres. fin. services Data Fin., Inc., 1972—. Bd. dirs. Fla. Jr. Coll. Found., pres., 1980-82; chmn. Jacksonville Recreation Bd., 1976-80; mem. Jacksonville Sports Commn., 1980. Served to capt. USAF, 1955-58. Heritage Heubner scholar, 1982; named Fla. Jr. Coll. Ins. Exec. of Yr., 1982. Mem. Fla. Gen. Agts. and Mgrs. Assn. (pres. 1977-78), Jacksonville Gen. Agts. and Mgrs. Assn., Jacksonville C.L.U. Assn. (pres. 1982-83; trustee, dir.), Jacksonville Underwriters Assn. (dir.), Fla. Assn. Life Underwriters (dir., chmn. com.), Estate Planning Council Jacksonville. Republican. Presbyterian. Clubs: San Jose Country, University. Home: 13250 Mandarin Rd Jacksonville FL 32223 Office: 820 Gulf Life Tower Suite 820 Jacksonville FL 32207

JACKSON, HORACE FRANKLIN, state official, accountant; b. Dillon, S.C., Oct. 1, 1934; s. Redden Haney and Daisy Belle (Moody) J.; B.S., U. S.C., 1961, M.B.A., 1971; m. Margie Jan Phillips, June 1, 1955; children—Margie Jan, Horace Darrin. Staff acct. J.W. Hunt & Co., C.P.A.s, 1961-64; staff auditor State Auditor S.C., Columbia, 1964-68, sr. budget analyst, 1968-70; dir. fin. S.C. Dept. Social Services, Columbia, 1970-72, dep. commr. fin. mgmt., 1973-75, dep. commr. fiscal ops., 1975-78, exec. asst. for fin. mgmt., 1978-80; fin. dir. S.C. Commn. on Aging, 1980—; mem. Gov.'s Task force on Nursing Home Reimbursement, 1969, on Medicaid, 1970, Gov.'s Health Planning Com., 1973, HEW Task Force on Welfare Cost Allocation, 1979-81. Served with AUS, 1957-61. Mem. S.C. State Employees Assn. (dir. 1976-77, 83—), Nat. Assn. Enrolled Agts., U. S.C. Alumni Assn. Methodist. Office: 915 Main St Columbia SC 29201

JACKSON, JAMES JOSEPH, JR., advertising executive; b. Santa Monica, Calif., Aug. 3, 1951; s. James Joseph and Mary Margaret (Lacy) J.; m. Nora Lee Cashin, June 26, 1982; 1 child, John Charles. B.A., U. San Francisco, 1973; student Lyndon B. Johnson Sch., U. Tex.-Austin, 1973-74. Dist. mgr. San Francisco Examiner Chronicle, 1969-73, 74-75; mgmt. trainee Phila. Inquirer, 1975-76; advt. rep. Austin Am. Statesman, 1977-78; realtor assoc., Austin, Tex., 1978-79; account exec. KTVV-TV, Austin, 1979-83; account exec. KHFI Radio, Austin, Tex., 1983-84; v.p. Robert Miller Advt., 1984—. Account exec., vol. United Way, 1983—; Mem. Austin-Travis County Republican Com., 1980. Episcopalian. Clubs: Austin Advertising, Austin Circle of Theaters. Author: Community Indicators Aids in Community Management, 1974. Home: 11405 Parkfield Dr Austin TX 78758 Office: 8200 Mopac Suite 155 Austin TX 78759

JACKSON, JANIE GORAB, librarian; b. Opelousas, La., Sept. 30, 1944; d. Hugh Doras and Marguerite (Mamalakis) Shultz; m. Leroy M. Jackson, Oct. 10, 1962 (dec. 1974); children—George Anthony, Jonathan James. B.A., U. S.W. La., 1967; M.L.S., La. State U., 1977. Tchr. English and speech Lafayette (La.) High Sch., 1967-69, librarian, 1978-82; tchr. English Scott Middle Sch., 1969-73; librarian Vermillion (La.) Elem. Sch., 1973-78, Paul Breaux Middle Sch., Lafayette, 1982—; chmn. sch. library dept. La. Bd. Elem. and Secondary Edn. Mem. ALA (nat. selection com. books for secondary schs.). Roman Catholic. Home: 502 Crawford St Lafayette LA 70506 Office: Paul Breaux Sch 1400 S Orange St Lafayette LA 70502

JACKSON, JOE LOUIS, educational administrator; b. Crystal Springs, Miss., Sept. 14, 1937; s. John H. and Eula Jackson; B.S. in Social Scis., Jackson (Miss.) State Coll., 1959; M.Ed. in Sch. Adminstrn., U. Ark., 1968; Advanced M.Ed. in Supervision and Adminstrn., U. Miss., 1972; m. Nora M. Jackson; children—Willie, Joseph, Jonathan, Leatha. Tchr., North Panola High Sch., Como, Miss., 1961-64; prin. Green Hill Sch., Sardis, Miss., 1964-74; program supr. North Panola Consol. Schs., Sardis, Miss., 1974—. Commr., Sardis Housing Authority, 1975—; treas. Sardis Community Center, 1970—. Cert. in edn., supervision and adminstrn., Miss. Mem. Order Eastern Star (state dir. edn.), Phi Beta Sigma, Phi Delta Kappa. Home: Davis Chapel Rd PO Box 291 Sardis MS 38666 Office: Hwy 51 N Sardis MS 38666

JACKSON, JOHN LESLIE, JR., energy company executive; B.S., U. Tex., 1958. In various engring. and prodn. positions Atlantic Richfield Co.; evaluation engr. H.J. Gruy & Assocs.; v.p. acquisitions Cenard Oil & Gas Co.; exec. v.p. Falcon Seaboard Inc. (merged into Diamond Shamrock Corp. 1979), 1969-79, also dir.; exec. v.p., unit pres. Diamond Shamrock Corp., Dallas, 1979—; dir. Republic Bank, Dallas. Bd. dirs. Berea Coll. Office: Diamond Shamrock Corp 717 N Harwood St Dallas TX 75201

JACKSON, JULIAN CURLEY, minister, marriage and family counselor; b. Sylvania, Ga., May 5, 1933; s. Sonny Jose and Iola (Reason) J.; m. Thelma Phronetta Watson, Mar. 14, 1953; children—Barbara Jackson Murray, Julian D., Mary Brigham. A.A., Miami-Dade Community Coll., 1971; B.S., Fla. Internat. Coll., 1974; M.A., Biscayne Coll., 1983; postgrad. N.Y. Theol. Sem., 1984—. Owner Jackson's Cleaner, Miami, Fla., 1962-67; mail courier Dade County Schs., Miami, 1965-74; social worker Miami Mental Health Ctr., 1975-78; project dir. New Horizons Mental Health Ctr., Miami, 1978-82; minister Ch. of God in Christ, Miami, 1960—, trustee, Memphis, 1972-80, dist. supt., Miami, 1971—. Home: 6890 NW 19th Ave Miami FL 33147 Office: Gamble Meml Ch of God in Christ 1898 NW 43rd St Miami Fla 33142

JACKSON, JULIUS LEE, clergyman; b. Beaumont, Tex., July 13, 1938; s. Oscar and Mary (Crochett) Green J.; m. JoAnn Bostic, Aug. 21, 1958 (div. Nov. 1977); children—Julius Lee, Jr., L'Tonya, Randy; m. Reda Jo Monroe, Sept. 12, 1981; stepchildren—Willis, Kelley, Keisha. Student Lamar U., 1964-67; A.D., Southwestern Theol. Sem., 1972; B.Th., Conroe Coll., 1973; D.D., New World Bible Inst., 1985, postgrad., 1987; postgrad. Tarrant County Jr. Coll., 1976-77, Tex. Wesleyan Coll., 1982, Princeton Theol. Sem., 1983, 85, Arlington Bible Coll., 1974-77, Bishop Coll., 1985. Ordained to ministry Baptist Ch., 1966. Pastor Lilly of the Valley Baptist Ch., Beaumont, 1968-70, Macedonia Bapt. Ch., Fort Worth, 1972—; bd. dirs. New World Bible Inst. Blytheville, Ark., 1985—, provost to pres., 1985—. Mem. adv. bd. Fort Worth State Sch.; mem. adv. bd. distributive edn. program Dunbar High Sch., Fort Worth; juror Grand Jury, Criminal Justice Tarrant County, Fort Worth, 1974, 84; mem. mgmt. com. Morningside Middle Sch., Fort Worth, 1985—; advisor Concerned Citizens for Quality Edn., 1985. Served to cpl. USMC, 1956-62. Recipient Nobel award F. Brooks and Gray, Fort Worth, 1977; Psycho Cybernetics award Dr. Maxwell Malt Miller Seminar, Houston, 1977; Progress award Ecclesiatical Christian awards, Atlanta, 1982. Mem. Bapt. Minister Alliance (courtesy com. 1983—), Black Pastor Assn. Tex. (exec. treas. 1983—), Zion Rest Dist. Assn. (1st vice moderator 1985—). Democrat. Baptist. Lodge: Masons. Avocations: tennis; running. Home: 7113 Kildee Ln Fort Worth TX 76133 Office: Macedonia Bapt Ch 2712 S Freeway Fort Worth TX 76104

JACKSON, (MARY) RUTH, orthopaedic surgeon; b. Jefferson, Iowa, Dec. 13, 1902; d. William Riley and Carolyn Arabelle (Babb) J.; B.A., U. Tex., 1924; M.D., Baylor U., 1928. Gen. intern Meml. Hosp., Worcester, Mass., 1928-29, resident in orthopaedic surgery, 1930-31; intern in orthopaedic surgery Univ. Hosps., U. Iowa, 1929-30; resident in orthopaedic surgery Tex. Scottish Rite Hosp. for Crippled Children, Dallas and asst. at Carrell-Driver-Girard Clinic, Dallas, 1931-32; pvt. practice medicine specializing in orthopaedic surgery, Dallas, 1932—; clin. instr. in orthopaedic surgery Baylor U., Dallas, 1936-43; hon. cons. orthopaedic surgeon Baylor U. Med. Center, Dallas, Parkland Meml. Hosp., Dallas; hon. asst. clin. prof. orthopaedic surgery Southwestern Med. Sch. of U. Tex., Dallas; lectr. in field. Diplomate Am. Bd. Orthopaedic Surgery. Fellow ACS, Internat. Coll. Surgeons; mem. Dallas County Med. Assn., Tex. Med. Assn., So. Med. Assn., AMA, Tex. Orthopaedic Assn., Tex. Rheumatism Assn., Southwestern Surg. Congress, Am. Acad. Orthopaedic Surgeons, Am. Orthopaedic Foot Soc., Am. Assn. for Study Headache, Am. Trauma Soc., Am. Assn. Automotive Medicine, Am. Soc. Contemporary Medicine and Surgery, Western Orthopaedic Assn., Law-Sci. Acad. Am., Pan-Am. Med. Assn. (diplomate sect. orthopaedic surgery), Royal Soc. Medicine (assoc.), Nat. Assn. Disability Examiners, Dallas C. of C., North Dallas C. of C., Kaufman C. of C. Republican. Methodist. Club: Zonta Internat. Author monograph: The Cervical Syndrome, 1956, 4th edit., 1977, Japanese transl, 1967; contbr. articles to profl. jours. Home: 4001 Turtle Creek Blvd Dallas TX 75219 Office: 3629 Fairmount Dallas TX 75219

JACKSON, MICHAEL LYNN, civil and structural engineer, consultant; b. Birmingham, Ala., Mar. 27, 1952; s. Marce L. and Mary Joyce (Bean) Ballinger J.; m. Joyce Hay Land, Mar. 30, 1974; children—William Blake, Jeffrey Craig. B.S. in Civil Engring., Auburn U., 1974; postgrad. U. Houston, 1977. Registered profl. engr., Tex. Structural engr. fed. govt. mktg. Fluor Engrs., Inc., Houston, 1974-81, prin. project engr., 1981-84; pres. exchange exec. U.S. Govt., Washington, 1983-84; prin. project engr. Fluor Engrs., Inc., Houston, 1984—; indsl. cons. Houston Area Research Ctr., The Woodlands, Tex., 1984-85; tech. cons. graphic design aids for structural systems. Mem. Chi Epsilon. Republican. Methodist. Club: Supervisors' (1st v.p. 1985—). Avocations: personal computing; photography; woodworking; youth sports. Home: 13223 Agarita Ln Houston TX 77083 Office: Fluor Engrs Inc 1 Fluor Dr Sugar Land TX 77478-3899

JACKSON, MONA BETHEL, educational administrator, consultant; b. Miami, Fla., Mar. 7, 1947; d. Charles E. Bethel and Olga Isabel (Goodman) Bethel Williams; m. Herman Jackson, Dec. 31, 1968; children—Keane Sean, Herman. B.S., Fla. A&M U., 1969; M.Ed., Fla. Atlantic U., 1973. Cert. tchr., Fla. Sci. tchr. Dade County pub. schs., Miami, 1970-74, sci. tchr./counselor, 1974-75, counselor, 1975-82, ednl. specialist, 1982-84, project mgr., 1984—; cons.; curriculum coordinator Perrine Crime Prevention Program, Miami, 1979-82. Author: (manual) Dollars and Cents: A Guide for Scholarship Applicants, 1980, Focus on Careers, 1984. Pres., Dade County Sickle Cell Found., 1983—; sec. bd. dirs. Haitian Refugee Ctr., Miami, 1983-85. Named Tchr. of Yr., Drew Jr. High Sch., 1972; recipient plaque Dade County Sickle Cell Found., 1981. Mem. Dade County Personnel and Guidance Assn. (pres. 1983-84, plaque 1984), Fla. Assn. Counseling and Devel. (pres.-elect 1985-86; plaque 1985), Fla. Assn. Sci. Tchrs., Phi Delta Kappa, Delta Sigma Theta. Democrat. Episcopalian. Sec. vestry Christ Episcopal Ch., 1984—. Home: 8970 SW 126th Terr Miami FL 33176

JACKSON, RANDALL C(ALVIN), lawyer; b. Baird, Tex., Mar. 21, 1919; s. Rupert and Anna (Faust) J.; J.D., U. Tex., 1946; B.B.A., 1941; m. Betty S. Johnson, June 18, 1955; 1 child, Randall Calvin. Admitted to Tex. bar, 1946, practiced in Baird, 1946-62, Abilene, 1962—; sr. partner firm Jackson & Jackson, 1949—; mem. Tex. Securities Bd., 1966-69; chmn. Abilene Spl. Housing Study Com. Former pres. bd. dirs. Boys Ranch, Abilene; former chmn. bd. regents Tex. Woman's U., 1961-66; mem. Tex. Dem. Exec. Com., 1960-64; former chmn. bd. trustees Sears Methodist Retirement Center. Enlisted USAC, 1942, disch. capt., 1946, assigned Exec. Office Statis. Control Unit, Guam. Fellow Am. Coll. Probate Counsel; mem. Southwestern Legal Found., Tex. Bar Found. (charter mem.), State Bar Tex. (chmn. legal bd. specialization), ABA, Callahan-Taylor County Bar Assn. (pres. 1979-80), Am. Judicature Soc., Am., Tex. (dir., chmn. planning com., pres. 1982), Tex. (pres. 1982), West Tex. (pres.), Sweetwater (dir.), Concho (dir.) hereford assns., Abilene Livestock Show Assn. (pres. 1979, 80-82), Am. Legion (past comdr.), Abilene C. of C. Methodist (chmn., dist. trustee). Clubs: Masons (32 deg.), Shriners; Headliners (Austin, Tex.); Abilene Petroleum, Abilene Country (Abilene). Home: Route 2 Box 703 Abilene TX 79601 Office: Bank of Commerce Bldg Abilene TX 79602

JACKSON, RICHARD LEE, lawyer, banker; b. Lima, Ohio, Jan. 21, 1931; s. Stanley H. and Cleta North J.; m. Sadie Lou Gibson, Dec. 26, 1953; children—Paul Edward, Janet Lynn, Martha Lee. B.A., Ohio State U., 1952, J.D., 1957; Nat. Grad. Trust Sch. degree, Northwestern U., 1969. Bar: Ohio 1958. Cert. fin. services counselor. Trust officer Huntington Nat. Bank of Columbus (Ohio), 1957-71, v.p. in charge trust dept., Lima, Ohio, 1971-75, v.p., trust officer-in-charge selected trusts, 1975-79; v.p., trust officer head estate, trust planning AmSouth Bank, Birmingham, Ala., 1979-82, officer in charge family group trusts, 1982—; mem. faculty Ohio Trust Sch., So. Trust Sch., Am. Inst. Banking, Ohio Legal Ctr. Inst., Nat. Grad. Trust Sch. Northwestern U. Chmn. bd. trustees Family, Childrens Bur., Columbus, 1971; bd. dirs., v.p. Lima Symphony, 1974; bd. dirs. Child, Family Bur., Lima, 1974. Served to lt. col. JAGC, U.S. Army; mem. Res. (ret.). Recipient Award Merit, Ohio Legal Ctr. Inst., Scout-O-Rama award Boy Scouts Am. Mem. ABA (real property, probate and trust com.), Ohio Bar Assn., Birmingham Bar Assn. (speakers com.), Estate Planning Council, Ohio State U. Alumni Assn., Phi Delta Phi, Phi Kappa Sigma. Baptist. Lodge: Kiwanis (pres. 1979-80, lt. gov.-elect 1985—). Contbr. articles to legal jours. Home: 409 Michael Ln Mountain Brook AL 35213 Office: AmSouth Bank NA Trust div POB 11426 Birmingham AL 35202

JACKSON, ROBERT EUGENE, JR., sugar and real estate executive; b. Memphis, Feb. 26, 1949; s. Robert Eugene and Della Lillian (Sevon) J.; A.A., Palm Beach Jr. Coll., 1970; B.S. in Bus. Adminstrn., U. Fla., 1973. Staff acct. Himes & Himes, C.P.A.s (now May Zime & Co.), West Palm Beach, Fla., 1973-74; asst. v.p. agrl. cos., treas. real estate cos. Osceola Farms Co., New Hope Sugar Co. and affiliated cos., Palm Beach, Fla., 1974-79, v.p. corp. planning Osceola Farms Co. and New Hope Sugar Co. and related cos., 1981—; pres., gen. mgr., co-owner Tennis Club Internat., 1980-81; v.p., fin. cons. to owner LaCroix Constrn. Co., 1980-81. Adv. bd. Goodwill Industries, West Palm Beach; bd. dirs. Thrift, Inc., Palm Beach; treas. Bethesda By the Sea Ch.; active Palm Beach Republican Club. C.P.A. Mem. Am. Inst. C.P.A.s, Fla. Inst. C.P.A.s, Nat. Assn. Accts., East Coast Estate Planning Council, Pi Kappa Alpha. Episcopalian. Clubs: Beach (jr. com. Palm Beach), Kiwanis. Home: 218 Seaspray Ave Box 2201 Palm Beach FL 33480 Office: 316 Royal Poinciana Plaza Box 1059 Palm Beach FL 33480

JACKSON, ROBERT HOLLAND, orthodontist; b. Memphis, June 12, 1944; s. Robert Lamar and Rebecca (Holland) J.; m. Betty Ann Carr, Dec. 16, 1972; children—Robert Brandon, Brooke Ann. B.S., Memphis State U., 1966; D.D.S., U. Tenn., 1969; M.S., 1972. Instr. U. Tenn., Memphis, 1972-74; practice dentistry specializing in orthodontics, Jonesboro, Ark., 1972—. Mem. ADA, Northeast Ark. Dist. Dental Soc. (pres. 1985—), Am. Assn. Orthodontists. Republican. Mem. Ch. of Christ. Clubs: Mallard (Jonesboro), Jubilation. Lodges: Elks, Rotary (bd. dirs. 1984—). Avocations: hunting; shooting; fishing; snow skiing; art collecting. Home: 2118 Paula Dr Jonesboro AR 72401 Office: Robert H Jackson DDS 911 Osler Dr Jonesboro AR 72401

JACKSON, ROBERT TOOMBS, physician; b. Cochran, Ga., Sept. 7, 1915; s. Robert Toombs and Eloise (Jones) J.; m. Ellen Holmes Carson, Aug. 10, 1946; children—Robert T., Ellen Taylor, Richard Montgomery. B.S., Mercer U., 1938; M.D., U. Ga., 1941. Diplomate Am. Bd. Radiology. Intern, U. Mich., Ann Arbor, 1941-42; gen. practice medicine, Washington, 1946-51; fellow radiology, 1st asst. diagnostic roentgenology Mayo Clinic, Rochester, Minn., 1951-54; assoc. radiology Bristol Meml. Hosp. (Tenn.), 1954-56, Rex Hosp., Raleigh, N.C., 1956—; chief cons. N.C. State U., 1974—, N.C. Dept. Corrections, 1974—. Served to maj. N.C., AUS, 1942-46. Decorated Army Commendation award with pendant. Mem. AMA, Am. Coll. Radiology, Radiol. Soc. N.Am., N.C. Radiol. Soc., Eastern Radiol. Soc., So. Conf. Radiologists, Raleigh Acad. Medicine (past pres.), Nuclear Med. Soc., Alumni Assn. Mayo Found. Methodist. Club: Carolina Country. Lodge: Masons. Home: 3347 Alamance Dr Raleigh NC 27609

JACKSON, SARAH ELIZABETH, nurse; b. Atlanta, Feb. 2, 1920; d. Agustus Bell and Ola Anna Lee (Reed) Glover; m. Fuller Lorenza Jackson, Feb. 14, 1939 (dec.); 1 child, Barbara Alaine Jackson Joiner. Grad. Grady Meml. Hosp. Nursing Sch. Atlanta, 1938. Staff nurse State Hosp., Milledgeville, Ga., 1938-39; nursery dir. Bethleham Ctr., Atlanta, 1940-41; owner nursery Fairburn Rd., Atlanta, 1958-59; founder Redales Model's, Atlanta, 1977-83; staff nurse McLendon Hosp., Atlanta, 1951-62, Hughes Spalding Meml. Ctr., Atlanta, 1962—. Recipient award Redale of Atlanta, 1977, 85. Mem. Black Women's Voters League. Democrat. Baptist. Home: 3000 Continental Colony TH D59 Atlanta GA 30331 Office: Hughes Spalding Community Hosp 35 Butler St SE Atlanta GA 30335

JACKSON, SHERYL SMITH, public relations executive; b. Atlanta, Sept. 30, 1956; d. Donald David and Gail Veronica (Duffy) Smith; m. Justin Carl Jackson, Jr., Oct. 29, 1978. B.A. in Journalism, Ga. State U., 1978. Editor, United Way of Met. Atlanta, 1978, communications assoc., 1978-81; sr. writer, press relations coordinator Blue Cross & Blue Shield of Ga., Atlanta, 1981; communications specialist Decatur Fed. Savs. & Loan Assn. (Ga.), 1981-83; dir. pub. info. Gwinnett Hosp. Systems, Lawrenceville, Ga., 1984—. Mem., chmn. spl. events task force Vol. Dekalb Adv. Bd. Mem. Women in Communications (v.p. fin. 1983, pres.-elect 1984), Pub. Relations Soc. Am., Sigma Delta Chi, Ga. State U. Alumni Assn. Office: PO Box 348 Lawrenceville GA 30246

JACKSON, THURMAN HINSON, JR., technical institute dean, educator; b. Brookwood, Ala., May 10, 1934; s. Thurman Hinson and Verna Maxine (Murray) J.; m. Marilyn Stewart, Sept. 19, 1963; children—Thurman Hinson III, Jason, Melissa. B.S. in Petroleum Geology, Miss. State U., 1957; M.S. in Sci., Memphis State U., 1966. Hydrologist, U.S. Geol. Survey, 1959-60; tchr., dept. chmn. Millington Central High Sch., Tenn., 1960-67; assoc. prof. physics, chmn. dept. State Tech. Inst., Memphis, 1967-70, div. head learning resource ctr., 1970-75, dir. adminstrv. affairs, 1975-78, acad. dean, prof. physics, 1978—. Consumer arbitrator Better Bus. Bur., Memphis. Served to cpl. USMC, 1952-54, U.S. Army, 1957-59. Mem. Am. Tech. Edn. Assn., Am. Vocat. Assn., Tenn. Vocat. Assn., Sigma Gamma Epsilon. Presbyterian. Avocation: jogging. Office: State Tech Inst-Memphis 5983 Macon Cove Memphis TN 38134

JACKSON, VIRGINIA FREDERICK, nurse; b. Nashville, May 4, 1934; d. Cecil Southworth and Beatrice (Pace) Frederick; m. Billy Wilson Jackson, Sept. 20, 1953 (div. 1965); children—Terry Frederick, Billy Wilson. A.A. in Nursing, Middle Tenn. State U., 1974; cert. nursing exec. mgmt. program Hosp. Corp. Am., Nashville, 1983. R.N., Tenn. Asst. operating room supr. Rutherford Hosp., Murfreesboro, Tenn., 1974-78; clin. asst. dept. nursing Middle Tenn. State U., Murfreesboro, 1978-80; asst. dir. nursing HCA Stones River Hosp., Woodbury, Tenn., 1980-82, dir. nursing, 1982—; chmn. Cannon County Am. Heart Assn., Woodbury, 1984; mem. Cannon County Child Protection Council, 1984-85. Dir. prodn. Cannon Community Playhouse, Woodbury, 1982—. Recipient Dr. Thomas Frist Humanitarian award Hosp. Corp. Am., 1981. Mem. Tenn. Hosp. Assn., Tenn. Nurses Assn. Methodist. Home: PO Box 326 Woodbury TN 37190 Office: HCA Stones River Hosp PO Box 458 Woodbury TN 37190

JACKSON, WALTER COLEMAN, III, clergyman, marriage therapist, educator; b. Chester, Pa., Mar. 21, 1933; s. Walter Coleman and Elsie Irene (Watson) J.; m. Jacqueline Jean Rhoads, Aug. 17, 1957; children—Jerri Leigh, Jeffrey Walter, Nanci Carol. B.A., U. Richmond, 1955; B.D., So. Baptist Theol. Sem., 1959, Th.M., 1961, Ph.D., 1968. Ordained to ministry, Baptist Ch., 1955; pastor chs., Va., Ky., 1954-64; chaplain Ky. Bapt. Hosp., Louisville, 1964-77, instr. sch. of Nursing, 1964-72; clin. instr. Louisville Presbyterian Theol. Sem., 1971-72; chaplain Bapt. Med. Ctr. Okla., Oklahoma City, 1977-81; prof. ministry So. Bapt. Theol. Sem., Louisville, 1982—. Diplomate Am. Assn. Pastoral Counselors; mem. Am. Assn. Marriage and Family Therapy (clin.; supr. 1981), Assn. Clin. Pastoral Edn. (supr. 1974), Coll. Chaplains, Am. Protestant Hosp. Assn., Louisville Assn. Mental Health (dir. 1976-77), Jefferson County Med. Soc. (physician clergy com.), Ky. Med. Assn. (com. religion and medicine, clergy cons.). Office: So Baptist Theol Sem 2825 Lexington Rd Louisville KY 40280

JACO, E. GARTLY, medical sociology educator; b. Memphis, Oct. 5, 1923; s. Oscar Hubert and Delzell (Simpson) J.; m. Adele Marie Bolles, May 28, 1947; children—Linda Dell, Jerry Monroe, Andrew Richard, John Douglas. B.A., U. Tex., 1949, M.A., 1950; postgrad. U. Chgo., 1951; Ph.D., Northwestern U., 1954. Teaching fellow dept. sociology U. Tex.-Austin, 1950, instr., 1952-55; teaching and research asst. dept. sociology Northwestern U., Evanston, Ill., 1950-52; assoc. prof. dept. preventive medicine and pub. health, dept. neurology and psychiatry, sch. nursing U. Tex. Med. Br., Galveston, 1955-59, prof. dept. preventive medicine and community health, 1978—, dir. div. med. sociology, 1957-59, dir. div. health behavior, 1978-79; assoc. Sch. Applied Social Sci., Western Res. U., 1959-62, assoc. dept. Psychiatry Sch. Medicine, 1959-62, assoc. prof. dept. sociology, 1959-62; assoc. prof., then prof. program in hosp. and health care adminstrn. Sch. Pub. Health, U. Minn., 1962-66; vis. prof. div. health adminstrn. Sch. Pub. Health, U. Calif. Health Sci. Ctr., Los Angeles, 1969-71; lectr. dept. psychiatry Loma Linda U. Sch. Medicine, 1966-75; vis. prof. dept. community and environ. medicine Calif. Coll. Medicine, U. Calif.-Irvine, 1974; adj. prof. dept. psychiatry Sch. Medicine, U. Tex. Health Scis. Ctr., San Antonio, 1976-78; prof. depts. health care adminstrn. and sociology Trinity U., San Antonio, 1976-78, dir. Ctr. for Profl. Devel. in Health Adminstrn., 1976-78; prof. dept. sociology U. Calif.-Riverside, 1966-78, chmn. dept. sociology, 1966-70; dir. lab. Socio-Environ. Studies, Cleve. Psychiat. Inst. and Hosp., 1959-61; research dir. St. Luke's Hosp., St. Paul, 1964-66; lectr., cons. in field. Author: The Social Epidemiology of Mental Disorders, 1960. Editor: Patients, Physicians and Illness: Sourcebook in Behavioral Science and Health, 1958, 72, 79. Co-founder, editor-in-chief Jour. Health and Human Behavior, 1960-66. Mem. editorial bd. jour. Inquiry. Editor Cap and Gown Press, Inc., 1981—. Contbr. articles, revs. to profl. publs., chpts. to books. Mem. research adv. com. Calif. State Dept. Mental Hygiene, 1968-70; mem. Tech. Com. on Health, 1970-71; del. White House Conf. on Aging, 1970-71; bd. dirs. Tex. Soc. for Aged, 1958-59. Served with USAF, 1943-46, PTO. Recipient James A. Hamilton Hosp. Adminstrs. Book award Am. Coll. Hosp. Adminstrs., 1974. Fellow Am. Sociol. Assn. (mem. council med. sociology sect. 1968-70), Am. Pub. Health Assn. (exec. council Com. on Social Sci. in Health 1978), Am. Orthopsychiat. Assn. (hon.); mem. AAAS, Am. Psychol. Assn., Internat. Sociol. Assn., Southwestern Sociol. Assn., Gerontol. Soc., Assn. Behavioral Sci., Med. Edn. Assn. Social Scis. and Health, Sigma Xi. Avocations: reading, golf, travel. Office: U Tex Med Br Dept Preventive Medicine and Community Health Galveston TX 77550

JACOB, BRUCE ROBERT, law educator, university dean and official; b. Chgo., Mar. 26, 1935; s. Edward Carl and Elsie Berthe (Hartmann) J.; m. Ann Wear, Sept. 8, 1962; children—Bruce Ledley, Lee Ann, Brian Edward. B.A., Fla. State U., 1957; J.D., Stetson U., 1959; LL.M., Northwestern U., 1965; S.J.D., Harvard U., 1980. Bar: Fla., 1959. Asst. atty. gen. Fla., Office Atty. Gen., Tallahassee, 1960-62; assoc. firm Holland, Bevis & Smith, Bartow and Lakeland, Fla., 1962-64; asst. prof. Emory U., Atlanta, 1965-68, assoc. prof., 1968-69; research assoc. Ctr. for Criminal Justice, Harvard U. Law Sch., 1969-70; staff atty. Community Legal Assistance Office, Cambridge, Mass., 1970-71; assoc. prof. Ohio State U., Columbus, 1971-73, prof., dir. clin. programs, 1973-78; dean, prof. Mercer U. Law Sch., Macon Ga., 1978-81; v.p., dean, prof. Stetson U. Coll. Law, St. Petersburg, Fla., 1981—. Contbr. articles to profl. jours. Mem. ABA, Am. Judicature Soc., Fla. Bar Assn. Democrat. Lodge: Rotary. Office: College Law Stetson U 1401 61st St S Saint Petersburg FL 33707

JACOBELLIS, MIKE, lawyer; b. Huntington Station, N.Y., Jan. 19, 1955; s. Nicholas Joseph and Phyllis (Evancie) J.; m. Amy Joanna Greer, June 10, 1978; children—Michael Greer, Joanna Marie. B.A., Cornell U., 1977; J.D., St. John U., Jamaica, N.Y., 1980. Bar: N.Y. 1981, Tex. 1981, U.S. Dist. Ct. (ea. dist.)

Tex. 1981, U.S. Ct. Appeals (5th cir.) 1984. Law clk. to judge U.S. Dist. Ct. (ea. dist.) Tex., Beaumont, 1980-82; ptnr. Tonahill, Hile, Leister & Jacobellis, Beaumont, 1982—. Editor, St. John's Law Rev. Mem. Assn. Trial Lawyers Am., Tex. Trial Lawyers Assn., Jefferson County Bar Assn. Home: 2494 Hazel Beaumont TX 77702 Office: Tonahill Hile Leister & Jacobellis 614 Goodhue Bldg Beaumont TX 77701

JACOBIUS, ARNOLD JOHN, library executive; b. Augsburg, Bavaria, Aug. 2, 1916; came to U.S., 1940; s. Salo and Frida (Sommerfeld) J.; m. Emmy Schöffel, June 25, 1947; children—Peter John, Susan Miryam. Student U. Milano, Italy, 1934-36; B.S., U. Pavia, Italy, 1938; postgrad. Columbia U., 1940-41, M.S. in Library Sci., 1951; Ph.D. in Germanistics, NYU, 1955. Bibliographer, Library of Congress, Washington, 1952-59, project dir., editor, 1959-66, field dir. Overseas Service, Wiesbaden, W.Ger., 1966-79; exec. dir. Academia Book Exhibits, Fairfax, Va., 1979—. Author: Carl Zuckmayer: Eine Bibliographie, 1971; Motive and Dramaturgie im Schauspiel Carl Zuckmayers, 1971; editor-in-chief: Aerospace Medicine and Biology; An Annotated Bibliography, 1952-61 (11 vols.), 1965-66; contbr. articles to profl. jours. Served with U.S. Army, 1942-46; ETO. Recipient Founders Day Achievement award N.Y. U., 1956; Superior Service award Library of Congress, Washington, 1979. Mem. ALA. Home: Fairfax VA

JACOBO, WINSTON WENDLE, business consultant, lawyer, agricultural reorganization consultant; b. Honolulu, Apr. 4, 1945; s. Primo M. and Julia (Rodriguez) Thomas J.; m. Deloris Greene, Apr. 10, 1976; children—Nicole, Primo M. B.A. in English, Jacksonville U., 1971; J.D., U. Fla., 1973. Bar: Fla. 1973, U.S. Dist. Ct. (mid. and no. dists.) Fla. 1977, U.S. Dist. Ct. (mid. dist.) Ga. 1979, U.S. Ct. Appeals (5th and 11th cirs.) 1978, U.S. Supreme Ct. 1979; diplomate Ct. Practice Inst. Asst. Pub. defender 3d Jud. Circuit, Lake City, Fla., 1975-77; assoc. Airth, Sellers & Lewis, Live Oak, Fla., 1977-78; agrl. cons., Crystal River, Leesburg, Clearwater, Fla., 1978-84; sole practice, Fruitland Park, Fla., 1984-85; assoc. Rumberger, Kirk, Caldwell, Cabanis & Burke, Orlando, Fla., 1985-86; prin., dir. Agri-Bus. Cons. Services, Inc., 1986—; co-owner Dairy Mgmt. Services, Inc. Served with USAF, 1963-67. Mem. Acad. Fla. Trial Lawyers, Assn. Trial Lawyers Am., ABA, Orange County Bar Assn. Democrat. Methodist. Home: 409 S Dixie Ave Fruitland Park FL 32731

JACOBS, ALEXANDER SAMUEL, retail shoe store executive; b. Petersburg, Va., Dec. 11, 1920; s. Max and Fay (Schoenbaum) J.; m. Rosalie Celia Want, July 29, 1943; children—James, Richard. B.S., U. Richmond, 1943. Pres., Standard James, Inc., Petersburg, Va., 1946—; adv. bd. Central Fidelity Bank of Petersburg, Va. Electric & Power Co. of Central Va. Pres. Petersburg Retail Mchts. Assn., 1982-83, bd. dirs., 1983; bd. dirs. Center City Assn., 1983; pres. Petersburg Gen. Hosp., 1976-78, 80-81, bd. dirs., 1983; bd. dirs., past pres. Southside Va. Emergency Crew, Petersburg YMCA; mem. Petersburg City Council, 1956-60. Served to lt. U.S. Navy, 1943-46. Named Young Man of Yr., Petersburg Jaycees, 1953; recipient Activity award, Achievement award USCG Aux., 1982; named Father of Yr., Petersburg, 1977. Clubs: Battlefield Park Swim (past pres., dir.), Lee Park Golf (past pres., dir.). Lodges: Elks, B'nai B'rith. Home: 421 Greenwood Dr Petersburg VA 23805 Office: 128 N Sycamore St Petersburg VA 23803

JACOBS, ELLEN DEBORAH, educator, glassblower, metalsmith; b. Chgo., Dec. 10, 1932; d. William Henry and Lucille Eugene (Hoover) J.; m. Charles M. Jacobs, July 7, 1957 (div. 1967). B.A., U. Chgo., 1951; M.S., Inst. Design, Ill. Inst. Tech., 1962; postgrad. Sch. Am. Craftsmen, Rochester Inst. Tech., 1967-68, U. Calif.-Berkeley, 1970, Art Inst. Chgo., 1952-83, others. Asst. art dir. Channel 11, WTTW, Chgo., 1956; instr. London, Kaiserlauten, Ger., 1957-59; metalsmith, designer, N.Y.C., 1960-69; asst. prof. art Wilkes Coll., Wilkes-Barre, Pa., 1969-72; prof. art Fla. Internat. U., Miami, Fla., 1972—; lectr. in field. Alexander White Hon. scholar, U. Chgo., 1948-51; 1st place, hon. mentions, Profl. Artist Guild shows, Miami, 1977, 78. Mem. Coll. Art Assn., Glass Art Soc., Soc. N. Am. Goldsmiths, Am. Craft Council, Artist Craftsmen of N.Y., Inst. Maya Studies, Common Cause, ACLU, NOW. Club: Sierra. Glass in collection of Corning Glass Museum, Cooper-Hewitt Mus., others; solo shows incl. Alaska, Chgo., N.Y., Pa., Del., Fla. Home: 3935 Kumquat Ave Coconut Grove Miami FL 33133 Office: Visual Arts Dept Fla Internat Univ Tamiami Trail Miami FL 33199

JACOBS, JEROME F., podiatric surgeon; b. Toronto, Ont., Can., Jan. 1, 1937; s. David and June (Kroft) J.; m. Vickie A. Bombalier, June 17, 1972; children—Jack, Eric. D.P.M., Ill. Coll. Podiatric Medicine, Chgo., 1964. Diplomate Am. Bd. Ambulatory Foot Surgery, Nat. Bd. Podiatry Examiners, Internat. Coll. Podiatric Laser Surgery. Intern, Ill. Coll. Podiatric Medicine and Surgery, 1964-65; pvt. practice podiatric medicine, specializing in foot surgery, Miami Beach, Fla., 1965—; mem. staff South Shore Hosp. and Med. Ctr., Miami Beach; cons. foot surgery VA Hosp., Miami; clin. instr. Ohio Coll. Podiatric Medicine, 1980; asst. prof. Coll. Podiatric Medicine and Surgery, U. Osteopathic Medicine and Human Sci., Des Moines, 1983; mem. faculty Dr. William M. Scholl Coll. Podiatric Medicine, 1982. Served with USAF, 1958-60. Fellow Acad. Ambulatory Foot Surgery (treas.), Am. Soc. Podiatric Medicine (trustee); mem. Fla Podiatry Assn. (2d v.p., mem. ins. ad hoc com.), Am. Assn. Hosp. Podiatrists, Am. Podiatry Assn., Dade County Podiatry Assn. Lodges: Masons, Shriners. Contbg. author: A Guide to Podiatric Hospital Procedures and Protocol. Contbr. articles to profl. jours. Office: 1688 Meridian Ave Suite 100 Miami Beach FL 33139 also 666 E 25th St Hialeah FL 33013

JACOBS, KEITH WILLIAM, psychologist, educator; b. Ames, Iowa, Feb. 24, 1944; s. Cyril W. and Sylvia Jacobs; B.A., U. No. Iowa, 1968; M.A., Eastern Ill. U., 1972; Ph.D., U. So. Miss., 1975. Adj. instr. psychology Natchez br. U. So. Miss., 1974-75; assoc. prof., chmn. psychology Loyola U., New Orleans, 1975-85, prof., chmn. dept., 1985—; lectr. psychology Our Lady of Holy Cross Coll., New Orleans, 1976-80; aux. faculty William Carey Coll. Sch. Nursing, New Orleans, 1979-80. Active ACLU; exec. bd. Oak Harbor Homeowners Assn., 1979-81. Served with U.S. Army, 1968-71. Fellow Am. Psychol. Assn.; mem. Am. Assn. Sex Educators, Counselors and Therapists (cert. sex educator and counselor), Southwestern Psychol. Assn., Midwestern Psychol. Assn., La. Acad. Scis., Southeastern Psychol. Assn., Sigma Xi. Contbr. articles to sci. publs. Home: PO Box 102 Pearlington MS 39572 Office: Dept Psychology Loyola U New Orleans LA 70118

JACOBS, RICHARD LEWIS, gasoline distributorship executive; b. Georgetown, Ky., Nov. 10, 1950; s. George Alexander Jacobs and Ellida (Sadler) Fri. B.A., Whittier Coll., 1972; student Internat. Study Program, U. Oslo, 1971; M.B.A., Vanderbilt U., 1981. Asst. to v.p. Whittier Coll. (Calif.), 1973-74, dir. of devel., 1974-76; v.p. River Oil Co., Memphis, 1976-81; pres. River Oil Co. of Jackson, Tenn., 1981—; sec. Compro, Inc., Touchstone Rwy. Supply Co.; mem. bds. River Oil Co., Memphis, Touchstone Ry. and Supply Co., Jackson, Rail Research, Jackson; mem. Nat. Oil Jobbers Council Planning Com. Past chmn. Tenn. Young Republican Fedn.; commr. Tenn. Civil Service Commn.; mem. Nat. Young Rep. Exec. Com.; vice chmn. Madison County Rep. Party; mem. Commitment Memphis; mem. adv. bd. Pub. Service Commn.; treas. Nat. Young Rep. Fedn.; del. Nat. Rep. Conv., 1984. Mem. Tenn. Oil Marketers Assn. (pres.), Jackson C. of C. (chmn. legis. com.), Jackson Area C. of C. Mem. Christian Ch. (Disciples of Christ). Home: 1010 Prospect Jackson TN 38301 Office: 1940 S Highland Jackson TN 38301

JACOBS, RICHARD OLIVER, lawyer, bank executive; b. Superior, Wis., May 7, 1931; s. Saul and Olive H. (Olson) J.; B.B.A., U. Wis., 1954; J.D. magna cum laude, Stetson U., 1967; m. Joanne Marie Swanson, Aug. 29, 1953; children—Julie, John. Life ins. sales rep. and mgr., 1956-66; admitted to Fla. bar, 1967; shareholder, founder firm Jacobs, Robbins, Gaynor, Burton, Hampp, Burns, Cole & Shasteen, P.A.; chmn., pres., dir. Fla. Park Banks, Inc., Park Bank Fla.; former lectr. ins. law Stetson U.; chmn. exec. com. tax sect. Fla. Bar, 1977-78. Trustee, Bayfront Med. Center, 1971-78, chmn., 1976-77; trustee Eckerd Coll., 1976-84, Stetson Coll. Law, 1982—. Served to 1st lt. U.S. Army, 1954-56. C.L.U. Mem. Am., Fla., St. Petersburg bar assns., Phi Beta Kappa, Phi Kappa Phi, Beta Gamma Sigma. Republican. Methodist. Co-author: Regulation of Financial Planners. Contbr. articles on tax and estate planning to trade jours. Home: 1742 Serpentine Dr S Saint Petersburg FL 33712 Office: 1 Plaza Pl NE Suite 300 Saint Petersburg FL 33701

JACOBS, WILLIE BERNARD, telephone equipment engineer; b. Arlington, Ga., Aug. 17, 1947; s. Sanford Jacobs and Lucile (Sellers) J.; m. Gloria Denise Howell, Nov. 25, 1972; children—Robin, Karla, Kandice. B.S., Fla. A. and M. U., 1971; M.Ednl. Adminstrn., U. Fla., 1974. Painter, Moore Dry Kiln, Jacksonville, Fla., 1967; porter May Cohens, Jacksonville, 1968; forklift operator Reliable Delivery, Lanhan, Md., 1970; camp counselor Alachua County Sch. Bd., Keystone Heights, Fla., 1972, asst. dir., Gainesville, 1971-72; salesman Sears, Gainesville, Fla., 1973; coach weightlifting Gainesville High Sch., 1973-76; supr. community Edn. Center, Santa Fe Community Coll., Gainesville, 1973-75; dean students Gainesville High Sch., 1972-76; instr. Pensacola (Fla.) Jr. Coll., 1976-78; Dimension and Horizon inventory adminstr. S.E. Fla., So. Bell, Fort Lauderdale, 1978-82; engr., assets assigner, 1982, network channel terminating equipment engr. SE Fla., 1982—. Vol., L. A. Lee br. YMCA, 1980-83. Recipient Award of Appreciation, Dillard High Sch. Booster Club, 1981. Home: 2110 Lou Dr W Jacksonville FL 32216 Office: 301 W Bay St Room 6JJ1 So Bell Tower Jacksonville FL 32201

JACOBSEN, REBECCA HANSON, psychologist; b. Dallas, Oreg., Mar. 1, 1949; d. Earl Willard and Virginia (Van Mourik) H.; m. Michael Anthony Jacobsen, Sept. 25, 1970; 1 child, Leif Peter. B.A., CCNY, 1972, M.S., 1974; M.S., U. Ga., 1980, Ph.D., 1982. Lic. psychologist, Ga. Asst. research scientist N.Y. State Psychiat. Inst., 1974-77; grad. teaching asst. U. Oreg., Eugene, 1978-79; psychology intern VA Med. Ctr., Durham, N.C., 1980-81; asst. prof. Med. Coll. Ga., Augusta, 1983—; clin. psychologist VA Med. Ctr., Augusta, 1982—; tng. fellow Ind. Consultation Ctr., Bronx, 1974-77. Contbr. articles to profl. jours. U. Ga. fellow, 1981-82. Mem. Am. Psychol. Assn., Ga. Psychol. Assn., Southeastern Psychol. Assn., Augusta Area Psychol. Assn., Psychologists in Pub. Service. Avocations: tennis; gourmet food; bird-watching; needlework. Office: VA Med Ctr Psychology Service 116BU Augusta GA 30910

JACOBSON, HELEN G. (MRS. DAVID JACOBSON), civic worker; b. San Antonio; d. Jac Elton and Rosetta (Dreyfus) Gugenheim; B.A., Hollins Coll.; m. David Jacobson, Nov. 6, 1938; children—Elizabeth Ann, Dorothy Jean Jacobson Miller. News, spl. events staff NBC, N.Y.C., 1933-38. First v.p. San Antonio, Bexar County council Girl Scouts U.S.A., 1957-63; Tex. state rep. UNICEF, 1964-69, hon. bd. dirs. U.S. Com. UNICEF, bd. dirs., 1970-80; chmn. Mayor's Commn. Status of Women, 1972-74; mem. Tex. coordinating com. Internat. Women's Year, 1977; mem. criminal justice planning com. Alamo Area Council Govts., chmn., 1975-77; pres. women's com. Ecumenical Center Religion and Health, 1975-77; bd. dirs. Nat. Fedn. Temple Sisterhoods, 1973-77, Temple Beth-El Sisterhood, mem. Commn. Social Action of Reform Judaism, 1973-77; bd. dirs. Community Guidance Center, chmn. bd., 1960-63; bd. dirs. Sunshine Cottage Sch. for Deaf Children, chmn. bd., 1952-54; pres. bd. trustees San Antonio Public Library, 1957-61; nat. trustee Nat. Council Crime and Delinquency, 1964-70; trustee San Antonio Mus. Assn., 1964-73; sec. Nat. Assembly Social Policy and Devel., 1969-73; pres. Community Welfare Council, 1968-70; bd. dirs. Foster Grandparents Bexar County, pres., 1968-69, v.p., 1970-73; mem. gov.'s steering com., del. 1970 White House Conf. on Children and Youth; bd. govs. Cancer Therapy and Research Found. South Tex.; pres. Central and South Tex. Coalition Juvenile Justice, 1977-79; chmn. women's campaign Jewish Fedn. San Antonio, 1980; bd. dirs., co-chmn. San Antonio chpt. NCCJ, 1981-84; bd. dirs. Youth Alternatives, Inc., Avance; chmn. campaign United Negro Coll. Fund, San Antonio, 1983, 84. Recipient Headliner award for civic work San Antonio chpt. Theta Sigma Phi (now Women in Communications, Inc.), 1958; Vol. Woman of Year, Express-News, 1959; Nat. Humanitarian award B'nai B'rith, 1975; Brotherhood award San Antonio chpt. NCCJ, 1970; Non-Govtl. Orgns. UNICEF Vol. of Year, 1977; honoree Jewish Nat. Hosp. and Research Center, 1978; Hannah G. Solomon award chpt. Nat. Council Jewish Women, 1979; Disting. Leadership award United Negro Coll. Fund, 1985. Mem. San Antonio Women's Fedn., Tex. Fedn. Women's Clubs (past bd. mem. Alamo dist.), Nat. Council Jewish Women, Symphony Soc. (women's com.). Club: Argyle. Home: 207 Beechwood Ln San Antonio TX 78216

JACOBSON, KENNETH ALLAN, cell biologist, educator; b. Milw., Oct. 29, 1941; s. Harold Ulrich and Ruth Ileen (Baumann) J.; m. Judith Ann Ruder, May 2, 1964; children—Jill, Joy, Julie. B.S. in Physics, U. Wis.-Madison, 1964, M.S. in Physics, 1966; Ph.D. in Biophys. Scis. SUNY-Buffalo, 1972. Materials scientist Dow Corning Corp., Midland, Mich., 1966-69; research asst. SUNY-Buffalo, 1969-72; cancer research scientist Roswell Park Meml. Inst., Buffalo, 1973-80; assoc. prof. U. N.C., Chapel Hill, 1980—; core mem. U. N.C. Cancer Research Ctr., Chapel Hill, 1980—; pres. Fluorescence Unltd., Durham, 1982—; bd. cons. Liposome Tech., Menlo Park, Calif., 1982—. Contbr. articles to profl. jours. Editorial bd. Am. Jour. Physiology, 1980-84. Bd. dirs., sec. Five Oaks Recreational Assn., Durham, 1982—. Mem. Am. Heart Assn. (established investigator 1977-82), Biophys. Soc., Am. Chem. Soc., AAAS. Avocations: tennis; biking; carpentry. Home: 4101 Trotter Ridge Durham NC 27707 Office: Univ N C Dept Anatomy 108 Swing Bldg 217H Chapel Hill NC 27514

JACOBSON, MERVIN VINCENT, manufacturer's representative; b. Preston, Minn., Feb. 14, 1919; s. Henry and Lydia Mae (Barnes) J.; m. Phyllis Helen Einwalter, Feb. 14, 1943 (div. 1958); 1 dau., Diane Elaine; m. Stella Margarita Lindstrom, Sept. 30, 1983. B.B.A., U. Minn., 1950; M.A., So. Meth. U., 1976; E.E. (hon.), Tex. A&M U., 1943. With radio stas. KATE, 1942-43, KRIS, 1945-47, KATE, 1947-49; chief engr. WCOW, 1949-50; aviation sales staff Collins Radio, 1950-60; pres. Jacobson Co., Dallas, 1960—. Lic. pilot. Mem. Inst. Radio Engrs. (assoc.), Internat. Relations Club, Antique Auto Club Am., Alpha Kappa Psi, Phi Theta Kappa, Captain's Forum. Office: PO Box 140715 Dallas TX 75214

JACOBSON, SIDNEY LEON, accountant; b. Portsmouth, Va., Oct. 6, 1938; s. Isaac and Rose (Markman) J.; B.S., Va. Poly. Inst., 1961; J.D., U. Va., 1966; m. Diane Cahoon, May 22, 1979; children—Valerie Lynn, Stephanie Keller. Acct., Peat, Marwick, Mitchell & Co., C.P.A., N.Y.C., 1961-62, M.R. Weiser & Co., C.P.A., 1962-63; admitted to Va. bar, 1966; asso. mem. firm Amato, Babalas, Breit, Cohen, Rutter & Friedman, Norfolk, Va., 1966-69, partner firm Babalas & Jacobson, Norfolk, 1969-71; partner firm Parker Rubinger & Jacobson, Virginia Beach, 1971-74; dir. tax services Norfolk office Laventhol & Horwath, C.P.A.s, 1974-75; prin. Sidney L. Jacobson, C.P.A., Virginia Beach, 1975-85; pres. Jacobson's Waranch P.C., Virginia Beach, 1985—; instr. Old Dominion U., 1967-68. Served with USCGR, 1955-67. Mem. Am. Inst. C.P.A.s, Va. Bar Assn., Norfolk Portsmouth Bar Assn. Republican. Zen layman. Contbr. articles to profl. jours. Office: 1604 Hilltop W Exec Center Suite 208 Virginia Beach VA 23451

JACQUES, RICHARD DOUGLAS, city official; b. Trenton, N.J., Dec. 7, 1949; s. Henry Pinkham and Dorothy (Killion) J.; B.A., Lynchburg Coll., 1971; M.S. in Public Adminstrn., George Washington U., 1978; m. Carolyn Wingfield, Feb. 9, 1974; children—Richard Douglas, Jaclyn Elizabeth. Asst. city planner City of Lynchburg (Va.), 1971, intergovtl. relations coordinator, 1971-74, staff asst. to city mgr., 1974-76, mgmt. services adminstr., 1976-78, dir. dept. community planning and devel., 1978—; adj. faculty Averett Coll.; vis. lectr. politics Randolph Macon Woman's Coll., 1981-82; vis. lectr. econs. Sweet Briar Coll., 1983-84; bd. v.p. Greater Lynchburg Transit Co., Inc.; v.p. Central Va. Spl. Transp. Co., Inc.; spl. liaison Va. Gen. Assembly, 1973. Ex-officio mem. Lynchburg Drug Abuse Task Force, 1972-74, Lynchburg Bicentennial Commn., 1972-76; bd. dirs. Central Va. Regional Health Planning Council, 1972-76; mem. bd. Va. Regional Med. Program, 1972-74; mem. adv. com. Lynchburg Overall Economic Devel. program, 1977—; sect. leader United Way, Lynchburg, 1977-78, div. leader, 1978—, bd. dirs., 1980, 81. Mem. Lynchburg Public Relations Assn., Greater Lynchburg Jaycees, Internat. City Mgmt. Assn., Nat. Council Urban Econ. Devel., Am. Planning Assn. Methodist. Office: City Hall PO Box 60 Lynchburg VA 24505

JACQUES, WILFRED JAMES, JR., marketing company executive; b. Chatham, Ont., Can., May 5, 1932; s. Wilfred James and Almeda (Buie) J.; m. Mary Aleece Strickland, Mar. 7, 1958; 1 son, Wilfred James III. Student U. Ga., 1950-51, LL.B., 1956; B.A., U. Western Ont., 1956; LL.M., NYU, 1964; postgrad. Advanced Mgmt. Program, Harvard U., 1959. Bar: Ga. 1957. With Deen & Jacques firm, Alma, Ga., 1957-63; house counsel Straus Duparquet Inc., N.Y.C., 1964-65; with Harrell Internat. Inc. & Subs., Westport, Conn., and Jacksonville, Fla., 1965-72, also sr. v.p., dir.; chmn. Jacques Co., Waycross, Ga. and Great Falls, Mont., 1973-77; assoc. prof. bus. U. No. Colo., Greeley, 1977-83, also chmn. dept. gen. bus.; assoc. prof. bus. and econs. Longwood Coll., Farmville, Va., 1983—, also head dept. Office: Dept Bus Longwood Coll Farmville VA 23901

JACYNA, GARRY MICHAEL, research scientist; b. Amsterdam, N.Y., Mar. 7, 1951; s. John Stephen and Lillian Ann (DeGroff) J.; B.S. in Physics, Rensselaer Poly. Inst., 1973, M.S. in Math., 1974, Ph.D. in Applied Math., 1977; m. Laura Frances Roche, May 1, 1982. Prin. research scientist Planning Systems, Inc., McLean, Va., 1977-84; prin. investigator communications engring. Sperry Corp. Tech. Ctr., Reston, Va., 1984—; assoc. prof. elec. engring. Cath. U. Am.; tech. cons. acoustics, radar, and signal processing. Mem. Acoustical Soc. Am., Soc. Indsl. and Applied Math., IEEE, Sigma Xi, Pi Mu Epsilon. Roman Catholic. Reviewer, contbr. to Jour. Acoustical Soc. Am.; reviewer IEEE. Home: 11319 Myrtle Ln Reston VA 22091 Office: 12010 Sunnse Valley Dr Reston VA 22091

JADLOW, JANICE WICKSTEAD, finance educator; b. Glen Ridge, N.J., Dec. 4, 1945; d. John Carson and Lucille (Forman) Wickstead; m. Joseph M. Jadlow, Aug. 30, 1969; children—Joanna Christine, Jennifer Lynn. B.A., Miami U., 1967; M.A., U. Va., 1969; Ph.D., Okla. State U., 1977. Economist Bd. Govs., Fed. Res. System, Washington, 1968-69; instr. Okla. State U., Stillwater, 1970-80, asst. prof. fin., 1984—. Sec. Skyline Sch. PTA, Stillwater, 1984-85. Mem. Am. Fin. Assn., Am. Econ. Assn., LWV. Republican. Methodist. Home: 24 Canyon Rim Dr Stillwater OK 74075 Office: Okla State U Coll Bus Stillwater OK 74078

JAEGER, BOI JON, health administration educator; b. Cin., May 17, 1936; s. Ludwig John and Sophie Margaret (Greisen) J.; div.; children—John Ashley, Robert Jeffrey, David Arthur. B.S., Duke U., 1957, M.H.A., 1964, Ph.D., 1971. Asst. adminstrv. dir. Duke Hosp., Durham, N.C., 1964-67; adminstrv. dir. Tulane Clinics, New Orleans, 1967-71; asst. prof. Tulane U.; cons. La. Dept. Hosps., New Orleans, 1968-71; assoc. prof., chmn. Duke U., 1972-79, prof., 1978—, bd. dirs. Univ. Program Health adminstrn., 1973-78, chmn., 1976-77. Author articles. Active Boy Scouts Am.; trustee Carolinas Hosp. and Health Services, 1972-78; active N.C. Gov. Efficiency Study Commn., 1973. Kellogg Found. scholar, 1966-71; Nat. Health Services Research Ctr. fellow, 1971-72. Fellow Am. Pub. Health Assn., Royal Soc. Health, Am. Coll. Hosp. Adminstrs.; mem. Mem. Group Mgmt. Assn., Am. Hosp. Assn. Office: Duke U Med Ctr Dept Health Adminstrn 154 Trent Dr Hall Box 3018 Durham NC 27710

JAFFE, ALAN A., psychologist; b. Bronx, N.Y., July 9, 1947; s. Jack and Ann (Chasen) J.; m. Rona Borreca, June 7, 1969; 1 child, Scott. B.A., C.W. Post Coll., L.I. U., 1969; M.A., New Sch. Social Research, 1971; Ph.D., Nova U., 1982. Staff psychologist Nova Clinic, Davie, Fla., 1978-79, Nova U. Clinic, Inc., Coral Springs, Fla., 1979-81; clin. assoc. Family Inst. Broward, Sunrise, Fla., 1982-83; clin. psychologist Clin. Psychology Inst., Sunrise, 1983-84, Alan A. Jaffe, Ph.D. and Assocs., P.A., Lauderhill, Fla., 1984—. Diplomate Am. Acad. Behavioral Medicine; mem. Am. Psychol. Assn., Fla. Psychol. Assn., Biofeedback Soc. Am., Fla. Assn. Behavioral Analysis. Office: Alan A Jaffe & Assocs PA 7451 W Oakland Park Blvd Lauderhill FL 33319

JAFFE, EUGENE L., economist, military logistician; b. N.Y.C., Apr. 10, 1929; s. Jack and Rose (Keller) J; 1 child, Maris Karyl. B.S., Purdue U., 1955; M.B.A., CUNY, 1965. Mil. logistician Mantech Internat., Alexandria, Va., 1976-80; cons. economist, 1980-83; ops. research analyst VA, Washington, 1983-85; ops. research analyst XMCO Inc., 1985—. Mem. exec. com. Alexandria City Republican party, Va., 1974-79. Served with U.S. Army, 1950-52. Recipient medal for civilian service in Vietnam, Dept. State, 1968. Mem. Washington Ops. Research Mgmt. Scis. Council, Soc. Logistics Engrs., Am. Econs. Assn., Am. Legion, Jewish War Vets. Clubs: Ski of Washington, Tennis Group (asst. editor 1984—) (Washington). Avocations: tennis; swimming.

JAFFE, HARRY J(ULIUS), Realtor; b. Birmingham, Ala., Oct. 25, 1906; s. Phillip and Lena (Friedman) J.; m. Helen Snyder, Nov. 1, 1926; children—Howard, Sidney, Perry Lee. Student Boston U., 1924-26. Founder, operator Harry Jaffe & Sons Auto Parts, Birmingham, 1926-76, ret., 1976; comml. Realtor, Molton Realty & Devel. Corp., Birmingham, 1976—; speaker Pres. Knesseth-Israel Synagogue, Birmingham, 1960; mem. nat. adminstrv. bd. Zionist Orgn. Am., 1955—. Recipient Key to City Miami (Fla.), 1960, Citizenship award Sertoma, 1959, Book of Golden Deeds award Hoover (Ala.) Exchange Club, 1982. Mem. Nat. Assn. Realtors. Club: The Club. Lodges: Lions (pres. club 1963-64), Toastmasters (founder Ala. club 1947, dist. pres. 1948-55), B'nai B'rith (pres. lodge 1973-74). Home: 200 Richmar Dr Birmingham AL 35213 Office: 1900 5th Ave N Suite 1520 Birmingham AL 35203

JAFFE, RICHARD PAUL, corporate executive, lawyer; b. New Haven, May 20, 1946; s. Samuel A. and Frances Diane (Molstein) J.; grad. The Choate Sch., 1963; B.A., Tufts U., 1968; M.B.A., Columbia U., 1971; J.D., Boston U., 1974; m. Jeanne Ellis, Aug. 18, 1968; children—Suzanne, Samuel Abraham. Bar: Mass. 1975, U.S. Dist. Ct. Mass., 1975, U.S. Tax Ct., 1975; assoc. law firm Arabian, Brankey, Chopelas and Eizman, Boston, 1975-78; ptnr., firm Arabian, Brankey, Jaffe & Kennedy, Boston, 1978-80; pres. The Jaffe Cos., Daytona Beach, Fla. and Boston, 1980—; instr. bus. adminstrn. Boston U., 1978-79. Mass. seminar leader The Problems of Drugs and Narcotics, 1967-70; guest speaker Govs' Conf. on Drug Dependency, Boston, 1968; del. N.H. Lakes Preservation Assn., 1978-80; pres. Temple Israel, Daytona Beach, 1983-85; v.p. central council United Synagogues Am., 1984—, mem. nat. bd. advisors, 1983—. Named Concerned Developer of Year New Eng. Heritage Deeds, 1976, Best Non-residential Developer of Year Ormond Beach C. of C., Fla., 1980. Fellow Acad. Internat. Law, 1972. Mem. ABA, Internat. Conf. Shopping Centers, Nat. Assn. Home Builders. Office: 2828 N Atlantic Ave Penthouse Suite Daytona Beach FL 32018 Office: 800 S Atlantic Ave Ormond Beach FL 32074

JAFFE, SYLVIA SARAH, art collector, former medical technologist; b. Detroit, May 16, 1917; d. Sam and Rose (Rosmarin) Turner; B.S. in Med. Tech., U. Wis., 1940; m. David Jaffe, Nov. 8, 1942. Med. technologist Watts Hosp. Lab., Durham, N.C., 1940-45; research hematology technologist in leukemia Sloan Kettering Meml. Hosp. Lab., N.Y.C., 1946-47; chief med. technologist in hematology Arlington (Va.) Hosp. Lab., 1948-55; chief technologist in diagnostic hematology Georgetown U. Hosp., Washington, 1959-70; self employed, collector 19th century art, 1970—. Mem. Am. Soc. Med. Technologists, Am. Soc. Clin. Pathologists (affiliate), Am. Women in Sci., Smithsonian Assocs., Corcoran Gallery of Art, Pa. Acad. Fine Arts, Nat. Trust for Historic Preservation, Washington Print Club, Boston Mus. Fine Arts, Nat. Mus. of Women in Arts, Wis. Alumni Assn. Democrat. Jewish. Club: Pioneer Women. Contbr. articles to profl. socs. Address: 1913 S Quincy St Arlington VA 22204

JAGASICH, PAUL ANTHONY, language educator, translator; b. Budapest, Hungary, Mar. 30, 1934; came to U.S., 1965, naturalized, 1971; s. Peter Kalman and Etelka (Tar) J.; m. Ea Jane Nagy, Oct. 15, 1960; children—Diana, Yvonne. M.A., U. N.C., 1970, 71, Ph.D., 1973; M.A., Middlebury Coll., 1983. Med. librarian Med. U., Budapest, 1958-61; major domo, sec. Motel Assn., Budapest, 1961-64; tchr. French and Russian, St. Bernard's Sch., Gladstone, N.J., 1966-68; grad. teaching asst. U. N.C., Chapel Hill, 1968-73; assoc. prof. fgn. langs. Hampden-Sydney Coll., Va., 1973—. Translator: The Casting of Bells, 1983 (Metthauer award 1985); Mozart in Prague, 1985; also short stories and poems. Mem. Am. Assn. Tchrs. German, Am. Translators Assn., Am. Literary Translators Assn., Am. Assn. Tchrs. Slavic and East European Langs., Phi Sigma Iota. Republican. Roman Catholic. Home: PO Box 81 Hampden-Sydney VA 23943 Office: Hampden-Sydney Coll College Rd Hampden-Sydney VA 23943

JAHANNES, JA ARTHUR, college administrator; b. Fredericksburg, Va., Aug. 25, 1942; s. Ja Arthur Jahannes and Frances Williams; children—Gloria, Naftal, Tkeban; m. Clara Aguero, June 6, 1984. B.A. cum laude, Lincoln U., 1964; M.A., Hampton Inst., 1966; Ph.D., U. Del., 1972. Lic. counseling psychologist, Va. Assoc. dir. devel. Lincoln U., Pa., 1968-69; dir. edn. Community Action Greater Wilmington, Newark, Del.; vis. lectr. Haile Selassie U., Ethiopia, 1972; head profl. studies Nat. Tchrs. Coll. Uganda, E. Africa., 1972-73; dean, dept. head Hampton Inst., Va., 1973-81; dean Sch. Humanities Social Sci., Savannah State Coll., 1981—; pres. New Found. Inst. Savannah, 1985; mng. dir. Jahannes & Co., Richmond, Va., 1978. Author: Post Doctoral Studies in United States, 1978; The Poets Song, 1981. Author: (play) One More Sunday, 1984, Ain't I Somethin', 1982, and Yet We Sing, 1986, La Dolorosa, 1986. Editor Melanon Jour., 1985. Exec. v.p. Operation Push, Savannah, 1984. Served to capt. USAF, 1964-69. Recipient Outstanding Young Man Am. award, 1969, Langston Hughes Cultural Arts award Lincoln U., 1981, Outstanding Tchr. Hampton U., 1977; scholar Lincoln U., 1960-64, Samuel Robinson Lincoln U., 1963; Atlantic Ctr. for Arts fellow, 1982. Mem.

Alpha Phi Alpha. Home: 2304 Noble Oaks Dr Savannah GA 31406 Office: Dean Sch Humanities Social Scis PO Box 20059 Savannah GA 31404

JAHN, BILLIE JANE, nurse; b. Byers, Tex., Dec. 12, 1921; d. Thomas Oscar and Molly Verona (Kennemer) Downing; student Scott and White Sch. Nursing, 1941-42, U. Mich., 1973-75; B.S. in Nursing, Wayne State U., 1971; M.S., East Tex. State U., 1976, Ph.D., 1982; m. Edward L. Jahn, Dec. 6, 1942; children—Antoinette R., James T., Thomas L., Edward L., Janette E. Staff nurse Warren Meml. Hosp., Centerline, Mich., 1957-61; supr. nursing service Mich. Dept. Mental Health, Northville, 1962-71, Franklin County (Tex.) Hosp., 1972-74; instr. nursing Paris (Tex.) Jr. Coll., 1975-80; nurse educator VA, Waco, Tex., 1981-82; exec. v.p., dir., sr. nursing cons. Dos Cabezas, Inc., Mt. Vernon, Waco and Temple, Tex., 1981—; cons. East Tex. State U., Texarkana, 1978—; adj. fawlty U. Tex. Arlington Sch. Nursing, 1985—; mem. dept. phys. medicine and rehab. Scott and White Hosp.; mem. nat. rev. bd. Rehab. Nursing Inst., 1986—. Vol., ARC, 1971—; den mother Boy Scouts Am., 1960-62; sec. PTA, Warren, Mich., 1960-62; v.p., Temple, Tex., 1957-58. Mem. AAAS, Nat. League Nursing, Tex. League Nursing, Nat. Assn. Rehab. Nurses, AAUP, Nat. Assn. Female Execs., Am. Assn. Curriculum and Supervision, Phi Delta Kappa, Kappa Delta Pi. Home: Mount Vernon TX 75457 Office: 2024 S 15th St Temple TX 76501

JAHODA, DIANE, inventor, physician; b. Tampa, Fla., Aug. 3, 1948; d. Thomas Joseph and Annie Rose (Yakicic) J. R.N., Tampa U., 1976; M.D., Universidad Central del Este (Dominican Republic), 1980. Cert. basic cardiac life support, advanced cardicac life support, advanced trauma life support. R.N. supr. Meml. Hosp., Las Cruces, N.Mex., 1972-74; nurse emergency room and critical care, El Paso, Tex., 1974-75; nurse, Tampa, 1975-76; resident in surgery Eastern Tenn. State U., Johnson City, 1981-82; physician emergency medicine, Atlanta, 1982—. Recipient Physicians Recognition award, 1984. Served to 1st lt. USAR, 1981-84. Mem. Am. Med. Women's Assn., Am. Coll. Emergency Physicians, Internat. Acad. Metabology, Soc. Ultramolecular Physicians, Internat. Acad. Bariatric Medicine, AAAS, Japan Am. Soc. Central Fla., Nat. Emergency Medicine Polit. Action Com., N.Y. Acad. Scis., Smithsonian Assocs. Nat., Tampa U. Alumni Assn. Democrat. Roman Catholic. Home: PO Box 1884 Athens GA 30603 also 12304 Oakleaf Ave Tampa FL 33612

JAI, JONI, automatic tube cleaner manufacturing company executive; b. Des Moines, Feb. 15, 1936; d. Mahlon Alonzo and Mary Jane (Cooper) Baldwin; student Orange Coast Coll., U. Minn.; m. Ken Jai, Apr. 24, 1967; children—Robert, Cindy, Troy, Aubrey, Mitchell, Tonya. Owner tax cons. and bookkeeping service, Calif., 1969; owner Global Heat Exchanger Inc., Beaumont, Tex., 1970—, sec.-treas., chmn. bd., 1970—; developer Riverside Marina seminar leader boiler maintenance. Mem. Republican Nat. Com., Rep. Presdl. Task Force; founder Citizens Against Narcotics, Orange County, Tex., 1985. Mem. Tex. Assn. Bus., U.S. Automobile Club, Nat. Assn. Stock Car Autoracing. Roman Catholic. Patentee automatic tube cleaner, clean and brush cleaning tool; co-patentee hydrolancer. Address: PO Box 1127 Beaumont TX 77704

JAIN, KAMAL CHANDRA, oil company executive; b. Ajmer, India, Sept. 11, 1939; came to U.S., 1961, naturalized, 1966; s. Manak Chand and Birdhi Devi (Fagiwala) J.; m. Prem Kumari, July 23, 1961; children—Aarti, Ravin. B.S. in Physics and Math., Agra U., 1957; B.S. in Chem. Engring., U. Bombay, 1961; M.S. in Chem. Engring., Northwestern U., 1962, Ph.D. in Chem. Engring., 1965. Research assoc. Argonne Nat. Lab., Ill., 1963-65; research engr. W.Va. Pulp Paper Co., Covington, Va., 1965-66; research physicist Shell Devel. Co., Houston, 1966-69, head geophys. interpretation research, 1974-76; sr. geophysicist, project leader Shell Oil Co., Denver, 1969-73, staff geophysicist, group leader spl. projects, Houston, 1976-79; pres. Venex Corp., Houston, 1979—. Editor: Concepts and Techniques in Oil and Gas Exploration, 1982. Contbr. articles to profl. jours. Nat. Merit scholar U. Bombay, 1957-61; Walter P. Murphy fellow Northwestern U., 1961-63, J.N. Tata Endowment scholar, 1961-63. Mem. Am. Assn. Petroleum Geologists, Soc. Profl. Well Log Analysts, Soc. Exploration Geophysicists (chmn. research com. 1980-82). Club: Greenspoint (Houston). Office: Venex Corp 12510 Donna Dr Houston TX 77067

JAIN, MAHENDRA KUMAR, mathematics educator, researcher; b. Muzaffarnagar, India, Jan. 4, 1929; came to U.S., 1967, naturalized, 1979; s. L. Mohar Singh and L. Sajan Mukhi (Jain) J.; m. Chandra Devi, Feb. 15, 1949; children—Shushil, Anil, Parshav, Dave. B.Sc., Lucknow U. (India), 1948, M.Sc., 1951, Ph.D., 1955; postdoctoral U. Wis., Johns Hopkins U. Lectr. M.J. Inter Coll., Asara, India, 1951-52, Vidyant Coll., Lucknow, India, 1952-55, H.D. Jain Coll., Arrah, India, 1955-58; asst. prof. Bihar Inst. Tech., Sindri, India, 1959-67; from research instr. to asst. prof. W. Va. U., Morgantown, 1967-70; prof. U. Tenn.-Martin, 1970—. Contbr. articles to profl. jours. Recipient Distinction in Math. award U.P. Bd., India, 1946; U.S. AID Postdoctoral Research scholarship, 1963. Mem. Am. Math. Soc., Bharata Ganita Parishad, Ramanujan Parishad (pres. 1956-57). Club: Lions (sec.-treas. 1980). Avocations: study of homeopathic medicines; bridge. Home: 201 Meadowbrook Dr Martin TN 38237 Office: U Tenn Dept Math and Computer Sci Martin TN 38238

JAINI, ASHOK KUMAR ATMARAM, ednl. adminstr.; b. Saigon, Vietnam, Apr. 3, 1945; came to U.S., 1970, naturalized, 1976; s. Atma Ram and Shila K. Jaini; B.Sc. in Math., Physics, and Chemistry, U. Paris, 1968, M.Sc. in Math. and Physics, 1978, Ph.D. in Bus. Adminstrn., 1975; M.Ed., Our Lady of Lake U., San Antonio, 1974; m. Yolanda Marie Jimenez, Dec. 31, 1971; children—Vinod K., Anup K., Rajendra K., Lachmi K., Radhika K., Lachmank. Asst. prin. Edgewood Ind. Sch. Dist., San Antonio, 1974-75; adj. prof. ednl. adminstrn. Tex. A&I U., Kingsville, 1975-80, univ. coordinator, 1975-76; asst. supt. schs. Crystal City (Tex.) Ind. Sch. Dist., 1978-79; supt. schs. Asherton (Tex.) Ind. Sch. Dist., 1978—; cons. in field. Mem. Nat. Sch. Bd. Assn., NEA, Am. Assn. Sch. Adminstrs., Assn. Supervision and Curriculum Devel., Nat. Assn. Gifted and Talented, Tex. Tchrs. Assn. (Friend of Edn. award 1980), Tex. Assn. Compensatory Edn., Tex. Assn. Sch. Adminstrs., Tex. Assn. Personnel Adminstrs., Tex. Assn. Bilingual Educators. Republican. Hindu. Clubs: Lions, Rotary. Author articles in field. Home: 109 S Gardenview St Castle Hills TX 78213 Office: Box 398 Asherton TX 78827

JAKLITSCH, JOSEPH JOHN, JR., technical publications consultant; b. Bklyn., Mar. 28, 1919; s. Joseph John and Josefa (Stonitsch) J.; m. Eleanor Mulligan, May 29, 1948; children—Gary, Diane. B.S., Pratt Inst., 1940. With planning dept. Brewster Aero. Corp., N.Y.C., 1940-41; test engr. ordnance dept. U.S. Army, 1941-44, editor, 1944-45; tech. editor ASME, N.Y.C., 1945-50, assoc. editor, 1950-55, acting editor, 1956, editor Mech. Engring. also Trans. ASME, 1957-81; editorial adv. com. Engrs. Joint Council, 1960-64; cons. editor Crowell-Collier Ednl. Corp., 1960-64; spl. cons. Barnhart World Book Dictionary, 1964-68; cons. editor-at-large Marcel-Dekker, Inc., 1980—; cons editor Shesidan Printing Co., Inc., 1983—; 1980; contbg. editor Am. Year Book, 1946-50, Collier's Year Book, 1951-59; assoc. editor Applied Mechanics Revs., 1948-56; info. com. Engrs. Joint Council, 1964-68, Profl. Devel. Adv. Council, Pratt Inst. Sch. Engring., 1976-80. Fellow ASME (Outstanding Leadership in Engring. award 1968); mem. N.Y. Bus. Press Editors. Clubs: Tamarack Assn. (N.J.); Walkill Country (Franklin, N.J.); Miles Grant Country (Stuart, Fla.); Martin Downs Country (Palm City, Fla.). Home: 2560 SW Egret Pond Circle Palm City FL 33490

JALBERT, LAWRENCE EDWARD, sales executive; b. San Diego, Dec. 1, 1943; s. Llewellyn Edward and Alice (Wood) J.; children—Shannon Rea, Leigh Erica; m. Cheryl Anne Morrison, May 11, 1985. Student Old Dominion U., Norfolk, Va., 1964-65. Lic. profl. diver, Fla. With Crofton Divers, Norfolk, Va., 1963-68; sales mgr. Cardinal Signs, Norfolk, 1968-73; owner, mgr. Window Displays, Ltd., Virginia Beach, Va., 1968-74; sales mgr. Monroe Transfers & Storage Co., Norfolk, 1973-74; ter. sales mgr. Johnson Wax Co., Racine, Wis., 1974—; cons. in advt. and infection control; diving tchr., 1963—. Author, narrator film Hosp. Infection Control, 1979. Bd. dirs. Virginia Beach Civic League. Fellow Worldwide Innopro. Mem. Edgar Cayce Found., Virginia Beach Divers (pres. 1961-63), Smithfield Flyers. Republican. Avocations: photography, diving, flying, canoeing, hiking. Address: 408 W Farmington Rd Virginia Beach VA 23454

JALONICK, GEORGE WASHINGTON, IV, interior plant service company executive; b. Dallas, Apr. 30, 1940; s. George Washington III and Dorothy Elizabeth (Cockrell) J.; m. Mary Lytle McDonough, Oct. 14, 1966; 1 dau., Mary Clare. B.B.A., U. Tex.-Austin, 1963. Asst. to pres. S.W. Airmotive Co., Dallas, 1963-69; owner Motion Picture Editors, Inc., Dallas, 1969-74; dir. retail sales Lambert Landscape Co., Dallas, 1974-75; owner Adam Whitney Inc., Dallas, 1978—. Bd. dirs. Am. Heart Assn., 1973-76, Boys Clubs of Dallas, 1974—, Cystic Fibrosis Found., Dallas, 1975-81, Hope Cottage Children's Bur., Inc., Dallas, 1973-79, Dallas Summer Musicals, 1984—; mem. U. Tex. at Dallas Devel. Bd., 1980—; mem. chancellor's council U. Tex., 1983—. Episcopalian. Clubs: Brook Hollow Golf, Idlewild, Terpsichorean. Home: 5712 Redwood Ln Dallas TX 75209 Office: Adam Whitney Inc 2231 Valdina St Dallas TX 75207

JAMAR, LOUIS GLENN, aerospace engineering company executive, engineer; b. Chgo., Apr. 28, 1937; s. Louis Maximillian and Evalyn Marie (Perry) J.; m. Jacquelyn Evans, Oct. 5, 1963; children—Heather Jean, Holly Anne. B.S., Mich. Tech. U., 1959; M.S.I.E., Tex. Tech U., 1966; Ph.D., Ohio State U., 1974. Registered profl. engr., Ohio, Calif. Commd. 2d lt. U.S. Air Force, 1959, advanced through grades to lt. col.; civil engring. officer, Kans., Tex., Vietnam, 1960-68; instr., dept. chief Air Force Inst. Tech., 1968-72; student, civil engring. officer, 1972-77; research mgr., chief advanced tech. div. Air Force Tech. Applications Center, 1977-80, ret., 1980; mgr. indsl. engring. United Space Boosters Inc. subs. United Techs. Corp., Kennedy Space Center Fla., 1981-84, dep. mgr. program support, 1984-85, asst. to exec. v.p. and gen. mgr., 1985—. Decorated Bronze Star. Mem. Nat. Assn. Corrosion Engrs. (cert.), Am. Inst. Indsl. Engrs., Sigma Xi, Alpha Pi Mu. Roman Catholic. Home: 1428 Gleneagles Way Rockledge FL 32955 Office: United Space Boosters Inc PO Box 21212 Kennedy Space Center FL 32899

JAMBOR, PAUL EMIL, mathematics educator; b. Olomouc, Czechoslovakia, Mar. 29, 1937; came to U.S., 1968, naturalized, 1983; s. Emil and Ludmila (Horinkova) J.; m. Virginia Lee Hamby, Feb. 18, 1984. M.S., Poly. Inst., Prague, Czechoslovakia, 1963; M.A., Columbia U., 1969; Ph.D., Charles U., Prague, 1973. Assoc. prof. Charles U., 1973-76; editor Math. Revs., Ann Arbor, Mich., 1977-80; lectr. U. Mich., Ann Arbor, 1977-80; assoc. prof. math. U. N.C.-Wilmington, 1981—. Contbr. articles to math. publs. Mem. Am. Math. Soc. Office: U NC Math Dept Wilmington NC 28406

JAMES, ARTHUR DARRYL, oil company executive; b. Rahway, N.J., Aug. 8, 1943; s. Arthur Daniel and Anne Marie J.; m. Lynn Ann Gnagy, May 10, 1980; children—Rebecca, Timothy; 1 child from previous marriage, Tiffany. B.S., Rutgers U., 1965, M.S., 1967. Prodn. geologist Exxon Co. U.S.A., New Orleans, 1970-73, exploration geologist, Midland, Tex., 1973-75; exploration geologist ESSO Norway, Stavanger, 1975-76, Exxon Co. U.S.A., Midland, 1976; staff geologist Southland Royalty Co., Midland, 1976, dist. geologist, 1977-82, exploration mgr., 1982—. Served to capt. AUS, 1967-70; Vietnam. Mem. Am. Assn. Petroleum Geologists, West Tex. Geol. Soc., Soc. Econ. Paleontologists and Mineralogists. Lodge: Lions. Avocations: skiing; flying. Home: 1429 Lanham St Midland TX 79701 Office: Southland Royalty Co 21 Desta Dr Midland TX 79705

JAMES, ARTHUR H., JR., safety and personnel administrator; b. Independence, Kans., Aug. 10, 1943; s. Arthur H. and Ann Sadler (Hamilton) J.; m. Linda Kay Linnenbringer, Aug. 12, 1967; children—Aaron H., Evan W. B.S., Central Mo. State Coll., 1971. Loss prevention engr. Lynn Ins. Group, Kansas City, Mo., 1971-73; air intelligence officer Tenn. Air N.G., Knoxville, 1974; mgr. nuclear and indsl. safety U.S. Nuclear, Inc., Oak Ridge, 1975-77; info. ctr. analyst Info. Ctr. for Energy Safety, Oak Ridge Nat. Lab., 1977-78; safety and personnel adminstr. Am. Limestone Co., Knoxville, 1978—. Instr. first aid and CPR, ARC, Knoxville, 1979—; referee, coach Am. Youth Soccer Orgn., Knoxville, 1980-85; vol. coach Bearden Middle Sch. and High Sch. soccer teams, Knoxville, 1984; asst. scoutmaster troop 20, Gt. Smoky Mountain council Boy Scouts Am., Knoxville, 1984—. Served with USAF, 1965-69, S.E. Asia; serving as maj. Air N.G., 1972—. Mem. Am. Soc. Safety Engrs. (chpt. sec. 1979-80), Tenn. Valley Personnel Assn., N.G. Assn. U.S., N.G. Assn. Tenn., Air Force Assn. Mem. United Ch. of Christ. Club: U.S. Parachute Assn. Home: 908 Red Saile Dr Knoxville TN 37909 Office: Am Limestone Co 2209 Blount Ave Knoxville TN 37920

JAMES, BRUCE HAMILTON, writer; b. Whiteman AFB, Mo., Oct. 24, 1957; s. Arthur Hauser and Ann (Hamilton) J.; m. Nancy Pamela Baum, Aug. 22, 1982; 1 child, Chaya Rachel. B.A. in Polit. Sci., George Washington U., 1979. Reporter, copyboy Colorado Springs Sun, Colo., 1974-78; writer Bennett Agy., Alexandria, Va., 1979-80, Close Up Found., Arlington, Va., 1981—; freelance writer, Arlington, 1981—. Author: Special Focus: Energy, 1982; Current Issues, 1985 (award of distinction Soc. Tech. Communication 1985). Contbr. articles to profl. jours. Crisis counselor Terros Hotline, Colorado Springs, 1977-79. Democrat. Jewish.

JAMES, DAVID WOODY, environmental consultant, educator; b. San Antonio, Jan. 5, 1954; s. Clarence E. and Anna L. (Moore) J.; m. Sherry Ann Pierce, Aug. 19, 1979 (div. June 1981); m. 2d, Ann Elizabeth Behl, May 21, 1982. Student San Antonio Coll., 1972-73; B.S. C.E., Tex. A&M U., 1978, M.S., 1984. Lab. technician City of San Antonio, 1969-71; operation/maintenance specialist Region VI, EPA, Dallas, 1974-75; lab. technician Tex. A&M U., College Station, 1976, plant technician, 1976-77, research asst., 1977-79; cons. Interspill, Inc., College Station, 1979, Civil Engring. Systems, Inc., College Station, 1979; project engr. Hays & Lindsey, Inc., Austin, 1980-82; trainer Environ. Tng. & Devel. Service, Austin, 1980—; pres., co-owner Envir-O-Spec, Inc., Austin, 1981—; instr. cert. tng. courses. Mem. adv. council legis. affairs Tex. State Senate, 1975. V.M. Ehlers Meml. Fund grantee, 1974-75. Mem. Water Pollution Control Fedn., Am. Water Works Assn., Tex. Water Utilities Assn., Capital Area Water and Wastewater Assn., Nat. Environ. Tng. Assn., ASCE, Nat. Soc. Profl. Engrs., Phi Theta Kappa. Author: From My Generation To Yours - With Love, 1971; contbr. articles to profl. jours. Office: Envir-O-Spec Inc PO Box 9942 Austin TX 78766

JAMES, DOLORES, investment and real estate executive; b. Miami, Fla., Nov. 14, 1946; d. Joseph George and Eunice Ann (Kehoe) Portell; m. Russell Wayland James (dec.); 1 dau., Kristy Ann. B.S., Ga. So. U., 1967; M.B.A., Barry Coll., 1968. Dir. comml. and resdl. leasing Keyes Co., Miami, Fla., 1974-78; property mgr., realtor/owner Dolores James Investments Inc., Coconut Grove, Fla., 1978—; realtor/owner Dolores James Cons., Inc., Coconut Grove, 1982—. Contbr. articles to profl. jours. Mem. MACH I, Coral Gables, 1979—, Met. Mus. Ctr. for Fine Arts, 1979—, Tiger Bay Polit. Club, Miami, 1980—; mem. steering com. Coconut Grove Polit. Action Com., 1983—; founder, mem. Manatee Bay Club, 1984. Mem. Soc. Profl. Women, Coral Gables Bd. Realtors, Miami Bd. Realtors, Coconut Grove C. of C. Republican. Roman Catholic. Clubs: Coral Gables Country, Grove Isle, 200. Office: Dolores James Investments Inc 2666 Tiger Tail Ave #115 Coconut Grove FL 33133

JAMES, EARL EUGENE, JR., aerospace engineering executive; b. Oklahoma City, Feb. 8, 1923; s. Earl Eugene and Mary Frances (Godwin) J.; m. Barbara Jane Marshall, Dec. 15, 1945 (dec. Feb. 2, 1982); children—Earl Eugene III, Jeffrey Allan; m. 2d, Vanita L. Nix, Apr. 23, 1983. Student Oklahoma City U., 1940-41; B.S., U. Okla., 1945; postgrad. Tex. Christian U., 1954-57; M.S., So. Meth. U., 1961. Asst. mgr. Rialto Theatre, 1939-42; with Consol. Vultee Aircraft Co., San Diego, 1946-49; with Convair, Ft. Worth, 1949—, group engr., 1955-57, test group engr., supr. fluid dynamics lab., 1957-81, engring. chief Fluid Dynamics Lab., 1981—. Asst. dist. commr. Boy Scouts Am., 1958-59; adviser Jr. Achievement, 1962-63; mem. sch. bd. Castleberry Ind. Sch. Dist. (Tex.), 1969-83; chmn. bd. N.W. br. YMCA, 1971. Served to lt. USNR, 1942-46; PTO. Fellow AIAA (assoc.); mem. Air Force Assn. (life), Gen. Dynamics Mgmt. Assn., Nat. Mgmt. Assn., Okla. U. Alumni Assn. (life), Tex. Congress Parents and Tchrs. (hon. life), Pi Kappa Alpha, Alpha Chi Sigma, Tau Omega. Methodist. Democrat. Clubs: Squaw Creek Golf, Camera. Lodge: Elks. Contbr. articles to profl. jours. Office: Fluid Dynamics Lab Mail Zone 5850 Box 748 Fort Worth TX 76101

JAMES, EDWARD MONROE, financial company executive; b. Cambridge, Md., Nov. 9, 1953; s. Edward Exodus and Eunice Vandella (Lake) J.; m. Constance Brooks, Dec. 31, 1977; 1 child, Edward Monroe. B.A., U. Md., 1975; M.S., N.C. A&T State U., 1977; J.D., Howard U., 1981. Record examiner intern Bd. for Correction of Naval Records, Washington, 1980; legis. intern Com. Finance and Revenue, Washington, 1980-81; adminstrv. aide Scotten Ins. Agy., Forestville, Md., 1981-83; reporter Equifax Services, Ind., Charlotte, N.C., 1984; market retirement rep. Future Security Services, Inc., Charlotte, 1985—. Vol. Hunt for Senate com., 1984. Mem. Nat. Assn. Counseling Devel., Internat. Platform Assn., Nat. Panel Consumer Arbitrators, Public Offenders Counselors Assn., Delta Theta Phi. Methodist. Club: Tuesday Morning Breakfast. Avocations: reading, kite flying. Home: 1315 Orvis St Charlotte NC 28216 Office: Future Security Services Inc Life Mid Am 560 Executive Center Dr 123 Charlotte NC 28212

JAMES, FELIX, history educator; b. Hurtsboro, Ala., Nov. 17, 1937; s. Leroy and Blanche (Clarke) J.; m. Florence Bernard Jacobs, Aug. 10, 1985; 1 child, Crystal Sharae. B.S., Fort Valley State Coll., 1962; M.A., Howard U., 1967; Ph.D., Ohio State U., 1972. Ordained to ministry N.T. Bapt. Ch., 1984. Tchr. social studies Columbia Pub. Schs. (S.C.), 1962-64; reserve book librarian Howard U., Washington, 1965-67; instr. history Tuskegee Inst. (Ala.), 1967-70; asst. prof. So. Ill. U., Carbondale, 1972-75; assoc. prof. So. U. in New Orleans, 1975-79, prof., 1979—. Mem. Taxicab Drivers Info. and Hospitality Com., 1983—; bd. dirs. So. Christian Leadership Conf. of La., 1983—. Mem. Internat. Platform Assn., Assn. Study Afro-Am. Life and History, Assn. Social and Behavioral Scientists, Orgn. Am. Historians. Democrat. Baptist. Lodge: Masons. Contbr. articles to profl. jours.

JAMES, FLOYD BENJAMINE, construction executive; b. Gibsland, La., Jan. 24, 1907; s. Thomas L. and Maggie (Hodges) J.; B.A., U. Tenn., 1927; m. Kathryn Ayres, June 12, 1928; children—Renna James Burkhalter, Floyd Benjamine, John, Tom. Sec., treas. Ruston (La.) Drilling Co., 1927-33; sec.-treas. T.L. James & Co., Ruston, 1933-44, pres., 1944-68, chmn. bd., 1968-84. Trustee La. Meth. Children's Home. Recipient Silver Beaver, Boy Scouts Am. 1955, Silver Antelope, 1961. Mem. Phi Kappa Phi, Sigma Chi. Methodist. Lodge: Kiwanis. Home: 1500 N Trenton St Ruston LA 71270 Office: PO Box O Ruston LA 71270

JAMES, GARY L., investment advisory firm executive, tax advisor; b. Bradford, Pa., Aug. 15, 1953; s. Donald G. and L. Dorothy (Head) J.; m. Lori Fuentes, Dec. 29, 1981; 1 dau., Kristie E. Ed. Coll. for Fin. Planning, 1981. Computer cons. with various cos., Dallas and Ft. Worth, 1973-79; exec. v.p., co-founder Fin. Devel. Group, Dallas, 1979-81; pres., owner Gary L. James R.I.A., Dallas, 1981—. Mem. Internat. Assn. Fin. Planners, Fin. Mgmt. Assn., Nat. Assn. Securities Dealers. Presbyterian. Club: Willow Bend Polo and Hunt (Plano, Tex.). Home: PO Box 191049 Dallas TX 75219 Office: Gary L James RIA PO Box 191049 Dallas TX 75219

JAMES, GENE A., farmers cooperative executive; b. 1932. B.S., Va. Poly. Inst., 1953. With So. States Coop. Inc., Richmond, Va., 1953—, trainee, then asst. mgr. Cumberland Coop., acting mgr., asst. mgr. farm supply warehouse, Roanoke, 1956-60, mgr. seed and farm supply warehouse, Clarksburg, 1960-66, product and promotional mgr. catalog service, 1966-69, regional mgr., Winchester, 1969-72, dir. planning, 1972-75, sr. v.p. ops., 1975-80, exec. v.p., gen. mgr., 1980-84, pres., chief exec. officer, 1984—; dir. CF Industries Inc., United Va. Bank, Nat. Council Farmer Coops, Texas City Refining Inc., Grad. Inst. Coop. Leadership. Office: Southern States Coop Inc PO Box 26234 Richmond VA 23206

JAMES, GUS JOHN, II, lawyer; b. Koma Yiolou, Cyprus, Dec. 29, 1938; s. John and Salome J.; m. Helen Alexion, July 25, 1964; children—Mary Margaret, Nicole. B.S. in bus., U. Richmond, 1962; J.D., Coll. William and Mary, 1966, LL.M. in taxation, 1967. Bar: Va. 1966. Assoc., Kaufman and Oberndorfer, Norfolk, Va., 1966-72, ptnr., 1972-76, mng. ptnr., 1976-81; mem. Kaufman & Canoles, Norfolk, 1982—, chmn. exec. com., 1982-84; lectr. in field Bd. dirs. Annunciation Greek Orthodox Ch., Norfolk, 1972-80, 81-85, pres. parish council, 1973-74, 84, chmn. Neptune Festival com., 1977-84, chmn. Azalea Festival com., 1976-84; bd. dirs. Med. Ctr. Hosps., Norfolk Symphony, Va. Orch. Group, Old Dominion U. Intercollegiate Found., Old Dominion U. Ednl. Found.; chmn. Old Dominion U. Soccer Com. Served with USAR, 1963-68. Mem. ABA, Va. Bar Assn., Norfolk-Portsmouth Bar Assn., Va. Assn. Hosp. Attys. Club: Order Ahepa. Editor in chief: William and Mary Law Rev., 1965-66. Home: 4137 Country Club Circle Virginia Beach VA 23455 Office: 2030 Sovran Center Norfolk VA 23510

JAMES, HARRY BLACKSHEAR, III, lawyer, educator; b. Savannah, Ga., June 11, 1951; s. Harry Blackshear and Alethia Eloria (Thornton) J.; m. Linda Strong, Oct. 9, 1975; children—Harry, Brandi. B.S., Savannah State Coll., 1972; J.D., George Washington U., 1975. Bar: Ga. 1979, U.S. Dist. Ct. (so. dist.) Ga. 1983, U.S. Ct. Mil. Appeals 1983, U.S. Ct. Appeals (11th cir.) 1983. Atty.-advisor U.S. Army, Redstone Arsenal, Ala., 1979-83; sole practice, Augusta, Ga., 1982—; adj. prof. Ala. A&M U., Huntsville, 1980-82; law clk. Dept. HEW, Washington, 1973. Contbr. articles to profl. jours. Pres. NAACP, Augusta-Richmond, 1985; alt. Democratic Nat. Conv., Miami, Fla., 1972; soccer coach YMCA, Augusta, 1984. Mem. Ga. Assn. Criminal Def. Lawyers, Augusta Bar Assn., Ga. Bar Assn., Ga. Trial Lawyers Assn. Baptist. Club: Young Dems. (pres. 1984). Office: Harry B James III 1101 Eleventh St Augusta, GA 30901

JAMES, LYNDEN NATHANIEL, county planner; b. Kingston, Jamaica, W.I., Mar. 28, 1940; came to U.S., 1967, naturalized, 1980; s. Nathan Arthur and Esmie Maud (Satchell) J.; A.A. in Acctg., Miami-Dade Community Coll., 1973; B.A. in Bus. Adminstrn., Fla. Internat. U., 1975; M.S.P.A., Pepperdine U., 1977; postgrad. in pub. adminstrn. Nova U., 1977-80; m. Otis Dorothia Downer, Nov. 7, 1962; children—John Mark, Janice Meloney. Fiscal officer Econ. Opportunity Program, Inc., Miami, Fla., 1967-73 asst. dir. concentrated employment program, 1973-80; asst. dir. fiscal affairs Office CETA Coordination, Metro Dade County (Fla.), dir. CETA-Pub. Service Employment Tng. Program, 1981-82, prin. planner Metro Dade County Community and Econ. Devel., 1979—; lectr. econs. Fla. Meml. Coll.; lectr. acctg. Miami Dade Community Coll. First v.p. Miami Gardens PTA, Miami, Fla.; capt. Combined Fla. Cricket Team. Recipient Key to City Miami, 1979, recognition West Indian Orgns. in Miami, 1979, spl. citation Mayor Metro Dade County, 1980, Internat. award of Excellence, Air Jamaica, 1980. Mem. Am. Soc. Pub. Adminstrn., Am. Mgmt. Assn., Metro Dade County Mgmt. and Profl. Assn., South Fla. Cricket Assn. (pres.). Clubs: W.I. Miami Sports, West Indian Am. Social (pres.), Optimists (sec. club). Author Dade County CETA man., 1974. Home: 18721 NW 42d Ct Miami FL 33055 Office: 90 SW 8th St Miami FL 33130

JAMES, MARGARET BRENDA, educator, counselor, intelligence and research analyst; b. Charlotte, N.C., July 26, 1948; d. Harry Carson and Evelyn Lodema (Deaton) James; m. Charles Mark Railey, Dec. 30, 1982. B.S. in Elem. Edn., Fla. State U., 1970; student Appalachian State U., 1975, U. Minn., 1977; M.S. in Human Services, Murray State U., 1985. Cert. tchr., N.C., Va. Tchr., sci. chmn. University Park Elem., Charlotte, 1970-76; teaching asst. U. Minn., Mpls., 1976-77; sci. resource tchr. Charlotte/Mecklenburg Sch. System, 1975-76, mem. environ. edn. com., 1975-76; tchr., substitute tchr. Roanoke Schs., Va., 1980; crypto-analyst U.S. Army, Ft. Campbell, Ky., 1983-85. Participating author: Shoe Box Science, 1974, environ. edn. resource book, 1975. Counselor Urban Ministries, Clarksville, Tenn., 1985; leader Hornet Nest council Girl Scouts Am., Charlotte, 1970-74, Monterey Bay council Boy Scouts Am., 1981-82. Recipient Army Achievement medal, 1984, Army Commendation medal, 1985. Served to sgt. U.S. Army, 1981-85; mem. USAR, 1985—. Mem. Non-Commd. Officers Assn., Am. Assn. for Counseling and Devel., Pi Lamda Theta, Phi Kappa Phi, Kappa Delta Pi. Lutheran. Avocations: guitar; trumpet; music composition; gardening; hiking.

JAMES, MILDRED HANNAH, hypnotist; b. Hopewell, Va., Oct. 18, 1918; d. Charles and Fannie (Enoch) Feldman; student Sch. Tech. Hypnosis, Ethical Hypnosis Tng. Center, Am. Inst. Hypnosis, Am. Guild Hypnotherapists; m. Albert W. James, Dec. 31, 1965; children by previous marriage—Shiela, Leslie, Andrea, David, Valerie, Kelly. Apprentice in hypnosis, 1959-60; practicing hypnotist, 1961—; pres., chmn. bd. Mildred H. James, Inc., Kent, Wash., 1976—; lectr., condr. seminars. Mem. Am. Inst. Hypnosis, Am. Guild Hypnotherapists, Hypnotists Union. Author weight reduction methods and smoking control methods; producer cassette tapes. Address: PO Box 1688 Eaton Park FL 33840

JAMES, PHYLLIS CAROL, hospital service administrator; b. Birmingham, Ala., Aug. 16, 1957; d. Harold Goode and Marie Therese (Flynt) Claiborne; m. David Scott James, Oct. 21, 1978; 1 child, Ruben Lee. Registered central service technician. Central service technician John F. Kennedy Hosp., Atlantis, Fla., 1975-79, asst. dir. central service, 1979-84, dir. central service, 1984—. Mem. Am. Soc. Hosp. Central Service Technicians (program planning com. 1982-83). Democrat. Roman Catholic. Avocation: collecting antiques. Office: John F Kennedy Hosp Inc PO Box 1489 Lake Worth FL 33460

JAMES, RICHARD E., appliance company executive; b. Glendale, Calif., Aug. 14, 1944; s. Uel A. and Mary (McLeod) J.; m. Jeanette Gay Wilson, Dec. 18, 1965; children—Scott, Melody, Ryan. B.S., Okla. Bapt. U., 1966; M.S., Purdue U., 1968, Ph.D., 1970. Various positions Gen. Motors, Detroit, 1970-76; with Gen. Electric Major Appliances, Louisville, 1977-84, region sales mgr., Dallas, 1984—; bus. instr. Wayne State U., Detroit, 1971-74. Contbr. articles to profl. jours. Chmn. budget planning St. Matthews Bapt. Ch., Louisville, 1981-82, vice chmn. deacons, 1983-84, bldg. com., 1982-84. NASA fellow, 1966-69; Okla. Bapt. U. scholar, 1962-66. Mem. Am. Statis. Assn. (chmn. mktg. subsect. 1981). Republican. Avocations: golf; tennis; racquetball; skiing. Home: 5614 Twin Brooks Dr Dallas TX 75252 Office: Gen Electric 8401 Carpenter Freeway Box 47471 Dallas TX 75247

JAMES, RONALD LANGFORD, dentist; b. Fort Lauderdale, Fla., Jan. 2, 1949; s. George Earl and Ruth Vera (Packer) J.; m. Yvonne Marie Whitson, Dec. 19, 1969. B.S. in Aerospace Engring., U. Fla., 1971, D.M.D., 1979. Commd. 2d lt. U.S. Air Force, 1971, advanced through grades to maj., 1981; missile maintenance officer, Cheyenne, Wyo., 1971-74, Great Falls, Mont., 1974-75; resident in gen. practice Eglin AFB, Fort Walton Beach, Fla., 1979-80; gen. dental officer Seymour Johnson AFB, Goldsboro, N.C., 1980-84; resigned, 1984; gen. dentist Alvin J. Fillastre, D.D.S., Pa., Lakeland, Fla., 1984-85; CPR instr. Am. Heart Assn., Goldsboro, 1981-84, Lakeland, 1984—. Active Soc. for Preservation and Encouragement of Barbershop Quartet Singing In Am., Inc., 1974—. Mem. Acad. Gen. Dentistry, ADA, Prosthodontic Study Group, Antique Automobile Club Am., Model A Restorer's Club. Republican. Methodist. Avocation: restoration of antique autos. Home: 5012 Grand Blvd Lakeland FL 33803 Office: 4406 S Florida Ave Suite 29 Lakeland FL 33803

JAMES, RONALD RUDELL, airline pilot; b. Amarillo, Tex., June 1956; s. Alfred Rudell and Bettye Faye (Cantrell) J. B.S. in Polit. Sci., (Army ROTC scholar; Superior Cadet 1975, 77, 78 Disting. Mil. Student 1978, Disting. Mil. Grad. 1978), W. Tex. State U., 1978. Commd. 2d lt. U.S. Army, 1978, advanced through grades to capt., 1981; various assignments, including 1st Bn. 20th Field Arty., Ft. Carson, Colo., 1978-83, resigned, 1983, now mem. Res.; mgr., pilot Amarillo Flying Service, 1983-86; pilot Mesa Airlines, 1986—. Mem. Res. Officers Assn., Aircraft Owners and Pilots Assn. Mem. Christian Ch. Home: 3411 Rusk Amarillo TX 79109 Office: Mesa Airlines Farmington NM 87401

JAMES, STEPHEN ELISHA, library science educator; b. Montgomery, Ala., May 19, 1942; s. Elisha and Hazel Agatha (Todd) J.; m. Janie, Apr. 5, 1964; children—Lydia Yvonne, Stephen Christopher. B.A., Case Western Res. U., 1970, M.S. in Library Sci., 1971; Ph.D., U. Wis., 1983. Librarian, Cleve. Pub. Library, 1969-73; assoc. prof. Atlanta U., 1976—. Editor: Measuring Quality Library Service (M.G. Fancher-Beeler), 1974. Contbr. articles to profl. jours. Mem. adv. bd. Library Quar., 1985-88; bd. dirs. Library Waves. Served with USN, 1962-66. Recipient commendation State of Ohio, 1972, City of East Point (Ga.), 1983. Mem. ALA, Ga. Library Assn., Southeastern Library Assn., Beta Phi Mu. Episcopalian. Club: Mensa. Home: 2890 Pine Valley Circle East Point GA 30344 Office: 223 James P Brawley Dr Atlanta GA 30314

JAMES, THOMAS, III, internist, pediatrician; b. Louisville, July 5, 1946; s. Thomas and Alice Wornell (Howry) J. B.A., Duke U., 1968; M.D., U. Ky., 1972. Diplomate Am. Bd. Internal Medicine, Am. Bd. Pediatrics. Med. resident Temple U. Hosp., 1972-74, U. Pa. Hosp., 1974-75; pediatric resident Children's Hosp. Phila., 1976-78; practice medicine specializing in internal medicine and pediatrics Health Care of Louisville, 1978-84, med. dir., 1979-84; med. dir. Health Am. of Va., Virginia Beach, 1984—; faculty U. Louisville Sch. Medicine, 1979—. Served with USPHS, 1974-76. Fellow ACP, Am. Acad. Pediatrics. Democrat. Episcopalian. Contbr. articles to profl. jours. Home: 401 College Pl Unit 21 Norfolk VA 23510 Office: 839 Poplar Hall Dr Norfolk VA 23502

JAMES, VAUGHAN STUART, leasing company executive; b. Barnsley, Eng., Dec. 30, 1951; s. Howard and Joan (Welsh) J.; m. Sandra Espat, Dec. 14, 1974; came to U.S. 1975. Grad. Britannia Royal Naval Acad., 1971. Commd. officer Royal Navy, 1970-75; dir. equipment Nopal Lines, Miami, Fla., 1975-80; v.p. Dana Equipment, Miami, 1980-82, Container Cons., Miami, 1982—; dir. Safe-Gard Corp., Dover, Del.; ptnr. Vangard, Miami. Bd. dirs. Emmanuel Fellowship, Miami, 1982-83. Home: 810 NE 159th St North Miami Beach FL 33162 Office: Container Consultants Inc 1015 North America Way Miami FL 33132

JAMES, WELDON BERNARD, writer, lecturer; b. St. Charles, S.C., Oct. 14, 1912; s. Lucian Adwell and Ada (Weldon) J.; m. Margaret, Lady North, Nov. 29, 1943; children—Sarah James DeBesche, Philip W., Charles R.G. B.A. cum laude, Furman U., 1933. Tchr., Parker High Sch., Greenville, S.C., 1933-34; writer travel series for several so. newspapers, 1934; reporter, columnist, editorial writer Greenville Piedmont, 1934-37; war corr. United Press, also PM newspaper, N.Y.C., 1937-41; Far East editor Collier's mag., 1946-48; assoc. editor, columnist Courier-Jour., Louisville, 1948-66; asst. adminstr. Nat. Credit Union Adminstrn., 1970-72; writer, lectr., 1972—. Press sec. to chmn. Democratic Nat. Com., 1952. Served to col. USMC, 1942-46, 50-52, 66-70; ETO, PTO, Vietnam. Pulitzer prize nominee, 1938; Nieman fellow, 1939-40; Carnegie fellow, 1960-61; recipient Disting. Alumnus award Furman U., 1975. Club: Nat. Press (Washington). Author: (with Omer Carmichael) The Louisville Story, 1957; (with others) Southern Schools: Problems and Progress, 1959; contbr. to pubs. including: Reader's Digest, Pageant, N.Y. Times Mag., Colliers. Home: 700 South View Terr Alexandria VA 22314

JAMES, WILLIAM CHANDLER, periodontist; b. High Point, N.C., Mar. 26, 1948; s. Chandler Carthell and Willie (Crump) J.; m. Linda Jean Webb, July 20, 1974; children—Lauren Nicole, Lindsey Elizabeth. B.S., U. N.C., 1971, D.D.S., 1974; M.S., 1976. Temporary staff dentist Pub. Health Service, Morgantown, W.Va., 1973 (summer); staff dentist Orange Chatham Comprehensive Health Service, Chapel Hill, N.C., 1974; practice dentistry specializing in periodontology, Charlotte, N.C., 1976—; ins. cons. Blue Cross Blue Shield, Durham, 1983—. Contbr. articles to periodontology jours. Pres., Charlotte Choral Soc., 1981-82, 85, chmn. bd. dirs., 1982-83, prodn. coordinator 25th, 26th, 30th, and 31st Singing Christmas Tree, 1979, 1980, 84, 85. Recipient Billy Pennel award So. Acad. Periodontology, 1976. Mem. Am. Acad. Periodontology (mem. council on dental care programs, 3d dist. advisor, dental health plans com. 1978—), So. Acad. Periodontology (chmn. dental health plans com. 1978—), N.C. Soc. Periodontists, N.C. Dental Soc. Democrat. Methodist. Clubs: Country Haven Tennis & Swim (Weddington, N.C.). Avocations: softball; singing; tennis; basketball; white-water rafting; snow skiing. Home: 3711 Spokeshave Ln Matthews NC 28105

JAMESON, PRESCILLA KAREN HOLMES, educator; b. Chgo., Sept. 4, 1925; d. Presley Dixon and Mildred Priscilla (Rufsvold) Holmes; A.B. in Speech, U. Mich., 1947, M.A. in Speech, 1953; postgrad. U. Va., James Madison U., George Washington U., George Mason U.; m. Dorence C. Jameson, Aug. 16, 1948; children—Scott Kelly, Terence Alan, Patrick Brian. Dir. drama, Mt. Morris, Mich., 1947; tchr. lang. arts, Albuquerque, 1950; pvt. practice speech pathology, 1959-63; tchr. pub. schs., Marietta, Ohio, 1966-67; speech pathologist, dept. human resources Child Growth and Devel. Center, Arlington, Va., 1967-68; dir. speech activities Washington Irving Intermediate Sch., Springfield, Va., 1969—, dir. gifted talented program, 1976-79; instr. Fairfax County Staff Devel. Mem. Polit. Action Com. for Edn., 1976-79; tchr. Sunday sch. class for exceptional children Grace Presbyterian Ch., 1970. Mem. United Teaching Professions, NEA, Va. Edn. Assn., Fairfax Edn. Assn. (sec., dir. 1977-78), Am. Speech and Hearing Assn., Council for Exceptional Children, AAUW (v.p. Springfield-Annandale br. 1961-63), Zeta Phi Eta, Alpha Delta Kappa. Republican. Home: 6024 Selwood Pl Springfield VA 22152 Office: 8100 Keene Mill Rd Springfield VA 22152

JAMGOTCH, NISH, JR., political science educator; b. Mpls., July 25, 1932. B.A. cum laude U. Minn., 1954; M.A. in Soviet Area Studies, 1956; Ph.D. in Polit. Sci., Claremont Grad. Sch., 1964. Asst. prof. polit. sci. U. N.C., Charlotte, 1966-69, assoc. prof., 1969-75, prof., 1975—. Ford Found. grantee, 1959; NDEA fellow, 1962-63, 63-64; research fellow Inst. Study of USSR, Munich, 1962; Hoover scholar Stanford U., 1966; assoc. Russian Research Ctr., Harvard U., 1967, 70; recipient Univ. award for excellence in teaching U. N.C., 1971. Mem. Am. Polit. Sci. Assn., Internat. Studies Assn. (sect. on U.S.-Soviet Relations), Am. Com. East-West Accord. Author: Soviet-East European Dialogue, 1968; author, editor: Thinking the Thinkable: Investment in Human Survival, 1978; Soviet Security in Flux, 1983; Sectors of Mutual Benefit in U.S.-Soviet Relations, 1985; author articles on Soviet affairs and U.S.-Soviet relations. Office: Dept Polit Sci U NC Charlotte NC 28223

JAMIL, MAZHAR, mathematics educator, researcher, consultant; b. Kamptee, Central, India, July 1, 1947; came to U.S., 1981; s. Anis and Rukayya (Khatoon) Khurshid; m. Meher Afroz Siddiqui, June 20, 1976; children—Rukhama, Madiha. B.S., U. Karachi, Pakistan, 1968, M.S., 1969; Diplom-Mathematiker, M.S., U. Aachen, Fed. Republic Germany, 1976; postgrad. U. Tex.-Arlington, 1982. Chmn. math. dept. Liaquat Coll., Karachi, Pakistan, 1969-71; lectr. dept. math. Karachi U., 1976-77, asst. prof. Inst. of Bus. Adminstrn., 1977-82; math. instr. Mountain View Coll., Dallas, 1982-84; instr. math. La. Sch. for Math., Sci. and the Arts, Natchitoches, 1984—; ednl. cons. Khurshid Acad., 1976-77. Author: Teach Yourself Algebra, 1971; Trignometry and Coordinate Geometry, 1972. Dir. Ahmed Ali Coaching Ctr., Saudabad, Pakistan, 1965-68, active C.P. and Berar Soc., Saudabad, 1965-69; treas. Turkish Lang. Soc., Karachi U., 1966-67. German Exchange Service scholar, 1972-76; U. Islamabad fellow, 1971-72. Mem. Math. Assn. Am., Am. Statis. Assn., La. Assn. Tchrs. of Math., Am. Math. Soc., Karachi Math. Assn., Acad. La. Sch. Math. Sci. and Arts (sponsor 1984—), Math. Soc. Muslim. Avocations: reading; writing; traveling. Home: 100 N Melrose Ave Apt 614 Natchitoches LA 71457 Office: Louisiana Sch for Math Sci and the Arts 715 College Ave Natchitoches LA 71457

JAMISON, ANNIE ADAMS, librarian; b. Gadsden, S.C., Nov. 23, 1934; d. Frank and Dorcas (Sims) Adams; m. Marion William Jamison Jr., Dec. 26, 1963; children—Marion William III, Markitta Anne, Mark Adams, Marlisa LeeNeel Dorcas. B.S., S.C. State Coll., 1956, M.S., 1963. Librarian, Orangeburg Sch. Dist. V., (S.C.), 1956-63, 66-73, media specialist, 1977—; librarian Dillard U., New Orleans, 1964-66. Mem. adv. com. Brookdale Mid. Sch., 1983—. Contbr. articles to profl. jours. Mem. ALA, S.C. Edn. Assn., S.C. Assn. Sch. Librarians, Orangeburg Dist. Five Edn. Assn., Jack and Jill of Am., Phi Delta Kappa, Delta Sigma Theta. Home: 1275 Goff St NE Orangeburg SC 29115

JAMISON, JOHN AMBLER, circuit judge; b. nr. Florence, S.C., May 14, 1916; s. John Wilson and Elizabeth Ambler (Fleming) J.; LL.B. cum laude, Cumberland U., Tenn., 1941; postgrad. George Washington U., 1944-45; grad. Indsl. Coll. Armed Forces, 1962; J.D., Samford U., 1969, LL.D. (hon.), 1983; m. Mildred Holley, Sept. 22, 1945. Admitted to S.C. bar, 1941, Va. bar, 1942, U.S. Supreme Ct. bar, 1945; atty. Va. Div. Motor Vehicles, Richmond, 1947-54; practiced law, Fredericksburg, Va., 1954-72; spl. acting judge County Cts. Stafford and King George Counties (Va.), Mcpl. Ct., Fredericksburg, 1956-72; judge 15th Va. Jud. Circuit, 1972—, chief judge, 1976—; dir., counsel Nat. Bank Fredericksburg, 1968-73. Mem. adv. bd. Gov.'s Hwy. Safety Commn., 1956-62; pres. Fredericksburg Rescue Squad, 1960-62, now hon. life mem.; hon. chmn. Fredericksburg Area Bicentennial Commn., 1975-77; chmn. bd. Fredericksburg Area Mental Hygiene Clinic, 1962-63; bd. dirs. Rappahannock Area Devel. Commn., 1960-66; mem. adv. bd. Cumberland Sch. Law; bd. visitors Coker Coll. Served from ensign to comdr. USN, 1941-46, Res., to 1976; comdg. officer Richmond Naval Res. Div., 1948-56; naval aide to govs. of Va., 1954-72. Recipient award S.C. Confederate War Centennial Commn., 1965; decorated UDC Cross Mil. Service. Mem. Am., S.C., Va., 15th Va. Jud. Circuit (pres. 1959-60, 69-70) bar assns., Cumberland Law Sch. Alumni Assn. (nat. pres. 1978-79), Jud. Conf. Va., Am. Judicature Soc., Am. Law Inst., Cumberland Order Jurisprudence, Res. Officers Assn. U.S. (life mem.), Mil. Order World Wars, Thomas Jefferson Inst. Religious Freedom (founding), SAR, Am. Legion (post comdr. 1951-52), Blue Key, Sigma Delta Kappa. Episcopalian (past warden, vestryman, lay reader). Clubs: Masons (32 deg.), Shriners, Jesters, Kiwanis (past dir.). Address: PO Drawer 29 Fredericksburg VA 22404

JAMISON, JOHN CALLISON, business educator, banker; b. Lafayette, Ind., July 12, 1934; s. John Ruger and Sara (Callison) J.; m. Carol Ann Sansone, July 7, 1979; children—Kelly Elizabeth, Deborah Louise. B.S. in Indsl. Econs., Purdue U., 1956; M.B.A., Harvard U., 1961. Assoc. corp. fin. Goldman, Sachs & Co., N.Y.C., 1961-69, ptnr., 1969-82, ltd. ptnr., 1983—; dir. Hershey Foods Corp., Pa. Bd. govs. Purdue Found., West Lafayette, Ind., 1979-83; mem. corp. Hurricane Island Outward Bound Sch., Rockland, Maine, 1984—; mem. Va. Gov.'s Adv. Com. on Merit Pay in Edn., 1984—; mem. vis. com. Harvard Grad. Sch. Edn., 1983—. Served to lt. USN, 1956-59; PTO. Named Old Master, Purdue U., 1977; Sagamore of the Wabash, Gov. Ind., 1982. Mem. Beta Gamma Sigma (hon.). Republican. Episcopalian. Club: Ocean Reef (Key Largo, Fla.). Lodge: Rotary. Office: Sch Bus Adminstrn Coll William and Mary Williamsburg VA 23185

JANCAUSKAS, DON, business executive; b. Hanau, Germany, July 16, 1946; came to U.S., 1949, naturalized, 1973; s. Paul and Stase J.; student Bentley Coll., 1964-65, U. Maine, 1965-66, Boston U., 1966, Northeastern U., 1966-67. With John Hancock Ins. Co., 1970—, sales mgr., Boston and Jacksonville, Fla., 1974-76, ednl. cons. to mktg. dept., Boston, 1976-78, asst. field v.p., Dallas, 1978-79, gen. agt. S. Tex., Corpus Christi, 1979—; regional dir. Profesco Corp., 1979—; pres. Corpus Christi Assocs., Inc., 1984—; dir. New Eng. Investors Trust. Served with U.S. Army, 1967-70. Mem. Gen. Agts. and Mgrs. Assn., Nat. Assn. Life Underwriters, VFW, Nat. Rifle Assn. (life). Office: 3319 Bali Corpus Christi TX 78418

JANER, ANN LOURDES, pharmacy educator, pharmacist, consultant; b. Scranton, Pa., Jan. 16, 1950; d. Albert Vincent and Lourdes Eileen (O'Hara) Costanzi; m. Edward John Janer, July 14, 1973; 1 child, Margaret Lourdes. B.S., Phila. Coll. Pharmacy and Sci., 1972; M.S., Temple U., 1975. Lic. pharmacist, Pa., Ala. Staff pharmacist Einstein Med. Ctr., Phila., 1972-73; clin. pharmacist Albert Einstein Med. Ctr., Phila., 1973-75; asst. prof. Auburn U. Sch. Pharmacy, Ala., 1975-81, assoc. prof., 1981—; mem. med. adv. bd. Central Ala. Home Health, Opelika, 1976—; reviewer U.S. Pharm. Conv.-Drug Info., Rockville, Md., 1983—. Mem. Am. Soc. Hosp. Pharmacists, Am. Assn. Colls. Pharmacy, Ala. Pharm. Assn., Ala. Soc. Hosp. Pharmacists, Kappa Epsilon Alumni (pres. 1984-85). Roman Catholic. Avocations: needlepoint; gardening. Home: 1806 Jollit Ave Opelika AL 36801 Office: Sch Pharmacy Auburn U Auburn University AL 36849

JANES, ROBERT HARRISON, JR., surgeon; b. Little Rock, Nov. 13, 1939; s. Robert Harrison and Fahy Helen (Mathers) J.; B.S., U. Ark., 1965, M.D., 1965; m. Patricia Mayes, June 30, 1962; children—Robert, Clayton, Matthew. Intern surgery U. Ark. Hosps., Little Rock, 1965-66, resident surgery, 1966-70; practice medicine, specializing in surgery Holt-Krock Clinic, Fort Smith, Ark., 1972—; mem. staff Sparks Regional Med. Center, chief surgery, 1977-78; mem. staff St. Edwards Mercy Med. Center; instr. surgery U. Ark., Little Rock, 1969-70, asst. clin. prof. surgery, 1976—. Pres. Sebastian County (Ark.) unit Am. Cancer Soc., 1975-76, bd. dirs. Ark. div., pres. Ark. div., 1978-79, 81-82, nat. bd. dirs., 1982—; bd. dirs. Ft. Smith Symphony, 1979—, treas., 1980-82, pres., 1982-83; bd. dirs. Broadway Theatre League Ft. Smith, 1981—. Served to maj., M.C., USAF, 1970-72. Diplomate Am. Bd. Surgery. Fellow ACS (commn. on cancer 1983—), Southwestern Surg. Congress; mem. AMA, Ark. Med. Soc., Lambda Chi Alpha. Methodist (adminstrv. bd. 1974-77). Clubs: Hardscrabble Country, Fort Smith Racquet, Town of Fort Smith; Red Apple Country (Eden Isle, Ark.); Oaklawn Jockey (Hot Springs, Ark.). Contbr. articles to profl. jours. Home: 3707 Old Oaks Ln Fort Smith AR 72903 Office: 1500 Dodson Ave Fort Smith AR 72901

JANN, WARREN WILLIAM, retirement and health care consultant; b. Chgo., July 9, 1939; s. Edward W. and Mildred (Barton) J.; B.S., North Tex. State U., 1968, M.S., 1983. Adminstrv. planner Gen. Dynamics, Ft. Worth, 1969-71; developer, adminstr., drug and alcohol programs, Hennepin County, Minn., 1971-75; developer mktg. and fin. plan for health maintenance orgn. Portland (Oreg.) Met. Health, 1973; pvt. practice retirement and health care cons., Ft. Worth, 1977—; dir. mgmt. services Kendal-Crosslands, 1985, Retirement Housing Corp., Dallas, 1986. cons. long term care facilities and program devel.; participant in devel. health maintenance orgns. in Tex. Recipient Disting. Student award North Tex. State U. Center for Studies in Aging, 1983. Mem. Gerontol. Soc., Am. Coll. Health Care Adminstrs., S.W. Soc. on Aging. Home and Office: 4371 Sandage Ave Fort Worth TX 76115

JANNEY, EDWARD LEE, structural engineer, educator; b. Roanoke, Va., June 3, 1951; s. Harless E. and Alma W. Janney; m. Faith Larue Bloodworth, Aug. 12, 1978; children—Nicholas Edward, Philip Kenton. B.S. in Civil Engring., Va. Poly. Inst. and State U., 1973. Registered profl. engr. Structural engr., head dept., assoc. Hayes, Seay, Mattern & Mattern, Roanoke, Va., 1973—; part-time instr. civil engring. tech. Va. Western Community Coll. Mem. ASCE, Va. Poly. Inst. and State U. Alumni Assn. Club: Hokie (Roanoke). Home: 120 Maple Dr Blue Ridge VA 24064

JANNIK, CAROL ANN, educational administrator; b. Rahway, N.J., Mar. 22, 1945; d. Carmen Albert and Helen Jane (Capone) Luca; m. Adam Alexander Jannik, June 11, 1966; children—Tracy Ann, Adam Alexander. B.S. magna cum laude, U. Ark., 1981; M.Edn., U. So. Miss., 1983. Adminstrn. asst. Princeton U., 1965-66; asst. to treas. Stevens Inst. Tech., 1966-67; asst. to dean engring. Ohio No. U., 1970-71; broker, salesman Continental, Chicago Heights, Ill., 1975-77; acad. advisor Tulane U., New Orleans, 1983—. Editor: Synthetic Leather, 1966. Environ. chmn. City of Lansing, Ill., 1972; trustee Thornton Community Coll., 1973, Prairie State Coll., 1976; vice-chmn. South Suburban Trustees Assn., Kankakee, Ill., 1973; mem. Mayor's Council, Lansing, 1972-73; mem. ednl. task force, ad hoc com. Crete/Monee Sch. Bd., Ill., 1975-77. Mem. NEA, Am. Personnel and Guidance Assn., Am. Assn. Counseling and Devel., Nat. Acad. Advising Assn., Am. Sch. Counselor Assn. Republican. Roman Catholic. Avocations: thoroughbred horse breeding; golfing. Home: 3860 3d St Metairie LA 70002 Office: Gibson Hall Room 200 Tulane U St Charles Ave New Orleans LA 70118

JANSEN, DONALD ORVILLE, lawyer; b. Odessa, Tex., Nov. 17, 1939; s. Orville Charles and Dolores Elizabeth (Olps) J.; children—Donald Orville, Lauren, Christine, David, Margaret. B.B.A., Loyola U., 1961, J.D. cum laude, 1963; LL.M., Georgetown U., 1966. Bar: La. 1963, Tex. 1965. Ptnr., Fulbright and Jaworski, Houston, 1966—. Served to capt. JAGC, U.S. Army, 1963-66. Named Outstanding Tex. Young Republican Man, Tex. Young Rep. Fedn., 1970. Fellow Am. Coll. Probate Counsel; mem. Fed. Bar Assn. (pres. Houston chpt. 1972), ABA, State Bar Tex., La. Bar Assn. Roman Catholic. Club: Serra (pres. 1984) (Houston). Home: 806 Magdalene St Houston TX 77024 Office: 800 MBank Bldg Houston TX 77002

JANSSEN, FELIX GERARD, building materials company executive; b. Netherlands, Aug. 18, 1925; s. Hendrik and Anna Christina (Sanders) J.; came to U.S., 1961, naturalized, 1966; B.S. in Mining and Mech. Engring., Hoge Technische Sch.; m. Irma Wouters, Aug. 20, 1949; 1 son, Robert Henry. Pres., U.S. Acoustics Corp., 1957—; pres., dir. Internat. Perlite Products, Inc., 1973—; chmn. bd. Internat. Sludge Reduction Inc., 1977—; dir. U.S. Environ. Products Inc., 1978—; partner Gen. Consulting Services, S.A., 1973—; cons. in acoustics. Served as capt. Royal Netherlands Air Force, 1944-56. Mem. Internat. Aeronautic Fedn., Water Pollution Control Fedn. Republican. Roman Catholic. Club: U.S. Power Squadron. Patentee in acoustical products and pollution control equipment and tech. Address: 20 Minnetonka Rd Sea Ranch Lakes Fort Lauderdale FL 33308

JANSSEN, LAWRENCE RAYMOND, architect; b. Jersey City, N.J., Aug. 20, 1943; s. Harry Arian and Dorothea Ann (Healy) J.; m. Nora Gaurys, June 11, 1977; children—Peter, Karen. B.A. in Philosophy, St. Stephen's Coll., 1967; B.F.A., R.I. Sch. Design, 1975, Profl. degree, 1975. Registered architect, Fla. Pvt. practice architecture, Coral Springs, Fla., 1983—. One man show of paintings and drawings Providence Coll., 1971; exhbn. of drawings Ward Nasse Gallery, Boston, N.Y.C.; commn. for mural Blue Cross Blue Shield, Boston, 1970; murals painted for Summerthing Program, Boston, 1969. City of Boston scholar, 1973-74, 74-75. Mem. AIA. Office: 7782 Wiles Rd Coral Springs FL 33065

JANTUNEN, KAUKO ILMARI, physician; b. Ruokolahti, Finland, Aug. 27, 1941; came to U.S., 1970, naturalized, 1978; s. Heimo and Helvi Sivia (Teppana) J.; M.D., U. Helsinki (Finland), 1967; m. Irene Marcarelli, Sept. 29, 1985; children—Pertti Tapio, Timo Juhani, Frank Kari. Gen. practice medicine, Kiihtelysvaara, Finland, 1967-69, Pajala, Sweden, 1969-70; intern St. Luke's Hosp., Fargo, N.D., 1970-71; practice family medicine, New York Mills, Minn., 1971-75, Lake Worth, Fla., 1975—; staff Drs. Hosp. Diplomate Am. Bd. Family Practice. Fellow Am. Acad. Family Physicians; mem. AMA. Finnish Pentecostal Ch. Address: 1622 S Dixie Hwy Lake Worth FL 33460

JAQUES, FRANK HESKETH, lawyer; b. Oklahoma City, Nov. 8, 1934; s. Robert Hesketh and Eula Hester (Shelton) J.; m. Frances Rebecca Ballard, Nov. 18, 1960; children—Robert H. II, John Fell. B.A. with distinction, U. Okla., 1956, LL.B., 1958. Bar: Okla. 1958, U.S. Dist. Ct. (ea. dist.) Okla., U.S. Dist. Ct. (we. dist.) Okla., U.S. Ct. Appeals (10th cir.), U.S. Supreme Ct. Mem. firm Lambert, Roberts & Jaques, Inc., and predecessor firms Kerr, Lambert, Conn & Roberts, Kerr, Lambert, Roberts, Lambert, Roberts & Lewis, Lambert, Roberts Jaques & Scrivner, Ada, Okla., 1961—; mem. bd. dirs. The Gloria Corp., Pre-Paid Legal Services, Inc, Okla. State Bank, Ada; judge Ct. of Appeals, Okla. Temporary Div. 23. Ex officio bd. dirs. Okla. Cardiovascular Inst.; past chmn. Heart Fund; former chmn. gifts com. Community Chest; active Okla. U. Assocs., pres. adv. council East Central U. Served to capt. USAF, 1958-61. Editor Okla. U. Law Rev. Mem. ABA, Okla. Bar Assn., Pontotoc County Bar Assn. (past pres.), Okla. Bd. Bar Examiners (past chmn.). Democrat. Presbyterian. Home: 114 E Kings Rd Ada OK 74820 Office: Lambert Roberts Jaques PO Box 130 Ada OK 74820

JAQUES, WILLIAM EVERETT, physician, educator; b. Newbury, Mass., July 11, 1917; s. Arthur Wellington and Helen Alice (Colby) J.; student U. N.H., 1935-38; M.D., C.M., McGill U., 1942; m. Betty Charlene Mansfield, Mar. 30, 1968; children—William, Roberta Gail, Alice Penelope, Judith Anne, Pamela Jane, Arthur William, David Everett. Intern, Bridgeport (Conn.) Hosp., 1943-44, resident pathology, 1946-47; resident pathology Mass. Meml. Hosp., Boston, 1947-49; instr. Harvard Med. Sch., 1949-53; resident Children's Med. Center, Boston, 1949-50, asst. pathologist, 1950-51; assoc. pathologist Peter Bent Brigham Hosp., Boston, 1951-53; asso. prof. pathology La. State U., 1953-57; prof., chmn. dept. pathology U. Okla. Med. Sch., 1957-65; mem. staff Univ. Hosp., Oklahoma City, 1957-65; vis. prof. Nat. Def. Med. Center, Taipei, Taiwan, 1965-66; prof., chmn. dept. pathology U. Ark. Med. Center, 1966-74; dir. pathology Nat. Center Toxicology Research, Jefferson, Ark., 1971-74; clin. prof. pathology U. Okla., Tulsa, 1974—; prof. pathology Okla. Coll. Osteo. Medicine and Surgery, Tulsa, 1974-81; prof. pathology Am. U. Carribbean, 1981-82, dean med. scis., 1982—. Mem. exec. com. Okla. div. Am. Cancer Soc., 1959-65. Served with armed forces, 1943-46. Mem. AMA, Am. Assn. Pathologists and Bacteriologists, Am. Soc. Exptl. Pathology, Am. Assn. Med. Colls., Internat. Acad. Pathology, Am. Coll. Angiology, Am. Soc. Colposcopy, Am. Legion, Sigma Xi, Alpha Omega Alpha. Co-author: Introduction to Colposcopy, 1960. Contbr. articles to profl. jours. Home: PO Box 1559 Tulsa OK 74101

JARCZEWSKI, PATRICIA, nursing educator; b. Colorado Springs, Colo., July 14, 1952; d. Francis Leo and Hazel Marie (Milliron) Holden; m. David W. Jarczewski, June 3, 1972; children—Delilah, Amanda. B.S., U. Mary Hardin Baylor, Belton, Tex., 1974; M.S., Tex. Woman's U., 1980. R.N., Tex. Nurse, Scott & White Hosp., Temple, Tex., 1973-74, VA, Temple, 1974-76; instr. nursing Central Tex. Coll., Killeen, 1976-81, dir. nursing div., 1981-85; asst. prof., chmn. nursing Eastern Ky. U., Richmond, 1985—. Mem. Tex. Nurses Assn. (bd. dirs. 1982-84), Am. Nurses Assn., Nat. League Nursing, Ky. Nurses Assn., Phi Delta Kappa, Sigma Theta Tau. Roman Catholic. Avocations: gourmet cooking; running. Office: Eastern Ky U 133 Windsor Dr Richmond KY 40475

JARDIEU, JANICE MARIE, university administrator; b. Herkimer, N.Y., Sept. 22, 1953; d. Joseph P. and Dorothy M. (DuBois) J. B.A., SUNY-Potsdam, 1975; M.A., Bowling Green State U., 1977. Residence hall dir. U. Tampa, Fla., 1977-78, dir. residence life and housing, 1978—. Mem. Am. Coll. Personnel Assn., Internat. Assn. Coll. and Univ. Housing Officers, Am. Assn. Counseling and Devel. Avocations: photography; golf. Office: U Tampa 401 W Kennedy Blvd Box 109F Tampa FL 33606

JARMAN, JACQULINE O'SHEA, graphic designer; b. Tulsa, May 2, 1939; d. Daniel Patrick and Thelma (Wheatley) O'Shea; m. George William Jarman, Dec. 28, 1966. Student Okla. U., 1958-62, Philbrook Art Inst., Tulsa, 1964. Graphic designer Arthur Zweck Bronner, Inc., Dallas, 1966-69; v.p., prodn. mgr. Big —D— Jamboree, Dallas, 1973-74; designer, artist Jacquline O'Shea Designs, Dallas, 1975—. Sec., Young Republicans, Tulsa, 1963-66; mem. women's com., chmn. art and decorations sale street fair Creative Learning Ctr., Dallas, 1983; aux. mem. Susan G. Komen Found., Dallas Mus. Fine Arts; Mem. Okla. U. Alumni (v.p. Dallas 1981-83, dir. 1983—), TACA, Inc, 500 Inc., Delta Gamma. Episcopalian. Home and Office: 4356 Potomac St Dallas TX 75205

JARRETT, ALAN, ophthalmologist; b. N.Y.C., Apr. 16, 1943; s. Jack and Allegra (Caspi) J.; m. Paula Rae Richman, Dec. 17, 1967; children—Jennifer Ann, Hillary. B.S. in Chemistry, U. Fla., 1965; M.D., U. Tenn., 1969.

Diplomate Am. Bd. Ophthalmology. Intern UCLA, 1969-70; resident in ophthalmology Baylor U., Houston, 1970-73, chief resident, 1973, instr., 1973—. Contbr. articles to profl. jours. Mem. AMA, Tex. Med. Assn., Tex. Ophthalmology Assn., Am. Acad. Ophthalmology. Republican. Jewish. Avocations: tennis; fishing; swimming. Office: 909 Frostwood #226 Houston TX 77024

JARRETT, JAMES LEO, health care administrator; b. Bristol, Va., Jan. 18, 1952; s. Leo Merle and Beatrice Marie (Pippen) J. B.S., E. Tenn. State U., 1974; M.S. in Health Administrn., Trinity U., 1980. Administrv. officer Hawley U.S. Army Hosp., Indpls., 1975-78; asst. to pres. Bapt. Med. Ctrs., Birmingham, Ala., 1980-81, dir. ambulatory care, 1981-82; asst. administr. Gulf Coast Med. Ctr., Wharton, Texas, 1982—. Served to lt. U.S. Army, 1974-78. Mem. Am. Coll. Hosp. Administrs., Am. Hosp. Assn., Birmingham C. of C. (pres. com. 1980-81). Presbyterian. Lodge: Rotary (bd. dirs. 1985—). Avocations: racquet sports; jogging. Home: 2017 Chapel Heights Wharton TX 77488 Office: Gulf Coast Med Ctr Box 3004 Wharton TX 77488

JARVIS, SCOTT EDWARD, lawyer; b. Winfield, Kans., Apr. 15, 1938; s. Chandler F. and Mary Scott (Nelson) J.; m. Sondra M. Brantley, June 1, 1961; children—Mary Ann, Cynthia Lee, Susan Kay, Catherine Lynn. A.B., Ft. Hays (Kans.) State U., 1962, postgrad. (fellow), 1962; J.D., Washburn U., 1966. Bar: Kans. 1966, Ohio 1974, N.C. 1982, U.S. Dist. Ct. Kans. 1966, U.S. Dist. Ct. (so. dist.) Ohio 1980, U.S. Dist. Ct. (we. dist.) N.C. 1982, U.S. Tax Ct. 1970, U.S. Ct. Mil. Appeals 1969, U.S. Ct. Appeals (8th cir.) 1969, U.S. Ct. Appeals (10th cir.) 1969, U.S. Supreme Ct. 1970. Sole practice Topeka, 1966-73, Sidney, Ohio, 1974-81, Asheville, N.C., 1981—; gen. counsel. The Way Internat., New Knoxville, Ohio, 1973-79; acting pres. Coll. Emporia (Kans.), 1974-75; asst. pros. atty. Shelby County (Ohio), 1975-77, pros. atty., 1977-81; asst. gen. counsel Buck Stove Corp., Asheville, N.C., 1981-83; judge protem Topeka Mcpl. Ct., 1967-73, Sidney (Ohio) Mcpl. Ct. intermittently 1974-78; lectr., instr. in field. Bd. dirs. Ballantree Homeowners Assn.; mem. adminstrv. bd. Skyland United Meth. Ch.; mem. Heritage Found., Am. Security Council; former bd. dirs. Shelby County ARC; former trustee Sidney-Shelby County Chamber Found., Inc.; past V.P., past pres. Botkins (Ohio) Area Community Club; mem. Ohio Unified Correctional Master Plan Adv. Com., 1977-81; mem. Ohio Law Enforcement Cons. Com., 1980. Recipient Police Service award Nat. Police Hall of Fame, 1980. Mem. Assn. Trial Lawyers Am., Ohio Acad. Trial Lawyers, N.C. Bar Assn., Ohio Bar Assn., Kans. Bar Assn., Fed. Bar Assn., ABA, Internat. Acad. Criminology, Delta Theta Phi, Sigma Alpha Epsilon, Clubs: Eagles, Elks, Moose. Home: 8 Elmwood Ln Asheville NC 28803 Office: PO Box 5421 Asheville NC 28813

JASNY, GEORGE ROMAN, corporate executive; b. Katowice, Poland, June 6, 1924; came to U.S., 1941; s. Maurice and Irene Jasny; m. Gloria Jones, June 23, 1951; children—Elizabeth Pruitt, Thomas Paul. B.S. in Chem. Engring., U. Wash., 1949; S.M. in Chem. Engring., MIT, 1952. Registered profl. engr., Tenn. With Nuclear div. Union Carbide Corp., Oak Ridge, 1950-84, v.p. engring. and computer scis., 1980-84; v.p. engring. and computer scis. Martin Marietta Energy Systems, Inc., 1984—. Chmn. bd. dirs. Oak Ridge Utilities Dist.; bd. dirs. Oak Ridge Hosp.; bd. engring. advisers Tenn. Tech. U.; adv. bd. Sch. Engring., U. Tenn., Knoxville. Served with USN, 1943-46. Fellow Am. Inst. Chem. Engrs.; mem. Nat. Acad. Engring., Nat. Soc. Profl. Engrs., Am. Soc. Engring. Mgmt. (pres.), AAAS, Sigma Xi, Tau Beta Pi. Democrat. Mem. United Ch. of Oak Ridge. Lodge: Rotary. Home: 106 Dixie Ln Oak Ridge TN 37830 Office: Martin Marietta Energy Systems PO Box Y Oak Ridge TN 37831

JASPER, NORMAN JOSHUA, JR., manufacturing company official; b. Shipman, Ill., July 30, 1933; s. Norman Joshua and Edith Ann (Green) J.; m. Virginia Elizabeth McCoy, Dec. 16, 1966; 1 dau., Angela Hope. Student Ball State U., 1951-52; B.S., Ill. State Normal Coll., 1955. Med. sales rep. RX div. Pennwalt Corp., Roanoke, Va., 1968-72, dist. mgr., 1972—. Contbr. articles to mil. jours. Served as parachutist, to capt. USMC, 1955-68; Vietnam. Decorated Bronze Star, Purple Heart with two stars. Mem. DAV (life; 1st jr. vice comdr.), VFW, Am. Legion, Mil. Order Purple Heart. Democrat. Methodist. Address: 4070 Blandfield Dr Vinton VA 24179

JASZCZAK, RONALD JACK, physicist, researcher, consultant; b. Chicago Heights, Ill., Aug. 23, 1942; s. Jacob and Julia (Gudowicz) J.; m. Nancy Jane Bober, Apr. 15, 1967; children—John, Monica. B.S. with highest honors, U. Fla., 1964, Ph.D., 1968. Staff physicist Oak Ridge Nat. 1969-71, AEC postdoctoral fellow, 1968-69; prin. research scientist Searle Diagnostics, Inc., 1971-73, sr. prin. research scientist, 1973, research group leader, 1973-77, chief scientist, 1977-79; assoc. prof. radiology Duke U. Med. Ctr., Durham, N.C., 1979—, assoc. prof. biomedical engring., founder, chmn. bd. dirs. Data Spectrum Corp., Chapel Hill, N.C., 1981—; cons. med. imaging systems Johnson and Johnson, Siemens, 1981—; sr. research fellow NIH, 1980-82; prin. investigator Nat. Cancer Inst. Grant, 1983-86. NASA fellow, 1964-67; U. Fla. fellow, 1967-68; RCA scholar, 1963-64. Mem. Soc. Nuclear Medicine (bd. govs. instrumentation council), Am. Phys. Soc., IEEE, AAAS, Am. Assn. Physicists in Medicine, Soc. Photo-Optical Instrumentation Engrs., Sigma Xi, Phi Beta Kappa, Phi Kappa Phi, Tau Sigma, Sigma Pi Sigma. Democrat. Roman Catholic. Contbr. articles to profl. jours.; patentee in field. Home: 2307 Honeysuckle Rd Chapel Hill NC 27514 Office: Duke U Med Ctr PO Box 3949 Durham NC 27710

JATRAS, STEPHEN JAMES, electronics executive; b. Mckeesport, Pa., Apr. 7, 1926; s. Andrew and Verna (Filakowski) J.; B.S. in Elec. Engring., Carnegie Inst. Tech., 1947; S.M., MIT, 1952; Sloan fellow Stanford Grad. Sch. Bus., 1958; children—Stephanie Ann, Andrew Anthony, Christopher Dale, Cindy Lou, Shawn James, Todd Charles. Dial systems engr. Stromberg Carlson Co., Rochester N.Y., 1947-48; instr. elec. engring. U. Mass., 1948-50; research engr. Mass. Inst. Tech., 1950-52; v.p. chief engr. Midwestern Instruments Co., Tulsa, 1952-56; v.p., gen. mgr. Lockheed Electronics div. Lockheed Aircraft Corp., 1956-65; pres., dir. Telex Corp., Tulsa, from 1965, chmn., chief exec. officer, 1981—; dir. D.G. O'Brien Inc., ONEOK, Inc., Fourth Nat. Bank, Tulsa. Chmn., Tulsa YMCA; mem. adv. bd. Salvation Army, Boy Scouts; trustee Carnegie Mellon U.; mem. adv. bd. St. John's Med. Ctr. Served with AUS, 1944-46. Mem. IEEE (sr.), Tulsa C. of C. (dir.), Sigma Xi, Tau Beta Pi. Home: 6123 S Florence Pl Tulsa OK 74136 Office: Box 1526 Tulsa OK 74101

JAY, JAMES ALBERT, insurance company executive; b. Superior, Wis., Aug. 24, 1916; s. Clarence William and Louie (Davies) J.; student pub. schs., Mpls.; m. Margie Hoffpauir, Dec. 23, 1941; 1 son, James A. Franchise with The Stauffer System of Calif., 1946-49; Ala. dist. mgr. Guaranty Savs. Life Ins. Co., Montgomery, Ala., 1949-51, state mgr. La., 1951—, dir., 1952—, La. gen. agent, 1964—; La. gen agt. Gen. United Life Ins. Co. of Des Moines (merged with Lincoln Liberty Life Ins. Co., Des Moines, with All Am. Life Ins. Co., Chgo. 1984), 1969—. Com. chmn. Attakapas council Boy Scouts Am., Alexandria, La., 1955, council commr., 1961-62, commr. Manchac dist., 1967—. Served as cpl. USMC, 1942-45, PTO. Decorated Purple Heart. Mem. Nat., Baton Rouge life underwriters assns., Gen. Agts. and Mgrs. Conf., C. of C., Internat. Platform Assn. Methodist. Elk. Home: 5919 Clematis Dr Baton Rouge LA 70808 Office: 2279 Main St Baton Rouge LA 70802

JAYANTY, RADHAKRISHNA MURTY, environmental scientist; b. Mukkamala, India, June 29, 1946; s. Somappa and Gouramma Jayanty; came to U.S., 1973; m. Lakshmi Svs, Dec. 25, 1978, children—Nagendra, Phanindra. M.S., Andhra U., Waltair, India, 1966; M.Engring., Pa. State U., 1975; Ph.D., U. Bradford (Eng.), 1972. Research assoc. Pa. State U., 1973-76; research scientist TRC-Environ. Cons., Inc., Hartford, Conn., 1976-78; sr. research chemist Research Triangle Inst., Research Triangle Park, N.C., 1978—. Mem. Air Pollution Control Assn., Am. Chem. Soc., Sigma Xi. Contbr. articles to profl. jours.

JAYNE, BENJAMIN A., university dean, forestry educator; b. Enid, Okla., Oct. 10, 1928; m. Betty Lu Bailey, Aug. 10, 1950; 3 children. B.S.F., U. Idaho, 1952; M.Forestry, 1953, D.F., 1955. Assoc. dean U. Wash., Seattle, 1968-72, dir. U. Wash., 1972-76; dean Sch. of Forestry and Environ. Studies, Duke U., Durham, N.C., 1976—; trustee Inst. of Ecology, 1978—. Editor: Wood & Fiber, Jour. of Soc. of Wood Sci. and Tech., 1968-72. NSF postdoctoral fellow U. Calif., 1961-62. Fellow Inst. of Wood Sci., Soc. Am. Foresters (mem. accreditation com. 1977-81); mem. Forest Products Research Soc. (sec. 1955-58, wood award 1955), Soc. Wood and Tech. (pres.-elect 1960-61), Soc. Wood Sci. and Tech. (mem. exec. bd. 1965-68, pres. 1968-69), Sigma Xi, Xi Sigma Pi. Home: 31118 Ridgview Dr Ocean Park WA 98640 Office: Duke U Sch Forestry and Environ Studies 214 Biol Scis Bldg Durham NC 27706

JEANES, OPEY DEW, college dean, chemistry educator; b. Wilson, N.C., Sept. 14, 1937; s. Lemmie Webster and Nola (Dew) J.; m. Virginia James, Apr. 14, 1963; children—Dale, James, Paul. B.A., Atlantic Christian Coll., 1959; M.A., George Peabody Coll., 1960; Ed.D., Va. Poly. Inst. and State U., 1977. Cert. tchr., N.C. Tchr. Wilson City Schs., N.C., 1960-61; prof. chemistry Chowan Coll., Murfreesboro, N.C., 1961-67; chmn. div. natural sci. John Tyler Community Coll., Chester, Va., 1967-79; v.p., dean Mt. Olive Coll., N.C., 1979—; cons. various colls. and state agys.; textbook reviewer various pub. cos. Contbr. articles to profl. jours. NSF fellow, 1962, 65. Mem. Assn. Acad. Deans So. States, Assn. Acad. Deans N.C., Phi Delta Kappa, Pi Sigma Eta. Democrat. Baptist. Lodge: Rotary. Avocation: woodworking. Home: 119 Club Knolls Rd Mount Olive NC 28365 Office: Mount Olive Coll Mount Olive NC 28365

JEFFCOAT, MARK RANDALL, religious organization executive; b. Columbia, S.C., Nov. 4, 1950; s. Alex Hoyt and Doris Elizabeth (Joyner) J.; m. Barbara Lynn Hamby, June 12, 1971; 1 children—Lisa Lynn, Jonathan Mark. B.A. in Journalism, U. S.C., 1973, postgrad., 1983-85. Minister of music and youth Siloam Bapt. Ch., Easley, S.C., 1974-76; minister of youth and adminstrn. Northside Bapt. Ch., West Columbia, S.C., 1976-81; assoc. office pub. relations Gen. Bd. of S.C. Bapt. Conv., 1981—; pres. ACTS of Columbia; condr. various workshops and clinics in youth ministry, recreation and communications. Mem. Pub. Relations Soc. Am., Bapt. Pub. Relations Assn. (honors competition award 1982), S.C. Bapt. Communicators Network, Assn. Edn. in Journalism and Mass Communication, Kappa Tau Alpha. Home: 1033 Hook Ave West Columbia SC 29169 Office: 907 Richland St Columbia SC 29201

JEFFERDS, JOSEPH CROSBY, JR., industrial machinery distributing company executive; b. Charleston, W.Va., June 24, 1919; s. Joseph Crosby and Agnes Atkinson (Arbuckle) J.; B.S. in Mech. Engring., MIT, 1940; Sc.D. (hon.), W.Va. Inst. Tech., 1969; m. Olivia Polk Evans, May 15, 1943; children—Joseph C. III, Marion Jefferds Sinclair, Olivia Polk, Robert Grosvenor. Trainee, Bethlehem Steel Co. (Pa.), 1940; v.p., dir. Kanawha Drug Co., Charleston, 1946-85, Distbr.'s Corp., Charleston, 1970—; pres. Jefferds Corp., Charleston, 1947—, Mech. Equipment Service Co., Charleston, 1952—; dir. Kanawha Banking & Trust Co., Bell Atlantic Corp., Intermountain Bankshares, Inc. Mem. W.Va. Bd. Edn., 1957-65, pres., 1963; trustee W.Va. Coll. Grad. Studies Found., W.Va. Inst. Tech. Found., Montgomery, Highland Hosp., Charleston; trustee U. Charleston. Served from 2d lt. to lt. col. AUS, 1941-46. Mem. Charleston Area C. of C. (pres. 1972), ASME, Am. Ordnance Assn., Am. Inst. Indsl. Engrs. Republican. Episcopalian. Clubs: Charleston Rotary (past pres.); Edgewood Country (past pres.). Author: A History of St. John's Episcopal Church, 1976; Captain Matthew Arbuckle. Home: 3 Scott Rd Charleston WV 25314 Office: PO Box 757 US Route 35 St Albans WV 25177

JEFFORDS, EDWARD ALAN, lawyer; b. Rector, Ark., Nov. 28, 1945; s. Roy Ezra and Sylvia Belle (Dickinson) J.; A.A., Victor Valley Coll., 1967; student U. Wis. Mgmt. Inst., 1977; B.A., SUNY-Albany, 1978; J.D., Baylor U. Sch. Law, 1985; m. Judith Ann Williams, Nov. 25, 1981; 1 son by previous marriage, Dana Alan. Editor, Auburn (Wash.) Globe-News, 1967; fine arts editor Tacoma News-Tribune, 1967-72; exec. dir. Ozark Inst., Eureka Springs, 1973-82; now asst. atty. gen. State of Tex. Served with USAF, 1963-67. Mem. Order of Barrister, Delta Theta Phi.

JEFFORDS, JEAN GARRETT, county official; b. Waycross, Ga., Feb. 8, 1921; d. Quillian Lemuel and Glenn Antoinette (Allen) Garrett; A.B., U. Ga., 1942; M.A. in Polit. Sci. (Univ. fellow), 1944; m. William Quintillus Jeffords, Jr., Oct. 15, 1954 (dec.); 1 son, Lawrence Garrett. With fgn. service Dept. State, Guatemala, 1945-48; asst. to dean Coll. Spl. and Continuation Studies, U. Md., College Park, 1948-49; prin. planner Jacksonville (Fla.) Area Planning Bd., 1965-74; planning dir. Central Fla. Regional Planning Council, Bartow, 1974-79; planning cons., after 1979; now supr. aging programs Collier County, Fla. Mem. Fla. Planning and Zoning Assn., Polk County Hist. Assn., Alpha Delta Pi. Democrat. Episcopalian. Author reports in field. Home: 4054 Kelly Rd Naples FL 33962 Office: Collier County Govt Complex Naples FL 33962

JEFFREYS, ELYSTAN GEOFFREY, geologist, oil company executive; b. N.Y.C., Apr. 26, 1926; s. Geoffrey and Georgene Frances Theodora (Littell) J.; Geol. Engr., Colo. Sch. Mines, 1951, grad. Econ. Evaluation and Investment Decision Methods, 1972; m. Pat Rumage, May 1, 1946; children—Jeri Lynn, David Powell; m. 2d, Peggi Villar, Feb. 28, 1975. Partner, G. Jeffreys & Son, 1951-53, Jeffreys and Launius, 1953-55; instr. structural geology U. So. Miss., 1955; pvt. practice petroleum exploration, 1954-77; exploration mgr. Arrowhead Exploration Co., Mobile and Brewton, Ala., 1977-83; cons. geologist, 1964—; pres., chmn. Major Oil Co., Jackson, Miss., 1961—. pres., chmn. bd. The Jeffreys Co., Inc., Mobile, Ala., 1985—. Served with 281st Combat Engrs., U.S. Army, 1944-46; ETO. Registered profl. engr., Miss.; registered land surveyor, Miss. Mem. Am. Assn. Petroleum Geologists, Ala. Petroleum Landman Assn., Gulf Coast Assn. Geol. Socs. (treas. 1960, cert. of service 1971), Soc. Petroleum Engrs. AIME, Ala. Petroleum Landman Assn., Am. Assn. Petroleum Landmen, Miss. Geol. Soc., New Orleans Geol. Soc., Soc. Ind. Profl. Earth Scientists, Ind. Petroleum Assn. Am., Soc. Ind. Profl. Earth Scientists, English Speaking Union, Mobile C. of C., Historic Mobile Preservation Soc., Mobile-Bristol Soc., 281st Engr. Bn. Assn. (treas.), Pi Kappa Alpha. Clubs: Athlestan, Shriners (Mobile); Capital City Petroleum (Jackson, Miss.); Masons (Jackson); Palm Beach (London). Home: 1810 Old Government St Mobile AL 36606 Office: 1509 Government St Suite 100 Mobile AL 36604 also 1440 Saratoga Bldg New Orleans LA 70112

JEFFRIES, JAMES RICHARD, dean, education consultant, speaker; b. Glasgow, Ky., Jan. 23, 1940; s. Delmar Clayborn and Annie Laverne (Medley) J.; m. Betty Joyce Meece, Apr. 3, 1959; children—Melody Logan, Timothy, Jamie Ann Coomer, Richard, Robert, Philip, Stephen. A.B., Lexington Baptist Coll., 1975; M.A., Morehead State U., 1976, M.H.E., 1977; M.R.E., Lexington Baptist Coll., 1978, D.D., 1981. Ordained Gospel minister. With Cin. Gas and Electric Co., 1958-67; pastor Emmanuel Baptist Ch., Winchester, Ky., 1967-70, Fincastle Baptist Ch., Ohio, 1970-74; Bapt. missionary Eastern Ky., 1974-76; instr. Lexington Baptist Coll., 1976—, acad. dean., 1979—. Bd. dirs. Blue Grass Baptist Sch.; host and tchr. Bapt. Focus, Bapt. Forum and Spiritual Life TV.; vol. counselor/tchr. Fed. Correctional Inst., Lexington. Served with U.S. Air N.G., 1956-61. Mem. Assn. Bus. Adminstrs. Christian Colls., Ky. Assn. Collegiate Registrars and Admissions Officers, So. Assn. Coll. Admission Officers, Nat. Audio-Visual Assn. Republican. Author: A Brief Bible Survey, 1980; co-editor: A Study Guide: Term Papers, Reports and Theses, 1981. Home: 713 Franklin Ave Lexington KY 40508 Office: Lexington Bapt Coll 163 N Ashland Ave Lexington KY 50402

JEFFRIS, RONALD DUANE, energy and fertilizer company executive; b. Gays, Ill., Aug. 30, 1937; s. Orval B. and Ola May (Henderson) J.; m. Myra Marie Edmonds, July 4, 1963. B.S. in Edn., Eastern Ill. U., 1959; M. Acctg. Sci., U. Ill., 1961. C.P.A., Ill., Okla. Auditor, Arthur Andersen & Co., Chgo., 1961-66; mgr. adminstrn. and credit USI Farm Chems., Danville, Ill., 1966-68; dir. tech. acctg. No. Ill. Gas Co., Aurora, 1968-73; controller Williams Cos., Tulsa, 1973—. Mem. Am. Inst. C.P.A.s, Okla. Soc. C.P.A.s. Office: One Williams Center Tulsa OK 74172

JELLICORSE, JOHN LEE, communications educator; b. Bristol, Tenn., Nov. 1, 1937; s. Harold Lee and Kathleen (Nickels) J.; m. Lenah Mary Lawrence, July 21, 1961 (div. 1980); 1 dau., Jennifer Lee. A.B., U. Tenn., 1959; Ph.D., Northwestern U., 1967. From instr. to assoc. prof. Northwestern U., Evanston, Ill., 1962-69; assoc. prof. U. Tenn., Knoxville, 1969-74; prof., head dept. communication and theatre U. N.C.-Greensboro, 1974—. Bd. dirs. Greensboro Community Theatre, Carolina Theatre Commn. Recipient Outstanding Tchr. award Northwestern U., 1968; So. Fellowships Fund fellow, 1959-62. Mem. Assn. for Communication Adminstrn., Am. Film Inst., So. Speech Communication Assn., Southeastern Theatre Conf., Carolinas Speech Communication Assn., Speech Communication Assn. for Recorded Sound Collections. Whitmanian. Conbtr. articles to profl. jours. Office: Dept Communication and Theatre UNC-Greensboro Greensboro NC 27412

JELLINEK, HAROLD LESTER, physician; b. N.Y.C., June 2, 1915; s. Henry and Edna (Comings) J.; B.S., N.Y. U., 1934; M.D., N.Y. Med Coll., 1939; m. Lucille Doris Jacobs (dec.); children—Hollis Maura, Leslie Ann; m. 2d, Jacqueline Margaret Rumley, Oct. 18, 1975. Intern, Morrisania City Hosp., N.Y.C., 1939-41, resident in internal medicine, 1946-47; practice medicine specializing in internal medicine, N.Y.C., 1941-42, 47-49; clin. asst. medicine Morrisania City Hosp., 1947-48, asst. vis. electrocardiographer, 1948-49; internist VA Center, Dayton, 1949-50; internist, cardiologist Golden Med. Group and Meml. Gen. Hosp., Elkins, W.Va., 1950-85; cons., 1985. Served to maj. AUS, 1942-46. Diplomate Am. Bd. Internal Medicine. Fellow Am. Coll. Cardiology, Am. Coll. Chest Physicians, Am. Coll. Angiology; mem. AMA, So. Med. Assn., Am. Soc. Internal Medicine, AAAS, Am. Heart Assn. (council clin. cardiology), Meml. Gen. Hosp. Assn. (dir. 1958-85, pres. bd. 1971-79, chmn. bd. 1979-84, bd. dirs. emeritus 1985—). Lodges: Masons, Elks. Home: 30 Boyd St Elkins WV 26241

JELSMA, EDWARD RICHARD, transportation consultant; b. Enid, Okla., Mar. 15, 1915; s. Edward Darwin and Orilla (Hackathorn) J.; B.S., Okla. State U., 1937, M.S., 1938; postgrad. Stanford U., 1939-40; Ph.D. (hon.), Colo. Christian Coll., 1973; m. Marjorie Marie Crain, Feb. 12, 1948 (dec. June 14, 1984); children—Schuyler, Richard, Lisa; m. Ericka C., Apr. 7, 1985. Asst. to tax counsel Standard Oil Co. Calif., San Francisco, 1940-41; dep. fiscal dir. Bur. Ordnance, U.S. Navy Dept., Washington, 1946-48, dep. fiscal dir. Navy Dept., 1948-49; engaged in citrus industry, 1949—; pres. Skyland Farms, 1967—, Agro Energy Corp., 1980—; profl. mem. Interstate and Fgn. Commerce Com., U.S. Senate, 1949-55; dir. bur. transport econs. and stats. ICC, 1955-58; pres. E.R. Jelsma & Assocs., transp. cons., 1958—; grad. asst. Okla. State U., 1937-38; instr. Northwestern State Coll., 1938-39, Am. U., 1946-49; guest lectr. U. Louisville, 1942-43. Rep. chmn. Lake County, 1983-87. Served from ensign to lt. comdr., USNR, 1940-52. Mem. Res. Officers Assn. (legis. chmn. for Fla. 1981—, pres. dept. Fla. 1983-84). Club: Masons (32 deg.). Author: Minimum Wage Legislation, 1938. Office: 1811 Morningside Dr Mount Dora FL 32757

JENKINS, ALBERT MILTON, JR., physician; b. Charleston, W.Va., Apr. 14, 1924; s. Albert Milton and Margaret Mitchell (McPeak) J.; m. Susan Ann Sheipline, Nov. 12, 1955; children—Virginia Mitchell, William Meredith. M.D., U. Cin., 1947. Diplomate Am. Bd. Radiology. Intern, U. Cin., 1947-48; resident radiologist Doctors Hosp., Emergency Hosp., Garfield Meml. Hosp., Washington, 1948-52; fellow in radiology, Washington, 1948-52; mem. med. staff Rex Hosp., Raleigh, N.C., 1953, Franklin Meml. Hosp., Louisburg, N.C., 1953, chief radiology Wake County Med. Ctr., Raleigh, N.C., 1960-66; sr. mem. Wake Radiology Cons. P.A., Raleigh, 1961—; asst. clin. prof. radiology U. N.C.-Chapel Hill, 1965—. Served with USN, 1942-50. Fellow Am. Coll. Radiology; mem. Wake County Med. Soc., N.C. Med. Soc., AMA, So. Med. Assn., Radiol. Soc. N. Am., N.C. Chess Assn., U.S. Chess Fedn., N.C. Art Soc., N.C. Symphony Soc., N.C. Mus. of History Assocs., N.C. Mus. Natural History Soc., Mordecai Sq. Hist. Soc., Raleigh Little Theater, Raleigh Chamber Music Guild. Home: 400 Scotland St Raleigh NC 27609 Office: 3821 Merton Dr Raleigh NC 27609

JENKINS, BOBBIE WHITFIELD, accountant; b. Guthrie, Ky., July 17, 1923; s. William Marshall and Leance (Rust) J.; B.S. in Commerce, U. Ky., 1951; postgrad. U.S. Air Force Air War Coll., 1972; m. Louise Stafford, May 22, 1946; 1 son, Marshall Whitfield. Asst. to chief acct. U. Ky., 1950-51; with Dept. Air Force, 1952-82, tech. adv. for fin. mgmt. Eastern Space and Missile Ctr., Patrick AFB, Fla., 1968-82, head acctg. dept., 1975-81; instr. Patrick AFB br. Rollins Coll., 1966-81. Served with USMC, 1943-44. C.P.A., Ohio, Fla. Mem. Am. Inst. C.P.A.s, Fla. Inst. C.P.A.s (com. mems. in industry, govt. and edn. 1983—), Fla. Assn. Acctg. Educators, Omicron Delta Epsilon. Democrat. Address: 117 Coral Reef Dr Satellite Beach FL 32937

JENKINS, CHARLES H., SR., grocery company executive; b. 1916. Mgr. Publix Markets Inc., 1945-53; with Publix Supermarkets Inc., 1953—, mgr., v.p., 1972-73, chmn. bd., 1973—. Address: Publix Supermarkets Inc 2040 George Jenkins Blvd Lakeland FL 33802*

JENKINS, CHARLES RILEY, aerospace co. exec.; b. Coffee Springs, Ala., Apr. 5, 1926; s. Charlie Morrell and Lessi Belle Jenkins; M.A., Midwestern U., 1973, Ph.D. (hon.), 1974; children—Charles Michael, Treasa Louise Friend. Buyer, Bomarc program, Boeing Co., Eglin AFB, Fla., 1959-60; buyer-supr. Minuteman missile, Cape Canaveral, Fla., 1961-65, Saturn program Kennedy Space Center, Fla., 1965-71; contracts adminstr. Boeing Services Internat., Inc., Kennedy Space Center, 1971-77, contracts mgr., 1977-81, contracts mgr. U.S. Army Nat. Tng. Center, Ft. Irwin, Calif., 1981-82. Served with U.S. Army, 1944-46; now col. Res. Mem. Res. Officers Assn. (pres.), Nat. Contract Mgmt. Assn., Nat. Guard Assn. U.S. Democrat. Baptist. Club: Masons. Home: 1155 N Courtney Pkwy Apt F-117 Merritt Island FL 32952 Office: Complex 34 Kennedy Space Center FL 32815

JENKINS, CLARA BARNES, educator; b. Franklinton, N.C.; d. Walter and Stella (Griffin) Barnes; B.S., Winston-Salem State U., 1939; M.A., N.C. Central U., 1947; Ed.D., U. Pitts., 1965; postgrad. N.Y. U., 1947-48, U. N.C.-Chapel Hill, N.C. Agrl. and Tech. State U.; m. Hugh Morris Jenkins, Dec. 24, 1949 (div. Feb. 1955). Faculty Fayetteville State U., 1945-53, Rust Coll., Holly Spring, Miss., 1953-58; asst. prof. Shaw U., 1958-64; now prof. edn. and psychology St. Paul's Coll., Lawrenceville, Va.; vis. prof. edn. Friendship Jr. Coll., Rock Hill, S.C., summer 1947, N.C. Agr. and Tech. State U., summers 1966-83. Former mem. bd. dirs. Winston-Salem State U. United Negro Coll. Fund Faculty fellow, 1963-64; grantee Am. Bapt. Conv., Valley Forge, Pa., 1963-64. Mem. AAUP, Nat. Soc. for Study Edn., NEA, AAUW, Am. Hist. Assn., Va. Edn. Assn., Am. Acad. Polit. and Social Sci., AAAS, Internat. Platform Assn., Doctoral Assn. Educators, Assn. Tchr. Educators, Marquis Biog. Library Soc., Am. Assn. for Higher Edn., Acad. Polit. Sci., Am. Psychol. Assn., History of Edn. Soc., Soc. for Research in Child Devel., Jean Piaget Soc., Philosophy of Edn. Soc., Soc. Profs. Edn., Kappa Delta Pi, Phi Eta Kappa, Phi Delta Kappa, Zeta Phi Beta. Episcopalian. Home: 920 Bridges St Henderson NC 27536 Office: St Pauls Coll Lawrenceville VA 23868

JENKINS, CLAUDE, III, fire chief; b. Cin., Oct. 3, 1947; s. Claude and Lillian (Manggrum) J.; m. Nancy Lee Adams, Mar. 19, 1971; children—Michelle, Claude. B.S., Central State U., Ohio, 1970; postgrad. U. Md., 1974, Nat. Fire Acad., 1983. Chief fire dept. Central State U., Wilberforce, Ohio, 1972-79, City of Albion, Mich., 1979-82, City of Greenville, Tex., 1982-85, City of Bryan, Tex., 1985—. Mem. Internat. Assn. Fire Chiefs. Roman Catholic. Lodges: Mason, K.C., Rotary. Home: 4101 Warwick Ln Bryan TX 77802 Office: City of Bryan PO Box 1000 Bryan TX 77805

JENKINS, DANIEL, electronics technician, insurance broker; b. Memphis, Sept. 10, 1937; s. Daniel and Irene (Bannister) J.; m. Ida Regine Powell, Nov. 21, 1959; (div. June 1970); children—Levane Rene, Shardon Fay Jenkins Raddick; m. 2d, Geneva Mason, Oct. 5, 1970; 1 dau., Charmain I. Student Wilberforce U., 1956-59; A.S. in Engring. Tech., J.S. Reynolds Community Coll., 1976; B.S. in Bus., Va. State U., 1983. Lic. ins. broker, Va. Electronic technician Philip Morris U.S.A., Richmond, Va., 1970—; ins. agt. Mut. of N.Y., Richmon, 1978-80; ins. broker Jefferson First, Richmond, 1980—; pres. Jefferson First Clearing House, Inc. and Assocs., Richmond, 1981-82; tchr. math. Richmond City Sch. System. Mem. adv. com. Urban Assistance Incentive Fund, 1979; mem. State Bd. for Community Colls., 1979-83; minority advisor to Congressman Thomas J. Bliley, Jr., 1981; candidate for city council City of Richmond, 1977. Served with USN, 1959-68. Recipient Disting. Service award 3d Dist. Republican Com. of Va., 1982. Mem. Alpha Phi Alpha. Republican. Baptist. Club: Richmond First. Home: 2918 Seminary Ave Richmond VA 23220 Office: PO Box 26603 Richmond VA 23261

JENKINS, DAVID ALAN, association executive; b. Corning, Iowa, Dec. 16, 1952; s. Roy Bennett and Patricia Sue (Burton) J.; m. Kim Renee Hooten, Mar. 17, 1979. B.M.E., U. Idaho, 1974; M.M., Ohio U., 1977. Gen. mgr. trainee Affiliated Home Ctrs., 1976-77; adminstrv. resident Methodist Hosps. Dallas, 1978-79, dir. communications, 1979-80, project coordinator, mktg. analyst, 1979-80; v.p. Oak Cliff C. of C., Dallas, 1980, acting gen. mgr., 1980-81, exec. v.p., 1981-82, pres., 1982-83; exec. v.p. Odessa C. of C., 1983—. Mem. Econ. Devel. Bd., City of Dallas; 1st v.p. U.S. Hwy. 67 Assn., 1983; mem. planning council Lakeview Reservoir; mem. Odessa Indsl. Devel. Corp., Odessa Health Facilities Corp.; bd. advisors Salvation Army; bd. dirs. local YMCA. Mem. U.S. C. of C., Dallas Area C. of C. (pres. 1982), Tex. C. of C. Execs., So. Assn. C. of C. Execs., East Tex. C. of C. Execs. Republican. Methodist. Home: 4800 Oakwood Apt 9A Odessa TX 79761 Office: 660 S Zang Dallas TX 75208

JENKINS, ED (EDGAR) LANIER, congressman; b. Towns County, Ga., Jan. 4, 1933; s. Charlie Swinfield and Evia Mae (Souther) J.; A.A., Young Harris Coll., 1951; LL.B., U. Ga., 1959; m. Beni Jo Thomasson, Dec. 27, 1959; children—Jan, Amy. Admitted to Ga. bar, 1959; adminstrv. asst. to Rep. Phil M. Landrum, 1959-62; asst. U.S. atty. No. Dist. Ga., 1963-65; sr. partner firm Jenkins & Landrum, Jasper, Ga., 1965-76; mem. 95th-99th Congresses from

9th Ga. Dist., 1977—. Served with USCG, 1952-55. Mem. Ga., Am. bar assns., Farm Bur., VFW, Am. Legion. Democrat. Baptist. Club: Lions. Office: 217 Cannon House Office Bldg Washington DC 20515

JENKINS, FRANCES OWENS, boutique executive; b. Leonard, Tex., Nov. 12, 1924; d. R. Melrose and Maureen (Durrett) Owens; m. William O. Jenkins (div. 1961). Student theatre arts East Tex. State U., 1939-42, Ind. U., 1945-48, U. Tenn., 1954-56. Fashion model Rogers Modeling Agy., Boston, 1950-52, Rich's, Knoxville, Tenn., 1955-60; owner, instr. Arts Sch. of Self-Improvement and Modeling, Knoxville, 1959-69; owner, pres. Fran Jenkins Boutique, Knoxville, 1964—; cons. Miss Am. Pageant, Knoxville, 1958-66. Actress Carousel Theatre, Knoxville, 1955-58. Office: Fran Jenkins Boutique 315 Mohican Homberg Sq Knoxville TN 37919

JENKINS, HARVEY CLARKE, art educator; b. Bamburg, S.C., Mar. 27, 1934; s. James Edgar Clark and Estelle (Brockington) J.; m. Fannie Williams, Aug. 13, 1961; children—Harvette, Harvey Jr., Harvil. B.A., Claflin Coll., 1958; M.A., Columbia U., 1959; Ph.D., U. Wis.-Madison, 1983. Art instr. Claflin Coll., 1959-63; photographer Collegiate Photography, Orangeburg, S.C., 1960-63; assoc. prof. art Fayetteville State U., N.C., 1963—; artist-in-residence, Fayetteville, 1958—; free lance photographer, Fayetteville, 1963—. Contbr. articles to profl. jours. Pres., Neighborhood Watch Assn., Fayetteville, 1982-84; sec. Mayor's Neighborhood Watch Council, 1983-84, Served with USAF, 1954-57. Named Most Eligible Bachelor, Ebony Mag., 1961; recipient U. Wis. Advanced Opportunity fellow, 1978-81. Mem. Nat. Art Edn. Assn., Nat. Conf. Artists, N.C. Cultural Arts Coalition, Fayetteville Art Guild, Arts Council of Fayetteville, Alpha Kappa Mu, Pi Lambda Theta, Phi Beta Sigma (pres. 1957-58). Democrat. Club: Wizard Racquet (pres. 1982—). Avocations: reading; writing; tennis; chess; aikido. Home: 727 Ashburton Dr Fayetteville NC 28301 Office: Fayetteville State U Murchison Rd Fayetteville NC 28301

JENKINS, HOLLY MAYNARD, sales administrator; b. Chgo., Dec. 18, 1953; d. John Sellman and Gloria (Mann) Maynard; m. Justin Heywood Jenkins, Nov. 19, 1979. A.A., St. Marys Coll., 1974; B.A., U. S.C., 1976. Sales rep. IBM, Greenville, S.C., 1977-79; account exec. Sta. WSPA-TV, Greenville, dir. devel. retail, Spartanburg, S.C., 1984-85, mgr. local sales, 1985, dir. regional sales, 1985—. Author: Caterin' to Charleston, 1981. Mem. Advt. Fedn. Am., Advt. Fedn. Greenville (pub. service award 1980-81), Advt. Fedn. Spartanburg (chmn. com. 1985—, bd. dirs. 1985—), Am. Women in Radio and TV, DAR, Huguenot Soc. of Founders in Colony of Va., Huguenot Soc. S.C., Daus. of Am. Colonists, Chi Omega. Avocations: cooking; hunting. Home: 303 Kings Mountain Dr Greer SC 29651 Office: WSPA-TV PO Box 1717 I 85 and I 26 Spartanburg SC 29301

JENKINS, JAMES MICHAEL, restaurant company executive; b. Los Angeles, Sept. 7, 1946; s. J.C. and Janet (Mae) Jenkins; m. Joan Eileen Gloden, Aug. 8, 1983; 1 dau. by previous marriage, Cheryl. Student, Calif. State U.-Northridge, 1964, 68-70. With S & A Restaurant Corp., Dallas, 1970-79, v.p., 1979-83, pres., 1983—, also dir.; exec. v.p., gen. mgr. Big Boy Restaurant System, 1985—; with Great Earth Vitamins, Inc., Irvine, Calif., 1979, Sambo's Restaurant Corp., Dallas., 1979; dir. Pace Fin. Mgmt. Inc., Genesis Venture Inc. Mem. Dallas Citizens Council, Tex. Assn. Taxpayers; vice chmn. Dallas Friday Group. Served with USAF, 1964-68. Mem. Am. Mgmt. Assn. Republican. Club: Toastmasters.

JENKINS, JENNIFER ELAINE, nursing administrator; b. Owatonna, Minn., Mar. 5, 1948; d. Ivor Neville and Anna May (Fuls) J.; m. William Demetri Theodorou, Sept. 10, 1983. R.N., Youngstown Hosp. Assn. Sch. Nursing, 1969; B.A. with honors in Biology, U. Tenn., 1978; M.B.A., Memphis State U., 1983. R.N., Tenn. Staff nurse, sr. instr. Harford Meml. Hosp. Sch., 1969-75; staff nurse, head nurse E. Tenn. Children's Hosp., Knoxville, 1975-77, dir. nursing, 1977-78; dir. profl. services So. Health Systems Home Health Agy., Memphis, 1984—; v.p. nursing LeBonheur Children's Med. Ctr., Memphis, 1978—; faculty mem. Creative Nursing Mgmt., Mpls., 1985; cons. nursing, Memphis, 1982—. Author: Flexible Concepts in Pediatrics, 1978. Editor: Assn. Care of Children in Health, 1984. Chairperson, Opening Ceremonies, Memphis in May Internat. Festival, 1984-85; v.p. Midsouth Eyebank, 1984—. Youngstown Hosp. Assn. scholar, 1969, Mem. Am. Soc. Nursing Service Adminstrs., Tenn. Soc. Nursing Service Adminstrs. (past pres.). Republican. Episcopalian. Office: LeBonheur Children's Med Ctr Children's Plaza Memphis TN 38103

JENKINS, JOHN FRANCIS, hospital biomedical engineer; b. Youngstown, Ohio, Aug. 10, 1946; s. Lloyd Garrison and Wilhemina Marie (Thompson) J.; m. Helen Annis Lovell, Jan. 17, 1968 (div. Jan. 1980); 1 child, Jeffrey; m. Terri Adele Tucker, May 10, 1980. A.A.S., DeVry Tech. Inst., Chgo., 1967. Dir. biomed. electronics Doctors Hosp., Washington, 1974-76, Arlington Hosp., Va., 1976-79; dir. biomed. engring., Youngstown Hosp. Assocs., Ohio, 1979-82; clin. equipment services supr. SunHealth Inc., Baton Rouge, 1982-85. Served with U.S. Army, 1967-71. Mem. Am. Soc. for Hosp. Engring., Assn. for Advancement of Med. Instrumentation, Nat. Fire Protection Assn., Am. Hosp. Assn. (mem. clin. engring. steering com. 1982-83), La. Hosp. Assn. Capital Area Med. Equipment Soc. (founder, pres. 1977-78). Republican. Methodist. Avocations: bowling; swimming; bike riding; tennis; racquetball.

JENKINS, MARIE HOOPER, manufacturing company executive, engineer; b. Alexandria, La., Apr. 22, 1929; d. Jesse Joseph and Katie B. Hooper; m. Charles Edward Jenkins, Jan. 28, 1950; children—Nancy Marie, Charles Edward. B.S. in Chem. Engring., U. Wash., 1956. Founder, prin. Decision Systems, Austin, Tex., 1975-76; chmn. bd., pres. NAPP Inc. and subsidiary LACE Engring., 1977—. Active Leadership Tex. program Tex. Found. for Women's Resources. Mem. Am. Inst. Chem. Engrs. (chmn. Mojave Desert sect.), Calif. Soc. Profl. Engrs. (founding sec., treas. Desert Empire chpt.), Tex. Soc. Profl. Engrs., Nat. Soc. Profl. Engrs., Leadership Tex. Alumni Assn. Episcopalian. Home: 2505 Dormarion Ln Austin TX 78703 Office: NAPP Inc & LACE Engring 2104 Kramer Ln Austin TX 78758

JENKINS, ROBERT ELLSWORTH, JR., biologist, conservation association executive; b. Lewistown, Pa., Sept. 30, 1942; s. Robert Ellsworth and Ellen Magdalena (Wesner) J.; m. Diane Alyce St. Pierre, Nov. 5, 1964; children—Heather Elizabeth, Robert Ellsworth. A.B. in Biology, Rutgers U., 1964; Ph.D. in Biology, Harvard U., 1970. Ecology advisor Nature Conservancy, Arlington, Va., 1970-72, v.p. sci., 1972—, dir. natural heritage programs, 1974—; mem. Fed. Com. Research Nat. Areas, Washington, 1970-73, Fed. Com. Ecol. Res., Washington, 1974—; mem. adv. council Ctr. for Plant Conservation, Boston, 1984—; mem. bd. Rare Animal Relief Effort, N.Y.C., 1975-78. Co-author: The Preservation of Natural Diversity, 1975. Contbr. articles on biol. conservation, info. mgmt. to profl. jours. Founder, chmn. Zero Population Growth, Mass., 1968-70; bd. dirs. Planned Parenthood League, Mass., 1970-73; mem. U.S. Nat. Com. UNESCO, Washington, 1972-74; mem. U.S. Man and Biosphere Com., Arlington, Va., 1978—; mem. adv. council Kai Moku Found., San Francisco, 1973-76. Orgn. Tropical Studies fellow, 1965; Richmond fellow, 1965-69; Population Council Demographic fellow, 1969-70; recipient Nat. Conservation award Am. Motors Corp., 1978. Fellow AAAS (mem. council 1971-75); mem. Am. Inst. Biol. Scis. (bd. govs. 1970—), Ecol. Soc. Am., Inst. for Conservational Biology (mem. sci. adv. bd. 1984—), Ctr. for Plant Conservation (sci. adv. bd. 1984—), Xerces Soc. (counsellor 1985—). Avocations: fly fishing; hunting; natural history; gardening. Home: RFD 1 Box 15 Warrenton VA 22198 Office: The Nature Conservancy 1800 N Kent St Suite 800 Arlington VA 22209

JENKINS, ROGER LANE, educator; b. June 16, 1946; B.S. in Bus. Adminstrn., Berea (Ky.) Coll., 1968; M.B.A., E. Tenn. State U., 1970; Ph.D., Ohio State U., 1976; m. Basia Matthews. Acct., Shell Oil Co., Tenn., 1965-66; asst. to treas. Berea Coll., 1966-68; auditor Kemper Ins., Chgo., 1967, 68; internat. acct. Eastman Kodak, 1969-76; instr. acctg. E. Tenn. State U., 1970-73; asst. dir. grad. bus. programs Ohio State U., 1973-76, asst. prof. mktg., 1977-78; asst. prof. U. Tenn., Knoxville, 1978-80, asso. prof., 1980—, also dean Grad. Bus. Programs; chmn. research Grad. Mgmt. Admissions council. Warren Wilson scholar, 1963-65; James S. Kemper scholar, 1966-68; Albert Herring fellow, 1976. Mem. Am. Mktg. Assn., So. Mktg. Assn., Midwest Mktg. Assn., Acad. Mktg. Sci. (program chmn. 1984, v.p. 1984-86), Assn. Consumer Research, Am. Inst. Decision Sci. (mktg. book rev. editor 1979-80), Acad. Internat. Bus. Office: 527 Stokely Mgmt Center University of Tennessee Knoxville TN 37916

JENKINS, RONALD BRADFORD, English educator; b. Rockingham, N.C., Nov. 14, 1941; s. Henry Clay and Eva Gray (Dowd) J.; m. Karen Tilden Davis, Mar. 10, 1973; children—Colby Bradford Holman, Drake Bradford Dorner. B.A., Wake Forest U., 1964; M.A., N.C. State U., 1970; Ph.D., U. N.C., 1976. Tchr. English, East So. Pines High Sch., Southern Pines, N.C., 1964-66; instr. Vardell Hall Jr. Coll., Red Springs, N.C., 1966-68; teaching asst. N.C. State U., Raleigh, N.C., 1968-70; instr. Winthrop Coll., Rock Hill, S.C., 1970-72; teaching asst. U. N.C., Chapel Hill, 1972-75, instr., 1975-76; asst. prof. English, Campbell U., Buies Creek, N.C., 1976-77, assoc. prof., 1977-78, Victor R. Small prof. English, 1978-79, chmn. dept. English, 1977-79; prof., chmn. dept. English and Speech, Ga. Coll., Milledgeville, 1979—. Author: Milton and the Theme of Fame, 1973; Henry Smith: England's Silver-Tongued Preacher, 1983; also articles on English and Am. lit. Recipient Disting. Grad. Faculty Publ. award Ga. Coll. Faculty, 1985. Mem. South Atlantic MLA, Southeastern Renaissance Conf., MLA Am., Renaissance Soc. Am., Phi Kappa Phi. Republican. Episcopalian. Lodge: Rotary. Avocations: reading; classical music; water sports. Home: 220 S Liberty St Milledgeville GA 31061 Office: Ga Coll Dept English and Speech Milledgeville GA 31061

JENKINS, TERRY SUSAN, geriatrics psychologist, program developer; b. Clifton Forge, Va., Sept. 24, 1949; d. Warren Edward and Gladys Belle (Dillard) Montgomery; m. Larry Richard Jenkins, June 5, 1971. B.A., Radford Coll., 1970; M.A., Va. Commonwealth U., 1977, Ph.D., 1982. Social worker Richmond Social Services, Va., 1971-77; geropsychologist Comprehensive Mental Health Services, Virginia Beach, 1977-84, supr. Older Adult Services, 1985—; adj. faculty dept. family medicine Eastern Va. Med. Sch., Norfolk, 1983—, dept. gerontology, Va. Commonwealth U., 1984—; co-dir. Dementia Ctr. Hampton Roads, Norfolk, 1983—; program cons. Parkinson's Disease Support Group, Virginia Beach, 1983—. Author: Mental Health and Aging: A Guide to In-Service Training, 1983. Bd. dirs. Lake Placid Civic League, Virginia Beach, 1985. Recipient Humanitarian award Alzheimer's Disease and Related Disorders Assn., 1983, Jefferson award Am. Inst. Pub. Services, 1984, Disting. Alumnus award Va. Commonwealth U., 1985. Mem. Am. Psychol. Assn. Avocation: music. Office: Comprehensive Mental Health Services Pembroke Three Suite 109 Virginia Beach VA 23462

JENNE, KENNETH CLARENCE, II, lawyer, state senator; b. New Haven, Dec. 1; s. Kenneth Clarence and Virginia J.; B.A. in Govt., Fla. Atlantic U., 1968; J.D., Fla. State U., 1972; m. Caroline Maslanka, Nov. 21, 1975; children—Sarah Elizabeth Anne, Evan Boyd. Bar: Fla. Asst. state atty. 17th Jud. Circuit, Broward County, Fla., 1972-74; exec. dir. Broward County Charter Commn., 1974; commr. County of Broward, from 1975, chmn., 1976; mem. Fla. State Senate, 1978—; partner Atkinson Golden Jenne Diner & Henry, P.A., Hollywood, Fla.; lectr. Nova U., Biscayne Coll.; dir. Cypress Savs. and Loan Assn. Bd. dirs. Salvation Army, Multiple Sclerosis Found., United Way. Served with USAR. Mem. Ft. Lauderdale C. of C. (dir.), Fla. Bar Assn., ABA, Am. Judicature Soc., Phi Alpha Delta, Phi Rho Pi, Omicron Delta Kappa. Democrat. Episcopalian. Club: Civitan. Home: 5001 Polk St Hollywood FL 33020 Office: 1946 Tyler St Hollywood FL 33020

JENNINGS, BETTY JEAN MC DONALD, educator, model, consultant; b. Houston, May 10, 1930; d. Ernest Bois and Jessie Leah (Tullis) Mc D.; m. James N. Jennings, June 1954 (div.); 1 child, Lesajean Mc Donald. B.S. in Home Econs. Prairie View U., 1949, M.Ed. in Adminstrn. and Supervision, 1958; M.A. equivalent in Costume Design, Pratt Inst., 1951. Cert. educator, supr., counselor, Tex. Instr. home econs. Wiley Coll., Marshall, Tex., 1953-56; tchr. needle trades, adult edn. Houston Ind. Sch. Dist., 1956-79, vocat. counselor, 1979-81, placement specialist, 1981-83, asst. dir. bus. and industry, 1983-84, asst. dir. vocat. curriculum devel., 1983—; mem. faculty, cons. Prairie View U., Tex., 1975-82; free-lance fashion show coordinator, Houston, 1956—; free-lance model, Houston, 1956—. Author poetry. Judge, Tex. Astro Bluebonnet Beauty Pageant, 1978-85; fashion coordinator Tex. Local and State Bluebonnet Beauty Contest, 1978-83; mem. Houston Election Campaign, 1981-83, 84-85. Recipient Woman of Yr. award Houston Fashion Guild, 1976; Outstanding Models' award Tom Kato Models Found., 1976; Outstanding Adminstrv. Service award Yates Faculty and Adminstrv. Staff, 1979; Dist. award Boy Scouts Am., 1979, 84. Mem. Houston Profl. Assn., NEA, Am. Vocat. Assn., Tex. Indsl. and Vocat. Assn., Iota Lambda Sigma, Epsilon Phi Tau, Delta Sigma Theta. Democrat. Baptist. Avocations: teaching; singing; travel; youth activities; acting. Home: 1317 Live Oak St Houston TX 77003 Office: Houston Ind Sch Dist Occupational and Continuing Edn Div 3830 Richmond Ave Houston TX 77027

JENNINGS, BRUCE MARTIN, III, oil well services company manager; b. Woodward, Okla., Aug. 25, 1947; s. Bruce M. and Ruby Bernice (Locke) J.; B.S., Tex. A&I U., 1970, M.A., 1974; m. Jennifer Littleton, Dec. 23, 1970; children—Beau Ryan, Tate Alan, Erica Lyn. Field chemist Halliburton Services, Corpus Christi, Tex., 1974-76; div. chemist S.W. Tex. div., Halliburton Services, 1976-79; mgr. research/devel. Nat. Cementers Corp., Grand Junction, Colo., 1979-80; mgr. U.S. ops. Am. Fracmaster Inc., Chanute, Kans., 1980-81; sta. mgr. Nat. Cementers Corp., 1981-83; tech. sales rep. Nat. Chems., Oklahoma City, 1983-84, mgr., 1984—; lectr. Served with USN, 1970-72. Rob & Bessie Welder Wildlife Found. grantee, 1970; Caeser Kleberg scholar, 1970. Mem. Soc. Petroleum Engrs. of AIME, Western Slope Oilfield Indsl. League, Am. Petroleum Inst., Nat. Rifle Assn. Republican. Presbyterian. Office: 3600 S Council Rd Oklahoma City OK 73179

JENNINGS, FRANK CLAY, author, publisher, printing company executive; b. Garrard County, Ky., June 30, 1913; s. Hamlet Manford and Jane (Reynolds) J.; student pub., pvt. schs. Ky.; m. Helen Maurine Music, Aug. 24, 1940. Area fin. officer Fed. Works Agy., Ky., 1935-41; chief wage adminstr. War Dept., Ft. Knox, 1942-46; free lance writer, 1947-49; assoc. editor Thoroughbred Record, 1950-51, mng. editor, 1952-54, exec. dir. Thoroughbred Record, Inc., gen. mgr. Thoroughbred Press, Inc., 1955-78, treas., 1957—; dir. v.p., treas. Record Pub. Co., Inc., 1963-80. Mem. Lexington Kennel Club, Throughbred Club Am., Thoroughbred Farm Mgrs., Blue Grass Sportsmens' League. Club: Lafayette. Home: 1715 Courtney Ave Lexington KY 40502 Office: PO Box 580 Lexington KY 40586

JENNINGS, J. BENNY, mayor. Mayor of Chesapeake, Va. Office: PO Box 15225 Chesapeake VA 23320*

JENNINGS, JOHN JAMES, waste management and investment consultant; b. N.Y.C., May 26, 1947; s. Michael J. and Catherine M. (Dugan) J.; B.S., St. John's U., 1968, M.B.A., 1970; cert. investment analysis N.Y. Inst. Fin., 1969; m. Wendy Christina Larson, June 7, 1975; 1 dau., Christina Laurel. Portfolio mgr., analyst G.A. Saxton & Co., Inc., N.Y.C., 1968-69; dir. mktg. Acad. Applied Motivation, 1970-72; exec. v.p. Entrepreneurial Devel. Corp., Inc., Amherst, N.Y., 1972-73, now dir.; pres. IWM, Inc., Orlando, Fla., 1973—; v.p. Indsl. Waste Services, Inc., 1981—; dir. Storybook Village, Inc., Indsl. Waste Mgmt., Inc., Jennings & Jennings Assos., Inc. Chmn., Citizens and Pvt. Bus. Awareness Com., 1977, 78, 79; mem. Pres.'s Conf. Ind. Bus. Recipient Tablet Cath. Action award, 1967, Human Relations award C.A.U.S.E., 1968; Motivator of Year award, 1972. Hon. fellow Truman Library Inst. Mem. Assn. Investment Brokers, Soc. Advancement Mgmt., Nat. Solid Waste Mgmt. Assn. (steering com.), Bus. Adminstrn. Soc. Seminole City Bd. Realtors, Smithsonian Assos. Roman Catholic. Office: 100 Amberwood Ct Longwood FL 32750

JENNINGS, JOSEPH ASHBY, banker; b. Richmond, Va., Aug. 12, 1920; s. Joseph Ashby and Leone (Bishop) J.; B.S., U. Richmond, 1949; grad. certificate Stonier Grad. Sch. Banking, Rutgers U., 1952; m. Anne Barrow Hatcher, Oct. 29, 1960; children—Joseph Ashby III, Ashby Anne. With United Va. Bank, Richmond, 1949—, v.p., 1956-66, sr. v.p., 1966-67, exec. v.p., 1967-71, pres., 1971, chmn. bd., 1972—, also dir.; vice chmn. bd. United Va. Bankshares, Inc., 1972-75, pres., 1975-76, chief adminstrv. officer, 1972-76, chmn. bd., chief exec. officer, 1976—; dir. Life Ins. Co. Va., Investors Mortgage Ins. Co., Va. Life Ins. Co. N.Y., Western Employers Ins. Co., United Va. Bankshares, Inc., Universal Leaf Tobacco Co. Trustee U. Richmond, Union Theol. Sem., Hollins Coll., Va. Found. Ind. Colls.; capital funds bd. United Givers Fund; mem. Va. Bus. Council; mem. pres.'s council Old Dominion U. Served with USAAF, 1942-46. Mem. Fin. Analysts Fedn. (past exec. v.p., dir.), Phi Beta Kappa, Omicron Delta Kappa, Phi Delta Theta, Beta Gamma Sigma. Presbyterian. Office: 919 E Main St Richmond VA 23219

JENNINGS, TONI, state senator; b. Orlando, Fla., May 17, 1949; B.A. cum laude, Wesleyan Coll., 1971; postgrad. Rollins Coll., 1972. Elem. sch. tchr., 1971-73; corp. officer Jack Jennings & Sons, Inc., 1973—; former mem. Fla. Ho. of Reps.; now mem. Fla. Senate; mem. Nat. Conf. State Legislators. Recipient Prominent Personality of Month award, 1980; Outstanding Service award Home Builders Assn. Mid Fla., 1980; Legislator of Yr. award Orange County Young Rep. Club, 1981; Freedom award for Excellence in State Govt., Women for Responsible Legislation, 1982; numerous other awards in recognition of outstanding legis. service. Mem. Assn. Builders and Contractors, Central Fla. Builders Exchange, Orlando-Winter Park Bd. Realtors, Kappa Delta Epsilon, Delta Kappa Gamma (hon.). Republican. Office: Fla Senate Office Bldg Tallahassee FL 32301

JENNISON, BEVERLY ANN, marriage and family counselor, educator; b. Texarkana, Ark., Dec. 11, 1945; d. Frank Luck and Florence Devin (Holmes) Berry; m. Raymond Ellis Jennison, June 30, 1979. B.A., E. Tex. State U., 1968, M.S., 1983. Tchr. spl. edn. Texarkana Ind. Sch. Dist., Ark., 1969-83; dir. Women in Need, Greenville, Tex., 1983—. Mem. Am. Sociol. Assn., Alpha Delta Phi. Episcopalian. Home: 3608 Henry St Greenville TX 75401 Office: Pediatric Clinic 4818 Wellington St Greenville TX 75401

JENSEN, JERRY KIRTLAND, industrial engineer, diversified company executive; b. Chgo., Sept. 27, 1947; s. Harry Dybdahl and Violet May (Novak) J. B.S. (John McMullen scholar 1965-69), Cornell U., 1969, M.Indsl. Engring., 1971. Cert. in prodn. and inventory mgmt. Pres., Jensen's Cinema 16, Western Springs, Ill., 1970—; indsl. engr. Gen. Foods, Chgo., 1970-72, sr. indsl. engr., 1972-73, prodn. scheduling supr., 1973-74, prodn. control mgr., 1974-76; mgmt. systems specialist Beatrice Foods Co., Chgo., 1976-77, operating services project mgr., 1977-79, mgr. indsl. engring., 1980-84; mgr. mfg. services Louver Drape div. Beatrice, Memphis, 1984-85, Memphis ops. mgr., 1985—; v.p., sec. Country Residential, Inc., Western Springs and Crystal Lake, Ill., 1978—. Author: (with Dr. Joel Ross) Productivity, People and Profits, 1981; contbr. (with Ted Olson) Productivity Improvement: Case Studies of Proven Practice, 1981. Film festivals chmn. Western Springs Recreation Commn., 1969-70, 73-84; active Theatre of Western Springs, 1983-84, Theatre of Memphis, 1984—. Mem. Am. Prodn. and Inventory Control Soc., Gt. Lakes English Springer Spaniel Breeders Assn. (pres. 1979-81), Am. Inst. Indsl. Engrs. (productivity com., v.p. services, Chgo. chpt.), Alpha Phi Omega, Beta Theta Pi. Club: Cornell. Office: Louver Drape div Beatrice Window Coverings 3921 Delp St Memphis TN 38118

JENSEN, OSCAR CHARLES, JR., college administrator; b. Balt., Mar. 11, 1935; s. Oscar Charles and Helen Ann (Hughes) J.; m. Elizabeth Kent, June 22, 1957; children—Melanie Lynn, Robert Allan, James Hall, Daniel Hughes. B.S., Towson State Coll., 1957; M.Ed., Western Md. Coll., 1961; D. Higher Edn., U. Md., 1972. Tchr. Balt. County Bd. Edn., Towson, Md., 1957-65; assoc. Md. State Tchrs. Assn., Balt., 1965-78; contract dir. Md. State Bd. Higher Edn., Annapolis, Md., 1978-79; v.p. Yankton Coll. (S.D.), 1979-84; dir. fin. and adminstrv. services W.Va. No. Community Coll., Wheeling, 1984—. Mem. Md. Gov.'s Com. on Sch. Fin., 1970, Mayor's Com. on Volunteerism, Balt., 1972-76. Recipient Citizenship award United Way of Md., 1977. Fellow Am. Sch. Health Assn.; mem. NEA (life), Md. Sch. Health Council (founding mem., chmn. 1972-76), Am. Assn. for Higher Edn., Nat. Assn. Coll. and Univ. Bus. Officers. Democrat. Episcopalian. Avocations: rug hooking; fishing. Home: 1328 Valley View Ave Wheeling WV 26003 Office: WVa No Community Coll College Square Wheeling WV 26003

JENSEN, RICHARD LELAND, research entomologist; b. Stanton, Nebr., June 1, 1937; s. Walter and Eva (Voelker) J.; B.S., Southeastern La. U., 1963; M.S., La. State U., 1968, Ph.D., 1971; m. Susanne Maria Dienhart, Aug. 22, 1959; children—Markus M., Christof M. Quality control chemist Allied Chem. Corp., 1963-65; research asso. La. State U., 1965-71, asst. prof. entomology, 1971-75; chmn. So. Regional Tech. Com. for Research on Soybeans, 1973-74; pres. Jensen Agrl. Cons., Inc., 1975—; agrl. cons. Claretian Fathers for Maya Indians, 1975—. Named to Crop Profls. Hall of Fame, 1983. Mem. Entomol. Soc. Am., Am. Registry Profl. Entomologists, La. Entomol. Soc., So. Weed Sci. Soc., Plant Growth Regulator Working Group, Nat. Alliance Ind. Crop Cons., La. Agrl. Cons. Assn. (pres. 1979), Baton Rouge Mental Health Assn., La. Arts and Scis. Assn., La. Agrl. Cons. Assn. (pres. 1979-80), La. Farm Bur. Assn., Am. Soybean Assn., La. Pathol. and Nematological Soc., Gamma Sigma Delta. Club: 13 (Southeastern La. U.). Contbr. to profl. jours.; book rev. editor. Home and office: 1125 Glenmore Ave Baton Rouge LA 70806 also PO Box 71 Lebeau LA 71345

JENSEN, WALTER EDWARD, JR., finance, insurance and law educator, lawyer; b. Chgo., Oct. 20, 1937. A.B., U. Colo., 1959; J.D., Ind. U., 1962, M.B.A., 1964; Ph.D. (Univ. fellow), Duke U., 1972. Bar: Ind. 1962, Ill. 1962, D.C. 1963, U.S. Tax Ct. 1982, U.S. Supreme Ct. 1967. Assoc. prof. Colo. State U., 1964-66; assoc. prof. Ill. State U., 1970-72; prof. bus. adminstrn. Va. Poly. Inst. and State U., beginning 1972, now prof. fin., ins. and law; with Inst. Advanced Legal Studies, U. London, 1983-84; prof. U.S. Air Force Grad. Mgmt. Program, Europe, 1977-78, 83-85; Duke U. legal research awardee, researcher, Guyana, Trinidad and Tobago, 1967; researcher U. London Inst. Advanced Legal Studies, London Sch. Econs. and Inst. Commonwealth Studies, summers, 1969, 71, 74, 76, winter 1972-73; Ford Found. research fellow Ind. U., 1963-64; faculty research fellow in econs. U. Tex., 1968; Bell Telephone fellow in econs. regulated pub. utilities U. Chgo., 1965. Recipient Teaching award Ind. U., 1964, Dissertation Travel award Duke U. Grad. sch., 1968; Ind. U. fellow, 1963, 74, scholar, 1963-64. Mem. D.C. Bar Assn., Ill. Bar Assn., Ind. bar Assn., ABA, Am. Polit. sci. Assn., Am. Soc. Internat. Law, Am. Judicature Soc., Am. Bus. Law Assn., Alpha Kappa Psi, Phi Alpha Delta, Pi Gamma Mu. Contbr. articles to profl. publs.; staff editor Am. Bus Law Jour., 1973—; vice chmn. assoc. editor for adminstrv. law sect. young lawyers Barrister (Law Notes), 1975-83; book rev. and manuscript editor Justice System Jour: A Mgmt. Rev., 1975—; staff editor Bus. Law Rev., 1975—. Home: PO Box 250 Blacksburg VA 24060 Office: VA Poly Inst and State U Blacksburg VA 24060

JENTZ, GAYLORD ADAIR, educator, author; b. Beloit, Wis., Aug 7, 1931; s. Merlyn Adair and Delva (Mullen) J.; B.A., U. Wis., 1953, J.D., 1957, M.B.A., 1958; m. JoAnn Mary Hornung, Aug. 6, 1955; children—Katherine Ann, Gary Adair, Loretta Ann, Rory Adair. Bar: Wis. 1957. Pvt. practice law, Madison, 1957-58; from instr. to asso. prof. bus. law U. Okla., 1958-65; vis. instr. to vis. prof. U. Wis. Law Sch., summers 1957-65; assoc. prof. U. Tex., 1965-68, prof., 1968—, Herbert D. Kelleher prof. bus. law, 1982—, chmn. gen. bus. dept., 1968-74, 80—. Served with AUS, 1953-55. Recipient Outstanding Tchr.'s award Tex. U. Coll. Bus., 1967, Jack G. Taylor Teaching Excellence award, 1971, Joe D. Beasley Teaching Excellence award, 1978; Outstanding Achievement in Edn. award Alpha Kappa Psi, 1979; Disting. Contbns. award CBA Found. Adv. Council, 1979; James C. Scarboro Meml. award Colo. Grad. Sch. Banking, 1983. Mem. Am. Arbitration Assn. (nat. panel 1966—), Am. Bus. Law Assn. (pres. 1971-72, Faculty award of excellence 1981), So. (pres. 1967) bus. law assns., Tex. Assn. Coll. Tchrs. (pres. Austin chpt. 1967-68, exec. com. 1969-70, state pres. 1971-72), SW Fedn. Adminstrv. Disciplines (v.p. 1979-80, pres. 1980-81), Wis. Bar Assn., Phi Kappa Phi (pres. 1983-84), Omicron Delta Kappa. Author: (with others) Business Law Text and Cases, 2d edit., 1968; Texas Uniform Commercial Code, 1967, rev. edit., 1975; (with others) Business Law Text and Cases, 1978, West's Business Law Text and Cases, 3d edit., 1986, West's Business Law: Alternate UCC Comprehensive Edition, 2d edit., 1984; dep. editor Social Sci. Quar., 1966-80, mem. editorial bd., 1980—; staff editor Am. Bus. Law Jour., 1967-69, editor-in-chief, 1969-74, adv. editor, 1974—; contbr. articles to profl. jours. Home: 4106 North Hills Dr Austin TX 78731

JERNER, R. CRAIG, metallurgical engineer, consultant; b. St. Louis, Oct. 12, 1938; s. Roland Axel and M. Marie (Hayes) J.; m. C. Elizabeth Johnson, June 7, 1957; children—Michael, Lisa, Stephen, Beth. B.S. in Metall. Engring., Washington U., St. Louis, 1961, M.S. in Metall. Engring., 1962; Ph.D. in Metallurgy, U. Denver, 1965. Registered profl. engr., Okla. Research assoc., metall. div. Research Inst., U. Denver, 1962-65; prof. metall. engring., U. Okla., Norman, 1965-78, asst. dean, grad. coll., 1971-72; chmn. bd., mem. sr. profl. staff S.W. Metall. Cons., Inc., Norman, 1973-79; pres., mem. sr. profl. staff Emtec Corp., Norman, 1979—. Contbr. articles to profl. jours. Served with U.S. Army, 1956-64. Mem. Am. Soc. Metals, AIME, ASTM, Acad. Forensic Sci. Registered Profl. Baptist. Home: 2816 Castlewood Dr Norman OK 73069 Office: Emtec Corp 3503 Charleston Rd Norman OK 73069

JERNIGAN, WARREN HAMILTON, civic worker; b. Pensacola, Fla., Apr. 25, 1937; s. William and Edna (Jones) J.; student George Washington U., 1959, U. Md., 1964-67; m. Helen Demirtashev, Jan. 31, 1959; children—Warren

Hamilton, Robert William. Doorman, U.S. Ho. of Reps., Washington, 1958-63, chief doorman, 1963-78, legis. asst. to Rep. Robert L.F. Sikes, 1967-77. Vice pres. Fla. Council Handicapped Orgns., Inc., chmn. membership com. 1980-81, sr. lobbyist on handicapped affairs to Fla. Legislature, 1980; pres. United Meth. Men, Arlington (Va.) United Meth. Ch., 1977-78, also former mem. several adminstrv. coms.; former instnl. rep. Boy Scouts Am., Cub Scouts Am.; pres. Patrick Henry Elem. Sch. PTA, 1977; asst. sgt.-at-arms, asst. doorkeeper Democratic Nat. Conv., 1972, 76; appeared in motion picture F.I.S.T.; chmn. Escambia County Dem. Exec. Com., 1980; mem. policy com. Fla. Gov.'s Conf. on Aging, 1980; mem. external equal access/equal opportunity com. Pensacola Jr. Coll.; vice chmn. Coordinating Council of Transp. Disadvantaged, 1979—; mem. Fla. Transp. Policy Study Commn.; Pensacola Mayor's rep. on handicapped affairs; mem. adv. com. on urban elderly and handicapped transp. Pensacola Urbanized Area Met. Planning Orgn.; chmn. subcom. sect. 504, Citizen Adv. Com. on Transp.; chmn. Subcom. on Transp. Facility Barriers to Handicapped Persons; pres. Pensacola Pen Wheels, Inc.; vice chmn. Gulf Coast Com. for Disabled Artists; treas. Pensacola Employ the Handicapped Council, 1980, pres., 1981; mem. adv. bd. for Escambia County, CETA; mem. adv. bd. West Fla. Hosp.; mem. exec. com., advancement chmn., dist. com. Boy Scouts Am., Pensacola, also mem. camping com. Gulf Coast council; leader Pensacola Scenic Pass 4-H Club; bd. dirs. Boy's Club Escambia County, Epilepsy Soc. N.W. Fla.; chmn. Housing for Handicapped Com., HRS Dist. 1; mem. Fla. Gov.'s Com. on Employe the Handicapped, 1981; del. White House Conf. on Aging, 1981; lobbyist Fla. State Coordinating Council, 1981; mem. pvt. sector research group Fla. Gov.'s Task Force on Sr. Citizens Employment and Volunteerism, 1983; mem. exec. bd., chmn. human service com. Job Partnership Tng. Act, 1983; mem. Fla. Commn. on Ethics, 1983; chmn. Gov.'s Commn. on Handicapped Concerns, 1983; chmn. S.E. region Pres.'s Com. on Employ The Handicapped; cons. Fla. State Coordinating Council on Transp. Disadvantaged. Recipient Service to Mankind award Sertoma Club, 1980; named Vol. of Yr., Pensacola, Fla., 1982. Mem. U.S. Ho. of Reps. Doormen's Soc. (founder, pres. 1969-77, editor-in-chief Threshold 1972-76, Exemplary Service award 1971, Meritorious Service to U.S. award 1975), Pensacola C. of C. (chmn. mass transit subcom., mem. comml. carriers task force, land use task force), Ensley/Cantonment C. of C. (dir., chmn. handicapped affairs), Bream Fisherman Assn. N.W. Fla., Assn. Worshipful Masters (pres. Washington 1977). Clubs: Pensacola Press (chmn. fin. com.); Masons, Scottish Rite.

JESSUP, HILLARY JEANNE, psychologist; b. Los Angeles, July 22, 1945; d. Clifford Magee and Jean (Lichty) May; m. George Terrill, May 15, 1971; 1 child, Jonathan. B.A., U. So. Calif., 1969, M.A., 1971; Ph.D., Tex. A&M U., 1980. Tchr. English and phys. edn. Centinela Valley Ind. Sch. Dist., Los Angeles, 1969-71; grad. asst. Tex. A&M U., College Station, 1972-74, 77-79, undergrad. counselor, 1979-81, profl. counselor, 1981—; counselor grades K-12 Sommerville Ind. Sch. Dist., Tex., 1974-77; cons. Wellness Inst., College Station, 1985—. Fund raiser Planned Parenthood, Bryan, Tex., 1984. Mem. Brazos Valley Psychol. Assn., Am. Psychol. Assn., Tex. Psychol. Assn., Brazos Valley Panhellenic Assn. (sec.-treas. 1982-84, v.p. 1984-85), Phi Delta Kappa (v.p. 1981-82, Achievement award 1982), Phi Delta Gamma (v.p. 1983-84), Alpha Phi (scholarship adviser Epsilon Omega chpt. 1982—). Clubs: Briarcrest Country, Aerofit (Bryan); Tex. A&M Women's Social (v.p. 1982-83). Avocations: travel; interior decorating; antique collecting; snow skiing. Home: 720 N Rosemary Dr Bryan TX 77802 Office: Acad Services Tex A&M U Acad Bldg Room 101 College Station TX 77843

JESSUP, JOE LEE, management consultant; b. Cordele, Ga., June 23, 1913; s. Horace Andrew and Elizabeth (Wilson) J.; B.S., U. Ala., 1936; M.B.A., Harvard U., 1941; LL.D., Chung-Ang U., Seoul, Korea, 1964; m. Genevieve Quirk Galloway, Aug. 29, 1946; 1 dau., Gail Elizabeth. Sales rep. Proctor & Gamble, 1937-40; liaison officer bur. pub. relations U.S. War Dept., 1941; spl. asst. and exec. asst. Far Eastern div. and office exports Bd. Econ. Welfare, 1942-43; exec. officer office deptl. adminstrn. Dept. State, 1946; exec. sec. adminstr.'s adv. council War Assets Adminstrn., 1946-48; v.p. sales Airkem Capitol & Service Co., 1948-49; pres. Joe L. Jessup & Co., 1957—; exec. v.p., gen. mgr. Hunter Labs., Inc., Fairfax, Va., 1965-69, also dir., mem. exec. com. to 1969; asso. prof. bus. adminstrn. George Washington U., 1949, prof., 1952-57, prof. emeritus, 1977—, asst. dean Sch. Govt., 1951-60; dir. Giant Food, Inc., Washington, 1971-75, mem. audit com., 1974-75; dir. Internat. Careers Inst., Inc., Los Angeles, 1972-73; coordinator resources mgmt. program U.S. Air Force, 1951-57; regional chmn. Harvard Bus. Sch. Fund, 1960-61; del. 10th Internat. Mgmt. Conf., Sao Paulo, Brazil, 1954, 11th, Paris, 1957, 12th, Sydney and Melbourne, Australia, 1960, 13th, N.Y.C., 1963, 14th, Rotterdam, Holland, 1966, 15th, Tokyo, 1970, 16th, Munich, Germany, 1973; mem. Md. Econ. Devel. Adv. Commn., 1973, 75. Nat. adv. council Center for Study of Presidency, N.Y.C., 1974—; mem. Arlington County (Va.) CSC, 1952-54; trustee Tng. Within Industry Found., Summit, N.J., 1954-58. Served from 2d lt. to lt. col. AUS, 1941-46. Decorated Bronze Star; recipient certificate of appreciation Sec. Air Force, 1957. Mem. Acad. Mgmt. Clubs: University (Washington); Coral Ridge Yacht, Tower (Ft. Lauderdale); Harvard (N.Y.C.). Home: 2801 NE 57th St Fort Lauderdale FL 33308

JETER, KATHERINE FEAGIN, enterostomal therapist, b. Langley, Va., Oct. 25, 1938; d. John A. and Katherine D. (Terrell) Feagin; m. John Randolph Jeter, Jr. Apr. 5, 1958; children—Sara Ann, John Randolph III, Stephen T. Student U. Tex., 1955-58; B.S. in Sociology, SUNY, 1977; M.A. in Counseling, Ball State U., 1977; Ed.D., George Washington U., 1981; cert. enterostomal therapy Emory U., Woodruff Med. Center, 1972. Enterostomal therapist Squier Urol. Clinic, Babies and Presbyn. Hosps., N.Y.C., 1968-72; practice enterostomal therapy, 1973-75; cons. Orange County (Calif.) Med. Center, U. Calif., Irvine, 1974-75; vis. prof. Volusia Acad. of Medicine, Daytona Beach, Fla., 1972, Halifax Hosp. Med. Center, Daytona Beach, 1973, John Hopkins Sch. Nursing, Balt., 1975, Tucson Med. Ctr., 1975, Handikappinstitutet, Bromma, Sweden, 1977; guest lectr. to various med. orgns. and schs., 1970—; now clin. asst. prof. urology Med. U. S.C., Charleston, also adj. prof. psychology U. S.C., Union; founder, pres. bd. dirs. HIP, Inc. Author: Count Your Blessings, 1965; Management of the Urinary Stoma, 1970; Urinary Ostomies: A Guidebook for Patients, 1972, rev. edit., 1977; These Special Children: The Ostomy Book for Parents of Children with Colostomies, Ilestomies, Urostomies, 1982; contbr. articles on rehab. of ostomy patients to profl. jours. Chmn. Pediatric Vols. for ARC, 1963-65. Named Mil. Wife of Yr., Western region U.S. Army Recruiting Command, 1973. Mem. United Ostomy Assn. (hon.), Volusia Acad. Medicine (hon.), Internat. Assn. Enterostomal Therapy (pres. Calif. div. 1973), Internat. Ostomy Assn., World Council Enterostomal Therapy, Am. Cancer Soc. (service com. Orange County unit 1974), Jr. League, Kappa Alpha Theta. Methodist. Home: 502 Park Dr Union SC 29379 Office: 128 Dillon Dr PO Box 8306 Spartanburg SC 29305

JETER, KATHERINE LESLIE BRASH, lawyer; b. Gulfport, Miss., July 24, 1921; d. Ralph Edward and Rosa Meta (Jacobs) Brash; B.A., Tulane U., 1943, J.D., 1945; m. Robert McLean Jeter, Jr., May 11, 1946. Admitted to La. bar, 1945; asso. mem. Montgomery, Fenner & Brown, New Orleans, 1945-46, Tucker, Jeter & Jackson, and predecessor firms, Shreveport, La., 1947—; judge pro tempore 1st Jud. Dist. Ct., Caddo Parrish, La., 1982-83. Pres., Little Theatre Shreveport, 1966-67, YWCA, 1963, LWV, 1950-51; treas. Am. Nat. Theatre and Acad., Shreveport, 1963; hon. consul of France in Shreveport, 1982—; 1st v.p. Shreveport Art Guild, 1973-74, pres., 1974-75. Mem. ABA, La. Bar Assn. Shreveport Bar Assn. (pres.-elect 1986), Public Affairs Research Council (trustee 1976-81, pub. affairs exec. com. 1981—), Nat. Assn. Women Lawyers, La. State Law Inst. (council), Jr. League Shreveport, Order of Coif, Phi Beta Kappa. Editor Tulane Law Rev., 1945. Home: 3959 Maryland Ave Shreveport LA 71106 Office: 905 La Tower 401 Edwards St Shreveport LA 71101

JEWELL, DONALD OLIVER, business psychologist, educator; b. Chgo., June 7, 1940; s. George Earl and Leanna Mae (Berdine) J.; m. Sandra Fuller Beldt, Dec. 4, 1981; 1 dau., Jennifer Elizabeth. B.S. in Psychology, Valparaiso U., 1962; Ph.D. in Psychology, So. Ill. U., 1967. Asst. instr. psychology So. Ill. U., Carbondale, 1962-64; instr., 1965-66; assoc. prof. psychology Purdue U., 1967-68; prof. mgmt. and urban life Ga. State U., Atlanta, 1968—; instr. Valparaiso U. (Ind.), 1964-65; pres., ptnr. The Mescon Group, Atlanta; organizational design cons. Mem. adv. bd. Ga. Consumer Services Program; chmn. bd. dirs. Lullwater Sch.; bd. dirs. United Way agys. EEOC Guidelines Program; chmn. tech. adv. bd. Ga. Peace Officers Selection and Tng. Council. NSF summer fellow. Mem. Am. Psychol. Assn., Am. Inst. Decision Scis., Sigma Xi. Author: Dynamic Incentive Systems, 1975; Women as a Management Resource, 1977, also numerous articles, abstracts, presentations and book chpts. Office: Georgia State U Atlanta GA 30303

JEWELL, HAROLD AARON, clinical psychologist; b. Newark, Jan. 7, 1941; s. Harold and Eleanor (Brandel) J.; m. May Christiansen, Aug. 18, 1975; children—Kerri, Jason. A.A., Orange County Community Coll., 1969; B.A., SUNY-New Paltz, 1971; M.S., Fairleigh Dickinson U., 1978; Ph.D., Calif. Sch. Profl. Psychology, 1982. Lic. psychologist, Tex. Psychology intern Calif. Men's Colony, San Luis Obispo, 1978-79, Madera Community Mental Hosp., Calif., 1979-80; drug rehab. counselor Baart Methadone Clinic, Fresno, Calif., 1980-82; staff psychologist Lubbock Mental Health/Mental Retardation, Tex., 1982-85, pvt. psychologist, 1985—; pvt. practice psychology, Lubbock, 1984—; health related affiliate Charter Plains Psychiat. Hosp., Lubbock, 1985—, West Tex. Hosp.; cons. Tex. Boys Ranch, Lubbock, 1985—. Served with U.S. Army, 1961-64. Mem. Am. Psychol. Assn., Lubbock Psychol. Assn., Nat. Health Service Provider. Baptist. Avocations: creative writing; camping; athletics.

JIMENEZ, ANDRES LAUREANO, psychiatrist; b. Ciego de Avila, Cuba, July 4, 1943; s. Armando A. and Juanita J.; B.S., Colegio de Belen, 1960; B.S., John Carroll U., 1967; M.S., Case Western Res. U., 1969; M.D., U. Miami, 1973; m. Lucila Venet, Aug. 19, 1967; children—Andres Francisco, Javier Eduardo, Cristina Elena. Intern, Jackson Meml. Hosp., Miami, Fla., 1973-74, resident in psychiatry, 1974-76; dir. geropsychiatric unit Cedars of Lebanon Health Care Center, Miami, 1977-78; chief psychiatrist Miami Mental Health Center, 1978; staff psychiatrist Douglas Gardens Geriatric Mental Health Center, Coral Gables, 1977-83; mem. panel Mental Health Adminstr.'s Program, 1980—; clin. instr. U. Miami Med. Sch., 1976—. Bd. dirs. Fellowship House, Miami, United Family and Childrens Services, Miami. Mem. Am. Psychiat. Assn., Am. Acad. Psychiatry and Law, Am. Assn. Geriatric Psychiatry. Roman Catholic. Office: 470 Biltmore Way Coral Gables FL 33134

JIMENEZ-TORRES, CARLOS FEDERICO, physician; b. Aguada, P.R., Oct. 19, 1921; s. Carlos Jimenez and Pura Torres; student U. P.R., 1936-39; M.D., George Washington U., 1943; postgrad. radiology U. Pa., 1948-49; m. Domitila Ferrer, June 18, 1949; children—Lorraine, Carlos Federico, Luis Javier, Pura Elaine, Janet Arlene. Intern, Fajardo Dist. Hosp., 1943-44; resident Presbyn. Hosp., Phila., 1949-51; physician VA Center and Hosp., San Juan, P.R., 1946-48; practice medicine specializing in radiology, Ponce, P.R., 1952—; instr. radiology U. Pa. Sch. Medicine, 1950-51; lectr. radiology U. P.R. Sch. Medicine, 1952—; asso. clin. prof. radiology Cath. U. P.R. Sch. Medicine, 1979—; cons. radiology Ponce Med. Center. Bd. dirs., past treas. Liceo Ponceno. Served with AUS, 1944-46. Diplomate Am. Bd. Radiology. Mem. Am., Pan Am., P.R. med. assns., Am. Coll. Radiology, P.R., Inter-Am. radiol. socs., Radiol. Soc. N.Am., Am. Legion, USCG Aux., U.S. Power Squadron. Roman Catholic. Clubs: KC, Lions (past dist. zone chmn., past pres. Ponce), Ponce Yacht (past commodore). Home: 16 Universidad St Ponce PR 00731 Office: Lorraine Bldg Ponce PR 00731

JO, JULIO CIPRIANO, mechanical contractor; b. Cienfuegos, Cuba, Sept. 26, 1942; s. Julio and Margarita (Nazco) J.; m. Kathryn F. Christian, Dec. 17, 1966; 1 son, Julio J. B.S. in Indsl. Engring., U. Ala., 1968. Sales engr. Johnson Controls, Inc., Milw. and Tampa, Fla., 1968-70; gen. mgr. Controles Joseco S.A. de C.V., Mexico City, 1970-73; pres. J & J Engring., Inc., Miami, 1973—. Mem. Planning Adv. Bd. of Dade County (Fla.). Mem. Am. Arbitration Assn., Inst. Indsl. Engrs., ASHRAE, Latin Builders Assn. (pres. 1982-84). Republican. Roman Catholic. Club: Ocean Reef (Key Largo, Fla.). Home: 12620 Ramiro St Coral Gables FL 33156 Office: 10460 SW 187th Terr Miami FL 33157

JOBE, TONY BRYSON, airline executive, lawyer; b. Washington, Aug. 29, 1943; s. William Theodore and Marguerite (Hendrickson) J.; m. Karen Elaine Forbes, May 4, 1982. B.A. in English, Southwestern U., Memphis, 1966; J.D., Tulane U., 1974. Bar: La. 1975. Prin. law firm Jobe & Assocs., New Orleans, 1975—; pres., chief exec. officer Air New Orleans, 1981—. Bd. dirs. New Orleans Ballet, 1981-83. Served to capt. (as pilot) USMC, 1967-71. Decorated D.F.C. Mem. Internat. Soc. Air Safety Investigators, ABA, Assn. Bar City N.Y., Assn. Trial Lawyers Am., Attys. Info. Exchange Group (exec. bd. 1979—). Republican. Presbyterian. Club: New Orleans Downtown Tennis. Office: Jobe & Assocs 427 Gravier St 3rd Floor New Orleans LA 70130

JOBE, WARREN YANCEY, electric utility company executive; b. Burlington, N.C., Nov. 12, 1940; s. Talmage Moton and Frances (Malone) J.; m. Sally Crumpler, June 6, 1964; children—Warren Yancey, Marshall Cooper. B.S. in Bus. Adminstrn., U. N.C.-Chapel Hill, 1963. C.P.A., N.C., Ga. Tax mgr. Arthur Andersen & Co., Charlotte and Atlanta, 1963-71; asst. comptroller dept. tax So. Co. Services, Inc., Atlanta, 1971-75; v.p., comptroller Ga. Power Co., Atlanta, 1975-81, sr. v.p., comptroller, 1981-83, sr. v.p., group exec., 1982, exec. v.p. fin., 1982—, also dir. Chmn. bd. mgmt. Ashford Dunwoody YMCA, 1983—. Mem. Am. Inst. C.P.A.s, N.C. Soc. C.P.A.s, Ga. Soc. C.P.A.s, Fin. Execs. Inst., Edison Electric Inst., Emory U. Mgmt. Conf. Bd. Methodist. Office: PO Box 4545 Atlanta GA 30302

JOE, HOWARD TONG, chemist; b. Kwangtung, China, Apr. 10, 1937; came to U.S., 1950; s. Shiu Chung and Toi Yuen (Wong) J.; B.S., U. Calif., Berkeley, 1960, M.S. (scholar), 1970; Ph.D., U. Houston, 1975; m. Catherine Wong, Sept. 6, 1961; children—John C., Ann C. Mem. faculty U. Houston, 1973; chief chemist Petroleum Analytical Lab., Odessa, Tex., 1972; sr. research analyst NASA, Johnson Space Center, Houston, 1975-76; sr. chemist supr. Mobay Chem. Corp., Baytown, Tex., 1976—. Mem. Am. Chem. Soc. Baptist. Home: 911 Edgebrook Dr Baytown TX 77521 Office: Mobay Chemical Corp West Bay Rd Baytown TX 77520

JOE, RAYMOND HING, computer scientist; b. Lambert, Miss., July 13, 1956; s. Denny Wong and Lucille Hain (Shing) J. B.S., U. Miss., 1983. Asst. office mgr. Kuhn's Big K Corp., Oxford, Miss., 1977-78, asst. office mgr., dept. mgr., 1979-80; dept. mgr., acting asst. store mgr. Wal-Mart Corp., Oxford, 1981; sr. programmer Advanced Mgmt. Systems, Inc., Booneville, Miss., 1981-83; with W.F. Bealls Corp., 1983—. Exec. trustee Alpha Sigma Found., 1983—. Joan Hallett and William King Self Meml. scholar Self Found., 1974. Mem. Assn. for Computing Machinery, U. Miss. Am.-Chinese Assn., Zeta Beta Tau. Roman Catholic. Home: 849 2d St Marks MS 38646 Office: PO Box 543 214-A W College St Booneville MS 38829

JOHANNESSON, PAUL, advertising executive; b. Dover, N.H., Aug. 12, 1951; s. Philip William and Norma Theresa (Couture) J.; B.S. Bus./Advt., B.S. Bus./Pub. Relations, Fla. State U., 1973. Copywriter, prodn. mgr. WFSO Radio, Pinellas Park, Fla., 1973-74; account exec. Media Design Advt., Clearwater, Fla., 1975-76; promotion dir. Trizec Ltd., Clearwater, 1977-78; chief exec. officer Johannesson, Reeser & Assocs., Inc., St. Petersburg, Fla., 1978-83; chief exec. officer Johannesson, Kirk & MaHarry, Inc.; pres. LEO Promotions, Inc., St. Petersburg, 1979, Wet Tortugas Charters, St. Petersburg, 1980. Mem. Am. Advt. Fedn. (pres.; Addy awards, Charlie awards), St. Petersburg Advt. Fedn. (pres., trustee), Am. Assn. Advt. Agys. Club: Fla. Ocean Racing Assn. Office: 1 Corporate Dr Suite 327 Clearwater FL 33520

JOHANSON, KNUT ARVID, JR., engring. exec.; b. St. Augustine, Fla., Feb. 27, 1936; s. Knut Arvid and Constance Elinor (Harrison) J.; B.S. in Elec. Engring. Tex. A&I U., 1959; M.S. in Chem. Engring., U. Houston, 1978; m. Eleanor Marie Friesen, Nov. 28, 1956; children—Michael James, David Bryan, Phillip Arvid. Registered profl. engr., La., Tex., Calif. Instrumentation engr. maintenance dept. Union Carbide Corp., Texas City, Tex., 1959-67, sr. control systems engr., Taft, La., 1967-72, control systems commissioning engr. UNIFOS plant, Stenningsund, Sweden, 1971, group leader systems engring. group, Port Lavaca, Tex., 1973—; instr. LaMarque Ind. Sch. Dist., 1964-66, Victoria Coll., 1977. Served with U. S. Army, 1960-61. Mem. Instrument Soc. Am. (dist. v.p., exec. bd. 1975-77). Baptist. Contbr. articles to profl. jours. Home: 201 Wearden Dr Victoria TX 77904 Office: PO Box 186 Port Lavaca TX 77979

JOHN, MARY WIDRIG, arts program administrator, theatrical producer; b. Green Bay, Wis., Dec. 6, 1925; d. Read E. and Thelma (Melville) Widrig; m. Richard Curtis John (div.); 1 son, Richard C., Jr. B.S. in Theater, Northwestern U., 1947; M.S. in Theater, U. Wis., 1948; Ph.D., NYU, 1965. Founder, pres., chmn. bd. Milw. Repertory Theatre, 1954-58; dir. Ballard Sch. Continuing Edn., N.Y.C., 1961-65; producer plays in N.Y.C., including: Phedre, 1966, Colette, 1970, Dear Oscar, 1972; v.p., nat. dir. arts programs, Northwood Inst., Dallas, 1973—; pres., chmn. Spear Arts Edn. Trust, adminstrv. v.p. Inst. Advanced Studies Theatre Arts; bd. dirs. Dallas Opera Bd. Past officer Dallas Women's Ctr.; founder, v.p., Wis. Arts Found.; spl. cons. Milw. Jr. League Children's Art Programs. Recipient Disting. Women Northwood Inst. award, 1973; Modern Spirit award Milw. Newspaper Guild, 1955. Mem. Am. Soc. Tng. and Devel., Actor's Equity Assn., Zeta Phi Eta, Alpha Kappa Delta, Theta Sigma Phi (Milw. chpt. Community Service award, 1955). Office: Northwood Inst 2906 Maple Ave Rm 211 Dallas TX 75201 also 61 Jane St #14D New York NY 10014

JOHNSEN, PETER HENRY, lawyer; b. Balt., Feb. 16, 1950; s. Henry E. and Marion E. (Kummen) J.; m. Margaret Ellen Irwin, Aug. 27, 1972; children—Henry Alexander, Thomas Christopher, Peter Carl. A.B. summa cum laude, Dartmouth Coll., 1972; M.B.A., U. Va., 1976, J.D., 1976. Bar: Ind. 1976, Md. 1979. Assoc. law firm Barnes, Hickam, Pantzer & Boyd, Indpls., 1976-79, asst. counsel, 1976-79; assoc. counsel Potomac Electric Power Co., Washington, 1979-80; assoc. gen. counsel Planning Research Corp., McLean, Va., 1982—; dir. Washington Met. Area Corp. Counsel Assn., 1984—, sec., 1986—; newsletter editor, 1981-83. Newsletter editor Nat. Republican Lawyers Assn., 1985—. Mem. ABA, Md. Bar Assn., Ind. Bar Assn., Order of Coif, Phi Beta Kappa. Home: 7954 Helmart Dr Laurel MD 20207 Office: Planning Research Corp 1500 Planning Research Dr McLean VA 22102

JOHNSON, ADA AUSTIN, Spanish language educator; b. Maxton, N.C., May 24, 1932; d. David McBryde and Ada (Livingstone) Austin; m. David Donovon Johnson, Aug. 14, 1954; children—Elizabeth, Harriet, McBryde, Ross, Eric. A.B., U. S.C., 1953; M.A., U. N.C., 1965; Ph.D., U. S.C., 1975; postgrad. in French, Sorbonne, France, 1984. Prof. Spanish, Bapt. Coll. at Charleston, 1967—; dir. Scholar's Forum, Charleston, 1984—. Mem. S. Atlantic MLA, S.C. Fgn. Lang. Tchrs. Assn., MLA, Hispanic Soc. Charleston, Am. Assn. Tchrs. Spanish and Portuguese. Office: Bapt Coll at Charleston Dept Fgn Lang PO Box 10087 Charleston SC 29411

JOHNSON, AILEEN SEACAT, teacher educator, consultant; b. Granada, Colo., Sept. 3, 1933; d. Forrest and Edna Mildred (Sundgren) Seacat; m. Howard Walter Johnson, Sept. 3, 1950 (div. 1972); children—Carolyn Kay Johnson Passamonte, Marsha May, Larry Wayne. A.A., Muskegon Community Coll., 1963; B.A., Western Mich. U., 1967; M.A., Ariz. State U., 1970, Ph.D., 1975. Cert. elem. tchr., elem. supr., prin., reading specialist, supt. Tchr., Phoenix Elem. No. 1, 1968-72; office mgr. Scottsdale Psychiat. Ctr., Ariz., 1973-74; coordinator/outreach Ariz. State U., Tempe, 1974-75; from asst. prof. to assoc. prof. Pan Am. U., Brownsville, 1975-81, chmn. dept. edn., 1981-84; assoc. prof. Sul Ross State U., Alpine, Tex., 1985—; cons. to Tex. schs. Author: Tecnicas De Investigacion Pedagogica, 1980. Contbr. articles to Jour. Exptl. Edn., Elem. Sch. Jour., other publs. Border State U. Consortium grantee, 1979-80; Pan Am. U. grantee, 1984; Tandy Corp. grantee, 1985; Tex. Dept. Human Resources grantee, 1986; Sul Ross State U. grantee, 1985. Mem. Internat. Reading Assn. (sec. Dena Gallic Chpt. 1980-85), Southmost Assn. for Edn. of Youth Children (founder, v.p. 1977-85), Assn. for Supervision and Curriculum Devel., Internat. Reading Assn., Nat. Assn. for Bilingual Edn., Alpha Delta Kappa, Kappa Delta Phi. Avocations: traveling; macrame; gardening. Home: 903 E Brown Alpine TX 79830 Office: Sul Ross State U Box C115 Alpine TX 79830

JOHNSON, ALCEE LABRANCHE, educator; b. Fernwood, Miss., July 22, 1905; s. Jonas Edward and Bertha (LaBranche) J.; student Alcorn Coll., 1925; A.B., Fisk U., 1927; M.A., Columbia U., 1956; postgrad. U. So. Calif., 1962; Hum.D. (hon.), Miss. Bapt. Sem., 1972; m. Thelma M. Wethers, Dec. 25, 1931; children—Joyce Johnson Bolden, Al Wethers. Instr., Prentiss (Miss.) Inst. Jr. Coll., 1927-30, dir. instrn., 1931-36, 37-71, pres., 1971-81, pres. emeritus, 1981—; Miss. state supr. Survey Vocat. Edn. and Guidance, Office Edn., Dept. Interior, Washington, 1936-37; chmn. bd. dirs. State Mut. Fed. Savs. & Loan Assn.; inst. rep. Heifer Project, Inc. Mem. Miss. Regional Med. Program, Merit Commn. Miss. Econ. Council, Phelps-Stokes Fund Conf. Edn. Leaders; former chmn. Western div. Boy Scouts Am., com. mem. JDC Mut. Fed. Credit Union, 1960—; del. White House Conf. on Aging, 1971; mem. Miss. Probation and Parole Bd., 1972-76; mem. Voters League, 1964—, past pres.; bd. dirs. So. Miss. Planning and Devel. Dist. So. Interracial Commn. grantee, 1930; recipient Silver Beaver award Boy Scouts Am., 1960. Mem. Am. (life), Miss. (past pres.), 6th Dist. (past pres.) tchrs. assns., NEA (life), NAACP (local coordinator), Jefferson Davis County, Miss. chambers commerce, Alpha Phi Alpha, Phi Delta Kappa. Mem. Ch. of Christ (trustee). Club: Masons (33 deg.). Home: PO Box 112 Prentiss MS 39474 Office: PO Box 1107 Prentiss MS 39474

JOHNSON, ALPHONSE LINDY, hotel executive, consulting company executive; b. Washington, Aug. 20, 1951; s. Leonard and Tersilla (Van Riet) J. Grad., St. Lawrence Coll. (Eng.), 1971; B.S., U. Houston, 1976. Mgmt. trainee Portman Intercontinental, London, 1971-72, Westin Oaks, Houston, 1976-78; cons. Laventhol & Horwath C.P.A., Houston, 1977-78; front office mgr. Adam's Mark Hotel, Houston, 1978-79; hotel mgr. Mansion on Turtle Creek, Dallas, 1979-84; dir. Rosewood Hotels Inc., Dallas, 1984—; pres. Teralin, Inc. Cons. Group, 1982—; guest lectr. U. Houston Sch. Hotel Mgmt., 1976-79. Bd. dirs. Lifescape Villas Condominium Assn., 1982-83. Mem. Dallas County Hotel Assn. (chmn. employer relations com. 1983-84). Club: U. Houston (pres. Dallas chpt. 1982-83). Office: Rosewood Hotels Inc 4950 Thanksgiving Tower Dallas TX 75201

JOHNSON, ANGELA CANDELLA, computer systems analyst; b. New Orleans, July 27, 1952; d. Vick Charles and Joan Emma (Garzotto) Candella; m. Donald Joseph Donnaud, Aug. 10, 1973 (div. 1981); m. 2d, Carl Henry Johnson, Nov. 12, 1983. B.S., U. New Orleans, 1974. Research chemist Gulf South Research Inst., New Orleans, 1974-79; assoc. sci. analyst programmer Middle South Services, Inc., New Orleans, 1979-80, sci. analyst programmer, 1980-82, systems analyst, 1982-85, sr. analyst programmer, 1985—. Contbr. articles to profl. jours. Mem. U. New Orleans Alumni Assn., Alpha Lambda Delta. Roman Catholic. Office: Middle South Services Inc 3510 General De Gaulle Dr PO Box 61300 New Orleans LA 70161

JOHNSON, AUBREY HERMAN, constrn. co. exec.; b. Nashville, Aug. 2, 1919; s. W. Herman and Maggie Bell (Harris) J.; m. Malvin Fuller, Jan. 19, 1952; children—William Harry, Gayle Alan, Mark Tyler, Belinda Belle. Pres., Nashville-Middle Tenn. Home Builders, Mt. Juliet, Tenn., 1957—; nat. rep. Home Builders, Nashville, 1962-63; pres. Belinda City, Inc., Mt. Juliet, Tenn., 1962—; chmn. Home Owners Warranty of Middle Tenn., Mt. Juliet, Tenn., 1980—. Mem., Donelson CD, 1956-57. Mem. Ch. of Christ. Home: 344 S Mount Juliet Rd Mount Juliet TN 37122 Office: Belinda Pkwy Mount Juliet TN 37122

JOHNSON, BENJAMIN CLARK, police chief; b. Osceola, Iowa, Aug. 6, 1946; s. Clark Eugene and Paula (Reinhart) J.; m. Paula Gay. A.A.S. in Law Enforcement, McGennan Community Coll., Waco, Tex., 1978. Advanced cert. lic. peace officer, Tex. Sgt., Beverly Hills Police Dept., Waco, 1980-85; chief of police Eagle Lake Police Dept., Tex., 1985—. Served as sgt. USMC, 1966-71, Vietnam. Mem. Internat. Assn. Chiefs Police, Tex. Police Assn., Am. Fedn. Police, Tex. Assn. Vietnam Vets (pres. 1984, Appreciation cert. 1984), VFW (Appreciation cert. 1984). Club: Lions (Eagle Lake). Home: 106 Church St Eagle Lake TX 77434 Office: Eagle Lake Police Dept PO Box 35 Eagle Lake TX 77434

JOHNSON, BENJAMIN LEIBOLD, education specialist, training analyst; b. Norborne, Mo., Nov. 23, 1950; s. Murrell Faxton and Chlora Pauline (Naylor) J.; B.A., Central Mo. State U., 1971, B.S., 1974, M.S., 1976. Tchr., Raytown and Independence (Mo.) Public Schs., 1974-76; with Wayne Regan, Inc., Realtors, Shawnee, Kans., 1976; tchr., chmn. dept. social studies, English, French, Breckenridge (Mo.) Public Schs., 1979-80; career intern edn. specialist Ft. Sill, Okla., 1980-82, tng. analyst Directorate of Tng. and Doctrine, 1982-85; staff and faculty devel. div. Directorate of Tng. and Doctrine, U.S. Army Engr. Sch., Ft. Belvoir, Va., 1985—; dept. chmn. social studies, English and French, also edn. specialist. Served with USNR, 1976-79. Mem. Assn. Am. Geographers, Nat. Council Social Studies, Am. Acad. Polit. and Social Scis., Nat. Space Inst., Nat. Council Tchrs. English, Am. Congress on Surveying and Mapping, Naval Enlisted Res. Assn., Assn. Supervision and Curriculum Devel., Acad. Sci. Fiction, Fantasy and Horror Films, Nat. Rifle Assn., N. Am. Darting Assn., Assn. U.S. Army, Am. Square Dance Soc. Clubs: Masons, Scottish Rite. Mem. Order DeMolay. Home: 7519 Republic Ct #201 Alexandria VA 22306

JOHNSON, BETTY JO, early childhood educator; b. Rankin County, Miss., Aug. 14, 1940; d. Louis and Louise (Hayes) J. A.A., Piney Woods Sch., 1960; B.A., Tougaloo Coll., 1964; M.S. in Edn., Jackson State U., 1971; Ed.D.,

Memphis State U., 1976. Tchr., Jackson Pub. Schs., Miss., 1964-66; grad. teaching asst. Jackson State U., 1970-71, Memphis State U., 1973-76; instr. LeMoyne-Owen Coll., Memphis, 1976; asst. prof. elem. edn. Ark. State U., 1976-77, dir. Early Childhood Edn. Ctr., 1977; prof. Shelby State Community Coll., Memphis, 1978—; curriculum specialist Headstart, Jackson, 1971-72; program evaluator Dept. Pub. Welfare, Jackson, 1972-73. Mem. exec. com. Mid-South Muscular Distrophy Assn., Memphis, 1982-84; bd. dirs. Community Day Care and Comprehensive Social Services, Memphis, 1984—; adv. council Comprehensive Employment and Tng. Adminstrn., Memphis, 1982-83, Memphis Bd. Edn. Child Care and Guidance, 1982—. Mem. Nat. Assn. Edn. Young Children, So. Assn. Children Under Six, Tenn. Assn. Young Children (bd. dirs. 1980-84, Cert. Appreciation, 1981), Memphis Assn. on Young Children (treas. 1981-83), Delta Sigma Theta (chpt. sec. 1971-73). Methodist. Office: Shelby State Community Coll Dept Edn PO Box 40568 Memphis TN 38174-0568

JOHNSON, BILLY GAINES, state official; b. Sparta, Tenn., Mar. 7, 1930; s. Loretta (Mills) J.; m. Mary Janet Goodwin, Aug. 21, 1949; 1 child, Michael Gaines. B.S., Tenn. Tech., 1958; M.S., U. Tenn., 1959; Ed.S., U. Va., 1982. Expediter Harvey Machine Co., Torrance, Calif., 1953-55; Tchr., athletic dir., head football coach John S. Battle High Sch., Bristol, Va., 1959-63; asst. supr. health and phys. edn. Va. State Dept. Edn., Richmond, 1963-67, supr. driver edn., 1967—; element dir. Va. State Dept. Transp. Author safety guides; also articles. Mem. Transp. Safety Bd., Va., 1978—; bd. dirs. Richmond Area Safety Council, 1978—; mem. adv. bd. Dept. Transp. Safety, Hwy. Safety Research Council. Served with USN, 1949-53, Korea. Recipient Outstanding Safety award State of Va., 1970. Mem. Am. Driver Traffic Safety Edn. Assn. (bd. dirs., Merit award 1979), AAHPER, Va. Assn. Driver Edn. and Traffic Safety (Appreciation plaque 1977), Va. Assn. Health, Phys. Edn. and Recreation, State Suprs. Driver Edn. and Traffic Safety, Va. Safety Assn. (bd. dirs., sec.-treas.). Clubs: Richmond Touchdown, Sparta Civitan, YMCA. Home: 3707 Brookside Rd Richmond VA 23225 Office: Va Dept Edn PO Box 6Q Richmond VA 23216

JOHNSON, BOBBY DALE, mechanical engineer; b. Lubbock, Tex., Oct. 3, 1952; s. Dale Lemuel and Roberta Dayle (Reynolds) J.; m. Mary Annette Giles, Mar. 2, 1974; children—Samuel Blake, Lacy Erin. B.S. cum laude in Math. Edn., La. Tech. U., 1975, B.S.M.E., 1977. Registered profl. engr., La., Tex. Mech. engr. Arco Chem. Co., Channelview, Tex., 1977-80; project engr. Panhandle Eastern Corp., Houston, 1980-81; project engr. Protech div. Merichem Co., Houston, 1981-82, sr. engr., 1982-83, engring. services mgr., 1984-85, prodn. mgr., 1986—. Mem. ASME. Baptist. Home: 323 Edgeton Ct Houston TX 77015 Office: Merichem Co 600 Travis St Suite 4800 Houston TX 77002

JOHNSON, CARLETON ALBERT, clinical psychologist, educator; b. New Bedford, Mass., Dec. 18, 1929; s. Albert Ernest and Laurianna Alice (Maynard) J.; B.S., U. Wis., 1952; M.S., N.Mex. Highlands U., 1957; research fellow U. Tex., 1962-64; Ph.D., Heed U., Hollywood, Fla., 1975; D.Sc. (hon.), 1983; m. Gail Joyce Gilbert, June 29, 1957; children—Gregory, Laury, Thor, April. Asst. prof. psychology Drake U., 1964-68; chief assessment officer Peace Corps, P.R., 1968-71; fgn. service officer, Afghanistan, 1971-72; chief psychologist Central Va. Mental Health Clinics, Lynchburg, 1972-84; asst. prof. Randolph Macon Woman's Coll.; assoc. prof. Lynchburg Coll.; behavioral sci. preceptor U. Va. Sch. Medicine, 1979-82, clin. asst. prof., 1982—; cons. Peace Corps, 1977—; cons. Lynchburg Gen.-Marshall Lodge Hosps., Inc., 1977—, mental health cons., 1984—. Charter mem. Lynchburg Preservation Trust, 1979—; nat. adv. Heed U.; bd. dirs. Taxi Found. Served with AUS, 1947-48. NIMH fellow, 1960-62. Mem. Am. Psychol. Assn., Assn. Advancement Behavior Therapy, Sigma Xi, Psi Chi. Home: 1000 Court St Lynchburg VA 24504 Office: 2524 Langhorne Rd Lynchburg VA 24501

JOHNSON, CAROLYN LEE, nurse; b. Amherst County, Va., Oct. 10, 1939; d. Lewis Franklin and Martha Catherine (Wilkerson) Lee; m. Ralph Edward Johnson, Aug. 31, 1959 (div. 1972); children—Donald Lewis, Kendall Lee. R.N., Va. Bapt. Hosp. Sch. Nursing, 1959; B.S., Lynchburg Coll., 1980, M.Ed., 1985. Staff nurse Va. Bapt. Hosp., Lynchburg, 1962-66, asst. operating room supr., 1967-73, surg. instr., 1973-82, mgr. central service, 1982—. Mem. Assn. Operating Room Nurses, Internat. Assn. Central Service Mgmt., Assn. Central Service Personnel, Kappa Delta Pi. Republican. Avocations: piano; reading; knitting. Office: Va Baptist Hosp 3300 Rivermont Ave Lynchburg VA 24503

JOHNSON, CARYLENE, natural food store executive; b. Clearwater, Fla., Aug. 30, 1947; d. Caryl Mallory and Lizzie Bell (Plumlee) J.; m. Wendell Ford, 1967 (div. 1972); 1 son, Clinton Wendell; stepchildren—Wendy Marie, Janet Rene. Student pub. schs., Dunedin, Fla. Proofing clk. 1st Nat. Bank Clearwater, 1965-67; clk. credit dept. Montgomery Wards, 1967-68; office mgr., bookkeeper W.C. Shepard & Son Contractors, Dunedin, 1968-74; clk. Caryl's Natural Foods, Inc., Clearwater, 1974-76, co-owner, pres., mgr., New Port Richey, Fla., 1978—; nutritional cons., lectr. Excelsior Health Spa, New Port Richey; lectr. local clubs. Bd. dirs. Pasco County Hosp. Mem. So. Health Orgn. (exec. sec., conv. dir., meeting planner), Nat. Nutritional Foods Assn. (conv. com.), West Pasco C. of C., Com. of 100. Contbr. to local TV mag. on nutrition TV Tempo; subject of article in Health Foods Retailing, 1981. Office: Caryl's Natural Foods Inc 6616 US Hwy 19 New Port Richey FL 33552

JOHNSON, CHARLES EDGAR, educator; b. Rochester, N.Y., July 6, 1919; s. Mason Frank and Ethel Clithero (Lyons) J.; B.S., SUNY, Geneseo, 1946; M.S., UCLA, 1948; M.Ed., U. Ill., 1950, Ed.D., 1952; m. Rita Irene Boyd, July 19, 1963. Tchr., Mt. Morris, N.Y., 1946-47, Geneseo, N.Y., 1948-49; asst. prof. U. Kans., Lawrence, 1951-55; asso. prof. U. Ill., Urbana, 1955-65; prof. edn. U. Ga., Athens, 1965—, asso. dir. Research and Devel. Center, 1965-68, dir. Ga. Ednl. Models, 1968-75, tchr. Assessment Project, 1976-81; ednl. researcher Spencer Press, Chgo., Grolier Inc., N.Y.C., 1958-62; vis. prof. U. P.R., 1963-64; cons. tchr. edn. Ministry of Edn., Indonesia, 1980, 82. Served with AUS, 1941-46. Recipient Cert. of Merit, U. Ga., 1980. Mem. Am. Edn. Research Assn., Assn. Supervision and Curriculum Devel., Phi Delta Kappa, Kappa Delta Pi (tchr. educator award for excellence 1979). Baptist. Clubs: Elks, Masons. Designer competency based tchr. edn. program model and Ga. tchr. performance assessment instruments; contbr. numerous articles in field to profl. jours.; editor Holiday Series, Garrard Pub. Co., Champaign, Ill., 1962—. Home: 245 Pine Forest Dr Athens GA 30606 Office: Coll Edn U Ga 427 Aderhold Hall Athens GA 30602

JOHNSON, CHARLES LENARD, human resources executive; b. Hurlock, Md., Mar. 23, 1942; s. Monroe S. and Rachel E. (Jolley) J.; m. Harriet Arhoda Rock, Aug. 6, 1967; 1 child, Rhonda Charlene. B.S., Morgan State U., 1964; M.A., Antioch U., 1979. Commd. 2d lt. U.S. Army, 1964, advanced through grades to capt., 1966; served in Vietnam, 1966-67; resigned, 1969; employee relations specialist Gen. electric Co., Bridgeport, Conn., 1969-70, mgr. employment, 1970-71, employee relations specialist, Columbia, Md., 1971-73; mgr. employee relations Washington Suburban San. Commn., Hyattsville, Md., 1973-76, mgr. labor relations, 1976-77, asst. to dir. engring., 1980-82; dir. employee/labor relations Johns Hopkins Med. Instns., Balt., 1980-82; v.p. human resources Regional Med. Ctr. at Memphis, 1982—. Bd. dirs. Memphis Urban League, 1982—, Blue Cross/Blue Shield, Memphis, 1982-83, Alliance for Progress, Memphis, 1982—; mem. health services adv. bd. Memphis State U., 1982—; legis. adv. Rep. Dist. 87, Memphis, 1982—; chmn. personnel com. Howard County Govt., Columbia, 1980-82; community adv. County Exec., Howard County, 1979-82; polit. adv. East Side Democratic Club, Balt., 1980-82.; grad. Leadership Memphis, 1985; active Boy Scouts Am.; mem. allocations com. United Way, 1983—. Democrat. Methodist. Home: 8720 Edney Ridge Dr Memphis TN 38018 Office: Regional Med Ctr 877 Jefferson Ave Memphis TN 38103

JOHNSON, CHARLES OWEN, retired lawyer; b. Monroe, La., Aug. 18, 1926; s. Clifford U. and Laura (Owen) J.; B.A., Tulane U., 1946, J.D., 1969; LL.B., Harvard U., 1948; LL.M., Columbia U., 1955. Admitted to La. bar, 1949, practiced in Monroe, 1949-50; mem. law editorial staff West Pub. Co., St. Paul, 1953; atty. Office of Chief Counsel, Internal Revenue Service, Washington, 1955-79, chief Ct. Appeals br. Tax Ct. Div., 1968-79. Served with AUS, 1950-52. Mem. Fed., La. bar assns., Nat. Lawyers Club, Soc. Colonial Wars (past dep. gov. D.C. soc.), SAR, S.R. (past pres. D.C. Soc.), Soc. War of 1812 (past pres. D.C. soc.), S.C.V., Soc. Colonial New Eng. (gov. gen. nat. soc.), Sons Union Vets., St. Andrew's Soc. Washington, Royal Soc. St. George, Sons and Daus. of Pilgrims (gov. La. br.), Huguenot Soc. S.C., Huguenot Soc. La. (pres.), Soc. Descs. Jersey Settlers, La. Colonials, Jamestowne Soc., Soc. Descs. Old Plymouth Colony, Order Ams. of Armorial Ancestry (past pres.), Soc. Descs. Colonial Clergy (chancellor gen.), Hereditary Order Descs. Colonial Govs. (past gov. gen.), Order Founders and Patriots of Am. (gov. La. Soc.), Order First Families Miss. 1699-1817 (gov. gen. 1967-69), Mil. Order Stars and Bars (past judge adv. gen.), Soc. Cin., Hereditary Order First Families of Mass. (registrar gen.), Nat., Va. geneal. socs., Miss., Va. hist. socs., Phi Beta Kappa. Clubs: Pendennis (charter mem.), Round Table, Plimsoll (New Orleans); Arts, Army and Navy (Washington). Lodges: Masons, K.T., Shriners, Order Eastern Star. Author: The Genealogy of Several Allied Families, 1961. Home: 1750 Saint Charles Ave Apt 325 New Orleans LA 70130

JOHNSON, CLARENCE EUGENE, agricultural engineer, educator; b. Elk City, Okla., Nov. 1, 1941; s. Arthur C. and Lena A. (Patterson) J. B.S., Okla. State U., 1963; M.S., Iowa State U., 1968, Ph.D., 1969. Registered profl. engr., Iowa. Grad. research asst., instr. Iowa State U., Ames, 1963-70; assoc. prof. S.D. State U., Brookings, 1970-77; research engr. U.S. Dept. Agr. Agrl. Research Service, Pendleton, Oreg., 1977-79; prof. Auburn U. (Ala.), 1979—. Mem. Am. Soc. Engring. Edn., Am. Soc. Agrl. Engrs., Nat. Soc. Profl. Engrs., Internat. Soil Tillage Research Orgn., Sigma Xi, Phi Kappa Phi, Omicron Delta Kappa, Gamma Sigma Delta, Alpha Zeta, Alpha Epsilon. Baptist. Author, co-author over 40 articles and tech. papers related to agrl. engring. Office: Auburn U Agricultural Engineering Dept Auburn AL 36849

JOHNSON, CLIFFORD ROBIN, roofing and insulation company executive; b. Oklahoma City, Apr. 7, 1952; s. Damon Ray and Donna Mae (Knox) J.; m. Marion Leanna Daves, June 19, 1971; children—David M., Jennifer M., Sarah M. B.S., Southwestern State Coll., 1974. Estimator, Empire Roofing and Insulation, Tulsa, 1973-81, pres., 1981—, chmn., chief exec. officer, pres., 1982—; Mem. Midwest Roofing Contractors Assn. (dir. 1978-80, 82-84, tech. and research com. 1985—), Okla. Roofing Contractors Assn. (pres. 1983), Tulsa Exec. Assn. (dir. 1984), Constrn. Specification Inst. (dir. Tulsa chapt. 1976-83), Bldg. Owners and Mgrs. Assn., Tulsa C. of C., Assoc. Gen. Contractors. Republican. Baptist. Avocations: sailing; scuba diving. Home: 5252 W 85th Tulsa OK 74131 Office: Empire Roofing & Insulation Co PO Box 480 Tulsa OK

JOHNSON, CLIFTON HERMAN, historian-archivist, research center director; b. Griffin, Ga., Sept. 13, 1921; s. John and Pearl (Parrish) J.; student U. Conn., 1943-44; B.A., U. N.C., 1948, Ph.D. 1959; M.A. U. Chgo., 1949; postgrad. U. Wis., 1951; m. Rosemary Brunst, Aug. 2, 1960; children—Charles, Robert, Virginia. Tutor, LeMoyne Coll., Memphis, 1950-53, asst. prof., 1953-56, prof., 1960-61, 63-66; asst. prof. East Carolina Coll., 1958-59; asst. librarian and archivist Fisk U., 1961-63; exec. dir. Amistad Research Center, New Orleans, 1966—. Bd. dirs. La. World Expn., 1980-82, Lillie Carroll Jackson Mus., 1978—, Countee Cullen Found., 1981—, Friends of Archives La., 1978—, La. Folklife Commn., 1982—. Served with AUS, 1940-45. Mem. So. Hist. Assn., Soc. Am. Archivists, Assn. for Study Negro Life and History, Orgn. Am. Historians, Nat. Assn. Human Rights Workers. Author: (with Carroll Barber) The American Negro: A Selected and Annotated Bibliography for High Schools and Junior Colleges, 1968; editor: God Struck Me Dead: Religious Conversions and Experiences and Autobiographies of Ex-Slaves, 1969. Office: 400 Esplanade Ave New Orleans LA 70116

JOHNSON, DALE LADSWORTH, educator; b. Sanish, N.D., Jan. 27, 1929; s. R. Kenneth and Mildred Louise (Christensen) J.; m. Carmen Acosta, Jan. 31, 1952; children—Jay Lawrence, Heidi Anna, Paul Kenneth. B.A., U. N.D., 1951; M.A., Kans. U., 1954, Ph.D., 1957. Staff psychologist VA Hosp., Houston, 1957-60, dir. patient tng. lab., 1960-64; assoc. prof. psychology U. Houston, 1966-69, prof., 1969—; cons. St. Joseph's Hosp., Houston, 1978—. Pres., Citizens Alliance for Mentally Ill, Houston, 1984-85. Fulbright Hayes fellow, Norway, 1973-74. Mem. Am. Psychol. Assn., Am. Ednl. Research Assn., Soc. Research in Child Devel., Nat. Alliance for Mentally Ill. Democrat. Quaker. Home: 2101 Dunstan Houston TX 77005 Office: Dept Psychology U Houston Houston TX 77004

JOHNSON, DAVID EDSEL, mathematics educator; b. Chatham, La., Aug. 16, 1927; s. Dave Ernest and Bessie (Morris) J.; m. Frances White, Jan. 24, 1959; children—Stephen, Nancy, Sandra, Katherine. B.S., B.A., La. Tech. U., 1949; M.S., Auburn U., 1952, Ph.D., 1958. Prof. math. La. Tech. U., Ruston, 1954-62; prof. elec. engring. La. State U., Baton Rouge, 1962-83; prof. math. Birmingham-So. Coll., Ala., 1983—. Author: Mathematical Methods in Engineering, 1982; Manual of Active Filter Design, 1983; Basic Electric Circuit Analysis, 1984; A Funny Thing Happened on the Way to the White House, 1984. Served with USN, 1945-46, U.S. Army, 1952-54. Recipient Disting. Faculty award La. State U., 1982. Mem. IEEE (sr.), Am. Math. Assn. Democrat. Presbyterian. Home: 3831 River View Dr Birmingham AL 35243 Office: Birmingham-So Coll Box A-32 Birmingham AL 35254

JOHNSON, DAVID GARLAND, metal building manufacturing company executive; b. Columbus, Miss., Mar. 27, 1945; s. David Henry and Annie Pearl (Bolton) J.; m. Edna Dianne Landrum, June 14, 1964; children—David G., Brent Layne. Student East Miss. Jr. Coll., Scooba, 1963-64. Supr., Mitchell Engring. Co., Columbus, Miss., 1964-69; supr. Gulf States Mfg., Inc., Starkville, Miss., 1969-72, estimator sales, 1972-74, sales coordinator, 1974-77, regional sales mgr., 1977-82; dist. sales mgr. for Varco-Pruden Steel bldgs., Miss. and La., 1982—. Served with USAR, 1967-72. Recipient Top Regional Mgr. award Gulf States Mfg., Inc., 1977-81, Sales with Builders in Top Five awards, 1977-81, Largest Sales Volume award Varco-Pruden Bldgs., 1982. Republican. Methodist. Home and Office: Starkville MS

JOHNSON, DAYSE MURPHY, language educator; b. Sedalia, Mo.; d. Antoine Lewis and Susie (Kinney) Murphy; B.A., Lincoln U., 1938; student U. Mo., Kansas City, summers 1958-59; M.A., La. Tech. U., 1971; m. James T. Johnson, July 4, 1944 (dec.); children—Rose Antoinette Johnson Thompson, James Tare. Tchr.-prin., public schs., Parkville, Mo., 1938; exec. dir. br. YWCA, St. Joseph, Mo., 1939-41; exec. dir. YWCA, Des Moines, 1941-44; sec. athletic dept. Grambling Coll., 1954-57, 61-67, mem. faculty, sec. to v.p. coll., 1961-67; tchr. Webster High Sch., Minden, La., 1957-61, Eden Gardens High Sch., Shreveport, 1967-69; asst. prof. English, Grambling State U. (La.), 1969—. Mem. com. YWCA, Kansas City, Mo., 1938-40; active Girl Scouts U.S.A., 1959-60. NDEA grantee, summer 1961. Mem. Nat. Council Tchrs. English, Assn. Supervision and Curriculum Devel., AAUP, La. Assn. Post-Secondary Lang. Arts, Grambling Voters League, Sigma Tau Delta. Democrat. Methodist. Club: Order Eastern Star. Home: 225 N Grand St Grambling LA 71245 Office: Grambling State U Grambling LA 71245

JOHNSON, DEAN FRAZIER, sociology educator; b. Dallas, Dec. 6, 1921; d. Clifton Lamar and Florence Marie (Montgomery) Frazier; m. A.G. Bauer, Jan. 16, 1945 (div. 1967); children—Marguerite Marie, John Montgomery. B.A., La. State U., 1942; Ph.D., 1976; M.A., Akron U., 1968. Sec. dept. speech La. State U., Baton Rouge, 1938-42; news editor KWKH and KTBS, Shreveport, La., 1942-43; substitute tchr. Stark County Pub. Schs., Ohio; woman's editor Ohio Broadcasting Co., Canton, 1959-66; grad. asst. Akron U., Ohio, 1966-67; pres. Northeast Research Inst., Monroe, La., 1972-73; asst. prof. sociology Northwestern State U. Natchitoches, La., 1974-80, assoc. prof., 1981—, chmn. Family Life Inst., 1975; participant various NSF seminars. Reviewer profl. jour. 1980-88. Editor newsletter field. Served to lt. USNR, 1942-46. Recipient Pacesetter award City of Monroe, 1970; Curia grant Northwestern U., 1981. Mem. Am. Sociol. Soc., So. Sociol. Assn., Southwest Social Sci. Assn., Soc. Study Social Problems (Pericles award 1980), Mid South Sociol. Assn. (sec. treas. 1980-83, reporter theme session 1979), Sociologists for Women in Society, Mensa, Alpha Kappa Delta, Phi Beta. Episcopalian. Avocations: golf; swimming; needlework; reading. Home: 303 Jefferson St Natchitoches LA 71457 Office: Dept History Social Sci Northwestern State U Natchitoches LA 71457

JOHNSON, DEBRA PORTER, insurance/financial consultant; b. Winnsboro, S.C., Oct. 5, 1955; d. Alex Herbert and Alma (Gardner) Porter. A.Music, U. S.C., 1975, postgrad., 1982—. Ins. underwriter Palmetto State Life Ins. Co., Columbia, S.C., 1974-75, word processing sec., 1975, supr. word processing dept., 1975; adminstrv. asst. to br. mgr. Assocs. Comml. Corp., Columbia, 1976, office mgr., 1976-77; paralegal McNair Law Firm, Columbia, 1977-78; tchr. piano and voice, 1978-80; gen. sec. Weldon Waites & Assocs., Columbia, 1980, adminstrv. asst. to pres., 1980-81, office mgr., 1981-83, bus. and fin. mgr., 1983; multi-line ins. and fin. cons. Prudential Ins. Co., Columbia, 1984—. Mem. Assn. Life Underwriters, Profl. Devel. for Women, Columbia C. of C. Club: M-7 (founding mem.). Home: 1107 Hagood Ave Columbia SC 29205

JOHNSON, DEWEY E(DWARD), dentist; b. Charleston, S.C., Mar. 19, 1935; s. Dewey Edward and Mabel (Momeier) J.; A.B. in Geology, U. N.C., 1957, D.D.S., 1961. Practice dentistry, Charleston, 1964—, assoc. to Stanley H. Karesh, D.D.S., 1970-76. Served to lt. USNR, 1961-63. Mem. Royal Soc. Health, Charleston C. of C. (cruise ship com. 1969), ADA, Charleston Dental Soc., Hibernian Soc., Charleston Museum, Internat. Platform Assn., Charleston Library Soc., S.C. Hist. Soc., Gibbes Art Gallery, Preservation Soc. of Charleston, Navy League of U.S., Phi Kappa Sigma, Sigma Gamma Epsilon, Psi Omega. Congregationalist. Club: Optimist. Home: 142 S Battery Charleston SC 29401 Office: Sergeant Jasper Bldg Charleston SC 29401

JOHNSON, DONALD (DON) WAYNE, lawyer; b. Memphis, Feb. 2, 1950; s. Hugh Don and Oline (Rowland) J.; m. Jan Marie Mullinax, May 12, 1972; 1 child, Scott Fitzgerald. Student Memphis State U., 1968, Lee Coll., 1968-72; J.D., Woodrow Wilson Coll. Law, 1975. Bar: Ga. 1975, U.S. Dist. Ct. (no. dist.) Ga. 1975, U.S. Ct. Appeals (5th cir.) 1976, U.S. Ct. Appeals (Fed. cir.) 1984, U.S. Tax Ct. 1978, U.S. Ct. Claims 1978, U.S. Ct. Appeals (11th cir.) 1984, U.S. Ct. Appeals (D.C. cir.) 1984, U.S. Ct. Appeals (9th cir.) 1984, U.S. Supreme Ct. 1979. Ptnr. Barnes & Johnson, Dalton, Ga., 1975-77, Johnson & Fain, Dalton, 1977-80; sole practice, Dalton, 1980—. Bd. dirs. Pathway Christian Sch., Dalton, 1978—; Jr. Achievement of Dalton, 1978-83, Dalton-Whitfield County Day Care Ctr., 1983—. Mem. Ga. Trial Lawyers Assn., Assn. Trial Lawyers Am., Ga. State Bar, ABA, Christian Legal Soc. Mem. Ch. of God. Office: 1600 Parkwood Circle Suite 220 Atlanta GA 30339

JOHNSON, DONALD LEROY, educational administrator; b. Mountain Home, Ark., Jan. 21, 1939; s. Roy Arthur and Blanche (Lewis) J.; m. Hazel LaVerne Deatherage, May 15, 1961; 1 child, Thomas. A.A., Southwest Baptist Jr. Coll., 1958; B.S. in Edn., Southwest Mo. State U., 1961, M.S., 1971; Ed.D., East Tex. State U., 1977. Cert. secondary tchr., prin., Mo. Asst. dir. fin. aids Southwest Mo. State U., Springfield, 1969-72; asst. dir. admissions East Tex. State U., Commerce, 1972-73, registrar, 1973-77; dean continuing edn. Ark. Tech. U., Russellville, 1978-81, dean grad. studies and continuing edn., 1981—. Contbr. articles to profl. jours. Bd. dirs. Pope County United Way, Russellville, 1983—, Pope County Unified Resource Council, Russellville, 1983—. Served to lt. USN, 1961-68. Mem. Russellville C. of C. (bd. dirs. 1981-84), Ark. Assn. for Community Service and Continuing Edn. (pres. 1985—), Ark. Grad. Deans Assn. (sec. 1981—), Assn. Continuing Higher Edn., Conf. So. Grad. Deans, Mid-South Regional Planning Bd. Advancement Exptl. Learning, Naval Res. Assn. Democrat. Methodist. Lodge: Rotary (pres. 1984-85). Avocations: gardening, reading, travel. Home: 2710 Camelot Dr Russellville AR 72801 Office: Ark Tech U Russellville AR 72801

JOHNSON, DOROTHY GULLEN, training and development specialist; b. San Gabriel, Calif., Sept. 19, 1931; d. Orin Clark Strathman and Frances Helen (Cosman) Strathman-Patrick; m. Richard Guerrier Johnson, Jan. 6, 1979 (dec. 1985); children—Joseph A. Gullen III, Carrol A. Gullen, Jocelyn E. Pinder, Elsa A. Johnson Rochier, Linda Azain. B.A. cum laude, 1972; M.B.A., 1985; M.A., U. No. Colo., 1974; Cert. therapist, family counselor, Fla.; cert. career counselor, Fla. Tng. program dir. T.A. Assocs., Miami, Fla., 1972-76; asst. dir. drug abuse program Cath. Services Bur., Miami, 1976-78; career devel. coordinator Miami Dade Community Coll., 1972-80; pres. Process Cons., Miami, 1983; tng., devel. coordinator Am. Bankers Ins. Group, Miami, 1983—. Author video tng. film. Mem. Am. Bus. Women's Assn. (pres., treas. 1979—), Civitan Internat. (bd. dirs., various offices 1972-81), Am. Soc. for Tng. Devel. (mem.-at-large com. chmn. 1972—). Republican. Lutheran. Avocations: writing; reading; bromiliads; learning; bridge. Home: 17171 SW 87th Court Miami FL 33157 Office: Am Bankers Ins Group 11222 Quail Roost Dr Miami FL 33157

JOHNSON, DUTCHIE ANTOINETTE, country administrator; b. Nov. 16, 1949; d. Fred Johnson and Rubye Nell (Ward) Johnson Lazier-Williams. Student Coppin State Coll., 1967-71, M.Ed., 1972; B.S., U. Md. and Coppin State Coll., 1971. Social worker Family Health Ctr., Miami, Fla., 1972-73; asst. prof. Fla. Meml. Coll., Miami, 1973-78; transit customer rep. Dade County Transit Agy., Miami, 1979-80, transit supr., 1980-81, chief community services, 1981—; cons. Nat. Drug Abuse, Rockville, Md., 1973-78; adj. prof. Miami Dade Community Coll., 1974-82, Nova U., Ft. Lauderdale, Fla., 1982-83. Greater Miami Urban League leadership fellow, 1982. Mem. Women's Transp. Seminar (bd. dirs. 1983—), Nat. Assn. Black Social Workers, Alpha Kappa Alpha. Democrat. Baptist. Club: Sophisticated Ladies (Miami). Lodge: Order Eastern Star. Home: 13000 NW 17 Ct Miami FL 33167

JOHNSON, EDGAR M., psychologist; b. Jacksonville, Fla., Oct. 29, 1941; s. James Mack Johnson and Dorothy (Vickers) Logue; m. Fatima Nunes, Sept. 9, 1967; children—Victoria C., David M. B.S. in Applied Psychology, Ga. Inst. Tech., 1964; M.S. in Exptl. Psychology, Tufts U., 1967, Ph.D. in Exptl. Psychology, 1969. Research psychologist U.S. Army Research Inst., Alexandria, Va., 1970-78, chief human factors sect., 1978-80, dir. systems research lab., 1980-82, tech. dir. U.S. Army Research Inst., chief psychologist U.S. Army, 1982—. Served to capt. U.S. Army, 1968-70. NDEA fellow, 1965-67. Fellow Am. Psychol. Assn., Human Factors Soc., Washington Acad. Sci. (Sci. Achievement award 1980); mem. IEEE (Franklin V. Taylor award 1984), Ergonomics Soc., Sigma Xi. Club: Cosmos (Washington). Home: 5314 Dunleer Ln Burke VA 22015 Office: US Army Research Inst 5001 Eisenhower Ave Alexandria VA 22333

JOHNSON, EDNA W., chemical company executive; b. Ada, Okla., June 5, 1945; d. Ralph Gordon and Wanda Patricia (Edwards) J. B.A., Okla. State U., 1967, B.S. in Chemistry, 1968; M.S. in Chemistry, U. Okla., 1970. Jr. chemist Acme Chem. Co., Bartlesville, Okla., 1970-72, sr. chemist, 1972-75; project chemist Werik Chem. Corp., Oklahoma City, 1975-78, chief chemist, 1978-80, asst. v.p. research and devel., 1980—, also dir.; cons. chemist, 1982—. Bd. dirs. S.W. Side YWCA, Oklahoma City, 1983—. Mem. Am. Chem. Soc., Am. Inst. Chemists, Sigma Xi. Democrat. Methodist. Address: Werik Chemical Corp 3532 NW 23d St Oklahoma City OK 73107

JOHNSON, EDWARD LEROY, geologist, consultant; b. Joplin, Mo., June 2, 1926; s. Guy Wesley and Georgia Etta (Nichols) J.; m. Lois Evelyn VanPool, Aug. 17, 1957; children—Paul Wesley, Robert VanPool. A.S., Joplin Jr. Coll., 1948; B.S., Mo. Sch. Mines, 1950. Cert. profl. geologist; registered profl. engr., Okla., cert. petroleum geologist. Exploration geologist Am. Zinc, Lead and Smelting Co., Metaline Falls, Wash., Mascot, Tenn. and Joplin, Mo., 1950-56; regional geologist U.S. Geol. Survey, Tulsa, 1956-80; cons. geologist L.R. Reeder & Assocs., Tulsa, 1980-81; chief geologist J.R. Wilson & Assocs., Tulsa, 1981-83; cons. geologist, Tulsa, 1983—; staff asst. Nat. Def. Exec. Res., 1971-80; pres. Nancy Oil & Royalty Co., Joplin, 1981-85; pres. Cresset Royalty Co., Tulsa, 1985—. Served with USN, 1944-46. Mem. AIME, Tulsa Geol. Soc. (newsletter editor 1965-66, treas. 1968-69, councilor 1974-76), Am. Assn. Petroleum Geologists, Am. Inst. Profl. Geologists (dist. rep. 1971-72, state pres. 1972-73, nat. exec. com. 1974). Republican. Avocations: hunting; fishing. Home and Office: 5816 E 57th St Tulsa OK 74135

JOHNSON, EDWARD ROY, librarian; b. Denver, Nov. 29, 1940; s. Burton Clifford and Bonnie Jean Johnson; B.A., U. Colo., 1964; M.A., U. Wis., 1966, Ph.D., 1974; m. Benita Irene Hulbert, June 14, 1964; 1 son, Elliot Hulbert. Library asst. U. Colo., 1964-65; reference librarian U. Iowa, 1966-67; bus. librarian 1967-69; asst. dean libraries Pa. State U., University Park, 1972-79; dir. libraries North Tex. State U., Denton, 1979—. HEW fellow, 1969-72. Mem. ALA, Southwestern Library Assn., Tex. Library Assn., AAUP, Oral History Assn., Am. Philatelic Soc., Phi Alpha Theta, Beta Phi Mu, Phi Kappa Phi. Clubs: Kiwanis, B'nai B'rith. Contbr. articles to profl. jours. Office: Library N Tex State U Denton TX 76203

JOHNSON, EDWIN ANTHONY, educational administrator; b. N.Y.C., Sept. 13, 1931; s. Alfred Anthony and Margaret Elizabeth (O'Gorman) J.; m. Fayetta Loise Wimmers, Apr. 25, 1959; children—Rosemary, Margaret, Edwin, Jr., Katherine, Donald. A.B., U. Miami, 1954; M.S., Barry U., Miami Shores, Fla., 1964; Ed.D., U. Ga., Athens, 1973. Tchr., Irish Christian Bros., New Rochelle, N.Y., 1955-58, Diocese of Miami, Ft. Lauderdale, Fla., 1958-60; tchr., counselor Broward Sch. Bd., Fort Lauderdale, 1960-64, supr., 1964-71, adminstr., 1971-74; dir. Seminole Community Coll., Sanford, Fla., 1974—; cons. U. Ga., 1976, U. North Fla., 1980-82, Council Non-Collegiate Edn., 1981; team mem. So. Assn. Coll. and Schs., 1984; presenter continuing edn. confs., 1966—. Mem. editorial staff Migrant Handbook, 1968; mem. editorial bd. Forum for Continuing Edn. Jour., 1979-80. Contbr. articles to profl. publs. Vice chmn. Seminole County Planning and Zoning Com., 1976-79; bd. dirs., chmn. fin. com. United Way, Seminole County, 1978—; pres. bd. Seminole County R.S.V.P., 1981-82. Publication scholar, 1953-54; Newspaper Fund fellow Wall St. Jour., 1960. Mem. Fla. Assn. Adult Adminstrs. (Hall of Fame, 1983), Nat. Assn. Pub. Continuing Adult Edn. I chmn. nomination and election com. 1964-82), Am. Assn. Adult and Continuing Edn. (bd. dirs.), Fla. Adult Edn. Assn. Avocation: tennis. Office: Seminole Community Coll Hwy 17-92 Sanford FL 32711

JOHNSON, ERIC EDWARD, applied statistics consultant; b. Omaha, May 9, 1918; s. Eric Sigfred and Ericka Charlotta (Erickson) J.; m. Audrey Lee Hall, June 27, 1947; children—Douglas, Alvin. B.S., Creighton U., 1940, M.S., 1941; postgrad. U. Tenn.-Oak Ridge, 1958-60. Analytical chemist Cudahy Packing Co., Omaha, 1942, Nat. Bur. Standards, Washington, 1943, Swift & Co., Chgo., 1947-55; statistician Union Carbide Corp., Oak Ridge, 1955-83; cons. applied stats. Martin Marietta Energy Systems, Inc., Oak Ridge, 1984—. Served with U.S. Army, 1944-46. Mem. Am. Statis. Assn., Math. Assn. Am., Am. Def. Preparedness Assn., Am. Soc. Quality Control (treas. Knoxville 1968-70). Republican. Mem. Church of Christ. Avocations: playing piano and organ; watercolor painting; ballroom dancing. Home: 101 Essex Ln Oak Ridge TN 37830 Office: Y-12 Bldg 9723-11A Oak Ridge TN 37830

JOHNSON, EURAL LEVORN, JR., pharmacist, mortician; b. Prentiss, Miss., May 24, 1955; s. Eural L. and Ruby (Kennedy) J. Diploma in Mortuary Sci., Gupton-Jones Sch., 1977; B.S. in Pharmacy, U. Miss., 1982. Registered pharmacist, Miss., La., funeral dir. and mortician, Miss. Asst. mgr. Treasury Drugs, Jackson, Miss., 1982-83; dir. pharmacy Madison-Yazoo-Leake Family Health Ctr., Canton, Miss., 1983-84; dir. pharm. services Madison Parish Hosp., Tallulah, La., 1985—. Mem. Am. Soc. Hosp. Pharmacists, Miss. Soc. Hosp. Pharmacists, Magnolia State Pharm. Soc. (pres. 1984, 85, Pres.'s award 1984, 85), Nat. Pharm. Assn. (dir. Zone II 1985—), Miss. Pharmacists Assn., Miss. Funeral Dirs. and Morticians Assn., Mensa, NAACP, Jackson Urban League, Jackson Jaycees, Pi Sigma Eta, Alpha Phi Alpha. Democrat. Baptist. Lodge: Masons. Avocations: tennis; numismatics; gardening; reading. Home: 3804 W Capitol St Jackson MS 39209 Office: Madison Parish Hosp Pharmacy #656 PO Box 1559 Tallulah LA 71282

JOHNSON, EVANS COMBS, history educator; b. Valley, Ala., Nov. 14, 1922; s. John Will and Cordelia Combs (Harrell) J.; m. Betty Drees, Jan. 28, 1958. A.B., U. Ala., 1943, M.A., 1947; Ph.D., U. N.C., 1953. Assoc. prof. history Huntingdon Coll., Montgomery, Ala., 1947-48; asst. prof. history Stetson U., DeLand, Fla., 1953-57, assoc. prof., 1957-69, prof., 1969—, chmn. dept. 1971—. Author: Oscar W. Underwood: A Political Biography, 1982 (James Sulzby award 1982). Served with USAAF, 1943-44. Mem. Phi Alpha Theta (chmn. manuscripts com. 1983—). Democrat. Episcopalian. Avocations: stock market; antique collecting. Home: 722 N Arlington St DeLand FL 32720 Office: Stetson U Dept History 1021 North Blvd DeLand FL 32720

JOHNSON, EVLYN LEE, guidance and counseling educator; b. Yoakum, Tex., Jan. 29, 1926; d. Roger Worden and Josie Anita (Porche) Lee; m. Richard Marion Johnson, Feb. 16, 1946 (div. Dec. 1963); 1 child, Sherilyn Marie Johnson Smith. Cert. tchr., counselor, Tex. B.S., Samuel Houston Coll.; M.A., U. Mich.; M.S., Prairie View A&M U.; Ph.D., Ind. State U. Nurse's aide Santa Rosa Hosp., San Antonio, 1947-50; vocat. nurse Good Samaritan Hosp., San Antonio, 1952-53; tchr. Douglas Jr. High Sch. San Antonio, 1953-64; instr. Prairie View A&M U., Tex., summers 1960-64, 67—, full time, 1964-66; mem. faculty Tex. So. U., Houston, 1967—, lab. supr., 1975—, assoc. prof. counseling, 1979—. Vestryman, usher St. Luke Evang. Episcopal Ch., Houston, 1967—. NDEA grantee, 1959-60; Ind. State U. fellow, 1971-72. Mem. Am. Assn. for Counseling and Devel., Am. Assn. for Counselor Edn. and Devel., Assn. for Multicultural Counseling and Devel., So. Assn. for Counselor Edn. and Supervision, Houston Assn. for Counseling and Devel., Tex. Soc. Coll. Tchrs. Edn., Phi Delta Kappa. Democrat. Avocations: vegetable gardening; lawn care; fishing. Office: Dept Guidance and Counseling Tex Southern U 3100 Cleburne St Houston TX 77004

JOHNSON, FARNHAM JAMES, rubber company executive; b. St. Paul, June 23, 1924; s. William Kendall and Mabel (Wirth) J.; B.S., U. Wis., 1948; student U. Mich., 1943-44; B. Fgn. Trade, Am. Grad. Sch. Internat. Mgmt., 1950, M. Internat. Mgmt., 1978; postgrad. U. Akron, 1977; m. Evelyn Porter Thompson, June 1, 1973 (dec. Aug. 1983); m. Paula Nan Wright, Sept. 28, 1986. Player, Chgo. Bears Football Team, 1947, Chgo. Rockets, 1948; internat. rep. Internat. B.F. Goodrich Co., Washington, 1950-51, mgr. Hawaii, 1951-53, internat. rep. Hague, 1954, gen. sales mgr. Goodrich Svenska Gummi A/B, Stockholm, 1955-57, asst. gen. mgr. Phillipines, 1958-61, mgr. internat. accounts N.Y.C. and Ohio, 1962-69, dir. export sales, Akron, 1970-74, dir. mktg. intelligence, 1974-80; dir. internat. div. Continental Conveyor & Equipment Co., Winfield, Ala., 1980—; dir. B.F. Goodrich of Japan Ltd., 1970-80. Bd. dirs. Better Boy's Assn. Philippines, 1958-61. Served with USMC, 1943-46. Mem. Rubber Export Assn. (bd. dirs. 1970-80), Soc. Automotive Engrs., Marine Corps Res. Officers Assn., Am. Legion, Delta Phi Epsilon, Sigma Phi Epsilon. Republican. Episcopalian. Clubs: Univ. (Akron), W. Club (Wis.), M Club (Mich.); Outrigger Canoe Club (Honolulu); Kiwanis, Elks. Office: Continental Conveyor & Equipment Co PO Box 400 Winfield AL 35594

JOHNSON, FAYE T., patient care center executive; b. Hampton, Va., June 4, 1945; d. Norman Thomas and Dolly Mae (Murphy) Tucker; m. Clarence V. Johnson, Feb. 20, 1963 (div. 1969); 1 child, Clifford Shane. Student Ga. State U., 1969-70, Kennesaw Coll., Ga., 1971-72, 75-76, No. Va. Community Coll., Annandale, 1973-74; cert. in programming IBM, Atlanta, 1978. Numerous acctg. positions, 1964-71; asst. to regional mgr. Babcock & Wilcox Constrn. Co., Atlanta, 1971-73, 74-75; adminstrv. asst. Lane Bryant Inc., Merrifield, Va., 1973-74; mgr. employee benefits, ins. Husky Industries Inc., Atlanta, 1975-80; mgr. employee relations Bunyon Enterprises, Atlanta, 1980-82; mgr. adminstrn. OXXO Inc., Houston, 1982-83; asst. to pres. The Energy Partnership, Atlanta, 1983-84; mgr. adminstrn. Am. Home Patient Ctr., Atlanta, 1984—; cons. small bus., Atlanta, 1976-81, 83—, gas and oil industry, Houston, 1982-83. Designer: Fashion Illustration. Producer-promoter musical recordings: (album) I Love You Dear Wine. Recipient numerous awards for excellence in field. Mem. Risk Ins. Mgmt. Soc., High Mus. Art, Nat. Assn. Female Execs., Smithsonian Assocs., Nat. Trust for Hist. Preservation. Republican. Mem. Pentecostal Ch. Club: Botanical Garden (Atlanta). Avocations: sailing; horseback riding; writing poetry; art; gardening. Home: 1512 Springleaf Circle Smyrna GA 30080 Office: Am Home Patient Ctrs Inc 8601 Dunwoody Pl Suite 504 Atlanta GA 30338

JOHNSON, FRANCES FLAHERTY, retired educator, career development specialist; b. Hamlet, N.C., Feb. 23, 1916; d. John Lawrence and Mary Elizabeth (Shortridge) Flaherty; m. Clifton Jerome Johnson, Nov. 27, 1940 (dec. 1953); 1 child, Carolyn Johnson Koch. B.S., State Tchrs. Coll., Fredricksburg, Va., 1936; Ed.M., U. N.C., 1958; postgrad. U. Oslo, 1963, U. Vienna, Austria, 1967. Tchr. Cumberland County Schs., Godwin, N.C., 1936-37; tchr. Aberdeen Schs., N.C., 1937-39, prin., 1939-41; counselor Fayetteville Schs., N.C., 1958-64, Winston-Salem Forsyth Schs., N.C., 1964-65; cons. Dept. Pub. Instruction, Raleigh, N.C., 1965-71; project dir. Dare-Hyde-Tyrrell Schs., Manteo, N.C., 1971-73; vocat. counselor Wake Schs., Raleigh, 1973-74; now ret. Contbg. mem. Smithsonian Inst., Washington, 1985—; active SITES and outreach programs. Mem. Am. Assn. for Adult and Continuing Edn. (del. for people-to-people visit to Soviet Union and to People's Republic China 1983), Am. Assn. for Counseling Devel., Asia Soc. Avocation: traveling.

JOHNSON, FRANK MINIS, JR., federal judge; b. Winston County, Ala., Oct. 30, 1918; s. Frank M. and Alabama (Long) J.; m. Ruth Jenkins, Jan. 16, 1938; 1 son, James Curtis (dec.). Grad., Gulf Coast Mil. Acad., Gulfport, Miss., 1935, Massey Bus. Coll., Birmingham, 1937; LL.B., U. Ala., 1943; LL.D. (hon.), U. Ala., 1977, Notre Dame U., 1973, Princeton U., 1974, Boston U., 1979, Yale U., 1980, J.D. (hon.), St. Michael's Coll., 1975. Bar: Ala. 1943. Mem. firm Curtis, Maddox & Johnson, 1946-53; U.S. atty. No. Dist. Ala., 1953-55; U.S. dist. judge Middle Dist. Ala., 1955-79; U.S. judge Ct. Appeals for 11th Circuit, Montgomery, Ala., 1979—; mem. Temporary Emergency Ct. Appeals of U.S., 1972-82; mem. rev. com. Jud. Conf., 1969-78, mem. jud. ethics com., 1978-85; mem. Spl. Com. on Habeas Corpus, 1971-78; chmn. Civil Rules Adv. Com., 1985 . Served from pvt. to capt. inf. AUS, 1943-46. Decorated Purple Heart with oak leaf cluster, Bronze Star. Mem. Ala. Acad. Honor. Office: US Court House PO Box 35 Montgomery AL 36101*

JOHNSON, FRANKLIN H., engineer; b. Athens, Tex., June 27, 1941; s. Benjamin Franklin and Hilbert M. (Elledge) J.; m. Dixie R. Hine, May 11, 1963; children—Brenda K., Carey A., Tracie S., Benjamin F. B.S.M.E., Ariz. State U., 1969; M.S.M.E., Okla. State U., 1971; Sc.D., Western State U., Doniphan, Mo., 1984. Profl. engr., Tex. Chief of safety, U.S. Air Force, 1959-79; safety engr. United Drilling Co., Tyler, Tex., 1979-80; pres. NSE, Tyler, 1981-84, System Engring. & Labs., Inc., Tyler, 1984—. Author regulation, guidline in field. Recipient Commendation Medal, USAF, 1976. Mem. Nat. Soc. Profl. Engrs. (dir. East Tex. 1984-85), Nat. Acad. Forensic Engring. (charter), Am. Soc. Safety Engrs. (profl.), Am. Nat. Standards Inst. Republican. Baptist. Avocations: art; cattle. Office: System Engring & Labs Inc Rt 7 Box 917 Tyler TX 75707

JOHNSON, FREDERICK DEAN, former food co. exec., cons.; b. Shreve, Ohio, Feb. 27, 1911; s. Harry H. and Grace Marcella (Cammarn) J.; A.B., Coll. Wooster (Ohio), 1935; m. Haulwen Elizabeth Richey, June 19, 1937; children—Frederick Dean II, Mary Haulwen, Grace Elizabeth. Dir. research Bama Co. (now Bama Products Borden Foods div. Borden Inc.), Birmingham, Ala., 1961-65, dir. research, Houston, 1965-76, dir. product devel. and tech. adviser, 1976-78, cons., 1978—; U.S. del. FAO/WHO Codex Alimentarius Commn. Processed Fruits and Vegetables, 1973, 74, 75. Bd. dirs. Afton Oaks Civic Club, 1967-70, 82—. Mem. Internat. Jelly and Preserve Assn. (chmn. quality control adv. com. 1969-73, chmn. standards com. 1973-76, citation and plaque 1974), Inst. Food Technologists (charter), Am. Chem. Soc. (past sec., chmn. Wooster sect.), AAAS. Republican (precinct chmn. 1981—). Presbyterian (ruling elder). Home: 4546 Shetland Ln Houston TX 77027

JOHNSON, GILBERT OSCAR, insurance agent; b. Chgo., May 3, 1910; s. Oscar F. and Ruth (Anderson) J.; m. Lylith M. Breitzka, Aug. 17, 1938; children—Bryan G., Dwight L., Kathryn Ruth, Lauralee. Student, Purdue U., 1931. C.L.U. Sec., treas. Crest Lawn Meml. Park, Atlanta, 1952-62; agt. Mut. Security Life Ins., Atlanta, 1962-63, gen. agt., 1963-73, agt., 1973—. Named to Million Dollar Round Table, Am. Assn. Life Underwriters, 1978. Mem. Am. Soc. C.L.U.s, Atlanta Estate Planning Council, Atlanta Life Underwriters Assn. Republican. Mem. Christian and Missionary Alliance. Home: 4437 Lake Breeze Dr Stone Mountain GA 30083 Office: Mut Security Life Ins Co 1791 Tullie Circle Suite 207 Atlanta GA 30329

JOHNSON, GILMER BROOKS, physician; b. Jackson, Miss., Sept. 12, 1916; s. Gilmer Brooks and Lena Leoti (Brown) J.; student Sul Ross State U., 1934-35, 46-47; B.S., Northwestern U., 1948, M.D., 1950; m. Avis Elizabeth Palmer, Oct. 9, 1942; children—Carolyn Jean, Gilmer Brooks, David Wallace. Intern, Baylor U. Med. Center, Dallas, 1951; practice family medicine, Plainview, Tex., 1952—; chief staff Central Plains Gen. Hosp., E. O. Nichols Meml. Hosp., Plainview; faculty (part-time) Tex. Tech U. Med. Sch.; med. cons. Mex. Rural Work Program. Trustee Central Plains Regional Hosp., 1983—; v.p. Hale County chpt. Am. Heart Assn. Served with AUS, 1936-46. Decorated Bronze Star. Diplomate Am. Bd. Family Practice. Fellow Am. Acad. Family Physicians (pres. chpt. 1976); mem. AMA (Physician's Recognition award 1970, 73, 76, 79, 82, 85), Hale-Briscoe-Floyd County Med. Soc. (pres. 1962-63), Los Hermanos de la Frontera (2d v.p.). Baptist (deacon). Home: 205 Yucca Terr Plainview TX 79072 Office: 814 W 8th St Plainview TX 79072

JOHNSON, GLEN ERIC, mechanical engineering educator, consultant; b. Rochester, N.Y., May 29, 1951; s. Ray Clifford and Helen Francis (Lindgren) J.; m. Kathryne Ann DeLoach, May 3, 1975; children—Edward Lindgren, Eric Anders. B.S. in Mech. Engring., Worcester Poly. Inst., 1973; M.S. in Mech. Engring., Ga. Inst. Tech., 1974; Ph.D., Vanderbilt U., 1978. Registered profl. engr., Va., Tenn. Mech. engr. Tenn. Eastman Co., Kingsport, 1974-76; asst. prof. mech. engring. Vanderbilt U., Nashville, 1978-79, assoc. prof. mech. engring., 1981—; asst. prof. mech. engring. U. Va., Charlottesville, 1979-81; cons. mech. design. President's fellow Ga. Inst. Tech., 1973-74; Harold Stirling Vanderbilt Grad. scholar Vanderbilt U., 1976-78. Mem. ASME (assoc. editor jours.), Am. Gear Mfrs. Assn., Acoustical Soc. Am., Math. Programming Soc., Soc. Automotive Engrs. (Ralph Teetor award 1984). Author numerous articles on optimization theory and mechanical design. Home: 235 Gloucester St Franklin TN 37064 Office: Box 8-B Vanderbilt U Nashville TN 37235

JOHNSON, GUS LAROY, marine chemist, safety consultant; b. Alexandria, La., Sept. 15, 1947; s. Samuel Joseph and Deanna (Campbell) J.; m. Carolyn Ann Mills, July 13, 1968; children—Rebecca Ann, Melissa Madene, Samuel Edward. B.S. in Chem. Engring., La. Tech. U., 1970; RTV electronics cert. San Jacinto Coll., 1975. Cert. marine chemist, Nat. Fire Protection Assn.; cert. safety profl., Bd. Cert. Safety Profls. Chemist Maintenance Engring. Corp., Houston, 1970-73; research chemist Exxon Research & Engring. Co., Baytown, Tex., 1973-78; marine chemist Marine Inspection Service, Pasadena, Tex., 1978—, pres., 1983—. Author: The Marine Chemist Professional, 1984. Mem. Nat. Fire Protection Assn., Am. Soc. Safety Engrs., Marine Chemists Assn., Tex. State Safety Assn., Marine Services Assn. Tex. Republican. Mem. Church of Christ. Avocations: fishing; camping; basketball; racquetball. Office: Marine Inspection Services PO Box 6232 Pasadena TX 77506

JOHNSON, HALLMAN TROY, engineering photographer; b. Gadsden, Ala., Jan. 30, 1925; s. Johnnie Jackson and Mabel Oyester (Story) J.; m. Lorena Elizabeth Cassenta, Feb. 7, 1953. Grad. high sch., Gadsden, 1943. Photographer, Gadsden Studio, 1941-42, P.C. Smith Studio, Gadsden, 1942-43; foreman and photographer Gadsden Photo, 1946-49; self-employed photographer Ala. Studio, Gadsden, 1949-60; engring. photographer Nat. Aeronautic and Space Adminstrn., Marshall Space Flight Ctr., Ala., 1960—; shop steward Am. Fedn. Gov't. Employees, Huntsville, Ala., 1982—. Developer of a method to accomplish better photographic results on motion pictures, 1977 (Outstanding Performance award 1977). State dept. chaplain Am. Legion of Ala., Montgomery, 1958-60; ordained deacon Bapt. Ch., 1949; dir. Mt. Zion Baptist Sunday Sch., Huntsville, 1975—. Served to sgt. USAF, 1943-46, ETO. Democrat. Club: Internat. Civitan (sec. 1949-60). Lodge: Masons. Avocations: religious work; gardening; flowers. Home: PO Box 273 Madison AL 35758

JOHNSON, HANSFORD FRED, dermatologist; b. Woburn, Mass., July 26, 1917; s. Hansford Duncan and Maudelle Blanche (Williams) J.; m. Ruth Elizabeth Daughtery, June 8, 1940 (dec. 1965); children—Jan Ellynn Johnson Ramsey, Hansford Frederic; m. 2d, Olla Carolyn Carter, Aug. 17, 1966; 1 dau., Carolyn Best. B.S., Wake Forest Coll., 1938, B.S. in Medicine, 1940; M.D., U. Md., 1942. Diplomate Am. Bd. Dermatology. Intern, Henry Ford Hosp., Detroit, 1942-43; resident U. Tex. Med. Br., Galveston, 1946-48; preceptee in dermatology Drs. Lehmann and Pipkin, San Antonio, 1948-49; practice medicine specializing in dermatology, Amarillo, Tex., 1949—; mem. staff VA Hosp., N.W. Tex. Hosp., St. Anthony's Hosp.; assoc. prof. U. Tex.-Galveston, 1948-49; assoc. clin. prof. Tex. Tech U., Lubbock. Vice pres. Amarillo Community Council, 1983; active Am. Cancer Soc.; vestry St. Andrew's Episcopal Ch.; bd. dirs. YMCA, City Bd. Health, Fine Arts Council. Served to capt. M.C., U.S. Army, 1943-46. Fellow Am. Acad. Dermatology, N.Am. Clin. Dermatologic Soc.; mem. AMA, Tex. Med. Assn., So. Med. Assn., Pacific Dermatol. Assn., Southwestern Dermatol. Assn. Panhandle Dist. Med. Soc. (pres. 1957), Potter County Med. Soc. (pres. 1960, membership chmn. exec. com. 1983), Tex. Dermatol. Soc. (pres. 1976), Amarillo C. of C. (pres. 1970). Club: Amarillo Country (pres. 1983-84). Lodge: Rotary. Office: 5 Medical Dr Amarillo TX 79106

JOHNSON, HARDWICK SMITH, educator; b. Millen, Ga., Aug. 13, 1958; s. Hardwick Smith and Louise (Joiner) J. B.A., Atlanta Christian Coll., 1981; M.Ed., Ga. So. Coll., 1984. Spl. edn. resource tchr. Claxton High Sch., Ga., 1983—; supervising tchr. Ga. So. Coll., Profl. Lab. Experiences, Statesboro, 1984—. Compiler: History of the Johnson Family, 1976. Named Tchr. of the Year, Council for Exceptional Children, Claxton, 1985. Mem. S.A.R. (v.p. chpt. 1985-86), Sons of Confederate Vets., Sons of the Am. Colonists, Council for Exceptional Children (pres.-elect), Ga. Assn. Educators (sch. rep. 1985—), NEA (sch. rep.). Republican. Christian Ch. Clubs: St. George's Soc. (Jacksonville, Fla.); Order of St. John of Jerusalem. Lodges: Masons, DeMolay (master councilor 1977-78). Avocations: genealogy and family research. Home: 106 1/2 Outland St Statesboro GA 30458 Office: Claxton High Sch North Clark St Claxton GA 30417

JOHNSON, HAROLD BENJAMIN, JR., educator; b. Hastings, Nebr., Mar. 17, 1931; s. Harold Benjamin and Patricia (Armstrong) J.; B.A., Cambridge U., 1953, M.A., 1960; Ph.D., U. Chgo., 1963. Lectr. U. Chgo., 1961-63, Yale, 1965-67; asso. prof. history U. Va., Charlottesville, 1969-81, scholar-in-residence, 1981—, dir. Latin Am. studies, 1971-73; vis. lectr. Universidade Nova de Lisboa (Portugal), 1983. Served with AUS, 1953-55. Social Sci. Research Council fellow, 1964; Ford Found. fellow, 1965-66; Fulbright Hayes fellow, 1968-69. Mem. Am. Hist. Assn., Conf. Latin Am. History, Phi Beta Kappa. Author: From Reconquest to Empire, 1970. Contbr. to Cambridge History of Latin America, profl. jours. Office: Randall Hall Univ Va Charlottesville VA 22903

JOHNSON, HERBERT ALAN, legal historian, educator; b. Jersey City, Jan. 10, 1934; s. Harry Oliver and Magdalena Gertrude (Diemer) J.; m. Barbara Arlene Balcerak, Sept. 24, 1955 (dec. Nov. 1980); children—Amanda Blair, Vanessa Paige; m. Jane McCue, June 4, 1983. A.B., Columbia U., 1955, M.A., 1961, Ph.D., 1965; LL.B., N.Y. Law Sch., 1960; Research asst. Columbia U., 1961-63; lectr. history Hunter Coll., City U. N.Y., 1964-65, asst. prof., 1965-67; asso. editor Papers of John Marshall, Inst. Early Am. History and Culture, Williamsburg, Va., 1967-70, co-editor, 1970-71, editor, 1971-77; prof. history and law U. S.C., Columbia, 1977—; lectr. history Coll. William and Mary, 1967-77. Mem. City of Williamsburg Bd. Adjustments and Appeals, 1971-77. Served with USAF, 1955-57. Recipient Paul S. Kerr history prize N.Y. State Hist. Assn., 1970; Am. Council Learned Socs. fellow, 1974-75; Liberty Fund fellow Inst. Humane Studies, 1981. Mem. Am. Hist. Assn. (chmn. Littleton-Griswold com. 1979-81), Assn. Am. Law Schs. (chmn. sect. legal history 1979), Am. Soc. Legal History (v.p. 1972-74, pres. 1974-75), Am. Law Inst., Selden Soc., Stair Soc., Osgoode Soc., Internat. Commn. Study of History of Parliamentary Instns. Author: The Law Merchant and Negotiable Instruments in Colonial New York 1664-1730, 1963; John Jay, 1745-1829, 1970; Imported Eighteenth-Century Law Treatises in American Libraries, 1700-1799, 1978; (with G.L. Haskins) History of the Supreme Court of the United States: Foundations of Power, John Marshall, 1801-1815, 1981; editor: (with C. T. Cullen) The Papers of John Marshall, vols. 1, 2, 1974, 77; South Carolina Legal History, 1980. Home: 615 LaBruce Ln Columbia SC 29205 Office: Gambrell Hall Dept History U SC Columbia SC 29208

JOHNSON, JAMES CALVIN, social work educator; b. Orange County, N.C., Oct. 6, 1929; s. James Parrish and Panthenia (Wiley) J.; m. Odessa Brooks, Mar. 22, 1929; children—Angela Renee, Shelton Keith, James Calvin III. B.S. magna cum laude N.C. A&T State U., 1962; M.S.W., U. N.C., 1968; J.D., N.C. Central U., 1974. Social worker Guilford County Dept. Social Services, 1962-69; assoc. prof. social work N.C. A&T State U., Greensboro, 1969—; protective social worker Guilford County Dept. Social Service Protective Service, 1970-73; mem. Cons. Council Social Work Edn., 1979-80, U. Ga. Sch. Social Work, 1982—. Southeastern regional rep. Third World Coalition; bd. dirs. Am. Friends Service Com.; candidate for major of Greensboro, 1983; chmn. Greensboro Human Relations Commn. Served with U.S. Army, 1951-55. Recipient Community award February One Soc., 1983; named Citizen of Yr., State Human Relations Commn., 1983; Order of Long Leaf Pine, Gov. of N.C. Mem. Nat. Assn. Social Workers, Nat. Council Social Work Edn., N.C. Council Social Workers, Alpha Delta Mu, Delta Theta Phi. Democrat. Methodist Episcopal. Club: Sertoma (dist. gov., Gold Coat award 1979). Author: Now Social Work Public and Private; Blacks Use of Difference in Social Work; Political Science in Black Universities is Dead; 1954 Brown vs Board of Education Twenty Years Later. Home: 2114 Edmond Dr Greensboro NC 27401 Office: Dept Sociology and Social Work A&T State U Greensboro NC 27411

JOHNSON, J(AMES) DONALD, JR., environmental chemist, educator; b. Inglewood, Calif., Aug. 1, 1935; s. James Donald and Mary Katherine (Biggs) J.; m. Elizabeth Joanne Wolf, Sept. 2, 1955; children—Christopher Robert, Katherine Donna. B.S., UCLA, 1957; Ph.D., U. N.C., 1962. Asst. prof. environ. scis. U. N.C., 1961-66, assoc. prof., 1966-71, prof., dir. program environ. chemistry and biology, dept. environ. scis. and engring., 1971-82; lectr. chemistry Wesleyan Coll., Rocky Mount, N.C., 1962-64; vis. prof. U. Gothenburg (Sweden), 1970-71; participant Nobel Symposium 20, Gothenburg, 1971; vis. scientist Swiss Fed. Water Lab., Zurich, 1982; cons. Nat. Sanitation Found. Am. Enka research fellow, 1959-60; R. J. Reynolds research fellow, 1970. Mem. Water Pollution Contro. Fedn., Am. Chem. Soc. (chmn. environ. chemistry div.), Am. Water Works Assn. (chmn. standard methods com., task group on chlorine residual 1978-83, chmn. disinfection research com. 1977-83), Nat. Acad. Scis.-Nat. Research Council safe dirnking water com. on disinfection 1977-79, 85-86), Sigma Xi. Author: Disinfection-Water and Wastewater, 1975. Club: Masons. Home: 720 Bradley Rd Chapel Hill NC 27514

JOHNSON, JAMES MCDADE, lawyer; b. Shreveport, La., Dec. 5, 1939; s. Leslie N. and Nell (McDade) J.; m. Glenda Roth, Jan. 27, 1962; children—Danielle Johnson Soufi, Kimberly Dawn. B.A., La. State U., 1962, J.D., 1964. Bar: La. 1964. First asst. dist. atty. 26th Jud. Dist. La., Minden, 1975-83; ptnr. Campbell, Campbell & Johnson, Minden, 1964—; asst. nat. legal counsel U.S. Jaycees, Tulsa, 1970-71, nat. legal counsel, 1971-72. Chmn. Minden Democratic Exec. Com., La., 1964-74. Named Outstanding Vice Pres. La. Jaycees, 1969. Mem. Assn. Trial Lawyers Am. Episcopalian. Office: Campbell Campbell & Johnson PO Box 834 Minden LA 71058

JOHNSON, JAMES WHITNEY, chiropractic physician; b. Watertown, S.D., Nov. 30, 1946; s. W.L. Mike and Irma (Opheim) M.; m. Resa Lynn Falk, Dec. 29, 1979; children—Tara Alyssa, David Ari. B.A., Newberry Coll., 1969; grad. Nat. Coll. Chiropractic, 1976. Assoc., Smith Chiropractic Clinic, South Sioux City, Nebr., 1976-77; dir., physician Cooper City Chiropractic Clinic, Cooper City, Fla., 1977—; instr. Nat. Coll. Chiropractic, Lombard, Ill., 1976. Served with AUS, 1969-71. Mem. Davie Cooper City C. of C. (pres.), Am. Chiropractic Assn., Fla. Chiropractic Assn., Broward County Chiropractic Assn., Internat. Assn. Preventive Medicine, Am. Chiropractic Assn. Council Sports Injuries, Cabinet Internationale (pres.), Nat. Coll. and Alumni Assn., Nat. Coll. Chiropractic. Clubs: Rotary (pres.), Optimist, Sportroom Athletic. Republican. Jewish. Home: 9760 NW 11th St Plantation FL 33322 Office: 9620 Griffin Rd Cooper City FL 33328

JOHNSON, JEFFREY LYNN, loss control consultant; b. McAllen, Tex., July 14, 1952; s. Nellis Lee and Mary Ellen (Kendrick) J.; m. Melinda Kay Rochester, Aug. 11, 1978; 1 child, Kari Lynn. B.S., Pan Am. U., 1974. Loss control rep. Hartford Ins. Co., Hartford, Conn., 1974, Houston, 1975-76, resident loss control rep., McAllen, Tex., 1976-78, loss control surveyor, 1978-81, loss control cons., 1981—; instr. defensive driving course, hunter safety course. Recipient gen. mgr.'s award Hartford Ins. Co., 1984. Mem. Am. Soc. Safety Engrs., Nat. Safety Council, Nat. Fire Protection Assn., Nat. Rifle Assn. (Leadership award 1981), Gulf Coast Conservation Assn. Baptist. Avocations: hunting; fishing; shooting; wildlife conservation. Home: Route 2 Box 1608-G McAllen TX 78504 Office: The Hartford PO Box 2228 McAllen TX 78502

JOHNSON, JIMMY RAY, recording studios and music publishing company executive; b. Sheffield, Ala., Feb. 4, 1943; s. Ray Warren and Hazel Elizabeth (Lewis) J.; children—Jimmy Ray, Jr., Kimberly Dawn; m. 2d Betsy West, Feb. 14, 1977; 1 dau., Alana. Student U. North Ala., 1962-65. Profl. guitar player Del-Rays, 1959-65; exec. asst., audio engr., studio musician Fame Rec. Studios, Muscle Shoals, Ala., mem. Muscle Shoals Sound Rhythm Sect., 1967—; ind. record producer, 1969—; pres. Jimmy Johnson Prodns., Sheffield, Ala., 1975—; pres. MSS Records, Inc., Sheffield, 1980-83; pres. Muscle Shoals Sound Studios, Inc. (Ala.), 1969—, Muscle Shoals Sound Pub. Co., 1969—. Mem. selection com., bd. govs. for Scotty awards 3-M Co., St. Paul, 1982-83. Mem. Muscle Shoals C. of C., Nat. Acad. Rec. Arts and Scis., Muscle Shoals Music Assn. (founding v.p. 1975; pres. 1979-82), Ala. Music Hall Fame (vice chmn. bd. dirs.), Soc. Profl. Audio Rec. Studios, Am. Rifle Assn., Tennessee Valley Hist. Soc., Am. Fedn. Musicians (local 256). Home: 109 Lakewood Dr Sheffield AL 35660 Office: 1000 Alabama Ave Sheffield AL 35660

JOHNSON, JOHN LEE, dentist; b. Raleigh, N.C., Jan. 14, 1949; s. Torrey Maynard and Janey Alice (Phillips) J.; m. Rebecca Rachel Morris, Dec. 18, 1971; children—Jessica Jane, Jennifer Rachel. B.S., Bob Jones U., 1971; D.D.S., U. N.C., 1976. Pvt. practice dentistry, Banner Elk, N.C., 1976—. Vice pres. Avery County Gideons, Newland, N.C., 1983-84, pres., 1985. Mem. ADA, N.C. Dental Soc., Tar Heel Dental Study Club (pres. 1979). Republican. Baptist. Lodge: Kiwanis (v.p. 1979). Avocations: skiing; tennis; camping; hiking; photography. Home and Office: PO Box 338 Banner Elk NC 28604

JOHNSON, JOHN PHILLIP, speech and hearing sciences educator; b. Macon, Ga., May 15, 1946; s. John Thomas and Anita (Faircloth) J.; m.

Barbara Jo Nyenhuis, Aug. 22, 1964; children—Michael, Scott, Traci, John Andrew. B.A., Fla. State U., 1967, M.S., 1969; Ph.D., Kent State U., 1975. Speech pathologist The Rehab. Ctr., Portsmouth, N.H., 1969-70; head speech pathology and audiology dept. Hillside Hosp., Warren, Ohio, 1971-73; asst. prof. speech Bowling Green State U., Ohio, 1975-77; assoc. prof. Lamar U., Beaumont, Tex., 1977-83, prof. chmn. dept. communication, 1983—; cons. speech pathologist St. Mary's Hosp., Port Arthur, Tex., 1981—, Neurol. Ctr., Beaumont, 1979—, Region V Sch. Dists., Beaumont, 1979—. Author: Nature and Treatment of Articulation Disorders, 1980. Contbr. articles to profl. jours. Active Leadership Beaumont, 1983-84. Recipient Outstanding Service award Wood County Ohio Children's Services Assn., 1977. Mem. Am. Speech Lang. Hearing Assn., Speech Communication Assn., Assn. Communication Adminstrn. Republican. Presbyterian. Avocation: golf. Home: 5925 Bicentennial Ln Beaumont TX 77706 Office: Lamar U PO Box 10050 Beaumont TX 77710

JOHNSON, JOHN ROBERT, petroleum company executive; b. Omaha, Apr. 17, 1936; s. Robert William and Hazel Marguerite (White) J.; B.S., Davidson Coll., 1958; m. Margaret Elizabeth Roberts, June 20, 1959; children—Robert Harle, Martha Elizabeth. With Johnson Oil Co. Inc., Morristown, Tenn., 1961—, pres., 1963—; dir. Lakeway Pubs., U.S. Bankshares, Inc., United So. Bank. Magistrate, Hamblen County Ct., 1968-78, chmn., 1971-72; elder 1st Presbyterian Ch., Morristown; pres. Hamblen County United Fund, 1969; pres. Great Smoky Mountain council Boy Scouts Am., 1977-78, 86; mayor Morristown, 1977—. Served to lt. U.S. Army, 1958-61. Recipient Distinguished Service award Morristown Jr. C. of C., 1966; named Tenn. Mayor of Yr., Tenn. Mcpl. League, 1983. Mem. Morristown C. of C. (pres. 1976), Tenn. Oil Marketers Assn. Democrat. Club: Rotary. Home: 505 Hale Ave Morristown TN 37814 Office: 1206 S Cumberland St Morristown TN 37814

JOHNSON, JOHNNY ALBERT, mathematics educator, researcher; b. El Paso, Tex., Mar. 6, 1938; s. Walter Albert and Lillian Ann (Martinets) J.; m. Betty Jean Smith, Aug. 21, 1955; children—Johnny Alden, Brenda Lynn. A.A., Community Coll., 1964; B.A. with honors, U. Calif.-Riverside, 1965, M.A., 1966, Ph.D., 1968. Asst. prof. U. Houston, 1968-72, assoc. prof., 1972-78, prof. math., 1978—; sr. engr. Jet Propulsion Lab.-Calif. Inst. Tech., Pasadena, 1969-71; assoc. mng. editor Houston Jour. Math., U. Houston, 1975-84, editor, 1984—. Contbr. articles to profl. jours. U. Houston grantee, 1969, 1978; NSF fellow, 1965-68. Mem. Math. Assn. Am., Am. Math. Soc. (reviewer), Pi Mu Epsilon. Home: 7802 La Roche Ln Houston TX 77036 Office: Dept Math U Houston University Park 4800 Calhoun Houston TX 77004

JOHNSON, JOSEPH BENJAMIN, university president; b. New Orleans, Sept. 16, 1934; s. Sidney Thomas and Lillie Mickens J.; B.S., Grambling State U., 1957; M.S., U. Colo., 1967, Ed.D., 1973; postgrad. Harvard U., 1975-76; m. Lula Young; children—Yolanda, Joseph, Juliet, Julie. Tchr., George Washington Carver High Sch., Shreveport, La., 1960-61, Booker T. Washington High Sch., Shreveport, 1962-63; with U. Colo., Boulder, 1969-77, exec. asst. to pres., 1975-77; pres. Grambling (La.) State U., 1977—. Mem. Task Force on Econ. Devel., State of La.; trustee Gulf South Research Inst.; mem. nat. adv. com. United Negro Coll. Fund's Dept. Employment and Tng. Devel.; mem. adv. com. Office for Advancement of Public Negro Colls.; mem. acad. adv. com. Black Entertainment TV; mem. La. State Fair. Served with U.S. Army, 1958-60, 61-62. Mem. Am. Assn. Adminstrs. Higher Edn., Am. Assn. Univ. Adminstrs., La. Assn. Educators, AAHPER, So. Assn. Colls. and Schs. (chmn. La. de.), Am. Council Edn., Am. Assn. State Colls. and Univs. (mem. humanities com., com. on acad. and student personnel), Nat. Assn. State Univs. and Land-Grant Colls., Nat. Assn. Equal Opportunity in Higher Edn. (vice chmn. bd. dirs.), La. Edn. Research Assn., Phi Delta Kappa, Kappa Alpha Psi, Kappa Delta Pi. Office: PO Box 607 Grambling LA 71245

JOHNSON, JOSEPH EDWARD, state senator; b. Raleigh, N.C., Oct. 17, 1941; s. Ira Edward and Grace (Ivey) J.; m. Jane Francum, Jan. 31, 1964; children—Jane Elizabeth, Kathryn Ivey, Susan Briles. Student N.C. State U., 1959-61; B.B.A., Wake Forest U., 1964, J.D., 1966. Mem. N.C. Ho. of Reps., 1975-76, 77-78, 79-80; mem. N.C. Senate, 1981—; chmn. pub. utilities and energy com., 1981; vice chmn. mfg., labor and commerce com., 1981; mem. appropriations com., appropriations com. on justice and pub. safety, banking com., election laws, judiciary II, law enforcement and crime control, sr. citizens affairs, state govt. coms., 1981. Mem. adminstrv. bd. Edenton St. United Meth. Ch., asst. supt., tchr. Sunday Sch. Served to 1st lt. M.P.C., U.S. Army, 1967-69. Mem. Wake County Bar Assn., N.C. Bar Assn., ABA, Alpha Kappa Psi, Phi Delta Phi. Democrat. Office: NC Senate State Capitol Raleigh NC 27611*

JOHNSON, JOSEPH TANNI, developer, builder; b. Bossier City, La., Aug. 7, 1934; s. George L. and Theresa (Dupuy) J.; m. Adaz Broussard, Mar. 10, 1956; children—Brent, Bruce. Student, Sch. Architecture, Tulane U., 1954, 55, 56, Centenary Coll., 1957. Owner, builder, developer Joseph T. Johnson Construction Co., Bossier City, La., 1957—; pres. Bossier Construction Co., Inc., 1966-68; sponsor and mortgagee various apartment complexes. Commr. Bossier Levee Bd., 1984; mem. bd. appeals Met. Planning Comm., 1980. Mem. Nat. Assn. Home Builders, Home Builders Assn. (Shreveport-Bossier chpt.), Home Owners Assn. (founder, pres. 1974-77), Bossier City Jaycees. Democrat. Episcopalian. Lodges: Elks, Lions, Exchange Club. Office: Joseph T Johnson Construction Co 2415 Montgomery Ln Bossier City LA 71111

JOHNSON, KAREN BREMER, dentist; b. Clark AFB, Philippines, Oct. 24, 1950; d. Charles and Eva-Ann (Dougherty) Bremer; 1 child, Kenneth Brandon. B.S. in Dental Hygiene, U. N.C., 1972, D.D.S., 1978. Practice dentistry, Creedmoor, N.C., 1978-80, Durham, N.C., 1980—; mem. dental faculty, U. N.C., Chapel Hill, 1978-80; mem. dental staff Durham County Gen. Hosp., 1983—. Mem. Acad. Gen. Dentistry, Acad. Implant Dentistry, ADA, N.C. Dental Assn., Durham C. of C., D.A.R. Avocations: raising and training horses, racquetball, swimming, bicycling, skiing. Office: 2702 S Miami Blvd Durham NC 27703

JOHNSON, KENNETH LEROY, retired air force officer, program management company executive; b. Chgo., Jan. 24, 1922; s. Stanley C. and Nell L. (Lundberg) J.; student Kans. State Coll., 1940-42, U. So. Calif., 1956-57; B.S., U. Omaha, 1959; m. Tran Thi Phuong, July 3, 1946; children—Jeffery John, Candy Ann, James John; children by previous marriage—Kenneth LeRoy, Terri Ann, Jeff J. Commd. U.S. Air Force, 1942, advanced through grades to col., 1960; ret., 1969; contract mgr. Pacific Architects & Engrs. Co., Vietnam, 1970-74; program mgr. Bell Helicopter Internat., Tehran, Iran, 1977-79. Decorated D.F.C. with oak leaf cluster, Purple Heart, Bronze Star, Air medal with seven oak leaf clusters, numerous others. Mem. Nat. Assn. Security Dealers. Republican. Lodge: Masons. Home: 3020 S Sheridan Wichita KS 67217

JOHNSON, KENNETH OSCAR, oil executive; b. Center City, Minn., Apr. 11, 1920; s. Oscar W. and Sigrid (Hollsten) J.; B.S. in Chem. Engring., U. Minn., 1942; m. Margery Wheeler, Apr. 18, 1945; 1 son, Eric W. With Exxon Corp. Houston, 1942-74, heavy fuels mgr. supply dept., 1968-72, wholesale fuels sales mgr., mktg. dept., 1972-74; chmn., chief exec. officer Belcher Oil Co., Miami, Fla., 1974—; dir. S.E. 1st Nat. Bank, Petroleum Industry Found. Mem. Nat. Petroleum Refiners Assn. (dir.). Clubs: Petroleum (Houston); Port Royal (Naples). Patentee in field. Home: 845 Admiralty Parade Naples FL 33940 Office: PO Box 525500 Miami FL 33152

JOHNSON, LADY BIRD (CLAUDIA ALTA TAYLOR, MRS. LYNDON BAINES JOHNSON), former first lady; b. Karnack, Tex., Dec. 22, 1912; d. Thomas Jefferson and Taylor; m. Lyndon Baines Johnson (36th Pres. U.S.), Nov. 17, 1934 (dec. 1973); children—Lynda Bird Johnson Robb, Luci Baines Johnson Turpin. B.A., U. Tex., 1933, B.J., 1934; LL.D., Tex. Woman's U., 1964; Litt.D., U. Tex., 1964, Middlebury (Vt.) Coll., 1967; L.H.D., Williams Coll., 1967, U. Ala., 1975; H.H.D., Southwestern U., 1967. Mgr. husband's congressional office, Washington, 1941-42; owner Tex. Broadcasting Corp., Austin, cattle rancher, Tex., 1943-73, also cotton and timberlands, Ala. Author: A White House Diary, 1970.; Narrator: TV prodn. A Visit to Washington with Mrs. Lyndon B. Johnson, 1965. Hon. chmn. numerous civic and charitable orgns., drives; founder Com. for More Beautiful Capital, 1965; mem. Adv. Council Nat. Parks, Historic Sites, Bldgs. and Monuments; mem. nat. com. Helen Keller World Crusade for Blind; hon. chmn. Town Lake Beautification Com., Austin, LBJ Meml. Grove, Washington; active environ., nat. beautification projects; hon. trustee Washington Gallery Modern Art; regent U. Tex. System, 1971-77; trustee Nat. Geog. Soc.; hon. co-chmn., founder Nat. Wildflowers Research Ctr., 1982. Recipient Togetherness award McCall's Mag., 1958, Crystal citation Fashion Group Phila., 1961, Distinguished Achievement award Washington Heart Assn., 1962, citation Nat. Assn. Colored Women's Clubs, 1962, Humanitarian award Ararat chpt. B'nai B'rith, Industry citation Am. Women in Radio and TV, 1963, Humanitarian citation Vols. Am., 1963; Conservation Service award Dept. Interior, 1974; named Woman of Year for quality of life Ladies Home Jour., 1975; Medal of Freedom Pres. Ford, 1977; numerous others. Mem. Federated Bus. and Profl. Women's Club (Bus. Woman's award 1961), AAUW (life mem. Tex. div.), Internat. Club U, Theta Sigma Phi (citation 1961), others. Episcopalian. Address: LBJ Library 2313 Red River Austin TX 78705*

JOHNSON, LILLIAN BEATRICE, sociologist, educator; b. Wilmington, N.C., Nov. 8, 1922; d. James Archie and Mary Gaston (Atkins) J. A.A., Peace Coll., 1940; B.R.E., Presbyterian Sch. Christian Edn., 1942; M.S., N.C. State U., 1965, Ph.D., 1972. Dir. Christian edn. First Presbyn. Ch., Pensacola, Fla., 1945-47, Greenwood, S.C., 1947-48, Durham, N.C., 1948-51; club dir. Army Spl. Services, No. Command, Japan, 1951-53; teenage dir. YWCA, Washington, 1953-56, assoc. exec. Honolulu, 1956-59, exec. dir. Tulsa, 1959-62; instr. N.C. State U., 1962-72; asst. prof. Greensboro Coll., 1972-75; mem. faculty sociology dept. Livingston U., 1975—, now prof. Election law commr. State of Ala. Mem. Am. Sociol. Assn., So. Sociol. Soc., Ala.-Miss. Sociol. Assn. (treas.), Nat. Council Family Relations, Ala. Council on Family Relations (v.p. 1981-83), Alpha Kappa Delta (treas. 1984-86). Home: Meadowbrook Dr Livingston AL 35470 Office: Livingston U Livingston AL 35470

JOHNSON, LOCH KINGSFORD, political science educator, researcher; b. Auckland, N.Z., Feb. 21, 1942; came to U.S., 1946; s. Roland and Kathleen Winifred (Frost) J.; m. Leena Sepp, Mar. 22, 1969; 1 child, Kristin Elizabeth. B.A., U. Calif.-Davis, 1965; Ph.D., U. Calif.-Riverside, 1969. Staff aide U.S. Senate, Washington, 1969-70, 75-77; asst. prof. Ohio U., Athens, 1971-75; staff dir. U.S. Ho. of Reps. Subcom., Washington, 1977-79; assoc. prof. dept. polit. sci., U. Ga., Athens, 1979—; adv. bd. Ctr. for Nat. Policy, Washington, 1980-85; cons. Nat. Security Council, Washington, 1980, U.S. Ho. of Reps. Fgn. Affairs Com., 1980, U.S. Dept. State, 1972. Author: The Making of International Agreement, 1984; Season of Inquiry, 1985; contbr. articles to profl. jours. in field. Active polit. campaigns, Calif., Idaho, 1968, 74; issues dir. Frank Church for Pres., Washington, 1976; debate advisor Jimmy Carter for Pres., Washington, 1980. Named Outstanding Tchr., Pi Sigma Alpha, U. Ga., 1980, 81, Outstanding Honors Prof., U. Ga., 1981, 82, 85; Haynes Found. fellow, 1966. Mem. Am. Polit. Sci. Assn. (Congl. fellow 1969), Internat. Studies Assn., Ga. Polit. Sci. Assn., Ctr. for Nat. Policy, Legis. Studies Group. Democrat. Presbyterian. Avocations: Orienteering; long distance running; drawing; backpacking; rugby. Office: Polit Sci Dept U Ga Baldwin Hall Athens GA 30602

JOHNSON, LOYD, agricultural engineer; b. Somerville, Ala., Mar. 18, 1927; s. Iley Benford and Ruth (Humphrey) J.; m. Ester Banegas, Dec. 24, 1952; children—Theresa Ann, Thomas Patrick, Loyd Carl. B.S., Auburn U., 1950, M.S., 1954. Registered profl. engr., Calif. Sr. project engr. United Fruit Co., Guatemala, Honduras, Panama, 1951-60; agrl. engr. Rockefeller Found., 1960-82, mem. research staff Internat. Rice Research Inst., Philippines, 1960-68, Centro Internacional de Agricultura Tropical, Colombia, 1968-77, Internat. Agrl. Devel. Service, Ecuador, 1977-81, Internat. Fertilizer Devel. Ctr., 1981-82; cons. agrl. engr. Internat. Agrl. Devel. Services, Bangladesh, 1982-83, Indonesia, 1984-85. Served with USNR, 1945-46. Mem. Am. Soc. Agrl. Engrs., Indian Soc. Agrl. Engrs. (life), Bangladesh Soc. Agrl. Engrs. Roman Catholic. Developed agrl. expt. sta. fields and research support facilities. Home: Route 3 Box 486 Somerville AL 35670

JOHNSON, MARK MATTHEW, museum administrator; b. Rochester, Minn., Dec. 10, 1950; s. Charles Michael Jr. and Jean Lee (Reid) J.; m. Amy Joy Schneider, Mar. 10, 1984. B.A., U. Wis.-Whitewater, 1974; cert. Art Mus. Studies, U. Ill., 1976, M.A., 1976. Teaching asst. art and design U. Ill., Urbana-Champaign, 1974-75; research asst. Krannert Art Mus., Champaign, 1975; lectr. fine arts Calumet Coll., Whiting, Ind., 1976-77; asst. mgr. World of Franklin and Jefferson Exhbn., Bicentennial Adminstrn. and Art Inst. Chgo., 1976; lectr. dept. mus. edn. Art Inst. Chgo., 1975-77; instr. Cuyahoga Community Coll., Cleve., 1977-81; asst. curator dept. art history and edn. Cleve. Mus. Art, 1977-81; asst. dir., keeper European collections Krannert Art Mus., 1981-85; dir. Muscarelle Mus. Art, Coll. William and Mary, Williamsburg, Va., 1985—. Author: Idea to Image: Preparatory Studies from the Renaissance to Impressionism, 1980. Mem. editorial adv. bd. Arts and Activities mag., 1977—. Research and travel grantee various museums. Mem. Coll. Art Assn., Am. Assn. Museums (edn. com.) Office: Muscarelle Mus Art Coll William and Mary Williamsburg VA 23185

JOHNSON, MARY ELIZABETH, music educator, pianist; b. Tyler, Tex., Mar. 29, 1933; d. Robert Edward and Mamie Oberia (Walters) Spaulding; B.F.A., So. Methodist U., 1955; pvt. study with Bomar Cramer, Dallas, 1964-69; m. George Devereaux Johnson, Mar. 31, 1955; children—Bradford D., Robin Elizabeth. Music tchr. Dallas Country Day Sch., 1955; tchr. Dayton (Ohio) pub. schs., 1956-57; pvt. tchr. piano Dallas, 1962—; profl. accompanist, Dallas, 1965—; duo-pianist, Dallas, 1965-86; sponsor-tchr. creative and performing arts program Dallas Ind. Sch. Dist., 1981-82. Named to honor roll Nat. Guild Piano Tchrs., 1971, Hall of Fame, Am. Coll. Musicians, 1981. Mem. Junior Pianists Guild (chmn. jr. recitals 1982-83, sr. recitals 1984-85), Nat. Guild Piano Tchrs. (cert.), Tex. Fedn. Music Clubs (historian 1974-76, state chmn. music service in the community 1971-73, dist. jr. counselor 1971-78, dist. chmn. music service in the community 1971-78; rec. sec. 5th dist. 1975-76, 1st v.p. 1977-78, jr. festival chmn. 1977-80, dist. chmn. Jr. Gold Cup awards 1980, 86, asst. chmn. North Dallas div. 5th dist. jr. festival 1981-82), Music Tchrs. Nat. Assn., Tex., Dallas music tchrs. assns., Music Study Club Dallas (chmn. piano program 1981-82), Schubert Study Club, Dallas Fedn. Music Clubs (del. 1969-78, 1st v.p. 1977), Daus. Republic Tex. (1st v.p. Bonham chpt. 1975-76), Alpha Delta Pi. Clubs: Melodie (pres. 1969-71, 3d v.p. 1977—, choral accompanist, counselor jr. club, historian, press sec. 1981-82), Kalista (v.p. 1984-85, pres. 1985-86), Jr. Melodie, Jr. Harmonie. Home: 3848 Cedarbrush Dr Dallas TX 75229

JOHNSON, MARY LYNN, chemistry educator, consultant; b. Pampa, Tex., Mar. 12, 1938; d. E. Ray and L. Hortense (Allison) Miller; m. James Jefferson Johnson, Jr., Aug. 17, 1957; children—Melinda Ann, James Jefferson III. Student, West Tex. State U., 1955-57; B.S. in Scis., U. Tex.-El Paso, 1958; M.S., N.Mex. State U., 1961; Ph.D., Pa. State U., 1970. Air pollution chemist El Paso City-County Health Dept., Tex., 1959-60, 61-63, Tex. State Health Dept., El Paso, 1963-64; air pollution spl. fellow USPHS, HEW, University Park, N.Mex., 1960-61, University Park, Pa., 1964-68; asst. prof. chemistry U. Tex.-Arlington, 1968-75; chemistry instr. Hockaday Sch., Dallas, 1975—, Brookhaven Coll., Dallas, 1979—; indsl. cons. combustion and air pollution problems, 1965-75. Contbr. articles to profl. jours. Mem. People to People Citizen Ambassadors. Mem. Am. Chem. Soc., Combustion Inst. Democrat. Presbyterian. Avocations: reading; antiques; piano. Home: 3004 Croydon Denton TX 76201 Office: Hockaday Sch 11600 Welch Rd Dallas TX 75229

JOHNSON, MERRITT W., college administrator; b. Longview, Tex., Nov. 9, 1934; s. Marshall B. and Virgie (Stokley) J.; m. Martha Del Collier, July 15, 1961 (div. Mar. 1972); children—Angela, Marshall; m. Georgia Diane Villyard, Mar. 15, 1974; 1 child, Ryan. B.S., Tex. A&M U., 1957; M.S., East Tex. State U., 1968. Wireline service technician Otis Engring., Longview, Tex., Shreveport, La., 1958-60; asst. mgr. B.F. Goodrich Co., Shreveport, 1960-63; tchr. Hallsville Ind. Sch., Tex., 1963-64; tchr. Kilgore Coll., Tex., 1964-74, dept. chmn., 1974-79, div. dir., 1979—. NSF study grantee Bklyn. Poly. Inst., 1971. Mem. Am. Soc. Engring. Edn., Nat. Assn. Corrosion Engrs., Tex. Indsl. Arts Assn., East Tex. Indsl. Arts Assn. Republican. Baptist. Clubs: Kilgore Coll. Employees Assn. (v.p. 1985-86); Deep East Tex. A&M, Tex. A&M Century (Longview). Avocations: golf; snow skiing; ranching. Home: 509 Cynthia St Longview TX 75601 Office: Kilgore Coll 1100 Broadway Kilgore TX 75662

JOHNSON, NOAH R., nuclear physicist; b. Kingsport, Tenn., Oct. 15, 1928; s. Noah R. Sr. and Alma L. (Lambert) J.; m. Rosemary McElroy, Aug. 19, 1950; children—Kurt, Gregory, Gwen. B.S., East Tenn. State U., 1950; Ph.D., Fla. State U., 1956. Research staff scientist Oak Ridge Nat. Lab., Tenn., 1956-62, sr. scientist, 1963-80, group leader, 1980—; vis. scientist Niels Bohr Inst., Copenhagen, 1962-63. Author (with others) Nuclear Chemistry, 1963. Editor: High Angular Momentum Properties of Nuclei, 1983. Contbr. articles to profl. jours. Guggenheim fellow 1962-63; Fulbright scholar 1962-63. Fellow Am. Phys. Soc.; mem. Am. Chem. Soc., Sigma Xi, Sigma Pi Sigma. Home: 997 W Outer Dr Oak Ridge TN 37830 Office: Oak Ridge Nat Lab Bldg 6000 Oak Ridge TN 37831

JOHNSON, NOTA, artist, educator; b. Maryville, Mo., Nov. 20, 1923; d. Sam and Eva (Papathanasopoulou) Gianacopoulos; divorced; children—Sharon Ann, Vicki Lyn Groom. B.A., Okla. State U., 1945; M.A., U. Tulsa, 1973. Art tchr. Meml. High Sch., Tulsa, 1968-70; art instr. Tulsa Jr. Coll., 1970—. Bd. dirs. Arts and Humanities Council Tulsa, 1976-81; com. mem. Visual Arts Com. Tulsa, 1976-81; v.p. So. Graphics Council, Statesboro, Ga., 1980-82. Prin. works include carved oak altar gates Greek Orthodox Ch., Tulsa, 1980, wood Byzantine cross, 1985. Recipient award Mus. Okla., 1979, Bartlesville Art Assn., 1976; Cin. Art Acad. scholar. Mem. Audubon Artists, Nat. Assn. Women Artists (membership com. 1978, awards 1980, 82, 84), Republican. Greek Orthodox. Club: Philoptohos (bd. dirs. 1984—) (Tulsa). Lodge: Daus. of Penelope (v.p., bd. dirs. 1982). Avocations: designing clothes; sports. Home and Studio: 1500 S Frisco St Tulsa OK 74119

JOHNSON, OTIS SAMUEL, social sciences educator; b. Savannah, Ga., Mar. 26, 1942. A.A., Armstrong State Coll., 1964; A.B., U. Ga., 1967; M.S.W., Atlanta U., 1969; Ph.D., Brandeis U., 1980. Dep. dir. Model Cities Program, Savannah, 1969-71; head dept. social scis. Savannah State Coll., 1980-84, head dept. social work, 1985—. Active Savannah Sickle Cell Com.; alderman City of Savannah, 1982—. Mem. NAACP, Acad. Cert. Social Workers, Assn. Study Afro-Am. Life and History, Nat. Assn. Social Workers (Ga. chapt., Social Worker of Yr. Southeast Ga. Unit 1984), Alpha Kappa Delta. Democrat. Baptist. Avocations: camping; bicycling. Home: 816 Maupas Ave Savannah GA 31401 Office: Savannah State Coll Dept Social Work and Applied Sociology PO Box 20537 Savannah GA 31404

JOHNSON, PATRICIA ANN, real estate agent; b. Springfield, Mo., Dec. 2, 1952; d. Elvis Eugene and Jean Alice (Cain) J.; B.S., U. Mo., Columbia, 1975. With Am. Nat. Ins. Co., Galveston, Tex., 1975-81, pub. asst., 1975-77, editor The Tower, 1977-80, editor The Tower and Star Bull. mag., 1980-81; assoc. Amelia Bullock Realtors, Inc., Austin, Tex., 1983—. Bd. govs. Upper Deck Theatre, Galveston, 1976, 80, chmn. governing bd., 1977-78, sec., 1978-80; bd. dirs. Galveston County unit Am. Cancer Soc., 1977-79, sec., 1978-79; bd. dirs. Paramount Theatre for Performing Arts, Austin, 1983—, Pebble Project, Austin, 1983—; mem. Jr. League of Austin, Inc. Presbyterian. Home: 10711 B Newmont Austin TX 78758 Office: 6907 Capital of Texas Hwy Suite 360 Austin TX 78731

JOHNSON, PAUL REYNOLD, economics educator; b. Bozeman, Mont., Feb. 23, 1929; s. Sherman E. and Evelyn (Hedin) J.; m. Eloise Johnston, Jan. 10, 1952; children—David R., Karen Johnson Dickerson, Paula M. A.B., Oberlin Coll., 1950; M.S., N.C. State U., 1953; Ph.D., U. Chgo., 1959. Asst. prof. U. Ky., Lexington, 1958-61, assoc. prof., 1961-62; economist U.S. Dept. Agr., Raleigh, 1962-63; prof. dept. econs. and bus. N.C. State U., Raleigh, 1963—; economist Rand Corp., Santa Monica, Calif., 1967-68. Author: (with others) Economics of World Grain Trade, 1978; Economics of the Tobacco Industry, 1984. Contbr. articles to profl. jours. Served to lt. USNR, 1953-56. Mem. Am. Econ. Assn., Am. Agrl. Econ. Assn., Am. Statis. Assn. Avocations: golf; reading. Home: 1520 Delmont Dr Raleigh NC 27607 Office: Dept Econs and Bus NC State U PO Box 8109 Raleigh NC 27695

JOHNSON, PETER MICHAEL, convenience stores marketing director; b. Mpls., Oct. 21, 1945; s. Raymond Lawrence and Evelyn Harriet (McGowan) J.; B.S., U. Minn., 1967; M.S., U. Calif., 1973; M.B.A., Emory U., 1982; m. Vivian Helen Langsdorf, Nov. 5, 1977. Mgr. quality control Feinberg Reuben Meats, Mpls., 1973-74; dir. product devel. Stewart Sandwich Co., Mpls., 1974-77; plant mgr. Pasquale Food Co., Birmingham, Ala., 1977-79; dir. product analysis and devel. Del Taco Corp. (W. R. Grace & Co.), Atlanta, 1979-81; dir. corp. fast food sales Nat. Convenience Stores, Houston, 1981-83; dir. mktg. Jitney Jungle, Inc., Jackson, Miss., 1983—; cons. in field. Pres. environ. commn., also mem. long-range planning commn. City of Crystal (Minn.), 1972-73. Served as officer, inf., U.S. Army, 1967-69. Mem. Inst. Food Technologists, Am. Assn. Cereal Chemists, Ry. and Locomotive Hist. Soc., Soc. Food Service Research, Internat. Food Service Assn. Home: 803 Euclid Ave Jackson MS Office: 440 N Mill St Jackson MS 39207

JOHNSON, RANDALL C., mortgage banker; b. Tulsa, Feb. 12, 1949; s. Clyde O. and Barbara (Wolf) J.; m. Frances E. Wigelius, Oct. 1, 1982; 1 son, Paul C. B.A., U. Miami, 1971. Cert. mortgage banker. Vice-pres. Baker Mortgage Co., Miami, Fla., 1971-75; regional mgr. Gen. Electric Credit Corp., Coral Gables, Fla., 1975-77; pres., chief exec. officer Arvida Mortgage Co., Clearwater, Fla., 1977—, also dir.; dir. Arvida Ins. Co.; mem. faculty Sch. Mortgage Banking, Washington, 1983—. Mem. Pinellas Com. of 100. Mem. Mortgage Bankers Assn. Fla. (bd. govs. 1980-83, chmn. legis. com. 1983-84, chmn. bd. polit. action com. 1982, sec.-treas. 1984-85), Mortgage Bankers Assn. Am. (legis. com. 1983-84, internal mgmt. com. 1981-84, cert. mortgage banker com. 1984—, state and local liaison com. 1984—), Clearwater C. of C., Soc. Real Estate Appraisers. Republican. Episcopalian. Clubs: Carlouel Yacht, Harborview, Rotary. Home: 5 Eastwood Ln Belleair FL 33516 Office: Arvida Mortgage Co 1307 US Hwy 19 S Clearwater FL 33546

JOHNSON, RICHARD ALVIN, electronics engineer; b. Edwardsville, Ill., July 8, 1934; s. William and Elma Marie (Blixen) J.; B.S.E.E., Mich. State U., 1963; m. Linda Covington, July 18, 1978; children—Richard Alan, Teresa Lynn, William Allen Covington. Electronic field engr. Gen. Dynamics/Electronics, 1960-65; systems engr. ITT Fed. Labs., 1965-66; program analyst Gen. Elec. Co., 1966-71; dir. Miss. State U. Research Center, 1971-74; v.p. AMCO Constrn. Co. Inc., Bay St Louis, Miss., 1974-76; sr. partner Johnson & Assos., 1976-77; sr. mem. tech. staff Arabian Am. Oil Co., 1977—. Lectr. mgmt. seminar Miss. State U.; adj. faculty U. So. Miss. Served with Signal Corps, AUS, 1955-58. Recipient tech. award in environ. sci. Am. Astronautical Soc., 1970. Mem. IEEE, Am. Mgmt. Assn., Am. Inst. Cons. Engrs. Author: (with others) Operations Management, 1972. Contbr. tech. articles to profl. jours. Home: 17 Poplar Circle Gulfport MS 39501 Office: Box 5734 Dhahran Saudi Arabia

JOHNSON, ROBERT ALAN, materials science educator; b. N.Y.C., Jan. 2, 1933; s. George E. and Betty (Durisek) J.; m. Joyce A. Wittenberger, June 19, 1954; children—Sharon L., Derek A., Todd A. A.B., Harvard U., 1954; Ph.D., Rensselaer Poly. Inst., 1962. Physicist, Brookhaven Nat. Lab., Upton, N.Y., 1962-69; prof. Univ. Va., Charlottesville, 1969—; researcher. Served with USN, 1954-57. Fellow Am. Phys. Soc.; mem. Metall. Soc. of AIME, AAAS, Sigma Xi. Contbr. author sci. publs. Home: Route 3 Box 253 Charlottesville VA 22901 Office: Materials Science Dept Thornton Hall U Va Charlottesville VA 22901

JOHNSON, ROBERT ALLEN, army officer; b. Massillon, Ohio, Oct. 28, 1934; s. Eugene and Lillian Narvella (Edwards) J.; m. Delina Merle Harvey, Dec. 1, 1956; children—Anita Ann, David Allen, Denise Michelle. B.S. in Radio Journalism, Kent State U., 1956. Commd. 2d lt. U.S. Army, 1957, advanced through grades to lt. col., 1971; comdr. 60th Postal Unit, Paris; comdr. Trf. Sta., Ft. Hamilton, N.Y.; chief adminstrv. services 2d Inf. Div., Korea; dep. AG, 9th Inf. Div., Vietnam; adj. gen. Ft. Jackson, S.C., Tokyo; chief adminstrv. systems Hdqrs. U.S. Army Forces Command, Ft. McPherson, Ga., 1978—. Mem. Forces Command Speakers Bur., 1975-77. Decorated Legion of Merit, Bronze Star, Meritorious Service medal, others. Mem. Assn. Info. Systems Profls. Mem. Christian Ch. (Disciples of Christ). Home: 4451 Sterling Forrest Dr Decatur GA 30034 Office: Headquarters US Army Forces Command Fort McPherson GA 30330

JOHNSON, ROBERT IVAR, marketing consultant, science writer; b. Chgo., Aug. 18, 1933; s. Ivar Carl and Anna Elena (Wirkula) J.; m. Patricia A. Horgan, June 30, 1962; children—Christine Anne, Selenie Anne. Diploma, Wright Jr. Coll., 1953; A.B., Northwestern U., 1957; postgrad. U. Mich., 1958-59. Research asst. Dearborn Obs., Northwestern U., 1953-54, 57; planetarium tech. Adler Planetarium and Astron. Mus., 1953-55, asst. dir., acting dir., 1959, dir., 1960-66; staff, Mus. Expdn. Observation Total Solar Eclipse, 1954, 63; dir. Kans. City Mus. History and Sci., 1966-70; exec. v.p., asst. sec., asst. treas., dir. Envirco, Inc., Northbrook, Ill., 1970-72; ptnr., exec. v.p. Tomorrow's Products Co., 1972-73; spectrographic observer U. Mich., 1958-59; adult edn. faculty Central YMCA, Chgo., 1959-61; lectr. astronomy Chgo. Acad. Scis., 1959-66, Chgo. Tchrs. Coll., 1960-66; spl. lectr. astronomy Ind. U., 1960-65; cons. Field Enterprises Ednl. Corp., 1960-66, Hubbard Sci. Co., 1961, Replogle Globe Co., 1962-63, 68, Compton's Ency., 1961-73, No. Ill. U., 1961-65, Ency. Brit. Films,

Inc., 1962-64, McGraw-Hill, Inc., 1963, Mus. Sci. and Tech., Tel Aviv, 1965-70, Rand McNally & Co., 1966, NSF Earth Sci. Curriculum Project, 1966, Coll. Am. Pathologists, 1970, 73-76, 79—, MCR, Inc., 1972-76, McCrone Research Inst., 1972-83, Frank J. Corbett, Inc., 1972-75, Johnson & Johnson Advt., 1972-83, Dynamic Mktg. Programs, Inc., 1972-73, McCrone Assocs., Inc., 1972-77, Yunker Industries, Inc., 1977—, Clay Enging. & Industries, Inc., 1977—, Sci. Teaching Aids Co., Inc., 1977—, Sonoscan Inc., 1977-83, F. E. Fryer Co., Inc., 1978-83, Andreas Assocs., Inc., 1979-80, Scott Abbott Mfg. Co., 1978—, Tech. Mktg. Group Ltd., 1979—, Intermatic, Inc., 1979-83, Sensidyne Inc., 1985—, CGM Services Inc., 1985—, others; ind. cons., 1970-83; cons. U. So. Fla. Office Devel., The Living Ctr. for Bibl. Studies and Archaeol. Studies, 1985—; dir. NSF Summer Inst. in Astronomy, 1963, 64, 65; ptnr. TBM Investments Co., 1964-65; tech. cons. Follett Pub. Co., 1966-68; mem. citizens adv. com. for natural scis. Lake Forest Coll., 1961-66; bd. advisers World Book Ency. Sci. Service, 1964-66; program adv. bd. Inter-Univ. Ctr., 1966-73; mem. Am. Nat. ICOM Com. Edn. and Cultural Action; cons. astronomy and allied scis., planetarium design and ednl. films prodn., various orgns. Author: Teachers Guide for the Celestial Globe, 1961, Astronomy-Our Solar System and Beyond, 1963, Galaxy Model Study Guide, 1963, The Story of the Moon, 1963, rev. edit., 1968, 2d edit., 1971, Celestial Planetarium Guide Book, 1964, Meteorite Kit Study Guide, 1968, Sundials, 1968; editor: Insight, 1972-77, Techniques, Instruments and Accessories for Microanalysts-A User's Manual, 1972-83; mem. editorial bd. Space Frontiers, 1962-66. Contbr. articles to profl. jours, other publs. Sci. fair judge high sch. div. Chgo. Bd. Edn., Parochial Schs., 1959-66; mem. U.S. com. for ednl. and cultural affairs Internat. Council Museums, 1966-70; mem. fine arts com. Ill. Sesquicentennial Commn., 1967-68; mem. Model Cities Com., Liberty Meml. Exhbn. Com., 1967-70; mem. Regional Health and Welfare Council, 1967-70, Kansas City Assembly on U.S. and Eastern Europe, 1968, NSF panel Summer Inst. for Secondary Schs., 1968-76, Midwest Mus. Conf., 1964-70; fin. com. Midwest Mus. Conf., 1967-70; mem. spl. events com. Kansas City Jewish Community Ctr., 1968-70; mem. Twin Lakes Bicentennial Com., 1976; v.p. Lakewood Sch. Parent Tchr. Orgn., 1976-77, pres., 1977-78, 80; bd. govs. Bacchus Cultural and Ednl. Found., 1968-70. Served with AUS, 1955-56; intelligence analyst; Chgo.-Gary Nike Def. Hdqrs. Recipient cert. for service Gary Pub. Schs., Ind., 1959, Indsl. Research 100 award, 1973; named One of 10 Outstanding Young Men Chgo. Jr. C. of C. and Industry, 1961. Fellow AAAS; mem. Am. Astron. Soc. (co-chmn. com. spl. events 1964), Chgo. Astron. Soc., Internat. Platform Assn., Chgo. Planetarium Soc., Chgo. Physics Club (dir., pres. 1960-66), Royal Astron. Soc. Can., Assn. Sci. Mus. Dirs., Chgo. Geog. Soc., Adult Edn. Council Greater Chgo. (speakers bur., dir.), Am. Assn. Museums (chmn. planetarium sect. 1962-66, program chmn. 1966), Nat. Adult Edn. Assn. (tours com. 1966), Golf Civic Assn., Northwestern U. Alumni Assn., Mu Beta Phi (hon.). Clubs: Execs. (Chgo.); Carriage.

JOHNSON, ROBERT MICHAEL, construction company executive, engineer; b. Springfield, Mass., Oct. 22, 1938; s. Ole W. and Virginia F. J.; m. Mary Richardson, Jan. 16, 1960 (dec. 1976); children—Kim, Jennifer, William, Judy; m. 2d, Virginia Hanggi, Oct. 9, 1976; children—Laura, Cindy. B.S. in Engring., Norwich U., 1959. Player Washington Redskins, 1959-61; clk. United Shoe Machinery, Boston, 1961-62; sales mgr. Indsl. Air Co., Newton, Mass., 1962-63, Atlanta, 1963-65, Birmingham, Ala., 1965-68; exec. Iron Mountain Enging., Inc., Birmingham, 1968-74; pres. JHK Systems, Inc., Birmingham, 1974—; dir. WRI Systems Internat.; officer, dir. WU's Agrl. Inc. Bd. dirs., mem. bowl game com. Nat. Football Found. Inc. Recipient Disting. Alumni award Norwich U., 1983; Mem. TAPPI, ASHRAE, Ala. Profl. Engrs. Roman Catholic. Clubs: Relay House, Riverchase Country (Birmingham). Lodge: Elks. Home: RD 1 PO Box 390 Leeds AL 35094 Office: JHU Systems Inc 2830 19th St S Birmingham AL 35209

JOHNSON, RUTH ALICE, small business owner; b. Oklahoma City, Dec. 10, 1917; d. George H. and Effie C. (Outler) Romberger; student Central State Coll., 1935-36, Hills Bus. Coll., 1936-37; student Jacques Gourmet Cooking Sch., 1977-78; m. William A. Johnson, Sept. 11, 1938 (dec. 1968); children—Jan Johnson Smith, Jerry, Judie Johnson Duncan, Jill Johnson Pence. Columnist Nichols Hills News, 1945-47; sec. vol. services Children's Meml. Hosp., Oklahoma City, 1969-70; supr. vol. services Hosps. of U. Okla., Oklahoma City, 1971-73; coordinator of vols. U. Hosp., 1973-74, Bapt. Med. Center, Oklahoma City, Okla. 1974-76; dir. vols. Deaconess Hosp., Oklahoma City, 1976-79; owner Antiqueville, Oklahoma City, 1980—. Girl scout leader Redland council Girl Scouts U.S., 1944-69; pres. Youth Study Club, Oklahoma City, 1947—; pres. West Nichols Hills PTA, 1960-61; pres. Christian Women's Fellowship Crown Heights Christian Ch., 1967-68, Sunday sch. tchr., 1954-56. Mem. Am. Hosp. Assn., Am. Soc. of Dirs. of Vols, Okla. Soc. for Dir. Vols. Compiler (girl scout guide) Our Treasure Chest, 1967. Club: La Connaissance Study (pres. 1983-84). Home: 1708 Guilford Ln Oklahoma City OK 73120 Office: 7626 N Western Oklahoma City OK

JOHNSON, SAM, judge; b. Hubbard, Tex., Nov. 17, 1920; s. Sam D. and Flora (Brown) J.; m. June Page, June 1, 1946; children—Page Johnson Harris, Janet Johnson Clements, Sam. J. B.B.A., Baylor U., 1946; LL.B., U. Tex., 1949. Bar: Tex. bar 1949. Former county atty. Hill County, Tex.; dist. atty. and dist. judge 66th Jud. Dist. of Hill County, Tex.; judge 14th Ct. Civil Appeals, Houston; assoc. justice Supreme Ct. Tex., Austin; now judge U.S. Ct. of Appeals for 5th Circuit.; Bd. dirs. Nat. Legal Aid and Defender Assn.; past bd. dirs. Houston Legal Found. Served with AUS, 1942-45. Recipient Disting. Alumnus award Baylor U., 1978-79. Mem. ABA (chmn. appellate judges conf., bd. govs., bd. govs. 1979-82), Baylor Ex-Students Assn. (pres. 1972-73). Democrat. Home: 1811 Exposition Blvd Austin TX 78703 Office: 999 American Bank Tower Austin TX 78701

JOHNSON, SANDRA BARTLETT, city official; b. Phoenix; d. Hartley and Alice C. (Johnson) Bartlett; m. Richard Anthony Johnson, May 1, 1965; 1 dau., Nicole Elizabeth. Student Fla. State U., 1958-61. Chem. Lab. tech. Agrl. Expt. Sta., U. Fla., Bradenton, 1963-65; chem. lab. tech. Coca-Cola Co., Atlanta, 1965-78, purchasing agt., tech. div., 1978-81, furnishing coordinator, 1981-83. Mem. city council City of Alpharetta (Ga.), 1980—. Mem. Nat. Assn. Purchasing Mgmt., Purchasing Mgmt. Assn., Ga. Mcpl. Assn., Am. Planning Assn., N. Fulton Council Local Govts. Episcopalian. Home: 240 Pebble Trail Alpharetta GA 30201

JOHNSON, STEPHANIE ROSE, nursing home administrator; b. Siler City, N.C., Apr. 10, 1958; d. Harvey Bynum and Willie (Davis) Johnson. B.A. in Bus. Mgmt., N.C. State U., 1980; M.A. in Counselor Edn. and Research, Appalachian State U., 1982. Coordinator ednl. programs Appalachian State U., Boone, N.C., 1981-82; residence hall dir. housing Ball State U., Muncie, Ind., 1982-84; student affairs coordinator, resident student devel. Fla. State U., Tallahassee, 1984-85; retirement/nursing home administr. Moravian Home, Inc., Winston-Salem, N.C., 1985—; mem. Staff Devel. Task Force. Mem. Rape Awareness Com., 1984. Mem. Am. Assn. Counseling and Devel., Am. Coll. Personnel Assn., Circle K Alumni Assn. Avocations: reading; walking; cross-stitch.

JOHNSON, THOMAS, economics educator; b. Hallitsville, Tex., Feb. 12, 1936; s. Lewis C. and Gladys (Gilmore) J.; m. Cleta Joy Anderson; children—David Eugene, Michael Joseph, Mark Alan. B.A., U. Tex., 1957; A.A., Navarro Jr. Coll., 1955; M.A., Tex. Christian U., 1962; M.E.S., N.C. State U., 1967, Ph.D., 1969. Engr., Convair, Ft. Worth, Tex., 1957-61, Ling-Temco Vought, Dallas, 1961-64; analyst Research Triangle Inst., Research Triangle Park, N.C., 1964-69; asst. prof. econs. and stats. So. Meth. U., Dallas, 1969-74, assoc. prof., 1974; prof. econs. and stats. N.C. State U., Raleigh, 1974—. Mem. Econometric Soc., Am. Econ. Assn., Am. Statis. Assn., Am. Agrl. Econs. Assn., Phi Theta Kappa, Phi Kappa Phi, Pi Mu Epsilon. Republican. Baptist. Author: Toward Economic Understanding, 1976. Contbr. articles to profl. jours. Home: 1217 Wellington Ln Cary NC 27511 Office: Dept Econs NC State U Raleigh NC 27695

JOHNSON, TRAVIS PHARON, police chief; b. Midland, Tex., Apr. 10, 1943; s. Wade Elliott Johnson and Leana Leata Johnson Crimes; m. Teresa Ann Tabor McQuerrey, Aug. 29, 1964 (div. Oct. 1976); 1 child, Kristin F. Johnson; m. Marcia Kelley, July 17, 1977; children—Eddie E. Pillers, Erica E. Pillers. B.S., Hardin-Simmons U., 1973. Patrolman, San Angelo Police Dept., Tex., 1964-74, sgt., 1974-79, chief of police, 1979—. Bd. dirs. Family Shelter, San Angelo, 1982—, Tex. Alcoholism Council, 1981—. Served with U.S. Army, 1966-68, Panama. Mem. Tex. Mcpl. Police Assn., Tex. Natcotic Officers Assn. (past pres.), Tex. Police Athletic Fedn. (bd. dirs. 1983—). Methodist. Club: Optimist. Lodges: Elks, Masons. Avocations: photography, skiing, hunting. Office: San Angelo Police Dept PO Box 5020 San Angelo TX 76902

JOHNSON, ULYSSES JOHANN, JR., educator, guidance counselor; b. Winter Haven, Fla., Aug. 11, 1929; s. Ulysses Johann and Hattie Lou (Thomas) J.; m. Thelma Mae Simmons, Aug. 9, 1967; children—Marcus Antonius, Melanie Aida. B.S., Fisk U., 1951; M.A., Denver U., 1955; Ed.S., Tenn. Inst. Tech., 1973. Tchr. phys. edn. and health Rochelle Jr. High Sch., Lakeland, Fla., 1951-52; dir. guidance Rochelle Sr. High Sch., Lakeland, 1955-69; dir. counseling Polk Community Coll., Winter Haven, Fla., 1969—. Chmn. boys state Dept. Fla., Am. Legion, Winter Haven, 1954—. Served with U.S. Army, 1952-54. Recipient cert. of appreciation Winter Haven Sr. High Sch., 1985. Mem. Fla. Assn. Community Colls. (past pres.), Am. Assn. for Counseling and Devel., NAACP, Kappa Delta Pi, Kappa Alpha Psi (Man of Yr. award 1975). Lodges: Masons (Speaker of Yr. award 1980), K.T. Democrat. Avocations: cycling; researching organizational histories. Home: 560 Lake Maude Dr NE Winter Haven FL 33881

JOHNSON, VANNETTE WILLIAM, physical education educator, athletic director; b. Little Rock, May 27, 1930; s. Charlie and Laura Delorius Johnson; m. Luella Bender, Jan. 28, 1952; children—Juliette, Alberta; m. 2d, Delois Verneka Davis, Aug. 8, 1959; children—Melanie, Leontyne. B.A., Ark. AM&N Coll., 1952; M.Ed., U. Ark., 1960, Ed.D., 1970. Asst. coach, tchr., Pine Bluff, Ark., 1952-57; asst. football coach, instr. Ark. AM&N Coll., Pine Bluff, 1957-62, dir. athletics, head football coach, 1962-73; dir. athletics, prof. U. Ark.-Pine Bluff, 1974-80, prof. health, phys. edn. and recreation, 1980—, chmn. dept., 1983—. Pres. Jefferson County Black Caucus; justice of peace, 1975—; mem. corp. bd. Jefferson Comprehensive Ctr.; commr. Pine Bluff Conv. Ctr. Mem. AAHPERD, Ark. High Sch. Coaches Assn., Nat. Assn. Intercollegiate Athletics (Coaches Assn.), Pine Bluff C. of C., Phi Delta Kappa, Alpha Kappa Mu, Kappa Delta Pi. Methodist. Club: 20th Century. Lodge: Elks. Home: 1905 Collegiate Dr Pine Bluff AR 71601 Office: U Ark N University Dr Pine Bluff AR 71601

JOHNSON, VERA POOLE, educational administrator; b. Lecompte, La., June 17, 1928; d. Murphy Archer and Dessie Irene (Chamberlain) Poole; B.S., La. Coll., 1960; M.Ed., La. State U., 1971; Ed.D., Northwestern State U., 1979; m. Aug. 11, 1946; children—Murphy Poole, George Gary, Robert Wayne, Randall Martin, Kayla Ann. Elem. math. tchr. Rapides Parish, 1969-70; elem. tchr. Allen Parish, Oberlin, La., 1970-73, helping tchr., 1974, reading coordinator Title I, 1974-85, co-dir. Chpt. 1, 1985—; condr. workshops, cons. in field. Mem. Internat. Reading Assn., La. Reading Assn., Assn. Supervision and Curriculum Devel., La. Assn. Sch. Execs., La. Assn. Sch. Suprs., La. Assn. Sch. Adminstrs. of Federally Assisted Programs, Phi Delta Kappa, Delta Kappa Gamma. Democrat. Mem. Church of Christ. Author: Efficiency of Three Classroom Methods for Achieving Automaticity in Oral Reading Performance, 1979; asst. editor: Epistle. Home: Route 1 Box 51-A Forest Hill LA 71430 Office: PO Drawer C Oberlin LA 70655

JOHNSON, VERNON EUGENE, history educator, educational administrator; b. Norfolk, Va., Oct. 25, 1930; s. Ellis Moses and Maude Louvenia (Wilkins) J.; A.B. with distinction, Va. State Coll., 1951; M.A., U. Pa., 1964; postgrad. Old Dominion U., 1977-78; advanced cert. in edn. Coll. William and Mary, 1979, Ed.D., 1982; diploma with honors U.S. Army Command and Gen. Staff Coll., 1968; m. Barbara Lucy Wynder, June 6, 1959; children—Kevin Bertram, Troy Eugene, Stacy Yvette. Commd. 2d lt. U.S. Army, 1951, advanced through grades to lt. col., 1966, ret., 1979; adminstr., adj. instr. Hampton (Va.) Inst., 1980—; adj. prof. Tidewater Va. Center, St. Leo Coll. of Fla., 1980—. Active Boys' Clubs. Decorated Legion of Merit with oak leaf cluster; recipient Brotherhood award, 1981, Jefferson Cup, 1982; named Man of Yr., 1981. Mem. Am. Assn. Higher Edn., Am. Hist. Assn., Nat. Hist. Assn., Assn. U.S. Army, Internat. Platform Assn., Alpha Kappa Mu, Phi Alpha Theta, Omega Psi Phi (3d dist. rep.). Methodist. Club: Beau Brummell Civic and Social. Office: Hampton Inst Stone Bldg Hampton VA 23668

JOHNSON, WALTER WILLIAM, financial consultant; b. Tampa, Fla., June 13, 1944; s. Howard T. and Alice (Jones) J.; m. Beth Lynn Exum, Apr. 25, 1981. B.S., La. State U., 1966. Mgmt. trainee program Firestone Tire and Rubber Co., Baton Rouge, 1966-70; with Roland Uymel & Assocs., New Orleans, 1970—, sr. assoc., fin. coordinator, 1974—; dir. Cresent Fed. Savs. and Loan. Mem. New Orleans Mus. Art, Thoroughbred Owners and Breeders Assn., New Orleans Met. Crime Assn., Preservation Resource Ctr. New Orleans, Tiger Boosters; dir. DelaSalle Alumni Assn.; mem. New Orleans Met. Crime Assn., 1981-83. Served with USCG, 1966-72. Mem. Internat. Assn. Fin. Planners, New Orleans Life Underwriters Assn. Roman Catholic. Club: Rivercenter Tennis (New Orleans). Office: 2475 Canal St Suite 100 New Orleans LA 70119

JOHNSON, WAYNE D., utility co. exec.; b. Winterset, Iowa, Sept. 20, 1932; s. Leslie E. and Ruth N. J.; m. Lynne Alice Brouwer, June 15, 1963; children—Christopher W., Kevin B. B.A., U. Nebr., 1954; LL.B., Harvard U., 1959. Bar: Ill. bar 1959. Asso. to partner firm Ross, Hardies, O'Keefe, Babcock & Parsons, Chgo., 1959-72; asst. gen. counsel Peoples Gas Co., Chgo., 1972-75; sr. v.p., gen. counsel Entex, Inc., Houston, 1975-78, pres., 1978—; dir. Simmons & Co. Served with U.S. Army, 1954-56. Woodrow Wilson fellow, 1954. Mem. Am. Bar Assn., Am., So. gas assns., Tex. Utilities Lawyers Assn. Clubs: Petroleum; Legal (Chgo.). Home: 710 Marchmont Houston TX 77024 Office: Entex Inc PO Box 2628 Houston TX 77252-2628

JOHNSON, WILLIAM BRUCE, retail executive, tattoo artist, investor; b. Coral Gables, Fla., Nov. 17, 1949; s. Robert Gerard and Josephine (Stromick) J. Grad. high sch., Coral Gables. Sign electrician Weiser Signs, Miami, Fla., 1974-75; mgr., kitchen stewart Ronnies, Inc., Orlando, Fla., 1975-79; owner, mgr. Tattoo Time #1, Maitland, Fla., 1979—; R & R Properties, Maitland, 1985—, Davey Jones Locker Restaurant, Orlando, 1985—, Cycledelic Choppers Motorcycle Supply, 1984—, Seven Seas Dry Cleaners, 1985, pres. Napson Inc. Served with USN, 1968-73. Mem. Nat. Tattoo Assn., European Tattoo Assn. (Deal, Eng.). Avocations: traveling; sailing; motorcycles; photography; guns. Office: Tattoo Time #1 9230 S US Hwy 17-92 Maitland FL 32751

JOHNSON, WILLIAM CLINT, III, economics educator, administrator; b. San Angelo, Tex., Nov. 26, 1941; s. William Clint Jr. and Mary Nell (Graston) J.; m. Ellen Elizabeth Sikes, July 11, 1964; children—David Edward, Stephen Craig, Susan Elizabeth. B.A. summa cum laude, Rice U., 1964; M.A., Vanderbilt U., 1969; D.B.A., Tex. Tech. U., 1975. Research assoc. Tex. Tech. U., Lubbock, 1972-75; assoc. prof. econs., chmn. dept. U. Central Ark., Conway, 1975-81, prof. and chmn. dept. econs. and fin., 1981—; cons. fin. feasibility analysis-health care and fin. instns., 1977—. Contbr. articles to profl. jours. Bd. dirs., facilities rev. com. Central Ark. Health Systems Agy., Inc., Little Rock, 1976-82; bd. dirs., chmn. fin. com. Human Services Ctr. of West Central Ark., Inc., Russellville, 1982—; chmn. Ark. Cert. of Need Appeals Commn., 1985—. U.S. Dept. Labor grantee, 1972. Mem. Am. Econ. Assn., So. Econ. Assn., Southwestern Econs. Assn. (pres. 1980-81), Southwestern Social Sci. Assn. (gen. program chmn. 1983—), Ark. Coll. Tchrs. of Econs. and Bus., Individual Investors Assn. Am., Phi Beta Kappa, Omicron Delta Epsilon, Beta Gamma Sigma. Democrat. Methodist. Lodge: Kiwanis. Avocation: piano. Home: 31 Forrest Ct Conway AR 72032 Office: Dept Econ and Fin U Central Ark PO Box U-1752 Conway AR 72032

JOHNSON, WILLIAM GRAY, petroleum geologist; b. Rotan, Tex., Aug. 24, 1946; s. William Robert and Hazel Jim (Gray) J.; m. Paquita Lee Glass, Sept. 9, 1968; 1 child, Timothy. B.S., U. Tex.-El Paso, 1969. Exploration geologist Union Oil Co., Midland, Tex., 1969-76; geologist Tex. Oil and Gas Corp., Midland, 1976-77, Watson & Cox Oil and Gas, Midland, 1977—. Mem. Am. Assn. Petroleum Geologists. Republican. Avocations: hunting; dirt bikes; photography; scuba diving; sailing. Home: 2807 Emerson Ln Midland TX 79705 Office: Watson & Cox Oil and Gas 303 Union Texas Plaza Midland TX 79701

JOHNSON, WILLIAM MICHAEL, physician; b. Olean, N.Y., Nov. 20, 1940; s. Loren Edward and Ann Elizabeth (Van Dyke) J.; m. Marlene Elsie Brill, June 26, 1965; children—Michael Scott, Susan Kim, Amy Marlene, Linda Marie. A.B., Stanford U., 1963, M.D., 1968; M.P.H., Harvard U., 1970, M. Indsl. Health, 1971. Diplomate Am. Bd. Internal Medicine, Am. Bd. Preventive Medicine. Intern, SUNY-Buffalo Hosps., 1968-69; resident in occupational medicine Harvard Sch. Public Health, Boston, 1969-71; acting dep. dir. div. field studies and clin. investigations Nat. Inst. Occupational Safety and Health Cin., 1971-73; resident in internal medicine U. Ariz. Hosps., Tucson, 1973-75, fellow in pulmonary disease, 1975-77; asst. prof. environ. health, adj. asst. prof. medicine U. Wash., Seattle, 1977-80; commd. lt. col. U.S. Army, 1980; chief pulmonary disease service Dwight David Eisenhower Army Med. Center, Fort Gordon, Ga., 1983, staff, 1980-83; asst. clin. prof. medicine Med. Coll. Ga., Augusta, 1981—. Served as surgeon USPHS, 1971-73. Fellow Am. Coll. Chest Physicians; mem. Am. Thoracic Soc., Soc. Occupational and Environ. Health, Am. Indsl. Hygiene Assn., N.Y. Acad. Scis. Contbr. articles on pulmonary disease and occupational cancer to profl. jours. Home: 2948 Foxhall Circle Augusta GA 30907 Office: Dwight D Eisenhower Army Med Center Fort Gordon GA 30905

JOHNSON, WILLIAM R., univ. adminstr.; b. Houston, Jan. 12, 1933; s. Ernest H. and Rosabelle (Thompson) J.; B.S., U. Houston, 1958, M.A., 1959; Ph.D., U. Okla., 1963; m. Freida Marilyn Kennedy, June 26, 1954; children—William Scott, Alison Gaye. Asso. prof. history Tex. Tech. U., Lubbock, 1968-76, asso. dean arts and scis., 1972-73, interim v.p. acad. affairs, 1973-75, v.p. acad. affairs, 1975-76; pres. Stephen F. Austin State U., Nacogdoches, Tex., 1976—. Served with USAF, 1951-55. Recipient L.R. Bryan Jr. award Tex. Gulf Coast Hist. Assn., 1961. Mem. Tex. Sr. Colls. and Univs. (chmn. council of pres.'s 1979-81), Am. Hist. Assn., Orgn. Am. Historians, Assn. Tex. Colls. and Univs. (pres. 1981-82). Methodist. Clubs: Rotary, Boosters. Author: A Short History of the Sugar Industry in Texas, 1961. Home: 505 E Starr Nacogdoches TX 75961 Office: Box 6078-SFA Station Nacogdoches TX 75962

JOHNSON, WILLIAM RAY, insurance company executive; b. West Union, Ohio, Feb. 12, 1930; s. A. Earl and Helen (Walker) J.; B.S. in Edn., Wilmington Coll., 1951; m. Anne Abrams, Mar. 27, 1954; children—Elizabeth Anne, William Randall. Tchr., theater dept. Miami U., Oxford, Ohio, 1951; div. mgr. Prudential Ins. Co. of Am., Waco, Tex., 1956-57, div. mgr., Houston, 1957-60; nat. tng. cons. Paul Revere Life Ins. Co., Dallas, 1960, gen. agt., 1960-65; health and accident ins. cons., Dallas, 1965-68; pres. MSP Service Corp., Dallas, 1974-83; partner Wiedeman & Johnson Cos., Dallas, 1965—, treas.-sec., 1967-79, pres., 1979—; dir. Cullen Frost Bank/Dallas, 1986—. Pres. bd. dirs. Suicide Prevention of Dallas, 1975-76; bd. dirs. Sr. Citizens of Greater Dallas, Inc., 1977-80, Dallas Child Guidance Clinic, 1977-83; mem. bishops adv. com. on planning and devel., Episcopal Diocese of Dallas, 1976-81, chmn. diocesan mission dept., 1983—, mem. exec. council, 1983—; sr. warden St. Michaels Episcopal Ch., 1979-81; mem. bd. theol. edn. Episcopal Ch., N.Y.C., 1982—; trustee Episcopal Theol. Sem. of SW, Austin, Tex., 1981—. Served to 1st lt. USAF, 1951-55. Clubs: Dallas City, Dallas Country. Office: 3626 N Hall St Suite 800 Dallas TX 75219

JOHNSON, WYLIE PIERSON, electric utility executive; b. Montgomery, Ala., Mar. 28, 1919; s. Seth and Neva (Carmichael) J.; m. Lurene Hall, Nov. 9, 1946; children—Barbara J. Hill, Melanie J. Atkinson, W. Benjamin Johnson. B.S. in Mech. Engring., Auburn U., 1942; postgrad. Cornell U., 1943, Ga. Inst. Tech., 1959. Registered profl. engr., Ala. Engr., Ala. Power Co., Montgomery, 1946-52, supr. transmission lines, Birmingham, 1952-58, supt. transmission, 1958-66, supt. spl. services, 1966-74, mgr. gen. services, 1974-76; ret. 1976; chmn. transmission and large substation com. Southeastern Electric Exchange, Atlanta, 1962-66. Contbr. articles to profl. jours. Chief insp. Election Ofcls., Montgomery, County, Ala., 1980—; pres. Pike Rd. Vol. Fire Dept. Bd., 1985—. Mem. IEEE (chmn. Ala. sect. 1962-63), ASME, Engrs. Club (chmn. budget and fin. 1961), Lambda Chi Alpha. Baptist. Clubs: Green Valley Country, The Club, Young Men's Bus. Lodges: Shriner, Exchange (pres. 1974-75). Avocation: wild life preservation. Home: 70 Robins Rd Pike Road AL 36064

JOHNSON-COUSIN, DANIELLE PAULETTE, language and literature educator; b. Geneva, Nov. 7, 1943; d. Edouard Henri and Suzanne Louise (Maurer) Cousin; m. Harry Morton Johnson, Jan. 25, 1970; 1 child, Eliza Suzanne. B.A., U. Alaska, 1966; M.A., Purdue U., 1968; Ph.D., U. Ill., 1977; postgrad. Oxford U., summer 1968, Northwestern U., 1968-69, U. Munich, 1970. Vis. lectr. U. Ill.-Urbana-Champaign, 1976-77; asst. prof. Amherst Coll., 1979-82; asst. prof. French, Andrew W. Mellon fellow Vanderbilt U., Nashville, 1982—, dir. Vanderbilt-in-France program, Aix-en-Pce, 1984-85. U. Mass. Oxford scholar, 1968; U. Ill. summer fellow, 1971, fellow, 1972-73; Inst. Advanced Studies in Humanities vis. hon. fellow U. Edinburgh (Scotland), summer 1979. Mem. MLA, S. Atlantic MLA, Am. Assn. Tchrs. of French, Assn. Suisse de Littérature comparative et générale, Soc. des Etudes Staëliennes (Paris), Soc. Suisse des Ecrivains, Assn. Suisse des Amis de Mme de Charrière (Neuchâtel), Soc. Benjamin Constant (Lausanne), Hist. Soc. Pa., Am. Soc. 18th-Century Studies. Contbr. articles to profl. jours. Home: 1809A Capers Ave Nashville TN 37212 Office: PO Box 6312-B Furman Hall 222 Dept French and Italian Vanderbilt U Nashville TN 37235

JOHNSON-JENSEN, KAREN SUE, computer systems analyst; b. Springfield, Mo., Mar. 7, 1955; d. E.E. Johnson and Jean Alice Cain. B.A., U. Tex. at Austin, 1977; postgrad. So. Meth. U., 1979—; m. John C. Jenson, Mar. 24, 1979. Lab. research asst. II Applied Research Labs., 1976-77; software design engr. Tex. Instruments Inc., from 1977, now mem. tech. staff for computer systems performance analysis for artificial intelligence research and applications. Campaign vol. Austin City Council, 1980-81, 82-83; blood fund co. coordinator Central Tex. Regional Blood Center, 1978—. Recipient Lifegiver award Central Tex. Regional Blood Center, 1979. Mem. Assn. Computing Machinery, IEEE, Mortar Bd., Alpha Chi Sigma, Pi Mu Epsilon. Presbyterian. Office: Computer Sci Lab Central Research Labs Tex Instrument Inc PO Box 226015 M/S 238 Dallas TX 75266

JOHNSTON, BARBARA ALICE, association executive; b. Onekama, Mich., Sept. 5, 1932; d. William Regal and Anice Juanita (Joseph) Guimond; m. Gerald Franklin Johnston, Dec. 19, 1953 (div. 1976); children—Linda Christine, Michael Carl, Scott Gerald, Bruce William. Student Albion Coll., 1950-51, Mich. State U., 1951-53. Needlework dir. Frederick and Nelson, Seattle, 1963-67; needlework designer, cons. Bucilla div. Armour-Dial Handcrafts, N.Y.C., 1971-80; needlework buyer, designer, cons. Rumplestiltskin's, Seattle, 1973-75; needlework designer, cons. Leisure Arts, Inc., Little Rock, 1976-82; hostess, script devel. TV series Needlecraft, KOCE-TV (recipient Emmy award), Huntington Beach, Calif., 1981; dir. consumer and retailer relations Nat. Needlework Assn., Austin, Tex., 1977—; dir. communications Women in Communications, Inc. Mem. Embroiderers Guild Am., Nat. Standards Council Am. Embroiderers, Counted Thread Soc. Am., Am. Needlepoint Guild, Nat. Embroidery Tchrs. Assn., Am. Stumpwork Soc., Austin Stitchery Guild, Austin Writers League.

JOHNSTON, CHARLENE WANNA, foundation executive; b. Miami, Fla., Oct. 22, 1949; d. Charles Motley and Mary Virginia (DeTardo) J. A.S. in Bus. Adminstrn., Webber Coll., 1985. Sec. to dir. Bok Tower Gardens, Lake Wales, Fla., 1969-75, adminstrv. asst. to dir., 1975-81, asst. sec.-treas., dir. pub. relations, 1981—, editor newsletter, 1984—. Mem. Fla. Pub. Relations Assn., UDC (pres. local chpt. 1985—), Lake Wales C. of C. (chmn. pub. relations council 1985—), Fla. Attractions Assn. Democrat. Methodist. Clubs: Lake Wales Garden; Horizon (Orlando, Fla.). Avocations: gardening; cooking; collecting antique china and rare books. Home: PO Box 787 Lake Wales FL 33853 Office: Bok Tower Gardens PO Drawer 3810 Lake Wales FL 33853

JOHNSTON, DAVID WHITE, JR., textile manufacturing company executive; b. Atlanta, Mar. 31, 1921; s. David White and Annie Kate (Johnston); m. Sally Onie Ingram, July 30, 1949; children—Elizabeth, David. B.S. in Indsl. Mgmt, Ga. Inst. Tech., 1942; postgrad., U. Western Ont., U. N.C. Plant mgr. Dominion Textile Co., Ltd., Drummondville, Que., Can., 1952-60, v.p. mfg., 1963-68; div. v.p. Deering Milliken Co., Spartanburg, S.C., 1960-64; v.p. mfg. Bibb Mfg. Co., Macon, Ga., 1968-70; chmn. bd., chief exec. officer Dan River Inc., Danville, Va., 1970—, also dir.; dir. Dibrrell Bros., Bank Va. Co., Liberty Life Ins. Co. Trustee Averett Coll., Danville; bd. dirs. Roman Eagle Nursing Home, Danville, Meml. Hosp., Danville; mem. adv. bd. Duke U. Hosp., Durham, N.C. Served to lt. USNR, 1942-46. Mem. Danville C. of C. (dir.). Presbyterian. Club: Danville Golf. Home: 134 Acorn Ln Danville VA 24541 Office: Dan River Inc 2291 Memorial Dr Danville VA 24543*

JOHNSTON, ELAINE CURRY, librarian; b. Hot Springs, Ark., Oct. 1, 1944; d. Aaron B. and Leta M. (Tisdale) C.; m. James Robert Johnston, Aug. 12, 1967; children—Gregory Joseph, James Scott. B.A., U. Ark., 1966; M.S. in L.S., U. Ky., 1981. Tchr. English Harrisburg (Ark.) High Sch., 1966-67, Raytown (Mo.) High Sch., 1967-70; ins. corr. Bus. Men's Assurance Co., Kansas City, Mo., 1970-71; reference librarian La. State Library, Baton Rouge, 1982—. Pres., corr. sec. Welcome Wagon Club, Bowling Green, Ky., 1973-75, corr. sec. treas., Louisville, 1977-79. Mem. ALA, La. Library Assn., Phi Beta Kappa, Beta Phi Mu, Alpha Delta Pi. Home: 17332 Chadsford Ave Baton Rouge LA 70817 Office: La State Library PO Box 131 Baton Rouge LA 70821

JOHNSTON, FLEMON CARDEN, JR., medical educator; b. Birmingham, Ala., Nov. 23, 1936; s. Flemon Carden and Lenora Nell (Peterson) J.; m. Susan Beehler, July 19, 1964; children—Wende, Heidi, Robert. B.S., U. Ala., 1957; M.D., Med. Coll. Ala., 1961. Diplomate Am. Bd. Pediatrics. Intern, Lackland AFB Hosp., San Antonio, 1961-62; resident in pediatrics Tulane Med. Sch.-Charity Hosp., New Orleans, 1964-66; fellow in pulmonary diseases Hosp. for Sick Children, London, 1966-67; practice pediatrics Kaiser Permanente Med. Group, Honolulu, 1967-70; pvt. practice pediatrics, Guntersville, Ala., 1970-74; assoc. prof. pediatrics Sch. Primary Med. Care, Huntsville, Ala., 1974-75; assoc. prof. pediatrics U. Ala. Med. Sch., Birmingham, 1975—. Served with USAF, 1962-64. Mem. Am. Acad. Pediatrics (chmn. Ala.), AMA, Med. Assn. Ala., Jefferson County Med. Soc., Jefferson County Pediatric Soc., Ambulatory Pediatric Assn., Am. Coll. Emergency Physicians. Home: 3208 Karl Daly Rd Birmingham AL 35210 Office: 1600 7th Ave S Birmingham AL 35233

JOHNSTON, GEORGE BURKE, English educator; b. Tuscaloosa, Ala., Sept. 8, 1907; s. George D. and Eleanor (McCorvey) J.; m. Mary Tabb Lancaster, Dec. 28, 1936; children—Elizabeth Carrington Johnston Lipscomb, Thomas McCorvey, George Burke, Mary Tabb. Instr. English, Va. Poly. Inst., Blacksburg, 1930-33, dean Sch. Applied Scis. and Bus. Adminstrn., 1950-61, dean Sch. Sci. and Gen. Studies, 1961-63, dean Coll. Arts and Scis., 1963-65, Miles prof. English, 1965-74, prof. emeritus, 1974—; instr. English, U. Ala., 1935-41, asst. prof., 1941-46, assoc. prof., 1946-50, prof., 1950, asst. dean Coll. Arts and Scis., 1946-50. Author: Ben Jonson: Poet, 1945; Reflections, 1965; Banked Fire, 1976. Editor: Poems of Ben Jonson, 1954; Alabama Historical Sketches (T.C. McCorvey) 1960; Poems by William Camden, 1975. Contbr. poems and articles to periodicals. Served as 2d lt. CA-Res., 1929, 1st lt., 1932; from 1st lt. to lt. col AUS, 1941-45. Mem. MLA, Phi Beta Kappa, Omicron Delta Kappa, Delta Kappa Epsilon, Alpha Kappa Psi, Phi Kappa Phi. Episcopalian. Home: 804 Gracelyn Ct Blacksburg VA 24060

JOHNSTON, JAMES BAKER, ecologist, administrator; b. Baton Rouge, Sept. 10, 1946; s. Troy James and Juanita (Baker) J.; m. Sherri Anne Watson, Dec. 20, 1970; children—Jamey, Stefanie, Robyn. B.S., La. State U., 1970; Ph.D., U. So. Miss., 1973. Cons. fisheries Miss. Marine Resources Council, Long Beach, 1973-74; oceanographer Bue. Land Mgmt., New Orleans, 1974-76; ecologist, supr. U.S. Fish and Wildlife Service, Dept. Interior, Slidell, La., 1976—; instr. Miss. State U., Bay St. Louis, 1976-78; cons. Environment Can., Halifax, N.S., Can., 1984—. Author sci. reports, jour. articles. Pres. Slidell Youth Soccer Club, 1982-83; asst. scoutmaster New Orleans area council Boy Scouts Am., Slidell, 1984—; Sunday Sch. tchr. First Bapt. Ch., Slidell, 1977—. Recipient Edward H. Hillard award Nat. Wildlife Fedn., 1972. Fellow Explorers Club (non-resident); mem. Coastal Soc., Ecol. Soc. Am. Republican. Lodge: Masons. Avocations: coin collecting; scuba diving; swimming; soccer. Home: 1454 Florida Ave Slidell LA 70458 Office: US Fish and Wildlife Service 1010 Gause Blvd Slidell LA 70458

JOHNSTON, J(OHN) BENNETT, senator; b. Shreveport, La., June 10, 1932; s. J. Bennett and Wilma (Lyon) J.; student Washington and Lee U., 1950-51, 52-53, U.S. Mil. Acad., 1951-52; LL.B., La. State U., 1956; m. Mary Gunn, 1956; children—J. Bennett III, Norman Hunter, Mary Lyon, Sarah Lee. Admitted to La. bar, 1956; U.S. senator from La., 1972—, mem. budget com., appropriations com., ranking minority mem. com. on energy and natural resources, subcom. energy and water devel.; chmn. Democratic Senatorial Campaign Com., 1975-77. Mem. La. Ho. of Reps., 1964-68, La. Senate, 1968-72. Former bd. dirs. Goodwill Industries. Served with U.S. Army, 1956-59. Mem. ABA, La. Bar Assn., Phi Delta Theta. Democrat. Baptist. Lodges: Masons, Shriners. Office: 136 Senate Hart Office Bldg Washington DC 20510

JOHNSTON, MICHAEL STEPHEN, police official; b. Tyler, Tex., July 22, 1948; s. Dave James and Dorothy Aileen (Brookshire) J.; m. Sharon Joyce Dowdell, Apr. 28, 1970; children—Michael Glen, Matthew Stephen. B.B.A. in Mgmt., U. Tex.-Arlington, 1970, M.A. in Urban Affairs, 1975. Cert. Advanced law enforcement, law enforcement instr., Tex. Police officer Arlington Police Dept., 1972-74, vice and narcotics detective, 1974-75, sgt., 1975-76, adminstrv. asst. to chief, 1976-78, dir. research and planning, 1978-83, dep. chief of police, 1983—; bd dirs., adv. com. Tarrant County Jr. Coll. Criminal Justice Ctr., Hurst, Tex., 1983-85; adj. prof. U. Tex., Arlington, since 1979—. Contbr. articles to prof. jours. Youth coach YMCA, Arlington, 1978-83; bd. dirs. Longhorn Explorer Posts Boy Scouts Am., 1983—. Served as sgt. U.S. Army, 1970-72. Decorated D.S.M.; named Outstanding Police Officer, Arlington Rotary Club, 1974; recipient Community Service award City of Arlington, 1975. Mem. North Tex. Police Chiefs Assn., North Tex. Police Planning Assn. (mem. exec. bd. 1984—), Tex. Police Chiefs Assn., Internat. Assn. Police Chiefs, U. Tex. at Arlington Maverick Club, U. Tex. at Arlington Alumni Assn. Republican. Presbyterian. Avocations: hunting; fishing; reading; philately; raising Angus cattle. Home: Route 6 Box 864 Burleson TX 76028 Office: Arlington Police Dept PO Box 1065 717 W Main St Arlington TX 76010

JOHNSTON, MURRAY LLOYD, JR., lawyer; b. Lake Charles, La., May 25, 1940; s. Murray Lloyd and Nancy Laura (Perry) J.; m. Jewel Anne Whittenburg, Sept. 4, 1965; children—Murray Lloyd III, Roy Austin. B.A., Austin Coll., 1962; J.D., U. Tex., 1965. Bar: Tex. 1965, U.S. Tax Ct. 1975. Adminstrv. asst. to dir. planning and to exec. dir. Tex. Water Devel. Bd., 1968; assoc. gen. counsel H.B. Zachry Co., San Antonio, 1967-75, sec., gen. counsel, 1975—; mng. ptnr. Johnston, Ralph, Reed & Cone, San Antonio, 1977—. Mem. Nat. Republican Senatorial Com.; mem. legal adv. bd. Nat. Legal Ctr. for Pub. Interest, Washington. Served to lt. comdr. USNR, 1967-78. Mem. San Antonio Estate Planners Council, ABA, San Antonio Bar Assn. (corp. chmn.), Am. Judicature Soc., Internat. Assn. Ins. Counsel. Methodist. Club: San Antonio Country. Home: 306 Kennedy St San Antonio TX 78209 Office: 2600 Tower Life Bldg San Antonio TX 78205

JOHNSTON, ROBERT CULLY, accountant; b. Derma, Miss., Aug. 6, 1916; s. Walter George and Cherrie Belle (Jones) J.; m. Margaret Jennie Baker, Apr. 19, 1947; children—Robert Baker, Margaret Michelle, David Bryan. B.S., Auburn U., 1939. Field rep. War Dept. and CSC, Atlanta, 1940-45; advt. mgr. Lee County Bull., Auburn, Ala., 1946-47; ins. clk. L.P. Baker Agy., Atlanta, 1948-50; promotion mgr., sales agt. B.E. Robuck, Inc., College Park, Ga., 1951-55; exec. dir. Home Builders Assn. Ala., Montgomery, 1956-60; acct. City of Atlanta, 1961-82; chmn. fin. com. Baptist Towers, Atlanta, 1981—. Maj. CAP, USAF Aux., 1971—. Mem. Airplane Owners and Pilots Assn. Democrat. Baptist (deacon). Lodge: Masons. Mng. editor Home Builder Mag., 1956-60.

JOHNSTON, RUTH LE ROY, nosologist, med. record adminstr.; b. Elizabeth, N.J., June 19, 1915; d. James Archibald and Frances Ione Davis (Austin) Le Roy; B.A., Bob Jones U., Greenville, S.C., 1945; postgrad. med. courses Emory U.; m. Earl Benton Johnston, Aug. 19, 1944 (dec.); 1 son, Jonathan Bruce (dec.). Various hosp. positions Atlanta, Asheville, N.C., 1948-55; chief med. record librarian VA Hosp., Richmond, Va., 1955-60, Wood, Wis., 1960, Hines, Ill., 1960-62; supervisory med. classification specialist, nosologist research and stats. Social Security Adminstrn., HEW, Balt., 1962-68; med. record cons. health data service Md. Blue Cross-Blue Shield, Balt., 1970-71; chief med. record adminstr. Good Samaritan Hosp., West Palm Beach, Fla., 1971-74; chief med. record adminstr. Gorgas Hosp., U.S. C.Z., Panama, 1974-77; library asst. North Palm Beach Public Library, 1978-80; lectr. in field, cons. Mem. Save the Panama Canal Club; 1st vice-chmn. bd. dirs. Paradise Harbour Condominium, 1973; charter mem. Republican Presdl. Task Force. Registered nat. med. record adminstr., nosologist. Recipient VA and civil service awards, 1960-68. Fellow Am. Biog. Inst. Research Assn. (life); mem. Va. (treas. 1957-58, pres. 1960), Md. (v.p. 1963), Fla., Am. med. record assns., Internat. Platform Assn., Audubon Soc., Nat. Assn. Fed. Ret. Employees, Am. Assn. Ret. Persons. Baptist. Home: 100 Paradise Harbor Blvd North Palm Beach FL 33408

JOHNSTON, SAMUEL MERRITT, sales executive; b. New Haven, Apr. 24, 1948; s. Wilbur Dexter and Elizabeth Merritt J.; B. Indsl. Engring. Tech., So. Tech. Inst., 1971; M.B.A., U. Utah, 1978; m. Marian Elizabeth Hayes, Oct. 23, 1971; children—Brandi, Elizabeth, Courtney Lynne. Methods engr. Tex. Instruments, Dallas, 1978-79; sales engr., UPA Tech., Inc., Syosset, N.Y., 1979, regional sales mgr., 1979-80 dir. Central and South Am., 1980-81, field sales mgr., 1980-84, dir. internat. sales, 1981-84; territory mgr. Micro Component Tech., St. Paul, 1984-85, key account mgr., 1985—. Pres., park Forest Homeowners' Assn., Plano, Tex., 1979-80. Served with USAF, 1971-78. Named Salesman of Year, UPA Tech., Inc., 1980. Mem. Am. Mgmt. Assn., Am. Electroplaters' Soc. Republican. Home: 3500 Remington Dr Plano TX 75023 Office: PO Box 1469 Plano TX 75074

JOHNSTON, THOMAS GIBSON, allergist; b. Dardanelle, Ark., Nov. 24, 1922; s. Thomas Glynn and Pauline (Gibson) J.; B.S., U. Ark., 1943, M.D., 1945; m. Amy Holcombe Ball, Nov. 14, 1963; children—Thomas Glenn, Marcella. Intern, U. Ark. Hosp., Little Rock, 1945; resident in internal medicine Gorgas Hosp., Ancon, Canal Zone, 1948-50, U. Mich. Hosp., 1950-51; now allergist Allergy Assos., P.A., Little Rock, asso. clin. prof., U. Ark.; cons. St. Vincent Infirmary, Baptist Hosp., Children's Hosp. Served with U.S. Army, 1947-49. Recipient Bela Shick award, 1959; diplomate Am. Bd. Allergy and Immunology. Mem. Am. Coll. Allergists (v.p. 1966), Am. Acad. Allergists, Am. Assn. Allergy and Clin. Immunology, AMA, Ark. Med. Assn., So. Med. Assn. (past chmn. allergy sect.), U. Ark. Med. Alumni Assn. (past pres.). Presbyterian. Contbr. articles in field to profl. jours. Home: 5315 Scenic Dr Little Rock AR 72207 Office: PO Box 5000 Hillcrest Sta Little Rock AR 72205

JOHNSTON, THOMAS MATKINS, engineering executive; b. Okmulgee, Okla., Dec. 8, 1921; s. Alexander and Lillian Grace (Matkins) J.; m. Esther Elizabeth Logan, June 7, 1943; children—Thomas Garrett, Robert Alexander, Hugh Samuel, Ann Logan. B.S., U.S. Mil. Acad., 1943; M.E., NYU, N.Y.C., 1949, postgrad., 1958-60; postgrad. MIT, 1960, Case Inst., 1962. Registered profl. engr., Mass. Instr. math. U.S. Mil. Acad., West Point, N.Y., 1949-52, lectr., 1969-71; mgr. systems analysis group RCA, Moorestown, N.J., 1958-67; mgr. info. systems dept. Raytheon Co., Bedford, Mass., 1967-71; chief tech. programs div. FAA, Dept. Transp., Washington, 1971-79; mgr. air traffic control systems Westinghouse Electric Co., Balt., 1979-81; pres. Enreal Enterprises, Inc., Mt. Vernon, Va., 1981—; lectr. math. U. Calif., 1954-55, U. Md., 1956-59, Am. U., Washington, 1956-59. Served to maj., C.E., U.S. Army, 1943-58. Decorated Bronze Star with oak leaf cluster. Fellow AAAS; mem. Ops. Research Soc. Home: 3720 Carriage House Ct Alexandria VA 22309 Office: PO Box 81 Mount Vernon VA 22121

JOHNSTONE, EDWARD H., U.S. district judge: b. 1922. J.D., U. Ky., 1949. Ptnr. firm Johnstone, Eldred & Paxton, Princeton, 1949-76; judge 56th circuit ct. Ky., 1976-77; U.S. dist. judge Western Ky., Paducah, 1977—. Mem. ABA, Ky. Bar Assn. Office: 219 Federal Bldg Paducah KY 42001

JOHNSTONE, WILLIAM OWEN, banker; b. Borger, Tex., Mar. 17, 1947; s. Leo Haskell and Mildred Christine (Owen) J.; m. Judith Ann Harley, Apr. 3, 1982; children—Megan Elizabeth, William Paul. B.A. in Econs., U. Okla., 1969, M.B.A., 1970. Vice pres. Fidelity Bank, N.A., Oklahoma City, 1970-78; pres. Union Bank and Trust Co., Oklahoma City, 1978-80, Union Bancorp., Inc., Oklahoma City, 1978-80; pres., chief exec. officer United Okla. Bankshares, Inc., Oklahoma City, 1980—; vice chmn., chief exec. officer United Okla. Bank, Oklahoma City, 1980—, also dir.; chmn. United Bankcard Assn., United Bankers Mortgage Corp., United Data Services, Inc., United Check Processing Ctr., Inc.; dir. United Bank Adv. Services, Inc., Post Oak Oil Co., Speck Homes, Inc., United Okla. Bankshares, Inc.; trustee Pvt. Enterprise Found. Bd. dirs. Arts Council Oklahoma City, Oklahoma County (Okla.) ARC, Okla. Polit. Action Com., Leadership Oklahoma City; trustee Ballet Okla., Inc.; bd. dirs., vice chmn. Okla. Bd. Pvt. Schs.; bd. advisors U. Okla.; pres. Okla. chpt. Nat. Sudden Infant Death Syndrome. Mem. Okla. Bankers Assn. (dir.), Am. Assn. Policy Advisors (dir.), Am. Bankers Assn. (exec. com. for housing and real estate), Young Pres. Orgn. Clubs: Econs., Young Men's Dinner, Men's Dinner, Masons, Quail Creek Golf and Country. Home: 12912 River Oaks Dr Oklahoma City OK 73142 Office: United Okla Bank PO Box 82427 Oklahoma City OK 73148

JOHR, BERNARDO MANUEL, surgeon; b. Bogota, Colombia, Oct. 12, 1950; came to U.S., 1976; s. Bert and Marga (Dampf) J. M.D., Rosario U., Bogota, 1974. Diplomate Am. Bd. Surgery. Intern, N.J. Coll. Medicine and Dentistry, Newark, 1976-77; surg. resident Mt. Sinai Hosp., Miami Beach, Fla., 1977-79, Maricopa County Gen. Hosp., Phoenix, 1979-82; vascular fellow Good Samaritan Hosp., Phoenix, 1982-83; gen. and vascular surgeon North Miami Gen. Hosp., Parkway Regional Med. Ctr., Humana Hosp. Biscayne, North Miami Beach, Fla., Miami Gen. Hosp., 1982—. Mem. AMA, Dade County Med. Assn. Office: Parkway Med Plaza 16800 NW 2d Ave Suite 303 North Miami Beach FL 33169

JOINER, EDWARD EARL, religious studies educator, minister; b. Colquitt, Ga., Apr. 25, 1924; s. John B. Sr. and Nancy Lula (Harrison) J.; m. Geraldine McCarty House, July 21, 1946; children—Edward Earl Jr., Paul Allen, Ann Eileen, John Andrew. A.B., Stetson U., 1949; B.D., So. Bapt. Theol. Sem., 1953, Th.M., 1954, Th.D., 1960. Ordained to ministry So. Bapt. Ch., 1947. Prof. religion Stetson U., DeLand Fla., 1955—. Author: A History of Florida Baptists, 1972; A Christian Considers Divorce and Remarriage, 1983. Contbr. articles to profl. jours. Curator Fla. Bapt. Hist. Soc., DeLand, 1975—. Served with U.S. Army, 1944-46. Mem. Am. Acad. Religion, Am. Soc. Christian Ethics. Democrat. Baptist. Lodge: Rotary. Avocations: backpacking; photography; fishing. Home: 735 N Sans Souci DeLand FL 32720 Office: Stetson U N Woodland Blvd DeLand FL 32720

JOKINEN, TEPPO KULLERVO, mechanical engineer; b. Finland, Oct. 14, 1938; came to U.S., 1968; s. Keijo and Salme (Lohko) J.; m. A. Mirjam Nieminen, May 26, 1940; children—Marko I., Anu M. B.S.M.E., Pori, Finland, 1967. Lic. pvt. pilot. Aircraft mechanic Finnair, Helsinki, 1962-65; prodn. mgr. Sumar Corp., Helsinki, 1967; process engr. Dixon Sintaloy, Stamford, Conn., 1968-71; chief process engr. Alcoa (APM), North Haven, Conn., 1971-73; service technician Gen. Electric Co., Lake Worth, Fla., 1973-77; pres. Palm Beach Engring., Inc., Lake Worth, 1977—. Served with Finnish Air Force, 1958-59. Mem. Nat. Assn. Home Builders, Air Force Assn. Club: Civitan (pres. 1983-84). Office: 3663 Boutwell Rd Lake Worth FL 33461

JOKL, ERNST F., clinical physiologist, educator; b. Breslau, Ger., Aug. 8, 1907; came to U.S., 1950, naturalized, 1958; s. Hans and Rose (Oelsner) J.; M.D., Beslau U., 1931; M.B., B.Ch., Witwatersrand U., Johannesburg, South Africa, 1936; m. Erica Lestmann, June 3, 1933; children—Marion Jokl Ball, Peter. Mem. faculty U. Ky. Coll. Medicine Lexington, prof. physiology, 1952—, disting. prof., 1964—; pres. research com. Internat. Council Sport and Phys. Edn., UNESCO, 1960—; Prince Philip lectr. Ho. of Lords, Eng., 1983, 85. Decorated Grand Cross Merit (Fed. Republic Ger.); recipient Brit. Commonwealth Research medal Harveian Soc., 1950; research fellow Nat. Library Medicine, Bethesda, Md., 1977; hon. prof. univs. Berlin and Frankfurt-/Main. Fellow Am. Coll. Cardiology; mem. AMA, Aerospace Med. Assn., N.Y. Acad. Medicine; hon. mem. Internat. Fedn. Sports Medicine. Club: Rotary. Author books, papers in field. Home: 340 Kingsway Dr Lexington KY 40502 Office: Coll Medicine Neurology and Sports Medicine U Ky Lexington KY 40506

JOKLIK, WOLFGANG KARL, scientist, educator; b. Vienna, Austria, Nov. 16, 1926; came to U.S., 1962; s. Karl Friedrich and Helene (Giessl) J.; m. Judith Vivien Nicholas, Apr. 9, 1955 (dec. Apr. 1975); children—Richard Gunther, Vivien Helene; m. 2d, Patricia Ann Hunter Downey, Apr. 23, 1977. B.Sc., Sydney U., 1947, M.Sc., 1948; Ph.D., Oxford U., 1952. Fellow Australian Nat. U., Canberra, 1954-62; assoc. prof. cell biology Albert Einstein Coll. Medicine, N.Y.C., 1962-65, prof., 1965-68; prof. dept. microbiology and immunology Duke U. Med. Ctr., Durham, N.C., 1968—; cons. NIH, Bethesda, Md., Am. Cancer Soc., N.Y.C. Sr. author, editor: Zinsser Microbiology, 18th edit., 1984; Virology, 1980, 2d edit., 1985, The Reoviridae, 1983. Editor-in-chief Virology, 1975—; assoc. editor Jour. Biol. Chemistry, 1977—. Mem. Nat. Acad. Scis., Inst. Medicine, Am. Soc. Virology (pres. 1981-83), Am. Soc. Microbiology (pres. virology div. 1979-81, divisional councillor 1982-84), Am. Soc. Biol. Chemists. Roman Catholic. Clubs: Hope Valley Country (Durham); Grandfather Golf and Country (Linville, N.C.). Avocations: tennis; golf; walking. Office: Duke Med Ctr 414 Jones Bldg PO Box 3020 Durham NC 27710

JOLLEY, SAMUEL DELANOR, JR., mathematics educator, consultant; b. Fort Valley, Ga., Feb. 1, 1941; s. Samuel Delanor J.; m. Jimmye Christine Hambry, Dec. 24, 1963; children—Terena A., Samuel D. III. B.S., Fort Valley State Coll. 1962; M.S., Atlanta U., 1965; Ed.D., Ind. U., 1974. Tchr. math Ballard-Hudson Sr. High Sch., Macon, Ga., 1962-67; instr. math. Fort Valley State Coll., Ga., 1967-70; grad. asst. Ind. Univ., Bloomington, 1970-74; assoc. prof. math. Fort Valley State, 1975-83, coordinator student tchrs., 1980—, prof. math., chmn. edn., 1983-85; dean sch. arts and scis., 1985—. cons. math. Bibb Bd. Edn., Macon, 1980—; researcher in field. Mem. exec. bd. Middle Ga. Area Planning Devel. Commn., 1978, bd. dirs., 1977—; chmn. Middle Ga. Area Agy. on Aging, Macon, 1978; mem. Mayor's Sr. Citizens task force, Macon, 1978, Macon Bibb County Coordinating Council, Macon, 1983—. Recipient research award NSF, 1963-64. So. Fellowships Funds fellow, 1973-74. Mem. Assn. Tchr. Educators, Math. Assn. Am., Nat. Edn. Assn., Nat. Council for Tchrs. of Math., Phi Delta Kappa (research rep., pres. 1984), Omega Psi Phi (pres. 1983). Democrat. Roman Catholic. Lodge: Masons (treas. 1980-83). Avocations: reading; swimming. Home: 3279 Commodore Dr Macon GA 31211 Office: Fort Valley State Coll 805 State College Drive Fort Valley Ga 31030

JOLLY, ANNA ELLEN, industrial hygienist; b. Louisville, June 10, 1954; d. John William and Evelyn (Gray) J.; m. Robert Coleman Thompson, Sept. 8, 1984. B.S. in Pub. Health, Eastern Ky. U., 1977; M.S. in Spl. Studies, George Washington U., 1980. Indsl. hygienist AT&T Techs. (formerly Western Electric), Richmond, Va., 1977—; del. Richmond Joint Engrs. Council, 1984-85. Mem. Am. Soc. Safety Engrs. (pres. 1984-85), Am. Indsl. Hygiene Assn. (pres. 1981-82). Democrat. Mem. United Ch. of Christ. Avocations: morris dancing; square dancing. Office: AT&T Techs 4500 S Laburnam Ave Richmond VA 23231

JOLLY, BRUCE OVERSTREET, retired newspaperman; b. Bay City, Tex., July 2, 1912; s. Irvin and Alice Gretchen (Overstreet) J.; m. Sarah Clark Tate Jeffress, Jan. 22, 1946; children—Bruce Overstreet, Jr., Edwin Jeffress. A.B. in English and Journalism, Franklin Coll., 1938. Reporter, Indpls. News, 1938-40, Post Tribune, Gary, Ind., 1940-42, 47-48; Washington corr. Daily News, Greensboro, N.C., 1949-65; with pub. relations dept. So. Ry., Washington, 1965-72. Author: The First Hundred Years, 1977; Keeping Up With Yesterday, 1985. Editor: The Brightness of His Presence, 1980. Bd. dirs. Sheltered Occupational Ctr. No. Va., Arlington, 1984—; mem. planning commn. N.C. Tercentenary Celebration, 1962. Served with USAF, 1942-46, CBI. Recipient Cert. of Merit, State of N.C., 1963; alumni citation Franklin Coll., 1977. Mem. Nat. Press Club, Soc. Profl. Journalists, Knights of the Round Table (pres. 1982-83). Episcopalian. Avocations: golf, swimming, travel. Home: 8359 Alvord St McLean VA 22102

JOLLY, E. GRADY, judge. Judge U.S. Ct. Appeals, 5th Circuit, Jackson, Miss. Office: PO Drawer 2368 Jackson MS 39205*

JOLLY, WILLIAM MONROE, hospital adminstrator; b. Richmond, Va., June 23, 1952; s. William Monroe Jr. and Marjorie (Oak) J. B.A., Coll. William and Mary, 1970-74; M.H.A., Med. Coll. Va., 1978. Lic. nursing home administr., Va. Asst. dir. Community Meml. Hosp., South Hill, Va., 1978-79; adminstr. St. Mary's Infant Home, Norfolk, Va., 1979—; dir. Independence Ctr., Inc., Norfolk Area Health Edn. Ctr., Sanctuary Inc. Preceptor nursing home adminstr.-in-tng. Program, Va. Dept. Commerce, 1982—. Mem. Va. Hosp. Assn., Am. Coll. Hosp. Adminstrs. Republican. Presbyterian. Avocations: stained glass crafts; running; swimming; racquetball. Home: 750-C W Ocean View Ave Norfolk VA 23503 Office: St Mary's Infant Home 317 Chapel St Norfolk VA 23504

JONES, ALBERT CECIL, consulting engineer; b. Montevallo, Ala., July 29, 1938; s. Albert Cecil and Thelma Evelyn (Hearn) J.; B.C.E., Auburn U., 1959; 1 son, Albert Cecil; m. Juanita S. Summers, Jan. 21, 1978. Bridge and bldg. supr. So. Ry., 1962-65; process engr. So. Ry., Atlanta, 1965-69; sr. design engr. Rust Engring., Birmingham, Ala., 1969-72; mgr., Harland Bartholomew & Assos., Birmingham, 1972-83, assoc. partner, 1974-83; pres. Cecil Jones & Assocs., Inc., 1983—. mem. faculty U. Ala., Birmingham, 1971-72. Served to 1st lt. C.E. AUS, 1960-62. Registered profl. engr., Ala., Ark., Fla., Ky., Miss., Ga., N.C. Mem. ASCE, Nat. Soc. Profl. Engrs., Inst. Traffic Engrs., Am. Pub. Works Assn. Clubs: The Club, Relay House. Lodges: Masons, Shriners. Home: 1525 Hidden Lake Dr Birmingham AL 35235 Office: 8933 Roebuck Blvd Suite E Birmingham AL 35206

JONES, ALBERT PEARSON, lawyer; b. Dallas, Tex., July 19, 1907; s. Dr. Bush and Ethel (Hatton) J.; student So. Meth. U., 1924; A.B., U. Tex., 1927, A.M., 1927, LL.B., 1930; m. Annette Lewis, Oct. 3, 1936; children—Dan Pearson, Lewis Avery. Admitted to Tex. bar, 1930, U.S. Ct. Appeals, U.S. Supreme Ct.; asso. Baker, Botts, Andrews & Wharton, Houston, 1930-43; mem. firm Helm & Jones, Houston 1943-62; prof. law U. Tex. at Austin, 1962-77, prof. emeritus, 1977—; adj. prof. law U. Houston Coll. Law, 1981; 1st asst. to atty. gen. State of Tex., 1963-64 (on leave). Trustee St. Lukes Hosp., 1949-62, Lulu Bryan Rambaud Charitable Trust, 1947-62. Fellow Am. Coll. Trial Lawyers; mem. State Bar Tex. (pres. 1950-51, dir. 8th congl. dist. 1948-50), Houston, Am. bar assns., Am. Law Inst. (life), Order of Coif, Phi Beta Kappa, Phi Delta Phi. Episcopalian. Home: 3195 Del Monte Houston TX 77019

JONES, ALBERTA GENENA, nurse; b. Okmulgee, Okla., Oct. 30, 1918; d. Riley Roy and Viola (Burgess) Richardson; m. Orvis James Jones, Mar. 2, 1940; children—Roy, James, Russell, Johnny. Student Okla. State U., 1974. Nurse aide Lake Drive Manor, Henryetta, Okla., 1970-73; dir. nursing Lake Drive Manor, Henryetta, 1974—. Named Outstanding Dist. Dep. Pres., Okla. Rebekah Assembly, 1982; mem. Bapt. Ch., Pharoah, Okla. Mem. Am. Assn. Mental Deficiency. Home: Route 1 Box 215 Henryetta OK 74437 Office: Lake Drive Nursing Home 600 Lake Rd Henryetta OK 74437

JONES, ALTON EDWIN, real estate executive; b. Augusta, Ga., Jan. 29, 1945; s. Oscar Edwin and Myrtis (Still) J.; m. Rebecca Jill Gatch, Feb. 14, 1970; children—Kevin Edwin, Julie Taylor. B.S., Citadel, 1967. Mng. gen. ptnr. Century 21 Tideland, Beaufort, S.C., 1978-80; pres. Century 21 Hilton Head, S.C., 1980-81; mng. gen. ptnr. Hilton Head Co. Realty, S.C., 1981—; pres. Hilton Head Mgmt., S.C., 1981—, Tideland Timesharing, 1981—; dir. Atlantic Savs. Bank, Hilton Head. Trustee, S.C. Coll., 1984-85, State Coll. Bd., 1983—; bd. dirs. Wexford Property Owners Assn., 1985. Bd. dirs. Coll. Charleston Found., 1984—. Mem. Nat. Assn. Corp. Relators. Democrat. Baptist. Clubs: Golf (New Albany, Ohio); Wexford Golf (Hilton Head). Avocations: Golf; fishing. Home: 17 Bridgetown Rd Hilton Head Island SC 29928 Office: Hilton Head Co Realty PO Box 7000 William Hilton Hwy Hilton Head Island SC 29938

JONES, ANDREW MELVIN, educator; b. Attala County, Miss., Mar. 10, 1932; s. Clint and Opal Irene (Peeler) J.; B.A., Miss. Coll., 1952; M.A., U. So. Miss., 1954; Ed.D., U. Miss., 1969; m. Elizabeth Reid, Dec. 20, 1959; children—Amy Elizabeth, John R. Tchr., French Camp (Miss.) Acad., 1952-53, tchr., prin., 1955-57; tchr. math. Weir (Miss.) High Sch., 1958; instr. U. Miss., Oxford, 1958-59, Miss. U. for Women, Columbus, 1959-69; prof. Delta State U., Cleveland, Miss., 1969— coordinator edn1. adminstrn., supervision and adult edn., 1983—. Pres. Miss. Youth Congress, 1961-85. Served with U.S. Army, 1957. Recipient Service Key, Phi Delta Kappa, 1961. Mem. NEA, Miss. Assn. Educators, Miss. Speech Communication Assn. (hon. life; pres. 1960-61, exec. sec. 1964-82), So. Speech Communication Assn., Miss. Assn. Sch. Adminstrs. Democrat. Baptist. Home: 809 Pecan St Cleveland MS 38732 Office: Drawer D-1 Delta State U Cleveland MS 38733

JONES, ARTHUR ROLAND, physics and astronomy educator; b. Liverpool, Eng., Oct 6, 1909; came to U.S., 1953; s. Arthur Holder and Alice Meredith (Hamer) J.; m. Hildegard Gronau, June 9, 1939. Master mariner, Nautical Coll., Liverpool, Eng., 1939; teaching diploma Alsager Coll., Cheshire, Eng., 1948. Cadet, 3d, 2d, 1st mate Mercantile Vessels, U.K., 1926-39 3d, 2d first officer Cunard, SS Line, U.K., 1939-45; tchr. Crayford Primary, London, 1948-52, Chislehurst Boys' Sch., London, 1952-53, Beaverd and Warwick High Schs., Va., 1953-55; lectr. physics and astronomy Va. Mil. Inst., Lexington, 1955-82; instr. Air Force Field Exercises, Va., 1955-70; officer in charge Forest Fire Fighting Cadets, Va., 1970-75; judge Va. Jr. Acad. Sci.; vis. scientist Va. Rec. sec., pres. Episcopalian Laymen's League, Lexington, Va., 1955—; scoutmaster, commr. Boy Scouts Am., Va., 1958—; dir., pres. Soc. for Prevention of Cruelty to Animals, Lexington, 1974-79. Recipient Citation and Plaque, USAF, 1966. Silver Beaver award Boy Scouts Am., 1970. Mem. Sci. Mus. Va., Lynchburg Astronomers, Planetary Soc., Southeastern Planetarian Soc., Sigma Pi Sigma. Avocations: writing; fencing; horse riding; sailing; swimming. Home: Route 1 Box 45 Huddleston VA 24104

JONES, BEN BLOCK, lawyer; b. Forrest City, Ark., Dec. 6, 1918; s. William Milton and Judith (Block) J.; 1 child, Ben Block II. LL.B., So. U., Memphis, 1946, Woodrow Wilson Coll. of Law, 1958; A.A., Hinds Jr. Coll., 1960; LL.B., U. Miss., 1962, J.D., 1968. Bar: Miss. 1962, Ark. 1968. Prin., owner Block Realty, Memphis, 1946-55, United Investments, Memphis, 1955-60, Benz, Jackson, Miss., 1946—, Jones Investments, Atlanta, 1946—; sole practice law, Jackson, 1962—. Mem. ABA, Miss. Bar Assn., Ark. State Bar, Hinds County Trial Lawyers (pres. 1972-73), Memphis Jaycees (dir. 1946), Civitan. Democrat. Baptist. Lodges: Masons, Shriners, Scottish Rite. Avocations: deep sea fishing; hunting. Office: PO Box 3672 Jackson MS 39207

JONES, BENJAMIN I, sanitarian; b. Newport News, Va., May 12, 1956; s. Joseph Alex and Yohlanda (Simmons) J.; m. Cynthia Marie Segar, Sept. 1, 1978. B.S., Western Carolina U., 1984. Cert. in occupational safety N.C.; cert. Nat. Registry Emergency Med. Technicians; registered sanitarian. Emergency med. technician Moody Funeral Home, Sylva, N.C., 1973-75, emergency med. tech., asst. funeral dir., 1981-84 operating room tech. Commanche County Meml. Hosp., Lawton, Okla., 1979-80; sanitarian Macon County Health Dept., Franklin, N.C., 1984—. Served with U.S. Army, 1976-80; W. Ger. Mem. Am. Soc. Safety Engrs., Western N.C. Pub. Health Assn., Nat. Environ. Health Assn., Democrat. Baptist. Avocations: photograhy, hiking, water skiing. Home: 140 Frazier Rd Franklin NC 28734 Office: Macon County Health Dept 5 W Main St Franklin NC 28734

JONES, BETTYE WRIGHT, education and reading educator; b. Savannah, Ga., Nov. 30, 1933; d. Walter and Carrie (Drayton) Wright; m. Howell Thomas Jones, Jr., Aug. 24, 1957; 1 dau., Caroline Annette Jones. B.S., Eastern Mich. U., 1956, M.A., 1967; M.Ed., Va. State U., 1982. Elem. tchr. Toledo pubs. schs., 1957-59, 62-64, Greensboro pub. schs., 1960-61, Lansing pub. schs., 1964-67, So. U. Lab. Sch., 1967-71, Matoaca Lab. Sch., 1971-80; asst. prof. edn. Univ. Ctr. for Reading Devel., Va. State U., Petersburg, 1980—; item writer Calif. Achievement Test, Calif. Test Bur., Mich. State U. Fellow Nat. Inst. Edn.; mem. Internat. Reading Assn., Va. State Reading Assn., Southside Council Reading Educators, Phi Delta Kappa, Kappa Delta Pi. Baptist. Club: Jack and Jill Am. (Petersburg). Office: Va State U 215 Harris Hall PO Box RR Petersburg VA 23803

JONES, BOYD CUSTIS, loss control manager, consultant; b. Richmond, Va., Feb. 1, 1941; s. Herman Boyd and Rebecca (Leatherbury) J.; m. Roberta Ramey, May 4, 1977; 1 child, D. Austin. Grad. high sch., Ashland, Va. Cert. safety profl., Ill. Loss control engr., cons. Kemper Ins., Va., 1966-82; v.p., mgr. loss control Alexander & Alexander of Va., Inc., Richmond, 1982—. Served with USNR, 1963-65. Mem. Am. Soc. Safety Engrs. (v.p. 1984-85, pres. 1986-87), Va. Chpt. of Am. Soc. Safety Engrs. (Merit award 1982-83), Am. Indsl. Hygiene Assn., Soc. Fire Prevention Engrs. Avocations: fishing; gardening; snow-skiing. Office: PO Box 1177 Federal Reserve Bank Bldg 701 E Byrd St Richmond VA 23209

JONES, CAROL POWELL, retired school administrator; b. East Orange, N.J., Aug. 9, 1917; d. Manassau James and Hettie (White) Powell; student St. Paul's Coll., 1937-39; B.S., Va. State Coll., 1947, M.S., 1962; postgrad. Hampton Inst., 1948, Columbia U., 1965; m. Willie Edwin Jones, Aug. 30, 1963 (dec. Dec. 1972). Tchr. elementary grades Buckingham County (Va.) Sch. Bd., 1939-60, elem. supr., 1960-79, supr. Title I Summer Program, 1966-72, coordinator Supplemental Skill Devel. Program, from 1974; ednl. television coordinator Buckingham County. Sec. bd dirs. Buckingham Community Action Program, 1965-69; pres. Womans Missionary and Ednl. Conv. Aux., Slate River Baptist Assn. Central Va.; bd. dirs. Bapt. Gen. Conv., 1982-85; 4-H leader; active Va. Lung Assn., Buckingham County Bicentennial Commn; life mem. Hist. Buckingham Inc. Recipient certificate of merit award Alpha Phi Alpha, 1975, numerous other achievement, appreciation and merit awards. Mem. NEA, Am., Va. assns. for supervision and curriculum devel., Va. Assn. Sch. Execs., St. Pauls, Va. State Coll. alumni assns., Fedn. Colored Womans Club (dist. pres. 1978-82, dir. 1979, fin. sec. 1980-84), NAACP (life), Buckingham Friends of Library. Home: Route 1 Box 88 Dillwyn VA 23936

JONES, CHARLES FREDERICK, ophthalmologist; b. Nashville, Apr. 5, 1949; s. Dallas Jackson and Virginia Lee (Hodgkins) J.; m. Janice Lynn Meyers, Dec. 14, 1974; children—Virginia Louise, Charles Frederick. B.S., Southwestern U.-Memphis, 1971; M.D., U. Tenn., 1974. Diplomate Am. Bd. Ophthalmology. Intern Meth. Hosp., Memphis, 1974-75; resident Tulane Med. Ctr., New Orleans, 1976-79; practice medicine specializing in ophthalmology, Mobile, Ala., 1979—; attending physician Providence Hosp., Mobile Infirmary, Mobile Surgery Ctr., Ala., 1979—. Fellow Am. Acad. Ophthalmology; mem. AMA, Ala. Acad. Ophthalmology, Ala. Med. Soc., Mobile County Med. Soc. Republican. Clubs: Mobile Country, Athelstan.

JONES, CHARLES MILLER, JR., physicist; b. Atlanta, Feb. 25, 1935; s. Charles Miller and Mattie (Ptomey) J.; m. Virginia Louise McClurkin, Mar. 16, 1957; children—Charles, Grace. B.S. in Physics, Ga. Inst. Tech., 1957; M.S., Rice U., 1959, Ph.D., 1961. Research assoc. Rice U., Houston, 1961-62; physicist Oak Ridge Nat. Lab., 1962-72, group leader, 1972-83, tech. dir., Holifield Heavy Ion Research Facility, 1983—. Contbr. articles to profl. jours. Mem. Am. Phys. Soc. Avocation: yacht racing. Office: Oak Ridge Nat Lab Bldg 6000 Oak Ridge TN 37831

JONES, CRAIG HALL, psychologist; b. Phila., May 2, 1950; s. Herbert S. and Gay Nell (Hall) J.; m. Patricia A. Tomori, June 20, 1970. B.A. in Psychology, Rutgers U., 1972; M.A., U. Kans., 1975; Ed.D. in Student Personnel, U. Miss., 1983. Cert. law enforcement instr., Ark. Commn. Law Enforcement Standards and Tng., 1982. Asst. instr. psychology U. Kans., Lawrence, 1975-77; assoc. prof. psychology Ark. State U., State University, 1977—. NIMH fellow, 1972-75. Mem. Am. Coll. Personnel Assn., Am. Assn. Counseling and Devel. Office: Box 925 State University AR 72467

JONES, DANIEL DAVID, biology educator, microbiological researcher; b. Olney, Ill., Feb. 23, 1943; s. Lloyd Lee and Thelma Leona (Lynch) J.; m. Karen Ruth Jones, June 7, 1965; children—Christine, Keith. B.S., Purdue U., 1965, M.S., 1967; Ph.D., Mich. State U., 1970. Asst. prof. biology U. Ala.-Birmingham, 1970-74, assoc. prof., 1974-83, chmn. dept. biology, 1981—; cons. U.S. Steel Corp., Monroeville, Pa., 1979-85. Water Resources Research Inst. grantee, 1979, 82-84. Mem. Am. Inst. Biol. Sci., Am. Assn. Plant Physiologists, Am. Soc. Microbiologists, Am. Soc. Microbiologists (chmn. policy com. Southeast br. 1981-83), Omicron Delta Kappa. Presbyterian. Club: Altadena. Contbr. articles in field to tech. jours. Home: 5038 Vale Ln Birmingham AL 35244 Office: U Ala Birmingham AL 35244

JONES, DAVID RANDOLPH, retired air force officer, psychiatrist; b. Cooperstown, N.Y., Sept. 2, 1934; s. Thomas Thweatt and Mary Cuyler (Scanlon) J.; m. Mary Mattison Brewer, June 16, 1954; children—Michael, Charles, Sara, Aline. B.S., Davidson (N.C.) Coll., 1954; M.D., Duke U., 1958; M.P.H., Harvard U., 1962. Diplomate Am. Bd. Preventive Medicine, Am. Bd. Psychiatry and Neurology. Commd. 2d lt. U.S. Air Force, 1956, advanced through grades to col., 1972; gen. rotating intern USAF Hosp., Lackland AFB, Tex., 1958-59, resident in psychiatry Wilford Hall USAF Med. Center, 1975-78; resident in aerospace medicine Brooks AFB, Tex., 1962-64; chief Aeromed. Services, Torrejon AFB, Spain, 1967-71; dep. comdr. to comdr. USAF Hosp., Randolph AFB, Tex., 1971-75; chief neuropsychiatry br. Clin. Services div. USAF Sch. Aerospace Medicine-Brooks AFB, Tex., 1978—; mil. cons. USAF Surgeon Gen., 1982; clin. assoc. prof. psychiatry Uniformed Services U. of Health Scis.-Bethesda, Md., 1980—; clin. asst. prof. psychiatry U. Tex. Health Scis. Center-San Antonio, 1979—. Patron, San Antonio Symphony, 1982—. Decorated Legion of Merit, Bronze Star, Air Medal with three oak leaf clusters, Commendation Medal with one oak leaf cluster; recipient Docere award USAF Sch. Aerospace Medicine, 1983. Fellow Am. Coll. Preventive Medicine, Aerospace Med. Assn.; mem. AMA, Am. Psychiat. Assn. (Falk fellow 1976), Tex. Med. Assn., Bexar County Med. Assn., Assn. USAF Flight Surgeons (pres. 1983), Assn. USAF Psychiatrists (sec.-treas. 1980). Presbyterian. Contbr. several med. articles to profl. publs., chpts. to books. Office: USAF Sch Aerospace Medicine Neuropsychiatry Br (NGN) Brooks AFB TX 78235

JONES, DONALD LEE, construction engineer; b. Buffalo, Dec. 26, 1932; m. Joan Dimenstien, Feb. 19, 1961; children—Helaine V., LeAnn A., Paula R., David L. A.A.S., NYU, 1953; B. Bldg. Constrn., U. Fla., Gainesville, 1959; M. Indsl. Engring., Pacific Western U., 1979, Ph.D. in Bus. Adminstrn., 1980. Lic. plumber, N.Y. Estimator, field engr. housing contractors, Buffalo, 1955-56; field engr. Turner Constrn. Co., Chgo., 1959; field engr., supt. Raymond Concrete Pile Co. div. Raymond Internat., Inc., Chgo., 1959, office mgr., N.Y.C., 1960, supt., engr., Jamaica, W.I., 1961, asst. mgr. N.Y. dist., 1962, dist. mgr., design and constrn. engr., Houston, 1962-64, regional mgr., Atlanta 1964-66, dist. mgr., Boston, 1966-71; founder D.L. Jones Subsurface Inv., JEM Mgmt. Corp., Boston, 1972-78; mgr., ptnr. Civil Engring., Inc., Boston, Universal Testing, Inc., Hill Internat., Inc., 1979—, Jocaro Trading, U.S.A., Boston. Served with USNR, 1949-60. Mem. Am. Arbitration Assn., Gargoyle, Am. Legion, Alpha Phi Omega. Home: 1510 N W 71st St Gainesville FL 32605

JONES, DORIS GREEN, social worker; b. Birmingham, Ala., Oct. 24, 1935; d. Irving and Lillie Mae (Walker) Green; m. John Thomas Jones, Oct. 11, 1963; 1 son, J. Irving. A.B., Samford U., 1958; M.R.E., New Orleans Sem., 1960; M.S.W., U. Ala., 1974. Dir. religious edn. Angier Ave. Bapt. Ch., Durham, N.C., 1960-63; promotional sec. First Bapt. Ch., Brewton, Ala., 1963-64; social worker Escambia County Dept. Pension and Security, 1964-68, Pike County Dept. Pensions and Security, 1968-72; supr. social services Chilton County Dept. Pension and Security, 1974-77; dir. Chilton County Dept. Pensions and Security, Clanton, Ala., 1977—. Mem. Am. Pub. Welfare Assn., Ala. State Employees Assn. (pres. Chilton County chpt.), Assn. County Dirs. Democrat. Baptist. Club: Pilot (2d v.p.) (Clanton, Ala.). Office: PO Box 446 Clanton AL 35045

JONES, ED, congressman; b. Yorkville, Tenn., Apr. 20, 1912; s. Will Frank and Hortense (Pipkin) J.; B.S., U. Tenn., 1934; postgrad. U. Wis., U. Mo.; D.Litt., Bethel Coll.; m. Llewellyn Wyatt, June 9, 1938; children—Mary Llew Jones McGuire (dec.), Jennifer Kinnard. Insp., Tenn. Dept. Agr., 1934-36; supr. Tenn. Dairy Products Assn., 1936-41; agrl. agt. Ill. Central R.R., West Tenn., 1941-48, Yorkville, 1953-69; commr. agr. State Tenn., 1949-52; asso. farm dir. Radio Sta. WMC, Memphis, 1952-69; pres. bd. dirs. Yorkville (Tenn.) Telephone Coop., 1950—; elected to U.S. Ho. Reps. in spl. election 7th Dist. Tenn., 1969; mem. 92d to 97th Congresses from 7th Dist. Tenn., 98th Congress from 8th Dist. Tenn. State chmn. Farmers for Kennedy-Johnson, 1961; pres. bd. trustees Bethel Coll., 1950-67. Named Man of Year, Progressive Farmer mag., 1952, 80, also Memphis Agrl. Club; recipient Disting. Alumnus award U. Tenn., Martin, 1980; award for service to agr. Gamma Sigma Delta, 1980; Disting. Service award Nat. Limestone Inst., 1979; Disting. Service award Nat. Assn. Conservation Dists., 1983; Disting. Service award Nat. Rural Electric Coop. Assn., 1985. Mem. 4-H (state farmer). Presbyterian (elder 1940—). Clubs: Masons, Shriners, Moose, Elks. Office: 108 Cannon House Office Bldg Washington DC 20515

JONES, EDDIE, professional sports team executive; b. Houston; m. Marilyn Jones; children—Wendy, Todd, Jeffrey. B.S. in Acctg., La. State U. Bus. mgr. New Orleans Saints, 1968-73, treas., 1973-77, v.p., 1977-78, exec. v.p., 1978-80, pres., 1982—; v.p. John Mecom Co., Houston, 1980-82. Served with USAF. Office: New Orleans Saints 1500 Poydras St New Orleans LA 70112*

JONES, EDWIN KERMIT, petrochem. cons.; b. Sacramento, Jan. 20, 1916; s. John Morgan and Selma Gertrude (King) J.; B.S. in Chem. Engring., Purdue U., 1937; m. Alice Catherine Welty, May 23, 1942; children—Nancy Lee, Linda Louise. Asst. to v.p. tech. service div. Universal Oil Products Co., Des Plaines, Ill., 1937-66; cons. Petroleum & Petrochem. Ind., worldwide, 1966-74; chief engr. chem. and environ. div. Catalytic Inc., Charlotte, N.C., 1974-77; mgr. process engring. div. Jacobs Engring., Houston, 1977-79; pres. Internat. Energy Cons., Inc., Sarasota, Fla., 1979—. Bd. dirs. Sears Sch., Kenilworth, Ill., 1966-72. Mem. Am. Petroleum Inst. Club: Bird Key Yacht. Editor Purdue Engr., 1936-37; contbr. articles to profl. jours.; patentee in field. Address: 275 Robin Dr Sarasota FL 33577

JONES, ELIZABETH COLLINS, utility company executive; b. Austin, Tex., Aug. 28, 1946; d. Talferd Gabriel and Ella Lee (Myers) Collins; m. Algie Jesuit Jones, Sept. 8, 1972. B.A., Prairie View A&M Coll., 1968. Records adminstr. Tenneco Inc., Houston, 1968-80; gen. supr. info. and records mgmt. Houston Lighting & Power Co., 1980—; lectr. Mem. Missouri City Transp. Com. (Tex.), 1979-82, Capital Improvement Com., 1984; adv. council U. Houston, 1981—, North Harris County Coll., 1982-83; Houston Community Coll., 1983—; Mem. Assn. Info. and Image Mgmt. (chpt. pres.), Assn. Records Mgrs. and Adminstrs. (mem. awards com.). Roman Catholic. Home: 1614 Oakbury Dr Missouri City TX 77489 Office: 611 Walker St Suite 2302 Houston TX 77002

JONES, ELIZABETH RIEKE (MRS. WAYNE VAN LEER JONES), club woman; b. Chgo., Oct. 15, 1903; d. Henry Edward and Vina Genevieve (Coulter) Rieke; A.B., Northwestern U., 1925; m. Wayne Van Leer Jones, Jan. 14, 1926; 1 son, Wayne Van Leer. Dir. Houston Grand Opera Assn., 1957-76, mem. pres.'s council, 1976—. Donor The Wayne V. and Elizabeth R. Jones Fine and Performing Arts Residential Coll., Northwestern U., 1980. Mem. Nat. Assistance League (nat. fin. com. 1970-72), Univ. Women's Alliance (pres. 1951-53, scholarship chmn. 1963-83), Houston Geol. Aux. (parliamentarian 1950-51, 60-61, 63-64), Kappa Kappa Gamma, Theta Sigma Phi. Republican. Presbyterian. Home: 5672 Longmont Dr Houston TX 77056

JONES, GENE ALAN, dental educator, dentist; b. Hodgenville, Ky., Dec. 21, 1924; s. Ben H. and Henritta B. (Baird) J.; m. Dorothy Burdette, Nov. 19, 1944; children—Janene L., S. Mark, Judy L., Timothy G. B.A., Coll. Anathoth, Indpls., 1964; D.D.S., Ind. U.-Indpls., 1962, M.S.D., 1980; B.S., Butler U., 1971. Records clk. Bidgeport Brass Co., Indpls., 1946-53; with purchase dept. Allison div. Gen. Motors Corp., Indpls., 1953-57; gen. practice dentistry, Danville, Ind., 1962-81; asst. prof. Sch. Dentistry, Ind. U.-Indpls., 1978-81; asst. prof. radiology U. Tenn.-Memphis, 1981—, head sect. dental radiology. Served to sgt. USAAF, 1943-45; PTO. Mem. ADA, Tenn. Dental Assn., Memphis Dental Soc., Am. Assn. Dental Schs., Am. Acad. Dental Radiology. Avocation: travel. Office: U Tenn Coll Dentistry 875 Union Ave Memphis TN 38163

JONES, GEORGE HILES, JR., association executive, insurance company executive; b. St. Louis, Mar. 17, 1932; s. George Hiles and Florence McCarty (Harris) J.; B.A., Birmingham-So. Coll., Birmingham, Ala., 1954; m. Mary Sue Poe, Nov. 11, 1973; 1 son, Robert W. Sales mgr. Ebsco Industries, Birmingham, 1954-57; exec. dir. Ala. Assn. Credit Execs., Birmingham, 1957-64; mgr. Ala.-Ga. Tire Dirs. Assn., Birmingham, 1966-69; pres. Assn. Mgmt. Services Inc., Leeds, Ala., 1969—; chmn. bd. Nat. Union Life Ins. Co., 1983—; mgr. Self Ins. Inst. Am. Mem. Ala. Council Assn. Execs., Ala. Soc. Profl. Benefit Adminstrs. (v.p.), Am. Soc. Assn. Execs. Episcopalian. Club: Relay House, Civitan. Editor Ala.-Ark.-La.-Miss. Tire Dealers Newsletters, 1969—, Ala.-Ark.-Ky.-Ga.-Miss.-Tenn. Auto Dismantler Newsletters, 1971—, Miss. Used Car Dealer Newsletter, 1971—, Ala. Auto Body Shop Newsletter, 1980—, Ala. Towing Assn. Newsletter, 1981. Office: 415 Parkway Dr Leeds AL 35094

JONES, GLENN WILLIAMSON, JR., investment banker, securities analyst; b. Nashville, Feb. 21, 1948; s. Glenn Williamson and Mary Lillian (Persons) J.; m. Mary Jane Hillard, Dec. 15, 1973; children—Madison Glenn, Logan Persons. B.A., Duke U., 1970; M.B.A., U. Chgo., 1972. Chartered fin. analyst. Securities analyst J.C. Bradford & Co., Nashville, 1972—. Mem. Nashville Soc. Fin. Analysts. Presbyterian. Avocations: Vanderbilt sports; cooking; bridge. Office: J C Bradford & Co 170 4th Ave N Nashville TN 37219

JONES, GRANT, state senator; b. Abilene, Tex., Nov. 11, 1922; s. Morgan and Jessie (Wilder) J.; B.B.A., So. Methodist U., 1947; M.B.A., Wharton Sch., U. Pa., 1948; Doctorate (hon.), Abilene Christian U., 1981; m. Anne Smith, Aug. 21, 1948; children—Morgan Andrew, Janet Elizabeth. Casualty underwriter Trezevant and Cochran, Dallas, 1950-54; ins. agt., Abilene, 1948-73; admitted to Tex. bar, 1974; pvt. practice law, also ind. ins. agt., 1954—; mem. Tex. Ho. of Reps. from 62d Dist., 1965-72, Tex. Senate from 24th Dist., 1973—. Served as pilot USAAF, World War II. C.P.C.U. Mem. Nat. Assn. Ins. Agts. (dir. 1963), Tex. Assn. Ins. Agts. (past pres.). Democrat. Methodist. Home: 2605 Pecan Dr Temple TX 76502 Office: PO Box 5138 Abilene TX 79608

JONES, J. MORGAN, business administration educator, statistical and marketing consultant; b. Dunsmuir, Calif., Oct. 29, 1939; s. J. Morgan and Beth (Kapke) J.; m. Judith Decherd, Aug. 6, 1966; children—David M., Laura K., Adam K. B.S. in Chem. Engring., Stanford U., 1960, M.B.A., 1963, M.S. in Stats., 1965, Ph.D. in Ops. Research, 1969. Asst. prof. Grad. Sch. Mgmt., UCLA, 1969-74, assoc. prof., 1974-82; vis. assoc. prof. Sloan Sch. Mgmt., MIT, 1974-75; assoc. prof. Sch. Bus. Adminstrn., U. N.C., 1982—; cons. So. Calif. Rapid Transit Dist., Los Angeles, 1978, Tosco Corp., Los Angeles, 1980, Mgmt. Analysis Ctr., Palo Alto, Calif., 1980, Burke Mktg. Research, Cin., 1984-85. Author: Introduction to Decision Theory, 1977. Contbr. articles to profl. jours. Recipient George H. Robbins Teaching award Grad. Sch. Mgmt. UCLA, 1971. Mem. Inst. Mgmt. Sci. (assoc. editor 1978—), Am. Statis. Assn., Assn. Consumer Research. Democrat. Avocation: choral singing. Office: Sch Bus Adminstrn U NC Chapel Hill NC 27514

JONES, JAMES LUTHER, III, corporate safety executive; b. New Bern, N.C., Apr. 29, 1946; s. James Luther Jr. and Hazel Marie (Waters) J.; m. Mary Helen Williams, Nov. 30, 1969; children—Sara Elizabeth, Katherine Marie. A.Graphic Arts, Chowan Coll., 1968; B.S., N.C. State U., 1974, M.E., 1975. Cert. tchr., N.C. Safety officer N.C. OSHA, Conover, 1976-79; corp. safety mgr. Roses Stores, Inc., Henderson, N.C., 1979—. First aid chmn. ARC, Henderson, 1982; bd. dirs. Mid-State Safety Council, Raleigh, N.C., 1979—. Served with USAF, 1968-72. Mem. Am. Soc. Safety Engrs., YMCA, Phi Kappa Phi. Democrat. Methodist. Lodge: Lions. Avocations: fishing; hunting; gardening. Home: 1718 Lynne Ave Henderson NC 27536 Office: Roses Stores Inc PO Box 947 Henderson NC 27536

JONES, JAMES PHILLIP, architect, design and building corporation executive, developer; b. Abbeville, S.C., Jan. 23, 1955; s. James Ben, Jr. and Barbara Olivia (Ashley) J.; m. Susan Marie Johnson, May 5, 1979; 1 child, Phillip Evan. B.S., Clemson U., 1977, B.Arch., 1979. Registered architect, S.C. Designer J. Alison Lee, AIA, Greenwood, S.C., 1978; designer W.E. Gilbert & Assocs., Inc., Greenwood, 1979-80, project mgr., 1980-82, archtl. group mgr., 1982-85; pres. Skillcraft, Inc., Abbeville, S.C., 1985—. Mem. AIA (S.C. chpt.), Ducks Unltd. Presbyterian. Avocations: bodybuilding; auto racing. Office: Skillcraft Inc PO Box 865 Abbeville SC 29620

JONES, JAMES R., congressman; b. Muskogee, Okla., May 5, 1939; A.B. in Journalism and Govt., U. Okla., 1961; LL.B., Georgetown U., 1964; m. Olivia Barclay, 1968; children—Geoffrey Gardner, Adam Winston. Admitted to Okla. bar, 1964; legislative asst. to Congressman Ed Edmondson, 1961-64; spl. asst. to Pres. Lyndon Johnson, 1965-69; mem. 93d-97th Congresses, 1st Dist. Okla., chmn. budget com. Served as capt. CIC, U.S. Army, 1964-65. Mem. Am., Okla., Tulsa bar assns., Am. Legion, Tulsa C. of C. Democrat. Rotarian. Home: Tulsa OK Office: 203 Cannon House Office Bldg Washington DC 20515

JONES, JANE SALMON, social services administrator, educator; b. Auburn, Ala., Nov. 9, 1929; d. William Davis and Eunice Helen (Bowman) Salmon; m. Robert Devan Jones, June 21, 1952; children—Sharon Jones Folmar, Robert D., Richard Carlton, Beverly Jones Ross. B.S. in Home Econs. Edn., Ala. Poly Inst. (now Auburn U.), 1951. Cert. tchr., Ala. Tchr. vocat. home econs. Baldwin County High Sch. (Ala.), 1951-52, 67-71; food service mgr. W.T. Grant, 1973-75; dir. Baldwin County Ret. Sr. Vol. Program, 1976—. Mem. Christian Charity League adv. bd.; vice-chmn. Community Resources Devel. Com., 1978—, Extension Service Home Econs. planning com. 1981, 82; judge Ala. Extension Service Sub-Dist. 4-H Roundup Food Awards, 1980, 81, 82; charter life mem. Baldwin Heritage Mus. Assn., Inc., bd. dirs., 1981-84. exec. sec., 1983: mem. North Baldwin Arts Council; residential div. chmn. North Baldwin United Fund, 1981, 82, 83; county memls. chmn. Baldwin County unit Am. Heart Assn., 1980, 81, 82, 83, 84, coordinator, 1980, 81, 82, 83, sec. 1983, 84; mem. adv. com. Project LIFT; tchr. Methodist Vacation Bible Sch., 1962-65, dir., 1966; mem. Bay Minette Infirmary Aux. and Council, 1984; bd. dirs. Community Action Agy. Baldwin and Escambia County, 1984; mem. Baldwin County Human Service Council. Mem. Nat. Assn. Female Execs., Nat. Assn. Ret. Sr. Vol. Program Dirs., Ala. Assn. Ret. Sr. Vol. Program Dirs. (treas., rec. sec. 1977-79, exec. bd. dirs. 1979-82, 84, budget com. 1979, edn. com. 1981, constn. and by-laws com. 1982-83, chmn. fin. 1983). Methodist. Club: Poplarville Garden (Miss.). Home: 705 E 7th St Bay Minette AL 36507 Office: 201-B City Hall PO Box 364 Bay Minette AL 36507

JONES, JANICE M., lawyer; b. Berkeley, Calif., Jan. 17, 1948; d. Frederick and Emily K. (Wilson) McCoy; m. Calvin William Sharpe, Apr. 13; children—Melanie, Adrienne. Asst. regional atty. Ford Motor Co., Dearborn, Mich., 1973-75; supervising atty. consumer protection div. Wayne County (Mich.) Prosecutor, Detroit, 1975-76; benefits atty. Montgomery Ward, Chgo., 1976-77, sr. atty., 1977-78; v.p., gen. counsel Booke & Co., Winston-Salem, N.C., 1978—; dir. BRIC, Inc., also sec.; lectr. U. Va. Law Sch.; adj. prof. Wake Forest Law Sch. Mem. Assn. Pvt. Pension and Welfare Plans (N.C. state chmn.), Am. Bar Assn., Mich. State Bar, Calif. Bar, Forsyth County Women Attys. (treas.), Delta Sigma Theta. Office: PO Box 66 Winston-Salem NC 27106

JONES, JEFFREY WALTON, chemical company executive; b. Rochester, N.Y., May 27, 1953; s. Robert Benson and Marjorie Ann (Ferrell) J.; m. Janis Lynn Obrien, Nov. 27, 1976; children—Ryan, Jeffrey. B.A., U. Puget Sound, 1975. Br. mgr. Jones Chems., Inc., San Diego, 1976-79, div. mgr., Houston, 1979-85, corp. v.p., 1985—. Mem. Chlorine Inst., Nat. Swimming Pool Inst., Nat. Assn. Chem. Distbrs., Beta Theta Pi. Republican. Methodist. Clubs: Kingwood Country, Deerwood. Home: 3727 Sandy Forks Dr Kingwood TX 77339 Office: Jones Chems Inc 1777 Haden Rd Houston TX 77015

JONES, JENKIN LLOYD, JR., newspaper editor; b. Tulsa, June 24, 1936; s. Jenkin Lloyd and Juanita Rose (Carlson) J.; B.A. in Polit. Sci., U. Colo., 1958; m. Carol Beatrice Jaros, June 27, 1959; children—Janette Lloyd Jones Strickland, Landon Lloyd. Sports writer Mpls. Tribune, 1959; reporter, news editor Anchorage Times, 1959-61; state capital corr. Tulsa Tribune, Oklahoma City, 1961-62, Washington corr., 1962-63, copy editor, Tulsa, 1963-64, chief copy desk, 1964-65, asst. city editor, 1965-66, asst. mng. editor, 1966-67, mng. editor, 1968-74, exec. editor, 1974—; v.p. Tulsa Tribune Co. Bd. dirs. Goodwill Industries Tulsa; Pulitzer Prize juror, 1982-83. Served with USAFR, 1958-64. Mem. AP Mng. Editors' Assn. (treas. 1984-86, past dir.), U. Tulsa Hurricane Club, Am. Soc. Newspaper Editors, Internat. Press Inst. Republican. Unitarian. Club: So. Hills Country. Home: 6447 S Louisville St Tulsa OK 74136 Office: PO Box 1770 315 Boulder Ave Tulsa OK 74102

JONES, JERRAULD C., lawyer; b. Norfolk, Va., July 22, 1954; s. Hilary Hewitt and Corrine J.; m. Lyn Michele Simmons, Apr. 20, 1985. B.A. cum laude, Princeton U., 1976; J.D., Washington and Lee U., 1980. Bar: Va. Law clk. Supreme Ct. of Va., Richmond, 1980-81; asst. commonwealth atty. Office of Commonwealth Atty., Norfolk, 1981-83; gen. ptnr. Jones and Carlson, Norfolk, 1983—. Bd. dirs. Med. Hosps., Norfolk, 1983—, Friends of Norfolk Juvenile Ct., 1982—; mem. Norfolk Indsl. Devel. Authority, 1985—; 1st vice chmn. Norfolk Democratic Com., 1984-85; mem. Norfolk Commn. on Parks and Recreation; pres. Broadcreek Shores Civic League, 1984-85; active United Way, Concerned Citizens for Polit. Action. Mem. ABA, Norfolk and Portsmouth Bar Assn., Old Doninion Bar Assn., Twin Cities Bar Assn., Nat. Dist. Attys. Assn. Episcopalian. Clubs: Torch (bd. dirs., exec. com. Norfolk), Princeton. Avocations: trumpet; piano; drums; languages; art and record collecting.

JONES, JOHN BOOTH, III, farm equipment dealer; b. DeRidder, La., Aug. 3, 1939; s. John Booth and Nona (Olds) J.; m. Florence Elizabeth Savarie, June 15, 1963; children—Christopher Ashley, Jeffrey Windham. B.S. in Bus. Adminstrn., La. State U., 1962. Sales rep. Exxon Corp., Searcy, Ark., 1967-69, sr. sales rep., Alexandria, La., 1969-74; pres. Jones Tractor & Equipment Inc., DeRidder, La., 1974—. Mem. DeRidder City Council, 1982—, pres., 1983—, liaison to Recreation commn., 1983—; v.p. library bd. trustees Beauregard Parish (La.), 1983; bd. dirs. Community Concerns Bd., DeRidder, 1983; chmn. La. Cleanest City Program, DeRidder, 1983. Served to capt. USAF, 1962-67. Mem. Deep South Farm Equipment Assn. Democrat. Episcopalian. Lodge: DeRidder Lions (dir. 1978, v.p. 1979). Home: 10 Ravenwood Dr DeRidder LA 70634 Office: Jones Tractor & Equipment Inc PO Box 207 DeRidder LA 70634

JONES, JOHN EDWARD, lawyer; b. Bainbridge, Ga., Mar. 24, 1943; s. Percy Price and Hilda Eloise (Tarpley) J.; m. Carolyn Kenn Morris, Aug. 21, 1965; children—Randall Edward, Julianne, Andrew John. B.A., Fla. State U., 1965; J.D., Stetson U., 1968. Bar: Fla. 1968, U.S. Dist. Ct. (mid. dist.) Fla. 1969, U.S. Supreme Ct. 1972. Law clk. U.S. Dist. Ct., Middle Dist. Fla., Tampa, 1968-69; ptnr. Carroll, Jones, Rooks & Owen, Casselberry, Fla., 1973-80; pres. John Edward Jones P.A., Casselberry, 1980—; dir. Seminole County Legal Referral Com., Altamonte Springs, Fla., 1976-78. Contbr. articles to profl. jours. Dir. Calvary Towers Housing Authority, 1984-86. Author: Reconciliation, 1983 (Gold Medallion award 1985). Served to lt. comdr., USNR. 1968-72. Paul Harris fellow; Charles Dana Scholar, 1968; named to Fla. State U. Hall of Fame, 1965. Mem. ABA, Seminole County Bar

Assn. (dir. 1978-79), Christian Legal Soc., Acad. Fla. Trial Lawyers, Am. Trial Lawyers Assn., Gold Key, Omicron Delta Kappa, Phi Delta Phi. Lodge: Rotary. Home: 450 Andrews Dr Longwood FL 32750 Office: PO Box 38 5200 S US Hwy 17-92 Casselberry FL 32707

JONES, JOHN LEWIS, JR., record services company executive, accountant, consultant; b. Atlanta, Aug. 13, 1939; s. John Lewis and Kathleen Cowart (Grogan) J.; m. Barbara Eason, Mar. 4, 1961; children—Barbara Joyce, John Lewis III. B.B.A., Mercer U., 1975. Asst. mgr. Singer Co., 1963-65; sales rep. Schering Corp., 1965-68; owner John's Interiors, 1968-70; controller Doctors Hosp., 1970-72; pvt. practice acctg., Atlanta, 1975-82; exec. dir. B & J Record Services, Inc., Atlanta, 1983—. Scoutmaster Boy Scouts Am., 1974-78. Served with U.S. Army, 1957-65. Named Outstanding Student in Bus. Adminstrn., Mercer U., Atlanta, 1975; recipient Order of Arrow, Boy Scouts Am., 1976, Wood Badge award, 1977. Mem. Am. Mgmt. Assn., Hosp. Fin. Mgrs. Assn., Ga. Hosp. Assn., Atlanta Radio Club. Republican.

JONES, JOHN RAY, educational administrator; b. Shawnee, Okla., Feb. 22, 1949; s. Kenneth and Lavona Cletis (Lumley) J.; m. Janna Lee Pool, Aug. 23, 1968; children—Kristin Lee, John Adam. B.E., East Central State U., 1971; M. Music Edn., U. Okla., 1976. Choral dir. Cushing Pub. Sch., Okla., 1971-76; dir. choral act Purcell Pub. Sch., Okla., 1976-80; prin. high sch. Noble Pub. Schs., Okla., 1980—. Condr., Cushing Community Chorale, 1972-76; music dir. 1st Bapt. Ch., Cushing, 1972-74; chmn. state curriculum com. State Dept. Edn., Okla., 1984-85; founder Rose Rock Festival, Noble, 1983. Named Outstanding Young Condr., Sea-Arama Music Festival, Galveston, Tex., 1973, 74. Mem. Okla. Assn. Secondary Sch. Prins. (Outstanding Secondary Sch. Adminstr. 1984-85), Nat. Assn. Secondary Sch. Prins., Nat. Fedn. Interscholastic Ofcls. Assn. (ofcl.), Assn. for Supervision and Curriculum Devel. Republican. Lodge: Kiwanis (Purcell pres. 1977-79). Avocations: golf; scuba diving; hunting. Office: Noble High Sch PO Box 519 Noble OK 73068

JONES, JOHN TILFORD, JR., broadcasting exec.; b. Dallas, Dec. 2, 1917; s. John Tilford and Margaret (Wilson) J.; student N.Mex. Mil. Inst., 1935-38, U. Tex. 1938-40; m. Winifred Ann Small, Oct. 20, 1945; children—Melissa Ann, Jesse Holman II, John Clinton. Pres. Houston Chronicle Pub. Co., 1949-66, Houston Consol. TV Co., 1954-67, Rusk Corp., 1965-83, Battleground Corp.; chmn. Rusk Corp., 1984—, Fischbach Corp.; dir. Am. Gen. Corp. Vice pres., dir. Tex. Med. Center, Inc. Served from lt. to capt. AUS, 1940-45; ETO. Presbyterian. Office: 712 Main St Houston TX 77002

JONES, JOHNNIE ANDERSON, lawyer; b. Laurel Hill, La., Nov. 30, 1919; s. Henry Edward and Sarah Ann (Coats) J.; m. Sebell Elizabeth Chase, June 1, 1948; children—Johnnie, Adair Darnell, Adal Dalcho, Ann Sarah Bythelda. B.S. in Psychology, So. U., Baton Rouge, 1949; J.D., 1953. Bar: La. 1953, U.S. Dist. Ct. (ea. and mid. dists.) La. 1953, U.S. Supreme Ct. 1961, U.S. Ct. Appeals (5th cir.) 1982, U.S. Dist. Ct. (we. dist.) La. 1985. Ins. agt. Universal Life Ins. Co., Baton Rouge, 1947-48; letter carrier U.S. Post Office, Baton Rouge, 1948-50; practice, Baton Rouge, 1953—; sr. lawyer Jones & Jones, Baton Rouge, 1975—; asst. parish atty. City-Parish Govt., Baton Rouge, 1969-72. Mem. La. Ho. of Reps., 1972-76; bd. dirs. La. Human Relations Council, Baton Rouge, 1984. Served with U.S. Army, 1942-46, ETO. Recipient Cert. of Appreciation, L.B. Johnson and H.H. Humphrey, Washington, 1964, Plaque, Alpha Kappa Alpha, 1972; named Most Outstanding Man of Yr., Mt. Zion First Bapt. Ch., Baton Rouge, 1970, Frontiersman of Yr., Frontiers Club Internat., Baton Rouge, 1962. Mem. Am. Judicature Soc., ABA, Nat. Bar Assn., Louis A. Marinet Legal Soc., Baton Rouge Bar Assn., Am. Legion, NAACP, Alpha Phi Alpha. Democrat. Baptist. Home 1438 N 32d St Baton Rouge LA 70802 Office: Jones & Jones 251 Florida St Suite 215 Baton Rouge LA 70801

JONES, JOSEPH BROOKE, nursing administrator; b. Aliceville, Ala., June 14, 1955; s. J.T. and Betty (Brooke) J.; m. Susan Glenn, June 25, 1976; children—Danah Suzanne, Jackson Brooke. L.P.N., N.W. Ala. State Tech. Coll., 1976; A.D.N., George C. Wallace State Community Coll., 1978. Staff nurse Pickens County Hosp., Carrollton, Ala., 1978-80, supr., 1980-81, intensive care unit supr., 1981-82, operating room supr., 1982-84, med. surg. coordinator, 1984, dir. nursing, 1984—. Mem. West Ala. Nursing Service Adminstrn., West Ala. Assn. Operating Room Nurses (pres. 1984—). Republican. Mem. Ch. of Christ. Avocations: water skiing; restoring old cars. Home: 1703 3d Ave NW Aliceville AL 35442 Office: Pickens County Hosp PO Box 478 Carrollton AL 35447

JONES, JUDITH ANNE CRAIG, nursing administrator, educator; b. Indpls., May 4, 1947; d. Kenneth Abbott and Mary Emma (Cody) Craig; m. Donald Rosswell Jones, Nov. 20, 1971; 1 dau., Christine Marie. B.S. in Nursing, Ind. U.-Bloomington, 1969; M.S. in Nursing, Ind. U.-Indpls., 1980. R.N. Asst. dir. infant units Riley Hosp for Children, Indpls., 1972-75, unit dir. toddlers 1975-77; maternal-child patient care coordinator Ochsner Found. Hosp., New Orleans, 1977-78, maternal-child patient care dir., 1978-81; dir. nursing All Saints Episcopal Hosp., Ft. Worth, 1981-82, assoc. hosp. dir., dir. nursing, 1982-85, sr. v.p. nursing, 1985—; instr. U. Tex.-Arlington, 1983—. Mem. Am. Orgn. Nurse Execs., Tex. Soc. Nursing Service Adminstrs., Fort Worth Area Dirs. Nursing (sec. 1983-84, pres. 1985-86), Dallas-Ft. Worth Nursing Dirs. Forum (v.p. 1984-85), Nurses Assn. Am. Coll. Obstetricians and Gynecologists. Methodist. Office: All Saints Episcopal Hosp 1400 8th Ave Box 31 Fort Worth TX 76101

JONES, JUDITH MUELLER, mathematics and science educator; b. Cin., Jan. 26, 1943; d. Harold Henry and Bernadine Winifred (Huenke) Mueller; m. Roy Carl Jones, Sept. 5, 1964; children—Roy, Janine, Robert, Richard. B.A. in Chemistry, Case Western Res. U., 1965; M.S. in Teaching, U. Fla., 1969. Instr. Coll. Orlando, Fla., 1969-70; prof. Valencia Community Coll., Orlando, 1975-82, chmn. dept., 1982—. Mem. Am. Chem. Soc., Nat. Sci. Tchrs. Assn., Com. Chemistry in Two Year Colls., Winter Park Jaycee Wives. Republican. Methodist. Avocation: bicycling. Office: Valencia Community Coll PO Box 3028 Orlando FL 32802

JONES, KENNETH RONALD, psychologist, researcher; b. Colorado Springs, Colo., May 29, 1958; s. E.R. and June Delores (Kern) J.; m. Gail Lynn Armstrong, May 28, 1983. A.D., Jackson County Jr. Coll., 1978; B.S., Millsaps Coll., 1980; M.A., U. So. Miss., 1986. Research asst., lab. coordinator U. So. Miss., Hattiesburg, 1981—. Contbr. chpt. to book. Mem. Am. Psychol. Assn. (assoc.), Soc. for Psychophysiol. Research (assoc.), Southeast Psychol. Assn., Miss. Psychol. Assn. Democrat. Lutheran. Avocations: sailing; scuba diving; beer brewing; culinary arts. Home: C105 Pinehaven Circle Hattiesburg MS 39406 Office: U So Miss Psychology Dept SS Box 5025 Hattiesburg MS 39406

JONES, LARRY LLOYD, quality engr.; b. Brookley AFB, Mobile, Ala., Oct. 2, 1953; s. Zelmer Lloyd and Katherine Krystine J.; B.S. in Biology, Birmingham-So. Coll., 1975; B.S. in Elec. Engring., U. Ala., Birmingham, 1979; m. Clare Adams, July 3, 1976; children—Erin Rainey, Brian Lloyd. Engring. asst. U. Ala., Birmingham, 1976-79; quality control engr. SONY Magnetic Products, Dothan, Ala., 1979-81, sr. quality control engr., 1981-82; quality engr. Baxter-Travenol Labs., Inc., Cleveland, Miss., 1982, sr. quality engr., 1982—. Summer scholar, 1971, leadership scholar, 1972. Mem. IEEE, Soc. Motion Picture and TV Engrs., Am. Soc. Quality Control, Tau Beta Pi. Baptist. Home: PO Box 1012 Cleveland MS 38732 Office: PO Box 1058 Hwy 61 N Cleveland MS 38732

JONES, LAURENCE R., JR., petrochemical company executive. Chmn., Pioneer Corp., Amarillo, Tex. Office: Pioneer Corp PO Box 511 Amarillo TX 79163*

JONES, LEON HERBERT (HERB), JR., artist; b. Norfolk, Va., Mar. 25, 1923; s. Leon Herbert and Edna May (Curling J.; student William and Mary Coll., 1942-44; m. Barbara Dean, Sept. 14, 1947; children—Robert Clair, Louis Herbert. Marine structural draftsman and designer Norfolk (Va.) Shipbuilding & Dry Dock Co., 1944-46; freelance comml. artist, 1946-49; prin. Herb Jones Realty, Norfolk, 1949-58; owner, mgr. Herb Jones Art Studio, Norfolk, 1958—; one-man shows: Norfolk Mus., 1968, Potomac Gallery, Alexandria, Va., 1979, Salisbury Gallery, 1979, Walter C. Rawls Mus., Courtland, Va., 1967, Virginia Beach Maritime Mus., 1983 Village Gallery, Virginia Beach, Va., 1984; group shows include: Chrysler Mus., Norfolk, 1973, 74, SUNY, Buffalo, 1966, Springfield (Mass.) Mus. Fine Arts, 1966, Mariners Mus., Newport News, Va., 1967-73, Va. Mus., Richmond, 1969, 71, Columbia (S.C.) Mus. Art, 1972, Winston-Salem (N.C.) Gallery Contemporary Art, 1970, 72, Norfolk Mus., 1963-69, Vladimir Arts, Winsbach, W. Ger., 1978, 79, Chesapeake Bay Maritime Mus., Md., Mobile Mus. Traveling Show, 1983, Knoxville World's Fair in Fine Arts, 1982, Art Buyers Caravan, Atlanta, 1982, Colonial Wild Fowl Festival, Williamsburg, Va., 1983, Chesapeake Jubilee (Va.) (award of excellence) 1984, Peninsula Fine Arts Festival, Newport News, 1984, Currituck Wildlife Show, N.C., 1984, Medley of Arts, Hampton, Va., 1984, Easton Nat. Wildfowl and Art Exhibit, Easton, Md., 1984; Mid-Atlantic Art Exhibit, Virginia Beach, Va., 1985, Chincoteague Island Easter Festival, Va., 1985, Harborfest Norfolk, Va., 1985; represented in permanent collections: Chrysler Mus., wardroom USS Skipjack, USS Iwo Jima, USS John F. Kennedy, USS Dwight D. Eisenhower, U. Va., Charlottesville, U.S. Treasury Dept., Library of Congress, Washington, Edenton Hist. Commn. (N.C.), also pvt. collections; commd. ltd. edit. print series Ducks Unltd., also Virginia Beach Maritime Mus. Recipient diploma di merito Universita delle Arti, 1981, also Gold Centaur award 1983; Cavalier of Arts, Acad. Bedriacense Calvatore, Italy, 1985; Oscar d'Italia, Acad. Italia Calvatore, 1985. Mem. Nat. Soc. Arts and Lit., Tidewater Artists Assn., Internat. Platform Assn., Virginia Beach Maritime Mus. (charter). Methodist. Home and Office: 238 Beck St Norfolk VA 23503

JONES, LONNIE LEE, nurse; b. Cotulla, Tex., Dec. 25, 1953; s. Charles Ray and Betty Jean (Wilson) J.; m. Paula Irene Benson, Sept. 10, 1981; children—Tahirih Denise, Eric Monroe, Dyami Patrick Eloy. A.A., Del Mar Coll. R.N., Tex. Gauger, Peet Oil Co., Refugio, Tex., 1976-77; oil field hand Expando Corp., Refugio, 1977-78; orderly Spohn Hosp., Corpus Christi, Tex., 1978-80, nurse, 1980-82; supr. Surg. ICU, Victoria Regional Med. Ctr. (Tex.), 1982—; supr. through Upjohn Corp., Goliad and area hosps., Victoria, 1982. Democrat. Baptist. Club: Nurses Book. Home: 510 Versailles St Victoria TX 77904

JONES, LOREAN ELECTA, federal probation officer, drug treatment specialist; b. Arlington, Tenn., June 29, 1938; d. Earnest and Alcorna (Harris) Matthews; m. Jimmie Jones Oct. 3, 1954 (dec. Sept. 1961); children—Gale D. Jones Carson and Dale J. (twins), Elna C. Jones Brunetti and Ervin C. (twins), Denise F. Jones Jimenez and Dennis R. (twins), Teresa Y. and Terry O. (dec.) (twins). A.A., Owen Coll., 1968; B.A., LeMoyne Owen Coll., Memphis, 1970; M.S., Memphis State U., 1977. Social worker Tenn. Dept. Mental Health, 1970-76; parole officer Tenn. Dept. Corrections, 1976-78; U.S. probation officer U.S. Dist. Ct., Memphis, 1978—; drug treatment specialist U.S. Dist. Ct. (we. dist.) Tenn., 1984—; hearing examiner U.S. Parole Commn. Western Dist. Tenn., 1980—. Trustee, Arlington Devel. Ctr., Tenn., 1972-73; mem. Black on Black Crime Task Force, 1979; mem. local bd. 38 Tenn. Selective Service, 1985—. Recipient Citizen of Week award Sta. WLOK, 1978. Mem. Operation PUSH, NAACP, Nat. Council Negro Women (historian 1983—), 100 Black Women, LeMoyne Owen Alumni Assn. (sec. 1983-85), Fed. Probation Officers Assn. (sec. treas. 1983-85), Am. Probation and Parole Assn., Am. Assn. Counseling and Devel., Nat. Alliance Bus. (youth motivating task force 1982-83). Democrat. Baptist. Avocations: reading; exercising; theatre. Home: 1520 Netherwood Ave Memphis TN 38106

JONES, LUTHER, mayor. Mayor of Corpus Christi. Office: PO Box 9277 Corpus Christi TX 78469*

JONES, MARGUERITE JACKSON, educator; b. Greenwood, Miss., Aug. 12, 1949; d. James and Mary G. (Reedy) Jackson; B.S., Miss. Valley State U., 1969; M.Ed., Miss. State U., 1974; Specialist in Community Coll. Teaching, Ark. State U., 1983; postgrad. U. Ark.; m. Algee Jones, Apr. 4, 1971; 1 dau., Stephanie Nerissa. Tchr. English, Henderson High Sch., Starkville, Miss., 1969-70; tchr. creative writing Miami (Fla.) Coral Park, 1970-71; tchr. English, head dept. Marion (Ark.) Sr. High Sch., 1971-78; tchr. East Ark. Community Coll., Forrest City, 1978-79; migrant edn. supr. Marion (Ark.) Sch. Dist., 1979-83; mem. faculty Draughons Coll., Memphis, 1978-83, State Tech. Inst., 1984—; cons. writing projects. Mem. Nat. Council Tchrs. English, Ark. Assn. Profl. Educators, Assn. Supervision and Curriculum Devel. Home: 3707 Stallion St Memphis TN 38116 Office: State Tech Inst 5983 Macon Cove Memphis TN 38134

JONES, MARTHA ELLEN, public relations firm executive; b. Detroit, Nov. 3, 1948; d. Robert Everett and Bess Alice (Johnson) J.; student Williams Coll., 1969; B.A., Vassar Coll., 1970. With radio/TV news dept. Burson Marsteller, N.Y.C., 1974; account exec. Hill & Knowlton, N.Y.C., 1975-78; dir. public relations and environ. affairs Fla. Phosphate Council, Lakeland, 1978-81; pres. Jones & Assos., Public Relations, Lakeland, 1981—. Commr. Edn. apointee Fla. Adv. Council on Sci. Edn., 1979, vice chmn., 1980-81, chmn., 1981-82; mem. Gov.'s Task Force on Phosphate-Related Radiation, 1979-80; trustee Learning Resource Center, Lakeland, 1979-82; bd. dirs. Campfire Inc., Lakeland, 1982-85; mem. Lakeland Young Life Council, 1985, Leadership Lakeland, 1985-86; del. Diocesan Conv., St. Stephen's Episcopal Ch., 1982—, lay reader, 1983—, mem. vestry, 1984-86; mem. adv. council Fla. Defenders of Environ., 1980, United Way, 1980, Hist. Lakeland, 1979-80, Fla. Assn. Sci. Tchrs., 1981. Recipient nat. 1st place Addy award Am. Advt. Fedn., 1978. Mem. Public Relations Soc. Am., Fla. Public Relations Assn. (bd. dirs. Polk chpt. 1983-84, awards 1979, 80, 82, All Fla. award 1982). Episcopalian. Club: Jr. League Greater Lakeland. Office: Jones & Assocs 4315 Highland Park Blvd PO Box 6555 Lakeland FL 33803

JONES, MARY ELIZABETH, school counselor; b. Lake Charles, La.; d. Annie Walter and Thelma (Griffin) J. B.S. in Recreation, So. U., 1969; M.A., 1977. Program dir. YWCA, Baton Rouge, 1969-72; instr. So. U., Baton Rouge, 1972-74, career counselor, 1974-84; student personnel officer Baton Rouge Vocat. Tech. Inst., 1984—, asst. test dir., 1984—; resource person Women's Skill Tng. Program, Baton Rouge, 1984—; advisor So. U. Tchrs. Job Fair, Baton Rouge, 1980—; judge, faculty advisor Vocat. Indsl. Clubs Am., Baton Rouge, 1984—. Bd. dirs. Battered Women's Program, Baton Rouge, 1985, also mem. exec. com., chmn. fin. and fundraising com.; sec. polit. action com. Scotlandville Area Adv. Council, Baton Rouge chmn. scholarship com., 1985. Recipient Community Services award Scotlandville Area Adv. Council, 1982. Mem. Nat. Family Opinion, Greater New Orleans Urban League, Smithsonian Assocs., Am. Assn. for Counseling and Devel., La. Sch. Counselors Assn., La. Vocation Assn., Nat. Assn. for Female Execs. Democrat. Roman Catholic. Avocations: traveling; reading; monogramming; hook rug weaving; interior design. Home: 1631 79th Ave Baton Rouge LA 70807

JONES, MARY VIRGINIA, mechanical engineer; b. Roanoke, Va., Sept. 19, 1940; d. James Bernard and Evangeline (Jamison) Jones. B.S. with honors in Mech. Engring., Va. Poly. Inst., 1962; M.S. in Mech. Engring., George Washington U., 1972, postgrad., 1972-73. Registered profl. engr., Va. Design engr. Atlantic Research Corp., Gainesville, Va., 1961-72, design team leader, 1972-77, chief engr. Multiple Launch Rocket Motor, 1977-81, head design engring. sect., 1981-83, chief mech. design group, 1982—. Mem. Va. State Bd. Architects, Engrs., Land Surveyors and Landscape Architects, 1982—, v.p., 1985, chmn. engring. sect., 1985, pres., 1986. Trustee Va. Poly. Inst., 1985—. Mem. Soc. Women Engrs. (membership chmn. 1979-80, v.p. 1981, pres. Balt.-Washington sect. 1982-84, sect. rep. 1985), ASME, AIAA Soc. Plastic's Engrs., NOW, Fedn. Orgns. Profl. Women (gov.), Omicron Delta Kappa, Phi Kappa Phi, Pi Tau Sigma, Tau Beta Pi. Methodist. Home: 3137 Stratford Ct Oakton VA 22124 Office: Atlantic Research Corp 7511 Wellington Rd Gainesville VA 22065

JONES, MAX KESLER, non-profit organization administrator; b. Hereford, Tex., May 9, 1938; s. Harold Kesler and Maudetha (Miller) J.; B.A., Tex. Christian U., 1960; M.Div., Yale U., 1964; m. Suzanne Smith, Sept. 8, 1962; children—Kinley Nan, Kyle Weldon, Lacey Suzanne. Ordained to ministry Christian Ch., 1964; pastor Christian Ch., Roswell, N.Mex., 1964-67; regional dir. Joint Action in Community Service, Austin, Tex., 1967-69; asst. dean Sch. Law, So. Meth. U., Dallas, 1969-71; dir. regional campaigns Tex. Christian U., Ft. Worth, 1971-74; pres. Ark. Council Ind. Colls. and Univs., Little Rock, 1974-78; pres. Tex. Ind. Coll. Fund, 1978-84; pres. Well Way Centers, Inc., 1984—; cons. on resource devel. Mem. bd. higher edn. Christian Ch. Mem. Nat. Benevolent Soc., Nat. Assn. Ind. Colls. and Univs., council for the Advancement and Support of Edn., Ind. Coll. Funds Am. (exec. com. 1981—), Nat. Soc. Fund Raising Execs. (bd. dirs.), Bridge Assn., Ft. Worth C. of C. Democrat. Club: Rotary. Office: 6536 Winifred St Fort Worth TX 76133

JONES, MELBA JOHNSON, accountant; b. Winnsboro, La., Jan. 24, 1933; d. Malcolm Malone and Lillie (McKaskle) Johnson; student N.E. La. U., 1951-52; grad. Sch. Acctg., Internat. Accts. Soc., 1967; m. Aubrey Jones, Oct. 11, 1952; children—Michael Aubrey, Gregory Alan. C.P.A., La. Office mgr. C.P.A. firm, Monroe, La., 1969-72; sole practice Melba Jones, C.P.A., Ruston, La., 1972-79; individual practice C.P.A., Ruston, 1980—. Adv. bd. N.E. La. Vocat. Sch. Recipient Citizenship award Am. Legion, 1952; C.P.A., La. Mem. Am. Inst. C.P.A.s, La. Soc. C.P.A.s, Bus. and Profl. Women's Club (named Outstanding Bus. Woman 1966), Ruston C. of C. Republican. Baptist. Address: 1221 Farmerville St PO Box 96 Ruston LA 71270

JONES, MICHAEL PAUL, philosophy educator; b. Anderson, Ind., Oct. 31, 1940; s. Calvin and Leotha Pearl (Kreeger) J. B.S., Purdue U., 1962; Ph.D., U. Tex., 1973. Instr. No. Ariz. U., Flagstaff, 1972-73; asst. prof. philosophy U. S.C., Columbia, 1973-74; assoc. prof. philosophy Western Carolina U., Cullowhee, N.C., 1974—. Editor: The Individual and Society, 1978. Mem. Am. Philos. Assn., So. Soc. Philosophy and Psychology. Home: PO Box D Webster NC 28788 Office: Dept Philosophy and Religion Western Carolina U Cullowhee NC 28723

JONES, NONA MAE, office manager; b. Kissimmee, Fla., Nov. 27, 1919; d. Arthur Eugene and Nina Mae (Sharpe) Jones; nursing home adminstr. licensure St. Petersburg Jr. Coll., 1972; 1 adopted dau., Sandra Jane Jones Dempsey. Bookkeeper, sales clk. H.B. Allen Firestone Store, Kissimmee, 1945-53; bookkeeper, key punch operator Tupperware Home Parties, Orlando, Fla., 1953-60; bookkeeper, office mgr. Cinderella Internat., Orlando, 1960-62; NCR operator/key punch Corporate Group Services, Orlando, 1963-68; bookkeeper, asst. adminstr. John Milton Nursing Home, Inc., Kissimmee, 1967-78, adminstr., 1978-80; office mgr./bookkeeper Robert L. Larson Contracting, Inc., Kissimmee, 1982—. Bd. dirs. Osceola County Mental Health Dept. Mem. Fla. Health Care Assn. (treas. dist. 3), C. of C. Osceola County. Mem. Christian Ch. (Disciples of Christ). Democrat. Home: PO Box 2312 809 N Brack St Kissimmee FL 32741 Office: Robert L Larson Contracting Inc PO Box 1647 South Hwy 17-92 Kissimmee FL 32742

JONES, OLIVER, JR., political science educator, consultant; b. Savannah, Ga., Aug. 6, 1947; s. Oliver and Jannie (Jenkins) J.; m. Vernita Christian, Sept. 2, 1967; children—Olivia, Deidra. B.S. in Polit. Sci., Savannah State U., 1970; M.A. in Polit. Sci., U. Ill., 1974, Ph.D. in Polit. Sci., 1979. Asst. prof. Rust Coll., Holly Springs, Miss., 1978-79; asst. prof. Fla. A&M U., Tallahassee, 1979—, chmn. polit. sci., 1980-82; chmn. bd. Frenchtown Devel., Tallahassee, 1984-85; dir. Ctr. Pub. Affairs Fla. Inst. Govt., Tallahassee, 1982—. Precinct committeeman Leon County Dem. Exec. Com.; Mondale del. Dem. Party Nat. Conv., San Francisco, 1984; campaign treas. Judy Curtain for Leon County Judge, Tallahassee, 1984; del. Dem. Party State Conv., 1982-84. Mem. Am. Polit. Sci. Assn., Acad. Polit. Sci., Am. Soc. Tng. and Devel., Am. Soc. Pub. Adminstrn., Transp. Research Bd. Democrat. Baptist. Avocations: boating; swimming; biking; racquetball; jogging. Home: 3612 Picket Ct Tallahassee FL 32301 Office: Ctr for Pub Affairs 412 Tucker Hall Tallahassee FL 32307

JONES, OMA PAUL, advertising agency executive; b. Crowell, Tex., Nov. 26, 1922; s. Latham Clements and Cleo Marjorie (Tefteller) J.; m. Irma E. Luckett, Mar. 21, 1945 (dec. 1981); children—Gail D. Jones Lenchan, Nancy Sue Jones Moore; m. Helen E. Enloe, Oct. 24, 1981. B.A. in Bus. and Advt., Tex. Christian U., 1951. Advt. mgr. All Ch. Press., Fort Worth, 1946-53, metroplex mgr., 1977-78; with nat. advt. dept. Dallas Morning News, 1953-66, Tarrant County advt. mgr., 1978-85; printing sales mgr. News Tex., Inc., Arlington, 1966-70; printing sales mgr. Arlington Plant, Capitol Cities Communication, 1971-76; owner, mgr. P&H Advt. Agy., 1986—. Served with USAF, 1943-46, PTO. Republican. Methodist. Lodge: Lions (sec., treas. Dallas 1957-58).

JONES, PAUL GRIFFIN, II, clergyman, lobbyist, denominational executive; b. Waynesville, Mo., Oct. 12, 1942; s. Paul Griffin and Era Frances (Foley) J.; m. Sandra Lee Poe, July 2, 1966; children—Stephanie Noel, Paul Griffin III, Mark David, Heather Elizabeth. B.A., Baylor U., 1964; M.Div., Southwestern Bapt. Theol. Sem., 1967, Th.D., 1976, Ph.D., 1978. Ordained to ministry So. Bapt. Ch., 1967; coordinator 4th St. Bapt. Mission, Waco, Tex., 1961-64; dir., instr. extension dept. So. Bapt. Conv. Sem., Ft. Worth, 1965-66; pastor Pleasant Valley Bapt. Ch., Olney, Tex., 1967-68; chaplain St. Francis Retirement Village, Crowley, Tex., 1968-70; dir. Bapt. Student Union, Tex. Christian U., Ft. Worth, 1970-80; dir. Bapt. Student Union, dir., chmn. dept. bibl. studies East Tex. State U., Commerce, 1980-81; exec. dir., treas. Christian Action Commn., Miss. Bapt. Conv., Jackson, 1982—; mem. Nat. Inst. Campus Ministry, 1978-82; Miss. Religious Leadership Conf., Jackson, 1982—; mem. adv. bd. Christian Life Commn., Nashville, 1982—. Author: Comprehensive Family Planning, 1975, Handbook for Group Leaders, 1981, Bible Speaks on Sex, Love and Marriage, 1982. Bd. dirs. Family Planning Soc., Ft. Worth, 1971-77, chmn. bd., 1973-77; mem. North Central Tex. Council Govts., Arlington, 1975, Bi-Racial Council, Ft. Worth, 1976-80, Am. Council on Family Relations, 1982, Am. Council on Alcohol Problems, 1982; mem. adv. bd. Middle Miss. council Girl Scouts U.S.A., 1982—. Scholar-in-ministry Southwestern Bapt. Theol. Sem., Ft. Worth, 1977-82; named Outstanding Young Man Am., U.S. Jr. C. of C., 1979; Good Shepherd award Boy Scouts Am. Home: 3 Dove Way Circle Clinton MS 39056 Office: Christian Action Commn Miss Bapt Conv 515 Mississippi St Jackson MS 39201

JONES, PAUL LAWRENCE, lawyer; b. Snow Hill, N.C., Mar. 15, 1948; s. LeRoy and Esther Belle (Harper) J.; m. Asonia Lynette Battle, June 14, 1980; 1 child, Krystle Paulette. B.S., N.C. Agrl. and Tech. State U., 1971; J.D., N.C. Central U., 1974. Bar: N.C. 1975, D.C. 1976, U.S. Tax Ct. 1976, U.S. Ct. Mil. Appeals 1976, U.S. Ct. Claims 1976, U.S. Dist. Ct. (ea. dist.) N.C. 1979, U.S. Supreme Ct. 1982. Atty., asst. clk. U.S. Supreme Ct., Washington, 1974-76; assoc. firm Beech & Pollock, Kinston, N.C., 1979-80; mng. atty. Eastern Carolina Legal Services, Wilson, N.C., 1980-82; ptnr. firm Beech & Jones, Kinston, 1982—. Mem. N.C. State Banking Commn., Raleigh, 1983; treas. Lenoir County Democratic Com., Kinston, 1983. Served as capt. JAGC, U.S. Army, 1976-79. Mem. ABA, N.C. Bar Assn., Assn. Trial Lawyers Am., N.C. Acad. Trial Lawyers, Lenoir County Bar Assn. (pres. 1983), Lenoir County C. of C. (bd. dirs. 1983), Phi Alpha Delta. Mem. African Methodist Episcopal Ch. Lodges: Rotary, Masons, Shriners. Home: 205 Summit Ave Kinston NC 28501 Office: Beech & Jones 308 S Queen St Kinston NC 28501

JONES, PHILLIP ROBERT, association executive, consultant; b. Palatka, Fla., Sept. 30, 1933; s. Robert Henry and Mary Frances (Brinson) J.; m. Malinda Usina, May 28, 1955; children—Michael, Cynthia, Laurie, Mark, Matthew. Dep. tax assessor St. John's County, St. Augustine, Fla., 1960-63; dept. mgr. U.S. Jaycees, Tulsa, 1963-64; exec. dir. Southeastern Fisheries, Tallahassee, 1964—; pres. R.P. Jones and Assocs., Tallahassee, 1981—; pres. South Devel. Corp., Tampa, Fla., 1976-78; chmn. Gulf Mgmt. Council, Tampa, 1979-80; advisor U.S. State Dept., Washington, 1965-80. Chmn. Boy Scouts Am., 1973-74; advisor Gov. and cabinet State of Fla., 1965—. Served with USMC, 1950-55. Recipient Founder's award Gulf Devel. Found., Tampa, 1978, Disting. Service award, 1982. Fellow Fla. Soc. Assn. Execs. (pres. 1977-78), Am. Soc. Assn. Execs. Democrat. Roman Catholic. Lodge: KC. Home: 1121 Lasswade Dr Tallahassee FL 32312 Office: Robert P Jones and Assocs 312 E Georgia St Tallahassee FL 32301

JONES, RALPH EDWARD, SR., counselor; b. Crescent City, Fla., Aug. 31, 1940; s. Ralph Boyd Jones and Lee Redner (Render) Phipps; m. Maria Arcelia Montmayor-Villareal, June 3, 1962; children—Ralph Edward Jr., Randall Edgar, Rosabel Arcelia. B. Gen. Studies, U. Nebr., 1972; M.A., Webster U., 1977; M.Ed., Sull Ross U., 1982; Ph.D., Columbia Pacific U., 1984. Lic. profl. counselor, Tex. Enlisted U.S. Air Force, 1958, advanced through grades to master sgt. (E-7), 1977, retired, 1979; dir., counselor Del Rio Mental Health Clinic, San Antonio State Hosp., Tex. Dept. Mental Health/Mental Retardation, Del Rio, 1979—; adj. instr. Park Coll., Del Rio, 1978—; pvt. practice Del Rio Counseling Assocs., 1982—. Mem. Tex. Mental Health Counselor Assn. (pres. 1983-84), Tex. Assn. for Counseling and Devel. (by-laws com. 1985—), Tex. Assn. Alcoholism and Drug Abuse Counselors (cert.). Democrat. Roman Catholic. Avocations: philately; camping; fishing. Home: 1406 Ave U Del Rio TX 78840 Office: Del Rio Mental Health Clinic 200 Bridge Del Rio TX 78840

JONES, RICHARD L., justice Alabama Supreme Court; b. Carrollton, Ala., Mar. 3, 1923; LL.B., U. Ala.; m. Jean Leslie; children—Rick, Marilyn, Leslie. Bar: Ala. Practiced law Aliceville, Ala., Bessemer, Ala., Birmingham, Ala.; assoc. justice Ala. Supreme Ct., Montgomery; mem. Uniform State Law Commn.; mem. Ala. Jud. Conf. and Code Revision Com. Elder, tchr. Shades Valley Presbyterian Ch. Served to col. USAR. Mem. Ala. Trial Lawyers Assn. (pres.). Office: PO Box 218 Montgomery AL 36101*

JONES, ROBERT ALEXANDER, II, aerospace company executive; b. Honolulu, Aug. 5, 1923; s. Nathaniel Alexander and Maryann Lyle (Muster) J.; B.S. in Indsl. Engring., Adelphi U., 1960; m. Barbara Helen Adams, Nov. 30, 1945; children—Penny Alexandra, Candace Adams, Cassandra Alice, Robert Alexander III, Wendy Ann. Chief, freight car estimating Am. Car & Foundry, Jersey City, 1948-50; mgr. material/prodn. control Am. Bosch, Garden City, N.Y., 1950-60; dir., v.p. mfg. Radiation Engring., Orlando, Fla., 1960-64; mgr. mfg. engring. Gen. Dynamics, East Camden, Ark., 1964-82; asst. prof. indsl. engring. Chaffey Coll., Ontario, Calif., 1973-79. Served with inf. U.S. Army, 1942-45, 50-52. Decorated Purple Heart. Mem. ASME, Am. Inst. Indsl. Engrs., Am. Soc. Tool Engrs., DAV. Republican. Clubs: Mason, Elks, Camden Country. Home: 650 Maple St Camden AR 71701 Office: General Dynamics East Camden AR 71701

JONES, ROBERT HOWARD, cardiothoracic surgeon, educator; b. Kansas City, Dec. 9, 1940; s. Norman and Ruth Alice (Maple) J.; m. Catherine Ann Peters, June 2, 1965; children—Julie Anne, Natalie Beth, David Bradley. B.S., Harding Coll., Searcy, Ark., 1961; M.D., John Hopkins Sch. Med., Balt., 1965. Diplomate Am. Bd. Surgery, Am. Bd. Thoracic Surgery. Successively intern, jr., sr. resident, chief resident instr. scholar Duke U. Med. Ctr., Durham, N.C., 1965-75, asst. prof. surgery, 1975-78, assoc. prof., 1978-82, asst. prof. radiology, 1977-82, Howard Hughes med. investigator, 1975-79, prof. surgery, assoc. prof. radiology, 1982—; cons. Baird Corp., 1979—; med. adv. bd. Cardiac Extension Inc., 1982—. Served to capt. M.C., USAF, 1966-68. NIH grantee, 1975-86. Mem. ACS, Am. Coll. Cardiology, Soc. Thoracic Surgeons, Soc. Nuclear Medicine, So. Surg. Assn., Am. Assn. Thoracic Surgery, Am. Heart Assn., Sigma Xi. Co-author, editor Quantitative Nuclear Cardiology, 1975; project dir. scinticor devel. 1980—. Office: PO Box 2986 Durham NC 27710

JONES, ROBERT NIELL, book import company executive; b. Big Spring, Tex., May 12, 1922; s. Sam P. and Lois (Niell) J.; m. Mary Alice Guerra, Dec. 3, 1944 (div. 1976); children—Robert, Shirley Maureen, David Bruce, Alexa Carole, Alice. B.S., U. Tex., 1947. Petroleum engr. trainee Magnolia Oil Co., Okla., Tex., 1947-48; petroleum engr. R.R. Commn., Tex., 1948-52; v.p., sales mgr. J&S Carburetor Co., Dallas, 1952-74; book importer Imported Books, Dallas, 1975—; translator, interpreter, Dallas, 1955-60; ptnr. Multilingual Translations, Dallas, 1970-73. Contbr. articles to profl. jours. Election judge, Dallas, 1964-66, election clk., 1960-72. Served with U.S. Army, 1944-46. Home and Office: PO Box 4414 2025 W Clarendon St Dallas TX 75208

JONES, ROBERT ROGERS, radio station executive; b. Pasadena, Tex., Aug. 22, 1938; s. William Presley and Lily Nadine (Rogers) J., Sr.; m. Gram Parsons, Nov. 3, 1984; stepchildren—Jennie Carol Johns, Felice Fuqua. Student, Baylor U., 1956-57, U. Houston, 1957-59, U. Tex., 1959, 76-79, 85. Owner, prin. Bob Jones Co., La Porte, Tex., 1959-68; ptnr. Property Investments, Houston, 1968-73; founder, dir. Houston Symphonette, Houston, 1972-75; music dir. Austin Chamber Orch., 1977-80; counselor Austin-Travis County Mental Health-Mental Retardation, 1982-84; minister of cultural affairs Sta. KMFA-FM Radio Sta., Austin, 1985—; cons. in field. Composer musical scores for children's productions. Mem. Tex. Assn. Alcoholism and Drug Abuse Counselors, Nat. Assn. Alcoholism and Drug Abuse Counselors. Episcopalian. Avocations: gardening; nutrition; jogging. Home: 2607 Sherwood Ln Austin TX 78704 Office: Capitol Broadcasting Assn Inc 3001 N Lamar Blvd Austin TX 78705

JONES, ROBERT ROLAND, JR., physicist; b. Houston, Sept. 1, 1942; d. Robert R. and Rubye Laura Frances (Burch) J.; children—Regina Renee, Robert R. III. B.S. in Physics, U. Tex.-Austin, 1967, B.A. in Math., 1967; M.A. in Physics, 1970; postgrad. U. Houston, Tex. So. U., 1960-61. Teaching and research asst. U. Tex., Austin, 1967-70; instr. physics and math. Houston Community Coll. and Lockheed Electronics, 1970-72; instr. physics and math. Tex. So. U. and Community Coll., 1972-74; teaching asst. U. Houston, 1974-76; teaching and research asst. Howard U., Washington, 1976-77; sr. engr. assoc. Lockheed Electronics, Inc., Houston, after 1978; now with Houston Ind. Sch. Dist.; owner, operator Trebore Industries, Trebore Medi-Ctr. Recipient Award of Merit, Greater Houston Sci. Fair, 1958; grantee Fisk U., Nashville, 1960; Worthing Scholar, Houston, 1960. Mem. Am. Phys. Soc., Am. Chem. Soc. (cert. of honor and plaque 1965), Sigma Pi Sigma. Republican. Baptist.

JONES, ROBERT WILLIAM, research physicist; b. Dyersburg, Tenn., Sept. 7, 1944; s. Robert Edward and Eloise (Stephenson) J.; m. Glenda Nelson, June 13, 1969; 1 son, Thomas Edmund. B.S., U. Ala., 1967, M.S., 1972, Ph.D., 1983. Physicist Teledyne/Brown Engring., Huntsville, Ala., 1968-70; teaching asst. U.Ala.-Huntsville, 1970-71; research physicist, mgr. optics tech. program U.S. Army Missile Command, Redstone Arsenal, Ala., 1971-83, project mgr. Strategic Def. Initiative, free electron laser device devel., 1983—. NSF fellow, 1968. Mem. Optical Soc. Am., Sigma Xi, Sigma Pi Sigma, Pi Mu Epsilon, Alpha Kappa Delta. Methodist. Patentee in field. Office: BMD Advanced Tech Ctr PO Box 1500 Huntsville AL 35807

JONES, ROBIN ROHRBOUGH, audiologist, educator; b. Weston, W.Va., Jan. 15, 1951; d. Otto Alonzo and Jo Ann (Gump) R.; B.S. magna cum laude, W.Va. U., 1972, M.S., 1973; 1 dau., Megan Nicole. Clin. audiologist Fairmont (W.Va.) Ear, Nose and Throat Assos., 1973-75; instr. audiology W.Va. U., Morgantown, 1975-79, asst. prof., 1979—, clin. dir., asst. chmn., 1976-83, hearing clinic coordinator, 1983—. Mem. Am. Speech-Lang.-Hearing Assn., Am. Auditory Soc., W.Va. Speech-Lang.-Hearing Assn. Home: Apt A-3 Bon Vista Apts Morgantown WV 26505 Office: 805 Allen Hall W VA U Morgantown WV 26506

JONES, ROSA LEE WRIGHT, school guidance counselor; b. Waynesboro, Ga., Sept. 16, 1938; d. George and Edith Arilee (Williams) Wright; m. Samuel Wyatt Jones III, Mar. 26, 1963; children—Alan Lenell, Arnold Myles. Student Bank St. Coll. Edn., N.Y.C., 1961-62; B.S., N.C. A&T State U., 1960, M.S., 1972; Headstart trainee, U. Ga., 1965; postgrad. U. N.C.-Greensboro, 1969-70. Tchr. Atlanta City Schs., 1964-65, 67-68, N.Y. Div. Day Care, Bklyn., 1961-65, Greensboro Headstart Program, 1968-70; ednl. dir. Greensboro City Schs., 1970-72, guidance counselor, 1973—; parent adv., trainer Advocacy Ctr. for Children's Edn. and Parent Tng., Piedmont Area, 1981—; guest presenter Bklyn. Coll. Guidance and Counseling Assn., 1985. Co-organizer McIver Serteen Club for Exceptional Students, 1978; co-developer Hayes-Taylor-McIver PEP Club, 1978; chmn. SE area Cancer Assn. drive, Greensboro, 1978; mem. Friends of Theatre, Kernersville, N.C., 1984; donation collector Easter Seals Assn., Cystic Fibrosis Assn., Greensboro. Recipient Lady of Yr. award Hayes-Taylor YMCA, Greensboro, 1977, Outstanding Cultural Arts Program award PTA Council N.C., 1977, Terry Sanford Creative Tchr. of Yr. award McIver Sch., Greensboro, 1975, award for membership recruitment Greensboro Assn. Retarded Citizens, 1979, Ben L. Smith Outstanding Educator of Yr. award Jonesboro Sch., Greensboro, 1981; citation Vol. for State Spl. Olympics, 1978, City U.-Bklyn. Coll. Guidance and Counseling Dept., 1985, others; Greensboro Woman's Club scholar, 1972; Greensboro Jr. League grantee, 1983. Mem. Am. Assn. for Counseling and Devel. (citation for outstanding work with exceptional children 1984), Am. Black Counselors (steering com.), N.C. Sch. Counseling Assn., Assn. Multicultural Counseling, N.C. Agrl. and Tech. State U. Alumni Assn., Jack and Jill Am. (membership com.), Delta Sigma Theta. Democrat. Episcopalian. Club: Pine Knolls Swim and Racquet. Avocations: bowling; golf; gardening; reading; crafts. Home: 1173 Pine Knolls Rd Kernersville NC 27284

JONES, RUBY DARLENE, home health care executive; b. Tahoka, Tex., Nov. 19, 1940; d. Arthur Benjamin and Renda Clementine (Mullings) Jones; student Lamar U., 1965, U. Tex., Austin, 1974; children—A.G. Thomas, Theresa Derickson, Karen Cotellesse. Nurse, Orange, Tex., 1966-69; charge nurse Jones Rest Home, Inc., Orange, 1969-74; partner England (Ark.) Flying Service, Inc., 1970-74, Delmar's Aerial Service, Kans. and Okla., 1970-74; Del Mar, Inc., Little Rock, 1975-76; charge nurse Bayshore Nursing Home, Inc., La Porte, Tex., 1976-80; regional adminstr. Home Health-Home Care, Inc., San Antonio, Tex., 1976-80, community relations dir., Orange, 1980-82, dir. community relations and devel. Tex. region, 1982—. Mem. Tex. Home Health Agys. Assn. (pub. affairs com.), Nat. Home Health Agys. Assn., Tex. Nursing Home Assn., Nat. Fedn. Practical Nurses, LWV, Nat. Assn. Female Execs., Pub. Relations Soc. Am., San Antonio Women's Credit Union. Home: 1001 28th St Orange TX 77630 Office: 3118 Edgar Brown Dr Orange TX 77630

JONES, SAMUEL B., JR., botany educator; b. Roswell, Ga., Dec. 18, 1933; s. Samuel B. and Belle J.; m. Carleen Arrington, June 26, 1955; children—Valerie, Velinda, Douglas. B.S., Auburn U., 1955, M.S., 1961; Ph.D., U. Ga., 1964. Instr., Auburn U., 1957-61; asst. prof. U. So. Miss., Hattiesburg, 1964-67; from asst. prof. to prof. botany U. Ga., Athens, 1967—; owner Piccadilly Farm Nursery, Bishop, Ga., 1975—. Author: Plant Systematics, 1979. Contbr. articles to profl. jours. Served to lt. col. USAR, 1955-81. Mem. Am. Soc. Plant Taxonomists, Internat. Assn. for Plant Taxonomy, Bot. Soc. Am., New Eng. Bot. Club, So. Appalachian Bot. Club, Phi Beta Kappa, Sigma Xi, Gamma Sigma Delta, Phi Kappa Phi. Avocations: gardening; hostas; wildflowers. Office: Dept of Botany U Ga Athens GA 30602

JONES, SAMUEL H., III, mathematics educator; b. Charleston, S.C., Dec. 18, 1938; s. Leon H. and Ruth B. (Twine) J. B.S. in Math., S.C. State Coll., 1959; M.A. in Math., The Citadel, 1972; grad. diploma in Math., Rutgers U., 1967. Cert. tchr. S.C. Math. tchr. Laing High Sch., Charleston, S.C., 1959-60; head math. dept. Georgetown High Sch., S.C., 1963—; cons. S.C. State Coll., Orangeburg, 1976. Served as lt. U.S. Army, 1960-62. Scholar S.C. State U., 1955-59, U. S.C., 1965, U. Maine, 1966. Mem. NEA (life), S.C. Edn. Assn. (del. 1968), Georgetown Edn. Assn. (past v.p., treas.), Nat. Council Tchrs. Math., Mu Alpha Theta, Delta Psi Omega. Democrat. Methodist. Avocations: serious reading; classical music. Office: Georgetown High Sch North St Georgetown SC 29440

JONES, SHARON LESTER, psychotherapist; b. Stuart, Fla., Mar. 26, 1944; d. Andrew Morrison and Dorothy Virginia (Atkinson) Lester; b. James Baker Jones, June 12, 1965; children—James Timothy, Jennifer Lynn. A.B. cum laude, U. Miami, 1966; M.A., U. Tulsa, 1980; postgrad. in family therapy, Houston Family Inst., 1980-82. Psychotherapist Interface Counseling Ctr., Houston, 1980—; Mem. Am. Assn. Marriage and Family Therapists, Houston Marriage and Family Therapist (sec. 1983-85), Nat. Council Family Relations, Am. Assn. Profl. Hypnotherapists, Assn. Neuro Linguistic Programming (master programmer 1983-85), Pi Beta Phi. Republican. Methodist. Avocations: jogging; raquetball; reading; camping. Office: Interface Counseling Ctr 5015 Westheimer Suite 3260 Houston TX 77056

JONES, SHARRON LEA, geologist; b. Dothan, Ala., Nov. 2, 1949; d. Fordyce Samuel and Louise (Arnette) Dowling; m. James Winston Jones, Aug. 26, 1978. B.A., U. Tex., 1972; M.S., Tex. A&M U., 1981. Tchr. biology and geology Pasadena I.S.D., South Houston, Tex., 1972-76; exploration geologist Tenneco Oil Co., Houston, 1978-80, Border Exploration, Houston, 1980-82; advanced geologist Getty Oil Co., Houston, 1982—. Mem. Am. Assn. Petroleum Geologists, Houston Geol. Soc., Phi Sigma, Alpha Lambda Delta. Baptist. Avocations: piano, hiking, boating. Home: 11215 Rippling Meadows Dr Houston TX 77064 Office: Texaco USA 6750 W Loop South Suite 400 Bellaire TX 77401

JONES, STANLEY E., engineering mechanics educator, consultant; b. Mt. Vernon, N.Y., July 20, 1939; s. E. Arthur and Helen (Jankowsky) J.; m. Miree Wood, Apr. 9, 1980; children—Lara Elaine, Robert Thomas. B.A., U. Del.-Newark, 1963, M.S., 1966, Ph.D., 1967. Tchr. Oxford Area High Sch., Pa., 1963-64; fellow U. Del.-Newark, 1965-66, NASA fellow, 1966-67; asst. prof. U. Ky., Lexington, 1967-73, assoc. prof., 1973-83, prof. engring. mechanics, 1983—; vis. lectr. Soc. for Indsl. and Applied Math., 1982-84; faculty fellow USAF, Eglin AFB, Fla., 1981. Author, co-author research papers. Research grantee Air Force Armament Lab., 1982-85, Air Force Office Sci. Research, 1976-80; NSF U.S.-Yugoslav Corp. grantee, 1983—; U.S. Water Resources Inst. grantee, 1984-85; Danforth Found. assoc., 1976-82; NASA fellow, 1970. Avocations: stamp collecting; bowling. Home: 4328 Calevares Dr Lexington KY 40514 Office: Dept Engring Mechanics U Ky Lexington KY 40506

JONES, STELLA PINKNEY, gynecologist and obstetrician, educator; b. Hasston, La., Jan. 16, 1946; d. Issac and Mamie Mae (Womsley) Pinkney; m. Harry Wade Jones. Dec. 26, 1965; children—; Brigette Nicolle, Kali Chantelle, Shaunna Dionne, Harry Pinkney. B.S. in Pharmacy, Tex. So. U., 1965; M.P.H., U. Tex., 1972; M.D., Tex. Technol. U., 1973. Registered pharmacist, Tex., Ga. Staff pharmacist Grady Hosp., Atlanta, 1965-67, Harris County Hosp. Dist., Houston, 1967-71; intern Charity Hosp., New Orleans, 1976-77, resident in ob-gyn, 1977-80; practice medicine specializing in ob-gyn, New Orleans, 1980—; clin. prof. ob-gyn Tulane U. Med. Sch., New Orleans, 1980—. Bd. dirs. Children's Bur. of New Orleans, Women in Mainstream. Mem. AMA, Am. Soc. Ob-Gyn, Tex. Pharm. Assn., NAACP, Urban League, New Orleans C. of C., Jack and Jill of Am., Delta Sigma Theta (Golden Life). Roman Catholic. Club: Crescent City Links. Home: 6941 Lake Willow Dr New Orleans LA 70126 Office: 2538 Tulane Ave New Orleans LA 70119

JONES, STEPHEN, lawyer; b. Lafayette, La., July 1, 1940; s. Leslie William and Gladys A. (William) J.; m. Virginia Hadden (div.); 1 son, John Chapman; m. Sherrel Alice Stephens, Dec. 27, 1973; children—Stephen Mark, Leslie Rachael, Edward St. Andrew. Student U. Tex. 1960-63; LL.B., U. Okla. 1966. Bar: Okla. Sec. Republican Minority Conf., Tex. Ho. of Reps., 1963; personal asst. to Richard M. Nixon, N.Y.C., 1964; adminstrv. asst. to Congressman Paul Findley, 1966-69; legal counsel to gov. of Okla., 1967; mem. U.S. del to North Atlantic Assembly, NATO, 1968; spl. U.S. atty. No. Dist. Okla., 1979; spl. prosecutor, spl. asst. dist. atty. State of Okla., 1977; judge Okla. Ct. Appeals, 1982; civil jury instrn. com. Okla. Supreme Ct., 1979-81; adv. com. ct. rules Okla. Ct. Criminal Appeals, 1980; now mng. ptnr. Jones & Jennings, Enid, Okla.; legis. counsel Congressman Donald Rumsfeld and spl. asst. Sen. Charles Percy, 1968; staff counsel Ho. of Reps. Impeachment Inquiry, 1974; gen. counsel Okla. chpt. ACLU, 1970-74. Acting chmn. Republican State Com., Okla., 1982; mem. vestry, sr. warden St. Matthews Episc. Ch. Mem. ABA, Okla. Bar Assn., Garfield County Bar Assn. Clubs: Capitol Hill, Nat. Lawyers (Washington); Whitehall (Oklahoma City); Oakwood Country (Enid). Contbr. articles profl. jours. Address: PO Box 472 Enid OK 73702

JONES, SUEJETTE ALBRITTON, retired educator; b. Kinston, N.C., Mar. 27, 1923; d. Clyde A. and Carrie (Jackson) Albritton; m. William Edward Jones, Mar. 15, 1946; 1 dau., Jocelyn Suejette. B.S. in Pub. Sch. Music, Va. State U., 1943; postgrad. U. Pa. Sch. Music, 1945, Winston-Salem State U., 1950-51, A&T State U., 1959-61, Shaw U., 1952, East Carolina U., 1970. Tchr. music, Greenville, N.C., 1943-45; clk. typist Navy Dept., Washington, 1945; interviewer N.C. Employment Security Commn., Kinston, 1946-47; tchr., choral dir. Bethel (N.C.) Union Sch., 1950-52; tchr. C.M. Eppes Sch., 1952-54, S. Greenville Sch., 1954-69, Eastern Elem. Sch., 1969-80; chorus accompanist, tchr. Wahl Coates Lab. Sch., East Carolina U., Greenville, 1980-85, ret., 1985. Mem. N.C. Assn. Educators, NEA, So. Assn. Colls. and Schs. (vis. com.), Delta Kappa Gamma, Tarboro Jubilee Singers, Greenville Choral Soc., Alpha Kappa Alpha. Episcopalian. Lodge: Daus. of Isis. Composer: O Isis Dear, 1956.

JONES, TERRI LYNN, advertising agency executive; b. Wagoner, Okla., Feb. 18, 1950; d. George R. and Dorothy Louise (Burress) J.; B.S. with honors in Communications, Phillips U., 1972; postgrad. Richland Coll., 1974-75, Brookhaven Coll., 1977-78. Media buyer Greene-Webb Assos., Dallas, 1972-73; writer, public relations exec. McCrary-Powell, Inc., Dallas, 1973-74; account service and research adminstr. Crume & Assos., Dallas, 1975; account supr., stockholder KCBN, Inc., 1975-79; v.p. Preston Square, Inc., 1978-79; pres. Jones Communications Group, Inc., Dallas, 1979—; guest instr. U. Dallas, Arlington, Tex., 1977-78. Vol., Am. Cancer Soc., 1976-77, Am. Heart Assn., 1977-78; bd. dirs. Big Bros. and Sisters of Met. Dallas, 1979-81, Campfire, Inc., Dallas, 1981-82. Recipient Spl. Judges award Southwest VTR and TV Festival, 1975; Golden Pyramid award Internat. Assn. Specialty Advt., 1977; 1st pl. advt. award (2) Savs. Instns. Mktg. Soc. Am., 1978; Golden Radio award Olney Savs., 1979; named Saleswoman of the Year, Big Bros. and Sisters of Met. Dallas, 1979. Mem. Am. Women in Radio and TV (pres. 1978-79, dir. 1979-80), Tex. Public Relations Assn. (Best of Tex. award, 1980, 81, Cert. of Merit 1980), Assn. Broadcasting Execs. of Tex., Nat. Assn. Female Execs., Internat. Assn. Bus. Communicators, Dallas Ad League (dir. 1982-83, recipient 2 Gold medals, Cert. of Merit 1980, various medals 1981). Republican. Mem. Disciples of Christ Ch. Home: 4651 Chapel Hill Rd Dallas TX 75214 Office: 4340 N Central Expressway Dallas TX 75206

JONES, TERRY LOZNICKA, nurse; b. Jacksonville, Fla., Oct. 23, 1950; d. George Frank and Zelna Beville (Woods) Loznicka; m. William Fredrick Jones, Oct. 27, 1973. A.S., Fla. Jr. Coll., Jacksonville, 1971; B.S.N., U. North Fla., Jacksonville, 1979, M.S. in Allied Health, 1982. R.N., Fla. Orthopedics clin. instr. St. Luke's Hosp., Jacksonville, 1971-81; clin. practice instr. neurology, orthopedics St. Vincent's Med. Ctr., Jacksonville, 1981-83; charge nurse neonatal convalescent care Grady Meml. Hosp., Atlanta, 1983—. Mem. Multiple Sclerosis Found., Am. Neurol. Found., Kappa Delta Pi. Democrat. Presbyterian. Home: 1800 Brandywine Ct Conyers GA 30208

JONES, THOMAS LANE, business executive, accountant; b. Jayton, Tex., June 8, 1927; s. Thomas Lemarcus and Itha (Lane) J.; B.S., Tex. A&M U., 1950; B.B.A., Lamar State Coll., 1956; m. Katherine Olivia Harris, Aug. 6, 1978; children—Laura Dudley, Thomas Lemarcus, Richard Hamilton. Mgr. plant systems Eastex, Inc., Beaumont, Tex., 1960-67; chief accountant Star Engraving Co., Houston, 1966-67; mgr. plant systems Rockwell Internat. Corp., 1967-71; v.p., dept. mgr. Cameron-Brown Co., Raleigh, N.C., 1977-81; asst. v.p., mgr. consolidation and merger First Union Corp., 1981—. Served with USN, 1945-47. C.P.A., N.C., 1962. Mem. N.C. Assn. C.P.A.s, Am. Inst. C.P.A.s, Tex. Soc. C.P.A.s. Democrat. Methodist. Home: 7001 Pleasant Dr Charlotte NC 28211 Office: 1st Union Plaza Charlotte NC 28288

JONES, TOM E(UGENE), county government public relations executive; b. Forrest City, Ark., Apr. 5, 1948; s. Robert Nall and Annie Lee (Trail) J.; m. Carolyn Elizabeth Hays, July 2, 1970; children—Emily, Adrienne. B.A. in Journalism, Memphis State U., 1970. Govtl. reporter Memphis Press-Scimitar, 1970-76; asst. to mayor Shelby County (Tenn.), Memphis, 1976—; mem. bd. Nat. Assn. Counties. Mem. United Way Membership Assembly, Memphis, 1982; mem. Shelby County Pub. Records Commn.; mem. Ctr. City Commn., Memphis, 1983—; mem. Leadership Memphis, 1983; bd. dirs. Memphis Arts Council, 1984-86. Recipient Memphis Press Club award, 1970. Mem. Pub. Relations Soc. Am., Nat. Assn. County Info. Officers (awards of excellence 1978-85), Memphis C. of C. (communications council 1981-85). Democrat. Methodist. Contbr. articles to various publs. Home: 3805 Gwyllim Cove Memphis TN 38115 Office: 160 N Mid-Am Mall Suite 850 Memphis TN 38103

JONES, VIRGINIA MCCLURKIN, social worker; b. Anniston, Ala., Mar. 13, 1935; d. Louie Walter and Virginia Keith (Beaver) McClurkin; m. Charles Miller Jones, Mar. 16, 1957; children—Charles Miller III, V. Grace. B.A., Agnes Scott Coll., 1957; M.A., U. Tenn., 1965, M.S. in Social Work, 1979. Instr. English, U. Tenn., Knoxville, 1967-71; religious edn. dir. Oak Ridge Unitarian Ch., 1972-73, 76-78; co-owner, mgr. The Bookstore, 1973-76; instr. English, Roane State Community Coll., 1975-80; clin. social worker Mountain Community Health Ctr., Coalfield, Tenn., 1980-83; pvt. practice clin. social work, Oak Ridge, 1980—. Mem. Nat. Assn. Social Workers, Oak Ridge Ministerial Assn., Soc. Psychoanalytic Psychotherapy. Democrat. Episcopalian. Club: Concord Yacht. Contbr. articles to newspapers. Office: Bacon & Howard 100 E Tennessee Ave Oak Ridge TN 37830

JONES, WALTER BEAMAN, congressman; b. Fayetteville, N.C., Aug. 19, 1913; s. Walter George and Fannie (Anderson) J.; m. Doris Long, Apr. 26, 1934 (dec.); children—Mrs. Dotdee Moye, Walter Beaman II; m. Elizabeth Fischer, Nov. 7, 1984. B.S., N.C. State U., 1934. Mem. N.C. Gen. Assembly, 1955-59; mem. N.C. Senate, 1965, 90th-98th Congresses from 1st Dist. N.C.; Dir. Security Savs. & Loan Assn., Farmville, N.C.; Mayor Farmville, 1949-53. Recipient Watchdog of Treasury award Nat. Assn. Businessmen, 1966; named Farmville Man of Year, 1955. Democrat. Baptist (deacon). Clubs: Mason (32 deg., Shriner), Elk, Rotarian, Moose. Office: Cannon Bldg Washington DC 20515*

JONES, WALTER HARRISON, chemist; b. Griffin, Sask., Can., Sept. 21, 1922; s. Arthur Frederick and Mildred Tracy (Walter) J.; B.S. with honors, UCLA, 1944, Ph.D. in Chemistry, 1948; m. Marion Claire Twomey, Oct. 25, 1959 (dec. Jan. 1976). Research chemist Dept. Agr., 1948-51, Los Alamos Sci. Lab., 1951-54; sr. research engr. N. Am. Aviation, 1954-56; mgr. chemistry dept. Ford Motor Co., 1956-60; sr. staff and program mgr. Inst. Def. Analyses, 1960-63; head propulsion dept. Aerospace Corp., 1963-64; sr. scientist, head advanced tech. Hughes Aircraft Co., 1964-68; prof. aero. systems, dir. Corpus Christi Center, U. W. Fla., Pensacola, 1969-75, prof. chemistry, 1975—; cons. pvt., fed. and state agys.; vis. prof. U. Toronto. Mem. Gov.'s Task Force on Energy, Regional Energy Action Com., Fla. State Energy Office, adv. com. Tampa Bay Regional Planning Council; judge regional and state sci. fairs. Fed. and state grantee; research corp. grantee; ASEE/ONR fellow. Fellow Am. Inst. Chemists; mem. Am. Astron. Soc., Am. Chem. Soc. (chmn. Pensacola sect.), N.Y. Acad. Scis., Am. Phys. Soc., AAUP, AAAS, Internat. Solar Energy Soc., AIAA, Combustion Inst., Am. Ordnance Assn., Air Force Assn., Philos. Soc. Washington, Pensacola C. of C., Phi Beta Kappa, Sigma Xi, Pi Mu Epsilon, Phi Lambda Upsilon, Alpha Mu Gamma, Alpha Chi Sigma. Author: (fiction) Prisms in the Pentagon, 1971; contbr. numerous articles tech. jours., chpts. in books. Patentee in field. Home: 2412 Oak Hills Circle Pensacola FL 32514 Office: Dept of Chemistry University of West Florida Pensacola FL 32514

JONES, WAYNE VAN LEER, consulting geologist, private investor; b. Chgo., June 18, 1902; s. Frank Edgar and Josephine Louella (Van Leer) J.; A.B., Northwestern U., 1923; m. Elizabeth Rieke, Jan. 14, 1926; 1 son, Wayne Van Leer, II. Accountant, then chief auditor Mission Oil Co., Kansas City, Mo., 1923-28; with F.E. Jones & Son, oil operators, Wichita, Kans., 1928-30; asst. mgr. Exchange Petroleum Co., Shreveport, La., 1930-34; geologist Midcontinent div. Tidewater Associated Oil Co., Houston, 1934-41, chief geologist, 1941-53; v.p. charge exploration Union Texas Natural Gas Corp. (formerly Union Sulphur & Oil Corp., Union Oil & Gas Corp. of La., merger Allied Chem. Corp., 1962, name now Union Tex. Petroleum Corp), Houston, 1953-59, sr. v.p., 1959-63; cons. geologist, Houston, 1963-72; pvt. investor, 1972—; mem. Am. Commn. Stratigraphic Nomenclature, 1947-53. Alumni regent Northwestern U., 1965-75, life regent, 1975—; mem. pres.'s council Houston Grand Opera Assn., 1976—. Mem. Am. Assn. Petroleum Geologists, geneal. socs. N.J., Md., Pa., N.Y. Geneal. and Biog. Soc., Soc. Genealogists (London), Houston Geol. Soc., Phi Beta Kappa, Sigma Xi, Sigma Alpha Epsilon. Clubs: Houston, Meml. Dr. Country (Houston). Author: Jacob Woodward Colladay and His Descendants, 1976; The Rieke Family of Bavenhausen and America, 1979. Donor Wayne V. and Elizabeth R. Jones Fine and Performing Arts Resdl. Coll., Northwestern U., 1980. Address: 5672 Longmont Dr Houston TX 77056

JONES, WILLIAM JOHN, music educator; b. Pontiac, Mich., Nov. 30, 1926; s. Percy Thomas and Evelyn Jessie (Bond) J.; m. Virginia Ann Lee, Aug. 8, 1953; children—Constance Ann, Evelyn Virginia, Glynis Lee, Cecilia Dorothy, Victoria Adeline. B.A., Taylor U., 1947; B.S. in Edn., Wayne U., 1948, M.A., 1949; Ph.D., Northwestern U., 1952. Tchr., Appalachian State Coll., Boone, N.C., 1954-61; instr., head dept. music Ferrum Jr. Coll., Va., 1961-63; prof., head dept. music Olivet Coll., Mich., 1963-65; prof., head dept. music U. South Ala., Mobile, 1965—; flutist Pontiac Symphony Orch., Mich., 1952-54, Battle Creek Symphony Orch., Mich., 1963-65, Mobile Symphony Orch., Ala., 1965-70. Nat. Endowment for Humanities grantee, 1978, 82. Mem. AAUP, Sonnenek Soc., Coll. Music Soc., Am. Musicological Soc., Music Educators Nat. Assn., Phi Mu Alpha. Methodist. Avocations: stamps, languages. Home: 1100 Goldsboro Ct Mobile AL 36608 Office: Music Dept Univ South Ala Mobile AL 36688

JONES, WILLIE CLYDE, college dean; b. Birmingham, Ala., Sept. 13, 1941; s. Robert Lee and Reaber Louise (Jackson) J.; m. Kay Frances Rice, Aug. 14, 1965; children—Errol Dewayne, Clyde Kennard Harriet Laquette. B.A., Miles Coll., 1963; M.Div., Interdenominational Theol. Ctr., 1967; M.A., U. Ala., 1971, Ed.D., 1974. Pastor St. Paul C.M.E. Ch., Jacksonville, Ala., 1964-66; intern Georgetown U., Washington, 1971; instr. Stillman Coll., Tuscaloosa, Ala., 1968, asst. dean students, 1969-70, asst. to pres., 1970-73, dean students, 1973—; cons. Nat. Alliance Businessmen, Birmingham, Assocs. for Instl. Devel. Inc., Birmingham. Author: Glossary of Educational Terms, 1973; Educational Financing: An Overview, 1973. Bd. dirs. Haitian Relief Fund, Birmingham, 1976—, Northport Zoning Bd. Adjustments, Northport, Ala., 1983—, Children Hands on Mus., Tuscaloosa, 1985. Research Tng. Ctr. grantee, 1972. Mem. Nat. Assn. Student Personnel Adminstrs., Ala. State Personnel Guidance Assn., Nat. Assn. Personnel Workers, Phi Delta Kappa,

Kappa Alpha Psi (Man of Yr. 1972). Democrat. Methodist. Lodge: Rotary (Rotoact Adv.). Avocation: fishing. Office: Stillman Coll PO Box 1430 Tuscaloosa AL 35403

JONES, WINONA NIGELS, library media specialist; b. St. Petersburg, Fla., Feb. 24, 1928; d. Eugene Arthur and Bertha Lillian (Dixon) Nigels; m. Charles Albert Jones, Nov. 26, 1944; children—Charles Eugene, Sharon Ann Jones Allworth, Caroline Winona Jones Pandorf. A.A., St. Petersburg Jr. Coll., 1965; B.S., U. South Fla., 1967, M.S., 1968; Advanced M.S., Fla. State U., 1980. Library media specialist Dunedin (Fla.) Comprehensive High Sch., 1967-76; library media specialist, chmn. dept. Fitzgerald Middle Sch., Largo, Fla., 1976—. Named Educator of Year, Pinellas County Sch. Bd. and Suncoast C. of C., 1983. Mem. Fla. Assn. Media in Edn. (pres.), ALA (com.), U. So. Fla. Alumni Assn., Assn. Ednl. Communication and Tech. (div. sch. media specialist, coms.), Am. Assn. Sch. Libraries (com.), Southeastern Library Assn., Fla. Library Assn., Assn. Supervision and Curriculum Devel., NEA, Fla. State Library Sci. Alumni, U. South Fla. Library Sci. Alumni Assn. (dir.), Phi Theta Kappa, Phi Ro Pi, Beta Phi Mu, Kappa Delta Pi, Delta Kappa Gamma. Democrat. Club: Inner Wheel (Palm Harbor, Fla.). Home: 911 Manning Rd Palm Harbor FL 33563 Office: 5410 118th Ave North Largo FL 33543

JONES Y DIEZ ARGUELLES, GASTÓN ROBERTO, educator; b. Cárdenas, Cuba, Dec. 6, 1910; came to U.S., 1963, naturalized, 1971; s. Guillermo Rafael Jones and María de Los Angeles Diez Arguelles; B.Letters and Scis., Matanzas Inst. Cuba, 1928; Dr. Law, U. Havana (Cuba), 1937; M.A., U. Ala., 1969; m. Dolores Carricarte, May 19, 1950. Practice law, Havana, 1937-60; mcpl. judge, Cuba, 1938-40; cons. atty. Cuban Treasury Dept., 1943-60; instr. dept. fgn. langs. Sacred Heart Coll., Cullman, Ala., 1965-70, St. Bernard Coll., Cullman, 1967-70; asst. prof. U. Ala., Birmingham, 1971-81. Mem. Nat. Bicentennial Com. for celebration of Nat. Fgn. Lang. Discovery Week, 1975-83. Mem. Am. Assn. Tchrs. Spanish and Portuguese (past pres. Ala. chpt., chmn. So. and mountain states regional pub. relations com. 1975-77, chmn. nat. public relations and publicity com. 1977-81), Ala. Assn. Fgn. Lang. Tchrs. (past dir., chmn. com. for advancement fgn. langs. in Ala. 1973-81), Birmingham-Cobán Ala.-Guatemala Partners of Americas (v.p. 1971-81), Sociedad Nacional Hispanica, Cuban Bar Assn. in Exile, Sigma Delta Pi, Omicron Delta Kappa. Roman Catholic. Clubs: Miami Rowing (Outstanding Contbn. award 1985), Coral Gables Country. Lodge: Cuban Rotary in Exile. Contbr. articles to profl. jours. Successfully promoting nat. campaign to make Americans aware of need for fgn. langs. in U.S. Home: 1311 SW 102d Ct Miami FL 33174

JORDAN, ARCHIBALD CURRIE, educator; b. Caldwell, N.C.; s. Archibald Currie and Octavia Graham (Stroud) J.; A.B. Duke U., postgrad. Law Sch.; A.M., Columbia U.; m. Jane Myers, Sept. 2, 1941; children—Ann Myers, Patsy Jane, Sally Rida, Julia Anna. Gen. Edn. Bd. fellow Columbia U.; admitted to N.C. bar; adviser N.C. Textbook Commn.; asst. prof. English, Duke U.; past pres., chmn. research com. N.C. English Teachers Council; judge N.C. high sch. English ann. award creative writing; v.p. Coll. English Assn. N.C., Va. and W.Va. Deacon, First Presbyterian Ch., Durham, N.C.; foreman Durham County Grand Jury (N.C.). Mem. AAAS, So. Atlantic Modern Lang. Assn., AAUP, Am. Dialect Soc., N.C. English Tchrs. Assn., Am., N.C. (award appreciation, spl. citation) bar assns., Council Basic Edn., Phi Delta Kappa, Kappa Delta Pi. Democrat. Author: Essentials of English Composition; College English Tests (forms A and B); College Handbook of Composition; Fundamentals of College Composition; How to Write Correctly; Everyday Grammar; A Comprehensive Examination in the Fundamentals of Correct English Usage, 1960; The Writer's Manual, 1963, rev. edit., 1967; asst. to editors So. Jour. Orthopaedic Surgery; editorial cons. Duke U. Med. Center, Am. Assn. Orthopaedic Surgeons, others. Address: Box 6006 Duke U Durham NC 27708

JORDAN, D.D., electric utility company executive; b. Corpus Christi, Tex., 1932; married. B.B.A., U. Tex., 1954; J.D., So. Tex. Coll. Law, 1969. With Houston Lighting & Power Co., 1956—, mgr. comml. sales, 1967-69, mgr. personnel relations, 1969-71, v.p., asst. to pres., 1971-73, group v.p., 1973-74, pres., 1974—, chief exec. officer, dir., 1977—; also pres., chief exec. officer Houston Industries, Inc.; dir. Great So. Corp., Hughes Tool Corp. Office: Houston Lighting & Power Co PO Box 1700 Houston TX 77001*

JORDAN, DANIEL PORTER, JR., history educator, administrator; b. Philadelphia, Miss., July 22, 1938; s. Daniel Porter and Mildred M. (Dobbs) J.; m. Lewellyn Lee Schmelzer, Dec. 18, 1961; children—Daniel P., Grace Dobbs, Katherine Lewellyn. B.A., U. Miss., 1960, M.A., 1962; Ph.D., U. Va., 1970. Various teaching positions overseas div. U. Md., 1962-65; mem. faculty U. Richmond (Va.), 1968-69, U. Va., summers, 1970-72; prof. history VA Commonwealth U., Richmond, 1969-84, dir. Stratford Hall Summer Sem., 1981—, acting chmn. history dept., 1976-77; dir. Thomas Jefferson Meml. Found. (Monticello), 1985—; cons. NEH, Nat. Geog. Mag., U.S. Nat. Park Service, Va. State Dept. Edn., U.S. Hist. Soc.; Sec. of Interior's adv. bd. Nat. Park Service, 1984—; mem. Lawn Adv. Bd. U. Va., 1985—; mem. rev. bd. Va. Hist. Landmarks Commn., 1981—, vice chmn., 1984—. Pres. Richmond Civil War Roundtable, 1983. Served with U.S. Army, 1962-65. Thomas Jefferson Found. fellow, 1965-68; recipient award of merit Am. Assn. for State and Local History, 1977. Mem. Va. Hist. Soc. (bd. dirs. 1986), So. Hist. Assn., Orgn. Am. Historians, Phi Beta Kappa, Omicron Delta Kappa, Sigma Chi. Methodist. Author: Political Leadership in Jefferson's Virginia, 1983; A Richmond Reader, 1733-1983, 1983. Contbr. numerous articles on history to profl. jours. Home and Office: Monticello PO Box 316 Charlottesville VA 22902

JORDAN, DON MAC, mathematics educator; b. Camden, S.C., Feb. 11, 1948; s. Burt Andrews and Ersie Stewart; stepson Frank L. and Nezzie (Roberts) J. B.A., U. S.C., 1966, M.S., 1968, Ph.D., 1973. Asst. prof. math. U. S.C., Columbia, 1973-78, assoc. prof. math., 1978—. Inventor teaching methods One on One Math., 1973-78, Murder on the Coliseum Express, 1978. Author: A Bushel and A Peck and A Hug Around the Neck, 1980. Recipient Innovation in Teaching award Internat. Soc. Individualized Instrn., 1981. Mem. Am. Math. Soc., U.S. Metric Assn. (eastern dir. 1984—), Math. Assn. Am., Nat. Council Tchrs. Math., S.C. Council Tchrs. Math., S.C. Acad. Scis., S.C. Jr. Acad. Scis. (bd. dirs. 1984—), Alpha Tau Omega (faculty adviser, Service award 1980). Club: Lettermen (U. S.C.). Avocations: sports, writing. Home: 2901 Monroe St Columbia SC 29205 Office: U S C Applied Profl Scis Columbia SC 29208

JORDAN, DUPREE, JR., small business owner, publisher, public relations executive, educator, consultant; b. Decatur, Ga., May 14, 1929; s. DuPree and Roslyn (Moncrief) J.; A.B., Mercer U., 1947; postgrad. Crozer Theol. Sem., 1948; M.Ed., Emory U., 1954; LL.B., Atlanta Law Sch., 1951, LL.D., 1963, D.Litt., 1971; postgrad. Nat. Inst. Pub. Affairs, 1967, Inst. Life-Long Learning, Harvard U., 1979, Inst. Ednl. Mgmt., 1981; m. Margaret Virginia Malone, Dec. 28, 1948; children—Margaret Jordan DeSear, DuPree III, Roslyn Jordan Whitworth, Terri Lee Chesser. Ordained to ministry Bapt. Ch., 1945; reporter Macon (Ga.) Telegraph, 1945-47, Chester (Pa.) Times, 1948-49; news dir. WVCH, Chester, 1948-49; asso. dir. Radio-TV Commn., So. Bapt. Conv., 1949-52, acting dir., 1952-53; tchr. Westminister Schs. and Atlanta div. U. Ga., 1953-55; pastor Duluth (Ga.) Bapt. Ch., 1953-54; editor, pub., owner West End Star, Atlanta Weekly newspaper, 1955-67; owner, pub. Piedmont Satellite, 1967-68, North DeKalb Record, Chamblee, 1956-64, Tri County Graphic, 1962-64; pres. Jordan & Jordan, advt. and pub. relations, 1954—, Jordan Enterprises, 1957—, Success Publs., Inc., 1969—; dir. Successful Selling Seminars; pres. Ga. Coll. for Leadership Devel., 1969—, Success Leaders Speakers Service, 1973—; dir. numerous corps. Mem. Gov.'s Com. for a World's Fair in Atlanta; mem. Rapid Transit Com. of 100; dir. pub. affairs for S. States Office Econ. Opportunity, 1965-69, spl. asst. to regional dir., 1967-69, nat. religious liaison dir., 1968; exec. dir. Assn. Pvt. Colls. and Univs. in Ga., 1970-82; mem. cons. staff Gov. Ga., 1962-66, 70-78; bd. dirs. Atlanta Girls Club, Boy Scouts Am., YMCA. Recipient numerous awards from various orgns., including Ga. Press Assn., Nat. Editorial Assn., Sigma Delta Chi, Jr. C. of C.; Distinguished Service award Office Econ. Opportunity, 1967; DuPree Jordan, Jr., Day proclaimed by Gov. Jimmy Carter, Dec. 18, 1973. Mem. Pub. Relations Soc. Am., Nat. Editorial Assn., Ga. Press Assn. (bd. mgrs.), Adminstrv. Mgmt. Soc. (dir. Atlanta chpt.), Am. Mgmt. Assn., Am. Soc. Pub. Adminstrn., Soc. Advancement Mgmt., Am. Soc. Tng. Dirs., Sales and Mktg. Execs. Internat., Assn. Mgmt. Cons., Inc., Nat. Assn. Ind. Colls. and Univs., State Assn. Execs. Council, AIM, Internat. Mgmt. Council, Mgmt. Assn. Atlanta, Am. Mktg. Assn., Ga., Internat. assns. bus. communicators, West End (pres. 1962), Chamblee-Doraville (pres. 1963) businessmen's assns., Ga., DeKalb County, Atlanta chambers commerce, Ga. State Chamber/Bus. and Industry Assn., Am., Ga. socs. assn. execs., Soc. Assn. Mgrs., Christian Council Met. Atlanta (pres. 1973), Nat. Press Club, Sales Exec. Club N.Y., Nat. Speakers Assn. (dir. 1982-84, nat. sec. 1983-84, exec. com. 1983-84), Meeting Planners Internat., So. Assn. Colls. and Schs. (chmn. state coll. execs.), Sigma Delta Chi (dir. Atlanta chpt. 1963). Home: 965 Oakhaven Dr Roswell GA 30075 Office: Lenox Sq 18737 Atlanta GA 30326

JORDAN, GEORGE E., art critic, historian; b. Ky., Oct. 29, 1940; s. William Ransom and Allie (Wells) J.; m. Casandra Springer, 1964 (div. 1972). B.F.A., Ringling Sch. Art, 1964; postgrad., East Tenn. State U., 1967. Curator Reece Mus., Johnson City, Tenn., 1966-68; bd. dirs. Huntsville Art League and Mus. Assn., Ala., 1969; curator, registrar New Orleans Mus. Art, 1970-72; art critic Times-Picayune, New Orleans, 1976-80; critic, free lance writer, 1980—; instr. art history and painting New Orleans Acad. Fine Arts, 1985—; specialist on artists who worked in La. 1780—. Contbg. editor Art and Auction mag., 1981-83. Mem. steering com. WYES-TV Pub. TV Art Auction, New Orleans, 1985. Avocations: music; theatre. Home and Office: 519 Saint Ann St New Orleans LA 70116

JORDAN, GEORGE LYMAN, JR., surgeon; b. Kinston, N.C., July 10, 1921; s. George L. and Sally (Herndon) J.; B.S., U. N.C., 1942; M.D., U. Pa., 1944; M.S. in Surgery, Tulane U., 1949; m. Florence Fischer Henszey, June 23, 1945; children—George Lyman III, Florence Elizabeth, Amy Henszey, Jacob Henszey. Intern Grady Meml. Hosp., Atlanta, Ga., 1944-45; fellow in surgery, Tulane U., New Orleans, La., 1947-49, Mayo Found., Rochester, Minn., 1949-52; practice medicine specializing in surgery Houston, 1952—; instr. in surgery Baylor U. Coll. of Medicine, Houston, 1952-54, asst. prof. surgery, 1954-57, assoc. prof., 1958-64, prof., 1964—, Disting. Service prof. surgery, 1978—; dep. chief of surgery Ben Taub Gen. Hosp., Houston, 1961-68; chief of the med. staff Harris County (Tex.) Hosp. Dist., Houston, 1968—; med. adviser to HEW, Social Security Adminstrn., region IV, 1965—; sr. cons. in surgery Nat. Inst. of Gen. Med. Scis., 1966; mem. surg. research tng. grants com. NIH, 1968-70; adviser Houston chpt. Nat. Found. for Ileitis and Colitis, Inc., 1974—. Chmn. commn. on edn. St. Paul's Meth. Ch., 1967-69, mem. adminstrv. bd., 1963—, chmn., 1978, chmn. council on ministries, 1973-74, chmn. pastor-parish relations com., 1977, charge lay leader, 1980-81, mem. worship com., 1983, trustee, 1984-86, vice chmn. bd. trustees, 1985, chmn. 1986. Served to capt., M.C., U.S. Army, 1945-47. Diplomate Am. Bd. Surgery (vice-chmn. 1975-77, dir. 1972-77), Am. Bd. Thoracic Surgery. Fellow A.C.S. (pres. southeastern Tex. chpt. 1966-67, gov. 1976-82, exec. com. 1977—, chmn. bd. govs. 1980-82, regent 1982—); mem. Am. (2d v.p. 1980), So. (pres. 1984), Western (dist. rep. on exec. com. 1976—, pres. 1984), Pan-Pacific surg. assns., Tex. (council mem. 1975-78, chmn. 1978, pres.-elect 1982, pres. 1983), Houston (pres. elect 1980, pres. 1981) surg. socs., Am. Assn. Surgery of Trauma, Soc. Surgery of the Alimentary Tract (pres. 1978, chmn. bd. trustees 1980, trustee 1981), Univ. Assn. for Emergency Med. Services, Am. Assn. Cancer Research (sec. southwestern sect. 1959-60), Tex., Pan Am. med. assns., AMA, Harris County Med. Soc., Harris County Unit, Am. Trauma Soc. (dir. 1974—), Am. Cancer Soc. (dir. Tex. div. 1966-68), Southwestern Surg. Congress, Internat. Cardiovascular Soc., Soc. Univ. Surgeons, Houston Gastroent. Soc., Soc. Exptl. Biology and Medicine, N.Y. Acad. Scis., Collegium Internat. Chirurgiae Digestivae, So. Soc. Clin. Investigation, Pancreas Club, Am. Soc. Exptl. Pathology, Assn. Advancement of Med. Instrumentation, Phi Beta Kappa, Alpha Omega Alpha. Methodist. Author: (with John M. Howard, M.D.) Surgical Diseases of the Pancreas, 1960; contbr. numerous articles to profl. jours.; editorial bd. Am. Jour. Surgery, 1968—, Advances in Surgery, 1971—. Home: 1748 North Blvd Houston TX 77098 Office: One Baylor Plaza Houston TX 77030

JORDAN, HENRY HELLMUT, JR., management consultant; b. Heidelberg, Germany, May 31, 1921; came to U.S., 1934, naturalized, 1940; s. Henry H. and Johanna (Narath) J.; student U. Cin., 1938-39; m. Hildegarde C. Dallmeyer, Mar. 11, 1942; children—Sandra, Michael, Patric, Henry Hellmut. Commd. 2d lt. U.S. Army, 1942, advanced through grades to maj., 1956; staff officer Ordnance Corps; ret., 1961; mgr. prodn. and inventory control Sperry Corp., N.Y.C., 1961-66, dir. quality control and field service engring., 1967-68; mgmt. cons. Wright Assos. Inc., N.Y.C., 1969-70; pres. Henry Jordan & Assos., N.Y.C., 1970-74; mng. partner Cons. Services Inc., Atlanta, 1975—; chmn. Center for Inventory Mgmt., Stone Mountain, Ga., 1975—; chmn. bd. Crugers Services Corp., Atlanta. Mem. Am. Inst. Indsl. Engrs. (sr.), Inst. Mgmt. Cons. (cert.), Am. Prodn. and Inventory Control Soc. (curricula and cert. council; Presdl. award of Merit 1974), Internat. Materials Mgmt. Soc., Am. Mgmt. Assn., Am. Radio Relay League, Aircraft Owners and Pilots Assn. Methodist. Club: Yacht of Hilton Head. Editorial bd. Jour. Prodn. and Inventory Mgmt.; editor: Production and Inventory Control Handbook, 1970; Cycle Counting for Record Accuracy, 1980; System Implementation Handbook, 1982. Home: 941 Carlisle Rd Stone Mountain GA 30083 Office: Koger Exec Center Oglethorpe Bldg Suite 174 Atlanta GA 30341

JORDAN, JAMES WYNDOL, educational adminstrator; b. Bennettsville, S.C., Apr. 11, 1948; s. Zaney and B. Christeen (Nolan) J.; m. Kay Lingle Jordan, July 12, 1980; children—Kathryn Ann, James Grant. B.S., U. S.C., 1971, postgrad., 1982-84; M.Edn., S.C. State Coll., 1983. Tchr., coach Richland County Sch. Dist. I, Columbia, S.C., 1971-80, tchr. coordinator curriculum, 1980-83; asst. prin. Buford High Sch., Lancaster, S.C., 1983-84, prin., 1984—; co-chmn. S.C. Student Safety Conf., Columbia, 1982-83; tchr. rep. Nat. Student Safety Project, 1977. Mem. Adminstrv. bd., chmn. evangelism com. Hopewell United Meth. Ch., Lancaster, S.C. Served with S.C. Army N.G., 1970-77. Mem. Assn. Supervision and Curriculum Devel., Nat. Assn. Secondary Sch. Prins., Nat. Assn. Sch. Adminstrs., S.C. Assn. Sch. Adminstrs., S.C. Assn. Secondary Sch. Prins. Clubs: Methodist Men's (Lancaster, S.C.). Lodges: Masons, Shriners. Avocations: golf; tennis; fishing; woodwork; sketching; sailing; cycling. Home: Route 6 Box 67A Lancaster SC 29720 Office: Buford High Sch Route 9 Lancaster SC 29720

JORDAN, JEFFREY LEE, agricultural economics educator, researcher; b. Belleville, Ill., July 6, 1954; s. Gerald J. and Margery (Piana) J.; m. Sherry A. Maddock, June 20, 1975. B.S. in Internat. Relations, Mich. State U., 1975, M.S. in Agrl. Econs., 1979, Ph.D. in Agrl. Econs., 1982. Instr. dept. sociology Adrian Coll., Mich., 1978-79; economist Office of Gov., Mich. 1978-80; research asst. in agrl. econs. Mich. State U., East Lansing, 1980-82; instr. econs. Lansing Community Coll., Mich., 1979-82, James Madison Coll., Mich. State U., 1982; asst. prof. agrl. econs. dept. Ga. Experiment Sta., U. Ga., 1982—. Columnist Griffin Daily News, Ga., 1984—. Editor Microcomputer software sect. So. Jour. Agrl. Econ., 1985—. Contbr. articles to profl. jours. Guest speaker Griffin Exchange Club, 1984. EPA grantee, 1984-85. Mem. Am. Agrl. Econs. Assn. (mem. econ. stats. com. 1984-85), Am. Econ. Assn., So. Agrl. Econs. Assn., Transp. Research Forum, Atlantic Econ. Soc. Democrat. Avocations: golf; piano; drums. Home: 108 Dungeness Rd Griffin GA 30223 Office: Ga Experiment Sta Dept Agrl Econs Experiment GA 30212

JORDAN, LUCIUS DONALD, JR., investor; b. Kosciusko, Miss., Sept. 12, 1929; s. Lucius Donald and Elva (Allen) J.; B.S., Miss. Coll., 1951; M.B.A., Harvard U., 1953; m. Marlene Drury, June 28, 1958; children—Cynthia, Jennifer, Lucius Donald III. Unit mgr. Procter & Gamble, Tex., Ga., 1955-59; dir. mktg. 1st Miss. Corp., Jackson, 1959-61; western regional mgr. Mead Johnson & Co., Tex. and Calif., 1961-68; v.p. nat. accounts Drackett Products Co., Cin., 1969; v.p. sales Internat. Distbrs. div. Plough Inc., Memphis, 1970-72; exec. v.p. Selective Mktg. Inc., Memphis, 1972-75; mng. ptnr. Jor-Lo Co., Memphis, 1975—. Mem. devel. council Baylor U.; deacon 2d Presbyterian Ch.; trustee Presbyn. Day Sch. Served with U.S. Army, 1953-55. Mem. SAR. Republican. Clubs: Harvard Alumni, Summit, Racquet (Memphis); Mill Creek Country (Salado, Tex.). Home: 2276 Wickerwood Cove Memphis TN 38138

JORDAN, MARTHA JEANNE, nurse; b. Clinton, Ind., Mar. 27, 1943; d. J. Lawrence and Sara C. (Farnsworth) Dempster; m. Sam A. Jordan, Dec. 12, 1970 (dec. Jan. 1980); 1 child, Thomas L. Assoc. Sci., Manatee Jr. Coll., 1982; R.N., Sarasota Meml. Hosp., 1982. Unit clk. Venice Hosp., Fla., 1977-82; nurse Sarasota Meml. Hosp., Fla., 1982—. Mem. Am. Assn. Critical Care Nurses. Republican. Mem. Christian Ch. Lodges: Order Eastern Star, Ind. Order Foresters, Internat. Order Job's Daus. Office: Sarasota Meml Hosp 1900 Arlington St Sarasota FL 33579

JORDAN, MICHAEL A., II, investment company executive; b. San Antonio, Feb. 20, 1947; s. Michael A. and Florence H. J.; B.S., MIT, 1969; M.B.A., Harvard U., 1973. Sr. fin. analyst Republic Nat. Bank, Dallas, 1975; founder Jordan Investments, Inc., Dallas, 1975; treas. Jordan Investments Inc.; pres. Pacific Broadcasting Corp. Served with Air N.G., 1972. Mem. MIT Alumni Assn. Clubs: University, Willow Bend Polo, Harvard Club of Dallas. Office: PO Box 801547 Dallas TX 75080

JORDAN, REGINALD CLEVELAND, environmental scientist; b. Washington, Mar. 12, 1946; s. Oscar Royce and Mary Elizabeth (Craver) J.; B.S., Salem Coll., 1968; M.S., Temple U., 1970; m. Gayle Anne Steger, June 8, 1968; children—Erin, Kelly, Megan. Chemist, Gillette Research Inst., Rockville, Md., 1968-69; chief lab. sect. Pa. Bur. Air Quality and Noise Control, Harrisburg, 1970-73; chief chemist Gen. Environments Corp., Springfield, Va., 1973-74; project scientist TRW Environ. Engring., McLean, Va., 1974-76; dep. program mgr. EPA Air Pollution Tng. Inst., 1976-79; mgr. quality assurance and environ. monitoring programs Northrop Services Inc., Research Triangle Park, N.C., 1979-84, mgr. environ. tech., 1984—; pres. EnviroScis., Inc., 1983—; adj. prof. environ. health Ctr. for Environ. Studies, Temple U. Diplomate Am. Acad. Indsl. Hygiene. Mem. Am. Indsl. Hygiene Assn., AAAS, N.C. Acad. Sci., Air Pollution Control Assn. (chmn. control programs adminstrn. div. 1979-83), Am. Mgmt. Assn. Club: Lions. Contbr. articles to profl. jours. Home: 3120 Julian Dr Raleigh NC 27604 Office: EnviroScis Inc 3509 Haworth Dr Suite 310 Raleigh NC 27609

JORDAN, ROBERT DULANEY, professional archivist; b. Kingsport, Tenn., Feb. 15, 1926; s. Oscar Delaney and Pauline Sarah (Williams) J.; m. Juanita Clark, Mar. 19, 1949; children—Robert Andrew, Amy Elizabeth. B.S. cum laude, East Tenn. State U., 1949, M.A., 1952. Lic. tchr., Tenn., Ohio, Fla. Tchr. 7th grade Sullivan County Bd. Edn., Blountville, Tenn., 1949-50; instr. Jr. High Sch., Kingsport Bd. Edn., 1950-53; jr. tool design engr. Brunswick Balke-Collender Co., Marion, Va., 1953; assoc. engr. Peter Kiewit & Sons and George Koch Sons, Portsmouth, Ohio, 1953-54; sr. engring. draftsman Mead Corp., Chillicothe, Ohio, 1954-65, corp. historian and archivist, Dayton, Ohio, 1965-68; archivist Ohio Hist. Soc., Columbus, 1968; prin. archivist Colo. State Archives, Denver, 1968-71; chief archives br. Los Angeles Fed. Archives and Records Ctr., Laguna Niguel, Calif., 1971-75; co-owner, mgr. family-owned dry cleaning bus., Hollywood, Fla., 1975-77; dir. Broward County Archives and Minutes Div., Ft. Lauderdale, Fla., 1977-80; engring. design draftsman Heinicke Instruments Co., Hollywood, 1981—; ptnr., sec., treas. Jordans of Fla., Inc., Hollywood, 1975-82. Cons. City of Lakewood (Calif.) Am. Bicentennial Com., 1974-75; cons. Broward County Hist. Commn., 1977-80. Served with USMC, 1944-46. Recipient 3 awards U.S. Gen. Services Adminstrn., 1971, 75; Commendation for excellent work in connection with move of Fed. Archives and Records Center from Bell, Calif. to Laguna Niguel, 1975; Nat. Achievement award Nat. Assn. Counties, 1980. Mem. Soc. Am. Archivists, Internat. Council Achivists, Internat. Assn. Paper Historians, Soc. Corp. Historians, Archivists and Librarians, Nat. Trust for Hist. Preservation, Am. Mgmt. Assn., Am. Assn. State and Local History, Soc. Calif. Archivists, C. of C., Nu Sigma Alpha, Mu Delta Kappa. Democrat. Ch. of Christ. Clubs: Men's T, Kingsport Country, Orangebrook Golf. Contbr. articles to profl. jours.

JORDAN, WILLIAM REYNIER VAN EVERA, SR., psychotherapist, poet; b. Kansas City, Mo.; s. Russell Clinger and Lois Eleanor (Van Evera) J.; m. Ruth Frauenheim, Dec. 1951 (dec. 1978); children—William, Michael, Paul. B.S. in Journalism cum laude, U. Fla., 1956; South Asia area specialist U. Pa., 1962; grad. Gen. Staff Coll., 1968; M.A. in Psychology, U. No. Colo., 1979. Served to cpl. U.S. Army, 1947-48, with Mil. Intelligence Res., 1948-51, to 1st lt. inf., 1951-54 re-entered 1957, advanced through grades to col., 1972; chief of plans and analysis psychol. ops. div. Mil. Assistance Command, Vietnam, 1970-71; group ops. officer, later spl. asst. to comdg. officer 902d Mil. Intelligence Group, Washington, 1971-72; ret., 1972; psychotherapist Juvenile Detention, Pensacola, Fla., 1976-77; vol. psychotherapist Colorado Springs Social Services Dept., Colo., 1977-78; psychotherapist Med. Clinic, Saint Petersburg, Fla., 1980-84, Epilepsy Found., Saint Petersburg, 1984-85, VA Mental Health Clinic, Bay Pines, Fla., 1985—; cons. Free Clinic, Saint Petersburg, 1984—. Author: Darkness and Shadows, 1975; More Than Friends, 1978; Heat Lightning, 1984; Peppermint Trees, 1985. Leader Rawalpindi council Boy Scouts Am., Pakistan, 1960-62, also troops at Ft. Bragg, N.C., Ft. Leavenworth, Kans., Ft. Holabird, Md., 1964-70; bd. dirs. YMCA, Dundalk, Md., 1969-71, Epilepsy Assn., Pensacola, Fla., 1975-77. Decorated Legion of Merit with oak leaf cluster; Cross of Gallantry with palm (Republic of Vietnam); named Vol. of Yr., Colorado Springs Social Services Dept., 1978. Fellow Internat. Council Sex Edn. and Parenting; mem. Internat. Acad. Profl. Counselors and Psychotherapists, Am. Psychol. Assn. (assoc.), Epilepsy Assn. Am. (pres.'s club), Am. Mental Health Counselors Assn. Democrat. Congregationalist. Avocation: photography. Home: 5311 Burlington Ave N Saint Petersburg FL 33710 Office: Suncoast Epilepsy Assn 9721 Executive Center Dr Saint Petersburg FL 33702

JORDRE, WILLIAM STARLING, retired mechanical engineer; b. Mantorville, Minn., June 1, 1906; s. John I. and Anna (Andrist) J.; m. Hazel E. Olson, Nov. 21, 1931; children—Starling Ann Jordre Kephart, Sue H. Jordre James, Diane Jordre Meyerratken, J. William, JoAnn. Student Antioch Coll., 1924-28; B.M.E., U. Minn., 1931. Erector, Babcock & Wilcox Co., Barberton, Ohio, 1931-38, dist. erection supt. Cin. office, 1938-43, Chgo. office, 1943-45; exec. v.p., dir. Oberle-Jordre Co., Inc., 1945-74; ret., 1974; dir. Crestview Lands, Inc. Chmn. bd. Trinity-St. Philips Found. Mem. Engring. Soc. Cin. (life), Nat., Ohio, socs. profl. engrs., ASME. Episcopalian. Clubs: Masons (32 deg.), Bankers. Home: 424 Herrington Woods Rd Harrodsburg KY 40330

JORGENSON, WALLACE JAMES, broadcasting executive; b. Mpls., Oct. 31, 1923; s. Peter and Adelia Henrietta (Bong) J.; student St. Olaf Coll., 1941-43, Gustavus Adolphus Coll., 1943; B.A., Bowling Green State U., 1944; L.H.D., Lenoir-Rhyne Coll., 1971; m. Solveig Elizabeth Tvedt, Feb. 24, 1945; children—Kristin, Peter, Mark, Philip, Lisa. Staff announcer Sta. WCAL, Northfield, Minn., 1941-43; sta. mgr. Sta. KTRF, Thief River Falls, Minn., 1946-48; with Sta. WBT, Charlotte, 1952-67, v.p., asst. gen. mgr., 1966-67; exec. v.p. Jefferson-Pilot Broadcasting Co., Charlotte, 1968-78, pres., 1978—, also dir.; dir. Jefferson-Pilot Corp.; chmn. Charlotte br. Fed. Res. Bank Richmond, 1985 Chmn. mgmt. com. Office for Communications, Lutheran Ch. in Am., 1978—; v.p., gen. chmn. United Way campaign, 1978, pres., 1984; bd. govs. ARC, 1977-83, chmn. Red Cross Centennial, 1981; trustee Lenoir-Rhyne Coll., 1963-81, chmn., 1971-77; bd. dirs. Central Piedmont Community Coll. Found, 1980—, Greater Charlotte Found., U. N.C.-Charlotte Found.; trustee N.C. Symphony; bd. visitors Davidson Coll., 1979—. Served with USMC, 1943-46. Recipient silver medal award Charlotte Advt. Club, 1975; Abe Lincoln award So. Baptist Conv., 1975; communications award N.C. Council Chs., 1976; Harriman award ARC, 1982; Earle Gluck Disting. Service award N.C. Assn. Broadcasters, 1981. Mem. Broadcast Pioneers, Nat. Assn. Broadcasters (dir. TV bd.), Am. Mgmt. Assn., N.C. Assn. Broadcasters, Assn. Maximum Service Telecasters (past chmn.), U.S. C. of C. (public affairs com.), Greater Charlotte C. of C. (past chmn.). Republican. Clubs: Quail Hollow Country. Charlotte City, Tower (chmn.). Home: 2742 Meade Ct Charlotte NC 28211 Office: 1 Julian Price Pl Charlotte NC 28208

JORY, VIRGINIA VICKERY, mathematician, research scientist; b. Union City, Ga., Jan. 4, 1934; d. Earl Lee and Mildred Louise (Nolan) Vickery; m. Philip Douglas Jory, July 11, 1953; children—Victoria Jory Dennard, Philip Douglas. B.S., Ga. Inst. Tec-., 1971, M.S., 1974, Ph.D., 1979. Supr. computers Northwestern U. Aerial Measurements Lab., Patuxent River, Md., 1954-55; programmer math. analysis dept. Lockheed-Ga., Marietta, 1956-58; research asst. U.S. Dist. Ct., Atlanta, 1976-80; instr. Sch. Math., Ga. Inst. Tech., Atlanta, 1979-80; research scientist Engring. Expt. Sta., Ga. Inst. Tech., Atlanta, 1980—; v.p., sec., bd. dirs. Jory Concrete Pumping Co., Atlanta, 1969—. Chmn., Ga. Tech. Com. on Handicapped, 1980-81; mem. Ga. Tech. Exec. Roundtable, 1980—. Recipient Book award Soc. Women Engrs., 1971. Mem. Rehab. Engring. Soc. N.Am., Am. Math. Soc., Math. Assn. Am., IEEE, Soc. Indsl. and Applied Math., N.Y. Acad. Scis., Sigma Xi, Pi Mu Epsilon (Math. award 1971), Phi Kappa Phi, Tau Beta Pi. Office: EES-STL-MSD Ga Inst Tech Atlanta Ga 30332

JOSEL, NATHAN, library director; b. New Orleans, Sept. 28, 1941; s. Nathan A. and Elise (Blummer) J.; B.A., Tulane U., 1963; M.S., La. State U., 1965; m. Jacqualine M. Nielsen, Dec. 15, 1979; children—Laura P., Nathan A. III. Various positions Enoch Pratt Free Library, 1965-69; head local history Memphis-Shelby County Public Library, 1969-71, head history and travel, 1971-74; asst. dir. Madison (Wis.) Public Library, 1974-80; dir. El Paso Public Library, 1980—; lectr. U. Wis. Library Sch. Commr., Shelby County (Tenn.) Hist. Records Commn., 1972-74, Shelby County Hist. Commn., 1973-74. Mem. ALA, Tex. Library Assn., SW Library Assn., Border Regional Library Assn. Contbr. chpts. to Reference Books for Small and Medium Libraries, 3d edit. Office: 501 N Oregon St El Paso TX 79901

JOSEPH, LURA ELLEN, exploration geologist; b. Tulsa, Jan. 24, 1947; d. Don Roscoe and Ruth Elizabeth (Hartman) J. Student St. Paul Bible Coll., 1965-67, Pan Am. Coll., 1967-68; B.A. in Anthropology, U. Okla., 1971, M.S., in Geology, 1981. Exploration geologist Getty Oil Co., Oklahoma City, 1977-84; geologist Harper Oil Co., Oklahoma City, 1984—. Author: (with others:) Hugo Reservoir I, 1971. Active adv. council New Life Ranch, Inc., Colcord, Okla.; mem. missions com. Met. Baptist Ch., Oklahoma City. Mem. Am. Assn. Petroleum Geologists, Oklahoma City Geol. Soc., Pan Am. Geol. Soc. (pres. 1967-68), Sigma Gamma Epsilon. Republican. Mem. Independent Evangelical Ch. Avocations: travel; photography; reading; art; ceramics.

JOSEPH, MARY, university administrator; b. Greensboro, N.C., June 27, 1952; d. Estelle (Sheheen) J.; m. Roy Steven Jones, Aug. 17, 1980; children—Jennifer F., Meredith A. B.S. in Speech Pathology, Appalachian State U., 1974, M.A. in Counseling, 1976; Ph.D. in Administrn., East Tenn. State U., 1984. Asst. dir. extension inst. Appalachian State U., Boone, N.C., 1976-81, dir., 1981-84, dir. ctr. mgmt. devel., 1984—; faculty Wilkes Community Coll., Wilkesboro, N.C., 1982-84. Pres. Watauga chpt. Am. Cancer Soc., Boone, 1982; mem. Watauga Council on Status of Women, 1983-85. Research fellow East Tenn. State U., 1979-80. Mem. ASTD, Assn. Continuing Higher Edn., State Employees Assn. N.C., (com.), Boone Profl. Women Assn. (Woman of Year award 1983, Outstanding Young Woman of Year award 1982, pres. 1985-86). Democrat. Roman Catholic. Office: Ctr Mgmt Devel Appalachian State U Boone NC 28608

JOSHI, MAHENDRA JAYANTILAL, telecommunication specialist; b. Bombay, India, Feb. 21, 1945; came to U.S., 1968; s. Jayantilal Pranshanker and Manjula (Shukla) J.; m. Asha Yajnik, Nov. 2, 1975; 1 son, Samir. B.E. in Elec. Engring., Maharaja Sayajiyao U., Baroda, India, 1967, B.E. in Mech. Engring., 1968; M.S.E.E., Ill. Inst. Tech., 1973; M.B.A. with distinction, Northwestern U., 1977. Registered profl. engr., N.C. Planning engr. Bell Labs., Naperville, Ill., 1968-72; software designer GTE Automatic Electric, Northlake, Ill., 1972-76; sr. systems engr. Rockwell Internat. Dallas, 1976-80; software mgr. Siemens Corp., Boca Raton, Fla., 1980-83; devel. mgr. IBM Corp., Research Triangle Park, N.C., 1983—. Govt. of India Open Merit scholar, 1962. Mem. IEEE, Bombay Astrological Soc. (cert. merit 1958), Am. Mgmt. Assn., Beta Gamma Sigma. Democrat. Hindu. Club: Toastmasters (Northlake). Home: 7208 Valley Lake Dr Raleigh NC 27612 Office: IBM Corp PO Box 12195 Research Triangle Park NC 27709

JOSHI, SURESH MEGHASHYAM, research engineer; b. Poona, India; came to U.S., 1969, naturalized 1982; s. Meghashyam and (Sulochana) J.; m. Shyamala, June 16, 1974; children—Sucharit, Sujay. B.S., Banaras U., India, 1967; M.S., Indian Inst. Tech., Kanpur, 1969; Ph.D., Rensselaer Poly. Inst., 1973. Engr., Stone & Webster Corp., Boston, 1972-73; research assoc. NASA, Hampton, Va., 1973-75, sr. research engr., 1983—; assoc. prof. Old Dominion U. Research Found., Norfolk, Va., 1975-83. Contbr. articles to profl. jours. Recipient Allen B. DuMont prize Rensselaer Poly. Inst., 1973; Group Achievement award NASA, 1977, Cert. of Recognition, 1981, Quality award, 1984. Mem. IEEE (sr.), AIAA (sr.) Avocation: amateur cartoonist. Office: NASA Langley Research Ctr Mail Stop 161 Hampton VA 23665

JOURARD, JOHNPAUL, human resource mgmt. cons.; b. Dallas, Nov. 11, 1939; s. PeterPaul and Carmelle Marie (Belmori) J.; m. Judy Lee Huck, Aug. 18, 1962. B.A., St. Mary's U., 1963; M.S.W., Our Lady of Lake Coll., 1967. Juvenile probation officer Bexar County Juvenile Probation Dept., San Antonio, 1962-65; planning dir. Community Welfare Council, 1967-70; assoc. exec. dir. Sr. Community Services, Inc., 1970-82; supr. Frontier Enterprises, 1982-83; exec. dir. San Antonio Alliance of Bus., 1983; exec. assoc. S.W. Cons. and Tng. Assocs., San Antonio, 1978—. Sec., past pres. Ednl. Arts Clearing House; founder, past pres. Tex. Assn. Sr. Ctrs. Mem. Nat. Council on Aging, Nat. Assn. Social Workers, Nat. Notary Assn., Nat. Assn. Pvt. Industry Councils, Nat. Alliance of Bus., Am. Soc. Tng. and Devel., Am. Mktg. Assn., Acad. Cert. Social Workers, Human Service Personnel Assn., St. Mary's U. Alumni Assn., Our Laky of Lake U. Alumni Assn., San Antonio C. of C., Soc. Fund Raising Execs. (past pres.), San Antonio Council Pres. Democrat. Roman Catholic. Lodge: Rotary. Contbr. articles to profl. jours. Home: 327 Craigmont Ln San Antonio TX 78213 Office: PO Box 12184 San Antonio TX 78212

JOWERS, SANDRA THOMAS, moving and storage company executive; b. Dallas, Oct. 4, 1950; d. Carl Dexter and Anita Lorraine (Garver) Thomas; m. Joseph Jacob Jowers. B.S. in Sociology, B.S. in Bus. Adminstrn., E. Tex. State U., 1972. Office mgr. Thomas Van & Storage, Inc., Dallas, 1972-74, pres., 1974—. Mem. Bus. and Profl. Women's Clubs (exec. del., young careerist chmn. 1980), S.W. Warehouse and Transfer Assn. (dir. 1979—; v.p. 1981), Dallas Movers Assn. (dir. 1974—, pres. 1979), Alpha Chi. Methodist. Home: 3408 Lakeside Dr Rockwall TX 75087 Office: 9201 Forest Ln Dallas TX 75243

JOYCE, DONALD FRANKLIN, academic library administrator, historian, consultant; b. Chgo., Nov. 4, 1938; s. Raleigh and Pearl (Jackson) J. B.A., Fisk U., Nashville, 1957; M.S., U. Ill.-Urbana, 1960; Ph.D., U. Chgo., 1978. Head br. librarian Chgo. Pub. Library, 1960-69, curator Harsh Collection of Afro-Am. History, 1969-81; coordinator downtown library, assoc. prof. Tenn. State U., Nashville, 1981—; cons. Nat. Endowment for the Humanities, Afro-Am. Pub. Co., Metro Books. Author: Gatekeepers of Black Culture, 1983; editor library catalogue; compiler bibliography; author book revs., articles. Chmn. essay contest DuSable Mus. of Afro-Am. History, Chgo., 1978-81. Mem. ALA, Tenn. Library Assn., Assn. Study of Afro-Am. Life and History. Democrat. Baptist. Home: 6 6 323 Forrest Park Rd Madison TN 37115 Office: Downtown Library Tenn State Univ 10th St and Charlotte Sts Nashville TN 37203

JOYCE, EDWARD JAMES, writer, editor, computer scientist; b. Pitts., Sept. 20, 1952; s. Edward James and Dolores L. (Czyzewski) J.; m. Judith Marie Hugenberg, Aug. 16, 1975. B.S. in Math., U. Pitts., 1974; M.S. in Computer Sci., Trinity U., 1978. Computer analyst Datapoint Corp., San Antonio, 1975-83; freelance writer, 1983—. Author: Modula-2: A Seatarer's Manual and Shipyard Guide, 1985. Contbr. articles to mags. Address: Route 9 Box 149 Charlottesville VA 22901

JOYCE, WILLIAM ROBERT, textile machinery company executive; b. Springfield, Ohio, Mar. 18, 1936; s. Robert Emmet and Christel Beatrice (Beekman) J.; m. Betty Arlene Provonsha, Aug. 29, 1959; children—Jennifer Lynn, Janet Cathleen. B.A. in Bus., Calif. Western U., 1982; M.B.A., Calif. Coast U., 1984. Cert. mfg. engring. technician Soc. Mfg. Engrs., 1975. Mgr. engring. Heinicke Instruments, Hollywood, Fla., 1964-68; div. mgr. Jensen Corp., Pompano Beach, Fla., 1969-72; pres. Textiles Supply, Inc., Gerton, N.C., 1972-80; v.p., gen. mgr. Tex-Fab, Inc., Gerton, N.C., 1980-82; pres. Tex-nology Systems, Inc., Gerton, N.C., 1982—; owner Corrib Enterprises, Automation Cons., Gerton, 1981—. Mem., co-founder Assoc. Woodland Owners N.C.; Upper Hickory Nut Gorge Vol. Fire Dept., Gerton. Served with USAF, 1958-64. Recipient innovative devel. award, 1985, award Optimist Club, 1953-54. Mem. Guild Master Craftsmen (internat. mem.) Nat. Rifle Assn., Soc. Mfg. Engrs., Am. Inst. Design and Drafting, Western Carolina Entrepeneurial Council. Republican. Baptist. Club: Gerton Community Civic. Patentee in field.

JOYNER, CASSANDRA LEE, volunteer program administrator, public relations/marketing specialist; b. Enfield, N.C., July 6, 1956; d. John Lewis and Llana (Lessane) J. B.A., Hampton Inst., 1978; M.P.A., Howard U., 1980. Grad. asst. Sch. Bus., Howard U., Washington, 1978-80, White House, Washington, 1979, Office of the Mayor, Washington, 1979-80; edn. cons. U.S. Dept. Edn., Washington, 1980-81; mktg. mgr. Green, Gladman & Assocs., Washington, 1981-84; coordinator Friends/N.C. Juvenile Services, Halifax, N.C., 1985—. TV co-host membership drive Sta. WHMM-TV Howard U., 1982-83. Mem. Mayor's Pub. Info. Com., Washington, 1981-82; city ward coordinator Congressman Walter Fauntroy, Washington, 1982; bd. dirs. Community Adv. Bd. Capitol Hill Hosp., Washington, 1982-83, John L. Joyner Scholarship Fund, Halifax/Northampton County, 1985-86. Grad. fellow Met. Washington Council Govts., 1979-80. Mem. Nat. Assn. Female Execs., Nat. Black M.B.A. Assn., Hampton Inst. Alumni (fundraising chmn. Halifax chpt. 1985-86), Howard U. Alumni, Pi Alpha Alpha, Delta Sigma Theta. Avocations: horseback riding; tennis; reading; jazz vocalist. Home: 416 Whitaker St Enfield NC 27823

JOYNER, JARVIS DONALD, JR., insurance safety engineer; b. Kinston, N.C., Jan. 20, 1955; s. Jarvis Donald and Hilda Martha (Speight) J.; m. Celia Harris, Feb. 18, 1978; 1 child, Ashley Margaret. B.S., East Carolina U., 1977. Loss control surveyor Fireman's Fund Ins. Co., Greensboro, N.C., 1977-79, loss control tech. adviser, San Rafael, Calif., 1979-80, Miami, Fla., 1980-84; loss control supr. Seibels, Bruce & Co., Orlando, Fla., 1984—. Bd. dirs., sec. Kingspoint Homeowner's Assn., Casselberry, Fla., 1985. Mem. Am. Soc. Safety Engrs., Fla. Affiliate of Ins. Safety Reps. Democrat. Methodist. Avocations: golf; woodworking. Home: 1634 Pinehurst Dr Casselberry FL 32707 Office: Seibels Bruce & Co 1300 N Semoran Blvd Orlando FL 32807

JOYNER, SYLVIA PETTIS, fundraiser; b. Galveston, Tex., Sept. 12, 1946; d. Louis James Pettis and Florence Gloria Lawton Cody; B.A., Tuskegee Inst., 1968; 1 son, Michael Pettis. Social service advisor Prichard (Ala.) Housing Authority, 1973-74; community rep. McDonald's of Mobile (Ala.), 1974-76; nat. VISTA worker, VISTA Spl. Project, Fedn. So. Coops., Epes, Ala., 1978; area devel. dir. United Negro Coll. Fund, Inc., Birmingham, Ala., 1978—. Bd. dirs. Vol. and Info. Center, 1980—, Birmingham Creative Dance Co., YWCA of Birmingham, Birmingham Festival of Arts, Coalition of 100 Black Women, Leadership Birmingham. Mem. Ala. Soc. Fund Raising Execs. (exec. com. 1980—), Urban League, NAACP, Nat. Assn. Young Children, Nat. Soc. Fundraisers, Alpha Kappa Alpha (Omicron Omega chpt.). Office: 1728 3rd Ave N Birmingham AL 35203

JREISAT, JAMIL ELIAS, public adminstration educator, consultant; b. Fuheis, Jordan, Apr. 9, 1935; came to U.S., 1960; s. Elias E. and Hanieh J. (Khory) J.; m. Andrea Brunais, July 9, 1977; children—Mark Ramsey, Leila Martine. B.A., Am. U., Washington, 1962; M.P.A., U. Pitts., 1963, Ph.D., 1968. Sr. ofcl. Govt. Jordan, 1957-60; lectr. pub. adminsrn. U. Pitts., 1967-68; prof. pub. adminstrn. U. South Fla., Tampa, 1968—, chmn. dept. polit. sci., 1976-80; vis. prof. U. Jordan, 1983, U. Riyad (Saudi Arabia), 1981-82. Mem. Am. Soc. Pub. Adminstrn., Am. Polit. Sci. Assn. Club: Middle East. Mem. editorial bd. Internat. Jour. Pub. Adminstrn., 1978; contbr. articles to profl. jours. Home: 9209 Hollyridge Pl Tampa FL 33617 Office: Pub Adminstrn Program U South Fla Tampa FL 33620

JUAREZ, ANTONIO, psychotherapist, consultant; b. El Paso, Tex., Nov. 6, 1952; s. Juan Antonio and Amelia (Rivas) J. B.S. in Psychology, U.Tex.-El Paso, 1976, M.A. in Clin. Psychology, 1982. Caseworker asst. El Paso Mental Health Ctr., 1978-79, caseworker III, 1982-83; clin. specialist S.W. Mental Health Ctr., Las Cruces, N.Mex., 1979-80; therapist, trainer S.W. Community House, El Paso, 1980-81; psychol. cons. El Paso Guidance Ctr., 1981-82, psychotherapist, 1983—; cons. Citizens and Students Together, El Paso, 1983—. Mem. Latin Am. com. N.Mex. State U., 1985. Served with USAF, 1972-76. Fellow N.Mex. State U., 1981. Mem. U.S.-Mex. Border Health Assn., El Paso Psychol. Assn. Democrat. Roman Catholic. Avocations: brown belt kenpo karate, playing violin, guitar and mandolin, YMCA barbell club. Home: 6032 Caprock 1802 El Paso TX 79912 Office: El Paso Guidance Ctr 1501 N Mesa St El Paso TX 79901

JUDD, DANIEL STEWART, financial and management consultant; cons.; b. West Asheville, N.C., Mar. 6, 1924; s. Oscar John and Mabel (Moyers) J.; student Berea (Ky.) Coll., 1941-43, U. Okla., 1943, U. N.C., Asheville, 1946; m. Margaret Norvelle Shipman, Dec. 8, 1946; children—Daniel Stewart, Mary Margaret Judd Wood, Oscar Herbert. Partner, Judd Furniture & Supply Co., West Asheville, 1949-54; owner Judd Supply Co., West Asheville, 1954-64; pvt. practice acctg., West Asheville, 1962-68; acct. Columbia (S.C.) Coll., 1968-73; fin. and mgmt. cons., Irmo, S.C., 1973—; instr. extension div. Asheville-Buncombe Tech Inst., 1966-67; dir. So. Bank & Trust Co., Irmo. Pres., Buncombe County (N.C.) Republican Club, 1950; sec. Buncombe County Rep. Exec. Com., 1954-60; chmn. 12th Dist. N.C. Rep. Com., 1960-62; dist. dir. 1960 Census for 11th congressional dist. N.C.; charter pres. Buncombe County Young Rep. Club; mem. Buncombe County Bd. Elections, 1948-50, N.C. Bd. Elections, 1961-62; trustee Lexington County Hosp. Served with Armed Forces, 1943-45. Decorated Bronze Star. Mem. Nat. Assn. Accts., Nat. Assn. Public Accts., S.C. Tax Council (pres. 1980-82), Berea Alumni Assn. (pres. Asheville chpt. 1957). Methodist (Sunday sch. tchr., adminstrv. bd., lay speaker, conf. del.). Clubs: Lions (pres. West Asheville 1955-56, pres. Seven Oaks club Columbia 1970-71, editor bulls. 1964-67, 68—), Masons, Mid-Carolina, Irmo Ruritan (pres. 1983). Home: 612 Old Friars Rd Columbia SC 29210 Office: PO Box 68 7349 Nursery Rd Irmo SC 29063

JUDICE, PHILIP CHARLES, oil exploration geologist; b. Crowley La., Nov. 1, 1958; s. Lee James and Gladys (Verrett) J. B.S. in Geology, U. S.W. La., 1980, M.S., 1981. Geotechnologist Union Tex. Petroleum Co., Lafayette, La., 1978-81; exploration geologist Conoco, Lafayette, 1981-83, Lea Exploration Inc., Lafayette, 1983—; asst. lectr. U. S.W. La., Lafayette, 1984; speaker judge Gulf Coast Assn. of Geol. Socs., Shreveport, La., 1984. Co-editor Lafayette Geol. Soc. Jour., 1984. Contbr. articles to profl. jours. Mem. Am. Assn. Petroleum Geologists, Lafayette Geol. Soc., Sigma Gamma Epsilon. Clubs: De Molay (master counselor 1975-76). Avocations: physical fitness, camping, karate, fishing, hunting. Home: 90 Luke Dr Apt 206-N Lafayette LA 70506 Office: Lea Exploration Inc 218 Heymann Blvd Layfayette LA 70503

JUDY, RICHARD H., airport executive; b. Heilwood, Pa., Oct. 16, 1931; s. Robert T. and Hannah Judy; m. Sonya Rogers; children—Dace J., Jolie L. B.S. in Bus. Adminstrn., U. Miami (Fla.). Dir. airport Dade County Aviation Dept., Miami, Fla. Mem. bldg. research bd., nat. research council Nat. Acad. Scis. Mem. Airport Operators Council Internat. (bd. dirs. Washington 1983—). Office: Dade County Aviation Dept PO Box 592075 Miami FL 33159

JUETT, DOROTHY FRANCES, state official; b. Owenton, Ky., Mar. 3, 1924; d. James William and Lula Bell (Grisham) J.; m. Daniel E. Hanbery, Feb. 17, 1944 (div. 1966). Student Georgetown Coll., 1942-44, U. Ky., 1959-60. Owner Ladies Ready to Wear, Owenton, 1947-51; sr. employment interviewer State of Ky., Lexington and Frankfort, 1954—. Mem. Internat. Assn. Employment Security, DAR (historian Owenton 1983-84, librarian 1984-85), Sigma Kappa. Democrat. Lodge: Order Eastern Star. Avocations: walking; horseback riding. Home: Route 6 115 W Adair St Owenton KY 40359 Office: Cabinet for Human Resources Dept Employment Services High and Metro Sts Frankfort KY 40601

JUKOFSKY, MICHAEL A., construction engineer; b. St. Louis, Dec. 1, 1948; s. S. Lawrence and Elizabeth Ann (Cushing) J.; m. Kerri Susan Crowe; children—Stacy, Joseph, Jeffrey. B.S. in Civil Engring., The Citadel, 1970. Assr. research engr. S.C. Hwy. Dept., Ridgeland, 1972-73; pres. M.A.J. Enterprises Inc., Hilton Head, S.C., 1974—, Seacoast Paving Inc., Hilton Head, 1978—. Served to 2d lt. USN, 1970-71. Mem. Nat. Assn. Home Builders (bd. dirs. 1983-84), Jr. C. of C. (v.p. Ridgeland sect. 1976-78). Republican. Jewish. Club; Rotary (Hilton Head). Avocations: running; photography; skiing. Home: 36 Dolphin Pt Ln Hilton Head SC 29928 Office: MAJ Enterprises Inc 148 P Spanish Wells Rd Box 1564 Hilton Head SC 20025

JULIAN, HAROLD EUGENE, foods company official; b. Boonville, Ind., July 8, 1926; s. Harold and Katherine J.; student Purdue U., 1958-59, Washington U., St. Louis, 1960-67, Columbia U., 1967-69; m. Lois Joel Thompson, Aug. 26, 1944; children—Danny Le, Deborah, Darlene, Donald. Partner supermarket chain, Evansville, Ind.; host TV program Julian's Food With Flair, Evansville, 1960-68; dir. tng. and corp. mgmt. devel. Wetterau Foods, St. Louis, 1968-70, dir. mktg. 3 affiliated cos., 1971-73, dir. new mktg. devel. and regional mgmt., Winter Haven, Fla., 1973-82, dir. tng. and corp. devel., 1982—; seminar specialist, dir. mktg. J. W. Allen Co.; cons. Served in USN, 1944-46; PTO, ETO. Recipient awards from Evansville Indsl. Found., Kiwanis, others. Mem. Food Mktg. Inst., Associated Retail Bakers Am., Am. Soc. Tng. and Devel., Retail Bakers Am. Clubs: Winter Haven (Fla.) Bass; United Bass Fishermen; Bass Angelers Soc.; Masons, Shriners. Author: Dairy Merchandising; Creative Grocery Merchandising; Public Relations Supermarket Management; Cash Control; others. Home and Office: 309 Suwanee Rd Winter Haven FL 33880

JUMPER, CHARLES FREDERICK, chemistry educator; b. Prosperity, S.C., Nov. 4, 1934; s. Keister O'Neal and Mattie Lee (Hendrix) J.; m. Peggy Harris, Mar. 19, 1967; 1 child. B.S., U. S.C., 1956, M.S., 1957; Ph.D., Fla. State U., 1961. Instr., U. S.C., 1960-61; research chemist Bell Telephone Labs., Murray Hill, N.J., 1961-62; asst. prof. chemistry The Citadel, Charleston, S.C., 1962-64, assoc. prof., 1964-69, prof., 1969—, head dept. chemistry, 1982—. Fellow NSF. Mem. Am. Chem. Soc., SiC. Hist. Soc., Sigma Xi, Phi Beta Kappa, Phi Kappa Phi. Republican. Lutheran. Contbr. articles to profl. jours. Office: The Citadel Charleston SC 29409

JUMPER, SIDNEY ROBERTS, geography educator; b. Gaston, S.C., Dec. 10, 1930; s. Sidney Parker and Gladys Corrine (Roberts) J.; m. Mary Joanne Scarcella, May 29, 1954; 1 dau., Kimberly. A.B., U. S.C., 1951, M.S., 1953; Ph.D., U. Tenn., 1960. Instr. U. S.C., 1952-53, U. Tenn., Knoxville, 1956-57; asst. prof. Tenn. Tech. U., Cookeville, 1957-60, assoc. prof., 1960-62, prof., 1962-67, dept. head., 1963-67; assoc. prof. U. Tenn., Knoxville, 1967-72, prof., 1972-77, head geography dept., 1977—. Served with U.S. Army, 1953-55. Mem. Assn. Am. Geographers, Nat. Geog. Soc., Sigma Xi. Democrat. Presbyterian. Author: (with Bell and Ralston) Economic Growth and Disparities: A World View, 1980; contbr. articles to profl. jours.

JUNG, RODNEY C., physician; b. New Orleans, Oct. 9, 1920; s. Frederick Charles and Clara (Cuevas) J.; B.S. in Zoology with honors, Tulane U., 1941, M.D., 1945, M.S. in Parasitology, 1950, Ph.D., 1953. Diplomate Am. Bd. Internal Medicine. Intern Charity Hosp. La., New Orleans 1945-46; dir. Hutchinson Meml. Clinic, 1948; asst. parasitology Tulane U., 1948-50, instr. tropical medicine, 1950-53, asst. prof., 1953-57, assoc. prof. tropical medicine, 1951-63, prof. tropical medicine, 1963-1975, clin. prof. tropical medicine, 1983—, head div. tropical medicine, 1960-63; health dir. City of New Orleans, 1963-70, 79-82; internist-in-charge Ill. Central Hosp., New Orleans, 1956-70; sr. vis. physician Charity Hosp., 1959—; sr. in internal medicine Touro Infirmary. Co-author: Clinical Parasitology, Animal Agents and Vectors of Disease; contbr. articles to profl. jours. Bd. dirs. S.E. La. Emergency Med. Services Council, 1977, med. dir. 1979—, pres. 1981-83; mem. commn. on parasitic disease Armed Forces Epidemiology Bd. Served as lt. (j.g.) M.C., USNR, 1946-48. John and Mary Markle scholar in med. sci.; Fellow ACP; mem. Am., Royal socs. tropical medicine and hygiene, Am. Soc. Parasitologists, La. State, Orleans Parish med. socs., Nat. Rifle Assn., La. Mosquito Control Assn., Am., La. socs. internal medicine, AMA, Brazilian Soc. Tropical Medicine (hon.), Irish Cultural Soc. New Orleans (founder, pres. 1980), Am. Def. Preparedness Assn., Phi Beta Kappa, Sigma Xi, Alpha Omega Alpha, Delta Omega. Presbyterian. Office: 3600 Chestnut New Orleans LA 70115

JUNGMAN, YOUNG FRANK, real estate broker; b. Houston, Mar. 18, 1929; s. J. Frank and Thelma Katherine (Young) J.; B.B.A., U. Tex., 1948, J.D., 1950; postgrad. U. Houston, Wichita State U., U. Ga., So. Methodist U.; m. Marilyn Virginia Skipwith, June 7, 1952; children—Robert Frank, John Skipwith. Sec.-treas., dir. Paul E. Wise Co., Inc., and affiliated cos., 1954-61; real estate broker, appraiser, cons., investor, Houston, 1961—. Admitted to Tex. bar, 1950, U.S. Supreme Ct. bar, 1954; instr. real estate U. Houston, 1970-73. Mem. Harris County Flood Control Task Force, 1975-77; mem. Harris County Democratic Exec. Com., 1978-80. Mem. Houston City Library Bd., 1965-76, v.p., 1973-76; mem. vestry Trinity Episcopal Ch., 1979-82. Served to 1st lt. USAF, 1951-53. Mem. Nat., Tex., Houston assns. realtors, Tex., Houston bar assns., Pi Kappa Alpha, Phi Alpha Delta. Mason (Shriner, 32 deg.). Home: 5325 Willers Way Houston TX 77056 Office: 5251 Westheimer Suite 350 Houston TX 77056

JUNK, PAUL JOSEPH, electric company executive; b. Chillicothe, Ohio, Dec. 15, 1933; s. Harold Clifton and Helen (Beath) J.; m. Gail LaVern Schneider, Jan. 26, 1955; children—Vicki, Paul Joseph, Gregory. B.S. in Commerce, Ohio U., 1962. Acct., Goodyear Atomic Corp., Piketon, Ohio, 1954-64; fin. officer Ohio State Hwy., Chillicothe, Ohio, 1964-67; constrn. audit mgr. Westinghouse Electric, Pitts., 1967-72; audit mgr. Ohio Brass Co., Mansfield, 1972-80; controller Ensign Electric Co., Huntington, W.Va., 1980—. Mem. Inst. Internal Auditors. Republican. Methodist. Clubs: Spring Valley Golf Course (Huntington, W.Va.). Lodge: Elks. Home: 224 St Clair Dr Chillicothe OH 45601 Office: Ensign Electric PO Box 7758 Huntington WV 25778

JUNKINS, JERRY R., electronics company executive; b. 1937; married. B.S.E.E., Iowa State U.; M.S., So. Methodist U. Successively mgr. mfg. control equipment group, mgr. mfg. radar systems div. Tex. Instruments, Inc. mgr. radar and digital systems div., 1977, corp. v.p., mgr. equipment group, 1977-82, exec. v.p., Dallas, 1982—. Office: Tex Instruments Inc PO Box 225474 Dallas TX 75265*

JUNOD, PATRICIA LEE, real estate broker; b. Jay County, Ind., Jan. 23, 1929; d. Willard Arthur and Dorothy Jeanette (Glendening) White; student pub. schs., Northville, Mich., 1947; m. Aubrey Sidney Junod, Sept. 26, 1947 (div.), remarried; children—Suzanne Junod Hopper, Lorayne Junod Evans, Andrew Arthur, Elizabeth Lee. Saleswoman, Juno Beach Realty Inc. (Fla.), 1960-65; broker-saleswoman Ketter Realty Co., Lake Park, Fla., 1966-67, Kenneth P. Foster Inc., West Palm Beach, 1967-71; pres., broker PGA Realty Inc., Palm Beach Gardens, Fla., 1971-79; pres. Heritage PGA Inc., 1970—. Mem. N. Palm Beach (Fla.) Planning and Zoning Bd., 1966-70; pres. Pal-Mar-Water Mgmt. Dist., Martin and Palm Beach County, 1972-78, South Indian River Drainage Dist. Mem. Nat., Fla. assns. realtors, No. Palm Beach County Bd. Realtors, Nat. Fedn. Ind. Bus., Palm Beach County Mental Health Assn., No. Palm Beach C. of C. Republican. Home: 941 Barlinton Circle Sunny Hills Chipley FL 32428 Office: 742 US 1 North Palm Beach FL 33408

JUREN, DENNIS FRANKLIN, petroleum company executive; b. Ellinger, Tex., Apr. 4, 1935; s. Daniel Arthur and Ellen Emily J.; m. Ruth Birmingham, Oct. 7, 1961; children—Patrick Edward, Ellen Emily, Anne Elizabeth. B.A. in Econs., U. Tex., 1968; M.B.A. in Fin., U. Houston, 1969. Mgr. supply Eastern States Petroleum Co., Houston, 1956-60; owner Bonded Petroleum Co., Houston, 1960-62; v.p. mktg. and supply Coastal States Petrochem. Co., Houston, 1962-70; pres. Tesoro Petroleum Corp., San Antonio, 1970—. Bd. dirs. YMCA, San Antonio, 1979. Served with U.S. Army, 1954-55. Mem. San Antonio C. of C. (dir. 1982), Nat. Petroleum Refiners Assn. (dir.), Am. Petroleum Inst. Methodist. Clubs: Oakhills Country, University. Lodge: Masons. Office: Tesoro Petroleum Corp 8700 Tesoro Dr San Antonio TX 78286

JURGENSEN, PAUL FRANCIS, physician; b. Savannah, Ga., June 21, 1938; s. Paul Frank and Mildred (Barrett) J.; m. Diane Marie Zinn, July 17, 1963; children—Margaret, Paul, Stephen, Neil. B.S. cum laude, Spring Hill Coll., 1960; M.D. magna cum laude, St. Louis U., 1964. Diplomate Am. Bd. Internal Medicine. Intern St. Louis U. Hosps., 1964-65, resident in internal medicine, 1964-68; fellow in infectious diseases U. Fla. Coll. Medicine, Gainesville, 1970-71; physician Paulsen Sq. Med. Assocs., Savannah, 1971—; mem. active staff Meml. Med. Center; cons. staff St. Joseph's Hosp.; clin. assoc. prof. medicine U. Fla., Med. Coll. Ga. Active Leadership Savannah, 1975. Served to lt. comdr. M.C., USN, 1968-70. Fellow ACP, Infectious Diseases Soc. Am. Roman Catholic. Contbr. articles to profl. jours. Office: PO Box 22069 Savannah GA 31403

JUSTICE, FRANK P., JR., corporation executive; b. Wanego, W.Va., May 5, 1938; m. Eva Mae Hartley, June 8, 1960; children—Kerry, Kelly, Kevin. B.S.

in Bus. Adminstrn., W.Va. State Coll.; M.B.A. in Fin., Marshall U.; postgrad. U. Louisville. Reporter, Dun & Bradstreet, Inc., Charleston, W.Va., 1960-63, reporting mgr., 1963-65, office mgr., Huntington, W.Va., 1966-68; domestic trade specialist Dept. Commerce, Charleston, 1968-70; pres., investment mgr. Equal Opportunity Fin., Inc., Ashland, Ky., 1970, adminstrv. asst. to v.p. personnel, 1973-74, adminstrv. asst. to v.p. external affairs, 1974-75, mgr. spl. projects, 1975-76, dir. pub. affairs, 1976-78; v.p. pub. relations Ashland Oil, Inc., 1978-82, corp. v.p., 1985—; v.p. Ashland Services Co., 1981-85. Cons., Ashland Tennis Commn., 1975—; mem. Ashland Human Rights Commn., 1978—; chmn. bd., 1980-83; dir. Tri-State Fair and Regatta, 1978-79; v.p., dir. Ky. Council Econ. Edn., 1978-79, chmn., 1982; pres. Greater Ashland Found., 1979-81; mem. Ky. Gov.'s Tourism Com.; vice chmn. Ashland Econ. Devel. Mem. Ashland Area C. of C. (pres. 1980, dir. 1978—), Ky. C. of C. (dir. 1978—, vice chmn. 1982, chmn. 1983, chmn. exec. com. 1984), Ky. Dist. Export Council (vice chmn. 1983), Pub. Affairs Council, Inc. (dir.), Pub. Relations Soc. Am. Club: Bellefonte Country (dir.). Office: PO Box 391 Ashland KY 41114

JUSTICE, RICHARD DOUGLAS, entrepreneur; b. Pikeville, Ky., Apr. 20, 1953; s. Perry Allen and Edna Jean (Gross) J.; m. Shirley Lynn Walker, Aug. 12, 1981; children—Richard Colby, Kerri Ann. Student, Transylvania Coll., 1972-75; B.A., U. Ky., 1972. Lic. funeral dir., Ky. Vice pres. Justice Funeral Home, Inc., Pikeville, 1975—, Justice Monument Sales, Inc., 1975—; pres. Baker Funeral Home, Inc., 1980—; v.p. Johns Creek Funeral Homes, Inc., 1981—; mng. ptnr. Octagon Devel., 1981—; dir. Syndicated Investment Co., Carter Brunning Paint, Appalachian Trading Co., Pikeville Nat. Bank bd. dirs. Pike County Bowl. Mem. Pike County C. of C. (chmn. bd.), Bldg. Owners and Mgrs. Assn., Bldg. Owners and Mgrs. Inst. Internat. Republican. Roman Catholic. Lodge: Kiwanis. Lodge: Masons, Shriner. Address: PO Box 3004 Pikeville KY 41501

JUSTICE, SUSANNE DOROTHY, medical administrator; b. Flushing, N.Y., Aug. 28, 1942; d. Edward H. and Dorothy E. (Scholl) Lane; m. Marion T. Justice, Feb. 17, 1962 (dec. Apr. 1980); children—Edward P., Jennifer L. Diploma Jackson Meml. Hosp. Sch. Nursing, 1963. R.N., Fla. Group nurse Mt. Sinai Hosp., Miami Beach, Fla., 1963-66, part-time group nurse, 1967-72; head nurse Jackson Meml. Hosp., Miami, Fla., 1966-67; hosp. coordinator to head coordinator Fla. Home Health Services, Miami, 1972-73; hosp. coordinator to assoc. dir. nursing Unicare, Inc., Miami, 1973-75; pres., adminstr. Medi-Health Fla., Inc., Ft. Lauderdale, 1975—; cons. home health care. Mem. Am. Pub. Health Assn., Nat. League Nursing, Nat. Assn. Home Care (dir. 1982), Nat. Assn. Home Health Agys. (dir. 1980-82), Fla. Assn. Home Health Agys. (dir. 1978-84, chairperson quality assurance com. 1980-83, v.p. 1982-83, pres. 1983-84, M.T. —Terry— Justice Meml. award 1980), Am. Acad. Med. Adminstrs. (sec.-treas. Fla. chpt. 1983-84), So. Fla. In Home Services Consortium (pres. 1981-83). Author: Quality Assurance Book, 1978; mem. editorial adv. bd. Caring mag., 1983; copyrighter Problem Oriented Rec. for Home Health Agys. Home: 465 NE 157th Terrace North Miami Beach FL 33162 Office: Medi-Health Fla Inc 3500 N State Rd 7 Suite 100 Fort Lauderdale FL 33319

JUSTICE, WILLIAM WAYNE, judge; b. Athens, Tex., Feb. 25, 1920; s. William Davis and Jackie May (Hanson) J.; LL.B., U. Tex., 1942; m. Sue Tom Ellen Rowan, Mar. 16, 1947; 1 dau., Ellen Rowan. Admitted to Tex. bar; partner firm Justice & Justice, Athens, 1946-61; city atty. Athens, 1948-50, 52-58; U.S. atty. Eastern Dist. Tex., 1961-68; U.S. dist. judge Eastern Dist. Tex., Tyler, 1968—, now chief judge. Vice pres. Young Democrats Tex., 1948; adv. council Dem. Nat. Com., 1954; alternate del. Dem. Nat. Conv., 1956; presdl. elector, 1960. Served to 1st lt. F.A., AUS, 1942-46; CBI. Mem. Am. Judicature Soc., VFW (past post comdr.). Baptist. Rotarian (pres. Athens 1961), Mason (K.T.). Office: Fed Bldg Tyler TX 75701*

JUSTINIANI, FEDERICO ROBERTO, physician; b. Havana, Cuba, Aug. 15, 1929; came to U.S., 1964, naturalized, 1969; s. Federico Luis and Margarita (Longa) J.; B.S., De La Salle Coll., Havana, 1947; M.D., Havana U., 1954; m. Maria Sarez, Nov. 29, 1955. Intern, resident in internal medicine Havana U. Hosp., 1955-61; practice medicine, Havana, 1961-64; intern St. Francis Hosp., Miami Beach, Fla., 1965; resident in internal medicine Mt. Sinai Hosp., Miami Beach, 1966-69, program coordinator residency in internal medicine, 1969-74; dir. med. edn. Mt. Sinai Med. Center, Miami Beach, 1974—; instr. medicine U. Miami, 1969-72, asst. prof., 1972-82, assoc. prof., 1982—. Diplomate Am. Bd. Internal Medicine. Fellow ACP; mem. AMA (Physicians' Recognition award 1969, 72, 76, 79, 82, 85), Fla., So., Dade County med. assns., Am. Soc. Internal Medicine, Am. Geriatrics Soc., Assn. Hosp. Med. Edn., Royal Soc. Medicine, Alliance for Continuing Med. Edn., Assn. Program Dirs. in Internal Medicine, Cuban Med. Assn. in Exile. Contbr. articles to profl. jours. Home: 9633 S W 11th Terr Miami FL 33174 Office: 4300 Alton Rd Miami Beach FL 33140

JUZWIK, THOMAS GREGORY, construction company executive; b. Charleston, W.Va., June 25, 1952; s. Stanley Francis and Julia Ann (Poindexter) J.; children—Stacey Lynn, Jamie Ryan. Student in Pre-Pharmacy, W.Va. State Coll., 1970-72. Mgr., supr. spl. projects Rite Aid Corp., Harrisburg, Pa., 1967-77; sales engr. Upton Constrn., Leon, W.Va., 1977-80; br. mgr., ptnr. Custom Facilities, Ind., 1980-82; pres., owner Consol. Constrn. Services, Inc., Nitro, W.Va., 1982—. Mem. Putnam County C. of C., W.Va. Contractors Assn. Republican. Methodist. Lodge: Moose. Avocation: golfing.

KAAKE, NORMAN BRADFORD, business executive, logistics specialist; b. Upper Darby, Pa., July 5, 1954; s. Norman Howard and Marjorie (Thurlow) K.; m. Kathy May Alexander, Dec. 27, 1983. B.A. in Polit. Sci., U. Maine, 1976. Restaurant mgr. That Seafood Place, Virginia Beach, Va., 1981; import/boarding mgr. Containership Agy., Inc., Norfolk, Va., 1982-84, equipment mgr., 1984—. Com. mem. Hampton Roads Steamship Trade Com., Norfolk, 1982—. Served to capt. U.S. Army, 1976-80. Mem. Hampton Roads Traffic Club. Republican. Avocations: antique collecting and refinishing; camping; downhill skiing; photography; reading. Office: Containership Agy Inc 7737 Hampton Blvd Norfolk VA 23505

KABACK, DAWN SAMARA, oil company researcher; b. Middletown, N.Y., Oct. 25, 1948; d. Erwin Rice and Genevieve Eleanor (Goldsmith) Kaback; m. Robert Eric Barnett, Jan. 1, 1985. B.S., SUNY-Stony Brook, 1970; M.S., U. Colo.-Boulder, 1972, Ph.D., 1977. Research scientist Conoco Inc., Ponca City, Okla., 1977-80, sr. research geochemist, 1980—. Author numerous tech. papers. N.Y. State Regents scholar, 1966-70; NSF grantee, 1973-76. Mem. Am. Assn. Petroleum Geologists, Soc. Econ. Paleontologists and Mineralogists, Indian Nations Sailing Assn. Avocations: sailing, swimming, skiing, aerobics, cooking. Home: 102 Roadrunner Ponca City OK 74604 Office: Conoco Inc PO Box 1267 Ponca City OK 74603

KADABA, PRASANNA VENKATARAMA, mechanical engineering educator; b. Gundlupet, Karnataka, India, July 4, 1931; s. K.V. Iyengar and K.V. Sharadamma; m. Usha Rani Rajgopal, Nov. 14, 1966; 1 son, Vaibhav. B.S. in Mech. Engring., U. Mysore (India), 1952, B.S. in Elec. Engring., 1954; M.S. in Mech. Engring., U. Ky., 1956; Ph.D. in Mech. Engring., Ill. Inst. Tech., 1964. With Borg-Warner R&D Ctr., Des-Plaines, Ill., 1963-67, Westinghouse R&D Ctr., Pitts., 1967-69; assoc. prof. mech. engring. Ga. Inst. Tech., Atlanta, 1969—; vis. prof. U. Carabobo, Valencia, Venezuela; cons. Nat. Bur. Standards, Md., Lawrence Berkeley Lab. (Calif.), NASA-Marshall Space Flight Ctr., Ala., NASA-Lewis Research Ctr., Cleve. Recipient Energy Action Service award Ga. Soc. Profl. Engrs., 1981. Mem. ASME, ASHRAE (Engr. of Yr. in Edn. Atlanta 1977, 80, Appreciation award 1985), Am. Soc. Engring. Edn., Soc. Am. Mil. Engrs., India-Am. Cultural Assn., Internat. Platform Assn., ASTM, Sigma Xi, Tau Beta Pi, Pi Tau Sigma, Vedanta Soc. Contbr. articles to profl. jours. Home: 2756 Carolyn Dr SE Smyrna GA 30080 Office: Sch Mech Engring Ga Inst Tech Atlanta GA 30332

KADANE, GEORGE EDWARD, oil and gas producer; b. Austin, Tex., June 28, 1939; s. Edward George and Hannah (Joseph) K.; m. Louise Fromme, Nov. 27, 1965; children—Edward George II, Matthew Byron. B.S., U. Okla.-Norman, 1961. Exploration geologist G. E. Kadane & Sons, Wichita Falls, Tex., 1962-65, exploration mgr., 1964-73; founder, pres., chief exec. officer Kadane Oil Co., Wichita Falls, 1974—; dir. MBank, Wichita, 1976—, mem. exec. com., 1981—. Bd. dirs. Wichita Falls YMCA, 1967-69, Boys Club of Am., 1982-83. Mem. Ind. Petroleum Assn. Am. (mem. exec. com. 1983—), North Tex. Oil and Gas Assn. (pres. 1980-82), Tex. Ind. Producers and Royalty Owners Assn. (mem. exec. com. 1979-85), Am. Assn. Petroleum Geologists, North Tex. Geol. Soc., Explorers Club. Republican. Roman Catholic. Office: Kadane Oil Co PO Drawer 1740 Wichita Falls TX 76307

KADISH, ALAN SAUL, physician; b. Bronx, N.Y., May 27, 1942; s. Jack and Bella K.; m. Mildred Isabel Diaz, Oct. 18, 1968; 1 son, Victor Manuel. B.S., CCNY, 1963; M.D., Albert Einstein Coll. Medicine, 1967. Diplomate Am. Bd. Internal Medicine. Intern, Lincoln Hosp., Bronx, 1967-68; resident, 1968-71; staff physician West Haven (Conn.) VA Hosp., 1975-77, Brooke Army Med. Ctr., San Antonio, 1977—; clin. instr. Yale U., New Haven, 1975-77. Served to lt. comdr. USN, 1971-73. Home: 6410 Jetty Dr San Antonio TX 78239 Office: Brooke Army Med Center San Antonio TX 78234

KADISH, KARL MITCHELL, chemistry educator; b. Detroit, Feb. 4, 1945; s. Murray Kadish and Jennie Shriman; m. Mary Frevel; children—Lesley Laura. B.S., U. Mich., 1967; Ph.D., Pa. State U., 1970. Vis. asst. prof. U. New Orleans, 1970-71; asst. prof. Calif. State U.-Fullerton, 1972-76; pres. Intersci. Cons. U.S.A., Midland, Mich., 1977—; assoc. prof. chemistry U. Houston, 1978-81, prof., 1981—; vis. prof. Ecole Superieur Chimie Industrielle de Lyon, France, 1984; vis. prof. U. Dijon, France, 1985. Editor: Electrochemical and Spectroelectrochemical Studies of Biological Redox Components, 1983. Contbr. over 150 articles to profl. jours., 1972—. Fulbright vis. lectr.-research scholar, Strasbourg, France, 1980-81. Mem. Am. Chem. Soc., Electrochem. Soc., Internat. Union Pure and Applied Chemistry (mem. Commn V.5), Sigma Xi, Phi Kappa Phi. Office: Dept Chemistry U Houston University Park Houston TX 77004

KADY, MICHAEL STANLEY, diversified manufacturing company executive; b. Ft. Wayne, Ind., June 10, 1949; s. Frank A. and Vera B. (Highley) K.; m. Linda S. McSherry, Jan. 23, 1971; children—Aaron A., Bradley C. B.S.M.E., Purdue U., 1972; M.B.A., Butler U., 1975. Registered profl. engr., Ind. Mfg. engr. chain div. FMC, Indpls., 1972-75, prodn. planning supr., 1975-76, prodn. mgr., 1976-78; planning analyst Cooper Industries, Inc., Houston, 1978-80, controller Portable Rig div., Dallas, 1980-82, dir. fin. Demco div., Oklahoma City, 1982-85; plant mgr. Nicholson/Cooper Steel, Greenville, Miss., 1985—; assoc. faculty mem. Ind. U.-Indpls., 1975-77. Bd. dirs. Greenville United Way. Mem. Greenville Area C. of C. (bd. dirs.), Fin. Execs. Inst. Republican. Roman Catholic. Club: Rotary (Greenville, Miss.). Office: Nicholson/Cooper Steel PO Box 958 Greenville MS 38701

KAESER, JOSEPH MICHAEL, technical consultant; b. Hamilton, Ohio, May 19, 1923; s. John and Hannah Ignatious (Cahalane) K.; student Coll. of Great Falls, 1951-52, U. Ala., 1943, U. Miss., 1952-53; m. Dailey Kathryn Merrill, Nov. 8, 1980; children by previous marriage—Sharon, John, Michael. Commd. 2d lt. USAF, 1943, advanced through grades to capt., 1951; served as sr. pilot, electronics staff officer, U.S. and overseas; separated; 1953; electronic design engr. Hayes Aircraft Corp., Birmingham, Ala., 1953-54; field project mgr. RCA, various locations, 1954-68; dir. field services N. and S. Am., Page Communications Engrs., Washington, 1968-70; program devel. mgr. Raytheon Corp., Burlington, Mass., and Sverdrup/ARO Corp., Washington, 1970-78; dir. internat. programs and market planning Computer Scis. Corp., Falls Church, Va., 1978-83; communications/mktg./mgmt. cons. Decorated Air medal with 2 oak leaf clusters; recipient Engr. of Yr. award Central Fla. sect. Inst. Radio Engrs., 1959. Fellow AIAA (assoc.); mem. IEEE (sr.), Soc. Flight Test Engrs., Internat. Test and Evaluation Assn. Baptist. Home: 912 Seneca Rd Great Falls VA 22066

KAGELER, WOODY VERNON, physician; b. Waco, Tex., June 15, 1945; s. Vernon Awalt and Vivian Marguerite (Wood) K.; m. Nancy Kathleen Bohn, Nov. 26, 1969; children—Brian Daniel, Kathleen Michelle. B.S. cum laude, Tex. Wesleyan Coll., 1967; M.D., U. Tex.-Galveston, 1971. Diplomate Am. Bd. Internal Medicine, Am. Bd. Pulmonary Disease. Intern John Peter Smith Hosp., Ft. Worth, 1971-72, resident, 1972-73, dir. pulmonary medicine, 1978—; resident U. Tex. Med. Sch., Houston, 1973-76; med. dir. respiratory therapy program Tarrant County Jr. Coll., 1980—. Vice-pres. St. Rita's Sch. Bd., Fort Worth, 1982-84, pres., 1984-85. Named Outstanding Clin. Prof., John Peter Smith Hosp. House Staff, 1980, 83. Fellow ACP, Am. Coll. Chest Physicians; mem. AMA, Am. Lung Assn., So. Med. Assn., Nu Sigma Nu, Alpha Chi. Office: 1500 S Main St Fort Worth TX 76104

KAGEN, HERBERT PAUL, chemistry educator, consultant, researcher; b. Worcester, Mass., May 6, 1929; s. Samuel Friedman and Sophie (Flax) K.; m. Pearl Sue Fellander, Dec. 30, 1956; children—Bradley, Beth, Michael, Ruth. S.B., MIT, 1952; M.S., U. R.I., 1954; Ph.D., Wayne State U., 1960. Research chemist MIT, Cambridge, summers 1951-53; spl. instr. chemistry Wayne State U., Detroit, 1962; assoc. prof. chemistry Detroit Inst. Tech., 1957-67; chmn. chemistry dept. W.Va. State Coll., Institute, 1967-73, dir. chem. tech., 1975—, prof. chemistry, 1967—; cons. various indsl. firms, 1960—. Author: Blood Platelets, 1962; Experiments in General Chemistry, 1965; Chemistry for Office Service Personnel, 1977. Precinct del. Democratic Party, Livonia Mich., 1959-67; mem. sch. bd., Livonia, 1959-67. Recipient various grants and fellowships; named Rear Adm., Cherry River Navy. Mem. Am. Chem. Soc. (nat. councillor 1972—, Outstanding Mem. award Kanawha Valley sect. 1974), AAUP (local officer), Nat. Sci. Tchrs. Assn., Sigma Xi, Phi Lambda Upsilon, Beta Kappa Chi. Jewish. Lodge: Masons. Avocations: philately; history. Home: 235 Sutherland Dr South Charleston WV 25303 Office: WV State Coll Institute WV 25112

KAHL, RICHARD LYN, banker; b. Richmond, Va., Feb. 28, 1953; s. Lloyd Raymond and Martha LaVerne (Pickering) K. B.S., Va. Commonwealth U., 1979. Loan officer So. Bank, Richmond, 1974-79; compliance examiner Fed. Res. Bank, Richmond, 1979-83; compliance officer Bank of Hallandale (Fla.), 1983—. Episcopalian. Office: Bank of Hallandale & Trust Co 801E Beach Blvd Hallandale FL 33009

KAHN, ALBERT MICHAEL, artist, designer; b. Gorky, Russia, July 4, 1917; s. Samson and Bertha (Kashket) K.; came to U.S., 1929, naturalized, 1942; grad. Pratt Inst., 1937, Art Students League, 1938; student U. Mexico, 1946, U. Lima Bellas Artes, 1949; m. Rose Menacer, Dec. 21, 1947 (div. 1970); children—Sharon Beth, Brenda Jo. Art dir. McCann Erickson Advt., 1947; mural painter, Mexico, 1948-50; graphic designer, Washington, 1950, San Francisco, 1951-54, 60-65; instr. San Francisco Art Sch., 1961-65; painter in Central and S.Am., 1955-59, in Europe and Israel, 1966-68; graphic cons. Matson Navigation Co., San Francisco, 1969-70; world painting tour, 1971; painter in Spain, 1972-73; painter, graphic artist Miami, Fla., 1974—; represented in permanent collections in museums in U.S., pvt. collections in U.S., Europe, S.Am., C.Am. Served with C.E., AUS, 1940-45. Decorated C.E. Commendation medal, U.S. Army C.E. Surg. Gen. commendation in graphics; recipient Art Dir.'s medal Washington, 1950, Art Dir.'s awards San Francisco, 1962, 63. Mem. Artists Equity Assn., Internat. Soc. Artists, Art Dir.'s Club of San Francisco, Nat. Soc. Published Poets, Nat. Writers Club, Am. Assn. Travel Editors, Nat. Geog. Soc. Jewish. Author: Requiem, 1970; travel editor Beach and Town mag. contbr. articles to profl. jours. Home: 5 Island Ave Miami Beach FL 33139

KAHN, BRUCE MEYER, lawyer; b. Memphis, Feb. 28, 1952; s. Sidney Louis, Jr. and Maxine March (Meyer) K. B.A., Trinity Coll., 1974; J.D., Tulane U., 1977. Bar: Tenn. 1977. Assoc., Buchignani & Greener, Memphis, 1977-80; ptnr. Goodman, Glazer, Greener, Schneider & McQuiston, Memphis, 1981—; sec.-treas., dir. Paper Products Co., 1984—. Mem. legal com. B'Nai B'Rith Home and Hosp. for Aged, Memphis, 1981-84, Temple Israel Synagogue, 1984—; vol. Memphis in May Internat. Festival, 1984—; chmn. Trinity Coll. Alumni Support Program, 1981-84; v.p. Temple Israel Brotherhood, 1984—. Mem. Memphis and Shelby County Bar Assn., Tenn. Bar Assn., ABA, Tax Watch Group, Greater Memphis Employee Benefits Council. Jewish. Club: Racquet of Memphis. Home: 4995 Normandy Ln Memphis TN 38117 Office: Goodman Glazer Greener Schneider & McQuiston 1500 First Tenn Bldg Memphis TN 38103

KAHN, CARI BETH, clinical psychologist; b. Chgo., Mar. 2, 1953; d. Harry S. and Doris (Silver) Kahn; B.A., U. Tex., Austin, 1974; Psy.D., Baylor U., 1978. Psychology resident U. Tex. Med. Br., Galveston, 1977-78; psychologist Girlstown U.S.A., Austin, Tex., 1980-82; pvt. practice clin. psychology, Austin, 1979—. Vol. counselor Rape Crisis Center; mem. adv. bd. Center Battered Women, 1980-82; bd. dirs. chpt. Am. Cancer Soc., 1981-82; mem. citizens adv. com. Travis County Juvenile Ct. Mem. Am. Soc. Clin. Hypnosis, Tex. Psychol. Assn., Am. Psychol. Assn., Am. Orthopsychiatry Assn., Phi Beta Kappa, Phi Kappa Phi. Office: 605 Baylor Austin TX 78703

KAHN, ELLIS IRVIN, lawyer; b. Charleston, S.C., Jan. 18, 1936; s. Robert and Estelle (Kaminski) K.; A.B., The Citadel, 1958; J.D., U. S.C., 1961; postgrad. So. Meth. U., 1962-63; m. Janice Weinstein, Aug. 11, 1963; children—Justin, David, Cynthia Anne. Admitted to S.C. bar, 1961, D.C. bar, 1978; law clk. U.S. Dist. Judge Robert W. Hemphill, Columbia, 1964-66; with firm Solomon, Kahn, Smith & Baumil, Charleston, 1966—. Mem. nat. council Am. Israel Pub. Affairs Com., 1982—. Served to capt. USAF, 1961-64. Diplomate Am. Bd. Profl. Liability Attys. Mem. ABA, S.C. State Bar, Internat. Soc. Barristers (diplomate), Nat. Bd. Trial Attys. (civil trial advocate), Am. (state committeeman 1970-74), S.C. (pres. 1976-77) trial lawyers assns., Phi Delta Phi (chpt. pres. 1960). Democrat. Jewish. Lodge: B'nai B'rith (pres. 1968-71). Editor The Brigadier, 1957-58. Home: 316 Confederate Circle Charleston SC 29407 Office: 39 Broad St Charleston SC 29402

KAHN, GORDON BARRY, judge; b. Mobile, Ala., Dec. 3, 1931; s. Al and Molly (Prince) K.; B.S., U. Ala., 1953, LL.B., 1958; LL.M., NYU, 1959; postgrad. U. London, 1957—; 1 son, Andrew Fortier. Bar: Ala. 1958. Practice in Mobile, 1959; mem. firm Lyons, Pipes & Cook, 1959-74; bankruptcy judge U.S. Dist. Ct. So. Ala., 1974—. Chmn. Mobile United Jewish Appeal, 1963-64; pres. Friends of Mobile Pub. Library; pres. Jewish Community Center of Mobile, 1974. Trustee Mobile Pub. Library, 1973-74; bd. dirs. Salvation Army Mobile, 1973-74, B'nai B'rith Home for Aged, Memphis, 1973-74. Served to 1st lt. U.S. Army, 1953-55. Mem. Ala., Mobile County bar assns. Jewish. Club: Athelstan. Lodge: Masons. Home: 230 S McGregor Ave Mobile AL 36608 Office: 314 US Courthouse Mobile AL 36602

KAHN, SIDNEY LAWRENCE, III, developer; b. Memphis, Aug. 13, 1946; s. Sidney L. and Maxine (Meyer) K.; B.A., Amherst Coll., 1968; M.B.A., Harvard Bus. Sch., 1972; m. Susan A. Merklas, Dec. 22, 1968; children—Susan Lani, Sidney Lowell, Sarah Lauren. Project mgr. U.S. Home Corp., Naples, Fla., 1972-73; exec. v.p. Planned Devel. Corp., Miami, Fla., 1974—; pres. Kahn-McKnight Co., Inc., Miami, 1976—, Lani's Shops, Inc.; v.p., dir. Brickell Assn., 1978—; dir., chmn. long range planning com., mem. investment com. Fla. Internat. Bank; mem. investment com., dir. South Fla., Inc. Adv. bd. Opportunities Industrialization Council, Miami, 1980-81; bd. dirs. Baptist Hosp. Found. Served to lt. USN, 1968-70. Lic. gen. contractor, Fla.; registered real estate broker, Fla. Mem. S. Dade C. of C. (pres. 1980-81), Greater Miami C. of C. (chmn. new bus. promotion task force), Builders Assn. S. Fla. (dir., chmn. Dade legis. com., exec. com.). Democrat. Clubs: Rotary (pres. 1978), Harvard Bus. Sch. (dir. 1980-81). Office: 1440 Brickell Ave Miami FL 33131

KAISER, CHARLES FREDERICK, psychologist, educator; b. N.Y.C., Dec. 30, 1942; s. Alexander and Etta K.; m. Judith Hammelburger, Aug. 21, 1966; children—Edward, Michael. B.S., CCNY, 1964, M.A., 1967; Ph.D., U. Houston, 1973. Asst. prof. Coll. Charleston, S.C., 1972-77, assoc. prof., 1977—; adj. prof. Med. U. S.C., 1981—. Contbr. articles to profl. jours. Bd. dirs. Mental Health Assn. Charleston Area, 1973-82, S.C. Lung Assn., 1975-83. Recipient award S.C. Lung Assn., 1977. Mem. Charleston Area Psychol. Assn. (pres. 1979), S.C. Psychol. Assn. (treas. 1979-81), Biofeedback Assn. S.C. (pres. 1981-84, sec. 1985), Biofeedback Soc. Am. (com. 1983-84), Southeastern Psychol. Assn. Avocation: softball. Office: Coll Charleston Psychology Dept Charleston SC 29424

KAISER, ELAINE JULIANN, communications executive; b. Miami, Feb. 12, 1949; d. Edward Joseph and Mary Jeannette (Foote) K. B.A., U. Ga., 1971. Adminstrv. asst. City of Miami Dept. Publicity and Tourism, 1968-69; assoc. dir. United Meth. Communications, Atlanta, 1971-73; pub. relations asst. Calhoun-Carroll Communications, Atlanta, 1973; sr. writer, press relations coordinator Blue Cross/Blue Shield, Atlanta, 1973-79, dir. pub. relations ARC, Atlanta, 1979-83; communications mgr. Provident Life & Accident Ins. Co., Chattanooga, 1983-84, communications dir., 1984—. Mem. campaign mktg. task force, mem. communications ops. com. United Way Met. Atlanta, 1979-83; mem. adv. council WXIA-TV, Atlanta, 1981-83. Recipient Good Guy award Ga. Bus. and Industry Assn., 1981. Mem. Am. Mktg. Assn., Internat. Assn. Bus. Communicators, Assn. Multi-Image, Pub. Relations Soc. Am. (pres. Ga. chpt. 1984),), Women in Communications, Inc. (leadership award Bernice McCullar chpt. 1982, pres. Ga. chpt. 1981-82, regional v.p. 1981-83, nat. v.p. programs 1983-85), Women's C. of C. of Atlanta (govt. affairs com. 1981, publicity com. 1980). Democrat. Roman Catholic. Home: 3131 Mountain Creek Rd Apt 14A-3 Chattanooga TN 37415 Office: Provident Life & Accident Ins Co Fountain Square Chattanooga TN 37402

KAISER, FRANK WILLIAM, III, oil company executive; b. Des Moines, June 16, 1944; s. Frank William, II and Barbara Ann (Smith) K.; B.A., U. Iowa, 1967; M.A., So. Ill. U., 1969; postgrad. Eastern Mich. U.; m. Joyce Ann Sayre, May 10, 1969; children—Kimberly Ann, Sean Stratton, Nicole Caroline. With Ford Motor Corp., Dearborn, Mich., 1971-75, labor relations mgr. gen. products group, 1973-75; adv. planning and devel. corp. staff Gulf Oil Corp., Pitts., 1976-80; dir. tng. and devel. Gulf Oil Chems. Co., Houston, 1980-82; employee relations exec. Tenneco Oil Co., Houston, 1983—. Served with USAR, 1969-71. Mem. Am. Soc. Personnel Adminstrn., Human Resources Planning Soc., Am. Soc. Tng. and Devel., Black Profls. Houston (dir. 1981—). Republican. Roman Catholic. Home: 15607 Winding Moss Dr Houston TX 77068 Office: PO Box 3766 Houston TX 77001

KAISER, ROBERT LEE, engineer; b. Louisville, June 28, 1935; s. Harlan K. and LaVerne (Peterson) K.; student U. Louisville, 1953-54, U. Ky., 1958-61; m. Margaret Siler; children—Robin Lee, Robert Lee. Draftsman, deisgner E.R. Ronald & Assos., Louisville, 1953-54, Thompson-Kissell Co., 1954-56; estimator, engr. George Pridemore & Son, Lexington, Ky., 1956-58; designer, engr., supr. Frankel & Curtis, Lexington, 1958-61; engr. Hugh Dillehay & Assos., 1961-65; owner, engr., operator K-Service, Inc., 1965-74; project engr. Mason & Hanger, Silas Mason Co., Inc., 1974-77; v.p. Webb-Dillehay Design Group, 1977-81; pres. Kaiser-Taulbee Assos., Inc., energy mgmt. cons., Lexington, 1981—; chmn., pres. Opportunity Workshop Lexington; vis. lectr. mech. engring. and Coll. Architecture, U. Ky. Mem. charter commn. merger Lexington-Fayette County govts.; mem. Gov.'s Task Force on Ednl. Constrn. Criteria, bd. dirs. chpt. Am. Cancer Soc. Registered profl. engr., Fla., Ind., Ky., N.Mex., Ariz., Ill. Mem. ASME, Nat., Ky. socs. profl. engrs., Lexington C. of C., ASHRAE (pres.-elect local chpt.), Assn. Energy Engrs. (pres. local chpt.). Episcopalian. Club: Rotary. Home: 401 Culpepper Rd Lexington KY 40502 Office: PO Box 480 Lexington KY 40585

KAISERMAN, NANCY JEANNE, nurse; b. Utica, N.Y., Mar. 28, 1944; d. Kenneth and Edna G. (Buck) Beagle; m. Maruice Kaiserman, Nov. 21, 1979. Diploma, A. Barton Hepburn Hosp.; student St. Edwards U., 1981—. R.N., N.Y., Fla., Tex. Charge nurse Oswego Hosp., N.Y., 1965-67; clinic nurse North Dade Clinic, Opalocka, Fla., 1967-69, supr., 1969-74; pvt. duty nurse Catalanos Registry, Miami, Fla., 1974-79; regional supr. Girling Health Care, Inc., Austin, 1980—. Recipient St. Lawrence County Scholastic award, 1962; St. Edwards U. scholar, 1983. Mem. Tex. Assn. Home Health Agencies (licensure and cert. com., nominating com.). Democrat. Episcopalian. Home: 1802 Lightfoot Round Rock TX 78664 Office: Girling Health Care Inc 4902 Grover St Austin TX 78765

KALAJIAN, JOHN LEO, city councilman, real estate investment company executive; b. Tubingen, Germany, Oct. 14, 1945; s. Paul Nubar and Araxi (Pashaian) K.; children—Jill, Matthew. Student Northeastern U., U. Fla. Staff anesthetist Venice Hosp., Venice, Fla., 1974-81; pres. D'J's Paper Clip, Inc., Venice, 1982-83; v.p. The Loveland Center, Venice, Fla., 1983-84, pres., 1984-85, dir., 1982—; v.p. Exceptional Industries, Venice, 1981-82. City councilman, Venice, 1978—, vice mayor, 1981; chmn. intergovtl. relations com. Fla. League Cities, Tallahassee, 1982-84; mem. exec. com. Sarasota County Republicans, 1979—. Served with USN, 1966-68. Mem. Pleasant Places Fla. Club: Sertoma (dir. 1983-84, pres.). Office: Combined Capital Corp 2100 S Tamiami Trail Venice FL 33595 also City of Venice 401 W Venice Ave Venice FL 33595

KALASHIAN, SUSAN WELLING, psychotherapist; b. Springfield, Ohio, Jan. 27, 1933; d. Clark Gardner and Ruth Amelia (Servis) Welling; m. William Buel, Sept. 14, 1957 (div. 1973); children—Stephen, Eric, Douglas; m. David Kalashian, Aug. 12, 1973. Student Miami U., Oxford, Ohio, 1951-54, Ohio State U., 1955-56, Northwestern U., 1962-63; B.A., U. South Fla., 1973; M.A., Goddard Coll., Plainfield, Vt., 1978; Ph.D., Internat. Coll., Los Angeles, 1980. Lic. marriage and family therapist, Fla. Psychometrist Hills Community Coll., Tampa, Fla., 1973-75; counselor Suicide-Crisis Ctr., Tampa, 1976-77; pvt. practice therapy, Tampa, 1978-79; sr. assoc. Kalashian & Assocs., Tampa, 1979-84; dir. East Tampa Ctr. Individual and Family Therapy, 1984—; bd. dirs. Forrest Terrace Home Health Agy., Tampa, 1982—, dir. family violence diversion program, Tampa, 1984—. Author: Before Divorce, 1985. Recipient cert. of appreciation Tampa Suicide Crisis Ctr., 1980. Mem. Am. Assn. for Counseling and Devel., Fla. Assn. for Counseling and Devel., Tampa Mental Health Assn. Avocations: writing; music; painting; physical activities; decorating. Office: East Tampa Ctr Individual and Family Therapy Lozano Bldg Suite 119 21st St at 4th St Tampa FL 33605

KALBFLEISCH, JOHN MCDOWELL, physician; b. Lawton, Okla., Nov. 15, 1930; s. George B. and Etta Lillian (McDowell) K.; Asso. Sci., Cameron A&M Coll., 1950; B.S., U. Okla., 1952, M.D., 1957; m. Jolie Harper, Dec. 29, 1961. Diplomate Am. Bd. Internal Medicine (Cardiovascular disease bd.). Intern, U. Va. Hosp., Charlottesville, 1957-58, fellow, 1961-62, NIH trainee in cardiovascular disease, 1964-65; resident VA Hosp. and U. Okla. Hosp., Oklahoma City, 1958-61; chief resident U. W.Va. Med. Center, Morgantown, 1960-61; practice medicine specializing in cardiology, Tulsa, 1969—; instr. medicine U. Okla. Med. Center, 1964-66, asst. prof. medicine, 1966-69, clin. asst. prof. medicine Tulsa br., 1969-72, clin. assoc. prof., 1972-78, clin. prof., 1978—; dir. cardiovascular services St. Francis Hosp., 1975—; mem. City of Tulsa Physician's Adv. Bd., 1979-82. Contbr. articles on cardiology to med. jours. Served with USPHS, 1962-64. Fellow A.C.P., Am. Coll. Cardiology (gov. Okla. 1978-81), Assn. Am. Med. Colls., Council on Clin. Cardiology, Am. Heart Assn.; mem. Okla. Heart Assn. (v.p. 1975-76), Okla. Cardiac Soc. (pres. 1976), Tulsa County Heart Assn. (dir. 1975-79, pres. 1974), Am. Fedn. Clin. Research, Am. Inst. Nutrition, Tulsa County Med. Soc., AMA, AAAS, Am. Soc. Internal Medicine, Okla. Soc. Internal Medicine (pres. 1985—), Tulsa Internists Soc. Republican. Presbyterian. Office: 6565 S Yale St Suite 310 Tulsa OK 74136

KALDOR, MICHAEL, geology educator; b. N.Y.C., Feb. 25, 1947; s. Leon and Helen (Kronick) K.; m. Kay Ellen Miller, June 30, 1972; children—Jonathan, Lindsay. B.S., Tulane U., 1967; M.A., SUNY-Buffalo, 1969; postgrad. Fla. State U., 1969-70. Grad. teaching asst. SUNY-Buffalo, 1967-69; NSF fellow Fla. State U., Tallahassee, 1969-70; asst. prof. geology Stetson U., Deland, Fla., 1970-71; sci. tchr. Everglades Sch. for Girls, Miami, Fla., 1972-75; assoc. prof. geology Miami Dade Community Coll., Miami, 1975—, chmn. dept. natural scis., 1978—; research geologist S.C. State Devel. Bd., Columbia, 1968. Mem. Am. Geol. Inst., Soc. Coll. Sci. Tchrs., Miami Geol. Soc., Nat. Sci. Tchrs. Assn., Nat. Assn. Geology Tchrs. Home: 12930 SW 116th Rd Miami FL 33186 Office: Miami Dade Community Coll 300 NE 2d Ave Miami FL 33132

KALDY, PATRICIA MARIE, physician; b. New Brunswick, N.J., Feb. 4, 1954; d. Alexander William and Ruthann (Bannier) K.; m. James Ely Taylor, Oct. 24, 1981. B.S. in Biology, B.A. in Math. summa cum laude, Lenoir Rhyne Coll., 1976; M.D., Bowman Gray Sch. Medicine, 1980. Fellow Am. Bd. Family Practice. Resident in family medicine Pitt County Meml. Hosp., Greenville, N.C., 1980-83; family practice medicine, Mt. Pleasant, N.C., 1983—; mem. staff Cabarrus Meml. Hosp. Recipient Cecilia Willard Sci. medal Lenoir Rhyne Coll., 1976, Fritz Math. medal, 1976, 1st Honor Grad. medal, 1976; Duke Endowment scholar, 1978. Mem. N.C. Med. Soc., AMA, Am. Acad. Family Physicians, Cabarrus County Med. Soc. Lutheran. Home: PO Box 1077 Mount Pleasant NC 28124 Office: PO Box 1058 Mount Pleasant NC 28124

KALE, HERBERT WILLIAM, II, ornithologist, consultant; b. Trenton, N.J., Dec. 24, 1931; s. Samuel Stewart Stryker and Julia Baker (Steward) K.; m. Charlotte Ross Jones, July 29, 1961 (div. Apr. 1982); children—Kathleen Elizabeth, Thomas Arthur, John Steward. B.S., Rutgers U., 1954; M.S., U. Ga.-Athens, 1961, Ph.D., 1964. Teaching and research asst. U. Ga., 1957-64; ornithologist Encephalitis Research Ctr., Tampa, Fla., 1964-66; vertebrate ecologist Fla. Med. Research Lab., Vero Beach, 1966-74; v.p. ornithol. research Fla. Audubon Soc., Maitland, 1974—. Served with U.S. Army, 1954-56, USAR, 1956-62. Recipient Fla. Wildlife Fedn. Gov. Conservation award, 1972; Outstanding Civic Service award Vero Beach Jr. Woman's Club, 1973; Disting. Service award Vero Beach Jaycees, 1974. Mem. Am. Ornithologists Union, Ecol. Soc. Am., Am. Soc. Mammalogists, Cooper Ornithol. Soc., Wilson Ornithol. Soc., Eastern Bird Banding Assn., Fla. Ornithol. Soc., Soc. Wetland Scientists, Fla. Acad. Sci., Colonial Waterbird Group, Fla. Audubon Soc. (named outstanding pres. 1973). Republican. Mem. United Ch. of Christ. Editor: Colonial Waterbirds, 1980—; assoc. editor: The Auk, 1971-84; contbr. articles to profl. jours. Home: 517 Peachtree Rd Apt 1 Orlando FL 32804 Office: 1101 Audubon Way Maitland FL 32751

KALEN, K. E., natural gas company executive; b. 1924. B.S., U. Mo., 1949. With Panhandle Eastern Pipeline Co., Houston, 1949—, asst. supt. compressor div., 1953-56, supt., 1956-60, asst. to v.p. transmission div., 1960-66, mgr. transmission, 1966-68, v.p. transmission, 1968-69, group v.p., 1969-83, pres., chief operating officer, dir., 1983—; group v.p. Panhandle Eastern Corp. Served to lt. USAF, 1943-46. Address: Panhandle Eastern Pipeline Co PO Box 1642 Houston TX 77001*

KALER, LEONARD MARVIN, pharmacist; b. Miami, Fla., Sept. 3, 1928; s. Calvin Harry and Dorothy N. (Atkins) K.; m. Joan Bornstein, May 30, 1957; children—Barry, Jody. A.A. in Humanity, U. Fla., 1950, B.S. in Pharmacy, 1952. Registered pharmacist, Fla., Ga., Tenn., Ky. Pharmacy mgr. Walgreen Drugs, Miami, Fla., 1954-56; owner, pharmacist Med. Arts Drugs, Miami, 1956—; dir. Profl. Devel. Corp., Miami, Assoc. Drugs, Miami; dir., v.p. Fla. Drugs, Miami, 1960-83; organizer, chmn. bd. Orange State Bank, 1982-85, now dir. Leader Boy Scouts Am., Miami, 1970-75, dist. supr., 1972-73; election treas. Fla. State Election, Miami, 1982; bd. dirs. Southeastern Coll. Osteo. Medicine. Served as 1st lt. M.C., U.S. Army, 1952-55. Recipient Silver Beaver award Boy Scouts Am., 1973. Mem. Am. Pharm. Assn., Fla. State Pharm. Assn., Dade County Pharm. Assn., Nat. Assn. Retail Pharmacists., Alpha Zeta Omega, Alpha Epsilon Pi. Democrat. Jewish. Club: Pharmacy (Miami). Avocations: fishing; bowling; bridge. Office: Med Arts Drugs 836 NW 183d St Miami FL 33169

KALIN, GEORGE BRUNO, pathologist, educator; b. Chgo., Feb. 22, 1948; s. Paul Peter and Rosemary (Nelson) K. B.S., U. Ill.-Chgo., 1970. Research asst. Rush-Presby.-St. Luke's Med. Ctr., Chgo., 1971-75; research asst. Northwestern Meml. Hosp., Chgo., 1975-78; instr. pathology, chief technologist E. Tenn. State U., Quillen-Dishner Coll. Medicine, Johnson City, 1978—; lectr. Tenn. Soc. Histotech. Mem. Nat. Soc. Histotech., Appalachian Regional Electron Microscopy Soc., Tenn. Soc. Histotech., Soc. Analytical Cytology, S. Central Flow Cytometry Assn., Sigma Xi. Roman Catholic. Contbr. articles to profl. jours. Home: 3514 Wildflower Ln Johnson City TN 37601 Office: E Tenn State U Quillen-Dishner Coll Medicine Dept Pathology PO Box 19540A Johnson City TN 37614

KALISH, KATHERINE MCAULAY, lawyer; b. Pinehurst, N.C., Aug. 6, 1945; d. Hugh Page and Exie Katherine (Beasley) McAulay; m. David Marcus Kalish, Jr., June 18, 1967; children—David Marcus, Page McAulay. B.A., Agnes Scott Coll., 1966; J.D., Walter F. George Sch. Law, 1979. Bar: Ga. 1979. Elem. sch. tchr. Clayton County, Jonesboro, Ga., 1966-67; in office claims adjuster C.N.A., Atlanta, 1967-68; customer account auditor So. Ry., Atlanta, 1968-69; asst. city atty. Macon, Ga., 1979-81; sole practice, Macon, 1981—. Mem. Career Women's Network of Macon, Temple Beth Israel Sisterhood, Macon; bd. dirs. Ctr. for Continuing Edn. Women, Macon, 1981—, Macon Fire and Police Pension Bd., 1983—. Mem. Macon Bar Assn., Ga. Bar Assn., ABA, YLS Coll. Placement and Forums Com., LWV. Democrat. Home: 4800 Mumford Rd Macon GA 31204 Office: 3110 Ridge Ave Macon GA 31204

KALISZEWSKI, CHARLES STANLEY, clergyman, international evangelist; b. Houston, July 18, 1950; s. Stanley Edward, Jr. and Charlene (Jackson) K.; m. Mary Suzanne Pierce, Jan. 8, 1972; children—Elizabeth Mary, Christopher Nathan. Student South Tex. Jr. Coll., 1969, Phillips U., 1970-71. Ordained to ministry Trinity Christian Ch., 1980, Jesus Hour Ministries, 1982, Full Gospel Evangelistic Assn., 1982. Internat. evangelist, Houston, 1970—; pres., founder Jesus Hour radio programs, Nacogdoches, Tex., 1975-76, Jesus Hour Ministries, Houston, 1982—; ch. cons. Jesus Hour Ministries, Tex., 1970—, Costa Rica, 1983, 84, Mex., Guatemala, 1981-84, Spain, 1984-85, Ghana, 1985. Contbr. religious articles to jours. Avocations: writing; travel; flying. Office: Jesus Hour Ministries 7311 Kite Hill Dr Houston TX 77041

KALLAND, KATHRYN JEAN, bookstore executive; b. Prineville, Oreg., Aug. 29, 1918; d. Charles Dow and Beth (Thomas) Morris; m. Earl Stanley Kalland, Aug. 30, 1936; children—Charles, Eric, Cheryl, Darlene. B.A., Western Bapt. Sem., 1953. Sec., Molly Mayfield Rocky Mountain News, Denver, 1956-64; librarian Denver Pub. Library, 1963-75; owner, mgr. Cape Coral Book & Bible, Fla., Mem. Christian Booksellers Assn., Cape Coral C. of C. Republican. Baptist. Avocation: reading. Home: 5360 Cobalt Ct Cape Coral FL 33904 Office: Cape Coral Book & Bible 1322 Cape Coral Pkwy Cape Coral FL 33904

KALLESTAD, JAMES STUART, lab. exec.; b. Mpls., Jan. 21, 1941; s. Hursel O. and Helen (Dela) K.; A.A. in Psychology, U. Minn., 1965, Asso. Liberal Arts in Chemistry, 1967, cert., 1971; cert. Advanced Mgmt. Research, Inc., 1969, 72, 73, Am. Mgmt. Assn., 1970. Co-founder, part owner Kallestad Labs., Inc., Mpls., 1968—, ops. controller, 1968-69, treas., 1969-70, mktg. mgr., 1970-72, dir. mktg., 1972-73, v.p. mktg., 1973-74, tech. salesman, 1975—; pres. Kallestad Properties, Inc., Miami, Kallestad Charters, Inc., Miami. Served with USMC, 1959-63. Mem. Am. Mktg. Assn., AAAS, Am. Mgmt. Assn., Nat. Contract Mgmt. Assn., U.S. Yacht Racing Union, Biscayne Bay Yacht Racing Assn., Performance Handicap Racing Fleet, Internat. Offshore Racing Assn., Fla. Ocean Racing Assn., So. Ocean Racing Conf. (award). Clubs: Coconut Grove Sailing; St. George Sports and Yacht (Bermuda). Home: 55 Holly Lane Wayzata MN 55447 Office: 1000 Lake Hazeltine Dr Chaska MN 55318

KALLSEN, THEODORE JOHN, emeritus English language educator; b. Jasper, Minn., Mar. 27, 1915; s. Bernhart H. and Irene (Wehrman) K.; B.S., Mankato State Coll., 1936; M.A., U. Iowa, 1940, Ph.D., 1949; m. Marvel J. Stordahl, Aug. 27, 1939; children—Carolyn Irene (Mrs. Harold Pate), Tonya Jo (Mrs. William Vining, Jr.). Various teaching positions, Minn., Mo., Iowa, 1936-49; asst. prof. integrated studies W.Va. U., Morgantown, 1949-55; prof. English, head dept. Stephen F. Austin State U., Nacogdoches, Tex., 1955-65, prof., dean Sch. Liberal Arts, 1965-76, disting. prof. English, 1976-80, emeritus, 1980—; cons. English curriculum pub. schs. Served to lt. (j.g.) USNR, 1944-46. Clubs: Piney Woods Country (past dir. Nacogdoches); East Tex. German-Am. Social (pres. 1974-76). Author: Modern Rhetoric and Usage, 1955; (with D.E. McCoy) Reading and Rhetoric: Order and Idea, 1963; Teachers' Use of Dictating Machines, 1965; Making, 1981; also traditional and concrete poetry, profl. articles. Home: 600 Bostwick Nacogdoches TX 75961

KALMIN, NORMAN DAVID, pathologist; b. Uitenhage, S. Africa, Aug. 28, 1946; came to U.S., 1976, naturalized, 1983; s. Elias and Ettye (Lazarus) K.; m. Jeanette Kaplan, July 4, 1971; children—Justine Rachel, Bruce Terrence. M.B. B.Ch., U. Witwatersrand, Johannesburg, S. Africa, 1971. Diplomate Am. Bd. Pathology. Intern, Johannesburg Gen. Group Hosps., 1972-73, house officer, 1973-74; practice family medicine, Germiston, S.Africa, 1974-75; resident in clin. pathology S.Africa Inst. Med. Research, Johannesburg, 1975-76, Erie County Lab., Buffalo, 1976-79; assoc. med. dir. ARC Blood Services, Atlanta, 1979-83; med. dir. South Tex. Regional Blood Bank, San Antonio, 1983—; asst. clin. prof. dept. pathology Emory U. Sch. Medicine, 1980-83; clin. asst. prof. pathology U. Tex. Health Sci. Ctr., San Antonio, 1983—; clin. assoc. prof. dept. med. tech. Ga. State U., 1983; assoc. prof. clin. hematology dept. med. tech. SUNY-Buffalo, 1976-78. ARC grantee, 1981-82, 83-84. Mem. Am. Assn. Blood Banks (insp. blood banks and transfusion services, 1981—), AMA, Tex. Med. Assn., Bexar County Med. Soc., Am. Soc. Clin. Pathology. Contbr. articles to profl. jours. Home: 114 Mossy Cup W San Antonio TX 78231 Office: Med Dir S Tex Regional Blood Bank 318 McCullough San Antonio TX 78212

KALUPA, FRANK B., educator; b. Princeton, Wis., Oct. 30, 1935; s. Franz B. and Erma Maude (Brewster) K.; B.S. in Philosophy, U. Wis. at Madison, 1969; M.A. in Journalism, U. So. Calif. at Los Angeles, 1971, Ph.D. in Communication, 1979; m. Nancy Elizabeth Pruitt, June 4, 1983; children—Mark Francis, Marni. News writer, editor Calif. and Wis. newspapers, 1960-66; dir. public communications Aerojet-Gen. Corp. Von Karman Ctr., Azusa, Calif., 1966-71; free lance writer-photojournalist, Europe, N. Africa, 1971-72; asst. prof. Sch. Journalism, Bowling Green (Ohio) State U., 1972-73; asst. prof. dept. communications Calif. State U., Fullerton, 1973-79, also head public relations; asso. prof. dept. journalism Iowa State U., 1979-80; asso. prof. journalism U. Ga., 1980-85; prof. communication U. Ala., 1985—, also chmn. dept. advt. and pub. relations. Served with USMC, 1954-57. Mem. Assn. Edn. in Journalism, Public Relations Soc. Am., Internat. Assn. Bus. Communicators, Internat. Communication Assn., Western Social Sci. Assn., Sigma Delta Chi.

KAMIEN, ISADORE ARTHUR, JR., department store executive, lawyer, researcher; b. Memphis, Dec. 11, 1914; s. Isadore Arthur and Rose (Michelson) K.; m. Eva Mintz Goldman, Sept. 14, 1944; children—Augusta Kamien Jacobs, Ian Arthur. A.B. with high honors in Polit. Sci., U. Ill., 1936, LL.B., 1939. Bar: Ill. 1939, Tenn. 1939. Assoc. Canada & Russell Law Firm, Memphis, 1939-40; researcher Anti-Defamation League of B'nai B'rith, Chgo., 1940-42; mgr. Kamien's Dept. Store, Cleveland, Miss., 1946-62, pres., 1962-80, chmn. bd., 1980—; dir. Cleveland Fed. Savs. Bank. Past pres. Adath Israel Congregation; trustee Bolivar County Econ. Devel. Dist., 1964-69; chmn. Cleveland Indsl. Devel. Found., 1966-67; organized, past pres. Cleve. C. of C. Served to 1st lt. U.S. Army, 1942-46. Recipient Bronze Tablet, U. Ill., 1936. Mem. Phi Beta Kappa, Phi Eta Sigma, Phi Kappa Phi. Club: Rotary (past pres.). Home: 1106 Farmer St Cleveland MS 38732 Office: Kamien's Dept Store 126 N Sharpe Ave Cleveland MS 38732

KAMINSKY, LAWRENCE EDWARD, apparel manufacturing executive; b. Fitzgerald, Ga., Nov. 29, 1938; s. Herman Richard and Annie (Cohen) K.; m. Sandra Elizabeth Brown, May 24, 1964 (dec. Aug. 1969); m. 2d, Nan Sherry Landsman, May 8, 1977; children—David, Samantha, Allison, George. B.B.A., Emory U., 1961. Pres., chmn. bd., chief exec. officer H.R. Kaminsky & Sons, Inc., Fitzgerald, Ga., 1961—; exec. v.p. H-K Corp., 1965-70; pres. Fitzgerald Investors, Inc., 1965-85; dir. Bank of Fitzgerald, Colony Bancorp. Mem. adv. staff to mayor of Fitzgerald, 1971—; mem. adv. council Ga. 8th Congl. Dist., 1976-82; chmn. Fitzgerald/Ben Hill County chpt. ARC 1978-79; bd. dirs. Alapaha area council Boy Scouts Am.; active Carter Inaugural Com., 1976, presdl. campaign, 1976, Bo Ginn for gov. campaign steering com., Ga.; pres. Fitzgerald Hebrew Congregation, 1972-73. Served with Air N.G., 1961-65. Recipient cert. of appreciation Ga. div. adv. council ARC, 1978-79. Mem. Fitzgerald C. of C. Democrat. Clubs: Standard (Atlanta); Spring Hill Country (Tifton); Lodges: Rotary, Elks. Home: Route 4 PO Box 501 Tifton GA 31794 Office: N Dixie Hwy Fitzgerald GA 31750

KAMMAN, WILLIAM, historian, educator; b. Geneva, Ind., Mar. 23, 1930; s. Harry August and Ruth Lois (Shoemaker) K.; A.B., Ind. U., 1952, Ph.D., 1962; M.A. (H. Bulkley scholar), Yale U., 1958; m. Nancy Ellen Prichard, Apr. 19, 1957; children—Frederick William, Elizabeth Ellen, David Paul. Tchr. pub. schs., Bloomington, Ind., 1955-57, 58-59; asst. prof. history North Tex. State U., 1962-66, assoc. prof., 1966-69, prof., 1969—, chmn. dept. history, 1977—. Mem. Denton (Tex.) Planning and Zoning Commn., 1976-79. Served with U.S. Army, 1952-54. Mem. Am. Hist. Assn., Orgn. Am. Historians, Soc. Historians Am. Fgn. Relations (exec. sec.-treas.), Phi Alpha Theta. Methodist. Author: A Search for Stability: United States Diplomacy Toward Nicaragua, 1925-1933, 1968; contbg. author: Makers of American Diplomacy, 1974, Ency. American Foreign Policy, 1978; Guide to American Foreign Relations Since 1700, 1983. Home: 2225 Scripture St Denton TX 76201 Office: History Dept North Tex State U Denton TX 76203

KAMMERER, OTTO WERNER, heavy machinery company executive; b. Mannheim, West Germany, Feb. 13, 1931; came to U.S., 1962; s. Otto and Rosa (Michel) K.; m. Mary Lou Riffel, Feb. 19, 1962. Mech. Engr., U. Tuebingen, 1953. Service technician Taeger Machinery Corp., Germany, 1953-57; service cons. SCM, Toronto, 1958-62; project mgr. DeBeers-Durban-South Africa, 1963-65; chief exec. Pilcco, Inc., Houston, 1966—. Bd. dirs. Muscular Dystrophy Assn.; mem. internat. com. Houston Livestock Show and Rodeo Assn. Republican. Roman Catholic. Clubs: Petroleum, Warwick, 100 (Houston). Patentee in field. Home: 503 Greenpark Dr Houston TX 77079 Office: 1111 Berry Rd Houston TX 77022 also PO Box 16099 Houston TX 77222

KAMPF, PAUL BERNARD, life insurance executive; b. N.Y.C., Aug. 19, 1920; s. Murray S. and Lillian G. Kampf; B.S., Davis and Elkins (W.Va.) Coll., 1942; M.S., Ind. U., 1948; postgrad. U. Mich.; m. Nan H. Haight, Aug. 26, 1951; children—Pamela Diane, Martha Nan, Paula Jo, Ward A. Football coach Kans. State U., Bradley U., Peoria, Ill., U. N.D., also Winnipeg (Can.) Blue Bombers profl. team, 1950-51; engaged in life ins. bus., 1951—; propr. Kampf Agy., Oklahoma City, 1961—, also pres. Bd. dirs. Oklahoma City Libraries, 1965; vestryman All Souls Episcopal Ch., Oklahoma City, 1975; pres. Brotherhood St. Andrews, 1977. Served with USMCR, 1942-45; PTO. Recipient Alumni award Davis and Elkins Coll., 1982. Charter mem. Soc. Underwriting Brokers Am. (past pres.), Risk Appraisal Forum; mem. Nat. Assn. Life Underwriters, Oklahoma City Life Underwriters Assn. (past dir.), Gen. Agts. and Mgrs. Club Oklahoma City. Republican. Clubs: Quail Creek Golf and Country, Petroleum, Beacon (Oklahoma City). Author articles; editor-pub. newsletter The Vital Margin, 1973—; contbr. articles to ins. jours. Address: Kampf Agy 601 Cravens Bldg Oklahoma City OK 73102

KAMPRATH, EUGENE JOHN, soil science educator; b. Seward, Nebr., Jan. 9, 1926; s. John Fred and Meta Katherine (Meyer) K.; m. Katherine Adair Arnold, Aug. 18, 1956; children—Sara, John. B.S. in Agronomy, U. Nebr., 1950, M.S. in Agronomy, 1952; Ph.D. in Agronomy, N.C. State U., 1955. Asst. prof. soil sci. N.C. State U., Raleigh, 1955-57, assoc. prof., 1958-63, prof., 1963-81, William Neal Reynolds prof. soil sci., 1981—; dir. soil testing div. N.C. Dept. Agr., 1958-63. Contbr. numerous articles on soil sci. to profl. jours. Fellow Am. Soc. Agronomy, Soil Sci. Soc. Am.; mem. Sigma Xi, Alpha Zeta, Gamma Sigma Delta. Democrat. Lutheran. Home: 101 Merwin Rd Raleigh NC 27606 Office: 3208 Williams Hall Dept Soil Sci NC State U Raleigh NC 27695

KAMPS, CAROLYN KAY, medical equipment executive; b. Pryor, Okla., Aug. 28, 1944; d. Cleburn Don and Carol Irene (Bavinger) McElroy; m. Dec. 22, 1970 (div.). B.A., Northeastern U., 1966; postgrad. Calif. State U.-Northridge, 1978. Tchr., counselor pub. schs., Manteca and Carmel, Calif., Los Angeles, 1966-78; artist, gallery owner The Co-op, Carmel, Calif., 1975-76; with Community Home Health Care Inc., Wagoner, Okla., 1980—; owner, corp. sec. Med. Rehab. Ctr., Inc., Wagoner, 1979—; cons. D.M.E. Hosps., Pvt. Orgns., Okla., N.Mex., 1983. Mem. panel State Medicare Senate Ad Hoc Com., Oklahoma City, 1982; speaker Community Action Resource Group, Tahlequah, Okla., 1981-82. State of Okla., Eastern Okla. Devel. Dist., grantee, 1982-83. Mem. Am. Quarter Horse Assn., Okla. Quarter Horse Assn., Nat. Cutting Horse Assn. Democrat. Baptist. Author, editor: How to Set Up a D.M.E. Business, 1982-83. Home: C Bar K Ranch Rural Route 2 PO Box 247 Wagoner OK 74467

KANAK, MARK THOMAS, marketing and advertising consultant; b. Hopewell, Va., Feb. 18, 1952; s. Marvin Cox and Elsie Ruth (Keener) K.; m. Gayle Martha Fraser, Feb. 27, 1982. B.A., Pfeiffer Coll., 1974. Sales service rep. NBC TV, N.Y.C., 1975-77; account exec. McDonald & Little, Advt., Jacksonville, Fla., 1977-78; mgr. mktg. Long John Silver's Orlando, Fla., 1979-81; dir. advt. Promotion Services, Inc., Atlanta, 1982-84; mktg. cons. WFYV-FM, 1985—. Republican. Methodist. Home: 3001 Cadiz Ave Jacksonville FL 32217 Office: 9090 Hogan Rd Jacksonville FL 32216

KANDIL, OSAMA ABD EL MOHSIN, engineering educator; b. Cairo, Oct. 25, 1944; came to U.S., 1971, naturalized, 1977; s. Abd El Mohsin and Attiat El-Sayed (El-Shazli) K.; B.S. in Mech. Engring., Cairo U., 1966; M.S. in Mech. Engring., Villanova U., 1972; Ph.D. in Engring. Mechanics, Va. Poly. Inst., 1974; m. Rawia Ahmed Fouad, Oct. 20, 1968; children—Dalya O., Tarek O. Instr. mech. engring. dept. Cairo U., 1966-70; grad. teaching asst. mech. engring. dept. Villanova (Pa.) U., 1971-72; grad. research asst. engring. sci. and mechanics dept. Va. Poly. Inst., Blacksburg, 1972-74, asst. prof. engring. sci. and mechanics dept., 1975-78; asso. prof. mech. engring. and mechanics dept. Old Dominion U., Norfolk, Va., 1978—; vis. prof. King Saud U., Riyadh, Saudi Arabia, 1983-84. NASA grantee, 1975-83, U.S. Army Research Office grantee, 1975-78, Naval Air Devel. Center grantee, 1980-81; NASA-Am. Soc. Engring. Edn. fellow, 1978-79. Mem. AIAA (tech. com. fluid dynamics), AAUP, Am. Acad. Mechanics, Am. Soc. Engring. Edn., Soc. Engring. Scis., Va. Acad. Scis., Sigma Xi, Phi Kappa Phi. Moslem. Contbr. articles to profl. jours. Home: 7212 Midfield St Norfolk VA 23505 Office: Mech Engring and Mechanics Dept Old Dominion U Norfolk VA 23508

KANDRUT, PHILIP STANLEY, configuration management engineer; b. Lawrence, Mass., Feb. 18, 1950; s. Stanley John and Gladys Mary (Rudis) K.; m. Patrice Lillian Dobson, Nov. 4, 1972; 1 child, Philip Edward. A. Acctg., Andover Jr. Coll., 1969; A.Computer Sci., Newburg Jr. Coll., 1971. Configuration mgmt. engr. Raytheon, Inc., West Andover, Mass., 1972-80, Northrop, Rosslyn, Va., 1980-82, Advanced Tech., Arlington, Va., 1982-83, Inter Systems, Annandale, Va., 1983-84, ROH, Inc., Arlington, 1984—. State of Mass. ednl. grantee, 1971. Mem. Callerlab, Nat. Def. Prepardenss Assn. Roman Catholic. Avocation: sports.

KANE, CHARLES JOSEPH, banker; b. Louisville, Jan. 2, 1920; s. Henry and Lillian (Berger) K.; m. Rosemary Wilder, Oct. 4, 1941; children—Charles Joseph, Michael. Grad., U. Louisville, 1951, Rutgers U. Grad. Sch. Banking, 1954, Columbia U. Comml. Banks Sr. Mgmt. Sch., 1959, Advanced Mgmt. Program Harvard U., 1966. With Citizens Fidelity Bank & Trust Co., Louisville, 1940—, v.p. charge banking, 1961-62, 1st v.p., 1962-67, exec. v.p., 1967-70, pres., 1970-74, also dir.; pres., dir. Third Nat. Bank, Nashville, 1975—, chmn., chief exec. officer, 1976—, Third Nat. Corp., Western Ky. Gas Co.; dir., mem. exec. com. Am. Gen. Corp.; dir. Hosp. Corp. Am., Nashville; past instr. U. Louisville. Author: Bank Financing of Small Loan Companies, 1954. Chmn. for Ky. Crusade for Freedom, 1957-58; bd. dirs. Children's Hosp., Vanderbilt U., Nashville. Served with AUS, 1942-45. Recipient Crusade for Freedom award, 1957; President's Citation for Outstanding Service U. Louisville, 1959; named Chief Exec. Officer of Yr. Advantage Mag. Mem. Assn. Res. City Bankers, Nashville Area C. of C. (past pres.), Am. Bankers Assn. (chmn. exec. com. comml. lending div.), Robert Morris Assocs., Newcomen Soc. Republican. Clubs: Louisville Country, Harvard Bus., Filson, Pendennis (Louisville); Union League (Chgo.); Belle Meade Country, Nashville City. Office: Third Nat Corp Third Nat Bank Bldg Nashville TN 37244*

KANE, SAM, meat company executive; b. Spisske Podhradie, Czechoslovakia, June 23, 1919; s. Leopold and Bertha (Narcisenfeld) Kannengiesser; grad. Rabbinical Coll. Galanta, 1939; m. Aranka Feldbrand, Jan. 15, 1946; children—Jerry, Harold Ira, Esther Barbara. Came to U.S., 1948, naturalized, 1953. Pres. Sam Kane Wholesale Meat, Inc., Corpus Christi, Tex., 1956—, Sam Kane Meat, Inc., Corpus Christi, 1956—, Sam Kane Packing Co., Corpus Christi, 1962—, Kane Enterprises, Inc. (merger Sam Kane Beef Processors Inc.), Corpus Christi, 1956—; dir. Guaranty Nat. Bank, Corpus Christi, First City Bank of Corpus Christi. Pres., Jewish Welfare Appeal, 1962—; v.p. Combined Jewish Appeal, 1968, chmn. bd., 1962-64; mem. regional bd. Anti-Defamation League, mem. nat. commn., chmn. Corpus Christi Area, nat. treas.; mem. world bd. Jewish Agy.; bd. dirs. Tex. Council Econ. Edn. nat. bd. dirs. United Jewish Appeal; mem. Tex. 2000 Commn. Recipient award chmn. bd. edn. B'nai Israel Synagogue, 1965; Israel Service award, 1966; Prime Minister Israel Peace medal, 1980, Koach award State of Israel, 1976, Brotherhood award Corpus Christi chpt. NCCJ, 1984, Torch of Liberty award Anti-Defamation League, 1984, award United Jewish Appeal. Mem. Assembly, Tex. Taxpayers Assn. Jewish (pres. synagogue 1964-65). Lodge: B'nai B'rith (named Outstanding Jewish Citizen 1969). Home: 27 Hewit Dr Corpus Christi TX 78404 Office: 9001 Leopard St Corpus Christi TX 78409

KANG, MANJIT SINGH, geneticist, plant breeder; b. Punjab, India, Mar. 3, 1948; came to U.S., 1969, naturalized 1976; s. Gurdit Singh and Parminder Kaur (Brah) K.; B.S. in Agr. with honors (India Council Agrl. Research scholar), Punjab Agrl. U., Ludhiana, India, 1968; M.S., So. Ill. U., Edwardsville, 1971, M.A. in Botany, Carbondale, 1977; Ph.D., U. Mo., Columbia, 1977; m. Georgia Anna Crocker, Feb. 13, 1971. Teaching asst. So. Ill. U., Edwardsville, 1969-71; research asst. plant and soil sci. So. Ill. U., Carbondale, 1971-72, preceptor plant and soil sci., 1972-74; grad. research asst. agronomy U. Mo., Columbia, 1974-77; research assoc. Center Biology of Natural Systems, Washington U., St. Louis, 1977; sr. plant breeder hybrid corn research sta. Cargill, Inc., St. Peter, Minn., 1977-78, research sta. mgr., 1979; research asso. agronomy U. Mo., 1980; asst. prof. genetics U. Fla. Agrl. Research and Edn.

Center, Belle Glade, 1981-85; assoc. prof. agronomy La. State U., Baton Rouge, 1986—. Mem. AAAS, Am. Soc. Agronomy, Am. Genetic Assn., Crop Sci. Soc. Am., Am. Soc. Sugar Cane Technologists, Internat. Soc. Plant Molecular Biology, Sigma Xi, Gamma Sigma Delta. Contbr. articles profl. jours. Home: 1422 Sharlo Baton Rouge LA 70820 Office: Dept Agronomy MB Sturgis Hall La State U Baton Rouge LA 70803

KANNADY, DONALD JOE, clergyman, nurse; b. Covington, Ky., Feb. 8, 1949; s. Joe Albert and Mary Katherine (Brashear) K.; m. Donna Sue Williams, Jan. 24, 1973; children—Donald Matthew, Mary Elizabeth. B.A., Cumberland Coll., 1972; M. Div., So. Baptist Sem., 1976; R.N. diploma Jewish Hosp., Cin., 1980. Ordained to ministry Baptist Ch., 1980. Pastor Pleasant Hill Bapt. Ch., Williamsburg, Ky., 1970-72, Madison Fellowship, Hamilton, Ohio, 1975-76, Oakland Bapt. Ch., Sparta, Ky., 1979-84, Stewartsville Baptist Ch., 1984—; attendant Grant County Hosp., Williamstown, Ky., 1976-79; nurse Booth Hosp., Florence, Ky., 1981—. Mem. exec. bd. Ten Mile Assn., Warsaw, Ky., 1979-84, brotherhood dir., 1980-84; pres. Glencoe PTA (Ky.), 1983-84, Gallatin County PTA, 1985-86; pres. Ministerial Assn. Cumberland Coll., 1971-72. Democrat. Home: Route 1 Box 242-B Glencoe KY 41046

KANSO, RIAYA MELHEM, real estate development and management executive; b. Beirut, Lebanon, Mar. 19, 1944; s. Melhem M. and Munira Youssef (Saab) K.; m. Bethina N. Mourtada, Sept. 19, 1977; 1 son, Maher. B.S., Am. U. Beirut, 1968. Group leader G.S.I./Tex. Instruments, Beirut, 1968-70, group leader, geophysicist, Croydon, Eng., 1971-72; regional mktg. coordinator 3M Middle East, Beirut, 1973-74; managing dir. Bin-Huraib Establishment, Riyadh, Saudi Arabia, 1975-76; exec. dir. Rossmore Internat., London, 1977-78; pres. Lenox Ctr. Inc., Atlanta, 1980—, pres., owner Maida Vale Corp., Atlanta. Sec. Am. Inst. Physics, Beirut, 1964, v.p., 1965; sr. advisor U.S. Congl. Adv. Bd., 1983; sustaining mem. Republican party. Mem. Bus. Council Ga., Sandy Springs C. of C. Home: 250 Landfall Rd Atlanta GA 30328 Office: Lenox Center Inc 6600 Powers Ferry Rd Suite 210 Atlanta GA 30339

KAPILOFF, MARK CARL, clothing company executive; b. Belfast, Maine, July 6, 1935; s. Lawrence E. and Ethel (Maisel) K.; B.A., Bowdoin Coll., 1957; m. Lillian Rodgers, Dec. 30, 1958; children—Marsha, Paula, Susan, Richard. Cutting foreman Neobel, Inc., Atlanta, 1957-58; gen. mgr. KYM Co., Jackson, Ga., 1958-73, pres., 1974—; pres. KYM Investment Corp., 1981—; sec. J. Bruce Mfg. Co., 1984—. Mem. adv. staff Griffin-Spalding County Vocat.-Tech. Sch. Served with U.S. Army, 1958. Mem. Am. Apparel Mfg. Assn. (apparel research com. 1979—), Butts County C. of C. (pres. 1983). Home: 840 Hillcrest Ave Griffin GA 30223 Office: 325 Alabama Blvd Jackson GA 30233

KAPLAN, ARNOLD AARON, physician; b. Chgo., Sept. 26, 1932; s. Al and Belle (Klebansky) K.; m. Barbara Riskin, June 23, 1957. B.S., U. Ill., 1955, M.D., 1960. Diplomate Am. Bd. Internal Medicine. Intern, Jackson Meml. Hosp., Miami, Fla., 1960-61, resident, 1961-63; fellow in nephrology VA Hosp., Miami, 1963-64; practice medicine, Miami, 1964—; staff mem. Parkway Gen. Hosp., 1964—, chief of medicine, 1970-71; staff mem. North Miami Gen. Hosp., 1964—, chief of staff, 1972-73; instr. internal medicine U. Miami. Past bd. dirs. Jewish Community Ctr. N. Dade, also past assoc. chmn. health and phys. edn. com. Recipient Spirit award Jewish Community Ctr., 1981. Mem. AMA, Am. Soc. Internal Medicine, Dade County Med. Assn., Am. Heart Assn., Fla. Med. Assn., Am. Physicians Fellowship, Fla. Heart Assn., Fla. Nephrology Assn. Club: Optimists. Address: 16800 NW 2d Ave North Miami Beach FL 33169

KAPLAN, BERTON HARRIS, medical educator; b. Winchester, Va., June 27, 1930; s. Rueben L. and Jennie G. (Rosenman) K.; m. Ellen Brauer, June 14, 1959; children—Daniel, Ron. B.S., Va. Poly. Inst., 1951; M.S., U. N.C., 1952, Ph.D. Mem. faculty U. N.C., Chapel Hill, 1960—, prof. epidemiology, 1972—. Author: Blue Ridge: A Mountain Community in Transition, 1971; (with Leighton and Wilson) Explorations in Social Psychiatry, 1976; contbr. articles to profl. jours. Bd. dirs. Carolina Friends Sch., 1982—. Served with USAF, 1952-54. Social Sci. Research Council fellow, 1965-66. Mem. AAAS, Soc. Epidemiol. Research, Am. Anthrop. Assn. Democrat. Jewish. Office: Sch of Pub Health U NC Chapel Hill NC 27514

KAPLAN, GLENN JEFF, chiropractor; b. Bronx, N.Y., Dec. 16, 1954; s. Leonard Abraham and Carole Eileen (Brown) K.; m. Barbara Rosenberg, June 24, 1979 (dec. Sept. 1983); m. Elizabeth Ann Marie Cobucci, June 28, 1986. Student SUNY Coll.-Cortland, 1972-74; B.A. in Biology, SUNY-Buffalo, 1976; D.Chiropractic, Life Chiropractic Coll., 1980. Lab. technician, field technician Eco Research Ecol. Research, site of Ginnae Nuclear Power Plant, Ontario, N.Y., 1976; instr. physiology and anatomy labs. Life Chiropractic Coll., Marietta, Ga., 1978-80; pvt. practice chiropractic Kaplan Clinic of Chiropractic, P.C., Duluth, Ga., 1980-84, 86—, also clinic dir.; speaker on health, nutrition, sports-related activities. Mem. Internat. Chiropractic Assn., Ga. Chiropractic Assn., Parker Chiropractic Research Found. Jewish. Office: 5270 Hwy 141 Norcross GA 30071

KAPLAN, JEFFREY DOUGLAS, public administrator; b. Miami Beach, Fla., Oct. 7, 1950; s. Bernard D. and Ruth (Bobrow) K.; m. Rae Epstein, Dec. 25, 1971; children—Hilary Ann, Lauren Jessica, Bernard Morris. B.A., Emory U., 1972; M.A., U. Miami, 1973. Program analyst I Metro-Dade County, Miami, 1973-75, adminstrv. officer III, 1975-80, spl. projects adminstr., 1980-81, asst. dir. Dept. Solid Waste Collection, 1981—. Local officer Fla. League of Anglers, Dade County, Fla., 1983. Mem. Am. Soc. Pub. Adminstrs., Pi Sigma Alpha. Democrat. Jewish. Home: 10743 SW 118 St Miami FL 33176 Office: Metro-Dade Dept Solid Waste Collection 8675 NW 53 St Miami FL 33166

KAPLAN, MICHAEL DAVID, health management executive; b. N.Y.C., Nov. 4, 1940; s. Harry J. and Rose K. Kaplan; B.A., Syracuse U., 1962, postgrad., 1963; postgrad. N.Y. U., 1964; m. Barbara Oberstein, Aug. 30, 1964; children—Jeremy Scott, Abigail Sarah. Polit. reporter AP, N.Y.C., 1965-69; v.p. mktg. First Healthcare Corp., Chgo., 1969-74; pres. Resource Dynamics, Inc., Chgo., 1974-79, also dir.; pres. Randmark Corp., Louisville, 1979—, also dir.; pres., dir. Pavilion Health Care Centers, Louisville, 1981—, Rand Mgmt. Corp., Peoria, 1981—; pres., dir. Pavilion Health Care North, Inc., 1981—, Pavilion Health Care South, Inc., 1981—, Pavilion Health Care West, Inc., 1981—, Pavilion Oaks of Peoria, Inc., 1981—, Pavilion Health Care Ctr. Louisville, Inc., 1984—, Richwoods Terrace of Peoria, Inc., 1981—, Central Dietary Systems, Inc., 1983—; lectr. Acad. Gerontol. Edn. and Devel. Bd. dirs. Louisville Jewish Community Fedn., Kenesth Israel Synagogue, Louisville, Bur. Jewish Edn., Louisville. Author: Comprehensive Guide to Health Care Marketing, 1974; Health Care Management in a Troubled Economy, 1979; contbr. articles to profl. jours.; contbg. editor Nursing Homes mag., 1978—. Home: 1801 Tyler Ln Louisville KY 40205 Office: 517 W Ormsby Ave Louisville KY 402032

KAPLAN, MURIEL SHEERR, sculptor; b. Phila., Aug. 15, 1924; d. Maurice J. and Lillian J. (Jamison) Sheerr; B.A., Cornell U., 1946; postgrad. Sarah Lawrence Coll., 1958-60, U. Calif. at Oxford (Eng.), summer 1971, U. Florence (Italy), summer 1973, Art Students League, N.Y.C., 1975-80, New Sch., N.Y.C., 1974-78, m. Murray S. Kaplan, June 3, 1946; children—Janet Belsky, James S., Jerrold, Amy Sheerr Eckman. Exhbns. at Women's Clubs in Westchester, 1954-60, Allied Artists Am., 1958-73, Nat. Assn. Women Artists, 1966-78, Bklyn. Museum, 1968, Sculptors Guild, 1972, Bergen County (N.J.) Mus., 1974; 2-person shows: Camino Real Gallery, Boca Raton, Fla., 1980, Norton Art Gallery, Palm Beach, Fla., 1980, Artist Guild, Palm Beach, Fla., 1986, Govt. Ctr. West Palm Beach, 1986; represented in permanent collections Jerusalem, Columbia U., Brandeis U., U. Tex., Barrington Art Mus., Delray Fla.; executed twin 30 foot cor-ten steel sculptures, Tarrytown, N.Y., 1972, 2 large rotating steel sculptures Art Park, Trans-Lux Corp., 1968, 70; art cons., interior designer, 1971—; sec. commn. to establish art mus. in Westchester, 1956; chmn. Westchester Creative Arts Festival, 1956. Bd. dirs. Fedn. Jewish Philanthropies, 1956; chmn. 1st WNET, Channel 13 Art Auction; mem. Com. for Art in Palm Beachs, 1984—. Recipient prizes Nat. Assn. Women Artists, 1966, Westchester Women's Club, 1955, 56, Allied Artists Am., 1969. Mem. Nat. Assn. Women Artists, Artists and Engrs. in Tech., Am. Portrait Soc. Democrat. Address: 339 Garden Rd Palm Beach FL 33480

KAPLAN, SIDNEY MARTIN, computer specialist; b. Balt., July 25, 1921; s. Maurice Lewis and Rose Diana (Monarch) K.; m. Irene Budlow, June 23, 1946; children—Phyllis, Ellen, David, Howard. Student Johns Hopkins U., 1939-43; B.S.E.E., U. Md., 1948; postgrad. Union Coll., 1948-51. Mgr. info. systems Gen. Electric Co., Ithaca, N.Y., 1948-56; pres. Systems, Inc., Piezo Tech., Inc. and Elmco, Inc., Orlando, Fla., 1956-80; ops. mgr. control systems Computer Scis. Corp., Falls Church, Va., 1980-85; cons. computer systems, Falls Church, Va., 1985—; cons. Mem. Fla. Commn. Higher Edn., Orlando, 1960-62. Served with U.S. Army, 1943-46. Mem. IEEE, AAAS, Sigma Xi, Phi Kappa Phi, Tau Beta Pi. Democrat. Jewish. Patentee in field. Office: 3001 Centreville Rd Herndon VA 22070

KAPNER, LEWIS, lawyer; b. West Palm Beach, Fla., May 21, 1937; s. Irving Michael and Mildred Leah (Pikelny) K.; m. Dawn Beth Grossman, Aug. 1964; children—Steven, Kimberly, Michael, Allison. B.A., U. Fla., 1958; postgrad. George Washington U. Law Sch., summer 1961, J.D. Stetson Law Sch., St. Petersburg, Fla., 1962. Bar: Fla., U.S. Supreme Ct., U.S. Dist. Ct. (so. dist.) Fla. Asst. county solicitor Palm Beach County, West Palm Beach, 1962-65; ptnr. Kapner & Kapner, West Palm Beach, 1965-67; gen. counsel County Legis. Delegation, Tallahassee, Fla., 1967; judge Juvenile and Domestic Relations Ct., West Palm Beach, 1967-73; judge Circuit Ct. Fla., West Palm Beach, 1973-84, chief judge, 1981-83; head marital and family law dept. Montgomery, Searcy & Denney, P.A.; mem. faculty Fla. Jud. Coll., Gainesville, 1979-83, dean, 1982-83; mem. faculty Nat. Jud. Coll., Reno, 1979—; mem. Supreme Ct. Commn. on Matrimonial Law, 1982—; adj. prof. law Nova U., Fort Lauderdale, Fla., 1982-84. Pres., Internat. Found. for Gifted Children, West Palm Beach, 1970-72. Served with USMC, 1959-60. Named one of five outstanding young men in Fla., Fla. Jaycees, 1972. Fellow Am. Acad. Matrimonial Lawyers (v.p. Fla. chpt. 1982—; Oustanding Fla. Judge award 1982); mem. Fla. Bar (chmn. family law sect. 1985-86). Jewish. Office: 2139 Palm Beach Lake Blvd West Palm Beach FL 33401

KARCH, ROBERT E., real estate and business executive; b. Bklyn., May 30, 1933; s. Charles H. and Etta R. (Becker) K.; A.B., Syracuse U., 1953, M.B.A., 1958; student in Russian, Army Lang. Sch., Monterey, Calif., 1953-54; m. Brenda Schechter, Sept. 7, 1958; children—Barry S., Karen D., Brian D. With Nationwide Beauty & Barber Supply Co., Syracuse, N.Y. and El Paso, Tex., 1956—, pres., 1966-74, chmn., 1974—, also dir.; sales mgr. Helen of Troy Corp., El Paso, 1974-76, v.p. sales and mktg., 1976-79, also dir.; v.p., dir. Bormex Constrn. Inc., 1980-81; real estate agt. Bonded Realty, 1979-81; pres. BKB Properties, 1979—; instr. investment real estate Acad. Real Estate, 1984—; lectr. in field. Pres. Syracuse Hebrew Day Sch., 1972-73. Served with U.S. Army, 1953-56. Lic. comml. pilot; lic. real estate broker, Tex., Colo., N.Mex. Mem. Beauty and Barber Supply Inst., Direct Mail/Mktg. Assn., Aircraft Owners and Pilots Assn., Jewish War Vets., El Paso Aviation Assn., El Paso Bd. Realtors, El Paso Apt. Assn., El Paso Comml. Investment Club, El Paso Property Exchangers Club, El Paso Aviation Assn., (pres. 1985), El Paso Investment Club. Clubs: Coronado Country, Lancers. Author: Data Processing for Beauty/Barber Dealers, 1968; also real estate investor's newsletter, 1981—, Property Mgmt. Newsletter, 1985—. Home: 6016 Torrey Pines El Paso TX 79912 Office: 10622A Montwood Dr Suite A El Paso TX 79935 also 2600 Erie Blvd E Syracuse NY 13224

KARCHER, BARBARA CORRENTI, sociologist, educator; b. New Orleans, Jan. 19, 1946; d. Alfred Francis Correnti and Betty Mae (Lockhart) C.; m. Charles Joseph Karcher, Aug. 31, 1968; 1 child, Elizabeth Marie. A.B., Loyola U., New Orleans, 1967; M.A., U. Ga., 1972, Ph.D., 1974. Instr. Ga. Inst. Tech., 1972-74; asst. prof. Kennesaw Coll., Marietta, Ga., 1974-79, assoc. prof. sociology, 1979—; chair regent's acad. com. on sociology, anthropology and social work State of Ga. Univ. System. NSF trainee, 1967-68. Mem. Am. Sociol. Assn., So. Sociol. Soc., Ga. Sociol. Assn. (sec.-treas.), Assn. Sociol. Study Religion, LaLeche League of East Cobb. Democrat. Roman Catholic. Contbr. articles to profl. jours. Home: 410 Arbor Trail Marietta GA 30067 Office: Kennesaw Coll Frey Lake Rd Marietta GA 30061

KARGES, HAROLD EARL, oil company executive, consultant; b. Wichita Falls, Tex., July 16, 1927; s. Carl Leslie and Anna Nelson (Johnson) K.; m. Nancy Katherine Hay, Oct. 8, 1948; children—Carl, Hardie, Wilson. B.A., Tex. Christian U., 1948. Registered profl. geologist, petroleum geologist, La., Miss. Subsurface geologist Shell Oil Co., Lake Charles, La., 1948-52, Jackson, Miss., 1952-55, cons. geologist, Jackson, 1955—; exploration mgr., v.p. Liberty Oil & Gas, New Roads, La., 1983—; dir. Miss. Mineral Resources Inst., University, 1979—; dir., v.p., pres. Love Petroleum Co., Jackson, 1965-79. Served with USN, 1945-46, PTO. Mem. Am. Assn. Petroleum Geologists, Am. Inst. Profl. Geologists, Soc. Econ. Paleontologists and Mineralogists, Palentol. Soc., Miss. Geol. Soc. Christian Scientist. Avocations: collecting fossils; golf. Home 1124 Star Rd Brandon MS 39042 Office: PO Box 1635 Jackson MS 39205

KARIM, SHIRAZ OMAR, hotel executive and administrator; b. Dar-Es-Salaam, Tanzania, East Africa, July 7, 1952; came to U.S., 1982; s. Kassamali Remtulla and Zaineb (Rahim) K. B.Comm., U. B.C.-Vancouver, 1975. Cert. hotel adminstr. Ednl. Inst. Am. Hotel and Motel Assn. Gen. acct., Tahsis Co. Ltd., Gold River, B.C., Can., 1975-76, cost acct., 1976-77, mill acct., 1977-78, sr. asst. to controller, Vancouver, 1979-81; asst. mgr. Wolray Hotels, Titusville, Fla., 1982, gen. mgr., Atlanta, 1983, v.p., 1983—. Mem. Canadian Property Mgrs. Assn., Soc. Mgmt. Accts. Republican. Muslim. Home: 2498 Parkdale Pl Atlanta GA 30305

KARLBERG, JOHN, transportation company executive; b. 1942. With Airco Indsl. Gases Inc., 1965-78, Sun Carriers Inc., 1979; sr. v.p., now pres., chief operating officer Jones Truck Lines, Springdale, Ark., 1980—, also dir. Office: Jones Truck Lines 610 E Emma-Office Springdale AR 72764*

KARNS, BARRY WAYNE, investment banker; b. Baton Rouge, Aug. 28, 1946; s. William G. and Margery N. (Lanehart) K.; m. Julie Josephine Goff, Aug. 2, 1969; children—David Adam, Julie Shannon, Shelby Allison. B.S. in B.A., La. State U., 1968, J.D., 1971. C.P.A., La.; bar: La. 1971. Asst. dir. La. State Bond Commn., 1973-78, dir., 1978-80; first asst. state treas. State of La., Baton Rouge, 1980-85; sr. v.p. Donaldson, Lufkin & Jenrette Securities Corp., Baton Rouge, 1985—; owner BWK Inc. d/b/a The Tinder Box, 1978—, K-Shirts, Inc. d/b/a T-Shirt Action, 1981—; treas. La Capitol Fed. Credit Union, 1979-86; lectr. Chmn., Dep. Sheriffs Supplemental Pay Bd., 1980-85; chmn. investment commn. La. Employees Retirement System, 1982-85; chmn. Kiwanis Found. Baton Rouge, Inc., 1980-84. La. State U. scholar, 1964-68. Mem. Phi Alpha Delta, Delta Sigma Pi. Democrat. Baptist. Club: Kiwanis. Office: Acadia Trace Bldg 2237 S Acadian Thruway Suite 705 Baton Rouge LA 70808

KARON, JOHN MARSHALL, statistician; b. Milw., Nov. 6, 1941; s. Morris and Vera Elizabeth (Block) K.; m. Kate Killebrew, Feb. 18, 1973; children—Amy, Sarah. B.A., Carleton Coll., 1963; M.S., Stanford U., 1965, Ph.D., 1968. Asst. prof. Syracuse U., N.Y., 1968-70, Colo. Coll., Colorado Springs, 1971-77; research asst. Stanford U., 1970; vis. lectr. Tel Aviv U., Israel, 1972-73; postdoctoral fellow research assoc. prof. U. N.C.-Chapel Hill, 1977-84; math. statistician Ctrs. for Disease Control, Atlanta, 1984—; cons. NIH, 1982—, FDA, 1985—. Contbr. articles to profl. jours. Mem. Am. Statis. Assn., Biometric Soc., AAAS. Home: 423 Blanton Rd Atlanta GA 30342 Office: Bldg 25 Ctrs for Disease Control Atlanta GA 30342

KARR, MARSHALL IVAN, developer, contractor, preservationist; b. Nashville, Dec. 19, 1951; s. Maurice J. and Joy R. Karr; m. Jacquelyn Roth, Aug. 23, 1980. B.A., U. Okla., 1974. Cert. proprety mgr. Vice pres. Jacques Miller Property Mgmt., Inc., Jacques Miller Devel., Inc., Nashville, 1982—, Jacques Miller Constrn., Inc., Nashville, 1982—; lectr., cons. in field. Bd. dirs. Met. Hist. Commn., Nashville, 1983-84; mem. Met. Bd. Zoning Appeals, 1984; mem. Mayor's Task Force to Rewrite Codes, Rehab. of Old Bldgs., Nashville, 1982-83, Mayor's Task Force Union Sta. Developer Selection Com., 1983. Mem. Nashville Area C. of C., Inst. Real Estate Mgmt. Club: Woodmont Country (dir.).

KARWINSKI, THOMAS FRANCIS, architect, city planner; b. Kearny, N.J., Dec. 21, 1948; s. Francis and Matylda (Stefanowicz) K. Student Bloomfield Coll., 1967-68, Essex County Coll., 1968-70; B.Arch., Pratt Inst. Sch. Architecture, 1974. Registered architect Nat. Council Designer Sidney Shelov, AIA Architect, N.Y.C., 1973-74; judiciary facilities cons. Space Mgmt. Cons, N.Y.C., 1974; architect, planner Arch. R. Winter FAIA, AICP, Mobile, Ala., 1974-84; architect, city planner Thomas F. Karwinski AIA Architect/Planner, Mobile, 1984—. Contbg. writer articles on historic restoration to newspaper, 1982. Appointed mem. Old Dauphin Way Historic Dist. Rev. Bd., Mobile, 1984—. Recipient Honor award Gulf States Region AIA, 1984, award for Excellence in Architecture Ala. Council AIA, 1984. Mem. AIA, Am. Planning Assn., Soc., Archtl. Historians, Nat. Council Archtl. Registration Bds. (cert.), Am. Inst. Cert. Planners (assoc.). Roman Catholic. Home and Office: 403 Conti St Mobile AL 36602

KASARDA, JOHN DALE, sociology educator and administrator, consultant; b. Wilkes-Barre, Pa., June 16, 1945; s. Edward and Stella (Sott) K.; m. Mary Ann Dudascik, Aug. 17, 1968; children—Jason, Kimberly. B.S., Cornell U., 1967, M.B.A., 1968; Ph.D., U. N.C., 1971, Asst. prof. U. Chgo., Ill., 1971-74; assoc. prof. Fla. Atlantic U., Boca Raton, 1974-76; prof. U. N.C., Chapel Hill, 1976—, chmn. dept. Sociology, 1980—; cons. Pres.'s Commn., Washington, 1980-81, HUD, Washington, 1981-82, USIA, Washington, 1982-83. Author: Contemporary Urban Ecology, 1977; The Organization and its Ecosystem, 1985. Contbr. articles to profl. jours. Mem. adv. bd. Taxpayers Edn. Found., Washington, 1982-83; adv. Staff of Senator John East, Washington, 1982—. Research grantee NSF, 1976, 79, 84. Mem. Internat. Sociol. Assn. (sec. gen. research com.). Republican. Home: 707 Gimghoul Rd Chapel Hill NC 27514

KASDORF, CHARLES ARTHUR, III, business economist; b. Chelsea, Mass., Aug. 6, 1943. B.A. in Psychology, Rice U., 1965, M.A. in Behavioral Sci., 1970; M.A. in Psychology, Brandeis U., 1969. Mgr. research Houston C. of C., 1974—. Mem. Am. C. of C. Researchers Assn. (pres. 1982-83, co-chmn. intercity cost of living index 1980—, editor newsletter 1979-80), Tex. Econ. and Demographic Assn. (editor newsletter). Office: Houston C of C Research Div 1100 Milam Bldg 25th Floor Houston TX 77002

KASEN, MARSHALL A., accounting firm executive; b. Newark, Jan. 22, 1943; s. Philip J. and Pearl (Gable) K.; m. Susan B. Lowing, Sept. 8, 1968; children—Jonathan, Peter. B.B.A., Pace U., 1968, postgrad. Rutgers U. C.P.A., N.Y., Fla. Acct., J.K. Lasser & Co., C.P.A.s, N.Y.C., 1968-72; asst. treas. Cavanagh Communities Corp., Miami, Fla., 1972-73; acct. Touche Ross & Co. C.P.A.s, Miami, 1973-77; ptnr. Steinberg, Strongin & Kasen P.A., C.P.A.s, Miami, 1977—; guest lectr. Fla. Internat. U., Miami; cons. to various firms, Miami, 1977-83; seminar leader continuing edn. seminars, 1975—. Mem. Fla. Inst. C.P.A.s (com. chmn. Dade County chpt. 1983), N.Y. State Soc. C.P.A.s. Office: Steinberg Strongin & Kasen PA 1395 Coral Way Miami FL 33145

KASHFI, MANSOUR SEID, petroleum geologist, consultant; b. Tehran, Iran, May 21, 1939; s. Mostafa Seid and Khadejeh (Abghari) K.; m. Mahroo Hoghoughi, Oct. 4, 1975; 1 child, David. B.S., Tehran U., Iran, 1962; M.S., Mich. State U., 1967; Ph.D., U. Tenn., Teaching asst. U. Tenn., Knoxville, 1967-71; sr. geologist Nat. Iran Oil Co., Tehran, 1971-78; assoc. prof. Pahlavi U., Shiraz, Iran, 1978-81; exploration mgr. Petroleum Corp. Jamaica, Kingston, 1981-82; petroleum geologist The Navajo Nation, Window Rock, Ariz., 1982-84; cons. geologist Associated Resource, Tulsa, 1984—. Author: Evolution of Oil Industry in Iran and the Middle East, 1981. Recipient Pahlavi medal Late Shah of Iran, Tehran, 1963. Mem. Am. Assn. Petroleum Geologists, Geol. Soc. Am. Home: PO Box 472921 Garland TX 75047

KASS, RAY ROBERT, artist, educator; b. Rockville Centre, N.Y., Jan. 25, 1944; s. Jacob James and Juliette Marie Antonette (VanDenLangenburgh) K.; m. Laurie B. Gunst, Aug. 1973 (div. 1978). B.A. in Philosophy, U. N.C., 1967, M.F.A. in Painting, 1969. Asst. prof. art Humboldt State U., Arcata, Calif., 1969-72; prof. Va. Poly. Inst., Blacksburg, 1976—; vis. curator Phillips Collection, Washington, 1980-84; bd. dirs. Mt. Lake Symposium of Va. Tech. Found., Blacksburg, 1983—. Author: Morris Graves: Vision of the Inner Eye, 1983. One-man shows at Allan Stone Gallery, N.Y.C., 1972, 75, 77, 81, 86, Osuna Gallery, Washington, 1979, 84, Addison Gallery Am. Art, Andover, Mass., 1974, Southeastern Ct. for Contemporary Art, Winston-Salem, N.C., 1980; also group shows; represented in permanent collections at U. Mass., Amherst, U. N.C., Boston Pub. Library, Roanoke Mus. Art, Va., others. Nat. Endowment for Arts individual artist's grantee, 1981; Va. Mus. Artists fellow Va. Mus. Fine Arts, Richmond, 1984-85. Mem. Jargon Soc. (bd. dirs. 1983—). Avocations: art criticism; gardening. Home: Route 2 Box 423 Christiansburg VA 24073 Office: Va Poly Inst Dept Art 201 Draper Rd Blacksburg VA 24061

KASSNER, HERBERT ALAN, government public information officer; b. Macon, Ga., June 9, 1927; s. Irving Edward and Rose Velma (Kessler) K.; student Davidson Coll., 1943-44; A.B., Mercer U., 1949; postgrad. U. Wis., 1967; children—David, Christopher, Karen. News reporter, news dir. Stas. WMAZ and WMAZ-TV, Macon, 1947-57; in advt. sales, 1957-59; public info. officer IV U.S. Army Corps, Jacksonville, Fla., 1959-61; public info. officer, asst. chief public affairs, Fort Rucker, Ala., 1961-69; chief public affairs office U.S. Army Engr., Lower Mississippi Valley div. Mississippi River Commn., 1969—. Bd. dirs. Warren County (Miss.) Dept. Public Welfare, 1973-83. Served with U.S. Army, 1945-46, 50-51; col. Res. ret. Decorated Meritorious Service medal, Army Commendation medal. Mem. Public Relations Soc. Am. (accredited; chmn. govt. sect.; past pres. Miss. chpt.), Soc. Am. Mil. Engrs., Assn. U.S. Army. Methodist. Office: PO Box 80 Vicksburg MS 39180

KASTEN, STANLEY HARVEY, sports association executive; b. Lakewood, N.J., Feb. 1, 1952; s. Nathan and Sylvia (Saltztreger) K.; m. Helen Weisz, Aug. 14, 1977; children—Alana Marie, Corey Richard. A.B., NYU, 1973; J.D., Columbia U., 1976. Exec. asst. Turner Broadcasting Co., Atlanta, 1976-77; in-house counsel Atlanta Braves, 1976-77; v.p., asst. gen. mgr. Atlanta Hawks, 1978-79, v.p., gen. mgr., 1980—, dir., 1980—; bd. govs. Nat. Basketball Assn., N.Y.C., 1978—. Bd. dirs. Police Athletic League, Atlanta, 1980-81. Mem. ABA, N.J. Bar Assn. Lodge: B'nai Brith Gate City (trustee 1982—). Office: Atlanta Hawks The Omni 100 Techwood Dr NW Atlanta GA 30303*

KASTL, JOHN DICK, optometrist; b. Brownfield, Tex., Apr. 8, 1951; s. Franklin Leon and Launis Pamelia (Passmore) K.; B.S. in Biology, Northeastern State U., Tahlequah, Okla., 1973; postgrad. Tulsa U., 1973; cert. in respiratory therapy U. Chgo., 1974; O.D., U. Houston, 1977; m. Barbara Darlene Simpson, Aug. 23, 1969; children—Jill Lynn, Amy Ann. Respiratory therapist St. Francis Hosp., Tulsa, 1973, St. Luke's Hosp., Houston, 1976, Tex. Children's Hosp., Houston, 1976, Tex. Heart Inst., Houston, 1976; pvt. practice optometry, Mannford, Okla., 1978—; CPR instr. Am. Heart Assn. Pres. bd. dirs. Golden Age Sr. Citizen Housing; pres. bd. trustees Mannford Pub. Library. Mem. Am. Optometric Assn., Okla. Optometric Assn., Mannford C. of C. Republican. Methodist. Club: Lions (v.p. Mannford). Home and Office: PO Box 810 Mannford OK 74044

KASVINSKY, PETER JOHN, biochemistry educator, researcher; b. Bridgeport, Conn., Dec. 7, 1942; s. Joseph Stephen and Irene Jenny (Kedves) K.; m. Elaine Joyce Amormino, Apr. 5, 1974; 1 son, Christopher John. B.S., Bucknell U., 1964; Ph.D., U. Vt., 1970. Instr. biochemistry Wayne State U. Sch. Medicine, 1972-74, U. Alta. (Can.), Edmonton, 1977-79, prof. asst., 1974-79; asst. prof. Marshall U. Sch. Medicine, Huntington, W.Va., 1979-82, assoc. prof., 1982—; mem. grad. faculty W.Va. U., 1980—. Mem. Huntington Galleries, 1980—. Served to capt. M.S.C., AUS, 1969-72. NIH grantee, 1981—. Mem. Am. Soc. Biol. Chemists, Am. Chem. Soc., AAAS, Can. Biochem. Soc., N.Y. Acad. Sci., Sigma Xi. Democrat. Roman Catholic. Contbr. articles to profl. jours.

KATZ, ANNETTE SARA, editor, journalist; b. Miami, Fla., Jan. 25, 1948; d. Harold Orville and Jean (Bulafkin) Van Dam; B.S. in Journalism, U. Fla., 1970; m. Stephen K. Katz, Feb. 26, 1978; 1 son, Matthew R. Reporter, Coral Gables (Fla.) Times, also The Guide, Coral Gables, 1970-71, women's editor, 1971-72, edn. editor, 1972-74; dir. communications United Tchrs. Dade County (Fla.), 1974—, publs. specialist, 1980—, editor UTD Today (named best union newspaper in Fla. 1981-82). Mem. Fla. Women's Polit. Caucus, 1970-71. Recipient Sch. Bell award Fla. Edn. Assn., 1973, 74; Number Two Suburban Journalist in U.S. award Suburban Newspapers Am., 1973; resolution City of Coral Gables, 1973; 1st place feature writing Union Press, 1975; State Union Press award, 1976, 77; award for disting. journalism Fla. Tchr. Press Assn., 1980; 1st place award Ednl. Press Assn. Am., 1983, 1st place feature writing, 1984; 1st place Internat. Labor Press, 1983; 1st place award Fla. Med. Assn., 1983; recognition award Union Tchr. Press Assn., 1983; outstanding recognition award Fla. Tchr. Union Press Assn., 1983, others. Mem. Women in Communications (corr. sec. 1972-73, rec. sec. 1973-77), Fla. Press Club, Sigma Delta Chi. Democrat. Jewish. Office: 2929 SW 3d Ave Miami FL 33129

KATZ, JAMES EVERETT, sociology educator; b. DeKalb, Ill., Sept. 24, 1948; s. Raymond and Frances R. (Rowe) K. B.A., No. Ill. U., DeKalb, 1971,

M.A., 1971; M.Ed., Rutgers U., 1976, Ph.D., 1974. Research fellow MIT, 1976-77, Harvard U., 1978-79; assoc. prof. Clarkson Coll., Potsdam, N.Y., 1979-81; profl. staff mem. U.S. Senate, Washington, 1982-83; asst. prof. LBJ Sch. of Pub. Affairs, U. Tex.-Austin, 1983—; cons. in field. Author, editor books. Contbr. articles to profl. jours. Chmn., Austin World Affairs Council, 1985—. Grantee Orgn. Econ. Coop. and Devel., 1973-74, Ctr. Computer and Info. Scis., 1974, Dantes, 1975, Ctr. for Edn. Research, 1981, Policy Research Inst., 1984, U.S. EPA, 1984, Univ. Research Inst., 1985; NSF fellow, 1976-77. Mem. Am. Heart Assn., Austin Christmas Bur., Austin World Affairs Council, Amnesty Internat., Ctr. Def. Info., Ctr. Sci. in Pub. Interest, Costeau Soc., Marbridge Farm (resident adv.), Nat. Wildlife Fund, Natural Resources Def. Council, People for Am. Way, Ctr. Statis. Scis., Domestic Policy Assn., Polit. Sociology Study Group, United Campuses to Prevent Nuclear War, Acad. Polit. Sci., Am. Acad. Polit. and Social Sci., AAAS, Am. Polit. Sci. Assn., Am. Profs. for Peace in Middle East, Am. Sociol. Assn., Am. Soc. Pub. Adminstrn., Audubon Soc. Sierra Club. Office: LBJ Sch of Pub Affairs U Texas Austin TX 78713

KATZ, LAWRENCE SHELDON, lawyer; b. Newark, Jan. 30, 1943; s. Edward Martin and Pearl Weiss K.; 1 son, Scott Michael. B.B.A., U. Miami, 1965, J.D., 1968, LL.M. Bar: Fla. 1968, U.S. Supreme Ct. 1971, U.S. Ct. Appeals (5th cir.) 1968, U.S. Dist. Ct. (so. dist.) Fla. 1968, U.S. Dist. Ct. (mid. dist.) Fla. 1980, U.S. Ct. Appeals (11th cir.) 1981. Practice, Miami Beach, Fla., 1967—; assoc. Hoffman & St. Jean, 1967-69, Jack R. Nageley, 1969-71; sole practice, 1971-73; ptnr. Swickle, Katz & Brotman, P.A., 1973-77; sole practice as Lawrence S. Katz, P.A., Inc. Miami Beach, Fla., 1977—; atty. Hialeah (Fla.) Fraternal Order of Police Lodge 12 and Dist. 6, 1974—; lectr. in criminal and internat. law. Asst. scoutmaster Troop 503, Boy Scouts Am., 1976-78; chmn. bd. dirs. Internat. Shooters Devel. Fund, 1978-83; mem. ho. of dels. U.S. Olympic Com., 1978-82; gen. counsel, chmn. adv. council U.S. Shooting Team, 1984—. Served to 2d lt. USAR. Mem. ABA (com. internat. criminal law 1971-83), Fed. Bar Assn., Inter-Am. Bar Assn., Am. Judicature Soc., Am. Soc. Internat. Law, Nat. Assn. Criminal Def. Lawyers (Presdl. award for exemplary service 1977, vice chmn by laws com. 1978-80, membership com. 1977-80, lawyers assistance com. 1983—), Acad. Fla. Trial Lawyers (dir. criminal law sect. 1974-79, sec. 1974-77, vice-chmn. 1977-78), Fla. Criminal Def. Attys. Assn. (dir. 1977-80, sec. 1978-80, v.p. 1980-81), Dade County Bar Assn., Lawyer-Pilots Bar Assn., Association Internationale de Droit Penal, Nat. Rifle Assn. (dir. 1977-84, chmn. legal action com. 1979-83). 1979-83). Club: Palmetto Rifle (pres. 1982—). Office: 1 Lincoln Rd Bldg Suite 219 Miami Beach FL 33139

KATZ, SAMUEL BENJAMIN, geologist; b. Bklyn., May 4, 1951; s. Oscar and Rose (Sobo) K.; m. Shelley Jane Regan, Mar. 11, 1984; 1 child, Aaron. B.S. in Geology Wayne State U., 1977; M.S. in Geology, SUNY, 1983; postgrad. U. Houston. Exploration geologist Marathon Oil Co., Houston, 1980—. Contbr. articles to profl. jours. Bd. dirs. Brotherhood Temple Emanuel, Houston, 1984—; asst. scoutmaster Sam Houston council Boy Scouts Am., 1984-85; coach Alief YMCA, Tex., 1983-84. Mem. Internat. Assn. Sedimentologists, Am. Assn. Petroleum Geologists, Soc. Economic Paleontologists and Mineralogists, Houston Geol. Soc., Sigma Xi (research grantee). Republican. Jewish. Club: Houston Bicycle. Avocations: bike riding, running, sailing, reading. Home: 9422 Meaux Houston TX 77031 Office: Marathon Oil Co PO Box 3128 Houston TX 77253

KATZ, WILLIAM DAVID, psychologist, psychoanalytic psychotherapist, educator; b. N.Y.C., Sept. 14, 1915; s. Charles and Esther (Dann) K. A.B., Bklyn. Coll., 1940; M.A., NYU, 1942, Ph.D., 1953. Diplomate Am. Acad. Behavioral Medicine. Clin. intern Hillside Hosp., 1950-53; pvt. practice as cons. psychologist and psychotherapist, N.Y., 1942—; cons. psychologist Human Relations Guidance Ctr., 1946-56; exec. dir. Civic Ctr. Clinic, Bklyn. Assn. Rehab. Offenders, Inc., 1951-55, Play Research Inst., Inc., 1953-57; psychotherapist Group for Community Guidance Ctrs., 1955-57; psychotherapist Mental Health Inst., 1957-59, assoc. dir., 1957, exec. dir., 1958; clin. assoc. Psychol. Service Center, N.Y.C., 1968—; supr. psychotherapy Met. Ctr. Mental Health, N.Y.C., 1969—; asst. prof. psychology L.I. U., 1958-64, assoc. prof., 1964-70, prof., 1970-82, prof. emeritus, 1982—, asst. chmn. psychology dept., 1963-72, 74-76, acting chmn., 1966, 75; prof. U.S. Army Chaplain Ctr. and Sch., Fort Wadsworth, 1970-77; psychotherapist Counseling & Psychotherapy Assocs., 1986—. Assoc. editor Am. Imago, 1978, Am. Psychol. Assn., 1950—; contbr. articles to profl. jours. Recipient Cross of Honor, La Fundacion Internat., Eloy Alfaro, 1964. Fellow Am. Internat. Acad. (cert. and medallion 1957), Assn. Applied Psychoanalysis (exec. sec. 1963-67, 78-79, pres. 1968-69, 74-75; mem. AAAS, Am. Acad. Polit. and Social Scis., Interam. Soc. Psychology, Am. Acad. Psychotherapists, AAUP, Soc. Clin. and Exptl. Hypnosis, Council Psychoanalytic Psychotherapists, Am. Psychol. Assn., N.Y. State Psychol. Assn., N.Y. Soc. Clin. Psychologists, Bklyn. Psychol. Assn. (pres. 1971-72), N.Y. Acad. Scis., S.I. Mental Health Soc., Nat. Register Health Services Provider in Psychology, Bklyn. Assn. Mental Health, Richmond County Psychol. Assn. (pres. 1975), NYU Alumni Assn., Psi Chi, Alpha Phi Omega, Tau Delta Phi. Lodges: KP, Masons, Shriners. Home: 116 Village Walk Dr Royal Palm Beach FL 33411

KATZEN, LAWRENCE B., physician; b. Miami Beach, Fla., June 11, 1949; s. Harry H. and Rose (Nash) K.; m. Jane Dormer, Mar. 26, 1976; children—Janine Toba, Harrison Craig. B.S., U. Miami (Fla.), 1970, M.D., 1974. Diplomate Am. Bd. Ophthalmology. Intern, Washington Hosp. Ctr., 1974-75; practice medicine specializing in emergency medicine, Salisbury, Md., 1975-77; resident in ophthalmology Washington Hosp. Ctr., 1977-80; fellow in ophthalmic plastic and reconstructive surgery U. Ill. Hosp./Michael Reese Hosp. Med. Ctr., Chgo., 1980-81; practice medicine specializing in ophthalmology and oculoplastic surgery, Miami Beach and Lake Worth, Fla., 1982—; mem. faculty Bascom Palmer Eye Inst., U. Miami Sch. Medicine, 1983—; mem. staff Ann Bates Leach Eye Hosp., Miami, Parkway Med. Ctr., Miami, JFK Meml. Hosp., Lake Worth, Fla. U. Miami scholar, 1966-67. Fellow Am. Soc. Ophthalmic Plastic and Reconstructive Surgery; mem. Am. Acad. Ophthalmology, AMA, Palm Beach County Med. Soc., Fla. Med. Assn. Jewish. Contbr. articles to profl. jours. Office: 2889 10th Ave N Lake Worth FL 33461 also 16400 NW 2d Ave North Miami Beach FL 33169

KATZMAN, GEORGE, international marketing specialist, educator; b. N.Y.C., Feb. 2, 1920; s. Hyman and Helen (Slotnick) K.; m. Ellen Delyse Shure, Sept. 23, 1951; children—Richard Alan, Susan Lea. Lic. real estate broker. Owner jewelry plant, N.Y.C., 1946-51; project engr., mgr. Am. Measuring Instruments Corp., Long Island City, N.Y., 1951-53; owner, operator non-ferrous plant, Miami, Fla., 1954-63; mktg. specialist, Miami, 1964-77; self-employed mktg. agt. for menswear and jewelry, S.E. U.S., 1975-76; adj. prof. internat. relations of Europe, Fla. Internat. U., Miami, 1975—; pres. European Mktg. Corp., Miami, Transatlantic Realty Corp., Miami, Fla., 1980—; Am. cons. Pouey, Inc., Paris, 1973—; lectr. on bus. mgmt., mktg., internat. relations, fgn. policy. Author: (monograph) Marketing in Western Europe: Guidelines for the American Businessman. Mem., lectr. S.E. Fla. Holocaust Commn., Fla. Internat. U., 1983-84. Served with U.S. Army, 1943-46; ETO. Democrat. Home: 850 NE 178th Terr North Miami Beach FL 33162 Office: Transatlantic Realty Corporation 850 NE 178th Terr North Miami Beach FL 33162

KATZMAN, MARTIN THEODORE, economics educator; b. Boston, July 15, 1941; s. Ira and Miriam D. (Waldman) K.; m. Arlene Rita Cohen, July 31, 1966; children—Douglas Paul, Karen Deborah, Sarah Allison, Julie Elizabeth. B.A. summa cum laude, Harvard U., 1963; Ph.D., Yale U., 1966. Asst. research economist Inst. Govt. and Pub. Affairs, UCLA, 1966-67; asst. dir. Office Analytical Studies, lectr. city planning U. Calif.-Berkeley, 1967-68; asst. prof. edn. Harvard U., 1968-70; Ford Found. vis. prof. econs. U. São Paulo (Brazil), 1970-72; assoc. prof. city planning Harvard U., 1972-77; prof. polit. economy U. Tex.-Dallas, 1977-80, prof. econs. and environ. scis., 1980—; cons. First Nat. Bank of Boston, Nat. Inst. Edn., U.S. Dept. Energy. Mem. Mass. Task Force on Capital Formation for Econ. Devel., 1976-77; mem. adv. com. gifted and talented Richardson Ind. Sch. Dist., 1977-78. Recipient research award Risk and Ins. Mgmt. Soc., 1985; Woodrow Wilson fellow, 1963-64; NSF fellow, 1964-66; Guggenheim fellow, 1980-81. Mem. Am. Econ. Assn., AAAS, Am. Risk and Ins. Assn., Phi Beta Kappa. Jewish. Author: Political Economy of Urban Schools, 1971; Cities and Frontiers in Brazil: Regional Dimensions of Economic Development (one of best acad. books of 1977 by Choice), 1977; Solar and Wind Energy, 1984; Chemical Catastrophes, 1985. Home: 7212 Dye Dr Dallas TX 75248 Office: U Tex PO Box 830688 Richardson TX 75083

KAUFFMAN, JAMES MILTON, special education educator, writer; b. Hannibal, Mo., Dec. 7, 1940; s. Nelson Edward and Christmas Carol (Miller) K.; m. Myrna Ellen Miller, Apr. 9, 1960; children—James Timothy, Melissa Ellen. B.S. in Edn., Goshen Coll., 1962; M.Ed., Washburn U., 1966; Ed. D. in Spl. Edn., U. Kans., 1969. Tchr. Southard Sch., children's div. Menninger Clinic, Topeka, 1962-64; tchr. Shawnee Heights Unified Sch. Dist., Tecumseh, Kans., 1964-67; asst. prof. spl. edn. Ill. State U., Normal, 1969-70; asst. prof. spl. edn U. Va., Charlottesville, 1970-73, assoc. prof. spl. edn., 1973-80, prof. spl. edn., 1980—, chmn. dept. spl., edn., 1977-81, assoc. dean research, 1981-84; mem. Ill. state com. emotionally disturbed and socially disturbed children, 1970-71; instr. in-service courses Charlottesville Pub. Schs., 1971-73; cons. ednl. behavior modification Western State Hosp., Staunton, Va., 1972-74, U. N.Mex., N.Mex. State Dept. Edn., 1974; mem. adv. bd. Adaptive Learning Environments Model Program, U. Pitts., 1979-82, mem. vis. com. to evaluate grad. programs, 1980; field reader Bur. Edn. for Handicapped, 1973-75, 77-78. U. Va. grantee, 1973; Bur. Edn. for Handicapped grantee, 1977-81. Mem. Am. Ednl. Research Assn., Council Exceptional Children, Assn. Advancement Behavior Therapy, Soc. Research Child Devel., Internat. Acad. Research in Learning Disabilities, Soc. Learning Disabilities and Remedial Edn. (pres. 1980-81). Author: (with J.S. Payne, G.B. Brown, R.M. Demott) Exceptional Children in Focus: Incidents, Concepts, and Issues in Special Education, 1974; (with G. Wallace) Teaching Children with Learning Problems, 1978; (with D.P. Hallahan) Introduction to Learning Disabilities: A Psychobehavioral Approach, 1976; (with D.P. Hallahan) Exceptional Children: Introduction to Special Education, 1978; Characteristics of Children's Behavior Disorders, 1981; editor: (with C.D. Lewis) Teaching Children with Behavior Disorders, 1974; (with J.S. Payne) Mental Retardation: Introduction and Personal Perspectives, 1975; (with D.P. Hallahan) Teaching Children with Learning Disabilities: Personal Perspectives, 1976; (with D.P. Hallahan) Handbook of Special Education, 1981; assoc. editor: Exceptional Children, 1973-76, Analysis and Intervention in Developmental Disabilities, 1979-83; editor Remedial and Spl. Edn. (jour.), 1979—; cons. editor Behavior Research of Severe Developmental Disabilities, 1979-80, Learning Disability Quar., 1981—; mem. editorial adv. bd. Jour. Learning Disabilities, 1976-80; contbr. chpts. to books, articles to profl. jours. Office: U Va 122 Ruffner Hall Charlottesville VA 22903

KAUFFMAN, JOHN HENRY, III, optometrist; b. Kittery, Maine, May 3, 1954; s. John Henry Jr. and Diana (Michaude) K.; m. Cynthia Sue Wilkerson, Apr. 30, 1983; 1 child, Jonathan Chase. A.A., Old Dominion U., 1975; O.D., So. Coll. Optometry, Memphis, 1979. Lic. optometrist, Va. Contact lens cons. AMSCO, Lombart Lenses Ltd., Norfolk, Va., 1979-80; sr. assoc. Richard S. Bartley & Assoc., Hampton, Va., 1980—, cons., 1982—. Author: (booklet) Instruction Manual Fitting Guide for AMSOF Contact Lenses, 1979. Mem. Am. Assn. Optometrists (sec.-treas. 1980—), Beta Sigma Kappa, Omega Dleta. Episcopalian. Avocations: golfing; fishing; tennis; billiards; bowling. Home: 7 Woodlake Circle Newport News VA 23606 Office: Richard S Bartley & Assoc 2310 Cunningham Dr Hampton VA 23666

KAUFFMANN, CAROL BROWN, paper converting company executive; b. Atlanta, Sept. 22, 1943; d. Matt Briggs and Carol Crystal (Beery) Brown; m. Norman Jacques, Oct. 31, 1970. Student Sophie Newcomb Coll., Tulane U., 1961-63; B.A. in Psychology and English, Ga. State U., 1965, postgrad., 1965-66. With pub. relations dept. Delta Air Lines, Inc., Atlanta, 1966-70; v.p., treas., owner, dir. NORCOM, Inc., Springfield, Mass., 1978-80, exec. v.p., treas., owner, dir., Atlanta, 1980—; career counselor Ga. State U., Atlanta; mem. editorial staff Peachtree Papers mag. Trustee Mary Brown Trust Fund. of Atlanta; mem. Republican Senatorial Club, Rep. Presdl. Task Force; pres. Women's Symphony League of Springfield, 1978. Presbyterian. Mem. Jr. League Atlanta, Hist. Oakland Cemetery, Ga. Mental Health Assn., Atlanta Zool. Soc. Home: 2565 Habersham Rd NW Atlanta GA 30305 Office: 6866 Jimmy Carter Blvd Norcross GA 30071

KAUFMAN, JAMES MARK, lawyer; b. Oklahoma City, Feb. 28, 1951; s. Milford James and Frances Aileen (Knight) K.; B.B.A., U. Okla., 1973, J.D., 1976; m. Vicki Jane Johnston, Aug. 18, 1973 (div. July 1985); children—Nathan Jay, Kaitlin Ann; m. Katheryn K. Kidd, Nov. 29, 1985; 1 child, Jordan Paige. Bar: Okla. 1976, U.S. Supreme Ct. 1983. Legal intern firm Carson & Trattner, Oklahoma City, 1975-77; assoc. firm Cheek, Cheek & Cheek, Oklahoma City, 1977-81, McKinney, Stringer & Webster, Oklahoma City, 1981-84; mem. firm Kaufman & Cheek, Oklahoma City, 1984—. Mem. Oklahoma County Bar Assn., Okla. Bar Assn., Sigma Chi. Club: Young Men's Dinner. Home: 2224 NW 120th St Oklahoma City OK 73120 Office: 3524 NW 56th St Suite 175 Oklahoma City OK 73112

KAUFMAN, JON ROSS, association executive; b. Los Angeles, Nov. 27, 1954; s. Joseph and Kay (LePon) K.; m. Maria S. Romero, July 10, 1981. Student pub. schs., Los Angeles; grad. Synanon Coll. Mgr. procurement Synanon Ch., Marin County, Calif., 1968-80, mktg. rep., Tulare County, Calif., 1980-82, dir. Synanon-Houston, 1983—. Republican. Jewish. Address: Synanon 5707 B Gardendale Dr Houston TX 77092

KAUFMAN, PHILIP RODNEY, safety engineer; b. Louisville, May 24, 1954; s. Alvin R. and Naomi J. (Miller) K.; m. Deborah Ann Kohls, May 31, 1975; 1 child, Vincent Rodney. B.S., Eastern Ky. U., 1976. Supr. fire loss prevention Louisville Gas & Electric Co., 1976—; asst. chief Pleasure Ridge Park Fire Dist., Jefferson County, Ky., 1972—; bd. advisers fire sci. program Jefferson Community Coll., 1982—. Instr./trainer Am. Heart Assn., 1979—; bd. dirs. St. Stephen United Ch. of Christ, 1981-84. Recipient cert. of appreciation Am. Heart Assn., 1979, Ky. State Fire Sch., 1980-85. Mem. Am. Soc. Safety Engrs., Jefferson County Alliance of Fire Chiefs (v.p. 1981—), Internat. Assn. Fire Chiefs, Internat. Soc. Fire Service Instrs., Ky. Firefighters Assn., Jefferson County Hazardous Materials Assn. Republican. Avocations: water sports; woodworking; electronics; autos. Home: 7403 Gaymont Dr Pleasure Ridge Park KY 40214 Office: Louisville Gas Co PO Box 32010 Louisville KY 40202

KAUFMAN, TOD J., state senator; b. Charleston, Oct. 15, 1952; s. Paul J. and Rose Jean K. B.A., Tufts U., 1975; postgrad. London Sch. Econs. and Polit. Sci., 1973-74; J.D., W.Va. U., 1980. Bar: W.Va. Paralegal, Convington & Burling, Washington, 1976-78; law clk. U.S. Tax Ct., Washington, 1979; ptnr. Kaufman & Ratliff, Charleston, 1980—; apptd. W.Va. Senate, 1982—, vice chmn. confirmations com. Bd. dirs. Women's Health Ctr.; founder Piedmont Tennis Program for Underprivileged. Mem. ABA, W.Va. Bar Assn., Kanawha County Bar Assn., W.Va. Trial Lawyers Assn. Club: Sierra, The Wilderness Soc. Office: W Va Senate Charleston WV 25305*

KAUFMANN, JAMES A., physician; b. Detroit, Dec. 15, 1923; s. Adolph and Dena (Lieberman) K.; children—Nancy Hope, Robert Scott. Student Vanderbilt U.; M.D., U. Tenn., 1947. Diplomate Am. Bd. Internal Medicine. Intern, Emory U. Service, Grady Meml. Hosp., Atlanta, 1947-48; resident in medicine Tufts U. Service, Pratt Diagnostic Hosp., New Eng. Med. Ctr., Boston, 1949-50, U. Louisville Service, Louisville Gen. Hosp., 1950-51; instr. Emory U. Sch. Medicine, 1952-57, assoc. in medicine, 1957—; practice medicine specializing in internal medicine, Atlanta; mem. staff Crawford W. Long Meml. Hosp.; pres. Kaufmann Diagnostic Clinic; cons. in medicine South Fulton Hosp., 1963-80, Psychiat. Inst. Atlanta, 1963—, Atlanta Fulton County Recreational Authority, 1979—; mem. staff Gov. Jimmy Carter, 1970-74, Gov. George Busbee, 1974-82. Contbr. articles in field to profl. jours. Chmn. bd. trustees Kaufmann Found., 1960-72; mem. southeastern regional bd. Anti-Defamation League, 1964—, vice chmn., 1981-84, chmn., 1984—; nat. vice chmn. Soc. Fellows, 1976—; active Am. Jewish Com., 1953—; active Democratic party Ga., 1960—, Fulton County Dem. party, 1960—, Century Club of Fulton County Dem. party, 1976—, mem. fin. com. Dem. Nat. Com., 1972—, vice chmn. Sam Nunn for Senate Com., 1972, treas. Senator Herman Talmadge Campaign Com., 1974; mem. Com. to Reorganize Comptroller Gen.'s Office, 1963-64; mem. Am. Israel Pub. Affairs Com., 1978—; mem. governing bd. Fulton County Heart Council, 1958-64; dir. med. program Ga. Gen. Assembly, 1970—; chmn. Council on Govtl. Affairs, 1970; mem. employment security agy. advisory council Ga. Dept. Labor, 1978—; sponsor Ga. Med. Polit. Action Com., 1970—; active Atlanta Symphony, 1965—, Nat. Jewish Welfare Bd., 1978—; mem. spl. gifts com. Atlanta Med. Heritage, 1981; chmn. physicians' div. United Way, 1981; bd. dirs. Civic Theater Atlanta, 1970; mem. patron's soc. Crawford W. Long Meml. Hosp., 1970—; trustee Ga. State U. Found., Morehouse Sch. Medicine; mem. Gov.'s Council Profl. Liability. Recipient Pres.'s award Morehouse Sch. Medicine, 1984; Outstanding Community Service award Christian Council Met. Atlanta, 1983, numerous others. Fellow Am. Coll. Chest Physicians (nat. com. on hypertension 1959-66), Am. Coll. Cardiology, Internat. Coll. Angiology; mem. ACP (life), Am. Soc. Internal Medicine (Disting. Internist award 1984), AMA, Med. Assn. Ga. (chmn. legis. com. 1973—, chmn. state com. on quackery 1970-77, mem. exec. com. 1979—, chmn. com. on physician/lawyer liaison 1983-84), So. Med. Assn., Med. Assn. Atlanta (trustee), Ga. Diabetes Assn., Atlanta Lung Assn., Ga. Lung Assn., DeKalb County Med. Soc., Nat. Tb Assn. (pres. 1956), Atlanta Tb Assn. (med. adv. bd. 1953-59, bd. dirs. 1959-63), Nat. Assn. Disability Examiners, Am. Heart Assn. (council clin. cardiology 1968—), Ga. Heart Assn., Am. Assn. for Respiratory Therapy, Am. Physicians Fellowship for Israel, Ga. Soc. Internal Medicine, Ga. Rehab. Assn., Ga. Soc. Respiratory Therapy, Am. Diabetes Assn., Am. Geriatric Soc., Am. Cancer Soc., Ga. Thoracic Soc., Am. Thoracic Soc., Am. Acad. Polit. and Social Sci., Jewish Hist. Soc. Am. (honor historian 1976—), NAACP (life, exec. bd. 1978—, co-chmn. polit. action com. Atlanta 1978—), Ga. C. of C. (state/nat. affairs task force 1982), Atlanta C. of C., Cobb County C. of C., Emory U. Alumni Assn. (bd. dirs.), U. Tenn. Coll. Medicine Alumni Assn., Lamplighter Soc. (Emory U.), Atlanta Bot. Soc., Zeta Beta Tau. Clubs: Atlanta Press, Braves 400, Commerce, Georgian, Stadium, Temple, Presidents (U. Tenn.). Lodge: B'nai B'rith (pres. Gate City lodge 1964-65, Silver mem. youth services Pres. club 1977—). Home: Apt 37-A-1 6640 Akers Mill Rd Atlanta GA 30339 Office: Kaufmann Diagnostic Clinic 565 W Peachtree St NE Atlanta GA 30308

KAUFMANN, ROBERT JOHN, physician; b. Chgo., Feb. 10, 1921; s. John H. and Anna (Schoenenberger) K.; A.B., James Millikin U., 1943; M.D., U. Ill., 1946; m. Majory Ann Magill, June 15, 1946; children—Suzanne (Mrs. Marc Tomlinson), Philip, Stephen, John, Thomas. Resident, MacNeal Meml. Hosp., 1949-51; physician, surgeon, adminstr. Pahala Hosp., Hawaii, 1951-58; med. dir. Maytag Co., Newton, Iowa, 1958-62; dir. Med. Services Am. Samoa, Dept. Interior, 1962-65; with AEC Health Found., Richland, Wash., 1965-66; pvt. practice medicine, Martinez, Calif., 1966-69; pres. staff Martinez Community Hosp., 1969; pvt. practice, Renton and Redmond, Wash., 1969-70; adminstrv. head emergency physicians Auburn (Wash.) Gen. Hosp., 1970-76, sec., med. staff, 1973-74, treas., 1972-76; tng. Brooks AFB Sch. Aerospace Medicine, 1976; dir. aerospace medicine Maxwell AFB, Ala., 1976-78; hosp. comdr. Wurtsmith AFB (Mich.) Hosp., 1978-81; mem. Physicians Evaluation Bd., Mil. Personnel Center, USAF, Randolph, Tex., 1981—; reviewing physician local draft bd., 1967-69; mem. planning bd. King County Puget Sound Health Planning Council, 1972-76. Mem. local council Boy Scouts Am., 1967-69. Served as lt. (j.g.) USNR, 1946-49; lt. col. to col., M.C., USAF, 1976—. Decorated Meritorious Serivce medal. Mem. Am., Indsl., Iowa, King County (com. emergency services) med. assns., Am. Geriatrics Soc., Pan Pacific Surg. Assn., Am. Coll. Emergency Physicians (charter mem. N.W. div. mem. chpt. exec. bd. 1972, sec. 1973-74), AMA, Assn. Mil. Surgeons U.S., Air Force Assn., Model Railroad Assn. (life), Renton Hist. Soc., U. Ill. Alumni Assn., James Milliken U. Alumni Assn., Ft. Steilecoom Running Club, Oreg. Road Runners, Marathon Runners Club, Sigma Zeta. Roman Catholic. Clubs: KC, Kiwanis. Home: 2 E Park Randolph AFB TX 78148 Office: Phys Evaluation Bd Mil Personnel Center USAAF Randolph TX

KAUGER, YVONNE, justice Oklahoma Supreme Court; b. Cordell, Okla., Aug. 3, 1937; m. Ned Bastow, May 8, 1982; 1 child, Jonna Sinclair. B.S. magna cum laude, Southwestern State U., Okla., 1958; J.D., Oklahoma City U., 1969. Bar: Okla. 1970. Cert. med. technologist. Med. technologist Med. Arts Lab., 1959-68; assoc. Rogers, Travis & Jordan, 1970-72; jud. asst. to Justice Ralph B. Hodges, Supreme Court Okla., 1972-84; justice Supreme Court Okla., Oklahoma City, 1984—; apptd. to Appellate Div. of the Ct. on the Judiciary; mem. dean's adv. com. Oklahoma City U. Sch. of Law. Founder, Gallery of the Plains Indians, Colony, Okla.; mem. State Capitol Preservation Commn., 1983-84; lifetime mem. Washita County Hist. Soc.; bd. dirs. Lyric Theatre, Inc., 1966—, pres., 1981; mem. St. Paul's Episc. Ch., St. Paul's Music Soc.; participant, organizer Jud. Day at Girl's State, 1976-80, keynote address Hall of Fame Banquet, 1984; past bd. dirs. Civic Music Soc., Okla. Theatre Ctr., Canterbury Choral Soc. Recipient Dean's award Oklahoma City U., 1969; included in Outstanding Young Women Am., 1967; named Byliner Honoree Women in Communications, 1984; adopted Cheyenne-Arapaho tribesonn ceremonial grounds Colony, 1984; named Woman of Yr. High Noon, 1985; recipient other honors. Mem. ABA (mem. law sch. accreditation com.), Okla. Bar Assn. (mem. law schs. com. 1977—), Washita County Bar Assn., Iota Tau Tau (1st place internat. scholarship award 1969), Delta Zeta. Office: Supreme Court of Oklahoma Room 204 State Capitol Oklahoma City OK 73105

KAVASS, IGOR IVAR, law educator, law librarian, consultant; b. Riga, Latvia, July 31, 1932; s. Nicolas and Iraida (Kushnarev) K.; m. Carmen Boada; children—Sybilla, Ariane, Lara, Veronica, Nicholas. LL.B. with honors, U. Melbourne (Australia), 1955. Bar: High Ct. Australia, Supreme Ct. Victoria (Australia), Supreme Ct. South Australia (Australia) 1957. Practice, Melbourne, 1956-59; sr. lectr. in law U. Adelaide (Australia) and U. Melbourne, 1959-66; vis. prof. law U. Ala., 1966-67; assoc. prof. law Monash U., Melbourne, 1967-68; prof. law, dir. Law Library, U. Ala., 1968-70; prof., law librarian Northwestern U., Chgo., 1970-72; prof., law librarian Duke U., Durham, N.C., 1972-75; prof., dir. Legal Info. Ctr. Vanderbilt U., Nashville, 1975—; vis. prof. Free U. Berlin, 1975; editorial cons. William S. Hein & Co., Buffalo; cons. legal research and info. Mem. Am. Assn. Advancement Slavic Studies, Am. Assn. Law Libraries, Am. Soc. Internat. Law, Assn. Am. Law Schs., Brit. Inst. Internat. and Comparative Law, Internat. Assn. Law Libraries (pres. 1976-83), Soc. Pub. Tchrs. Law (U.K.), Order of Coif. Author numerous books, including: (with Michael Blake) United States Legislation on Foreign Relations and International Commerce, 1789-1979 (Am. Soc. Internat. Law cert. Merit 1979), 5 vols., 1977, 78, 84; (with B.A. Christensen) A Guide to North Carolina Legal Research, 1973; (with Adolf Sprudzs) A Guide to the United States Treaties in Force, 1982, and ann. updates; contbr. articles to profl. publs.; editor books, including: International Military Law and History Reprint Series, 1972—; editor pub. Internat. Assn. Law Libraries Newsletter, 1976-79. Office: Vanderbilt U Sch Law Nashville TN 37240

KAWAGUCHI, HARRY HARUMITSU, psychologist; b. Watsonville, Calif., Oct. 14, 1928; s. Kikuzo and Kino (Tanaka) K.; B.A., U. Tex., 1953, M.A., 1957; m. Meredith Ferguson, Apr. 22, 1977. Clin. psychologist Austin (Tex.) State Hosp., 1961-73; pvt. practice clin. psychology, Austin, 1973—; cons. Tex. Vocat. Rehab. Assn., Tex. Com. on Alcoholism. Bd. dirs. Salvation Army Youth Center. Mem. Tex. Psychol. Assn., Assn. Advancement of Psychology, Am. Psychol. Assn., Council for Nat. Register for Health Service Providers in Psychology, Internat. Platform Assn. Democrat. Episcopalian. Home: 5009 Westview Dr Austin TX 78731 Office: 1600 W 38th St Suite 400-7 Austin TX 78731

KAWAMURA, KAZUHIKO, electrical engineering educator; b. Nagoya, Japan, Feb. 4, 1939; came to U.S., 1964, naturalized, 1981; s. Eizo and Nobuko (Tani) K.; m. Ethel Ruth Perisho, Jan. 2, 1971. B.E.E., Waseda U., Tokyo, 1963; M.S. in E.E., U. Calif., Berkeley, 1966; Ph.D., U. Mich.-Ann Arbor, 1972. Lectr., U. Mich.-Dearborn, 1972-73; specialist Ford Motor Co., Dearborn, Mich., 1973; researcher Battelle Columbus Lab., Columbus, Ohio, 1973-78, prin. researcher, 1978-81; invited prof. Kyoto U., Japan, 1980; assoc. prof. Sch. Engring. Vanderbilt U., Nashville, 1981—, assoc. dir. Ctr. for Intelligent Systems, 1985—. Mem. AAAS, Soc. Gen. Systems Research, IEEE, Soc. Risk Analysis, AAAI, Robotics Internat. Office: Box 1674 Sta B Vanderbilt U Nashville TN 37235

KAY, JOE ELDRED, food marketing executive; b. Lakeland, Fla., Mar. 1, 1931; s. Sidney Christopher and Elva (Coleman) K.; m. Dionne O'Brien, Mar. 11, 1956 (div. 1973); children—Jeffrey James, Sandra Leigh, Jon Christopher. B.S.B.A., The Citadel, 1953. In various sales positions Scott Paper Co., Atlanta, 1960-61, Orlando, Fla., 1961-63, Atlanta, 1963-65, Charlotte, N.C., 1965-67, Phila., 1967-69, Atlanta, 1969-71; regional mgr. A.E. Staley Co., Atlanta, 1971-75, eastern sales mgr., 1976-81; mgr. so. region H. P. Hood Co., Atlanta, 1981-83; dir. sales and mktg. So. region Williams Foods Inc., Atlanta, 1983—. Served to capt. U.S. Army, 1953-60; ETO. Republican. Episcopalian.

KAYE, BERNARD L., plastic surgeon, musician; b. New Haven, Conn., Sept. 12, 1927; s. Reubin and Anne Kaye; m. Joyce Bailey; children—Robert Scott, Debra Hollis. B.A., Yale U., 1949; M.D., Harvard U., 1955; D.M.D., Harvard Sch. Dental Medicine, 1953. Diplomate Am. Bd. Plastic Surgery. Pvt. practice plastic surgery, Jacksonville, Fla., 1962—; asst. clin. prof. surgery, U. Fla., 1970-76, clin. prof. surgery, 1976—; past chief plastic surgery service Baptist Med. Ctr., Jacksonville, Fla. Past v.p. Jacksonville Safety Council; bd. dirs. Jacksonville Symphony Assn.; prin. saxophonist Jacksonville Symphony Orch.; 1st saxophonist Jacksonville Starlight Symphonette. Served to lt. sr. grade USCG, 1956-58. Recipient Best Faculty award Plastic Surgery Ednl. Found.

(2); Beale award for best paper Duval County Med. Soc. (2). Mem. Am. Soc. Aethetic Plastic Surgery (past pres.), Am. Soc. Plastic and Reconstructive Surgeons, Fla. Soc. Plastic and Reconstructive Surgeons (past pres.), N.E. Fla. Soc. Plastic Surgery (past pres.); fellow ACS, Am. Assn. Plastic Surgeons. Clubs: River, Ponte Vedra, Deerwood, Sawgrass (Jacksonville). Contbr. articles to profl. jours. Office: Suite 702 820 Prudential Dr Jacksonville FL 32207

KAYE, HELEN LOUISE, speech pathologist; b. Newark, June 2, 1945; d. Frank William Juliana and Florence Louise (Trano) J.; m. Graham Ross Donaldson, Aug. 24, 1968 (dec.); 1 son, Christopher Eric; m. Bryce William Kaye, Dec. 19, 1981. A.B., Douglass Coll., 1967; M.Ed., Pa. State U., 1968. Speech pathologist Children's Hosp., Halifax, N.S., 1968-72, Peel and Halton Counties Home Care, Ont., 1972-79; lectr. speech N.C. State U., Raleigh, 1980; speech pathologist Gov. Morehead Sch. for Blind, Raleigh, 1980-83, coordinator multihandicapped program, 1983—; clin. supr. internship programs U. N.C.-Chapel Hill, N.C. State U., Raleigh. Active Assn. Retarded Citizens, N.C. Orgn. Advancement Visually Impaired. Mem. Am. Speech, Hearing and Lang. Assn., N.C. Speech, Hearing and Lang. Assn., Assn. Edn. Visually Impaired, Sigma Alpha Eta. Democrat. Unitarian. Club: Capital Area Speech Pathologists. Home: 421 Warren Ave Cary NC 27511 Office: Gov Morehead Sch for Blind 301 Ashe Ave Raleigh NC 27606

KAYE, MARTIN BERNARD, chemical company executive; b. Norfolk, Va., July 13, 1948; s. Nathan and Shirley Jean (Nicholson) K. B.S. in Adminstrn. and Mgmt. Sci., Carnegie-Mellon U., 1971, M.B.A. in Indsl. Adminstrn., 1971. Corp. planning analyst Bankers Trust Co., N.Y.C., 1971-73; fin. analyst Freeport-McMoran, Inc., N.Y.C., 1974-77; adminstrv. coordinator Freeport Queensland Nickel, Inc., New Orleans, 1977-78; asst. v.p. fin. Freeport Chem. Co., Uncle Sam, La., 1978-84; dir. planning and analysis Chems. Group, Freeport-McMoran, Inc., New Orleans, 1984—; also gt. dane breeder. Carnegie-Mellon U. fellow, 1970. Mem. Data Processing Mgmt. Assn., Gt. Dane Club Am., Phi Kappa Phi. Home: 824 Vintage Dr Kenner LA 70065 Office: Freeport McMoran Inc 1615 Poydras St New Orleans LA

KAYE, NEAL WALLACE, SR., brewery executive, travel agency executive; b. Meridian, Miss., Sept. 15, 1916; s. Frank and Sara (Mashburn) K.; m. Ruth Hammond Drew, Mar. 21, 1938 (dec. 1975); children—Patricia Kaye Frankland, Neal W.; m. Betty Hunt, June 24, 1978. B.A. in Bus. Adminstrn., U. Ga., 1937. Mgr. sales adminstrn. Jos. B. Schlitz Brewing Co., Milw., 1947-68; owner, operator Schlitz West Palm Beach Distbrs. (Fla.), 1968; chmn. bd. Neal W. Kaye, Inc., New Orleans, 1969—, Coy Internat. Corp., New Orleans, 1981—, Dixie Brewing Co., Inc., 1983—; pres. Let's Go, Inc., New Orleans, 1983—. Bd. dirs. met. area com. New Orleans Jazz and Heritage Found.; active New Orleans Tourist and Conv. Commn. Served to lt. USN, 1942-47. Mem. Nat. Beer Wholesalers' Assn. (past pres.), Beer Industry League La., Navy League U.S. Clubs: Internat. House, City (New Orleans), Pendennis, New Orleans Country. Office: Dixie Brewing Co Inc 2537 Tulane Ave New Orleans LA 70119

KAYE, RACHEL, computer, capital equipment leasing company executive, educator; b. Broken Bow, Okla., Sept. 16, 1937; d. Manuel and Iris Erma (Harvey) Y'Barra; m. Harvey J. Kupferberg, Feb. 24, 1962 (div. 1974); children—Elisabeth Dana, Eric David. B.A. in Bus. Adminstrn., Goddard Coll., 1976. Tng. dir. Mayor's Office Manpower, Balt., 1977-78, mgr. adminstrv. services, 1978-80; dir. adminstrv. services Univ. Research Corp., Chevy Chase, Md., 1980-81; dir. adminstrn. Finalco, Inc., McLean, Va., 1981-82, asst. v.p. adminstrn., 1982-83, v.p., 1983—; bd. dirs. Vision House, 1982—; adj. prof. bus. adminstrn. Community Coll. Balt., 1979—; mgmt. cons. to pvt. cos., 1970-81. Mem. Nat. Assn. Female Execs., Am. Mgmt. Assn., Am. Soc. Tng. and Devel., Am. Soc. Pub. Adminstrn. Home: 6678 Midhill Pl Falls Church VA 22043 Office: Finalco Inc 8200 Greensboro Dr McLean VA 22102

KAYE, SIDNEY, toxicologist, educator; b. Bklyn., Mar. 10, 1912; s. Isaac and Ida (Lefkowitz) Kozinsky; B.S., N.Y. U., 1935, M.S., 1939; Ph.D., Med. Coll. Va., 1956; m. Carmen Maria Jimenez Calzada, June 7, 1951; children—Cynthia Susan, Frederic Joseph. Toxicoldgist, St. Louis Police, 1946-47; instr. Washington U., St. Louis, 1946-47; state toxicologist State of Va., 1947-62; assoc. prof. Med. Coll. Va., Richmond, 1947-62; state toxicologist, P.R., 1962—; assoc. dir. Inst. Legal Medicine, prof. emeritus toxicology, pathology, pharmacology and legal medicine U. P.R., San Juan, 1962—; cons. to U.S. Army, VA; adj. prof. Caribe U.; coordinator Poison Control Center, Va., 1950-62, P.R., 1962—; lectr. in field. Served to col. Med. Service, U.S. Army, 1941-46. Decorated Army Commendation medal, Legion of Merit; recipient cert. of appreciation U.S. CD, P.R. CD, Indsl. Coll. Armed Forces; diplomate Am. Bd. Clin. Chemistry, Am. Bd. Toxicology. Mem. Nat. Safety Council, Am. Acad. Forensic Scis. (founding, recipient award of merit), Soc. Toxicolog (founding), Pan Am. Med. Assn. (Latin Am. v.p. taxicology), Soc. Mil. Surgeons (life), Sigma Xi (founding pres. P.R.). Contbr. chpts. on toxicology, to books, articles to profl. jours. Author: Emergency Toxicology, 4th edit., 1979. Office: GPO Box 5067 Inst Forensic Med San Juan PR 00936

KAYS, B. THOMAS, dentist, educator; b. Kansas City, Mo., July 2, 1944; s. Benjamin C. and Mary C. (Shelton) K.; m. Claudia Johnson, Aug. 14, 1982; children—Mary Trinette, B. Charles, Tadd Wright McKellar. B.S., the Citadel, 1966, M.Ed., 1981; D.D.S., U. Iowa, 1970. Gen. practice dentistry, Charleston, S.C., 1972—; asst. clin. prof. Med. U. S.C., Charleston, 1972—. Bd. dirs. Omega Ins. Co., Psi Omega Found. Served to capt. USAF, 1970-72. Fellow Internat. Coll. Dentists; mem. ADA, S.C. Dental Assn. (v.p. 1984-85, pres. 1986—, directing sec. 1983-84), Coastal Dist. Dental Soc., Charleston Dental Soc., Psi Omega (nat. pres. 1983-84). Republican. Episcopalian. Avocations: sailboat racing; photography. Home: 12 Casa Bianca Dr Charleston SC 29407 Office: 1040 Savannah Hwy Charleston SC 29407

KAZAKS, PETER A., physics educator; b. Riga, Latvia, Feb. 22, 1940; s. Aleksander and Sigrida (Meijers) K.; m. Alexandra Garrison Hazen, Sept. 8, 1968; children—Julia, Emily, Karl, Kristopher, Hazen. B.Sc. with honors, McGill U., 1962; M.S., Yale U., 1963; Ph.D. in Physics, U. Calif.-Davis, 1968. Postdoctoral research assoc. Ohio U., Athens, 1968-70; asst. prof. physics St. Laurence U., 1970-73; asst. to assoc., then prof. New Coll., U. South Fla., Sarasota, 1973—, chmn. div. natural scis., 1979—. Grantee NSF, 1972-73, Research Corp., 1974-75, 75-76; Computer Sci. Devel. grantee. Mem. Am. Physics Soc. Contbr. articles to profl. jours. Office: Div Natural Sciences New College U South Fla Sarasota FL 34243

KAZOR, WALTER ROBERT, mechanical engineer; b. Avonmore, Pa., Apr. 16, 1922; s. Steven Stanley and Josephine (Lestic) K.; B.S. in Mech. Engring., Pa. State U., 1943; M.S., U. Pitts., 1953, M.Letters in Econs. and Indsl. Mgmt., 1957; m. Gloria Rosalind Roma, Aug. 10, 1946; children—Steven Edward, Christopher Paul, Kathleen Mary Jo. Research engr. Gulf Oil Corp., Pitts., 1946-57; with Westinghouse Electric Corp., 1957-84, quality assurance mgr. breeder reactor components project, Tampa, Fla., 1977-81, mgr. nuclear service center, Tampa, 1981-84; pres. Integrated Quality Systems Corp., Mgmt. Quality Assurance Cons., St. Petersburg, Fla., 1984-86; quality assurance specialist in nuclear waste mgmt. Sci. Applications Internat. Corp., Las Vegas, 1986—; cons., guest lectr. in field. Bd. dirs. New Kensington (Pa.) council Boy Scouts Am., 1958-62. Served with USNR, 1944-46. Registered profl. engr., Pa. Mem. ASME, Am. Soc. Quality Control. Republican. Roman Catholic. Club: Lions (past pres. clubs). Author, patentee in field. Home: 1120 88th Ave N Saint Petersburg FL 33702

KEAGY, DOROTHY KEAGY, marketing communications executive; b. Waltham, Mass., March 3, 1945; d. Albert Stanley and Bertha (Bluestein) Rouffa; m. Robert Keagy, Aug. 6, 1966 (div.); children—Meredith, Brian; m. Timothy Bishop, July 10, 1982. Student U. Ill., 1963-65, Pratt Inst., N.Y.C., 1965-66. Mgr. depts. Neiman-Marcus, Lou Lattimore, Tex., 1970-75; freelance writer Dallas Morning News, 1975-76; editor Dallas Fashion Showcase, 1976-78; bur. chief, regional editor Women's Wear Daily, Dallas, 1978-84; dir. mktg. communications Dallas Apparel Mart, Trammel Crow Co., 1984—. Mem. Tacassociates, Dallas, 1982-83. Recipient Editorial award Dallas Apparel Mart, Braniff Internat. Bambi award, 1980. Mem. Fashion Group Dallas, Sigma Delta Phi. Contbr. mag. articles to publs. Office: 2300 Stemmons St Dallas TX 75207

KEARL, MICHAEL CHARLES, sociology and gerontology educator; b. Seattle, Jan. 21, 1949; s. J. Alten and Cordelia Ann (Rankin) K.; m. Joan Woolf, Aug. 17, 1974; 1 child, Frank Rankin. B.A., Dartmouth Coll., 1971; Ph.D., Stanford U., 1976. Vis. prof. U. Tex.-San Antonio, 1976-77; asst. prof. sociology and gerontology Trinity U., San Antonio, 1977-82, assoc. prof., 1982—; cons. San Antonio State Hosp., 1980, Adv. Task Force for Tex. Gov's Com. in Aging, Austin, 1976-77. Contbr. articles to profl. publs. Bd. dirs. St. Benedict's Hospice, San Antonio, 1980-81; mem. Tex. Bd. Morticians, Austin, 1981—. Mem. Am. Sociol. Assn., Gerontology Soc. Am., Assn. Sociology of Religion, Soc. Sci. Study of Religion, S.W. Social Sci. Assn. Democrat. Home: 1702 Talcott San Antonio TX 78232 Office: Trinity U 715 Stadium Dr San Antonio TX 78284

KEARNEY, RICHARD JAMES, chemical marketing consultant; b. Kansas City, Mo., Aug. 25, 1927; s. Emmett Leo and Irene Elizabeth (Ruddock) K.; B.S. in Chem. Engring., U. Mich., 1951; m. Caroline Hamilton Archer, Sept. 19, 1953; children—Caroline Hamilton, Richard James. Chem. purchasing agt. Hercules, Inc., Wilmington, Del., 1954-62; chmn. bd., pres., sr. v.p. Kearney Chems. Inc., Tampa, Fla., 1962-80; sr. v.p. Royster Chems., Inc., 1980-82; chem. mktg. Cons., Tampa, 1982—. Served with USNR, 1945-46, to 1st lt. AUS, 1951-53; Korea. Mem. Am. Chem. Soc., Pershing Rifles, Scabbard and Blade Honor Soc., Decorative Arts Soc., Tampa Arts Mus., Sigma Chi. Episcopalian. Clubs: U. Mich. Pres.'s, Tampa Yacht and Country, Tower, Bath. Office: 4301 El Prado Tampa FL 33629

KEARNEY, WILLIAM EDWARD, petroleum geologist; b. San Antonio, May 18, 1928; s. William Edward and Loda Genevieve (Revard) K.; m. Elizabeth Jean Stremmel, Dec. 23, 1949; children—Dale Edward, Sheryl Lynn Kearney Sanders. B.S., Okla. State U., 1952. Dist. prodn. geologist, Seaboard Oil Co., Corpus Christi, Tex., 1952-58; dist. exploitation geologist Texaco, Inc., Corpus Christi, 1958-61; cons. geologist, San Antonio, 1961-64; dist. geologist Crown Petroleum Corp., Houston, 1964-68; sr. staff geologist The Analysts, Inc., Houston, 1968-73; regional geologist Pennzoil/Pogo, Houston, 1973-76; offshore dist. exploration mgr. Am. Natural Resources, Houston, 1976-79; div. mgr. Paragon Resources, Inc., Houston, 1979-80; v.p. exploration Shield Resources, Inc., Houston, 1980-82; sr. explorationist Daniel Oil Co., Houston, 1982-83; v.p. exploration Convest Energy Corp., 1983-85; cons., Navasota, Tex., 1985—. Active local ch., scouting, PTA groups. Served with USN, 1946-48. Mem. Houston Geol. Soc., Am. Assn. Petroleum Geologists. Republican. Methodist. Avocations: ranching, hunting, fishing, golf. Home and Office: Route 1 Box 406 Navasota TX 77868

KEARNS, GREGORY LEE, clinical pharmacologist, researcher; b. St. Louis, June 3, 1954; s. Noel Wesley and Jacqueline Virginia (Byrds) K.; m. Franicine Storm, Sept. 1, 1979; 1 child, Justin Hadley. B.S. in Pharmacy, St. Louis Coll. of Pharmacy, 1977; Pharm.D., U. Cin., 1979. Instr., pharmacology and pediatrics La. State U. Sch. of Med., Shreveport, 1981-83; asst. prof. pharm. and pediatrics U. Ark. Med. Sci., Little Rock, 1983—; cons. La. State U. Poison Control Ctr., Shreveport, 1980-82, Poison and Drug Info. Ctr. U. Ark. Med. Sci., Little Rock, 1983—; head clin. pharmacokinetic monitor service Ark. Childrens Hosp., Little Rock, 1983—. Contbr. articles to profl. jours. Chmn. Bd. of Christian Life-Rose Hill Ch. of The Nazarene, Little Rock, 1983-85. Served to capt. USAFR, 1982—. Recipient Young Investigator award So. Soc. Ped. Research, 1982, Found. Research award U. Ark. Med. Scis., 1984. Mem. Am. Pharm. Assn., Acad. Pharm. Scis., Assn. Mil. Surgeons U.S., Sigma Xi, Rho Chi. Club: B.A.S.S. (Little Rock). Avocations: fishing; computer programming; flying. Office: Dept of Pediatrics Slot 522 Univ Ark Med Sci 4301 W Markham Little Rock AR 72205

KEATING, DANIEL GRIFFITH, banker; b. St. Louis, Feb. 10, 1944; s. Anthony Francis and Anne (Martin) K.; m. Kathryn Shields, Dec. 30, 1967; children—Matthew, Bryan. B.S., Tulsa U., 1967; M.B.A., U. Okla., 1972. Vice pres. Bank of Okla., Tulsa, 1976-80; v.p. First Nat. Bank, Tulsa, 1980-82, sr. v.p., 1982—. Underwriting mem. Lloyd's of London, 1979—. Bd. dirs. Tulsa Civic Ballet, 1972, Jr. Achievement, 1981; assoc. trustee Hillcrest Med. Ctr., 1981. Served to lt. col. USMC, 1967. Mem. Tulsa County Hist. Soc. (bd. dirs.). Republican. Roman Catholic. Home: 1392 E 27th St Tulsa OK 74114 Office: First Nat Bank Box 1 5th and Boston Tulsa OK 74193

KEATING, JEROME FRANCIS, transportation executive, personnel administrator, educator; b. Chgo., July 24, 1938; s. James Basil and Dorothy Mildred (Kettner) K.; m. Janet Anne Gelineau, Apr. 2, 1970 (div. Dec. 1982); children—Jerome G., Doranne M., Marcelle J. B.A. in English, U. Notre Dame, 1961; M.A. in Counseling and Theology, Holy Cross Coll., 1965; M.A. in English, U. Notre Dame, 1966; Ph.D. in Humanities, Syracuse U., 1972. Cert. tchr., U. Mich. Prof., Bishop Coll., Dallas, 1975-79; assoc. dir. Opportunity to Learn and Earn, Dallas, 1979-80; dir. Dallas Trade Sch., 1980-81; mem. quality and mfg. tng. staff Otis Engring., Dallas, 1981-82; tng. mgr. Lehigh Steck, Warlick, Dallas, 1982-84; assessment and tng. supr. Dallas Transit Systems, 1984—. Art critic Tex. Happenings mag., 1983-84. Author: (play) Dallas 1840-1900, 1984. Contbr. book revs. and articles to Dallas Morning News, Dallas Times Herald. Bd. dirs. Goals for Dallas, 1978-80, 84-85, Dallas Visual Art Soc., 1979-81. NEH grantee, 1974-82. Mem. Am. Soc. for Tng. and Devel., Addison Community Theatre (pres. 1976-78). Democrat. Roman Catholic. Club: Sons of St. Patrick (pres. 1983-84). Avocations: jogging; photography; free lance writing. Home: PO Box 683 Carrollton TX 75006 Office: Dallas Transit System 101 N Peak Dallas TX 75226

KEATY, THOMAS ST. PAUL, II, lawyer; b. Baton Rouge, Jan. 3, 1943; s. Thomas St. Paul and Alicia Armshaw (Burk) K.; m. Sherrie Kerr, Feb. 4, 1966; children—Thomas St. Paul III, Emily Elizabeth Kerr-Keaty. B.S., U. Southwestern La., 1966; J.S., Tulane U., 1972. Bar: La. 1972, U.S. Dist. Ct. (ea. dist.) La. 1972, U.S. Dist. Ct. (we. dist.) La. 1975, U.S. Dist. Ct. (mid. dist.) La. 1984, U.S. Dist. Ct. (so. dist.) Tex. 1980, U.S. Dist. Ct. (we. dist.) Tex. 1983, U.S. Ct. Appeals (5th cir.) 1975, U.S. Ct. Customs and Patent Appeals 1975. Ptnr. Keaty & Keaty, New Orleans; instr. Tulane U.; dir. Fed. Bar Assn. New Orleans, 1983-85. Mem. ABA, La. State Bar Assn., La. Trial Lawyers Assn., Am. Patent Law Soc., San Francisco Patent Law Soc., La. Engring. Soc., Am. Soc. Chem. Engrs. Roman Catholic. Author: What the U.S. Businessman should know about Patents, U.S. and Foreign, 1979. Office: Keaty & Keaty 1818 Internat Trade Mart New Orleans LA 70130

KECK, GEORGE RUSSELL, music educator; b. Rogers, Ark., Aug. 15, 1942; s. Wayland and Veba Viola (Bland) K.; m. Ouida Anne Eppinette, July 29, 1972. B. Mus., U. Ark., 1965, M. Mus., 1968; Ph.D., U. Iowa, 1982. Teaching asst. U. Ark., Fayetteville, 1965-68; pub. sch. tchr., Portage, Ind., 1968-69; assoc. prof. Ouachita U., Arkadelphia, Ark., 1969—; lectr., Washington Hist. State Park, Ark., 1983—. Author: Pre-1875 American Imprint Sheet Music, 1982. Mem. Am. Musicol. Soc., Sonneck Soc., Coll. Mus. Soc., Ark. State Mus. Tchrs. Assn. (bd. dirs. 1970—), Pi Kappa Lambda, Phi Mu Alpha Sinfonia. Presbyterian. Democrat. Office: Ouachita Baptist U Box 3711 Arkadelphia AR 71923

KEE, CAROLYN CROWELL, nursing educator, b. Colchester, Vt., Mar. 12, 1943; d. Harold Warren and Eunice (Drummond) Crowell; m. Kenneth Roger Kee, Dec. 7, 1963; children—Jennifer Beth, Kevin David. B.S. U. R.I., 1963; M.N., Emory U., 1975; Ph.D., Ga. State U., 1984. Discharge coordinator Vis. Nurse Assn., San Jose, Calif., 1966-67, team leader, Atlanta, 1968-69, supr., 1972-74; charge nurse, part-time supr. Piedmont Hosp., Atlanta, 1971-72; asst. prof. nursing Ga. State U., Atlanta, 1975-84, assoc. prof., 1984—; chmn., mem. various coms. sch. nursing workshop presentations. Bd. dirs., sec. chair personnel com. Dekalb Community Council on Aging, Decatur, Ga., 1980—. Recipient Outstanding Merit award Intersorority Council, Ga. State U., 1981. Mem. Am. Nurses Assn., Am. Sociol. Assn., Ga. Nurses Assn., Ga. Sociol. Assn., Gerontol. Soc. Am., Sigma Theta Tau, Alpha Kappa Delta. Republican. Baptist. Avocations: gardening; camping. Office: Ga State U University Plaza Atlanta GA 30303

KEEBLER, EUGENE M., college dean; m. Dorcas Longley; children—Candace K. Thompson, Christina. B.S. in History, Edn., English, U. So. Miss., 1945; B.D. in Old and New Testament, New Orleans Bapt. Theol. Sem., 1949, Th.D. in Biblical Archaeology, 1953; Ph.D. in Edn. Adminstrn. and Psychology, U. So. Miss., 1962; postgrad. Fla. State U., 1959-60. Tutor Union Bapt. Theol. Sem., 1945-48; fellow dept. Biblical Archaeology New Orleans Bapt. Theol. Sem., 1950-51; asst. to pres. Clarke Coll., Newton, Miss., 1951-54; dean, registrar, prof. Bible Norman Coll., Norman Park, Ga., 1954-62; dean Gardner-Webb Coll., Boiling Springs, N.C., Louisiana Coll., Pineville, La., 1963-64; acad. v.p., dean U. Corpus Christi, Tex., 1964-65, Mobile Coll., Ala., 1965-84, Palm Beach Atlantic Coll., West Palm Beach, Fla., 1984—; acad. v.p., dean E.M. Keebler Chair of Biblical Faith, Studies, and Practice, Mobile Coll., 1981; cons. Am. Assn. Sch. Adminstrs.; gov.'s adv. body to Higher Edn. Facility Commn.; private coll. rep. Am. Am. Coll. Testing in Ala. and State Dept. Edn. Commn.; interim pastor. Vice chmn. bd. dirs. Mus. Bd., Mobile; chmn. Am's. Jr. Miss Scholarship Achievement Com., 1965-81, mem. Found. 1977-81; rep. State Ala. Sister Cities Internat. Office: Palm Beach Atlantic Coll 1101 S Olive Ave West Palm Beach FL 33401

KEEDY, HUGH FORREST, engineering educator; b. Berkeley Springs, W.Va., Sept. 22, 1926; s. Lester B. and Letha (Swaim) K.; m. Marjorie June Bomer, Aug. 22, 1948; children—Bruce Kevin, Susan Gayle. B.S., George Peabody Coll., 1951, M.A., 1952; M.S., U. Mich., 1962, Ph.D., 1967. Prof. engring. sci. Vanderbilt U., Nashville, 1951—. Tech. editor Lawrence Livermore Nat. Lab., Calif., 1980-81; co-author textbook: Fundamental Principles and Applications of Fluid Mechanics, 1979. Recipient Excellence in Teaching award, Western Electric Co., 1977. Mem. Soc. Tech. Communication, Am. Soc. Engring. Edn. (pres. Southeastern sect. 1984-85). Office: Vanderbilt U Box 1686 Station B Nashville TN 37235

KEEFE, SUSAN EMLEY, anthropology educator; b. Spokane, Wash., Dec. 1, 1947; d. Ivan Thomas and Palma Teresa (Plett) Emley; m. Thomas Keelin Keefe, Sept. 3, 1970; 1 dau., Megan Mansfield Emley. B.A., U. Calif.-Santa Barbara, 1969, M.A., 1971, Ph.D., 1974. Research assoc. Social Process Research Inst., U. Calif.-Santa Barbara, 1974-78; asst. prof. anthropology Appalachian State U., Boone, N.C., 1978-82, assoc. prof., 1982—; cons. to mental health services, social services. Sec.-treas. bd. dirs. Blue Ridge Crafts Edn. Fund, 1982-83. NIMH grantee, 1974-79, NSF grantee, 1983-84, grad. trainee, 1971-72; Woodrow Wilson fellow, 1972-73. Fellow Am. Anthrop. Assn., Soc. Applied Anthropology; mem. Soc. Urban Anthropology (treas. 1983-85), AAAS, So. Anthrop. Soc., Soc. Med. Anthropology, LWV. Democrat. Editor: (with J. Manuel Casas) Family and Mental Health in the Mexican American Community; contbr. articles to profl. jours. Home: PO Box 949 Blowing Rock NC 28605 Office: Dept Anthropology Appalachian State U Boone NC 28608

KEEGAN, JOHN EUGENE, architect; b. Teaneck, N.J., Aug. 9, 1926; s. James Francis and Mary Agnes Keegan; m. Jane Keirce Ryan, July 5, 1957 (dec. 1961); children—Mary Jane, John; m. 2d, Margaret Mary Maggelet, June 26, 1970; 1 son, Neil. Cert. of Architecture, Cooper Union, 1953; B.Arch., M.Arch., Yale U., 1955. Registered architect, Va. Project architect Perkins & Will, Washington, 1963-65, Wm. H. Metcalf, Washington, 1965-68; pres. John Keegan Assoc., Falls Church, Va., 1968—. Archtl. works featured in Liturgical Arts mag., Washington Post, Archtl. Record, Washington Star. Del. Fairfax County Republican Com., Va., 1985—. Served with AC, USN, 1944-46; ATO. Recipient 1st award Catholic Art Soc., N.Y., 1957; 1st alt. traveling fellow Yale U., 1955. Mem. AIA (dir. Washington 1971-73, chmn. edn. com. No. Va. chpt. 1985—, design award 1977, 80), Am. Arbitration Assn. (arbitrator 1973—), Soc. Am. Mil. Engrs. (sustaining), Falls Church C. of C. Republican. Roman Catholic. Clubs: Maryland Yacht (sail fleet capt. 1976—), U.S. Power Squadron (chmn. sail 1979—). Lodge: Rotary. Avocation: sailing. Home: 3428 Surry Ln Falls Church VA 22042 Office: John Keegan Assoc PC 100 W Great Falls St Falls Church VA 22046

KEELER, BARBARA, nurse, consultant; b. Paris, Tex., Apr. 2, 1951; d. Bruce L. and Regina (Jeckot) Sanders; m. Gregory A. Failing, Oct. 15, 1976 (div. Jan. 1980); m. Richard A. Keeler, Feb. 12, 1982; 1 child, Stephen A. A.N., Angelo State U., 1976; B.S. in Nursing, U. Tex. Health Sci. Ctr.-San Antonio, 1978; M.Sc. in Hosp. Adminstrn., S.W. Tex. State U., 1983. R.N., Tex. Staff nurse operating room Med. Ctr. Hosp., San Antonio, 1976-79, asst. supr. operating room, 1979-80, supr. operating room, 1980—, supr. gen. surgery unit, 1984-85; cons. infection control, design to operating rooms; cons. Marmon MOK Architets, San Antonio, 1984-85; speaker on leadership to nursing students, 1983, 84, 85. Treas. Architects Aux., San Antonio, 1984, 85; sec. San Antonio Scuba Club, 1985; bd. dirs. Homeowners Assn., San Antonio, 1985. Mem. Assn. Operating Room Nurses (chmn. ways and means 1984, corr. sec. 1985), Sigma Theta Tau. Republican. Roman Catholic. Avocations: scuba diving; snow skiing; ballet; piano; tennis. Home: 12434 Wandering Trail San Antonio TX 78249 Office: Med Ctr Hosp 4105 Medical Dr San Antonio TX 78284

KEENAN, ANTHONY LEE, trucking company executive; b. Greenwood, S.C., Mar. 18, 1949; s. Arthur Lee and Betty (Hart) K.; m. Cheryl Toney, Dec. 31, 1985. B.A., W.Ga. Coll., 1973; postgrad. Woodrow Wilson Coll. Law, 1975-79. Pres. Keenan, Inc., Decatur, Ga., 1975—; v.p. All Day Leasing Co., Decatur, 1977—; pres. United Trucker's Services, Conyers, Ga., 1978—; exec. dir. Ind. Trucker's United Co., Conley, Ga., 1979-80. Mem. White House Task Force to Develop Motor Carrier Act of 1980, 1979-80. Mem. Aircraft Owners and Pilots Assn. Lodges: Elks, Moose.

KEENAN, DAVID HENRY, mental health director, clinical psychologist, social worker; b. Jacksonville, N.C., Mar. 2, 1949; s. Lawrence Williard and Katherine (McMorrow) K. B.A., U. Va., 1972; M.S.W., Norfolk State U., 1979; Ed.D., W.Va. U., 1982. Lic. clin. psychologist and social worker, Va. Social worker USPHS, Portsmouth, Va., 1978-79, health service worker, Morgantown, W.Va., 1979-82; mental health dir. Chesapeake City, Va., 1982—; chmn. region V Mental Health Council, Va., 1982—, mem. exec. com., 1983—. Bd. dirs. Pendleton Project, Virginia Beach, Va. 1984. USPHS scholar, 1980. Mem. Am. Psychol. Assn., Am. Assn. Marital and Family Therapy, Nat. Assn. Social Workers (lic.), Am. Assn. Mental Health Adminstrs. Democrat. Roman Catholic. Club: Tidewater Tennis (Norfolk). Avocations: tennis, swimming. Home: 1245 Westover Ave B6 Norfolk VA 23507 Office: Human Services Bldg 4715 Bainbridge Blvd Chesapeake VA 23320

KEENE, NANCY, public relations executive; b. Altoona, Pa., July 14, 1951; d. Frank J. and Mary F. (Romagnino) Vetakis; m. Kenneth D. Kuehn, Aug. 19, 1972 (div. July 1981). B.S., Indiana U. Pa., 1972. Tchr. lang. arts Altoona (Pa.) Area Sch. Dist., 1972; exec. asst. Crown Zellerbach Corp., Newark, Del., 1972-73; mgr. pub. relations projects Snelling & Snelling, Inc., Paoli, Pa., 1973-76; pub. relations dir. Northwood Inst., Midland, Mich., Dallas, 1976-80; v.p. pub. relations Keller-Crescent/S.W., Dallas, 1981-85; dir. mktg. communications Infomart, Dallas, 1985—. Mem. Women in Communications, Inc., Pub. Relations Soc. Am., Dallas Ad League, TACA. Republican. Roman Catholic. Club: 500, Inc. Columnist, Adweek/S.W. Office: Infomart 1950 Stemmons Freeway Dallas TX 75207

KEENEY, ARTHUR HAIL, medical educator and administrator, ophthalmologist; b. Louisville, Jan. 20, 1920; s. Arthur Hale and Eugenia (Hail) K.; m. Virginia Tripp, Dec. 27, 1942; children—Steven Harris, Lee Douglas, Martha Blackledge Keeney Heyburn. B.S., Coll. William and Mary, 1941; M.D., U. Louisville, 1944; D.Sc., U. Pa., 1955. Diplomate Am. Bd. Ophthalmology (assoc. examiner 1960-84). Intern, Louisville Gen. Hosp., 1944-46; resident in ophthalmology Wills Eye Hosp., Phila., 1949-51, ophthalmologist in chief, 1965-73; instr. U. Louisville, 1951-58, asst. prof. ophthalmology, 1958-63, assoc. prof., 1963-65, prof., . Sch. Medicine, 1973-80, dean emeritus and disting. prof. ophthalmology, 1980—, interim chmn. ophthalmology, 1983—; prof., chmn. ophthalmology Temple U., 1966-72; profl. adv. com. Nat. Soc. Prevention of Blindness, 1954-64, dir., 1981—, mem. exec. com., 1984—; sec-treas. Nat. Com. Research in Ophthalmology and Blindness, 1964-78; vision study sect. neurol. and sensory disease control program Nat. Center Chronic Disease Control, USPHS, 1966-69; med. cons. Project Head Start, 1968—; chmn. com. on ophthalmic standards Am. Nat. Standards Inst., 1970-85; mem. Ky. med. rev. bd. driver limitation program State of Ky., 1974—; med. adv. bd. Recording for Blind, 1976-80, Nat. Aid to Visually Handicapped, 1970-79; hon. pres. 2d symposium Internat. Congress Diagnostic Ultrasound in Ophthalmology, Czechoslovakia, 1967; pres. 4th Internat. Congress Ultrasonography in Ophthalmology, Phila., 1968. Mem. Phila. Dist. Bd. Health and Welfare Council, 1967-69, Nat. Council to Combat Blindness, 1967-85; adv. bd., assoc. trustee U. Pa. Sch. Social Work, 1968-73; exec. bd. Old Ky. Home council Boy Scouts Am., 1976-79; life trustee James Graham Brown Found., 1978—. Served to capt., U.S. Army, 1942-47. Recipient Allstate Safety Crusade award, 1965, Lucien Howe Gold medal SUNY-Buffalo, 1973, Silver Tray Faculty award U. Louisville Sch. Medicine Class of 1979, 1979, Patrick R. O'Connor Meml. award, 1983. Fellow Am. Assn. History of Medicine, Am. Ophthal. Soc., Am. Acad. Ophthalmology and Otolaryngology (chmn. com. ophthalmic instruments and devices, bd. councillors 1981-83, v.p. 1985—; award of merit 1973, sr. award of merit 1984), Coll. Physicians of Phila., Pa. Acad. Ophthalmology and Otolaryngology (v.p. 1973), Am. Soc. Ophthalmic Ultrasound (hon.); mem. AMA, AAAS, Am. Com. Optical and Visual Physiology, Columbian Soc. Ophthamology, Assn. Univ. Profs. Ophthalmology, Louisville Eye and Ear Soc. (pres. 1956), Ky. Eye, Ear, Nose and Throat Soc. (pres. 1958), Am. Assn. Automotive Medicine (pres. 1967), Hellenic Ophthal. Soc., Joint Comm. Allied Health Personnel in Ophthalmology (v.p. 1985-86), Louisville Acad. Ophthalmology, Ky. Acad. Eye Physicians and Surgeons (pres. 1984), Ky. Surg. Soc., Ill. Soc. Ophthalmology and Otolaryngology (hon.), Phi Chi. Republican. Presbyterian. Clubs: Salmagundi, Louisville Country, Filson (Louisville). Editor: (with V.T. Keeney) Dyslexia: Diagnosis and Management of Reading Disorders, 1968; (with K. Gitter, D. Meyer and L.K. Sarin) Ophthalmic Ultrasound, 1969; assoc. editor Am. Jour. Ophthalmology, 1965-81, cons. bd., 1981—; editorial bd. Investigative Ophthalmology, 1969-73, Ophthalmology Excerpta Medica, 1974—, Sight Saving, 1982—; contbr. numerous articles to profl. jours., chpts. in books. Home: 4018 Glenview Ave Glenview KY 40025 Office: 301 E Muhammad Ali Blvd Louisville KY 40202

KEENEY, WILLIAM EDWIN, JR., space systems co. exec.; b. Clarinda, Iowa, Aug. 22, 1930; s. William Edwin and Dorothy LaVerne (Enerson) K.; B.B.A., U. Nebr., 1952, B.E.E., 1958; m. L. Eileen Faull, Oct. 3, 1980. With AC Electronics div. Gen. Motors, Milw., 1959-67, successively as systems engr., engring. supr., systems engring. group head; with Perkin-Elmer Corp., Wilton, Ct., 1967-77, successively as spacecraft cabin analyzer program mgr., test equipment sect. mgr., systems integration sect. mgr., systems engring. dept. mgr., solid state sensor camera program mgr.; dir. govt. orbital payloads Harris Corp., Melbourne, Fla., 1977-81; v.p. engring. Indsl. Drive div. Kollmorgan Corp., Raford, Va., 1981—; asst. prof. U. Notre Dame, South Bend, Ind., 1954-56. Mem. Danbury (Conn.) City Council, 1973-77; bd. dir. Assn. Religious Communities, Danbury; chmn. com. Conn. council Boy Scouts Am. Served to lt. USN, 1952-56. Mem. IEEE, Smithsonian Instn., Air Force Assn. Democrat. Presbyterian. Lodge: Kiwanis (pres.). Book reviewer Jour. Astronautical Scis., 1976—. Home: 108 Buckeye Ln Radford VA 24141 Office: 201 Rock Rd Radford VA 24141

KEESEE, KONRAD KENT, real estate company executive; b. Wichita, Kans., Oct. 25, 1934; s. Oscar Leo and Evelyn (Briscoe) K.; m. Joan Kirkpatrick, May 10, 1960 (div. Oct. 1965); 1 child, Christian Kirkpatrick; m. Frances Searle, Nov. 13, 1970. B.A., Okla. U., 1956. Pres., Keesee & Co., Inc., Oklahoma City, 1960—; rep. Sotheby's Internat. Realty for Okla. Active Okla. Heritage Assn., Okla. Mus. Art. Mem. Nat. Assn. Real Estate Bds., Okla. Bd. Realtors, Oklahoma City C. of C. Office: Keesee & Co Inc 6421 Avondale Dr Oklahoma City OK 73116

KEGLEY, CHARLES WILLIAM, JR., political science educator, author; b. Evanston, Ill., Mar. 5, 1944; s. Charles William and Elizabeth Euphemia (Meck) K.; m. Ann Curry Taylor, Apr. 1, 1966 (div.); 1 child, Suzanne Taylor; m. 2d, Pamela Ann Holcomb, July 6, 1975; B.A., Am. U., 1966; Ph.D., Syracuse U., 1971. Asst. prof. Sch. Fgn. Service, Georgetown U., 1971-72; prof., chmn. dept. govt. and internat. studies, dir. Byrnes Internat. Ctr., U. S.C., 1972—, holder chair internat. studies, 1985; vis. prof. U. Tex., 1976. Recipient Disting. Alumni award Am. U., 1984; R.M. Davis scholar, 1962-66; Maxwell fellow, 1968-69, 70-71; N.Y. State Regents fellow, 1969-70; Fulbright sr. scholar, 1978; Russell research awardee in humanities and social scis., 1982. Mem. Am. Polit. Sci. Assn., Am. Soc. Internat. Law, Am. Soc. Advancement Sci., Internat. Polit. Sci. Assn., Internat. Studies Assn. (assoc. dir.), Midwest Polit. Sci. Assn., Peace Sci. Soc., Peace Research Soc., So. Polit. Sci. Assn., Pi Sigma Alpha, Omicron Delta Kappa, Delta Tau Kappa. Lutheran. Author: A General Empirical Typology of Foreign Policy Behavior, 1973; co-author, co-editor (with William Coplin): A Multi-Method Introduction to International Politics: Observation, Explanation and Prescription, 1971, Analyzing International Relations: A Multi-Method Introduction, 1975; co-author: (with Eugene R. Wittkopf) American Foreign Policy: Pattern and Process, 1979, 2d edit., 1982, 3d edit., 1986, 3d edit., 1986, World Politics: Trend and Transformation, 1981, 2d edit., 1985; editor: (with Robert W. Gregg) After Vietnam: The Future of American Foreign Policy, 1971; (with Gregory A. Raymond, Robert M. Rood, Richard A. Skinner) International Events and the Comparative Analysis of Foreign Policy, 1975; (with Patrick J. McGowan) Challenges to America: U.S. Foreign Policy in the 1980's, 1979, (with Patrick McGowan) Threats, Weapons, and Foreign Policy, 1980, The Political Economy of Foreign Policy, 1981, Foreign Policy: USA/USSR, 1983; (with Eugene R. Wittkopf) Perspectives on American Foreign Policy, 1983, The Global Agenda: Issues and Perspectives, 1984; (with Patrick McGowan) Foreign Policy and the Modern World System, 1983; (with Eugene R. Wittkopf) The Nuclear Reader: Strategy, Weapons, War, 1985; (with Hermann and Rosenau) New Directions in the Study of Foreign Policy, 1986; contbr. chpts. to books, articles to profl. jours. Home: 1829 Senate St 17-E Columbia SC 29201 Office: 702 Byrnes Internat Ctr U SC Columbia SC 29208

KEHOE, JAMES W., U.S. district judge; b. 1925. A.A., U. Fla., 1947, LL.B., 1950. Individual practice law, 1950-52; with firm Worley, Kehoe & Willard, 1952-55; asst. county solicitor Dade County, Fla., 1955-57; with firm Milton R. Wasman, 1957-61; judge Civil Record Ct., Miami, Fla., 1961-63; judge 11th Jud. Circuit Ct., 1963-77, 3d Dist. Ct. Appeals, 1977-79; U.S. dist. judge So. Fla., Miami, 1979—. Mem. ABA, Fla. Bar Assn. Office: PO Box 013097 Flagler Sta Miami FL 33101*

KEHOE, ROBERT EMMET, publishing and venture capital exec.; b. Scranton, Pa., June 23, 1943; s. Michael Francis and Eleanor Theresa K.; B.S., U. Fla., 1968; m. Mimi Buxbaum, Sept. 1, 1968; children—Kelly Sue, Kimberly Ann. Gen. mgr. Wilmar Inc., Charlotte, N.C., 1968-71; v.p. Synetics, Inc., Charlotte, N.C., 1971-74; v.p., gen. mgr. Trend Publs., Inc., Tampa, 1974-80, also dir.; pres. Key Energy Systems, Inc., Tampa, 1980—, corp. v.p. Key Energy Enterprises, Inc., Tampa, 1981—; pres., dir. Trident Sci. Corp., Tampa and N.Y.C., 1981-83; pres. Pubs. Resource Orgn., 1983—; chmn., pres. Conf. Resource Ctr., 1983—; cons. communications and bus. field. Served with AUS, 1964-66. Mem. Assn. Area Bus. Publs. (1st pres.), Club: Exchange. Lectr., speaker So. and sunbelt economy, venture capital and bus. mgmt. Office: PO Box 25313 Tampa FL 33622

KEIL, CHARLES EMANUEL, corporation executive; b. N.Y.C., Aug. 27, 1936; s. E. William and Marie Katherine (Diebold) K.; m. Patricia Ann O'Toole, Dec. 21, 1970; children—Brett, Morgan. A.B., Bklyn. Coll., 1964, postgrad., 1964-65. Sales mgr. Columbian Bronze Corp., Freeport, N.Y., 1960-66; sr. v.p., pub., mng. dir. Marine Engring.-Log Group, Simmons Boardman Pub. Co., N.Y.C., 1966-78; sr. v.p. Thomas Internat. Pub. Co., N.Y.C., 1978-80; pres. Gen. Synergistics Corp., Boca Raton, Fla., 1980-82; pres., dir. spl. projects Tech. Pub. Co., Boca Raton, 1983—. Served with USNCR, 1956-58, Mem. Soc. Naval Architects and Marine Engrs., IEEE, Walter Badgehot Soc., Internat. Soc. Philos. Enquiry, Propeller Club of U.S., Mensa. Home: 671 Elm Tree Ln Boca Raton FL 33432 Office: Arvida Park of Commerce Boca Raton FL 33431

KEILLER, JAMES BRUCE, college dean, clergyman; b. Racine, Wis., Nov. 21, 1938; s. James Allen and Grace (Modder) K.; diploma Beulah Heights Bible Coll., 1957; B.A., William Carter Coll., 1963, Ed.D. (hon.), 1973; LL.B., Blackstone Sch. Law, 1964; M.A., Evang. Theol. Sem., 1965, B.D., 1966, Th.D., 1968; M.A. in Ednl. Adminstrn., Atlanta U., 1977; Ph.D. cand., Ga. State U.; m. Darsel Lee Bundy, Feb. 8, 1959; 1 dau., Susanne Elizabeth. Ordained to ministry Internat. Pentecostal Assemblies, 1957; pastor Maranatha Temple, Boston, 1957-58, Midland (Mich.) Full Gospel Ch., 1958-64; v.p. acad. dean Beulah Heights Bible Coll., Atlanta, 1964—, trustee, 1964—; nat. dir. youth and Sunday sch. dept. Internat. Pentecostal Assemblies, 1958-64, dir. world missions, Atlanta, 1964-76, youth commn., 1958-64, missions com., 1964-76, exec. bd., 1964-76, missionary editor Bridegroom's Messenger, 1964—; dir. global missions Internat. Pentecostal Ch. of Christ, 1976—, mem. exec. com., 1976—; mem. exec. bd. Mt. Paran Christian Sch. Mem. Republican Presdl. Task Force; mem. Nat. Rep. Senatorial Com., Am. Tax Reduction Movement, Moral Majority Found., So. Ctr. Internat. Studies. Named Alumnus of Year, William Carter Coll., 1965. Mem. Woodmen of World, So. Accrediting Assn. Bible Colls. (exec. sec.), Christian Mgmt. Assn., Soc. Pentecostal Studies, Acad. Polit. Sci., Ind. Order Foresters, Evang. Theol. Soc. Club: Kiwanis (lt. 1986-87). Home: 892 Berne St SE Atlanta GA 30316 Office: 906 Berne St SE Atlanta GA 30316

KEIRNS, HARRY DAYTON, data processing cmpany executive; b. Akron, Ohio, Jan. 25, 1938; s. Harry Austin and Charlotte June (Betz) K.; student Akron U., 1957-68; m. Nancy Cogar, Feb. 20, 1957, children—Susan Marie, Katherine Ann, Roberta Diana; m. Nancy Ann Nabinger, May 6, 1978; children—Phaedra Ann, Alicia Marie. Mgr. systems devel. B.F. Goodrich Tire Co., Akron, 1967-70; pres. Automated Graphic Tech., Champaign, Ill., 1970-71; dir. software and data processing Gould Inc., Boston, 1972; systems mgr. B.F. Goodrich Tire Co., Akron, 1972-78; pres. Community Tech., Champaign, 1979-80; pres. KMW Systems Corp., Austin, Tex., 1975-83, chmn. bd., 1975—, also dir.; chmn. bd. Ultra Systems Design, 1985—. Systems analyst Little Hoover Commn., Summit County, Ohio, 1969. Served with USNR, 1956, 57. Mem. Assn. Computing Machinery, Data Processing Mgmt. Assn. (cert. in data processing), Mensa, Am. Contract Bridge League. Home: 609 Rocky River Rd West Lake Hills TX 78746 Office: 8307 Hwy 71 W Austin TX 78735

KEISER, ALAN FRANK, coal geologist; b. Plymouth, Ind., June 30, 1938; s. Cecil Leroy and Ruth Arlene (Stine) K. A.B. in German, Manchester Coll., 1963; A.M. in Geology, Ind. U., 1971. Vol., U.S. Peace Corps, Cebu, Philippines, 1963-65; geol. asst. Westfield Minerals, Perth, West Australia, 1966-67; computer Ray Geophys., Perth, 1967-68; geol. asst. Cominco Am., Spokane, Wash., 1970; coal geologist Amax Coal Co., Indpls., 1971, Cravat Coal Co., Cadiz, Ohio, 1972-73, W.Va., Geol. Survey, Morgantown, W.Va., 1973—. Mem. Am. Inst. Mining Engrs., Am. Assn. Petroleum Geologists. Home: 324 Barrickman Morgantown WV 26505 Office: WVa Geol Survey PO Box 879 Morgantown WV 26507

KEITER, AARON, lawyer; b. Phila., May 26, 1946; s. Joseph and Lisa (Brahen) K.; B.S., Pa. State U., 1968; M.B.A., Widener Coll., 1973; J.D., U. Houston, 1976; m. Eileen Marsha Brown, Sept. 16, 1972; children—Justin Alan, Ashley Rochelle. Trader investment div. Phila. Nat. Bank, 1972-73; admitted to Tex. bar, 1976; tax specialist Coopers & Lybrand, Houston, 1976-77; gen. counsel Jetero Corp., Houston, 1977-79, Allison/Walker Interests, Inc., Houston, 1979-81; partner firm Goldberg & Keiter, Houston, 1981-83; sr. ptnr. Keiter, Blustein, DuBois & Krocker, Houston, 1983-85; ptnr. Keiter & Blustein, P.C., Houston, 1985—; mem. faculty U. Houston Law Sch., 1975-76. Served with U.S. Army, 1968-72; maj. Res. Decorated Bronze Star, Air medal; recipient Am. Jurisprudence award, 1974; Sutherland scholar, 1964-66; ROTC scholar, 1966-68. Mem. Am. Bar Assn., State Bar Tex., Houston Bar Assn., Tex. Young Lawyers Assn., Am. Trial Lawyers Assn. Republican. Jewish. Club: Houston City. Home: 7907 Deer Meadow Dr Houston TX 77071 Office: Loop Central III 4828 Loop Central Dr Suite 500 Houston TX 77081

KEITH, DONALD MORTON, retired army officer, research center director; b. Chgo., Apr. 24, 1935; s. Myron and Jennette (Porter) K.; m. Phyllis Beryl Markuson, Mar. 24, 1963; children—Nina Susan, Paula Dorit. B.B.A. cum laude, U. Wis., 1956; postgrad. U. Hawaii, 1957-58; M.B.A. summa cum laude, Monmouth Coll., Long Branch, N.J., 1973; postgrad. NYU, 1974. Enlisted U.S. Army Res., 1954, commd. 2d lt. U.S. Army, 1956, advanced through grades to lt. col., 1971; dep. comdr. U.S. Army Security Agy. Material Support Command and dir. Nat. Maintenance Point, 1974-77, ret., 1977; telecommunications engr. and logistics mgr. CALCULON Corp., cons., Washington, 1977—; chmn. bd. dirs., exec. dir. Center for Study of Multiple Birth, Northwestern U. Med. Sch., 1977—; research asst. Am. Assn. Gynecol. Laparoscopists, 1973-78, staff asst. sci. program com., 1973-78; participant symposia. Decorated Bronze Star (2), Meritorious Service medal, numerous others; Armed Forces Communications Electronics Assn. scholar, 1957; cert. profl. logistician, profl. resource mgr. Fellow Internat. Soc. Twin Studies, Soc. Advanced Med. Systems, Soc. Logistics Engrs. (chmn. tech. communications workshop 1978); mem. Am. Pub. Health Assn., Am. Assn. Gynecol. Laparoscopists (assoc.), Am. Coll. Hosp. Adminstrs. (assoc.), Am. Hosp. Assn., Assn. U.S. Army, World Population Soc. (charter). Lodge: Masons. Home: 1415 Green Run Ln Reston VA 22090

KEITH, JAMES MELVIN, clergyman; b. Jackson, Miss., June 22, 1943; s. Hardy Melvin and Mary Frances (Walton) K.; B.A., Miss. Coll., 1966; M.Div., Southwestern Bapt. Theol. Sem., 1969, Th.D., 1975; m. Saundra Elaine Gordon, Aug. 20, 1966; children—James Scott, Gordon Todd, Kristin Elaine. Ordained to ministry So. Baptist Conv., 1967; pastor Antelope Bapt. Ch. (Tex.), 1967-69, 1st Bapt. Ch., Blum, Tex., 1970-71, 1st Bapt. Ch., McGregor, Tex., 1971-72, 1st Bapt. Ch., San Marcos, Tex., 1972-74, 1st Bapt. Ch., Laurel, Miss., 1974-77, 1st Bapt. Ch., Gulfport, Miss., 1977—; chaplain U.S. Ho. of Reps., 1981; grad. asst. dept. preaching Southwestern Bapt. Theol. Sem., 1970-72; adj. prof. O.T., William Carey Coll., 1977; adj. prof. homiletics William Carey Coll., 1978, preaching New Orleans Baptist Theol. Sem., 1982; pres. Jones County Bapt. Pastors Conf., 1975-76. Trustee, William Carey Coll., 1976-79, 79-82, chmn. bd. trustees, 1980, 81. Mem. Miss. Bapt. Conv. (chmn. order of bus. com. 1978, mem. com. on coms. 1980), Miss. Coll. Ministerial Alumni Assn. (pres. 1977-78), Southwestern Bapt. Theol. Sem. Alumni (pres. 1980). Home: 29 Bayou View Dr Gulfport MS 39501 Office: PO Drawer 70 Gulfport MS 39501

KEITH, L'TANYA CASSANDRA, association executive; b. Atlanta, Dec. 4, 1955; d. Harold Anderson and Katherine (Griffin) K. B.A., Barnard Coll., Columbia U., 1977. Cert. mediator. Newsletter coordinator Econ. Opportunity Atlanta Dunbar Ctr., 1974-79; data assessor Sears and Roebuck, Atlanta, 1975; asst. to regional dir., tribunal adminstr., program coordinator, graphic designer Am. Arbitration Assn., Atlanta, 1978—; mem. nat. panel consumer arbitrators Better Bus. Bur., Atlanta, 1983—. Mem. Foster Parents Plan Support Group, Atlanta. Author: An Analysis of Criminal Law, 1973. Mem. Indsl. Relations Research Assn., AAUW, Barnard Alumnae. Office: Am Arbitration Assn Colony Sq Mall 1197 Peachtree St NE Atlanta GA 30361

KEITH, ROBERT EUGENE, educational administrator; b. Troy, Ala., Feb. 25, 1926; s. William Jonah and Pearlena (Culpepper) K.; m. Lily Anne King, Mar. 30, 1949; children—William Adger, Jan Capers, Olivia Leigh. B.S.E.E., U. S.C., 1971, M.Ed., 1972. Owner, mgr. K&K Mobile Park, Bradenton, Fla., 1957-68; asst. prof. distributive edn. Abraham Baldwin Agrl. Coll., Tifton, Ga., 1972-77, asst. dir. continuing edn., 1977-79, dir. continuing edn., 1979—. Del., White House Conf. on Aging, Jacksonville, Fla., 1981; bd. dirs. Tift County unit Am. Heart Assn., 1978—. Mem. Ga. Adult Edn. Assn., Assn. Continuing Higher Edn., Am. Assn. Adult and Continuing Edn., Tift County C. of C. (bd. dirs. 1985). Recipient Dedicated Service award Tifton Golden Age Club, 1980, 84, 85, Dedicated Service awards Distributive Edn. Clubs Am., 1972, 74; grantee Ga. Endowment for Humanities, 1981. Served as sgt. USMC, 1944-46. Democrat. Methodist. Lodge: Kiwanis (pres. 1976-77, bd. dirs. 1973-75, 78-83). Avocations: Reading; traveling; woodworking. Office: Continuing Edn Dept Abraham Baldwin Agrl Coll ABAC Sta Box 12 Tifton GA 31793

KEITHLEY, BRADFORD G., utility executive; b. Macomb, Ill., Nov. 23, 1951; s. S. Irish and Joan G. Keithley; m. Sarah J. Ruebush, May 24, 1975. B.S. with honors, U. Tulsa, 1973; J.D., U. Va., 1976. Bar: Va. 1976, D.C. 1978, Okla. 1978. Ptnr. Hall, Estill, Hardwick, Gable, Collingsworth & Nelson, Tulsa, Okla., 1978-84; v.p., gen. counsel Arkla, Inc., 1984—. Served with USAF, 1976-78. Mem. Fed. Energy Bar Assn., ABA, Va. State Bar Assn., D.C. Bar Assn., Okla. Bar Assn. Democrat. Episcopalian. Office: 525 Milam St Shreveport LA 71120

KEITHLEY, JAMES STUART, advertising and film director; b. Chgo., Oct. 30, 1938; m. Mary Helen Ruiz, Oct. 9, 1959; children—Jayme Ann, Scott James. Student U. Ill.; B.A. in English, Drake U., 1959. Writer, Earle Ludgin Co., Chgo., 1963-65; sr. writer Post Keyes Gardner Inc., Chgo., 1965-67; creative supr. Lee King & Ptnrs., Chgo., 1967-72, assoc. creative dir., 1977-81; assoc. creative dir. Campbell Mithun Inc., Chgo., 1972-76; v.p., creative dir. Nader-Lief, Chgo., 1976-77; assoc. creative dir. Green & Burkhard, Atlanta, 1981; v.p., creative group supr. Cargill, Wilson & Acree Inc., Atlanta, 1981—, pres., creative dir. Keithley & Assocs., 1985—. Served with U.S. Army, 1960-62. Recipient awards including: Chicago 4 (19 awards), certs. of distinction N.Y.-Art Direction Mag., 1971, 72, 79, 82, 83, 85, 6 awards and Silver Medal Art Dirs.' Club N.Y., Campaign award Chgo. Internat. Film Festival, 1975, 6 awards Chgo. Ad Club, Am. Inst. Graphic Arts Cert. of Excellence, 1980, 7 awards Hollywood Radio and TV Soc. Internat. Broadcasting awards, 5 awards, cert. of excellence Communications Art Mag., 7 Andy awards, Advt. Club N.Y., 1980-83, 3 awards One Show of N.Y., 7 awards, 4 statuettes CLIO awards N.Y. Advt. accounts include Jovan Bath Oil, Wish-Bone Salad Dressing, Old Fitzgerald Bourbon, Inland Steel, Jim Beam, Internat. Harvester, Ovaltine, Wyler Foods Div. Borden, Inc., Thomas J. Lipton Co. Home: 1101 Cumberland Ct Smyrna GA 30080

KELEHEAR, CAROLE MARCHBANKS SPANN, legal assistant; b. Morehead City, N.C., Oct. 2, 1945; d. William Blythe and Gladys Ophelia (Wilson) Marchbanks; m. Henry M. Spann, June 5, 1966 (div. 1978); children—Lisa Carole, Elaine Mabry; m. Zachariah Lockwood Kelehear, Sept. 15, 1985. Student Winthrop Coll., 1963-64; grad. Draughon's Bus. Coll., 1965; cert. in med. terminology Greensville Tech. Edn. Coll., 1972; grad. Millie Lewis Modeling Sch. Cert. med. asst. Office mgr. S.C. Appalachian Adv. Commn., Greenville, 1964-68, Wood-Bergheer & Co., Newport Beach and Palm Springs, Calif., 1970-72; asst. to Dr. J. Ernest Lathem, Lathem & McCoy, P.A., Greenville, 1972-75, Robert E. McNair, McNair, Konduros, Corley, Singletary and Dibble Law Firm, Columbia, S.C., 1975-77; office mgr. Dr. James B. Knowles, Greenville, 1977-78, Constangy, Brooks & Smith, Columbia, 1978-83; legal asst. to sr. ptnr. Bethea, Jordan & Griffin, P.A., Hilton Head Island, S.C., 1983—; notary pub. Ladies aux. vol. Greenville Gen. Hosp., 1966-72, South Coast Hosp., Laguna Beach, Calif., 1973, St. Francis Hosp, Greenville, 1974-76, Hilton Head Hosp., 1983—. Mem. Hilton Head Hosp. Aux., Profl. Women's Assn. Hilton Head Island, Am. Bus. Women's Assn., Nat. Assn. Female Execs. Home: PO Box 1174 Hilton Head Island SC 29925

KELL, JOSEPH FOSTER, JR., neurosurgeon; b. Salina, Kans., Feb. 19, 1918; s. Joseph Foster and Martha Emma (Mitchel) K.; m. Rita Clare Ryan, Apr. 6, 1946; children—Josephine Ann, Mary Margaret, Thomas Raymond, John Ryan. B.A., U. Kans., 1940; M.D., Yale U., 1943; M.S., Med. Coll. Va., 1950. Diplomate Am. Bd. Neurol. Surgery. Intern, U. Va., Charlottesville, 1944-45; resident in neurosurgery Med. Coll. Va., 1949-52; practice medicine, specializing in neurosurgery, Richmond, Va., 1955—; asst. clin. prof. neurol. surgery Med. Coll. Va., Richmond, 1962-76, assoc. clin. prof. surgery, 1976-84, clin. prof., 1984—; chief staff St. Mary's Hosp., 1968-69. Served to capt. M.C., U.S. Army, 1946-48. Fellow ACS; mem. Neurosurg. Soc. Va. (pres. 1978-80), AMA, Congress Neurol. Surgeons, Med. Soc. Va., Am. Assn. Neurol. Surgeons, So. Neurosurg. Soc., So. Med. Assn., Neurosurg. Soc. Va., Sigma Chi. Presbyterian. Contbr. articles to profl. jours. Home: 7102 Chandler Dr Richmond VA 23229 Office: 7702 Parham Rd Suite G Richmond VA 23229

KELLEHER, HERBERT DAVID, lawyer, airline executive; b. Camden, N.J., Mar. 12, 1931; s. Harry and Ruth (Moore) K.; m. Joan Negley, Sept. 9, 1955; children—Julie, Michael, Ruth, David. B.A. cum laude (Olin scholar), Wesleyan U., 1953; LL.B. cum laude (Root Tilden scholar), NYU, 1956. Bar: N.J. 1957, Tex. 1962. Clk. N.J. Supreme Ct., 1956-59; assoc. Lum, Biunno & Tompkins, Newark, 1959-61; ptnr. Matthews, Nowlin, Macfarlane & Barrett, San Antonio, 1961-69; sr. ptnr. Oppenheimer, Rosenberg, Kelleher & Wheatley, Inc., San Antonio, 1969—; founder, gen. counsel, pres. chmn., dir. S.W. Airlines Co., Dallas, 1967—; dir. May Petroleum, Inc., Dallas, Merc. Tex. Corp. Chmn. adv. bus. council Trinity U., San Antonio; vice chmn. bus. adv. council U. Tex. Sch. Bus.; campaign coordinator Connally for Gov., 1961, 63, 65; Bexar County dir. Bentsen for Senator, 1970, 76, state co chmn., 1975-76; chmn. Senate Dist. 19 Democratic Com., 1968-70; del. Dem. Nat. Conv., 1964, 68; mem. state steering com. Bentsen for Pres., 1975-76; pres. bd. trustees St. Mary's Hall, San Antonio; pres. Travelers Aid Soc., San Antonio. Named Chief Exec. Officer of Yr., The Fin. World, 1982, Best Chief Exec. Regional Airline Industry Wall St. Transcript, 1982; Recipient Fin. Mgmt. award Air Transport World, 1982. Fellow Tex. Bar Found. (life); mem. ABA, San Antonio, N.J. bar assns., State Bar Tex., San Antonio C. of C. (dir.), Order of Alamo, Tex. Cavaliers. Home: 144 Thelma Dr San Antonio TX 78212 Office: SW Airlines Co PO Box 37611 Dallas TX 75235*

KELLEHER, JEAN HUDGIN, graphic designer; b. Sharon, Pa., May 30, 1943; s. Lawrence M. and Margaret W. (Williams) Hudgin; m. John Joseph Kelleher, Aug. 28, 1968; children—John L., James M., Jill E. B.Art Edn., Miami U., Oxford, Ohio, 1965. Art tchr. Mad River Schs. (Ohio), 1965-69; art dir./graphic designer, pres. Jean Kelleher Assocs., Lilburn, Ga., 1979—. Mem. Assn. Women Entrepreneurs (bd. dirs.), Atlanta Artists Guild (v.p.), Bus. and Profl. Advt. Assn. Republican. Episcopalian. Home and Office: 387 Angie Ct Lilburn GA 30247

KELLER, E. W. (WAYNE), state senator, lawyer; b. Bonners Ferry, Idaho, Sept. 25, 1936; s. Logan M. and Allie B. (McPherson) K.; m. Marsha M. Huffman, July 11, 1958; children—Trenton Wayne, Rachel Elizabeth. B.A., U. Okla., 1958, LL.B., 1960. Bar: Okla. 1960. Mem. Keller & Fernald, Oklahoma City, 1960—; mem. Okla. Senate, 1973—, asst. minority floor leader 1984. Mem. ABA, Okla. Bar Assn., Oklahoma County Bar Assn., Okla. Trial Lawyers, Assn., Am. Trial Lawyers Assn. Served to capt. U.S. Army. Republican. Methodist. Club: Young Men's Exec. (Oklahoma City). Office: Oklahoma State Capitol Oklahoma City OK 73105

KELLER, ROBERT TERRY, management educator; b. Bronx, N.Y., June 26, 1943; s. Ben and Lucille G.K.; m. Phyllis Meltz, July 3, 1966; children—Mark B., Michelle N. B.S., U. Ill., 1965; M.B.A., SUNY, Buffalo, 1967; Ph.D., Pa. State U., 1972. Indsl. relations adminstr. Westinghouse Electric Corp., Edison, N.J., 1967-68; personnel adminstr. Westvaco Corp., N.Y.C., 1968-69; instr. mgmt. Pa. State U., University Park, 1969-72; asst. prof. U. Houston, 1972-77, assoc. prof., 1977-81; prof. mgmt. La. State U., Baton Rouge, 1981—, chmn. dept. mgmt., 1985—. NSF grantee, 1976-78. Mem. Am. Inst. Decision Scis., Acad. Mgmt. Contbr. articles to profl. jours.

KELLEY, EDWARD LIVINGSTON, safety engineer; b. St. Louis, Aug. 8, 1939; s. Harry C. and Marguerite M. (Kunkel) K.; m. Olivia Ann Lock, June 5, 1965; children—Edward Lawrence, Steven Christopher. B.S. in Chem. Engring., Northwestern U., 1962; M.Engring. Adminstrn., Washington U., St. Louis, 1967. Registered profl. engr., Mo.; cert. safety profl. Chem. engr. Mallinckrodt, Inc., St. Louis, 1962-66, safety engr., 1966-73; group safety engr. chem. group FMC Corp., Phila., 1973-77, group safety mgr., 1977-79; staff safety engr. Kerr-McGee Corp., Oklahoma City, 1979-80, sr. staff safety engr., 1980—; career speaker pub. schs. Webelos leader Boy Scouts Am., 1980; mem. Oklahomans for Energy and Jobs, Inc., 1981—. Scholar, Northwestern U., 1957, Washington U., 1957. Mem. Am. Soc. Safety Engrs., Nat. Safety Council (exec. com. chem. sect. 1981—, gen. chmn. 1984-85, William H. Cameron award 1984, 85). Republican. Methodist. Avocations: computers; photography; music; travel. Office: Kerr-McGee 123 Robert S Kerr Ave Oklahoma City OK 73125

KELLEY, ELLEN QUINN, educator; b. Dothan, Ala., Aug. 25, 1933; s. Floyed Willis, Sr., and Pennie (Mullins) K. B.A., Samford U., Birmingham, Ala., 1957. Cert. tchr., Fla. Tchr. phys. edn. Dade County Pub. Schs., Hialeah (Fla.) High Sch., 1957—, head dept., 1978—; cheerleading sponsor North-South Shrine Game, Orange Bowl, Fla., 1964; counselor Miami Herald-Camp for Underprivileged Children, 1963; vice chmn. Fla. Commn. Edn., 1970, Fla. profl. rev. panel, 1968-74. Named Tchr. of Yr., Hialeah High Sch., 1982; recipient Community Service award Hialeah-Miami Springs Kiwanis Club, 1960. Mem. Fla. Assn. Health and Phys. Edn. (v.p. 1970, Honor award 1973), AAHPER (sec. exec. bd. So. dist. 1974), Dade County Assn. Health and Phys. Edn. (pres. 1970), Delta Psi Kappa. Democrat. Baptist. Office: Hialeah High Sch 251 Throughbred Dr Hialeah FL 33012

KELLEY, EVERETTE EUGENE, retailing executive; b. Hartford, Kans., July 27, 1938; s. Joseph Leo and Lelia Elizabeth (Hartenbower) K.; m. Peggy L. Clapham, Apr. 25, 1959; children—Kimaley Kay, Barbara Lynn, Janet Marie. B.S. in Bus., Kans. State Tchrs. Coll., 1960. C.P.A., Ill. With Arthur Andersen & Co., Chgo., 1960-69; v.p. fin. Cunningham Drug Stores, Detroit, 1969-71; controller City Products Corp., 1975-76; sr. asst. controller Household Fin. Corp., Chgo., 1976-83; exec. v.p., chief operating officer Moore Handley Inc., Birmingham, Ala.; pres. TAC Corp., Birmingham, 1983—. Mem. Am. Inst. C.P.A.s, Fin. Exec. Inst. (pres. Birmingham chpt. 1982-83). Clubs: Vestavia Country (fin. com.). Home: 105 Sharpsburg Circle Birmingham AL 35213 Office: PO Box 6685 Birmingham AL 35210

KELLEY, GEORGE LARRY, building contractor; b. Little Rock, 1916. B.S. in Civil Engring., U. Ark., 1938. Civil engr. Manhattan Constrn. Co., 1937-42; engring. foreman G.W. May Constrn. Co., 1946-47; with Pickens-Bond Constrn. Co., Little Rock, 1951—, v.p., 1958-74, pres., chief exec. officer now chmn. bd., chief exec. officer, also dir. Served with USN, 1942-46. Office: Pickens-Bond Constrn Co 400 Atkins Corp Bldg Little Rock AR 72203

KELLEY, GORDON RANDOLPH, II, automobile agency executive; b. Kinston, N.C., Dec. 19, 1952; s. John Henry Kelley and Dorothy Massey; m. Molly Patrick, May 30, 1981; 1 son, Gordon Randolph III. B.A., U. N.C., 1975, postgrad. Gen. Motors Inst., Flint, Mich., 1976, Gen. Motors U. Automotive Mgmt., 1984. Salesman, Massey Motor Co., Kinston, 1975-78, sales mgr., 1978-82, co-owner, v.p., gen. mgr., 1982—. Bd. dirs. United Way,

Kinston, 1981, Heart Fund, Kinston, 1985. Mem. Vanguard Olds Sales Orgn., Kinston Auto Dealers Assn. (sec.-treas. 1980-81, pres. 1981-82). Republican. Episcopalian. Lodge: Rotary. Avocations: sailing; golf; football; basketball fan. Home: 1500 Greenbriar Rd Kinston NC 28501 Office: Massey Motor Co 2900 W Vernon Ave Kinston NC 28501

KELLEY, HOWARD WELLS, JR., television executive; b. Jacksonville, Fla., Mar. 3, 1942; s. Howard Wells and Mary (Koniowka) Kelley; m. Ann Jennifer Helm, Aug. 1, 1964; children—Shannon C., Adam F. B.S. in Broadcasting, U. Fla., 1964; P.M.D., Harvard Bus. Sch., 1981. Chief announcer Sta. WRUF Radio, Gainesville, Fla., 1962-63; news dir. Sta. WPDQ Radio, Jacksonville, 1963-64; reporter, producer, news dir. Sta. WTLV-TV 12 Jacksonville, 1964—, v.p., gen. mgr., 1981—; dir. Quanta Corp., Salt Lake City; dir. strategic planning Harte-Hanks Communications, San Antonio. Contbg. editor: Longman's Dictionary of Mass Media and Communications, 1980; The Non-Profit Organization Handbook, 1982. Bd. dirs. Police Athletic League, 1983. Recipient Red Barber award U. Fla., 1964, spl. commendation AMA, 1976. Mem. Nat. Assn. Broadcasters, Soc. Profl. Journalists, Radio and TV News Dirs. Assn., Jacksonville C. of C. (v.p. 1983-84). Democrat. Episcopalian. Club: River (Jacksonville). Lodge: Rotary.

KELLEY, JAMES HAROLD, floor covering products company executive; b. Greenville, S.C., June 11, 1939; s. Clyde C. and Gladys Irene (Carter) K.; m. Frances Dowling, Aug. 2, 1958; children—J. Bryan, C. Blake, Dana E. Student N. Greenville Jr. Coll., 1958-59; B.A., LaSalle Ext. U., 1968; postgrad. Ohio State U., 1981. Field rep. Gen. Motors Acceptance Corp., Greenville, 1960-66; with Orders Distributing Co., Inc., Greenville, 1967—, asst. to pres., 1972-75, v.p. adminstrn., 1975-79, exec. v.p., 1979-83, sr. v.p., 1983—. Served with U.S. Army, 1957. Nat. Assn. Floor Covering Distbrs. scholar, 1981. Baptist. Home: 100 Meridian Ave Taylors SC 29687 Office: 501 Congaree Rd Greenville SC 29607

KELLEY, MARY ANTOINETTE, retirement and pension plan consulting firm executive; b. Columbus, Ohio, Aug. 19, 1933; d. Anthony Charles Fasone and Ernestine (Stilwell) Leckrone; m. John Maurice Kelley, Jan. 24, 1953; children—Diane Elizabeth Garrison, Victoria Lenore Trumbetic, Nina Marie Trott, Jacquelynne, Frances Ann. Student St. Francis Hosp., 1951-53. Sec.-treas. Marsh, Mead, Hill & Assocs. Inc., Washington, 1967-70; mgr. R. L. Frank, Columbus, Ohio, 1963-66; exec. v.p. D.L. Mead & Assocs., Inc., 1970—; pres. Automated Retirement Plans Inc., Washington, 1978—. Editor: (newsletter) Dominews, 1984. Mem. fin. com. Montclair Property Owners Assn., Dumfries, Va., 1983-85. Mem. Am. Soc. Pension Actuaries (examination com. 1982, 85, instr. examination course 1985), Bus. and Profl. Women/Va. (state fin. chmn., program planning com. 1984—, pres. Old Dominion chpt. 1982, Va. State speakoff winner 1981, nat. speakoff participant 1981). Republican. Roman Catholic. Club: Montclair Arts (Dumfries) (pres. 1980-81, 82-83). Avocation: needlepoint. Office: Automated Retirement Plans Inc 6320 Augusta Dr Suite 300 Springfield VA 22150

KELLEY, MARY ELLEN, nursing administrator, educator, consultant; b. Cin., Feb. 17, 1950; d. Joseph E. and Clara Margaret (Vonderheide) Williams; m. William Robert Kelley, Dec. 28, 1974; 1 child, Bridget Katrina. B.S. in Nursing, Mt. St. Joseph Coll., 1974; M.Ed., Xavier U., 1977; M.S. in Nursing, U. Cin., 1984. Registered nurse, Ohio, Ky. Instr. nursing Christ Hosp., Cin., 1976-77; psychotherapist U. Med. Ctr., Cin., 1977-83, vol. debate team, 1985; asst. prof. nursing Thomas More Coll., Crestview Hills, Ky., 1977-83, chmn., dir. nursing program, 1983—, trustee, 1984—; cons. Health Improvement Systems Inc., Cin., 1983—. Vol. Cin. Fine Arts Fund Raising Com., 1983-84, Nat. Cancer Research Inst., 1985. Recipient Outstanding Nurse in Ky. award Ky. Nurses Assn., 1984. Mem. Am. Nurses Assn., Ohio Nurses Assn., (chmn. pub. relations com.), Nat. League for Nursing, Ky. Assn. Baccalaureate and Higher Degree Program Deans, Women in Academia, Women in Bus., Sigma Theta Tau. Republican. Roman Catholic. Office: Thomas More Coll 2771 Turkeyfoot Rd Crestview Hills KY 41017

KELLEY, MARY PALMER, landscape architect; b. Jacksonville, Fla., Apr. 26, 1954; d. James Palmer and Shirley (Talbot) Kelley; m. Hugh Graham Dargan, Mar. 31, 1985. B.A. in Botany, U. Tenn., 1976; M.Landscape Architecture, La. State U., 1982. Dir. edn. Cheekwood Bot. Gardens, Nashville, 1977-78, botanist, 1976-77; landscape architect Miller, Wihry, and Lee, Nashville, 1981-85, Hugh Dargan Assocs., Columbia, S.C., 1984—; pres. Garden History Assocs., Columbia, 1984—. Author: The Early English Kitchen Garden, 1982 (award Am. Soc. Landscape Architecture 1982); The Early American Kitchen Garden. Councilman Historic Elmwood Park Neighborhood Assn., 1985; singer Palmetto Pipers, 1984—. Herb Soc. Am. scholar, 1980; English Speaking Union Nashville fellow, 1984. Mem. Am. Soc. Landscape Architects, Jr. League Am. Episcopalian. Avocations: horses; restoring old houses; cultivating perennials; glazing. Home: PO Box 12606 Columbia SC 29211 Office: Hugh Dargan Assocs Inc PO Box 12606 Columbia SC 29211

KELLEY, SAM LYNN, state official; b. Alvarado, Tex., July 29, 1934; s. Samuel Albert and Annie Bill (Prestridge) K.; m. Mary Kate Wendler, Nov. 15, 1958; children—Sam L. Jr., Kerry, Karen, Timothy, Michelle, Michael. B.A., No. Tex. State U., 1955; LL.B., U. Tex., 1958. Asst. dist. atty. Dist. Atty's Office, Lubbock, Tex., 1960-62; assoc. Crenshaw, Dupree & Milam, Lubbock, 1962-64; asst. atty. gen. State of Tex., Austin, 1964-70; consumer credit commr. Office of Consumer Credit Commn., Austin, 1970—. Served to with U.S. Army, 1958-60. Mem. Nat. Assn. Consumer Credit Adminstrs., Delta Theta Phi. Home: 4820 Highway 290 W Austin TX 78735 Office: Consumer Credit Commn 1011 San Jacinto Blvd Austin TX 78701

KELLEY, SHELIA CRAWFORD, pharmacist; b. Griffin, Ga., Mar. 20, 1953; d. Edgar Rollin and Ellen Asenith (Busbin) Crawford; m. Tony Reginald Kelley, June 9, 1972; 1 child, Matthew Ryan. B.S. in Pharmacy, U. Ga., 1975. Intern St. Mary's Hosp., Athens, Ga., 1975-76, staff pharmacist, 1976-77; staff pharmacist DeKalb Gen. Hosp., Decatur, Ga., 1977-78; staff pharmacist St. Anthony's Med. Ctr., St. Louis, 1978-80, sr. staff pharmacist, 1980-83; staff pharmacist DeKalb Gen. Hosp., Decatur, Ga., 1984—; nursing home cons. St. Anthony's Med. Ctr., St. Louis, 1980-81. Lutheran. Avocations: snow and water skiing; sewing; needlework; reading. Home: 2838 Wood Hollow Ln Jonesboro GA 30236

KELLOGG, CHARLES GARY, civil engineer; b. Des Moines, July 14, 1948; s. Charles Leonard and Patricia (Johnson) K.; m. Linda Louise Pries, Sept. 5, 1970; children—Karees, Tait. B.S. in Civil Engring. with distinction, Iowa State U., 1970, M.S. in Soil Engring., 1972. Registered profl. engr., N.J., Fla. Grad. asst. Iowa State U., Ames, 1970-72; structural designer George L. Levin, Mpls., 1973; engr. in tng. Iowa Dept. Transp., Ames, 1973-76; personal and mgmt. cons., Ames, Iowa and New Brunswick, N.J., 1976-80; civil engr. Epstein-Johnson, Plainfield, N.J., 1980-81; structural engr. Herbert A. Wiener, Newark, 1981; sr. engr. Jones, Edmunds & Assocs., Gainesville, Fla., 1981-83; regional engr. Universal Engring. and Testing, Gainesville, 1983—; engring. cons. North Fla. Drainage Task Force. Recipient Donald T. Davidson award Iowa State U., 1972; Gibbs Cook scholar, 1968, 69. Mem. Am. Concrete Inst., Fla. Engring. Soc. (emergency assistance team), Fla. Inst. Cons. Engrs., Nat. Soc. Profl. Engrs., ASCE (accreditation team), Tau Beta Pi.

KELLOGG, JOHN RICHARD, dentist; b. San Antonio, Sept. 16, 1949; s. Joseph Warner and Eleanor (West) K.; children—Joseph Edward, Ann Claire; m. Karen Valentine, Feb. 14, 1984. B.S. in Chemistry, U. Tex., 1972; D.D.S., Emory U., 1976. With faculty U. Tex., San Antonio, 1980-82; cons. Bus. and Profl. Assocs., Houston, 1982; practice dentistry, San Antonio, 1976—. Active San Antonio Urban council, 1985, San Antonio Health and Emergency com., 1985; elder Alamo Heights Presby. Ch., 1985 pres. Day Sch. bd., 1986. Mem. San Antonio Dental Soc. (chmn. dental emergency com. 1981—, chmn. United Way 1982), Am. Acad. Gen. Dentistry, ADA. Avocations: music; computers, computer programming. Office: O'Brien and Kellogg 935 Eventide St San Antonio TX 78209

KELLY, ED, educational administrator. Supt. of schs. Little Rock. Office: W Markham and Izard Sts Little Rock AR 72201*

KELLY, HUGH J., oil and gas drilling company executive; b. 1925; married. LL.B., La. State U., 1950. Atty., 1950-51; with Calif. Co., 1951-57; with Ocean Drilling and Exploration Co., 1957—, v.p., sec., 1966-71, sr. v.p., sec., 1971-74, pres., New Orleans, 1974—, now also chief exec. officer, also dir. Served with AC, U.S. Army, 1942-45. Office: Ocean Drilling & Exploration Co 1600 Canal St New Orleans LA 70161*

KELLY, KENNETH KARL, accountant; b. Lexington, Ky., Feb. 5, 1942; s. Woodrow Wilson and Valiere Elizabeth (Smith) K.; m. Wandalee Dick, June 30, 1960 (div.); m. Zena Ann Paul, May 31, 1968; children—Vivian Renee, Kenneth Karl II, Darin Paul, Christopher Marc. B.S., Cumberland Coll., 1970. C.P.A., Ky., Tenn., Ind. Acct. Pritchard Mooney, C.P.A., 1970-75; pvt. practice acctg., Somerset, Ky., 1975—. Served with USN, 1959-63. Mem. Ky. Soc. C.P.A.s, Tenn. Soc. C.P.A.s. Republican. Baptist. Lodge: Masons.

KELLY, MARGARET RICAUD, educator; b. Dillon, S.C., Mar. 22, 1910; d. Robert Barry and Lulu Mowry (Crosland) Ricaud; A.B., Winthrop Coll., 1931; postgrad. Duke, 1931, U. Miami, 1937, U. Fla., 1938, U. N.C., 1950, 52, 53, U. S.C., 1954, Coker Coll., 1954-55; m. John Quinton Maynard, Jan. 1, 1936; m. 2d, Thomas W. Kelly, Sept. 12, 1950. Tchr. high sch., Elizabethtown, N.C., 1931-32; prin. Ebenezer Sch., Bennettsville, S.C., 1932-35; tchr. public schs., Homestead, Fla., 1937-39; tchr. Fletcher Meml. Sch., McColl, S.C., 1940-46; 67-69; attendance tchr. Marlboro County Schs., Bennettsville, 1946-50; tchr. elementary sch., Tabor City, N.C., 1950-51; tchr. public schs., Cordova, N.C., 1951-56, Society Hill, S.C., 1956-67; tchr. spl. edn. Blenheim (S.C.) primary schs., 1970-73; individual tutor, Bennettsville, 1973-77. Registered genealogist. Mem. Nat., S.C. edn. assns., Marlboro County Tchrs. (past chmn. pub. relations), S.C., Marlborough hist. socs., Mental Health Assn. Marlboro County, Marlboro Arts Council, Nat. Geneal. Soc., South Carolinian Soc., Colonial Dames 17th Century (registrar 1979-83), Magna Charta Dames, United Daus. Confederacy (pres. chpt. 1983—), Most Noble Order of Garter, S.C. Ret. Tchrs. Assn., Am. Assn. Ret. Persons, French Huguenot Soc., Colonial Order of Crown, Nat. Soc. Poetry, Bethea Family Assn., Pee Dee Queue. Author: Jack and the Flying Saucer, 1973; Poems by Margaret Ricaud Kelly, 1974; The Ricaud Family, a genealogical history, 1976; A Short History of Marlboro County 1600-1979, 1979; Colonel Harlee, 3 vols., rev. edit., 1984. Contbr. poetry to anthologies, 1972—, articles to various local newspapers. Home: 402 Fayetteville Ave Bennettsville SC 29512

KELLY, MARION, retail executive; b. Chgo., June 20, 1954; d. Stanton Wolf and Judith Anne (Bolnick) Brody; m. Edward William Kelly, Mar. 18, 1979. B.A., Kenyon Coll., 1976. Freelance illustrator, Chgo., 1973-79; freelance illustrator, courtroom illustrator, Winston-Salem, N.C., High Point, N.C., 1979-81; owner, mgr. Rainbow News, Winston-Salem, 1981—; acting exec. officer Rainbow Properties. Democrat. Jewish. Avocation: art. Office: Rainbow News Ltd 712 Brookstown Ave Winston-Salem NC 27101-2513

KELLY, THOMAS ALLEN, newspaper editor; b. Allentown, Pa., May 13, 1936; s. Thomas Allen and Mary Naomi (Snyder) K.; m. Barbara Jean Koch, Dec. 21, 1957 (div. July 1973); children—Christopher Jon (dec.), Michael Patrick, David Allen; m. Donna Jean Robertson, Nov. 16, 1974; 1 son, Thomas Glenn. B.J., Lehigh U., 1958. Copyboy, reporter Call-Chronicle Newspapers, Allentown, 1954-58; reporter, copy editor Fla. Pub. Co., Jacksonville, 1958-61; sports editor Times Pub. Co., St. Petersburg, Fla., 1961-73; mng. editor Palm Beach Newspapers, Inc., West Palm Beach, Fla., 1973-76; editor The Palm Beach Post, West Palm Beach, 1976—. Bd. dirs. Palm Beach County Community Found., 1981—, Palm Beach County Council of the Arts, 1981-82, Palm Beach Festival, 1980-82. Recipient Myrtle Wreath award Palm Beach County Hadassah, 1979. Mem. Fla. Sports Writers Assn. (pres. 1966-67), Fla. Soc. Newspaper Editors (dir.), Am. Soc. Newspaper Editors, AP Mng. Editors, Democrat. Lutheran. Clubs: Forum, Mayacoo Lakes Country (West Palm Beach). Home: 927 Paseo Andorra West Palm Beach FL 33405 Office: 2751 S Dixie Hwy West Palm Beach FL 33405

KELLY, THOMAS C., archbishop; b. Rochester, N.Y., July 14, 1931; s. Thomas A. and Katherine Eleanor (Fisher) K.; A.B., Providence Coll., 1953; S.T.L., Dominican House Studies, Washington, 1959; J.C.D., U. St. Thomas, Rome, 1962; S.T.D. (hon.), Providence Coll., 1979; L.H.D. (hon.), Spalding Coll., Louisville, 1983. Joined Dominican Order Preachers, 1951, ordained priest Roman Catholic Ch., 1958; sec. Dominican Provincial, N.Y.C., 1962-65; sec. to apostolic del., Washington, 1965-71; asso. gen. sec. Nat. Conf. Cath. Bishops, Washington, 1971-77; gen. sec. Nat. Conf. Cath. Bishops and U.S. Cath. Conf., 1977-82; aux. bishop Archdiocese Washington, 1977-82; archbishop of Louisville, 1982—. Mem. Canon Law Soc. Am. Address: Archdiocese of Louisville 212 E College St Louisville KY 40203

KELLY, WILLIAM GLENN, health organization administrator; b. Dallas, Feb. 1, 1943; s. Denzil Carl and Florace Louisa (Crain) K.; m. Donna Gay Laney, Dec. 20, 1969; children—James Michael, Steven Wayne. B.B.A., U. Tex., 1967; M.B.A., Midwestern U., 1971. Asst. adminstr. John B. Chester Hosp., Dallas, 1971-79; adminstr. Panola Gen. Hosp., Carthage, Tex., 1979-85, Blue Cross and Blue Shield of Tex. Inc., 1985—. Organizing com. Am. Cancer Soc., Carthage, 1985; emergency med. services com. East Tex. Council Govts., Kilgore, Tex., 1983; United Way of Metropolitan Dallas, 1973, 75, 77; mem. pub. service div. campaign, hosp. com. Served to staff sgt. USAF, 1967-71. Mem. Am. Hosp. Assn., Tex. Hosp. Assn. (pub. hosp. ops. com. 1985). Democrat. Lodge: Rotary (pres. 1982-83). Avocation: church youth work. Home: 8727 Point Park #1311 Houston TX 77095 Office: Blue Cross and Blue Shield of Tex Inc 2950 North Loop W Suite 1030 Houston TX 77092

KELSEY, ALICE MURPHREE, college administrator; b. Pickens, S.C., Sept. 13, 1938; d. J. Hoke and S. Naomi (Jones) Murphree; m. Walter Brice Kelsey, Jr., Sept. 22, 1962; children—Alisa, Fran, Glenda. B.A., Winthrop Coll., 1959; postgrad. Furman U., 1961; M.A., S.C. Coll., 1977. Counselor, dir. student affairs Orangeburg-Calhoun Tech. Coll., S.C., 1977—. Active Presbyn. Ch., Orangeburg, 1967—; pres. Orangeburg Winthrop Coll. Alumni, 1970; sec. Assn. Parents and Tchrs Willington High Sch., Orangeburg, 1976; vice-regent DAR, 1976-82, chmn. good citizens com., 1982-85. Recipient Outstanding Leadership award Orangeburg-Calhoun Tech. Coll., 1978, 79, 80, 81, 82, 83, 84, 85. Mem. Am. Assn. Counseling and Devel., Am. Coll. Personnel Assn., S.C. Assn. Counseling and Devel., S.C. Assn. Measurement and Evaluation in Guidance, S.C. Tech. Edn. Assn. Republican. Club: Orangeburg Country. Avocations: tennis; golf; music. Home: 630 Rutledge St Orangeburg SC 29115 Office: Orangeburg-Calhoun Tech Coll 3250 St Matthews Rd NE Orangeburg SC 29115

KELSEY, CLYDE EASTMAN, JR., educator; b. Wadena, Minn., Mar. 30, 1924; s. Clyde Eastman and Lorraine (Lamb) K.; m. Betty Jean Williams, Apr. 1, 1949; children—Becky Kelsey Marcin, Nancy Kelsey Dawson. B.A., U. Tex.-El Paso, 1948; M.A., U. Tulsa, 1951; Ph.D., U. Denver, 1960; hon. degree U. de Oriente (Venezuela), 1969. Dir. counseling bur. U. Tex.-El Paso, 1951-61, prof., head depts. philosophy and psychology, 1961-62; dean students, dir. Inter-Am. Inst., 1962-66; Ford Found. program adviser Venezuela, 1966-69; vice chancellor pub. affairs U. Denver, 1969-72; v.p. devel. and univ. relations Tex. Tech U., Lubbock, 1972-80, prof. edn., 1981—; lectr. 4th Army U.S., 1961-65; cons. U.S. Dept. State, Peace Corps, 1961-66. Mem. adv. bd. Kans. Wesleyan Coll., 1969-71; v.p. Colo. Ptnrs. of Alliance, 1971-73; bd. dirs. El Paso Mental Health Assn., 1951-58, pres., 1953-55; bd. dirs. El Paso Sch. Retarded Children, 1952-57, pres., 1953-55; bd. dirs. Lubbock Goodwill Industries, 1972-83, v.p., 1973-77, pres., 1978-80; sr. research fellow Nat. Ctr. for Higher Edn. Mgmt. Systems, Boulder, Colo., 1983—. Served with USNR, 1942-45. Decorated Order San Carlos, Republic of Colombia, 1964; recipient Disting. Alumni Service award U. Denver, 1972; Fulbright scholar, Colombia, 1960-61. Fellow Tex. Acad. Sci.; mem. Am. Psychol. Assn., Tex. Psychol. Assn., AAAS, Am. Ednl. Research Assn. Contbr. articles to profl. jours. Home: 3307 A 74th St Lubbock TX 79423 Office: PO Box 4560 Lubbock TX 79409

KELSOE, LYNDA CAROL, aerospace engineer, computer scientist; b. Birmingham, Ala., Apr. 5, 1943; d. Johnny Willard and Marjorie Nanette (Wallace) Simmons; B.S., U. Montevallo, 1966; student U. Ala., 1968; B.S., Stevens Inst. Bus. Tech., 1971; M.A., U. Houston, 1977, M.A., 1979; m. Neal Marshall Kelsoe, July 18, 1981. Tchr. English, Birmingham (Ala.) Pub. Schs., 1966-70; programmer Bell Telephone Labs., Whippany, N.J., 1971-74; sci. programmer Lockheed Electronics, Houston, 1973-74; programmer analyst IBM, Houston, 1974-76, Lockheed Electronics, Houston, 1977-78; sr. analyst Computer Scis. Corp., Houston, 1978-82; corp. staff Jefferson Assocs., Inc., Houston, 1982; project mgr. Intermetrics Inc., Houston, 1982-86; mgr. Booz, Allen & Hamilton, 1986—. Councilwoman City of El Lago (Tex.). Lic. pvt. pilot. Mem. Assn. Computing Machinery, Nat. Mgmt. Assn., AIAA, Nat. Assn. Female Execs., Graphics Exchange. Home: 206 Yacht Club Ln Seabrook TX 77586 Office: 17625 El Camino Real Houston TX 77058

KEMBLE, CHARLES ROBERT, university system chancellor; b. Oskaloosa, Iowa, Aug. 17, 1925; s. Roy H. and Pauline (Hoover) K.; m. Helen Elizabeth Elfstrom, July 3, 1949; children—Christopher, Keith Eilene, Cynthia Kemble Lawshe, Geoffrey, Carol Lynn. Student Kans. U., 1943, Cornell U., 1945; B.S., U.S. Mil. Acad., 1949; M.A., U. Pa., 1956; Ph.D., George Washington U., 1966. Commd. 2d lt. U.S. Army, 1949, advanced through grades to col., 1970; asst. prof. U.S. Mil. Acad., 1956-60; exec. asst. dir. ops. Joint Chiefs of Staff, 1961-64; assoc. prof. English, dir. Am. studies U.S. Mil. Acad., 1966-72; ret., 1972; pres. N.Mex. Mil. Inst., 1972-77; chancellor Lamar U., Beaumont, Tex., 1977—; dir. 1st City Bank, Beaumont. Author: The Image of the American Army Officer, 1973; co-editor: John Brown's Body (Benet), 1968. Decorated Legion of Merit, Bronze Star, others. Mem. Am. Studies Assn., MLA, Assn. U.S. Army, Ret. Officers Assn., Beaumont C. of C. (dir.). Lodge: Rotary. Office: Office of Chancellor Lamar U Sta Box 11900 Beaumont TX 77710

KEMLER, JUDITH ANN-CARSON, educator; b. Mt. Vernon, Tex., July 22, 1950; d. James Elton and Tennie (Couch) Carson; student Sam Houston State U., 1968-69; B.S., U. Houston, 1975; M.S., U.Houston, Clear Lake City, 1979; children—Brian Webb, Heather Kristina, Shelley Sea. Ins. claims examiner European Exchange System, Munich, 1969-71; programmer, sec. elec. engring. dept. U. Houston, 1973-75; tchr. Pasadena (Tex.) Ind. Sch. Dist., 1976—, tchr. math. J. Frank Dobie High Sch., 1976—; mem. faculty San Jacinto Jr. Coll., 1980—; reviewer secondary algebra book Prindle-Webber Pubs., 1979-80. Active Boy Scouts Am. Mem. San Jacinto Area Council Tchrs. Math. (pres. 1979-81, 3d v.p. in charge newsletter 1981-83), NEA, Tex. Council Tchrs. Math., Nat. Council Tchrs. Math., Tex. Tchrs. Assn., Pasadena Tchrs. Assn., Assn. Supervision and Curriculum Devel., PTA. Clubs: Burke Meadows Civic, Antique Clock Assn. Home: 1214 Kenwick St Pasadena TX 77504 Office: 11111 Beamer St Houston TX 77089

KEMM, JAMES OSWALD, retired public relations executive, writer; b. Springfield, Mo., May 6, 1921; s. Oswald Fred and Vivian Beatrice (Baldridge) K.; m. Betty Ann Harner, June 12, 1947; children—Nancy, Kathleen, Martha. Student Southwest Mo. State Coll., 1939-42; B.Journalism, U. Mo., 1947; postgrad. U. Pa., 1947-48. Newswriter, Sta. KTTS, Springfield, Mo., 1942; asst. prof. Rider Coll., Trenton, N.J., 1947-49; copyreader Springfield Newspapers, Inc., 1949-52; dist. rep. Oil Info. Com., Am. Petroleum Inst., Kansas City, Mo., 1952-53, sr. dist. rep., Tulsa, 1953-58; exec. mgr. Okla. Petroleum Council, Tulsa, 1958-82; exec. v.p. pub. relations Okla.-Kans. Oil & Gas Assn., Tulsa, 1982-83; cons. and freelance writer, Tulsa, 1983—. Bd. dirs. Okla. Hist. Soc., 1983—; chmn. Okla. Gov.'s Council on Tourist Devel., 1964-66, vice chmn., 1967-70; bd. dirs. Okla. Hwy. Users Fedn., Goodwill Industries of Tulsa; mem. communications com. Tulsa Area United Way; elder First Presbyterian Ch., Tulsa. Served with U.S. Army, 1942-45. Recipient Cert. of Appreciation, Okla. Petroleum Council, 1972; Appreciation award Okla.-Kans. Oil and Gas Assn., 1983. Mem. Pub. Relations Soc. Am. (accredited; pres. Okla. chpt. 1959-60, Silver Link award as Pub. Relations Profl. of Yr., Tulsa chpt. 1980), Tulsa Soc. Assn. Execs. (pres. 1965), Am. Soc. Assn. Execs. (award of merit for mgmt. achievement 1977), Okla. Soc. Assn. Execs., Assn. Petroleum Writers, Sigma Delta Chi (past pres. Eastern Okla. chpt.). Republican. Clubs: Petroleum Club of Tulsa, Tulsa Press. Author: Let's Talk Petroleum, 1958. Home: 1609 E 55th St Tulsa OK 74105

KEMP, BETTY RUTH, librarian; b. Tishomingo, Okla., May 5, 1930; d. Raymond Herrell and Mamie Melvina (Hughes) K.; B.A.L.S., U. Okla., 1952; M.S., Fla. State U., 1965. Extramural loan librarian U. Tex., Austin, 1952-55; librarian lit. and history dept. Dallas Public Library, 1955-56, head Oaklawn Br., 1956-60, head Walnut Hill Br., 1960-64; dir. Cherokee Regional Library, LaFayette, Ga., 1965-74; dir. Lee County Library, hdqrs. Lee-Itawamba Library System, Tupelo, Miss., 1975—; bd. library commrs. State of Miss., 1979-83, chmn., 1979-80. Active LWV, United Meth. Women. Mem. ALA, Southeastern Library Assn., Miss. Library Assn., Beta Phi Mu. Democrat. Club: AAUW. Home: 2112 President Tupelo MS 38801 Office: 219 Madison Tupelo MS 38801

KEMP, EDGAR RAY, JR., retail executive; b. Corsicana, Tex., Sept. 15, 1924; s. Edgar Ray and Earla Mae (Brennan) K.; m. Margaret Ellen Letzig, Sept. 17, 1949; children—William R., Daniel B., Ellen C., Michael E. B.B.A., U. Ark., 1948. C.P.A., Ark. Pvt. practice acctg., 1948-58; treas. M. M. Cohn Co., 1958-63; vice chmn. Dillard Dept. Stores, Inc., Little Rock, 1963—, also vice chmn., chief adminstrv. officer; chmn. Little Rock br. Fed. Res. Bank of St. Louis. Served with USAAF, 1943-45; Served with USAF, 1951-52. Mem. Am. Inst. Accts., Nat. Assn. Accts., Sigma Chi, Alpha Kappa Psi. Roman Catholic. Office: Dillard Dept Stores Inc 900 W Capitol St Little Rock AR 72201*

KEMP, EMORY LELAND, civil engineering educator; b. Chgo., Oct. 1, 1931; s. Emory Leland and Anita Maye (Hucker) K.; m. Janet Karen Dodd, July 26, 1958; children—Mark, Alison, Geoffrey. B.S. with high honors, U. Ill., 1952, Ph.D., 1962; diploma Imperial Coll. Sci. and Tech., London, 1955; M.S.E., U. London, 1958. Registered profl. engr., W.Va. Asst. engr. Ill. State Water Survey, Urbana, 1952; structural engr. Sir Bruce White Wolfe Barry and Ptnrs., Ove Arup and Ptnrs., London, 1956-59; instr. dept. theoretical and applied mechanics U. Ill., Urbana, 1959-62; assoc. prof. dept. civil engring. W.Va. U., Morgantown, 1962-66, prof., 1966—, chmn. dept., 1967-74, dir. program for history, sci. and tech., 1975. Served with U.S. Army, 1952-54. Fulbright fellow, 1955; Am. Council Learned Socs. fellow, 1975-76, U.K.; Regent's fellow Smithsonian Instn., 1983-84. Fellow Inst. Civil Engrs., ASCE, Am. Concrete Inst.; mem. Inst. Structural Engrs., Soc. Indsl. Archeology, Am. Soc. Engring. Edn., Newcomen Soc., Phi Kappa Phi, Tau Beta Pi, Chi Epsilon. Methodist. Home: 429 Riley St Morgantown WV 26505 Office: W Va U G14 Woodburn Hall Town Campus Morgantown WV 26506

KEMP, JAMES DILLON, animal science educator; b. Pickett, Ky., Feb. 6, 1923; s. George Talbott and Mattie Coleman (Whitlock) K.; m. Helen Gertrude Walker, Dec. 21, 1947; children—Bonnie Kay, James Walker. B.S., U. Ky., 1948, M.S., 1949; Ph.D., U. Ill., 1952. Asst. prof. animal sci. U. Ky., Lexington, 1952-56, assoc. prof., 1956-60, prof., 1960—, coordinator food sci. sect., 1966—, trustee, 1983—; cons. U.S. Dept. Agr., N.E. Agrl. Ctr., Thailand, 1974. Served as 2d lt., AC, U.S. Army, 1943-45. Decorated Air medal; recipient U. Ky. Cooper Research award, 1974; Fulbright research scholar, N.Z., 1964. Fellow Inst. Food Technologists; mem. Am. Meat Sci. Assn. (teaching award 1968, Signal Service award 1977), Am. Soc. Animal Sci. (meats research award 1971). Republican. Methodist. Lodge: Lions. Contbr. numerous articles to profl. jours. World Book Ency. Home: 778 Hildeen Rd Lexington KY 40502 Office: 209 Agr Sci Bldg S U Ky Lexington KY 40546

KEMP, MARILYN BAREFIELD, college administrator, educator; b. Gilbertown, Ala., Feb. 10, 1941; d. Andrew Jackson and Eunice (Moseley) Barefield; children—Stephanie, Cecil, Dale. B.A., U. Southwestern La., 1963; M.Ed., U. New Orleans, 1978, postgrad., 1978-82, 82—. Cert. tchr., counselor, prin., supr. Tchr., St. Bernard Sch. System, Chalmette, La., 1963-82; counselor, coordinator student services St. Bernard Parish Community Coll., Chalmette, 1982-83, dir. student services, 1983—. Contbr. poems to publs. Participant St. Bernard Trade Show, 1982—; vol. mental health unit Juvenile Probation Unit, Recreational Dept., Chalmette, New Life, New Orleans. Mem. Am. Assn. Counseling and Devel., Mid-South Ednl. Research, Delta Kappa Gamma, Phi Delta Kappa, Kappa Delta Phi. Democrat. Roman Catholic. Avocations: Reading; creative writing; research; exercise; music. Office: St Bernard Parish Community College 1100 E Judge Perez Dr Chalmette LA 70043

KEMP, MAURY PAGE, financial executive; b. El Paso, Tex., Nov. 25, 1929; s. Roland Gordon and Nora (Henderson) K.; m. Jean Jones, Mar. 30, 1955; children—Diane, Maury Page, Jr. B.B.A., U. Tex.-El Paso, 1952. Founder, chmn. Kemp Ford Inc., El Paso, 1957—, Lone Star Growth Corp., El Paso, 1970—; past owner Main Lincoln-Mercury, San Antonio, Mesilla Valley Lincoln-Mercury, Las Cruces, N. Mex., Selby Motors, Tucson, various car dealerships in Colo., Ariz., N. Mex., Tex., 1964-84; founder First Fin. Enterprises, El Paso, 1980, chmn. bd., 1980—; chmn. bd. First Fin. Banking Center, El Paso, First Service Life Ins. Co., Security Southwest Life Ins. Co., Knickerbocker Life Ins. Co. Past. pres. bd. trustees El Paso Museum Art; bd. dirs. El Paso Indsl. Devel. Bd., Tex. Ind. Coll. Fund, El Paso Renaissance 400, El Paso Arts Alliance, El Paso Cancer Treatment Ctr.; past bd. dirs. United Fund, El Paso Boys Club, El Paso Symphony Assn., Goodwill Industries, El Paso Better Bus. Bur.; mem. vestry St. Clement's Episcopal Ch., El Paso.

Served with U.S. Army, 1952-54. Recipient Bus. Leadership and Achievement award, U. Tex.-El Paso, 1980, Outstanding Student award, 1985. Mem. Nat. Automobile Dealers Assn. (past alternate chmn.), Ford Dealers Advt. Fund (past chmn.), Tex. Automobile Dealers Assn. (past dir.), El Paso New Car Dealers Assn. (pres.) Employers Assn. El Paso. Clubs: El Paso Country, Coronado Country, The El Paso, Internat. of El Paso; Dallas, Northwood Country (Dallas); Thunderbird Country (Rancho Mirage, Calif.); The Argyle (San Antonio). Office: First Fin Enterprises 500 N Mesa El Paso TX 79901

KEMP, ROLAND CONNOR, lawyer; b. Dallas, May 29, 1943; s. William Thomas and Martha Bell (Arney) K.; m. Carol Ann DeRosa, Dec. 12, 1966; children—Thomas Roland, Patrick Michael. B.A., Baylor U., 1965, postgrad., 1966; J.D., U. Tex.-Austin, 1972. Bar: Tex. 1972, U.S. Dist. Ct. (so. dist.) Tex. 1973, U.S. Ct. Apls. (5th cir.) 1973, U.S. Sup. Ct. 1976. Law clk. U.S. Dist. Ct. So. Dist. Tex., Houston, 1972-74; assoc. Schlanger, Cook, Cohn & Mills, Houston, 1974-76; assoc. Fred Parks & Assocs., Houston, 1977-80; sole practice, Houston, 1980—. Chmn. bd. dirs. Timberlane Mcpl. Utility Dist., Harris County, Tex., 1973. Served to capt. USAF, 1966-70. Mem. ABA, State Bar Tex., Houston Bar Assn., Phi Delta Phi. Presbyterian. Club: Inns Ct. (Houston). Office: 14450 TC Jester Blvd Suite 160 Houston TX 77014

KEMP, STEPHEN FRANK, pediatric endocrinologist, educator; b. Newport, Oreg., Mar. 21, 1947; s. Frank Shirley and Charla Mae (Wait) K. B.A., U. Oreg., 1969; Ph.D. in Biochemistry, U. Chgo., 1974, M.D., 1976. Diplomate Am. Bd. Pediatrics. Intern Stanford U., 1976-77, resident in pediatrics, 1977-78; postdoctoral fellow in pediatric endocrinology, 1978-80; asst. prof. pediatrics and chief pediatric endocrinology U. South Ala., Mobile, 1980-84; asst. prof. pediatrics U. Ark. for Med Sci., 1984-85, assoc. prof. pediatrics and biochemistry, 1985—. Vice pres. Ala. affiliate Am. Diabetes Assn., 1982-84, chmn. youth com. Ark. affiliate, mem. camp com. Recipient NIH postdoctoral nat. research service award, 1978-80. Mem. Med. Assn. State Ala., Am. Fedn. Clin. Research, Southern Soc. Pediatric Research, Endocrine Soc. Democrat. Episcopalian. Contbr. articles to profl. jours. Home: 8 Victoria Circle Maumelle AR 72118 Office: Dept Pediatrics U Ark for Med Sci 4301 W Markham Little Rock AR 72205

KEMP, TEDDY MAURICE, therapist, health center administrator; b. LaFayette, Ga., Aug. 31, 1950; s. George Everett and Mary Ellen (Evans) K.; m. Martha Francina Cook, Jan. 29, 1977. A.B., U. Ga., 1976, M.S.W., 1978, M.P.A., 1982. Lic. marriage and family therapist. Project coordinator Family Counselling Service, Athens, Ga., 1978-81; founder, dir. N.E. Ga. Employee Assistance Program, Athens, Ga., 1980-81; dir. human resources and employee relations Mental Health Resource Ctr., Jacksonville, Fla., 1981—; founder, dir. RP/M Systems, Jacksonville, 1982—; pvt. practice marriage family therapy. Bd. dirs. Central Crisis Ctr., Jacksonville. Served with AUS, 1969-72; Vietnam. Mem. Fla. Occupational Program Com., Occupational Program Cons. Assn., Am. Assn. Marriage/Family Therapy, South Council C. of C. Home: Rt 2 Box 553 Yulee FL 32097 Office: 4237 Salisbury Rd Suite 111 Jacksonville FL 32216

KEMPER, J. ALLEN, accounting firm executive, tax/business consultant; b. Ft. Worth, Oct. 15, 1939; s. J. Marvin and Ruby Alice (Botts) K.; m. Ida Layland, Feb. 5, 1982; children—Kevin, Bryan. B.B.A., West Tex. State Coll., 1962. C.P.A., Tex. Owner, J. Allen Kemper, C.P.A.s, Midland, Tex., 1982—. Served to capt. AUS, 1963-64. Mem. Am. Inst. C.P.A.s, Tex. Soc. C.P.A.s. Home: 3241 Preston St Midland TX 79707 Office: J Allen Kemper CPA Suite 214 4305 N Garfield St Midland TX 79705

KEMPER, MARLYN J., librarian, historian; b. Balt., Mar. 26, 1943; d. Louis and Augusta Louise (Jacobs) Janofsky; m. Bennett I. Kemper, Aug. 1, 1965; children—Alex Randall, Gari Hament, Jason Myles. B.A., Finch Coll., 1964; M.A. in Anthropology, Temple U., Phila., 1970; M.A. in Library Sci., U. S. Fla., 1983. Dir., Hist. Broward County Preservation Bd., Hollywood, Fla., 1979—; automated systems librarian Broward County Main Library, Ft. Lauderdale, Fla., 1983—. Pub. info. officer Broward County Hist. Commn., 1975-79. Recipient Judge L. Clayton Nance award, 1977; Boward County Hist. Commn. award, 1979. Mem. ALA, Am. Soc. for Info. Sci., Spl. Libraries Assn., Orgn. Am. Historians, Associated Info. Mgrs., Beta Phi Mu, Phi Kappa Phi. Democrat. Jewish. Author: A Comprehensive Documented History of the City of Pompano Beach, 1982 A Comprehensive History of Dania 1983, Hallandale, 1984, Deerfield Beach, 1985; author weekly columns Ft. Lauderdale News, 1975-76, 77-79; contbr. articles to profl. jours. Home: 2845 NE 35th St Fort Lauderdale FL 33306 Office: Broward County Main Library 100 S Andrews Ave Fort Lauderdale FL 33301

KEMPTHORNE, RICHARD LEWIS, construction industry executive; b. Orange, N.J., Jan. 7, 1927; s. James Lewis and Eleanor (McKelvey) K.; Asso. Bus. Adminstrn., Nichols Coll., 1949; B.S., Syracuse U., 1951; m. Alice Clair Prost, Feb. 26, 1949; children—James Lewis III, Ann. Vice pres. Sprayed Insulation Inc., Newark, 1951-53; head Columbia Acoustics & Fireproofing Co., Stanhope, N.J., 1954-56; chief exec., sec.-treas. Fla. Insulation & Fireproofing Co., Miami, 1957-65; pres., dir. Sprayed Fibers, Inc., Miami, 1963-71, Spraydon Overseas Corp., Miami, 1966-71; v.p. Tex. Fireproofing Co., Houston, 1960-63; pres., dir. Sprayon Research Corp., Ft. Lauderdale, Fla., 1964—; pres., dir. Midwest Sprayon Corp., Miami, 1966-71; pres. Sprayon Internat. Inc., N.Y.C., 1971-73; pres., dir. Spraydon Corp., 1974—, Spraydon Corp. Ltd., 1974—; pres. Am. Energy Products Corp., 1977-81; acoustical, computer cons. Mem. bd. elections Young Republicans of Miami, 1958—. Pres. Miami Shores Prep. Sch., 1968-72. Served with USNR, 1944-46. Mem. Am. Soc. Testing Materials, Nat. Fireprotection Assn., Internat. Assn. Walls and Ceilings Contractors, Amateur Athletic Union. Clubs: Miami Shores Country (pres. swimming assn. 1964-67); Marine Bay. Patentee in field. Address: 5701 Bayview Dr Fort Lauderdale FL 33308

KENADJIAN, BERDJ, economist, author; b. Istanbul, Turkey, May 29, 1930; came to U.S. 1946, naturalized 1954; s. Aram N. and Adrine (Stambolian) K.; m. Barbara G. Glenn, May 15, 1955; 1 child, Clarence Glenn. B.B.A. in Bus. Adminstrn., U. Mich., 1951; A.M. in Econ., Harvard U., 1954, Ph.D. in Econ., 1957. Chmn. dept. econ. and bus. adminstrn. Wofford Coll., Spartanburg, S.C., 1957-59; asst. dir. ops. analysis div. Dept. HEW, 1964-67; dep. dir. Ctr. Priority Analysis Nat. Planning Assn., Washington, 1969-70; chief econ. estimates and studies sect. IRS, Washington, 1970-80, chief economist compliance estimates, 1980—; cons. to gov. of Fed. Reserve Bd., 1961; mem. editorial com. of Statis. Reporter, 1975-80. Author: Economics of the New Age, 1973. Author, editor quar. bull. The Word on Government, 1974—. Contbr. articles to profl. jours. Organizer, bd. dirs. Friendship Circle, 1960-62; exec. com. of council of Lutheran Ch. of the Reformation, 1960-63; pres. New Age Action Group, Alexandria, Va., 1974—. Served with U.S. Army, 1954-56. Recipient Achievement award U.S. Treasury Dept. Mem. Am. Econ. Assn., Soc. Govt. Economics, Nat. Economists Club (rapporteur 1977—), Beta Gamma Sigma, Phi Kappa Phi. Methodist. Club: Conservative (Alexandria). Home: 910 Crescent Dr Alexandria VA 22302

KENDALL, GEORGE CHARLES, JR., information systems executive; consultant; b. Rahway, N.J., June 18, 1938; s. George Charles and Etta Francis (Van Pelt) K.; m. Emmalu Mary Moody, June 23, 1979; 1 son, George Charles III. Student Stanford U., 1956; B.B.A. in Fin., U. Tex. Austin, 1960. Dir. internat. ops. Corp. S., Dallas, 1967-70; mgr. software devel. Gen. Computer Systems, Dallas, 1970-74; v.p. info. resources and revenue mgmt. St. John Med. Ctr., Tulsa, 1974—; cons. People's Republic China, 1981—. Served to capt. U.S. Army, 1960-61. Unitarian. Author tech. papers. Home: 3041 W 55th Pl Tulsa OK 74107 Office: St John Med Ctr 1923 S Utica Ave Tulsa OK 74104

KENDALL, WILLIAM SIMMS, educator; b. Wharton, Tex., Mar. 7, 1937; s. William Edward and Johnnie (Lee) K.; m. Virginia Ruth Breeding, Dec. 12, 1964; children—Kevin Edward, Keith Lamont. B.A., Prairie View A&M Coll., 1960, M.Ed., 1967; Ed.D., U. Houston, 1974; postgrad. U. No. Colo., 1981. Tchr., LaGrange Pub. Schs. (Tex.), 1962-65, Victoria Pub. Schs. (Tex.), 1965-68, Houston Pub. Schs., 1968-74; asst. prof. dept. spl. edn. Prairie View A&M U. (Tex.), 1974-78, dir. spl. edn. programs, 1978—; cons. in spl. edn. Served with U.S. Army, 1960-62. Recipient Edn. award HEW, 1974. Mem. Am. Assn. Mental Deficiency, Council for Exceptional Children, Orton Soc., Assn. for Supervision and Curriculum Devel., Assn. for Children and Adults with Learning Disabilities. Contbr. articles to profl. jours. Home: 1046 Creekmont Dr Houston TX 77091 Office: Prairie View A&M U Prairie View TX 77446

KENDER, WALTER JOHN, university official, educator; b. Camden, N.J., Dec. 20, 1935; s. Walter and Martha Kender; m. Carole Adele Holm, May 26, 1957; children—David Walter, Lily Carole. B.S., Delaware Valley Coll., 1957; M.S., Rutgers U., 1959, Ph.D., 1962. Asst. prof. U. Maine, Orono, 1962-66, assoc. prof., 1966-69; assoc. prof. Cornell U.-Geneva, N.Y., 1969-75, prof., 1975-82, chmn. dept. pomology, Ithaca, N.Y., 1975-82; head dept. pomology and viticulture N.Y. State Agrl. Expt. Sta., Geneva, 1972-82; dir. Citrus Research and Edn. Ctr., U. Fla.-Lake Alfred, 1982—. Fellow Am. Soc. for Hort. Sci.; mem. AAAS, Am. Pomol. Soc., Internat. Soc. for Hort Sci., Sigma Xi. Democrat. Roman Catholic. Mem. editorial bd. AVI Press; contbr. numerous articles to sci. jours. Home: 40 Club Ct Haines City FL 33844 Office: Citrus Research and Edn Ctr 700 Experiment Station Rd Lake Alfred FL 33850

KENDERDINE, JOHN MARSHALL, manufacturing company executive; b. Ft. Worth, Dec. 6, 1912; s. Robert Leonard and Caroline (Raab) K.; B.S. in Petroleum Engring., Tex. A. and M. Coll., 1934; grad. Army War Coll., 1953, Advanced Mgmt. Program, Harvard, 1959, Exec. Decision Inst., 1962; m. Su Anne Carroll, Feb. 26, 1937; children—James Marshall, Su C. Brackman. Petroleum engr. Gulf Oil Corp., 1934-37; br. mgr. Norvell-Wilder Supply Co., Midland, Tex., 1938-41; commd. 1st lt. U.S. Army, 1941, advanced through grades to brig. gen., 1962; mil. logistician in France, Germany and U.S., World War II; spl. asst. to adminstr. War Assets Adminstrn., 1946; mil. staff and command assignments, 1947-60; joint petroleum officer Europe, 1961; exec. dir. supply ops. Def. Supply Agy., 1962-65; comdr. Def. Indsl. Supply Center, Phila., 1965-66, Def. Personnel Support Center, Phila., 1966-67; ret., 1967; v.p. spl. tech. Scott Paper Co., Phila., 1967-70; pres. C.F. Adams, Inc., Ft. Worth, 1970—. Decorated D.S.M., Legion of Merit, Joint Service Commendation medal, Commendation ribbon with 3 oak leaf clusters. Registered profl. engr., Tex. Mem. Soc. Logistics Engrs., Def. Supply Assn., Assn. U.S. Army, Airline Passengers Assn. (adv. bd.), West Tex. C. of C. (dir. 1985), Am. Mgmt. Assn. Club: Petroleum. Contbr. articles on handling and safety of aviation fuels, especially turbine fuels to profl. jours. Home: 3212 Chapparal Ln Fort Worth TX 76109 Office: Box 253 Fort Worth TX 76101

KENDRICK, DANIEL FREDERICK, III, real estate investment executive; b. Waco, Tex., May 14, 1950; s. Edward Storey and Martha Anna (Wiman) K. Vice pres. E. Kendrick & Sons, Atlanta, 1970-74; fin. analyst First Nat. of Atlanta, 1974-76; sr. fin. analyst Johnstown Properties, Atlanta, 1976-79; sr. fin. officer Home Ins.-City Investing, N.Y., 1979-80; v.p., regional dir. Krupp Realty, Boston, Mass., 1980-82; v.p. portfolio mgmt. Murray Properties, Dallas, 1982—; officer, dir. various real estate ltd. partnerships. Mem. Internat. Council shopping Ctrs. Democrat. Presbyterian. Office: Murray Properties 5520 LBJ Freeway Suite 600 Dallas TX 75240

KENDRICK, DAVID ANDREW, economist; b. Gatesville, Tex., Nov. 14, 1937; s. Andrew Green and Nina Alice (Murray) K.; B.A., U. Tex., 1960; Ph.D., MIT, 1965; m. Gail Tidd, July 4, 1964; children—Ann, Colin. Asst. prof. Harvard U., 1966-70; vis. scholar Stanford U., 1969-70; vis. prof. MIT, 1978-79; prof. econs. U. Tex.-Austin, 1970—. Served with U.S. Army, 1960-61. Woodrow Wilson fellow, 1960; Ford faculty fellow, 1969. Mem. Econometric Soc., Am. Econs. Assn., Soc. Econ. Dynamics Control. Author: Stochastic Control Economic Models, 1981; (with P. Dixon and S. Bowles) Notes and Problems in Microeconomic Theory, 1980; (with A. Stoutiesdijk) The Planning of Industrial Investment Programs, 1978. Home: 7209 Lamplight Ln Austin TX 78731 Office: Dept Econs BEB400 U Tex Austin TX 78712

KENDRICK, GARLAND LEE, consulting mechanical engineer; b. Ft. Hall, Idaho, May 24, 1918; s. Luther Garland and Mary Eula K.; m. Margaret Louise Mullen, June 10, 1963; children—Lynne, Kay, Joyce, Stephen, Randolph, Kimberly. B.S. in Mech. Engring., Ga. Inst. Tech., 1941. Registered profl. engr., Va., Md., D.C. Prin. Lee Kendrick & Assocs., 1952, Kendrick & Redinger, 1959-67, Vosbeck, Vosbeck, Kendrick, Redinger, Alexandria, Va., 1967-74, Office of Lee Kendrick, Falls Church, Va., 1974—. Served to lt. comdr. USN, 1941-45. Decorated Bronze Star medal. Mem. Am. Council Cons. Engrs., Constrn. Specifications Inst., ASHRAE. Author: Design Manual for Heating, Ventilation, Plumbing and Air Conditioning Systems, 1970; Energy Construction and Management, 1977; Specification Manual for Heating, Ventilating and Air Conditioning, 1970. Home: 3808 Hemlock Way Fairfax VA 22030 Office: 8401 Arlington Blvd Fairfax VA 22031

KENDRICK, RICHARD LOFTON, university administrator, consultant; b. Washington, Nov. 19, 1944; s. Hilary Herbert and Blanche (Lofton) K.; m. Anne Ritchie, Mar. 5, 1966; children—Shawn Elizabeth, Christopher Robert. B.S. in Bus. and Mktg., Va. Poly. Inst., 1971; postgrad. U. Ky., 1978-80. Adminstr., U.S. Army Security Agy., Washington, 1965-69; with credit, sales and adminstrv. depts U.S. Plywood-Champion Internat., Pa., N.C. and Va., 1971-77; purchasing dir. James Madison U., Harrisonburg, Va., 1977-78, fin. officer, 1978—; fin. cons.; credit cons. to plywood and lumber industry; home builder, designer World War II dioramas. Leader, treas. Boy Scouts Am., Harrisonburg, 1977—; mem. ch. com. Sterling Methodist Ch., 1975-77. Served with U.S. Army, 1965-69. Recipient New Idea award U.S. Plywood-Champion Internat., 1972; named Profl. Pub. Buyer, Nat. Inst. Govt. Purchasers, 1977. Mem. Am. Mktg. Assn., Nat. Assn. Accts., Nat. Assn. Coll. and Univ. Bus. Officers, Fin. Officers of State Colls. and Univs., So. Assn. Coll. and Univ. Bus. Officers, Internat. Platform Assn. Clubs: Exchange (Harrisonburg); Square Dance (Sterling, Va.). Home: 1059 Bobwhite Pl Harrisonburg VA 22801 Office: James Madison U S Main St Harrisonburg VA 22807

KENDRICK, WALTER MOFFETT, JR., college administrator; b. Dublin, Ga., Jan. 21, 1924; s. Walter Moffett and Annie L. (McDuffie) K.; m. Helen C. Youngblood, Aug. 1, 1951; children—Katherine Virginia, Walter Moffett III, Laura Ann. B.A., Emory U., 1948. Cert. chamber exec. Advt. mgr. News-Banner, Baxley, Ga., 1948-50; mgr. Jesup C. of C., Ga., 1950-54, Valdosta C. of C., Ga., 1954-56, Ocala C. of C., Fla., 1956-57; sales rep. Talley Box Co., Ocala, 1957-59; exec. v.p. Gainesville C. of C., Ga., 1959-64, exec. v.p. Greenville C. of C., S.C., 1964-67; v.p. devel. Furman U., Greenville, 1964—; cons. to non-profit orgns., 1981—. Bd. dirs. Greenville Little Theatre, 1965-67, Greenville Civic Chorale, 1969-73, Furman-Greenville Fine Arts Assn., 1983—. Served to maj. USAFR, 1943-75. Mem. St. Andrews Soc. Upper S.C., Council Advancement and Support of Edn. Methodist. Clubs: Greenville Country (bd. govs. 1966-69), Commerce (Greenville). Avocations: golf; hunting; fishing; fine arts. Home: 4 Rock Creek Ct Greenville SC 29605 Office: Furman U Poinsett Hwy Greenville SC 29613

KENELLY, JOHN WILLIS, JR., mathematician, educator; b. Bogalusa, La., Nov. 22, 1935; s. John Willis and Erma (Whittom) K.; m. Charmaine Voss, Aug. 12, 1956; children—Deidre Ammie, John Trent. B.S., Southeastern La. U., 1957; M.S., U. Miss., 1957; Ph.D., U. Fla., 1961. Instr., U. Fla., 1959-61; prof. U. Southwestern La., 1961-63; assoc. prof. Clemson U., S.C., 1963-68, prof. math., 1969-85, Alumni prof. math., 1985—, head dept., 1969-77; prof. math., chmn. dept. U. New Orleans, 1968-69; vis. prof. U.S. Mil. Acad., 1982-83; research investigator NASA; mem. com. undergrad. programs Math. Cons.'s Bur., 1968—; chief reader advanced placement program in math. Ednl. Testing Service, 1975-79, chmn. math. scis. adv. com., 1983—, chmn. acad. affairs council, 1985—; chmn. calculus devel. com. Coll. Bd., 1979-83; mem. math adv. com., 1981—; dir. Clemson area S.C. Nat. Bank. Author: Informal Logic, 1967; contbr. articles to profl. jours.; referee Pacific Jour. Math. Mem. Math. Assn. Am. (vis. lectr. 1969—, bd. govs. 1985—, chmn. com. on placement exams. 1985—), Am. Math. Soc., Nat. Council Tchrs. Math., Ops. Research Soc. Am., Inst. Mgmt. Sci. Unitarian (pres. Clemson Fellowship). Lodge: Rotary. Home: 327 Woodland Way Clemson SC 29631

KENIG, SYLVIA, sociology educator, evaluation researcher; b. Harrisburg, Pa., Sept. 5, 1949; d. Isadore Joel and Esther (Liebowitz) K.; m. Arthur Charles Nielsen III, May 28, 1972 (div. 1977). B.A. cum laude, Goucher Coll., 1971; M.A., U. Conn., 1972, Ph.D., 1981. Researcher Nat. Hospice Study, Brown U., Providence, 1981-82; evaluation researcher Community Council of Hartford, Conn., 1982-83; asst. prof. sociology Clemson U., S.C., 1983—, cons. on evaluation Sch. Nursing, 1984—; mem. Task Force on Volunteerism, Strom Thurmond Inst., 1984—; mem. plan com. and mental health plan com. Health Systems Agy., Hartford, 1980-83. Author evaluation reports. Co-founder women's caucus, U. Conn. Health Ctr., 1979, Brookwood Tenants' Assn., Rocky Hill, Conn., 1983, Citizens for Real Majority, Clemson, 1985; commr. Rocky Hill Fair Rent Commn., 1983; founder Faculty Women's Caucus, Clemson, 1985; mem. LWV, Clemson, Alliance for Peace, Clemson. Grad. fellow, 1978-81; U.S. Dept. Edn. grantee, 1978; Kellogg Found. grantee; univ. research grantee, Clemson U. Mem. Am. Sociol. Assn. (med. sociol. council 1978-79, one of 1st two grad. student mems.), So. Sociol. Soc., AAUP, NOW, Phi Kappa Phi. Avocation: magic. Office: Dept Sociology Martin Hall Clemson U Clemson SC 29631

KENKEL, WILLIAM FRANCIS, sociologist, educator, author; b. E. Hyattsville, Md., 1925; m. Marion Scott, 1947; children—Stephen, Philip, Donald, Kenneth, Kathryn. B.A. in Sociology, U. Md., 1949, M.A., 1950; Ph.D., Ohio State U., 1952. Research assoc. Air Force project Ohio State U., Columbus, 1952-53; asst. prof., Iowa State U., 1954-57, assoc. prof., 1957-60, prof. in charge sociology, 1960-66, head dept. sociology, anthropology, 1966-67; prof. dept. sociology U. Ky., Lexington, 1967—, chmn. dept. sociology, 1970-76, dir. grad. study sociology, 1968-70, pres. Nat. Council Family Relations, 1967-68. Served with USMC, 1943-44. Mem. Nat. Council Family Relations (former pres., chmn. fin. com., exec. com., bd. publs.), Anthropologists, Sociologists Ky. (pres. 1975-76), North Central Sociol. Assn. (v.p. 1980-81), Am. Sociol. Assn. (counselor family sect. 1982-84, regional research coms.), So. Sociol. Assn. (chmn. family sect. 1977, 79), Mid South Sociol. Assn. (chmn. family sect. 1977, 80), Author (with John F. Cuber) Social Stratification in the United States, 1954; (with John F. Cuber, Robert Harper) Problems of American Society, edit., 1964; The Family in Perspective, 5th edit., 1985; Society in Action, 2d edit., 1980; contbr. numerous articles to jours., books.

KENNEDY, BOB, baseball executive; m. Claire Kennedy; children—Robert Jr., Terry, Coleen, Christine, Kathleen. Baseball player with Chgo. White Sox, Cleve. Indians, Balt. Orioles, Detroit Tigers, Bklyn. Dodgers, 1939-57; asst. farm dir. Cleve. Indians, 1959-61; mgr. Chgo. Cubs, 1963-65, Oakland A's, 1968; dir. player personnel St. Louis Cardinals, 1969-76; gen. mgr. Chgo. Cubs, 1977-81; spl. asst. Houston Astros, 1981, v.p. baseball ops., 1982—. Address: Houston Astros Astro Dome PO Box 288 Houston TX 77001*

KENNEDY, DAVID STEWART, federal judge; b. Reagan, Tenn., Apr. 9, 1944; s. Charles Elco and Ethelyn (Stewart) K.; m. Patricia Kelly, June 18, 1977. B.A., Memphis State U., 1967, J.D., 1970. Bar: Tenn. 1971. "AV" rating with Martindale-Hubbell. Law clk. U.S. Dist. Courts (western dist.) Tenn., 1970-71; sole practice law, mem. pvt. panel bankruptcy trustees, Memphis, 1971-73, 76-80; adminstrv. asst., chief clk. U.S. Bankruptcy Court (western dist.) Tenn., 1974-76; judge, 1980—; adj. prof. Cecil C. Humphreys Sch. Law, Memphis State U. Contbr. articles to profl. publs. Mem. ABA, Tenn. Bar. Assn., Memphis-Shelby County Bar Assn., Nat. Conf. Bankruptcy Judges, Cecil C Humphreys Sch. Law Alumni Nat. Council (pres.). Office: US Bankruptcy Court Suite 1200 969 Madison St Memphis TN 38104

KENNEDY, JOSEPH EVERETT, accountant, state senator; b. Claxton, Ga., Oct. 8, 1930; s. Jesse Gordon and Nannie Byrd (DuPree) K.; student Ga. Mil. Coll., 1949; m. Lalah Jane, 1953; children—Debra, Cliff, Adam. Pvt. practice acctg.; mem. Ga. Senate, now pres. protem. Chmn. bd. deacons First Baptist Ch. Served to capt. U.S. Army, 1950-53. Decorated Bronze Star. Named outstanding young man of yr. Claxton Jaycees, 1962. Mem. Am. Legion, VFW. Clubs: Rotary, Mason. Office: Ga State Senate Atlanta GA 30334*

KENNEDY, KEITH FURNIVAL, packaging company executive, lawyer; b. New London, Conn., Nov. 1, 1925; s. Joseph Reilly and Madeleine (Mason) K.; m. Joan Ruth Canfield, Feb. 11, 1956; children—Joseph Keith, Austin Robert, Thomas Canfield, Richard Furnival. B.S., Yale U., 1949; LL.B., Harvard U., 1953. Bar: N.Y. 1955. Atty., Vick Chem. Co., 1953-54, 58-60; sec., dir. personnel J.T. Baker Chem. Co., 1955-58; with Riegel Paper Corp., 1960-71; sr. v.p., dir. Rexham Corp., Charlotte, N.C., 1972—; dir. Laminex, Inc., Schiller Industries, Inc., Brittains-Riegel Ltd. Capt. Scarsdale Vol. Fire Co. 3, 1966-70; bd. dirs., sec. Adoption service Westchester, 1966-84, pres., 1971-73; adv. council Coll. New Rochelle, 1974-77; bd. dirs. Calvary Hosp., N.Y.C., 1977-85, vice-chmn., 1982-85; bd. visitors Mercy Hosp., Charlotte, 1985—. Served to 1st lt. AUS, 1943-46, 51-52. Mem. Assn. Bar City N.Y., Am. Soc. Corp. Secs., St. Andrews Soc N.Y., Chi Phi. Roman Catholic. Clubs: Union League, Economic of N.Y., Yale (N.Y.C.); Larchmont Yacht (N.Y.); Niantic Bay Yacht (Conn.). Home: 1441 Carmel Rd Charlotte NC 28226 Office: 7315 Pineville-Matthews Rd Charlotte NC 28211

KENNEDY, MARC J., lawyer, corporation executive; b. Newburgh, N.Y., Mar. 2, 1945; s. Warren G. and Frances F. (Levinson) K.; m. Debra L. Shaw, Apr. 19, 1986. B.A. cum laude, Syracuse U., 1967; J.D., U. Mich., 1970. Bar: N.Y. 1971. Assoc., Davies, Hardy, Ives & Lawther, N.Y.C., 1971-72, London, Buttenweiser & Chalif, N.Y.C., 1972-73, Silberfeld, Danziger & Bangser, N.Y.C., 1973; counsel Occidental Crude Sales, Inc., N.Y.C., 1974-75; v.p., gen. counsel Internat. Ore & Fertilizer Corp., N.Y.C., 1975-82, Occidental Chem. Agrl. Products, Inc., Tampa, Fla., 1982—; asst. gen. counsel Occidental Chem. Corp., Houston, 1982; faculty Columbia Pacific U., San Francisco, 1980—. Trustee Bar Harbor Festival Corp., N.Y.C., 1974—; mem. com. for planned giving N.Y. Foundling Hosp., N.Y.C., 1977—; post advisor Explorer post Boy Scouts Am., N.Y.C., 1976-78; bd. dirs. Am. Opera Repertory Co., 1982-85. Mem. ABA, Internat. Bar Assn., Am. Soc. Internat. Law, Maritime Law Assn., N.Y. State Bar Assn., Assn. Bar City N.Y. Home: 690 Island Way 1101 Clearwater FL 33515 Office: 5404 Cypress Center Dr 210 Tampa FL 33609

KENNEDY, MARY ELIZABETH, mental health regional manager; b. San Antonio, July 25, 1938; d. Byron Daniel and Katherine Daugherty (Hodson) K. B.A., Austin Coll., Sherman, Tex., 1960; M.C.E., Presbyn. Sch. Christian Edn., Richmond, Va., 1962; M.S.W., Tulane U., New Orleans, 1972. Dir. Christian edn. St. Andrew's Presbyn. Ch., Beaumont, Tex., 1962-68, Pulaski Heights Presbyn. Ch., Little Rock, Ark., 1968-71; social worker Irish Channel Mental Health Clinic, New Orleans, 1973-74; adminstr. Central City Mental Health Clinic, New Orleans, 1974-79; mgr. New Orleans Mental Health Center, 1979-81, mental health regional mgr., 1981—; field instr. and mem. continuing edn. adv. bd. Tulane U. Sch. Social Work. Mem. St. Louis Cathedral Concert Choir and Chantez (madrigal group), New Orleans Inst. Performing Arts Chorale. NIMH grantee, 1975. Mem. Nat. Assn. Social Workers, Acad. Cert. Social Workers (cert.), Am. Mgmt. Assn., La. Assn. Mental Health and Substance Abuse Adminstrs. Office: Region I Mgr 914 Richard St New Orleans LA 70130

KENNEDY, WALLACE ALBERT, educator; b. Montverde, Fla., Apr. 2, 1929; s. George Leslie and Elizabeth Lucy (Bible) K.; m. Patricia Burghard, June 30, 1950; children—Lois, Wally B., Lucy, Lora. A.B., Fla. State U., 1951, M.A., 1952, Ph.D., 1956. Diplomate in clin. psychology. Dir. grad. tng. in psychology, prof. psychology Fla. State U., Tallahassee, 1958—; pvt. practice Psychology Assocs. of Tallahassee, 1976—. Author: Child Psychology, 1971, 2d edit. 1975. Contbr. articles to profl. jours. Served with U.S. Army, 1947-49. Recipient Disting. Service award, Fla. Psychol. Assn., 1971, 76. Fellow Am. Psychol. Assn. (council of reps. 1972-75, 78-81); mem. Southeastern Psychol. Assn. (pres. 1968-69), Fla. Psychol. Assn. (pres. 1967-68). Democrat. Presbyterian. Avocations: gardening. Home: Rt 5 Box 3855 Tallahassee FL 32301 Office: Psychology Assocs 103 Salem Ct Tallahassee FL 32301-2810

KENNER, MARY ELLEN, marketing consultant; b. Darlington, Wis., Jan. 7, 1941; d. Horace James and Adean Elizabeth (McDonald) Smith; B.S., Marquette U., 1963, M.S. in Bus. Adminstrn., 1966; m. John Miller Kenner, Sept. 27, 1975. Fashion dir. spl. events Federated Store, Milw., 1962-63; mktg. ofcl. Ohio Bell and Wis. Telephone Cos., 1963-66; coll. mktg. instr. Milw. Inst. Tech., 1966-67; advt. positions AT & T and Wis. Telephone Co., 1967-78; advt. dir. No. States Power Co., Mpls., 1978-83; pres. Kenner Enterprises. Steering com. 1st Conf. Consumerism. Recipient Clio award, 1974, Effie award, 1978, 79, 81. Mem. Minn. Advt. Fedn., Minn. Center Arts, Milw. Advt. Club (dir. 1969-72, sec. 1973-76), Edison Electric Inst., Marquette U. Alumni Assn. Roman Catholic. Club: Belleek Collectors. Home: 1145 Forest Rd Niceville FL 32578

KENNETT, JOSEPH RALSTON, clinical psychologist; b. Little Rock, Aug. 4, 1930; s. H. Lester and Helen Josephine (Strickler) K.; m. Anne McKeever Darby, Nov. 7, 1962; children—Joanne Gwynne, James Ralston, Richard Joseph. B.S., U. Houston, 1956, M.S., 1961, Ph.D., 1962. Lic. psychologist. Psychologist, Baylor Coll. Medicine, Houston, 1961-63; chief psychologist Houston Child Guidance Ctr., 1963-64; pvt. practice psychology, Houston, 1964—; instr. Baylor Coll. Medicine, Houston, 1962-72, asst. prof. psychology, 1972—; owner, dir. Acad. Devel. Services, Houston, 1973-76, cons., 1976-80. Served with U.S. Army, 1950-53. Mem. Tex. Psychol. Assn. (parliamentarian 1972), Houston Psychol. Assn. (pres. 1973-74, ethics com. 1975, 76-84).

Presbyterian. Avocations: books; music; tennis; sailing. Office: 50 Briar Hollow Ln 575 East Houston TX 77027

KENNEY, D. GREGORY, financial consultant; b. Cumberland, Md., July 11, 1954; s. Donald Walter and Carol Fay (Shanholtz) K.; m. Amy Thal, Aug. 9, 1981. B.S., W.Va. U., 1976. Asst. mgr., sales asst. Ramada Inn, Morgantown, W.Va., 1977-78; sales and engring. asst. Pinzone Communications, Newbury, Ohio, 1978-79; ops. mgr. NorthAm., Philips Lighting, Miami, Fla., 1979-84; with elec. distbr. sales Wesco, Ft. Lauderdale, Fla., 1985; corp. tax credit cons. Ameriserv of Fla., Ft. Lauderdale, 1985—. Contbg. mem. Nat. Rifle Assn., Washington, 1978-82, Alumni Family Boy Scouts Am., Springfield, Ill., 1984; polit. chmn. Embarcadero Condominium Assn., Ft. Lauderdale, 1985. Mem. W.Va. U. Alumni Assn., U.S. Olympic Soc., Amateur Golfers Assn. Republican. Club: U.S. Table Tennis Assn. Lodge: Moose. Avocations: golf; bicycling; tennis; football; softball. Home: 5250 NE 6th Ave Fort Lauderdale FL 33334

KENSON, DAVID LEE, educator, coach; b. Cleve., July 18, 1947; s. Joseph Carl and June Elaine (Trapnell) Kencson; m. Sharyn Laurine Kenson, Sept. 5, 1966; 1 son, Kelly David. A.B.A., U. Cin., 1968, B.S., 1970, M.Ed., 1971. Football coach North Coll. Hill High Sch., Cin., 1971-74, The Bolles Sch., Jacksonville, Fla., 1974-79; tng. dir., dist. mgr. Sterling Investors Corp., Lakeland, Fla., 1979-82, v.p., 1982-83; v.p. Excellex Securities Corp., Tampa, Fla., 1983; football coach Fletcher High Sch., Neptune Beach, Fla., 1984—. Address: 1757 El Camino Rd 3 Jacksonville FL 32216

KENT, BARTIS MILTON, physician; b. Terrell, Tex., June 23, 1925; s. Bartis William and Annie (Smalley) K.; student So. Meth. U., 1942-44; M.D., Baylor U., 1948; m. Ann L. Kiel, July 6, 1954; children—Susan Ruth, Martha Lucille, Bartis Michael. Intern, Jefferson Davis Hosp., Houston, 1948-49; resident pathology Mass. Meml. Hosps., Boston, 1951; resident in internal medicine Baylor U., 1953-56; indsl. physician Humble Oil Co., Houston, 1949-51; instr. dept. medicine U. Iowa, 1956-58; staff physician Iowa City VA Hosp., 1956-58; practice medicine specializing in internal medicine, Muskogee, Okla., 1958—; cons. Muskogee VA Hosp.; clin. asst. prof. medicine U. Okla. Sch. Medicine, 1975—. Chmn., Muskogee County chpt. Am. Nat. Red Cross, 1963-65. Served with USAF, 1951-53. Decorated Air medal. Diplomate Am. Bd. Internal Medicine. Mem. A.C.P., Indsl. Med. Assn., Soc. Nuclear Medicine, Am. Fedn. Clin. Research, Am. Heart Assn., Aerospace Medicine Assn., Am., Okla. socs. internal medicine, Muskogee C. of C. Methodist. Mason (Shriner). Home: 800 N 45th St Muskogee OK 74401 Office: 211 S 36th St Muskogee OK 74401

KENT, ROBERT TAYLOR, geologist; b. Wills Point, Tex., May 27, 1943; s. Oscar Wylie and Izora Lorene (Bedingfield) K.; m. Suzie Lee Berryhill, Jan. 5, 1968; children—Mitchell Gregory, Elizabeth. B.S. in Geology, U. Tex.-Austin, 1972. Cert. profl. geol. scientist. Environ. health supr. Austin-Travis County Health Dept., Austin, Tex., 1972-74; geologist Tex. Water Quality Bd., Austin, 1974-77; chief subsurface disposal br. Tex. Dept. Water Resources, Austin, 1977-78; v.p. Underground Resource Mgmt., Austin, 1978—, also dir. Adv. com. ground water protection tng. Tex. A&M U., 1981; cons. Ministry of Environment, Ont., Can., 1982-83, Capital Area Planning Council, 1979. Served with USAF, 1961-66. Mem. Geol. Soc. Am., Am. Assn. Petroleum Geologists, Nat. Water Well Assn., Am. Inst. Profl. Geologists, Soc. Petroleum Engrs. of AIME, Corpus Christi Geologic Soc., Austin Geologic Soc., Internat. Assn. Hydrogeologists. Contbr. articles to profl. jours. Office: 508 Powell St Austin TX 78703

KENT, SHERMAN TECUMSEH, museum administrator, educator; b. New Haven, Conn., Nov. 1, 1941; s. Sherman and Elizabeth (Gregory) K.; m. Laura Lee, Dec. 22, 1969; children—Thacher Lee, Hector Pillow, Henry Haskell, Ogden Gregory. B.A., Yale U., 1964; M.S., U. Mich., 1969. Dir. edn. Acad. Nat. Scis. Phila., 1971-76; exec. dir. Omniplex, Oklahoma City, 1976—. Served with U.S. Army, 1965-67. Mem. Wilderness Soc. Democrat. Home: Route 4 PO Box 420 Oklahoma City OK 73111 Office: Omniplex 2100 NE 52d St Oklahoma City OK 73111

KENTROS, GEORGE ARTHUR, dental educator; b. Worcester, Mass., Mar. 7, 1922; D.M.D., Tufts Univ., 1945. Prof. dentistry U. Ala., Birmingham, 1976—, asst. dean, 1976-80; vice-chmn. hosp. dentistry Univ. Hosp., Birmingham, 1976—, div. gen. practice residency, 1976—; cons. in field. Fellow Am. Coll. Dentists, Am. Assn. Hosp. Dentists (pres. 1981), Internat. Coll. Dentists. Office: Dent Sch Univ Sta Birmingham AL 35294

KEOUGH, DONALD RAYMOND, beverage and entertainment executive; b. Maurice, Iowa, Sept. 4, 1926; s. Leo H. and Veronica (Henkels) K.; B.S., Creighton U., 1949, LL.D. (hon.), 1982; LL.D. (hon.), U. Notre Dame, 1985; m. Marilyn Mulhall, Sept. 10, 1949; children—Kathleen Anne, Mary Shayla, Michael Leo, Patrick John, Eileen Tracy, Clarke Robert. With Butter-Nut Foods Co., Omaha, 1950-61, Duncan Foods Co., Houston, 1961-67; v.p., dir. mktg. foods div. The Coca-Cola Co., 1967-71, pres. div., 1971-73, exec. v.p. Coca-Cola USA, Atlanta, 1973-74, pres., 1974-76, exec. v.p. Coca-Cola Co., 1976-79, sr. exec. v.p., 1980-81, pres., chief operating officer, dir., 1981—; dir. IBM World Trade Americas/Far East Corp., Tex. Commerce Bancshares, Inc. Mem. pres.'s council Creighton U.; trustee U. Notre Dame, Spelman Coll., The Lovett Sch., Agnes Scott Coll. Served with USNR, 1944-46. Clubs: Capital City, Piedmont Driving Commerce (Atlanta). Office: 310 North Ave NW PO Drawer 1734 Atlanta GA 30301

KEPHART, DONALD RALPH, restaurant company executive; b. Orange, N.J., Nov. 7, 1948; s. Ralph S. and Josephine Mary (Golas) K.; B.A. in Psychology, Fairleigh Dickinson U., 1971; M.A. in Psychology, Montclair State Coll., 1972. Tng. specialist Institiut Teknoloji Mara, Shah Alam, Selangor, Malaysia, 1972-75; tng. cons. Innovative Scis., Inc., Stamford, Conn., 1975-76, Nat. Tng. Systems, New Brunswick, N.J., 1976-78; mgr. tng. and devel. L'Eggs Products, Winston-Salem, N.C., 1978-83; mgr. mgmt. devel. Blount Internat. Ltd., 1983-84; regional tng. mgr. Denny's Inc., Arlington, Tex., 1984—. Mem. Am. Soc. Tng. and Devel., Am. Mgmt. Assn., Internat. Assn. Bus. Communicators, Nat. Soc. for Performance and Instrn. Home: 1204 Alder Dr Apt 1504 Arlington TX 76012 Office: 801 Ave H East Suite 116 Arlington TX 76011

KEPHART, EARL LAWRENCE, nurse; b. Madera, Pa., Dec. 15, 1919; s. Lawrence and Cora (Lockett) K.; R.N., Pa. Hosp., 1943; B.S. in Edn., U. Pa., 1949; M.Ed., U. Va., 1959; m. Harriet Hosmer, Nov. 29, 1944; 1 child, Larry Herbert. Head nurse, then instr. Pa. Hosp., 1943-49; mem. nursing staff VA, 1949-84; chief nursing service VA Med. Center, Shreveport, 1973-84. Active local Boy Scouts Am. Served with AUS, 1944-45. Mem. Am. Soc. Hosp. Nursing Service Adminstrs., Assn. Mil. Surgeons U.S., Am. Radio Relay League, Sigma Theta Tau, Kappa Phi Kappa. Republican. Presbyterian. Author ednl. TV material. Home: 2106 Cynthia Ln Shreveport LA 71118

KEPHART, LARRY ROBERT, architect; b. Clearfield, Pa., Sept. 1, 1949; s. Robert Joseph and Nora Elizabeth (Livergood) K. Student Pa. State U., 1967-69. Registered architect, D.C. Drafter RCP Architects, Johnstown, Pa., 1970-72; office mgr. R. William Clayton Jr., Ft. Lauderdale, Fla., 1972-80; project architect C.F. McKirihan, Fort Lauderdale, 1980-81, A. Nicholas Hosking, Fort Lauderdale, 1981-82, Randall F. Keller, Ft. Lauderdale, 1982-83; architect, head research and devel. Vander Ploeg & Assocs., Boca Raton, Fla., 1983—; vis. lectr. Fort Lauderdale Art Inst., 1984. Bd. dirs. Rotary Club Ft. Lauderdale N., 1980. Lodge: Masons. Avocations: golf; military gaming. Home: 2830 NE 2d Ave Pompano FL 33064 Office: Vander Ploeg & Assocs 1700 N Dixie Hwy Boca Raton FL 33432

KEPNER, THEODORE STANLEY, electronics engineer; b. Columbus, Ohio, Nov. 6, 1921; s. Paul R. and Theresea F. (Dropiewski) K.; student U. Melbourne, 1951; m. Frances C. Hobbs, July 28, 1947; children—Pele Dianne, Gina, Yolanda. Geophys. engr. Robert Ray Houston, 1946-47; electronics engr., Australia, 1951-53; nuclear reactor elec. engr. Oil Refinery, Munitions Factory, Sydney, Australia, 1953-57; communications engr. Mutual Telephone, Honolulu, 1948-51; elec. engr. constrn. USAF Spanish Bases, Madrid, Zaragoza, 1957-60; quality engring. supr. GTE-Sylvania Western div. Mountain View, Calif., 1962-78; Gen. Telephone Internat., mgr. Project Electronique Grand Public, Sidi Bel Abbes, Algeria, 1978-80; cons. Power Ignition Co., Houston, from 1980; now sr. quality assurance engr. Gould Inc., S.E.L. div., Ft. Lauderdale, Fla. now cons. Automatic Devices of P.R. Served to 2d lt. U.S. Army, 1951-52, USN, 1941-45. Registered profl. engr., Calif. Mem. IEEE, Assn. Old Crows. Democrat. Patentee in field. Address: care Gould Computer System De Puerto Rico PO Box 698 Humacao PR 00661

KEPNER, WOODY, public relations executive; b. Millersburg, Pa., June 30, 1920; s. E. Elwood and Charlotte (Dressler) K.; m. Palma M. Brown, Feb. 10, 1943; children—Linda Louise Kepner Henke, Dawn Annette Kepner Kendrick, Tana Lee Kepner Tracy. Grad. pub. schs., Millersburg, Pa. Free-lance reporter Williamsport Grit (Pa.), Harrisburg Telegraph (Pa.), Harrisburg Patriot-News, Harrisburg Sunday Courier, 1935-41; reporter, feature and spl. events writer, photo editor, news editor, news bur. mgr. Miami Publicity Dept. (Fla.), 1945-53, dir., 1953-57; pres. Woody Kepner Assocs., Inc., Miami, 1957—. Vice pres. United Fund Met. Miami, 1963. Served with USN, 1942-45. Mem. Pub. Relations Soc. Am. (Silver Anvil award 1957), Fla. Pub. Relations Assn., Greater Miami C. of C. Lutheran. Clubs: Bankers, Cricket. Office: Woody Kepner Assocs Inc 9200 S Dadeland Blvd Suite 300 Miami FL 33156

KEPPLE, THOMAS RAY, JR., college administrator; b. Pitts., Mar. 19, 1948; s. Thomas Ray and Virginia Grace (Hudson) K.; m. Jane Donaldson, Aug. 22, 1977 (dec. 1977); m. Daney Daniel, Mar. 22, 1978. B.A., Westminster Coll., 1970; M.B.A., Syracuse U., 1973, Ed.D., 1984. Dir. tech. tng. Morse div. Borg-Warner Corp., Ithaca, N.Y., 1970-73; dir. adminstrv. services Rhodes Coll., Memphis, 1975-81, dean adminstrv. services, 1981—. Exec. com. Vollintive Evergreen Community Assn., Memphis, 1976-85, pres., 1981; active Memphis Metro Tech. Council, 1985. Mem. Internat. Soc. Planning and Strategic Mgmt. (v.p. communications 1984-85, pres.-elect. 1985-86), Nat. Assn. Coll. and Univ. Bus. Officers, Am. Assn. Higher Edn., Memphis Acad. Forum (pres. 1985-86), Coll. and Univ. Personnel Assn. Presbyterian. Club: U. Tenn. Ctr. Health Scis. Faculty. Avocations: swimming; oil painting. Home: 1895 Jackson Memphis TN 38107 Office: Rhodes Coll 2000 N Parkway Memphis TN 38112

KERBY, ROBERT BROWNING, non-profit foundation executive; b. Waynesboro, Va., Oct. 21, 1938; s. Guy Albert and Josephine (Carpenter) K. B.S. in Bus. Adminstrn., Va. Poly. Inst., 1960; postgrad. U. Richmond, 1964, Va. Commonwealth U., 1965, U. Va., 1968. Rep. mfrs. Josten Co., Owatonna, Minn., 1960-67; gen. sales mgr. Sta. WANV, Waynesboro, 1967; tech. editor Gen. Electric Co., Waynesboro, 1967-72; v.p., chief exec. officer Fishburne Hudgins Ednl. Found., Inc., Waynesboro, 1972—; advisor Sovran Bank, Waynesboro, 1982—. Designer, author: (catalogue) Military School, 1981 (1st place award Printers Assn. Va.'s, 1982). Bd. dirs., chmn. Waynesboro Redevel. Housing Authority, 1970-72; pres. Alumni Assn. Offices, 1960-71; chmn. publicity Robinson for Congress, 1970; chmn. fund raising and adv. bd. Salvation Army, 1967-68. Mem. SAR, Quarter Century Wireless Assn., Am. Radio Relay League. Republican. Methodist. Office: Fishburne Mil Sch PO Box 988 225 Wayne Ave Waynesboro VA 22980-0722

KERCHER, JOHN WESLEY, III, management consultant; b. Dayton, Ohio, Mar. 23, 1941; s. John Wesley and F. Elizabeth (Blakeslee) K.; B.A., Ohio Wesleyan U., 1963; M.B.A. (Bus. Found. fellow), U. N.C., 1964; m. Diane M. Grotz, Sept. 7, 1963; children—Lee Elizabeth, John Wesley, IV. With Price Waterhouse, 1964—, mgr., Pitts., 1971-74, partner, Tampa, Fla., 1974—. Bd. dirs. Pitts. Symphony Soc., 1973-74; bd. dirs. Fla. Gulf Coast Symphony, 1974-83, pres., 1979-80, mem. exec. com., 1974-81, chmn. fund raising dr., 1976-78, chmn. nominating com., 1980-82; chmn. bd. fellows U. Tampa, also trustee; treas., mem. exec. com. Tampa Bay Performing Arts Center. C.P.A., Fla., others. Mem. Am. Inst. C.P.A.s, Fla. C.P.A. Soc. (past chmn. state/local govt. relations, mgmt. services com.), Inst. Mgmt. Cons. (cert.), Ohio Wesleyan Alumni Assn., Tampa C. of C. Republican. Episcopalian. Clubs: Tampa Yacht and Country, Tower of Tampa, Univ. Home: 5142 San Jose St Tampa FL 33629 Office: PO Box 2640 Tampa FL 33601

KERGE, CHRISTIAN JOSEPH, real estate development and building company executive; b. Washington, July 5, 1950; s. Mitri Moses and Alice Marie (Skaff) K.; m. Sonia Esther Diez, Dec. 15, 1970; children—Alice Marie, Teresa Marie, Rita Marie. Ed. schs., Largo, Md. Jr. acct. Pan Am. Health Orgn./WHO, Washington, 1969-71; pres. K & M Assocs., Inc., Alexandria, Va., 1971-75; pres., chief exec. officer Creative Enterprises, Ltd., Falls Church, Va., 1975—; adv. bd. dir. Community Bank and Trust, Sterling, Va., 1983—; dir. Gateway Properties, Inc., Springfield, Va., 1973—. Recipient Bus. Improvement award, City of Falls Church, 1978. Mem. No. Va. Builders Assn. (fin. com.). Republican. Greek Orthodox. Avocations: Model train collecting; golf; bicycling; chess. Office: Creative Enterprises Ltd 100 A E Fairfax St Suite 201 Falls Church VA 22046

KERLEY, AVERY JAMES, education educator, administrator; b. Pikeville, Tenn., Apr. 27, 1950; s. Ulysses Archie and Hazel Ruth (Matthews) K.; m. Donna Marie Hassoun, Dec. 30, 1973; children—James Joseph, Rachael Marie. B.S., Tenn. Tech. U., 1976; M.A.T., The Citadel, 1978; Ph.D., Fla. State U., 1982. Acct. Fairfield Glade Corp., Tenn., 1972-74; tchr. Charleston County Sch. System, S.C., 1976-79; trainer and educator Fed. Emergency Mgmt. Agy., Valdosta State Coll., Thomasville, Ga., 1982-83; coll. tchr., head edn. Union Coll., Barbourville, Ky., 1983—; trainer, leadership seminars for adminstrs. and suprs., 1985—; cons. human relations Tallahassee, Fla., 1982-83. Vice chmn. Young Reps., Cookeville, Tenn., 1975. Served with USN, 1970-72. S.C. Press scholar, 1977; recipient Disting. Service award Miss. Emergency Agy., 1983. Mem. Ky. Assn. Tchr. Educators (presented papers annual meeting 1984), Ky. Assn. Colls. for Tchr. Educators (newsletter com. 1983—), Assn. Tchr. Educators, Phi Kappa Phi, Phi Delta Kappa (coms., research 1983—). Republican. Methodist. Home: HC 81-860 Barbourville KY 40906 Office: Union College Barbourville KY 40906

KERN, CLIFFORD HAROLD, JR., lawyer; b. New Orleans, Dec. 2, 1915; s. Clifford Harold and Sadie Judith (Schwartz) K.; m. Nettie Cahn Hirsch, June 14, 1947; children—Clifford Harold III, Jay H. LL.B., Tulane U., 1938, J.D., 1969. Bar: La. 1939, U.S. Dist. Ct. (ea. dist.) La. Ptnr. Kuhner & Kern, New Orleans, 1939-46; asst. to pres., treas., sec., v.p. Imperial Shoe Store Inc., New Orleans, 1946-77; assoc. Dresner & Dresner, New Orleans, 1977—. Pres. Sugar Bowl Football Classic, 1974-75, chmn. bd., 1983-84. Served as lt. comdr., submarine service USN, 1941-46. Elected to Football Hall of Fame, 1977. Mem. La. State Bar Assn., New Orleans Bar Assn., New Orleans C. of C., Mil. Order World Wars, Navy League U.S. Home: 69 Versailles Blvd New Orleans LA 70125 Office: Dresner & Dresner 1204 First NBC Bldg New Orleans LA 70112

KERN, JOHN JEROME, magazine editor; b. Washington, Jan. 21, 1925; s. Irving Gerard and Margaret Alice (Burke) K.; m. Mary Teresa Spasaro, Aug. 19, 1949; children—John Frederick, Mary Catherine, James Patrick, Thomas Michael. Student Villanova U., 1943-44, 46-47, U. Pa., 1944-45; B.A., Cath. U. Am., 1949; M.A., George Washington U., 1953. Photogrammetric engr. U.S. Naval Hydrographic Office, Suitland, Md., 1949-59; cartographer Hdqrs. Dept. Army Chief of Engrs. Office, Washington, 1959-69; topographic scientist Def. Mapping Agy. Topographic Ctr., Brookmont, Md., 1969-74; mng. editor Soc. Am. Mil. Engrs., Washington and Alexandria, Va., 1974-78; editor The Mil. Engr. mag., Alexandria, 1978—. Pres. Greater Colesville Citizens Assn., 1975-76; pres. Springwood Area Citizens Group, 1967-75. Served with USNR, 1943-46. Mem. Soc. Am. Mil. Engrs. Republican. Roman Catholic. Club: Ocean Pines (Berlin, Md.). Home: 302 Springloch Rd Box 4193 Silver Spring MD 20904 Office: 607 Prince St Alexandria VA 22314

KERNER, MARTIN, freight forwarding company executive, consultant; b. N.Y.C., Oct. 9, 1947; s. Paul Kerner and Alma Lillian (Harris) Kerner Gottlieb; m. Mary Katharine Porretto, Apr. 8, 1977 (div. May 1982). B.S., U. Houston, 1970. Asst. traffic mgr. Sta. KHOU-TV, Houston, 1967-72, S.W. Trading Co., Houston, 1972-75; projects mgr. Hudsons Internat., Houston, 1975-78; mgr. J. Sierra & Co., Houston, 1978-79, McLean Cargo Specialists, Inc., Houston, 1979—. Mem. Interam. C. of C., Sharpstown Civic Assn. Democrat. Jewish. Lodge: B'nai B'rith (Houston). Office: McLean Cargo Specialists Inc PO Box 60469 AMF Houston TX 77205

KERNODLE, RUTH LYNCH, sociology educator, gerontologist; b. Washington, July 30, 1922; d. William Aubrey and Ethel (Williams) Lynch; m. Rigdon Wayne Kernodle, Feb. 22, 1945; children—Michael, Kathryn. B.A., Madison Coll., 1942; M.A., U. N.C., 1944. Research assoc. Hampton Rds. War Studies, Williamsburg, Va., 1945-49; lectr. Coll. William and Mary, Williamsburg, 1949-54; with social service dept. Eastern State Hosp., Williamsburg, 1954-68; assoc. prof. sociology Christopher Newport Coll., Newport News, Va., 1968—. Contbr. articles to profl. jours. Chmn. Mental Health Services, Williamsburg, 1970-74; mem. Social Services Bd., Williamsburg, 1984—; v.p. Va. Assn. Aging, 1978. Named Outstanding Gerontology Educator of Yr., Va. Assn. Aging 1983. Mem. Gerontol. Soc. Am., So. Sociol. Soc. Democrat. Avocations: tennis; hiking. Home: 108 Governors Dr Williamsburg VA 23185 Office: Christopher Newport Coll 50 Shoe Ln Newport News VA 23606

KERNS, DAVID VINCENT, lawyer; b. Salt Lake City, Jan. 29, 1917; s. Clinton Bowen and Ella Mae (Young) K.; m. Dorothea Boyd, Sept. 5, 1942; children—David V., Clinton Boyd. B.Ph., Emory U., 1937; J.D., U. Fla., 1939. Bar: Fla. 1939, U.S. Dist. Ct. (mid. dist.) Fla. 1939, U.S. Dist. Ct. (so. dist.) Fla. 1978, U.S. Dist. Ct. (no. dist.) Fla., U.S. Ct. Appeals (11th cir.) 1981. Assoc. Sutton & Reeves, Tampa, Fla., 1939-41, Fowler & White, Tampa, 1945-47; ptnr. Moran & Kerns, Tampa, 1948-49; resident atty. Fla. Road Dept., 1949-53; research asst. Supreme Ct. Fla., 1953-58; dir. Fla. Legis. Reference Bur., 1958-68, Fla. Legis. Service Bur., 1968-71, Fla. Legis. Library Services, 1971-73; gen. counsel Fla. Dept. Adminstrn., 1973-82; mem. Fla. Career Service Commn., 1983—. Contbr. articles to profl. jours. Served with U.S. Army, 1941-45. Mem. Fla. Govt. Bar Assn. (pres. 1966, J. Ernest Webb Meml. award 1982), Fla. Bar (bd. govs. 1978-84), Tallahassee Bar Assn. Democrat. Methodist. Club: Capital City Country. Home: 418 Vinnedge Ride Tallahassee FL 32303

KERNS, ROBERT LOUIS, educator; b. Cedar Rapids, Iowa, May 1, 1929; s. William Edward and Nellie (Sawyer) K.; B.A., U. Iowa, 1956; M.A., Syracuse U., 1970; m. Jean Adair Slater, May 20, 1961; children—William Patrick, Heather. Photographer, Davenport (Iowa) Democrat, 1956; photographer, pictorial editor Cedar Rapids (Iowa) Gazette, 1958-59; dir. public relations photography Goodyear Tire and Rubber Co., Akron, Ohio, 1960-64; prof. Syracuse (N.Y.) U., 1964-72; prof. U. South Fla., Tampa, 1972—. coordinator visual communications, dept. mass communications; dir. workshops, cons. in field. Trustee Carrollwood Recreation Dist. Served with USAF, 1951-56. Recipient Don Christianson Meml. award for outstanding journalism in Iowa, 1950. Mem. Assn. for Edn. in Journalism, Internat. Assn. Bus. Communicators (pres. Suncoast chpt. 1977-78), Am. Soc. for Tng. and Devel. (dir.), World Futurists Soc., Sigma Delta Chi. Presbyterian (elder). Club: Masons. Author: Photography With a Purpose, 1980; Creative News Photography, 1961; patentee Kerns camera strap; lectr. in field; recent photo shows: Marjorie Kinnan Rawlings in Retrospect, 1979, The Quiet Moments, 1978; Jamaica, 1983. Home: 10503 Orange Grove Dr Tampa FL 33618 Office: Mass Communications Dept Univ South Florida Tampa FL 33620

KERR, ALVA RAE, association executive, writer, editor; b. Borger, Tex., July 29, 1926; d. Rene Lawerence and Georgia Margaret (Jones) McDonald; m. Gary Karp, Jan. 23, 1946 (dec. 1969); children—Pamela Karp Olifant, Victoria, Richard; m. Glenn Enevold Kerr, Nov. 18, 1977. Student U. of Ams., Mex., summer 1970; B.A., U. Houston, 1972; M.A., George Washington U., 1975. Real estate broker Coldwell Banker Realtors, McLean, Va., 1975-83, writer, editor, D.C. area, 1984; writer, editor Nat. Capital chpt. Multiple Sclerosis Soc., Washington, 1985—; corr. sec. UN World Com. Decade of Disabled Persons, Washington, 1985—; lectr. Nat. Security Agy., Fort Meade, Md., 1983, Somerset Civic Assn., Fairfax, Va., 1983, B'nai Brith, McLean, 1984, also others. Vol. spl. asst. on community program Nat. Orgn. on Disability, Washington, 1985—. Mem. No. Va. Bd. Realtors (Million Dollar Sales Agt. award 1983), Nat. Assn. Realtors, Va. Assn. Realtors, Phi Delta Gamma (pres. 1984-86). Avocations: piano; writing; theatre; lectures; concerts. Home: 9804 Limoges Dr Fairfax VA 22032

KERR, BAINE PERKINS, oil co. exec.; b. Rusk, Tex., Aug. 24, 1919; s. James Herman and Myrta Blake (Perkins) K.; B.A., LL.B., U. Tex. at Austin, 1942; m. Mildred Pickett Caldwell, June 13, 1942; children—Baine Perkins, John Caldwell, James Robinson, Mary Blake. Admitted to Tex. bar, 1942; practiced in Houston, 1945-77; partner firm Baker & Botts, 1955-77; dir. Pennzoil Co., Houston, 1964—, chmn. exec. com., 1972—, pres., 1977—. Bd. govs. (adv.) William Marsh Rice U., Houston; adv. bd. Marine Mil. Acad., Harlingen, Tex.; trustee Interferon Found.; mem. adv. council Coll. Natural Scis. Found., U. Tex. at Austin. Served with USMCR, 1942-45. Mem. Chancellors, Order of Coif, Phi Beta Kappa, Phi Eta Sigma, Phi Delta Theta, Phi Delta Phi. Office: PO Box 2967 Houston TX 77001

KERR, JOHN MARTIN, engineering development executive; b. Normal, Ill., Jan. 31, 1934; s. Edgar Steele and Vera Belle (Martin) K.; m. Virginia M. Grille, Sept. 1, 1956; children—Sharon, John Jr., Patricia, Mary Anne. B.S. in Engring., U. Ill., 1956; M.B.A., Lynchburg Coll., 1973. Engr. Oak Ridge Nat. Lab., 1956-61; engr. Babcock & Wilcox, Lynchburg, Va., 1961-67, supr., 1967-70, mgr. engring. devel., 1970—. Patentee nuclear fuel rod (3); contbr. articles to profl. jours. Fellow Am. Ceramic Soc. (div. chair 1975-76); mem. Soc. Mfg. Engrs. (sr.), ASTM (subcom. chair 1956-81; award 1981). Republican. Presbyterian. Club: Ruritan (pres. 1979, zone gov. 1980). Avocation: fishing. Office: Babcock & Wilcox-LRC Mt Athos PO Box 11165 Lynchburg VA 24506

KERR, JOHN WARD, JR., public accountant; b. Fort Monroe, Va., July 30, 1937; s. John Ward and Florence (Bricker) K.; B.B.A., Old Dominion U., 1960; J.D., George Washington U., 1965; m. Carole Anne Alexander, Jan. 18, 1958; children—Katherine Lynne, John Ward III, Elizabeth Carole. CPA. Appellate conferee and field agt. IRS, Washington, 1960-65; tax mgr. Coopers & Lybrand, Richmond, 1965-69; tax mgr. Peat, Marwick, Mitchell & Co., Richmond, 1969-72; tax coordinator J.K. Lasser & Co., Jacksonville, Fla., 1972-73; tax ptnr. Goodman & Co., Norfolk, Va., 1973—; past mem. Va. State Bd. Accountancy; prof. taxation Old Dominion U., Norfolk, U. Va.; prof. real estate taxation U. Va. C.P.A., Va., Fla. Mem. Am. Inst. C.P.A.'s, Va. Soc. C.P.A.'s (past tax com. chmn.), Am., Va. bar assns., Nat. Assn. Accountants, Fed. Govt. Accountants Assn., Alpha Kappa Psi, Pi Kappa Alpha, Phi Alpha Delta. Presbyterian. Clubs: Harbor (Norfolk); Town Point; Kiwanis; Bull and Bear (Richmond). Home: 1160 Revere Point Rd Virginia Beach VA 23455 Office: SMA Tower Norfolk VA 23415

KERR, JOSEPH CHESTER, judge; b. McKeesport, Pa.; s. Joseph Chester and Corinne (Ulm) K.; m. Dorothy Sample Brockmann, Oct. 7, 1944 (div. 1974); children—David, Wayne, Deborah, Scott; m. Karen Lynn Adams, Jan. 25, 1974; children—Kevin, Brian. B.S., Washington and Jefferson U., 1943; LL.B., U. Pitts., 1949. Bar: Pa. 1949, Fla. 1965, U.S. Dist. Ct. (mid. dist.) Fla. 1968. Mgr. contracts Martin Marietta, Orlando, Fla., 1957-68; sole practice law, Orlando, Fla., 1968-70; judge Juvenile Ct., Orange County, Fla., 1970-72; sole practice law, Kissimee, Fla., 1972-82; judge, Osceola County, State of Fla., Kissimee, 1983—. Contbr. articles to mags. Served to lt. USNR, 1943-46, 50-52. Mem. Fla. Bar Assn., Osceola County Bar Assn., Nat. Contract Mgmt. Assn. Republican. Presbyterian. Lodges: Masons, Kiwanis (past pres.). Home: 1472 Skyline Dr Kissimmee FL 32743

KERR, R. MICHAEL, radio/TV and film production company executive; b. Tyler, Tex., July 12, 1950; s. Donald Milton and Clarice (Green) K. A.S., Kilgore Coll., 1970; B.A. in Telecommunications, Tex. Tech U., 1976. News corr., TV host Am. Forces Radio and TV Network, Pentagon, Washington, 1972-75; pub. affairs officer USN Office Info., Dallas, 1978—; pres. KERCO, Kilgore, Tex., 1971—, pres., dir. pub. relations, corp. pilot, 1977—, fin. mgmt. cons., 1983—; NASA and USN judge East Tex. Regional Sci. fair, Kilgore, 1978—; speaker USN Sea Power Programs, Washington, 1979—; audio/visual cons. World's Richest Acre, Kilgore, 1980—; host, co-producer USN films, 1981. Chmn. publicity Rangerette Showcase Mus., Kilgore Coll., 1980—; vol. in pub. relations, docent East Tex. Oil Mus., Kilgore, 1980—; mem. Republican Presdl. Task Force, Washington, 1981—; chmn. city-wide dir. Kilgore council Boy Scouts Am., 1981. Served to lt. USN. Decorated Joint Service commendation; recipient Office of Sec. Def. award, 1975, cert. recognition Nat. Rep. Congl. Com., 1982, 83. Mem. Advt. Pub. Relations Orgn. East Tex. (dir. 1982-84, also program dir.), Assoc. Gen. Contractors (dir. 1980-82, audio/visual dir., service award 1980). Methodist. Lodge: Rotary. Office: KERCO 916 Broadway Kilgore TX 75662

KERSTEN, JOHN CHARLES, lawyer; b. Richmond, Va., Dec. 14, 1940; s. Harold Charles and Katherine Ellen (Dunning) K.; m. GeorgeAnn Williamson (div. 1971); m. Leilani Ann O'Keefe, Apr. 10, 1973; 1 child, Katherine Elizabeth. Student Duke U., 1957-59; B.A., U. Miami, Fla., 1962, J.D., 1965. Bar: Fla. 1965, N.C. 1982. Assoc. Kirsch & Spellacy, Ft. Lauderdale, Fla., 1965-66; ptnr. Sheffey & Kersten, Ft. Lauderdale, 1967-69, Duffy, Sladon & Kersten, Ft. Lauderdale, 1969-71, Friedrich, Kersten & Blackwell, Ft. Lauderdale, 1972-80, Alley, Killian & Kersten, P.A., Waynesville, N.C.,

1982—; asst. city atty. City of Ft. Lauderdale, 1967-68. Mem. Fla. Bar, N.C. Bar, Assn. Trial Lawyers Am., N.C. Trial Lawyers Assn. Lodge: Waynesville Rotary. Avocations; golf; hunting. Home: 554 Camp Branch Rd Waynesville NC 28786 Office: Alley Killian & Kersten PA 437 N Main St Waynesville NC 28786

KERSTETTER, WILLIAM CARL, educational administrator, counselor; b. Shamokin, Pa., May 22, 1946; s. William Carl and Grace Beatrice (Mast) K.; m. Donna Dunn, Feb. 14, 1971; children—Wendy Sue, Jonathan David. B.A., Bloomsburg State Coll., 1968, M.Ed., 1972; M.Ed., Pa. State U., 1981. Instr., U. Alaska, Fairbanks, 1968-69; tchr., coach So. Area Sch. Dist., Catawissa, Pa., 1969-81; instr. counseling Pa. State U., University Park, 1981-83; dir. guidance McCallie Sch., Chattanooga, 1983—; cons. substance abuse, leadership tng., peer counseling to schs., industry; pvt. practice counseling. Mem. adminstrv. bd., family life coordinator, mem. fin. com., mem. pastor/parish com. United Methodist Ch. Named Tchr. of Yr., Faculty Student Adminstrn. South Area, 1974. Mem. Am. Coll. Personnel Assn., Am. Assn. Counseling and Devel., Nat. Employment Counselors Assn., Assn. Non-White Concerns in Counseling, Assn. Counseling Educators and Supervision, Nat. Vocat. Counseling Assn., Assn. Humanistic Edn. and Devel., Assn. for Specialists in Group Work, Am. Sch. Counselors Assn., Assn. for Measurement and Evaluation in Guidance, Assn. Religious and Value Issues in Counseling, Phi Delta Kappa. Episcopalian. Avocations: hiking; reading; gardening; woodworking. Home: 319-321 West St Bloomsburg PA 17815 Office: McCallie Sch 2850 McCallie Ave Chattanooga TN 37404

KESLER, ROBERT MILTON, radiologist; b. Salem, Va., July 30, 1927; s. William Furman and Myrtle Harris (Crosswhite) K.; m. Susan Connelly Lanier, Apr. 1, 1953; children—Robert Milton, Mary Elizabeth, Catherine Hale, Susan Connelly. B.S., Va. Mil. Inst., 1950; M.D., U. Va., 1954. Diplomate Am. Bd. Radiology. Intern, Walter Reed Army Hosp., Washington, 1954-55; gen. med. officer 1360th U.S. Air Force Hosp., Orlando, Fla., 1955-57; gen. practice medicine, Lake County, Fla., 1958-59; resident in radiology McGuire VA Hosp. and Med. Coll. Va., Richmond, 1959-61; fellow in radiation therapy Mt. Sinai Hosp., N.Y.C., 1961-62; practice medicine specializing in radiology, Norfolk, Va., 1962—; mem. staff Med. Ctr. Hosps., Children's Hosp. of the Kings' Daughters; asst. prof. radiology Eastern Va. Med. Sch., Norfolk. Past pres. Norfolk Acad. Medicine; bd. dirs. Va. Med. Polit. Action Com. Served with USNR, 1945-46; served to capt. M.C., USAFR, 1954-57. Mem. Med. Soc. Va. (former del.), Norfolk Acad. Medicine, AMA, Am. Coll. Radiology, Tidewater Radiology Soc., Radiol. Soc. N.Am., Am. Legion. Episcopalian. Club: Norfolk Yacht and Country.

KESSLER, HAROLD, commercial real estate developer and broker, mortgage broker; b. N.Y.C., Aug. 31, 1947; s. Isidore and Rose (Lefkowitz) K.; m. Eddyse Ilene Hershbein, Aug. 8, 1971; children—Lee Ryan, Cari Sarina. B.A., U. South Fla., 1969; M.B.A., Eastern Mich. U., 1972. Engr., Ford Motor Co., Detroit, 1969-77; dist. sales mgr. Am. Motors Corp., Miami, Fla., 1977-79; real estate broker Kessler Group, Inc., Miami, 1979-81, real estate developer, 1981—. Mem. Kendall-Perrine Bd. Realtors (Million Dollar Sales award 1979), Miami Bd. Realtors, Coral Gables Bd. Realtors, Homestead Bd. Realtors, South Miami-Kendall C. of C., Hialeah-Miami Springs C. of C., NACPAC, South Fla. Hist. Soc., Mus. Sci., Dade County Zool. Soc. Democrat. Jewish. Office: Kessler Group Inc 10771 SW 104th St Miami FL 33176

KESSLER, MARION, insurance executive; b. Belle Rose, La., Feb. 8, 1906; s. Sam and Selma (Schwartz) K.; m. Martha Newburger, Jan. 10, 1928. A.B., Tulane U., 1927. Pres. Kessler Ins. Agy., New Orleans, 1935-62; chmn. bd. Kessler-Bodenheimer Inc., New Orleans, 1962-78; chmn. bd. Corroom & Black La., New Orleans, 1978—. Campaign chmn. bldg. fund drive Jewish Community Center, 1962; asst. campaign chmn. Tulane Endowment Fund Drive, 1962; chmn. Temple Sinai Bldg. Fund, 1964; chmn. fund raising drive New Orleans, Nat. Multiple Sclerosis Soc.; past mem. athletic adv. bd. Tulane U.; past mem. ins. adv. com. Tulane U.; past bd. dirs. Internat. House.; chmn. div. United Fund drive; past bd. dirs. Met. Crime Commn.; past mem. ins. adv. com. Orleans Parish Sch. Bd.; first pres., organizer, fund raising chmn. Jr. Achievement Greater New Orleans; organizer, 1st pres., bd. dirs. Goodwill Industries Greater New Orleans Area, Inc.; campaign chmn. fund raising drive Boys' Clubs Am. Greater New Orleans, 1969, also bd. dirs., Man of Yr., 1973; campaign chmn. drive Am. Cancer Soc., 1976; campaign chmn. Protestant Home for Babies, 1978; campaign chmn. fund raising Inst. Human Understanding, One of Ten Most Outstanding Persons, 1977; mem. bd. Soc. Prevention Cruelty to Animals. Served to capt. USAF, 1943-46. Recipient Weiss award NCCJ, 1972; Nat. Pioneer award Jr. Achievement, 1980; named Ins. Man of Yr., Casualty and Surety Assn. New Orleans, 1977. Mem. New Orleans Ins. Exchange, New Orleans C. of C. Republican. Jewish. Club: Lakewood Country. Home: 7040 Coliseum St New Orleans LA 70118 Office: 1539 Jackson Ave New Orleans LA 70130

KESTER, MONTY CHARLES, mathematics educator; b. Odell, Tex., Jan. 22, 1940; s. Charles Marvin and Ida Perlina Pearl (Towry) K.; m. Phyllis Ann Smith, Mar. 21, 1964; children—Charles Melvin, David Lynn. B.A., McMurry Coll., Abilene, Tex., 1962; M.S. in Math., Okla. State U., 1965, Ed.D., 1972; postgrad. U. Ark., 1967, 68. Grad. teaching asst. Okla. State U., Stillwater, 1963-66, 1970-72; mem. math. faculty Tyler Jr. Coll., Tex., 1966-67; asst. prof. Ark. Coll., Batesville, 1967-70; asst. prof., head math. dept. John Brown U., Siloam Springs, Ark., 1972-75; mem. math. faculty Lee Coll., Baytown, Tex., 1975—; speaker in field. Researcher (with P. Kester): What's All This Monkey Business?, 1981. Textbook reviewer: Tex. State Bd. Edn., 1977-84. Contbr. articles to profl. publs. Asst. scout leader Raven dist. and Sam Houston area council Boy Scouts Am., Baytown, 1978-84. Active John Brown Univ. Ch. and Alliance Bible Ch. Nat. Bur. Standards grantee, 1962-63; NSF fellow, 1979. Mem. Math. Assn. Am. (5th Biennial N. Central sect. seminar 1985), Nat. Council Tchrs. Math., Am. Math. Assn. for Two-Year Colls., Tex. Jr. Coll. Tchrs. Assn., Creation Research Soc., Sigma Pi Sigma, Pi Mu Epsilon, Phi Kappa Phi. Republican. Avocations: camping; canoeing; backpacking; reading. Home: PO Box 397 Baytown TX 77522 Office: Dept Math Lee Coll Baytown TX 77520

KETCHAM, ALFRED SCHUTT, surgeon, educator; b. Newark, N.Y., Oct. 7, 1924; s. Colston Esty and Ellen (Schutt) K.; m. Elsie Jane Chase, July 13, 1946; children—Sue Ellen, Wendy Jane, Sally Lin, Jill Ann, Jeff Terry, Dana Kay. B.S., Hobert Coll., 1945, Sc.D., 1970; M.D., U. Rochester, 1949. Intern, U.S. Naval Med. Ctr., Bethesda, Md., 1949-50; resident in surgery USPHS Hosp., San Francisco, 1950-52, Seattle, 1952-55; chief surgery USPHS Indian Hosp., Talihina, Okla., 1955-57; sr. investigator Nat. Cancer Inst., NIH, Bethesda, 1957-62, chief surgery, 1962-74, clin. dir., assoc. sci. dir. for clin. research, 1970-74; prof. surgery, chief. div. oncology, dept. surgery U. Miami Sch. Medicine, 1974—, Am. Cancer Soc. prof. clin. oncology, 1974—; cons. oncology Walter Reed Army Med. Ctr., Washington, Nat. Naval Med. Ctr. Active mem. breast cancer task force Am. Cancer Soc. Recipient Meritorious Service medal HEW, 1970. Mem. AMA, USPHS Clin. Soc., European Soc. Cancer Research, Soc. Head and Neck Surgeons (past pres.), James Ewing Soc., Am. Surg. Assn., So. Surg. Soc., ACS, Am. Radium Soc. (past pres.), Am. Assn. Cancer Research, Soc. Pelvic Surgeons, Am. Fedn. Clin. Oncologic Socs. (pres. bd. govs.), Am. Soc. Clin. Oncology, Theta Delta Chi. Assoc. editor Jour. Surg. Oncology, Am. Jour. Surgery; cons. editor Jour. Thonatology, Jour. Breast; editorial bd. Internat. Advances in Surg. Oncology; contbr. articles to profl. jours. Home: 1120 San Pedro Ave Coral Gables FL 33156 Office: Dept Surgery U Miami Sch Medicine Miami FL 33101

KETELSEN, JAMES LEE, diversified industry exec.; b. Davenport, Ia., Nov. 14, 1930; s. Ernest Henry and Helen (Schumann) K.; B.S., Northwestern U., 1952; m. Joan Velde, Feb. 22, 1953; children—James V., Lee. Accountant Price Waterhouse & Co., C.P.A.'s, Chgo., 1955-59; v.p. finance, treas. J.I. Case Co., Racine, Wis., 1962-68, pres., chief exec. officer, 1968-72; exec. v.p. Tenneco Inc., Houston, 1972—, chmn. bd., chief exec. officer, 1978—, also dir.; dir. Sara Lee Corp., Morgan Guaranty Trust Co. Bd. dirs. Am. Petroleum Inst.; trustee Northwestern U., Conf. Bd. Served to lt. USNR, 1952-55. C.P.A., Tex., Ill. Mem. Chi Psi. Clubs: River Oaks Country, Petroleum (Houston). Office: 1010 Milam St Houston TX 77001

KETNER, RALPH WRIGHT, retail food executive; b. Salisbury, N.C., Sept. 20, 1920; s. George Robert and Effie Viola (Yost) K.; student Tri-State Coll., 1937-39; m. Anne Blizzard, Mar. 22, 1980; children—Linda, Robert. Gen. mgr. Excel Grocery, Salisbury, 1950-56; head grocery buyer Winn Dixie Co., Raleigh, N.C., 1956-57; pres., treas. Food Lion Stores Inc., Salisbury, 1957-81, chmn. bd., chief exec. officer, 1981—; v.p. Save-Rite, Inc.; dir. Security Bank and Trust Co., Rose's Inc. Mem. adv. bd. Salvation Army; past bd. dirs. Rowan County (N.C.) Vocat. Rehab.; mem. adv. com. distbrv. edn. N.C.; mem. N.C. adv. bd., hon. life mem. DECA; mem. N.C. Devel. Fund, 4-H Clubs. Served with U.S. Army, 1942-46. Recipient N.C. Grocery of Yr. award, 1972-73; named N.C. Retailer of Yr., 1977; Paul Harris fellow. Mem. Salisbury-Rowan C. of C. (past dir.), N.C. Food Dealers (past pres., dir.), Mchts. Assn. (past pres.), Am. Legion Clubs: Asparagus, Rotary, Elks, Moose. Holder copyright on inventory form. Home: 333 Richmond Rd Salisbury NC 28144 Office: PO Box 1330 Harrison Rd Salisbury NC 28144

KETTLER, KARL KINAUD, pharmacist; b. New Orleans, Feb. 9, 1943; s. Karl Kinaud and Louise Elizabeth (Morrison) K.; m. Janis Louise Pyka, Feb. 24, 1968 (div. Feb. 1980); children—Laura Lynn, Kristin Marlene. B.S. in Pharmacy, Northeast La. U., 1968. Registered pharmacist, Tex., La. Staff pharmacist Brooke Army Med. Ctr., Fort Sam Houston, Tex., 1974-83; clinic pharmacist 574th Med. detachment, Stuttgart, Fed. Republic Germany, 1983-84; staff pharmacist Northeast Bapt. Hosp., San Antonio, 1984—. Mem. Central Tex. Soc. Hosp. Pharmacists, Kappa Psi. Republican. Roman Catholic. Avocations: motorcycling; hunting; fishing. Home: 603 Royal Ct San Antonio TX 78228 Office: Northeast Baptist Hosp Villge Dr San Antonio TX 78286

KEUSCH, KENNETH DAVID, diagnostic radiologist; b. N.Y.C., Feb. 23, 1935; s. Harry and Ida (Grobifker) K.; m. Joyce Carol Maken; children—Kathy Dale, Jordan Matthew. A.B., NYU, 1955, postgrad., 1958-59; M.D., U. Miami, 1963. Diplomate Am. Bd. Radiology, Am. Bd. Nuclear Medicine. Med. intern Jackson Meml. Hosp., Fla., 1963-64, resident in radiology, 1964-66, 68-69; instr. histology NYU Dental Coll., N.Y.C., 1958-59; radiologist Cedars Med. Ctr., Miami, Fla., 1969—; instr. radiology U. Miami, 1969-75, clin. asst. prof., 1975-84, clin. assoc. prof., 1984—; chief nuclear medicine Cedars Med. Ctr., Miami, 1969—, chief interventional radiology, 1975—. Served to capt. U.S. Army, 1966-68, Japan. NYU fellow, 1958-59; U. Miami fellow, 1968. Mem. Greater Miami Radiol. Assn. (pres. 1976-77), Am. Coll. Radiology, Am. Coll. Nuclear Physicians, Alpha Omega Alpha. Jewish. Lodge: Masons. Avocations: woodworking, art history, contemporary art collecting. Office: Cedars Med Ctr 1400 NW 12 Ave Miami FL 33136

KEVORKIAN, RICHARD, artist; b. Dearborn, Mich., Aug. 24, 1937; s. Kay and Stana (Bedeian) K.; B.F.A., Richmond Profl. Inst., 1961; M.F.A. in Painting, Calif. Coll. Arts and Crafts, 1962; m. Salpy Bouroujian; children—Anna, Raffi, Soseh and Ellina (twins). Instr. drawing and painting Richard Bland Coll., Petersburg, Va., 1961-64; instr. dept. fine arts Va. Commonwealth U., Richmond, 1962-66, asst. prof. dept. painting and printmaking, 1967-69, asso. prof., 1969-77, prof., 1977—, chmn. dept., 1969-81; exhbns. include: Birmingham (Ala.) Mus. Art, 1977, Greenville County (S.C.) Mus. Art 1977, Southeastern Center Contemporary Art, Winston-Salem, N.C., 1977, 78, Hunter Mus. Art, Chattanooga, 1978, Va. Mus. Fine Art, 1983, U. Tenn., Knoxville, 1983. Mem. selection bd. for visual arts Va. Center for Creative Arts, Sweet Briar. Served with N.G., 1955-63. NEA individual sr. artists grantee, 1972; Va. Commonwealth U. Sch. Arts faculty creative reserach grantee, 1974; Nat. Endowment for Arts/Southeastern Center Contemporary Arts grantee, 1976; Guggenheim fellow, 1978. Mem. Va. Cultural Laureate Soc. (bd. dirs.). Office: Painting and Printmaking Dept VA Commonwealth U 325 N Harrison St Richmond VA 23284

KEY, JAMES DAVID, orthopedic surgeon; b. Slaughter Ranch, Post, Tex., Mar. 5, 1939; s. James Orman and Sybil Pauline (Stewart) K.; m. Janice Omega Coke, June 22, 1963 (div. 1983); children—Cynthia Lynne, Amy Janet, James David. A.S., Lubbock Christian Coll., 1959; B.A., Harding Coll., 1961; M.D., U. Tenn., 1966. Intern, Wilford Hall USAF Hosp., 1966; resident Ochsner Found. Hosp., New Orleans, 1969-73; fellow Bapt. Hosp., 1973-74; commd. 2d lt. U.S. Air Force, 1965, advanced through grades to col., 1976; flight surgeon Vietnamese Pilot Tng. Squadron, 3389th, 1966-69; flight surgeon Air Force Acad., Colorado Springs, Colo., 1969, surgeon, 1969-70; pres. Key Clinics Associated and Sports Medicine Clinics Am., Dallas, 1979—; dir. City Bank, Carrollton; teaching fellow Mary Sherman Bone Pathology Lab., Oschner Found., New Orleans, 1971. Hexcel Fiber Corp. grantee, 1976-84. Fellow Am. Acad. Neurol. and Orthopedics Surgeons (dir. Coll. Sports Medicine, sec. 1982, v.p. 1983, pres. elect. 1988), N.Am. Arthoscopic Assn. (charter), Am. Coll. Sports Medicine (dir. rehab. sect.), Internat. Arthoscopic Surg. Soc., Riordan Hand Surgeon Soc., Tex. Med. Assn., Dallas County Med. Soc., Alpha Omega Alpha. Republican. Mem. Ch. of Christ. Clubs: University, Brookhaven Country (Dallas). Patentee in field. Home: 14502 Park Lake Ct Dallas TX 75234 Office: 10 Medical Pkwy Suite 106 Dallas TX 75234

KEY, JOE WAYNE, consulting engineer; b. Vernon, Tex., Nov. 22, 1934; s. Joseph N. and Ruby P. (Emerick) K.; m. Virginia M. Smith, May 31, 1958; children—Pam, Brenda. B.A., Rice U., 1958, M.S., 1960. Registered profl. engr., Tex. Engr., Brown & Root, Inc., Houston, 1959-60; project mgr. Fluor Ocean Services, Houston, 1968-71; prin. design engr. Offshore Co., Houston, 1971-72; chmn. bd., pres. Ocean Resources Engring., Inc., Houston, 1972-81; pres. Key Ocean Services, Inc., Magnolia, Tex., 1982-84, project dir. combustion engring.-offshore prodn. systems, 1984—. Contbr. articles to profl. jours.; patentee in field. Pres. bd. dirs. Westbury Christian Sch., Houston, 1974-76; chmn. bd. dirs. Christian Schs. Greater Houston, 1976-78; bd. dirs. Inst. for Storm Research, 1983-84. Pres. Clear Creek Forest Property Owners Assn., Magnolia, Tex., 1984-85. Served to lt. comdr. USN, 1960-68. Decorated Navy Commendation medal with star. Fellow Soc. Naval Architects and Marine Engrs. (Blakely Smith medal 1983); mem. ASCE, Nat. Soc. Profl. Engrs., Tex. Soc. Profl. Engrs., Rice Engring. Alumni Assn. (awards com. 1982-85). Republican. Mem. Ch. of Christ. Home and Office: 732 Pelican St Magnolia TX 77355

KEYSER, CAMERON POWELL, public relations executive; b. Charleston, W.Va., Sept. 6, 1950; s. Harry C. and Rosalie V. (Barlow) K.; m. Ronda Ann Walker, May 5, 1973; children—Christopher Patrick, Ashley Lynn. B.S., SUNY, 1978. Press aide John D. Rockefeller IV, 1971-72; morning news anchorman Sta. WPTF, Raleigh, N.C., 1974-75; news dir. Sta. WSOC, Charlotte, N.C., 1975-77; news anchorman Sta. WBT, Charlotte, 1977-78; dir. info. services Pfeiffer Coll. Misenheimer, N.C., 1978-79; pubs./pub. info. officer Charlotte-Mecklenburg Schs., Charlotte, 1979-84, chmn. employee assistance program, 1982-84; dir. devel., pub. affairs Providence Day Sch., Charlotte, 1984—. Bd. dirs. McClintock Woods Neighborhood Assn., 1980—; bd. trustees United Way. Served with USAR, 1970-76. Recipient Green Eyeshade, Sigma Delta Chi, 1977; Freedoms Found. at Valley Forge Honor Cert., 1980; Bronze medal Internat. Film and TV Festival of N.Y., 1980; Golden Mike award Am. Legion Aux., 1981; Award of Excellence, Nat. Sch. Pub. Relations Assn., 1981. Mem. Radio-TV News Dirs. Assn., Nat. Sch. Pub. Relations Assn., Ednl. Press Assn. Am., Charlotte Pub. Relations Soc. (dir.), Sigma Delta Chi. Democrat. Baptist. Office: 5800 Sardis Rd Charlotte NC 28226

KEYSERLING, HARRIET H., state legislator; b. N.Y.C., Apr. 4, 1922; d. Isadore and Pauline Hirschfeld; m. Ben Herbert Keyserling, June 24, 1944; children—Judy, Billy, Paul, Beth. B.A. in Econs., Barnard Coll., 1943. Mem. S.C. Ho. of Reps., 1977—, mem. joint legis. energy com., 1982—, com. for purpose of ofcl. consultation with fed. govt. concerning away-from-reactor storage facility for spent nuclear fuel; mem. adv. panel on nuclear waste disposal office of Tech. Assessment of U.S. Congress, 1979-82; mem. exec. com. Nat. Conf. State Legislatures, 1979-82, vice chmn. com. on energy, 1982, chmn. women's network, 1981-82; mem. adv. com. to U.S. Commn. on Civil Rights. At-large mem. Beaufort County Council, 1975-77; chmn. S.C. Task Force on Arts. Mem. S.C. Women in Govt. (founder). Democrat. *

KHAN, WINSTON, physics educator; b. Port-of Spain, Trinidad, Mar. 12, 1934; s. Amarnath and Safeeran (Mohammed) K.; m. Joan Acklima, Dec. 22, 1961; children—Alima, Selina, Shereeza, Winston, Jr. Alim. B.Sc., U. London, 1956, M.Sc., 1958; diploma in Math. and Physics, U. Birmingham, 1961, Ph.D., 1964. Chmn. dept. math., lectr. U. W.I., Trinidad, 1964-69; assoc. prof. math., dir. math. dept. U. P.R., Cayey, 1970-72; assoc. prof. physics U. P.R., Mayaguez, 1974, prof., 1975—; dir. U.S. Army grant for U. P.R., 1981—. Contbr. papers to profl. publs. NSF grantee, 1970-72, 1981-84. Mem. Internat. Assn. Math. Modelling, Am. Phys. Soc., Am. Math. Soc., Soc. Indsl. Applied Math., AAAS, Acad. Scis. Home: Calle Uroyan AD4 Mayaguez PR 00709 Office: U PR Dept Physics and Math Mayaguez PR 00708

KHARE, MOHAN, chemist; b. Varanasi, India, May 15, 1942; s. Dwarka Nath and Rampyari Devi Khare Srivastava; came to U.S., 1967, naturalized, 1971; B.Sc., Banaras Hindu U., 1961, M.Sc., 1963, Ph.D., 1967; m. Meena K., Nov. 23, 1973; 1 son, Rohit. Research assoc. U. Md., College Park, 1967-69, Oreg. State U., Corvallis, 1969-70; sr. research asso. Cornell U., Ithaca, N.Y., 1970-78; analytical specialist Hydroscience Inc., Knoxville, Tenn., 1978-80; tech. specialist IT Enviroscience, Knoxville, from 1980; later with EA Engring., Sci. and Tech., Sparks, Md. Mem. AAAS, Am. Chem. Soc. Contbr. articles to profl. jours. Office: EA Engring Sci and Tech 15 Loveton Circle Sparks MD 21152

KHEIR, SONIA MIKHAIL, pathologist; b. Cairo, Egypt, Dec. 19, 1947; came to U.S., 1973; d. Labib and Esther (Nashid) Mikhail; P.N.S., Cairo U., 1967, M.B.B.Ch. with honors, 1972; m. Nagi A. Kheir, Nov. 21, 1973; children—John, Michael, Susan Elizabeth Intern, Cairo U. Hosp. and Clinics, 1972-73; resident in pathology U. Ala., Birmingham, 1974-78, fellow in surg. pathology, 1978-79, asst. prof. pathology, 1979-83, assoc. prof., 1983—. Ednl. Council for Fgn. Med. Grads. grantee, 1973; lic. physician, Ala.; diplomate Am. Bd. Pathology. Mem. Ala. Assn. Pathology, Ala. Dermatologic Soc., ACP, Birmingham Assn. Resident Pathologists (chmn. 1976-77). Baptist. Contbr. articles to profl. jours. Office: 619 19th St S Birmingham AL 35233

KHORRAM, SIAMAK, remote sensing and image processing educator, computer graphics researcher, engineering consultant; b. Kerman, Iran, Oct. 14, 1946; s. Bahman and Touran (Jahanshahi) K.; m. Raquel J. Khorram, June 12, 1952. M.Sc., U. Tehran, 1967; M.Sc., U. Calif.-Davis, 1974, Ph.D., 1975. Assoc. specialist Space Scis. Lab., U. Calif.-Berkeley, 1975-78, asst. research photogrammetrist, 1980-84; assoc. prof. forestry and elec. and computer engring., dir. Univ. Systems Analysis and Control Ctr., N.C. State U., Raleigh, 1980-84, prof., 1984—, dir. computer graphics ctr., 1983—; dir. Free Trade Zone Authority Services, Inc., Washington, 1982—; cons. computer systems integration, software engring. Recipient Top Student award U. Tehran, 1967, 1st Class Medal of Edn., Ministry Edn. and Culture Iran, 1969; Disting. Research Scientist plaque Italian Navy League. U. Calif. scholar. Mem. AAAS, Am. Soc. Photogrammetry, Am. Water Resources Assn., Calif. Remote Sensing Council, Sigma Xi. Contbr. 50 articles to tech. jours., chpts. in books.

KHOSRAVI, HORMOZ, physician, ultrasonographist; b. Yazd, Iran, Jan. 4, 1943; s. Khosrow and Bano (Idon) K.; m. Nooshazar Khalvaty, June 21, 1973. B.S., Am. Coll. Iran, 1961; M.D., U. Tehran, 1968. Diplomate Am. Bd. Ob-Gyn. Resident in ob-gyn, W.Va. U., Wheeling, 1973-77; fellow in diagnostic ultrasound Ohio Valley Med. Ctr., Magee Women's Hosp. Pitts., Johns Hopkins Hosp., Balt., 1974-75; practice medicine specializing in ob-gyn, Jacksonville, Fla., 1978—; chair dept. ob-gyn Meth. Hosp, Jacksonville; mem. staff St. LuKe's, Bapt. hosps., both Jacksonville. Served to capt. Iranian Navy, 1968-70. Fellow Am. Coll. Obstetricians and Gynecologists; mem. Duval County Med. Soc., Duval County Ob-Gyn. Soc., Fla. Med. Assn., Am. Assn. Gynecol. Laparoscopists, Am. Fertility Soc. Zoriastin. Home: 3265 Front Rd Jacksonville FL 32217 Office: 580 W 8th St #6005 Jacksonville FL 32209

KHOURI, JUDITH LYNN, petroleum company librarian; b. Tonkawa, Okla., Mar. 27, 1938; d. Charlie Clark and Irene Elizabeth (Ladusau) Musselman; m. Leon Wayne Wyckoff, Dec. 24, 1957 (div. 1977); children—Perri Lisa, Michael Ann, Mathew Wayne, Paul Andrew. Student No. Okla. Jr. Coll., 1956-58, Okla. State U., 1981—. Data conversion operator Conoco, Inc., Ponca City Okla., 1964-68, Mountain States Bankcard, Denver, 1968-69; data conversion operator Conoco, Inc., Ponca City, 1969-71, tape librarian, 1971—. Pres. Methodist Youth fellowship, Tonkawa, 1955; active Rainbow Girls, Tonkawa, 1953-56. U. Okla. Scholarship-Leadership Enrichment Program participant, 1985. Mem. Okla. State U. Geol. Soc., Am. Assn. Petroleum Geologists (student mem.), Ponca City Computer Assn. Republican. Home: 807 W Knapp Stillwater OK 74075 Office: Conoco Inc 1000 S Pine St Ponca City OK 74001

KHOURI, PHILIPPE JOHN, psychiatrist, educator, researcher; b. Fontainbleau, France, Oct. 5, 1947; came to U.S., 1972, naturalized, 1983; s. John Stetson and Odette Jean (Plantier) K.; m. Randa Rousse Philippe, Apr. 1972; children—Sani-Philippe, Daniel John. B.A., Am. U. Beirut, 1967, M.D., 1972. Diplomate Am. Bd. Psychiatry and Neurology. Intern, Am. U. Beirut Med. Center, 1971-72; resident, U. Rochester Strong Meml. Hosp., 1972-73, U. Tenn. Affiliated Hosp., 1973-75; research assoc./staff psychiatrist NIH, Bethesda, Md., 1975-77; asst. prof. dept. psychiatry, Georgetown U., Washington, 1977-80; assoc. vis. prof. Am. U. Beirut, 1979; assoc. prof., dir. residency tng. dept. psychiatry, U. Tenn. Health Sci. Center, Memphis, 1982—; cons. Va Med. Center, Memphis. Recipient Sandoz award, 1975. Mem. Am. Psychiatric Assn., Am. Psychopath. Assn., N.Y. Acad. Scis., Am. Soc. Biol. Psychiatry, AAAS, Sigma Xi. Christian Ch. Office: 66 N Pauline St Suite 633 Memphis TN 38105

KHOUZAM, NAGUI NASSIF, physician, educator; b. Cairo, Egypt, May 26, 1927; came to U.S., 1969, naturalized, 1974; s. Nassif Yassa and Nathalie (Issa) K.; m. Desiree Victor Chaker, Apr. 16, 1955; children—Nevine, Nadine, Nelly, Nayer, Nermine. B.S., St. Joseph Coll., 1945, M.S., 1947; M.D., Cairo U., 1952. Lic. physician, Fla. Pvt. practice gen. surgery, Winter Garden, Fla., 1974—; attending physician, surgeon Orlando (Fla.) Regional Med. Ctr., 1974—, West Orange Meml. Hosp., Winter Garden, 1974. Recipient numerous awards AMA, 1969-84. Fellow Am. Soc. Abdominal Surgeons, Internat. Coll. Surgeons, Internat. Acad. Proctology; mem. Fla. Med. Assn., Orange County Med. Soc., McClure Surg. Soc., Fla. Assn. Gen. Surgeons. Home: 710 Valencia Shores Winter Garden FL 32787 Office: 54 E Plant St Winter Garden FL 32787

KHULLAR, GURDEEP SINGH, gerontology educator, researcher; b. Lamore, Punjab, Pakistan, Nov. 6, 1945; came to U.S., 1975; s. Durga Dass and Kaushalya D. (Puri) K.; m. Neelam Tangri, Dec. 9, 1972; children—Anuradha, Denesh. Ph.D. in Lit., Panjab U., Chandigarh, India, 1973, M.A. in English, 1974; M.S. in Sociology, East Tex. State U., 1976; Ph.D. in Sociology North Tex. State U., 1981. Cert. gerontology specialist, Tex. Asst. prof. G.N. Coll., Firozpur, Pb. India, 1971-74; Howard Payne U., Brownwood, Tex., 1977-78; asst. instr. East Tex. State U., Commerce, 1975-76; teaching fellow North Tex. State U., Denton, 1978-81; assoc. prof. gerontology U. Ark., Pine Bluff, 1981—; cons. Kahn Jewellers, Pine Bluff, 1984—, Pine Bluff Nursing Home, 1982-84. Author: Indian Middle Ages, 1985. Contbr. articles to profl. jours. Mem. Am. Sociol. Assn. Hindu. Lodge: Rotary. Home: 6905 White Oak Cove Pine Bluff AR 71602 Office: Univ Ark Dept Social Behavioral Scis N University Dr Pine Bluff AR 71601

KHURI, ANDRE ILIAS, statistics educator; b. Damascus, Syria, Mar. 1, 1940; s. Elias Boulos and Rosette (Khalil Shami) K.; came to U.S., 1966; m. Ronnie Lee Gross, Oct. 11, 1970; children—Marcus, Roxanne. B.S., Damascus U., 1963; M.S., Am. U. Beirut, 1966; Ph.D., U. Fla., 1969; Ph.D., Va. Poly. Inst., 1976. Asst. prof. math. Middle East Tech. U., Ankara, Turkey, 1970-71; asst. prof. math. Beirut Univ. Coll., 1971-73; asst. prof. stats. U. Fla., Gainesville, 1976-82, assoc. prof. stats., 1982—. Assoc. editor Technometrics, Washington, 1983—; contbr. articles to profl. jours. Recipient Boyd Harshbarger award Va. Poly. Inst., 1974. Mem. Am. Statis. Assn., Phi Kappa Phi. Greek Orthodox. Avocations: fishing, camping. Home: 5827 NW 54th Way Gainesville FL 32606 Office: Dept Stats Univ Fla Gainesville FL 32611

KICKLITER, GEORGE PAUL, lawyer; b. Tampa, Fla., Nov. 12, 1933; s. Paul Revere and Lucy Lucille (Hall) K.; B.S. in Bus. Mgmt. cum laude, U. Tampa, 1976; J.D., Stetson U., 1978; m. Shirley Jean Spivey, Mar. 19, 1955; children—Kim Leigh, Karen Iris. Enlisted in U.S. Air Force, 1951, commd. 2d lt., 1954, advanced through grades to lt. col., 1971; B-47 navigator and bombadier, 1956-58; fighter pilot, 1959-74; Vietnam combat pilot, 1969; ret., 1975; admitted to Fla. bar, 1979; individual practice law, Tampa, 1979-82; exec. USAA Ins. Co., 1983; asst. state atty., Hillsborough County, Fla., 1984—. Decorated Bronze Star, Air medal, Meritorious Service medal; lic. comml. pilot. Mem. Ret. Officers Assn., Hillsborough County Bar Assn., Am. Bar Assn., Assn. Trial Lawyers Am., Fla. Sheriffs Assn., Democrat. Baptist. Club: University (Tampa). Office: Suite 670 Lincoln Pointe 2502 Rocky Point Dr Tampa FL 33607

KICLITER, E(RNEST) EARL, JR., anatomy educator; b. Fort Pierce, Fla., June 19, 1945; s. Ernest Earl and Betty Lloyd (Winn) K.; m. Veronica Pelaez, Oct. 23, 1967 (div. 1978). Student Emory U., 1963-64; A.B., U. Fla., 1968; Ph.D., SUNY-Syracuse, 1973. Postdoctoral fellow in neurosurgery U. Va., Charlottesville, 1972-74; asst. prof. neuroanatomy and physiology U. Ill., Urbana, 1974-77; assoc. prof. anatomy U. P.R., Med. Scis. Campus, San Juan, 1977-84, prof., 1984—. Fellow NSF, 1967, Ford Found., 1967-68, NIH,

1968-74; grantee: NIH, 1976—, Nat. Acad. Sci., 1976. Fellow AAAS; mem. Am. Assn. Anatomists, Assn. Research in Vision and Ophthalmology, Cajal Club, J.B. Johnston Club, Soc. Neuroscience, Sigma Xi. Contbr. articles to profl. jours.; research in comparative structure and function of vertebrate visual systems, neuronal plasticity and color vision. Office: Lab Neurobiology Blvd Del Valle 201 San Juan PR 00901

KIDD, NANCY VAN TRIES, psychologist; b. Huntingdon, Pa., June 5, 1933; d. Samuel Musser and Pauline (Haupt) Van Tries; children—Linda A. Rowley Tawfik, Joseph J. Rowley, III, Bruce W. Rowley; m. J. Thomas Kidd, May 23, 1970. B.A. in Journalism, Pa. State U., 1955, Ed.D. in Counseling Psychology, 1977; Ed.M., Temple U., 1969. Lic. psychologist, Va., Pa. Assoc. prof. psychology and counseling Community Coll. R.I., 1973-82; counselor Ariz. Counseling Ctr., Phoenix, 1983; psychologist Counseling Psychol. Services, Richmond, Va., 1984; psychologist, dir. Psychol. Counseling Resources, Richmond, 1985—; career counselor, speaker Women's Resource Ctr., U. Richmond, 1984—; mem. adj. faculty women's studies U. Richmond, 1985, Glendale Coll., Phoenix, 1983-84, Providence Coll., 1977-81; cons. in field. Trustee Pa. State U., University Park, 1983—. Mem. Am. Psychol. Assn., Va. Psychol. Assn., Va. Counseling psychology Assn. (exec. bd., legis. officer 1984—), Acad. Family Mediators, Richmond Mediation Network (charter). Home: 2122 Stuart Ave Richmond VA 23220 Office: Psychol Counseling Resources 122 Granite Ave Richmond VA 23226

KIDD, REBECCA (LOUISE) MONTGOMERY, artist; b. Muncie, Ind., Nov. 29, 1942; d. Joe Bucklyn and Mary Marguerite (Mark) Montgomery; corr. student comml. art, Famous Artists Schs.; m. Ben Roy Kidd, Apr. 10, 1964; children—Daniel Ben, Diana Piper. Painter in oils and pastels; portrait painter and drawer, 1962-81, 83—, character painter, 1966—, outdoor scene, still life, floral painter, 1969—; children's story illustrator, 1972-74; miniature painter, 1974-82; restorer of old houses, 1972-81; adaptor of master's paintings, 1974-82; film illustrator, 1975; Am. Indian painter, 1975-81; trading pin designer, 1977, 78; lithographer, 1977; monotype printmaker, 1978—. One-woman show: Roadside Gallery, 1982; group shows include: Roadside Gallery, Melfa, Va., 1977—, The Gallery, Ct. Plaza, Salisbury, Md., 1977—, Queens Coll., U. Cambridge (Eng.), 1982. Mem. exec. com. Quality Edn. of Accomack County, 1979-80. Mem. Eastern Shore Va. Art League (chmn. constn. and by-laws com. 1979, dir. 1982), Visual Artists and Galleries Assn., Internat. Platform Assn. (merit and popular choice art awards 1984). Address: 9 Lake St Onancock VA 23417

KIDD, THORNTON LENOIR, JR., physician; b. San Antonio, Aug. 3, 1932; s. Thornton Lenoir and Lillian Beatrice (Watts) K.; m. Billie Eugenia Rekoff, Aug. 26, 1961; 1 dau., Sharlyn Gail. Student, San Antonio Coll., 1950-51, Trinity U., 1951-52; student U. Tex., 1952-53, M.D., 1957. Diplomate Am. Bd. Pediatrics, Am. Bd. Allergy and Immunology. Intern, Brackenridge Hosp., Austin, Tex., 1957-58; resident U. Tex. Med. Br.-Galveston, 1958-60, fellow in allergy, 1960-61 practice medicine specializing in allergy, Austin, 1963-64, Pasadena, Tex., 1964—; mem. staffs Bayshore Hosp., Southmore Hosp. Served to lt. comdr. USPHS, 1961-63. Mem. Am. Coll. Allergists, Am. Assn. Cert. Allergists, Am. Acad. Pediatrics, Am. Coll. Chest Physicians, AMA, So. Med. Assn., Houston Allergy Soc., Asthma and Allergy Found. Am., Houston Pediatric Soc., Internat. Corr. Soc. Allergy, Tex. Med. Assn., Am. Assn. Clin. Immunology and Allergy, Am. Acad. Allergy. Republican. Baptist.

KIDD, WILLIAM MATTHEW, judge; b. Burnsville, W.Va., June 15, 1918; s. Robert H. and Henrietta (Hornor) K.; student Glenville State Coll., 1936-38; J.D., W.Va. U., 1950; m. Madelyn Conrad, June 28, 1943; 1 dau., Madelyn Sue Kidd Shipe. Tchr. elem. schs., 1938-41, 45-46; admitted to W.Va. bar, 1950; mem. W.Va. Ho. of Dels., 1950-52; practice law, 1952-74; circuit judge 14th Jud. Circuit, Bluefield, W.Va., 1974-79, chief judge, 1976-79; U.S. dist. judge No. Dist. W.Va., Bluefield, 1979—. Prosc. atty. Braxton County (W.Va.), 1962-70. Served with USN, 1942-45. Mem. W.Va. Jud. Assn., Am. Judicature Soc., U.S. 4th Circuit Jud. Assn., Phi Alpha Delta. Home: 1901 Jefferson St Seville Manor #6 Bluefield WV 24701 Office: PO Box 4010 Federal Station Bluefield WV 24701

KIELY, DAN RAY, real estate development executive; b. Ft. Sill, Okla., Jan. 2, 1944; s. William Robert and Leona Maxine (Ross) K.; B.A. in Psychology, U. Colo., 1966; m. J.D., Stanford U., 1969; m. Lucianne Holt, June 11, 1966; children—Jefferson Ray, Matthew Ray. Admitted to Colo. bar, 1969, Va. bar, 1973, D.C. bar, 1970; asso. firm Holme, Roberts and Owen, Denver, 1969-70; pres. DeRand Equity Group, Arlington, Va., 1973—; chmn. Bankwest Indsl. Bank, Strasburg, Colo., 1984—, Monte Vista Indsl. Bank, Colo., 1984—; dir. DeRand Corp. and affiliates; trustee DeRand Real Estate Investment Trust; speaker, lectr. in field. Deacon, McLean (Va.) Baptist Ch., 1977-80. Served as officer, USAR, 1969-73. Decorated Legion of Merit; cert. property mgr. Mem. Nat. Bd. Realtors, Inst. Real Estate Mgmt., Nat. Assn. Rev. Appraisers, Internat. Council Shopping Centers, Nat. Assn. Real Estate Investment Trusts, Am. Bar Assn., Colo. Bar Assn., D.C. Bar Assn. Club: Chesterbrook Swim and Tennis (dir. 1980). Office: 2201 Wilson Blvd Arlington VA 22101

KIGHT, HENRY TOM, investment company executive; b. Oklahoma City, Mar. 2, 1939; s. Henry Tom and Thelma (Heenan) K.; children—Kristi Lee, H. Tom IV. Student U. Miami (Fla.) 1957; B.B.A., Oklahoma City U., 1961. Pres. H. Tom Kight III, Investments, Oklahoma City. Roman Catholic. Club: Oklahoma City Golf and Country. Home: PO Box 20430 Oklahoma City OK 73156

KIHLE, DONALD ARTHUR, lawyer; b. Noonan, N.D., Apr. 4, 1934; s. John Arthur and Linnie Wilhelmena (Ljunggren) K.; B.S. in Indsl. Engring., U. N.D. at Grand Forks, 1957; J.D., U. Okla. at Norman, 1967; m. Judith Ann Hudson, July 18, 1965; children—Kevin, Kirsten, Kathryn, Kurte. Engr. trainee Continental Pipe Line Co., Ponca City, Okla., 1957, staff engr., 1960-61, 63-64, sr. staff engr., 1964-65; project engr. Oasis Oil Co., Libya, Inc., Tripoli, Libya, 1961-62, sr. project engr., 1962-63; admitted to Okla. bar, 1967; asso. firm Huffman, Arrington, Scheurich & Kincaid, Tulsa, 1967-71, ptnr., 1971-78; ptnr. firm Huffman, Arrington, Kihle, Gaberino & Dunn, Tulsa, 1971—. Trustee Undercroft Montessori Sch., Inc., Tulsa, 1973-79; Chmn. Eagle dist. com. 1984-85, asst. scoutmaster Boy Scouts Am. Served to 1st lt. AUS, 1957-59. Mem. ABA, Okla. Bar Assn. (chmn. state law day 1982-84; Golden Gavel award), Tulsa County Bar Assn., Order of Coif, Sigma Tau, Sigma Chi, Phi Delta Phi. Clubs: Tulsa, So. Hills Country. Bd. editors Okla. Law Rev., 1965-67. Home: 4717 S Lewis Ct Tulsa OK 74105 Office: 1000 One OK Plaza Tulsa OK 74103

KILBORNE, GEORGE BRIGGS, investment company executive; b. N.Y.C., Oct. 7, 1930; s. Robert Stewart and Barbara Briggs K.; B.A., Yale U., 1952; m. Lucie Wheeler Peck, Nov. 12, 1960 (div. 1978); children—George Briggs, Kim McNeil, Sarah Skinner. Vice pres. William Skinner & Sons, N.Y.C., 1955-60; pres. Bus. Research Co., Birmingham, Mich., 1961-74, Creative Capital of Mich., Inc., Birmingham, 1962-70; partner Comac Co., 1968-70; chmn., pres. First Citizen Bank, Troy, Mich., 1970-74; engaged in real estate investing and cons., Palm Beach, Fla., 1975-79; mng. dir. corp. acquisitions Bessemer Securities Corp., N.Y.C., 1980-84; pres. Bay Street Corp., Palm Beach, Fla., 1984—; chmn. State Bank of Mich., Coopersville, 1966-67, Muskegon (Mich.) Bank & Trust, 1967-68, Bank of Lansing (Mich.), 1968-69; vice chmn. Creative Capital Corp., N.Y.C., 1968-70, Hockey Club of Pitts., 1968-70; dir. Watts Regulator Co., Lawrence, Mass., 1981-84, Diversified Communications, Inc., Portland, Maine. Bd. dirs. Oakland (Mich.) unit. Am. Cancer Soc., 1973-74; mem. Republican Com., Dist. 13, Palm Beach County, Fla., 1976-80; mem. Palm Beach County Rep. Exec. Com., 1976-80; bd. dirs. Palm Beach Rep. Club, 1977-80. Served to lt. (j.g.) USN, 1953-55. Recipient Disting. Service award First Citizen Bank, Troy, 1974, Midwest Assn. Small Bus. Investment Cos., 1970. Mem. Nat. Assn. Small Bus. Investment Cos. (gov. 1967-70, mem. exec. com. 1967, pres. Midwest assn. 1970), Soc. Mayflower Descs., Clubs: Yale of the Palm Beaches (pres. 1979-80), Bath and Tennis (Palm Beach, Fla.); Wianno (Mass.) Yacht, Wianno. Office: Bay Street Corp 205 Worth Ave Palm Beach FL 33480

KILBORNE, ROBERT STEWART, retired business executive; b. N.Y.C., Aug. 1, 1905; s. Robert Stewart and Katharine (Skinner) K.; student Yale U., 1923-25; m. Barbara Briggs, Nov. 28, 1925 (dec. 1968); children—Belle (Mrs. Richard S. Taylor), Robert Stewart III (dec.) George Briggs; m. Jane Lowes, May 2, 1969. Joined William Skinner & Sons (Mass. Common Law Trust), N.Y.C., 1925, pres. subs. Truhu Fabrics Corp., 1933, v.p. William Skinner & Sons, 1941, trustee, 1945-61, pres., 1947-61; dir. The Equitable Life Assurance Soc. U.S., 1946-77. Commr. of conservation N.Y. State Conservation Dept., 1966-70; spl. asst. to Gov. on conservation affairs, 1970-72; mem. industry adv. com. OPA, Washington, 1943-46, OPS, 1951-53; mem. adv. com. Research and Devel. br. Mil. Planning Div., Office Q.M. Gen., Washington 1943-49, synthetic br. Broad Woven Fabrics div. Quartermaster Assn., Washington, 1951-61; chmn. Saratoga Springs Commn., 1966-70; alt. to gov. N.Y. State for Delaware River Basin Commn., 1966-71; bd. dirs. Saratoga Performing Arts Center, 1966-72, Gt. Lakes Commn., 1966-77, Hudson River Valley Commn., 1966-77, Interstate Oil Compact Commn., 1966-70, State Air Pollution Control Bd., 1966-70, commr. N.Y. State Taconic Park Commn., 1963-76; trustee Arthur W. Butler Meml. Sanctuary, 1967-77; bd. dirs. Union Theol. Sem., 1950-66; pres. Humane Soc. of South Coastal Ga., 1982-84; state advisor U.S. Congl. Adv. Bd., 1984—; bd. dirs. Sea Island Property Owners Assn., 1979-81, v.p., 1980, pres., 1980-81; elder Presbyterian Ch.; mem. adv. com. Map Internat., 1985—; life mem. Rep. Nat. Com., 1983—. Mem. Mem. Am. Cotton Mfrs. Inst., Inc. (dir. 1958-62), Nat. Fedn. Textiles, Inc. (dir. 1949-58, pres. 1954-55), Am. Arbitration Assn., Am. Textile Mfrs. Inst. (hon. dir. 1962—), Soc. Mayflower Descs. (bd. assts. 1968-72), Bedford Hist. Soc. (dir. 1971-78), New Eng. Soc. of N.Y., Nat. Aero. Assn., OX5 Pioneers, Coastal Ga. Hist. Soc., Delta Kappa Epsilon. Republican. Clubs: Sea Island Golf, Yale, Wings (N.Y.C.). Home: 137 W Cherokee Rd Sea Island GA 31561

KILBOURNE, DEANE EARLE, geologist; b. Leslie, Mich., Feb. 6, 1918; s. Hubert Lynn and Dorothy May (Mudge) K.; m. Jeanne Louise Bridges, Feb. 27, 1954. B.S., Mich. State U., 1941, M.S., 1947; Ph.D., U. Ariz., 1967. Geologist, Texaco, Inc., Casper, Wyo., 1947-62, Enserch Exploration, Midland, Tex., 1975-76; dist. geologist Am. Trading & Prodn. Corp., Midland, 1978—. Contbr. articles to profl. jours. Served as cpl. USAF, 1942-45, ETO. Mem. Am. Assn. Petroleum Geologists, Sigma Xi. Republican. Avocation: golfing.

KILBY, DAVID KENT, food service management executive, consultant; b. Adrian, Mich., Apr. 21, 1937; s. Kenneth Frank and Cleone A. Kilby; m. Karen R. Farr, July 14, 1958; children—Kurt, Susan, Michael, Keith. B.S., Eastern Mich. U., 1967. Cert. contractor Adesis Synergistic Systems. Gen. mgr., v.p. Domino's Pizza Inc., Ann Arbor, Mich., 1967-70, 78-81; dir. franchising, v.p. Domino's Pizza Franchise, Gainesville, Fla., 1970-76, Original Pizzaman, Gainesville, 1976-78; v.p. Snelling & Snelling Inc., Sarasota, Fla., 1981; pres. David K. Kilby & Assocs., Sarasota, 1981—; chmn. bd. Pizza Pronto, Sarasota, 1982-85; franchise mgr. Arby's, Atlanta, 1982-83; cons. Sunkiss Products, Melbourne, Fla., 1983, McGinnis Restaurant Group, London, Ont. Can., 1985, Gt. Am. Pizza Delivery Co., Sarasota, 1985. Chmn. City Planning Commn., Ypsilanti, Mich., 1966-68; mem. County Planning Commn. Washtenaw County, Mich., 1967-68. Served with U.S. Army, 1958-60. Republican. Avocation: sports. Home: 5770 Midnight Pass Rd 208C Sarasota FL 34242 Office: David K Kilby & Assocs 5053 Ocean Blvd Suite 118 Sarasota FL 34242

KILCULLEN, MARY ANN, army officer; b. Tucson, Feb. 11, 1956; d. William Joseph and Phyllis (O'Brien) K.; m. John Edward Martin, June 28, 1985; 1 child, Kirstin Meischel Kilcullen. B.S., Ariz. State U., 1981. Commd. 2d lt. F.A., U.S. Army, 1981, advanced through ranks to capt., 1984; with Tactical Intelligence, Babenhausen, Federal Republic of Germany, 1984-85; Field Artillery advance course student Alpha Battery Officer Student Bn., Fort Sill, Okla., 1985-86; tactical intelligence officer 212th F.A. Brigade, Ft. Sill, 1986—. Mem. Res. Officer Assn., Assn. U.S. Army, F.A. Assn. Democrat. Roman Catholic. Avocations: sailing; water skiing; writing poetry; photography. Home: 7204 SW Drakestone Blvd Lawton OK 73505 Office: S-2 212th Field Artillery Brigade Fort Sill OK 73505

KILGORE, DONALD GIBSON, JR., pathologist; b. Dallas, Nov. 21, 1927; s. Donald Gibson and Gladys (Watson) K.; student So. Methodist U., 1943-45; M.D., Southwestern Med. Coll., U. Tex., 1949; m. Jean Upchurch Augur, Aug. 23, 1952; children—Michael Augur, Stephen Bassett, Phillip Arthur, Geoffrey Scott, Sharon Louise. Intern, Parkland Meml. Hosp., Dallas, 1949-50; resident pathology Charity Hosp. La., New Orleans, also Tulane, 1950-54; asst. pathologist Charity Hosp., 1952-54; pathologist Greenville (S.C.) Hosp. System, 1956—, dir. labs. Greenville Meml. Hosp., 1972—; dir. labs. Greenville Hosp. System, 1984—; cons. pathologist St. Francis, Shriners hosps., Greenville, Easley Baptist Hosp.; pres. Pathology Assocs. Greenville, 1983—; vis. lectr. Clemson U., 1963—; asst. prof. pathology Med. U. S.C., 1968—. Bd. dirs. Greenville County United Fund, 1966-74, Greenville Community Council, 1968-71, Friends of Greenville County Library, 1966-74; trustee Sch. Dist. Greenville County, 1970—; bd. govs. S.C. Patient Compensation Fund, 1977—; patron Greenville Mus. Art, Greenville Little Theatre, 1956—. Served to capt. USAF, 1954-56. Recipient Distinguished Service award S.C. Hosp. Assn., 1976. Diplomate Am. Bd. Pathology, Dermatopathology, Blood Banking. Fellow Coll. Am. Pathologists (assemblyman for S.C. 1968-71), Am. Soc. Clin. Pathologists (councilor S.C. 1959-62), Am. Soc. Dermatopathology; mem. Am. Assn. Blood Banks (adv. council 1962-67, insp. committeeman Southeast dist. 1965—), AMA (ho. of dels. 1978—), So. Med. Assn., S.C. Med. Assn. (exec. council 1969-76, 78—, pres. 1974-75; A.H. Robins award 1985), Am. Soc. Cytology, Am. Coll. Nuclear Medicine, Nat. Assn. Med. Examiners, S.C. Inst. Med. Edn. and Research (pres. 1974-80), S.C. Soc. Pathologists (pres. 1969-72), Richard III Soc. (co-chmn. Am. br, 1966-75), Soc. Ancient Numismatics (charter), Am. (life), Blue Ridge (life), Royal (life) numis. assns., Preservation Soc. Charleston, S.C. Hist. Soc., Friends of Tewkesbury Abbey (life), Canterbury Cathedral Trust in Am., Greenville County Hist. Soc. (life), Am. Numis. Soc., Mensa, S.C. Congress Parents and Tchrs. (life), Greenville County Dental Soc. (hon. life), Greater Greenville C. of C. (ednl. task force 1962-70, chmn. 1965-70), U.S. Power Squadron, Soc. Med. Friends of Wine, Wine Acad. Am., Soc. Wine Educators Les Amis du Vin (hon. life mem., v.p. Greenville chpt. 1971—), Clan MacDuff Soc. Am. (exec. council 1980—), St. Andrews Soc. Upper S.C., Phi Eta Sigma, Phi Chi. Democrat. Presbyn. (ruling elder 1969—). Rotarian (sr. active mem., dir. 1970-72). Clubs: Commerce, Poinsett, Greenville Country, Thirty-Nine (pres. 1981-82), Western S.C. Torch (pres. 1964-65), Chandon. Home: 129 Rockingham Rd Greenville SC 29607 Office: 8 Memorial Medical Ct Greenville SC 29605

KILGORE, JOE MADISON, laywer; b. Brown County, Tex., Dec. 10, 1918; s. William Henry and Myrtle (Armstrong) K.; m. Patricia Jane Redman, July 28, 1945; children—Mark, Dean, Bill, Shannon. Student Westmoreland Coll., 1935-36; grad. U. Tex., 1941. Bar: Tex. 1946; Sole practice, Edinburg, Tex., 1946-55; ptnr. McGinnis, Lochridge & Kilgore, Austin, Tex., 1965—; mem. Tex. Ho. of Reps., 1946-55; del. Tex. Democratic State Conv., 1947-66; mem. U.S. Congress from 15th Dist., Tex., 1955-65; del. Dem. Nat. Conv., 1956-60, 68; chmn. bd. Republic Bank Austin; sr. chmn. Tex. Regional Bancshares, McAllen; dir Republic Bank Corp., Dallas, Tex. State Bank, McAllen, Harlingen State Bank; former chmn. bd. Live Oak Energy; chmn. adv. com. Tex. Legis. Conf., 1975-80; dir. Southwestern Legal Found., 1981-85. Regent, U. Tex., 1967-73; mem. council Adminstrv. Conf. U.S., 1968-72; active U. Tex. Centennial Commn., 1981-83; bd. visitors M.D. Anderson Hosp. and Tumor Inst., 1975-78; mem. investment com. Meth. Home; mem. exec. council U. Tex. Ex-Students Assn.; trustee Scott and White Meml. Hosp., Scott, Sherwood and Brindley Found., 1983—; bd. dirs. Tex. Research League, 1981—, mem. exec. com., 1983—; former bd. dirs. Wesley Found., S.W. Tex. Conf., United Meth. Found. Served to maj. gen. USAAF, World War II. Decorated Silver Star, Legion of Merit, D.F.C., Air Medal with 2 oak leaf clusters, others. Fellow ABA, Tex. Bar Found.; mem. Travis County Bar Assn., State Bar Tex. (vice chmn. legis. com. 1967-68). Methodist. Home: 3311 River Rd Austin TX 78703 Office: 1300 Capitol Ctr 919 Congress Ave Austin TX 78701

KILLIAN, GEORGE SHADRICK, veterinarian; b. DeKalb County, Ala., Aug. 23, 1922; s. George Shake and Bessie (Burt) K.; m. Delta Virginia Payton, Oct. 14, 1950; children—Donna Virginia Killian Boone, Rhonda George Killian Callahan, Angela Kay Killian Shugart, Vicki Frances. D.V.M., Auburn U., 1948. Lic. veterinarian, Ala. General practice vet. medicine, DeKalb County-Ft. Payne, Ala., 1948-53, 55—. Pres. Ft. Payne PTA council, 1968-70. Served as pfc. U.S. Army, 1942-44; to capt. U.S. Army, 1953-55. Mem. AVMA, Ala. Vet. Med. Assn. (pres. 1969-70), Ft. Payne C. of C. (pres. 1971-72), Northeast Ala. Vet. Med. Assn., Ala. Cattlemen's Assn. (pres. 1983-84), DeKalb County Cattlemen's Assn. (pres. 1978-79), Southeastern Livestock Exposition, Soc. Theriogenology, Nat. Fedn. Ind. Bus., DeKalb Auburn Club (past pres.), Auburn Alpha Psi Alumni Assn. (past pres.). Democrat. Baptist. Contbr. articles to profl. jours. Home: PO Box 576 Fort Payne AL 35967 Office: 1112 Chitwood Ave Fort Payne AL 35967

KILLIAN, GRANT ARAM, psychologist; b. Cambridge, Mass., Nov. 3, 1949; s. Lee Gary and Ann (Mazmanian) K. Student Harvard U., 1967-69; B.A., New Coll., Sarasota, Fla., 1972; M.A., U. Chgo., 1975, Ph.D., 1981. Lic. psychologist, Fla. Research fellow U. Chgo., 1975-77; researcher Ill. State Psychol. Inst., 1977-80, intern, 1980-81; psychologist St. Elizabeth Hosp., Washington, 1981-82; clin. psychologist, Coral Springs, Fla., 1982—; asst. prof. psychology Nova U., Fort Lauderdale, 1982—; bd. advisors Test Corp. Am., Kansas City, Mo., 1985. Contbr. articles to profl. jours. Recipient Noyes Found. award U. Chgo., 1974-78, Nat. Research Service award U. Chgo., 1977-78. Mem. Nat. Register of Health Service Providers in Psychology, Am. Psychol. Assn., Fla. Psychol. Assn. Club: Broward Bus. Home: 2202 Cypress Bend Dr S #805 Pompano Beach FL 33069 Office: 9319 W Sample Rd Suite 200 Coral Springs FL 33069

KILLORIN, EDWARD WYLLY, lawyer, tree farmer; b. Savannah, Ga., Oct. 16, 1928; s. Joseph Ignatius and Myrtle (Bell) K.; B.S., Spring Hill Coll., Mobile, 1952; LL.B. magna cum laude, U. Ga., 1957; m. Virginia Melson Ware, June 15, 1957; children—Robert Ware, Edward Wylly, Joseph Rigdon. Admitted to Ga. bar, 1956; practice in Atlanta, 1957—; ptnr. firm Gambrell, Russell, Killorin & Forbes, 1964-78; sr. ptnr. firm Killorin & Schroder, 1978—; lectr. Inst. Continuing Legal Edn. Ga., 1967—. Dir. Ga. 1st Realty Inc. Chmn., Gov.'s Adv. Com. on Coordination State and Local Govt., 1973, Gov.'s Legal Adv. Council for Workmen's Compensation, 1974-76; bd. regents Spring Hill Coll., 1975-82, trustee, 1981—. Served with AUS, 1946-47, 52-54. Mem. ABA, Internat., Ga. (chmn. jud. compensation com. 1976-77, chmn. legis. com. 1977-78), Atlanta (editor Atlanta Lawyer 1967-70, exec. com. 1971-74, chmn. legislation com. 1978-80) bar assns., Am. Judicature Soc., Lawyers Club Atlanta, Atlanta Legal Aid Soc. (adv. com. 1966-70, dir. 1971-74), Nat. Legal Aid and Defender Assn., Internat. Assn. Ins. Counsel (chmn. environ. law com. 1976-78), Atlanta Lawyers Found., Ga. Def. Lawyers Assn. (dir. 1972-80), Ga. C. of C. (chmn. govtl. dept. 1970-75, chmn. workmen's compensation com. 1979—), Def. Research Inst. (Ga. chmn. 1970-71), Spring Hill Coll. Alumni Assn. (nat. pres. 1972-74), High Mus. Art, Ga. Forestry Assn. (bd. dirs. 1969—, pres. 1977-79, chmn. bd. 1979-81), Am. Forestry Assn., Demosthenian Lit. Soc. (pres. 1957), Sphinx, Blue Key, Gridiron, Phi Beta Kappa, Phi Beta Kappa Assos., Phi Kappa Phi, Phi Delta Phi, Phi Omega. Clubs: Capital City, Peachtree Golf, Commerce (Atlanta); Oglethorpe (Savannah). Roman Catholic. Contbr. articles to legal jours. Home: 436 Blackland Rd NW Atlanta GA 30342 Office: Cain Tower Peachtree Center Atlanta GA 30303

KILLOUGH, MARY LEE, retired artist; b. Retrop, Okla., Mar. 19, 1907; d. Henry Irving and Emma Francis (Dillard) Devin; m. John Harve Killough, Nov. 13, 1937 (dec. May 1966); 1 child, Charles William. Grad. high sch. Rocky Ind. Sch. Dist., Okla., 1930; cosmetology cert. Chgo. Beauty Sch., Tulsa, 1931; diploma in Apt. Mgmt., Tarrant Apt. Assn., Fort Worth, 1972; Elderhostel diploma, N. Tex. State U., 1983; student Weatherford Jr. Coll., 1967-68; cert. in floral design El Centro Jr. Coll., Dallas, 1970-71. Registered cosmetologist. Owner/operator Beauty Shop, Rocky, Okla., 1931-36; seamstress, dept. head Granbury Dress Co., Tex., 1952-56; seamstress Maybelle Sports Wear, 1958-64; floral designer Wolfe's Nursery, Dallas, 1970-71; apt. mgr. Hildring Place Apts., Fort Worth, 1972-73, Oakwood Apts., Tulsa, 1973-74; receptionist Oral Roberts U., Tulsa, 1975-76; ret. vol. artist Sr. Citizens Groups, Tex., 1981—; dir. arts and crafts Shanley Sr. Ctr., Granbury, 1979-80; instr. in oils Tex. Agrl. Extension Service, Brownwood, 1981—, Prud Ranch, Fort Davis, Tex., 1985—. Com. mem. Extension Council/Life Learning, Granbury, 1981-85; elder, Sunday sch. tchr. 1st Presbyterian Ch., Granbury; room mother Granbury Pub. Schs., 1952-62; bd. dirs. local high sch. Booster Club; telephone, fin. mem. Hood County Democrats, Granbury, 1960—; county dir. March of Dimes, 1954-64, ARC, 1942-44; mem. Hood County Com. on Aging, 1983—; mem. Regional Aging Adv. Com., 1985—. Mem. Granbury C. of C. (beautification com. mem. 1984—), Am. Assn. Ret. Persons (charter mem. Granby chpt.), Lake Granbury Art Assn. Lodge: Eastern Star (worthy matron 1942-43), Rainbow Girls (mother advisor 1968-69). Avocation: designing and creating clothes. Home: Route 3 Box 552 A Granbury TX 76048

KILLOUGH, NORMA JEANNE (HOOD), office management and insurance firm executive, antiques and collectibles store executive; b. Dallas, Aug. 18, 1928; d. Charles Ernest and Lillie Ethel (Sharp) H.; m. Doyle Laverne Hart, June 19, 1945 (div. 1957); children—La Dolle Gene, Melody Darlin; m. Joe Burns Killough, Feb. 4, 1958 (dec. May 1978). Student Draughon's Bus. Coll., Dallas, 1945, 59-60, Tyler Comml. Coll., 1969-72. Musician, singer Musical Hart Group, U.S., Can., 1945-57; sec., acct. SEDCO, Dallas, 1960-62, Thompson, Knight, Simmons & Bullion, Dallas, 1962-69; owner, operator The Barn Antiques, Tyler, Tex., 1976—; owner, operator office mgmt., ins. and bookkeeping firm, Tyler, 1978—; organist, Tyler area, 1969—; organ tchr., Tyler area, 1975—. Coordinator Religious and Civic Outreach for Tyler Elderly and Handicapped, 1973—; active in fund raising Democratic Party; active LWV, Dem. Nat. Com., Nat. Com. for Effective Congress, Common Cause. Mem. Bethesda Fellowship (founder and pres. 1979—). Avocations: music; choir; study and restoration of antiques; gardening. Home: 1719 Kimwood Tyler TX 75703

KILPATRICK, CHARLES OTIS, newspaper editor, publisher; b. Fairview, Okla., June 16, 1922; s. John E. and Myrtle (Arant) K.; m. Margie Ada Partin, June 3, 1944; children—Kent Fairles, Millicent Kye, Mark Kevin. B.A., Stephen F. Austin State Coll., 1942. With daily newspapers, Nacogdoches, Tex., 1940-42, with Daily Sentinel, Nacogdoches, 1946-48, Courier-Times, Tyler, Tex., 1948-49; regional editor Tyler Morning Telegraph, 1949, mng. editor, 1949-50; mem. staff Evening News, San Antonio, 1950-51; Sunday Editor San Antonio Express, 1951-54; asst. mng. editor Evening News, 1954-55, mng. editor, 1955-56; asst. exec. editor San Antonio Express and San Antonio News, 1957-58, exec. editor, 1958, v.p., 1971; pub. San Antonio Express, 1971-72, San Antonio Express and News, 1972—. Pulitzer prize journalism juror, 1963, 64, 67, 71, 75. Bd. dirs. Incarnate Word Coll., United Way, San Antonio Indsl. Found., San Antonio Festival; trustee Southwest Research Center; pres. Goodwill Rehab. Service, 1983-84. Served as comdg. officer 14th Inf. Bn., USMCR; lt. col. Res. Mem. Tex. A.P. Mng. Editors Assn. (pres. 1963), C. of C. (dir.), Am. Soc. Newspaper Editors, Tex. Daily Newspaper Assn. (pres. 1983), San Antonio Symphony Soc. (pres. 1984-86). Episcopalian. Home: 2019 E Lawndale Dr San Antonio TX 78209 Office: Express-News Corp Ave E at 3d St San Antonio TX 78206

KILPATRICK, GEORGE H., banker; b. Denver, Apr. 20, 1936; s. George Harrington and Margaret M. (Wall) K.; m. Dorothy Ray Winter, June 13, 1959; children—Robin, Jeffrey. B.S. in Finance with honors, U. Colo., 1959. Credit analyst, gen. banking officer Interfirst Bank Dallas, N.A., 1960-70, asst. cashier, 1962-64; asst. v.p. Inter First Bank, 1964-67, v.p., 1967-70, sr. v.p., 1970-73, exec. v.p., chief operating officer, dir. Interfirst Bank Houston N.A. (N.A.), 1973; pres. Inter First Bank Houston (N.A.), 1973-79; exec. v.p. Interfirst Corp., 1979-85; chief credit adminstrn. officer, 1985—. Bd. mgrs. Harris County Hosp. Dist., 1975-79. Mem. Robert Morris Assos. (bd. regents loan mgmt. seminar 1973, 74), Beta Gamma Sigma, Sigma Chi. Methodist. Club: Dallas Country. Office: 901 Main St Dallas TX 75283

KILPATRICK, JEREMY, mathematics educator; b. Fairfield, Iowa, Sept. 21, 1935; s. Walter Phillips and Catherine Bernice (Johnson) K.; m. Carlene Joan Friedrichsen, Aug. 26, 1962; children—Judson Carl, Barton Phillips. A.A., Chaffey Coll., Ontario, Calif., 1954; A.B. in Math., U. Calif.-Berkeley, 1956, A.M., in Edn., 1960; M.S. in Math., Stanford U., 1962, Ph.D. in Edn., 1967. Tchr., math. and sci. Garfield Jr. High Sch., Berkeley, Calif., 1957-60; research asst. Sch. Math. Study Group, Stanford U., 1962-67; asst. prof. Tchrs. Coll., Columbia U., 1967-70, assoc. prof., 1970-75; prof. of math. edn. U. Ga., Athens, 1975—; vis. lecttr. U. Cambridge, England, 1973-74; guest prof. Institut fur Didaktik der Mathematik, Bielefeld, FRG, 1976; cons. Coll. Bd. and Nat. Assessment of Ednl. Progress. Mem. Nat. Council of Tchr. of Math., Math. Assn. Am., Am. Ednl. Research Assn., Nat. Council on Measurement in Edn., Nat. Council of Suprs. of Math., Ga. Council of Tchrs. of Math. Author: (with George Polya) The Stanford Mathematics Problem Book, 1974; Editor: (with Izaak Wirszup, et. al.) Soviet Studies in the Psychology of Learning and Teaching Mathematics (14 vols.), 1969-75, The Psychology of Mathematical Abilities in Schoolchildren (V.A. Krutetskii), 1976; (with Geoffrey Howson and Christine Keitel) Curriculum Development in Mathematics, 1981, Jour. for Research in Math. Educn. 1982—. Home: 227 Woodlawn Ave Athens GA 30606 Office: 105 Aderhold Hall U Ga Athens GA 30602

KILPATRICK, JOHN AARON, computer company executive; b. Norfolk, Va., Jan. 7, 1954; s. Marion Calvin and Maude Elaine (Simms) K.; m. Lynnda Christina Peterson, Aug. 19, 1978; children—Lynnda Madonna, Jonathan Simms. B.S., U. S.C., 1976, M.B.A., 1981. Bus. mgr. J. Allen Shumaker Builders, Columbia, S.C., 1979-81; stockbroker Dean Witter Reynolds, Columbia, 1981-83; teaching assoc. U. S.C., Columbia, 1982-83; v.p., co-owner Carolina Microsystems, Columbia, 1983—. Fin. chmn. Com. to Re-elect Pat Antley County Auditor, Columbia, 1982. Mem. Nat. Assn. Accts. (past dir.), Homebuilders Assn. Midlands, Greater Columbia C. of C., Omicron Delta Kappa. Republican. Episcopalian. Home: 1827 Ingelwood Dr Columbia SC 29204

KIM, CHURL SUK, business company executive; b. Chinhae, S. Korea, Aug. 6, 1930; came to U.S., 1956, naturalized, 1969; s. Buhmsool Kim and Mallim Joo; m. Sookwon Lee, May 19, 1978; 1 child, Stella. B.A., So. Ill. U., 1959, M.A., 1961; Ph.D., U. Okla., 1970. Asst. prof. math. Lindenwood Coll., St. Charles, Mo., 1961-63, Northwest Mo. State Coll., 1965-66, Ind. U. Southeast-New Albany, 1970-74, chmn., assoc. prof. math., 1975-79; co-dir. Southeast Ind. Regional Sci. Fair, 1975-79; chief exec. officer Ophir of Memphis, Inc., 1983—. USAF fellow, 1968-70. Mem. Math. Assn. Am. Republican. Roman Catholic. Lodge: Rotary. Home: 1793 Brierbrook Rd Germantown TN 38138 Office: Ophir of Memphis Inc 113 S Main St Memphis TN 38103

KIM, HAK YOUN, economics educator; b. Seoul, Korea, Feb. 22, 1947; came to U.S., 1975; s. Kwan Sik and Bok Nam (Choe) K.; m. Jae Jang, Sept. 10, 1976; children—Raymond, Stanley. B.A., Sogang U., Seoul, 1973; M.A., U. Cin., 1979, Ph.D., 1982. Teaching asst. U. Cin., 1975-77, research cons., 1977-79, instr., 1978-79, research assoc., 1981-83; asst. prof. econs. Western Ky. U., Bowling Green, 1983—; research economist EPA, Cin., 1978-81. Contbr. articles to profl. jours. Served with Korean Army, 1968-71. Decorated D.S.M.; Univ. scholar Sogang U., 1972; research grantee EPA, 1981-83. Mem. Am. Econ. Assn., Soc. for Econ. Dynamics and Control. Baptist. Home: 1664 Normal Dr Bowling Green KY 42101 Office: Western Ky U Dept of Econs Bowling Green KY 42101

KIM, HONG NACK, political science educator; b. Youngchun, Korea, Aug. 20, 1933; came to U.S., 1956, naturalized, 1973; s. Sang Do and Nam Jo (Sung) K.; m. Boohi Suh, Mar. 26, 1967; children—Michael, Jeffrey, Brian Kim. B.A., Seoul Nat. U., Korea, 1956; M.A., Georgetown U., 1960, Ph.D., 1965. Lectr. Georgetown U., Washington, 1965-66; asst. prof. North Tex. State U., Denton, 1966-67, asst. prof., 1967-72, assoc. prof., 1972-77; prof. polit. sci. W.Va. U., Morgantown, 1977—. Editor: Political Studies Rev., 1984—; co-editor: Korean Reunification: New Perspectives and Approaches, 1984. Pres. Korean Assn. W.V., 1981-82; chmn. Assn. Korean Polit. Scientists North Am., 1983—. Recipient Fulbright-Hays Faculty Research Abroad Grants, U.S. Dept. Edn., 1979, 82; Outstanding Research award W.Va. U., 1985. Mem. Am. Polit. Sci. Assn., Assn. Asian Studies. Democrat. Presbyterian. Editor: Asian Forum, 1972-74; author Scholars Guide to Washington, D.C. for East Asian Studies 1979; co-editor: Essays in Political Science, 1972; contbr. articles to various publs. Home: 1270 Braewick Dr Morgantown WV 26505 Office: Dept of Polit Sci West Va U Morgantown WV 26506

KIM, YOUNG JEH, political science educator; b. Seoul, Republic of Korea, Jan. 24, 1939; s. Chul Soo and Soon Rae Kim; m. Ock Joo Han, Dec. 22, 1968; children—Michelle, Peter, Charlie. B.A., Kon-Kuk U., Seoul, 1962; M.A., U. Cin., 1968; Ph.D., U. Tenn., 1977. Asst. prof. polit. sci. Alcorn State U., Lorman, Miss., 1968-74, 77-81, assoc. prof., 1981—; teaching asst. U. Tenn.-Knoxville, 1974-77. Author: Korea's Future and East Asian Politics, 1977; Roads for Korea's Future Unification, 1980; Korean Reunification, 1984. Guest editor Asian Profile, Dec. 1983; mem. internat. editorial adv. com. Asian Research Service, Hong Kong, 1985. Grantee U.S. Dept. Edn., 1985, Lilly Found., 1985. Fellow Internat. Ctr. for Asian Studies; mem. Am. Polit. Sci. Assn., So. Polit. Sci. Assn., Miss. Polit. Sci. Assn., Assn. for Asian Studies. Baptist. Avocations: Golf; skiing. Home: 109 Traceside Dr Natchez MS 39120 Office: Alcorn State U Lorman MS 39096

KIMBALL, ALLAN CURTIS, editor; b. Burlington, Vt., July 27, 1946; s. Wayne Curtis and Ursula Amanda (Chicoine) K.; m. Rita Dianne Ramsey, Dec. 8, 1979. B.A., U. Houston, 1975. City editor Pasadena Citizen (Tex.), 1975-76, mng. editor, 1978-84; tech. writer Schlumberger Well Services, Houston, 1976-78; features copy editor Houston Chronicle, 1984—. Col., Tex. Army, Houston, 1982—. Recipient Column Writing in Tex. award Tex. Editors, 1982; Community Service award Tex. Gulf Coast Press Assn., 1979. Mem. Investigative Reporters and Editors Assn., Sigma Delta Chi. Home: 7619 Hereford St Houston TX 77087 Office: Houston Chronicle PO Box 4260 Houston TX 77210

KIMBALL, AUBREY PIERCE, biochemistry educator; b. Lufkin, Tex., Oct. 20, 1926; s. Aubrey Joseph and Eula Bernice (Pixley) K.; B.S., U. Houston, 1958, Ph.D., 1961; postdoctoral Stanford Research Inst., 1961-62; m. Kay Tabor, Mar. 29, 1975; children by previous marriage—Kathleen, Erin, Lisa. Research biochemist Stanford Research Inst., 1962-67; assoc. prof. biochemistry U. Houston, 1967-72, prof., 1972—, planning dir. central campus cancer program, 1976-81, chmn. dept. biophys. scis., 1977-78. Served with USNR, 1944-46, 50-52. Roche fellow, 1952-54. Grantee Robert A. Welch, 1968-85, NIH, 1969-85. Fellow Am. Inst. Chemists, N.Y. Acad. Scis.; mem. Am. Chem. Soc., Am. Assn. Cancer Research, Soc. Exptl. Biology and Medicine, Am. Soc. Biol. Chemists, S.W. Sci. Forum (dir., pres.), AAAS, Sigma Xi (pres. U. Houston chpt.). Editor: (with J. Oro') Prebiotic and Biochemical Evolution, 1972. Contbr. articles to sci. jours. Home: 1501 Bonnie Brae Houston TX 77006

KIMBALL, CURTIS R., trust banker; b. Grand Rapids, Mich., Dec. 21, 1950; s. Rollin Hibbard and Jane Ann (Walterman) K.; m. Marilyn M. Quaderer. B.A., Duke U., 1972; M.B.A., Emory U., 1984. Comml. lending and trust portfolio mgr. Wachovia Bank and Trust Co., N.A., Winston-Salem, N.C., 1972-81; v.p., trust mgr. bus. owner services group Citizens and So. Nat. Bank, Atlanta, 1981—; dir. Hen House Interstate, St. Louis, 1982—. Active Midtown Bus. Assn., Atlanta, 1982—. Fellow Inst. Chartered Fin. Analysts; sr. mem. Am. Soc. Appraisers (pres. Atlanta chpt. 1985-86). Republican. Episcopalian. Avocations: running; fencing; tennis. Office: Citizens and So Nat Bank 33 North Ave Suite 1150 Atlanta GA 30308

KIMBLE, GLADYS AUGUSTA LEE, nurse, civic worker; b. Niagara Falls, Can., June 28, 1906; d. William and Florence Augusta Baker (Buckton) Lee; R.N., Christ Hosp., Jersey City, 1929; B.S., Columbia U. Tchrs. Coll., 1938, M.A., 1948; m. George Edmond Kimble, Jan. 5, 1952. Nurse, Willard Parker Hosp., N.Y.C., 1931; asst. and supervisory relief nurse Margaret Hague Maternity Hosp., Jersey City, 1931-37; staff nurse, relief supr. Manhattan Eye, Ear and Throat Hosp., N.Y.C., 1937-38; sr. staff, asst. nurse supr. Vis. Nurse Service, N.Y.C., 1938-41; sr. public health nurse USPHS, Little Rock, 1941-43; public health supr. Providence (R.I.) Dist. Nursing Assn., 1943-46; edn. dir. Jersey City Public Health Nursing Service, 1946-49, also instr. Seton Hall U., N.J., 1947-48; public health nurse cons. U.S. Inst. Inter-Am. Affairs, Brazil, 1949-51; dir. public health dept. Englewood (N.J.) Hosp., 1951-53; nurse coordinator exchange visitor nurse program Overlook Hosp., Summit, N.J., 1964-71; mem. Ladies Oriental Shrine of N.Am., 1978—. Recipient woman of year award Essex County Bus. and Profl. Women, 1968. Fellow Am. Public Health Assn.; mem. Sarasota Geneal. Soc. (charter mem.), Somerset and Dorset Family History Soc., AAUW. Episcopalian. Home: 4540 Bee Ridge Rd #12 Sarasota FL 33583

KIMBROUGH, EVELYN SUE, environmental engineer; b. Nashville, Aug. 30, 1954; d. George Robert and Irene K.; A.A., Martin Coll., 1974; B.S., Vanderbilt U., 1976. Environ. scientist U.S. EPA, Research Triangle Park, N.C., 1977—. Methodist. Club: Order of Eastern Star. Home: 700 Morreene Rd R-8 Durham NC 27705 Office: MD-14 Research Triangle Park NC 27711

KIMBROUGH, JAMES DANIEL, university dean; b. Fairfax, Ala., Sept. 22, 1937; s. Keener Patterson and Alethia (Gibson) K.; m. Carol Sanders, Aug. 5, 1960; children—James Daniel, Janet Kimbrough Murray. B.S., Jacksonville State U., 1959, M.S., 1964; Ed.D., U. Ala., 1972. Tchr. lic., Ala.; adminstr.'s lic., Ala. Tchr. De Kalb County Schs., Decatur, Ga., 1959-64; prin., supt. sch. Ft. McClellan Sch., Ala., 1964-69; prof. edn. Troy State U., Ala., 1972-81, dean Sch. Edn., 1981—; trustee So. Assn. Colls. and Schs., 1983—; mem. Ala. Edn. Adv. Com., 1983—; mem. governing bd. Ala. Edn. Leadership Hall of Fame, Troy, 1982—. Trustee Truman Pierce Inst., Auburn, Ala., 1983—; mem. Troy Day Care Adv. Bd., 1975—, Pike County Edn. Adv. Com., 1980—. NDEA fellow, 1969-72. Mem. NEA, Ala. Assn. Colls. for Tchr. Edn. (pres. 1983—), Assn. Tchr. Educators (pres. southeast region 1984—), Kappa Delta Pi (treas. 1982—), Phi Delta Kappa (exec. sec. 1982—). Democrat. Baptist. Avocations: landscaping; water sports; traveling. Home: 300 Pine Forest Circle Troy AL 36081 Office: Troy State U 206 McCartha Hall Troy AL 36082

KIMBROUGH, WILLIAM EDWARD, lawyer; b. Birmingham, Ala., Dec. 27, 1949; s. James Edward and Elizabeth (Emfinger) K.; m. Lynne Barnes, Aug. 2, 1980; 1 child, Mary Ellen. B.A., U. South Ala., 1975; J.D., Jones Law Sch., Montgomery, Ala., 1979. Bar: Ala. 1979, U.S. Dist. Ct. (so. dist.) Ala. 1980, U.S. Ct. Appeals (11th cir.) 1983. Claims rep. Ala. Dept. Veterans Affairs, Montgomery, 1976-79; sole practice, Thomasville, Ala., 1979—; mcpl. judge City of Thomasville, 1980—, Town of Grove Hill, Ala., 1981—. Bd. dirs. Friends of Thomasville Adjustment Ctr., 1983—. Served with U.S. Army, 1972-74. Recipient award of merit Ala. Dept. Veterans Affairs, 1979. Mem. ABA, Ala. Bar Assn., Assn. Trial Lawyers Am., Ala. Trial Lawyers Assn., Ala. Lawyer Referral Service (trustee 1981-83), Thomasville C. of C. Democrat. Methodist. Club: Pineview Country (bd. dirs. 1984—). Lodges: Masons, Am. Legion (post comdr. 1981—). Home: 234 Old Hwy 5 N Thomasville AL 36784 Office: 12 W Front St Thomasville AL 36784

KIMMEL, ELLEN BISHOP, psychology and educational psychology educator, consultant; b. Knoxville, Sept. 16, 1939; d. Archer W. and Mary Ellen Bishop; m. Herbert D. Kimmel, Dec. 30, 1961 (div.); children—Elinor, Ann, Jean, Tracy. B.A., U. Tenn., 1961; M.A. in Psychology, U. Fla., 1962, Ph.D., 1965. Asst. prof. psychology Ohio U., 1965-68; asst. prof. dept. ednl. psychology U. South Fla., Tampa, 1971-72, dir. div. univ. studies, 1972-73, assoc. prof. dept. ednl. psychology, 1972-75, prof. dept. ednl. psychology and dept. psychology Coll. Social and Behavioral Scis., 1975—; dir. Women and Adminstrn. Inst.; disting. vis. prof. Simon Fraser U., Vancouver, B.C., Can., 1980-81; cons. industry, service agys., retail and ednl. orgns. Mem. Hillsborough County Commn. on Status of Women, Gov.'s Com. on Status of Women, 1978—, Commn. on Juvenile Delinquency. Recipient Outstanding Prof. award U. South Fla., 1978; Gov.'s award for outstanding service to State of Fla., 1975; various other awards and honors; recipient 7 fed. research grants, 4 univ. devel. and research grants. Fellow Am. Psychol. Assn. (exec. com.); mem. Southeastern Psychol. Assn. (pres. 1978-80), Good Govt. Soc. Women's Polit. Caucus, NOW. Democrat. Club: Athena. Contbr. chpts. to books, articles to profl. jours. Home: 11925 Riverhills Dr Tampa FL 33617 Office: U South Fla FAO 268 Tampa FL 33620

KIMMONS, DAVID BENTLEY, computer operations administrator; b. Ft. Worth, Sept. 29, 1955; s. Wylie M. and Sarah E. (Christopher) Kimmons; m. Karen L. Richards, Oct. 15, 1977; 1 dau., Aimee L. Student Heiskell Sch., 1984. Arcade shop technician Six Flags Over Tex., Arlington, 1973-74; arcade shop foreman Cedar Point, Sandusky, Ohio, 1974-79; computer technician Marietta Coll. (Ohio), 1979-83; dir. computer ops. Sophisticated Data Research, Atlanta, 1983—. Roman Catholic. Lodge: K.C. Home: 4870 Twin Lakes Trail Doraville GA 30360 Office: Sophisticated Data Research 2251 Perimeter Park Dr Atlanta GA 30341

KIMMONS, JAMES FELIX, accountant; b. Eastman, Ga., July 31, 1948; s. Jacob Felix and Maggie Maria (McCranie) K.; m. Linda Sue Murphy, Aug. 14, 1965; children—James Felix, Keith H., Linda M., Susan R. A.A., Middle Ga. Coll., 1970; B.S., Ga. Southwestern Coll., 1971. C.P.A., Ga. Bookkeeper Heart of Ga. Community Action Council, Inc., Eastman, 1971, fiscal officer, controller, 1971-73; staff acct. Walker, Meadors and Vickers, C.P.A.s, Hawkinsville, Ga., 1973-75, audit mgr., sr. acct., 1975-77, ptnr., 1977; sole practice acctg., Eastman, Ga., 1978—. Sec., Dodge County Band Boosters, 1982-83. Mem. Am. Inst. C.P.A.s, Ga. Soc. C.P.A.s (mem. profl. ethics com. 1979—), Acctg. Research Assn., Middle Ga. Coll. Alumni Assn., Ga. Southwestern Coll. Alumni Assn. Baptist. Lodges: Masons (past master 1974); Shriners (pres. 1980, 82), Lions, Rotary. Home: Route 3 Eastman GA 31023 Office: 303 4th Ave NE Eastman GA 31023

KINCAID, EUGENE D., III, lawyer; b. Uvalde, Tex., Mar. 7, 1941; s. Eugene D. and Lochie M. (Mundine) K. B.A., Baylor U., 1962; J.D., U. Tex.-Austin, 1966. Bar: Tex. 1966. Briefing atty. Tex. Ct. Criminal Appeals, 1967-68; asst. city atty. San Antonio, 1969; atty. Tex. Water Rights Commn., Austin, 1970-71; sole practice, Uvalde, 1971—; exec. v.p. EDK Ranches, Inc., AVK Ranch Co., Inc. Chmn. Uvalde Housing Authority, 1972-80. Mem. State Bar Tex., Border Dist. Bar Assn., Uvalde Bar Assn. (pres. 1972), Uvalde Arts Council, Magna Charta Barons, Pi Sigma Alpha, Sigma Delta Pi. Republican. Anglican. Clubs: Uvalde Country. Office: 243 N Getty PO Box 1769 Uvalde TX 78801

KINCAID, JOHN, political science educator; b. Phila., May 5, 1946; s. John and Louise M. (Berger) K.; m. Dee Elaine Muesse, Jan. 10, 1981; 1 child, Karen Louise. B.A., Temple U., 1967, Ph.D., 1981; M.A., U. Wis., 1968. Instr., St. Peter's Coll., Jersey City, 1969-70; dir. Phoenix Peace Ctr., Ariz., 1970-72; v.p., treas. Pentagon Papers Fund for Civil Liberties, Los Angeles, 1972-73; instr. Temple U., Phila., 1975-79; assoc. prof. North Tex. State U., Denton, 1979—; research fellow Ctr. for Study Federalism, Phila., 1982-85; cons. White House, Washington, 1981-82, U.S. Adv. Commn. on Intergovtl. Relations, Washington, 1983—. Editor and contbr.: Political Culture, Public Policy and the American States, 1982; Covenant, Polity, and Constitutionalism, 1983; The Covenant Connection: Federal Theology and the Origins of Modern Politics, 1985. Editor: The Covenant Letter, 1979—; Publius: The Journal of Federalism, 1981—; assoc. editor: State Government and Politics book series, 1983—. Contbr. articles to profl. jours. Recipient numerous grants NEH, 1979—, North Tex. State U., Nat. Inst. Edn. Mem. Southwestern Polit. Sci. Assn. (v.p., program chmn. 1984-85), Am. Polit. Sci. Assn., Am. Acad. Polit. and Social Sci., Acad. Polit. Sci., Nat. Mcpl. League, Pres.'s Research Group, Soc. for Values in Higher Edn. Episcopalian. Avocation: stamp collecting. Office: North Texas State Univ Dept Polit Sci Denton TX 76203-5338

KINCHEN, LEON JOSEPH, financial corporation executive, financial planner; b. Prairieville, La., Mar. 14, 1938; s. Jackson Alexander and Bessie (Brignac) K.; m. Jennifer Kelly Miller, May 2, 1967 (div. 1971); 1 son, Lance Joseph; m. Nancy Huval, Jan. 17, 1983; children—Molly Christina, Melanie Catherine. B.S., U. Southwestern La., 1964; postgrad. Loyola Law Sch., New Orleans, 1972-73. C.L.U.; cert. fin. planner; registered investment adviser; registered prin. Nat. Assn. Securities Dealers; lic. realtor. Salesman, Liberty Mut. Ins., Baton Rouge, 1964-67; propr. Taxes and Fin. Planning Services, Inc., Lafayette, La., 1976—; founder, owner Bottomline Money Mgmt., Inc., Lafayette, 1982. Author: Financial Planners Ency., 1983. Mem. Internat. Assn. Fin. Planners, Am. Soc. C.L.U.s, Nat. Assn. Securities Dealers, Nat. Life Underwriters Assn., Lafayette Council on Estate Planning, Registry of Fin. Personnel Practitioners, Greater Lafayette C. of C. Republican. Roman Catholic. Clubs: Oakbourne Country, Country of La. Home: 204 Mitze Dr Lafayette LA 70507 Office: Taxes & Fin Planning Services Inc 710 Hugh Wallis Rd Suite 201 Lafayette LA 70508 also 7908 Wrenwood Blvd Suite B Baton Rouge LA 70809

KINDER, BILL NYE, psychology educator; b. Christiansburg, Va., Oct. 30, 1946; s. Rodney P. and Juanita S. (Altizer) K.; m. Carole Waite, Dec. 30, 1972; children—Christopher W., Laura N. B.S., Va. Tech., 1969; Ph.D., U. S.C., 1975. Instr. psychology U. Tex. Med. Sch., Galveston, 1975-76; asst. prof. U. South Fla., Tampa, 1976-81, assoc. prof. psychology, 1981—, acting dir. clin. psychology, 1984-85. Author: (with others) Human Sexuality: Current Perspectives, 1980. Contbr. articles to profl. jours. Mem. Am. Psychol. Assn., Soc. Personality Assessment, AAAS, Am. Assn. Sex Educators, Counselors and Therapists. Office: U South Fla Dept Psychology Tampa FL 33620

KINDER, RAY JERMAIN, museum curator; b. Chgo., June 23, 1925; s. Pierre Jermain and Gertrude Sylvia (Spaller) K.; A.B. magna cum laude, Lawrence Coll., 1949; A.M., U. Chgo., 1955, Ph.D., 1975. Library technician U. Chgo., 1950-55, archivist, 1955-60, adminstrv. asst., 1960-64; asst. prof. history Meth. Coll., Fayetteville, N.C., 1965-75; mus. curator, installation historian, Ft. Stewart, Ga., 1977—. Com. mem. Civic Music Assn., Fayetteville, 1966-75; mem. Community Chorus, Fayetteville, 1967-75; active in Civic Orch., Fayetteville, 1967-75, Humane Soc., Fayetteville, 1968—, Hinesville, 1985—; active Civic Theatre, Fayetteville. Served to T-5 AUS, 1944-46, ETO. Recipient Outstanding Service award Ft. Stewart, Ga., 1980, 81, Exceptional Service award, 1984. Mem. Orgn. Am. Historians, Econ. History Assn., Soc. History of Tech., North Am. Conf. Brit. Studies. Anglican. Avocations: music; tennis; water sports; target shooting; skiing. Home: 622 Ogden St Hinesville GA 31313 Office: 24th Infantry Div and Fort Stewart Mus Attn AFZP-PTO-PM Fort Stewart GA 31314-5082

KING, ALGIN BRADDY, coll. dean; b. Latta, S.C., Jan. 19, 1926; s. Dewey Algin and Elizabeth (Braddy) K.; B.A. in Retailing and Polit. Sci. (W.T. Grant Retailing scholar) cum laude, U. S.C., 1947; M.S., N.Y.U., 1953; Ph.D., Ohio State U., 1966; m. Joyce Heisick, Aug. 21, 1976; children—Drucilla Ratcliff, Martha Louise. Exec. trainee Sears, Roebuck & Co., 1948-48; instr. retailing U. S.C., 1948-51; chief econ. analysis br. dist. OPS, 1951-53; exec. dir. Columbia (S.C.) Mchts. Assn., 1953-54; asst. prof. Tex. A&M U., 1954-55; mem. faculty Coll. William and Mary, 1955-72, prof. bus. adminstrn., 1959-72, dir. Bur. Bus. Research, 1959-63, assoc. dean Sch. Bus. Adminstrn., 1968-72; prof., dean Sch. Bus., Central Conn. State Coll., Avon, 1972-73; prof., head dept. bus. and econs. Madison Coll., 1973-74; prof., dean Sch. Bus., Western Carolina U., Cullowhee, 1974-76; prof. mktg. and mgmt. Christopher Newport Coll., Newport News, Va., 1976—, dean sch. bus. adminstrn. and econs., 1977—; pres. Algin B. King and Assos., 1980—; teaching asst. Ohio State U., 1963-64; professorial lectr. George Washington U.; mgmt. cons. CSC, U.S. Army. Mem. fin. resource group Conn. Council Higher Edn., 1972-73. Mem. U.S. Sales and Mktg. Execs. Club, Am. Mktg. Assn., Acad. Mgmt., Acad. Mktg. Sci., Am. Inst. Decision Scis., Phi Beta Kappa. Independent. Methodist. Mason, Rotarian. Author: (with others) Hampton Waterfront Economic Study, 1967; The Source Book of Economics, 1973; (with others) Management Perceptions, 1976; also chpts. in books, articles. Home: 103 N Will Scarlet Ln Williamsburg VA 23185

KING, ARNOLD KIMSEY, JR., clergyman, nursing home executive; b. Durham, N.C., May 7, 1931; s. Arnold Kimsey and Edna May (Coates) K.; m. Marjorie Jean Fisher, June 22, 1952; children—Leslie Diane, Carole Jean, Arnold Kimsey III, Julia Paige. B.A., U. N.C., 1955; M.Div., Duke U., 1959; D.D., Am. Bible Inst., 1971. Ordained deacon Methodist Ch., 1956, elder, 1959; lic. hotel adminstr., nursing home adminstr. N.C. Enlisted U.S. Air Force, 1951, served as staff sgt., various assignments in psychol. training, bus. adminstrn., mgmt.; minister, organizer Aldersgate Methodist Ch., Chapel Hill, N.C., 1955-61; assoc. pastor Edenton St. Methodist Ch., Raleigh, N.C., 1961-64; pastor Ahoskie (N.C.) United Methodist Ch., 1964-70; pastor Woodland (N.C.) United Methodist Ch., 1970-74; sec. N.C. Annual Conf., United Methodist Ch., Raleigh, 1972-74; asst. adminstr. Methodist Retirement Homes Inc., Durham, 1974-75, adminstr. Methodist Retirement Homes Inc., Durham, 1975—; mem. N.C. Commn. on Health Services Mem. Young Democrats Club, N.C. Gov.'s Com. on Aging, United Fund, Am. Cancer Soc.; councilman Town of Woodland, 1972-74; trustee, mem. exec. com. Goodwill Industries, Durham, 1974-78; theol. adv. Internat. Yr. of Handicapped. Named Tar Heel of Week, Raleigh (N.C.) News and Observer, 1969. Mem. N.C. Bd. Examiners of Nursing Home Adminstrs., N.C. Hist. Assn. (past pres. United Methodist Conf.), Am. Acad. Med. Adminstrn., Am. Coll. Health Care Adminstrs., Am. Assn. Non-Profit Homes for Aging, N.C. Assn. Non-Profit Homes for Aging, Am. Hotel and Motel Assn., Paralyzed Vets. Am., Nat. Paraplegia Found., Methodist Found., N.C. Conf. Bd. Ministerial Tng. and Qualifications, N.C. Conf. Bd. Evangelism (past pres., v.p.), Mensa, Lambda Chi Alpha. Lodges: Kiwanis, Rotary, Optimists, Masons, Shriners. Contbr. to U.S. Air Force manuals; contbr. articles to profl. jours.; contbr. N.C. Christian Advocate Weekly, 1973—; lectr. to profl. confs. Home: 5315 Yardley Terr Durham NC 27707

KING, ARTHUR THOMAS, economics educator, retired air force officer; b. Greensboro, Ala., Feb. 10, 1938; s. Harvey James and Elizabeth (Williams) K.; m. Rosa Marie Bryant, June 24, 1962; children—Donald, Kevin. B.S. in Biology, Tuskegee Inst., 1962; M.S. in Econs., S.D. State U., 1971; Ph.D. in Econs., U. Colo., 1977. Commd. 2d lt. U.S. Air Force, 1962, advanced through grades to lt. col., 1979; asst. prof. econs. U.S. Air Force Acad., 1970-74; ops. planner, Davis-Monthan AFB, Tucson, 1975-76, strategic planner/energy economist, Wright-Patterson AFB. Ohio, 1977-79; assoc. prof. econs. Air Force Inst. Tech., 1979-82, ret., 1982; assoc. prof. econs. Baylor U., Waco, Tex., 1982—. Mem. Am. Econ. Assn., Nat. Econ. Assn., Soc. Govt. Economists, Air Force Assn. Baptist. Author articles in field. Home: 212 Whitehall Dr Waco TX 76710 Office: Dept Econs Baylor U Waco TX 76798

KING, BERT THOMAS, research administrator; b. N.Y.C., Mar. 28, 1927; s. Norbert T. King and Rose J. (Kacin) King Elwell; m. Margaret MacKinnon, Aug. 26, 1950 (div. Nov. 1982); children—Cheryl, Douglas, Jeffrey. B.S., Rutgers U., 1950; M.S., Yale U., 1952, Ph.D., 1955. Lic. psychologist, Conn. Research psychologist U.S. Navy Submarine Base, New London, Conn., 1956-58; dir. tng. div. U.S. Navy Personnel Research, Washington, 1958-60; social sci. analyst USIA, Washington, 1960-63; dir. psychology dept. USN Personnel Research, Washington, 1963-65; program mgr. Office of Naval Research, Washington, 1965—; lectr. various colls. and univs. Editor: Attitudes, Conflict and Social Change, 1972; Managerial Control and Industrial Democracy, 1977. Contbr. articles to profl. jours. Served with USN, 1945-46. Woodrow Wilson fellow, 1950-52. Fellow Am. Psychol. Assn. (com. head 1980-83); mem. D.C. Psychol. Assn. (com. head 1985—), Phi Beta Kappa, Sigma Xi. Unitarian. Avocations: music; dancing. Home: 4023 Byrd Rd Kensington MD 20895 Office: Office of Naval Research 800 N Quincy St Arlington VA 22217

KING, CHARLES GORDON, electric equipment manufacturing company sales executive; b. Atlanta, Sept. 9, 1939; s. Clinton Brown and Majorie (Clements) K.; m. Janice Lynell Carter, June 19, 1959; children—Barry, Gerald, Cynthia. Salesman ITE-Imperial, Nashville, 1964-72, dist. sales mgr., Richmond, Va., 1972-78; area sales mgr. Gould/ITE, Atlanta, 1978-80; nat. sales mgr. Crouse-Hinds, Charlottesville, Va., 1980—. Baptist. Office: Crouse-Hinds of Cooper Industries Route 660 Earlysville VA 22936

KING, CHARLES HENRY, civil engineer; b. Sumter, S.C., Aug. 19, 1944; s. Malcolm Edmund and Audrey Elizabeth (Watson) K.; m. Mary Donna Stewart, May 29, 1971; children—Matthew Charles, Seth Edmund. B.S. in C.E., Clemson U., 1966, M.S. in C.E., 1967; grad. Air Command and Staff Coll., Air U., Maxwell AFB, 1982. Registered profl. engr., Tenn. Supervisory bldgs. engr. Gen. Telephone Co., Durham, N.C., 1971-72; resident contracting officer U.S. Army Corps Engrs., MacDill AFB, Fla., 1976, Fort Rucker, Ala., 1976, Holston Army Ammunition Plant, Kingsport, Tenn., 1977-78; asst. chief contract adminstrn. Arnold Air Force Sta., Tenn., 1978-84; area engr., resident contracting officer C.E., Tenn. Area office, 1985—. Served to capt. USAF, 1967-71, lt. col. USAFR. NSF Fellow, 1967. Mem. ASCE, Am. Soc. Mil. Engrs., Reserve Officers Assn., Air Force Assn., Tau Beta Pi, Phi Kappa Phi. Baptist. Office: AEDC Area Engrs Office Arnold Air Force Station TN 37389

KING, CHARLES MARK, dentist, teacher; b. Fort Benning, Ga., Mar. 15, 1952; s. Charles Ray and Marilyn Anita (Alexander) K.; m. Debra Jean Hood, Sept. 28, 1974; children—Kelley Michelle, Kevin Marcus. B.S., U. Ala., 1973, M.S., 1977, D.M.D., 1981. Lab. technician Med. Lab. Assn., Birmingham, Ala., 1973-74; research asst. dept. surgery Univ. Hosp., Birmingham, 1974-76, dept. anesthesiology, 1976-78; gen. practice dentistry, Birmingham, 1981—; clin. instr. U. Ala. Sch. Dentistry, Birmingham, 1982—; mem. bd. advisors Dist. Dental Assts. Soc., 1984—. Contbr. articles to profl. jours. Named Best Clin. Instr., Student Body U. Ala. Sch. Dentistry 1985. Mem. ADA, Ala. Dental Assn., 7th Dist. Dental Soc., Acad. Gen. Dentistry, Soc. Mil. Surgeons U.S., Delta Sigma Delta. Republican. Baptist. Lodges: Sertoma, Masons, Avocations: archery; martial arts; hunting; water sports; reading. Office: 5620 Chalkville Rd Birmingham AL 35235

KING, CHARLES MCDONALD, JR., hospital management company executive, consultant; b. Canton, Ohio, June 14, 1934; s. Charles McDonald and Marjorie Olive (Blazer) K.; m. Anna Marie Starkey, June 3, 1956; children—Jeffrey Luis, Gregory Alan. B.S. in Pharmacy, U. Toledo, 1956; M.S. in Pharmacy, Phila. Coll. Pharmacy and Sci., 1958; postgrad. in Bus. Adminstrn., Tenn. State U. Registered pharmacist, Ohio, Minn. Resident in pharmacy Thomas Jefferson U. Hosp., Phila., 1958, asst. dir. pharmacy service, 1962-64; dir. pharmacy services Barbeton Citizens Hosp. (Ohio), 1960-62; instr. Phila. Coll. Pharmacy and Sci., 1962-64; dir. dept. pharmacy U. Ala., Birmingham, 1964-73; mgr. pharmacy services Med. Delivery Systems Div., Becton, Dickinson & Co., Rutherford, N.J., 1973-74; dir. pharmacy services U. Minn. Hosps., Mpls., 1974-77, dir. grad. studies in hosp. pharmacy, asst. prof. Coll. Pharmacy, U. Minn., 1974-77; mgr. pharmacy services Hosp. Affiliates Internat., Nashville, 1977-78, corp. dir. clin. services and pharmacy services,

1978-80, dir. div. client services Central Div., 1980-81; dir. Gen. Services, Hosp. Corp. Am., 1981-83, asst. v.p. adminstrv. services, 1983—; adj. faculty U. Tenn. and Auburn U.; mem. hosp. adv. bd. Roche Labs., 1968-70; mem. adv. com. nursing home unit dose systems State of Minn., 1975-76; mem. adv. panel on hosp. practices U.S. Pharmacopia, 1971-73. Served with USPHS, 1958-60. Am. Found. for Pharm. Edn. fellow, 1956-58. Mem. Adminstrv. Mgmt. Soc., Am. Mgmt. Assn., Am. Soc. Hosp. Pharmacists (spl. interest group adminstrv. pharmacy practice, bd. dirs.), Southeastern Soc. Hosp. Pharmacists (pres. 1969-70), Tenn. Soc. Hosp. Pharmacists, Rho Chi, Phi Kappa Phi, Kappa Psi. Lodges: Masons, Blue Lodge, Scottish Rite, Shriners. Cons. editor Am. Jour. Hosp. Pharmacy, 1978-79; mem. editorial bd. Aspen Systems, Topics in Hosp. Pharmacy Mgmt., 1980—; contbr. articles in field to profl. publs., papers to profl. confs. Home: 213 Countryside Dr Franklin TN 37064 Office: 4525 Harding Rd Nashville TN 37205

KING, CLYDE RICHARD, educator, writer; b. Gorman, Tex., Jan. 14, 1924; s. Clyde Stewart and Mary Alice (Neill) K.; A.S., John Tarleton State Coll., 1943; B.A., U. Okla., 1948, M.A., 1949; Ph.D., Baylor U., 1962. Dir. news service, instr. journalism Mary Hardin-Baylor Coll., Belton, Tex., 1950; asst. prof. English, Tarleton State Coll., Stephenville, Tex., 1951; dir. news service, instr. journalism East Tex. State Coll., Commerce, 1952-56; asst. prof., assoc. prof. U. Tex., Austin, 1956-62, prof. journalism, 1965-81, mem. faculty adv. com. U. Tex. Press, 1977-80; free-lance writer, 1948—. Mem. Winedale Adv. Com., 1969-71; pres. bd. Stephenville Hist. House Mus., 1976-79, 83—; mem. Cross Timbers Fine Arts Council; mem. adminstrv. bd. First Meth. Ch., Stephenville, 1982—. Served with AUS, 1943-45; ETO. Research grantee U. Tex., 1960. Mem. Tex., West Tex. hist. assns., Sigma Delta Chi, Sigma Phi Epsilon. Lodge: Masons (32 deg.). Author: Ghost Towns of Texas, 1953; Wagons East, 1965; Mañana with Memories, 1964; Watchmen on the Walls, 1967; Susanna Dickinson: Messenger of the Alamo, 1976; We Sing Their Harvest Songs, 1980; A Birthday in Texas, 1980; The Lady Cannoneer, 1981. Editor: Letters from Fort Sill, 1886-1887, 1971; Victorian Lady on the Texas Frontier, 1971, Brit. edit., 1972; Fred Gipson: Before Old Yeller, 1980. Home: 830 Alexander Rd Stephenville TX 76401

KING, CONSTANCIO YUZON, surgeon; b. Philippines, Sept. 1, 1934; s. Alfonso M. and Consrcia G. (Yuzon); M.D., U. Santo Tomas, Manila, 1959; m. Rosalinda de la Rosa, Mar. 17, 1962; children—Annabel, Raymund, Grace. Adj. resident surgeon U. Santo Tomas Hosp., 1960, resident surgeon, 1962-66, chief resident, 1965-66, vis. prof., 1976; surg. resident Columbus Hosp., Cabrini Med. Center, N.Y.C., 1967-70; cardiovascular surg. resident N.Y. U. Hosp., 1969; attending surgeon emergency dept. Columbus Hosp., 1970, attending in surgery, 1971; staff VA Med. Center, Los Angeles, 1971; chief surg. service VA Med. Center, Amarillo, Tex., 1972-74, 79—, chief vascular surgery, 1983—, chmn. tumor bd., 1983, HSRO/Utilization Com.; asst. clin. prof. surgery Tex. Tech U. Sch. Medicine, 1981—. Bd. dirs. Amarillo Area Acad. Health Center Corp., 1973-76, Potter-Randall div. Am. Heart Assn., 1984—; pres. St. Joseph's Sch. Bd., Amarillo, 1975-77. Fellow A.C.S., Am. Coll. Angiology, Am. Soc. Abdominal Surgeons, Internat. Coll. Surgeons, Assn. Clin. Scientists, Royal Soc. Health; mem. Assn. Mil. Surgeons, Pan-Pacific Surg. Assn., Am. Inst. Ultrasound in Medicine, Amarillo Surg. Soc. Roman Catholic. Clubs: Mercedes Benz, Nat. Rifle Assn. Contbr. article to profl. jours. Home: 3717 Farwell Dr Puckett Pl Amarillo TX 79109 Office: Surg Service Suite VA Med Center 6010 Amarillo Blvd Amarillo TX 79106

KING, DAMON D., hospital administrator; b. Huntingdon, Tenn., Sept. 9, 1934; s. V.L. and Quincye (Smith) K.; m. Janet Hudson, Dec. 31, 1959; children—David G., DeAnn, Robin K. B.S., U. Tenn., 1957; cert., Ga. State U., 1960. Adminstr. Walton County Hosp., Monroe, Ga., 1961-65, Hall County Hosp., Gainesville, Ga., 1965-68, Med. Ctr. Central Ga., Macon, 1968—, chmn. bd. Shared Services So. Hosps., Inc., Atlanta, 1983—; exec. com. Blue Cross/Blue Shield, Columbus, Ga., 1961—. Served to 1st lt. U.S. Army, 1957-61. Fellow Am. Coll. Hosp. Adminstrs. mem. Ga. Hosp. Assn. (dir. 1966-68, treas., pres. 1969), N.E. Ga. Hosp. Dist. Assn. (pres. 1965). Lodges: Rotary (dir. 1975); Kiwanis (sec. 1967, Gainesville; pres. elect 1964, Monroe). Home: 587 Taylor Ct Macon GA 31204 Office: Med Ctr Central Ga 777 Hemlock St PO Box 6000 Macon GA 31208

KING, DAVID WARREN, psychologist, professor of psychology; b. Corsicana, Tex., Nov. 8, 1947; s. David Warren and Claudie Maxine (Steele) K.; m. Sherry Lynn Purvis, Apr. 6, 1968; children—Christopher Kamal, Stephen Bishare. B.A., Tex. Tech. U., 1969; M.A., Ariz. State U., 1974, Ph.D., 1977. Lic., cert. Tex. State Bd. of Examiners of Psychologists. Asst. prof. psychology Beirut U. Coll., Lebanon, 1978-80; chmn. dept. psychology Howard Payne U., Brownwood, Tex., 1980-84, dean of social scis., 1984; assoc. prof. psychology Tanta U., Egypt, 1983; chief psychologist Tex. Dept. of Corrections Retrieve Unit, Angleton, 1985—. Co-editor El-Raida newsletter Women's Studies in the Arab World, 1978. Contbr. articles to profl. jours. Mem. Am.-Arab Anti-Discrimination Com., Houston, 1983-85. Fulbright Scholar, 1982-83. Mem. World Fedn. for Mental Health, Internat. Council of Psychologists, Internat. Assn. for Cross-Cultural Psychology, Am. Psychol. Assn., Tex. Assn. for Middle East Scholars. Avocations: amateur radio, travel. Home: 603 Magnolia Lake Jackson TX 77566 Office: Retrieve Unit Tex Dept Corrections Route 4 Box 1500 Angleton TX 77515

KING, DEBORAH ANN, nurse; b. Enterprise, Ala., Mar. 5, 1953; d. Wilson Robertson II and Mae (Nichols) Robertson Davis; m. John David King, Jan. 2, 1978; children—James Christopher, Amanda Elizabeth. A.N., Wallace Community Coll., 1973. R.N., Ala. Nurse's aide Dale County Hosp., Ozark, Ala., 1970-73, charge nurse, 1973-74; charge nurse, staff nurse Southeast Ala. Med. Ctr., Dothan, 1974-79, head nurse emergency dept., 1979—; chmn. Code 4 Com., Dothan, 1983—, Community Awareness Com., Dothan, 1984—; mem. MAST Community Group, Dothan, 1984; mem. Emergency Doctors Com., Dothan, 1984—. Mem. Emergeny Nurses Assn., Am. Nurses Found. Democrat. Mem. Ch. of Christ. Home: 206 Aspen Circle Dothan AL 36303 Office: SE Ala Med Ctr PO Box 6487 Dothan AL 36302

KING, EDWARD WILLIAM, transportation company executive; b. North Fork, W.Va., Jan. 29, 1923; s. Edward Ward and Myrtle (Charlton) K.; m. Mary Elizabeth Preston, Oct. 31, 1947 (div. 1976); children—Edward William, Elizabeth King Griffin, Mary King Sullivan; m. Martha Lee Corns Mather, Apr. 7, 1977. Ed. Va. Poly. Inst., Washington and Lee U., U. Tenn.-Knoxville. Pres., treas. Mason & Dixon Lines, Inc., Kingsport, Tenn., until 1974, chmn. bd., treas., 1974—; pres., treas. Crown Enterprises, Inc.; treas. Mason & Dixon Tank Lines, Inc.; chmn. Regular Common Carrier Conf., 1966-67; dir. Kingsport Nat. Bank, Kingsport Fed. Savs. & Loan. Seal sale chmn. Sullivan County TB Assn.; mem. Kingsport Bd. Edn.; dir., sec.-treas. Holston Valley Hosp., 1956-79; trustee East Tenn. State U. Found. Named Young Man of Yr., Kingsport Jaycees, 1958. Mem. Am. Trucking Assn. (Tenn. v.p., trustee, ATA Found.), Trucking Employers, Tenn. Motor Transport Assn. (pres. 1957-58), Kingsport C. of C. (v.p.). Presbyterian. Clubs: Ridgefields Country (Kingsport); Kingsport Civitan (pres.). Office: Mason & Dixon Lines Inc Eastman Rd Kingsport TN 37664*

KING, ELTON RAY, communications company executive; b. Canton, Miss., July 31, 1946; s. Troy Lee and Estelle (Slade) K.; m. Patsy Sheryl Lomax, Jan. 28, 1966; children—Karol Nichole, Kristopher Elton. B.S.E.E., Miss. State U., 1968. Registered profl. engr., Ala. Engr., South Central Bell Telephone Co., Jackson, Miss., 1968-75, dist. mgr., Jackson and Hattiesburg, Miss., 1975-78, div. mgr., Jackson, 1978-80, gen. mgr. residence, 1980-81, gen. mgr. distbn., 1981-83, asst. v.p., Birmingham, Ala., 1983; gen. mgr. Network Planning and Engring. La. Unit chmn. United Givers Fund/United Way, Jackson, 1978, sect. chmn., 1979, co. chmn., 1980. Served with USAF, 1964-70. Mem. IEEE, Miss. Engring. Soc., Nat. Soc. Profl. Engrs. Republican. Baptist. Lodges: Hattiesburg Kiwanis, Jackson Lions. Home: 218 Evangeline Dr Mandeville LA 70448

KING, ERIKA IRENE, painter, specialist in collage; b. Phila., May 8, 1942; d. Ernest R. and Hildegard (Saul) Herbster; m. William Donald King, Aug. 17, 1972 (div. June 1978). Student Earlham Coll., 1960-62, Kunst Gewerbeschule, Lucerne, Switzerland, 1962-63, Ecole des Beaux Arts, Paris, 1963-64. Dir., Grove House Art Gallery, Miami, Fla., 1972-74; ptnr., dir. Miller and King Gallery, Miami, 1974-77; art columnist Lowe Mus. Mag., 1982-85; represented by galleries and art cons., N.Y.C., Miami, Chgo., Detroit, Atlanta, Washington, Boston, Dallas, 1977-85. One-man shows include Galeria El Bosco, Madrid, 1966, Woodstock Gallery, London, 1967; exhibited in group shows N.Y.C., San Francisco, Miami, New Orleans, Chgo., Caracas, Washington, Atlanta, 1970-85; represented in numerous pub. and pvt. collections. Mem. Artists Speak for Peace, Miami, bd. dirs. Mets., Coral Gables, Fla., 1977-80, Lowe Mus., 1980-82. Mem. Met. Mus. and Art Ctrs (various art awards), Miami Ctr. for Fine Arts, Whitney Mus. Am. Art., Nat. Found. Women in Arts. Democrat. Clubs: Grove Isle, Ensign Bitters (Coconut Grove, Fla.). Avocations: foreign languages; boating. Home and office: Box 715 Coconut Grove FL 33133

KING, FREDERIC WAYNE, museum director, zoologist; b. West Palm Beach, Fla., May 20, 1936; s. Frederic Worthington and Vera Hilda (Ashburner) K.; B.S., U. Fla., 1957, M.S., 1961; Ph.D., U. Miami (Fla.), 1966; m. Sharon Ray Frances Ryther, Sept. 20, 1965. Postdoctoral research asso. Fla. State Mus., Gainesville, 1966-67; asso. curator to curator herpetology N.Y. Zool. Soc., Bronx, 1967-75, chmn. edn. program, 1971-73, dir. conservation and environ. edn., 1973-75, dir. zoology and conservation, 1975-79; dir. Fla. State Mus., Gainesville, 1979—; prof. zoology, wildlife and Latin Am. studies U. Fla., 1979—. Fellow Herpetologists League; mem. Am. Soc. Ichthyologists and Herpetologists (gov. 1975-77, 79-83, chmn. com. environ. quality, 1973-75), Am. Assn. Mus., Internat. Council Mus., Soc. Study Amphibians and Reptiles, Am. Assn. Zool. Parks and Aquariums (chmn. wildlife conservation com. 1972-74), Am. Alligator Council, Internat. Union Conservation of Nature and Natural Resources (dep. chmn. species survival commn. 1978—, chmn. crocodile specialist group 1973-79, 81—), Assn. Systematics Collections (treas. 1981-84, v.p. 1984-85, pres. 1985—), Am. Com. Internat. Conservation (dir. 1975—, vice-chmn. 1976-78, chmn. 1978-81), Caribbean Conservation Corp. (chmn. conservation com. 1973-81), N.Y. Zool. Soc. (sci. fellow 1970—, conservation fellow 1979—), Rare Animal Relief Effort (trustee 1979-81), Sierra Club (internat. earthcare center adv. com. 1977—, tropical forest adv. com. 1977—). Decorated officer Order Golden Ark, 1981; recipient Am. Motors Corp. Conservation award, 1975. Contbr. articles to profl. jours.; speaker in field; mem. adv. panel Internat. Zoo Yearbook, 1972-79. Address: Fla State Mus U Fla Gainesville FL 32611

KING, HENRY HAYES, JR., business executive; b. Shreveport, La., July 12, 1932; s. Henry Hayes and Vashti Estell (Bullock) K.; m. Beverly Ann Farmer, June 16, 1956; children—Beverly Lynn, Thomas Bradford, David Earl. B.A., La. State U., 1956; postgrad., South Tex. Coll. Law, 1962; grad. Advanced Mgmt. Program, Harvard U., 1976. With Tex. Eastern Transmission Corp., Houston, 1958-76, dir. employee relations, 1971-72, dir. public relations, 1972-73, gen. mgr. human relations, 1973-74, gen. mgr. corp. adminstrv. staff, 1974, v.p. corp. adminstrv. staff, 1974-76; v.p. adminstrn. Tex. Eastern Corp., Houston, 1976-80, sr. v.p., chief adminstrv. officer, 1980-82, exec. v.p., 1982—. Bd. dirs. Jr. Achievement, Greater Houston Conv. and Visitors Council, Tex. Research League. Served to capt., inf. U.S. Army, 1956-58. Mem. Am. Compensation Assn., Am. Gas Assn., Am. Mgmt. Assn., Am. Soc. Personnel Adminstrn., Houston Personnel Assn., Houston World Trade Assn., Interstate Natural Gas Assn. Am., Nat. Assn. Corp. Dirs., Public Relations Soc. Am. Republican. Methodist. Clubs: Astrodome, Columns, Houston, Houston Center, Houston Racquet. Office: Tex Eastern Corp PO Box 2521 Houston TX 77001*

KING, JAMES LAWRENCE, federal judge; b. Miami, Fla., Dec. 20, 1927; s. James Lawrence and Viola (Clodfelter) K.; m. Mary Frances Kapa, June 1, 1961; children—Lawrence Daniel, Kathryn Ann, Karen Ann, Mary Virginia. B.A in Edn., U. Fla., 1949; LL.B., 1953. Bar: Fla. 1953. Assoc. Sibley & Davis, Miami, 1953-57; ptnr. Sibley, Giblin, King & Levenson, Miami, 1957-64; judge 11th Jud. Cir., Dade County, Miami, 1964-70; judge U.S. Dist. Ct. (so. dist.) Fla., Miami, 1970—, chief judge, 1984—; temporary assoc. justice Supreme Ct. Fla., 1965; temporary assoc. judge 2d, 3d, 4th Dist. Ct. Appeals, 1965-68; temporary judge U.S. Ct. Appeals (5th cir.), 1977, 78; chief judge U.S. Dist. Ct. for C.Z., 1977-78; mem. adv. commn. jud. activities Jud. Conf. U.S., 1973-76, mem. joint commn. code of jud. conduct, 1974-76, mem. commn. to consider standards for admission to practice in fed. cts., 1976-79, mem. com. on bankruptcy legislation, 1977-78, 11th cir. rep., 1984-85; mem. U.S. team studying English Civil Jud. Procedures, London, 1974. Mem. state exec. council U. Fla., 1956-59; mem. Bd. Control Fla. Governing State Univs. and Colls., 1964. Served to 1st lt. USAF, 1953-55. Recipient Outstanding Alumnus award U. Fla. Law Rev., 1980; elected to U. Fla. Hall of Fame. Mem. ABA, Am. Law Inst., Fla. Bar (pres. jr. bar sect. 1963-64, bd. govs. 1958-63, award of merit Young Lawyers sect. 1967), Inst. Jud. Adminstrn., Fla. Blue Key, Pi Kappa Tau, Phi Delta Phi. Democrat. Office: US Courthouse 301 N Miami Ave Miami FL 33128

KING, JEAN DOSTER, public relations executive; b. Monroe, Ga., Nov. 1, 1937; d. Jake Monroe and Flora Jean Doster; student U. Ala., Tuscaloosa, 1955-58; children—Jean Christiana King Whatley Donna Carole King. Editor, writer Mobile Press Register, 1963-69; dir. public affairs Delchamps, Inc., Mobile, 1969-77; pres., owner Jean King & Assos. Public Relations/Advt., Mobile, 1977—; mem. consumers affairs com. Food Mktg. Inst., 1970-77; chmn. Mobile County Nutrition Council, 1974-76. Publicity dir. Mobile County chpt. Nat. Found.-March of Dimes, 1964-68, also sec. bd. dirs.; mem., chmn. com. Mobile Bicentennial Community Com., 1975-76; bd. dirs. Sr. Citizens Services Mobile County, 1976-79; sec. bd. dirs. Mobile Public Parks and Recreation Bd., 1977-79; sec. Med. Clinic Bd. Mobile, 1985-87; mem. curriculum study com. Mobile County Public Sch. System, 1976; nat. civic chmn. U.S. Singletons, 1971-73, nat. mem.-at-large, 1971-73. Mem. Public Relations Soc. Am. (dir. Ala. chpt. 1979—), Women's Bus. Ownership Council SBA, Am. Advt. Fedn., Public Relations Council Ala. (pres. 1973-74), So. Public Relations Fedn. (charter mem., dir. 1972-76), Better Bus. Bur. S. Ala./N.W. Fla. (dir. 1973-77). Baptist. Home: 2316 E High Point Dr N Mobile AL 36609 Office: 716 Oak Circle Dr E Mobile AL 36609

KING, JERRY ALLAN, air transportation executive; b. San Antonio, Dec. 16, 1952; s. Roy Roxie and Angela (Hernandez) K.; m. Cynthia Lanford, Aug. 11, 1979 (div. 1983). B.B.A., Southwest Tex. State U., 1976. With mktg. dept. Western Union, Houston, 1976-77; with truck div. Southland Corp., Arlington, Tex., 1978-79, Memphis, 1979; dist. dealer mgr. Ryder Trucks, San Antonio, 1979-80; v.p. Assoc. Air Ctr., Dallas, 1983—; pres. Boca Inc., investments, 1982—. Chmn. Town of Addison Zoning Commn., 1982—. Mem. Nat. Bus. Aircraft Assn., Helicopter Internat. Assn., Alpha Kappa Psi. Republican. Episcopalian. Lodge: Rotary.

KING, JON BRADLEY, architectural construction manager, construction consultant; b. Abilene, Tex., July 17, 1942; s. Jack L. and Bessie Alene King; m. Holley Kathryn Purcell, Aug. 17, 1963; children—Jay Lawrence, Jim Steven, Jack Jeffrey. B.S. in Architecture, Tex. A&M U., 1965. Cert. profl. engr., Tex. Project supt. Warrior Constrn., Inc., Houston, 1968-71; project coordinator Hunt Building Corp., El Paso, 1971-73; project mgr. Leavell Devel. Co., El Paso, 1973-74; v.p., project mgr. Wilmac Constrn., Inc., Houston, 1974-78; pres. King & Assocs., Houston, 1978—; trustee King Trust Estate, Abilene, 1979—; v.p. Key Devel. Co., Houston, 1981—; v.p., dir. Key Devel. Co., Houston. Cubmaster, Sam Houston Area council Boy Scouts Am., 1974, scoutmaster, 1977-82, commr., 1976-81, bd. dirs., 1981. Served to capt. U.S. Army, 1965-68; served to maj. USAR, 1968-73. Recipient awards Eagle Scout award Boy Scouts Am., 1956, Explorer Silver award, 1958, Vigil Honor award, 1959, Silver Beaver award 1982. Fellow Am. Inst. Constructors; mem. Bldg. Ofcls. Assn. Tex. (bldg. ofcl. 1975—). Republican. Baptist (mem. sanctuary choir). Lodge: Masons. Home: 29100 Cedarwood Dr Spring TX 77381 Office: King & Assocs Inc 4422 FM 1960 West 100 Houston TX 77068

KING, JOSEPH DAIN, air force officer; b. Pitts., Oct. 3, 1939; s. Joseph James and Carolyn Jane (Dain) K.; m. Jean Stewart Thomas, Sept. 16, 1961; children—Steven John, Kristin Elizabeth. B.S. in Bus. magna cum laude, U. Md., 1974; M.B.A. in Mgmt., Eastern N.Mex. U., 1976. Commd. officer USAF, 1959, advanced through grades to lt. col., 1976; radar navigator SAC, Mont., Calif., Asia, 1959-69; flight comdr., Eng., N.Mex., 1970-77; chief current ops., Cannon AFB, N.Mex., 1977-78, wing exec. officer, 1978-80; comdr., dept. chmn. Air Force ROTC, Riverdale, N.Y., 1980-84; plans officer Tactical Air Control Ctr. Squadron, Shaw AFB, S.C., 1984—; adj. prof. Eastern N.Mex. U., Portales, 1976-79; prof. aerospace studies Manhattan Coll., Riverdale, 1980-84; advisor, moderator Soc. Am. Mil. Engrs., N.Y., 1980-84. Parish pres. Holy Name Soc., Glasgow, Mont., 1967-68; post advisor Allegheny council Boy Scouts Am., Pitts., 1958-59. Decorated Air medals; recipient Eagle Scout award Allegheny council Boy Scouts Am., 1957. Mem. Air Force Assn., Phi Kappa Phi, Alpha Sigma Lambda. Republican. Roman Catholic. Clubs: Early Ford V-8 (Calif.); Sumter Philatelic Soc. (S.C.). Lodge: Order of Arrow. Avocations: automobilia; philately. Home: 5625 B Persimmon St Shaw AFB SC 29152 Office: 507 Tactical Air Control Ctr Squadron Shaw AFB SC 29152

KING, KATHLEEN OLDENBURG, advertising agency executive; b. Wausau, Wis., Sept. 25, 1946; d. Harvey Kenneth and Alice Victoria (Ahlbom) Oldenburg; m. Robert Allen King, Feb. 25, 1978; 1 son, Travis Mitchell. Student St. Cloud State U., 1964-66. Prodn. mgr. Food Fair Markets, Los Angeles, 1966-70; art dir. Rio Hondo Valley Pub., Los Angeles, 1970-72; graphics cons., Los Angeles, 1970-74, Nat. Football League Properties, Los Angeles, 1974-78; mktg. dir. Vorwerk USA, Atlanta, 1979-80; creative dir. Informatics Gen. Corp., MCS Div., Atlanta, 1980-82; pres., owner Olio 2 Advt., Atlanta, 1982—; advt./pub. relations cons. United Way volunteer, 1970-74; active Air Force Sergeant's Aux., 1980—. Mem. Alpha Xi Delta. Republican. Contbr. articles to profl. jours.; art dir., title producer film The Ark of Noah, 1974. Home: 4546 Windsor Oaks Ct Marietta GA 30066 Office: PO Box 6432 Marietta GA 30065

KING, LAURISTON RACKLIFFE, marine research administrator, marine educator; b. Hartford, Conn., Mar. 24, 1943; s. Carl Clinton and Dawn Ardele (Dunphy) K.; m. Geraldine Bartley, June 12, 1965; children—Christopher Garrett, Paul Gregory, Brendan Carl. B.A., Tufts U., 1965; M.A., U. Conn., 1967, Ph.D., 1971. Inter-agy. liaison officer NSF, Washington, 1972-76; program mgr. marine sci. affairs, 1976-78; dep. dir. sea-grant coll. program Tex. A&M U., College Station, 1978—; cons. White House Office of Sci. and Tech. Policy, Washington, 1979-82. Author: Washington Lobbyists for Higher Education, 1975. Contbr. articles to profl. jours. Recipient Dissertation Research award NSF, 1968, postdoctoral fellowship award Woods Hole Oceanographic Instn., Mass., 1971-72; research grantee Tex. A&M Sea Grant Coll. Program, College Station, 1985. Mem. AAAS, Am. Polit. Sci. Assn., So. Polit. Sci. Assn. (best conv. paper award 1983), Marine Tech. Soc. Democrat. Methodist. Club: Royal Oaks Raquet (Bryan, Tex.). Avocations: jogging; reading; gardening. Office: Sea Grant Program Tex A & M U College Station TX 77843

KING, LOWELL RESTELL, pediatric urologist, educator; b. Salem, Ohio, Feb. 28, 1932; s. Lowell Waldo and Vesta Ethelwyn (Snyder) K.; m. Mary Elizabeth Hill, July 9, 1960; children—Andrew R., Erika L. B.A., Johns Hopkins U., 1953, M.D., 1956. Diplomate Am. Bd. Urology (examiner, past trustee). Intern Johns Hopkins U., Balt., 1956-57; resident in urology Johns Hopkins U., 1957-62; chmn. div. urology Children's Meml. Hosp., Chgo., 1963-81; prof. urology Northwestern U., Chgo., 1963-81; prof. urology, head sect. pediatric urology Duke U., Durham, N.C., 1981—. Warden Episcopal Ch. of Our Savior, Chgo., 1977-81. Mem. Am. Acad. Pediatrics (co-founder, past pres. sect. urology), Soc. Pediatric Urology (past pres.), Am. Urol. Assn., N.C. Med. Soc., N.C. Urol. Soc., ACS, Am. Assn. Genitourinary Surgeons, Clin. Soc. Genitourinary Surgeons, Soc. Univ. Urologists, Durham Wildlife Club. Republican. Club: Chgo. Athletic Assn. Contbr. numerous articles to profl. jours.; author chpts. in texts. Co-editor Clinical Pediatric Urology, 1976, 2d edit., 1984; Bladder Reconstruction and Continent Urinary Diversion, 1986. Office: Duke Univ Med Ctr PO Box 3831 Durham NC 27710

KING, LULA TASSIN, social work educator; b. New Orleans, Sept. 15, 1941; d. August and Henrietta (Clark) Tassin; m. Joe King, Aug. 23, 1969; 1 child, Tareson. B.A., So. U., 1963; M.A., Atlanta U., 1966; M.S.W., Mich., 1973, Ph.D., 1975. Mem. faculty Tuskegee Inst., Ala., 1966-69, Ft. Valley State U., Ga., 1969-70, Jackson State U., Jackson, Miss., 1975—. Mem. bd. dirs. United Way, Jackson, 1982. Mem. Nat. Assn. Social Work, Council on Social Work Edn., Nat. Council on Family Relations. Democrat. Roman Catholic. Home: 921 Wynwood Dr Jackson MS 39209 Office: Jackson State U 1325 Lynch St Jackson MS 39217

KING, MARJORIE SOMMERLYN, medical photographer; b. Conway, S.C., June 22, 1925; s. Bernard St. Lawrence and Mary Essie (Lupo) Sommerlyn; student Coker Coll., 1943-45; m. John L. King, Jan. 11, 1945; children—John Bernard, William Lawrence, Mary Elizabeth. Photopprinter for editor bus. pages Miami Daily News, 1954; owner, operator King's Portrait Studio, Conway, S.C., 1956-58; clk. bacteriol. lab. Jackson Meml. Hosp., Miami, 1963-65; photo lab. technician biomed. communications dept. U. Miami Med. Sch., 1965-67, photo lab. technician II, 1967-70, photographer III trainee, 1970-72, photographer III, 1973-76, photographer III supr., 1977-80; ret., 1985; owner M.S. King Enterprises, 1985—. Den mother Boy Scouts Am. Recipient Golden Key award Boy Scouts Am., 1957. Mem. Biol. Photog. Assn., DAR, UDC. Democrat. Episcopalian. Clubs: Miami Yacht, Coconut Grove Sailing (C gull pres.), West End Pool Aquatic (pres.). Home: 8035 SW 17th St Miami FL 33155 Office: PO Box 520875 Miami FL 33152

KING, PAUL HARVEY, engineering educator; b. Ft. Wayne, Ind., Sept. 4, 1941; s. Arthur Ward and Mildred Elizabeth (Kahse) K.; m. Carolyn Sue McGhee; 1 child, Paul Erin; m. Margaret-Gail Ruhl; children—Kelsey, Sarah-Melissa; m. Betty Sue Freeman, Mar. 27, 1982; 1 child, Elizabeth Chance. B.S., Case Inst. Tech., 1963, M.S., 1965; Ph.D., Vanderbilt U., 1968. Registered prof. engr., Tenn. Assoc. prof. biomed. and mech. engring. Vanderbilt U., 1965—; research scientist Oak Ridge Associated Univs., 1968-69. cons. in field. Contbr. aticles to profl. jours. Patentee multi-crystal tomography. Organizer, mem. Williamson County Rescue Squad, Franklin, Tenn., 1979-81. Mem. Am. Soc. Engring. Edn., Assn. for Advancement of Med. Instrumentation, Sigma Xi, Mensa. Republican. Unitarian. Avocations: photography; gardening. Home: 432 Rembrandt Dr Old Hickory TN 37138 Office: Electrical and Biomedical Engineering Vanderbilt U PO Box 1631 Station B Nashville TN 37235

KING, RICHARD FRANCIS, safety engineer; b. West Point, N.Y., July 19, 1948; s. John Rochford and Mary Catherine (Martindale) K.; m. Susan Kathleen Ashley, Sept. 16, 1968; children—Kristan, Tara. B.A., Black Hills State Coll., 1971; postgrad. U. S.D., 1971-73, Mine Safety and Health Acad., 1975-76. Miner 1st class Homestake Mining Co., Lead, S.D., 1966-76; parole agt. S.D. Div. Corrections, Sioux Falls, 1975-76; supr. mine safety Mine Safety Health Adminstrn., U.S. Dept. Labor, Denver, 1975-82; loss control mgr. Black & Veatch, Engrs., Architects, Orlando, Fla., 1982—. Mem. Western S.D. Crime Commn., Rapid City, 1974. Recipient Spl. Achievement award U.S. Dept. Interior, 1977, U.S. Dept. Labor, 1978-80, Outstanding Mgr. award Dept. Labor, 1981. Mem. Am. Soc. Safety Engrs., Colo. Safety Assn., Central Fla. Safety Assn., Fla. Bus. Round Table. Republican. Roman Catholic. Club: Synergist (Orlando). Lodge: Elks. Avocations: coin collecting, boating. Home: 4118 Teriwood Ave Orlando FL 32806 Office: Black & Veatch Engrs Architects PO Box 27519 Orlando FL 32867

KING, ROBERT HARLEN, college administrator, educator; b. McCook, Nebr., Feb. 2, 1935; s. Floyd E. and Lola M. (Banta) K.; m. Sandra Lee Cooney, 1961; children—Paul Daniel, Jennifer Ann. B.A., Harvard U., 1957; postgrad. Edinburgh U., Scotland, 1957-58; B.D., Ph.D., Yale U., 1965; postdoctoral Oxford U., Eng., 1967-68. Asst. instr. Yale U., New Haven, 1961-63; prof. philosophy and religion DePauw U., Greencastle, Ind., 1963-80, asst. to pres., 1977-79; v.p., acad. dean Millsaps Coll., Jackson, Miss., 1980—. Author: Meaning of God, 1973; editor: Christian Theology, 1982, Readings in Christian Theology, 1985; contbr. articles to profl. jours. Danforth fellow, 1957-62, Rotary fellow, 1957-58, NEH jr. fellow, 1967-68. Mem. Am. Acad. Religion, Am. Assn. Higher Edn., Soc. Values Higher Edn., Phi Beta Kappa. Methodist. Avocations: golf; travel. Home: Millsaps Coll 1701 N State St Jackson MS 39210

KING, ROBERT HOWARD, publisher; b. Excelsior Springs, Mo., June 28, 1921; s. Howard and Nancy Eaton (Henry) K.; student Kenyon Coll., Gambier, Ohio, 1942; m. Marjorie Kerr, Feb. 26, 1966; children—John McFeeley, Mary Nan, Sarah Ann. Vice pres. sales Ency. Brit., Chgo., 1946-61; pres. Spencer Internat. Press, Chgo., 1961-66; v.p. Dill Clitherow & Co., Palatine, Ill., 1966-68; pres. Time-Life Libraries, Palatine, 1968-79; chmn. bd., chief exec. officer World Book-Childcraft Internat., Inc., Chgo., 1979-83, vice chmn., 1983—; past pres. consumer Mktg. Services Inc., 1983. Chmn. bd. Direct Selling Ednl. Found. Served to capt. AUS, 1942-46. Mem. Direct Selling Assn. (past chmn. bd.), World Fedn. Direct Selling Assns. (past chmn. bd.), Sales and Mktg. Execs. Internat., Clubs: Meadow; Chicago, Chgo. Yacht; Arts (Chgo.); Lighthouse Point Yacht (Fla.); Ocean Reef (Key Largo, Fla.). Home: 3750 NE 26th Ave Lighthouse Point FL 33064 Office: 3440 Hollywood Blvd Suite 320 Hollywood FL 33021

KING, ROBERT LEE, biology educator; b. Whiteville, N.C., Aug. 11, 1938; s. Malcolm M. and Minnie (Brown) K.; m. Janis Pigott, Dec. 22, 1960; children—Robert LeRoy, Gina Dawn, John Malcolm. A.B., Elon Coll., 1960; M.A., Appalachian State Coll., 1961. Assoc. prof. biology Coll. of Albemarle, Elizabeth City, N.C., 1961-65; prof. biology Southeastern Community Coll., Whiteville, 1965—, chmn. sci. div., 1965—, pres. coll. faculty senate, 1979. Lodges: Civitan (pres. 1978), Masons (chaplain 1967-68). Avocations: organic gardening, photography. Home: 215 Ole Farm Trail Whiteville NC 28472 Office: Southeastern Community Coll PO Box 151 Whiteville NC 28472

KING, ROBERT LEROY, business administration educator, college administrator; b. Decatur, Ga., Jan. 22, 1931; s. John Todd and Charlotte (Stringer) K.; m. Helen Butler Leaptrott, Mar. 25, 1956; children—Robert Todd, Keith Alan, John Christopher. B.B.A., U. Ga., 1952; M.A., Mich. State U., 1953, Ph.D., 1960. Asst. prof. mktg. U. S.C., Columbia, 1957-61, assoc. prof., 1961-65; prof. mktg. Va. Poly. Inst. and State U., Blacksburg, 1965-82, head dept., 1969-76; prof. bus. adminstrn., head dept. The Citadel, Charleston, S.C., 1982-85, Robert A. Jolley prof. bus. adminstrn., 1985—; cons. in field; vis. researcher Warsaw Tech. U., Acad. Econs. in Wroclaw (Poland); overseas tchr. in field. Served to maj. USAR, 1953-76. Grantee Ford Found., 1964-65, Va. Poly. Inst. and State U., 1979-82, Citadel Devel. Found., 1982-86. Mem. Am. Acad. Advt., Am. Mktg. Assn., Acad. Mktg. Sci., Assn. for Consumer Research, Acad. Internat. Bus., Am. Assn. for Advancement Slavic Studies, So. Conf. Slavic Studies, So. Mktg. Assn. Baptist. Contbr. numerous articles in bus. adminstrn. to profl. jours; author: An Annotated Index to the Proceedings of the American Marketing Association Educators' Conferences, 1973, 80; Procs: Southern Marketing Association 1973 Conference, 1974; Marketing and the New Science of Planning, 1969. Book rev. editor Jour. Advt. Home: 639 McCutchen St Charleston SC 29412 Office: Dept Bus Adminstrn The Citadel Charleston SC 29409

KING, ROLLIN WHITE, executive recruiting consultant; b. Cleve., Apr. 10, 1931; s. Warren Griffin and Elizabeth (White) K.; student Cornell U., Ithaca, N.Y., 1950-54; B.A., Western Res. U., 1955; M.B.A., Harvard U., 1962; m. Mary Ella Ownby Dewar, July 5, 1976; children—Rollin White, Edward Prescott. Mem. mgmt. staff NSA, Washington, 1955-60; v.p. King, Pitman Co., investment counsel, San Antonio, 1962-63; pres. Southwest Airlines, Inc., San Antonio, 1963-68; founder, 1st pres., dir. Southwest Airlines Co., Dallas, 1967—; partner King Investments Co., Dallas, 1978—; exec. dir. Russell Reynolds Assocs., Inc., Dallas, 1983—; cons. air transp. Dept. Communication Royal Thai Govt., Bangkok, 1969. Served with AUS, 1956-58. Clubs: Brook Hollow Golf; Dallas, Dallas Gun; Wings (N.Y.C.). Home: 4417 S Versailles Dallas TX 75205 Office: 1900 LTV Center 2001 Ross Ave Dallas TX 75201

KING, THOMAS WADE, former air force officer, telephone company representative; b. Dalton, Ga., Jan. 11, 1938; s. Thomas Ford and Bertha Evelyn (Wade) K.; m. Elizabeth Anne Robinson, Dec. 21, 1965; children—Christopher Robinson, Sarah Caroline. B.S. in Social Sci./Econs., Fla. State U., 1962; M.A. in Speech Communication, U. Okla., 1973. Commd. 2d lt., U.S. Air Force, 1962, advanced through grades to maj., 1977; hosp. adminstr. USAF Hosp., Wiesbaden, W.Ger., 1964-67, O'Hare Internat. Airport, Chgo., 1967-69; pub. affairs officer Aerospace Med. Div., Brooks AFB, Tex., 1970-73, Kwang Ju Air Base, Korea, 1973-74, 463d Tactical Airlift Wing, Dyess AFB, Tex., 1974-75, 437th Mil. Airlift Wing, Charleston (S.C.) AFB, 1975-78, 20th N.Am. Air Def. Region, Ft. Lee (Va.) Air Force Sta., 1979-80; with Internal Info. div. Tactical Air Command Office Pub. Affairs, Langley AFB, Va., 1981-82, chief community relations, 1983; ret., 1983; community relations rep. Continental Telephone of Va., Mechanicsville, 1984—. Pres. Booker Elem. PTA, 1981-83; com. chmn. Boy Scouts Am., Langley AFB, 1982-83, Mechanicsville, 1984—; mem. coms. Richmond, Charleston chambers of commerce, 1977-80, active United Way Vol. Action Ctr., 1978, San Antonio Alamo Regional Sci. Fair, 1971-72; exec. Korean-Am. Friendship Council, Gwang San County, Korea, 1974; mem. Trident 2000 Land-Use Adv. Council, Charleston, 1977. Decorated Meritorious Service medal with 2 oak leaf clusters, Air Force Commendation medal with oak leaf cluster; citation Mil. Airlift Command, 1979; named Pacific Air Forces Pub. Affairs Officer of Yr., 1974. Mem. Pub. Relations Soc. Am., Richmond Pub. Relations Assn., Charleston Advt. Fedn. (dir. 1978). Methodist. Home: 610 Thrasher Way Mechanicsville VA 23111 Office: Continental Telephone of Va PO Box 900 Mechanicsville VA 23111

KING, WALTER BLACKBURN, JR., physician, surgeon; b. Seguin, Tex., Feb. 13, 1916; s. Walter B. and Ida C. (Stamps) K.; m. Anna Margaret Willoughby, June 7, 1941; children—Anne W. King Wood, Walter B. III, Margaret M. King Hendrix. B.A., Baylor U., 1936; M.D., U. Tex.-Galveston, 1940. Diplomate Am. Bd. Surgery. Intern, Kans. City (Mo.) Gen. Hosp., 1940-41; resident in pathology U. Tex. Med. Br.-Galveston, 1946, resident in surgery, 1946-50; practice gen. surgery, Waco, Tex., 1950—; mem. staff Hillcrest Baptist Med. Center, 1950—, chief of staff, 1956; mem. staff Providence Hosp., 1950—, chief of staff, 1965. Served to maj. M.C., AUS, 1941-45; PTO. Mem. McLennan County Med. Soc. (pres. 1969), Tex. Med. Assn., So. Med. Assn., AMA, ACS (pres. N. Tex. chpt. 1984), Tex. Surg. Soc. (pres. 1967), Southwestern Surg. Congress, Singleton Surg. Soc. (pres. 1965), So. Surg. Assn. Contbr. articles to med. jours. Home: 2323 Cedar Ridge Rd Waco TX 76708 Office: Hillcrest Med Tower Suite 205 3115 Pine Ave Waco TX 76708

KINI, SARVOTHAM, physician, surgeon; b. Mangalore, India, Dec. 18, 1944; came to U.S., 1971; s. Upendra and Sumitra (Shendy) K.; m. Shyamala Kamath, Oct. 25, 1970; children—Sunil, Rajesh. M.B. B.S., Karnataka Med. Coll., Hubli, India, 1967. Diplomate Am. Bd. Surgery. Practice medicine specializing in surgery, McKenzie, Tenn., 1977-78, Humboldt, Tenn., 1978-80, Hendersonville, Tenn., 1980-85, Nashville, 1985—. Fellow ACS, Internat. Coll. Surgeons, Southeastern Surg. Soc. Hindu. Avocations: tennis, photography. Home: 94 Valleybrook Dr Hendersonville TN 37075 Office: Miller Med Group 1616 Hayes St Nashville TN 37203

KINLOCH, GRAHAM CHARLES, sociology educator; b. Mutare, Zimbabwe, Oct. 29, 1943; s. Denis Thomas and Isabel Mary (Donaldson) K.; m. Beverley Gale Smith, Dec. 12, 1964; children—Marc, Andrew. B.A., U. Otago, 1963; M.S., Purdue U., 1966, Ph.D., 1968. Lectr. sociology U. Natal, 1968, sr. lectr., 1969-70; asst. prof. sociology U. Hawaii, 1970-71; assoc. prof. Fla. State U., Tallahassee, 1971-75, prof., 1975—. Grantee U. Natal Research Com., 1968-69, U. Hawaii Research Council, 1970-71, Am. Philos. Soc., 1972-74; recipient Best Tchr. award, dept. sociology Fla. State U., 1983. Mem. So. Sociol. Soc., Pi Gamma Mu, Delta Tau Kappa. Author: The Dynamics of Race Relations, 1974; Sociological Theory, 1977; Racial Conflict in Rhodesia, 1978; The Sociology of Minority Group Relations, 1979; Ideology and Contemporary Sociological Theory, 1981; Race and Ethnic relations: An Annotated Bibliography, 1984. Contbr. articles and revs. to profl. jours. Office: Fla State U Sociology Dept Tallahassee FL 32306

KINNE, FRANCES BARTLETT, university president; b. Story City, Iowa, May 23; d. Charles Morton and Bertha (Olson) Bartlett; student edn. U. No. Iowa, 1936; B.Mus.Edn., Drake U., 1940, M. Mus. Edn., 1944, D.F.A. (hon.), 1981; Ph.D. cum laude, U. Frankfurt (Germany), 1957; L.H.D. (hon.), Wagner Coll., S.I., N.Y.; LL.D. (hon.), Lenore Rhyne Coll., N.C.; m. Harry L. Kinne, Jr., June 24, 1948. Tchr. music kelley (Iowa) Consol. Sch., 1936-37; music supr. Boxholm (Iowa) Consol. Sch., 1937-40, Des Moines pub. schs., 1940-43; sr. hostess Camp Crowder, Mo., 1943-46; recreation dir. VA, Wadsworth, Kans., 1946-48; lectr. music, English, also Western culture Tsuda Coll., Tokyo, 1949-50; music cons. U.S. Army Gen. Hdqrs., Tokyo, 1950-51; mem. faculty Jacksonville U., 1958—, prof. music and humanities, 1963—, dean Coll. Fine Arts, 1961—, interim pres., 1979, pres., 1979—, Disting. Univ. prof., 1961-62; dir., mem. salary rev. com. Barnett Banks of Fla. Mem. adv. council Nat. Soc. Arts and Letters; bd. dirs. Assn. Am. Colls., Jacksonville Symphony-Women's Guild, Drake U.; trustee Greater Jacksonville Com. Found., Ballet Repertory Group of Jacksonville; mem. bd., exec. com. Found. for Sight; bd. govs. Gator Bowl Assn.; charter mem. adv. bd. Greater Jacksonville Community Found.; mem. U.S. Senate Edn. Adv. Com.; resource mem. Heritage Found.; mem. panel to assess sch. busing Duval County; mem. adv. com. Arts Assembly Festival; mem. Commn. on Recreation and Culture, Mayor's Commn. Status of Women. Recipient hon. awards Bus. and Profl. Women's Clubs, 1962; Disting. Service award Drake U., 1966; 1st Fla. Gov.'s award for achievement in arts, 1972; EVE award in edn., 1973, named Eve of the Decade, 1970-80; Arts Assembly Individual award, 1978-79; Brotherhood award NCCJ, 1981; Roast award Soc. for Prevention of Blindness, 1980; Top Mgmt. award Jacksonville Sales and Mktg. Execs., 1981; Disting. Service award U. No. Iowa; Burton C. Bryan Meml. award; Day in her honor Women's Club of Jacksonville and other orgns.; named to Internat. Inner Wheel, River Club Hall of Fame; Paul Harris fellow Rotary Found. Mem. AAUW, Nat., Fla. music tchrs. assns., Assn. Am. Colls. (chmn. exec. com., chm. resolutions com.), Ind. Colls. and Univs. of Fla. (vice chmn.), Music Educators Nat. Conf., Fla. Music Edn. Assn. (past dir.), Friday Musicale, Fla. Coll. Music Edn. Assn. (past pres., v.p.), Delius Assn. of Fla., Fla. Council of Arts, Nat. Assn. Schs. Music (past chmn. region 7), Jacksonville C. of C. (dir., speakers bur., past gov., chmn. fine arts com., mem. com. of 100), Internat. Council Fine Arts Deans (past chmn., chmn. fed. liaison com.), Jacksonville Women's Network, Order Eastern Star, P.E.O., Green Key (hon.), Navy League U.S., Inner Wheel (hon.), Alpha Xi Delta, Mu Phi Epsilon (judge Internat. Music Edn. award), Alpha Psi Omega (hon.), Alpha Kappa Psi (hon.), Omicron Delta Kappa, Beta Gamma Sigma (hon.). Clubs: St. John's Dinner (past pres.), Women's of Jacksonville (program com.). Author: A Comparative Study of British Traditional and American Indigenous Ballads, 1958; Music, Moon and Man, 1970; contbr. chpt. to book, articles to profl. jours. Home: 7304 Arrow Point Trail S Jacksonville FL 32211

KINNER, CLARA WEBB, public relations executive; b. Lexington, Ky., Dec. 5, 1946; d. Earl Warnock and Delia (Webb) Kinner; m. Dan L. Lamkin, June 1, 1968 (div. Jan. 1985). B.A., U. Ky., 1974. Staff asst. Ky. Fried Chicken Co., Louisville, 1974-75, mgr. press relations, dir. pub. affairs, 1981—; exec. dir. Louisville Zool. Soc., 1976-78; account exec., account supr. Jack Guthrie & Assocs., Louisville, 1978-81. Recipient Tribute to Women in Internat. Industry award Nat. YWCA, 1984. Mem. Women in Communication (hon. mention Clarion award 1979), Pub. Relations Soc. Am., LWV, Louisville Area C. of C., Leadership La., Third Century. Democrat. Methodist. Home: PO Box 32070 Louisville KY 40232 Office: 1441 Gardiner Ln Louisville KY 40232

KINNEY, ABBOTT FORD, radio broadcasting exec.; b. Los Angeles, Nov. 11, 1909; s. Gilbert Earl and Mabel (Ford) K.; student Ark. Coll., 1923, 26, 27; m. Dorothy Lucille Jeffers, Sept. 19, 1943; children—Colleen, Joyce, Rosemary. Editor Dermott News, 1934-39; partner Delta Drug Co., 1940-49; pres., gen. mgr. S.E. Ark. Broadcasters, Inc., Dermott and McGhee, 1951—; corr. Comml. Appeal, Memphis, Ark. Gazette, Little Rock, 1935-53; research early aeronautics Inst. Aero. Scis., 1941; castor bean prodn., 1941-42; mem. bd. McGhee-Dermott Indsl. Devel. Corp. Mem. Ark. Geol. and Conservation Commn., 1959-63, Ark. State Planning Commn. 1963—; mem. Miss. River Parkway Commn.; exec. bd. DeSoto Area Council Boy Scouts Am.; past pres. Hosp. Adv. Bd.; mem. Chicot Fair Assn. Bd., Park Commn.; chmn. Chicot County Library Bd. Recipient Silver Beaver award Boy Scouts Am.; State Community Leader Ark. C. of C., 1968, Man of Year, 1978. Mem. Nat. Assn. Radio and TV Broadcasters, Ark. Broadcasters Assn. Ark. (charter mem. Ark. Econ. Council), S.E. Ark. (charter) chambers commerce, Ark. Hist. Assn. (charter), Am. Numis. Assn., AIM, Chicot County Hist. Soc. (charter). Rotarian (past pres., sec.). Adv. editorial bd. Internat. Broadcasters Soc. Home: PO Box 111 Dermott AR 71638 Office: Dermott AR 71638 also McGhee AR 71654

KINSER, DONALD LEROY, materials science educator; b. Loudon, Tenn., Sept. 28, 1941; s. Fred D. and Annie (Watkins) K.; m. Barbara Lange, June 10, 1964; children—Elizabeth, Cynthia. B.S., U. Fla., 1964, Ph.D., 1968. Asst. prof. materials sci. Vanderbilt U., Nashville, 1968-71, assoc. prof., 1971-76, prof., 1976—; cons. in field. Contbr. articles to profl. publs. Patentee in field. Recipient NATO Sr. Postdoctoral award, 1973, Cert. Recognition NASA, 1976, 80. Mem. AAAS, Am. Ceramic Soc., Am Soc. Engring. Edn., Soc. Glass Tech., Internat. Soc. Optical Engring., Internat. Soc. Hybrid Microelectronics, Nat. Inst. Ceramic Engrs., Nat. Soc. Profl. Engrs., Sigma Xi, Sigma Tau. Home: 1306 Winchester Rd Brentwood TN 37027 Office: Vanderbilt U Box 1689-B Nashville TN 37235

KINSEY, ROBERT CHARLES, food broker, consultant; b. Amarillo, Tex., Aug. 8, 1940; s. Delbert Colonel and Gracie Louise (Whiteside) K.; children—Robert Cayton, Michael Sterling, Lezlie Denise. Student Eastern N.Mex. U., 1962-63, West Tex. State U., 1966—; B.B.A. in Mktg., Tex. Tech U., 1967. Warehouse foreman refinery Holly Sugar Corp., Hereford, Tex., 1964-66, mktg. rep., product mgr., Colorado Springs, 1967-70, western distbn. mgr., San Mateo, Calif., 1970-71; asst. prodn. mgr. See's Candies, South San Francisco, Calif., 1971-73; co-owner, sec., treas., v.p. Oliver Taylor Co., Dallas, 1973-83; owner Kinsington Ltd., Dallas, 1983—. Mem. No. Tex. chpt. Nat. Multiple Sclerosis Soc. Mem. Dallas Food Broker Assn. (pres. 1982), Nat. Food Brokers Assn. (regional rep. 1983), Tex. Retail Grocers Assn., Tex. Bottlers Assn., Allied Food Club. Club: Los Rios Country.

KINSLEY, GERALD WENDALL, geologist; b. Crocker, Mo., Dec. 10, 1932; s. Ray Noah and Minnie May (Daniels) K.; m. Norma Louise Carmack, May 28, 1955; children—Stephen C., Gregory A., Pamela D. B.A. in Geology, U. Mo.-Columbia, 1958, M.A. in Geology, 1960. Geologist, Texaco, Inc., Jackson, Miss., 1960-62, dist. devel. geologist, 1962-63, exploration geologist, 1963-68, dist. computer geologist, New Orleans, 1968-70; gen. ptnr., exploration geologist Janoex Co., Jackson, 1970; exploration geologist Lone Star Producing Co., Jackson, 1970-72; dist. geologist, exploration mgr. 1972-74; ind. cons. geologist, Jackson, 1974-80; pres., chmn. Kinsley Corp., Jackson, 1980—. Bd. dirs. Southwest YMCA, Jackson, 1972-74; chmn. bd. deacons Alta Woods Baptist Ch., Jackson, 1984—. Served to cpl. U.S. Army, 1953-55. Fellow U. Mo., 1958-60. Mem. Am. Assn. Petroleum Geologists (ho. of dels. 1974, cert.), Miss. Geol. Soc., Miss. Assn. Petroleum Landmen, Jackson Geophys. Soc. Republican. Clubs: Capital City Petroleum, Shady Oaks Country (Jackson). Lodge: Masons. Avocations: golfing; skiing; fishing; traveling. Home: 547 Heatherwood Dr Jackson MS 39212 Office: Kinsley Corp 515 Yazoo St Jackson MS 39201

KINZEY, OUIDA BLACKERBY, retired mathematics educator, photographer, photo journalist; b. Leeds, Ala., Feb. 6, 1922; d. George W. and Kate (Spruiell) Blackerby; m. William Thomas Kinzey, Feb. 6, 1943. A.B., Birmingham So. Coll., 1942, Ed.M., 1959; advanced profl. diploma U. Ala., 1964. Math. tchr. Phillips High Sch., Birmingham, Ala., 1942-44, Humes High Sch., Memphis, 1944-45; chmn. math. dept. Woodlawn High Sch., Birmingham, 1945-69; assoc. prof. math. Birmingham So. Coll., 1969-84, prof. emeritus, 1984—, dir. vis. profs. program, 1971-75; cons., lectr., speaker, workshop dir. throughout SE. Author audio-visual text Creative Teaching Mathematically, 1973; author, photographer of photographic essays. Photographic exhibit one man shows include Birmingham-So. Coll., 1984, Samford U., 1984, Med. Ctr. E., 1985. Grantee NSF, 1959, 61, 64, 71, Kellogg Found., 1978, Mellon Found., 1980, 81, 84, Title III, 1982; recipient Grand Nat. award NEA/Kodak, 1984; named Outstanding Educator of Am., 1972. Mem. Ala. Assn. Coll. Tchrs. Math., Ala. Acad. Sci., United Daus. Confederacy, AAUW, Nat. Council Tchrs. Math., Math. Assn. Am., Ala. Edn. Assn., Ala. Poetry Soc. Ala. Writers' Conclave, Am. Math. Soc., Nat. League Am. PEN Women, Phi Beta Kappa, Kappa Delta Pi, Delta Kappa Gamma, Kappa Delta Epsilon, Kappa Mu Epsilon, Theta Sigma Lambda, Delta Phi Alpha, Alpha Lambda Delta. Club: Speech Arts (pres., v.p., sec., treas.). Democrat. Methodist. Avocations: Photography; rock and Indian artifact collector; antique collector. Home: 1413 Swallow Ln Birmingham AL 35213 Office: Birmingham So Coll Box A-32 800 8th Ave W Birmingham AL 35254

KIPFER, DIANA LYNN, art director, graphic designer; b. Houston, Feb. 15, 1957; d. Allen Russel and Jane Alice (Rogers) Matthews; m. Joe Edwin, Kipfer, July 18, 1981. B.S. in Advt., U. Tex.-Austin, 1979. Sec., Tex. Dept. Labor and Standards, Austin, 1978; asst. art dir. Page Advt., Austin, 1979; art dir. West & Co., Advt., San Antonio, 1979; art dir. Smitherman Graphic Design, Austin, 1980-82; owner, art dir., designer Diana Kipfer Advt. & Design, Austin, 1982—. Recipient award of excellence Dallas Soc. Visual Communications, 1978; cert. of excellence Houston Ad Dirs. Club, 1978; award of excellence Dallas Soc. Visual Communications, 1979; award of merit Austin Advt. Club, 1980, 81, 83, Gold award, 1982, best of show and gold Addy award for brochure design, 1985; merit awards for internal publs. Best of Austin show, 1983, for color photography, cover design and overall publ., 1984, best award for poster design, merit award for color photography, merit award for internal publ. design, 1985; Mitchell A. Wilder award Tex. Assn. Mus. Mem. Am. Inst. Graphic Artists, Austin Graphic Arts Soc. (silver medal for brochure design 1985), Internat. Assn. Bus. Communicators. Democrat. Episcopalian. Home and office: 5307 Peacedale Ln Austin TX 78723

KIPLEY, DONALD E., hardware products company executive; b. 1923. Student, DePauw U., 1950, Harvard U., 1974. With U.S. Navy, 1943-45; with Gardner-Denver Co., 1951-79 as v.p., gen. mgr. indsl. machine div.; pres. Cooper Industries Machine Group, Houston, 1980-81, v.p. ops., 1981-82, exec. v.p. ops., drilling equipment, 1982—. Address: Cooper Industries Inc PO Box 4446 Houston TX 77210*

KIPP, GERALD BURTON, government official; b. Moline, Ill., July 27, 1937; s. Conrad W. Kipp and Ruth Elizabeth (Giles) Lindbeck; m. Gretchen Gay, Dec. 17, 1959; children—Kelly Kay, Jacquelyn. B.A., St. Ambrose Coll., 1962; postgrad. La. State U., 1973-74; M.A., Central Mich. U., 1980. Cert. profl. contract mgr. Bus. agt. Meatcutters Union, Davenport, Iowa, 1966-74; owner, mgr. meat market, Moline, 1966; contract specialist U.S. Army, Rock Island, Ill., 1966-72, chief contract mgmt., 1972-83; dir. contract div. U.S. Navy, Charleston, S.C., 1983—. Med. Fed. Execs. Assn. Lodge: Elks. Avocations: tennis; fishing; hunting; water sports. Home: 150 Mellard Dr Goose Creek SC 29445 Office: So Div Naval Facilities Engring Command 2155 Eagle Dr Charleston SC 29411-0068

KIPP, PATRICIA THOMPSON, public relations practitioner; b. Portsmouth, Va., Aug. 1, 1949; d. Lewis Henry and Anne Elizabeth (Hill) Thompson; m. Larry J. Kipp, Jan. 15, 1982. B.A., U. South Fla., 1984. Asst. buyer Vogue Shops, Jacksonville, Fla., 1970; retail fashion buyer Purcells, Inc., Jacksonville, 1973; sales mgr. Casual Corner, Jacksonville, 1974; pub. affairs asst. Gen. Telephone Co. Fla., Tampa, 1979, pub. affairs rep., 1980, sr. pub. affairs rep., 1981; pres., owner Kipp & Assocs., Inc., Pub. Relations, Tampa, Fla., 1982—; pres. Kipp & Assocs., Interior Design & Devel. Mem. Friends of the Arts, Tampa Com. of 100, Tampa Mus., pub. relations com. Mus. Sci. and Industry. Recipient Award of Merit, 1980, Award of Excellence, 1981, 82, Internat. Assn. Bus. Communicators. Mem. Pub. Relations Soc. Am. (dir. local chpt.), Internat. Assn. Bus. Communicators (dist. v.p., past pres. and dir. local chpt.), Nat. Assn. Women Bus. Owners. Lodge: Order of Rainbow for Girls (Jacksonville, Fla.). Creator numerous brochures, posters, video programs, 1979—. Home: 12514 Clendenning Drive Tampa FL 33624 Office: Kipp & Assocs One Tampa City Ctr 19th Floor Tampa FL 33602

KIRALY, BRUCE ALEXANDER, optometrist; b. Cleve., Mar. 29, 1952; s. Alexander William and Helen Judith (Daroczy) K. B.S. in Chem. Engring., Purdue U., 1974; O.D., U. Ala., 1982. Lic. optometrist, Va. Staff engr. Standard Oil Co. Ohio, Cleve., 1974-77; staff process engr. Columbia Nitrogen Corp., Augusta, Ga., 1977-78; pvt. practice optometry, Richmond, Va., 1982—. Active Meals on Wheels. Mem. Am. Optometric Soc., Va. Optometric Soc., Richmond Optometric Soc. Presbyterian. Lodge: Lions. Office: 3601 Grove Ave Richmond VA 23221

KIRBY, DAVID D., oil company executive, optometrist; b. Shreveport, La., June 14, 1950; s. Charles D. and Mable M. (Louviere) K. B.S. in Pre-medicine, Northeast La. U., 1973; O.D., So. Coll., 1980. Owner, operator Kirby Oil Co., Hosston, La., 1980—; low vision coordinator Shreveport Eye Research Found., 1981—. Mem. Hosston Vol. Fire Dept., 1975—. Mem. Am. Optometric Assn., Optometric Extension Program, Better Vision Inst., La. State Assn. Optometrists, Beta Sigma Kappa. Republican. Baptist. Avocations: gardening; tennis; singing. Home: PO Box 355 Hosston LA 71043 Office: 2751 Virginia Ave Suite 3B Shreveport LA 71103

KIRBY, JAMES EDWARD, management consultant; b. Spartanburg, S.C., Mar. 2, 1948; s. James Thomas and Margaret Jeanette (Frady) K.; m. Jayne Kellett, Aug. 15, 1970; children—James Edward, Thomas Price. B.S. in Bus. Adminstrn., U. N.C., 1970; M.B.A.,, Emory U., 1977. Staff cons. Kurt Salmon Assocs., Atlanta, 1977-83, prin., 1983—. Served to lt. USN, 1970-75. Republican. Home: 3743 Fir Ct Marietta GA 30066 Office: Kurt Salmon Assocs 400 Colony Sq Atlanta GA 30361

KIRBY, RITA MAYE KNOWLES (MRS. CARLTON BEDFORD WATTS), real estate management company executive; b. Dalhart, Tex., Sept. 10, 1941; d. Luby F. and Jonnie Reta Knowles; student Frank Phillips Jr. Coll., Borger, Tex.; m. Jerry W. Kirby, May 6, 1961 (div. 1976); children—Michael, Daniel; m. 2d, Carlton Bedford Watts, Aug. 12, 1983. Property mgr. Villa France Apts., Irving, Tex., 1971-72; mgmt. v.p. First Property Mgmt. Corp., Chgo. and Dallas, 1972-80; v.p. ops. S & S Properties, Inc., Dallas, 1980—; pres., mng. ptnr. Capital Concept Mgmt. Corp., Dallas, 1980—. Mem. Dallas Apt. Assn. (dir. 1979-85, sec.-treas. 1981-82, 1st v.p. 1982-83, pres. 1983-84), Tex. Apt. Assn. (dir. 1979—, chmn. edn. com. 1981), Nat. Apt. Assn. (dir. 1978-85, chmn. edn. com. 1980-81, chmn. Nat. Apt. Mgmt. Accreditation Bd. 1980, 85, regional v.p. 1983). Baptist. Author: Community Directors Guide, 1975; co-author: Property Evaluation and Takeover, 1982. Home: 1606 W Shady Grove Irving TX 75060 Office: 4825 LB Johnson Dallas TX

KIRBY, WILLIAM BRADLEY, gas company executive; b. Wilmington, N.C., Jan. 28, 1944; s. William E. and Louise (Daughtry) K.; m. Dinah Bulla, Sept. 29, 1972 (div. 1982); 1 son, William Bradley; m. Sue Williams, 1984. Student Wilmington Coll., 1963-68. With Central Gas & Appliance Inc., Asheboro, N.C., 1968—, now pres.; pres. Guilford Gas Inc., 1979—; owner Kirby Motor Lines, 1980—, Lake Country Estates, 1982—; dir. various cos. Mem. N.C. Liquid Propane Gas Assn. (dir.), Nat. Liquid Propane Gas Assn., Southeastern Liquid Propane Gas Assn. (pres.), S.C. Liquid Propane Gas Assn. Democrat. Presbyterian. Lodges: Masons, Shriners. Home: 2014 Lake County Dr Asheboro NC 27203 Office: 72S Pineview St PO Box 1066 Asheboro NC 27203

KIREILIS, THOMAS VYTAUTAS, army officer; b. Amberg, Bavaria, Fed. Republic Germany, Sept. 20, 1950; came to U.S., 1956, naturalized, 1963; s. Edward Robert and Arija (Gulbitis) K.; m. Althea Antoinette Lambert, June 29, 1973; 1 child, Regan. B.A. in Polit. Sci., Huron Coll., 1973. Commd. 2d lt. U.S. Army, 1974, advanced through grades to capt., 1980; chief phys. security sect. Provost Marshal Office, Fort Devens, Mass., 1978-80; chief plans div. Provost Marshal Office V Corps, Frankfurt, Fed. Republic Germany, 1981; comdr. Hdqrs. and Hdqrs. Co. 2d Mil. Police Group, Frankfurt, 1981, 503d Mil. Police Co., Frankfurt, 1982-83, Criminal Investigation Div., Fort Belvoir Field Office, Va., 1984—. Republican. Roman Catholic. Lodge: K.C. Avocations: skiing; scuba diving; running; white water rafting. Home: 8705 Parry Ln Alexandria VA 22308 Office: Fort Belvoir Field Office USACIDC Fort Belvoir VA 22060

KIRK, EDWARD LEE, educator; b. Benjamin, Tex., Aug. 9, 1923; s. Oliver Lee Kirk and Glorena Aldine (Taylor) Lindsey Kirk; m. Lois Yuneva Bass, July 6, 1945; children—Oliver Frank, Sandra Jeanne. B.S., Abilene Christian U., 1945, M.S., 1957. Seismologist, Atlantic Refining Co., Tex., 1945-47; tchr., adminstr. Benjamin pub. schs., 1947-54; assoc. prof. Abilene Christian U., Tex., 1955—. Contbr. articles to profl. jours. Recipient awards Freedoms Found. Valley Forge; Liberty Bell award Abilene Bar Assn., others. Mem. Phi Delta Kappa (pres. 1970). Club: Abilene Civitan. Avocations: clock restoration; antique woodwork. Home: 1773 Cedar Crest Dr Abilene TX 79601 Office: Abilene Christian U ACU Station Box 8010 Abilene TX 79699

KIRK, HOWARD WARD, educator; b. Indpls., Feb. 18, 1923; s. Howard Ward and Edith Bell K.; B.S., Butler U., 1948; M.A., Stetson U., 1951; Ph.D., Fla. State U., 1969; m. Vonnie Jean Hart, July 13, 1968; children—Shirley Elizabeth, Richard Allen. Math. tchr. Lake County High Schs., 1948-51; diversified coop. tng. coordinator Manatee County High Sch., 1951-56; owner, operator Kirk Bldg. Supply, Inc., 1956-64; mid-mgmt. coordinator St. Petersburg (Fla.) Jr. Coll., 1964-66; tchr., educator U. S. Fla., Tampa, 1966-67; curriculum specialist Fla. State Dept. Edn., Tallahassee, 1967-68; prof. tchr. edn. U. W. Fla., Pensacola, 1968—; mgmt. cons. Westinghouse Electric Corp., 1969—. Bd. dirs., Manatee County Boys Club; cons. Am. Council Edn. Served with USN, 1942-45. Mem. Am. Arbitration Assn., Am. Vocat. Assn., AAUP, Fla. Assn. Vocat. Edn., Sales and Mktg. Execs. Republican. Methodist. Clubs: Lions (tail twister, v.p.), Masons (past master), Shriners. Home: 8502 Punta Lora Pensacola FL 32514 Office: U W Fla Pensacola FL 32504

KIRK, ROBERT L., aerospace company executive; m. Elise Kuhl, July 2, 1955; 3 children. B.S., Purdue U., 1952. Engr. Rockwell Internat., 1955-58, Litton Industries, Inc., Calif., Washington, Switzerland, 1955-58; v.p. ITT, N.Y.C., 1967-77; pres., chief exec. officer LTV Aerospace and Def. Co., Dallas, 1977—; dir. 1st City Bank of Dallas. Trustee SW Research Inst., Falcon Found.; bd. dirs. Air Force Acad. Found. Served with USN, 1952-55. Recipient Disting. Pub. Service award HHS. Fellow AIAA (assoc.); mem. Aerospace

Industries Assn. (chmn. bd. govs. 1986), Am. Def. Preparedness Assn. (bd dirs.). Office: PO Box 225003 Dallas TX 75265

KIRKHAM, ANN L. KNECHT, nurse educator, consultant, researcher, author; b. Rapid City, S.D., June 16, 1936; d. Clem and Ruth (Slocomb) Knecht; m. Dan H. Kirkham, Sept. 20, 1959; children—Matthew, Kathy Jane. B.S., U. Wyo., 1958; M.S., Tex. Woman's U., 1971; postgrad. U. Tex.-Austin. Registered nurse, Wyo. Surg. staff nurse Bennett-Clarkson Meml. Hosp., Rapid City, S.D., 1958, Univ. Minn. Hosps., 1959; pub. health nurse Hennepin County, Minn., 1959; operating room nurse Presbyn. Hosp., Denver, 1959-60; obstet. nurse, Denver, 1960-62; faculty Tex. Woman's Univ., Dallas, 1972-75; asst. prof. Tex. Christian U., Ft. Worth, 1975—; cons., psychiat. mental health nursing. Bd. dirs. Rape Crisis Tarrant County Inc.; mem. profl. adv. com. Tarrant County Mental Health; mem. Ft. Worth Police Dept. Sexual Assault Com. Grantee Tex. Christian U.; recipient Outstanding Nurse award Sigma Theta Tau, 1983. Mem. Am. Nurses' Assn., Tex. Nurses' Assn., Mental Health Assn. Clubs: P.E.O. Episcopalian. Contbg. author publs. in field. Home: 7809 Bayshore Ct Fort Worth TX 76179 Office: Harris Coll Nursing Texas Christian Fort Worth TX 76129

KIRKLAND, DARREL OWEN, financial executive; b. Los Angeles, June 26, 1939; s. Edmund Wilbur and Ellen Maxine (Hunter) K.; m. Elizabeth Wyatt-Brown, July 1, 1966; children—Hunter Quinatd, Grayson Alexandra. B.S. in Engring., U. Houston, 1966, M.S., 1969; B.B.A., U. Tex.-Austin, 1963. Registered profl. engr., Tex. Mktg. specialist Exxon Corp., Houston, 1965-70; sr. mgr. MRI Systems Corp., Austin, Tex., 1970-73; v.p. CPI Microwave, Austin, 1974-76; owner Darrel O. Kirkland Co., Austin, 1977-82; v.p. MCI Telecommunications, Washington, 1982-83; pres. Comquest Inc., Austin, 1983—; chmn. bd. S.W. Tex. Pub. Broadcasting Council. Author: Parameters of Solubility, 1968; producer movie: Worldwide Control of Mosquito, 1969. Served to 1st lt. U.S. Army, 1962-68. Mem. Tex. Soc. Profl. Engrs., Tex. Ind. Producers and Royalty Owners Assn. Republican. Episcopalian. Club: Austin. Address: 2600 Plumcreek St Austin TX 78703

KIRKLAND, MARJORIE CREWS, university dean; b. Echo. Ala., July 18, 1928; d. Lunie Thomas and Sallie Jo (Johnson) Crews; m. Joe Ed Kirkland, Sept. 15, 1948; children—Deborah Gale, Joe Ed Jr. B.S., U. Ala., 1950; M.Ed., Auburn U., 1960, Ed.D., 1966. Tchr., Dothan City Sch., Ala., 1958-64; counselor Auburn U., 1964-65; dir. grad. studies Troy State U., Ft. Rucker, Ala., 1966-70, dean of counseling, 1970-81, dean of edn., Dothan, Ala., 1981—. Mem. Wiregrass Mental Health Bd., Dothan, 1975-85. Named Ala. Woman of Achievement, Ala. Bus. and Profl. Women's Club, 1977. Mem. NEA, Ala. Edn. Assn., Ala. Assn. Colls. of Tchr. Edn., Phi Kappa Phi. Baptist. Avocations: reading; traveling; genealogy; gardening. Home: Rt 2 Newville AL 36353 Office: Troy State Univ Dothan AL 36301

KIRKMAN, ELLEN ELIZABETH, mathematics educator, researcher; b. St. Paul, July 28, 1948; d. Thomas William and Ruth Mary (Kolthoff) K. M.S. in Statistics, Mich. State U., 1975, Ph.D., 1975. Alfred Brauer instr. Wake Forest U., Winston-Salem, N.C., 1975-78, asst. prof., 1978-81, assoc. prof. math., 1981—. Contbr. articles to profl. jours. Reynolds grantee, 1984. Mem. Am. Math. Assn., Math. Soc. Am., Am. Statis Assn. Democrat. Baptist. Office: Wake Forest Univ Box 7311 Winston Salem NC 27109

KIRKPATRICK, ARNOLD HADEN, thoroughbred racing and breeding executive; b. Lexington, Ky., Feb. 14, 1941; s. L. Haden and Anne (Robertson) K.; m. Jane Carol Glober, Feb. 13, 1965 (div. 1977); 1 dau., Joyce Elaine; m. Sally Anne Battin, Sept. 4, 1977; children—Sara Arden, Haden Keith. B.A., Tulane U., 1965. Pres., editor, pub. The Thoroughbred Record, Lexington, 1965-76; v.p. Spendthrift Farm, thoroughbred racing and breeding farm, Lexington, 1980—; pres. Latonia Race Course, thoroughbred race track, Cin., 1981—; mem. racing adv. com. Am. Horse Council, 1976-80. Bd. dirs. Lexington Philharm. Soc., 1974-77. Recipient Eclipse award for best mag. writing, 1983. Mem. Am. Horse Publs. (founding pres.), Morris Animal Found. (trustee), Thoroughbred Racing Assn. (dir.). Republican. Episcopalian. Editor: The History of Thoroughbred Racing in America; contbr. numerous articles on horses to periodicals and mags. Home and office: Spendthrift Farm PO Box 996 Lexington KY 40588

KIRKPATRICK, GEORGE GRIER, JR., state legislator, real estate investor; b. Gainesville, Fla, Dec. 24, 1938; m. Monika Godzewski; children—Catherine Grace, George Grier III. B.S. in Psychology, Davidson Coll., 1962. Owner, ptnr. Kirkpatrick Builders of Gainesville; ptnr. 441 Properties, Gainesville, KK & PP Properties, La Fontana Apts., N.W. Past mem. Realty of Gainesville; officer NCF Gen. Contractors, Inc.; dir. High Springs Bank; mem. Fla. Senate, 1980—. Past mem. bd. dirs. United Fund; vice chmn. Gainesville Drug Control Found.; seminar speaker Leadership Gainesville; active Crime Trac, Inc.; v.p., then pres. Santa Fe Community Coll. Endowment Corp.; vice chmn. Nat. Home Builders Task Force on Fed. Clean Water Act; chmn. area fund drive Boy Scouts Am.; Served with Mil. Police, AUS, 1962-65. Recipient service award U. Fla., 1981, Gator Medal of Honor, 1981, cert. of appreciation Ocala Lions Club, 1981, City of Gainesville, 1984; award Gainesville Bd. Realtors, 1981, 82; numerous awards for legis. activities including Fla. Farm Bur., Fla. League Hosps., Fla. Student Assn., Fla. Agrl. Research Inst., Fla. Sheriffs Assn., Marion Correctional Instn., Alachua County Med. Soc., Fla. Assn. Soil and Conservation Dists., Alliance North Fla. Ednl. Employees, Unified Sportsmen Fla., Fla. Med. Assn., Physicians of Fla., Fla. Cattlemen's Assn., Fla. Assn. Funeral Dirs., Gainesville Police Dept., Fla. Aquaculture Assn., Fla. Assn. Home Health Agys., Fla. Regional Planning Council Assn., numerous others. Mem. U.S. C. of C., Fla. C. of C., Lafayette County C. of C., Putnam County C. of C., Gainesville C. of C. (past bd. dirs., v.p. econ. devel. 1978), Gainesville Area C. of C. (past chmn. com. of 100), Am. Legion, VFW, Unified Sportsmen of Fla., Cousteau Soc., Ducks Unltd., Common Cause, LWV, Fla. Home Builders Assn. (Builder of yr. award 1981, past area v.p. and bd. dirs.), Nat. Home Builders Assn. (life bd. dirs.; chmn. coordinating com. for nat. sensible growth environ. com.), Home Builders Assn. Gainesville (past sec., v.p., pres.), Fla. Farm Bur., Nat. Conf. State Legislators, Nat. Fedn. Ind. Bus., Fla. Fox Hunters Assn., Gold Era of Gator Football (hon.), Fellowship Christian Athletes, Nat. Rifle Assn., Alachua County Cattlemen's Assn., Fla. Blue Key (hon.), Sigma Chi (life). Presbyterian. Clubs: Sierra, Gator Touchdown, Gainesville Quarterback, Gator Boosters, Gator Scholarship Boosters, Gator Tip-Off. Lodge: Alachua Lions. Office: c/o State Senate Tallahassee FL 32304

KIRKPATRICK, GERALD LEE, petroleum geologist; b. Olean, N.Y., Nov. 19, 1958; s. James Wellington and Marion (Fitzgerald) K.; m. Karen L. Johns, July 26, 1980 (div. 1985). B.A., cum laude, Muskingum Coll., 1980; M.S., Fla. State U., 1982. Asst. geologist Coastal Petroleum Co., Tallahassee, Fla., 1980-82; sr. petroleum geologist Amoco Prodn. Co., New Orleans, 1982—. Contbr. articles to profl. jours. Mem. Am. Assn. Petroleum Geologists (jr. mem.), New Orleans Geol. Soc., Sigma Xi. Republican. American Baptist. Avocations: scuba diving; bicycle racing; outdoor activities. Office: Amoco Production Co PO Box 50879 New Orleans LA 70150

KIRKPATRICK, WILLIAM ELLIS, public relations director, consultant; b. Louisville, Miss., Dec. 22, 1935; s. William Lee and Gussie Mae (Ellis) K.; m. Wilma Virginia LaVigne; 1 fosterchild, David Wayne LaVigne; 1 dau., Kathrine Mae. B.S. U. So. Miss., 1958, M.S., 1964. Dir. student activities, student union U. So. Miss., Hattiesburg, 1958-72, dir. pub. relations, 1972—; cons. in field. Cons. United Methodist Ch., Miss., 1984—; bd. dirs. Centennial Activities, Hattiesburg, 1982; mem. Mayor's Adv. Com. on Cable TV, Hattiesburg, 1982—. Mem. Pub. Relations Soc. Am., Council Advancement and Support Edn. Democrat. Clubs: Gulf Coast Ad, Civitan. Avocations: camping; traveling; creative graphic design. Office: U So Miss So Sta Box 5016 Hattiesburg MS 39406

KIRMSE, WILLIAM ANDREWS, hotel executive; b. N.Y.C., June 16, 1944; s. William Albert and Jane (Andrews) K.; m. Matinee Goh Mary, Oct. 9, 1971; children—David, Christopher. B.S. in Hotel Adminstrn., Cornell U., 1967; M.B.A., Columbia U., 1979. Exec. trainee, cost controller Hotel Ivoire Inter-Continental, Abidjan, West Africa, 1967, cost controller food and beverage, asst. mgr. food and beverage, 1967-68; asst. sales mgr. Ducor Inter-Continental, Monrovia, Liberia, 1968; corp. ops. analyst IHC Corp. Hdqrs., N.Y.C., 1968-70, dir. ops./planning, 1977-78; asst. to pres. Pacific-/Asia div. IHC, Bangkok, Thailand, 1970-72; resident mgr. Hotel Bali Beach Inter-Continental, Bali, Indonesia, 1972-74; gen. mgr. Hotel Inter-Continental, Rawalpindi, Islamabad, Pakistan, 1974-76; gen. mgr. Hotel Inter-Continental, Miami, Fla., 1978-81, Hotel St. Anthony Inter-Continental, San Antonio, 1981—. Dep. sheriff Bexar County (Tex.); hon. ambassador Dade County (Fla.); bd. dirs. San Antonio Parks Found; St. Philip's Coll. of Hotel and Restaurant Mgmt. Served with USAF, 1963-67. Mem. San Antonio Hotel and Motel Assn. (dir.), Cornell Soc. Hotelmen, Chaine des Rotisseurs, Am. Mgmt. Assn., San Antonio Restaurant Assn., Hotel Sales Mgmt. Assn. Republican. Episcopalian. Clubs: Plaza, University, St. Anthony, Woodlake Country, Oak Hills Country. Lodge: Rotary (past v.p.). Office: 300 East Travis San Antonio TX 78205

KIRSCH, THOMAS JOHN, personnel manager, consultant; b. Phila., Nov. 19, 1940; s. Stanley J. and Frances (Mitros) K.; m. Patricia Mary Atmore, Dec. 28, 1963; children—Thomas J., Jr., Patrice A., Christina M. B.S., LaSalle U., 1962, M.B.A., 1979. Wage, salary adminstr. RCA Tech. Products, Cherry Hill, N.J., 1967-68, employee, labor relations/employment adminstr., 1968-69, benefits mgr., RCA Service Co., 1969-72, mgr. orgn. devel., employee relations, RCA Parts & Accessories, Deptford, N.J., 1972-77, mgr. orgn. devel., employee services and safety RCA Distbr. and Spl. Products Div., Deptford, N.J., 1977-81; mgr. tng., mgmt. devel. E-Systems, Inc., Greenville, Tex., 1981-84, mgr. staffing and personnel devel., 1984—; regional adv. Inst. Mgmt. Studies, San Francisco, 1983—; cons. U. Tex. Human Resource Devel. adv. council, Austin, 1984—; mem. adv. bd. Paris Jr. Coll., Tex., 1982—; liaison officer Air Force Acad., Colorado Springs, Colo., 1982—; adj. prof. Glassboro State Coll., 1979-80. Pres. Point Royal Property Owners Assn., Rockwall, Tex., 1983-84, West Lake Civic Club, Rockwall, 1983-84; bd. dirs. United Way Gloucester County, N.J., 1980. Served to maj. USAFR, 1963—. Mem. Am. Soc. for Tng. Devel., OD Network, LaSalle U. Alumni Assn. (bd. dirs. 1974-83), Air Force Assn., Reserve Officers Assn. Avocations: tennis; travel; flying; photography. Office: Staffing and Personnel Devel Majors Field Greenville TX 75401

KIRSCHBERG, NANCY JEANNE MILLER, occupational health nurse; b. Great Bend, Kans., Oct. 29, 1948; d. Merle Eugene and Eunice Mena Maria (Fischer) Miller; student nursing Barnes Hosp., St. Louis, 1966-68; R.N., St. Luke's Hosp., Denver, 1970; m. Morris Joseph Kirschberg, Dec. 28, 1974; children—Sarah Anne, Rachel Morissa. Staff nurse St. Luke's Hosp., 1970-72, Audie Murphy VA Hosp., San Antonio, 1974-75, Community Hosp., San Antonio, 1975-77; occupational health nurse Columbia Industries, San Antonio, 1977, health and safety mgr., 1977-85, health and safety cons., 1985—; speaker profl. and civic orgns. Served to 1st lt., Nurses Corps, USAF, 1972-74. Mem. Am. Assn. Occupational Health Nurses, Tex. Assn. Occupational Health Nurses (dir. 1979-81), San Antonio Assn. Occupational Health Nurses (pres. 1978-81), Am. Soc. Safety Engrs., Tex. Safety Assn., Hadassah (corr. sec. 1986—). Jewish. Home: 3500 Hunters Sound San Antonio TX 78230 Office: 5005 West Ave San Antonio TX 78213

KIRSCHNER, SIDNEY, corporate executive; b. 1934. B.S.M.E., N.Mex. Inst. Mining and Tech., 1956. Engr., Aerojet-Gen. Corp., 1956-60; dir. engring. Aerospace Corp., 1960-63; asst. to pres. Curtiss-Wright Corp., 1963-67; pres. Electro Dynamic, 1967-73; group v.p. Nat. Service Industries, Atlanta, Ga., 1973-77, exec. v.p., chief operating officer, 1977-79, pres., chief operating officer, dir., 1979—. Office: Nat Service Industries 1180 Peachtree St NE Atlanta GA 30357

KIRSNER, MILDRED DOROTHY, librarian; b. Bklyn., Nov. 4, 1923; d. Isadore and Ida (Rosen) Warshofsky; m. Robert Kirsner, Apr. 11, 1947; children—Steven and David (twins), Barbara, Kenneth, Tamara. B.A., U. Cin., 1946; B.L.S., Pratt Inst., 1947. Asst. librarian Inst. for Advanced Study, Princeton, N.J., 1947-49; reference librarian Miami Dade Community Coll., Miami, Fla., 1972—, coordinator, library instr., 1981—; cons. to library U. Madrid, Spain, 1983. Mem. Community Bd. Hillel, Miami, 1981. Mem. ALA, Assn. Coll. and Research Libraries (sect. sec. 1983-84), Dade County Library Assn. (chmn. sect. 1979-81), Fla. Library Assn. (chmn. sect. 1981), Fla. Assn. Coll. and Research Libraries (bd. dirs. 1984-85), Fla. Assn. Community Colls. Jewish. Home: 500 Alminar St Coral Gables FL 33146 Office: Miami Dade Community Coll 11011 SW 104th St Miami FL 33176

KIRTLEY, DAVID WARREN, petroleum geologist; b. Enid, Okla., Nov. 6, 1927; s. Edwin Lankford and Olina (Talla) K.; children—David L., Nancy J., Mary D., James L.; m. Sandra Lee Montgomery, July 2, 1977; 1 child, Dean A. B.A., Phillips U., Enid, 1950; M.S. Fla. State U., 1966, Ph.D., 1974. Cert. profl. geologist. Geologist H.E. Lillibridge Oil Properties, Enid, 1950-51, Sinclair Oil and Gas Corp, Ardmore, Okla., 1951-53, Midstates Oil Corp., Oklahoma City, 1953-54; owner, operator D.W. Kirtley & Assocs., Oklahoma City, 1955—. Serviced with USN, 1943-45, PTO. Mem. Am. Assn. Petroleum Geologists, Geol. Soc. Am., Soc. Exploration Geophysicists, Biol. Soc. Washington, Soc. Econ. Paleontologists and Mineralogists. Office: D W Kirtley & Assocs 2601 NW Expressway Oklahoma City OK 73112

KIRTLEY, PAUL WILLIAM, educational administrator, public relations consultant; b. San Francisco, June 10, 1947; s. Edwin Lankford and Edna Mae (Curtis) K. B.Journalism and Pub. Relations, U. Tex., 1979. Coordinator mgmt. devel. programs Grad. Sch. Bus., U. Tex., Austin, 1970-80; dir. adminstrn. Permian Basin Grad. Ctr., Midland, Tex., 1980-85; founder Omnetech Internat., Austin, Tex.; dir. graphic layout and design for numerous small businesses throughout Permian Basin and Central Tex. region; lectr. on creativity and innovation. Founder of Disting. Keynote Speaker and Brown-Bag Lecture Series of Permian Basin Grad. Ctr. Served with U.S. Army, 1967-69. Decorated Army Commendation medal. Mem. Am. Soc. Tng. and Devel., Pub. Relations Soc. Am., Midland C. of C. (mem. edn. com.), N.Am. Catamaran Racing Assn., Mensa, Sigma Delta Chi. Mem. Christian Ch. (Disciples of Christ).

KISER, KENNETH KING, wax manufacturing company executive, safety consultant; b. Concord, N.C., July 5, 1930; s. Lawrence King and Margaret (Hudson) K.; children—Kenneth K., Jr., Susan Kiser Bradford, Charles; m. Margaret Ellen Jones, Aug. 28, 1976; children—Karen Ellen, Margaret Carol. B.S., Appalachian State U., 1951. Indsl. engr. trainee Cannon Mills, Concord, N.C., 1951-53; indsl. engr. Am. Efird Mills, Albemarle and Whitnel, N.C., 1953-56; plant mgr. Kohler and Campbell Piano Co., Granite Falls, N.C., 1956-65; tax supr. Caldwell County, Lenoir, N.C., 1965-67; pres., owner Wax-Crafters, Inc., Concord, N.C., 1967—; mem. N.C. Ho. of Reps., 1973-74; chmn. N.C. OSHA Review Bd., Raleigh, 1973-79, 85—; safety cons. Electrical Service Co., Hickory, N.C., Guy Frye & Sons, Inc., Hickory. Inventor: round-square hole wax disc for textile industry, 1981. Pres. Western Piedmont Safety Council, Lenoir, N.C., 1962-63; campaign chmn. Holshouser for Gov. Ga., 1972; Rep. chmn. Caldwell County, 1975-77; campaign chmn. Martin for Gov. N.C., 1984, Reagan-Bush re-election com., Cabarrus County, N.C., 1984; chmn. Cabarrus County Bd. Elections, 1985—. Recipient Presidential invitation Pres's. Conf. Occupational Safety, 1962, 500 Club Placque N.C. Rep. Party, 1973. Mem. Am. Soc. Safety Engrs., Am. Inst. Indsl. Engrs., Appalachian State U. Alumni Council, Piedmont Personnel Assn. (pres. 1954-55). Methodist. Lodge: Lions. Avocations: boating; hunting; fishing. Home and Office: 2 S Union St Concord NC 28025

KISER, ROBERT WAYNE, chemistry educator; b. Rock Island, Ill., Apr. 26, 1932; s. Jay Clifford and Margaret Wilhelmina (Lutz) K.; m. Barbara Marie Hatje, May 29, 1954; children—Mark David, Scott Alan; Ann Marie. B.A., St. Ambrose Coll., 1953; M.S., Purdue U., 1955, Ph.D., 1958. Asst. prof. chemistry Kans. State U., Manhattan, 1957-62, assoc prof. chemistry, 1962-66, prof. chemistry, 1966-67; chmn. dept. chemistry U. Ky., Lexington, 1968-72, dir. Mass Spectrometry Ctr., 1967—, prof. chemistry, 1967—; cons. Radiochemistry, Inc., 1957-58; Batelle Meml. Inst., Columbus, Ohio, 1963-68, Midwest Research Inst., Kans. City, Mo., 1967-80. Author: Introduction to Mass Spectrometry and Its Applications, 1965; Tables of Ionization Potentials, 1960; author (with Meloan) Problems and Experiments in Instrumental Analysis, 1963. Recipient Alumni Merit award St. Ambrose Coll., Davenport, Iowa, 1971; Honorary Citizen award City of Louisville, Ky., 1970; summer faculty fellow NASA, 1975-77. Fellow Am. Phys. Soc., Chem. Soc. London; mem. Mass Spectrometry Soc. Japan, Am. Soc. for Mass Spectrometry, Am. Chem. Soc., Phi Lambda Upsilon, Phi Kappa Phi, Sigma Xi, Alpha Chi Sigma. Home: 781 Glendover Rd Lexington KY 40502

KISER, S. CURTIS, state senator, lawyer; b. Oskaloosa, Iowa, June 17, 1944; s. Ira M. and E. Jean (Raley) K.; m. Sara Margaret Hess, Aug. 27, 1966; children—Jennifer Lynn, Kevin Curtis. B.A., U. Iowa, 1967; J.D., Fla. State U., 1970. Bar: Fla. 1970. Asst. legal counsel to gov. of Fla., 1970; assoc. mcpl. judge, Dunedin, Fla., 1971-72; sole practice, Clearwater, Fla., 1979—; mem. Fla. Ho. of Reps., 1972-82; mem. Fla. Senate, 1985—; dir. Bank of St. Pete, St. Petersburg, Fla.; mem. Electoral Coll., 1980. Bd. dirs. Palm Harbor Youth Recreation League, 1984-85; pres. Indian Bluff Island Civic Assn., 1972-73. Recipient Tiger award Fla. Edn. Assn., 1977, Award for Services to Children, Juvenile Welfare Bd., 1977, Friend of Edn. award Pinellas Classroom Tchrs. Assn., 1977, Outstanding Legislator award Fla. Common Cause, 1980. Mem. Dunedin C. of C., Dunedin Jaycees, ABA, Fla. Bar Assn., Clearwater Bar Assn., Greater Pinellas Young Republicans, Fla. State U. Law Sch. Alumni Assn. (bd. dirs.). Presbyterian. Office: 121 N Osceola Ave Clearwater FL 33516

KISH, ZAVEN AVEDIS, oriental rug company executive; b. Hadjin, Turkey, July 17, 1911; came to U.S., 1929, naturalized, 1939; s. Avedis H. and Marie (Tufunkjian) K.; student Columbia U., 1929-30; m. Susan Griffin, Aug. 16, 1936; 1 child, Ruth Marie. With Lowenstein's Dept. Store, Memphis, 1930-36; owner oriental rug dept. Goldsmith's Dept. Store, Memphis, 1937-74; pres. Zaven A. Kish Oriental Rug Co., Memphis, 1980—; appraiser, lectr. in field. Mem. Oriental Rug Retailers of Am. (a founder). Republican. Episcopalian. Clubs: Civitan, Masons (Shriner). Home: 24 Belleair Dr Memphis TN 38104 Office:; 97 N Tillman Memphis TN 38104

KISSIAH, RICHARD CLARK, lawyer; b. Chattanooga, Oct. 15, 1952; s. Joseph Lloyd and Delphia (Blevins) K.; m. Carolyn Brandt, June 12, 1976; children—Kristin Ann, Jennifer Claire. Student Coll. of William and Mary, Williamsburg, Va., 1971-73; B.A. cum laude, Johns Hopkins U., 1975; J.D., Emory U., 1978. Bar: Ga. 1978. Assoc., Haynsworth, Baldwin & Miles, Greenville, S.C., 1978-79, Swift, Currie, McGhee & Hiers, Atlanta, 1979-82; ptnr. Drew, Eckl & Farnham, Atlanta, 1982—. Republican. Baptist. Home: 2186 Tanglewood Rd Decatur GA 30033 Office: Drew Eckl & Farnham PO Box 7600 1400 W Peachtree St NW Atlanta GA 30357

KISSINGER, DAVID L., insurance company executive; b. Richland, Mo., July 18, 1939; s. James B. and Elizabeth K.; m. Barbara S. Mosley, Feb. 3, 1963; children—Deborah, Timothy. A.A. Southwest Bapt. Coll., 1959; B.S., Hardin-Simmons U., 1961. Tchr., coach Bowling Green Schs. (Mo.), 1962-66; agt., mgr. State Farm Ins., Columbia, Mo., 1966-74; assoc. regional dir. Am. Nat. Ins. Co., Galveston, Tex.; asst. dir., then exec. v.p., dir. Ordinary Agy.; sr. v.p. mktg. Durham Life Ins. Co., Raleigh, N.C., 1985—; dir. Life Ins. Mktg. and Research. Mem. Nat. Assn. Life Underwriters, Life Ins. Mktg. and Research Assn. Baptist. Home: 11004 Pacer Ct Raleigh NC 27614 Office: PO Box 27807 Raleigh NC 27611

KISSLING, GRACE ELIZABETH, biometry educator; b. Montgomery, Ala., Dec. 21, 1955; s. Robert Emmons and Martha Elizabeth (Eidson) K. B.S. in Applied Math., Ga. Inst. Tech., 1977; Ph.D., U. N.C., 1981. Health statistician Nat. Inst. Occupational Safety and Health, Chapel Hill, N.C., 1980; asst. prof. biometry La. State U. Med. Ctr., New Orleans, 1981—. Contbr. articles to med. jours. Nat. Research Service fellow, Chapel Hill, N.C., 1977-81. Mem. Am. Statis. Assn., Biometric Soc., AAAS, Sigma Xi, Tau Beta Sigma, Phi Eta Sigma, Phi Kappa Phi, Pi Mu Epsilon. Office: Dept Biometry and Genetics La State U Med Ctr 1901 Perdido St New Orleans LA 70112

KISTLER, WILLIAM A., JR., drilling equipment company executive; b. Wichita Falls, Tex., 1926; married. B.S.M.E., U. Houston, 1950; M.S.M.E., Rice U., 1953. Lab. technician-devel. engring. Hughes Tool Co., Houston, 1947-58, field engr., 1958-60, asst. v.p.-mfg. product mgr., 1960-66, v.p.-mfg., 1966-75, exec. v.p.-ops., 1975-80, corp. exec. v.p., pres. Drilling Tools and Equipment group, 1980-82, pres., chief operating officer, 1982—, also dir.; dir. Gt. So. Life Ins. Corp., Tex. Commerce Bank, Greenway Plaza N.A. Served to lt. (j.g.) USN, 1943-47. Mem. Nat. Assn. Mfrs. (dir.). Office: Hughes Tool Co 6500 Tex Commerce Tower Houston TX 77002*

KIT, SAUL, molecular biology educator; b. Passaic, N.J., Nov. 25, 1920; s. Isadore and Minnie (Dardick) K.; m. Dorothy Anken, Sept. 28, 1945; children—Sally, Malon, Gordon. B.A. with highest honors, U. Calif.-Berkeley, 1948, Ph.D., 1951. Successively research biochemist, asst., assoc. and biochemist, chief sect. nucleoprotein metabolism U. Tex. M.D. Anderson Hosp. and Tumor Inst., Houston, 1953-62; asst. prof., assoc. prof., vis. prof. Baylor U. Coll. Medicine, Houston, 1956-62, prof. biochemistry, head div. biochem. virology, 1962—; vis. prof. U. Buenos Aires, 1971; Am. Acad. Microbiology Latin Am. vis. prof. Instituto Venezolano de Investigaciones, Caracas, 1971; disting. vis. prof. La Trobe U., Bundoora, Melbourne, Australia, 1982; cancer virology panel USPHS, 1961-62; mem. delegation U.S.-Soviet Health Exchange in Virology, 1967; sci. cons. Miles Labs., Elkhart, Ind., 1969-72; chmn. pathobiol. chemistry study sect. USPHS, 1975-79, cons., 1970—; chmn. research adv. bd. Novagene, Inc., Houston, 1983—. Served with USAAF, 1942-46. Abraham Rosenberg predoctoral fellow, 1949-50; Polio Found. and Nat. Cancer Inst. postdoctoral fellow, 1952; recipient Research Career award USPHS, 1963—; research grantee USPHS, Am. Cancer Soc., Leukemia Soc., NSF, 1952—. Mem. Am. Assn. Cancer Research, Am. Soc. Biol. Chemists, Am. Soc. Cell Biology (past pres.), Am. Soc. Microbiology, Am. Soc. Virology, Argentine Soc. Virology (corr.). Jewish. Editorial bd. Intervirology, 1972—, Internat. Jour. Cancer, 1964—; editorial bd., assoc. editor Cancer Research, 1960-79; editorial cons. numerous sci. publs.; contbr. numerous articles to sci. jours. Home: 11935 Wink Dr Houston TX 77024 Office: One Baylor Plaza Room 250E Houston TX 77030

KITCHENS, JAMES LESTER, health physicist; b. Atlanta, Dec. 5, 1948; s. Charles Dillon and Elsie Pauline (Lester) K.; m. Ruth Alice Keister, Oct. 21, 1972 (div. 1976); m. Brenda Elaine Epperly, May 22, 1981; 1 child, Elaine Allyson. B.S. in Chemistry, U. Ga., 1973; postgrad., Ga. State U., 1974-77. Chem. technologist Story Chem. Corp., Athens, Ga., 1972-73; environ. scientist Environ. Protection Div., State of Ga., Atlanta, 1973-77; chemist Bionetics Corp., Athens, 1977-80; radiation safety officer U. Ga., Athens, 1980—. Recipient Environ. Safety Officer of Yr. award U. Ga., 1983. Mem. Health Physics Soc. (pres. elect 1985-86), Am. Soc. Safety Engrs., Air Pollution Control Assn., Am. Conf. Govtl. Indsl. Hygienists. Democrat. Baptist. Avocations: music, photography, metal working, anthropology, gardening. Home: PO Box 2466-UGA Sta Athens GA 30612 Office: U Ga Pub Safety Bldg Athens GA 30602

KITCHENS, PAUL, pharmacist, drug and variety store executive, consultant; b. Waco, Tex., May 26, 1953; s. Travis Eugene and Delores Grace (Stough) K.; m. Patricia Perryman, Dec. 26, 1971; children—Sarah Kate, Joseph, Samuel. Student U. Ark., 1971, Temple Jr. Coll., Tex., 1972-73, Tex. Tech U., 1973-74; B.S. in Pharmacy with honors, U. Tex., 1976. Registered pharmacist, Tex. Pharmacist/extern Tarrytown Pharmacy, Austin, Tex., 1974-75; research statistician U. Tex. Coll. Pharmacy, Austin, 1975-77; pharmacist/intern St. David's Hosp., Austin, 1976-77; pharmacist, mgr. Circle Drug, Waco, Tex., 1977, See Right Drug, Moody, Tex., 1977-79; pharmacist, owner, operator Moody Drug & Variety, 1979—; pharm. cons. Moody Care Ctr., 1977—; instr. emergency medicine Moody and McGregor vol. ambulance assns., Tex., 1979-82; spl. fair judge Heart of Tex. Regional Sci. Fair, Waco, 1980, 82. Co-author: Drugs of the Bible, 1976. Co-dir. Moody Centennial Com., 1981-82; new trustee trainer Tex. Assn. Sch. Bds., Austin, 1983—; co-group leader Central Tex. chpt. The Compassionate Friends, 1985—; treas., worship chmn. Moody-Leon United Methodist Ch., 1980—; pres. bd. trustees Moody Ind. Sch. Dist., 1980—. Recipient Golden Timepiece award Abbott Labs., 1981, cert. appreciation Tex. Assn. Sch. Bds., 1983, Tex. Dept. Health, 1985; named to Outstanding Young Men Am., U.S. Jaycees, 1982. Mem. Heart of Tex. Pharm. Assn. (bd. dirs. 1981—), Tex. Pharm. Assn. (sects. cons. pharmacist and pharmacy mgmt.), Am. Pharm. Assn. (divs. cons. pharmacy and clin. pharmacy), Nat. Assn. Retail Druggists, Moody C. of C. (pres. 1978-80, Ex-Pres. plaque 1980). Lodge: Lions (past local 1st, 2d and 3d v.p.). Avocations: farm-ranch; tennis; golf; travel. Home: 303 8th St Moody TX 76557 Office: Moody Drug & Variety 500 Ave E Moody TX 76557

KITTENBACHER, RALF WERNER, petroleum geologist, photographer; b. Berg, W. Ger., Apr. 13, 1954, came to U.S., 1973; s. Paul Ewald and Gusti (Riedlinger) K.; m. Nancy I. Beun, Feb. 5, 1983; 1 child, Laura Ann. B.S., U. Tex.-Arlington, 1977; M.S., U. Tex.-Dallas, 1982. Geologist, Delhi Oil Co., Dallas, 1973-79; sr. devel. geologist Placid Oil Co., Dallas, 1979-81; sr. exploration geologist Universal Resources Co., Dallas, 1981-83, Resource Reconnaissance, Dallas, 1982-84; chief geologist Chapman Energy Inc., Dallas, 1984—; owner, cons. High Sierra Petroquest, Dallas, 1982—; owner, mgr. Texana Photography, Dallas, 1979—. Mem. Dallas Geol. Soc. (Disting. Service award 1982), Soc. Profl. Well Log Analysts (pres.), Soc. Petroleum Engrs., Am.

Assn. Petroleum Geologists (Southwest sect. house del. 1984—), Pi Sigma Epsilon (pres. 1975-83). Republican. Methodist Avocations: naturalist; camping; photography. Home: 2905 O'Henry Dr Garland TX 75042 Office: Chapman Energy Inc 6350 LBJ Freeway # 115 W Dallas TX 75240

KITTINGER, CAROL ANN, nurse; b. Detroit, May 24, 1946; d. Junior Claude Gordon and Betty Corenne (Wheeler) Gordon; m. William Henry Harrell, Jan. 6, 1963 (div. 1966); children—Tonya Lynn, Tammy Lynn; m. Ronald Nall Kittinger, Apr. 5, 1970 (div. 1980). Lic. practical nurse cert. Madisonville Vocat. Sch. (Ky.), 1968; emergency med. technician cert. Hopkinsville Vocat. Sch., 1979. Nurse's aide Hopkings County Hosp., Madisonville, 1966-67; practical nurse Sr. Citizens Nursing Home, Madisonville, 1968-70, Dawson Health Care Nursing Home, Dawson Springs, Ky, 1976-79, New Dawson Nursing Home, Dawson Springs, 1980-82; emergency med. technician Med. Ctr. Ambulance, Madisonville, 1981-83; practical nurse Outwood Care Inc., Dawson Springs, 1982—; Vol. emergency med. technician squad, Dawson Springs, 1978-85; mem. Dawson Springs Vol. Fire Dept., 1978-82. Recipient Vol. Activist award Gov. John Y. Brown, 1982; Behavior Modification I award Exception Outwood Campus, Dawson Springs, 1982; St. Ives Homemakers scholar, 1968; Dept. Ky. Ladies Aus. VFW scholar, 1968. Home: 517 W Keigan St Dawson Springs KY 42408 Office: Outwood Care Inc Hwy 109 Dawson Springs KY 42408

KITTLE, ROBERT EARL, educational administrator; b. Flemington, W.Va., Jan. 10, 1935; s. Bertsel and Ruth (Ball) K.; B.A. in Elem. Edn., Alderson-Broaddus Coll., 1957; M.A. in Adminstrn., Marshall U., 1966, suprs. degree, 1973; m. Marianna Arthur; children—Marian, Matthew. Prin. Taylor County Schs., 1957-62; tchr. Kanawha County Schs., Charleston, W.Va., 1962-65, prin., 1965-69, dir. elem. schs., 1969-72, dir. planning and accountability, 1972-73, asst. supt. dept. instrnl. programs Div. Curriculum and Instrn., 1972-78, supt. schs., 1979-84; supt. schs. Randolph County Schs., 1984-85, Harrison County Schs., 1985—. Bd. trustees Children's Coll., W.Va. State Coll.; mem. Jr. Achievement. Mem. Am. Assn. Sch. Adminstrs., Nat. Assn. Elem. Sch. Prins., W.Va. Assn. Sch. Adminstrs. (exec. com.), Charleston Alliance Businessmen. Baptist. Clubs: Elks, Lions, Rotary, Masons, Shriners. Office: PO Box 1370 Clarksburg WV 26301

KITTRELL, CHARLES MINOR, II, petroleum company executive; b. Gregory, Ark., 1926; married. B.S., U. Ark. With Phillips Petroleum Co., 1950—, mgr. N.Y. office, 1958-63, mgr. supply and transp. dept., 1963-66, v.p. supply and transp., 1966-71, sr. v.p., 1971-74, exec. v.p., Bartlesville, Okla., 1974—, also dir. Office: Phillips Petroleum Co 17 Phillips Bldg Bartlesville OK 74004

KITTS, THOMAS RICHARD, oil well services company executive; b. Washington, Jan. 15, 1947; s. William Thomas and Dorothy Beatrice (Conner) K.; m. Wanda Ann Fodrin, May 16, 1971 (div. May 1983); children—Tod Randall, Kelly Rianne. Student in mktg. U. Houston, 1968-70; B.S. in Geology, Lamar U., 1973. Field engr. Schlumberger, Hobbs, N.Mex., 1974-78, recruiting engr., Houston, 1978-79; sr. sales engr. Go Wireline Services, Amarillo, Tex., 1979-83; div. sales mgr. Gearhart Industries, Amarillo, 1983—. Contbr. articles to profl. jours. Served with U.S. Army, 1971-72. Mem. Soc. Petroleum Engrs. (chpt. sec. 1981-82, vice chmn. 1982-83, chmn. 1983-84, dir. 1984-86), Am. Assn. Petroleum Geologists, Soc. Profl. Well Log Analysts (chpt. pres. 1985-86). Republican. Avocations: skiing; racquetball; soccer; hunting; fishing. Office: Gearhart Industries 2209 W 7th St Suite 200-B Amarillo TX 79106

KIZER, CHARLES ANDREW, evangelist; b. Huntington, Tenn., July 17, 1949; s. Charles Freddie and Mackey Ruth (Cole) K.; m. Mary Jane Colvett, Aug. 2, 1969; children—Drew, Ashley, MacKenzie, Barton. B.S., U. Tenn., 1971; cert. Brown Trail Sch. Preaching, 1979. Evangelist, Bedford Ch. of Christ, Tex., 1979-82, Howe Ch. of Christ, Tex., 1982—; dean, instr. Brown Trail Sch. of Preaching, Hurst, Tex., 1979-82. Mem. Bd. Parks and Recreation, Howe, 1983-84; com. chmn. Grayson County Lectrs. Com., Grayson County, Tex., 1984-85. Served with USAR, 1971-77. Club: Lions (pres. 1984-85). Avocations: music; guitar; voice. Home: Route 2 Box 218 Howe TX 75059 Office: Ch of Christ PO Box 275 Howe TX 75059

KIZER, LEWIS BOND, optometrist; b. Milan, Tenn., Oct. 7, 1953; s. Jerry Dudley and Margaret Bond (Conner) K.; m. Jane Hayden, July 10, 1976; children—Hope, Charity, Lewis Jr. B.S., U. Tenn., 1975; postgrad. Memphis State U., 1976; O.D., So. Coll. Optometry, 1980. Assoc. Jewell & Kizer, Milan, Tenn., 1980-82; gen. practice optometry, 1982—. Mem. Student Vol. in Optometric Services to Humanity, Memphis, 1978-79, Milan Jaycees, 1980-83; elder Presbyterian Ch. Lodge: Lions (King Lion 1985). Avocations: hunting; fishing. Home: Route 2 Box 367 Milan TN 38358 Office: PO Box 548 Milan TN 38358

KJORLIEN, CLARENCE JOHN, textile manufacturing company executive; b. 1916. B.A., Concordia Coll. (Minn.), 1938. Vice pres. Lenox Inc., 1954-67; v.p. mktg. consumer products div. West Point-Pepperell Inc. (Ga.), 1967-69, pres. consumer products div., 1969-79, sr. v.p. household fabrics, 1979—, pres., chief operating officer, dir.; dir. Sealy Inc. Served to lt. USN, 1941-46. Office: West Point-Pepperell Inc 400 W 10th St West Point GA 31833*

KLAERNER, CURTIS MAURICE, former oil company executive; b. Fredericksburg, Tex., Sept. 7, 1920; s. Elgin and Irene (Wagner) K.; B.S. in Chem. Engring., U. Tex., 1942; grad. program sr. execs. MIT, 1956; m. Aileen E. Eitt, Sept. 4, 1942; children—Sherilyn Kay, Curtis Elgin. Process engr., then chief process engr. Magnolia Petroleum Co., 1942-53; refinery mgr., then mgr. Eastern region mfg. Socony Mobil Oil Co., 1953-59; regional exec., then regional v.p. Mobil Internat. Oil Co., 1959-61; pres. Mobil Inner Europe, Geneva, Switzerland, 1962-65; corp. v.p. charge marine transp. and internat. sales Socony Mobil Oil Co., 1965-69; exec. v.p. internat. div. Mobil Oil Corp., 1969-72, pres., 1972-79, also exec. v.p., dir., mem. exec. com. corp.; vice chmn., dir. Commonwealth Oil Refining Co., San Antonio, 1979, pres., chief operating officer, 1979-82; founder, pres. Klaerner Enterprises, Inc.; vice chmn., dir. Weed Instrument Co.; dir. Nat. Petroleum Ltd., West Indies Oil Co., Belgian Refining Co. Inc., Encino Oil Co. Bd. dirs. Nat. Fgn. Trade Council; mem. U. Tex. Engring. Found. Mem. Council Fgn. Relations, Brit. Am. Soc. (dir.), Internat. C. of C. (trustee U.S. chamber), German-Am. C. of C. (dir., vice chmn.), Phi Eta Sigma, Omega Chi Epsilon, Phi Kappa Sigma. Republican. Episcopalian. Clubs: Union League, Pinnacle, Circumnavigators (N.Y.C.); Oak Hills Country, Giraud (San Antonio).

KLAMON, LAWRENCE PAINE, diversified conglomerate exec.; b. St. Louis, Mar. 17, 1937; s. Joseph Martin and Rose (Schimel) K.; A.B., Washington U., St. Louis, 1958; J.D., Yale U., 1961; children—Stephen Robert, Karen Jean, Lawrence Paine; m. Ann Estes, Mar. 1980. Confidential asst. Office Sec. Def., Washington, 1961-62, spl. asst. to gen. counsel, 1962-63; admitted to N.Y. bar, 1964; asso. Cravath, Swaine & Moore, N.Y.C., 1963-67; v.p., gen. counsel Fuqua Industries, Inc., Atlanta, 1967-73, sr. v.p. fin. and adminstrn., 1971-81, pres., 1981—; dir. Pier 1, Inc., Triton Group, Ltd. Mem. ABA, Assn. Bar City N.Y., Phi Beta Kappa, Order of Coif, Omicron Delta Kappa. Bd. editors Yale Law Jour., 1959-61. Home: 2665 Dellwood Dr NW Atlanta GA 30305 Office: 4900 Ga Pacific Center Atlanta GA 30303

KLANS, VALERIE MARIE, respiratory therapist; b. Chgo., Aug. 20, 1950; s. Robert Edward and Mary Ann (Zidarich) K. A.S., Triton Coll., 1976. Registered respiratory therapist. Staff therapist MacNeal Meml. Hosp., Berwyn, Ill., 1976, supr. respiratory therapy, 1976-81; critical care coordinator Mt. Sinai Med. Ctr., Miami Beach, Fla., 1981—; clin. instr. Triton Coll., 1981; clin. coordinator Med. Careers Inst., Chgo., 1980; clin. tutor Met. Group Hosp., Chgo., 1976-80. Contbr. articles to profl. jours. Bd. dirs. Sea Camp for Children Cystic Fibrosis, Key Largo, Fla., 1983, coordinating therapist, 1983; instr. CPR, Jewish Community Ctrs., North Miami, 1981. Mem. Internat. Assn. Quality Circles (v.p. Miami Dade chpt. 1983, bd. dirs. 1982-83), Fla. Com. Respiratory Therapy Edn. (sec. 1983-84), Fla. Soc. Respiratory Therapy (dir. chpt. affairs 1983-84, v.p., dir. 1985-86). Roman Catholic. Home: 12555 Biscayne Blvd Apt 834 North Miami FL 33181 Office: Mt Sinai Med Center 4300 Alton Rd Miami Beach FL 33140

KLASHAK, ALPHEUS RICHARD, safety engineer, consultant; b. Coleman, Mich., Jan. 31, 1929; s. Frederick William and Louise Caroline (Braum) K.; m. Peggy B. Klasnak, June 1983; 1 child by previous marriage, Robert William. Cert. safety engr., Calif. Farmer, Coleman, Mich., 1952-53; lab. technician Dow Corning Corp., Midland, 1953-56; job coordinator Reserve Mining Co., Silver Bay, Minn., 1956-62; safety mgr. Hunkin-Conkey, Cleve., 1962-72, Associated Gen. Contractors of Colo., 1972-76; pres. Ask Safety Cons., Ada, Okla., 1976—, Denver, 1976-83; expert witness, constrn. and mining. Served with USAFR, 1958-67. Mem. Am. Soc. Safety Engrs. (pres. Colo. chpt. 1975-76), Nat. Safety Council Constrn. (gen. chmn. 1974-75), Dept. Consumer Affairs (profl. engr.). Democrat. Avocations: hunting; fishing; flying; family. Home: 2600 Arlington Blvd Ada OK 74820 Office: Ask Safety Cons PO Box 1332 Ada OK 74820

KLEBBA, ROBERT HAROLD, orthopedic company executive; b. Mt. Vernon, Ill., Dec. 1, 1928; s. B.A. and Lucille O. (Morgan) K.; m. Lois J. McGuire, Dec. 16, 1950; 1 son, Robert Steven. Student Glendale City Coll., 1952, 53. With United Mfg. Co., Pasadena, Calif., 1951-78; exec. v.p., dir. Durr-Fillauer Orthopedics, Chattanooga, 1978—.

KLECK, GARY DAVID, educator; b. Elmhurst, Ill., Mar. 2, 1951; s. William Gordon and Joyce (Edwards) K.; m. Diane Gomez, June 20, 1981; 1 child, Matthew. A.B., U. Ill., 1973, M.A., 1975, Ph.D., 1979. Teaching/research asst. U. Ill., Urbana, 1975-78; asst. prof. Sch. Criminology, Fla. State U., Tallahassee, 1978-84, assoc. prof., 1984—. Contbr. articles to profl. jours. U. Ill. Found. fellow in sociology, 1974. Mem. Am. Sociol. Assn., Am. Soc. Criminology. Democrat. Home: 1003 Piedmont Dr Tallahassee FL 32312 Office: Sch Criminology Fla State Univ Tallahassee FL 32306

KLEEMAN, ROBERT HERBERT, retired oral surgeon; b. Bklyn., Feb. 4, 1931; s. Louis and Rae (Schwartz) K.; m. Elaine Gerviro, Dec. 3, 1982; 1 child by previous marriage, Robert Joseph. Grad. Pennington Sch., 1949; B.S., L.I. U., 1952; D.D.S., Loyola U., 1956; postgrad. in oral surgery NYU, 1956-57. Intern in oral surgery Queens Gen. Hosp. Ctr., 1957-58, attending dentist, 1958-63, guest lectr. spl. radiation procedure course, 1958-62; practice dentistry specializing in oral surgery, Riverdale, N.Y., 1959-82; ret., 1982; attending dentist St. Agatha Home for Children, 1958-62; corp. exec. Beta Internat., Inc., Interglobal Investment Ltd. Exhibited XIII Internat. Dental Congress, Cologne, W.Ger., 1962; exhibited art Bronxville Theater, 1963, YM-YWHA of Mid-Westchester, 1978. Scenic prodn. designer Actors Conservatory Theatre, Ardsley, N.Y., Harrison (N.Y.) Players, Inc. Fellow Am. Endodontic Soc.; mem. ADA, Am. Dental Soc. Anesthesiology, Internat. Acad. Orthdontics, Am. Soc. Dentistry for Children, Am. Sch. Health Assn., Royal Soc. Health, Am. Orthodontic Soc., N.Y. Artists Equity Assn., Am. Theatre Assn., Sr. Golfers Assn. Am., Am. Philatelic Soc., New Rochelle Art Assn. Address: 25 Edinburgh Dr Palm Beach Gardens FL 33418

KLEIN, BENJAMIN GARRETT, mathematics educator, consultant; b. Durham, N.C., Jan. 24, 1942; s. James Raymond and Lenetta Mae (Garrett) K.; m. Rosemary Therese McAndrew, June 19, 1971; children—David Garrett, Peter Raymond. B.A., U. Rochester, 1963; M.A., Yale U., 1965, Ph.D., 1968. Lectr., asst. prof. NYU, N.Y.C., 1967-71; asst. prof. to prof. math. Davidson Coll., N.C., 1971—; cons. N.C. Dept. Pub. Instrn., Raleigh, 1981—. Elder, Davidson Coll. Presbyterian Ch., 1981-83. Mem. Am. Math. Soc., Math. Assn. Am., N.C. Council Tchrs. of Math. Democrat. Home: 705 Greenway St Davidson NC 28036 Office: Dept Math Davidson Coll Davidson NC 28036

KLEIN, BERNARD, publisher, author; b. N.Y.C., Sept. 20, 1921; s. Joseph J. and Anna (Wolfe) K.; B.A., Coll. City N.Y., 1942; m. Betty Stecher, Feb. 17, 1946; children—Cheryl Rona, Barry Todd, Cindy Ann. Founder, pres. U.S. List Co., N.Y.C., 1946—; founder, pres., chief editor B. Klein Publs., Coral Springs, Fla., 1953—. Cons. on direct mail advt. and reference book pub. to pubs. and industry, 1950—. Served with AUS, 1942-45; ETO. Mem. Direct Mail Advt. Assn. Mason. Author: Guide to American Directories, Guide to American Educational Directories, Mail Order Business Directory, Directory of College Media, Directory of Coll. Stores, Ency. of Am. Indian, all pub. biennially, 1954—. Home: 7309 Corkwood Terr Tamarac FL 33321 Office: PO Box 8503 Coral Springs FL 33065

KLEIN, CHARLES KENNETH, shipbuilding company executive; b. Phila., Aug. 27, 1939; s. Charles F. and Margaret I. (Walsh) K.; m. Gail P. Heagen, Oct. 23, 1982. B.A. summa cum laude in Mgmt., St. Leo Coll., 1983; M.S. in Human Resource Mgmt., Golden Gate U., 1985, M.S. in Human Resource Mgmt., 1985. Lic. nuclear plant operator, 1960; cert. hazard control mgr., safety exec. safety exec. Enlisted U.S. Navy, 1958, advanced through grades to chief warrant officer 2, 1974, ret., 1978; dir. safety Newport News Shipbuilding, 1978—. Bd. dirs., exec. com., vice chmn. Citizens Adv. Bd. Peninsula Va. Alcohol Safety Action Program, 1978—; mem. Newport News Republican Com. Decorated Navy Commendation medal. Mem. Nat. Safety Council (mem. exec. com. marine sect., marine constrn. and repair), Va. Safety Assn. (dir.), Shipbuilders Council Am. (chmn. lead working group, chmn. safety and health com. on carcinogen policy), Va. Mfrs. Assn. (mem. safety/health com.), Soc. Naval Architects and Marine Engrs., Soc. Mfg. Engrs., Am. Soc. Safety Engrs., Nat. Safety Mgmt. Soc., Nat. Soc. to Prevent Blindness, Am. Inst. Indsl. Engrs. Republican. Lutheran. Clubs: Warwick Yacht and Country, Propeller of Port of Hampton Rds. Lodge: Masons. Home: 15 Blacksmythe Ln Newport News VA 23602 Office: 4101 Washington Ave Newport News VA 23607

KLEIN, HARVEY ALLEN, clinical psychologist; b. Bronx, N.Y., Feb. 15, 1947; s. Sidney and Beatrice (Rauch) K.; m. Marilyn Penn; children—Michael, Jason, Jeffrey. B.A., SUNY-Stony Brook, 1968; M.S., St. John's U., 1970; Ph.D., U. Ga., 1972. Diplomate Am. Bd. Profl. Psychology. Psychologist I, Norristown State Hosp., Pa., 1972-73; asst. chief psychology service Bklyn. VA Outpatient Clinic, 1978-82, chief Day Treatment Ctr., 1975-82; pvt. practice psychology, Staten Island, N.Y., 1975-82; assoc. psychologist Atlantic Ctr. for Human Resource Devel., Hobe Sound, Fla., 1985—; pvt. practice psychology, West Palm Beach, Fla., 1983—; cons. psychologist Parent Child Study Ctr., West Palm Beach, 1983—; cons. psychologist Human Sexuality Ctr., Lakeland, Fla., 1984—, Western Communities Med. Ctr., West Palm Beach, 1985—. Mem. Am. Psychol. Assn., Fla. Psychol. Assn., Fla. Mental Health Assn., Richmond County Psychol. Assn. (pres. 1980-81), Phi Delta Kappa, Psi Chi. Home: 13133 Doubletree Circle Wellington FL 33414 Office: 12765 Forest Hill Blvd Suite 1307 Wellington West Palm Beach FL 33414

KLEIN, JOAN ELIZABETH, pharmacist; b. Phila., Nov. 5, 1959; d. Clarence Thomas and Dorothea Lillian (Kraft) Skaudis; m. William Fenton Klein, June 18, 1983. A.S., Delaware County Community Coll., Media, Pa., 1979; B.S. in Pharmacy, Temple U., 1982. Lic. in real estate sales, Ga. Pharmacist Crozer-Chester Med. Ctr., Chester, Pa., 1982-83, Univ. Hosp., Augusta, Ga., 1983—. Mem. Am. Soc. Hosp. Pharmacists, Am. Pharm. Assn., Lambda Kappa Sigma (alumni). Home: 621 Dennis Dr Martinez GA 30907 Office: Univ Hosp 1350 Walton Way Augusta GA 30910

KLEIN, JOHN JACOB, economics educator; b. Chgo., Aug. 30, 1929; s. John and Mathilda (Keller) K.; m. Sylvia Elvine Knauss, Nov. 25, 1953; 1 child, Leslie R. B.A., Northwestern U., 1950; A.M., U. Chgo., 1952, Ph.D., 1955. Asst. prof. Okla. State U., Stillwater, Okla., 1957-60; assoc. prof. to prof. econs. Fordham U., Bronx, N.Y., 1960-67; prof. econs. Ga. State U., Atlanta, 1967—. Author: Money and the Economy (6th edition) 1986; Studies in the Quantity Theory of Money, 1956. Contbr. editor Wall St. Review of Books, 1974—. Contbr. articles to profl. jours. Served with U.S. Army, 1955-57. Mem. Am. Econ. Assn., So. Econ. Assn., Am. Fin. Assn., History of Polit. Economy Soc., Phi Beta Kappa, Pi Mu Epsilon. Republican. Avocations: music; gardening. Home: 855 Oakhaven Dr Roswell GA 30075 Office: Ga State U University Plaza Atlanta GA 30303

KLEIN, LEONARD, optometrist; b. N.Y.C., May 4, 1925; s. Aaron and Lena (Lurie) K.; m. Marcia M. Margolis, Aug. 2, 1945 (dec. 1983); children—Lynn Schimmel, James A.; m. Marilyn R. Posnansky, Oct. 22, 1983. B.S., Columbia U. Pvt. practice optometry, Louisville, Ky.; pres. Ky. Vis. Services, Louisville, 1975-79, also dir. Commr. City of Meadowview, Louisville, 1981-84. Served with U.S. Army, 1943-46, ETO. Mem. Louisville Optometric Assn. (pres. 1975-76), Ky. Optometric Assn. (3d v.p. 1976-77, Optometrist of Yr. 1973). Avocation: golf.

KLEIN, MILTON MARTIN, history educator; b. N.Y.C., Aug. 15, 1917; s. Edward I. and Margaret (Greenfield) K.; m. Margaret Kerr Gordon, Aug. 25, 1963; children—Edward Gordon, Peter Gordon. B.S.S., City Coll. N.Y., 1937, M.S., 1939; Ph.D., Columbia U., 1954. Tchr. social studies N.Y.C. Pub. Schs., 1947-57; lectr. history Columbia U., 1954-58; prof. history, chmn. dept. L.I. U., 1958-62, dean Coll. Liberal Arts and Sci., 1962-66; dean Grad. Studies and Research SUNY, Fredonia, 1966-69; prof. history U. Tenn., Knoxville, 1969-85, Lindsay Young prof., 1980-85, prof. emeritus, 1985—; Fulbright prof. history U. Canterbury, Christchurch, N.Z., 1962; Walter E. Meyer vis. prof. NYU, 1976-77. Served to lt. col. USAF, 1942-46. Decorated Army Commendation medal with oak leaf cluster. Recipient Kerr History prize N.Y. State Hist. Assn., 1975; U. Tenn. Alumni Outstanding Teaching award, 1974, Mortar Bd. Outstanding Faculty award, 1979; fellow Fund for Advancement of Edn., 1955-56, Lilly Found., 1961. Mem. Am. Soc. Legal History (pres. 1980-82), Southeast Am. Soc. Eighteenth-Century Studies (pres. 1984-85), AAUP (nat. council 1977-80). Author: Social Studies for the Academically Talented Student, 1960; The Politics of Diversity: Essays in the History of Colonial New York, 1974; New York in the American Revolution: A Bibliography, 1974; (with others) Twilight of British Rule in Revolutionary America, 1983. Editor: The Independent Reflector, 1963; New York: The Centennial Years, 1676-1976, 1976; Courts and Law in Early New York, 1978. Gen. editor: A History of the American Colonies, 1973-86.

KLEIN, RICK, mayor. Mayor of Amarillo, Tex. Office: PO Box 1971 Amarillo TX 79186*

KLEIN, ROBERT ALLAN, chemical company executive; b. Chambersburg, Pa., Nov. 30, 1947; s. Paul and Edith (Pupik) K.; m. Nancy J. Edsall, June 15, 1969 (div. 1980); m. Linda J. Field, Nov. 19, 1983. B.S. in Chemistry, Clarkson U., 1969; M.S. in Econs., Rice U., 1974, Ph.D., 1976. Research engr. Shell Oil, Houston, 1969-72, corp. economist, 1975-77; bus. mgr. Conoco Chems., Houston, 1977-82; mgr. mktg. Vista Chem., Houston, 1982—. Councilman Stoneycreek Homeowners Assn., Houston, 1984-85. Union Carbide scholar, 1965-69; Rice fellow, 1972-75. Mem. Am. Econ. Assn., So. Econ. Assn. Republican. Jewish. Club: Clear Lake Sailing (commodore 1973-74) (Houston). Avocations: sailing; running; tennis. Home: 12011 Naughton St Houston TX 77024

KLEIN, ROBERT LAWRENCE, international public relations executive; b. Houston, Mar. 3, 1948; s. Irving Robert and Mary (Dover) K.; m. Jacquie D. Rentz, July 9, 1949. B.Jour., U. Tex., 1971. Graphic designer Office Econ. Opportunity, HEW, Houston, 1972-74; adminstrv. asst. to mayor City of Houston, 1974-76; pres. Klein Communications Inc., Houston, 1976-83; v.p. GCI Pub. Relations, Houston, 1983—; mng. dir. GCI Intelligence; speaker on internat. trade, mktg., pub. relations, pub. affairs for U.S. Dept. Commerce seminars; mem. dist. export council U.S. Dept. Commerce, 1980—; mem. adv. bd. SBA, South Tex.; chmn. Venezuela Briefing for Internat. Trade Week. Contbr. articles to various bus. publs. Mem. Houston Interam. C. of C. (co-founder, dir., past pres. 2 terms), Japan Am. Soc., Norwegian Am. C. of C. Office: 1111 North Loop West Suite 520 Houston TX 77008

KLEIN, ROBERTA PHYLLIS, writer; b. Columbus, Ohio, Dec. 26, 1934; d. Arthur Ezra and Anne Dorothy (Shrut) Krum Sternberg; m. Joseph Klein, Jan. 25, 1953 (div. 1969); children—Kenneth, Wendy, Ronald, Karyn, Valerie; m. Joseph Klein, Mar. 17, 1970. Student U. Pitts., 1952-53, Miami-Dade Community Coll., Miami, 1964-65, U. Miami, 1975-76. Copywriter, account exec. Azen and Assocs., Ft. Lauderdale, Fla., 1977-80; exec. editor Fla. Designers Quar., Miami, 1978-83; editor-in-chief On Design mag., 1983-84; dir. Sunshine State Bank, South Miami, Fla., 1978-85; design writer Sunshine Mag., Ft. Lauderdale News, 1984—; contbg. editor So. Accents Mag., Atlanta; lectr. Purdue U., Ill., Inst. Bus. Designers, Miami, Orlando, Am. Soc. Interior Designers, Miami, Atlanta, Jacksonville, 1980-83. Contbr. feature articles to mags. Active Am. Heart Assn., Miami, Palm Beach Festival Assn., Fla., Ctr. for Fine Arts, Miami, Zool. Soc., Miami. Recipient Editorial awards Am. Soc. Interior Designers, Miami/Ft. Lauderdale, 1978, Inst. Bus. Designers, Fla. chpt., Miami, 1979, Interior Design Guild, Miami, 1981; Editorial/Pictorial award AIA, Miami/Ft. Lauderdale chpt., 1980, Addy awards, 1977, 85. Democrat. Jewish. Club: Fiction Writers (Boca Raton, Fla.). Avocations: tennis; fishing; cooking; concerts; theatre. Home and Office: 6000 Alton Rd Miami Beach FL 33140

KLEINBERG, HOWARD J., newspaper editor; b. N.Y.C., Oct. 23, 1932; s. Benjamin and Ruth (Wile) K.; student pub. schs.; m. Natalie Bernstein, Feb. 22, 1953; children—Linda Kleinberg Landy, Eliot, Eileen, David. Mem. staff Miami (Fla.) News, 1950-65, 66—, mng. editor, 1968-76, editor, 1976—; pub. relations exec. Hank Meyer Assos., Miami, 1965-66. Author: Miami: The Way We Were, 1985. Served with AUS, 1953-55; Korea. Recipient 1st place Editorial Writing, Fla. Edn. Assn., 1985. Mem. Am. Soc. Newspaper Editors, Inter-Am. Press Assn. Office: Box 615 Miami News Miami FL 33152

KLEIN-GILLIGAN, BONNEE, advertising executive; b. Pitts., May 27, 1954; d. James J. and Patricia R. (Redrick) Klein; m. James Vincent Gilligan, July 4, 1981. Diploma in graphic arts, York Acad. Arts, 1975. Art. dir. Imaging Systems Corp., Derry, Pa., 1978-81; advt. mgr. Pelikan, Inc., Franklin, Tenn., 1981-84; pres., owner Personal Expressions Advt., 1983—. Freelance designer, 1975-85. Recipient plaque Office Mag., 1978, Office World News Mag., 1981; Best Read Ad award Geyers' Dealer Topics Mag., 1982. Mem. Am. Advt. Fedn., Nashville C. of C. Office; 164 8th Ave N Nashville TN 37203

KLEINPETER, ROBERT LAWRENCE, lawyer; b. Baton Rouge, Sept. 28, 1924; s. George Buffinton and Ethel (McDaniel) K.; m. Rachel Beth Williams, June 19, 1951; children—Melanie Anne, Robert Loren. B.A. La. State U. 1950, J.D. 1950. Bar: La. 1950. Assoc. Sanders, Miller, Downing, Rubin & Kean, Baton Rouge, 1948, 49; spl. agt. FBI, 1950-52; ptnr. Kantrow, Spaht, West & Kleinpeter, Baton Rouge, 1952-61, Kantrow, Spaht & Kleinpeter, Baton Rouge, 1961-65; sole practice Baton Rouge, 1965-75; ptnr. Kleinpeter, Kleinpeter & Kleinpeter, Baton Rouge, 1975—; part-time inst. La. State U. Law Sch.; mem. adv. com. La. Law Inst. Mem. exec. com. Boy Scouts Am.; chmn. profl. div. United Givers Fund. Served with USAAF. Fellow Am. Coll. Trial Lawyers, Am. Bd. Criminal Lawyers, Internat. Soc. Barristers; mem. La. State Bar Assn., ABA, Internat. Assn. Ins. Counsel. Republican. Baptist. Clubs: Rotary Internat. (Paul Harris fellow), Masons. Home: 944 E River Oaks Baton Rouge LA 70815 Office: 6233 Harry Dr PO Box 66443 Baton Rouge LA 70896

KLEINSCHMIDT, WILLIAM EDWARD, business consultant; educator; b. Highland Park, Ill., Feb. 5, 1951; s. Edward Ernst and Marie Jeannette K.; B.B.A., U. Miami, 1973, M.S., 1975, cert. acctg., 1975, doctoral candidate, 1978—; M.B.A., Barry U., 1979. Computer office mgr. U. Miami (Fla.), 1971-75; pres. Kleinschmidt Enterprises, 1976-78; co-owner Kleinschmidt Teletypewriter Communications Co.; instr., coordinator bus. seminars, spl. asst. to v.p. bus. affairs, spl. asst. to controller Barry U., Miami Shores, Fla., 1977-80; asst. dir., adult edn. program Miami Edn. Consortium-Embry Riddle Aero. U., Daytona Beach, Fla., 1977-78. Co-founder, co-chmn. ann. bus. conf. Barry U., 1978-80; asst. mgr. local polit. election Dade County, 1972-73; vol. com. dir. Archbishop's Charities Dr., 1969-73; vol. com. dir. United Way Dade County, 1974-75. North Shores Optimist Club scholar, 1969; recipient letter of appreciation U.S. Pres., 1968, Pres.'s Appreciation cert. Barry U., 1978, numerous other awards, appreciation letters and citations. Mem. Am. Acctg. Assn., AAUP, Fla. Inst. C.P.A.s, Armed Forces Communications and Electronics Assn., Armed Forces Communications and Electronics Assn., Assn. Systems Mgmt., Cath. Forensic League, Gold Coast Unltd., Orchid Soc., U. Miami Gen. Alumni Assn., Barry U. Gen. Alumni Assn., Miami Shores C. of C., Beta Alpha Psi. Roman Catholic. Clubs: KC; Fraternal Order Police Booster State of Fla. Author: (with E. Tomeski) Study Guide for Fundamentals of Computers in Business, 1979, Acknowledgement Fundamentals of Computers in Business, 1979, Essentials of Computers in Business, 1980, Study Guide for Essentials of Computers in Business, 1980. Address: PO Box 2644 Miami Beach FL 33140

KLEINSORGE, WILLIAM PETER, metallurgical engineer; b. San Francisco, Feb. 10, 1941; s. William P. Kleinsorge; m. Kathryn Deane Vincent, Nov. 14, 1966; children—Elizabeth Louise, Victoria Anne. B.S. in Metall. Engring., U. Nev.-Reno, 1964. Registered profl. engr., S.C., Calif. Welding engr. Mare Island Naval Shipyard, Vallejo, Calif., 1965-69, Charleston-Naval Shipyard, 1969-70; supervisory welding engr. U.S. Naval Ship Repair Facility, Republic of the Philippines, Subic Bay, 1970-72; head welding engr. Charleston Naval Shipyard, 72-79; metall. engr. U.S. Nuclear Regulatory Commn., Atlanta, 1979—; cons. in field. Served with U.S. Army N.G., 1965-72. Mem. Am. Soc. Metals, Am. Welding Soc., Am. Soc. Mil., Engrs. Lodge: Mason.

KLEIN-WOMACK, BARBARA ANN, demographer, research specialist; b. Akron, Ohio, Feb. 23, 1958; d. Henry Albert, Sr., and Cora Betty (Sain) Klein; m. Scott Raymond Womack, Aug. 20, 1983. B.A. in Sociology, Kent State U., 1980; postgrad. U. Akron, 1980-82, M.A. in Sociology, 1984; postgrad. U. Tex., 1982. Research and teaching asst. U. Akron, 1980-82; research asst. U. Tex., Austin, 1982; pvt. practice cons., Corpus Christi, Tex., 1983-84; planning cons. Resource Mgmt. Co., Corpus Christi, 1984; research assoc. Research & Planning Cons., Inc., Austin, 1985, RAM Assocs., Austin, 1986—; cons. Ctr. for Bus. and Econ. Research Corpus Christi State U., 1983-84, Evans Wyatt Advt., Corpus Christi, 1984, Mc Murrey Co., Austin, 1985. Author article, abstract. Active Church and Society, Corpus Christi, 1984-85. NIH Merit Scholar for Demographic Trainees, 1982. Mem. Am. Sociol. Assn., Tex. Econ. and Demographic Assn., Alpha Kappa Delta. Avocations: watercolor painting; photography. Office: RAM Assocs 4017 Victory Dr Suite 130 Austin TX 78704

KLEMPERER, W. DAVID, forest economics educator, consultant; b. Boston, Feb. 26, 1937; s. Friedrich W. and Ingeborg (Klink) K.; m. Marilyn Lupton, Feb. 1962 (div. 1981); children—Mark, Kurt, Nathan, Kristen. B.S., Syracuse U., 1962; M.F., Oregon State U., 1966, Ph.D., 1971. County extension forester Wash. State U., Tacoma, 1962-67; forest economist Assn. Oreg. Industries, Salem, 1970-74; cons. forest economist, Salem, 1974-76; assoc. prof. forest econs. Va Poly. Inst. and State U., Blacksburg, 1976—. Contbr. articles to profl. jours., also book chpts. Bd. dirs. Inst. Forest Analysis Policy and Planning, Washington, 1983—; adv. bd. Internat. Devel. Inst., Washington, 1983—. Mem. Am. Econ. Assn., Soc. Am. Foresters (chmn. tax com. 1977-78, sci. and tech. bd. 1982-83), Internat. Union Forestry Research Orgn. (chmn. econ. group 1982-84), XI Sigma Pi. Avocations: violin; photography; skiing; music; bicycling. Office: Va Poly Inst and State U Forestry Dept Blacksburg VA 24061

KLIEFOTH, A(RTHUR) BERNHARD, III, neurosurgeon; b. San Antonio, Nov. 26, 1942; s. Arthur Bernhard, Jr. and Pauline (Grey) K.; m. Ingrid R. Kunde, Apr. 22, 1968; children—Karena, Tanya. A.B. in Chemistry, Princeton U., 1965; M.D. U. Tex., 1970. Diplomate Am. Bd. Neurol. Surgery. Intern, Naval Hosp., Oakland, Calif., 1970-71; resident gen. surgery Naval Hosp., San Diego, 1972-73; neurosurg. tng. Washington U., St. Louis, 1973-78; commd. ensign U.S. Navy, 1969, advanced through grades to comdr., 1977; staff neurosurgeon Naval Regional Med. Ctr., Oakland, 1978-81; resigned, 1981; capt. USNR, 1985; practice medicine specializing in neurosurgery, Knoxville, Tenn., 1981—; mem. staff U. Tenn. Hosp., St. Mary's Hosp. Fellow ACS, Stroke Council Am. Heart Assn.; mem. AMA, Am. Assn. Neurol. Surgeons, Congress Neurol. Surgeons, So. Neurol. Soc., So. Med. Assn., Soc. Med. Cons. to Armed Forces, Assn. Mil. Surgeons U.S. Office: 1928 Alcoa Hwy Suite 119 Knoxville TN 37920

KLINE, CATHY JEAN, personnel management educator; b. Toledo, Sept. 12, 1950; d. William Raymond and Betty Ann (Moldenhauer) Jackson; m. John Henry Kline Jr., Dec. 26, 1982; 1 child, Shaun William. B.A. in Psychology, George Washington U., 1972; M.S. in Behavioral Mgmt., U. Tex.-Dallas, 1979, Ph.D. in Mgmt. Sci., 1982. Personnel asst. Fed. Nat. Mortgage Assn., Phila., 1973-75; instr. U. Tex. Dallas, 1981-82; asst. prof. U. Tex., Arlington, 1982-85. Contbr. articles to profl. jours. Mem. Acad. Mgmt., Am. Psychol. Assn., Psi Chi Democrat. Avocations: bridge; tennis.

KLINE, EDWARD SAMUEL, biochemist; b. Phila., June 26, 1924; s. Morris and Bessie K.; m. Bernice Shirley, Aug. 27, 1950; children—Andrew Phillip, Matthew Theodore. B.A., U. Pa., 1948; M.S., George Washington U., 1955, Ph.D., 1961. Assoc. prof. biochemistry dept. Med. Coll. Va., Va. Commonwealth U., Richmond, 1968—. Served with U.S. Army, 1943-45. Recipient merit award U.S. Govt., 1960; NSF fellow, 1961-63. Mem. AAAS, Va. Acad. Scis., Sigma Xi. Patentee in field. Office: Biochemistry Dept Box 614 Med Coll Va Richmond VA 23298

KLINE, HARRY BYRD, lecture bureau executive public speaker; b. Nevada, Mo.; s. George W. and Bonnie M. (Garrett) K.; B.S., Phillips U.; m. Marian K. Shimeall (dec. Feb. 1968); children—Jerome W., Madelyn K.; m. Dorothy Champlin May, Nov. 26, 1968. Tchr. pub. speaking and debate Enid (Okla.) High Sch.; pastor First Christian Ch., Hobart, Okla. and Port Arthur, Tex.; organizer, dir. Little Theatre, Port Arthur; owner/dir. So. Sch. Assemblies, 1930-57, Harry Byrd Kline Celebrity Service, 1957-74; lectr. current issues, 1974—; owner/developer Flamingo Bay Retirement Village, Pine Island, Fla., pres. Laymen's League of Tex. Christian Chs., 1948-51. Mem. Internat. Platform Assn. (life, pres. 1951-52, Outstanding Service award 1958, 70), Greater Pine Island C. of C. (pres. 1962, 64, 66), SAR. Mem. Christian Ch. Home: 5516 Williamstown Rd Dallas TX 75230

KLINE, JUDITH ELLEN, osteopathic physician, pharmacist; b. Allentown, Pa., Jan. 29, 1939; d. Edgar Laubach and Ellen Pauline (Wolf) K. B.Sci. and Pharmacy, Phila. Coll. Pharmacy and Sci., 1962; D.Osteo. Medicine, Phila. Coll. Osteo. Medicine, 1968. Practicing pharmacist, Allentown, 1962-64, Phila., 1964-68; rotating intern Sun Coast Hosp., Largo, Fla., 1968-69, emergency room physician, 1969-70; emergency room physician Met. Gen. Hosp., Pinellas Park, Fla., 1969-72; practice medicine specializing in osteopathy, St. Petersburg, Fla., 1972—; chief staff Met. Gen. Hosp., St. Petersburg, 1973-74, St. Petersburg Osteo. Hosp., 1974-75. Mem. Sun Coast Better Bus. Bur., St. Petersburg, 1985; staff physician St. Petersburg Free Clinic, 1971-76. Mem. Am. Osteo. Assn., Fla. Osteo. Med. Assn., Am. Bariatric Soc., St. Petersburg C. of C., Delta Omega, Lambda Kappa Sigma. Republican. Club: Palm Harbor Rep. Avocations: gardening, reading, music, swimming, boating, tennis. Office: 8000 4th St N 101A Saint Petersburg FL 33702

KLINEBAUER, JAMES JOSEPH, biomedical engineer, field engineer; b. Detroit, Jan. 23, 1949; s. Jerome C. and Marjorie (Flynn) Kline; m. Anne Marie Bauer, Aug. 31, 1979; children—Adam, Helene. B.S. in Bus. Adminstrn., Ferris State Coll., 1981; A.A.S. in Biomed. Engring., Da Costa Coll., 1985. Engring. supr. Lady of Sea Hosp., Galliano, La., 1982-84; asst. engr., chief biomed. technician Doctors Hosp. of Jefferson, Metairie, La., 1984—; cons. Hill-Rom, Batesville, Ind., 1984—. Foster parent Lafourche Social Services, 1985; core group leader lay ministry Holy Savior Parish, Lockport, La., 1985. Served with USMC, 1967-77. Mem. ASHRAE, Am. Hosp. Assn. (engring. sect.), Am. Assn. Med. Instrumentation, VFW. Roman Catholic. Avocations: bowling; racquetball; swimming. Home: 323 Belle Vue Lockport LA 70374

KLINETOBE, MICHAEL LEE, sales manager; b. Pasco, Wash., Sept. 18, 1953; s. Lee M. and Sally A. (Schmitt) K.; m. Celia L. Scholefield, Feb. 13, 1982; 1 son, Patrick Michael. B.S., San Diego State U., 1975; Realtor Realty World, San Diego, 1975-77; sales rep. to regional mgr. Hanes Knitwear Consol. Foods, Calif., N.Mex., Tex., Colo., Mo., Ill., New England, N.C., 1977-83; sales mgr., Winston-Salem, N.C., 1983—. Active Young Republicans, 1975-80. Named Sales Rep. of Yr. Hanes Knitwear Consol. Foods, 1980. Mem. Gen. Mdse. Distbr. Council, Nat. Assn. Service Merchandisers, Nat. Food Broker Assn., Lambda Chi Alpha Alumni Assn. Roman Catholic. Home: 2600 St Johns Pl Winston-Salem NC 27106 Office: Hanes Knitwear Consol Foods PO Box 3019 Winston-Salem NC 27102

KLING, WILLIAM, JR., radio executive; b. Huntsville, Ala., Nov. 8, 1954; s. William and Margaret (Rothschild) K. Student The Principia, 1970-73, North Ala. Coll. Commerce, 1971, New Coll., 1973-76, Ala. A&M U., 1983—. Asst. press sec. to U.S. Senator John Sparkman, Washington, 1974; job program evaluator CETA, Huntsville, Ala., 1977; news dir. Sta. WLRH, pub. radio, Huntsville, 1978—. Media cons. United Way; pub. relations chmn. Am. Cancer Soc.; pres. Madison County Young Democrats; mem. steering com. Ala. Young Dems., 1980-81; mem. Madison County Dem. Exec. Com., Ala. Election Law Commn. Recipient Ala. Legislature commendation, Congl. Record commendation, 1981; winner Ala. investigative reporting competition, 1980; Douglas L. Cannon Med. Reporter award Ala. Med. Assn., 1983, Ron Autry Meml. award Ala. AP, 1983; named hon lt. col. Ala. Militia, hon. Ky. col. Mem. Ala. AP Broadcasters Assn., Pub. Relations Council Ala., Pub. Broadcasting News Producers Assn., Huntsville/Madison County C. of C., Friends of Pub. Radio, U.S. Capitol Hist. Soc., Huntsville Jaycees, Randolph Sch. Alumni Assn. (pres. 1980-82), Delta Tau Delta. Christian Scientist. Club: Huntsville Press (pres.). Office: 222 Holmes Ave E Huntsville AL 35801

KLINGBIEL, PAUL HERMAN, information science consultant; b. Watertown, Wis., Nov. 3, 1919; s. Herman Carl and Elsa Helen (Zilisch) K.; Ph.B., U. Chgo., 1948, B.S., 1950; M.A., Am. U., 1966; m. Mildred Louise Wells, Nov. 30, 1968; stepchildren—Alice J. Blessley, Jo Ann Grayson. Abstractor, Armed Services Tech. Info. Agy., Dept. Def., Washington, 1953-58, editor Tech. Abstract Bull., 1958-60, dir. Office of Lexicography, 1960-66; phys. sci. adminstr., linguistics research Def. Documentation Center, 1966-79; sr. cons. Aspen Systems Corp., 1979-81; systems analyst PRC Data Services Co., Linthicum Heights, Md., 1981-82; lectr. Am. U., Washington, 1966-69; cons. div. med. scis. Nat. Acad. Scis., 1969-70. Served with AUS, 1943-46. Recipient Meritorious Civilian Service award, 1974, Disting. Career award, 1979. Mem. Assn. Computational Linguistics. Lutheran. Contbr. articles to profl. jours. Research in field of computational linguistics. Home: 2435 Sumatran Way Clearwater FL 33575

KLINGMEYER, FAYE MICHENER, librarian, dog breeder; b. Orrville, Ohio, June 21, 1913; d. Karl William and Verna Mae (Meese) Michener; m. George A. Klingmeyer, June 21, 1938 (div. 1958); 1 son, Kerry Alan. B.S., Coll. Wooster, 1936; B.S. in Library Sci., Case Western Res. U., 1938, M.S. in Library Sci., 1955. Librarian Cleve. Pub. Schs., 1938-53, Dade County Pub. Schs., Miami, Fla., 1954-79; breeder Basenji dogs, Miami, Fort Lauderdale, 1968—; cons., McGraw Hill Pub. Co., Ency. Sci., Ency. World Biography. Editor Fort Lauderdale Dog Club newsletter, 1985—, Southeastern U.S. Basenji Club newsletter, 1979-83. Mem. com. NCCJ. NAACP, 1951-54; del. UNESCO, 1953. NCCJ scholar U. Chgo., 1952. Mem. Basenji Club Am., Basenji Club SE U.S. (pres. 1980-84). Democrat. Clubs: Fort Lauderdale Dog, Collectors' Guild. Avocations: writing poetry; needlework; gourmet cooking; opera and musical performances. Home: 14021 SW 37th Ct Davie FL 33330

KLOESS, LAWRENCE HERMAN, JR., lawyer; b. Mamaroneck, N.Y., Jan. 30, 1927; s. Lawrence Herman and Harriette Adelia (Holly) K.; A.B., U. Ala., 1954, J.D., 1956; grad. Air Command and Staff Coll., 1974, Air War Coll., 1976, Indsl. Coll. Armed Forces, 1977; m. Eugenia Underwood, Sept. 27, 1952; children—Lawrence H. III, Price Mentzel, Branch Donelson, David Holly. Served to col. Judge Adv. Gen. Corps U.S. Air Force Res., Maxwell (Ala.) AFB, 1954—; admitted to Ala. bar, 1956, U.S. Dist. Ct. bar, 1956, U.S. Ct. Appeals 5th Circuit bar, 1957, U.S. Ct. Appeals 11th Circuit bar, 1982, U.S. Supreme Ct. bar, 1971, U.S. Ct. Mil. Appeals bar, 1971; individual practice law, Birmingham, Ala., 1956-60, 62-66; corporate counsel Bankers Fire and Marine Ins. Co., Birmingham, 1960-62; dist. counsel U.S. VA, Montgomery, Ala., 1966—; v.p. AQS Pharm. Labs. Exec. com. Citizens' Conf. Ala. Cts., Inc. 1973—; mem. Ala. Election Law Commn., 1979—; vestrymen Episcopal Ch. Holy Comforter, Montgomery, 1971-74, del. diocesan conv., 1973; mem. del. assembly United Appeal, 1972, 77; adv. bd. Salvation Army, 1980—, vice chmn., 1981—; mem. Ala. 2d Dist. Congl. Com., 1980—; trustee Ala. Law Found. Inc., 1984—. Recipient Cert. of Merit, Montgomery Area C. of C., 1972, 78; Spl. Achievement award VA, 1973; Outstanding Meritorius Service award Res. Officers Assn. U.S., 1975, named to Brigade of Vols., 1976; Outstanding Alumni award Theta Chi, 1976, 81; Air Force Commendation award, 1973; Outstanding Judge Advocate award, 1977, 79; U.S. Meritorious Ser. award, 1978, 82; named hon. Ky. col. Mem. ABA (nat. conf. bar presidents 1981—), Ala., Montgomery Fed. (pres. 1973), Montgomery County (chmn. bd. dirs. 1977, pres. 1981), Birmingham bar assns., Ala. Res. Officers Assn. (pres. 1982—), Ala. (judge adv. 1977), Montgomery (pres. 1977) res. officers assns., Farrah Law Soc., Sigma Delta Kappa (pres. 1956). Clubs: Montgomery Country, Capital City, Maxwell-Gunter Officers, Rotary (pres. 1979, dist. rep. 1980, Paul Harris fellow), U. Ala. Century. Contbr. articles to legal jours.; mem. editorial adv. bd. The Ala. Lawyer, 1972—, chmn., 1975-79; editor Montgomery County Bar Jour., 1979-81. Home: 3174 Highfield Dr Montgomery AL 36111 Office: 234 Aronov Bldg 474 S Court St Montgomery AL 36104

KLOHN, FRANKLIN JAMES, JR., clinical psychologist, educator; b. Galion, Ohio, Aug. 8, 1951; s. Franklin James and Ruth (Dorchester) K.; m. Suzanne M. Clark, Dec. 28, 1981; children—Katherine, Suzanne. B.S., U. Dubuque, 1974; M.S., Central Mo. State U., 1978; Ph.D., Calif. Sch. Profl. Psychology, 1984. Lic. clin. psychologist, S.C. Psychology intern Calif. Dept. Corrections, San Louis Obispo, 1981-82, Fresno Community Hosp. Med. Ctr., 1982-84; crisis counselor Valley Med. Ctr., Fresno, 1983-84; instr. Carl Sandburg Coll., Galesburg, Ill., 1978-85; psychologist IV, Galesburg Mental Health Ctr., 1977-85; child and adolescent clin. psychologist S.C. State Hosp., Columbia, 1985—; clin. psychologist in pvt. practice, 1986—; cons. psychologist S.C. Vocat. Rehab. Dept., 1986—; dir. conf. ctr. Central Mo. State U., Warrensburg, 1976-77; adolescent counselor Mercy Med. Ctr., Dubuque, Iowa, 1973-76; cons. Knox Warren Spl. Edn., Galesburg, 1985; group cons. Family Action Support Team, Fresno Community Med. Ctr., 1982-84; cons. N.E. Iowa council Boy Scouts Am., Dubuque, 1971-76. Mem. Am. Psychol. Assn., Assn. for Advancement Behavior Therapy, Assn. for Advancement Psychology, Assn. Behavioral Analysis, S.C. Psychol. Assn., Midwest Psychol. Assn., Southeastern Psychol. Assn., Psi Chi. Episcopalian. Home: 5005 Village Creek Dr Columbia SC 29210 Office: SC State Hosp Children and Adolescent Unit 2100 Bull St Columbia SC 29202

KLOPMAN, WILLIAM A., mfg. co. exec.; b. 1921; grad. Williams Coll.; married. With Burlington Industries Inc., 1946—, pres. Klopman Mills div., 1963-71, group v.p. parent co., Greensboro, N.C., 1971-72, exec. v.p., 1972-74, pres., mem. exec. fin. com. and mgmt. policy com., 1974-76, pres., 1976-78, chmn. bd., chief exec. officer, 1976—, also dir. Served with USN, 1942-45. Office: Burlington Industries Inc 3330 W Friendly Ave Greensboro NC 27420

KLOSS, EDWARD BAILLIE, interior designer; b. Oakland, Calif., July 16, 1949; s. Richard Gilbert and Doris (Hair) K.; m. Cynthia Anne Walsh, Oct. 21, 1978; children—Beckwith Charles, Georgia Cody. B.Interior Design, Auburn U., 1971. Staff designer Lang's Interiors, Opelika, Ala, 1971-72; assoc. Alan L. Ferry Designers, Atlanta, 1972-79; assoc. dir. design New S. Drawing Co., 1979-81; v.p. Davis-Kloss, Inc., Atlanta, 1981—; design instr. Am. Coll. for Applied Arts, 1978-80; continuing edn. instr. Am. Coll. for Applied Arts, 1979—. Contbr. articles in field. Recipient Atlanta Urban Design Commn. award of Excellence, 1975, 79. Mem. Atlanta C. of C., High Mus. Art, Inst. Bus. Designers, Illuminating Engring. Soc. Avocations: woodworking; painting; sailing; skiing; photography. Office: Davis-Kloss Inc 1375 Peachtree St Atlanta GA 30309

KLOSZEWSKI, STANLEY R., insurance brokerage executive; b. Erie, Pa., Feb. 26, 1939; s. Stanley F. and Nora S. (Skinner) K.; m. Sylvia M. Albert, June 11, 1960; children—Lisa Marie, Steven Albert. B.S. in Physics, Edinboro U., Pa., 1967; M.B.A., U. Hartford, Conn., 1974. Engring. account exec. Travelers Ins. Co., 1969-74; dir. Great Am. Ins. Co., Cin., 1974-80; risk mgmt. cons., safety engr. Risk Mgmt. Planning, Tampa, Fla., 1981-82; exec. v.p. Jordan Robert & Co., Tampa, 1982-83; v.p. ops. Poe & Assocs., Tampa, 1983—. Mem. Am. Soc. Safety Engrs. Republican. Avocations: fishing; sports; antique car restoration. Home: 2777 Northcote Dr Palm Harbor FL 33563 Office: Poe & Assocs 702 N Franklin St Tampa FL 33602

KLOTZ, HERBERT WERNER, business executive; b. Berlin, Feb. 24, 1917; came to U.S., 1937, naturalized, 1944; s. Herbert and Gertrude (Koppel) K.; m. Patricia Radford Hopkins, Apr. 3, 1954; children—Radford Werner, Leslie Ritchie, James Taylor. B.A., Zuoz (Switzerland) Coll., 1935; student U. Zurich (Switzerland), 1935-36. With Smith, Barney & Co., and predecessor, N.Y.C., 1937-42, W.E. Hutton & Co., N.Y.C., 1946-48; engaged in mgmt. personal investments, 1949-52; with Winslow, Douglas & McEvoy, N.Y.C., 1953-54; pres., treas. Tex. Securities Corp., N.Y.C., 1957; with Alex Brown & Sons, Washington, 1957-60; spl. asst. to sec. commerce, 1961, dep. to sec. commerce, 1961-62, asst. sec. commerce for adminstrn., 1962-65; exec. v.p. Am. Growth Investment Co., 1966-67; dir. Govt. Systems Center, Kurt Salmon Assos., Inc.; mgmt. cons., 1968-69; pres. Quest Research Corp., McLean, Va., 1970-81, chmn., 1970—; chmn. bd., pres. Questech, Inc., McLean, 1981—; chmn. bd. Dynamic Engring., Inc., Newport News, Va., 1976, DHR, Inc., Washington, 1978—, Engring. Resources, Inc., McLean, 1978—. Bd. dirs. Washington Internat. Horse Show, Inc., 1970-83; asso. dir. Nat. Com. Bus. and Profl. Men and Women for Kennedy-Johnson, 1960. Served to 1st lt. AUS, 1942-45; maj. Res. ret. Democrat. Episcopalian. Clubs: 1925 F St., Met., Fed. City (Washington); Warrenton Hunt, Fauquier, (Warrenton, Va.). Home: 1401 Langley Pl McLean VA 22101 Office: 6858 Old Dominion Dr McLean VA 22101

KLOTZ, KENNETH AMBROSE, oil co. exec.; b. Mpls., Apr. 8, 1945; s. Ambrose Anthony and Katherine Elisabeth K.; B.A., Winona State U., 1967; M.B.A., North Tex. State U., 1978; m. Rose Marie Alejos, Nov. 14, 1970; children—Nicole Denise, Jason Kyle, Jamie Dihann. Programmer, Univac, St. Paul, 1967-68; sr. data processing officer Republic Nat. Bank, Dallas, 1970-78; mgr. corp. systems div. Tesoro Petroleum Corp., San Antonio, 1978-83; dir. mgmt. info. services Pride Refining Inc., Abilene, Tex., 1983—. Officer Boy Scouts Am. Served with AUS, 1968-70. Mem. Assn. Systems Mgmt. (pres. San Antonio 1980-81). Republican. Roman Catholic. Home: 18 Cypress Point Abilene TX 79604 Office: PO Box 3237 Abilene TX 79604

KLUCHIN, ALLEN JAMES, geophysicist; b. New Orleans, July 6, 1951; s. Paul William and Anna May Henrietta (Gerdes) K.; m. Susan Jean Mattingly (div. Oct. 1984); m. Barbara Frances Gottlob, July 3, 1985. 1975. Geophysicist U.S. Geol. Survey, New Orleans, 1975-80; exploration geophysicist Gulf Oil Co., New Orleans, 1980-81; geophysicist Getty Oil Co., New Orleans, 1981-84; geophysicist interpreter Texaco U.S.A., New Orleans, 1984—. Mem. Am. Assn. Petroleum Geologists, Soc. Exploration Geophysicists, Southeastern Geophys. Soc., New Orleans Geol. Soc. Republican. Roman Catholic. Avocations: gardening, carpentry. Home: 767 River Rd L Saint Rose LA 70087

KLUSMEYER, PAUL WADE, microbiologist; b. Americus, Mo., Dec. 10, 1919; s. Oscar Charles and Mabel Clare (Cundiff) K.; m. Shirley Maxine Thomas, Sept. 3, 1950; 1 dau., Paula Sue. B.S., U. Mo., 1949, M.S., 1950. Milk insp. City of St. Joseph (Mo.), 1950-53; county sanitarian, Jefferson County, Mo., 1953-54; bacteriology lab. technician Mo. Div. Health, Jefferson City, 1954-58; bacteriologist Henningsen Foods, Springfield, Mo., 1958-69; microbiologist Wilson Foods Corp., Oklahoma City, 1969—. Served with AUS, 1942-45. Decorated Purple Heart, Combat ribbon with three stars. Mem. Am. Public Health Assn., Am. Soc. Microbiology, Internat. Assn. Milk, Food and Environ. Sanitarians, Inst. Food Technologist (treas. Okla. sect. 1979—). Republican. Methodist. Home: 1808 Guilford Ln Oklahoma City OK 73120 Office: 4545 N Lincoln Blvd Oklahoma City OK 73105

KLUTTS, WILLIAM ALONZO, newspaper editor; b. Ripley, Tenn., June 26, 1928; s. Alonzo and Helen (Given) K; B.A. with honors, U. Chgo., 1947, postgrad. 1947-49. With Chgo. bur. AP, 1945-49; edtior The Lauderdale Co. Enterprise, Ripley, Tenn., 1949—; co-pub., 1949-65, pub., 1965—; v.p., dir. Ripley Devel. Corp.; vice chmn. Ripley Housing Authority, 1962-66, chmn. 1966-72; exec. dir. 1972-84; N.Am. membership sec., council mem., Pvt. Libraries Assn., 1978—. Mem. nat. council Boy Scouts Am., 1957; mem. West Tenn. Council, 1955-67; pres. 1958; pres. Consol. Charities, Inc., 1955—; trustee Lauderdale Co. Library, chmn., 1982—; trustee Union U., Jackson Tenn., 1960-65; mem. adv. council Tenn. Civil War Centennial Commn., 1960-65. Served with U.S. Army, 1950-52, capt. USAR; served to lt. comdr. USNR, 1966-78. Coroner Lauderdale County, 1956-79; exec. sec. W. Tenn. Mayors Conf., 1961-79. Winner 24 U. Tenn. press awards. Mem. Am. Hist. Soc. (life), West Tenn. Hist. Soc. (life, v.p.), Tenn. Press Assn., Tenn. Future Farmers (hon.), Ripley C. of C. (pres. 1954). Baptist (deacon, trustee). Lodge: Rotary (pres. 1957, Paul Harris fellow 1983—). Contbr. hist. articles to profl. jours. Home: 157 Lake Dr Ripley TN 38063 Office: 145 E Jackson Ripley TN 38063

KNAPHEIDE, LILLIAN ANNE, educator; b. Hempstead, Tex., May 19, 1952; d. Fredrick C. and Mary Anne (Christian) Wiesner; student Sam Houston State U., 1970-71, Tex. Tech U., 1971-72; B.S. in Edn., U. Houston, 1976; postgrad. in edn. Tex. A&M U., 1979, Prairie View A&M U., 1981—; m. William M. Knapheide, Sept. 30, 1972; children—Christy Anne, Donna Anne. Title I math. tchr. Holleman Elem. Sch., Waller, Tex., 1978—. Mem. Assn. Tex. Profl. Educators (pres. Waller County 1982-83, 84-85, regional membership com. 1983-84, state del. 1983, 84), Assn. Compensatory Educators Tex. Methodist. Club: Order Eastern Star. Home: PO Box 548 Waller TX 77484

KNAPP, GAYLE, molecular biologist, educator; b. Norwich, N.Y., July 31, 1949; d. Carlton Morgan and Annette Rose (Giza) Knapp. A.B. in Chemistry, Barnard Coll., 1971; Ph.D. in Biochemistry, U. Ill., 1977. Postdoctoral fellow U. Calif., San Diego, 1977-81; asst. prof. microbiology, U. Ala. at Birmingham, 1981—, assoc. scientist Comprehensive Cancer Ctr., U. Ala., Birmingham, 1983—. Mem. Am. Chem. Soc., Am. Soc. Microbiologists, Sigma Xi. Office: 801 Sch Dentistry Bldg Dept Microbiology Univ Ala Birmingham AL 35294

KNAPP, RICHARD S., planetarium director, film producer and director, educator; b. Sept. 16, 1942; married; 6 children. B.A. in History and Geography, Stetson U., 1964; M.A. in Geography, U. N.C., 1975. Edn1. asst. Morehead Planetarium, 1965-68, asst. dir., 1968-73, chmn., 1973-77; dir. Davis Planetarium, 1977—; co-founder, v.p. Cinema-360, Inc., 1981-84, film dir., co-producer The Space Shuttle: An American Adventure; adj. faculty: U. N.C., 1966-70, Miss. State U., 1981—, Jackson State U., 1982—; feature writer, syndicated columnist Newspaper Enterprise Assn., 1974-77; lectr., author writings in field. Recipient Gold medal Internat. Film and TV Festival of N.Y., 1985, Disting. Merit award City of Jackson, Miss., 1985. Mem. Internat. Planetarium Soc. (council 1976), Southeastern Planetarium Assn. (pres. 1975, Spl. Achievement award 1977), Am. Assn. Mus. (accreditation com.), Gamma Theta Upsilon. Lutheran (elder, stewardship chmn.).

KNAPP, S. MAGNET, painter, sculptor, enamelist; b. N.Y.C., July 18, 1909; d. Lewis and Annie (Silver) Magnet; m. George J. Knapp, Aug. 24, 1934 (dec. 1978); 1 son, Malcolm. Teaching cert. tng. N.Y. Tchr. Tng. Coll., 1926-29; student CCNY, 1930-38, Bklyn. Mus. Art Sch., 1943-48, Sculpture Ctr., N.Y.C., 1941-43. One-woman shows: Roberson Meml. Ctr., Binghamton, N.Y., 1963, Marist Coll., Poughkeepsie, N.Y., 1969, Donan Gallery, N.Y.C., 1971, Hollywood Mus. Art., Fla., 1974; group shows include: Bklyn. Mus., 1947-60, Corcoran Gallery, Washington, Balt. Mus., 1956, 58, 61, Butler Inst. Art, Silvermine Guild, Conn., 1965; represented in permanent collections Ga. Mus. Art, Norfolk Mus. Art, Riverside Mus. Art, Kew Gardens Civic Ctr., N.Y., also pvt. collections. Recipient award for painting Balt. Mus., 1956, 58, 61, Silvermine Guild, 1965, Am. Heritage, 1975. Mem. Nat. Assn. Women Artists (arranged U.S.-Japan exchange exhbn. 1960, U.S.-Argentina exhbn. 1963, pres. 1965-67, award for painting 1980), Soc. Painters in Casein and Acrylic (treas. 1958-60), Artists Equity. Avocations: collecting prints, Tiffany glass, Galle glass. Home: 162 Somerset H West Palm Beach FL 33417

KNAUER, WILLIAM JEROME, JR., ophthalmologist, educator; b. Jacksonville, Fla., Aug. 7, 1924. Student U. Fla., 1942-44; M.D., George Washington U., 1948. Diplomate Am. Bd. Ophthalmology, 1953. Intern Emory U., Atlanta, 1948-49; resident Johns Hopkins Hosp. Wilmer Eye Inst., Balt., 1949-52, 54-56; pvt. practice ophthalmology, Jacksonville, Fla., 1956—, chief dept. ophthalmology St. Vincent's Med. Ctr., Jacksonville, 1961-75, chief med. and dental staff, 1975-76, presently mem. staff; mem. staff Riverside Hosp., Jacksonville; mem. courtesy staff Bapt. Meml., St. Luke's, Univ. hosps., Jacksonville; instr. ophthalmology U. Fla., Gainesville. Bd. dirs. Young Life, 1969-71; vestryman St. Mark's Episcopal Ch., 1957-70; bd. dirs. Mental Health Assn., 1959-62; trustee Bartram Sch., 1972-74; exec. com. United Fund; mem. Com. 100 and 2 per cent Club, Jacksonville. Fellow Am. Bd. Ophthalmology, Am. Acad. Ophthalmology and Otolaryngology, ACS, Soc. Eye Surgeons; mem. Am. Soc. Contemporary Ophthalmology, Duval County Med. Soc. (sec. 1958), Fla. Med. Assn., AMA, So. Med. Assn., Internat. Glaucoma Congress, Duval County Soc. Ophthalmology (pres. 1958), Fla. Soc. Ophthalmology, Found. for Sight (chmn., bd. dirs.), Assn. Cryosurgery, Am. Intraocular Lens Implant Soc., U.S. Eye Study Club (pres. 1973), Soc. Cons. Clin. Ophthalmologists, Contact Lens Assn. Am., Smith-Reed Russell Soc., William Beaumont Soc., Sigma Alpha Epsilon. Clubs: Rotary (bd. dirs. 1982-84), Ye Mystic Revelers (capt. 1974, king 1980), Fla. Yacht, Timuquana Country (bd. govs. 1967-69), Ponte Vedra, River, Tournament Players Championship Assn. Contbr. articles to med. jours. Office: 2535 Riverside Ave Jacksonville FL 32204

KNAUF, JANINE BERNICE, educator; b. Rochester, N.Y., Apr. 10, 1945; d. William Charles and Ila May (Hauss) Knauf; S.B., MIT, 1967; M.B.A., Rutgers U., 1971; M.Ph. Columbia U., 1979, Ph.D., 1981; 1 son, Christopher Robert Burgess. Research engr. Northrop/Norair, Hawthorne, Calif., 1965-66; sci. research engr. Rockwell Internat., Los Angeles, 1967-68; acct. Knauf and Knauf, Rochester, 1968-69, 76-78; lectr. mgmt. dept. Poly. Inst. N.Y., 1972-73; asst. prof. info. systems Rutgers U., Newark, N.J., 1973-80; asst. prof. acctg. Fla. State U., Tallahassee, 1980—; computer cons. Keefe, Bruyette & Woods, Inc., N.Y.C., 1978—; fin. edn. cons. Internat. Paper Co., 1980. C.P.A., N.Y., Fla. Mem. Am. Inst. C.P.A.s, Fla. Inst. C.P.A.s, N.Y. State, Am. Woman's Soc. C.P.A.s, Soc. Women Engrs., Internat. Platform Assn., AIAA, Am. Acctg. Assn., Aircraft Owners and Pilots Assn., Beta Gamma Sigma, Sigma Gamma Tau. Office: Fla State U Tallahassee FL 32306

KNAUSS, STEPHEN CHARLES, civil engineer; b. Poughkeepsie, N.Y., Dec. 14, 1949; s. Howard Cope and Jeanne (Cassese) K.; m. Elizabeth Brunger, June

7, 1975; children—Daniel Alan, Amanda Elaine. B.S. in Civil Engring., Cornell U., 1972, M.E. in Civil Engring., 1973. Registered profl. engr., N.C., Fla. Staff engr. Law Engring., Washington, 1973; instr. soil and geology sect. U.S. Army Engr. Sch., Fort Belvoir, Va., 1974-75; staff engr. Soils and Material Engrs., Raleigh, N.C., 1975-76; staff engr. Pitts. Testing Lab., Durham, N.C., 1976-77, br. mgr., 1977-79, dist. mgr. Tampa, Fla., 1979—. Served to 1st lt. U.S. Army, 1973. Mem. ASCE, ASTM, Soc. Mil. Engrs., Am. Concrete Inst. (pres. Fla. Suncoast chpt.), Fla. Engring. Soc. (v.p. Tampa chpt.), Tampa C. of C. (mem. com. of 100). Office: 512 N Delaware Ave Tampa FL 33606

KNETEN, SUSAN BURTON, oil company executive, geologic consultant; b. Conway, Ark., May 4, 1944; d. Dan. and Irene (Mizell) B.; m. William Rogers Mays, Jr., June 1, 1963 (div. 1978); children—Chapman Rogers Mays, Emily Montague Mays; m. Norval Charles Kneten, Jan. 6, 1979; 1 child, Craig C. B.S. in Geology, Tex. Christian U., 1976. Geologist, Atlantic Richfield, Lafayette, La., 1978-79, Dallas, 1979-81; cons. in geology, Ft. Worth, 1981—; pres. Kneten Oil Co., Ft. Worth, 1984—. Mem. exec. com. I-CARE, Inc., Ft. Worth, 1983-85; chmn. Southside Sector Planning Council, Ft. Worth, 1983. Mem. Am. Assn. Petroleum Geologists (del., alt. del. 1982-85), Ft. Worth Geol. Soc. (sec. 1984-85), Dallas Geol. Soc., Appalachian Geol. Soc., Network for Exec. Women (pres. 1983-85), Roundtable of Ft. Worth, Petroleum Club. Republican. Methodist. Clubs: Woman's, Woman's Wednesday (Ft. Worth). Avocations: gardening; traveling; knitting. Office: Kneten Oil Co Inc PO Box 2017 Fort Worth TX 76113

KNIESNER, THOMAS JOHN, economics educator; b. Cleve., Apr. 22, 1947; s. Harry William and Grace (Russo) K.; m. Deborah A. Freund, Jan. 3, 1981; m. Cheryl Segrist, Dec. 26, 1970 (div. July 1979). B.A. cum laude, Ohio State U., 1969, M.A., 1971, Ph.D., 1974. Asst. prof. econs. U. N.C., Chapel Hill, 1974-79, assoc. prof., 1979—; sr. staff economist Council Econ. Advisers, Exec. Office Pres., Washington, 1982-83; vis. prof. Inst. Policy Scis., Duke U., 1983-84; cons. Rand Corp., U.S. Dept. Energy, Research Triangle Inst. Co-author: Labor Economics, Theory, Evidence and Policy, 1983, 3d edit.; contbr. articles, revs. to profl. jours. Fellow Ford Found., 1969, Ohio State U., 1970, 74. Mem. Am. Econ. Assn., Econometric Soc., Phi Beta Kappa. Avocations: clarinetist; classical chamber music. Office: Dept Econs U NC Chapel Hill NC 27514

KNIGHT, ELIZABETH DALE, educator; b. Greenville, S.C., Nov. 22, 1959; d. Charles Hood and Margaret (Williamson) K. A.A. in Fashion Merchandising, Anderson Coll., 1979; B.A. in Edn., U. S.C.-Spartanburg, 1982, M.Ed., U. S.C.-Columbia, 1986. Tchr. Haynsworth Pvt. Sch., Greenville, 1983-84, Dacusville, S.C., 1984-85, Palmetto Primary Sch., Williamston, S.C., 1985—. Mem. Am. Assn. Counseling Devel., S.C. Assn. Counseling Devel., S.C. Edn. Assn., NEA, S.C. Bd. Realtors, Nat. Bd. Realtors. Baptist. Avocations: swimming; biking. Home: 471 E Parkins Mill Rd Greenville SC 29607 Office: Palmetto Primary Rogers Rd Williamston SC 29697

KNIGHT, ERICA (MADELEINE KAY BAR-SADEH), writer; b. N.Y.C., Jan. 16, 1946; d. Harry and Anne (Zinns) Kay; div.; 1 son, Danny Bar-Sadeh. B.A. cum laude, Boston U., 1967; M.A., U. Miami, 1974; cert. in English lang. and lit. Sorbonne, Paris, 1968; diploma in Hebraic lang. and studies U. Tel Aviv, 1970. Poet writer, model, N.Y.C., Boston, Tel Aviv and Miami, Fla., 1965-78; instr. U. Tel Aviv, 1969-72, U. Miami, 1972-78; media dir. Garber & Goodman Advt., Inc., Miami, 1978-79; advt. exec. Beber Silverstein & Ptnrs., Inc., Miami, 1979-80; 1980; pres. Erica Knight Assocs., Inc., Miami, 1981—; cons. Mem. Am. Assn. Advt. Execs., Ad Fedn. Club Miami, Assn. Poetry Therapy. Clubs: Executive Travellers, Ionosphere. Contbr. articles and poetry to jours.

KNIGHT, JAMES ALBERT, research scientist, consultant, educator; b. La Grange, Ga., Oct. 16, 1920; s. James Albert and Evelyn (Brooks) K.; m. Marian Kemper Krape, Oct. 2, 1948; children—Marcia, Kent, Craig. B.S., Wofford Coll., 1942; M.S., Ga. Inst. Tech., 1944; Ph.D., Pa. State U., 1950. Asst. prof. Ga. Inst. Tech., Atlanta, 1950-53, assoc. prof., 1953-62, research prof., 1962-73, prin. research scientist, 1973—; cons. Nat. Bur. Standards, Washington, 1978—, FAO, Rome, 1984—. Patentee thermochem. conversion of biomass to syngas, 1985; author tech. articles. Served with U.S. Army, 1944-46. Procter & Gamble fellow, 1947-50. Mem. Am. Chem. Soc., AAAS, Phi Beta Kappa, Sigma Xi. Lutheran. Avocations: gardening; tennis; photography. Home: 2117 Kodiak Dr NE Atlanta GA 30345 Office: Ga Tech Research Inst Ga Inst Tech 225 North Ave NW Atlanta GA 30332

KNIGHT, JERRY GLENN, fire chief, educator; b. St. Petersburg, Fla., Jan. 11, 1938; s. Elias David and Pebble Virginia (Sneed) K.; m. Constance O. Becker, Sept. 16, 1961; children—Bryan Keith, Steven Glenn. B.A. in Pub. Safety Adminstrn., Eckerd Coll., 1985. Mem., officer St. Petersburg Fire Dept., 1959-80, fire chief, 1983—; fire chief Largo Fire Dept., Fla., 1980-83; adj. instr. St. Petersburg Jr. Coll., 1975, Nat. Fire Acad., Emmittsburg, Md., 1978-80; cons. U.S. Fire Adminstrn., Washington, 1976, Fla. Dept. Health and Rehab. Services, 1984. Mem. Emergency Med. Services Adv. Council, Pinellas County, Fla., 1974—. Served with USCG, 1955-59. Mem. Internat. Fire Chiefs Assn., Southeastern Fire Chiefs Assn., Fla. Fire Chiefs Assn., Pinellas County Fire Chiefs Assn. (pres. 1984—). Democrat. Episcopalian. Club: N.E. Exchange (St. Petersburg). Lodge: Masons. Avocations: boats; fishing; family camping. Office: St Petersburg Fire Dept 1429 Arlington Ave N Saint Petersburg FL 33705

KNIGHT, JOHN FRANCIS, insurance company executive; b. N.Y.C., Sept. 30, 1919; s. Samuel F. and Abigail (Sullivan) K.; m. Marilyn Rockefeller, Oct. 30, 1948; children—Jeffrey J., Melanie J., John Mark, Jane M., James M. B.B.A. cum laude, St. John's U., 1952. With Republic Fin. Services Inc. Republic Ins. Group, Dallas, 1939—, agy. supr., 1950-56, asst. v.p., 1956-60, v.p., 1960-67, sr. v.p., 1967-69, exec. v.p., 1969-71, sr. exec. v.p., 1971-72, pres., 1972-83, vice chmn. bd., 1983—, also dir.; adv. dir. Fidelity-N.Y., Floral Park, N.Y. Served to maj. AUS, 1942-46. Decorated Bronze Star. Mem. Ins. Club Dallas. Home: 16 Coolidge St Malverne NY 11565 Office: 2727 Turtle Creek Blvd Dallas TX 75219

KNIGHT, JULIA EDWARDS, retired educational administrator; b. DeWitt County, Tex., Feb. 24, 1921; d. Nathan and Susie (Wimbish) Edwards; B.A., Huston-Tillotson U., 1942; M.A., Our Lady of the Lake U., 1957; postgrad. Our Lady of the Lake U., Trinity U.; m. Levi M. Knight, Apr. 14, 1951; 1 dau., Linda Myra. Tchr. English, Aycock High Sch., 1946-51; elem. tchr. Edgewood Ind. Sch. Dist., San Antonio, 1951-65; prin. Johnson Elem. Sch., San Antonio, 1966-82. Trustee San Antonio Public Libraries, 1977—; active LWV; del. Democratic Senatorial Dist. Conv., 1980; former pres., chmn. bd. Miller Child Devel. Center; active Tex. Coalition of Black Democrats, Community Workers Council; mem. exec. com. San Antonio br. NAACP; bd. dirs., vice-chmn. Eastside San Antonio Econ. Devel. Council; mem. United San Antonio Edn. Study Com.; trustee, steward, supt. Sunday sch. Emmanuel African Methodist Episcopal Ch.; mem. human resources exec com. San Antonio Area Council Govts.; bd. dirs. San Antonio Indsl. Devel. Authority. Hon. life mem. Tex. Congress PTAs; recipient Outstanding Black Woman's award S.W. 10th Episcopal dist. A.M.E. Ch. Mem. NEA, Tex. Tchrs. Assn., Edgewood Adminstrs. Assn., Elem. Prins. and Suprs. Assn., Friends of Library, Friends of Goodwill Industries, Nat. Council Negro Women, Alpha Tau Omega, Alpha Kappa Alpha. Club: Urban Elite Garden. Home: 4330 Eulalee Dr San Antonio TX 78220

KNIGHT, KEITH MATHIAS, hospital administrator; b. Miami, Fla. Aug. 26, 1949; s. Donald and Carmen Elizabeth (Schank) K.; m. Sandra Kay Bloomster, Mar. 19, 1977; 1 child, Keith Mathias, Jr. R.N., Jackson Meml. Hosp., 1971; A.S. in Bus. Adminstrn., Miami Dade Jr. Coll., 1976; B.B.A., U. Fla., 1978. Hosp. orderly Hialeah Hosp., Fla., 1965-68, staff nurse in emergency, 1973-75; staff nurse in emergency Palmetto Gen. Hosp., Hialeah, 1975-76; asst. v.p. Lee Meml. Hosps., Fort Myers, Fla., 1978—. Mem. Dem. Com., Fort Myers, 1980. Served to 1st lt. U.S. Army, 1971-73. Mem. Ambulatory Services Assn. Fla. (pres. 1985-87). Roman Catholic. Club: Windward Fleet (Fort Myers). Avocations: sailing; flying; music; sports. Office: Lee Meml Hosp 2776 Cleveland Ave Fort Myers FL 33902

KNIGHT, LYDIA FRANCES, librarian; b. Chattanooga, Tenn., Jan. 28, 1956; d. Charles Franklin and Mary Frances (Cashion) K. A.A., Dalton (Ga.) Jr. Coll., 1977; B.A., U. Tenn.-Chattanooga, 1979; M.L.S., George Peabody Coll., 1981. Library clk. U. Tenn.-Chattanooga, 1979-80; library grad. asst. Country Music Found. Library and Media Ctr., Nashville, 1980-81; librarian Tri-Cities State Tech. Inst., Blountville, Tenn., 1981—. Editor: The Armarius, 1982—. John C. Winslow fellow, 1980-81. Mem. ALA, Tenn. Library Assn. (bylaws and procedures com. 1985—, editorial adv. bd. Tenn. Librarian 1985—), Southeastern Library Assn., Am. Tech. Edn. Assn., Boone Tree Library Assn. (pres. 1982-84). Democrat. Presbyterian. Home: Route 17 Lakeshore Apt 32 Johnson City TN 37601 Office: Tri-Cities State Tech Inst PO Box 246 Blountville TN 37617

KNIGHT, MARY LUCILLE, convalescent center administrator; b. Enid, Okla., Dec. 5, 1938; d. Otis Stanley and Mary Ellen (Record) Kile; m. E. Harmon Knight, Apr. 30, 1962; children—Sherri, Fran, Cathy. Med. asst. Dr. Fred Thomas, Dallas, 1963-67; x-ray asst., physicians' asst. Prevost Meml. Hosp., Donaldsonville, La., 1967-72; asst. adminstr. Archusa Convalescent Center, Quitman, Miss., 1976—, sec. bd. dirs., 1976-78. Lic. adminstr. Mem. Miss. Nursing Home Assn. Republican. Baptist. Home: 10 Betty Circle Quitman MS 39355 Office: Hwy 511 E Quitman MS 39355

KNIGHT, ROBERT JACKSON, JR., research horticulturist, plant explorer, educator; b. Clearwater, Fla., May 24, 1926; s. Robert Jackson and Marguerite Munroe (Wooddell) K. B.S. in Agr., U. Fla., Gainesville, 1951, Ph.D. in Biology, U. Va., Charlottesville, 1958. Researcher Agrl. Research Service, U.S. Dept. Agr., Beltsville, Md., 1958-61, Carbondale, Ill., 1961-62, Miami, Fla., 1962, research horticulturist specializing in 1958—(since); courtesy prof. fruit crops dept. U. Fla., Gainesville, biology dept. Fla. Internat. U., Miami; cons. tropical, subtropical pomology; pres. Fla. chpt. The Nature Conservancy, 1971, bd. mem., 1972-74. Served with U.S. Army, 1944-46. Decorated Combat Infantry badge; Hume fellow Fedn. Garden Clubs, 1951-52, Du Pont Blandy Farm fellow U. Va., 1953-58; recipient Fleming Research award, U. Va., 1957. Mem. Am. Soc. Hort. Sci., Am. Genetic Assn., Am. Pomological Soc., AAAS, Fla. State Hort. Soc. (best paper award Krome meml. sect. 1975), Sigma Xi, Alpha Zeta. Democrat. Presbyterian. Clubs: Country of Coral Gables (Fla.), Flamingo Dinner (Coral Gables), Sword, Marlin (Miami). Led plant explorations in Thailand, Brazil, Mexico, Malaysia, released new varities of fruit; contbr. Contbr. chpt. to book, numerous research papers, articles to publs. Home: 19620 Franjo Rd Miami FL 33157 Office: 13601 Old Cutler Rd Miami FL 33158

KNOBLAUCH, MARILYN DEATRICK, realtor; b. N.Y.C., May 4, 1945; d. Robert Sayres and Margaret Elizabeth (Butterworth) D.; m. Peter Knoblauch, Apr. 1, 1967; children—Michael P., Patricia L., Scott M., David P. R.N. diploma Holy Name Sch. Nursing, Teaneck, N.J., 1966. R.N., Fla., N.J. Pediatric charge nurse Naples Community Hosp. (Fla.), 1976-78, head nurse/supr., 1978-82; realtor assoc., Propr. Properties of Naples, Inc. 1982-83, Realtor, ptnr., 1983—. Leader Gulf Coast council Girl Scouts U.S.A., 1976; Cub Scout leader Southwest council Boy Scouts Am., 1977-81. Catholic Daus. Am. scholar, 1963-66. Mem. Nat. Assn. Realtors, Naples Area Bd. Realtors, Women's Council Realtors (pres. 1984—). Roman Catholic. Home: 6800 6th Ave SW Naples FL 33999

KNOLLE, MARY ANNE, human resources company executive; b. Kilgore, Tex., Jan. 7, 1941; d. Evert Eric and Frances Leone (Scott) Ericson; B.A., North Tex. State U., 1962; M.A., U. Tex., Austin, 1968; postgrad. UCLA, 1964-66, U. Houston, 1974-76; m. Jon W. Knolle; children—Clay Claflin, Sunny Claflin, Sara Ann Knolle, Evelyn Knolle. Editor co. publs. Gt. S.W. Life Ins. Co., 1962; prof. U. Balt., 1968, Miami (Fla.) Dade Coll., 1968, Savannah (Ga.) State Coll., 1969, U. Houston, 1972-76; dir. public relations Alvin (Tex.) Coll., 1970-72; founder, pres. Panorama Programs, Houston, 1972-76; mgmt. devel. tng. coordinator Brown & Root, Inc., Houston, 1970-79; div. founder, mgr. mgmt. and organizational devel. systems Diversified Human Resources Group, Inc., Houston, 1979—; founder, pres. Panorama Mgmt. Inst., Houston, 1979—; cons. moot ct. U. Tex. Law Sch., 1965—. Regional speech contest judge Houston Jaycees. Recipient Blockbuster award United Way, 1979. Mem. Am. Soc. Tng. and Devel., Houston C. of C. (chmn. edn. com.), Alpha Delta Pi (pres. alumnae). Presbyterian. Club: Houston Indoor Tennis. Office: 12307 Broken Arrow Houston TX 77024

KNOPP, ANTHONY KEITH, history educator; b. St. Paul, Apr. 15, 1940; s. Keith Kenneth and Mary (FitzGibbon) K.; m. Margueritte F. Callicotte, June 8, 1963 (div. 1979); 1 child, Katrina Anne; m. Martha C. Valdez, May 12, 1985. B.A., Coll. St. Thomas, 1962, M.A.T., 1963; M.A., U. Minn., 1966; Ph.D., Tex. Tech. U., 1973. Instr. history San Antonio Coll., 1966-68, 71-72; asst. prof., asst. dean Coll. St. Thomas, St. Paul, 1972-76; instr., chmn. social sci. dept. Tex. Southmost Coll., Brownsville, 1976—; dir. Tex. Com. Humanities grant for Tex. Revolution; part-time instr. grad. courses Pan Am. U., Brownsville. NEH summer seminar fellow, 1980. Mem. Latin Am. Studies Assn., Tex. Jr. Coll. Tchrs. Assn., Soc. for History Edn., Brownsville Hist. Assn. (bd. dirs.), Phi Alpha Theta. Republican. Contbr. articles to profl. jours. Home: 642 W Levee St Brownsville TX 78520 Office: 80 Fort Brown Brownsville TX 78520

KNORPP, J. RONALD, utility executive; b. Louisville, July 26, 1936; s. John Henry and Corrine (Wirth) K.; m. Shirley Ann Scott, Nov. 18, 1963; children—Rhonda, Rachele, Eric, Kevin. B.A., Bellarmine Coll., Louisville, 1958; M.B.A. summa cum laude, Clemson-Furman univs., 1973. C.P.A., Ky. Acct., Humphrey Robinson & Co., Louisville, 1959-66; v.p. subs. Liberty Corp., Greenville, S.C., 1966-72; v.p. fin. Fla. Gas Co., Winter Park, 1973—; exec. v.p., chief fin. officer Fla. Gas Transmission Co., Winter Park; adminstrv. bd. Sun First Nat. Bank, Orlando, Fla., 1978—. Mem. parish council, fin. com. St. Mary Magdalen Roman Catholic Ch., Orlando, 1977—; bd. dirs. Central Fla. chpt. Leukemia Soc. Am., 1976—; trustee Winter Park Meml. Hosp., 1978—. Served with USMCR, 1958-63. Mem. Am. Inst. C.P.A.s, Am. Gas Assn., Interstate Natural Gas Assn., Am. Mgmt. Assn. Republican. Office: Fla Gas Transmission Co 1560 Orange Ave Winter Park FL 32790*

KNOTTNERUS, JOHN DAVID, sociology educator; b. Alton, Ill., Dec. 23, 1946; s. John Henry and Lois Marian (Moles) K. B.A., Beloit Coll., 1969; M.A., So. Ill. U., 1975, Ph.D., 1981. Asst. prof. sociology U. Tampa, Fla., 1981—. Contbr. articles to profl. jours. Regional dir. Fla. Council on Family Relations, Tampa Bay area, 1984—, bd. dirs., State of Fla., 1984—; mem. steering com. Tampa Bay Family Conf., 1986. Served with M.C., U.S. Army, 1969-71. U. Tampa faculty devel. fellow, 1982, 83, 85, 86. Mem. Am. Sociol. Assn., So. Sociol. Assn., Fla. Council on Family Relations, Phi Kappa Phi, Sigma Alpha Epsilon. Democrat. Baptist. Avocations: jogging; reading; hiking; travel; music. Home: 141 E Davis Blvd Apt 211 Tampa FL 33606 Office: Div of Social Sci U Tampa Tampa FL 33606

KNOTTS, GLENN R(ICHARD), university educator; b. East Chicago, Ind., May 16, 1934; s. V. Raymond and Opal Ione (Alexander) K.; B.S., Purdue U., 1956, M.S., 1960, Ph.D., 1968; M.S., Ind. U., 1964; Dr. Med. Sci. (hon.), Union Coll., 1975; Sc.D. (hon.), Ricker Coll., 1975. Mem. profl. staff Bapt. Meml. Hosp., San Antonio, 1957-60; instr. chemistry San Antonio (Tex.) Coll., 1958-60; adminstrv. asst. AMA, Chgo., 1960-61, research asso., 1961-62, dir. advt. evaluation, div. sci. activities, 1963-69; exec. dir. Am. Sch. Health Assn., Kent, Ohio, 1969-72; vis. disting. prof. health sci. Kent State U., 1969-72, prof., mem. grad. faculty dept. allied health scis., 1972-75, coordinator grad. studies and research, 1975; editor-in-chief, prof. med. journalism U. Tex. System Cancer Center M.D. Anderson Hosp. and Tumor Inst., Houston, 1975-85, head dept. med. info. and publs., 1975-79, dir. div. ednl. resources, 1979-82; dir. devel. U. Texas Health Sci. Ctr., Houston, 1985—; vis. prof. health edn. Madison (Va.) Coll., summer, 1965, Union (Ky.) Coll., summers 1965, 66, 69, Utah State U., 1965; vis. lectr. Ind. U., 1965-66; vis. lectr. pharmacology Purdue U., 1968-69; vis. prof. Pahlavi U. Med. Sch., Iran, summer, 1970; adj. prof. dept. allied health scis. Kent State U., 1975—; prof. dept. biomed. communications U. Tex. Sch. Allied Health Scis., Houston, 1976—; prof. dept. behavioral scis. U. Tex. Sch. Public Health, 1977—; prof. U. Tex. Grad. Sch. Biomed. Scis., 1983—; adj. prof. journalism U. Tex., Austin, 1984—; cons. health scis. communications, 1969—; pres. Health Scis. Inst., 1973—; mem. exec. com. Internat. Union Sch. and Univ. Health and Medicine, Paris, 1969—. Bd. dirs. Med. Arts Pub. Found., Houston, 1977-80; mem. adv. bd. World Meetings Inc., 1971—. Served with U.S. Army, 1956-58. Recipient Gold medal French-Am. Allergy Soc., 1973. Fellow Am. Public Health Assn., Am. Sch. Health Assn. (mem. exec. com. 1968-72, editor Jour. Sch. Health 1975-76, Disting. Service award 1973), Am. Inst. Chemists, Royal Soc. Health; mem. Internat. Union Health Edn., AAHPER, Am. Acad. Pharm. Scis., Am. Med. Writers Assn., Am. Pharm. Assn., AAUP, Am. Chem. Soc., AAAS, AMA, Purdue U. Alumni Assn., Ind. U. Alumni Assn., Union Coll. Alumni Assn., Ricker Coll. Alumni Assn., Sigma Xi, Rho Chi, Sigma Delta Chi, Eta Sigma Gamma, Phi Delta Kappa, Kappa Psi. Republican. Presbyterian. Clubs: Marines Meml. (San Francisco); Warwick (Houston); Univ. Faculty, Drs. (Houston). Lodge: Rotary. Co-author various texts and filmstrips on health sci.; contbr. numerous articles to profl. jours.; cons. editor Clin. Pediatrics, 1971—; contbg. editor Annals of Allergy, 1972—; exec. editor Cancer Bull., 1976-85; mem. numerous editorial bds. Home: 2600 Bellefontaine Houston TX 77025 Office: U Tex Health Sci Ctr at Houston PO Box 20036 Houston TX 77225

KNOTTS, ULYSSES SIMEON, JR., business educator; b. Augusta, Ga., Nov. 18, 1924; s. Ulysses Simeon and Daisy Iona (Gleaton) K.; m. Barbara Florence Dunham, Apr. 28, 1950; children—Deborah Joyce Knotts Callahan, Cassandra Dunham Knotts Mott, Ulysses Simeon III, Robert Edward. B.B.A. in Acctg., U. Ga., 1948; M.L. in Econs., U. Pitts., 1957; Ph.D. in Econs., U. Nebr., 1971. Commd. 2d lt. U.S. Air Force, 1948, advanced through grades to lt. col., 1966; various duties from aircraft comdr. strategic jet bombardment aircraft to ops. officer at all levels of command; final assignment as chief Program Mgmt. Br., Hdqrs. SAC, Offutt AFB, Nebr., ret., 1969; prof. bus. Central Mich. U., Mt. Pleasant, 1971-77; prof. mgmt. Ga. So. Coll., Statesboro, 1977—; pres. Hospital Systems, Inc., 1982—; cons., seminar leader in field; dir. PROSEM, Inc. Mem. diocesan council Episcopal Diocese of Ga., 1980-83; sr. warden Trinity Epis. Ch., 1979-81. Mem. Assn. for Bus. Simulation and Exptl. Learning, Am. Inst. for Decision Scis. (Southeastern chpt.) Southeastern Inst. Mgmt. Scis., So. Mgmt. Assn., Beta Gamma Sigma, Omicron Delta Epsilon, Sigma Iota Epsilon. Republican. Author: (with Leo G. Parrish) The Hospital Simulator: HOSPSIM, 1981; (with Ernest W. Swift) Management Science for Management Decisions, 1978; also monograph. Contbr. articles to bus. and mgmt. to profl. jours. Home: 34 Golf Club Circle Statesboro GA 30458 Office: Dept Mgmt LB 8152 Ga So Coll Statesboro GA 30460

KNOWLES, MALCOLM SHEPHERD, educator; b. Livingston, Mont., Aug. 24, 1913; s. Albert Dixon and Marian (Straton) K.; m. Hulda Elisabet Fornell, Aug. 20, 1935; children—Eric Stuart, Barbara Elisabeth Knowles Harti. A.B., Harvard U., 1934, M.A., U. Chgo., 1949, Ph.D., 1960; D.Sc. (hon.), Lowell Tech. Inst., 1975. Dep. adminstr. Nat. Youth Adminstrn. Mass., Boston, 1935-40; dir. adult edn. YMCA, Boston, 1940-43, dir. USO, Detroit, 1943-44, exec. sec., Chgo., 1946-51; exec. dir. Adult Edn. Assn. U.S., Chgo., 1951-59; prof. edn. Boston U., 1959-74, N.C. State U., 1974-79; mem. Task Force on Lifelong Edn., UNESCO Inst. Edn., 1972—; dir. Leadership Resources, Inc., 1962-67, Project Assos., Washington, 1967-78; cons. on tng. Democratic Nat. Com., 1956-60; cons. Office Consumer Affairs, Office of Pres., 1972-73, IBM, Polaroid, Steel Co. Can., Westinghouse Corp., AT&T, United Airlines, Mass. Dept. Mental Health, NIMH, Overseas Edn. Fund, Nat. Council Chs., Girl Scouts U.S.A., U.S. depts. Labor, Justice, Post Office, HEW, Urban League, various schs. and univs., others. Mem. adv. council Franklin Pierce Coll., Rindge, N.H., 1969—; bd. visitors Nat. Def. U. Served with USNR, 1944-46. Recipient Delbert Clark award W. Ga. Coll., Carrollton, 1967; Nat. Tng. Labs. Inst. for Applied Behavioral Sci. fellow, 1969—. Mem. Adult Edn. Assn. U.S., AAUP, Authors Guild. Club: Harvard of Boston. Author: Informal Adult Education, 1950; (with Hulda Knowles) How to Develop Better Leaders, 1955, Introduction to Group Dynamics, 1959; The Adult Education Movement in the U.S., 1962; Higher Adult Education in the U.S., 1969; The Modern Practice of Adult Education: Andragogy vs. Pedagogy, 1980; The Adult Learner: A Neglected Species, 1984; Self-Directed Learning: A Guide for Learners and Teachers, 1975; A History of Adult Education in the U.S., 1977; Andragogy in Action, 1984; Editor Handbook of Adult Education in the U.S., 1960. Contbr. articles to profl. jours. Host TV series The Dynamics of Leadership, NET, 1962; And Now We Are People, Group W Network, 1969. Home: 1506 Delmont Dr Raleigh NC 27606

KNOWLES, PHYLLIS BRADFUTE, title insurance company executive; b. Cin., Oct. 16, 1927; d. Fred Lott and Mary (White) Bradfute; m. Harry V. Knowles, Aug. 24, 1950 (div. 1973); children—Pamela A. Fleizach, Debra A. B.A., Barnard Coll., 1950. Exec. sec. Carrie Chapman Catt Meml., N.Y.C., 1950-53; pres. Quinbee & Bradfute Internat. Promotions, Eastchester, N.Y., 1957-75; exec. mgr. Urban Developers, Phila., 1975-79; v.p., chief exec. officer Gibraltar Title & Escrow Co. of Boca Raton, Fla., 1979—. Author: Records of the Town of Eastchester, 1969. Pres. LWV, Eastchester, 1954-56, Eastchester Hist. Soc., 1965-76; treas. West County Hist. Soc., 1970-76; treas. Univ. Arts League, Phila., 1977-79. Mem. Nat. Assn. Notaries. Republican. Methodist. Club: Boca West. Avocations: Doll house building; historian; lecturer. Home: 1626 Bridgewood Dr Boca Raton FL 33434 Office: Gibraltar Title & Escrow Co of Boca Raton 301 Crawford Blvd Boca Raton FL 33432

KNOWLES, ROBERT LEVIS, producer, theatre manager, educator; b. Ft. Pierce, Fla., June 22, 1925; s. Thomas Camden and Lillie Drew (Garnto) K.; m. Nancy Entrekin, June 6, 1954; children—Susan Johnston, Melissa Robin Miner. B.A., Stetson U., 1949; M.A., U. Fla., 1950. Prof. theatre Auburn U., Ala., 1952-55, 56-66; actor, N.Y.C., 1955-56; mng. dir. Theatre Jacksonville, Fla., 1967-80; prodn. coordinator The Lost Colony, Manteo, N.C., 1968-80, assoc. producer, gen. mgr., 1980—; v.p. Southeastern Theatre Conf., 1972-73, pres., 1973-74. Author: Use of Tape Recorder for Sound in Theatre, 1955. Bd. dirs. Dare County Tourist Bur., Manteo, N.C., 1980—. Served to sgt. U.S. Army, 1943-46, ETO. Recipient Suzanne Davis award for Disting. Service to So. Theatre, 1985. Mem. Actors Equity, SAG, Southeastern Theatre Conf., N.C. Assn. Profl. Theatres, Phi Sigma Soc., Phi Kappa Phi, Sigma Nu. Office: The Lost Colony PO Box 40 Manteo NC 27954

KNOWLTON, WILLIAM ALLEN, former army officer, corporate director, consultant; b. Weston, Mass., June 19, 1920; s. Frank Warren and Isabelle (Riese) K.; m. Marjorie Adams Downey, Nov. 27, 1943; children—William Allen, Davis Downey, Timothy Riese, Hollister Knowlton Petraeus. B.S., U.S. Mil. Acad., 1943; M.A., Columbia U., 1957; LL.D. (hon.), U. Akron, 1972. Commd. 2d lt. U.S. Army, 1943, advanced through grades to gen., 1976; assigned 7th Armored Div., World War II, Army General Staff, 1947-49, SHAPE, France, 1951-54; assoc. prof. social scis. U.S. Mil. Acad., 1955-58; bn. comdr. 3d Armored Cav. Regiment, 1958-59; mil. attache, Tunisia, 1961-63; brig. comdr., Ft. Knox, Ky., 1963-64; assigned Office Chief Staff, U.S. Army, 1964-65; mil. asst. to spl. asst. to sec. and dep. sec. def. Office Sec. Def., 1965-66; sec. Joint Staff, dir. pacification support, also dep. asst. chief staff for civil ops. and revolutionary devel. support U.S. Mil. Assistance Command, Vietnam, 1966-67; asst. div. comdr. 9th Inf. Div., Vietnam, 1968; sec. gen. staff Office Chief Staff, U.S. Army, 1968-70; supt. U.S. Mil. Acad., 1970-74; chief staff hdqrs. U.S. European Command, Stuttgart, Germany, 1974-76; comdr. Allied Land Forces S.E. Europe, Izmir, Turkey, 1976-77; U.S. rep NATO Mil. Com., Brussels, Belgium, 1977-80; ret., 1980; internat. cons., 1980—; sr. assoc. Burdeshaw Assocs. Ltd., 1981—; sr. fellow Inst. Higher Def. Studies Nat. Def. U., 1984—; dir. Chubb Corp., Fed. Ins. Co., Vigilant Ins. Co. Trustee Davis and Elkins Coll., 1982—. Decorated Def. and Army D.S.M., Silver Star with 2 oak leaf clusters, Legion of Merit with oak leaf cluster, D.F.C., Bronze Star with V device, Air medal with 9 oak leaf clusters, Army Commendation medal with oak leaf cluster; Knight Comdr. Cross Order of Merit (Ger.); officer Legion of Honor (France); Belgian and Vietnamese decorations; recipient George Washington honor medal Freedoms Found. at Valley Forge, 1957, 58. Mem. Am. Mil. Inst., Am. Mgmt. Assns., Nat. Assn. Corp. Dirs., Council Fgn. Relations, Am. Acad. Polit. and Social Sci., Acad. Polit. Sci., Soc. Mayflower Descendants, SR, Soc. Colonial Wars. Clubs: Univ. (N.Y.C.); Army and Navy (Washington). Contbr. to Ency. Americana and nat. mags. Home: 4520 4th Rd N Arlington VA 22203

KNOX, JOANNA MAURICE, general contractor; b. Phila., Jan. 1, 1925; d. Joseph and Annie M. (Myers) Zuchelli; m. Eugene C. Kiger, Oct. 13, 1944 (div. 1951); m. Walter B. Knox, Apr. 3, 1952; children—Eugene C., Barbara Knox Betts. Student, U. Ga., 1969, U. South Fla., 1974-75, U. North Fla., 1978-79, U. Central Fla., 1982. Asst. architect staff Ga. State U., Atlanta, 1966-68; v.p., mgr. Empire State Chair, Atlanta, 1969-71; v.p. constrn. Equity Fin., Chgo., 1979-81; sr. engr. constrn. Fed. Express, Memphis, 1981-83; pres. Constrn. Design Real Estate, Inc., Mt. Dora, Fla., 1984—. Designer interior Central Bank and Trust, 1971 (appeared mag., award 1971). Candidate for mayor Mt. Dora, 1983; mem. planning and zoning bd., Mt. Dora, 1984, Council of 50. Mem. C. of C. (bd. dirs.). Home: 302 W 6th Ave Mount Dora FL 32757 Office: Construction Design Real Estate Inc 717 N Donnelly St Mount Dora FL

KOCH, FRANCES ANN, nurse; b. Spur, Tex., Apr. 13, 1939; d. T.J. and Mary Frances (Van Meter) Taylor; R.N., B.S., Tex. Christian U., 1961; postgrad. Tex. Tech. U., summer 1958, nights 1967-68; M.S. in Nursing (USPHS grantee), U. Ariz., 1971; m. Stuart Alan Koch, Mar. 20, 1970; children—Lesleigh, Brett, Todd. Operating room supr. W.Tex. Hosp., Lubbock, 1961-69; operating room supr., instr. nursing Coll. Medicine, U. Ariz., Tucson, 1970-73; sch. nurse Torrejon AFB, Madrid, Spain, 1974-75; dir. operating room Seton Med. Center, Austin, Tex., 1975-79; dir. surg. services Scott & White Meml. Hosp., Temple, Tex., 1979-85; dir. operating room services Spohn Hosp., Corpus Christi, Tex., 1985—; clin. instr. U. Mary Hardin Baylor Coll. Nursing, 1981; adv. com. operating room tech. program Pima County Jr. Coll., Austin Community Coll. Nursing cons. Am. Cancer Soc., Lubbock, 1968, profl. edn. com., Ariz., 1972. Cert. nurse operating room. Mem. Assn. Operating Room Nurses (pres. Central Tex. 1981-82, pub. chpt. newsletter 1979-82, nat. subcom. recommended practice 1981), Tex. Assn. Operating Room Nurses (pres.-elect 1981-82, pres. 1982-83, dir. 1979-81), Assn. Advancement of Med. Instrumentation (pres. regional council 1983, nominating com. 1983), Am. Nurses Assn., Sigma Theta Tau. Republican. Methodist. Instr. continuing edn. for operating room nurses, U. Ariz., 1972, speaker on subject nat. congress Assn. Operating Room Nurses, 1974. Home: 14105 White Cap Corpus Christi TX 78418 Office: 600 Elizabeth St Corpus Christi TX 78404

KOCH, JANET SUE, human resource development consultant; b. Spring Valley, Ill., Oct. 29, 1945; d. Lawrence Elton and Arlene Marie (Dagner) Myers; B.S., U. Ill., 1967; postgrad. Tex. So. U., S.W. Tex. State U.; 1 son, Jon Robert. Program analyst regional office OEO, Austin, Tex., 1967-68; center dir. YWCA Head Start Program, San Antonio, 1968-70; successively service rep., tng. technician, mgr. mortgagee services, mgr. ins. edn., mgr. ednl. devel., mgr. on-th-job tng. unit United Services Automobile Assn., San Antonio, 1970-84; pres. Koch and Assocs., San Antonio, 1984—; guest speaker profl. meetings; guest speaker Trinity U., U. Tex. San Antonio, St. Phillip's Coll., San Antonio Coll. Mem. adv. com. Tex. Dept. Human Resources, San Antonio, 1984. Named Boss of Yr., Office Ednl. Assn. of South San Antonio High Sch., 1981. Vocat. Office Edn. of Harlandale High Sch., 1979; cert. profl. ins. woman. Mem. Nat. Assn. Ins. Women (pres. 1978-79, exec. bd. chpt.), Am. Soc. Tng. and Devel. (rep. Women's Network 1978-81, pres. San Antonio chpt. 1984, leadership devel. chmn. 1981-83, nat. chmn. Women's Network 1981-82, regional rep. career devel. div. 1985-86).

KOCHAKIAN, CHARLES DANIEL, endocrinologist, educator, researcher; b. Haverhill, Mass., Nov. 18, 1908; s. Daniel S. and Haigoohee (Nalbandian) K.; m. B. Irene Armstrong, July 27, 1940; 1 child, Charles P. A.B., Boston U., 1930, A.M., 1931; Ph.D., U. Rochester, 1936. From instr. to assoc. prof. U. Rochester, N.Y., 1936-50; prof. research biochemistry U. Okla., Oklahoma City, 1951-57; head biochemistry and endocrinology Okla. Med. Research Found., Oklahoma City, 1951-57, coordinator research, 1953-55; dir., prof. exptl. endocrinology U. Ala., Birmingham, 1961-79, prof. emeritus, 1979; chmn. screening Commn. Steroid Hormones, AMA, 1952-57; mem. commn. growth NRC, 1949-51. Author, editor: How It Was: Anabolic Action of Steroids, 1984. Editor: Anabolic Androenic Steroids, 1976. Contbr. numerous articles to profl. jours. Elder Westminster Presbyn. Ch., Oklahoma City, Southminster Presbyn. Ch., Birmingham, Mt. Brook Presbyn. Ch., Birmingham. Recipient Claude Bernard medal U. Montreal, 1950; Endocrine medal Osaka Endocrine Soc. Japan, 1962; Collegium Disting. Alumni award Boston U. Fellow AAAS; mem. Am. Chem. Soc. Endocrine Soc., Am. Soc. Biol. Chemists, Am. Physiol. Soc., Jefferson County Div. Ala. Am. Cancer Soc. Club: The Club. Avocations: photography; traveling; gardening; golf; tennis. Home: 3617 Oakdale Rd Birmingham AL 35223 Office: U Ala Sch Medicine University Station Birmingham AL 35294

KOCHER, ERIC GLENN, lawyer; b. Brussels, Feb. 29, 1948; s. Eric and Margaret (Helburn) K. B.A. in Polit. Sci., Am. U., 1969; J.D., Boston Coll., 1972. Bar: Ga. 1972. Mem. staff U.S. Senator Edward M. Kennedy, Washington, 1966-69; mem. staff press sect. Presdl. Campaign of Robert F. Kennedy, Washington, 1968; mng. atty. Brunswick (Ga.) Legal Aid Soc., 1972-73; atty. Glynn County Pub. Defenders Office, Brunswick, 1973-75; sole practice, Brunswick, 1975-77; pub. defender Brunswick Jud. Circuit, 1976-78; mng. atty. Ga. Legal Services Program, Gainsville Regional Office, 1978-82; dir. Pro Bono Project, State Bar Ga., Atlanta, 1982-84, chmn. legal aid com., 1984—; ptnr. Kocher, Wilson, Korschun & Cobb, Atlanta, 1984— dir. Coalition for Legal Services, 1981-84. First v.p. St. Simons (Ga.) Concerned Citizens Assn., 1974-75, pres., 1975-76; mem. Mental Health Adv. Council for 6 county area, Ga., 1974-76, chmn., 1975-76; bd. dirs. Lawyers Alliance for Nuclear Arms Control, 1984—, Interfaith vol. Lawyers, 1984—; mem. profl. adv. bd. Patterns Drug Counseling Center, Brunswick, 1973-74; bd. dirs. Ga. Clearinghouse on Prisons and Jails, 1973-75, Ctr. for Law and Edn., 1985—, Seven Stages Theatre, 1986—. Mem. ACLU, Nat. Assn. Criminal Def. Lawyers, Nat. Legal Aid and Defender Assn., ABA, Brunswick Bar Assn. (dir. 1975-76, pres. young lawyers sect. 1974-75), State Bar Ga. (exec. council young lawyers sect. 1974-76), Atlanta Bar Assn., St. Simons Island Players. Adv. bd. Nat. Clearinghouse Rev., 1979-81. Home: PO Box 8623 Atlanta GA 30306 Office: Kocher Wilson Korschun & Cobb Suite 500 1422 W Peachtree St Atlanta GA 30309

KOEHLER, WALTER HERMAN, JR., bakery executive; North Little Rock, Jan. 13, 1924; s. Walter Herman and Eva M. (Siepiela) K.; B.S.C., St. Louis U., 1947; postgrad. Harvard U., 1945; m. Mary Evelyn Troillett, June 8, 1948; children—Daniel W., Robert M., Ralph E. With Koehler Bakery Co., North Little Rock, 1947—, pres., 1955—, chmn., 1983—; pres. Kitty Koehler's Kitchens, Inc., North Little Rock, 1965—; pres. Compko, Inc., North Little Rock, 1977—; dir. First Am. Nat. Bank, North Little Rock. Mem. exec. com. ARC, 1977-80, v.p., 1977-80, chpt. chmn., 1983-84. Served to lt. (j.g.) USNR, 1943-46. Mem. Am. Soc. Bakery Engrs., Retail Bakers Am. Clubs: Rotary (dist. gov. 1972-73); K.C.; The Little Rock; North Hills Country; Elks. Home: 32 Heritage Park Circle North Little Rock AR 72116 Office: 5902 Warden Rd North Little Rock AR 72116

KOELLA, CARL OHM, JR., lawyer, state senator; b. Blount County, Tenn., Oct. 10, 1933; s. Carl Ohm and Betty (Zoller) K.; B.S. in Bus. Adminstrn., U. Tenn., LL.L.B., 1960; m. Maribel Watson; children—Carl, Richard, Abby, Laura. Admitted to Tenn. bar; individual practice law, 1960-72; partner Koella & Dixon, Maryville, 1972—; mem. Tenn. Senate, 1972—, past chmn. rules com., asst. minority leader, sec. judiciary com., mem. commerce and labor com., state and local govt. com. Bd. dirs. Peninsula Psychiat. Hosps., Inc.; past chmn. Blount County Republican Party; del. Tenn. Constl. Conv., 1964. Served to capt. U.S. Army. Named State Senator of Yr., Youngs Ams. for Freedom, 1979, 80. Mem. Am. Judicature Soc., ABA, Tenn. Bar Assn., Am. Legion. Presbyterian. Club: Maryville Kiwanis. Address: PO Box 6 Maryville TN 37801

KOEN, OTTIS VAUGHN, writer, photographer, educator; b. Mills County, Tex., Nov. 15, 1906; s. Clairborne and Rosa (Qualls) K.; B.A., Tex. Technol. U., 1929; M.A., Columbia U., 1932; postgrad. U. Tex., 1935-82; m. Margaret Branch, Jan. 30, 1937; children—Billy Vaughn, Beverly Koen La Grone. Free-lance writer, 1925—; tchr. gen. sci. Lubbock (Tex.) Public Schs., 1929-30; tchr., prin. Ft. Davis (Tex.) Public Schs., 1932-35; tchr., head English dept. Mt. Pleasant (Tex.) Public Schs., 1935-36; tchr., adminstr. Graham (Tex.) Public Schs., 1937-42; owner, operator photog. bus., Austin, Tex., 1945-68; tchr. Austin Public Schs., 1979-80, 82-84, Santa Maria (Tex.) Public Sch., 1980-81, La Joya (Tex.) Public Schs., 1981-82; freelance photographer. Author: The Glory Trail, 1975; The Dignity of Man, 1984; contbr. articles to newspapers and mags. including Tex. Outlook. Past chmn. bd. deacons Univ. Presbyterian Ch., Austin. Served with USN, 1944-45. Mem. Austin Photographers Assn. (past pres.). Club: Rotary (past pres. Graham, past sec. Austin, past gov. dist. 587). Rotarian, Profl. Photographer.

KOENIG, DANIEL DEAN, college dean; b. Freelandville, Ind., Feb. 1, 1944; s. Walter G. and Ruby M. (Stone) K. B.S. in Edn., Ind. U., 1967; M.S., Purdue U., 1973; postgrad. U. S.C.-Columbia, 1981—. Tchr. math. and history Kankakee Valley Schs., Demotte, Ind., 1967-75; media specialist Eastern Handrock Schs., Charlottesville, Ind., 1975-77; dir., dean learning resources div. Piedmont Tech. Coll., Greenwood, S.C., 1977—. Contbr. articles to profl. jours. Counselor, Christian Haven Home for Boys, Wheatfield, Ind., 1968-69; foster parent Jasper County Welfare, Renselaer, Ind., 1969-75. Mem. Kankakee Valley Tchrs. Assn. (pres. 1972-73), Ind. State Tchrs. Assn., S.C. Library Assn. (roundtable chmn. 1978-79), Assn. for Ednl. Communications and Tech. S.C. (pres. 1981-82, editor newsletter 1978-81, Southeastern regional rep. 1984—). Home: 101 Cypress Hollow Greenwood SC 29646 Office: Piedmont Tech Coll PO Drawer 1467 Emerald Rd Greenwood SC 29648

KOEPNICK, RICHARD BORLAND, geologist; b. Dayton, Ohio, Feb. 5, 1944; B.S. in Geology, U. Colo., 1967; M.S., U. Kans., 1969, Ph.D., 1976. Asst. prof. geology Williams Coll., Williamstown, Mass., 1975-77; research geologist Mobil Research and Devel. Corp., Dallas, 1977-79, sr. research geologist, 1979-85, assoc. geology, 1985—. Contbr. articles to sci. jours. Mem. Soc. Econ. Paleontologists and Minerologists, Am. Assn. Petroleum Geologists, Sigma Xi. Office: Mobil Research and Devel Corp 13777 Midway Rd Dallas TX 75234

KOGER, MARVIN, animal genetics educator; b. Coalgate, Okla., May 18, 1915; s. James Ebben and Mary Armenda (Edwards) K.; m. Nina Stewart; children by previous marriage—Thomas M., Dorothy Elizabeth, Marva Jo, David Charles. B.S., N.Mex. State U., 1939; M.S., Kans. State U., 1940; Ph.D., U. Mo., 1943. Mem. faculty N.Mex. State U., 1943-51, asst. prof., 1943-47, assoc. prof., 1948-51; prof. animal breeding and genetics U. Fla., Gainesville, 1951-84. Recipient Beef Research Pioneer award Beef Improvement Fedn., 1977. Fellow Am. Soc. Animal Sci. (disting. service award 1979, Rockefeller Prentice Meml. award 1981); mem. Am. Genetics Assn. Presbyterian. Lodge: Rotary. Editor: Crossbreeding Beef Cattle, 1973; contbr. articles to profl. jours. Office: 202C Animal Sci Bldg U Fla Gainesville FL 32611

KOHL, DORA DIERKS (MRS. CHARLES WILLIAM KOHL, JR.), bookkeeper; b. Sugar Land, Tex., Aug. 7, 1922; d. Hans Fritz and Elizabeth Amelia (Pilz) Dierks; student pub. schs.; m. Charles William Kohl, Jr., Feb. 27, 1944; 1 son, Charles Johann. With Marshall Canning Co., Sugar Land, 1939-45, Montgomery Ward, Denver, 1945-46; with Liberty County Fed. Savs. & Loan Assn., Liberty, Tex., 1951-85, treas., controller, 1972-77, v.p. personnel, 1977-79, v.p., adminstrv. asst., 1979-85; bookkeeper Black Gold Press, Liberty, 1983—. Sec., Liberty chpt. Am. Cancer Soc. Mem. Am. Savs. and Loan Inst. (pres. Beaumont chpt.), Nat. Soc. Controllers and Financial Officers. Home: 2001 Magnolia St Liberty TX 77575 Office: 400 Main St Liberty TX 77575

KOHL, JOHN PRESTON, management educator; b. Allentown, Pa., Dec. 26, 1942; s. Claude Evan and Edna Lenoir (Woodland) K.; m. Nancy Ann Christensen, Mar. 11, 1967; children—John P. Jr., Mark C. B.A., Moravian Coll., 1964; M.Div., Yale U., 1967; M.S. in Mgmt., Am. Tech. U., 1974. M.S. in Counseling, 1976; Ph.D. in Bus. Adminstrn., Pa. State U., 1982. Ordained to ministry United Ch. of Christ, 1967. Minister, Christ Congl. Ch., New Smyrna Beach, Fla., 1968-71, First Congl. Ch., Hutchinson, Minn., 1971-73; instr. Pa. State U., University Park, 1978-82; asst. prof. mgmt. U. Tex., El Paso, 1982-85; assoc. prof. mgmt. San Jose State U., Calif., 1985—; cons. in field. Served to capt. U.S. Army, 1973-78; to maj. USAR, 1978—. Decorated Nat. Def. Service medal, Meritorious Service medal, Army Commendation medal. Mem. Acad. Mgmt. Contbr. articles to profl. publs. Home: 855 DeLeon Dr El Paso TX 79912 Office: San Jose State U San Jose CA

KOHLBERG, JEROME, JR., lawyer, business executive; b. N.Y.C., 1925. Grad., Swarthmore Coll., 1946; J.D., Columbia U., 1950. Bar: N.Y. Sr. ptnr. Kohlberg, Kravis, Roberts & Co., N.Y.C.; chmn. Houdaille Industries, Inc., chmn. exec. com.; dir. Sterndent Corp. Office: Houdaille Industries Inc One Financial Plaza Fort Lauderdale FL 33394*

KOHLBRY, JOAN CHARLOTTE, newspaper promotions director; b. St. Louis, July 5, 1936; d. Gordon Edward and Hildegarde Charlotte (Ruecker) K. Student Washington U., 1956-59, Fontbonne Coll., 1956-57. Office clk. Brentwood Auto Service, Brentwood, Mo., 1959-64; service sec. E.M. Stivers Lincoln-Mercury, Rock Hill, Mo., 1964-70, Sam Galloway Ford, Ft. Myers, Fla., 1970-71; head title, billing dept. Bill Branch Chevrolet, Fort Myers, 1971-73; exec. sec. to editor Ft. Myers News-Press, 1974-81, asst. dir. promotions, pub. relations, 1981—; Contbr. articles to newspapers. Bd. mem. Sr. Aides Program, Ft. Myers, 1984—; bd. dirs. Lee County Humane Soc., Ft. Myers, 1984; chmn. Fla. Statue Liberty Com., Ft. Meyers, 1984—; mem. Lee County Young Democrats, 1975-76; chief fundraiser Lend-a-hand Fund, Ft. Myers, 1981—, mem. planning com. Celebrity Tennis Tournament; planner, implementer Heart of Gold awards, Ft. Myers, 1981—, Fla. Pub. Service awards, 1974—. Mem. South Fla. Advt. Fedn., Am. Bus. Women's Assn., Profl. Secs. Internat. Presbyterian. Avocations: sewing; reading; gardening; swimming; writing. Home: 526 NE 15th Pl Cape Coral FL 33904 Office: Fort Myers News-Press 2442 Anderson Ave Fort Myers FL 33901

KOHLENBERG, EILEEN MIERAS, nurse educator, administrator; b. Sioux City, Iowa, Apr. 10, 1954; d. Howard Charles and Esther Rosellaa (Van Roekel) Mieras; m. Randy Bryan Kohlenberg, Mar. 17, 1979; B.S. in Psychology, B.S. in Nursing, Morningside Coll., 1977; M.S. in Nursing, U. Tex.-Austin, 1982; postgrad., 1984. R.N., Iowa, Nebr., N.C. Registered nurse Marian Health Ctr., Sioux City, 1977-79; instr. nursing Morningside Coll., Sioux City, 1979-83, chmn. nursing edn., 1983-85, dir. workshops in microcomputers, testing and phys. assessment of geron., 1984-85, coordinator Sci. and Tech. Forum, 1983; mem. faculty Sch. of Nursing U. N.C., Greensboro, 1985—. Organist, pianist Sioux City Symphony, 1983—. Mem. Iowa Nurses' Assn. (sec., dir. 1980—), Iowa League Nursing, AAUW (treas., by-laws chmn. local chpt.), Briar Cliff Honor Soc. (community nurse leader 1984—). Episcopalian. Clubs: Morningside (pres. 1983-84), Women's. Avocations: organist, seamstress. Home: 2700 Cottage Pl Greensboro NC 27405 Office: Univ NC Sch Nursing Greensboro NC 27412

KOHLER, LARRY WALTER, fast food company executive; b. Lakeview, Mich., Sept. 27, 1945; s. Ora E. and Marjorie T. (Dutmers) K.; m. Paige N. Bernhardt, Feb. 28, 1970; 1 child, Brek Andrew. Student Mich. State U., 1969. Restaurant and dist. mgr. Burger King Corp., Detroit, 1970-76, regional gen. mgr., Cleve., 1976-77, regional v.p., Boston, 1977-80, sr. v.p., div. mgr., Miami, 1980-82, exec. v.p. ops., 1982—; lectr. Tufts U., 1977-80, U. Wis.-Stout, 1983. Served with U.S. Army, 1968-70. Decorated Bronze Star. Mem. Nat. Restaurant Assn. Republican. Roman Catholic. Home: 17740 SW 7th Ave Miami Fl 33157 Office: Burger King Corp 7360 N Kendall Dr Miami FL 33156*

KOHLHASE, JANET ELLEN, economics educator; b. Buffalo, Apr. 4, 1953; d. William Lawrence and Margaret Hulda (Heick) K.; m. Steven G. Craig, Aug. 21, 1982. B.A., U. Ill., 1975; M.A., U. Pa., 1977, Ph.D., 1980. Asst. prof. Mich. State U., East Lansing, 1980-82; vis. asst. prof. U. Houston, 1982-83, asst. prof. dept. econs., 1983—. Contbr. articles to publs. in field. Recipient Bronze Plaque award U. Ill., 1975. Mem. Am. Econs Assn., Econometric Soc., Regional Sci. Assn. (treas. 1980—), Nat. Tax Assn., Nat. Tax Inst. Office: Dept Econs Univ Houston University Park Houston TX 77004

KOHNERT-NICHOLSON, JILL ILENE, abstract company assistant; b. Mpls., June 18, 1950; d. Carl Creighton and June Ilene K.; m. George A. Nicholson, Apr. 14, 1984. Student So. Methodist U., 1968-69; student U. Tex., 1970; B.A., U. Houston, 1972. Exec. sec. real estate and archtl. firms, Houston, Dallas, Austin, Tex., 1972-75; exec. asst. to exec. dir. State Bar Tex., Austin, 1975-77; exec. dir. Tex. Lawyers Ins. Exchange, Austin, 1978-81; exec. asst. Tex. Commerce Bank, Austin, 1981-83; adminstrv. asst. GSD&M Advt., Austin, 1983-84; exec. asst. to pres. Lawyers Title & Abstract Co., Austin, 1985—. Mem. Zachary Scott Theatre Guild, Austin, 1979—, Laguna Gloria Art Mus. Guild, 1981; mem. Austin Bus. Forum, 1981. Lic. securities dealer, Tex. Mem. Exec. Women Internat., Nat. Assn. Female Execs., Am. Inst. Banking, PEO. Club: Pilot. Home: 6908 Moonmont St Austin TX 78745 Office: Lawyers Title & Abstract Co 1250 Capital of Tex Hwy S Bldg One Suite 260 Austin TX 78746

KOHRS, CHARLOTTE ANN CURTIS, librarian; b. Talco, Tex., Nov. 7, 1938; d. Houston Pink and Juanita E. (Smith) Kelley; A.A., Ventura Coll., 1968, U. Houston, 1980; m. Richard H. Kohrs, Jan. 2, 1981; children—Carla E. Curtis, Peggy L. Curtis; stepchildren—Cynthia J. Kohrs, Douglas William Kohrs, Librarian, tech. standards rep. Raytheon Co., Goleta, Calif., 1970-76; supr. info. services Peat, Marwick, Mitchell & Co., Houston, 1977—. Sec., Republican County Central Com., Santa Barbara, 1973-76; bd. dirs. Santa Barbara Young Reps., 1972-76; mem. adv. bd. Goleta Valley Girls Club, 1975-76. Mem. Spl. Library Assn. (editor bus. and fin. div. newsletter 1982-84, chmn. bus. and fin. div. 1985-86), Am. Soc. Info. Sci., Southwest Assn. Law Librarians. Home: 2301 Lakenheath Dr Dickinson TX 77539 Office: 3000 Republic Bank Ctr Houston TX 77002

KOKENZIE, HENRY FAYETTE, county official; b. Gray's Landing, Pa., July 13, 1918; s. John and Antonia (Philimonova) K.; B.A., U. Denver, 1948; m. Irene Mildred Owens, May 24, 1941; children—Henry Fayette, Antoinette I., John R., Nicholas A. Bus. mgr. athletics U. Denver, 1948-49; dep. clk. Mcpl. Ct. Savannah (Ga.), 1952-58; mgr. truck sales Key West Ford, Inc. (Fla.), 1961-72; dir. vets. affairs Monroe County, Key West, 1972—; exec. sec. Vets. Council Monroe County, 1972—. Mem. Monroe County Democratic Exec. Com., 1960-69. Served to capt. U.S. Army, 1939-46. Recipient Thomas H. Gignillat award, Savannah, 1958. Mem. Fla. Pub. Relations Assn. (pres. Fla. Keys/Conch chpt. 1977-78), County Vets. Service Officers Assn. Fla. (pres. 1977-79), Assn. Naval Aviation, Navy League U.S. (life), DAV (life, Savannah chpt. comdr. 1955-56, Key West chpt. comdr. 1971-72, adjutant 1972—), Ret. Officers Assn. (life; pres. chpt. 1981-82), Noncommd. Officers Assn. (life), Nat. Assn. Civilian Conservation Corps Alumni, Nat. Am. Legion Press Assn., Am. Legion (post comdr. 1981—), Key West C. of C., AMVETS (life), Mil. Order World Wars, Internat. Platform Assn. (life patron), Phi Beta Kappa, Omicron Delta Kappa, Pi Gamma Mu. Roman Catholic. Clubs: Elks, Kiwanis, Moose (Key West). Home: 3413 Riviera Dr Key West FL 33040 Office: Pub Service Bldg Stock Island Key West FL 33040

KOLAR, MARY JANE, association executive; b. Benton, Ill., Aug. 9, 1941; d. Thomas Haskell and Mary Jane (Sanders) Burnett; B.A. with high honors, So. Ill. U., 1963, M.A. with highest honors, 1964; m. Otto Michael Kolar, Aug. 13, 1966; children—Robin Lynn, Deon Michael. Tchr. pub. schs., Benton and Zeigler, Ill., 1960-63; grad. asst. and grad. fellow So. Ill. U., Carbondale, 1963-64; instr. Ridgewood High Sch., Norridge, Ill., 1964-67, Maine Twp. High Sch., Des Plaines, Ill., 1967-70; freelance writer, Chgo., 1970-71; cons. Contractor Promotions, Chgo., 1970-71; ednl. coordinator Am. Dietetic Assn., Chgo., 1971-72; dir. profl. devel. Am. Dental Hygienists Assn., Chgo., 1972-78; dir. Learning Center div. Am. Coll. Cardiology, Bethesda, Md., 1978-80; dir. edn. Nat. Moving and Storage Assn., Alexandria, Va., 1980-82; exec. dir. Women in Communications, Inc., Austin, Tex., 1982—; cons., speaker various profl. assns., ednl. instns. and fed. agys. Troopleader, Girl Scouts U.S.A., 1970-71; adminstrv. bd. mem. Prince of Peace Ch., Elk Grove Village, Ill., 1972-76; edn. com. mem. St. Paul's Ch., Chgo., 1977-79; mem. adv. council Accrediting Commn., Assn. of Ind. Colls. and Schs., 1980—; mem. centennial com. U. Tex.-Austin. Fellow Am. Soc. Allied Health Professions (dir. 1978-79); mem. Am. Soc. Assn. Execs. (cert. assn. exec.; dir. edn. sect. 1977—, chmn. edn. com., 1983, bd. dirs. 1983—, Educator of Yr. award 1978), Greater Washington Soc. Assn. Execs. (edn. com. 1981-82), Tex. Soc. Assn. Execs., Am. Bus. Women's Assn., Ill. Hist. Soc., Kellogg Nat. Com. on Allied Health Edn., Women in Communications (newsletter editor, legis. and career reentry chmn., chmn. ERA task force, dir. Washington profl. chpt.), So. Ill. U. Alumni Assn. (bd. govs. 1977-80, pres.-elect Washington chpt. 1981), Phi Beta Kappa (Commencement prize), Phi Kappa Phi, Kappa Delta Pi, Alpha Lambda Delta, Pi Lambda Theta. Clubs: Triton Wives Service Orgn. (program chair 1971-72), Nat. Women's Polit. Caucus, Tex. Women's Polit. Caucus, So. Christian Leadership Conf. Contbr. articles to profl. jours., chpts. to books. Home: 7117 Woodhollow Dr Apt 1621 Austin TX 78731 Office: PO Box 9561 Austin TX 78766

KOLASA, KATHRYN MARIANNE, food and nutrition educator, consultant; b. Detroit, July 26, 1949; d. Marion J. and Blanche Ann (Gasiorowski) K.; m. Patrick Noud Kelly, Jan. 3, 1983. B.S., Mich. State U., 1970; Ph.D., U. Tenn., 1974. Test kitchen home economist Kellogg Co., 1971; instr. dept. food sci. and food systems adminstrn. U. Tenn.-Knoxville, 1973-74; asst. prof. dept. food sci. and human nutrition Mich. State U., East Lansing, 1974-76, assoc. prof., 1976-82; prof., chmn. food, nutrition and instn. mgmt. Sch. Home Econs., East Carolina U., Greenville, N.C., 1982—; mem. subcom. food and nutrition bd. Nat. Acad. Scis. on Uses of the RDA, 1981-83; cons. food and nutrition. Recipient grants in nutrition and food service, 1974—; Kellogg nat. fellow, 1985-88. Mem. Soc. Nutrition Edn. (pres.), Am. Instn. Nutrition, Inst. Food Technologists, Com. on Nutritional Anthropology, Am. Dietetic Assn., N.C. Home Econs. Assn. Roman Catholic. Author: (with Ann Bass and Lou Wakefield) Community Nutrition and Individual Food Behavior, 1978. Home: Box 1772 Greenville NC 27834 Office: Dept Food Nutrition and Instn Mgmt Sch Home Econs East Carolina U Greenville NC 27834

KOLB, DAVID ALLEN, chiropractor, homeopath, herbalist, nutrition consultant, acupuncturist; b. El Paso, Tex., May 14, 1946; s. David Crocket Kolb and Ann Laura (Thrash) Kolb Swingle; m. Barbara Paul Carey, May 3, 1980; 1 child, Aaron Scott. A.A.S., U. Odessa, 1967; B.A., U. Tex., 1971; D.Chiropractic magna cum laude, Palmer Coll. Chiropractic, 1979; postgrad. in homeopathy Occidental Inst. Research Found., Bellingham, Wash., 1980; postgrad. in acupuncture Nat. Coll. Chiropractic, Lombard, Ill., 1983, 84, Peoples Republic China, 1984. Computer operator Dallas Bank Commerce, 1969; computer operator Tex. Instruments, Austin and Dallas, Tex., 1970-72, computer programmer, 1972-73; researcher on meditation Maharishi U., Santa Barbara, Calif., 1973-74; computer operator Austin Nat. Bank, Tex., 1974; computer programmer Tex. Water Resources, Austin, 1974-75; chiropractor Profl. Healthcare Services, Inc., Austin, 1979—. Mem. Am. Chiropractic Assn., Tex. Chiropractic Assn., Travis County Chiropractic Soc., Internat. Found. Homeopathy, Occidental Inst. Research Found., Pi Tau Delta. Avocations: hiking; camping; jogging; swimming; science fiction. Office: Profl Healthcare Services Inc 1004 W 31st St Austin TX 78705

KOLBECK, RALPH CARL, physiology and cardiology educator; b. Wausau, Wis., Sept. 2, 1944; s. John and Elma L. (Kersten) K.; m. Donna Jean Belling, July 16, 1966; children—Lisa Jean, John Carl. B.A. in Physiology, U. Minn., 1966, Ph.D. in Physiology, 1970. Teaching asst. physiology U. Minn., Mpls., 1966-67, lectr., 1968-73, postdoctoral fellow, 1970-73; instr. medicine Med. Coll. Ga., Augusta, 1973-76, asst. prof., 1976-80, assoc. prof. medicine and physiology, 1980—. Scoutmaster, Ga./Carolina council Boy Scouts Am.; fin. chmn. Sci. Fair Am.; active Am. Heart Assn. Recipient Investigatorship award Am. Heart Assn., 1977-82; grantee NIH, Ga. Heart Assn., Am. Heart Assn., Am. Lung Assn. Mem. AAAS, Am. Assn. Lab. Animal Sci., Am. Physiol. Soc., Am. Fedn. Clin. Research, Soc. Exptl. Biol. Medicine (Southeast sect.), Sigma Xi. Contbr. numerous articles to profl. jours. Home: 3235 Winding Wood Pl Augusta GA 30907 Office: Dept Medicine Med Coll GA Augusta GA 30912

KOLBESON, MARILYN ELIZABETH, advertising agency executive, artist; b. Cin., June 9, 1930; d. Henry Dilg and Carolyn J. (Brown) Hopf; children—Michael Llen, Kenneth Ray, Patrick James, Pamela Sue Kolbeson Lang, James Allan. Student U. Cin., 1947, 48, 50; grad. Silva Mind Control. Sales and mktg. mgr. Cox Patrick United Van Lines, 1977-80, Creative Incentives, Houston, 1980-81; pres. Ad Sense, Inc., Houston, 1981—; lectr., cons. in field; artist, pub. speaker. Mem. adv. bd. Alief Ind. Sch. Dist., 1981—, pres., 1983-85; bd. dirs., v.p. Santa Maria Hostel, 1983—; founder, pres. Mind Force, Houston, 1978—. Mem. Houston Advt. Specialty Assn. (treas. 1985-86, bd. dirs. 1985—v.p. 1986—), Service Coop. Assn., Cultural Arts Soc. Houston, Greater Houston Conv. and Visitors Council (loaned exec. 1986—), Gallaria C. of C., West Houston C. of C., Pasadena. C. of C., Am. Inst. for Achievement. Republican. Christian Scientist. Clubs: Toastmasters (club pres. 1977, area gov. 1978), Rosicrucians, Grand (v.p. 1986—), Achievers Group, Regency. Office: 800 Post Oak Blvd #81 Houston TX 77056

KOLESZAR, GEORGE EDMUND, research analyst, former air force officer; b. Newark, Nov. 22, 1941; s. George Emil and Alice Angela (Nugent) K.; B.S., N.J. Inst. Tech., 1963; M.S., U. Mo., 1969; Ph.D., Ohio State U., 1975; m. Irene Marie Hauck, July 13, 1963; children—Loretta Marie, John Edmund, Jean Margaret, Mary Ellen. Commd. 2d lt. U.S. Air Force, 1963, advanced through grades to lt. col., 1979; elec. engr., research and devel. ops. NSA, Ft. George G. Meade, Md., 1963-68; chief signal analysis br. European Def. Analysis Center, Wiesbaden, W. Ger., 1969-73; instr. supr., telecommunications systems staff officer course, coordinator, telecommunications mgmt. program, adj. faculty U. So. Miss., Biloxi, 1975-78; chief System Integration Office, Def. Communications Agy., Washington, 1978-81; project officer Orgn. Joint Chiefs of Staff, Washington, 1981-83; research staff mem. Inst. Def. Analyses, Alexandria, Va., 1983—. Judge, Fairfax County (Va.) Regional Sci. Fairs, 1979—. Mem. AAAS, IEEE, Armed Forces Communications Electronics Assn., Sigma Xi, Air Force Assn. Home: 2500 Bristol Circle Woodbridge VA 22192 Office: Inst Def Analyses 1801 N Beauregard St Alexandria VA 22311

KOLLAER, JIM C., real estate executive, architect; b. Amarillo, Tex., Jan. 5, 1943; s. Walter W. and Margaret M. Kollaer; m. Sally Ann Hawkins, Aug. 6, 1966; 1 son, Andrew N. Student, Amarillo (Tex.) Coll., 1960-62, La. State U., 1962-65; B.Arch., Tex. Tech U., 1969. Lic. architect, Tex.; lic. broker, Tex. Vice pres., dir. urban design RKA Inc. Assoc., Dallas, 1969-75; v.p., dir. mktg. CRS Inc., Houston, 1977-80, sr. planner, 1975-76, assoc., 1976-77; pres. Houston div. Henry Miller Co., Houston, 1980—, exec. v.p. Holding Co., 1980—; dir. HMSCO; cons. and lectr. in field. Sr. fellow Am. Leadership Forum; bd. dirs. Tex. Bus. Hall of Fame. Named Young Architect of Yr., Dallas, 1974. Mem. AIA, Tex. Soc. Architects, Urban Land Inst., Houston Bd. Realtors (dir.), Tex. Assn. Realtors, Nat. Assn. Realtors, Nat. Assn. Corp. Real Estate Execs., Houston C. of C. (chmn. internat. bus. com. 1983-84), Houston World Trade Assn. (bd. dirs.), Houston Lyceum. Republican. Presbyterian. Clubs: Houstonian, Houston, Univ. Office: 3000 Post Oak Blvd 1750 Houston TX 77056

KOLSKY, ALLAN, real estate development company executive; b. Bklyn., June 30, 1932; s. Jack R. and Lee (Wolf) K.; m. Phyllis Lillian South, Jan. 17, 1970; children—Bruce, Mark, Diane. Student pub. schs., New Brunswick, N.J. Lic. real estate broker, N.Y. Real estate and home builder, Sunrise Estates, Nanuet, N.Y., 1955-59; self employed in real estate and comml. devel., New Brunswick, N.J., 1960-69; v.p. real estate and real estate dir. Lionel Leisure, Phila., Fla., Ga., N.Y., N.J., 1970-74; exec. v.p., Wolf Corp., N.Y.C., 1975-78; pres. Redevco Corp., Hialeah, Fla., 1978—; pres., dir. Redevco Mgmt. Corp., Redevco Devel. Corp., Tamiami Ctr., Inc., Redevco II, Inc.; mng. ptnr. Redevco Assocs., 1985—, Plaza South Assocs., Las Tiendas Assocs., Trail Plaza Assocs.; Hon. dir. Assn. Advancement of Mentally Handicapped, Miami, Fla., 1983-; nat. adv. bd. Research and Devel. Inst. for Nat. Assn. Retarded Citizens, Dallas, 1983—; dir.-at-large Fla. Assn. for Retarded Citizens, 1986—. Served with USAF, 1952-53. Mem. C. of C., Better Bus. Bur., Internat. Council Shopping Centers, Am. Soc. Notaries, Nat. Rifle Assn. Clubs: U.S. Senatorial; Turnberry Yacht and Racquet (Miami). Office: 2000 W Commercial Blvd Suite 232 Fort Lauderdale FL 33309

KOLT, ROBERT PAUL, musicologist, conductor; b. Valley Forge, Pa., Feb. 22, 1953; s. Paul Joseph and Lee (Ireland) K. B.A., Mary Washington Coll., 1979; M.A., Radford U., 1981: postgrad. North Tex. State U., Asst. condr. No. Va. Symphony, Sterling, 1976-77; condr. Radford Chamber Orchestra, Va., 1979-80; co-editor in chief Southwest Jour. Music, Denton, Tex., 1984—; research asst. Doctoral Dissertations Music, Denton, 1982—. Served to E-3 USAF, 1972-74. Mem. Am. Musicological Soc., Sonneck Soc., Alpha Phi Sigma, Phi Kappa Phi. Avocation: music. Home: PO Box 7504 NT Station Denton TX 76203 Office: PO Box 13377 NT Station Denton TX 76203

KOMECHAK, MARILYN GILBERT, psychologist, author; b. Wabash, Ind., Aug. 28, 1936; d. Russell and Evelyn (Snyder) Gilbert; m. George J. Komechak, Aug. 23, 1958; children—Kimberly, Gilbert. B.S., Purdue U., 1958; B.S., Tex. Christian U., 1966, M.Ed., 1968; Ph.D., North Tex. State U., 1975. Child specialist Child Study Ctr., Ft. Worth, 1968-74; assoc. dir. CBS Sch. Community Service, North Tex. State U., Denton, 1974-77; pvt. practice psychology, Ft. Worth, 1977—; instr. counselor edn., Tex. Christian U., 1977-78, instr. psychology, 1977-78; instr. criminal justice div. U. Tex. at Arlington, 1977-78. Author: Getting Yourself Together, 1982; contbr. articles to profl. jours. Named to Hon. Bd. Trustees, Olympiads of Knowledge, Ft. Worth, 1982. Mem. Am. Physiol. Assn., Tex. Physiol. Assn., Tarrant County Physiol. Assn., Psi Chi. Episcopalian. Avocations: short story and poetry writing. Office: Suite 7 5280 Trail Lake Dr Fort Worth TX 76133

KOMKOV, VADIM, mathematics educator and administrator, consultant, researcher; b. Moscow, Aug. 18; came to U.S., 1957; s. Boris D. and Eugenia (Romanov) K.; m. Joyce Radford; children—Valerie Hill, Stephanie, Andrea, Leon, Michael. M.S., Warsaw Poly. Inst., 1948; Ph.D., U. Utah, 1964. Prof., U. Wis., Madison, 1964-65, Fla. State U., 1965-70, Tex. Tech U., 1970-77; editor Math. Reviews, Ann Arbor, Mich., 1977-80; chmn. dept. math. W.Va. U., 1980-83; disting. prof., chmn. dept. math. Winthrop Coll., Rock Hill, S.C., 1983—. Author: Optimal Control, 1973; co-author: Design Sensitivity for Structural Systems, 1985; Variational Principles, 1986; editor: Problems of Elastic Stability, 1981; Sensitivity of Functionals, 1984. Served with RAF, 1942-46. Democrat. Avocation: fencing. Home: 132 Neely Ct Rock Hill SC 29733 Office: Winthrop College Rock Hill SC 29733

KOMORN, ROBERT MELVIN, head and neck surgeon; b. Detroit, June 24, 1939; s. William and Gertrude (Katzman) K.; M.D., U. Mich., 1964; m. Judith Gail Katz, Aug. 21, 1961; children—Sherri Lynne, Deborah Susan, Janet Elizabeth. Intern, Sinai Hosp., Detroit, 1964-65; resident in otolaryngology U. Mich. Hosp., Ann Arbor, 1966-70; chief otolaryngology sect. VA Hosp., Houston, 1970-74; practice medicine specializing in head and neck surgery-otolaryngology, Houston; mem. staff Methodist, St. Joseph, St. Luke's, Tex. Children's hosps.; chief otolaryngology, dir. audio-vestibular lab. St. Joseph Hosp.; asst. prof. otolaryngology Baylor U. Coll. Medicine, 1970-74, clin. asst. prof., 1974—. Diplomate Am. Bd. Ophthalmology and Otolaryngology. Fellow A.C.S., Am. Acad. Otolaryngology, Soc. Univ. Otolaryngologists, Am. Soc. Head and Neck Surgery, Am. Acad. Facial Plastic and Reconstructive Surgery; mem. AMA, Tex. Med. Assn., Harris County Med. Soc., Tex. Otolaryn. Assn., Houston Otolaryn. Soc. (pres. 1976-77), Alpha Omega Alpha, Phi Kappa Phi. Contbr. chpts. to books, articles to med. jours. Home: 5219 Loch Lomond St Houston TX 77096 Office: 6560 Fannin Suite 1228 Houston TX 77030

KOMOSA, ADAM ANTHONY, educator; b. Pitts., Aug. 24, 1913; s. Simon and Kathrine K.; diploma Advanced Inf. Officers Sch., 1947; certificate The Army Signal Sch., 1952; diploma Air Groun Ops. Sch., 1952; A.A., U. Fla., 1960; B.A., Fla. State U., 1962, M.A., 1963; Ph.D., Inter-Am. U., 1967; m. Naomi Evlyn Beard, Feb. 11, 1949; children—Katherine Louise, Adam Anthony. Enlisted in U.S. Army, 1932, advanced through grades to lt. col., 1951; radio operator, China, 1935-38; parachute inf. co. comdr, plans and tng officer, World War II, 1942-46; sr. regtl. adviser Korean Mil. Adv. Group, 1950-52; gen. staff officer plans and ops., 1956-58; camp dir. nat. rifle and pistol matches, Camp Perry, Ohio, 1957. ret., 1958; prof. history No. Mich. U., 1968-78, prof. emeritus, 1978—; adv. Am. Security Council. Mem. steering com. Adair County Sharing and Learning Experience, Free SOS Learning Networks; contbr., critic All-Ky. City Com.; mem. steering com. Mich. UN Day, 1970. Decorated Croix de Guerre with palm (France); Fouragerre (Belgium); knight comdr. Order of Polonia Restituta; Silver Star, Bronze Star with oak leaf cluster, Purple Heart, others; recipient cert. of appreciation U.S. Army Chief of Staff, 1957; Presdl. commendation Republic of Korea, 1951; cert. of Merit, Korean Army, 1951; cert. of Recognition, Polish Guard, 1955; named hon. citizen Sainte-Mere Eglise, France, 1984, to Hall of Fame of Parachuting. Mem. Am. Assn. Advancement of Slavic Studies, Polish Am. Hist. Assn., Kosciuszko Found., Adair County Ret. Educators Assn. (pres.), Soc. Wireless Pioneers, Phi Kappa Phi, Phi Alpha Theta, Alpha Kappa Psi. Club: Pinewood Country. Lodges: Rotary (pres.) (Columbia); Elks. Author: Third Flank Over Sicily, 1963; La Batalla de la Angostura, 1967. Home: Circle K Acres Route 1 Box 294 Columbia KY 42728

KONDONASSIS, ALEXANDER JOHN, economics educator; b. Kozani, Greece, Feb. 8, 1928; s. John and Eve (Hatzistylianou) K.; children—John, Yolanda. A.B., DePauw U., 1952; M.A., Ind. U., 1953, Ph.D., 1956. Teaching assoc., lectr. Ind. U., Bloomington, 1954-58; asst. prof., assoc. prof., prof. Okla. U., Norman, 1958-70, chmn. dept. econs., 1961-71, dir. advanced program in econs. Okla. U., Norman, 1971—, David Ross Boyd prof. econs., 1971—, also dir. div. econs.; Fulbright prof. Athens Sch. Econs. (Greece), 1965-66; dir. Am. Bank Commerce, Oklahoma City. Edward Rector scholar, 1948-52; Fulbright scholar, 1965-66; recipient Regents award Okla. U., 1964; Teaching award Merrick Found., 1977; Rector Scholar Alumni Achievement award DePauw U., 1977. Mem. Am. Econ. Assn., So. Econ. Assn., Southwestern Social Sci. Assn. (pres. 1983-84), Mo. Valley Econ. Assn. (pres. 1983-84), Beta Gamma Sigma, Phi Beta Kappa. Lodge: Lions (pres. 1981-82). Contbr. articles in field to profl. jours.

KONE, JAMES STANDIFER, II, petrochemical equipment company sales executive; b. Denison, Tex., June 7, 1912; s. James Standifer and May Evans K.; m. Ruthelma Koller, Oct. 5, 1946; 1 son, James S. III. B.S., Austin Coll., 1933. Jr. staff engr., various oil companies, 1933-38; with Manning Maxwell Moore, Inc., Bridgeport, Conn., 1938-42, 49-51; mktg. agt. Malcolm Black & Co., N.Y.C., 1945-49; founder, chmn. James S. Kone & Co., Amarillo, Tex., 1951—. Pres., Panhandle Plains Hist. Soc., 1976-77. Served with USN, 1942-46. Mem. Instrument Soc. Am., Gas Processors Suppliers Assn. (pres. 1964-65). Episcopalian. Club: Westerners. Lodge: Rotary (pres. 1971-72). Home: 4105 Julie Dr Amarillo TX 79109 Office: PO Box 1109 Amarillo TX 79105

KONETZNI, ALBERT H. (ALKO), artist, character licensing company executive; b. Bklyn., May 19, 1915; s. Anton Albert and Wilma J. (Heuer) K.; m. Adeline Elizabeth Gurgie, Mar. 14, 1943; children—Albert H., Douglas W., Gary, Karen. Grad. Pratt Inst., 1936. Advt. asst. Gertz Dept. Stores, L.I., N.Y., 1935-37; art dir. Splty. Press, N.Y.C., 1937-39, Personna Blade Co./Pal Blade Co., N.Y.C., 1939-53; account exec., artist/creative idea man Walt Disney Co., N.Y.C., 1953-80; cons. in mdse. Ringling Bros. and Barnum & Bailey Circus, Washington, 1980—; cons., lectr., photographer in field. Works exhibited: N.Y.C. Mus. Modern Art, 1952, Acad. Notre Dame de Namur, Villanova, Pa., 1979. On cover Golden Years mag., 1984. Served with U.S. Army, 1932-33. Recipient poster award Am. Soc. for Prevention Cruelty to Animals, 1931; product design citation Aladdin Industries, 1972; numerous photog. awards including N.Y. Jour. Am. award, 1947, Revere Camera, 1952. Mem. Pratt Inst. Alumni Assn., Navy League. Republican. Lutheran. Club: Golden Ears. Lodge: Elks. Address: 4180 Bowling Green Circle Sarasota FL 33583

KONG, LOK KING, obstretrician, gynecologist; b. Malaysia, May 28, 1938; came to U.S., 1969; s. Ah Lok and Kwee Choon (Teoh) K.; m. Ai Choo Ling, July 14, 1967; children—Li Sheng, Li Kuo, Lin Min. M.D., Nat. Taiwan U., 1969. Intern City Hosp. of N.Y., N.Y.C., 1970, resident in internal medicine, 1971; resident in ob-gyn, 1971-74; gynecology, oncology fellow N.Y. Infirmary, N.Y.C., 1976; chief gynecologist USPHS Hosp., N.Y.C., 1974-75, 77; practice medicine specializing in ob-gyn, Murphy, N.C., 1978—; dir. dept ob-gyn Murphy Med. Ctr.; owner, mgr. motel and restaurant. Fellow Am. Coll. Obstetrics and Gynecology (jr.); mem. AMA, Murphy C. of C. Democrat. Office: Profl Bldg Suite 64E Murphy NC 28906

KONTOGIORGIS, MICHAEL THEODORE, clergyman; b. Boston, May 15, 1948; s. Theodore Michael and Panagiota (Andriopoulos) K.; m. Vicki Betty George, Aug. 27, 1972; children—Kristen, Patricia, Megan. B.A., Hellenic Coll., 1970; M.Div., Holy Cross Greek Orthodox Sch. Theology, 1973, S.T.M., 1974. Ordained deacon Greek Orthodox Ch., 1972, priest, 1973; driving instr. Cleve. Circle Auto Sch., Brookline, Mass., 1969-71; coordinator United Shoppers Assn., Randolph, Mass., 1971-73; asst. to dean Annunciation Greek Orthodox Cathedral of New Eng., Boston, 1973-75; parish priest Holy Trinity Greek Orthodox Ch., Orlando, Fla., 1975—; dir. Greek Orthodox Youth Actionline, Orlando, 1981, Greek Orthodox Altar Boys Workshop, Brooksville, Fla., 1981-83; chmn. Youth Commn., Greek Orthodox Diocese Atlanta, 1981-83; mem. Presbyters Council, Greek Orthodox Archdiocese North and South Am., N.Y.C., 1983—; co-producer, dir. Grecian Echoes radio program, Orlando, 1978; chaplain Orlando Police Dept., 1978-79; bd. dirs. Olympic Village, 1977-84, 1st v.p., 1979-83, pres., 1983-84. Author: The Altar Boy's Guidebook, 1981; editor weekly ch. newsletter Harbinger, 1975—. Named Sakellarios, Greek Orthodox Archdiocese North and S.Am., 1980; recipient Pectoral Cross and plaque for 10th anniversary of ordination Holy Trinity Greek Orthodox Ch., 1983. Mem. Greek Orthdox Clergy Assn. (sec. Atlanta Diocese 1981-83, pres. 1983—), Orthodox Clergy Fellowship North and Central Fla. (sec. 1982—), Holy Cross Greek Orthodox Sch. Theology Alumni Assn. Home: 106 Valencia Loop Altamonte Springs FL 32714 Office: Holy Trinity Greek Orthodox Ch 1217 Trinity Woods Ln Maitland FL 32751

KONTZ, MARY MARGARET, nurse, educator; b. St. Paul, Dec. 13, 1955; d. Milo James and Loretta Margaret (Winkler) K. B.S. in Nursing, U. Miami, Coral Gables, Fla., 1978, M.S.N., 1984. R.N., Fla. Mem. surg. staff Mercy Hosp., Miami, 1978-79; mem. emergency staff Parkway Hosp., Miami, 1979-80; mem. faculty Jackson Meml. Hosp., Miami, 1980-86, asst. dir. nursing edn., 1986—; cons. nursing diagnosis/documentation community hosps., Miami, 1982—. Mem. N. Am. Nursing Diagnosis Assn. (program com. southern region, Fla. State rep.), Am. Nurses Assn., Fla. Nurses Assn., Sigma Theta Tau. Home: 9301 SW 92 Ave #315-B Miami FL 33176 Office: Jackson Meml Hosp 1611 NW 12 Ave Miami FL 33136

KOONCE, KENNETH LOWELL, experimental statistics educator; b. Lake Charles, La., Sept. 6, 1939; s. George A. and Alice S. Koonce; m. Judy G. Deroven; children—Steven, David, William. B.S. in Agr., U. of S.W. La., 1961; M.S. in Animal Breeding, La. State U., 1963; Ph.D. in Statis. Genetics, N.C. State U., 1968. Instr. N.C. State U., Raleigh, 1967; asst. prof. exptl. statis. La. State U., Baton Rouge, 1967-71, assoc. prof., 1971-76, prof., 1976—, head dept., 1982—. Mem. Am. Statis. Assn., Biometrics Soc., Am. Soc. Animal Sci. Office: Dept Exptl Stats La State U 161 Agriculture Administration Bldg Baton Rouge LA 70803

KOONTZ, LESLIE LESTER, coal sales company executive; b. Charleston, W.Va., Apr. 25, 1928; s. Leslie Lester and Mary Martha (Otey) K.; B.S., W.Va. U., 1950; postgrad. U. Toledo, 1951; m. Brenda Copley Koontz, Dec. 24, 1968; children—Kelly, Michael Ann; 1 son from previous marriage, Mark Timothy. With Island Creek Coal Co., Huntington, W.Va., 1951-58, asst. div. mgr., 1956-58; asst. v.p. N. Am. Coal Corp., Cleve., 1958-60; asst. to pres. Sovereign Pocahontas Co., Cleve., 1960-66; mgr. sales Pickands, Mather & Co., Cleve., 1966-67; with Osborne Mining Co., Bluefield, W.Va., 1967-69; pres. Osborne-Koontz Coal Sales Co., 1969—; pres. B&C Oil Co.; pres. Koontz Coal Sales Co., Matewan, W.Va.; pres. Kelly Oil Co., Tug River Co.; pres. Mabley Coals, Inc.; v.p. Red Jacket Coal Corp.; dir. Allegheny Coal and Land Co., Sandy Delta Coal & Dock Co. Served with USNR, 1944-46. Mem. Tug Valley C. of C. (dir.), W.Va. Gasoline Dealers Assn., Nat. Oil Dealers Assn., Tau Kappa Epsilon. Democrat. Episcopalian. Clubs: Tug Valley Country, Guyan Golf and Country, Duck Woods Golf, Elks, Moose. Office: Mate St Matewan WV 25678

KOPP, OTTO CHARLES, geology educator, researcher, consultant; b. Bklyn., July 22, 1929; s. Frank H. and Hattie M. (Gruhn) K.; m. Helen Eleanor Shotkowski, Sept. 4, 1954; children—Michael A., Patricia A., Mary B., Paul B. B.S., U. Notre Dame (Ind.), 1951; M.A., Columbia U., 1955, Ph.D., 1958. Research asst. Columbia U., 1955-58; asst. prof. dept. geol. scis. U. Tenn., Knoxville, 1958-63, assoc. prof., 1963-68, prof. geol. scis., 1968—; cons. and adj. research participant, Oak Ridge Nat. Lab., 1959—; geol. cons. Served with U.S. Army, 1951-54. Recipient Centennial of Sci. award U. Notre Dame, 1965; Disting. Prof. award, Am. Fedn. Mineral. Socs., 1976. Fellow Mineral. Soc. Am., Geol. Soc. Am.; mem. Soc. Econ. Geologists, Nat. Assn. Geology Tchrs. (exec. sec. 1981-84), AIME, Tenn. Acad. Sci., Sigma Xi. Contbr. scholarly writings in field to sci. publs. Home: 5808 Meadow Glen Dr Knoxville TN 37919 Office: Dept Geol Scis Univ Tenn Knoxville TN 37916

KOPPEL, HAROLD EUGENE, auditor, accountant; b. Wilkensburg, Pa., Jan. 1, 1942; s. Harold Elwood and Clara Louise (Palmer) K.; m. Eunice Diane Godwin, Sept. 19, 1964 (div.); m. Patricia Virginia Lee Riley, Jan. 27, 1979; children—Harold Eugene, James Jarrod, Jason Adam; 1 stepson, Greg Roberts. A.A., Daytona Beach Community Coll., 1966; B.Gen. Studies, Rollins Coll., 1970; M.B.A., Stetson Univ., 1974. Teller, Barnett Bank Deland, Fla., 1962-66; auditor, asst. dir. fin. Sch. Bd. Volusia County (Fla.), 1966-74; auditor gen. State of Fla., 1974-80; dir. fin. Lake County Bd. County Commrs., 1980-81; dir. fin. Sch. Bd. Lake County, Fla., 1981-84; auditor Auditor Gen. State of Fla., Orlando, 1985—. Served with USN, 1959-62. Mem. Am. Inst. C.P.A.s, Fla. Inst. C.P.A.s. Republican. Baptist. Home: 29506 Highway 44 Eustis FL 32726 Office: 400 W Robinson Orlando FL 32801

KOPPER, HANS-HARALD, man-made fiber and chemical company executive; b. Sobotka, Poland, Aug. 21, 1930; s. Erich and Erika (Peschken) K.; m. Brigitte Eleonore Sauer, Mar. 22, 1963. Student U. Goettinger, Germany, 1949-55; diplom-chemistry, U. Hamburg, Germany, 1956, Ph.D. Chemistry, 1958. Research assoc. Princeton U., 1958-60; research and devel. positions BASF AG, Ludwigshafen, 1960-69, tech. dir. fertilizer div., 1969-79; pres., chief exec. officer Badische Corp., Williamsburg, Va., 1979-85; exec. v.p. BASF Corp., also pres. Fibers div., 1986—. Office: BASF Fibers PO Drawer D Williamsburg VA 23187

KOPRIVA, SHARON ORTMAN, visual artist, educator; b. Houston, Feb. 11, 1948; d. Lowell and Rosalie (Cusimano) Ortman; m. Gustav A. Kopriva, June 12, 1971. B.S.A.E., U. Houston, 1971, M.F.A., 1982; postgrad. Tex. Tech. U., 1977, Art Students League N.Y., 1979, Mus. Fine Arts Houston, 1976. Tchr. art Houston and Aldine Ind. Sch. Dists., 1971-79; fine art teaching fellow U. Houston, 1981; adminstrv. rep. Orange Show Found., 1982—; one woman shows include: Brazosport Fine Arts Center, Lake Jackson, Tex., 1980, Graham Gallery, Houston, 1986; exhibited in group shows: Am. Acad. Arts and Letters, N.Y.C., 1980, U. Houston, 1982, Houston Mus. Art, 1985, Allan Stone Gallery, N.Y.C., 1985, Houston Sch. Mus. Fine Arts, 1985, P.S.I., N.Y.C., 1985; represented in permanent collections: Monsanto Chem. Co., Houston, Dow Chem. U.S.A., Plaquemine, La., United Energy Resources, Houston. Recipient 1st place, Art League of Houston, 1978; Houston Festival, Houston Pub. Library work grantee, 1980; Best of Show, Brazosport Fine Arts Center, 1979, 80. Contbr. articles to profl. jours.

KORCHIN, JUDITH MIRIAM, lawyer; b. Kew Gardens, N.Y., Apr. 28, 1949; d. Arthur Walter and Mena (Levisohn) Goldstein; m. Paul Maury Korchin, June 10, 1972; 1 son, Brian Edward. B.A. with high honors, U. Fla., 1971; J.D. with honors, 1974. Law clk. to U.S. Dist. Judge, 1974-76; assoc., Steel, Hector & Davis, Miami, Fla., 1976-81; ptnr., 1981—. Bd. dirs. Fla. Film & Recording Inst., 1982—; mem. U. Fla. Law Ctr. Council, 1980-83; pres. alumni bd. U. Fla. Law Rev., 1983. Mem. Dade County Bar Assn. (treas. 1982, sec. 1983, 3d v.p. 1984, 2d v.p. 1985, bd. dirs. 1981-82), Fla. Bar (vice chmn. jud. nominating commn. com. 1982, mem. civil procedure rules com. 1984—), Order of Coif, Phi Beta Kappa, Phi Kappa Phi. Exec. editor, contbg. author U. Fla. Law Rev., 1973-74. Office: Steel Hector & Davis 4000 Southeast Financial Ctr Miami FL 33131

KORDELL, JAMES LEROY, computer specialist, systems analyst; b. Detroit, July 25, 1946; s. George and Lorrine B. Kordell; m. Helen L. Van Amber, July 23, 1975; 1 son, James M.; 1 stepson, W. David Van Amber. Student, South Fla. Coll. Automation, Sarasota, 1966-68. Vice pres. South Fla. Coll. Automation, 1967-69; sr. analyst Automated Systems Corp., Sarasota, 1969-75, data processing mgr., 1979-81, sr. analyst, 1982—; with Gulf Contracting, Inc., Sarasota, 1975-79; asst. data processing mgr. Eaton Corp., Sarasota, 1981-82. Mem. Data Processing Mgmt. Assn. Republican. Presbyterian. Home: 3923 Lancaster Dr Sarasota FL 34241 Office: 8527 Whitfield Park Loop Sarasota FL 33580

KORDISCH, MARY SCHROLLER, educator; b. Marysville, Kans., Jan. 23, 1921; d. Rudolph Frank and Ida Theresa Schroller; B.S., Kans. State U., 1943, M.S., 1944; postgrad., Fort Hays State Tchrs. Coll., 1953, U. Houston, 1965, La. State U., 1968, McNeese State U., 1975; children—Sherry, Terry, Foster C., Stanley Ray, Steven A. Tchr. public schs., Marysville, Kans., 1937-40; instr. zoology Kans. State U., Manhattan, 1940-44; elem. tchr., Maplewood, La., 1953-55, LaCrosse, Kans., 1955-56, Lake Charles, La., 1956-57; faculty McNeese State U., Lake Charles, La., 1957—, asso. prof. zoology 1974—. Mem. AAAS, Am. Bus. Women Assn. (woman of yr. award 1981), Sigma Xi, Phi Alpha Mu, Phi Lambda Chi. Democrat. Mem. Christian Ch. Clubs: Order of Eastern Star, Rebekah. Co-author zoology and anatomy manuals. Office: McNeese State U Biology Dept Lake Charles LA 70609

KORGEN, BENJAMIN JEFFRY, physical oceanographer; b. Duluth, Minn., Jan. 6, 1931; s. Benne Hanson and Helen Louise (Slattum) K.; B.S., U. Minn., 1956; M.A., U. Mich., 1958; Ph.D., Oreg. State U., 1969; m. Judith Kay Waggoner, Aug. 15, 1959; children—Susan Kay, Jeffry David, James Matthew. Phys. oceanographer U. N.C., Chapel Hill, 1969-74, asst. prof., 1969-74; cons. in oceanography, Sandwich, Mass., 1974-78; cons. Harper & Row Pubs., 1972-74, Thermonetics Corp., San Diego, 1972-74; textbook writer Allyn & Bacon, Boston, 1974-78; oceanographer U.S. Naval Oceanographic Office, 1978—; adj. assoc. prof. Tulane U., 1978—; adv. com. Miss.-Ala. Sea Grant Consortium, 1978-81, textbook writer Jones & Bartlett, Boston, 1985—. Served with USN, 1951-54. U. Mich. grad. fellow, 1957-58; NSF grantee, 1965; Office Naval Research fellow, 1966-69; Office Naval Research-NSF grantee, 1968-69; NSF grantee, 1969-70; U. N.C. Research Council grantee, 1969-72; N.C. Bd. Sci. and Tech. grantee, 1971-72; Naval Oceanographic Office contractee, 1971-73. Mem. Am. Soc. Limnology and Oceanography, Internat. Oceanographic Found., Am. Geophys. Union, AAAS, Geol. Soc. Am., Woods Hole Assocs. Contbr. articles in field to profl. jours. Home: 219 Lodor Dr Slidell LA 70458

KORNEMANN, WILLIAM EDWARD, II, air force officer; b. Washington, Jan. 5, 1946; s. William Edward and Rosalie Ann (Novak) K.; B.S. in Engring., U.S. Air Force Acad., 1967. Commd. 2nd lt. U.S. Air Force, 1967, advanced through grades to lt. col., 1983—; instr. pilot MC-130 90 Spl. Ops. Squadron, Nha Trang Air Base Vietnam, 1970-71; exchange pilot with German Air Force (C-160) 61st Mil. Alft Wing, Landsberg Air Base, Frg., 1972-75; staff officer mil. affairs Hdqrs. U.S. Air Force, Pentagon, Washington, 1975-79; mil. asst. Asst. Sec. Air Force, Manpower, Res. Affairs and Installations, Pentagon, Washington, 1979-80; asst. air attache' Am. Embassy, Bonn Fed. Rep. of Germany, 1980-83; chief tactical ops. 463 Tactical Airlift Wing, Dyess Air Force Base, Abilene, Tex., 1983—. Pres. Raiders Football Assn., Pop Warner League, Abilene, 1984—. Decorated D.F.C., Def. Meritorious Service medal, Meritorious Service medal with one oak leaf cluster, Air medal with four clusters, Gallantry Cross with palm Rep. of Vietnam. Republican. Methodist. Club: Daedalians. Avocations: jogging; reading. Home: 5557 Piping Rock Dr Abilene TX 79606 Office: Chief Tactical Ops 463 TAW Dyess Air Force Base Abilene TX 79601

KORNFELD, ITZCHAK EHUD, geologist; b. Tel-Aviv, Israel, Feb. 21, 1953; came to U.S., 1962, naturalized, 1968; s. Abraham M. and Helena (Rozdzial) K.; m. Maria Linda Barracca, June 14, 1981; 1 child. B.S., Bklyn. Coll., 1976, M.S., 1980. Research scientist Research Council N.Y., N.Y.C., 1976-78, Bur. Econ. Geology, State of Tex., Austin, 1978-79; cons. EPA, N.Y.C., 1980; sr. geologist Fred C. Hart Assocs., Newark, 1980-81; project mgr. Texaco Inc., New Orleans, 1981—; lectr., cons. in field. Contbr. articles to profl. jours. Coordinator, United Way, New Orleans, 1983—; vol. Sta. WWNO, 1984—; bd. dirs. Congregation Beth Israel, 1983—, Young Leadership Conf., 1984—. Grantee Geol. Soc. Am., 1977, Sigma Xi, 1977. Mem. Am. Assn. Petroleum Geologists (regional coordinator cross-sect. com. 1984-85), Am. Geophys. Union, Geol. Soc. Am., New Orleans Geol. Soc. (chmn. computer application com. 1984), Internat. Assn. Sedimentologists, Soc. Econ. Mineralogists and Paleontologists. Avocations: music; wine tasting; car racing; gardening. Office: Texaco Inc PO Box 60252 New Orleans LA 70160

KORNMEIER, RICHARD KARL, accountant, real estate broker; b. Providence, Apr. 28, 1946; s. Frank John and Marion (Drury) K.; m. Linda Jean Adams, May 6, 1967; children—Richard Karl, Jamie Lynn. B.A., Fla. State U., 1969, M.Accountancy, 1970. C.P.A., Fla.; real estate broker, Fla. Acct., Price Waterhouse, Miami, Fla., 1970-72; owner pub. acctg. firm, Ft. Lauderdale, Fla., 1972-78; instr. Broward Community Coll., 1971-74; sr. v.p. Stiles Corp., 1978-85; pres. Jeko Real Estate Devel., Jeko Realty, 1985—; dir., officer Stiles Property Mgmt. Co., Stiles Constrn. Co., Architecture 6400 Inc., R.T.W.D. Enterprises, Inc.; dir., lectr. pastoral ministries. Mem. adv. bd. Miami region SBA, 1980-82; del. White House Conf. on Small Bus., 1979; adviser bd. govs. Barry Coll., 1978—; exec. council Nova U., 1977-81, treas., 1979-81; mem. acctg. bd. Broward Community Coll., 1973-75; mem. Republican Nat. Com., 1978-86; mem. Met. Planning Council, Broward County, Fla., 1979-81; mem. Com. of 100 Broward Indsl. Bd., 1979-81; mem. South Fla. Racing Commn., 1983. Recipient Wall St. Jour. award, 1969; Price Waterhouse fellow, 1970-71. Mem. Am. Inst. C.P.A.s, Fla. Soc. C.P.A.s, Fla. State Bd. Realtors, Oakland Park-Wilton C. of C. (pres. 1980-81), Ft. Lauderdale C. of C. (ambassador 1977-79), Oakland Park Hist. Soc. (v.p. 1980), South Fla. Mfrs. Assn. Baptist. Columnist, Krause Publs., 1982—. Editor Internat. Jour. Antique Car Collecting, 1974-77. Contbr. articles to profl. jours. Office: 6400 N Andrews Ave Fort Lauderdale FL 33309

KORNRUMPH, JOAN O., educational guidance counselor; b. Duluth, Minn., Oct. 1, 1933; d. George and Hilia Sophia (Hemming) Ylen; m. Ralph E. Kornrumph, Feb. 29, 1964; 1 child, Michael David. B.A., Northland Coll., 1955; M.B.A., U. Ala., 1969; M.A. in Edn., U. Alaska, 1968. specialist in Edn., Rollins Coll., 1976. Life cert. English tchr., Wis.; cert. counselor, Fla. English tchr. Eagle River High Sch., Wis., 1955-58; asst. to program dir. YMCA, Mpls., 1958-59; commd. 2d lt. U. S. Air Force, 1959, advanced through grades to capt., 1966; comdr. Hdqrs. Squadron, Hamilton AFB, Calif., 1959-61, Norton AFB, Calif., 1961-63; comdr. hdqrs. Alaskan Communications Region, sect. Elmendorf AFB, Alaska, 1965-67; substitute tchr., East Grand Forks, N.D., 1969-70; guidance counselor Lyman High Sch., Longwood, Fla., 1970—, mem. Seminole County Curriculum Com.; mem. Fla. State Homebound/Hospitalized Steering Com. 1983—. Author: 919 SOG (USAFR) History, 1980-84; editor Lyman Guidance Newsletter, 1984—. Served USAFR, 1974-84. Named hon. admissions counselor U.S. Naval Acad., 1985. Mem. Am. Assn. Counseling and Devel. (participant Counselors Role in Excellence in Edn., Orlando 1985), Seminole County Assn. Counseling and Devel. (past pres.), Seminole County Tchrs. Assn. (past sec.), NEA, Profl. Bus. Women, WAF Ret. Officers Assn., Phi Delta Kappa, Kappa Delta Pi. Democrat. Lutheran. Clubs: Tops, Holiday Spa. Avocations: Health and fitness; literature. Home: 10634

Eastview Dr Orlando FL 32817 Office: Lyman High School 1141 SE Lake Ave Longwood FL 32750

KORTE, CHARLES DAVIS, university studies educator; b. State College, Pa., May 7, 1943; s. Edwerth E. and Ann F. (Hannum) K.; m. Margaret A. Roberts, Aug. 21, 1965; children—Margaret C., Jeffrey E. B.A., Miami U., Oxford, Ohio, 1965; Ph.D., Harvard U., 1969. Asst. prof. Vassar Coll., Poughkeepsie, N.Y., 1969-75; lectr. psychology U. St. Andrews (Scotland), 1975-79; assoc. prof. univ. studies N.C. State U., Raleigh, 1979—. Mem. Hillsborough Citizens Adv. Council. Mem. Soc. Psychol. Study of Social Problems, Soc. Personality and Social Psychology. Democrat. Lutheran. Contbr. articles to profl. jours. Office: North Carolina State University Raleigh NC 27650

KORTH, CHARLOTTE WILLIAMS, furniture and interior design firm executive; b. Milw., Nov. 16, 1920; d. Lewis C. and Marguerite Peil Brooks; student U. Wis., 1941; m. Robert Lee Williams, Jr., Oct. 25, 1944 (dec.); children—Patricia Williams Williams, Melissa Williams O'Rourke, R. Brooks; m. Fred Korth, Aug. 23, 1980. Owner, chief exec. officer, chmn. bd. Charlotte's Inc., El Paso, Tex., 1951—; pres. Paso del Norte Design, Inc., El Paso, 1978—; mem. adv. bd. Mountain Bell Telephone Co., 1976-79; dir. First City Nat. Bank. Mem. women's com. El Paso Symphony Guild; charter mem. Com. of 200; mem. adv. bd. El Paso Community Coll.; mem. Renaissance 400, El Paso. Recipient Silver plaque Gifts and Decorative Accessories mag., 1978; named Woman of Year, Women's Polit. Caucus, 1979, Outstanding Woman Entrepreneur El Paso, Am. Bus. Women's Assn., 1979. Mem. Am. Soc. Interior Designers (dir. Tex. 1977-82), El Paso C. of C. (dir. 1976—), El Paso Women's C. of C., Delta Gamma. Roman Catholic. Clubs: Santa Teresa (N.Mex.) Country; Coronado Country, El Paso, Internat. (El Paso). Home: 1054 Torrey Pines El Paso TX 79912 also 4200 Massachusetts Ave NW Apt #101 Washington DC 20016 Office: Charlotte's Fine Furniture Pepper Tree Sq 5411 N Mesa St El Paso TX 79912

KORZENIOWSKI, ANDRZEJ, mathematics educator; b. Strzelce, Opolskie, Poland, Apr. 15, 1951; came to U.S., 1981; permanent resident; s. Jozef Maksymilian and Maria (Ledwolorz) K.; m. Teodozja Cecylia Rawicka, Aug. 28, 1976; children—Edgar Maria, Samson Oscar. M.S., Wroclaw U., Poland, 1974, Ph.D., 1978. Asst. to sr. asst. to asst. prof. Wroclaw U., 1974-81; vis. asst. prof. So. Ill. U., Carbondale, 1981-83; asst. prof. U. Tex., Arlington, 1983—. Recipient Teaching award Wroclaw U., 1977, Research award, 1978; Internat. Research and Exchange Bd. grantee, 1982. Mem. Polish Math. Soc. (Research award 1979), Polish Ministry Sci. (Research award 1980), Am. Math. Soc. Roman Catholic. Avocation: classical guitar. Office: U Tex at Arlington Dept Math Arlington TX 76019

KOSHUBA, WALTER JOSEPH, consulting metallurgical engineering firm executive; b. St. Paul, Aug. 22, 1917; s. John and Pauline (Rychley) K.; B.Metall. Engring., U. Minn., 1940; m. Renella J. Waaland, Sept. 8, 1945; children—Walter Joseph, Mykola J. Supt. research engring. Allis Chalmers Mfg. Co., Milw., 1940-46; gen. supt. Solar Aircraft Co., Des Moines, 1946-47; head materials sect. NEPA div. Fairchild Engine & Airplane Corp., Oak Ridge, 1947-51; head metall., ceramic engring. aircraft nuclear propulsion div. Gen. Electric Co., Cin., 1951-56, mgr. tech. prodn., 1956-61; mgr. Nuclear div. Beryllium Corp. (name now Kawecki-Berylco Industries, Inc.), Hazleton, Pa., 1961-64, gen. mgr. div., 1964-65, mgr. alloy div., 1965-71, mgr. mfg. tech., 1971-72; mgr. facilities and equipment engring. United Nuclear Corp. Naval Reactors div., 1972-74; v.p. engring. and constrn. Uranium Recovery Corp., Mulberry, Fla., 1974-79, v.p. spl. projects, 1979-83; pres. Walter J. Koshuba & Assocs., Cons. Engrs., Highland City, Fla., 1983—. Mem. Hazleton Indsl. Council. Fellow Am. Inst. Chemists; mem. Pa. Mfrs. Assn., Am. Soc. Metals (chmn. Cin.), Am. Inst. Mining, Metall. and Petroleum Engrs., Am. Ceramic Soc., Am. Powder Metallurgy Inst., Inst. Ceramic Engrs., Am. Nuclear Soc. Home: 3621 Dan Unie Ln Lakeland FL 33803 Office: Walter J Koshuba & Assocs Box 963 Highland City FL 33846

KOSLOWSKI, GERALD JOHN, sales engineer; b. Green Bay, Wis., Nov. 11, 1945; s. Leo Donald and Genevive (Wicker) K.; m. Diane Marie Radomski, June 5, 1964; children—Kaylynn Marie, Scott Anthony, Kevin John. B.C.E., Marquette U., 1969. Designer draftsman Allis Chalmers, West Allis, Wis., 1963-66; shoring engr. Safway Steel Products, Milw., 1966-70, sales engr., Washington, 1970-76; sales mgr. Able Equipment, Greensboro, N.C., 1976-79; v.p. Strickland Systems, Jacksonville, Fla., 1979—; lectr. in field; condr. concrete shoring seminars. Recipient numerous sales awards. Mem. Assn. Gen. Contractors, Am. Concrete Inst., Am. Precast Inst., Jacksonville Internat. Trade Assn., Am. Scaffolding and Shoring Inst., Secret Cove Civic Assn., Police Benevolent Soc., Jacksonville C. of C., Secret Cove Bowling Assn. (pres.). Roman Catholic. Contbr. articles to profl. jours. Office: 233 Tresca Rd Jacksonville FL 32211

KOSS, MARK T., lawyer; b. Bklyn., Apr. 24, 1954; s. Theodore and Katherine (Misnick) K.; m. Jeanette Marian Hirst, Aug. 9, 1980; 1 child, Michael Theodore. B.S. in Econs. and Fin., Fairleigh Dickinson U., 1976; J.D., Oklahoma City U., 1980. Bar: Okla. 1980, U.S. Dist. Ct. (we. dist.) Okla. 1982, U.S. Ct. Appeals (10th cir.) 1984. Assoc. Berry & Berry, Oklahoma City, 1979-81; atty. Hadson Petroleum Corp., Oklahoma City, 1981-82; sole practice, Oklahoma City, 1982-85; ptnr. Hamilton & Koss, Oklahoma City, 1985—; hearing examiner Ethics and Merit Commn., Oklahoma City, 1982—. UN Cultural Exchange student and USSR, 1974. Mem. Okla. Trial Lawyers Assn., Assn. Trial Lawyers Am., ABA, Okla. Bar Assn. (pub. info. commn. Oklahoma City, 1980—). Democrat. Episcopalian. Club: Young Men's Dinner. Home: 10305 Basswood Canyon Rd Oklahoma City OK 73132

KOSSACK, CARL FREDERICK, statistics educator; b. Chgo., May 30, 1915; s. Walter Edward and Elizabeth Marie (Jost) K.; m. Elizabeth Ayres, June 24, 1940; children—Barbara L., Charles A., Edgar W., Howard W., Kenneth A., William S. B.A., UCLA, 1935, M.A., 1936; Ph.D., U. Mich., 1939. Asst. prof. U. Oreg., Eugene, 1938-50; prof., head dept. math. and stats. Purdue U., North Lafayette, Ind., 1950-59; univ. rep. IBM, Yorktown Heights, N.Y., 1959-63; dir. lab. for computer sci. Grad. Research Ctr. of Southwest, Dallas, 1963-65; prof., head dept. stats. and computer sci. U. Ga., Athens, 1965-80, prof. emeritus, 1980—. Fellow Am. Statis. Assn.; mem. Am. Math. Soc., Phi Kappa Phi, Phi Kappa Delta. Democrat. Congregationalist. Home: Rt 1 Box 332 Huli GA 30646

KOSTOCH, ARLENE JOAN, college instructional administrator; b. Cumberland, Wis., Oct. 27, 1936; d. Arlo Walter and Agnes Otilda (Johnson) Thorsness; m. Walter Bernard Kostoch Jr., Dec. 28, 1957; children—Kristin, Karin, Walter B. III, Karla. B.S. in Nursing, St. Olaf Coll., 1958; M.S., Tex. A&I, 1976; Ph.D., U. Tex., 1981. Registered nurse. Staff nurse various hosps., Tex., Minn., 1958-70; instr. Del Mar Coll., Corpus Christi, Tex., 1970-75, asst. prof., 1975-80, assoc. prof. nurse edn., chmn. dept., 1980-85, dean occupational edn. and tech., 1985—; coordinating bd. cons. Ad Hoc Vis. Team, 1981—; mem. admissions com. dept. nursing Corpus Christi State U., 1980—, adv. council, 1980—. Bd. dirs. Am. Cancer Soc., 1985, ARC, 1983—; mem. adv. bd. Hill Haven Community, 1981—; tchr. sex edn., health edn. Trinity Luth. Ch., 1976-78; camp nurse, leader Paisano council Girl Scouts U.S.A., 1971-75; active Community Health Fair, 1982—. Mem. Tex. Jr. Coll. Tchrs. Assn., Del Mar Edn. Assn. (spl. projects com. 1980-81, trip com. 1982—, audit com. 1983), Am. Nurses Assn., Tex. Nurses Assn. (dist. 17 sec. 1982—), Nat. League Nursing, Tex. League Nursing, Orgn. Advancement Assoc. Degree Nursing, Sigma Theta Tau, Phi Kappa Phi, Phi Delta Kappa. Lutheran. Avocations: boating; archeological expeditions. Home: 14001 Jackfish Corpus Christi TX 78418 Office: Del Mar Coll Office of Dean Occupational Edn and Tech Corpus Christi TX 78404

KOSTRZEWA, RICHARD MICHAEL, pharmacology educator; b. Trenton, N.J., July 22, 1943; s. John Walter and Wladyslosa (Wnuk) K.; m. Florence Agnes Palmer, Sept. 4, 1965; children—Theresa, Richard, Joseph, Maria, Krystyna, Thomas, John Palmer, Francis, Roseanna. B.S., Phila. Coll. Pharmacy and Sci., 1965, M.S., 1967; Ph.D., U. Pa., 1971. Research pharmacologist VA Hosp., New Orleans, 1971-75; asst. prof. pharmacology Tulane Med. Center-New Orleans, 1972-76; asst. prof. physiology La. State U. Med. Center-New Orleans, 1975-78; assoc. prof., then prof. pharmacology East Tenn. State U. Med. Sch.-Johnson City, 1978—. Mem. exec. com. Appalachian March of Dimes, Johnson City, Tenn., 1980—. Recipient Research award East Tenn. State U. Found., 1981. Mem. Am. Soc. Pharmacology, Soc. Neurosci., Histochem. Soc., AAAS, Sigma Xi. Roman Catholic. Mem. editorial adv. bd.: Peptides, 1980—; contbr. sci. articles to profl. publs. Office: East Tenn State Univ PO Box 19810A Johnson City TN 37614

KOSZALKA, ELIZABETH MACFARLAN, clinical psychologist; b. Arlington, Va., Aug. 7, 1950; d. Walker Joynes and Luta (Chappell) Macfarlan; m. George W. Koszalka, June 3, 1972; children—Erica Diane, Amy Elizabeth. B.A., William and Mary Coll., 1972; Ph.D., U. N.C., 1976. Lic. psychologist, N.C. Staff psychologist Human Resource Cons., Chapel Hill, N.C., 1975—. Mem. Am. Soc. Clin. Hypnosis, Am. Psychol. Assn., N.C. Psychol. Assn., N.C. Soc. Clin. Hypnosis. Home: Route 3 Box 166-3 Apex NC 27502 Office: Human Resource Cons 104 S Estes Dr Chapel Hill NC 27514

KOSZTARAB, MICHAEL, entomologist, researcher; b. Bucharest, Romania, July 7, 1927; came to U.S., 1957; s. Michael and Berta (Albert) K.; m. Matilda Pinter, Oct. 21, 1953; 1 dau., Eva K. J.D.; B.S., Hungarian U. Agr. Sci., Budapest, 1951; Ph.D., Ohio State U., 1962. Extension asst. Hungarian State Bur. Plant Protection Budapest, 1947-50; asst. prof. Hungarian U. Agrl. Scis., Budapest, 1951-56; cons. entomologist Insect Control and Research, Inc., Balt., 1957-58, asst. dir. research, 1959-60; assoc. prof. Va. Poly. Inst. and State U., Blacksburg, Va., 1962-68, prof. entomology, 1968—; chmn. planning com. Nat. Biol. Survey, 1984—. Recipient W. E. Wine Faculty Achievement award, 1967. Fellow Va. Acad. Sci.; mem. Hungarian Entomol. Soc. (hon.), Entomol. Soc. Am., Soc. Systematic Zoology, Entomol. Soc. Washington, Fla. Entomol. Soc., Soc. Systematic Zoology. Club: Cosmos (Washington). Author: Scale Insects of Hungary, 1978; contbr. articles to profl. jours.

KOTHMANN, GLENN HAROLD, state senator; b. San Antonio, May 30, 1928; s. Wilkes John and Lillie (Mertz) K.; B.S., Tex. A&M U., 1950. Mem. Tex. State Legislature, 1957-58, 61-66, 69-70; mem. Tex. State Senate, 1971—, pres. pro-tempore, 1975, vice-chmn. state affairs com., mem. intergovtl. relations com., natural resources com., chmn. subcom. on elections. Served as maj. gen. Tex. Army N.G. Democrat. Address: 4610 Sea Breeze San Antonio TX 78220

KOTLARSKI, IGNACY ICCHAK, statistics and mathematics educator; b. Warsaw, Poland, July 29, 1923; came to U.S., 1969, naturalized, 1974. Docent Tech. U. Warsaw, 1967; D., U. Wroclaw, Poland, 1961. Clk., Normalization Com., Warsaw, 1950-53; asst. Math. Inst., Warsaw, 1953-54; asst. adj. Army Tech. Acad., Warsaw, 1953-59; adj. Tech. U. Warsaw, 1954-68; prof. stats. and math. Okla. State U., Stillwater, 1969—. Home: 2723 Pioneer Trail Stillwater OK 74074 Office: Dept Stats and Dept Math Okla State U Stillwater OK 74078

KOTTI, KOSTA SPIRO, chemist; b. Hochisht, Albania, Aug. 13, 1927; came to U.S., 1938; s. Spiro C. and Olga (Pema) K.; m. Patricia S. Kneale, Sept. 11, 1954; children—Douglas K., James D., Thomas S., William P., Carol O. B.S. in Chemistry, U. Akron. Chemist, Dana plant duPont Co. (Ind.), 1951-53, Savannah River plant, Aiken, S.C., 1953-54, prodn. supr., 1955-72, accountability and budget dir., 1972-81, planning coordinator, 1981—. Bd. dirs. Ga.-Carolina council Boy Scouts Am., 1980-83. Served with USN, 1945-46. Republican. Greek Orthodox. Club: Exchange (treas. S.C. 1976-78). Home: 811 Jackson Ave North Augusta SC 29841 Office: duPont Co Savannah River Plant Aiken SC 29808

KOTWAL, KEKI RUSI, prosthodontist; b. Bombay, India, Jan. 5, 1939; came to U.S., 1961; s. Rusi T. and Arnavaz R. (Shroff) K.; m. Marie Catherine Cox Graham, Aug. 31, 1962; children—Nevil Eric, Russ Steven. B.D.S., U. Bombay, 1960; M.S. in Prosthodontics, U. Ala., 1963, D.M.D., 1965. Lic. dentist, D.C.; diplomate Am. Bd. Prosthodontics. Practice dentistry, Bombay, 1960-61; commd. capt. U.S. Army, 1965, advanced through grades to col., 1979; clinic chief, prosthodontist Schofield Barracks, Hawaii, 1981-84; chief dental clinic, chief dept. dentistry William Beaumont Army Med. Ctr., El Paso, 1984—, also dir. prosthodontic residency program and cons. Contbr. articles to profl. jours. Recipient award Surgeon Gen., 1983. Fellow Am. Coll. Prosthodontists; mem. ADA, Fedn. Prosthodontic Orgns. Home: 4501 RJ Lunn Ct El Paso TX 79924 Office: William Beaumont Army Med Ctr El Paso TX 79920

KOTZEBUE, ROBERT WILLIAM, SR., retired air conditioning company executive; b. Moulton, Tex., Mar. 28, 1909; s. George William and Adelia (Helmcamp) K.; ed. high sch., Frigidaire Air Conditioning Engring. Schs., 1934-36; m. Mary Lou Wanek, May 18, 1929; children—Robert William, Kenneth Lee. Mgr. air conditioning dept. Straus-Frank Co., San Antonio, 1934-41; partner Bell-Kotzebue Co., Inc., wholesale distbrs., San Antonio, 1945-60; operator Kotzebue Distbg. Co., San Antonio, 1960-84, chmn. bd., 1968-84, ret. Served to capt., C.E., U.S. Army, 1941-45. Registered profl. engr. Tex. Mem. San Antonio Power Squadron (comdr. 1971-72), ASHRAE (life). Republican. Lutheran. Clubs: Oak Hills Country, St. Anthony. Home: 149 Lou-Jon Circle San Antonio TX 78213 Office: 1031 NE IH 410 PO Box 17369 San Antonio TX 78217

KOUTRAS, PHOEBUS, thoracic and cardiovascular surgeon; b. Athens, Greece, Aug. 31, 1932; s. Demetrius and Helen (Kongos) K.; came to U.S., 1965, naturalized, 1977; M.D., U. Athens, 1958; m. Helen Nicolacopoulos, Sept. 4, 1960; children—Elena, Jim, Charles. Intern, Trumbull Meml. Hosp., Warren, Ohio, 1965-66; resident in thoracic and cardiovascular surgery Southwestern Med. Sch., 1967-69; fellow in cardiovascular surgery Baylor Hosp., Dallas, 1971-72; practice medicine, specializing in thoracic and cardiovascular surgery, Midland, Tex., 1973-74, Garland, Tex., 1974—; mem. staffs Garland Meml. Hosp., Garland Community Hosp., Med. City Dallas Hosp., Richardson Med. Center, Plano Gen. Hosp., Baylor U. Med. Center. Diplomate Am. Bd. Surgery, Am. Bd. Thoracic Surgery. Fellow A.C.S., Mem. Am., Tex. med. assns., Dallas County Med. Soc., Am. Coll. Angiology, Am. Coll. Cardiology, Soc. Clin. Vascular Surgery, So. Thoracic Surg. Assn. Contbr. articles to med. jours. Office: 618 Clara Barton Blvd Garland TX 75042

KOVAC, JOSEPH BERNARD, retail executive; b. McKeesport, Pa., June 1, 1947; s. Joseph Albert and Elizabeth (Jacko) K.; m. Patricia Groene, June 21, 1980; 1 child, Kimberly Lynn. B.S., Slippery Rock State Coll., 1969. Men's wear buyer Kaufmann's Dept. Store, Pitts., 1969-73; women's wear buyer Woodward & Lothrop, Washington, 1973-75; sales exec. I. C. Isaacs & Co., Balt., 1975-77; gen. mgr. Micada Distbrs., Virginia Beach, Va., 1977-84; mdse. mgr. Farm Fresh Inc., Norfolk, Va., 1984—; cons. Old Dominion U. Distributive Edn. Program, Norfolk, Va., 1980-82, Kempsville Sr. High Distributive Edn. Program, Virginia Beach, 1977—. Creative dir. TV comml., 1979-83, radio comml., 1979-83; editor newsletter, 1981. Recipient Speaker's award Dale Carnegie Inst., 1979, Grad. Asst. award, 1980; cert. of Appreciation Kempsville Sr. High Sch., Virginia Beach, 1979. Mem. Retail Merchants Assn. Roman Catholic. Clubs: Eagles Social (Virginia Beach); Debate (Slippery Rock; v.p. 1968). Home: 1705 Dancers Ct Virginia Beach VA 23464 Office: Farm Fresh Inc 3487 Inventors Rd Norfolk VA 23502

KOVACHEVICH, ELIZABETH A., judge; b. Canton, Ill., Dec. 14, 1936; d. Dan and Emilie (Kuchan) Kovachevich. B.B.A. magna cum laude in Fin., U. Miami; J.D., Stetson U. Bar: Fla. 1961, U.S. Dist. Ct. (mid. and so. dists.) Fla. 1961, U.S. Ct. Appeals (5th cir.) 1961, U.S. Supreme Ct. 1968. Research and adminstrv. aide Pinellas County Legis. Del. Fla., 1961; gen. practice, St. Petersburg, Fla., 1961-62; assoc. DiVito & Speer, St. Petersburg, 1961-62; house counsel Rieck & Fleece Guilders Supplies, Inc., St. Petersburg, 1962—; sole practice, St. Petersburg, 1962-73; judge 6th Jud. Cir., Pinellas and Pasco Counties, Fla., 1973-82; judge U.S. Dist. Ct. (mid. dist.) Fla., St. Petersburg, 1982—; chmn. St. Petersburg Profl. Legal Project - Days in Court -, 1967. Bd. regents State of Fla., 1970-72; legal advisor, bd. dirs. Young Women's Residence, Inc., 1968; mem. Fla. Gov.'s Commn. on Status of Women, 1968-71; mem. Pres.'s Commn. on White House Fellowships, 1973-77; mem. def. adv. com. on Women in Service, Dept. Def., 1973-76; Fla. conf. publicity chmn. 18th Nat. Republican Women's Conf., Atlanta, 1971; lifetime mem. Children's Hosp. Guild, YWCA of St. Petersburg; charter mem. Golden Notes, St. Petersburg Symphony; bd. dirs. Abilities Inc. Fla. Rehab. Ctr., 1977-80. Recipient Disting. Alumni award Stetson U., 1970; Woman of Yr. award Fla. Fedn. Bus. and Profl. Women, 1981; Ann. Ben C. Willard Meml. award Stetson Lawyers Assn., 1983; numerous other awards. Mem. St. Petersburg Bar Assn. (chmn. bench and bar com., sec 1969), ABA, Fla. Bar Assn., Pinellas County Trial Lawyers Assn., Assn. Trial Lawyers Am., Am. Judicature Soc. Home: 2459 Woodlawn Circle E St Petersburg FL 33704 Office: U S Dist Ct 635 U S Courthouse 80 N Hughey Ave Orlando FL 32801

KOVACS-LONG, JUDITH, counselor, consultant; b. Lorain, Ohio, Oct. 30, 1941; d. Gasper Aloysis and Margaret Eleanor (Cawley) K.; m. William John Long, Aug. 10, 1963; children—Randolph William, Erin Elizabeth. B.A., Miami U., Oxford, Ohio, 1963; M.A., Western Mich. U., 1979. Lic. profl. counselor; nat. cert. counselor. English tchr. Lorain City Schs., Ohio, 1963-66; instr. Glen Oaks Community Coll., Centreville, Mich., 1977-79; instr., counselor, cons. Ctr. Women's Services Western Mich. U., Kalamazoo, 1978-79; instr., counselor Women's Program San Antonio Coll., Tex., 1980—, Ctr. Counseling and Health Services, San Antonio, 1982-83; pvt. practice counselor, cons., New Braunfels, Tex., 1983—; coordinator, chmn. Ann. Women's Forum, New Braunfels, 1980; counselor Bexar County Womens Ctr., San Antonio, 1979-80. Exec. com., dir. edn. Hospice, New Braunfels, 1983—; co-ordinator Chem. People Project, New Braunfels, 1983; active in Supts. Parent Adv. Com., 1983—, Adv. Com. Community Edn., 1983—; coordinator Profl. Women's Network, New Braunfels, 1983—. Mem. Am. Assn. Counseling and Devel., Am. Mental Health Counselors Assn., Assn. Humanistic Edn. and Devel., AAUW (v.p. chpt. 1974-77, Project Renew grantee 1977, Agt. of Change award 1979), Tex. Assn. Counseling and Devel., Gamma Phi Beta. Office: 685 Floral Circle New Braunfles TX 78130

KOVARIK, DANIEL CHARLES, petroleum geologist, consultant; b. Patchogue, N.Y., Jan. 15, 1958; s. Vincent Joseph and Mary Anne (Kriklava) K.; m. Colleen Ann Smith, July 11, 1981. B.S., SUNY-Stony Brook, 1980. Wellsite geologist Exploration Services, Inc., Midland, Tex., 1981-83, 84; geologists, ops. mgr., pres., 1983-84; petroleum geologists Midland, 1984—; cons. geologist, Midland, 1984—. Mem. Geol. Soc. Am., Am. Assn. Petroleum Geologists, West Tex. Geol. Soc. Republican. Roman Catholic. Home: 3600 N Midland Dr #8-H Midland TX 79707

KOWNSLAR, ALLAN OWEN, history educator; b. Wichita Falls, Tex., Sept. 5, 1935; s. Dorsey Taylor and Ruth Lorene (Jackson) K.; m. Marguerite Louise Hanicak, Aug. 19, 1961; children—Donald Taylor, Edward Jonathan. B.A. in History, Trinity U., 1957, M.A. in History, 1960; D.A. in History, Carnegie-Mellon U., 1969; postgrad. McCormick Theol. Sem., 1958-59, U. Mass., 1963-65. Tchr. pub. schs., San Antonio, 1957-59, Amherst, Mass., 1961-67; research historian Carnegie-Mellon U., Pitts., 1967-70; prof. history Trinity U., San Antonio, 1972—; cons. in field. Mem. Andrew Carnegie Soc., Nat. Council for Social Studies, Tex. Council for Social Studies. Democrat. Presbyterian. Author: Contemporary Social Issues and the Teaching of American History, 1978; Tips for Teaching About the Bicentennial, 1975; Studies in Environmental Folkliterature, two vols., 1976; Using Newspapers to Develop Critical Thinking Skills, 1980; Teaching Critical Thinking, 1981; co-author: Inquiring About American History, 1972, People and Our World: A Study of World History, 1977, rev., 1980; American Government: The Great Experiment, 1979; Civics: Citizens and Society, 1980; sr. author, editor: Dealing with Contemporary Issues in Social Studies Education: Use of the Inquiry Process and Basic Questioning Strategies for the Secondary Level, 1981; Teaching Basic Thinking Skills in Social Studies Instruction, 1982; contbr. numerous articles to profl. publs. Home: 7922 Thornhill St San Antonio TX 78209 Office: Trinity U History Dept 715 Stadium Dr San Antonio TX 78284

KRACKE, ROBERT RUSSELL, lawyer; b. Decatur, Ga., Feb. 27, 1938; s. Roy Rachford and Virginia Carolyn (Minter) K.; student Birmingham So. Coll.; B.A., Samford U., 1962; J.D., Cumberland Sch. Law, 1965; m. Barbara Anne Pilgrim, Dec. 18, 1965; children—Shannon Ruth, Robert Russell, Rebecca Anne, Susan Lynn. Admitted to Ala. bar, 1965; individual practice law Birmingham, Ala., 1965—; ptnr. firm Kracke, Thompson & Ellis. Mem. Jefferson County Dem. exec. com., 1972—; deacon Ind. Presbyn. Ch., Birmingham, 1973-76, pres. adult choir, 1968—; 1st v.p., trustee, mem. exec. bd. Birmingham Civic Opera Assn.; bd. dirs. Jefferson County Assn. Retarded Citizens; bd. dirs., founding pres. Birmingham chpt. Juvenile Diabetes Found. Served with USNR, 1955-57. Mem. Birmingham (chmn. law library, law day 1976), Ala., Am. (award merit law day 1976) bar assns., Am. Judicature Soc., Ala. Hist. Assn., Phi Alpha Delta (pres. chpt. 1964-65), Sigma Alpha Epsilon. Democrat. Clubs: Downtown, Relay House. Lodge: Rotary (treas., dir. Shades Valley club; Paul Harris fellow). Editor, Birmingham Bar Bull., 1974—; bd. editors Ala. Lawyer. Contbr. articles to profl. publs. Home: 4410 Briarglen Dr Birmingham AL 35243 also Deerwood Lake Harpersville AL 35078 Office: 2220 Highland Ave Birmingham AL 35205

KRAEHE, MARY ALICE, librarian, educator; b. Mpls., Oct. 1, 1924; d. Laurence and Elizabeth (Folds) Eggleston; m. Enno Edward Kraehe, May 25, 1946; children—Laurence Adams, Claudia. B.A., U. Minn., 1945; M.S., U. Ky., 1963. Library asst. U. Ky. Library, Lexington, 1956-64; out-of-print librarian U. N.C., Chapel Hill, 1964-68; out-of-print librarian U. Va. Library, Charlottesville, 1970—, asst. prof., 1974—, African bibliographer, 1976—; book reviewer African Book Pub. Record, 1983—. Author: African Languages: A Guide to the Library Collection of the University of Virginia, rev. edit., 1986. Mem. Archives Libraries Com. (sec. exec. bd. 1981-85, exec. bd. 1986—), African Studies Assn., ALA, Va. Library Assn., Southeastern Regional Seminar African Studies, LWV, Colonial Dames, Kappa Kappa Gamma, Beta Phi Mu. Club: Blue Ridge Swim (sec. 1977-83). Home: 130 Bennington Rd Charlottesville VA 22901 Office: Collection Devel Dept U Va Library Charlottesville VA 22901

KRAKEL, DEAN, museum administrator, consultant, historian; b. Ault, Colo., July 3, 1923; s. Eldon A. and Gretta (Cross) K.; m. Iris Lesh, June, 1947; children—Ira Dean, Jennie L., Jack R. B.A., No. Colo. U., 1950; M.A. in History, U. Denver, 1952; D.H.L. (hon.), U. Colo., 1976. Asst. curator Colo. State Hist. Soc., Denver, 1950-52; dir., archivist U. Wyo. Library, Laramie, 1952-56; dep. dir. Mus. and Fine Arts Program, U.S. Air Force Acad., Colo., 1956-61; exec. dir. Thomas Gilcrage Inst., Tulsa, 1961-64; dir., exec. v.p. Nat. Cowboy Hall of Fame, Oklahoma City, 1964—; dir. Anti Metric Soc., 1976—. Author: South Plate Country, 1952; Saga of Tom Horn, 1952; James Boren: A Study in Discipline, 1968; Tom Ryan, 1971; End of The Trail: The Odyessey of a Statue, 1973; Adventures In Western Art, 1977; Mitch: On the Tail of the Old West, 1981; Schwering: Painting On the Square, 1981. Served with USN, 1943-46. Recipient Am. Heritage award No. Colo. U., 1978; Gari Melcher Medal for Arts N.Y. Art Soc., 1985. Mem. Nat. Cowboy Hall of Fame (trustees' gold medal award, 1975). Avocation: art appraisal. Home: Route One Box 160J Oklahoma City OK 73111 Office: Nat Cowboy Hall of Fame 1700 NE 63d St Oklahoma City OK 73111

KRAMER, ERROL D, business executive; b. Grand Rapids, Mich., Mar. 17, 1940; s. Jack Dowie and Thelma Ardene K.; B.S. in Tech., U. Houston, 1977; m. Lillian Annette Holcomb, May 27, 1961; children—Lisa Renee, Ramona Lois. Supr. purchasing Texsteam Corp., Houston, 1960-77; with W-K-M div. ACF Industries, Inc., Houston, 1977-84, purchasing mgr., 1979-84; purchasing mgr. G.H. Bettis Co., 1984—; owner, pres. E.D. Kramer Enterprises, Inc. distbrs. S.M.I. motivation and self-devel. cassette tapes, 1983—; materials mgr. S.W. Electronics, Inc., Stafford, Tex.; instr. Continuing Edn. Coll., U. Houston, 1978—. Vol. uniform patrolman Missouri City Police, 1978—. Cert. purchasing mgr.; named Profl. Devel. Man of Year, Nat. Assn. Purchasing Mgmt., 1977-78. Mem. Purchasing Mgmt. Assn. Houston (pres. 1982-83 James O. Cox award 1977-78). Methodist. Clubs: United Meth. Men (pres. 1981-82), Communities Recreation (pres. 1981-82), Toastmasters. Home: 942 Circle Bend Missouri City TX 77489 Office: 18703 GH Circle Box 508 Waller TX 77484

KRAMER, RICHARD DOUGLAS, aerospace engineer; b. Durham, N.C., Aug. 27, 1946; s. Richard Andrew and Ruby Nell (Kelly) K.; m. Carolyn Manette Hancock, June 23, 1973; children—William Andrew, Douglas Ryan. B.Aerospace Engring., Auburn U., 1969; M.S., U. Ala., 1976; M.S. in Indsl. Engring., U. Ala.-Huntsville, 1982, Ph.D. in Mech. Engring., 1982. Aerospace engr. NASA, Marshall Space Flight Ctr., Huntsville, 1969-82; sr. systems engr. Teledyne Brown Engring., Huntsville, 1982-83; sr. staff scientist SRS Technologies, Huntsville, 1983—; tchr. physics and engring. Calhoun Jr. Coll., 1982-83, U. Ala.-Huntsville, 1982-83, So. Inst. Tech., 1983. Served with U.S. Army, 1971-72, maj. Res. Recipient Dirs. Commendation, Marshall Space Flight Ctr., 1972. Mem. Res. Officers Assn., ASME, AIAA. Baptist. Home: 1302 Aldridge Dr SE Huntsville AL 35803

KRANTZ, GARY HOWARD, criminal justice training executive; b. Youngstown, Ohio, Sept. 4, 1950; s. Marvin Alan and Florence (Lewin) K.; m. Mary Jane Cecile, June 5, 1976; children—Donald Alan, Ryan Michael. B.S., Youngstown State U., 1973; M.S., Biscayne Coll., 1979. Cert. police instr., Fla., Va. Police officer Metro-Dade Police Dept., Miami, Fla., 1973-84, curriculum developer, 1981-84; exec. dir. Central Shenandoah Criminal Justice Tng. Ctr., Waynesboro, Va., 1984—; cons., Miami, Va., 1982—. Mem. Am. Soc. Tng. and Devel., Internat. Assn. Chiefs of Police (assoc.). Lodges: Lions, Elks. Avocations: woodworking; bowling; golf; fishing. Office: Central Shenandoah Criminal Justice Training 325 Pine Ave Waynesboro VA 22980

KRASLOW, DAVID, newspaperman, author; b. N.Y.C., Apr. 16, 1926; s. Frank and Goldie (Sirota) K.; B.A., U. Miami (Fla.), 1948; m. Bernice Schonfeld, Sept. 18, 1949; children—Ellen Anne, Karen Leah, Susan Beth. Sports writer Miami News, 1947-48, successively sports writer, reporter, Washington corr. Miami Herald, 1948-63; with Los Angeles Times, 1963-72, Washington corr., news editor Washington Bur., then chief Washington Bur., 1970-72; asst. mng. editor Washington Star-News, 1972-74; Washington Bur. chief Cox Newspapers, 1974-77; pub. Miami News, 1977—. Bd. dirs. New World Festival of Arts; trustee Center for Fine Arts, Miami; trustee U. Miami; mem. Orange Bowl Com. Served with USAAF, 1944-46. Recipient George Polk award, 1969; Raymond Clapper award, 1969; Dumont award, 1969; Nieman fellow Harvard U., 1961-62. Mem. InterAm. Press Assn. (bd. dirs.), Am. Newspaper Pubs. Assn., Sigma Delta Chi. Jewish. Clubs: Gridiron, Federal City (Washington); Miami, City, New World Center (Miami). Co-author: A Certain Evil, 1965; The Secret Search for Peace in Vietnam, 1968. Office: Miami News PO Box 615 Miami FL 33152

KRASNICK, ARTHUR ROBERT, hotel, restaurant, country club consultant; b. Bronx, N.Y., June 29, 1932; s. Harry and May Krasnick; m. Josephine Flores, May 25, 1963 (div.); children—Allison Maria, Robert John. Student in psychology, CCNY, 1953; postgrad. in hotel mgmt. Lewis Hotel Sch., 1962. Cert. profl. cons. Co-owner, exec. v.p. San Juan Weekly, 1970; dir. restaurant ops. Riviana Foods, Miami, Fla., 1975-76; dir. catering banquets Opryland Hotel, Nashville, 1977-81; internal cons. Coral Gables Country Club, (Fla.), 1982-83; gen. mgr. Emerald Hills Country Club, Hollywood, Fla., 1983—; pres. Associated Food & Beverage Cons., Miami, 1982-83; dir. Cons. Inc., Miami, 1983—. Mem. Fla. Restaurant Assn., Fla. Hotel Assn. Home: 950 NW 199 St Miami FL 33169

KRASNOW, MARK, lawyer; b. Chgo., Jan. 26, 1951; s. Robert and Florance (Siegel) K. A.B., U. Miami, Fla., 1972, J.D., 1975. Bar: Fla. 1975, U.S. Dist. Ct. (so. dist.) Fla. 1975, U.S. Ct. Appeals (5th cir.) 1975, U.S. Ct. Appeals (11th cir.) 1975. Ptnr. Weinstein & Krasnow, Miami, 1976-79, Lida & Krasnow, Miami, 1979-80; sole practice, Miami, 1980—; lectr. U. Miami, 1978—. Mem. ABA, Assn. Trial Lawyers Am., Fla. Bar Assn., Fla. Trial Lawyers Assn., Fla. Criminal Def. Assn., Omicron Delta Kappa. Lodge: Iron Arrow. Office: 9000 SW 87th Ct Miami FL 33176

KRATER, CLETUS ANTHONY, JR., financial executive; b. St. Louis, June 9, 1950; s. Cletus A. and Katherine Pearl (Dambacher) K.; m. Rosalie E. Eckstorm, June 30, 1982; 1 son, Travis Anthony; 1 stepson, Ian Lucas Morrissey. B.S., U.S. Mil. Acad., 1973. Dist. mgr. H & R Block Ft. Myers, Fla., 1978-80; pres. Internat. Tax Services, Inc., Ft. Myers, 1980—. Served to lt. U.S. Army, 1973-76.

KRATHEN, DAVID HOWARD, lawyer; b. Phila., Nov. 17, 1946; s. Morris S. and Lillian E. K.; m. Francine Ellen, Oct. 21, 1973; children—Richard, Stefanie, Michael. B.B.A., U. Miami, Fla., 1969, J.D., 1972. Bar: Fla. 1972, D.C. 1972, N.Y. 1984, U.S. Supreme Ct. 1976. Atty. advisor ICC, Washington, 1972-73; asst. pub. defender 17th Jud. Cir., Ft. Lauderdale, Fla., 1973-74; ptnr. Glass, Krathen, Rastatter, Stark & Tarlowe, Ft. Lauderdale, 1974-78, Krathen & Sperry, P.A., Ft. Lauderdale, 1978-84, David H. Krathen, P.A., 1984—; mem. Fla. Bar Grievance Com. 17 C, 1982-85, Jud. Adminstrn., Selection and Tenure Com., 1982—; mem. 4th Dist. Ct. of Appeal Jud. Nominating Commn., 1983—. Mem. Acad. Fla. Trial Lawyers (diplomate), Broward County Trial Lawyers Assn. (dir. 1983-84, sec. 1984-85, v.p. 1985-86, pres. elect 1986—), Assn. Trial Lawyers Am. Office: 524 S Andrews Ave Suite 301 N Fort Lauderdale FL 33301

KRAUS, RICHARD STUART, oil company safety advisor; b. Chgo., Mar. 26, 1934; s. Paul P. and Margaret (Goldblatt) K.; m. Leona Breit, Dec. 21, 1958; children—Lawrence Jacob, Robert Steven. B.S. in Civil Engring., Purdue U., 1956. Cert. safety profl.; cert. dir. motor safety; registered profl. engr. Comml. marketing rep. Mobil Oil Corp., Chgo., Cleve., 1959-67, heating oil mgr., Detroit, 1967-68, asst. to fleet sales mgr., 1969, asst. real estate mgr. Great Lakes Div., Chgo., 1970-73, safety mgr. Central Region, Schaumburg, Ill., 1974-80, sr. safety advisor U.S. Div., Fairfax, Va., 1980—; industry mem. nat. fire code com. Nat. Fire Protection Assn., Boston, 1980—; mem. safety commn. Nat. Petroleum Refiners Assn., Washington, 1980—, Pvt. Truck Council Am., Washington, 1976—. Author: (with others) Motor Fleet Safety, Supervision, Principles and Practices, 1984. Mem. Morton Grove Planning Com., Ill., 1970-76. Served to 1st lt. U.S. Army, 1956-58. Mem. Nat. Com. for Motor Fleet Supr. Tng. (chmn. nat. cert. bd., mem. exec. bd. 1980—), Petroleum Sect. of Nat. Safety Council (chmn. ops., mem. exec. com. 1981—, exec. com., mem.-at-large Indsl. Div.) Am. Petroleum Inst. (com safety and fire protection, coordinator codes and consensus standards 1982—). Avocation: golf. Office: Mobil Oil Corp 3225 Gallows Rd Fairfax VA 22037

KRAUS, VIRGIL KELLY, geologist, oil company executive; b. Pecos, Tex., Mar. 13, 1928; s. Kirk Kelly and Jessie Mae (Shaum) K.; student U. Tex., 1946-49; B.S. in Geology, U. Houston, 1956; m. Jane Lee Muir, Aug. 8, 1951; children—Kenneth W., Linda Gayle. Geologist, Dow Chem. Co., Houston, 1956-72, chief geologist, 1972-73; chief geologist Buttes Gas & Oil Co., Houston, 1973-76; geologist, partner Chapman Oil Co., Houston, 1976—; pres. Chapman Internat. Oil Co., Tex-Lou Co., Transgas Co.; dir. Lou-Tex Trust Co., Allied Oil Co., Transgas Co., Giant Piper Explorations, Inc.; v.p. Chapman Oil Co. Israel. Mem. Am. Assn. Petroleum Geologists, Houston Geol. Soc. Republican. Methodist. Clubs: Houston Met. Racquet, Houston. Home: 10803 Pine Bayou Houston TX 77024 Office: 808 Travis Houston TX 77002

KRAUSE, ERWIN KOERPS, micropaleontologist, paleoecologist; b. San Antonio, Oct. 16 1923; s. Erwin Emil and Clara Ida (Koerps) K.; m. Edna Marie Bible, Nov. 26, 1953 (div.); m. Naomi Ruth McFarland, Sept. 22, 1972. B.S. in Geology, U. Tex., 1949, M.A., 1954. Research assoc. Bur. Econ. Geology, Austin, Tex., 1949-50; geologist J.E. Elliott, Austin, 1951-52, Shell Oil Co., Corpus Christi, Tex., 1954-64; mining geologist Dow Chem. Co., Coahuila, Mex., 1953; research scientist Sinclair Oil and Gas Co., Tulsa, 1965-69; sr. paleontol. assoc. Arco Exploration Co., Houston, 1969-85. Author, asst. editor: Occurrence of Oil and Gas in Northeast Texas, 1951. Author: Pelecypoda From Type Locality Stone City Beds of Texas, 1957; Stone City Beds, 1960; (with others) Correlation Chart, Roadlog, 1963. Water safety instr. ARC, Corpus Christi, 1957-63; scoutmaster, advisor Gulf Coast council Boy Scouts Am., 1955-65, chmn. tng., 1960-65. Served to staff sgt. USAAF, 1943-45, ETO. Mem. Am. Assn. Petroleum Geologists (mem. field trip com. 1979), Am. Inst. Profl. Geologists, Houston Geol. Soc., Soc. Econ. Paleontologists and Minerologists (chmn. nominating com. Gulf coast sect. 1979), Gulf Coast Assn. Geol. Soc. (judge 1979). Avocations: photography; travel; opera; audio-video. Home: 5731 Darnell Houston TX 77096

KRAUSE, ROBERT DALE, government executive, consultant; b. Port Huron, Mich., July 2, 1923; s. Ernst Karl and Pearl Athena (Bedwell) K.; m. Maxine Ann Driscoll, Jan. 15, 1946. B.A., Western Mich. U., 1948; M.P.A., U. Mich., 1950. Mgmt. analyst AEC, Oak Ridge, 1951-55; personnel dir. City of Kenosha (Wis.), 1955-56; chief classification and pay, Milw. City Service, 1956-65; personnel br. chief AID, Washington, 1965-67; personnel dir. City of Hartford (Conn.), 1967-77; dir. human resources City of Miami (Fla.), 1977—; cons. to various orgns., 1967—; lectr. U. Conn., 1972-77, Fla. Internat. U., Miami, 1982-83. Co-chmn. New Eng. Task Force Labor Relations, Hartford, 1969-70; mem. Adv. Com. Personnel and Manpower, Washington, 1971-72; mem. Conn. Adv. Council on Intergovtl. Personnel Act, Hartford, Conn., 1971-75; mem. Task Force, Strategies for Future, Nat. Tng. and Devel. Service, Washington, 1977. Recipient C. H. Cushman award Eastern Region Internat. Personnel Mgmt. Assn., 1982. Named Boss of Yr., Nat. Secs. Assn., Hartford, Conn., 1973. Mem. Internat. personnel Mgmt. Assn. (pres. 1979), Nat. Pub. Employees Labor Relations Assn. (founder 1972), Am. Soc. Pub. Adminstrs. (chpt. pres. 1965). Democrat. Home: 531 Tibidabo Ave Coral Gables FL 33143 Office: Dept of Human Resources 1145 NW 11th St Miami FL 33136

KRAUSS, HENRY FREDERICK, JR., optometrist; b. Sewickley, Pa., Apr. 10, 1952; s. Henry Frederick and Mirella Anna (Guerrieri) K.; m. Sally Winston Miller, July 5, 1975; children—Molly Anne, Henry Neil, Malinda Paige. B.S., Centre Coll. Ky., 1976; O.D., U. Houston, 1980. Optometrist, owner Eye Care Assocs., Richardson, Tex., 1980—; v.p. ProComp Systems Inc., Albuquerque, 1983—; ptnr. K-W Distbrs., Dallas, 1983—, Summit Seminars, Richardson, 1985—. Mem. Am. Optometric Assn., Tex. Optometric Assn. (Young Optometrist of Yr. award 1985), North Tex. Optometric Assn. (pres. 1983-84), Am. Optometric Found., Vision Ednl. Found., Better Vision Inst., Am. Pub. Health Assn. (vision care sect.). Republican. Mormon. Avocations: golf; tennis; photography. Office: Eye Care Assocs 1207 Hampshire Ln #101 Richardson TX 75080

KRAVITCH, PHYLLIS, judge; b. Savannah, Ga., Aug. 23, 1920; d. Aaron and Ella (Wiseman) K.; B.A., Goucher Coll., 1941, LL.D., 1981; LL.B., U. Pa., 1943. Admitted to Ga. bar, 1943, U.S. Dist. Ct. bar, 1944, U.S. Supreme Ct. bar, 1948, U.S. Circuit Ct. Appeals bar, 1962; practice law, Savannah, 1944-76; judge Superior Ct., Eastern Jud. Circuit of Ga., 1977-79; judge U.S. Ct. Appeals, 5th circuit (now 11th circuit), Atlanta, 1979—. Trustee, Inst. Continuing Legal Edn. in Ga., 1979-82; mem. Bd. of Edn., Chatham County, Ga., 1949-55. Recipient Hannah G. Solomon award Nat. Council of Jewish Women, 1978. Fellow Am. Bar Found.; mem. ABA, Savannah Bar Assn. (pres. 1976), State Bar of Ga., Am. Judicature Soc., Am. Law Inst. Office: PO Box 8085 Savannah GA

KRAYBILL, RICHARD REIST, chemical engineer; b. Dover, N.H., July 31, 1920; s. Henry Reist and Mary Ruth (Grove) K.; m. Jean Carolyn Gilbert, Aug. 8, 1945; children—Mary, Virginia, Anne, Elizabeth. B.Chem. Engring., Purdue U., 1942; M.S., U. Mich., 1943, Ph.D. (Am. Cyanamid fellow, Horace Rackham fellow), 1953. Lab. asst. Am. Viscose Corp., Parkersburg, W.Va., 1941; asst. research engr. Calif. Research Corp., El Segundo, 1944-46; asst. prof. chem. engring. U. Rochester (N.Y.), 1950-55, assoc. prof., 1955-67, sr. lectr. Univ. Coll. Liberal and Applied Studies, 1978-79; tech. assoc. Eastman Kodak Co., Rochester, 1967-83; cons. in field. Contbr. articles to profl. jours. Fellow Am. Inst. Chem. Engrs.; mem. AAAS, Am. Soc. for Engring. Edn., Soc. Rheology, Soc. Plastics Engrs. (tech. vols. com. 1971—, best paper award 1964), Am. Chem. Soc., Sigma Xi, Alpha Phi Omega, Phi Kappa Phi, Triangle. Clubs: Bass Lake Sailing (Pentwater, Mich.); Island Yacht (Clearwater, Fla.); Shipwatch Yacht and Tennis (Largo, Fla.); Pentwater Yacht. Home: 1704 Laurie Ln Belleair FL 33516

KREAGER, DAVID JAY, JR., lawyer; b. Tulsa, Apr. 28, 1929; s. David Jay and Ethel Mae (Martin) K.; B.A. with honors, Tex. A. and M. U., 1950; J.D. with honors, U. Tex., 1953; m. Ann Fleetwood, Mar. 22, 1949; children—David, Michael, Cameron, Heather, Gretchen, Paige. Admitted to Tex. bar, 1953, since practiced in Beaumont; partner firm Orgain, Bell and Tucker, pres., 1983-84. Cert. civil trial and personal injury trial Tex. Bd. Legal Specialization. Mem. Beaumont Civil Service Commn., 1961-70. Mem. Tex. Bar Found. (chmn. bd. trustees 1977-79), State Bar Tex. (dir. 1973-76), Am., Jefferson County (pres. 1960-61) bar assns., Tex. Assn. Def. Counsel (cert., dir. 1977-80), Am. Judicature Soc., Fedn. Ins. Counsel, Internat. Assn. Ins. Counsel, Nat. Bd. Trial Advocacy, Coll. State Bar Tex., Order of Coif. Presbyterian. Club: Rotary. Home: 1245 Nottingham Ln Beaumont TX 77706 Office: PO Box 1751 Beaumont TX 77704

KREAMER, KAREN SUE, psychotherapist, model; b. Montgomery, Ala., May 13, 1956; d. Charles Cooper and Betty Sue (Sanford) K.; m. Jeffrey S. Jones, Mar. 18, 1977 (div. June 1982). B.S. in Family and Child Devel., Auburn U., 1978; M.A. in Guidance and Counseling, U. Ala., 1979. Nat. cert. counselor, lic. profl. counselor. Dir. pub. relations Women's Med. Ctr., Birmingham, Ala., 1978-79; dir. counseling Summit Med. Ctr., Birmingham, 1979-81; sole practice Vestavia Counseling Ctr., Birmingham, 1981-82; dir. Campus Counseling Ctr. U. Ala., Birmingham, 1982-84; pvt. practice Hubbard Inst., Birmingham, Sumiton, Ala., 1984-85, Kreamer & Assocs., Birmingham, Graysville, Ala., 1985—; cons. Summit Med. Ctr., Birmingham, 1981—; model e'lan/Casablancas, Birmingham, 1982—. Author: Holistic Weight Loss, 1985. Author and producer of audio tapes. Volunteer Donald Stewart Senate Campaign, Birmingham, 1980, John Buccanon Senate Campaign, Birmingham 1980, Project Uplift, Auburn, Ala., 1978; actress ARC Pub. Service Announcement, Birmingham, 1985. Recipient Spl. Citation, ARC, 1985; named Miss Southeastern Regional, Am. Fedn. Women's Bodybuilders. Mem. Am. Mental Health Counselors Assn., Am. Assn. Counseling and Devel., Ala. Mental Health Counselors Assn., Ala. Assn. Counseling and Devel., Ala. Council Family Relations, Nat. Fedn. Bus. and Profl. Women, AAUW, Auburn Alumni Assn. Episcopalian. Avocations: nutrition science; sewing; skiing; bodybuilding; aerobics. Home: 715 Chalet Dr Birmingham AL 35209 Office: Kreamer & Assocs PC 1451 Main St Graysville AL 35073 also: 1222 14th Ave S Suite 212 Birmingham AL 35205

KREDITOR, MARK HOWARD, direct marketing executive; b. Glen Cove, N.Y., Nov. 10, 1958; s. Larry X. and Marlene Rene (Moskowitz) K. B.S. in Mktg. and Small Bus. with high honors, Northeastern U., 1981. Pres., Samigee Sales Co., Boston 1977-81; pres., chief exec. officer Dallas Get There First Inc., 1981—; dir. mktg. and pub. relations Blue ribbon Foods, Dallas, 1982-84, Houston Internat. Mgmt. Co., 1984-85. Publicity dir. Dallas White Rock Marathon, 1983. Mem. Dallas Advt. League, AD 2, Alpha Mu Alpha, Betta Gamma Sigma. Club: Gross Country (Dallas). Composer mus. Ballet Theatre, Northeastern U., 1981. Home: 11107 Hillcrest Dallas TX 75230 Office: GTF Inc 12830 Hillcrest Suite 111 Dallas TX 75230

KREEGER, SAUNDRA SUE, musician; b. Baird, Tex., Mar. 10, 1939; d. George Robert and Jessie Lynn (Briley) Owen; m. July 5, 1958; children—Gary, Victor. Student Southwestern Assembly of God Coll., Waxahachie, Tex., 1957-58, Tex. Tech. U., 1962—. Pvt. tchr. piano and organ, Lubbock, Tex., 1964-65; organizer and tchr. deaf, Austin, Tex., 1965-70, Temple, Tex., 1970-72; organizer, promoter 3 statewide ann. deaf camps, Tex.; owner Artworld Internat., Dallas, 1977-84; pianist City Music Club, Electra, Tex.; music dir. and/or keyboardist various Assembly of God Chs., Tex.; music chmn. Christian Profl./Bus. Women, Dallas; scorer and arranger music for ch. choirs. Mem. Bus. and Profl. Women, Dallas Apt. Assn., Dallas C. of C., Tex. Mus. Assn., Nat. Assn. Female Execs. Republican. Office: PO Box 2292 Mesquite TX 75149

KREMSER, JANET GORDON, nursing administrator; b. Oceanside, N.Y., May 17, 1941; d. Lennox Albert and H. Jacquelin (Merrill) Gordon; m. Robert H. Kremser, Nov. 19, 1977; 1 child, David G. B.S. in Edn., SUMY, 1963; M.P.S. in Health Care Adminstrn., L.I.U., 1975. Registered nurse, N.Y., La. Nursing instr. and adminstr., N.Y., 1963-75; asst. dir. nursing Temple U. Hosp., Phila., 1976-77, Tulane Med. Ctr., New Orleans, 1978-79, Mercy Hosp., New Orleans, 1980; spl. projects dir. Eye Ear Inst. La., New Orleans, 1981; inst. Jefferson Parish Vocat. Tech. Sch., Metairie, La., 1982-85; dir. nursing Norman Care Ctr., New Orleans, 1985—; CPR instr. Am. Heart Assn., New Orleans; cons. U. New Orleans, 1983. Coordinator Neighborhood Watch Program, New Orleans; mem. New Orleans Non-Police Anti-Crime Commn. New Orleans. Mem. Am. Sch. Health Assn., Am. Soc. Tng. and Devel. (sec. 1983, bd. dirs. for community projects 1984). Presbyterian. Avocations: medical investigator; pre-publication book reviewer. Home: 7810 Sandpiper Dr New Orleans LA 70128 Office: Norman Care Ctr Lake Forest Blvd New Orleans LA 70128

KRENEK, RICHARD FRANK, real estate broker and developer; b. Cleve., Oct. 7, 1940; s. Frank John and Helen Marie (Aron) K.; B.Engring. Sci., Cleve. State U., 1966; M.S., Ohio State U., 1967, Ph.D., 1970; m. Geraldine Ann Ulicky, July 6, 1963; children—Richard, Robert. Devel. engr. Lewis Research Center, NASA, Cleve., 1966; research asso. Systems Research Group, Ohio State U., 1966-70; asst. prof. Sch. Indsl. Engring., U. Okla., 1970-72; v.p. OMEC, Inc., Norman, Okla., 1972-73, pres., 1973-78; asso. prof. U. Okla., 1979-82; v.p., dir. Bio-Cide Chem., Inc., 1982, pres., 1983; pres. RFK Properties, Inc., 1983—. Bd. dirs. Cleveland County chpt. ARC, 1976—, chmn. bldg. fund drive, 1976, 1st vice chmn. chpt., 1977-78, chpt. chmn., 1979-81; mem. Okla. region blood services, Tulsa county chpt. ARC, bd. dirs., 1979-81, mem. exec. com., 1979-80; chmn. Norman chmn. Norman Parking Authority Com., 1975-76, Norman Polit. Action Com., 1977. Served with AUS, 1958-61. Registered profl. engr., Okla. Mem. Nat. Soc. Profl. Engrs., Okla. Soc. Profl. Engrs. (v.p. Canadian Valley chpt. 1979-80, pres. 1980-81, state dir. 1980-83), Am. Inst. Indsl. Engrs., Human Factors Soc., Norman C. of C. (dir. 1975-77), Nat. Assn. Realtors, Okla. Assn. Realtors, Norman Bd. Realtors, Sigma Xi, Tau Beta Pi, Alpha Pi Mu, Pi Mu Epsilon. Republican. Clubs: Norman Rotary (dir. 1975-79, chmn. funds com. 1975-78, pres. 1978-79), University. Home: 4209 Oxford Way Norman OK 73069 Office: 3625 W Main St Norman OK 73069

KRESHON, MARTIN JOHN, ophthalmologist; b. East Liverpool, Ohio, Nov. 11, 1929; s. James I. and Elizabeth (Maroni) K.; m. Jerri May Jerome, Aug. 31, 1952; children—Kathy, Susan, Karol, Martin John, Michael, Amy Lou, Elizabeth, John. B.S. cum laude, Geneva Coll., 1950; M.D., Marquette U., 1954. Diplomate Am. Bd. Ophthalmology. Rotating intern Hamot Hosp., Erie, Pa., 1954-55; resident in ophthalmology Duke U. Hosp., Durham, N.C., 1957-60; practice medicine specializing in ophthamology, Charlotte, N.C., 1961; mem. staff Charlotte Eye, Ear, Nose and Throat Hosp., Meml. Hosp., Mercy Hosp.; assoc. clin. prof. Duke U., 1961—; dir. Piedmont Eye Clinic, Charlotte. Bd. dirs. N.C. Cancer Soc., Mecklenburg Assn. for Blind, Piedmont Sci. Fair, N.C. Eye Bank. Served to capt. U.S. Army, 1955-57. Mem. Am. Acad. Ophthamology and Otolaryngology, N.C. Med. Soc., Mecklenburg County Med. Soc., Am. Assn. Ophthamology, So. Med. Soc., N.C. Soc. Ophthamology (pres. 1977-78). Lodge: Lions. Contbr. articles to med. jours. Home: 260 Cherokee Rd Charlotte NC 28207 Office: Charlotte EENT Hosp 1600 E Third St Charlotte NC 28204

KRESS, RANDY LEE, oilfield geologist, consultant; b. Waterloo, Iowa, Aug. 19, 1955; s. Harold Wayne and Shirley Jean (Gissel) K.; m. Beverly Ann Joplin, Mar. 19, 1982; 1 child, Cassandra Ann. B.S. in Earth Scis., Iowa State U., 1978. Applied drilling tech. engr. NL Baroid, Houston, 1978-81; logging geologist Tech. Drilling Services, Oklahoma City, 1981-82, SENS-ANOM Inc., Oklahoma City, 1982; self employed geologist, Bethany, Okla., 1982—. Mem. Am. Assn. Petroleum Geologists. Republican. Baptist. Avocations: hiking; hunting; fishing; rock hound; gardening. Home and Office: 6207 NW 34th St Bethany OK 73008

KRESSIN, EILEEN KAY, telephone company sales executive; b. Port Washington, Wis., July 1, 1950; d. Harold Frederick and Emma Helen (Nierode) K. B.S.B.A. in Mktg., Central Mo. State U., 1974. Directory rep. Southwestern Bell Yellow Pages, Kansas City, Mo., 1975-76, supr. directory sales, 1976-78, staff mgr. directory premises tng., St. Louis, 1978-80, dist. mgr. directory telephone sales and clerical, Kansas City, 1980-81, dist. mgr. directory sales, Oklahoma City, 1981—; lectr. bus. Central Mo. State U. Organist, tchr. Sunday sch. Lutheran Ch. Named Miss. Exec., Central Mo. State U. Sch. Bus., 1973. Mem. Am. Mktg. Assn. (v.p. St. Louis chpt. 1980). Republican. Author tng. manual. Office: 909 S Meridian St Room 300 Oklahoma City OK 73108

KRETCHMAR, RUTH GOLDMAN, artist; b. Little Rock, Apr. 18, 1918; d. Abraham Joseph and Augusta (Finger) Goldman; B.S., U. Ill., 1939; B.A., U. Ark., 1968; m. Lee Kretchmar, 1940 (dec. July 5, 1976); 1 son, Kent. Art cons. Main Galleries, Little Rock, 1969-70; exhibited one-man shows: Ark. Arts Center, 1972, 73, 74, 75, 76, Little Rock Arts and Crafts Design Fair, 1973-74, 1st Nat. Bank of Little Rock, 1976; exhibited group shows: Spar Nat. Art Exhbn., Shreveport, La., 1973, S.E. Ark. Arts and Scis. Center, Pine Bluff, 1973, U. Little Rock, 1974-75, Columbus (Ga.) Mus. Arts and Scis., 1978, Ark. Arts Center Traveling exhibit, 1978, Worthen Bank Show, 1985, Ark. Ter. Exhibit, 1985; represented in permanent collections: 1st Comml Bank of Little Rock, 1st Am. Bank of North Little Rock. Mem. budget com. United Fund, 1954; mem. State White House Conf. Children and Youth, 1960; mem. nat. bd. women's com. Brandeis U., 1969-71; bd. dirs. Jewish Fedn. of Little Rock, 1985-86. Mem. Mid-So. Water Colorists (dir. 1985-86), So. Watercolor Soc., AAUW (work rep. mag. cover 1979). Home and Studio: 2 Beverly Pl Little Rock AR 72207

KRICHEV, ALAN, psychologist, mental health organization administrator; b. Phila., June 25, 1943; s. Max and Anna Belle (Vederman) K.; m. Pamela Jane Morris, June 3, 1972; children—Jennifer Ann, Jessica Naomi, Jonathan Edward. B.A., Susquehanna U., 1965; M.A., U.N.H., 1968; Ph.D., U. Windsor, Ont., Can., 1972. Licensed psychologist, cert. mental health adminstr. Chief psychologist Lakehead Bd. Edn., Thunder Bay, Ont., 1972-77; asst. clin. dir. New Mex. State Hosp., Las Vegas, 1977-79; asst. exec. dir., chief treatment services Marshall-Jackson Mental Health Ctr., Guntersville, Ala., 1979-86; private practice in psychology, 1975—; adj. prof. Lakehead U., Thunder Bay, Ont., 1972-77, Am. Inst. Psychotherapy, Huntsville, Ala., 1980—. Contbr. articles to profl. jours. Bd. dirs. Children's Aid Soc., Thunder Bay, 1975-77. Mem. Am. Psychol. Assn., Ala. Psychol. Assn., Ala. Lic. Psychologists Assn., Assn. Mental Health Adminstrs. Lodge: Rotary. Avocations: racquetball, model railroading, camping. Office: Stress Control Services 1507-B Rainbow Dr Gadsden AL 35901

KRIDEL, MICHAEL STEPHEN, accountant; b. East Orange, N.J., Dec. 20, 1951; s. Myron Meyer and Gloria Jean (Morris) K.; B.B.A., George Washington U., 1974; m. Susan Renee Rose, Jan. 1, 1980; 1 son, Jeremy; m. Nancy Elaine Kridel, July 6, 1984. Staff acct. Raymond A. Bookman, C.P.A., North Miami Beach, Fla., 1974-77, Gurland & Goldberg, C.P.A.s, Hallandale, Fla., 1977-78; pvt. practice acctg., Miami, 1978—. Bd. dirs. Found. for Learning, Inc. C.P.A., Fla. Mem. Am. Inst. C.P.A.s, Am. Mgmt. Assn., Fla. Inst. C.P.A.s, North Dade C. of C., Greater Miami Jr. C. of C., North Dade Estate Planning Council, Sigma Nu. Clubs: North Miami Beach Lions, KP. Home: 12256 NW 13th Ct Pembroke Pines FL 3302 Office: 6151 Miramar Pkwy Suite 317 Miramar FL 33023

KRIEGER, ROBERT EDWARD, publisher; b. Chgo., Apr. 6, 1925; s. Nicholas Francis and Clara Maude (Larson) K.; m. Maxine Donalda Spooner, June 21, 1947; children—Robert Edward, Donald Eric, Thomas Eliot. Formerly exec. with multi-corp. book and pub. firms; chmn. bd., pres., dir. R.E. Krieger Pub. Co., Inc., Malabar, Fla., 1969—. Served with USCG, 1943-46; ETO. Mem. ALA, Am. Pubs. Assn., Am. Assn. History of Medicine, Scholarly Pubs. Assn., Melbourne C. of C., Palm Bay C. of C. Republican. Methodist. Club: Masons. Home: 970 SW Meadowbrook Rd Palm Bay FL 32905 Office: Krieger Dr Malabar FL 32950

KRIEGER, ROBERT LEE, JR., management consultant, educator; b. Louisville, Nov. 13, 1946; s. Robert Lee and June Elise (Waters) K. B.B.A., Memphis State U., 1968, M.B.A., 1969. Adminstrv. asst. to mayor City of Memphis, 1969-72; dir. devel. programs Memphis State U., 1972-74; cons. pvt. practice, Memphis, 1974-76; exec. v.p. Randall Howard & Assocs., Memphis, 1976—; faculty Memphis State U. Coll. Bus., 1984—; speaker numerous profl. groups. Mem. Republican Presdl. Task Force, Washington, 1980—; mem. Rep. Nat. Adv. Com., Washington, 1972—; mem. U.S. Olympic Soc., Boulder, Colo., 1968—. Recipient U.S. Treasury award U.S. Dept. Treasury, 1971; Nat. Presdl. medal of Merit, Rep. Presdl. Task Force, 1984; Pres.'s award Memphis Cotton Carnival Assn., 1968—. Mem. Data Processing Mgmt. Assn., Am. Mgmt. Assn., Am. Film Guild, Alpha Delta Sigma. Episcopalian. Clubs: Mensa, Memphis State Alumni. Avocations: writing; bowling; photography; travel; movies. Home: 2948 Dalebrook St Memphis TN 38127 Office: Randall Howard & Assoc Inc 5353 Flowering Peach Memphis TN 38115

KRIER, CYNDI TAYLOR, lawyer, state senator; b. Beeville, Tex., July 12, 1950; d. Robert Stevens and Mary (McGuffin) T; m. Joseph R. Krier. B.J. in Journalism, U. Tex., Austin, 1971, J.D., 1975. Bar: Tex. 1975. Staff atty., exec. asst. to U.S. Senator John Tower, Washington, 1975-76, dir. state office, Houston, 1976-77, staff atty., 1977-78; campaign coordinator Texans for Tower, San Antonio, 1977-78; ptnr. Lang, Cross, Ladon, Boldrick & Green, P.C., San Antonio, 1979—; mem. Tex. Senate, 1985—. Mem. dean's council U. Tex. Law Sch., Austin, 1980-84, dist. dir., 1982-84; mem. Tex. Gov.'s Task Force on Equal Opportunities for Women and Minorities, 1981-82; mem. programs ops.: health support services United Way, 1982-84, chmn., 1984; vice chmn. Bexar County Republican Com., 1979-81; del. precinct, dist. and state Rep. convs., 1978, 80, 82; mem. Task Force on Equal Opportunities, 1981-82; mem. adv. panel Tex. Election Code, 1980; sec. Vol. Ctr. of San Antonio, 1983-84,. bd. dirs., 1983—; bd. dirs. San Antonio Little Theatre, 1983-84. Mem. U. Tex. Ex-Students Assn. (life), Friar Soc., Greater San Antonio C. of C. (bd. dirs.). Episcopalian. Club: Oakes (San Antonio). Office: 301 S Frio San Antonio TX 78207

KRISCH, ADOLPH OSCAR, hotel executive; b. N.Y.C., June 3, 1916; s. Samuel J. and Miriam (Weinstein) K.; m. Heidrun Ilsa Feller, June 16, 1966; children—Victoria (Mrs. James Mills), Juliana (Mrs. Martin L. Weiss). Student, Roanoke Coll., 1933-34, U. Va., 1934-37. With various retail jewelers, 1936-57; chmn. bd. Am. Motor Inns Inc., Roanoke, Va., 1957—. Served with U.S. Army, 1943-44. Mem. Internat. Assn. Holiday Inns (dir., pres. 1969).

Home: 5128 Grossbow Circle SW Roanoke VA 24014 Office: Am Motor Inns Inc 1917 Franklin Rd SW Roanoke VA 24014*

KRISCH, JOEL, motel executive; b. Roanoke, Va., June 23, 1924; s. Samuel J. and Miriam (Weinstein) K.; m. Nancy Jane Scher, Jan. 2, 1950; children—Kathryn Jane Krisch Loeb, Linda Scher Krisch Vinson, Samuel J. II. Student Va. Poly. Inst., 1941-43. Partner bus. firm, Roanoke, 1946-57, exec. officer motel corps., 1957-62; pres. Am. Motor Inns, Inc., Roanoke, 1962—; dir. Sidney's, Inc., Roanoke. Bd. dirs. Va. Poly. Inst., State U. Ednl. Found., Airline Passengers Assn., Dallas. Trustee Goucher Coll., Balt. Served with AUS, 1943-45. Mem. Roanoke Valley C. of C. (dir.). Jewish. Club: Hunting Hills Country (Roanoke). Lodges: Masons, Shriners, B'nai B'rith. Office: Am Motor Inns Inc 1917 Franklin Rd SW Roanoke VA 24014*

KRISE, EDWARD FISHER, retired army officer; b. Detroit, June 28, 1924; s. W. Gomer and Dorothy (Fisher) K.; A.B., Brown U., 1949; M.A., U. Chgo., 1950, Ph.D., 1958; m. Elizabeth Ann Bradt, Aug. 5, 1948; children—Patricia Lynn Krise Kane, Thomas Warren. Chief social work service Walter Reed Gen. Hosp., 1964-65; chief personnel services div. Hdqrs. USCONARC, 1965-69; dir. Race Relations Inst., Dept. Def., 1970-72; owner, master sailing yacht on charter in W.I., 1975-81; asso. prof. U. Md., 1973-75. Exec. com. Beaufort County (S.C.) Democratic Com. Served with U.S. Army, 1942-73, col. (ret.). Decorated Silver Star, Legion of Merit with oak leaf cluster, Meritorious Service medal, Bronze Star, Purple Heart. Mem. Nat. Assn. Social Workers, Acad. Cert. Social Workers, Ret. Officers Assn., Ranger Bns. Assn. World War II, Ex Prisoners of War, SAR, Sigma Nu. Democrat. Presbyterian. Clubs: Annapolis Yacht. Home: 28 Pine Land Rd Hilton Head Island SC 29928

KRISHEN, KUMAR, research technologist; b. Kashmir, India, June 22, 1939; came to U.S., 1964, naturalized, 1976; s. Srikanth and Dhanwate Bhat; B.A. with highest merit in Math. and Physics, Jammu and Kashmir U., India, 1959; B.Tech., Calcutta U., 1962, M.Tech., 1963; M.S. in Elec. Engring., Kans. State U., 1966, Ph.D. with distinction, 1969; m. Vijay Lakshmi Raina, Sept. 12, 1961; children—Lovely, Sweetie, Anjala. Asst. prof. elec. engring. dept. Kans. State U., Manhattan, 1968-69; staff scientist and engr. Lockheed Electronics Co., Inc., Houston, 1969-76; mgr. microwave program NASA, Johnson Space Center, Houston, Tex., 1977-78, mgr. advanced microwave programs, 1976-78, coordinator advanced programs expt. systems div., 1981; mgr. research and devel., tracking div., 1981—; lectr. U. Houston Grad. Center, 1980; adj. assoc. prof. Rice U., 1985—; research adv. NRC; coordinator The Krishen Trio Performers, 1969—; founder Krishen Found. for Arts and Scis. Pres., Hindu Worship Soc., 1970-72, 74, 79-80, 83. Recipient Gold and Silver medals Calcutta U.; Outstanding Performance and Superior Performance awards NASA, 1979, 82, 84, 85; Govt. India Merit scholar, 1959-61. Mem. IEEE, AIAA, Am. Soc. Engring. Edn., Radio Physics and Electronics Assn. India, Sigma Xi, Phi Kappa Phi, Eta Kappa Nu. Contbr. articles on radar tech. and geophys. research to sci. publs. Home: 4127 Long Grove Dr Seabrook TX 77586 Office: Code EE4 NASA Johnson Space Center Houston TX 77058

KRISHNAMURTHY, POOVAMBUR SUNDARESAN, cardiologist; b. Kumbakonam, India, Aug. 25, 1940; came to U.S., 1971; s. Sundaresan Poovambur and Parvatham Viswanathan Iyer; m. Minal Khanderao Parelkar, June 4, 1969; children—Mina Shabnam, Sarita. M.B., B.S., Bombay U., 1964, M.D., 1968. Diplomate Am. Bd. Internal Medicine; cert. subsplty. cardiovascular diseases. Resident Jewish Hosp. Med. Ctr., Bklyn., 1971-75; practice medicine specializing in cardiology, Perry, Fla., 1976—; mem. staff Drs. Meml. Hosp. Fellow Am. Coll. Cardiology, Coll. Chest Physicians, Council Clin. Cardiology; mem. AMA, Fla. Med. Assn. Democrat. Lodge: Rotary. Office: 402 E Ash St Perry FL 32347

KRISTOFEK, DAISY REA, dietitian; b. Valley Falls, Kans., Jan. 20, 1925; d. Harry Benton and Edith May (Mallory) Martin; B.A., U. Kans., 1951; M.S., State U. Iowa, 1953; m. Andrew Kristofek, June 16, 1953; children—Jo Andrea, Jacqueline Kay, Andrew, Margaret Fae. Elem. sch. tchr., Kans., 1942-43, jr. high sch. tchr., 1946-47; chief dietitian King's Mountain Hosp., Bristol, Va., 1952-53; therapeutic dietitian, tchr. R.N. program Meml. Hosp., Johnson City, Tenn., 1954-56, cons., 1956-76, clin. and adminstrv. dietitian, 1976-78; dir. dietetic services successor Johnson City Med. Center Hosp., 1980—; mem. Sullins Coll., Bristol, 1956-76, trustee, 1968-76; guest lectr., cons. in field; bd. advisers Sch. Applied Sci. and Tech., E. Tenn. State U., also mem. spl. adv. com. dept. econs. Recipient Victor B. Cook award Sullins Coll., 1976. Mem. Am. Dietetic Assn., Am. Soc. Parenteral and Enteral Nutrition, Nutrition Today Soc., TriCities Dietetic Assn. (dir.), Va. Dietetic Assn., Bus. and Profl. Women's Club. Democrat. Methodist. Home: 600 Garden Ln Bristol VA 24201 Office: 400 State of Franklin Rd Johnson City TN 37601

KRISTOFF, KIM C., architectural company executive; b. Dayton, Ohio, Jan. 22, 1948; d. Joseph M. and Charlene L. (Seigle) K.; m. Jeri J. Combs, June 3, 1971. B. Arch., U. Notre Dame, 1971. Registered architect, Va., Washington. Assoc. architect Weihe/Black/Jeffries/Strassman and Dove, Washington, 1971-75; dir. archtl. design Hunter Miller and Assocs., Alexandria, Va., 1975-76; pres. KH and Assocs., Falls Church, Va., 1976-78, Pace Group, Inc., McLean, Va., 1978; Pace Design, Inc., McLean, 1978—, Design Resource Internat., McLean, 1980—, Pace Constrn., Inc., McLean, 1981—, Tandem Assocs., Inc., McLean, 1984—; v.p. Pace Mgmt., Inc., McLean, 1985—. Patentee space wall, 1980; contbr. articles to profl. jours. Mem. AIA, Nat. Assn. Office and Indsl. Parks, Urban Land Inst., Fairfax County C. of C., Constrn. Specification Inst. Avocations: artist; illustrator. Office: Pace Group Inc 6820 Elm St McLean VA 22101

KRISTOFFERSON, KARL ERIC, writer; b. Jacksonville, Fla., Mar. 3, 1929; s. Gustave Edward and Oma Nancy (Reynolds) K.; A.A., Jacksonville U., 1961; B.S. with honors in Journalism, U. Fla., 1963; m. Barbara Elaine Dalton, Jan. 22, 1954; children—Karol, Paul, Scott. Motion picture film booker Paramount Pictures, Warner Bros. Pictures and United Artists, 1954-59; engring. writer Pratt & Whitney Aircraft Co., West Palm Beach, Fla., 1963; publs. supr. Ling-Temco-Vought Ops., also Boeing Co., Kennedy Space Center, Fla., 1964-72; chief public affairs IRS Dist. Hdqrs., Greensboro, N.C., 1972-74; chief writer/editor NASA Public Affairs, Kennedy Space Center, 1974—; free-lance writer for TV, motion pictures and maj. nat. mags. and publs., 1960—; regular assignment writer Reader's Digest. Served with USAF, 1950-53; Korea. Decorated Air medal; recipient Apollo Achievement award NASA, 1969; Aviation Space Writers Assn. award for articles writing, 1974. Mem. Sigma Delta Chi, Phi Kappa Phi, Kappa Tau Alpha. Democrat. Lutheran. Office: PA-EAB Kennedy Space Center FL 32899

KROL, JOSEPH, engineer, emeritus educator, underwriter; b. Warsaw, Poland, Jan. 14, 1911; s. Kazimierz and Feliksa (Tokarzewski) K.; M.S., Warsaw (Poland) Inst. Tech., 1937; Ph.D. U. London (Eng.), 1947; m. Evelyn Swingland, Apr. 15, 1952. Came, to U.S., 1956, naturalized, 1962. Tech. officer with directorate ammunition prodn. Brit. Ministry of Supply, London, Eng., 1941-45; research scientist U. London, 1946-47; cons. engr., Montreal, Que., Can., 1948-51; asso. prof. mech. engring. U. Manitoba (Can.), 1951-56; prof. indsl. engring. Ga. Inst. Tech., Atlanta, 1956-79, prof. emeritus indsl. and systems engring., 1980—; mem. Lloyd's of London. Recipient George Stephenson prize, 1951. Registered profl. engr., Ga. Fellow Instn. Mech. Engrs.; mem. ASME, Engring. Inst. Can., Corp. Profl. Engrs. Que., Am. Econ. Assn., Instrument Soc. Am., AAUP, N.Y. Acad. Scis., U.S. Naval Inst., AAAS, Am. Statis. Assn., Econometric Soc., Inst. Mgmt. Scis., Sigma Xi. Author articles on engring. and mgmt. subjects.

KRONENFELD, JENNIE JACOBS, public health administrator; b. Hampton, Va., Aug. 11, 1949; d. Harry and Bessie (Pear) J.; m. Michael Reed Kronenfeld, Sept. 8, 1970; children—Shaun Jacobs, Jeffrey Brian. B.A., U. N.C., 1971; M.A., Brown U., 1972, Ph.D., 1976. Asst. prof. U. Ala., 1975-80; assoc. prof. Sch. of Pub. Health, U. S.C., Columbia, 1980-85, prof., 1985:13 ; scientist Multi-purpose Arthritis Ctr. & Diabetes Research & Tng. Ctr., 1978-80; vis. faculty Princeton U., 1982. Co-editor: Social and Economic Impact of Coronary Artery Disease, 1980; U.S. Health Policy, 1984. Mem. mgmt. task force Carolina Health Style Project, Columbia, 1982—. Assoc. editor Jour. Health and Social Behavior, 1983-85. Mem. Am. Sociol. Assn., Assn. Social Scientists in Health (council mem. 1979-84), So. Sociol. Soc. (com. mem.), NOW. Democrat. Jewish. Avocations: gardening; boating. Office: Dept Health Administrn Sch Pub Health U SC Columbia SC 29208

KROPP, JAMES HERBERT, SR., real estate company executive; b. N.Y.C., Feb. 24, 1949; s. Herbert H. and Agatha (Tell) K.; m. Linda Budziloski, July 4, 1969; children—Jamie, Jody, Jennifer. B.B.A., St. Francis Coll., 1971; postgrad., NYU Grad. Sch. Bus., 1971-73. C.P.A., N.Y. Mgr. Arthur Young & Co., C.P.A.s, N.Y.C., 1973-79; asst. controller Dillon Read & Co., N.Y.C., 1979-81; v.p., treas.-controller Morgan Stanley Realty, Inc., N.Y.C., 1981-85; exec. v.p. The Harlon Group, Raleigh, N.C., 1985—. Mem. N.Y. State Soc. C.P.A.s, Am. Inst. C.P.A.s (real estate acctg. com.), Real Estate Bd. N.Y., Fin. Execs. Inst. (N.C. chpt.). Republican. Home: 2020 Aurora Dr Raleigh NC 27609 Office: Harlon Cos 5510 Six Forks Rd Raleigh NC 27609

KRUDOP, JAMES DEAS, college dean; b. Andalusia, Ala., Jan. 18, 1947; s. Bellaire and Sara Frances K.; m. Hollace Moore, Sept. 6, 1970; children—Ashley Frances, Hadyn Lorraine. B.S., Auburn U., 1969; M.A., U. Ala., 1973, Ph.D., 1975. Speech and English tchr. Andalusia City Sch. system, 1969-71; dir. sch. relations Birmingham-So. Coll., 1974-78; dean L. B. Wallace State Jr. Coll., Andalusia. Exec. dir. LBW Community Arts Council, 1981-82; sec. troop 46 com. Boy Scouts Am., 1978-80; vol. Andalusia United Way, 1980-82; mem. Andalusia City Council, 1980—; acad. judge Covington County Jr. Miss Program, 1981-83. Recipient Appreciation plaque Student Govt. Assn. Lurleen B. Wallace State Jr. Coll., 1979, Achievement cert. So. Assn. Student Fin. Aid Adminstrs., 1978, Recognition cert. U. Ala., 1974. Mem. Andalusia Area C. of C. (bd. dirs. 1979-84, pres. 1984), Nat. Eagle Scout Assn., Ala. Jr. and Community Coll. Assn. (exec. com. 1982-84, parlaimentarian 1983-84), Ala. Jr. and Community Coll. Deans of Students Assn. (pres. 1981-82), Ala. Coll. Personnel Assn. (pres. 1982-83), Ala. Assn. Student Fin. Aid Adminstrs., So. Assn. Student Fin. Aid Adminstrs., Ala. Assn. Collegiate Registrars and Admissions Officers (exec. com. 1977-78), Ala. Coll. Public Relations Assn. (pres. 1977-78), Am. Assn. Univ. Adminstrs., Internat. Edn. Assn. (v.p. 1974), Speech Communication Assn. Am. Lodge: Rotary (pres. 1985-86). Office: LB Wallace Stat Jr Coll PO Drawer 1418 Andalusia AL 36420

KRUEGER, GEORGE EDWARD, dentist, prosthodontist; b. Chgo., Mar. 10, 1921; s. Alonzo and Elizabeth Olive (Matthews) K.; D.D.S., Northwestern U., 1943; M.S. in Clin. Dentistry, Prosthodontics, Marquette U., 1967; m. Joan Eileen Fellows, Aug. 6, 1949; children—Leila Krueger Zschau and George (twins), Leslie Bertha, Lydia Swalchick and Laura Brock (twins), Gerard, Gregory, Gordon. Asst. clin. prof. Marquette U., Milw., 1967-72, asso. clin. prof., 1972; prosthetic cons. U.S. Navy Hosp., Great Lakes, Ill., 1968-72. Served with USNR, 1943-46, ret. Res., 1956. Diplomate Am. Bd. Prosthodontics. Fellow Am. Coll. Prosthodontists, Am. Coll. Dentists; mem. ADA, Fla. Dental Assn., Am. Prosthodontic Soc., Fla. Prosthodontic Assn. (pres. 1977-78), Am. Equilibration Soc., West Coast Dist. Dental Soc., Pierre Fauchard Acad., Am. Equilibration Soc. (life), Fedn. Dentaire Internationale. Roman Catholic. Clubs: K.C. (4 deg.), Serra (dist. gov. 1979-80). Home: 8269 33d Ave N Saint Petersburg FL 33710 Office: 6740 Crosswinds Dr N Suite F Saint Petersburg FL 33710

KRUG, ADELE JENSEN (MRS. WALTER JOHN KRUG), former library science educator; b. Thief River Falls, Minn., Mar. 30, 1908; d. Anton Martin Hulbert and Tillie Manspand (Johnson) Jensen; B.A., Gallaudet Coll., 1930; M.S., Cath. U. Am., 1961; m. Walter John Krug, June 18, 1932 (dec. May 1962); children—Janice Krug Riley, Diana Krug Armstrong, Walter F., Warren J. Instr., R.I. Sch. for Deaf, 1930-32; instr. library sci. Gallaudet Coll., Washington, 1955-63, asst. prof., 1963-67, asso. prof., 1967-75. Pres., Stuart Jr. High Sch. PTA, Washington, 1954-56, McKinley High Sch. PTA, 1956-57. Mem. Conv. Am. Instrs. Deaf, Nat. Assn. of Deaf, D.C. Women's Aux., Nat. Luth. Home, Phi Kappa Zeta (nat. alumnae pres. 1954-60). Contbr. to Am. Anns. of Deaf. Home: Crystal Sq W 511 1515 S Jefferson Davis Hwy Arlington VA 22202

KRUG, SANDRA WILLIS, lawyer; b. Dallas; d. Fred R. and Lois E. Willis; children—Michael W., Jill E. B.E., North Tex. State U., 1956; postgrad. U. Colo., 1970; J.D., Oklahoma City U., 1978. Bar: Okla. 1979, U.S. Dist. Ct. (we. dist.) Okla. 1980, Tex. 1980. With staff Oklahoma County Dist. Atty., Oklahoma City, 1979; sole practice, Oklahoma City, 1980—; counsel Okla. Dept. Mines, Oklahoma City. Contbr. articles to profl. jours. Bd. dirs. Okla. Women Bus. Owners, 1983—. Mem. Oklahoma City Republican Womens Club, Okla. Bar Assn., Tex. Bar Assn., AAUW, Oklahoma City Womens Forum. Office: 6301 N Meridian Suite B Oklahoma City OK 73112

KRUGER, DENNIS G., registered nurse; b. Jackson, Minn., Feb. 22, 1946; s. Benjamin Henry and Lois Lila (Wolff) K. Diploma in nursing Sioux Valley Hosp., 1967. Commd. 2d lt. U.S. Army, 1966, advanced through grades to maj., 1979; staff nurse 312th Evacuation Hosp., Chulai-Viet Nam, 1968-70; head nurse Walter Reed Hosp., Washington, 1970-71, McAfee Health Clinic, White Sands, N.Mex., 1975-77, DDEAMC, Augusta, Ga., 1977-79; staff nurse USAH Augsburg, Ger., 1972-75; asst. head nurse Univ. Hosp., Augusta, 1980—; sexuality counselor Univ. Hosp., 1982—. Decorated Bronze Star; recipient Army Achievement medal, 1984. Mem. Oncology Nursing Soc., Nat. League for Nursing, Assn. Operating Room Nurses, Chu Lai Med. Soc., Res. Officers Assn. Baptist. Avocations: reading. Home: Box 5948 Augusta GA 30906 Office: Univ Hosp 1350 Walton Way Augusta GA 30910

KRUGER, MELVIN IRVIN, roofing and sheet metal contracting company executive; b. Eastman, Ga., Apr. 30, 1929; s. David S. and Elsie (Schwartz) K.; m. Beverly Diane Safer, June 15, 1952; children—Lynn, Steven, Gail. J.D., U. Ga., 1952. Bar: Ga. 1952. Sec.-treas. L.E. Schwartz & Son, Inc., Macon, Ga., 1957-67, v.p., 1967-75, pres., 1975—; mem. adv. bd. Celotex Corp., 1971-74, Manville Corp., 1974-77, Owens Corning Fiberglas Corp., 1978-82; mem. faculty Roofing Industry Ednl., Inst., chmn. bd. regents, 1979-80; pres. Southeastern Roofing Contractors Bd., 1971. Bd. trustees Macon United Way, 1975-78. Recipient Boone Noblitt award Roofing and Sheet Metal Contractors Assn. Ga., 1969; J.A. Piper award Nat. Roofing Contractors Assn., 1980. Mem. Roofing and Sheet Metal Contractors Assn. Ga. (pres. 1969-70), Nat. Roofing Contractors Assn. (pres. 1978-79), Greater Macon C. of C. (dir. 1978-81, v.p. 1982, pres. elect 1983, pres. 1984), U.S. C. of C. (mem. council small bus. 1979-82). Lodge: Rotary (Macon). Home: 566 Taylor Ct Macon GA 31204 Office: 279 Reid St Macon GA 31206

KRUKONES, MICHAEL GEORGE, political science educator; b. Chgo., Nov. 3, 1944; s. George Henry and Bernice Barbara (Rozenski) K. B.S., Loyola U., Chgo., 1966; M.A., U. Minn., 1969; Ph.D., Miami U., Oxford, Ohio, 1979. Instr. U. Wis.-River Falls, 1969-72; research assoc. Computer Horizons, Chgo., 1973; teaching fellow Miami U., 1973-76; asst. prof. Ball State U., Muncie, Ind., 1976-79; assoc. prof. polit. sci. Bellarmine Coll., Louisville, 1979-85, prof., 1985—. Author: Promises and Performance: Presidential Campaigns as Policy Predictors, 1984. Contbr. articles to profl. jours. Bd. dirs. Highlands Ct. Inc., Louisville, 1983—. Mem. AAUP, Am. Polit. Sci. Assn., Midwest Polit. Sci. Assn., Acad. Polit. Sci., Am. Acad. Polit. and Social Sci., Ctr. Study of Presidency. Democrat. Roman Catholic. Avocations: classical music, theater, reading. Office: Bellarmine Coll Dept Polit Sci Newburg Rd Louisville KY 40205

KRUMM, GEORGE WARDEN, microbiologist; b. West Monroe, La., Sept. 7, 1939; s. Chester Wilbur and Cena Pauline (Taylor-Wanless) K.; m. Barbara Nell Norris, Aug. 8, 1964; children—Curtis Wayne, Eric Paul. B.S., Northwestern State U., 1961, M.S., 1964. Microbiologist FDA, New Orleans, 1964-65, Phila., 1965-67; with Dept. Agriculture, 1967—, microbiologist Food Safety Quality Service, Microbiology Div., Beltsville, Md., 1967-74; microbiologist-in-charge Food Safety Inspection Service, Eastern Lab., Athens, Ga., 1974—. Republican. Baptist. Lodge: Lions. Avocations: gardening, camping. Home: 1000 Kings Ct Watkinsville GA 30677 Office: Eastern Lab Food Safety Inspection Service USDA PO Box 6085 Athens GA 30604

KRUSE, HEEREN SAMUEL EILTS, architect; b. St. Louis, Oct. 20, 1911; s. Samuel Andrew and Geraldine (Eilts) K.; m. Ada Juanita Medcalf, 1936 (div. 1942); m. Mary Ruth Owens, Dec. 21, 1945; children—Mary Katherine, David Samuel Owens, Candice Serena. B.Arch., U. Ill., 1933, postgrad., 1934; student Beaux Arts Inst. Design, 1929-34, Bauhaus Sch. Design, 1935, Taliesin Seminars, 1935; grad., Command and Gen. Staff Sch., 1945. Draftsman George Fred Keck, Chgo., 1934-35; sec.-treas. Harford Field, Inc., architect, Hinsdale, Ill., 1935-36; master graphic arts Lake Forest (Ill.) Acad., 1936; architect E.A. Gruensfeld, Jr., Chgo., 1936-38; gen. practice, Chgo. and Centralia, Ill., 1939-42; architect William E. Kittle, Robert Law Weed & Assoc., also Nims, Inc., 1947-51; ptnr. Watson & Deutschman, 1951-60; v.p. Watson, Deutschman & Kruse, architect and engrs., Miami, Fla., 1961-74, Watson, Deutschman, Kruse & Lyon Inc., architects, engrs., 1974—, pres., 1976; instr. Miami Draftsmen's Club, 1959-62; lectr., adj. prof., prof. Clemson U., U. Miami, U. Waterloo, 1967—; city planner, Plantation, Fla., 1971—. Projects include Young Sch, Salem Twp., Ill., 1941, Yoyogi Chapel, and New Town, Tokyo, Japan, 1946, U.S. Post Office, Biscayne Annex, Miami, 1956, Cutler Ridge Jr. High Sch, 1960, U. Miami Library, 1961, Fla. Atlantic U, 1963, Miami Springs Sr. High Sch, 1964, Computing Ctr., U. Miami, 1965, Triton Towers, Miami Beach, 1967, Victoria Hosp, 1973, Dade County Detention and Treatment Center, 1974, Miami Beach Conv. Ctr., Pan Am. World Airways Flight Tng. Acad, Miami, 1980. Mem. Welfare Bldg. Council. Mem. bd. Children's Home Soc. of Florida, asst. treas., 1959, pres., 1974-76; mem. adv. bd. LWV; chmn. adv. bd. U. N.C. Served to col., C.E. AUS, 1942-46. Medalist Beaux Arts Inst. Design, 1933. Fellow AIA (dir. Fla. region 1967-69, past exec. com., gold medal Fla. chpt. 1969, silver medal Fla. South chpt. 1981, bursar Coll. of Fellows); mem. Fla. Assn. Architects (sec. 1957, pres. 1958, dir. 1959-63, 80-83, pres. found. 1972-76, 83—), Soc. Am. Mil. Engrs., Fla. Planning and Zoning Assn., Constrn. Specifications Inst. (chpt. pres. 1974-75), Am. Planning Assn., Am. Inst. Cert. Planners, Alpha Rho Chi. Office: Watson-Deutschman/Druse & Lyon Architects 1600 NW LeJeune Rd Miami FL 33126*

KRUSE, RICHARD HARRY, microbiologist; b. Gilman, Vt., June 3, 1927; s. Harry John and Carla Methyne (Hansen) K.; student Duke U., 1944-45; B.S., U. Richmond, 1952; m. Eloise Christenberry, Oct. 31, 1948; 1 dau., Cynthia Jo. Microbiologist indsl. health and safety div., Fort Detrick, Md., 1953-63, chief research sect., 1963-72; dir. mycology lab. State Mycology Center, Paris, Ky., 1973-77; pres. MEDI, Inc., Lexington, Ky., 1977—. Served with U.S. Army, 1946-49. Mem. Am. Soc. Microbiology, Internat. Soc. Human and Animal Mycology, S.C. Assn. Clin. Microbiology, Southeastern Assn. Clin. Microbiology, So. Assn. Clin. Microbiology, Med. Mycological Soc. Am., Sigma Xi. Baptist. Contbr. articles to profl. jours. Home: Bourbon Arabians 717 Lloyd Rd Georgetown KY 40324 Office: Box 11486 Lexington KY 40576

KRYSIAK, MARGARET ANNE, librarian; b. Cleve., Jan. 4, 1933; d. Edward A. and Anna (Molinski) Krysiak; m. Stanley Goscinski, Oct. 2, 1954; children—Laurence, Michael, Mary Elisabeth. B.A., U. Fla., Gainesville, 1976, postgrad., 1977-80; M.S., Fla. State U., Tallahasse, 1981. Library aide Riley Ave. Sch., Calverton, N.Y., 1966-68; tech. asst. U. Fla. Library, 1982-83, asst. librarian., 1983—. Mem. Cleve. Orch. Chorus, 1956-58. Mem. ALA, Med. Library Assn., Phi Beta Kappa, Beta Phi Mu, Sigma Tau Sigma. Club: Polish Singers Alliance (sec. 1951-55). Home: 1519 NE 12th St Gainesville FL 32601 Office: 131 Library W U Fla Gainesville FL 32611

KUBIAK, MATTHEW CHRISTOPHER, library administrator; b. London, Jan. 4, 1947; came to U.S., 1951, naturalized, 1959; s. Klemens W. and Stefaniak (Jamiolkowska) K.; m. Christine N.R. Sterner, Sept. 9, 1984; 1 child, Andrew Stephen. Student Heidelberg Coll., 1965-67; B.A., U. Mich., 1969; A.M.L.S., U. Mich., 1973. Reference librarian Mich. State U., East Lansing, 1972-73; head tech. services Peoria (Ill.) Pub. Library, 1973-76, head of branches, 1976; asst. dir. Weir Pub. Library, Weirton, W.Va., 1977-80; dir. West Fla. Regional Library System, Pensacola, 1980—; mem. faculty Ill. Central Coll., East Peoria, 1975-76, W.Va. No. Coll., Weirton, 1979; mem. info. and referral bd. Escambia County, 1981-83. Mem. Escambia County Democratic Exec. Com., 1982—, mem. steering com., 1984-86, audit com. 1986—; mem. Pensacola Arts Council, 1980—; mem. Habitat for Humanity. Served with USAR, 1969-75. Recipient U. West Fla. Upward Bound Outstanding Contbn. award, 1982; Fla. Jaycees Outstanding Chmn. award, 1982; Jr. League of Pensacola Info. and Referral Valuable Service award, 1981; LWV Rose award, 1983. Mem. ALA, Pub. Library Assn., Southeastern Library Assn., Fla. Library Assn., Am. Soc. Pub. Adminstrn., Library Adminstrn. and Mgmt. Assn., West Fla. Library Assn. Democrat. Contbr. articles to profl. jours. Club: Optimists. Office: 200 W Gregory St Pensacola FL 32501

KUBIET, LEO L., newspaper advertising and marketing executive; b. Fairmont, W. Va., Apr. 11, 1924; s. Joseph J. and Laura Agnes (Bucy) K.; m. M. Jean Metz, Sept. 14, 1945; children—Lawrence Michael, Martin Alan. B.A. in Journalism and English, Fairmont State Coll., 1949; postgrad. U. Mich., 1950, Wayne State U., 1952, U. Detroit, 1953. With The News, Detroit, 1950-68; retail advt. mgr. St. Petersburg Times and Evening Ind., Fla., 1968-70, advt. mgr. in charge classified, co-op, gen. and retail advt., 1970-75, advt. dir., 1975—, dir., 1976—, v.p. advt., 1986—; dir. Modern Graphic Arts, Fla. Trend Mags., Inc. Mem. advt. adv. council U. Fla.; bd. govs. St. Petersburg Area C. of C., 1980-83; bd. dirs. Fla. Orch. Served with USNR, 1942-46. Mem. Internat. Newspaper Advt. and Mktg. Execs. (past pres.), So. Region Adv. Council, Am. Press Inst., St. Petersburg Advt. Fedn. (bd. dirs. Silver medal 1977), St. Petersburg Sales and Mktg. Execs., Inc. (past pres.), Newspaper Advt. Bur. Am. Newspaper Pubs. Assn. (plans com.). Office: St Petersburg Times 490 1st Ave S St Petersburg FL 33701

KUCEWICZ, JOHN CASIMIR, JR., geologist; b. Boston, Nov. 26, 1950; s. John Casimir and Erma Leti (Summarsell) K.; m. Emma Louise Parent, May 26, 1978; 1 child, Hilary Anne. Student U. New Orleans, 1975-78, 85—, SUNY-Oneonta, 1968-72. Geol. asst. Texaco Inc., New Orleans, 1975-78; geol. specialist CNG Producing Co., New Orleans, 1978—. Adult leader 4H, Picayune, Miss., 1985—; industry liaison Explorers, Boy Scouts Am., New Orleans, 1978-81. Mem. Potential Gas Com. (Gulf Coast chmn. 1983-85, tech. advisor 1985—), Am. Assn. Petroleum Geologists (jr.), New Orleans Geol. Soc., Corpus Christi Geol. Soc. Mem. Worldwide Ch. of God. Avocations: Rose gardening; travel; photography. Office: CNG Producing Co 3100 One Canal Pl New Orleans LA 70130

KUCK, JOHN FREDERICK READ, biochemist, eye researcher, educator; b. Savannah, Ga., Jan. 27, 1918; s. John Frederick Read and Helen Louise (Van Horne) K.; m. Kathryn Donnan, Sept. 4, 1949; children—Kay, Jack, Martha, Andrew, Mary. B.S., Va. Poly. Inst., 1939, M.S., 1940; Ph.D., U. N.C., 1951. Chemist. nat. adv. com. NASA, Cleve., 1940-45; prof. chemistry Ill. Benedictine Coll., Lisle, Ill., 1950-51; research assoc. Wayne U. surgery dept., Detroit, 1951-57; research assoc. Kresge Eye Inst., Detroit, 1957-63; asst. prof. Emory U., Atlanta, 1963-68, assoc. prof., 1968-78, prof. ophthalmology, 1978—. Mem. Am. Chem. Soc., AAAS, Assn. Research Vision and Ophthalmology, Sigma Xi. Home: 1964 N Decatur Rd NE Atlanta GA 30307 Office: Emory U Eye Research Lab Atlanta GA 30322

KUDLATY, FRANK, educational administrator. Supt. of schs. Waco, Tex. Office: Box 27 Waco TX 76703*

KUEHN, RONALD LEGG, JR., natural resources and energy executive; b. Bklyn., Apr. 6, 1935; s. Ronald L. K.; m. Kathleen Moriarty, Feb. 15, 1958; children—Kathleen, Kelly, Erin, Coleen, Shannon. B.S., Fordham U., 1957, LL.B., 1964. Assoc. atty. Hughes Hubbard & Reed, 1964-68; exec. v.p., gen. counsel Allied Artists Pictures, 1968-70; sec., asst. gen. counsel So. Natural Gas Co., 1971-73, v.p., gen. counsel, sec., 1973-76; sr. v.p. So. Natural Resources, Inc., 1980, sec., 1973-76, gen. counsel, sec., 1976-79; v.p. Sonat, Inc., Birmingham, Ala., 1979-80, sr. v.p., 1980-81, pres., chief operating officer, 1981-84, pres., chief exec. officer, 1984—, also dir.; chmn. bd. Teleco Oilfield Services Inc.; dir. Sonat Offshore Drilling Co., Sonat Exploration Co., Sonat Marine, Union Carbide Corp. Bd. dirs. Birmingham Area council Boy Scouts Am.; gen. co-chmn. United Way, 1983; nat. trustee Boys Clubs Am.; trustee Birmingham So. Coll. Served to 1st lt., U.S. Army, 1958. Mem. Am. Soc. Corp. Secs., ABA, N.Y. State Bar Assn., Assn. Bar City N.Y., Interstate Natural Gas Assn. Am. Roman Catholic. Lodge: Birmingham Rotary. Office: 1900 5th Ave N Birmingham AL 35203

KUEHNE, BENEDICT P., lawyer; b. Merced, Calif., Mar. 24, 1954; s. Ben and Jean T. Kuehne; m. Lynne A. Auerbach, Nov. 17, 1984. B.A. cum laude, U. Miami, 1974, J.D. cum laude, 1977; postgrad. Fla. Atlantic U., 1979—. Bar: Fla. 1977, D.C. 1978, U.S. Ct. Appeals (5th cir.) 1977, U.S. Dist. Ct. (so. and mid. dists.) Fla. 1977, U.S. Ct. Appeals (4th cir.) 1980, U.S. Ct. Appeals (7th and 11th cirs.) 1981, U.S. Ct. Appeals (9th and D.C. cirs.) 1982, U.S. Supreme Ct. 1981, U.S. Dist. Ct. (so. dist.) Ala. 1983, U.S. Ct. Appeals (2d, 3d, 6th and 8th cirs.). Asst. atty. gen. State of Fla., West Palm Beach, 1977-79, spl. asst. state atty. 15th Jud. Cir., 1978-80; assoc. Bierman, Sonnett, Shohat & Sale, P.A., Miami and Ft. Lauderdale, Fla., 1980—; lectr. in field. Editor U. Miami Jour. Internat. Law, 1975-77. Contbr. articles to profl. jours. Bd. dirs. U. Miami Law Alumni Assn., Coral Gables, 1980—; bd. dirs. Coconut Grove Assn., Fla. 1983—, 1st v.p. 1985; ; gen. counsel Fla. Young Democrats, 1984-85, polit. v.p. 1983-84; pres. Dade County Young Dems. Fla., 1982-83, bd. dirs., 1983-84; co-chmn. Young Dems. of Am. Nat. Conv., 1985, chmn. jud. council, 1985. Named one of Outstanding Young Men of Am., 1980, 82. Mem. Fla. Bar Assn. (edn. com. criminal law sect.), Fla. Criminal Def. Attys. Assn.

(chmn. brief bank com., bd. dirs. 1985, Cert. of Merit 1984) Pub. Interest Law Bank (Award of Merit 1984), Dade County Bar Assn., Greater Miami Jewish Fedn. (atty.'s div.), Nat. Eagle Scout Orgn. Home: PO Box 013329 Miami FL 33101 Office: Bierman Sonnett Shohat & Sale PA 200 SE First St #500 Miami FL 33131

KUENZLER, EDWARD JULIAN, environmental biologist, educator; b. West Palm Beach, Fla., Nov. 11, 1929; s. Edward and Flora Caroline (Jeske) K.; m. Jutta Gertraud Koslowski, Sept. 4, 1965; children—Doreen Friederika, Dirk Edward. B.S., U. Fla., 1951; M.S., U. Ga., 1953, Ph.D., 1959. Asst.-assoc. scientist Woods Hole (Mass.) Oceanographic Inst., 1959-65; assoc. prof. environ. biology U. N.C., Chapel Hill, 1965-71, prof., 1972—; program dir. biol. oceanography NSF, 1971-72; mem. panel Nat. Acad. Scis., 1974-75; chmn. curriculum in marine scis. U. N.C.-Chapel Hill, 1968-71, 72-73, program area dir. environ. chemistry and biology dept. environ. scis. and engring., 1980-83; dep. chmn. dept. environ. scis. and engring., 1984—; mem. N.C. Gov.'s Tech. Coordinating Com., 1968-70; mem. N.C. Comml. and Sports Fisheries Adv. Com., 1975-77; mem. N.C. Div. Health Services Com. on Mosquito Control, 1980-81; advisor U.S. C.E. on Open Marsh Water Mgmt. for Mosquito Control, 1981-83. Served from 2d lt. to capt. USAF, 1951-54. Research grantee AEC, 1962-70, NOAA Office Sea Grants, 1971-73, Office Water Research and Tech., 1970-84. Mem. Ecol. Soc. Am., Phycol. Soc. Am., Am. Soc. Limnology and Oceanography, Estuarine Research Fedn., N.C. Acad. Sci. (treas. 1982-85). Republican. Methodist. Contbr. articles to profl. jours. Home: Route 1 Box 277 Chapel Hill NC 27514 Office: Dept Environ Scis and Engring U NC Chapel Hill NC 27514

KUGHN, JAMES CURTIS, JR., college administrator; b. Washington, Pa., May 27, 1944; s. James Curtis Sr. and Florence (Bromley) K.; m. Kristine Helen Krajack, Jan. 28, 1967; children—Christopher James, Allison Marie. B.S., California U. Pa., 1966; M.A., W.Va. U., 1968. Tchr. Trinity High Sch., Washington, Pa., 1966-68; asst. dir. admissions Washington Jefferson Coll., Washington, Pa., 1968-72, asst. dir. devel., 1973-74; v.p. for devel. and pub. relations Salem Coll., W.Va., 1974-77; v.p. devel. and publs. Randolph-Macon Woman's coll., Lynchburg, Va., 1977—. Bd. dirs. Meals on Wheels, Lynchburg. Mem. Nat. Soc. for Fund Raising Execs., Council for Advancement Support Edn. (U.S. Steel award, 1980), Lynchburg Estate Planners, C. of C., Delta Sigma Phi. Republican. Lodge: Kiwanis (bd. dirs.). Avocations: tennis; skiing; travel. Home: 3015 Sedgewick Dr Lynchburg VA 24503 Office: Randolph-Macon Woman's Coll 2500 Rivermont Ave Lynchburg VA 24503

KUHLER, RENALDO GILLET, illustrator, museum official; b. Teaneck, N.J., Nov. 21, 1931; s. Otto August and Simonne L. (Gillet) K.; B.A., U. Colo., 1961. Curator of history, exhibit and miniature diorama preparer Eastern Wash. State Hist. Soc. Mus., Spokane, 1962-67; museum artist-illustrator N.C. State Mus. Natural History, Raleigh, 1969—; designer, executor of art work for sci. illustrations, awards, brochures, pamphlets and periodicals Dept. Agr. and Mus., N.C., 1972-74; designer 36 illustrations for Handbook of Reptiles and Amphibians of Florida, Part 1 (Ray E. Ashton), 1981; designer many fish illustrations for Atlas of North American Fresh Water Fishes (by Carter Gilbert, David Lee), 1980; designed and executed models from laminated paper. Mem. Nat. Trust Historic Preservation. Democrat. Illustrator: American Firearms and the Changing Frontier (Waldo E. Rosebush), 1962-67. Office: Box 27647 Raleigh NC 27611

KUHLMAN, KARL MENNINGER, transportation company executive; b. Norman, Okla., Sept. 28, 1940; s. John Henry and Inez (Menninger) K.; m. Barbara Dean Burch, June 30, 1962; children—Kay Denene, Alex Clay. Supr. Warehouse Ford Motor Co., Carrollton, Tex., 1964-69; pres., chief exec. officer Yellow Cab Dallas, Inc., 1969—, Surtran Taxicabs, Inc., Dallas, 1973—; mem., past chmn. taxicab adv. com. Tex. Dept. Hwys. and Public Transp., Bd. dirs. Lakehill Prep. Sch., Dallas. Mem. Tex. Taxicab Owners Assn., Dallas Citizens Council, Dallas C. of C., North Tex. Commn., Better Bus. Bur., Tex. Motor Transp. Assn., Internat. Taxicab Assn. Democrat. Methodist. Club: Lakewood Country. Home: 6318 Highgate Ln Dallas TX 75214 Office: 1610 S Ervay St Dallas TX 75215

KUHLMAN, ROBERT PHILLIP, business consultant; b. Wadsworth, Ohio, Feb. 13, 1946; s. Myron George and Ruth Irene (Miller) K. B.S., U. Tex.-Austin, 1969; M.B.A., Stanford U., 1974. Asst. to pres., gen. mgr. Anthony Industries, San Francisco, 1974-75; asst. regional mgr. Kaiser Health Plan, Honolulu, 1975-81; v.p. CIGNA Health Plan, Miami, 1981-82; chief exec. officer, pres. North Tex. Med. Care, Inc., Denton, Tex., 1982-83; owner gen. bus. services Dallas, 1983—; dir. DFW Restaurants, Inc. Home: 5636 Spring Valley Rd Apt 20-A Dallas TX 75240 Office: 14902 Preston Rd Suite 212 Dallas TX 75240

KUHN, JAMES E., lawyer; b. Hammond, La., Oct. 31, 1946; s. Eton Percy and Mildred Louise (McDaniel) K.; m. Cheryl Aucoin, Dec. 27, 1969; children—James M., Jennifer L. Bar: Southeastern La. U., 1968; J.D., Loyola U. of South, 1973. Bar: La. 1973. Asst. dist. atty. 21st Jud. Dist. La., 1979—. Mem. ABA, La. State Bar Assn., 21st Jud. Bar Assn., Livingston Parish Bar Assn., Assn. Trial Lawyers Am., La. Trial Lawyers Assn., La. Assn. Def. Counsel, Delta Theta Phi. Home: 8178 Hermitage Dr Denham Springs LA 70726 Office: 217 Hermitage Dr Denham Springs LA 70726

KUIC, VUKAN, educator; b. Sarajevo, Yugoslavia, Feb. 17, 1923; came to U.S., 1950, naturalized, 1956; s. Simeon and Aglaja (Homiuka) K.; m. Louise Helen Cobb, Aug. 31, 1957; children—Angela, Sonja, Mira, Tanja, Simeon, Elena. M.A., U. Colo., 1953; Ph.D., U. Chgo., 1958. Instr., U. Ala., Tuscaloosa, 1956-58, asst. prof., 1958-63, assoc. prof., 1963-66; prof. dept. govt. and internat. studies U. S.C., Columbia, 1966—; vis. fellow Center for Study of Dem. Instns., Santa Barbara, Calif., 1965-66; research assoc. Center for Study of Federalism, Temple U., Phila., 1976. Mem. So. Polit. Sci. Assn., World Future Soc., Am. Maritain Assn. Contbr. articles to profl. jours. Home: 745 Westover Rd Columbia SC 29210 Office: 324 Gambrell Hall U SC Columbia SC 29208

KULINSKI, STEPHEN EDWARD, interior architect; b. Balt., Aug. 20, 1955; s. Paul Dominic and Christine (Armstrong) K.; m. Fredricka Strumpf, Aug. 6, 1983. B.Design, U. Fla., 1977; M.B.A., U. North Fla., 1983. Sr. designer Reynolds, Smith & Hills, Jacksonville, Fla., 1977-80, project mgr., 1980-83; project dir. Gresham, Smith & Ptnrs., Nashville, 1983-84, dir. interior architecture, 1984—, assoc., 1985—. Mem. bd. visitors U. Tenn., Knoxville, 1985. Mem. Nashville C. of C. Republican. Home: 1209 Brenner Dr Nashville TN 37221 Office: Gresham Smith and Ptnrs 3310 West End Ave Nashville TN 37202

KULKA, RICHARD ALAN, survey research methodologist; b. Cleve., July 29, 1945; s. James Maurice Kulka and Shirley (Grossman) Gelband; m. Linda Mary Sachen, Apr. 26, 1968; children—Sean Christopher, James Evan. B.A. with honors, Tulane U., 1967; M.A. in Sociology, U. Mich., 1969, Ph.D. in Social Psychology, 1975. Teaching fellow, trainee depts. of psychology and Sociology U. Mich., Ann Arbor, 1967-69, asst. study dir. Survey Research Ctr., Mich., 1973-75, study dir., 1975-80; psychol. research assoc. HQ VIII Airborne, Ft. Bragg, N.C., 1971-72; sr. survey methodologist Research Triangle Inst., Research Triangle Park, N.C., 1980—. Author: (with others) The Inner American, 1981; (with others) Mental Health in America, 1981. Woodrow Wilson Nat. fellow Ford Found, 1967-68. Mem. Am. Assn. Pub. Opinion Research, Am. Mktg. Assn., Am. Psychol. Assn., Am. Sociol. Assn., Am. Statis. Assn., Phi Beta Kappa. Home: 101 Huntington Dr Chapel Hill NC 27514 Office: Ctr Survey Research Research Triangle Inst PO Box 12194 Research Triangle Park NC 27709

KULKARNI, KISHORE GANESH, economics educator, consultant; b. Poona, Maharashtra, India; Oct. 31, 1953; came to U.S., 1976; s. Ganesh Y. and Sindhu G. Dhekane; m. Jayu K., Aug. 17, 1980; 1 child, Lina. B.A., U. Poona, India, 1974, M.A., 1976; M.A., U. Pitts., 1978, Ph.D., 1982. Teaching asst. U. Pitts., 1976-78, teaching fellow, 1978-80, asst. prof., Johnstown, Pa., 1981-82; asst. prof. U. Central Ark., Conway, 1982—. Contbr. articles to profl. jours. Research fellow Winrock Internat., Morrilton, Ark., 1984—; recipient K. Shinde prize, Poona, India, 1974, First prize, essay competition, Forum of Free Enterprise, Bombay, India, 1975, Rama Watumull Fund award, Honolulu, 1977. Mem. Am. Econ. Assn., Southwestern Econ. Assn., So. Econ. Assn., Assn. Indian Econ. Studies. Avocation: tennis. Home: 2512 College St Conway AR 72032

KULL, RICHARD LANCE, information resources training director, consultant; b. Castle AFB, Calif., Sept. 11, 1949; s. George Howard and Gladys Irene (Woodall) K.; m. Claire Elizabeth Beck, Oct. 28, 1972; children—Elizabeth, Matthew, Christina, Deborah. A.A., Pensacola Jr. Coll., 1970; B.S., U. W.Fla., 1975, M.B.A., 1976. Programmer Potomac Research, Inc., Pensacola, Fla., 1975-76; sr. programmer Am. Enka, Inc., N.C., 1976-78; systems analyst Westinghouse, Inc., Asheville, N.C., 1978-80; programming mgr. Siecor, Inc., Hickory, N.C., 1980-81; edn. cons. Deltak, Inc., Charlotte, N.C., 1981-82; data processing tng. dir. Dan River, Inc., Danville, Va., 1982—; chmn. adv. bd. Danville Community Coll., Danville, 1983—; cons. tng. various orgns. in Southeast, 1980—; presenter seminars on data processing management, tng. and gen. mgmt. Pres. Home Sch. Assn. Sacred Heart Sch., Danville, 1984—; adv. Post 358 Blue Ridge Mountain council Boy Scouts Am., Danville, 1983—, unit commr., 1983—; edn. chmn. internat. mgmt. council Danville chpt. YMCA, 1985-86. Served with USMC, 1970-73. Recipient Individual Performance award Data Processing Mgmt. Assn., 1984, Silver Scout award Gulf Coast council Boy Scouts Am., 1965. Mem. Am. Soc. for Tng. Devel., W. Piedmont Chpt. Data Processing Mgmt. Assn. (program chmn. 1984-85, pres. 1985), Triad Data Processing Educators Council (chmn. 1983-85), Optimist Internat. Republican. Roman Catholic. Lodge: KC. Avocations: microcomputers; woodcarving; leatherwork; camping; gardening. Home: 633 Timberlake Dr Danville VA 24540 Office: Dan River Inc PO Box 261 Danville VA 24543

KULP, MARILYN JEAN, association executive; b. Phila., July 28, 1941; d. William Thomas and Eleanor May (Hasher) Miller; m. Louis F. Kulp III, July 2, 1966; children—William Scott, June Marie. Student Phila. Modeling Sch., 1956, various tech. courses. Mem. quality control Paramount Packaging Corp., Chalfont, Pa., 1963-64; mem. electricy and design engring. dept. Selas Corp., Dresher, Pa., 1964-66; asst. staff dir. Adminstrv. Mgmt. Soc., Willow Grove, Pa., 1966-69; mgr. Abington Assns., Pa., 1973-79; exec. dir. Assn. for Multi-Image Internat., Inc., Tampa, 1974—. Recipient Media All-Star award, Audio Visual Communications, 1984. Republican. Presbyterian. Avocations: sports; music; traveling. Office: Assn for Multi-Image Internat Inc 8019 N Himes Ave Sutie 401 Tampa FL 33614

KULP, RICHARD WAYNE, mathmatics educator, consultant; b. Norfolk, Va., Nov. 4, 1943; s. William Vernon and Ruth Crawford (Hudson) K.; m. Alice Faye Owens, July 22, 1966; children—Richard Wayne Jr., Jonathan Lance. B.S., Fla. State U., 1964, M.S., 1967; Ph.D., Tex. Tech U., 1976. Mathematician, Ballistic Systems Div., Norton AFB, Calif., 1964; naviagtor USAF Flying Orgns., 1965-80; asst. prof. Air Force Inst. Tech., Wright-Patterson AFB, Ohio. 1977-80, assoc. prof., 1981-84, David Lipscomb Coll., Nashville, 1984; cons. in field. Contbr. articles to profl. jours. Served to lt. col. USAF, 1964-84. Decorated D.F.C., Air medal with 4 oak leaf clusters, Meritorious service medal with 1 oak leaf cluster; recipient Joint Services Commendation medal USAF, 1972. Mem. Am. Statis. Assn. Republican. Avocation: golf. Office: David Lipscomb Coll PO Box 4233 Nashville TN 37203

KULP, SAMUEL LESTER, computer systems educator; b. Mishawaka, Ind., Nov. 23, 1942; s. Lester Charles and Frances Bernice (Chamness) K.; B.S., Purdue U., 1970; m. Constance Lenora White, June 26, 1965. Systems programmer Purdue U. adminstrv. data processing center, West Lafayette, Ind., 1969-70; info. analyst Eli Lilly and Co., Indpls., 1970-73; sr. programmer analyst Am. United Life Ins. Co., Indpls., 1973-78, EDP tng. coordinator, 1978-79; data systems analyst So. Bell Telephone Co., Atlanta, 1979-83; data base instr. Cullinet Software, Atlanta, 1983-84; tng. specialist Mgmt. Sci. Am., 1985; tech. tng. specialist Consultec, Inc., 1986—. Scoutmaster, leadership devel. chmn., dist. commr. Boy Scouts Am. (recipient Eagle award, Scouters Key, Commr.'s Key, Dist. Award of Merit, vigil mem. Order of Arrow, Silver Beaver award). Mem. Assn. Computing Machinery (past treas. Central Ind. chpt.), Atlanta Council Computer Edn. Support and Services (v.p.), Am. Soc. Tng. and Devel., Nat. Eagle Scout Assn., Cousteau Soc., Profl. Assn. Diving Instrs. Baptist. Home: 160 Leeward Ln Roswell GA 30076

KULP, TIMOTHY CLAY, lawyer; b. Columbia, S.C., Sept. 24, 1952; s. Francis Clay and Annie Mae (Graham) K. B.A., U. S.C., 1975, J.D., 1978. Bar: S.C. 1978, U.S. Dist. Ct. S.C. 1983. Asst. solicitor 5th Circuit S.C., Columbia, 1978; spl. agt. FBI, Miami, Fla., 1978-80; asst. solicitor 9th Circuit, Charleston, S.C., 1980-82; legal counsel, city prosecutor Charleston Police Dept., 1982—. Mem. Nat. Dist. Attys. Assn., Charleston County Bar Assn. Baptist. Office: 180 Lockwood Blvd Charleston SC 29403

KUMAR, KRISHNA, physics educator; b. Meerut, India, July 14, 1936; came to U.S., 1956, naturalized, 1966; s. Rangi and Susheil (Devi) Lal; m. Katharine Johnson, May 1, 1960; children—Jai Robert, Raj David. B.Sc. in Physics, Chemistry and Math., Agra U., 1953, M.Sc. in Physics, 1955; M.S. in Physics, Carnegie Mellon U., 1959, Ph.D. in Physics, Carnegie Mellon U., 1964. Research assoc. Mich. State U., 1963-66, MIT, 1966-67, research fellow Niels Bohr Inst., Copenhagen, 1967-69; physicist Oak Ridge Nat. Lab., 1969-71; assoc. prof. Vanderbilt U., Nashville, 1971-77; fgn. collaborator AEC of France, Paris, 1977-79; Nordita prof. U. Bergen, Norway, 1979-80; prof. physics Tenn. Tech. U., Cookeville, 1980-82, Univ. prof. physics, 1983—; lectr. in field; cons. various research labs. Sec., India Assn., Pitts., 1958-59. Recipient gold medal Agra U., 1955; NSF research grantee, 1972-75. Mem. AAAS, Am. Phys. Soc., N.Y. Acad. Scis., Planetary Soc., Sigma Pi Sigma, Sigma Xi. Republican. Hindu. Lodge: Rotary. Author: Nuclear Models and the Search for Unity in Nuclear Physics, 1984; contbr. articles to profl. jours, books. Home: 1248 N Franklin Ave Cookeville TN 38501 Office: Box 5051 Tenn Tech U Cookeville TN 38505

KUMAR, MADHURENDU BHUSHAN, geologist; b. Khagaria, India, Jan. 4, 1942; came to U.S., 1969, naturalized, 1971; s. Sita Ram Prabhas and Bhavani Devi K.; A.I.S.M., Indian Sch. Mines, Dhanbad, India, 1962; M.Sc., Ranchi U., Ranchi, Bihar, India, 1962; Ph.D., La. State U., 1972; m. Sharda Swarnkar, July 7, 1965; children—Madhuresh, Vinita. Instr., Indian Sch. Mines, 1962-63; sci. office Dept. Atomic Energy, New Delhi, 1963; geologist Oil India Ltd., 1963-69; grad. teaching and research asst. dept. geology La. State U., 1969-72, research asso. Inst. Environ. Studies, summers 1975, 77, 76, sr. research asso. Inst. Environ. Studies, 1978-82; sr. investigator geohydrology, salt dome project Dept. Energy, 1978-82; geologist supr. oil and gas div. Office of Conservation, La. Dept. Natural Resources, 1982—. Cons. and exploration geologist, 1972-74; mem. faculty dept. geology and geography Hunter Coll., CUNY, 1974-77; mem. faculty dept. geology La. State U., 1977-78, U. Southwestern La., spring 1979, dept. civil engring. So. U., Baton Rouge, 1978-82; cons. in field. Recipient Sir Henry Hayden medal Mining, Metall. and Geol. Inst. India, 1962, Disting. Alumni award Indian Sch. Mines, 1978. Fellow Geol. Soc. Am.; mem. Am. Assn. Petroleum Geologists (cert. petroleum geologist), Am. Inst. Profl. Geologists (cert. profl. geol. scientist), Soc. Petroleum Engrs., Sigma Xi. Research, publs. on subsurface petroleum geology, computerized mapping, geopressured reservoirs, geothermal and geopressure patterns, salt dome tectonics, geohydrology of salt mines. Home: 7744 Wimbledon Ave Baton Rouge LA 70810 Office: La Dept Natural Resources Oil and Gas Div PO Box 44275 Capitol Sta Baton Rouge LA 70804

KUNDU, MADAN MOHAN, rehabilitation counseling educator; b. Calcutta, India, June 3, 1946, came to U.S., 1970; s. Narayan C. and Labanayamayee Kundu; m. Pravati Chakraborty, Nov. 17, 1972; 1 child, Uma. B.S. with distinction, U. Calcutta, 1966; M.A. in Rehab. Counseling, Mich. State U., 1976, Ph.D., 1983. Cert. rehab. counselor. Rehab. asst. counseling, research asst. Blind Boy's Acad., Ramakrishna Mission, Calcutta, 1964-70, rehab. counselor, 1972-75; placement trainer Mich. Vocat. Rehab. Services, Mich. State U., East Lansing, 1976; vocat. rehab. intern State of Mich. Vocat. Rehab. Services, Lansing, 1976; internat. rehab. and spl. edn. research asst. Mich. State U., East Lansing, 1976-79; rehab. analyst La. State U., Baton Rouge, 1979-80; math. instr., 1980-81; research fellow Mich. State U., East Lansing, 1982-83; coordinator, asst. prof. rehab. counseling So. U., Baton Rouge, 1984—; cons. Internat. Rescue Com., Bangladesh, 1971-74; speaker Headstart Handicap Conf., La., 1979, Rehab. Counselor Educator Forum, 1984, Am. Assn. Counseling and Devel. conv., 1985; adminstr., monitor Bd. Rehab. Cert., 1984—; bd. dirs. Nat. Council Rehab. Edn. Contbr. articles to profl. jours. Delta Gamma Found. scholar, Ohio, 1976; scholar Watumul Found., Hawaii, 1970, Brit. Council, 1971, Internat. Eye Found., 1971, Council Internat. Programs for Youth Leaders and Social Workers, 1971; Fulbright fellow, 1970-71; grantee Mich. State U., 1976-79, Russell Sage Found., 1983. Mem. Am. Assn. Counseling and Devel., Am. Rehab. Counseling Assn., Am. Psychol. Assn., Council Exceptional Children, La. Rehab. Assn. (treas. 1985), Nat. Rehab. Assn. (del. La. 1984), Nat. Rehab. Counseling Assn. (research award 1984), Am. Rehab. Counseling Assn., Nat. Assn. Rehab. Instrs., La. Rehab. Assn., Rho Chi Sigma (founding pres. Alpha Zeta). Home: 312 Chippenham Baton Rouge LA 70808

KUNSTEL, JAMES V., groceries company executive; b. 1931. With Nat. Food Stores, 1952-68, Super Valu Inc., Hopkins, Minn., 1968-70, Allied Supermarkets, Tulsa, 1970-77; chmn. bd., pres., chief exec. officer, dir. Scrivner Inc., Oklahoma City, 1983—. Address: Scrivner Inc 1301 SE 59th Oklahoma City OK 73126*

KUNTZ, HAL GOGGAN, petroleum exploration company executive; b. San Antonio, Tex., Dec. 29, 1937; s. Peter A. and Jean M. (Goggan) K.; B.S.E., Princeton U., 1960; M.B.A., Oklahoma City U., 1972; m. Vesta M. Kuntz; children—Hal Goggan II, Peter V, Michael B. Line and staff positions Mobil Oil Corp., Dallas, Oklahoma City and New Orleans, 1963-74; co-founder CLK Corp., New Orleans and Houston, 1974, pres., chief exec. officer, dir., 1974—; pres. IPEX Co.; gen. partner Gulf Coast Exploration Co.; mng. ptnr. CLK Prodn. Co., 1980—, CLK Oil & Gas Co., 1984—. Served with U.S. Army, 1960-63. Winner amateur golf tournaments, 1955, 56, 63. Mem. Am. Mgmt. Assn., Nat. Small Bus. Assn., Am. Assn. Petroleum Geologists, Inter-Am. Soc., Soc. Exploration Geophysicists, Aircraft Owners and Pilots Assn., Houston Mus. Fine Arts, Houston Opera Soc. (governing bd.), Condrs. Circle of Houston Symphony. Republican. Roman Catholic. Clubs: Presidents, Argyle, Houston City, Univ., Order of Alamo. Office: First City Tower Suite 1400 1001 Fannin Houston TX 77002

KUO, HUI-HSIUNG, mathematics educator; b. Tachia, Taichung, Taiwan, Oct. 21, 1941; came to U.S., 1966; s. Kin-sueh and Fan-Po (Wang) K.; m. Fukuko Tanaka, Apr. 19, 1969; children—Isaac Ji, Henry Gene. B.A., Taiwan U., 1965; M.A., Cornell U., 1968, Ph.D., 1970. Vis. mem. Courant Inst., N.Y.C., 1970-71; asst. prof. U. Va., Charlottesville, 1971-75; vis. asst. prof. SUNY-Buffalo, 1975-76; assoc. prof. math. Wayne State U., Detroit, 1976-77; assoc. prof. La. State U., Baton Rouge, 1977-82, prof. math., 1982—. Author: Gaussian Measures, 1975; also articles. Editor: Stochastic Differential Equations, 1984. NSF grantee, 1972-77, 78-84; Japan Soc. Promotion of Sci. fellow, 1984; NSF research visitor, Warsaw, Poland, 1980. Mem. Am. Math. Soc., Math. Soc. Japan, Sigma Xi. Democrat. Presbyterian. Home: 7436 Shrewsbury Ave Baton Rouge LA 70808 Office: Dept Math La State U Baton Rouge LA 70803

KUPFERLE, NICHOLAS HENRY, III, hospital administrator; b. Fort Worth, Nov. 20, 1949; s. Nicholas Henry, Jr. and Doris Gene (Jaco) K.; m. Glenda Ann Golly, May 18, 1974. B.S., Tex. A&M U., 1972; M.S., Trinity U., 1976. Adminstrv. resident Arlington Meml. Hosp., Tex., 1974-75; field cons. Am. Hosp. Assn., Des Moines, 1975-77; asst. adminstr. Tarrant County Hosp. Dist., Fort Worth, 1977-78, Pasadena Bayshore Hosp., Tex., 1978-82; adminstr. Eastwood Hosp., El Paso, Tex., 1982-83, Meml. Hosp., Cleburne, Tex., 1983—. Contbr. articles to profl. jours. Chmn. 1st United Meth. Ch., Cleburne, 1985—, Johnson County chpt. ARC, 1984—. Mem. Tex. Hosp. Assn. (alt. del. dist. V 1984—), Am. Coll. Hosp. Adminstrs., Am. Hosp. Assn. Republican. Methodist. Club: Riverview Country. Lodge: Kiwanis. Avocations: golfing; music; hunting; fishing. Home: 1202 A Nolan River Rd Cleburne TX 76031 Office: Meml Hosp 1600 N Main St Cleburne TX 76031

KUPPERS, JAMES RICHARD, retired chemistry educator, consultant; b. Newland, Ind., Aug. 4, 1920; s. Herman Jacob and Gladys Caroline (Harlow) K.; m. Faith Channell Farnham, Mar. 13, 1944; children—James F., Theresa H., Kathryn C., Mary S. B.S., U. Fla., 1943; M.S., La. State U., 1947; Ph.D., U. Fla., 1957. Assoc. biochemist United Fruit Co., Panama, Costa Rica, Honduras, 1947-54; research chemist E. I. duPont de Nemours, Inc., Kinston, N.C., 1957-60; assoc. prof. Pfeiffer Coll., 1960-64; prof. chemistry dept. U. N.C., Charlotte, 1964-85. Served to lt. (j.g.) USNR, 1943-46. Mem. Am. Chem. Soc., N.Y. Acad. Scis., Sigma Xi. Contbr. articles to profl. jours.; patentee in field. Home: 3207 Connecticut Ave Charlotte NC 28205 Office: Chemistry Dept U NC Charlotte NC 28223

KUPRIS, MARTIN ANTHONY, architect; b. Wilkes-Barre, Pa., Jan. 19, 1954; s. Goodwin Anthony and Elizabeth Ann (Fioti) K. B.A., Columbia U., 1975, M.Arch., 1978. Designer, Davis, Brody & Assocs., N.Y.C., 1978-81; dir. specifications Ehrenkrantz Group, N.Y.C., 1981-83; dir. specifications Clark, Tribble, Charlotte, N.C., 1983-85; dir. specifications Little & Assocs., Charlotte, 1985—; pres. Kupris Assocs., Charlotte, 1983—. Arbitrator, Am. Arbitration Assn., 1984—. Treas., 3 Parks Democrats, Inc., N.Y.C., 1982-83; mem. N.Y. County Democratic Com., 1982-83; pres. Soc. Traditional Roman Catholics, 1984—; pres. Com. for Cath. Unity, Charlotte, 1985—. William F. Kinne fellow, 1977. Mem. Mensa, Constrn. Specifications Inst. (v.p. 1984—), AIA, Practicing Law Inst., Nat. Fire Protection Assn., ASTM. Republican. Avocations: cooking; running; classical music. Home: 1304 Wembley Dr Charlotte NC 28205 Office: Little & Assocs 5815 Westpark Dr Charlotte NC 28210

KURAITIS, VYTENIS PETRAS, compensation consultant; b. Hanau, Fed. Republic Germany, Feb. 3, 1948; came to U.S., 1950; s. Algirdas C. and Tamara (Visockis) K.; m. Joan Kantner Parsons, Sept. 15, 1973; children—Kristina Kantner, Anne Parsons. B.A., U. Ill., 1970. Mgr. personnel planning and devel. Leaseway, Corp., Cleve., 1977-80; sr. cons. Peat, Marwick, Mitchell & Co., Cleve., 1980-82; dir. compensation and benefits Nordson, Amherst, Ohio, 1982-84; cons. prin. A.S. Hansen, Inc., Houston, 1984—. Contbr. articles to profl. jours. Avocations: squash; racquetball; tennis. Home: 5418 Sycamore Kingwood TX 77345

KURIE, ANDREW EDMUNDS, mining geologist; b. Dallas, May 30, 1932; s. Charles Winfred and Katherine Doyle (Edmunds) K.; B.S. in Geology, Sul Ross State Coll., Alpine, Tex., 1954; M.A. in Geology, U. Tex. at Austin, 1956; m. Judith Ann Hankins, Feb. 14, 1970; children—Andrea, Mary Kay, Michael, Thomas, Teresa. Petroleum geologist Pure Oil Co., Fort Worth, 1956-63; geologist Utah State Dept. Hwys., Salt Lake City, 1964-67; mining geologist LaDomincia S.A. de C.V., Marathon, Tex., 1968-85, exploration supt., 1972-76, mgr. mines and exploration, 1977-85; cons. mining geologist, 1985—. Cert. profl. geologist. Fellow AAAS; mem. Geol. Soc. Am., Am. Assn. Petroleum Geologists, Am. Inst. Profl. Geologists, Explorers Club. Editor: West Tex. Geol. Soc. Membership Directory, 1962; contbr. articles to profl. jours. Home: 610 N Ave D Marathon TX 79842 Office: PO Box 386 Marathon TX 79842

KURKA, DONALD FRANK, art administrator, painter; b. Chgo., July 29, 1930; s. Anton Joseph and Rose Barbara (Jicka) K.; m. Nance Feibel, July 29, 1953; children—Mara, Karel. B.F.A. magna cum laude, Syracuse U., 1952; M.F.A., Sch. of Art Inst., Chgo., 1956; Ph.D., NYU, 1968. Dir. arts, crafts U.S. Army Spl. Services, Yong DungPo, Korea, 1953-54; art specialist Plainedge (N.Y.) Pub. Schs., 1956-59; instr. design, drawing and painting Adelphi U., Garden City, N.Y., 1959-61, Hofstra U., Hempstead, N.Y., 1960-66, Suffolk Community Coll., Selden, N.Y., 1965-67, instr. drawing, painting Harborfields (N.Y.) Pub. Schs., 1959-67, dist. dir. arts, humanities, 1967-69; assoc. prof. art Southampton Coll., Long Island U., 1969-70, dir. Grad. and Undergrad. Div. Edn., 1970-73, dir. Div. Fine Arts, 1973-77; dir. Summer Program, Mus. Modern Art, Amagansett, N.Y., 1969-71; head dept. art U. Tenn.-Knoxville, 1977—. One man shows include U. Tenn.-Knoxville, 1978, Slocum Gallery, East Tenn. State U., 1979, Hunter Mus., Chattanooga, 1981; Rose Art Center, Morristown, Tenn., 1982, Mayor's Gallery, Knoxville, 1982; exhibited in numerous group shows; represented in permanent collections Library Congress, L.I.U., also pvt. collections. Bd. dirs. Knoxville Symphony, Dulin Gallery of Art, Arts Council Greater Knoxville, Tenn. State Mus. Served with U.S. Army, 1952-54; Korea. Recipient numerous awards for painting including: Founders Day award NYU, 1968, Knoxville Mayor's award, 1981, Knoxville Council Arts award, 1982. Mem. Coll. Art Assn. Nat. Council Art Adminstrs., Southeastern Coll. Art Assn., Tau Sigma Kappa, Kappa Delta Pi. Office: Dept Art U Tenn Knoxville TN 37916

KURKE, DAVID SAMUEL, high tech executive, industrial psychologist; b. Havre de Grace, Md., Apr. 22, 1955; s. Martin Ira Kurke and Joy Barbara (Edinger) Kurke Joseph; m. Kathleen Marie Tighe, Feb. 22, 1986. B.S. cum laude, Va. Poly. and State U., 1979. Research scientist Allen Corp. Am., Alexandria, Va., 1979-82; prin. scientist/mgr. edn. and tng. tech. Pacer Systems, Inc., Arlington, Va., 1982-85; v.p. tech. ops. Tech. Corp. Am., Falls Church, Va., 1985—. Mem. exec. bd. Arlington Area Young Republicans,

1980-82; mem. Republican Nat. Com., Washington, 1980—, mem. Presdl. inaugural com., 1980-81; scoutmaster Boy Scouts Am., Washington, 1978; sr. counselor peer counselor program Va. Poly. Inst. and State U., 1974-75, chmn. univ. advisors com., 1978, co-chmn. student-faculty com. on psychology dept. affairs, 1977-78. Recipient Presdl. Achievement award Rep. Nat. Com., 1982; named Outstanding Sr. of Year, Va. Poly. Inst. and State U., 1979. Mem. Am. Soc. Tng. and Devel., Human Factors Soc., Soc. for Applied Learning Tech., Human Factors Soc. Computer Tech. Group, Mensa, Psi Chi. Jewish. Avocations: bicycling; backpacking; restoring antique cars; renovating old homes. Home: 1814 Ontario Pl NW Washington DC 20009 Office: Technology Corp of Am 3027 Rosemary Ln Falls Church VA 22042

KURRELMEIER, HERMAN MARTIN, grain and seed company executive; b. St. Paul, Nov. 28, 1929; s. Herman A. and Gertrude D. (Paulson) K.; m. Gayle Jupp, July 11, 1953; children—Kelly M. Kurrelmeier Bradham, K. Shawn Kurrelmeier Kelsay, L. Bryn Kurrelmeier Fortune, M. Kristin Kurrelmeier Golden, Herman A. B.M.E., U. Minn., 1952; M.B.A., U. Akron, 1974. Registered profl. engr., Tenn. Engring. trainee Quaker Oats Co., Cedar Rapids, Iowa, 1952, engr., St. Joseph, Mo., 1955-56, mgr. engring. and maintenance dept., Chattanooga, 1956-61, sr. milling engr., Chgo., 1961-62, plant supr., Sherman, Tex., 1962-65, plant mgr., Evanston, Ill., 1965-67, Akron, Ohio, 1967-72; planning and services mgr. Ill. Cereal Mills, Inc., Paris, 1972, v.p. mfg., 1972-82, dir., 1973-84; pres. Gurley's Inc., Selma, N.C., 1982—. Elder 1st Presbyn. Ch., Smithfield, N.C., 1983—; pres. Johnston County Agri-Bus. Council, 1985; bd. dirs. Tuscarora council Boy Scouts of Am., Goldsboro, N.C., 1982—; past pres., bd. dirs. Paris YMCA. Served with U.S. Army, 1953-55. Mem. ASME, Assn. Operative Millers, Southeastern Grain and Feed Assn. (bd. dirs. 1984—), Paris C. of C. (past pres., bd. dirs.). Lodge: Rotary (dir. 1983-85).

KURTTS, MARY ALTA, hospital nursing administrator; b. Birmingham, Ala., Aug. 20, 1936; d. William Hugh and Alta Mae (Mewbourne) Walker; m. Raymond Edward Kurtts, June 8, 1957; children—Karen Leigh Kurtts Alley, Laura Kathleen. Diploma, St. Vincent's Hosp. Sch. Nursing, Birmingham, 1957; student U. Ala.-Birmingham. R.N., Ala. Staff nurse VA Hosp., Birmingham, 1961-63, head nurse surg. service, 1963-65; head nurse surg. intensive care unit U. Ala. Hosps., Birmingham, 1966-67, dir. cardiovascular surg. nursing, 1967-70, dir. profl. standards rev. orgn./quality assurance, 1974—; dir. nursing service Medictrs. Am., Inc., Birmingham, 1971-74. Mem. exec. com. Birmingham Regional Health Systems Agy., 1976-82, sec. bd. dirs., chmn. nominating com., 1979-80, chmn. appropriateness rev. com., 1980-82; mem. Ala. Statewide Health Coordinating Council, 1976-81, vice chmn., 1979-80, chmn., 1980-81; bd. dirs. Family Med. Services, 1982—. Mem. Am. Nurses Assn., Ala. State Nurses Assn. (dist. 3 pres. 1975-76, Nurse of Year in Dist. 1973), Nat. Assn. Quality Assurance Profls., Nat. League for Nursing. Republican. Roman Catholic. Home: 448 Indian Crest Dr Helena AL 35080 Office: Dept Med Care Review U Ala Hosps 619 S 19th St Birmingham AL 35233

KURTZ, ANN WHITE, foreign languages educator; b. New Bedford, Mass.; d. Robert Clarke and Dorothy (Onthank) White; m. Lawrence A. Kurtz, Nov. 24, 1943; (divorced); children—Lawrence A. Kurtz, III, Margareta Kurtz Robens. A.B., Wellesley Coll., 1942; M.A., U. Md., 1951, Ph.D., 1956. Asst. prof. dept. fgn. langs. Old Dominion U., Norfolk, Va., 1960-63, U. Calif., Santa Barbara, 1963-65; lectr. U. Coll., Dublin, Ireland, 1971-74; assoc. prof. Damavand Coll., Tehran, Iran, 1975-79; chmn., prof. fgn. langs. dept. fgn. langs. Meredith Coll., Raleigh, N.C., 1979—; project dir. Fulbright Seminar, Japan, 1985; dir. summer study for Meredith students, 1981, 83. Author: America at a Glance, 1970. Translator: Kyoto, the Soul of Japan. Author: (poetry) Hibiscus Lei, 1949. Served to lt. (j.g.) USNR, 1942-44. Fulbright grantee, 1965; Fulbright seminar awardee, 1982. Mem. Am. Assn. Tchrs. German, Am. Assn. Tchrs. French, South Atlantic MLA, Phi Kappa Phi. Clubs: Tokyo Wellesley (pres. 1968-70), Japan-Am. Women's (v.p. 1969-70). Avocations: music; writing. Home: 1110 A Schaub Dr Raleigh NC 27606 Office: Meredith Coll Dept Fgn Langs Raleigh NC 27611

KURTZ, EDWIN BERNARD, biology educator, researcher; b. Wichita, Kans., Aug. 11, 1926; s. Edwin B. and Florence (Warner) K.; m. Lois L. Leecing, June 12, 1952 (dec. July 1984); children—Kathryn, Jane. B.S., U. Ariz., 1948, M.S., 1949; Ph.D., Calif. Inst. Tech., 1952. From asst. prof. to prof. U. Ariz., Tucson, 1951-68; prof., chmn. dept. Kans. State Tchrs. Coll., Emporia, 1968-72; prof. biology, chmn. dept. biology U. Tex.-Permian Basin, Odessa, 1972—. Author books, including: Adventures in Living Plants, 1965; Modules for Contemporary Natural Science I and II, 1978; also articles. Pres. Planned Parenthood of Permian Basin, Odessa, 1982-83. Recipient Amoco Found. Outstanding Tchr. award, 1982; NRC-AEC fellow Calif. Inst. Tech., Pasadena, 1949-51. Fellow AAAS (asst. dir. edn. 1964-67), Sigma Xi; mem. Phi Beta Kappa, Phi Kappa Phi. Unitarian. Avocation: gardening. Home: 3010 Windsor Odessa TX 79762 Office: U Tex-Permian Basin Odessa TX 79762

KURTZ, MYERS RICHARD, hospital administrator; b. Schaefferstown, Pa., June 18, 1924; div.; 1 child, Ronald Hayden. B.S., U. Md., 1958; M.B.A., Ind. U., 1963. Commd. 2d lt. U.S. Army, 1951, advanced through grades to lt. col., 1951-67; affiliation adminstr. N.Y. U. Med. Ctr., N.Y.C., 1967-69; exec. dir. Ephrata Community Hosp., Pa., 1969-76; supt. Longview State Hosp., Cin., 1976-79; asst. dir. Ohio Dept. Mental Health and Mental Retardation, Columbus, 1979-81, dir., 1981-82; sr. v.p. Metropolitan Gen. Hosp., Cleve., 1982-83; supt. chief exec. officer Central State Hosp., Milledgeville, Ga., 1983—. Adv. bd. Youth Devel. Ctr., Milledgeville, 1984—; bd. dirs. Milledgeville C. of C., 1984—. Decorated Soldiers Medal, Army Commendation Medal, Legion of Merit. Fellow Royal Soc. Health; mem. Am. Coll. Hosp. Adminstrs., Am. Hosp. Assn., Retired Officers Assn., Sigma Iota Epsilon. Club: Milledgeville Country. Lodges: Masons, Elks, Rotary (com. 1984—). Avocations: golf; hunting; sports. Home: 164 Annex Dr Milledgeville GA 31061 Office: Central State Hosp Swint Ave Milledgeville GA 31062

KURTZ-PAUL, DIANE, medical records transcription company executive; b. N.Y.C., Dec. 27, 1944; d. Abraham Herbert and Lillian Helen (Reis) Kurtz; m. Ronald David Paul, Jan. 12, 1974; 1 dau., Amy Deborah. Student pub. schs., North Miami, Fla. Free-lance med. transcriptionist, Miami, Fla., 1962-70; br. mgr. Med. Transcription Co., Miami, 1970-73; pres. All Points Transcribers, Inc., North Miami Beach, 1973—. Office: All Points Transcribers Inc 995 N Miami Beach Blvd North Miami Beach FL 33162

KURZER, MARTIN JOEL, lawyer; b. Milw., May 6, 1938; s. Louis and Clare (Steinberg) K.; m. Joy Ann Smith, June 16, 1963; children—Sandra Lois, Jody Renee. B.B.A., U. Wis.-Milw., 1960; J.D. cum laude, Marquette U., 1968; LL.M. in Taxation, U. Miami, 1971. Bar: Wis. 1968, Fla. 1968. Assoc. Blackwell, Walker, Gray, Powers, Flick, & Hoehl, Miami, Fla., 1968-72, jr. ptnr., 1973-77, gen. ptnr., 1978—; adj. prof. law, grad. tax dept. U. Miami, 1976-80; lectr. seminars and orgns. Author monthly column Health notes. Served to capt. USAF, 1960-69. Mem. Greater Miami Tax Inst. (sec. 1979, treas. 1980, 1st v.p. 1981, pres. 1982), Am. Assn. Atty.-C.P.A.s (dir. 1978—, treas. 1981-82, sec. 1982-83, v.p. 1983-84, 1st v.p. 1984-85), Nat. Health Lawyers Assn., Healthcare Fin. Mgmt. Assn., Fla. Assn. Atty.-C.P.A.s (dir. 1975—, v.p. 1975-81, exec. v.p. 1981—), S. Fla. Employee Benefits Council (sec. 1979-80), Fla. Bar Assn. (chmn. com. on relations with Fla. Inst. C.P.A.s 1981-82), ABA, Dade County Bar Assn., State Bar Wis., Fed. Bar Assn., Nat. Health Lawyers Assn., Am. Inst. C.P.A.s, Am. Soc. Hosp. Attys., Fla. Assn. Hosp. Attys., Fla. Inst. C.P.A.s. Jewish. Clubs: Miami, Miami Shores Country (adminstrn. bd. 1976). Home: 1532 NE 104th St Miami Shores FL 33138 Office: 2400 AmeriFirst Bldg One SE 3rd Ave Miami FL 33131

KUSCH, POLYKARP, physicist; b. Blankenburg, Germany, Jan. 26, 1911; s. John Matthias and Henrietta (van der Haas) K.; came to U.S., 1912, naturalized, 1922; B.S., Case Inst. Tech., 1931; D.Sc. 1956; M.S. U. Ill., 1933; Ph.D. 1936; D.Sc., 1961; D.Sc., Ohio State U., 1959; D.Sc., Colby Coll., 1961, Gustavus Adolphus Coll., St. Peter, Minn., 1963, Yeshiva U., 1976, Incarnate Word Coll., 1980, Columbia U., 1983; m. Edith Starr McRoberts, Aug. 12, 1935 (dec. 1959); children—Kathryn, Judith, Sara; m. Betty Jane Pezzoni, 1960; children—Diana, Maria. Engaged as asst. U. Ill. 1931-36; asst. U. Minn., 1936-37; instr. Columbia U., 1937-41, asso. prof. physics, 1946-49, prof., 1949-72, chmn. dept. physics, 1949-52, 60-63, acad. v.p. and provost, 1969-72; engr. Westinghouse, 1941-42; research asso. Columbia U., 1942-44; mem. tech. staff Bell Telephone Labs., 1944-46; prof. physics U. Tex.-Dallas, 1972—, Eugene McDermott prof., 1974-80, Regental prof., 1980-82, Regental prof. emeritus, 1982—. Recipient Nobel prize in physics, 1955; fellow Center for Advanced Study in Behavioral Sciences, 1964-65; Illini achievement award U. Ill., 1975. Fellow Am. Phys. Soc., AAAS; mem. Am. Acad. Arts and Scis., Am. Philos. Soc., Nat. Acad. Scis. Democrat. Research in atomic molecular and nuclear physics. Office: Dept Physics U Tex PO Box 830688 Richardson TX 75083

KUSHNER, LAWRENCE MAURICE, physical chemist; b. N.Y.C., Sept. 20, 1924; s. Hyman Tobias and Mary (Malkin) K.; m. Shirley Brown, June 24, 1972; m. Mildred Vernick, June 23, 1946; (div. Jan. 1970); children—Robb Adam, Leslie Meryl. B.S., Queens Coll., 1945; A.M., Princeton U., 1947, Ph.D., 1949. With Nat. Bur. Standards, Washington, 1948-73, 77-80, chief metal physics sect., 1956-61, chief metallurgy div., 1961-66, dep. dir. Inst. for Applied Tech., 1966-68, dep. dir., 1969-73; commr. U.S. Consumer Product Safety Commn., 1973-77; cons. scientist The Mitre Corp., McLean, Va., 1980—; adj. prof. engring. and pub. policy Carnegie Mellon U., Pitts., 1981—. Contbr. articles to profl. jours. Served with AUS, 1942-43. Fellow AAAS; mem. ASTM Materials (hon. life), Am. Chem. Soc., Fed. Profl. and Exec. Assn., Sigma Xi. Avocations: Photography, golf, travel. Office: Mitre Corp 1820 Dolley Madison Blvd McLean VA 22102

KUTAL, CHARLES RONALD, chemistry educator, researcher; b. Chgo., Aug. 9, 1944; s. Charles George and Mildred Marie (David) K.; m. Judy Gombos, Apr. 20, 1974; B.S. cum laude, Knox Coll., 1965; M.S., U. Ill.-Urbana, 1968, Ph.D., 1970. Postdoctoral research assoc. U. So. Calif., 1970-72; NRC fellow Aerospace Research Lab., Dayton, Ohio, 1972-73; instr. U. Ga.-Athens, 1973-75, asst. prof. chemistry, 1975-79, assoc. prof., 1979-85, prof., 1985—. Mem. Am. Chem. Soc. (Named Chemist of Year, N.E. Ga. Sect. 1979), AAAS, Inter-Am. Photochem. Soc., Sigma Xi (recipient Creative Research award U. Ga. chpt. 1979). Co-editor: Solar Energy: Chemical Conversion and Storage, 1979; contbr. articles to profl. jours. Office: Dept Chemistry U Ga Athens GA 30602

KUTCHER, FRANK EDWARD, JR., printing company executive; b. Teaneck, N.J., Dec. 20, 1927; s. Frank Edward and Helen Marie (Crowley) K.; m. Elizabeth Vespaziani, Jan. 19, 1952; children—Kenneth, Karen, Kristin. B.S. cum laude, Fairleigh Dickinson U., 1953. Mgmt. cons. Peat, Marwick, Mitchell & Co., Inc., 1961-63; controller Celanese Plastics Co., 1963-65, Pfister Chem. Co., Ridgefield, N.J., 1965-67; v.p. fin. Litton Industries, N.Y.C., 1967-70; v.p., controller McCall Pub. Co., Norton Simon, Inc., N.Y.C., 1970-73, also dir.; chmn., pres., chief operating officer Foote & Davies, Inc., Doraville, Ga., 1973—, also dir.; pres. Foote & Davies/Lincoln (Nebr.), 1978—; pres. Foote & Davies Transport Co., Doraville, 1973—; chmn. pres., chief exec. officer FDI Holdings, Inc., Doraville, 1985—. Served with USN, 1945-46. Mem. Graphic Arts Tech. Found. (bd. dirs. 1982—), Fin. Execs. Inst., Nat. Assn. Accts., Mensa. Clubs: Atlanta Athletic, Commerce, Ashford (Atlanta); Atrium (N.Y.C.). Office: Foote & Davies Inc 3101 McCall Dr Doraville GA 30340

KUTELL, MICHAEL ALLEN, hematologist; b. N.Y.C., Dec. 24, 1940; s. Jesse and Mildred Julie (Dahlman) K.; m. Harriet Beitch, Aug. 29, 1960; children—Fredric, Adam, Benjamin. B.A., Alfred U., 1961; M.D., Jefferson Med. Coll., 1965. Diplomate Am. Bd. Internal Medicine. Intern, Kings County Hosp., Bklyn., 1965-66, resident, 1966-69; resident Baylor Med. Coll., Houston, 1969-71; practice medicine, specializing in internal medicine, hematology Internal Medicine Assocs., Miami Springs, Fla., 1971—; dir. med. edn. Hialeah Hosp., Fla., 1974—, chief internal medicine, 1980-82. Trustee, Leukemia Soc. Am., Miami, 1973—; bd. dirs. Am. Cancer Soc., Miami, 1978—, mem. profl. edn. com., 1978—; cubmaster Boy Scouts Am., Miami, 1977-80. Served to capt. USAF, 1967-69. Recipient Mosby award Jefferson Med. Coll., 1965; Nat. Cancer Inst. grantee, 1967. Mem. Am. Soc. Hematology, ACP, Am. Soc. Clin. Oncology, Am. Soc. Internal Medicine, Dade County Med. Soc. Republican. Jewish. Avocations: marathon running; reading; fishing. Home: 14517 SW 83 St Miami FL 33183 Office: Internal Medicine Assocs 232 Westward Dr Miami Springs FL 33166

KUYKENDALL, JERRY DEAN, advertising agency executive; b. Cushing, Okla., Sept. 25, 1941; s. Charles and Velma R. (Senft) K.; m. Mary Ann Williams, July 26, 1964; children—Kristian, Kyle. Student pub. schs., Olney, Ill. Prop boy, cameraman, projectionist, dir. comml. coordinator, to gen. sales mgr. Sta. WKYT-TV, Lexington, Ky., 1960-75; pres. Kuykendall & Co., Lexington, 1978—, Paddock Pub. Inc., Lexington, 1979—; pub. Lexington: As It Was, 1981; Keeneland mag., 1979—, Red Mile mag., 1983—. Bd. dirs. Better Bus. Bur., Lexington, 1970-71; chmn. Antioch Ch., 1983-84. Served with USAR, 1958-66. Mem. C. of C., U. Ky. Fellows, also others. Democrat. Mem. Christian Ch. Clubs: Lafayette, Thoroughbred of Am., Kenneland Assn., Spindletop Hall. Office: 904 N Broadway Lexington KY 40505

KUYKENDALL, PATRICIA ANNE, hospital administrator, nurse; b. Kewanee, Ill., Mar. 27, 1935; d. Samuel Burton and Theresa Marie (McEnroe) Ensley; m. James Kennith Kuykendall, Jan. 18, 1972; 1 child, Jay Kirk. B.S.N., Incarnate Word Coll., San Antonio, 1960; M.S.N., St. Louis U., 1965. Asst. dir. nursing Barnes Hosp., St. Louis, 1965-69, dir. staff devel., 1969-74; program dir. Nat. Cancer Inst. program M.D. Anderson Hosp., Houston, 1974-77; dir. nursing U. Tex. Med. Br. Hosps., Galveston, 1977-80, exec. dir., 1980—. Bd. dirs. Hospice Group, Galveston, 1985-86. Named to Leadership Tex., Tex. Women's Resources, Austin, 1984; Johnson & Johnson-Wharton Sch. fellow U. Pa., Phila., 1983. Mem. Am. Hosp. Assn., Am. Soc. Nursing Service Adminstrn., Tex. Hosp. Assn., U. Tex. Med. Br. Women's Faculty Assn., Am. Bus. Women's Assn. (local treas. 1984-85), Sigma Theta Tau (local treas. 1977-79). Home: 15542 Edenvale Friendswood TX 77546 Office: U Tex Med Br 8th and Mechanic Galveston TX 77550

KUYKENDALL, RONALD EDWARD, lawyer; b. Lincolnton, N.C., Dec. 24, 1952; s. Ellis Clingman Jr. and Dorothy Mae (Leatherman) K.; m. Julie Elizabeth Maconaughay, Mar. 28, 1981; children—Erin Elizabeth, Laura Anne. B.A. with distinction, U. Va., 1975; J.D., U. Richmond, 1978. Bar: Va. 1978, U.S. Dist. Ct. Va. 1978, U.S. Ct. Appeals (4th cir.) 1978, U.S. Supreme Ct. 1981. Law clk. to presiding justice Va. Supreme Ct., Richmond, 1978-79; assoc. Parker, Pillard & Brown, P.C., Richmond, 1979-82; assoc. Minor & Lemons, P.C., Richmond, 1982-83; ptnr., Minor & Kuykendall, P.C., Richmond, 1984—. Mem. Law Rev., Moot Ct. Bd., U. Richmond. Mem. Assn. Trial Lawyers Am., Va. Trial Lawyers Assn., Richmond Trial Lawyers Assn., Va. Bar Assn., Henrico County Bar Assn., Richmond Bar Assn., ABA (litigation and gen. practice sects.), Christian Legal Soc., Baptist. Office: Minor & Kuykendall PC 8001 W Broad St Richmond VA 23229

KVINTA, CHARLES JAMES, lawyer; b. Hallettsville, Tex., Feb. 16, 1932; s. John F. and Emily P. (Strauss) K.; B.A., U. Tex., 1954, LL.B., 1959; m. Margie N. Brenek, Oct. 9, 1954; children—Charles James, Sherri A., Kenneth E., Chris E. Bar: Tex. 1959. Pvt. practice, Yoakum, 1960—; city atty. Yoakum, 1977—; cons. to industry. Founder Bluebonnet Youth Ranch, 1968, pres., 1968-75; mem. St. Joseph's Cath. Sch. Bd., 1970; chmn. fund raising campaign Boy Scouts Am.; 1968—, pres., Yoakum Ind. Sch. Dist., mem. 1975-83; dir., mgr. Yoakum Little League, Yoakum Teenage League. Served as 1st lt. AUS, 1954-55. Recipient Outstanding Service award Sons of Hermann, Yoakum Little League, Bluebonnet Youth Ranch; Appreciation award Yoakum Lions Club, Vocat. FFA, Am. Cancer Soc., Boy Scouts Am.; Outstanding Service award Athletic Dept., Yoakum Ind. Sch. Dist. Mem. State Bar Tex., Yoakum C. of C. (dir.), Am. Legion. Democrat. Club: KC. Home: 713 Coke St Yoakum TX 77995 Office: 413 W Grand St Yoakum TX 77995

KWASHA, H. CHARLES, consulting actuary; b. Providence, Dec. 2, 1906; s. Barned and Lena (Lisker) K.; m. Sylvia I. Herman, Aug. 20, 1939; children—Linda Dianne, Bruce Charles, Robert Dexter. A.B., Brown U., 1928. Mem. faculty Brown U., 1929; actuary Travelers Ins. Co., 1929-37; head pension dept. Marsh and McLennan, Inc., 1937-44; organized firm, cons. actuarial work H. Charles Kwasha, cons. actuary, 1944; ptnr. Kwasha Lipton, 1947—. Mem. Soc. Actuaries, Phi Beta Kappa, Sigma Xi. Phi Beta Kappa. Author articles on employee retirement, employee benefit programs. Office: Kwasha Lipton 9999 NE 2d Ave Suite 118 Miami Shores FL 33138

KYKER, CHRIS WHITE, state official; b. Temple, Tex., Mar. 30, 1925; d. Labon Edmondson and Grace Mae (Wrye) White; m. Rex Paxton Kyker, Sept. 1, 1946; children—Jerilyn Kyker Pfeifer, Robert Paxton, Melinda Lea Kyker Fullerton, Jan Christi Kyker Bryan, Richard Morris. B.A., Abilene Christian U., 1946, M.S., 1959, M.A., 1960. Instr. Abilene (Tex.) Christian U., 1946-50, part-time, 1954-63; guest lectr. Hardin-Simmons U., Abilene, 1970-74; exec. dir. Abilene Assn. for Mental Health, 1963-74; dir. West Central Tex. Council of Govts., Area Agy. on Aging, Abilene, 1974-79; exec. dir. Tex. Gov.'s Com. on Aging, Austin, 1979-81; exec. dir. Tex. Dept. on Aging, Austin, 1981-84; program specialist family and children services Tex. Dept. Human Services, 1984—; lectr. in field: Tex. coordinator White House Conf. on Aging, 1981; pres. Nat. Mental Health Assn. Staff Council, 1974, Tex. Mental Health Assn. Staff Council, 1973, Tex. Assn. of Area Agy. on Aging Dirs., 1976. Recipient Alumni award Abilene Christian U., 1980. Mem. S.W. Soc. on Aging (charter bd. dirs. and treas. 1978-82), Nat. Assn. State Units on Aging (chmn. staff devel. and discretionary grants 1983). Mem. Ch. of Christ. Office: PO Box 2960 Austin TX 78769

KYRA, artist, educator; b. Harbin, China (parents Am. citizens); B.F.A., Ariz. State U., 1973; M.F.A., Fla. State U., 1975. Mem. faculty Broward Community Coll., Pembroke Pines, Fla., 1975—, dept. chmn. humanities, 1981-83, gallery dir., 1981—; mem. faculty Miami-Dade Community Coll., 1975, Barry U., Miami, Fla., 1981-82; lectr. and cons. in field; one-woman shows Artful Dodger Gallery, Tallahassee, 1975, Bainbridge Jr. Coll., 1975, The Gallery, Fla. State U., 1975, William D. Pawley Creative Arts Ctr., 1976, Womanart Gallery, N.Y.C., 1977, 78, An Alternative Gallery, Miami, 1979, A.I.R. Gallery, N.Y.C., 1979, Art and Culture Ctr. Hollywood, 1980, Fla. Atlantic U. Library, Boca Raton, 1981, Broward Community Coll., 1982, Fine Arts Gallery, Broward Community Coll., 1977, 1982, The Gallery, Bailey Hall, 1983; exhibited in group shows Gallery 741, 1975, Burdines Gallery, 1975, Boca Raton Ctr. for Arts, 1976, Grove House, 1976, 81, Lowe Art Mus., 1976, U. Miami, 1977, Avery Fisher Hall, Lincoln Ctr., 1977, Soho 20 Gallery, 1977, Womanart Gallery, 1977, An Alternative Gallery, 1978, Grove House South Gallery, 1978, Jeanne Taylor Gallery, 1978, Long Galleries, 1978, Womanart Galleries, 1978, Broward Art Guild, 1979, Hanson Galleries, 1980, Aventura Libary, 1980, Lowe-Levinson Gallery, 1980, Alain Bilhaud Gallery, 1981, Barry U., 1981, Nova U., 1982, Mus. Art, Ft. Lauderdale, 1982, Continuum Gallery, 1982, Broward Community Coll., 1983, Art and Culture Ctr. of Hollywood, 1983, numerous others. Fla. Art Council fellow 1982-83; Broward Art in Pub. Places Commn. for So. Regional Courthouse, Hollywood, 1981; named Outstanding Artist of S.E., Am. Art/S.E., 1978; Gene Segal award Sta. WPBT-TV, 1981, Ltd. Edit. award, 1980, 1st Nationwide Savs. award, 1982, numerous juried arts awards. Mem. Women's Caucus for Art (dir. Fla. chpt.), Coalition Women's Art Orgns. (nat. dir.), Fla. Assn. Community Colls., AAUP (dir. Fla. chpt.), Coll. Art Assn. Am., Democrat. Contbr. articles to profl. jours. Home: PO Box 6735 Hollywood FL 33021 Office: Broward Community Coll 7200 Hollywood Blvd Pembroke Pines FL 33024

KYZAR, OLLIE JEANETTE, educator; b. Brookhaven, Miss., Oct. 7, 1933; d. Marcel Wooden and Annie Leona (Brister) Grice; m. Reese Eugene Kyzar, June 16, 1953. B.S. in Edn., Delta State Coll., 1960, postgrad., 1972-74, 79-81; postgrad. U. So. Miss., 1960-61, 65-66, 69-70, U. Miss., 1961-63. Tchr. English, Fielding L. Wright High Sch., Rolling Fork, Miss., 1960-61; tchr. Fielding L. Wright Elem. Sch., Rolling Fork, 1961-70; homebound tchr. Rolling Fork Elem. Sch., 1970-73, tchr. reading and math., 1973-84, resource tchr. computer assisted instrn., 1984—; evaluator Nat. Council Accreditation Tchr. Edn., Washington, 1982—; mem. supt.'s adv. bd., Rolling Fork, 1981-83; mem. steering com. on sch. evaluation So. Assn. Colls. and Schs., 1962-73. Sunday sch. tchr., former dir. Acteens, mem. Womens Missionary Union, 1st Baptis Ch. Rolling Fork, 1959. Mem. Smithsonian Instn. (assoc.), Nat. Trust Historic Preservation, Fielding L. Wright Tchrs. Assn. (pres. 1966-67), Rolling Fork Assn. Educators (pres. 1977-78, 81-82, Disting. Service award 1978, 82), Miss. Assn. Educators (workshop presenter 1982-84), NEA, Miss. Ednl. Computing Assn., Internat. Reading Assn., Miss. Reading Assn., Kappa Delta Pi. Avocations: reading; listening to music; walking; riding bicycle. Home: 105 N 2nd St Rolling Fork MS 39159 Office: Rolling Fork Elem Sch 600 South Pkwy Rolling Fork MS 39159

LABEN, JOYCE KEMP, nursing educator; b. Elgin, Ill., Mar. 2, 1936; d. Berton John and Lois Elizabeth (Heath) Kemp; B.S.N., U. Mich., 1957; M.S.N., U. Calif., San Francisco, 1963; J.D., Suffolk U., 1969; m. Robert J. Laben, Feb. 27, 1971. Nurse, U. Calif. San Francisco Med. Center, 1957-59, 61-62; surg./office nurse, San Francisco, 1960-61; instr. Boston State Hosp., 1964-65; asst. prof. Sch. Nursing, Boston U., 1965-70; assoc. prof. Sch. Nursing, Vanderbilt U., Nashville, 1970-78, prof., 1978—, chmn. behavioral scis. as applied to nursing, 1975-81, acting asso. dean undergrad. studies, 1981-82, asso. dean undergrad. studies, 1982—, pres. women's faculty orgn., 1980-81. Dir. forensic services sect. Tenn. Dept. Mental Health, Nashville, 1972-74; cons. Tenn. Dept. Mental Health/Mental Retardation, 1974—, others; mem. task force panel Pres.' Commn. on Mental Health, 1977. Bd. dirs., v.p. Opportunity House, Nashville, 1973-80; bd. dirs. Nat. Commn. on Confidentiality of Health Records, 1976-79. Recipient Cert. of Spl. Recognition, Tenn. Dept. Mental Health, 1974; Mem. Am. Nurses Assn. (spl. recognition award 1980), mem. council advanced practitioners in psychiat./mental health nursing, AAUP, Am. Orthopsychiat. Assn., Am. Assn. Nurse-Attys., Am. Soc. Law and Medicine. Contbr. articles to profl. jours. Home: 301 Tanglewood Dr Mount Juliet TN 37122 Office: Godchaux Hall Vanderbilt U Nashville TN 37240

LABOON, JOE T., utility executive; b. Monroe, Ga., 1920. B.M.E., Ga. Inst. Tech., 1948; LL.B., Woodrow Wilson Coll. Law, 1952. With Atlanta Gas Light Co., 1939—, v.p., 1962-74, sr. v.p., 1974-76, pres., 1976-80, pres., chief exec. officer, 1980—, also dir.; dir. John H. Harland Co., First Nat Bank Atlanta. Office: 235 Peachtree St NE Atlanta GA 30302

LABORDE, JOHN P., corporate executive; b. Marskville, La., 1923. B.S., La. State U., 1944, LL.B., 1949. Practice law, 1949-56; pres., chief exec. officer Tidewater Marine Service Inc. subs. Tidewater Inc., New Orleans, 1956-69, chmn., pres., chief exec. officer, 1969-80, chmn., chief exec. officer, 1980—, chmn. bd., chief exec. officer, parent co., New Orleans, also dir.; dir. Hibernia Nat. Bank, New Orleans, Am. Bankers Ins. Group Inc., United Energy Resources Inc. Served to capt. U.S. Army, 1944-47. Office: Tidewater Inc 1440 Canal St New Orleans LA 70112*

LABORDE, MARY PURCELL, club woman, retired educator; b. Pelican, La., May 19, 1905; d. George Dowell and Ela Lee (Browne) Purcell; Christian culture diploma M.E. Ch. S., 1922; Lic. instr. Mansfield (L.I.) Female Coll., 1923; postgrad. La. State U., 1924, 45, Centenary Coll., 1925-26; cert. N.Y. Sch. Interior Decorating, 1931; B.A., Nicholls State Coll.; m. Joseph Gaston LaBorde, Apr. 24, 1926; 1 son, Joseph Newton. Tchr., Caldwell Parish, La., 1923-25, S. Highlands Sch., Shreveport, La., 1925-26, Lady of Mercy Sch., Baton Rouge, 1958-60, St. Theresa's Sch., Shreveport, 1960-61, Trinity Elem. Sch., Baton Rouge, 1969-70; active in glee club, ch. and club music; 2d v.p. UDC, Henry W. Allen chpt., Baton Rouge, 1960-61, 3d v.p. Martha Ried chpt., 1954-57; bd. dirs. Emma Gayle McFadden chpt. Children of Confederacy, Jacksonville, Fla., 1955-57, dir. John McGrath chpt., Baton Rouge, 1958-60, organizing dir. G.B. Saucier chpt., 1974-76; mem. and del. Katherine Livingston chpt. DAR, Jacksonville, 1949-52, del. nat. congress, 1950-63, treas. Kan Yuk Sa, 1955-57, del. state conf., 1964; chmn. music La. 6th dist. La. Fedn. Women's Clubs, 1974-76; organized Jr. Nat. Soc. Sons and Daus. of Pilgrims; active Gray Ladies ARC; mem. Confederate Mus., Richmond, Va., 1971-72; hostess Found. for Hist. La., 1965-71. Recipient awards (2) Nat. Soc. So. Dames Am., 1966; Medal of Mert, Presidential Task Force, 1984. Mem. Descs. Knights of Garter, Plantagenet Soc., Ams. Royal Descent, Nat. Trust Hist. Preservation, Magna Charta Dames (v.p. La. Soc. 1967-69, rec. sec. 1974—), Nat. Soc. Sons. and Daus. of Pilgrims (gov. La. br. 1962-64, nat. rec. sec. 1965-66, del. nat. congress 1963, del. Gen. Ct., state registrar 1968-70), Nat. Soc. So. Dames (award 1966, charter; La. eye bank chmn. 1964-65, v.p. La. 1964-65, award of merit 1967), UDC (nat. com. preservation hist. sites and records 1967-68, nat. and state geneal. records, 1967-69, rec. sec. H.W. Allen chpt. 1966-67, chmn. music 1967-68), W.S.C.S., Tchrs. Assn., La. Parliamentarins, Nat. Assn. Parliamentarians, First Families of Am., 1974-75, Huguenot Soc. La. (compiled handbook; state registrar 1975-77), Marquis Biog. Library Soc. (adv.), Washington Family Descs., Tex. Geneal. Soc., Epsilon Sigma Omicron (chpt. book reviewer 1974-77). Methodist (youth dir.). Clubs: Music, Baton Rouge Women's, Baton Rouge Music, Order of Crown, High Heritage. Home: 11645 Archery Dr Baton Rouge LA 70815

LABORDE, PEGGY LYNN, antique furniture consultant, microbiologist; b. New Orleans, Nov. 20, 1951; d. Lyle Yves and Elvera Theresa (Messina) LeCorgne; m. John P. Laborde, Sept. 21, 1974; children—Eric Lanning, Blayne Yves. B.S. in Med. Tech. cum laude, Loyola U., New Orleans, 1973. Lic. med. technologist. Hematologist, night advisor Hotel Dieu Hosp., New Orleans, 1972-73, Touro Hosp., New Orleans, 1973; microbiologist St. Joseph Hosp.,

Houston, 1974-76; technologist New Orleans Blood Bank, 1976-77; antique furniture cons., New Orleans, 1980—; docent Hermann-Grima Hist. Home, New Orleans, 1982-83. Bd. dirs. Juenesse D' Orleans, 1982—; v.p. adminstrn., treas. Symphony, New Orleans, 1982-85; co-chmn. childrens hosp. fundraiser, New Orleans, 1986; merchandising co-chmn. Sta. WLAE Pub. Broadcasting, New Orleans, 1985; com. head City Park, Cystic Fibrosis Found., Audubon Zoo, St. Elizabeth's Guild; mem. adv. bd. antique show Multiple Sclerosis Soc., 1983; mem. Spl. Donors com. United Way, 1985; 1st v.p. Patrons of Vatican Mus. of South, Inc., 1985. Mem. Jr. League (chmn. computer services 1983-84), Am. Assn. Clin. Pathologists, Cardinal Key Soc., Classy Assets Investment (treas. 1982-83, 84-85), Delta Epsilon Sigma; Beta Epsilon Upsilon. Democrat. Roman Catholic. Avocations: golf; horticultural work; swimming.

LA BRECQUE, RICHARD THEODORE, educator; b. Quincy, Mass., Jan. 23, 1933; s. Richard Theodore and Edith Knowlton (Haslett) La B.; divorced; children—Leslie, Margaret. B.S., Boston U., 1959, Ed.D., 1971; M.A.T., Harvard U., 1960. Tng. officer U.S. C.E., Ft. Belvoir, Va., 1961-63, GSA, Washington, 1963-65; employee devel. officer AID, Washington, 1965-68; asst. prof. edn. Salem State U., Mass., 1968-70; asst. prof. U. Ky., Lexington, 1970-75, assoc. prof., 1975—. Co-author: Culture As Education, 1977; also articles. Served with USN, 1951-55. Vis. scholar U. London, 1976, 84. Fellow Philosophy of Edn. Soc., Philosophy of Edn. Soc. Gt. Brit.; mem. Am. Ednl. Research Assn., Am. Ednl. Studies Assn., John Dewey Soc. Democrat. Unitarian. Avocations: boating; photgraphy. Home: 439 Carlisle Ave Lexington KY 40505 Office: U Ky Coll Edn Lexington KY 40506

LABUDDE, ROBERT ARTHUR, software company executive, engineering company executive; b. Flint, Mich., May 28, 1947; s. Verne M. and Adeline M. (Essa) LaB.; m. Constance M. Miller, Apr. 11, 1969; children—Philip V., Zina M. B.S., U. Mich., 1969; Ph.D., U. Wis., 1973. Lectr. computer sci. U. Wis., Madison, 1973; asst. scientist Math. Research Ctr., Madison, 1973-74; instr. applied math. MIT, Cambridge, 1974-75; asst. prof. Old Dominion U., Norfolk, Va., 1976-79; exec. v.p. LaBudde Engring. Corp., Westlake Village, Calif., 1983—; pres., chmn. bd. Least Cost Formulations, Ltd., Virginia Beach, Va., 1979—; sec. ERB Leasing Co., Inc., Westlake Village, Calif., 1983—; tech. cons. IBM Corp., Atlanta, 1975-78; cons. Allied Corp., Morristown, N.J., 1977-78, Burroughs Corp., Westlake Village, Calif., 1980-82, Optical Coating Labs., Inc., Santa Rosa, Calif., 1982-83, Digital Design Labs., Norfolk, Va., 1979. Author computer programs; contbr. articles to profl. jours. Patentee in field. Mem. Soc. Indsl. and Applied Math., Assn. Computing Machinery, AAAS, Assn. Ofcl. Analytical Chemists, Inst. Food Technologists, Phi Beta Kappa, Sigma Xi, Phi Kappa Phi, Phi Lambda Upsilon. Office: Least Cost Formulations Ltd 821 Hialeah Dr Virginia Beach VA 23464

LACAFF, REGINA MAE KIRKLAND, educator; b. Twin Falls, Idaho, Oct. 4, 1946; d. Troy Leonard and Rose (Spreier) K.; B.A., Ariz. State U., 1968; M.A., U. Central Fla., 1980; m. William King Lacaff, Nov. 23, 1968. Tchr. Carver Elem. Sch., Little Rock, 1970-73, Montessori Sch., Calabasas, Calif., 1973-75, Dawson Sch., Columbus, Ga., 1975-77; math. remediation tchr. Stonewall Jackson Jr. High Sch., Orlando, Fla., 1978, tchr. math., 1978-82, chmn. faculty-staff relations, 1978-80, guidance com. chmn., 1980-81, tennis coach, 1980-82; owner La Math Tutoring Service. Mem. Nat. Council Tchrs. Math., Fla. Council Tchrs. Math., Orange County Council Tchrs. Math., Fla. League Middle Schs., Council Elem. Math. Specialists, Okla. State Alumni Assn., Fla. Teaching Profession, NEA, Assn. Supervision and Curriculum Devel., U. Central Fla. Alumni Assn., Kappa Delta Pi, Delta Kappa Gamma, Kappa Delta. Home: 208 Sweet Gum Way Longwood FL 32750 Office: Financial Security Corp Am 341 N Maitland Ave Maitland FL 32751

LACANCELLERA, GEORGE, architectural technology consultant, lecturer, educator; b. N.Y.C., Apr. 5, 1930; s. George Lacancellera and Maria (Parcelluzzi) Lacancellera Lofaro; m. Virginia Joan Trolan, Feb. 22, 1958; 1 child, Maria Julia. Ph.D. in Architecture, Kensington U., 1983. Archtl. engr. various archtl.-engring. firms, N.Y.C., 1950-60; assoc. E.D. Stone & Assocs., N.Y.C., 1960-69; archtl. tech. cons. George Lacancellera, Inc., Boca Raton, Fla., 1969—; adj. prof. Kensington U., Glendale, Calif., 1984—; lectr. Fla. Atlantic U., Boca Raton, 1984—. Co-editor: Dictionary of Architecture, 1975. Bd. dirs. Boca Raton Acad., 1979. Served with USNG, 1951-62. Recipient awards Constrn. Specifications Inst., 1974—. Assoc. mem. AIA. Republican. Roman Catholic. Avocations: photography; gardening; boating; travel. Home: 230 E Camino Real Boca Raton FL 33432

LACAYO, RAUL ANTONIO, financial institutions consultant; b. Managua, Nicaragua, Apr. 12, 1949; came to U.S., Jan. 10, 1982; s. Raul Gonzalo and Myriam (Solorzano) L.; m. Leslie, June 23, 1984. B.A., Duke U., 1970; M.A., Yale U., 1971; postgrad., Cornell U., 1971-73. Dir. fin. dept. Central Bank of Nicaragua, Managua, 1974-78; gen. mgr., chief exec. officer Azucarera Monte Rosa, Managua, 1978-81; investments mgr. Agropecuaria Miravalle, San José, Costa Rica, Miami 1981-83; econ. cons. Totalbank Corp., Miami, Fla., 1983-84; sr. cons. Deloitte Haskins & Sells, Miami, 1984—; dir. Nicaragua AM Pvt. Enterprise Council, Miami, 1985—; bd. dirs. Nicaragua Inst. for Devel., Managua, 1978, 80. Central Bank of Nicaragua fellow, Managua, 1971-73. Mem. Econ. Soc. of South Fla., Internat. Ctr. of Fla. Roman Catholic. Avocations: scuba diving; tennis.

LACERDA, GAYLE QUINN, training specialist; b. Galveston, Tex., Mar. 30, 1948; d. Ryce J. and Vivian L. (Henry) Byrd; m. Ernest Lee Quinn, Jan. 20, 1965 (div. June 1972); children—Rhonda Elizabeth, Lisa Bayle; m. David A. Lacerda, May 13, 1977. Student Coll. Mainland, Tex., 1977-81. Program dir. Gulf Coast Mental Health/Mental Retardation, Galveston, Tex., 1977-79, U. Tex. Med. Bd., Galveston, 1979-81; staff coordinator Career Works, Inc., Ft. Worth, 1981-82; personnel specialist City of Arlington, Tex., 1983—; cons. in field. Chair, Arlington Task Force Drugs and Alcohol, 1984. Mem. Am. Soc. Tng. and Devel. (v.p. chpt. devel. 1984—). Avocations: running; skiing. Home: 4312 Willow Bend Dr Arlington TX 76017 Office: PO Box 231 Arlington TX 76010

LACEY, NEAL, JR., architect; b. Dallas, Jan. 12, 1931; s. Neal Terry and Julia (Walker) L.; m. Sarah Anne Luger, Sept. 13, 1958; children—Nelson Karl, Anne Paxton, John Andrew. B.A., Rice U., 1952, B.S. with distinction, 1953; M.Arch., U. Tex., 1954. Lic. architect, Tex. Ptnr., Pierce, Lacey Architects, Dallas, 1963-78, PLM Design, Inc., Dallas, 1978—. Trustee St. Mark's Sch. of Tex., Dallas, 1976—; bd. govs. Rice U., Houston, 1982—. Recipient Awards of Merit for bldg. designs. Mem. Tex. Soc. Architects (12 awards), AIA (Dallas chpt). Office: PLM Design Inc 2001 Ross Ave Dallas TX 75201

LACKEY, LARRY ALTON, lawyer; b. Galax, Va., Aug. 24, 1940; s. Alton and Reba Mae (Phipps) L.; B.S. in Accountancy, Southeastern U., 1962, postgrad. in Bus. Adminstrn., 1962; LL.D., (hon.), Midwestern U., 1963; diploma in advanced accountancy La Salle U., Chgo., 1965, LL.B., 1965; Ph.D. in Bus. Adminstrn., Calif. Pacific U., 1977; m. Ilene Jane Minhinnett, June 7, 1963; children—Larry Alton, Teresa Ann, Lisa Marie. Asst. proof dept. Riggs Nat. Bank, Washington, 1958-59, bookkeeper corp. accounts, also comml. accounts teller, 1959, asst. head teller, 1959-60; asst. head teller, then head teller and head note teller, also br. asst. Old Dominion Bank, Arlington, Va., 1960-61; pub. acct., bus. mgmt. analyst, Washington, 1961-68; dir. accounting, treas. W.W. Chambers Co. Inc., undertaking, Washington, 1968-69; exec. v.p., gen. mgr. Old Dominion Casket Co. Inc., Washington, 1969-70; sr. ops. analyst Macke Corp., vending and food service, Washington, 1970-71, asst. dir. corp. taxes, 1970-71; bd. dirs. Hamilton Bank & Trust Co., 1973-75; pub. accountant, tax analyst, bus. mgmt. counselor, efficiency analyst firm Mervin G. Hall Co., Oakton, Va., 1971, founder Bus. Mgmt. Services div., fin. analysis, 1971; chmn. bd. dirs. Internat. Moving & Storage Co. Inc.; pres., chmn. bd. dirs. Key Investment Corp.; sec., dir., founder, ALA Corp., nat. automotive system chain, 1975. Instr. Boyd Sch. of Bus., 1969-71, also trustee; spl. lectr. pub. high schs., Arlington County, Va., 1970-72; spl. cons. Commonwealth Doctors Hosp., Fairfax, Va., 1973—; founder, pres. Bus. Mgmt. Inst., 1978—. Treas., v.p. Camp Springs (Md.) Civic Assn., 1971-73; sec.-treas. Camp Springs Boys Club, 1971-73; baseball asst. Little League, Annandale, Va., 1974-76; trustee Calif. Pacific U., 1977—. Mem. Annandale Jaycees. Republican. Roman Catholic. Author: How To Start A Small Business, 1971.

LACKLAND, THEODORE HOWARD, lawyer; b. Chgo., Dec. 4, 1943; s. Richard and Cora Lee (Sanders) L.; m. Dorothy Ann Gerald, Jan. 2, 1970; 1 child, Jennifer Noel. B.S., Loyola U., Chgo., 1965; M.A., Howard U., 1967; J.D., Columbia U., 1975. Bar: N.J. 1975, N.Y. 1975, U.S. Dist. Ct. N.J. 1975, Ga. 1982, U.S. Tax Ct. 1983, U.S. Supreme Ct. 1979, U.S. Dist. Ct. (no. dist.) Ga. 1982, U.S. Dist. Ct. (mid. dist.) Ga. 1985. Assoc. Dewey, Ballantine, Bushby, Palmer & Wood, N.Y.C., 1975-78; asst. U.S. atty. Dist. N.J., Newark, 1978-81; ptnr. Arnall Golden & Gregory, Atlanta, 1981—. Contbr. articles to profl. jours. Adv. dir. Atlanta Bus. Devel. Ctr., Minority Bus. Devel. Council, Atlanta, 1983—, Leadership Atlanta, 1986. Served with U.S. Army, 1967-71. Decorated Bronze Star (2), Purple Heart, Air Medal, Army Commendation medal. Mem. ABA, N.J. Bar Assn., Ga. Bar Assn., Fed. Bar Assn., Gate City Bar Assn. Democrat. Roman Catholic. Home: 4400 Oak Ln Marietta GA 30062 Office: Arnall Golden & Gregory 55 Park Pl Atlanta GA 30335

LACOMBA, ERNESTO ALEJANDRO, mathematics educator, researcher; b. Mexico City, Mex., Dec. 2, 1945; s. Antonio and Catalina (Zamora) L.; m. Ruth Susana Krivorucoff, June 27, 1971; 1 child, Rossana. B.A. in Engring., Polytech. Inst., Mexico City, 1966, B.A. in Physics and Math., 1968; Ph.D. in Math., U. Calif.-Berkeley, 1972. Lectr. Poly. Inst., Mexico City, 1966-68; asst. Mex. Oil Inst., Mexico City, 1967-68; asst. prof. U. Brasilia, Brazil, 1972-73; assoc. researcher U. Nacional de Mex., Mexico City, 1973-74; vis. researcher U. Dijon, France, 1980-81; prof. math. U. Autónoma Metropolitana, Mexico City, 1974—, coordinator master degree program, 1976-80, 82-85, research team dir., 1984—. Contbr. chpts. to books, articles to profl. jours. Mem. Mex. Com. Mathematicians to Free Massera, Mexico City, 1978-84. Tufts U. fellow, 1972-73; grantee Conacyt, 1976—; grantee Ministry Pub. Edn., 1984-85, Nat. Research fellow, 1984-87; recipient Hon. Mention for research OAS, 1985. Mem. Sociedad Mathemática Mexicana (rev. papers editor 1978-84, mem. grant assignment com. 1985), Am. Math. Soc., Math. Assn. Am., Academia de la Investigación Científica, Sigma Xi. Jewish. Avocations: baking bread; gardening; hiking; traveling. Home: Jalcomulco 4 Col La Presilla Mexico DF Mexico 10510 Office: U Autónoma Metropolitana Dept Math Apdo Postal 55-534 Mexico DF 09340 Mexico

LACOMBE, RAYMOND DANIEL, banking executive, economist, consultant; b. N.Y.C., Sept. 22, 1925; s. Edward and Marie (Schwang) LaC.; m. Doris Jean Colelli. B.B.A., CUNY, 1949, M.B.A., 1950; Ph.D., NYU, 1957. Economist UN, N.Y.C., 1950-53; dept. mgr. U.S. Dept. Def., Dover, N.J., 1953-56; mgr. research dept. Am. Ins. Assn., N.Y., 1956-65; v.p., economist Amerifirst, Miami, Fla., 1965-81, Barnett Bank, Miami, 1981-83; sr. v.p., economist Profl. Savs. Bank, Coral Gables, Fla., 1983—; dir., exec. v.p. Econ. Soc., 1973—; dir. Air Ride Craft, Miami, 1980—. Contbr. articles to profl. jours. SUNY scholar, 1949. Republican. Roman Catholic. Club: Miami Shores Country (pres. 1979). Avocations: reading; music; tennis. Home: 1500 NE 105 St Miami Shores FL 33138 Office: Profl Savings Bank 3001 Ponce de Leon Blvd Coral Gables FL 33134

LACY, ALLEN WAYNE, economics educator; b. Huntsville, Ala., Oct. 14, 1938; s. Allen Luther and Betty Isabelle (Sharp) L.; m. Nancy Jean Cira, Apr. 2, 1960; children—Valerie Lynn Lacy Allen, Stuart Scott. B.S., Auburn U., 1966, M.S., 1968; Ph.D., Iowa State U., 1971. Grad. asst. Auburn U., Ala., 1966-68, asst. prof. econs., 1971-76; instr. Iowa State U., Ames, 1968-71; spl. instr. Central Coll., Pella, Iowa, 1971; prof., head dept. econs. Auburn U.-Montgomery, Ala., 1976—; cons. to business. Editor: Ala. Bus. and Econs. Reports, 1977-82. Served with USAF, 1961-65. Recipient Faculty Service award Alumni Auburn U. at Montgomery, 1981. Mem. Am. Econ. Assn., So. Econs. Assn., Mid-South Acad. Economists, Ala. Acad. Sci. (chmn. 1975-78), Central Ala. Purchasing Mgmt. Assn., Phi Kappa Phi, Omicron Delta Epsilon. Avocations: amateur dramatics; jogging. Home: 415 N Moye Dr Montgomery AL 36109 Office: Dept Econs Auburn U at Montgomery Montgomery AL 36193

LACY, MILDRED PAULINE, fashion company executive; b. Kilgore, Tex., Apr. 12, 1936; d. Paul Burleson Jones and Irma Nola (DeRamus) Doggett; m. Eugene Shirley Lacy, Dec. 28, 1954; children—Sheri Dews, I. Lance. Student numerous home courses, 1961—. Legal sec. Neal & Girrand Law Firm, Hobbs, N. Mex., 1953-54; bookkeeper Randall & Hebbard Gen. Ins. Agts., Jacksonville, Fla., 1955-58; exec. sec., personel mgr. Home Savs., Houston, 1959-60; co-owner, mgr. The Toggery Shoe Salon, Kilgore, 1963; The Toggery Ladies Speciality Store, Kilgore, 1968; co-owner, exec. v.p. Kilgore Toggery Inc., 1968—; style show producer, dir. numerous orgns.; fashion cons. Leader Girl Scouts Am., 1962-69, East Tex. council Boy Scouts Am., 1967-69; tchr. Methodist Ch., 1963-70; chmn. edn. for family living PTA, 1965-67, v.p., 1965-67; benefit coordinator numerous orgns. Recipient Outstanding Leader award Girl Scouts Am., 1965, Year Book award PTA Tex., 1966, Promotion and Pub. Relations award Helene Sidel, 1979, Gold Belt award Alexis Kirk, 1981; silk pump named Pauline's Pet, Stewart Weitzman (shoe designer), 1986. Mem. Tex. Retailers Assn., Community Concert Assn., Nat. Assn. Female Execs., Smithsonian Inst., Kilgore C. of C. Clubs: Roy H. Laird Country, Summit. Avocations: investments; reading; home computer; gardening; swimming. Home: 1210 Brook Dr Kilgore TX 75662 Office: The Togegry Inc 104 N Kilgore St Kilgore TX 75662

LACY, ROSCOE DELIAS, JR., industrial supply company executive; b. Elizabeth City, N.C., Mar. 2, 1940; s. Roscoe D. and Maggie (Chappell) L.; student public schs., Elizabeth City; m. Luna O'Nella Meads, Dec. 3, 1960; children—Sandra, Beverly, Pam, Robert. With Miles Jennings Inc., Elizabeth City, 1962—, gen. mgr., v.p., treas., 1967—; dir. Northeastern Savs. & Loan; chmn. bd. Skills, Inc. Pres., Albemarle Area Devel. Assn. Mem. Nat. Fedn. Indsl. Businesses, Nat. Welding Soc., So. Instn. Indsl. Distributors, So. Hardware Assn., U.S. C. of C., Elizabeth City C. of C. Republican. Presbyterian. Club: Rotary. Home: Rural Route 1 Box 18 Elizabeth City NC 27909 Office: 1111 Halstead Blvd Elizabeth City NC 27909

LACY, WILLIAM BARKSDALE, sociology educator; b. Wellsville, N.Y., Apr. 17, 1942; s. Edred Earle and Gertrude (Tucker) L.; m. Laura Jane Robinson, July 23, 1966; children—Donovan Burke, Kristin Marguerite. B.S., Cornell U., 1964; M.A., Colgate U., 1965; M.A., U. Mich., 1971, Ph.D., 1975. Dir. upperclass housing Colgate U., 1967-69; asst. prof. U. Ky., Lexington, 1974-80, assoc. prof. sociology, 1980-85, prof. sociology, 1985—, assoc. chair dept., 1983-85, dir. Coll. Arts and Sci. Interdisciplinary Program on Food, Environ., Agr. and Soc. in Transition, univ. acad. ombudsman, co-chmn. com. agrl. research policy; cons. Brazilian Agrl. Research Corp., 1983-84. Co-author/editor two books on sci., agr. and food; author articles for profl. jours.; assoc. editor Rural Sociology. Sec. 78th Legis. Dist. Democratic Party, 1978-80. NSF grantee, 1981-85; Ford Found. grantee, 1981—; U.S. AID grantee, 1979—; W. Kellogg Found grantee, 1985—. Mem. Am. Sociol. Assn., AAAS, Rural Sociol. Soc. Office: Scovell Hall University of Kentucky Lexington KY 40506

LADHA, SHAFIK HASSANALI, industrial company executive; b. Bujumbura, Burundi, July 19, 1946; came to U.S., 1979; s. Hassanali and Nurbanu Ladha; married; children—Ally, Farouk, Salima. Student, Ecole Belge, 1954-60; H.H., Aga Khan High Sch., 1963; student U. Cambridge, 1964. Co-founder, pres. Ladha Trading, Zaire, 1965—, Milan, 1974—; ptnr. Ladha Motors, Osaka, Japan, 1968-73, Ladha Leather Industries, Kinshasa, Zaire, 1973—, Ladex Italia Import/Export Co., Milan, 1974-79, Ladha Hotels Ltd., Atlanta, 1979—, Ladha Fashions, Atlanta, 1981-82, Ladha Properties, Atlanta, 1982—; pres. Ladha Group Cos., U.S., Europe, Africa, Can. Decorated knight Govt. Zaire, 1976; granted hon. title Adm. of Ga. Navy, State of Ga., 1980. Mem. World Trade Club, Belgian C. of C. Office: 70 Houston St Ladha Downtown Hotel Suite 700 Atlanta GA 30303

LADNER, PHILIP DALE, accountant; b. New Orleans, Jan. 21, 1956; s. Christian Levy, Jr. and Violet Mae (Capdepon) L.; m. Anna Marie Martin, May 18, 1979; 1 dau., Jamie Lynn. B.S. in Bus. Adminstrn. cum laude, U. Southwestern La., 1977. C.P.A., La. Acct., Voorhies, Davis & Clostio, C.P.A.s, Lafayette, La., 1977-78; practice acctg., Lafayette, 1979—; fin. advisor oil-related cos. Mem. Soc. La. C.P.A.s, Am. Inst. C.P.A.s, Greater Lafayette C. of C. Democrat. Roman Catholic. Lodge: KC. Home: 208 Julian Circle Lafayette LA 70507 Office: PO Box 90365 Lafayette LA 70509

LAFAYE, CARY DUPRE, librarian; b. Horry County, S.C., June 22, 1945; d. Moffatt Barmore and Helen Elizabeth (Cappelmann) DuPre; m. Angus Bird Lafaye, Mar. 21, 1970; 1 dau., Helen Cary. B.A. cum laude, U.S.C., 1967, M. Librarianship, 1973. Reading, history tchr. Moultrie Jr. High Sch., Mount Pleasant, S.C., 1967-69; tchr. French, history Irmo High Sch. (S.C.), 1969-71; library asst. U.S.C., Columbia, 1971-72; librarian Richland County Pub. Library-Cooper Br., Columbia, S.C., 1973-74; reference librarian Midlands Tech. Coll., Beltline Library, Columbia, 1975 . Mem. Ala. S.C. Library Assn., Southeastern Library Assn., Phi Beta Kappa, Beta Phi Mu (chpt. pres. 1983—), Kappa Delta. Home: 1412 Haynsworth Rd Columbia SC 29205 Office: Midlands Tech Coll Beltline Library PO Drawer 2408 Columbia SC 29202

LAFFRE, RANDALL O'CONNELL, JR., dentist; b. Mobile, Ala., Oct. 4, 1925; s. Randall O'Connell and Miriam (Dorgan) L.; m. Elizabeth Beavers Hollis, Sept. 29, 1945; children—Miriam, Renee, Cheri. D.M.D., U. Ala., 1952. Diplomate Am. Bd. Dentistry. Practice dentistry, Mobile, 1952—. Served to lt. (j.g.) USN, 1943-46. Fellow Am. Coll. Dentists, Ala. Dental Assn.; mem. ADA. Episcopalian. Avocations: photography; fishing. Home: 263 College Ln Mobile AL 36608 Office: R O Laffre Jr DMD 3475 Springhill Ave Mobile AL 36608

LAFITTE, RONALD YANCY, pharmacist, consultant; b. Shreveport, La., Jan. 24, 1950; s. L.E. and O.L. (Yancy) LaF. B.S. in Zoology, La. State U., 1972; B.S. in Pharmacy, N.E. State U., 1976; postgrad. S.W. Theol. Sem., Fort Worth, 1973. Registered pharmacist. Tchr. high sch. math./sci. Southside Acad., Shreveport, La., 1973; pharmacy mgr. Medic-Pharmacies, Shreveport, 1976, Thriftyway Pharm., DeRidder, La., 1976-78; chief inpatient pharmacy BJAC Hosp., Fort Polk, La., 1978-82; dir. pharmacy Beauregard Hosp., DeRidder, La., 1982—; cons. pharmacy Leesville Gen. Hosp., La., 1982. Mem. Am. Soc. Hosp. Pharmacists, La. Soc. Hosp. Pharmacists. Republican. Baptist. Avocations: jogging; gardening; reading. Office: Beauregard Meml Hosp 600 S Pine St DeRidder LA 70634

LAFLEUR, KENNETH CHARLES, ophthalmologist; b. Lawtell, La., Aug. 22, 1941; s. Abram George and Mary Irene (Olivier) L.; m. Patricia Ione McNamara, Aug 3, 1963; children—James Mathew, Suzanne Annette, Caroline Marie. B.S., U. So. La., 1963; M.D., Tulane U., 1966. Diplomate Am. Bd. Ophthalmology. Intern, Hermann Hosp., Houston, 1966-67; ophthalmology resident U. Tex., 1970-73; practice medicine specializing in ophthalmology, Opelousas, La., 1972—; clin. asst. prof. La. State U. Eye Ctr., New Orleans, 1983—. Trustee, St. Landry Roman Catholic Ch., Opeloussas, 1979—. Served to maj. U.S. Army Med. Corps, 1970-72. Fellow Am. Acad. Ophthalmology, Soc. Mil. Ophthalmologists; mem. Am. Intraocular Implant Soc. Lodges: Elks, K.C. (Knight of Yr. award 1984). Avocation: fishing. Office: 526 Prudhomme Ln Opelousas LA 70570

LAFLEUR, YVONNE, retailer/designer; b. Bakersfield, Calif., Apr. 14, 1947; d. Conroy Farrell and Cecile (LaFleur) Owens; m. James Charles Walsh, June 9, 1981; children—Joseph, Elizabeth Louisiana, Mary Jane Melisande. B.S. in Fashion Merchandising, La. State U., 1969. Chief exec. officer Yvonne LaFleur/New Orleans and predecessor cos., 19—; creator fragrance Yvonne LaFleur, 1981. Recipient Amita award for bus., 1981. Mem. Fashion Group. Roman Catholic. Home: 1325 Cadiz St New Orleans LA 70115 Office: 8131 Hampson St New Orleans LA 70118

LAFLURE, ERNEST JAMES, oil company executive, oil and gas exploration geologist; b. Glens Falls, N.Y., Oct. 2, 1953; s. Joseph Ernest and Ruth (Leggat) LaF.; m. Dorothy Marie Drobny, Nov. 22, 1980. Student Rensselaer Polytechnic Inst., 1972-74; B.A. summa cum laude (Dept. Scholar) in Geology, SUNY-Potsdam, 1976; M.A. in Geology, SUNY-Binghamton, 1978. Geol. cons. O'Hara Township, Pitts., 1977-78; research asst. SUNY-Binghamton, 1977-78; exploration geologist Shell Oil Co., New Orleans, 1978-82; project leader Shell Western Exploration and Prodn., New Orleans, 1982-84, province leader Shell Offshore Inc, New Orleans, 1984—. Contbr. papers to profl. jours. Mem. Audabon Zoo, New Orleans, 1984—, Shell PAC, New Orleans, 1983—. Citizens to Re-Elect the Pres., Washington, 1984, Citizens for Legal Reform, Washington, 1984—. Recipient Sci. award Bausch and Lomb, 1972; Nat. Assn. Geology Tchrs. Scholar, 1975; recipient Spl. Recognition award Shell Oil Co., 1985. Mem. Am. Assn. Petroleum Geologists (judge 1985), New Orleans Geol. Soc. (judge 1983), Nat. Geog. Soc. Methodist. Avocations: skiing; tennis; history and archeology. Home: 1500 Mithra St New Orleans LA 70122 Office: Shell Offshore Inc PO Box 61933 New Orleans LA 70161

LA FORGE, RAYMOND BERNARD, JR., marketing consultant; b. Jersey City, Mar. 22, 1933; s. Raymond Bernard and Irene Veronica (Koeffler) LaF.; B.S. in Bus. Adminstrn., Monmouth Coll., West Long Branch, N.J., 1959; m. Sheridan J. Willie, Mar. 2, 1968; children—Raymond Bernard III, Ashley Alexandra. Salesman to sales mgr. West Side Fgn. Cars, Asbury Park, N.J., 1957-59; with Dun & Bradstreet, Inc., 1960—, fin. analyst, N.Y.C., 1960-64, with salesman credit service, 1964-67, with salesman mktg. services, 1967-79, mgr. South Fla. mktg. service div., 1972—, mem. pres.'s adv. council, 1979. Former mem. Miami Jaycees, recipient cert. of appreciation. Recipient cert. of appreciation Lindsey Hopkins Export Sch., 1960, Elliott Blood Bank, 1977. Mem. Am. Mktg. Assn. S. Fla. (dir., former v.p. and treas.). Republican. Clubs: Country of Coral Gables, Racquet, Shriners, Masons, Allapattah Rotary (past pres.). Home: 3275 Riviera Dr Coral Gables FL 33134 Office: 2050 Coral Way Miami FL 33145

LAGEDROST, HUGH LEROY, architect; b. Dayton, Ohio, June 9, 1923; s. Fred and Kathryn (Geran) L.; m. Jo Ann Elde, Dec. 17, 1983; children—Reed, Susan, Scott, Jill, Kelly, Holly, Eric. Ph.D., Hamilton State U., 1953. Head engr. Monsanto Chem., 1945-47; chief architect Brown & Assoc., Dayton, Ohio, 1947-54, Great Southwest Devel., San Antonio, 1956-72; architect Assoc. Architects, San Antonio, 1972—; real estate inspector Nat. Assn. Realtors, Boerne, Tex., 1982—; real estate appraiser Tex. Assn. Realtors, 1984—. Author: Teach Them Early, 1984. Prin. works include Down to Earth Homes. Mem. Nat. Council Archtl. Registration, San Antonio, 1985—. Recipient Best Arch. Design award Great Southwest Devel. Corp., 1980. Mem. Am. Inst. Real Estate Appraisers. Republican. Mormon. Club: Nat. Republican Club (Washington); Mercator Internat. (Dayton). Lodge: Rotary (bd. dirs. 1973). Avocations: aviation pilot; oils artists; watercolors and pencil amateur cartoonist.

LA GRECA, ANNETTE MARIE, clinical psychologist, psychology and pediatrics educator; b. N.Y.C., Dec. 22, 1950; d. Frank and Betty (Guzzio) La Greca. B.S. summa cum laude, Fordham U., 1972; M.S. in Psychology, Purdue U., 1975, Ph.D., 1978. Lic. psychologist, Fla. Clin. caseworker Cath. Home Bur., N.Y.C., 1972-73; from asst. to prof. psychology and pediatrics U. Miami, Coral Gables, Fla., 1978—, coordinator clin. child/pediatric tng., 1982—, dir. clin. psychology Mailman Ctr. Child Devel., 1984—; cons. Montanari Residential Treatment Ctr., Hialeah, Fla. Mem. editorial bd. Jour. Abnormal Child Psychology, Jour. Pediatric Psychology; Bd. dirs. OASIS Parent Resource Ctr., Chapel Hill, N.C., 1977-78, community alternatives program Assn. for Retarded Citizens, Dade County (Fla.), 1980—. NIMH fellow, 1975-78; NIH fellow, 1976-77; NIH Biomed. grantee, 1978-79, 80-82; Kennedy Found. grantee, 1982; Squibb-Novo grantee, 1983-86. Mem. Am. Psychol. Assn., Soc. Pediatric Psychology, Am. Diabetes Assn., Southeastern Psychol. Assn., Phi Beta Kappa, Kappa Gamma Pi. Contbr. chpts. to books, articles to profl. jours. Office: PO Box 248185 Dept Psychology U Miami Coral Gables FL 33124

LA GRONE, WILLIAM TAYLOR, lawyer; b. Browndell, Tex., Jan. 19, 1914; s. William Taylor and Lena Enola Westmorland LaG.; B.A., U. Tex., 1936, LL.B., 1939, J.D., 1971; m. Alta Mae Atteberry, Oct. 12, 1940; children—Linda Lee, Alta Eloise, Suzanne. Admitted to Tex. bar, 1939; practiced in Houston, 1939-52, Dallas, 1952—; v.p., gen. counsel Jake L. Hamon, Oil and Gas Operator, Dallas, 1952-79; pres. CNR Resources, Inc., 1979-81; chmn. bd., chief exec. officer LaGrone Exploration, Inc., 1981—; atty. Dallas Crime Commn., 1953-56. Served to col. AUS, 1940-46. Mem. Am., Tex., Dallas bar assns., Tex. Mid-Continent Oil and Gas Assn., Dallas Petroleum Landmen Assn. (pres. 1955-56), Ind. Producers Assn. Am., Tex. Ind. Producers and Royalty Owners Assn., Am. Assn. Petroleum Landmen, Ind. Producers Assn. Am. Methodist. Clubs: Northwood, Petroleum (Dallas). Home: 6308 Woodstream Ct Dallas TX 75240 Office: Two Hillcrest Green 12700 Hillcrest Rd Suite 507 Dallas TX 75230

LAGUERUELA, EARLINE, advertising executive; b. Rio Piedras, P.R., Apr. 8, 1952; d. Rafael F. and Lisette (Ortiz) Veve; B.A., Manhattanville Coll., 1973; student U. Geneva, 1971; m. Jan. 29, 1972. Vice pres. Velsweet Internat. Ltd., Laredo, Tex., 1973-75; v.p. Burgundy Woods, Inc., San Antonio, 1975-77; pres., dir. Sounds and Creations, Inc., San Antonio; dir. Burgundy Woods, Inc. Am. Mktg. Assn., Pub. Relations Soc. Am., San Antonio Advt. Fedn. Office: 8961 Tesoro Dr Suite 403 San Antonio TX 78217

LAHAYE, LEON CLAUDE, ophthalmologist; b. Arnaudville, La., Apr. 17, 1952; s. Francis and Adrienne (Regard) LaH.; children—Lainie, Lance. B.S. in Biology and Chemistry, U. Southwestern La., 1974; M.D., La. State U., 1978. Diplomate Am. Bd. Ophthalmology. Rotating surg. intern Charity Hosp., New Orleans, 1978-79; resident in ophthalmology dept ophthalmology John Sealy Hosp., U. Tex. Med. Br., Galveston, 1979-82; practice medicine specializing in ophthalmology, LaHaye Eye Clinic; sec.-treas. exec. com. Doctor's Hosp., Opelousas, 1984-85. Fellow Am. Acad. Ophthalmology; mem. La. State Med. Soc., So. Med. Assn., La. State Ophthalmology Assn., St. Landry Parish Med. Soc., AMA, Tex. State Ophthalmology Assn. Republican. Home: 6651 I-49 South Opelousas LA 70570 Office: LaHaye Eye Clinic 121 Ventre Blvd Suite 8 Opelousas LA 70570

LAHOUSE, THOMAS MICHAEL, exploration geophysicist; b. Springfield, Mass., Jan. 30, 1956; s. Edmund Joseph and Mary Josephine (Sessa) LaH.; m. Anita Belle Simmons, Mar. 28, 1981. Student St. Mary's U., San Antonio, 1974-75; B.S., Tex. A & M U., 1978. Geophysicist, ARCO Oil & Gas Co., Dallas, 1978-81; geophys. ops. supr. ARCO Exploration Co., Houston, 1981-85; dist. exploration mgr. ARCO Exploration & Tech. Co., Houston, 1985—. Vol., Campaign for Houston, 1985; tape ministry coordinator Spring Branch Community Ch., Houston, 1981-84, small group coordinator, 1985. Mem. Soc. Exploration Geophysicists, Am. Assn. Petroleum Geologists. Republican. Avocations: hiking; basketball; tennis. Office: ARCO Exploration Co PO Box 1346 Houston TX 77251

LAING, MALCOLM BRIAN, consulting geologist; b. Toronto, Ont., Can., Apr. 4, 1955; s. Alexander Duncan and Joan (Dawson) L.; m. Vicki Lynne. B.S. in Geology, Tex. Christian U., 1978. Geologist Electro-Seise, Inc., Ft. Worth, 1978-79, Exploration Logging Co., Houston, 1979-80, Thomas-Powell Royalty Co., Ft. Worth, 1980-82, Lentex Petroleum Inc., Abilene, Tex., 1982-84; cons., 1984—. Mem. Am. Assn. Petroleum Geologists, Soc. Petroleum Engrs., Drillsite Suprs. Assn., Soc. Profl. Well Log Analysts, Geol. Soc. Abilene. Republican. Baptist. Club: Petroleum (Ft. Worth). Home: 2802 Broken Bough Abilene TX 79606 Office: 209 S Danville Suite 108 Bldg A Abilene TX 79605

LAING, ROBERT SCOTT, lawyer; b. Chgo., Aug. 7, 1952; s. Robert Bruce and Mary Edith (Lindsay) L.; m. Barbara Jean Myking, Dec. 20, 1981. B.A. magna cum laude, Fla. Technol. U., 1973; J.D., U. Fla., 1976. Bar: Ohio 1977, Fla. 1977, U.S. Dist. Ct. (so. dist.) Fla. 1978. Asst. pub. defender Pub. Defender's Office, Bartow, Fla., 1975-76, Vero Beach, Fla., 1976; asst. state atty. State's Atty.'s Office, West Palm Beach, Fla., 1976-77; sole practice, West Palm Beach, 1977—; dir., pres. Am. Internat. Corp., West Palm Beach, 1980—; resident agt. Mason Realty & Internat. Investment Inc., West Palm Beach, 1980—, Landscape Concepts, Inc., Ft. Lauderdale, Fla., 1980—; dir. Barrel of Gold, Inc., West Palm Beach, 1980—. Contbr. numerous articles to profl. jours. Bd. dirs. Gainesville Cultural Commn. (Fla.), 1974-75; committeeman Fla. Democratic Party, Lakeland, 1976; mem. City Utilities Bd., Vero Beach, Fla., 1976; campaign chmn. Alan Becker for Fla. Atty. Gen. Mem. Assn. Trial Lawyers Am., Fla. Bar Assn. (chmn. gen. practice sect. 1980-81, chmn. fed. practice com. criminal law sect. 1982-83), ABA (vice chmn. criminal practice com., gen. practice sect. 1983—), Acad. Fla. Trial Lawyers. Independent Democrat. Presbyterian. Office: Law Offices R Scott Laing 900 Harvey Bldg Ocean Side West Palm Beach FL 33401

LAING, SUSAN JO, audiovisual library coordinator, health educator; b. Minot, N.D., Sept. 25, 1950; d. John Francis Laing and Evelyn (Nelson) May; m. Clint E. Bruess, Aug. 16, 1981. B.S., U. Oreg., 1972, M.S., 1981. Cert. health educator, Ala. Health edn. tchr., health team leader S. Lane Sch. Dist., Cottage Grove, Oreg., 1972-77; health edn. specialist Oreg. Dept. Edn., Salem, 1977-79; dist. health edn. specialist North Slope Borough Sch. Dist., Barrow, Ala., 1979-81; coordinator Multi-Media Health Lib. Lister Hill Library, U. Ala.-Birmingham, 1982—. Author: Instructor's Resource Manual for Decisions for Health, 1984. Mem. Health Educators Assn. Ala. (pres.), Greater Birmingham Am. Soc. for Tng. and Devel. (v.p. membership), Assn. for Advancement Health Edn. (mem. editorial bd.), Health Scis. Communications Assn., Ala. Pub. Health Assn., Am. Soc. for Tng. and Devel., Ala. Assn. for Health, Phys. Edn., Recreation and Dance, Eta Sigma Gamma. Avocations: running; gardening; sewing; traveling. Office: Multi-Media Health Lib Lister Hill Library U Ala-Birmingham Birmingham AL 35294

LAIR, PATRICK HENRY, school administrator; b. Stanford, Ky., May 28, 1950; s. Henry Clark and Helen (Herrington) L.; m. Lisa Maas, Nov. 24, 1972; children—Bryson Patrick, Larkin Shea. B.S., Western Ky. U., 1972, M.A., 1975, postgrad. in ednl. adminstrn., 1975-77. Tchr. Parker-Bennett Elem. Sch., Bowling Green, Ky., 1972-75; L.C. Curry Elem. Sch., Bowling Green, 1975-77; prin. Scott County Sch., Georgetown, 1977-85, 85—. Active Senate Bill Adv. Com., State Legislature, Frankfort, Ky., summer 1984; pres. Royal Spring Fed. Credit Union, Georgetown, 1983-85. Mem. Nat. Orgn. Legal Problems Edn., Ky. Middle Sch. Assn., Ky. Assn. Sch. Adminstrs. Assn. Supervision and Curriculum Devel. Republican. Roman Catholic.

LAIRD, ANGUS MCKENZIE, author, journalist; b. Opp, Ala., Oct. 9, 1903; s. John Henry and Ada (Zorn) L.; A.B., U. Fla., 1927, M.A., 1928; postgrad. Syracuse U., 1928-29, U. Chgo., 1930-31; m. Myra Adelia Doyle, June 8, 1938 (dec. 1981); children—Victoria Mell Laird Ackerman, Nan McKenzie. Teaching fellow Syracuse U., 1928-29; prof. history and polit. sci. U. Fla., Gainesville, 1929-30, 37-46, U. Denver, 1931-37; dir. Fla. Merit System, Tallahassee, 1946-60; pres. Huesack Enterprises, Inc.; editor Wakulla News, 1967-71; founder St. Andrews Press. Pres., Fla. Heritage Found., 1973-76; coordinator award program Fla. Press Club, 1977; trustee St. Andrews Soc.; bd. dirs. Monticello Opera, 1976-82. Recipient citation Fla. Cabinet, 1961. Mem. Fla. Public Health Assn. (pres. 1955), Fla. Public Personnel Assn. (pres. 1953), Public Personnel Assn. U.S. and Can. (hon.; exec. council 1958-60), Fla. Heritage Found. (pres. 1973-76), Friends of Library Fla. State U. (pres. 1974-76). Author: City Manager Government in Florida, 1929; (with Wilson K. Doyle) Government and Administration in Florida, 1955; Centennial History of Kappa Sigma, 1969; My Brothers: Wallace and Roy, 1977; Like I Saw It, 1981. Home: 3304 Rue de Lafitte Tallahassee FL 32303

LAKE, KELLY ORLAN, educator, consultant; b. Fort Wayne, Ind., Aug. 28, 1952; d. Francis Orlando and Christie Delight (Allen) L. B.A. in Sociology, Ind. U., 1976; M.A. in Counseling Psychology, Ball State U., 1978. Cert. Montessori presch. tchr., Ill. Clin. therapist, child and adolescent program Porter-Starke Services, Valparaiso, Ind., 1981-83; pvt. therapist, Valparaiso, 1983-84; exec. dir. Y Kids Koffeehaus, Valparaiso, 1983-84; Montessori dir. Chesterton Montessori, Ind., 1983-84, Montessori Children's House of Chapel Hill, Durham, N.C., 1984—. Membership chmn. Christian Community Action, Valparaiso, 1982, bd. dirs., 1983. Mem. Am. Montessori Soc., Am. Assn. for Counseling and Devel., Am. Mental Health Counselors Assn., Nat. Assn. for Edn. Young Child. Democrat. Methodist. Avocations: recreational sports; the arts; outdoors; spending time with friends. Home: B-12 The Villages Carrboro NC 27510 Office: Montessori Children's House of Chapel Hill 4512 Pope Rd Durham NC 27707

LAKE, LARRY WAYNE, petroleum engineer; b. Del Norte, Colo., Jan. 31, 1946; s. Ralph Wayne and Ina Belle (Card) L.; B.S., Ariz. State U., 1967; Ph.D., Rice U., 1973; m. Carole Sue Holmes, Mar. 22, 1975; children—Leslie Sue, Jeffrey Wayne. Prodn. engr. Motorola Co., Phoenix, 1968-70; sr. research engr. Shell Devel. Co., Houston, 1973-78; Halliburton prof. petroleum engring. U. Tex., Austin, 1978—; cons. enhanced oil recovery AMOCO, Mobil Oil, Core Labs, Intera. Recipient U. Tex. Engring. Found. award, 1979; Disting. Faculty Adv. award U. Tex., 1981; registered profl. engr., Tex. Mem. Soc. Mining Engrs., Soc. Petroleum Engrs. (mem. editorial rev. com., author video, Disting. Achievement award 1981), Am. Inst. Chem. Engrs., Sigma Xi, Tau Beta Pi, Pi Epsilon Tau. Baptist. Home: 4003 Edgefield Ct Austin TX 78731 Office: CPE 4108 U Tex Austin TX 78712

LAKE, ROBERT CAMPBELL, JR., lawyer, state senator; b. Whitmire, S.C., Dec. 27, 1925; s. Robert Campbell and Susan Gaston (Howze) L.; LL.B., U. S.C., 1949; LL.D., Newberry Coll., 1981; m. Carolyn Young Gray, July 5, 1955; children—Robert Campbell III, Samuel Young, Linda (dec.). Practice law, Whitmire; chmn. adv. bd. First Fed. Savs. & Loan Assn. of Newberry (S.C.); mem. S.C. Senate, 1969-85, chmn. ethics com., 1980-84. Bd. dirs. United Fund; elder, moderator Presbyn. Ch.; mem. Jr. Coll. Study Com., 1966-67; pres. County Devel. Bd., 1965-67, Jr. C. of C., 1953; chmn. bldg. com. Whitmire Presbyn. Ch., 1966; mem. So. Regional Edn. Bd., also mem. exec. com.; trustee Winthrop Coll., 1977. Served with U.S. Army, 1944-45. Mem. Farm Bur., Blue Key. Democrat. Club: Shriners (potentate 1972). Office: Box 338 Whitmire SC 29178

LAKE, ROBIN ANNE, nurse; b. Memphis, Sept. 10, 1954; d. Charles Wayne and Helen (Galloway) Roberts; m. Robert Michael Lake, Nov. 23, 1973; children—Summer Rochelle, Robert Michael II. A.S. in Nursing, Phillips County Community Coll., 1974; student U. Ark., 1977, Ind. U. Purdue U.-Indpls., 1979-82. R.N., Ind., Ark, Tenn.; cert. poison info. specialist. Nurse Northwest Miss. Regional Med. Ctr., Clarksdale, Miss., 1974-75, Bapt. Med. Ctr., Little Rock, 1975-77; nurse, patient care mgr. Meth. Hosp., Indpls., 1978-82, mem. delivery model coordinating com., 1980-81; nurse, patient care mgr. Meth. Hosp., Memphis, 1981; nurse intravenous therapy Bapt. Meml. Hosp., Memphis, 1983—; distbr. Fay Swafford Originals, 1985—; nurse, poison info. specialist Ind. Poison Ctr. Indpls., 1982-83; Contbr. numerous articles to various med. publs. Democratic election clk., Indpls., 1978. Mem. Am. Diabetes Assn., Nat. Intravenous Therapy Assn., Creative Writing Orgn. (v.p. 1981), Am. Assn. Poison Control Ctrs., Mid-South Creative Writing Club (v.p. 1981). Home: 4243 Hobson Rd Memphis TN 38128

LAKER, JOSEPH ALPHONSE, history educator; b. Indpls., Mar. 17, 1941; s. Alphonse Joseph and Anna Catherine (Riegel) L. B.A. in History, Marian Coll., 1963; M.A. in History, Ind. U., 1967, Ph.D., 1975. Instr. St. Olaf Coll., Northfield, Minn., 1967-70, Ind. U., Bloomington, 1970-71, 72-74; asst. prof. Wheeling Coll., W. Va., 1974-81, assoc. prof. history, 1981—. Mem. Assn. Asian Students, Econ. History Assn., W. Va. Hist. Soc. Democrat. Roman Catholic. Avocations: tennis; golf; reading mystery stories. Office: Wheeling Coll 316 Washington Ave Wheeling WV 26003

LAKICS, CHRISTOPHER JOHN, state official, systems analyst; b. Toledo, Feb. 22, 1960; s. Walter Gilbert and Rose Barbara (Warrington) L. B.S., Tex. A&M U., 1983. Electronics draftsman Amscor Corp., Angleton, Tex., 1978-79; research asst. Cyclotron Inst., College Station, Tex., 1979-80; designer/draftsman Brown & Root, Inc., Houston, 1980-82; computer graphics operator 3D/Internat., Inc., Houston, 1982; systems analyst Tex. State Engring. Extension Service, College Station, 1982—; mem. TAMU Microcomputer Users Group, College Station, 1983—. Mem. Century Singers, College Station, 1979-80. Mem. Data Processing Mgmt. Assn., ACM, Nat. Space Inst. Author: (poem) That Cold Friday Night (2d pl. award Detroit News), 1977, That Little Monster (3d pl. award Quill & Scroll), 1978. Office: Tex Engring Extension Service FE Drawer K College Station TX 77843

LAL, RAVINDRA B., physics educator, researcher; b. Agra, India, Oct. 5, 1935; came to U.S., 1964; s. Avadh B. and Randha Pyari L.; m. Usha Mathur, Nov. 21, 1962; 1 child, Amit. B.S., Agra U., 1955, M.S., 1958, Ph.D., 1963. Asst. prof. physics Indian Inst. Tech., New Delhi, 1968-70; sr. research assoc. U. Ala., Huntsville, 1971-73; assoc. prof. physics Paine Coll., Augusta, Ga., 1973-75; prof. physics Ala. A&M U., Huntsville, 1975—. Prin. investigator NASA research contract, 1985; contbr. articles to profl. jours. Trustee Huntsville India Assn. 1964—, mem., 1985—. Mem. Am. Phys. Soc., Am. Assn. Crystal Growth, Sigma Xi. Office: Ala A&M Univ PO Box 71 Huntsville AL 36762

LALLINGER, E. MICHAEL, savings and loan association executive; b. St. Louis, Aug. 17, 1915; s. Michael N. and Clara (Neiderhoff) L.; m. Johnetta Claire Ward, Jan. 14, 1948; children—Michael John, John Ward, Mary Jeanne. Student Jefferson Coll., St. Louis, 1937. With RFC, 1941-51, asst. mgr. Dallas office, 1950-51; asst. regional commr. IRS, Dallas, 1952-56; exec. v.p. Gibraltar Savs. Assn., Houston, 1956-63, pres., 1963-80, chmn. bd., chief exec. officer, 1980—; also dir.; pres., chief exec. officer, dir Imperial Corp. Am., 1980—; dir. First Internat. Bank, Houston, Fed. Home Loan Mortgage Corp., Washington; tchr. individual and corp. tax acctg. Jefferson Coll., 1939-40. Served to capt., inf. AUS, 1942-46; ETO. Decorated Silver Star, Bronze Star, Purple Heart; Order Leopold, Belgium; Croix de Guerre, France). Mem. Nat. League Insured Savs. Assn., U.S. Savs. and Loan League, U.S. C. of C., Houston C. of C. Home: 21 Briar Hollow Ln 802 Houston TX 77027 Office: Gibraltar Savs Assn 13401 North Freeway Houston TX 77060*

LALLY, RALPH CHARLES, publisher; b. New Orleans, Dec. 5, 1946; s. John and Mildred (Bertrand) L.; m. Carol Pearce, Nov. 23, 1968; children—Carol Ann, Leslie Ann. B.A., U. Southwestern La., 1971. Gen. mgr. Automatic Vending Co., Lafayette, La., 1968-71; exec. v.p., gen. mgr. Operators Sales, Inc., New Orleans, 1971-74; pub., editor Skibird Pub. Co., Inc., New Orleans, 1974—. Democrat. Roman Catholic. Lodge: K.C. (grand knight 1973). Office: Skybird Pub Co Inc 6600 Fleur de Lis St New Orleans LA 70124

LALLY, TIM DOUGLAS PATRICK, English language educator; b. Los Angeles, Nov. 11, 1942; s. Thomas William Jr. and Ferne Constance (Sears) L.; m. Marie Louise Therese Kessel, Sept. 26, 1973; 1 child, Nicole Claire. A.B. magna cum laude, Harvard Coll., 1968; A.M., SUNY-Stony Brook, 1972, Ph.D., 1980. Instr. English, Bowling Green State U., Ohio, 1976-80; asst. prof. U. South Ala., Mobile, 1980-84, assoc. prof. English, 1984—; pres. Faculty Senate, U. South Ala., Mobile, 1983-84. Editor Jour. Advanced Composition U. South Ala., 1980—. Served to sgt. 101st Airborne Div., U.S. Army, 1961-64. SUNY-Stony Brook grad. fellow, 1970-76; Harvard Club Rocky Mountains scholar, 1964-68. Mem. Ala. Council Tchrs. English (dir. 1983—), Ala. Council Coll. and U. Faculty Presidents (pres. 1984-85), Mod. Lang. Assn., Medieval Acad. Am., Nat. Council Tchrs. English, Conf. Coll. Composition and Communication, Early English Text Soc. Episcopalian. Club: Harvard (Mobile). Home: 1120 Montauk Ave Mobile AL 36604 Office: U South Ala Dept English Mobile AL 36688

LAM, CHAN F., biomedical engineering educator, computer consultant; b. Kwangtung, China, Oct. 23, 1943; came to U.S., 1961; s. Wing-Cheong and Choy (Chan) L.; m. Carolina Po Lam, Sept. 18, 1967; children—Shirley, Ken. B.S., Calif. State Poly. Coll., 1965; M.S. in Mech. Engring., Clemson U., 1967, Ph.D. in Elec. Engring., 1970. Asst. prof. dept. biometry Med. U. S.C., Charleston, 1970-75, assoc. prof. dept. biometry, 1975-80, prof., 1980—, dir. ops., chief programming Research Data Processing Ctr., 1971-72, dir. Time Share, Hybrid Computation Lab., 1975-79, dir. Biometry Computer Ctr., 1979-86. Treas. Cooper Estates Civic Club, 1972-74. Research grantee State S.C., 1972-75. Mem. IEEE (sr., chmn. coastal S.C. sect. 1975), Soc. Math. Biology, Pattern Recognition, Assn. Computing Machinery. Author: Techniques for Analysis and Modeling of Enzyme Kinetic Mechanisms, 1981; contbr. articles, abstracts to publs. Home: 1097 Cottingham Dr Mt Pleasant SC 29464 Office: Dept Biometry Med U SC Charleston SC 29425

LAMALIE, ROBERT EUGENE, executive search executive; b. Fremont, Ohio, June 3, 1931; s. Glen E. and Mildred M. (Hetrick) L.; B.A., Capital U., 1954; postgrad. in bus. adminstrn. Western Res. U., 1958; m. Dorothy M. Zilles, June 20, 1953; children—Deborah, Dawn, Elaine. Personnel mgr. Am. Greetings Corp., Cleve., 1956-59; asst. dir. profl. recruiting Xerox Corp., Rochester, N.Y., 1959-62; mgr. profl. recruiting and orgn. planning The Glidden Co., Cleve., 1962-65; assoc. exec. search Booz, Allen & Hamilton, Inc., Cleve., 1965-67; pres. Lamalie Assocs., Inc., Tampa, Fla., 1967—. Served with U.S. Army, 1954-56. Mem. Assn. Exec. Search Cons. (dir.). Office: Lamalie Assocs Inc 13920 N Dale Mabry Hwy Tampa FL 33618

LAMAR, SONDRA GAIL, college public relations administrator, writer; b. Ft. Smith, Ark., May 21, 1947; d. Odes Farel and Pearl Mae (Geoates) Cradduck; m. Stephen Edward Fritchey, June 1964 (div. 1967); 1 child, Jon Michael; m. Edward Eugene Waldrop, Apr. 1968 (div. Feb. 1978); 1 child, Shane Ed; m. Charles Garet LaMar, Aug. 20, 1981; 1 dau., Kristin Elaine. Student Little Rock U., 1966. Reporter Ark. Democrat, Little Rock, 1966; reporter S.W. Times Record, Ft. Smith, 1966-68, 69, 71-72; edn. writer Lawton Constn., Okla., 1968-69; reporter Pine Bluff News, Ark., 1970; traffic and news dir. Stas. KFAY-KKEG, Fayetteville, Ark., 1971; dir. pub. info. Westark Community Coll., Ft. Smith, 1972—. Contbr. articles to Christian Single mag. Past mem. promotions com. Old Ft. Days Ark.-Okla. Rodeo; single adult spl. cons. Baptist Sunday Sch. Bd. Recipient spl. citation Ark. Edn. Assn., 1967; First Place award Internat. Reading Assn. competition, 1969; award of excellence Ark. Advt. Fedn. ADDY Awards, 1981; various competition awards Council for Advancement and Support of Edn., 1983, 84, 85; award of excellence Univ. and Coll. Designers Assn., 1983; named to Outstanding Young Women Am., U.S. Jaycees, 1979; named one of five Women of Day, Bus. and Profl. Women's Club, 1982. Mem. Ft. Smith-Van Buren Advt. Fedn. (pres. 1981-82, ADDY award 1983, 84, awards of Excellence 1983, 84), Nat. Council Community Relations, Am. Advt. Fedn. (co-chmn. edn. com. 10th dist. 1981-82). Avocation: graphology. Office: Westark Community Coll PO Box 3649 Fort Smith AR 72913

LAMB, LESTER LEWIS, hospital administrator; b. Winchester, Va., Aug. 11, 1932; s. Lester Lewis and Nina Elizabeth (Higgs) L.; m. Mary Lou Watson, Aug. 11, 1956; children—Melissa, Amy, Elizabeth. B.A., Richmond Coll., 1955, postgrad., 1955-56; M.H.A., Med. Coll. Va., 1958. Asst. dir. admissions, hosp. div. Med. Coll. Va., Richmond, 1956, adminstrv. resident, 1957; adminstrv. resident Shenandoah County Meml. Hosp., Woodstock, Va., 1957, Washington County Hosp., Hagerstown, Md., 1957-58; adminstr. Hampshire Meml. Hosp., Romney, W.Va., 1958-59, Marmet Hosp. Inc. (W.Va.), 1959-60; asst. dir. U. Va. Hosp., Charlottesville, 1961; adminstr. R.J. Reynolds-Patrick County Meml. Hosp., Stuart, Va., 1961-64, Shenandoah County Meml. Hosp., Woodstock, 1965-69, Mary Greely Meml. Hosp., Ames, Iowa, 1969-70; exec. dir. Radford Community Hosp. (Va.), 1970-81, pres., 1981—; guest lectr., adj. asst. prof. Radford U. (Va.), 1980-81; chmn. Va. Hosp. Underwriters, Inc.; vice chmn. Va. Hosp. Shared Services. Mem. exec. bd. Episcopal Diocese of S.W. Va., also lay reader, pres. convocation; mem. Va. Gov.'s Health Services Cost Rev. Commn., 1978-82. Fellow Am. Coll. Hosp. Adminstrs., Royal Soc. Health; mem. Va. Hosp. Assn. (pres. 1981-82), Med. Coll. Va. Hosp. Adminstrn. Alumni Assn. (sec., pres.), Roanoke Area Hosp. Council (pres. 1974), Psi Chi. Club: Rotary (past pres.). Home: 116 Greenbrier Dr Radford VA 24141 Office: Radford Community Hosp Radford VA 24141

LAMB, RICHARD WILLIAM, construction company executive; b. Aberdeen, S.D., May 8, 1934; s. George Dewey and Cora Matilda (Bailey) L.; m. Noreen Judith Marino, May 22, 1954; children—Stephan Mitchell, Mark Christopher. Engring. Sci. degree, Humprheys Coll., 1960. Adminstrv. mgr. ETS-Hokin Corp., San Francisco, 1960-66; contracts mgr. Hughes Aircraft, Cape Kennedy, Fla., 1967-70; constrn. cons., Washington, 1971-79; exec. v.p. Constrn. Cons. Internat. Corp., Washington, 1980—. Served with USN, 1952-56; Korea. Mem. Am. Arbitration Assn., Am. Assn. Cost Engrs. Republican. Roman Catholic. Office: 8133 Leesburg Pike Suite 260 Vienna VA 22180

LAMB, ROBERT REID, petroleum geologist; b. Kewanee, Ill., Apr. 22, 1923; s. Walter Thomas and Hannah Marie (Anderson) L.; m. Nancy Marie Brant, Oct. 8, 1944; children—Evelyn Louise, Reid Allen, Paul Montgomery. B.S., U. Ill., 1947, M.S., 1948. Geologist Atlantic Richfield Co., Wyo., N.D., La., 1948-55; div. geologist Diversa, Inc., New Orleans, 1955-65; v.p. Homa Oil & Gas Co., New Orleans, 1965-71, also dir.; v.p. Hughston & Lamb, Inc., Dallas, 1971-79; pres. Robert R. Lamb, Inc., Dallas, 1979—; founder, dir. Preston North Nat. Bank, Dallas, 1983—. Pres. Behrman High Sch. PTA, New Orleans, 1969—; v.p. Alice Harte Elem. Sch. PTA, New Orleans, 1967—. Served with U.S. Army, 1942-43. Mem. Am. Assn. Petroleum Geologists (cert.), Dallas Geol. Soc., New Orleans Geol. Soc., Soc. Ind. Profl. Earth Scientists (chmn. Dallas chpt. 1984-85). Republican. Methodist. Lodges: Masons, Shriners. Home: 7430 Oakbluff Dr Dallas TX 75240 Office: Robert R Lamb Inc 419 Meadows Bldg Dallas TX 75206

LAMBERT, C ROGER, history educator; b. Decatur, Tex., Aug. 8, 1933; s. Charlie C. and Ida Mae (Tate) L.; m. Janna Sue Walker. B.A., North Tex. State U., 1954, M.A., 1955; Ph.D., U. Okla., 1962. Instr. history Del Mar Coll., Corpus Christi, Tex., 1961-64; assoc. prof. Angelo State U., San Angelo, Tex., 1964-66; prof. Ark. State U., Jonesboro, 1966—, chmn. dept. history, 1982—. Contbr. articles on agrl. and social history to profl. jours. Mem. Orgn. Am. Historians, Agrl. History soc., Ark. Coll. History Tchrs. (bd. dirs. 1984—). Avocation: gardening. Home: 1425 Haven St Jonesboro AR 72401 Office: Ark State U Box 1890 State University AR 72467

LAMBERT, CAROL ANN, audiologist; b. Easton, Pa., June 15, 1947; d. Harry and Clara (Miller) L.; B.A., U. Tulsa, 1972, M.A., 1977; m. Michael Read Minshall, Mar. 19, 1973; 1 child, Eugene Read. Audiologist, Tulsa Otolaryngology, Inc., and U. Tulsa, 1977-78; speech reading instr. Tulsa Speech and Hearing Assn., 1977-78; audiologist Ear, Nose and Throat Consultants, Inc., Tulsa, 1978-83; audiologist U. Tulsa, 1983—; cons. audiologist Springer Clinic, 1979-80; cons. Okla. State Dept. Health, Tulsa Scottish Rite Center for Childhood Lang.Disorders, At Risk Parent-Child Program; adj. asst. prof. U. Tulsa, 1981-82. Active women's ctr. project Jr. League of Tulsa. vol. Philbrook Art Ctr., Tulsa Opera Guild. Mem. Am. Speech and Hearing Assn. (cert. in audiology), Acad. Dispensing Audiologists, Okla. Speech and Hearing Assn. (past sec.), Okla. Council for the Hearing Impaired, Acad. of Audiology, Tulsa Assn. Speech Pathologists and Audiologists (past pres.), Tulsa Speech and Hearing Assn. (past dir.). Office: 6355 E Skelly Dr Tulsa OK 74135

LAMBERT, DENNIS EDSON, investment company executive; b. Kansas City, Mo., Jan. 16, 1941; s. Paul McKinley and Della Mae (Rogers) L. A.B., William Jewell Coll., 1963; M.P.A., NYU, 1966; grad. Fed. Exec. Inst., 1975. Chief city council staff Kansas City, Mo., 1972-73, asst. to the city mgr., 1973-76; exec. asst. Hon. E. Thomas Coleman, Kansas City, Mo., 1977-82; exec. v.p. Cardinal Capital Corp., Dallas, 1982—. Served to capt. USAF, 1967-71. Decorated Commendation medal. Mem. Sigma Nu. Republican.

LAMBERT, GUSSIE, book company executive; b. Avery, Tex., Nov. 22, 1914; s. Livingston Stark Lambert and Pearl Kistler; m. Ruth Burns, Dec. 27, 1941; 1 child, Mary Beth Lambert Brednich. B.A., Ark. State Coll., 1945. Minister, Ch. of Christ, Rush Springs, Okla., 1939-41, Portland Ave. Ch. of Christ, Shreveport, La., 1945-54, Creswell Ave. Ch. of Christ, Shreveport, 1954-64; pub. Lambert House Inc., Shreveport, 1954—. Democrat.

LAMBERT, JOHN LARUE, college administrator; b. Jarratt, Va., Nov. 21, 1949; s. John Irvin and Alice Mabel (Presley) L.; m. Susan Kimberly Green, Oct. 24, 1981; 1 child, Laura Tillman. A.S. in Bus. Adminstrn., J. Sargeant Reynolds Coll., Richmond, Va., 1976; B.A. in Religion, Centenary Coll., Shreveport, La., 1978; M.A. in Edn., La. Tech. U., Ruston, 1985. Radio announcer Sta. WHEO, Stuart, Va., 1968-69; patient account mgr. Greensville County Hosp., Emporia, Va., 1974-75; dir. fin. aid Centenary Coll. La., Shreveport, 1978-79, dir. admissions, 1979-84, dir. enrollment planning, 1984—; bd. dirs. Modern Miss Scholarship Pageant, Celina, Tenn., 1983—; cons. Collegiate Consulting Service, Shreveport, 1985. Editor, producer slide show The Pride is Catching, 1984 (U.S. Film Festival Silver award 1984). Bd. dirs. Shreveport ARC, 1978; moderator leadership groups St. Mark's Episcopal Ch., Shreveport, 1985. Mem. Nat. Assn. Fgn. Student Adminstrs. (chmn. La. chpt. 1985-86), Am. Assn. Counseling and Devel., Nat. Assn. Coll. Admissions Counselors, So. Assn. Coll. Admissions Counselors, La. Assn. Fin. Aid Adminstrs. (legis. chmn. 1979—), Omicron Delta Kappa, Tau Kappa Epsilon. Lodge: Kiwanis. Avocations: travel; reading; gardening; bicycling. Home: 920 Kirby Pl Shreveport LA 71104 Office: Centenary Coll La 2911 Centenary Blvd Shreveport LA 71104

LAMBERT, PHILLIP EDWARD, accountant; b. Jacksonville, Fla., Apr. 18, 1948; s. William Melvin and Monte (Welch) L. B.A., U. Fla., 1970; M.P.A., Ga. State U., 1974. C.P.A., Fla. Staff acct. Wolf & Co. C.P.A.s, Atlanta, 1974-77; sr. acct. Alexander Grant & Co. C.P.A.s, Atlanta, 1977-78; sr. fin. specialist Martin Marietta Corp., Orlando, Fla., 1978-82; controller Martin Electronics, Inc., Perry, Fla., 1982—; adj. instr. acctg. Valencia Community Coll., 1980-82. Contbr. article to profl. jour. Served with USNR, 1970-76. Mem. Nat. Assn. Accts. Republican. Lutheran. Club: Kiwanis (Perry). Home: PO Box 921 Perry FL 32347 Office: Martin Electronics Inc Route 1 Box 700 Perry FL 32347

LAMBIRD, PERRY ALBERT, pathologist; b. Reno, Feb. 7, 1939; s. Clifford D. and Florence T. (Knowlton) L.; B.A. with great distinction, Stanford U., 1958; M.D., Johns Hopkins U., 1962; M.B.A. with high honors, Oklahoma City U., 1973; m. Mona Sue Salyer, July 30, 1960; children—Allison Thayer, Jennifer Salyer, Elizabeth Gard, Susannah Johnson. Intern, Johns Hopkins Hosp., Balt., 1962-63, jr. asst. resident in pathology, 1965-66, asst. resident in pathology, 1966-68, chief resident pathologist, 1968-69; practice medicine specializing in pathology, Oklahoma City, 1969—; asso. pathologist Med. Arts Lab., 1969-70, pathologist, 1970—; cons. pathologist, dep. med. examiner Office State Med. Examiner Okla., 1969—; mem. staff Hosp. U. Okla., Presbyn. Hosp., Children's Meml. Hosp., St. Anthony Hosp., South Community Hosp., Mercy Health Center; cons. pathologist Okla. Breast Cancer Control Network, Okla. Med. Research Found., 1975-80; spl. cons. Rees Assoc., Oklahoma City, 1975—; clin. assoc. prof. pathology U. Okla., 1970—, clin. assoc. prof. orthopedic surgery, 1970—; asst. prof. Sch. Mgmt. and Bus. Scis., Oklahoma

City U., 1973-82; reviewer So. Med. Jour., 1974-82, Jour. AMA, 1983—, Diagnostic Cytopathology, 1985—; propr. Lambird Mgmt. Cons. Services, Oklahoma City, 1974—. Chmn., Oklahoma County Citizens for Reagan, 1976, 84. bd. regents Uniformed Services U. of the Health Scis., 1982—; exec. com. Republican Com. Oklahoma County, 1973-79; del. Rep. Nat. Conv., 1976, alt. del., 1984; bd. dirs. Oklahoma City chpt. ARC, 1976-83, CAP Found., 1984—, Community Action Program Oklahoma City, 1976-79, Hist. Preservation, Inc., 1970—, Okla. Found. Peer Rev., 1979-85; bd. dirs. Okla. Symphony Orch., 1972—, pres., 1974-75, chmn. bd., 1975-77, chmn. adv. com., 1977-79; trustee Ballet Okla., pres., 1978-79; trustee Westminister Day Sch., 1973-83; trustee Phi Beta Kappa Assn. Oklahoma City, 1976-83, pres., 1982-83; mem. U.S. Ho. of Reps. Taskforce on Entitlements and Human Assistance Programs, 1983—. Served with USPHS, 1963-65. Recipient Exec. Leadership award Oklahoma City U., 1976; named Outstanding Young Man, Oklahoma City Jaycees, 1972, Outstanding Young Oklahomans award (3), 1973; Outstanding Young Am. award U.S. Jaycees, 1974; Outstanding Pathologist award Am. Pathol. Found., 1984. also various med. soc. awards. Diplomate Am. Bd. Pathology. Fellow Coll. Am. Pathologists (ho. of dels. 1978-84, vice chmn. nat. legis. coms. 1982-84, bd. govs. 1984—, exec. com. 1985—, chmn. council pathology practice 1985—), Am. Soc. Clin. Pathologists; mem. Am. Pathology Found. (dir. 1978-83, v.p. 1980-81, pres. 1982-83), Internat. Acad. Pathology, Okla. Assn. Pathologists (sec. 1973-74, pres. 1983-84), So. Med. Assn., Am. Assn. Pathologists, Okla. Med. Assn. (chmn. council govt. activities 1976—, ho. of dels. 1973—, trustee 1974—), AMA (path. sect. council 1979-80, ho. of dels. 1980—, council on med. service 1985—), Oklahoma City Clin. Soc., Oklahoma County Med. Soc. (dir. 1976-78, 80-83, pres. 1983, v.p. 1977-78, 81), Johns Hopkins Med. and Surg. Assn., Am. Soc. Cytology, Osler Soc. Oklahoma City, Okla. Soc. Cytopathology (pres. 1982-83), Fedn. Am. Socs. Exptl. Biology, N.Y. Acad. Scis., Phi Beta Kappa, Alpha Omega Alpha. Methodist. Contbr. articles on pathology to profl. jours. Home: 419 NW 14th St Oklahoma City OK 73103 Office: 100 Pasteur Bldg 1111 N Lee St Oklahoma City OK 73103

LAMENSDORF, HUGH, urologist; b. Greenville, Miss., July 20, 1936; s. Jerome Hugh and Rosann (Mundt) L.; m. Louise Faye Doernberg, July 6, 1958; children—Jerome Stewart, Marilyn Elizabeth, Bradley Hugh, Jonathan Louis. B.S., Tulane U., 1958, M.D., 1961. Diplomate Am. Bd. Urology. Intern, U. Miss. Hosp., Jackson, 1961-62; resident in urology Ochsner Found. Hosp., New Orleans, 1962-66; mem. staff Urology Clinic, Ft. Worth, 1968—; chief staff Med. Plaza Hosp., Ft. Worth; asst. prof. surgery Southwestern Med. Sch., Dallas. Pres. TEXPAC; active Van Cliburn Soc., Ft. Worth Jewish Fedn., Knights of Vine; v.p. Beth El Congregation. Served to capt. USAF, 1966-68. Mem. Am. Urol. Assn., Am. Assn. Clin. Urologists, ACS, Am. Fertility Soc., Soc. for Pediatric Urology, Am. Acad. Pediatrics, Tex. Surg. Soc., Tex. Urol. Soc. (pres. 1975), AMA (del. from Tex.), Tex. Med. Assn., Tarrant County Med. Assn. (pres. 1986), Pan Am. Med. Assn. (council). Republican. Home: 1424 Shady Oaks Ln Fort Worth TX 76107 Office: 1415 Pennsylvania Ave Fort Worth TX 76109

LAMMLEIN, DAVID RAYMOND, oil company executive; b. St. Louis, Mar. 21, 1945; s. Raymond William and Rose Mary (Woltering) L.; m. Leslie Peterson, Nov. 28, 1975; children—David Hunter, John Forrest. B.S. in Geophys. Engring., St. Louis U., 1967; Ph.D. in Geophysics, Columbia U., 1973; postgrad. in exec. mgmt. Harvard U., 1984. Registered geophysicist, Calif. Exploration geophysicist Gulf Oil Corp., Houston, 1968-69; asst. prof. U. Tex., Galveston, 1972-75; exploration mgr. Pennzoil Co., Houston, 1975—; adj. prof. U. Houston, 1975—. Contbr. 33 articles to profl. jours. Mem. Am. Assn. Petroleum Geologists, Am. Geophys. Union (reviewer publs.), Soc. Exploration Geophysicists (reviewer publs.), Geophys. Soc. Houston, Houston Geol. Soc. Republican. Roman Catholic. Clubs: Harvard, Athletic (Houston). Avocations: racquetball; fishing; softball; chess. Home: 5650 Olympia St Houston TX 77056 Office: Pennzoil Co PO Box 2967 711 Louisiana St Houston TX 77252-2967

LAMOND, CORA PEELER, home economics educator, consultant; b. Shannon, Miss., Apr. 7, 1927; d. Alric Arnold and Mary Katherine (Brandon) Peeler; m. John Franklin Lamond, June 5, 1949; children—Heather Lee, Mary Charlotte, John Fleming. B.S. in Edn., Miss. Delta U., 1948; M.A. in Adminstrn., Memphis State U., 1958; guidance cert. William and Mary U., 1973. Cert. tchr., Va. Tchr., Arcola High Sch., Miss., 1948-49, Juanita High Sch., Nebr., 1949-51, White Sta. High Sch., Memphis, 1960-63, Frost and Cooper Inst., Fairfax, Va., 1964—; TV personality Sta. WKNO-TV, Memphis, 1958-60; comparative edn. cons. Am. U., Washington, 1972-80. Contbr. articles to popular mags. Sec., treas. Memphis Civic Assn., 1955-60; del. Republican Conv., Richmond, Va., 1980; elder Clifton Presbyn. Ch., Va., 1978-82. Mem. NEA, Va. Edn. Assn. (com. mem. 1983-85), Fairfax Edn. Assn. (dept. and com. chmn. 1978-85), Fairfax Home Econs. Assn. (com. chmn. 1980-85). Clubs: Clifton Book; Capital Yacht, Chantilly Country. Avocations: travel consultant; swim team judge; sewing judge; sailing; outdoor education. Home: 13300 Johnny Moore Ln Clifton VA 22024 Office: Cooper Inst Sch Fairfax County Schs 977 Balls Hill Rd McLean VA 22101

LAMONT, ALICE, accountant, consultant; b. Houston, July 19; d. Harold and Bessie Bliss (Knight) L. B.Sc., Mont. State U.; M.B.A. in Taxation, Golden Gate U., 1982. Tchr. London Central High Sch., 1971-80; acct. Signetics, Sunnyvale, Calif., 1980-82, Metcalf, Frix & Co., Atlanta, 1983-84; propr. Alice Lamont Ltd., 1985—. Mem. AAUW (life), Ga. Soc. C.P.A.s. (assoc.), EDP Auditors, Inst. Internal Auditors. Episcopalian. Club: Atlanta Woman's.

LAMOUNTAIN, DIANNE MARIE, consultant, human resources, trainer; b. Boston, Aug. 26, 1948; d. Armand Achile and Rose Ann (Beaudoin) Beauchemin; m. Dennis Michael LaMountain, Oct. 25, 1969. B.A., R.I. Coll., 1972; M.S., Cornell U., 1977. Program assoc. United Way or Greater Richmond, Va., 1975-76, research cons. Va. State Crime Commn., Richmond, 1976-79; exec. dir. Greater Richmond Child Advocacy of Richmond, 1979-81; project assoc. Va. Commonwealth U., Richmond, 1981-82; prin., cons. LaMountain & Assocs., Richmond, Va., 1982—. Mem., sec. Richmond Youth Services Commn., 1981—; grad. Leadership Met. Richmond, 1984; pres. bd. dirs. Carrillon Civic Assn., Richmond, 1985. Recipient Outstanding Child Advocate Va. Commn. for Children, 1982. Mem. Am. Soc. for Tng. and Devel. (com. chmn. 1983—), Richmond Profl. Women's Network. Democrat. Roman Catholic. Home: 3114 Bute Ln Richmond VA 23221 Office: LaMountain & Assocs 3114 Bute Ln Richmond VA 23221

LAMOUREUX, WILLIAM A., poet; b. Montreal, Que., Can., Aug. 15, 1938; s. William C. and Beatrice (Benoit) L.; B.A., Tufts U., 1964; postgrad. Boston U., 1964-65, U. Hawaii, 1974; came to U.S., 1938, naturalized, 1953. Partner, Lamoureux Funeral Home, Gardner, Mass., 1949-76; founder, propr. Librairie Francaise, Santurce, P.R., 1970-73; broker-salesman J.M. Urner Inc., Realtors, Honolulu, 1974-76; broker-salesman Portner & Portner, Inc., Realtors, Hollywood, Fla., 1978-82; right-of-way agent Fla. Dept. Transp., 1978-80; works include: (poetry) La lumiere se retire du bord de la terrasse....., 1960; Comme je traversais le pays des licornes, 1961; Un oranger, supreme emeraude, 1962. Republican. Roman Catholic. Home and office: 6 Lantana Ln Sewall's Point Stuart FL 33494

LAMPE, HENRY O., stockbroker; b. Bremen, Germany, Apr. 8, 1927 (parents U.S. citizens); s. Henry D. and Dorothea C. (Gatje) L.; m. Virginia Harvey, July 18, 1953 (dec. 1984). B.S. with honors, Am. U., 1952. Investigator pub. safety Office Mil. Govt., Berlin, 1947-49; methods examiner Bur. Consular Affairs, Dept. State, 1952-53; investigator USIA, Office of Security, 1953-55; budget examiner Resources and Civil Works div. Bur. Budget, Washington, 1955-58; v.p., br. mgr. Birely & Co., Washington and Arlington, Va., 1959-66; v.p. Thomson McKinnon Securities Inc., Arlington, 1967—; dir. Home Health Equipment Co., Med.-Tech, Inc.; cons., lectr. in field. Co-author: Faculty Handbook, George Mason U., 1985. Mem., past chmn. Arlington Com. of 100, 1963—; mem. Va. Legislature, 1970-72; trustee Arlington Hosp., 1976-86, pres., 1982-85; bd. visitors George Mason U., 1980—; vice chmn. Home Health Services No. Va., 1984—. Served with USN, 1945-46. Recipient merit citation U.S. Office Mil. Govt., Berlin, 1949; named Arlington County Man of Yr., 1985. Mem. Arlington C. of C. (bd. dirs. 1985), Bond Club of Washington. Republican. Lutheran. Clubs: Bull and Bear (Richmond); Lions (Arlington). Avocation: gardening. Home: 2914 N Greencastle St Arlington VA 22207 Office: Thomson McKinnon Securities Inc 3030 Clarendon Blvd Arlington VA 22201

LAMPE, RICHARD MICHAEL, pediatrician, army officer; b. Covington, Ky., June 28, 1944; s. Victor H. and Marie E. (Sipple) L.; m. Janice Suzanne Simon, Aug. 31, 1968; children—Jill, Christopher, Charles, Craig. A.B., Thomas More Coll., 1964; M.D., Marquette U., 1968. Diplomate Am. Bd. Pediatrics. Intern, Walter Reed Gen. Hosp., Washington, 1968-69, resident in pediatrics, 1970-72; commd. capt. U.S. Army, 1968, advanced through grades to col., 1982; asst. chief pediatric dept. William Beaumont Army Med. Ctr., El Paso, Tex., 1982—. Recipient Ogden Bruton award Uniformed Services Pediatric Seminar, 1983. Mem. Am. Acad. Pediatrics, So. Soc. Pediatric Research, Ambulatory Pediatric Assn., Tex. Infectious Disease Soc. Roman Catholic.

LAMPERT, ROBERT EDWARD, educational administrator, medical ethics consultant; b. Muncie, Ind., June 24, 1939; s. William Joseph and Helen Agnes (McDonald) L. B.A., Cardinal Glennon Coll., 1961; M.A., U. Notre Dame, 1972; Ph.D., St. Louis U., 1978. Ordained priest, Roman Catholic Ch., 1965. Asst. prof. Christian ethics U. St. Thomas, Houston, 1975-78, Washington Theol. Union, Silver Spring, Md., 1978; co-dir. Benedictine Health Resource Ctr., San Antonio, 1984—; acad. dean Oblate Sch. Theology, San Antonio, 1979—; med. ethics cons. Seton Med. Ctr., Austin, Tex., 1979—, Spohn Hosp., Corpus Christi, Tex., 1984—. Mem. Cath. Theol. Soc., Am. Soc. Christian Ethics. Avocation: passenger train history in U.S. Home: 3803 Barrington 6-C San Antonio TX 78217 Office: Oblate Sch Sch Theology 285 Oblate Dr San Antonio TX 78216

LAMPERT, SCOTT IRVING, ophthalmologist; b. Phila., Aug. 28, 1948; s. Harold J. and Selma Irene (Heitzer) L.; m. Ellen M. Graboyes, Sept. 5, 1971 (div. 1976); m. Judy Lynn Morris, June 2, 1978; children—Samantha, Adam, Alexandra. B.A., U. Pa., 1970; M.D., Thomas Jefferson U., 1974. Intern Grady Meml. Hosp. Atlanta, 1974-75; resident in ophthalmology Thomas Jefferson U., Phila., 1976-79; retina and vitreous fellow U. Pa., Phila., 1979-80; practice medicine specializing in ophthalmology, Atlanta, 1980—; dir. Diabetes Assn. Atlanta, 1983—. Fellow Am. Acad. Ophthalmology; mem. Ga. Soc. Ophthalmology, Atlanta Ophthal. Soc., AMA, Med. Assn. Ga., Med. Assn. Atlanta. Avocations: music (saxophone); swimming. Office: 3280 Howell Mill Rd NW Atlanta GA 30327

LAMPLEY, DONNA JEAN, cardiopulmonary nurse, physician assistant; b. Bethesda, Md., July 7, 1953; d. Eulan Lyman and Mary Jane (Hanks) Lampley. Diploma in Nursing, Methodist Hosp. Sch. Nursing, 1973; Diploma in Cardiopulmonary Perfusion, Tex. Heart Inst., 1979; postgrad. Memphis State U., 1982-84. Charge nurse psychiatry Naval Regional Med. Ctr., Jacksonville, Fla., 1974-76; staff nurse ICU, Methodist Hosp. of Central Memphis, 1976-78; cardiopulmonary nurse-perfusionist Surg. Group for Thoracic and Cardiovascular Diseases, Memphis, 1979—; clin. instr. U. Tenn. Sch. Perfusion Tech., Memphis, 1980-82. Served to lt. j.g., USNR, 1974-76. Mem. Am. Soc. Extracorporeal Tech., Am. Assn. Critical Care Nurses, Golden Key Honor Soc., Pi Epsilon Iota. Democrat. Presbyterian. Home: 4507 Sequoia St Memphis TN 38117 Office: The Surg Group for Thoracic and Cardiovascular Diseases PC Suite 340 1325 Eastmoreland Memphis TN 38104

LAMY, M(ARY) REBECCA, land developer, former govt. ofcl.; b. Ft. Bragg, N.C., Nov. 21, 1929; d. Charles Joseph and Sarah Esther (Koonce) L.; B.A., U. N.C., Greensboro, 1952. Procurement analyst Air Force MIPR Mgmt. Office, Washington, 1958-60, procurement and fiscal officer, 1960-68; budget analyst Naval Air Systems Command, Washington, 1968-69, indsl. specialist, 1969-71; indsl. specialist A.D.T.C., Eglin AFB, Fla., 1971-74, Def. Logistics Agy., Alexandria, Va., 1974-81; logistics mgmt. specialist Strategic Systems Project Office, Dept. Navy, Washington, 1981-82; procurement analyst Hdqrs. Dept. Army, Washington, 1982-85. Recipient Outstanding Performance awards U.S. Air Force, 1956, 65, 72, 73; Quality award Def. Logistics Agy., 1979, Outstanding Performance award, 1978, 79, Exceptional Service award, 1983, 84; Comdr.'s award Hdqrs. Dept. Army, 1985; others. Mem. U. N.C. at Greensboro. Alumni Assn. Office: PO Box 1494 Jacksonville NC 28541

LA NASA, JOSEPH ALOYSIUS, JR., physician; b. New Orleans, Nov. 5, 1942; s. Joseph Aloysius and Leola (Dalton) LaN.; B.S., U. Notre Dame, 1964; M.D., La. State U., 1968; m. Wanda Anne Garcia, June 15, 1968; children—Joseph Aloysius III, Connie Lee, Jonathan Andrew. Intern, Charity Hosp., New Orleans, 1968-69, resident in urology, 1971-75; fellow in infertility UCLA, others, 1975; mem. faculty La. State U. Med. Center, New Orleans, 1975—, assoc. prof. urology, 1979—, chmn. dept. urology, 1979-82, dir. fertility lab. and semen bank, 1975-82; chief surgery, bd. dirs. River Parishes Med. Ctr. Hosp., La Place, La. 1982—; mem. staff So. Bapt. Hosp., St. Jude Hosp., Patron Acad. Sacred Heart; mem. New Orleans Opera Guild, Metairie Park Country Day Assn. Served with AUS, 1969-71. Diplomate Am. Bd. Urology. Mem. Am. Urol. Assn., La. Urol. Soc. (pres. 1976-77), Am. Fertility Soc., La. State U. Urology Alumni Assn. (pres. 1977-81), So. Med. Assn. (pres. urology sect. 1980-81), Am. Soc. Andrology, Notre Dame Club New Orleans. Democrat. Roman Catholic. Clubs: Children Carnival of New Orleans, Endymion Carnival Orgn., Valencia, Ormond Country. Home: 10 Villere Pl Destrehan LA 70047 Office: 501 Rue de Sante Suite 2 La Place LA 70068

LANCASTER, CARL HERBERT, JR., architect; b. Jasper, Ala., Feb. 1, 1913; s. Carl Herbert and Hattie (Anderson) L.; m. Dorothy Edward Heisler, Dec. 31, 1946; children—Carl H. III, Hilda Annette, Dorothy Susan, Winston Churchill. B. Arch., Auburn U., 1947. Registered architect, Ala. Sr. draftsman Sherlock, Smith & Adams, Montgomery, 1947-48; prin. Carl Herbert Lancaster Architect, Montgomery, 1948—. Prin works include mcpl. complex, Jackson, Ala., 1983, Chaplains Sch., Maxwell AFB, 1983, Tyson Manor House, 1985. Adj. Thomas Goode Jones Camp Sons Confederate Vets., Montgomery, 1985; sec., treas. Taxpayers Def. Fund, Montgomery, 1985; pres. Keep Montgomery Beautiful, 1980. Served with USN, 1942-45, PTO. Mem. Scarab, Alpha Rho Chi. Mem. Ind. Methodist Ch. Clubs: Toastmasters (Montgomery) (pres.), Creative Writers (Montgomery) (bull. editor). Avocations: Creative writing; sketching; gardening; camping; reading. Office: 469 S McDonough St Montgomery AL 36104

LANCASTER, CARROLL TOWNES, JR., marketing executive; b. Waco, Tex., Mar. 14, 1929; s. Carroll T. and Beatrice (Hollaman) L.; student U. Tex., 1948-51, 52-53; m. Catherine Virginia Frommel, May 29, 1954; children—Loren Thomas, Barbara, Beverly, John Tracy. Sales coordinator Union Tank div. Butler Mfg. Co., Houston, 1954-56, sales rep., New Orleans, 1956-57, br. mgr., 1957-60; asst. to exec. v.p. Maloney-Crawford Mfg. Co., Tulsa, 1960-62; mktg. cons., sr. assoc. Market/Product Facts, Tulsa, 1962-63; market devel. asst. Norriseal Controls div. Dover Corp., Houston, 1963-66; area dir. Arthritis Found., Houston, 1966-69, dir. S.W. div., 1969-70; exec. dir. United Cerebral Palsy Tex. Gulf Coast, 1971-74; exec. dir. Leukemia Soc. Am., Gulf Coast, 1974-76, Lancaster & Assocs., 1976—. Christian edn. tchr., 1966-70, supr., 1971, asst. youth football coach, Bellaire, 1967-68, 70-71; mem. Houston-Galveston Area Health Commn. Study Group, 1972-76, co-chmn., 1976; dir., essayist Tex. Low Vision Council, 1976-79, sec.-treas., 1978-81, pres., 1981-84; del. Houston Interfaith Sponsoring Com., 1979-81; bd. dirs. Council Chs. Greater Houston, 1966-68, v.p., 1968. Served with USNR, 1946-48, 51-52. Recipient award for securing free blood for indigent Harris County Hosp. Dist., 1968. Mem. Am. Mktg. Assn., SAR, Huguenot Soc., San Marcos Acad. Ex-Students' Assn. (pres. 1982-84), Delta Sigma Phi. Episcopalian (vestryman 1975-78). Home: 4901 Holly St Bellaire TX 77401 Office: PO Box 745 Bellaire TX 77401

LANCASTER, EDD TURNER, sign manufacturing company executive; b. Centerville, Tenn., Aug. 7, 1933; s. Samuel Benjamin and Mary Elizabeth (Harper) L.; m. Bette Cordell, Aug. 31, 1951 (div. 1983); children—Deborah S., Lynda K., Steven E. Student pub. schs., Nashville. With gen. acctg. dept. Neuhoff Packing Co. div. Swift and Co., Nashville, 1952-62; with Swift & Co., Chgo., 1962-63, Rivers Mfg. Corp., Centerville, Tenn., 1963-65; with Tencon Co., Centerville, 1965—, pres., chief exec. officer, 1980—; dir. Nat. Electric Sign Assn. Republican. Mem. Ch. of Christ. Home: Rural Route 2 Hwy 100 Centerville TN 37033 Office: Tencon Co 400 Rivers Rd Centerville TN 37033

LANCASTER, JOANNE RUSSELL, legal secretary; b. Raleigh, N.C., Mar. 31, 1938; d. Robert Milton and Lillian Russell (Stuart) Clements; student Trident Tech. Sch., 1975-77; B.S. in B.A., Baptist Coll., Charleston, S.C., 1985; m. Rondel Alexander Lancaster, Dec. 20, 1975; children by previous marriage—Debra Ann Kerce Jones, Spencer Tracy Kerce, Jr. Sec., 1st. Baptist Ch., Johns Island, S.C., 1963-65, tchr. kindergarten, 1966-67; legal sec. Office of John C. Conway, Charleston, S.C., 1974; clk.-typist Profl. Staff Office, Med. U. S.C., Charleston, 1974-75; clk. County of Charleston, 1967-73, ct. reporter, sec. to master in equity Charleston County, 1975-76, document clk., 1984-85; legal sec. Michael T. Bolus & Deborah K. Lewis, Charleston, 1985—; adminstrv. sec. Neighborhood Legal Assistance Program, Inc., Charleston, 1976-79, program adminstrv. sec., 1976-79, adminstrv. sec., Summerville, S.C., 1979-84. Baptist. Home: Route 4 Box 663 Moncks Corner SC 29461 Office: 5861 Rivers Ave Suite 213 Charleston SC 29418

LANCE, WILLIAM MICHAEL, architect, furniture designer; b. Oklahoma City, Aug. 23, 1937; s. William Jewell and Lois Elizabeth (Primm) L.; m. Mary Elizabeth Merrett, June 9, 1962; children—Kathryn Anne, Sara Ellen. B.A. in Arch., U. Tex., 1961. Registered architect, Tex. Assoc. O'Neil Ford & Assocs., San Antonio, 1961-69; ptnr. O'Neill, Perez, Lance & Larcade, San Antonio, 1969-73, Lance, Larcade & Bechtol, San Antonio, 1973—. Co-winner Internat. Competition Chair 1977, AIA, 1977. Democrat. Methodist. Avocations: kinetic sculpture; furniture design and prototype fabrications. Home: 1818 E Pyron Rd San Antonio TX 78223 Office: Lance Larcade & Bechtol Architects 235 E Commerce St San Antonio TX 78205

LANCIO, JERRY WILLIAM, educator; b. Dallas, Pa., Sept. 4, 1940; s. William G. and Alberta R. (Hofmeister) L. A.A.S., No. Va. Community Coll., 1968; B.S., Va. Commonwealth U., 1970; M.S., Va. Poly. Inst. and State U., 1975. Cert. tchr., Va., Fla. Office mgr. Xerox Corp., Rockville, Md., 1965-66; bus. tchr. Loudoun County Pub. Sch., Leesburg, Va., 1970-80; bus. prof. Fla. Keys Community Coll., Key West, 1980—; cons. internal control Key West Navy Fed. Credit Union, Fla.; chmn. student activities com. Fla. Keys Community Coll., Key West, 1983-84, chmn. faculty grievance com. 1984, chmn. salary com., 1984; faculty commn. rep. Fla. Assn. Community Colls., 1984. Democrat. Avocations: producer, director. Home: 1521 5th St Key West FL 33040 Office: Fla Keys Community Coll 1 Jr College Rd Key West FL 33040

LAND, DEANNA KAY, university dean; b. Prairie Grove, Ark., Apr. 10, 1945; d. Frank Reed and Betty Mae (Hankins) Briggs Crum; m. James Robert Land, Nov. 26, 1964; children—Tracy Annette, James Robert. B.S. in Edn., Northeastern State U., Tahlequah, Okla., 1967, M.Ed., 1974; postgrad U. Okla., 1985—. Sec. div. health, phys. edn. and recreation Northeastern State U., 1967-69, sec. to dean students, 1970-74, asst. dir. residential life, 1974-77, residential life coordinator, 1977-78; tchr. bus. Stroud High Sch., Okla., 1969-70; assoc. dean students Central State U., Edmond, Okla., 1978—. Pres., Oklahoma County Womens Democratic Com., Oklahoma City, 1982-83; bd. dirs. Edmond Jr. Cotillion, 1984-86. Mem. Okla. Coll. Personnel Assn. (pres. 1985—), Am. Coll. Personnel Assn. (state del. 1984-85), Okla. Assn. Counseling and Devel. (bd. dirs. 1985—), Nat. Assn. Student Personnel Adminstrs., S.W. Assn. Student Personnel Adminstrs., Okla. Assn. Univ. Deans, Am. Bus. Womens Assn. (scholarship chmn. Oklahoma City 1981-82), Okla. Women in Edn. Baptist. Lodge: Elk Ladies. Office: Central State U 100 N University Dr Edmond OK 73034

LAND, JOHN CALHOUN, III, lawyer, state senator; b. Manning, S.C., Jan. 25, 1941; s. John Calhoun, Jr. and Anna Abbott (Weisiger) L.; m. Marie Mercogliano, Oct. 23, 1965; children—John Calhoun IV, Frances Ricci, William Ceth. Student vocat. forestry U. Fla., 1960-62; B.S., U. S.C., 1965, J.D., 1968. Bar: S.C. 1968. Mem. Land, Turbeville and Parker P.A., Manning, 1968—; mem. S.C. Ho. of Reps., 1975-76, mem. S.C. Senate, 1977—. Sec. Clarendon County Democratic Com., 1968-70; commr. S.C. Hwys. and Pub. Transp., 1971-74. Mem. ABA, Clarendon County Bar Assn., S.C. Bar Assn., S.C. Trial Lawyers Assn. Avocations: hunting; fishing. Office: Land Turbeville and Parker PA PO Drawer G Manning SC 29102

LAND, KENNETH CARL, sociology educator, demographer, statistician, consultant; b. Llano, Tex., Aug. 19, 1942; s. Otto Carl and Tillie (Lindemann) L.; m. Jacqueline Yvette Apere, Mar. 22, 1969; 1 child, Kristoffer Carl. B.A., Tex. Luth. Coll., 1964; M.A., U. Tex., 1966, Ph.D., 1969. Staff assoc. Russell Sage Found., N.Y.C, 1969-73; lectr. Columbia U., N.Y.C., 1970-73; assoc. prof. U. Ill.-Urbana, 1973-76, prof., 1976-81; prof. sociology U. Tex.-Austin, 1981-86; prof., chmn. dept. sociology Duke U., Durham, N.C., 1986—. Editor: Social Indicator Models, 1975; Social Accounting Systems, 1981; Multidimensional Mathematical Demography, 1982; Contbr. articles to profl. jours. Fellow Am. Statis. Assn.; mem. Sociol. Research Assn., Am. Sociol. Assn., Population Assn. Am., Am. Soc. Criminology. Lutheran. Office: Duke U Dept Sociology Durham NC 27706

LAND, MARGARET FOSTER, statistics consultant; b. Norman, Okla., Feb. 20, 1939; m. Hugh C. Land, May 24, 1957 (dec. 1968); children—Peter Colman, David Foster, Stephanie Ruth. Asst. prof. math. N.W. State U. La., Natchitoches, 1967-70; asst. prof., statistics cons. N.Mex. State U., Las Cruces, 1977-80; teaching assoc. Okla. State U., Stillwater, 1970-77, 80-81; assoc. prof., cons. Tex. A&I U., Kingsville, 1981—; cons. statistician, 1979—. State del. Tex. Republican Party, Ft. Worth, 1984, Corpus Christi, 1984; county del. Tex. Med. Assn. Aux., Ft. Worth, 1984. Fulbright grantee, Venezuela, 1986. Mem. Am. Statis. Assn. (mem. subcom. on statis. cons. edn. 1984—), Biometrics Soc., Soc. Indsl. and Applied Math., Am. Soc. Quality Control, Mensa, Audubon Soc. Lutheran. Clubs: Intertel, Triple Nine. Avocations: running, birding, horticulture, parrots, miniature pinschers. Home: 1800 Newell St Alice TX 78332 Office: Dept Math Tex A&I U Box 172 Kingsville TX 78363

LANDAU, JEFFREY ALLEN, counselor, educator; b. N.Y.C., Dec. 10, 1959; s. Charles David and Joan L.; m. Kristin Kae Adamson, Aug. 3, 1985. B.S., Fla. State U., 1981, M.S., 1984, postgrad., 1984—. Counselor Psychol. and Family Cons., Tallahassee, 1979—; counselor Apalachee Mental Health Ctr., Tallahassee, 1979-81, crisis counselor, 1982-84; counselor Intensive Crisis Counseling Service, Tallahassee, 1982-84; trainer Telephone Counseling and Referral Service, Tallahassee, 1982-84; faculty Tallahassee Community Coll., 1983—. Mem. Am. Assn. Counseling and Devel., Lambda Chi Alpha. Office: Psychol and Family Cons 1254 Ocala Rd Tallahassee FL 32304

LANDAU, SOL, clergyman, educator-counselor; b. Berlin, Germany, June 21, 1920; s. Ezekiel and Helene (Grynberg) L.; B.A., Bklyn. Coll., 1949; M.Hebrew Lit., Rabbi, Jewish Theol. Sem., 1951, D.D., 1977; M.A., N.Y. U., 1958; Ph.D., Fla. State U., 1977; m. Gabriela Mayer, Jan. 14, 1951; children—Ezra M., Tamara A. Rabbi, 1951; rabbi Whitestone (N.Y.) Hebrew Center, 1952-56; co-rabbi Park Synagogue, Cleve., 1956-60, 63-65; rabbi Beth Hillel Congregation, Wilmette, Ill., 1960-63, Beth David Congregation, Miami, Fla., 1965-81; pres., exec. Midlife Service Found., Inc., 1981—. Chaplain Homestead Air Force Base, 1974-77; adj. prof. psychology U. Miami, 1979-85. Pres., Dade County Mental Health Assn., 1973-81; pres. Dade County Youth Adv. Bd. Served with AUS, 1942-45. Recipient Jerusalem award, citation City Miami, award Dade County Mental Health Assn.; Rabbinic Community award Fedn. Welfare Council, 1976. Fellow Jewish Acad. Arts and Sci.; mem. Rabbinical Assembly (pres. S.E. Region), Rabbinical Assn. Greater Miami (pres. 1976-77, 80-81), AAUP, Am. Assn. Counseling and Devel., Orthopsychiat Assn., Adult Edn. Assn., Jewish War Vets. Author: Christian-Jewish Relations; Length of Our Days; Bridging Two Worlds; Turning Points. Home: 3 Grove Isle Dr Miami FL 33133 Office: 9100 S Dadeland Blvd Suite 1163 Miami FL 33156

LANDER, GERALD HAROLD, accounting educator, consultant; b. Wayland, N.Y., Nov. 1, 1942; s. Harold LeRoy and Catherine Christina (Isaman) L.; m. Catherine Elaine Faulkner, June 30, 1962 (div. Nov. 1974). B.A. in Econs., SUNY-Geneseo, 1971; M.B.A. in Acctg., Rochester Inst. Tech., 1975; D.B.A. in Acctg., U. Ky., 1980. C.P.A., Fla. Mgr. Agway Inc., Syracuse, N.Y., 1961-64; consumer credit loan officer First Trust Union Bank, Wellsville, N.Y., 1964-66; sr. acct. Deloitte Haskins & Sells, Rochester, N.Y., 1972-75; instr. Eastern Mich. U., Ypsilanti, 1975-77; asst. prof. Fla. State U., Tallahassee, 1980-81; assoc. prof. acctg. U. South Fla., Tampa, 1981—; cons. in field; instr. continuing edn. and profl. edn. Fla. Inst. C.P.A.s. Served with U.S. Army, 1966-68. Named Outstanding Faculty Mem., Bryant and Stratton Bus. Inst., 1975, U. Ky., 1979, U. South Fla., 1982; Deloitte Haskins & Sells fellow, 1979. Mem. Am. Acctg. Assn., Assn. Govt. Accts., Nat. Assn. Accts., Am. Inst. C.P.A.s, Fla. Inst. C.P.A.s, Omicron Delta Epsilon, Beta Alpha Psi. Contbr. articles to profl. jours. Home: 6365 Bahia Del Mar Blvd Apt J-406 Saint Petersburg FL 33715 Office: College of Business University of South Florida Tampa FL 33620

LANDESZ, J. KARL, architect; b. Teheran, Iran, June 5, 1938; came to U.S., 1957; s. Karoly Landesz and Maria Soos; m. Joan Shillington (div. 1972); 1 son, William C. Student Tech. Sch. Bldg. Constrn., Budapest, Hungary, 1952-56. Assoc. mgr. prodn. Horowitz and Seigel Assocs., Inc., Silver Spring, Md., 1962-65; assoc. Madis Valge Assocs., Silver Spring, 1965-74; project mgr.

Chatelain, Samperton and Carcaterra, Washington, 1974-76; sr. architect DMJM, Washington and Balt., 1976-78; project architect Harry Weese & Assocs., Miami, Fla., 1978-82, asst. mgr., 1982—. Served with U.S. Army, 1959-61. Office: Harry Weese & Assocs 44 W Flagler St Miami FL 33130

LANDIS, DAVID ANDREW, educator, coach; b. Harrisburg, Pa., Nov. 7, 1957; s. Samuel Wayne and Ona Elaine (Bowman) L. B.S. Ed., Univ. Ga., 1980. Teaching cert. Asst. coach wrestling athletic dept. Univ. Ga., Athens, 1979-80; asst. mgr. Am. Fitness Ctr., Atlanta, 1980; restaurant mgr. Western Sizzlin Steak House, Atlanta, Athens, 1980-82; food service mgr. Kada Kitchens, Atlanta, 1982-83; tchr., coach DeKalb County Schs., Atlanta, 1983—. Sponsor Key Club Lakeside High Sch., 1983-84. Mem. Christian Ch. Home: 71 Thrasher St Norcross GA 30071 Office: Lakeside High Sch-DeKalb County 3801 Briarcliff Rd Atlanta GA 30071

LANDOLT, ARLO UDELL, astronomer, educator; b. Highland, Ill., Sept. 29, 1935; s. Arlo Melvin and Vesta (Kraus) L.; m. Eunice Jean Casper, June 8, 1966; children—Linda, Barbara, Vicky, Debra, Jennifer. B.A., Miami U.-Oxford, Ohio, 1955; M.A., Ind. U., 1960, Ph.D., 1962. Research and teaching asst. Ind. U., 1955-56, 58-62; asst. prof. La. State U., Baton Rouge, 1962-65, assoc. prof., 1965-68, prof., 1968—, dir. Obs., 1970—, acting chmn. dept. physics and astronomy, summers 1972, 73, pres. faculty senate, 1979-80; program dir. NSF astronomy sect., 1975-76; guest investigator Vanderbilt U. Dyer Obs., Ind. U. Goethe Link Obs., Kitt Peak Nat. Obs., Tucson, Cerro Tololo Inter-Am. Obs., La Serena, Chile; mem. 1st wintering-over party Internat. Geophys. Yr. Amundson-Scott S. Pole Sta., Antarctica, 1957. Mem. AAAS (sec. astronomy sect. 1970-78), Am. Astronomy Soc. (sec. 1980—, mem. vis. prof. program), Astron. Soc. Pacific, Royal Astron. Soc. Eng., Internat. Astron. Union (Organizing com. Commn. 25), Am. Polar Soc., Explorer's Club, Sigma Xi, Pi Mu Epsilon. Office: Dept Physics and Astronomy La State U Baton Rouge LA 70803

LANDON, FORREST MALCOLM, editor; b. Pontiac, Mich., Sept. 24, 1933; s. Eleanor (Stevens) Smith; m. Barbara Patrick, Sept. 25, 1955; children—Jeffrey W., Tracy A. Student Hartwick Coll., Oneonta, N.Y., 1951-53; B.J., U. Mo., 1955. Reporter, anchorman Sta. WDBJ AM-FM-TV, 1955-59; news dir. Sta. WDBJ AM-FM, Roanoke, Va., 1959-64; assoc. editor editorial page Roanoke World-News, 1964-67; editor editorial page Roanoke Times, 1967-71, assoc. editor, 1971-74, night mng. editor, mng. editor, 1974-82, exec. editor, 1982—, v.p., 1984—; tchr. journalism Hollins Coll., 1970-74, host weekly forum Sta. WBRA-TV, 1968-79. Mem. Am. Soc. Newspaper Editors, Sigma Delta Chi. Club: Torch. Office: Roanoke Times & World News 201-209 W Campbell Ave PO Box 2491 Roanoke VA 24010

LANDON, JOHN WILLIAM, social worker, educator, author; b. Marlette, Mich., Mar. 24, 1937; s. Norman A. and Merle Irene (Lawrason) L. B.A., Taylor U., 1959; M.Div., Northwestern U., Christian Theol. Sem., 1962; M.S.W., Ind. U., 1966; Ph.D. in Social Sci., Ball State U., 1972. Regional supr. Iowa Dept. Social Welfare, Des Moines, 1965-67; acting chmn. dept. sociology Marion (Ind.) Coll., 1967-69; asst. prof. sociology and social work Ball State U., Muncie, Ind., 1969-71; asst. prof. social work, coordinator base courses Coll. Social Professions U. Ky., Lexington, 1971-73, assoc. prof., coordinator undergrad. program in social work Coll. Social Professions, 1974—, coordinator Undergrad. Program in Social Work Coll. of Social Work, 1974-85, assoc. dean, 1985—; dir. social work edn. Taylor U., Upland, Ind., 1973-74. Author: From These Men, 1966; Jesse Crawford, Poet of the Organ, Wizard of the Mighty Wurlitzer, 1974; Behold the Mighty Wurlitzer, The History of the Theatre Pipe Organ, 1983; The Development of Social Welfare, 1986. Mem. Am. Sociol. Assn., Council Social Work in Edn., Am. Acad. Social Sci., Ind. Acad. Social Sci., AAUP, Nat. Assn. Christians in Social Work, Am. Guild Organists, Am. Theatre Organ Soc. Home: 809 Celia Lane Lexington KY 40504 Office: U Ky Coll Social Work Lexington KY 40506

LANDON, ROBERT KIRKWOOD, insurance company executive; b. N.Y.C., Apr. 27, 1929; s. Kirk A. and Edith (Ungar) L.; student U. Va., 1946-48; B.S., Ga. Inst. Tech., 1950; m. Beulah Pair, Mar. 19, 1965; children—Chris Joseph, Kathleen Adele Staley, Kellyann Spears. With Am. Bankers Life Assurance Co., Miami, Fla., 1952—, pres., 1960-74, chmn., chief exec. officer, 1974—, chmn. bd., chief exec. officer Am. Bankers Ins. Group Inc., Miami; pres. Landon Corp., Dover, Del., 1971—. Trustee Kirk A. and Dorothy P. Landon Found., from 1969. Served to lt. (j.g.) USNR, 1950-53. Mem. Met. Mus. and Art Centers, Council Internat. Visitors, World Bus. Council, Scabbard and Blade. Phi Gamma Delta. Office: 11222 Quail Roost Dr Miami FL 33157

LANDRAM, CHRISTINA LOUELLA, librarian; b. Paragould, Ark., Dec. 10, 1922; d. James Ralph and Bertie Louella (Jordan) Oliver; m. Robert Ellis Landram, Aug. 7, 1948; 1 son, Mark Owen. B.A., Tex. Woman's U., 1945, B.L.S., 1946, M.L.S., 1951. Preliminary cataloger Library of Congress, Washington, 1946-48; cataloger U.S. Info. Ctr., Tokyo, Japan, 1948-50, U.S. Dept. Agr., Washington, 1953-54; librarian Yokota AFB, Yokota, Japan, 1954-55; librarian St. Mary's Hosp., West Palm Beach, Fla., 1957-59; librarian Jacksonville (Ark.) High Sch., 1959-61; coordinator Shelby County Libraries, Memphis, 1961-63; head catalog dept. Ga. State U. Library, 1963—. Contbr. articles to library jours. Mem. Ga. Library Assn. (chmn. resources and tech. services sect. 1969-71), Metro-Atlanta Library Assn. (pres. 1967-68), ALA (chmn. cataloging norms 1979-80, nominating com. 1977-78), Southeastern Library Assn. (mem. govtl. relations com. 1975-78). Presbyterian. Home: 1478 Leafmore Ridge Decatur GA 30033 Office: Pullen Library Ga State U 100 Decatur St SE Atlanta GA 30303

LANDRENEAU, RODNEY EDMUND, JR., surgeon; b. Mamou, La., Jan. 17, 1929; s. Rodney Edmund and Blanche (Savoy) L.; M.D., La. State U., 1951; m. Colleen Fraser, June 4, 1952; children—Rodney Jerome, Michael Douglas, Denise Margaret, Melany Patricia, Fraser Edmund, Edythe Blanche. Intern, Charity Hosp., New Orleans, 1951-52, resident, 1952-54, 56-58; practice medicine specializing in surgery, Eunice, La., 1958—; pres., dir. Eunice Med. Center, Inc., 1960—; mem. staff Moosa Meml. Hosp., Eunice, 1958—, chief med. staff; vis. staff Opelousas Gen. Hosp., 1958—; asso. faculty La. State U.-Eunice; cons., staff Lafayette (La.) Charity Hosp.; cons. staff surgery Savoy Meml. Hosp., Mamou; pres. Eunice Med. Center, Inc.; dir. Acadiana Bank & Trust Co.; mem. La. State Hosp. Bd., 1972—. Mem. Evangeline council Boy Scouts Am.; bd. dirs. Moosa Meml. Hosp., Eunice, 1986—; pres. St. Edmund's Scholastic Boosters' Club, 1986—. Served with M.C., AUS, 1954-56. Recipient Physician's Recognition award AMA, 1978-83. Diplomate Am. Bd. Surgery. Fellow Internat. Coll. Surgeons (regional bd.), ACS (local chmn. com. trauma, instr.), Southeastern Surg. Congress, Pan Pacific Surg. Congress; mem. Am. Bd. Abdominal Surgeons, Am. Geriatrics Soc., St. Edmunds Athletic Assn., St. Edmunds High Sch. Scholastic Booster's Club, St. Landry Hist. Soc. (v.p. chpt.), St. Landry Parish Med. Soc. (pres. 1969-71), Am. Legion, SCV, SAR, Eunice C. of C. (bd. dirs.) Alpha Omega Alpha. Democrat. Roman Catholic. Home: 1113 Williams St Eunice LA 70535 Office: 301 N Duson St Eunice LA 70535

LANDRITH, GEORGE CLAY, business exec.; b. Los Angeles, Nov. 29, 1915; s. William George and Mary (Wickersham) L.; student pub. schs.; m. Frances Jordan, Oct. 28, 1935; children—Nicholas J., George Clay. Vice pres. Thomas L. Dawson, gen. contracting, Kansas City, Mo., 1934-39; owner, operator Landrith Constrn. Co., Alexandria, Va., 1939-45; owner Belle View Apts., Alexandria, 1947—; dir. 1st Commonwealth Ins. Co., Richmond, Va., Gt. Lake Ins. Co., Elgin, Ill. Mem. Va. Hwy. Commn., 1962-70; mem. Fairfax County Planning Commn., 1948-60, bd. Fairfax County Suprs., 1960, Richmond Met. Authority, 1966-70, Va. Met. Areas. Transp. Study Commn.; bd. dirs. Alexandria Community Health Center, 1953-54, Alexandria Boys Club, 1958-62; mem. dist. council Salvation Army, 1958-62; sponsor Alexandria Little League, 1953-75; dir. trustees Fairfax County Hosp., 1957-59; trustee Ind. Colls. Va., 1974-79; treas., Fairfax County Democratic Com., 1948-49; trustee George Mason Coll., Fairfax, Va. Mem. Fairfax County C. of C. (dir. 1953, 71). Clubs: Belle Haven Country (Alexandria); Commonwealth (Richmond); Farmington Country (Charlottesville, Va.). Home: 6109 Edgewood Terr Alexandria VA 22307

LANDRON, JOSÉ MANUEL, personnel executive, management consultant, educator; b. Santurce, P.R., Feb. 4, 1936; s. José M. and Blanca R. (Villamil) L.; B.S., Clemson U., 1963; m. Judith A. Baralt, Oct. 5, 1974; children—Lindy Aurora, Bianca Alexandra, Jose Guillermo. Engring. trainee Ralston Purina Co., Oklahoma City, 1963; regional dir. Economic Devel. Adminstr., Arecibo, P.R., 1964-68; personnel mgr. Blue Bell of P.R., Inc., Mayaguez, 1968; regional dir. Cooperative Devel. Adminstrn., Arecibo, P.R., 1969-71; personnel mgr., pub. relations dir. Caribe Motors Rio Piedras, P.R., 1971-73; dir. adminstrn. ITT Aetna Corp., Hato Rey, P.R., 1973-74; dir. indsl. relations Gulf and Western Caguas, P.R., 1974; personnel mgr., asst. dir. Personnel Div., Matsushita Electric of P.R., Rio Piedras, P.R., 1975-83, adminstrv. asst., 1983—; instr. govt. employee program P.R. Office Labor Relations, 1979—; mem. evaluation com. P.R. Pvt. Industry Council, 1979—; mem. P.R. Vocat. Tng. Council, 1979—. Active various charitable orgns.; vice chmn. Pvt. Industry Council, Nat. Alliance Businessmen; advisor, Jr. Achievement, 1971-72. Recipient United Funds Award of Merit, 1972; citation, Jr. Achievement of P.R., 1970-71; named Employer's Rep. for the Year, Sec. of Edn. of P.R., 1972. Mem. Am. Soc. Personnel Adminstrn., Profl. Soc. for Accident Prevention of P.R., Engrs. Soc. for Accident Prevention. Roman Catholic. Author: Manual for Personnel Procedures, 1972; Responsibilites of Good Supervisors, 1972; contbr. articles to profl. jours. Home: 275 Larrinaga St Urb Baldrich Hato Rey PR 00918 Office: PO Box 184 Caguas PR 00625

LANDRUM, CHARLES VERNON, constrn. company executive; b. New Orleans, Sept. 5, 1941; s. Vernon C. and Berma B.L.; student Jones County Jr. Coll., 1960-62; m. Sherry A. Leach, June 12, 1982; children—Sandra J., Charles Vernon II, Jim, Allyson Taylor. Gen. mgr. Comml. Machine & Welding, Laurel, Miss., 1965-72; chief exec. officer Comml. Constrn. Co., Inc., Laurel, 1972—; pres., chief exec. officer Comml. Trucking Co., Inc., 1979—; partner, chief exec. officer Comml. Pipeline Constrn. Co., 1980—; pres., chief exec. officer Comml. Inspection Services, Inc., 1981—; pres., chief exec. officer LaSalle, Inc., 1981—. Mem. Miss. Oilmens Invitational, Am. Petroleum Inst., Oilfield Haulers Assn., Nat. Cattlemen's Assn. Baptist. Clubs: Masons, Duck Unltd., Dixie Golf. Home: Rural Route 8 Laurel MS 39440 Office: 1939 Herbert Ave Laurel MS 39440

LANDRY, JANE LORENZ, architect; b. San Antonio, Feb. 12, 1936; d. John Henry and Lulie Amanda (Sample) L.; m. Duane Eugene Landry, Sept. 8, 1956; children—Rachel, Claire, Ellyn, Jean. Student U. Tex., 1952-55, Yale U., 1955-56; B.Arch., U. Pa., 1957. Registered architect, Tex. Draftsman Wade, Gibson, & Martin, Corpus Christi, Tex., 1958-59; project architect O'Neil Ford & Assoc., San Antonio, 1959-65; prin. Duane Landry, Architect, San Antonio, 1965-68, Dallas, 1968-76; ptnr. Landry & Landry, Architects & Planners, Dallas, 1976—, Meyer, Landry & Landry, Architects & Planners, Dallas, 1977-80; instr. San Antonio Coll., 1965. Mem. Liturgical Commn. Diocese of Dallas. Mem. AIA (mem. hist. resources com., design awards Dallas chpt. 1970, 75, 76, 77, 80), Tex. Soc. Architects (design award 1969, 81), Roman Catholic. Office: Landry & Landry Architects & Planners Suite 1419 608 N Saint Paul St Dallas TX 75201

LANDRY, RONALD JUDE, lawyer, state senator; b. Lutcher, La., May 30, 1943; s. Ambroise Harry and Althae (Clement) L.; B.A., Nicholls State U.; J.D., La. State U.; m. Mary Ellen Hebert, Aug. 14, 1965; children—Christopher Benton, Lauryn Elizabeth. Admitted to La. bar; asso. firm Becnel & Kliebert, Gramercy, La., 1969-77; individual practice law, LaPlace, La.; mem. La. Senate, 1976—. Active Tri Parish area Cub Scouts Boy Scouts Am. Mem. La. State U. Alumni Assn., LaPlace Jaycees, La. Assn. Deaf. Clubs: KC, Lions. Democrat. Roman Catholic. Address: PO Box 789 LaPlace LA 70068*

LANDRY, TOM (THOMAS WADE), profl. football coach; b. Mission, Tex., Sept. 11, 1924; s. Ray and Ruth (Coffman) L.; m. Alicia Wiggs, Jan. 28, 1949; children—Thomas, Kitty, Lisa. B.S., U. Tex., 1949; degree indsl. engring., U. Houston, 1952. Player N.Y. Yankees All-Am. Football Conf., 1949; player N.Y. Giants, 1950-53, player-coach, 1954-55, defensive coach, 1956-59; head coach Dallas Cowboys, 1960—. First v.p. Nat. Fellowship Christian Athletes, chmn. bd. Dallas chpt.; bd. govs. Dallas Town North YMCA. Served with USAAF, World War II. Named to All-Pro team, 1954. Methodist (bd. govs.). Address: care Dallas Cowboys 6116 N Central Expressway Dallas TX 75206*

LANDRY, WALTER JOSEPH, lawyer; b. Willswood, La., Jan. 23, 1931; s. John Theodore and Lelia Lucille (Peltier) L.; m. Carolyn Margaret Kruschke, Nov. 24, 1962; children—Celeste, John, Joseph, Catherine, Walter Jr., James. B.S.M.E., U. Notre Dame, 1952; J.D., Tulane U., 1958; M.A., Am. U., 1969, Ph.D., 1975. Bar: La. 1958, U.S. Supreme Ct. 1961. Legis. asst. to U.S. Sen. Russell B. Long, Washington, 1956-57, sole practice law, New Orleans, 1958-61; foreign service officer Dept. State, 1961-70; mem., action officer U.S. del. to San Jose Conf., Am. Conv. on Human Rights, 1969; ptnr. Landry, Poteet and Landry, Lafayette, La., 1974-79, Poteet & Landry, 1979—; asst. prof. U. Southwestern La., 1970-74; chmn. U.S. Lang. Policy Conf., Chgo., 1983; pres. Fedn. Am. Cultural and Lang. Communities, Inc., 1984—. Contbr. articles to Human Rights Jour., Hemispherica, other profl. publs. Editor: La. Donkey, 1977-79. Mem. Lafayette Parish Democratic Exec. Com., 1971—, chmn., 1976-83; mem. Dem. State Central Com. La., 1971—, former state co-chmn. affirmative action, 1975-76; counsel Bill of Rights Com. La. Constnl. Conv., 1973-74; del. Dem. Nat. Mid-Term Conf., 1974, 78, alt. del. Dem. Nat. Conv., 1980; organizer La. Assn. Parish Dem. Exec. Coms., 1976-77, pres., 1977-78; chmn. Dem. Caucus, 7th Congl. Dist. La., 1985—; pres. Hamilton PTA, La., 1973-74. Served to maj. USMCR, 1952—; Korea. Mem. Internat. Relations Assn. of Acadiana (pres. 1974-75), ABA (chmn. internat. law working group 1971-76), Internat. Good Neighbor Council (organizer, pres. Acadiana chpt. 1978-81). Lodge: Rotary. Home: 501 Tulane Ave Lafayette LA 70503 Office: Poteet & Landry Attys Poteet & Landry Bldg 708 W University Lafayette LA 70501

LANDURETH, LEWIS JAMES (JIM), audio visual service manager; b. Houston, Apr. 17, 1943; s. Lewis James and Iola Ruth (Hill) L.; m. Libbie Elaine Schobel, May 21, 1971; 1 child, James Bradley. B.S., U. Houston, 1966; M.S., U. So. Calif., 1969. Tchr. Houston Sch. Dist., 1966-69; coordinator instructional systems Houston Baptist U., 1969-72, adj. faculty, 1969—; mgr. audio visual services Meml. Care Systems, Houston, 1972—; cons. various hosps., Houston Sch. Dist., 1967-69, Helene Fuld Health Trust, N.Y.C., 1971—; producer various video tapes on healthcare, 1969—. Coordinator Houston Tchrs. Assn. citizenship com., 1968-69. Mem. Internat. T.V. Assn., (treas. 1978, 85), Am. Assn. Tng. Devel. (editor 1977-78), chmn. awards com. 1978). Republican. Episcopalian. Club: Houston Yacht. Avocations: sailing; hiking; running. Home: 12411 Trebeau Ct Houston TX 77031 Office: Meml Care Systems 6440 High Star St Houston TX 77074

LANDY, BURTON AARON, lawyer; b. Chgo., Aug. 16, 1929; s. Louis J. and Clara (Ernstein) L.; m. Eleonora M. Simmel, Aug. 4, 1957; children—Michael Simmel, Alisa Anne. B.S., Northwestern U., 1950; J.D., U. Miami, 1952; student Nat. U. Mexico, 1948; scholar U. Havana, 1951; fellow Inter-Am. Acad. Comparative Law, Havana, Cuba, 1955-56. Admitted to Fla. bar, 1952; gen. practice law in internat. field, Miami, 1955—; ptnr. firm Ammerman & Landy, 1957-63, Paul, Landy, Beiley & Harper, P.A., and predecessor firm, 1964—; lectr. Latin Am. bus. law U. Miami Sch. Law, 1972-75, also Internat. Law Confs. Contbg. editor Economic Developments Lawyer of the Americas, 1969-74. Contbr. articles to legal jours. Mem. Nat. Conf. on Fgn. Aspects of U.S. Nat. Security, Washington, 1958; mem. organizing com. Miami regional conf. Com. for Internat. Econ. Growth, 1958; mem. U.S. Dept. Commerce Regional Export Expansion Council, 1969-74, mem. Dist. Export Council, 1978—; mem. Fla. Council Internat. Devel., 1977—, vice chmn., 1985—; mem. exec. com. U. Miami Citizens Bd., 1977—; chmn. Fla.-S.E. U.S.-Japan Assn.; mem. adv. com. 1st Miami Trade Fair of Ams., 1978; dir., v.p. Greater Miami Fgn. Trade Zone, Inc.; mem. organizing com., lectr. 4 Inter-Am. Aviation Law Confs.; bd. dirs. Inter-Am. Bar Legal Found.; participant Aquaculture Symposium Sci. and Man of the Ams., Mexico City, Fla. Gov.'s Econ. Mission to Japan and Hong Kong, 1978; mem. bd. exec. advisors, internat. adv. bd., vis. com. U. Miami Sch. Bus.; mem. internat. fin. council Office Comptroller Fla.; bd. dirs. Simon Bolivar Found., 1984—. Served with JAGC, USAF, 1952-54, Korea, 1953-54; maj. USAF Res. Hon. mem. Bar Republic South Korea, 1954, hon. consul gen.; mem. Inter-Am. (asst. sec.-gen. 1957-59, treas. 11th conf. 1959, co-chmn. jr. bar sect. 1963-65, mem. council 1969—, exec. com. 1975—, pres. 1982-84), Am. (chmn. com. arrangements internat. and comparative law sect. 1964-65), Spanish-Am., Fla. (vice chmn. adminstrv. law com. 1965, vice chmn. internat. and comparative law com. 1967-68, chmn. aero. law com. 1968-69), Dade County (chmn. fgn. laws and langs. com. 1964-65) bar assns., Internat. Center Fla. (pres. 1981), World Peace Through Law Center, Miami Com. Fgn. Relations, Instituto Ibero Americano de Derecho Aeronautico, Am. Soc. Internat. Law, Council Internat. Visitors, Am. Fgn. Law Assn. (pres. Miami 1958), Greater Miami C. of C., Phi Alpha Delta. Home: 6255 Old Cutler Rd Miami FL 33156 Office: Penthouse Peninsula Fed Bldg Miami FL 33131

LANDY, LOIS CLOUSE, educator, counselor; b. Pitts., June 12, 1947; d. Raymond Walter and Loretta (Smith) Clouse; m. Robert Charles Landy, Dec. 20, 1969; 1 child, Robert Raymond. B.S., Pa. State U., 1969; M.Edn, Trenton State Coll., 1974; Edn. Specialist, Ga. So. Coll., 1980. Cert. sch. counselor, elem. tchr., Ga., Fla., N.J. Tchr. Penn Hills Sch. System, Pa., 1969-70, Chatham County Pub. Sch., Savannah, Ga., 1970-72, Camden City Sch., N.J., 1972-75; counselor, tchr. Voluisa County Schs., Daytona Beach, Fla., 1975-77; tchr. J.G. Smith Elem., Savannah, 1977-78; counselor Penn Ave and Whitney Schs., Savannah, 1978-81, Hesse Elem. Sch., Savannah, 1981—. Author: Child Support, 1984. Vol. counselor Rape Crisis Ctr., Savannah, 1978-81. Named Tchr. of Yr., Enterprise Elem. Sch. 1977-78. One of Outstanding Young Women Am., 1981. Mem. Ga. Sch. Counselors Assn. (2nd v.p. 1983-85, Counselor of Yr. 1979-80, Profl. Writer of Yr. 1980-81), Chatham County Counselors Assn. (chmn. 1979-80), Alpha Delta Kappa, Delta Kappa Gamma, Phi Delta Kappa. Avocations: running; swimming. Home: 204 Maria Rd Savannah GA 31410 Office: Hesse Elem Sch 9116 Whitfield Ave Savannah GA 31406

LANE, ALVIN HUEY, JR., management consultant; b. Dallas, May 2, 1942; s. Alvin Huey and Marianne (Halsell) L.; m. Melanie Kadane, June 21, 1963; children—Alvin Huey III, Michael, Lance, Marianne. B.A., Rice U., 1964, B.S., 1965. With Procter & Gamble, Dallas, 1964-68, Ernst & Whinney, Dallas, 1968-69, Balanced Investment Dynamics, Inc., Dallas, 1969-72; sr. v.p., fin., sec. Dr Pepper Co., Dallas, 1972-83; pres. Lane & Assocs., 1983—; chmn. bd. PICS Investment Co., Dallas; dir. Republic Bank-Greenville Ave., Dallas Trustee Baylor Coll. Dentistry, Dallas. Club: Lakewood Country. Home: 3415 Colgate St Dallas TX 75225 Office: 5950 Bershire Lane Suite 920 Lockbox 50 Dallas TX 75225

LANE, BERNARD BELL, furniture company executive; b. Lynchburg, Va., Nov. 23, 1928; s. Edward Hudson and Myrtle Clyde (Bell) L.; B.S., U.S. Naval Acad., 1950; m. Minnie Matthews Bassett, June 7, 1950; children—William R., Lucy H., Douglas B., Bernard Bell. With Lane Co., Altavista, Va., 1954—, v.p., then exec. v.p., 1960-76, pres., chmn. exec. com., 1976-81, chmn. bd., 1981—, dir., 1956—. Bd. dirs. Va. Poly. Inst. and State U. Ednl. Found., 1968-76; mem. Gov. Va. Adv. Bd. Indsl. Devel., 1970-82, Gov. Va. Adv. Bd. Revenue Estimates, 1977—; chmn. com. urol. research endowment and devel. Duke U. Med. Center, 1974-82, mem. com., 1974—; bd. dirs. Food for the Hungry, Scottsdale, Ariz., 1985—. Served as officer USAF, 1950-53. Methodist. Home: 302 Myrtle Ln Altavista VA 24517

LANE, BETTY, home economics educator, tree farmer; b. Statesboro, Ga., Mar. 19, 1929; d. Emory Speer and Mary Louise (Jones) L.; m. Frank Fleming Clark, Apr. 11, 1951 (div. 1952). B.S., Ga. Coll., 1949; M.Ed., U. Ga., 1956; Ph.D., Fla. State U., 1962. Secondary tchr. Jefferson County, Louisville, Ga., 1949-51, Chatham County, Savannah, Ga., 1952-53, Bulloch County, Statesboro, 1953-57; asst. prof. Ga. So. Coll., Statesboro, 1957-59, assoc. prof., 1959-64, prof. home econs., 1964—, head div. home econs., 1958—; mem. adv. bd. Willingway Alcohol and Substance Abuse, Statesboro, 1984—; mem. adv. council Ogeechee Home Health Agy., Statesboro, 1982—. Mem. Semicentquintinary Commn., Bulloch County, 1983; mem. historic resources adv. council Area Planning and Devel. Commn., Baxley, Ga., 1980—; bd. dirs. Bulloch County unit Ga. Heart Assn., Statesboro, 1984—, Bulloch Hist. Soc., Statesboro, 1984—. Recipient Friends of Extension award Ga. Assn. Extension Home Economists, 1979. Mem. Ga. Home Econs. Assn. (pres. 1973-74, Outstanding Home Economist award 1978), Nat. Council Home Econs. Adminstrn. (exec. bd. 1974-75), Am. Home Econs. Assn., AAUW, Univ. System Ga. (chmn. acad. com. on home econs. 1977-78), Ga. Future Homemakers Am. (hon.), Daus. Am. Colonists (chpt. regent), Phi Upsilon Omicron, Omicron Nu. Baptist. Club: Altrusa Internat. Avocation: genealogy. Office: Ga So Coll Div Home Econs LC Box 8034 Statesboro GA 30460

LANE, C. B., baked goods products executive; b. El Paso, Tex., 1924. Grad., Tex. A&M U., 1945. With Campbell Taggart, Inc., Dallas, 1947—, v.p., treas., then chmn. exec. com., v.p., treas., 1947-70, pres., 1970-72, vice chmn. bd., 1972, then pres., now pres., chief exec. officer, dir. Office: Campbell Taggart Inc 6211 Lemmon Ave PO Box 222640 Dallas TX 75222*

LANE, CLEVE WILSON, JR., management executive; b. Kim, Colo., Mar. 22, 1934; s. Cleve Wilson and Patricia Ada (Crain) L.; m. Shirley Sherrene Aten, Feb. 22, 1955 (div. 1968); children—Mark W., Gary Q.; m. Beverly Jean Hargrove, Aug. 24, 1970; 1 dau., Kimball. B.S., W. Tex. State U., 1963; M.A., U. Redlands, 1967; Ed.D., N.C. State U., 1971. Prof. English, Ariz. Western Coll., 1969-70; research assoc. N.C. State U., 1970-71; dir. adult edn. San Diego County Probation Dept., 1972-74; program dir. Teledyne Econ. Devel. Co., Los Angeles, 1974-78; pres. Training and Mgmt. Resources, Inc., Atlanta, 1978—; cons. in field. Nat. adv. com. Job Corps, 1982-83; mem. Mayor's Adv. Com. on Juvenile Delinquency, Los Angeles, 1977-78. Served with U.S. Army, 1954-56. Mem. Am. Mgmt. Assn., Adult Edn. Assn. Democrat. Unitarian. Contbr. articles to profl. jours. Home: 9300 Huntcliff Trace Atlanta GA 30338 Office: 8515 Dunwoody Pl Atlanta GA 30338

LANE, DANIEL MCNEEL, physician; b. Ft. Sam Houston, Tex., Jan. 25, 1936; s. Samuel Hartman and Mary Maverick (McNeel) L.; student U. Tex., 1953-57; M.D., Southwestern Med. Sch., Dallas, 1961; M.S., U. Tenn., 1967; Ph.D., U. Okla., 1973; m. Carolyn Ann Spruiell, Nov. 28, 1958; children—Linda Ann, Daniel McNeel, Maury Spruiell, Oleta Katherine. Intern, Children's Med. Center, Dallas, 1961-62, resident pediatrics, 1962-63; chief pediatric resident U. Miss., Jackson, 1963-64; fellow hematology U. Tenn., Memphis, 1964-66; asst. prof. pediatrics U. Okla., Oklahoma City, 1966-72, clin. asst. prof., 1974-83, clin. assoc. prof., 1984—; assoc. prof. pediatrics Tulane Med. Sch., New Orleans, 1972-73; head hematology-oncology dept., mem. pediatrics dept. Oklahoma City Clinic, 1973-79; dir. clin. investigation Presbyn. Hosp., Oklahoma City, 1975-77; pvt. practice medicine specializing in hematology-oncology, Oklahoma City, 1973—; staff Langston Med. Clinic; pres. Old Guthrie Proper Assocs., Inc., Guthrie, Okla. Nat. trustee Nat. Hemophilia Found., 1966-68, Okla. pres., 1966-67. USPHS fellow pediatric hematology, 1965-66; Nat. Heart and Lung Inst. spl. research fellow, 1969-72. Diplomate Am. Bd. Pediatrics with sub-splty. Bd. Pediatric Oncology-Hematology. Fellow Am. Acad. Pediatrics; mem. Am., Okla. med. assns., Oklahoma County Med. Soc., Am. Soc. Clin. Oncology, Am. Fedn. Clin. Research, So. Soc. Pediatric Research, Am. Assn. Cancer Edn., Am. Soc. Hematology. Clubs: Oklahoma City Golf and Country, Oklahoma City Tennis (pres. 1969-72). Contbr. articles to profl. jours. Home: 1504 Guilford Lane Oklahoma City OK 73120 Office: Langston Med Clinic 3200 W Wilshire St Oklahoma City OK 73116

LANE, DONALD WILSON, geologist; b. Fayetteville, Tenn., June 23, 1934; s. Carl Wilson and Martha Elizabeth (Smith) L.; m. Joanne Eloise Eaker, June 25, 1960; children—Marjorie Elizabeth, Jennifer Susan, Jonathon Christopher. B.A., Dartmouth Coll., 1956; M.S., U. Ill., 1958; Ph.D., Rice U., 1961. Geologist, Tenneco Oil Co., Houston, 1960-70, Wyo. Geolog. Survey, Laramie, 1970-73; mgr. exploration geology Mich.-Wis. Pipeline, Houston, 1973-76; cons. geologist, Houston, 1976-85; sr. geologist Britoil Ventures, Inc., Houston, 1985—. Contbr. articles to profl. jours. Fellow Geolog. Soc. of Am.; mem. Am. Assn. Petroleum Geologists, Soc. Econ. Paleontology and Mineralogy, Soc. Ind. Earth Scientists, Houston Geol. Soc. Avocations: sailing; photography; tennis; golf. Home: 12214 Mossycup Houston TX 77024 Office: Britoil Ventures Inc 1360 Post Oak Blvd Houston TX 77056

LANE, ELEANOR BASDEN, state official; b. Burgaw, N.C., Feb. 13, 1938; d. William C. and Lela P. (Bostic) Basden; m. William N. Lane, Oct. 23, 1955; 1 dau., Deborah A. Student, U. N.C.-Wilmington, 1977-80. Cert. med. asst., Am. Assn. Med. Assistance, 1980; cert. E.M.T., 1981. Med. asst. Med. Clinic Drs. John T. Dees & H. Peedin, Burgaw, N.C., 1960-75; part-time instr. EMT program Cape Fear Tech. Sch., Wilmington, N.C., 1979-80; magistrate Pender County, Burgaw, N.C., 1980—; ins. examiner Phys. Data Service, Winston-Salem, 1983; partner Reades Restaurant, Burgaw, 1978—. Recipient Founders award N.C. Heart Assn., 1968. Mem. N.C. Magistrate Assn., N.C. State Employees Assn., N.C. Assn. Rescue Squad, Nat. Assn. Rescue Squad, Pender County Rescue Squad, Surf City Police Aux., U. N.C.-Wilmington Alumni Assn. Democrat. Methodist. Address: E Wilmington St Burgaw NC 28425

LANE, FRANK BENJAMIN, hematologist, clinical researcher; b. Little Rock, Jan. 23, 1940; s. Frank B. and Elizabeth S. (Stancil) L.; m. Gail Anna Ingalls, Oct. 1968 (div. May 1972); m. 2d, Debra A. Crum, Aug. 17, 1979. B.S.,

U. Md., 1961; M.D., Temple U., 1965. Diplomate Am. Bd. Internal Medicine, Am. Bd. Hematology. Intern, Tampa Gen. Hosp. (Fla.), 1965-66; resident in internal medicine U. Mo., Columbia, 1966-67, U. Miami (Fla.), 1967-68; chief med. resident Tampa Gen. Hosp. (Fla.), 1968-69; fellow in hematology/oncology U. Wash., Seattle, 1971-74; assoc. prof. medicine U. South Fla., 1974-75; practice medicine specializing in internal medicine, hematology and oncology, Tampa and Brandon, Fla., 1974—; chief dept. hematology Tampa Gen. Hosp., 1984—; lectr. and researcher in field. Served to maj. M.C., U.S. Army, 1969-71. U. Wash. Sch. Medicine grantee, 1970-71. Mem. Am. Soc. Hematology, Am. Soc. Clin. Oncology, Fla. Soc. Clin. Oncology, Internat. Soc. Hematology, Am. Coll. Medicine, Am. Coll. Internal Medicine, So. Med. Soc., Southeastern Research Inst., N.Y. Acad. Sci., Am. Soc. Prevention of Cancer, Fla. Med. Assn., Hillsborough County Med. Assn. Contbr. to Brit. Jour. Hematology, 1975.

LANE, GARRY STEPHEN, customer engineer; b. Detroit, Mich., Feb. 7, 1957; s. John Thomas Sr. and Evelyn Louise (Sweeney) L.; m. Pamela Lilaine Lane, Apr. 30, 1977 (div. 1980); 1 son, Garry Stephen II. Student Miss. Gulf Coast Coll., 1976, 78, Riverside City Coll., 1979-80, Air Force Community Coll., 1976-83. Customer engr. Wang Labs., Atlanta, 1980—; pres. Lanenal III, Inc., Atlanta, 1982—. Inventor electronic timepiece, 1983. Served with USAF, 1974-80, Ga. Air Guard, 1980—. Democrat. Mem. Christian Ch.

LANE, GEORGE HOLMAN, JR., newspaper publisher; b. Lewisburg, Tenn., Oct. 18, 1945; s. George Holman and Martha Frances (Ross) L.; m. Sue Carol Colbert, Mar. 26, 1976; children—Lee Anna, Cynthia Lynn, Nathan George. Corr. Miami Herald, Ft. Myers, Fla., 1963-64; editor, pub. Northside Citizen, North Ft. Myers, 1964-65; news/photo stringer S.W. Fla., UPI, 1965; news reporter/corr. WINK News, Ft. Myers, 1967-74; bur. chief St. Petersburg Times, Punta Gorda, Fla., 1967-74; legis. aide Fla. State Legislature, Ft. Myers and Tallahassee, 1974-75; gen. mgr., advt. dir. Sunshine Newspaper, Arcadia, Fla., 1976; gen. mgr., pub. Desoto Shopping Guide, Arcadia, 1976-83; pub./gen. mgr. Desoto County Times, 1983—; ptnr. Big Red Q Quickprint Ctr., Arcadia, 1981—. Author: A Pictorial History of Arcadia and Desoto County, 1984; editor hist. papers in Southwest Fla. history, 1980-83. Pres. Southwest Floridiana, Arcadia, 1980—; chmn. Desoto County Republican Com., 1977—, precinct 10 committeeman, 1980—, mem. state com., 1980-83; chmn. Desoto County Hist. Commn., 1976—; mem. DeSoto High Sch. Adv. Com., 1983—; chmn. Arcadia/DeSoto County Centennial Celebration Com., 1985-87; chmn. Main Street Arcadia Com., 1984—; co-founder, charter v.p. Save Our School Com., 1985—; chmn. pub. relations com. Fla. Rep. Party, 1984-86; mem. citizens adv. com. Desoto Meml. Hosp., 1981—; bd. dirs. March of Dimes, 1981-85; mem. vestry St. Edmunds Ch., 1978-80. Recipient Disting. Service award DeSoto Historic Commn. Mem. Downtown Assn. Arcadia (pres. 1981-82), Desoto County C. of C. (Citizen of Yr. 1983, pres. 1982-83), Fla. Advt. Pubs. Assn., Fla. Press Assn., Nat. Assn. Advt. Pubs., Nat. Fedn. Ind. Bus., Charlotte Harbor Area Hist. Soc., Peace River Valley Hist. Soc., Fla. Hist. Soc., Ducks Unltd. Republican. Episcopalian. Clubs: Arcadia Country, others. Lodges: Odd Fellows, Moose, Rotary (pres. 1983-84, outstanding service award 1978-80), Elks. Home: 910 SW Nineth Ln Arcadia FL 33821 Office: Desoto County Times 128 W Oak St Arcadia FL 33821

LANE, HAROLD MILTON, dentist; b. Williamsburg, Ky., June 22, 1934; s. Glaude Lester Lane and Dorothy Glen (Schultz) Lane Ross; m. Barbara Jean Pearson, Dec. 27, 1960; children—Claudia Jean Lane Cooter, Monica Patrice. D.D.S., U. Tenn.-Memphis, 1962. Practice dentistry, Elizabethton, Tenn., 1962—. Served to cpl. U.S. Army, 1953-56; Korea. Fellow Acad. Gen. Dentistry (mastership 1985); mem. First Dist. Dental Soc. (pres.-elect), Tenn. Dental Assn. (council on continuing edn.), ADA, Southeastern Acad. Prosthodontics, Carter County C. of C. (pres. 1971). Republican. Baptist. Lodges: Kiwanis (pres. local club 1966), Elks (exalted ruler 1967-68). Home: 501 Paty Pl Elizabethton TN 37643 Office: 210 N Sycamore St Elizabethton TN 37643

LANE, HAROLD RICHARD, oil company executive; b. Danville, Ill., Mar. 7, 1942; s. Charles Edward and Naomi Helen (Holden) L.; m. Sherry Ellen Fennell, June 15, 1968; children—Christopher Richard, Erich Thomas. B.S., U. Ill., 1964; M.S., U. Iowa, 1966, Ph.D., 1969. Jr. research scientist Pan Am. Research Ctr., Tulsa, 1965-69; research scientist Amoco Research Ctr., Tulsa, 1969-76, sr. research scientist, 1976-77, staff research scientist, 1978-81, research assoc., 1981-84, research supr. II, 1984—; titular mem. Subcommn. on Carboniferous Stratigraphy, 1983—, chmn. Mid-Carboniferous Boundary Working Group, 1983—. Editor, contbg. author: Paleoenvironmental Setting of Waulsortian Facies, 1982; Toward a Boundary in the Middle of the Carboniferous, 1985. Pres., Park Plaza East Homeowners Assn., Tulsa, 1975-76. Fellow Alexander von Humboldt Found., Fed. Republic Germany, 1977-78. Mem. Am. Assn. Petroleum Geologists, Paleontol. Soc. Democrat. Avocations: boating, skiing, fishing. Home: 2826 E 27th Pl Tulsa OK 74114 Office: Amoco Research Ctr 4502 E 41st St PO Box 3385 Tulsa OK 74102

LANE, JANE PALMER, guidance counselor; b. Oelwein, Iowa, Feb. 5, 1941; d. Donald D. and Mary (McKibben) Palmer; m. Gerald W. Lane, Apr. 21, 1963; 1 child, Janise Mary. B.A., U. Iowa, 1962; M.Ed., Va. Commonwealth U., 1978. Tchr. Pub. Schs., Westerly, R.I., 1962-63, Frances Asbury Sch., Hampton, Va., 1968-71, Hugh Mercer Sch., Fredericksburg, Va., 1971-83; guidance counselor Spotsylvania Sch. System, Va., 1983—. Mem. Am. Assn. for Counseling and Devel., Am. Sch. Counselor Assn., Va. Counselors Assn., Stratford Personnel and Guidance Assn., NEA, Va. Edn. Assn., Spotsylvania Edn. Assn., Internat. Platform Assn., DAR, Phi Delta Kappa. Clubs: Toastmistress (pres. 1984-85), Fredericksburg Ski (Fredericksburg). Lodge: Lioness. Home: 403 Tulip Poplar Ln Fredericksburg VA 22401

LANE, JOHN, administrative judge; b. N.Y.C., Sept. 8, 1940; s. John and Mary Keyes (McCloskey) L.; m. Penelope Jeanne Sichol, Sept. 18, 1965; children—Jennifer, Gregory, Sharon, David, Alexander. A.B., Coll. Holy Cross, 1961; LL.B., Fordham U., 1964. Bar: N.Y. 1964, D.C., 1967, U.S. Claims Ct. 1968, U.S. Ct. Appeals (D.C. cir.) 1968, U.S. Supreme Ct. 1968. Assoc. firm Sullivan & Cromwell, N.Y.C., 1964-65, Sellers, Conner & Cuneo, Washington, 1968-70, Reavis, Pogue, Neal & Rose, Washington, 1970-72; atty.-adviser office of gen. counsel Sec. of Air Force, Washington, 1965-68; adminstrv. judge Armed Services Bd. Contract Appeals, Alexandria, Va., 1972—; spl. adviser statutory studies group Commn. on Govt. Procurement, Washington, 1970-72. Editor-in-chief Fordham Law Rev., 1963-64; contbr. articles to profl. jours. Chmn. lawyers' com. D.C., United Givers Fund, 1972. Served to capt. USAF, 1965-68. Recipient Gibbons Meml. award United Givers Fund, Washington, 1972. Mem. ABA (chmn. com. on current fed. procurement statutes, regulations and forms, sec. pub. contract law, 1972-73, sr. editor Pub. Contract Law Jour. 1977-78), Nat. Contract Mgmt. Assn. (officer Washington chpt. 1970-72), Fed. Bar Assn., N.Y. State Bar Assn. Republican. Roman Catholic. Lodge: K.C. Home: 913 Dalebrook Dr Alexandria VA 22308 Office: Armed Services Bd Contract Appeals 200 Stovall St Alexandria VA 22332

LANE, JOHN WILLIAM, radiologist; b. Doniphan, Mo., July 20, 1923; s. Arthur Lee and Virlie Lee (Rogers) L.; m. Louise Featherston, Feb. 21, 1947; children—John W., Jr., Rebecca Lane Larson, Gregory C. Student Ark. Polytech. Coll., 1941-42; B. Med. Sci., U. Ark., M.D., 1947. Diplomate Am. Bd. Radiology, Am. Bd. Nuclear Medicine. Intern, Scott White Clinic, Temple, Tex., 1947-48; resident in radiology U. Ark. Med. Ctr., Little Rock, 1956-58, radiology instr., 1958-59, asst. prof., 1959-60; assoc. clin. prof., 1970—. gen. practice medicine Ethyl Corp., Baton Rouge, 1949-51; asst. prof. U. Colo. Med. Ctr., Denver, 1960-61; staff radiologist Bapt. Med. Ctr., Little Rock, 1961—, chief radiology dept., 1970-83; practice medicine specializing in radiology Radiology Cons., Little Rock, 1961—. Contbr. articles to med. jours. Served with U.S. Army, 1943-46, USAF, 1951-56. Fellow Am. Coll. Radiology; mem. Am. Coll. Nuclear Physicians, AMA, Am. Roentgen Ray Soc., Radiol. Soc. N.Am., Soc. Nuclear Medicine. Republican. Mem. Christian Ch. Clubs: Grande Maumelle Sailing (commodore 1977-78), Little Rock Chamber Music Soc. (pres. 1975-76). Avocations: sailing; photography; painting; music; wine. Home: 2916 Shenandoah Valley Dr Little Rock AR 72212 Office: Radiology Cons 1100 Medical Towers St Little Rock AR 72205

LANE, KEITH ANTON, pharm. co. exec.; b. Borger, Tex., Mar. 23, 1933; s. Keith Anton and Loyce Catherine (Landis) L.; A.A., Frank Phillips Coll., 1953; B.B.A., N. Tex. State U., 1955; postgrad. Mgmt. Devel. Program, Harvard U. Grad. Sch. Bus., 1978—, Imede Sch. Bus. U. Lausanne (Switzerland), 1978; m. Kathleen Dotzel, Jan. 29, 1983; children—Kent, Kimberly, Keith III, Ryan Kristin. Sales rep. Alcon Labs., Inc., Fort Worth, 1959-63, dist. mgr., 1963-68, field sales mgr., 1968-70, nat. sales mgr. splty. div., 1970-71, dir. mktg. Owen div., 1971-73, gen. mgr. Owen div., 1973-7S, corp. v.p. parent co., 1975—, exec. v.p. Owen and Cosmetic divs., 1975-82, v.p., gen. mgr. Profl. Products div., 1982—; pres. Dermatol. Products Tex., Inc., 1981—; lectr. Tex. Christian U. Grad. Sch. Bus. Named High Sch. All Am. in basketball, 1951. Mem. Am. Mgmt. Assn. (course dir. in sales mgmt.), Phi Kappa Sigma. Baptist. Home: 3013 Overton Park Dr E Fort Worth TX 76109 Office: Alcon Labs Inc PO Box 1959 Fort Worth TX 76101

LANE, PAMELA ADAMS, pharmacist; b. Bogalusa, La., Apr. 12, 1957; d. Malcolm Fielding and Elaine Helen (Haik) Adams; m. James Michael Lane, Jan. 24, 1981; 1 child, Justin Adam. B.S. in Pharmacy, N.E. La. U., 1978. Staff pharmacist Washington-St. Tammany Hosp., Bogalusa, La., 1979-80; staff pharmacist West Fla. Hosp., Pensacola, 1980-81, pharm. supr., 1981—, mem. instn. rev. com., 1983—. Mem. Am. Pharm. Assn., N.W. Fla. Soc. Hosp. Pharmacists. Democrat. Roman Catholic. Avocations: scuba diving; water skiing; snow skiing. Home: 808 Heatherwood Way Pace FL 32570 Office: West Fla Regional Med Ctr 8383 N Davis Hwy Pensacola FL 32514

LANE, SHARI, psychotherapist, consultant; b. Cleve., July 13, 1945; d. William A. and Vera Olga (Leibersberger) Piekney; 1 child, Tara Chandra Limpert. B.A., U. S.C., 1967; cert. secondary English, U. N.C., 1968; M.Ed., U. Houston, 1976. Instr., co-developer, adult communications lab., instr. lit., composition Central Piedmont Community Coll., Charlotte, N.C., 1969-71; tchr. curriculum design Montrobac Montessori Sch., Stamford, Conn., 1974-75; trainer, counselor Victoria Women's Ctr., Tex., 1975-78; women's editor, broadcaster, pub. relations Sta. KNAL and KVIC, Victoria, 1975-78; instr. interdisciplinary and humanities dept. U. Houston-Victoria, 1975-78; dir. new options pilot program State of Tex., 1977-79; coordinator mgmt. and planning Austin Mental Health/Mental Retardation Ctr., Tex., 1979-81; dir. cons. services MOHR Devel., 1982; counselor, adminstrv. coordinator APLE Found., 1982-83; psychotherapist, cons. interpersonal conflict resolution for individuals and instns., specializing in substance abuse and co-dependency, Houston, 1983—; speaker Mental Health Assn., Houston, 1983—. Contbr. articles to profl. publs. Mem. LWV, NOW, Am. Assn. for Counseling and Devel. Office: 6666 Harwin St Suite 400 Houston TX 77036

LANE, WILLIAM BRADLEY, postmaster; b. Kyrock, Ky., Oct. 31, 1926; s. Ernest E. and Clorene (Musick) L.; m. Mary Pearl Stratton, Mar. 21, 1946 (div. 1984); children—Rebecca Lane Goad, William B. Student U. Louisville, 1943; grad. Diesel Engine Sch., 1948. Farmer, Lanes' Farm, Sweeden, Ky., 1946-85; mcht. Lane's Store, Sweeden, 1949-85; postmaster Sweeden Post Office, 1961—; mem. and sec. Edmonson County Soil Conservation Dist., Brownsville, Ky., 1962—. Mem. Edmonson County Selective Service Draft Bd., Bowling Green Area Selective Service Draft Bd., Ky., 1981—. Served as pfc. AAF, 1950-52. Democrat. Baptist. Lodge: Masons. Home: Sweeden KY 42285

LANEWALA, MOHAMMED ALI, chemical company executive, consultant; b. Dohad, India; came to U.S., 1961, naturalized, 1982; s. Jafarbhai and Ranibai (Balamkhan) L.; m. Emma Jean France, Aug. 10, 1968; children—Rani Joy, Shirin Anne. B.S. with honors, Calcutta U., India, 1956, M.S., 1959; M.S., Toronto U., Can., 1961; Ph.D., NYU, 1967. Devel. engr. Union Carbide Corp., Tonawanda, N.Y., 1964-67, project engr., 1967-69, sr. staff engr., Tarrytown, N.Y., 1969-77, computer tech. coordinator, Chickasaw, Ala., 1977-84, cons., 1984—. Patentee in field; contbr. articles to profl. jours. Loaned exec. United Way of Mobile County, 1983-84. Recipient Sir P.C. Ray Gold medal, Calcutta U., 1956; J. Henry Mason award NYU, 1964, Founders Day award, 1968. Mem. ASTM, Internat. Mgmt. Council. Democrat. Islam. Clubs: India Assn. (Mobile) (pres. 1981-82), Southcoast Mensa (pres. 1984-85). Avocations: electronics; computers; tennis; table tennis; music. Office: Union Carbide Corp POB 11486 Chickasaw AL 36611

LANEY, DAVID BRUCE, statistician; b. Anniston, Ala., July 6, 1946; s. Cecil D. and Joyce (Henson) L.; m. Helen Dudley Vines, July 2, 1967; children: Christopher David, Michael Dudley. B.S. in Applied Math., Ga. Inst. Tech., 1967, M.S. in Info. Sci., 1968. Grad. research asst. Ga. Inst. Tech., Atlanta, 1967-69; statistician South Central Bell, Birmingham, Ala., 1969-72, dist. mgr. stats., 1975-84; statistician AT&T, N.Y.C., 1973-74; ops. mgr. stats and econometrics BellSouth Services, Birmingham, 1985—; instr. Oglethorpe Coll., Atlanta, 1969; instr. math. dept. U. Ala.-Birmingham, intermittently 1969—; speaker on career opportunites in math. Chmn. Transit Adv. Group, Birmingham, 1983. Served with U.S. Army Res., 1969-76. Mem. Am. Statis. Assn., Bell Companies Bus. Research Group (chmn. 1984—). Methodist. Avocation: personal computers; drama. Office: BellSouth Services 1876 Data Dr Room N-404 Birmingham AL 35244

LANEY, JAMES THOMAS, university president; b. Wilson, Ark., Dec. 24, 1927; s. Thomas Mann and Mary (Hughey) L.; B.A., Yale U., 1950, B.D., 1954, Ph.D. (D.C. Macintosh fellow 1965-66), 1966; D.D., Fla. So. Coll., 1977; L.H.D., Southwestern at Memphis, 1979; D.Hum., Mercer U., 1980; LL.D., De Pauw U., 1985; m. Berta Joan Radford, Dec. 20, 1949; children—Berta Joan Vaughan, James T., Arthur Radford, Mary Ruth Laney Reilly, Susan Elizabeth Castle. Chaplain, Choate Sch., Wallingford, Conn., 1953-55; Ordained to ministry Methodist ch., 1955; asst. lectr. Yale Div. Sch., 1954-55; pastor St. Paul Methodist Ch., Cin., 1955-58; sec. student Christian movement, prof. Yonsei U., Seoul, Korea, 1959-64; asst. prof. Christian ethics Vanderbilt U. Div. Sch., 1966-69; dean Candler Sch. Theology, Emory U., 1969-77, pres. univ., 1977—; vis. prof. Harvard Div. Sch., 1974; dir. Trust Co. of Ga., Coca-Cola Co. Pres. Nashville Community Relations Council, 1968-69; mem. Yale U. Council, 1985—. Bd. dirs. Fund Theol. Edn., Christian Higher Edn. in Asia, Atlanta Symphony, 1979—; chmn. overseers com. to visit Harvard Div. Sch., 1980—; chmn. soc. dist. Rhodes Scholarship Com. Served with AUS, 1946-48. Selected for Leadership, Atlanta, 1970-71. Fellow Soc. Religion in Higher Edn.; mem. Am. Soc. Christian Ethics, Atlanta C. of C. (dir.), Phi Beta Kappa, Omicron Delta Kappa. Author: (with J.M. Gustafson) On Being Responsible, 1968; also essays. Home: 1463 Clifton Rd Atlanta GA 30329 Office: Emory U Atlanta GA 30322

LANEY, RAY STANLEY, economics educator; b. Eastland, Tex., Mar. 2, 1937; s. L. G. and Lilah (O'Brien) L.; m. Billie B. Johnson, Nov. 19, 1960; 1 child, Johnsa Lynn. B.B.A., U. Tex., 1959; M.S., East Tex. State U., 1962, Ph.D., 1969. Instr. S. Tex. Coll., Houston, 1962-63, Alvin Jr. Coll., Tex., 1963-66; grad. asst. East Tex. State U., Commerce, 1966-69; dept. mgr. div. bus. and mgmt. Central Tex. Coll., Killeen, 1969—. Mem. Tex. Jr. Coll. Tchrs. Assn., Mid-Mgmt. Tchrs. Assn., Killeen C. of C. (dir. 1981-82). Republican. Methodist. Home: 1701 Halbert St Killeen TX 76541 Office: Central Tex Coll Hwy 190W Killeen TX 76541

LANFORD, HERBERT ALVIN, JR., state official; b. Spartanburg, S.C., Feb. 19, 1948; s. Herbert Alvin and Ruth (Thomason) L.; B.A., Wofford Coll., 1970; postgrad. U. S.C., 1970-71, U. Okla., 1972-74; grad. Leadership S.C., Leadership Columbia. Legis. asst. U.S. Forest Service, Washington, 1971; long range planning asst. City of Spartanburg, 1972; asst. adj./cts. and bd. officer Tng. Command, Ft. Ord, Calif., 1972-74; field investigator, sr. investigator and chief investigator conciliator S.C. Human Affairs Commn., Columbia, 1974-78, dir. extended investigations div., 1978—. Mem. task force program Nat. Alliance Bus. Youth Motivation, 1980—; mem. supervision com. S.C. State Employees Credit Union, 1981—; sustaining mem. 2nd Regiment, S.C. Line, Continental Establishment, 1981—, Republican Nat. Com., 1981—, Nat. Rep. Congl. Com., 1981—, S.C. Rep. Com., 1981—; mem. Rep. Presdl. Task Force, 1981—. Served with U.S. Army, 1972-74; capt. Res. Decorated Army Commendation medal, Nat. Def. Service medal; recipient Pres.'s award, S.C. State Employees Assn. Richland/Lexington chpt., 1980, chpt. Disting. Service award, 1980, chpt. cert. of recognition and appreciation, 1980, chpt. Outstanding State Employee award, 1981; cert. of commendation, Nat. Alliance of Bus., 1981. Mem. Am. Soc. Pub. Adminstrn. (council S.C. chpt. 1980-83, chpt. pres. 1983-84; Pres.'s award 1983), S.C. State Employees Assn. (dir. 1979—, membership chmn. Richland/Lexington chpt. 1979-80, sec. 1980-81, pres. 1981-82; Outstanding Employee award 1984), Nat. Assn. Human Rights Workers, Internat. Personnel Mgmt. Assn., S.C. Wildlife Fedn. (spl. award vol. service 1984, chpt. pres. 1983-84, dir. 1984—, exec. com. 1985— Conservation Educator of Yr. award 1984), Southeastern Conf. Pub. Adminstrn. (dir. 1983—), S.C. Shooting Assn. (dir. 1981-83, pres. 1986—), Trout Unltd. (chpt. bd. dirs. 1985—), N.C. Rifle and Pistol Assn., Fla. State High Power Rifle Assn., Nat. Rifle Assn. (Outstanding State Citizen award 1984), Res. Officers Assn. U.S., Palmetto State Marksman's Assn., Riverbanks Zool. Soc., Friends of S.C. State Mus., Richland County Game and Fish Assn., Nat. Wildlife Fedn., Nature Conservancy, S.C. Bow Hunters Assn., Carolina Practical Shooting League, Ducks Unltd., Wildlife Action Inc., Calif. Rifle and Pistol Assn., Citizens Against Violent Crimes, Second Amendment Found., Citizens Com. Right to Keep and Bear Arms. Baptist. Club: Silver Elephant.

LANG, DAVID, oil company executive; b. Palestine, Tex., Sept. 1, 1939; s. Turner and Olga (Coats) L.; m. Ruth Ann Lundy, Nov. 19, 1960; children—Michael David, Brian Douglas. A.A., Henderson County Jr. Coll., Athens, Tex., 1959; B.A., Tex. Wesleyan Coll., Ft. Worth, 1969. Indsl. engr. LTV, Dallas, 1966-70; mgr. indsl. engrng. Can Tex Industries, Mineral Wells, Tex., 1970-74; plant mgr. Weatherford Oil Tool Co., (Tex.), 1974-77; pres. Flo-Drill, Inc., Mineral Wells, 1977-80; gen. mgr. Weatherford Float Equipment Co., 1980—. Patentee in field. Bd. dirs. Happy Hills Children's Farm, Granbury, Tex., 1982-83; pres. Wolters Indsl. Assn., 1983-84; nat. affairs chmn. Region V, Tex. Assn. Bus., 1982-83. Served with USAF, 1960-64. Mem. Soc. Mfg. Engrs., Mineral Wells C. of C. (dir. 1982-83). Baptist. Home: 3150 Mineral Wells Hwy Weatherford TX 76086 Office: Weatherford Float Equipment PO Box 1364 Mineral Wells TX 76067

LANG, DENNIS CHARLES, marine insurance broker, consultant; b. Los Angeles, July 21, 1941; s. Chester Charles and Alice Marie (Ryan) L.; m. Joan Mary Schadewald, Jan. 22, 1963 (div. Jan. 1976); children—Dennis Charles, Kristine Marie, Michele Renee; m. 2d, Susan Jewel Bass, Feb. 7, 1981; 1 son, Tanner Christian. A.A., Los Angeles City Coll., 1965; Bus. Adminstrn., U. Calif.-Irvine, 1969; postgrad. in law Western States U., 1971. Spl. agt. Marine Office Am., Los Angeles, 1963-69; v.p., bd. dirs., marine mgr. Robert F. Driver Co., San Diego, 1969-80; br. mgr., v.p., large account producer Fred S. James, San Diego, 1980-81; v.p. oil and gas prodn. Emett & Chandler, Houston, 1981-82; exec. v.p., mgr. oil and gas prodn. Republic Hogg Robinson, San Diego, Los Angeles, 1982-83; pres. Dennis Lang, risk cons., Houston, 1983—; now sr. account exec. for Tex. and N.Mex., Carriers Ins. Co., Des Moines; cons. to ins., oil, and gas industries. Mem. Balboa Park Cultural Funding Com., 1976-79; commr. San Diego County Park and Recreation, 1973-76, San Diego Community Coll., 1975-81. Served with USN, 1959-63. Named Outstanding Young Man of Chula Vista, C. of C., 1972; recipient Disting. Service award Calif. Jaycees, 1972. Mem. Nat. Assn. Ins. Agts., Ind. Ins. Agts. and Brokers Assn. (dir. 1969-82), San Diego Agts. and Brokers Assn., Nat. Automobile Mktg. Assocs. (dir.), Navy League, Internat. Platform Assn. Democrat. Methodist. Clubs: Jaycees (v.p., dir., outstanding new Jaycee 1970-71) (Chula Vista, Calif.); Toastmasters (dir. 1973-76); Propellor of U.S. (I Day chmn. 1969-82). Lodge: Sertoma (dir. 1973-76). Contbr. articles in field to profl. jours. Office: PO Box 683 Colleyville TX 76034

LANG, JEAN MCKINNEY, editor, educator; b. Cherokee, Iowa, Nov. 6, 1921; d. Roy Clarence and Verna Harvey (Smith) McKinney; B.S., Iowa State U., 1945; M.A., Ohio State U., 1969; postgrad. U. South Fla., 1972; 1 dau., Barbara Jean Wilcox. Merchandiser, jewelry buyer Rike-Kumler Co., Dayton, Ohio, 1952-59, Met. Co., Dayton, 1959-64; tchr. DeVilbiss High Sch., Toledo, 1966-67; chmn. dept. retailing Webber Coll., Babson Park, Fla., 1967-72; asso. editor Wet Set Illustrated, 1972-75; sr. editor Pleasure Boating, Largo, Fla., 1975—; tchr. bus. adminstrn. St. Petersburg (Fla.) Jr. Coll., 1974—. Presdl. appointee Nat. Boating Safety Adv. Council. Recipient recognition Nat. Retail Mchts. Assn., 1971; cert. of appreciation U.S. Power Squadron, 1976, Webber Coll., 1972. Mem. Greater Tampa C. of C., AAUW, Tampa Aux. Power Squadron, U.S. Coast Guard Aux., Sales and Mktg. Execs. Tampa (Pres.'s award 1973), Fla. Outdoor Writers Assn., Am. Mktg. Assn., Gulf Coast Symphony, Internat. Platform Assn., Fla. Council Yacht Clubs, Chi Omega. Republican. Presbyterian. Clubs: Toledo Yacht (hon.), Tampa Yacht and Country. First woman to cruise solo from Fla. to Lake Erie in single-engine inboard, 1969, to be accepted into Fla. Council Yacht Clubs; yachting accomplishments published in The Ensign, Lakeland Boating, Yachting, Boote mags. Office: PO Box 402 Largo FL 33540

LANG, JULIUS W., management consultant; b. Granite City, Ill., Mar. 2, 1919; s. Julius F. and Ruby (Coppedge) L.; student U. Mo., 1936-39; m. Billie Ruth Flemming Rhame, Dec. 27, 1968; children—Ronald, Donna Ruth, Cheryl, Robert. Owner, pub. Court News and Printing Co., Beaumont, Tex., 1950-57; sales mgr. Western Gear Co., 1957-65; gen. mgr. Sam White Leasing Co., Houston, 1965-69; pres. J.W. Lang/Assos., Houston, 1939—; mem. faculty U. Houston, 1971—; seminar leader Am. Mgmt. Assn., 1979—. Mem. council Sam Houston Area council Boy Scouts Am. Served with USAAF, 1942-46; CBI. Recipient Silver Beaver award Boy Scouts Am. Mem. Adminstrv. Mgmt. Soc. (Diamond merit award 1976), Sales and Mktg. Execs., Am. Soc. Tng. and Devel., Houston C. of C. Republican. Episcopalian. Club: Toastmasters. Author articles in field. Home: 13426 Agarita Lane Houston TX 77083

LANG, LILLIAN OWEN, accountant; b. Yorkville, Tenn., Oct. 8, 1915; d. Hugh Preston and Susan (Davis) Owen; student U. Tenn. Extension, 1956-62, Memphis State U., 1963-64, Memphis Acad. Arts, 1965-66; 1 son, John Sanford. Shipping clk. Buckeye Cellulose Corp., 1943-46; x-ray technician Memphis and Shelby County Health Dept., 1948-56; acctg. clk. Purex Corp., 1957-59; bookkeeper Electrolock, Inc., 1959-62; sec.-treas. Allied Bruce Terminix Cos., Inc., Mobile, Ala., 1962-80, v.p., 1980-86, also dir.; pvt. practice acctg., Memphis, 1986—; former dir. dir. affiliated corps. Leasing of Mobile, Inc., Terminix Services of Tupelo (Miss.). Lic. pub. acct.; enrolled agt. IRS. Mem. Nat. Assn. Pub. Accts., Am. Soc. Women Accts. (pres. Mobile chpt. 1977-78, dir. S.E. area 1979-81), DAR. Mem. Disciples of Christ. Home: 45 S Idlewild St Apt 901 Memphis TN 38104 Office: 45 S Idlewild #901 Memphis TN 38104

LANG, PAMELA RENATA, physician; b. Budapest, Hungary, Oct. 21, 1954; d. Alexander Sander and Rosalie (Baan) Haraszti; m. Stephen I.B. Lang, Dec. 8, 1979. A.A., Emory U., 1974; M.D., Semmelieis U., Budapest, 1980, postgrad., 1980-81. Diplomate Edinl. Commn. Fgn. Med. Graduates. Intern Semmelweis U., 1979-80, resident, 1980-81; epidemic intelligence service officer div. reproductive health, pregnancy epidemiology br., Ctrs. for Disease Control, Atlanta, 1982-84; resident in family practice Meth. Med. Ctr., Birmingham, Ala., 1984—. Served with USPHS, 1982-84. Bd. dirs. Am. Hungarian Fedn., Newark, 1982-82; mem. Hungarian Cultural Fedn., Atlanta, 1976—. Mem. AMA, Am. Pub. Health Assn., Assn. Planned Parenthood Profls., U.S. Commd. Officers Assn. Democrat. Baptist. Home: 1624 N 25th St Birmingham AL 35234 Office: Methodist Medical Center Birmingham AL

LANGBEIN, CHARLES EDWARD, JR., consulting mechanical engineer; b. Akron, Ohio, May 12, 1930; s. Charles E. and Josephine M. (Tregler) L.; m. Anne T. Canouse, Apr. 12, 1958; children—Mary Ann, Joan. B.M.E., U. Fla., 1956. Application engr. Worthington Corp., New Jersey, Pa., 1956-59; mech. engr. LECO, Lakeland Fla., 1959-60; project engr. Internat. Mining and Chem. Co., Bartow, Fla., 1960-62; cons. engr. Langbein and Bell, Engrs., Inc., 1962—; cons. to State of Fla. Chmn. Regional Energy Action Com. region VII, 1978-79, chmn. Polk County (Fla.) Mech. Bd., 1982. Served with USNR, 1952-54. Fellow Fla. Engring Soc. (continuing profl. devel. cert.), Nat. Soc. Profl. Engrs., ASHRAE, Am. Soc. Plumbing Engrs., Tampa C. of C. (award of merit) Club: K.C. Author: School Design for Energy Conservation, 1974; contbr. articles to profl. jours. Home: 120 Parkside Dr SE Winterhaven FL 33880 Office: Langbein and Bell Inc 2920 Winter Lake Rd Lakeland FL 33801

LANGDALE, GEORGE WILFRED, research soil scientist, soil conservationist; b. Walterboro, S.C., Sept. 14, 1930; s. Benjamin Hayward and Hazel Ruth (Smith) L.; m. Eugenia Miles Boatwright, Aug. 28, 1955. B.S., Clemson Univ., 1957, M.S., 1961; post grad. N.C. State Univ., 1963-64; Ph.D., Univ. Ga., 1969. Research soil scientist U.S. Dept. Agr., Agrl. Research Service, S.C., Ga., Tex., 1957—; cons. tillage and soil fertility. Contbr. articles to profl. jours. Served with inf. U.S. Army, 1951-53, Korea. Kellogg fellow Agr. Policy Inst., 1963-64. Fellow Soil Conservation Soc. Am. (chpt. pres. Tex. 1970-71); mem. Am. Soc. Agronomy, Soil Sci. Soc. Am., World Assn. Soil and Water Conservation, Internat. Soil Sci. Soc., Sigma Xi. Baptist. Avocations: organic gardening, small game hunting. Home: 125 Orchard Knob Ln Athens GA 30605 Office: USDA Agr Research Service Box 555 Watkinsville GA 30677

LANGDALE, NOAH NOEL, JR., coll. pres.; b. Valdosta, Ga., Mar. 29, 1920; s. Noah Noel and Jessie Katharine (Catledge) L.; A.B., U. Ala., 1941, LL.D., 1959, LL.B., Harvard, 1948, M.B.A., 1950, m. Alice Elizabeth Cabaniss, Jan. 8, 1944; 1 son, Noah Michael. Asst. football coach U. Ala., 1942; admitted to Ga. bar, 1951, and practiced in Valdosta, 1951-57; instr., then asst. prof. econs.

and social studies, chmn. dept. accounting, econs., secretarial sci., bus. adminstrn. Valdosta State Coll., 1954-57; pres. Ga. State U., Atlanta, 1957—. Dir. Guardian Life Ins. Co. Am. Past mem. U.S. Adv. Commn. Ednl. Exchange; mem. pres.' commn. NCAA. Served to lt. (s.g.) USNR, 1942-46. Recipient 1st Georgian of Year award Ga. Assn. Broadcasters, 1962; Silver Anniversary All-Am. award Sports Illustrated, 1966; Mrytle Wreath award Hadassah, 1970; Salesman of Yr. award Sales and Marketing Execs. of Atlanta, 1975; Silver Knight of Mgmt. award Lockheed-Ga. chpt. Nat. Mgmt. Assn., 1978; Humanitarian award Nat. Jewish Hosp./Nat. Asthma Center, 1980. Mem. Am., Ga. bar assns., Ga. Assn. Colls. (pres. 1962-63), SAR (past v.p. Ga.), Gridiron Soc., Phi Beta Kappa, Omicron Delta Kappa, Delta Chi, Phi Kappa Phi. Methodist. Rotarian. Club: Capital City (Atlanta). Home: 3807 Tuxedo Rd NW Atlanta GA 30305 Office: Ga State Univ University Plaza Atlanta GA 30303

LANGDON, RONALD BRUCE, neurobiology researcher, educator; b. Northville, Mich., July 12, 1950. Student U. Mich. Sch. Medicine, 1971-73, Sch. Grad. Studies, 1975-76; B.S. in Zoology with high honors, Mich. State U., 1977; Ph.D. in Biology U. Calif.-Santa Barbara, 1984. Lab asst. U. Mich. lab medicinal chemistry Sch. Pharmacy, 1974, research asst., 1974-76, research assoc., 1976, research assoc. I dept. pharmacology Sch. Medicine, 1976-77; teaching asst. dept. biol. sci. U. Calif., Santa Barbara, 1977-80; NOAA trainee, 1980-83; research assoc. dept. anatomy Vanderbilt U. Sch. Medicine, Nashville, 1983-85, dept. cell biology, 1985—. Contbr. articles to profl. jours. U. Calif. Regents' fellow, 1978-79, Nat. Eye Inst. postdoctoral fellow 1984—. Mem. AAAS, N.Y. Acad. Scis., Soc. Neurosci., Am. Mus. Natural History, Assn. Research in Vision and Ophthalmology, Barnard-Seyfert Astron. Soc. Club: Nashville Country Dancers. Avocations: journalism; music; folk dancing; astronomy; natural history. Office: Dept Cell Biology Vanderbilt Univ Sch Medicine Nashville TN 37232

LANGEWISCH, CAROLYN DIANE, nurse epidemiologist; b. Tulsa, May 27, 1940; d. Melvin William and Clara Ida (Dempsey) L. B.S. in Nursing, Tex. Woman's U., 1963. R.N., Tex. Staff nurse Dallas County Pub. Health Dept., 1963-64; nurse evening charge nursery Baylor Med. Ctr., Dallas, 1964; staff nurse, asst. supv. I.V. dept. Wadley Blood Bank, Dallas, 1965-69; nurse epidemiologist St. Paul Med. Ctr., Dallas, 1969—; dir. Cert. Bd. Infection Control, 1982—, chmn. numerous coms.; cons. on infection control. Co-author patient info. pamphlet on isolation, 1978. Mem. Assn. for Practitioners of Infection Control (corr. sec. 1972-74, Service Above Beyond Call Duty award 1973), Assn. for Practitioners Infection Control (sec. Dallas-Ft. Worth Regional chpt. 1973, bd. dirs. 1976-77). Avocations: tennis; gardening. Office: St Paul Med Ctr 5909 Harry Hines Blvd Dallas TX 75235

LANGFORD, ROBERT LOUIS, trading company executive; b. Louisville, May 22, 1944; s. Louis Y. and Hazel (Martin) L.; m. Patricia Rogers, Sept. 3, 1966 (div. July 1979); 1 son, Christopher. B.S., Western Ky. U., 1967; M.A., Webster Coll., St. Louis, 1976. Buyer maj. appliances Gen. Electric Co., Louisville, 1969-74, contracting agt. steel, 1974-76, mgr. purchasing range, 1976-78, mgr. purchasing home laundry, 1978-79, mgr. commodity purchasing internat., 1979-82; pres. World Buying Service, Louisville, 1982—; dir. Aerial Promotions. Served to 1st lt. U.S. Army, 1967-69; Vietnam. Mem. Purchasing Mgmt. Assn. Louisville, Ky. Import/Export Assn., VFW. Democrat. Home: 10341 Timberwood Circle Louisville KY 40223 Office: World Buying Service PO Box 43369 Louisville KY 40243

LANGLAND, ELIZABETH, English literature educator; b. Iowa City, Aug. 11, 1948. B.A. summa cum laude with honors in English, Barnard Coll., 1970; M.A. in English Lit., U. Chgo., 1971, Ph.D. in English Lit., 1975. Asst. prof. dept. English Vanderbilt U., Nashville, 1975-82; assoc. prof., chmn. dept. English, Converse Coll., Spartanburg, S.C., 1982-85; assoc. prof. English, U. Fla., Gainesville, 1985—. Woodrow Wilson fellow, Ford Found. fellow, 1970-74; Assoc. Alumnae of Barnard Coll. Grad. fellow, 1970-71; recipient Sidney Miner Poetry prize, 1970. Mem. MLA, Nat. Women's Studies Assn. South Atlantic Modern Lang. Assn. Author: (with Abel and Hirsch) The Voyage In: Fictions of Female Development, 1983; (with Walter Gove) A Feminist Perspective in the Academy: The Difference It Makes, 1983; Society in the Novel, 1984; contbr. articles to lit. jours.; editorial cons. U. Ga. Press, So. Ill. U. Press, U. N.C. Press, Soundings. Home: 3902 NW 20th Ln Gainesville FL 32605 Office: Dept English U Fla Gainesville FL 32611

LANGLEY, EUGENE LOYLE, telecommunications company executive; b. Beaver, Okla., Aug. 23, 1924; s. Frank and Mable L.; m. Alena D. Jones; children—Larry, Danny F. Student U. Wyo., 1942-43, U. Kans., 1962-63, NYU, 1968, Columbia U., 1971. With Gen. Telephone Co. of S.W., 1948-61, pres., 1981—; gen. mgr. plant Gen. Telephone Co. of Pa., 1961-65; plant dir. Gen. Telephone Co. of Fla., 1965-66, v.p. ops., 1966-74; pres. Gen. Telephone Co. Ky., Lexington, 1974-78; pres. Gen. Telephone Co. S.E., Durham, N.C., 1978-81; dir. Tex. Commerce Bank, San Angelo. Vice pres. United Way of Durham County, 1980; mem. exec. com. Concho Valley council Boy Scouts Am., 1983; chmn. United Way of Tom Green County, 1984; bd. visitors Duke U. Served with Signal Corps, U.S. Army, 1942-46. Recipient Silver Beaver award Boy Scouts Am., Tampa, 1971. Presbyterian. Clubs: San Angelo Country, Bentwood Country, University. Lodges: Masons, Shriners. Office: PO Box 1001 San Angelo TX 76902

LANGLEY, ROBERT ARCHIE, scientist; b. Athens, Ga., Oct. 21, 1937; s. Archie and Mary V. (Burch) L.; m. Sara Leith Haizlip, Dec. 21, 1959 (div.); children—Laura, Anne, David; m. Anna Carol Lampe, May 29, 1982 (div.). B.S., Ga. Inst. Tech., 1959, M.S., 1960, Ph.D., 1963. Staff scientist Oak Ridge Nat. Lab., 1964-67, 1977—, Sandia Nat. Lab., Albuquerque, 1967-77, IAEA, Vienna, 1979-80. Served to capt. USAF, 1962-65. Mem. Am. Phys. Soc., Am. Vacuum Soc., Sigma Xi, Sigma Pi Sigma. Author: Surface Analysis Using High Energy Ion Beams, 1982; holder 2 patents; contbr. numerous articles to profl. jours. Home: 103 Balsam St Oak Ridge TN 37830 Office: Oak Ridge Nat Lab Fusion Energy Div PO Box Y Oak Ridge TN 37830

LANGLEY, ROLAND LOUIS, public relations and advertising company executive; b. New Orleans, Dec. 31, 1955; s. Christopher and Christina (Jenkins) Bell; m. Evelyn Delores Richards, July 16, 1983. B.S., U. Ala.-Huntsville, 1980. Sports editor Limestone Reporter, Athens, Ala., 1974-75, editor, 1975-76; sports writer Huntsville News, 1976-78, sports editor, 1978-80; v.p. Dixie Graphics Inc., Decatur, Ala., 1978-81, pres., owner, 1981—. Contbr. articles to profl. jours. Mem. Decatur Conv. and Tourism Bur., Decatur C. of C., Cullman C. of C. Republican. Mem. Assembly of God Ch. Avocations: reading; sports; photography. Office: Dixie Graphics Inc PO Box 1127 Decatur AL 35602

LANGLEY, WELBORN JAMES, physician; b. Westbrook, Tex., Sept. 12, 1926; s. Floyd Alford and Frances Willie (Cunningham) L.; B.A., Baylor U., 1953; M.D., Southwestern U., 1957; m. Dorothy Jean Lee; children—Beverly Jo (Mrs. Jack Mcdowell), Debbie Jean, Roger James, Brenda Diane, Rebecca Jane. Intern Baylor U. Hosp., 1958; resident surgery Harris Hosp., 1959; family practice physician, Dallas, 1969—. Served with AUS, 1944-50. Mem. AMA, Tex., Dallas County med. assns. Independent. Mem. Ch. of Christ. Office: 7777 Forest Ln Dallas TX 75230

LANGLINAIS, JOSEPH WILLIS, theology educator, minister; b. San Antonio, Aug. 12, 1922; s. Joseph Willis and Marie Nellie (St. Julien) L. B.S. in Edn., U. Dayton, 1943; S.T.B. in Theology, U. Fribourg, Switzerland, 1950, S.T.L. in Theology, 1952, S.T.D. in Theology, 1954. Dir. Marynook Novitiate, Galesville, Wis., 1959-63; dean arts and scis. St. Mary's U., San Antonio, 1964-75, acad. v.p., 1975-81, chmn. dept. theology, 1981-83, dir. instl. self-study, 1982-84, now prof. theology. Contbr. articles to profl. jours. Pres. United Service Orgn., San Antonio, 1983-85; bd. dirs. Torch Internat., San Antonio, 1977-82. Mem. Cath. Theology Soc. Am., Southwest Archaeol. Soc. (pres. 1985—), Mariological Soc. Am., Soc. Sci. Study Religion. Republican. Avocations: gardening; archaeology; chess. Home: 1 Camino Santa Maria San Antonio TX 78284 Office: St Mary's U 1 Camino Santa Maria San Antonio TX 78284

LANGLOIS, BRUCE EDWARD, animal sciences educator; b. Berlin, N.H., Sept. 16, 1937; s. Edward F. and Bernice L. (Erickson) L.; m. Valerie LaMontagne, Aug. 13, 1960; children—Kim Ann, Cynthia. B.S., U. N.H., 1959; Ph.D., Purdue U., 1962. Grad. asst. Purdue U., West Lafayette, Ind., 1959-62, postdoctoral fellow, 1962-64; asst. prof. U. Ky., Lexington, 1964-67, assoc. prof., 1967-74, prof. animal scis., 1974—. Reviewer Jour. Food Protection, 1985-88. Contbr. articles to profl. jours. Recipient Outstanding Research in Agrl. award U. Ky., 1985. Mem. Am. Dairy Sci. Assn., Am. Soc. Microbiology, Internat. Assn. Milk Food Environmentalist Sanitarians (cert. merit 1982), Ky. Assn. Milk Food Environ. Sanitarians (pres. 1981-83), Gamma Sigma Delta. Office: U Ky Dept Animal Scis 204 Agrl Sci Ctr S Lexington KY 40546

LANGLOIS, VALERIE LAMONTAGNE, educator, coach; b. Berlin, N.H., May 18, 1937; d. Alphonse Joseph and Leona Martha (Hayes) LaMontagne; m. Bruce E. Langlois, Aug. 13, 1960; children—Kim Ann, Cynthia Leona. B.Ed., Plymouth (N.H.) State Coll., 1959; M.A., U. Ky., 1969. Tchr., coach Berlin (N.H.) High Sch., 1959-60; tchr. Crouch and Elston Elem. Sch., Lafayette, Ind., 1960-63, East Tipp High Sch., Lafayette, 1962-63, Paris (Ky.) High Sch., 1967-68; tchr., coach Bryan Station Sr. High Sch., Lexington, Ky., 1969—; coach championship basketball and softball teams; coach Pony Tail Softball, 1970-76, Recreation Girls' Basketball, Lexington, 1975-76. Ky. col.; recipient cert of honor in basketball Midway (Ky.) Coll., 1975. Mem. Ky. State Coaches Assn., Girls Coaches Assn., Delta Pi Epsilon. Democrat. Roman Catholic. Home: 1813 Barwick Dr Lexington KY 40505 Office: Bryan Station Senior High School Edgeworth Dr Lexington KY 40505

LANGSDON, JOHN KINNARD, JR., mfg. co. exec.; b. Columbia, Tenn., Feb. 6, 1934; s. John Kinnard and Ree (Coleman) L.; B.Engring., Vanderbilt U., 1955; postgrad. U. Wash., 1955-56, U. Tenn., 1958; m. Bonnie Jean Strong, Sept. 3, 1955; children—Valerie Langsdon Wilson, John Kinnard, Rosemarie (Mrs. John. K. Overstreet), James David, Joseph William. With Columbia Machine Works, Columbia, 1946-53, chief engr., 1958-59, plant mgr., 1959-69, pres., chmn. bd., 1969—; chemist DuPont Co., Columbia, 1954; research asst. Monsanto Co., Columbia, 1954; chem. engr. Union Carbide Nuclear Co., Oak Ridge, 1955; tchr. Central High, Columbia, 1956. Dist. commr. Boy Scouts Am., 1966-81, exec. bd. Middle Tenn. council, 1977—; bd. dirs. Jr. Achievement, 1972-79, Moury County United Givers Fund, 1975-79. Recipient Silver Beaver award Boy Scouts Am., 1976; named Outstanding Rotarian, 1976; Paul Harris fellow, 1979. Mem. Moury County C. of C. (sec.-treas. 1974-75, Salesman of the Yr. 1982), ASME, Am. Inst. Chem. Engrs. Republican. Ch. of Christ. Club: Rotary (dir. 1964-66, pres. 1982—). Patentee in field. Home: 307 N Hardin Dr Columbia TN 38401 Office: PO Box 1018 Columbia TN 38401

LANGSTON, GEORGE CALHOUN, textile company executive; b. Anderson, S.C., Apr. 20, 1930; s. Judson B. and Lula Mae (Gibson) L.; m. Jo Ann Harbert, Apr. 6, 1952; children—Andrew Dale, George Michael, Lisa Ann. B.S. in Acctg., U. S.C., 1951. Vice pres. Milliken & Co., Spartanburg, S.C., 1955-79, also dir. Milliken Service Corp.; v.p. info. services div. J. P. Stevens & Co., Inc., Greer, S.C., 1979—. Served to 1st lt. U.S. Army, 1951-54. Mem. Fin. Execs. Inst., Am. Prodn. and Inventory Control Soc., Soc. Info. Services Mgmt. Republican. Baptist. Club: Country (Spartanburg, S.C.). Lodge: Rotary.

LANGSTON, JAMES LELAND, electronics engineer; b. Atlanta, Tex., July 26, 1942; s. Paul T. and Vernie D. (Bridges) L. B.S.E.E., So. Meth. U., 1966, postgrad., 1966-67. Registered profl. engr., Tex. Technician, Collins Radio, Richardson, Tex., 1961-65, design engr., 1965-67, lead engr., 1967-70, sr. engr., 1970-71; sr. engr. Tex. Instruments, Dallas, 1971-73, project engr., 1973-75, system engr., 1975-78, mem. tech. staff, 1978-82, sr. mem. tech. staff, 1982—. Jr. Achievement advisor Highland Park High Sch., 1981. Recipient Group Achievement award NASA, 1976, Cash award and cert. of appreciation, 1979, Pub. Service award medal, 1981. Contbr. articles in field to profl. jours. Office: 13500 N Cent Expressway PO Box 660246 MS 3648 Dallas TX 75266

LANIER, JAMES OLANDA, lawyer, banker, state legislator; b. Newbern, Tenn., Sept. 8, 1931; s. James Parker and Robbye (Sullivan) L.; student U. Tenn., 1949, U. Tenn. Jr. Coll., 1950-51; B.S., Memphis State Coll., 1955; J.D., Memphis State U., 1969; m. Carolyn Holland, June 1, 1950; children—James Elton, Donna Kay, Robbye Ann (dec.), Amy Claire. Indsl. engr. Milan (Tenn.) Arsenal, 1953-54; social worker Dept. Pub. Welfare, Memphis, 1955-57, sr. social worker, appeals examiner, 1957-58; dir. surplus Commodities, Dyer County, Tenn., 1958; pres., gen. mgr. Main Sporting Goods, Inc., Dyersburg, 1959-62; tech. engr. Milan Ordnance Plant, 1961-63; spl. investigator Tenn. Dept. Pub. Welfare, Nashville, 1963-67; ins. adjuster U.S. Fidelity & Guaranty Co., 1967-69; pvt. practice law, Dyersburg, 1969—; county atty. Dyer County, 1972—; admitted to U.S. Supreme Ct. bar, 1975; pres. Lanier Enterprises, Inc., Dyersburg, West Tenn. Inc., Dyersburg; pres. Dukedom Bank (Tenn.), 1979-80, chmn. bd., 1980—; pres. Freightmasters, Inc., Union City, Tenn., 1981—; referee Dyer County Juvenile Ct., 1985—. Mem. Tenn. Ho. of Reps., 1959-62, 71-80, chmn. com. on agr., 1961-62, chmn. com. on state and local govt., 1973-77, chmn. W. Tenn. Democratic House Caucus, 1975-80, chmn. com. on calendar and rules, 1977-78; chmn. Tenn. Tollway Authority, 1975-80; chmn., hearing officer Tenn. Med. Malpractice Rev. Bd., 1979-83; state campaign coordinator Lamar Alexander for Gov., 1978; dir. Dyer County Levee and Drainage Dist., Obion-Forked Deer Basin Authority, 1979—; pres. Dyer County chpt. Muscular Dystrophy Assns. Am., 1958-60; mem. exec. com. West Tenn. council Boy Scouts Am., 1981—. Mem. Tenn. Law Enforcement Officers Assn., Am., Dyersburg-Dyer County (sec.-treas.) bar assns., Tenn. Bar Assn. (ho. of dels. 1983-85), Am., Tenn. trial lawyers assns., Am. Judicature Soc., Dyer County C. of C., Memphis State U. Alumni Assn. (nat. dir. 1976—), Sigma Delta Kappa (pres. 1967-68), Kappa Sigma. Democrat (W. Tenn. pres. Young Democrats of Tenn. 1957-63). Mem. Ch. of Christ. Moose (jr. gov. 1959-60, gov. 1960-62, chmn. com. civic affairs, recipient fellowship degree and gov.'s award of merit 1963), Elk. Clubs: Dyersburg Kiwanis, Dyersburg Country. Home: Route 4 Box 349 Nauvoo Dyersburg TN 38024 Office: Lanier Bldg 208 N Mill St Dyersburg TN 38024

LANIER, JOHN HICKS, apparel executive; b. Nashville, Apr. 12, 1940; s. Sartain and Claudia Gwynn (Whitson) L.; B.A., Vanderbilt U., 1962; M.B.A., Harvard U., 1964; m. Jane M. Darden, Oct. 15, 1966; children—Jay, Liza, Stephen. Pres., chmn. Oxford Industries, Inc., Atlanta; dir. Crawford & Co., Trust Co. of Ga. Assocs. Trustee, Westminster Schs., Henrietta Egleston Hosp. for Children; bd. dirs. Piedmont Med. Ctr., Atlanta. Served with USAFR, 1964-65. Mem. Am. Apparel Mfrs. Assn. (dir.). Republican. Office: 222 Piedmont Ave NE Atlanta GA 30308

LANIER, JOSEPH L., JR., textile manufacturing company executive; b. Lanett, Ala., 1932. B.S., Washington and Lee U., 1954; postgrad. Harvard U. Grad. Sch. Bus. Adminstrn., 1955. Mgmt. trainee West Point-Pepperell Inc. (Ga.), 1957-59, asst. mgr. Fairfax Mill, 1959-62, v.p., 1962-64, v.p. new product planning devel. ops., 1964-66, v.p. mfg. indsl. fabrics div., 1966-68, pres. indsl. fabrics div., 1968, dir., 1968-69, exec. v.p., 1969-74, pres., 1974-75, pres., chief operating officer, 1975-79, chmn. bd., chief exec. officer, dir., 1979—. Served to lt. U.S. Army, 1955-57. Office: West Point-Pepperell Inc 400 W 10th St West Point GA 31833

LANIER, THURMAN WAYNE, dentist; b. Batesville, Ark., Sept. 19, 1932; s. Luther Thurman and Ethel Lavinia (Settle) L.; m. Helen Lorene Barnes, Sept. 4, 1955; children—Lance Littleton, Tara Kaay. B.S. in Edn., U. Ark., 1958; D.M.D., Washington U., St. Louis, 1962. Gen. practice dentistry, Fort Smith, Ark., 1962—. Editor Ark. Dental Jour., 1965-75. Trustee Westark Community Coll., 1972-82; chmn. Ark. Ednl. TV Commn., 1982—. Served to capt. Dental Corps, USN, 1951-54, Korea. Fellow Am. Coll. Dentists; mem. Ark. Dental Assn. (pres. 1980-81), Am. Assn. Dental Editors (pres. 1973-74), ADA, Assn. Mil. Surgeons, Ft. Smith C. of C. (bd. dirs. 1971, 72), Xi Psi Phi (pres. Tau chpt. 1961-62). Club: Exchange (pres. Ft. Smith 1971-72). Lodge: Masons. Home: Rural Route 1 Box 1147 Greenwood AR 72936 Office: 5422 Euper Ln Fort Smith AR 92703

LANKFORD, ROBERT J., insurance company executive; b. Edwardsville, Ill., Apr. 18, 1929; s. James M. and Wilma I. L.; student U. Ill., 1948; B.B.A., So. Meth. U., 1950; cert. in estate planning Am. Coll. Life Underwriters, 1966, postgrad. cert. in acctg. and bus. eval., 1977, cert. in advanced pension planning, 1978, cert. in bus. tax planning, 1979, postgrad. cert. in exec. benefit planning, 1980, others; m. LaVern Olney, Dec. 29, 1959; children—Bruce, Craig, Leigh, Stuart. Sales rep., Haughton Pub. Co., Dallas, 1950; agent New Eng. Mut. Life Ins. Co., Dallas, 1950; instr. personal fin. Bishop Coll., Dallas, 1970-71; mem. spl. task force com. investigating problems in sale of ins. in Tex., 1976-77; owner, pres. Bus. & Estate Analysts; bd. govs. Dallas Estate Planning Council, 1979-81; mem. policyholder's service com. New Eng. Life Leaders Assn. Bd. dirs. So. Meth. U., YMCA, 1956-66, Downtown Br. YMCA, 1958-60; chmn. Dallas County Blood Security Program, 1968. Recipient Vanguard award New Eng. Life, 1975; C.L.U. Mem. Nat. Assn. Life Underwriters and C.L.U.s, Dallas Assn. Life Underwriters (dir. 1968-76) Dallas Estate Planning Council (gov. 1966-68, 79-81), Million Dollar Round Table (life), New Eng. Life's Leaders Assn., New Eng. Life's Hall of Fame. Republican. Presbyterian. Club: Willow Bend Polo and Hunt. Contbr. articles in field to The Pilots Log, Flitcraft Mag., 1966. Home: 4228 Caruth Blvd Dallas TX 75225 Office: PO Box 12607 Dallas TX 75225

LANKTON, CAROL AGNES HICKS, therapist, author; b. Greenville, Miss., Aug. 24, 1950; d. Morris Adron and Agnes Ware (Stanfield); m. Stephen Ryan Lankton, Sept. 22, 1979; children—Shawn Michael, Alicia Michelle. B.A. in Psychology, U. Ala., 1972; M.A. in Psychology, U. W. Fla., 1976. Staff psychologist NW Fla. Mental Health Ctr., Panama City, 1972-79; co-dir., trainer, cons., pvt. practice Matrix Communications and Learning System, Gulf Breeze, Fla., 1979—; adj. faculty dept. psychology U. West Fla., 1986—. Author: The Answer Within: A Clinical Framework of Ericksonian Hypnotherapy, 1983; Enchantment and Intervention in the Family, 1986. Founding editorial bd. mem. The Ericksonian Monographs, 1984. Mem. Am. Assn. Marriage and Family Therapy, Am. Acad. Psychotherapists, Am. Psychol. Assn. (assoc.), Internat. Transactional Analysis Assn. Avocations: scuba diving, gardening, photography, music. Office: PO Box 958 Gulf Breeze FL 32561

LANOUE, JOHN LONG, religious organization administrator; b. Beaumont, Tex., Sept. 25, 1934; s. John Charles and Ruth Irene (Long) LaN.; m. Kaywin Joan Baldwin, Dec. 18, 1954; children—John Long, Lydia Kaywin. B.A., Stephen F. Austin U., 1957; M.Div., Southwestern Bapt. Theol. Sem., 1960; postgrad U. Houston, 1963, U. Tex.-Tyler, 1980-81. Cert. expedition leader Nat. Outdoor Leadership Sch. Ordained to ministry Baptist Ch., 1954; pastor churches, Tex., 1954-60, West Frankfort, Ill., 1960-62; campus minister U. Houston, 1962-69; state youth coordinator Bapt. Gen. Conv. Tex., Dallas, 1969-73; outdoor edn. cons. Bapt. Sunday Sch. Bd., Nashville, 1973-81; dir. Royal Ambassadors and Bapt. Young Men, Bapt. Gen. Conv. Tex., Dallas, 1981—. Dir. mobile unit disaster relief, Dallas, 1981—. Mem. Christian Camping Internat., Am. Camping Assn., NRA. Republican. Home: Rt 5 Box 221 Tyler TX 75706 Office: 511N Akard Suite 1129 Dallas TX 75201

LANOUX, SIGRED BOYD, chemistry educator; b. New Orleans, Nov. 1, 1931; s. Nelson Joseph and Lucille (Speyrer) L.; m. Emily Ann Broussard, Jan. 9, 1954; children—Yvonne Marie, Jeannine Marie. B.S., U. Southwestern La., 1957; Ph.D., Tulane U., 1962. Research assoc. U. Ill.-Champaign, 1961-62; research chemist E.I. Dupont de Nemours Co., Chattanooga, Tenn., 1962-66; asst. prof. chemistry U. Southwestern La., Lafayette, 1966-72, assoc. prof., 1972-74, prof., 1974—, head dept., 1972—; research chemist USDA, New Orleans, 1969, 71. Contbr. articles to sci. publs. Patentee in field. Bd. dirs. Cathedral Carmel Schs., Lafayette, 1974-76; pres. Bayou council Girl Scouts U.S., 1976-81. Served as sgt. U.S. Army, 1951-53. Fellow Am. Inst. Chemists; mem. Am. Chem. Soc., La. Acad. Sci. (pres. 1972-73, treas. 1982—), Sigma Xi. Roman Catholic. Democrat. Home: 104 Ridgewood St Lafayette LA 70506 Office: U Southwestern La PO Box 44370 Lafayette LA 70504

LANSING, ALLAN MEREDITH, surgeon, medical administrator; b. St. Catherines, Ont., Can., Sept. 12, 1929; s. George Clayton and Annie Irene (Scott) L., m. Donna Joanne Alford, Aug. 25, 1951; children—Ann Meredith, Peter Scott, Michele Elizabeth. M.D. magna cum laude, U. Western Ont., 1953, Ph.D. in Physiology, 1957. NRC research fellow in physiology U. Western Ont., Can., 1955-57, resident in surgery, 1954-55, 57-58; intern Victoria Hosp., London, Ont., 1953-54; resident in surgery U. Ill. Research and Ednl. Hosp., Chgo., 1958-59; fellow in surgery Prebyn.-St. Luke's Hosp., Chgo., 1959-60, Baylor U., Houston, 1960, Children's Hosp., Boston, 1961; asst. prof. surgery U. Western Ont., 1961-63, asst. prof. physiology, 1961-63; assoc. prof. surgery U. Louisville, 1963-69, prof., 1969-76, clin. prof., 1976-84, chief cardiovascular surgery, 1967-72; chmn. and dir. Humana Heart Inst. Internat., Louisville, 1983—; chmn. bd. Heart Internat. Found., Inc., Louisville, 1985—; chief cardiac surgery Jewish Hosp., Louisville, 1965-84; dir. pediatric cardiac surgery Kosair-Children's Hosp., Louisville, 1963-83; surgeon-in-chief End-Stage Renal Disease Program for Western Ky., 1964-83; staff physician Commn. for Handicapped Children in Ky., 1963—. Contbr. articles to profl. jours. Trustee Bellarmine Coll., Louisville, Transylvania U., Lexington; bd. dirs. Kentuckiana Mended Hearts, Inc., Nat. Kidney Found. Met. Louisville and Western Ky. Wilhelmina McIntosh scholar, 1948; U. Western Ont. Bd. Govs. scholar, 1947, 48, 49; B'nai B'rith scholar, 1951; recipient CIBA prize, 1952; John and Mary Markle scholar, 1961-66; Am. Legion Community Service award, 1966; Hon. Ky. Col., 1966; named Disting. Citizen of Louisville, 1981; Nat. Humanitarian award Nat. Jewish Hosp. and Research Ctr./Nat. Asthma Ctr., 1983; others. Fellow Royal Coll. Surgeons Can., ACS, Am. Coll. Cardiology; mem. Ky. Med. Assn., Louisville Pediatric Soc., Louisville Surg. Soc., Central Surg. Assn., Innominate Soc., Soc. Univ. Surgeons, Inernat. Surg. Soc., Alpha Omega Alpha, Sigma Xi, others. Office: Humana Heart Inst One Audubon Plaza Louisville KY 40217

LANTRIP, J(OE) GARY, petroleum geologist; b. Dallas, Aug. 3, 1952; s. Bobby Joe and Donna Harlene (Belk) L.; m. Sandra Gail Wofford, Sept. 15, 1979; children—Kristen Nicole, Jonathan Tyler. B.S. in Geology, U. Tex.-Arlington, 1978. Geologist Hunt Energy, Dallas, 1975; logging engr. Gearhart Industries, Fort Worth, 1978-80; geologist, log analyst REO Devel, Tulsa, 1980-82; geologist, cons. Marmac Resources, Los Angeles, 1982—; geologist, Arlington, Tex., 1983—; cons. micro-computer software, 1984. Mem. Am. Assn. Petroleum Geologists, Soc. Petroleum Engrs. Republican. Avocation: scuba diving. Office: J Gary Lantrip Petroleum Geologist 408 Hillcrest St Arlington TX 76010

LA PAZ, IRENE MCGOVERN, city official; b. Havana, Cuba, Sept. 9, 1932; came to U.S., 1960; d. Francis and Irene (Diaz) McGovern; m. George La Paz, June 8, 1954; children—Mayra, Marlen, George. Student U. Tampa, 1977, U. South Fla., 1977. With City of Tampa Sanitation Dept., 1961—, sanitation asst. dir., 1973-83, adminstrv. and fiscal mgr., 1983—. Mem. Govtl. Refuse Collection and Disposal Assn. (past chpt. pres.), Am. Pub. Works Assn. (past br. chmn. West Coast). Democrat. Roman Catholic. Office: 4010 W Spruce St Tampa FL 33607

LAPINER, BETTY JANE, securities broker and dealer; b. Mason City, Iowa, Nov. 16, 1926; d. Nathan and Dora Mae (Richer) L.; div.; children—Carolyn, Judd. Student MacMurray Coll. Women, 1943-44, U. Minn., 1944-47, U. No. Iowa, 1961-62, So. Meth. U., 1966-67. Pres., H&M Land Co., 1951-63; asst. v.p. Ramco Industries, 1959-68; investment exec., registered rep. Drexel Burnham Lambert, 1977-78, Shearson Loeb Rhoades Inc., N.Y.C., 1978-80; v.p. adminstrn. Jon-R Assocs., Inc., N.Y., 1980-81; investment exec. Dominick and Dominick, Inc., N.Y.C., 1981-82; securities broker-dealer B. J. Lapiner Co., Louisville, Ky., 1982—. Assoc. dir., mem. exec. com., mem. profl. adv. bd. The Found. Thanatology; leader seminar on death Columbia U.; pres. 67 Park Owners Corp., N.Y.C., 1979-81. Mem. Nat. Assn. Securities Dealers. Address: 1424 S 4th St Louisville KY 40208

LAPORTE, CRAIG AISTON, lawyer; b. Worcester, Mass., Apr. 9, 1953; s. Philip A. and Birgit (Ekengren) L.; m. Arndrea S. Bowman, June 20, 1980; 1 child, Stephen Kyle. B.S. in Broadcasting, U. Fla., 1975; J.D. magna cum laude, Stetson U., 1983. Bar: Fla. 1983, U.S. Dist. Ct. (mid. dist.) Fla. 1983. Dep., pilot Pasco County Sheriff's Office, New Port Richey, Fla., 1975-81; assoc. Riley & Proly, Port Richey, 1983—. Served to 2d lt. USAF, 1971-75. Mem. Assn. Trial Lawyers Am., Fla. Trial Lawyers Assn., West Pasco County Bar Assn., ABA, Fla. Bar Assn., Phi Delta Phi. Republican. Office: 202 Oak Trail Way Port Richey FL 33568

LAPP, ROGER JAMES, pharmacist; b. Buffalo, Jan. 29, 1933; s. Roger Vincent and Georgia James (Saemenes) L.; student Mich. State U., 1952-53; B.S. in Pharmacy, U. Buffalo, 1957; m. Judith Bure, Mar. 30, 1956; children—Eric Roger, Mark Frederick. Pharmacist intern Nobb Hill Pharmacy, Buffalo, 1956-57; pharm. intern Buffalo Gen. Hosp., 1957, pharm. resident, 1958; pharmacy mgr., Morton Plant Hosp., Clearwater, Fla., 1960-84, dir. profl. and extension services, 1984—; preceptor Sch. Pharmacy, U. Fla., Fla. A&M U.; tchr. profl. seminars. Mem. Human Rights Advocacy Com. for Pinellas and Pasco Counties (Fla.), 1973-83, chmn., 1973-81; pres. Upper Pinellas Assn. Mental Retardation Assns., 1970-72, bd. dirs., 1969-78; pres. Am. Cancer Soc., Pinellas County, 1979-82, bd. dirs., 1971—; pres. Pinellas Epilepsy Found., 1978-79; v.p. Fla. Assn. Retarded, 1971-75, sr. v.p., 1979-81;

bd. dirs. Christian Care Found. for Mentally Handicapped, 1983—, pres., 1985-86. Served with U.S. Army, 1958-60. Named Man of Yr., Upper Pinellas Assn. Retarded, 1970; recipient Nat. Bowl of Hygeia, Fla. Pharm. Assn. and A.H. Robins Co., 1975, Smith award Kiwanis Club, Clearwater Beach, 1978, cert. of merit for public edn. Am. Cancer Soc., 1978, Citizen Health award Clearwater Sun, 1981. Mem. Am. Soc. Hosp. Pharmacists, Fla. Soc. Hosp. Pharmacists (pres. 1972-73, chmn. bd. 1973-74, dir. 1970-78, 79-81; President's award 1982 Hosp. Pharmacist of Yr. 1975), Fellowship Christian Pharmacists (bd. dirs. 1983—), Fla. Pham. Assn. (award for public relations 1981), Pinellas Soc. Pharmacists (pres. 1982, dir. 1979—, exec. sec. 1983—), S.W. Fla. Soc. Hosp. Pharmacists (pres. 1966-67 dir. 1967-70), Fla. Assn. Retarded Citizens (v.p. 1971-75, Brother hood award 1975, Pres.'s award 1978, exec. v.p. 1979-81), Gideons Internat. Republican. Baptist. Author: Antibiotics, 1974, 5th rev. edit., 1983; contbr. articles to pharmacy and mgmt. jours., chpt. to book. Home: 1998 Temple Terr Clearwater FL 33546 Office: 323 Jeffords St Clearwater FL 33516

LAPPE, DONNIE GENE, lawyer; b. Brownwood, Tex., Nov. 19, 1955; s. Alfred Stewart and Muriel (Parsons) L. B.A., Howard Payne U., 1977; J.D., Baylor U., 1980. Bar: Tex. 1980, U.S. Dist. Ct. (no. dist.) Tex. 1981, U.S. Ct. Appeals (5th cir.) 1981, U.S. Supreme Ct. 1984. Ptnr. Lappe & Lappe, Brownwood, 1980—; pro tem county atty. Mills County, 1985—; city atty. City of Earlg, Tex., 1985—; participating atty. Tex. Legal Aid. Author of poetry pub. in lit. mags. Mem. ABA, Tex. Bar Assn., Brown County Bar Assn. (sec.-treas. 1982-84), Comml. Law League Am., Pi Gamma Mu, Alpha Lambda Delta, Alpha Chi. Democrat. Mem. Ch. of Christ. Lodge: Lions. Home: 2111 Ave C Brownwood TX 76801 Office: Lappe & Lappe 305 N Fisk St Brownwood TX 76801

LAPPIN, CARL WELLINGTON, educator, publishing executive, consultant; b. Sewanee, Tenn., Mar. 1, 1928; s. Delbert Brown and Lillian Elizabeth (Conry) L.; B.S., Middle Tenn. State Coll., 1950; M.S., U. Tenn., 1956. Tchr., prin. Monteagle (Tenn.) Elem. Sch., 1950-53; tchr. Knoxville (Tenn.) City Schs., 1955-57; underwriter Am. Mut. Ins. Co., Atlanta, 1957-58; tchr., supr. instrn. Westminster Schs., Atlanta, 1958-61; prin. Shook Sch., Tracy City, Tenn., 1961-62; prin. Dependent Sch., Wheelus AFB, Tripoli, Libya, 1962-63; textbook cons., dir. Instructional Materials Reference Center, Am. Printing House for the Blind, Louisville, 1963-84; textbook cons., 1984—. Served with U.S. Army, 1953-55. Recipient award Calif. Transcribers and Educators, 1981. Mem. Nat. Braille Assn. (v.p. 1983-85), Council Exceptional Children, Assn. Edn. and Rehab. of the Blind and Visually Impaired Calif. Transcribers and Educators of Visually Handicapped. Republican. Mem. Church of Christ. Editor: Nat. Braille Assn. Bull. 1968-69; field editor; Teaching Exceptional Children, 1976-86; contbr. articles to profl. publs. Home: 5100 Brownsboro Rd Louisville KY 40222 Office: 1839 Frankfort Ave Louisville KY 40206

LAPUZ-DE LA PENA, ERLINDA LARON, physician, pathologist, educator; b. Manila, P.I., Nov. 26, 1933; d. Eriberto Mallari and Teodora Quiero (Laron) Lapuz; M.D., U. Santo Tomas, 1957; m. Cordell De La Pena, Apr. 1, 1957; children—Leslie, Nina, Cordell. Intern, St. John's Hosp., Lowell, Mass., 1959-60; attending physician Tewksbury (Mass.) Hosp., 1960-63; resident in pathology Mercy Hosp., Pitts., 1967-71; instr. pathology U. Pitts. Med. Sch., 1967-71; chief lab. service VA Hosp., Clarksburg, W.Va., 1971—, chief staff, 1983—; courtesy staff United Hosp. Center; asst. prof. pathology W.Va. U. Sch. Medicine, 1981—; asst. prof. Coll. Nursing, Salem (W.Va.) Coll., 1978, Coll. Nursing and Physician Assts., Alderson Broadus Coll., Phillipi, W.Va. Diplomate Am. Bd. Pathology. Fellow Coll. Am. Pathologists, Am. Soc. Clin. Pathology; mem. AMA, W.Va. Med. Assn., W.Va., Assn. Pathologists (bd. dirs. 1983—, pres.-elect 1985-86). Roman Catholic. Club: Clarksburg Country. Contbr. articles med. jours. Home: 209 Candlelight Dr Clarksburg WV 26301 Office: Veterans Administration Hospital Clarksburg WV 26301

LAQUER, THOMAS EUGENE, gem broker, telemarketing consultant; b. Barcelona, Spain, Jan. 21, 1944; came to Can., 1946; s. Joseph and Elizabeth (Garterberg) L.; m. Edith, Mar. 15, 1968 (div. May 1972); m. 2d, Linda Susan Goodfellow, Sept. 9, 1979. Sales mgr. Durham Securities, Toronto, Ont., Can., 1965-68; v.p. L. J. Forset, Germany, Italy, 1968-72; pres. Lintel Investments, Toronto, 1972-75; pres. Telmgmt. Corp., Miami, Fla., 1975—, Anglo Union Corp., Miami, 1977—. Mem. Presdl. Council Fitness, 1981. Lodges: Rotary (dir. 1981, 83-84) (Key Biscayne, Fla.), Masons, Shriners.

LARCHE, JAMES CLIFFORD, II, professional society administrator; b. Mobile, Ala., Nov. 27, 1946; s. James Clifford and Alma (Dunn) L.; m. Mary Cecilia Whelchel, June 6, 1969 (div. 1972). A.B., Ga. State U., 1974. Claims examiner Employees' Retirement System, Atlanta, 1969-73, div. dir., 1973-84, dep. dir., 1985—; with Nat. Conf. State Social Security Adminstrs., Atlanta, 1973—, regional v.p., 1978-80, sec., 1980-82, first v.p., 1982-83, pres., 1983-84, chmn. fed.-state procedures com., 1984-85. Served with N.G., 1968-74. Roman Catholic. Home: PO Box 38056 Atlanta GA 30334 Office: Nat Conf State Social Security Adminstrs Two Northside 75 Suite 400 Atlanta GA 30318

LARDENT, CHARLES LEWIS, JR., psychologist, educator; b. Birmingham, Ala., July 2, 1935; s. Charles Lewis and Lillian Dorothy (Childs) L.; B.S., U. Montevallo (Ala.), 1961; M.B.A., Ga. State U., 1969, Ph.D., 1977; M.Mil. Art and Sci., U.S. Army Command Gen. Staff Coll., 1976; m. Edna Louise Shaver, June 28, 1969; children—Renee R., Margot Susette. Mgr., Sears, Roebuck & Co., Atlanta, 1961-66; psychol. counselor Ga. Rehab. Services, 1966-71; research asso., teaching asst. Ga. State U., 1971-75; asso. prof. mgmt. Troy (Ala.) State U., Europe, 1977-80; prof. leadership and mgmt. Air War Coll., Maxwell AFB, Ala., 1980—; pres. HUMRAD, Inc., 1984—; cons. in field, 1976—. Served with USAR, 1957, 59-61, 75-77. Decorated Meritorious Service medal, Army Commendation medal; fellow Rehab. Services Adminstrn., 1970; Army Research Inst. Behavioral and Social Scis. grantee, 1975. Mem. Am. Psychol. Assn., Acad. Mgmt., Nat. Rehab. Counselors Assn., Res. Officers Assn., Huguenot Soc., Sigma Phi Epsilon. Republican. Club: Capital City (Montgomery, Ala.). Author army reports, papers in field. Home: 502 Camellia Ct Millbrook AL 36054 Office: Air War Coll/EDRL Maxwell AFB AL 36112

LARGEN, JOHN WILLIAM, psychologist; b. Johnson City, Tenn., Nov. 5, 1950; s. John William and Mary (Fouraker) L.; m. Janet Lee Burns, July 27, 1975; 1 child, William. B.A., Rutgers Coll., 1973; M.A., Montclair State Coll., 1975; Ph.D., U. Houston, 1980. Lic. psychologist, Tex. Clin. neuro-psychologist Tex. Research Inst. Mental Scis., Houston, 1980-84, Kelsey Seybold Clinic, Houston, 1984—; adj. clin. asst., prof. psychology U. Houston, 1982—. Contbr. articles to profl. jours. Mem. Am. Psychol. Assn., Internat. Neuropsychol. Soc., Biofeedback Soc. Am. (Citation Award for Sci. Merit 1978, 79, 80), Biofeedback Soc. Tex. (pres. 1983-85), Biofeedback Soc. Harris County (co-founder, pres., 1979-80), Tex. Psychol. Assn. Methodist. Clubs: Apple Users Group (Houston). Home: 3519 Cave Springs Dr Kingwood TX 77339 Office: Kelsey-Seybold Clinic 6624 Fannin St Houston TX 77030

LARKAM, BEVERLEY MCCOSHAM, clinical social worker; b. Vancouver, Can., Mar. 3, 1928; d. William Howard and Marjorie Isabel (Jerome) McCosham; came to U.S., 1951; asso. Royal Conservatory Music, U. Toronto, 1948; B.A., U. B.C., 1949, B.S.W., 1950, M.S.W., 1951; children—Elizabeth, Charles, Daphne, Peter, John. Psychiat. social worker Brackenridge Hosp., 1952-54; chmn. dept. sr. high sch. Univ. Presbyn. Ch., Austin, Tex., 1952-55, mem. Christian edn. com., 1961-67, mem. community orgn. to establish classes for mentally retarded children, 1966-68, bd. dirs. developing and organizing nursery sch., 1967-70; social worker Counseling-Psychol. Services Center, U. Tex., 1971-72; psychiatric social worker, chief supr. adult mental health, children's mental health Human Devel. Center-South, Austin, 1972-79; pvt. practice marriage and family therapy, sex therapy and individual and group psychotherapy, Austin, 1975—; field supr. Sch. Social Work U. Tex.; cons. in field. Mem. City of Austin Commn. for Women, 1978-85, emeritus, 1985—; bd. dirs. Nat. Assn. Commns. for Women, 1985—. Cert. social worker, advanced clin. practitioner, Tex. Mem. Am. Assn. Marriage and Family Therapy (approved supr.), Am. Assn. Sex Educators, Counselors and Therapists (cert. sex therapist), Am., Southwestern group psychotherapy socs., Acad. Cert. Social Workers, Nat. Assn. Social Workers, Acad. Family Mediators (assoc.), Soc. Clin. and Exptl. Hypnosis, Nat. Registry. Health Providers in Clin. Social Work, Tex. Council Family Relations, Am. Orthopsychiat. Assn., Soc. Sci. Study of Sex, PEO. Presbyterian. Home and Office: 2102 Raleigh Ave Austin TX 78703

LARKIN, MICHAEL CONWAY, land developer; b. Shreveport, La., Apr. 3, 1956; s. James Lincoln and Arshula Joymae (Washburn) L.; m. Eija Riitta Laine, Jan. 9, 1983. B.S. in Bus. Adminstrn., La. Tech. U., 1978. Vice-pres., Larkin Builders, Inc., Bossier City, La., 1978—. Fund raiser Norwell council Boy Scouts Am., Shreveport, 1979—; commr. Bossier Parish Levee Bd., 1984—. Mem. Bossier City Jaycees (Jaycee of Quarter award 1979), Holiday In Dixie Diplomats, Nat. Fedn. Ind. Bus., Shreveport-Bossier Bd. Realtors, Homebuilders Assn. Shreveport-Bossier (bd. dirs. 1984—). Republican. Roman Catholic. Avocations: cross country bicycling; flying; scuba diving. Home: PO Box 5233 Bossier City LA 71171 Office: Larkin Builders Inc 322 Green Acres Blvd Bossier City LA 71111

LARKIN, WILLIAM THOMAS, clergyman; b. Mt. Morris, N.Y., Mar. 31, 1923; s. William Thomas and Julia Ann (Beuerlein) L.; B.A., St. Bernard's Coll., Rochester, N.Y., 1944; postgrad. St. Bernard's Theol. Sem., 1942-47; D. Theology, U. St. Thomas, Rome, 1949. Ordained to ministry Roman Cath. Ch., 1947; pastor Christ the King Ch., Jacksonville, Fla., 1954-67, St. Cecelia Ch., Clearwater, Fla., 1967-79; vicar gen. Diocese of St. Petersburg, Fla., 1968-79, bishop, 1979—. Office: 6363 9th Ave N Saint Petersburg FL 33710

LARMER, GRAHAM CHESTER, accounting firm executive; b. Abingdon, Va., Nov. 16, 1949; s. Chester Hollan and Bertha (Smith) L.; m. Teresa Widener, Mar. 5, 1972 (div. 1980); m. 2d, Sabrina Leonard, June 27, 1981; 1 son, Graham Chester. B.S. in Acctg. and Bus. Adminstrn. and Mktg. cum laude, East Tenn. State U., 1972. C.P.A. Staff acct., mgr. Mgmt. Adv. Services Dept., Andrews, Burket and Co., C.P.A.s (now Deliotte, Haskins & Sells), Roanoke, Va., 1972-75; controller and asst. treas. Ga. Bonded Fibers, Inc., Buena Vista, Va., 1975-76; pres., chief exec. officer Larmer, Young & Co., P.C. (successor of Faine, Harrell, Larmer and Co., C.P.A.s, and Faine, Larmer and Co., C.P.A.s), Roanoke, 1976—; part time instr. Nat. Bus. Coll., Roanoke, 1974-76. Mem. Am. Inst. C.P.A.s, Va. Soc. C.P.A.s. Republican. Methodist. Home: 5123 Crossbow Circle SW Roanoke VA 24014 Office: PO Drawer 12505 Roanoke VA 24026

LAROCHE, KARL, JR., motion picture and television producer and director, film production executive, audio-visual consultant; b. Stamford, Conn., Mar. 2, 1927; s. Karl and Martha (Meisel) LaR.; m. Clarrissa Worcester Dey, III, Nov. 15, 1952; children—Andre John, Michelle Dey. Student, Art Ctr. Sch., Los Angeles, 1947-49; student Personnel Mgmt., Rollins Coll., 1956-57. Staff engr. Sta. WSRR, Stamford, 1943-45; Sta. WSTC, Stamford, 1947; v.p. Fla. Photo, Inc., Miami, 1950-51; staff photographer Fairchild Aerial Surveys, Inc., N.Y.C., 1952-54; motion picture and aerial photographer RCA Service Co., Missile Test Project, Cocoa, Fla., 1954-56, motion picture dir., RCA, 1957-58, adminstr. photog. services Ballistic Missile Early Warning System Project, Riverton, N.J., Thule, Greenland and Clear, Alaska, 1958-60, motion picture dir. Redstone Pictorial Services, Huntsville, Ala., 1960-64, mgr. film prodn. services, 1964-68; v.p., exec. producer Zapel Studios, Inc., Chgo., 1968-70; mgr. film prodn. and services A.B. Dick Co., Niles, Ill., 1970-72; v.p., exec. producer Bill Stokes Assocs., Dallas, 1972; v.p. prodn. and corp. exec. v.p. Continental Film Prodns. Corp., Chattanooga, 1972-83; audiovisual producer, creative staff corporate communications dept. Provident Cos., Chattanooga, 1983—. Bd. dirs. Lutheran Sch., East Ridge, Tenn., 1977—. Served with USNR, 1945-46. Mem. Soc. Motion Picture & TV Engrs., Soc. Photog. Scientists & Engrs., Am. Soc. Photogrammetry, Am. Rocket Soc., AIAA. Republican. Lutheran. Home: 101 Nancy Ln Route 5 Ringgold GA 30736 Office: Provident Cos Corp Communications Fountain Sq Chattanooga TN 37402

LAROCHE, SHIRLEY SUE, clinical psychologist; b. Fosterville, Tenn., June 21, 1936; d. Powell Maganan and Sophia Sue (Coop) Brothers; B.S., Middle Tenn. State U., 1958, M.A., 1965; Ph.D., U. N.Mex., 1973; m. Richard Frederick LaRoche, 1969; children—Norman Louis, Timothy, Shea. Tchr. public schs., Virginia Beach, Va., 1961-62; tchr., dir. Sch. for the Gifted, Murfreesboro, Tenn., 1965-68; psychol. counselor public schs., Albuquerque, 1968-74; adj. prof. U. Mex., 1974; staff clin. psychologist, chief psychology tng. Murfreesboro VA Med. Center, 1974—; adj. prof. Middle Tenn. State U., 1975—. Dir., Rutherford County Council for Rape and Sexual Abuse; dir. Am. League Women Voters, 1979—; personnel relations rep. Rutherford County Arts and Humanities Council. Recipient superior performance award, 1983, 84. Mem. Am. Psychol. Assn., Southeastern Psychol. Assn., Tenn. Psychol. Assn., AAUW (pres. Murfreesboro br. 1975-77), DAR. Democrat. Roman Catholic. Home: Route 11 Betty Ford Rd Murfreesboro TN 37130 Office: VA Med Center Lebanon Rd Murfreesboro TN 37130

LARRÉ, GAY LYNN HARMANN, micropaleontologist; b. New Orleans, May 3, 1944; d. August Frank and Violet Grace (Ebert) Harmann; m. Randall Francis Larré, Jan. 19, 1973. B.S., Newcomb-Tulane U., 1966; postgrad. U. Wash., 1967-70, Tulane U., 1969, U. New Orleans, 1973. Asst. curator-paleontologist Tulane U., New Orleans, 1963-66; micropaleontologist Texaco, Inc., New Orleans, 1966-79; sr. micropaleontologist U.S. Dept. Interior, New Orleans, 1979—. Vol. Audubon Zool. Soc., New Orleans, 1973, Jefferson Parish Animal Shelter, Metairie, La., 1973, Alter Guild-Grace Luth. Ch., New Orleans, 1985. Mayor's scholar City of New Orleans, Newcomb/Tulane, 1962, NSF undergrad. grantee Tulane U., 1964, 65; recipient Spl. Achievement awards U.S. Dept. Interior, Metairie, 1981, 83. Mem. Am. Assn. Petroleum Geologists, New Orleans Geol. Soc., Alpha Delta Pi. Clubs: The La. Nature and Sci. Ctr., Jefferson Soc. Prevention Cruelty to Animals (Metairie). Avocations: day hiking; vol. work with animals; cooking; gardening; reading. Home: 2009 Madison St Metairie LA 70001 Office: US Dept Interior MMS 3301 Causeway Blvd Metairie LA 70002

LARSEN, BRYAN, microbiologist, educator; b. Omaha, Jan. 26, 1949; s. Norman Louis and Shirley Lorraine (Bryan) L.; m. Nancy Esther Nettleton, July 19, 1969; children—Erik Bryan, Jeremy Todd. B.S., U. Iowa, 1971, M.S., 1973, Ph.D., 1976. Research asst. scientist U. Iowa, Iowa City, 1976-80, asso. research scientist, 1980-81; asst. prof. obstetrics and gynecology and asst. prof. microbiology Marshall U., Huntington, W.Va., 1981-84, assoc. prof., 1984—; chief analytical services Microbiol. Cons., Inc., Huntington, 1984—; cons. in field regarding pharm. products toxic shock syndrome. Contbr. articles to books and profl. jours. Served to capt., USAR, 1981—. Freedom's Found. awardee, Freedom's Found. Valley Forge, 1972; Freedom's Found. Award and Bronze medal, 1973; NIH fellow, 1978. Mem. Am. Soc. Microbiology, Infectious Disease Soc. for Obstetrics and Gynecology, N.Y. Acad. Sci., Infectious Disease Soc. Am., Soc. Gynecologic Investigation. Republican. Baptist.

LARSEN, JOHN MATHUE, JR., psychologist, educator; b. Ackley, Iowa, Aug. 8, 1922; s. John Mathue and Helen (Morgan) L.; m. M. Suzanne Wetmore, Oct. 17, 1949; children—Mary Christine Quillen, Mathue L., Marn Suzanne, John Morgan. Diploma Ellsworth Jr. Coll., 1942; B.S., Iowa State U., 1948, M.S., 1959; Ph.D., Purdue U., 1963. Lic. psychologist, Tenn. From asst. to full prof. mgmt. U. Tenn., Knoxville, 1963—, dir. indsl. and orgnl. psychology program, 1970—; mem. Tenn. Bd. Examiners in Psychology, 1969-70, 73— exec., 1975-77, chmn., 1977-78; cons. in field. Served with USAAF, 1942-45; ETO. Decorated Silver Star, Air medals with 9 clusters, Purple Heart. Mem. Tenn. Valley Personnel Assn., Am. Soc. Tng. and Devel., Tenn. Psychol. Assn. (pres. 1980-81), Southeastern Psychol. Assn., Am. Psychol. Assn., Acad. Mgmt., Beta Gamma Sigma, Phi Kappa Phi. Lodge: Masons. Home: 524 Bardon Rd Knoxville TN 37919 Office: 413 SMC Coll Bus Adminstrn U Tenn Knoxville TN 37996

LARSEN, MARTIN RAYMOND, refrigeration company executive; b. New Brunswick, N.J., July 30, 1949; s. Raymond Martin and Margaret (Dudik) L.; student U. Miami, 1967-72, Rutgers U., 1969, Miami Dade Community Coll., 1974-76, Broward County Community Coll., 1979-80, Nova U., 1983—. Comptroller, So. Farm Supermarket, Inc., Miami, Fla., 1970-77, Cambronne Enterprises, Inc., Miami, 1977-79; asst. comptroller Seacoast Appliance Distbrs., Inc., Miami, 1979-80; comptroller, Graves Refrigeration Co., Miami, 1980—; chief fin. officer Graves Corp., 1980—; dir., v.p. Distributor Computer Services Corp. div. Graves Corp., Miami, 1980—; dir. Bill Kress & Co., Inc., Paradise Prodns. Unltd. Mem. Am. Mgmt. Assn., Nat. Assn. Accts. Democrat. Roman Catholic. Home: 651 SW 98th Terr Pembroke Pines FL 33025 Office: 2400 NW 23 St Miami FL 33142

LARSEN, RALPH IRVING, environ. research engr.; b. Corvallis, Oreg., Nov. 26, 1928; s. Walter Winfred and Nellie Lyle (Gellatly) L.; B.S. in Civil Engring., Oreg. State U., 1950; M.S., Harvard U., 1955, Ph.D. in Air Pollution and Indsl. Hygiene, 1957; m. Betty Lois Garner, Oct. 14, 1950; children—Karen Larsen Cleeton, Eric, Kristine Larsen Burns, Jan Alan. San. engr. div. water pollution control USPHS, Washington, 1950-54; chief tech. service state and community service sect. Nat. Air Pollution Control Adminstrn., Cin., 1957-61; with EPA and Nat. Air Pollution Control Adminstrn., 1961—, environ. research engr., environ. ops. br., meteorology and assessment div., Research Triangle Park, N.C., 1971—; adj. lectr. Inst. Air Pollution Tng., 1969—; Falls of Neuse community rep. City of Raleigh (N.C.), 1974—. Recipient Commendation medal USPHS, 1979. Mem. Air Pollution Control Assn. (editorial bd. jour.), Research Soc. Am., Conf. Fed. Environ. Engrs., USPHS Commd. Officers Assn. (past br. pres.). Republican. Mem. Christian and Missionary Alliance Ch. (elder). Contbr. numerous articles to profl. jours. Home: 4012 Colby Dr Raleigh NC 27609 Office: MD-80 EPA Research Triangle Park NC 27711

LARSEN, RUSSELL DAVID, chemistry educator; b. Muskegon, Mich., June 6, 1936; s. Russell D., Sr. and Hilda (Bloomquist) L.; m. Juanita Bargahiser, Aug. 17, 1958; children—Erik David, Susan Ingrid. B.A., Kalamazoo Coll., 1957; Ph.D., Kent State U., 1964; postdoctoral study Princeton U., 1964-65, Rice U., 1965-66. Asst. prof. Ill. Inst. Tech., Chgo., 1966-72, Tex. A&M U., College Station, Tex., 1972-76; vis. assoc. prof. U. Nev.-Reno, 1976-77; assoc. prof. U. Mich., Ann Arbor, 1977-83, Tex. Tech. U., Lubbock, 1983—. Mem. Am. Chem. Soc., Am. Phys. Soc., Am. Statis. Assn., AAAS, IEEE, Triangle (hon. mem.). Home: 3604 97th St Lubbock TX 79423 Office: Dept Chemistry Tex Tech U 79409

LARSON, ALLEN LEO, telephone company official; b. Buffalo, Mar. 10, 1946; s. Allen Howard and Lulu Belle L.; B.A. in History cum laude, SUNY-Buffalo, 1973; m. Linda Joyce Anger, July 27, 1 son, Andrew Jay. Personnel mgr. RJR Foods Inc., Lockport, N.Y., 1973-75, South Brunswick, N.J., 1975-77, supr. employee devel. Corp. RJR Foods Inc., Winston-Salem, N.C., 1977-78, personnel devel. mgr., 1978-79; dir. labor relations and safety Continental Telephone, Atlanta, 1979-82; dir. mgmt. and organizational devel. Continental Telecom Inc., 1982—; designer Personnel Mgmt. Seminar, U.S. Ind. Telephone Assn., 1981, 82. Instr. job-finding, interviewing skills YWCA, Urban League, Niagara County, N.Y., 1973-74; loaned exec. United Way Niagara County, 1973, 74; mem. Personnel Policies Forum, Bur. Nat. Affairs, 1981-82. Served with USMC, 1969-70. Recipient award of appreciation Raritan Valley Regional C. of C., 1977. Mem. Am. Soc. Personnel Adminstrn. (nat. com. employee-labor relations 1981-82), Am. Soc. Tng. and Devel. Designer wage and salary survey Raritan Valley (N.J.) Regional C. of C., 1976; editor, reviewer Safety and Health Reference Handbook, 1979; contbr. article to personnel publ. Home: 3340 Woodleaf Way Marietta GA 30062 Office: 245 Perimeter Center Pkwy Atlanta GA 30346

LARSON, ARVID GUNNAR, electrical engineer; b. Chgo., July 26, 1937; s. Arvid G. and Marion Edith (Parker) L.; m. Gladys Lorraine Anderson, June 6, 1959; 1 son, Gregory Monte. B.S. in Elec. Engring., Ill. Inst. Tech., Chgo., 1959; M.S. in Elec. Engring., Stanford (Calif.) U., 1966, Ph.D. in Elec. Engring., 1973. Registered profl. engr., Calif., Va. Research engr. Stanford Research Inst., Menlo Park, Calif., 1964-74; mgr. advanced research Planning Research Corp., McLean, Va., 1974-78; project mgr. System Planning Corp., Arlington, Va., 1978-80; mgr. Washington div. Advanced Research and Applications Corp., Vienna, Va., 1980-85; v.p. Analytical Disciplines Inc., Vienna, 1985—. Chmn. bd. dirs. Electronics and Aerospace Systems Conf., 1982-84; bd. dirs. Research Inst. in Info. Scis and Engring., 1978—; bd. advisers George Mason U., Fairfax, Va., 1980—; chmn. 3d NATO Advanced Study Inst. in Info. Scis., 1978. Served to lt. USN, 1959-63. Fellow IEEE (chmn. def. research and devel. com. 1985—, chmn. No. Va. sect. 1986—, Centennial medal 1984); mem. Armed Forces Communications and Electronics Assn., Sigma Xi. Club: Cosmos. Author: Information Science in Action: System Design, 1983; contbr. numerous elec. engring. articles to profl. publs. Home: 6921 Espey Ln McLean VA 22101 Office: 2070 Chain Bridge Rd Suite 400 Vienna VA 22180

LARSON, DAVID RICHARD, university administrator, accountant, educator; b. Mpls., Oct. 8, 1944; s. James Freeman and Jean Elizabeth (Rahders) L.; m. Betty Jane Sump, Sept. 15, 1973. B.S., U. Minn., 1967; M.B.A., U. Tenn., 1969. C.P.A., Tenn. Asst. to treas. U. Tenn., Knoxville, 1969, asst. to vice chancellor bus. and fin., Chattanooga, 1967-73, asst. vice chancellor bus. and fin., 1973-75, vice chancellor bus. and fin., 1975-82, vice chancellor adminstrn. and fin., 1982—, asst. prof. acctg., 1983—. Chmn. Downtown Housing Task Force I, Chattanooga, 1985; asst. treas. Chattanooga Symphony Opera, 1984-85; mem. assoc. commn. United Way, Chattanooga, 1980-85; bd. dirs. Better Bus. Bur., Chattanooga, 1983-85. Mem. Am. Inst. C.P.A.s (mem. com. 1981-84), Tenn. Soc. C.P.A.s (com. chmn. 1981-83), Golden Key, Beta Alpha Psi. Lodge: Rotary. Home: 816 Brynewood Park Ln Chattanooga TN 37415 Office: U Tenn 615 McCallie Ave Chattanooga TN 37403

LARSON, KERMIT DEAN, accounting educator; b. Algona, Iowa, Apr. 7, 1939; s. Loren L. and Hansena Laurena (Andersen) L.; m. Nancy Lynne Weber, June 17, 1961; children—Julie Renee, Timothy Dean, Cynthia Lynne. A.A., Ft. Dodge Jr. Coll., 1960; B.B.A., U. Iowa, 1962, M.B.A., 1963; D.B.A., U. Colo., 1966. C.P.A., Tex. Mem. faculty U. Tex., Austin, 1966—, Arthur Andersen & Co. Alumni prof., 1975—, chmn. dept. acctg., 1971-75; vis. assoc. prof. Tulane U., New Orleans, 1970-71; cons. sales tax audit litigation, pvt. anti-trust litigation, expropriation ins. arbitration. Mem. Am. Acctg. Assn. (v.p. 1978-79). Am. Fin. Assn., Am. Inst. C.P.A.s, Tex. Soc. C.P.A.s, Beta Gamma Sigma, Beta Alpha Psi. Baptist. Author: (with Griffin et al.) Advanced Accounting, 5th edit., 1985; (with W.W. Pyle) Fundamental Accounting Principles, 10th edit., 1984; (with W.W. Pyle) Financial Accounting, 3d edit., 1986; contbr. numerous articles in field of fin. acctg. to profl. jours. Home: 1310 Falcon Ledge Austin TX 78746 Office: Dept Acctg Univ Tex Austin TX 78712

LARSON, LEONARD GILES, optometrist, electronics engineer; b. Auburn, Mass., Sept. 21, 1943; s. Hugo B. and Eva B. (Giles) L.; m. Diane Marie Dicenso, Apr. 20, 1968; children—Troy Michael, Craig Robert, Mark Andrew. B.S., Northeastern U., 1966, M.S. in Elec. Engring., 1967, Ph.D. in Elec. Engring., 1970; O.D., New Eng. Coll. Optometry, 1982. Lic. optometrist, Va., Mass.; diagnostic pharm. agts. cert., Va. Elec. engr. Def. Communications Agy., Washington, 1972-80; pvt. practice optometry, Fairfax, Va., 1982—. Contbr. articles to tech. jours. Mem. adv. council Christian Stewardship Ministries, Fairfax, 1984—; youth ministry vol. Truro Episcopal Ch., Fairfax, 1983—. Served to capt. U.S. Army, 1970-72. Mem. Am. Optometric Assn., No. Va. Optometric Soc., Va. Optometric Assn., IEEE (sr.), Tau Beta Pi, Eta Kappa Nu, Phi Kappa Phi. Avocations: stamp collecting, soccer, golf, softball, basketball. Office: 9844-B Main St Fairfax VA 22031

LARSON, RICHARD FRANCIS, sociology educator; b. Yakima, Wash., Apr. 2, 1931; s. Renus Matthew and Helen Mary (Snyder) L.; m. Celine M. Krupka, Apr. 6, 1968. B.A., Seattle U., 1957; M.A., U. Wash., 1958; Ph.D., U. Notre Dame, 1961. Asst. prof. sociology U. Ala., 1961-62, U. R.I., 1962-64; assoc. prof. sociology Okla. State U., 1964-67, U. Mo.-St. Louis, 1967-68; prof. sociology U. Fla., 1968-73; prof., chmn. dept. sociology Calif. State U.-Hayward, 1973-78; prof. sociology, head sociology dept. Clemson U. (S.C.), 1978—. Served with USN, 1950-54. Mem. AAUP, Am. Sociol. Assn., Soc. for Study of Social Problems, Soc. for Sci. Study Religion. Roman Catholic. Co-author: Introductory Sociology, 1973, 3d edit., 1980; Statistics— A Tool for the Social Sciences, 1974, 3d edit., 1983; Readings for Introducing Sociology, 1982; The Sociology of Social Problems, 8th edit., 1985. Home: 223 N Clemson Ave Clemson SC 29631 Office: 0-303 Martin Hall Clemson U Clemson SC 29631

LARTIGUE, PIUS CARROLL, ednl. adminstr., clergyman; b. Baton Rouge, Dec. 22, 1928; s. Carroll Louis and Gladys Marie (Ourso) L.; B.A., St. Joseph Sem. Coll., 1953; M.S. in Library Sci., Cath. U. Am., 1956; B.S., Loyola U., New Orleans, 1960; M.A., Loyola U., Chgo., 1967. Ordained priest Roman Cath. Ch., 1953; mem. faculty St. Joseph Sem. Coll., St. Benedict, La., 1955—, acad. dean, 1967-71, 72-75, treas., 1975-78, pres.-rector, 1980—; prior St. Joseph Abbey, St. Benedict, 1971-80, bus. officer, 1976-80. Mem. Am. Psychol. Assn., Am. Cath. Edn. Assn. Democrat. Office: St Joseph Seminary College St Benedict LA 70457

LA SALLE, ARTHUR EDWARD, historic foundation executive; b. New Orleans, Aug. 9, 1930; s. Rene Charles and Jeanne Matilda (Senac) La S.; divorced; children—Carl Alan, Adam David, Jeanne Ambre Victoria. Student Holy Name of Jesus Coll. Founder, pres. Am. R.R. Equipment Assn., Asheville, N.C., 1960—; founder Trains of Yesterday Mus., Hilliard, Fla., 1964-73; owner, restorer Brush Hill mansion, Irwin, Pa., 1973-77; lessee, restorer Springfield mansion, Fayette, Miss., 1977—; founder, pres. Hist. Springfield Found., Fayette, 1977—; cons. Smithsonian Instn., 1959, 75,

Japanese Nat. Rys., Tokyo, 1968, Henry Ford Mus., 1975 City of Natchez, Miss., 1985, Old South Soc., Church Hill, Miss., 1985—; cons. in field; lectr. in field. Contbr. articles to profl. jours. Mem. Ry. and Locomotive Hist. Soc., Nat. Trust for Historic Preservation, Natchez Hist. Soc. Club: Natchez Garden. Avocations: historical preservation and study; writing; painting. Home and office: Route 1 Box 201 Springfield Plantation Fayette MS 39069

LASHBROOK, PAUL N., lawyer; b. Hillsboro, Wis., Oct. 6, 1940; s. Jack W. and Ruth E. (Raisch) L.; m. Bonnie L. Hayes, May 23, 1964. B.A., Asbury Coll., 1962; M.Ed., Fla. Atlantic U., 1974; J.D., Nova U., 1982. Bar: Fla. 1984. Prodn. engr. Oxford Paper Co., West Carrollton, Ohio, part-time 1960-63; tchr. White Oak Schs., Mowrystown, Ohio, 1963-64, Fairfield Schs., Ohio, 1964-66, Forest Park Schs., Ohio, 1966-69, Broward County Schs., Fort Lauderdale, Fla., 1969-80; sole practice, Fort Lauderdale, 1984—. Recipient Book award Nova U., 1982. Mem. Broward County Bar Assn., Fla. Bar Assn., ABA, Assn. Trial Lawyers Am., Antique Auto Club Am. (pres., chmn. bd. Fort Lauderdale region 1970-84, counsel 1984), Rolls Royce Owners Club, Cadillac-LaSalle Club, Phi Alpha Delta, Phi Delta Kappa. Republican. Methodist. Office: 315 SE 7th St Suite 200 Fort Lauderdale FL 33301

LASHLEE, FRANK P., state senator; b. Camden, Tenn., June 30, 1937; married. Student Murray State U.; B.S., U. Tenn.; LL.B., YMCA Law Sch.; LL.B., LaSalle U. Mem. 88th-92d Tenn. Gen. Assembly, Nashville; owner, mgr. ins. agy. Served with USMCR. Mem. U. Tenn. Alumni Assn., PTA, Am. Legion, Lambda Chi Alpha. Democrat. Methodist. Clubs: Camden Quarter-back, Magic Valley Gold and Country. Lodges: Elks, Masons, Shriners. Office: Tenn Senate War Meml Bldg Nashville TN 37219*

LASHLEE, ROBERT WILEY, continuing education executive; b. Memphis, Aug. 8, 1935; s. T.W. and Etta Hester (Gassaway) L.; m. Kristi June Deaver, Jan. 12, 1956; children—Robert W., Jr., Pamela Denise. A.A., Ark. State U., 1976; B.S., U. Central Ark., 1977, M.S., 1981; postgrad., U. Ark., 1982—. Enlisted U.S. Marine Corps, 1953, served active duty until 1973; dir. pub. info. Ark. State U., Beebe, 1974—. Alderman, City of Beebe, 1977. Mem. Ark. Assn. Coll. Admissions officers (mem. com. 1979, 81), Ark. Assn. Community Service and Continuing Edn. (mem. com. 1984—), Phi Beta Lambda, Gamma Beta Phi. Lodge: Masons, Shriners. Avocations: coaching; football; bowling; computers; photography. Office: Ark State U Beebe PO Drawer H Beebe AR 72012

LASKER, ESTHER WOOL, former educator; b. Boston, Dec. 15, 1929; d. Irving B. and Anna W. (Wolper) Wool; m. Norman Lawrence Lasker, Dec. 17, 1950; children—Amy Lasker Shumrak, Brenda. B.S., Boston U., 1951; M.Ed., Fla. Atlantic U., 1971; postgrad. Nova U., 1981-82. Cert. tchr., Fla. Drama and English tchr. Booker High Sch., Sarasota, Fla., 1965-66; tchr. English, Miami (Fla.) Central High Sch., 1968-70; tchr. English, TV and movies Hialeah-Miami Lakes Sr. High Sch., 1970-80; spl. assignment tchr. to Mariel refugees, 1980-82; tchr. remedial reading Palm Springs Jr. High Sch., Miami, 1982-84; group sales coordinator, travel agt., 1984—. Pres. Woman's Am. ORT, Brookline, Mass., 1953, 55, Sisterhood of Temple Beth Shalom, Sarasota, 1964-65. Democrat. Jewish.

LASSEIGNE, PAUL WALTER, JR., pharmacist; b. Rayne, La., Jan. 8, 1942; s. Paul Walter and Dorothy Amelia (Castille) L.; m. Carolyn Ann Region, July 6, 1968; children—C. Wesley, Stephen R. B.S., Northeast La. U., 1963, M.S., 1973. Registered pharmacist, La. Pharmacist Kemper Drugs, Mansfield, La., 1963-65, VA Hosp., Shreveport, La., 1969-73; chief pharmacist Bapt. Hosp., Alexandria, La., 1966-69; supervisory pharmacist VA Med. Ctr., Decatur, Ga., 1973-74, VA Hosp., Columbia, S.C., 1974-84, VA Hosp., Little Rock, 1984—; adj. asst. prof. pharmacy U. S.C., Columbia, 1975-84. Chief Y-Indian Guides Fedn., Columbia, 1980; vice-chmn. adv. council 7 Oaks Elem. Sch., Columbia, 1982; bd. dirs. Gardendale Crime Watch, Columbia, 1983. Mem. Southeastern Soc. Hosp. Pharmacists (sec.-treas. 1984-87), Am. Soc. Hosp. Pharmacists, S.C. Soc. Hosp. Pharmacists, Civitan, Jaycees, Kappa Psi, Omicron Delta Kappa, Rho Chi. Home: 7013 Incas Dr North Little Rock AR 72116 Office: John L McClellan Meml VA Hosp 4300 W 7th St Little Rock AR 72205

LASSETER, DAWSON FRANKLIN, oil and gas consultant; b. Three Rivers, Tex., Feb. 25, 1949; s. Norman William and Minnie Faye (Shumate) L.; m. Sandra Lynn Camren, June 23, 1972; children—Jennifer Renea, Nathan William. B.S. in Geol. Engring., U. Okla., 1972. Registered profl. engr., Okla., Tex.; cert. profl. geol. scientist. Reservoir engr., staff geologist Mustang Fuel Corp., Oklahoma City, 1972-76; reservoir engr. Ramsey Engring., Oklahoma City, 1976; dist. reservoir engr., proration engr. Tex. Oil & Gas Corp., Oklahoma City, 1976-79; v.p. exploration and engring. GEC Prodn. Co., Norman, Tex., 1979-82; pres., founder Geol. Engring. Cons., Norman, 1979—. Recipient James K. Anderson award U. Okla., 1972. Mem. Soc. Petroleum Engrs., Am. Assn. Petroleum Geologists, Am. Inst. Profl. Geol. Scientists, Soc. Ind. Petroleum Exploration Scientists, Nat. Soc. Profl. Engrs., Okla. Soc. Profl. Engrs. Republican. Baptist. Home: 1155 Merrymen Green Norman OK 73069 Office: 330 W Grey St Suite 320 Norman OK 73070

LASSETER, KENNETH CARLYLE, pharmacologist; b. Jacksonville Fla., Aug. 12, 1942; s. James and Retta (Shad) L.; B.S., Stetson U., 1963; M.D., U. Fla., 1967; m. Kathy G. Marks, Aug. 6, 1977; children—Kenneth C. III, Susan, Frank L. Intern, resident in medicine U. Ky. Med. Center, 1967-71; asst. prof., asso. prof. pharmacology and medicine U. Miami Med. Sch., 1971-81, clin. asso. prof., 1981—; dir. Clin. Pharmacology Assos., Inc., Miami, 1981—. Served with USAR, 1971-76. Recipient William B. Peck Sci. Research award Interstate Postgrad. Med. Assn., 1976, research award Alpha Omega Alpha, 1967. Fellow Am. Coll. Clin. Pharmacology; mem. Am. Soc. Pharmacology and Exptl. Therapeutics, Am. Soc. Clin. Pharmacology, ACP, Sigma Xi. Republican. Contbr. articles to profl. jours. Home: 13260 Coronado Dr North Miami FL 33181 Office: 2060 NW 22d Ave Miami FL 33142

LASSITER, ALLEN DREW, investment banking executive; b. Winston-Salem, N.C., June 24, 1948; s. James Harrison and Allene L. B.A., U. N.C., 1970; M.B.A., Wharton Sch. Fin. U. Pa., 1974. With loan adminstrn. officer Wachovia Bank & Trust, Charlotte, N.C., 1970-71; with Smith Barney Harris Upham & Co., Inc., Dallas, 1973—, mgr. Dallas corporate fin., 1979—, 1st v.p., 1980—. Clubs: The Brook, Doubles (N.Y.C.); City (Dallas). Home: 3921 Hanover St Dallas TX 75221 Office: 5300 First International Bldg Dallas TX 75270

LASSITER, RONALD CORBETT, oil company executive; b. Houston, Aug. 2, 1932; s. Mance and Pauline Marie (Lloyd) L.; m. Ella Lee Moechel, Dec. 26, 1951; children—Rona Lee, James Mance, Jennifer Lynn, Lynda Fay. B.A., Rice U., 1955; M.B.A., Harvard U., 1964. Sr. v.p. Zapata Corp., Houston, 1970-71, exec. v.p., 1971-77, sr. exec. v.p., 1977-78, pres., chief operating officer, 1978-83, pres. chief exec. officer, 1983-86, chmn. bd., chief exec. officer, 1986—; also dir. Zapata Off-Shore, Inc., Zapata Exploration Co., Zapata Haynie Corp., Pesquera Zapata, S.A., Zapata Gulf Marine Corp. Mem. Soc. Mining Engrs. AIME, Petroleum Club Houston. Club: Athletic (Houston). Office: Zapata Tower Houston TX 77210-4240

LASTER, STANLEY JERRAL, geophysicist; b. Fittstown, Okla., June 28, 1937; s. Stanley L.D. and Dola Bell (Stacy) L.; m. Susan Zane, Mar. 18, 1960; children—David, Kevin, Michael, Cynthia. B.S. in Engring. Physics, U. Tulsa, 1959; M.S. in Solid State Physics, So. Meth. U., 1962; Ph.D. in Geophysics, MIT, 1970. Geophysicist research Tex. Instruments, Dallas, 1959-74; assoc. prof. U. Tulsa, Okla., 1974-80; mgr. geophysics research Mobil Research and Devel. Corp., Dallas, 1980-83, research scientist, 1983—; cons. Amoco Prodn. Research, Tulsa, 1974-75, 78-80. Mem. Soc. Exploration Geophysicists (assoc. editor 1984-85), Seismol. Soc. Am., Am. Assn. Petroleum Geologists, Dallas Geophys. Soc., Archeol. Inst. Am. Republican. Home: 7608 Cliffbrook Dr Dallas TX 75240

LASTINGER, ALLEN LANE, JR., banker; b. Atmore, Ala., Aug. 16, 1942; s. Allen Lane and Sue Belle (Bevis) L.; m. Shirley Delores Taylor, May 1, 1965; children—Randall Lane, Lindsey Kathleen, Amy Delores. B.B.A., U. Fla., 1965, 1971; postgrad. Stonier Grad. Sch. Banking, Rutgers U., 1979-81; A.M.P., Harvard U., 1982. Fin. analyst Barnett Banks Fla., Inc., Jacksonville, 1971-75, asst. v.p., 1975; pres., chief exec. officer Barnett Bank, Gainesville, Fla., 1976-80; exec. v.p. community banking Barnett Banks Fla., 1980-82, sr. exec. v.p. community banking, 1982-84, vice-chmn., 1984—; dir. Barnett Banks of Fla., Inc. Bd. dirs. U. Fla. Found. Served with USN, 1966-70. Mem. Fla. C. of C. (bd. dirs.). Republican. Methodist. Office: 100 Laura St Jacksonville FL 32202

LASTRA, JESUS L., dentist; b. La Salud, Havana, Cuba, Jan. 5, 1928; came to U.S., 1961, naturalized, 1968; s. Patricio and Antonia (Martinez) L.; B.S., Inst. Havana, 1947; D.D.S., Havana U., 1952; D.M.D., U. Ala., 1966; m. Silvia M. Lopez, Aug. 6, 1950; children—Idalia, Teresa. Practice dentistry, Havana, 1952-61; instr. crown and bridge U. Havana, 1952-59, prof., 1959-61, prof. Summer Sch., 1956; instr., research asso. U. Ala., 1966-68; clin. asst. prof. U. Miami Sch. Medicine, 1968—; practice dentistry, Miami, Fla., 1968—. Fellow Acad. Gen. Dentistry (master), Internat. Coll. Dentists, Am. Coll. Dentists; mem. Am., Mexican, Cuban (past v.p., sec. sci. com.), Havana dental assns., Internat. Assn. Dental Research, Am. Prosthodontic Soc., Latin Am. Dental Study Club (pres. 1973-74), S.E. Fla. Acad. Gen. Dentistry (pres. 1978-79), Greater Miami Dental Soc. (pres. 1982-83), Dade County Dental Research Clinic (pres. 1981-82), Delta Sigma Delta. Lion (pres. 1972-73). Club: Cuban Sertoma (pres. 1979-80). Contbr. articles to profl. jours. Home: 2100 SW 21st Terr Miami FL 33145 Office: 2150 SW 21st Ave Miami FL 33145

LATHAM, ALICE FRANCES PATTERSON, public health nurse; b. Macon, Ga., Dec. 18, 1916; d. Frank Waters and Ruby (Dews) Patterson; R.N., Charity Hosp. Sch. Nursing, New Orleans, 1937; student George Peabody Coll. Tchrs., 1938-39; B.S. in Public Health Nursing, U. N.C., 1954; M.P.H., Johns Hopkins U., 1966; m. William Joseph Latham, July 21, 1940 (dec. 1981); children—Jo Alice Latham Ziegler, Marynette Latham Stephens, Lauruby Latham Gold; m. Sidney Dumas Herndon, Apr. 26, 1985. Staff public health nurse assigned spl. venereal disease study USPHS, Darien, Ga., 1939-40; county public health nurse Bacon County, Alma, 1940-41; USPHS spl. venereal disease project, Glynn County, Brunswick, 1943-47; county public health nurse Glyn County, 1949-51, Ware County, Waycross, 1951-52; public health nurse supr. Wayne-Long-Brantley-Liberty Counties, Jesup, 1954-56; dir. public health nursing Wayne-Long-Appling Bacon-Pierce Counties, Jesup 1956-70, dist. chief of nursing S.E. health dist., 1970-79, exec. dir. health dept. home care services, 1968-80; cons. health planning and devel., home health programs. Bd. dirs. Wayne County Mental Health Assn., 1959, 60, 61, v.p., 1982—; bd. dirs. Wayne County Tb Assn., 1958-62, Health Dept. Home Care Services, 1980—; a non-alcoholic organizer Jesup group Alcoholics Anonymous, 1962-63; mem. Ga. Community Health Task Force, 1974-76; vestry person St. Paul's Episcopal Ch., Jesup, Ga., 1979—; adv. council Ware Meml. Hosp. Sch. Practical Nursing, Waycross, Ga., 1958; bd. dirs. S.E. Ga. Health Systems Agy. Inc., 1975-82, mem. exec. com., 1975-76, 78-81. Recipient recognition Gen. Service Bd., Alcoholics Anonymous, Inc. Fellow Am. Public Health Assn.; mem. Am., 8th Dist. (pres. 1954-58, dir. 1960-62, 1st v.p. 1962), Ga. (exec. bd. 1954-58, continuing edn. program rev. com. 1980—) nurses assns., Ga. Public Health Assn. (chmn. nursing sect. 1956-57), Ga. Assn. for Dist. Chiefs of Nursing (pres. 1975-77). Contbr. to state nursing manuals. Home: Route 6 Box 46 Brunswick GA 31520

LATHAM, JAMES PARKER, geographer, educator; b. Collingdale, Pa., June 2, 1918; s. William Harry and Martha (Curry) L.; B.S., U. Pa., 1949, M.S., 1950, M.A. in Econs., 1951, Ph.D., 1959; m. Eloise McDaniel, Mar. 7, 1945. Lectr. geography and industry Wharton Sch., U. Pa., 1951-59; asst. prof. geography Bowling Green (Ohio) State U., 1959-61, assoc. prof., 1961-64; prof., chmn. dept. geography Fla. Atlantic U., Boca Raton, 1964-70, prof., dir. Remote Sensing Lab., 1970—; prin. investigator Office Naval Research project, 1965-74, U.S. Geol. Survey project, 1967-70, 78-80; mem. com. remote sensing NRC, 1973-78. Mem. Bowling Green City Planning Commn., 1963-64, Beach Park Devel. Com., Boca Raton, 1967. Served with USAAF, 1942-46; maj. M.I., U.S. Army Res., 1947-71. Mem. Assn. Am. Geographers, Fla. Soc. Geographers (pres. 1966-67), AAAS, Am. Planning Assn., Am. Soc. Photogrammetry (pres. Fla. region 1970-72, nat. dir., mem. exec. com. 1971-74), Phi Kappa Phi. Methodist. Club: Kiwanis. Editor, The Darby Progress, 1946-51; contbr. articles to profl. jours. Home: 830 NE 69th St Boca Raton FL 33431

LATHAM, RICHARD CARLTON, oil and gas producer; b. Longview, Tex., Mar. 31, 1941; s. R. Sidney and Iris Lorraine (Anderson) L.; m. Linda Carolyn Jones, Dec. 28, 1963 (div. June 1975); 1 son, A. Carter. B.A., U. Va., 1964; postgrad. Sch. Law, So. Meth. U., 1964-65. Promotion dir. Petroleum Engr. Pub. Co., Dallas, 1965-67; account exec. Wyatt & Williams Advt., Dallas, 1967-69; ind. oil and gas producer, Dallas, 1969—; dir. Pan Am. Produce Co.; pres. Druid Properties, Inc.; rancher, Douglassville, Tex., 1980—. Bd. govs. U.S. Polo Assn., 1972-79, sec., 1973-75; bd. dirs. Cystic Fibrosis Found. Republican. Clubs: Brook Hollow Golf, Dallas Gun, Dallas Safari (Dallas); Farmington Country (Charlottesville, Va.); Garden of Gods (Colorado Springs, Colo.). Home: 4659 S Versailles Dallas TX 75209 Office: 3525 Cedar Springs St Dallas TX 75219

LATHEM, BETTY BROOKS, administrative assistant; b. Griffin, Ga., Aug. 16, 1931; d. Raymond England and Annie Ezelle (Chappell) Brooks; m. Charles Malcolm Lathem, July 18, 1950; children—Charles Thomas, Richard Lee, Betty Kathryn. Student pub. schs., Griffin. With So. Bell Telephone Co., Griffin, Ga., 1949-50, J.D. Jewell, Inc., Gainesville, Ga., 1950-54; part-time sec., various cos., Gainesville, 1954-59; with Jacobs, Matthews & Parker, Architects, Gainesville, 1959-69; self-employed ind. sec., Gainesville, 1969-70; adminstrv. asst. Internat. Mgmt., Gainesville, 1970—, specialist in orgn., research and preparation of bus. and profl. books and articles for publ.; ptnr. poultry farm; owner Windfield Crafts. Active various charitable orgns. Democrat. Baptist. Home and Office: Baker Circle Box 1477 Clermont GA 30527 Office: PO Box 1477 Clermont GA 30527

LATHROP, GERTRUDE ADAMS, chemist, consultant; b. Norwich, Conn., Apr. 28, 1921; d. William Barrows and Lena (Adams) Lathrop; B.S., U. Conn., 1944; M.A., Tex. Woman's U., 1953, Ph.D., 1955. Devel. chemist textiles Alexander Smith & Sons Carpet Co., Yonkers, N.Y., 1944-52; research asso. textiles Tex. Women's U., 1952-56; chief chemist Glasgo Finishing Plant div. United Mchts. & Mfrs., Inc. (Conn.), 1956-57, chief chemist Old Fort Finishing Plant div. (N.C.), 1957-63; research chemist U.M.R.C., 1963-64; lab. and warranty mgr. automotive div. Collins & Aikman Corp., Albemarle, N.C., 1964-78; chief chemist, lab. dir. Old Fort Finishing Plant United Mchts., 1979-82. Recipient Textile Tech. Centennial Yr. Disting. Alumni award U. Conn., 1981. Mem. Am. Chem. Soc., Am. Assn. Textile Chemists and Colorists (sect. treas., vice chmn. 1963-64, research chmn. 1962; Charles H. Stone scholarship com., chmn. 1975-79), ASTM (chmn. transp. fabrics on flammability com. 1973-75), Bus. and Profl. Women's Club (pres. chpt. 1974-76, Career Woman of Year award 1979, 80), Iota Sigma Pi. Home: 301 Mountain St Black Mountain NC 28711

LATIMER, MARGARET KINARD, political science educator; b. Anderson, S.C., May 20, 1926; d. Francis Marion and Anna Rice (Sloan) Kinard; m. Paul Henry Latimer, Aug. 16, 1952; children—Margaret, Marianne, Susan. B.A. magna cum laude, Agnes Scott Coll., 1947; M.A., Vanderbilt U., 1948; postgrad. U. Ill., 1953-54. Editorial asst. Inst. Early Am. History & Culture, Williamsburg, Va., 1948; asst. editor William & Mary Quar., Williamsburg, 1948-51, assoc. editor, 1952; asst. editor Engring. Experiment Sta. U. Ill., 1952-55; instr. to assoc. prof. polit. sci. Auburn U., Ala., 1966—; cons. Joint Ctr. Polit. Studies, Washington, 1984—, U.S. Commn. Civil Rights, Washington, 1982-83, So. Poverty Law Ctr. Montgomery, Ala., 1985—, local news media on elections, 1983—. Contbr. articles to profl. jours. Recipient Research award Ala. Press Assn. 1982. Mem. Am. Polit. Sci. Assn., So. Polit. Sci. Assn., Midwest Polit. Sci. Assn., Southwest Polit. Sci. Assn., Ala. Polit. Sci. Assn., LWV (bd. dirs. Ala. 1960), Phi Beta Kappa, Pi Sigma Alpha (Outstanding Prof. award 1981). Presbyterian. Home: 530 Forestdale Dr Auburn AL 36830 Office: Auburn U Dept Polit Sci Auburn AL 36830

LATIMER, ROBERT ALLEN, pulmonary physician; b. Plainfield, N.J., Mar. 7, 1948; s. Robert Byars and Elizabeth Margaret (Brandeis) L.; m. Cindy Ann Harlan, Sept. 9, 1977; 1 son, Robert Hays. B.A., Colgate U., 1970; M.S., Rutgers U., 1973; M.D., Washington U., St. Louis, 1975. Diplomate Am. Bd. Internal Medicine. Intern, U. Ala. Hosps. and Clinics, Birmingham, 1975-76, resident in internal medicine, 1976-78, fellow in pulmonary medicine, 1978-80; practice medicine specializing in pulmonary medicine, Dothan, Ala., 1980—; pres. Pulmonary Assocs.; med. dir. respiratory therapy Flowers Hosp., S.E. Ala. Med. Ctr.; chief of medicine Flowers Hosp., 1982; S.E. Ala. rep. Ala. Lung Assn. Mem. Houston County Med. Soc., AMA. Home: 1118 Appian Way Dothan AL 36303 Office: 509 W Main St Dothan AL 36301

LATIN, DONALD EDWARD, corporate finance consultant; b. Oak Park, Ill., Oct. 28, 1930; s. Louis H. and Lillian H. (Himmelblau) L.; B.S. in Bus. Adminstrn., Northwestern U., 1952, M.B.A. with distinction, 1953; m. Mary H. Buttler, Apr. 27, 1957; children—Lynne, Richard. Analyst, Cruttenden, Podesta & Miller, Chgo., 1956-62; v.p. Walston & Co., Inc., Chgo., 1963-73; sr. assoc. Bacon, Whipple & Co., Chgo., 1973-76; v.p., mgr. corp. fin. dept. Rauscher Pierce Refsnes Inc., Dallas, 1976-80, sr. v.p., 1980-83; exec. v.p., chief fin. officer Dallas Fed. Savs., 1983-85; pres. D. Latin & Co., Inc., 1986—. Chmn. Commuter Bus Com., Northbrook, Ill., 1975-76. Served with U.S. Army, 1954-56. Mem. Inst. Chartered Fin. Analysts, Dallas Assn. Investment Analysts, Ins. Club Dallas (dir., treas.), Beta Gamma Sigma, Beta Alpha Psi. Presbyterian. Home: 12 Carmarthen Ct Dallas TX 75225 Office: D Latin & Co Inc 3208 Southland Ctr Dallas TX 75201

LATIOLAIS, MINNIE FITZGERALD, nurse, hospital administrator; b. Vivian, La., Dec. 26, 1921; d. Thomas Ambrose and Mildred Surita (Nagle) Fitzgerald; R.N., Touro Infirmary, New Orleans, 1943; m. Joseph C. Latiolais, Jr., July 19, 1947; children—Felisa, Diana, Sylvia, Mary, Amelia, Joseph Clifton, III. Asst. dir. nurses Ochsner Clinic and Ochsner Found. Hosp., New Orleans, 1943-47; supr. Lafayette (La.) Gen. Hosp., 1960-64; adminstrv. asst., supr. operating room Abbeville (La.) Gen. Hosp., 1964-68; gen. mgr., neurol. surg. nurse J. Robert Rivet, neurol. surgeon, Lafayette, 1968-78; hosp. cons. assoc. B.J. Landry & Assocs., hosps. cons., Lafayette, 1979—; dir. nursing Acadia St. Landry Hosp., Church Point, 1981-82; supr. supplies, processing and distbn. Univ. Med. Center, Lafayette, 1982—; bd. dirs. S.W. La. Rehab. Assn., 1975—, pres., 1979-80; mem. Mid-La. Health Systems Agy., 1977-82, project rev. chmn., 1978-80; bd. dirs. Acadica Regional Clearing House. Mem. Am. Nurses Assn., La. State Nurses Assn., Lafayette Dist. Nurses Assn. (pres. 1967-69). Roman Catholic. Clubs: Lafayette Woman's, Lafayette Garden. Home: 507 E Vermilion St Apt C Lafayette LA 70501

LATONI, ALFONSO RAFAEL, sociology educator; b. Coral Gables, Fla., Feb. 9, 1958; s. Alfonso and Olga (Rodriguez) L.; m. Raquel Leonor Brailowsky, Jan. 25, 1984. B.A. in Polit. Sci., U. P.R., 1979; M.A., Georgetown U., 1981. Research asst. Smithsonian Instn., Washington, 1979; asst. fgn. student advisor Georgetown U., Washington, 1980-81; teaching fellow dept. sociology Boston Coll., 1982-83; prof. sociology Interamerican U. P.R., San German, 1983—, cons. for planning new courses, 1983—, assoc. dean studies, 1985—. Mem. Arts and Cultural Workshop, Adjuntas, P.R., 1984—; tchr. Labor inst. for Worker Edn., Mayaguez, 1983; asst. organizer United Elec. Radio & Machine Workers of Am., Boston, 1982. U. P.R. grad. presdl. scholar, 1979; Boston Coll. grantee, 1982, 83. Mem. Am. Sociol. Assn., Latin Am. Sociol. Assn., Soc. Intercultural Edn., Tng. and Research, Union Radical Polit. Econs., Phi Delta Kappa. Socialist. Avocations: camping; hiking; reading; gardening; woodwork. Home: Carr 101 KM 3 8 BO Lajas Lajas PR 00667 Office: Interamerican U of PR Office Dean of Studies San German PR 00753

LATSHAW, TRENT BEDFORD, dilling company executive; b. Memphis, May 22, 1953; s. Russell E. and Gladys (Brown) L. B.S. in Petroleum Engring., Tex. A&M U., 1975. Petroleum engr. Parker Drilling Co., Anchorage, 1975-77; drilling engr. Arco Oil & Gas Co., Anchorage, 1977-78; drilling cons., Anchorage, 1978-80; pres. Latshaw Drilling Co., Houston, 1981—. Mem. Soc. Petroleum Engrs., Aircraft Owners and Pilots Assn. Office: PO Box 488 Alief TX 77411

LATTA, CAROL JEAN, educational association executive; b. Hartford, Conn., May 30, 1948; d. Johnson Brown Jr. and Esther Cook (Perry) L. B.A. Wesleyan Coll., 1970. Adminstrv. asst. Security Mgmt. Co., Atlanta, 1970-71; adminstrv. coordinator, office mgr. Planned Projects, Inc., Atlanta, 1971-73; adminstrv. coordinator, office mgr. Research Group, Inc., Atlanta, 1973-77, corp. sec. of bd., 1974-77; assoc. exec. dir. Am. Inst. Decision Scis., Atlanta, 1977—; corp. sec., treas. of bd. Planned Projects, Inc., Atlanta, 1972-73; participant, grad. Exec. Mgmt. supervisory Seminar, Ga. State U., Atlanta, 1980. Sec., treas. various campaign coms. Mem. Am. Inst. for Decision Scis. (disting. service award 1984), Ga. Soc. Assn. Execs., Meeting Planners Internat., Atlanta Book Club. Democrat. Avocations: reading; languages; sailing; tennis. Home: 136 Peachtree Memorial Dr NW Atlanta GA 30309 Office: Am Inst Decision Scis University Plaza Atlanta GA 30303

LATTA, DIANA LENNOX, interior designer; b. Lahaina, Maui, Hawaii, Aug. 5, 1936; d. D. Stewart and Jean Marjorie (Anderson) Lennox; m. Arthur McKee Latta, Jan. 26, 1957 (dec.); children—Mary-Stewart, Marion Latta Davidson. Grad. The Bishop's Sch., La Jolla, Calif., 1954; student U. Wash., 1954-56. Dir., Vero Beach (Fla.) br. of Wellington Hall, Ltd., Thomasville, N.C., 1970-72; asst. to chief designer Rablen-West Interiors, Vero Beach, 1972-75; design and adminstrv. asst. to pres. Design Studio Archtl. & Interior Design Concepts, Inc., Vero Beach, 1975-83; owner, operator The Designery, Vero Beach, 1983—. Mem. Indian River Meml. Hosp. Women's Aux., Vero Beach, 1957-70, chmn. Charity Ball, 1960, v.p., 1962-64; leading actress in Vero Beach Theatre Guild prodns.: The Laughmaker, 1964, Oklahoma, 1966; model for Holly Fashion Show, Vero Beach, 1962-69; mem. adv. bd. Indian River County 4-H Horsemaster's Club, 1973-76; bd. dirs. Vero Beach Mut. Concert Assn., 1973-76, chmn. hospitality com. 1974; bd. dirs. Vero Beach Theatre Guild, 1964. Mem. Internat. Platform Assn., Republican Women Aware. Kappa Kappa Gamma. Republican. Episcopalian. Club: Riomar Bay Yacht (club tennis champion 1964, 66, chmn. tennis com. 1964-66). Home and Office: 555 Honeysuckle Ln Vero Beach FL 32963

LATTING, JEAN ELIZABETH, social work educator; b. Memphis, Dec. 25, 1944; d. A. A. Latting and Marietta Ish Bass; 1 dau., Dnika Najuma Njeri Jones. B.A., Douglass Coll., 1965; M.S., Columbia U. Sch. Social Work, 1971; D.P.H., U. N.C., 1980. Cert. social worker. Caseworker Kingsbridge Welfare Ctr., N.Y.C., 1965-67; welfare services coordinator Hamilton Madison House, N.Y.C., 1967-69; dir. Dept. Human Services, U. N.C., Chapel Hill, 1972-74, prin. investigator dissertation research, 1977-79; profl. fellow Bush Inst. Child and Family Policy, Frank Porter Graham Child Devel. Inst., Chapel Hill, 1978-79; asst. prof. Grad. Sch. Social Work, U. Houston, 1979—; cons. in social work and orgn. devel. Contbr. articles to profl. jours. Mem. Houston Ind. Sch. Dist. Magnet Sch. Task Force, 1980-81. Urban Leadership Tng. Program fellow, Columbia U., 1977-79. Mem. Am. Soc. Trainers and Developers, Nat. Assn. Social Workers, Nat. Assn. Black Social Workers. Home: 6035 Sunridge Way Houston TX 77087 Office: Grad Sch Social Work U Houston Houston TX 77004

LATTU, ANDREW CHARLES, geologist, petroleum company executive; b. San Francisco, Jan. 21, 1944; s. Charles Albert and Rosemary Leigh (Andrews) L.; m. Nancy Corbett Nokes, Dec. 14, 1969; children—Lisa, Stephanie, Robert. B.A., U. Mont., 1966; M.S. El Paso, U. Tex. 1976. Geologist Marathon Oil Co., Midland, Tex., 1970-75; sr. geologist Tex. Pacific Oil Co., Midland, 1975-76; exploration mgr. Harvey Yates Co., Midland, 1976-81; div. mgr. Delta Drilling Co., Midland, 1981-82; pres. Corbett Petroleum Co., Midland, 1982—. Served to capt. U.S. Army, 1966-69, Vietnam Mem. Am. Assn. Petroleum Geologists, Soc. Ind. Profl. Earth Scientists. Republican. Presbyterian. Clubs: Toastmasters (Midland), Midland Chess (pres. 1973-76). Avocations: chess, stamp collecting, rock collecting. Home: 2401 Northtown Ct Midland TX 79705 Office: Corbett Petroleum Inc PO Box 3453 Midland TX 79702

LATTURE, JAMES PAUL, JR., association executive; b. Tulsa, Aug. 10, 1946; s. J. Paul and Ernestine Faye (McLemore) L.; m. Sandra Kay Pearce, Feb. 3, 1967; children—James Paul III, Brian Scott. B.S. in Bus. Adminstrn., U. Ark., 1968; M.B.A., Northeast La. U., 1969. Cert. chamber exec.; cert. indsl. developer. Mgr. research Tulsa C. of C., 1969-71; asst. mgr. Lake Charles C. of C., La., 1971; internat. cons. Ark. Indsl. Devel. Commn., Little Rock, 1971-75; exec. v.p. Joplin C. of C., Mo., 1975-80; exec. v.p. Wichita Falls Bd. Commerce and Industry, Tex., 1980-83; exec. v.p. Jackson C. of C., 1983—. Bd. dirs. Miss. chpt. ARC, Jackson, 1985; treas. Jackson Conv. and Visitors Bur., 1985, Central Miss. Growth Found., Jackson, 1985; mem. exec. com. Pvt. Industry Council, Jackson, 1985. Mem. Am. C. of C. Execs. (bd. dirs. 1985-86), Am. Indsl. Devel. Council, So. Indsl. Devel. Council, So. Assn. C. of C. Execs. (treas. 1986, v.p. 1987, pres. 1988), Miss. Assn. C. of C. Execs. (treas. 1985, v.p. 1986, pres. 1987). Methodist. Lodge: Rotary. Avocations: golf; boating. Office: Jackson C of C PO Box 22548 Jackson MS 39225

LAUBE-MORGAN, JERRI M., university dean, nursing educator; b. Terre Haute, Ind., July 1, 1928; d. George J. and M. Martell (McBride) DeWald; m. William B. Laube, Aug. 8, 1947 (dec. Feb. 1979); children—Stephen William, Joan Martelle; m. C.J. Morgan, Feb. 14, 1983. B.S. in Nursing and Psychology,

U. Tenn., 1961; M.S. in Nursing, U. Colo., 1969; Ph.D., Tex. Woman's U., 1974. Instr. St. Joseph Sch. Nursing, Memphis, 1957-62, St. Paul Sch. Nursing, Dallas, 1962-67; asst. prof. nursing Baylor U., 1969-72; assoc. prof. nursing Ind. U.-Indpls., 1972-74, prof., chairperson dept. psychol. mental health Sch. Nursing, 1974-80; adj. prof. psychology Purdue U.-Indpls., 1976-80; prof. nursing, dean Sch. Nursing, U. So. Miss., 1980—, project dir. psychiat. nursing, cross-cultural mental health nursing, 1980-83; project dir. NIMH, 1975-82. Contbr. articles to profl. jours. Fellow Am. Acad. Nursing; mem. Am. Nurses' Assn., Council Specialists in Psychiat./Mental Health Nursing, Am. Psychol. Assn., Am. Group Psychotherapy Assn., Am. Assn. Marriage and Family Therapists, Nat. League for Nursing, Sigma Theta Tau. Episcopalian. Club: Altrusa. Home: 710 Edgewood Dr Hattiesburg MS 39401 Office: U So Miss Sch Nursing So Sta Box 5095 Hattiesburg MS 39406

LAUBER, JOSEPH LINCOLN, publisher's rep.; b. Rock Island, Ill., Feb. 12, 1924; s. Joseph Harold and Margaret Juliane (Underhill) L.; B.A., St. Ambrose Coll., Davenport, Iowa, 1951; M.A., U. Iowa, 1952; postgrad. East Tex. State U.; m. Hilda Liska Zimmerman, June 10, 1960. Tchr., prin. schs., Iowa and Ill., 1952-57; from salesman to nat. sales mgr. Economy Co., Oklahoma City, 1957-71; dir. mktg. Lyons & Carnahan, Chgo., 1971-72; regional sales mgr. Benefic Press, Westchester, Ill., 1972-75; sales rep. Cambridge Book Co., Tex., 1975-80; self-employed rep. for ednl. pubs., Tex., 1981—; chmn. bd., chief exec. officer J.B. Harber Pub., Inc., Houston, 1980—. Served with AUS, 1943-46. Mem. Am. Soc. Tng. and Devel., Nat. Assn. Profl. Continuing Adult Edn., Tex. Textbook Pubs. Assn., Phi Delta Kappa. Republican. Episcopalian. Address: 4714 Country Club View Baytown TX 77521

LAUDER, JEAN MILES, anatomy educator, research scientist, neurobiologist; b. Haverhill, Mass., June 29, 1945; d. Robert William and Frances (Miles) L.; m. Helmut Krebs, Nov. 28, 1974. B.A., U. Maine, 1967; Ph.D., Purdue U., 1972. Staff fellow NIMH, Washington, 1972-74; research assoc. U. Conn., Storrs, 1974-76, asst. prof. in residence, 1976-78; assoc. prof. anatomy U. N.C., Chapel Hill, 1978—. Recipient Research Career Devel. award NIH, 1980-85; NIH grantee, 1976-85. Mem. Internat. Soc. Psychoneuroendocrinology (Curt P. Richter prize 1983), Internat. Soc. Devel. Neurosci., AAAS, Am. Assn. Anatomists, Soc. Neurosci., Am. Soc. Cell Biology, Sigma Xi. Club: Cajal. Contbr. articles to profl. jours. Home: 106 Marion Way Chapel Hill NC 27514 Office: 108 Swing Bldg U NC Sch Medicine Chapel Hill NC 27514

LAUDER, VALARIE ANNE, writer, editor, public relations director, consultant; b. Detroit, Mar. 1, 1926; d. William Jay and Murza Valerie (Mann) L. A.A., Stephens Coll., 1944. Feature writer and columnist Chgo. Daily News, 1944-52; lectr. Sch. Assembly Service and Redpath Bur., Chicago and Rochester, N.Y., 1952-55; free lance writer, 1955—; sch. editor Ingenue Mag., 1961-62; editor-in-chief Scholastic Roto, 1962-63; pub. relations dir. U. N.C., Chapel Hill, 1975-81, dir. Lipid Research Clinics Program, communications dir. Ctr. for Women, lectr. Sch. Journalism, 1980—; chmn. student writing project Ford Times, 1981-86; mem. nat. fund raising bd. Kennedy Ctr., 1962-63; pub. relations dir. Am. Dance Festival, Duke U., 1982-83. Dir. Chapel Hill Hist. Soc., 1981-85; active Chapel Hill Preservation Soc., Univ. Woman's Club, Chapel Hill Woman's Club. Recipient 1st prize Nat. Fedn. Press Women, 1981; 2 1st place awards N.C. Press Club, 1984, 8 awards, 1983; 1st place award Women's Press Club N.C., 1982, 3 awards, 1981; 1st place award Ill. Women's Press Assn., 1951, 3 1st place awards, 1950. Mem. Pub. Relations Soc. Am. (treas. N.C. chpt. 1982, sec. 1983, v.p. 1984, pres. 1986), N.C. Press Club (2d v.p. 1983-85, 3d v.p. 1981-83, pres. 1985) N.C. Press Women, Women in Communications, Inc., DAR, Soc. Mayflower Descendants. Episcopalian. Contbg. editor So. Accents; contbr. to Ford Times; contbr. articles to jours. in field. Office: Howell Hall 021A UNC Chapel Hill NC 27514

LAUDERDALE, MICHAEL LYNN, social psychologist, educator; b. Hobart, Okla., Dec. 9, 1941; s. Tommie Lee and Almeta Carolyn (Cantrall) L.; B.A., U. Okla., 1963, M.S., 1964, Ph.D., 1967; m. Camille Teresa Contreras, Dec. 28, 1966; children—Gregory, Lynn Marisa Lauren. Lectr. psychology U. Okla., Norman, 1966-67; asst. prof. psychology N.Mex. State U., Las Cruces, 1967-69; asst. prof. social work U. Tex., Austin, 1970-74, asso. prof., 1974—, dir. continuing edn. Sch. Social Work, 1970, dir. Research Center, Sch. Social Work, 1981; cons. in field. NIMH predoctoral fellow, 1964-67. Bd. dirs. S.W. Center Child Abuse and Neglect, 1975—. Research grants aging. Mem. Am. Psychol. Assn., Council Social Work Edn., Am. Sociol. Assn. Methodist. Author: (with others), Community Development, 1970, Planning for Change, 1970, Service Delivery Systems, 1970; Burnout: Strategies for Personal and Organizational Life-Speculation on Evolving Paradigms, 1982; editor: Social Service Improvement Series, 10 vols., 1970-71; contbr. chpts. to books, articles to profl. jours. Home: 4510 Spanish Oak Trail Austin TX 78731 Office: 2609 University Ave U Tex Austin TX 78712

LAUER, DWIGHT KEITH, forester; b. Anchorage, Alaska, July 19, 1956; s. Robert David and Joan Marie (Mark) L.; m. Susan Denese Stenger, June 13, 1981; 1 child, Christopher. Student U. Md., 1974-76; B.S. in Forestry, N.C. State U., 1978; M.S. in Forestry, U. Ga., 1983. Research forester ITT Rayonier, Inc., Yulee, Fla., 1981—. Mem. Soc. Am. Foresters, Am. Statis. Assn., Biometric Soc., Xi Sigma Pi, Gamma Sigma Delta. Republican. Roman Catholic. Home: 15 N 18th St Fernandina Beach FL 32034 Office: ITT Rayonier Inc Morgan Research Ctr PO Box 437 Yulee FL 32092

LAUGHERY, JACK ARNOLD, restaurant chain executive; b. Guthrie Center, Iowa, Feb. 25, 1935; s. Gerald Reve and Mildred Eva (Ansberry) L.; B.C.S., U. Iowa, 1957; grad. exec. program U. N.C., Chapel Hill, 1976; m. Helen Herboth, Sept. 14, 1968; children—Brenda, Kelly, Christine, Sarah. Salesman, Conn. Gen. Ins. Co., 1957-62; with Sandy's Systems, 1962-72, pres., 1969-72, chief operating officer, 1970-72, chief exec. officer, 1971-72, exec. v.p. Hardee's Food Systems, Inc., Rocky Mount, N.C., 1972-73, pres., 1973—, chief operating officer, 1973-75, chief exec. officer, 1975—, chmn., 1980—, also dir.; dir. First Union Nat. Bank, Charlotte, N.C., First Union Nat. Bank, Charlotte. Bd. dirs. Wesleyan Coll., Rocky Mount; chmn. Nash County Jobs for Progress, Nash County Indsl. Devel. Commn. Served with AUS. 1957-60. Recipient Gold Plate award IFMA, 1981; named Boss of Yr., N.C. Jaycees, 1983. Mem. Nat. (dir. 1977—), N.C. (dir. 1975—) restaurant assns., Rocky Mount C. of C. (dir. 1976—, pres. 1985), Am. Mgmt. Assn. Republican. Episcopalian. Home: 150 Hunter Hill Rd Rocky Mount NC 27801 Office: Hardee's Food Systems Inc PO Box 1619 Rocky Mount NC 27801

LAUNER, ROBERT LIONEL, government administrator, researcher; b. Port Arthur, Tex., July 23, 1935; s. George Otto and Emilie Marie (Wagner) L.; m. Jane Norton Aldrich, Aug. 20, 1958 (div. 1970); children—Sharon Elizabeth, Matthew Robert, Philip Eric; m. Ellen Louise Good, July 2, 1971; 1 child, Michael Scott. B.A. in Math., U. Tex., 1962, M.A. in Math., 1964; Ph.D. in Stats., Va. Poly. Inst. State U., 1971. Assoc. research scientist Tex. Nuclear Corp., Austin, 1960-64; instr. U.S. Naval Acad., Annapolis, Md., 1964-67; asst. prof. math., stats. Radford Coll., Va., 1969-70; statistician Army Research Office, Petersburg, Va., 1970-76; program mgr. U.S. Army Research Office, Research Triangle Park, N.C., 1976-82, asst. dir. math. div., 1982—; adj. assoc. prof. N.C. State U., Raleigh, 1977—; vis. prof. U. Richmond, Va., 1970-75; adj. prof. Va. Poly. Inst. State U., Richmond, 1971-75; mem. tech. staff Bell Telephone Labs., Whippany, N.J., summer 1970. Editor: Robustness in Statistics, 1979; Modern Data Analysis, 1982; Reliability in the Acquisition Process, 1983. Served to lt. comdr. USNR, 1955-67. Fellow Am. Stats. Assn.; mem. Am. Soc. for Quality Control. Avocations: piano; tennis; whittling; camping. Office: US Army Research Box 12211 Research Triangle Park NC

LAURENT, ANTHONY IRVIN, JR., hospital pharmacist; b. New Orleans, Sept. 18, 1957; s. Anthony Irvin and Dolores (Payton) L.; m. Lisa Maria Wilson, May 29, 1982. B.S. in Pharmacy, Xavier U., New Orleans, 1980; postgrad. U. New Orleans. Lic. Pharmacist, La., Tex. Staff pharmacist Ochsner Hosp., New Orleans, 1980-82, pharmacy supr., 1982-84; dir. pharmacy Humana Women's Hosp., New Orleans, 1984—. Mem. Southeast La. Soc. Hosp. Pharmacists (sec.-treas. 1984—), Kappa Psi (chpt. pres. 1979-80, Outstanding Mem. 1980), Chi Delta Mu. Democrat. Roman Catholic. Avocations: music; photography; woodworking. Home: 4943 Papania Dr New Orleans LA 70127 Office: Humana Women's Hosp 6000 Bullard Ave New Orleans LA 70127

LAURI, JOHN PETER, hospital administrator; b. Marquette, Mich., Apr. 25, 1946; s. T.J. and Elsie Elizabeth (Storstrang) L.; m. Cynthia Judith Barr, June 22, 1968; children—Brian Barr, Christian Matthew. B.A., Morehead State U., 1968; M.A. in Health Care Adminstrn., George Washington U., 1972. High sch. tchr. Roseville Pub. Schs., Mich., 1968-70; adminstrv. resident Bapt. Med. Ctrs., Birmingham, Ala., 1971-72; asst. adminstr. Foote Meml. Hosp., Jackson, Mich., 1972-73, assoc. adminstr., 1973-78; adminstr. Miami Heart Inst., Miami Beach, Fla., 1978—; adj. prof. grad. program U. Miami, 1982—. Mem. Miami Beach Health Adv. Bd., 1984—, Rediscover Miami Beach Task Force, 1984—. Mem. Am. Coll. Hosp. Adminstrs., Am. Hosp. Assn., Fla. Hosp. Assn. (bd. dirs. 1984-85), South Fla. Hosp. Assn. (chmn. 1982-83), Greater Miami C. of C., Miami Beach C. of C. Republican. Presbyterian. Club: LaGorce Country (Miami Beach). Avocations: golf; tennis; boating. Home: 268 NE 102d St Miami Shores FL 33138 Office: Miami Heart Inst 4701 N Meridian Ave Miami Beach FL 33140

LAURIER, FRANCISCO HERMINIO, architectural and interior designer; b. Havana, Cuba, May 2, 1942; s. Francisco Herminio and Olga (Esquijarosa) Lorie. B.Arch., Pratt Inst., 1969. Project mgr. Pan Am., N.Y.C., 1969-73; pres. Laurier & Assocs., Miami, Fla., 1974-79, F.H. Laurier Design Group, Inc., Miami, 1984—; chmn., mem. interior design adv. bd. Internat. Fine Arts Coll., Miami, 1985—, trustee, 1985; advisor Cuban Mus., 1985—, AIBC Fin. Corp. Contbr. articles to profl. jours Chmn. spl. projects Miami's For Me, 1985, chmn. artistic design, 1984; exec. v.p. Greater Miami Symphony, 1984—, Miami Symphony, 1983-84, pres. Latin Orange Festival Council, 1986—. Recipient Award of Honor for contribution to edn., Designers & Decorators Guild, 1978. Mem. Interam. Businessman Assn. Democrat. Roman Catholic. Club: Bankers (gov. 1984—). Avocations: art collecting; sailing. Home: 3817 S Le Jeune Rd Coconut Grove Miami FL 33146 Office: FH Laurier Design Group Inc 5825 Sunset Dr Suite 208 South Miami FL 33143

LAUTENSCHLAGER, GARY JOSEPH, psychology educator, consultant; b. Chgo., Mar. 21, 1949; s. George Frederick and Bernadette (Spaeth) L.; m. Karen Kathleen Keszycki, Apr. 1, 1973; children—Erica Rae, Rene Erin. Student Bradley U., 1967-68; B.A., U. Ill.-Chgo., 1972, Ph.D., 1982; M.S., San Diego State U., 1976. Instr. U. Ill., Chgo., 1979-82; asst. prof. psychology U. Ga., Athens, 1982—; cons. Rehab. Inst., Chgo., 1978-80, Northwestern Med. Sch., Chgo., 1980-81, Organizational Cons., Inc., Chgo., 1981-82, Augusta VA Hosp., Ga., 1984—. Contbr. articles to profl. jours. NIMH fellow, 1976-78. Mem. Am. Psychol. Assn. (div. 14, divs. 5, 8), Southeast Psychol. Assn. Avocations: guitar, reading; running; softball. Home: 105 Flannigan Pl Athens GA 30605 Office: Psychology Dept U Ga Athens GA 30602

LAUVER, DAVID HALEY, public relations executive; b. Knoxville, Tenn., Oct. 25, 1949; s. Murl Haley and Teresa (Sivils) L.; m. Susan Jeanne Scarbrough, July 22, 1979. B.S. in Communications, U. Tenn., 1971. Reporter Knoxville News-Sentinel, 1970; congl. journalism intern, staff U.S. Senator Strom Thurmond, 1971; press aide, legis. asst. to U.S. Senator Howard Baker, 1972-75; dir. pub. relations U. Tenn., Knoxville, 1975-85; exec. communications coordinator TVA, 1985—. Pub. info. chmn. Southeastern 1st Amendment Congress, 1982. Mem. E. Tenn. Soc. Profl. Journalists (service award 1981, pres. 1982-83), Pub. Relations Soc. Am. (pres. Vol. chpt. 1984-85), U. Tenn. Nat. Alumni Assn. (pres. Washington-Balt. chpt. 1974-75), Sigma Delta Chi, Kappa Tau Alpha, Omicron Delta Kappa, Phi Kappa Phi. Methodist. Lodge: Kiwanis (dir. Knoxville club 1977-79). Home: 4224 Valencia Rd Knoxville TN 37919 Office: TVA Info Office 400 W Summit Hill Dr Knoxville TN 37902

LAVELLE, BRIAN FRANCIS DAVID, lawyer; b. Cleve., Aug. 16, 1941; s. Gerald John and Mary Josephine (O'Callaghan) L.; m. Sara Hill, Sept. 10, 1966; children—S. Elizabeth, B. Francis D., Catherine H. B.A., U. Va., 1963; J.D., Vanderbilt U., 1966; LL.M. in Taxation, N.Y.U., 1969. Bar: N.C. 1966, Ohio 1968. Assoc. VanWinkle Buck, Wall, Starnes & Davis, Asheville, N.C., 1968-74, ptnr., 1974—; lectr. continuing edn. N.C. Bar Found., Wake Forest U. Estate Planning Inst., Am. Coll. Probate Counsel, Hartford Tax Inst., Duke U. Estate Planning Inst. Trustee Asheville Country Day Sch., 1981—, sec., 1982-85; vice chmn. Buncombe County Indsl. Facilities and Pollution Control Authority, 1976-82; mem. exec. bd. Asheville Tax Study Group, 1981—, chmn., 1984; bd. advs. U.N.C. Annual Tax Inst., 1981—. Served as capt. Judge Adv. Gen. USAF, 1966-67. Mem. N.C. Bar Assn. (bd. govs. 1979-82, councillor tax sect. 1979-83, councillor estate planning law sect. 1982—), ABA, Am. Coll. Probate Counsel (state chmn. 1982-85, regent 1984—), N.C. State Bar (splty. com. on estate planning and probate law 1984—). Episcopalian (clk. vestry All Souls Ch.). Clubs: Rotary of Asheville, Biltmore Forest Country. Contbr. articles on law to profl. jours. Home: 45 Brookside Rd Asheville NC 28803 Office: 18 Church St PO Box 7376 Asheville NC 28807

LAVENDER, ABRAHAM DONALD, clinical sociologist, educator; b. New Zion, S.C., Nov. 14, 1940; s. William Maxcy and Velma (Floyd) L. B.A., U. S.C., 1963, M.A., 1964; Ph.D., U. Md., 1972. Prof. sociology St. Mary's Coll., St. Mary's City, Md., 1972-74, U. Md., College Park, 1974-77, U. Miami, Coral Gables, Fla., 1977-83; pvt. practice clin. sociologist, Miami, Fla., 1983—; pres. Clin. Sociologists of South Fla., Inc., 1985—. Author: A Coat of Many Colors, 1977; Ethic Women and Feminist Values, 1985; assoc. Jour. Ethnic Studies, 1981—; contbr. articles to profl. jours. Mem. com. Greater Miami Jewish Fedn., 1981—. Served to capt. USAF, 1964-68. Named Outstanding Prof., U. Miami, 1981, 83. Mem. Am. Sociol. Assn., Clin. Sociology Assn., So. Sociol. Soc., Assn. for Sociol. Study Jewry (v.p. 1983-85), Assn. Humanist Sociology (regional rep. 1982-84), NOW, Phi Beta Kappa (pres. alumni assn. South Fla. 1983—), Phi Kappa Phi, Alpha Kappa Delta, Psi Chi. Democrat. Jewish.

LAVENDER, ROBERT EUGENE, chief justice Okla. Supreme Ct.; b. Muskogee, Okla., July 19, 1926; s. Harold James and Vergene Irene (Martin) L.; LL.B., U. Tulsa, 1953; grad. Appellate Judges Seminar, 1967, Nat. Coll. State Trial Judges, 1970; m. Maxine Knight, Dec. 22, 1945; children—Linda (Mrs. Dean Courter), Robert K., Debra (Mrs. Thomas Merrill), William J. Admitted to Okla. bar, 1953; with Mass. Bonding & Ins. Co., Tulsa, 1951-53, U.S. Fidelity & Guaranty Co., Tulsa, 1953-54; asst. city atty., Tulsa, 1954-55; practice, Tulsa, 1955-60, Claremore, Okla., 1960-65; justice Okla. Supreme Ct., 1965—, now chief justice; guest lectr. Okla. U., Oklahoma City U., Tulsa U. law schs. Republican committeeman Rogers County, 1961-62. Served with USNR, 1944-46. Mem. ABA, Okla., Rogers County bar assns., Am. Judicature Soc., Okla. Jud. Conf., Phi Alpha Delta (hon.). Methodist (adminstrv. bd.). Mason (32 deg.). Home: 2910 Kerry Ln Oklahoma City OK 73120 Office: Room 208 State Capitol Bldg Oklahoma City OK 73105

LAVERY, WILLIAM EDWARD, univ. pres.; b. Geneseo, N.Y., Nov. 20, 1930; s. John Raymond and Mary Irene (O'Brien) L.; m. Peggy J. Johnson, Apr. 7, 1956; children—Debra, Kevin, Lori, Mary. B.S., Mich. State U., 1953; M.A., George Washington U., 1959; Ph.D., U. Wis., 1962. Tchr. Clarence (N.Y.) Central High Sch., 1953-54; asst. to adminstr. Fed. Extension Service Dept. Agr., Washington, 1956-66; dir. adminstrn.-extension div. Va. Polytech. Inst. and State U., Blacksburg, 1966-68, v.p. finance, 1968-73, exec. v.p., 1973-75, pres., 1975—; AID cons. to, El Salvador, 1969; Dir. Dominion Bankshores Corp. Mem. United Fund-Community Fedn., 1968-72; Bd. dirs. Montgomery County Hosp. Served with AUS, 1954-56. Kellogg Found. fellow, 1960-62. Mem. Omicron Delta Kappa, Epsilon Sigma Phi, Phi Kappa Phi, Phi Delta Kappa. Club: Rotary (Blacksburg). Office: Office of Pres Va Polytechnic Inst and State U Blacksburg VA 24061*

LAVIN, THOMAS CHARLES, addiction counselor; b. Peoria, Ill., Feb. 20, 1950; s. Thomas James and Dorothy May (O'Brien) L.; m. Glenda Ray Enos, July 1, 1977; children—Rachel, John Michael. B.A., U. Detroit, 1980. Clin. dir. Cypress Hosp., Lafayette, La., 1981-82; pres. Journey, Inc., Lafayette, 1981—; exec. dir. New Life Network Found., Lafayette, 1983—; dist. rep. Western Diocese, Lafayette, 1982-84; dist. rep. La. Task Force on Substance Abuse, Lafayette, 1984—; vice-chmn. Cert. Examining Bd. La., Lafayette, 1984-85. Author: Journey for Awareness, 1981; Continuing Care Program, 1983; Pathways of Spiritual Growth, 1985; Relationships and Transformations, 1985. Mem. La. Assn. Substance Abuse Counselors and Trainers (vice-chmn. 1984-85), Substance Abuse Counselors of Acadiana (v.p. 1983-84), Nat. Assn. Substance Abuse Counselors, Am. Assn. Counseling and Devel. Avocations: cycling, canoeing. Home: 210 Lyons St Lafayette LA 70506 Office: New Life Network Found PO Box 5015 Lafayette LA 70502

LAVINGTON, MICHAEL R., corporate executive; b. 1943. Student, Cambridge U., Columbia U., Lancaster U. Cons., Arthur Andersen & Co., 1968-70; exec. dir. Ralli Australia Pty. Ltd., 1970-71; exec. v.p., dir. Kay Corp., Alexandria, Va., 1972—. Office: Kay Corp 320 King St Alexandria VA 22314

LAW, JAPHET SEBASTIAN, engineering educator; b. Shanghai, China, Nov. 28, 1951; came to U.S., 1969; s. Ching-Sun and Lai-Yuk (Chan) L.; m. Debra Yu-yu Chiu, Nov. 24, 1974; 1 son, Bertrand Japhet. Ph.D., U. Tex., 1976. Asst. instr. U. Tex., Austin, 1975-76; asst. prof. St. Mary's U., San Antonio, 1977; sr. engr. McDonnell Douglas, Houston, 1978; ops. research analyst Ford Aerospace Co., Houston, 1979-80; asst. prof. dept. indsl. engring. U. Houston, 1980—, dir. ops. research, 1983—, dir. grad. studies, 1983—; research assoc. health delivery study Dept. Transp.; research assoc. MX missile research Dept. Def. Mem. Am. Inst. Indsl. Engrs., Ops. Research Soc. Am., Soc. Logistic Engrs., Tau Beta Pi, Alpha Pi Mu. Contbr. articles to profl. jours. Home: 10131 Sagemill Dr Houston TX 77089 Office: Department of Industrial Engineering University of Houston Houston TX 70004

LAW, JOSEPH GILLESPIE, JR., psychologist; b. Mobile, Ala., Feb. 8, 1947; s. Joseph Gillespie and Elma Idonia (Antoine) L.; m. Pamela McFerrin, Dec. 5, 1975; children—Joseph, Jonathan. B.S., Spring Hill Coll., 1969; M.S., U. South Ala., 1976; Ed.D., Auburn U., 1981. Lic. psychologist, Tenn. Psychologist Dept. Mental Health, Eufaula, Ala., 1976-78; sch. psychologist Opelika City Schs., Ala., 1978-80; intern VA Mental Ctr., Tuskegee, Ala., 1980-81; team leader VA Vet. Ctr., Mobile, Ala., 1981—; cons. psychologist Ala. Bd. Polygraph Examiners, 1978—. Contbr. articles to profl. jours. Served to capt. U.S. Army, 1969-73. Named Employee of Yr., VA Med. Ctr., 1984; recipient Cert. of Recognition, Miss. Coast Assn. Fed. Adminstrs., 1984. Mem. Am. Psychol. Assn., Ala. Psychol. Assn., Am. Mental Health Counselors Assn. Methodist. Avocation: astronomy. Office: Vet Ctr 110 Marine St Mobile AL 36604

LAW, RALPH AREGOOD, chemist; b. Little Rock, Nov. 20, 1927; s. Ralph Aregood and Frances Louise (Weber) L.; B.A. in Chemistry, U. Ark., 1950; m. Frances Carolyn Adair, Aug. 4, 1973; children by previous marriage—David, Leslie, Brian. Chemist, Coca-Cola Co., Atlanta, 1955-60, Pennsalt Chem. Corp., Indsl. Mfg., Dallas, 1960-64; chief chemist Core Labs, Inc., Indsl. Water Tech., Dallas, 1964-71, Ecology Audits, Inc., subs. Core Labs., Inc., after 1974; then div. mgr., chief chemist water services Dallas Chem. Lab., Core Labs., Inc.; chem. engring. supr. Herman Blum, Cons. Engrs., Dallas, 1971-74; cons. in field. Served with USN, 1946-48. Mem. Am. Chem. Soc., Water Pollution Control Fedn., Nat., Tex. rifle assns. Republican. Episcopalian. Home: 1934 Rambling Ridge Ln Carrollton TX 75007 Office: 11061 Shady Trail Dallas TX 75229

LAWHON, TOMMIE COLLINS MONTGOMERY, home economics educator; b. Shelby County, Tex., Mar. 15; d. Marland Walker and Lillian (Tinsley) Collins; m. David Baldwin Montgomery, Mar. 31, 1962 (dec. Aug. 1964); m. John Lawhon, III, Aug. 27, 1967; 1 child, David Collins. B.S., Baylor U., Waco, 1954; M.Home Econs. Edn., Tex. Woman's U., 1964, Ph.D., 1966. Cert. vocat. home econs., Tex. Tchr., Victoria Pub. Schs. (Tex.), 1954-55; stewardess, supr. Am. Airlines, Dallas/Ft. Worth, 1955-62; prof. home econs. Eastern Ky. U., Richmond, 1966-67; prof. North Tex. State U., Denton, 1968—, profl. presenter Profl. Devel. Inst., 1981—. North Tex. State U. chmn. United Way, Denton, 1980-81; crusade chmn. Am. Cancer Soc., Denton County, Tex., 1982-83; chmn. nominating com. First Baptist Ch., Denton, 1983-85. Recipient Honor Prof. award North Tex. State U., 1975, Fessor Graham award, 1980; Presdl. award Tex. Council Family Relations, 1979; Service award Am. Cancer Soc., 1983; Outstanding Home Econs. Alumni award Baylor U., 1985. Mem. Tex. Council Family Relations (pres. 1977-79), Denton Assn. Edn. of Young Children (pres. 1970-72, 84-86), Tex. Home Econs. Assn., Nat. Council Family Relations, Alpha Iota/Phi Upsilon Omicron (advisor 1970-82). Democrat. Clubs: Tri D Baylor University (parliamentarian 1952-53, v.p. 1953-54), Grad. Tex. Woman's U. (pres. 1965-66). Author: (with Jessie Bateman) Children Are Artists, 1971; (with Barbara Krishnan) Hidden Hazards for Children and Families, 1982; editor: What to do With Children, 1974; (with Velma Schmidt) Field Trips for Children, 1984; contbr. articles to profl. jours. Office: North Texas State Univ Sch Home Econs Denton TX 76203

LAWHORN, JESS SHERMAN, finance company executive; b. Cin., Jan. 20, 1933; s. Jess Sherman and Dorothy E. (Riggs) L.; B.B.A. in Marketing and Econs., U. Miami, 1953; postgrad. Sch. Mortgage Banking Northwestern U., 1960-63, Mich. State U., 1969-70; m. Hilda D. Foxworth, Oct. 12, 1957; 1 son, Jess S. Officer, dir. Shaw Bros. Shipping Co., Miami, Fla., 1964-68, Shaw Marine Co., 1964-68; officer Lon Worth Crow Co., Miami, 1958-64, 69-71; Lon Worth Crow Realty Co., Miami, 1970-71; officer Southeast Mortgage Co., Miami, 1971-81, dir., 1971—; sr. v.p. Southeast First Nat. Bank Miami, 1981-82; sr. v.p. Southeast Bank N.A., 1982—; pres. Semco Services, Inc., 1974-81. Lectr. mortgage banking U. Ga., 1973—, So. Meth. U., 1973—, Mich. State U., 1973—. Chmn. United Fund Div. Recipient Outstanding Mortgage Bankers award, Fla., 1978, nat., 1983. Served to 1st lt. USAF, 1954-56. Mem. Econ. Soc. South Fla., Fla. Bankers Assn. (com. chmn. 1974-75, div. chmn. 1975-76), Fla. Mortgage Bankers Assn. (dir. 1975-76, pres. 1978-79), Mortgage Bankers Assn. Am. (cert.; chmn. edn. com. 1982, chmn. CMB com. 1984), C. of C., SAR, Soc. Real Estate Appraisers (pres. Greater Miami chpt. 1966), Marine Council Greater Miami (pres. 1968-69). Order Founders and Patriots Am., Sigma Alpha Epsilon. Clubs: Rotary, Riviera Country, University, Miami. Home: 500 Perugia Ave Coral Gables FL 33146 Office: 100 S Biscayne Blvd Miami FL 33131

LAWLER, PETER AUGUSTINE, political science educator; b. Alexandria, Va., July 30, 1951; s. Thomas C. and Patricia Ann (Fullerton) L.; m. Rita Kay Schnuck, Sept. 6, 1979; 1 child, Catherine Mary. B.A., Allentown Coll., 1973; M.A., U. Va., 1975, Ph.D., 1978. Instr. Fla. So. Coll., Lakeland, 1978-79; asst. prof. Berry Coll., Mt. Berry, Ga., 1979-83, assoc. prof. polit. sci., 1983—. Editor: American Political Rhetoric, 1982. Contbr. articles to profl. jours. Grantee Lilly Found. 1983, 85, Claremont Inst. 1985, Mellon Found, 1981, NEH. Mem. Am. Polit. Sci. Assn. (grantee 1980), Ga. Polit. Sci. Assn. Roman Catholic. Home: 308 E 5th Ave Rome GA 30161 Office: Berry Coll Box 118 Mount Berry GA 30161

LAWRENCE, DAVID MICHAEL, legal educator; b. Portland, Oreg., Dec. 26, 1943; s. Robert A. and Maude (Davis) L.; m. Alice Oviatt, June 18, 1966. A.B., Princeton U., 1965; J.D., Harvard U., 1968. Asst. prof. Inst. Govt., U. N.C., Chapel Hill, 1968-71, assoc. prof., 1971-76, prof. pub. law and govt., 1976—; counsel N.C. Local Govt. Study Commn., 1972-73, N.C. Open Meetings Study Commn., 1978-79. Recipient N.Y. Herald Prize, Princeton U., 1965. Mem. N.C. State Bar. Democrat. Club: Campus Princeton U. Contbr. law articles to profl. jours. Office: Knapp Bldg 059A U NC Chapel Hill NC 27514

LAWRENCE, JOHN HAROLD, health care executive, consultant; b. Richmond, Va., Sept. 28, 1942; s. John Henry and Hellen Margaret (Clark) L. Student Va. Commonwealth U., Richmond, 1959, Concord Coll., Athens, W.Va., 1961. Lic. pilot FAA. Investigator Va. Dept. Profl. Registration, 1962-66; v.p. Harry A. Stroh Assocs., custodial systems cons., Princeton, N.J., 1966-68; contract cons. P.R. Port Authority and P.R. Pub. Bldg. Authority, 1968-72, Health Dept. U.S. Virgin Islands; pres. Service De P.R., Inc., San Juan, 1972-73; dir. environ. services and property control Riverside Health Care Systems, Newport News, Va., 1973—; cons. custodial and bldg. mgmt. systems. Bd. dirs., past pres. Riverside Health Care Credit Union. Mem. Environ. Mgmt. Assn. (pres. So. regional chpt., pres. Tidewater chpt.). Republican. Episcopalian. Home: 215 Chesapeake Ave Newport News VA 23607 Office: Riverside Hosp J Clyde Morris Blvd Newport News VA 23601

LAWRENCE, KEVIN DONAT, grocery chain executive; b. Bennington, Vt., Jan. 31, 1956; s. Lionel Theberge and Rita Pearl (Cyr) Crow; m. Kathy Lynn Albury, July 27, 1974; children—Kevin Donat, Kyle Daniel. Student Northeastern Okla. A&M U., 1977-79, Fla. State U., 1979-80. Gen. mgr. Community TV of Miami (Okla.), 1977-79; hardlines mgr. Albertson's Southco, Tallahassee, 1979-81; pricing analyst Kroger Co., Atlanta, 1981—; gen. mgr. Dando Enterprises, Atlanta, 1981—. Fin. sponsor Jimmy Carter for Pres. campaign, Tallahassee, 1980. Served with USN, 1976-77. Northeastern Okla. A&M scholar, 1977. Democrat. Methodist. Home: 4451 Briarcliff Rd Atlanta GA 30345

LAWRENCE, MICHAEL EDWARD, religious publishing executive; b. Maysville, Ky., Feb. 28, 1955; s. Riley Edward and Lillian Jean (O'Daire) L.; B.A., Lambuth Coll., 1977; Cert. in Book Publishing, NYU, 1977; M.B.A., Middle Tenn. State U., 1982. Mgmt. trainee Abingdon Press/The United Methodist Pub. House, Nashville, 1977-78, asst. to multi-media resources mgr., 1978-79, product devel. supr., 1979-81, supplies and product devel. mgr., 1981-82, planning and devel. mgr., 1982-83, asst. mgr. ops. dept., 1983-84, dir.

fin. and ops., 1984-85, exec. editor trade books, 1985—. Home: 2024 Convent Pl Nashville TN 37212 Office: 201 8th Ave S Nashville TN 37202

LAWRENCE, ROBERT DE TREVILLE, III, wine growers association executive; b. Atlanta, June 21, 1915; m. Lelia Aiken Turner, Sept. 15, 1944; children—R. de Treville, IV, Lelia Randolph Lawrence Clark, Caro McDonald Lawrence Slingluff. A.B. in Journalism, U. Ga., 1937. Commd. 2d lt. U.S. Army, 1941, advanced through ranks to lt. col., 1951; served in World War II, China, Burma, India; served in Korean War; ret., 1975; founder Vinifera Wine Growers Assn., The Plains, Va., 1973—, pres., editor quar. jour., 1973—. Mem. Am. Soc. Enologists. Republican. Episcopalian. Avocations: conservation; preservation; hunting; fishing; tennis. Home: Highbury Farm The Plains VA 22171

LAWRENCE, TELETÉ ZORAYDA, speech and voice pathologist, educator; b. Worcester, Mass., Aug. 5, 1910; d. James Newton and Cora Valeria (Hester) Lester; A.B. cum laude, U. Calif., Berkeley, 1932; M.A., Tex. Christian U., 1963; pvt. study voice with Edgar Schofield, N.Y.C., 1936-41, drama with Enrica Clay Dillon, N.Y.C., 1937-40; m. Ernest Lawrence, Oct. 9, 1939; children—James Lester, Valerie Alma. Mem. Am. Lyric Theatre, 1939—; instr. speech Sch. Fine Arts, Tex. Christian U., Ft. Worth, 1959-66, asst. prof., 1966-71, asso. prof., 1971-75, prof., 1975-76, emeritus prof., 1976—; specialist disorders of voice and related therapeutic procedures; pvt. practice speech and voice therapy, 1960—; cons. voice disorders. Participant, contbr. numerous internat. congresses, 1965—, including Congress Internat. Assn. Sci. Study of Mental Deficiency, Montpellier, France, 1967, Semmelweis Anniversary Week Acad. Scis., Budapest, Hungary, 1968, Internat. Congress Logopedics and Phoniatrics, Sch. Medicine, U. Buenos Aires (Argentina), 1971, Lucerne, Switzerland, 1974, Copenhagen, 1977, Washington, 1980, Internat. Congress Phonetic Scis., Charles U., Prague, Czechoslovakia, 1967, McGill U., Montreal, Que., Can., 1971, U. Leeds (Eng.), 1975, Third World Congress of Phoneticans, Tokyo, 1976. Bd. dirs. Sunshine Haven, home for retarded children, 1957-59; gen. chmn. Ft. Worth and Tarrant County, Nat. Retarded Children's Week, 1954; mem. family and child welfare div. Community Council of Ft. Worth and Tarrant County, 1955-57; mem. health and hosp. div., 1959-60; mem. women's com. Ft. Worth chpt. NCCJ, 1956-59; exec. v.p. Fine Arts Found. Guild of Tex. Christian U., 1955-56, exec. sec., 1956-58, financial sec., 1958-59. Tex. Christian U. faculty research grantee, 1961, on leave to Gt. Britain, Western Europe, Hungary, 1968. Fellow Internat. Soc. Phonetic Scis.; mem. Nat. Council Chs. (bd. dirs. joint com. missionary edn. Pacific Coast area, 1952-55), United Ch. Women of Ft. Worth (chmn. Christian world missions dept. 1955-57, pres., 1957-59), Ft. Worth Area Council Chs. (v.p. 1955-57, exec. com. 1957-59, dir. 1959-60), U. Calif. Alumni Assn. (life), Am. Speech, Lang. and Hearing Assn. (life; cert.), Tex. Speech and Hearing Assn., Ft. Worth Council for Retarded Children, Speech Communication Assn. Am. (sec. speech and hearing disorders interest group 1962, 63), American Dialect Soc., A.A.U.P., Phoenetic Soc. Japan, Internat. Assn. Logopedics and Phoniatrics, Phi Beta Kappa (charter mem.; pres. Delta of Tex. chpt. 1973-74), Delta Zeta, Psi Chi, Sigma Alpha Eta. Republican. Mem. Christian Ch. Clubs: Woman's of Fort Worth; Women of Rotary. Author: Handbook for Instructors of Voice and Diction, 1968. Contbr. articles to profl. publs. Home: 3860 South Hills Circle Fort Worth TX 76109

LAWRENCE, THOMAS ALBERT, clergyman, social services administrator; b. Portsmouth, N.H., Apr. 10, 1919; s. William John and Emily Jane (Thomas) L.; m. Amy Jane Snow, June 9, 1946; children—Sharon Jane, Thomas Albert. B.A., U. Mass., 1952; M.Div., Bangor Theol. Sem., 1952; postgrad. Union Sem., 1958-60. Ordained to ministry United Ch. of Christ, 1952. With Millers Falls Congl. Ch., Mass., 1950-56; minister of edn. Wellesley Congl. Ch., Mass., 1956-59, 1st Central Ch., Omaha, 1959-60, United Ch. of Christ, Fla. Conf., 1960-74, Penn West Conf., 1974-80; dir. community relations, employee assistance program Tri-County Alcoholism Rehab. Services, Inc., Winter Haven, Fla., 1980—. Editor: Fla. Occupational Program Com. Newsletter, 1982-83. Mem. Fla. Occupational Program Com. (bd. dirs. 1981-84), Fla. Pub. Relations Soc. (bd. dirs. Dick Pope chpt. 1981-84). Democrat. Lodge: Masons. Home: PO Box 1414 Avon Park FL 33825

LAWRENCE, WILLIAM HOMER, science educator, researcher; b. Magnet Cove, Ark., Mar. 20, 1928; s. William Horten and Iva Myrtle (Wright) L.; m. Ella S. Elbourn, Sept. 18, 1954 (div. 1973); children—Karyn (Edwards), Bill, Thomas, Stephanie. B.S. in Pharmacy, Coll. of the Ozarks, 1950, Pharm.D. (hon.), 1981; M.S., U. Md., 1952, Ph.D. in Pharmacology, 1955. Diplomate in Gen. Toxicology. Instr. nursing U. Md., Balt., 1951; asst. prof. pharmacology and physiology U. Houston, 1956-60, assoc. prof., 1960-66; assoc. prof. pharmacy U. Tenn.-Memphis, 1966-73, prof. drug and material toxicology, 1973-83, prof. med. chemistry, 1983—; asst. dir. Materials Sci. Toxicology Labs., Memphis, 1967-75, assoc. dir., 1975—. Editorial bd. sci. jours., 1978—. Contbr. articles to prof. jours. Served with U.S. Army, 1956-57. Grantee NIH, NASA, and numerous health orgns. Mem. AAAS, Am. Pharm. Assn., Soc. Toxicology. Office: Dept Med Chem Coll Pharmacy U Tenn Ctr Health Scis 800 Madison Ave Memphis TN 38163

LAWRENCE-BERREY, ROBERT EDMOND, pathologist; b. Calgary, Alta., Can., Oct. 8, 1934; s. Jack Edmond and Ruth Evelyn (Eiseman) L.-B.; came to U.S., 1946, naturalized, 1958; B.A. in Chemistry, Whitman Coll., 1956; M.D., U. Wash., 1962; m. Shirley Anne Davis, Feb. 23, 1962; children—Ruth Elizabeth, Robert Edmond, Julia Anne. Intern in pathology Good Samaritan Hosp. and Med. Center, Portland, Oreg., 1962-63, resident in anat. and clin. pathology, 1963-66, staff pathologist, 1968-71; practice medicine specializing in pathology, Portland, 1968-72, Parkersburg, W.Va., 1972—; staff pathologist Salem (Oreg.) Meml. Hosp., 1971, Providence Hosp., Portland, 1971-72; pathologist, dir. Gen. Consultants Med. Labs., Inc., Parkersburg, 1972—; pres. L.-B. & J. Investments, Inc., 1972—, Gen. Cons. Inc., 1976—; clin. instr. clin. pathology U. Oreg. Med. Sch., Portland, 1970-72; clin. instr. Sch. Med. Tech., Parkersburg Community Coll., 1972—; cons. pathologist, dir. labs. Guernsey Meml. Hosp., Cambridge, Ohio, 1972—, Barnesville (Ohio) Hosp. Assn., 1972-80, Selby Gen. Hosp., Marietta, Ohio, 1972—, Calhoun Gen. Hosp., Grantsville, W.Va., 1972-83; cons.-adviser Sch. Med. Tech., Jefferson County (Ohio) Tech. Inst., 1974—; Bishop of La. Council, Polk Meml. Episcopal Mission, 1967-68; mem. fin. com. St. Bartholomew's Episc. Ch., Beaverton, Oreg., 1971-72; trustee Parkersburg Community Coll. Found., 1975—, pres., 1979—; bd. dirs. Mid Ohio Valley chpt. ARC, 1981—, treas., 1982—. Served with M.C., U.S. Army, 1966-68. Diplomate Am. Bd. Pathology. Fellow Am. Soc. Clin. Pathologists, Coll. Am. Pathologists; mem. Am. Soc. Nuclear Medicine, Parkersburg Acad. Medicine, Am. Soc. Cytology, Oreg. Pathologists Assns., W.Va. Med. Assn., AMA, Alpha Kappa Kappa, Phi Delta Theta. Club: Rotary (chmn. Rotary Found. com. 1980—) (Parkersburg). Home: 30 Oakwood Estate Parkersburg WV 26101 Office: PO Box 1229 1217 Ann St Parkersburg WV 26101

LAWSON, DAVESENE WIGGINS-SPELLMAN, business educator, consultant; b. Durham, N.C., Nov. 24, 1937; d. David Lee and Nixola (Burnette) Wiggins; m. Charles Gilbert Spellman, May 4, 1963 (div. 1965); 1 child, Daryl Paul; m. James Ranaldo Lawson, Mar. 24, 1984; 1 child, Querida Denise. B.S. in Commerce, N.C. Central U., 1960, M.S., 1972; Ed.D., U. N.C.-Greensboro, 1980. Acctg. clk. N.C. Central U., Durham, 1960-63, sec. to v.p. for fin., 1963-71, adminstrv. asst. in devel., 1971-73, assoc. prof., dept. chmn. bus. edn., 1974-84, assoc. prof., program coordinator bus. edn., 1984—; exec. dir. search for chancellor, 1985; instr. Durham Tech. Inst., 1973-74. Sec., bd. dirs. City-Wide United Way, Durham, 1973; chmn. City-Wide PTA Com., Durham, 1976; bd. dirs. Triangle Hospice, Durham, 1983—, sec., 1985—; mem. adv. council N.C. Bus. Office Edn., Raleigh, 1983—. Mem. Nat. Bus. Edn. Assn., So. Bus. Edn. Assn. (chmn. basic bus. div. 1984-85), N.C. Bus. Edn. Assn. (pres. 1984-85, bd. dirs. 1979—), Delta Pi Epsilon, Delta Sigma Theta. Club: Quettes (pres. 1985—). Avocations: bowling, singing. Home: 1906 University Dr Durham NC 27707 Office: NC Central U Dept Bus Edn Durham NC 27707

LAWSON, JIMMIE DON, mathematics educator; b. Waukegan, Ill., Dec. 6, 1942; s. Maurice Lestel and Ida Lois (Lee) L.; m. Laura Jane Miller, Sept. 1, 1964; children—Michal Lynette, John Kevin. B.S., Harding U., 1964; Ph.D., U. Tenn., 1967. Asst. prof. U. Tenn.-Knoxville, 1967-68; asst. prof. La. State U., Baton Rouge, 1968-70, assoc. prof., 1971-76, prof. math. dept., 1976—. Author: A Compendium of Continuous Lattices, 1980. Contbr. articles to profl. jours. Alexander Humboldt Found. fellow, 1980-81; hon. Fulbright fellow, 1980-81. Mem. Am. Math. Soc., Am. Sci. Affiliation. Democrat. Mem. Ch. of Christ. Home: 8275 Menlo Dr Baton Rouge LA 70808 Office: Math Dept La State U Baton Rouge LA 70803

LAWSON, MARION EDWARD, dentist; b. Clinton, S.C., Aug. 12, 1921; s. Lonnie Thompson and Mary Frances (Sumner); m. Frances Elizabeth Coop, Aug. 26, 1962. B.S., Furman U., 1941; D.D.S., Emory U., 1946. Gen. practice dentistry, Clinton, 1946—. Served to capt. U.S. Army, 1951-53. Mem. Clinton C. of C., ADA, S.C. Dental Assn. (bd. dirs., del.), So. Acad. Oral Surgery, So. Assn. Instl. Dentistry, Hopewell Game Conservation Club (pres.). Baptist (chmn. bd. deacons). Clubs: Wadsworth Community (pres.). Lodge: Lions. Avocations: hunting; horses; cattle. Home: Route 3 Box 336 Clinton SC 29325 Office: 200 S Broad St Clinton SC 29325

LAWSON, STEVEN F., history educator, historian; b. N.Y.C., June 14, 1945; s. Murray and Ceil (Parker) L. B.A., CCNY, 1966; M.A., Columbia U., 1967, Ph.D., 1974. Instr. U. South Fla., 1972-74, asst. prof., 1974-78, assoc. prof., 1978—, chmn. dept., 1983—. Author: Black Ballots, 1976 (Phi Alpha Theta award 1977); In Pursuit of Power, 1985. Editor: (microfilm) Civil Rights During the Johnson Administration, 1984. Grantee NEH, Am. Council Learned Socs. Mem. Am. Hist. Assn., Orgn. Am. Historians, So. Hist. Assn. Home: 7801 Garrison St Tampa FL 33617 Office: Dept History U South Fla Tampa FL 33620

LAWSON, THEODORE EARL, company executive; b. Portland, Oreg., Apr. 29, 1941; s. Earl Loraine and Vera Minnie (Heitschmidt) L.; B.A., U. Kans., 1963; M.S.T., Portland State U., 1970; children by previous marriage—Michael L., Larry D., Kristin L., Jay E. Gen. mgr., Portland Civic Theater, 1969-70; manpower specialist Oreg. Employment Div., Portland, 1970-72; asso. project dir. Oreg. Med. Assn., Portland, 1972-74, dir. sci. affairs, 1974-75, exec. sec. Oreg. Soc. Internal Medicine, 1972-75, exec. sec. West Coast Allergy Soc., 1973-75; exec. dir. Spokane County Med. Soc., 1975-79, Tex. Dental Assn., 1979-82; project mgr. The Horne Co., 1983-84; property mgr. Trammell Crow Co., 1984-85; mgr. bldg. ops. Watson-Casey Cos., 1985—. Mem. blue ribbon com. on health care Multnomah County Commrs., 1973-75. Served with USAF, 1963-68; Vietnam. Recipient George Washington medal Freedom Found., 1966. Mem. Am. Assn. Med. Soc. Execs., Am. Soc. Assn. Execs., Tex. Soc. Assn. Execs., Bldg. Owners and Mgrs. Assn. (pres. Austin chpt. 1985, bd. dirs. Tex.), Air Force Assn. Republican. Baptist. Toastmaster. Home: 1510 W North Loop Suite 1022 Austin TX 78756 Office: 816 Congress Ave Suite 1200 Austin TX 78701

LAWSON, THOMAS SEAY, JR., lawyer; b. Montgomery, Ala., Oct. 30, 1935; s. Thomas Seay and Rose Darrington (Gunter) L.; m. Sarah Hunter Clayton, May 27, 1961; children—Rose Gunter, Gladys Robinson, Thomas Seay. A.B., U. Ala., 1957, LL.B., 1963. Bar: Ala. 1963, U.S. Supreme Ct. 1969. Law clk. to chief judge U.S. Dist. Ct. (no. dist.) Ala., 1963-64; assoc. Steiner, Crum & Baker, Montgomery, 1964-68; ptnr. Capell, Howard, Knabe & Cobbs, Montgomery, 1968—, asst. dist. atty. 15th jud. cir. of Ala., 1969-70; mem. lawyers adv. com. U.S. Ct. Appeals (11th cir.), 1980-84. Pres. The Lighthouse, 1978-79; trustee Ala. Law Sch. Found. Served to lt. USNR, 1957-60. Mem. ABA, Fed. Bar Assn., Ala. State Bar (pres. young lawyers sect. 1970-71), Montgomery County Bar Assn. (pres. 1980), Am. Judicature Soc., Eleventh Cir. Hist. Soc. (trustee). Democrat. Episcopalian. Clubs: Montgomery Country, Capital City (Montgomery). Home: 1262 Glen Grattan Montgomery AL 36111 Office: PO Box 2069 Montgomery AL 36197

LAWTON, ROBERT JAMES, school administrator, counselor; b. Orlando, Fla., July 15, 1929; s. Thomas Willingham and Charlotte (Lee) L. B.S., Fla. So. U., 1950; M.A., U. Del., 1956; Ed.D., U. Va., 1970. Instr., Fla. So. Coll., 1950-51; tchr. high sch., Lakeland, Fla., 1950-52; asst. headmaster Pennington Sch., N.J., 1956-64; coll. counselor Peddie Sch., Hightstown, N.J., 1954-69; supt., headmaster Miller Sch., Va., 1969-84, pres., supt., 1984—. U. Va. fellow 1967-68. Mem. AAUP, Phi Delta Kappa. Avocations: reading; music. Home: PO Drawer A Miller School VA 22901 Office: Miller Sch PO Drawer A Miller School VA 22901

LAWVER, JAMES EVERETT, retired minerals and chemical corporation executive; b. Denver, May 28, 1919; s. Edgar Alfred and Emma Elizabeth (Wilber) L.; m. Sinharinha Maria Tome, Dec. 21, 1946; children—Joyce Esther, Joseph West. B.S. in Metall. Engring., Colo. Sch. Mines, 1943, Sc.D., 1956. Registered profl. engr., Minn., Fla. Mining engr. Braden Copper Co., Chile, 1943-45; mining engr. Bur. Strategic Warfare, Brazil, 1944-45; research engr., sect. leader Internat. Minerals and Chem. Corp., Mulberry, Fla., 1946-53, mgr. minerals processing research dept., 1956-62; dir. minerals resources research ctr., prof., assoc. head civil and mineral engring. dept. U. Minn., Mpls., 1962-75; tech. mgr. Internat. Minerals & Chem. Corp., Bartow, Fla., 1975-78, ret., 1978. Recipient Robert H. Richards award AIME, 1980; Disting. Mem. award Soc. Mining Engrs. of AIME, 1980; named Engr. of Yr., Ridge chpt. Fla. Engring. Soc., 1981; Fla. Engr. of Yr., Fla. sect. AIME, 1981. Mem. Am. Inst. Mining, Metall. and Petroleum Engrs., AAUP, Brit. Instn. Mining and Metallurgy, Electrostatic Soc. Am., Nat. Soc. Profl. Engrs., Am. Nuclear Soc., Sigma Xi, Tau Beta Pi. Contbr. articles to various publs. Patentee in field. Home: 6334 Oak Sq E Lakeland FL 33803

LAWYER, PHILIP STERLING, army administrator, b. Boston, Dec. 23, 1947; s. John and Alice (Brewer) L.; m. Ruth Eleanor Ho, July 7, 1969; 1 child, Tamara. B.S., N.Y. State U., 1980; M.Ed., U. Okla., 1982. Fed. police officer C.Z., Cristobal, 1970-82; safety officer Marine Bur., Panama Canal, 1982-85; tng. instr. U.S. Army Alcohol and Drug Prevention Control Program, Ft. Davis, Panama, 1985—; tchr., counselor drug abusers; ednl. counselor. Emergency med. technician Panama Canal, 1979—; CPR-first aid instr. ARC, 1982—; defensive driving instr. Nat. Safety Council, 1982—. Served as sgt. U.S. Army, 1966-69. Recipient numerous awards for meritorious service, U.S. Govt. Mem. Am. Soc. Safety Engrs., Fed. Criminal Investigation Assn., Am. Law Enforcement Officers Assn., Am. Police Acad., Internat. Acad. Criminology. Home: PSC Box 774 APO Miami FL 34005 Office: 193d Infantry Brigade Pan ADAPCP Atlantic Office: APO Miami FL 34005

LAXSON, RUTH KNIGHT, visual artist; b. Roanoke, Ala., July 16, 1924; d. Edward Wilts and Ruby Malinda (Dunson) Knight; m. Claude Roland King, Nov. 29, 1942 (div. 1947); 1 son, Claude Roland; m. Robert Earl Laxson, Jan. 31, 1953. Student Auburn U., 1943, Atlanta Coll. Art, 1959-65. One-woman shows: Some Earthly Ideas, Atlanta Artworkers Coalition Gallery, 1980, Emory U., Atlanta, 1984, Quinlan Art Ctr., Gainesville, Ga., 1985; represented by Galerie Illien, Atlanta, 1968-76, Heath Gallery, Atlanta, 1976—, Artworks, Los Angeles, 1980—, Hand in Hand Gallery, N.Y.C., 1984—; group shows include: Getler/Pall Gallery, N.Y.C., 1980-81, New in '82, Ctr. Book Arts, N.Y.C., 1982, Breaking the Bindings, U. Wis., 1983; leader workshops and seminars; represented in permanent collections: Ga. Council Arts and Humanities, Delta Air Lines, Emory U.; author/artist: Power Poem, Mus. Modern Art, N.Y.C., 1982; Earth Score, Sackner Collection Visual Poetry, Miami, Fla., 1983; Playfulness Works, Franklin Furnace Archive, N.Y.C., 1983; also narrative works in libraries including Sch. Art Inst. Chgo., Va. Commonwealth U. Active High Mus. Art, Atlanta. NEA grantee, 1980. Mem. Nexus, Franklin Furnace, Atlanta Coll. Art Alumni Assn. Presbyterian. Home: 2298 Drew Valley Rd NE Atlanta GA 30319 Office: PO Box 9731 Atlanta GA 30319

LAY, WILLIAM EDWARD, JR., insurance company executive; b. Easton, Md., May 11, 1926; s. William Edward and Mildred (Woodford) L.; m. Elizabeth Miller, Aug. 15, 1949; children—Susan, John, Robert, Jane, Anne. B.A., Furman U., 1949; postgrad. U.N.C., 1976. With Liberty Life Ins. Co., Greenville, S.C., 1949—, sr. v.p. adminstrn., 1978-81, dir., 1974—; v.p. adminstrn. Liberty Corp., 1974—. Served with USN, 1942-45. Mem. Am. Mgmt. Assn., Life Office Mgmt. Assn., Adminstrv. Mgmt. Soc. Methodist. Clubs: Poinsett, Paladin. Office: PO Box 789 Greenville SC 29602

LAYMAN, FRED DALE, biblical literature educator; b. Marshfield, Mo., Sept. 27, 1931; s. Lee R. and Winnie A. (Thomas) L.; m. Donna J. Roberts, Aug. 2, 1952; 1 child, Steven. A.B., Asbury Coll., 1954; B.D., Asbury Theol. Sem., 1956; Th.M., Princeton Theol. Sem., 1957; Ph.D., U. Iowa, 1972. Prof. bibl. lit. Friends U., Wichita, Kans., 1957-64, Asbury Coll., Wilmore, Ky., 1967-68, Asbury Theol. Sem., Wilmore, 1968—. Contbr. articles to profl. jours. Vice chmn. Planning and Zoning Commn., Nicholasville, Ky., 1977-85. Mem. Soc. Bibl. Lit. Methodist. Avocations: music; sports. Office: Asbury Theol Sem Wilmore KY 40390

LAYMAN, MAYA LINK, clinical psychologist, school psychologist; b. Chgo., Aug. 26, 1949; d. Milton N. Brutten and Yolanda I. Molnar; m. Allen F. Layman, Jan. 19, 1980; 1 child, Hillary Claire. B.A., McGill U., 1971; M.S., Hahnemann U., 1974; Ph.D., U. Va., 1982. Lic. clin. psychologist, Va.; cert. sch. psychologist. Psychologist "B" Western State Hosp., Staunton, Va., 1976-78, spl. edn. tchr., 1981-82; intern Blue Ridge Mental Health Clinic, Stanardsville, Va., 1978-79; clin. program cons. T.R.E.E.S./Augusta County Schs., Fisherville, Va., 1982-83; practice of clin. psychology Shenandoah Valley Med. Ctr., Spottswood, Va., 1984-85; clin. sch. psychologist Augusta County Schs., Fishersville, 1983-85; cons. Valley Pastoral Counseling Ctr., Staunton, 1985; pvt. practice in clin. psychology specializing in adolescents, 1984-85; clin. psychologist Neurol. Rehab. Assocs., Waynesboro, Va., 1985—. Mem. bd. Office of Youth Services, Waynesboro, Va., 1982-83. Mem. Va. Psychol. Assn. (chmn. membership com. 1984-86, chmn. edn. and tng. com. 1986—), Am. Psychol. Assn., Am. Assn. Pastoral Counselors, Va. Acad. Clin. Psychologists. Democrat. Episcopalian. Home: 1040 Fairway Dr Waynesboro VA 22980 Office: PO Box 1303 Waynesboro VA 22980

LAYMAN, REBECCA SUE, food products executive; b. Camp Zama, Japan, Apr. 6, 1958; d. David Eugene and Caroline Jean (Thompson) L. B.B.A. in Fin., S.W. Tex. State U., 1983. Day mgr. Mr. Gattis, Austin, Tex., 1976-77; asst. mgr. Burger King, Huntsville, Tex., 1978-80; retail sales/ops. mgr. House of Jeans, San Marcos, Tex., 1981-82, Zippers, San Marcos, 1982-83; sales rep. Frito Lay, Austin, 1984—. Author poetry collection: Reflections, 1976. Recipient Sportsmanship award Kwanis Club, 1969. Mem. Fin. Mgmt. Assn. Home: 303 Doefield Leander TX 78641 Office: Frito Lay 9806 Middlefiskville Rd Austin TX 78753

LAYMON, CYNTHIA J., artist, art educator; b. Gary, Ind., Feb. 17, 1948; d. Michael and Norma (MacLaverty) Semanchik; m. Terrance E. Laymon, 1972. B.A., Ind. U., 1970; M.F.A., So. Ill. U., 1977. Asst. prof. art Lake Erie Coll., Painesville, Ohio, 1977-79; assoc. prof. U. N.C.-Greensboro, 1979—; exhibited in one man shows including: Weatherspoon Gallery, Greensboro, N.C., 1982, C. Corcoran Gallery, Muskegon, Mich., 1983; group shows include: Columbus (Ohio) Mus. Fine Arts, 1975, 77, Gathering Gallery, Kansas City, Mo., 1979, Green Hill Gallery, Greensboro, 1982, mus. in Spain and Morocco, 1982-83, Redding (Calif.) Mus., 1983, Ga. State Art Gallery, 1984, Mindscape Galleries, Chgo., 1984-85, Iowa Arts Ctr., 1984, N.C. Art Mus., 1984, Roanoke Art Mus., 1984, Tampa Art Mus., 1985, Soc. Arts and Crafts, Boston, 1985, Longwood Coll., Va., 1985. Recipient Best of Show award Columbus Inst. for Contemporary Art, 1978; Merit award Survey of Ill. Fiber, Lakeview Mus., Peoria, 1978, Handweavers Guild of Am. award, 1978; Belding Lily award North/South Carolina Fibers Competition, Charlotte, 1980, award of excellence, 1980, Am. and Efrid Mills award, 1981. Mem. Am. Craft Council, Surface Design Conf., N.C. Fiber Art Assn. (treas. 1979-81). Office: Art Department University of North Carolina Greensboro NC 27412

LAYNE, JAMES NATHANIEL, mammalogist, research administrator; b. Chgo., May 16, 1926; s. Leslie Joy and Harriet Barbara (Hausman) L.; m. Lois Virginia Linderoth, Aug. 26, 1950; children—Linda Carrie, Kimberly, Jamie, Susan, Rachel. Student Chgo. City Jr. Coll., 1946-47; B.A., Cornell U., 1947-50; Ph.D., 1954. Grad. teaching asst. Cornell U., Ithaca, N.Y., 1950-54; asst. prof. zoology So. Ill. U., Carbondale, 1954-55; asst. prof. biology U. Fla., Gainesville, 1955-59, assoc. prof. biology, 1959-63; assoc. prof. vertebrate zoology Cornell U., Ithaca, N.Y., 1963-67; dir. research Archbold Biol. Sta., Lake Placid, Fla., 1967-76, exec. dir., 1967-85, sr. research biologist, 1976—; vis. scientist Nat. Inst. Neurol. Disorders and Blindness, Cayo Santiago, P.R., summers 1961, 62; adj. prof. zoology U. South Fla., Tampa, 1963—; cons. WHO, 1969; research assoc. Fla. Dept. Agr., Gainesville, 1970—; research assoc. Am. Mus. Natural History, 1982—. Served with USAF, 1944-46. Recipient C. Hart Merriam award Am. Soc. Mammalogists, 1976. Mem. Am. Soc. Mammalogists, AAAS, Am. Soc. Zoologists, Am. Soc. Naturalists, Ecol. Soc. Am., Phi Beta Kappa, Sigma Xi, Phi Kappa Phi, Phi Sigma. Contbr. articles to sci. jours. Home: PO Box 1022 Lake Placid FL 33852 Office: PO Box 2057 Lake Placid FL 33852

LAYNE, JOHN FRANCIS, accountant; b. Milw., Mar. 25, 1928; s. Lawrence E. and Blanche E. (Tetzlaff) L.; A.A., Valencia Jr. Coll., 1971; B.S.B.A., U. Central Fla., 1972; m. Esther A. Ornberg, Mar. 10, 1951; children—Loretta E., John W., Mark L. Enlisted U.S. Air Force, 1948, advanced through grades to chief warrant officer-4, 1964; test controller, systems devel. Air Proving Ground Center, Eglin AFB, 1962-65; standardization/evaluation controller USAF, Far East, Okinawa and Vietnam, 1966-70; ret., 1970; acct. Electric Specialty, Orlando, Fla., 1971-74, controller, 1975-77; fin. field rep. Tupperware div. Dart, Orlando, 1978—. Vice pres. Central Fla. Assn. Sq. Dancers, 1977-78, pres., 1978-79; chmn. 1978 Fla. Sq. Dance Conv.; active Fla. Fedn. Sq. Dancers, 1978-82, pres., 1982-83. Decorated Bronze Star; recipient citation for excellence Boy Scouts Am., 1968, Am. Square Dance Soc., 1983. Mem. Nat. Accts. Assn., Nat. Soc. Public Accts., Nat. Assn. Enrolled Agts. Home: 328 Stewart St Marble Falls TX 78654 Office: PO Box 7922 Horseshoe Bay TX 78654

LAYNE, LARRY THOMAS, osteopathic physician, educator; b. Kimper, Ky., July 30, 1946; s. Alonzo and Annah Lee (May) L.; m. Jeanne Louise Cain, Aug. 31, 1968; children—Laura Lee, Marjorie Ann, Arthur Thomas. B.S. in Chemistry cum laude, Harding Coll., 1969; postgrad. U. Mo.-Kansas City, 1969-72; D.O., Kansas City Coll. of Osteo. Med., 1976. Diplomate Nat. Bd. Examiners Osteo. Physicians and Surgeons. Intern Pontiac Osteo. Hosp., Mich., 1976-77; emergency room physician Helen Keller Meml. Hosp., Sheffield, Ala., 1979—; physician adviser, instr. for emergency med. technicians II program Northwest Ala. State Jr. Coll., Tuscumbia, 1983—; gen. practice medicine Waterloo Primary Health Care Clinic, Ala., 1979—, Ford Motor Co., Muscle Shoals, Ala., 1981-82; physician adviser, tchr. for emergency med. technicians II course Northwest Ala. Jr. Coll., 1983-84; mem. staff Helen Keller Meml. Hosp., Sheffield, Ala., 1977—, Shoals Hosp., Sheffield, 1977-79. Mem. PTO, Muscle Shoals, 1983—; patrol chmn. Broadway Neighborhood Watch, Muscle Shoals, 1982-84. Served to 1st lt. USPHS, 1977-79. NDEA Title IV grad. fellow U.S. Dept. of Edn., 1969-72. Mem. Am. Osteo. Assn., Am. Coll. of Osteo. Emergency Physicians, Med. Assn. of Ala., Colbert County Med. Soc. (sec., treas. 1981—), Am. Heart Assn. Mem. Ch. of Christ. Lodge: Lions. Avocations: camping; bowling; gardening; travelling. Home and Office: 408 SW Clark Ave Muscle Shoals AL 35661

LAYTON, ROBERT GLENN, radiologist; b. Bklyn., Oct. 14, 1946; s. Irving and Charlotte (Bell) L.; m. Judith Helene Bohrer, May 31, 1969; children—Andrew, Julia. B.S., Union Coll., 1968; M.D., Boston U., 1972. Diplomate Am. Bd. Radiology. Resident in radiology, Boston City Hosp., 1972-75; jr. attending radiologist L.I. Jewish Hosp., Hillside, N.Y., 1975-76; staff radiologist Cedars Med. Ctr., Miami, Fla., 1978—; radiologist Highland Park Gen. Hosp., Miami, 1978. Pres., Michael-Ann Russell Jewish Community Ctr., Miami, 1980-82; bd. dirs. Jewish Community Ctrs. S. Fla., 1982—; trustee Temple Sinai of North Dade, North Miami Beach, 1982—, v.p., 1985—. Served to maj. USAF, 1976-78. Mem. AMA, Am. Coll. Radiology, Am. Inst. Ultrasound in Medicine, Miami Radiol. Soc., Begg Soc., Alpha Omega Alpha. Jewish. Home: 21120 NE 23rd Ct North Miami Beach FL 33180 Office: Dept Radiology Cedars Med Center 1400 NW 12th Ave Miami FL 33136

LAZAR, WILLIAM JOEL (BILLY JOE), aviation and marine insurance specialist, sports and entertainment promoter; b. N.Y.C., July 4, 1957; s. William and Carmen L. Lazar. Student County Coll. of Morris, 1977-79; A.S. in Bus. Adminstrn., Seton Hall U., 1976; postgrad. Daytona Beach Community Coll., 1982. Lic. ins. agent, Fla.; lic. aircraft pilot. Recovery mgr. aviation dept. Am. Nat. Bank & Trust of N.J., Morristown, 1976-79; aviation and marine agt. Air-Sur, Inc., Ormond Beach, Fla., 1980—; promoter Sun Ray Prodns., Daytona Beach, Fla., 1982—; Youth coordinator senatorial campaign, Morris County, N.J., 1974; mem. Inst. for Polit. and Legal Edn. of Republican Party. Mem. Fla. Assn. Ins. Agts., Fla. Air Taxi Assn., Black Belt Profl. Kickboxing Assn., Aircraft Owners and Pilots Assn., World Tae Kwon Do Fedn. Home: 7 Bristol Ln Ormond Beach FL 32074 Office: Air-Sur Inc 595 N Nova Rd Suite 209 Ormond Beach FL 32074

LAZO, LUIS REID, industrial executive; b. N.Y.C., Feb. 28, 1931; s. William Cornelius and Mary Elizabeth (Kent) L.; m. Patricia Blount, July 16, 1954; children—Kenneth, Peter, Michael. B.A. in Physics and Math., Middlebury Coll., 1951; S.B. in Mech. Engring., MIT, 1953. From mgr. systems planning to sr. project engr. TRW, Inc., Cleve., 1953-63; dir. corp. planning, pres., chief exec. officer Transport Dynamics Inc. subs. Lear-Siegler, Inc., Santa Ana, Calif., 1963-70; pres. FM4 Corp., Cleve. and Boca Raton, Fla., 1970-75; pres. Internat. Engring. Group, Inc., McGill Co., I.S.C. Co., Houston, 1975-78; pres. Newport News Indsl. Corp., Newport News Offshore Systems Corp. subs. Newport News Shipbldg. Co. (Va.), 1978—. Pres. bd. trustees Harbor Day

Sch., Corona del Mar, Calif.; chmn. bd. trustees Pub. Library Mentor (Ohio), 1958-63; bd. dirs. Va. Stage Co., 1980-83; pres. bd. trustees Festival Williamsburg, Inc., 1983—. Mem. Soc. Naval Architects and Marine Engrs., Atomic Indsl. Forum (dir.), Delta Upsilon. Republican. Club: Propeller. Patentee in field. Home: 25 Whittaker's Mill Williamsburg VA 23185 Office: Newport News Indsl Corp 230 41st St Newport News VA 23607

LAZO, ROBERT LINDEN, book store executive; b. South Bend, Ind., Mar. 17, 1954; s. Robert Martin and Rosemarie (Walsh) L.; m. Theresa Moxley Stone, May 23, 1981. B.S., Va. Tech. State U., 1976, M.A., 1978. Teaching asst., engr. Va. Tech. State U., Blacksburg, 1977-78; program advisor Retired Sr. Volunteer Program, Christiansburg, Va., 1978-79; tech. editor Sci. Applications, Inc., McLean, Va., 1980-83; bookseller, owner Blue Ridge Books, Wytheville, Va., 1983—. Pres. Citizens Peace, Wytheville, 1983-84. Mem. Merchants Assn. (dir. 1984—). Democrat. Avocation: writing. Office: Blue Ridge Books 148 W Main St Wytheville VA 24382

LAZOR, JOHN DAVID, consulting geologist, oil and gas exploration; b. Scranton, Pa., July 22, 1941; s. John Paul Lazor and Doroth-Rae (Crowl) Dugan; m. Barbara Jean Stevens, June 11, 1967; children—Jennifer Rae, Michael David. B.A., Coll. of Wooster, 1966; M.A., Ind. U., 1968, Ph.D., 1971. Geol. mgr., exploration geologist Cities Service Co., Midland, Tex., Houston, 1975-79; v.p. Beaumont Energy, Houston, 1979-80; exploration geologist Texaco, Inc., Houston, 1973-75; Am. Coastal Energy, Houston, 1980-81; pres. Lazor Petroleum, Houston, 1981-82; exploration geologist Valero Producing Co., Houston, 1982-84; cons. geologist D.B.W. C.B. Hamill, Houston, Tex., 1984—; asst. prof. Ind. U., Gary, Inc., 1972-73, Washington and Lee U., Lexington, Va., 1971-72. Bd. dirs. Westland YMCA, 1983-84. Served with U.S. Army, 1959-62; Korea. Mem. Soc. Econ. Paleontologists and Minerologists, Am. Inst. Profl. Geolists, Am. Assn. Petroleum Geologists, Houston Geol. Soc. (chmn. entertainment com. 1984—), Tobacco Root Geol. Soc. (charter Mem.). Presbyterian. Avocations: hunting; fishing; photography. Home: 7719 Burning Hills Houston TX 77071

LEA, ALFRED SCOTT, physician; b. Houston, Aug. 18, 1950; s. Walker Alfred and Beverly Barbara (Hayes) L.; B.S. cum laude, Baylor U., 1972, M.D. with honors, Baylor Coll. Medicine, 1975; m. Patricia Ann Hufnall, Jan. 4, 1975; children—Melissa Marie, Scott Townsend. Intern, Baylor Affiliated Hosps., Houston, 1976-77, resident in medicine, 1977-79; chief resident in internal medicine Ben Taub Gen. Hosp., 1979-80; instr. internal medicine, fellow in infectious diseases Baylor Coll. Medicine, 1980-82; mem. med. staff Hillcrest Bapt. Hosp., Providence Hosp., VA Med. Ctr. (all Waco, Tex.); med. dir. Amicable Life Ins. Co., 1982—; mem. faculty Mc Lennan County Med. Edn. and Research Found., 1982—. Diplomate Am. Bd. Internal Medicine, Am. Bd. Infectious Disease. Mem. AMA (recipient Physicians' Recognition award 1981), ACP, Am. Soc. Microbiology. Episcopalian. Lodge: Rotary. Home: 1241 Woodland W Waco TX 76710 Office: 1700 Providence Dr Waco TX 76708

LEA, SUZANNE MOORE, physics educator; b. Waxahachie, Tex., Jan. 27, 1944; d. Wallace C. and Josephine M. (Lumpkins) Moore; m. Michael David Lea, June 14, 1964; children—Katharine Alexandra, Michael David. B.A. cum laude, Rice U., 1964; M.S. in Physics, Ohio State U., 1966; Ph.D. in Physics, Duke U., 1970. Instr. physics Davidson County Community Coll., Lexington, N.C., 1970-77, instr. physics, 1978-79; vis. asst. prof. physics U. N.C.-Greensboro, 1977-78, 83-84, research assoc., 1978-83, adj. assoc. prof., 1984—; asst. prof. physics Livingstone Coll., Salisbury, N.C., 1979-82, assoc. prof., 1982-85, chmn. physics dept., 1979-85. Nat. Merit scholar, 1960-64; NSF grantee, 1980-83, 85-87. Mem. Am. Phys. Soc., Am. Assn. Physics Tchrs. (pres. So. Atlantic Coast Sect. 1981-82, mem. exec. com. So. Atlantic Coast sect. 1982-83), N.C. Acad. Sci., Am. Astron. Soc., N.C. Assn. Astronomers. Democrat. Episcopalian. Contbr. articles to profl. jours. Home: 205 Oakwood Dr Thomasville NC 27360 Office: Physics Dept U NC Greensboro NC 27412

LEACH, CHARLES SELLERS, merchant, farmer; b. Jackson, Tenn., Jan. 17, 1926; s. Wendall Clifford and Ruth Maybell (Evans) L.; B.A., U. Mich., 1947; student Milligan Coll., 1944-45, Central Mich. Coll., 1945-46; m. Mary Sophia May, July 23, 1949; children—Jim, John, Robert, Charlie. Owner, operator Leach's Music & TV, also Radio Shack, Paris, Tenn., 1950—; leader orch., Paris, Tenn., 1951-68; farmer, Paris, 1968—. Served to lt. comdr., USNR, 1944-68. Mem. Paris-Henry County C. of C., Downtown Businessman Assn. Paris, Jackson Symphony Orch., Tennessee Valley, Am. polled hereford assns., Am. Quarter Horse Assn., Ret. Officers Assn. Roman Catholic. Clubs: Rotary (v.p. Paris 1971-72, pres. 1985-86), Paris Elks, Henry County Saddle (pres. 1977). Home: Route 4 Paris TN 38242 Office: 122 E Washington St Paris TN 38242

LEACH, RICHARD MAXWELL, psychologist, writer; b. Childress, Tex., Feb. 10, 1909; s. John Reuben and Cora Lee (Curd) L.; m. Lelia Page, Jan. 17, 1931 (dec. 1976); children—Beth Tatum, Max Jr., Leslie Prather; m. Lavoy Burke Miller, July 10, 1977. Faculty Abilene Christian U., 1942-72; pvt. practice psychology, Lamesa, Tex., 1972—. Mem. Am. Psychol. Assn., Tex. Psychol. Assn. Democrat. Mem. Ch. of Christ. Author: Like Stars Shining Brightly, 1950; College, Classroom, Campus and You, 1955; Christianity and Mental Health, 1960; His Way in His Words, 1963; Sex and the Christian, 1971. Contbr. articles to profl. jours. Home and Office: 1011 N 13th St Lamesa TX 79331

LEACH, ROBERT ALAN, chiropractor, author, researcher; b. Des Moines, Dec. 2, 1955; s. Joseph Stanley and Thelma Maxine (Strubhar) L.; m. Vicki Elaine Hughes, Apr. 24, 1979; children—Robert Alan, Zachariah Michael. A.A., Phoenix Coll., 1975; D. Chiropractic, Life Chiropractic Coll., 1978. Diplomate Nat. Bd. Chiropractic Examiners. Pres., Leach Chiropractic Clinic, Inc., Starkville, Miss., 1979—. Fellow Internat. Coll. Chiropractic (hon.); mem. Am. Chiropractic Assn., Miss. Associated Chiropractors (chmn. com. on research, chmn. com. on continuing edn.). Author: The Chiropractic Theories-A Synopsis of Scientific Research, 1980. Office: 415 Hwy 82 E Box 1313 Starkville MS 39759

LEACY, CHARLES RICHARD, librarian, educator; b. Cambridge, Mass., July 15, 1935; s. Charles Bernard Leacy and Dorothy Janice (Leavitt) LaForge. B.A., Boston U., 1959; M.A., Emory U., 1965. Cert. librarian. Head govt. documents and maps dept. Price Gilbert Meml. Library, Ga. Inst. Tech., Atlanta, 1964—, instr. 1964-72, asst. prof., 1972-76, assoc. prof., 1976—; project dir. Inventor Info. Resource Ctr., 1980-83; mem. depository library council to pub. printer, U.S. Govt. Printing Office, Washington, 1980-83; mem. ad hoc com. on depository library access to fed. automated data bases, 1983—. Contbr. papers to profl. meetings. Mem. ALA, Ga. Library Assn. Democrat. Episcopalian. Home: 1145 W Peachtree St NE Atlanta GA 30309 Office: Price Gilbert Meml Library Ga Inst Tech 225 N Ave Atlanta GA 30334

LEADBETTER, BRUCE C., investment company executive; b. Hugo, Colo., Sept. 4, 1938; s. Merton King and Edith (Cline) L.; student U. Ariz., 1956-57, Mexico City Coll., 1957, No. Ariz. U., 1958-60; divorced; children—Reagan Jessica, Tiffany Amber. Pres., dir. Post Co., Dallas, 1968—; chmn. Exec. Investment Corp., 1966-69; pres. Summit Properties, Inc., 1966—, Kona-Post Corp., 1969—, Aspen-Post Corp., 1969—, The Post Corp., 1969—; pres. Astraea Co., 1982—; chmn. exec. com. Braniff, Inc., 1983—. dir. Tres Vidas En La Playa Inc., Levitz Furniture Co.; chmn., dir. Stores Trading Group, 1978—. Bd. dirs. Salvation Army, 1971-74, March of Dimes, 1982—. Mem. Am. Assn. Small Bus., N. Ariz. Bd. Realtors (pres. 1961-65), Nat. Assn. Ind. Businessmen, Practising Law Inst. Named Outstanding Businessman of Ariz., 1972; hon. citizen Tex., 1966; nominee for Man of Year, Dallas, 1965. Republican. Episcopalian. Clubs: Phoenix Country, Tres Vidas Country. Address: 8140 Walnut Hill Ln Dallas TX 75231

LEAFE, JOSEPH A., mayor. Mayor of Norfolk, Va. Office: 1109 City Hall Bldg Norfolk VA 23501*

LEAGUE, PATRICIA ANNETTE, government researcher, genealogist; b. Kansas City, Mo., Sept. 14, 1948; d. Archie William and Ida Margaret (Wood) League. Student U. Va., 1966-74, Marymount Coll., 1977, Va. Theol. Sem., 1979—. Translator and guide Office Pub. Relations, Dulles Internat. Airport, summer 1966; adminstrv. asst. Fed. govt. agy., 1967-70, research Soviet Studies, 1970—. Active Washington Cathedral Assn., 1965—, Fairfax Hosp. Assn., 1965—, Ct. of Camelot, 1965—. Recipient Service award YWCA Ft. Worth, 1963. Mem. Am. Assn. Advancement Slavic Studies, DAR. Episcopalian. Author: Theories of Education, 1969; A Contemporary Theodicy, 1979; William de Edington: Reluctant Archbishop, 1980; Ties That Bind: Family Celebrations, 1984. Home: 3715 King Arthur Rd Annandale VA 22003 Office: PO Box 6194 McLean VA 22006

LEAL, JOSÉ GILBERTO, educational adminstrator; b. Benavides, Tex., Aug. 5, 1946; s. Juan G. and Maria (Canales) L.; m. Norma Oliveira, Nov. 2, 1968; children—Gilbert, Michael, Ricardo. B.S., North Tex. State U., 1968; M.Edn., Pan Am. U., 1974; postgrad. East Tex. State U., 1981—. Tchr., coach Brownsville Ind. Sch. Dist., Tex., 1968-69; instr. adult basic edn. Tex. State Tech. Inst., Harlingen, 1969-70, dir. admissions, 1970-72, dean student services, 1972-78, campus pres., 1978—; mem. reaffirmation com. So. Assn. Colls. and Schs., Catawba Valley Tech. Coll., Hickory, N.C., 1984, mem. Miami-Dade Community Coll., Miami, Fla., 1985. Mem. sch. bd. Harlingen Ind. Sch. Dist., 1977-80, v.p., 1979-80; mem. adv. com. Inter-First Bank, Harlingen, 1983—; mem. Valley Bapt. Med. Ctr. Found., Harlingen, 1984-85; mem. exec. bd. Boy Scouts Am., Harlingen, 1984-85. Served with Army N.G., 1969-75. Named to Region 1 Honor Bd., Region 1 Edn. Service Ctr., Edinburgh; recipient Cert. of Merit and Excellence, Cameron County Commrs. Ct., Brownsville, 1983. Mem. Am. Vocat. Assn., Tex. Tech Soc. Democrat. Roman Catholic. Club: Civitan (pres. 1976-77). Lodge: Rotary. Avocations: bowling; swimming; cooking; hunting. Office: Tex State Tech Inst PO Box 2628 Harlingen TX 78550

LEAMON, PHIL HARRIS, software company executive; b. Huntsville, Ala., June 8, 1953; s. Annie Pearl (Jacobs) L.; m. Judy Hiner, June 8, 1984; children—Victoria, Christabelle. B.B.A., SUNY-Albany, 1982; M.B.A., So. Meth. U., 1984; M.S. in Mgmt., Columbia Pacific U., 1984. MIS analyst Dept. Army, Washington, 1971-80; ops. supr. Lawson Enterprises, Dallas, 1983-84; product program mgr. UCCL Software Corp., Dallas, 1984—. Served with U.S. Army, 1971-80. Recipient Chmn. of Bd. award UCEL Corp., 1984. Mem. Am. Cons. League, Am. Soc. Tng. and Devel., Nat. Soc. Sales Tng. Execs. Home: 4103 Lawngate Dr Dallas TX 75252

LEATH, JAMES MARVIN, Congressman; b. Henderson, Tex., May 6, 1931; student Kilgore Jr. Coll.; B.B.A., U. Tex., 1954; m. Alta Ruth Neill, 1954; children—Thomas, Jim (dec.). Freshman line coach U. Tex., Austin, 1953-54; football and track coach Henderson High Sch., 1957-59; salesman, 1959-62; banker, from 1962; officer, dir. 5 Tex. banks, 2 mfg. cos.; spl. asst. to Rep. W.R. Poage, 1972-74; mem. 96th Congress from 11th Dist. Tex. Active in community and indsl. devel. in central Tex. Served with U.S. Army, 1954-56. Democrat. Presbyterian (elder). Office: Room 336 Cannon House Office Bldg Washington DC 20515

LEATHERMAN, HUGH KENNETH, SR., state senator, business exec.; b. Lincoln County, N.C., Apr. 14, 1931; s. John Bingham and Ada Annis (Gantt) L.; B.S. in Civil Engring., N.C. State U., Raleigh, 1953; m. Jean Helms, Nov. 11, 1978; children—Sheila Dianne, Hugh Kenneth, Karen Ann, Joyce Lynn, Amy Jean, Sarah Ada. Engr., then sec. Florence Concrete Products Inc. (S.C.), 1955-72, pres., 1972—; pres. Ebb Tide Inc., Myrtle Beach, S.C., 1972—, Atlantic Investments Inc., Myrtle Beach, 1970—, Leisure Inns Inc., Charleston, S.C., 1975—, Pee Dee Block Inc., Marion, S.C., 1975—, Mid-Lands Broadcasting Corp., 1979—; sec. Hugh-Stan Inc., Myrtle Beach, 1974—. Commr. S.C. Dept. Consumer Affairs; mem. S.C. Senate, 1980—. Named Legislator of Yr., 1982. Baptist. Home: Timberlane Dr Country Club of SC Florence SC 29501 Office: PO Box 5506 Florence SC 29502

LEATHERS, RAMSEY BARTHELL, clerk Tennessee Supreme Court; b. Nashville, Oct. 8, 1920; s. John Rucker and Sadie Florence (DeJarnatt) L.; m. Ardis Maurine Freeman, May 8, 1943; children—Ramsey B., Karen Elaine Reddy, Raymond Swen. L.L.B., Cumberland U., 1949. Bar: Tenn. 1949, U.S. Supreme Ct. 1980. Probate master Davidson County Ct., Nashville, 1950-63; clk. Middle Div., Supreme Ct. Tenn., Nashville, 1963—. Served with USAAF, 1941-46. Mem. Nashville Bar Assn., Tenn. Bar Assn. Democrat. Episcopalian. Club: Exchange. Lodges: Masons, Shriners, Elks. Home: 983 Windrowe Dr Nashville TN 37205 Office: 100 Supreme Ct Bldg 7th and Charlotte Sts Nashville TN 37219

LEAVELL, LANDRUM PINSON, II, seminary president, clergyman, educator; b. Ripley, Tenn., Nov. 26, 1926; s. Leonard O. and Annie Glenn (Elias); m. Jo Ann Paris, July 28, 1953; children—Landrum Pinson III, Ann Paris, Roland Q. II, David E. A.B., Mercer U., 1948; B.D., New Orleans Bapt. Theol. Sem., 1951, Th.D., 1954. Pastor Union Bapt. Ch., Magnolia, Miss., Crosby Bapt. Ch. (Miss.), First Bapt. Ch., Charleston, Miss., First Bapt. Ch., Gulfport, Miss., First Bapt. Ch., Wichita Falls, Tex., 1963-75; pres. New Orleans Bapt. Theol. Sem., 1975—. Recipient George Washington Honor medal Freedoms Found., Valley Forge, Pa., 1968. Mem. New Orleans C. of C. Lodge: Rotary. Author: Angels, Angels, Angels, 1973; Sermons for Celebrating, 1978; Twelve Who Followed Jesus, 1975; The Devil and His Domain, 1973; For Prodigals and Other Sinners, 1973; God's Spirit in You, 1974; The Harvest of the Spirit, 1976; John's Letters: Light for Living, 1970; Evangelism: Christ's Imperative Commission, 1979; The Doctrine of the Holy Spirit, 1983. Home: 4111 Seminary Pl New Orleans LA 70126 Office: 3939 Gentilly Blvd New Orleans LA 70126

LEAVITT, HERBERT DOUGLAS, educational administrator; b. Morgantown, Ind., Mar. 14, 1920; s. Herbert Douglas and Irene Edna (Arbegust) L.; m. Gladys Joyce McKoy, Dec. 20, 1948; children—Laurence Douglas, Carole Joy. B.S., Ind. U.-Bloomington, 1948, M.S., 1956, D. Health and Safety, 1964. Tchr., coach Fla. pub. schs., 1948-55; field rep. Ind. Heart Assn., Bloomington, 1956-58, program dir., Indpls., 1958-62; head recreation curriculum Ga. Southern Coll., Statesboro, 1962-68, div. chmn. Health, Phys. Edn. and Recreation, 1968-80, dean Sch. Health, Phys. Edn., Recreation and Nursing, 1980—; bd. dirs. Ga. Bd. Recreation Examiners, Atlanta, 1967-80, chmn. 1967-71. Bd. dirs. Statesboro Recreation Dept., 1972—. Served to sgt. USAF, 1941-45. Recipient Outstanding Recreation Service award Ga. So. Coll., 1967; named Prof. of Yr., Delta Phi Kappa, 1976. Mem. Ga. Recreations and Park Soc. (pres. 1976-77), Profl. of Yr. award 1970), Am. Alliance for Health, Phys. Edn., Recreation and Dance. Democrat. Club: Forest Heights Country (Statesboro) (bd. dirs. 1982—). Lodge: Rotary. Avocations: golf; gardening. Home: 101 Chelsea Circle Statesboro GA 30458 Office: Ga So Coll L B 8073 GSC Statesboro GA 30460

LEAVITT, JOSEPH, orchestral administrator, educator; b. Chelsea, Mass.; s. Abraham and Mildred (Leavitt) L.; m. Sally Elissa, Aug. 30, 1942; children—Howard R., Joan E. Grad. New Eng. Conservatory Music, 1940; student Boston U., 1940-41, Manhattan Sch. Music, 1945-46; A.B., Am. U., 1954; seminars Harvard U. Bus. Sch., 1978-79. Prin. musician Nat. Symphony Orch., Washington, 1949-69, utility pianist, then asst. mgr., until 1969; gen. mgr. N.J. Symphony Orch., Newark, 1969-71; exec. dir., exec. producer Wolf Trap Nat. Park for Performing Arts, Vienna, Va., 1970-73; exec. dir. Balt. Symphony Orch., 1973-84; exec. v.p. Philharm. Orch. of Fla., Ft. Lauderdale, 1984—; chief instr. arts mgmt. U. Md., 1974-76; adj. prof. mgmt. Goucher Coll., 1977-83; former field reader HEW Program for gifted and talented. Author: Reading by Recognition, 1960; The Rhythms of Contemporary Music, 1963. Bd. dirs. Md. Council for Dance, Balt.; mem. Mayor's Adv. Commn. on Art and Culture; mem. exec. com. Regional Cultural Commn. Served to lt. sgt. USAAF, 1942-45. Mem. Internat. Soc. Performing Arts Adminstrs. (dir.), Boston Musicians Assn., Associated Musicians Greater N.Y. Lodge: Rotary (past dir. and chmn. public relations com. Balt.). Office: 1430 N Federal Hwy Fort Lauderdale FL 33304

LEAVITT, MARY JANICE DEIMEL, educator, civic worker; b. Washington, Aug. 21, 1924; d. Henry L. and Ruth (Grady) Deimel; B.A., Am. U., Washington, 1946; postgrad. U. Md., 1963-65, U. Va., 1965-67, George Washington U., 1966-67; m. Robert Walker Leavitt, Mar. 30, 1945; children—Michael Deimel, Robert Walker, Caroline Ann (Mrs. Joseph Paul Snyder). Tchr., Rothery Sch., Arlington, Va., 1947; dir. Sunnyside, Children's House, Washington, 1949; asst. dir. Coop. Sch. for Handicapped Children, Arlington, 1962, dir., Arlington, Springfield, Va., 1963-66; tchr. mentally retarded children Fairfax (Va.) County Public Schs., 1966-68; asst. dir. Burgundy Farm Country Day Sch., Alexandria, Va., 1968-69; tchr. specific learning problem children Accotink Acad., Springfield, Va., 1970-80, now substitute tchr.; also substitute tchr. Children's Achievement Center, McLean, Va., Psychiat. Inst., Washington, 1976-82, Dominion Psychiat. Treatment Center-Devel. Sch., 1980-84; tchr. Home-bound and Substitute Tchrs. program Fairfax County (Va.) Schs., 1979—; asst. research specialist Ednl. Research Service, Inc., Rosslyn, Va., 1974-76. Den mother Nat. Capital Area Cub Scouts, Boy Scouts Am., 1962; troop fund raising chmn. Nat. Capitol council Girl Scouts U.S.A., 1968-69; capt. amblyopia team No. Va. chpt. Delta Gamma Alumnae, 1969; fund raiser Martha Movement, 1977-78; mem. edn. subcom. Va. Commn. Children and Youth, 1973-74; docent Sully Plantation, Fairfax County Park Authority, Fairfax, 1981—; mem. No. Va. Widowed Persons Service, 1983—, sec., 1983-85; vol. Prevention of Blindness Soc., 1980—. Recipient award Nat. Assn. for Retarded Children, 1975. Mem. Assn. Part-Time Profls. (co-chmn. Va. local groups 1980, job devel. mem. 1981-82), Smithsonian Resident Assocs., Older Women's League, AAUW (co-chmn. met. area mass media com. 1973-75, v.p. Alexandria br. 1974-76, fellowship chmn. 1979, mem. Name Grantee Ednl. Found. Springfield-Annandale br. 1980, historian 1980-82, cultural co-chmn. Springfield/Annandale br. 1983-84), Delta Gamma (treas. 1974-76, pres. alumnae chpt. 1977-79, found. chmn. 1979-80). Roman Catholic. Club: Arlington Hall Officer's. Home: 7129 Rolling Forest Ave Springfield VA 22152

LEAZER, GARY HERBERT, religious agency executive; b. Keokuk, Iowa, Dec. 14, 1944; s. Herbert Horace and Delphia Mae (Rube) L.; m. Ruth Marie Bilbo, Aug. 23, 1969; children—David Bilbo, Sonya Lorraine. B.A., Miss. Coll., 1971; M.Div., Southwestern Bapt. Theol. Sem., 1974, Ph.D., 1981; grad. student U. Iowa, 1984. Ordained to ministry Bapt. Ch., 1979; asst. dir. for sects and new religious movements Interfaith Witness Dept., Home Mission Bd. of So. Bapt. Conv., Atlanta, 1979—; teaching fellow Southwestern Bapt. Theol. Sem., Fort Worth, Tex., 1976; adj. prof. Midwestern Bapt. Theol. Sem., Kansas City, Mo., 1979. Served with U.S. Navy, 1965-69. Mem. Am. Acad. Religion, Assn. Bapt. Profs. Religion. Baptist. Contbr. articles to various denominational mags. Office: 1350 Spring St NW Atlanta GA 30367

LEBARON, EDWARD WAYNE, JR., professional football team executive; b. San Rafael, Calif., Jan. 7, 1930; s. Edward Wayne and Mabel Butler (Sims) LeB.; m. Doralee M. Le Baron, June 4, 1954; children—Edward Wayne, William Bruce, Richard Wilson. B.A., Coll. Pacific, 1950; LL.B., George Washington U., 1959. Football quarterback Washington Redskins, 1952-59; admitted to Calif. bar, 1960, Tex. bar, 1960, Nev. bar, 1967; with Dallas Cowboys, 1960-63; exec. v.p. Nevada Cement Co., 1964-65; mem. firm Wynne & Wynne, Dallas, 1960-63; mem. firm Bible, McDonald & Carano, Reno, 1966-68; mem. firm Laxalt & Berry, Carson City, Nev., 1969-70; partner firm Jones, Jones, Bell, LeBaron and Brown, Las Vegas, Nev., 1970-76; gen. mgr. Atlanta Falcons Football team, 1977-82, exec. v.p., 1982—; dir. Tom Brown, Inc., Ormand Industries; partner LeBaron Ranches. Served with USMC, 1950-52. Decorated Purple Heart, Bronze Star. Named Sportsman of Year in Ga., 1978-79. Mem. ABA. Republican. Clubs: Commerce, Capital City. Office: I-85 at Suwanee Rd Suwanee GA 30174*

LEBAUER, SAM MORGENSTERN, physician; b. Greensboro, N.C., July 4, 1938; s. Sidney Ferring and Sophie (Morgenstern) LeB.; B.A., Duke U., 1961; M.D., U. Va., 1967; m. Joan Luchs, June 22, 1963; children—Cynthia Anne, Karen Elizabeth. Intern in medicine Sinai Hosp., Balt., 1968-69; resident Ohio State U., Columbus, 1969-70, gastroentology fellow, 1970-71; resident in gastroenterology Walter Reed Army Med. Center, 1971-74; practice medicine specializing in gastroenterology, Greensboro, 1974—; clin. asst. prof. Sch. Medicine, U. N.C.; mem. staff Cone Hosp., Greensboro. Trustee, Greensboro City Council; bd. dirs. L. Richardson Hosp., Eastern Music Festival, United Jewish Appeal, Goodwill Industries, Temple Emanuel, Greensboro. Mem. Guilford County Med. Soc., Greensboro Med. Soc., ACP, N.C. Soc. Internal Medicine, Am. Soc. Gastrointestinal Endoscopy. Republican. Jewish. Clubs: Woodmont Country (Washington); Greensboro Country. Home: 1519 Burlwood Dr Greensboro NC 27410 Office: 1409 Pembroke St Greensboro NC 27408

LEBLANC, JOSEPH URLAN, management engineering executive; b. Couteaux, La., Mar. 17, 1937; s. A. Bernard and Levie (Broussard) LeB.; m. Elizabeth Holder, June 11, 1960; children—Mark J., Kathleen A. B.S., Southwestern La. Inst., 1959; M. Computing Sci., Tex. A&M U., 1969, M. Engring., 1972, M.B.A., 1972, D. Engring., 1981. Registered profl. engr., Tex.; cert. data processor. Program analyst Aero Chart and Info. Ctr., St. Louis, 1960-63; test and evaluation specialist 465L Systems Program Office, Bedford, Mass., 1963-64; research and devel. mgr. Electronics Systems, Bedford, 1964-66; lead systems analyst Humble Oil & Refining, Houston, 1966-68; cons. Tex. A&M U., College Station, 1968-70, program mgr. BLM program office, 1978-81; ops. mgr. Tex. Data Ctr., Bryan, 1971-72; exec. dir. Master Planning Assocs., College Station, 1972-77; project mgr. Brown & Root, Inc., Houston, 1977-78; prin., dir. LeBlanc Cons. Services, College Station, 1981—. Pres., bd. dirs. St. Mary Cath. Ch., College Station, 1968-81; mem. Town Meeting Com., Bryan-College Station, 1976; mem. Communication Com., College Station, 1979-83; tour dir. Internat. Youth Festival Trip, College Station, 1981-82. Served to lt. col. USAFR, 1983—. Tex. A&M U. fellow, 1970-71. Mem. Nat. Soc. Profl. Engrs., Tex. Soc. Profl. Engrs., Inst. Indsl. Engrs., Project Mgmt. Inst., Am. Assn. Cost Engrs., Am. Soc. Mgmt. Engring., Res. Officers Assn., Inst. Cert. Computer Profls., Upsilon Pi Epsilon, Alpha Pi Mu, Sigma Pi Epsilon. Republican. Avocations: travel; hunting; sports; camping; cooking. Home: 902 Holik Dr S College Station TX 77840-3022

LEBLANC, LARRY JOSEPH, management educator; b. New Orleans, July 21, 1947; s. J. Wilfred and Mary (Lachin) LeB.; m. Marguerite Jarreau, Sept. 6, 1969; children—Aimee, Sara. B.S., Loyola U., New Orleans, 1969; M.S., Northwestern U., 1971, Ph.D., 1973. Assoc. prof. So. Meth. U., Dallas, 1973-80; assoc. prof. Owen Grad. Sch. Mgmt., Vanderbilt U., Nashville, 1980—; cons. Dr. Pepper Co., Dallas, 1977, U.S. Army Inventory Research Office, Phila., 1979-82, Trailways, Dallas, 1979, Miss. Chem. Co., Yazoo City, 1980-81, U.S. Dept. Transp., 1981-83; vis. prof. U. Chile, Santiago, 1978, Linkoping Inst. Tech., Sweden, 1980, U. Ulm, Fed. Republic Germany, 1981-82, 84-85, Technion, Haifa, Israel, 1984. Author: (with L. Cooper, U. Bhat) Introduction to Operations Research Models, 1977. Contbr. articles to profl. jours. Editorial adv. bd. Transp. Research, 1973—. Served to capt. U.S. Army, 1972-73. Research grantee NSF, 1980-83, U.S. Dept. Transp., 1979-80. Mem. Inst. Mgmt. Scis., Ops. Research Soc. Am. (chmn. transp. sci. sect. 1984—). Republican. Roman Catholic. Avocations: instrument flying, skin diving, photography, jogging. Home: 424 Manor View Ln Brentwood TN 37027 Office: Owen Grad Sch of Mgmt 401 21st Ave S Nashville TN 37203

LE BLANC, LEONA LACY, mental health center administrator; b. Scott, La., July 15, 1935; d. Percy and Rena Marie (Breaux) Lacy; student S.W. La. Vocat. Sch., Port Arthur Coll., U. Southwestern La., La. State U.; m. Thomas Clayton LeBlanc, Feb. 19, 1955; children—Thomas, Michael, Holly. Various secretarial and office positions, 1956-60; staff mem. Acadiana Mental Health Center, Lafayette, La., 1960—, adminstrv. asst., 1973-75, exec. asst., 1976-81, bus. adminstr., 1981—. Active local PTA; religious instr. Roman Catholic Ch., 1963-67, Reach Program instr., reader, 1983—. Recipient Dunbar award La. Civil Service League, 1980. Mem. La. Personnel Council, La. Hosp. Assn. Soc. Personnel Dirs., La. Assn. Retarded Citizens (dir., membership chmn. Lafayette chpt. 1979-81), Profl. Secs. Internat. (pres. Azalea chpt. 1976-77). Democrat. Office: 400 St Julien St Lafayette LA 70506

LEBLANC, SHARON ANNE, geophysicist; b. Balt., Oct. 2, 1957; d. Dalex Joseph and Eleanor Jane (Navarria) LeB. B.S., Pa. State U., 1979. Geophysicist Texaco, Inc., Bellaire, Tex., 1979-84, New Orleans, 1984—. Mem. Bread for the World, Washington, 1985. Mem. Assn. Am. Petroleum Geologists, Assn. Women Geoscientists. Democrat. Mem. Vineyard Christian Fellowship. Club: Bibl. Archaeology (Washington). Avocations: ballet; hiking; horseback-riding; photography; camping; backpacking. Office: Texaco Inc PO Box 60252 New Orleans LA 70160

LEBOUEF, CATHY FAKIER, auditor; b. Houma, La., Oct. 11, 1956; d. Richard George and Barbara Jean (Gaidry) Fakier; m. Ronald Joseph LeBouef, Jr., Apr. 26, 1985. B.S. in Acctg., Nicholls State U., 1978. With Terrebonne Bank & Trust Co., Houma, 1978—, EDP auditor, 1981—. Loaned exec. United Way, Houma, 1981. Mem. Nat. Assn. Bank Women, Bank Adminstrn. Inst. (cert. in bank EDP auditing), Inst. Internal Auditors, Vandebilt Catholic High Sch. Alumni Assn., Delta Zeta. Democrat. Roman Catholic. Club: Krewe of Aphrodite (Houma). Avocations: racquetball; golf; water skiing; photography. Home: 921 School St Houma LA 70360 Office: Terrebonne Bank & Trust Co 720 E Main St Houma LA 70360

LEBOWITZ, JACOB, biochemistry educator; b. N.Y.C., Oct. 20, 1935; s. Morris and Minnie (Gross) L.; m. Ellen Perlman, Apr. 2, 1967 (div. 1974); m. Candace Ridington, June 1, 1978. B.S. in Chemistry, Bklyn. Coll., 1957; Ph.D. in Chemistry Purdue U., 1962. Postdoctoral fellow Calif. Inst. Tech., Pasadena, 1962-66; from asst. prof. to assoc. prof. Syracuse U., N.Y., 1966-74; from assoc. prof. to prof. microbiology U. Ala.-Birmingham, 1974—. Contbr. articles to profl. jours. Recipient Research Career Devel. award Nat. Cancer Inst., 1972-77; Am. Cancer Soc. scholar, 1982-83. Mem. Am. Soc. Biol. Chemists, Am. Soc. Microbiology, AAAS, Fedn. Am. Scientists. Democrat. Office: U Ala-Birmingham 520 CHSB Birmingham AL 35294

LECKLITNER, MYRON LYNN, nuclear physician; b. Canton, Ohio, June 16, 1942; s. Myron Devoy and Margaret (Koon) L.; m. Carol Vance, Sept. 1979; 1 child, Tonja Ann. B.S. in Acctg., Pa. State U., 1964; B.S. in Chemistry and Biology, U. Ala., 1970, M.D., 1974. Diplomate Am. Bd. Nuclear Medicine. Intern Lloyd Noland Hosp., Birmingham, Ala., 1974-75, resident in internal medicine, 1975-77; resident in nuclear medicine, U. Ala.-Birmingham, 1977-79; asst. prof. U. Tex.-San Antonio, 1979-83; assoc. prof. U. South Ala., Mobile, 1983—, dir. diagnostic imaging div., 1984—. Contbr. chpts. to books, articles to profl. jours. Served to capt. U.S. Army, 1964-67. Decorated Bronze Star medal, 1966, Army Commendation medal, 1966, Air medal, 1966. Mem. Am. Coll. Nuclear Physicians (vice chmn. fin. com. 1985—, vice chmn. membership com. 1985—), Ala. Soc. Nuclear Medicine (pres. 1985-86). Avocation: photography. Home: 5505 Oak Park Ct Mobile AL 36609 Office: U South Ala Dept Radiology 2451 Fillingim St MSN 301 Mobile AL 36617

LECKY, WILLIAM RALSTON, III, electrical engineer; b. Richmond, Va., July 8, 1940; s. William Ralston and Allene (Pace) L.; B.S. in Elec. Engring., Va. Poly. Inst., 1963; m. Susan Evans Hearn, June 6, 1964; children—Jennifer Jill, Kathryn Pace, Susan Arrington. Assoc. engr., plant engring. Mobile (Ala.) Mill, Internat. Paper Co., 1963-64, project engr., 1966-68, sr. project engr., central design engring., 1968-74, design engr., 1974-76, sr. design engr., 1976-78, supr. engring. sers. Natchez (Miss.) Mill, 1978-81, supt. maintenance and engring., 1981, supt. operational services, 1981-83, mgr. operational services, 1983-86, mgr. maintenance services, 1986—. Adviser, Jr. Achievement, 1967-68; active United Fund Canvass, 1971-72; v.p. Mobile Soap Box Derby, Inc., 1972-73. Bd. dirs. Greater Gulf State Fair, Inc., 1972-77, chmn. bd., 1977, chief engr., mgr. constrn. new fair grounds, 1973-74, pres. Greater Gulf State Fair, 1975. Served to 1st lt. U.S. Army, 1964-66. Registered profl. engr., Miss., Ala. Mem. IEEE (sr. mem., sect. treas. 1971-72, sec. 1972-73, vice chmn. 1973-74, chmn. 1974-75), Va. Tech. Alumni Assn., Mobile Jr. C. of C. (sec. 1971-72, bd. dirs. 1974, 75, 77), Natchez C. of C., Omicron Delta Kappa. Baptist. Clubs: Belwood Country, Delta Yacht (commodore 1981). Home: #1 Village Pl Natchez MS 39120 Office: PO Box 311 Natchez MS 39120

LE CORGNE, RICHARD KENNETH, insurance company official, consultant sales and investments; b. New Orleans, Nov. 2, 1943; s. Earl Raymond and Isabelle Marie (de los Reyes) Le C.; m. Mary Ellen Smyer, Dec. 17, 1966; children—Richard Kenneth, Michelle Elizabeth. B.A., U. New Orleans, 1965. Vice pres. Tele Tector of La., New Orleans, 1969-71; trainer, agt. Mut. of N.Y., New Orleans, 1971-77; sales mgr. Life of Va., New Orleans, 1977-79; unit supr. Provident Mut. Life Ins. Co., New Orleans, 1979-80; agy. supr. Conn. Mut. Life Ins. Co., New Orleans, 1981-84; gen. agt. CM Alliance, New Orleans, 1984—. Contbr. articles to profl. jours. Ambassador Life Underwriters Polit. Action Com., 1983-86; bd. dirs. Lafreniere Park Found., Metairie, La., 1985-86; pres. Friends of Lafreniere Park, Metairie, 1985-86. Mem. New Orleans Life Underwriters Assn. (dir. 1983-86), New Orleans Gen. Agts. and Mgrs. Assn. (bd. dirs. 1985-87), Assn. C.L.U.s (bd. dirs. New Orleans chpt. 1985—), New Orleans Life Underwriters Assn. (chmn. legis. com. 1983—), New Orleans Health Underwriters Assn. Democrat. Roman Catholic. Avocations: tennis; the arts; fishing; photography; art. Home: 328 E Livingston Pl Metairie LA 70005 Office: CM Alliance 3636 One Shell Sq New Orleans LA 70139

LECRONE-CHURCH, SALLY CAROLINE, educator; b. Wewoka, Okla., July 23, 1934; d. Elvis Avir and Geneva Cloe (Holmes) Miller; B.S., U. Okla., 1961, M.Ed., 1971; m. Gerlad D. Church, Feb. 14, 1981 (div.); children—David, Pamela (dec.), Greg, Jeffrey, Molly. Tchr. emotionally disturbed children in Okla., 1961-73; mem. psychology staff Phil Smalley Children's Center, Norman, Okla., 1973—, prin., 1976—; assoc. prof. Oklahoma City U., 1974-76; instr. U. Okla., 1981—; owner LeCrone-Church Enterprises, car leasing. Cons., speaker, trainer in field. Adv. bd. Norman Alcohol Info. Center; bd. dirs. Wonder House Day Care Center, Norman, Cleveland County Mental Health Assn. Worry Clinic, 1978. Mem. Nat. Assn. Female Execs., Nat. Council Exceptional Children, NEA, Okla. Women in Edn. Adminstrn., Okla. Sch. Psychologists Assn., Okla. Group Process Soc., Okla. Edn. Assn., Nat. Council Children with Behavior Disorders, Nat. Council Adminstrs. Spl. Edn., Nat. Council Ednl. Diagnostic Services, Okla. Profls. for Emotionally Disturbed Profl. Educators Norman, Nat. Council Accreditation of Tchr. Edn. (evaluator), Hi-Noon Bus. and Profl. Women, Norman C. of C., Gamma Phi Beta, Phi Delta Kappa, Sigma Beta Phi. Democrat. Episcopalian. Home: 1429 Homeland St Norman OK 73069 Office: Box 1008 Norman OK 73070

LEDBETTER, PAUL MARK, lawyer; b. San Francisco, Oct. 14, 1947; s. John Paul and Joyce (Mayo) L.; m. Jerald Ann Broyles, Sept. 18, 1971; children—Paul Mark, Sarah Broyles. B.A. in English, Ouachita Bapt. U., 1970; J.D., U. Ark., 1973. Bar: Ark. 1974, U.S. Dist. Ct. (ea. dist.) Ark. 1974, U.S. Ct. Appeals (8th cir.) 1974. Assoc. Frierson, Walker, Snellgrove & Laser, Jonesboro, Ark., 1974-77, ptnr., 1977-82; pres. Mark Ledbetter, P.A., Jonesboro, 1982—. Co-founder St. Mark's Episcopal Day Sch., Jonesboro, 1978; mem. vestry St. Mark's Episcopal Ch., 1979; mem. Forum Commn. City of Jonesboro, 1978-80. Conservation Found. grantee, 1976; Rotary Internat. grantee, Japan, 1979. Mem. Ark. Bar Assn. (mem. tort reform com. 1980, ho. of dels. 1979-80), Ark. Trial Lawyers Assn. (chmn. amicus curiae com. 1980-81, gov. 1980—), Jonesboro C. of C. (bd. dirs. 1978-80). Democrat. Episcopalian. Office: 402 S Main St Jonesboro AR 72401 also 7th Floor Cotton Exchange Bldg 65 Union Ave Memphis TN

LEDBETTER, RICKEY GLENN, food company executive; b. Anniston, Ala., Sept. 5, 1957; s. Truby L. and Doris Lorene (Mullinex) L.; m. Sabrina Dean Summers, Aug. 19, 1976; children—Lindsey Jane, Tyler Ross. B.S. in Human Resource Mgmt., U. Ala., 1982. Chief process operator Monsanto Co., Anniston, Ala., 1977-84; mgr. edn. and tng. Flowers Industries, Inc., Thomasville, Ga., 1984—. Mem. Am. Soc. Personnel Adminstrn., Am. Soc. Tng. and Devel., Am. Mgmt. Assn. Republican. Presbyterian. Office: Flowers Industries Inc US 19 S Thomasville GA 31792-1338

LEDBETTER-STRAIGHT, NORA KATHLEEN, insurance company executive; b. Gary, Ind., May 11, 1934; d. Jacob F. and Nora I. (Bollen) Moser; student U. Houston, 1954-58; m. Robert L. Straight, Aug. 9, 1975; 1 dau., Cindy Kathleen Ledbetter Baurax. Vice pres. Hindman Mortgage Co., Inc., Houston, 1960-70, also mng. ptnr. Assocs. Ins. Agy.; corp. sec. N.Am. Mortgage Co., Houston, 1970—; pres. N.Am. Ins. Agy., 1970—; v.p., sec. Better Bodies of Tex., Inc., 1983—; ins. counselor Houston Apt. Assn., 1978—, dir. product service council, 1981—. C.P.C.U.; cert. Ins. Inst. Am., Soc. Cert. Ins. Counselors. Mem. Ind. Ins. Agts. Am., Soc. Cert. Ins. Counselors, Soc. C.P.C.U.s, Community Assocs. Inst. (dir. 1976-80), Ind. Ins. Agts. Tex., Ind. Ins. Agts. Houston (dir. 1974-78). Republican. Methodist. Author curriculum materials in field. Office: 900 Threadneedle Houston TX 77079

LEDEBUR, LINAS VOCKROTH, JR., lawyer, trust company executive; b. New Brighton, Pa., June 18, 1925; s. Linas Vockroth and Mae McCabe L.; student Geneva Coll., 1943, 45-46, Muhlenberg Coll., 1943; LL.B., J.D., U. Pitts, 1949; m. Connie Ryan, July 3, 1969; children—Gary, Sally, Nancy, Sandra. Bar: Pa. 1950. Ptnr. firm Ledebur, McClain & Ledebur, New Brighton, 1950-63; trust mktg. mgr. Valley Nat. Bank Ariz., 1963-72; ptnr. firm Ledebur & Ledebur, then Ledebur, Petrush & Young, New Brighton, 1972-76; sr. v.p., mgr. state trust div. Fla. Nat. Banks of Fla. Inc., 1976-81; sr. v.p. Fla. Nat. Bank, Jacksonville, 1977-81; sr. v.p. R. Rowlin & Assocs., Jacksonville and Tucson, 1981-82; pres. Northeastern Trust Co. of Fla., N.A., 1982-86; exec. v.p. PNCTRUST Co. of Fla., N.A., 1986—; lectr. in field. Chmn. Beaver County chpt. Nat. Found.-March of Dimes, 1950-63; chmn. com. on corrections Pa. Citizens Assn., 1958-63; dir., counsel Beaver County Mental Health Assn., 1960-63; bd. dirs. ARC, Maricopa County, Ariz., 1970-72. Served with USMC, 1943-45, 51-53. Recipient Partner in Sci. award Salk Inst. Mem. ABA, Pa. Bar Assn., Central Ariz. Estate Planning Council (past pres.), Fla. Bankers Assn. Republican. Clubs: Vero Beach Yacht, Moorings (Vero Beach, Fla.); University, Ponte Vedra. Home: 2102 Via Fuentes Vero Beach FL 32963 Office: 3003 Cardinal Dr PO Box 4026 Vero Beach FL 32964

LEDERBERG, AMY RUTH, psychology educator; b. N.Y.C., Feb. 5, 1953; d. Philip Michael and Yvette (Brown) L. B.A., Smith Coll., 1974; Ph.D., U. Minn., 1981. Asst. prof. psychology U. Tex.-Dallas, Richardson, 1981—. Mem. Am. Psychol. Assn., Soc. for Research in Child Devel. Office: Dept Psychology GR 41 U Tex-Dallas Richardson TX 75080

LEDERMAN, JOANN VOLK, marriage, family and group therapist, consultant; b. N.Y.C., Jan. 9, 1942; d. Cecil Sussman and Audrey Elaine (Morgen) V.; m. Alan Lederman, Aug. 4, 1963; children—Elizabeth, Michael, John. B.S., Syracuse U., 1962; M.S., U. Miami, Fla., 1979; postgrad. Psychoanalytic Inst., 1981. Lic. marriage and family therapist; cert. marriage and family specialist. Researcher, writer Sta. WTVJ, Miami, Fla., 1979-80; psychotherapist Epilepsy Found., Miami, 1979-81; psychol. cons. P.M. Mag., Miami, 1981-83; psychotherapist Family Life Ctr., Miami, 1981-82; pvt. practice marriage and family therapy South Miami Psychology Assocs., Miami, 1982—, dir. edn., 1982—, clin. dir., 1982—; assertion trainer U. Miami, 1980-81. Author, facilitator workshop series. Trustee Palmer Sch., Miami, 1985—; bd. dirs. Temple Beth Am Day Sch., Miami, 1975-80; fundraiser Epilepsy Found., Miami, 1979-81. Mem. Am. Assn. Counseling and Devel., Am. Assn. Marriage and Family Therapists, Assn. Specialists in Group Work, Fla. Assn. Marriage and Family Therapists, African Art Soc. (pres. 1984—). Clubs: King's Bay (Miami); Ocean Reef (Key Largo, Fla.). Avocations: scuba diving; skiing; painting. Home: 5860 SW 117th St Miami FL 33156 Office: South Miami Psychology Assocs 7800 Red Rd Suite 205A Miami FL 33143

LEDOCK, ARTHUR H., JR., physician's assistant; b. Jacksonville, Fla., Feb. 15, 1922; s. Arthur H. and Lydia LeD.; B.S., U. S.C., 1941; m. Gertrude Walker, June 4, 1961; children—Lynda, Elizabeth, James, Cynthia, Carol Ann. Physician's asst. VA, Augusta, Ga., 1953-61, Dept. Justice, Montgomery, Ala., 1969-72; physician's asst. State of Miss., Meridian, 1972-79, East Miss. State Hosp., Meridian, 1972—. Served with USNR, 1941-46. Decorated Silver Star, Purple Heart medal. Democrat. Mem. Pentecostal Holiness Ch. Address: PO Box 48 Quitman MS 39355

LEDOUX, JACK, author, ret. race track exec.; b. Orlando, Fla., Oct. 4, 1928; s. Leonard K. and Louise (Downs) L.; B.S. in Journalism, U. Fla., 1950; m. Lenita C. Riles, Sept. 22, 1981; children—Michele, Lance, Stephen, Lola. Sportswriter, columnist Orlando Sentinel-Star, 1948-53; pub. relations dir. Sarasota, Daytona Beach (Fla.) Kennel Clubs, 1953-55; gen. mgr., corp. sec. Sanford-Orlando Kennel Club, 1955-72; gen. mgr., exec. v.p. Black Hills Kennel Club, Rapid City, S.D., 1964-71; pres., co-owner Exec. Travel, Winter Park, Fla., 1977—, Triex Enterprises, Inc., Winter Park, 1977—; ind. editorial columnist, free-lance writer, 1972—; dir. Center Stage. Mem. Fla. Golf Assn. (chmn. adv. com. 1964-65, dir., pres.), Am. Greyhound Track Operators Assn. (publ. and supervisory com. Am. Greyhound Racing Ency., pub. 1963; nat. pres.), World Racing Fedn. (chmn.), World Greyhound Racing Fedn. (pres.), U. Fla. Alumni Assn. (past pres. Sarasota County chpt.), Sigma Delta Chi, Theta Chi. Democrat. Clubs: Univ., Country; Winter Park (Fla.) Racquet. Home: PO Box 2127 Winter Park FL 32790

LEDOUX, JOHN CLARENCE, law enforcement official; b. Muskogee, Okla. Oct. 19, 1944; s. Clarence Watson and Nedra Ruth (Dayton) LeD.; m. Anne Marie Sommervold, Aug. 8, 1970; children—Matthew Watson, Justin William Clay. B.A., U. Md., 1967; M. Criminal Justice, Auburn U., 1977, Ed.D., 1980. Spl. agt. FBI, Albany, N.Y., 1971, Binghamton, N.Y., 1972, Opelika, Ala., 1972-80, supervisory spl. agt., Quantico, Va., 1980—. Author: (with others) A Study of Factors Influencing the Continuing Education of Law Enforcement Officers, 1942. Editor Law Enforcement Tng. Network, 1983—. Mem. Stafford County Parks and Recreation Commn., Stafford, Va., 1982—, chmn., 1983, 85, 86. Served to capt. USMC, 1967-71, Vietnam. Recipient Jeffersonian award U. Va., 1982. Mem. Am. Soc. for Tng. and Devel., Acad. Criminal Justice Scis., Assn. for Devel. of Computer-Based Instructional Systems. Lutheran. Club: Stafford Soccer (coach 1983—). Avocations: Tae Kwan Do; soccer; tennis; magic. Office: Econ and Fin Crimes Tng Unit FBI Acad Quantico VA 22135

LE DUC, ALBERT LOUIS, JR., college administrator; b. Montgomery, Ala., Feb. 1, 1937; s. Albert Louis and Rachel Nancy (Wineinger) LeD.; student Duke U., 1954-55; B.A., Fla. State U., 1958, M.S., 1960; m. Ellen Heath, June 18, 1960; children—Albert Louis III, Charles Andrew. Civilian mathematician Army Rocket Guided Missile Agy., Huntsville, Ala., 1958, 59; mathematician analyst RCA Service Co., Patrick AFB, Fla., 1960-63, programming leader, 1963-67, project mgr., Eglin AFB, Fla., 1967-69, mktg. adminstr., Cherry Hill, N.J., 1969-71; tech. dir. Ind. U., Bloomington, 1971-77; dir. analysis programming Miami-Dade Community Coll., Miami, Fla., 1977-81, dir. computer services planning and analysis, 1981—; part-time instr. Fla. State U., 1958-60, Brevard Engring. Coll., 1961-62, Ind. U., 1972-77. Bd. dirs. Coll. and Univ. Machine Records Conf., 1979-85. Mem. Assn. Computing Machinery (Best Paper award 1973). Author: The Computer for Managers, 1972. Home: 10321 SW 107th St Miami FL 33176 Office: 11011 SW 104th St Miami FL 33176

LEE, ALFRED HARRISON, III, clergyman; b. Estelline, Tex., Mar. 11, 1932; s. Alfred Harrison and Lillie Mae (Thompson) L. B.A., Tex. Christian U., 1954; M.A., U. Ala., 1955; M.Div., Episcopal Theol. Sch., 1959. Ordained to ministry Episcopal Ch., 1959. Instr., U. Ala., 1955-56; priest in charge Karkloof Parish, Natal, South Africa, 1959-61; met. sec. United Soc. Christian Lit., London, 1962-65; hon. chaplain St. Bride's, London, 1964—; rector St. Luke's, Denison, Tex., 1965-70, Christ Ch., Dallas, 1970—; dean No. Deanery, 1967-70, Dallas Deanery, 1971-74, 83-84; chmn. Commn. on Ministry, 1971-83. Trustee, Deaconess Crow Found., 1970—, Episcopal Sem., Austin, 1980-83; bd. dirs. ARC, Dallas, 1975—. Republican. Episcopalian. Club: Athenaeum (London). Author: Window on Asia, 1963; Agony of Africa, 1964. Office: 534 W 10th St Dallas TX 75208

LEE, ANDRE L., hospital administrator; b. Detroit, Aug. 14, 1943; s. Clyde and Laura D. (Davis) L.; m. Katrina (div.); children—Andre, Bryan, Tracey, Robyn. B.S., Mich. State U., 1966; M.P.A., Cornell U., 1972; D.P.A., Nova U., Fort Lauderdale, 1978. Cert. med. technologist Am. Soc. Clin. Pathologists. Adminstr., Highland Park Hosp., Mich., 1972-76; adminstr. Sumby Hosp., River Rouge, Mich., 1976-78; asst. adminstr. St. Joseph Hosp., Fort Wayne, Ind., 1978-81; adminstr. Hubbard Hosp., Nashville, 1981—; asst. prof. Shaw Coll., Detroit, 1976-77; assoc. prof. Ind. U. Grad. Sch., Fort Wayne, 1978-80; adj. prof. Eastern U., Ann Arbor, Mich., 1976-78; asst. prof. Meharry Med. Coll., Nashville, 1981—. Author: Teach Your Child Healthy Habits, 1978; newspaper/cartoonist: Frost Illustrated, 1978-79. Contr. articles to profl. jours. Served to capt. U.S. Army, 1968-70. Fellow Am. Coll. Hosp. Adminstrn. (numerous coms.), Am. Acad. Med. Adminstrn. (state bd. dirs. 1981—); mem. Nat. Assn. Health Sci. Execs. (pres. 1985), NAACP. Methodist. Club: Optimist (River Rouge). Avocation: cartooning. Home: 7528 Rolling River Pkwy Nashville TN 37221 Office: Hubbard Hosp 1005 18th Ave N Nashville TN 37208

LEE, ANITA ANN, college administrator, counselor; b. Pine Bluff, Ark., Mar. 31, 1954; d. James Laurns and Velma Gean (Reynolds) L.; m. Charles Douglas Flynn, Oct. 26, 1985. Student NE La. State U., 1972-73; B.S. in Edn., U. Ark., 1976, M.S. in Higher Edn., 1977; postgrad. U. Va., 1981—. Asst. dir. Office of Residence Life, La. State U., Baton Rouge, 1977-81; housing coordinator Washington Ctr., 1983-84; research asst. U. Va., Charlottesville, 1981—. Contbg. author: Directory of Campus Business Linkages, 1983. Mem. Am. Coll. Personnel Assn., Phi Delta Kappa. Democrat. Baptist. Avocations: travel; cooking. Home: 4102 Hazel St Pine Bluff AR 71603

LEE, ANITA MARIE, pharmaceutical company official, educator; b. Sanford, N.C., Apr. 29, 1951; d. Julian Cornell and Ruth Agnes (Stewart) L. B.S., Cheyney (Pa.) State U. 1973; postgrad. Ga. State U., 1978. Cert. tchr., Ga. Tchr., Archdiocese of Phila., 1973-76, Phila. Bd. Edn., 1976-77; dir. edn. Lou Hudson Youth Devel. Program, Atlanta, 1982-83; cons., 1983; asst. dir. Nat. Football League Players Assn., Washington, 1979-82; tchr. Fulton County Bd. Edn., Atlanta, 1977-83; pharm. rep., Ga., 1983—. Contbr. articles to profl. jours. Bd. dirs. Ga. Assn. Retarded Citizens, Atlanta, 1983. Recipient award of appreciation Nat. Football League Players Assn., 1980; cert. of appreciation Mayor Maynard Jackson, Atlanta, 1981. Mem. Nat. Assn. Pharm. Reps., Ga. Assn. Educators, NEA, AAUW, NAACP. Democrat. Methodist. Home: 1522 Shoreham Dr Apt E College Park GA 30349

LEE, ANNE NATALIE, nurse; b. Bklyn.; d. Taras Pavlovich and Maria (Jukovskaya) Dubovick; B.A., Hunter Coll., 1940; M.A., N.Y.U., 1948; R.N., McLean Hosp.-Mass. Gen. Hosp. Sch. Nursing, Waverly, 1946; M.S., Boston U., 1958; m. Henry Lee, Feb. 20, 1945; adopted children—Alice, Jennifer, Philip. Pvt. duty nurse, N.Y.C., 1946-48; staff nurse Vis. Nurse Service, 1947-48; staff nurse health dept. Schoharie Co., N.Y., 1948-51; supervising nurse N.Y. Dept. Health, Syracuse, 1951-53, cons. hosp. nursing, Albany, 1958-63, cons. nurse in service edn., 1963-75, dir. Bur. of Hosp. Nursing Services, 1975-80; cons. nursing services and adminstrn., 1980—; dir., coordinator nursing service instr. program co-sponsored N.Y. State Dept. Health, N.Y. State Hosp., Assn., N.Y. State League Nursing, N.Y. State Nurses Assn., 1954-57; sometimes lectr. Mem. Sigma Theta Tau. Contbr. articles to profl. jours. Home and Office: 1149 Hillsboro Mile Hillsboro Beach FL 33062

LEE, BETTY REDDING, architect; b. Shreveport, La., Dec. 6, 1919; d. Joseph Alsop and Mary (Byrd) Redding; student La. State U., 1936-37, 37-38, U. Calif. War Extension Coll., San Diego, 1942-43; student Centenary Coll., 1937; grad. Roofing Industry Ednl. Inst., 1980, 81, 82; m. Frank Cayce Lee, Nov. 22, 1940 (dec. Aug. 1978); children—Cayce Redding, Clifton Monroe, Mary Byrd (Mrs. Kent Ray). Sheetmetal worker Consol.-Vultee, San Diego, 1942; engring. draftsman, 1943-45; jr. to sr. archtl. draftsman Bodman & Murrell, Baton Rouge, 1945-55; sr. archtl. draftsman to architect Post & Harelson, Baton Rouge, 1955-60; asso. architect G. Ross Murrell, Jr., Baton Rouge, 1960-66; staff architect Charles E. Schwing & Assos., Baton Rouge, 1966-71, Kenneth C. Landry, Baton Rouge, 1971, 73-74; design draftsman Rayner & McKenzie, Baton Rouge, 1972-73; cons. architect and planner, div. engring. and cons. services, La. Dept. Health and Human Resources, Baton Rouge, 1974—; architect La. Dept. Facility Planning and Control, 1982—; founding mem. La. Inst. Bldg. Scis., 1980—. Mem. La. Assn. Children with Learning Disabilities, 1970-71, Multiple Sclerosis Soc., 1963-82, CPA Aux., 1960-69, PTA, 1953-66; troop leader Brownies and Girl Scouts U.S.A., 1959-60; asst. den mother Cub Scouts, 1955-57. Licensed architect, real estate counselor, La. Mem. AIA, La. Architects Assn., Nat. Fire Protection Assn., Constrn. Specifications Inst. (charter mem. Baton Rouge chpt.), Miss. Roofing Contractors Assn. (hon.), ASTM, Nat. Roofing Contractors Assn., La. Inst. Bldg. Scis. (founding mem.), Jr. League Baton Rouge. Baton Rouge Caledonian Soc., DAR, Kappa Delta. Democrat. Episcopalian. Clubs: Fais Do Do, Le Salon du Livre. Co-author: Building Owners Guide for Protecting and Maintaining Built-Up Roofing Systems, 1981. Designed typical La. country store for La. Arts and Sci. Center Mus. Home: 1994 Longwood Dr Baton Rouge LA 70808 Office: Box 44095 Capitol Station Baton Rouge LA 70804

LEE, CLAUDE RONALD, dentist, educator; b. Kenova, W.Va., July 1, 1942; s. James Mason and Virginia Kathryn (Howell) L.; m. Lucretia Ann Mellon, June 14, 1969; 1 child, Jenna Elizabeth. B.A. in Chemistry, U. Ky., 1964; D.M.D., U. Ky., 1969. Staff dentist VA Hosp., Ft. Wayne, Ind., 1971-78; sr. staff dentist VA Med. Ctr., Huntington, W.Va., 1978—; clin. instr. W.Va. U. Dental Sch., Morgantown, 1979—. Mem. ADA, Ky. Dental Assn., Eastern Dental Soc. Democrat. Mem. Ch. of God. Avocations: computer programming; religious teaching. Home: 2829 Crestview Dr Catlettsburg KY 41129 Office: VA Med Ctr Spring Valley Dr Huntington WV 25704

LEE, DAN M., state supreme court justice; b. Petal, Miss., Apr. 19, 1926; m. Mary Alice Gray; children—Sheron Lee Anderson, Dan M. Grad. U. So. Miss.; J.D., Jackson Sch. Law. Bar: Miss. 1948. Pvt. practice, 1948-71; county judge, 1971-77; judge 7th cir. dist. Hinds and Yazoo Counties, 1977-82; justice Miss. Supreme Ct., Jackson, 1982—; mem. Miss. Oil and Gas Bd., 1968-71, Interstate Oil Compact Commn., 1968-71. Served with A.C., USN, World War II. Mem. Hinds Bar Assn., Miss. Bar Assn., ABA, Miss. Cir. Ct. Judges Assn., Am. Judicature Soc., Aircraft Owners and Pilots Assn. Baptist. Office: Miss Supreme Ct Supreme Ct Bldg Jackson MS 39205*

LEE, DAVID MYRON, pharmacist; b. Jackson, Miss., July 10, 1956; s. George Myron and Dorothy (Ware) L.; m. Wanda Dee Kelly, May 21, 1976; children—Zachary David, Adam Wayne, Nicholas Alan. B.A., U. Miss., 1981, B.S., 1981. Lic. pharmacist La., Miss., Ark. Staff pharmacist Meth. Hosp., Hattiesburg, Miss., 1981; asst. mgr. Treasury Drugs, Pearl, Miss., 1981, Revco Drug Stores Inc., Magee, Miss., 1981; dir. pharmacy HPI Health Care Services, Collins, Miss., 1982-83, Louisville, Miss., 1983-84, regional coordinator ops. Newhebron, Miss., 1984—. Mem. Miss. Pharm. Assn., Miss. Soc. Hosp. Pharmacists, Am. Soc. Hosp. Pharmacists. Baptist. Club: Newhebron Civic. Lodge: Newhebron 508 (sr. warden 1985). Avocations: golf; football; fishing. Home: PO Box 182 Newhebron MS 39140 Office: HPI Health Care Services Inc 5775 Peachtree Dunwoody Rd Atlanta GA 30342

LEE, DIANA MANG, biochemist; b. Mukden, China, Oct. 10, 1932; D. Chen Yin Chung and Lin (Lin) Chung; m. Fu Chu Lee, Jan. 30, 1960; 1 dau., Amy J. B.S., Nat. Taiwan U., 1955; M.S., Utah State U., 1960; postgrad. U. Chgo., 1960-61; Ph.D., U. Okla., 1967. Supr. clin. lab. dept. biochemistry Presbyn. St. Luke's Hosp., Chgo., 1961-64; sr. investigator cardiovascular sect. Okla. Med. Research Found., Oklahoma City, 1967-71, asst. mem. cardiovascular research program, 1971-75, assoc. mem. lipoprotein and atherosclerosis research program, 1975—; assoc. prof. dept. biochemistry and molecular biol. U. Okla. Grantee NIH. Mem. Am. Chem. Soc., AAAS, Council on Arteriosclerosis of Am. Heart Assn., Am. Oil Chemists Soc, N.Y. Acad. Scis., Am. Soc. Biol. Chemists, Sigma Xi. Assoc. editor Artery; reviewer for Biochemistry, Jour. Lipid Research and Atherosclerosis; editor Biochimica Biophys. Acta. Research on structure of low density lipoproteins and apolipoprotein B. Office: 825 NE 13th St Oklahoma City OK 73104

LEE, DONALD WILLIAM, mechanical engineer, researcher; b. Buffalo, N.Y., Nov. 4, 1947; s. Robert Arthur and Elizabeth Anne (Kinkead) L.; m. Veronica Mary Martin, June 15, 1971 (div. 1975); m. Sandra Kaye Stout, Nov. 18, 1979; children—Eric Franklin, Andrew Robert. B.S.M.E., Clarkson Coll. Tech., 1969, M.S. in Engring. Sci., 1973; Ph.D. in Applied Mech., U. Mich., 1977. Registered profl. engr., Mich., Tenn. Product design engr. Ford Motor Co., Dearborn, Mich., 1969-70; teaching asst. Clarkson Coll. Tech., Potsdam, N.Y., 1970-71; instr. Wayne State U., Detroit, 1975-76; researcher, teaching asst. U. Mich., Ann Arbor, Mich., 1971-76; research assoc. Oak Ridge Nat. Lab., Tenn., 1977-82, research staff, 1982—. Mem. Am. Phys. Soc., ASCE, ASME, East Tenn. Brewers Guild (sec. 1980-82), Sigma Xi. Democrat. Methodist. Avocations: homebrewing; gardening. Home: Route 6 Box 418 Lenoir City TN 37771 Office: Oak Ridge Nat Lab PO Box X Oak Ridge TN 37831

LEE, ELIZABETH BOBBITT, architect; b. Lumberton, N.C., July 9, 1928; d. William Osborne and Catharine Wilder (Bobbitt) Lee. Student Salem Coll., 1945-47; B.Arch., N.C. State Coll., 1952. Assoc. William Coleman, Architect, Kingston, N.C., 1952-55; Skidmore, Owens & Merrill, N.Y.C., 1955-56; prin. Elizabeth B. Lee, FAIA, Architect, Lumberton, N.C., 1956-73, 82—; sr. ptnr. Lee & Thompson, Architects, Lumberton, 1973-82. Bd. dirs. Robeson Little Theatre, Lumberton, 1977-80, N.C. Dance Theatre, Winston-Salem, N.C., 1980—, Robeson County Community Concerts, Lumberton, 1980—; trustee N.C. State U., Raleigh, 1983—. Recipient cert. recognition Randolph E. Dumont Design Program, 1970. Fellow AIA (nat. dir. 1983—; officeholder N.C. chpt., eastern sect. N.C. chpt., S. Atlantic Regional Council); mem. N.C. Design Found., N.C. Archtl. Found. (pres. 1982-83), Lumberton Jr. Service League (pres. 1968), N.C. State Alumni Assn. (bd. dirs. 1982-85), Phi Kappa Phi. Democrat. Presbyterian. Home: 906 Chestnut St Lumberton NC 28358 Office: PO Box 1067 Lumberton NC 28359

LEE, FRANK BARNWELL, SR., surgeon; b. Scranton, S.C., Aug. 26, 1918; s. David Lamar and Margaret (Barnwell) L.; m. Eddie McCravy; children—Frank Barnwell, Edward McCravy, Margaret Eugenia Lee Rhea. B.S., U. S.C.; M.D., Med. Coll. S.C., 1942. Intern Orange Meml. Hosp., N.J., 1942; resident Garfield Meml. Hosp., Washington, 1943, Watts Hosp., Durham, N.C., 1944; adminstr. Florence Gen. Hosp., S.C., 1949-84; private practice specializing in surgery, Florence, 1949—; mem. staff Florence Gen. Hosp. Home: 629 Park Ave Florence SC 29501 Office: 512 S Irby St Po Box F-8600 Florence SC 29501

LEE, GERALD ROY, computer analyst, consultant; b. Tulsa, Aug. 18, 1954; s. Harold Daniel and Joyce (Inks) L. B.S. in Math. and Stats., Okla. State U., 1976. Computer programmer James Richards Assn., Dallas, 1976; programmer Nat. Data Commn., Dallas, 1977-78; computer analyst Tex. Instruments, Inc., Dallas, 1978—. Republican. Methodist. Avocations: reading; bicycling; music;

raising my dog. Home: 3807 Clover Hill Ln Carrollton TX 75007 Office: Tex Instruments Inc PO Box 660246 M/5 8276 Dallas TX 75266

LEE, JAMES GILLIS, corporate executive; b. Panama City, Fla., 1927. Student, U.S. Merchant Marine Acad., 1949. Chief engr. Lykes Steamship Co., 1949-52, compusation engr., 1952-55; with Eatex Pulp & Paper, 1955-60, Tenn. River Pulp & Paper, 1960-67, Pineville Kraft Co., 1967-68, Continental Can Co., 1968-75; exec. v.p. Georgia Kraft Co., Rome, Ga., 1975—. Office: Georgia Kraft Co 1700 Redmond Circle Rome GA 30161

LEE, LINDA SUSAN, educator, college dean; b. Hendersonville, N.C., Feb. 21, 1950; d. Richard Sieben and Marjorie Jane (Weeter) Lee; B.S. in Home Econs., U. Tenn., Knoxville, 1972; student East Tenn. State U., 1971; postgrad. in Edn., Furman U., 1973-78; M.Ed. in Early Childhood Edn., U. S.C., 1980. Tchr. Greenville (S.C.) County Schs., 1972-73, Anderson (S.C.) Sch. Dist. I, 1973-75; coordinator, Mobile Day Care Tng. Project, S.C. Appalachian Health Council, 1975-77; child devel. specialist and project dir. Project Little Kids, Greenville County Library, 1977-79; coordinator Title XX Child Devel. Tng. Project, Greenville Tech. Coll., 1979-80, dept. head and instr. child devel., 1980-83, dean allied health scis., 1982—; cons. Project TOT, Anderson County Library and Library Parenting Project, Greenville County Library. Bd. dirs. Greenville County chpt. ARC. Recipient Project Little Kids award of merit Southeastern Library Assn., 1978, Outstanding Service award HEW, 1979. Mem. Am. Soc. Allied Health Professions, Kappa Delta Pi, Delta Kappa Gamma. Home: 22 Lynchester Rd Greenville SC 29615 Office: PO Box 5616 Station B Greenville Technical College Greenville SC 29606

LEE, MARGARET JANE, computer systems administrator; b. La Habana, Cuba, Sept. 21, 1952; came to U.S., 1961; d. Bernardo P. González and Margarita E. (Villaverde) Seixas; m. Glenn M. Lee, Oct. 3, 1971 (div. 1979). B.S. in Biology (scholar), U. Miami, Coral Gables, 1974, A.B. in Psychology, 1974, M.S. in Mgmt. Sci., 1977. Psychology technician Mailman Ctr. for Child Devel., U. Miami Sch. Medicine, 1975-76, grad. research asst. dept. psychiatry Univ. Health Service, 1976-77, programmer/analyst Comprehensive Cancer Ctr., 1977-80, database analyst Fla. Cancer Data System, 1980-81, system mgr. dept. pathology, 1981—; cons. in field. Mem. IEEE Computer Soc., COSTAR Users Group, MUMPS Users Group, DEC Users Soc., Fla. Native Plant Soc. Club: Everglades Bicycle (sec. 1984) (Miami). Home: PO Box 162708 Miami FL 33116

LEE, MARYAT (MARY ATTAWAY LEE), playwright, producer, director, painter; b. Covington, Ky., May 26, 1923; d. DeWitt Collins and Grace Barbee (Dyer) Lee; student Northwestern U., 1940-41; B.A., Wellesley Coll., 1945; student Middlebury Coll., summer 1944; postgrad. Union Theol. Sem., 1949-50, Columbia U., 1949-51, M.A., 1955; m. David Phillips Foulkes-Taylor, July 4, 1957 (dec. Sept. 1966). Engaged in film editing, 1946-48; instr. Wesleyan Coll., Macon, Ga., 1948-49; transcriber and oral history project Columbia U., 1950-51; asst. to Margaret Mead, 1952-53; writer, dir. DOPE!, a street play, 1951 (pub. in Best Short Plays of 1952-53); producer, founder, playwright Soul and Latin Theater, 1968-70, trustee, pres., 1969-70; mem. faculty New Sch. for Social Research, 1965-70; founder, playwright, producer EcoTheater, 1975—; adj. faculty W.Va. Coll. Grad. Studies, 1978—; fellow Va. Center for Creative Arts, Sweet Briar, 1979, 86; co-dir. drama and writing workshops Fed. Reformatory for Women, 1972-75; adv. panel Expansion Arts program Nat. Endowment Arts, 1973-75. Recipient CAP's award; nat. recognition award Am. the Beautiful Fund, 1985. Rockefeller Found., 1973, DJB Found., 1974. Mem. Dramatists Guild. Author (plays): Kairos, 1954; Clytemnestra, 1957; Love In 57th Street Gallery, 1960; Four Men & A Monster, 1967, 80; The Tightrope Walker, 1963, 67; Meat Hansom, 1962; FUSE, 1971, 80; (street plays) DOPE!, 1951, Day to Day, After the Fashion Show, The Classroom, Luba; (rural indigenous plays) Ole Miz Dacey, John Henry, The Hinton Play; participating playwright Office for Advanced Drama Research, 1967-74; contbr. articles to profl. publs. Developed 1st modern street theater. Home: 343 Church St Lewisburg WV 24901

LEE, MIN SHIU, research scientist, polymer engineer, material science consultant; b. Taipei, Taiwan, June 30, 1940; s. Thoan Chip and Ping Hsuey (Chen) L.; m. Amy Yen-Mei Su, Apr. 16, 1966; children—Terri Sue, David Marshall. B.S., Nat. Taiwan U., 1962; M.S., N.Mex. Highland U., 1966; Ph.D., Case Western Res. U., 1969. Sr. research chemist FMC Corp., Princeton, N.J., 1969-72; sr. research scientist Avicon Corp., Princeton, 1972-76; sr. research scientist Jelco Lab., Johnson & Johnson Co., Raritan, N.J., 1976-79, mgr. material research and sci. services, 1979-80, mgr. material and process devel., research and devel. Critikon, Inc. div., Tampa, Fla., 1980-83, staff cons., 1983—. Contbr. to profl. jours. Chmn. Taiwan Christian Fellowship of Central Jersey, 1972-74; treas. Univ. Chinese Sch. of Princeton, 1977-78; pres. Chinese Christian Ch. in Bay Areas, Fla., 1982—. Served to 2d lt. Chinese Army, 1962-64. Recipient award Nat. Def. Ministry, 1963; Inst. Sci. Research fellow, 1964-66; chemistry fellow Case Western Res. U., 1966-67. Mem. Am. Chem. Soc., N.Y. Acad. Scis., AAAS, Am. Assn. for Med. Instrumentation and Biomaterials (Johnson & Johnson polymer subcom.), Sigma Xi. Office: PO Box 22800 Tampa FL 33630

LEE, M(ONHÉ) HOWARD, research physicist, educator; b. Pusan, Korea, May 21, 1937; came to U.S., 1953, naturalized, 1973; s. Sang-Hun and Ho-Jung (Park) L.; m. Margaret Frances Kendig, Feb. 26, 1967; 1 child, Jennifer Katharine. B.S., U. Pa., 1959, Ph.D., 1967. Instr., U. Alta., Edmonton, Can., 1967-69; research assoc. MIT, Cambridge, Mass., 1969-73; prof. physics U. Ga., Athens, 1973—; vis. prof. U. Louvain, Belgium, 1976, Fulbright prof., 1979; vis. AID prof. Seoul Nat. U., Korea, 1980. Contbr. articles to sci. jours. Recipient Michael award for sci. U. Ga., 1976; Fulbright-Hays sr. research scholar, 1979; recipient Creative Research medal U. Ga., 1984. Mem. Am. Phys. Soc. Avocation: flower gardening. Home: 275 Sandstone Dr Athens GA 30605 Office: Dept Physics U Ga Athens GA 30602

LEE, MOO HEE, pediatrician, pediatric cardiologist; b. Pusan, Korea, Mar. 8, 1942; came to U.S., 1966; s. Sang Mook and Sang Kyung (Oh) L.; m. Jung Won Han, Aug. 8, 1970; children—Michael Jaiwhan, Michelle Nayung, Monica Unjin. B.S., Yonsei U., Seoul, Korea, 1962, M.D., 1966. Intern, Salem Hosp. (Mass.), 1966-67; resident in pediatrics, U. Man., Winnipeg, Can., 1967-69; fellow in pediatric cardiology Case Western Res. U., Cleve., 1969-71; research fellow in cardiovascular physiology Mt. Sinai Hosp., 1971-72; asst. prof. pediatrics and pediatric cardiology, Med. Coll. Ga., Augusta, 1973-75; pediatric cardiologist and pediatrician, Atlanta Heart and Lung Clinic, P.C., Crippled Children's Cardiac Clinic, Atlanta, South Atlanta Pediatrics, P.A., Riverdale, Ga., 1975—. Contbr. articles to profl. jours. including Am. Jour. Cardiology, Circulation, Circulation Research, Am. Jour. Physiology, Jour. of Pediatrics, Pediatrics, Jour. of Electrophysiology. Am. Heart Assn. cardiovascular research fellow, 1972. Fellow Am. Coll. Cardiology; mem. AMA, Med. Assn. Ga., Am. Acad. Pediatrics (Ga. chpt.), Am. Heart Assn. Republican. Methodist. Club: Lions. Home: 1071 Helmer Rd Riverdale GA 30296 Office: South Atlanta Pediatrics PA 251 Medical Way Riverdale GA 30274

LEE, NELDA S., art dealer, appraiser, film producer; b. Gorman, Tex., July 3, 1941; d. Olan C. and Onis Lee; A.A. in Art (Franklin Lindsay Found. grantee), Tarleton State U. (Tex.), 1961; B.A. in Fine Arts, North Tex. State U., 1963; postgrad. Tex. Tech U., 1964, San Miguel de Allende Art Inst., Mex., 1965; 1 dau., Jeanna Lea Pool. Head dept. art Ector High Sch., Odessa, Tex., 1963-68; in art gallery bus., 1967—; owner Mega-Tex. Prodns., film producers; exhibited paintings throughout U.S. and Mex., including Tex. Fine Arts Assn.; pres. Mega-Tex Movie Prodn. Co. Bd. dirs. Odessa YMCA, 1970, Am. Heart Assn., Odessa, 1975; fund raiser Easter Seal Telethon, Odessa, 1978-79; bd. dirs. Ector County (Tex.) Cultural Center, 1979—; bd. dirs., mem. acquisition com. Permian Basin Presdl. Mus., Odessa, 1978; sponsor mem. Mus. of S.W., Midland, Tex.; bd. dirs., chmn. acquisition com. Odessa Art Mus., 1979—; pres. Ector County Democratic Women's Club, 1975; active various congl. and senatorial campaigns. Recipient Designer-Craftsman award El Paso Mus. Fine Arts, 1964; spl. award Odessa YMCA, 1968. Mem. Am. Soc. Appraisers (sr. mem.; cert.), Appraisers Assn. Am. (cert.), Appraisers of Fine Arts Soc. (cert.), Nat. Soc. Lit. and Arts, Tex. Assn. Art Dealers (pres. 1978-81), Odessa C. of C. (life), Better Bus. Bur. Club: Tarleton State U. Century. Contbr. articles to profl. jours. Office: PO Box 6385 Odessa TX 79767

LEE, NORMAN RAY, utility exec.; b. Grayson, La., Oct. 24, 1924; s. John Wesley and Lillie Ellen (Bozone) L.; B.S., Calif. Inst. Tech., Pasadena, 1947; grad. Advanced Mgmt. Program, Harvard U., 1967; m. Nell Ray, Jan. 15, 1950; children—Norman Ray, Rebecca Nell. Engr., Standard Oil Co. Calif., 1946-47, Allis-Chalmers Co., Milw., 1947-48; with Gulf States Utilities Co., 1949—, sr. v.p., then exec. v.p., 1970-73, pres., Beaumont, Tex., 1973—, also dir.; dir. Tex. Commerce Bank, Beaumont. Campaign chmn. United Way Beaumont, 1978, 1st v.p., 1979. Served with USNR, 1943-46, 51-52. Registered profl. engr., Tex. Mem. Beaumont C. of C. (pres. 1979). Methodist. Club: Beaumont Rotary (past dir.). Office: PO Box 2951 Beaumont TX 77704

LEE, PHILIP W., computer services education and training analyst; b. Los Angeles, Apr. 2, 1954; s. Joseph H. and Pauline A. (Davis) L. B.A., U. Calif.-Santa Barbara, 1975; M.B.A., U.Calif.-Irvine, 1977; postgrad., UCLA, 1977. Systems programmer assoc. ITT Gilfillan, Van Nuys, Calif., 1977-81; part time instr. Los Angeles City Coll., 1980-81; computer services edn. and tng. analyst Aramco Services Co., Houston, 1981—; instr. in field. Calif. State fellow, 1975-77. Mem. Black MBA Assn. (membership chmn.), Am. Prodn. and Inventory Control Soc. (bd. dirs. affiliate 1978-79), Am. Soc. Tng. and Devel., Data Trainers Soc. Baptist. Office: 500 Dallas Houston TX 77001

LEE, PUI LUEN, civil engineer; b. Hong Kong, Mar. 7, 1952; s. Kon L. and Lai Yu (Wang) L.; came to U.S., 1974. Student Tex. A&M U., 1974-76; B.Sc. in Civil Engring., U. Man. (Can.), 1978; M.Sc. in Civil Engring., Ga. Inst. Tech., 1979. Registered profl. engr., Ga. Structural engr. Engring. Tech., Atlanta, 1979, Nuclear Structures, Inc., Atlanta, 1980—. Mem. ASCE, Inst. Civil Engrs. in Britain. Office: 4470 Chamblee Dunwoody Rd Suite 150 Atlanta GA 30338

LEE, RICHARD JAMES, lawyer, accountant; b. Newark, Nov. 26, 1947; s. Joseph James and Estelle (Musa) L.; m. Linda Ann Giancola, children—Teresa Dawn, Andrea Renee. B.S.C., U. Louisville, 1972, J.D., 1975; LL.M. in Taxation, U. Miami, 1978. Bar: Fla. 1977, U.S. Tax Ct. 1977. Sr. tax specialist Peat, Marwick, Mitchell & Co., C.P.A.s, Miami, 1975-76; assoc. Tew, Critchlow, Sonberg, Scott & Traum, P.A., Miami, 1976-79; assoc. Schwartz, Nash, Heckerling, Tescher & Kantor, P.A., Miami, 1979-82; prin. Richard J. Lee, P.A., Coral Gables and Fort Lauderdale, Fla., 1982—. Mem. Fla. Bar Assn. (tax sect. com.), ABA, Club: Sports Car of Am. Home: 10231 SW 128th Ave Miami FL 33186 Office: Richard J Lee PA 2655 LeJeune Rd 5th Fl Coral Gables FL 33134 also 4301 N Federal Hwy Suite 104 Fort Lauderdale FL 33308

LEE, ROBERT E., mathematics educator, consultant, author; b. Covington, Ky., Dec. 7, 1919; s. Dewitt Collins and Grace Barbee (Dyer) L.; m. Mary Dean Lott, May 27, 1944 (dec.); children—Mary Dean, Robert Lott. B.A., Washington and Lee U., 1941; M.A., Vanderbilt U., 1942; D.Ed., U. Fla., 1950. Instr. math. U. Fla., Gainesville, 1946-48; dir. research and stats. dept. edn., Tallahassee, 1950-54; asst. dean Berry Coll., Rome, Ga., 1954-56; pres. Ga. Coll., Milledgeville, 1956-67; acad. v.p. U. West Fla., Pensacola, 1967-69, prof. math. and stats., 1969—. Pres. Rotary Club of Milledgeville, 1959. Served with USNR, 1942-46. Recipient Disting. Tchr. award U. West Fla., 1983. Mem. Nat. Council Tchrs. Math., Ga. Assn. Colls. (pres. 1958), Am. Assn. State Colls. and Univs. (governing bd. 1967), Internat. Platform Assn. Democrat. Presbyterian. Club: W.Fla. Toastmasters (pres. 1982). Author: The Mathematics and Mysteries of the Great Pyramid, 1981. Home: 8853 Scenic Hills Dr Pensacola FL 32514 Office: U West Fla Pensacola FL 32514

LEE, ROBERT EDWARD, optometrist; b. Vicksburg, Miss., Mar. 11, 1947; s. Robert Edward and Artimease (Montgomery) L.; m. Ruthetta Bankston, Aug. 11, 1973; children—Ruben Edward, Rayford Eugene, Reginald Earl. B.S. in Physics, Tougaloo Coll., 1969; D. Optometry, Ind. U., 1978. Mktg. analyst Gen. Motors Corp., Dayton, Ohio, 1971-72, purchasing analyst, 1972-73, prodn. buyer, 1973-74; practice optometry, Meridian, Miss., 1978-81, Gautier, Miss., 1984—; prof. Army External Program, San Antonio, 1981-84. Active Community Action, Bloomington, Ind., 1975, Meridian, 1978, San Antonio, 1982. Served as cpl. USMC, 1969-71, to capt. U.S. Army, 1981-84. Recipient Community Service award First Union Headstart, Meridian, 1979, Service plaque U. Houston, 1984. Mem. Miss. Optometric Assn., Nat. Optometric Assn., Council on Sports Vision, Armed Forces Officers Soc., NAACP, Omega Epsilon Phi, Alpha Phi Alpha. Baptist. Lodge: Masons. Club: Esquire (Vicksburg). Avocations: public speaking; singing; sports activities, including track, basketball, coaching. Home: 6000 Hollis St Moss Point MS 39563 Office: Singing River Mall 1210 Hwy 90-W Gautier MS 39553

LEE, ROBERT THOMAS, dentist; b. San Antonio, Oct. 31, 1947; s. Thomas J. and May L. Lee; m. Donna Marie Keegan Aug. 1, 1981; 1 dau., Danielle; 1 step-dau., Tonya. B.A., U. Tex., 1969, D.D.S., 1973. Pvt. practice, San Antonio, 1976—; pres. and dir. Lee Dental Ctrs. and Lee Dental Care, San Antonio; dir. Helotes State Bank. Dir. Whispering Oaks Homeowners Assn.; pres. Elm Creek Homeowners Assn. Served as capt. USAF, 1973-75. Mem. ADA, Acad. Gen. Dentistry, Am. Orthodontic Soc., Tex. Dental Assn., Leon Valley Bus. and Profl. Assn. (pres.). Baptist. Club: Dominion Country.

LEE, ROY DOUGLAS, JR., university administrator; b. PeWee Valley, Ky., Aug. 18, 1948; s. Roy Douglas and Dorothy Leora (Moore) L.; m. Carmen Kathrene Daley, May 27, 1972; children—Amanda Adair, Meredith Moore. A.B., Eastern Ky. U., 1973; M.Ed., U. Louisville, 1978. Cert. tchr., Ky. Classroom instr. Oldham County High Sch., Buckner, Ky., 1973-78; coordinator residence life Ga. Coll., Milledgeville, 1979-82; asst. dir. Tulane U., New Orleans, 1982-85; asst. dean of students Ga. State U., Atlanta, 1985—; cons. time mgmt., student activities. Writer grant proposals for Louisville Zool. Gardens, 1979. Mem. So. Assn. Coll. Student Affairs (newsletter bd. 1984, 85, membership com. 1981, local arrangements com. 1985). Democrat. Baptist. Lodge: Masons. Avocations: photography, bluegrass music. Home: 71G Trevitt Dr Stone Mountain GA 30083 Office: Room 458 Student Ctr Ga State U Atlanta GA 30303

LEE, ROY NOBLE, justice state supreme court; b. Madison County, Miss., Oct. 19, 1915; m. Sue Epting; 5 children. B.A. with distinction, Miss. Coll., 1938, LL.B., Cumberland U., 1939. Bar: Miss. 1939. Spl. agt. FBI, 1942-44; dist. atty. 8th Circuit Ct. Dist., 1951-64; circuit judge 8th Circuit Ct. Dist., 1964-75; justice Miss. State Supreme Ct., Jackson, 1975—. Trustee Miss. Coll. Served to ensign USNR, 1944-46. Mem. Miss. Bar Assn., Am. Judicature Soc., Am. Legion (past post comdr.), VFW (past dist. comdr.), Soc. Former FBI Agents. Baptist. Lodges: Masons; Shriners; Woodmen of World. Office: Mississippi Supreme Court Gartin Bldg Jackson MS 39205*

LEE, SEUNG-DONG LEIGH, economics and statistics educator; b. Andong, Korea, May 2, 1947; s. Eung-Rak and Jeung-Kyo (Lee) L.; m. Soon Duk Song, Nov. 26, 1977; children—Lyndon, Michelle. B.A., Korea U., 1970; M.A., Korea U., 1974; M.A. in Econs., So. Meth. U., 1976, Ph.D. in Econs., 1979. Teaching asst. Korea U., Seoul, 1970-72; instr. Korea Mil. Acad., Seoul, 1972-74; research asst. So. Meth. U., Dallas, 1974-76, teaching asst., 1976-79; asst. prof. econs. and stats. U. Ala.-Birmingham, 1979—. Assoc. editor Rev. of Regional Studies, 1979—. Research economist Urban Ala. Bus. Newsletter, 1984—. Contbr. articles to profl. jours. Mem. Am. Econ. Assn., Can. Econ. Assn., Korean Scientists and Engrs. Assn. in Am., Korean Assn. Greater Birmingham (pres. 1985—), Omicron Delta Epsilon. Avocations: golf; tennis; jogging. Office: Dept Econs U Ala-Birmingham University Station Birmingham AL 35294

LEE, SUNG JAE, mathematician, educator; b. Kim-Jae, Jeonbuk, Korea, Jan., 17, 1942; came to U.S., 1966; s. Man-Chul and Bundong (Choi) L.; m. Whei-Mei Chen, Feb. 28, 1971; children—Ann, John Jungan, Susan. B.S. in Math., Jeonbuk Nat. U., 1965; M.A. in Math., Boston Coll., 1968; Ph.D. in Math., McMaster U., 1972. Postdoctoral fellow U. Guelph, Ont., Can., 1972-74, asst. prof., 1974-76; research assoc. Queens U., Kingston, Ont., Can., 1974-76, U. Alta., Edmonton, 1976-78; asst. prof. Pan Am. U., Edinburg, Tex., 1979-81; assoc. prof. math. dept. U. South Fla., Tampa, 1981-86, prof., 1986—. Assoc. editor Honam Math. Jour., Jeonju, Jeonbuk, 1983—. Contbr. research articles to profl. jours. Scholar Jeonbuk Nat. U., 1961-65; teachng fellow Boston Coll., 1966-68; Ont. Govt. fellow, 1968-69; teaching asst. McMaster U., 1969-72. Mem. Am. Math. soc. (reviewer Math. Revs. 1976—), Korean Scientists and Engrs. Assn. Am. Avocations: running, chess. Home: 7601 Sanibel Circle N Tampa Fl 33617 Office: Math Dept U South Fla Fowler Ave Tampa FL 33620

LEE, TERRY MARCUS, osteopathic physician; b. Independence, Mo. Dec. 5, 1950; s. Marcus Leroy and Eleanor M. (Campbell) L.; m. Lana K. Pacey, May 28, 1972; children—Christopher Marcus, Phillip Scott, Carolyn Joy. B.A., U. Kans., 1973; D.O., Kansas City Coll. of Osteo. Medicine and Surgery, 1977. Intern Okla. Osteo. Hosp., Tulsa, 1977-78; staff physician Wellington Hosp. and Clinic, Kans., 1978-80; gen. practice medicine Lee Family Clinic, Inc., Durant, Okla., 1980—; mem. staff, chief of staff Bryan Meml. Hosp., Durant, 1984-85, dir. of med. edn., 1982-84; mem. Okla. State Com. on Standards for Peer Rev., 1984, Regional Profl. Rev. Orgn. Rev. Team, 1981—, U.S. Health Adv. Com., 1985—. Pres. Wellington Jacees, 1978-79, Durant Jaycees, 1981-82. Recipient Outstanding Young Oklahoman award Okla. Jaycees, 1985, Gt. Am. Family award U.S. Jaycees, 1983. Mem. Am. Osteo. Assn., Am. Coll. of Osteo. Gen. Practitioners, Am. Coll. of Gen. Practice, Okla. Osteo. Assn. (v.p. Southeastern Okla. dist. 1984-85), Durant C. of C. (bd. dirs. 1982—). Republican. Methodist. Lodges: Rotary (bd. dirs. 1982-83), Elks. Avocations: aviation; photography. Home: 101 Rollingwood Hills Durant OK 74701 Office: Lee Family Clinic Inc 16th and University Sts Box 1610 Durant OK 74702-1610

LEE, TIMOTHY ALLEN, oil company geologist, consultant geologist; b. Memphis, July 17, 1956; s. Walter A. and Rosalie Grace (Hehr) L.; m. Betty L. DeLorge, Feb. 14, 1982. B.S. in Geology, Tenn. Tech. U., 1980. Geologist, NSF, Washington, 1979-80, Trans Tenn. Energy, Crossville, Tenn., 1980-83, Miller Petroleum, Livingston, Tenn., 1984—. Mem. Am. Assn. Petroleum Geologist, Geol. Soc. Am. Lutheran. Avocation: golf. Home: Route 14 Box 485 Crossville TN 38555 Office: Miller Petroleum Inc Box 478 Livingston TX 38570

LEE, TOM STEWART, district judge, Southern District of Mississippi; b. Jackson, Miss., Apr. 8, 1941; s. Percy Mercer and Claudia (Stewart) L.; m. Norma Ruth Robbins, Aug. 14, 1966; children—Elizabeth Robbins, Tom Stewart. B.A., Miss. Coll., 1963; J.D., U. Miss., 1965. Bar: Miss. 1965. Mem. firm Lee & Lee, Forest, Miss., 1965-84; U.S. dist. judge So. Dist. Miss., Jackson, 1984—. Served as capt. USAR, 1965-73. Recipient D.M. Nelson Jr. Meml. Scholarship Trophy, 1963, Frederick P. Hamel award, 1964. Mem. Phi Alpha Delta, Omicron Delta Kappa. Baptist. Avocations: tennis; basketball; football. Office: US Dist Ct 245 E Capitol St PO Drawer 22846 Jackson MS 39225-2846

LEE, VIVIAN FOSTER, nurse; b. East Tallassee, Ala., Sept. 30, 1945; d. James Dewey and Cora Geneva (Railey) Foster; m. Joseph Dale Lee, Oct. 4, 1963; children—Shannon LaDale Setzer, Joseph Dale II. Practical Nursing Cert., Opelika Vocat. Sch., 1973; Assoc. Sci. Nursing, Troy State U., 1977, B.S. in Nursing cum laude, 1984, postgrad., 1984—. Staff licensed practical nurse East Ala. Med. Ctr., Opelika, 1974-77, Community Hosp., Tallassee, 1974-77; staff nurse, 1977-78; office nurse pvt. practice, Opelika, 1978-83; div. head emergency room, psychiatry East Ala. Med. Ctr., Opelika, 1983—; bd. dirs. Lee County Stop Child Abuse Now, Opelika, 1985. Mem. Nat. Assn. Alcoholism and Drug Abuse Counselors, Ala. State Nurses Assn., Am. Nurses Assn., Am. Heart Assn. (instr. 1984-85), Gamma Beta Phi, Alpha Sigma Lambda. Democrat. Baptist. Avocations: cross stitching; camping; reading; scuba diving. Home: Route 1 Box 109 Cusseta AL 36852 Office: E Ala Med Ctr 2000 Pepperell Pkwy Opelika AL 36801

LEE, W. BARRY, pharmacist; b. Danville, Va., Dec. 20, 1947; s. A. B. and Dorothy (Hammond) L.; m. Linda Leigh Poston, Mar. 10, 1973; children—Hunter, Christine. B.S. in Pharmacy, U. S.C., 1971; M.B.A., U. Tampa, 1979. Clin. pharmacist VA Med. Ctr., Tampa, Fla., 1974-77, supervisory pharmacist, 1977-79; chief pharmacy VA Med. Ctr., Beckley, W.Va., 1979-83; dir. pharmacy service Colonia Hosp., Terrell, Tex., 1983—. Bd. dirs. Welcome to Terrell Com., 1984—, Am. Heart Assn., Terrell, 1985—. Mem. Am. Soc. Hosp. Pharmacists, Tex. Soc. Hosp. Pharmacists. Presbyterian. Avocations: water skiing; racquetball; reading. Home: 709 Eulalia Dr Terrell TX 75160

LEE, WALTER C., educational administrator. Supt. of schs. Shreveport, La. Office: PO Box 37000 Shreveport LA 71130*

LEE, WILLIAM CHALKER, optometrist; b. Ocala, Fla., May 15, 1933; s. Robert Edward and Edna (Chalker) L.; A.B., Duke U., 1955; B.S., Pa. Coll. Optometry, 1962, O.D., 1963; m. Gwen Marie Clark, June 13, 1958; children—Kristin, Diane, William Chalker, Jason. Optometrist, Bayshore, Swanson, Sowers, Lee & Yager, Orlando, Fla., 1963—; pres. Lee Contact Lens Labs., Inc. Served with U.S. Army, 1956-59. Fellow Am. Acad. Optometry (diplomate in contact lens); mem. Am. Optometric Assn., Fla. Optometric Assn., So. Council Optometrists, Soc. Contact Lens Specialists. Roman Catholic. Club: Rotary. Contbr. articles to profl. jours. Home: 1621 Chinook Trail Maitland FL 32751 Office: Bayshore Swanson Sowers Lee & Yager 214 E Marks St Orlando FL 32803

LEE, WILLIAM CLEMENT, III, corporate patent attorney; b. Atlanta, July 17, 1948; s. William Clement Jr. and Barbara Anne (Wilson) L.; m. Mary Reed Evans, Apr. 16, 1982. B.S., U. Ga., 1970, M.S., 1974; J.D., Emory U., 1977. Bar: Ga. 1977, U.S. Patent Office 1980, U.S. Dist. Ct. (no., mid., so. dists.) Ga., U.S. Ct. Appeals (5th, 11th, fed. cirs.), U.S. Claims Ct., U.S. Tax Ct., U.S. Supreme Ct. Sole practice, Bremen, Ga., 1978-80; asst. sec. U. Ga. Research Found., Inc., Athens, 1981-84; patent atty., asst. to v.p. research, U. Ga., Athens, 1980-84; patent staff counsel The Coca-Cola Co., Atlanta, 1984—. Served with U.S. Army Res., 1970-76. Mem. Atlanta Bar Assn., Ga. Bar Assn., ABA, Am. Intellectual Property Law Assn., Licensing Execs. Soc., Am. Corp. Counsel Assn., Am. Judicature Soc., Phi Delta Phi, Delta Tau Delta (Outstanding Alumnus award 1981). Home: 2344 Woodward Way NW Atlanta GA 30305 Office: Coca Cola Co PO Drawer 1734 Atlanta GA 30301

LEE, WILLIAM JOHN, petroleum engineering educator, consultant; b. Lubbock, Tex., Jan. 16, 1936; s. William Preston and Bonnie Lee (Cook) L.; m. Phyllis Ann Bass, June 10, 1962; children—Anne Preston, Mary Denise. B.Chem. Engring., Ga. Inst. Tech., 1959, M.S. in Chem. Engring., 1961, Ph.D. in Chem. Engring., 1963. Registered profl. engr., Tex., Miss. Sr. research specialist Exxon Prodn. Research Co., Houston, 1962-68; assoc. prof. petroleum engring. Miss. State U., Starkville, 1968-71; tech. advisor Exxon Co., Houston, 1971-77; prof. petroleum engring. Tex. A. and M. U., College Station, 1977—; sr. v.p. engring. S.A. Holditch & Assocs., Inc., College Station, 1979—. Author: Well Testing, 1982. Recipient award of excellence Halliburton Edn. Found., 1982, Meritorious Engring. Teaching award Tenneco, Inc., 1982, Disting. Teaching award Assn. Former Students, Tex. A. and M. U., College Station, 1983. Mem. Soc. Petroleum Engrs. (chmn. edn. and accreditation com. 1985-86, disting. lectr. 1980, disting. faculty achievement award 1982). Presbyterian. Avocation: investments. Home: PO Box 483 College Station TX 77841 Office: Tex A and M U Petroleum Engring Dept College Station TX 77843

LEE, WILLIAM MALCOLM, building materials company executive; b. Atlanta, Sept. 25, 1941; s. Clarence Gordon and Florabel (McGoogan) L.; B.A., Emory U., 1963; postgrad. Ga. State U., 1963-64; children—William Malcolm, Elizabeth Shannon; m. Patricia J. Sanders, 1983; 1 stepson, Charles Loren Hicks. Dist. counselor Atlanta Newspapers, Inc., Atlanta, 1963-65; sales rep., sales mgr. GAF Corp., N.Y.C., 1965-69; corp. v.p. Builder Marts of Am., Inc., Greenville, S.C., 1969-82; with Aid/man Computer Systems subs. BMA, 1983—, v.p., 1984—. Lay reader, vestry mem. Episcopal Ch. of the Redeemer. Mem. Nat. Lumber and Bldg. Material Dealers Assn., Greenville C. of C. Republican. Episcopalian. Home: 3 Parrish Ct Greenville SC 29607 Office: PO Box 1417 Greenville SC 29602

LEE, WILLIAM STATES, utility executive; b. Charlotte, N.C., June 23, 1929; s. William States and Sarah (Everett) L.; B.S. in Engring. magna cum laude, Princeton U., 1951; m. Janet Fleming Rumberger, Nov. 24, 1951; children—Lisa, States, Helen. With Duke Power Co., Charlotte, 1955—, engring. mgr., 1962-65, v.p. engring., 1965-71, sr. v.p. engring. and constrn., 1971-75, exec. v.p., 1976-78, pres., chief operating officer, 1978-82, chmn., chief exec. officer, 1982—, dir., 1968—, mem. exec. com., 1971—, fin. com., 1978—. Mem. U.S. Com. on Large Dams, 1963—; bd. dirs. United Community Services; bd. advisors Engring. Sch., U. N.C., Charlotte; trustee Queens Coll. Served with C.E., USNR, 1951-54. Registered profl. engr., N.C., S.C. Fellow ASME (George Westinghouse Gold medal 1972), ASCE; mem. Nat. Acad. Engring., Inst. Nuclear Power Ops. (chmn. 1979—), Nat. Soc. Profl. Engrs. (Outstanding Engr. in U.S. award 1980), Am. Nuclear Soc., Charlotte C. of C. (chmn. 1979), Phi Beta Kappa, Tau Beta Pi. Presbyterian (ruling elder). Office: 422 S Church St Charlotte NC 28242

LEEDOM, JOHN NESBETT, distribution company executive, state senator; b. Dallas, July 27, 1921; s. Floyd H. and Gladys Lorraine (Nesbett) L.; m. Betty Lee Harvey, Mar. 17, 1956; children—Jo Ann, Judy, Eddie Kennedy, Danny Kennedy, Linda, John Nesbett. B.S.E.E., Rice U., 1943. Engr., Naval Research Lab., Washington, 1943-45; asst. sales mgr. Sprague Products Co., North Adams, Mass., 1945-50; founder, pres. Wholesale Electronic Supply, Inc., Dallas, 1950—; sec.-treas., dir. Ginger Patch, Inc., 1973—; dir. Promade Nat. Bank; mem. Tex. Senate, 1980—. Chmn. Dallas County Republican Com., 1962-66, mem. state exec. com., 1966-68; mem. Dallas City Council, 1975-80. Served to lt. (j.g.), USNR, 1943-45. Mem. Nat. Electronic Distbrs. Assn. (pres. 1971-72), Nat. Assn. Wholesale Distbrs. (pres. 1972-73), IEEE, Mil. Order World Wars, Navy League, Tau Beta Pi. Office: 2809 Ross Ave Dallas TX 75201

LEEDS, ROBERT, dentist; b. Newark, Sept. 8, 1930; s. William David and Gertrude (Greene) L.; m. Joyce Sumner, Nov. 28, 1960; children—Deborah Joyce, Robin Elizabeth. A.A., U. Fla., 1950; D.D.S., Emory U., 1954. Gen. practice dentistry, Miami, Fla. Patentee herpes simplex method of therapy. Served to maj. USAF, 1954-56. Mem. ADA, East Coast Dental Assn., Miami Dental Soc., South Dade Dental Soc. Club: Coral Gables Country (Fla.). Lodges: Shriners, Masons. Avocations: sailing; water skiing; snow skiing. Office: 6437 Bird Rd Miami FL 33155

LEEDS, ROBERT LEWIS, JR., business educator, consultant; b. N.Y.C., Feb. 9, 1930; s. Robert Lewis and Elisabeth (Bandler) L.; m. Irene Osterweil, June 9, 1958 (div. 1981); children—Leslie Anne; m. Joan Wrigley, Sept. 27, 1984. Robert Lewis. B.A., Amherst Coll., 1951; M.B.A., U. Pa., 1953. With Manhattan Industries (formerly Manhattan Shirt Co.), N.Y.C., 1953-76, v.p. mktg., 1958-65, exec. v.p., 1965-66, chmn., chief exec. officer, 1965-74; v.p. corp. devel. Benrus Co., N.Y.C., 1976-78; prin. Robert L. Leeds and Assocs., N.Y.C., 1978-81; assoc. dir. exec. M.B.A. program U. South Fla., Tampa, 1982—, disting. lectr. in mktg. and mgmt., 1985—; instr. Bklyn. Coll., Hunter Coll., Marymount Coll., Pace U., 1979-81; bd. dirs. Manhattan Industries, Inc., Vera Cos., Frost Bros., Yves St. Laurent Menswear, 1957-74; adv. bd. Mfrs. Hanover Trust Co., 1973-74; pres., chmn. Men's Fashion Assn. Am., 1968-69. Served to 1st lt. USAF, 1953-55.

LEEDS, STEVEN FRANK, portfolio manager; b. Flushing, N.Y., Nov. 3, 1947; s. Robert Sol and Roberta Vera (Mistlin) L.; m. Karen Anne Cole, Nov. 20, 1969 (div. 1978); m. Linda Eve Nadelman, Aug. 1, 1982. B.S. in Edn., U. Ala., 1969, M.B.A., 1973. Gen. acct. Am. Hosp. Supply, Milledgeville, Ga., 1974-75; registered rep. Kidder, Peabody & Co., Ft. Lauderdale, Fla., 1975-78; trust investment officer Sun Banks, Ft. Lauderdale, 1978-82; sr. investment officer Southeast Bank, Miami, Fla., 1982-85; sr. trust investment officer Landmark 1st Nat. Bank, Ft. Lauderdale, 1985—. Served to 1st lt. U.S. Army, 1969-71. Mem. Fin. Analysts Soc. South Fla. Republican. Clubs: Bond (pres. 1984-85), (Ft. Lauderdale); Gulfstream Sailing; Seven Seas Cruising Assn. (La.). Avocations: sailing; running; photography; flying; scuba diving. Home: 1217 Avocado Isle Fort Lauderdale FL 33315 Office: Landmark 1st Nat Bank 1 Financial Plaza Fort Lauderdale FL 33310

LEEMIS, LAWRENCE MARK, industrial engineering educator, researcher; b. Mpls., June 27, 1957; s. Arthur Henry and Ivah Lucille (Turner) L. B.S. in Math., Purdue U., 1978, M.S. in Applied Math., 1980, Ph.D. in Ops. Research, 1984. Computer operator Oak Brook Data Ctr., Ill., 1977; program cons. Argonne Nat. Lab., Ill., 1979; lectr. Baylor U., Waco, Tex., 1980; v.p. programming Nisus Corp., West Lafayette, Ind., 1981; grad. instr. Purdue U., West Lafayette, 1981-84; asst. prof. indsl. engring. U. Okla., Norman, 1984—; cons. Delco Electronics, Kokomo, Ind., 1983, Leemis Mktg., Oak Brook, 1980-83, Dunn & Hargitt, West Lafayette, 1978. Big bro. Big Bros./Big Sisters Program, Lafayette, Ind., 1978-84. Recipient Grandon H. Griffith award U. Okla., 1985, Estus Magoon award Purdue U., 1982, 83, 84; David Ross fellow, 1982. Mem. Am. Statis. Assn., Inst. Indsl. Engrs., Ops. Research Soc. Am., Omega Rho (sec. 1983-84). Home: 803 Red Bird Ln Norman OK 73072 Office: U Okla 202 W Boyd St Suite 124 Norman OK 73019

LEEPER, DORIS MARIE, sculptor, painter; b. Charlotte, N.C., Apr. 4, 1929; d. Ernest R. Leeper and Pauline A. (Fry) Leeper Harrison. B.A., Duke U., 1951. With graphic arts dept. Charlotte Engraving, 1951-55; artist, salesperson So. Engraving, Atlanta, 1955-61; mem. adv. panels Fla. Arts Council, 1975-85. One-woman shows include Hunter Mus. Art, Chattanooga, 1968, 75, 79, Jacksonville Art Mus., Fla., 1968, 76, Mint Mus. Art, Charlotte, 1968, 76, Duke U. Mus., Durham, N.C., 1969, High Mus. Art, Atlanta, 1975, Greenville County Mus. Art, S.C., 1976, Columbia Mus. Art, S.C., 1976, Ringling Mus. Art, Sarasota, Fla., 1976, Miss. Mus. Art, Jackson, 1979, Mus. Arts and Scis., Daytona Beach, Fla., 1980, LeMoyne Art Found., Tallahassee, 1980, Anniston Mus., Natural History, Ala., 1980; group shows include Jacksonville Art Mus., 1971-72, 72, Albright-Knox Gallery, Buffalo, 1972-73, Miss. Mus. Art, 1978, Am. Acad. and Inst. Arts and Letters, N.Y.C., 1979, N. Miami Mus., Fla., 1984, Ctr. Arts, Vero Beach, Fla., 1986; commns. include Fla. State Legis. Bldg., IBM, Atlanta, Orlando Internat. Airport, Fla., others; represented in permanent collections Hunter Mus. Art, Chattanooga, Jacksonville Art Mus., Columbus Mus. Art, Ohio, Duke U., Durham, Greenville County Mus. Art, Ill. Wesleyan U., Mint Mus. Art, Miss. Mus. Art, Mus. Arts and Scis., Daytona Beach, Nat. Mus. Am. Art, Washington, Stetson U., Deland, Fla., U. S. Fla., Tampa, Wadsworth Athenaeum, Hartford, Conn., others. Founder Atlantic Ctr. for Arts, New Smyrna Beach, Fla., 1977-78, trustee, 1979—; trustee Mus. Arts and Scis., Daytona Beach, 1977-78, Fla. Conservation Found., 1981-85; mem. adv. commn. Canaveral Nat. Seashore, 1975-85; bd. dirs. Coastal Ednl. Broadcasters, Inc., New Smyrna Beach, 1983—. Nat. Endowment Arts fellow, 1972; Fla. Fine Arts Council fellow, 1977; Rockefeller Found. fellow, 1977. Republican. Avocations: reading; tennis; environmental affairs. Home: River Rd Box 2093 Canaveral National Seashore FL 32070

LEEPER, JOHN PALMER, museum exec.; b. Denison, Tex., Feb. 4, 1921; s. John Palmer and Maryanne (Platter) L.; B.Journalism, So. Methodist U., 1942; M.A. in Art History, Harvard, 1947; m. Blanche Wheeler Magurn, Sept. 18, 1948; 1 dau., Maryanne M. Keeper W.A. Clark Collection, Corcoran Gallery Art, Washington, 1948, asst. dir. gallery, 1949-50; dir. Pasadena (Calif.) Art Inst., 1950-53; dir. Marion Koogler McNay Art Inst., San Antonio, 1954—. Instr. Dexter Sch., Boston, 1947-48; lectr. Pasadena Sch. Fine Arts, 1952-53, U. So. Calif., Los Angeles, 1952, Trinity U., San Antonio, 1957-59. Pres. San Antonio Little Theatre. Trustee San Antonio Art Inst. Served with USAAF, 1942-45. Mem. Am. Assn. Museums, Assn. Art Mus. Dirs., Tex. Soc. Arts and Letters (hon.). Club: Harvard (San Antonio).

LEES-HALEY, PAUL RUSSELL, psychologist, business consultant; b. Shreveport, La., Nov. 25, 1946; s. Foster Alexander and Anne Katherine (Moon) Haley; m. Cheryl Elaine Lees, May 9, 1970; 1 child, Savannah Hunter. B.S., U. Tenn., 1970, Ph.D., 1978. Lic. psychologist; cert. vocat. expert. Pvt. practice psychology and cons. Huntsville, Ala., 1978—; pres., v.p., bd. dirs. various cos. Contbr. articles to profl. jours. Mem. Am. Psychol. Assn., Southeastern Psychol. Assn., Ala. Psychol. Assn., Phi Beta Kappa. Republican. Home: Five Old Chimney Rd Huntsville AL 35801 Office: Lees-Haley Inc PO Box 864 Huntsville AL 35801

LEESON, TERESITA BAYTAN, school counselor; b. Havana, Cuba, Mar. 25, 1943; d. Rogaciano Ganive and Carmen (Lateulade) Baytan; m. John Joseph Leeson, Dec. 20, 1969; children—Carina Marie, Ben Albert. B.A., U. Miami, 1965, M.A., 1973; Ph.D., U. Fla., 1985. Tchr., Dade County Sch. System, Miami, 1967-72, Bishop Kenny High Sch., Jacksonville, 1975-76; resource specialist Duval County Sch. System, Jacksonville, 1977-82; tchr. Seminole County Sch. System, Longwood, Fla., 1983-84; counselor Orange County Sch. Systems, Orlando, 1984—. Cons. cross-cultural counseling. Mem. Am. Assn. Counseling and Devel., Fla. Assn. Counseling and Devel., Orange County Assn. Counseling and Devel., Jr. High League, Sigma Alpha Iota, Sigma Delta Pi, Kappa Delta Pi. Democrat. Roman Catholic. Avocations: Piano; tennis; reading; swimming. Home: 1204 Augusta National Blvd Winter Springs FL 32708 Office: Stonewall Jackson Jr High Sch 1103 Stonewall Jackson Rd Orlando FL 32807

LEETARU, HANNES EDMUND, geologist; b. N.Y.C., June 21, 1953; s. Edmund Eduard and Ilse (Kopper) L.; B.S. in Geology cum laude, SUNY, Fredonia, 1975; M.S., Syracuse (N.Y.) U., 1979; m. Marilyn Elizabeth King, July 1, 1978; 1 son, Kalev. Exploration geologist Getty Oil Co., Houston, 1978-84, Champlin Petroleum, Houston, 1984—. Grantee Sigma Xi, 1976. Mem. Am. Assn. Petroleum Geologists, Am. Soc. Photogrammetry. Lutheran. Home: 7426 San Pablo St Houston TX 77083 Office: 4 Allen Ctr 1400 Smith St Suite 1500 Houston TX 77002

LEFEBER, EDWARD JAMES, physician; b. Wauwatosa, Wis., June 1, 1911; s. Cornelius George and May (McCord) L.; 1936; m. Ellie Hancock Weisiger, June 4, 1938; children—Edward James, Robert Randolph, John Courtney, Ann Elizabeth, Donald Louis, Nancy Ellen. B.S., U. Wis., 1934, M.D., 1936. Intern, resident in medicine Med. Coll. Va. Hosps., Richmond, 1936-40; mem. faculty Med. Br., U. Tex., Galveston, 1940—, clin. asso. prof. medicine, 1951-83, clin. prof. medicine and family practice, 1983—, dir. Student Health Service, 1943-46; practice medicine, specializing in internal medicine Internal Medicine Assos., Galveston, 1948—; chief out-patient service Galveston office Houston Regional Office, VA, 1946-48; cons. gastroenterology USPHS Hosp., Galveston, 1952-53; pres. staff St. Mary's Infirmary, Galveston, 1961; mem. adv. com. on nursing home affairs Tex. Dept. Health, 1976-82. Bd. dirs. Galveston chpt. ARC, 1958-78; mem. Galveston Civic Orch., 1957-60; mem. Tex. Bd. Licensure for Nursing Home Adminstrs., 1979—; bd. dirs. Moody House, 1964-65, 67-71, med. dir. Diplomate Am. Bd. Internal Medicine. Fellow ACP; mem. Galveston County Med. Soc. (pres. 1954, sec.-treas. 1948-53), AMA, Tex., So. med. assns., Am., Tex. (pres. 1977) socs. internal medicine, Am. Soc. Gastro-Intestinal Endoscopy, Tex. Club Internists, Phi Chi. Episcopalian (past vestryman). Club: Masons. Home: 2927 Bernardo de Galvez Galveston TX 77550 Office: Sealy Smith Profl Bldg 200 University Blvd Galveston TX 77550

LEFEMINE, ARMAND ANGELO, thoracic surgeon, educator; b. Windsor Licks, Conn., Sept. 14, 1926; s. Vito and Mary (Casarola) L.; m. Natalie Jenckes, June 10, 1952; children—Stephen, Linda, David, Carolyn. B.S., Holy Cross Coll., 1948; M.D., Harvard U., 1952. Diplomate Am. Bd. Surgery, Am. Bd. Thoracic Surgery. Intern USPHS Hosp., Brighton, Mass., 1952-53; resident Boston VA Hosp., 1953-57, Rutland Heights VA Hosp., 1957-58, Peter Bent Brigham Hosp.-Mt. Auburn Hosp., 1958-60; assoc. in surgery Peter Bent Brigham Hosp., Boston, 1960-66; staff surgeon Hartford Hosp., Conn., 1966-69; chief cardiothoracic surgery St. Elizabeth Hosp., Boston, 1969-78; chief surgery VA Med. Ctr., Johnson City, Tenn., 1978, prof. surgery, 1978—; assoc. chmn. dept. surgery East Tenn. State U., Johnson City, 1983—. Author: Surgery and Acquired Lesions of the Heart and Pericardum, 1978. Contbr. articles to profl. jours. Served with USN, 1944-45. Grantee Conn. Heart Assn. 1966-67, Tenn. affiliate Am. Heart Assn. 1979-80, Mass. Heart Assn. 1971-72, VA merit rev., 1984—. Fellow ACS; mem. Am. Assn. Thoracic Surgery, Soc. Thoracic Surgeons, Internat. Coll. Vascular Surgeons. Roman Catholic. Avocation: painting. Office: VA Med Ctr Mountain Home TN 37684

LEFEVER, MICHAEL GRANT, criminologist; b. Lancaster, Pa., Sept. 12, 1947; s. Norwood Grant and Frances (Gillespie) LeF. B.A. in English, Presbyn. Coll., 1969; M.P.A., U. S.C., 1976. Claims rep. Underwriters Adjusting Co., Columbia, S.C., 1972-73; project adminstr. CATAYTIC, Inc., Charlotte, N.C., 1973-75; dept. dir. S.C. Dept. Juvenile Placement and Aftercare, Columbia, 1977-81, dir., 1981; asst. commr. for adminstrn. S.C. Dept. Youth Services, Columbia, 1981-82, dep. commr., 1982—; mem. Gov.'s Juvenile Justice Adv. Council, Columbia, 1981—; chmn. Serious and Violent Offender Study Com., Columbia, 1981—; cons. Gov.'s Children Coordinating Cabinet, Columbia, 1981—. Committeeman Richland County Democratic Party, Columbia, 1978-81; pres. Palmetto State Alumni chpt. Theta Chi, Columbia, 1973-83, Columbia Area Alumni Assn., Presbyn. Coll., Columbia, 1979; v.p. Windcrest Villas Homeowners Assn., North Myrtle Beach, S.C., 1983—. Served with U.S. Army, 1970-71. Recipient Outstanding Young Alumnus award Presbyn. Coll. Alumni Assn., Clinton, S.C., 1981. Mem. Nat. Youth Work Alliance (chmn. 1982-83), S.C. Youth Workers Assn. (bd. dirs. 1979-83). Democrat. Lodge: Rotary. Home: 4127 Devine St Columbia SC 29205 Office: SC Dept Youth Services PO Box 7367 Columbia SC 29202

LEFEVRE, CHARLENE, motor club executive, fashion consultant; b. Richland, Tex., Oct. 18, 1924; d. William Rufus and Sophie (Sherrard) Fetty; m. Deward Forrest LeFevre, Aug. 23, 1942; children—Susan Elaine LeFevre Freitas, Biff Forrest. Grad. Wortham High Sch., 1942. Mng. dir. Wortham Jour., Tex., 1955-66; dir. auto travel Southwest Motor Club, Dallas, 1967—. Named Top Tex. Travel Counselor, Am. Automobile Assn., 1969. Mem. Discover Tex. Assn., Tex. Tourist Devel. Assn. Methodist. Avocations: fashion creating; bridge; golf; tennis. Home: 11323 Earlywood St Dallas TX 75218 Office: Southwest Motor Club 4425 N Central St Dallas TX 75218

LEFEVRE, GERALDINE, librarian; b. Seminole, Okla., Nov. 18, 1925; d. Herman Cecil and Mary Elizabeth (Hill) Sullivan; widowed; 1 dau., Kathleen. B.A. in Library Sci.; M.L.S., U. Okla., 1947. Children's librarian San Antonio Pub. Library, 1950-55, librarian-in-charge, 1955-61, children's coordinator, 1961-70, asst. library dir., 1970—; past chmn. Tex. Library System, San Antonio; mem. technician adv. bd. San Antonio Coll. Library, 1983; mem. San Antonio Council of Presidents, 1978-80; bd. dirs. Beautify San Antonio. Recipient award of appreciation San Antonio Ind. Tchrs. Council, 1979, award of appreciation San Antonio Youth Orgn., 1979, Spl. Recognition award San Antonio Council of Presidents, 1979. Mem. Bexar Library Assn. (chmn. 1960-61, Julia Grothaus award 1982), Tex. Library Assn. (past chmn. dist. 10, chmn. local arrangements 1982), ALA, Friends of San Antonio Pub. Library, Adminstrv. Mgmt. Assn. of San Antonio. Clubs: Women's Breakfast, Knife and Fork (San Antonio), Zonta (pres. San Antonio, 1978-80). Home: 15118 Circle Oak San Antonio TX 78232 Office: Pub Library San Antonio TX

LEFEVRE, RICHARD J., art educator, graphic designer, illustrator; b. Rochester, N.Y., Feb. 11, 1931; s. Harold John and Mary Lou (Geitener) LeF.; m. Shirley Bryant, June 14, 1952 (div. 1976); children—Corey J., Amy J., Geoffrey P.; m. Carol Ann Summers, Dec. 11, 1976. A.A.S., Rochester Inst. Tech., 1952, B.S., 1955, M.F.A., 1967. Designer, Todd Co., Rochester, 1954-55, S.M. Crossett, Rochester, 1955-58, LeFevre Studios Inc., Rochester, 1958-65; prof. art U. Tenn., Knoxville, 1967—; free lance designer, Knoxville, 1967—; also painter. Adviser Tenn. Arts Commn., Nashville, 1973-75, Knoxville, 1981. Served with USN, 1952-54. Recipient over 50 awards in painting and design. Episcopalian. Avocation: folk singing with guitar. Home: PO Box 281 Seymour TN 37865

LEFFLER, CHARLES WILLIAM, physiology and biophysics educator; b. Cleve., May 21, 1947; s. William Bain and Marjorie Adele (Smith) L.; m. Robin Davis Burke, Aug. 23, 1968; 1 dau., Noelle Burke. Student DePauw U., 1965-68; B.S., U. Miami, 1969; M.S., U. Fla., 1971, Ph.D., 1974. Postdoctoral fellow dept. physiology U. Fla., Gainesville, 1974-76; asst. prof. physiology and biophysics U. Louisville Sch. Medicine, 1976-77; asst. prof. physiology and biophysics U. Tenn. Ctr. for Health Scis., Memphis, 1977-81, assoc. prof., 1981—; established investigator Am. Heart Assn., 1982—. Grad. council fellow U. Fla., 1973-74. Mem. Am. Physiol. Soc., Soc. for Exptl. Biology and Medicine, Am. Soc. Zoologists, Cardiopulmonary Council of Am. Heart Assn., Phi Beta Kappa. Contbr. articles to profl. publs. Office: 894 Union Ave NA427 Memphis TN 38163

LEFLER, MICHAEL DOUGLAS, personnel and job service specialist; b. Memphis, June 3, 1946; s. Bourton Douglas and Allie (Beard) L.; m. Margaret Clay, June 21, 1971. Student Christian Bros. Coll., 1965; B.A., Memphis State U., 1974; postgrad. in bus. adminstrn. Old Dominion U., 1975. Accredited personnel specialist. Engring. aide Pickering Egnrs., Memphis, 1963-64; stock clk. Sears Roebuck Co., Memphis, 1965-66, quality control insp., 1970-71, customer service mgr., 1972-73, personnel asst., 1973-74; employment specialist N.C. Job Service, Ahoskie, 1976—; instr. bus. R-C Tech. Coll., Ahoskie, 1977—. Graphic artist: History of Reynoldson Ch., 1980; coll. logo of Roanoke-Chowan Tech. Coll., 1981. Cons., Gates County Hist. Soc. (N.C.), 1983. Served with USAF, 1966-70; Korea. Recipient Presdl. Achievement award Republican Nat. Com., 1982; Cert. Appreciation Employment Security Commn., 1982. Mem. Econ. Research Inst. Am. (RIA Supr. award 1981), Internat. Assn. Personnel in Employment Service (v.p. 1982, edn. chmn. vet. services 1981, 82), DAV (vets. service officer 1980-83). Club: Gates Hunt (N.C.; sec.-treas. 1978-83). Home: Route 2 Box 172 Gates NC 27937 Office: 717 E Memorial Dr Ahoskie NC 27910

LEFLER, WADE HAMPTON, JR., ophthalmologist; b. Statesville, N.C., Feb. 27, 1937; s. Wade Hampton and Eunice Trudye (Chilcoat) L.; A.B., U. N.C., Chapel Hill, 1959; M.D., Bowman Gray Sch. Medicine, 1963; m. Katherine Webb Davis, Apr. 1, 1961; children—Elizabeth Ashley, Rosemary Kirsten. Med. intern N.Y. Hosp., Cornell Med. Center, 1963-64; resident in ophthalmology Duke U. Med. Center, 1966-69; practice medicine specializing in ophthalmology, Hickory, N.C., 1969—; partner Graystone Eye, Ear, Nose, Throat Center, Hickory, 1974—; clin. asso. prof. ophthalmology Duke Med. Center, 1969—; mem. staff Catawba Meml. Hosp., Hickory, Glenn R. Frye Meml. Hosp., Hickory, Western Carolina Center, Morganton, N.C., Duke Eye Center, Durham, N.C., Broughton Hosp., Morganton, N.C., Oteen VA Hosp., Asheville, N.C. Served to capt. M.C., U.S. Army, 1964-66. Duke U. Med. Center grantee, 1968-70; diplomate Am. Acad. Ophthalmology. Mem. AMA, N.C. Med. Soc., Catawba County Med. Soc., Phi Beta Kappa, Alpha Omega Alpha. Presbyterian. Club: Lake Hickory Country. Home: 1260 6th St NW Hickory NC 28601 Office: PO Box 2588 Hickory NC 28603

LEFLORE, BYRON LOUIS, banker; b. San Antonio, Feb. 6, 1936; s. Louis and Margaret (Byron) LeF.; m. Kathryn Barragan, June 22, 1962; children—Byron Louis, Elizabeth Barragan, James Milo, Campbell Joseph. B.B.A., U. Tex., 1958; grad. Grad. Sch. Credit and Fin. Mgmt., Harvard U., 1973. Asst. v.p. Mission City Bank, San Antonio, 1959-60, v.p., 1960-69, exec. v.p., 1969; v.p. Nat. Bank Commerce, San Antonio, 1969-71, sr. v.p., 1971-73; exec. v.p. Bexar County Nat. Bank, San Antonio, 1973-74, pres., chief exec. officer, 1974-81; chmn. bd. Republic Bank San Antonio, 1981-82; pres., chief exec. officer Jefferson State Bank, 1982—. Chmn. adv. council Coll. Bus., U. Tex.-San Antonio; bd. dirs. Centro 21 Task Force, San Antonio Econ. Devel. Council, Downtown, Inc.; trustee Incarnate Word Coll.; mem. San Antonio Air Force Community Council; mem. Alamo Heights Planning and Zoning Commn.; mem. Greater San Antonio Mil. Affairs Steering Com.; mem. Fiesta San Antonio Commn. Recipient award Am. Petroleum Credit Assn., 1973; Archbishop Francis J. Furey medal, 1973. Mem. Bank Adminstrn. Inst. (bd. dirs. San Antonio chpt.), Tex. Bankers Assn. (dist. chmn.), San Antonio C. of C. Roman Catholic. Clubs: St. Anthony, Conopus. San Antonio German, Tex. Cavaliers, Order of Alamo, Town. Office: PO Box 5190 2900 Fredericksburg Rd San Antonio TX 78284

LEFTWICH, RICHARD HENRY, economics educator; b. Burden, Kans. Feb. 1, 1920; s. Rush F. and Nellie (Batliff) L.; m. Maxine Ellen Dieterich, Mar. 11, 1945; children—Judith E. (dec.), Gregory V., Bradley R. B.A., Southwestern Coll., 1941; M.A., U. Chgo., 1948, Ph.D., 1950; From asst. prof. to assoc. prof. econs. Okla. State U., Stillwater, 1948-55, prof., 1955-75, head dept., 1966-75, regent prof., 1975—, dir. Market Economy Edn. Ctr., 1980—. Ford Found. faculty research fellow, 1959-60; vis. prof. U. Chgo., 1962-63; disting. vis. prof. Am. U., Cairo, 1977, Tunghai U., Taiwan, 1981; mem. GRE advanced econs. com., Ednl. Testing Service, 1969-75, chmn. GRE advanced econs. com., 1972-75. Author: The Price System and Resource Allocation, 1955, 9th edit., 1985; An Introduction to Economic Thinking, 1969; A Basic Framework for Economics, 1980, 2d edit., 1984; Productivity in Encyclopedia Americana, 1980; (with Ansel M. Sharp) The Economics of Social Issues, 1974, 7th edit., 1986. Served with USAAF, 1942-45. Decorated Bronze Star; recipient Amoco' Found. outstanding tchr. award, 1980; Merrick Found. teaching award, 1981; Freedoms Found. Leavy award, 1982. Mem. Am. Econs. Assn., Midwestern Econ. Assn. (pres. 1977), So. Econ. Assn. (pres. 1965), Southwestern Econs. Assn. (pres. 1985), Southwestern Social Sci. Assn., Western Social Sci. Assn. (pres. 1973), Beta Gamma Sigma (disting. scholar 1977-78). Home: 818 W Knapp Ave Stillwater OK 74075 Office: Dept Econs Okla State U Stillwater OK 74078

LEGAN, HARRY LEWIS, orthodontic educator; b. St. Paul, Sept. 16, 1948; s. Leo Theodore and Charlotte June (Most) L.; m. Robertanne Turner, Mar. 27, 1982. B.S., U. Minn.-Mpls., 1969, B.A., 1969, D.D.S., 1973; Orthodontic cert. U. Conn., 1977. Asst. prof. surgery U. Tex. Southwestern Med. Sch., Dallas, 1977-83, assoc. prof. surgery, 1983—, dir. orthodontics Health Sci. Ctr. at Dallas, 1977—; orthodontic cons. VA Med. Ctr., Dallas, 1977—, Children's Med. Ctr. Craniofacial Deformities Team, Dallas, 1978—; research cons. U. Conn., Farmington, 1982—. Contbr. chpts. to books, articles to profl. jours. Research fellow NIH, 1974-77; research grantee U. Tex., Dallas, 1978. Mem. Am. Assn. Orthodontists, Southwestern Soc. Orthodontists, ADA, Internat. Assn. for Dental Research, Am. Cleft Palate Assn., Sadi Fontaine Acad. (hon.), Sociedad Colombiana de Ortodoncia (hon.), Sierra Club, Smithsonian Assocs. Avocations: tennis, travel, hiking, farming, reading. Office: Southwestern Med Sch Orthodontic Sect 5323 Harry Hines Blvd Dallas TX 75235

LEGARD, EDWIN NEEL, JR., oil company executive, consultant; b. Marion, Va., May 21, 1938; s. Edwin Neel and Louise Kathryn (Johnston) LeG.; m. Betty Lacy Lyle, July 13, 1963; children—Michelle, Renee, Nicole. Student Va. Poly Inst. and State U., Blacksburg, 1956-58; B.A. in Econs., Emory and Henry Coll., Emory, Va., 1961. Supr. mfg. E.I. duPont de Nemours & Co., Waynesboro, Va., 1966-69; account exec., asst. br. mgr. duPont Walston, Inc., Roanoke, Va., 1969-74; pres. LeGard & Assocs., Roanoke, 1974-80, LeGard Petroleum Co., Roanoke, 1975—. Pres. Cave Spring United Meth. Ch. choir; precinct chmn. Roanoke County Democratic Com.; mem. Roanoke County Pollution Control Bd. Served to comdr. USNR, 1962-83. Recipient Joint Services Commendation medal, 1982. Mem. Va. Oil and Gas Assn., Navy League, Naval Res. Assn., Res. Officers Assn. Lodges: Masons, Shriners. Home: 3946 Sandpiper Dr SW Roanoke VA 24018 Office: LeGard Petroleum Co 4502 Starkey Rd SW Roanoke VA 24014

LEGÉ, CYNTHIA VERRET, nurse; b. Lake Charles, La., Nov. 5, 1955; d. Robert Edgar and Eva Eugenia (Stewart) Verret; student U. Southwestern La., 1973-76; A.S. in Nursing, La. State U., Eunice, 1978; m. Larry Michael Legé, Mar. 1, 1980; children—Christopher Michael, Ann Michelle. Nurse, Am. Legion Hosp., Crowley, La., 1978-79; dir. nursing Lafayette (La.) Guest House, 1979-81; dir. nursing Crowley Town and Country Nursing Home (La.), 1981-83, adminstr., 1983—. Mem. La. Health Care Assn. Dirs. of Nurses (pres. 1981—), Am. Nursing Assn., Bus. and Profl. Women. Democrat. Methodist. Office: PO Box 1274 Crowley LA 70526

LEGG, REAGAN HOUSTON, lawyer; b. Kaufman, Tex., Nov. 18, 1924; s. Edward and Mary Alva (Coon) L.; m. Norma Jean Eden, July 16, 1949 (div. 1976); children—John, Ellen, Emily, Reagan Houston. B.B.A., U. Tex., 1947, LL.B., 1948. Bar: Tex. 1948. Sole practice, Midland, Tex., 1949-51; county atty. Midland County, Tex., 1951-55; ptnr. firm Legg, Saxe and Baskin, Midland, 1955-81, Legg, Aldridge & Carr, Midland, 1981-84. Pres. bd. govs. Midland Community Theatre, 1965-66; pres. Leadership Midland Program, 1978-80; trustee Midland Symphony Assn., 1961-63, Midland Coll., 1970-86, chmn., 1972-75; pres. United Fund, 1953, U. Tex. Ex-Students Assn., 1953; dir. Permian Basin Regional Planning Commn., 1978-85. Recipient Leadership award M. Dale Ensign Community Coll., 1977; named Boss of Yr., Midland Legal Secs. Assn., 1968. Served to lt. (j.g.) USN, 1943-46. Fellow Tex. Bar Found.; mem. ABA, State Bar Tex. (chmn. com. group legal services 1965-72, grievance com. 1975-77, Tex. Trial Lawyers Assn., Am. Judicature Soc., Midland County Bar Assn. (pres. 1966-67), Nat. Assn. Community Coll. Trustees (pres. 1982-83), Tex. Assn. Community Coll. Adminstrs. and Trustees (pres. 1981), Midland C. of C. (dir. 1968-73). Democrat. Methodist. Club: Midland Country. Lodges: Masons, Shriners. Home: 2007 Boyd Midland TX 79705 Office: 1000 Midland Savs Bldg Midland TX 79701

LEGORY, JAMES PATTON, computer executive, consultant, real estate investor; b. Crockett, Tex., July 12, 1940; s. Joe Gus and Bessie Louise (Patton) LeG.; m. Mary Clay Huff, Oct. 13, 1938; children—John, Jennifer, Laura, Martha. B.B.A., U. Tex., 1964; LL.B., Mt. Vernon Sch. Law, 1968; J.D., U. Balt., 1970. Congl. aide, Washington, 1964-66; nat. govt. sales mgr. Dennison Mfg. Co., Washington, 1966-71; nat. sales mgr. SCM Corp., Washington, 1971-72; pres., chmn. Fed. Mktg. Corp., Falls Church, Va., 1972-74; fed. mktg. mgr. EAI Corp., Washington, 1974-76; Dept. Def. mktg. mgr. Perkin-Elmer Corp., McLean, Va., 1976-78; v.p., dir., a founder, gen. counsel Computer & Info. Scis. Corp., Fairfax, Va., 1979—; dir. KRICIS Corp.; cons.; tchr. Served with USNG, 1956-63. U. Tex. scholar, 1959; hon. Tex. ranger. Mem. Inter-Am. Bar Assn. (sr.), Nat. Contract Mgmt. Assn., Am. Mktg. Assn., Antique Oldsmobile Club Am. (past state dir.), SAR, Old Crows. Methodist. Home and office: 8823 Southwick St Fairfax VA 22031

LEGRAND, HARRY ELWOOD, geologist; b. Concord, N.C., May 19, 1917; s. William Pleasant and Nancy Elizabeth (White) LeG.; B.S., U. N.C., 1938; m. Undine Nye, Dec. 23, 1945; children—Harry, Jr., Edmund. With U.S. Geol. Survey, 1946-74, dist. geologist water resources div., Raleigh, N.C., 1949-57, chief radiohydrology sect., Washington, 1960-62, research geologist, Raleigh, 1962-74; cons. geologist, Raleigh, 1974—. Served with AUS, 1941-46. Decorated Bronze star. Fellow Geol. Soc. Am.; mem. Am. Water Resources, Internat. Assn. Hydrogeologists (chmn. nat. com. 1972), Am. Geophys. Union, Soc. Econ. Geologists, Am. Assn. Petroleum Geologists, Am. Inst. Mining

Engrs., Nat. Water Well Assn. (dir.). Author 2 books; contbr. articles to profl. jours. Address: 331 Yadkin Dr Raleigh NC 27609

LEHEW, JAMES DUDLEY, advertising agency executive; b. Hillsboro, Tex., Sept. 30, 1935; s. J.D. and Jimmie Corine Lehew; m. Dorothy Ann Harkins, Apr. 20, 1963; children—Lisa Catherine, Stephanie Lynn, Patrick LaCaffinie, Leigh Corinne. Student La. State U., La. Coll., 1954-59. Reporter, Baton Rouge Morning Advocate, 1960; reporter A.P., Baton Rouge, 1961, Miami, 1961, New Orleans, 1961, reporter, editor, Jackson, Miss., 1962-64, reporter, editor, supr., Atlanta, 1964-68, supr., Boston, 1968-72, supr., exec., N.Y.C., 1972-78; owner Impact III, pub. relations, Jackson, Miss., 1978-79; exec. v.p. G. Williams & Assocs., Jackson, 1979—. Bd. dirs. Miss. div. ARC, Miss. chpt. Epilepsy Found. Am. Recipient Broadcast Writing award A.P. Broadcasters Assn., 1966, 67; Addy award Am. Advt. Fedn., 1983. Mem. Pub. Relations Soc. Am. (pres.), Pub. Relations Assn. Miss. (pres.), So. Pub. Relations Fedn. (bd. dirs.), Sales and Mktg. Execs. Internat. (bd. dirs. Jackson), World's Fair Council (bd. dirs.). Home: 1004 Tanglewood St Clinton MS 39056 Office: G Williams & Assocs Bldg E The Quarter Jackson MS 39216

LEHIGH, GEORGE EDWARD, medical group administrator, management executive; b. Graettinger, Iowa, Feb. 3, 1927; s. Earl F. and Rachel F. (Baker) L.; student N.D. State U., 1944-45, W.Va. U., 1945; B.A., Buena Vista Coll., 1948; postgrad. Drake U., 1949, 50; m. Karla Bair; children—Bruce V., Susan Paige. Tchr. secondary schs., Iowa, 1953-54; prin. secondary schs., Iowa and Minn., 1948-51, 57-58; jr. exec. World Ins. Co., 1951-54; field cons. Profl. Mgmt. Midwest, Waterloo, Iowa, 1954-57; bus. adminstr. Mankato (Minn.) Clinic, 1958-70; adminstr. Austin (Tex.) Diagnostic Clinic, 1970-75, Jackson Clinic, P.A., Jackson, Tenn., 1975-77; exec. adminstr. Thomas-Davis Clinic, P.C., Tucson, 1977-80; dir. adminstrn. law firm Brown, Maroney, Rose, Baker & Barber, Austin, Tex., 1980-82; exec. adminstr. Capitol Anesthesiology Assn., Austin, 1982—; pres. A.P.S. Practice Mgmt., Inc., 1984-85; dir., treas. Profl. Health Services, Inc., Tucson, 1977-80; dir. Richardson Securities, Inc., A.P.S. Practice Mgmt., Inc. Bd. dirs. Credit Bur., Mankato, 1960-70, pres., 1967. Fellow Am. Coll. Med. Group Adminstrs.; mem. Med. Group Mgmt. Assn., Austin-Central Tex. Assn. Legal Adminstrs. (pres. 1981-82), Anesthesia Adminstrn. Assembly (chmn. 1983-85). Republican. Methodist. Club: Kiwanis. Office: 1005 W 38th St Suite 200 Austin TX 78705

LEHMAN, MALCOLM E., management educator; b. Danville, Pa., May 15, 1942; s. Malcom E. and Mary Ann (Labalaukis) L.; m. Mary Ann Dauksha, Sept. 5, 1964. B.S., U. Mo.-Columbia, 1971, M.Ed., 1975; postgrad. U. Ark., 1983—. Instr. U. Mo.-Columbia, 1972-75; asst. prof. Boise State U., Idaho, 1975-78, assoc. prof., 1978-79; asst. prof. U. Ark. Med. Sci. Campus, Little Rock, 1979-80; instr. supr./mgmt. devel. Bapt. Med. System, Little Rock, 1980—, facilitator, coordinator quality circle program, 1983—; mem. adj. faculty Webster U., Little Rock AFB, Jacksonville, Ark., 1983—. Contbr. articles, reviews to profl. publs. Mem. sch. bd. Our Lady Fatima Elem. Sch., Benton, Ark., 1984—. Mem. Ark. Soc. Tng. and Devel. (cert. Appreciation 1984, Outstanding New Mem. of Yr. 1985), Am. Soc. Tng. and Devel., Internat. Assn. Quality Circles (cert. facilitator), Am. Assn. Adult and Continuing Edn. Republican. Roman Catholic. Avocations: saxophone; canoeing; hiking; camping; gardening. Home: 12407 Coleen Dr Little Rock AR 72212 Office: Human Resource Devel Dept Baptist Med System 9601 Interstate 630 Exit 7 Little Rock AR 72205

LEHMAN, WILLIAM, congressman; b. Selma, Ala., Oct. 5, 1913; s. Maurice M. and Corinne L. (Leva) L.; m. Joan Feibelman, 1939; children—William, Kathy Lehman Weiner (dec.), Tom. Owner car sales and finance bus., Miami, Fla., 1936-41, 46-66; owner William Lehman Buick, North Miami Beach, 1966-72; tchr. Dade County Public Schs., Miami-Dade County Community Coll., 1963-66; mem. 93d-99th Congresses from 17th Dist. Fla., 1973—, mem. com. on appropriations, chmn. subcom. on transp., mem. select com. on children, youth and families. Mem. Dade County Sch. Bd., Miami, 1966-72, chmn., 1971-72; mem. U.S. Holocaust Meml. Council. Named Humanitarian of Year, Am. Jewish Com., 1972. Democrat. Office: 2347 Rayburn House Office Bldg Washington DC 20515*

LEHMANN, ROBERT PAUL, ophthalmologist; b. Massilon, Ohio, Aug. 18, 1947; s. Albert P. and June Faye (Stegkamper) L.; m. Charlene Janina Manley, May 13, 1968 (div. 1984); children—Charles, Lara, Emily, Angelique. B.S., Marquette U., 1969; M.D., Med. Coll. Wis., 1973. Diplomate Am. Bd. Ophthalmology. Physician, Nacogdoches Med. Ctr. Hosp., Tex., 1977—, Nacogdoches Meml. Hosp., 1977—; clin. investigator Ioptex, Iolab, Coopervision. Fellow Am. Acad. Ophthalmology; mem. ACS, Am. Intraocular Implant Soc. Episcopalian. Avocation: outdoor sports. Home: Route 7 Box 1320 Nacogdoches TX 75961 Office: 4848 NE Stallings Dr Suite 102 Nacogdoches TX 75961

LEHNER, JOHN MICHAEL, architect; b. Queens, N.Y., Aug. 20, 1929; s. George and Margareta (Ott) L.; m. Carolyn Albergmina, Apr. 27, 1975; children—Raymond, Annmarie Lehner, Debbie, Donna Maggiore. Student architecture, SUNY, 1969-71, N.Y. Structural Inst., 1966-69, Inst. of Design and Constrn. 1953-54. Registered architect, N.Y., Va., Md. Project architect A.H. Salkowitz AIA, Jamica, N.Y., 1953-69, Lathrop Douglass FAIA, N.Y., 1969-72; v.p. design Lerner Corp., Wheaton, Md., 1972-75; prin. John M. Lehner, AIA, Sterling, Va., 1975-76, 1981—; constrn. project mgr. C.B.I. Fairmac Corp., Arlington, Va., 1976-78, Rouse Co., Columbia, Md., 1978-80, Arcade Square Ltd., Dayton, Ohio, 1980-81; ptnr. Pence/Petrie Properties, Inc., McLean, Va., 1983—. Mem. adv. bd. Loudoun City Parks and Recreation, Leesburg, Va., 1980-83; mem. adv. plannng bd. West Loudoun Citizens, Leesburg, 1981-83. Served with U.S. Army, 1948-52. Recipient Cert. of Appreciation Arcade Sq. Bd. of Dirs., 1981. Mem. AIA (Queens and N.Y. State chpts.), N.Y. Soc. Architects, Sterling Park Jaycees (recipient outstanding com. service award 1978). Avocations: stamp collecting; fishing Home: 119 Evergreen St Sterling VA 22170 Home: 119 Evergreen St Sterling VA 22170 Office: Pence/Petrie Properties 1360 Beverly Rd McLean VA 22101

LEHR, EDWIN ERVIN, college administrator; b. Baytown, Tex., Nov. 2, 1933; s. Edd and Carrie (Burns) L.; m. Dovie Jo May, Dec. 26, 1964; children—Edwin E., Lynda Irene, Holly Lynn. B.A. in History, Sam Houston State Tchrs. Coll., Huntsville, Tex., 1956, M.A. in History and Govt., 1961; Ph.D. in Econ. History, Tex. Christian U., Ft. Worth, 1972. Cert. secondary tchr., Tex. Tchr., Goose Creek Ind. Sch. Dist., Baytown, 1957-61; tchr. San Jacinto Coll., Houston, 1961-68, head dept., 1968-70, 71-72, dir. Clear Creek Extension, 1973-74, v.p. North campus, 1974-80, pres., 1980—; dir. Northshore Bank. Chmn. planning and zoning City of Deer Park, Tex., 1967-68, 71-73, councilman, 1969-70, 73-74; pres. North Channel Emergency Med. Service, Harris County, Tex., 1981-82, 82-83; dir. Northshore YMCA, Houston, 1980-83. Served with USAR, 1955-63. Recipient Geissenbier Meml. award U.S. Jaycees, 1968; Outstanding Young Educator award Deer Park Jaycees, 1968; Acme Brick Co. grantee, 1971. Mem. Southwestern Social Sci. Assn., Tex. Jr. Coll. Tchrs. Assn., Tex. Pub. Community Jr. Coll. Assn., Tex. Hist. Assn., Deer Park Jaycees (pres. 1967-68), North Channel Area C. of C. (pres. 1977-78), East Tex. C. of C. (dir. 1982—), Phi Theta Kappa, Phi Alpha Theta, Pi Gamma Nu, Phi Delta Kappa, Sigma Delta Nu. Democrat. Baptist. Lodges: Rotary, Masons (Houston). Author: From Kiln to Conglomerate: A History of the Acme Brick Company, 1972. Office: 5800 Uvalde St Houston TX 77049

LEHRER, KENNETH EUGENE, realtor; b. N.Y.C., Apr. 17, 1946; s. Charles Carlton and Evelyn Estelle (Rosenfeld) L.; B.S., NYU, 1967, M.B.A., 1969, M.A., 1972, D.Pub. Adminstrn., 1980; m. Myrna Sue Newman, Apr. 4, 1981. Asst. treas. Bankers Trust Co., N.Y.C., 1970-73; dir. devel. Coventry Devel. Corp., N.Y.C., 1974-77; asst. v.p. Affiliated Capital Corp., Houston, 1977-80; dir. fin. Allison/Walker Interests, Houston, 1980-82; v.p. real estate devel. Lehrer Devel. and Investments, 1982—. Pres. Cornerstone Mcpl. Utilities Dist., 1978-85. Mem. Am. Horse Show Assn., Nat. Steeplechase and Hunt Assn. (life), U.S. Tennis Assn. (life), Am. Real Estate and Urban Econs. Assn., Nat. Assn. Bus. Economists, New York Univ. Money Marketeers, NYU Alumni Fedn. (dir. 1974-77), Tex. Republicans Assn. Clubs: Atrium, N.Y. U. (N.Y.C.); Jockey (Miami, Fla.); Lakeway World of Tennis (Austin, Tex.). Home: 5555 Del Monte Dr #802 Houston TX 77056 Office: 5718 Westheimer Rd Suite 1515 Houston TX 77057

LEIBOLD, MARY LOUISE, librarian, book seller; b. Wheeling, W.Va., Apr. 10, 1916; d. William Oliver, Jr. and Marie (Brandfass) McCluskey; m. Robert Waltner Leibold, June 26, 1942; children—David, Stephen, Richard, Robert Waltner. Student Duke U., 1936-37; A.B., Conn. Coll., 1938; M.A., U. Pitts., 1941; M.A. in L.S., U. Wis.-Madison, 1966. Cert. English tchr. English tchr. Ohio County Schs., Wheeling, 1941-42, 65; asst. librarian Wheeling Coll., 1962-64; librarian West Liberty State Coll., Wheeling, 1966-71; owner, mgr. Goldberry's Book Store, Wheeling, 1978-81; acquisitions librarian Vance Meml. Ch. Library, Wheeling, 1982—. Pres., Wheeling Area LWV, 1969, bd. dirs. W.Va., 1971-73; bd. dirs. Florence Crittenton Home, Salvation Army, YWCA (all Wheeling). Mem. ALA, Beta Phi Mu, Pi Beta Phi Alumnae (pres. Wheeling). Republican. Presbyterian. Home: RD 4 Cloverfields Wheeling WV 26003

LEIBSON, CHARLES M., state supreme court justice; b. Louisville, June 30, 1929; m. Margaret Leibson. LL.B. cum laude, U. Louisville, 1952. Bar: Ky. 1952. Ptnr. firm Leibson & Leibson, 1954-70, Leibson & McCarthy, 1970-75; judge Ky. Cir. Ct., Louisville, 1976-82; assoc. justice Ky. Supreme Ct., Louisville, 1982—; lectr. courtroom law U. Louisville Sch. Law, 1969-82; co-chmn. Louisville Law-Sci. Found., 1969-71; bd. advisors Ct. Practice Inst., 1972—. Served to 1st lt. JAGC, U.S. Army, 1952-54. Fellow Internat. Acad. Trial Lawyers (founder); mem. Assn. Trial Lawyers Am. (gov. 1968-71, named outstanding state trial judge 1980, outstanding state appellate judge 1985), Internat. Acad. Trial Judges, Internat. Circle Advs. Ky. Assn. Trial Attys. (pres. 1965). Office: Kentucky Supreme Court Capitol Bldg Frankfort KY 40601

LEIBSON, DAVID JAY, lawyer, law educator, consultant; b. Louisville, Mar. 18, 1944; s. Albert and Dorothy Alise (Reibert) L.; m. Phyllis Arion Dobrin, Aug. 18, 1968. B.A. cum laude, Vanderbilt U., 1966; J.D. cum laude, U. Louisville, 1969; LL.M., Harvard U., 1979. Bar: Ky. 1969. Assoc., Leibson and Franklin, 1970-72; instr. law U. Louisville, 1971-72, asst. prof., 1972-75, assoc. prof., 1975-77, prof., 1977—, assoc. dean, 1985—; vis. prof. U. Pacific, 1978-79; lectr., cons. in comml. law field; cons. Spl. Study Commn. Uniform Comml. Code, Ky. Legislature. Vice pres. Louisville Jewish Community Ctr.; bd. dirs. Jewish Community Fedn. Mem. Ky. Bar Assn., Brandeis Soc., Phi Kappa Phi. Club: Standard Country (Louisville). Author: (with Nowka) The Uniform Commercial Code of Kentucky, 1983; contbr. articles to profl. jours. Office: U Louisville Sch of Law Louisville KY 40292

LEICHNETZ, GEORGE ROBERT, anatomy educator; b. Buffalo, Oct. 15, 1942; s. George and Alberta G. (Black) L.; m. Athalie Joan Arhcibald, Sept. 2, 1967; children—Keri Elizabeth, Geoffrey Scott, Joel Ethan. B.S. in Zoology, Wheaton Coll., 1964; M.S. in Anatomy, Ohio State U., 1966, Ph.D. in Anatomy, 1970. Instr. Ohio State U., Columbus, 1969-70; asst. prof. anatomy Med. Coll. Va., Va. Commonwealth U., Richmond, 1970-78, assoc. prof., 1978-85, prof., 1985—. Contbr. articles to profl. publs. Vocalist, Chorus of Alumni and Friends of U. Richmond, 1978—; bass soloist Sing Along Messiah, Va. Ctr. for Performing Arts, Richmond, 1984, 85. NSF grantee, 1978—. Mem. Am. Assn. Anatomists, Cajal Club Neuroanatomy, Soc. Neurosci. Republican. Baptist. Home: 2200 Banstead Rd Midlothian VA 23113 Office: Med Coll Va Va Commonwealth U Dept Anatomy Box 709 Richmond VA 23298

LEIDY, ROSS BENNETT, research scientist, educator; b. Newark, Ohio, June 1, 1939; s. Myron Willis and Marigold Olga (Hall) L.; m. Nancy Elaine Antoine, May 1, 1971; B.S. in Physiology, Tex. A&M U., 1963, M.S. in Radiation Biology, 1966; Ph.D. in Biochemistry, Auburn U., 1972. Chemist Dow Chem. Co., Freeport, Tex., 1960-61, Pennwalt Chem. Co., Bryan, Tex., 1961-63; grad. research asst. Radiation Biology Labs., Tex. A&M U., College Station, 1963-66; instr. U.S. Army Chem. Ctr. and Sch., Ft. McClellan, Ala., 1966-68; grad. research asst. biochemistry Auburn U. (Ala.), 1968-72; NIH research fellow N.C. State U., Raleigh, 1972-73, sr. research scientist Pesticide Residue Research Lab., 1974—; supr. Pesticide Residue Lab. Dept. Human Resources, State of N.C., Raleigh, 1973-74; cons., mem. faculty toxicology program crop sci. dept. N.C. State U. Served to lt. col. Chem. Corps, USAR, 1963—. Mem. N.Y. Acad. Scis., N.C. Acad. Scis., N.C. Entomol. Soc., Sigma Xi. Contbr. tech. reports, articles and textbook chpts. to profl. lit. Home: 5128 Norman Pl Raleigh NC 27606 Office: Pesticide Residue Lab N C State U 3709 Hilsborough St Raleigh NC 27607

LEIGH, BEVERLY EUGENE, oil company executive; b. Savannah, Ga., Jan. 5, 1924; s. Herbert David and Pauline C. (Rehm) L.; m. Mary Pindar, Dec. 22, 1944 (dec. Feb. 1968); children—John David II, Julia Montgomery Leigh West; m. Elizabeth LeHardy, Jan. 30, 1971. Student U. Ga., 1944-45, Ga. Sch. Tech., 1946-48. Treas., Colonial Oil Industries, Savannah, 1957—, exec. v.p., 1971—. Chmn. Savannah Transit Authority. Office: Colonial Oil Industries Inc N Lathrop Ave Savannah GA 31402

LEIGH, TIMOTHY YARBROUGH, nursing home adminstr.; b. Tallahassee, Dec. 30, 1955; s. Giles Yarbrough and Christine (Brantley) L.; B.S. cum laude, Western Ky. U., 1977; m. Carol Tinkle, Sept. 8, 1979. Sales rep. Gen. Med. Corp., Tampa, Fla., 1977-78; staff asst. to dean, Coll. Applied Arts and Health, Western Ky. U., 1978; adminstr. Cedars of Lebanon Rest Home, Inc., Lebanon, Ky., 1978-79; adminstr. Green Valley Personal Care Home, Carrollton, Ky., 1979-80; exec. dir. Parkway Med. Center, Louisville, 1980—; regional mgr. managed nursing home ops. United Med. Corp., 1981—; v.p. Health Concepts Corp., Louisville, 1983—. Mem. peer rev. com. Ky. Assn. Health Care Facilities. Bd. dirs. Lincoln-Cumberland Area Health Edn. System, 1978-79; mem. No. Ky. Subarea Health Council Edn. Com., 1979-80; co-chmn. Carrollton All Kentucky City Program, 1979-80; mem. Carroll County Meml. Hosp. Physician Recruitment Com., 1979-80. Mem. Ky. Assn. Health Care Facilities (mem. edn. com., non-proprietary com.), Carroll County Louisville chambers commerce, Am. Coll. Nursing Home Adminstrs. (sec. Ky. chpt. 1981-82, v.p. 1982-83, pres. 1983-84), Pi Sigma Alpha. Republican. Mem. Ch. of Christ. Office: Health Concept Corp 109 Daventry Ln Louisville KY 40223

LEINBACH, LAURENCE BRICKENSTEIN, radiologist, educator; b. Winston-Salem, N.C., Feb. 22, 1926; s. Clarence Theodore and Margaret Catherine (Brickenstein) L.; m. Kathryn Lou McNair, June 18, 1949; children—Elizabeth, Margaret, Kathryn, Laurence. A.B., U.N.C., 1948; M.D., Harvard U., 1952. Lic. physician N.C. 1952; diplomate Am. Bd. Radiology. Intern Harvard Med. Service, Boston, 1952-53, asst. resident in medicine, 1953-54; resident in radiology Peter Bent Brigham Hosp., Boston, 1954-57; teaching fellow in medicine Harvard Med. Sch., Boston City Hosp., 1953-54, instr. in radiology Peter Bent Brigham Hosp., 1956-57; instr. radiology Bowman Gray Sch. Medicine, 1957-63, asst. prof., 1963-66, assoc. prof., 1966-79, prof., 1979—, mem. resident selection com., radiology dept., 1970-73, chmn., 1972-73. Bd. dirs. Bowman Gray Found., Forsyth County Heart Assn. Served with USAAF, 1944-46. Fellow Am. Coll. Radiology (guest examiner 1975-79); mem. AMA, Med. Soc. State N.C., Forsyth County Med. Soc., N.C. Heart Assn., Am. Roentgen Ray Soc., Assn. Univ. Radiologists, Radiol. Soc. N.Am., Eastern Radiol. Soc. (bd. dirs. 1971-73, sec. 1978-81, pres. 1981-82). Contbr. articles and abstracts to profl. publs. Home: 1060 Kenleigh Circle Winston-Salem NC 27106 Office: Bowman Gray Sch of Medicine Dept Radiology Winston-Salem NC 27103

LEINER, MELISSA GAYLE, financial planner, consultant; b. Salinas, Calif., Feb. 20, 1953; d. Fred B. and Helen G. (Gertner) L.; B.A., Skidmore Coll., 1975. Sales asst. Paine Webber Jackson & Curtis, N.Y.C., 1976, Kidder Peabody, Washington, 1977-78; fin. cons., fin. planner Shearson Am. Express, McLean, Va., from 1978; now v.p., fin. cons. Shearson Lehman Am. Express. Active United Jewish Appeal, Nat. Council Jewish Women. Cert. fin. planner. Mem. Internat. Assn. Fin. Planners, Stockbrokers Soc., Skidmore Coll. Alumni Assn. Club: Skidmore Coll. Alumni (pres. Washington area). Office: Shearson 8260 Greensboro Dr McLean VA 22102

LEISK, JAMES CLARK, petroleum consultant; b. Waldo, Ark., May 3, 1929; s. William Charles and Julia Evelyn (Fincher) L.; B.S. in Petroleum Engring., La. State U., 1951; m. Anna Glen Gute, June 25, 1955; children—Julia Ann, Catherine Glen. With Union Producing Co., 1953-67, field drilling and prodn. supt., Tinsley, Miss., 1963-67; dist. petroleum engr., then sr. engr. Pennzoil Producing Co., 1967-72; cons. T.W. McGuire & Assos., Inc., Shreveport, 1972-78, Caddo Oil Co., Inc., 1978-82; ind. petroleum cons., 1982—. Served as 2d lt. C.E., AUS, 1951-52. Mem. Soc. Petroleum Engrs., Am. Petroleum Inst. (com. on standardization of prodn. equipment), U.S. Power Squadrons, Delta Kappa Epsilon. Republican. Baptist. Club: Shreveport Yacht. Home and Office: 4026 Gilbert Shreveport LA 71106

LEIST, JACK LESLIE, building contractor; b. Miami, Fla., Nov. 23, 1944; s. Clayton Eugene and Dorothy (Mock) L.; m. Evelyn Carole Reedy, Feb. 4, 1967; children—Deanna Dawn, Loretta Ann. Pres. Ocala Commerce Indsl. Plaza, 1984-85, CI Developers, Inc., Ocala, Fla., 1984-85; owner, mgr. J.L. Leist Constrn., Ocala, 1980—; trustee local Apprenticeship, Ocala, 1984-85; chmn. Constrn. Adv. Com., Ocala, 1983—. Mem. alt. fin. com. Marion County Commn., 1985—, State Homeowners Warranty Program, Fla., 1984-85. Served with USCG, 1965-69. Mem. Marion County Home Builders Assn. (pres. 1984; 1st place award luxury home 1983, 84), Marion County C. of C., Fla. Home Builders Assn. (state dir. 1984-85), Nat. Home Builders Assn. (nat. dir. 1985; Builder of Yr. 1985). Lodges: Kiwanis, Elks. Home: 4055 SE 24th Terr Ocala FL 32671 Office: 1558 SW 7th Rd Ocala FL 32674

LEITCH, ALMA MAY, city ofcl.; b. Fredericksburg, Va., Nov. 24, 1924; d. Maurice Andrew Doggett and Nora May (Spicer) L.; grad. James Monroe High Sch., Fredericksburg; various specialized courses U. Va., Va. Poly. Inst. Dep. commnr. revenue City of Fredericksburg, 1946-69, commr. revenue, 1970—; mem. Va. Adv. Legis. Council, 1977-78; mem. subcom. Commonwealth Va. Revenue Resources and Econ. Commn., 1978. Bd. dirs. Fredericksburg chpt. ARC, 1960—, chmn., 1969; sec. Democratic Com. Fredericksburg, 1964; bd. dirs. Rappahannock United Way for Fredericksburg, Spotsylvania, and Stafford counties, pres., 1979. Recipient various service awards; Outstanding Citizenship award Fredericksburg Area C. of C., 1979. Mem. Commrs. Revenue Assn. Va. (pres. 1979-80), Va. Govtl. Employees Assn. (dir.-at-large 1979-81), League No. Va. Commrs. Revenue (pres. 1972), Va. Assn. Local Exec. Constl. Officers (exec. com.), Internat. Assn. Assessing Officers, Va. Assn. Assessing Officers, Historic Fredericksburg Found., Bus. and Profl. Women's Club. Club: Ann Page Garden (pres. 1980-82, Mary B. Benoit award 1977), Altrusa. Home: 511 Hanover St Fredericksburg VA 22401 Office: City Hall Fredericksburg VA 22401

LEITCH, HUGH JOHN, architect; b. Battle Creek, Mich., Nov. 22, 1920; s. Reginald Genge and Catherine Margaret (Matthews) L.; m. Erin Louise Herrington, Nov. 28, 1944; m. Lacy J. Taylor, Oct. 7, 1972; children—Christine Leitch Fast, Joan Leitch Gillson, Loretto Leitch Martin, Mary. Registered architect, Fla., Ala. Ptnr., Hart & Leitch, Architects, Pensacola, Fla., 1952-57; owner, operator Hugh J. Leitch, Architect, Pensacola, 1958—; dir. Sun Bank N.W. Fla. Former mem. Archtl. Rev. Bd., City of Pensacola; former mem. Hist. Pensacola Preservation Bd. Served to lt. (j.g.) USN, 1942-46. Named Boss of Yr., Nat. Secs. Assn., 1979-80. Mem. AIA (4 archtl. excellence awards Fla. N.W. chpt. 1975, award of honor in architecture Fla. Assn., 1979). Republican. Club: Pensacola Country (pres. 1980-82). Avocations: music; golf. Home: 1103 E Jackson St Pensacola FL 32501 Office: Hugh J Leitch Architect PA 227-A E Intendencia St Pensacola FL 32501

LEKOUDIS, SPYRIDON GEORGE, aerospace engineering educator; b. Komotini, Greece, July 13, 1949; came to U.S., 1972; s. George P. and Loukia (Exarchou) L.; m. Helen Miliotis, Dec. 8, 1979; 1 son, George. B.S. in Mech. Engring., Nat. Tech. U. Greece, 1972; M.S., Va. Poly. Inst. and State U., 1973, Ph.D., 1977. Cons., Lockheed Ga., 1977-79; mem. faculty Ga. Inst. Tech., Atlanta, 1980—, assoc. prof. aerospace engring., 1983—; cons. in field. Office: Sch Aerospace Engring Ga Inst Tech Atlanta GA 30332

LELAND, GEORGE THOMAS (MICKEY LELAND), congressman; b. Lubbock, Tex., Nov. 27, 1944; s. George Thomas and Alice Rains (Lewis) L. B.S. in Pharmacy, Tex. So. U., 1970. Instr. clin. pharmacy Tex. So. U., 1970-71; mem. Tex. Ho. of Reps., 1973-78, vice chmn. pub. welfare subcom., 1975-76, mem. appropriations com., legis. budget bd., 1977-78; mem. 96th-99th U.S. Congresses from 18th Dist. Tex., former freshman whip. Co-chmn. Nat. Black-Hispanic Democratic Coalition, 1978—; mem. Dem. Nat. Com., 1976—, Tex. Dem. Black Caucus. Office: US House of Reps 419 Cannon House Office Bldg Washington DC 20515*

LELAND, JOSEPH JAMES, dentist; b. Pampa, Tex., Mar. 17, 1941; s. Everett Eugene and Martella Marie (Howell) L.; m. Janiece Billingsley, Jan. 19, 1962; children—James Michael, Mark Patrick. B.S., West Tex. State U., 1963; D.D.S., Baylor U., 1967. Practice dentistry, Amarillo, Tex., 1969—. Served as capt. U.S. Army, 1967-69. Mem. ADA, Tex. Dental Assn., Panhandle Dist. Dental Soc. Baptist. Home: 3321 Lombard Amarillo TX 79106 Office: 7201 W 34th Amarillo TX 79109

LELAND, MARIAN BELL, school administrator; b. Phila., Apr. 3, 1936; d. Thomas Porter and Margaret (McDermott) Bell; m. James Morrison Leland, Jr., June 21, 1958; children—Pamela Jane, James Morrison. B.S. in Chemistry, Limestone Coll., 1958; M.Ed., U. S.C., 1973. Head dept. sci. Orangeburg-Calhoun TEC, S.C., 1968-70; head of upper sch. Hammond Acad., Columbia, S.C., 1971-77, Wildewood Sch., Columbia, 1978-79; headmistress Ashley Hall Sch., Charleston, S.C., 1979-84; dir. student affairs U. S.C. Sch. Medicine, Columbia, 1984—; exec. dir. Palmetto Assn. Ind. Schs., Columbia, 1984-85; cons. to ind. schs., Columbia, 1984—. Mem. adv. bd. Mary Baldwin Coll., Staunton, Va., 1980-83, Higher Edn. Consortium, Charleston, 1982-84; mem. adv. bd., dean grad. edn. The Citadel, Charleston, 1981-84; bd. dirs. Charleston Mus., 1981-84. Mem. Nat. Assn. Prins. Schs. for Girls, Headmistress Assn. of East, Delta Kappa Gamma. Republican. Presbyterian. Avocations: reading; walking; sewing; art. Home: 270 Berry Tree Ln Columbia SC 29223 Office: U SC Sch Medicine Garners Ferry Rd Columbia SC 29208

LELEK, ANDRZEJ STANISLAW, mathematics educator; b. Radom, Poland, Nov. 3, 1934; came to U.S., 1970; s. Franciszek and Janina (Dziubinska) L.; m. Zofia Teresa Dumanska, Aug. 8, 1959 (div. 1977); m. Wilma Lydia Mast, May 3, 1980; children—Nathaniel, Doris. Ph.D., U. Wroclaw, Poland, 1959. Assoc. prof. math. Polish Acad. Sci., 1964-70; prof. math. U. Houston, 1970—. Author: Sets, 1966. Editor Houston Jour. Math., 1975—, mng. editor, 1981-84. Contbr. articles to profl. publs. Mem. Am. Math. Soc. Roman Catholic. Office: Dept Math U Houston Houston TX 77004

LELI, DANO ANTHONY, neuropsychologist, educator; b. S.I., N.Y., July 22, 1947; s. Peter and Viola (Troisi) L.; m. Patricia Gaile Percy, June 1, 1972; children—David Anthony, Shannon Marguerite. B.A., U. Central Fla., 1972, M.S., 1974; Ph.D., U. South Fla., 1978. Postdoctoral fellow in clin. neuropsychology U. Ala.-Birmingham Med. Sch., 1978-79, asst. prof. dept. psychology, 1980—, asst. prof. dept. psychiatry, 1981—, research asst. prof. dept. neurology, 1979—, dir. clin. neuropsychology lab., 1979—, assoc. scholar Ctr. for Aging, 1984—; adv. cons. NIH-NINCDS; ad hoc reviewer Jour. Cons. and Clin. Psychology. Contbr. articles to profl. publs. Served with USAF, 1968-70. Grantee U. Ala., 1982-83, Cerebrovascular Disease Research Ctr., 1983—. Mem. Ala. Psychol. Assn., AAAS, Internat. Neuropsychol. Soc., Assn. Lic. Psychologists in Ala., Birmingham Regional Assn. Lic. Psychologists, Am. Psychol. Assn., Southeastern Psychol. Assn., Assn. for Advancement of Behavior Therapy (behavioral neuropsychology spl. interest group), Psi Chi. Democrat. Office: U Ala Med Sch Dept Neurology Birmingham AL 35294

LEMAISTRE, CHARLES AUBREY, university president, physician; b. Lockhart, Ala., Feb. 10, 1924; s. John Wesley and Edith (McLeod) LeM.; B.A., U. Ala., 1943; M.D., Cornell U., 1947; LL.D. (hon.), Austin Coll., 1970, U. Ala., 1971; D.Sc. (hon.), U. Dallas, 1978, Southwestern U., 1981; m. Joyce Trapp, June 3, 1952; children—Charles Frederick, William Sidney, Joyce Anne, Helen Jean. Intern, then resident medicine N.Y. Hosp., 1947-49; research fellow infectious diseases Cornell U. Med. Coll., N.Y.C., 1949-51, mem. faculty, 1951-54, asst. prof. medicine, 1953-54; mem. faculty Emory U. Sch. Medicine, Atlanta, 1954-59, prof. preventive medicine, chmn. dept., 1957-59; prof. medicine U. Tex. Southwestern Med. Sch., 1959-78, assoc. dean, 1965-66; vice chancellor health affairs U. Tex. System, Austin, 1966-68, exec. vice chancellor, 1968-69, dep. chancellor, 1969-70, chancellor, 1971-78, pres. U. Tex. System Cancer Center, Houston, 1978—; cons. on epidemiology Communicable Disease Center, USPHS, 1953—; cons. on medicine VA, Tuskegee, Ala., 1954-59, area med. cons. Atlanta area, 1958-59; vis. staff physician Grady Meml. Hosp., Atlanta, 1954-59, Emory U. Hosp., 1954-59, Parkland Meml. Hosp., Dallas, 1959-66; med. dir. Woodlawn Hosp., Dallas, 1959-65; mem. Surgeon Gen. Adv. Com. Smoking and Health, 1963-64; mem. AMA-Edn. Research Found. com. research tobacco and health, 1964-66; chmn. Gov. Tex. Com. Tb Eradication, 1963-64; cons. internal medicine Baylor U. Med. Center, Dallas, 1962-66, St. Paul Hosp., Dallas, 1966—; cons. div. hosp. and med. facilities USPHS, 1966—; mem. N.Y.C. Task Force on Tb, 1967-68; cons. Bur. Health and Manpower, HEW, 1967-70; mem. Tex. Legislature Dept. Health, Edn. and Welfare, 1967; mem. Tex. Legislature Com. on Organ Transplantation, 1968, Carnegie Commn. Non-Traditional Study, 1971-73; mem. com. fed.

health programs Assn. Am. Med. Colls., 1967; Am. Cancer Soc.; mem. Pres.'s Commn. White House Fellows, 1971; mem. Nat. Commn. Smoking and Public Policy, 1977-80, med. dir. at large, 1978-81, mem. com. on tobacco and cancer, 1977—, vice chmn., 1981-82, chmn., 1982-83, mem. med. and sci. com., 1978-80, 81-82, chmn., 1982-83, mem. profl. edn. com., 1978—, bd. dirs., mem. exec. com., 1978-82, mem. public issues com., 1978—, chmn. Nat. Conf. on Smoking or Health, 1981, mem. med. and sci. exec. com., 1980—, mem. awards com., 1981—, dir.-at-large, 1981—, pres. 1986; mem. med. and sci. com. Tex. div. Am. Cancer Soc., 1974—, public edn. com., 1976—, chmn. study com. on tobacco and cancer, 1976, bd. dirs., mem. exec. com., 1977—, med. dir.-at-large, 1977—, chmn. target 5 com., 1977; nat. panelist identification program for advancement women in higher edn. adminstrn. Am. Council Edn., 1977—; dir. United Savs. of Tex., Houston Natural Gas Corp., United Fin. Group, Am. Physicians Group, Inc. Chmn. steering com. Presbyn. Physicians for Fgn. Missions, 1960-62; mem. Ministers Cons. Clinic, Dallas, 1960-62; mem. bd. commrs. Nat. Commn. on Accrediting, 1973-76; mem. joint task force on continuing competence in pharmacy Am. Pharm. Assn.-Am. Assn. Colls. in Pharmacy, 1973-74. Bd. dirs. Ga. Tb Assn., 1955-59; trustee Biol. Humanics Found., Dallas, 1973-84; bd. dirs. Damon Runyon-Walter Winchell Cancer Fund, 1976—, chmn. exec. com., v.p., 1978-79, pres., 1979-83; bd. trustees Austin Coll., 1979-83, Stillman Coll., 1978-84. Recipient Alumni award of distinction Cornell U., 1978, Disting. Alumnus award U. Ala. Sch. Medicine, 1982. Mem. Am. (v.p. 1964-65), So. (pres. 1963-64) thoracic socs., Nat. Tb Assn., Am., Internat. Assn. for Study Lung Cancer, Am. Soc. Clin. Oncology, Tex. Hosp. Assn., Tex., Ga. med. assns., Central Soc. Clin. Research, Dallas Clin. Soc., Philos. Soc. Tex. (pres. 1980-81), Houston C. of C. (chmn. health com. 1979-80, dir. 1979—), Alpha Omega Alpha. Presbyterian. (deacon 1959-62). Contbg. author: A Textbook of Medicine, 10 and 11th edits., 1963; Pharmacology in Medicine, 1958. Translating author: The Tubercle Bacillus, 1955; editorial bd. Am. Rev. Respiratory Diseases, 1955-58; contbr. articles to med. jours. Office: University of Texas System Cancer Center Tex Med Center 6723 Bertner Ave Houston TX 77030

LEMANN, THOMAS BERTHELOT, lawyer; b. New Orleans, Jan. 3, 1926; s. Monte M. and Nettie E. (Hyman) L.; m. Barbara M. London, Apr. 14, 1951; children—Nicholas B., Nancy E. A.B. summa cum laude, Harvard U., 1949, LL.B., 1952; M.C.L., Tulane U., 1953. Bar: La. 1953. Assoc. firm Monroe & Lemann, New Orleans, 1953-58, ptnr., 1958—; dir. B. Lemann & Bro., Mermentau Mineral & Land Co., Lastarmco, Inc., Longue Vue Found., Zemurray Found. Contbr. articles to profl. publs. Mem. council La. State Law Inst., sec. trust adv. com.; chmn. Mayor's Cultural Resources Com., 1970-75; pres. Arts Council Greater New Orleans, 1975-80; mem. vis. com. art museums Harvard U., 1974-80; trustee Metairie Park Country Day Sch., 1956-71, pres., 1967-70; trustee New Orleans Philharm. Symphony Soc., 1956-78, Flint-Goodridge Hosp., 1960-70, La. Civil Service League, pres., 1974-76. Served with U.S. Army, 1944-46; PTO. Mem. ABA, La. Bar Assn. (bd. govs. 1977-78), New Orleans Bar Assn., Assn. Bar City N.Y., Am. Law Inst., Soc. Bartolus, Phi Beta Kappa. Jewish. Clubs: New Orleans Country, Wyvern (New Orleans); Harvard (N.Y.C.). Home: 6020 Garfield St New Orleans LA 70118 Office: 1424 Whitney Bank Bldg New Orleans LA 70130

LEMASTER, SHERRY RENEE, college administrator; b. Lexington, Ky., June 25, 1953; d. John William and Mary Charles (Thompson) LeM. B.S., U. Ky., 1975, M.S., 1984, postgrad. Cert. fund raising exec. Cert. technician in virology, serology Central Ky. Animal Disease Diagnostic Lab., Lexington, 1976-77; grant, environ. specialist Commonwealth Ky. Dept. for Natural Resources and Environ. Protection, Frankfurt, 1977-78; coordinator student activities Murray State U., Ky., 1978-80; dean students Midway Coll., Ky., 1980-81, v.p. for devel., alumnae affairs, 1981—. Ambassador, U. Ky. Coll. Agr., 1977—; chmn. Midway chpt. Am. Heart Assn., 1981, co-chmn. Woodford County chpt., 1983; mem. adminstrv. bd. First United Meth. Ch., 1982-84; mem. Council for Advancement and Support Edn., 1981—, chmn. Ky. conf., 1982; planning com. Nat. Disciples Devel. Execs. Conf., 1984. Named Ky. col., hon. sec. state. Mem. Am. Council on Edn. (state planning com. 1984—, instl. rep. 1980—), Nat. Soc. Fund Raising Execs. (bd. dirs. Lexington chpt. 1985—), Nat. Assn. Female Execs., Greater Lexington Area C. of C., Ky. Assn. Women Deans, Adminstrs. and Counselors (editor Newsletter 1981), U. Ky. Alumni Assn. (life), Gen. Fedn. Womens Clubs, P.E.O., Ninety-Nines, Pi Beta Phi Nat. Alumnae Assn. (alumnae province pres. 1980-81, sec. bd. dirs. Ky. Beta chpt. house assn. 1982-84), Alpha Kappa Psi Alumnae Assn. (charter Murray chpt.). Club: Lexington Zonta (bd. dirs., Amelia Earhart Fellowship awards dist. chmn. 1984—, Keeneland Day chmn. 1983, Amelia Earhart com. chmn. 1983). Avocations: needlecrafts; aerobics; piano; racquetball; hot air ballooning. Office: Midway Coll Stephens St Midway KY 40347

LEMBERG, FRED L., marketing consultant; b. Detroit, July 18, 1935; s. Ben and Carolyn (Goodman) L.; children—Natalie, Ivy. Pres., Western Concession Corp., San Antonio, 1968-69, Concession Devel. Corp., N.Y.C., 1970-78; trainer, speaker, cons., 1979-81; pres. The P.E.P. Connection/Personal Devel. Courses, 1982; cons., editor Multi-Level Inquirer, 1982—; founder The Winning Ways Mktg. Group. Served with U.S. Army, 1956-57. Mem. Nat. Assn. Multi-Level Mktg., Internat. Platform Assn. Republican. Jewish. Author: The Winning Ways of Multi-Level Marketing, 1983. Office: 12121 Northwest Freeway Suite 366 Houston TX 77092

LEMBERG, LOUIS, cardiologist, educator; b. Chgo., Dec. 27, 1916; s. Morris and Frances Lemberg; m. Dorothy Feinstein, 1940; (dec. 1969); children—Gerald, Laura Bott; m. 2d, Miriam Mayer, Jan. 29, 1971. B.S., U. Ill.-Chgo., 1938, M.D., 1940. Intern Mt. Sinai Hosp., Chgo., 1940-41, resident, 1945-48; prof. clin. cardiology U. Miami Sch. Medicine (Fla.), 1970—, dir. coronary care unit; chief cardiology Mercy Hosp.; chief staff Nat. Children's Cardiac Hosp.; cons. cardiology VA Hosp., Miami, 1953-64; dir. courses in coronary care for practicing physician, Master Approach to Cardiovascular Problems, cardiology update for intensive care nurses. Served to maj. AUS, 1941-55; ETO. Recipient U. St. Torres (Phillippines) Luis Guerrero hon. lectr. award, 1973; Recognition award U. Miami Sch. Medicine; Key to City of Miami Beach, Fla. Fellow ACP, Am. Coll. Cardiology (editorial bd. jour.); mem. Heart Assn. Greater Miami (pres.), Fla. Heart Assn. (pres.), Am. Heart Assn. (fellow Council Clin. Cardiology), AMA (Physician's Recognition award 1970-86). Democrat. Jewish. Clubs: Palm Bay, Westview Country (Miami). Author: Vectorcardiography, 1969, 2d edit., 1975; Electrophysiology of Pacing and Cardioversion, 1969. Editor-in-chief Current Concepts in Cardiovascular Disorders, 1984—. Contbr. to med. publs. Pioneer in devel. Demand Pacemaker, 1964. Home: 1 Palm Bay Plaza 18 Miami FL 33138 Office: 3661 S Miami Ave Suite 805 Miami FL 33133

LEMBO, PHILIP JOSEPH, architect; b. Chgo., Apr. 8, 1935; s. Anthony and Rose (Savage) L.; m. Elaine Barbera Klodnicki, Jan. 26, 1967; 1 son, Scott A. B.A. in Arch., U. Ill., 1958. Registered architect, Ill., Fla. Project architect Ezra Gordon-Jack Levin & Assocs., Chgo., 1961, 71, Ferry & Henderson, Chgo., 1972-73, S. Guy Fishman & Assocs., Northbrook, Ill., 1973-75; ptnr. Lembo/Wimmer AIA, Architects and Planners, Elmhurst, Ill., 1976-78; project architect P. Marich Assocs., Clearwater, Fla., 1978-81; prin. Lembo & Assocs., Architects and Planners, Palm Harbor, Fla., 1981—; cons., project architect, team mem. or prin. architect on works including; Newberry Plaza, Chgo., 1971, Kimbark Townhouses, Chgo. (award), 1966, 1st Fed. of Chgo. br. banking facilities, 1976-78, South Commons Urban Renewal Project, Chgo. 1965, 67, 71; planning cons. St. Anthony's Hosp., St. Petersburg, Fla., 1979. Mem. Appearance Control Commn., Buffalo Grove, Ill., 1972-76. Served with U.S. Army, 1958-60. Recipient J. McLaren White award U. Ill., 1958, Appreciation award, City of Buffalo Grove, 1976. Mem. U. Ill. Alumni Assn. (life), Nat. Trust Historic Preservation. Specialist multi-story constrn., resdl., office bldgs. and fin. instns. Office: PO Box 282 Palm Harbor FL 33563

LE MIEUX, HENRY FISHER, construction executive; b. Greenville, Miss., Aug. 20, 1926; s. Frederic Alexander and Elizabeth (Fisher) LeM.; B.E. in Elec. Engring., Tulane U., 1946, B.S. in Civil Engring., 1949; m. Marjorie Elizabeth Hunter, May 7, 1954; children—Michelle E., Jolie M., Babette A., Henry Fisher. Engr., field supt. Raymond Internat., Inc., 1949-51, dist. mgr., New Orleans, 1951-57, asst. v.p., New Orleans, N.Y.C. and London, 1957-65, dir., N.Y.C., 1965—; v.p., gen. mgr. Raymond Concrete Pile div., 1965-68, pres., 1968-78, chief exec. officer, 1970—, chmn. bd., 1976—, also officer, dir. subs. cos.; dir. Hughes Tool Co., Houston. Mem. adv. bd. Tulane U. Engring. Sch., Tulane U. Grad. Sch. Bus. Adminstrn., also mem. pres.'s council; mem. adv. bd. U. Houston Bus. Sch.; mem. So. regional adv. bd. Inst. Internat. Edn. Served to lt. (j.g.) USNR, 1944-46. Registered profl. engr., Fla., La., N.Y. Mem. ASCE, ASTM, Moles, Beavers, Pan Am. Soc. U.S., Houston C. of C. (dir.). Episcopalian. Clubs: Plimsoll, So. Yacht (New Orleans); Ramada, River Oaks Country, Houston, Warwick, Univ. (Houston); Sky (N.Y.C.); Ocean Reef (Key Largo). Address: PO Box 27456 Houston TX 77227

LEMLEY, K(ENT) CHRISTOPHER, advertising agency executive; b. Ft. Myers, Fla., Oct. 10, 1946; s. Kermit Roosevelt and Maelee (Hollandsworth) L.; B.A., Furman U., 1968; M.B.A., Ga. State U., 1973. Media trainee Tucker Wayne & Co., Atlanta, 1968-69; sr. speechwriter, aide to gov. State of Ga., Atlanta, 1969; account exec. Stein Printing Co., Atlanta, 1970-73, Liller, Neal, Battle & Lindsey, Atlanta, 1973-77; sr. account exec. Cargill, Wilson & Acree, Atlanta, 1977-79, account supr., 1979-83, v.p., 1983-85; prin., chief exec. officer Lemley & Assocs., 1985-86; dir. Cargill & Assocs., 1986—; arbitrator Atlanta Better Bus. Bur. Chief of staff CAP, 1970-74; mem. Atlanta Symphony Orch. League, 1978—. Recipient several awards for copywriting and mktg. Mem. Am. Mktg. Assn. (dir. chpt. 1977-79), Am. Advt. Fedn., Pub. Utilities Communicators Assn., Bus. Profl. Advt. Assn., Am. Film Inst., Aircraft Owners and Pilots Assn., Savs. and Loan Mktg. Assn., Atlanta Broadcast Execs., U.S. Yacht Racing Union. Episcopalian. Club: Variety Internat. Home: 2862 Ridgemore Rd NW Atlanta GA 30318 Office: Cargill & Assocs 400 Colony Sq Suite 1101 Atlanta GA 30361

LEMMA, SCHLEY DEE, school administrator; b. Ranger, Tex., Nov. 14, 1925; s. Burnice Schley and Monnie (Culpepper) L.; B.S., Howard Payne U., 1952, M.Ed., 1957; student U. Tex., 1963, 68, Corpus Christi State U., 1975, 77; m. Mary Joyce Swinney, Aug. 21, 1948; children—Schley Dee, Cindy Luann, Robin Gay, Amy Carol. Tchr., Brownwood (Tex.) Jr. High Sch., 1953-56; juvenile probation officer Bexar County Juvenile Ct., San Antonio, 1956-57; prin. Northside Jr. High Schs., San Antonio, 1957-66; prin. Tuloso-Midway High Sch., Corpus Christi, Tex., 1966-75; curriculum dir. Tuloso-Midway Ind. Sch. Dist., Corpus Christi, 1975-82, adminstrv. asst., 1982—; cons. Served with USMMR, 1943-46. Recipient Silver Beaver award Boy Scouts Am. Mem. Am. Assn. Suprs. and Curriculum Dirs., Tex. Assn. Suprs. and Curriculum Dirs., Tex. Assn. Sch. Adminstrs., Tex. Assn. Secondary Sch. Prins., Assn. Compensatory Educators, Assn. Compensatory Educators Tex., Tex. State Tchrs. Assn., Phi Delta Kappa. Baptist. Club: Masons. Home: 4233 Western Dr Corpus Christi TX 78410 Office: 1902 Lodge Rd Corpus Christi TX 78409

LEMMON, HARRY THOMAS, judge; b. Morgan City, La., Dec. 11, 1930; s. Earl Anthony and Gertrude Jeanette (Blum) L.; m. Mary Ann Vial, Dec. 2, 1961; children—Andrew, Lauren, Roslyn, Carla, Jake, Patrick. B.S., Southwestern La. Inst. (now U. Southwestern La.), 1952; J.D., Loyola U., New Orleans, 1962. Bar: La. Ptnr., Vial, Vial & Lemmon, Hahnville, La., 1963-70; judge U.S. Ct. Appeals 4th cir., La., 1970-80; assoc. justice Supreme Ct. La., New Orleans, 1980—; lectr. in field; chmn. bd. govs. La. Judicial Coll. Served with U.S. Army, 1954-56. Mem. ABA, La. State Bar Assn., Am. Judicature Soc., Soc. Bartolus, Henri Capitant Assn. Roman Catholic. Office: La Supreme Ct 301 Loyola Ave New Orleans LA 70112

LEMOINE, HELEN LOUISE, nurse; b. Millford, Tex., Feb. 20, 1929; d. Chester Randolph and Ina Louise (Dotson) Riddels; R.N., Parkland Hosp. Sch. Nursing, 1951; m. Louis M. Escude, Dec. 26, 1950; children—Annette, Escude, Michael Escude, Donna Escude McInnis; m. 2nd Albert L. Lemoine, Dec. 21, 1980. Staff nurse Wichita Falls Clinic Hosp., 1952, McConnell and Dupree Clinic and Hosp., Bunkie, La., 1955-65, Bayou Vista Manor Nursing Home, Bunkie, 1965; dir. nursing Avoyelles Manor Nursing Home, DuPont, La., 1966—. Mem. La. Health Care Assoc. Dirs. of Nursing in Action (region rep.), Am. Legion Aux., Cath. Daus. Am. Democrat. Roman Catholic. Club: Nurses Book, Altar Soc. Home: Route 1 Box 597-A Cottonport LA 71327 Office: Route 1 PO Box 215 Plaucheville LA 71362

LEMONS, JACK E., biomaterials educator, consultant, researcher; b. St. Petersburg, Fla., Jan. 20, 1937; s. John E. and Florence E. (Collier) L.; m. Benta Sorensen, Dec. 24, 1938; children—Paul Eric, Hans David. B.S., U. Fla., 1962, M.S., 1963, Ph.D., 1968. Asst. in research U. Fla., 1962-68; chief phys. metallurgy So. Research Inst., 1968-70; asst. prof. materials engring. Clemson U., 1970-71; instr. biomaterials U. Ala.-Birmingham, 1970-73, assoc. prof., 1973-76, prof., 1976—, chmn. dept. biomaterials, 1978—. Recipient several fed., state and indsl. grants. Mem. Soc. for Biomaterials, ASTM, Internat. Assn. for Dental Research, Am. Soc. for Metals. Republican. Lutheran. Contbr. numerous articles and abstracts to profl. jours. Office: U Ala-Birmingham Dept Biomaterials SDB-49/UAB Birmingham AL 35294

LENCHNER, VICTOR, pediatric dentist; b. Bklyn., Feb. 7, 1925; s. Herman and Molly Hildreth (Gerber) L.; m. Rose Shermer, July 18, 1948; children—Douglas Roy, Julie Claire. D.D.S., NYU, 1948; M.S. in Psychology, U. Miami, Fla., 1969. Diplomate Am. Bd. Pedodontics. Gen. practice dentistry, Bklyn., 1948-50; practice dentistry specializing in pedodontics, Miami Beach, Fla., 1953—; chmn. pedodontics Mt. Sinai Hosp., Miami Beach, 1957—; cons. pediatric dentistry Miami Children's Hosp., Coral Gables, Fla., 1960—; examiner Am. Bd. Pedodontics, 1973-80, chmn., 1979-80; cons. Dept. Profl. Regulations, Fla., 1983—; vis. asst. prof. pedodontics Boston U., 1980—. Author: What You Should Know About Your Child's Teeth, 1971; The Answer Book, Answers to Questions About Your Child's Dental Health, 1984. Contbg. author: Behavior Management in Dentistry for Children, 1975. Served to capt. USAR, 1951-53. Recipient Alumni Gold medal NYU Coll. Dentistry, 1948, award of Excellence Fla. Soc. Dentistry for Children, 1976, Thomas P. Hinman Lecture medallion 1981, Humanitarian award Miami Beach Dental Soc., 1981. Fellow Am. Coll. Dentists, Am. Acad. Pediatric Dentistry (bd. dirs. 1981-84); mem. Am. Soc. Dentistry for Children (pres. 1962-63), Southeastern Soc. Pedodontics (pres. 1975-76), Fla. Soc. Pedodontics (pres. 1981-82), Fla. Soc. Dentistry for Children (pres. 1959-60), Miami Beach Dental Soc. (pres. 1969-70), Psi Chi, Lambda Tau Lambda. Home: 1315 Daytonia Rd Miami Beach FL 33141 Office: 1185 71st St Miami Beach FL 33141 also 5458 Town Ctr Rd Boca Raton FL 33431

LENDRUM, JAMES BARTLEY, business executive; b. Wilkes-Barre, Pa., 1926; A.B., U. Pa., 1949, A.M., 1950; married. With Hosp. Food Mgmt. Co., 1953-56, Master Vibrator Co., 1956-63; div. gen. mgr. Massey-Ferguson Inc., 1963-67; with Gen. Portland Inc., 1967—, v.p., gen. mgr. Fla. div., 1969, v.p., gen. mgr. Peninsular div., 1970-74, v.p. ops., 1974, exec. v.p., 1975, pres., chief exec. officer, 1976-79, chmn., chief exec. officer, 1979-81, chmn., pres., chief exec. officer, 1981—; also dir. Office: 12700 Park Central Pl PO Box 324 Dallas TX 75221

LENHART, LOWELL CORDELL, hospital administrator, consultant; b. Oklahoma City, Jan. 19, 1940; s. Herbert William and Helen Nancy Lenhart; m. Sharen Annette Gambill, Jan. 21, 1961; 1 child, Lance Christian. B.S., Central State U., 1963; M.S., Okla. State U., 1967; Ph.D., Okla. U., 1976. Tech. dir. service outcome measurement project Div. Rehab. Services, Oklahoma City, 1968-70; research utilization supr. Dept. Pub. Welfare, Oklahoma City, 1970-72; program evaluation supr. Dept. Instns., Oklahoma City, 1972-74; coordinator dept. mgmt. services Dept. Human Services, Oklahoma City, 1974-79; dep. adminstr. O'Donoghue Rehab. Inst., Oklahoma City, 1979-81, adminstr., 1981—; cons. in field. Contbr. articles to profl. jours. Pres. Okla. Ptnrs. of Americas, 1981-82; mem. Oklahoma City Alliance for Safer Cities, 1975-76; cons. Community Workshop, 1978-79. Mem. Am. Coll. Hosp. Adminstrs., Am. Hosp. Assn., Okla. Hosp. Assn., Nat. Rehab. Assn. Okla. Rehab. Assn. (bd. dirs.). Democrat. Lodge: Rotary. Avocations: renovation of historic homes; snow skiing; gardening; writing. Home: 4100 Harvey Pkwy Oklahoma City OK 73188 Office: State of Okla Teaching Hosps PO Box 26307 Oklahoma City OK 73126

LENNON, CHARLES WOODBURY, II, trade association executive; b. Washington, N.C., Oct. 16, 1934; s. Charles Downing and Helen Louise (Wilkinson) L.; student Va. Mil. Inst., 1952-53; grad. Inst. for Orgn. Mgmt., U. Notre Dame, 1977; m. Shirley Anne Clore, Mar. 27, 1971; 1 son, Sean Patrick. With Dun & Bradstreet, Richmond, Va., 1957-59; self-employed in pub. relations and sales, candy industry, Richmond, 1959-66; exec. mgr. Va. Assn. Plumbing-Heating-Cooling Contractors, Richmond, 1966-69; exec. officer Hydro Mech. Contractors Assn., Fort Lauderdale, Fla., 1969-75; exec. dir. Air Conditioning Contractors Assn. and Mech. Contractors Assn. So. Fla., Miami, 1975-80; exec. v.p. Greater Pompano Beach (Fla.) C. of C., 1980-83; exec. dir. Builders Assn. South Fla., Miami, 1983—. Mem. Broward County Charter Commn., 1974-78, vice chmn., 1975-76, chmn., 1976; mem. Progress for Broward County, chmn., 1973-74; mem. Broward County Personnel Rev. Bd., 1975-80, Ft. Lauderdale Com. Performing Arts. Bd. dirs. Broward County United Way Family Service Agy., 1972-78, pres., 1975—; mem. Broward County Consumer Affairs Bd., 1979—, vice chmn., 1980-81. bd. dirs. Fork Union Mil. Acad. Served with U.S. Army, 1953-57; Korea. Named Man of Year, W.Va. Wholesalers Assn., 1965, 66, Nat. Candy Wholesalers Assn., 1966. Mem. Am. (designated certified assn. exec. 1976), Fla. socs. assn. execs., Constrn. Industry Mgmt. Council Broward County, Constrn. Industry Advisory Council So. Fla., Am. Arbitration Assn. (panel of arbitrators 1976—), U. Notre Dame Alumni Assn. Club: Notre Dame of Greater Miami (v.p. 1980-81). Contbr. articles to profl. jours. Home: 2406 NE 13th Ct Fort Lauderdale FL 33304 Office: 15225 NW 77th Ave Miami Lakes FL 33014

LENNOX, EDWARD NEWMAN, industrial corporation executive; b. New Orleans, July 27, 1925; s. Joseph Andrew and May Alice (Newman) L.; B.B.A., Tulane U., 1949; m. Joan Marie Landry, Sept. 3, 1949; children—Katherine Sarah, Anne Victoria, Mary Elizabeth, Laura Joan. Mktg. service clk. Shell Oil Co., New Orleans, 1949; with W.M. Chambers Truck Line, Inc., 1950-60, exec. v.p., 1954-60; v.p. Radcliff Materials, Inc., New Orleans, 1961-71, So. Industries Corp., New Orleans, 1971—; pres. Tidelands Industries, Inc., 1982-85; v.p. pub. affairs Oravo Natural Resources Co., 1982—; dir. Home Savs. & Loan Assn., 1979—, pres., 1982—, chmn. bd., 1984—. Mem. La. Bd. Hwys., 1965-67; chmn. New Orleans Aviation Bd., 1960-67; bd. mem. Travelers Aid Soc., 1966-68; pres. Met. New Orleans Safety Council, 1969-71. Pres. bd. Levee Commrs. of Orleans Levee Dist., 1969-72; bd. dirs. Constrn. Industry Legislative Council, 1968—, Miss. Valley Assn., 1969-72; mem. Ala. Gov.'s Adv. Council on Econs., 1971-72, La. Gov.'s Adv. Com. on River Area Transp. and Planning Study, 1971-72; del. La. Constnl. Conv., 1973; bus. and fin. adviser Congregation Sisters of Immaculate Conception, New Orleans. Bd. dirs., mem. exec. com. Methodist Hosp., 1963-81, bd. dirs. emeritus, 1981—; bd. govs. La. Civil Service League, 1974—, pres., 1977-78; adv. bd. Morality in Media of La., Inc., 1975-76; bd. dirs. New Orleans, Boys' Clubs Greater New Orleans, Inc., 1973-79, Americanism Forum, Inc., 1975-77, Met. Area Com., 1967-79; bd. dirs. Goodwill Industries Greater New Orleans Area, 1981—, mem. exec. bd., 1975-79, treas., 1984, 2d v.p., 1978, 79, 85; mem. career advisement com. Tulane Grad. Sch. Bus. Adminstrn., 1972; bd. dirs. Tragedy Fund, Inc., 1976—, La. Polit. Action Council; bd. govs. Water Resources Congress, 1981—; mem. Citizens Adv. Com. for Air Quality-Transp. Planning, 1980, New Orleans Bd. Trade, 1971—; trustee La. Ind. Coll. Fund, 1980—, chmn., 1981-83; vice chmn. Transp. Task Force Goals for La., 1969-72; mem. Loving Cup selection com. Times-Picayune, 1972. Served to capt. AUS, 1943-46. Recipient Industry Service award Asso. Gen. Contractors Am., 1967; New Orleans Jr. C. of C. award, 1960; certificate of merit. City New Orleans, 1964, 67; certificate Constrn. Industry Assn. New Orleans, 1972; Monte M. Lemann award La. Civil Service League, 1976; named hon. citizen, Jacksonville, Fla. Mem. La. Tank Truck Carriers (pres. 1954-55), La. Motor Transport Assn. (pres. 1963-64, dir. 1981-82), La. Good Roads Assn. (exec. com. 1972-74), Am. (v.p. 1956-62), Ala. (v.p. 1956-60) trucking assns., NAM (public affairs steering com. So. div. 1979—), So. Concrete Masonry Assn. (pres. 1963-68), Greater New Orleans Ready Mixed Concrete Assn. (pres. 1966-68), Pub. Affairs Research Council La. (area v.p. 1972-73, trustee 1970-79), La. Shell Producers Assn. (pres. 1966-68), C. of C. New Orleans Area (pres. elect 1973, area v.p. external affairs 1969-72), Mobile Area C. of C., Lakeshore Property Owners Assn. (bd. dirs. 1974—, pres. 1976, 77, 79, 80), Internat. House (bd. dirs. 1977-79), Tulane Alumni Assn. Clubs: Metairie Country (bd. govs. 1976-82, pres. 1980-81), Traffic (New Orleans); Tulane Alumni T. Home: 862 Topaz St New Orleans LA 70124 Office: 110 James Dr W Suite 110 Saint Rose LA 70087

LENTZ, JOHN DENLEY, periodontist; b. Lancaster, Pa., July 6, 1947; s. Merideth Clyde and Dorothy (Darlington) L. B.S., Auburn U., 1969; D.D.S., Med. Coll. Va., 1975, cert. periodontics, 1980. Pvt. practice periodontia, Abingdon, Va., 1980—; bd. dirs. Highland Enterprises, Abingdon, 1984—. Treas. Washington County Hist. Preservation Found., Abingdon, 1983-85; bd. dirs. Highlands Festival, 1984-85. Recipient Outstanding Pres. award Capital Dist. Kiwanis Club, 1983-84. Mem. Am. Acad. Periodontology, ADA, Va. Dental Assn. (necrology com. 1982-84), S.W. Va. Dental Soc. (pres. 1985-86), Va. Soc. Periodontists, Washington County Dental Soc. Episcopalian. Home: PO Box 182 Abingdon VA 24210

LEON, BENJAMIN JOSEPH, engineering educator, consultant; b. Austin, Tex., Mar. 20, 1932; s. Harry J. and Ernestine (Franklin) L.; m. Maxine Murphy, Jan. 26, 1954; children—Nathaniel, Victoria, Jennifer, Theresa. B.S., U. Tex., 1954; S.M., MIT, 1957, Sc.D., 1959. Registered profl. engr., Ky. Mem. tech. staff MIT, Lincoln Labs., Lexington, 1954-59; mem. tech. staff Hughes Research Labs., Malibu, Calif., 1959-62; assoc. prof. Sch. Elec. Engring., Purdue U., West Lafayette, Ind., 1962-65, prof. elec. engring., 1965-80; prof., chmn. elec. engring. U. Ky., Lexington, 1980-84, prof., 1984—. NSF fellow, 1956-57; recipient Cert. of Merit, Tau Beta Pi, 1967. Fellow IEEE (v.p. 1979-80, trans. editor 1967-69, newsletter editor 1981-85), AAUP (chmn. univ. governance com. U. Ky. chpt. 1982-83, sec. 1984-86). Internat. Electrotech. Commn. (U.S. nat. com. tech. advisor terminology 1976-81), Am. Assn. Engring. Socs. (mem. ednl. affairs council planning com. 1980). Unitarian. Author: Lumped Systems, 1968; Basic Linear Networks (with P.A. Wintz), 1970; contbr. articles to profl. jours.; patentee in field. Home: 1831 Nicholasville Rd Lexington KY 40503 Office: Dept Elec Engring U Ky Lexington KY 40506

LEONARD, ANGELA MICHELE, researcher, writer; b. Washington, June 26, 1954; d. Walter Jewell and Betty (Singleton) Leonard; A.B., Harvard U., 1976, postgrad. (fellow), 1978-81; postgrad. Howard U., 1977-78; M.L.S. (fellow), Vanderbilt U., 1982. Tchr., Cambridge (Mass.) Public Schs., 1974-75, Atlanta Urban Corps, 1975, Boston Public Schs., 1977; with Newton (Mass.) South High Sch. Library, 1971-72, Widener Library, 1974-75, Fogg Fine Arts Library, Harvard U., 1975; writer, cons. Seigenthaler Assocs., Nashville, 1979—; instr. Trevecca Nazarene Coll., 1979, Nashville State Tech. Inst., 1980-81; researcher learning library program Fisk U. Library, 1981—; free-lance writer; astrologer, play dir. Mem. ALA, NAACP, Urban League Nashville, Alpha Kappa Alpha. Roman Catholic. Contbr. articles, stories to mags. Address: 1604 Jackson St Nashville TN 37208

LEONARD, BYRDIE A. LARKIN, political science educator; b. Tuskegee Institute, Ala.; d. Charles Haile and Lula (Berry) Larkin; 1 child, Seve Mwangi Leonard. B.S., Ala. State U., 1973; M.A., Atlanta U., 1975, Ph.D., 1982. Instr. Atlanta Jr. Coll., 1975-77; assigned supply tchr. Atlanta Pub. Sch. System, 1977; asst. prof. dept. polit. sci. Ala. State U., Montgomery, 1977-82, acting chairperson, 1982-85; seminar participant Dept. State Scholar Diplomat Conf., Washington, 1981; inst. participant Am. Judicature Soc., Chgo., 1984; planning cons. Congress Human Services, Montgomery, 1985. Analyst, Ala. Edn. Network's Focus, Montgomery, 1983; speaker First Bapt. Ch. Women's Day, Montgomery, 1984; analyst WVAS Ala. State's Radio, Montgomery, 1984. Ala. State U. scholar 1969-73; Fulbright scholar 1985; grad. awards Atlanta. U., Ohio State U., Notre Dame U., 1973. Mem. Ala. Conf. Polit. Scientists, Pi Gamma Mu, Alpha Kappa Mu, Alpha Kappa Alpha. Avocations: recreational activities; reading; creative writing. Office: Ala State U Dept Polit Sci 915 S Jackson St Montgomery AL 36195

LEONARD, GARY JUDE, pharmacist, restauranteur; b. New Orleans, Nov. 7, 1956; s. Leroy John and Lois (Sunseri) L.; m. Susan Tingstrom, Jan. 19, 1985. Student Loyola U., New Orleans, 1974-76; B.S. in Pharmacy, Xavier U., 1979. Registered pharmacist, La. Owner, pharmacist Sunseri's Pharmacy, New Orleans, 1983—; owner, mgr. Columbo's Restaurant, New Orleans, 1984—. Mem. Alliance for Good Govt., New Orleans, 1984—, Elwood Civic Assn., 1984—. Mem. La. Pharmacist Assn., Am. Pharm. Assn., Nat. Assn. Retail Druggists, New Orleans C. of C. (state legis. com. 1982—, nat. legis. com. 1982—), Jaycees. Republican. Roman Catholic. Avocations: politics; health; art collections. Home: 2829 Wabash St New Orleans LA 70114 Office: Sunseri's Pharmacy 4400 Gen Meyer Ave New Orleans LA 70114

LEONARD, GUY MEYERS, JR., international holding company executive; b. Bluefield, W.Va., Sept. 22, 1926; s. Guy Meyers and Mabel (Bonham) L.; A.B., Morris Harvey Coll., 1949; B.Div., Southwestern Bapt. Sem., 1952; S.T.M., Harvard U., 1957; m. Pat Kirby, June 28, 1949; children—Calvin David, Dinah Lynn. Commd. ensign U.S. Navy, 1952, advanced through grades to capt., 1968, ret., 1972; dir. research and devel. Ency. Britannica Ednl. Corp., Chgo., 1972-76; pres. Communication Programming Services, Inc., Charleston, S.C., 1976—; pres., chief exec. officer First Don Trading Co., 1982; chmn., chief exec. officer Transocean Ltd., internat. holding co., 1982—; cons.

Ency. Britannica, Home Mission Bd. and Brotherhood Commn. So. Bapt. Conv. Sec., U.S. Power Squadron, Charleston, 1969; chmn. Spl. Commn. on Drug Abuse for Armed Forces, 1970-72; active Conn. council Boy Scouts Am., 1959-62. Served with USN, 1943-46. Decorated Legion of Merit, Meritorious Service medal, Navy Commendation medal; recipient Disting. Service award City of Louisville, 1963. Mem. Harvard Club S.C., C. of C., Trident Chamber (Charleston), Navy League U.S., Ret. Officers Assn. Club: Kiwanis (spl. projects chmn., 1964-65). Designer, produced with Harvard U. and sta. WGBH, Boston, mediated coll. curriculum leading to B.S. degree for use by naval personel. Office: Suite 20 1023 Wappou Rd Charleston SC 29407

LEONARD, PATRICIA LYNN, university administrator, educator; b. Rockeville Center, N.Y., May 28, 1955; s. John Thomas and Grace Lillian (Foster) L. B.A. in Social Work and Secondary Edn., Coll. Misericordia, Dallas, Pa., 1977; M.A. in Coll. Student Personnel Adminstrn., Mich. State U., 1979. Residence coordinator U. N.C., Charlotte, 1979-80; area coordinator, instr. Miami U., Oxford, Ohio, 1980-83; assoc. dean students U. N.C., Wilmington, 1983—; cons. Rape Task Force, Wilmington, 1983—. Mem. Am. Assn. Counseling and Devel., Am. Coll. Personnel Assn., So. Assn. Coll. Student Affairs, Nat. Assn. Fgn. Student Advisors, N.C. Assn. Women Deans Adminstrs. and Counselors, Alpha Delta Mu, Phi Delta Kappa. Avocations: running, softball. Office: U NC 601 S College Rd Wilmington NC 28403

LEONARD, RAYMOND LOUIS, trucking company executive, musician; b. Miami, Fla., Sept. 8, 1950; s. Talbert Armlon and Lucy Elizabeth (Setzler) L.; m. Janice Taylor, Aug. 25, 1973; 1 son, Raymond Matthew. Student bus. adminstrn. and music, Belhaven Coll., intermittantly, 1968-73. With Leonard Bros. Trucking Co., Inc., Miami, Fla., 1973-84, terminal mgr., 1973-75, regional mgr., 1975-78, dir. govt. sales, 1978-79, exec. v.p., 1979-84, dir., 1973-84; pres. Intermodal Logistics, Inc., South Miami, Fla., 1985—; chmn. bd. Munitions Carriers Conf., Washington, 1983-84, pres., 1982-83, bd. dirs., 1979-84; dir. SLO Transport Corp., Miami. Served with U.S. Army, 1970-76. Piano scholar, Belhaven Coll., 1968-70; winner 1st place solo and ensemble awards trumpet and piano, Fla. Band Masters Assn., 1966-68. Mem. Am. Trucking Assn. (sales and mktg. council), Fla. Trucking Assn., Nat. Def. Transp. Assn. Specialized Carriers and Rigging Assn., Traffic Clubs Internat., Fla. C. of C., Zool. Soc. Fla., Delta Nu Alpha, Phi Mu Alpha Sinfonia. Democrat. Presbyterian. Club: Mus. Sci. Century (Miami). Lodge: Miami Rotary. Office: Intermodal Logistics Inc PO Box 43-2155 South Miami FL 33243

LEONARD, RAYMOND WESLEY, retired civil and sanitary engineer; b. Lexington, N.C., Dec. 12, 1909; s. John Wesley and Clara Ada (Swing) L.; B.S. in Civil, Sanitary and Hwy. Engring., N.C. State U., 1932; M.P.H. (fellow), Yale U., 1947; m. Gladys Jane DeHart, June 14, 1934; children—Baxter C. J. and James R. W. (twins). Various engring. assignments N.C. State Hwy., TVA, N.C. State Bd. Health, until 1936; engr. U.S. Geol. Survey, Asheville, N.C. and Pitts., 1936-45, 46-63, C.E., Wilmington, N.C., 1946-63, C.E. and Mississippi River Commn., Vicksburg, Miss., 1963-73; ret., 1973. Registered profl. engr., Vt., Miss. Fellow Royal Soc. Health; mem. N.C. Engrs. Soc., Nat. Soc. Profl. Engrs., ASCE, Am. Assn. Sanitary Engrs. Interam. Assn. Sanitary Engrs., Am. Public Health Assn., Tau Beta Pi, Phi Kappa Phi. Lutheran. Clubs: Companion of St. Patrick, Masons, Shriners, Eastern Star. Home: PO Drawer HH Bryson City NC 28713

LEONARD, ROBIN ANN, publishing company executive; b. San Diego, Mar. 5, 1957; d. John Dunbar and Dorothy Ann (Jones) Leonard. B.A. in Bus. Adminstrn., U. Houston, 1979. Account exec. Houston Chronicle, 1979-81; sales mgr. Houston City Mag., 1981—; marketing cons. Spoons Restaurants Inc., Houston and Calif., 1982—. Mem. Houston C. of C., Am. Mktg. Assn. (past pres.), Advt. Fedn. Houston. Club: Raveneaux Country (Houston). Office: 1800 West Loop S Suite 1450 Houston TX 77027

LEONARD, TIM D., state senator, lawyer; b. Jan. 22, 1940; B.A., J.D., U. Okla. Bar: Okla. Navy White House mil. aide, 1966-67; asst. atty. gen. Okla., 1968-70; mem. Okla. Senate, 1979—, now minority leader. Republican. Office: PO Box 879 Beaver OK 73932

LEONSIS, THEODORE JOHN, publishing company executive; b. Vero Beach, Fla., Jan. 8, 1956. B.A. magna cum laude, Georgetown U., 1976; postgrad. Suffolk U. Law Sch., 1980. Copywriter, advt. mgr. Wang Labs., Inc., 1976-78, corp. publicity/pub. relations dir., 1978-81; dir. mktg. communications Harris Corp., Melbourne, Fla., 1981-83; exec. v.p. Redgate Pub. Co., Vero Beach, Fla., 1983—, also dir.; pres. Redgate Communications Corp., 1986—; founder Collegiate Entrepreneurs Fund; dir. Preview Media Inc., Brevard Venture Fund. Chmn. United Fund campaign, Wang Labs. Inc., 1980; bd. dirs. Big Bros. Brevard County, 1981. Brevard Art Ctr. and Mus., Brevard Council of Arts, 1981, Juvenile Employment Project, Lowell, Mass., Merrimack Regional Theatre. Mem. Pub. Relations Soc. Am. (cert.), Publicity Club Boston, Bus. Profl. Advt. Adminstrs., Am. Mktg. Assn. Contbr. articles to profl. jours.; pub., editor-in-chief LIST, LISTLETTER, Macintosh Buyers Guide, Apple II Buyers Guide, Wang Solutions, Amiga Buyers Guide, FYI (Harris Corp. mag.), book/software series, 1983—. Home: 490 Sea Oak Dr Johns Island Vero Beach FL 32963 Office: Redgate Pub Co 3381 Ocean Dr Vero Beach FL 32963

LEON-SOTOMAYOR, JOSE R., lawyer, educator; b. Ponce, P.R., Aug. 27, 1930; s. Jose León and Olga Del C. Sotomayor; m. Carmen D. Ribas-Rivera, Dec. 11, 1954; children—Jose R., Teresa, Allen L., Carlos J., Carmen L., Candida M., David A., Juan E., Glorimar, Carmen D., Olga G. B.S.M.E., U. P.R., 1954; J.D. magna cum laude, Catholic U. of P.R., 1970. Bar: P.R. 1970, U.S. Dist. Ct. P.R. 1973, U.S. Supreme Ct., 1985. Sole practice, Ponce, 1970-77, 1977—; assoc. prof. Sch. of Law, Catholic U. of P.R., Ponce, 1977—; spl. cons., v.p. fin. affairs, 1977-84; cons. and lectr. in law. Author: Casebook on Notarial Law, 1984; Puerto Rican Property Law Manual, 1984. Contbr. articles to profl. jours. Bd. dirs., trustee Ponce Med. Sch. Found., 1979—; legal cons. Com. on Civil Legislation, Ho. of Reps. of Legislature P.R., 1982—. Served to capt. USAF. Decorated Knight Equestrian Order Holy Sepulcher Jerusalem. Recipient Am. Jurisprudence award, 1970; P.R. Bar Assn. award, 1970, Ponce Bar Assn. award, 1970, Outstanding Alumni award Catholic U. P.R., 1983. Mem. Assn. Trial Lawyers Am., ASME, P.R. Bar Assn., Coll. Engrs. and Surveyors P.R., Phi Alpha Delta, Nu Sigma Beta. Republican. Roman Catholic. Clubs: Deportivo de Ponce (treas. 1975-77, v.p. 1977-78), Ponce Yacht & Fishing, William's Shooting. Lodge: K.C. Home: 334 St 2 La Rambla Ponce PR 00731 Office: Marvesa Bldg Office Suite 203 Rambla Ponce PR 00731

LEOPOLD, LOUIS, aerospace electronics engr.; b. Boston, Mar. 8, 1918; s. Nathan and Mary (Meyers) L.; B.S., U. Mich., 1941, Ill. Inst. Tech., 1958; postgrad. U. Chgo., 1949-51; m. Wilma Erika Miron, Dec. 27, 1947; children—Robert Louis, Laurence Scott. Electronics devel. engr. Magnecord, Inc., Chgo., 1952-53; sr. electronics project engr., group leader Motorola, Inc., 1953-59; electronics aero. research engr. communications system Project Mercury, NASA, Langley Field, Va., 1950-60, head antennas and microwave systems Project Apollo, Manned Spacecraft Center, Houston, 1961-67; NASA rep. for Project Mercury, McDonnell Aircraft Corp., St. Louis, 1960-61; mgr. NASA office, Apollo High Gain and LEM Steerable High Gain Antennas, Dalmo Victor Co., Belmont, Cal., 1968-69; asst. mgr. NASA Apollo Lunar Orbital Missions, S-band Transponder and Bistatic Radar Expts., 1969-73, mgr. antenna and microwave systems study Space Solar Power Satellite and Space Base Station, Johnson Space Center, Houston, 1973—. Cons. AMA, Chgo., 1957-59, Motorola, Inc., Thompson Ramo Wooldridge, Inc., 1956-59. Served to capt. USAAF, 1942-46. Recipient NASA Achievement awards, 1963-75. Mem. AIAA, IEEE (chmn. aerospace group 1964-65), AAAS, Ill. Acad. Sci., U. Mich. Union, St. Louis Engrs. Club, U. Mich. Alumni Assn. (dir. Houston 1967-68). Home: 7751 El Rancho St Houston TX 77087 Office: NASA Johnson Space Center Houston TX 77058

LEOPOLD, RALPH BRUCE, leasing company executive; b. New Orleans, Sept. 16, 1953; s. Ivan Ralph and Cecile (Rosenthal) L. B.S., La. State U., 1975; postgrad. Tulane U., 1979-80. Salesman, P.B.R., Inc., New Orleans, 1970-74, v.p., dir., 1974-81, founder, pres. mfg. div., 1974-81; pres., chief exec. officer Port-O-Let Internat., Inc., New Orleans, 1981-84, also dir.; pres., dir. Pac-Van Corp., 1984—; sales assoc. Latter-Blum Inc., 1984—; dir. Skyway Travel Inc., PBR, Inc., LEPCO, Inc. Mem. Jewish Children's Service; mem. adv. com. World's Fair. Mem. Internat. Franchise Assn., Portable Sanitation Assn., Associated Gen. Contractors, Fla. C. of C., Jacksonville C. of C., Com. 100, Southside Businessmen's Assn., Internat. Trade Com., New Orleans C. of C., Westbank Bus. Council, U. New Orleans Alumni Assn. Clubs: University (Jacksonville); YMCA (New Orleans). Editor: Port-O-Letter, 1981-84. Home: 4801 Rue Laurent Metairie LA 70002 Office: 1615 Poydras St 16th Floor New Orleans LA 70118

LEOPOLDO, FRANK CHARLES, sales and marketing executive; b. Phila., Jan. 1, 1949; s. Frederick John and Edith Frances (Principato) L.; m. Nancy Marie Pizzutillo, Jan. 17, 1951; 1 son, Frederick John. Student bus. adminstrn. St. Joseph's U., Phila., 1966-71; student Glassboro State Coll., 1971. Ops. mgr. Leopoldo Motel Corp., Wildwood, N.J., 1972-74; food service exec. Longchamps Inc., N.Y.C., 1974-75, Bambergers, Newark, 1975-78; food service dir. Burdines Dept. Stores, Miami, Fla., 1978-84; dir. sales and mktg. Exotic Gardens Inc., Ft. Lauderdale, Fla., 1984—. Served with USNR, 1967-74. Mem. Nat. Restaurant Assn., Fla. Restaurant Assn. Home: 2525 Polk St Apt 202 Hollywood FL 33020 Office: 5815 Ravenswood Rd Fort Lauderdale FL 33312

LEPCHITZ, MICHAEL, lawyer; b. Radford, Va., June 27, 1953; s. Morris and Helen (Kemp) L.; m. Nathalynn Tucker, June 27, 1981; 1 child, Zachary Butler. B.S. in Edn., U. Va., 1976; J.D., Washington and Lee U., 1979. Bar: Va. 1979, U.S. Dist. Ct. (we. dist.) Va. 1979, U.S. Ct. Appeals (4th cir.) 1979. Assoc. William Rogers McCall, Bristol, Va., 1980-82; sole practice, Radford, 1982—. Mem. Va. State Bar Assn. (law day com.), Bristol Bar Assn. (law day com.), ABA, Assn. Trial Lawyers Am., Floyd-Montgomery-Radford Bar Assn. (chmn. law day com. 1984). Home: PO Box 2923 Radford VA 24143

LEPPEL, KAREN, economics educator; b. Stratford, N.J., Oct. 22, 1954; d. Leon and Ruth Sara (Rosenberg) L. A.B. in Math. and Econs., Douglass Coll., New Brunswick, N.J., 1976; M.A. in Econs., Princeton U., 1978, Ph.D., 1980. Coadjutant, Douglass Coll., 1980; asst. prof. econs. U. N.C.-Greensboro, 1980—. Contbr. articles to profl. jours. Mem. Am. Econ. Assn., Atlantic Econ. Soc., Greensboro Single Faculty Assn. (founder 1981), Com. on the Status of Women in the Econs. Profession, Phi Beta Kappa, Pi Mu Epsilon, Omicron Delta Epsilon. Democrat. Avocations: reading, bicycling, cooking, movies. Office: U NC Dept Econs Greensboro NC 27412

LERCHBACKER, ALAN BERNARD, naval officer; b. Cleve., Apr. 20, 1952; s. Bernard Cyril and Eileen Florence (Horn) L.; children—Scott, Susan. B.S. in Mech. Engring., U.S. Naval Acad., 1974; M.S. in Mech. Engring., Naval Postgrad. Sch., 1980. Registered profl. engr., Calif. Commd. ensign U.S. Navy, 1974, advanced through grades to lt. comdr., 1982; repair officer USS John F. Kennedy, 1975-79; sr. ship supt. docking officer, diving officer Charleston Naval Shipyard (S.C.), 1980-83; Atlantic fleet diving and salvage officer, Norfolk, Va., 1983—. Decorated Navy Marine Corps Medal for Heroism, Navy Achievement medal. Mem. Am. Soc. Naval Engrs. Mormon. Home: Room 158 Orexler Manor NAB Little Creek Norfolk VA 23521

LERMAN, SIDNEY, ophthalmologist, educator; b. Montreal, Que., Can., Oct. 6, 1927; s. Aaron and Rachel (Sivak) L.; m. Marilyn Frank, Apr. 14, 1957; children—Lora Rachel, Mark Jonas. B.S., McGill U., Montreal, 1948, M.D., 1952; M.S., U. Rochester, 1961. Cert. Royal Coll. Physicians and Surgeons Can.; diplomate Am. Bd. Ophthalmology. Intern Montreal Gen. Hosp., 1952-53, resident in ophthalmology, 1953-55; instr. ophthalmology, dir. ophthalmic research U. Rochester (N.Y.), 1957-60, assoc. prof. ophthalmology and biochemistry, 1962-68; prof. ophthalmology and biochemistry, dir. ophthalmic research dept. McGill U., Montreal, 1968-71; prof. ophthalmology Emory U., Atlanta, 1975—. Mem. Am. Acad. Ophthalmology, Assn. Research in Vision and Ophthalmology, Am. Chem. Soc., Am. Soc. Biol. Chemists, Am. Soc. Photobiology, Internat. Soc. Eye Research, Oxford Ophthal. Congress. Author: Glaucoma, 1961; Cataracts, 1964; Basic Ophthalmology, 1966; Radiant Energy and the Eye, 1980; contbr. numerous articles to sci. jours. Home: 1648 Musket Ridge NW Atlanta GA 30327 Office: 1708 Haygood Dr NE Atlanta GA 30322

LERNER, MICHAEL HARVEY, dentist; b. Huntington, W.Va., Jan. 19, 1943; s. Leonard Allen and Marjorie (Cohen) L.; m. Freda Grace Miller, Aug. 2, 1964; children—Neil William, Marc Louis, Shayna Elaine. B.A. magna cum laude, Marshall U., 1964; D.M.D., U. Ky., 1967; M.S. in Dentistry and Pedodontics, Ind. U., 1969. Gen. practice dentistry, Lexington, Ky. Bull. editor Lexington B'nai B'rith, 1972—, pres., 1974-75; trustee Temple Adath Israel, Lexington, 1984—. Mem. ADA, Ky. Dental Assn., Am. Orthodontic Soc., Am. Endodontic Soc., Am. Soc. Dentistry for Children. Democrat. Jewish. Avocations: jazz piano; graphic design. Home: 3403 Thistleton Dr Lexington KY 40502 Office: 114 B Stone Rd Lexington KY 40503

LERNER, NORMAN CONRAD, communications company executive; b. N.Y.C., Feb. 13, 1936; s. Irving and Florence L.; m. Ina Roslyn Goldman, Sept. 6, 1959; children—Sheila, Julie. B.S.E.E., MIT, 1957; M.B.A., Columbia U., 1961; Ph.D., Am. U., 1968. Lic. profl. engr. Design engr. RCA Corp., Camden, N.J., 1957-58; mgr. field engring. Merit Light and Power, N.Y.C., 1958-61; asst. to pres. Associated Testing Labs., Wayne, N.J., 1961-62; program ITT, Arlington, Va., 1962-65; project mgr. MITRE Corp., Arlington, 1965-68; dir. Computer Scis. Corp., Falls Church, Va., 1968-71; cons. Exec. Office of Pres., Office Telecommunications Policy, Washington, 1971-72; pres. TRANSCOMM, Inc., Falls Church, 1971—; assoc. prof. George Washington U., Washington, 1971. Contbr. articles to profl. jours. Served to maj. USAR, 1957-66. Grad. fellow Columbia U., 1958-59. Mem. Am. Econ. Assn., Nat. Assn. Bus. Economists, IEEE, Nat. Soc. Profl. Engrs. Home: 4527 Pickett Rd Fairfax VA 22032 Office: TRANSCOMM Inc 6521 Arlington Blvd Falls Church VA 22042

LESAGE, ROBERT GORDON, optometrist; b. Chgo., Aug. 4, 1947; s. Gordon Bennett and Elizabeth Anne (Lee) LeS.; m. Bonnie Faye Johnson, Jan. 9, 1971; children—Colin Charles, Michelle Ruth. A.A., Manatee Jr. Coll., 1967; B.A., Fla. State U., 1969; B.S., U. Houston, 1973, O.D., 1973. Child vision cons. Harris County Ind. Sch. Dist., Houston, 1972-73; assoc. Dr. Arthur T. Young, Cape Coral, Fla., 1973-78; pvt. practice optometry, Sanibel, 1975—, Ft. Myers, Fla., 1978—. Mem. S.W. Fla. Health Planning Council, 1974—. Mem. Am. Optometric Assn., S.W. Fla. Optometric Assn., Fla. Optometric Assn. (pres. 1983-84), Fla. State U. Alumni Assn., Phi Theta Upsilon, Tau Kappa Epsilon (alumni sec. 1971-82, v.p. 1983-84). Democrat. Methodist. Club: Rotary (pres. Cape Coral 1982-83, dist. rep. 1983-84). Home: 5254 Skylark Ct Cape Coral FL 33904 Office: 28 San Carlos Blvd Suite 11 Gulf Point Sq Fort Myers FL 33908 also 7 Perwinkle Way Sanibel FL 33957

LESCH, JAMES RICHARD, manufacturing company executive; b. Apache, Okla., July 13, 1921; s. Emil W. and Rose (Stenger) L.; B.S. in Mech. Engring., U. Okla., 1946; m. Zelma Lee Meeks, Sept. 10, 1942; children—James Richard, Jack Wayne, Terry Alan, Steven Andrew. With Hughes Tool Co., Houston, 1946—, v.p. product planning and adminstrn. services, 1962-68, dir., 1964—, sr. v.p., gen. mgr., 1968-72, pres., chief operating officer, 1972-79, pres., chief exec. officer, 1979—, chmn. bd., 1981—, dir., officer subs.'s, dir. Raymond Internat., Tex. Commerce Bank. Trustee United Fund, Houston and Harris County Tex. Trustee South Tex. Coll. Law, engring. found. adv. council U. Tex. at Austin; bd. dirs. Meth. Hosp., Gulf Coast div. Tex. Soc. Prevention Blindness; nat. adv. bd. Goodwill Industries Am.; exec. com. Center Internat. Bus. Served with U.S. Army, 1942-45. Named to U. Okla. Engring. Hall of Fame, 1971. Mem. Petroleum Equipment Suppliers Assn. (pres. 1979). Am. Petroleum Inst., Tex. Mid-Continent Oil and Gas Assn. (exec. com.), Internat. Assn. Drilling Contractors, Nat. Ocean Ind. Assn., Houston Dist. Export Council, Nomads, Houston C. of C. (dir. 1968—, chmn. 1977-78). Jr. Achievement of S.E. Tex. (pres. 1973-74). Methodist. Clubs: Masons, Houston Met. Racquet, 25 Yr. of Petroleum Industry, Petroleum, Houston, Lakeside Country (Houston). Office: PO Box 2539 Houston TX 77001

LESHER, JACK LEITER, JR., dermatologist; b. Carlisle, Pa., June 11, 1948; s. Jack Leiter and Margaret (Farriday) L.; m. Patricia Smith, Dec. 28, 1974 (dec. 1981); m. Catherine Knight, Apr. 9, 1983. A.B., Bucknell U., 1970; B.M.Sc., Emory U., 1974; M.D., Med. Coll. Ga., 1981. Diplomate Nat. Bd. Med. Examiners. Med. lab. technician Carlisle Hosp., Pa., 1970-72; physician's assoc. Emory U., Atlanta, 1973-74, Dade City Med. Ctr., Fla., 1975-76; intern Med. Coll. Ga., Augusta, 1981-82, resident, 1982-84, chief resident, 1984, asst. prof. dermatology, 1985—; speaker in field. Contbr. articles to profl. publs. Co-chmn. Augusta Skin Cancer Program, Augusta, 1985. Recipient Merck award Merck, Sharpe and Dohme, 1981, 2d place resident award Med. Coll. Ga., 1983, 1st place resident award Med. Coll. Ga., 1984. Mem. Augusta Dermatol. Soc., Richmond County Med. Soc., Ga. Soc. Dermatologists, Med. Assn. Ga., Am. Acad. Dermatology, AMA, Alpha Omega Alpha. Democrat. Methodist. Avocations: wildlife conservation; museums; spy novels. Office: Dept Demmatology Med Coll Ga 1521 Pope Ave Augusta GA 30912

LESHER, MARIE PALMISANO, sculptor, painter; b. Reading, Pa., Sept. 20, 1919; d. John and Carmela (Napoli) Palmisano; m. Sam O'Neal Carter, Mar. 1, 1952 (dec. 1958); m. Arthur C. Lesher, Jr., Sept. 2, 1960. Student Berte Fashion Studio, Phila., 1940-43, Mus. Fine Arts Sch., Houston, 1963, U. Houston, 1964. Advt. mgr., art dir. Lowenstein's, Memphis, 1945-46, Levy's, Houston, 1946-50, Sakowitz, Houston, 1950-52, Battelstein's, Houston, 1959-60; instr. Sculptors Workshop, Houston, 1972-73; free lance sculptor, painter, Houston, 1960—. Solo exhbns. include: bronze sculpture, Beaumont Art Mus., 1973, Longview Mus., 1973, McAllen Internat. Mus., 1976, watercolors, Wichita Falls Art Assn., 1985, Goethe Inst., Houston, 1985. Recipient Art Archives award Smithsonian Instn., 1974—; Matrix award Women in Communications, 1973; art-in-embassy exhibits, U.S. Dept. State, Europe, Africa, S.Am., 1976—. Mem. Fashion Group of Houston (charter), Art League of Houston (charter), Artists Equity of N.Y., Knickerbocker Artists N.Y., Watercolor Art Soc. Houston, Tex. Soc. Sculptors (dir. 1973-78). Avocations: Travel; investments; photography. Home: 10130 Shady River Rd Houston TX 77042

LESIKAR, GEORGE J., anesthesiologist; b. New Braunfels, Tex., Sept. 27, 1942; s. George and Imogene (Hancock) L.; B.S., Trinity U., San Antonio, 1964; M.D., U. Tex.-Galveston, 1968; m. Jerri Joan Allamon, June 22, 1968; children—George Jay, Dean Alan, Keith Laddie. Intern, Brooke Gen. Hosp., San Antonio, 1968-69; resident in anesthesia Brooke Gen. Hosp., Fort Sam Houston, Tex., 1969-72; staff anesthesiologist Scott & White Clinic, Temple, Tex., 1975-78; staff anesthesiologist St. Francis Hosp., Tulsa, 1978—, chmn. dept., 1985—. 2d v.p. Assoc. Anesthesiologists, Inc., Tulsa, 1981-85; pres., 1985—. Served with M.C., AUS, 1967-75. Diplomate Am. Bd. Anesthesiology. Mem. AMA, Okla. Med. Assn., Am. Soc. Anesthesiologists. Republican. Episcopalian. Home: 7606 S Quebec Ave Tulsa OK 74136 Office: 6202 S Lewis St Suite 150 Tulsa OK 74136

LESIKAR, RAYMOND VINCENT, educator, writer, consultant; b. Rogers, Tex., June 29, 1922; s. Vince E. and Albina Julia (Stanislaw) L.; m. Lu Clay Allen, July 7, 1945; children—Patricia A. Lesikar King, Raymond V. B.B.A., U. Tex.-Austin, 1947, M.B.A., 1948, Ph.D., 1954. With Douglas Aircraft Co., 1941-42, Sears Roebuck & Co., 1947; faculty various univs., 1948-54; faculty La. State U., Baton Rouge, 1954-59, prof. bus. adminstrn., 1959, chmn. dept. mgmt., 1959-77, dean coll. bus. adminstrn., 1963-64, 72-73, prof. emeritus, 1977—; adj. prof. U. Tex., Austin, 1977-79; prof., chmn. dept. mgmt. N. Tex. State U., Denton, 1979—; cons., writer. Served to capt. AUS, 1943-46. Mem. Am. Bus. Communication Assn. (pres. 1961), Southwest Fedn. Adminstrv. Disciplines, Southwest Social Sci. Assn. (pres. 1967), Acad. Mgmt., Internat. Soc. Gen. Semantics, Beta Gamma Sigma, Sigma Iota Epsilon, Phi Kappa Phi. Clubs: Denton Country. Contbg. author publs. in field. Home: Route 1 PO Box 19-A Argyle TX 76226 Office: North Texas State U Coll of Bus Administration Denton TX 76203

LESLIE, FRED WELDON, space scientist; b. Ancon, Panama, C.Z., Dec. 19, 1951; s. Grady Weldon and Golden Lucille (Bateman) L. B.S. with honors in Engring. Sci., U. Tex., 1974; M.S. in Meteorology, U. Okla., 1977, Ph.D. in Meteorology, 1979. Research asst. Ctr. Nuclear Studies, Austin, Tex., 1972-73; teaching asst. U. Tex., Austin, 1973-74, U. Okla., Norman, 1974-75; research asst., 1975-79; postdoctoral research assoc. Purdue U., West Lafayette, Ind., 1979-80; vis. scientist NASA Marshall Space Flight Ctr., Huntsville, Ala., 1980, research scientist, 1980—, instrument scientist, co-investigator, astronaut instr. for Spacelab 3. Demonstration parachute jumper for civic orgns. Huntsville, 1980-83; exhbn. parachute jumper for Shriner burned children, 1982. Recipient NASA Group Achievement award, 1981, Cert. Appreciation, 1982. Mem. Am. Phys. Soc., Am. Geophys. Union, Am. Meteorol. Soc., U.S. Parachute Assn. (Gold Wings 1979, 12 Hour badge 1981). Clubs: Health, Scuba, Sports Parachute (Huntsville); NASA Flying. Contbr. articles to profl. publs. Home: 1030 Sharpsburg Dr Huntsville AL 35803 Office: NASA Marshall Space Flight Center Mail Code ED42 Huntsville AL 35812

LESLIE, HENRY ARTHUR, banker; b. Troy, Ala., Oct. 15, 1921; s. James B. and Alice (Minchener) L.; B.S., U. Ala., 1942, J.D., 1948; J.S.D., Yale U., 1959; grad. Sch. Banking, Rutgers U., 1964; m. Anita Doyle, Apr. 5, 1943; children—Anita Lucinda Leslie Cochrane, Henry Arthur. Bar: Ala. 1948. Asst. prof. bus. law U. Ala., 1948-50, 52-54, prof. law, asst. dean Sch. Law, 1954-59; v.p. trust officer Birmingham Trust Nat. Bank (Ala.), 1959-64; sr. v.p., trust officer Union Bank & Trust Co., Montgomery, Ala., 1964-73, sr. v.p., 1973-76, exec. v.p., 1976-78, pres., chief exec. officer, 1978—, dir., 1973—; dir. Birmingham br. Fed. Res. Bank, 1st Fin. Mgmt. Corp., Atlanta. Pres., Downtown Unltd., 1983-84; atty. Water Improvement Commn. Ala., 1971-75; bd. dirs. Pike County Mus., Montgomery Mus. Fine Arts, Ala. Shakespeare Theatre, Blue and Grey Tennis Assn.; chmn. bd. trustees Humana East Hosp., 1984—; mem. Ala. Oil and Gas Bd., 1984—; trustee Ala. Assn. Ind. Colls. Served to capt. AUS, 1942-46; to lt. col. JAGC, Res. Decorated Bronze Star. Mem. ABA, Ala. Bar Assn., Am. Bankers Assn., Ala. Bankers Assn. (trust div. pres. 1963-65), Ind. Bankers Ala. (chmn. 1984), Ind. Bankers Assn. Am. (dir. 1984—), Farrah Order Jurisprudence (pres. 1973), Newcomen Soc. N.Am., Montgomery C. of C. (dir.), Delta Sigma Pi, Phi Delta Phi, Omicron Delta Kappa, Pi Kappa Phi. Episcopalian (sr. warden). Clubs: Maxwell Officers, Montgomery Country, Capital City (dir.). Lodge: Kiwanis. Contbr. articles to profl. jours. Home: 3332 Boxwood Dr Montgomery AL 36111 Office: Union Bank & Trust Co 60 Commerce St Montgomery AL 36104

LESLIE, RICHARD MCLAUGHLIN, lawyer; b. Chgo., Oct. 31, 1936; s. Richard S. and Belle (McLaughlin) L.; m. Nancy Lomax; children—Saralynn, Richard, Lance. B.A., U. Fla., 1958; J.D., U. Mich., 1961. Assoc. Jacobs & McKenna, Chgo., 1961-63; assoc. Louis G. Davidson, Chgo., 1963; assoc., then ptnr. Shutts & Bowen, Miami, Fla., 1964—; adj. prof. trial advocacy program U. Miami Law Sch., 1979—. Served with U.S. Army; to capt. USAR. Mem. ABA (past chmn. trial techniques com. trial and ins. practice sect.), Fla. Def. Lawyers Assn. (pres.-elect), Fedn. Ins. Counsel (chmn. com.), Maritime Law Assn. U.S. (arrangements com.), Fla. Bar Assn. (admiralty com.), Ill. Bar Assn., Average Adjustors Assn., Phi Delta Theta, Delta Theta Phi. Mem. United Ch. of Christ. Home: 4116 Pinta Ct Coral Gables FL 33146 Office: 1500 Edward Ball Bldg Miami Center 100 Chopin Plaza Miami FL 33131

LESSARD, CHARLES STEPHEN, educator, former air force officer, electrical engineer; b. Panama City, Panama, Jan. 21, 1936; s. Stephen C. and Adelina Maria Lessard; B.S. in Elec. Engring., Tex. A&M U., 1958; grad U.S. Air Force Squadron Officers Sch., 1962; M.S. in Elec. Engring., Air Force Inst. Tech., 1967; Ph.D. in Biomed. Engring., Marquette U., 1972; grad. U.S. Air Force Command and Staff Coll., Air U., 1974, Air War Coll., 1976; m. Martha Louise Meath, May 13, 1960; children—Stephen C., Catherine A., Joseph P., Daniel P. Commd. 2d lt. USAF, 1958, advanced through grades to lt. col., 1974; pilot strategic bombers and fighter interceptors, 1958-64; devel. engr. of precision electronic instruments, Kelly AFB, Tex., 1967-68; chief biomed. engring. research Sch. of Aerospace Medicine, Brooks AFB, Tex., 1968-70; research scientist Aerospace Med. Research Labs., Wright-Patterson AFB, Dayton, Ohio, 1972-74; dir. combat grande field office Electronics Systems Div., Torrejon Airbase, Spain, 1974-80; asst. chief biodynamics and bioengring. div. Aerospace Med. Research Labs., Wright-Patterson AFB, Dayton, Ohio, 1980-81; ret., 1981; prof. evening div. San Antonio Coll., 1967-69; adj. prof. Air Force Inst. Tech., Wright-Patterson AFB, Dayton, 1972-74; asso. prof. biomed. engring. Tex. A&M U., College Station, 1981—. Bond Drive and Fed. campaign fund chmn., 1963, 72, 73; mgr. Little League Baseball, Ramey AFB, P.R., 1963; coach of basketball, baseball, and football St. Helen's Elementary Sch., Dayton, Ohio, 1972, 73, 74. Recipient Research and Devel. Tech. Achievement award Air Force Systems Command, 1970; Commendation medal U.S. Air Force, 1970, Meritorious Service medal, 1974, 80, 81; Aero. Meritorious Cross with white distinction of 1st class Spanish Air Force; registered profl. engr., Tex. Mem. IEEE, Neuroelectric Soc., Soc. for Psychophysiol. Research, Aerospace Med. Assn., Tau Beta Phi, Phi Eta Sigma, Eta Kappa Nu. Designer automatic electronic analysis of EEG. Home: 1805 Shadowood Dr College Station TX 77840 Office: Biomed Engring Indsl Engring Dept Tex A&M U College Station TX 77844

LESSARD, RAYMOND W., bishop, Roman Catholic Ch. Ordained priest, 1956, consecrated bishop, 1973, bishop diocese of, Savannah, Ga., 1973—. Office: 225 Abercorn St PO Box 8789 Savannah GA 31412*

LESSENBERRY, ROBERT ADAMS, retail executive; b. Glasgow, Ky., May 7, 1926; s. Robert Long and Hugh Barret (Adams) L.; m. Mary Lloyd Howard, Dec. 26, 1946; children—Robert Howard, Hugh Barret Adams, Leigh Langford. B.A., Centre Coll. of Ky., 1950. Owner, Lessenberry Realty, Glasgow, 1954—; ptnr. Parkview Devel. Co., Glasgow, 1959-80, owner, 1980—; owner Lessenberry Real Estate, Glasgow, 1968; pres. Lessenberry Devel. Co., Inc., Glasgow, 1969—; ptnr. Lessenberry Enterprises, Glasgow, 1972—; pres. Lessenberry Bldg. Centre, Inc., Glasgow, 1953—, Lessenberry Electric & Plumbing, Inc., 1973; pres. The Glasgow Ry. Co., 1965—, also dir., treas. Elder, First Presbyn. Ch., Glasgow, 1952—, tchr. sch., 1963-67, choir dir. 1953-68; vice chmn. exec. council Louisville Presbytery, 1962-66; pres., trustee Westminster Terr. Presbyn. Home for Sr. Citizens and Health Care Ctr., Louisville, 1968-79, 83—; bd. dirs. Barren County (Ky.) Red Cross; pres. Glasgow Community Concert Assn., 1953-58; mem. Glasgow City Council, 1962-66, chmn. fin. 1962-66, mayor, 1966-68, chmn. water commn., 1966-68, dir. mcpl. housing, 1966-68; dir. Barren River Area Devel. Council, 1968-72; chmn. Glasgow Urban Renewal and Community Devel. Agy., 1979-81; trustee Ky. Ind. Coll. Fund, 1972-80. Served with AUS, 1944-46, to capt., 1950-53. Decorated Bronze Star with cluster; named hon. citizen Metro Nashville. Mem. Glasgow C. of C. (dir. 1972-74), Glasgow-Barren County Bd. Realtors (dir. 1979—), Ind.-Ky. Hardware Assn. (pres. 1981, dir. 1975—), Nat. Lumber and Bldg. Material Dealers Assn. (dir. 1977-80), Ky. Retail Lumber Dealers Assn. (pres. 1973—), Hardware Wholesalers, Inc. (pres. 1978—), Sigma Chi, Omicron Delta Kappa. Lodge: Rotary (dir., past pres.), Masons, Shriners. Office: 1010 W Main St Glasgow KY 42141

LESSER, CHARLES HUBER, archivist; b. DuBois, Pa., Mar. 15, 1944; s. Ray Clyde and Mary Ann (Huber) L. B.A., Pa. State U., 1966, M.A., 1968; Ph.D., U. Mich., 1974. Supr. research, research editor Am. Revolution bicentennial project William L. Clements Library, U. Mich., Ann Arbor, 1972-75; asst. dir. archives and publs. S.C. Dept. Archives and History, Columbia, 1975—. Mem. Soc. Am. Archivists (chmn. govt. records profl. affinity group 1981-82), So. Hist. Assn., Orgn. Am. Historians, Am. Hist. Assn., Assn. Documentary Editing. Author: The Sinews of Indpendence: Monthly Strength Reports of the Continental Army, 1976; (with J. Todd White) Fighters for Independence: A Guide to Sources of Biographical Information on Soldiers and Sailors of the American Revolution, 1977. Office: PO Box 11669 Capitol Station Columbia SC 29211

LESSER, JOSEPH M., physician; b. N.Y.C., July 5, 1927; s. Philip and Ida Lesser; divorced; 1 child, Judith. B.S., U. Ga., 1949; Ph.D. in Chemistry, Temple U., 1965, M.D., 1969. Diplomate Am. Bd. Internal Medicine. Intern, Phila. Gen. Hosp., 1969-70; resident Temple U., Phila., 1970-72; practice internal medicine, Atlanta, 1973—. Office: 116 Cade St Hartwell GA 30643

LESTER, LANE PATMAN, biology educator, computer programmer; b. Miami, Fla., Oct. 16, 1938; s. Ralph Ingram and Myrtis Olivia (Sharman) L.; m. Gail Lee Attaway, Dec. 13, 1958; children—Kenneth Lane, Lee Ann, Jennifer Paige. B.S.E., U. Fla., 1963; M.S., Purdue U., 1967, Ph.D., 1971. Biology tchr. Evans High Sch., Orlando, Fla., 1963-67; asst. prof. biology U. Tenn., Chattanooga, 1970-73; mini-course developer Biol. Scis. Curriculum Study, Boulder, 1973-74; prof. biology Christian Heritage Coll., El Cajon, Calif., 1974-75; prof. biology Liberty Baptist U., Lynchburg, Va., 1979—. NDEA fellow, 1967-70. Mem. Va. Assn. for Biology Edn., Creation Research Soc., Sigma Xi. Republican. Baptist. Author: (with J.N. Hefley) Cloning: Miracle or Menace?, 1980; (with R.G. Bohlin) The Natural Limits to Biological Change, 1984; contbr. articles to profl. jours. Office: Liberty U Creation Studies Lynchburg VA 24506

LESTER, ROY DAVID, lawyer; b. Middletown, Ohio, Jan. 16, 1949; s. Edgel Celsus and Norma Marie (Elam) L.; 1 child, Justin David. B.S., Western Ky. U., 1970; J.D., U. Ky., 1975. Bar: Ky. 1975, U.S. Tax Ct. 1979, U.S. Dist. Ct. (ea. dist.) Ky. 1976, U.S. Supreme Ct. 1979. Agt. Mut. Benefit Life, Louisville, 1970-72; ptnr. Stoll, Keenon & Park, Lexington, 1975—; dir. Almahurst Farm, Lexington. Contbr. articles to profl. jours. Bd. dirs., past pres. Lakeview Estates Lake Assn., Lexington, 1982—. Served with USNG, 1970-76. Mem. Fayette County Bar Assn. (auditor 1984), Order of Coif. Republican. Roman Catholic. Club: YMCA (Lexington). Home: 2060 Norborne Dr Lexington KY 40502 Office: Stoll Keenon & Park 1000 First Security Plaza Lexington KY 40507

LESTMANN, PHILLIP EDWARD, mathematics educator, marketing executive; b. Pasadena, Calif., Sept. 25, 1951; s. Henry Eugene and Dorothy Alyene (Pryor) L.; m. Darlene Faith Roodzant, June 16, 1973; children—Keri-Lynn, Kristi Marie, Kati Elise, Kalani Leigh. B.S., Biola U., 1972; Ph.D., U. So. Calif., 1977. Teaching asst. U. So. Calif., Los Angeles, 1972-77; asst. prof. Bryan Coll., Dayton, Tenn., 1977-82, assoc. prof. math., 1982—. Contbr. articles to profl. jours. Orgn. chmn. Rhea County Christian Action Council, Tenn., 1984-85; elder Grace Bible Ch., Dayton, 1979-82, 84—; mem. Christian Businessmen's Com., Dayton, 1984—; campaign worker campaigns Rhea County, 1982, 84. Mem. Math. Assn. Am. (com. on math. applications). Republican. Avocations: Personal evangelism and discipleship; reading; net sports. Home: 1619 N Oak St Dayton TN 37321 Office: Bryan Coll Box 7615 Dayton TN 37321

LETCHER, HARVEY D., recruiting company executive; b. Dallas, Jan. 2, 1942; s. Harvey D. and Dee Louise (Holloman) L.; m. Shirley JoAn Robinson, June 9, 1961; children—Deanna Jill, Harvey D. III. B.S. in Bus. Adminstrn., North Tex. State U., 1964. Grad. cert. Am. Inst. Banking. With InterFirst Bank, Dallas N.A., 1963-69; v.p. Univ. Computing Co., Dallas, 1971-77; v.p. Inforex Inc., Boston, 1977-78; dir., fin. cons. Coopers & Lybrand, Houston, 1978-80; v.p., dir. Intercomp Inc., Houston, 1980-82; ptnr., v.p. Korn Ferry Internat., Houston, 1982-85; sr. v.p., mgr. Houston office Paul R. Ray & Co., Inc., 1986—; adv. dir. Comml. Nat. Bank, Dallas Bd. dirs., v.p. Wimbledon Estates Homeowners Assn., Spring, Tex., 1983; chmn. Houston chpt. Am. Heart Assn., 1984; bd. dirs. Arts for Everyone, 1986. Mem. Am. Mgmt. Assn., Pleasant Grove C. of C. (dir. 1973-74), Assn. Corp. Growth (pres. Houston chpt. 1984-85, past pres. 1985-86), Downtown Houston Assn. (charter), Republican. Baptist. Club: Kiwanis (S.E. Dallas chpt. dir. 1972). Lodges: Masons, Rotary, Shriners. Home: 6706 Robinwick Ct Spring TX 77379 Office: 1010 Lamar Suite 990 Houston TX 77002

LETCHWORTH, GEORGE ALLEN, psychology educator; b. Liberty, Mo., Jan. 20, 1940; s. Harry Frances and Martha Ann (Sams) L.; m. Frances Leivo Everett, May 8, 1975; children—Mark, Christopher. B.A., Okla. Baptist U., 1962; M.S. U. Okla., 1965, Ph.D., 1968. Research specialist Okla. Rehab. Services, Oklahoma City, 1966-67; asst. prof. Okla. Baptist U., Shawnee, 1967-69; assoc. prof. U. Okla., Norman, 1969—; mem. Okla. State Bd. Examiners, 1976-79, chmn. bd., 1979. Mem. Okla. Psychol. Assn. (pres. 1978-79), Am. Psychol. Assn., Southwestern Psychol. Assn., Am. Edn. Research Assn. Home: Rt 5 Box 109 Stillwater OK 74074 Office: U Okla 820 Van Vleet Oual Norman OK 73019

LETIZIA, CHARLES JOSEPH, architect; b. N.Y.C., Sept. 7, 1954; s. Charles J Joseph and Helen (Amato) L. B.S. in Design, U. Fla., 1976, M.A. in Architecture, 1978. Registered architect, Fla., Ga., S.C., N.C., Tenn. Architect, designer Leon Jay Meyer & Assoc., Savannah, Ga., 1977-80; staff architect Mid-State Devel., Longwood, Fla., 1980-81; architect., v.p. Master Design Group, Inc., North Palm Beach, Fla., 1981-82; sr. design architect Reynolds, Smith & Hills, Inc., North Palm Beach, 1982-84; architect, pres. Island Designs, Inc., Riviera Beach, Fla., 1984—; v.p. Island Contractors of Palm Beaches Inc., Riviera Beach, 1984—; prof. Savannah Coll. Art, Ga., 1979-80. Mem. Fla. Homebuilders Assn., North Palm Beach County C. of C., North Palm Beach 1 Palm Beach Gardens Jaycees. Roman Catholic. Avocations: golf; tennis, skiing; scuba diving; boating. Home: 905 Lakeshore Dr Apt 202 Lake Park FL 33403 Office: Island Design Inc 2603 N Ocean Ave Suite L Riviera Beach FL 33404

LETTERI, WILLIAM MICHAEL, corporate executive, tax consultant; b. Bklyn., Jan. 16, 1957; s. William Frederick and Winifred Reginia (Tarpey) L.; m. Nancy Ann Florac, Aug. 5, 1978. B.S., Cornell U., 1980. Acct., Maxfield, Randolph & Carpenter, Ithaca, N.Y., 1980-81; acct. Hantzman, Wiebel & Co., Charlottesville, Va., 1981-82; corp. adminstr. Central Va. Psychiat. Assocs., Inc., Charlottesville, 1982—; v.p., treas. Lafayette Acad., Inc., Charlottesville, 1983—; tax cons., 1982—; exec. ptnr. Va. Ventures, Ltd., Charlottesville, 1983—. Mem. Va. Soc. C.P.A.s, Health Care Fin. Mgmt. Assn. Club: Holiday Health and Racquet. Home: 1092 Towne Ln Charlottesville VA 22901 Office: 2101 Arlington Blvd Charlottesville VA 22903

LETTS, HUBERT WINFRED, writer, publisher; b. Inez, Tex., Aug. 18, 1913; s. Henry Frank and Totsy Clara (Spencer) L., Sr.; m. Clarris Lissie Bright, Oct. 9, 1938; children—Betty Louise Letts Arnold, Janet Gail Letts Slay. B.B.A., U. Tex., 1970. Clk., U.S. Post Office, Corpus Christi, 1937-48, supr., supt., 1948-68; office mgr. Carlton Constrn. Co., Texas City, Tex., 1971-72; constrn. supr. Hospitality Mgmt. Corp., Dallas, 1973-74; writer, pub. Home Pub. Co., Corpus Christi, 1975—. Author: West of the Blue Ridge, 1982; Free Market Economics, 1983; Yankee Land to Dixie Land, 1986. Contbr. articles to profl. jours. Candidate for U.S. Congress from 14th Dist., Tex., 1968. Served with U.S. N.G., 1937-40. Mem. Am. Econ. Assn., Assn. for Comparative Econ. Studies, SAR, Portairs Businessmen's Assn. (pres. 1967). Democrat. Lodge: Kiwanis (pres. 1966). Avocations: hunting, genealogy. Home and office: 1037 McClendon St Corpus Christi TX 78404

LETTS, THOMAS CLINTON, farmer, rancher, retired educator; b. El Campo, Tex., Mar. 15, 1911; s. Henry Frank and Clara (Spencer) L.; student U. Houston, 1935-36, 47-48; B.S., Sam Houston State U., 1937; M.S., Tex. A. and M. U., 1945, postgrad., 1948-52; m. Margaret Evelyn McDaniel, Oct. 27, 1934; 1 dau., Margaret Sue Letts Hopper. Tchr., prin., supt. public schs., Tex., 1929-42; clk. War Dept., 1942; work unit conservationist U.S. Dept. Agr., 1943-46; asso. prof. Sam Houston State U., 1946-58; agriculturist FOA, Tel Aviv, 1953-54; educationist ICA, Taipei, Taiwan, 1955-57, elem. edn. adviser, Asuncion, Paraguay, 1958-60; tchr. ednl. adviser USOM, Tegucigalpa, Honduras, 1960-62; elem. edn. adviser AID, Recife, Brazil, 1963-65; area devel. officer USOM, Dinh Turong Province, Vietnam, 1965, agrl. edn. officer AID, Saigon, Vietnam, 1966-71; farmer, rancher Walker and Williamson Counties, Tex., 1971—; sr. Congressional intern, 1980. Exec. com. Wharton County Inter-Scholastic League, 1935-37; chmn. Tex. joint legis. com. Nat. Ret. Tchrs. Assn./Am. Assn. Ret. Persons, 1980-81; nat. del. White House Conf. on Aging, 1981; bd. dirs. Trinity River Authority, 1983—, Grand Person's Ctr., Huntsville-Walker County, 1984—. Mem. Tex. Tchrs. Assn. (pres. dist. VI ret. tchrs. sect.), Tex. Ret. Tchrs. (parliamentarian), Huntsville-Walker County Assn. (pres. 1977), Walker County C. of C. (dir. 1946-49), Kappa Delta Pi. Clubs: Rotary (past pres.); Vocational Agriculture (past pres.). Home: Route 5 Box 388 Huntsville TX 77340

LETZSCH, WALTER STEPHEN, agronomist; b. Chgo., Sept. 6, 1942; s. Walter Sitz and Lavinia Dorthy (Meister) L.; B.S., U. Ill., 1971; M.S., U. Ga., 1978, postgrad., 1978—. Research asst. U. Ga., Athens, 1972; jr. high sci. tchr. Burke County Sch. Bd., Waynesboro, Ga., 1975-76; lab. asst. U. Ga., Athens, 1977, agrl. research asst. III, 1977-83, research coordinator I, 1983—. Cert. profl. soil scientist. Mem. Internat. Soil Sci. Soc., Am. Soc. Agronomy, Soil Sci. Soc. Am., Soc. Econ. Paleontologists and Mineralogists, Council Agrl. Sci. and Tech., Zionist Orgn. Am. Jewish. Contbr. articles to profl. jours. Home: 11 Cloverhurst Ct #4 Athens GA 30605 Office: U Ga Dept Agronomy Athens GA 30602

LEUNG, WING HAI, chemistry educator; b. Hong Kong, July 29, 1937; came to U.S., 1969; s. Ju-Dug and Ping-Fan (Yu) L.; m. Lai-Yin Kwan, Aug. 12, 1965; children—Kar-Woo, Kar-Hong, Kar-Peck. Ph.D., U. Miami, 1974. Sr. chemist GAF Corp., Binghamton, N.Y., 1976-77; research scientist Clinton Corn Corp. (Iowa), 1977-78; asst. prof. Hampton (Va.) U., 1978-82, assoc. prof. chemistry, 1982—. Mem. U.S. Congl. Adv. Bd., 1983. NASA research grantee, 1982. Mem. Am. Chem. Soc., Am. Geophys. Union, Sigma Xi. Home: 701 C Orchard Rd Hampton VA 23669 Office: PO Box 6422 Hampton U Hampton VA 23668

LEUTHARD, JOY LYNNE, social service agency executive, social worker; b. Denver, Mar. 28, 1952; d. John Joseph and Garnett Edwana (Ferry) L.; m. Thomas Wayne Gillock, Nov. 9, 1985. B.A., Colo. State U., 1974; M.S., Okla. State U., 1976. Lic. social work assoc. Okla. Juvenile diversion counselor Ponca City Police, Okla., 1976-78; youth and family counselor Kay County Youth Services, Ponca City, 1978-81; program dir. YWCA Rape Crisis Ctr., Oklahoma City, 1981-82; sexual assault program dir. Women's Resource Ctr., Norman, Okla., 1982-85; state rape prevention coordinator Okla. Dept. Mental Health, 1982-85; exec. dir. Tri-City Youth and Family Ctr., Choctaw, Okla., 1985—; instr. Okla. State U., Stillwater, 1982-83. Author and editor: (with others) Sexual Assault: A Guide for Professionals, 1983. Editor directory Oklahoma Directory of Sexual Assault Services, 1983. Bd. dirs. Okla. Assn. Youth Services; mem. women's adv. council Okla. Dept. Mental Health. Mem. Bus. and Profl. Women, Women's Polit. Caucus, NOW, Nat. Assn. Social Workers, Am. Assn. Counseling and Devel., Am. Mental Health Counselors Assn., Nat. Council Crime and Delinquency, Am. Correctional Assn., Nat. Coalition Against Sexual Assault. Democrat. Avocations: horses; music; theater; ballet; reading; gardening. Home: 14380 SE 15th St Choctaw OK 73020 Office: Tri-City Youth and Family Ctr Inc 14625 NE 23d St PO Box 695 Choctaw OK 73020

LEUZE, REX ERNEST, chemical engineer; b. Sabetha, Kans., Mar. 7, 1922; s. Ernest Jacob and Madelyn Iola (Newman) L.; m. Ruth Imogene Morris, June 19, 1948; children—Michael Rex, Robert Morris, Thomas Ernest. B.S. in Chem. Engring., Kans. State U., 1944; M.S., U. Tenn., 1956. Analytical chemist Monsanto Chem. Co., Monsanto, Ill., 1944-45; radio-chem. analyst Clinton Lab., Oak Ridge, 1945-46; process devel. engr. Oak Ridge Nat. Lab., 1946-49, process devel. problem leader, 1949-63, asst. sect. chief, 1963-76, exptl. engring. sect. head, 1976-81, pilot plant sect. head, 1981—. Served with U.S. Army, 1945-46. Recipient IR-100 award Fabrication Process for Nuclear Fuel, 1979. Fellow Am. Inst. Chemists; mem. Am. Nuclear Soc., Am. Chem. Soc., AAAS, Internat. Union Pure and Applied Chemistry, Sigma Xi, Phi Kappa Phi. Baptist. Contbr. articles to profl. jours.; patentee in field. Home: 517 W 5th Ave Lenoir City TN 37771 Office: PO Box X Oak Ridge TN 37830

LE VAN, DANIEL HAYDEN, business exec.; b. Savannah, Ga., Mar. 29, 1924; s. Daniel Hayden and Ruth (Harner) Le V.; B.A., Harvard U., 1950; student Babson Inst., 1950-51. Dir., Colonial Gas Co., Overseas Properties Ltd., N.Y.C. Served with AUS, 1943-46. Clubs: Harvard (N.Y.C. and Boston). Home: Box 158 DeLeon Springs FL 32028

LEVERENZ, JULIA BULKELEY, university administrator; b. Princeton, N.J., Nov. 3, 1947; d. Humboldt Walter and Edith Ruggles (Langmuir) L.; m. Charles Leslie Britt, Jr., May 9, 1979. A.B., Dickinson Coll., 1969; Certificat Pratique, U. Paris, 1968; M.B.A., Coll. William and Mary, 1982. Research asst. Research Triangle Inst., Raleigh, N.C., 1970-75; asst. to vice pres. Ashland Chem. Co., Columbus, Ohio, 1975-76; dir. sponsored program Coll. William and Mary, Williamsburg, 1976-78, dir. Women in Bus., 1978-84, dir. Ctr. for Exec. Devel., 1984—. Contbr. articles to profl. jours. Vice pres. Peninsula Women's Network, Newport News, Va., 1982-83, dir., 1979-80, 81-82; pres. The Forum of Williamsburg, 1979—. Mem. Nat. Assn. Female Execs. (network dir. 1982—), Am. Soc. Tng. and Devel., Phi Beta Kappa, Beta Gamma Sigma. Avocations: sailing, licensed private pilot. Office: Ctr for Exec Devel Coll William and Mary PO Box JD Williamsburg VA 23187

LEVEY, DOUGLAS POKORNY, retail company executive; b. New Orleans, Mar. 26, 1926; s. Ralph Pokorny and Sadie (Dannenbaum) L.; m. Mary Ramsey, Aug. 27, 1949; children—Sherman Douglas, Helen Colt. B.B.A., Tulane U., 1948. Treas. M. Pokorny & Sons. Ltd., New Orleans, 1953-58, pres., 1958-78, chmn. bd., 1978—. Served with USCG, 1944-46. Mem. Nat. Shoe Retail Assn., Nat. Retail Merchants Assn., Better Bus. Bur., New Orleans C. of C. Mem. First Ch. of Christ Scientist. Clubs: Vista Shores, Sertoma. Lodges: Kiwanis. Home: 60 N Lark St New Orleans LA 70124 Office: 124 St Charles St New Orleans LA 70130

LEVIN, BERNARD, physician; b. Johannesburg, S. Africa, Apr. 1, 1942; came to U.S. 1966, naturalized 1974; m. Ronelle DuBrow; children—Adam, Katherine. M.D., U. Witwatersrand, 1964. Resident, Presbyn. St. Lukes Hosp., Chgo., 1966-68; research fellow U. Chgo., 1968-71; fellow NIH-U. Chgo., 1971-72; instr. medicine U. Chgo., 1971-73, asst. prof. medicine, 1973-78, assoc. prof., 1979-84; prof. med., chief sect. gastrointestinal oncology and digestive diseases, M.D. Anderson Hosp., Houston, 1984—; mem. large bowel cancer working group Nat. Cancer Inst., 1984-85; vis. prof. U. Iowa, 1983; cons. spl. study sect. Nat. Cancer Inst., 1976-84, others; mem. nat. adv. com. on colorectal cancer Am. Cancer Soc., 1983—. Contbr. articles to profl. jours. Recipient Outstanding Med. Resident award Presbyn. St. Luke's Hosp., 1968; USPHS grantee, 1976-80; Melamid Found. Gift, U. Chgo., 1978-83; NCI grantee, 1980-84, others. Mem. AAAS, Am. Gastroenterol. Assn., Am. Soc. Gastrointestinal Endoscopy, ACP, Am. Pancreatic Assn., Am. Soc. Clin. Oncology, Sigma Xi. Jewish. Address: M D Anderson Hosp 6723 Bertner Ave Houston TX 77030

LEVIN, DAVID HAROLD, lawyer; b. Pensacola, Fla., Nov. 19, 1928; s. Abe Irvin and Rose (Lefkowitz) L.; A.B., Duke, 1949; J.D., U. Fla., 1952; m. Sue Williams, Aug. 15, 1985; 1 dau., Lisa Ann. Admitted to Fla. bar, 1952, since practiced in Pensacola; asst. county solicitor, 1952; asso. Robinson, Roark & Hopkins, 1954-55; sr. partner Levin, Warfield, Middlebrooks, Mabie, Thomas, Mayes & Mitchell, 1955—. Past pres., dir. Gator Boosters, Inc. Crusade chmn. Pensacola chpt. Am. Cancer Soc., 1964-65, pres., 1966-67; bd. dirs. Pensacola chpt. Am. Heart Assn., 1966-69; chmn. Pensacola United Jewish Appeal, 1967-68; chmn. Fla. Pollution Control Bd., 1971-74. Bd. dirs. U. Fla. Found., Inc. Served to capt. USAF, 1952-54. Fellow Fla. Trial Lawyers Assn.; mem. Am., Fla. (chmn. family law sect., 1980-81) bar assns., Am. Trial Lawyers Assn., Am. Acad. Matrimonial Lawyers (sec.-treas. Fla. chpt. 1980-81, bd. mgrs., v.p. 1983-84, pres. elect), Am. Legion, Pensacola U. Fla. Alumni Assn. (pres. 1960). Lodges: Masons (32 deg.), Shriners. Home: 3632 Menendez St Pensacola FL 32503 Office: 9th Floor Seville Tower Pensacola FL 32501

LEVIN, DONALD NORMAN, classics educator; b. Rochester, N.Y., Feb. 1, 1927; s. Harry and Rose (Chatman) L.; m. Barbara Lila Bieber, June 12, 1949; children—William Mark, Amy Beth. A.B., Cornell U., 1949, A.M., 1952; A.M., Harvard U., 1954, Ph.D., 1957. From instr. to asst. prof. Washington U., St. Louis, 1956-59; asst. prof. Mount Holyoke Coll., South Hadley, Mass., 1959-63; assoc. prof. classics Rice U., Houston, 1963-68, prof., 1968—. Served with USN, 1945-46. Mem. Am. Philological Assn., Archaeol. Inst. Am., Vergilian Soc., Soc. Ancient Greek Philosophy, Classical Assn. of the Middlewest and South, Am. Soc. Papyrologists, Tex. Classical Assn., Houston Area Tchrs. Fgn. Langs. Democrat. Jewish. Author: Apollonius Argonautica Reexamined: The Neglected First and Second Books, 1971; contbr. articles to profl. jours. Home: 4986 Dumfries St Houston TX 77096 Office: Dept Classics Rice U Houston TX 77001

LEVIN, MERWYN ELLIOT, educational administrator; b. Cleve., Feb. 14, 1930; s. Louis Moses and Lillian (Baron) L.; B.S., Ohio State U., 1951; M.Ed., Kent State U., 1955; postgrad. Western Res. U., 1956, Lehigh U., 1958, Boston U., 1958; m. Marcia Lea Grumet, June 8, 1952; children—Karen Beth, Debra Lynn, Sandra Kay. Tchr. Oakwood Park Sch., Lorain, Ohio, 1951, Belvoir Elem. Sch., University Heights, Ohio, 1953-56; adminstrv. asst. Brith Sholom Community Center, Bethlehem, Pa., 1956-58; exec. dir., youth dir. Temple Beth El, Fall River, Mass., 1958-59; exec. dir. Congregation Shearith Israel, Dallas, 1959-61; tchr. Coral Park Elem. Sch., Miami, Fla., 1962-67; asst. prin. Drew Elem. Sch., Miami, 1967-68, Gladeview Elem. Sch., Miami, 1968-70, Lillie C. Evans Elem. Sch., Miami, 1970-73; asst. prin. Gladeview Elem. Sch., Miami, 1973-77, Poinciana Park Community Sch., Miami, 1977-79, West Little River Elem. Sch., Miami, 1979-82, Nathan B. Young Elem. Sch., Opa Locka, Fla., 1982-83; interim prin. Melrose Elem. Sch., Miami, 1983; prin. Comstock Elem. Sch., Miami, 1983—; asst. prin. summer sessions various schs. Co-organizer, founding pres. men's B'nai Brith Lodge, 1955-56; v.p. Congregation B'nai Israel, 1973; chmn. edn. com. Temple Or Olom, 1971-72; ednl. dir. Temple Beth Sholom Religious Sch., Miami Beach, Fla., 1968-70; chmn. edn. South Dade Hebrew Acad., 1972-75; chmn. community edn. com. Northwest Area Parent Adv. Com. Dade County, 1975-78. Served with USMC, 1951-53. Mem. NEA (life), Fla. Assn. Sch. Adminstrs., Dade County Sch. Adminstrs. Assn., Assn. Supervision and Curriculum Devel., Phi Delta Kappa. Club: Afro-Am. Kiwanis. Home: 15610 Bull Run Rd Apt 509 Miami Lakes FL 33014 Office: 2420 NW 18th Ave Miami FL 33142

LEVIN, MILDRED LENORE, children's bookstore executive; b. Nashville, Oct. 1, 1933; d. Aaron Herman and Rose Marie (Stuart) Block; m. Jack Lee Levin, Aug. 30, 1953; children—Janis Levin Fields, Linda Levin Hyson, Karen Marie. B.A., U. N.C.-Greensboro, 1967, MLS., 1980. Cert. secondary tchr., cert. media coordinator, N.C. Library asst. Pub. Library, San Antonio, 1954-55; social rehab. dir. Phoenix Club-Mental Health, Greensboro, N.C., 1967-68; owner B. Dolphin Ltd., Greensboro, 1983—. Librarian B'nai Shalom Day Sch., Greensboro, 1974-80. Mem. Nat. Council Jewish Women (life), Hadassah (life). Democrat. Jewish. Avocations: travel; books. Office: 211-A State St Greensboro NC 27408

LEVIN, WILLIAM COHN, physician, university president; b. Waco, Tex., Mar. 2, 1917; s. Samuel P. and Jeanette (Cohn) Lipson; B.A., U. Tex., 1938, M.D., 1941; m. Edna Seinsheimer, June 23, 1941; children—Gerry Lee Levin Hornstein, Carol Lynn Levin. Intern, Michael Reese Hosp., Chgo., 1941-42; resident John Sealy Hosp., Galveston, Tex., 1942-44; mem. staff U. Tex. Med. Br. Hosps., Galveston, 1944—, asso. prof. internal medicine, 1948-65, prof., 1965—, also Warmoth prof. hematology; pres. U. Tex., Galveston, 1974—. Past mem. cancer clin. investigation rev. com. Nat. Cancer Inst.; trustee Menil Found., 1976-83, Houston-Galveston Psychoanalytic Found., 1975-78. Served to lt. col., M.C., U.S. Army. Recipient Nicholas and Katherine Leone award for adminstrv. excellence, 1977; decorated comdr. Ordre des Palmes Académiques (France). Diplomate Am. Bd. Internal Medicine. Fellow ACP, Internat. Soc. Hematology; mem. Tex. Club Internists (hon. 1977), Phi Beta Kappa, Sigma Xi, Alpha Omega Alpha. Home: 1301 Harbor View Dr Galveston TX 77550 Office: Office Pres U Tex Galveston TX 77550

LEVINE, HAROLD, lawyer; b. Newark, Apr. 30, 1931; s. Rubin and Gussie (Lifshitz) L.; B.S., Purdue U., 1954; J.D. with distinction, George Washington U., 1958; m. Maria Cristina; children—Linda Ellen, Brenda Sue, Jill Anne, Louise Abby, Charles A., Cristina Gussie II, Harold Rubin II. Marine engr., naval architect Navy Dept., Washington, 1954-55; patent examiner U.S. Patent Office, Washington, 1955-58; admitted to Va. bar, 1958, D.C. bar, 1959, Mass. bar, 1959, Tex. bar, 1972; with Tex. Instruments, Inc., 1959-77, asst. v.p., gen. patent counsel, Dallas, 1972-77; ptnr. firm Sigalos & Levine, Dallas, 1977—; chmn. bd. Vanguard Security Inc., 1977—, Tex. Am. Realty Corp., 1977—. Mem. Nat. Assn. Mfrs., Am. Mfrs. Assn., Am. Patent Law Assn., Am. Bar Assn., Tex. Bar Assn., Dallas-Ft. Worth Patent Law Assn., Dallas Bar Assn., Pacific Indsl. Property Assn. (pres. 1975-77), Electronic Industries Assn., U.S. C. of C., Alpha Epsilon Pi, Phi Alpha Delta. Club: Kiwanis. Contbg. author electronics book; editor George Washington U. Law Rev., 1956-57; contbr. articles to profl. jours. Office: Sigalos & Levine 1300 Republic Bank Tower Dallas TX 75201

LEVINE, HYMAN ISRAEL, retired chemical company executive; b. Bklyn., Aug. 11, 1909; s. Joseph and Dora (Alpert) L.; student Columbia U. Sch. Pharmacy, 1931; m. Gertrude Sendrowitz, Mar. 25, 1944; 1 son, Theodore. Owner, mgr. Adams & Nassau Pharmacy, Bklyn., 1931-46, Chelsea Pharmacy, N.Y.C., 1946-49; pres., founder Ruger Chem. Co. Inc., N.Y.C., 1949—; pres. Amend Drug & Chem. Co. Inc., Irvington, N.J., 1965—, GLS Realty Co., 1971—, A & R Sales Corp., 1974—, 500 Chancellor Ave., 1976—. Served with USAAF, 1941. Mem. Drug, Chem., Allied Trades. Jewish. Club: B'nai B'rith. Home: 3039 Harwood Dr Deerfield Beach FL 33441

LEVINE, JACK HARVEY, real estate investor, general contractor; b. Coral Gables, Fla., Nov. 25, 1952; s. Murray I. and Eileen F. (Lauretz) Levine Seitlin. B.S. in C.E. cum laude, U. Miami, 1973. Cert. gen. contractor, Fla.; registered mortgage broker, Fla., lic. real estate broker, Fla. Gen. ptnr. LFK Properties, South Miami, Fla., 1979—; pres. Levine Mgmt., Inc., South Miami, 1980—; pres. Levine Realty, Inc., South Miami, 1981—; gen. ptnr. Columbia Properties, South Miami, 1981—, Highland Park Properties, South Miami, 1980—, Ludlum Sq. Profl. Assocs., South Miami, 1979—; gen. ptnr. Challenger Airport Properties, South Miami, 1982—; owner Levine Properties, South Miami, 1973—. Mem. Camp Judaea Com., Atlanta, 1977—; bd. dirs. Greater Miami Jewish Fedn., Miami, 1979-81, 82—; mem. citizens bd. U. Miami, Coral Gables, 1982—; mem. United Jewish Appeal-Young Leadership Cabinet, N.Y.C., 1981—; mem. Joshua Soc. Nat. Action Com.-Polit. Action Com., Miami, 1981—. Recipient Stanley C. Myers Pres. Leadership award Greater Miami Jewish Fedn., 1983. Mem. Bldrs. Assn. South Fla., ASCE, Tau Beta Pi. Jewish. Lodge: B'nai B'rith (treas. 1981-82), v.p. 1979-81). Office: Levine Properties 7901 Ludlam Rd South Miami FL 33143

LEVINE, JANE SHEILA, nurse, medical personnel organization executive, insurance brokerage consultants; b. Bklyn., Jan. 2, 1946; d. Irving Richard and Ann (Odell) Levine; grad. Bellevue Sch. Nursing, 1966; student Am. U., 1966-67, Marymount Manhattan Coll., 1967, Fla. Internat. U., 1976-78. Staff nurse Washington Hosp. Center, 1966; nurse N.Y. Office, Paramount Pictures,

1967-68; operating room nurse Beth Israel Hosp., N.Y.C., 1968-70; public health nurse Bellevue Hosp., N.Y.C., 1970-74; regional rep. N.Y. State Nurses Assn., 1974-75; asst. dir. nursing Parkway Gen. Hosp., Miami, Fla., 1975-77; dir. Staff Builders, Miami, 1977-78; v.p. for nursing Westchester Gen. Hosp., Miami, 1978-80; dir. nursing services Med. Personnel Pool Am., 1981—; founder Elder Designs Inc., 1982-85; agt., health, life and fin. counsel Equitable Life Assurance, Miami, 1986—; brokerage cons. Springfield/Monarch Ins. Brokers; mem. Com. for Protection Human Rights in Research Greater Miami Area. Mem. Am. Nurses Assn., Fla. Nurses Assn., South Fla. Hosp. Assn. (council dirs. nursing service), Fla. Soc. for Hosp. Nursing Service Adminstrs. Home: 671 NE 195th St North Miami Beach FL 33179 Office: 1637 NE 18th Ave North Miami Beach FL 33162

LE VINE, JEROME EDWARD, ophthalmologist, educator; b. Pitts., Mar. 23, 1923; s. Harry Robert and Marian Dorothy (Finesilver) L.; m. Marilyn Tobey Hiedovitz, Apr. 14, 1957; children—Loren Robert, Beau Jay, Janice Lynn. Student, U. Pitts., 1940-42, 44; M.D., Hahnemann Med. Sch., Phila., 1949; postgrad. in ophthalmology U. Pa., 1951-52. Intern, St. Francis Hosp., Pitts., 1949-50; resident in ophthalmology Jefferson U. Med. Sch. Hosp., Phila., 1952-54; ophthalmologist Leech Farm VA Hosp., Pitts., 1955-59; chief eye dept. Stanocola Clinic, Baton Rouge, 1959-64; sole practice medicine specializing in ophthalmology, Baton Rouge, 1959—; cons. La. State U., East La. State Hosp. Infirmary, Villa Feliciana Geriatric Hosp., disability dept. Social Security Adminstrn., div. blind La. State Pub. Welfare dept., VA outpatient clinic; mem. staff Our Lady of the Lake Hosp., Baton Rouge Gen. Hosp., Dixon Women's Hosp.; instr. spl. edn. U. Southeastern La., 1971. Served with MC, AUS, 1942-44. Fellow Am. Geriatric Soc., Royal Soc. Health; mem. La. Eye Ear Nose and Throat Soc., New Orleans Acad. Ophthalmology, Inst. Glaucoma Research, AMA, So. Med. Assn., Internat. Med. Assn., Indsl. Medicine Assn., La. Med. Soc., Baton Rouge Parish Med. Soc., Pi Lambda Phi, Phi Delta Epsilon. Democrat. Jewish. Office: 4560 North Blvd Baton Rouge LA 70806

LEVINE, KENNETH CHARLES, soft drink company executive; b. N.Y.C., Mar. 19, 1945; s. Lawrence and Adele (Friedman) L.; m. Susan Jane Bursten, Aug. 14, 1966; children—David, Craig. B.S. in Math., U. Fla., 1966; M.A. in Actuarial Sci., Ga. State U., 1968. Instr. quantitative methods Ga. State U., Atlanta, 1968-72; mgr. mgmt. sci. C&S Nat. Bank, Atlanta, 1972-74; asst. v.p., mgr. mgmt. info. dept. 1st Nat. Bank Atlanta, 1974-75; mktg. mgr. ADP-Cyphernetics, Atlanta, 1975-76; mgr. sales forecasting Coca-Cola USA, Atlanta, 1976-80, market planning mgr., 1980-82, nat. account exec. fountain sales dept., 1982—; founder and chmn. S.E. Econ. Project, Atlanta, 1972-74. Contbg. author: Cost Accountant's Handbook, 1979; contbr. articles to profl. jours. Vice pres. Lockridge Forest Civic Assn., Atlanta, 1982-84. Recipient Men's B Singles Tennis championship Coca-Cola USA, 1983. Mem. Inst. Mgmt. Scis. (chmn. Atlanta chpt. 1975-76; service award 1979), Am. Inst. Decision Scis. (charter), Am. Mktg. Assn., Crest Mfg. Assn. (steering com. chmn. 1982-85), Alpha Iota Delta. Jewish. Home 455 Sassafras Ln Roswell GA 30076

LEVINGSTON, ERNEST LEE, engring. co. exec.; b. Pineville, La., Nov. 7, 1921; s. Vernon Lee and Adele (Miller) L.; B.S. in Mech. Engring., La. State U., 1960; m. Kathleen Bernice Bordelon, June 23, 1944; children—David Lewis, Jeanne Evelyn (Mrs. Andy Woltz), James Lee. Gen. foreman T. Miller & Sons, Lake Charles, La., 1939-42; sr. engr., sect. head Cities Service Refining Corp., Lake Charles, 1946-57; group leader Bovay Engrs., Baton Rouge, 1957-59; chief engr. Augenstein Constrn. Co., Lake Charles, 1959-60; pres. Levingston Engrs., Inc., Lake Charles, 1961—. Mem. Lake Charles Planning and Zoning Commn., 1965-70; mem. adv. bd. Sowela Tech. Inst., 1969—; mem. Regional Export Expansion Council, 1969-70, chmn. code com. 1966—; chmn. coordinating and adv. com. for Ward 1, Calcasieu Parish, La., 1976-77; bd. dirs. Lake Charles Meml. Hosp.; mem. La. Commerce and Industry Bd., 1979—. Served with USNR, 1942-46. Named Jaycee Boss of Yr., 1972; registered profl. engr., La., Tex., Miss., Ark., Tenn., Pa., Md., Del., N.J., D.C., Okla. Mem. La. Engring. Soc. (pres. 1967-68, state dir. 1967-68), Lake Charles C. of C. (dir. 1969-73), Inst. Cert. Engring. Technicians (exam. com., trustee). Baptist (deacon 1955—). Clubs: Lake Charles Quarter Horse (pres. 1966—), Rotary. Home: Levinwood Rd Lake Charles LA Office: PO Box 1865 Lake Charles LA 70602

LEVINSON, JON ROBERT, corporation executive; b. Cin., Nov. 1, 1949; s. Robert Edward and Phyllis Ann (Goldsmith) L.; m. Lori Ann Malkasian, Mar. 27, 1976; children—Loren Ariel, Jamie Rae. B.S., Jacksonville U., 1971. Acct., Harold Lawlor, C.P.A., Pompano Beach, Fla., 1972-73; controller Sanford Industries, Pompano Beach, 1973-74; tax mgr. Visual Graphics Corp., Tamarac, Fla., 1974-75; tax mgr. Landmark Banking Corp., Ft. Lauderdale, 1975-76; pres. Engineered Air Corp., Ft. Lauderdale, 1977—; v.p. REL Enterprises, Inc., Boca Raton, Fla., 1982—; lectr. Fla. Small Bus. Devel. Ctr. Mem. bus. adv. bd. Jr. Achievement, 1981-84, bd. dirs., 1984—; pres. Boca Raton Youth Baseball/Softball Assn., 1977. Mem. Nat. Assn. Accts., Internat. Assn. Hospitality Accts., ASHRAE, Energy Mgmt. Contractors Assn., Solar Energy Industries Assn., Alpha Micro Users Soc., Ft. Lauderdale/Broward County C. of C. (chmn. West Broward div. 1984, bd. dirs. 1983, v.p. area councils 1984, bd. dirs. polit. action com.). Republican. Jewish. Clubs: Tower, Commerce (pres. 1980-82, chmn. bd. 1982-83). Home: 943 Evergreen Dr Delray Beach FL 33444 Office: 1016 NE 45th St Fort Lauderdale FL 33334

LEVINSON, MARK BRADLEY, corporate secretary, financial manager; b. Dallas, June 1, 1956; s. Lewis S. and Adele Lillian (Friedlander) L. B.S. in Profl. Geology, La. State U., 1978, postgrad. Washington campus, summer 1982; M.Profl. Acctg. (teaching asst.), U. Tex.-Austin, 1984. Geologist, U.S. Geol. Survey, Metairie, La., 1978-80; with controller's dept. Arco Oil & Gas Co., Dallas, 1980; credit analyst First Nat. Bank Chgo., Dallas, 1981; owner, operator Bradley's Word Factory, Austin and Dallas, 1981-83, 84—; bus. analyst Diamond Shamrock Corp., Dallas, 1983-84; controller, sec./treas., mgr. fin. and adminstrn. Brice Foods, Inc., I Can't Believe It's Yogurt, Inc. Active Shakespeare Festival Dallas; vol. Dallas Area Rapid Transit, Channel 13 KERA Pub. Auction; mem. Dallas Mus. Art; exec. mem. Arts Dist. Friends, Dallas; mem. Tex. Posse. Mem. Am. Assn. Petroleum Geologists, Assn. M.B.A. Execs., La. State U. Alumni Assn., La. State U. Letterman's Club, U. Tex-Austin Coll. Bus. Adminstrn. Century Club (adv. Council), Big D Beat, Inc. Zeta Beta Tau. Jewish. Clubs: Lone Star Masters Swim (Dallas); Brookhaven Country; U. Tex.-Austin Metroplex Grad. Bus. (pres. 1984-85); Internat. Athletic. Home: 3529 Townsend Dr Dallas TX 75229

LEVINSON, RICHARD MURRAY, community health educator; b. New London, Conn., Apr. 1, 1942; s. Robert I. and Sophia Tyba (Rakosky) L.; m. Linda Ellen Hollander, Apr. 14, 1966; children—Daryl, Hollande, Jennefer. B.A., U. Conn., 1964; M.A., U. Wis., 1966, Ph.D., 1975. Instr. Ind. U., Bloomington, 1970-72; asst. prof. Emory U., Atlanta, 1972-79, assoc. prof. community health, 1979—. Assoc. editor Am. Sociologist Jour., 1979-82, Jour. Health Social Behavior, 1983—. Contbr. articles to profl. jours. Fellow Danforth Found., 1976, Robert Wood Johnson Found., 1983. Mem. Am. Pub. Health Assn., So. Sociol. Soc., Am. Sociol. Assn., Soc. for Study Social Problems, Ga. Sociol. Assn. (pres. 1982-83). Home: 4208 St Marie Court Stone Mountain GA 30083 Office: MPH Program Emory U Sch Medicine 735 Gatewood Rd Atlanta GA 30322

LEVITAN, LEWIS JAY, endodontist; b. San Antonio, Jan. 22, 1947; s. Mort and Helen (Lehwald) L.; m. Ileene Joyce Sagor, June 4, 1967; children—Lisa Kay, Lon Jared. B.A. in Zoology, U. Tex.-Austin, 1968; D.D.S., U. Iowa Coll. Dentistry, 1972; Cert. Adv. Grad. Study in Dentistry in Endodontics, Boston U. Sch. Grad. Dentistry, 1976. Cert. specialist in endodontics. Gen. practice dentistry, Attleboro, Mass., 1974-76; practice dentistry specializing in endodontics, San Antonio, 1976—; clin. instr., prof. U. Tex. Dental Sch., San Antonio, 1977-78; lectr. Tex. Dental Assn. Annual Session, San Antonio, 1983. Contbr. articles to profl. jours. Examiner Health-O-Rama, San Antonio, 1981. Served to capt. USAF, 1972-74. Recipient Appreciation for Hiring cert. Health Occupations Careers Clark High Sch., 1985. Mem. San Antonio Dist. Dental Soc. (appreciation for serving cert. 1979), Tex. Dental Assn., Am. Dental Assn., Am. Assn. of Endodontists. Republican. Jewish. Clubs: D.D.D. Golf Assn. (San Antonio) (pres. 1982-83, v.p. 1981-82, appreciation for serving cert. 1983), Tapatio Springs Country. Avocations: golf; fishing. Office: 7300 Blanco Rd Ste 402 San Antonio TX 78216

LEVITT, MICHAEL KENT, psychiatrist; b. Detroit, May 6, 1941; m. Mary Ritchie, Oct. 25, 1974; children—Hollis, Lisa, Blair, Jonathan, Erin. B.A. in Zoology, U. Mich., 1962, M.D., 1966. Sr. med. student extern in child psychiatry Hawthorn Ctr., Northville, Mich., 1965; intern Sinai Hosp., Detroit, Wayne State U. Sch. Medicine, 1966-67; resident in psychiatry Albert Einstein Coll. Medicine, Mcpl. Hosp. Center, Bronx, N.Y., 1967-71; practice medicine specializing in psychotherapy, Ann Arbor, Mich., 1973-74; practice medicine specializing in psychiatry Tri-County Mental Health Services, P.C., Ann Arbor, Mich., 1975-81, Hickory, N.C., 1981—; mem. staff Sinai Hosp. of Detroit, Mt. Carmel Mercy Hosp., 1975-81, Catawba Meml. Hosp., Hickory Meml. Hosp., Glenn R. Frye Meml. Hosp., 1981—; mem. faculty dept. psychiatry Div. Youth Services, U. Mich. Med. Sch., Ann Arbor, 1973-74, Wayne State U. Sch. Medicine, 1975-81, Lenoir Rhyne Coll., Catawba Valley Tech. Coll., 1981—; dir. Parent/Youth Devel. Services, Farmington Hills, Mich., 1975; assoc. dir. Pain Rehab. Ctr., Glenn R. Frye Meml. Hosp., 1981—; med. dir. Adolescent Inpatient Psychiat. Services, Hickory Meml. Hosp., 1981—; cons. to pub. schs., community agencies and clinics. Mem. task force Catawba County Rape Crisis, 1981—, Catawba County Child Abuse and Neglect, 1981—; mem. Mayor's Human Relations Com., Hickory, N.C., 1981—; mem. com. for the prevention of child abuse and neglect State of N.C., 1981—; bd. dirs. N.C. chpt. Nat. Com. for the Prevention of Child Abuse and Neglect, 1981—; bd. dirs., mem. com. on pals, com. on future planning, com. for programs and policies Family Guidance Ctr., 1981—; Sunday sch. tchr., mem. youth ministry com. Holy Trinity Lutheran Ch., 1981—; bd. dirs. Premature Infant Found. of Catawba County, 1981—. Served to major USAF, 1971-73. Mem. Am. Psychiat. Assn, Am. Acad. Child Psychiatry, Am. Soc. Adolescent Psychiatry, Mich. Psychiat. Soc., Mich. Soc. for Adolescent Psychiatry, Detroit Pediatric Soc., Mich. Soc. for Mental Health, Am. Soc. Clin. Hypnosis, Mich. Assn. for Infant Mental Health (mem. Selma Frabergaa-ward com.), Internat. Assn. for Infant Mental Health, Am. Acad. Psychosomatic Medicine, Am. Med. Record Assn. (assoc., com. for mental health records), Assn. for Advancement of Behavior Therapy, Am. Orthopsychiatric Assn., Oakland County Med. Soc. (mental health com. 1981), Mich. Council Child Psychiatry, Am. Group Psychotherapy Assn., Soc. Air Force Psychiatrists, Mich. State Med. Soc., Assn. for the Advancement of Psychotherapy, N.C. Med. Soc., Catawba County Med. Assn., N.C. Neuropsychiat. Assn., N.C. Council Child Psychiatry, Nat. Stepfamilies of Am. Found., Inc., C. of C. (family life edn. com.), Phi Delta Epsilon. Club: Kiwanis (dir.). Office: Michael Kevitt MD 104 Third Ave NW Hickory NC 28601

LEVITT, PHILLIP RUSSELL, periodontist; b. Cheyenne, Wyo., July 29, 1926; s. Max P. and Alys (Weinstein) L.; m. Nina Rosenthal, Feb. 27, 1955; children—Gail M., Ronald A., Jeffery M. B.A., U. Colo., 1950; postgrad. U. Wyo., 1950-51; D.D.S., Northwestern U., 1954; cert. Periodontics, U. Ala., 1960. Gen. practice dentistry, Denver, 1955-58; practice dentistry specializing in periodontics, Birmingham, Ala., 1961—; mem. staff Bryce Hosp., Tuscaloosa, Ala., 1960-63. Served to cpl. U.S. Army, 1944-46; maj. Ala. N.G., 1959-63. Mem. Am. Acad. Periodontology, ADA, Ala. Dental Assn., Birmingham Dist. Dental Soc., So. Acad. Periodontology, Alpha Omega. Jewish. Office: 1000 S 19th St Birmingham AL 35205

LEVITT, PRESTON CURTIS, lawyer; b. Queens Village, N.Y., July 23, 1950; s. Leon and Meryl Barbara (Rosenstock) L.; m. Maddy Charlene Domenitz, July 1, 1973; children—Taryn Audra, Brandon Ross. B.S., Am. U., 1972; J.D., Bklyn. Law Sch., 1975; LL.M., NYU, 1980. Bar: N.Y. 1976, Fla. 1977, U.S. Dist. Ct. (ea. and so. dists.) N.Y. 1976, U.S. Dist. Ct. (so. dist.) Fla. 1980, U.S. Ct. Claims 1980, U.S. Tax Ct. 1976, U.S. Ct. Appeals (5th cir.) 1980. Sr. tax acct. Arthur Young & Co., N.Y.C., 1975-80; mem. firm E.T. Hunter, Hollywood, Fla., 1980-81; sr. ptnr. Brydger & Levitt, P.A., Ft. Lauderdale, Fla., 1981—; dir. Atlantic Services Group Inc., Ft. Lauderdale. Bd. dirs. Vis. Nurses Assn., Fort Lauderdale, 1983—. Mem. Fla. Bar Assn., Broward County Bar Assn., Am. Inst. Banking (bd. dirs. 1981—), Fraternal Order Police, Tau Epsilon Phi. Jewish. Office: Brydger & Levitt PA 7770 W Oakland Park Blvd Fort Lauderdale FL 33321

LEVITT, ROBERT ALAN, clinical neuropsychologist; b. Balt., Nov. 9, 1938; s. George and Ruth (Feinman) L.; m. Phyllis Feldman, Dec. 21, 1958. B.S. in Pharmacy, U. Fla., 1961, M.S. in Psychology, 1963, Ph.D., 1965. From asst. prof. to prof. psychology So. Ill. U., Carbondale, 1967-77; prof., chmn. dept. U. Ala., Birmingham, 1977-82; vis. prof. dept. neurology Med. Coll. Ga., Augusta, 1982-83; clin. neuropsychology practice, Miami, 1983—; adj. prof. Fla. Atlantic U., Nova U., 1984—. Author: Physiological Psychology, 1981; Psychopharmacology, 1975. Contbr. articles to profl. jours. NIMH grantee, 1968-74. Fellow Am. Psychol. Assn. (cert.); mem. Internat. Neuropsychol. Soc., Nat. Acad. Neuropsychologists, S.E. Psychol. Assn. Fla. Psychol. Assn. Democrat. Jewish. Home: 5415 Collins Ave PH-E Miami Beach FL 33140 Office: Neurologic Cons 1841 NE 45 St Fort Lauderdale FL 33308

LEVITT, RONALD L., public relations consulting executive; b. Rochester, N.Y., Mar. 23, 1931; s. Maurice and Pearl (Altman) L.; m. Geraldine Rita Wortsman, June 20, 1954; children—Lynn Barbara, Howard Jay. A.B., U. Miami, 1956. Staff corr. UP, 1956-59; news dir., accounts supr. Mandell/Newman, 1959-60; pres. Ronald Levitt Assocs., Inc., pub. relations cons., Coral Gables, Fla., 1961—; asst. sec. of state State of Fla., 1978-81; lectr. pub. relations colls. throughout U.S.; guest lectr. in field. Vice pres. Miami Symphony. Served with U.S. Navy, 1950-54. Recipient Dept. Def. award 1953; service awards Pub. Relations Soc. Am., 1966, 67, 68, 69. Mem. Pub. Relations Soc. Am. (pres. Fla. 1966, chmn. S.E. dist. 1968-70), Internat. Platform Assn., Am. Assn. Polit. Cons., Fla. Pub. Relations Assn., Internat. Assn. Bus. Communicators, Sigma Delta Xi. Clubs: Miami Press, U. Miami Alumni, Palm Bay, Bankers. Contbr. articles to mags. Office: 141 Sevilla Ave Coral Gables FL 33134

LEVITZ, ELIZABETH JONES, travel executive; b. Baton Rouge, Apr. 12, 1941; d. Bob Reiley and Elizabeth Marguerite (Reeves) Jones; student Tulane U., 1959-61, Sorbonne, Paris, 1961-62; 1 son by previous marriage, John S. Coulter. With E. F. Hutton & Co., Inc., Baton Rouge, 1965-68; pres. Aero Charter Inc., Miami, Fla., 1976-82, also dir.; mng. dir. Trophy Hunter Safaris Inc.; curator internat. exhibits N.C. State Mus. Natural History, also mem. dir.'s council. dir. Blairstown Land, Inc. Pres. women's com., pres. Big Bros. Am., 1979-80, bd. dirs., 1978-80; mem. Children in Distress; bd. advisors Pine Crest Sch., 1979—, mem. Tower Council, 1980—; bd. dirs. Am. Heart Assn. Fellow Royal Geog. Soc.; mem. Anglo-Am. Art Mus., Am. Cancer Soc., Hakluyt Soc. (Eng.), Internat. Oceanographic Found., Internat. Profl. Hunters Assn., Internat. Game Fish Assn., Game Conservation Internat., Found. N.Am. Wild Sheep, Ducks Unltd. (sponsor), Kappa Alpha Theta. Methodist. Clubs: Safari Club Internat., Mzuri Safari Cat Cay, Chub Cay (Bahamas); Les Ambassadeurs (Eng.); Palm Bay, Surf, Jockey (Miami); Ocean Reef (Key Largo, Fla.); Dallas Safari. Home: Tower 1 1000 Quayside Terr Miami FL 33138

LEVY, ALEXANDRO GUSTAVO, exploration geologist; b. Santiago, Chile, Mar. 27, 1954; came to U.S., 1968, naturalized, 1978; s. Jorge A. and Sylvia E. (Salazar) L.; m. Penny Lorraine DeMent, May 17, 1980; 1 child, Laura Michelle. B.S. in Geology, U. Fla., 1975, M.S., 1977. Assoc. geologist Phillips Petroleum Co., Houston, 1978-80; exploration geologist Sohio Petroleum Co., Houston, 1980-82, area geologist, 1982—. Mem. Am. Assn. Petroleum Geologist, Houston Geol. Soc., Phi Kappa Phi. Republican. Clubs: Tex. Mariners Cruising Assn., Jensen Owner Assn. Avocations: sailing; sport cars; hiking; camping. Office: Sohio Petroleum Co 9401 SW Freeway Suite 1200 Houston TX 77074

LEVY, HAROLD BERNARD, pediatrician; b. Shreveport, La., Apr. 27, 1918; s. Phillip and Ida (Sperling) L.; m. Betty Ann Friedenthal, Nov. 29, 1942; children—James, Charles, Roger, Judy Levy Ganucheau. B.S., La. State U., 1937; M.D., 1940. Diplomate Am. Bd. Pediatrics. Intern, Tri-State Hosp., Shreveport, 1940-41; resident in pediatrics Shreveport Charity Hosp., 1946-48; practice medicine specializing in pediatrics, Shreveport, La., 1948—; co-med. dir. Caddo Found. for Exceptional Children, 1953—; founder, dir. spl. clinic for learning disabilities La. Handicapped Children's Services, 1955—; clin. assoc. prof. pediatrics La. State U. Med. Sch., Shreveport, 1973—; faculty mem. Nat. Coll. Juvenile Justice, Reno, 1975—; mem. staff Schumpert, Willis-Knighton, Doctors, La. State U. hosps.; Pres., Shreveport Summer Theater, 1953; pres. Caddo-Bossier Safety Council, 1959-60. Served to maj. M.C., USAAF, 1942-46. Recipient Brotherhood citation NCCJ, 1976; Spl. recognition award La. Assn. Children with Learning Disabilities, 1976; Axson-Choppin award La. Pub. Health Assn., 1983. Mem. Am. Acad. Cerebral Palsy and Devel. Medicine (pres. 1983), Am. Acad. Pediatrics, La. Med. Soc., So. Med. Assn., AMA, Orton Dyslexia Soc., Sigma Xi. Republican. Jewish. Club: East Ridge Country. Author: Square Pegs, Round Holes, The Learning Disabled Child in the Classroom and at Home, 1973; contbr. articles to profl. jours. Home: 6026 Dillingham Ave Shreveport LA 71106 Office: 6300 Line Ave Shreveport LA 71106

LEVY, HOWARD I., wholesale merchandise company executive; b. 1939. J.D., Vanderbilt U., 1965. With Service Merchandise Co., Nashville, Tenn., 1966—, v.p., 1967-75, sr. v.p., 1975-77, exec. v.p., 1977—. Office: Service Merchandise Co 1283 Murfreesboro Rd Nashville TN 37204

LEVY, IRVIN L., diversified company executive; b. Dallas, 1929; married. B.B.A., So. Methodist U., 1950. With NCH Corp. (formerly Nat. Chemsearch Corp.), Irving, Tex., 1946—, now pres., also dir. Office: NCH Corp 2727 Chemsearch Blvd Irving TX 75061*

LEVY, ISAAC JACK, Hispanic studies educator; b. Rhodes, Greece, Dec. 21, 1928; s. Jack and Catherine (Mussafir) L.; m. Judy Ann Bearsch, June 16, 1961 (div. 1978); children—Catherine Ann, Michael Jack; m. Rosemary Zumwalt, Jan. 1, 1984. B.A., Emory U., 1957; M.A., U. Iowa, 1959; Ph.D., U. Mich., 1966. Research asst. U. Iowa, Iowa City, 1957-59; teaching asst. U. Mich., Ann Arbor, 1959-63; prof. Hispanic studies U. S.C., Columbia, 1963—; vis. prof. Purdue U., summer 1961, Tex. Tech. U., 1963. Served with U.S. Army, 1949-50, 50-52. Grantee U. S.C., 1965, 66, 67, 69, 81, 82, 84, Lucius N. Littauer Found., 1968, 82, Atlanta Jewish Fedn., 1982, Or Veshalom Congregation, 1982, Nat. Council Jewish Culture, 1984. Mem. South Atlantic MLA, Am. Assn. Tchrs. Spanish and Portuguese (Quixote award S. C. chpt. 1975), Am. Soc. Sephardic Studies (Founders award 1973), S.C. Conf. Fgn. Lang. Tchrs. (State Merit award 1971), Sigma Delta Pi (Order of Don Quixote 1968). Jewish. Contbr. books and articles on Hispanic and Sephardic studies to profl. lit.

LEVY, JACK HEYMANN, radiologist; b. Norwood, Ga., Aug. 15, 1913; s. Samuel Abraham and Clara Libby (Zelkin) L.; m. Marilyn Brand, May 23, 1976; 1 dau., Sue-Robin. M.D., U. Ga., 1936. Intern, Jewish Hosps. of St. Louis, 1936-37; resident in radiology and pathology Univ. Hosps., Augusta, Ga., 1937-38; resident in radiology Mount Sinai Hosp., N.Y.C., 1938-40, attending radiologist, 1940-46; asst. prof. clin. radiology Yale U. Sch. Medicine, New Haven, 1946-47; assoc. prof. clin. radiology Med. Coll. Ga., Augusta, 1947—; practice medicine specializing in radiology, Augusta, 1947—; chmn. dept. radiology St. Joseph Hosp., Augusta, 1974—; mem. med. staffs Univ. Hosp., Doctors Hosp., Augusta. Mem. U.S. Senatorial Bus. Adv. Bd., 1981—. Served to maj. M.C., AUS, 1942-46. Fellow Am. Coll. Radiology, Royal Soc. Health; mem. Radiol. Soc. N.Am., Am. Assn. Physicians and Surgeons, So. Med. Assn., Ga. Radiol. Soc., Med. Assn. Ga. Club: Pinnacle. Contbr. articles to med. jours. Home: 3062 Hillsdale Dr Augusta GA 30909 Office: 1450 Winter St Augusta GA 30910

LEVY, JOHN BRUCE, mortgage banker; b. Portland, Maine, July 15, 1947; s. Laurence H. and Nancy (Galeski) L.; m. Judith Brown, June 17, 1949; children—Shana, Bram. B.A., Harvard U., 1969; M.B.A., Ga. State U., 1977. Sr. v.p. Sovran Mortgage Corp., Richmond, Va., 1983—; sr. v.p., originator, dir. Barron's/John B. Levy & Co. Nat. Mortgage Survey, 1983. Served to lt. USN, 1972. Contbr. articles to profl. publs. Home: 7310 Normandy Dr Richmond VA 23229 Office: 1512 Willow Lawn Dr Richmond VA 23230

LEVY, MAURICE, medical college administrator, educator, researcher; b. Chgo., Aug. 15, 1933; s. Eugene and Jean Belle (Anshel) L.; m. Loris Belle Rissman, Sept. 11, 1955; children—Arden Lynn, Andrea Hilary, James Michael. B.S., U. Ill., 1956, Ed.M., 1959; Ed.D., U. Ga., 1968. Asst. prof. Ga. State U.-Atlanta, 1968-69; postdoctoral fellow U. So. Calif., Los Angeles, 1969-70; assoc. prof. Med. Coll. Ga., Augusta, 1970-73, prof. ednl. research, dir., 1976—; prof., dir. So. Ill. U. Sch. Medicine, Springfield, 1973-76. Author: Introduction to Pediatric Cardiology, 1975; Physical Assistants Exam Review, 1980. Bd. dirs. Am. Cancer Soc., Springfield, Ill., 1974, Health Info. Services, Virginia Beach, Va., 1982—; trustee Augusta County Day Sch., 1972-80; chmn. Med. Coll. Ga. United Fund, Augusta, 1980. Recipient Outstanding Sci. Exec. award Am. Acad. Family Practice, 1974; Gold Cert. award Am. Acad. Pediatrics, 1973; Boss of Yr. award Am. Bus. Women's Assn., 1978. Mem. Am. Acad. Phys. Assts. (bd. advisors 1975—; Significant Contbns. award 1980-83), Health Scis. Commn. Assn. Jewish. Clubs: Augusta Track, Torch (vice chmn. 1972-73). Home: 703 Woodgate Ct Augusta GA 30909 Office: Med Coll Ga 1120 15th St Augusta GA 30912

LEVY, ROBERT ISAAC, osteopathic physician; b. N.Y.C., Oct. 17, 1954; s. Jack and Irma Sandra (Rudack) L. B.S. in Chemistry, U. Miami, 1976; D.O., Coll. Osteo. Medicine and Surgery, 1980. Diplomate Am. Bd. Osteo. Medicine. Intern John F. Kennedy Hosp., Cherry Hill, N.J., 1980-81, resident internal medicine Met. Hosp., Phila., 1981-82, general practice Delaware Valley Med. Ctr., Bristol, Pa., 1982-83; practice osteo. medicine, Port St. Lucie, Fla., 1983—; mem. staff Port St. Lucie Hosp., 1983—. Bd. dirs. Am. Cancer Soc., St. Lucie County, 1984—, Port St. Lucie Ambulance Vol. Squad, 1983—. Mem. Am. Osteo. Assn., Fla. Osteo. Med. Assn., St. Lucie Okeechobee Med. Soc. Home: 3149 Morningside Blvd Port St Lucie FL 33452 Office: 1701 SE Hillmore Dr Suite 16 Port St Lucie FL 33452

LEVY, SUZANNE JEANNE, writer, editor, television producer; b. Arlington, Va., Nov. 8, 1956; d. Louis James Levy and Jeanne Dorothy Collins. B.S. in Mass Communications, Va. Commonwealth U., 1979. Assoc. producer The Lawmakers, Sta. WETA-TV, Washington, 1980-84; writer, editor, videodisc producer Kinton, Inc., Bailey's Crossroads, Va., 1984—. Author short stories, poems. Democrat. Avocations: Washington Redskins; songwriting; music; movies. Home: 16 W Forrest St Alexandria VA 22305 Office: Kinton Inc 5707 Seminary Rd Bailey's Crossroads VA 22041

LEW, SALVADOR, radio station executive; b. Camajuani, Las Villas, Cuba, Mar. 6, 1929; came to U.S., 1961; s. Berko and Clara (Lewinowicz) L.; 1 child, Esther Maria. J.D. magna cum laude, U. Havana, 1952. Editor Sch. Mural Newspaper, Camajuani, Cuba, 1941-43; pres. youth sect. and nat. sec. Cuban People's Party, Cuba, 1948-53; Latin Am. cons. Walters, Moore & Costanzo, Miami, Fla., 1961-72; news dir. Sta. WMIE and Sta. WQBA, Miami, 1961-70; gen. mgr., news dir. Sta. WRHC, Miami, 1973—. Trustee United Way, 1985—; mem. adv. bd. U. Miami Sch. Music, 1985—. Recipient Lincoln Marti award Sec. HEW, 1964; FBI Award for Community Services, 1983; community service awards various orgns., 1973-84. Mem. Cuban Lawyers Assn. Exile. Jewish. Office: WRHC Radio 330 SW 27th Ave Miami FL 33135

LEWANDOWSKI, EDMUND D., artist, educator; b. Milw., July 3, 1914; s. Frank and Sally Helen (Kowalski) L.; m. Dolores Helen Bingenheimer, July 29, 1939. Diploma Layton Sch. Art, Milw., 1936. Faculty, Layton Sch. Art, 1947-49, pres., 1954-72; prof. painting Fla. State U., Tallahassee, 1949-52, head dept. art, 1951-54; chmn. dept. art Winthrop Coll., Rock Hill, S.C., 1973—; interim dir. Milw. Art Inst., 1955-56. One man shows include: Layton Art Gallery, 1935, Warsaw Acad. Arts, Poland, 1936, Fla. State U., 1950, Fairweather-Hardin Gallery, Chgo., 1973, 78, Sid Deutsch Gallery, N.Y.C., 1983; group exhbns. include: Art Inst. Chgo., 1936, 37, 41, 42, 49, 54, Mus. Modern Art, N.Y.C., 1937, 43, Downtown Gallery, N.Y.C., 1937, 41, 46, 48, 50, 53, 58, Musée Du Jeu De Paume, Paris, 1938, Met. Mus. Art, 1941, 42, Whitney Mus. Am. Art, 1946, 50, 52, 53, Corcoran Gallery Art, 1947, 57, Alan Gallery, N.Y.C., 1953, 54, 55, 56, 57, others, 1935-83. Commns. include: Portrait of Pope Pius XI, 1935, murals U.S. Maritime Commn., 1939, post office murals, 1939, 40, First Wis. Center, Milw., 1973, mosaic murals: Marquette U., 1953, St. Patrick's Ch., Menasha, Wis., 1954, Flint Art Ctr., 1957, Allen Bradley Co., 1958, Employers Ins. of Wausau, 1968, Vets. Meml., Milw. War Meml., 1976, St. Luke's Hosp., Milw., 1979; designer commemorative stamp Poland's Mellennium, U.S. Post Office, 1966, stainless steel fountain Badger Meter Co., Brown Deer, Wis., 1967, Milw. Civic Ctr., 1970, bicentennial graphics Polish-Am. Bicentennial, Polish Nat. Alliance, Chgo., 1975. Rep. museums including Addison Gallery, Milw. Art Ctr., Mus. Modern Art, N.Y.C., Chgo. Art Mus., Atlanta Art Mus., Mus. Fine Arts, Krakow, Poland, Bklyn. Mus., Grand Rapids Art Gallery, Corcoran Gallery Am. Art, Milw. Art Inst., Mus. Fine Arts, Boston, U. Wis., Marquette U., Karakowa Sch. Fine Art, Poland, Warsaw Acad. Arts, Poland, Winthrop Coll., Ford Motor Co., N.Y.C., Gen. Motors, Detroit, Gen. Electric Co., Shell Oil Co., N.J., Barclays Bank Internat., Chgo., Container Corp. Am., S.C. Arts Commn., U.S. Treasury Dept., Polish Govt. Collection, also pvt. collections. Represented in books: New Horizons in American Art, 1936; Modern Art in America, 1940; American Realists and Magic Realists, 1943; Abstract Painting and Sculptures in America, 1951; American Watercolors, Drawings and Prints,

1952; The Precisionist View of American Art, 1960; Images of America, 1982. Served as artist-corr. USAAF, 1942-46, Europe. Recipient Man of Yr. award Formost Civic Assn., Milw., 1972; Disting. Prof. award Winthrop Coll., 1979; Algernon Sydney Sullivan award Winthrop Coll., 1982, others. Mem. Wis. Art Tchrs. Assn. (life hon.), Nat. Soc. Art Dirs. (hon.), Illustrators and Designers, Milw. (hon.), Alpha Eta Kappa Phi (life hon.). Republican. Roman Catholic. Avocations: Travel; swimming; nature trails; historical documentations. Home: 537 Meadowbrook Ln Rock Hill SC 29730 Office: Art Dept Winthrop Coll Rock Hill SC 29733

LEWANDOWSKI, RAYMOND CASIMIR, JR., physician; b. Berwyn, Ill., Jan. 14, 1944; s. Raymond C. and Adele (Anderson) L.; B.A. with honors, Gustavus Adolphus Coll., 1966; M.D., U. Ill., 1970; postgrad. U. Minn., 1971-72; m. J. Clarise Little, Nov. 21, 1980; children by previous marriage—Raymond III, Bryan, Ian, Meagan, Aaron; 1 stepson, Anthony Raposa. Cert. Am. Bd. Med. Genetics. Intern, Hennepin County Gen. Hosp., Mpls., 1970-71; resident in pediatrics U. Minn. Hosp., Mpls., 1971-72; NIH fellow med. genetics U. Minn., 1974-76; practice medicine specializing in pediatrics and genetics, Laredo, Harlingen, Corpus Christi, Edinburg and Brownsville, Tex., 1980—; mem. staff Brownsville Med. Center, Valley Community Hosp., Spohn Hosp., Meml. Hosp. (both Corpus Christi); exec. v.p. Driscoll Found. Children's Hosp., Corpus Christi, 1983—; med. geneticist Tex. Dept. Mental Health and Mental Retardation, Denton, 1976-77, dir. clin. services, 1978-80, cons., 1980—; cons. genetics Tex. Dept. Human Resources, 1979—; guest lectr. genetics Driscoll Children's Hosp., 1977—, Fairbault (Minn.) State Hosp., 1974-76; lectr. genetics dept. pediatrics U. Minn., 1974-76; mem. adv. bd. Interagy. Council Early Childhood Intervention. Served with M.C., USN, 1972-74. Mem. AMA, Tex. Med. Assn., Nueces County Med. Soc., Tex. Genetics Soc. (program chmn. 1977-78). Contbr. articles on med. genetics to sci. jours. Home: 5521 Wooldridge Corpus Christi TX 78413 Office: PO Box 6530 Corpus Christi TX 78411

LEWELLYN, JESS WILLIAM, rancher, real estate developer; b. Cedar Hill, Tex., Sept. 1, 1933; s. J.R. and Earlene (Burns) L.; B.S. in Mech. Engring., U. Tex. at Austin, 1960; student Arlington State Coll., 1958, Tex. Wesleyan Coll., 1953; m. Ann Truitt, Aug. 5, 1955; children—Debbie Jane, Jess William. Project engr. Texas Instruments, Dallas, 1959-64; mgr. mfg. Beta Corp. subsidiary Koppers, Dallas, 1964-67; dir. mfg. Gulf Aerospace Corp., Houston, 1967-69; dir. mfg. Volkswagen Products Corp., Fort Worth, Tex., 1969-76; gen. mgr. Royal Mfg. Co., Grand Prairie, Tex., 1976-77; chmn. bd., pres. Glass Center of Hurst, Inc. (Tex.), Metroplex Glass Center, Inc., Arlington, Tex., Metroplex Metal Products, Inc., Hurst, after 1977; founder, chmn. bd., pres. Lewellyn Industries, Inc. Fund raiser, Abilene Christian Coll., 1967-68. Served with AUS, 1953-55. Mem. Tex. Soc. Profl. Engrs., ASME. Republican. Mem. Ch. of Christ (elder). Club: Lions. Office: 280 W Euless Blvd Euless TX 76039

LEWIS, ALTON BARNEY, JR., lawyer; b. Greenwood, Miss., Feb. 4, 1949; s. Alton Barney and Marion (Huber) L.; m. Elizabeth Brock Montgomery, Oct. 5, 1974 (div. 1984); 1 child, Jordan Montgomery. B.A. in Econs., U. Miss., 1971, B.S. in Mech. Engring., 1971; J.D., Memphis State U., 1979. Bar: La. 1979, U.S. Ct. Appeals (5th cir.) 1980, U.S. Dist. Ct. (ea. dist.) La. 1980. Ops. mgr. Nat. Art Co., Greenwood, Miss., 1971-74; chief engr. dept. pub. works Shreveport Dept. Pub. Works, La., 1974; plant mgr. L.O.A. Inc., Hughes, Ark., 1974-76; v.p. ops. Pearl Enterprises, Inc., Memphis, 1976-80; ptnr. Pittman, Matheny, Lewis & Moody, Hammond, La., 1980-84; sole practice, Hammond, 1984-85; ptnr. Lewis & Moody, Hammond, 1985—; dir. Tangi Broadcasting Co., Hammond, 1982-84, Strother Broadcasting N. Mex., Roswell, 1984, Strother Broadcasting La., 1984. Pres. Mental Health Assn. Tangipahoa Parish, Hammond, 1982-84; bd. dirs. La. Mental Health Assn., New Orleans, 1983-84. Served to 1st lt. U.S. Army, 1972-74. Recipient Am. Jurisprudence award Mathew Bender Corp., 1976, 79; Outstanding Young Men Am. award, 1982. Mem. ABA, Am. Trial Lawyers Assn., La. Bar Assn., 21st Jud. Dist. Bar Assn., La. Assn. Def. Counsel, Tau Beta Pi. Democrat. Baptist. Home: 1001 N General Pershing Hammond LA 70401 Office: 906 Fagan Dr Suite 3B Hammond LA 70401

LEWIS, ANDREW M., diversified company executive; b. 1946. B.A., Harvard U., 1967; postgrad. MIT. With Best Products Co. Inc., Richmond, Va., 1969—, exec. v.p., 1972-74, pres., chief operating officer, 1976—, also dir. Office: Best Products Co Inc Parham Rd & I-95 Richmond VA 23260

LEWIS, AUBREY JAMES, dentist; b. Ancon, C.Z., Dec. 29, 1922; s. James Franklin and Mabel Louise (McBlane) L.; m. Mildred Eunice Proctor, Nov. 15, 1947 (div. 1959); children—Donald Aubrey, Ronald James, Edward Charles, Jayne Mildred; m. Clyde Willis, Dec. 31, 1962. A.A., Balboa Coll., C.Z.; D.D.S., U. Pa. Dental intern Fla. State Hosp., Chattahoochee, 1947; sr. dentist Fla. State Hosp., Arcadia, 1947-48; gen. practice dentistry, Arcadia, 1948-50, 52-61, Orlando, Fla., 1961—. Mem. Nat. Rep. Senatorial Com., 1984—, Presdl. Task Force, 1984—; state advisor U.S. Congl. Adv. Bd., Orlando, 1984—. Served with USN, 1950-52. Recipient Presdl. Achievement award Rep. Nat. Com., 1984, Medal of Merit, Presdl. Task Force, 1984; Cert. of Recognition, Nat. Rep. Congl. Com., 1983-84. Mem. ADA, Fla. State Dental Assn., Orange County Dental Soc., Central Dist. Dental Soc., Xi Psi Phi. Democrat. Baptist. Lodges: Kiwanis, K.P., DeMolay. Avocations: sailing; archery. Home and office: 2901 Corrine Dr Orlando FL 32803

LEWIS, BARRY THOMAS, business educator; b. Fort Worth, Jan. 9, 1946; s. Barry Thomas and Lola Mae (Levi) L.; m. Linda Ilene Griffith, Oct. 13, 1967; children—Barrett Dean, Brian Thomas, Becca Lynn. B.A. in Bus. Adminstrn., Tex. Tech U.; M.A. in Acctg., Ph.D. in Bus., U. Mo. Instr., U. Houston, 1975-76, U. Mont., Missoula, 1976-78; asst. prof. acctg. U. Mo., Columbia, 1978-84; head dept. acctg. La. State U., Shreveport, 1984—; treas. System Solutions, Warrensburg, Mo., 1981-84. Contbr. articles to profl. jours. Mem. Friends of Fgn. Students, Mo., 1980-83. Served to cpl. USMC, 1965-67. Mem. Nat. Assn. Accts., Internat. Auditors Assn., Am. Assn. Accts., Warrensburg Jaycees (Outstanding Young Men Am. 1980). Democrat. Mem. Ch. of Christ. Club: Officers (Whiteman AFB, Mo.). Lodge: Lions (KnobNoster, Mo.). Home: 9238 Hillside Ave Shreveport LA 71118 Office: La State U 8515 Youree Dr Shreveport LA 71115

LEWIS, BARTLETT BOWERS, socioeconomic analyst, statistician; b. Asheville, N.C., Aug. 31, 1946; s. Rex Tilman and Elizabeth Watson (Bowers) L.; m. Doreen Iris Mattes, Sept. 1, 1984. B.S., N.C. State U., 1968; M.Stats., U. Fla., 1971. Analytical engr. Pratt & Whitney Aircraft Corp., East Hartford, Conn., 1968-69; reliability engr. Martin Marietta Aerospace Corp., Orlando, Fla., 1971-72; photographer, Gainesville, Fla., 1972-74; asst. in research U. Fla., Gainesville, 1974-80; chief socioecon. analysis Atlanta Regional Commn., 1980—. Contbr. articles to profl. jours. Mem. Am. Statis. Assn., Population Assn. Am., So. Regional Demographic Group, So. Regional Sci. Assn., Atlanta Econs. Club. Democrat. Avocation: photography. Home: 4855 Fieldgreen Dr Stone Mountain GA 30088 Office: Atlanta Regional Commn 100 Edgewood Ave NE Suite 1801 Atlanta GA 30335

LEWIS, BYRON CRAIG, management information sciences educator, researcher; b. Brooksville, Fla., Nov. 2, 1944; s. Willie Burgess and Mary Eloise (Rush) L. B.S., U. Fla., 1966; M.S., U. Conn., 1971; Ph.D., Va. Poly. Inst., 1977. Asst. prof. Western Carolina U., Cullowhee, N.C., 1977-78; dir. acad. computing, research assoc. Clemson U., S.C., 1978-79; asst. prof. Auburn U., Ala., 1979-84; assoc. prof. mgmt. info. systems Ga. State U., Atlanta, 1984—; head computer info. systems dept. Troy State U., Ft. Benning, Ga., 1983-84. Contbr. articles to profl. jours. Served with U.S. Army, 1966-69. Mem. Inst. Math. Stats., N.Y. Acad. Scis., Am. Statis. Assn., Am. Inst. Decision Scis. Presbyterian. Home: 3431 Valley Brook Pl Decatur GA 30033 Office: Ga State U Dept Decision Scis Atlanta GA 30303

LEWIS, CARLOS EDWIN, chemist; b. Winston-Salem, N.C., June 7, 1940; s. Lee Craig and Annie Hazel (McDade) L.; m. Norma Ann Hester, Mar. 6, 1965. Student Mars Hill Jr. Coll., 1958-59, High Point Coll., 1959-60; B.S., U. N.C., 1971. With R.J. Reynolds Tobacco Co., Winston Salem, N.C., 1962—, assoc. chemist, 1977-82, research chemist, 1982—, analytical sect. mgr., 1983—; forensic cons. Vice pres. Southwest urban growth com. Winston Salem Arts Council, 1975—. Served with U.S. Army, 1961-67. Mem. Am. Chem. Soc., U. N.C. Alumni Assn., Tobacco Chemists Assn., Sigma Xi, Kappa Psi, Republican. Methodist. Contbr. articles to profl. jours. Office: RJ Reynolds Chestnut St Bldg 26-1 Winston Salem NC 27102

LEWIS, DAVID KENT, forest economist, researcher; b. Madison, Wis., June 11, 1938; s. Wayne Cuthbert and Margaret Caldew (Caldwell) L.; m. Judith Lynn Grover, July 8, 1962; children—Lynn Renee, Anne Elizabeth, Evan David. B.S., U. Minn., 1960; M.Forestry, Yale U., 1966; D.Phil., Oxford U., Eng., 1976. Registered profl. forester, Okla. Forester, Weyerhaeuser Co., Klamath Falls, Oreg., 1963-65, silviculturist, Centralia, Wash., 1967-76, tech. planner, Federal Way, Wash., 1976-80, project mgr. strategic planning, Tacoma, Wash., 1980-82; assoc. prof. dept. forestry Okla. State U., Stillwater, 1982—. Served with USAR, 1961-63; served to capt. USAR, 1960-70. H. Schmidt scholar, 1960; Yale U. fellow, 1965-66; recipient Profl. award Weyerhaeuser Co., 1979. Mem. Soc. Am. Foresters, Am. Econs. Assn. Republican. Lutheran. Club: Exchange (Stillwater). Avocations: Cycling, cross country skiing. Office: Dept Forestry Okla State Univ Stillwater OK 74078

LEWIS, DIANNE BOARDLEY, educational administrator; b. Tallahassee, May 22, 1949; d. John Wilkerson and Barbara Ann (Baker) Boardley; B.S. with honors, Hampton Inst., 1971; M.Ed., U. Ill., 1973; postgrad. Hampton U., Old Dominion U., children—Nichole Reshan, Raegan Latrese. Elem. tchr. Greensboro (N.C.) Public Schs., 1971-72; tchr. Newport News (Va.) Public Schs., 1973-77, asst. prin., 1977-79, 80-82, acting prin., 1979-80; elem. prin. Williamsburg, Va., 1982—; guest lectr. Coll. William and Mary, Williamsburg. Mem. Nat. Assn. Elem. Sch. Prins., Nat. Assn. Edn. Young Children, Assn. Supervision and Curriculum Devel., Nat. Alliance Black Sch. Educators, Hampton Crusade for Votes League, Black Child Inst. Democrat. Roman Catholic. Home: 239 Breckinridge Ct Hampton VA 23666 Office: Scotland St Williamsburg VA 23185

LEWIS, EDWARD EUGENE, bridge contracting executive; b. Millen, Ga., Jan. 8, 1940; s. Edward E. Lewis and Grace (Joyner) Dailey; m. Rebecca Ruth Whatley, Dec. 22, 1963; children—Gary E., Brent A., Kent A. A.S. in Civil Tech., So. Tech. Inst., 1960. Civil technologist Hwy. Dept., Atlanta, 1960-69; v.p. Shepherd Constrn. Co., Atlanta, 1969-83; exec. v.p. Rogers Bridge Co., Atlanta, 1983—. Pres. Fulton County Bd. Edn., Atlanta, 1980—; active Rainbow Park Bapt. Ch. Served with U.S. Army, 1961-67. Recipient Service award Gov. George Busbee, 1975, Key to City, Millen, Ga., 1974, Outstanding Young Man Am. award, 1977, others. Home: 2405 Roxburgh Dr Roswell GA 30076 Office: Fulton County Bd Edn 786 Cleveland Ave SW Atlanta GA 30315

LEWIS, EDWARD SHELDON, chemistry educator; b. Berkeley, Calif., May 7, 1920; s. Gilbert Newton and Mary Hinckley (Sheldon) L.; m. Fofo Catsinas, Dec. 21, 1955; children—Richard Peter, Gregory Gilbert. B.S., U. Calif.-Berkeley, 1940; M.A., Ph.D., Harvard U., 1947. Postdoctoral fellow UCLA, 1947-48; asst. prof. Rice Inst., Houston, 1948-52, assoc. prof., 1952-59, prof. chemistry, 1959—, chmn. dept. chemistry, 1963-67, 80-85; vis. prof. U. Southampton, 1957, Oxford U., 1967, U. Kent, Canterbury, 1977. Served with USNR, 1944-46. Guggenheim fellow, 1966; recipient Southeastern Tex. sect. Am. Chem. Soc. award, 1977. Mem. Am. Chemistry Soc., Royal Soc. Chemistry. Editor: Investigation of Rates and Mechanisms of Reactions, 1974; contbr. numerous articles to profl. jours. Home: 5651 Chevy Chase Houston TX 77056 Office: Dept Chemistry Rice U PO Box 1892 Houston TX 77251

LEWIS, ELIZABETH MATTHEW, artist, writer, researcher; b. Charleston, S.C., Dec. 3, 1916; d. Charles Frederick and Margaret Eloise MacIntosh (Tyler) Matthew; m. John Chase Lewis, Feb. 24, 1950 (dec. 1963); 1 son, Christopher Tyler Sweetman Lewis. Student Cornwall Tech. Coll., 1964, U. London, 1964; B.A., Purdue U., 1965; M.L.S., Pratt Art Inst., 1967; Ed.D., Columbia Tech. Coll., 1974; cert. Inst. in Arts Adminstrn., Harvard U., 1977. Tchr. Miami Art Sch. (Fla.), 1949-51; instr. Ind. U.-Kokomo, 1952-57; v.p. Lewis Workshop Studios, Ind. and Mich., 1951-63; curator of slides dept. art CUNY, N.Y.C., 1971; sr. lectr. fine arts, art librarian U.S. Mil. Acad., West Point, N.Y., 1968-78; dir. Lyon Prodns. Ltd., Highland Falls, N.Y. and Ft. Lauderdale, Fla., 1972—; one man shows include: Hollywood Art Mus. (Fla.) and Hallandale, Fla., 1983, also retrospectives LaFayette and Ft. Wayne, Ind., 1964, Miami and Ft. Lauderdale, 1965; exhibited in group shows in Ind., Mich. and N.Y., 1950-71; designer, dir. video programs in graphic arts; producer color film Sun Song: the Art of John DeGroot (award Fla. Film Festival 1982); designer, fabricator stained glass panels. Election ofcl. Broward County (Fla.), 1982. Served with U.S. Mcht. Marines, 1943-45. Mem. Am. Craft Council, Coll. Art Assn., Artists Equity (bd. dirs. Fla. chpt.), Stained Glass Assn. Am., AAUP, others. Patentee graphics retrieval systems, 1978. Contbr. articles to profl. jours. Home and Office: 1500 NE 18th Ave Fort Lauderdale FL 33304

LEWIS, ERNEST CROSBY, lawyer, state legislator; b. Mar. 4, 1934; s. Ernest Van and Nell (Brooks) L.; m. Cleo Brooks; children—Lisa, Allyson, Ernest Crosby, Jr., Gage. LL.B., U. S.C., 1958. Bar: S.C. Ptnr. firm Lewis, Lewis, Bruce & Truslow, P.A., Columbia, S.C., 1958—; mem. S.C. Ho. of Reps., 1961-64, 83—; pres. Palmetto Title Corp. Past mem. bd. visitors The Citadel; trustee Med. Coll. S.C., Columbia Coll.; vice-chmn. S.C. State Bd. Edn.; founding mem., 1st v.p. Assn. State Dem. Chairmen; chmn. S.C. Dem. party. Served to capt. U.S. Army. Mem. ABA, S.C. Bar Assn., S.C. Trial Lawyers Assn., Phi Alpha Delta. Methodist.

LEWIS, FLETCHER SHERWOOD, petroleum engineer, geologist; b. North Tonawanda, N.Y., Oct. 11, 1948; s. Kenneth John and Doris (Dollen) L. B.S. in Geology, U. Nebr., 1970; M.S. Geology, U. Oreg., 1975; M.S. in Petroleum Engring., U. Okla., 1978. Staff geologist Willamette Western Co., Coos Bay, Oreg., 1974; engr. reservoir No. Natural Gas, Omaha, 1975-77; engr. reservoir and prodn. Grace Petroleum, Oklahoma City, 1977-79; chief engr. Eason Oil Co., Oklahoma City, 1979-81; prin. Fletcher Lewis Engring., Oklahoma City, 1981—; v.p. Hydrostatic Engring., Oklahoma City, 1984—. Mem. Okla. Interstate Oil Compact Commn. Mem. Soc. Petroleum Engrs (chmn. 1982-83), Am. Petroleum Inst., Am. Assn. Petroleum Geologists. Avocations: gardening; rock collecting. Office: 5001 N Pennsylvania St #300 Oklahoma City OK 73112

LEWIS, FLOYD WALLACE, electric utility executive; b. Lincoln County, Miss., Sept. 23, 1925; s. Thomas Cassidy and Lizzie (Lofton) L.; B.B.A., Tulane U., 1945, LL.B., 1949; m. Jimmie Etoile Slawson, Dec. 27, 1949; children—Floyd Wallace, Gail, Julie, Ann, Carol, Michael Paul. Bar: La. 1949. With New Orleans Pub. Service, Inc., 1949-62, v.p., chief fin. officer, 1960-62; v.p. Ark. Power & Light Co., Little Rock, 1962-63, sr. v.p., 1963-67; exec. v.p., dir. La. Power & Light Co., New Orleans, 1967-68, pres., 1968-70, chief exec. officer, 1968-71, chmn. bd., 1970-72; pres. Middle South Utilities, Inc., 1970—, dir., chief exec. officer, 1972—, chmn., 1979—; pres., dir. Middle South Services, Inc., New Orleans, 1970-75, chmn., 1975—; pres., dir. Middle South Energy, Inc., 1974—; chmn. bd., dir. System Fuels, Inc., 1972—, Electec, Inc., 1984—; dir. New Orleans br. Fed. Res. Bank, 1974-75, chmn., 1975; dir. Fed. Res. Bank Atlanta, 1978-81, New Orleans Pub. Service Inc., Ark. Power & Light Co., La. Power & Light Co., Miss. Power & Light Co. Mem. adv. com. Elec. Cos. Advt. Program, 1969-72, chmn., 1970-71; mem. electric utility adv. com. Fed. Energy Adminstrn., 1973-77; chmn. Edison Electric Inst., 1976-77, exec. com., 1974-78, chmn. policy com. nuclear power, 1974-75, utility nuclear power oversight com., 1979-81; chmn. Electric Power Research Inst., 1979-81; dir. Am. Nuclear Energy Council, 1979—, Atomic Indsl. Forum, 1980, vice chmn., 1983—; mem. exec. com. Assn. Edison Illuminating Cos., 1973-81, 83—; mem. coal adv. com. Dept. Interior, 1976-78. Deacon, Baptist Ch., 1950—; mem. Bus. Roundtable, 1975—; vice chmn. campaign United Fund, New Orleans, 1970, chmn., 1971; bd. dirs. New Orleans Symphony Soc., 1974, Pub. Affairs Research Council La.; trustee New Orleans Bapt. Sem. Found., 1969—, pres., 1974-76; trustee New Orleans Bapt. Theol. Sem., 1954-62, 68-76, v.p., 1970-75; trustee Com. Econ. Devel., 1973—; bd. adminstrs. Tulane U., 1973—, bd. visitors, 1968-71, bd. govs. Med. Ctr., 1969-73, vice chmn., 1969-71, chmn. alumni adv. council Grad. Sch. Bus., 1970-73; v.p. Internat. House, 1970; trustee Com. Better La., 1975—, sr. v.p., 1976-77, pres., 1977-78; trustee La. Coll., 1984—; trustee Alton Ochsner Med. Found., 1976—, exec. com., 1977—; bd. dirs. U.S. Com. for Energy Awareness, 1982—, chmn., 1984—. Served to ensign USNR, 1945-46. Recipient Outstanding Alumni award Coll. Bus. Adminstrn., Tulane U., 1970, Disting. Alumnus award Univ., 1983; Silver Beaver, Silver Antelope awards Boy Scouts Am. Mem. ABA, La. Bar Assn., Tulane Alumni Assn. (exec. com., treas. 1970), U.S. C. of C. (dir. 1981—), New Orleans Area C. of C. (v.p. 1970, dir. 1970-73), Order of Coif, Beta Gamma Sigma, Omicron Delta Kappa, Beta Theta Pi, Phi Delta Phi. Office: 225 Baronne St New Orleans LA 70161

LEWIS, FORBES DOWNER, computer science educator, researcher; b. New Haven, Apr. 15, 1942; s. Taylor Downer Lewis and Clara (Bartholow) Hall. B.S., Cornell U., 1967, M.S., 1969, Ph.D., 1970. Asst. prof. Harvard U., Cambridge, Mass., 1970-75; assoc. prof. SUNY-Albany, 1975-78; assoc. prof. U. Ky., Lexington, 1978-83, prof. computer sci., 1983—. Contbr. articles to profl. jours. Served with U.S. Army, 1960-63. Mem. Assn. for Computing Machinery, Assn. for Symbolic Logis, Soc. for Indsl. Applied Math., IEEE. Home: 3548 Merrick Ct Lexington KY 40502 Office: Dept Computer Sci U Ky Lexington KY 40506

LEWIS, FRANCES AARONSON, retail company executive; b. Bklyn., June 27, 1922; d. Nathaniel Bernard L. and Lillian (Beller) Aaronson; m. Sydney Lewis, Sept. 3, 1942; children—Sydney, Andrew M., Susan Lewis Butler. B.A., U. Mich., 1942; D.H.L. hon., Va. Union U., 1977, H.H.D., Va. Commonwealth U., 1983. Cert. diamond evaluator and appraisor Gemological Inst. Am. Entrepreneur, founder Best Products Co., Inc., Richmond, Va., 1957—. Trustee Va. Environ. Endowment, Richmond, 1978—; mem. Richmond Pub. Sch. Bd., 1980—; mem. legis. affairs com. C. of C. Richmond, 1981—; mem. exhbns. com. Va. Mus. Fine Art, Richmond, 1982—; mem. Va. State Fedn. Block Grant com. City of Richmond, 1983. Recipient Disting. Virginian award State of Va., 1972, ann. award Federated Arts Council, Richmond, 1976, Jackson Davis award for Disting. Service to High Edn., Va., 1978, Thomas Jefferson award State of Va., 1978. Mem. Va. Retail Mchts. Assn. (award for Retailer of Yr. 1982), Beta Gamma Sigma, DAR (Medal of Honor 1983). Democrat. Jewish. Office: Best Products Company PO Box 26303 Richmond VA 23260*

LEWIS, FRANK LEROY, electrical engineering educator; b. Wurzburg, Fed. Reublic Germany, May 11, 1949; came to U.S., May 1966; s. Frank Leroy and Ruth Evangeline (Shirley) L. B.A. in Elec. Engring. and Physics, Rice U., 1971, M.E.E., 1971; M.S. in Aerosystems, U. Western Fla., 1977; Ph.D. in Elec. Engring., Ga. Inst. Tech., 1981. Cons. Lockheed, Marietta, Ga., 1983—. Author: Optimal Control, 1985; Optimal Estimation, 1985. Contbr. articles to profl. jours. Grantee NSF, 1982-84. Mem. IEEE, Systems and Controls Soc., ETA Kappa Nu (teaching award 1981), Sigma Xi (Excellence in Ph.D. research award 1981, Jr. Faculty in Engring. award 1984). Home: 835 Glendale Terr Apt 6 Atlanta GA 30308 Office: Sch Elec Engring Ga Inst Tech Atlanta GA 30332

LEWIS, GEORGE MCKOY, banker; b. Valley Mills, Tex., Aug. 3, 1902; s. Samuel Knight and Mary Rebecca (Barrett) L.; B.S., Tex. A&M U., 1924; M.B.A., Harvard U., 1927; postgrad. U. Chgo., 1929-30; m. Mary Gregory Bunting, Feb. 10, 1940. Mem. staff U.S. Dept. Agr., 1924-25; staff Bur. Bus. Research, U. Tex., 1927-29; Inst. Meat Packing fellow U. Chgo., 1929-30; dir. mktg. Am. Meat Inst., Chgo., 1939-57, v.p., 1950-63, v.p., dir. Am. Meat Inst. Found., 1957-63; vice chmn. bd., economist Jefferson State Bank, San Antonio, 1963—. Established and endowed George M. and Mary B. Lewis Scholarship Fund, Tex. A&M U., 1983. Mem. SAR, Sons Tex. Republic. Mason (Shriner). Clubs: Quadrangle, Union League, University of Chicago, South Shore Country (Chgo.); Argyle (San Antonio). Home: 715 Wiltshire Ave San Antonio TX 78209 Office: Jefferson State Bank San Antonio TX 78284

LEWIS, GEORGE RAY, real estate company executive; b. San Francisco, May 7, 1937; s. Millard and Dorothy (Ray) L.; m. Carolyn Cantwell, Sept. 28, 1968; children—Dorothy, James Millard. A.B., Princeton U., 1959; M.B.A., Harvard U., 1961. Contract negoatiator TRW Inc., Manhattan Beach, Calif., 1964-65; asst. v.p. Recognition Equipment Co., Dallas, 1966-67; gen. mgr. Ranch Foods, Dallas, 1967-70; v.p. Ike Harris & Co., Dallas, 1970-73; pres. George Lewis, Inc., Dallas, 1973—. Served to 1st lt. USAF, 1960-64. Mem. Nat. Homebuilders Assn., Tex. Homebuilders Assn., Dallas Home and Apt. Builders Assn., Park Cities Redevel. League (chmn. 1984—). Clubs: Chevy Chase (Washington); Brook Hollow Golf (Dallas); Kook Kreek (Athens, Tex.). Avocations: skiing; hiking; golf; gardening; reading. Home: 3604 Princeton Dallas TX 75205 Office: George Lewis Inc 6517 Hillcrest Suite 211 Dallas TX 75205

LEWIS, GERALD, state government official; b. Birmingham, Ala., Mar. 31, 1934; s. Bernard and Molly L.; m. Mary Lewis; children—Patty, Beth, Susan. B.A., Harvard U., 1955, J.D., 1960. Bar: Fla. 19. Practice law, Miami, Fla., 1960-66; mem. Fla. Ho. of Reps., 1966-70, Fla. Senate, 1970-72; asst. states atty. 11th Jud. Circuit, also asst. county atty. Dade County, Fla., 1972-74; comptroller State of Fla., Tallahassee, 1974—. State chmn. Am. Cancer Soc., state employee's div. Heart Fund Drive; trustee Conf. State Bank Suprs. Schs. Served with U.S. Army, 1955-57. Recipient Disting. Service award South Fla. Pub. Service Soc., 1975; Humanitarian award United Cerebral Palsy of Miami, 1975. Mem. ABA, Fla. Bar Assn., Dade County Bar Assn. Democrat. Jewish. Club: Harvard (Tallahassee). Office: Plaza Level The Capitol Tallahassee FL 32301

LEWIS, GLADYS SHERMAN, nurse, educator; b. Wynnewood, Okla., Mar. 20, 1933; d. Andrew and Minnie Elva (Halsey) Sherman; R.N., St. Anthony's Sch. Nursing, 1953; student Okla. Baptist U., 1953-55; A.B., Tex. Christian U., 1956; postgrad. Southwestern Bapt. Theol. Sem., 1959-60, Escuela de Idiomas, San Jose, Costa Rica, 1960-61; M.A., Central State U., Edmond, Okla., 1985; m. Wilbur Curtis Lewis, Jan. 28, 1955; children—Karen, David, Leanne, Cristen. Mem. nursing staff various facilities, Okla., Tex., 1953-57; instr. nursing, med. missionary Baptist Hosp., Asuncion, Paraguay, 1961-70, missionary nurse So. Bapt. Fgn. Mission Bd. Mobile Clinic, 1968-70, mem. staff, 1972-73; vice chmn. edn. commn. Paraguay Bapt. Conv., 1962-65; sec. bd. trustees Bapt. Hosp., Paraguay, 1962-65; chmn. personnel com., handbook and policy book officer Bapt. Mission in Paraguay, 1967-70; trustee Southwestern Bapt. Theol. Sem., Ft. Worth, 1974—, chmn. student affairs com., 1976-78, vice chmn. bd., 1977-79; partner Las Amigas Tours; writer, conference leader, campus lectr., 1959—. Active Democratic party; leader Girl Scouts U.S.A., 1965-75; Okla. co-chmn. Nat. Religious Com. for Equal Rights Amendment, 1977-80; tour host Meier Internat. Study League. Recognized for disaster relief work in Honduras, Fgn. Mission Bd., So. Bapt. Conv., 1975; named Woman of Yr., Midwest City, 1979; Outstanding Grad. Student, Central State U., 1984-85. Mem. Nat. Women's Polit. Caucus, Okla. Women's Polit. Caucus, AAUW, Evang. Women's Caucus, Am. Nurses Assn., Internat., Am. colls. surgeons women's auxiliaries, Okla. State, Okla. County med. auxiliaries. Author: On Earth As It Is Two Dreams and a Promise, 1983; also religious instructional texts in English and Spanish; contbr. articles to So. Bapt. and secular periodicals; columnist Royal Service, Christian Med. Soc. News and Reports; editor Sooner Physician's Heartbeat. Home and office: 14501 N Western Ave Edmond OK 73013

LEWIS, GORDON DEPEW, government administrator, forest economist; b. Charlottesville, Va., July 22, 1929; s. Chauncey Depew and Clarice Undine (Laughon) L.; m. Yoshie Mukaida, June 16, 1954. B.S., Va. Polytech. Inst., 1951; M.F., Duke U., 1957; Ph.D., Mich. State U., 1961. Asst. prof. forest econs. U. Mont., Missoula, 1959-62; project leader Southeastern Forest Expt. Sta., U.S. Forest Service, Asheville, N.C., 1962-66, br. chief Washington, 1966-71, program mgr. Rocky Mountain Forest Expt. Sta., Ft. Collins, Colo., 1971-81, asst. dir. Southeastern Forest Expt. Sta., Asheville, N.C., 1981—. Served to cpl. C.E., U.S. Army, 1951-53. Mem. Soc. Am. Foresters, Am. Econ. Assn., Sigma Xi. Republican. Office: 200 Weaver Blvd Asheville NC 28804

LEWIS, GRADY CAROL, educational administrator, consultant; b. Grimesland, N.C., Aug. 27, 1941; d. Lemuel Worley and Eva Mae (Creech) Gaskins; div. 1966; 1 son, Stephen Jacob. B.S. in Vocat. Home Econs., East Carolina U., 1963; M.Ed. in Ednl. Media, U. N.C., 1972. Vocat. home econs. tchr. Currituck County Schs., N.C., 1963-65; sch. librarian Alamance County Schs., N.C., 1965-67; media specialist Burlington City Schs., N.C., 1967-71; dir. media services Ravenscroft Sch., Raleigh, N.C., 1971-75; dir. sch. media programs div. N.C. Dept. Pub. Instruction, Raleigh, 1975—. Developer staff tng. materials. Ednl. Policy Program fellow, 1984. Mem. East Carolina U. Library Sci. Profl. Soc. (hon. life mem.), Phi Delta Kappa (v.p. 1982-84, service award 1984). Democrat. Avocations: boating; oriental cooking; needlework. Home: 11437 Norwood Rd Raleigh NC 27612 Office: NC Dept Pub Instruction Edenton and Salisbury Sts Raleigh NC 27611

LEWIS, HAROLD E(UGENE), association executive; b. Dodge City, Kans., July 7, 1933; s. Eugene Paul and stepson Gladys M. (Davis) L.; m. Fern E. Showbarger, June 8, 1953; children—Carla Lewis Gleason, Annette Lewis Fields, Eldon, Monica Lewis Morgan, Bonita. B.S. in Edn., Pittsburg (Kans.) State U., 1956, M.S. in Vocat. Tech. Edn., 1965. Cert. secondary tchr., Kans.; accredited conf. mgr.; cert. assn. exec. Am. Soc. Assn. Execs. Secondary and jr. high sch. tchr., 1956-68; prodn. and design supr. Adventure Line Mfg. Co., Parsons, Kans., 1960-63; asst., then acting state supr. trade and indsl. edn.

Kans. Dept. Edn., 1968-74; dir. U.S. Skill Olympics, exec. officer Vocat. Indsl. Clubs Am., Leesburg, Va., 1974—; organizer Internat. Skill Olympics, Atlanta, 1981; leader workshops and tng. confs. on vocat. edn.; ofcl. rep. of U.S., Internat. Orgn. for Promotion of Vocat. Edn., 1982—. Pres. Topeka chpt. Gideons Internat., 1968-71; assoc. Parsons YMCA, 1960-65; bd. dirs. Nat. Safety Council, 1985—. Recipient Disting. Service award Kans. Vocat. Indsl. Clubs Am., 1974; annual award for nat. project, Nat. Assn. Industry Edn. Cooperation, 1980. Mem. Am. Vocat. Assn., Kans. Vocat. Assn., Nat. Assn. Trade and Indsl. Edn., Nat. Assn. Industry Edn. Cooperation (ann. award 1980), Am. Welding Soc. (edn. com., 1983—). Mem. Ch. of Nazarene. Office: PO Box 3000 Leesburg VA 22075

LEWIS, HAROLD GREGG, economist, educator; b. Homer, Mich., May 9, 1914; s. Clayton Arthur and Florence (Gregg) L.; m. Julia Catherine Elliott, Dec. 14, 1938; children—Peter Elliott, John Gregg, Scott Porter. Student Port Huron Jr. Coll., 1932-34; A.B., U. Chgo., 1936, Ph.D., 1947. Inst. econs. U. Chgo., 1939-43, asst. prof., 1945-49, assoc. prof., 1949-57, prof., 1957-75; prof. econs. Duke U., 1975-84; asst. dir. wage stblzn. WLB, 1943-45. Author: Union Relative Wage Effects, 1986. Contbr. articles to profl. jours. Served with USAAF, 1945. Mem. Am. Econ. Assn., Phi Beta Kappa. Home: 102 Longwood Pl Chapel Hill NC 27514

LEWIS, HARVEY DELLMOND, JR., clergyman, educator; b. Florence, Tex., Jan. 29, 1918; s. Harvey Dellmond and Rosell Hawkins (Whittenberg) L.; m. Marie Frances Fuscia, Feb. 19, 1945; children—Olan Harvey, Rosell Marie Lewis Carr, Frances Ann Lewis Smith. B.A., Baylor U., 1939; Th.M., Southwestern Bapt. Theol. Sem., 1942; D.D. (hon.), Univ. Mary Hardin Baylor, 1980. Ordained to ministry So. Bapt. Conv., 1937. Pastor Calvary Bapt. Ch., Port Acres, Tex., 1946-48, First Bapt. Ch., Cleveland, Tex., 1948-51, First Bapt. Ch., Kerrville, Tex., 1951-55, Harlandale Bapt. Ch., San Antonio, 1955-58, First Bapt. Ch., Mt. Pleasant, Tex., 1958-63, Central Bapt. Ch., Marshall, Tex., 1963-76; dir. planned giving East Tex. Bapt. U., Marshall, 1976-85, acting pres., 1985—; moderator Tryon Evergreen Assn., Bapt. Gen. Conv., 1949-51; trustee San Marcos Bapt. Acad., Tex., 1955-60, East Tex. Bapt. U., 1959-68, 70-77, Mex. Bapt. Bible Inst., San Antonio, 1955-58. Served chaplain USAAF, 1942-46. Mem. Marshall C. of C. Lodge: Masons (32 degree). Home: 3401 Indian Springs Marshall TX 75670 Office: East Tex Bapt Univ 1209 N Grove Marshall TX 75670

LEWIS, HENRY, III, clinical pharmacist, college dean, educator; b. Tallahassee, Jan. 22, 1950; s. Henry and Evelyn L.; m. Rita Ann Lewis, Dec. 24, 1977. Assoc. dir. pharmacy Bayfront Med. Ctr., St. Petersburg, Fla., 1972-74; asst. dean clin. affairs Fla. A&M U. Coll. Pharmacy, Tallahassee, 1978—, assoc. prof. clin. pharmacy, 1978—; mem. grad. record exam. bd. Minority Grad. Edn. Com. Bd. dirs. C.K. Steele Jaycees, Tallahassee, Leon County chpt. Am. Cancer Soc. (Fla.). Recipient Kappa Psi Meritorious award; named Tchr. of Yr., Fla. A&M U., 1976; grantee Grad. and Profl. Opportunities Program, Dept. Edn., 1979-84, Dept. Health and Rehab. Services, 1982-84, Fla. Bd. Regents, 1982-84. Mem. Am. Pharm. Assn., Fla. Pharmacy Assn., Am. Assn. Colls. Pharmacy, Rho Chi. Contbr. articles to profl. jours. Home: 1277 E Orange Ave Tallahassee FL 32301 Office: Coll Pharmacy Fla A&M U Tallahassee FL 32307

LEWIS, HENRY FIELDING, JR., investment company executive; b. Patterson, La., Nov. 2, 1930; s. Henry Fielding and Margaret Elizabeth (Peterman) L.; student U. So. La., 1948, Southeastern U., 1949; m. Gladys Louise Darby, Feb. 11, 1949; 1 child, Paula Lewis Holmes. Lumber inspector May Bros. Cypress Co., Franklin, La., 1949-51; with Columbian Carbon Co., Franklin, 1953-56; pres. Franklin Bldg. Materials, Inc., 1958-71; pub. Franklin Post, after 1971, also editorial writer; mng. ptnr. LBD Investors; owner Fielding Lewis Investments free lance writer; dir. La. Landowners Assn., Riggs Land Co., Inc., Kyle-Peterman Group, Inc., Cour-Win Corp. Pres. West St. Mary Parish Port Commn.; mem. Gov's. Commn. on Atchafalaya Basin, La. Coastal Commn., St. Mary Parish Democratic Com., La. State Boxing Commn., del. La. State Dem. Conv., 1986. Served with USAF, 1948-49. Episcopalian. Clubs: Jackson Bayou Wildlife Protectors, Duck Hunters. Contbr. articles on land use and floodway to profl. jours. and mags. Office: 810 Iberia St Franklin LA 70538

LEWIS, HOWARTH LISTER, JR., architect; b. N.Y.C., June 13, 1934; s. Howarth Lister and Edith Sophia (Braakman) L.; m. Dianna J. Moore, June 8, 1957; children—Kimberly Jean, Gregory Howarth, Jeffery Christopher. B.Arch., U. Fla., 1957. Registered architect, Fla. Chief designer Howard Chilton Architects, Palm Beach, Fla., 1957-60; ptnr. Peacock & Lewis Architects/Planners, West Palm Beach, Fla., 1960—; pres. Gallery Worth Ave, Inc.; chmn. bd. Formula Racing Sailboats Inc. Chmn. constrn. industry bd., Palm Beach County, 1974, 77; chmn. parks and recreation West Palm Beach, 1976; bd. zoning appeals West Palm Beach, 1977-80; mem. bldg. bd., Lake Worth, Fla., 1979—. Mem. AIA (Pulara award Fla. assn. 1971). Republican. Episcopalian. Clubs: Mayacoo Country, Highlands Country (N.C.); Fraternal Order Police Assocs. Home: 15 Harbor Dr Lake Worth FL 33460 Office: 501 S Flagler Dr West Palm Beach FL 33401

LEWIS, JAMES CRAIGER, real estate development company executive; b. Birmingham, Ala., Feb. 4, 1922; s. Taylor Bright and Agnes (Craiger) L.; m. Mary Hatfield, June 30, 1950; children—James Hatfield, Elizabeth Anne. B.S.M.E., U. Ala.-Tuscaloosa, 1948. Pres. Lewis Investment Co., Inc., Birmingham, 1960—; dir. City Nat. Bank, Birmingham, 1965-80, Southland Bankcorp., Mobile, Ala., 1976-80. Trustee Cumberland Coll., Lebanon, Tenn., 1965—. Served to capt. USAF, 1942-52. Mem. Birmingham Assn. Home Builders (pres. 1964), Ala. Home Builders Assn. (pres. 1966), Birmingham C. of C., Newcomer Soc. Republican. Club: Toastmasters (pres. Birmingham 1961). Avocations: flying; skiing; golf; tennis. Home: 3040 Weatherton Dr Birmingham AL 35223 Office: Lewis Investment Co Inc 2101 Magnolia Ave S Birmingham AL 35205

LEWIS, JAMES WOODROW, state chief justice; b. Darlington County, S.C., Mar. 8, 1912; s. W. J. and Mary Aletha (Bryant) L.; A.B., U. S.C., 1932; m. Alice Lee, Dec. 26, 1936; 1 dau., Barbara (Mrs. Olin D. Haynes). Admitted to S.C. bar, 1935; mem. S.C. Hwy. Commn., 1936-40; mem. S.C. Ho. of Reps. from Darlington County, 1935-36, 43-45; judge 4th Jud. Circuit S.C., 1945-61; asso. justice Supreme Ct. S.C., 1961-75, chief justice, 1975—. Address: PO Box 53 Darlington SC 29532

LEWIS, JANA LEE, elementary school principal; b. Corbin, Ky., Oct. 23, 1933; d. Elias E. and Mary S. (Hill) Gabbard; A.B., Berea (Ky.) Coll., 1955; M.A., E. Tenn. State U., 1970, Ed.S., 1978; m. Alan E. Lewis, June 9, 1954; children—Bradley Eugene, Karen Janine. Caseworker, Knoxville (Tenn.) Children's Bur., 1956-59; tchr. Hawkins County (Ky.) Schs., 1959-61; tchr. Kingsport (Tenn.) City Schs., 1962-64, 66-73, prin., 1973—; prin. Lincoln Sch., 1973—. Mem. Council Exceptional Children, Am. Assn. Sch. Adminstrs., Nat. Elem. Prins. Assn., Adminstrv. Mgmt. Soc., Assn. Supervision and Curriculum Devel., Phi Delta Kappa. Home: 2513 Essex Dr Kingsport TN 37660 Office: Lincoln School Summer St Kingsport TN 37664

LEWIS, JANE ELIZABETH, business executive; b. Montgomery, Ala., Sept. 24, 1957; d. Howard Jackson and Cecile Anne (Westmoreland) L. B.S. in Journalism, U. Fla., 1980. Pub. affairs asst. Fed. Emergency Mgmt. Agy., Atlanta, 1980; editor, writer Equifax, Inc., Atlanta, 1980-81; printing cons., art designer, Atlanta Printing Co., 1981-82; editor, employee info. specialist Atlanta Gas Light Co., 1982-85; employee communications coordinator HBO & Co., Atlanta, 1985—. Mem. com. young careers group High Mus. Art, Atlanta. Mem. Internat. Assn. Bus. Communicators (bd. dirs.), Women in Communications (bd. dirs.). Republican. Presbyterian. Office: HBO & Co 301 Perimeter Center N Atlanta GA 30346

LEWIS, J(EWELLE) DEAN, lawyer; b. Alexandria, Va., May 6, 1948; d. Miller Benjamin, Sr. and Edna (Apperson) L.; m. Larry H. Lohman, Aug. 28, 1976; 1 child, Gregory Scott. B.A., Mary Washington Coll., 1970; J.D., Coll. William and Mary, 1973. Bar: Va. 1973, U.S. Dist. Ct. (ea. dist.) Va. 1974, U.S. Bankruptcy Ct. 1974. Law clk. to judges Circuit Ct. Arlington County, Va., 1973; sole practice, Stafford, Va., 1974—; commr. in chancery Circuit Ct. Stafford County, 1974—, asst. commr. accounts, 1980—; Spotsylvania County and City of Fredericksburg Circuit Cts., Va., 1974—; trustee in bankruptcy U.S. Dist. Ct. (ea. dist.) Va., 1974; substitute judge 15th Jud. Circuit, 1985—. Legal adviser Dumfries-Triangle Vol. Rescue Squad. Mem. ABA, Va. Bar Assn., Va. State Bar Assn., Fredericksburg Bar Assn., 15th Jud. Circuit Bar Assn., Phi Delta Phi. Democrat. Home: 221 Braehead Dr Fredericksburg VA 22401 Office: PO Box 356 Stafford VA 22554

LEWIS, LLOYD ROLAND, JR., utility company executive, public speaker, personal development consultant; b. Madison, Wis., Oct. 11, 1943; s. Lloyd Roland and Vera Mae (Joslin) L.; m. Shirley Lou Keisler, Apr. 9, 1966; children—Todd Roland, Mark Stanley. B.S., U. S.C., 1966; M.B.A., 1978, M.S. in Bus. Adminstrn., 1982. Tng. coordinator S.C. Electric & Gas Co., Columbia, 1978-79, staff devel. analyst, 1979-81, dir. organizational planning and devel., 1981-82, dir. human resources planning and devel., 1982-83, supr., 1983-84, coordinator organizational design, 1984—; cons. Teepak, Inc., Columbia, 1984—. Gov.-elect Civitan Internat. S.C. dist., 1984-85, gov., 1985—. Served to capt. U.S. Air Force, 1966-71. Named Outstanding Lt. Gov., S.C. dist. Civitan, 1982-83, recipient District Honor Key, 1983-84. Mem. Beta Gamma Sigma. Republican. So. Baptist. Lodge: Cayce W. Columbia Civitan (pres.-elect 1980-81, pres. 1981-82). Avocations: jogging; tennis; reading; stamp collecting; collecting old books. Home: 2767 Naples Pass West Columbia SC 29169 Office: SC Electric and Gas Co 1426 Main St Columbia SC 29201

LEWIS, MARY LOU, ophthalmologist, educator; b. Evanston, Ill., May 27, 1942; d. Thomas A. and Mary Catherine (Carter) Jenkins; m. Jackson Hall Lewis, Dec. 4, 1971. B.S., U. Iowa, 1964, M.D., 1967. Diplomate Am. Bd. Ophthalmology. Intern, Jackson Meml. Hosp., Miami, Fla., 1967-68; resident U. Calif., San Francisco, 1968-71; fellow Bascom Palmer Eye Inst., Miami, 1971-72, assoc. prof., 1972—; vis. prof. U. South Fla., Tampa, 1982, Northwestern U., Chgo., 1983. Contbr. articles to profl. jours., chpts. to books. Mem. Heed Soc., Macula Soc., Fla. Med. Soc., Dade County Med. Assn., Miami Ophthalmol. Soc., Frederick C. Cordes Soc., Pan Am. Assn. Ophthalmology, Bascom Palmer Eye Inst. Alumni Assn. Republican. Avocation: sailing. Office: Bascom Palmer Eye Inst 900 NW 17th St Miami FL 33136

LEWIS, MORRIS, JR., wholesale and retail grocery executive; b. Lexington, Miss., Apr. 19, 1911; s. Morris and Julia (Herrman) L.; B.S. in Econs., U. Pa., 1932; m. Frederica Lantor, Nov. 21, 1933; children—Morris III, Julia (Mrs. Gerald W. Miller). With Lewis Grocer Co., Indianola, Miss., 1932—, pres. 1937-69, chmn. bd., 1969—; pres. Sunflower Stores, Indianola, 1948-69, chmn. bd., 1969—; v.p., dir. Super Valu Stores, Inc, Hopkins, Minn., 1965-70, chmn. bd., 1970-76, chmn. exec. com., 1976-83; dir. Peoples Bank of Indianola; dir. mem. exec. com. Columbus & Greenville R.R. Mem. Nat. council Boy Scouts Am., also dir., past pres. Delta council, Silver Beaver award; past trustee Millsaps Coll., Jackson. Served to maj. AUS, World War II. Named Indianola Citizen of Year, Indianola C. of C., 1954. Mem. Nat.-Am. Wholesale Grocers Assn. (past nat. pres., past chmn. bd.), Miss. C. of C. (past pres.). Rotarian (past pres.). Office: Hwy 49W Indianola MS 38751

LEWIS, NORMA JEAN, nursing administrator; b. Kennett, Mo., Apr. 16, 1948; d. H.D. Sample, Jr. and Willa (Raney) Lassiter; children—Mark, Laura, Jason. A.A.S.N., Ark. State U., 1978. R.N. Nursing supr. obstetrics Dunklin County Meml. Hosp., Kennett, 1978-79; clinic and home health nurse Ark. Dept. Health, Corning, 1979-82; home health dir. Corning Community Hosp., 1982-83, dir. nursing service, 1983—. Recipient Outstanding Services award Ark. Dept. Health, 1981. Mem. Ark. Pub. Health Assn., Ark. Soc. Hosp. Nursing Service Dirs. Mem. Ch. of Christ. Avocations: reading, softball, swimming, canoeing, camping. Office: Corning Community Hosp PO Box 158 Corning AR 72422

LEWIS, PAUL SCHMID, marine tanker broker; b. Tarrytown, N.Y., Apr. 26, 1938; s. George Alexander, Jr. and Emma Rose (Schmid) L.; m. Donna Marie Carabine, Aug. 8, 1964; children—Paul, Kristin, Stephen. B.S. in Marine Transp., SUNY Maritime Coll.-Fort Schuyler, 1960. Lic. 2d mate U.S. Coast Guard. Pilot, FAA, 1962; dir. marine chartering dept. Gulf Oil Corp., N.Y.C., 1963-72; v.p. C.J. Thibodeaux & Co., Houston, 1972—. Served to lt. USNR, 1960-64. Roman Catholic. Clubs: Houston, Plaza. Lodge: K.C. Home: 1819 Grand Valley Houston TX 77090

LEWIS, PHILLIP VERNON, management educator; b. Eastland, Tex., Mar. 27, 1942; s. Walter Vernon and Doris Mintie (Nelmns) L.; m. Marilyn Hermann, Dec. 14, 1963; children—P. Brook, Blair E. B.S., Abilene Christian Coll., 1964; M.A., U. Denver, 1966; Ed.D., U. Houston, 1970. Instr., No. Ariz. U., Flagstaff, 1966-68; prof. bus. communication Okla. State U., Stillwater, 1970-82; prof. mgmt. Abilene Christian U., Tex., 1982—; mgmt. trainee S & Q Clothiers, Abilene, 1961-64; teller 1st Nat. Bank, Westminster, Colo., 1965-66. Author: Organizational Communication, 1975, 2d edit., 1980; Managing Human Relations, 1983. Fellow Am. Bus. Communication Assn. (pres. 1984); mem. Acad. Mgmt. Republican. Mem. Ch. of Christ. Home: 734 Scott Pl Abilene TX 79601 Office: Abilene Christian U Box 7819 Abilene TX 79699

LEWIS, RICHARD STANLEY, writer, editorial consultant; b. Pitts., Jan. 8, 1916; s. S. Morton and Mary (Lefstein) L.; m. Louise Gertrude Silberstein, June 8, 1938; children—Jonathan, David. B.A., Pa. State U., 1937. City editor Indpls. Times, 1947-49; chief investigator St. Louis Star Times, 1949-51; asst. city editor, sci. editor Chgo. Sun-Times, 1951-68; editor Bull. Atomic Scientists, 1968-74; author: The Other Child, 1960; The Other Child Grows Up, 1977; A Continent for Science, 1964; Appointment on the Moon, 1969; The Voyages of Apollo, 1974; The Nuclear Power Rebellion, 1972; From Vinland to Mars, 1976; editor: Frozen Future, 1972; prin. author The New Ency. of Space Exploration, 1983; The Voyages of Columbia, 1984. City councilman, dep. mayor Indialantic, Fla., 1980-82. Served with AUS, 1943-46. Fellow Brit. Interplanetary Soc.; mem. Nat. Press Club, Authors Guild. Address: 1401 S Magnolia Dr Indialantic FL 32903

LEWIS, ROBERT HUGH, JR., oral and maxillofacial surgeon; b. Jackson, Tenn., Nov. 3, 1950; s. Robert Hugh and Elizabeth (Durio) L.; m. Mary Elizabeth Bovine, Jan. 20, 1979; children—Amanda Elizabeth, Laureen Rebecca, Paul Robert. B.S., U. Tenn., 1972; D.D.S., U. Tenn.-Memphis, 1976. Diplomate Am. Bd. Oral and Maxillofacial Surgery. Intern, City of Memphis Hosp., 1977-78, resident, 1978-80; pvt. practice oral and maxillofacial surgery, Rogers, Ark., 1980—; mem. staff St. Mary-Rogers Meml. Hosp. Contbr. articles to profl. jours. Bd. dirs. Benton County Adult Devel. Ctr., Ark., 1982—. Fellow Am. Assn. Oral and Maxillofacial Surgery; mem. ADA, Am. Soc. Dental Anesthesiology, Ark. Soc. Oral and Maxillofacial Surgery, Ark. Dental Assn. Home: 3 Canterbury Ln Rogers AR 72756 Office: 615 W Oak St Rogers AR 72756

LEWIS, ROBERT WILLIAM, JR., pharmacist executive; b. Baton Rouge, May 29, 1934; s. Robert William and Lucille (Tregre) L.; m. Jacqueline Couture, June 13, 1959; children—Lori Elizabeth Lewis Clattenburg, Robert William III. B.S. in Pharmacy, U. Miss., 1961; Pharm.D. (hon.), La. Pharmacy Assn., 1982. Registered pharmacist La., Ala., N.C., Ill., Kans., Ga., Miss., Tex. Sr. v.p. Medi-Save Pharmacies, Baton Rouge, 1963—; pharmacist City Drugs Co. DeRidder, La., 1962-63; dir. River City Fed. Savs. Bank, Baton Rouge, 1980—. Chmn. St. Patrick's Bd. of Edn., Baton Rouge, 1974; bd. dirs. Boy Scouts Am., Baton Rouge, 1975. Served with U.S. Army, 1958-60. Mem. Am. Pharm. Assn., Am. Soc. Cons. Pharmacists, Am. Inst. History of Pharmacy, La. Pharmacy Assn. (pres. 1985-86), Baton Rouge Pharm. Soc. (treas. 1972-73), Baton Rouge Roundtable. Democrat. Roman Catholic. Club: Sherwood Forest Country (Baton Rouge). Lodges: K.C., Rotary Internat. Avocations: reading historical novels; travel; jogging; gardening; genealogy. Home: 2367 Woodland Ridge Blvd Baton Rouge LA 70816 Office: Medi-Save Pharmacies Inc PO Box 1631 Baton Rouge LA 70821

LEWIS, STEPHEN DALE, business education educator; b. Grimsley, Tenn., Oct. 13, 1947; s. Stanton David and Lou Neil (Davis) L.; m. Linda Kay Clark, Mar. 25, 1965; children—Stephen Clark, Erin Nicole. B.S. in Bus. Adminstrn., Tenn. Tech. U., 1974; M.Ed., Memphis State U., 1975; Ph.D., U. N.D., 1977. Assembler, Frigidaire div. Gen. Motors, Dayton, Ohio, 1966-71; grad. asst. Memphis State U., 1974-75; grad. teaching asst. U. N.D., Grand Forks, 1975-77; prof. bus. edn. Middle Tenn. State U., Murfreesboro, 1977—. Author: Secretarial Administration and Management, 1985. Middle Tenn. State U. grantee, 1985. Mem. Nat. Bus. Edn. Assn. (award 1973), So. Bus. Edn. Assn., Tenn. Bus. Edn. Assn. (sec. 1980-81, pres. 1983), Assn. Bus. Communication, Adminstrv. Mgmt. Soc. (faculty sponsor 1983—), Delta Pi Epsilon (research found. bd. 1982-84, sec. 1983). Home: 2603 Regency Park Dr Murfreesboro TN 37130 Office: Middle Tenn State U PO Box 152 Murfreesboro TN 37132

LEWIS, SYDNEY, retail company executive; b. Richmond, Va., Oct. 24, 1919; s. Julius Beryl and Dora (Lewis) L.; B.A., Washington and Lee U., 1940, postgrad. in law, 1940-42; postgrad. bus. adminstrn., Harvard, 1942-43, in law, George Washington U., 1946; m. Frances Aaronson, Sept. 3, 1942; children—Sydney Jr., Andrew Marc, Susan (Mrs. Dixon Butler). Admitted to Va. bar, 1942, D.C. bar, 1947; v.p. New Standard Pub. Co. Inc., Richmond, 1947-58, pres., 1958—, also dir.; founding pres., chmn. Best Products Co. Inc., Richmond, 1951—, also dir. Pres. Richmond Jewish Community Council, 1953—. Trustee, Washington and Lee U., Lexington, Va., Va. Union Univ., Richmond, Hirshorn Mus., Washington, 1976—, Inst. Contemporary Art, Phila., 1975—, Sch. Visual Arts, Boston U., 1976—, Va. Environ. Endowment Fund, Va. Found. for Humanities and Public Policy, Va. Mus. Fine Arts, 1980—. Hebrew Union Coll., Cin.; mem. bd. assos. U. Richmond. Recipient Disting. Virginian award, 1972; nat. honoree award Beta Gamma Sigma, 1976; ann. award Federated Arts Council of Richmond, 1976; Jackson Davis award for disting. service to higher edn. in Va., 1978; Thomas Jefferson award for public service, 1978. Club: Lakeside Country. Office: PO Box 26303 Richmond VA 23260

LEWIS, TANDY GIDDENS, JR., stockbroker, disc jockey; b. Shreveport, La., Apr. 6, 1958; s. Tandy Giddens and Emily Greene (Randolph) L. B.A., U. of South, 1980; postgrad. U. Tex., 1981. Account exec. E.F. Hutton & Co., Shreveport, 1981—; owner, operator Living for the Weekend, disc jockey service and booking agy., Shreveport, 1981—. Mem. Shreveport Leadership Council, Shreveport Sports Found. Mem. Broadmoor Jaycees (bd. dirs. 1982-85), Ducks Unltd. (Shreveport com.). Republican. Episcopalian. Clubs: Shreveport Country (jr. mem.); Century (Sewanee, Tenn.); E.F. Hutton Blue Chip. Avocations: tennis; running; music. Home: 4156 Maryland Ave Shreveport LA 71106 Office: EF Hutton & Co 415 Texas St Shreveport LA 71101

LEWIS, TOM, U.S. Congressman; b. Phila., Oct. 26, 1924. Ed., Palm Beach Jr. Coll., U. Fla. Corp. exec. Pratt and Whitney Aircraft, 1957-73; mayor/councilman North Palm Beach (Fla.), 1964-71; realtor Marion V. Lewis Inc. Realtors, 1972-82; mem. Fla. House of Reps., 1972-80, Fla. Senate, 1980-82; mem. 98th Congress from 12th Dist. Fla. Served with USAF, World War II, Korea. Address: Room 1313 Longworth House Office Bldg Washington DC 20515*

LEWIS, WALTER LAUGHN, lawyer, former air force officer; b. Charlottesville, Va., Aug. 22, 1924; s. Chauncey DePew and Clarice Undine (Laughon) L.; m. Karen Irvine, Sept. 22, 1956; children—Karen Hotchkiss, Robin Laughn. B.A., U. Va., 1947, J.D., 1950; postgrad. Acad. Internat. Law, The Hague, Netherlands, 1964, George Washington U. Law Sch., 1967-69, LL.M., 1969. Bar: Va. 1949, U.S. Ct. Mil. Appeals 1953, U.S. Supreme Ct. 1953, N.C. 1983. Commd. officer U.S. Air Force, 1950, advanced through grades to col.; with Judge Adv. Gen.'s dept. 1950-80; dep. dir. internat. law U.S. Air Forces in Europe, 1962-65; mem. Air Force Bd. Rev. (Ct. Mil. Rev.), 1965-67; staff judge adv. Air Force Missile Devel. Center, Holloman AFB, N.Mex., 1969-70; legal officer U.S. Embassy, Bangkok, Thailand, 1971-72; chief mil. justice div. Office of Judge Adv. Gen., Washington, 1972-77, dir. U.S. Air Force Judiciary, 1977-79; vice comdr. Air Force Legal Services Center, Washington, 1979-80, ret., 1980; chmn. rules adv. com. U.S. Ct. Mil. Appeals, Washington, 1981—; assoc. Everett & Hancock, Durham, N.C., 1983-84. Served with USAAF, 1943-45. Decorated Legion of Merit with oak leaf cluster, Air Force Commendation medal with 3 oak leaf clusters, Air Medal with four oak leaf clusters. Mem. ABA (standing com. on mil. law 1986, com. on criminal justice and mil. 1983-85), Va. Bar Assn., Fed. Bar Assn., Interam. Bar Assn., Am. Judicature Soc., Mil. Law Inst. (pres. 1986—), Delta Theta Phi. Presbyterian. Clubs: Nat. Lawyers, Mason, Shriners. Home: 2674 N Upshur St Arlington VA 22207

LEWIS, WILBUR CURTIS, surgeon; b. Okmulgee, Okla., Sept. 10, 1930; s. Charles D. and Eula Alice (Cole) L.; B.S., Okla. Baptist U., 1952; M.D., Okla. U., 1955; m. Gladys Sherman, Jan. 28, 1955; children—Karen Kay, Mark David, Leanne Gwynneth, Cristen Sue. Intern, Harris Hosp., Ft. Worth, 1955-56; resident in surgery VA Hosp., Dallas, 1956-57, Univ. Hosp., Oklahoma City, 1965-67; med. missionary So. Bapt. Conv., Costa Rica and Paraguay, 1959-70; practice medicine specializing in surgery, Oklahoma City and Midwest City, Okla., 1970—; ordained to ministry So. Bapt. Conv., 1953; pastor chs., Okla., Paraguay; leader med. disaster relief team, Honduras, 1975, Guatemala, 1976, Dominican Republic, 1977; mem. staff Midwest City, Bapt., Deaconess, Mercy, St. Anthony hosps., Oklahoma City (Okla.) Hosp. Served as capt. USAF, 1957-59. Diplomate Am. Bd. Family Practice. Fellow ACS, Internat. Coll. Surgeons, Am. Soc. Abdominal Surgeons; mem. AMA, Christian Med. Soc., Oklahoma City Surg. Soc., Am. Burn Assn., Internat. Soc. Burn Injuries, Oklahoma City Clin. Soc., Midwest City C. of C. (past pres.). Democrat. Home: 14501 N Western Ave Edmond OK 73034 Office: 3141 NW Expy Oklahoma City OK 73112

LEWIS, WILLIAM HEADLEY, JR., manufacturing company official; b. Washington, Sept. 29, 1934; s. William Headley and Lois Maude (Bradshaw) L.; B.S. in Metall. Engring., Va. Poly. Inst., 1956; postgrad. Grad. Sch. Bus. Adminstrn., Emory U., 1978; m. Carol Elizabeth Cheek, Apr. 22, 1967; children—Teresa Lynne, Bret Cameron, Charles William, Kevin Marcus. Research engr. Lockheed-Ga. Co., Marietta, 1956-57, sr. research engr., 1960-63, research group engr., 1963-72, research and devel. program mgr., 1972-79, mgr. engring. tech. services, 1979-83; dir. engring. Lockheed Getex Div., 1983-86; gen. mgr. inspection systems div. Lockheed Air Terminal, Inc., 1986—; chmn. Lockheed Corp. Task Force on NDE, 1980—; mem. com. on compressive fracture Nat. Acad. Sci., 1981-83; mem. com. to study advanced tech. in improving reliability and maintainability of future weapon systems Office Sec. of Def., 1982-83; dir. Applied Tech. Services, Inc., SafeTran Corp.; lectr. grad. studies and continuing edn. Union Coll., Schenectady, 1977-82. Served to 1st lt. USAF, 1957-60. Registered profl. engr., Calif. Fellow Am. Soc. for Non-destructive Testing (cert.; nat. dir. 1976-78, chmn. nat. tech. council 1977-78, chmn. aerospace com. 1972-74, nat. nominating com. 1984-85); mem. AIAA; Am. Soc. for Metals, Nat. Mgmt. Assn. Editor: Prevention of Structural Failures: The Role of Fracture Mechanics, Failure Analysis, and NDT, 1978; patentee detection apparatus for structural failure in aircraft. Home: 1205 W Nancy Creek Dr Atlanta GA 30319 Office: 1100 Circle 75 Pkwy Suite 945 Atlanta GA 30339

LEWIS-BRENT, LANA JANE, retail food company executive; b. Panama City, Fla., May 29, 1946; d. Luther Darius and Leona Mae (Jhonson) L.; m. Paul Richard Brent, Sept. 5, 1971; 1 child, Jensen Lewis. Student Stetson U., 1966-68. Payroll bookkeeper, data processing coordinator Sunshine-Jr. Stores, Inc., Panama City, Fla., 1968-71; dir. pub. relations, 1971-75, sr. v.p., 1975-82, pres., chief exec. officer, 1982—; dir. First Nat. Bank, Panama City, Retail Grocers Assn. of Fla. Founding mem. LWV, Bay County, Panama City, 1976—; bd. dirs. United Way of Bay County, 1981—; Bay Med. Ctr. Found., 1985—; mem. Bay Arts and Humanities Council, 1980—; mem. Gov.'s Pub. Facilities Financing Commn., 1984, Gov.'s Regional Interstate Banking Adv. Com., 1984; vice chmn. Seven and Eight to Build Fla., 1984. Named Woman Grocer of Yr., Nat. Grocers Assn., 1983. Mem. Food Mktg. Inst., Nat. Grocers Assn., Nat. Assn. Convenience Stores, Com. of 200, Fla. Women's Network, Fla. C. of C. (bd. dirs. 1983—). Democrat. Clubs: St. Andrews Yacht (Panama City), Bay Point Country. Office: Sunshine-Jr Stores Inc 17th St and June Ave Panama City FL 32401

LEYDEN, DENNIS ROGER, university dean; b. Jersey City, Aug. 21, 1933; s. Cornelius Joseph Leyden and Theresa (Napiorski) Leyden Boardingham; m. Anna Trifon, Dec. 4, 1954; children—Dennis Patrick, Julia Anne Leyden-Ingram. B.S., Clemson U., 1959; Ph.D., U. Va., 1976. Dir. Bur. Bus. Research, W.Va., U., Morgantown, 1972-82, prof. econs., 1981-82; dean Coll. Bus., Miss. State U., Mississippi State, 1982—; sr. ptnr. FEC Assocs., Tucson, 1971—; cons. Inst. for Tech. Devel., Jackson, Miss., 1985—. Author: The Differential Effects of Changing to a Value-Added Tax in an Open Economy, 1982. Contbr. articles to profl. jours. Bd. dirs. Miss. Econ. Council, 1984—; mem. Bus. and Tech. Task Force, Biloxi, Miss., 1984—; mem. adv. bd. Miss. State Ctr. for Econ. Edn., Jackson, 1984—. Nat. Def. fellow U. Va., 1959-62. Mem. Am. Econ. Assn., Phi Kappa Phi, Beta Gamma Sigma. Lodge: Rotary. Avocations: sailing; music; flying; carpentry. Home: 1106 Yorkshire St Starkville MS 39759 Office: College of Business Miss State U PO Drawer 5288 Mississippi State MS 39762

LEYSIEFFER, FREDERICK WALTER, statistics educator; b. Milw., Jan. 30, 1933; s. Walter and Charlotte Margaret (Martins) L.; m. Annelise Carlsen, Aug. 6, 1964; children—Kirsten, Suzanne, Beth. B.A., U. Wis., 1955, M.A., 1956; Ph.D., U. Mich., 1964. Asst. prof. stats. Fla. State U., Tallahassee, 1964-70, assoc. prof., 1970-82, prof., 1982—, chmn. dept. stats., 1981—. Served to capt. U.S. Army, 1961-62. Mem. Am. Statis. Assn., Inst. Math. Stats., Math. Assn. Am., Am. Math. Soc., AAAS. Home: 3720 Lifford Circle Tallahassee FL 32308 Office: Dept Stats Fla State U Tallahassee FL 32306

LIANG, JOSEPH JEN YIN, mathematics educator; b. China; came to U.S., 1960, naturalized, 1971; s. Tung-Tsai and Shu (Chou) L.; m. Diana Fang, June 12, 1965; children—Patrick, Michael. B.A. in Econs., Mat. Taiwan U., Taipei, 1958; M.A. in Math., U. Detroit, 1962; Ph.D. in Math., Ohio State U., 1969. Postdoctoral research fellow Calif. Inst. Tech., Pasadena, 1969-70, vis. assoc., 1975, 77; asst. prof. math. U. South Fla., Tampa, 1970-72, assoc. prof., 1972-77, prof., 1978—; vis. research prof. Nat. Tsing Hua U., Hsinchu, Taiwan, 1983; dir. summer Hollsborough County U. South Fla. Gifted Program, 1979—. Contbr. articles to profl. publs. Grantee NSF, 1977, 78, Tex. Instruments, 1982, Tandy Inc., 1981, Hillsborough County, 1979—. Mem. Math. Assn. Am., Am. Math. Soc., Sigma Xi. Office: U S Fla Dept Math Tampa FL 33620

LIARDON, CAROL MOORE, librarian; b. Beaulaville, N.C., Mar. 20, 1941; d. Lebasker and Gladoylene (Williams) Moore; m. Fredrick M. Liardon, Apr. 18, 1981; children—Kenneth Roberts, Priscilla Oralene. B.S., Oral Roberts U., 1972; M.L.S., Okla. U.-Norman, 1977. Nurse, Greenville Gen. Hosp., S.C., 1961-62; substitute tchr. Tulsa County Schs., 1972-73; tchr. sci. Bixby Pub. Schs., Okla., 1973-77; health scis. librarian Oral Roberts U., Tulsa, 1977—; cons. City of Faith Med. & Research Ctr. Library, 1981-82, Eastern State Hosp. Library, Vinita, Okla., 1982—; adv. com. Med. Books in China, Downey, Calif., 1982—. Vol. March of Dimes Telerama, Tulsa, 1980. Mem. Nat. Wildlife Fedn., Med. Library Assn., Okla. Health Scis. Library Assn., Nat. Assn. Women Deans, Adminstrs. and Counselors. Club: Civitan (bd. dirs. 1981-82). Office: Oral Roberts U 7777 S Lewis St Tulsa OK 74171

LIBBY, GARY RUSSELL, museum administrator, college educator art history; b. Boston, June 7, 1944; s. Charles W. and Sylvia (Phillips) L. A.A., U. Fla., 1966, B.A., 1968, M.A., 1970; M.A., Tulane U., 1972. Teaching asst. Tulane U., New Orleans, 1970-72; instr. Stetson U., Deland, Fla., 1972-73, asst. prof., 1973-77; dir. Mus. of Arts and Scis., Daytona Beach, Fla., 1977—; vis. prof. Stetson U., 1977—. Editor: Stokely Webster, 1985, Mus. Mag., 1977—; contbg. editor S.W. Art Mag., 1978-84; contbr. articles to profl. jours. Trustee Art League, Daytona Beach, 1979—, Atlantic Ctr. for Arts, New Smyrna Beach, Fla., 1982-83; v.p. Volusia County Arts Council (Fla.), 1983-84. NDEA fellow, 1970-72. Mem. Volusia County Arts Council, Fla. Art Mus. Dirs. Assn., Am. Soc. Appraisers. Avocations: writing; art criticism. Home: 419 Jessamine Blvd Daytona Beach FL 32018 Office: Mus of Arts and Sci 1040 Museumn Blvd Daytona Beach FL 32014

LICARIONE, BERNARD WILLIAM, juvenile corrections trainer; b. Houston, Dec. 31, 1950; s. William Junior and Kathleen (McElgun) L.; m. Margaret Mary Higgins, Jan. 25, 1974. B.A., U. St. Thomas, 1972; M.A., Loyola U., 1975. Cert. profl. counselor, Tex.; cert. juvenile probation officer, Tex.; cert. correctional trainer, Tex.; cert. child care adminstr., Tex. Tchr., St. Pius High Sch., Houston, 1973-76; program dir. Deep East Council of Govt., Nacogdoches, Tex., 1976-78; asst. dir. Parole, Tex. Youth Council, Austin, Tex., 1978-81; tng. coordinator S.W. Tex. State U., San Marcos, 1981-82; dir. tng. Tex. Juvenile Probation Commn., Austin, 1982—. Mem. Tex. Juvenile Detention Assn. (v.p. 1984—, bd. dirs. 1982-84), Tex. Corrections Assn. (regional chmn. 1984—), Am. Assn. Correctional Tng. Personnel (v.p. 1984—). Roman Catholic. Office: Tex Juvenile Probation Commn PO Box 13547 Austin TX 78711

LICH, GLEN ERNST, educator; b. Fredericksburg, Tex., Nov. 5, 1948; s. Ernst Perry and Thelma Olive (Woolfley) L.; student U. Vienna, (Austria), 1969-70; B.A., Southwestern U., 1971; M.A., U. Tex., 1976; M.A., S.W. Tex. State U., 1978; Ph.D., Tex. Christian U., 1984; grad. U.S. Army Command and Gen. Staff Coll., 1984; m. Lera Patrick Tyler, Sept. 5, 1970; children—James Ernst Lich-Tyler, Stephen Woolfley Lich-Tyler, Elizabeth Erin Lich-Tyler. Instr., S.W. Tex. State U., 1977-79, U. New Orleans, 1979-80; asst. prof. English and German, Schreiner Coll., 1980—, head program for accelerated coll. enrollment, 1980—; cons. in field. Lay reader St. Peter's Ch., Kerrville, Tex. Served to 1st lt. U.S. Army, 1972-75. NEH research grantee, 1978; guest W.Ger. govt. to study German-Am. cultural exchange, 1983. Mem. MLA, South Central MLA (sect. officer 1977—), Am. Studies Assn., Am. Folklore Assn., Am. Assn. Tchrs. German, Nat. Council Tchrs. English, Tex. Folklore Soc., Tex. State Hist. Assn., Western Assn. German Studies, Soc. German-Am. Studies (asso. editor yearbook 1981—), Pi Kappa Alpha. Author: The German Texans, 1981; editor: (with Dona B. Reeves) Retrospect and Retrieval: The German Element in Review; Essays on Cultural Preservation, 1978; German Culture in Texas: A Free Earth, 1980; The Cabin Book, 1985; Texas Country: The Changing Rural Scene, 1986; assoc. editor Jour. German-Am. Studies, 1977-80; contbr. articles to profl. publs. Home: Westland Pl 718 Jackson Rd Kerrville TX 78028 Office: Schreiner Coll Kerrville TX 78028

LICHT, IRA, museum director, art historian; b. N.Y.C., Dec. 24, 1928; s. Louis William and Rae (Price) L. B.S., Columbia U., 1964, M.A., 1967. Asst. prof. art history U. Rochester, 1970-74; curator Mus. Contemporary Art, Chgo., 1974-76; vis. lectr. art history U. Ill., Chgo., 1975; coordinator Art in Pub. Places and Visual Arts on the Performing Arts Nat. Endowment for Arts, Washington, 1976-78; dir. Lowe Art Mus. U. Miami, Coral Gables, 1978—; grad. fellow Columbia U., 1966. Author: catalog and exhbns. Bodyworks, 1974, Hans Bellmer, 1975, Robert Irwin, 1975; exhbns. Roy Lichtenstein: Recent Work, 1979, The Art of Opinion, 1979, Morris Hirshfield, 1980, Jade East and West, 1980, Fabrications, 1980, Roger Fenton's Crimean War Photographs, 1981, Pre-Columbian Ceramics from Eucador, 1981. Mem. Assn. Art Mus. Dirs., Am. Assn. Mus., Fla. Art Mus. Dirs. Assn. (v.p.), Cultural Execs. Council (v.p.). Home: 1 Grove Isle Dr Coconut Grove FL 33133 Office: Lowe Art Mus 1301 Stanford Dr Coral Gables FL 33146*

LICHTENBERG, JOSEPH MINOR, trade association executive; b. Cin., Oct. 28, 1941; s. Harry Louis and Lucille Charlotte (Minor) L.; m. Carolyn L. Helman, Aug. 21, 1964; children—Sara Minor, Elizabeth Helman. B.S. in Journalism, Ohio U., 1963; M.S. in Bus., 1966. Mgr. communications Whirlpool Corp., St. Joseph, Mich., 1966-69; corp. mgr. communications The Kroger Co., Cin., 1969-76, dir. pub. affairs, Atlanta, 1977-83; pres. Nat. Pasta Assn., Washington, 1983—. Vice chmn. Atlanta Pub. Broadcasting Assn., 1978-82; exec. bd. Leadership Atlanta, 1979-82. Served to 1st lt. U.S. Army, 1964-66. Recipient Harper award, Ga. Retail Assn., 1982; Hearst Writing award, W.R. Hearst Found., 1963. Mem. Pub. Relations Soc. Am., U.S. C. of C. (bd. regents Inst. Orgn. Mgmt. 1985—), Am. Soc. Assn. Execs., Greater Washington Soc. Assn. Execs. (chief exec. officer com.), Pa. Retail Assn. (dir. 1971-78), Ga. Retail Assn. (chmn. bd. 1981-82), Ohio U. Alumni Assn. (bd. dirs., 1985—). Republican. Clubs: University (Washington); Cincinnatus (Cin.). Home: 6512 Anna Marie Ct McLean VA 22102 Office: Nat Pasta Assn 1901 N Fort Myer Dr Arlington VA 22209

LICHTIGER, MONTE, physician, anesthesiologist, educator; b. Bronx, N.Y., July 12, 1939; s. Manuel and Sylvia Lichtiger; m. Barbara Zucker, Aug. 25, 1962; children—Shari Beth, Marcie Dawn, Adam Brett. A.B., Columbia U., 1961; M.D., Albert Einstein Coll. Medicine, 1965. Staff USAF Wilfred Hall Hosp., San Antonio, 1969-71; instr. U. Miami, Fla., 1969, asst. prof., 1971-74, clin. assoc. prof., 1974-83, clin. prof., 1983—; clin. asst. prof. U. Tex.-San Antonio, 1969-71. NIH fellow in anesthesiology U. Miami (Fla.), 1966-69. Served with USAF, 1969-71. Vice chmn. anesthesiology dept. Mt. Sinai Med. Ctr., Miami, Fla. Mem. Am. Soc. Anesthesiologists, Fla. Soc. Anesthesiologists, So. Med. Assn. Jewish. Author: Introduction to the Practice of Anesthesia, 1975, 2d edit., 1978; revs. editor Clin. Revs. in Anesthesiology, Current Revs. for Nurse Anesthetists. Office: Mt Sinai Medical Ctr 4300 Alton Rd Miami Beach FL 33140

LICK, DALE WESLEY, mathematician, college president; b. Marlette, Mich., Jan. 7, 1938; s. John R. and Florence M. (Baxter) L.; B.S. with honors, Mich. State U., 1958, M.S. in Math., 1959; Ph.D. in Math., U. Calif., Riverside, 1965; m. Marilyn Kay Foster, Sept. 15, 1956; children—Kitty, Diana, Ronald. Research asst. physics Mich. State U., East Lansing, summer, 1958, teaching asst. math., summer, 1959; instr., chmn. dept. math. Port Huron (Mich.) Jr. Coll., 1959-60; asst. to comptroller Mich. Bell Telephone Co., Detroit, 1961; instr. math. U. Redlands (Calif.), 1961-63; teaching asst. math. U. Calif., Riverside, 1964-65; asst. prof. math. U. Tenn., Knoxville, 1965-67, assoc. prof., 1968-69; assoc. prof., head dept. math. Drexel U., Phila., 1969-72; adj. assoc. prof. dept. pharmacology Med. Sch., Temple U., Phila., 1969-72; v.p. acad. affairs Russell Sage Coll., Troy, N.Y., 1972-74; prof. math. and computing scis. Old Dominion U., Norfolk, Va., 1974-76, also dean Sch. Scis. and Health Professions; prof. math. and computer sci. Ga. So. Coll., Statesboro, 1978—, pres., 1978—; textbook and manuscript reviewer for Appleton-Century Crofts, Bogden and Quigley, Macmillan and Prentice-Hall, 1966—; cons. Va. Health Planning and Resources Devel. Agy., 1976-78, Norfolk State U., Va., 1977, U. Central Fla., 1977; proposal reviewer divs. higher edn. in sci. and public understanding of sci. NSF, 1972—; appeared in interviews, discussions and spl. topic presentations various radio and TV programs, 1974—; mem. faculty 7 day tng. programs series in health adminstrn., 1977-79; guest lectr. various conf. and symposia on health care and interinstnl. cooperation, 1975—. Mem. community adv. bd. Willingway Hosp., Statesboro, 1978—; bd. dirs. Statesboro/Coll. Symphony, 1978—, Norfolk Shipbldg. Sch., 1977-78, Health Care Centers Am., Virginia Beach, Va., 1975-78, Eastern Va. Health Systems Agy., 1976-78; bd. dirs. Assembly Against Hunger and Malnutrition, 1977-78, pres., 1977-78. Mem. Am. Math. Soc., Math. Assn. Am. (joint com. on meetings 1974-76), Am. Assn. Univ. Adminstrs. (nominating com. 1975), Am. Soc. Allied Health Professions, AAUP, Am. Assn. Higher Edn., AAAS, Sigma Xi, Phi Kappa Phi, Pi Mu Epsilon. Mem. Reorganized Latter-day Saints Ch. Lodge: Rotary. Author: Fundamentals of Algebra, 1970; contbr. articles on math. to sci. jours., articles on edn. and health care to profl. publs. Office: Georgia Southern College Statesboro GA 30460

LIDDELL, BOBBY (MCCOY), JR., minister; b. Birmingham, Ala., Sept. 15, 1952; s. Bobby M. and Stella Earcell (Gant) L.; m. Cathy Joan Loe, Aug. 18, 1972; children—Anthony Allen, Nathan Gant, Keri Jayne. Cert. Memphis Sch. Preaching, 1979; B.A., Ala. Christian Sch. Religion, 1984, postgrad., 1984-86. Ordained to ministry Ch. of Christ, 1979. Electrician, contractor Little, Moore and Walter Constrn., Birmingham, 1972-77; minister Central Ch. of Christ, Winfield, Ala., 1979-83, Parrish Ch. of Christ, Ala., 1983—; instr. Sch. of World Evangelism, Guin, Ala., 1980; dir. Campaign for Christ, Winfield, Ala., 1981, Parrish, 1984; speaker Daily Radio Broadcast, Parrish, 1984—. Assoc. editor: (monthly publ.) The Christian Sentinel, 1979-83. Contbr. articles to religious publs. Active Walker County and Parrish PTAs; bd. dirs. Indian Creek Youth Camp. Mem. Memphis Sch. Preaching Alumni Assn., Ala. Christian Sch. Religion Alumni Assn. (v.p.). Republican. Avocations: Woodworking; volunteer work; photography. Home: Box 118 White St Parrish AL 35580 Office: Parrish Church of Christ White St Parrish AL 35580

LIDER, MARGARET MAY, communications company executive; b. Paterson, N.J., Sept. 24, 1943; d. Thomas Joseph and Lillian Mary (Strassburg) May; m. Militon S. Lider, Sept. 6, 1979. B.Mus., Boston U., 1965, M.Mus., 1966; postgrad. Harvard U., 1972-73; grad. Leadership Palm Beach County, 1985. Mgr., Boston U. Youth Symphony Orch., 1967-69; mgr. pub. relations Handel & Haydn Soc., Boston, 1969-72; pres., founder Cultural Communications Assocs., Inc., Boca Raton, Fla., 1973—; pres. Premiere TV Prodns., Inc., Boca Raton; exec. dir. Arts Boston, 1978; cultural editor Boca Raton Shiny Sheet, 1979; radio producer Arts News, Sta. WXEL-FM, West Palm Beach, Fla., 1982, co-producer, co-host Centerstage weekly program Sta. WXEL-TV, 1983—; teaching assoc. music Boston U., 1967-69; cons. Mass. Council Arts and Humanities, 1973-79. Bd. dirs., arts info. chmn. Palm Beach County Council Arts, 1983; fin. mem. bd. dirs. Palm Beach County Citizen for the Arts; bd. mem. Harvard Pierian Found.; sec. bd. Friends of Boca Raton Pops; pub. relations bd. Caldwell Playhouse; mem. bd. Boca Raton Mayor's Com. Community Affairs, 1984—; bd. dirs. Philharm. Orch. of Fla., Vol. Ctr. of Palm Beach County; adv. bd. Singing Pines Mus. Named Woman of Yr., Brandeis U. Nat. Women's Com., 1983; recipient Sword of Honor, Sigma Alpha Iota, 1965; Key to City, Boca Raton City Council, 1983. Mem. Pub. Relations Soc. Am., Women in Communications, Nat. Soc. Arts and Letters, Am. Symphony Orch. League, Music Guild Boca Raton, NOW, LWV, Women in Radio and TV Broadcasting, Fla. Free Lance Writers Assn., Pi Kappa Lambda, Sigma Alpha Iota. Democrat. Methodist. Author: Getting Into Ink and On the Air, 1973: Backstage at the White House, 1976. Columnist Palm Beach Life Mag., 1984—; media columnist Boca Raton Life, 1984—. Home: 600 S Ocean Blvd Apt 1508 Boca Raton FL 33432 Office: PO Box 1296 Boca Raton FL 33432

LIEBER, BETTE RAE, hospital public relations executive; b. Houston, Dec. 24, 1927; d. Henry C. and Leona (Lindsey) Hassler; m. Robert Louis Lieber, Nov. 1, 1943; children—Robert Milton, Betty Lynn, John Lindsey, Carole Anne. Student U. Houston, 1964-67. Writer on space program ABC-TV, N.Y.C., 1964-72; editorial asst., then assoc. editor Offshore mag., 1968-69; asst. to editor Houston Post, 1969-70; editor Apt. Directory and Data Ctr., 1970-71; editor Houston Chronicle, 1972-75; dept. head Twelve Oaks Hosp., Houston, 1976-81; dir. pub. relations/mktg. Meml. City Med. Ctr., Houston, 1981-85; owner Lieber Cos., advt./pub. relations. Area chmn. Cancer Crusade; pres. Sam Houston Parents Assn., 1978-80. Named Outstanding Woman, YWCA, 1981, Outstanding Bus. Women in Houston, Fedn. Houston Profl. Women, 1984. Mem. Pub. Relations Soc. Am., Women in Communications, Tex. Pub. Relations Assn., Tex. Hosp. Soc. for Hosp. Pub. Relations, Assn. for Vol. Adminstrn., Spring Branch/Meml. C. of C. Club: Houston Press. Home: 3103 Virginia St Houston TX 77098 Office: 3103 Virginia Houston TX 77098

LIEBERMAN, MELVYN, physiologist, educator; b. Bklyn., Feb. 4, 1938; B.A. in Zoology, Cornell U., 1959; Ph.D. in Physiology, SUNY Downstate Med. Center, Bklyn., 1964; married; 2 children. Lectr., lab. instr. dept. biology Queens Coll., City U. N.Y., 1960, 63-64; teaching asst. dept. physiology SUNY Downstate Med. Center, 1960-64; postdoctoral fellow dept. embryology Carnegie Inst. Washington, Balt., 1964-65, Instituto de Biofisica, U. Federal do Rio de Janeiro (Brazil), 1965-67; postdoctoral fellow div. biomed. engring. Duke, 1967, research asso. dept. physiology and pharmacology, 1967-68, asst. prof. Duke U. Med. Center, 1968-73, asso. prof., 1973-78, prof., 1978—, dir. grad. studies, 1977-80; coordinator U.S.-Japan Coop. Sci. Program Conf., Tokyo, 1974, U.S.-Brazil Coop. Sci. Program Conf., Rio de Janeiro, 1980, Gordon Conf.-Muscle, 1979; vis. investigator Jan Swammerdam Inst., U. Amsterdam (Netherlands), 1975; cons. Macy Found., 1970, NIH, 1972-83, physiology study sect., 1980-84, NSF, 1974-75, 78, others; mem. research rev. com. N.Y. Heart Assn., 1980—, participant numerous sci. symposia; established investigator Am. Heart Assn., 1971-76. Mem. AAAS, Am. Heart Assn. (basic sci. council 1963, del. to assembly 1982), Am. Physiol. Soc. (Porter devel. com. 1974-77, ednl. materials rev. bd. 1975—, councillor cell physiol. sect. 1984—), Biophys. Soc., Cardiac Muscle Soc., Internat. Soc. for Heart Research, N.C. Heart Assn. (research rev. subcom. 1972-75, chmn. 1975-76, mem. research com. 1983-84), Soc. Gen. Physiologists (sec. 1969-71, rep. NRC 1971-74, pres. 1981-82), Tissue Culture Assn. Co-editor: Developmental and Physiological Correlates of Cardiac Muscle, 1975; Excitable Cells in Tissue Culture, 1981; Normal and Abnormal Conduction of the Heart, 1982; Electrogenic Transport: Fundamental Principles and Physiological Implications, 1984; assoc. editor Am. Jour. Physiology/Cell, 1981—; mem. editorial adv. bd. Experientia, 1982—; editorial cons. Jour. Applied Physiology, Circulation Research, Jour. Gen. Physiology, Devel. Biology, Jour. Molecular Cell Cardiology, Jour. Pharm. Exptl. Therapeutics, Life Scis., Am. Jour. Physiology, Circulation, Science, Jour. Cell Biology, Pflugers Archiv, Fedn. Proc., Cell Motility, Molecular Pharm.; contbr. numerous articles to profl. jours. Home: 1110 Woodburn Rd Durham NC 27705

LIEBMANN, SEYMOUR W., construction company executive; b. N.Y.C., Nov 1, 1928; s. Isidor W. and Etta (Waltzer) L.; m. Hinda Adam, Sept. 20, 1959; children—Peter Adam, David W. B.S. in Mech. Engring., Clarkson U., (formerly Clarkson Coll. Tech.), 1948; grad. Indsl. Coll. Armed Forces, 1963, Command and Gen. Staff Coll., 1966, Army War Coll., 1971. Registered profl. engr., N.Y., Mass., Ga. Area engr. constrn. div. E.I. DuPont de Nemours & Co., Inc., 1952-54; constrn. planner Lummus Co., 1954-56; prin. mech. engr. Perini Corp., 1956-62; v.p. Boston Based Contractors, 1962-66; v.p. A.R. Abrams, Inc., Atlanta, 1967-74, pres., 1974-78, also dir.; founder Liebmann Assocs., Inc., constrn. cons., Atlanta, 1979—; mem. nat. adv. bd. Am. Security Council. Mem. Author: Military Engineer Field Notes, 1953; Prestressing Miter Gate Diagonals, 1960. Contbr. articles to publs. USO Council, Atlanta, 1968—, v.p., 1978, mem. exec. com., 1975-79; mem. Nat. UN Day Com., 1975; judge sci. fairs Atlanta City Pub. Schs., 1979-86; asst. scoutmaster troop 298 Atlanta area council Boy Scouts Am., 1980-86, explorer adviser, 1982, mem. Order of Arrow, 1983, unit commr. North Atlanta dist. Atlanta Area council, 1985—, mem. faculty Coll. Commrs., 1985, asst. trek advisor 1st Order of Arrow Philmont Trek, 1985; mem. alumni adv. com. Clarkson Coll. Tech., 1981—; vice chmn., mem. exec. bd., zoning chmn. Neighborhood Planning Unit A, City of Atlanta, 1982—. Served to 1st lt. C.E., AUS, 1948-52; col. Res. ret. Recipient U.S. Army Res. medal, 1975; decorated Legion of Merit, Meritorious Service medal; elected to Old Guard of Gate City Guard, Atlanta, 1979; recipient cert. of achievement Dept. Army, 1978; USO nat. award of recognition, 1979. Fellow Soc. Am. Mil. Engrs. (dir., program chmn. Atlanta post 1980-81, v.p. 1982, pres. 1983, bd. dirs. 1986-87, nat. award of merit 1983); mem. Soc. First U.S. Inf., Res. Officers Assn. U.S., Nat., Ga. socs. profl. engrs., Assn. U.S. Army, Def. Preparedness Assn., Am. Arbitration Assn. (panel constrn. arbitrators 1979—, constrn. adv. com. 1984), Mil. Order World Wars, Clarkson Coll. Alumni Assn. (bd. govs. 1983—, Golden Knight award for disting. service 1983), U.S. Army War Coll. Alumni Assn. (life mem.), U.S. Army War Coll. Found. (life mem.), Atlanta C. of C. Republican. Jewish. Clubs: Engrs. of Boston; Masons (32 deg.), Shriners, Elks; Civitan (Atlanta); Ft. McPherson Officers; Ga. Appalachian Trail. Home: 3260 Rilman Dr NW Atlanta GA 30327 Office: 6520 Powers Ferry Rd Suite 200 Atlanta GA 30339

LIEBOWITZ, ERROL EMANUEL, psychologist; b. N.Y.C., Mar. 25, 1954; s. Solomon and Ernestine (Lowy) L.; m. Robyn Lee Friedman, June 22, 1980. B.A., CCNY, 1975; Ph.D., Ohio U., 1982. Lic. clin. psychologist, Va. Postdoctoral fellow U. Va. Med. Ctr., Charlottesville, 1981-82; psychologist Multimodal Therapy Inst., Virginia Beach, Va., 1982-85; psychologist Tidewater Psychotherapy Services, Virginia Beach, 1985—; research dir. Athens Mental Health Ctr., Ohio, 1973-75. Editor chess mag. Knight Moves, 1983— (4 nat. awards). Mem. Am. Psychol. Assn., Am. Diabetes Assn. (bd. dirs. Tidewater chpt. 1983), Phi Kappa Phi. Avocations: chess (Ohio state champion 1979, Va. state champion 1981); guitar. Office: Tidewater Psychotherapy Services 256-G N Witchduck Rd Virginia Beach VA 23462

LIEBTAG, BENFORD GUSTAV (BEN), III, cons. engr.; b. Pitts., Sept. 20, 1941; s. Benford Gustav and Alice Mildred (Hunt) L.; B.S. in Elec. Engring., U. Pitts., 1964; m. Cynthia Taylor Creighton, Aug. 22, 1964; children—Cindy, Ben. Sr. heating and air-conditioning engr. Duquesne Light Co., Pitts., 1964-79; dir. energy mgmt. Van Wagenen and Searcy, Inc., Jacksonville, Fla., 1979-80, v.p., 1980-81; pres. Liebtag, Robinson, and Wingfield, Inc., Jacksonville, 1981—. Mem. ASHRAE (award of merit, disting. service award), Assn. Energy Engrs. Methodist. Lodges: Masons, Kiwanis. Home: 4134 Old Mill Cove Trail E Jacksonville FL 32211 Office: 1840 Southside Blvd Bldg 3 Suite A Jacksonville FL 32216

LIEDTKE, JOHN HUGH, petroleum company executive; b. Tulsa, Feb. 10, 1922; B.A., Amherst Coll., 1942; postgrad. Harvard Grad. Sch., Bus. Adminstrn., 1943; LL.B., U. Tex., 1947; m. Betty Lyn; children—Karen, Kristin, John Hugh, Blake, Kathryn. Chmn., chief exec. officer Pennzoil Co., Houston. Trustee Houston United Fund, Kinkaid Sch., Houston, Rice U., Baylor Coll. Medicine, U.S. Naval Acad. Found., Lawrence Acad.; council overseers Jesse H. Jones Grad. Sch. Adminstrn. Rice U. Mem. Tex. Mid-Continent Oil and Gas Assn. (dir.), Am. Petroleum Inst. (dir.), Nat. Petroleum Council (dir.), Houston C. of C. (dir.), Beta Theta Pi, Phi Alpha Delta. Clubs: Houston Country, Ramada, Pennhills, Bradford (Pa.) Country; Rolling Rock (Ligonier, Pa.), Racquet (Midland), Calgary (Alta., Can.) Petroleum. Office: PO Box 2967 Houston TX 77252

LIENHARD, JOHN HENRY, mechanical engineering educator; b. St. Paul, Aug. 17, 1930; s. John Henry and Catherine Edith Lienhard; m. Carol Ann Bratton, June 20, 1959; children—John Henry, Andrew Joseph. A.S., Multnomah Jr. Coll., 1949; B.S., Oreg. State Coll., 1951; M.S. in M.E., U. Wash.-Seattle, 1953; Ph.D. in Mech. Engring., U. Calif.-Berkeley, 1961. Assoc. prof. mech. engring. Wash. State U., Pullman, 1961-67; prof. mech. engring. dept. U. Ky., Lexington, 1967-80; Clyde chair prof. U. Utah, Salt Lake City, summer 1981; prof. mech. engring. dept. U. Houston, 1980—. Fellow ASME (heat transfer meml. award, Charles Russ Richards award). Episcopalian. Author 2 textbooks, also numerous articles in profl. jours. Home: 3719 Durhill St Houston TX 77025 Office: Mech Engring Dept U Houston Houston TX 77004

LIGHT, ALFRED ROBERT, lawyer, political scientist; b. Atlanta, Dec. 14, 1949; s. Alfred M. Jr. and Margaret Francis (Asbury) L.; m. Mollie Sue Hall, May 28, 1977; children—Joseph Robert, Gregory Andrew. Student Ga. Inst. Tech., 1967-69; B.A. with highest honors, Johns Hopkins U., 1971; Ph.D., U. N.C., 1976; J.D. cum laude, Harvard U., 1981. Bar: D.C. 1981, Va. 1982. Tax clk. IRS, 1967; lab. technician Custom Farm Services Soils Testing Lab., 1968; warehouse asst. State of Ga. Mines, Mining and Geology, 1970; clk.-typist systems mgmt. div., def. contract adminstrv. services region Def. Supply Agy., Atlanta, 1971, research and teaching asst. dept. polit. sci. U. N.C., Chapel Hill, 1971-74; research asst. Inst. Research in Social Sci., 1975-77; program analyst Office of Sec. Def., 1974; asst. prof. polit. sci., research scientist Ctr. Energy Research, Tex. Tech U., Lubbock, 1977-78; research asst. grad. sch. edn., Harvard U., 1978-79; assoc. Butler, Binion, Rice, Cook & Knapp, Houston, summer 1980, Bracewell & Patterson, Washington, summer 1980, Hunton & Williams, Richmond, Va., 1981—. Active Cystic Fibrosis Found., Neighborhood Crime Watch, First Bapt. Ch. Served to capt. USAR, 1971-85. Grantee NSF, Inst. Evaluation Research, U. Mass., Ctr. Energy Research, Tex. Tech U.; recipient William Anderson award Am. Polit. Sci. Assn.; Julius Turner award Johns Hopkins U. Mem. ABA, Am. Soc. Pub. Adminstrn., Am. Polit. Sci. Assn., Va. State Bar Assn., Richmond Bar Assn., So. Polit. Sci. Assn., Phi Beta Kappa, Phi Eta Sigma, Pi Sigma Alpha. Democrat. Baptist. Contbr. articles to profl. jours. Address: 2308 Park Ave Richmond VA 23220 Office: Hunton & Williams PO Box 1535 707 E Main St Richmond VA 23212

LIGHT, ARTHUR HEATH, bishop; s. Alexander Heath and Mary Watkins (Nelson) L.; B.A., Hampden-Sydney Coll., 1951; M.Div., Va. Theol. Sem., 1954, D.Div., 1970; D.Div., St. Paul's Coll., 1979; m. Sarah Ann Jones, June 12, 1954; children—William Alexander, Philip Nelson, John Page, Sarah Heath. Ordained to ministry as priest Episcopal Ch., 1955; rector West Mecklenburg Cure, Boydton, Va., 1954-58, Christ Ch., Elizabeth City, N.C., 1958-63, St. Marys Ch., Kinston, N.C., 1963-67, Christ and St. Luke's Ch., Norfolk, Va., 1967-79; bishop Diocese of Southwestern Va., Roanoke, 1979—. Bd. dirs. United Communities Fund, 1969-79, Norfolk Seamen's Friends Soc., 1969-79, Tidewater Assembly on Family Life, 1970-79, Friends of Juvenile Ct., 1975-79, Va. Inst. Pastoral Care, 1971-72; bd. dirs., mem. exec. com. Va. Council Chs., 1979—; bd. dirs. Roanoke Valley Council of Community Services, 1980-83, Virginians Organized for Informed Community Effort (VOICE), 1981—; bd. dirs. Appalachian People's Service Orgn., 1981—, pres., 1981-85. mem. bio-med. ethics com. Eastern Va. Med. Sch., 1973-79; trustee Va. Episcopal Sch., Lynchburg, Episcopal High Sch., Alexandria, Va. Theol. Sem., Alexandria, Boys' Home, Covington, Stuart Hall Sch., Staunton, St. Paul's Coll., Lawrenceville, 1979—; pres. Province III, Episcopal Ch., 1984—; mem. Presiding Bishop's Council of Advice, 1985—. Democrat. Office: 1000 1st St SW Roanoke VA 24009

LIGHTCAP, TRACY LEE RAMSAY, researcher, statistician; b. Atlanta, Mar. 31, 1946; s. Leonard Lowe and Myrtle (Seckinger) L.; m. Ann Margaret Pointer, Mar. 20, 1976; 1 child, Allen Inman Pointer. B.A., U. of South, 1969; M.A., U. S.C., 1974; Ph.D., Emory U., 1980. Instr., LaGrange Coll., Ga., 1977-78, Emory U., Oxford, Ga., 1978-80; research assoc. Adminstrv. Office of Cts., Jud. Council Ga., Atlanta, 1981—, cons., 1980-81. Contbr. articles to profl. jours. Active Morningside-Lenox Park Neighborhood Assn., Atlanta, 1978—. Mem. Am. Polit. Sci. Assn., Pi Sigma Alpha (pres. chpt. 1972-74). Democrat. Episcopalian. Clubs: Cherokee Town and Country, Brookwood Hills Country. Avocations: microcomputer programming; reading; weight training. Office: Adminstrv Office of Cts Suite 550 224 Washington St Atlanta GA 30334

LIGHTY, ROBIN GREG, geology educator; b. Harrisburg, Pa., Nov. 13, 1951; s. Raymond Greek and Dorothy Louise (Pinkerton) L.; m. Kathe Ann Wege, Apr. 30, 1977. B.S. with honors, Fla. Atlantic U., 1975; M.S. in Geology, Duke U., 1977; Ph.D., U. N.C., 1986. Field geologist Chevron Resources Co., Denver, 1977; geol. cons. Cities Service Co., Belize and Bahamas, 1980; research geologist, Tulsa, 1980-83; asst. prof. geology Tex. A&M U., College Station, 1983—; dir. Ctr. for Tropical Marine Research. Author Internat. Reef Symposium Procs., 1977, 83. Contbr. articles to profl. jours. Vis. research fellow Smithsonian Instn., 1977. Mem. Geol. Soc. Am., Am. Assn. Petroleum Geologists, Soc. Econ. Paleontologists and Mineralogists, Internat. Assn. Sedimentologists, Internat. Soc. Reef Studies, Am. Geophys. Union, Sigma Xi. Office: Ctr Tropical Marine Research Box E College Station TX 77841

LIGON, HELEN HAILEY, educator; b. Lott, Tex., Feb. 7, 1921; d. Rolla Will and Bobbye A. (Ruble) Hailey; B.S., Tex. Women's U., Denton, 1942, M.A., 1945; Ph.D., Tex. A & M U., 1976; m. William Grady Ligon, Jr., July 26, 1941; 1 son, William Grady III. Instr., Tex. Women's U., 1942-45; secondary tchr. Lott Pub. Schs., 1947-52, Marlin (Tex.) Pub. Schs., 1952-55; asst. to contracting officer Phillips Petroleum Co., McGregor, Tex., 1955-56; sec. to factory mgr. Gen. Tire Co., Waco, Tex., 1956-58; instr. Hankamer Sch. Bus., Baylor U., Waco, 1958-60, asst. prof., 1960-62, asso. prof., 1962-77, prof. statistics and mgmt. info. systems, 1977—, dir. Casey Computer Center, 1962—. Named Most Popular Bus. Prof., Baylor U., 1962, 67, 78, Outstanding Baylor Faculty Woman, 1967, Outstanding Faculty Mem., 1979. Mem. Data Processing Mgmt. Assn., Assn. Computing Machinery, Soc. Mgmt. Info. Systems, Am. Statis. Assn., Beta Gamma Sigma, Delta Kappa Gamma (local pres. 1967-68, mem. state com. for research 1977-78), Sigma Iota Epsilon. Democrat. Presbyterian. Office: Box 6278 Waco TX 76706

LIHANI, JOHN, Spanish literature and linguistics educator; b. Hnusta, Czecho-Slovakia, Mar. 24, 1927; came to U.S., 1937, naturalized, 1944; s. John and Susanna (Jablonska) L.; m. Emily G. Kolesar, Sept. 9, 1950; children—J. Brian, Robert P., David L. B.S., Case-Western Res. U., 1948; M.A., Ohio State U., 1950; Ph.D., U. Tex., 1954. Teaching fellow Tulane U., New Orleans, 1950-51; teaching fellow, then instr. U. Tex., Austin, 1951-54; instr., then asst. prof. Yale U., New Haven, 1954-62; Fulbright prof. Instituto Caro y Cuervo, Bogota, Colombia, 1965-66; assoc. prof. U. Pitts., 1962-69; prof. Spanish lit. and linguistics U. Ky., Lexington, 1969—. Author: El lenguaje de Lucas Fernandez, 1973; Lucas Fernandez, 1973; Bartolome de Torres Naharro, 1979. Founding editor La Coronica Jour., 1972; co-editor Bull. of Comediantes Jour., 1973—. Grantee Internat. Research Exchanges Bd., 1974; Morse fellow Yale U., 1960-61. Mem. MLA (editor, assoc. editor div. publs.), Am. Assn. Tchrs. Spanish Portuguese, Linguistic Soc. Am., Phi Beta Kappa. Club: Slovak Garden (Winter Park, Fla.). Avocations: writer; lecturer; traveler; multilingual knowledge; languages. Home: 825 Cahaba Rd Lexington KY 40502 Office: Dept Spanish Italian U Ky Lexington KY 40506

LIKES, DAVID HENRY, educator, retired air force officer; b. N.Y.C., Aug. 4, 1914; s. Slyvan Henry and Mamie (Leopold) L.; B.A., Johns Hopkins, 1936; postgrad. Harvard U., 1938-39; M.A. (Univ. fellow), Georgetown U., 1948, Ph.D., 1949; m. Grace Ann McWilliams, Feb. 28, 1948 (dec. Dec. 1971); children—David McWilliams, Lawrence Andrew; m. 2d, Adeline Lee Stuckey, July 15, 1972; stepchildren—Elizabeth Stuckey Bright, Lauren Stuckey Glass. Commd. 2d lt. USAF, 1941, advanced through grades to col., 1945; mem. U.S. Mil. North African Mission, Cairo, 1942; assigned Desert Air task force, component USAF Middle East 9th Air Force, USAF Middle East, Egypt, 1942-43; mem. Overlord planning staff, London, Eng., 1943-44; assigned 1st Airborne Army, 1944-45; mem. mil. del. Potsdam (E. Ger.) Conf., 1945; assigned War Plan div. USAF, 1948-51; mem. standing group NATO, Washington, 1951-52, U.S. Naval War Coll., 1952-53; mem. U.S. Mission to NATO, Paris, 1953-56; mil. air staff planner War Plans Div. Air Staff, Washington, 1956-58; dep. dir. NSC Affairs, Office Sec. Def., 1958-59; mem. faculty Nat. War Coll., 1959-61; mem. Aero. Space Studies Inst., Maxwell AFB, Ala., 1961-63; ret., 1963; prof., chmn. dept. internat. studies Southwestern at Memphis, 1963—; cons. Inst. Internat. Studies U. S.C., Islamic and Arabian Devel. Studies Duke U., Durham, N.C.; Ford Found. postdoctoral research fellow Duke U., 1967-68; research fellow Center Middle Eastern Studies, Harvard U., 1975-76; guest lectr. Am. Studies Conf., Tamkang, Taipei, Taiwan, 1980, Inst. Study U.S.A. and Can., Acad. Scis. USSR, 1981; lectr. Inst. Fgn. Policy and Nat. Security, Seoul, 1980. Bd. govs. Internat. Group, English Speaking Union. Mem. Polit. Sci. Assn., Assn. Asian Studies, Middle East Studies Assn., Inst. Naval Procs., Am. Acad. Polit. Sci., Internat. Studies Assn., Air Force Assn., Ret. Officers Assn., UN Assn. (bd. dirs. Chpt. 1980-83), Nat. Trust Historic Preservation, English Speaking Union, Gold Key Soc., Omicron Delta Kappa, Pi Sigma Alpha. Clubs: Willowbrook Country (Tyler, Tex.); Harvard (Dallas). Lodge: Rotary. Author: Guerilla Warfare World War II, 1963; Organization of Defense Department, 1963. Contbr. articles to profl. jours.

LILES, DANIEL ALAN, state official; b. Asheville, N.C., Feb. 8, 1949; s. James Carlton and Anna Laura (McCurry) L.; m. Brenda Charlene Honeycutt, Sept. 15, 1979; 1 dau., Amy Elizabeth. Student, U. N.C.-Asheville, 1970-71, B.S., 1978. Accredited personnel specialist. Proof dept. supr. Wachovia Bank & Trust Co., Asheville, 1971-74; asst. v.p., br. mgr. Pinehurst Mortgage & Loan Co., Asheville, 1974-75; personnel specialist U.S. Dept. Commerce, Winston-Salem, N.C., 1978-80; disabled vets. outreach specialist N.C. Employment Security Commn., Winston-Salem, 1980—. Mem. Winston-Salem's Mayoral Com. for Handicapped, 1980—. Served with U.S. Army, 1967-70. Decorated Air medal, Purple Heart. Mem. Am. Soc. Personnel Adminstrs., Internat. Assn. Personnel in Employment Service, N.C. State Employees Assn., Exptl. Aircraft Assn., Aircraft Owners and Pilots Assn., Am. Legion, VFW, DAV (Humanitarian Service award 1980), Nat. Wheelchair Aviators Assn. (bd. dirs. 1983—), Triad Viet-Nam Vets. Assn. (bd. dirs. 1980—). Democrat. Episcopalian. Office: NC Employment Security Commn 630 W 6th St Winston-Salem NC 27101

LILES, FRANCES ROSE, computer project executive; b. Richmond, Va., Jan. 4, 1943; d. Milford Kenyon and Helen Frances (Boston) L.; student Coll. William and Mary, 1961-63; B.A., U. Toledo, 1965; postgrad. Va. Poly. Inst., Am. Grad. U. Adminstr., AID, Dept. of State, Washington, 1965-67; research analyst Def. Intelligence Agy., Lisbon, Portugal, Madrid and Washington, 1968-75; mgr. Spanish programs Jet Engine Group, Gen. Elec. Co., Madrid, 1976; proposal mgr. corp. mktg. Atlantic Research Corp., Alexandria, Va., 1977-82; sr. mem. adv. staff Computer Scis. Corp., Falls Church, Va., 1982—. Chmn. youth com. Am. Embassy, Lisbon, 1968-70. Mem. Nat. Fedn. Bus. and Profl. Women (chmn.), Women in Info. Processing, Nat. Assn. Female Execs., Data Processing Mgmt. Assn., Internat. Platform Assn., NOW, Mu Phi Epsilon, Sigma Delta Pi, Pi Beta Phi. Episcopalian. Home: 4638 N 23d St Arlington VA 22207 Office: 6565 Arlington Blvd Falls Church VA 22046

LILLARD, GERALD PATRIC, geophysicist; b. Fort Worth, July 12, 1950; s. George Pierce Jr. and Evora Jean (Griffin) L.; m. Janice Elaine Gordy, Mar. 4, 1973; children—Christina Dawn, Carrie Suzanne. B.S., U. Tex.-Arlington, 1972. Exploration geophysicist Mobil Oil Corp., Dallas, 1973-77; dist. geophysicist Tex. Oil & Gas Co., Oklahoma City, 1977-80; div. geophysicist Fla. Exploration Co., Jackson, Miss., 1980-83; dist. geophysicist Moore McCormack Energy Co., Houston, 1983—. Genealogic distinction: Lollards, Huguenots Honore de Balzac, George Washington, James Monroe, Robert E. Lee, Will Rogers, others. Mem. Am. Assn. Petroleum Geologists, Soc. Exploration Geophysicists, Geophys. Soc. Houston, Tex. Soc. Sons Am. Revolution. Democrat. Baptist. Home: 1315 Deerfield Rd Richmond TX 77469 Office: Moore McCormack Energy Inc 2950 N Loop West Suite 1045 Houston TX 77092

LILLELEHT, LEMBIT UNO, educator; b. Parnu, Estonia, Mar. 9, 1930; came to U.S., 1949, naturalized 1954; s. Paul August and Julie (Jensen) L.; m. Karen Van Doren, Aug. 20, 1960; children—Erica, Mark Lembit. B.Ch.E. with honors and distinction, U. Del., 1953; M.S.E., Princeton U., 1955; Ph.D., U. Ill., 1962. Chem. engr. E.I. duPont de Nemours & Co., Inc., Wilmington, Del., 1953-57; asst. prof. U. Alta. (Can.), Edmonton, 1960-62, assoc. prof., 1962-66; process engr. Canadian Chem. Co., Edmonton, 1962; vis. assoc. prof. Solar Energy Research Inst., Golden, Colo., 1978-79; asso. prof. chem. engring. U. Va., Charlottesville, 1966—; ptnr. Assoc. Environ. Cons., Charlottesville, 1972—. USIA expert lectr. on solar energy overseas, 1978, 79; U. Va. Sesquicentennial research assoc., 1978-79. Mem. AAAS, Am. Inst. Chem. Engrs., Am. Chem. Soc., Internat. Solar Energy Soc., Va. Acad. Sci., Sigma Xi, Tau Beta Pi, Omicron Delta Kappa, Phi Kappa Phi. Democrat. Contbr. articles to profl. jours. Home: Route 2 Box 374 Charlottesville VA 22901 Office: Thornton Hall Univ Va Charlottesville VA 22901

LILLY, ARNYS CLIFTON, JR., physicist; b. Beckley, W. Va., June 3, 1934; s. Arnys Clifton and Ella Vay (McKeehan) L.; m. Agnes Madelynn Micou, June 9, 1956; children—Greg Alan, Diane Renee, James Clifton. B.S. in Petroleum Engring., Va. Poly. Inst., 1957; M.S. in Physics, Carnegie-Mellon U., 1963. Research physicist Gulf Research and Devel. Co., Pitts., 1957-65; prin. scientist Philip Morris Research Ctr., Richmond, Va., 1965—, research fellow, 1984. Mem. Am. Phys. Soc., Sigma Xi. Contbr. articles to physics jours.; patentee in field. Home: 4733 Hopkins Rd Richmond VA 23234 Office: Philip Morris Research Center 4201 Commerce Rd Richmond VA 23234

LILLY, BOB A., rancher, commissioner; b. Foard City, Tex., May 16, 1919; s. Amos Willis and Johnnie Marion (Traweek) L.; student John Tarleton Coll., 1936-38; B.S., Tex. A&M U., 1940; m. Ruth L. McBurney, Dec. 21, 1939; children—Michele Bock, Niki (Mrs. Joe L. Lockwood). County agrl. agt. Cameron County, Tex., 1943-45, Starr County Tex., 1945-46, Ft. Bend County, Tex., 1947, Calhoun County, Tex., 1948-51; legis. dir. Tex. Farm Bur., 1951-63, N. Tex. Milk Producers, Inc., Arlington, 1963-67; asst. to gen. mgr., legis. dir., sec. polit. arm Associated Milk Producers, San Antonio, 1967-74; dir. Tex. Fedn. Coops., 1972-74; chmn. Tex. Animal Health Commn., 1972, commr., 1973-75; commr. Tex. Rural Devel. Commn., 1971-73; bd. dirs. Tex. Feed and Fertilizer Law, 1961-71; cons. Tex. Dept. Agr.; agrl. cons. govtl. regulatory agys. and lending agys.; dir. Nat. Animal Health Commn., 1972—; mem. legis. com. Nat. Milk Producers, 1970—; pres., dir. Rural Water Corp. Mem. Tex. Lt. Gov.'s Water Research Com., 1973—. Served with USAAF, 1940-43. Mem. Nat. Animal Health Assn., Interstate Milk Shippers Assn. (dir.). Democrat. Club: Masons. Home: Route 1 Box 150 Zephyr TX 76890 Office: GPM Bldg San Antonio TX 78216

LILLY, EDWARD GUERRANT, JR., utility company executive; b. Lexington, Ky., Oct. 29, 1925; s. Edward Guerrant and Elisabeth Read (Fraser) L.; m. Nancy Estes Cobb, Nov. 25, 1961; children—Penelope Read, Edward Guerrant III, Collier Cobb, Steven Clay. Student U. Va., 1944-45; B.S., Davidson Coll., 1948; M.B.A., U. Pa., 1949. Credit analyst Citizens & So. Nat. Bank, Charleston, S.C., 1949-50; asst. v.p. Wachovia Bank & Trust Co., Charlotte, N.C., 1952-55, v.p., loan adminstrv. officer, Wilmington, N.C., 1956-60, sr. v.p., area exec., Kinston, N.C., 1961-62, sr. v.p., area exec., Durham, N.C., 1963-70, sr. v.p., mgr. trust investment services dept., Winston-Salem, N.C., 1970-71; sr. v.p., group exec. fin. Carolina Power & Light Co., Raleigh, N.C., 1971-76, sr. v.p., chief fin. officer, 1976-81, exec. v.p., chief fin. officer, 1981—, dir., 1971—; dir. Wachovia Bank & Trust Co., Raleigh. Trustee Davidson Coll., Peace Coll., Raleigh; bd. visitors U. N.C.; bd. dirs. Research Triangle Found., Research Triangle Park, N.C.; mem. Bus. Found. N.C., Chapel Hill, 1972-74. Served to lt. USNR, 1950-52. Mem. Edison Electric Inst. (exec. com. fin. and econ. div.), Southeastern Electric Exchange. Presbyterian. Lodge: Rotary. Office: PO Box 1551 411 Fayetteville St Mall Raleigh NC 27609

LILLY, LARRY EUGENE, coal company executive; b. Beckley, W.Va., Dec. 28, 1947; s. Jonathan Dott and Goldie Mae (Meador) L.; m. Delma Jean Wood, Nov. 4, 1965; 1 son, Larry Eugene. Student Auto Diesel and Welding Coll., Nashville, 1965-66. Deep mine supt. in charge total project Double A Coal Co., Pineville, W.Va., 1975-76; gen. job supt. Philpott Coal Corp., Daniels, W.Va., 1977-78; pres. W.Va., Excavating, Glen Morgan, 1974-75; pres. Lilly Augering Co., Inc., Beaver, W.Va., 1978-80; v.p. in charge ops. To-Lar Coal Corp., Big Stone Gap, Va., 1980—; v.p. T&L Augering Corp., Big Stone Gap. Republican. Baptist. Home: 202 Briarwood Ln Beaver WV 25813 Office: To-Lar Coal Corp PO Drawer L Big Stone Gap VA 24219

LIM, DANIEL VAN, microbiology educator; b. Houston, Apr. 15, 1948; s. Don H. and Lucy (Toy) L.; m. Carol Sue Lee, Sept. 2, 1973. B.A. in Biology, Rice U., 1970; Ph.D. in Microbiology, Tex. A&M U., 1973. Postdoctoral fellow Baylor Coll. Medicine, 1973-76; asst. prof. U South Fla., Tampa, 1976-81, assoc. prof. microbiology, 1981—; cons. in field. Inventor bacteriological broth. Recipient Outstanding Ph.D. Dissertation in U.S. award Phi Sigma, 1974. Fellow Am. Acad. Microbiology; mem. Inter-Am. Soc. Chemotherapy (v.p. 1982—), Am. Soc. Microbiology (Carski award com. 1983-86), Internat. Soc. Chemotherapy. Home: 11713 Palmer Dr Tampa FL 33624 Office: Dept Biology U South Florida Tampa FL 33620

LI MANDRI, SALVATORE, engineering company executive; b. Milan, Italy, July 20, 1952; s. Vincenzo and Angela Maria (Ardizzone) Li M.; m. Marie Varine Smith, May 16, 1981. B.S. in Engring. Tech. and Electronics, U. Ark., 1986. Draftsman Harvey Engring. Co., Hot Springs, Ark., 1975-77, jr. programmer, 1977-80, sr. programmer, Little Rock, 1980—. Served to 2d lt. Italian Army, 1972-74. Avocations: tennis; guitar; electronics; chess. Home: 601 Higdon #248 Hot Springs AR 71913 Office: Harvey Engring 1701 S Shakelford Little Rock AR 72204

LIN, PING-HUANG, analytical chemist; b. Taichung, Taiwan, Sept. 2, 1943; came to U.S., 1969, naturalized, 1981; s. Wu-Chang and Chen-Tsai L.; B.S., Nat. Cheng-Kung U., Taiwan, 1966; M.S., U. Nebr., 1971, Ph.D., 1973; m. Shiow-Jean Shyr, June 5, 1971; children—Alice, Grace, Connie. Research fellow U. Toronto, Canada, 1973-74; research assoc. M.I.T., 1974-75; sr. scientist, mass spectrometrist Radian Corp., Austin, Tex., 1975-81; research specialist Exxon Prodn. Research Co., Houston, 1981—. Served to 2d lt. Chinese Air Force, 1966-67. NSF Grad. Summer fellow, 1970; 3M Corp. Grad. fellow, 1971-72; named Hon. Nebr. Citizen, 1973. Mem. Am. Chem. Soc., Am. Soc. Mass Spectrometry, Am. Assn. Petroleum Geologists, Phi Lambda Upsilon. Contbr. articles to profl. jours. Home: 11626 Trailmont Dr Houston TX 77077 Office: Exxon Prodn Research Co PO Box 2189 Houston TX 77001

LINCOLN, RODERICK MARC, training supervisor, historical archivist; b. Port Sulphur, La., May 30, 1950; s. Hays Marc and Marjorie (Garlington) L.; m. Leslie Jean McCutcheon, June 7, 1975; 1 child, Jennifer Leslie. B.A. in Psychology, Southeastern La. U., 1973. Dist. exec. Boy Scouts Am., Baton Rouge, 1973-76; sales rep. Mercury Freight Lines, Baton Rouge, 1976-79; personnel asst. Freeport Chem. Co., Uncle Sam, La., 1979, Freeport Sulphur Co., New Orleans, 1979-85; supr. tng. Freeport McMoRan, Inc., New Orleans, 1985—; historic site cons. U.S. Corp. of Engrs., New Orleans, 1982—; expert hist. site cons. R. Christopher Goodwin Archeologists, New Orleans, 1983—. Author, videographer numerous tng. programs, 1982—. Contbg. author Jour. Deep Delta Geneal. Quar., 1982—. Co. chmn. United Way of New Orleans, 1979, 81, 84, Blood Ctr. of Southeast La., 1984; dist. commr. Istrouma Area council Boy Scouts Am., 1976-78; counselor Jr. Achievement of New Orleans, 1979-80; instr. ARC, 1981-85. Served with USAFR, 1970-77. Mem. Am. Soc. Tng. and Devel., Gulf Coast Safety and Tng. Orgn., Plaquemines Hist. Soc. (v.p. 1982—, organizer hist. collection 1983), Deep Delta Geneal. Soc. (pres. 1982-83, 84—), Mayflower Soc., Sigma Tau Gamma. Roman Catholic. Avocations: archival research; genealogy. Home: 5414 MacArthur Blvd New Orleans LA 70114 Office: Freeport McMoRan Inc 1615 Poydras New Orleans LA 70130

LIND, JAMES PETER, computer sci. cons., b. Chgo., June 8, 1932; s. James and Mabel Antoinette (Nelson) L.; B.A. (Nat. Def. Transp. scholar), U. Minn., 1954, M.A.P.A., 1965. Mgmt. analyst Bur. Employment Security, Dept. Labor, Washington, 1965-66; dean of men U. Bridgeport (Conn.), 1966-68; sr. budget analyst Montgomery County (Md.), Rockville, 1968-72; dir. planning Office of Gov. S.C., Columbia, 1972-73; sr. cons. Northrop Services, Arlington, Va., 1973-75; v.p.-fin. Ability Devel. Services, Washington, 1975-76, dir., 1975—; sr. program analyst Social Rehab. Services, HEW, Washington, 1976-77; dept. mgr. Computer Scis. Corp., Falls Church, Va., 1977—; dir. Mid-Atlantic Capital Corp. Contbr. articles to adminstrn. jours. Ward officer Democratic Farmer Labor Party, Mpls., 1959-65. Served to 1st lt. U.S. Army, 1955-58. Mem. Am. Soc. Pub. Adminstrs., Internat. City Mgmt. Assn., Internat. Platform Assn., World Future Soc., Am. Inst. Planners. Democrat. Presbyterian. Home: Apt 1416 5375 Duke St Alexandria VA 22304 Office: 6565 Arlington Blvd Falls Church VA 22046

LINDAHL, MARY WETHERBEE, psychologist; b. Greenville, Miss., Oct. 19, 1941; d. Donald Gist and Virginia Elizabeth (LaRochelle) Wetherbee; m. Frederick William Lindahl, Oct. 9, 1971; children—George, Virginia, Kristine. B.A., Wellesley Coll., 1963; M.S.W., Simmons Coll., 1965; Ph.D., U. Chgo., 1984. Lic. ind. practitioner clin. social work, Mass.; lic. practicing psychologist, N.C. Supr., therapist Tufts New Eng. Med. Ctr., Boston, 1968-78; pvt. practice psychotherapy, Boston, 1970-78, Homewood, Ill., 1978-84, Durham, N.C., 1985—; field supr. U. Chgo., 1981-82; therapist Family Service and Mental Health of South Cook County, Homewood, 1982-84; clin. psychologist Durham City Schs., 1984—; postdoctoral fellow Duke U., Durham, 1985—, Ctr. for Continuing Edn., 1985—; clin. cons. to bd. deacons Flossmoor Community Ch. (Ill.), 1981-84. Mem. com. on ch. and society Epworth United Methodist Ch., Durham, 1984-85. NIMH trainee, 1978, 79; Woodrow Wilson Found. fellow, 1983. Mem. Nat. Assn. Social Workers, Acad. Cert. Social Workers, Am. Psychol. Assn., N.C. Psychol. Assn. Avocations: piano; choir. Home: 4306 Malvern Rd Durham NC 27707

LINDAMOOD, MARY ORLENA, nurse; b. St. Petersburg, Fla., Jan. 27, 1946; d. Otis Dean and Evva Mabel (Mullins) L. B.S. in Nursing, Med. Coll. Pa., 1967; M.S. in Nursing, Med. Coll. Va., 1975. Charge nurse Med. Coll. Va., Richmond, 1967-68, asst. head nurse, 1968-69, cardiopulmonary resuscitation team coordinator, 1968-73, asst. dir. nursing, 1975-78, assoc. dir. 1978—; clin. instr. Va. Commonwealth U. Sch. Pharmacy, Richmond, 1976-84, clin. assoc. Sch. Nursing, 1981-84, asst. prof., 1984—; cons. in field. Mem. editorial bd. Dimensions in Critical Care Jour., 1983-84. Contbr. articles to profl. jours. Bd. dirs. Providence Green Homewoners Assn., Richmond, 1985—. Mem. Am. Nurses' Assn., Am. Assn. Critical Care Nurses (treas. 1978-80), Am. Lung Assn., Am. Heart Assn., Sigma Theta Tau. Episcopalian. Office: Box 7 MCV Sta Richmond VA 23298-0001

LINDBERG, DAVID SEAMAN, educational administrator; b. Merrill, Wis., July 17, 1929; s. Clifford Harvey and Dorothy Jo Lindberg; B.S. in Med. Tech., Wis. State U., Stevens Point, 1958; M.Ed., U. Fla., 1969, Ed.D., 1970; m. Frances Eleanor Cortelyou, Dec. 27, 1951; children—David Seaman, John Edward, Martha Joan. Med. technologist Marshfield (Wis.) Clinic, 1958-66; research asst. U. Fla. Teaching Hosp., Gainesville, 1966; supervisory med. technologist VA Hosp., Gainesville, 1967-68; asst. prof. health related professions and med. tech. U. Fla., Gainesville, 1971-74; asst. dean Sch. Allied Health Professions, La. State U. Med. Center, New Orleans, 1974-77, assoc. dean for acad. affairs, 1977—; cons. med. lab. continuing edn. and accreditation. Chmn. adminstrv. bd. Fitzgerald United Meth. Ch., Covington, La., 1977-80; mem. Naval Res. Med. Policy Bd., 1977-78; founder, pres. Fla. Tech-ucation Found., 1969-72; del. Fla. Health Planning Council, 1969-73; treas., bd. trustees Med. Lab. Tech. Polit. Action Com., 1976-77; Surgeon Gen., Naval Order of U.S., 1985-86. Served with USN, 1950-54. Lic. lab. dir., Fla. Mem. Am. Soc. for Med. Tech. (Profl. Achievement award in edn. 1974, Outstanding Service award 1974, 75, 76, Silver award 1973, pres. Fla. div. 1973-74), Am. Soc. Allied Health Professions, Am. Soc. Clin. Pathologists, Assn. Mil. Surgeons U.S., Naval Res. Assn. Author: Introduction to the Profession of Medical Technology, 4th edit., 1979; mem. editorial bd. Am. Jour. Med. Tech., 1977-82; contbr. articles to profl. jours. Home: Rural Route 4 Box 131 Covington LA 70433 Office: 1900 Gravier St New Orleans LA 70112

LINDBERG, FRANCIS LAURENCE, JR., ins. holding co. exec.; b. Jacksonville, Fla., Mar. 13, 1948; s. Francis Laurence and Mildred (Parrish) L.; student Eckerd Coll., 1965-66; B.A., Jacksonville U., 1969; M.B.A., U. N. Fla., 1976; m. Alexis Jean Parker, Nov. 12, 1983; 1 dau., Kristen Anne. Actuarial analyst Gulf Life Ins. Co., Jacksonville, 1967-72, group actuarial asst., 1972-73; asst. actuary Am. Heritage Life Ins. Co., Jacksonville, 1973-77; asst. sec.-treas., prin. acctg. officer Atlantic Am. Corp., Atlanta, 1977—. Mem. Nat. Assn. Accts., Am. Inst. C.P.A.s, Ga. Soc. C.P.A.s, Southeastern Ins. Tax Forum, Pi Kappa Phi. Republican. Episcopalian. Clubs: Ponte Vedra, Ansley Golf. Home: 3 Pendleton Pl NW Atlanta GA 30342 Office: 4370 Peachtree Rd NE Atlanta GA 30319

LINDBERG, STEVEN ERIC, geochemist; b. Waukegan, Ill., May 9, 1947; s. Donald W. and Betty (Schmidt) L.; m. Margaret Kay Caulk, June 21, 1969; 1 dau., Kristina Ann. B.S., Duke U., 1969; M.S., Fla. State U., 1973, Ph.D., 1979. Tchr., Antioch Upper Grade Ctr. (Ill.), 1969-71; grad. fellow Fla. State U., 1971-74; staff geochemist Environ. Scis. div. Oak Ridge Nat. Lab., 1974—, mem. exec. com. Nat. Atmospheric Deposition Program, 1981—. Recipient Environ. Sci. Achievement award Oak Ridge Nat. Lab., 1984; NSF Predoctoral award, 1968; Sigma Xi grantee, 1972; NDEA fellow, 1971-74; numerous other research grants, 1975—. Mem. Nat. Wildlife Fedn. (environ. conservation fellow 1974-75), Air Pollution Control Assn., Internat. Assn. Aerobiology. Contbr. articles to books and tech. jours. Office: Bldg 1505 Environmental Scis Div Oak Ridge Nat Lab Oak Ridge TN 37830

LINDENMUTH, RICHARD ALAN, telecommunications company executive; b. Phila., Dec. 28, 1944; s. Ralph Lester and Evelyn Josephine (Zimmerman) Dedel L.; m. Christine Louise Ulmer, Sept. 7, 1968; children—Michael, Carol Anne. B.A. in Internat. Affairs, U. Colo., 1970; M.B.A., Wharton Sch., U. Pa., 1971. Gen. mgr. North and West Africa Singer, Beirut, Lebanon, 1972-77; dir. internat. ops. Bendix Corp., Southfield, Mich., 1978-80; pres. Lexar Bus. Communications, Inc., Woodland Hills, Calif., 1980-82; v.p., gen. mgr. Imaging Systems div. Burroughs Corp., Danbury, Conn., 1982-83; pres. Bus. and Consumer Communications div. ITT, Raleigh, N.C., 1983—. Mem. nat. adv. bd. Ctr. Study Presidency, N.Y.C., 1982—; bd. dirs. Internat. Trade, Raleigh, 1983—; cons. on middle east U.S. Govt., 1982-83. Served with USN, 1962-66. Republican. Presbyterian. Club: Capital City (Raleigh). Avocations: flying; sailing; travel; tennis. Home: 312 Dunwoody Dr Raleigh NC 27609 Office: ITT 6131 Falls of Neuse Rd Raleigh NC

LINDER, ALICE DEISSLER, environmental education and science consultant; b. Freeman, S.D., July 22, 1930; d. William and Adeline (Schrag) Deissler; m. Ira M. Linder, Dec. 23, 1951; children—Terry, William. B.S. in Chemistry, Nebr. Wesleyan U., 1950; postgrad. Holyoke Hosp. Sch. Med. Tech., 1951; M.A., Winthrop Coll., 1962. Registered med. technologist. Tchr. gen. sci., biology and advanced biology, also dept. chmn. Rock Hill Sch. Dist., S.C., 1957-68, coordinator sci. and math., 1968-69, tchr. biology and advanced biology, dept. chmn., 1969-71; environ. edn. and sci. cons. S.C. Dept. Edn., Columbia. Author, editor: Basic Science-Environmental Skills, 1970, Science Education, K-12, Administrator's Planning Guide, 1972, The Energy Book, 1975, Environmental Education, A Source Book for Educators, 1976, Resources for Environmental Education, 1977, The School Site, An Environment for Learning, 1977, Back to the Basics with an Environmental Education Program, 1978, Environmental Studies, A Course for High School, 1979, Energy Savers, 1981, Staff Development, Environmental Education, 1981. Commr. Lexington County Soil and Water Conservation Dist., 1983. Recipient Outstanding Biology Tchr. of Yr. award, 1966-67; S.C. Wildlife Fedn. Conservation Educator of Yr. award, 1975; Outstanding Conservation Citizen award Soil Conservation Soc., 1980; Water Resources Commn. award, 1981; Order of Palmetto award Gov. S.C., 1982. Mem. Conservation Edn. Assn. (bd. dirs., v.p. 1982-84), Nat. Sci. Tchrs. Assn., Nat. Assn. Conservation Dists. (edn. and youth com.), S.C. Wildlife Fedn., S.C. Environ. Edn. Assn., S.C. Assn. Naturalists, S.C. Friends of Mus., Am. S.C. Assn. Supervision and Curriculum Devel., S.C. Natural Resources Edn. Council. Methodist.

LINDER, JERRY LEROY, dentist; b. Omaha, Jan. 28, 1939; s. Arthur Leroy and Mary Marie (Rogers) L.; m. Sharon Irene Kirch, June 6, 1964; children—Jerry Leroy, Jr., Cindy Sue. Student Creighton U., 1956-58, Washington U., St. Louis, 1958-60; D.D.S., U. Nebr., 1964. Mem. Clay County Health Adv. Com., Fla., 1974-82; dist. chmn. North Fla. council Boy Scouts Am., 1980-83, adv. bd., 1983-86; bd. dirs. Am. Cancer Soc., Clay County, Fla., 1984-85. Served to lt. comdr. USN, 1964-67. Recipient Silver Beaver award Boy Scouts Am., 1985. Mem. ADA, Fla. Dental Assn., N.E. Dist. Dental Soc., Clay County Dental Soc. (pres. 1980-81). Presbyterian. Lodge: Rotary (Paul Harris fellow 1983); Masons: Shriners. Home: 2475 Dogwood Ln Orange Park FL 32073

LINDERMAN, EDWARD LEE, human resources executive; b. Norman, Okla., Nov. 3, 1950; s. Edward Lee and Jean (Boyd) L.; m. Linda Kay Rosenbloom Bates, June 25, 1983; stepchildren—Tamara, Robert Rosenbloom. B.A., Bucknell U., 1973. Salesman, Zia Agy., Santa Fe, N.Mex., 1973-74; owner The Haven Restaurant, Santa Fe, 1974-76; mgr. Village Inn Pancake House, Santa Fe, 1976-78, v.p. ops., 1978-81; area rep., instr. Dale Carnegie Courses, El Paso, 1981—; human resources dir. Whataburger of El Paso, 1984—. Tona Lema Meml. scholar, 1969. Mem. Am. Soc. Tng. and Devel., Am. Mgmt. Assn., Nat. Soc. for Performance & Instrn., Nat. Assn. for Mgmt. Republican. Methodist. Lodge: Kiwanis. Avocations: golf; skiing. Home: 1010 Marilissa Ln Las Cruces NM 88005 Office: Whataburger of El Paso Inc 9400 Montana El Paso TX 79925

LINDLEY, DONA LOU, real estate broker; b. Shattuck, Okla., Jan. 28, 1936; d. Albert and Georgia Ima (Gillespie) Hartley; student real estate courses; m. George W. Lindley, Feb. 3, 1954; children—Wyliea Lindley Edens, George W., David L., Nancy Chloe, Dona Lisa. Owner, broker Lindley Land & Cattle Co., Ozark, Ark., 1972—; co-owner Bobby's Beauty Shop and Boutique, Ozark. Pres. Band Boosters; mem. Ozark Sch. Bd.; leader 4-H Club; active Extension Club, PTA, Girl Scouts U.S.A. designated G.R.I. (grad Realtors Inst.), C.R.S. (cert. residential specialist). Mem. Ozark C. of C. (dir. 1975-76), Nat. Fedn. Small Bus., Nat. Assn. Real Estate, Ark. Real Estate Assn., Ark. Real Estate Polit. Edn. Assn., Farm Bur., Smithsonian Assos., Bus. and Profl. Women's Club. Home: Parker Plantation Ozark AR 72949 Office: Box 531 Ozark AR 72949

LINDOERFER, JOANNE SHEAHAN, psychologist, educator; b. Antioch, Ill., Apr. 25, 1945; d. Joseph and Mary Jayne Sheahan; m. Dennis Lindoerfer, May 15, 1971 (div. Oct. 1977); 1 child, Mark. B.S. cum laude, Loyola U., Chgo., 1967; Ph.D., U. Tex., 1980. Lic. psychologist, Tex. Psychotherapist Mental Health-Mental Retardation, Beaumont Tex., 1976-80; counselor Lamar U., Beaumont, 1980-82, asst. prof., 1982—; psychotherapist, Beaumont, 1984—; cons. in field. Bd. dirs. Mental Health Assn., Beaumont, 1983—; com. mem. Juvenile Fire Prevention Assn., Beaumont, 1985. Mem. Am. Psychol. Assn., Southwestern Psychol. Assn., Tex. Psychol. Assn. Roman Catholic. Home: 3520 Kipling Dr Beaumont TX 77706 Office: Psychology Dept Lamar U Box 10036 Beaumont TX 77710

LINDOW, LESTER WILLIAM, former telecasters organization executive; b. Milw., Apr. 11, 1913; B.A. in Journalism, U. Wis., 1934; m. Baroness Andree de Verdor, Dec. 7, 1946; 1 child, Suzanne Helene Lindow Gordon. Asso. editor Advt. Almanac, Hearst Newspapers, N.Y.C., 1934-35; with comml. dept. sta. WCAE, Pitts., 1935-36, nat. sales mgr., 1936-38, comml. mgr., asst. to gen. mgr., 1938-40; sec., gen. mgr. WFBM, Inc., Indpls., 1940-42; gen. mgr. stas. WRNY and WRNY-FM, Rochester, N.Y., 1946-47; sec., gen. mgr. Trebit Corp. operators sta. WFDF, Flint, Mich., 1947-60, sec., dir. 1948-60, v.p., 1954-60; sec.-treas. Landsmore Corp., 1952-57, v.p., 1954-57; mem. exec. com. NBC Radio Affiliates, 1955-57, chmn. exec. com., 1956-57; exec. dir. Assn. Maximum Service Telecasters, Inc., 1957-77, pres., 1977-78, also dir., asst. sec.-treas.; v.p., dir. Grelin Broadcasting Inc., sta. WWRI, West Warwick, R.I., 1957-69, Radio Buffalo, Inc., stas. WWOL and WWOL-FM, N.Y. 1959-62. Treas., dir. ARC, 1953-56, nat. fund vice chmn. for Mich., 1956-57, bd. dirs. Palm Beach County chpt., 1981—; bd. dirs., mem. exec. com., chmn. budget and fiscal com. Radio Free Europe/Radio Liberty, Inc., Washington. Served from 1st lt. to lt. col. U.S. Army, 1942-46; apptd. to Gen. Staff Corps, War Dept., 1946-47; col. Res. ret. Mem. Mich. Assn. Broadcasters, Mich. AP Broadcasters' Assn. (dir.), Res. Officers Assn., Armed Forces Broadcasters Assn. (dir. 1982—), Nat. Assn. Radio and TV Broadcasters (dir. AM radio com.), Radio Advt. Bur. (Mich. chmn.), AP Radio Programming Com. N.Y.C., Assn. Profl. Broadcasting Edn. (dir.), AP Radio and TV Assn. (v.p., dir.), TV Allocations Study Orgn. (alt. dir.), Union U. Wis., U. Wis. Alumni Assn., Nat. Broadcasters Club of Washington (pres. 1964-65, gov. 1959-61, chmn. bd. 1965-66), Internat. Radio and TV Soc., Radio-TV Pioneers, Palm Beach Civic Assn., Ret. Officers Assn., English Speaking Union, Scabbard and Blade, Iron Cross, White Spades, Alpha Chi Rho, Sigma Delta Chi. Clubs: Flint Golf; Radio Executives (N.Y.C.); Nat. Broadcasters, Congressional Country, Internat. (Washington); Beach, Pundits (Palm Beach, Fla.); Elks, Rotary (pres.). Home: La Bonne Vie Apt 406-7 3475 S Ocean Blvd Palm Beach FL 33480

LINDSAY, COTTON MATHER, economics educator; b. Atlanta, June 17, 1940; s. Paul Leonard and Elizabeth (Mather) L.; m. Bonnie Sue McClay, Jan. 19, 1963 (div. 1976); children—Paul Mather, Jefferson Davis; m. Mary Featherstone Osler, May 14, 1977. B.B.A., U. Ga., 1962; Ph.D., U. Va., 1968. From asst. to assoc. prof. econs. UCLA, 1969-80, prof. econs., 1980-81; prof. econs. Emory U., Atlanta, 1981-84; J. Wilson Newman prof. managerial econs. Clemson U., S.C., 1984—. Author: Veterans Administration Hospitals, 1975; Equal Pay for Comparable Work, 1980; National Health Issues: The British Experience, 1980; Applied Price Theory, 1984. Mem. Health Policy Adv. Com. to candidate Ronald Reagan, 1980. Served to 1st lt. USAF, 1962-65. NSF Postdoctoral fellow, London Sch. Econs., 1968-69; Nat. fellow, Hoover Inst., Stanford U., 1975-76. Mem. Am. Econ. Assn., So. Econs. Assn., Pub. Choice Soc., Mont Pelerin Soc. Republican. Episcopalian. Home: 131 Folger St Clemson SC 29631

LINDSAY, ROBERT FORREST, geologist; b. Ogden, Utah, Nov. 9, 1948; s. Wallace Robert and Martha Lucille (Ramsay) L.; m. Deborah Marie Mischel, May 8, 1973; children—Jared, Julie, Janet, Jacob. B.S., Weber State Coll., Ogden, 1974; M.S., Brigham Young U., Provo, Utah, 1976. Geologist, supr. enhanced oil recovery Gulf Oil Exploration and Prodn. Co., Oklahoma City, 1976-83, sr. project geologist, Houston, 1983-85; carbonate petrographer Chevron U.S.A., Denver, 1985—; editor Oklahoma City Geol. Soc., 1981-83. Contbg. author books: 4th International Williston Basin Symposium, 1982; American Association Petroleum Geologists Memoir-Williston Basin, 1986; Scanning Electron Microscopy in Geology, 1986; Carbonate Petroleum Reservoirs, 1985. Mem. Geol. Soc. Am., Am. Assn. Petroleum Geologists, Soc. Econ. Paleontologists and Mineralogists.

LINDSEY, BARBARA JOAN, medical technology educator; b. Welland, Ont., Can., Nov. 5, 1950; d. Alvin Maurice Michael and Jean Mildred (White) M.; m. Kenneth Ray Lindsey, Apr. 16, 1982. R.T., Mohawk Coll., Hamilton, Ont., 1971; M.S., Va. Commonwealth U./Med. Coll. Va., 1977. Med. technologist Welland County Gen. Hosp., Ont., Can., 1971-72; asst. master Mohawk Coll., dept. med. tech., Hamilton, 1972-73; med. technologist Children's Hosp. Pitts., 1973-74, Bethesda Hosp., Zanesville, Ohio, 1974-75; assoc. prof. dept. med. tech. Sch. Allied Health Professions, Va. Commonwealth U./Med. Coll. Va., Richmond, 1975—; co-owner Profl. Med. Labs., Inc., Petersburg, Va., cons. A.D. Williams grantee, 1979-80. Mem. Am. Soc. Med. Tech. (region II council mem 1979-82), Va. Soc. Med. Tech. (pres. 1980-81), Richmond Soc. Med. Tech. (treas. 1979-80, 85-86), Am. Soc. Clin. Pathology. Lutheran. Contbr. articles to profl. jours. Office: Dept Med Tech MCV Sta Box 583 Va Commonwealth U/Med Coll Va Richmond VA 23298

LINDSEY, CHERYL ANN, nurse; b. Jasper, Ga., Feb. 5, 1958; d. Tom A. and Ruth (Cline) L. Grad. med. office asst. Pickens Vo-Tech Sch., 1977, in practical nursing, 1978; A.D. in Nursing, Kennesaw Coll., 1980. R.N. Nursing supr. Pickens Gen. Hosp., Jasper, 1980-83; cardiac care nurse R.T. Jones Hosp., Canton, Ga., 1983; nurse Met. Hosp., Atlanta, 1984—; CPR instr. ARC, Atlanta, 1982—. Baptist. Lodge: Order Eastern Star. Office: 3223 Howell Mill Rd NW Atlanta GA 30327

LINDSEY, DAVID MARTIN, accountant, management consultant; b. Norfolk, Va., Jan. 14, 1947; s. Thomas A. and Edith (Gordon) L.; m. De Anne Carol Melworth; children—Rachel E., Jay Michael. B.A., Gallaudet Coll., 1973; M.B.A., Columbia Pacific U., 1983, Ph.D., 1983. Pres., chief corp. officer David M. Lindsey & Assocs., Ltd., Virginia Beach, Va., 1978—; pres., chief corp. officer Generic Systems, Inc., Virginia Beach, 1979—, Assoc. Cable Services, Ltd., Virginia Beach, 1982—; lectr. tax law and acctg. Tidewater Community Coll. Mem. Republican Nat. Com., U.S. Congl. Adv. Bd. Mem. Nat. Soc. C.P.A.s, Va. Soc. C.P.A.s. Lodge: Masons. Home: 5368 Providence Rd Virginia Beach VA 23464 Office: 5368 Providence Rd Virginia Beach VA 23464

LINDSEY, DOTTYE JEAN, educator; b. Temple Hill, Ky., Nov. 4, 1929; d. Jesse D. and Ethel Ellen (Bailey) Nuckols; B.S., Western Ky. U., 1953, M.A., 1959; m. Willard W. Lindsey, June 14, 1952 (div.). Owner, Bonanza Restaurant, Charleston, W.Va., 1965; tchr. remedial reading Alice Waller Elem. Sch., Louisville, 1967-75, tchr., 1953-67, 1975—, contact person for remedial reading, 1968—; profl. model Cosmo/Casablancas Internat., Louisville, 1984—. Bn. sponsor ROTC Western Ky. U., 1950. Named Miss Ky., 1951. Mem. NEA, Ky. Edn. Assn., Jefferson County Tchrs. Assn., various polit. action coms., Internat. Reading Assn., Am. Childhood Edn. Assn., Met. Louisville Women's Polit. Caucus (treas. 1980-84). Democrat. Baptist.

LINDSEY, EDWARD MICAJAH, dentist, farmer; b. Boaz, Ala., Oct. 4, 1920; s. Joseph E. and Exa (Cook) L.; m. Geneva Hendricks, Sept. 5, 1949; children—Cenda Lindsey Price, John M., Rebecca A. Lindsey Gerlach, Edward Micajah Jr. Student Snead Jr. Coll., 1938-39; D.M.D., U. Louisville, 1950. Gen. practice dentistry, Gadsden, Ala., 1950—; also farmer. Pres. Gadsden Hist. Soc., 1960, Ala. Archeol. Assn., Birmingham, 1965. Mem. 5th Dist. Dental Soc. (pres. 1972), Ala. Dental Assn. (bd. dental examiners 1974-80, pres. bd. 1980, mem. dental coms.), Pierre Fauchard Soc., Am. Bd. Dental Examiners. Methodist. Avocations: reading; archaeology; history. Home: 173 Azalea Dr Gadsden AL 35901 Office: 313 S 5th St Gadsden AL 35901

LINDSEY, MARK SHAW, architect; b. Richmond, Va., Dec. 29, 1958. B.Arch., Va. Poly. Inst., 1982. Registered architect, Va. Draftsman, J.V. Ciucci Architects, Richmond, 1980-81; designer S.A.L. Architects, 1981, Baskerville & Son, 1982; project architect SWA Architects, Inc., Richmond, 1982-85; designer, project architect Baskervill & Son Architects & Engrs., Inc., Richmond, 1985—. Contbr. articles to mags. Recipient Ctrs. of Excellence award for design of Celebration Sta., Nat. Mall Monitor, 1985; Alice Sundy prize AIA, 1984. Mem. Va. Poly. Inst. Alumni Assn., Va. Solar Energy Assn. Avocations: skiing; sailing. Home: 807 G Georgianna Ct Richmond VA 23236 Office: PO Box 5516 Richmond VA 23220

LINDSEY, RONALD WAYNE, pharmacist; b. Nashville, May 27, 1950; s. William J. and Mildred C. (Evans) L.; m. Victoria Frances Dantzler, Aug. 26, 1973; children—William Brandon, Steven Michael, Christopher Wayne. B.S. in Biology, U. S.C., Columbia, 1972, B.S. in Pharmacy, 1976, M.S. in Pharm. Practice, 1986. Assoc. dir. pharmacy Bapt. Med. Ctr., Columbia, S.C., 1972—. Mem. Nat. Conservative Polit. Action Com., Washington, 1984—. Mem. Am. Soc. Hosp. Pharmacist, S.C. Soc. Hosp. Pharmacists, S.C. Pharm. Assn. Republican. Baptist. Avocations: photography; reading; basketball; gardening. Office: Bapt Med Ctr Taylor at Marion Columbia SC 29220

LINDSTROM, ERIC EVERETT, ophthalmologist; b. Helena, Mont., Nov. 28, 1936; s. Everett Harry and Nan Augusta (Johnson) L.; B.S., Wheaton Coll., 1958; M.D., U. Md., 1963; M.P.H., Harvard U., 1966; m. Nancy Jo Alexander, July 24, 1960; children—Laura Ann, Eric Everett. Intern, Madigan Army Med. Center, Tacoma, Wash., 1963-64; resident in aerospace medicine Sch. Aerospace Medicine, Brooks AFB, Tex., 1966-68, resident in ophthalmology Brooke Army Med. Center, Ft. Sam Houston, Tex., 1972-75; surgeon 12th combat aviation group U.S. Army, Vietnam, 1968-69, chief profl. services and aviation medicine Beach Army Hosp., Ft. Wolters, Tex., 1969-72; asst. chief ophthalmology clinic Madigan Army Med. Center, Tacoma, 1975-76; now with Laurel (Miss.) Eye Center; med. dir. Palo Pinto County (Tex.) Mental Health Clinic., 1970-72; cons. Tex. State Rehab. Com., 1971-72; flight surgeon Miss. Air N.G. Deacon, First Bapt. Ch., Laurel, 1978—. Trustee Jones County Community Hosp. Decorated Bronze Star, Air medal with 2 oak leaf clusters, Meritorious Service medal. Diplomate Am. Bd. Preventive Medicine, Am. Bd. Ophthalmology. Fellow Am. Coll. Preventive Medicine, Aerospace Med. Assn. (assoc.), Am. Acad. Ophthalmology, ACS; mem. AMA, Miss. Med. Assn., Miss. EENT Assn., South Miss. Med. Soc., La.-Miss. EENT Assn., Flying Physicians Assn., Soc. Mil. Ophthalmologists, Soc. of USAF Flight Surgeons, Alliance of Air N.G. Flight Surgeons, Aircraft Owners and Pilots Assn., Nu Sigma Nu. Club: Kiwanis. Home: 809 Cherry Ln Laurel MS 39440 Office: Laurel Eye Center PO Box 2907 Laurel MS 39442

LINDSTROM, ROBERT LEE, counselor, consultant, lecturer; b. Tucson, Apr. 3, 1940; s. Olaf Reginald and Eleanor Rose (Moore) L.; A.S. magna cum laude, Blue Ridge Community Coll., 1974; B.A., James Madison U., 1975, M.Ed., 1976. Heavy equipment operator R.G. Foster & Co., Wadley, Ga., 1963-67; sales rep. IBM, Waynesboro, Va., 1967-70; partner Lindstrom & Co., New Market, Va., 1970-72; counselor Operation PAR, Clearwater, Fla., 1977-79; time-out room specialist PASS Project, Pinellas County (Fla.) Sch. Bd., 1979; pvt. practice counseling; owner, operator Indian Rocks Beach SCUBA Sch. (Fla.), 1980-84, Alpha Divers, 1985—. Served with AUS, 1958-61. Cert. tchr., guidance counselor, Fla.; lic. capt.; cert. aquanaut. Mem. Am. Personnel and Guidance Assn., Am. Mental Health Counselors Assn., Cousteau Soc., Profl. Assn. Diving Instrs., Phi Theta Kappa. Office: PO Box 9267 Treasure Island FL 33740

LINE, JOHN PAUL, mathematics educator; b. Pontiac, Mich., Mar. 2, 1929; s. Paul Benjamin and Dortha Bernice (Thompson) L.; m. Frances Carlton Winn, Sept. 7, 1957; children—Paul, Carl, Mark, John. B.S., U. Mich., 1950, M.S., 1951. Instr. Oberlin (Ohio) Coll., 1955, U. Rochester, N.Y., 1955-56; asst. prof. Ga. Inst. Tech., Atlanta, 1956-62, assoc. prof. math., 1962—. Mem. Am. Math. Soc., Math. Assn. Am., AAUP, Ga. State Square Dancers Assn., Inc., Sigma Xi. Presbyterian. Club: Merry Mixers Square Dance (Atlanta). Home: 1170 Old Coach Rd Stone Mountain GA 30083 Office: 263 Skiles Ga Inst Tech Atlanta GA 30332

LINEBACK, DAVID RAY, food science educator; b. Russellville, Ind., June 7, 1934; s. Clyde and Betty Louise (Reed) L.; m. Patricia Lee Jones, June 17, 1956; children—Linda Lee, D. Scott, Karen Louise. B.S., Purdue U., 1956; Ph.D., Ohio State U., 1962. Postdoctoral fellow dept. chemistry U. Alta., Edmonton, Can., 1962-64; instr. dept. biochemistry and nutrition U. Nebr., Lincoln, 1964-65, asst. prof., 1965-69; assoc. prof. grain sci. and industry Kans. State U., Manhattan, 1969-74, prof., 1974-76, asst. dept. head, instrn. dept. grain sci. and industry, 1971-76; prof. and head dept. food sci. Pa. State U., University Pk., 1976-80, N.C. State U., Raleigh, 1980—. Contbr. articles to profl. jours. Served to 1st lt. U.S. Army, 1957-58. Recipient award of merit Japanese Soc. Starch Sci., 1985. Fellow Inst. Food Technologists (chmn. carbohydrate div. 1980-81, grad. award jury 1982, Carolina, Va. sect. 1982-83, Kansas City sect. 1973-74, food sci. adminstrs. 1983-85, sci. lectr. 1979-83, mem. nominations and elections com. 1984—, long range planning com. 1982—, chmn. 1985—); mem. Am. Assn. Cereal Chemists (chmn. bd. 1984-85, pres. 1983-84, bd. dirs. 1982-85, mem. long range planning com. 1978-80, 1982-85), League Internat. Food Edn. (bd. dirs. 1983—, vice chmn. 1985—), Nat. Acad. Scis. (com. food protection 1983-85), Wheat Industry Council (nutrition advisor 1982—), Sigma Xi (pres. Kans. State U. chapt. 1973-74), Phi Tau Sigma (pres. 1985—). Office: NC State U Dept Food Sci Box 7624 Raleigh NC 27695-7624

LINEBACK, JERRY A., geologist; b. Ottawa, Kans., Oct. 25, 1938; s. Charles E. and Edna P. (Scott) L.; m. Mary C. Price, June 28, 1969; children—Nathan C., Benjamin I., Daniel J. B.S., U. Kans., 1960, M.S., 1961; Ph.D., Ind. U., 1964. Geologist Ill. State Geol. Survey, Urbana, 1964-81; sr. geologist Robertson Research (US) Inc., Houston, 1981—. Fellow Geol. Soc. Am.; mem. Am. Assn. Petroleum Geologists, Soc. Econ. Paleontologists and Mineralogists. Mormon. Avocations: gardening; monitoring internat. shortwave radio broadcasting. Home: 115 Wroxton St Conroe TX 77304 Office: Robertson Research (US) Inc 16730 Hedgecroft St Suite 306 Houston TX 77060

LINEBAUGH, GEORGE PHILLIPS, III, banker, former TV journalist; b. Nashville, Apr. 2, 1956; s. George Phillips, Jr. and Ann Hamilton (Harsh) L.; B.A. in Radio-TV, Abilene (Tex.) Christian U., 1980; postgrad. U. of South, Western Ky. U. Program dir. Sta. WLBQ, Morgantown, Ky., 1977; studio cameraman Stas. KRBC/KACB-TV, Abilene, 1979; spotting/scoring asst. to assoc. producer Profl. Golf Assn. golf tour CBS Sports, N.Y.C., 1979; TV news reporter Stas. KRBC/KACB, 1979; adminstrv. clk. TV drama series/serials BBC, London, 1980, TV news intern, 1980; account exec. Stas. WYCQ/-WHAL, Shelbyville, Tenn., 1981; TV news reporter, editor Sta. WTVF, Nashville, 1981-83; TV news reporter, anchor Sta. WTVK, Knoxville, Tenn., 1983-84; teller/counselor Leader Fed. Savs. and Loan Assn., Nashville, 1984-85; asst. trust officer 1st Am. Trust Co., 1985—. Mem. Nashville Jr. C. of C. Methodist. Clubs: Bachelor's of Nashville, Cumberland, Sewanee of Nashville, Nashville, Md. Farms Raquet and County. Home: Route 9 Brentwood TN 37027 Office: Leader Fed Savs and Loan Assn 3325 West End Ave Nashville TN 37203

LINEBERGER, MARILYN HAZZARD, clinical psychologist, educator; b. Abbeville, S.C., Dec. 10, 1952; d. Sanders and Louise (Lomax) Hazzard; m. Frank James Lineberger, Jr., Sept. 1, 1979; 1 child, Winsheket Nicole. B.A., U. S.C., 1975; M.S., U. Ga., 1977, Ph.D., 1979. Lic. clin. psychologist, Ga. Research and clin. asst. U. Ga., Athens, 1975-79; asst. prof. clin. psychology Kent State U., Ohio, 1979-80, Emory U., Atlanta, 1980—; pvt. practice clin. psychology, Atlanta, 1980—; cons. various orgns., Atlanta, 1980—. Contbr. chpt. to book, articles to profl. jours. Vol. Big Bro./Big Sister Program, Atlanta, 1980-81, YMCA, Atlanta, 1985. Mem. Am. Psychol. Assn., Assn. for Advancement of Behavior Therapy (chmn. black spl. interest group 1981-83), Assn. Black Psychologists, Ga. Psychol. Assn., Phi Beta Kappa. Democrat. Methodist. Avocations: writing and reading poetry and short stories; running; aerobics; chess; backgammon. Home: 3668 Crossvale Rd Lithonia GA 30058 Office: Dept Psychology Emory U Atlanta GA 30322

LINES, SHELLEY BRYANT, English language educator; b. Bozeman, Mont., May 7, 1944; d. George Albert and Thelma (McRay) Bryant; B.A., Mont. State U., 1966; postgrad. Jones Coll., 1978, Am. Inst. Banking, Orlando, 1981-83, Fla. So. U., Lakeland, 1984; children—Matthew M., Carter W. Sec., Credit Bur. Gallatin County (Mont.), 1962-66; tchr. Southbury (Conn.) High Sch., 1967-70; instr. English, psychology and speech dean adminstrn., Jones Sr. Coll. Bus., Orlando, Fla., 1973-77; asst. v.p., dir. tng. Barnett Bank of Central Fla., N.A., 1979-84; prof. English and mgmt. So. Coll., Orlando, 1984—. Mem. adv. com. Vocat.-Tech. Sch., Orlando. Mem. NEA, Am. Soc. Tng. and Devel., Am. Inst. Banking (instr.), Winter Park C. of C., Mont. State U. Alumni, Delta Gamma. Home: 2053 Hounds Lake Dr Winter Park FL 32792 Office: 250 Park Ave S Winter Park FL 32789

LINGERFELT, ALAN THOMAS, civil engineer, real estate executive; b. Richmond, Va., Sept. 10, 1954; s. Luther Harold and Mildred Juanita (Corvin) L.; m. Gwendolynn Montes Ferguson, Aug. 9, 1975; children—Jonathan Ryan, Justin Michael, Daniel Kenton. B.S.C.E., Va. Poly. Inst., State U., 1976; M.B.A., Va. Commonwealth U., 1980. Cert. profl. engr., Va. Founder, pres. Lingerfelt & Assoc., Inc., Richmond, 1977—, Lingerfelt Devel. Corp., 1978—, founder, v.p. Lingerfelt Mgmt. Corp., 1980—. Mem. Children's Hosp. Building Fund Raising Campaign, Nat. Right to Work Com., Am. Security Council, Derbyshire Baptist Ch. Recipient Eagle Scout award Boy Scouts Am., 1972. Mem. Nat. Soc. Profl. Engrs., ASCE (pres. central Va. chpt. 1979, dir. Va. sect. 1982-83), Am. Cons. Engrs. Council, Constrn. Specifications Inst., Am. Water Works Assn., Water Pollution Control Fedn., Am. Pub. Works Assn., Richmond Joint Engrs. Council (found. chmn. 1979), Va. Soc. Profl. Engrs. (polit. action com. 1981-83, dir. bd. trustees, chmn. pvt. practice sect. central chpt. 1981-82), Inst. Real Estate Mgmt., Nat. Assn. Indsl. and Office Parks (pres. Va. chpt. 1982, outstanding service award 1982), Richmond Real Estate Group, Richmond Board Realtors, Urban Land Inst. W. Richmond Bus. Men's Assn., Jaycees (outstanding young man Am. award 1982). Assoc. Gen. Contractors Va., Inc. Clubs: Westwood Racquet, Downtown (Richmond), Va. Power Boat Assn., Skidmore Hunt, Engrs. (Richmond), 2001 Supper. Lodge: Rotary Internat. Home: 355 N Mooreland Rd Richmond VA 23229 Office: PO Box 8570 Richmond VA 23226

LINGLE, JOSEPH RICHARD, JR., chief of police; b. Hattiesburg, Miss., Sept. 7, 1952; s. J. R. and Kathern Ann (Young) L.; m. Lena Breaux, 1977 (div. 1980); m. Mary E. Gorman, Jan. 18, 1980. Cert., cert. instr. Tex. Commn. on Law Enforcement. Spl. officer New Orleans Police Dept., 1971-74; asst. chief police Big Sandy Police Dept., Tex., 1974-77, chief of police, 1979—; asst. chief police Hawkins Police Dept., Tex., 1977-78; patrolman Gladewater Police Dept., Tex., 1978-79; staff artist East Tex. Police Acad., East Tex. Police Chiefs Assn., Tex. Police Chiefs Assn., 1980—. Scouting coordinator Big Sandy council Boy Scouts Am. Recipient Merit award for Excellent Arrest, Am. Law Enforcement Assn.; Felony Arrest commendation, Am. Law Enforcement Assn., 2 Felony Arrest Commendations Big Sandy Police Dept.; named hon. dep. dir. La. Patrol Service, hon. capt. New Orleans Police Dept., hon. dep. sheriff Upsham County, Tex. Mem. Internat. Assn. Chiefs Police, Am. Law Enforcement Officers Assn., East Tex. Police Chiefs Assn., Tex. Law Enforcement Officers Assn., Nat. Sheriffs Assn., Tex. Sheriffs Assn., Tex. Police Assn., Tex. Police Chiefs Assn., Am. Police Hall of Fame (hon. bd. dirs.), Am. Fedn. Police (v.p. Tex.), East Tex. Council Govts. (criminal justice adv. com.). Republican. Office: Big Sandy Police Dept Box 461 Big Sandy TX 75755

LINGLE, KENDALL IDE, urban generalist, consultant; b. Chgo., June 30, 1910; s. Bowman Church and Bertha (Kendall) L.; m. Mary Bruce, Jan. 4, 1936 (dec. Jan. 1982); 1 son, Bowman Church, II. B.S., Princeton U., 1933. Exec. dir. various civic orgns. in Ill., 1935-40; chief personnel and tng. Ill. Dept. Pub. Health, 1940-41; field staff cons. Pub. Adminstrn. Service, 1941-45; active in civic and charitable affairs in Chgo. and nationally, 1945—; mem. Mayor's Adv. Com. on Youth Welfare, Chgo., 1948-59, exec. com., 1953-59; chmn. bd. mgrs., bd. dirs. Old Peoples Home of Chgo., 1948-58; mem. com. on aging and pub. affairs com. Met. Welfare Council of Chgo., 1948-65; mem. first nat. com. on aging Nat. Social Welfare Assembly, 1948-50; mem. Chgo. Commn. Youth Welfare, 1959-69; mem. adv. com. Chgo. Dept. Human Resources, 1969-74. Trustee New Coll., Sarasota, Fla., 1970-79; trustee Fund for Advancement of Camping, 1970—, nat. chmn., 1974-85; trustee, Am. Camping Assn., 1974-84; bd. dirs., 1974-84; project dir. Internat. Consortium on Alternatives for Youth-at-Risk, 1979—; mem. community resources com. Nat. Council Juvenile and Family Ct. Judges. Recipient Hedley Dimock award Am. Camping Assn., 1980. Mem. Nat. Soc. Internships and Experiential Edn., Internat. Personnel Mgmt. Assn., Internat. City Mgmt. Assn., Am. Soc. Public Adminstrn., Govtl. Research Assn., Internat. Union of Local Authorities, Nat. Juvenile Restitution Assn., Am. Corrections Assn., Nat. Council on Crime and Delinquency, Fla. Assn. Alternative Sch. Educators, Nat. Dist. Attys. Assn., Assn. Family Counseling in Juvenile and Family Cts., Am. Polit. Sci. Assn., Nat. Mcpl. League, Fla. Assn. Alternative Sch. Educators, Adult Edn. Assn. U.S., Am. Acad. Polit. and Social Sci. Presbyterian. Clubs: Saddle and Cycle, Casino, Econ., Monroe, Rotary, Chgo. Yacht, Univ. (Chgo.); Princeton (N.Y.C., Sarasota); Elm (Princeton U.); Venice (Fla.) Yacht; Mission Valley Golf and Country, Field. Home: 316 N Casey Key Osprey FL 33559 Office: 4500 N Tamiami Trail PO Box 3006 Sarasota FL 33578 also Suite 1818 36 State St Chicago IL 60603

LINK, MELVIN ROBERT, otolaryngologist; b. Paris, Ky., Aug. 8, 1916; s. Robert and Annie B. (English) L.; m. Margaret Swope, Aug. 15, 1942 (div. Dec. 1970); children—Robert S., Richard M., Jane F.; m. 2d, Evelyne Johnson, Aug. 21, 1976. A.B., Transylvania U., 1938; M.D., U. Louisville, 1942. Diplomate Am. Bd. Otolaryngology. Intern U.S. Naval Hosp., Bethesda, Md., 1942-43; resident in otolaryngology Columbia-Presbyn. Med. Ctr., N.Y.C., 1947-50; practice medicine specializing in otolaryngology, Charlotte, N.C., 1950—; mem. staffs Mercy Hosp., Presbyn. Hosp. Served to lt., M.C., USN, 1942-47. Decorated Bronze Star. Mem. Am. Acad. Bronchoesophagology, AMA, So. Med. Assn., N.C. Med. Assn., Am. Acad. Otolaryngology-Head and Neck Surgery. Republican. Lutheran. Club: Charlotte City. Office: 2107 E 7th St Charlotte NC 28204

LINKER, RITA YVONNE, librarian; b. Johnson City, Tenn., Mar. 22, 1938; d. Gordon Buford and Mary Grace (Scott) Stinson; m. Eustace Sloop Linker, Aug. 16, 1958; 1 dau., Yvonne Hall. B.S., East Tenn. State U., 1959; M.L.S., Emory U., 1977. Tchr., Rome City Schs. (Ga.), 1963-64; reference librarian Tri-County Regional Library System, Rome, 1975-80; dir. Chattooga County Library, Summerville, Ga., 1980—. Bd. dirs. Regional Ednl. Service Agt., 1986-88. Mem. ALA, Ga. Library Assn. (sec. pub. library div. 1987), Southeastern Library Assn., Bus. and Profl. Women (sec. 1983-84, 2d v.p. 1984-85, 1st v.p. 1985-86, pres. 1986-87). Mem. Ch. of Christ. Home: PO Box 305 Adairsville GA 30103 Office: Chattooga County Library 200 S Commerce St Summerville GA 30747

LINN, ROBERT ALLEN, chemical company executive, lawyer; b. Akron, Ohio, June 9, 1932; s. Robert Albertus and Rita Marie (Hogl) L.; m. Eileen Marie Ryan, Nov. 22, 1956 (div. 1986); children—Nancy Ann, Thomas Patrick, Michael Joseph, Mary Lisa. B.S. in Chemistry, Xavier U., Cin., 1954, M.S., 1956; postgrad. Wayne State U., 1956-58; LL.B., U. Detroit, 1961; M.B.A., Mich. State U., 1980. Bar: Mich. 1961, U.S. Dist. Ct. (ea. dist.) Mich. 1962, U.S. Patent & Trademark Office, 1963. Toxicologist, Wayne County, Detroit, 1957-61; patent atty. Ethyl Corp., Ferndale, Mich., 1961-64, mgr. patent sect., 1964-80, economist, Baton Rouge, 1980-81, dir. corp. bus. devel., Richmond, Va., 1981-86, patent atty., Baton Rouge, La., 1986—. Contbr. articles to profl. jours. Mem. Product Devel. and Mgmt. Assn. (pres. 1984-85, Cresheim award for best conf. paper 1982), Assn. Corp. Growth, Am. Intellectual Property Assn. Episcopalian. Office: Ethyl Corp 451 Florida Blvd Baton Rouge LA 70801

LINNARTZ, ROY, educational administrator; b. San Antonio, Jan. 2, 1947; s. Erich George and Ophila (McGraw) L.; m. Frances Faye Wiemers, Aug. 30, 1969; children—Roy Neal, Deborah Lauren. B.S., Southwest Tex. State U., 1969, M.Ed., 1974. Tchr., Comal Ind. Sch. Dist., New Braunfels, Tex., 1969-75, asst. prin., 1976-79, prin., 1979—; dir. Baese Realty Inc., New Braunfels; adviser state curriculum project, 1972. Vice chmn. zoning bd. adjustments and appeals City of New Braunfels, 1978-83; election judge Comal County, Tex., 1978-83. Recipient Outstanding Regional Tchr. award Tex. Indsl. Arts Assn., 1972, Am. Indsl. Arts Assn., 1974, Disting. Teaching award Tex. Indsl. Arts Assn., 1974. Mem. Tex. State Tchrs. Assn. (life mem., pres. local chpt. 1973), Tex. Assn. Secondary Sch. Prins., Tex. Bd. Realtors, New Braunfels Bd. Realtors, Phi Delta Kappa. Lutheran. Office: Canyon Middle Sch 1275 Hwy 81 E New Braunfels TX 78130

LINNEY, JEAN ANN, psychology educator, researcher; b. Floral Park, N.Y., July 18, 1950; d. John Joseph and Henrietta Francis (Hahn) L.; m. Michael Jeffery Schoen, Nov. 25, 1978; 1 child, Ryan Linney. B.A. cum laude, William Smith Coll., 1972; M.A., U. Ill., 1976, Ph.D., 1978. Research asst., undergrad. supr. Vols. in Schs. Program U. Ill., Urbana, 1972-73, co-dir., supr. vols., 1974-75; research assoc., 1975-76; program cons. Gemini House, Champaign, Ill., 1974-75; program cons. Crisis Intervention Service, Good Samaritan Mental Health Ctr., Dayton, Ohio, 1976-77; evaluation dir. Middletown Area Mental Health Ctr., Ohio, 1976-77; psychology instr. Miami U., Oxford, Ohio, 1976-77; evaluation dir. Parents Plus, U. Va., Charlottesville, 1978-79, evaluation cons. Offender Aid and Restoration, 1983, co-dir., faculty supr.

undergrad. internship program, 1979-83, asst. prof. psychology, 1977-83; evaluation dir., program cons. Theatrically Related Employment Experience, Barboursville, Va., 1980-81; sr. research assoc. Nat. Acad. Scis., Washington, 1980-81, cons., 1982; program cons. S.C. Dept. Youth Services, Columbia, S.C., 1983—; asst. prof. psychology, U. S.C., Columbia, 1983—. Editorial bd. Am. Jour. Community Psychology, 1979-82, 85—; reviewer Am. Jour. Community Psychology, Child Devel., Profl. Psychology: Research and Practice, Policy Studies Rev.; chmn. profl. symposia, confs. in field; contbr. articles to profl. publs., papers to profl. confs. U.S., Can. Bd. mem. Midlands Kidney Found., Columbia, 1984—. Recipient Welker Meml. award, William Smith Coll., 1972; USPHS trainee in psychology, 1972-73. Mem. Am. Psychol. Assn. (div. 27 sec.-treas. 1982-85, co-chmn. Task Force on Women 1983—, mem. coms.), Soc. for Psychol. Study of Social Issues (Social Issues Dissertation award 1979), Southeastern Psychol. Assn. Democrat. Roman Catholic. Office: Dept Psychology Univ SC Columbia SC 29208

LINNEY, PAUL ALVIN, architect; b. New Albany, Ind., June 22, 1943; s. Eugene Knott and Edith Clola (Wright) L.; B.Arch. (alt. Ryerson traveling fellow), U. Ill., 1967; m. Kathy Loots, Nov. 27, 1976; 1 son, Paul Alvin II. Designer, archtl. firms in Louisville and Atlanta, 1967-73; pres. Med. Facilities Devel. Corp., Atlanta, 1973-75, Paul Linney & Assos./Architects, Inc., Atlanta, 1975—; prin. works include Urban Med. Hosp., Atlanta, 1972, Sumter Meml. Hosp., Ala., 1979, Macon County Med. Center, Ga., 1981, Ormond Beach Hosp. (Fla.), 1982, Emergency Trauma Ctr., Roswell, Ga., 1982, Mary E. Dickerson Meml. Hosp., Jasper, Tex., 1983, South Haven Med. Ctr. (Miss.), 1983, New Boston Doctors Bldg. (Tex.), 1983, N.E. Med. Ctr., Houston, 1983, Urban Med. Profl. Bldg., Atlanta, 1983, Kleman Leach Clinic, Albany, Ga., 1983; renovation Doctors Meml. Hosp., 1979, Physicians and Surgeons Hosp., Atlanta, 1978; cons. hosp. and med. related design, 1975—. Counselor Henderson (Ky.) Jr. Achievement, 1969-70. Scoutmaster, Boy Scouts Am., 1969-70; founder, chmn. bd. Accelerated Acads., Inc., 1985; pres. Acad. Early Learning, 1985. Recipient God and Country award, Order of Arrow Boy Scouts Am. Mem. AIA (honor award designer Eastern Ky. U. phys. edn. bldg. and stadium 1971), Gargoyle Soc. Republican. Methodist. Clubs: Sierra, Green Peace. Home: 3867 Wieuca Rd Atlatna GA 30342 Office: 1000 Circle 75 Pkwy Atlanta GA 30339

LINNSTAEDTER, JERRY LEROY, mathematics educator; b. Lindale, Tex., July 25, 1937; s. Leroy and Bonnie (Lyon) L.; m. Julia Woods McCulley, Jan. 30, 1962; children—Jean Elizabeth, Joan Margaret, Jane Katherine. B.A., Tex. A&M U., 1959, M.S., 1961; Ph.D., Vanderbilt U., 1970. Instr. Northeast La. State U., Monroe, 1961-63, Vanderbilt U., Nashville, 1963-68; prof. math., chmn. dept. math., computer sci. and physics Ark. State U., State University, 1968—; research assoc., asst. NASA, Huntsville, Ala. and Cambridge, Mass., 1962-68; prin. investigator NASA, Cambridge, 1969-71; state commr. IMPAC, Little Rock, 1983-86; dir. IMPAC Systems, Inc., Little Rock. Contbr. articles to profl. jours. Mem. Am. Math. Soc., Math. Assn. Am., Ark. Acad. Sci. (chmn. math. sect. 1972-73), Nat. Council Tchrs. Math., Ark. Council Tchrs. Math. (pres. 1980-82), Northeast Ark. Council Tchrs. Math. (pres. 1974-77), Sigma Xi, Phi Delta Kappa, Phi Kappa Phi, Kappa Mu Epsilon. Democrat. So. Baptist. Home: Route 2 Box 2297 Jonesboro AR 72401 Office: Ark State Univ PO Box 70 State University AR 72467

LINOFF, MARIAN GOTTLIEB, psychologist; b. Mpls., Feb. 17, 1937; d. Jack and Anne (Meirowitz) Gottlieb; m. Alan Lee Linoff, June 17, 1956 (div. 1968); children—Joseph, Deborah, Gordon; m. Thomas Elton Thornton, July 8, 1984. B.A., U. Minn., 1961, M.A., 1963; Ph.D., U. Miami, 1972. Lic. psychologist, Fla. Psychologist VA Med. Ctr., Miami, 1971—; cons. Nat. Humanities Faculty, U. Miami Ctr., 1976-79, Nat. Drug Abuse Tng., 1974-78; specialist in geropsychology and aging. Mem. County Employ Handicapped, Miami, 1980-85. NIMH fellow, 1969-71; recipient Outstanding Performance award VA, 1983, 84, 85. Mem. Am. Psychol. Assn., Gerontol. Soc. Am., Biofeedback Soc. Am. Jewish. Research on geropsychology. Office: VA Med Ctr 116B Miami FL 33158

LINSCOMB, ALSIE, geologist; b. Beaumont, Tex., July 28, 1924; s. Leonard and Olivia (Boudreaux) L.; m. Louise Elizabeth Holt, Aug. 31, 1948; children—Alsie Parkholt, Mary Louise, James Stephen. B.S. in Geology, U. Tex., 1951. Exploration geologist Standard Oil Co. of Tex., San Antonio, 1951-57, devel. geologist, Corpus Christi, Tex., 1957-61; area petroleum geologist Central State Gas Prodn. Co., Corpus Christi, 1961-67; petroleum geologist Suburban Propane Gas Co., San Antonio, 1970-76; div. geologist Sigmor Corp., San Antonio, 1976-83, cons. geologist, San Antonio, 1967-70, 83—. Elder, Ch. of Christ, San Antonio, 1973—. Served to cpl. U.S. Army, 1943-46, ETO. Decorated Bronze Star with oak leaf cluster. Mem. South Tex. Geol. Soc. (sec. 1976-77), Am. Assn. Petroleum Geologists. Republican. Club: Petroleum. Avocations: hunting, fishing, travel. Office: Alsie Linscomb Oil and Gas Interests Petroleum Ctr 900 NE Loop 410 San Antonio TX 78209

LINSEY, GEORGE ALAN, retail healthcare executive, optometrist; b. N.Y.C., Aug. 21, 1947; s. Jack and Sylvia (Shapiro) L.; m. Barbara Ann Schenker, Mar. 27, 1983. B.S., L.I. U., 1968; O.D., Pa. Coll. Optometry, 1973. Pres. Vision Care Assocs., Harrisburg, Pa., 1973-78; chief exec. officer Dental Health Services, Tampa, Fla., 1981—, also dir.; chmn. bd. G. & D. Eyecare, Tampa, 1985—, also dir. Named to Outstanding Young Men Am., U.S. Jaycees, 1978. Mem. Assn. Group Practice Dentistry, Am. Optometric Assn. Republican. Jewish. Avocations: investments; tennis; fishing. Home: 13930 Shady Shores Dr Tampa FL 33612 Office: 6302 Benjamin Rd Tampa FL 33614

LINVILLE, JEWELL IRENE, business educator, consultant; b. Qualls, Okla., Oct. 30, 1941; d. Curtis and Eunice Alta (Walker) Holderby; m. Paul Wildon Linville, Dec. 27, 1959; children—Paula Dawn, Curtis Weldon. B.S. in Edn., Northeastern State Coll., 1961; M.S. in Edn., Northeastern Okla. State U., 1976; Ed.D., U. Ark., 1982. Service rep. Southwestern Bell Telephone Co., 1961-63; bus. instr. Granby High Sch., Mo., 1963-64; acct. Linville Jewelry, Tahlequah, Okla., 1964-68; bus. instr. Midwest Bible Coll., Stanberry, Mo., 1968-72; acct. Christian Challenge Sch., Wichita, Kans., 1973-74; bus. instr. Muskogee High Sch., Okla., 1974-78; assoc. prof. bus. Northeastern Okla. State U., Tahlequah, 1978—; cons. Community Action Agy., Wichita, 1974; pvt. practice as cons. and seminar presentor, 1974—. Contbr. articles to profl. and Christian pubs. Rep. Cancer Soc. Tahlequah; mem. com. U.S. Dept. Edn., 1984-85. Mem. Am. Bus. Communications Assn., AAUW, Nat. Bus. Edn. Assn., Okla. Bus. Edn. Assn. (area rep. 1983-85, zone sec., v.p., pres.), Am. Vocat. Assn., Tahlequah C. of C. (sec.), Delta Kappa Gamma, Delta Phi Epsilon, others. Democrat. Mem. Ch. of God (Seventh Day). Office: Northeastern Okla State U Tahlequah OK 74464

LIPKIN, DAVID LAWRENCE, physician; b. Bklyn., Mar. 9, 1938; s. Herman and Celia (Granate) L.; m. Nicole Van Laere, Sept. 23, 1962; children—Lawrence, Elline, Diane. A.B. in Biology, Clark U., Worcester, Mass., 1957; M.D., Catholic U. Louvain (Belgium), 1964. Diplomate Am. Bd. Phys. Medicine and Rehab. Intern, Lutheran Med. Ctr., Bklyn., 1963-64; resident in pediatrics N.J. Coll. Medicine, Jersey City, 1964-66; resident rehab. medicine Albert Einstein Coll. Medicine, Bronx, N.Y., 1966-68, chief resident, 1968-69; clin. instr. U. Miami, 1974-80, clin. asst. prof., 1980—; med. dir. rehab. Parkway Regional Med. Center Humana Hosp., Biscayne, Fla., 1974—; med. dir. Bon Secours Hosp., North Miami, Fla., 1984—; cons. in field. Chmn. stroke com. Am. Heart Assn., Monroe and Dade Counties, Fla., 1980-82. NIH fellow, 1966-69. Mem. Dade County Med. Assn., Fla. Med. Assn., Fla. Soc. Phys. Medicine and Rehab. (pres. 1976-78), Am. Rheumatism Assn., Am. Acad. Phys. Medicine and Rehab. Fla. Rheumatology Soc., So. Soc. Phys. Medicine and Rehab. Home: 20411 NE 22d Pl North Miami Beach FL 33199

LIPMAN, BERNARD SYLVESTER, physician; b. St. Joseph, Mo., June 14, 1920; s. Harry and Sarah (Kross) L.; B.A., Washington U., 1941, M.D., 1944; m. Leslie Joy Garber, Apr. 23, 1949; children—Lawrence A., Robert B., Bradford C., William L. Intern, Barnes Hosp., St. Louis, 1943-44, resident in medicine, 1944-45, 47-48; resident in medicine Yale U., 1948-49; asst. in medicine, teaching fellow cardiology Washington U. Sch. Medicine, St. Louis, 1949-50; instr. medicine Emory U., Atlanta, 1950-56, asso. in medicine, 1956-61, asst. prof. medicine, 1961-65, asso. prof. medicine, 1965-73, prof. clin. medicine (cardiology), 1973—; guest lectr. cardiology U. Tenn., 1958, U. Minn., 1959, 73; dir. heart sta. St. Joseph Hosp., Atlanta, 1965—; co-dir. Giddings Heart Clinic, Atlanta, 1970-75. Co-trustee, Albert Steiner Meml. Fund. Served to capt., M.C., AUS, 1945-47. Recipient Maimonides award Israel Bonds, 1982; Nat. Heart Inst. grantee, 1949. Diplomate Am. Bd. Internal Medicine. Fellow ACP, Am. Coll. Cardiology; mem. Council Clin. Cardiology, Am. Heart Assn., Am. Fedn. Clin. Research, Altanta Med. Assn., Am. Soc. Internal Medicine, N.Y. Acad. Sci., Phi Beta Kappa, Sigma Xi, Alpha Omega Alpha. Author: Clinical Electrocardiography, 7th edit., 1984. Contbr. articles to profl. jours. Office: 3280 Howell Mill Rd NW Atlanta GA 30327

LIPMAN, IRA ACKERMAN, security service co. exec.; b. Little Rock, Nov. 15, 1940; s. Mark and Belle (Ackerman) L.; student Ohio Wesleyan U., 1958-60; LL.D., John Marshall U., 1970; m. Barbara Ellen Kelly Couch, July 5, 1970; children—Gustave K., Joshua S, M Benjamin. Salesman and exec. Mark Lipman Service, Inc., Memphis, 1960-63; pres. Guardsmark, Inc., Memphis, 1963—, chief exec. officer, 1966—, chmn. bd., 1968—. Mem. young leadership cabinet United Jewish Appeal, 1973-78, Pres.'s Council, Memphis State U., 1975—, S.E. regional campaign cabinet, 1980; bd. dirs. NCCJ, Memphis chpt., 1980-85, life bd. 1985—, nat. trustee, 1980—, exec. com., 1981—, Humanitarian of yr. award 1985); bd. dirs. Nat. Council on Crime and Delinquency, 1975, mem. exec. com., 1976, chmn. fin. com., treas., 1978-79, vice chmn., 1982—; bd. dirs. Greater Memphis Council on Crime and Delinquency, 1976-78; met. chmn. Nat. Alliance Businessmen, 1970-71; mem. environ. security com., pvt. security adv. council Law Enforcement Assistance Adminstrn., 1975-76; bd. dirs. Tenn. Ind. Colls. Fund, 1977-79, mem. exec. com., 1978-79; trustee Memphis Acad. Arts, 1977-81, Brooks Meml. Art Gallery, Memphis Brooks Mus. Art, 1980-83; mem. Future Memphis, 1979—, bd. dirs., 1980—; mem. exec. bd. Chickasaw council Boy Scouts Am., 1978-81, adv. council, 1982—; Group II chmn. United Way Greater Memphis, 1982—, gen. campaign chmn., 1985-86; Shelby County chmn. U.S. Savs. Bonds, 1976; mem. Union of Am. Hebrew Congregations, Task Force on Reform Jewish Outreach, 1979-83; chmn. trustees campaign com. Simon Wiesenthal Ctr., 1983, also trustee; trustee Yeshiva U., 1982—; bd. dirs. Nat. Alliance Against Violence, 1983-85; mem. conf. planning com., 2d Nat. Law Enforcement Explorer Conf., 1980—; bd. overseers B'nai B'rith Internat., 1980—; mem. Visual Arts Council, Memphis State U., 1980—; bd. dirs. Memphis Jewish Fedn., 1974-83, Memphis Jewish Community Center, 1974, Memphis-Shelby County unit Am. Cancer Soc., 1980-81, Memphis Orchestral Soc., 1980-81, Gov.'s Jobs for High Sch. Grads. Program, 1980-83; ambassador for Tenn., 1981—. Entrepreneurial fellow Memphis State U., 1976; Named one of 10 Best Corp. Chief Execs. of Achievement, Gallagher Pres.'s Report, 1974. Mem. Internat. Assn. Chiefs Police, Am. Soc. Criminology, Internat. Soc. Criminology, Am. Soc. Indsl. Security (cert. protection profl.). Republican. Clubs: Economic (dir. 1980-85, v.p. 1983-84, pres. 1984-85, chmn. exec. com. 1984-85), Racquet, Summit, Delta, Petroleum, Ridgeway Country, Christian Bros. Coll. President's, 100 of Memphis (dir.) (Memphis); Internat. (Washington). Author: How to Protect Yourself from Crime, 1975, 81; contbr. articles to jours. and newspapers. Office: 10 Rockefeller Plaza 12th Floor New York NY 10005 also 22 S 2d St Memphis TN 38103

LIPOFF, NORMAN HAROLD, lawyer; b. N.Y.C., Dec. 9, 1936; s. Benjamin and Anna (Lippow) L.; m. Nancy B. Bressler, June 12, 1960; children—Ann, Elise. B.S.B.A., U. Fla., 1958, J.D. with honors, 1961; LL.M. in Taxation, NYU, 1962. Assoc., Carlton, Fields, Ward, Emmanuel, Smith & Cutler, Tampa, Fla., 1962-70; ptnr. Greenberg, Traurig, Askew, Hoffman, Lipoff, Rosen & Quentel, Miami, Fla., 1970—. Pres., Greater Miami Jewish Fedn.; nat. vice chmn., treas. United Jewish Appeal; nat. chmn. Endowment Fund Devel. of Council of Jewish Fedns.; bd. govs. Tel-Aviv U., Jewish Agy. for Israel; mem. citizens bd. U. Miami; bd. dirs. U. Fla. Found.; trustee Law Ctr. Assn., U. Fla. Coll. Law. Recipient Pres.'s Leadership award Greater Miami Jewish Fedn., 1972; Pres.'s award Tel Aviv U., 1982. Mem. ABA (tax sect.), Fla. Bar Assn. (chmn. tax sect. 1972). Democrat. Home: Three Grove Isle Dr 1009 Coconut Grove FL 33133 Office: 1401 Brickell Ave PH 11 Miami FL 33131

LIPPA, BARBARA JEAN, planning official; b. Rochester, N.Y., Sept. 3, 1952; d. Frank and Joan Patricia (Vitello) Lippa; B.S., SUNY, Brockport, 1974; M.A., George Washington U., 1977, M.S.A., 1983. Legis. intern Com. on Human Resources, U.S. Senate, Washington, 1974; edn. cons., 1974; cons. Nat. Adv. Council on Indian Edn., 1974; staff Nat. Adv. Council on Edn. of Disadvantaged Children, Washington, 1974-77; planning aide Fairfax County (Va.) Planning Commn., 1978-79; dep. exec. dir. Fairfax County Planning Commn., 1979—. Religious edn. tchr. Roman Cath. Ch., Alexandria, 1974-80, coordinator Bible sch., 1977. Recipient award for excellence HEW, 1975, Unusual Ability increment County of Fairfax, Va.; 1982. Mem. Am. Planning Assn., Nat. Assn. Exec. Women, Zonta Intenat. Home: 14436 Manassas Gap Ct Centreville VA 22020 Office: 10th Floor 4100 Chain Bridge Rd Fairfax VA 22320

LIPPER, STEVEN, psychiatrist, educator; b. Boston, July 17, 1943; s. Philip and Tillie (Levine) L.; m. Susan Fay Shapiro, July 27, 1969; children—Rachel Margaret, Charles Nathan. A.B. magna cum laude, Harvard Coll., 1964; postgrad. Yale U. Sch. Medicine, 1964-65, 67-68; Ph.D., Boston U., 1970, M.D., 1972. Diplomate Nat. Bd. Med. Examiners. Resident in psychiatry N.C. Meml. Hosp., Chapel Hill, 1972-75; clin. assoc. NIMH, Bethesda, Md., 1975-77; staff psychiatrist VA Med. Ctr., Ann Arbor, Mich., 1977-82; asst. prof. psychiatry U. Mich. Med. Sch., Ann Arbor, 1977-80, assoc. prof., 1980-82; staff psychiatrist VA Med. Ctr., Durham, N.C., 1982—; assoc. prof. psychiatry Duke U., Durham, 1982—. Served with USPHS, 1975-77. Recipient John M. Murray prize in psychiatry, 1972; Anclote Manor award in psychiatry N.C. Meml. Hosp. Dept. Psychiatry, 1975. Mem. Am. Psychiat. Assn. N.C. Neuropsychiat. Assn., Am. Psychosomatic Soc., AAAS, Fedn. Am. Scientists, N.Y. Acad. Scis., Phi Beta Kappa, Sigma Xi, Alpha Omega Alpha. Contbr. chpts. to books, articles to profl. jours. Office: Psychiatry Service VA Med Ctr 508 Fulton St Durham NC 27705

LIPPMAN, MERVIN ROBERT, physician, educator; b. N.Y.C., Apr. 10, 1922; s. Nathan I. and Fannie Lippman; m. Elaine P. Levant, Jan. 25, 1949 (div. Mar. 1964); children—Ellen Joy Bellerose, Andrew E.; m. Sydney Altschuler, June 25, 1964; children—Linda Patterson, Cathie Bourne. B.A., U. Tex., 1943; D.O., Chgo. Coll. Osteo. Medicine, 1949. Am. Coll. Osteo. Gen. Practice. Intern Kansas City Coll. Osteo. Medicine Hosp. and Conley Maternity Hosp., 1949-50; gen. practice osteo. medicine, Kansas City, Mo., 1950-75, Sarasota, Fla., 1975—; assoc. prof. family practice N.Y. Coll. Osteopathy, W. Va., Coll. Osteopathy. Served to lt. comdr. USN, 1943-46, PTO. Fellow Am. Coll. Gen. Practitioners, Am. Acad. Family Practice (Physicians award 1982-85); mem. Am. Osteo. Assn., Fla. Osteo. Med. Assn., Sigma Sigma Phi. Republican. Jewish. Lodges: Masons, Shriners, Rotary. Avocations: golf, photography. Home: 1255 Gulf Stream Ave Sarasota FL 33577 Office: 2831 Ringling Blvd Sarasota FL 33577

LIPSCOMB, OSCAR HUGH, archbishop; b. Mobile, Ala., Sept. 21, 1931; s. Oscar and Margaret (Saunders) L.; student St. Bernard Coll., Cullman, Ala., 1949-51, N. Am. Coll., Rome; S.T.L., Gregorian U., Rome, 1957; Ph.D., Cath. U. Am., 1963. Ordained priest Roman Catholic Ch., 1956; asst. pastor St. Mary Parish, Mobile, 1959-65; vice chancellor Diocese of Mobile-Birmingham, 1963-66, chancellor, 1966-80; archbishop of Mobile, 1980—; tchr. McGill Inst., Mobile, 1959-60, 61-62; pastor St. Patrick Parish, Mobile, 1966-71; lectr. history Spring Hill Coll., Mobile, 1971-72; asst. pastor St. Matthew Parish, Mobile, 1971-79; asst. pastor Cathedral of Immaculate Conception, Mobile, 1979-80; pres. Cath. Housing Mobile, Inc.; pres. Mobile Senate of Priests, 1978-80; trustee Trustee, Pontifical N. Am. Coll., Rome, Cath. U. Am., 1983; mem. bd. Notre Dame Sem., New Orleans. Pres. Mobile Mus. Bd., 1966-76; trustee Ala. Dept. Archives and History, 1979—. Mem. Ala. Hist. Assn. (pres. 1971-72, exec. com. 1981), So. Hist. Assn., Am. Cath. Hist. Assn. Author: The Administration of John Quinlan, Second Bishop of Mobile, 1859-1883, 1967. Address: 400 Government St Mobile AL 36602

LIPSCOMB, STEPHEN LEON, mathematics educator; b. Junior, W.Va., Jan. 31, 1944; s. David Leon and Dema Ann (Alkire) L.; m. Patrecia Ann Skidmore, Sept. 15, 1962; children—Stephen Leon, Darrin Joel. B.Ed., Fairmont State Coll., 1965; M.Math., W.Va. U., 1967; Ph.D. in Math., U. Va., 1973. High sch. tchr. and coach, Rehoboth Beach, Del., 1967-68; sr. mathematician Naval Surface Weapons Ctr., Dahgren, Va., 1968-83; eminent scholar in math. Mary Washington Coll., Fredericksburg, Va., 1983-84, chmn. dept. math. sci. and physics, 1984—; adj. prof. math. Va. Poly. Inst. and State U. Solved imbedding problem for finite-dimensional metric spaces, 1975; generalized Uryshon's theorem, 1976; conceived new group of graph used to count reconstructions, 1984; developed first thrust integral program for U.S. Navy; author papers in field. Mem. Am. Math. Soc. Home: 10 Eden Dr King George VA 22485 Office: Dept Math Sci and Physics Mary Washington Coll Fredericksburg VA 22401

LIPSHY, BRUCE A., jewelry company executive; b. 1941; B.B.A., U. Tex., 1963, LL.B., 1965. Partner firm Stalcup, Johnson, Lipshy & Williams, 1965-71; v.p. gen. corp. mgmt. affairs Zale Corp., Dallas, 1971-72, sr. v.p. adminstrn., 1972-77, exec. v.p., 1977-78, pres., chief operating officer, 1978—, also dir.; dir. Interfirst Bank, Dallas. Bd. dirs. Temple Shalom, Dallas United Way, Dallas Central unit Am. Cancer Soc., Goodwill Industries; former bd. dirs. Dallas Home for the Jewish Aged, Spl. Care Sch., Tex. Research League. Mem. State Bar Tex., Dallas Bar Assn., Young Pres.'s Orgn., Dallas Assembly. Office: Zale Corp 3000 Diamond Park Dr Dallas TX 75247

LIPTAK, ROBERT WILLIAM, manufacturing company executive; b. Reading, Pa., Apr. 6, 1939; s. William Steven and Ruth Elizabeth (Adam) L.; B.S., Albright Coll., 1962; M.S., Columbia U., 1979; m. Maryellen Chelius, Jan. 28, 1961; children—Julia C., Robert William, John B., Katherine L. Mgr., Price Waterhouse & Co., N.Y.C., 1962-75; dir. fin. controls Babcock & Wilcox Co., N.Y.C., 1975-78; exec. asst. to pres. fin. Babcock & Wilcox, 1978-80; sr. v.p. fin. and adminstrn. Bigelow Sanford Inc., Greenville, S.C., 1980—. Treas., Charles T. King Student Loan Fund, Millburn/Short Hills, N.J., 1974-79; trustee, pres. Maplewood Club, 1972-80. C.P.A., N.J., N.Y. Mem. Am. Inst. C.P.A.s, N.J. Soc. C.P.A.s, N.Y. Soc. C.P.A.s, Fin. Execs. Inst., Nat. Assn. Accts. (pres. 1976-77, nat. dir. 1979-81, nat. v.p. 1983-84, chmn. edn. com. 1984—). Roman Catholic. Clubs: Greenville Country, Maplewood. Office: PO Box 3089 Greenville SC 29602

LIPTON, RICHARD JAY, steel products manufacturing company executive; b. Atlanta, Mar. 31, 1949; s. Nathan and Bernice (Berman) L.; m. Beth Yates, Sept. 12, 1972; 1 dau., Lauren Beth; m. 2d, Claudia Ann McCabe; 1 son, Zachary Richard. Student U. Tenn.-Knoxville, 1967-68, Ga. State U.-Atlanta, 1968-71. Account exec. Beamm Lipton Co., Atlanta, 1968-71; exec. v.p. LLL Corp., Atlanta, 1971-74; pres. Oxylance Corp., Atlanta, 1974—; lectr. Emory U., Atlanta, 1979-83; dir. Hi-Fi Buys, Atlanta. Mem. Democratic Nat. Com., Washington, 1979-80; sponsor Atlanta Defamation League, 1979-83. Recipient Small Bus. Person of the Yr. award Small Bus. Adminstrn., 1979. Mem. White House Conf. on Small Bus. Jewish. Clubs: Standard, Jewish Community Ctr. (Atlanta). Home: 2400 Bohler Rd Atlanta GA 30327 Office: Oxylance Corp 2400 Tower Pl Atlanta GA 30326

LIRETTE, TERRY JOSEPH, respiratory therapist, nurse, medical technology consultant; b. New Orleans, Sept. 28, 1940; s. Wilton Joseph and Louella Maria (Chauvin) L.; m. Alice Roddy, June 6, 1961; children—Angela, Mark, Eileen. Student U. Chgo., 1970, Hinds Jr. Coll., 1967-68, Nicholls State U., 1968-82, Ottawa U. Kansas City, 1985-86. Registered respiratory therapist, cardiology technologist, emergency med. technologist; cert. respiratory therapy technician; lic. practiced nurse. Staff Terrebonne Gen. Hosp., Houma, La., 1961-66, staff nurse respiratory therapy, 1966-67, tech. dir. cardio-respiratory care, program dir. sch. respiratory therapy, 1969-79, tech. dir. cardio-respiratory care, 1983—; program dir. respiratory therapy tech. Nicholls State U., 1979-83; pres. Wee Care Nursery, Inc., Houma, 1978—; v.p. Health Care Systems, Houma, 1983—; pres. Parish Home Oxygen Supply, Houma, 1984—; Bd. Med. Advisers Respiratory Therapy Licensure, 1986—. Bd. dirs. Am. Heart Assn. La., 1973—, Am. Lung Assn. La., 1973—, La. State Bd. La. Fedn. Lic. Practical Nurses, 1973-74, Bayou chpt. March of Dimes, 1983—. Served with USN, 1958-68. Recipient Disting. Citizenship award Nueces County Med. Soc., Corpus Christi, 1962; cert. of Appreciation La. Heart Assn., 1976, 77, 78, 79, 80, 81, 82, 83, 84; Most Successful Sem. award La. Soc., 1979; Personality of Week award Houma Courrier, 1979; Vol. of Yr. award March of Dimes, 1984. Mem. Am. Assn. Respiratory Therapy (bd. dirs. 1973-75, pres. 1977, 85), La. Fedn. Lic. Practical Nurses (bd. dirs. 1973—), Am. Cardiology Tech. Assn., La. Lung Assn., La. Heart Assn. Democrat. Roman Catholic. Avocations: fishing; hunting; work around house. Home: 505 Oaklawn Dr Houma LA 70363 Office: Terrebonne Gen Med Ctr 936 E Main St Houma LA 70361

LIS, ANTHONY STANLEY, educator; b. Easthampton, Mass., Aug. 11, 1918; s. Antoni and Anna Barbara (Karczmarczyk) L.; B.S., Mass. State Coll. at Salem, 1950; M.S., Okla. State U., 1950-51; Ph.D., U. Minn., 1961; m. Jane Ann Mikus, June 25, 1951 (dec.); children—Anthony Stanley, Judith Ann, Sandra Jane; m. 2d Sophie Ann Pobieglo, June 24, 1983. Instr. to asst. prof. bus. edn. Okla. State U., 1950-54; asst. prof. to asso. prof. bus. communication U. Tulsa, 1956-62; asso. prof. to prof. bus. adminstrn. U. Okla., 1962—; vis. prof. bus. adminstrn. Central Sch. Planning/Stats., Warsaw, Poland, 1984; cons. to bus., govtl. agencies. Participant, 2d Congress Scholars of Polish Descent, Warsaw and Cracow, 1979. Served with U.S. Army, 1937-40, to lt. col. AUS, 1942-46. Decorated Bronze Star; Faculty fellow Joint Econ. Found., 1954. Mem. Adminstrv. Mgmt. Soc., Am. Bus. Communication Assn. (nat. dir.), Southwestern Social Sci. Assn. (gen. program chmn. 1963-76), Am. Assn. Advancement Slavic Studies, Polish Am. Hist. Assn. Roman Catholic. Lion. Home: 1827 Peter Pan St Norman OK 73072

LISCOM, CLAYTON LEE, investment counselor; b. Goodrich, Mich., Mar. 21, 1947; s. Paul William and Mary Maxine (McKenzie) L.; m. Patricia Denise Mulcrone, Nov. 28, 1970; children—Craig Patrick, Ryan Michael. B. Indsl. Engr., Gen. Motors Inst., 1970; M.B.A., U. Mich., 1974. Chartered fin. analyst. Indsl. engr. Buick Motors Gen. Motors Corp., Flint, Mich., 1970-73; sr. fin. analyst Treas. Staff Gen. Motors, Detroit, 1977-78; portfolio mgr. Genesee Bank, Flint, 1973-77, dir. research, 1978-82; dir. equity research First Nat. Bank, Oklahoma City, 1982-84; chief adminstrv. officer First Investment Mgmt., Oklahoma City, 1984—; sec. program chmn. Fin. Analysts Soc. Okla., 1984—. Author: Visual Man-Computer Interface, 1970. Fellow Fin. Analysts Fedn. Republican. Methodist. Club: Greens Country. Avocations: golf, tennis. Home: 6209 Lansbrook Ct Oklahoma City OK 73127 Office: First Investment Mgmt 120 N Robinson Oklahoma City OK 73125

LISS, MILTON, financial services company executive; b. Bklyn., Sept. 19, 1943; s. Morris and Florence (Bormanstein) L.; m. Trina Gale Botler, June 29, 1969; children—William Jay, Bari Ann. B.A., Bklyn. Coll., 1967. Vice pres. Fin. Ind. Group, San Diego, 1974-75, Lincoln Annarino, Fort Worth, 1975-78; exec. v.p. Annarino Liss and Assocs., Fort Worth, 1978-81; v.p. Sidney W. Fairchild Co., Houston, 1981—. Mem. Nat. Assn. Health Underwriters. Jewish. Office: Sidney Fairchild Co 3100 Eastside St Houston TX 77098

LISTER, IRVIN CANON, chiropracter; b. Birmingham, Ala., Oct. 18, 1933; s. Robert Hood and Ruth (Griffin) L.; m. Bonnie Sanders, May, 1985; children by previous marriage—Elizabeth Ann, David Canon, Linda Diane. Student, U. Tuscaloosa, 1951-52, Del Mar Coll. 1953-54, Tulane U., 1954-55, B.S., William and Mary Coll., 1955-57; D.Chiropractic, Logan Chiropractic Coll., St. Louis, 1961; postgrad. La. State U., 1974, Tex. Chiropractic Coll., 1976-78. Lic. chiropractor, Fla., La. Gen. practice chiropractic medicine, Lafayette, La., 1961—; mem. La. Chiropractic Peer Rev. Bd., 1981-83, La. Bd. Chiropractic Examiners, 1983—, Fedn. Chiropractic Licensing Bds.; cons., lectr. in field. Served with Hosp. Corps, USN, 1952-56. Mem. Chiropractic Assn. La. (past pres., dir.), Internat. Chiropractors Assn., Am. Chiropractic Assn., Parker Chiropractic Research Found. Baptist. Lodge: Lions (Lafayette Lion of Yr. 1961). Presenter paper Soviet-Am. Exchange Tour, 1977. Office: 1444 Bertrand Dr Lafayette LA 70506

LITTELL, WILLIAM JON, psychologist; b. Liberal, Kans., Apr. 11, 1935; s. William Delmas and Eunice (Ipson) L.; m. Ann Bigbee, Apr. 5, 1959; children—James S., William J. B.M.E., U. Kans., 1957, M.M.E., 1961, Ph.D., 1973. Sales mgr. Bigbee Motors, Inc., Topeka, 1962-64; area mgr. Russ Hannibal Assocs., Topeka, 1964-68; cons. psychologist Rohrer Hibler & Replogle, Houston, 1973-77; prin. William J. Littell, Cons. Psychologist and Mgmt. Cons., Houston, 1977—. Bd. dirs. Meadowbriar Home for Children; mem. diocesan council Episcopal Ch., Houston, 1978-79. Served with U.S. Army, 1957-59. Mem. Am. Psychol. Assn., Houston Psychol. Assn., Am. Soc. Profl. Cons. Home: 10815 Dunbrook Dr Houston TX 77070 Office: 1000 FM 1960 W Suite 200 Houston TX 77090

LITTEN, DONALD DOUGLAS, lawyer; b. New Market, Va., Mar. 24, 1930; s. Raye Zirkle and Georgia Grace (Swartz) L.; m. Frances Ann Minor, Dec. 23, 1949; children—Ann Litten Menefee, Donald D., Jonathan J. Ed. James Madison U. Bar: Va. 1957, U.S. Dist. Ct. (we. dist.) Va. 1958, Va. Supreme Ct. 1958. Assoc., George D. Conrad, Harrisonburg, Va., 1957-61; jr. ptnr. Conrad and Litten, Harrisonburg, 1961-68; ptnr. Conrad, Litten and Sipe, Harrisonburg, 1968-80; mng. ptnr. Litten, Sipe and Miller, Harrisonburg, 1980—; chmn. regional bd. First Am. Bank; dir. Rockingham Mut. Ins. Co., Valley Nat. Bank, Rockingham Meml. Hosp., 1972-84, Hokeli Ltd. Pres. Massanutten

Property Owners Assn. Inc., 1985—; bd. visitors James Madison U., 1980-83. Served with USN, 1947-49. Recipient Disting. Service award Va. Jaycees, 1962. Mem. ABA, Assn. Trial Lawyers, Nat. Inst. Mcpl. Law Officers. Home: 101 McGuffin Pl Bridgewater VA 22812 Office: PO Box 712 Harrisonburg VA 22801

LITTLE, F. A., JR., federal judge; b. 1936. B.A., Tulane U., 1958, LL.B., 1961. Assoc. Chaffe, McCall, Phillips, Toler & Sarpy, New Orleans, 1961-65; assoc. Gold, Little, Simon, Weems & Bruser, Ltd., 1965-69, ptnr., 1969-84; judge U.S. Dist. Ct. for Western Dist. La., Alexandria, 1984—. Fellow Am. Coll. Probate Counsel; mem. La. Bar Assn., Alexandria Bar Assn. (pres.). Office: Box 1031 Alexandria LA 71309*

LITTLE, FREED SEBASTIAN, petroleum equipment mfg. co. exec.; b. Ft. Smith, Ark., May 4, 1926; s. Jess Edward and Floy Kimbrough (Witt) L.; B.A., U. Ark., 1950; m. Jana V. Jones, Dec. 9, 1951 (div.); 1 son, Mark McKenna. With Gilbarco Inc., Houston, 1964—, central area mgr., Chgo., 1969-73, Western regional mgr., Houston, 1974—. Served with USAAF, 1945-46. Mem. Am. Petroleum Inst., Petroleum Equipment Inst., Am. Mgmt. Assn., Sigma Alpha Epsilon. Presbyterian. Clubs: Houston City, Memorial Dr. Country. Home: 10121 Valley Forge Houston TX 77042 Office: 6405 Richmond Ave Suite 300 Houston TX 77057

LITTLE, HERBERT TIMOTHY, computer services executive; b. Amonate, Va., June 23, 1941; s. Herbert Floyd and Edythe (Bausell) L.; m. Judy Melchor, Aug. 31, 1964; children—Herbert Timothy, Whitney Jo. B.S., Hampden-Sydney Coll., 1964. Analyst, Dept. Def., Fort Meade, Md., 1965-69; computer analyst City of Portsmouth, Va., 1969-72, asst. dir., 1972-81, dir. computer services, 1981—; cons. Bert Systems, Portsmouth, 1971-78. Named Boss of Yr., Assn. City Secs., 1982. Mem. Data Processing Mgmt. Assn. (pres. 1978-79), Tidewater Community Coll. (adv. bd. 1984-86), Employee Credit Union (pres., 1979-80). Methodist. Avocations: reading; sports. Office: City of Portsmouth 801 Crawford St Portsmouth VA 23704

LITTLE, MARTHA LOUISE, clinical psychologist; b. Evansville, Ind., Mar. 28, 1914; d. Harry Wilson Sr. and Dora (Haussermann) Little. B.A., Wellesley Coll., 1935; M.A. in French, Middlebury French Sch., 1942; Cert. Applied Psychiatry for Tchrs., Washington Sch. Psychiatry, 1955; M.A. in Clin. Psychology, Catholic U. Am., 1958, Ph.D., 1967. Lic. clin. psychologist, Fla., Ill., Ohio; Diplomate in clin. psychology Am. Bd. Profl. Psychology, Clin. psychologist, research asst, NIMH, Bethesda, Md., 1955; trainee VA, Washington, Balt., 1955-57; intern Columbus Psychiatric Clinic (Ohio), 1957-58; staff psychologist Dayton State Hosp. (Ohio), 1958-59; State of Ohio stipendiary, Washington, 1959-63; staff psychologist Fairfax-Falls Church Mental Health Ctr. (Va.), 1961-63, Adult Psychiat. Clinic, Dayton, 1963-66; supervising clin. psychologist Oneida County, Utica, N.Y., 1966-68; chief clin. psychologist Sinnissippi Mental Health Ctr., Dixon, Ill., 1966-68; pvt. practice psychology, Dixon, 1968-78, Sarasota, Fla., 1978—; clin. instr. U. South Fla. Sch. Medicine, 1979-82. Mem. Am. Psychol. Assn., Fla. Psychol. Assn. (pres. Sarasota-Manatee div. Lower West Coast chpt. 1981), Am. Group Psychotherapy Assn., Internat. Assn. Group Psychotherapy. Unitarian. Clubs: Altrusa, Wellesley (Sarasota). Home: 800 Ben Franklin Dr #104 Sarasota FL 33577 Office: 635 S Orange Ave Sarasota FL 33577

LITTLE, ROBERT COLBY, medical educator, scientist; b. Norwalk, Ohio, June 2, 1920; s. Edwin Robert and Eleanor Thresher (Colby) L.; m. Claire Campbell Means, Jan. 20, 1945; children—William C., Edwin C. A.B., Denison U., 1942; M.D., Western Res. U., 1944, M.S., 1948. Intern, Grace Hosp., Detroit, 1944-45; postdoctoral fellow physiology Western Res. U., 1947-48; resident VA Hosp., Cleve., 1949-51; asst. prof. physiology Sch. Medicine, U. Tenn., Memphis, 1950-52, assoc. prof., 1952-54, assoc. prof. medicine, 1953-54; research participant Oak Ridge Inst. Nuclear Studies (Tenn.), summer 1952; dir. clin. research Research div. Mead Johnson and Co., Evanston, Ind., 1954-57; head Cardiopulmonary Labs., Scott, Sherwood and Brindley Found., Temple, Tex., 1957-58; lectr. physiology U. Tex. Postgrad. Sch. Medicine, Temple, 1957-58; prof. physiology, asst. prof. medicine Seton Hall Coll. Medicine and Dentistry, Jersey City, 1958-64, acting chmn. dept. physiology, 1961-63; prof., chmn. dept. physiology, asst. prof. medicine Ohio State U. Coll. Medicine, Columbus, 1964-73; prof., chmn. dept. physiology, prof. medicine Med. Coll. Ga., Augusta, 1973—; lectr. medicine U. Louisville, 1955-57. Served to capt. M.C., U.S. Army, 1943-47. Mem. Am. Physiol. Soc., So. Soc. Clin. Investigation, Soc. Exptl. Biology and Medicine, Am. Fedn. for Clin. Research, Am. Heart Assn., Ga. Acad. Sci., AMA, Internat. Soc. for Cardiac Research. Author: Physiology of the Heart and Circulation, 1977, 3d edit., 1985; Physiology of Atrial Pacemaker and Conductive Tissues, 1980; contbr. articles to profl. jours. Home: 44 Plantation Hills Dr Evans GA 30809 Office: Dept Physiology Med Coll Ga Augusta GA 30912

LITTLE, ROBERT NARVAEZ, JR., physics educator; b. Houston, Mar. 11, 1913; s. Robert Narvaez and Lillian Forrest (Kinney) L.; m. Betty Jo Browning, June 1, 1942; children—Scott Robert, Emily Browning. Student, U. Tex.-Austin, 1929-32; B.A. with honors in Math., Rice U., 1935, M.A. in Physics, 1942, Ph.D. in Physics, 1943. Seismologist Shell Oil Co., Houston, 1936-40; mem. faculty dept. physics U. Oreg., Eugene, 1943-44, U. Tex., 1946—, Universidad del Valle, Guatemale, 1977, Universidad Nacional de Education a Distancia, Madrid, 1981; chief nuclear physics Gen. Dynamics, Ft. Worth, 1953-55, cons., 1955-60. Author: Motion and Matter, 4th edit., 1984. Contbr. articles to profl. publs. Recipient Dedication of R.N. Little Lab. Physics, Universidad Nacional Autonoma de Honduras, 1981, Diploma de Reconocimiento, Universidad de el Salvador, 1984. Fellow Am. Phys. Soc., Tex. Acad. Sci.; mem. Am. Assn. Physics Tchrs. (Disting Service award 1973, Outstanding Contbns. to Higher Edn. Tex. award 1978), Sociedad Centro-Americano de Fisica, Groupe Internat. des Recherches sur L'Enseignement de la Physique. Home: 3928 Balcones Dr Austin TX 78731 Office: U Tex Physics Dept Austin TX 78712

LITTLE, SELBY FRANCIS, III, information services official; b. Panama, C.Z., Nov. 11, 1953; s. Selby F., Jr., and Anne S. Little; m. Linda K. Earnest, Aug. 23, 1975; children—Stephanie, Jeffrey. B.S. in Econs., Tex. A&M U., 1975, M.B.A., 1976. C.P.A., Tex., 1978. Fin. analyst Internat. Service Corp., Ft. Worth, 1976-78; fin. planning mgr. Docutel Corp., Irving Tex., 1978-81; sr. mgmt. cons. Ernst & Whinney, Dallas, 1981; asst. treas. UCCEL Corp., Dallas, 1981-83, treas., 1984—, v.p. subs. Open Systems, Inc., Mpls., 1983-84. Mem. Am. Inst. C.P.A.s, Tex. Soc. C.P.A.s, Assn. Corp. Growth, Fin. Execs. Inst. Office: UCCEL Tower Exchange Park Dallas TX 75235

LITTLEFIELD, WILLIAM MITCHELL, technical documentation executive; b. Pine Bluff, Ark., Nov. 24, 1919; s. Oscar Porter and Clara Beatrice (King) L.; m. Grace Ann Clement, Sept. 5, 1942; children—Jay Mitchell, Pamela Ann, Craig Porter. Student, Advt. Art, Nashville, 1936-38, Art Inst. Chgo., 1948, U. Mass., 1948-50. Graphic designer Montgomery Ward, Chgo., 1945-50; pres. Adart, Pittsfield, Mass., 1950-51; art dir. Fris Advt., Albany, N.Y., 1951-52; prodn. artist Hearst Corp., Albany, 1952-58; advt. exec. Sprague Electric Co., North Adams, Mass., 1958-70; dir. communications Faultfinders, Latham, N.Y., 1970-72; cons. Tech. Documentation, Arlington, Va., 1972—. Author: Holography, 1971. Contbr. articles to profl. jours. Leader Air Scouts, Latham, 1953-54. Served to maj. USAF, 1941-54. Club: Advt. Art (Nashville) (pres. 1936-38). Avocations: art; photography; travel; woodworking.

LITTLEJOHN, MARK HAYS, radiologist, b. Detroit, Apr. 11, 1936; s. Maurice Mark and Elizabeth Dowell (Metcalf) L.; m. Mary Jane Schrock, Dec. 29, 1961 (div. 1983); children—M. Hays. Sara J.; m. Karla Ann McGinnis, Apr. 16, 1983; 1 stepchild, Bradford D. Schwartz. B.S., Northwestern U., 1958, M.D., 1961. Diplomate Am. Bd. Radiology, Am. Bd. Nuclear Medicine. Intern, Luth. Hosp., Ft. Wayne, Ind., 1961-62; resident VA Research Hosp., Chgo., Northwestern U. Med. Sch., Chgo., 1962-65; staff radiologist Ireland Army Hosp., Ft. Knox, Ky., 1965-66, chief radiology, 1966-67; staff radiologist St. Mary Nazareth Hosp., Chgo., 1968-80, chief nuclear medicine, 1975-80; dir. dept. radiology Cannon Meml. Hosp., Banner Elk, N.C., 1980—; cons. 1st U.S. Army, 1966-67. Served to capt. U.S. Army, 1965-67. Mem. AMA (Physician's Recognition award 1971, 74, 77, 80, 84), Am. Coll. Nuclear Physicians, (charter), Am. Coll. Nuclear Medicine (charter), Am. Inst. Ultrasound in Medicine, Radiology, Soc. N.Am., Soc. Nuclear Medicine, Pi Kappa Epsilon. Avocations: sculpture; painting. Home: Box 188 Hound Ears Club Blowing Rock NC 28605 Office: Box 1167 Banner Elk NC 28604

LITTLETON, BETTY CAROL, building management company executive, medical technologist; b. Paris, Ky., Sept. 25, 1946; d. Rex Beach and Agnes Evelyn (Whalen) Littleton. B.S. in Med. Tech., Eastern Ky., U., 1973. Cert. med. technologist. Tchr. med. tech. and med. assts., Charron-Williams Coll., Ft. Lauderdale, Fla. and Ft. Lauderdale Med. Coll., 1974-76; med. sales rep. Upjohn Med. Co., Kalamazoo, 1976-79; co-owner, pres. HeLP Enterprises Profl. Distbn., Inc., Crescent Springs, Ky., 1979—. Recipient Med. Exhibit award, Upjohn Med. Co., 1977, 78. Mem. Am. Soc. Notaries, Am. Bus. Women's Assn. (hon. state treas. 1980—). Democrat. Office: 2643 Crescent Springs Rd Crescent Springs KY 41017

LITTLETON, ISAAC THOMAS, III, librarian; b. Hartsville, Tenn., Jan. 28, 1921; s. Isaac Thomas and Bessie (Lowe) L.; m. Dorothy Young, Aug. 12, 1949; children—Sally Lowe, Thomas Young, Elizabeth. A.B., U. N.C., 1943; M.A., U. Tenn., 1950; M.L.S., U. Ill., 1951, Ph.D., 1968. With D.H. Hill Library, N.C. State U., Raleigh, 1959—, dir., 1967—; instr. Peabody Library Sch., Nashville, 1958; cons. in field. Author: Bibliographic Organization and Use of the Literature of Agricultural Economics, 1967; State Systems of Higher Education and Libraries, 1977. Editor: North Carolina Union List of Scientific Serials, 1965-67. Served to lt. (j.g.) USNR, 1943-46. Council on Library Resources fellow, 1976-77. Mem. ALA, N.C. Library Assn. (2d v.p. 1972-74), Southeastern Library Assn. (exec. bd. 1974-78), Spl. Libraries Assn., Assn. Southeastern Research Libraries (chmn. 1971-72), Southeastern Library Network (bd. dirs. 1973-74, 83—, chmn. 1985-86), Beta Phi Mu, Phi Kappa Phi. Office: NC State U PO Box 7111 Raleigh NC 27695

LITTLETON, JESSE TALBOT, III, radiology educator, consultant; b. Corning, N.Y., Apr. 27, 1917; s. Jesse Talbot and Bessie (Cook) L.; m. Martha Morrow, Apr. 17, 1943; children—Christine, Joanne, James, Robert, Denise. Student Emory and Henry Coll., 1934-35, Johns Hopkins U., 1935-39; M.D., Syracuse U., 1943. Intern, Buffalo Gen. Hosp., 1943-44; resident in medicine Robert Packer Hosp., Sayre, Pa., 1946-47, resident in surgery, 1947-48, resident in radiology, 1948-51, staff radiologist, 1951-53, chmn. dept. radiology, 1953-76; clin. prof. dept. medicine Hahnemann Med. Sch., Phila., 1955-63, prof. dept. radiology, 1972-77; prof. dept. radiology U. South Ala., Mobile, 1977—; cons. x-ray industry. Served to capt. AUS, 1943-46. Fellow Am. Coll. Radiology; mem. AMA, Bradford County Med. Soc., Pa. Med. Soc., Am. Cancer Soc., Research Soc. Am., N.Y. Acad. Scis., Pa. Radiol. Soc., Am. Roentgen Ray Soc., Inter-Am. Coll. Radiology, Assn. Univ. Radiologists, French Soc. Neuroradiology, Ala. Acad. Radiology, Med. Assn. State Ala., Med. Soc. Mobile County, So. Radiol. Conf., Am. Soc. Head and Neck Radiology, Soc. Thoracic Radiologists, Ala. Wildlife Assn., Ruffed Grouse Soc. N.Am., Found. for N.Am. Wild Sheep, Ducks Unltd. Republican. Methodist. Club: Country of Mobile. Designed radiology devices; importer 1st pluridirectional tomographic device; pioneer in sheet film seriography; developer dedicated system for radiography of acutely traumatized patients; author 2 books; contbr. chpts. to books, articles to profl. jours. Home: 5504 Churchill Downs Ave Theodore AL 36582 Office: U South Ala Med Ctr 2451 Fillingim St Mobile AL 36617

LITTLETON, VANCE, educational administrator. Supt. of schs. Corpus Christi, Tex. Office: Box 110 Corpus Christi TX 78403*

LITTON, LURA ADELINE, consumer products marketing executive; b. Columbus, Ga., Dec. 19, 1955; d. Robert Benton and Margaret (Easom) L. A.B. in Biology and Govt., Sweet Briar Coll., 1978. Adminstrv. mgr. Blue Bell, Inc., Greensboro, N.C., 1979-80, designer, 1980-81, advt. and traffic mgr., 1981-82, assoc. mgr. consumer promotions, 1982-84; mktg. asst. mgr. R.J. Reynolds Tobacco Co., Winston-Salem, N.C., 1984-85; mktg. mgr. Alba-Waldensian, Inc., Valdese, N.C., 1985—. Leader Jr. Achievement, Greensboro, 1979-82; fund agt. Class of 1978, Sweet Briar Coll., 1983—. Ednl. grantee Ednl. Expdns. Internat., 1974, 75. Mem. Assn. Nat. Advertisers, Promotion Mktg. Assn. Am., Am. Mgmt. Assn., Sweet Briar Coll. Alumnae Assn. (chpt. pres. 1980-81, alumnae rep. 1981-82, class fund agt. 1983—). Republican. Episcopalian. Avocations: tennis; piano; bird watching. Home: PO Box 458 Valdese NC 28690 Office: Alba-Waldensian Inc PO Box 100 201 St Germain St SW Valdese NC 28690

LITWIN, ALEXANDER ANDREW, JR., navy nurse corps officer; b. Amityville, N.Y., Nov. 12, 1952; s. Alexander Andrew and Ruth Jesse (Lear) Litwin; m. Carolyn Julia Gross, Mar. 19, 1971; children—Christopher Matthew, Kimberly Anne. Nursing diploma Central Islip Psychiat. Ctr., 1973; A.A., Los Angeles Met. Coll., 1981; B.S. in Nursing, Corpus Christi State U., 1984. Staff nurse coronary care unit Brookhaven Meml. Hosp., Patchogue, N.Y., 1973-74; commd. officer Nurse Corps, U.S. Navy, 1974, advanced through grades to lt. comdr.; staff nurse intensive care unit Naval Aerospace Regional Med. Ctr., Pensacola, Fla., 1974-76; charge nurse intensive care unit Naval Regional Med. Ctr., Camp Lejeune, N.C., 1976-79, Naval Hosp., Roosevelt Roads, P.R., 1979-82; charge nurse med. unit, night nursing supr. Naval Hosp., Jacksonville, Fla., 1982—. Author: Education in Coronary Heart Disease, 1982. Commr. Youth Soccer Program, Roosevelt Roads, 1979-82. Mem. Am. Assn. Critical Care Nurses, Baccalaureat Orgn. Registered Nurses, Assn. Mil. Surgeons U.S. Republican. Lutheran. Club: Fla. Striders Track (Orange Park, Fla.). Home: 2371 Kirkwall St Orange Park FL 32073

LIU, AN-YEN, psychologist, educator; b. Ming-hsiung, Taiwan, Oct. 15, 1941; came to U.S., 1966, naturalized, 1976; s. Hsea and Hsiu-Chu (Chang) L.; m. Mei Mei Chien, Aug. 19, 1969; children—Gilbert, Geofrey, Gerald. B.Ed., Taiwan Normal U., Taipei, 1963; M.A., NE Mo. State U., 1967; Ph.D., Iowa State U., 1971. Tchr., registrar Shih-Lin High Sch., Taipei, 1965-66; instr. Woodward State Hosp. Sch., Iowa, 1967-68; research asst. Iowa State U., Ames, 1968-71; mem. faculty SW Community Coll., Creston, Iowa, 1971-73; from asst. to assoc. prof. Jackson State U., Miss., 1973-81, prof. psychology, 1981—. Author: Psychology, 1978; Social Psychology, 1984; also articles in ednl. and psychol. jours. Troop program instr. Andrew Jackson council Boy Scouts Am., 1983-84, mem. advancement rev. bd., 1985. Served as 2d lt. Chinese Army, 1964-65, Taiwan. Mem. Am. Psychol. Assn., Am. Ednl. Research Assn., Psychometric Soc. Avocations: gardening; landscaping. Home: 113 Pebble Brook Dr Clinton MS 39056 Office: Jackson State U Jackson MS 39217

LIU, CHARLES CHUNG-CHA, engineering educator; b. Ping-Tung, Taiwan, Oct. 6, 1953; came to U.S., 1977; s. Lian-Chyan and Sheue-Er (Chien) L.; m. Ing-Ing Tsai, Aug. 19, 1979; 1 son, Alexander Charles. B.S.C.E., Nat. Taiwan U., 1975; M.S.C.E., Purdue U., 1979, Ph.D., 1982. Instr. Chinese Army Engr. Sch., Taipei, Taiwan, 1975-77; grad. instr. Sch. Civil Engring. Purdue U., West Lafayette, Ind., 1977-82; asst. prof. civil engring. Tenn. State U., Nashville, 1982—. Mem. Inst. Transp. Engrs., Ops. Research Soc. Am., Transp. Research Bd., ASCE, Sigma Xi, Omega Rho. Contbr. articles to profl. jours. Office: Dept Civil Engring Tennessee State U Nashville TN 37203

LIU, TSAI-SHENG, software development engineer; b. Kaohsiung, China, July 29, 1937; came to U.S., 1971, naturalized, 1983; s. Wan-Chang and Pai-Tsai (Lin) L.; m. Li-Hua Cheng, Apr. 1, 1961; children—Lin-Lin, Hao-Tse, Hao-Yuang, Mo-Lin. B.S., Taiwan Normal U., 1963; M.S., Nat. Tsing Hua U., 1965; Ph.D., U. Okla., 1974. Instr. U. Okla., Norman, 1975-76; asst. prof. U. Sci. and Arts Okla., Chickasha, 1976-80; programmer, analyst Computer Sci. Corp., Houston, 1980-82; devel. engr. Anadrill, Schlumberger, Sugarland, Tex., 1982—. Contbr. articles to profl. jours. Fullbright scholar U. Wash., 1967. Mem. Math. Assn. Am., Am. Math. Soc., IEEE, Sigma Xi. Avocation: fishing. Home: 11907 Blair Meadow Stafford TX 77477 Office: Anadrill Schlumberger 200 Macco Blvd Sugarland TX 77478

LIVAUDAIS, MARCE, JR., federal judge; b. New Orleans, Mar. 3, 1925; m. Carol Black; children—Julie, Marc, Durel. B.A., Tulane U., 1945, J.D., 1949. Assoc. Boswell & Loeb, New Orleans, 1949-50, 52-56; ptnr. Boswell, Loeb & Livaudais, 1956-60, Loeb & Livaudais, 1960-67, 71-77, Loeb, Dillon & Livaudais, 1967-71; U.S. magistrate, 1977-84; judge U.S. Dist. Ct. for Eastern Dist. La., New Orleans, 1984—. Mem. Am. Judicature Soc. Office: US Courthouse 500 Camp St Room C-313 New Orleans LA 70130*

LIVELY, H(OWARD) RANDOLPH, JR., retail company executive; b. Atlanta, Ga., Nov. 24, 1934; s. Howard R. Sr. and Nelle (Everett) L.; m. Barbara Fortun, June 3, 1958 (div. Apr. 1975); children—Bonnie, Dana, Andrea, Mindy, John; m. Fran Antone, Apr. 3, 1976. B.A., La. State U., 1957. Cert. consumer credit exec. With Sears Roebuck and Co., 1960-81, asst. credit mgr., New Orleans, 1960-63, statis. analyst, Atlanta, 1963-64, credit field supr., 1964-66, asst. gen. credit mgr., 1966-69, spl. research asst., Chgo., 1969-71, dir. public affairs, 1971-77, gen. credit mgr. Southwest Territory, Dallas, 1978-80, gen. credit mgr. Eastern Territory, Phila., 1981; pres. Jewelers Fin. Services Div., Zale Corp., Dallas, 1981-84, exec. v.p. Zale Corp., Dallas, 1984-85, chief exec. officer Fine Jewelers Guild div., 1986—; chmn. bd. First Bank/Las Colinas, Irving, Tex.; pres. Merchants Research Council, Chgo., 1982-84. Contbr. articles in field to profl. publs. Exec. advisor (indsl. film) A Day at the Fair 1975 (Best Indsl. Film Indsl. Film Producers Assn. 1977). Chmn., Zale PAC, 1983—; mem. legis. com. Am. Retail Fedn., 1972—; mem. Ill. State Electronic Funds Transfer Study Commn., 1976-77. Served to E-5 U.S. Army, 1957-59. Recipient Disting. Service to Retail Industry award Merchants Research Council, 1977; President's Cup Zale Corp., 1984. Mem. Credit Research Ctr. Purdue U. (exec. com. 1985—), mem. Columbia U. Fin. Services Mgmt. Program Alumni Assn., Nat. Retail Merchants Assn. (chmn. credit mgmt. div. 1984—, bd. dirs. 1985—), Internat. Credit Assn. (bd. dirs. 1982—). Republican. Methodist. Clubs: Las Colinas Sports, La Cima (Irving, Tex.). Avocations: home computing; swimming. Office: Zale Corp 901 W Walnut Hill Ln Irving TX 75038

LIVELY, PIERCE, federal judge; b. Louisville, Aug. 17, 1921; s. Henry Thad and Ruby Durrett (Keating) L.; m. Amelia Harrington, May 25, 1946; children—Susan, Katherine, Thad. A.B., Centre Coll., Ky., 1943; LL.B., U. Va., 1948. Bar: Ky. 1948. Individual practice law, Danville, Ky., 1949-57; mem. firm Lively and Rodes, Danville, 1957-72; judge U.S. Ct. Appeals (6th cir.), Cin., 1972—, chief judge, 1983—; Mem. Ky. Commn. on Economy and Efficiency in Govt., 1963-65, Ky. Jud. Advisory Com., 1972. Trustee Centre Coll. Served with USNR, 1943-46. Mem. Am. Bar Assn., Am. Judicature Soc., Order of Coif, Raven Soc., Phi Beta Kappa, Omicron Delta Kappa. Presbyterian. Office: Fed Bldg Danville KY 40422 also Room 626 US Courthouse Cincinnati OH 45202

LIVINGOOD, AGNES DYER, public systems analyst, chemist; b. N.Y.C., Feb. 25, 1925; d. Harry Wing and Agnes (Schasse) Dyer; m. Marvin Duane Livingood, Apr. 17, 1949; children—Christopher, Winifred, Matthew, Abigail. B.S., Ursinus Coll., 1944; M.B.A., U. Louisville, 1970, postgrad., doctoral student in pub. systems analysis, 1972—. Phys. chemist Interchem. Corp., 1944-45; grad. research asst., Mich. State U., 1945-48; freelance tech. writer, 1950-60; chmn. research and pub. fin. coms. Mayor's Adv. Com. for Community Devel., Louisville, Ky., 1964-70; asst. project dir., then dir. urban systems modelling studies, U. Louisville Urban Studies Ctr., 1968-73, dir. pub. systems analysis, 1973—; co-ptnr. RCI Ltd., engring. and systems cons. firm., Louisville; cons. on health planning to State of Ky. Chmn. Wilmington chpt. LWV (Ky.), 1956, Louisville chpt., 1966, nat. conv. del., 1966, 67; sr. warden St. John's Episcopal Ch., 1983. Recipient cert. Louisville mayor's Com., 1970; appreciations Ky. Assn. County Ofcls. Mem. Am. Pub. Health Assn., Am. Trauma Soc. (sec. Ky. sect.), Ky. Pub. Health Assn., MEDICS, Inc., Inst. Mgmt. Sci., County Judges' Assn. (hon.), Sigma Xi (assoc.). Republican. Home: 2603 Landor Ave Louisville KY 40205 Office: RCI Ltd 2603 Landor Ave Louisville KY 40205

LIVINGSTON, CRAIG RAYMOND, architect; b. Teaneck, N.J., May 17, 1953; s. Raymond Paul and Margaret Theresa (Kennedy) L.; m. Maura Terese Hurley, Aug. 27, 1977; children—Matthew Craig, Meghan Elizabeth. A.A.S., SUNY-Farmingdale, 1973; B. Arch., Pratt Inst., 1976. Regis. architect, Vt., Fla., N.Y. Architect Skidmore, Owings & Merrill, N.Y.C., 1976-79, Edward D. Stone & Assocs., N.Y.C., 1979-80, I.M. Pei & Ptnrs., N.Y.C., 1980-82; ptnr. HSCL Architects, West Palm Beach, Fla., 1982-83; pres. Siteworks Architects and Planners Inc., Boynton Beach, Fla., 1983—. Designer Harbor Towers and Marina, 1983, Forum Shoppes, 1985, United Artists Cinema, 1985, Boynton W. Exec. Ctr., 1985. Active Boynton C. of C., 1984—, Econ. Devel. Com., 1984—. Mem. AIA, Fla. Assn. Architects, N.Y. Soc. Architects. Office: Siteworks Architects and Planners Inc 639 E Ocean Ave Boynton Beach FL 33435

LIVINGSTON, EDWARD REESE, JR., design and graphic consultant; b. Norfolk, Va., Sept. 5, 1947; s. Edward Reese and Mary Dolnar (Knight) L.; m. Elizabeth Macy Williams, Aug. 25, 1984. Student Old Dominion U., U. Central Fla. Project mgr. Shriver-Holland Architects, Norfolk, 1979-80; prodn. mgr. Fugleberg-Koch Architects, Orlando, Fla., 1980-81, W.R. Frizzell Architects, Winter Park, Fla., 1981-82; project mgr. Burgh Assocs. Architects, Charlottesville, Va., 1982-83, Eisenman-Robertson Architects, Charlottesville, 1983—; ptnr., prin. Total Corp. Identity, Charlottesville, 1983—. Graphic designer: Virginia Voters Registration Handbook, 1983. Bd. dirs. Winter Park Jaycees, 1982. Mem. AAIA (assoc.). Baptist. Clubs: Am. Sports Car, Tidewater Austin Healy. Office: Dale Hamilton & Assocs 700 Nat Bank Bldg Charlottesville VA 22901

LIVINGSTON, GEORGE HERBERT, clergyman, Old Testament educator; b. Russell, Iowa, July 27, 1916; s. George Wendell and Clara Lutheria (Baker) L.; m. Maria Gertruida Saarloos, Aug. 12, 1937; children—Burton George, Nellie Maria, David Herbert. B.A. in Religion, Wessington Springs Coll., 1937; A.B., Kletzing Coll., 1945; B.D., Asbury Theol. Sem., 1948; Ph.D., Drew U., 1955. Ordained to ministry Free Meth. Ch. Pastor, Free Meth. Ch., Beaver Dam and Birchwood, Wis., 1937-39, Free Meth. Ch., Marion, Cedar Rapids and Oskaloosa, Iowa, 1939-45, United Meth. Ch., Lynchburg, Ohio, 1947-48, United Meth. Ch., Callicon, N.Y., 1948-51; dean Wessington Springs Coll., S.D., 1951-53; prof. O.T., Asbury Theol. Sem., Wilmore, Ky., 1953—; dir. Inst. Holy Land Studies, Jerusalem, 1959, chmn. assoc. schs., 1964-74; field supr. Archeol. Expedition to Ai, Deir Diwan, Israel, 1966, 68. Author: Genesis, Aldersgate Bibl. Series, 1961, Jeremiah, Aldersgate Bibl. Series, 1963; the Pentateuch in its Cultural Environment, 1974. Contbr. articles to profl. publs. Recipient Higher Edn. award Free Meth. Ch., 1979. Mem. Am. Schs. Oriental Research, Evang. Theol. Soc., Wesleyan Theol. Soc., Nat. Assn. Profs. of Hebrew, Theta Phi. Republican. Office: Asbury Theol Sem N Lexington Ave Wilmore KY 40390

LIVINGSTON, JAMES ARCHIBALD, JR., insurance executive; b. Macon, Ga., Aug. 8, 1918; s. James Archibald and Hazel (Wiley) L.; A.B., U. Mich., 1939, M.B.A., 1940; m. Margaret Gresham, July 15, 1947; children—Mary Margaret, James Archibald III, Katherine, Elizabeth. With Met. Life Ins. Co., 1939-40, Nat. Life & Accident Ins. Co., Nashville, 1940-44; with Liberty Nat. Life Ins. Co., Birmingham, Ala., 1944—, chief actuary, 1965—, v.p., 1960-73, sr. v.p. in charge ins. operations, dir., 1973-80, exec. v.p., 1980—; dir. Liberty Nat. Fire Ins. Co., Brown Service Funeral Homes Co. Pres., Jefferson Tb Sanatorium Soc., 1965, Birmingham br. English Speaking Union, 1967; bd. dirs. Lake Shore Hosp., 1979, YMCA, 1979—; vestryman Ch. of Advent Episcopal, 1976-78. Served with USNR, World War II. Fellow Soc. Actuaries; mem. Internat. Soc. Actuaries, Am. Acad. Actuaries, Southeastern Actuaries Club (past pres.), Birmingham C. of C. (chmn. cultural affairs com. 1981), St. Andrews Soc. Middle South. Clubs: Downtown, Redstone, Birmingham Country, Mountain Brook. Lodge: Rotary (dir. 1976-78). Home: 12 Country Club Rd Birmingham AL 35213 Office: 301 S 20th St Birmingham AL 35233

LIVINGSTON, JOHN CHARLES, real estate and financial executive, lawyer; b. Waynesboro, Va., Jan. 15, 1943; s. John Lawrence and Muriel (Bishop) L.; m. Margaret Proud Moore, Aug. 12, 1963; children—Kimberly, Jennifer, Katherine. B.S., N.C. State U., 1965; postgrad. Sch. Law, U. N.C.-Chapel Hill, 1969-70; J.D., Georgetown U., 1972. Bar: Va. 1973, D.C. 1973. Assoc. Steptoe & Johnson, Washington, 1972-75; counsel Cameron-Brown Investment Group (predecessor to Sunstates Corp.), Raleigh, N.C., 1975-81, pres. and chief exec. officer Sunstates Corp., 1981-84; also dir.; chmn., chief exec. officer Guaranty Savs. & Loan, Fayetteville, N.C., 1984—, North State Savs. & Loan Corp., Greenville, N.C., 1985—. Served to capt. USMC, 1965-69. Mem. Nat. Assn. Real Estate Investment Trusts, Va. Bar Assn., D.C. Bar Assn., VFW. Republican. Episcopalian. Office: 320 Green St Fayetteville NC 28302

LIVINGSTON, MARGARET MORROW GRESHAM, civic leader; b. Birmingham, Ala., Aug. 16, 1924; d. Owen Garside and Katherine Molton (Morrow) Gresham; grad. The Baldwin Sch., Phila., 1942; A.B., Vassar Coll., 1945; M.A., U. Ala., 1946; m. James Archibald Livingston, Jr., July 16, 1947; children—Mary Margaret, James Archibald, Katherine Wiley, Elizabeth Gresham. Tutor in math., 1949-55; substitute elem., secondary sch. tchr., 1953-60; judge arts and crafts shows, founder edn. program Birmingham Mus. Art, 1962, acting dir., 1978-79, 81, chmn. bd. dirs., 1978—, sec. bd. dirs. 1978—, co-editor bulletin, 1970-75, pres. bd. dirs., 1971—, chmn. bd. Birmingham Mus. Art Edn. Council, 1968—; bd. dirs., past pres. Children's

Aid Soc., 1959-81, treas., 1950, v.p., 1951; mem. arts com. Birmingham Civic Center Authority, 1970—; bd. dirs. U. Ala. Art Gallery, Birmingham, 1978—, Altamont Sch., Birmingham, 1959—, Greater Birmingham Arts Alliance, 1979-81. Mem. Am. Assn. Mus. (trustees com., edn. com., public relations com.), Internat. Com. of Mus. (edn. com. 1981—), Am. Fedn. Arts, So. Assn. Mus. Episcopalian. Clubs: Jr. League, English Speaking Union, Colonial Dames of Commonwealth of Va., Linly Heflin Unit, Ala. State Tennis Assn. Co-editor Spain Rehabilitation Arts Catalog, 1976-77. Home: 12 Country Club Rd Birmingham AL 35213 Office: Birmingham Mus of Art 2000 8th Ave N Birmingham AL 35203

LIVINGSTON, PHILIP HENRY, physician; b. Columbus, Ga., Sept. 14, 1905; s. Sol and Zelda (Smullian) L.; B.S., Emory U., 1926, M.D. with honors, 1929; m. Jean Doris Wicksman, May 24, 1942 (dec. June 7, 1977); children—Richard, Ann, Dean. Intern, Jewish Hosp., St. Louis, 1929-30, resident, 1931-33; resident Michael Reese Hosp., Chgo., resident, 1930-31; practice medicine specializing in cardiology, Chattanooga, 1933-83; ret., 1983. Bd. dirs. Allied Arts Council, Chattanooga; elected squire Quar. Ct., 1966, 72. Served to lt. col. M.C., AUS, 1942-45. Diplomate Am. Bd. Internal Medicine. Fellow ACP, Am. Coll. Cardiology, Am. Coll. Angiology, Am. Coll. Clin. Cardiology; mem. AMA, Am. Diabetes Assn., Am. Acad. Medicine, Vienna, N.Y. acads. sci. Democrat. Unitarian. Clubs: Kiwanis, Torch. Home: 1718 Minnekahda Rd Chattanooga TN 37405

LIVINGSTON, RALPH, chemist; b. Keene, N.H., May 16, 1919; s. David Israel and Annie Gertrude (Finkelstein) L.; m. Zelda Becker, Oct. 24, 1943 (div. 1968); children—Beverly Jean, Sally Maura, Donna Ruth, Stuart Aaron. B.S., U. N.H., 1940, M.S., 1941; D.Sc., U. Cin., 1943. Chemist, Manhattan project U. Chgo., 1943-45; chemist Oak Ridge (Tenn.) Nat. Lab., 1945-84, assoc. dir. chemistry div., 1965-74, group leader, 1945-84, cons., 1984—, Union Carbide Corporate research fellow, 1979—; prof. chemistry U. Tenn., Knoxville, 1964-76. Bd. dirs. Oak Ridge Civic Music Assn., 1968-71, pres., 1970; pres. Oak Ridge Community Art Ctr., 1972-73. John Simon Guggenheim fellow, 1960-61; Fulbright research scholar in France, 1960-61. Mem. Am. Chem. Soc., Am. Phys. Soc., AAAS, Internat. Soc. Magnetic Resonance, Sigma Xi. Mem. editorial bd. Magnetic Resonance Reviews, 1971—, The Jour. Magnetic Resonance, 1971-84; contbr. articles to profl. jours.; patentee in field. Home: 144 Westlook Circle Oak Ridge TN 37830 Office: Oak Ridge Nat Lab PO Box X Oak Ridge TN 37830

LIVINGSTON, ROBERT L., JR., congressman; b. Colorado Springs, Colo., Apr. 30, 1943; s. Robert L. and Dorothy (Godwin) L.; B.A., Tulane U., 1967, J.D., 1968; LL.D. (hon.), Our Lady of Holy Cross Coll., 1981; m. Bonnie Robichaux, 1965; children—Robert L. III, Richard, David, Su Shan. Bar: La. 1968. Asst. U.S. atty., New Orleans, 1970-73; asst. dist. atty. Orleans Parish, 1974-75; asst. atty. gen. La., 1975-76; mem. firm Livingston & Powers, New Orleans, 1976-77; mem. 95th-99th congresses from 1st Dist. La.; mem. Am. del. to observe elections in El Salvador, 1982, 84; mem. Am. del. to observe elections in the Philippines, 1986; mem. Presdl. Commn. Fgn. Aid, 1983. Vice chmn. Orleans Parish Republican Exec. Com., 1974-76. Served with USN, 1961-63, USNR, 1961-67. Named Outstanding Asst. U.S. Atty., 1973. Mem. ABA, La. Bar Assn. (ho. of dels. 1977), New Orleans Bar Assn., La. Trial Lawyers Assn. Episcopalian. Clubs: Masons, Young Men's Bus. Office: 2437 Rayburn House Office Bldg Washington DC 20515

LIVINGSTON, RONALD PAUL, osteopathic physician; b. Comanche, Tex., Nov. 28, 1947; s. John Bernice and Ruby Jo (McCoy) L.; m. Paula Gay Mask, June 6, 1979; children—Tiffany, Nicole, Kassadii, Cari, Sloane. B.S., Tarleton State U., 1970; D.O., Tex. Coll. Osteo. Medicine, 1974. Diplomate Am. Bd. Osteo. Medicine. Intern Stevens Park Hosp., Dallas, 1974-75; gen. practice osteo. medicine, Comanche, Tex., 1975—; team physician Commanche High Sch., 1975—. Mem. Am. Acad. Gen. Practice, Am. Osteo. Assn., Tex. Osteo. Med. Assn., Tex. Med. Assn., Tex. Coll. Osteo. Medicine Alumni Assn. (pres. 1976-77), Sigma Sigma Phi. Republican. Methodist. Avocations: reading, jogging, fishing. Home: Route 3 Fox Creek Dr Comanche TX 76442 Office: Doctors Med Clinic 105 Valley Forge Comanche TX 76442

LIVINGSTON, WILLIAM SAMUEL, university dean and official; b. Ironton, Ohio, July 1, 1920; s. Samuel George and Bata Elkins L.; m. Lana Sanor, July 10, 1943; children—Stephen, David. B.A., Ohio State U., 1943, M.A., 1943; Ph.D., Yale U., 1950. Asst. prof. govt. U. Tex., Austin, 1949-54, assoc. prof., 1954-61, prof., 1961—, Jo Anne Christian Centennial prof. in Brit. studies, 1982—, chmn. dept. govt., 1965-69, asst. dean Grad. Sch., 1954-58, chmn. grad. assembly, 1965-68, chmn. faculty senate, 1973-79, vice chancellor acad. programs U. Tex. System, 1969-71, v.p. dean grad. studies, 1979—; vis. prof. Yale U., 1955-56, Duke U., 1960-61; USIS lectr., U.K., India, 1977. Author: Federalism and Constitutional Change, 1956; contbg. author: World Pressures on American Foreign Policy, 1962; Teaching Political Science, 1965; Federalism: Infinite Variety in Theory and Practice, 1968; Britain at the Polls, 1979, 81; editor: The Presidency and Congress: A Shifting Balance of Power, 1979; co-editor: Australia, New Zealand and the Pacific Islands Since the First World War, 1979; editor, contbg. author: Federalism in the Commonwealth, 1963; A Prospect of Liberal Democracy, 1979; book rev. editor Jour. Politics, 1965-68, editor in chief, 1968-72; mem. editorial bd. Polit. Sci. Quar., 1972-80, Publius Jour. Federalism, 1971—; mem. bd. editors P.S., 1976-78, chmn., 1978-81. Served to 1st lt., FA, AUS, 1943-45. Decorated Bronze Star, Purple Heart; recipient Teaching Excellence award, 1959; Ford Found. fellow, 1952-53, Guggenheim fellow, 1959-60. Mem. Am. Polit. Sci. Assn. (exec. council, adminstrv. com. 1972-74, chmn. nominating com. 1973-74, 78-79), So. Polit. Sci. Assn. (exec. council 1964-67, pres. 1974-75), Southwestern Polit. Sci. Assn. (pres. 1973-74), Brit. Polit. Sci. Assn., Can. Polit. Sci. Assn., Hansard Soc. London, Royal Commonwealth Soc. London, Philos. Soc. Tex., Austin Soc. Pub. Adminstrn. (pres. 1973-74), Southwestern Social Sci. Assn. (pres. 1977-78), Phi Beta Kappa, Omicron Delta Kappa, Phi Gamma Delta, Pi Sigma Alpha (nat. council 1976-84, nat. pres. 1980-82). Home: 3203 Greenlee Dr Austin TX 78703

LLADO, SARAH EMILIA, clinical psychologist; b. Rio Piedras, P.R., Dec. 30, 1949; d. Juan E. Llado and Sara J. Escudero. B.A. cum laude, U. P.R., 1971; M.S. with distinction, Caribbean Ctr. for Advanced Studies, 1976. Clin. psychologist Mental Health Ctr., Humacao, P.R., 1975-81, Lucy Lopez-Roig Assn., Hato Rey, P.R., 1982—; clin. supr. Caribbean Ctr. for Advanced Studies, Santurce, P.R., 1984—; instr. InterAm. U., Bayamon, P.R., 1985—. Fellow Am. Psychol. Assn.; mem. Assn. de Psicologos de P.R., Nat. Hispanic Psychol. Assn. Home: Calle 1 D2 Altos de la Fuente Caguas PR 00625 Office: Lucy Lopez Roig Assoc Domenech 400 Hato Rey PR 00918

LLANO, CESAREO, services company executive; b. Havana, July 22, 1939; came to U.S., 1961; s. Cesareo and Sara (Jiminez) L.; m. Elena Cano, Aug. 25, 1962; children—Cesareo Enrique, Eduardo. B.B.A., Villanova U., Havana, 1962. Mgr. El Boton, Havana, 1957-61; exec. v.p. Frontier Freight Forwarders, Miami, 1961-76; pres. Stair Cargo Services Inc., Miami, 1976—. Mem. Fla. Custom Brokers and Forwarders Assn. (bd. dirs., past v.p., past pres.), Nat. Custom Brokers and Forwarders Assn. (adv. bd.). Republican. Roman Catholic. Club: Big Five (Miami). Home: 7425 Los Pinos Blvd Coral Gables FL 33143 Office: Stair Cargo Services Inc 9020 NW 12th St Miami FL 33172

LLANOS, LUIS SOCORRO, safety and health professional; b. St. Croix, V.I., June 30, 1940; s. Felix and Eulogia (Encarnacion) L.; m. Joycelyn Louise Bough, Oct. 23, 1964; children—Elaine Eulogia, Luis Socorro, Eric Andre Farid. Student Christiansted, V.I. schs. Cert. hazard control mgr. Compliance officer Div. Occupational Safety and Health, V.I. Dept. Labor, 1973-74, chief compliance officer, 1974-76, supervisory compliance officer, 1976-77, asst. dir., 1977-80, asst. commr., St. Croix, 1980—; mem. pub. Employee Relations Bd., V.I., 1983, Vocat. Ednl. Adv. Council, V.I., 1984, V.I. Tax Rev. Bd., 1979. Elected mem. Holy Cross Parish Council, St. Croix, 1982; mem. Holy Cross choir, 1958. Served with U.S. Army, 1962-64. Mem. Am. Soc. Safety Engrs., State Occupational Safety and Health Dirs. Assn., Vets. of Safety. Democrat. Roman Catholic. Lodge: KC (charter St. Croix, treas. 1974-75). Avocations: photography; classic guitar; choir. Office: Govt of VI of USA Dept Labor Div Occupational Safety and Health Room 207 Govt Complex Frederiksted Saint Croix VI 00840

LLOYD, MARILYN, congresswoman; b. Fort Smith, Ark., Jan. 3; d. James Edgar and Iva Mae (Higginbotham) Laird; m. Joseph P. Bouquard; children—Nancy Lloyd Smithson, Mari, Mort II, Deborah Lloyd Riley. Grad., Shorter Coll., 1963. Mem. 94th-98th congresses from 3d Tenn. Dist. Office: 2334 Rayburn House Office Bldg Washington DC 20515*

LLOYD, MARILYN HOLASEK, stress consultant, nurse educator; b. Cleve., Feb. 16, 1946; d. William John and Mildred (Chylik) Holasek; m. T. Stacy Lloyd Jr., Aug. 23, 1974; children—William, Holly. R.N., Lutheran Med. Ctr., 1967; B. Liberal Studies, Mary Washington Coll., 1979. Registered nurse, Ohio, Va. Psychiatric nurse Mt. Sinai Hosp., Cleve., 1967-69; ob-gyn nurse, patient advocate Pratt Med. Ctr., Fredericksburg, Va., 1969-74; pvt. practice as cons. Coping Unlimited, Fredericksburg, 1982—; adj. faculty Germanna Community Coll., U. Va. Extension, Mary Washington Coll. Past pres., bd. dirs. Mental Health Assn., Fredericksburg, 1976-83. Named Most Valuable Vol. in field mental health, Fredericksburg, 1979. Fellow Am. Stress Inst.; mem. Bus. Profl. Women's Club, Am. Soc. Tng. Devel., Am. Assn. Female Execs., Fredericksburg C. of C. Presbyterian. Avocation: playing piano. Home: 215 Braehead Dr Fredericksburg VA 22401 Office: Coping Unltd PO Box 3576 Fredericksburg VA 22402

LLOYD, MILTON HAROLD, chemist; b. Des Moines, Mar. 27, 1925; s. Raymond Lloyd and Helen (Brunner) Johnson; m. Naomi Irene Stull, May 19, 1943; children—Carol McAmis, Mark A., Arlene A. B.S., Creighton U., 1950, M.S., 1954. Product devel. chemist Tidy House Products Co., Omaha, 1950-56; sr. research chemist group leader Oak Ridge Nat. Lab., Tenn., 1956—. Author: (with others) Progress in Nuclear Energy Series III, 1969. Contbr. articles to profl. jours. Patentee in field. Served to tech. sgt. U.S. Army, 1943-45. Recipient 100 award Indsl. Research Devel. 1979. Mem. Am. Chem. Soc., AAAS, N.Y. Acad. Sci. Republican. Episcopalian. Avocation: model railroading. Home: 111 Locust Ln Oak Ridge TN 37830 Office: Oak Ridge Nat Lab PO Box X Oak Ridge TN 37831

LLOYD, RALPH WALDO, college president emeritus; b. Friendsville, Tenn., Oct. 6, 1892; s. Henry Baldwin and Maud (Jones) L.; m. Margaret Anderson Bell, June 21, 1917; children—John Vernon, Hal Baldwin, Ruth Bell Lloyd Kramer, Louise Margaret Lloyd Palm. B.A., Maryville (Tenn.) Coll., 1915, D.D., 1929; B.D., McCormick Theol. Sem., 1924; LL.D., Centre Coll., 1940, U. Chattanooga, 1953; Litt.D., Lake Forest Coll., 1954, Westminster Coll., 1955; L.H.D., Lincoln Meml. U., 1955; S.T.D., Blackburn Coll., 1955; Pd.D., Monmouth Coll., 1961. Ordained to ministry Presbyterian Ch. U.S.A., 1923. Instr., athletic coach Westminster Coll., Salt Lake City, 1915-17, asst. to pres., 1918-19; with Fulton Sylphon Mfg. Co., Knoxville, Tenn., 1920-21; supply First Presbyn. Ch., Ossian, Ind., 1922-23; pastor First Ch., Murphysboro, Ill., 1924-26. Edgewood Ch., Pitts., 1926-30; pres. Maryville Coll., 1930-61, now pres. emeritus; moderator Presbytery of Cairo (Ill.), 1926, Presbytery of Union, 1932-33, Synod of Mid-South, 1944-46; gen. council Presbyn. Synod Tenn., 1931-40, chmn., 1940-42; mem. permanent commn. inter-ch. relations Presbyn. Ch. U.S.A., 1938-58, chmn., 1941-58, moderator gen. assembly, 1954-55; mem. Presbyn. Ch. U.S.A. deputation to China, 1946; chmn. com. lay edn. Presbyn. Council on Theol. Edn., 1943-48; mem. commn. on ecumenical mission and relations United Presbyn. Ch. U.S.A., 1959-60. Author: The Presbyterian Colleges Today, 1948; The Christian College in America, 1951; The World Alliance of Reformed Churches, 1956; Maryville College - A History of 150 Years, 1969; Westminster United Presbyterian Church (Bradenton, Fla.) - A History of 50 Years, 1974; contbr. articles to religious jours. Mem. So. area bd. YMCA, 1939-54; mem. Nat. Council Commn. Student Work, 1939-42, chmn. So. area, 1942-45, pres. So. area council, 1946-48; Am. sec. World Alliance Presbyn. and Ref. Chs., 1951-59, pres., 1959-64; mem. central com. World Council Chs., 1951-61; gen. bd. Nat. Council Chs., 1950-60; pres. Affiliated Ind. Colls. Tenn., Inc., 1958-61; v.p. Nat. Conf. Ch. Related Colls., 1937, pres., 1938; pres. Pan-Presbyn. Coll. Union, 1938, Presbyn. Coll. Union, 1943, Tenn. Coll. Assn., 1942-43; mem. commn. insts. higher edn. So. Assn. Colls. and Secondary Schs., 1940-47; del. Presbyn. Ch. in U.S.A., World Council Chs., Amsterdam, 1948, Evanston, 1954, New Delhi, 1961. Served to 1st lt. U.S. Army, 1917-18. Address: 5916 Riverview Blvd Bradenton FL 33529

LLOYD, SAM ROBERT, training and development consulting company executive; b. Poteau, Okla., May 20, 1940; s. Sam Henderson and Lela Mae (Robertson) L.; m. Carolyn Ann McDonald, Aug. 12, 1960 (div. 1973); children—Stephen Robert, Marc David; m. 2d, Christine Emma Berthelot, Mar. 5, 1983. B.S., Okla. State U., 1962, M.B.A., 1967; Ph.D., Washington U., St. Louis. Agt., tng. supr. John Hancock Life Ins. Co., Oklahoma City, 1962-64; ptnr. Sommers-Lloyd Ins. Agy., Poteau, Okla., 1964-65; instr. bus. Okla. State U., 1966-68; instr. mktg. St. Louis U., 1969-70; asst. dean Sch. Bus., U. Mo.-St. Louis, 1970-77; dir. Mgmt. Ctr., So. Meth. U., 1977; pres., co-founder Success Systems, Inc., Dallas, 1977—. Mem. ASTD, Adminstrv. Mgmt. Soc. (past pres. St. Louis chpt.), Am. Soc. Personnel Adminstrn., Dallas Personnel Assn. Office: Success Systems Inc PO Box 31622 Dallas TX 75231

LLOYD, WINSTON DALE, chemistry educator, consultant; b. Pensacola, Fla., Sept. 9, 1929; s. Elmer Bruce and Inez (Herrington) L.; m. Luella Jean Rote, Jan. 19, 1958; children—Pamela D. Powell, Donald G., Craig W. B.S., Fla. State U., 1951; Ph.D., U. Washington, 1956. Organic chemist Dow Chem. Co., Midland, Mich., 1956-58, Dept. Agr., Olustee, Fla., 1959-62; prof. chemistry U. Tex.-El Paso, 1962—. Contbr. articles to profl. jours. Mem. Am. Chem. Soc., Sigma Xi. Home: 4312 Larchmont El Paso TX 79902 Office: Dept Chemistry U Tex-El Paso El Paso TX 79968

LLOYD-JONES, ESTHER MCDONALD, retired graduate education educator, corporation executive; b. Lockport, Ill., Jan. 11, 1901; d. Leon Emerson and Augusta Claire (Rudd) McDonald; m. Silas L. Lloyd-Jones (dec.), June 12, 1924; children—Joanne, Donald. B.A. summa cum laude, Northwestern U., 1923; M.A., Columbia U., 1924, Ph.D., 1929; LL.D., (hon.), Elmira Coll., 1955, Pratt Inst., 1978; D.Sc. in Edn. (hon.), Boston U., 1961; L.H.D., (hon.), Long Island U., 1963. Assoc. dir. personnel Northwestern U., Evanston, Ill., 1924-26; prof., chmn. dept., Columbia U. Tchrs. Coll., N.Y.C., 1926-66; disting. prof. U.S. Internat. U., San Diego, 1966-76; pres. Lloyd-Jones Farms, Inc., Warren, Ind., 1978—; cons. various orgns., 1976—. Author books, articles to profl. jours. Recipient Disting. Alumni award Columbia U., also numerous other awards; grantee Ford Found., U.S. Office Edn., NIMH. Fellow Nat. Vocat. Assn., Am. Psychol. Assn.; mem. Nat. Assn. for Women Deans, Adminstrs. Counselors, Am. Sociol. Assn., Internat. Psychol. Assn., Am. Assn. for Counseling Devel., Am. Coll. Personnel Assn. (pres. 1935-37), Kathyrn S. Phillips Trust (pres. 1974—). Republican. Episcopalian. Avocations: music; economics; agriculture. Home: 10622 Pagewood Dr Dallas TX 75230 also B62 Beaver Lake Franklin NJ 07416

LOAR, WARREN NELSON, III, hosp. adminstr.; b. Okmulgee, Okla., Nov. 29, 1927; s. Warren Nelson and Frederica Inez (Morton) L.; B.S., U.S. Naval Acad., 1950; M.B.A., U. So. Calif., 1966; M.H.A., Ga. State U., 1973; m. Betty Ann Propp, June 10, 1950 (dec.); m. 2d, Barbara Schuster Cox, July 10, 1968; children—Warren Nelson IV, Michael G., Andrew S., Frederica L.; stepchildren—Conde T. Cox, Prentiss E. Cox. Commd. 2d lt. USAF, 1950, advanced through grades to lt. col., 1966; pilot and aircraft comdr. SAC, 1950-67, chief propulsion br., Offutt AFB, Nebr., 1967-70; tactical airlift liaison officer Mil. Region III, Vietnam, 1970-71; ret., 1971; asst. adminstr. St. Mary's Hosp., Athens, Ga., 1973-76; adminstr. U. Ga. Health Services, Athens, 1976—. Decorated Bronze Star, Air medal with 2 oak leaf clusters. Mem. Air Force Assn., Am. Coll. Hosp. Adminstrs. Am. Mgmt. Assn., Ga. Hosp. Assn. Office: Health Service Herty Dr Athens GA 30602

LOBSTEIN, DENNIS DAVID, health and physical education exercise psychobiologist; b. Los Angeles, Sept. 18, 1953; s. Otto Ervin and Miriam Thelma (Goldberg) L. B.A., Purdue U., 1976, M.S., 1981, Ph.D., 1983. Paramedic Emergency Service, Lafayette, Ind., 1973-78; instr. Purdue U., Lafayette, 1978-81, Wabash Coll., Crawfordsville, Ind., 1982; asst. prof. Lamar U., Beaumont, Tex., 1983-86; prof., dir. Human Performance Lab., U. N.Mex., 1986—; cons. Southeast Tex. Industry, Beaumont, 1983—; lectr. Hosp. Clinics, Beaumont, 1983—; coordinator fitness research, Beaumont, 1983—; del. sports medicine, Peoples Republic China, 1985—. Contbr. articles to profl. jours. Nominee Gov.'s Commn. Physical Fitness, 1985. Fellow Am. Coll. Sports Medicine; mem. AAHPERD, AAAS, Am. Psychol. Assn., Soc. Neurosci., Internat. Soc. Psychoneuroendocrinology, Sigma Xi. Avocations: Asian fitness systems; Oriental philosophy. Office: Dept Health and Phys Edn U NMex Albuquerque NM 87131

LOBUE, MARIE, economics educator, researcher, consultant; b. Hammond, La., Jan. 6, 1950; d. Roe Joseph and Mary (Bencaz) L.; m. William Rabiega, May 29, 1972 (div. June 1977). M.S. in Econs., So. Ill. U., Carbondale, 1973; Ph.D. in Econs., Fla. State U., 1979. Research asst. So. Ill. U., Carbondale, 1972-74; part-time instr. Fla. State U., Tallahassee, 1974-76; instr. U. Nev., Reno, 1976-78; chief researcher Urban Planners, New Orleans, 1978-79; assoc. prof. dept. econs., fin. U. New Orleans, 1979—; presentor papers at confs. Contbr. articles to profl. jours. Reviewer acad. papers So. Econ. Jour., Macroecon. Jour., Midsouth Jour. of Econ. Active mem. Amnesty Internat., New Orleans, ACLU. NSF grantee, 1971; U. New Orleans research grantee, 1982. Mem. Com. on Status of Women in Econs. Profession, Am. Econ. Assn., So. Econ. Assn., Eastern Econ. Assn., Southwestern Social Sci. Assn. Avocations: tennis; jazz singing. Home: 820 Spain St New Orleans LA 70117 Office: Dept Econs-Finance U New Orleans Lakefront New Orleans LA 70148

LOCK, AARON CHARLES, JR., civil engineer, consultant; b. Altus, Okla., Jan. 10, 1925; s. Aaron Charles and Ada (Martin) L.; m. Jessie Lee Morgans, Mar. 5, 1946; 1 child, Phyllis Ann Lock Gregory. A.A., NE Okla. A&M U., 1948; B.C.E., Okla. State U., 1952. Lic. profl. engr., Okla., Tenn. Civil engr. U.S. Corps Engrs., Tulsa, 1952-56; city engr. City of Claremore, Okla., 1956-58, City of Cushing, Okla., 1958-61, City of Stillwater, Okla., 1961-65; mgmt. cons. U. Tenn., Memphis, 1965-73, cons. pub. works and engring., 1973—. Editor Tenn. Pub. Works newsletter, 1975-82. Author curriculum materials. Served as sgt. U.S. Army, 1943-46, ETO. Mem. Am. Pub. Works Assn. (sec. 1980—, recipient Harry S. Swearingin award 1983), Tenn. Water Quality Mgmt. Assn., Gideons Internat. (v.p. 1973). Democrat. Baptist (deacon, Sunday sch. tchr.). Lodges: Lions (pres. 1978-80), Masons. Avocations: gardening; photography; woodworking.

LOCKE, BENJAMIN CLARK, medical computing consultant; b. N.Y.C., June 21, 1942; s. Edwin Allen Locke and Dorothy (Clark) Ramer; m. Dana Burlingame, May 30, 1981; 1 child, Benjamin Burlingame. B.A., Harvard U., 1969; M.S. in Mgmt., MIT, 1980. Tech. adminstrv. dir. renal div. Peter Bent Brigham Hosp., Boston, 1967-80; pres. Trowbridge Cons. Co., Cambridge, Mass., 1980-81; tech. staff MITRE Corp., McLean, Va., 1981—; cons. in field. Author: Hospital Information Systems, 1982. Fellow Soc. Advanced Med. Systems; mem. AAAS, Am. Assn. Clin. Histocompatibility Testing (Parliamentarian 1974-79), Am. Assn. Med. Systems and Informatics (founding mem.). Clubs: Harvard, MIT (Washington). Office: MITRE Corp 1820 Dolley Madison Blvd McLean VA 22102

LOCKE, ELIZABETH HUGHES, foundation administrator; b. Norfolk, Va., June 30, 1939; d. George Morris and Sallie Epps (Moss) Hughes; m. John Rae Locke, Jr., Sept. 13, 1958 (div. 1981); children—John Rae III, Sallie Curtis. B.A. magna cum laude with honors in English, Duke U., 1964, Ph.D., 1972; M.A., U. N.C., 1966. Instr. English, U. N.C., Chapel Hill, 1970-72; vis. prof. English, Duke U., Durham, N.C., 1972-73, dir. univ. pubs., 1973-79; corp. contbns. officer Bethlehem Steel Corp., Pa., 1979-82; dir. edn. div. and communications Duke Endowment, Charlotte, N.C., 1982—; pres. Communications Philanthropy, Washington, 1983—; v.p. Charlotte Area Donors Forum, 1983—; mem. communications com. Council on Founds., Washington, 1985—. Editor: Duke Encounters, 1977; Prospectus for Change: American Private Higher Education, 1985. Pres., Jr. League, Durham, 1976, Hist. Preservation Soc., Durham, 1977; v.p. Sch. of Arts, Charlotte; mem. adv. bd. N.C. Civil Rights Commn., Atlanta. Recipient Leadership award Charlotte C. of C., 1984; Danforth fellow, 1972. Mem. Phi Beta Kappa. Democrat. Episcopalian. Club: Charlotte Athletic. Office: Duke Endowment 200 S Tryon St Charlotte NC 28202

LOCKE, PAUL WOODROW, JR., chief of police; b. Anniston, Ala., June 23, 1947; s. Paul Woodrow and Ethel Louise (Hargrove) L.; m. Nancy Louise Steele, Mar. 28, 1968; children—John Paul, Donna Kay. Student Auburn U., 1965-69, Jacksonville State U., 1969-72. Patrolman, Oxford Police Dept., Ala., 1969-72; chief dep. Talladega Sheriff, Ala., 1972-77; chief of detectives Talladega Police Dept., 1977-81; chief of police, Jacksonville Police Dept., Ala., 1981—; cons. N.E. Ala. Police Acad., Jacksonville, 1981—, Coll. Criminal Justice Jacksonville State U., 1981—. Mem. Ala. Assn. Chiefs of Police, Ala. Police Officers Assn. (v.p. 1982-83), Calhoun County Law Enforcement Assn. (pres. 1983-84), FBI Nat. Acad. Assocs., Fraternal Order of Police, Internat. Assn. Chiefs of Police, Internat. Assn. for Identification. Club: Exchange. Lodge: Masons. Home: 903 N 5th Ave Jacksonville AL 36265 Office: Jacksonville Police Dept 116 E Ladiga St Jacksonville AL 36265

LOCKER, JAMES JOSEPH, restaurant manager; b. Toledo, July 17, 1957; s. James Wall and Mary Elizabeth (Byrne) L. B.B.A., U. Miami, 1981. Gen. mgr. Bagel Emporium, Coral Gables, Fla., 1981—; party cons. Myra Jacobs Party Planners, Coral Gables, 1980—. Mem. Internat. Assn. Catering Profls. Roman Catholic. Home: 8365 B SW 107th Ave Miami FL 33173 Office: Bagel Emporium 1238 S Dixie Hwy Coral Gables FL 33173

LOCKETT, LENORA COLMAN, library administrator; b. Franklin, La., Dec. 19, 1938; d. Noah James and Landora (Landry) Colman; m. Nolan James Lockett, June 23, 1973; children—Terrence Duane, Tale Dayan, B.A., So. U., Baton Rouge, 1960; M.S.L.S., La. State U., 1967. Librarian Tangiopahoa Parish Schs., Kentwood, La., 1960-67, Orleans Parish Schs., 1967-70, Delgado Community Coll., New Orleans, 1970-76; library dir., 1976-82, dir. libraries, 1982—. Mem. ALA, La. Library Assn., Greater New Orleans Library Club (sec. 1977-78), Southeast La. Library Network (exec. bd. 1975-81), Kappa Delta Phi, Phi Delta Kappa. Democrat. Baptist. Home: 2059 Mirabeau Ave New Orleans LA 70122 Office: Delgado Community Coll 615 City Park Ave New Orleans LA 70119

LOCKEY, RICHARD F., allergist, immunologist, internist; b. Lancaster, Pa., Jan. 15, 1940; s. Stephen Daniel and Anna (Funk) L.; m. Carol Lee, July 3, 1982; children—Brian Christopher, Keith Edward. B.S., Haverford Coll., 1961; M.D., Temple U., 1965; M.S., U. Mich., 1972. Straight med. intern, Temple U. Med. Sch., Phila., 1965-66; asst. resident in internal medicine, Univ. Hosp., U. Mich., Ann Arbor, 1966-67, resident in internal medicine, 1966-68, fellow in allergy and immunology, 1969-70; asst. prof. medicine U.S. Fla. Coll. Medicine, Tampa, 1973-77, assoc. prof. medicine, 1977-83, asst. dir. div. allergy and immunology, 1979-82, dir. div. allergy and immunology, 1982—, prof. medicine, 1983—, prof. pediatrics, 1983—; asst. chief sect. allergy and immunology VA Hosp., Tampa, 1973-82; chief James A. Haley VA Hosp., Tampa, 1982—. Author or co-author articles in field. Served to maj. M.C., USAF, 1971-73. Disting. Visitor, Ann. Meeting, Coll. Medicine, Costa Rica, 1979; Claude P. Brown Meml. Lectr. Assn. Clin. Scientists, 1981. Fellow ACP; mem. Am. Acad. Allergy and Immunology (chmn. undergrad. and grad. edn. com. 1982—, mem. com. on occupational lung disease 1982—, chmn. com. on standardization of allergic extracts 1983—), Fla. Allergy and Immunology Soc. (pres. 1981-82), Southeastern Allergy Assn., AMA, Hillsborough County Med. Soc., Fla. Med. Soc., Fla. West Coast Allergy and Immunology Jour. Club (founder, pres. 1975-80), Am. Assn. Cert. Allergists, Internat. Assn. Aerobiology, AAAS, Fla. Thoracic Soc., John M. Sheldon U. of Mich. Allergy Soc. (pres. 1980-82), Alpha Omega Alpha. Clubs: Carrollwood, Village. Avocations: antique tool collecting; hiking; backpacking; photography; tennis. Home: 3909 Northampton Way Tampa FL 33624 Office: 13801 N 30th St Tampa FL 33612

LOCKHART, MADGE CLEMENTS, educator; b. Soddy, Tenn., May 22, 1920; d. James Arlie and Ollie (Sparks) Clements; student East Tenn. U., 1938-39; B.S., U. Tenn., Chattanooga and Knoxville, 1955, M.Ed., 1962; m. Andre J. Lockhart, Apr. 24, 1942 (div. 1973); children—Andrew, Jacque West, Janice Watson, Jill Smith, Jacqueline. Elem. tchr. Tenn. and Ga., 1947-60, Brainerd High Sch., Chattanooga, 1960-64, Cleveland (Tenn.) City Schs., 1966-82; owner, operator Lockhart's Learning Center, Inc., Cleveland and Chattanooga, 1975—; co-founder Down Center, Hamilton County, Tenn., 1974, Hermes, residential, day care and workshops orgn., 1972. Pres., Cleveland Assn. Retarded Citizens, 1970, state v.p., 1976; pres. Cleveland Creative Arts Guild, 1980, Cherokee Easter Seal Soc., 1973-76; bd. dirs. Tenn. Easter Seal Soc., 1974-77, 80-83, recipient awards; chair Bradley County Internat. Yr. of Child; pres. Hermes, Inc., 1973-79. Recipient Service to Mankind award Sertoma, 1978. Gov.'s for service to handicapped, 1979. Mem. NEA (life), Tenn. Edn. Assn., Am. Assn. Rehab. Therapy, Cleveland Edn. Assn., Council Exceptional Children, Tenn. Conf. Social Welfare, Bradley-Cleveland C. of C. Clubs: Byliners, Fantastiks. Mem. Ch. of Christ. Contbr. articles to profl. jours. and newspapers; writer poetry, short stories and fiction. Home: 3007 Oakland Dr Cleveland TN 37311 Office: 1212 Greenslake Rd Chattanooga TN 37412

LOCKHART, VERDREE, government official; b. Louisville, Ga., Oct. 21, 1924; s. Fred Douglas and Minnie Belle (Roberson) L.; m. Louise Howard, Aug. 5, 1950; children—Verdree II, Vera Louise, Fernandez, Abigail. B.S. in Agrl. Edn., Tuskegee Inst., 1949; M.A. in Adminstrn. and Supervision, Atlanta U., 1957, Ph.D. in Guidance and Counseling, 1975; postgrad. in guidance and counseling George Peabody Coll., 1960. Cert. nursing home adminstr., prin., counselor. Tchr., counselor Jefferson County High Sch., Louisville, 1949-63; edn. cons. Ga. Dept. Edn., Atlanta, 1963-80; trustee Atlanta U., 1975-81, v.p., 1981-82; dean of edn. Phillips Coll., Atlanta, 1984-85; regional insp. U.S. EPA, Atlanta, 1985—. Treas., bd. dirs. Atlanta br. NAACP, 1970—; mem. forest resource council Tuskegee Inst., 1972—; asst. commr. Atlanta area council Boy Scouts Am., 1972—. Served to master sgt. U.S. Army, 1943-46, PTO. Recipient Ga. Gov.'s Medallion award Exec. Br. Ga., 1967-68, Silver Beaver award Boy Scouts Am., 1970; named Tchr. of Yr., Ga. C. of C., 1957. Mem. Am. Coll. Personnel Assn., Assn. Counseling and Devel., Alpha Phi Alpha (Alumni Bro. of Yr. 1980), Phi Delta Kappa. Democrat. Baptist. Home: 2964 Peek Rd NW Atlanta GA 30318 Office: US EPA 345 Courtland St Atlanta GA 30365

LOCKWOOD, FRANCES MANN, clinical psychologist; b. Washington, June 20, 1946; d. Ernest Daniel Mann and Thelma Gertrude (Gheen) Hubert; m. Bruce Robert Lockwood, May 10, 1975; children—Kathleen Gail, Karen Ann. B.A., Westhampton Coll., U. Richmond, 1968; M.A., U. Tenn., 1971, Ph.D., 1973. Lic. psychologist, Tenn., Va. Intern. VA Hosp., Memphis, 1971-72; staff psychologist children's youth program Helen Ross McNabb Ctr., Knoxville, Tenn., 1973-75; staff psychologist, asst. dir. psychology Commonwealth Psychiat. Ctr., Richmond, Va., 1975-77; clin. psychologist in pvt. practice, Arlington and Alexandria, Va., 1978-81, Jackson, Tenn., 1982—; mem. Child Abuse Rev. Team, Madison County, Tenn., 1985. Mem. steering com. Jackson chpt. Assn. Children With Learning Disabilities, 1985; mem. Leadership Jackson, 1985. Mem. Tenn. Psychol. Assn. (ins. com. 1984—), Southeastern Psychol. Assn., Am. Psychol. Assn., Tenn. Soc. Clin. Psychology, Jackson Area C. of C. Psi Chi (Book award 1968). Club: Jackson Bus. and Profl. Women's (2d v.p. 1985). Home: 148 Laurie Circle Jackson TN 38305 Office: 36 Brentshire Sq Suite B Jackson TN 38305

LODOWSKI, RUTH ELLEN, physician; b. Dallas, Feb. 15, 1951; s. Charles Harry and Genevieve (Gowaty) L.; B.S., U. Tex., Austin, 1972; M.B.A., North Tex. State U., Denton, 1976; M.D., U. Tex., 1986. Resident asst., then head resident Castilian Dormitory, Austin, Tex., 1971-72, head resident, 1972-73; singer self-employed band Austin, 1972-74; bank teller Greenville Ave. Bank, Dallas, 1974-75; employment interviewer Tex. Employment Commn., Grand Prairie, 1975-76; personnel intern U.S. Dept. Justice, Seagoville, Tex., 1976-77; personnel asst. Army and Air Force Exchange Service, San Antonio, 1977-78; staffing adminstr. personnel adminstrn. dept. Tex. Instruments Inc., Dallas, 1978-81. Active, YWCA, ARC; bd. dirs. Children, Inc., for mentally retarded. Recipient Top 10 Medal of Honor, Kiwanis Internat., 1969. Mem. Am. Soc. Personnel Adminstrn., Dallas Personnel Assn., AMA, Tex. Med. Assn., Sigma Alpha Eta. Clubs: Tex. Exes, S.W. Assn. Oriental Dancers. Home: 715 Green Hill Rd Dallas TX 75232

LODWICK, MICHAEL WAYNE, lawyer; b. New Orleans, Sept. 21, 1946; s. Frank Tillman Jr. and Grace Evelyn (Hilty) L.; m. Donna Peirce, June 15, 1968; children—Sarah Peirce, Jane Durborow, Elizabeth Hilty. B.A., La. State U., 1968; M.A., Tulane U., 1972, Ph.D., 1976; J.D., Loyola U., New Orleans, 1981. Bar: U.S. Dist. Ct. (ea. dist.) La. 1981, U.S. Ct. Appeals (5th cir.) 1981, U.S. Ct. Appeals (D.C. cir.) 1982. Instr. to asst. prof. Tulane U., New Orleans, 1976-78; assoc. Barham & Churchill, New Orleans, 1981-83, O'Neil, Eichin & Miller, New Orleans, 1983—. Editor Plantation Soc. in Americas jour., 1979-83. Editor-in-chief Loyola Law Rev., 1980-81. Contrbr. articles to profl. jours. Mem. New Orleans Symphony Chorus, 1985—. Tulane U. fellow, 1970-72; recipient Loyola U. Law Rev. Honor award, 1981, Loyola Law Alumni award, 1981. Mem. ABA, La. State Bar Assn., New Orleans Bar Assn., Maritime Law Assn. U.S., Assn. Trial Lawyers Am. Clubs: U.S. Swimming, Green Wave Swim (pres. 1984-85). Home: 7726 Cohn St New Orleans LA 70118 Office: O'Neil Eichin & Miller 1 Poydras Plaza Suite 2600 New Orleans LA 70113

LOE, EMMETT BAXTER, social worker; b. Haskell County, Tex., Dec. 28, 1924; s. Stephen Rals and Ellie Lorene (Baker) L.; m. Ruby Nell Ketchersid, Sept. 12, 1946; children—Ronald Wayne, Karen June, Kimberley Grant, Melinda Michelle. Student, Howard Payne U., 1964-66, Amarillo, Coll., 1970-71, West Tex. State U., 1971-72. Ordained to ministry Ch. of Christ, 1961. With Amerada Petroleum Corp., Gaines County, Tex., 1950-61; pastor chs. Brownwood, Tex., 1961-66, Odessa, Tex., 1966-69; chmn. bd. John Abraham Relief Fund, Amarillo, Tex., 1985—; lectr. in field. Bd. dirs. Southwestern Bible Inst., San Angelo, Tex., 1980-83. Served with USN, 1944-46. Mem. Evang. Council for Fin. Accountability, Amarillo Ministerial Alliance (pres.), Christian Ministries Mgmt. Assn., Internat. Platform Assn. Republican. Lodge: Rotary (pres. 1978-79). Editor Gospel Tidings mag., 1965-75. Home: 2521 Walnut St Amarillo TX 79107 Office: 4606 River Dr Amarillo TX 79107

LOEFFLER, THOMAS G., congressman; b. Fredericksburg, Tex., Aug. 1, 1946; s. Gilbert and Marie Loeffler; B.B.A., U. Tex., 1968, J.D., 1971; m. Kathy Crawford; children—Lance, Cullen, Lauren. Bar: Tex. 1971. Legal counsel U.S. Dept. Commerce, 1971-72; chief legis. counsel to U.S. Senator John Tower of Tex., 1972-74; dep. for congressional affairs FEA, 1974-75; spl. asst. for legis. affairs to Pres. Gerald Ford, 1975-77; Washington counsel Tenneco Inc., 1977; pvt. practice law, 1977-78; mem. 96th-99th Congresses from 21st Dist. Tex. Mem. Am. Bar Assn., Tex. Bar Assn., D.C. Bar Assn. Republican. Lutheran. Office: Room 1212 Longworth House Office Bldg Washington DC 20515

LOEHLE, BETTY BARNES, artist, painter; b. Montgomery, Ala., Mar. 21, 1923; d. Harry McGuinn and Elizabeth (Fowler) B.; m. Richard E. Loehle, Aug. 16, 1947; children—Craig Edward, Alan David, Bruce Barnes, Lynn Elizabeth. Student Auburn U., Harris Sch. Art, Nashville, 1942-46, Evanston Art Ctr., 1964-68. Layout artist Atlanta Art Studios, 1970-75; free lance designer, painter, Atlanta, 1975-80; full time painter, Atlanta, 1980—; dir., publicity chmn., exhibition chmn. Ga. Watercolor Soc., 1981-85; pres. Artists Assocs. Gallery, Atlanta, 1977-79, sec., 1985—. Represented by Artists Assocs. Gallery, Abstein Gallery of Art, Atlanta, Little House on Linden Gallery, Birmingham, Ala., Gallery Contemporanea, Jacksonville, Fla., Virginia Miller Galleries, Coral Gables, Fla. Entries judge Arts Festival of Atlanta, 1974; chmn. Unitarian Ch. Art Com., Atlanta, 1973-76. Recipient Purchase award Decatur Sesquicentennial, Ga., 1974, Hunter Mus. of Art, Chattanooga, 1977, Ga. Council for the Arts, Atlanta, 1977, 1980. Mem. DeKalb Council for the Arts, Ga. Watercolor Soc. (signature mem.; merit awards 1980, 82, 83), So. Watercolor Soc. (signature mem.; silver award 1979, merit award 1980), Ky. Watercolor Soc. (artist mem.). Club: Atlanta Artist (exhbn. chmn. 1972-74). Home: 2608 River Oak Dr Decatur GA 30033

LOESER, WILLIAM RICHARD, bookstore owner; b. Chgo., Sept. 26, 1942; s. William Henry and Virginia Josephine (Bressman) L.; m. Barbara L. Mahaffey, Aug. 29, 1975 (div. Jan. 1978). B.A., U. Houston, 1964. Corr. clk. Pub. Health Service, Washington, 1965-66; office mgr. Phoenix Mut. Life Ins Co., Hartford, Conn., 1966-73, mgr., pension services, 1973-75; pension cons. Guardian Life Ins. Co., N.Y.C., 1975-78; owner, operator Keith & Martin Book Shop (name changed to Book Shop Inc. 1985), Chapel Hill, N.C., 1979—, pres., 1985—. Democrat. Club: Durham Bibliophiles. Avocations: reading; baseball. Home: 100 Pine St Carrboro NC 27510 Office: The Book Shop Inc 400 W Franklin St Chapel Hill NC 27514

LOFTON, JEROME, JR., devel. engr.; b. Goldsboro, N.C., Dec. 2, 1954; s. Jerome and Essie Lucille (Johnson) L.; B.S.E.E., N.C. State U., 1976. Engr., Research Triangle Inst., Research Triangle Park, N.C., 1975; engring. group leader Communications div. Motorola Inc., Plantation, Fla., 1976—. Mem. IEEE, Nat. Soc. Profl. Engrs., Alpha Phi Alpha. Home: 550 SW 38th Terr Fort Lauderdale FL 33312 Office: 8000 W Sunrise Blvd Plantation FL 33322

LOFTUS, DONALD GREGORY, hospital administrator; b. St. Louis, Aug. 17, 1943; s. Charles J. and Mary A. Loftus; m. Kala Rae Gilmour, Sept. 10, 1966; children—Kelly Anne, Kyle Andrew. B.S., Ind. U., 1965; M.S., Trinity U., 1969. Adminstrv. extern Bloomington Hosp. (Ind.), 1964-65; unit mgr. dept. adminstrv. medicine Presbyn.-St. Luke's Hosp., Chgo., 1965-67; grad. asst. health resources planning unit Tex. Hosp. Assn., San Antonio, 1968; adminstrv. resident Ind. U. Med. Ctr., Indpls., 1968; asst. adminstr. Graham Hosp., Canton, Ill., 1969-73; adminstr. Franklin Hosp., Benton, Ill., 1973-74; exec. v.p. Holy Family Hosp., Des Plaines, Ill., 1974-76; pres., chief exec. officer Appleton Meml. Hosp. (Wis.), 1977-80, United Health Services, Appleton, 1980-83, St. Joseph Hosp., Fort Worth, 1983, St. Joseph Health Corp., 1984—; rep. Outagamie Community Blood Bank, 1977-79; mem. instructional workshop adv. com. Tri-State Hosp. Assembly, 1976-78; dir. Valley Bank; assoc. clin. prof. U. Wis. Med. Sch., Madison. Hosp. rep. Gov.'s Prison Health Care Adv. Com., State of Wis., 1977-79; bd. dirs. Lake Winnebago Health Systems Agy., 1977—, Dallas-Ft. Worth Hosp. Council, 1984—, Tex. Conf. Cath. Health Facilities, 1985—. Fellow Am. Coll. Hosp. Adminstrs.; mem. Wis. Hosp. Assn. (mem. com. on planning 1978-82), Am. Acad. Polit. and Social Sci., Sigma Iota Epsilon. Office: St Joseph Hosp 1401 S Main St Fort Worth TX 76104

LOFTUS, JAMES FRANCIS, exploration geophysicist; b. Rhinebeck, N.Y., Dec. 8, 1952; s. James Francis and Agnes Marie (Cavanaugh) L.; m. Iva Lorraine Light, July 16, 1977 (div. 1981), 1 child, Seamus Eugene; m. Patricia Louise Wright, May 14, 1983. B.S. in Geology, U. Rochester, N.Y., 1975; M.S. in Geology and Geophysics, Boston Coll., 1979. Petroleum geophysicist Amoco Prodn. Co., New Orleans, 1977-81; geophysicist Mobil Exploration Co., Metairie, La., 1981-82; advanced geophysicist Marathon Oil Co., Houston, 1983—. Assoc. editor Southeastern Geophys Soc. newsletter, New Orleans, 1979-80, editor, 1980-81. Contbr. articles to newspapers. Democratic candidate for town council Rhinebeck, N.Y., 1973; deed restriction committeeman Silvermill Homeowners' Assn., Katy, Tex., 1985. Mem. Soc. Exploration Geophysicists, Am. Assn. Petroleum Geologists, Geophys. Soc. Houston. Roman Catholic. Avocations: writing fiction, reading, chess, playing keyboard instruments. Office: Marathon Oil Co PO Box 3128 Houston TX 77253

LOFTUS, ROBERT EARL, cataract and ocular implant surgery consultant; b. Belvedere, Ill., Aug. 5, 1922; s. Frederick Charles and Bertha Belle (Allen) L.; m. Marjorie Lucille Miller, June 30, 1945; children—Steven Robert, Charles Webber, David Kendall, Barbara Dianne. B.S., Lawrence Coll., Appleton, Wis., 1944; Ph.D., U. Chgo., 1947; Litt.D., U. Barcelona (Spain), 1977. Midwest regional mgr. Warren-Teed Co., Mpls., 1950-64; eastern divisional mgr. Wesley-Jessen, Chgo., 1964-72; dir. ednl. services House of Vision, Chgo., 1972-74, Cavitron Surg. Systems, Atlanta, 1974-79; asst. to pres. Intermedica/Intraocular, Inc., Pasadena, Calif., 1979—; cons. Charing Cross Med. Ctr., London, 1975-79, Lucknow Med. Ctr. (India), 1978, Goethe U., Frankfurt, W.Ger., 1977, Soc. Ophthalmology, Rio de Janiero, 1983, others. Served with U.S. Army, 1943. Recipient citations Lions Club, 1977, 76, Soc. Venezuelan Opthalmology, 1983. Mem. Halum-Arnold Eye Found. (v.p. 1981-85, dir. 1981—), Phi Kappa Tau. Republican.

LOGAN, JOHN A., association executive. Pres., Lubbock C. of C., Tex. Office: Lubbock C of C 1120 14th St PO Box 561 Lubbock TX 79408*

LOGGINS, BOBBY GENE, meat company executive; b. Tyler, Tex., Oct. 17, 1955; s. Bobbie Daniel and Dorthey Gene Loggins; m. Linda Ella Sides, June 1, 1974; children—Lisa, Lindy. B.A. in Bus. Adminstrn., Bapt. Christian Coll., 1982, LL.D., 1983. Sales rep. Loggins Meat Co., Inc., Tyler, 1974-76, in plant supr., 1976-78, v.p. transp. and in-house sales, 1978-80, exec. v.p. distbn. and purchasing, 1980-84, pres., 1984—; sec.-treas. Landmark Oil Co., Inc., 1980-83; mem. bus. devel. bd. First Nat. Bank Whitehorse. Gen. advisor vocat. edn. Tyler Pub. Sch. Dist.; bd. deacons. Central Baptist Ch., 1977—. Named Lone Star Farmer, 1973; Outstanding Vocat. Student, Rotary Club, 1972. Club: Central Bapt. Century.

LOGGINS, EDWARD M., JR., corporate executive; b. 1930. B.S. in E.E., U. Tex., 1958. With Gulf States Utilities Co., Beaumont, Tex., 1958—, supr. comml. and indsl. sales, Baton Rouge, 1964-69, dir. indsl. sales, 1969-71, supt. Sabine Power Sta., 1971-75, prodn. mgr., then mgr. Western div., 1975-77, v.p. tech. services, 1977-78, v.p., 1978-79, sr. v.p. adminstrv. services, 1979-80, exec. v.p., 1980—. Served with USAF, 1951-54. Office: Gulf States Utilities Co 285 Liberty St Beaumont TX 77704*

LOHMAN, T. E., oil and gas company executive; b. 1937; married. B.S., Tex. A&M U., 1959. Engr., Pan Am. Petroleum Corp., 1959-62; dist. engr. Tex. Oil & Gas Corp., 1962-65, process engr., 1965-67, asst. v.p., 1967-68, v.p., 1968-72, sr. v.p., 1972-76, sr. v.p., mgr. gas gathering and processing, 1976-81, exec. v.p. gas gathering, Dallas, 1981—; asst. to pres. Nat. Fuels Corp., 1964-65. Served to capt. U.S. Army, 1959-66. Office: Tex Oil & Gas Corp 1507 Pacific Dallas TX 75201*

LOHMANN, JULIA ELISE, engineering firm and oil production company executive; b. Pauls Valley, Okla., Nov. 18, 1939; d. King James and Margaret Huntley (Shumate) Davenport; m. James A. Stine, Aug. 19, 1959 (div. 1972); m. 2d, Phillip Jay Lohmann, June 1, 1973; children—John Allen Stine, Sandra Elise Stine. Co-owner, decorater Stine Constrn. Co., 1959-72; co-owner, dir. Jasper & Lohmann Engrs., 1974-79, Apex Energy, Inc., Norman, Okla., 1979—; co-owner Lohmann & Assocs., Inc., Norman, 1979—. Active Boy Scouts Am., P.T.A., Hosp. Vols. Assn. Recipient award Am. Legion, 1959. Mem. Am. Petroleum Inst., DAR, C. of C. Republican. Methodist. Office: 1215 Crossroads Blvd Suite 100 Norman OK 73069

LOHMANN, KEITH HENRY, police department official, consultant; b. Brookhaven, N.Y., Dec. 26, 1955; s. Henry August and June Dorothy (Friberg) L.; m. Margaret Lynch, Mar. 31, 1984. A.S. in Law Enforcement, Guilford Coll., 1977, B.S. in Adminstrn. of Justice, 1981. Ops. mgr. H. Lohmann and Son, Brookhaven, 1973-75, 81-82; ops. supr. Powers Detective and Patrol, Greensboro, N.C., 1975-81; pub. safety officer Chapel Hill Police Dept., N.C., 1982-84, police planner, 1984—; security cons. Hotel Europa, Inc., Chapel Hill, 1982-83. Mem. Nat. Assn. Police Planners, Am. Soc. Pub. Adminstrn., N.C. Assn. Law Enforcement Planners. Lutheran. Avocations: golf; tennis; snow skiing; snowmobiling. Office: Chapel Hill Police Dept 828 Airport Rd Chapel Hill NC 27514

LOHSEN, ARTHUR KENNETH, electrical construction company executive; b. Jersey City, Mar. 11, 1942; s. Arthur Claude and Viola (Burke) L.; m. JoAnn Dorothy Strub, Aug. 29, 1964; children—Arthur Charles, Lynda Anne. Grad. in E.E., Newark Coll. Engring., 1965. Elec. engr. Syska & Hennessy Cons. Engrs., N.Y.C., 1963-65, chief elec. engr., Washington, 1966-71; br. mgr. Howard P. Foley Co., Washington, 1972-81; v.p. Preconstrn. Service Corp., Washington, 1982-85, F.B. Harding Inc., 1985—. Membership chmn. Washington Bldg. Congress, 1982. Mem. Fairfax County (Va.) C. of C. Republican. Lutheran. Home: 4801 Reston Ln Bowie MD 20715 Office: FB Harding Inc 4302 Howard Ave Kensington MD 20895

LOISELLE, LARRY DALE, personnel adminstrator; b. Milw., Dec. 18, 1942; s. Virgil Willis and Erma Clara (Oestreich) L.; m. Karen Suzanne Van Sluyters, Oct. 16, 1974; children—Christy Cherie, Timothy Christopher, Thomas Christopher, Michael Christopher. Collection mgr. Gen. Electric Credit Corp., Lansing, Mich., 1970-71; employment and contract service rep., personnel methods technician Mich. Employment Security Commn., Lansing, 1971; asst. personnel dir. Dept. Mgmt. and Budget, Lansing, 1971-76, model eval. program coordinator Office Criminal Justice Programs, 1976; personnel technician, personnel and staff devel. div. Tex. Edn. Agy., Austin, 1976-78, asst. dir. personnel adminstrn. and staff devel. div., 1978-81, dir. personnel adminstrn. and staff devel. div., 1981—; mem. personnel subcom. Tex. State Govt. Effectiveness Program, Office Gov., 1979-83, mem. adv. council working com. statewide personnel project, 1980-81, staff coordinators com., 1983—; mem. industry coop. com. Tex. State Tech. Inst. Computer Sci. Tech. Sch., 1980—. Served with USAF, 1966-69. Mem. Tex. State Personnel Adminstrs. Assn. Avocations: travel; camping; fishing; hunting; dog breeding. Home: Route 2 Box 75-G Manor TX 78653 Office: Tex Edn Agy 201 E 11th St Austin TX 78653

LOLLAR, PERRY DURANT, coal company executive; b. Jasper, Ala., Mar. 8, 1941; s. Ezra Clay and Margaret (Myers) L.; m. Jean Gober, Aug. 21, 1965; children—Lori Michelle, Elizabeth Dixon. B.S., Samford U., 1965; M.A., U. Ala., 1975, A.A., 1976. Biology tchr. Jasper City Bd. Edn. (Ala.), 1966-69, 72-78; case worker Dept. Pensions, Jasper, 1969-70; heavy equipment operator Pratt Coal Co., Birmingham, Ala., 1970-72; gen. supt. Dime Coal Co., Inc. subs. Coal Systems Inc., Birmingham, 1978—. Democrat. Baptist. Home: 200 Forest Ln Jasper AL 35501 Office: Dime Coal Co Inc RR3 Box 285 Phil Campbell AL 35581

LOMASON, WILLIAM KEITHLEDGE, automotive company executive; b. Detroit, 1910; s. Harry A. and Elizabeth (Bennett) L.; m. Neva C. Wigle, 1930 (dec.); m. 2d, Ruth M. Martin, 1970. A.B., U. Mich., 1932, A.M., 1933. With Douglas & Lomason Co., Detroit, 1934—, treas., 1943-52, v.p., 1945-50, pres., 1950-75, chmn. bd., chief exec. officer, 1975—, also dir.; dir. Mich. Mut. Liability Co. Pres. Ga. Bus. and Industry Assn., 1963-64; dir., exec. com. Nat. Right to Work Com. Mem. Nat. Assn. Mfrs. (indsl. relations com.), Am. Electroplaters Soc., Engring. Soc. Detroit, Alpha Chi Rho. Episcopalian. Home: 831 Fairfield Rd NW Atlanta GA 30327 Office: 24600 Hallwood Ct Farmington Hills MI 48018 and PO Box 20783 AMF Atlanta Airport GA 30320

LOMAX, DAN WADE, pharmacist; b. Monroe, La., Dec. 29, 1945; s. John Tillman and Marjorie (Kelly) L.; m. Molly Duncan, Mar. 2, 1974; children—Molly Duncan, Dan Kelly, William Joseph. B.S. in Pharmacy, U. Miss., 1969. Registered pharmacist, Miss., Ala. Pharmacist, Eckerd Drugs, Mobile, Ala., 1972-74; owner, pharmacist Lomax Discount Drugs, Waynesboro, Miss., 1975—. Alderman City of Waynesboro, 1976-85. Mem. U. Miss. Alumni Assn., Miss. Pharmacists Assn. (chmn. local chpt. 1984—), Wayne County C. of C. Methodist. Club: Little Theater (Waynesboro). Lodge: Rotary. Avocations: swimming; carpentry.

LOMAX, JOHN HARVARD, financial company executive; b. Macon, Ga., Mar. 28, 1924; s. John H. and Regis (Garrity) L.; m. Ann E. Davis, Dec. 30, 1947; children—John Harvey, Jan Lomax Teal. B.B.A., cum laude, U. Ga., 1948. Trainee, Joseph E. Seagram Co., Louisville, 1948-49; personnel dir. Schwob Mfg. Co., Columbus, Ga., 1949-51; personnel and pub. relations dir. Burlington Mills, Gastonia, N.C., 1951-54; personnel dir. Allstate Ins. Co., Charlotte, N.C., 1954-59; exec. v.p. Am. Credit Corp., Charlotte, 1959-76, Assocs. Corp. of N.Am., Dallas, 1976—; dir. Interfirst Bank, Irving, Tex., Gen. Telephone Co. of Southwest. Bd. trustees St. Paul Hosp., Dallas, Dallas Summer Mus., Dallas br. Tex. Soc. to Prevent Blindness; bd. advisors Internat. Airline Passengers Assn. Served to capt. USAF, 1942-46; with USAFR, 1946-55. Mem. Am. Fin. Services Assn. Clubs: Lancers, Northwood (Dallas). Home: 4215 Glenaire Dr Dallas TX 75229 Office: PO Box 660237 Dallas TX 75266

LOMELO, JOHN, JR., mayor; b. Orange, N.J., Mar. 22, 1928; s. John and Dorothy L.; m. Virginia, 1948; 1 dau., Martha. Grad. high sch. Mayor and chief exec. officer City of Sunrise (Fla.), 1967—. Treas., Broward County League of Cities, 1970-72, pres., from 1972; mem. legis. com. Fla. League Cities, bd. dirs., 1973, mem. resolutions com., 1972, 73; mem. com. community devel. Nat. League Cities, 1973. Mem. adv. com. Sch. Pub. Adminstrn., Broward Community Coll.; mem. community adv. bd. Lauderdale Lakes Med. Ctr.; chmn. Broward County Democratic Exec. Com., 1980; mem. Broward County Tourist Devel. Council, 1980. Served in USN. Recipient State of Israel Scroll of Honor, 1974; named Law Enforcement Mayor, Scotland Yard, 1975; Man of Yr., Italian-Am. Civic Orgns. Broward County, 1975, 76; Humanitarian award Brotherhood of Temple Beth Israel, 1976; cert. of appreciation Jewish War Vets., 1974; award Free Sons of Israel, 1975; award B'Nai B'rith Century Club; NATO Forces award, 1978; Voice of Democracy award VFW, 1978; cert. of appreciation Am. Police Acad., 1979; Idealism award City of Hope, 1980; Humanitarian award Deborah Hosp. Fond Found., 1981; Good Govt. award Sunrise/Lauderhill Jaycees, 1982; Broward Press Corps award, 1982; Spirit of Life award City of Hope, 1983. Mem. Fla. Peace Officers Assn., Am. Police Acad., Broward County Chiefs of Police Assn., West Broward Jaycees, Smithsonian Assocs., Jewish War Vets (assoc.), Notary Pub. Assn. Fla. Club: Optimists (charter). Lodges: Kiwanis (charter), KP (charter), Fraternal Order of Police Assocs. (treas. 1970), others. Lutheran. Office: 10770 W Oakland Park Blvd Sunrise FL 33321*

LOMENZO, JOHN RAYMOND, insurance company executive; b. Cape Charles, Va., May 14, 1926; s. John Raymond and Helen Ora (Shackelford) L.; m. Anita Carol Dehnert, Dec. 23, 1971; 1 child, Tiffany. Student, U. Richmond, 1947-50. Western regional mgr. nat. accounts Aetna Life & Casualty Ins. Co., Los Angeles, 1958-72; v.p. Alexander & Alexander, Los Angeles, 1972-74; v.p. nat. field ops. Interstate Nat. Corp., Chgo., 1974-79; pres., chief exec. officer Tex. Med. Liability Trust, Austin, 1979—. Mem. Nat. Republican Com., 1981—. Served with USAF, 1944-46. Mem. Am. Assn. Individual Investors, Soc. C.P.C.U.s, Physicians Ins. Assn. Am., Soc. Medicine and Law, Am. Morgan Horse Assn. Episcopalian. Home: Route 2 Box 39B Bertram TX 78605 Office: PO Box 14746 Austin TX 78761

LOMICKA, WILLIAM HENRY, business executive; b. Irwin, Pa., Mar. 9, 1937; s. William and Carabel L.; m. Carol L. Williams, Feb. 14, 1979; 1 son, Edward W. B.A., Coll. of Wooster, 1959; M.B.A., U. Pa., 1962. Sr. securities analyst Guardian Life, N.Y.C., 1962-65; treasury services mgr. L.B. Foster, Pitts., 1966-68, Welch Foods, Westfield, N.Y., 1969-70; asst. treas. Ashland Oil, Inc. (Ky.), 1970-75; v.p. fin., treas. Humana, Inc., Louisville, 1975-82, sr. v.p. fin., 1982— dir. Clayton Homes, Inc., Knoxville, Tenn., Calumet Industries, Inc. Bd. dirs. Louisville chpt. ARC, Ky. Opera Assn. Served with USAR, 1962-68. Home: 573 Sunnyside Dr Louisville KY 40206 Office: 1800 1st National Tower Louisville KY 40201

LONG, ALFRED B., oil co. exec.; b. Galveston, Tex., Aug. 4, 1909; s. Jessie A. and Ada (Beckwith) L.; student S. Park Jr. Coll., 1928-29, Lamar U., 1947-56, U. Tex., 1941; m. Sylvia V. Thomas, Oct. 29, 1932; 1 dau., Kathleen Sylvia Long Pearson. With Sun Oil Co., Beaumont, Tex., 1931—, driller geophys. dept., surveyor engring. dept., engr. operating dept., engr. prodn. lab., 1931-59, regional supr., 1960-69, now ret.; ind. oil cons., Beaumont, 1969—; mem. tech. adv. group Oil and Gas Drilling Inst., Lamar U. Mem. Jefferson County Program Planning Com., 1964. Mem. Soc. Petroleum Engrs., Am. Assn. Petroleum Geologists, IEEE, Houston Geol. Soc., Gulf Coast Engring. and Sci. Soc. (treas. 1962-65, recipient cert. for outstanding service to engring. profession), Am. Petroleum Inst., Soc. Wireless Pioneers, U.S. Power Squadron. Inventor various oil well devices. Address: PO Box 7266 Beaumont TX 77706

LONG, CATHY, congresswoman; b. Dayton, Ohio, Feb. 24, 1924; m. Gillis W. Long (dec.); children—George Harrison, Janis Catherine. B.A., La. State U., 1948. Del., Democratic Nat. Convs., 1980, 84; mem. 99th U.S. Congress from 8th dist. La. Mem. La. State Dem. Fin. Council, Nat. Council Sr. Citizens, Nat. Trust for Hist. Preservation. Office: US House of Reps Office of House Members Washington DC 20515*

LONG, CECIL LANIER, systems analyst; b. Philadelphia, Miss., Dec. 8, 1938; s. John Cecil and Sudie Elizabeth (Fulton) L.; m. Wanda Jo Lyle, May 30, 1963; children—John Andrew, Dana Elizabeth. B.A. in Chemistry, Miss. So. Coll., 1961; postgrad. U. So. Miss., 1971-72; M.S. in Elec. Engring., Southeast Inst. Tech., 1983. Quality control mgr. Johnson & Johnson Co., Chicago, 1963-65; supr., prodn. supt. May Alumnium Inc., El Campo, Tex., 1965-68; chemist Dow Chem. Co., Russellville, Ark., 1969-70; prodn. supr. Armstrong Rubber Co., Natchez, Miss., 1970-73; quality assurance mgr. Coyne Cylinder Co., Huntsville, Ala., 1973-79; systems analyst Delta Research Inc., Huntsville, 1979—. Served to 1st. lt. U.S. Army, 1961-63. Recipient disting. service award U. So. Miss., 1983. Mem. Am. Security Council, Am. Def. Preparedness Assn., Jaycees (past officer El Campo), Nat. Rifle Assn., U. So. Miss. Alumni Assn. (Huntsville chpt. pres. 1982-83), Kappa Alpha. Republican. Baptist. Club: Exchange. Lodge: Masons. Patentee in field. Home: 12112 Chicamauga Trail Huntsville AL 35803 Office: Delta Research Inc 2109 Clinton Ave SW Suite 414 Huntsville AL 35805

LONG, CHARLES FARRELL, insurance company executive; b. Charlottesville, Va., Nov. 19, 1933; s. Cicel Early and Ruth Elizabeth (Shifflett) L.; C.L.U., The Am. Coll., 1972; m. Ann Tilley, May 28, 1960; children—C. Farrell, Linda. Founder, pres. Casualty Underwriters Inc., Charlottesville, 1959-72, Group Underwriters Inc., Charlottesville, 1959—; trustee P.A.I. Ins. Trust. Mem. Assay Commn. U.S., 1975; bd. dirs. Heart Assn. Served with U.S. Navy, 1954-58. Mem. Central Va. Estate Planning Council, Am. Soc. C.L.U.s, Central Va. C.L.U.s Assn. (dir.), Va. Press Assn., Va. Assn. Life Underwriters. Creator Queen's medal for Queen Elizabeth, 1976. Home: 1400 W Leigh Dr Charlottesville VA 22901 Office: Madison Park Charlottesville VA 22901

LONG, CHARLES JOSEPH, neuropsychologist, psychology educator; b. Caruthersville, Mo., Dec. 25, 1935; s. Charles Roby and Alice Louis (Luten) L.; m. Rosemary Flack; children—Charles, Jr., Steve, Ken, Greg, Chris, Jon, Jen, Melissa. B.S., Memphis State U., 1957, M.A., 1960; Ph.D., Vanderbilt U.,

Nashville, 1963. Diplomate Am. Bd. Profl. Neuropsychology. Faculty Memphis State U., Tenn., 1967—, prof. psychology, 1976—. Contbr. articles to profl. jours. Mem. Am. Psychol. Assn., Nat. Acad. Neuropsychology, Internat. Neuropsychology Assn., Southeastern Psychol. Assn. Avocations: computers, sailing. Home: 1308 Hayne Memphis TN 38119 Office: Dept of Psychology Memphis State U Memphis TN 38152

LONG, ELDON WAYNE, college executive; b. Denton, Tex., Sept. 9, 1925; s. Joseph Bailey and Zola Bland (Howard) L.; m. Charlene Frances Lang, July 20, 1945; children—Sherrie Ellen, Terry Wayne, Charla Jayne, James Howard. B.S., North Tex. State U., 1949, M.Ed., 1962. Coach, tchr. Harlingen Ind. Sch. Dist., Tex., 1949-60; coach Del Mar Coll., Corpus Christi, Tex., 1960-66, student personnel dir., 1966-71, dean of students, 1971-85, v.p. student services, 1985—. Served as sgt. U.S. Army, 1945-47. Mem. Tex. Assn. Coll. and Univ. Student Personnel Adminstrs., Jr. Coll. Student Personnel Assn. Tex. (bd. dirs. 1983—, Service award 1985), Tex. Assn. Community Colls. (chief student affairs adminstrn.). Lodge: Rotary. Avocations: hunting, fishing. Home: 324 California St Corpus Christi TX 78411 Office: Del Mar Coll Baldwin and Ayers Sts Corpus Christi TX 78404

LONG, EUGENE THOMAS, III, philosophy educator, administrator; b. Richmond, Va., Mar. 16, 1935; s. Eugene Thomas and Emily Joyce (Barker) L.; m. Carolyn Macleod, June 25, 1960; children—Scott, Kathryn. B.A., Randolph-Macon Coll., Ashland, Va., 1957; B.D., Duke U., 1960; Ph.D., U. Glasgow (Scotland), 1964. Asst. prof. philosophy Randolph-Macon Coll., 1964-67, assoc. prof., 1967-70; assoc. prof., U. S.C., Columbia, 1970-73, prof., 1973—, chmn. dept., 1972—. Mem. S.C. Com. for Humanities, 1980-85. Recipient Research award NEH, 1968, Duke U./U. N.C. Coop. Program in Humanities, 1968-69. Mem. Soc. Philosophy in Religion (pres. 1980-81), Metaphys. Soc. Am. (sec. treas. 1977-81), So. Soc. Philosophy and Psychology (exec. council 1976-79), Am. Philos. Assn. (sec. treas. eastern div. 1985—). Author: Jaspers and Bultmann, 1968; Existence, Being and God, 1985; contbr., editor: God, Secularization & History, 1974, Experience, Reason & God, 1980; assoc. editor Internat. Jour. Philosophy of Religion, 1975—, So. Jour. Philosophy, 1978—; co-editor: God and Temporality, 1984; mem. adv. editorial bd. The Works of William James, 1974—; contbr. articles to profl. jours. Office: Dept Philosophy Univ SC Columbia SC 29208

LONG, GERALD H., tobacco company executive; b. Mineola, N.Y., 1928; grad. Adelphi U., 1952; postgrad. N.Y. U., 1962. With R.J. Reynolds Tobacco Co., Winston-Salem, N.C., 1969—, exec. v.p., mem. exec. com., 1979-81, pres., chief exec. officer, 1981—, also dir. Office: R J Reynolds Tobacco Co 4th and Main Sts Box 2959 Winston-Salem NC 27102

LONG, HENRY SPROTT, architect; b. Jasper, Ala., June 30, 1914; s. Edgar William and Ruth (Lacy) L.; m. Margaret Preacher, June 28, 1941; children—Ruth Adelaide Long Karpeles, Henry Sprott, Jr. B.Arch., Ga. Inst. Tech., 1935. Pvt. practice architecture Henry Sprott Long, Architect, Birmingham, 1939-41; prin. Henry Sprott Long & Assocs., Architects, Birmingham, 1945—. Served with AUS, 1942-45. Mem. AIA, Nat. Trust for Historic Preservation. Presbyterian. Clubs: Country Club of Birmingham, Mountain Brook, Ponte Vedra, Rotary of Birmingham. Home: 3217 Pine Ridge Rd Birmingham AL 35213 Office: 3016 Clairmont Ave Birmingham AL 35205

LONG, JOHN MALOY, university dean, music educator; b. Guntersville, Ala., Dec. 28, 1925; s. Sam James and Lilian (Letson) L.; B.S., Jacksonville State U., 1949, LL.D. (hon.), 1971; M.A., U. Ala., 1964; m. Mary Lynn Adams, July 7, 1950; children—John Maloy, Deborra Lynn. Dir. bands Oneonta (Ala.) High Sch., 1949-50, Ft. Payne (Ala.) High Sch., 1950-55, Robert E. Lee High Sch., Montgomery, Ala., 1955-65; dir. bands Troy (Ala.) State U., 1965—, chmn. music dept., 1969, dean Sch. Fine Arts, 1971, dean Coll. Arts and Scis., 1972—; chmn. bd. dirs. Nat. Band Assn. Hall of Fame for Disting. Condrs. Mem. Ala. Hist. Commn., 1974—; mem. Troy City Bd. Edn., 1972—, chmn., 1976—. Served with AUS, 1944-46. Recipient citation of excellence Nat. Band Assn., 1972; Disting. Citizens Service award City of Montgomery, 1964; Cert. of Appreciation, State of Ala., 1964; named one of 10 top band dirs. in U.S., Sch. Musician mag., 1969; new music bldg. at Troy State U. named in his honor, 1975; Outstanding Music Educator, Ala. Music Edn. Assn., 1983-84. Mem. Am. Bandmaster Assn., Am. Sch. Band Dirs. Assn. (state pres. 1968-72), Coll. Band Dirs. Nat. Assn. (state pres.), Omicron Delta Kappa, Phi Mu Alpha, Phi Beta Mu, Phi Delta Kappa, Kappa Kappa Psi (Nat. Disting. Service to Music award 1979; dist. gov. 1979-83, nat. trustee 1981-83), Delta Chi. Democrat. Methodist. Clubs: Masons, Rotary. Contbr. articles to mags. Office: Office of Dean Coll Arts and Scis Troy State U Troy AL 36081

LONG, KATHLEEN WEBB, legal administrator, office design consultant; b. Shreveport, La., Dec. 31, 1945; d. Gilbert E. Henry and Anne (Wigley) Henry-Tidwell; m. William M. Long, Mar. 18, 1971. B.A. magna cum laude, Sophie Newcomb Coll., Tulane U., 1977; postgrad. Loyola U., 1977-78. Various positions Deutsch Kerrigan & Stiles, New Orleans, 1972-78, supr. legal assts., 1978-80; adminstr. Goldberg Evans & Katzman, Harrisburg, Pa., 1980-82, Carroll & Halberg, Miami, Fla., 1982—; pres. Practical Approach to Office Systems, Miami, 1984—; space design cons. Levenshon & Co., Miami, 1984, Gerald D. Hines Mgmt. Offices S.E. Bank Bldg., Miami, 1984; guest lectr. 15th Ann. Law Office Mgmt. Workshops, Inst. Continuing Legal Edn. Mem. ACLU, Fla., 1984—; bd. dirs. Chiron Bus. Sch., Miami, 1983-84. Mem. Assn. Legal Adminstrs. (chmn. ednl. com. South Fla. chpt. 1983-84), ABA, Am. Mgmt. Assn., Nat. Assn. Female Execs. Avocations: cinema; travel Office: Carroll & Halberg PA 2701 S Bayshore Dr Miami FL 33133

LONG, LARRY NEIL, applied organizational psychologist, program evaluator; b. Bloomington, Ind., Sept. 17, 1952; s. Keith Robert and Eleanor Helene (Szur) L.; m. Helena Lay, Jan. 21, 1982; 1 child, Allison Michelle. B.A. in Psychology, Indiana U. of Pa., 1974; M.A. in Indsl. and Orgnl. Psychology, U. Nebr., 1979; postgrad. U. Tenn., 1977—. Internal cons. TVA, Knoxville, 1979-80, personnel staff officer, 1980-82, quality assurance specialist, 1982-85, supr. project mgmt. tng., 1985—; cons. Orgnl. Measures, Knoxville, 1982—. Pres. Concord Woods Homeowners Assn., Knoxville, 1980—. Mem. Am. Mgmt. Assn, Acad. Mgmt., Am. Psychol. Assn. Republican. Presbyterian. Avocation: skydiving. Office: TVA 9-177-SB-K 400 W Summit Hill Knoxville TN 37902

LONG, LEWIS MCCLELLAN K(ENNEDY), psychologist, consultant; b. Porto Alegre, Brazil, Nov. 19, 1923 (parents Am. citizens); s. Frank Millard and Eula Lee (Kennedy) L.; m. Barbara Dietterich, Dec. 27, 1952 (dec. Mar. 1976); children—Mark, Susan, David, Stephen; m. Alice Deaton, Mar. 24, 1979. B.A., U. Okla., 1947, B.S., 1950, M.S., 1949; M.A., Harvard U., 1953, Ph.D., 1956; M.B.P.A., Southeastern U., 1981. Diplomate Am. Bd. Profl. Psychology. Instr. Roanoke Coll., Salem, Va., 1948-49; psychologist U. Ark. Med. Ctr., Little Rock, 1956-57, NIMH, Peace Corps, VISTA, 1967-81; pvt. practice psychology, Little Rock, 1957-63, Alexandria, Va., 1981—; part-time instr. George Mason U., Fairfax, Va., 1981-82, U. Va., 1963-65; cons. various orgns., 1964—. Author: (with others) Staffing for Better Schools, 1967. Contbr. articles to profl. jours. Planning chmn. Alexandria Youth Commn., 1984—; pres. Stephen Foster PTA, Alexandria, 1968-69; mem. ch. bd. Mt. Vernon Unitarian Ch., Alexandria, 1970-73; v.p. Mt. Vernon Community Mental Health Ctr., 1976-79. Served to lt. USN, 1943-46, PTO. Charles Smith scholar Harvard U., 1952; U.S. Dept. of State fellow, 1952. Mem. Am. Psychol. Assn., Am. Sociol. Assn., No. Va. Soc. Clin. Psychologists, D.C. Sociol. Soc., Va. Acad. Psychologists. Clubs: Harvard (Washington), U. Okla. (life). Avocations: art, magic, reading, sports. Home: 213 S Alfred St Alexandria VA 22314

LONG, LINDA ANN, public affairs consultant; b. Durham, N.C., Feb. 8, 1952; d. Grover Cleveland and Ellen (Parnell) L. B.A., U. Del., 1974; J.D., Widener U., 1979. Lobbyist Legis. Services, Inc., Dover, Del., 1977-79; mem. campaign staff Connally for Pres. Com., Arlington, Va., 1979-80; exec. dir. Reagan-Bush Com.-Del., Wilmington, 1980; spl. asst. for legis. affairs Gov. Pierre S. duPont, Iv.-Del., 1981; regional rep. pub. affairs, Gulf Oil Corp., Phila., 1981-83, area dir. pub. affairs, dir. Gulfpac-Gulf Oil Corp., Pitts., 1983-84; loaned exec. pub. affairs NASA, Washington, 1984-85; pres. Long Cons., Inc., Washington, 1985—; mem. com. on pub. relations Am. Petroleum Inst., eastern region, 1981-84. Asst. to chmn. Republican Nat. Com., 1984, 86—, Rep. Nat. Conv., Dallas, 1984; mem. Rep. Bus. Council, Wilmington, 1982-83, Gov. Commn. on Women-Speaker's Bur., Wilmington, 1981-83. Baptist. Club: Capitol Hill. Avocations: landscape painting; duck decoys; photography; golf; gardening. Home: 7716 Asterella Ct Springfield VA 22152 Office: Suite 800 1211 Connecticut Ave NW Washington DC 20036

LONG, MARIA-TERESA ELIZABETH, financial planner; b. St. Louis, July 10, 1947; d. Terry and Mary-Louise Katharyn (Madden) Butler; B.S., N.E. Mo. State U., 1972; M.A., Washington U., 1973; m. Ellery Long, Sept. 21, 1975; 1 child, Korté. Dir. guidance Kinloch (Mo.) High Sch., 1973-74; vocat. counselor Ferguson-Florissant Sch. Dist., Ferguson, Mo., 1974-79; fin. planner Met. Life Ins. Co., St. Louis, 1979-82, Prudential Ins. Co., Houston, 1982—. Bd. dirs. Urban League Met. St. Louis, 1976—. Washington U. grantee, 1973. Mem. Am. Personnel and Guidance Assn., NEA (del., sec. 1976-77), Florissant-Ferguson Community Tchrs. Assn. (sec. 1976-77), Am. Vocat. Assn., Nat. Assn. Life Underwriters, Assn. Profl. Negotiations Teams, Delta Sigma Theta. Roman Catholic. Office: 7001 Corporate Dr Houston TX 77036

LONG, MARTHA LIVINGSTON, nurse, infection control practitioner; b. Rantoul, Ill., Dec. 6, 1937; d. James H. and Dorvis (Loy) Livingston; m. John E. Long, Oct. 18, 1963; 1 child, John Earl. Nursing diploma Canton Hosp. Tng. Sch., Ill., 1959; cert. Ctr. Disease Control, Atlanta, 1976; cert. advanced epidemiology U. Va., 1978. Psychiat. nurse Galesburg State Research Hosp., Ill., 1959-63; staff nurse Smyth County Community Hosp., Marion, Va., 1964-67, central sterile supply supr., 1967-70, obstetrics supr., 1971-74, infection control practitioner, 1975—; healthcare speaker Smyth County Schs., 1980—. Author Nosocomial News, 1984—. Mem. Va. Assn. Practitioners Infection Control (nominating com. 1981-82), Assn. Practitioners of Infection Control (nat. com. 1977—), Appalachian Soc. Infection Control (chmn. Southwest Va. chpt. 1982—). Democrat. Mem. Ch. of Nazarene. Avocations: reading; speaking. Home: Rural Route 2 Box 42 Marion VA 24354 Office: Smyth County Community Hosp PO Box 880 Marion VA 24354

LONG, NEAL BASIL, economics educator, energy economics consultant; b. Plymouth, Ind., Dec. 7, 1936; s. Neal Basil Long and Bessie Amanda (Dague) Brundige; m. Marilyn Kleinschmidt, June 13, 1959; children—Gregory Neal, Michael Basil. A.B. in Econs., Ind. U., 1959, Ph.D. in Econs., 1964; M.A. in Econs., U. N.C., 1960. Asst. prof. U. Colo., Boulder, 1963-64, Ohio U., Athens, 1964-65, Ind. U., South Bend, 1965-70; assoc. prof. Youngstown State U., Ohio, 1970-74; prof. econs., dept. chmn. Stetson U., DeLand, Fla., 1974—; sabbatical leave Fla. Solar Energy Ctr., Cape Canaveral, 1984-85, econ. cons., 1985. Co-author: Basic Statistics, 1975. Contbr. articles to publs. Bd. dirs. Sugar 'n' Spice Day Care Ctr., DeLand, 1978—; precinct man Democratic Party Volusia County, Fla., 1984—. Mem. Am. Econs. Assn., So. Econs. Assn., Fedn. Am. Scientists, AAUP, Am. Soc. Pub. Adminstrn. Mem. Ch. of Brethren. Avocations: gardening; volleyball. Home: 560 S Ridgewood Ave DeLand FL 32720 Office: Stetson U Woodland Blvd DeLand FL 32720

LONG, ROBERT ALLEN, clinical research scientist; b. Kingman, Ariz., Aug. 17, 1941; s. Frederick McMullin and Mary Helen (Meng) L.; m. Sharon LaRae Suckow, June 8, 1963; children—Christopher, Rebecca, Gretchen. B.A., Portland State U., 1964; Ph.D., U. Utah, 1970. Synthetic organic chemist ICN-Pharmaceuticals Inc., Irvine, Calif., 1970-76, clin. research assoc., 1976-77; clin. research scientist Burroughs Wellcome Co., Research Triangle Pk., N.C., 1977-83, sr. clin. research scientist, 1983—. Contbr. articles to profl. jours. Patentee in field. Mem. Am. Chem. Soc. (medicinal chemistry sect.), Drug Info. Assn., Am. Pharm. Assn., Acad. Pharm. Scis., Am. Soc. Clin. Pharmacology and Therapeutics. Republican. Lutheran. Avocations: fishing; gardening; reading. Office: Burroughs Wellcome Co 3030 Cornwallis Rd Research Triangle Park NC 27709

LONG, ROBERT RICHARD, banker; b. Atmore, Ala., Mar. 4, 1937; s. Robert Richard and Vivian (Crook) L.; m. Jane Hamilton Hancock, June 22, 1968; children—Robert Richard, Caroline Tison. B.S., Auburn U., 1959; M.B.A., Harvard U., 1967. Trainee, then group v.p., Trust Co. Bank, Atlanta; pres.; exec. v.p. Trust Co. Bank, Savannah, Ga. Pres., Am. Cancer Soc.; treas. Atlanta Arts Alliance. Served with U.S. Army, 1959-61. Episcopalian. Clubs: Piedmont Driving, Oglethorpe (Savannah). Home: 119 Brighton Rd Atlanta GA 30309 Office: PO Box 4418 25 Park Pl Atlanta GA 30302

LONG, ROY KAMPTON, construction management company executive, consultant; b. Athens, Ga., May 8, 1956; s. Ralph and Juanita Amelia (Mitchell) L.; m. Adrienne Rene Berry, Mar. 25, 1978; children—Raymond Moses, LaShawne Rene, Jonathan Edward. B.S. in Architecture, Pa. State U., 1978. Staff engr. D.D.R. Internat., Atlanta, 1978-79, project engr., 1979-81, project mgr., 1981-83, sr. mgr., 1983—; project mgr. engring. dept. Mass. Port Authority, 1985—; cons. constrn. Mem. Project Mgmt. Inst. Democrat. Baptist. Office: DDR Internat Inc 3340 Peachtree Rd NE Suite 2200 Atlanta GA 30326

LONG, RUSSELL B(ILLIU), U.S. senator; b. Shreveport, La., Nov. 3, 1918; s. Huey Pierce and Rose (McConnell) L.; B.A., La. State U., 1939, LL.B., 1942; m. Carolyn Bason, Dec. 23, 1969; children by previous marriage—Katherine (Mrs. John C. Gilmore), Pamela Rust Long McCardell. Bar: La. 1942. Practiced law, Baton Rouge, 1946-47; exec. counsel to gov. La., May-June, 1948; elected to U.S. Senate from La. for unexpired term ending 1950, reelected, 1950—, asst. majority leader, 1965-68; mem. Democratic steering com.; del. Dem. Nat. Conv., 1952. Served to lt. USNR, 1942-45; MTO, NATO. Mem. Am. Legion, Order of Coif, Delta Kappa Epsilon, Pi Delta Phi, Tau Kappa Alpha, Omicron Delta Kappa. Clubs: Elks, Lions. Home: Baton Rouge LA Office: Senate Office Bldg Washington DC 20510

LONG, RUTH YALE, nutrition counselor, writer; b. Oklahoma City, Jan. 7, 1914; d. Bertram Sheldon and Mabel Frances (Jones) Yale; m. William Retzer Long, Aug. 31, 1934; children—William Yale, Thomas Robert. Student Rice U., 1931-32; B.S., U. Houston, 1961, M.Ed., 1962; M.S., Tex. So. U., 1976; M.P.H., U. Tex. Sch. Pub. Health; Ph.D., 1978. With advt. dept. Bellaire Texan Newspaper, 1955-59; English tchr. Westbury High Sch., Houston, 1960-75; writer Psychiat. Bull., Houston, 1970-75; nutritionist Nutrition Edn. Assn., Houston, 1975—, pres., founder 1977—. Author: (home study course) Nutrition, 1979; (cookbook) Switchover, 1979; Crackdown On Cancer, 1980. Contbr. articles to profl. jours. Recipient Outstanding Sci. Research award Internat. Coll. Applied Nutrition, 1977. Mem. Internat. Acad. Preventive Medicine, Internat. Acad. for Med. Preventics, Internat. Coll. Applied Nutrition, Internat. Acad. Nutritional Cons., Houston Tchrs. Assn. Episcopalian. Clubs: Rice Women's (Houston) (treas. 1975-76). Avocations: cooking, writing. Home and Office: 3647 Glen Haven Houston TX 77025

LONG, SHIRLEY DOBBINS, designer, author, artist; b. Guilford County, N.C.; B.S. in Math., U. N.C., 1964; postgrad. U. Mich. 1966-69, 75-76; m. Bruce E. Long, Dec. 1967 (dec. Jan. 1969). Corp. exec. Long, Inc., Radley Run, Inc., deAnne Designs, Ltd., Antiquity Designs, Ltd. Mem. Internat. Platform Assn., Art Guild Assn. Author: Wentworth Place; Return to Wentworth Place. Home and Office: PO Box 5582 Emerywood Sta High Point NC 27262

LONG, STANLEY PAUL, safety engineer; b. Ponca City, Okla., Oct. 27, 1951; s. Paul Adrain and Viola Lenora (Revard) L.; m. Linda Sue McCroskey, June 4, 1971; children—Kendell, Steven. Student Okla. State Tech. Coll., 1969-71; grad. Basic Firefighting Acad., Okla. State U., 1975. Cert. fire service instr., Okla. Firefighter City of Ponca City, 1975-83; owner, operator S & L Fire Protection Co., Ponca City, 1975-83; safety specialist Conoco Inc., Ponca City, 1983-85, sr. safety specialist, 1985—. Cubmaster Boy Scouts Am., Ponca City, 1983-85; coach Ponca City Soccer Assn., 1984—. Mem. Nat. Fire Protection Assn. (indsl. div.), Am. Soc. Safety Engrs., Am. Bus. Clubs (pres. Ponca City 1984-85). Democrat. Methodist. Avocations: fishing; camping; raquetball. Home: 2225 John St Ponca City OK 74601 Office: Conoco Inc PO Box 1267 Ponca City OK 74603

LONG, STUART ALLEN, electrical engineering educator; b. Phila., Mar. 6, 1945; s. Jeb Menefee and Oma (Payne) L.; m. Judy Kay Mixion, June 7, 1969; children—Meredith, Garrett. B.A., Rice U., 1967, M.Elec.Engring., 1968; Ph.D., Harvard U., 1974. Aerosystems engr. Gen. Dynamics Corp., Ft. Worth, 1968-69; teaching fellow, research asst. Harvard U., Cambridge, Mass., 1969-74; research assoc. Los Alamos Sci. Lab., 1970-71; asst. prof. elec. engring. U. Houston, 1974-81, assoc. prof., 1981-85, prof., 1985—, chmn. dept. elec. engring., 1981—. Mem. IEEE, Antennas and Propagation Soc., Internat. Union Radio Sci. (Commn. B 1980—). Contbr. articles to profl. jours. Office: Dept Elec Engring U Houston Houston TX 77004

LONG, WILLIAM DAVID, food company executive; b. Crisfield, Md., Sept. 20, 1929; s. Thomas Berry and Etta (Luettinger) L.; student Va. Poly. Inst., 1947-50; m. Barbara Russell, July 15, 1959; children—Lisa Bea, William David, Beauregard Thomas. Pres., Long Farms, Inc., Apopka, Fla., 1961—, Long & Scott Farms, Inc., Apopka, 1964—, Apopka Properties, Inc., 1967—; pres. Apopka Devel. Co., 1970—, All-Gator Carrot Co., Apopka, 1979—, Ag-Care Inc., Apopka, 1980, Lust & Long Precooler Inc., Apopka, 1960—; v.p. Long Farms North Inc., Apopka, dir. Tucker State Bank, Winter Garden, Fla.; chmn. bd. Fla. Fed. Savs. & Loan, 1979—; v.p. Zellwood Sweet Corn Exchange (Fla.). Vice pres. Orange County Farm Bur., 1967-74, pres., 1974—; pres., dir. Zellwood Drainage and Water Control Dist., 1985—; mem. Orange County Air and Water Pollution Control, 1970—; mem. Gov.'s Migratory Labor Com., 1967—; bd. dirs. NW Orange County Little League, 1979-80. Named Outstanding Young Farmer Orange County, Orlando Jr. C. of C., 1964, 65, Outstanding Young Farmer Fla. Jr. C. of C., 1965, 1964, 65, one of four outstanding young farmers in U.S., Nat. Jr. C. of C. and Nat. L.P. Gas Assn., 1966, Ford Found. award in vegetable crop mgmt., 1968; recipient Spl. Resolution 2782 for being selected one of four outstanding young farmers in U.S., Fla. Ho. of Reps., 1965. Mem. Fla. Fruit and Vegetable Growers Assn. (dir., conv. chmn. 1980), C. of C. (agr. com.). Presbyterian (elder 1974—). Clubs: New Smyrna Beach Yacht, Masons (32 deg.), Shriners, Jesters, Elks, Zellwood (Fla.) Country (pres.). Home: 2860 E Green Acre Rd Apopka FL 32703 Office: PO Drawer 729 Apopka FL 32703

LONGENECKER, LEE (SHIRLEY) H., writer; b. Summit, N.J., Nov. 16, 1925; s. William Hetherington and Leila (Sisty) H.; m. John Mortimer Longenecker, Sept. 13, 1947; children—Sandi, Craig, Bruce, Lynn. B.A., U. Pa., 1947; postgrad. West Chester State Coll., Pa., 1962-64. Columnist, women's editor County Leader Newspaper, Newtown Square, Pa., 1956-60; instr. English, Phila. Coll. Bible, 1964-74; corr. Convenience Store News, 1979—; editor Currents publ. Christian Writers League Am., Harlingen, Tex., 1983—; writing instr., dir.; columnist Longview Morning Jour. (Tex.), 1983-84. Mem. Republican party Tex. Mem. Tex. Press Women, Nat. Press Women, Christian Writers League E. Tex. (pres. 1982-84), Kappa Alpha Theta Alumni. Mem. Christian and Missionary Alliance. Author: (with Jack Henry) Employee Theft Tracks, 1981, Deliveryman Theft Tracks, 1981; Refunding-52 Hints for 52 Weeks, 1981. Columnist Kilgore (Tex.) News Herald.

LONGINO, LOYCE WHITE, financial analyst; b. Texas City, Tex., Oct. 1, 1944; d. Delbert Loy and Emma Barr (Walker) W.; m. Charles F. Longino, Jr., July 11, 1964; children—Laura Elizabeth, Charles F. B.A., U. N.C.-Chapel Hill, 1966; postgrad. U. Miami. Asst. grant writer Office Devel., U. Miami and Inst. Aging, 1978; grants mgr. dept. psychology U. Miami, 1980, dir. research office devel., 1981; exec. dir. Miami Choral Soc., 1983-85; fin. analyst U. Miami, 1985—; bd. dirs. Cultural Execs. Council, 1983. Convener div. on adminstrn. Riviera Presbyn. Ch., 1982, elder, 1980. Mem. Am. Assn. Counseling and Devel. Presbyterian.

LONGLEY, BENJAMIN LEHMANN, life insurance company executive, state senator; b. LaGrange, Ga., Aug. 7, 1930; s. Julian McLauren and Mary Bowen (Robertson) L.; B.A. in Econs., Bus. Adminstrn., Vanderbilt U., 1951; m. Anne E. Hayes, Oct. 26, 1957; children—Mary Elizabeth, Amy Lauren. Comptroller, Hardwick Stove Co., Cleveland, Tenn., 1954-59, asst. sec., 1959-66; agent Provident Life and Accident Ins. Co., Chattanooga, 1966-77, gen. agent, 1977-83; pres. Income Plans, Inc., Cleveland; mem. Tenn. Ho. of Reps., 1966-78; mem. Tenn. Senate, 1978—, sec. com. on gen. welfare, health and human resources; dir. Cherokee Valley Fed. Bank. Bd. dirs. ARC, Cleveland, 1961-66; pres. Bradley County (Tenn.) Young Republicans, 1960-62, county congressional Republican mgr., 1962-64; chmn. Rep. 3d Congl. Dist., 1964-68; bd. dirs. Cleveland State Community Coll. Found. Served with U.S. Army, 1951-54. Mem. Cleveland Jaycees (dir. 1956-62), Nat. Life Underwriters Assn., Tenn. Life Underwriters Assn., Cleveland Life Underwriters Assn., Nat. Soc. State Legislators, Million Dollar Round Table (life), Am. Legion. Methodist. Club: Elks.

LONGO, MARGARET FAY, surgeon; b. Alexandria, La., July 4, 1936; d. Joseph Phillip and Mary Margaret (Cangelosi) L. B.A., Our Lady of Lake Coll., 1958; M.D., La. State U., 1962. Diplomate Am. Bd. Surgery. Intern, house staff Confederate Meml. Med. Ctr., Shreveport, La., 1962-63; surg. resident St. Mary's Hosp., Rochester, Minn., 1963-66, Rochester (Minn.) Meth. Hosp., 1963-66, 67; asst. surg. cons. Mayo Clinic, Rochester, 1967; mem. active surg. staff Lafayette (La.) Gen. Hosp., 1968—, chmn. dept. surgery, 1971; mem. active surg. staff Our Lady of Lourdes Hosp., Lafayette, 1974—; mem. vis. surg. staff Lafayette Charity Hosp., 1968-72; critical care cons. on trauma Acadiana Emergency Med. Services Council, 1977-79. Chmn. med. div. United Givers Fund, 1971, 83; co-chmn. Acadian Right to Life Com., 1974; mem. Acadiana Arts Council, 1977-79; bd. dirs. Lafayette Natural History Mus. Assn., 1978-81, 81-84; bd. dirs. Emergency Med. Services Council, 1978-83; bd. dirs. United Givers Fund Lafayette, Inc., 1979—; advisor Acadiana chpt. Am. Assn. Med. Assts., 1978-83; mem. Bayou council Girl Scouts U.S.A., 1982—; mem. med. adv. com. Hospice Acadiana, 1983—; mem. Trustees' Acad., Our Lady of the Lake Coll., 1981—. Recipient Best Original Research award Tex. Acad. Sci., 1956, cert. of merit award, 1956; Minn. Surg. Essay award Minn. Surg. Soc., 1966; Surg. Travel award Mayo Found.-Mayo Clinic, 1967; Physician's Recognition award AMA, 1974-77, 78-80, 80-83; Outstanding Alumni award Our Lady of Lake, U. San Antonio, 1976; scholastic scholar, Our Lady of Lake Coll., 1954-58. Fellow ACS (pres. La. chpt. 1983-84); mem. AAAS (hon.), Priestley Soc. (dir. 1977-80, pres. 1982-83), Undersea Med. Soc., Doctors Mayo Soc., So. Med. Assn., Southeastern Surg. Congress, La. Med. Soc., Minn. Med. Soc., Surg. Assn. La. (dir. 1976-79), Lafayette Parish Med. Soc., Mayo Clinic Alumni Assn. (v.p. 1983-85). Roman Catholic. Contbr. articles to profl. jours. Office: 1101 S College Rd Suite 305 Lafayette LA 70503

LONGSWORTH, CHARLES R., foundation executive; b. Fort Wayne, Ind., Aug. 21, 1929; s. Maurice A. and Marjorie K. L.; m. Polly Ormsby, June 30, 1956; children—Amy Porter, Elizabeth King, Laura Cramer, Anne Graybill. B.A., Amherst Coll., 1951; M.B.A., Harvard U., 1953. Mktg. trainee Campbell Soup Co., Camden, N.J., 1955-58; account exec. Ogilvy & Mather, Inc., N.Y.C., 1958-60; asst. to pres. Amherst (Mass.) Coll., 1960-65; chmn. edn. trust Hampshire Coll., Amherst, 1966, v.p., sec., 1966-71, pres., 1971-77; pres., chief operating officer Colonial Williamsburg Found. (Va.), 1977-79; pres., chief exec. officer Colonial Williamsburg Found., 1979—; dir. Houghton Mifflin, Flight Safety Inc. Author: (with others) The Making of a College, 1966; contbr. articles to profl. jours. Trustee Amherst Coll., Colonial Williamsburg Found., Nat. Trust Hist. Preservation; bd. dirs. Center for Public Resources, Coll. William and Mary Sch. Bus. Adminstrn. Served to lt. USMC, 1953-55. Mem. Phi Beta Kappa Assocs. (dir.). Clubs: University, Century Assn. (N.Y.C.); Commonwealth, Forum (Richmond, Va.). Home: Coke-Garrett House Williamsburg VA 23185 Office: Colonial Williamsburg Found Williamsburg VA 23185

LONGYEAR, REY MORGAN, music educator; b. Boston, Dec. 10, 1930; s. John Munro, Jr. and Wanda Rae (Archambeau) L.; m. Katherine Marie Eide, Apr. 11, 1959. B.A. with high honors, Los Angeles State Coll., 1951; M.A., U. N.C., 1954; Ph.D., Cornell U., 1957. Band dir. Edgewood High Sch., Md., 1957-58; assoc. prof. U. So. Miss., Hattiesburg, 1958-63, U. Tenn., Knoxville, 1963-64; prof. music U. Ky., Lexington, 1964—. Author: Schiller and Music, 1966; 19th-Century Romanticism in Music, 1973. Author and editor: Mattei, Zingarelli: Selected Symphonies, 1980; The Northern Italian Symphony, 1982; The Symphony in Naples, 1800-1840, 1983. Timpanist, Knoxville Symphony Orch., 1963-64. Served with U.S. Army 1948-49. Guggenheim fellow, 1971; grantee Am. Council Learned Socs., 1964, Australian Humanities Commn., 1979, NEH, 1984. Mem. Am. Musicol. Soc. (council 1971-73), Coll. Music Soc. (life), Univ. Profs. for Acad. Order (bd. dirs. 1981-83), Internat. Musicol. Soc., Società italiana di musicologia, Gesellschaft für Musikforschung. Republican. Roman Catholic. Home: 656 Berry Ln Lexington KY 40502 Office: U Ky Sch Music Lexington KY 40506

LOOMIS, JACQUELINE CHALMERS, photographer; b. Hong Kong, Mar. 9, 1930 (parents Am. citizens); d. Earl John and Jennie Bell (Sherwood) Chalmers; m. Charles Judson Williams III, Dec. 2, 1950 (div. Aug. 1973); children—Charles Judson IV, John C., David F., Robert W.; m. Henry Loomis, Jan. 19, 1974; stepchildren—Henry S., Mary Loomis Hankinson, Lucy F., Gordon M. Student U. Oreg., 1948-50, Nat. Geog. Soc., 1978-79, Winona Sch. Profl. Photography, 1979, Sch. Photo Journalism, U. Mo., 1979. Pres., J. Sherwood Chalmers-Photographer, Middleburg, Va., 1979—, Windward Corp., Middleburg, 1984—; pub. in Nat. Geog., mag. and books, Fortune Mag., Am. Shotgunner Mag., Living Bird Quar., Orvis News, 1980—, Frontiers Internat., 1979—; executed photo murals McLean, Va. and Washington, 1981, others. Bd. dirs., exec. com., sec. bd. dirs. Washington Opera,

1976—; bd. dirs., exec. com., rep. to Corp. for Pub. Broadcasting, Nat. Friends Pub. Broadcasting, 1970-73; bd. dirs. Pub. Broadcasting Service, 1972-73; trustee WJCT TV, Jacksonville, Fla., 1965-73, exec. com., chmn., 1965-66; bd. dir. Jacksonville Art Mus., 1968-70, treas., 1968; bd. dirs. Jacksonville Council Arts, 1969-72, co-chmn. Arts Festival, 1970, chmn., 1971; bd. dirs. Planned Parenthood North Fla., 1968-69; treas. league shop Jr. League Jacksonville, 1970. Recipient Cultural Arts award Jacksonville Council Arts, 1971, award Easton Waterfowl Festival, 1982, 84, Virginia Beach Waterfowl Festival, 1983. Mem. Profl. Photographers Am. (merit award 1982), Southeastern Profl. Photographers, Photo Soc. Am., Am. Soc. Picture Profls., Jr. League of Jackson. Republican. Presbyterian. Clubs: Fla. Yacht (Jacksonville); Amelia Island (Fla.) Plantation; Center Habor Yacht (Brooklin Maine). Office: Route 1 Box 122 Middleburg VA 22117

LOOMIS, RAYMOND CLEMONS, JR., oil company executive, lawyer; b. Houston, May 4, 1949; s. Raymond C. and Pamela (Woods) L.; m. Gina Marie Forlano, May 14, 1977; 1 child, Anna. B.S. in Geology, Sul Ross State U., 1977; J.D., U. Dayton, 1985. Bar: Tex. 1985. Self-employed land broker, Houston, 1971-74; petroleum landman Texas City Refining Inc., Tex., 1974-76, Mitchell Energy, Houston, 1978-79, SONAT Exploration, Houston, 1979-80, Towner Petroleum Co., Houston, 1980-82; pres. Loomis & McKenney, P.C., Houston, 1985—. Bd. dirs. Clear Creek Basin Authority, Harris County, Tex., 1971-72. Recipient Am. Jurisprudence award, 1983. Mem. Houston Assn. Petroleum Landmen, Am. Assn. Petroleum Landmen, Houston Geol. Soc., Am. Assn. Petroleum Geologists. Club: Houston Petroleum of Houston. Office: Loomis & McKenney PC Cornerstone Towers 450 3707 FM 1960 W Houston TX 77068

LOONEY, JAKE WAYNE, college dean; b. Mena, Ark., June 29, 1944; s. Lee and Eunice (Cooper) L.; m. Era Brown Furr, Jan. 31, 1965; 1 child, Jason. B.S.A., U. Ark., 1966; M.S., U. Mo., 1968; J.D., U. Mo.-Kansas City, 1971, M.S., 1976. Bar: Ark., 1972, Mo., 1972, Va., 1977. Sole practice, Mena, 1973-75; asst. prof. Va. Tech. U., Blacksburg, 1975-78, Kans. State U., Manhattan, 1979-80; dir. agrl. law program U. Ark., Fayetteville, 1980-82, dean law, 1982—. Author: Estate Planning for Farmers, 1977; Estate Planning for Business Owners, 1979; Business Management for Farmers, 1983; (with others) Agricultural Law: Principles and Cases, 1981. Mem. Am. Agrl. Law Assn. (pres. 1983-84), ABA, Ark. Bar Assn. (Golden Gavel award 1982), Am. Agrl. Econs. Assn., Fayetteville C. of C. (com.). Democrat. Methodist. Lodge: Rotary. Avocations: travel; reading. Home: Route 1 Box 399 Fayetteville AR 72703 Office: Sch Law U Ark Fayetteville AR 72701

LOONEY, STEPHEN WARWICK, mathematics and statistics educator; b. Atlanta, Sept. 6, 1952; s. William Jarrell and Minnie Hannah (Ivie) L.; m. Teresa McVeigh, Aug. 24, 1980. B.S. in Math., U. Ga., 1974; M.S. in Math., U. Va., 1976; Ph.D. in Statistics, U. Ga., 1980. Chief statis. analyst Northeast Ga. Health Dist., Athens, 1979-80; vis. fellow Health & Welfare Can., Ottawa, 1980-81; asst. prof. quantitative bus. analysis La. State U., Baton Rouge, 1981—. Contbr. articles to profl. jours. Mem. Am. Statis. Assn., Royal Statis. Soc., Biometric Soc., Internat. Assn. Statis. Computing. Methodist. Avocations: racquetball; music; natural history. Office: La State U Quantitative Bus Analysis Dept Room 3190 CEBA Bldg Baton Rouge LA 70803

LOOSE, ROGER RAY, optometrist; b. Scottsbluff, Nebr., Feb. 23, 1947; s. Carl and Rose (Schnell) L.; m. Janet Lee Thelen, Aug. 29, 1970; children—Gregory, Brenda. B.S., So. Coll. Optometry, 1979, O.D., 1979. Practice optometry, Wiggins, Miss., 1980—. Served with AUS, 1967-69. Mem. Am. Optometric Assn., Miss. Optometric Assn. Lodge: Lions (pres.). Home: Route 3 Box 317 Perkinston MS 39573 Office: 313 S Parker St Wiggins MS 39577

LOPATKA, MANFRED, architect; b. Breslau, Germany, Apr. 28, 1923; came to U.S. 1949, naturalized, 1955; s. Erwin and Berta Emma (Heintze) L.; m. Evelyn Rosel Peritz, July 15, 1950; children—Susan E., Michael I., John E., Adi D. Student in city planning Technische Hochschule, Brelau, Germany, 1943; B.S. in Architecture, State Bldg. Acad., Luebeck, Germany, 1949. Registered architect, Fla. Architect Lopatka & McQuaig, Winter Park, Fla., 1958-72; architect, pres. Lopatka, McQuaig & Assoc., Winter Park, 1972-83, Lopatka, Murdock, Jammal & Parsons, Inc., 1983—. Chmn. Winter Park Bd. Adjustments and Appeals, 1983, mem., 1985. Named hon. mem. Civil Engring. Corps., U.S. Navy, 1976, Service Sch. Command Commanding Officer SSC, U.S. Navy, 1979. Mem. Soc. Am. Mil. Engrs. Republican. Episcopalian. Avocation: travel. Home: 1151 Washington Ave Winter Park FL 32789

LOPEZ, ANTONIO M., JR., mathematician, scientist, educator; b. Miami, Fla., Feb. 14, 1949; s. Antonio M. and Esperanza (Montesinoes) L.; m. Michele Colonel, May 23, 1970; children—Jeannine, Tammy. B.S., Loyola U, New Orleans, 1970; M.S. in Math., Clemson U., 1973, Ph.D., 1976. Asst. prof. math. Loyola U., New Orleans, 1976-80, assoc. prof., 1980—, chmn. dept., 1982—; cons. La. Dept. Edn., 1984—; dir. Microcomputer Summer Camp, New Orleans, 1982-84; software reviewer Math. Tchr., 1983—; reviewer NSF, 1985. Editor: Computer Programming in the Basic Language, 1981; Computer Literacy, 1986. Contbr. articles to profl. jours. NDEA fellow, 1970-72. Mem. Am. Math. Soc., Math. Assn. Am., Assn. Computing Machinery, Data Processing Mgmt. Assn., Res. Officers Assn. Roman Catholic. Avocations: jogging; racquetball. Office: Loyola U Box 51 New Orleans LA 70118

LOPEZ, GENARO, biology educator; b. Brownsville, Tex., Jan. 24, 1947; s. Genaro Velasco and Carmen (Coronado) L.; m. Lee Cecelia Tole, June 23, 1972; children—G. Daniel, Adriana. B.S., Tex. Tech U., 1970; Ph.D., Cornell U., 1975. Research asst. Cornell U., Ithaca, N.Y., 1970-75; state extension entomologist Tex. Agr. Extension Service, College Station, 1975-76; instr. biology Tex. Southmost Coll., Brownsville, 1976—. Contbr. articles to profl. jours. Mem. Gulf Coast Coalition for Pub. Health, Brownsville, 1982—. Served with USNG, 1970-76. Writing grantee NSF, 1980. Mem. Gulf Coast Conservation Assn., Nat. Wildlife Assn., Phi Theta Kappa (sponsor hon. soc. 1985). Roman Catholic. Avocations: running; fishing; custom rod building; Volvo restoration. Home: 110 Ebony Ave Brownsville TX 78520 Office: Tex Southmost Coll 80 Ft Brown Brownsville TX 78520

LOPEZ, GEORGE JOAQUIN, architect; b. Havana, Cuba, Dec. 24, 1948; came to U.S., 1960, naturalized, 1980; s. Rafael Enrique and Caridad (Martinez) L.; m. Maria Eugenia de la Torre, Dec. 26, 1970; children—Nicole Lilliam, George Andrew. A.A., Miami-Dade Jr. Coll., 1970; B.Arch., U. Fla., 1973. Registered architect, Fla. Sr. planner Sverdup & Parcel, Inc., Gainesville, Fla., 1973-74; planner, archtl. designer BMPT Architects, Miami, Fla., 1974-75; archtl. designer, project mgr. Morton & Wolfberg, Arch., 1977; architect, designer Charles Sieger & Assocs., 1977-78; architect, project mgr. BKV Architects, 1978-83; architect, owner, prin. Archtl. Office George J. Lopez & Assocs., Miami, 1983—; adj. prof. Fla. Internat. U., 1984—. Pres. adv. bd. St. Luke's Ctr., 1984; mem. Miami Citizens Against Crime, 1985—. Fellow Nat. Trust Hist. Preservation. Republican. Roman Catholic. Office: 7245 SW 87th Ave Suite 102 Miami FL 33173

LOPEZ, GLORIA, pediatrician; b. Pinar del Rio, Cuba, Mar. 27, 1952; came to U.S., 1970; d. Ismael and Dalia (Regalado) Piedra; m. Rolando Lopez, July 5, 1973; children—Rolando, Ricardo. A.A., Miami Dade Coll., 1973; med. diplomate Universidad Autonoma de Guadalajara (Mex.), 1977. Resident in pediatrics Miami Children's Hosp., Coral Gables, Fla., 1979-82; pediatrician high risk neonates Northshore Hosp., North Miami, Fla., 1982-83; practice gen. pediatrics, Coral Gables, 1983—. Mem. AMA. Republican. Office: 747 Ponce de Leon Blvd Suite 607 Coral Gables FL 33154

LOPEZ, LIONEL, petroleum geologist, consultant; b. Callao, Lima, Peru, June 18, 1957; came to U.S., 1976; s. Carlos and Antonina (Cruz) L. Student, U. N.C., 1978-79, U. Tex., 1980-81; B.S., St. Mary's U., 1981. Cert. petroleum geologist. Well site geologist Service Well, San Antonio, 1980-81; analytical well site geologist Analytical Logging, Houston, 1982-83; ops. mgr. Apex Logging, Fort Worth, 1983—. Full tuition scholar St. Mary's U., San Antonio, 1976; x-ray diffraction grantee NASA, Houston, 1978. Mem. Am. Assn. Petroleum Geologists (jr.). Mem. Ch. of Christ. Avocations: mountain climbing; racquetball. Home: 1616 Weyland Dr Apt 2068 Fort Worth TX 76118

LOPEZ-JIMÉNEZ, ILIA ENID, Spanish educator; b. Aguadilla, P.R., Dec. 8, 1952; d. Galileo Lopez and Lucila (Jimenez) Campos. B.A., U. P.R.-Mayaguez, 1973; M.A., U. Paris, Sorbonne, 1975, Ph.D., U. Paris III and Paris VIII, 1980. Prof. Spanish, U. P.R., Rio Piedras, 1980—, prof. Spanish composition, 1983-84, prof. Spanish linguistics, 1984—. Author publs. in field. U. P.R. grantee, 1981. Mem. Am. Assn. Tchrs. Spanish and Portuguese (treas. 1984-85), Am. Bus. Communications Assn., Instituto Internacional de Literatura Hispanoam., MLA. Avocation: gymnastics. Home: Box 21964 Univ Sta San Juan PR 0093-1964 Office: U Puerto Rico Facultad de Adminstrn de Empresas Dept Espanol Comercial Alpartado A-F Rio Piedras PR

LOPOPOLO, ROBERT JOHN, general contractor; b. Queens, N.Y. Feb. 5, 1954; s. Dominic and Eleanor (Porpora) L. B.S., Northeastern U., 1978. Cert. gen. contractor, Fla. Mgr. Melville Corp., Woonsocket, R.I., 1975-79; pres. J&L Contracting Co., Boston, 1979-81, R.J. Lopopolo & Co. Inc. Boca Raton, Fla., 1981—. Mem. bus. unit group Boca Mus. Art. Mem. Boca Raton C. of C. Republican. Roman Catholic. Home: 141 SE 12th Ct Pompano Beach FL 33060 Office: R J Lopopolo & Co Inc 1700 N Dixie Hwy Suite 143 Boca Raton FL 33432

LOPREATO, JOSEPH, sociology educator, author; b. Stefanaconi, Italy, July 13, 1928; s. Frank and Marianna (Pavone) L.; m. Carolyn H. Prestopino, July 18, 1954 (div. 1971); children—Gregory F., Marisa S.; m. Sally A. Cook, Aug. 24, 1972 (div. 1978). B.A. in Sociology, U. Conn., 1956; Ph.D. in Sociology, Yale U., 1960. Asst. prof. sociology U. Mass., Amherst, 1960-62; vis. lectr. U. Rome, 1962-64; assoc. prof. U. Conn., Storrs, 1964-66; prof. Sociology U. Tex.-Austin, 1966—, chmn. dept. sociology, 1969-72; vis. prof. U. Catania, Italy, 1974, U. Calabria, Italy, 1980; mem. steering com. Council European Studies, Columbia U., 1977-80. Mem. Nat. Italian-Am. Com. for U.S.A. Bicentennial; mem. exec. com. Congress Italian Politics, 1977-80. Served to cpl. U.S. Army, 1952-54. Fulbright Faculty Research fellow, 1962-64, 1973-74; Social Sci. Research Council Faculty Research fellow, 1963-64; NSF Faculty Research fellow, 1965-68. Mem. Internat. Sociol. Assn., Am. Sociol. Assn., Am. Biol. Assn. Roman Catholic. Author: Vilfredo Pareto, 1965; Peasants No More, 1967; Italian Americans, 1970; Class, Conflict, and Mobility, 1972; Social Stratification, 1974; The Sociology of Vilfredo Pareto, 1975; La Stratificazione Sociale negli Stati Uniti, 1977; Human Nature and Biocultural Evolution, 1984. Office: Dept of Sociology Univ of Tex Austin TX 78712

LORCH, SUE CAROL, English educator; b. Shelbyville, Ky., Sept. 10, 1946; d. James F. and Caroline (Wakefield) L. B.A. cum laude, U. Ky., 1968; postgrad. U. London, 1973; Ph.D., U. Louisville, 1976. Tchr., Louisville Pub. schs., 1968-70; dir. Writing Ctr., U. Louisville, 1976-77; assoc. prof., head English dept. U. S.C., Aiken, 1977—. Named hon. Ky. Col., 1973; English-Speaking Union fellow, 1973; S.C. Com. for Humanities grantee, 1978, 79, 81; NEH grantee, 1983. Mem. MLA, South Atlantic Modern Lang. Assn., Conf. Coll. Composition and Communication, Nat. Council Tchrs. of English, NOW. Democrat. Presbyterian. Author: Basic Writing: A Practical Approach, 1981, 2d edit., 1984; also articles. Home: 1309 S Boundary Ave SE Aiken SC 29801 Office: English Dept U SC Aiken SC 29801

LORD, FONCHEN USHER (MRS. WILLIAM WALCOTT LORD), artist; b. St. Louis; d. Roland Green and Florence (Richardson) Usher; A.B., Radcliffe Coll., Harvard U., 1933; M.A., Washington U., St. Louis, 1935; m. William Walcott Lord, June 12, 1935; children—Fonya Lord DeLong, William Pepperell, Carter Usher, Elizabeth Usher Lord Hillman, Exhibited invitational one-man shows Stetson U., Deland, Fla., 1969, W.Va. Wesleyan Coll., 1970, Avanti Galleries, N.Y.C., 1970, Miami Mus. Modern Art, 1970, Broward Community Coll., Ft. Lauderdale, 1971, Polk Public Mus., 1972, 78, Trend House Gallery, 1972, Fla. So. Coll., 1974, 82, Lakeland Civic Center Complex, Theatre Gallery, 1974—, Miller-King Gallery, Miami, 1975, 76, Artists Gallery, Madeira Beach, Fla., 1978, Russell B. Hicken Fine Arts Ltd., 1979, U. Tampa, 1982, Polk Community Coll., 1984; exhibited in group shows at Columbia Mus. Art, Columbus Mus. Arts and Crafts, Birmingham Mus. Art, Atlanta High Mus., Norton Gallery, Dulin Gallery Art, Ringling Mus. Art, Butler Inst. Am. Art, Jacksonville Art Mus., many others; represented in permanent collections: Fla. Ho. of Reps., City of Lakeland Civic Center, Miami Mus. Modern Art, Wesleyan Coll., Lowe Mus., Fla. So. Coll., Polk Pub. Mus., Daytona Mus. Arts and Scis., New Coll., Sarasota, Fla. Pres., Palm Island Corp., Bartow, Fla., 1954-64, Braden River Ranchettes, Bartow, 1964-71; asst. treas. Paris Tanning Co., South Paris, Maine, 1944-48; artist-in-residence Fusion Dance Co., Miami, 1976-82. Recipient Merit award Fla. State Fair, 1964; Clearwater Art Seminar award, 1961, 63; Sunshine Art Festival award, 1962; Ridge Art ann. competition awards 1963, 65, 66, 67, 70, 73, 85; Chautauqua Nat. award, 1968; award Festival of States Ann., 1965; Sarasota Art Assn. juried awards, 1971, 73, 74, 80, 81, 82, 85; Cape Coral Nat. award, 1973; Fla. Artist Group awards, 1972, 78, 80, 82, 83. Fellow Royal Soc. Arts (London); mem. Fla. Artists Group, Zeta Tau Alpha. Episcopalian. Home: 4305 Oakglen Rd Lakeland FL 33803

LORD, JEFFREY ALLAN, veterinarian; b. San Antonio, Apr. 10, 1950; s. Sidney Crane and Edna Earl (Etheridge) L.; m. Twyla Ann Toler, Sept. 29, 1973. B.S., Tex. A&M U., 1971, D.V.M., 1973. Staff veterinarian Pigott Animal Hosp., San Antonio, 1973-77; pres. Nacogdoches Road Veterinarian Hosp., Inc., San Antonio, 1977—; v.p. Emergency Pet Clinic, San Antonio, 1985—. Mem. AVMA, Tex. Vet. Med. Assn., Bexar County Vet. Med. Assn. (ethics and grievence com. 1984-85). Republican. Club: Alamo Yacht (Canyon Lake, Tex.). Avocations: sailing; hunting. Office: 14039 Nacogdoches Rd San Antonio TX 78247

LORD, LOUISE FALLAW, insurance company executive; b. Augusta, Ga., Oct. 14, 1926; d. Fletcher Lee and Allie Mae (Sanders) Fallaw; m. John E. Lord, Feb. 14, 1947 (div. Feb. 1955); children—Carol Ruth Lord White, Frances Elaine Lord Lamar. Student pub. schs., Augusta. Cert. profl. ins. woman. Bookkeeper property mgmt. Sherman & Henstreet, Augusta, 1958-64, ins. underwriter, 1964-80, account exec. and corp. sec.-treas., 1980—. Named Ins. Woman of Yr. Ga. State Ins. Women, 1983-84. Mem. Ins. Women of Augusta (pres. 1970, 78, named Ins. Woman of Yr. 1966, 69, 79), Ind. Ins. Agts. of Augusta (sec. 1974-80), CSRA Ins. Assn. (pres. 1982), Nat. Assn. Ins. Women (internat.), Augusta Geneal. Soc. (sec. 1981). Republican. Methodist. Home: 1806 Hampton Ave Augusta GA 30904 Office: Sherman & Henstreet Inc 123 8th St Augusta GA 30901

LORD, PRISCILLA SAWYER, author; b. Woburn, Mass.; d. Frank Hayward and Emelyn (Strang) Sawyer; A.B., Boston U., 1933; m. Philip Hosmer Lord, Feb. 10, 1938; children—Beverly, Roberta (Mrs. William H. Moore, Jr.). Readers' adviser Woburn Public Library, 1933-38; story teller Book Reviewer, 1933—. Bd. dirs. Mass. Soc. Univ. Edn. for Women, 1965—; active Girl Scouts U.S.A.; vol. chmn. scholarship com., past v.p. Marblehead Hosp. Aid Assn. Named to Boston U. Collegium Disting. Alumni, 1975. Mem. Herb Soc. Am. (nat. bd., historian, chmn. New Eng. unit), Mass. Descs. of Mayflower, Nat. Soc. Colonial Dames Am., Alpha Gamma Delta. Clubs: Marblehead Garden (past pres.), Winter Garden (past pres.). Author: (with Daniel J. Foley) Easter Garland, 1963; The Folk Arts and Crafts of New England, 2d edit., 1975; The Eagle, 1968; Easter The World Over, 1970; (with Virginia Clegg Gamage) Marblehead: The Spirit of '76 Lives Here, 2d edit., 1975, The Lure of Marblehead, 1973, rev. edit., 1980; The History of the Herb Society of America, 1981-82; The Basket of Herbs, 1983; Under the Golden Cod, 1984. Contbr. articles to periodicals. Home: Dennett Rd Marblehead Neck MA 01945 Office: The Maritimes-C23 2051 NE Ocean Blvd Stuart FL 33494

LORD, WILLIAM GROGAN, financial holding company executive; b. Hearne, Tex., Oct. 21, 1914; s. Otis G. and Erminee G. Lord; L.H.D. (hon.), Southwestern U., Georgetown, Tex., 1967; children—Roger Griffin, Sharon Lord Rydel. Chmn. bd., pres. TeleCom Corp., Houston, 1958—; sr. chmn. First Tex. Bancorp, Inc., Georgetown, 1971—; sr. chmn. bd. 4-L Ranches, Inc., Florence, Tex., 1977—; adv. dir. Citizens State Bank, Georgetown, 1970—; dir. Merc. Tex. Corp., Frozen Food Express Industries, Inc. (both Dallas). Trustee, mem. exec. com., vice chmn. bd. Southwestern U., 1958. Served to 1st lt. F.A., AUS, World War II. Decorated Purple Heart, Air medal with 4 oak leaf clusters; named Most Worthy Citizen, Georgetown C. of C., 1971. Mem. Nat. Assn. Small Bus. Investment Cos. (past pres.), Regional Assn. Small Bus. Investment Cos. Republican. Methodist. Clubs: Ramada, River Oaks Country (Houston); Austin, Headliners (Austin, Tex.); St. Anthony (San Antonio). Home: 1111 Carolina Houston TX 77010 Office: 3000 Clay Suite 2100 Houston TX 77002

LORENZ, HANS ERNEST, photographer; b. Karlsbad, Czechoslovakia, Sept. 11, 1940; s. Hugo and Maria (Gareis) L.; came to U.S., 1950, naturalized, 1954; B.A., Okla. Baptist U., 1962; m. Pamela Marie Carswell, May 27, 1978. Tchr. pub. schs., Prince George County, Va., 1964-65; sr. curatorial photographer Colonial Williamsburg Found., Williamsburg, Va., 1965—. Served with USN, 1962-64. Mem. Profl. Photographers Am., Am. Numismatic Assn. Baptist. Photographs contbr. to numerous books in field of 18th century antiques. Home: PO Box 336 Williamsburg VA 23187 Office: Curator Photog Studio Dept Collections Colonial Williamsburg Found Williamsburg VA 23185

LORENZO, FRANCISCO A., airline executive; b. N.Y.C., May 19, 1940; s. Olegario and Ana (Mateos) L.; B.A., Columbia U., 1961; M.B.A., Harvard U., 1963; m. Sharon Neill Murray, Oct. 14, 1972. Fin. analyst TWA, 1963-65; mgr. fin. analysis Eastern Airlines, 1965-66; founder, chmn. bd. Lorenzo, Carney & Co., fin. advisers, N.Y.C., from 1966; chmn. bd. Jet Capital Corp., fin. advisers, Houston, from 1969; pres. Tex. Internat. Airlines, Inc., Houston, 1972-80, chmn. exec. com., from 1980, pres. Tex. Air Corp., 1980—; chmn N.Y. Airlines, from 1980; chmn., chief exec. officer Continental Airlines, 1981—. Office: 4040 MCorp Plaza Houston TX 77002

LORENZO, JOHN JOSEPH, restaurant equipment company executive; b. Bklyn., Sept. 4, 1933; s. Daniel Michael Lorenzo and Angelina (Carlino) Giardina; m. Yolanda Rose Caruso, Feb. 5, 1956 (dec. Nov. 1969); 1 child, Lana; m. Charlotte Anne Webb Pollard, Feb. 6, 1971; 1 child, Michael; stepchildren—David, James, Donald. Student Drake's Sch. Drafting, 1951-52, Bklyn. Coll., 1957-58. Draftsman Am. Homes, Inc., N.Y.C., 1952-53, Bastian Blessing Co., N.Y.C., 1957-62; draftsman, designer Straus Duparquet Inc., N.Y.C., 1962-68; v.p., designer C.W. Robbins, Inc., Miami, Fla., 1968-78; pres., owner Commemorative Designs Inc., Miami, 1975—. Served with USN, 1953-57. Democrat. Roman Catholic. Home: 14368 NE 3d Ct Miami FL 33161 Office: Commemorative Designs Inc 15706 NW 2d Ave Miami FL 33169

LORENZO SÉNCHEZ-BRETÓN, GLADYS, psychologist; b. Guanabacoa, Havana, Cuba, Oct. 6, 1934; came to U.S., 1974; d. Bernabe and Graciella (Sanchez-Breton) Lorenzo; m. Sola Arturo, July 5, 1958; children—Sola Arturo, Gladys de Jesus. M.Edn., U. Havana-Cuba, 1971, M.Psychology, 1971; Ed.D. in Edn., U. Havana, 1970; Ph.D. in Psychology, Complutense U. of Madrid, 1974. Prof. U. Havana, Cuba, 1959-61; prof. Internat. Ctr. Psychology, Madrid, 1970-74; clin. psychologist Hunt Point Multi-Service Ctr., Bronx, 1975-79; faculty prof. St. Thomas U., Miami, Fla., 1980—; adj. prof. Caribbean Ctr. Advanced Studies; cons. clin. psychologist Mailman Ctr. U. of Miami, 1983—; clin. psychologist Youth and Family Devel., Miami, 1980—. Named Prof. of Yr., St. Thomas U., 1981-82. Mem. Am. Psychol. Assn. (bd. ethnic minority affairs), Interam. Psychol Assn., Internat. Neuropsychol. Soc., Nat. Hispanic Psychol. Assn. (chmn. 1983-84), Hispanic Psychol. Assn. South Fla. (pres.). Republican. Roman Catholic. Avocations: music, aerobic dance, swimming. Address: 4375 W 10th Ln Hialeah FL 33012

LORETTA, JAMES MICHAEL, trading company executive, consultant; b. Torreon, Coahuila, Mexico, Aug. 27, 1946; s. Frank Bernard and Eleanor (Butterly) L.; m. Susan Burton, June 30, 1973. B.S. in Bus. Adminstrn., Xavier U., 1969. Store mgr. Firestone, Indpls., 1971-76; dist. mgr. Clark Equipment Co., Buchanan, Mich., 1976-79; marketing mgr. U.S. Airmotive, Miami, Fla., 1979-83; sales dir. ATP Internat., Inc., Miami, 1983—. Mem. Cursillos in Christianity, Miami, 1981; pres. Parish Council, St. Louis Catholic Ch., Miami, 1983; mem. bd. Kairos Prison Ministry, Miami, 1982. Served with U.S. Army, 1969-71; Vietnam. Mem. Internat. Material Mgmt. Soc. Home: 10801 SW 126th Ave Miami FL 33186 Office: ATP Internat Inc 6890 NW 4th Ct Miami FL 33138

LOREY, WILL(IS) EDWARD, II, management consultant; b. St. Clair Shores, Mich., Apr. 14, 1926; s. Willis Edward and Myrle Agnus (Bollenbacker) L.; B.S. in Edn., S.E. Mo. State U., 1950; M.S. in Edn., Columbia U., 1979, Ph.D. in Indsl. Psychology, 1980; children—Sandra, Sara, Marcia, Melissa; m. Legurisha Sue Gray, Jan. 21, 1983; children—Mark, Wade, Donna. Served as enlisted man U.S. Marine Corps, 1943-46; commd. 2d lt. U.S. Air Force, 1950, advanced through grades to col., 1967, ret., 1970; mgr. tng. dept. Blue Cross/Blue Shield, Washington, 1970-76; dir. human resources The Drawing Board, Dallas, 1976-78; mgr. human resources Bell Ops. Corp. div. Bell Helicopter Co., Euless, Tex., 1978-79; pres. Lorey Assos., mgmt. cons., Smithfield, Tex., 1979—; course leader Am. Mgmt. Assns., 1979—; adj. prof. Richland Coll., N. Lake Coll., Dallas. Co. chmn. U.S. Savs. Bonds, 1978-79, United Way, 1978-79. Decorated Bronze Star with oak leaf cluster, Joint Services Commendation medal, Air Force Commendation medal with oak leaf cluster, Army Commendation medal. Mem. Am. Soc. Tng. and Devel. (dir., past pres. Dallas chpt), Soc. Humanistic Mgmt. (past pres.), Internat. Platform Assn., Dallas Personnel Assn., Ret. Officers Assn. Republican. Methodist. Club: Alpine Ski. Contbr. articles to profl. jours. Home and Office: 740 Bandit Trail Smithfield TX 76180

LOSSER, STEVEN VERN, association administrator; b. Salt Lake City, Utah, May 27, 1950; s. Vern and Doris G. (Swanson) L.; m. Kathy L. Burback, Sept. 2, 1972; 1 child, Erik. B.S., Colo. State U., 1972, M.S., 1976. Instr. mktg. and econs. U. Ark., Little Rock, 1978-82, market analyst, 1978-82; mktg. rep. Armstrong World Industries, Little Rock, 1976-78; project mgr. Ga. Inst. Tech., Atlanta, 1982-83; exec. dir. Nat. Dimension Mfrs. Assn., Atlanta, 1983—; cons. in field, Little Rock, Atlanta, 1978—. Contbr. articles to profl. jours. Mem. Am. Soc. Assn. Execs. (presentor annual mgmt. conf. 1984), Am. Mktg. Assn., Toastmasters Internat. (ednl. v.p. 1981, pres. 1982, competent toastmaster 1982). Home: 3761 Cara Ln Marietta GA 30062 Office: Nat Dimension Mfrs Assn 101 Village Pkway Suite 202 Marietta GA 30067

LOSTON, ADENA WILLIAMS, college administrator; b. Vicksburg, Miss., Nov. 13, 1952; d. Tommie Lee and Frances Pearline (Miller) Williams; m. Gilbert Loston, Jr., Aug. 12, 1978 (div.); 1 child, Gilbert Williams, III. B.S., Alcorn State U., Lorman, Miss., 1973; M.Ed., Bowling Green State U., 1974, Ph.D., 1979. Instr. Ark. State U., 1974-76; supr. Southwestern Bell Telephone, Houston, 1976-77; teaching fellow, coordinator fed. proposal Bowling Green State U., Ohio, 1977-79; instr. Houston Community Coll., 1979-82, supr. office occupations, 1982—; adj. instr. U. Houston-D.C., 1980-82; adj. asst. prof. Tex. So. U., Houston, 1984—; cons. in field. Contbr. articles to profl. jours. First v.p. Houston League of Bus. & Profl. Women, 1984-85; treas. Community Orgn. for Polit. Effectiveness. Mem. Am. Soc. Tng. and Devel., Am. Assn. Higher Edn., Nat. Bus. Edn. Assn., Tex. Bus. Edn. Assn., Sigma Gamma Rho (named outstanding Educator 1984), Alpha Kappa Alpha, Mu Kappa Omega, Alcorn Alumni Chpt. (corr. sec. 1984—). Home: 8402 Blue Quail Dr Missouri City TX 77489 Office: Houston Community Coll System 1215 Holman Room 202 Houston TX 77004

LOTT, JOHN BERTRAND, English educator, university dean; b. Aberdeen, Miss., June 27, 1933; m. Sandra Ward; children—Anna, Bertrand, Ward. B.A. with highest honors, Millsaps Coll., 1955; M.A., Vanderbilt U., 1956, Ph.D., 1961. Asst. prof. English, U. Montevallo, Ala., 1959-61, assoc. prof., 1961-64, prof., 1964—, chmn. English dept., 1962-79, dean Coll. Arts and Scis., 1979—. Preparer TV programs in English lit. Past chmn. bd. dirs. First United Methodist Ch., Montevallo Area Services Ctr.; mem. Planning and Zoning Bd., City of Montevallo; treas. Montevallo High Sch. Band Boosters. Mem. Assn. Coll. English Tchrs. Ala., (past pres.), Ala. Council Tchrs. English, Ala. Edn. Assn. (past pres.), South Atlantic Modern Lang. Assn., Nat. Council Tchrs. English, MLA. Office: U Montevallo Sta 13 Montevallo AL 35115

LOTT, SARAH KATHERYN, architect; b. San Antonio, Nov. 23, 1952; d. Harry and Cornelia (Rotramel) L.; m. John Michael Bernardoni, May 22, 1981. B.Arch. with honors, U. Tex., 1974. Registered architect, Tex. Intern architect Scudder & Wadsworth, Austin, Tex., 1972-73, Martin & Ortega, San Antonio, 1974-76; designer Century Planners, Laredo, Tex., 1976-77; architect 3D Internat., Austin, Tex., 1977-79; assoc. Lundgren & Assocs., Austin, 1979-81; v.p. Am. Design Group, Austin, 1981-84, ptnr., 1984—. Trustee Creative Rapid Learning Ctr., Austin, 1984-85. Mem. Soc. Mktg. Profl. Services (sec. 1984-85), AIA, Tex. Soc. Architects. Baptist. Avocations: travel; skiing; water sports. Office: Am Design Group 1250 Capitol of Texas Hwy S Bldg 1 Suite 290 Austin TX 78746

LOTT, TRENT, congressman; b. Grenada, Miss., Oct. 9, 1941; s. Chester P. and Iona (Watson) L.; B.P.A., U. Miss., 1963, J.D., 1967; m. Patricia E. Thompson, Dec. 27, 1964; children—Chester T., Jr., Tyler Elizabeth. Bar:

Miss. 1967. Assoc., Bryan & Gordon, Pascagoula, 1967; adminstrv. asst. to Congressman William M. Colmer, 1968-72; mem. 93d-98th Congresses from 5th Dist. Miss., chmn. Ho. Republican Research Com., 96th Congress, elected Ho. Rep. whip 97th and 98th Congresses. Field rep. U. Miss., 1963-65; acting alumni sec. Ole Miss Alumni Assn., 1966-67; vice chmn. platform com. Republican Nat. Conv., 1980, chmn., 1984. Mem. ABA, Jackson County Bar Assn., Sigma Nu, Phi Alpha Delta. Baptist. Club: Masons. Office: 2400 Rayburn House Office Bldg Washington DC 20515

LOTT, WYNELL BEARD, test administrator, energy consultant; b. Laurel, Miss., June 9, 1940; d. Clinton Eugene and Myrtle Lee (Turner) Beard; m. James Alford Lott, June 8, 1958; children—James Derek, Douglas Eugene, Donald Alford, John Darwin. Student Jones County Jr. Coll., Ellisville, Miss., 1957-58, William Carey Coll., Hattiesburg, Miss., 1975-76. Sec., treas. Plainview Farm, Seminary, Miss., 1963-65; vol. Action, Washington, 1976; test adminstr. U.S. Office of Personnel Mgmt., Huntsville, Ala., 1979—; vice pres. L&M Rabbitry & Processing, Inc., Moselle, Miss., 1981—; area dir. Time Energy Systems Inc., Houston, 1981—; pres. Energy Controls Inc., Moselle, Miss., 1981—, chmn., 1981—. Recipient Letter of Appreciation U.S. Office Personnel Mgmt., 1983, U.S. Dept. Def. 1983. Mem. Nat. Assn. Female Execs., Am. Legion Aux. Democrat. Roman Catholic. Club: Petal Recreation Inc. (sec. treas. 1977-78). Home: Route 1 Box 29 Moselle MS 39459

LOTTERHOS, JULIUS LIEB, JR., lawyer; b. Crystal Springs, Miss., Dec. 8, 1918; s. Julius Lieb and Bessie (East) L.; student Copiah-Lincoln Jr. Coll., 1937-38, U. Miss., 1938-39; LL.B., Jackson Sch. Law, 1949; m. Ruth Norrell Hollingsworth, Aug. 27, 1939; children—Julius Lieb, Joseph Edward. Chief office dep. sheriff and tax collector Copiah County (Miss.), 1939-40; office mgr. Hammond Box Co. (La.), 1940-44; supr. bus. enterprises, div. rehab. blind Miss. Dept. Pub. Welfare, Jackson, 1947-51; admitted to Miss. bar, 1949; partner firm Henley, Lotterhos and Henley, Hazlehurst and Jackson, Miss., 1951—; spl. judge 14th Circuit Ct. Dist. Miss., 1967, 71-73; atty. Copiah County, 1952—, City of Crystal Springs, 1957-69. Del., Miss. Democratic Conv., 1952, 56, 60, 64, 68, 72; trustee Crystal Springs Sch., 1956-68; trustee Belhaven Coll., 1966—, chmn., 1970-72. Served with USNR, 1944-46. Mem. Copiah County (pres. 1967), Miss. (commr. 1964-65), Am. bar assns., Am. Judicature Soc., Comml. Law League Am. (chmn. 5th region 1971-72), Am., Miss. trial lawyers assns., Miss. Oil and Gas Lawyers Assn., Mid-Continent Oil and Gas Assn., Am. Soc. Hosp. Attys., Am. Soc. Law and Medicine, Nat. Assn. Civil County Attys., Miss. Bd. Suprs. Attys. Assn. (pres. 1975-76), C. of C., Miss. Econ. Council, Am. Legion, Sigma Delta Kappa. Presbyterian. Clubs: Lions, Univ., Rolling Hills, Masons (32 deg.), Shriners. Home: 435 Mathis Rd Crystal Springs MS 39059 Office: 141 S Caldwell Dr Hazlehurst MS 39083

LOTZ, AILEEN ROBERTS, government consultant; b. Orange, N.J., Dec. 11, 1924; d. Paul R. and Aileen (Jeandron) Roberts; children—Alexandra Virginia, David William. B.A., U. Miami, 1971. Exec. dir. Miami Beach Taxpayers Assn., 1954-60; exec. dir. Govt. Research Council, Miami, Fla. 1960-66; sr. adminstrv. asst. to mgr. Dade County, Miami, 1966-72; dir. Dade County Dept. Human Resources, 1975-82; cons. to local govt., 1982—. Candidate Fla. Ho. of Reps., 1974. Mem. Internat. City Mgmt. Assn., Am. Soc. Pub. Adminstrn. Democrat. Author: Metropolitan Dade County: Two-Tier Government in Action, 1984; author articles in field. Address: 6950 SW 71st Ct South Miami FL 33143

LOTZ, MICHAEL JAY, pathologist, medical educator; b. N.Y.C., Feb. 4, 1948; s. Herbert R. and Evelyn I. (Purmell) L.; m. Willemina M. Reichgelt, Aug. 27, 1969; 1 dau., Margot. A.B., Columbia U., 1968, M.D., 1972. Diplomate Am. Bd. Pathology. Resident in pathology Nat. Cancer Inst., NIH, Bethesda, Md., 1972-74; resident physician Clin. Center, NIH, Bethesda, 1974-76; instr. Columbia U., N.Y.C., 1976-78; med. dir. Met. Path. Lab., Hackensack, N.J., 1976-77; asst. prof. pathology U. South Fla., Tampa, 1978-82, assoc. prof., 1982-84, dir. Clin. Labs., 1978-84, assoc. prof. comprehensive medicine, 1982-84; mem. faculty Coll. Am. Pathologists, Profl. Lab. Mgmt. Inst., Chgo., 1980-82; assoc. clin. prof. pathology Brown U., Providence, R.I., 1984—; assoc. pathologist Miriam Hosp., Providence, 1984—. Served to lt. comdr. USPHS, 1972-76. Recipient Meierhof award Columbia U., 1972; pathobiology fellow, 1971-72. Mem. Internat. Acad. Pathology, Am. Soc. Clin. Pathologists, Coll. Am. Pathologists, Assn. Clin. Scientists. Contbr. articles to profl. pubs. Home and Office: 164 Summit Ave Providence RI 02906

LOTZ, WALTER JOHN, JR., pharmacist; b. New Orleans, July 27, 1946; s. Walter John and Helen (Healy) L.; m. Suzanne Marie Chaffin, Nov. 11, 1970; children—Daniel Joseph, Colleen Marie. B.S. in Pharmacy, NE La. U., 1969. Cert. pharmacist, La., Colo. Staff pharmacist K&B Drug Store, New Orleans, 1969-72; asst. dir. pharmacy Lakewood Hosp., Morgan City, La., 1972-80, dir. pharmacy, 1980-84, Dr.'s Hosp. of Jefferson, Metairie, La., 1984—; pres. Lakemed, Inc., Mandeville, La., 1982—. Treas. Lamaze Assn. Childbirth Edn., Morgan City, 1980-83. Mem. Am. Soc. Hosp. Pharmacists, La. Soc. Hosp. Pharmacists (chmn. 1983). Democrat. Roman Catholic. Avocations: camping; snow skiing; photography. Home: 2321 Tortoise Dr Mandeville LA 70448 Office: Drs Hosp of Jefferson 4320 Honma Blvd Metairie LA 70006

LOUDEN, GEORGE MALCOLM, financial executive; b. Waco, Tex., Mar. 9, 1945. B.A. in Acctg., Tex. Christian U., 1967. C.P.A., Tex. Chief fin. officer Walsh and Watts Inc., F. Howard Walsh, Fleming Found., Walsh Found.; pres. First Tex. Trust Corp.; dir. Ridglea Nat. Bank, Overton Bankshares. Trustee Tex. Christian U., chmn. endowment com., chmn. intercollegiate athletic com.; trustee Tex. Boys Choir; past pres. Panther Boys Club, Fort Worth; bd. dirs. Cotton Bowl Athletic Assn., Trinity Valley Sch., Univ. Pl., Arts Council Fort Worth and Tarrant County Inc.; past pres., bd. dirs. Fort Worth Ballet Assn.; treas. Dorothy Shaw Bell choir. Named Mr. Tex. Christian U., 1967; recipient Pres.' award Tex. Christian U., 1979, Valuable Alumnus award, 1982. Mem. Fin. Exec. Inst., Am. Inst. C.P.A.s, Tex. Soc. C.P.A.s, Soc. La. C.P.A.s, Nat. Assn. Accts., Mid Continent Oil and Gas Assn., Ind. Producers Assn. Am., Estate Taxation Council, Petroleum Accts. Soc., Tex. Christian U. Alumni Assn. (past pres.), Kappa Sigma (alumni advisor). Clubs: Petroleum, Steeplechase, Fort Worth, Rivercrest Country, City, Shady Oaks Country. Office: 1007 Interfirst Ft Worth Bldg Fort Worth TX 76102

LOUDENSLAGER, LARRY NEAL, safety and environmental coordinator; b. Thomas, Okla., Aug. 19, 1949; s. Samuel Grover and Twila Mae (Valentine) L.; m. Diana Carrol Reber, June 27, 1969; children—Kimberly, Larry Neal, Lori. B.A., Southwestern Okla. State U., 1972, M. Ed., 1976. Cert. tchr., Okla. Art and indsl. arts instr. Okeene Pub. Schs., Okla., 1972-78; system operator Delhi Gas Pipeline, Canton, Okla., 1978-80, safety technician, 1980-82, dist. safety environ. coordinator, Fort Smith, Ark., 1983—; dist. safety environ. coordinator Ozark Gas Pipeline, Fort Smith, 1982—, TXO Prodn., 1984—; dir. Ark. One-Call System, Little Rock. Feature artist Western Plains Library System, 1971; designer tng. aids trailer. Inventor emergency exit security latch. Asst. scoutmaster Gt. Salt Plains council Boy Scouts Am., Okeene, 1976-77; mem. sch. bd. Okeene Pub. Schs., 1981-82. Mem. Okla. Air Nat. Guard (hon.), Am. Soc. Safety Engrs. Lodge: Masons.

LOUDERMILK, ROMELLE QUARLES, nurse, consultant; b. Walhalla, S.C., July 21, 1944; d. Melvin James and Blanche Quarles; m. Raymond Albert Loudermilk, Sept. 12, 1964; children—Michael, LeAnn. A.A., Lander Coll., 1964. Cert. in infection control. Home health nurse Laurens County Health Dept., S.C., 1965-66, 68-72, Oconee County Health Dept., Seneca, S.C., 1973-75; staff nurse Oconee Meml. Hosp., 1976-78, infection control nurse, 1978—; cons. instr. Tri-county Tec, Pendleton, S.C., 1985—. Recipient Lee Cobb award Lander Coll., 1964. Mem. S.C. Hosp. Assn. (sec., v.p., pres. 1984—), Nat. Intravenous Assn., Assn. Practitioners in Infection Control, Palmetto div. of Nat. Infection Control Orgn. Mem. Pentecostal Ch. of God. Avocations: sewing; needlepoint; farming. Home: Route 2 Box 726 Walhalla SC 29691 Office: Oconee Meml Hosp PO Box 858 Seneca SC 29678

LOUGHLIN, MARY ANNE ELIZABETH, TV news anchor; b. Biddeford, Maine, July 30, 1956; d. John Francis and Jacqueline Anne (LaLonde) L.; B.S., Fla. State U., 1977. Reporter, Sta. WFSU-FM, Tallahassee, 1976; news anchor/producer Sta. WECA-TV, Tallahassee, 1977-81; producer/show host Sta. WTBS-TV, Atlanta, 1981-84; news anchor, producer Cable News Network, Atlanta, 1983—. Recipient Woman at Work Broadcast award Nat. Commn. on Working Women, 1982. Mem. Women in Cable, Women in Communications, Am. Women in Radio and TV (Woman of Achievement award 1982, 84). Roman Catholic. Office: 1050 Techwood Dr NW Atlanta GA 30318

LOUIS, PAUL ADOLPH, lawyer; b. Key West, Fla., Oct. 22, 1922; s. Louis and Rose Leah (Weinstein) L.; B.A., Va. Mil. Inst., Lexington, 1947; LL.B., U. Miami (Fla.), 1950, J.D., 1967; m. Nancy Ann Lapof, Dec. 28, 1971; children—Louis Benson, IV, Connor Cristina and Marshall Dore (twins). Bar: Fla. 1950; cert. civil trial lawyer, Fla. Bar. Asst. state atty., 1955-57, atty. Beverage Dept. Fla., 1957-60; spl. asst. atty. gen. State of Fla., 1970-71; partner firm Sinclair, Louis, Siegel, Heath, Nussbaum & Zavertnik, P.A., Miami, 1960—; mem. Fed. Jud. Nominating Commn., 1977-80; mem. peer rev. com. U.S. Dist. Ct. (so. dist.) Fla., 1983—; mem. Dade County Health Facilities Authority, 1979—. Founder mem. Palm Springs Gen. Hosp. Scholarship Com., 1968. Served to maj. USAAF, 1943-45; ETO. Decorated Air medal with five oak leaf clusters, Bronze Star (7), Purple Heart. Mem. Am., Fla. (bd. govs. 1970-74), Dade County (dir. 1954-55, 66-69) bar assns., Assn. Trial Lawyers Am., Trial Bar of U.S. Dist. Ct. of So. Dist. Fla., Am. Judicature Soc., Va. Mil. Inst. Alumni Assn. Democrat. Jewish. Clubs: Miami; Palm Bay. Author: Defamation, How Far Can You Go, Trial and Tort Trends, 1969; contbr. chpts. to Fla. Family Law, 1967, 72. Home: 4411 Palm Ln Miami FL 33137 Office: 1125 A I Dupont Bldg 169 E Flagler St Miami FL 33131

LOUKIDES, GEORGE, rare book dealer; b. Plainfield, N.J., July 28, 1930; s. George and Stamatia (Chronis) L.; B.A., McGill U., 1952; M.A., U. Denver, 1954, Columbia U., 1957. Guidance counselor, asst. prin., supr. classes emotionally handicapped children N.Y.C. Bd. Edn., 1956-77; rare book dealer Old Mill Books, Charleston, S.C., 1962—. Bd. dirs. Footlight Players, Charleston Opera Co., Charleston. Home and office: PO Box 12353 Charleston SC 29412

LOURIE, ISADORE EDWARD, lawyer; b. St. George, S.C., Aug. 4, 1932; s. Louis and Anne (Friedman) L.; m. Susan Reiner, Nov. 29, 1959; children—Lance, Joel, Neal. B.S., U. S.C., 1953, J.D., 1956. Bar: S.C. 1956, D.C. 1972. Sr. ptnr. Lourie, Curlee, Barrett and Popowski, Columbia, S.C., 1957—. Active S.C. Nat. Democratic Com.; mem. S.C. Ho. of Reps., Columbia, 1965-72; mem. S.C. Senate, 1973—, chmn. transp. com., mem. judiciary, corrective penology, labor, commerce, industry coms., chmn. legis. study com. on worker's compensation and pub. transp. Recipient S.C. Young Man of Yr. award Jaycees, 1966, Legislator of Yr. award S.C. Young Democrats, 1978, S.C. Trial Lawyers Assn., 1981, S.C. Civil Liberties Union, 1984. Mem. Assn. Trial Lawyers Am., S.C. Trial Lawyers Assn. Jewish. Home: 6308 Westshore Rd Columbia SC 29207 Office: PO Box 142 Columbia SC 20292

LOVALLO, MICHAEL DANIEL, architect, real estate developer; b. Torrington, Conn., Sept. 10, 1926; s. Daniel Michael and Clara (Eanniello) L.; m. Thelma Elaine Hricko, Jan. 18, 1947 (div. 1965); children—Michael John, Kim Anne Lovallo Robbins; m. 2d, Virginia Carolyn Emmert, Apr. 3, 1965. Cert. Hartford Tech. Inst., 1949, Hartford State Tech. Sch., 1957; student Yale U., 1958. Registered architect, Pa., Md., Va., Ky., W.Va. From draftsman to job capt. Joseph Stein, AIA, Waterbury, Conn., 1948-56; asst. to architect Thomas C. Babbitt, AIA, Torrington, Conn., 1956-64; project architect Howard Weinreich, AIA, Stamford, Conn., 1964-65; job capt. Robert C. Bennett, AIA, Morgantown, W.Va., 1965-66; project architect L.D. Schmidt & Sons, Inc.-Architects/Engrs., Fairmont, W.Va., 1966-70; freelance architect, Morgantown, 1970-73; office mgr. Whalen King Assocs., AIA, Clarksburg, W.Va. and Beckley, W.Va., 1973-76; chief architect Holley, Kenney, Schott div. BCI, Beckley and Pitts., 1976-81; prin., ptnr. Lovallo/Houchins Assocs., Beckley, 1981-84; guest lectr. W.Va. U. Sch. Landscape Architecture, 1972-73. Served with USMC, 1945-46. Mem. W.Va. Soc. Architects (pres. 1980-81), AIA, of the Nat. Inst. Bldg. Scis. (pres. W.Va. Cons. Council 1980), Torrington Jaycees (past pres.). Republican. Mormon. Lodges: Suncrest Kiwanis, Elks. Home: Route 1 Box 37B Shady Spring WV 25918 Office: Lovallo & Assocs Route 1 Box 37 B Shady Spring WV 25918

LOVE, BEN F., banker; b. 1924; B.B.A., U. Tex., 1947; married. Founder Gift-Wraps, Inc (merged with Gibson Greeting Card Co. 1960), 1948-62, pres. Gift-Wraps Inc. div. Gibson Greeting Card Co., 1962-65; pres. River Oaks Bank & Trust Co., Houston, 1965-67; sr. v.p. Tex. Commerce Bank Nat. Assn., 1967-68, exec. v.p., dir., 1968-69, pres., dir., 1969-72, chmn. bd., chief exec. officer, 1972-77, sr. chmn., chief exec. officer, 1977-80; pres. Tex. Commerce Bancshares, Inc., 1971-72, chmn. bd., chief exec. officer, 1972—; dir. Burlington No. Inc. Cox Enterprises, Inc., Proler Internat. Corp., Hughes Tool Co., Tex. Commerce Bank-Austin, Tex. Commerce Bank-Houston; internat. adv. bd. Pan Am. World Airways. Office: Tex Commerce Bancshares Inc 600 Travis St Houston TX 77002

LOVE, GORDON LEE, pathologist, researcher; b. Concord, Calif., Dec. 11, 1951; s. Curtis and Violet (Cota) L.; m. Margaret Fuller, Jan. 12, 1985. B.S., La. Tech. U., 1973; M.D., Tulane Med. Sch., 1978. Diplomate Am. Bd. Pathology. Resident in pathology Charity Hosp., New Orleans, 1978-83, vis. pathologist, 1984—; staff pathologist VA Hosp., New Orleans, 1983—; instr. pathology La. State U. Med. Sch., New Orleans, 1984—. Contbr. articles to profl. jours. Fellow Coll. Am. Pathologists; mem. Internat. Acad. Pathologists, Am. Soc. for Microbiologist. Republican. Baptist. Avocation: computing. Home: 1540 Aviators D New Orleans LA 70122 Office: VA Med Ctr 1601 Perdido St New Orleans LA 70146

LOVE, JAMES FRANKLIN, JR., textile company executive; b. Lincolnton, N.C., Apr. 26, 1921; s. James Franklin and Margaret Marion (Dover) L.; m. Georgia Mack Antley Keeter, June 12, 1943 (dec. May 1982); children—James Franklin III, Margaret Marion Love Guin. B.S. in Bus. Adminstrn, The Citadel, 1942; postgrad., Advanced Mgmt. U. Va., 1966. Mfg. supr. trainee Dover Mills, Shelby, N.C., 1946-50; sec., supt. Marion Yarn Mills, Boiling Springs, N.C., 1951-53; with Am. & Efird Mills, Inc., Mt. Holly, N.C., 1953—, exec. v.p., 1971-73, pres., 1973—. Pres. N.C. Tennis Found.; Bd. dirs. Gaston County YMCA, United Way Gaston County; bd. visitors Sacred Heart Coll. Served to maj. USAAF, 1942-46. Mem. Thread Inst. (ex-officio mem. exec. com.), Am. Yarn Spinners Assn. (budget com., internat. trade com.), Am. Textile Mfrs. Inst. (adv. bd. internat. trade com.), Nat. Cotton Council (mfrs. del.). Presbyterian. Clubs: Charlotte (N.C.); Athletic, Charlotte City, Gaston Country, Olde Providence Racquet, Southampton Racquet; Rotary (Mt. Holly) (past pres. local club). Home: PO Box 826 Mount Holly NC 28120 Office: PO Box 507 Mount Holly NC 28120*

LOVE, JEFFREY BENTON, lawyer; b. Houston, Oct. 4, 1949; s. Benton Fooshee and Margaret (McKean) L.; m. Katherine Brownlee, Dec. 30, 1972; children—Benton Fooshee, III, Elizabeth Houston. B.A., Vanderbilt U., 1971; J.D., U. Tex. Sch. Law, 1976. Bar: Tex. 1976. Assoc. Liddell, Sapp, Zivley, Brown & LaBoon, Houston, 1976-81, ptnr., 1982—; dir. Tex. Commerce Bank-River Oaks Nat. Assn., Kinark Corp.; hon. consul gen. Sweden in Tex., 1983—. Pres. Sunrisers Houston Breakfast Assn., Houston, 1979; dir. exec. com. Houston Grand Opera Assn., Houston, 1979—; dir., chmn. Children's Fund, Inc., Houston, 1981-82; bd. dirs. Tex. Bus. Hall of Fame Found., 1985—. Mem. ABA, Houston C. of C., Houston Bar Assn., Tex. Bar Assn., Swedish Am. Trade Assn. (bd. dirs. 1983—), U. Tex. Law Alumni Assn. (bd. dirs. 1981—, pres.-elect 1985—), Phi Delta Theta Alumni Assn. Presbyterian. Clubs: River Oaks, Allegro, Houston (Houston). Home: 2038 Timberlane Houston TX 77027 Office: Liddell Sapp Zivley and LaBoon 3400 Texas Commerce Tower Houston TX 77002

LOVE, JOSEPH WILLIAM, JR., realtor, retired oil company executive; b. Tulsa, Mar. 31, 1928; s. Joseph William and Eva Elizabeth (Henderson) L.; B.S. in Bus. Adminstrn., U. Tulsa, 1949; postgrad. U. Houston, 1957-60. Various mgmt. positions Union Tex. Petroleum Corp., 1956-84; founder, chmn. Bill Love Enterprises, Inc., Cedarcrest Retreat Ctr., Inc., Love Meml. Found., Inc. Served to capt. USAF, 1951-55, Decorated Air medal; lic. real estate broker, Tex. Mem. Nat. Assn. Bus. Economists, North San Jacinto C. of C. (pres. 1986), Huntsville Bd. Realtors, Tex. Assn. Realtors, Nat. Assn. Realtors, Aircraft Owners and Pilots Assn. Sigma Phi Epsilon. Methodist. Lodge: Lions. Home: Governor's Point PO Box 387 Pointblank TX 77364 Office: PO Box 810 Pointblank TX 77364

LOVE, NORMAN DON, educator; b. Childress, Tex., May 15, 1946; s. Norman A. and Clydie L. (Glover) L.; B.A. in History, Midwestern State U., 1973, M.A., 1978; doctoral program U. Ky., 1977—, mgmt. seminars Am. Inst. Banking, 1981, El Paso Nat. Bank, 1981, Am. Mgmt. Assn., 1984; m. Leticia Figueroa, Mar. 27, 1981; children—Norman Don, Jason Marc. Cert. first aid instr. ARC; cert. CPR instr. Am. Heart Assn. Teaching asst. Am. history Midwestern State U., Wichita Falls, 1975-77; intern Wichita Falls Mus. and Art Center, 1976-77, curator history exhibit, 1976-77: teaching asst. Am. history U. Ky., Lexington, 1977-79, instr., 1979-80; mgmt. trainee, supr. armored car dept./cash vault El Paso (Tex.) Nat. Bank, 1980-81, credit officer and mgr. credit dept., 1982-83; asst dir. staff devel. Vernon (Tex.) State Hosp., Tex. Dept. Mental Health/Mental Retardation, 1983-84, instr. prevention and mgmt. aggressive behavior, 1983-84; instr. El Paso County Community Coll., 1985—; curator World War I poster art collection King Library, 1978. Served with USAF, 1969-73. Phi Alpha Theta scholar, 1976-77. Home: 716 W Yandell Apt 18 El Paso TX 79902 Office: El Paso County Community Coll El Paso TX 79998

LOVE, ROBERT HUGH, mechanical engineer; b. Gaffney, S.C., Aug. 19, 1957; s. Bascomb Richard and Sara Brown L. B.S. in Mech. Engring., Clemson U., 1980. Jr. project engr. S.P.W. Indsl. Piping, Inc., Gaffney, 1979; constrn. engr. E.I. duPont de Nemours, Inc., Florence, S.C., 1980-81, constrn. area engr., 1981-83, research engr., 1983—, now research engr. Mem. ASME, Clemson U. Alumni Assn., Sigma Nu. Methodist. Home: 118 Woodmill Rd Brandywine Hundred Wilmington DE 19809 Office: PO Box 3886 Philadelphia PA 19146

LOVE, TERRENCE LESTER, real estate consultant; b. Covington, Va., Feb. 6, 1937; s. James Harold and Patsy (King) L.; B.Arch., Va. Inst. Tech., 1961; M.B.A., Ga. State U., 1969, Ph.D., 1971; m. Valerie Gay LeCraw, Nov. 20, 1965; children—Terrence Lester, Jennifer M. Designer, Bodin & Lamberson, Atlanta, 1962-63; architect Aeck Assocs., Atlanta, 1963-65; urban planner Adley Assocs., Atlanta, 1965-69; mem. faculty Ga. State U., Atlanta, 1969-73; chmn. bd. Land Devel. Analysts, Atlanta, 1973—; prof. Coll. Arch. Ga. Inst. Tech., Atlanta, 1967-84; pres. First Land Collaborative, Inc., Atlanta, 1973—. Elder Trinity Presbyterian Ch. Served with AUS, 1961-62. Mem. Am. Inst. Real Estate Appraisers, Am. Inst. Cert. Planners, Soc. Real Estate Appraisers. Contbr. articles to profl. jours. Home: 675 River Chase Point NW Atlanta GA 30328 Office: 180 Allen Rd Suite 310 N Atlanta GA 30328

LOVELACE, (BYRON) KEITH, management consultant; lawyer; b. Vernon, Tex., Feb. 15, 1935; s. Joseph Edward and Hattie Pearl (Brians) L.; B.S. in Chem. Engring., U. Tex., Austin, 1958, M.S., 1961, Ph.D., 1973; J.D., S. Tex. Coll. Law, 1978; m. Sandra Alene Daniel, June 17, 1961; children—Kirk Daniel, Bethany Alene, Amy Kathleen. Research and devel. engr. Core Labs., Dallas, 1960-61; with Tex. Instruments, Inc., Dallas and Houston, 1961-78, mgr. process control for advanced tech., 1969-70, reliability mgr. metal oxide semicondr. (MOS) div., 1971-75, MOS reliability dir., 1975-78; pres. P-V-T Inc., Houston, 1978-80, Mgmt. Resources Internat., 1980—; admitted to Tex. bar. Served with U.S. Army, 1953. Tex. Instruments fellow, 1965-68; FMC Corp. fellow, 1958-60; Eastern States Petroleum and Chem. scholar, 1957-58; Ethyl Corp. scholar, 1956-57. Mem. Am. Chem. Soc. (award 1958), Am. Inst. Chem. Engrs., Soc. Petroleum Engrs. (vice chmn. reservoir group 1979-80), Am. Bar Assn., State Bar Tex., Trial Lawyers Am., Tau Beta Pi (chpt. v.p. 1958-59), Omega Chi Epsilon. Contbr. articles to profl. jours. Patentee in field. Home: 11580 S Kirkwood Rd Houston TX 77477 Office: 7324 SW Freeway Suite 800 PO Box 37175 Houston TX 77237

LOVELESS, HOMER JACKSON, JR., public utility executive; b. Searcy, Ark., Feb. 24, 1931; s. Homer Jackson and Mary Esther (Stewart) L.; m. Beverly Jane Morrow, Feb. 16, 1951; children—David Wayne, Alan Jackson. B.S., Memphis State U., 1956. C.P.A., Tex., 1962. Dist. controller Montgomery Ward & Co., Detroit, 1956-65; bus. info. mgr. Fieldcrest Mills, Inc., Eden, N.C., 1965-68; controller, sec. Piedmont Shirt Co., Greenville, S.C., 1968-70; controller Profl. Golf Co., Chattanooga, 1970, Modern Maid Homes, Inc., Chattanooga, 1970-72; controller Electric Power Bd. Chattanooga, 1972—. Served with C.E., U.S. Army, 1952-53. Mem. Am. Inst. C.P.A.s, Am. Pub. Power Assn., Fin. Execs. Inst., C. of C., Pi Kappa Alpha. Methodist. Club: Valleybrook Golf and Country. Lodge: Kiwanis. Home: 812 Brynewood Park Ln Chattanooga TN 37415 Office: 537 Cherry St Chattanooga TN 37402

LOVELL, RUTH MOSES, jewelry designer; b. Arab, Ala., Jan. 12, 1943; d. Clifton Morgan and June Evelyn (Oden) Moses; m. Donald G. Lovell, Nov. 23, 1969 (div. 1975). B.S., Auburn U., 1964; postgrad. Pa. State U., 1971. Systems analyst Dept. Army and Dept. Treasury, 1965-73; spl. agt. U.S. Treasury Dept., 1973-82; dir. SASC, Tampa, Fla., 1977-82; pres., chmn. bd. Houseware Rentals, Inc., Tampa, 1982—, RML Designs, Inc., Tampa, 1983—, Incahoots Designs, Tampa, 1983—. Recipient various awards for jewelry design. Mem. Gatlinburg Craftsmen Tenn., Art Assn. N.C., Eastern Shore Art Assn., Virginia Beach Art Assn., ALA. Office: PO Box 10098 Tampa FL 33679

LOVELL, SAVAGE MARKETTE (S. MARK LOVELL), corporation executive, investor; b. Brookhaven, Miss., Apr. 26, 1935; s. George Carroll and Bessie Maude (Marr) L.; B.A., Baylor U., 1958; LL.B., So. Meth. U., 1966; m. Sarah Ann Quinn, June 9 1938; children—Kimberly Ann, Jennifer Ellen, Betty Allison, Jeffery Markette. Engr., Pierce Enterprises, Dallas, 1958-59; engr., dir. quality control, contracts adminstr., legal counsel, div. mgr. Baifield Industries, 1959-67; real estate investor, Shreveport, La., 1967—; chmn. bd. Temtex Industries, 1971, Tex. Clay Industries, 1970; chmn. bd., pres. Quinn-L Corp., 1972—; pres. Q-L Corp. (name changed to Braxton Corp.), 1977—; chmn. bd. Quinn-L Fin. Corp., 1977—; pres. SML, Inc., 1978—, Quinn-L Capital, Inc., 1982—; chmn. bd. Claridge Corp., 1982—; pres. Nashville Feature and Music, Inc., 1980—, Crestmed Corp., 1983—; cons. Former bd. dirs. Shreveport A.R.C., Shreveport Jr. Achievement; past pres., bd. dirs. Shreveport Civic Opera. Mem. Am., Dallas, Tex. bar assns., Shreveport C. of C. (past dir.). Democrat. Baptist. Home: 3851 Betty Virginia Circle Shreveport LA 71106 Office: 3003 Knight St Shreveport LA 71105

LOVESY, (THOMAS) CRAIG, SR., mag. exec.; b. Alexandria, La., Dec. 2, 1921; s. Charles Lewis and Mae Odel (Jameson) L.; student Ark. Poly. Coll., Russellville, 1939-42; m. Doris Jean Sublett, Sept. 6, 1941: children—Jean Anne, Thomas Craig, Mary Lou. Owner, Craig Lovesy Photog. Service, Russellville, 1945-49; editor, mgr. Tribune and Advertiser newspapers, Russellville, 1949-55, Daily and Weekly Courier Dem. newspapers, Russellville, 1955-57; dir. mail subscription promotion mgr. Cowles Communications, Look mag., Des Moines, 1957-72; asst. dir. Creative Services div. Nat. Wildlife Fedn., Washington, 1972-75; subscription dir. The Mother Earth News, Hendersonville, N.C., from 1976, now v.p., dir. Communications and Subscriptions; judge nat. dir. mail promotion contest Direct Mail Mktg. Assn., 1970, conv. panel speaker, 1975, 81. Served with USAAF, 1942-45. Recipient George Washington medal Freedoms Found., 1953. Mem. Direct Mail Mktg. Assn. Office: 105 Stoney Mountain Rd Hendersonville NC 28739

LOVICK, GINA PACITA, petroleum geologist, consultant; b. Chgo., Oct. 18, 1953; d. Casey and Diane Donella (McKenzie-Field) Present; m. Robert Gregg Lovick, Mar. 14, 1975. B.S. in Agr., Purdue U., 1974; M.S. in Geosci., U. Tex.-Arlington, 1977. Chief geologist Spindletop Oil and Gas, Dallas, 1977-80; mgr. exploration Vanguard Exploration, Dallas, 1980, Gage and Co., Fort Worth, 1980-81; cons. petroleum geologist, Grapevine, Tex., 1981—. Contbr. articles to profl. jours. Mem. Am. Assn. Petroleum Geologists, Dallas Geol. Soc., Purdue Alumni Assn. (life). Avocation: equestrian jumping. Home and Office: 814 Yellowstone Dr Grapevine TX 76051

LOVING, GEORGE GILMER, JR., retired air force officer, botanical gardens administrator; b. Roanoke, Va., Aug. 7, 1923; s. George Gilmer and Ora Page (Carr) L.; m. Mary Ambler Thomasson, Jan. 15, 1945; children—Cary Ambler, Betty Page. Student, Lynchburg Coll., 1941; B.A., U. Ala., 1960; M.A. in Internat. Affairs, George Washington U., 1965; grad., Air War Coll., 1965. Commd. 2d lt. U.S. Army Air Force, 1943; advanced through grades to lt. gen. U.S. Air Force, 1975; fighter pilot, test pilot, operations officer, fighter squadron comdr., 1943-55, U.S. adviser, Republic of China, 1960-62; staff planner, Washington, 1965-69, dir. plans, 1973-75, Joint Chiefs Staff rep. for mut. and balanced force reductions, Washington, 1975; comdr., Izmir, Turkey, 1975-77, Japan, Yokota Air Base, Japan, 1977-79, ret., 1979; cons. RAND Corp., 1979-80; exec. dir. Marie Selby Bot. Gardens, Sarasota, Fla., 1980—. Decorated D.S.M. with 2 oak leaf clusters, Silver Star medal, Legion of Merit, D.F.C. with oak leaf cluster, Silver Star medal, Legion of Merit, D.F.C. with oak leaf cluster, Meritorious Service medal, Air Force Commendation medal, Air medal with 25 oak leaf clusters; N.Y.C. Council on Fgn. Relations fellow, 1969-70. Mem. Am. Fighter Aces Assn. Episcopalian. Club: Sarasota Yacht. Address: 539 Commonwealth Ln Sarasota FL 33581*

LOVOY, SHARON WILLIAMS, federal agency administrator; b. Birmingham, Ala., Nov. 24, 1952; d. Robert Cleve and Elizabeth Maria (Jones) Williams; m. John Anthony Lovoy, Apr. 7, 1979. B.S. in Secondary Edn., Auburn U., 1974. Taxpayer service rep. IRS, Birmingham, 1975, adminstrv. intern, Atlanta, 1975-78, employee relations specialist, 1978-79, chief Tng. and Devel. Br., 1979—; cons. Baxter and Assoc., Birmingham, 1984—. Mem. com. for opening ceremony Birmingham City Library, 1984. Recipient Sustained Superior Performance award IRS, 1982, 84, High Quality Increase award, 1983. Mem. Am. Soc. for Tng. and Devel. (membership chmn. 1981, treas. 1982, exec. bd. 1983—, Mem. of Yr. 1982). Roman Catholic. Avocations: gourmet cooking; sailing; calligraphy; reading; aerobics. Home: 2333 Farley Terr Birmingham AL 35226 Office: IRS Tng Br 500 22d St S Birmingham AL 35223

LOWARY, THOMAS B., pipe company executive; b. 1923; married. B.S., U. Okla., 1948. With Mobil Oil Co., 1948-51; with Vinson Supply Co., 1951—, now chmn. bd., chief exec. officer, Tulsa, also dir. Served with U.S. Army, 1944-48. Office: Vinson Supply Co 220 N Boston Tulsa OK 74101*

LOWDERMILK, ROBERT ELBERT, III, minister, religious educator; b. Greensboro, N.C., July 9, 1951; s. Robert Elbert Jr. and Virginia (Overby) L.; m. Ellen Currie Sapp, July 14, 1973. A.B., Guilford Coll., 1973; M.Div., Duke U., 1976; D. Ministry, Southeastern Bapt. Theol. Sem., 1981. Ordained to ministry United Methodist Ch. College chaplain High Point Coll., N.C., 1976-79, dean of students, 1979-82; campus minister, dean of student devel. Catawba Coll., Salisbury, N.C., 1983-84, campus minister, asst. prof. religion, 1984—; chmn. div. campus ministry Bd. of Higher Edn. and Campus Ministry, Western N.C. Conf. United Meth. Ch., 1984—. Contbr. materials to The Upper Room, Ch. Sch. Today. Recipient L. E. Moody award High Point Coll., 1978, Algernon Sydney Sullivan award Catawba Coll., 1985. Mem. Am. Coll. Personnel Assn., Inst. Soc., Ethics, and Life Scis., Assn. for Counseling and Devel., U.S. Field Hockey Assn. (SE sect. umpiring chmn. 1983—). Avocations: field hockey officiating; piano; organ; calligraphy. Home: 707 Wiltshire Village Salisbury NC 28144 Office: Campus Minister's Office Catawba College 2300 West Innes St Salisbury NC 28144

LOWE, ALAN DENNIS, architect; b. Atlanta, May 24, 1953; s. Linzsey and Naomi Jane (White) L.; m. Melonye Dawn Bartlett, June 9, 1979; 1 child, Jonathan Daniel. Student Ga. Inst. Tech., 1971-72; B.S. in Bible Education, Columbia Bible Coll., 1975; postgrad. Southwestern Bapt. Theol. Sem., 1976-77; B.S. in Architecture, Ga. Inst. Tech., 1980; student New Orleans Bapt. Theol. Sem., 1985-86. Interim ministerial asst. College Park Second Bapt. Ch., Ga., 1976; constrn. supt. Woodland Homes, Inc., Jonesboro, Ga., 1977; archtl. draftsman Tipton Masterson Assocs., Atlanta, 1978-80; archtl. apprentice John J. Harte Assocs., Inc., Atlanta, 1981; design/devel. cons. Continental Fin. Corp., Marietta, Ga., 1981-83; cons., mgr. computer drafting, archtl. apprentice Zachary W. Henderson, AIA, Inc., Roswell, Ga., 1983-85; archtl./design cons. Clinton M. Day Cos., Inc., Norcross, Ga., 1984-85, C.P. Day Devel. Co., Norcross, 1985; photographer Zachary W. Henderson, AIA, Inc., Roswell, Ga., 1983-85. Deacon Dunwoody Bapt. Ch., Ga., 1984-85; singer Messengers Quartet, 1981-83; vice-chmn. deacons, dir. Single Adults, College Park Second Bapt. Ch., 1970-83; chmn. zoning com., v.p. Terramont Homeowners Assn., Inc., Roswell, Ga., 1984-85. Recipient Design and Detailing Excellence award Zachary W. Henderson, AIA, Inc., Atlanta, 1983. Republican. Avocations: music; antique car restoration; reading; photography.

LOWE, CHARLES ERWIN, safety engineer; b. Toronto, Ohio, Oct. 31, 1930; s. John Charles and Esther Eliza (Brandfass) L.; m. Helen Huson, 1952; children—John, Jeffery; m. Ethel May Franks, May 27, 1970; children—Robin, Daniel, Michael, Laura. Student, Bremerton Jr. Olympic Coll., 1952-54. Safety engr. United Engrs. and Constrn. Co., Phila., 1965-74; mech. supt. Ford, Bacon & Davis, Monroe, La., 1974-75; safety dir. Cajun Electric Co., New Roads, La., 1975-79; owner, operator Lowe Enterprises, Ventress, La., 1979-82; safety supr. Raymond Kaiser Engrs., Oakland, Calif., 1982—. Served with USN, 1948-52, Korea. Recipient Dist. Achievement award Kiwanis Internat., 1980. Mem. Am. Soc. Safety Engrs. Republican. Avocations: flying single engine airplane; golf; woodworking.

LOWE, PAMELA SUZANNE POWELL, educational coordinator; b. Chattanooga, Tenn., June 5, 1955; d. Giles Ernest and Burma Lee (Jones) Powell; m. Joseph Edward Lowe, Dec. 16, 1977 (div.); 1 son, Taylor Edward. B.S.N., U. Tenn.-Chattanooga, 1977, M.Ed., 1982. Cert. critical care nurse. Staff nurse ICU, Red Bank Community Hosp., Chattanooga, 1977-78, head nurse ICU, 1978-80, ednl. coordinator, 1980-84; asst. dir. nursing Meml. Hosp., Chattanooga, 1984—; adj. faculty mem. Chattanooga State Tech. Community Coll., 1981—; guest instr. Sequatchie Gen. Hosp., Dunlap, Tenn., 1980-84; adj. faculty Chattanooga Paramedic Program, 1981-82, U. Tenn., Chattanooga, 1986. Mem. Am. Assn. Critical Care Nurses, Sigma Theta Tau. Republican. Baptist. Author: A Beginner's Guide to EKG, 1982; Basic Electrocardiography, 1983. Office: Meml Hosp 2500 Citico Ave Chattanooga TN 37404

LOWE, RALPH STEPHEN, physician; b. El Paso, Jan. 19, 1947; s. Ralph Leroy and Martha Ann (Satterwhite) L.; B.S., U. Tex., El Paso, 1968; M.D., U. Tex., San Antonio, 1973; m. Helen Mellado, Dec. 22, 1969; children—Stephanie, Elizabeth, Sarah. Commd. lt. U.S. Air Force, 1972, advanced through grades to maj., 1980; resident in internal medicine Wilford Hall USAF Med. Center, San Antonio, 1973-76, fellow in allergy and clin. immunology, 1976-78, instr. alin. allergy physicians tng. course, 1976-78; staff allergist Keesler USAF Med. Center, Biloxi, Miss., 1978-80. Diplomate Am. Bd. Internal Medicine, Am. Bd. Allergy and Immunology. Mem. AMA, Assn. Mil. Allergists, A.C.P., Am. Acad. Allergy, Am. Coll. Allergists. Roman Catholic. Contbr. articles to profl. jours. Office: 10470 Vista del Sol Suite 100 El Paso TX 79925 also 6927 N Mesa Suite D El Paso TX

LOWE, REID HARRISON, funeral home executive; b. Asheville, N.C., June 18, 1922; s. Oscar Cleveland and Mary Knox Bess Lowe; m. Helen Maxwell, Apr. 1943; children—Judy A., Steven H., Susan Lowe Auterhoff. A.S., Biltmore Coll., 1941; student Coe Coll., 1943; D.Mortuary Sci. cum laude, Gupton-Jones Coll. Mortuary Sci., 1946. Apprentice embalmer Bess Funeral Home, Miami, Fla., 1941-43, mgr., funeral dir., 1945-58; owner Reid Lowe Funeral Home, Miami, 1958—; owner, pres. Lowe-Hanks Funeral Homes, Inc., Hialeah, Fla., 1961—; pres. Virlen, Inc., Miami, 1958—; dir. First State Bank of Miami, Southeast Planners, Inc., Keyes City Ins. Agy.; chmn. bd. Grove Park Crematory, 1978-82; commr. Fla. Med. Examiners Commn., 1972—; mem. adv. bd. mortuary sci. dept. Dade Community Coll., 1962—. Bd. dirs. Loch Lomond Property Owners Assn., 1975-80. Served with USAAF, 1943-45. Mem. Nat. Funeral Dirs. Assn., Fla. Funeral Dirs. Assn., Flying Funeral Dirs. Assn., Aircraft Owners and Pilots Assn., Fla. Assn. Med. Examiners (hon.), Air Force Assn., Hialeah-Miami Springs C. of C., Mil. Order World Wars, Ret. Officers Assn., VFW, Am. Legion. Baptist. Clubs: Miami Acacia, Allapattah Exchange, Glades Flying (dir. 1962-80), Army-Navy, Mahi Golf, Oasis. Lodges: Moose, Masons, Shriners, Jesters, Circus Saints and Sinners, Lions. Home: 15902 Kilmarnock Dr Miami Lakes FL 33014 Office: Lowe-Hanks Funeral Homes 4850 Palm Ave Hialeah FL 33012

LOWE, ROBERT CHARLES, lawyer; b. New Orleans, July 3, 1949; s. Carl Randall and Antonia (Morgan) L.; m. Theresa Louise Acree, Feb. 4, 1978. 1 child, Nicholas Stafford. B.A., U. New Orleans, 1971; J.D., La. State U., 1975. Bar: La. 1975, U.S. Dist. Ct. (ea. dist.) La. 1975, U.S. Ct. Appeals (5th cir.) 1980, U.S. Dist. Ct. (we. dist.) La. 1978, U.S. Supreme Ct. 1982. Assoc. Sessions, Fishman, Rosenson, Snellings and Boisfontaine, New Orleans, 1975-80; ptnr. Sessions, Fishman, Rosenson, Boisfontaine, Nathan and Winn, 1980—. Author: Louisiana Divorce, 1984. Contbr. articles to profl. jours. Mem. La. Law Rev., 1974-75. Mem. ABA, La. State Bar Assn. (chmn. family law sect. 1984-85), La. Assn. Def. Counsel, New Orleans Bar Assn., Order of Coif, Phi Kappa Phi. Home: 9421 Roslyn Dr River Ridge LA 70123 Office: Sessions Fishman Rosenson Boisfontaine Nathan and Winn 601 Poydras St 25th Floor New Orleans LA 70130

LOWE, ROBERT CHARLES, pharmacist; b. Mountain City, Tenn., Aug. 5, 1947; s. Charles Clinton and Gertrude (Butler) L.; m. Elizabeth Emily Brown, Oct. 11, 1975; 1 child, Elizabeth Lea. B.A. in Chemistry, Milligan Coll., Tenn., 1969; B.S. in Pharmacy, U. Tenn., 1972, D.Pharmacy, 1973. Pharmacist, mgr. South Roan Pharmacy, Johnson City, Tenn., 1973-74; pharmacist Broughton Hosp., Morganton, N.C., 1974-79, dir. pharmacy services, 1981—; asst. dir. pharmacy Cherry Hosp., Goldsboro, N.C., 1979-81; methodology improvement cons. div. mental health State of N.C., 1984—; mem. N.C. Drug Adv. Com., 1981—. Mem. Am. Soc. Hosp. Pharmacists, N.C. Soc. Hosp. Pharmacists. Methodist. Avocations: golf, tennis, fishing. Office: Broughton Hosp Pharmacy 1000 S Sterling St Morganton NC 28655

LOWE, ROBERT WYLIE, orthopedic surgeon; b. Lexington, Ky., Oct. 28, 1937; s. John Wylie and Pearl (Brown) L.; m. Sara Herr, Aug. 23, 1963; children—Mary Cassel, Robert Wylie, Jenny Rebecca, John Daniel. B.S., Morehead State Coll. (Ky.), 1959; M.D., Vanderbilt U., 1964. Cert. Am. Bd. Orthopedic Surgery. Intern, Vanderbilt Univ. Hosps., 1964-65, gen. surgery, 1965-66, resident in orthopedic surgery 1966-69; ptnr. Scott, Carythorne, Lowe, Mullen & Foster, Huntington, W.Va., 1971—; med. dir. Cerebral Palsy Council of Cobell County (W.Va.), 1971-84. Contbr. articles to profl. jours. Served to maj. U.S. Army, 1969-71. Recipient Richmond Cerebral Palsy award Am. Acad. Cerebral Palsy, 1970; Outstanding Alumnus award Morehead State U., 1973. Fellow ACS; mem. Am. Acad. Orthopedic Surgeons, So. Med. Assn., Cabell County Med. Soc. (pres. 1984), Am. Orthopedic Soc. Sports Medicine. Republican. Presbyterian. Lodge: Rotary. Home: 1860 McCoy Rd Huntington WV 25701 Office: 2828 1st Ave Huntington WV 25701 also 3 Woodland Pl Paintsville KY also 2000 Carter Ave Ashland KY

LOWENSTEIN, CHARLES DOUGLAS, educational services company executive; b. Bayonne, N.J., Apr. 22, 1942; s. Irving Eric and Barbara (Goldenberg) L.; B.S. in Commerce and Econs., U. Vt., 1963; m. Leslie Ann Diamond, Sept. 5, 1965; children—Lee Jay, Andrea Michelle, Evan Mitchell and Jaron David (twins). Supt. Lowenstein Metals Inc., Newark, 1964-67; registered prin. Penn Securities Co., East Orange, N.J., 1967-68; asst. dir. Nelson Sch. Securities, Mountainside, N.J., 1968-69; v.p. sales Ga. Internat. Securities Co., Atlanta, 1969-70; pres. Investment Tng. Inst., Inc., Atlanta, 1969—; tng. cons. Wiesenberger Services, Inc., N.Y.C., 1971-76. Mem. task force to design new industry tng. standards Nat. Assn. Securities Dealers, 1971; bd. regents Coll. for Financial Planning, Denver, 1972-73; pres. Atlanta dist. Zionist Orgn. Am.; nat. vice chmn. United Jewish Appeal; v.p. Union Orthodox Jewish Congregations; mem. Sabra Soc.; bd. dirs. Atlanta Jewish Community Center, 1977-82; bd. dirs. Yeshiva High Sch. of Atlanta, 1977-78, fin. sec., 1978-79, v.p., 1979-82, pres., 1982-84; bd. dirs., mem. exec. com. Atlanta Jewish Fedn., chmn. leadership devel. com., 1984-86, Atlanta Men's ORT, Atlanta Chabad-Lubavitch, Atlanta Bur. Jewish Edn., 1977-82; trustee Congregation Beth Jacob; mem. young leadership cabinet United Jewish Appeal, 1980-82, mem. exec. com., 1982-84; Atlanta chmn. Israel Bonds, 1983-84, also mem. nat. campaign cabinet. Served with AUS, 1963. Mem. Internat. Assn. Fin. Planners (dir. 1973-74), Jaycees, Nat. Assn. Securities Schs. (pres. 1974-76), Ga. Security Dealers Assn., Nat. R.R. Hist. Soc., Tau Epsilon Phi. Home: 1050 Burton Dr Atlanta GA 30329 Office: 3569 Habersham at Northlake Tucker GA 30084

LOWENSTEIN, GEORGE WOLFGANG, retired physician, UN consultant; b. Ger., Apr. 18, 1890; s. Julius Max and Augusta Victoria (Klettschoff) L.; student Royal William Coll., Germany, 1909, Friedrich William U., Ger., 1919, London Sch. Tropical Hygiene and Medicine, 1939; m. Johanna Sabath, Nov. 27, 1923; children—Peter F. Lansing (dec.) and Ruth Edith Gallagher (twins). Dir. public health Berlin Neubabelsberg, 1920-22; dir. public health and welfare Berlin, 1923-33; pvt. practice medicine, Berlin, 1933-38, Chgo., 1940-46, Chebeague and Dark Harbor, Maine, 1947-58; instr. Berlin Acad. Prevention of Infant Mortality, Postgrad. Acad. Physicians; permanent cons. Internat. Abolitionists Fedn. at ECOSOC, UN, 1947—; lectr. Morton Plant Hosp., Clearwater, also Clearwater campus St. Petersburg Jr. Coll.; guest prof. U. Bremen, Berlin, 1981-82. Served with German Army, 1914-18. Decorated Cross Merit I Class, Germany, 1965; recipient Commendation awards Pres. U.S., 1945, 70; 65 Year Gold Service Pin, AMA and ARC, 1985; Service to Mankind award Sertoma, 1972, 73; Sport award Pres. Carter, 1977; Musicologist award Richey Symphony, 1979; others. Fellow Am. Acad. Family Physicians (charter, life, 35-yr. service award 1984), AAAS, Am. Coll. Sport Medicine (emeritus, charter, life), Am. Pub. Health Assn. (life, 40-yr. service award 1984), Brit. Soc. (emeritus); mem. German Assn. History of Medicine (life), Acad. Mental Retardation (charter life), Am. Pub. Health Assn. (life), Fla. Health Assn. (life), Fla. Pub. Health Assn. (life), Brit. Public Health Assn. (life), AMA (hon.), Am. Assn. Mil. Surgeons (life), Steuben Soc., Richey Symphony Soc. (musicologist, charter), World Peace Through World Law Center. Clubs: City (Chgo. chmn. hygiene sect. 1944-46), Rotary (Harris fellow 1980), Masons, Shriners (comdr., life v.p.; 32 deg.). Co-author: Public Health Between the Time of Imperium and National Socialism; The Destruction of Public Health Reforms of the First German Republic, 1985, others. Contbr. 300 articles and revs. to books and med. jours. Home: 2470 Rhodesian Dr #34 Clearwater FL 33515

LOWENSTEIN, IRWIN LANG, retail furniture chain executive; b. Louisville, Aug. 17, 1935; s. Stanley Ben and Fannie Georgie (Lang) L.; m. Joel Annette Dampf, June 15, 1957; children—Jo-Anne, Suzanne, Ruth, Ellen, Stanley. B.A., Vanderbilt U., 1957. Pres. Biederman Furniture, St. Louis, 1971-72, Duchess Furniture, Florence, Ky., 1972—, Crossroads Furniture, Houston, 1972-77, Rhodes, Inc., Atlanta, 1977—. Served with U.S. Army, 1957. Mem. Nat. Home Furnishings Assn., Young Presidents Orgn. Republican. Jewish. Club: Standard (Atlanta). Home: 6275 Old Hickory Point NW Atlanta GA 30328 Office: 1800 Century Blvd Suite 1000 Atlanta GA 30345*

LOWERY, FRED MAURICE, management educator; b. Jacksonville, Tex., Oct. 8, 1941; s. Fred and Grace (Johnston) L.; m. Astrid Hildegard Stoppe, Dec. 23, 1961; children—Fred M., Jr., John Robert, Julie E. B.S., Bryant Coll., 1967; M.B.A., North Tex. State U., 1978; Ph.D., Calif. Coast U., 1983. Personnel mgr. Army and Air Force Exchange Service, Ft. Bragg, N.C., 1972-76, employee devel. specialist, Dallas, 1976-79; tng. coordinator Atlantic Richfield Co., Houston, 1979-80, sr. advisor, Los Angeles, 1980-81; sr. adminstr. Tenneco Oil Co., Houston, 1981-83, tng. mgr., 1983—; pres. Tenneco Fed. Credit Union, 1985—, dir. 1982—; adj. prof. U. Houston, Clear Lake City, Tex., 1980—; adv. human resources U. Tex., Austin, 1983-85. Contbr. articles to photog. mags. Pres. Maurice Music Pub. Co., 1984. Served as maj. Tex. State Guard, 1967—. Recipient Civilian Service medal U.S. Dept. State, 1972, George M. Parks award Bryant Coll., 1967. Mem. Am. Soc. for Tng. Devel. (dir. industry group 1983-85, plaque 1985), Acad. Mgmt., Am. Petroleum Inst., Houston Oil Tng. Dirs. (vice chmn. 1984-85). Republican. Lutheran. Avocation: photography. Office: Tenneco Oil Co 1010 Milam St Houston TX 77002

LOWMAN, RODNEY LEWIS, psychologist, educator; b. Oklahoma City, Feb. 10, 1949; s. Raymond Paul and Olga Lowman; m. Linda Richardson, July 21, 1979. B.A. in Psychology, U. Okla., 1973; B.S. in Bus., Okla. State U., 1969; M.A. in Psychology, Mich. State U., 1975, Ph.D. in Psychology, 1979. Lic. psychologist, Tex. Asst. prof. psychology, asst. research scientist Inst. Social Research, mem. staff funded research project Office Personnel Mgmt., U. Mich., Ann Arbor, 1979-82; asst. prof., dir. designate Ph.D. program cons. psychology N. Tex. State U., Denton, 1982—; dir. corp. assistance program and evaluation and treatment team Houston Child Guidance Ctr., 1985—; pres. Lowman, Richardson & Assocs., Fort Worth, 1982—, Dallas/Fort Worth Orgnl. Psychology Group, 1984-85; cons. in field. Contbr. articles to profl. jours. Served to capt. USAF, 1969-72. Rochester Area Hosp. Corps. grantee, 1981-82. Mem. Am. Psychol. Assn., Soc. Indsl. and Organizational Psychology (head com. profl. affairs of clin. psychology sect.). Home: 2532 6th Ave Fort Worth TX 76110 Office: Houston Child Guidance Ctr 3214 Austin St Houston TX 77004

LOWNDES, JOHN FOY, lawyer; b. Medford, Mass., Jan. 1, 1931; s. Charles L. B. and Dorothy Foy L.; children: Elizabeth Anne, Amy Scott, John Patrick, Joseph Edward; m. Rita Davies, Aug. 18, 1983. B.A., Duke U., 1953, LL.B., 1958. Bar: Fla. 1958. Practice, Daytona Beach, Fla., 1958; practice, Orlando, Fla., 1959-69; sr. ptnr., chmn. bd. dirs. Lowndes, Drosdick, Doster, Kantor & Reed, P.A., Orlando, 1969—; chmn. bd. dirs. Atlantic Bank Orlando, 1979-82; mem. adv. bd. Atlantic Nat. Bank Fla., 1982—. Trustee Loch Haven Art Ctr.; bd. visitors Duke U.; mem. adv. bd. Coll. Bus. Adminstrs. U. Central Fla. Served to capt. USMC, 1953-55. Mem. So. Fed. Tax Inst. (founding trustee). Republican. Roman Catholic. Clubs: Orlando Country, Citrus, University (Orlando, Fla.). Office: Lowndes Drosdick Doster Kantor & Reed PA Box 2809 Orlando FL 32802

LOWREY, E. JAMES, food service company executive; b. Lubbock, Tex., Feb. 21, 1928; s. E. J. and Sarah Ruth (Cooper) L.; m. Stella Jean Oates, Apr. 28, 1950; children—Jane Lynwood Tierney, Ernest James. B.B.A., U. Tex., 1949. C.P.A., Tex. With Howard T. Cox & Co., Austin, Tex., 1949-51; ptnr. Frazer & Torbet, Austin, 1951-55, 59-70; with Elgin-Butler Brick Co., Austin, 1955-59; sr. v.p.-fiduciary River Oaks Bank & Trust Co., Houston, 1971-73; exec. v.p. fin. and adminstrn. Sysco Corp., Houston, 1978—, v.p. fin., treas., 1973-76, sr. v.p. adminstrn. and fin., 1976-78, also dir.; dir. Tex. Commerce Bank-Tanglewood, Houston, 1983—. Mem. Am. Inst. C.P.A.s, Tex. Soc. C.P.A.s (pres. Houston chpt. 1970-71). Republican. Presbyterian. Office: Sysco Corp 1177 W Loop S Houston TX 77027

LOWREY, ROBERT ALLEN, geography and human resources consultant, researcher; b. Oxford, Miss., Sept. 20, 1936; s. Edwin Stovall and Anna Jane (Allen) L.; m. Patricia Ann Dusch, May 11, 1974. B.A., U. Miss., 1958, M.A., 1963; Ph.D., Johns Hopkins U., 1969. Project dir. CONSAD Research Corp., Pitts., 1969-74, sr. researcher, part-time 1974-81; cons., Rockdale, Tex., 1981—; research asst. Nat. Bur. Standards, Washington, 1967-68. Author: (with others) A Study of Public Works Investment in the United States, 1980, A Subject Reference: Benefit Cost Analysis of Toxic Substances, 1977. Actor Rockdale Community Players, 1983. Mem. AAAS, Am. Statis. Assn., Rockdale Tennis Assn. Avocations: horticulture; camping. Home and Office: 1400 Yokley Rd Rockdale TX 76567

LOWREY, RUSSELL HARMON, orthodontist; b. Montgomery, Ala., Mar. 21, 1942; s. Allen Benjamin and Lillian (Russell) L.; m. Sherry Delane McCain, May 25, 1968. B.S. in Physics, U. Ala., 1963, D.M.D. with honors, 1967, cert. orthodontics, 1971. Practice dentistry specializing in orthodontics, Huntsville, Ala., 1971—. Served to capt. USAF, 1967-69. Mem. ADA, Am. Assn. Orthodontists, So. Soc. Orthodontists, Ala. Orthodontic Assn. Republican. Baptist. Avocation: computers. Home: 2706 Downing St Huntsville AL 35801 Office: 2319 Whitesburg Dr Huntsville AL 35801

LOWRIE, ALLEN, geologist; b. Washington, Dec. 30, 1937; s. Allen and Mary (Green) L.; m. Mildred C. McDaniel, Feb. 2, 1985; 1 child from previous marriage, Tanya Anne. B.A., Columbia U., 1962. Cert. Assn. Profl. Geol. Scientists. Geologist, Lamont Doherty Geol. Obs., Palisades, N.Y., 1963-68; geologist U.S. Naval Oceanographic Office, NSTL Station, Miss., 1968-81, oceanographer, 1983—; geologist Mobil Oil Corp., New Orleans, 1981-83; cons. Mobil Research & Devel. Corp., Dallas, Sci. Applications Inc., McLean, Va., Geo-Cons Internat., Inc., Kenner, La., Seagull Internat. Exploration Inc., Houston, Planning Systems, Inc., Slidell, La., Corporacion Miners de Cerro Colorado, Panama City, Hotel Drotama, Santa Marta, Colombia, others. Contbr. articles to profl. jours. Mem. Am. Assn. Petroleum Geologists, Soc. Econ. Paleontologists and Mineralogists, N.Y. Acad. Scis., Am. Geophys. Union, Miss. Acad. Sci., Naval Inst., Sierra Club, Sigma Xi. Episcopalian. Avocations: reading; hiking; ranching. Home: RFD 1 Box 164 Salem Community Goss Rd Picayune MS 39466

LOWRY, JANET ELIZABETH HUBER, sociology educator, researcher; b. Chgo., Feb. 12, 1950; d. William Alfred and Jane McAfee (Parker) Huber; m. Thomas Andrew Lowry, June 4, 1971; children—Katharine, Peter. B.A. in Math., Hanover Coll., 1971; M.A. in Sociology, U. N.C., 1973, Ph.D. in Sociology, 1976. Instr., asst. Kirkland Coll., Clinton, N.Y., 1975-78; asst. prof. sociology Hamilton Coll., Clinton, 1978-83, Austin Coll., Sherman, Tex., 1983—. Bd. dirs. Clinton Child Care Ctr., N.Y., 1979-82; del. Tex. Democratic Conv., 1984; pres. Coll. Child Care Ctr., Sherman, 1984-86; mem. Jefferson PTA, Sherman, 1983—. NIMH fellow, 1971-75; grantee Hamilton Coll., 1981-83, City of Utica Bur. Sr. Citizens, 1982; Huber grantee Kirkland Coll. 1976-77. Mem. Am. Sociol. Assn., Gerontol. Soc. Am., Southwestern Social Sci. Assn., Population Assn. Am., SW Soc. Aging. Presbyterian. Avocations: swimming; softball; sailing; knitting. Home: 1008 N Harrison Ave Sherman TX 75090 Office: Austin Coll Box 1641 900 N Grand Ave Sherman TX 75090

LOWRY, LEO ELMO, former petroleum exec.; b. Utopia, Kans., Dec. 4, 1916; s. Nim Roderick and Marticia (Veach) L.; B.A., Okla. A&M Coll., 1937; m. Elizabeth Watson, Sept. 5, 1940; children—Richard Clark, John Christopher, Janet Kaye. With Creole Petroleum Corp., Caracas, Venezuela, 1937-71, exec. v.p., 1961-64, pres., 1964-71; pres. Esso Inter-Am., Inc., Coral Gables, Fla., 1971-77.

LOWRY, MICHAEL BRADFORD, architect; b. Norfolk, Va., Sept. 4, 1950; s. Bradford and Margaret (Bullard) L. B.S. with honors, N.C. State U., 1972; M.Arch., Ga. Inst. Tech., 1977. Project architect Dennis & Dennis, Macon, Ga., 1977-79, John J. Harte, Atlanta, 1979-80; project architect Cooper, Carry & Assocs., Atlanta, 1980—. Mem. AIA. Republican. Baptist. Lodge: Sandy Springs Optimists (sec.-treas. 1980-82, pres. 1982-83, lt. gov. 1983-84). Home: 1310 Woodcliff Dr Dunwoody GA 30338 Office: 3520 Piedmont Rd Suite 200 Atlanta GA 30305

LOY, JOHN WOOTEN, retired laboratory administrator; b. Knoxville, Tenn., Aug. 31, 1919; s. John Wooten and Martha (Hawkins) L.; m. Dorothy Ina Spann, May 30, 1945; 1 child, Martha Denise. Services coordinator Oak Ridge Nat. Labs., 1943-85; ret., 1985. Republican. Presbyterian. Lodge: Masons. Active in devel. of atomic bomb. Avocation: sports. Home: 3113 Lafayette Rd Knoxville TN 37921

LOY, SAMUEL ELLSWORTH, III, drilling contractor; b. Muskogee, Okla., Dec. 2, 1932; s. Samuel Ellsworth and Wahlelle (Parks) L.; B.S. in Mech. Engring., Okla. State U., 1954; m. Mary Sue Sprague, Apr. 5, 1954; children—Stephen, Charles, Samuel, Mark. Drilling ops. mgr. Exxon Co., U.S.A., Houston, 1954-78; v.p., gen. mgr. Progress Drilling and Marine, Houston, 1978-80; v.p., gen. mgr. ATCO Drilling Inc., Houston, 1980-81, pres. ATCO Energy Inc., 1981—. Served to 1st lt. U.S. Army, 1955-57. Recipient Bausch and Lomb Sci. award, 1950; registered profl. engr., Tex., Okla. Mem. Internat. Assn. Drilling Contractors (dir.), Soc. Petroleum Engrs. (disting. lectr. 1983-84), Am. Petroleum Inst. (prodn. exec. com.), Blue Key, Sigma Chi, Pi Mu Epsilon, Pi Tau Sigma, Sigma Tau. Republican. Club: University. Patentee in field. Home: 2910 Manila Houston TX 77043 Office: 10590 Westoffice Dr Houston TX 77042

LOYD, HAROLD JAMES, economics educator; b. Springfield, Mo., July 20, 1944; s. Claud H. and Esther Loyd; m. Rowena Sharp, Dec. 15, 1971. B.S., SW Mo. State U., 1966; M.S., U. Mo., 1968, Ph.D., 1971. Prof. econs., chmn. div. bus. Abraham Baldwin Agrl. Coll., Tifton, Ga. Mem. Tifton C. of C., Ga. Bus. Edn. Assn., Ga. Assn. Econ. Educators. Mem. Assembly of God Ch. Club: Toastmasters (pres. 1973). Lodge: Kiwanis (pres. 1980, sec. 1982—). Office: Dept Bus Administrn Abraham Baldwin Agrl Coll Moore Hwy Tifton GA 31794

LOYD, LOYE CARROLL, glass company executive; b. Yantis, Tex., May 19, 1926; s. Edward M. and Ava (Gilbreath) L.; student So. Meth. U., 1948-51; m. Barbara Ray, Feb. 16, 1952; children—Stanley Alan, Terry Ray. Mgr., Mid-West Glass Co., Midland, Tex., 1955-62; pres. Glasco Glass Co., Inc., Midland, 1962—, Temple Glass & Mirror Co., Inc. (Tex.), 1969—, Bell Glass & Mirror Co., Killeen, Tex., 1970—, El Paso Glass & Mirror Co., Inc. (Tex.), 1970—, Killeen Glass & Mirror Co., 1974—; sec.-treas. Barber Glass & Mirror Co., Inc., Big Spring, Tex., 1968—; dir. Tex. Glass Distbrs., Inc., Ft. Worth, Glass Shack, Inc., Midland; pres. Odessa Glass & Mirror Co., Inc. (Tex.); dir. Eastex Glass Co. Inc., Nacogdoches, Tex., Western Glass & Mirror Co., El Paso, Glass Wholesalers, Inc., Houston, Big Spring Auto Glass Co., Inc., City Auto Glass Co., Inc., Hobbs, N.Mex., Mid-West Door & Window Co., Inc., Midland, Tex., Odessa Door & Window Co., Inc. (Tex.), Stockton Glass & Mirror Co., Inc., Ft. Stockton, Tex., Ave. Glass Co., Inc., Temple, Tex., City Glass & Mirror Co., Hobbs, N.Mex., Quality Glass & Mirror Co., Big Spring, Tex., Tyler Mirror & Glass Co. (Tex.). Served with USNR, 1943-46. Mem. Assembly of God Ch. Club: Rotary (sec. 1965-66). Home: 2503 Dartmouth Midland TX 79705 Office: 24 W Industrial Loop Midland TX 79701

LOYD, OLIVER HERBERT, emergency medicine and aerospace medicine physician; researcher; b. Dec. 23, 1945; s. Oliver Cornelius and Glenda Ione (Diggins) L.; m. Donna Louise Hutton, July 7, 1975; children—Tara Louise, Olivia Brooke, Haley Hutton. B.A. in Zoology, W.Va. U., 1967, M.D., 1976; M.P.H., Johns Hopkins U., 1980. Intern U. Ky., 1976-77, resident in emergency medicine, 1977-78; resident in aerospace medicine Wright State U., 1981-83; emergency medicine physician, Kings Daus. Hosp., Ashland, Ky., 1978-83, St. Elizabeth Hosp., Dayton, Ohio, 1981-82, Miami Valley Hosp., Dayton, 1981-83, St. Elizabeth Hosp., Beaumont, Tex., 1983—; research on application CPR techniques in space Kennedy Space Ctr., Fla., 1983—. Served to capt. USAF, 1967-72; mem. Res. Decorated D.F.C. (2), Air medal (15),

Purple Heart. Mem. Aerospace Med. Assn., Am. Coll. Emergency Physicians. Home: 4750 Dunleith St Beaumont TX 77706

LOZIER, CYNTHIA WOOLEY, physician; b. Mobile, Ala., Sept. 10, 1948; d. Samuel Oliphant and Mary Emma (Chambers) Wooley; m. Phillip Blocker, Feb. 18, 1966 (div. June 1972); m. Mark Davis Lozier, Dec. 15, 1978; children—Darren, Nancy, Joshua. B.S. in Chemistry, U. South Ala., 1974, M.D., 1979. Intern in surgery U. South Ala., Mobile, 1979-80; physician, med. dir. Mostellar Med. Clinic, Bayou La Batre, Ala., 1980-83; practice gen. medicine, Mobile, 1983—; assoc. dir. Famlicare Med. Ctr., 1986; mem. staff Knollwood Park Hosp., Springhill Meml. Hosp., Mobile Infirmary, Doctors Hosp.; mem. staff dept. community medicine U. Ala.-Birmingham; med. dir. Grandbay Nursing Home, Midsouth Home Health Assn., 1983-84. Served with USPHS, 1980-83. Recipient Commd. Officer award USPHS, 1982, Outstanding Career Woman award, 1984. Mem. AMA, Med. Assn. State Ala., Mobile County Med. Soc., So. Med. Assn., Mobile C. of C. Roman Catholic. Club: Zonta. Office: Cynthia W Lozier MD 3401 Medical Park Dr Mobile AL 36609

LUBOW, JAY ALAN, architectural-interior designer, urban planner; b. Bethpage, N.Y., July 10, 1957; s. Murray Harry and Marion (Wald) L. B.S. in design, Clemson U., 1979; M.Arch., U. Mich., 1982, M.Urban Planning, 1982. Assoc. designer LSK Designs, Inc., N.Y.C., 1979-80; sr. assoc. Enplanar, Inc., New Orleans, 1983-85; pres. Spatial Effects, New Orleans, 1984—; assoc. designer Hershberg & Assocs., Inc., New Orleans, 1985—; interior cons. MIA Assocs., Inc., Garden City, N.Y., 1983; urban cons. Planning Dept. Ann Arbor, Mich., 1982. Mem. Am. Soc. Interior Designers (assoc.). Jewish. Avocations: furniture and lighting design; painting; writing. Home and Office: 605 Julia St Apt B New Orleans LA 70130

LUBRANT, BARRY MICHAEL, controller, accountant; b. West Point, N.Y., Sept. 19, 1952; s. Anthony John and Jeanne (Cina) L.; m. Gail Baird, Nov. 27, 1983. B.B.A. in Acctg., U. Ga., 1977. C.P.A., Ga. Staff acct. Wolf & Co., C.P.A.s, Atlanta, 1977-78; sr. acct. Anderson, Hunt & Co., C.P.A.s, Atlanta, 1978-79; ops. analyst Dart & Kraft Inc., Atlanta, 1979-83; controller North Ga. Rendering Co., Cumming, 1983—; income and estate tax cons., Atlanta, 1978—. Mem. Am. Inst. C.P.A.s, Ga. Soc. C.P.A.s, Acad. Internat. Bus. Republican. Home: 315 Wood Creek Ct Roswell GA 30076 Office: North Ga Rendering Co Route 12 Box 490 Cumming GA 30130

LUCAS, AUBREY KEITH, university pres.; b. State Line, Miss., July 12, 1934; s. Keith Caldwell and Audelle Margaret (Robertson) L.; B.S., U. So. Miss., 1955, M.A., 1956; Ph.D., Fla. State U., 1966; m. Ella Frances Ginn, Dec. 19, 1955; children—Margaret Frances, Keith Godbold (dec.), Martha Carol, Alan Douglas, Mark Christopher. Asst. dir. reading clinic U. So. Miss., 1955-56, dir. admissions, 1957-61, registrar, 1963-69, dean Grad. Sch., 1970-71; instr. Hinds Jr. Coll., Raymond, Miss., 1956-57; pres. Delta State Coll., Cleveland, Miss., 1971-75, U. So. Miss., Hattiesburg, 1975—; bd. dirs. Am. Assn. State Colls. and Univs., 1983—, chmn.-elect, 1984-85; bd. dirs. Am. Council on Edn., 1983-85; Miss. rep. So. Regional Edn. Bd., mem. exec. bd., 1983—; bd. dirs. Pine Burr area Boy Scouts Am.; past chmn. Miss. Arts Commn.; past Miss. crusade chmn. Am. Cancer Soc.; conf. lay leader United Meth. Ch., 1980—. Mem. Newcomen Soc. N.Am., PTO, Hattiesburg C. of C. (dir.), Miss. Assn. Colls. (pres. 1979-80), Miss. Forestry Assn., Miss. Econs. Council (chmn. 1982-83), Omicron Delta Kappa, Phi Kappa Phi, Pi Gamma Mu, Pi Tau Chi, Kappa Delta Pi, Phi Delta Kappa, Kappa Pi, Sigma Phi Epsilon, Phi Theta Kappa (hon. mem. nat. bd.). Clubs: Red Red Rose, Hub City Kiwanis. Author: The Mississippi Legislature and Mississippi Public Higher Education, 1890-1960; contbg. author: A History of Mississippi, 1973. Address: Box 5001 So Sta U So Miss Hattiesburg MS 39406

LUCAS, FRED VANCE, university administrator, pathology educator; b. Grand Junction, Colo., Feb. 7, 1922; s. Lee H. and Katharine W. (Vance) L.; m. Rebecca Ross Dudley, Dec. 21, 1948; children—Fred Vance, Katherine Dudley Lucas Volk. A.B., U. Calif., 1942; M.D., U. Rochester, 1950. Diplomate Am. Bd. Anatomic and Clin. Pathology. Intern, Strong Meml. Hosp., Rochester, N.Y., 1950-51, resident in pathology, 1951-54; vet. postgrad. fellow in pathology U. Rochester, 1950-51, asst. in pathology, 1951-53, Lilly fellow in pathology, 1953-54, instr. pathology, 1953-54, asst. prof., 1954-55; assoc. prof. pathology Columbia U. Coll. Physicians and Surgeons, N.Y.C., 1955-60; assoc. attending pathologist Presbyn. Hosp., N.Y.C., 1955-60; prof., chmn. dept. pathology U. Mo. Sch. Medicine, Columbia, 1960-77, research assoc. Space Sci. Research Ctr., 1964-70; prof. pathology Vanderbilt U., Nashville, 1977—, dir. med. services, assoc. dean Sch. Medicine, 1977-79, acting exec. dir. hosp., 1977, 81-83, assoc. chancellor for med. affairs, 1979—; cons. USPHS-NIH, 1967, U.S. AID-AMA, Vietnam Med. Edn. Project, 1967-75; cons., vis. scientist Health Services and Mental Health Adminstrn., Washington, 1969-71, cons., 1972-75; cons. Nat. Acad. Sci., Washington, 1975-77; del. World Health Assembly, Geneva, 1971; bd. dirs. Univs. Assoc. for Research and Edn. in Pathology, Bethesda, Md., 1972-79. Served with AUS, 1942-46. Recipient Lederle Faculty award, 1954-56; Columbia U. Disting. Service award, 1967; Edn. and Social Affairs medal South Vietnam, 1968, Student Exec. Com. Service award U. Mo., 1975. Fellow Am. Soc. Clin. Pathologists, Am. Coll. Pathologists (state commr. for Mo. and Ark. inspection and accreditation program 1975-77); mem. Am. Pathology Assn., Internat. Acad. Pathology, Harvey Soc., Sigma Xi. Democrat. Roman Catholic. Home: Apt 302 Box 48 3901 Harding Rd Nashville TN 37205 Office: D-3300 Medical Center North Vanderbilt U Nashville TN 37232

LUCAS, GEORGE HOYT, JR., marketing educator; b. Kansas City, Mo., Nov. 7, 1953; s. George H. and Dorothy B. (Harmon) L.; m. Linda Jo Curia, July 4, 1981. B.S., U. Mo., 1976, M.B.A., 1979, Ph.D., 1983. Sales rep. Am. Hosp. Supply Corp., Corpus Christi, and Kansas City, Mo., 1976-77; area sales rep. Pitney Bowers Corp., Kansas City, Mo., 1977; asst. prof. mktg. Tex. A&M U., College Station, 1982—. Contbr. articles to profl. jours. Mem. Am. Mktg. Assn., Acad. Mktg. Sci., Am. Inst. for Decision Scis., Omicron Delta Epsilon. Methodist. Home: 1302 Van Horn Dr College Station TX 77840 Office: Tex A&M U Mktg Dept College Station TX 77843

LUCAS, J. J., ednl. adminstr.; b. Prentiss, Miss., June 16, 1932; s. Frank and Josephine R. (Stephens) L.; B.S., Alcorn State U., 1958; M.S., Bradley U., 1960; S.Ed., U. Ill., 1974; Ph.D., U. Mo., 1978. Tchr. indsl. arts Bay St. Louis Schs., 1958-61; coordinator vocat. edn. Columbus (Miss.) Schs., 1961-67; dir. vocat. tech. edn. Utica (Miss.) Jr. Coll., 1968-71; dir. vocat. tech. edn. Copiah Lincoln Jr. Coll., Fayette, Miss., 1971-79; dir. vocat. tech. edn. Holmes County Schs., Lexington, Miss., 1979—. Served with U.S. Army, 1954-56. Mem. Am. Vocat. Assn., Nat. Assn. Advancement Black Ams. in Vocat. Edn., Miss. Assn. Vocat. Educators, NEA, AAUP, ACLU, NAACP, Phi Delta Kappa. Democrat. Baptist. Club: Masons, Elks. Home: PO Box 932 Brookhaven MS 39601

LUCE, CHARLES MCCABE, public relations consultant; b. Port Huron, Mich., Mar. 11, 1931; s. Charles M. and Dorothy Jessie (Martin) L.; m. Dorothea M. Leveille, June 12, 1954; children—Stephen, Elizabeth, William, Cynthia, David, Mark (dec.). B.S., U.S. Mil. Acad., 1954; M.A. in Pub. Relations, U. Wis., 1968. Commd. 2d. lt., inf., U.S. Army, 1954, advanced through grades to lt. col., 1968, ret., 1974; dir. pub. affairs and exec. asst. to state commr. S.C. Dept. Mental Retardation, Columbia, 1974-82; owner, prin. Charles M. Luce & Assocs., pub. relations cons., Columbia, 1982—. Chmn. adv. bd. Fairwold Ctr., Columbia, 1980—. Decorated Bronze Star, Air medal, Vietnamese Cross of Gallentry. Mem. Pub. Relations Soc. Am. (accredited), Am. Assn. Mental Deficiency (exec. bd. southeastern region), S.C. Pub. Relations Soc. (exec. bd.). Roman Catholic. Home: 3502 Deerfield Dr Columbia SC 29204 Office: PO Box 4711 Columbia SC 29240

LUCHT, SONDRA MOORE, state senator; b. Stumptown, W.Va., Dec. 12, 1942; d. Arthur Jackson and Lucille (Cain) Moore II; m. William Lucht; 1 son, Carl Joseph. B.A., Glenville State Coll.; M.A., Marshall U.; postgrad. James Madison U. Mem. W. Va. Senate, Charleston, 1982—. Mem. NOW (pres. W.Va. 1977-82). Democrat. Office: W VA Senate State Capitol Charleston WV 25305*

LUCIER, JAMES ALFRED, advertising executive; b. Grand Forks, N.D., Feb. 5, 1920; s. Alfred Joseph and Mildred Perry (Fahar) L.; B.A., U. Minn., 1946; postgrad. So. Meth. U., 1965; m. Catherine Belle Stiles, June 11, 1961; children—John, Jane, James Alfred. Sales exec. Ft. Smith (Ark.) Times, 1946-47; sales mgr. Sta. KRKN, Ft. Smith, 1947-48; dir. advt. Fayetteville (Ark.) Times, 1948-51; sales exec. San Antonio Express, 1952-53; mgr. Sunday mag. Dallas Times, 1953-65; dir. advt. and pub. relations Home Furniture Co., Dallas, 1965-81; dir. sales and advt. Smith Furniture Co., Dallas, 1981-85; mktg. dir. Southwest Home Furnishings Assn., 1985—; owner Lucier Assos. Advt., Dallas, 1965—. Unit chmn. United Way, 1965—; precinct chmn. Democratic Party, 1974—; mem. bd. Dem. Com. of Rep. Govt., 1974-80; pres., bd. dirs. Dallas council USO; mem. Greater Dallas Sesquicentennial Com., 1982—. Served with inf., AUS, 1942-44, USAAF, 1944-45, USAF, 1951-52. Decorated Air medal with 2 oak leaf clusters. Mem. Retail Furniture Assn. Greater Dallas (pres. 1971-72, 83-84, dir. 1968-85), Retail Furniture Assn. S.W. (dir. 1977-79), Dallas C. of C., Sigma Delta Chi, Theta Chi. Episcopalian (vestry 1976-79). Clubs: Exchange (pres. E.Dallas 1967, pres. Tex. dist. 1969-70, nat. dir. 1970-72, chmn. nat. edn. com. 1974-76, nat. fin. com. 1977-79, nat. pub. relations com. 1980-81, 84-85), U. Minn. Alumni (past pres.), Vagabond, Dallas Magic (past pres.). Home: 6942 Meadow Lake Dallas TX 75214 Office: 110 World Trade Ctr PO Box 581207 Dallas TX 75258

LUCK, RICHARD STUART, rehabilitation counseling educator; b. Richmond, Va., Apr. 8, 1944; s. Stuart Mercer and Mildred Woodlon (Schultz) L.; m. Ann Dudley Brooks, June 16, 1973. B.A., U. Richmond, 1966; M.S., Va. Commonwealth U., 1968, Ed.D., U. Va., 1975. Lic. profl. counselor, Va.; cert. rehab. counselor; nat. cert. counselor. Dir. regional rehab. continuing edn. program Va. Commonwealth U., Fishersville, 1977-82, asst. prof. rehab. counseling, Richmond, 1976-82, assoc. prof., 1982—; assoc. PSI Therapy Ctr., Richmond, 1983—; allied health prof. Charter Westbrook Hosp., Richmond, 1983—. Co-editor: (with W. Emener and S. Smits) Rehabilitation Administration and Supervision, 1981. Active mem. Ptnrs. of Ams., 1985. Recipient Rehab. Manpower award Nat. Rehab. Assn. Mid-Atlantic Region, 1981. Mem. Am. Psychol. Assn., Am. Assn. Counseling and Devel., Am. Rehab. Counseling Assn., Va. Counseling Psychol. Assn., Nat. Vocat. Guidance Assn., Assn. of Psychol. Type, Roadrunners Club, Nat. Assn. Watch and Clock Collectors. Episcopalian. Avocations: watch and clock collecting; running; hunting; fishing; sailing. Office: Va Commonwealth U 921 W Franklin St Richmond VA 23284

LUCKHARDT, JACK HENRY, JR., safety engineer; b. Balt., May 20, 1955; s. Jack Henry and Melba Christine (Potz) L.; m. Virginia Joan Pupillo, Aug. 6, 1977; children—Jack Henry III, Karolyn Marie. B.S., U. Md., 1978. Cert. safety profl., Fla. Safety engr. Maritime Co., Arlington, Va., 1976-78; supt. safety Taylor Bros., Inc., Evansville, Ind., 1978-80; exec. loss control rep. Argonaut Ins. Co., Phoenix, 1980-83; loss control. rep. Cigna Corp., Tampa, Fla., 1983; corp. safety mgr. Keller Industries, Inc., Miami, Fla., 1984—. Active Kingsville Vol. Fire Co., Md., 1972-79; instr. ARC, Balt., 1975-77. Mem. Am. Soc. Safety Engrs. (pres. S. Fla. chpt. 1985—). Republican. Lutheran. Avocations: flying; music. Office: Keller Industries Inc 18000 State Rd 9 Miami FL 33162

LUCKHARDT, MILDRED COOK, home economics educator; b. Pa., Aug. 3, 1919; d. John Quincy Adams and Etta Mae (Beatty) Cook; children—Joan, John, Louis, Wade. B.S., Carnegie-Mellon U., 1941, M.S., 1966; Ph.D., U. Pitts., 1972. Tchr., Pitts. Pub. Schs., 1961-72; assoc. prof. edn. Manchester Coll., North Manchester, Ind., 1973-75; faculty home econs. U. W.Va., Morgantown, 1975-76; faculty, head dept. East Tex. State U., Commerce, 1976—. U. Pitts.-Women's grantee, 1972. Mem. AAUW (pres. 1978-79), Assn. Devel. Computer Based Instrl. Systems, Assn. Adminstrn. Home Econs., Nat. Council Adminstr. Home Econs., Am. Home Econs. Assn., Tex. Home Econs. Assn., Vocat. Homemaking Assn. Tex. Am. Vocat. Assn., Am. Research Assn., ACLU, Tex. Abortion Rights League, Phi Kappa Delta. Democrat. Presbyterian. Author: Everyone Guesses, 1974. Home: 5811 Pineland Dr #7131 Dallas TX 75231 Office: Dept Home Econs East Tex State U Commerce TX 75428

LUCKSINGER, HENRY CHARLES, JR., periodontist; b. Austin, Tex., Dec. 16, 1934; s. Henry Charles and Mary (Holt) L.; m. Annette Smith, July 28, 1956; children—Laurie Ann, Henry Clay. D.D.S., U. Tex.-Houston, 1957; postgrad. Georgetown U., 1964-65. Gen. practice dentistry, Austin, 1957-58; commd. capt. U.S. Army, 1958, advanced through grades to col., 1973; served with Dental Corps, Heidelberg, Fed. Republic Germany, 1958-61, Vietnam, 1968-69; periodontal resident Letterman Army Gen. Hosp., 1972-74; dentist Tex. Dept. Correction, Gatesville, 1981—. Mem. Am. Acad. Periodontology, ADA. Republican. Methodist. Home: PO Box 1609 Trinity TX 75862

LUDEMAN, DOUGLAS HENRY, banker; b. Bklyn., Oct. 2, 1930; s. Henry Frederick and Florence (Smith) L.; B.S. in Applied Econs., Yale U., 1952; certificate Stonier Grad. Sch. Banking; Rutgers U., 1972; m. Mary Joanne Dancy, June 15, 1952; children—Douglas Henry, Daniel J. Stock trader Ohio Co., Columbus, 1956; securities trader and analyst First Nat. Bank, Miami, Fla., 1957-59, mgr. bond dept., 1959-60; mgr. municipal bond dept. South Fla. region Goodbody & Co., Miami, 1960-64; regional instl. sales Hayden Stone, Inc., Ft. Lauderdale, Fla., 1965; with United Va. Bank, Richmond, 1965-76, v.p., 1969-71, sr. v.p., 1971, exec. v.p., 1972-76, vice chmn., 1976-78; exec. v.p. United Va. Bankshares, Inc., 1976-78, pres., 1978—; pres. United Va. Bank, 1980—; dir. UV Mortgage Corp., UV Leasing Corp., Lane Co., Altavista, Va.; mem. Gov.'s Adv. Bd. Revenue Estimates, vice pres. United Way Greater Richmond; bd. dirs. Central Richmond Assn., Valentine Mus.; bd. dirs. Mary Baldwin Coll.; rector, bd. dirs. Va. Commonwealth U. Served with AUS, 1952-54; Korea. Decorated Bronze Star. Mem. Assn. Res. City Bankers, Am. Bankers Assn., Va. Bankers Assn., Nat. Alliance Businessmen. Phi Gamma Delta, Beta Gamma Sigma. Clubs: Richmond First, Forum, Country of Va., Soc. Va. Creepers, Yale Va. Author: The Investment Ments of Big City Bonds, 1972. Office: United Va Bank Box 26665 Richmond VA 23261

LUDENIA, KRISTA, psychologist, health facility administrator; b. Alexandria, Minn., Dec. 20, 1942; d. Dell John and Ethel Agnes (Balder) Ludenia; children—Peter Jonathan, John Thomas, Kristin Ashley. B.A., B.S., Quincy Coll., 1967; M.S., Ind. U., 1969; Ph.D., U. Mo., 1972. Asst. chief alcohol and drug unit VA Med. Ctr., Danville, Ill., 1972-74; clin. psychologist VA Med. Ctr., St. Cloud, Minn., 1974-76, coordinator mental hygiene clinic, 1976-78; chief psychology service VA Med. Ctr., Wichita, Kans., 1978-80; chief psychology service, VA Med. Ctr., Bay Pines, Fla., 1980-82; health systems adminstr. VA Med. Ctr., St. Louis, 1982-84; assoc. med. ctr. dir. VA Med. Ctr., Danville, Ill., 1984—. Recipient Outstanding Student award Quincy Coll., 1967; Dir.'s Commendation for EEO, 1978; Leadership award VA, 1978, 1979; VA Dir.'s Commendation, 1981, 1982. Mem. Am. Psychol. Assn., Nat. Register Health Care Providers. Office: VA Med Ctr Danville IL 61832

LUDWIG, ALLEN CLARENCE, chemical engineer, researcher; b. San Antonio, Nov. 3, 1938; s. Frederick and Eleanora Johanna (Wolff) L.; m. Mary Jo Grothues, Nov. 26, 1960; children—Amy, Allen, Theresa, Elizabeth. B.S. in Chem. Engring., Tex. A&M U., 1960. Registered profl. engr., Tex. Engring. trainee Humble Oil, Pleasanton, Tex., 1959; engr. Monsanto, Texas City, 1960; research chemist U.S. Air Force, Sacramento, 1960-63; engr. SW Research Inst., San Antonio, 1963—; cons. UN, Guatemala, 1969, Agy. for Internat. Devel., Colombia, Panama, Tanzania, Botswana, 1974-77. Author: Elemental Sulfur, 1965. Contbr. articles to profl. jours. Patentee in field. Chmn. St. Luke's Fed. Credit Union Com., San Antonio, 1971—. Served to 1st lt. USAF, 1960-63. Recipient Top 20 Award of Merit Materials Engring., 1981. Mem. Tex. Soc. Profl. Engrs. Roman Catholic. Avocations: hunting; fishing; leatherwork. Home: 5914 Brenda Ln San Antonio TX 78240 Office: SW Research Inst 6220 Culebra Road San Antonio TX 78284

LUDWIG, RAY W., educator; b. Rio, W.Va., June 10, 1941. A.B. in Secondary Edn., Shepherd Coll., Shepherdstown, W.Va., 1964; A.M. in Secondary Adminstrn., W.Va. U., Morgantown, 1966, M.A. in Guidance and Counseling, 1972. Tchr. math. Ohio County Schs., Wheeling, W.Va., 1964-67; tchr. math., asst. prin. Berkeley Springs (W.Va.) High Sch., 1967-68; math. specialist Region II Curriculum Improvement Center, Shepherdstown, 1968-69; dir. spl. projects, coordinator secondary edn. Hardy County Schs., Moorefield, W.Va., 1969-76, English tchr., 1976—. Mem. Nat. W.Va., Hardy County (pres. 1977-78) edn. assns., Assn. for Supervision and Curriculum Devel., Hardy County Tchrs. Assn. (v.p. 1977-78). Certified in secondary edn., secondary adminstrn., counseling and guidance, W.Va. Home: PO Box 570 Moorefield WV 26836 Office: Moorefield High Sch Moorefield WV 26836

LUEDKE, GEORGE WILLIAM, psychiatrist; b. Oak Park, Ill., Nov. 10, 1945; s. William John and Charlyne Faith (Thompson) L.; m. Janet Grace Lauchnor, Dec. 27, 1967 (div. Dec. 1985); children—Benjamin, Katherine, Brian. B.A., Lehigh U., 1967; M.D., Yale U., 1976. Diplomate Am. Bd. Psychiatry and Neurology. Intern U. Pa. Hosp., 1976-77, resident, 1977-80; practice medicine specializing in adolescent and adult psychiatry Assocs. in Psychiatry and Counseling Ltd., Roanoke, 1980—; clin. asst. prof. U. Va., 1983—; chief psychiatry Roanoke Meml. Hosp., Va., 1984-85. Served to capt. USAF, 1969-73. Mem. AMA, Am. Psychiat. Assn., So. Med. Assn., Med. Soc. Va., Psychiat. Soc. Va. (pres. SW chpt.), Roanoke Acad. Medicine, Phi Beta Kappa. Office: Assocs in Psychiatry and Counseling Ltd 1112 2d St SW Roanoke VA 24016

LUEKEN, PATTY WATSON, dietitian, business executive; b. Fayetteville, Ark., Oct. 20, 1953; d. Lavon Verdon and Evelyn Lucille (Bates) Watson; B.S., U. Ark., 1975, M.B.A., 1981; m. Thomas Whitten Lueken, Jan. 27, 1979. Adminstrv. dietitian VA Hosp., North Little Rock, 1976-77; dir. dietetics Central Bapt. Hosp., Little Rock, 1977-80; founder, prin. PAL Assocs.; asst. v.p. Multi Mgmt. Services, Inc., 1984—; with Cons. Dietitians in Health Care Facilities; adj. instr. Henderson State U., Arkadelphia, Ark. Mem. Am. Dietetic Assn. (sec. mgmt. practice group 1985-87), Am. Soc. Hosp. Food Service Adminstrs., Ark. Dietetic Assn. (Young Dietitian of Yr. 1982-83; treas. 1978-80, pres. 1982-83), Alpha Delta Pi. Baptist. Office: 9601 Interstate 630 Little Rock AR 72205

LUFKIN, GAIL ELLEN, insurance company executive; b. LaPorte, Ind., Mar. 4, 1946; d. Edward R. and Dorothy Mae (Wallace) Trigg. B.S., U. S.C., 1966, M.S., 1972; M.B.A., U. Ala.-Birmingham, 1984. Instr. U. S.C., Columbia, 1971-73; mgr. tng. and devel. Blue Cross and Blue Shield, Columbia, 1972-76, dir. tng. and devel., Birmingham, 1976-79, mgr. dept. human resources, 1979-82, v.p. human resources 1983—. Chmn. funding and fin. Childcare Task Force, United Way, Birmingham, 1983-84, bd. dirs., chmn. personnel com. Childcare Resources of Jefferson, Shelby and Walker counties, 1984—; v.p. membership, pres. FORUM, Birmingham, 1984—; mem. adv. bd. Masters in Pub. and Pvt. Mgmt. program Birmingham So. Coll., 1953—. Mem. Am. Soc. Personnel Adminstrs. (v.p. program 1983-84, pres.-elect 1984-85), Am. Compensation Assn., Am. Soc. Tng. and Devel. (human resources exec. council Greater Birmingham chpt.), Birmingham C. of C. (chmn. pub. affairs com. 1985-86, chmn. edn. com. 1985-86), Beta Gamma Sigma, Omicron Delta Epsilon. Clubs: Civitan (founding pres. local chpt. 1984-85), Young Men's Bus. Club (Birmingham) (chmn. Radio Day 1984, chmn. Citizen of Yr. luncheon 1984). Avocations: reading; music; astronomy and astrophysics; volleyball. Office: Blue Cross and Blue Shield of Ala 450 Riverchase Pkwy E Birmingham AL 35298

LUGER, MICHAEL IAN, economics planning and public policy educator, consultant, researcher; b. Phila., Feb. 24, 1950; s. Charles and Anne (Kurland) L.; m. Laura June Bernstein, June 27, 1976; children—Jason David, Emily Diane. A.B. in Architecture and Urban Planning, Princeton U., 1972, M.P.A. in Pub. and Internat. Affairs, 1976; M.C.P. in City and Regional Planning U. Calif.-Berkeley, 1978, Ph.D. in Econs., 1981. Dir. planning Model Cities Bur., Scranton, Pa., 1972-73; profl. officer Greater London Council, 1973-74; cons. Urban Inst., Washington, 1975-76, 85, Berkeley Planning Assocs. (Calif.), 1977, Approach Assocs., Oakland, Calif., 1978, Nat. Ctr. for Econ. Alternatives, Washington, 1979, World Bank, 1986; asst. prof. pub. policy studies and econs. Duke U., Durham, N.C., 1980—, dir. Ctr. for N.C. Policy Research and Planning, 1980-83, dir. grad. studies Dept. Pub. Policy Studies, 1984-85 ; vis. asst. prof., research assoc. dept. econs., Bur. Econ. and Bus. Research, U. Md., College Park, 1983-84; participant White House Conf. on Productivity, 1983. Bd. advisers Nat. Govs. Assn. Ctr. for Governorship and State Policymaking, 1981—; mem. Durham Mayor's Task Force on Transp., 1983; mem. Gov.'s Task Force on Sci. and Tech., 1983-84; mem. North Central Durham Planning Com., 1983-85. Recipient Duke U. Research Council award, 1981-83, 85; U.S. Dept. Labor research grantee, 1983-85; Employment and Tng. Adminstrn. fellow, 1979-80; NSF fellow, 1975-78. Mem. Am. Econs. Assn., Nat. Tax Assn., Assn. Pub. Policy Analysis and Mgmt., Regional Sci. Assn. Jewish. Contbr. articles to profl. jours. Home: 1714 Vista St Durham NC 27701 Office: 4785 Duke Station Durham NC 27706

LUGG, JOSEPHINE ARNS, rehabilitation consultant, psychologist; b. N.Y.C., July 6, 1910; d. Arthur and Sara Isabel (Giles) Arns; m. George Wilson Lugg Sept. 14, 1965 (div. Sept. 1969). Tchr. cert. Phila. Normal Sch., 1932; B.S. in Edn., Temple U., 1935, Ed.M. in Counseling and Guidance, 1953. Ed.D., 1958. Lic. psychologist, Fla.; cert. profl. psychologist. Tchr. elem. pub. and pvt. schs., Phila. area, 1932-38; social case worker Pa. Dept. Pub. Assistance, Phila., 1937-42; head of ballistics unit U.S. Army Ordinance, Phila., 1942-43; employment counselor and employer relations rep Pa. State Employement Service, Phila., 1943-56; dir. vocat. rehab. United Cerebral Palsy, Phila., 1956-59, Miami, Fla., 1959-61; dir. rehab. Goodwill Industries of S. Fla., Miami, 1961-80; rehab. cons. Goodwill Industries Inc. of Broward County, Ft. Lauderdale, Fla., 1980—. Bd. dirs. Epilepsy Found. So. Fla., Miami, 1978—; bd. dirs. treas. Good Living, Inc., Ft. Lauderdale, 1981—; 1st v.p. bd. dirs. Democratic Women's Club of Broward County, 1985—; bd. dirs. UNA/USA, Broward County Chpt., 1984—, bd. dirs., treas. UNA/USA Greater Miami Chpt., 1982—; mem. adv. bd. Goodwill Industries of So. Fla., Inc., Miami, 1980—. Recipient Fellowship award Inst. Phys. Medicine and Sch. Edn., NYU, 1956; named Outstanding Rehab Profl. Dade County Employment of the Handicapped Fla., 1968; recipient Trail Blazer award Women's Com. of One Hundred, Dade County, 1981; award Goodwill Industries of S. Fla., 1981; Humanitarian award Goodwill Industries of Broward County, 1983. Mem. Dade County Psychol. Assn. (sec. 1960-73, treas. 1960-77, award 1978), Am. Psychol. Assn., AAUW, Audubon Soc. Lutheran. Club: Hibiscus (Miami). Lodge: Zonta (pres. Miami chpt. 1976-78, mem. Ft. Lauderdale chpt.). Home: 2424 NE 9th St Apt 303 Fort Lauderdale FL 33304 Office: Goodwill Industries of Broward County 1830 S Federal Hwy Fort Lauderdale FL 33316

LUGO, LONI GRIMECK, insurance company executive; b. Stockton, Calif., Jan. 9, 1948; s. Adam E. and Helen V. (Vega) L.; student psychology Del Mar Coll., 1975-77, U. Corpus Christi (Tex.), 1977-78; diaconate candidate U. Dallas; m. Delpha Gonzales, Oct. 24, 1970; children—Joseph Louis, William Anthony. Sales agt. Allstate Ins. Co., Corpus Christi, 1973-74, asst. dist. sales mgr., 1974-75, dist. sales mgr., 1975-79, sr. dist. sales mgr., Dallas, 1979-80, sales tng. mgr., Irving, Tex., 1980-83, field sales mgr., San Antonio, 1983—; instr. mgmt., U. Corpus Christi, 1978. Bd. dirs. Corpus Christi Little League, 1978; instr. Corpus Christi Jr. C. of C., 1977. Mem. Nat. Assn. Life Underwriters, Am. Soc. Trainers and Developers, Mexican Am. C. of C. Home: 14414 Dark Star San Antonio TX 78248 Office: 10909 Wurzbach San Antonio TX 78230

LUI, KUNG-JONG, statistician; b. Taipei, Republic of China, June 22, 1953; came to U.S., 1976; s. Shung-Wu Lu and Li-Chin Chen; m. Jen-Mei Tung; children—Chen-Hwa, Chen-Hsiang. B.S., Fu-Jen U., Taiwan, 1975; M.A., UCLA, 1977, M.S., 1979, Ph.D., 1982. Teaching asst. UCLA, 1979-82, postdoctoral scholar, 1982-83; statistician Ctrs. for Disease Control, Atlanta, 1983—. Inventor in field. Mem. Am. Statis. Assn. Republican. Avocations: swimming; table tennis. Home: 8555 Colony Club Dr Alpharetta GA 30201 Office: Ctrs for Disease Control 1600 Cliffton Rd NE Atlanta GA 30333

LUIGS, CHARLES RUSSELL, business executive; b. Evansville, Ind., Apr. 4, 1933; s. Charles Anthony and Agnes A. (Russell) L.; m. Mary M. McClaine, Sept. 7, 1957; children—Charles Edwin, James Russell, Carol Lynn, Susan Nadine, Michael Alan. B.S. in Petroleum Engring., U. Tex., 1957; student, St. Edwards U., 1951-52. With U.S. Industries (various locations), 1957-76, v.p., 1969-71, exec. v.p., 1971-74, pres., 1974-76, dir., 1971-76; pres., chief exec. officer, dir. Global Marine, Inc., 1977—, chmn. bd., 1982—; dir. Hydril Co. Mem. Internat. Assn. Drilling Contractors (dir.), Nat. Soc. Profl. Engrs., AIME. Clubs: Houstonian, Houston, Westlake (Houston). Home: PO Box 4577 Houston TX 77210 Office: 811 W 7th St Los Angeles CA 90017 also 777 Eldridge Houston TX 77079*

LUIKART, WILLIAM MCCOLLAM, physician; b. Baton Rouge, Aug. 20, 1921; s. Carl Bryan and Helen Carmelite (Coons) L.; B.S., La. State U., 1943, M.D., 1945; m. Nancy Irene Bird, June 22, 1946; children—William M., Carl S., Nancy B., Helen I. Resident in internal medicine La. State U., 1948-51; practice medicine, Baton Rouge, 1954—; prof. medicine La. State U.; bd. dirs. Am. Heart Assn.; nat. adv. bd. Vols. Am.; mem. state adv. council La. High Blood Pressure Control Program. Served to lt. (j.g.), M.C., USNR. Diplomate Am. Bd. Internal Medicine. Decorated Pro Ecclesia et Pro Pontifice (Vatican); recipient Merit award Am. Heart Assn. Fellow Am. Coll. Cardiology, Council Clin. Cardiology of Am. Heart Assn., Royal Soc. Health; mem. Am. Diabetes Assn., So. Med. Assn., La. Med. Soc. (chmn. com. hypertension, hosp. com.), Cath. Physicians Guild, Nat. Ritual Com., Sigma Chi. Republican. Roman

Catholic. Contbr. articles to med jours. Home: 913 Richland Ave Baton Rouge LA 70806 Office: 4730 North Blvd Baton Rouge LA 70806

LUIS, JUAN FRANCISCO, governor Virgin Islands; b. Viegues, P.R., July 10, 1940; ed. U. P.R.; m. Luz Maria Luis; children—Juan Francisco, Carlota Amalia. Formerly tchr. public schs.; indsl. relations mgr. Litwin Corp.; acct. Burns Internat.; personnel mgr., controller Estate Carlton Hotel; adminstr. personnel office V.I. Dept. Health; V.I. dist. senator, 1972-74; lt. gov. V.I., 1975-78, gov., 1978—. Served in U.S. Army. Mem. Ind. Movement. Office: Office Gov. Govt House Charlotte Amalie VI 00801*

LUISI, KATHY ANN, insurance executive; b. N.Y.C., Sept. 14 1951; d. Anthony John and Frances Mary (Miceli) Luisi; m. Nelson N. D'Antonio, June 2, 1973 (div.). B.A. cum laude, St. Johns U., 1972. Vice pres. EBCO Internat. of Fla., Inc., North Miami, 1973-82, pres., 1982—; broker Ins. Exchange of Ams., Miami, 1982. Sustaining mem. Nat. Republican Congl. Com., Washington, 1982-83. Mem. Fla. Assn. Ins. Agts., Profl. Ins. Agts. Roman Catholic. Office: Ebco Internat of Fla Inc 12550 Biscayne Blvd Suite 404 North Miami FL 33181

LUKAS, GAZE ELMER, accountant; b. Austria, Hungary, Nov. 9, 1907; s. Victor and Theresa (Dinzenberger) L.; came to U.S., 1909, naturalized, 1920; B.S. in Accountancy, U. Ill., 1930, M.S., 1933, J.D., 1956; m. Frances Adelaide Lyman, Nov. 25, 1932; 1 son, Victor Thomas. Instr. U. Ill., Urbana, 1930-35, asst. prof., 1954-55, asso. prof., 1955-56, prof., 1956-69, prof. emeritus, 1969—; dir. fin. U.S. Farm Security Adminstrn., Washington, 1935-42; chief accountant UNRRA, Washington, 1945-46; chief of renegotiation Quartermaster Gen.'s Office, Fgn. Service, State Dept., Rome, New Delhi, 1947-54; partner Paul M. Green & Assos., Bus. Edn. Cons., Champaign, Ill., 1955-68; Elmer Fox vis. prof. accounting Wichita (Kans.) State U., 1970-71; vis. prof. accounting Fla. Tech. U., Orlando, 1968-70, Fla. Atlantic U., Boca Raton, 1971-72; comptroller Palm Beach Atlantic Coll., West Palm Beach, Fla., 1979-81, cons., 1981-85. Mem. County Audit Adv. Bd. of Ill., 1962-68, chmn., 1964-66, recipient pub. service award, 1968. Served to maj. AUS, 1942-45; ETO. Decorated Bronze Star; recipient Meritorious Civilian Service award Q.M. Gen., 1947, Americanism medal Nat. Soc. DAR, 1986. C.P.A., Ill. Mem. Am. Inst. C.P.A.'s, Ill. C.P.A. Soc. (life), Appraisers Assn. Am., Order of Coif, Beta Gamma Sigma, Beta Alpha Psi, Pi Kappa Phi, Phi Eta Sigma, Sigma Alpha Epsilon, Phi Delta Phi, Alpha Kappa Psi. Contbr. articles to profl. jours. Address: 719 Lori Dr #19-210 Palm Springs FL 33461

LUKAT, ROBERT NORTON, manufacturing company executive; b. Terre Haute, Ind., Feb. 7, 1946; s. Robert Timon and Emily Lucile (Ward) L.; m. Suzanne Gilbert Berry, June 22, 1968; children—Robert Berry, Reed Morgan. Student Hampden Sydney Coll., 1964-66; B.Chem. Engring., Ga. Inst. Tech., 1969, M.S. in Metallurgy, 1970. Metallurgist, So. Saw Service, Atlanta, 1972-73, sr. engr., 1973-76, dir. product planning and promotion, 1976-78, gen. mgr., 1978-80, v.p., gen. mgr., 1980—. Mem. Am. Soc. Metals, Am. Welding Soc., Meat Industry Suppliers Assn., Meat Industry and Equipment Assn., Am. Meat Inst., Meat Industry Mfrs. Inst. Presbyterian. Club: South River Hunting. Home: 5843 Foxfield Trail Rex GA 30273 Office: 1594 Evans Dr SW Atlanta GA 30310

LUKIN, PENNY ROSEN, psychologist; b. N.Y.C., May 30, 1949; d. Rishon Seymour Rosen and Marion (Dancis) Dragoon; m. Barry Frederick Beck, Apr. 7, 1979; 1 child, Sonja Lukin-Beck. B.A., Brown U., 1971; M.A., SUNY-Buffalo, 1974, Ph.D., 1979. Lic. psychologist, Ga., Fla. Sr. counselor, dir. Storefront Counseling Ctr., Buffalo, 1978; intern Child and Adolescent Psychol. Ctr., Buffalo, 1978-79; asst. prof. psychology Ga. Southwestern Coll., Americus, 1979-82; clin. psychologist, Americus, Ga., 1980-83, Winter Park and Longwood, Fla., 1983—. Contbr. articles to profl. jours. Mem. Bach Festival Choir, Orlando, Fla., 1983-84; bd. dirs. Profl. Women's Network, Orlando, 1983—. Mem. Am. Psychol. Assn., Ga. Psychol. Assn. (chairperson family and childrens services 1982-83), Southeastern Psychol. Assn., Fla. Psychol. Assn. (pres. Central chpt. 1985-86), Bus. and Profl. Women, Phi Beta Kappa. Club: Oviedo Women's (Fla.). Avocations: singing; tennis; swimming; hiking; skiing. Home: 924 Woodcrest Way Oviedo FL 32765 Office: 210 Lake Ctr 1250 S US Hwy Longwood FL 32750

LUKSIC, MLADEN, mathematician, engineering consultant; b. Zagreb, Yugoslavia, May 20, 1955; came to U.S., 1979; s. Ivan and Ernestine (Drager) L.; m. Robin Jeanneanne Lucky, July 6, 1985. B.S., Zagreb Music Sch., 1974; B.S., U. Zagreb, 1978; M.S., Va. Poly. Inst., 1981; Ph.D., Tex. Tech U., 1984. Engr., cons. Geotehnika, Zagreb, 1978-83; research asst. Va. Poly. Inst., Blacksburg, 1979-82; research asst. Tex. Tech U., Lubbock, 1982-84, asst. prof., 1984-85, U. Tex.-San Antonio, 1985—; engr., cons. UN Geophysics Inst., River Sava Direction, Zagreb, 1979-83. Contbr. articles to profl. jours. Mem. Soc. Indsl. and Applied Math., Am. Math. Soc. Avocations: music, tennis. Office: U Tex Div Math Computer Sci and Systems Design San Antonio TX 78285

LUNA, EUGENE IRVING, III, university administrator, training and development consultant; b. Eden, N.C., Sept. 27, 1949; s. Eugene Irving and Martha Elizabeth (Thacker) L.; m. Shelia Jean Bolick, June 5, 1982. B.A., Roanoke Coll., 1971; G.R.I., U. N.C., 1974; M.A., Appalachian State U., 1981; postgrad. U. Fla., 1984—. Lic. real estate broker, N.C. Realtor, salesman Wall Realtors, Eden, 1971-74, v.p., 1974-79; residence life coordinator Appalachian State U., Boone, N.C., 1981-83; asst. dir. housing U. Fla., Gainesville, 1983—; cons. Nat. Exec. Housekeepers Assn., Gainesville. Mem. traffic planning com. City of Eden, 1976; chmn. United Way, Eden, 1977; pres. Eden Bd. Realtors, 1978. Mem. Nat. Assn. Student Personnel Adminstrs., Am. Assn. Counseling and Devel., Assn. Coll. Personnel Adminstrn. Baptist. Avocations: golf; badminton, tennis; hang-gliding; sailing. Office: U Fla Div Housing Gainesville FL 32611

LUND, JULIE ANN, interior designer, consultant, showroom designer; b. Annapolis, Md., Aug. 26, 1946; d. John Alfred and Lois Eileen (Wallace) Lee; m. Dennis Gust Lund, Aug. 20, 1967; children—Wendy Ann, Kimberly Ann. Student Russell Sage Coll., 1964-66, Phila. Coll. Art, 1970-73; B.S. in Housing and Interior Design, Central State U., Edmond, Okla., 1977. Head interior designer John G. Gann, Huntsville, Ala., 1975; interior designer Myers Haus Interiors, Edmond, Okla., 1977-79; instr. phys. fitness Aerobic D'Lite, Charlotte, N.C., 1980-82; sr. staff interior designer Exclusively Contemporary, Charlotte, 1982-85; furniture showroom designer, High Point, N.C., 1985—; owner, interior designer Julie A. Lund, Interior Design, Matthews, N.C., 1983—. Designer So. Living Show, 1983, 84, 85, 86, Sophisticated Contemporaries, 1985. Mem. Am. Soc. Interior Designers (designer ASID House Necessary Room, Charlotte 1984, dining terr. 1985, and Pinehurst Castle 1984). Republican. Avocations: horseback riding; sailing; snow skiing; running. Office: Julie A Lund Interior Design 3023 Shallowood Ln Matthews NC 28105

LUNDBERG, GUSTAVE HAROLD, mathematician, educator; b. Fremont, Nebr., Sept. 5, 1901; s. Gustave Emil and Clara (Lindquist) L.; B.S., Midland Coll., 1924; M.A., Colo. State Coll., 1937, Vanderbilt U., 1942; Ph.D., George Peabody Coll., 1951; m. Hazel Alice Glenny, Oct. 30, 1939. Instr. Vanderbilt U., Nashville, 1942-45, asst. prof., 1945-53, asso. prof., 1953-56, prof. applied math., 1956-67, prof. emeritus, 1967—; prof. math. Austin Peay State U., 1967-72; faculty participant Boeing Airplane Co., summers 1955-56; research participant Oak Ridge Nat. Lab., summer 1957; faculty George Peabody Coll., summers 1961-62. Mem. Am. Math. Assn., AAAS, Engring. Assn. Nashville, Tenn. Acad. Sci. (pres. 1969), Sigma Xi, Phi Delta Kappa. Editor: Jour. Tenn. Acad. Sci., 1963-66; contbr. articles to profl. jours. Home: 2001 21st Ave S Nashville TN 37212

LUNDBERG, PAULA KATHLEEN, psychologist, educator, researcher; b. Cin., Feb. 27, 1949; d. Christian Walter and Alma Amelia (Bock) Hirsch; m. Charles Andrew, Nov. 6, 1971 (div. 1981). Student Western Coll. for Women, 1967-70; B.S. in Chemistry, Xavier U., 1976; M.A. in Psychology, U. Cin., 1978, Ph.D. in Phys. Psychology, 1980. Spectroscopist Merrell-Nat. Labs., Cin., 1970-73, research asst., 1973-76; research asst. Sleep Lab., Cin., 1976-78; postdoctoral fellow Washington U., St. Louis, 1980-83; asst. prof. psychology U. Tex.-Tyler, 1983—, Hudnall prof., 1985—; specialist in counseling and testing services, Tyler, 1984—; dir. behavioral modification Human Devel. Ctr., Tyler, 1984—. Contbr. articles to profl. jours. Sec., treas., bd. dirs. Smith County Council on Alcoholism and Drug Abuse, Tyler, 1984—; group therapy leader Parents Anonymous, Tyler, 1985; bd. dirs. Smith County chpt. Am. Heart Assn., Tyler, 1984—. Research grantee U. Tex., 1983—. Mem. N.Y. Acad. Scis., Soc. for Neurosci., Am. Psychol. Assn., SW Psychol. Assn., AAAS, Sigma Xi. Lutheran. Avocations: jogging, gardening, canoeing. Home: 2612 S Robertson St Tyler TX 75701 Office: Dept Psychology U Tex 3900 University Blvd Tyler TX 75701

LUNDIN, ROBERT WILLIAM, psychology educator; b. Chgo., Apr. 28, 1920; s. Adolph E. and Agnes (King) L. m. Margaret Waitt, Aug. 8, 1952; children—Sara Jane, Robert King. A.B., DePauw U., 1942; M.A., Ind. U., 1943, Ph.D., 1947. Lic. psychologist, Tenn. Asst. prof. Denison U., Granville, Ohio, 1947-49; assoc. prof. Hamilton Coll., Clinton, N.Y., 1949-64; William R. Kennan, Jr. prof. psychology U. South, Sewanee, Tenn., 1964—; dept. chmn., 1964—. Fellow Am. Psychol. Assn.; mem. S.E. Psychol. Assn., Sigma Xi. Republican. Episcopalian. Club: Ecce Quo Bonum. Author: Personality: An Experimental Approach, 1961; Principles of Psychopathology, 1965; The Study of Behavior, 1965; An Objective Psychology of Music, 1953, rev. edit., 1967, 3d edit., 1985; Personality: A Behavioral Analysis, 1969, rev. edit., 1974, trans. into Portuguese, for Brazilian edit., 1972, 1978; Personality, 1973, trans., 1980; Theories and Systems of Psychology, 1972, rev. edit., 1979, 3d. edit., 1985; contbr. numerous articles to profl. jours.; assoc. editor The Psychological Record. Home: Green's View Rd Sewanee TN 37375 Office: University of the South Sewanee TN 37375

LUNDRIGAN, PAUL JOHN, fine arts educator, administrator; b. N.Y.C., Nov. 26, 1936; s. John Edward and Gladys Emily (Makatura) L.; m. Carol Jean Barrett, Aug. 22, 1964; children—Jeffrey Paul, Erik John, Jennifer Ann. B.A., CUNY-Hunter, 1965; M.F.A., CUNY-Bklyn., 1969; Ph.D., So. Ill. U., 1985. Lectr., technician CUNY-Bklyn., 1966-68; instr. Concord Coll., Athens, W. Va., 1969-72; asst. prof. Coll. Santa Fe, N.Mex., 1972-74, Orange County Community Coll., Middletown, N.Y., 1975; asst. prof., chmn. dept. fine arts High Point Coll., N.C., 1980—. Dir., performer various plays and musicals. Mem. bd. edn. Christ The King Roman Catholic Ch., High Point, 1984—. Served with USAF, 1956-60. Mem. Triad Theater League, N.C. Theater Conf., Acad. Leader, Assn. for Supervision and Curriculum Devel., Speech Communication Assn. Avocations: canoeing; camping; carpentry; painting; dancing. Office: Dept Fine Arts High Point Coll Montlieu Ave High Point NC 27262

LUNNEY, CAROL ANN, college administrator; b. Mpls., Feb. 26, 1943; d. Victor Herbert and Bernice P. (Leiter) Muckenhirn; m. Gerald Hugh Lunney, Aug. 19, 1966; children—Michael Joseph, Colleen Marie, Peter Alan. B.A., U. Minn., 1964; M.S., L.I. U., 1972. Cert. counselor. Social worker Holyoke Day Nursery, Mass., 1966-67; placement cons. C.W. Post Coll., Greenvale, N.Y., 1971-72; dir. Ctr. for Advising and Career Services, Centre Coll., Danville, Ky., 1973—; presenter profl. conf. Ch. organist, Danville. Mem. Am. Coll. Personnel Assn., Coll. Personnel Assn. Ky. (bd. dirs. 1983—), Ky. Coll. Placement Assn. (newsletter editor 1984-85), Nat. Assn. Student Personnel Adminstrs. Home: 2036 Old Lexington Rd Danville KY 40422 Office: Centre Coll Walnut St Danville KY 40422

LUNNEY, DAVID CLYDE, chemistry educator; b. Charleston, S.C., Mar. 7, 1935; s. John Wilberforce and Pearle Bethea (Turbeville) L.; m. Carol Ann Zalewski, Dec. 13, 1970. B.S., U. S.C., 1959, Ph.D., 1965. Registered profl. engr., N.C. Asst. prof. U. S.C., Columbia, 1965-66; research assoc. Duke U., Durham, N.C., 1966-68; asst. prof. East Carolina U., Greenville, N.C., 1968-74, assoc. prof., 1974-80, prof., 1980—. Contbr. articles to profl. jours. Served with USAF, 1953-56. Postdoctoral fellow NIH, 1966-68; grad. fellow NSF, 1961-65. Mem. IEEE, Am. Chem. Soc., Audio Engring. Soc., Phi Beta Kappa. Office: East Carolina U Chemistry Dept Greenville NC 27834

LUNNON, BETTY SHEEHAN (MRS. JAMES LUNNON), ret. librarian; b. Montgomery, Ala., May 29, 1908; d. Merrill Ashurst and Martha (Guice) Sheehan; student U. Ala., 1928, 30, 32-34; A.B., George Washington U., 1938; M.A., Appalachian State Tchrs. Coll., 1959; m. David White, Nov. 27, 1927 (div. 1936); m. James Lunnon, May 13, 1939 (dec. Nov. 1954); 1 dau., Penelope Anne Lunnon Fleeger. Tchr., librarian Hayneville (Ala.) Public Sch., 1927-29, Seale (Ala.) Public Sch., 1929-31, Dadeville (Ala.) Public Sch., 1931-32; case worker Ala. Dept. Public Welfare, Fed. Emergency Relief Adminstrn., 1933-35; statis. cataloger U.S. Govt., 1937-38; librarian Miami Edison Sr. High Sch., 1938-42, Fairlawn Elem. Sch., 1952-54; supr. Dade County Sch. Libraries, Miami, 1954-68; supr. libraries Dept. Edn., Pago Pago, Am. Samoa, 1968-73; librarian Cushman Sch., Miami, Fla., 1974-81, Gulliver Acad., 1982-83; asst. prof. U. Miami, summer 1960, evening sch., 1961, 63-66; prof. summer workshop Drexel Inst., 1965; library com. cons. Field Enterprises Ednl. Corp. Gray Lady ARC, 1949-52; bd. dirs. Fla. Hearing and Speech Center, 1962-63. Mem. AAUW (br. v.p. 1950-51), DAR, NEA, Fla. Edn. Assn., ALA (nat. chmn. sch. library suprs. 1966-67), Fla. Library Assn. (pres. 1961-62), Dade County Sch. Library Assn. (pres. 1953), Am. (dir. southeastern states 1962-64, chmn. suprs. sect. 1966-67, dir. 1962-64), Fla. (pres. 1956) assns. sch. librarians, Kappa Delta Pi, Delta Kappa Gamma. Club: Quota (lt. gov. 27th dist.). Author: Jacarezinho Vadico, 1946; Two Shoes, 1951; contbr. articles to profl. jours. Home: 222 Blue Cove Dr Dunnellon FL 32630

LUNSFORD, DONALD WAYNE, clergyman; b. Boss, Mo., Apr. 26, 1938; s. Donald Arthur and Aileen (Nelson) L.; m. Beverly Ann Stratemeyer, July 31, 1960; children—Mark Dwayne, Angela Dawn. Student Southwestern U., 1955-58, Pioneer Theol. Sem., 1958-60. Ordained to ministry Ill. Dist. Assemblies of God Ch., 1957, Gen. Council of Assemblies of God, 1961. Founding pastor Assemblies of God Ch., Evansville, Ind., 1960-63, 1st Assembly of God Ch., Colorado Springs, 1971-80, Clearwater, Fla., 1980—; evangelist Assemblies of God, Springfield, Mo., 1963-71; asst. dist. supt. Rocky Mountain dist. Assemblies of God., 1978-80; gen. presbyter Gen. Council Assemblies of God, 1978-80; exec. presbyter Peninsular Fla. Dist., Lakeland, 1983—. Contbr. articles to religious jours. Home: 1739 S Greenwood Ave Clearwater FL 33516

LUNSFORD, JAMES FRANKLIN, real estate executive; b. Beeville, Tex., Dec. 7, 1939; s. Jess Monroe and Ethel Elizabeth (Davis) L. B.B.A., Baylor U., Waco, Tex., 1963. Asst. v.p. Dallas Fed. Savs. & Loan Assn., Dallas, 1964-65; v.p., dir. internat. div. Henry S. Miller Co. Realtors, Dallas, 1966-82; pres., owner Lunsford Interests, Inc., Dallas, 1982—, Lunsford Property Co., Dallas, 1982—. Sponsor, Tex. Heart Assn. Served with USAFR, 1963-67. Mem. Delta Sigma Pi. Baptist. Clubs: Tersichorean, Calyx, Dervish (Dallas); Giraud (San Antonio). Office: 3131 Turtle Creek Blvd Suite 222 Dallas TX 75219

LUPPENS, JAMES ALAN, geologist; b. Toledo, Oct. 30, 1946; s. Maximillian F. and Louise M. (Kauffmann) L.; m. Suzanne Boyd, Sept. 14, 1968; 1 child, Jonathan M. B.S. in Geology, Toledo U., 1968, M.S. in Geology, 1970; postgrad., N.Mex. Tech. U., 1971-73. Coal geologist Phillips Petroleum Co., Casper, Wyo., 1973-74; area geologist Phillips Coal Co., Tyler, Tex., 1974-82, chief geologist, Richardson, Tex., 1982—. Co-Author: Fieldguide Book to the Gulf Coast Lignite Region, 1982. Contbr. articles to profl. jours. Cubmaster Circle 10 council Boy Scouts of Am., Plano, Tex., 1980—. Mem. Am. Assn. Petroleum Geologist, ASTM (task group, chmn. com. 1979—). Republican. Avocations: woodworking; sports. Office: Phillips Coal Co 2929 N Central Expressway Richardson TX 75080

LUPTON, MARY HOSMER, owner, operator rare book search service; b. Olympia, Wash., Jan. 2, 1914; d. Kenneth Winthrop and Mary Louise (Wheeler) Hosmer; m. Keith Brahe Wiley, Oct. 12, 1940 (dec. Apr. 1955); children—Sarah Hosmer Wiley Guise, Victoria Brahe Wiley; m. Thomas George Lupton, Nov. 27, 1965; 1 stepson, Andrew Henshaw. Student Gunston Hall Jr. Coll., 1932-33; B.S. in Edn., U. Va., 1940; Ptnr., Wakefield Press, Earlysville, Va., 1940-55; owner, operator Wakefield Forest Bookshop, Earlysville, 1955-65, Forest Bookshop, Charlottesville, 1965—, Wakefield Forest Tree Farm, 1955-85. Corr. sec. Charlottesville-Albemarle Civic League, 1963-64; sec. Instructive Vis. Nurses Assn., Charlottesville, 1961-62; chmn. pub. info. Charlottesville chpt. Va. Mus. Fine Arts, 1970-77; mem. writers' adv. panel Va. Center for Creative Arts, 1973-75, chmn. pub. info., 1976-77; mem. Albemarle County Forestry Com., 1961-62; bd. dirs. Charlottesville-Albemarle Mental Health Assn., 1980-82. Mem. AAUW, DAR (Am. Heritage com. chmn. 1983—), New Eng. Hist. Geneal. Soc., Conn. Soc. Genealogists, Va., Albemarle County hist. socs., Va. Soc. Mayflower Descs. (asst. state historian 1979-82), LWV, Soc. Mayflower Descs., Am. Soc. Psychical Research, Brit. Soc. Psychical Research, Nature Conservancy, Va. Forestry Assn., Chi Omega. Mem. Soc. of Friends. Address: La Casita Blanca PO Box 5206 Charlottesville VA 22905-0206

LUSAS, EDMUND WILLIAM, food processing research executive; b. Woodbury, Conn., Nov. 25, 1931; s. Anton Frank and Damicele Ann (Kasputis) L.; m. Jeannine Marie Muller, Feb. 2, 1957; children—Daniel, Ann, Paul. B.S., U. Conn., 1954; M.S., Iowa State U., 1955; Ph.D., U. Wis., 1958; M.B.A., U. Chgo., 1972. Project leader Quaker Oats Research Labs., Barrington, Ill., 1958-61, mgr. canned pet foods research, 1961-67, mgr. pet foods research, 1967-72, mgr. sci. services, 1972-77; assoc. dir. Food Protein Research and Devel. Ctr., Tex. A&M U., College Station, 1977-78, dir., 1978—. Contbr. articles to jours., chpts. to books. Assoc. editor Jour. Am. Oil Chem. Soc., 1980—. Fund raiser YMCA, Crystal Lake, Ill., 1970-77, chmn. fin. com., 1977. Recipient F.N. Peters research award Quaker Oats Co., 1968. Mem. Am. Oil Chemists Soc., Inst. Food Technologists (Gen. Foods research fellow 1956, 57), Am. Chem. Soc., Am. Assn. Cereal Chemists, Am. Soc. Agrl. Engrs., Nutrition Today Soc., Guayule Soc. Am., Sigma Xi, Phi Tau Sigma. Avocation: fishing. Home: 3504 Old Oaks St Bryan TX 77802 Office: Food Protein Research and Devel Ctr Tex A&M U FM 183 College Station TX 77803

LUSHBAUGH, CLARENCE CHANCELLUM, pathologist, radiation researcher; b. Covington, Ky., Mar. 15, 1916; s. Clarence Chancellum and Florence Barton (Van Slyck) L.; m. Mary Helen Chism, Sept. 5, 1942 (div. 1963); children—William Burton, Robert Chism, Nancy Elizabeth; m. Dorothy Bess Hale, Sept. 30, 1963. Student in pre-medicine, U. Cin., 1934-37; B.S. in Anatomy, U. Chgo., 1938, Ph.D. in Pathology, 1942, M.D., 1948. Instr. pathology U. Chgo., 1942-46, asst. prof., 1946-49; sect. head in pathology UCLA, Los Alamos, 1949-63; pathologist Los Alamos Hosp., 1949-63; sr. scientist Oak Ridge Assoc. Univs., 1963-74, div. chair, asst. chair., 1974—; mem. path B study sect. DRG-NIH, Bethesda, Md., 1961-65; sect. com. 14 NCRP, Bethesda, 1968-74; mem. safety com. 47 WHO-IAEA, Bethesda, and Vienna, Austria, 1978; research study sect. RRD-NIH, Bethesda, 1979-83; cons. and lectr. in field. Contbr. chpts. to books, articles to profl. jours.; participant, lectr. numerous profl. confs. and seminars in pathology and radiation research. Recipient Disting. Sci. Achievement award Health Physics Soc., 1984; West Region Landauer award Am. Assn. Physicists in Medicine, 1985. Mem. AMA, Am. Occupational Medicine Assn., Health Physics Soc., Soc. Nuclear Medicine, Tenn. Med. Assn. Avocations: stained glass. Home: Route 1 Box 374 Clinton TN 37716 Office: Oak Ridge Associated Univs PO Box 117 Oak Ridge TN 37831

LUSK, GLENNA RAE KNIGHT (MRS. EDWIN BRUCE LUSK), librarian; b. Franklinton, La., Aug. 16, 1935; d. Otis Harvey and Lou Zelle (Bahm) Knight; B.S., La. State U., 1956, M.S., 1963; m. John Earle Uhler, Jr., May 26, 1956; children—Anne Knight, Camille Allana; m. Edwin Bruce Lusk, Nov. 28, 1970. Asst. librarian Iberville Parish Library, Plaquemine, La., 1956-57, 1962-68; tchr. Iberville Parish Pub. Schs., Plaquemine, 1957-59, Plaquemines Parish Pub. Schs., Buras, La., 1959-61; dir. Iberville Parish Library, 1969—; mem. La. State Bd. Library Examiners, 1979—, chmn., 1983. Mem. Iberville Parish Econ. Devel. Council, Plaquemine, 1970-71; sec. Iberville Parish Bicentennial Commn., 1973—; mem. La. Bicentennial Commn., 1974. Mem. La. (sect. chmn. 1967-68), Riverland (sec. 1973-74) libraries assns., Capital Area Libraries (chmn. com. 1972-74). Democrat. Episcopalian. Author: (with John E. Uhler, Jr.) Cajun Country Cookin', 1966; Rochester Clarke Bibliography of Louisiana Cookery, 1966; Royal Recipes from the Cajun Country, 1969; Iberville Parish, 1970. Home: 206 Pecan Tree Ln Plaquemine LA 70764 Office: 1501 J Gerald Berret Blvd Plaquemine LA 70764

LUSK, JULIE TAPIN, college dean; b. Cin., Sept. 1, 1953; d. Thomas Phillip and Angela (Raubolt) Tapin; m. W. David Lusk. B.A. in Edn., Marshall U., 1975; M.A. in Edn., Va. Tech. U., 1978. Lic. profl. counselor, W.Va.; nat. cert. counselor. Awareness counselor Ednl. Awareness Talent Search Project, W.Va. Bd. Regents, Charleston, 1975-77; child care worker Mental Health Services, Roanoke, Va., 1977-78; spl. services counselor Va. Western Community Coll., Roanoke, 1978-80, dir. spl. services, 1980-82; asst. dean student affairs, instr. Roanoke Coll., Salem, Va., 1982—; guest speaker Nat. Wellness Conf., Stevens Point, Wis., 1985; cons. J. Sergeant Reynolds Community Coll., Richmond, Va. Editor, author: Handibook-Reference Manual for Personnel Working with Handicapped Students, 1982. Mem. steering com. Health Promotion and Risk Reduction Com., Roanoke, 1984-85; mem. Mayor's Com. on Handicapped Employment, Roanoke. Mem. Am. Assn. Counseling and Devel., Am. Coll. Personnel Assn. (bd. dirs. Commn. VI 1983—), Ctr. for Sci. in Pub. Interest, Va. Coll. Placement Assn. Avocations: Hatha yoga; flute. Office: Roanoke Coll Salem VA 24153

LUSKIN, PAUL BANSECH, lawyer, business exec.; b. Balt., June 19, 1948; s. Joseph and Mildred Luskin; m. Marie Reitzes, June 6, 1971; children: Shana, Diana. B.A., U. Miami; J.D., U. Balt., 1975. Bar: Fla. 1975, U.S. Dist. Ct. Fla. 1979. Sole practice, Hollywood, Fla., 1975—; pres. Luskin's Inc., Hollywood, 1976—, also gen. counsel; dir. Sight and Sound Inc.; anti-trust cons. to various firms. Bd. dirs. Broward County chpt. ARC. Recipient Golden award, 1978, 79, 80, Hollywood Benevolent award, 1981; A.O.C. Achievement award U.S. Ho. of Reps. Adv. Com.; named Retailer of Yr., 1980, Dealer of Yr., 1981, 82. Mem. Broward Bd. Attys., SAE Dealer Inventor Circle, Tau Kappa Epsilon, Phi Delta Pi. Republican. Designer audio receiver. Home: 2831 Palmer Ct Hollywood FL 33022 Office: 4150 N 28th Terr Hollywood FL 33022

LUSKY, MALVERN DAVID, accountant, management and finance consultant; b. San Antonio, Oct. 27, 1947; s. Herman A. and Louise Adelle (Pincus) L.; B.J., U. Tex., Austin, 1970; postgrad. U. Houston, 1973-74; m. Judy Kaplan, Dec. 21, 1969; children—Lauren Jennifer, Benjamin Joseph. Internal auditor Sakowitz, Inc., Houston, 1975-76. ops. mgr. nat. mail order div., 1976-77; auditor United Fund Houston and Harris County, Houston, 1977-78; audit supr. Am. Savs. & Loan Assn., Houston, 1978-79; mgmt. cons. bus. and non-profit orgns., 1976—; Del., 13th Senatorial Dist. Democratic Conv., 1974, 76, State Dem. Conv., 1976; treas. Harris County Dems., 1976-78, mem. Harris County Dem. Exec. Com., 1976—, active mem. election coms. several polit. candidates, 1974—; bd. dirs. Northbrook Homeowners Assn., 1975-77; mem. City of Houston Transp. Adv. Group, 1977—. C.P.A. Mem. Inst. Internal Auditors, Am. Inst. C.P.A.s, Tex. State Soc. C.P.A.s. Jewish. Home: 6107 Hummingbird St Houston TX 77096 Office: Malvern D Lusky CPA 9660 Hillcroft Suite 422 Houston TX 77096

LUSSKY, WARREN ALFRED, librarian, educator, consultant; b. Chgo., Apr. 16, 1919; s. Arthur W. and Alma (Proegler) L.; B.A., U. Colo., 1946; M.A., U. Denver, 1948; student U. Ill., 1941-42;; m. Mildred Joann Island, June 12, 1948. Asst. librarian Pacific Luth. Coll., Parkland, Wash., 1948-49; librarian Hopkins Transp. Library, Stanford, 1950, Rocky Mountain Coll., Billings, Mont., 1950-55; head librarian Nebr. Wesleyan U., Lincoln, 1955-56; dir. library, assoc. prof. Tex. Luth. Coll., Sequin, 1956—; library cons.; mem. accrediting team Tex. Edn. Agy., 1961, 84. 84 Mem. Am., Tex. (dist. vice chmn. 1965, chmn. 1966), S.W. library assns., Council Research and Acad. Libraries (dir. 1968—, pres. 1976-78), prin. contbr. to design new Tex. Luth. Coll. Library; research and publs. on design and functions coll. library bldgs. Home: 357 Irvington Dr San Antonio TX 78209 Office: Tex Luth Coll Library Seguin TX 78155

LUSZKI, MARGARET BARRON, psychologist; b. Washington, Mar. 24, 1907; d. Charles Henry Butler and Helena L. Johnson; m. Edward M. Barron, Nov. 29, 1930 (dec. 1944); m. Walter Aloise Luszki, Mar. 15, 1950. A.B., U. Mich., 1928, Ph.D., 1951; M.A., U. Md., 1930; postgrad. Cath. U. Am. Sch. Social Work, 1939-40, Washington Sch. Psychiatry, 1945-47, MIT, 1947-48. Employee counselor Social Security Bd. and FSA, 1939-43; chief employee relations sect. HEW, 1943-50; lectr. U.S. Dept. Agr. Grad. Sch., 1945-47; Am. U., 1951; project coordinator work confs. in mental health research Nat. Tng. Labs., 1951-57; cons. student personal adjustment Paine Coll., Augusta, Ga., 1957-58; psychologist VA Hosp., Augusta, 1958-59, clin. psychologist, vocat. counselor, Ann Arbor, 1961-66, clin. psychologist, Charleston, S.C., 1966-72; psychol. cons. Crippled Children's div. Ga. Dept. Health, 1958-59; study dir. Research Ctr. for Group Dynamics, Inst. Social Research, U. Mich., Ann Arbor, 1960-61, research assoc. Ctr. Research on Utilization of Sci. Knowledge, Inst. Social Research, 1961-66; assoc. psychiatry dept. psychiatry and behavioral scis. Med. U. S.C., Charleston, 1968-72, clin. assoc. in psychiatry, 1972—; cons. psychologist, Charleston, 1966—. Author: Interdisciplinary Team Research: Methods and Problems, 1958; (with Fox and Schmuck) Diagnosing Classroom Learning Environments, 1966; (with Walter A. Luszki) How to Test Your Dog's IQ, 1980, How to Test Your Cat's IQ, 1984. Contbr. articles to profl. jours. Founder, bd. dirs. Goodwill Industries of Lower S.C., Inc., 1975—; charter mem. Folly Island Residents Assn., 1984. Fellow Am.

Psychol. Assn., Soc. Psychol. Study Social Issues, Am. Sociol. Assn. Unitarian. Democrat. Avocations: dog psychology; dog breeding and showing. Home: 502 E Indian Ave Box 72 Folly Beach SC 29439 Office: 165 Maple St Charleston SC 29403

LUTCHE, MICHAEL WILMER, city administrator; b. Balt., May 27, 1946; s. Wilmer Charles and Bertha Alvina (Leyko) L.; m. Bondurant Hilands, June 29, 1974; children—Michele Elizabeth, Anne Morgan. B.A., George Peabody Coll. of Vanderbilt U., 1968; M.P.A., U. Tenn.-Knoxville and Middle Tenn. State U., 1975; mgmt. tng. program Internat. City Mgrs. Assn., 1977. Lic. single engine pilot FAA. Tchr., Christ the King Sch., Nashville, 1968-69; fiscal analyst Tenn. Ho. of Reps., Nashville, 1969-70; sales rep. Sun Life of Can., Nashville, 1971-72, Armour-Dial, Inc., Nashville, 1972-73; personnel cons. Tenn. Dept. Personnel, Nashville, 1973-77; dir. personnel City of Morristown, Tenn., 1977-78, asst. city adminstr., 1978—; pres., bd. dirs. Morristown Employees Credit Union; instr. U. Tenn. Inst. for Pub. Service; 1st pres. Govtl. Info. Systems of Tenn., 1985-86. Bd. dirs. Morristown Girls Club; chmn. govt. div. United Way, 1979-80, 83; mem. Nashville Recruiting Dist. Adv. Council Naval Programs, 1986—. Served with U.S. Navy, 71. Named Jr. Officer of Yr., 14th Naval Res. Intelligence Area, 1984. Mem. Pub. Employers-Employees Assn. (pres. Tenn. chpt. 1981-83), U.S. Naval Inst., Res. Officers Assn., Naval Res. Assn., Air Force Assn., Smithsonian Assocs., Aircraft Owners and Pilots Assn., Am. Soc. Pub. Adminstrn. (pres. Tenn. chpt. 1977), Internat. Personnel Mgmt. Assn. (pres. Tenn. chpt. 1979-80), Lakeway Personnel Mgmt. Assn. (chpt. v.p. 1979). Roman Catholic. Lodge: Rotary. Publs. adv. bd. So. Jour. Pub. Adminstrn., 1977-78. Home: 1505 Country Club Dr Morristown TN 37814 Office: PO Box 1499 Morristown TN 37816

LUTEN, JOSEPH RANDLE, JR., dentist; b. Little Rock, May 2, 1925; s. Joseph Randle and Dora H. Luten; children—Betsy Luten Kemp, Randy, Tommy. Student Washington U., St. Louis, 1942-43; D.M.D., U. Louisville, 1947. Practice gen. dentistry, Little Rock, 1950-51, 75—, specializing in pedodontics, Little Rock, 1950-51, 53-74; cons. Childrens Convalescent Ctr., Jacksonville, Ark., 1953-59; mem. staff Ark. Childrens Hosp., 1949—, St. Vincents Infirmary, 1949—, Meml. Hosp., 1962-65; cons. med. examiner State Crime Lab., 1982—. Contbr. articles to profl. jours. Mem. exec. bd. Quapaw council Boy Scouts Am., 1970—. Served to 1st lt. Dental Corps, U.S. Army 1951-53; to col. Res. Recipient numerous awards Boy Scouts Am. including Eagle Scout award, 1939, Order of Arrow award, 1965, Koskalakas award, 1970, Tng. award, 1967, Scouters Key, 1969, Wood Badge award, 1969, Silver Beaver award, 1970, Brotherhood award, 1984. Fellow Am. Acad. Pedodontics, Internat. Coll. Dentists, Acad. Gen. Dentistry; mem. Central Dist. Dental Soc., Ark. State Dental Assn., ADA, Am. Orthodontic Soc., Little Rock C. of C. (bd. dirs. 1956-58, v.p. 1950), Am. Numismatic Assn., Delta Sigma Delta. Clubs: Town Club (Little Rock), Twinkletoes Dance, Pleasant Valley Country, Little Rock. Lodges: Masons, Kiwanis. Home: 9600 Warren Rd Little Rock AR 72209 Office: 6600 Baseline Rd Little Rock AR 72209

LUTER, JOSEPH WILLIAMSON, III, meat packing company executive; b. Smithfield, Va., 1939. B.B.A., Wake Forest Coll., 1962. Pres., Smithfield Packing Co., Arlington, Va., 1964-69; pres. Bryce Mountain Resort Inc., 1969-75; with Smithfield Foods Inc., Arlington, 1975—, pres., chief exec. officer, 1975-77, chmn. bd., chief exec. officer, 1977—. Office: Smithfield Foods Inc 1777 N Kent St Arlington VA 22209

LUTEY, JOHN KENT, govt. ofcl.; b. Butte, Mont., Sept. 19, 1902; s. William John and Martha Louise (Williams) L.; student Wharton Sch., U. Pa., 1920-74; m. Agnes Theresa Sakal, Sept. 28, 1949; children—Iona Theresa, Vanessa Louise. With Henningsen Produce Co., Fed. Inc., U.S.A., Shanghai, China, 1925-40; founder, pres., dir. Kibon S.A., Sao Paulo and Rio de Janeiro, Brazil, 1940-62; dir. div. industry AID, Brazil, 1964-66; spl. ambassador of Iceland for inaguration Pres. Kubitschek of Brazil, 1956. Bd. dirs. Inst.-Brazil U.S., 1956-58; pres. Strangers Hosp., Rio de Janeiro, 1950-51; hon. consul of Iceland in Brazil, 1949-56, hon. consul gen., 1956-62. Decorated knight comdr. Order Falcon, 1953; grand knight Order Falcon, 1956 (Iceland). Mem. Am. C. of C. for Brazil (pres. 1951, permanent dir. 1952—), Am. Soc. Rio de Janeiro (pres. 1948). Methodist. Home: 400 Seasage Dr Delray Beach FL 33444

LUTKEN, DONALD C., utility co. exec.; b. Jackson, Miss., Mar. 26, 1924; s. Peter Koch and Erma (Curry) L.; student Miss. State U.; B.S., U.S. Naval Acad., 1946; m. Melissa Turner, June 11, 1946; children—Melissa (Mrs. Hugo Newcomb, Jr.), Isabel Poteat (Mrs. W.L. Eggart), Donald C., Lucie T. (Mrs. David Morgan). Edwin Poteat. With Miss. Power & Light Co., 1949—, exec. v.p. operations, 1969-70, pres., 1970—, chief exec. officer, 1971—; dir. Middle South Utilities, Inc., Miss. Power & Light Co., Unifirst Fed. Savs. & Loan Assn., Southeastern Electric Exchange, Southwest Power Pool. Miss. chmn. payroll U.S. Savs. Bond div. Treasury Dept. Mem. exec. bd. Andrew Jackson council Boy Scouts Am., v.p. S.E. region Area IV. Trustee Belhaven Coll., So. Research Inst., Miss. Found. Ind. Colls., bd. dirs. Central Miss. Growth Found. Served with USNR, 1946-49. Mem. Jackson C. of C., Jackson Symphony League, Newcomen Soc., Miss. State U. Alumni Found., Nat. Assn. Electric Cos., Miss. Soc. Profl. Engrs., ASME, IEEE, Edison Electric Inst., Miss. Mfrs. Assn., Miss. Econ. Assn., Miss. Hist. Soc. Presbyn. (past deacon). Rotarian. Clubs: Jackson Country, University, Capital City Petroleum (Jackson). Home: Route 2 Box 250 Sub Rosa Jackson MS 39209 Office: PO Box 1640 Jackson MS 39209

LUTMAN, SUSAN SODINI, librarian, children's literature educator; b. Natrona Heights, Pa., Aug. 28, 1952; d. Vincent J. and Betty Louise (Cole) Sodini; m. John Carl Lutman, Aug. 28, 1982. B.S. in Edn., Clarion State Coll. (Pa.), 1974; cert. Indiana U. of Pa., 1975-77; M.L.S., U. Pitts., 1981. Librarian, Penns Manor Area Sch. Dist., Clymer, Pa., 1974-81; evening supr. Western Psychiat. Inst. and Clinic Library, Pitts., 1980-81; staff librarian reference dept. Carnegie Library, Pitts., 1981; asst. librarian pub. services Alderson-Broaddus Coll., Philippi, W.Va., 1981—, instr. children's lit., 1981—. Pres., Clymer PTA, 1977-79; cadette leader Girl Scouts U.S.A., Clymer, 1978-79. Mem. ALA, W.Va. Library Assn., Beta Phi Mu, Tau Beta Sigma. Republican. Methodist. Club: Alderson-Broaddus Faculty-Staff (sec.-treas.). Address: Alderson-Broaddus Coll Box 45 Philippi WV 26416

LUTWACK, PATRICIA ANN, psychotherapist, administrator; b. Buffalo, Apr. 2, 1943; d. Maurice Robert and Mary Joseph (Mosher) L. B.A., Boston U., 1967, M.A., 1974; M.Ed., U. Miami, 1978; Ph.D. in Psychology, nat. cert. in gerontology, U. Fla., 1984. Researcher Staub, Warmbold Assocs., Brussels, 1970-73; asst. to dir. personnel Sheraton Corp., Boston, 1973-75; research asst. U. Miami, Coral Gables, Fla., 1976-77; teaching asst. U. Fla., Gainesville, 1977-80; dir. programs and research Holocaust Meml. Ctr., Fla. Internat. U., Miami, 1981—. Author: Effective Coping Strategies Used in Nazi Concentration Camps, 1984; also research articles. Recipient Excellence in Teaching awards Fed. Loan Res. Officers Assn., 1978, Dade County Mental Health, 1976, Excellence in Counseling award Dade County Mental Health, 1976. Mem. Am. Psychol. Assn. Democrat. Home: 19135 NW 64th Ct Miami FL 33015 Office: Holocaust Meml Ctr Fla Internat Univ NE 151st St and Biscayne Blvd North Miami FL 33181

LUTZ, MATTHEW CHARLES, geologist, oil company executive; b. Bunkie, La., Mar. 28, 1934; s. John Matthew and Maxie Mae (Andrus) L.; m. Patricia Dawnn Feazel, Apr. 11, 1953; children—Matt, Jr., Cyndy, Tracey, Clay. B.S., U. Southwestern La., 1956. Various geol. profl. positions Tidewater-Getty Oil Co., 1956-71; asst. dist. geologist Getty Oil Co., Houston, 1971-73, dist. geologist, Midland, Tex., 1973-78, central div. geologist, Tulsa, 1978-80, offshore dist. exploration mgr., Houston, 1980, so. div. exploration mgr., Houston, 1980-82, gen. mgr. offshore exploration and prodn., Houston, 1982-83, exploration mgr. so. div., Houston, 1983-84; sr. v.p. exploration Enserch Exploration Inc., Dallas, 1984—, also dir.; dir. Enserch Internat. Exploration Inc., Dallas, Enserch Processing Inc., Dallas, 1984—. Mem. Am. Assn. Petroleum Geologists, Houston Geol. Soc., Dallas Geol. Soc., Mid-Continent Oil Gas Assn., Am. Petroleum Inst., Independent Petroleum Assn. Am. Democrat. Baptist. Clubs: Dallas Petroleum, Las Colinas Sports. Avocations: travel; golf. Office: Enserch Exploration Inc 1817 Wood St Dallas TX 75201

LYDAY, JOHN REED, petroleum geologist; b. Port Arthur, Tex., Dec. 29, 1951; s. Pete E. and Ruth (Merwin) L.; m. Dyrika Diane Weeks, May 12, 1978 (div. 1983); 1 child, Dustin Reed. B.S. in Geology, Lamar U., 1975; M.S. in Geology, U. Tulsa, 1978. Geologist Santa Fe Energy Co., Amarillo, Tex., 1977-81; sr. geologist Pioneer Prodn. Corp., Amarillo, Denver, 1981-85; sr. geologist Meridian Oil Inc., Amarillo, 1985—. Contbr. articles to profl. publs. Mem. Am. Assn. Petroleum Geologists (chmn. tech. program mid-continent conv. 1985, A.I. Levorsen Meml. award 1985) Geol. Soc. Am., Panhandle Geol. Soc. (program chmn. 1983-84, sec. 1984-85), Rocky Mountain Assn. Geologists, Oklahoma City Geol. Soc. Avocations: photography; tennis; music. Home: 4003 Tucson St Amarillo TX 79109 Office: Meridian Oil Inc 1616 S Kentucky Suite C-300 Amarillo TX 79102

LYLE, JEAN STUART, social worker; b. Rock Hill, S.C., Jan. 13, 1912; d. David and Martha (Nash) L.; B.A., U. S.C., 1949; M.S. in Social Work, Columbia U., 1951. Recreation dir. City of Rock Hill, 1938-44; commd. 1st lt. Med. Service Corps, U.S. Army, 1951, advanced through grades to lt. col., 1966; asst. chief social worker, Ft. Benning, Ga., 1951-55; chief social worker Fort Jay, N.Y., 1955-58, Fort McClellan, Ala., 1958-62, female inpatient service Walter Reed Gen. Hosp., Washington, 1962-66; dir. Army Community Service, U.S. Army, Hawaii, 1966-68, Walter Reed Army Med. Center, 1968-70; cons. group work to Med. Field Service Sch., Fort Sam Houston, Tex., 1969; ret., 1970; dir. vol. services S.C. Dept. Health and Environ. Control, Columbia, 1970-74; pvt. practice social work, Rock Hill, 1974—; tchr. and supr. social work students Catholic U. Am., Washington, 1960-62. Decorated Legion of Merit; recipient Community Service award U.S. Army, 1968. Mem. Nat. Assn. Social Workers, Acad. Cert. Social Workers. Democrat. Address: PO Box 2553 Rock Hill SC 29730

LYLE, ROBERT EDWARD, chemist; b. Atlanta, Jan. 26, 1926; s. Robert Edward and Adaline (Cason) L.; m. Gloria Gilbert, Aug. 28, 1947. B.A., Emory U., 1945, M.S., 1946; Ph.D., U. Wis.-Madison, 1949. Asst. prof. Oberlin Coll., Ohio, 1949-51; asst. prof. U. N.H., Durham, 1951-53, assoc. prof., 1953-57, prof., 1957-76; prof., chmn. dept. chemistry N. Tex. State U., Denton, 1977-79; v.p. chemistry, chem. engr. SW Research Inst., San Antonio, 1979—; vis. prof. U. Va., Charlottesville, 1973-74, U. Grenoble, France, 1976; adj. prof. Bowdoin Coll., Brunswick, Maine, 1975-77. Mem. editorial bd. Current Abstracts Chemistry, 1976—. USPHS fellow Oxford U., Eng., 1965; recipient honor scroll award Mass. chpt. Am. Inst. Chemistry, 1971. Mem. Am. Chem. Soc. (medicinal chemistry div., councilor 1965-84, 86—), Phi Beta Kappa, Sigma Xi. Methodist. Home: 12814 Kings Forest St San Antonio TX 78230 Office: SW Research Inst 6220 Culebra Rd San Antonio TX 78284

LYLE, SAMUEL PATTERSON, ret. agrl. engr.; b. Memphis, Mo., Feb. 12, 1892; s. Edward Gerard and Jeanetta Wilson (Patterson) L.; B.S., Kans. State U., 1921; M.S. in Agrl. Engring., Iowa State U., 1922; m. Besse Maude MacQueen, Dec. 26, 1921 (dec.); children—Samuel Patterson (dec.), Marion Elizabeth Lyle Fowler, Alice Louise Lyle Cockrill. Head agrl. engring. dept. Ark. A&M Coll., 1922-24; head agrl. engring. dept. U. Ga., 1924-30; sr. engr. Fed. Extension Service, Dept. Agr., Washington 1930-40, prin. scientist in charge specialists, 1941-57, dir. agrl. programs div., 1958-62. Served with USAAF, 1917-19. Fellow Am. Soc. Agrl. Engrs. (pres. 1938-39; John Deere Gold medal); mem. AAAS (life), Am. Soc. Engring. Edn., Nat. Safety Council, Nat. Inst. Farm Safety, Farm Safety (hon. life), Orgn. Profl. Employees Dept. Agrl., Nat. Assn. Ret. Fed. Employees, Soil Conservation Soc. Am., Council Agrl. Sci. and Tech., Vets. World War I, VFW, Sigma Xi, Phi Kappa Phi, Epsilon Sigma Phi, Gamma Sigma Delta. Methodist. Contbr. numerous articles to profl. jours. Home: 218 Spring St Huntingdon TN 38344

LYLES, ALBERT MARION, educational administrator, English educator; b. Kendrick, Fla., July 28, 1926; s. Edwin Franklin and Berta Marguerite (Guthery) L.; m. Lillian Mae Hendricks, Sept. 8, 1955; children—Lawrence Alan, Stephen Louis. A.B., Union Coll., 1948; A.M., U. Pa., 1949; Ph.D., Rutgers U., 1957. Instr. English, U. Mo., Columbia, 1949-51; instr. to assoc. prof. U. Tenn., Knoxville, 1953-70; asst. prof. English, Auburn U., Ala., 1956-57; chmn. English dept. Va. Commonwealth U., Richmond, 1970-74, assoc. dean arts and scis., 1974-81; dean Coll. Arts and Scis., Winthrop Coll., Rock Hill, S.C., 1981—. Author: Methodism Mocked, 1960; Hodges Collection of William Congreve, 1970. Served with U.S. Army, 1944-46, ETO. Am. Council Learned Socs. grantee, 1965. Mem. Am. Soc. 18th Century Studies, Am. Assn. Higher Edn. Home: 5041 Wedgewood Dr Charlotte NC 28210 Office: Arts and Scis Winthrop Coll Rock Hill SC 29733

LYNCH, CATHERINE GORES, social work administrator; b. Waynesboro, Pa., Nov. 23, 1943; d. Landis and Pamela (Whitmarsh) Gores; B.A. magna cum laude and honors, Bryn Mawr Coll., 1965; Fulbright scholar, Universidad Central de Venezuela, Caracas, 1965-66; postgrad. (Lehman fellow), Cornell U., 1966-67; m. Joseph C. Keefe, Nov. 29, 1981; children—Shannon Maria, Lisa Alison, Gregory T. Keefe, Michael D. Keefe. Mayor's intern, Human Resources Adminstrn., N.Y.C., 1967; research asst. Orgn. for Social and Tech. Innovation, Cambridge, Mass., 1967-69; cons. Ford Found., Bogota, Colombia, 1970; staff Nat. Housing Census, Nat. Bur. Statistics, Bogotá, 1971; evaluator Foster Parent Plan, Bogotá, 1973; research staff FEDESARROLLO, Bogotá, 1973-74; dir. Dade County Advocates for Victims, Miami, Fla., 1974—; guest lectr. local univs. Participant, co-chmn. various task forces rape, child abuse, incest, family violence, elderly victims of crime, nat., state, local levels, 1974—; developer workshops in field; mem. gov.'s task force on victims and witnesses, gov.'s task force on sex offenders and their victims. Recipient various public service awards including WINZ Citizen of Day, 1979; Outstanding Achievement award Fla. Network Victim Witness Services, 1982; cert. police instr. Mem. Nat. Orgn. of Victim Assistance Programs (bd. dirs. 1977-83; Outstanding Program award 1984). Fla. Network of Victim/Witness Programs (bd. dirs., treas., 1980-81), Nat. Assn. Social Workers, Am. Soc. Public Adminstrs., Dade County Fedn. Health and Welfare Workers, Fla. Assn. Health and Social Services (Dade County chpt., treas., 1979-80). Contbr. writings in field to publs. Office: 1515 NW 7th St Suite 213 Miami FL 33125

LYNCH, JAMES CHARLES, security guard company executive; b. Newark, Jan. 15, 1919; s. Bernard and Bridget (Fitzsimmons) L.; B.S. in Bus. Adminstrn., Rutgers U., 1940; cert. Indsl. Coll. of Armed Forces, 1964; m. Mary Delia Powell, June 29, 1959; 1 child, Brian Joseph; 1 stepdau., Maria Nannette. Insp., P. Ballantyne & Son, Newark, 1940-42; investigator Retail Credit Co., Newark, 1946; night mgr. Robert Richter Hotel, Miami Beach, 1946-47, night auditor, 1947-48; hotel asst. mgr. Sans Souci Hotel, Miami Beach, Fla., 1948-50; chief Intelligence and Security div. Redstone (Ala.) Arsenal, 1950-60; security adv. NATO Hawk Prodn. Orgn., Paris, 1960, security program chief, until 1964; security specialist U.S. Army Missile Command, Redstone Arsenal, 1964-68; chief Security Office, U.S. Army Safeguard Systems Command, Huntsville, Ala., 1968-72; pres., chmn. bd., chief exec. officer Asset Protection Assos., Inc., Huntsville, Ala., 1973—; guest lectr. U. Ala., Birmingham, 1979-80, Jefferson State U., Birmingham, 1979-80. Bd. dirs. A.S.I.S. Found., Inc., Washington., 1983-84. Served with U.S. Army, 1942-46, 50-52; ETO. Decorated Silver Star with oak leaf cluster, Bronze Star with oak leaf cluster, Purple Heart. Cert. protection profl., 1978. Mem. Huntsville-Madison County C. of C. (chmn. internat. trade com. 1976-78), Am. Soc. Indsl. Security (past dir., past nat. treas.), Assn. U.S. Army, Smithsonian Assos., Am. Security Council, VFW, Am. Legion, Security and Intelligence Assn. Republican. Roman Catholic. Clubs: Huntsville Country, Burning Tree Country, Elks, KC. Contbr. articles to profl. jours. Home: 403 Zandale Dr Huntsville AL 35801 Office: 101 Governor's Dr Suite 406 Huntsville AL 35801

LYNCH, JOHN ELLSWORTH, hospital administrator; b. Fargo, N.D., June 8, 1935; s. John Joseph and Mary Louise (Paulson) L.; B.S. in Bus. Adminstrn., U. N.D., 1959; M.B.A., U. Mo., 1969; D.P.A., Nova U., 1980; LL.D. (hon.), Campbell U., 1983; m. Beth Margaret Pallas, July 14, 1956; children—John Ellsworth, Michael, Kevin. Fin. mgr. U.S. Steel Corp., Chgo., 1959-63; controller Decatur (Ill.) and Macon County Hosp., 1963-65; asst. exec. dir. Research Hosp. and Med. Center, Kansas City, Mo., 1965-70; pres., chief exec. officer N.C. Baptist Hosps., Winston-Salem, 1970—; chmn. fin. com., dir. 1st Home Fed. Savs. and Loan Assn.; chmn., dir. Piedmont Assoc. Industries, Inc.; Mem. hon. life mem. Forsyth County chpt. ARC; bd. dirs. Sun Alliance; bd. dirs. Amos Cottage; bd. dirs., treas., mem. exec. com. United Way. Served with AUS, 1954-57. Mem. Am. Coll. Hosp. Adminstrs., N.C. Hosp. Assn. (trustee, mem. budget com., council on mgmt.), Beta Gamma Sigma, Beta Alpha Psi. Republican. Baptist. Lodge: Rotary. Office: 300 S Hawthorne Rd Winston-Salem NC 27103

LYNCH, KINNEY LEE, insurance company executive; b. Detroit, Apr. 4, 1945; s. James Edward and Hazel (Weber) L.; m. Jayne Echtenkamp, Nov. 29, 1969; children—Gretchen, Heather. Student, U. Oreg., 1963-66; B.A., U. Nebr., 1970. Gen. agt. Penn Mutual, Chgo., 1975-82; regional agy. mgr. Jefferson Standard Life, Washington, 1982—. Mem. Gen. Agts. and Mgrs. Assn. (Nat. Mgmt. award-life and quality), C.L.U. Assn. Republican. Home: 10316 Yellow Pine Dr Vienna VA Office: Jefferson Standard 1655 N Ft Myer Dr #300 Arlington VA 22209

LYNCH, MARK NORRIS, commercial sound contracting company executive, electro-acoustic engineer; b. Pitts., June 13, 1950; s. Vincent Patrick and Dolores Mae (Dickey) L.; m. Pamela Jean Divis, Jan. 7, 1982. A.S., Bucks County Community Coll., 1970; B.S.E.E., Temple U., 1972. Pres. Quality Sound, Fayetteville, N.C., 1978—; dir. The Track, Inc., Fayetteville, Comml. Entertainment Corp., Fayetteville, AJC Leasing Co., Fayetteville; sec. Flite Lease, Inc., Dillion, S.C., 1982—; sec.-treas. C.A. Cook Corp., 1984—. Com. mem. Cumberland County Mixed Beverage Commn. (N.C.), 1979. Served with U.S. Army, 1972-78; Korea. Recipient Service award March of Dimes, Fayetteville, 1977, Presdl. Achievement award Pres. Reagan, 1981, cert. of appreciation Gov. N.C., 1982. Mem. Audio Engring. Soc., Vietnam Vets. Am. (sec.-treas. 1978-80). Office: Quality Sound Enterprise Inc 833 Bragg Blvd Fayetteville NC 28301

LYNCH, MARY BRITTEN, artist, educator; b. Pruden, Ky., Sept. 30, 1931; d. Fred Clarence and Mary Virginia (Strange) Hill; m. James Walton Lynch, Oct. 6, 1956; 1 child, Holly Kristen. B.A., U. Tenn.-Chattanooga, 1956. Art instr. Hunter Mus. Art, Chattanooga, 1954-56, 65-75; Chattanooga Christian High Sch., Chattanooga, 1979-85; apptd. panel mem. Tenn. Arts Commn., 1972-76. Exhibited in group shows throughout U.S., 1974-77; represented by Art S., Inc., Washington and Montgomery, Ala. Founder Tenn. Watercolor Soc., 1969, Lenoir City Spring Arts Festival, Tenn., 1963; v.p. Hamilton County Republican Women's Club, 1969; bd. dirs. Chattanooga Symphony Guild, 1968-73, Little Miss Mag Day Nursery, 1977-85, Chattanooga Nature Ctr., 1983-84. Recipient numerous purchase and cash awards Tenn. State Mus., 1974-78. Mem. Nat. Watercolor Soc., Nat. Assn. Women Artists (medal of honor 1973). Episcopalian. Avocation: high sch. tennis coach. Home: 1505 Woodnymph Trail Lookout Mountain TN 37350

LYNCH, REGINALD SHELDON, fast food company official; b. Charleston, W.Va., Dec. 13, 1937; s. Bernard Grey and Eileene Louise (Burks) L.; B.S., Hampden-Sydney Coll., 1959; m. Doris Ann Davis, Sept. 27, 1966; children—Reginald Sheldon, Deborah, Lisa, Pamela. Vice pres. Four Flags Internat., Inc., Mpls., 1964-66, Sveden House Internat., Mpls., 1966-69; pres., chief exec. officer The White House, Mpls., 1969-70; regional mgr. Church's Fried Chicken, Inc., St. Louis, 1970-78; pres. Reggie's Fried Chicken, Inc., St. Louis, 1978-80; nat. dir. mktg. Church's Fried Chicken, Inc., San Antonio, 1981—; guest lectr. St. Louis Community Coll. at Forest Park, 1980. Bd. dirs. Martin Luther King Jr. Meml. Fund. Mem. Am. Mktg. Assn., Pub. Relations Soc. Am., Minn. Restaurant Assn. (past dir.), Mo. Restaurant Assn. (pres. St. Louis chpt. 1981), Nat. Restaurant Assn. (exec. mem.), Foodservice Execs. Assn., NAACP (patron), Congress of Racial Equality (patron), Nat. Eagle Scout Assn. Democrat. Baptist. Contbr. articles to profl. jours. Office: 355 Spencer Ln PO Box BH001 San Antonio TX 78284

LYNCH, RUSSELL VINCENT, oil and gas company executive; b. N.Y.C., Nov. 14, 1922; s. Francis R.V. and Helen Adams (Barrett) L.; B.A., Yale U., 1947; m. Nell Orand, Oct. 4, 1958; children—C. Bruton, Peter Francis, Joseph Barrett Orand; children by previous marriage—Rose P., R. Vincent, Alexander P. Chmn., chief exec. officer Lane-Wood, Inc., Dallas, 1962-75, dir., 1975—; owner, mng. partner R.V. Lynch & Co., Dallas, 1975—; chmn. bd. Riata Oil & Gas Co., Inc., 1978—, Lynch Locke Corp., 1980—; dir. Richardson Savs. Bank. Past sr. warden St. Michael's and All Angels Ch.; past pres. Episcopal Retreat and Conf. Center, Flower Mound, Tex. Served with USNR, 1942-45. Decorated Air medal. Episcopalian. Clubs: Houston; Brook Hollow Golf, Links (N.Y.C.); City (Dallas); Fishers Island Country (N.Y.); Chevy Chase (Washington). Home: 9436 Meadowbrook St Dallas TX 75220 Office: 1600 One Main Pl Dallas TX 75202

LYNCH, WALTER KENNETH, textile engineering educator; b. Lincoln County, N.C., Apr. 17, 1929; s. Walter R. and Eva (Kiser) L.; m. Martha Anne Jeffreys, Aug. 18, 1951; children—Carol, Kaye. B.S., N.C. State U., 1959, M.S., 1966; Ph.D., U. Leeds (Eng.), 1971. Head dept. Superior Yarn Mills, Mount Holly, Inc., 1952-56; textile engr. Union Carbide Corp., South Charleston, W.Va., 1959-62; instr., asst. prof., assoc. prof. N.C. State U., Raleigh, 1964-75; prof., head dept. textile engring. Auburn (Ala.) U., 1975—; vis. lectr. U. Leeds 1969-71. Burlington Industries scholar, 1957-59. Mem. Rayon Acetate Council (chmn. bd. dirs.), Nat. Council Textile Edn. (pres.), Textile Quality Control Assn., Assn. Textile Technologists, Am. Assn. Textile Chemists and Colorists, Acad. Mgmt. Methodist. Club: Saugahatchee Country. Lodge: Lions (sec.). Office: Textile Engring Dept Auburn Univ Auburn AL 36849

LYNCH, WILLIAM WRIGHT, JR., real estate developer; b. Dallas, Aug. 26, 1936; s. William W. and Martha (Hirsch) L.; B.S. in E.E., Ariz. U., 1959; M.B.A., Stanford U., 1962; m. Sandra McVay, June 11, 1960; children—Mary Margaret, Katherine. Pres., Ins. Bldg. Corp., Dallas, 1965-84, also ptnr. Cimarron Properties Corp., 1972-83; pres. Argus Realty Corp., 1984—; ptnr. Encino Co., 1985—; dir. Llano, Inc., 1967-83, Broadmoor Properties, Inc., 1974-84 N.Mex. Elec. Service Co., 1969-83, Hobbs Gas Co., 1971-83, Ins. Bldg. Corp., 1965-84 Lynch Properties Corp. Bd. dirs. Dallas Civic Music, 1970-77, Ednl. Opportunities, Inc., 1973—, Dallas Symphony Orch., 1966-74; trustee Lynch Found., 1983—. Served with AUS, 1959-60. Mem. Blue Key, Tau Beta Pi, Pi Mu Epsilon. Republican. Episcopalian. Clubs: Brook Hollow Golf, Dallas, Chaparral, Verandah. Home: 3604 Haynie Ave Dallas TX 75205 Office: 1845 Woodall Rodgers Freeway Suite 1600 Dallas TX 75201

LYNES, CYNTHIA JANE, educator; b. Savannah, Mar. 2, 1956; d. Lee Moore and Rosalyn Jane (Copeland) Dickerson; m. Daniel Neill Lynes, Jr., June 21, 1975; 1 son, Daniel Lee. B.S., Armstrong State Coll., 1978, M.Ed., 1984. Tchr., coach Chatham Bd. Edn., Savannah, 1978—. Mem. AAHPERD, Ga. Assn. Health, Phys. Edn., Recreation and Dance, NEA. Democrat. Baptist. Clubs: Meldrim Civics, Meldrim Athletic. Address: Route 1 Box 435 Bloomingdale GA 31302

LYNN, C(HARLES) STEPHEN, fast food chain executive; b. LaGrange, Ga., July 27, 1947; s. Charles Hubert and Norma Lee (Battey) L.; m. Milah Faith Pass, Sept. 4, 1976. B.S. in Indsl. Engring., Tenn. Tech. U., 1970; M.B.A., U. Louisville, 1973. Indsl. engr. Brown & Williamson Tobacco, Louisville, 1970-73; dir. dist. div. Ky. Fried Chicken Corp., Louisville, 1973-77; pres., chief exec. officer MarQuest, Inc. subs. Century 21 Real Estate Corp., 1978-80, v.p. prodn. cont. and service div. Century 21 Real Estate Corp., 1978-80; exec. v.p., chief operating officer The Burtson Corp., Marina Del Rey, Calif., 1980-83; pres., chief exec. officer Sonic Industries, Inc., Oklahoma City, 1983—; also dir.; dir. Century Bank, Oklahoma City, Med. Adv. Group, Inc., Oklahoma City. Bd. dirs. Salvation Army, Oklahoma City, 1984—. Mem. Inst. Indsl. Engrs. (sr. mem., pres. Louisville chpt. 1973), Nat. Restaurant Assn., Assn. M.B.A.s, Pres. Assn. of Am. Mgmt. Assn., Internat. Franchise Assn. Republican. Presbyterian. Avocations: reading; tennis; basketball; watching movies; sports. Office: Sonic Industries Inc 6800 N Bryant St Oklahoma City OK 73121-4444

LYNN, GERI DUNLAP, educator; b. Odessa, Tex., Sept. 30, 1954; d. Jerry Cecil and Laquita Adelia (Whisenhunt) Dunlap; m. A. Dale Lynn, June 18, 1983. Student Odessa Coll., 1972-74; B.S.Ed., U. Tex., 1982. Lic. tchr., Tex. Child care worker emotionally disturbed adolescents Mary Lee Sch., Austin, Tex., 1979-81; homebound tchr. Balcones Coop., Austin, 1982; tchr. severe and profound unit Round Rock (Tex.) High Sch., 1982—; tchr. sign lang. Vol., Tex. Spl. Olympics, 1982—, coach, mem. planning com., 1983—, head coach bowling, basketball and gymnastics, 1983—, head coach soccer and track & field, 1984—; vol. deaf and blind children Tex. Lions, 1981—; Hattie Hewlitt Found. scholar, 1979-81. Mem. Tex. Soc. Autistic Citizens. Address: 18504 Lakeview Dr E Jonestown TX 78641

LYNN, HENRY SHARPE, investment banker; b. Pitts., July 16, 1907; s. Albert Maxfield and Ethel Hansell (Sharpe) L.; A.B., Princeton U., 1928; M.B.A., Harvard U., 1930; m. Fariss Gambrill, Feb. 4, 1942; children—Henry Sharpe, George Gambrill. Clk., salesman Sterne, Agee & Leach, Inc., Birmingham, 1930-40, partner, 1951-63, v.p., treas., 1963-67, pres., 1967-76, chmn. exec. com., 1976-82, vice chmn. bd., 1982—, also dir.; asst. v.p., then v.p. Birmingham Trust Nat. Bank, 1940-51. Past bd. dirs., v.p. Jefferson County (Ala.) Coordinating Council; vice chmn. Jefferson County Health Council; bd. dirs. Jefferson Family Counseling Assn.; pres., trustee Jefferson Tb Sanatorium. Served to lt. comdr. USNR, 1942-45. Mem. N.Y. Stock Exchange, Soc. of Cin., Order St. John of Jerusalem, SCW, SR, SAR, Soc. War 1812.

Republican. Episcopalian. Clubs: Mountain Brook, Birmingham Country, Shoal Creek, Redstone, Downtown, Relay House (Birmingham); Boston (New Orleans); Princeton, Racquet and Tennis (N.Y.C.). Home: 2878 Shook Hill Rd Birmingham AL 35223 Office: 1500 First National-Southern Natural Bldg Birmingham AL 35203

LYNNE, GARY DEAN, agricultural economics educator, consultant; b. Harvey, N.D., Apr. 10, 1944; s. Gordon and Dorothy (Lowe) L.; m. Judy A. Hagen, June 6, 1965; children—Jill A., Erica M. B.S., N.D. State U., 1966, M.S., 1969; Ph.D., Oreg. State U., 1974. Staff asst. N.D. State U., Fargo, N.D., 1967-69; water resource economist Water Inst., Fargo, 1969-70; asst. prof. U. Fla., Gainesville, 1974-79, assoc. prof., 1979—; soil and water conservation cons. Contbr. articles to profl. jours. Treas., mem. ch. council Univ. Luth. Ch., Gainesville, 1976-78; treas., v.p. bd., pres. Gator Exchange Club, Gainesville, 1977-85. Recipient numerous grants from state and fed. agys., 1975—. Mem. Am. Agrl. Econs. Assn., Am. Econs. Assn., Assn. Environ. and Resource Econs., Western Agrl. Econs. Assn., So. Agrl. Econs. Assn. Democrat. Lutheran. Club: Hogtown Hackers (Gainesville). Avocations: computers; sports cars; camping. Office: McCarty 1157 U Fla Gainesville FL 32611

LYNNE, SEYBOURN HARRIS, judge; b. Decatur, Ala., July 25, 1907; s. Seybourn Arthur and Annie Leigh (Harris) L.; B.S., Ala. Polytechnic Inst., 1927; LL.B., U. Ala., 1930, LL.D., 1973; m. Katherine Donaldson Brandau, June 16, 1937; 1 dau., Katherine Roberta. Admitted to Ala. bar, 1930; gen. practice law, Decatur, Ala., 1930-34; judge Morgan (Ala.) County Ct., 1934-41, 8th Jud. Circuit Ct. Ala., 1941-42, U.S. Dist. Ct. No. Dist. Ala., 1946—, chief judge, 1953-73, sr. judge, 1973—. Served to lt. col., JAGC, U.S. Army, 1942-46. Decorated Bronze Star; named to Ala. Acad. Honor, 1978. Mem. Ala., Am. bar assns., Blue Key, Scabbard and Blade, Pi Kappa Alpha, Phi Kappa Phi, Phi Delta Phi, Omicron Delta Kappa, Alpha Phi Epsilon. Democrat. Baptist. Kiwanian (dist. gov. Ala. dist. 1938). Clubs: Birmingham Country, Univ. of Ala. A. Home: 3323 Briarcliff Rd Birmingham AL 35223 Office: Federal Bldg Birmingham AL 35203

LYON, DORIS ELAINE, commercial credit manager, insurance underwriter; b. Ft. Belvoir, Va., Nov. 18, 1947; d. Robert Belie and Geneva N (Legate) Wilson; m. Robert B. Lyon, III, Nov. 4, 1968; children—Jacquelyn Denise, Robert B. Student U. Okla., 1965-67, Wichita State U., 1974-75. Regional ins. auditor U.S. Fidelity & Guaranty Co., Oklahoma City, 1967-68; ins. underwriter Ancel-Earp-McEldowney & McWilliams, Inc., Oklahoma City, 1968-71; comml. credit mgr. TexChron, Inc., San Antonio, 1978—; con. to wholesale jewelry distbrs. Adv. Vocat. Occupational Edn. Program. Republican. Episcopalian.

LYON, MARTHA SUE, naval officer, research engineer; b. Louisville, Oct. 3, 1935; d. Harry Bowman and Erma (Moreland) L.; B.A. in Chemistry, U. Louisville, 1959; M.Ed. in Math., Northeastern Ill. U., 1974. Cert. tchr., Ill., Ky. Commd. ensign U.S. Navy, 1965, advanced through grades to comdr., 1983; instr. instrumentation chemistry Northwestern U., Evanston, Ill., 1968-70; chemistry tchr. gifted math. Waukegan pub. schs., Ill., 1971-75; phys. scientist Library of Congress, 1975-76; research engr. Lockheed Missiles & Space Co., 1976-77; instr., assoc. chmn. dept. physics U.S. Naval Acad., 1977-79; analyst Systems Analysis div. Office of Chief of Naval Ops., 1980-81; comdg. Officer Naval Res. Ctr., Stockton, Calif., 1981-83; mem. faculty Def. Intelligence Coll., 1983-85; project mgr. Naval Electronic Systems Command, 1985—. Decorated Def. Meritorious Service medal, Navy Achievement medal; Am. Heart Assn. grantee, 1960-62; NSF grantee, 1971-72. Mem. Soc. Women Engrs., Am. Statis. Assn., Ops. Research Soc. Am., Assn. Old Crows, Armed Forces Communications and Electronics Assn., Am. Soc. Photogrammetry, Internat. Conf. Women Engrs. and Scientists (protocol chair), Am. Assn. Engring. Socs. (pub. affairs council), Mensa, Zeta Tau Alpha, Delta Phi Alpha. Lodge: Order Eastern Star. Avocation: music. Home: 8102 Sleepy View Ln Springfield VA 22153

LYON, PAULA SNELL, nursing educator; b. Dothan, Ala., Mar. 2, 1952; d. Jack Borland and Paula Jalane (Kelly) Snell; m. Benjamin Rex Lyon, Feb. 23, 1974; children—Kelly, Jacquelyn. B.S.N., U. Ala., 1973, M.S.N., 1981. R.N., Ala., Fla. Staff nurse CICU, Univ. Hosp., Birmingham, Ala., 1974, staff/charge nurse, 1975-76; staff psychiat. unit VA Hosp., Tuscaloosa, Ala., 1974-75; instr. nursing Wallace Community Coll., Dothan, Ala., 1976—, faculty adv. Wallace Assn. Nursing Students, 1982—. Mem. Am. Nurses Assn., NEA, Ala. Jr. and Community Coll. Assn. Baptist. Address: 804 Wimbledon Dr Dothan AL 36301 Office: G C Wallace State Community Coll Dothan AL 36301

LYON, SHERMAN ORWIG, rubber and chemical company executive; b. Greenwich, Conn., Sept. 4, 1939; s. James R. and June K. (Orwig) L.; m. Nell Collar, June 15, 1968; children—Jeffrey, Michelle. B.S. in Chem. Engring., Purdue U., 1961; postgrad. exec. program Stanford U., 1978. Processing engr., prodn. supt. Monsanto Co., St. Louis, 1961-69, mktg. mgr., 1969-72; gen. mgr. chem. div. Mallinckrodt, Inc., St. Louis, 1972-78, v.p. specialty chemicals, 1978-80; group v.p. Celanese Corp., Chatham, N.J., 1980-82; pres. Copolymer Rubber and Chem. Corp., Baton Rouge, 1982—; sr. v.p. Armstrong Corp., New Haven, 1983—; pres. N.Am. sect. Internat. Inst. Synthetic Rubber Producers, Houston, 1985—; dir. City Nat. Bank Baton Rouge. Bd. dirs. Woman's Hosp. Found., Baton Rouge, 1985-88, Baton Rouge United Way, 1985-88; trustee Gulf South Research Inst., Baton Rouge, 1983-89. Recipient Iron Key, Purdue U., 1961. Mem. Baton Rouge C. of C. (bd. dirs. 1984-87), Am. Inst. Chem. Engrs., Omicron Delta Kappa (founding mem. Purdue chpt.), Sigma Phi Epsilon (sec.), Tau Beta Pi. Republican. Clubs: Baton Rouge Country, City, Camelot (Baton Rouge). Office: Copolymer Rubber & Chem Corp PO Box 2591 Baton Rouge LA 70821

LYONS, CLAUDIA JANE, nurse, educator; b. Springhill, La., May 25, 1951; d. Claude Behnke and Gwendolyn Jane (McDonald) Dreher; m. Tommy Eugene Lyons, Aug. 28, 1973; children—Michael Eugene, John Gabriel. B.S. with honors in Nursing, Northwestern State U. La., 1973. R.N., La., Ark. Staff nurse Community Hosp., Springhill, La., 1973-77; pub. health nurse Webster Parrish, Springhill, 1977-80; dir. nurses Taylor (Ark.) Nursing Home, 1980-81; instr. nursing So. Ark. U., Magnolia, 1982—, mem. curriculum com., 1982-83, chmn. admissions com., 1983—. So. State Coll. scholar, Magnolia, Ark., 1969-70. Mem. Am. Nurses Assn., Sigma Theta Tau. Baptist. Home: Route 1 Box 395 Taylor AR 71861 Office: So Ark U PO Box 1323 Magnolia AR 71753

LYONS, DONALD WALLACE, university library administrator; b. Lexington, Ky., Dec. 11, 1945; s. Joseph Bailey and Sam Ella (Turner) L.; m. Myra Lucretia Briggs, June 28, 1969; children—Donald Wallace, Reginald. A.B., Ky. State U., 1968; M.S.L.S., U. Ky., 1971. Cert. tchr., Ky., Mich. Tchr. Detroit Pub. Schs., 1968-69, Fayette County Pub. Schs. (Ky.), 1969-74; library asst. Ky. State U. Frankfort, 1971-72, asst. librarian, 1972-74, assoc. dir., 1975, dir. libraries, 1976—, supervising tchr., 1969-73; supervising tchr. Eastern Ky. U., Richmond, 1972; bd. dirs. Jesse Stuart Found., 1978-84. Compiler bibliography: African and African Am. Lit., 1972; editor, compiler various newsletters. Vice pres. Russell Elem. Sch. Parent-Tchr. Orgn., Lexington, 1983—, Pres., 1981-83. Recipient Disting. Service award Russell Elem. Sch. Parent-Tchr. Orgn., 1983. Mem. ALA, Ky. Library Assn., State Assisted Acad. Library Council Ky. (chmn. 1980-81), 1890 Land-grant Coll. Library Dirs. Assn. (treas. 1984—), NAACP, Alpha Phi Alpha (sec. 1975-81, 83—, pres. 1982, Man of Yr. 1982). F Democrat. Methodist. Lodges: Lions (treas. 1980—, Outstanding Lion of Yr. 1982), Kiwanis (Club Cup 1964) (Lexington). Home: 517 Collier Ct Lexington KY 40505 Office: Blazer Library Ky State U Frankfort KY 40601

LYONS, JAMES EDWARD, university administrator; b. Kershaw, S.C., Oct. 21, 1928; s. Lacey and Jannie Louise (Jones) L.; B.S., 1958. M.B.A., 1960; Ph.D., Clayton U., 1961; D.Sc. (hon.), Fla. Inst. Tech., 1978; L.H.D. (hon.), Nathaniel Hawthorne Coll., Antrim, N.H., 1982; m. Ollie Mae Brown, Sept. 7, 1957; children—James Edward, Katherine Brown. Gen. mgr. Chevrolet-Cadillac and Nat. Auto Leasing Co., Melbourne, Fla., 1958-62; owner Pontiac, Chevrolet, GMC Truck, MG and Austin Healey dealerships, Gainesville, Fla., 1962-64; pres. chmn. bd. Central Supply Industries, Lake Wales, Fla., 1964-68; chmn., chief exec. officer Leasetran Corp., Winter Haven, Fla., 1968-81; chmn. Fla. Inst. Tech., 1976—; chmn. dir. Jacksonville br. Fed. Res. Bank of Atlanta, 1972-79. Chmn., Alliance with Colombia, 1970-73; mem. Fla. Council of 100, 1971—; mem. adv. bd. Fla. State U., Tallahassee, 1975—, U. Fla. Grad Sch. Bus., 1974—; chmn. bd. trustees Fla. Inst. Tech., 1971—. Served with USAAF, 1945-48; with USAF, 1948-50. Recipient Champion of Higher Edn. award from pres. of 17 Fla. univs., 1978. Fellow Soc. Univ. Fellows; mem. Air Force Assn. (life air council 1980—), Missile and Space Pioneer. Democrat. Research in aeros. history sonic range. Home: 2905 S Vasser St Melbourne FL 32901 Office: 150 W University Blvd Melbourne FL 32901

LYONS, PAUL CHRISTOPHER, government geologist, educator; b. Cambridge, Mass., Oct. 1, 1938; s. Maurice and Abby (Brennan) L.; m. Arlene D'Addieco, July 24, 1963; children—Sheryl, Russell, Crystal, Sandra, Jennifer. A.A., Boston U., 1963, A.B., 1964, A.M., 1969, Ph.D., 1964. Tchr. earth sci., Boston area high schs., 1964-68; instr. sci. Boston U., 1968-69, asst. prof., 1969-75; research assoc. Boston Coll., 1976-77; geologist U.S. Geol. Survey, Reston, Va., 1977—. Served with USN, 1956-59. Boston U. research grantee, 1972-73. Mem. Geol. Soc. Am. (editor spl. paper on coal-forming basins of U.S.), Am. Assn. Petroleum Geologists, Geol. Soc. Washington, Paleontol. Research Inst., Bot. Soc. Am. Co-editor Studies in New England Geology, 1976. Home: 11904 Escalante Ct Reston VA 22091 Office: US Geol Survey 956 Nat Ctr Reston VA 22092

LYSHER, MARY RITA, educator, field hockey coach; b. Niagara Falls, N.Y., July 28, 1956; d. Charles Wesley and Anna Mary (Leonard) F. A.A., Essex Community Coll., Balt., 1977; B.S., James Madison U., Harrisonburg, Va., 1979. Cert. in spl. edn. and mental retardation, Va. Fine jewelry sales rep. Hochschild/Kohn, Balt., 1975-77, J.C. Penney's, Fredericksburg, Va., 1981-82; sales rep. Paul's Bakery, Fredericksburg, 1982-85, also spl. edn. tchr., softball coach Fredericksburg City Schs., 1979-85, field hockey coach, 1980—; mem. U.S. lacrosse team, Balt., 1977, Harrisonburg, 1978, U.S. Collegiate Touring Team, Eng., 1978. Recipient James H. Newpher award Essex Community Coll., 1977, award Council Exceptional Children. Mem. Va. Edn. Assn., NEA, Fredericksburg Edn. Assn., Women's Field Hockey Assn., Va. High Sch. Coaches Assn., Nat. High Sch. Coaches Assn. Democrat. Roman Catholic. Home: 309 Patterson Ave Fredericksburg VA 22401 Office: Hugh Mercer Sch Fredericksburg VA 22401

LYSINGER, REX JACKSON, gas distribution company executive; b. Pitts., Aug. 14, 1937; s. W. Mark and Clare Ann (Long) L.; B.S. in Indsl. Engring., U. Pitts., 1959; m. Jodene Elizabeth Scott, Sept. 19, 1958; children—Teri Jo, Beth Ann, Rex Jay, Holly Sue. Engr., staff asst. E. Ohio Gas Co., Cleve., 1959-64, asst. dist. supt., 1964-65; v.p., engr., cons., mgr. Stone & Webster, N.Y.C., 1965-74, v.p., Houston, 1974-75; v.p. corp. planning Ala. Gas Corp., Birmingham, 1975-77, pres., dir., 1977—; pres., dir. Alagasco Energy Co., Inc., chmn. bd., pres., chief exec. officer Alagasco Inc., Ala. Gas Corp. and subs.; dir. Birmingham, South Trust Bank Ala. N.A. Bd. dirs. Met. Devel. Bd. Birmingham, 1978, Ala. Safety Council, Inc.; bd. dirs. Bapt. Hosp. Found. Served with USAR, 1960-61. Mem. Am. Gas Assn. (bd. dirs. 1983), Inst. Gas Tech. (bd. dirs. 1982), So. (dir. 1978-81) gas assns., Young Presidents Orgn., Birmingham Area C. of C. (dir. 1980—, pres. 1984), Newcomen Soc. Clubs: Downtown, Relay House, Birmingham Country, Rotary. Office: 2021 6th Ave N Birmingham AL 35203

LYTLE, ERNEST JAMES, JR., mathematician, industrial statistician; b. East Lake Weir, Fla., June 28, 1913; s. Ernest J. and Caroline (Pasteur) L.; m. Florence George, Feb. 19, 1941 (dec. Sept. 1980); children—Ernest, Caroline, J. Stephen; m. 2d, Shirley Gragg Young, Jan. 22, 1983. B.S. with honors, U. Fla., 1935, M.A., 1940, Ph.D., 1956. Cert. tchr., Fla. Tchr., coach Fellowship High Schl, Ocala, Fla., 1935-36, 37-39, prin., 1939-40; contact officer VA, Bay Pines, Fla., 1945-46; instr. math. U. Fla., Gainesville, 1946-50, 52-56, research asst., 1952-56, assoc. research prof., 1957-59, prof. grad. extension courses, 1963-68; assoc. engr. math. analysis and group head IBM Corp., Poughkeepsie, N.Y., 1956-57; staff mathematician Radiation Inc., Orlando, Fla., 1959-61; design engr. and staff mathematician Martin-Marietta Corp., Orlando, 1961-68; prof. math. sci. dept. U. Central Fla., Orlando, 1968-74 chmn. dept., 1974-75, prof. emeritus, 1975—; cons. mathematician Wood-Ivey Systems Co., Winter Park, Fla., 1974-82. Served with AUS, 1941-45, 50-52; to lt. col. USAR, 1934-62. Mem. Am. Math. Assn., Statis. Assn., Fla. Blue Key, Sigma Xi, Kappa Phi Kappa, Kappa Delta Pi. Democrat. Episcopalian. Home: 2107 Whitehall Dr Winter Park FL 32792

LYTLE, MICHAEL ALLEN, university official, consultant; b. Salina, Kans., Oct. 22, 1946; s. Milton Earl and Geraldine Faye (Young) L.; m. Bjorg Lindqvist, Mar. 12, 1984; 1 child, Eric Alexander. B.A., Ind. U., 1973; grad. cert. Sam Houston State U., Huntsville, Tex., 1977; M.Ed., Tex. A&M U., 1978; Substitute high sch. tchr., Butler County, Kans., 1969; instr. criminal justice Cleveland State Community Coll., Tenn., 1974-77; adj. instr. criminal justice U. Tenn., Chattanooga, 1975-76; teaching asst. Tex. A&M U., 1977-80, intern adminstrv. asst. Office Vice Chancellor Legal Affairs and Gen. Counsel, Tex. A&M U. System 1980, staff asso. Office Chancellor, 1980-81, asst. to chancellor, 1981-83, asst. dir. govt. relations, 1983-84, spl. asst. to Chancellor for fed. relations, 1984—; rep. legis. network Nat. Assn. State Univs. and Land-Grant Colls.; instl. rep. Research Univs. Network; chmn. fed. relations com. Tex. A&M Univ. System; exec. dir. Tex. Com. for Employer of Guard and Res.; mem. militarily critical techs. adv. com. U.S. Internat. Trade Adminstrn.; bd. advisers Ctr. Internat. Bus. Studies Tex. A&M U.; res. asst. army attache to Republic of Ireland, 1985—. Contbr. articles to profl. jours. Served with USAR, 1970-72; Vietnam. Decorated Bronze Star, Army Commendation medal with 2d oak leaf cluster; Inter-Univ. Seminar Armed Forces and Soc. fellow, 1979; assoc. Ctr. NATO Studies, Kent State U. Mem. Nat. Assn. State Univs. and Land-Grant Colls. (vet. affairs and nat. service com.). Policy Studies Orgn., Internat. Studies Assn., Am. Assn. Univ. Adminstr., Am. Soc. for Pub. Adminstrn., Res. Officers Assn., Am. Def. Preparedness Assn., Phi Delta Kappa. Republican. Episcopalian. Club: Army and Navy. Home: 402-C Fall Circle College Station TX 77840 Office: Office of Chancellor Tex A&M U System College Station TX 77883

MA, LI-CHEN, sociology educator; b. Xian, China, May 10, 1941; came to U.S., 1968, naturalized, 1979; s. Ho-Tze and Chin-fin (Lin) Ma; m. sue Ann Lee; children—Serena L., Jennifer L. B.S., Nat. Taiwan U., Taipei, 1963, M.S., 1967; Ph.D., U. Ga., 1972. Grad. asst. U. Ga., Athens, 1968-72, research assoc., 1970; asst. prof. sociology Lamar U., Beaumont, Tex., 1972-80, assoc. prof., 1980—; vis. prof. Nat. Taiwan U., 1983; chmn. subcom. on edn. Mayor's Correct Count Census, Beaumont, 1980. Contbr. articles to profl. jours. Grantee Lamar Bd. Regents, 1977, Lamar Research Council, 1981-82, 82-83, Nat. Sci. Council, Taiwan, 1983. Mem. Am. Sociol. Assn., Southwestern Sociol Assn. (fin. com. 1984—), Midsouth Sociol. Assn., So. Sociol. Soc., Assn. Chinese Am. Profls. (chmn. social sci. com. 1984—). Avocations: travel, camping, outdoors, sports. Office: Lamar U Dept Sociology Social Work and Criminal Justice Beaumont TX 77710

MABRY, NELLOISE JOHNSON, former educator; b. Valdosta, Ga., Sept. 8, 1921; d. Hansford Duncan and Maudelle (Williams) Johnson; student Bethel Woman's Coll., 1938-39, Wesleyan Conservatory, 1941; A.B., Mercer U., 1943, M.Ed., 1949; m. William Herbert Mabry, Mar. 5, 1942 (div. Nov. 1947); 1 son, William Herbert. Tchr., Cynthia H. Weir Elem. Sch., Macon, Ga., 1950-80. Mem. NEA, Ga., Bibb edn. assns., Ga. Assn. for Childhood Edn. (state pres. 1964-66), Delta Kappa Gamma (chpt. scrapbook chmn. 1966-68, chpt. program chmn. 1974-76, chpt. chmn. personal growth and services 1980-82, chpt. social chmn. 1982-84, 2d v.p. chpt. 1984-86, state dir. 3d dist. 1985—), Alpha Delta Pi, Alpha Psi Omega. Democrat. Baptist. Home: 1575 Adams St Macon GA 31204

MABRY, PAUL DAVIS, psychobiologist, researcher, educator; b. Meridian, Miss., Sept. 28, 1943; s. Paul Davis and Frances Elizabeth (Thigpen) M. B.S., Millsaps Coll., Jackson, Miss., 1965; M.S., U. Miss., 1967, Ph.D., 1970. Research trainee dept. neurosurgery U. Miss. Med. Ctr., Jackson, 1966, predoctoral research fellow, 1969-70; research asst. dept. psychology U. Miss., University, 1967-69; research assoc. neurosci. and behavior program Princeton U., N.J., 1970-76; chmn. dept. psychology, head div. behavioral and natural scis. Sacred Heart Coll., Belmont, N.C., 1976—. Contbr. articles to profl. jours. NIMH fellow, 1969. Mem. Soc. for Neurosci., Am. Psychol. Assn., Eastern Psychol. Assn., AAAS, Sigma Xi. Home: 6500 Carsdale Pl Charlotte NC 28210 Office: Dept Psychology Sacred Heart Coll Belmont NC 28012

MABRY, RICHARD LEE, otolaryngologist; b. Decatur, Tex., July 7, 1936; s. George D. and Ina Rachel (Lambert) M.; m. Cynthia Ann Surovik, July 17, 1959; children—Allen, Brian, Ann Elizabeth. B.A., North Tex. State U., 1956; M.D., U. Tex. Southwestern Med. Sch., 1960. Diplomate Am. Bd. Otolaryngology-Head and Neck Surgery. Intern VA Hosp., Dallas, 1960-61, resident, 1961, 64-67; practice medicine specializing in otolaryngology, Dallas, 1968—; mem. staff Meth. Hosp. of Dallas; clin. assoc. prof. otolaryngology U. Tex. Health Sci. Center, Dallas, 1968—; cons. Dallas VA Hosp., 1968—; mem. expert adv. panel otolaryngology U.S. Pharmacopoiea. Mem. Dallas Pub. Health Adv. Bd. Served to capt. M.C., USAF, 1962-64. Decorated Air Force Commendation medal. Mem. Am. Acad. Otolaryngology-Head and Neck Surgery (chmn. com. med. devices and drugs instr. postgrad. courses 1978—), Tex. Otolaryngological Assn., Tex. Soc. Ophthalmology and Otolaryngology, So. Med. Assn., Tex. Med. Assn., Dallas County Med. Soc., Dallas Acad. Otolaryngology. Baptist (deacon). Contbr. articles to profl. jours. Office: 3450 W Wheatland Rd Suite 260 Dallas TX 75211

MABSON, ROBERT LANGLEY, clergyman; b. New Orleans, Apr. 17, 1931; s. Eugene Beall and Eva Louise (Lea) M.; m. Minnie Augusta Lewis, Dec. 22, 1953; children—Lewis, Susan Jane, Laura Lea. B.A., Tulane U., 1952; postgrad. Union Theol. Sem., 1952-55; M. Religious Edn., Pres. Sch. Christian Edn., 1955; M.S., La. State U., 1964. Ordained to ministry Presbyterian Ch., 1955. Pastor Mt. Pleasant Presbyn. Ch., Sinks Grove, W.Va., 1955-57; dir. Christian edn. Barbee Larger Parish, Perry, Mo., 1957-59; pastor First Presbyn. Ch., Talihina, Okla., 1959-63; chaplain USPHS Hosp., 1959-63; head librarian, prof. Methodist Coll., Fayetteville, N.C., 1964-66; pastor Eastland Presbyn. Ch., Memphis, 1966-78, asst. librarian Memphis Theol. Sem., 1967-74; chaplain Calvary Colony Alcoholic Rehab. Ctr., also Kings Daus. and Sons Home, Memphis, 1979-83; pastor Ebenezer Presbyn. Ch., Strong, Ark., 1983-84, Sulphur Springs Cumberland Presbyn. Ch., Louann, Ark., 1984—; mem. Presbyn. Council Evangelism, 1959-63; mem. Covenant Presbytery, stated clk., moderator, 1973-75. Author: Presbyterian Missionary Labors in Kiamichi Valley, Oklahoma, 1850-1960. Recipient Congl. Community Service award, 1975. Address: PO Box 92 Mount Holly AR 71758

MACALPINE, ROBERT THOMAS, periodontist; b. Los Angeles, Jan. 5, 1949; s. Orville Duncan and Leone (Dufty) MacA.; m. Gail Yvonne Anderson, Dec. 31, 1978; children—Jill, Trent. B.A., So. Coll., 1971; M.P.H., D.D.S., Loma Linda U., 1977, cert. in periodontics, 1981. Practice dentistry ltd. to periodontics/periodontology, Asheville, N.C., 1982—. Contbr. articles to profl. jours. Mem. Am. Acad. Periodontology, So. Acad. Periodontology, N.C. Soc. Periodontists, Buncombe County Dental Soc., Phi Alpha Theta. Home: 28 Maple Ridge Ln Asheville NC 28806 Office: 1061 Haywood Rd Asheville NC 28806

MACAULAY, ALEXANDER STEPHENS, lawyer, state senator; b. Fort Moultrie, Sullivan Islands, Jan. 31, 1942; s. Neill Webster and Eliza (Barron) M.; m. Maria Locke Boineau; children—Maria Locke, Alexander Stephens, Jr., B.A., The Citadel, 1963; J.D., U. S.C., 1970. Bar: S.C. Ptnr. Miley and Macaulay, Walhalla, S.C.; asst. atty. gen. State of S.C., 1970-72; mem. S.C. Senate, 1981—. Mem. S.C. Bd. Edn., 1979-80; bd. dirs. United Way of Oconee County; bd. visitors Clemson U., 1980, Med. U. S.C., 1984; deacon, edler Walhalla Presbyn. Ch. Served with M.I., U.S. Army, Vietnam. Decorated Bronze Star, Air medal. Mem. Oconee County Bar Assn. (pres. 1980). Democrat. Lodges: Rotary, Sertoma. Office: Miley and Macaulay Box 343 West Union SC 29696*

MACAULEY, JOHN CHAPMAN WILSON, public relations executive; b. Princeton, N.J., May 23, 1952; s. Michael and Barbara Jones (Cart) M.; m. Margaret Anne Long, Mar. 24, 1979; children—James Edward, Margaret Wilson. B.A. in Journalism, U. N.C., 1974. News dir. U. N.C. TV, Chapel Hill, 1973; staff reporter Sta. WCHL, Chapel Hill, 1973-74; sports reporter The Sentinel, Winston-Salem, N.C., 1974-78; asst. pub. relations rep. R.J. Reynolds Tobacco Co., Winston-Salem, 1978-80, pub. relations rep., 1981-84, sr. pub. relations rep., 1985—; pub. address announcer for football and basketball Wake Forest U. Active Moravian Ch., Winston-Salem. Recipient Disting. Service award for devel. of high sch. athletics in N.C., Forsyth Country Day Sch. Republican. Home: 1407 Reynolda Rd Winston-Salem NC 27104 Office: Reynolds Tobacco Internat Reynolds Plaza Complex Winston-Salem NC 27102

MACCALLUM, ANNE WHICHARD, nurse, educator, administrator; b. Portsmouth, Va., Nov. 29, 1944; d. Murray P. and Ida Lee (Allen) Whichard; m. M. Reid MacCallum, Sept. 12, 1964; 1 child, Bruce. Student Va. Commonwealth U., 1962-64, M.S., 1978; B.S. in Nursing, Old Dominion U., 1969. Registered nurse, Va. Nursing instr. Norfolk Tech. Vocat. Ctr., Va., 1969-71, Chesapeake Tech. Ctr., Va., 1971-73, Norfolk Gen. Hosp., 1973-76, 1978-81; coordinator patient edn. and discharge planning Children's Hosp. of King's Daughters, Norfolk, 1981-83, assoc. dir. nursing, 1983-85, dir. edn. and profl. devel., 1985—. Mem. Assn. for Care Children's Health, Am. Nurses Assn. Va. Nurses Assn. (dist. bd. dirs. 1980-83, dist. pres. 1984—, chmn. council dist. presidents 1986—), Va. Nurses Assn. Maternal Health Profl. Practice Group (chmn. dist. 1979-80, state nominating chmn. 1981), Soc. for Health Edn. Tng., Sigma Theta Tau. Methodist. Club: Back River Yacht. Avocation: sailing. Office: Children's Hosp of King's Daughters 800 W Olney Rd Norfolk VA

MACDANIEL, SHERMAN PAINE, investment banker, stockbroker; b. San Antonio, Nov. 10, 1934; s. Gibbs and Virginia (Paine) M.; m. Kendall Bradshaw, Dec. 26, 1956; children—Sherman, Jr., Anne Chickering, Sara Macdaniel. B.B.A., U. Tex., 1956, M.B.A., 1957. Vice pres. Dominick & Dominick, Houston, 1968-70; v.p., br. mgr. Jesup & Lamont, Houston, 1970-74; v.p. White, Weld & Co., Houston, 1974-78, Merrill Lynch, Houston, 1978; Donaldson, Lufkin & Jenrette, Houston, 1978—; dir. Questronics, Inc., Salt Lake City. Pres., Winedale Council Winedale Hist. Soc., Tex., 1984—; bd. dirs. Planned Parenthood, Houston, 1970-74. Served capt. Fin. Corps., U.S. Army, 1957-61. Mem. Houston Soc. Fin. Analysts (program com. 1968—), Forum Club Houston, Chgo. Bd. Trade (registered rep.), German Club, Beta Theta Pi. Republican. Presbyterian. Clubs: Coronado (Houston); Argyle, San Antonio (San Antonio). Avocations: traveling; skiing. Home: 14971 Bramblewood St Houston TX 77079 Office: Donaldson Lufkin & Jenrette Securities Corp 3200 Inter First Plaza Houston TX

MACDONALD, CHARLES GORDON, international relations educator, consultant; b. Ravenna, Ohio, Apr. 17, 1947; s. Gordon Howard and Rose Eileen (Wright) MacD.; m. Martha Jane Furgiuele, Jan. 22, 1972; 1 child, Thomas Charles. B.A. in Internat. Affairs, Fla. State U., 1969; M.A. in Fgn. Affairs, U. Va., 1971, Ph.D. in Fgn. Affairs, 1976. Assoc. prof. internat. relations Fla. Internat. U., North Miami, 1977—; vis. asst. prof. U. Va., Charlottesville, 1979-80. Author: Iran, Saudi Arabia, and Law of the Sea, 1980; Crises and Issues in the Middle East, in press; (with others) Revolution in Iran: A Reappraisal, 1982. Contbr. articles to profl. jours. Mem. Miami Com. Fgn. Relations, 1985. Served to capt. USAF, 1971-73. Fellow Woodrow Wilson Found., 1969-70, NDEA, 1969-74, Higher Edn. Act., 1974-75, NEH, summer 1983. Mem. Am. Soc. Internat. Law, Am. Profs. for Peace in Middle East, Internat. Studies Assn., Middle East Inst., Middle East Studies Assn., Soc. Iranian Studies, Res. Officers Assn. Home: 111 NW 77 Way Pembroke Pines FL 33024 Office: Fla Internat U Dept Internat Relations Bay Vista Campus North Miami FL 33181

MACDONALD, GORDON JAMES FRASER, geophysicist; b. Mexico City, July 30, 1929; came to U.S., 1951, naturalized, 1955; s. Gordon James and Josephine (Bennett) MacD.; m. Betty Ann Kipniss; children by previous marriage—Gordon James, Maureen E., Michael A., Bruce S. A.B. summa cum laude, Harvrd U., 1950, M.A., 1952, Ph.D., 1954. Exec. v.p. Inst. Def. Analyses, 1967-68; bd. trustees The Mitre Corp., McLean, Va., 1968-70, 72-77, exec. com., 1972-77, chief scientist, 1979-83, v.p., chief scientist, 1983—; prof. physics and geophysics U. Calif., Santa Barbara, 1968-70, vice chancellor for research and grad. affairs, 1968-70; mem. Council on Environ. Quality, Exec. Office of Pres., Washington, 1970-72; bd. dirs. Inst. for Congress, 1974-78, Environ. Law Inst., 1975—; mem. adv. council Gas Research Inst., 1976-79; Henry R. Luce Third Century prof. environ. studies and policy and dir. environ. studies program Dartmouth Coll., 1972-79, adj. prof. environ. studies, 1979—; jr. fellow Harvard U., 1952-54; asst. prof. geology and geophysics MIT, 1954-55, assoc. prof., 1955-58; staff assoc. Geophys. Lab., Carnegie Inst. Tech., 1955-58; prof. geophysics UCLA, 1958-68, dir. Atmospheric Research Lab., 1960-66; staff assoc. NASA, 1960-61; Fulbright lectr. Ecole d'Ete de Physique Theorique, Les Houches, France, 1962; lectr. Italian Phys. Soc. Summer Sch. on Space Physics, Varenna, 1962; mem. corp. Woods Hole Oceanographic Instn., 1964-76; cons. editor MIT Press., 1972—; tech. adv. bd. Dept. Commerce, 1964-66; mem. Def. Sci. Bd., Dept. Def., 1966-70, Air Force Sci. Adv. Bd., 1968, Air Force Office Sci. Research Physics Research Evaluation Group, 1964-66; mem. spl. study group on noise and sonic boom in relation to man Dept. Interior, 1967-68; cons. for sci. and tech. study Dept. State, 1976, adv. com. on sci. and fgn. affairs, 1973-74; chmn. Commn. Natural Resources, Nat. Acad. Sci., Nat. Acad. Engring./NRC, 1973-77, chmn. div. earth scis., 1969-70, many other coms.; adv. panel for weather modification NSF, 1964-67, chmn. adv. com. atmospheric scis., 1977-80; adv. panel on nuclear effects Office Tech. Assessment, 1975-77, mem. many panels on Pres.'s Sci. Adv. Com., 1965-70. Recipient Am. Acad. Arts and Scis. Monograph prize, 1959; Fulbright fellow, 1962; James B. Macelwane award, Am. Geophys. Union, 1965. Fellow Am. Geophys. Union, AAAS Am. Meteorol. Soc., Geol. Soc. Am., Royal Astron. Soc.; mem. Nat. Acad. Sci., Am. Acad. Arts and Scis., Am. Philos. Soc., Council on Fgn. Relations, Am. Assn. Petroleum Geologists, Am. Astron. Soc., Am. Math. Soc., Am. Mineral. Soc., Geochem. Soc. Am., N.Y. Acad. Sci., Seismological Soc. Am., Soc. Indsl. and Applied Math. (bd. dirs. Inst. for Math. and Soc. 1975-77), Sigma Xi. Assoc. editor Jour. Atmospheric Scis., 1962-64, editor, 1964-70; editor Revs. of Geophysics, 1962-70; assoc. editor Jour. Geophys. Research, 1960-70, Sci., 1964-69, Space Sci. Revs., 1963—, Bolettino di Geofisica Teorica ad Applicata 1968—, Jour. Def. Research, 1969-70, The Moon, 1970—; contbr. articles to profl. jours. Office: 1820 Dolley Madison Blvd McLean VA 22102

MACDONALD, LINDA LORRAINE, public relations specialst; b. Galveston, Tex., Aug. 29, 1947; d. George Henry and Lorraine Irene (LaCoume) Saenz; m. William Keith Macdonald, July 11, 1970; children—Keitha Lorraine, Kenneth Lawrence. B.A., Sam Houston State U., 1969. Informational writer U. Tex. Med. Br., Galveston, 1969-71, editor publs., 1971-73, asst. dir. pub. info. office, 1973-76, assoc. dir., 1976-79, dir. info., 1979—; cons. pub. relations, Galveston, 1980—. Vice-pres. pub. relations United Way Galveston, 1982—; 84; dir. communications Trinity Episcopal Sch., 1979—. Recipient Nat. Gold award United Way, 1983. Mem. Council Advancement and Support Edn. (mag. award 1983), Tex. Soc. Hosp. Pub. Relations Dirs., Galveston Cultural Arts, Galveston Hist. Found. Episcopalian. Club: Noon Opti-Mrs (pres. 1978-79). Home: 4801 Crockett Blvd Galveston TX 77550 Office: U Tex Med Br Adminstrn Bldg Galveston TX 77550

MACDONALD, ROBERT ALAN, language educator; b. Salamanca, N.Y., Mar. 25, 1927; s. Guy E. and Hildur V. (Helene) MacD. B.A., U. Buffalo, 1948; M.A., U. Wis., 1949, Ph.D., 1958. Asst. prof. U. Richmond, Va., 1955-61, assoc. prof., 1961-67, prof. Spanish, 1967—; ofcl. project reviewer NEH, Washington, 1977—, Social Sci. and Humanities Research Council, Ottawa, Ont., Can., 1981—. Editor Bull. of Fgn. Lang. Assn. Va., 1962-67, 72—Contbr. articles to profl. jours. Served with U.S. Army, 1946-47, 51-53. A. L. Markham traveling fellow U. Wis., 1958-59; Am. Council Learned Socs. fellow, 1976; fellow and grantee U. Richmond, 1958-84; named Cultural Laureate of Va., 1977; recipient Disting. Service award Fgn. Lang. Assn. Va., 1981. Mem. Acad. Am. Research Historians on Medieval Spain, Am. Assn. Tchrs. of Spanish and Portuguese (past pres. state chpt.), AAUP (past pres. local chpt.), Am. Council on Teaching Fgn. Langs., Medieval Acad. Am., MLA. Club: Torch (Richmond). Office: U Richmond PO Box 278 Richmond VA 23173

MACDONALD, ROBERT DICKSON, business executive; b. South Bend, Ind., Mar. 14, 1937; s. Charles A. and Dorothy (Dickson) MacD.; B.S. in Mktg., Northwestern U., 1959; m. Anita Olson, Sept. 23, 1960; children—William Robert, Scott Robert. Account exec. Needham, Harper & Steers, Chgo., 1961-66; account exec. Leo Burnett Co., Chgo., 1966-68; gen. mgr. Roblee div. Brown Shoe Co., St. Louis, 1968-77, gen. mgr. Roblee and Pedwin divs., 1977-80, sales rep. S.E. region Mound City div., 1980-83; pres. Excalibur Enterprises, Inc., Atlanta, 1983-84; sr. v.p. mktg. Buypass the System, Atlanta, 1984—. Served with USMC, 1959-60. Mem. Nat. Shoe Retailers Assn., (mem. men's style com. 1976-80), Nat. Shoe Travelers Assn., Southeastern Shoe Travelers Assn., Phi Kappa Psi. Clubs: Horseshoe Bend Country.

MACDONALD, ROSS BANKS, corporate planner; b. Dayton, Ohio, May 29, 1934; s. Chisholm Nicholson and Mary Louise (Banks) M.; B.S., Yale U., 1955; M.S., U. Tex., 1957; m. Hope Hollister, June 23, 1956; 1 dau., Laura Hollister; m. 2d, Lynne Cameron Andrews, Sept. 25, 1965 (div.); children—Chisholm Andrew, Cameron Ross. With Chase Manhattan Bank, 1957-61; research analyst Reynolds Securities, Inc., 1961-64; pres. Optronics Tech., Inc., N.Y.C., 1964-68; pres. Ross B. Macdonald & Co., Ltd., 1964-73; chmn. bd. Clinicare Corp., Milw., 1973-74; pres. Macdonald Assos., Inc., Houston, 1974—; cons. Internat. Semmental, Inc. Pres. Met. Houston Hockey Assn., 1978—. Mem. Planning Execs. Inst., N. Am. Soc. Corp. Planners. Republican. Clubs: Masons, Shriners. Office: PO Box 42888-231 Houston TX 77042

MAC DONALD, THOMAS COOK, JR., lawyer; b. Atlanta, Oct. 11, 1929; s. Thomas Cook and Mary (Morgan) MacD.; B.S. with high honors, U. Fla., 1951, LL.B. with high honors, 1953; m. Gay Anne Everiss, June 30, 1956; children—Margaret Anne, Thomas William. Admitted to Fla. bar, 1953; practiced in Tampa, 1953—; mem. firm Shackleford, Farrior, Stallings & Evans, 1953—; dir. Jim Walter Corp.; legis. counsel Gov. of Fla., 1963; del. 5th Circuit Jud. Conf., 1969-81; mem. Supreme Ct. Com. on Jud. Ethics, 1976. Mem. Fla. Student Scholarship and Loan Commn., 1963-67, Hillsborough County Pub. Edn. Study Commn., 1965, Fla. Jud. Qualifications Commn., 1983—. Bd. dirs. Shands Teaching Hosp., Inc. (U. Fla.), 1981—, U. Fla. Found., Inc.; trustee Univ. Community Hosp., Tampa, 1968-78. Served to 1st lt. Judge Adv. Gen. Corps, USAF, 1953-55. Recipient Disting. Alumnus award U. Fla., 1976. Fellow Am. Bar Found., Am. Coll. Trial Lawyers; mem. Am. Law Inst., Am. Bar Assn. (com. on ethics and profl. responsibility 1970-76), Fla. Bar (mem. com. on profl. ethics 1964-72, chmn. 1966-70, bd. govs. 1970-74), Fla. West Coast Sports Assn. (sec. 1965-80), U. Fla. Nat. Alumni Assn. (pres. 1973), Phi Kappa Phi, Phi Delta Phi, Fla. Blue Key, Kappa Alpha. Episcopalian (lay reader 1961—). Home: 1904 Holly Ln Tampa FL 33629 Office: PO Box 3324 Tampa FL 33601

MACDOUGALL, ROBERT DOUGLAS, geologist; b. McVille, N.D., Jan. 2, 1922; s. Rollo Dixon and Nettie Corinne (Syvertson) MacD.; m. Ingrid Margarete Heemann, Sept. 30, 1961; children—Jerome W., James F. Student N.D. State Sch. of Sci., 1939-41, U. N.D., 1946-47; B.A., U. Mont., 1949; M.S., U. Minn., 1952. Surface geologist Arabian Am. Oil Co., Saudi Arabia, 1952-56, subsurface geologist, 1956-59; cons. geologist, N.D. and Mont., 1959-62; geologist U.S. Geol. Survey, Washington, 1962-70, Metairie, La., 1970-82, Minerals Mgmt. Service, Metairie, 1982—. Bd. dirs., treas., coach 4th Ward Recreation Assn., Mandeville, La., 1971-81; dist. dir. Dixie Youth Baseball, 1980-82. Served with USNR, 1942-46, PTO. Fellow Royal Geog. Soc.; mem. Am. Assn. Petroleum Geologists, New Orleans Geol. Soc., Mensa. Club: Ponchartrain Yacht (Mandeville). Home: 646 Oak St Mandeville LA 70448

MACE, CARROLL EDWARD, Spanish language educator; b. Neosho, Mo., Dec. 5, 1926; s. Rector Tolle and Beatrice (Dunkeson) M. B.A., Drury Coll., 1949; M.A., Tulane U., 1952, Ph.D., 1965. Prof. Spanish, Xavier U. La., New Orleans, 1975—. Author: Two Spanish-Quiche Dance-Dramas of Rabinal, 1971. United Negro College Fund scholar, 1985. Roman Catholic. Office: Xavier U La 7325 Palmetto St New Orleans LA 70125

MACFADDEN, ARTHUR ROSS, educator; b. N.Y.C., Dec. 20, 1921; s. William James and Mabel (Ross) MacF.; m. Cynthia Neal, June 23, 1944; children—Gaylord Neal, Arthur Ross, Jr. B.S., Johns Hopkins U., 1964; M.B.A., U. Tenn.-Chattanooga, 1969; Ed.D., U. Tenn.-Knoxville, 1974. Commd. 2d lt. USAF, 1942, advanced through grades to lt. col., 1970, ret., 1970; prof. mgmt. Chattanooga State Tech. Community Coll., 1970—, bus. mgr., 1976-78, dean adminstrv. services, 1978-80, dean fin. adminstrn., 1980-83. Investment officer Chattanooga State Found., 1980—; mem. Armed Forces Celebration Mil. Project Office, Chattanooga, 1984. Jimmy Doolittle fellow Aerospace Edn. Found., 1983; recipient Exceptional Service award Air Force Assn., 1983. Episcopalian. Clubs: Lookout Mountain Fairyland, Privateer Yacht. Avocations: aircraft pilot, sailing, quarter horses, travel. Home: 1101 Fleetwood Ave Lookout Mountain TN 37350 Office: Chattanooga State Tech Community Coll 4501 Amnicola Hwy Chattanooga TN 37406

MACGILVRAY, DANIEL FRANK, architect, educator; b. Kankakee, Ill., Sept. 13, 1944; s. George Alexander and Gretchen Rose (Allie) M.; m. Patricia Dale Harville, Aug. 12, 1966; children—Eric Andrew, Brian Christopher, Katherine Erin Melanie. B. Arch., U. Ill., 1967, M. Arch., 1969; cert. U. Rome, 1969. Registered architect Md., Tex. Sr. designer, planner Walton, Madden, Cooper, Riverdale, Md., 1972-75; cts. project adminstr. Nat. Clearinghouse, Champaign, Ill., 1975-77; asst. prof. Tex. A&M U., College Station, 1977-80, asst. dean, 1980-85, assoc. dean, 1985—, assoc. prof. architecture, 1982—; architect, College Station, 1977—. Prin. works include elem. sch., Laurel, Md., 1972 (award 1973), elem. middle sch., Columbia, Md., 1974 (award 1975). Mem. Zoning Bd. Adjustment, College Station, 1981-84; chmn. Northgate Planning Com., College Station, 1983; mem. planning and zoning commn., College Station, 1984—; pres. College Station Assn. Gifted and Talented, 1985—. Served to lt. USNR, 1970-72. Martin Roche fellow 1968-69; acad. study leave Tex. A&M U., Egypt, Turkey, Greece, 1985. Mem. Nat. Trust Hist. Preservation. Methodist. Avocations: philately; watercolor painting; jogging; history. Office: Tex A&M U Dept Environ Design Coll Architecture College Station TX 77843

MACH, WILLIAM HOWARD, meteorology educator; b. Hamilton, Tex., July 16, 1945; s. William Howard Mach and Effie Mae (Laney) M.; m. Diane Lynn Sivertson, June, 1968; 1 child, Melissae Diane. B.S. in Physics, U. Wash., 1969, M.S., 1972; Ph.D. in Meteorology, Pa. State U., 1978. Asst. prof. dept. Meteorology Fla. State U., Tallahassee, 1978-83, assoc. prof., 1983—. Contbr. articles to profl. jours. Office: Dept of Meteorology 404 Love FSU Tallahassee FL 32306

MACHAC, QUENTIN JOSEPH, safety professional; b. Yoakum, Tex., Nov. 14, 1928; s. Joseph and Glenna Mary (Brown) M.; m. Ella Reimer, June 1, 1950; children—Joella (dec.), Terry, Nancy. Student U. Tex., 1946-47. Newspaper editor Malec Pub. Co., Yoakum and East Bernard, Tex., 1947-52; with Shell Oil Co., Tex., 1952—, Shell gas processing plants, 1952-68, region safety rep. Shell Exploration and Prodn. Tex., 1968-78, sr. safety rep. Shell Oil Co. (Corp.), Houston, 1978—; curriculum adv. Houston Community Coll. System, 1983-85. Author tng. manuals and coordinator audio-visual tng. programs. Bd. mgrs. Nottingham Forest Townhome Assn., Houston, 1979-80, pres., 1980; v.p. Westbury Civic Club, 1975. Mem. Am. Soc. Safety Engrs. (chpt. pres. 1983-84, chpt. Safety Profl. of Yr. award 1984-85, regional conf. chmn. 1986; regional safety profl. of year award 1986). Methodist. Avocation: home building. Office: Shell Oil Co One Shell Plaza 900 Louisiana Houston TX 77002

MACHADO, PRISCILLA HELENE, political science educator; b. Dallas, Jan. 20, 1957; d. Gaston Gerardo and A. Elaine (Sutts) M. B.A., Baylor U., 1979, M.A., 1980; Ph.D., U. Tex.-Austin, 1986. Teaching asst. govt. dept. U. Tex.-Austin, 1982-85, asst. instr., 1985-86; spl. asst. to Sec. of State, Austin, 1982; legis. aide to speaker Tex. Ho. of Reps., Austin, 1982-83; legis. aide to Rep. Mike Toomey, 1983-85; statistician, demographer Morrison & Guinn Redistricting, Waco, Tex., 1981-82; jud. intern U.S. Supreme Ct., Washington, 1985. Mem. Am. Polit. Sci. Assn., Pi Sigma Alpha, Phi Alpha Theta, Pi Beta Phi, Phi Kappa Phi. Republican. Roman Catholic. Home: 3607 B Summit Bend Austin TX 78759 Office: U Tex 536 Burdine Hall Austin TX 78712

MACHAN, JAMES ROBERT, internist; b. Niagara Falls, N.Y., July 3, 1924; s. James Andrew and Mildred Alvira (Goodison) M.; m. Barbara Mary Blay, Apr. 23, 1949; Susan Sarah Elizabeth Machan Zysko, James Andrew, Sarah Jane Machan Hobbs. M.D. cum laude, U. Western Ont., 1948. Jr. intern, then sr. intern Victoria Hosp., London, Ont., Can., 1949-52; sr. intern Westminster Hosp., London, 1953-54; staff Hammersmith Hosp., London, Eng., 1955-56, Brompton Rd. Chest Hosp., London, Eng., 1957; practice medicine specializing in internal medicine, Fredericksburg, Va. Fellow Royal Coll. Physicians, ACP; mem. AMA, Ont. Med. Soc., Can. Med. Soc., Delta Upsilon, Alpha Omega Alpha. Episcopalian. Office: 2300 Charles St Fredericksburg VA 22401

MACHANIC, MINDY ROBIN, environmental designer, educator, consultant, writer, photographer; b. N.Y.C., June 21, 1950; d. Harmon Jack Machanic and Helen Jewel (Wolf) Mamolen. B.F.A., San Francisco Art Inst., 1973; B.S., U. State N.Y., 1983; M. Planning, U. So. Calif., 1980; M.A., Calif. State U.-Los Angeles, 1984. Exec. dir. YWCA of U. So. Calif., Los Angeles, 1980-81; instr. UCLA Extension, 1980, Calif. State U.-Northridge, 1982, Otis Art Inst. of Parsons Sch., Los Angeles, 1979-82; facility planner-analyst Steinmann, Grayson, Smylie, Los Angeles, 1981-82; asst. prof., program coordinator environ. design program Sch. of Art, E. Carolina U., Greenville, N.C., 1984—; research asst. HUD, San Francisco, 1975, adminstrv. program analyst Nat. Flood Ins. Program, Washington, 1978; program coordinator Pacific Am. Inst., Los Angeles, 1982-83; mgmt. analyst IRS, Los Angeles, 1983; pres., prin. City Arts, Los Angeles, 1978-84, Greenville, N.C., 1984—; movie reviewer Daily Reflector, Greenville, N.C., 1985; vol. cons., student coordinator design project City of Greenville and E. Carolina U., Greenville, 1984—, Hollywood Revitalization Com. and Otis/Parsons, Los Angeles, 1979. Contbr. articles and book revs. to profl. jours. One-man shows include Lycoming Coll., Pa., 1974; exhibited in group shows So. Exposure Gallery, San Francisco, 1974, 75, Barnsdall Park Mcpl. Gallery, Los Angeles, 1981, Gray Gallery, E. Carolina U., 1984, 85, 86, Community Council for Arts, Kinston, N.C., 1985. Mem. Environ. Design Research Assn., Indsl. Design Soc. Am., Inst. Bus. Designers, Nat. Trust for Historic Preservation, N.C. Am. Planning Assn., Sierra Club, Greenville Area Preservation Assn., Popular Culture Assn., Am. Film Inst. Democrat. Jewish. Avocations: gardening; music; reading; old-house renovations. Home: 302 Lewis St Greenville NC 27834 Office: Environ Design Program E Carolina U Sch Art Greenville NC 27834

MACHANIC, ROGER, real estate developer; b. Burlington, Vt., Mar. 11, 1933; A.B. in Econs. cum laude, Harvard U., 1955; m. Grace Wishart Manly, Apr. 20, 1963; children—Bruce Manly, Laura Manly. Founder, past owner, Devel. Resources Inc.; now chmn. Omsco Inc., Montgomery Real Estate Corp. (all Alexandria, Va.). Bd. dirs. Alexandria Symphony; trustee George Mason U. Found. Served with U.S. Army, 1956-57. Mem. Alexandria C. of C. (past pres.), Va. C. of C. (v.p., bd. dirs.), Alexandria Bldg. Industry Assn. (pres.), No. Va. Builders Assn. (dir. 1967-70). Clubs: Belle Haven Country, Rotary (Alexandria); Harvard (Washington) (N.Y.C.). Home: 430 S Fairfax St ALexandria VA 22314 Office: 218 N Lee St Suite 300 Alexandria VA 22314

MACHOVEC, FRANK J., psychologist; b. Balt., May 16, 1930, s. James Joseph and Theresa Anna MacH.; m. Evelyn Mary Stultz, May 5, 1951; 1 child, Frank. B.A., U. Md., 1964; M.A., Loyola U., Balt., 1965; Ph.D., Fielding Inst., 1979. Lic. clin. psychologist, Va., N.C., Man., Can.; diplomate Am. Bd. Psychol. Hypnosis. Asst. dir. New Sch. Psychotherapy, Washington, 1970-71; chief psychologist Victoria Hosp., Winnipeg, Man., 1973-75, Alta. Mental Health, Lethbridge, Can., 1975-77; staff psychologist Alaska Psychiat. Inst., Anchorage, 1977-79, State Hosp. South, Blackfoot, Idaho, 1979-81; dir. psychol. services S. Va. Mental Health Inst., Danville, 1981—; dir. Ctr. for Study of Self, Danville, 1984—; dir. quality assurance Va. Dept. Mental Health. supr. Am. Assn. Marriage and Family Therapy, 1973—. Contbr. articles to profl. jours. Served with USMC, 1950-52. Fellow Am. Coll. Psychology; mem. Am. Psychol. Assn. (Nat. Cert. Recognition 1982), Va. Psychol. Assn., Soc. Clin. and Exptl. Hypnosis, Internat. Rorschach Soc. Republican. Lodge: Masons. Avocations: lapidary; winemaking; travel; ham radio.

MACICA, JOSEPH MILES, industrial manufacturing company official, planning consultant; b. Baroda, Mich., Oct. 2, 1936; s. Joseph Miraslav and Helen Antonia (Cesnak) M. Student Western Mich. U., 1959-60, Bates Coll., Lewiston, Maine, 1963; B.S.B.A. in Indsl. Mgmt., U. Fla., 1965. European tour condr. Olson Travel Orgn., Chgo., 1965-66; asst. to pres. Basic C Corp., Bridgman, Mich., 1967-68; mgr. telecontrol hydraulics div. Bendix, St. Joseph, Mich., 1968-74, product coordinator engine controls div., Newport News, Va., 1974-76, planner, 1976-80, supr. prodn. control, 1980-81; sr. planner, supr. prodn. control Bendix Electronic Controls div. Allied Automotive, Newport News, 1981-85; planner internat. trade zone ops. Bendix Electronics-Global, 1985—. Pres. bd. dirs. Sonoma Woods Condo, Newport News, 1978—. Served with U.S. Army, 1955-57. Recipient Rescue and Lifesaving commendation Tanzanian Nat. Parks. Mem. Phi Kappa Phi, Beta Gamma Sigma. Club: Twin City Camera (St. Joseph) (pres. 1972-73). Home: 1441 Ventura Way Newport News VA 23602 Office: Bendix Electronic Controls Div Allied Automotive 615 Bland Blvd Newport News VA 23602

MACINNES, DAVID FENTON, JR., chemistry educator, researcher; b. Abington, Pa., Mar. 19, 1943; s. David F. and Emma Kathleen (O'Neill) MacI.; m. Barbara Ellen Hardy, June 26, 1973; children—Colin, Breanyn, Gavin. B.A., Earlham Coll., 1965; M.A. Princeton U., 1970, Ph.D., 1972. Chemistry tchr. Westtown Sch., Pa., 1970-73; asst. prof. Guilford Coll., Greensboro, N.C., 1973-82, assoc. prof. chemistry, 1982—; postdoctoral fellow U. Pa., Phila., 1980-81; vis. assoc. chemist Brookhaven Nat. Lab., Upton, N.Y., 1982. Author: Laboratory Manual for Chemical Principles, 1985. Contbr. articles to profl. jours. Grantee Lindbergh Soc., 1982-83. Mem. Am. Chem. Soc. (chmn. N.C. sect. 1986, Dolittle award 1981), Nat. Sci. Tchrs. Assn., N.C. Acad. Scis., Sigma Xi (bd. dirs. local chpt. 1985). Mem. Society of Friends. Office: Chemistry Dept Guilford Coll Greensboro NC 27410

MACK, CONNIE (CORNELIUS MCGILLICUDDY), III, congressman; b. Phila., Oct. 29, 1940; s. Cornelius M. and Susan (Sheppard) McGillicuddy; m. Ludie Priscilla, Sept. 11, 1960; children—Debra Lynn McGillicuddy Elam, Cornelius Harvey. Grad., U. Fla. Mgmt. tng. Sun Bank, Ft. Myers, Fla., 1966-68; v.p. bus. devel. First Nat. Bank, Ft. Myers, 1968-71; sr. v.p., dir. Sun Bank, Cape Coral, Fla., 1971-75; pres., dir. Fla. Nat. Bank, Cape Coral, 1972-82; mem. U.S. Ho. of Reps., Washington, 1983—; dir. Fed. Res. Bd., Miami, 1981-82. Bd. dirs., chmn. Palmer Drug Abuse Program, Cape Coral; bd. dirs. Cape Coral Hosp. Named most effective freshman Ho. of Reps., U.S. News and World Report. Mem. Met. Ft. Myers C. of C., Cape Coral C. of C. Republican. Roman Catholic. Office: 504 Cannon House Office Bldg Washington DC 20515

MACK, D., JR., educational administrator. Supt. of schs. Charleston, S.C. Office: 103 Calhoun St Charleston SC 29409*

MACK, GARNETT LLOYD, educator; b. Chase City, Va., Apr. 26, 1931; s. Garnet and Susanna (Gayle) M.; B.A., Storer Coll., Harpers Ferry, W.Va., 1954; postgrad. Ohio State U., 1955; M.A., George Washington U., 1966, M.Philosophy, 1969, Ph.D. (So. Fellowships fellow), 1972; postgrad. Rydal Mt. Summer Sch., Eng., 1972, Emory U., summer 1975; m. Janice Deros McManus, June 1, 1963; children—Luis Garnett, Lloyd Joseph; foster children—Johnnie L. Beale, Billy J. Robinson. Instr. English, Va. State U., Petersburg, 1964-67, asst. prof., 1967-71, asso. prof., 1971-73, prof., 1973—, coordinator grad. studies English, 1972—, editor Scip Anglia, dept. English newsletter, 1973-79; lectr. English and Am. civilization George Washington U., summers 1968-70; edn1. specialist U.S. Dept. Agr. Research Center, Beltsville, Md., summer 1971; exec. dir. Mack's Secretarial Services; notary public. Tutor, vol. worker Children's Home of Va. Baptists, Inc., Petersburg, 1972—, editor New Horizons newsletter; active Bapt. Home Improvement Assn., Big Bros.; founder, pres. James Alexander Gayle Meml. Fellowship Fund, Inc., 1976—; founder, exec. dir. Susanna Gayle Mack Community Center, Ettrick, Va., 1981—; deacon Shiloh Bapt. Ch., Petersburg, Va., 1982—, sec. bd. deacons; sec. pastor's adv. com. D.Min. program Pitts. Theol. Sem. Served with AUS, 1956-58; mem. Res. (ret.). Mem. MLA, Am. Studies Assn. (nat. Am. studies faculty), Wordsworth-Coleridge Assn., Am. Lit. Assn., South Atlantic Modern Lang. Assn., Coll. Lang. Assn., Comparative Lit. Assn., African Lit. Assn., Shakespeare Assn., Internat. Shakespeare Congress. Democrat. Presbyn. Home: 6900 Hickory Rd Petersburg VA 23803 Office: Va State U Box 376 Petersburg VA 23803

MACK, JEFFREY EDWARD, psychotherapist; b. Middletown, Del., Apr. 12, 1945; s. Samuel and Jessie (Green) M.; m. Sima Beryl Stoltz, Jan. 1, 1966; children—Reid Philip, Tracy Inez. A.A. in Psychology, Miami Dade Community Coll., 1974; B.A., Fla. Internat. U., 1975; M.Ed., U. Miami (Fla.), 1977. Lic. mental health counselor, marriage and family therapist, Fla. Activities supr. Sunrise Sch. for Retarded, Miami, 1974; health service counselor Treatment Alternatives to Street Crime, 1974-79; clin. health service counselor S. Dade Alcohol Edn. Ctr., Miami, 1979—; pvt. practice psychotherapy, Miami, 1980—; mem. adv. com. for human services internship program U. Miami; presenter alcohol/drug abuse workshops. Mem. Am. Mental Health Counselors Assn., Am. Personnel and Guidance Assn., Am. Psychol. Assn., Fla. Mental Health Counselors Assn. Jewish. Home: 9941 Kendale Blvd Miami FL 33176 Office: 7995 SW 112th St Miami FL 33156

MACK, LESLIE EUGENE, research administrator, hydrogeologist; b. Winchester, Mass., June 24, 1929; s. Clifton Eugene and Louise Franklin (Upton) M.; m. Greta Sonia Stangeland, May 28, 1954 (div. 1970); children—Karen, Laura, Glenn, Jeanette; m. Nancy Jane Mann, Dec. 14, 1970. B.A. in Geology, Duke U., 1951; M.A. in Geology, U. Kans., 1957, Ph.D., 1959; J.D., U. Ark., 1964. Cert. hydrogeologist. Water mgmt. cons. Rockwin Fund, Inc., Fayetteville, Ark., 1959-70; v.p. Resources, Inc., Little Rock, 1970-73; sr. hydrologist Dames & Moore, Washington, 1973-75; asst. dir. exploration Am. Petroleum Inst., Washington, 1975-80; dir. water resources research ctr. U. Ark., Fayetteville, 1980—; water mgmt. cons., Fayetteville, 1959—. Author: Water Law in Arkansas, 1964; also articles. Served to lt. (j.g.) USNR, 1951-53, Korea. Mem. Am. Water Resources Assn. (bd. dirs. 1970-72), Nat. Water Well Assn. (bd. dirs. 1966-70), Internat. Water Resources Assn., Am. Assn. Petroleum Geologists, Am. Inst. Hydrology. Avocation: Woodworking. Office: Water Resources Research Ctr U Ark 223 Ozark Hall Fayetteville AR 72701

MACK, MAZIE NELL, guidance counselor; b. Bryan, Tex., July 19, 1936; d. William and Clara Bell (Hersey) Smith; m. Emanuel Mack, Dec. 23, 1959; children—Cedric Emanuel, Melanie Jeannine. B.A., Fisk U., 1957; M.Ed., Prairie View A&M U., 1972. Lic. profl. counselor; nat. cert. counselor. Tchr. pub. schs., Bryan, 1957-60, 62-64, Freeport, Tex., 1964-65; prodn. clk. Dow Chem. Co., Freeport, 1965-68; tchr. Brazosport Ind. Sch. Dist., Freeport, 1968-74, guidance counselor, 1974—. Campaign mgr. Emanual Mack for City Council campaign, 1974-85; bd. dirs. Brazosport Meml. Day Care Ctr., Lake Jackson, Tex., 1971-74. Mem. Brazosport Edn. Assn. (pres. 1974-75, Human Relations award 1984), Brazoria Assn. Counseling and Devel. (pres. 1978-79; Counselor of Yr. 1985), Tex. Assn. Counseling and Devel. (dir. 1983-86; Disting. Service award 1984, Outstanding Counselor 1985), Delta Kappa Gamma. Baptist. Avocation: church music. Home: 22 N Ave F Freeport TX 77541 Office: PO Drawer Z Freeport TX 77541

MACK, THEODORE, lawyer; b. Ft. Worth, Mar. 5, 1936; s. Henry and Norma (Harris) M.; A.B. cum laude, Harvard, 1958, J.D., 1961; m. Ellen Feinknopf, June 19, 1960; children—Katherine Norma, Elizabeth Ellen, Alexandra. Bar: Tex. 1961, U.S. Supreme Ct. 1971. Assoc., Mack & Mack, Fort Worth, 1961-62, ptnr., 1963-70; ptnr., shareholder Wynn, Brown, Mack, Renfro & Thompson, and predecessors, 1970—. Dir. So. Plow Co., Dallas, 1966—, v.p., 1968—, sec., 1976—. Bd. dirs. Jewish Fedn. Fort Worth, 1965-72, sec., 1967-68, 3d v.p., 1968-69; bd. dirs. Suicide Prevention of Tarrant County, Tex., 1963-64, Tarrant County Sr. Citizens Center, Inc., 1969-81, Family and Individual Services Assn. Met. Tarrant County, 1981-84; trustee Ft. Worth Country Day Sch., 1976-82; participant Leadership Ft. Worth, 1973-74. Fellow Tex. Bar Found.; mem. ABA, Fort Worth/Tarrant County Bar Assn. (editor Bar News 1963-64), State Bar Tex. (chmn. dist. grievance com. 1973), Harvard Alumni Assn., Harvard Law Sch. Assn. (v.p. 1977), Harvard Law Sch. Fund (class agt. 1973-80), Harvard Law Sch. Assn. Tex. (dir. 1970-73, treas. 1973-74, sec. 1974-75, v.p. 1975-76, pres. 1976-77). Democrat. Jewish (dir. congregation 1964-73, sec. 1968-69, 72-73, pres. 1975-77). Club: Rotary (Ft. Worth). Home: 2817 Harlanwood Dr Fort Worth TX 76109 Office: 1800 First City Bank Tower Fort Worth TX 76102

MACK, VERNELLE MARIE, insurance agent; b. Durham, N.C., Feb. 21, 1950; d. James and Magdaline (Cates) Mack; m. Howard Snells III, Feb. 20, 1977 (div.); Vocalist, USO, S.E. Asia, 1968-74; clk. N.C. Meml. Hosp., 1974-76; vocalist Dynamic Upsetters Bank, Cary, N.C., 1976-78; ins. claim adjuster Blue Cross/Blue Shield, Durham, N.C., 1978-80; ins. agt. Ind. Life & Agy., Durham, from 1978; ins. agt., area coordinator Winston Mut. Life Ins. Co., Winston Salem, N.C., 1980-82, dist. mgr., Raleigh, N.C., from 1982; now mgr. Final Expense Ins., House of Reeves Funeral Home, Sale and Service Life Ins. Div., 1980—; vocalist Square Biz Show and Dance Band, 1982—. Named Agt. of Yr., Ind. Life Ins. Co., 1978. Democrat. Baptist. Home: 2217 Watkins St Raleigh NC 27604 Office: 3314 Apex Hwy Durham NC 27713

MACKALL, WILTON BENJAMIN, hospital public relations administrator; b. Crafton, Pa., Jan. 14, 1920; s. Benjamin William and Elizabeth (Rigley) M.; m. Julia Davis, Aug. 29, 1959. Student St. Petersburg Jr. Coll., 1952-53. With U.S. VA, St. Petersburg, Fla., 1945-48; vet. service officer State of Fla., St. Petersburg, 1948-72, state dir., 1972-78; community relations officer VA, Bay Pines, Fla., 1978—. Served with USAF. Recipient Samuel Rose award, Va. Central Office, 1982; Silver medal of merit Nat. Vets and Fgn. Wars, 1979; D.A.V. Service Commn. award, 1985; Amvets Service Commn. award, 1985, others. Mem. Am. Legion (life), D.A.V. (life), Amvets, V.F.W. (life). Republican. Lutheran. Lodge: Masons. Avocations: driving; fishing. Home: 7524 Garden Dr N Saint Petersburg FL 33710 Office: US Vets Adminstrn Med Center Seminole Blvd Bay Pines PL 33504

MACKAY, KENNETH HOOD, congressman; b. Ocala, Fla., Mar. 22, 1933; m. Anne Selph; children—Ken, John, Ben, Andy. B.S., B.A., U. Fla., 1954, LL.B., 1961. Bar: Fla. 1961. Sole practice, Daytona Beach, Fla.; mem. 98th Congress from 5th Dist. Fla. Mem. Fla. Ho. of Reps., 1968-74, Fla. State Senate, 1974-80; candidate for U.S. Senate, 1980; elder Ft. King Presbyterian Ch. Served to capt. USAF, 1955-58. Recipient Community Coll. Legis.

Leadership award, 1976, Nat. Legis. Service award, 1977, award for improving criminal justice Fla. Council Crime and Delinquency, 1979. Mem. ABA. Democrat. Lodges: Kiwanis; Elks. Office: 503 Cannon House Office Bldg Washington DC 20515*

MACKEL-VANDERSTEENHOVEN, ANNE MARIE, immunologist; b. Atlanta, June 28, 1956; d. Donald C. and Rose Rita (Donahue) M.; m. Jacob Jan Vandersteenhoven, Aug. 6, 1983. B.S., U. Fla., 1978; Ph.D., Med. U. S.C., 1982. Immunology researcher U. Fla., Gainesville, 1977-78; instr. Coll. of Charleston (S.C.), 1979; grad. researcher Med. U. S.C., Charleston, 1978-82, research assoc., 1982-84. S.C. grad. scholar, 1978-82; Med. U. S.C., research grantee, 1981. Mem. Sigma Xi. Contbr. articles to profl. jours.

MACKENZIE, DUNCAN THOMAS, III, petroleum geologist, executive, consultant; b. Detroit, Jan. 15, 1952; s. Duncan Thomas and Virginia Etta (Baldwin) MacK.; m. Sandra Kay Thompson, June 12, 1982; 1 child, Katharine Minta. Student Alma Coll., Mich., 1970-72; B.S. in Geology, La. State U., 1974; M.S., Fla. State U., 1977. Prodn. geologist Chevron U.S.A., New Orleans, 1977-79, exploration geologist, 1979-80; cons. geologist DeGolyer & MacNaughton, Dallas, 1980—, v.p., 1984. Chmn. Neighborhood Crime Watch, Dallas, 1984-85. Recipient Antarctic Service medal NSF, 1977. Mem. Am. Assn. Petroleum Geologists, Geol. Soc. Am., Soc. Petroleum Engrs., Soc. Exploration Geophysicists. Republican. Methodist. Avocations: travel; photography; genealogy; swimming. Home: 6930 S Ridge St Dallas TX 75214 Office: DeGolyer and MacNaughton One Energy Sq Dallas TX 75206

MAC KENZIE, JAMES DONALD, clergyman; b. Detroit, Nov. 17, 1924; s. James and Ida (Conklin) M.; student Moody Bible Inst., 1946-49, Union Theol. Sem., 1952; m. Elsie Joan Kerr, May 7, 1960; children—Janet Eileen, Kayly Kathleen, Christy Carol, Kenneth Kerr. Ordained to ministry Presbyn. Ch., 1953; pastor Calvary Ch., Swan Quarter, N.C., 1952-60, Kirkwood Ch., Kannapolis, N.C., 1960-64, Barbecue and Olivia Ch., Olivia, N.C., 1964-71, Elise Ch., Robbins, N.C., 1971—. Historian, Fayetteville Presbytery, 1975—, moderator, 1978, chmn. com. on hist. matters, 1983—. Founder, Conf. on Celtic Studies, Campbell Coll., Buies Creek, N.C., 1972—; councillor Conf. on Scottish Studies (Can.), 1968-75. Served with AUS, 1943-45; ETO. Decorated Purple Heart, Bronze Star; named Robbins Area Citizen, 1983. Mem. N.C. Presbyn. Hist. Soc. (pres. 1972-74, Author's award 1970, 75), Harnett Hist. Soc. (pres. 1968-71, Distinguished Service award 1970), Irish Uilleann Pipers Soc., Gaelic Soc. of Inverness, An Comunn Gaidhelach (life). Author: Colorful Heritage, 1970. Editor: The Uilleann Piper, 1974—. Contbr. articles to profl. jours. Home: PO Box 867 Robbins NC 27325

MACKENZIE, JOHN A., U.S. district judge; b. 1917. LL.B., Washington and Lee U., 1939. Practiced law, 1939-67; mem. Va. Gen. Assembly, 1954-58; assoc. judge Portsmouth Mcpl. Ct., 1952-62, U.S. dist. ct. judge, Eastern Va., 1967—. Mem. ABA, Va. Bar Assn. Office: Room 319 US Courthouse Norfolk VA 23510*

MAC KENZIE, MALCOLM ROBERT, personnel management consultant; b. Revere, Mass., Oct. 12, 1924; s. Malcolm John and Helen Margaret (Pelrine) MacK.; m. Chieko Yoshida, Nov. 4, 1954; 1 child, Kenneth Andrew. Dep. civilian personnel dir. U.S. Army, Camp Zama, Japan, 1959-63, civilian personnel dir., Fort Shafter, Honolulu, 1963-65, chief employee mgmt. U.S. Army Pacific Hdqrs., 1965-69, civilian personnel dir. electronics command, Fort Monmouth, N.J., 1969-76; command civilian personnel mgr. Naval Edn. and Tng., Naval Air Sta, Pensacola, Fla., 1976-81; personnel mgmt. cons., Gulf Breeze, Fla., 1981—. Mem. Human Rights Advocacy Com., Dist. I, Pensacola, 1982-84; asst. dist. dir. Fla. Spl. Olympics, Pensacola, 1983—; bd. dirs. Pensacola Penwheels, Employ the Handicapped, Pensacola, 1983—; pres. Pensacola Spl. Steppers retarded dancers, 1983; mem. Fla. Gov.'s Com. on Employment of Handicapped, 1983; co-chmn. com. for handicapable dancers United Square Dancers Am., 1984—; pres. Assn. Retarded Citizens-Escambia, Pensacola, 1985-87, exec. v.p. advocacy, 1985-86. Served to ensign USNR, 1943-45, PTO. Recipient Commemorative medallion Tokyo Met. Govt., 1963, cert. Appreciation, Chief of Staff, Ground Office, Defense Agy., Japan, 1963, dir. fgn. affairs. Kanagawa Prefecture, Japan, 1963, dir. fgn. affairs, Saitama Prefecture, Japan, 1963. Mem. Internat. Personnel Mgmt. Assn. (pres. far east chpt. 1960-63, Honolulu chpt. 1964-65, N.J. chpt. 1973-74), Am. Soc. Pub. Adminstrn., Fed. Personnel Council Pacific (chmn. 1965-66), Fed. Personnel Council N.J. (chmn. 1972-73), Gulf State Fed. Personnel Council (vice-chmn. 1980-81), Indsl. Relations Research Assn., Am. Soc. Tng. and Devel., Fla. Pub. Personnel Assn., Eastern Regional Orgn. for Pub. Adminstrn., Am. Arbitration Assn. (mem. comml. and trade panels). Democrat. Roman Catholic. Lodge: Elks. (treas. 1976-78). Avocations: bowling; golf; Boy Scouts. Home and Office: 2652 Venetian Way PO Box 280 Gulf Breeze FL 32561

MAC KENZIE, MELISSA TAYLOR, musician, music tchr.; b. Brownsville, Tenn., Sept. 23, 1925; d. Lee Bond and Rose Eleanor (Harwood) Taylor; B.A., Peabody Coll., 1946, postgrad., 1946; postgrad. Memphis State U., summers 69-70; div.; 1 dau., Donna Reid. Soprano, Memphis Open Air Theatre, summer 1948; soprano Episcopal Actors' Guild of N.Y., 1949-51, Am. Theatre Wing, N.Y.C., 1949-51; concert singer, 1948—; pvt. tchr. piano, voice and organ, 1953—; tchr. music edn. Haywood County Bd. Edn., Brownsville, 1953—; soprano soloist, dir. music Temple Adas Israel, Brownsville, 1952—; dir. music Gay Valley Camp, Brevard, N.C., summers 1959-62; chmn.-elect Grace Moore Opera Scholarship, 1966—; mem. Tenn. Bicentennial Com., 1976. Mem. Nat. Fedn. Music Clubs, Tenn. Fedn. Music Clubs (parliamentarian, v.p.), Nat. Guild Piano Tchrs. (faculty, accredited music tchr.), Am. Coll. Musicians (Hall of Fame 1969), Tenn. Music Tchrs. Assn. (v.p., program chmn. West Tenn. div.), DAR (chmn. Am. music, regent David Craig chpt.), Wednesday Morning Musicale Brownsville (pres.), Rehearsal Club Alumnae Assn. N.Y., UDC, Haywood County Hist. Soc., Alpha Delta Kappa (pres.-elect Iota chpt.). Home: 647 W Main St Brownsville TN 38012

MAC KENZIE, ROLAND REDUS, realty exec.; b. Washington, Mar. 13, 1907; s. Albert Redus and Mary J. (Hummer) MacK.; grad. Brown U., 1929; m. Louise Parker Fownes, May 11, 1940; children—Clark Fownes, Margot Fownes. Rep. U.S. Walker Cup Golf Team, 1926, 28-30; with Dupont Laundry, Washington, 1930-32; pres., dir. Shamrock Properties, Inc., Balt., 1938—, pres. Shamrock Realty Co., Greentree Realty Co., Towson, Md., Scottish Devel. Corp. Presbyn. Clubs: Country of N.C., Foxfire Golf and Country, Pinehurst Country (Pinehurst, N.C.); Gulf Stream Golf (Del Ray Beach); Elkridge-Greenspring (Balt.). Home: Polo Dr Gulfstream FL 33444 also McCaskill Rd Pinehurst NC 28374 also Garrison MD 21055 Office: MacKenzie Bldg Southern Pines NC 28387

MACKERCHER, PETER ANGUS, II, physician; b. Ponca City, Okla., June 27, 1946; s. Peter Angus and Marie (Wright) MacK.; m. Ellen A. Cooper, Mar. 28, 1951; children—Rachel Kathleen, Peter Angus III. B.A., Westminster Coll., 1968; M.D., U. Mo.-Columbia, 1972. Diplomate Am. Bd. Internal Medicine. Intern U. Mo., Columbia, 1972-73, resident in internal medicine, 1973-75; fellow in gastroenterology U. Mo., 1975-77; practice medicine specializing in gastroenterology and internal medicine, Mountain Home, Ark., 1979—. Served to lt. comdr. M.C., USN, 1977-79. Mem. Am. Soc. Gastrointestinal Endoscopists, AMA, Am. Med. Soc. on Alcoholism, Am. Soc. Internal Medicine. Presbyterian. Home: PO Box 329 Mountain Home AR 72653 Office: 402 S College Mountain Home AR 72653

MACKEY, LENORA JARVIS, social services administrator, social worker; b. Powells Point, N.C., Oct. 14, 1944; d. William Columbus and Martha Ann (Case) Jarvis; m. Claudie James Mackey, May 28, 1966; 1 child: Hasani Jabari Mackey. B.S., Elizabeth City State U., 1966; Cert. in Community Orgn., Columbia U. Sch. Social Work, 1973. Cert. social worker, N.C. Caseworker, N.Y.C. Dept. Social Services, Bklyn., 1966-72; community organizer N.Y. Dept. Social Services, 1972-74; protective services worker Spl. Services for Children, Jamaica, N.Y., 1975-77; living-learning specialist Elizabeth City State U., N.C., 1978-79, coordinator living-learning program, 1979-82; dir. Correlation of Youth Services program, Currituck County Involvement Council, N.C., 1983—. Editor: (newspaper) Viking Yard, 1980-82. Bd. dirs. Elizabeth City Boys Club, 1983—, Am. Cancer Soc., Elizabeth City, 1984—; mem. Pasquotank Action Council, Elizabeth City, 1984—, NAACP, 1985—. Recipient Outstanding Services award Elizabeth City State U. Gen. Alumni Assn., 1981, Meritorious Achievement award Jack & Jill of Am. Inc., 1982, Gov.'s Vol. award State of N.C., 1984, 85. Mem. Assn. Black Social Workers, Am. Assn. Counseling and Devel., Nat. Assn. Univ. Women, Elizabeth City Bus. and Profl. Women's Club, Alpha Kappa Alpha. Democrat. Clubs: Elizabeth City State U. Booster (pres. 1979-82, Most Outstanding Booster award 1982), Jack & Jill of Am. Inc. (pres. 1980-82), Pasquotank County Homemakers Extension Assn. (2d v.p. 1982-84). Home: 2213 Meads St Elizabeth City NC 27909 Office: Correlation of Youth Services PO Box 118 Currituck NC 27929

MACKEY, WILLIAM STURGES, JR., consultant; b. St. Louis, May 27, 1921; s. William Sturges and Dorothy Francis (Allison) M.; m. Margaret Powell, Dec. 10, 1943; children—Dorothy Mackey Lurie, John Powell, James Wescott. B.A., Rice U., 1943; M.B.A., U. Tex., 1950. Assoc. prof. acctg. Rice U., Houston, 1946-62; v.p., treas. Mandrel Industries, Houston, 1962-66; v.p. fin. Tex. Internat. Airlines, Houston, 1966-69; chmn., chief exec. officer Lifemark Corp., Houston, 1969-84; dir. MBank Houston, Spaw-Glass, Inc., Whole Foods Market, Inc., Curaflex Health Services, HEI Corp., Am. Constructors Co., Inc., Am. Nat. Funds Group. Served to 1st lt. USAAF, 1943-46. Mem. Am. Inst. C.P.A.s, Tex. Soc. C.P.A.s, Rice U. Council Acctg., Houston Philos. Soc. Episcopalian. Clubs: Houston, Lakeside Country, Forum (dir.). Home: 2011 Albans St Houston TX 77005 Office: 221 Norfolk Houston TX 77098

MACKIERNAN, MEREDITH ANNE, computer programmer; b. Hartford, Conn., Mar. 22, 1949; d. Duncan Winchester and Mamie Vivian (Joyner) M. B.S., Fla. So. Coll., 1971; M.S. in Math., Ga. So. U., 1973, postgrad., 1975; postgrad. Clemson U., 1975-80. Instr. Emanuel County Jr. Coll., Swainsboro, Ga., 1973-75, Spartansburg, S.C., 1977-78; sr. assoc. programmer IBM, Tampa, Fla., 1980—. Co-developer software system Series 1 SNA Gateway, 1984. Recipient award IBM, 1982, 84. Fellow Phi Kappa Phi; mem. Am. Math. Soc. Democrat. Methodist. Avocations: bicycling; growing roses; reading; sewing. Home: 2048 Ronald Circle Seffner FL 33584

MACKIN, BERNARD JOHN, natural resource company executive; b. Dallas, Sept. 5, 1917; s. James Stephen and Martha (Dettmann) M.; B.B.A., U. Tex.; also LL.B.; m. Elizabeth Storie, July 12, 1946. Admitted to Tex. bar; asso. firm Baker & Botts, Houston, 1946-52, mem. firm, 1952-79, sr. mem., 1979; chmn. bd., chief exec. officer Zapata Corp., Houston, 1979—; dir. Tenneco Inc., Houston, Houston Nat. Bank. Served to maj., inf. U.S. Army, 1941-46. Decorated Bronze Star. Mem. Internat. Bar Assn., Am. Bar Assn., Tex. Bar Assn., various bus. and trade assns. Roman Catholic. Clubs: Houston Country, Tejas, Remada (Houston); Recess (N.Y.C.). Office: PO Box 4241 Houston TX 77210

MAC KINNON, LEITA KECK, marketing director; b. Ralls, Tex., May 4, 1939; d. Clarence D. and Vergie (Russell) Mc Candless; student Tex. Inst. Tech., 1961-62, U. Houston, 1970-74; m. Robert L. Mac Kinnon, Feb. 4, 1974; children—Rhonda Dixon Smith, Brenda Nicholson Kees. Salesperson, Century 21 N.W. Properties Co., Houston, 1970-76, Century 21 Regional Properties Co., Houston, 1976-79; owner, mgr. Century 21 Pin Oak Properties, Houston, 1979-81; mktg. dir. So. Title Co., 1979-81, Tex. Am. Title, 1981-83, Guardian Title, 1983-84, United Title Co., 1984—; tchr. real estate. Cert. broker, Tex. Mem. Women's Council Houston Bd. Realtors, Nat. Assn. Realtors. Democrat. Baptist. Home: 9166 Larston Houston TX 77055

MACKLE, FRANCIS (FRANK) ELLIOTT, housing development co. executive; b. Bethesda, Md., Sept. 6, 1944; s. Francis Elliott and Virginia (Steward) M.; B.A. in Civil Engring., U. Notre Dame, 1966; m. Loretta McCaughan, Aug. 14, 1965; children—Francis Elliott, Laura Theresa, Thomas Patrick, John Christopher, Virginia Lee. With Deltona Corp., Miami, Fla., 1966—, v.p. mfg., 1969-72, v.p. constrn. and devel., 1972-75, sr. v.p., exec. v.p., 1975-79, pres., chief operating officer, 1979—. Pres., dir. Boystown of Fla. Mem. Fla. C. of C. (dir.). Roman Catholic. Office: 3250 SW 3d Ave Miami FL 33129*

MACKLIN, HARRIET JOHNSON, housing, community development consultant; b. New Haven, Feb. 12, 1944; d. Harry Cherman and Estella Maxine (William) Johnson; children—Germaine, Monique. B.S., Fla. A & M U., 1965. Resource program dir. New Haven Pub. Schs., 1967-72; housing dir. NAACP, N.Y.C., 1973-75; program technician Ga. Residential Fin. Authority, Atlanta, 1976, program dir., 1977-81, spl. asst., 1982; chief exec. officer First Rural Services, Atlanta, 1982—. Author: Donay Harewood NAACP Technical Assistance Workbook, 1980. Housing chmn. LWV, Atlanta, 1974; vice chmn. Atlanta Regional Commn., Atlanta, 1976; chmn. Met. Fair Housing Services, Atlanta, 1978-82; legis. chmn. Ga. Housing Coalition, Atlanta, 1982-84; v.p. Nat. Leased Housing, Washington, 1981-84; pres. Housing Assistance Council, Washington, 1983—. Named Woman of Yr., Am. Bus. Women Am., Mableton, Ga., 1981. Ford Found. fellow, 1976; Leadership Atlanta fellow, 1980. Mem. Nat. Fedn. Housing Counselors (v.p. 1977), NAACP, Nat. Council Negro Women (chmn. 1979). Democrat. Office: First Rural Services Inc 1655 Peachtree St Suite 1009 Atlanta GA 30309

MACLEAN, CHARLES BERNARD, human resource and health consultant; b. Ann Arbor, Mich., Oct. 12, 1945; s. Harold McKenzie and Marie Clare (Coshenet) M. B.S., Wis. State U.-Oshkosh, 1967; M.S., Mich. State U., 1969, Ph.D., 1973. Cert. profl. counselor, Tex. Dir. med. edn. Am. Coll. Emergency Physicians, 1974-81; exec. dir. Soc. Tchrs. Emergency Medicine, Dallas, 1978-81; pres. Applied Foresight, Dallas, 1978—; ptnr. Inman, Maclean & Gaddy, Dallas, 1983—. Author, co-author publs. in field. Coordinator Project Restart, Dallas, 1984; coordinator Holiday Project, Dallas, 1983—; com. chmn. Polo and Pops Cancer Benefit, 1985—; mem. steering com. Highland Village celebration Tex. Sesquicentennial. Mem. Am. Soc. Tng. and Devel. (v.p. profl. devel. 1984), Nat. Eagle Scout Assn., Psi Chi, Delta Tau Kappa, Psi Delta Kappa, Delta Sigma Phi (chpt. Man of Yr. 1967). Avocations: sailing; dancing; backpacking; puns; dining. Office: Inman Maclean & Gaddy 4307 Newton Ct Suite 11 Dallas TX 75219-3133

MACLENNAN, JOHN MEDLAND, manufacturers agent; b. Detroit, Oct. 4, 1925; s. John Kaye and Blanche (Medland) MacL.; m. Billie Bonnadine Bourland, May 15, 1948; children—Jacqueline, John, Kevin, Brian, William, James. Student, U. N.C., 1943, James Millikin U., 1947-47. Tool designer Hoodaille Industries, Decatur, Ill., 1948-56; sales rep. Grigoleit Co., Decatur, 1956-64; owner, pres. MacLennan Assocs., Inc., Signal Mountain, Tenn., 1964—. Served with USMC, 1943-49. Democrat. Episcopalian. Clubs: Walden, Signal Mountain. Office: Box 4365 Chattanooga TN 37405

MACLIN, ALICE NYSTROM, English language educator; b. Cadillac, Mich., May 18, 1928; d. George Herbert and Minnie Marguerite (Harwood) Nystrom; m. Harry T. Maclin, Aug. 30, 1947; children—Susan Maclin Box, Catherine Maclin Boyles, Gregory, Ruth Maclin Golley. B.A., So. Meth. U., Dallas, 1949, M.A., 1950. Instr. English, So. Meth. U., 1949-51; ednl. missionary, Belgian Congo (now Zaire), 1954-60; lectr. Internat. Press Inst., Nairobi, Kenya, 1963-65; lectr. All-Africa Conf. Chs. Tng. Ctr., 1965-71; tchr. lang. Nairobi Internat. Sch., 1970-71; assoc. prof. English and ESL Dekalb Coll., Clarkston, Ga., 1972—, also dir. ESL program. Bd. dirs. Westlands Sch., Nairobi, 1964-69; bd. adjudicators Villa Internat., Atlanta, 1974-81; bd. global ministries North Ga. United Meth. Ch., 1974-78; mem. com. for vols. in mission United Meth. Ch., 1981-84. Nat. Endowment for Humanities fellow, 1978. Mem. Tchrs. of English to Speakers of Other Langs. Internat., Ga. Tchrs. of English to Speakers of Other Langs., Nat. Assn. for Fgn. Student Affairs, AAUP, Am. Assn. Higher Edn., South Atlantic MLA, Phi Beta Kappa, Delta Kappa Gamma. Author: Useful Swahili, 1972; Reference Guide to English, 1981.

MACMILLAN, C(HARLES) J(AMES) B(ARR), philosophy of education educator; b. Auburn, N.Y., Apr. 30, 1935; s. John Walker and Margaret Ethel (Barr) M.; m. Joan T. Reinberg, June 15, 1958; children—Ann Tyler, Tyler Lash. B.A., Cornell U., 1957, Ph.D., 1965; M.A. with distinction, Colgate U., 1960. Acting asst. prof. UCLA, 1962-64; asst. prof. Temple U., Phila., 1964-68, assoc. prof., 1968-70; assoc. prof. philosophy of edn. Fla. State U., Tallahassee, 1970-84, prof., 1984—. Bd. dirs. Betton Hills Neighborhood Assn., 1973—. Mem. Fla. Philos. Assn., Southeast Philosophy of Edn. Soc. (pres. 1973), Philosophy of Edn. Soc. (sec., treas. 1980-82, pres. 1983-84), Am. Ednl. Research Assn. Club: Sturgeon Lake Sailing (Ontario). Editor: Psychological Concepts and Education, 1967; Concepts of Teaching: Philosophical Essays, 1968; contbr. articles to profl. lit. Home: 2316 Armistead Rd Tallahassee FL 32312 Office: Fla State U 306 Stone Bldg Tallahassee FL 32306

MACMINN, RICHARD DEAN, finance educator; b. Vancouver, Wash., Sept. 5, 1946; s. James Lewis and Lola Alice (Merritt) MacM.; m. Carole Ann Grimm, June 22, 1969; children—Sarah, Mark. B.A., UCLA, 1967; M.A., U. Ill., 1973, Ph.D., 1978. Asst. prof. econs. SUNY-Binghamton 1977-81; asst. prof. finance U. Tex.-Austin, 1981—. Contbr. articles to profl. jours. Served to capt. USAF, 1967-71. Recipient research awards U. Tex., 1983, 84, 85. Mem. Am. Econ. Assn., Am. Fin. Assn., Am. Risk and Ins. Assn., So. Econ. Assn., SW Fin. Assn. Presbyterian. Avocations: reading; running; racquetball; tennis. Office: U Tex Dept Fin Austin TX 78712

MACMULLEN, JEAN ALEXANDRIA STEWART, nursing service administrator; b. N.Y.C., Feb. 21, 1945; d. John Douglas and Isabella Stewart (Park) MacM. Diploma in Nursing, Lenox Hill Hosp., 1965; B. Nursing, Adelphi U., 1969, M.S. in Nursing, 1971; M.A. in Anthropology, U. South Fla., 1978. Tng. dir. renal diseases R.M.P., N.Y.C., 1971-72; clin. specialist VA, Tampa, Fla., 1972-76, nursing coordinator, 1976-82, assoc. chief nursing, Gainesville, Fla., 1982; clin. assoc. U. S. Fla., Tampa, 1979-82, adj. faculty U. Fla., Gainesville, 1982—. Contbr. articles to profl. jours. Recipient Jane Tingley Scholarship award Lenox Hill Hosp. Alumni, 1969. Mem. Am. Nurses Assn., Am. Nephrology Nurses Assn. (Fla. pres. 1973-74), Sigma Theta Tau, Lambda Alpha. Republican. Episcopalian. Avocations: swimming; raising orchids. Office: VA Med Ctr Archer Rd Gainesville FL 32602

MAC NABB, GEORGE MALCOLM, internist; b. Newnan, Ga., May 8, 1941; s. George Malcolm and Ella Gay (Parks) MacN.; B.A., Emory U., 1962, M.D., 1966; m. Michele Patricia Ney, Jan. 5, 1984; children—Mary Lisa, Amy St. Clair, Benjamin Howell, Kathryn Patricia. Intern, Emory U., Atlanta, 1966-67, resident in internal medicine, 1970-72, fellow, 1972-73; practice medicine, specializing in internal medicine, Newnan, Ga., 1973—; chief of staff Beaulieu Skilled Care Nursing Facility, 1973—; chief med. staff Newnan Hosp., 1981—; chief of medicine Humana Hosp., Newnan. Served to lt. comdr. USN, 1967-70. Diplomate Am. Bd. Internal Medicine. Mem. AMA, Med. Assn. Ga., Coweta County Med. Soc. (pres. 1981—), Am. Heart Assn., Am. Diabetic Assn., Assn. Mil. Surgeons U.S. Home: 1 Pine Knoll Newnan GA 30263 Office: 58 Hospital Rd Newnan GA 30263

MACNAUGHTON, DONALD SINCLAIR, hospital ownership and management company executive; b. Schenectady, July 14, 1917; s. William and Marion (Colquhoun) MacN.; A.B., Syracuse U., 1939, LL.B., 1948; m. Winifred Thomas, Apr. 10, 1941; children—Donald, David. Tchr. history Pulaski (N.Y.) Acad. and Central Sch., 1939-42; admitted to N.Y. bar, 1948; pvt. practice, Pulaski, 1948-54; dep. supt. ins. N.Y. State, 1954-55; with Prudential Ins. Co. Am., 1955-78, pres., chief exec. officer, 1969-70, chmn. bd., chief exec. officer, 1970-78, now dir.; chmn. exec. com., former chmn. bd., Hosp. Corp. Am., Nashville; dir. Exxon Corp., Prudential Ins. Co. Am., Third Nat. Corp. Chmn. bd. trustees Meharry Med. Coll., Vanderbilt U. Served as 1st lt. with AC, U.S. Army, 1942-46. Mem. Bus. Council. Clubs: Eastward Ho!, El Dorado, Links, Belle Meade. Home: Nashville TN 37205 Office: HCA Park Plaza Nashville TN 37203

MACNUTT, LAMAR A., dentist; b. Pontiac, Mich., Jan. 21, 1934; s. Omar Edwin and Cora Eleanor (Sweet) M.; m. Janet Ann Burwell, June 27, 1959; children—Alicia Ann, Marla Jean, Lori Shannon, Roberta Jo, Amy Lynn. Student U. Mich., 1951-54, D.D.S., 1958. Gen. practice dentistry, Clearwater, Fla., 1959—. Pres. bd. Quest Inn, Clearwater, 1983; commr. Bd. Parks and Recreation, Clearwater, 1982-85. Fellow Fla. Dental Soc.; mem. Acad. Gen. Dentistry, ADA, Am. Soc. Preventive Dentistry. Republican. Presbyterian. Lodge: Kiwanis. Avocation: marathon runner. Home: 322 Magnolia Dr Clearwater FL 33516 Office: 1947 Drew St Clearwater FL 33575

MACON, JAMES BARBOUR, III, neurological surgeon; b. Richmond, Va., Mar. 23, 1947; s. James Barbour and Marion (Pate) M.; m. Caroline Sprague Stewart, Aug. 31, 1972; children—James Barbour IV, Charles Sprague, Peter Randolph. A.B. magna cum laude, Princeton U., 1968; M.D. cum laude, Harvard U., 1974. Diplomate Am. Bd. Neurol. Surgery. Intern in surgery Stanford U. Med. Ctr., Palo Alto, Calif., 1974-75; resident in neurosurgery Mass. Gen. Hosp., Boston, 1977-82; practice medicine specializing in neurol. surgery, Louisville, 1982—; clin. advisor Neurosci. Ctr. of Excellence, Humana Hosp. Audubon, Louisville, 1985—. Contbr. articles to profl. jours. Served to lt. comdr. USPHS, 1975-77. Recipient Neurosurgery Resident Research award, New Eng. Neurosurg. Soc., 1980, 81, 82; Fulbright scholar, Paris, 1968-69. Mem. Internat. Assn. for Study of Pain, Congress Neurol. Surgeons, Mass. Med. Soc., Ky. Med. Assn., Jefferson County Med. Soc. Clubs: Ivy (Princeton, N.J.); Dedham Country (Mass.). Home: 548 Barberry Ln Louisville KY 40206 Office: Jelsma Jelsma and Macon PSC 420 Audubon Medical Plaza Louisville KY 40217

MACOR, VALENTINO, golf professional, manager; b. Latisana, Italy, May 23, 1936; came to U.S., 1948; s. Victor and Marcella Mafalda (Buffon) M.; m. Jandira Pereira Barbosa, Apr. 8, 1965 (div.); 1 son, Janval; m. 2d, Teresa Marita Erb, Nov. 27, 1983. B.B.A., U. Miami, 1973. Acct. Fla. Power and Light, Coral Gables, Fla., 1960-62; golf profl. Granada Golf Club, Coral Gables, 1962—. Vice pres. Jr. Orange Bowl, Coral Gables, 1983; mem. steering com. U. Miami Athletic Fedn., Coral Gables, 1983; treas., dir. Coral Gables Ambassadors, 1983. Served with USAF, 1955-59. Mem. Profl. Golfers Am. Republican. Roman Catholic. Clubs: Country of Coral Gables. Lodge: Kiwanis Internat. (v.p., dir. 1983) (Coral Gables). Home: 1414 San Benito Coral Gables FL 33134

MADDEN, LLOYD WILLIS, petroleum geologist; b. Lewis, Kans., Aug. 27, 1918; s. Oscar Thomas and Grace (Schuffelburger) M.; m. Shirley A. Bergstrom, Sept. 10, 1950; children—Deborah Kay, Steven Douglas, Kim Ashley, Victoria Angela. Geol. Engr. Colo. Assoc. Sch. Mines, 1941; student in physics U. Chgo.; M.S. in Physics, UCLA, 1942. Geologists, Shell Oil Co., San Antonio, 1946-47, Corpus Christi, Tex., 1947-49, Wichita Falls, Tex., 1949-52; dist. mgr. McElroy Ranch Co., Midland, Tex., 1952-65; dist. geologist Mobil Oil Corp., Midland, 1965-76; cons. Resources Investment Corp., Denver, 1976-82, Internat. Oil and Gas Corp., Houston, Vinson Exploration Co., Midland, 1983—. Served to maj. USAAF, 1940-46. Mem. Am. Assn. Petroleum Geologists, Tau Beta Pi. Republican. Methodist. Lodge: Masons. Home: 1804 N H St Midland TX 79705 Office: Cons Geologist 600 Western United Life Bldg Midland TX 79701

MADDOX, ALVA HUGH, state supreme court justice; b. Andalusia, Ala., Apr. 17, 1930; s. Christopher Columbus and Audie Lodella (Freeman) M.; A.B. in Journalism, U. Ala., 1952, LL.B., 1957; m. Virginia Ann Roberts, June 14, 1958; children—Robert Hugh, Patricia Jane. With Florala (Ala.) News, 1947-48, Treasurer's Office, U. Ala., 1949-52, 54-56; admitted to Ala. bar, 1957; law clk. Ct. Appeals of Ala., 1957; atty. field examiner VA, Montgomery, Ala., 1958; law clk. U.S. Dist. Ct., Montgomery, 1959-60; practiced in Montgomery, 1961-64; circuit judge 15th Jud. Circuit, Montgomery, 1963, asst. dist. atty., 1964; legal adviser to Gov. George Wallace of Ala., 1965-67, to Gov. Lurleen B. Wallace of Ala., 1967-68, to Gov. Albert P. Brewer of Ala., 1968-69; asso. justice Supreme Ct. Ala., Montgomery, 1969—; mem. Jud. Planning Commn. Permanent Study Commn. on the Judiciary. Active Youth Legislature, Montgomery Baptist Hosp. Found. Bd. dirs. YMCA, Montgomery. Served with USAF, 1952-54. Mem. Am., Ala. bar assns., Ala. Law Inst., Farrah Law Soc., Inst. Jud. Adminstrn., Am. Judicature Soc. Arnold Air Soc., Pershing Rifles, Jasons, Quadrangle, Omicron Delta Kappa, Phi Alpha Delta, Sigma Delta Chi. Democrat. Baptist (deacon). Clubs: Kiwanis, Maxwell AFB Open Mess, Oak Hollow Country, Blue and Grey Cols. Home: 3137 Hathaway Pl Montgomery AL 36111 Office: PO Box 218 Montgomery AL 36101

MADDOX, GEORGE LAMAR, JR., medical sociology educator; b. McComb, Miss., July 2, 1925; s. George Lamar and Dimple (McEwen) M.; m. Evelyn Godbold, June 9, 1946; children—Patricia Maddox Ashmore, George David. B.A., Millsaps Coll., 1949, D.Sc. (hon.), 1984; M.A., Boston U., 1952; Ph.D., Mich. State U., 1956. Mem. faculty Millsaps Coll., Jackson, Miss., 1952-59; prof. med. sociology Duke U., Durham, N.C., 1959—, dir. Ctr. for Aging, 1972-82, chair Univ. Council on Aging, 1982—; founding mem. nat. adv. council NIA/NIH, 1975-80; dir. AARP/Scudder Stevens & Clark, N.Y.C. Author: Inflation and Economic Well Being of the Elderly, 1984. Editor: Ency. of Aging, 1986. Trustee Wesley Homes, Inc., Atlanta, 1980-85. Served with inf. U.S. Army, 1943-45; ETO, PTO. Kent-Danforth fellow, 1954; Russell Sage fellow, 1960-61; USPHS fellow U. London, 1968-69. Fellow Am. Sociol. Assn. (sect. chair 1983-84), Gerontol. Soc. Am. (pres. 1978-79; Kleemeier research award 1985), So. Sociol. Soc. (v.p. 1977-78); mem. Internat. Assn. Gerontology (v.p., sec. 1984—; Sandoz research prize 1983). Methodist. Lodge: Rotary. Home: 2750 McDowell St Durham NC 27705 Office: Duke U Box 2920 Durham NC 27710

MADDOX, JUNE CURRY, guidance counselor; b. Gadsden, Ala., June 6, 1934; d. Clyde Almuth and Grace Elizabeth (Storey) Curry; m. William Gordon Maddox, Aug. 4, 1956; B.S., Auburn U., 1956; M.Ed., U. S.C., 1971. Elem. tchr., Ala., N.C. and S.C., 1956-70; middle sch. counselor Ridge Spring Middle Sch., S.C., 1972-73; guidance dir. Eddy Jr. High Sch., Columbus, Ga., 1977—. Co-author: Recipes for Preventive Guidance, 1981 (Co-Writer of Yr. award Ga. Sch. Counselors Assn. 1981); guide for programs for exceptional children. Mem. Ga. Sch. Counselors Assn. (2d v.p. 1981-82, sec. 1982-83, conf. coordinator 1985-86, Jr. High Counselor of Yr. 1983), Am. Sch. Counselors Assn. (Jr. High Counselor of Yr. award 1984), Ga. Assn. Educators, NEA, DAR, United Daus. Confederacy, Porcelain Artist Guild, Phi Delta Kappa. Methodist. Avocation: porcelain art. Office: Eddy Jr High Sch 2100 S Lumpkin Rd Columbus GA 31903

MADDOX, RAY REGINALD, pharmacist, administrator; b. Savannah, Ga., Jan. 18, 1949; s. Bonnie Rowe, Jr. and Bessie (Boatright) M.; m. Carol Jean Joyce, Aug. 1, 1970 (div. 1974); m. Brenda Kay Moody, Dec. 14, 1974; children—Cory Evan, Brian Chadwick. B.S. in Pharmacy, U. Ga., 1972; Pharm.D., U. Ky., 1977. Registered pharmacist Ga., S.C. Hosp. pharmacy resident Med. U. Hosp. of S.C., Charleston, 1972-73, clin. pharmacist, 1977-82, dir. clin. pharmacokinetic services, 1977-82, asst. prof. clin. pharmacy, 1977-81, assoc. prof., 1981-82, asst. prof. lab. medicine, 1980-82; staff pharmacist St. Joseph's Hosp., Savannah, 1973-74; clin. pharmacy resident Chandler Med. Ctr., U. Ky., Lexington, 1974-77; exec. v.p. Drug Therapy Cons., Inc., Charleston, 1981-85, also chmn. bd.; assoc. dir. clin. and ednl. services dept. pharmacy Emory U. Hosp., Atlanta, 1982-84, acting dir. pharm. services, 1984-85, dir. pharm. services, 1985—; researcher, presenter, cons. in field. Mem. Am. Soc. Hosp. Pharmacists (chmn. spl. interest group in clin. pharmacokinetics practice 1982, 83, clin. pharmacokinetic fellowship selection panel 1983-85, mem. adminstrv. adv. working group for edn. 1984-85), Atlanta Acad. Instnl. Pharmacists, Ga. Soc. Hosp. Pharmacists (legis. affairs com. 1983, chmn. canvas com. 1984, dirs. dist. IV 1984—), Southeastern Soc. Hosp. Pharmacists, Am. Assn. Colls. of Pharmacy (del. alt council faculties 1980), Am. Coll. Clin. Pharmacists (credentials com. 1981-83). Baptist. Avocation: reading historical fiction. Home: 1366 Cedar Park Pl Stone Mountain GA 30083 Office: Dept Pharmacy Emory Hosp 1364 Clifton Rd NE Atlanta GA 30302

MADDOX, ROBERT NOTT, chemical engineer, educator; b. Winslow, Ark., Sept. 29, 1925; s. R.L. and Mabel (Nott) M.; m. Paula Robinson, Oct. 6, 1951; children—Deirdre O'Neil, Robert Dozier. Student, Iowa State Coll., 1944-45; B.S., U. Ark., 1948; M.S., U. Okla. 1950; Ph.D., Okla. State U., 1955. Registered profl. engr., Okla. Mem. faculty Sch. Chem. Engring., Okla. State U., 1950-51, 52-58, prof., head dept. 1958-77, Leonard F. Sheerar prof., 1976, dir. phys. properties lab., 1976—; design engr. process div. Black, Sivalls & Bryson, Inc., Oklahoma City, 1951-52; adminstrv. v.p., tech. dir. Fluid Properties Research, Inc.; chem. engring. cons. Author numerous tech. papers. Served with USNR, 1944-45. Fellow Am. Inst. Chem. Engrs. (chpt. pres. 1956-57, Andre Wilkins Meml. award 1981); mem. Nat. Soc. Profl. Engrs., Okla. Soc. Profl. Engrs. (chpt. pres. 1961-62, bd. dirs. 1966-68, Engr. of Yr. 1972), Am. Soc. Engring. Edn., Am. Inst. Mining Engrs., Soc. Petroleum Engrs., Am. Chem. Soc. (treas. indsl. and engring. chemistry div. 1966-68, chmn. div. 1970, Stewart award 1971), Gas Processors Assn. (editoral adv. bd. engring. data book 1972—, Hanlon award 1985), Sigma Xi, Omega Chi Epsilon (nat. pres. 1968-70), Tau Beta Pi, Alpha Chi Sigma, Omicron Delta Kappa, Sigma Nu (high council 1966-70, regent 1972-74). Episcopalian (lay reader, vestryman). Lodges: Elks, Masons. Home: 1201 Fairway Dr Stillwater OK 74074

MADDOX, TOM SMITH, JR., ophthalmologist; b. Greenville, Ky., Sept. 28, 1943; s. Tom Smith and Maryanna (Jenkins) M.; m. Jackie C. Calhoun, July 15, 1967; children—Tom, Jeffrey, Austin. B.A., Murray State U. 1965; M.D., U. Ky., 1969. Intern Charity Hosp., New Orleans, 1969-70; resident U. Ky., Lexington, 1970-73; chief ophthalmology U.S. Navy, Charleston, S.C., 1973-75; practice medicine specializing in ophthalmology, Owensboro, Ky., 1975—; staff ophthalmologist Owensboro-Daviess County Hosp., Mercy Hosp., Owensboro Ambulatory Surgery Ctr. Contbr. articles to profl. jours. Mem. Owensboro Ind. Bd. Edn., 1980—, Ky. Sch. Bd. Assn., 1980—. Served to lt. comdr. USN, 1973-75. Fellow Am. Acad. Ophthalmology; mem. Am. Intraocular Implant Soc., Ky. Med. Assn., AMA, Daviess County Med. Soc., Ky. Acad. Eye Physicians and Surgeons (pres. 1985—). Democrat. Mem. Disciples of Christ. Lodge: Kiwanis (pres 1980-81). Avocations: jogging; golf; photography. Home: 1210 Griffith Ave Owensboro KY 42301 Office: Ophthalmic Cons 2816 Veach Rd Owensboro KY 42301

MADDUX, JAMES FREDERICK, physician; b. Sycamore, Ga., Aug. 17, 1916; s. Creed Taylor and Ida (Nussell) M.; m. Agnes Griffin; children—James Michael, Frederick Taylor, John Stephen, Mary Bernadette. M.D., U. Ga., 1941. Diplomate Am. Bd. Psychiatry and Neurology. Intern, USPHS Hosp., Balt., 1941-42; resident in psychiatry USPHS Hosp., Fort Worth, 1942-43, Colo. Psychopathic Hosp., Denver, 1946-48; med. officer USPHS, 1942-69; various clin. psychiatry and mental health adminstrv. positions, 1942-62, chief NIMH Clin. Research Ctr., Fort Worth, 1962-69; ret., 1969; prof. psychiatry U. Tex. Health Sci. Ctr., San Antonio, 1969—. Author: (with D.P. Desmond) Careers of Opiod Users, 1981. Contbr. numerous articles to profl. jours. Served to lt. comdr. USCG, 1943-46. Fellow AMA, Am. Psychiat. Assn. (life), Am. Orthopsychiat. Assn. (life.). Democrat. Home: 6608 Adair Dr San Antonio TX 78238 Office: 7703 Floyd Curl Dr San Antonio TX 78284

MADEJ, THADDEUS ANDREW, car dealership executive; b. Chgo., Aug. 21, 1936; s. Walter Victor and Sophie D. (Janiga) M.; m. Madelyn Marie Sinclair, Nov. 16, 1957. B.S. in Bus. Adminstrn., Roosevelt U., 1961, M.S. in Bus. Adminstrn., 1965. Market rep. mgr. Ford Motor Co., Chgo., 1964-74; gen. mgr. Marshall White Ford, Chgo., 1974-76; gen. mgr. Courtesy Ford Inc., Miami, Fla., 1976-85; gen. mgr. Potamkin Chrysler Plymouth, Miami, 1985—. Served with USMC, 1954-57. Recipient Trainee of Yr. award Ford Motor Co., 1970, Employee of Yr. award Ford Motor Co., 1971, Dept. Mgr. award Ford Motor Co., 1974, Nat. Sales Mgr. award Marshall White Ford, 1975. Mem. Soc. Profl. Sales Mgrs. (v.p. 1975-84, award 1982, 83, 84). Republican. Roman Catholic. Avocation: weight lifting. Home: 12294 SW 103d Ct Miami FL 33176 Office: Potamkin Chrysler Plymouth 57th Ave & Palmetto Expy Miami FL 33014

MADER, JON TERRY, physician; b. Madison, Wis., Mar. 21, 1944; s. John Henry and Louise E. (Hancock) M.; B.A., Wabash Coll., 1966; M.D., Ind. U., 1970; m. Joan Eileen Piper, Nov. 29, 1969; children—Travis Jon, Amy Eileen, Bret Mark. Intern, U. Tex. Med. Br., Galveston, 1970-71, resident in internal medicine, 1971-73, fellow in infectious disease, 1973-74, 76-77, instr., 1977-78, asst. prof. dept. internal medicine, 1978-82, assoc. prof., 1982—, mem. med. staff, 1977-78; chief hyperbaric medicine, div. marine medicine Marine Biomed. Inst., Galveston, 1979—, mem., 1977—; trainee in hyperbaric oxygenation therapy NASA Manned Spacecraft Center, Houston, 1973; bd. advisors Ocean Corp., Houston; med. advisor, dir. Nautilus Corp., Houston. Served with M.C., USN, 1974-76. Diplomate Am. Bd. Internal Medicine, Am. Bd. Infectious Disease. recipient numerous fellowships and grants. Fellow ACP; mem. Am. Soc. Microbiology, Undersea Med. Soc. (pres. Gulf Coast chpt.), Am. Fedn. Clin. Research, Can. Infectious Disease Soc., Infectious Disease Soc. Am., Soc. for Exptl. Biology and Medicine. Episcopalian. Contbr. articles to profl. jours. Home: 1015 Church St Galveston TX 77550 Office: Dept Internal Medicine Div Infectious Diseases U Tex Med Br Galveston TX 77550

MADEWELL, CARL EDWARD, economist, federal agency executive, researcher; b. Spencer, Tenn., May 11, 1935; s. Erastis E. and Annie Lee (McCoy) M.; m. Dorothy Jean Hollingsworth, Aug. 15, 1958; children—Allen Edward, Jared Lee. B.S. in Agrl. Edn., Tenn. Tech. U., 1957; M.S. in Agrl. Econs., U. Tenn., 1960; M.A. in Resource Econs., U. Wis.-Madison, 1968. Inspector Ohio Rubber Co., Willoughby, 1957-58; research asst. U. Tenn., Knoxville, 1959; mktg. specialist U.S. Dept. Agr., Balt., 1960-62; economist TVA, Muscle Shoals, Ala., 1962—. Contbr. articles to profl. jours. Leader Tenn. Valley council Boy Scouts Am., Florence, Ala., 1974-83; coach Underwood Little League Baseball, Football, Florence, 1974-83. Served with U.S. Army, 1958-59. Tenn. Farmer Coop. scholar, 1954; U. Wis. grantee, 1965. Mem. Am. Econ. Assn., Am. Agrl. Econ. Assn., Am. Mktg. Assn., So. Agrl. Workers Assn., So. Agrl. Econs. Assn., Exchange Club, TVA Muscle Shoals Nat. Mgmt. Assn. Republican. Baptist. Avocations: golf; softball; fishing; hunting; gardening. Home: Route 2 Box 197-B Killen AL 35645 Office: TVA Econs Mktg Branch F-122 NFDC Muscle Shoals AL 35660

MADIGAN, ELINOR MARIA, mathematics and computer technology educator, consultant; b. Munich, Bavaria, Fed. Republic Germany, Oct. 22, 1950; d. Paul Dello and Gertruda Maria (Kowolik) Maxam; m. Thomas Raymond Madigan, Jan. 8, 1972; children—Jennifer, Michael. A.A., Brevard Community Coll., 1970; B.S., Fla. Inst. Tech., 1973, M.S., 1980. Tchr. Melbourne High Sch., Fla., 1973-74; adj. faculty Fla. Inst. Tech. Melbourne, 1976-80; instr. Martin County High Sch., Stuart, Fla., 1981-82; asst. prof. math., computer tech. Fla. Inst. Tech., Jensen Beach, 1982—; cons. micro computers, Stuart, 1982—. Mem. Math. Assn. Am. Avocations; collecting old math. books; cooking. Office: Fla Inst Tech 1707 Indian River Dr Jensen Beach FL 33457

MADIGAN, RICHARD ALLEN, museum director; b. Corning, N.Y., Oct. 29, 1937; s. Myles L. and Rebekah M. (Bacon) M.; A.B., Drew U., 1959; m. Mary Jean Smith, June 11, 1960 (div. 1975); children—Richard Allen, Dana Smith, Reese Jennings; m. 2d, Alice Sturrock, Sept. 6, 1975 (div. May 1978); m. 3d, Cara Montgomery, Aug. 5, 1978; 1 son, James Myles. Pub. contact rep. Corning Glass Center, 1959, supr. visitor relations, 1959-60; dir. Andrew Dickson White Mus. Art, Cornell U., 1960-63; asst. dir., asst. sec. Corcoran Gallery Art, Washington, 1963-67; dir. N. Tex. Museums Resources Council, 1967-68, Bklyn. Children's Mus., 1968-69; exec. dir. Wave Hill Center Environ. Studies, 1969-74; instr. anthropology dept. Lehman Coll., 1968-74; dir. Norton Gallery and Sch. Art, West Palm Beach Fla., 1974—; sec. Norton Gallery and Sch. of Art, Inc., 1974—; past instr. art dept. George Washington U.; bd. dirs. Palm Beach Festival; lectr. Fgn. Service Inst., Dept. State. Mem. Am. Assn. Museums (chmn. coll. and univ. museums sect. 1962-63), Museums Council N.Y.C. (chmn. 1970-71), Fla. Art Mus. Dirs. Assn. (pres. 1978-79, 83-84), S.E. Museums Conf. (dir.), Assn. Art Mus. Dirs., Palm Beach C. of C. (dir. 1979—), West Palm Beach C. of C. (dir. 1981-82). Author: The Sculpture of Michael Schreck, 1983. Address: 5656 Upland Way West Palm Beach FL 33409

MADORY, JAMES RICHARD, hospital administrator, former air force officer; b. Staten Island, N.Y., June 11, 1940; s. Eugene and Agnes (Gerner) M.; m. Karen James Clifford, Sept. 26, 1964; children—James E., Lynn Anne, Scott J., Elizabeth Anne, Joseph M. B.S., Syracuse U., 1964; M.H.A., Med. Coll. Va., 1971. Enlisted U.S. Air Force, 1958, commd. 2d lt., 1964, advanced through grades to maj., 1978; adminstr. Charleston Clinic, S.C., 1971-74, Beale Hosp., Calif., 1974-77; assoc. adminstr. Shaw Regional Hosp., S.C., 1977-79; ret., 1979; asst. adminstr. Raleigh Gen. Hosp., Beckley, W.Va., 1979-81; adminstr., dir., sec. bd. Chesterfield Gen. Hosp., Cheraw, S.C., 1981—; mem. adv. bd. Cheraw Nursing Home, 1984-85. Contbr. articles to profl. publs. Chmn. bd. W.Va. Kidney Found., Charleston, 1980-81; chmn. youth bd. S.C. TB and Respiratory Disease Assn., Charleston, 1972-73; county chmn. Easter Seal Soc., Chesterfield County, S.C., 1984-85; campaign crusade chmn. Am. Cancer Soc., Chesterfield County, 1985-86. Decorated Bronze Star, Vietnamese Cross of Gallantry, Vietnamese Medal of Honor. Fellow Am. Coll. Hosp. Adminstrs.; mem. S.C. Hosp. Assn. (com. on legislation 1984-86), Cheraw C. of C. (bd. dirs. 1982-83). Republican. Roman Catholic. Lodge: Rotary (pres. 1984-85). Office: Chesterfield Gen Hosp PO Box 151 Cheraw SC 29520

MADRY, MAUDE HOLT, hospital administrator; b. Thomaston, Ala., Aug. 3, 1949; d. Henry James and Naomi Ruth (Burrwell) Holt; m. LeRay Madry, Nov. 26, 1979; 1 son, Andre D. B.S., Ala. A&M U., 1976, M.B.A., cert. in health adminstrn., U. Miami, 1983. Account clk. Rochester Telephone Co. (N.Y.), 1972, 76; supr. Allstate Ins., Rochester, 1976-77; asst. adminstr. Jackson Meml. Hosp., Miami, Fla., 1978—; instr. word processing. Mem. Dade Club Bus. and Profl. Women, YWCA Women-in-Mgmt. Network, Nat. Assn. Female Execs., NAACP. Democrat. Lodge: Order Eastern Star. Office: 1611 NW 12th Ave Miami FL 33012

MADURA, DANIEL RICHARD, social service agency executive, financial consultant; b. East Chicago, Ind., Apr. 7, 1945; s. Joseph Edward and Mary Margaret (Zatorski) M.; m. Carol Jean Natili, Apr. 30, 1983; children—Andrew, Megan. B.A., U. Idaho, 1968; M.A., U. S. Fla., 1975. Tchr., Keswick Christian, St. Petersburg, Fla., 1976-77; licensing specialist State of Fla., Largo, 1977-78, social worker, Clearwater, 1978-80, with grants mgmt., Largo, 1980-82; chief fin. officer Gulf Coast Jewish Family Services, St. Petersburg, 1982—; fin. cons. Jasmine Med. Ctr., Port Richey, Fla., 1984—. Campaign mgr. for City Treas., Calumet City, Ill., 1968; Eucharistic minister St. Patricks Catholic Ch., Largo, 1984—. Served with U.S. Army, 1968-70. Mem. Am. Mgmt. Assn., Comptrollers, Adminstrs., Bus. Mgrs. of Mental Health, Alcohol, Drug Abuse and Non Profit Orgns. (charter), Uparc Jaycees (sponsor). Democrat. Lodge: K.C. (chancelor 1983—). Home: 9212 Rustic Pines Blvd Seminole FL 33542 Office: Gulf Coast Jewish Family Services 8167 Elbow Ln N Saint Petersburg FL 33710

MADUZIA, EDWARD W., automotive company executive; b. New Orleans, Aug. 3, 1951; s. James Michael and Bertha Agnes (Townsend) M.; m. Laura Elizabeth Reede, June 10, 1975; children—Elizabeth Laura, Jason Kenneth. B.S., La. State U., 1973, M.S., 1974; postgrad. U. Tex., 1974-75. Acct. Cambridge Bus. Supply House, Baton Rouge, 1975-78, auditor, 1978-79; sr. acct. Werik Motor Co., Avondale, La., 1979-80, jr. comptroller, 1980-82, comptroller, 1982—; dir. Holmes Bus. Services Co., New Orleans. Cubmaster Boy Scouts Am., 1984—. Mem. Am. Def. Preparedness Assn., Am. Security Council, Am. Accts. Assn., Sigma Tau Phi. Baptist. Republican. Lodges: Masons, Shriners, Elks. Office: Werik Motor Co 137 Nicolle Blvd Avondale LA 70094

MAEHL, WILLIAM HENRY, JR., university administrator, history educator; b. Chicago Heights, Ill., June 13, 1930; s. William Henry and Marvel (Carlson) M.; m. Audrey Mae Ellsworth, Aug. 25, 1962; 1 child, Christine Amanda. B.A., U. Minn., 1950, M.A., 1951; Ph.D., U. Chgo., 1957. Asst. prof. Montclair State Coll., N.J., 1957-58, Washington Coll., Chestertown, Md., 1958-59; asst. prof. history U. Okla., Norman, 1959-64, assoc. prof., 1964-70, prof., 1970-76, dean, 1976-79, vice provost, 1979—; vis. fellow Wolfson Coll., Oxford, Eng., 1975. Editor: Reform Bill of 1832, 1967; Reminiscense of Chartist, 1983. Contbr. articles to profl. jours. Editor Continuum Jour., 1980-83. Leverhulme Research fellow, 1961-62; Am. Philos. Soc. grantee; Fulbright scholar, 1955-56. Fellow Royal Hist. Soc.; mem. Am. History Assn., S. Conf. on Brit. Studies (pres. 1982-84), Soc. for Study Labour History, Nat. Univ. Continuing Edn. Assn. Home: 2601 Meadowbrook Dr Norman OK 73072 Office: U Okla 1700 Asp Ave Room 111 Norman OK 73037

MAERCKLEIN, DOUGLAS RICHARD, geologist; b. Sheboygan, Wis., Oct. 22, 1949; s. Richard Charles and Cathren (Holtz) M.; m. Kathleen Louise Phillips, Oct. 1, 1979; children—Kimberley Louise, Felicia Kathleen. B.S., U. Wis.-Eau Claire, 1972; M.S., U. Wis.-Milw., 1974. Geologist, Texaco Inc., Midland, Tex., 1974-77, Kewanee Oil Co., Tulsa, 1977-78, Cotton Petroleum, Tulsa, 1978-80, Whitmar Exploration, Tulsa, 1980-82, KWB Oil Property Mgmt., Tulsa, 1982-84, Keener Oil Co., Tulsa, 1984—. Mem. Am. Assn. Petroleum Geologists, Geol. Soc. Am., Tulsa Geol. Soc. Clubs: Tulsa, Tulsa Running. Avocation: competitive running. Office: Keener Oil Co #406 320 S Boston Ave Tulsa OK 74103

MAGEE, LYMAN ABBOTT, microbiology educator and administrator; b. Bogalusa, La., Apr. 10, 1926; s. Donies Eldridge and Novie Gertrude (Pierce) M.; m. Betty Joyce Upton, Apr. 21, 1957; children—Esther Margaret, David Donies. B.S. in Chemistry, La. Coll., 1946; M.S., La. State U., 1954, Ph.D. in Microbiology, 1958. Sr. analyst Cities Service Corp., Lake Charles, La., 1947-48; asst. prof. chemistry La. Coll., Pineville, 1948-51, acting chmn. dept., 1948-49, asst. dean of men, 1950, dean of men, 1956; instr. microbiology La. State U., Baton Rouge, 1956; Hite fellow in cancer research M.D. Anderson Hosp. and Tumor Inst., Houston, 1958-59; instr., NIH fellow U. Miss. Sch. Medicine, 1959-61; assoc. prof. microbiology U. Miss., Oxford, 1961-65, prof., 1965—, chmn. dept. biology, 1969-76, asst. dean Coll. Liberal Arts, 1979-85, assoc. dean, 1985—. 1971-72. NSF Faculty Research Participation grantee Valley Forge Space Ctr., Gen. Electric Co., 1975. Fellow Nat. Inst. Allergy and Infectious Diseases, Am. Acad. Microbiology, Am. Soc. Microbiology (pres. South Central br. 1969-71); mem. Miss. Acad. Scis. (pres. 1984-85), Sigma Xi, Phi Kappa Phi, Delta Psi. Baptist. Contbr. numerous articles to profl. jours.

MAGGIO, CAROLYN OUBRE, pharmacist, state government official; b. Donaldsonville, La., Apr. 23, 1941; d. Waldron Ledmond and Emily Cecilia (Rivault) O.; m. Nickie Charles Maggio, June 22, 1963; children—Brent Michael, Nicole Anne. B.S. in Pharmacy, Northeast La. U., 1963. Retail pharmacist Andrews Rexall Drugs, Baton Rouge, La., 1963-66; pharmaceutical cons. La. Dept Pub. Welfare, Baton Rouge, 1966-78 pharmaceutical cons., program mgr. La. Dept. Health and Human Resources, 1978-81, asst. dir. med. assistance program, 1981-82, dir. med. assistance program, 1982-84, asst. div. dir., 1984—; drug procurement adv. council mem. La. Div. Adminstrn., Baton Rouge, 1983—; continuing edn. faculty mem. Northeast La. U. and Xavier U., 1984; continuing edn. presentor La. Pharmacist Asssn., 1985. Canvasser, March of Dimes, Baton Rouge, 1984. Named Alumnus Pharmacist of Yr., Northeast La. U. Sch. Pharmacy, Monroe, 1984; recipient La. Bd. Pharmacy Resolution of Commendation, 1985. Mem. Am. Pharmaceutical Assn., La. Pharmacists Assn., Kappa Epsilon. Democrat. Roman Catholic. Avocations: gardening; sewing. Home: 11024 Bellarbor Dr Baton Rouge LA 70815

MAGID, ANDY ROY, mathematics educator; b. St. Paul, May 4, 1944; s. William Eli and Marion Ethel (Mintz) M.; m. Carol Ann King, Aug. 21, 1966; children—Sarah, Samuel. B.A., U. Calif.-Berkeley, 1966; Ph.D., Northwestern U., 1969. Instr. Columbia U., 1969-72; prof. math. U. Okla., Norman, 1972—. Author: The Separable Galois Theory of Commutative Rings, 1974; Module Categories of Analytic Groups, 1983; Applied Matrix Models, 1985. Mem. Am. Math. Soc., Math. Assn. Am., Sigma Xi. Democrat. Jewish. Home: 1025 Connelly Norman OK 73072 Office: U Okla Norman OK 73019

MAGILL, MARCIA NOREEN, instructional technologist, consultant; b. Providence, Feb. 10, 1950; s. Robert Andrew and Geraldine Adair (Scopes) Kulzer; m. Wayne Alan Magill, June 27, 1970; children—Karen Malia, Michael Wayne. B.A., U. Hawaii, 1973, B.Ed., 1973; M.Ed., U. Va., 1984, Ed.S., 1985. Master tchr., math. curriculum adviser and developer Big Bend Community Coll., Grafenwohr, Fed. Republic Germany, 1981-83; math. tchr. of gifted U. Va., Charlottesville, 1984; instructional design cons. Children's Rehab. Ctr., Charlottesville, 1984, U. Va. Med. Ctr. Resource Ctr., Charlottesville, 1984-85; instructional developer for ASEC, Orlando, Fla., 1985—. Pres. Protestant Women of Chapel, Grafenwohr, 1982; mem. adv. com. for elem. sch., Grafenwohr, 1982. Mem. Am. Soc. for Tng. and Devel., Nat. Soc. for Performance and Instrn. Republican. Avocations: running; racquetball; stenciling; theorem painting.

MAGINNIS, GORDON HOBSON, real estate executive, investor; b. New Orleans, Sept. 21, 1928; s. Donald Ambrose and Ruth (Hobson) M. Student U. of South, Sewannee, Tenn., 1947-48, U. Calif.-Berkeley, 1952-54. Co-owner McDougall's Travel Service, Inc., New Orleans, 1961-72; with Parrish Travel Centre, Ltd., New Orleans, 1973-83; realtor Martha Ann Samuel, Inc., New Orleans, 1980—. Vestryman, treas. St. Anna's Episcopal Ch. Served with USN, 1948-52. Mem. Nat. Assn. Realtors, Orleans Parish Bd. Realtors, New Orleans Mus. Art, La. Landmarks Soc., Friends of Cabildo, Preservation Resource Ctr., Nat. Trust for Historic Preservation, Patio Planters, Spring Fiesta Assn. Republican. Home: 831 Dauphine St New Orleans LA 70116 Office: 1521 Washington Ave New Orleans LA 70130

MAGLIERO, ANTHONY JOSEPH, knowledge engineer; b. Boston, Feb. 11, 1952; s. Antonio Joseph and Bessie Joanne (Tolios) M.; m. Jean Ann Pull, Apr. 16, 1983. B.S., Suffolk U., 1975; M.A., U. Tex.-Arlington, 1979, Ph.D., 1981. Postdoctoral fellow U. Ill., Champaign, 1981-82; sr. staff scientist Applied Sci. Assocs., Inc., Valencia, Pa., 1982-84; knowledge engr., Software Architecture & Engring., Inc., Arlington, Va., 1984—. Mem. Am. Psychol. Assn., Cognitive Sci. Soc., Am. Assn. Artificial Intelligence, Human Factors Soc. Avocations: basketball; chess; running. Office: Software Architecture & Engring Inc 1500 Wilson Blvd Suite 800 Arlington VA 22209

MAGOON, ROBERT CORNELIUS, ophthalmologist; b. N.Y.C., Apr. 4, 1934; s. Neil Twerdin and Rose M.; m. Andrea Lynn Ruskin, June 11, 1958 (div. Apr. 1975); children—Eric Troy, Arden Renee; m. Nancy Amelia Parker, Mar. 16, 1978. B.S., U. Fla., 1955; M.D., U. Miami, 1959. Diplomate Am. Bd. Ophthalmology. Intern, Jackson Meml. Hosp., Miami, Fla., 1959-60; resident Harlem Eye and Ear Hosp., N.Y.C., 1960-62, U. Miami, 1962-63; practice medicine specializing in ophthalmology, Miami Beach, Fla., 1963—; mem. staff Mt. Sinai Med. Ctr., also chmn. dept. ophthalmology; mem. staff Bascom Palmer Eye Inst., Anne Bates Leach Eye Hosp. Bd. dirs. Am. Powerboat Assn. Fellow ACS; mem. Miami Ophthalmology Soc., Fla. Soc. Ophthalmology, Am. Soc. Ophthalmology and Otolaryngology, Am. acad. Ophthalmologists. Club: Palm Bay (Miami). Nat. power boat racing champion, 1968, 70, 71, 72, 73. Home: 1535 W 27 St Sunset Island 2 Miami Beach FL 33140 Office: 1688 Meridian Ave Suite 921 Miami Beach FL 33139

MAGRATH, LAWRENCE KAY, biology educator; b. Garnett, Kans., Mar. 28, 1943; s. Charles Jerome and Ruth (Richardson) M. B.S. in Edn., Emporia State U., 1967, M.S., 1969; Ph.D., U. Kans., 1973. Asst. instr. biology U. Kans., Lawrence, 1970-72; instr. botany, acting curator herbarium Okla. State U., Stillwater, 1972; prof. biology, curator herbarium U. Sci. and Arts Okla., Chickasha, 1972—; sec., treas. bd. trustees Flora Okla. Inc., Oklahoma City, 1983—. Contbr. articles to profl. jours. Mem. Okla. Republican Dist. Com., 1983-84, treas. dist. 4, 1984—; mem. Okla. Rep. State Com., 1985—; treas. Grady County Rep. Com., Chickasha, 1984-85. Kans. Acad. Sci. grantee, 1969; U. Sci. and Arts Okla. grantee, 1982, 83. Mem. Internat. Assn. Plant Taxonomists, Am. Soc. Plant Taxonomists, Kans. Acad. Sci., Am. Inst. Biol. Sci., Higher Edn. Alumni Council Okla., Bot. Soc. Am., Calif. Bot. Soc., New Eng. Bot Club, Southwestern Assn. Naturalists, Am. Orchid Soc., Asociacion Mexicana de Orquideologia A.C., Okla. Soc. Med. Tech. Educators, Okla. Acad. Sci. (exec. council 1982-84, rec. sec. 1984), Okla. Orchid Soc. (v.p. Oklahoma City 1983-85), Sigma Xi, Beta Beta Beta, Kappa Delta Pi (v.p. Iota chpt. 1967, faculty sponsor Pi Omega chpt. 1985). Republican. Avocations: book collecting; gardening; landscaping; raising orchids. Home: 416 S 13th St Chickasha OK 73018 Office: U Sci and Arts Okla 17th and Grand Ave Chickasha OK 73018

MAGUIRE, CHARLOTTE EDWARDS, physician; b. Richmond, Ind., Sept. 1, 1918; d. Joel Blaine and Lydia (Betscher) Edwards; student Stetson U., 1936-38, U. Wichita, 1938-39; B.S., Memphis Tchrs. Coll., 1940; M.D., U. Ark., 1944; m. Raymer Francis Maguire, Sept. 1, 1948 (dec.); children—Barbara, Thomas Clair II. Intern Orange Meml. Hosp., Orlando, Fla., 1944-46; resident Bellevue Hosp. and Med. Center, N.Y.U., N.Y.C., 1955; instr. nurses Orange Meml. Hosp., 1947-57, staff mem., 1946-48; staff mem. Fla. Sanatarium and Hosp., Orlando, 1946-56, Holiday House and Hosp., Orlando, 1950-62; mem. courtesy and cons. staff West Orange Meml. Hosp., Winter Garden, Fla., 1952-67; active staff, chief dept. pediatrics Mercy Hosp., Orlando, 1965-68; med. dir. med. services and basic care Fla. Dept. Health and Rehab. Services, 1975-84; med. exec. dir., med. services, dept. worker's compensation Fla. Dept. Labor, Tallahassee, 1984—; chief of staff physicians and dentists Central Fla. div. Children's Home Soc. of Fla., 1947-56; dir. Orlando Child Health Clinic, 1949-58; engaged in pvt. practice, medicine, Orlando, 1946-68; asst. regional dir. HEW, 1970-72; pediatric cons. Fla. Crippled Children's Commn., 1952-70, dir., 1968-70; med. dir. Office Med. Services and Basic Care, sr. physician Office of Asst. Sec. Ops., Fla. Dept. Health and Rehab. Services; clin. prof. dept. pediatrics U. Fla. Coll. Medicine, Gainesville, 1980—. Mem. profl. adv. com. Fla. Center for Clin. Services at U. Fla., 1952-60; del. to Mid-century White House Conf. on Children and Youth, 1950; U.S. del. from Nat. Soc. for Crippled Children to World Congress for Welfare of Cripples, Inc., London, Eng., 1957; pres. of corp. Eccleston-Callahan Hosp. for Colored Crippled Children, 1956-58; sec. Fla. chpt. Nat. Doctors' Com. for Improved Med. Services, 1951-52; med. adv. com. Gateway Sch. for Mentally Retarded, 1959-62; bd. dirs. Forest Park Sch. for Spl. Edn. Crippled Children, 1949-54, mem. med. adv. com., 1955-68, chmn. 1957—; mem. Fla. Adv. Council for Mentally Retarded, 1965-70; dir. central Fla. poison control Orange Meml. Hosp.; mem. orgn. com., chmn. com. for admission and selection policies Camp Challenge; participant 12th session Fed. Exec. Inst., 1971; del. White House Conf. on Aging, 1980. Mem. Nat. Rehab. Assn., Am. Congress Phys. Medicine and Rehab., Fla., Central Fla. (dir. 1949-58, pres. 1956-57) socs. crippled children and adults, Am. Assn. Cleft Palate, Fla. Soc. Crippled Children (trustee 1951-57, v.p. 1956-57, profl. adv. com. 1957-68), Mental Health Assn. Orange County (charter mem.; pres. 1949-50, dir. 1947-52, chmn. exec. com. 1950-52, dir. 1963-65), Fla. Orange County heart assns., AMA, Am. Med. Women's Assn., Am. Acad. Med. Dirs., So. Fla. (chmn. com. on mental retardation), Orange County med. assns., Fla. Orlando pediatric socs., Fla. Cleft Palate Assn. (counselor-at-large, sec.). Club: Governors. Home: 2013 E Randolph Circle Tallahassee FL 32312 Office: 1321 Executive Center Dr E Tallahassee FL 32301

MAGUIRE, JACK RUSSELL, writer, columnist; b. Denison, Tex., Apr. 10, 1920; s. Jeff Edward and Elizabeth (Russell) M.; student N. Tex. State Coll., 1940-41; B.J., U. Tex., Austin, 1944; m. Patsy Jean Horton, Aug. 11, 1946;

children—Jack Russell, Kevin Maguire. Reporter AP, Austin, 1943-44; public relations rep. M.-K.-T. R.R., St. Louis, 1945-50, T.P. & P. Ry., Dallas, 1950-51; dir. public relations Tex. Ins. Adv. Assn., Austin, 1950-56; exec. dir. U. Tex. Ex-Students Assn., 1956-76; exec. dir. U. Tex. Inst. Texan Cultures, San Antonio, 1976-83; public relations cons., Austin, 1950-76. Trustee Ednl. Projects for Edn., Inc., Washington, S.W. Research Inst.; mem. Tex. Sesquicentennial Commn. Recipient Master Publicist award San Antonio Advt. Fedn., 1979. Mem. Am. Ry. Mag. Editors Assn., Public Relations Soc. Am., Am. Soc. Assn. Execs., Philos. Soc. Tex., Sigma Delta Chi. Presbyterian. Clubs: Rotary, Torch, Headliner, Argyle. Author: Talk of Texas, 1973; Texas: Amazing, but True, 1982; co-author: The Governors Who Lived The Mansion, 1984; editor: A President's Country. Columnist: Talk of Texas, Texas Yesterday; contbr. articles to profl. jours. Address: PO Box 1097 Fredericksburg TX 78624

MAGURNO, RICHARD PETER, airline executive, lawyer; b. Suffern, N.Y., June 29, 1945; s. Eugene and Rose (Foresta) M. B.S., Georgetown U., 1964; M.S., U. Wis.-Madison, 1965; J.D. Fordham U., 1968. Bar: N.Y. 1970, Fla. 1982. Atty., Eastern Air Lines, Inc., 1970-72, sr. atty., 1973-76, gen. atty., 1977-79, dir. legal affairs, 1980, legal v.p., asst. sec., 1980-83, sr. legal v.p., sec., 1984—; dir. Airline Tariff Pub. Co.; sec. Dorado Beach Devel. Co., Dorado Beach Estates, Eastern Air Lines of P.R. Mem. planning com. Good Samaritan Hosp., Rockland County Dem. Com. Served with U.S. Peace Corps, 1968-69. Mem. ABA, Fla. Bar Assn., Bar Assn. City of N.Y. Roman Catholic. Home: 2575 South Bayshore Drive Coconut Grove FL 33133 Office: Eastern Air Lines Miami International Airport Miami FL 33148

MAGYAR, MARY ELLEN, nurse. Diploma, Youngstown Hosp. Assn. Sch. Nursing, 1962; B.S., Villa Marie Coll., 1979; M.S. in Nursing, U. Tex., 1981. Staff nurse operating suite and med. unit Youngstown Hosp. Assn., Ohio, 1962-63, asst. head nurse, 1965-66; charge nurse psychiat. women's admission Woodside Receiving Hosp., Youngstown, 1963-64; staff nurse premature nursery Children's Med. Ctr.-East Bay, Oakland, Calif., 1964-65; staff nurse surg. area Kaiser Hosp., Fontana, Calif., 1965; shift supr. Warren Gen. Hosp., Ohio, 1966-68; asst. head nurse surg. area San Antonio Community Hosp., Upland, Calif., 1968-71; clin. charge nurse I rehab. neurol. care, intensive and coronary care Riverside Gen. Hosp.-Med. Ctr., Calif., 1971-72; vocat. nursing instr. Calif. Instn. for Women, Dept. Corrections, Frontera, 1972; dir. inservice Richmond Heights Gen. Hosp., Ohio, 1973-75; staff devel. instr. St. Vincent Health Ctr., Erie, Pa., 1975-80; clin. nurse specialist med./surg. areas Lynchburg Gen.-Marshall Lodge Hosps., Inc., Va., 1981-82, dir. surg. services, 1982—. Mem. Am. Nurses Assn. (div. on practice), Am. Assn. Critical Care Nurses, Nat. League for Nursing (hosp. and long-term care nursing services), Va. Orgn. Nurse Execs., Assn. Operating Room Nurses, Sigma Theta Tau, Eta Zi, Phi Kappa Phi. Home: 709 Pearl St Lynchburg VA 24504 Office: Lynchburg Gen-Marshall Lodge Hosps Inc Tate Springs Rd Lynchburg VA 24506

MAGYAR, STEPHEN VINCENT, JR., safety engineer, administrator; b. Bethlehem, Pa., Nov. 6, 1942; s. Stephen Vincent and Marie (Greuters) M.; m. Mary Scutt, Oct. 24, 1964; children—Stephen, Sonya, Stacy, Melissa. B.A., Moravian Coll., 1966; M.A., Rider Coll., 1971; M.B.A., Fairleigh Dickinson U., 1974. Cert. safety profl. Adminstr. safety RCA Corp., Camden, N.J.; former safety dir. Cooper Industries, Sunnyvale, Tex.; former safety, personnel dir. Climate Control Co., Hutchins, Tex.; supr. safety E-Systems, Greenville, Tex., 1984—; pres. S. Jersey Indsl. Safety Council, Haddon Field, N.J., 1979; bd. mgrs. N.J. State Self-Insurers Assn., 1976-79. Contbr. articles to profl. mags. First aid instr. ARC, Pa., and N.J., 1968-74, bd. dirs., mem. exec. com., 1975-79; v.p. Parks and Recreation Commn., Delran, N.J., 1974-79; team mgr. Little League, Colt League, N.J., N.Y. and Tex., 1975-83; vol. probation counselor Camden County Probation Dept., Camden, 1976-78. Mem. Am. Soc. Safety Engrs. (Tech. Writing Excellence award 1983-84), Vets. of Safety Internat. Roman Catholic. Avocations: table tennis; construction trades; creative writing; public speaking. Home: 4925 Willowhaven Circle Garland TX 75043 Office: E-Systems PO Box 1056 Greenville TX 75401

MAHADY, CATHERINE MARY, nun, college administrator, consultant; b. Bklyn., Jan. 3, 1936; d. Daniel James and Margaret Mary (McMurray) M. B.A. in History, Regis Coll., 1965; M.A. in Social Scis., Bklyn. Coll., 1972; M.B.A., Bellarmine Coll., 1987. Joined Ky. Dominicans, Roman Catholic Ch., 1955. Tchr. Dominican Acad., Plainville, Mass., 1957-67; prin. St. Simon Jude Acad., Bklyn., 1967-73; asst. to supt. schs. Diocese of Bklyn. and Queens, 1973-75; pres. St. Catharine Coll., Springfield, Ky., 1975-83; v.p. adminstrn. and bus. Pikeville Coll., Ky., 1983—. Mem. Council Ind. Ky. Colls. and Univs. (pres. 1981-83, sec./treas. 1977-79, v.p. 1979-81), Coll. and Univ. Bus. Officers, Phi Theta Kappa (hon. fellow). Democrat. Avocations: jogging; reading; travel. Home: 212 Bank St Apt 1 Pikeville KY 41501 Office: Office VP for Adminstrn and Bus Pikeville Coll Pikeville KY 41501

MAHANEY, LOU ANN, mathematics educator; b. Houma, La., Dec. 13, 1940; d. Olvin Frank and Helen (Hafer) Sebesta; m. Merle Parks Mahaney, III, Oct. 4, 1961; children—Merle Parks IV, Hollie Kathleen, Heather Louise. B.A., Tex. Woman's U., 1962; M.A., U. Tex.-Arlington, 1980, Ph.D., 1984. Cert. tchr., Tex. Tchr., tutor, translator Alexander Smith Acad., Fort Worth, 1974-75; grad. teaching assoc. U. Tex. Arlington, 1978-82, asst. instr., 1982-83; asst. prof. math. Dallas Baptist U., 1983-85, assoc. prof., 1985—. Chmn. Apoyo tours com., Fort Worth, 1975-76; mem. bd. parish edn. Faith Lutheran Ch., Fort Worth, 1973; vol. Mothers March, Girl Scouts, Maifest, Fort Worth, 1968—. Mem. Math. Assn. Am., Am. Math. Soc., Jr. Woman's Club (pres. Shakespeare sect. 1976), Mortarboard Club, Student Fin. Council of Tex. Woman's U. (pres. 1961-62). Republican. Avocations: theatre; music; bridge. Home: 4903 Racquet Club Dr Arlington TX 76017 Office: Dallas Bapt U 7777 W Kiest Dallas TX 75211

MAHDI, SYED IQBAL, economics educator, researcher, consultant; b. Hyderabad, India, Oct. 4, 1938; came to U.S., 1964, naturalized, 1977; s. Syed Mahmood and Qamar Jahan Mahdi; m. Zehra Parveen, July 4, 1968; children—Asima, Reshma. B.A. in Econs., Osmania U., Hyderabad, 1959, M.A. in Econ. Stats., 1963; M.A. in Econs., U. Mass., 1967, Ph.D. in Econs., 1976; cert. in computer programming, Honeywell Inst. Info. Scis., 1972. Instr. U. Wis.-Milw., 1967; from instr. to asst. prof. St. Anselm's Coll., Manchester, N.H., 1968-72; asst. prof. Bryant Coll., Smithfield, R.I., 1972-75; assoc. prof. econs. Benedict Coll., Columbia, S.C., 1975-78, prof. econs., head dept., 1978—, dir. Econ. Devel. Tech. Assistance Ctr., 1983-84; cons. to minority bus. Econ. Devel. Ctr., 1983-84. Recipient Econ. Issues Essay award Nat. Economist Club, 1979; NEH grantee, 1981; GE Found. postdoctoral fellow, 1983; grantee Urban Mass Transp. Adminstrn., 1984, Dept. Transp., 1985—. Mem. Am. Econ. Assn., So. Econ. Assn., Econ. Awareness Club (advisor). Islam. Avocations: travel; reading; chess; bridge. Office: Benedict Coll Columbia SC 29204

MAHER, JAMES EARL, emergency management agency executive, former marine corps officer; b. Sioux Falls, S.D., Oct. 21, 1929; s. James Earl and Anna Margeruite (Tovik) M.; m. Elizabeth Brown, Dec. 22, 1951; children—Anna Louise, Mary Elizabeth, Sandra Davis, James Earl, Patricia Jean. B.A. in Edn., U. Miss., 1951; M.Pub.Adminstrn., Miss. Coll., 1980, M.B.A., 1981. Commd. 2d lt., U.S. Marine Corps, 1951, advanced through grades to lt. col., 1971; ret., 1971; ops. officer Miss. Civil Def. Council, Jackson, 1972-80; exec. dir. Miss. Emergency Mgmt. Agy., Jackson, 1980—; dir., vice chmn. Central U.S. Earthquake Consortium, Marion, Ill., 1983—. Editor: The Marine Reserve, A History, 1966. Creator advt. art Marine Corps Reserve. Decorated Bronze Star; recipient award Point of Purchase Advt. Inst., 1967. Fellow Nat. Assn. Search and Rescue (bd. dirs. 1977-79); mem. Nat. Emergency Mgmt. Assn. (v.p.), Marine Corps Assn. Presbyterian. Avocations: computer science; model building; history. Office: Miss Emergency Mgmt Agy 1410 Riverside Dr Jackson MS 39216

MAHLE, PATSY BEGHTEL, clergywoman, pastoral counselor; b. Huntington, Ind., Jan. 9, 1942; d. Fred Andress and Lila Margaret (Bradford) Beghtel; m. Ralph Jerry Mahle, Feb. 24, 1961; children—Christine, Jerry Bradford. Student, Carnegie Coll., 1959-61, Perkins Sch. Theology, 1982—. Med. technologist Middletown Hosp. (Ohio), 1962-67, Physician and Surgeon Clinic, Dallas, 1972-77; advanced resident for chaplaincy in emergency area Parkland Meml. Hosp., Dallas, 1978-79, mem. pastoral care dept., 1979-83, staff chaplain emergency area, 1980—. Mem. Am. Assn. Clin. Pastoral Educators, Assn. Pastoral Counselors. Methodist. Home: 3810 Old Faithful Irving TX 75062 Office: 5201 Harry Hines Blvd Dallas TX 75235

MAHLMANN, JOHN JAMES, educational association administrator; b. Washington, Jan. 21, 1942; s. Charles Victor and Mary Elizabeth (Deye) M.; m. Ning Ning Chang, Feb. 5, 1972; 1 child, Justin Geeng Ming. B.F.A., Boston U., 1962, M.F.A., 1963; postgrad. U. Notre Dame, summer 1962; Ed.D., Pa. State U., 1970. Grad. asst. Boston U., 1962-63, instr., supr. student tchrs., dir. masters degree candidates, 1964-66; grad. asst., research asst. Pa. State U., 1963-64, instr., 1966-67, dir. gallery, art edn. dept., 1966-67; asst. prof. Tex. Tech Coll., 1967-69, chmn. tenure and promotions com.; dir. publs., asst. exec. sec. Nat. Art Edn. Assn., Washington, 1969-71, exec. sec., 1971-82, also tour dir. to Japan and Orient; exec. dir. Music Educators Nat. Conf., Reston, Va., 1983—; instr. drawing Lubbock Art Assn., Tex.; asst. debate coach, asst. coordinator forensics Boston U. Exhibited at Boston U., Pa. State U., Harvard U., Tex. Tech U., Salem State Coll., Mass., Botolph Gallery, Boston, Inst. Contemporary Art, Boston, Barncellar Gallery, Orleans, Mass., State Gallery, State College, Pa., Halls Gallery, Lubbock, Lubbock Art Assn., Loft Gallery, San Antonio, Llano Estacado Art Assn., Hobbs, N.Mex., Purdue U., Cushing Gallery, Dallas, Religious Art Exhbn., Cranbrook Acad. Art, Bloomfield Hills, Mich., Upstairs Gallery, Arlington, Tex., SW Tex. State Coll., San Marcos. Editor Art Edn., 1970-81, Art Tchr., 1971-80; exec. editor Design mag. Contbr. articles to publs. Bd. dirs. Sino-Am. Cultural Soc., Washington, 1985. Mem. Music Educators Nat. Conf., Nat. Art Edn. Assn., Reston Bd. Commerce, Phi Delta Kappa. Club: Rotary. Office: Music Educators Nat Conf 1902 Association Dr Reston VA 22091

MAHOD, ADNAN MOHD, counselor, researcher; b. Irbid, Jordan, July 31, 1955; s. Mohd Daoud Mahod and Amna (Ahmad) Al-Masri. B.A. in Edn., U. Jordan, Amman, 1978; M.A. in Clin. Psychology, Tex. So. U., 1981. Cert. counselor. Therapist St. Joseph Hosp., Houston, 1980-81; counselor Bellaire Hosp., Houston, 1981—. Mem. Am. Assn. for Counseling and Devel., Am. Psychol. Assn. (assoc.), Assn. of Muslim Social Scientists, Assn. for Counselor Edn. and Supervision, Am. Mental Health Counselors Assn. Avocations: chess; travel; photography. Home: PO Box 771323 Houston TX 77215

MAHON, ELDON BROOKS, U.S. judge; b. Loraine, Tex., Apr. 9, 1918; s. John Bryan and Nola May (Muns) M.; B.A., McMurry Coll., 1939; LL.B., U. Tex., 1942; m. Nova Lee Groom, June 1, 1941; children—Jana, Martha, Brad. Admitted to Tex. bar, 1942; law clk. Tex. Supreme Ct., 1945-46; county atty. Mitchell County, Tex., 1947; dist. atty. 32d Jud. Dist. Tex., 1948-60, dist. judge, 1960-63; v.p. Tex. Electric Service Co., Ft. Worth, 1963-64; practiced law, Abilene, Tex., 1964-68; U.S. atty. No. Dist. Tex., Ft. Worth, 1968; now judge U.S. Dist. Ct. for No. Tex., Ft. Worth. Pres. W. Tex. council Girl Scouts U.S.A., 1966-68. Trustee McMurry Coll. Served with USAAF, 1942-45. Named an outstanding Tex. prosecutor Tex. Law Enforcement Found., 1957. Mem. Am., Fed., Ft. Worth-Tarrant County bar assns., Am. Judicature Assn., State Bar Tex. Methodist (past del. confs.). Home: 4167 Sarita St Fort Worth TX 76109 Office: US Dist Court 403 US Courthouse Fort Worth TX 76102

MAHONEY, JEROME, business executive, consultant; b. Boston, Aug. 31, 1947; s. William Joseph and Anne Frances (Smolski) M.; m. Phyllis Jeanne Wilhelm, Dec. 29, 1973; children—Mark Jerome, Lauren Jeanne. B.S., Calif. Maritime Acad., 1968. Ship's officer United Fruit Co., San Francisco, 1968-69, Grace Lines, N.Y.C., 1969-70; compass adjuster Baker, Lyman & Co., New Orleans, 1970-72, pres., Houston, 1972—; cons. Lockheed Shipbldg., Seattle, 1984—. Recipient recognition award for contbn. to marine industry Tex. A&M U., 1984. Mem. Marine Services Assn. Tex. (chmn. scholarships, dir. 1980), Propellor Club of U.S., Better Bus. Bur., Houston C. of C. Club: Chancellor's (Houston). Avocation: sailing.

MAHONEY, JOHN JOSEPH, business executive, educator; b. Chattanooga, Nov. 9, 1921; s. John J. and Helen M. (Armstrong) M.; m. Elizabeth Dubose Porcher, June 25, 1949. B.S. in Commerce, The Citadel, 1946; M.S. in Indsl. Mgmt., Ga. Inst. Tech., 1967. Instr. dept. bus. adminstrn. The Citadel, Charleston, S.C., 1947-50, asst. prof., 1967—; founder, pres., gen. mgr. Carolinga Vending Inc., 1947-67, Shamrock System, Inc., 1960-67; dir. Charles F. Cates & Sons, Inc., Pickle Co., Faison, S.C., also mem. exec. com.; founder, v.p., treas., dir. Cons. to Bus., Inc. (formerly Mahoney Cons., Inc.); dir. Aunt Jane Foods, Inc.; S.C. steering com. White House Conf. on Small Bus., vice chmn. S.C. del. Ordained permanent deacon Roman Catholic Ch., 1979; procurator, advocate diocesan tribunal Diocese of Charleston, mem. Bishop's Com. on Vocations; pres. Cath. Charities, 1958—; bd. dirs. Charleston C. of C., Charleston Devel. Bd., 1957-60, United Fund, Charleston, 1955-56, Family Agy., Charleston, 1956-60, South Found., Confederate Meml. Assn.; chmn. Pres.'s Export Expansion Council. Served to 1st lt. AUS, 1943-46, capt. Res. Decorated Order So. Cross; recipient Disting. Service award Jaycees, 1956. Fellow Found. Econ. Edn.; mem. Acad. Mgmt., So. Mgmt. Assn., Irish-Am. Cultural Inst. (life), Fellowship Cath. Scholars, Charleston Trident C. of C., Confederate Hist. Assn. Belgium (chargé d'affaires, S.C.), Univ. Profs. for Acad. Order (bd. dirs. 1985), O'Mahoney Record Soc., Sons Confederate Vets. Assn. Pvt. Enterprise (chaplain S.C. div.), Fund for Conservative Majority (bd. govs.). Republican. Clubs: Carolina Yacht, Hibernian Soc. Office: The Citadel Charleston SC 29409 also 276 East Bay Ct Charleston SC 29401

MAHONEY, LARY STUART, real estate development company executive, architect; b. Jacksonville, Fla., Oct. 10, 1951; s. Willard George and Jean Louise (Worley) M. B.Arch., Ga. Inst. Tech., 1974; postgrad. Swiss Fed. Inst. Tech., Zurich, 1974-75; grad. diploma in architecture Archtl. Assn. Sch. Architecture, London, 1978. Lic. architect, Calif., Ga. Architect Craig Combs and Assocs., Newport Beach, Calif., 1976, Ken Himes and Assocs., Santa Ana, Calif., 1976-77, Langdon and Wilson Architects, Newport Beach, 1978-79, Heery & Heery Architects & Engrs. Inc., Atlanta, 1979-84; project mgr., constrn. mgr. Ackerman & Co., Atlanta, 1984-85; devel. mgr. D.L. Smith Realty, 1985—. Mem. selection com. for scholars World Student Fund, Atlanta, 1975—. Recipient design citation Progressive Architecture, 1983; World Student Fund scholar Swiss Fedn. Inst. Tech., 1974-75. Mem. Nat. Council Archtl. Registration, Nat. Trust for Hist. Preservation, High Mus. of Art. Presbyterian. Home: 1150 Collier Rd Apt C-8 Atlanta GA 30318 Office: DL Smith Realty PO Box 47010 Atlanta GA 30362

MAHONEY, MICHAEL PATRICK, public relations and advertising executive, educator; b. Tampa, Fla., Feb. 17, 1951; s. Robert Eugene and Margaret Effie (Breland) M.; m. Mary Ellen Kawaky, Oct. 20, 1973; children—Michael Patrick, Matthew John. B.A. in Speech Communications, U. South Fla., 1973, B.A. in Mass Communications, 1974. With Seald-Sweet Growers, Inc., Tampa, Fla., 1974-76, Citrus & Vegetable Mag., Tampa, 1974-76; dir. pub. relations S.W. Fla. Blood Bank, Tampa, 1976-85; pres. Profl. Writing Services, Inc., Tampa, 1980—; adj. prof. mass communications U. South Fla., Tampa; exec. dir. Tampa Tiger Bay Club, 1983—. Author: The Path to Excellence, 1983; contbr. writings to publs. including Citrus and Vegetable mag., Communique, Tampa Tribune, Living in Florida Year Round. Mem. Fla. Mag. Assn., Pub. Relations Soc. Am. (accredited; pres. Central Fla. chpt. 1985), Tampa C. of C. (internal promotions council 1978—), Am. Assn. Blood Banks, Fla. Assn. Blood Banks. Roman Catholic. Club: Tiger Bay of Tampa. Home: 3147 Lakestone Dr Tampa FL 33618

MAHOOD, RAMONA MADSON, library science educator; b. Brigham City, Utah, June 7, 1933; d. Stanley Johnson and Effie (Webb) Madson; m. Harry Richard Mahood, Dec. 21, 1962. B.S., Utah State U., 1955; M.S., U. Ill., 1959, Cert. Advanced Study, 1971. Lic. stock broker. Reference librarian Weber State Coll., 1955-62; asst. prof. library sci. Memphis State U., 1964—; broker Cooper St. Group Securities. Mem. ALA, Assn. Library and Info. Sci. Edn., Children's Lit. Assn., Southeastern Library Assn., Spl. Libraries Assn., Tenn. Library Assn., Tenn. Govt. Documents Orgn., Beta Phi Mu, Delta Kappa Gamma, Phi Kappa Phi. Co-editor (with Millicent Lenz) Young Adult Literature: Background and Criticism, ALA, 1980; contbr. articles to profl. jours. Home: 3528 Lily Ln Memphis TN 38111 Office: Dept Curriculum and Instruction Memphis State U Memphis TN 38152

MAI, HUNG THE, civil engineer; b. Cantho, South Vietnam, May 16, 1950; came to U.S., 1979; s. Truyen Van and Nguyet Thi (Nguyen) M.; m. Chi Kim Mai, Apr. 6, 1975; 1 child, Tu Mai. B.S.C.E. with 1st class honors, Nat. Inst. Tech., Saigon, 1973. Registered profl. engr., Fla., Calif. Chief engring. sect. Saigon Met. Water and Sewer Authority, 1973-78; civil engr. Sam O. Hirota, Inc., Honolulu, 1979-80; project engr. Greenleaf-Telesca, Inc., Miami, Fla., 1980-83; project mgr. Tomasino & Assocs., Inc., Tampa, Fla., 1983-85; cons. engr., 1985—. Mem. ASCE, Fla. Engring. Soc., Nat. Soc. Profl. Engrs. Buddhist. Home: 11018 Ashbourne Circle Tampa FL 33624 Office: PO Box 2059 Tampa FL 33601

MAI, KLAUS L., chemical engineer, research company executive; b. Changsha, China, Mar. 7, 1930; s. Ludwig H. and Ilse (Behrend) M.; m. Helen Martinchek, July 14, 1957; children—Martin, Michael, Mark, Matthew. B.S. in Chem. Engring., Gonzaga U., 1951; M.S. in Chem. Engring., U. Wash., 1952, Ph.D. in Chem. Engring., 1955. With Shell Chem. Co., Houston, 1969—, gen. mgr. indsl. chem. and polymers div., 1972-74, exec. v.p., 1977-81, pres. Shell Devel. Co., Houston, 1981—, dir. Shell Cos. Found., Houston, 1981—. Trustee S.W. Research Inst., San Antonio, 1982—; bd. govs. St. Joseph Hosp.; mem. U.S. nat. com. World Petroleum Congress. Recipient Alumni Merit award Gonzaga U., 1982. Fellow Am. Inst. Chem. Engrs. (bd. dirs.); mem. Council for Chem. Research (Chmn. 1985—), Am. Chem. Soc. (adv. bd. 1984—), AAAS, Am. Petroleum Inst., Indsl. Research Inst., Houston Area Research Council (bd. dirs., exec. com.), Tex. Gov.'s Sci. and Tech. Council, Sigma Xi, Tau Beta Phi. Clubs: Lakeside Country, Petroleum (Houston). Contbr. articles on chem. engring. to profl. jours.; patentee in field. Home: 403 Kari Ct Houston TX 77024 Office: PO Box 2463 Houston TX 77001

MAIB, DONALD EUGENE, insurance company executive; b. Lawton, Okla., May 15, 1943; s. Ernest V. and Katherine (Fewell) M.; m. Rachel E. Rakes, Feb. 12, 1963 (div. 1975); children—Kimberly L., Donald E.; m. Thelma L. Moore, Apr. 9, 1976; children—Misty L., Moriah Victoria. Student U. Okla., 1961-64. Mgr., Retail, F. W. Woolworth, Memphis, 1964-68; sales mgr. Nat. Life, Nashville, 1968-83; pres. Am. Insurors, Gallatin, Tenn., 1983—; sec.-treas. Tri-County Underwriters, Gallatin, 1972-78; cons. in field. Contbr. articles to profl. jours. Mgr. Youth T-Ball, Gallatin, Tenn., 1980-84; scoutmaster Boy Scouts Am., 1980-81; lectr. in field. Mem. Nat. Assn. Life Underwriters (Nat. Sales Achievement award 1968, 85), Million Dollar Round Table, Gen. Agts. and Mgrs. Assn. (Agt. of Year 1978, 80), Sales and Mktg. Execs. Internat. (Sales award 1978, 80). Republican. Baptist. Avocations: writing; baseball; youth group. Home: Route 3 Douglas Bend Rd PO Box 1685 Gallatin TN 37066-1685 Office: American Insurors PO Box 551 Hendersonville TN 37077-0551

MAIER, KURT WILLIAM, lawyer; b. Louisville, Ky., Apr. 26, 1954; s. G. George and Martha Clark (Fowler) M.; m. Paula Lynn Metzger, July 24, 1976; children—Mark Bohannan, Cole Martin. B.A., Denison U., 1976; J.D., U. Ky., 1979. Bar: Ky. 1979, U.S. Dist. Ct. (we. dist.) Ky. 1979. mem. English, Lucas, Priest & Owsley, Bowling Green, Ky., 1979—. Mem. Bowling Green Bar Assn. (sec. 1982), Ky. Bar Assn., ABA, Ky. Acad. Trial Attys., Assn. Trial Lawyers Am., Bowling Green-Warren County Jaycees, Bowling Green-Warren County C. of C., U. Ky Alumni Assn., Ky. Cols. Democrat. Roman Catholic. Home: 1525 Sherwood Dr Bowling Green KY 42101 Office: English Lucas Priest & Owsley PO Box 770 1110 College St Bowling Green KY 42101

MAIER, ROBERT HENRY, metals company executive; b. Greenville, Tex., Nov. 19, 1932; s. William Lokey and Charlsie Lorraine (Nation) M.; B.A., So. Meth. U., 1964; m. Ruth Jean Chapman, Mar. 1, 1968; children—Alice Silberman, Joy Kupp. Personnel dir. Atlantic Richfield Co., Dallas, 1954-69; v.p. adminstrn. ETMF Freight System, Dallas, 1969-78; chief personnel officer Varo, Inc., Garland, Tex., 1978-80; corp. v.p. adminstrn. Comml. Metals Co., Dallas, 1980—. Mem. Am. Soc. Personnel Adminstrn., Am. Soc. Advancement of Mgmt. (chpt. pres.), Dallas Personnel Assn. Republican. Clubs: Rotary, Masons. Office: Comml Metals Co 7800 Stemmons Freeway Dallas TX 75247

MAIER, SIBYL CHAUVIN, draftsman; b. Raceland, La., Nov. 25, 1945; d. Fay Joseph and Agatha Mary (Robichaux) Chauvin; m. Douglas Andrew Maier, Aug. 1, 1964; children—Michael Anthony, Michelle Anne, Mark Anthony. Student La. State U., 1963, Nicholl's State U., 1963-64. Draftsman, Houma, La., 1969—; owner Residential Drafting Service, Houma. Mem. Houma Jr. Aux., 1980-85, assoc. life, 1985—; vol. Terrebonne Parish Council on Aging. Democrat. Roman Catholic. Address: 3344 Little Bayou Black Dr Houma LA 70360

MAILHOS, JOSEPH LEEMAN, industrial engineer; b. Elizabeth, La., Mar. 28, 1936; s. Joseph Eugene and Thelma (Prescott) M.; m. Nelwyn Elizabeth Soileau, June 1, 1959 (div. 1965); children—David Joe, Jolié Camele, Lizabeth, Mathew Leeman. Various positions with Rust Engring., Birmingham, Ala., 1953-54, Combustion Engring. Co., Valdosta, Ga., 1954, Daniels Constrn. Co., Greenville, S.C., 1956, Alpha Constrn. Co., Valdosta, 1957, Bowater Carolina Corp., Catawba, S.C., 1958-60, Continental Can Co., Augusta, Ga., 1960-63, Calcasieu Paper Co., Elizabeth, La., 1965-69; heavy equipment operator Boyles Constrn. Co., Sumpter, S.C., 1955; chem. plant foreman Celanese Chem. Co., Bay City, Tex., 1963-65; with Penrod Drilling Co., Lafayette, La., 1975-76; dist. sales mgr. pulp and paper equipment Voigt England Co., Birmingham, 1969-75; staff engr. Brown & Root Engring., Houston, 1976-83; sales engr. Gen. Electric Co., Baton Rouge, 1983—. Served with USNR, 1953-61. Mem. TAPPI, Paper Industry Mgmt. Assn., Aircraft Owners and Pilots Assn., Epsilon Phi Tau. Democrat. Baptist. Club: Nat. L (La. State U.). Office: 8312 Florida Blvd Suite 108B Baton Rouge LA 70806

MAILHOT, RAYMOND BERNARD, educator; b. Crosby, Minn., Nov. 17, 1929; s. Arthur Joseph and Ida Caroline (Carlson) M.; B.B.A., U. Minn., 1954; B.S. with high scholastic honors, St. Cloud (Minn.) State U., 1974; M.S., Eastern Mich. U., 1978; postgrad. Ala. A&M U., 1977-81; m. Linda Belle Peace, Feb. 20, 1971; children—Michelle, Rochelle, Raymond Bernard, Richard. Mgmt. trainee Montgomery Ward & Co., 1954-58; civilian adminstrv. asst. Signal Corps, U. Mich., 1958-65; chief forms mgmt. div. U.S. Army Tank-Automotive Command, Warren, Mich., 1965-67; computer control analyst IRS Data Center, Detroit, 1967-68; acting exec. officer Motor Vehicle Pollution Control Lab., Ann Arbor, Mich., 1968-72; mgr. Spalding Hotel, Crosby, Minn., 1972-73; tchr. Skyline High Sch., Scottsboro, Ala., 1974-81, 83—; dir., tchr. Skyline Headstart Ctr., 1982-83; tchr. migrant program, 1983-84, cons. early edn. programs, 1982—; treas. AnLyn Inc., 1972-73; cons. lang. arts assessment team Ala. Dept. Edn., 1977-78. Served with USAF, 1947-51. Recipient Quality Performance award U.S. Army, 1961, Sustained Superior award, 1962. Mem. Internat. Reading Assn., NEA, Assn. Supervision and Curriculum Devel., Ala. Reading Assn. (cert. of appreciation 1978), Ala. Edn. Assn., Jackson County Edn. Assn. (faculty rep.), Sequoyah Reading Council (past pres.). Methodist. Mem. editorial adv. bd. Ala. Reader, 1975-81. Home: Route 1 Scottsboro AL 35768

MAIN, EDNA DEWEY, educator; b. Hyannis, Mass., Sept. 1, 1940; d. Seth Bradford and Edna Wilhelmina (Wright) Dewey; m. Donald John Main, Sept. 9, 1961; children—Alison Teresa, Susan Christine, Steven Donald. Degree in Merchandising, Tobe-Coburn Sch., 1960; B.A.Ed., U. North Fla., 1974, M.A.Ed., 1979, M.Adminstrn. and Supervision, 1983. Asst. buyer Abraham & Straus, Bklyn., 1960-61; asst. mdse. mgr. Interstate Dept. Stores, N.Y.C., 1962-63; tchr. Holiday Hill Elem. Sch., Jacksonville, Fla., 1974—; mem. adv. council Coll. Edn., U. North Fla., 1982—, instr. summer sci. inst., 1984, 85; instr. U. South Fla., 1981. Rep., United Way, 1981-83; tchr. rep., chpt. leader White House Young Astronaut Program, 1984-85; mem. supervisory com. Ednl. Community Credit Union. Mem. Nat. Sci. Tchrs. Assn. (sci. tchrs. achievement recognition award 1983), Assn. Supervision and Curriculum Devel., Council Elem. Sci. Internat., Fla. Assn. Sci. Tchrs., Phi Kappa Phi, Phi Delta Kappa, Delta Kappa Gamma, Kappa Delta Pi. Republican. Episcopalian. Office: 6900 Altama Rd Jacksonville FL 32216

MAIN, T(OM) TALMAGE, JR., petroleum consultant; b. Hamilton, Tex., Jan. 9, 1922; s. Tom Talmage and Doris (Williams) M.; A.A., Tyler Tex. Jr. Coll., 1941; B.B.A., U. Tex., Austin, 1947; M.Sc., Tex. Tech. U., 1950; postgrad. Jackson (Miss.) Sch. Law, 1955-59; m. (Virginia) Sue Pingree, Feb. 26, 1955; children—Deborah Sue, Steven Talmage. Field rep. Bur. Bus. Research, U. Tex., Austin, 1947; asst. to dist. traffic mgr. Phillips Petroleum Co., Houston, 1947-49; geologist Sun Oil Co., Dallas, 1952-59; geologist, asst. v.p., trust officer Merc. Nat. Bank at Dallas, 1959-80; v.p. Gt. Am. Exploration Corp., 1980-82; dir. Dorchester Petroleum Co. Mem. Circle Ten council Boy Scouts Am.; mem. bd. adjustment Town of Highland Park; sec., treas. Dallas County Tex. Vets. Service Bd.; bd. assoc. Reform Theol. Sem., Jackson, Miss., 1981-85. Served to col. USAR, 1942-46; ETO; 50-52; Korea. Decorated Legion of Merit, Bronze Star, Meritorious Service medal; Medaille de Liberée (France); Presdl. citation (Korea). Mem. U.S. Res. Officers Assn. (life; dept. pres. 1976-77, nat. councilman 1977-78, nat. treas. 1978-80), Assn. U.S. Army (life; pres. chpt. 1970), Mil. Order World Wars (perpetual; comdr. chpt. 1973-74), Highland Park (Tex.) Community League (exec. com. 1966—, treas. 1975—), Knight Order of San Jacinto (Knight comdr. 1985-86), Sons Republic of Tex. (life; pres. 1973-75), Dallas, Am. (cert. petroleum landman) assns. petroleum landmen, Dallas Geol. Soc., Am. Assn. Petroleum Geologists (cert. petroleum geologist), Dallas Mil. Ball Corp. (founder; dir., sec. 1965—), United Service Orgn. (council 1970-73), Dallas Cares, Dallas C. of C., Nat. Mil. Intelligence Assn. (charter dir. 1974-76), Sigma Gamma Epsilon, Sigma Delta Kappa. Club: Dervish (Dallas). Presbyterian (elder, clk. session 1980-82). Home: 4564 Arcady Ave Dallas TX 75205

MAINOR, RAYFER EARL'E, writer, educator; b. Seattle, Mar. 25, 1954; s. Henry and Rosetta (Manning) M.; m. Treva Jeanette Gainer, Dec. 15, 1983; 1 dau., Sarah Jean; 1 foster son, David. B.A., Paul Quinn Coll., Waco, Tex., 1978; M.Ed., Tex. State U.-Prairie View, 1980; A.B.D., Okla. State U.-Stillwater, 1984. Cert. Inst. of Theatre Arts and Creative Writing, 1969. Dir. fine arts Paul Quinn Coll., 1977-78; researcher Gov.'s Criminal Justice Div., Austin, 1978-79; counselor, coordinator McLennan Community Coll., Waco, 1979-80; grad. research asst. Okla. State U., 1980-81; counselor, prof. Langston U. (Okla.), 1981-83; student devel. specialist Oklahoma City Community Coll., 1983—; prof. English, U. Redlands (Calif.), 1977-78; intake supr. People Coordinated Services, Los Angeles, 1976-77; counselor Calif. State Dept. Corrections, Los Angeles, 1970-75. Author: (play) Two, But Not of a King, 1969; (poetry) Tribute to Blackness (Vassie D. Wright Authors award Assn. for Study of Afro-Am. Life and History), To Mister or Sarah Jean: A Love Story, 1984 (Quinn & Quill Humanitarian award). Organizer Oklahomans for Jesse Jackson, Oklahoma City; bd. dirs. Okla. Hist. Soc.-Capitol Complex, Oklahoma City. Recipient Poet Laureate award Mayor of Langston, 1979; Melvin B. Tolson award Omega Psi Phi, 1980; Golden Laurel Wreath award United Poet Laureates Internat., 1981; Internat. Who's Who in Poetry awards, 1982, 83, 84. Mem. Los Angeles Mcpl. Arts Dept., Nat. Newtork Poets, Nat. Black Writers Conf., World Poetry Soc., Unted Poet Laureate Internat., Alpha Phi Alpha. Democrat. Mem. Ch. of God. Clubs: Internat. Poetry Soc. (Youlgrave, Eng.); Central Studi e Scambi (Rome).

MAISEY, JUDITH MEWSHAW, counselor; b. Lebanon, Pa., Nov. 14, 1939; d. Charles Thomas and Geraldine (Ray) Mewshaw; m. Terry Mercer Maisey, June 20, 1959; children—Mary Kealoha, Michael Terrence, Melissa Marguerite, Michele Christine, Melanie Regina. B.A. summa cum laude, U. N.H., 1961; M.Ed., Midwestern State U., 1976. Lic. profl. counselor, Tex.; nat. cert. counselor. Counselor, Miss. County Community Coll., Blytheville, Ark., 1976-79, Nat. Coll., Rapid City, S.D., 1979-83, St. Mary's U., San Antonio, 1983—; part-time instr. Park Coll., Blytheville AFB, 1976-79. Lector St. Francis Assisi Parish, San Antonio, 1984—; lay eucharistic minister, lector Ellsworth AFB Parish, S.D., 1979-83. Recipient Outstanding Faculty Mem. award Nat. Coll., 1981. Mem. Am. Assn. Counseling Devel., Am. Coll. Personnel Assn. Roman Catholic. Avocations: cross-country skiing; star gazing; downhill skiing; hiking; swimming. Home: 2930 Meadow Circle San Antonio TX 78231 Office: St Mary's U Counseling Ctr One Camino Santa Maria San Antonio TX 78284

MAJESKI, JAMES ANTHONY, transplantation surgeon; b. Newark, Jan. 29, 1945; s. Anthony Andrew and Irene Teresa Majeski; m. Elizabeth Watts Durst, June 16, 1973; children—Elizabeth, James Anthony, Marie. B.S., The Citadel, 1966; M.S., U. S.C., 1968; Ph.D., Med. U. S.C., 1971, M.D., 1974. Research fellow pathology Med. U. S.C., Charleston, 1972-74; intern U. Cin., 1974-75, resident in surgery, 1975-80, fellow in transplantation surgery, 1980-81; asst. prof. surgery Med. U. S.C., 1981—. Served with USAFR, 1966-71. NSF fellow, 1968; scholar Health Professions, 1971; Mosby award, 1973; recipient Jefferson award S.C. Acad. Sci., 1972; Mead Johnson award, 1972. Mem. AMA, So. Med. Assn., Am. Soc. Transplant Surgeons, Assn. Acad. Surgery, Sigma Xi. Contbr. numerous articles to sci. jours. and textbooks; editor transplantation surgery sect Reference and Index Services, Inc., 1976—. Home: Box 721 Sullivan's Island SC 29482 Office: Dept Surgery Med U SC Charleston SC 29425

MAJEWSKI, DONALD PHILLIP, aerospace engineer; b. Buffalo, May 1, 1952; s. Daniel Harry and Regina Teresa (Bujalski) M. A.S., Erie Community Coll., 1972; B.S., SUNY-Buffalo, 1974, M.S., 1983; M.B.A., U. Dallas, 1985. N.Y. State intern mgr. cert., 1975; cert. quality engr. Computer operator Mfrs. and Traders Trust Co., Amherst, N.Y., 1978-79; jr. engr. Ecology and Environ., Inc., Cheektowaga, N.Y., 1979-80; aerodynamics engr. Bell Aerospace Textron, Inc., Niagara Falls, N.Y., 1980-82; sr. engr. E Systems Inc., Greenville, Tex., 1982—; founder Triamar Inst., Buffalo, 1980—. Mem. Grosvenor Soc. Buffalo. Mem. AIAA (pub. policy officer Niagara Frontier sect. 1981-82), Nat. Soc. Profl. Engrs., Aircraft Owners and Pilots Assn., Nat. Pilots Assn. Roman Catholic. Home: 5007 Utah St Greenville TX 75401 Office: CBN-86 PO Box 1056 Greenville TX 75401

MAJID, JOHNATHAN, architect, building design company executive; b. Peshawar, Pakistan, Mar. 20, 1950; came to U.S., 1970; s. John Abdul and Khela Majid; m. Linda Maureen Majid, divorced; 1 child, Joshua. B.S. in Architecture, M.S., Okla. State U. Archtl. engrng. exec. Unidyne Co., Edmond, Okla., 1978-79; pres. Under-Ground & Solar Homes, Inc., Oklahoma City, 1980—; conducted seminars on energy Gov.'s Energy Com., Oklahoma City, 1981, 82. Avocations: sail boating; aerobics; camping. Home: 1205 NW 34th St Oklahoma City OK 73118 Office: 3324 N Classen Blvd Oklahoma City OK 73118

MAJOR, ROBERT WAYNE, physics educator, researcher; b. Newark, Ohio, Sept. 5, 1937; s. Charles Leslie and Leah (Jones) M.; m. Helen Smith; children—Maurice Lee, Diane Louise. B.S., Denison U., 1958; M.S., Iowa State U., 1960; Ph.D., Va. Poly. Inst., 1966. Assoc. prof. U. Richmond, Va., 1968-74, prof., 1974-80, R.E. Lovin prof. physics, 1980—; summer research participant Oak Ridge Nat. Lab., 1973, 80. Grantee NASA, 1970, Research Corp., 1979, U.S. Navy, 1982, 83, 84, 85. Mem. Am. Inst. Physics, Va. Acad. Scis. (chmn. physics and math sect. 1975), Sigma Xi, Sigma Pi Sigma, Omicron Delta Kappa. Office: Dept Physics U Richmond Richmond VA 23173

MAJOR, THOMAS DANIEL, real estate company executive; b. Pasadena, Calif., Feb. 26, 1946; s. Thomas Derhm and Bethel Hope (Quesnell) M.; m. Sherryl Wilson, Oct. 21, 1971; children—Brooke Cannon, Lauren Daniele. B.S., Whittier Coll., 1967. Sales rep. Eastman Kodak, Birmingham, Ala., 1969-70, New Orleans, 1970-71, Mpls., 1972-76, key account rep., Atlanta, 1976-78, mgr. dealer sales, 1978-80, dir. bus. planning, Rochester, N.Y., 1980-82; dir. new home sales Buckhead Brokers, Atlanta, 1983—, pres., owner subs. Major Concepts Inc., homebuilders, 1982—. Mem. Ga. Home Builders Assn., Sales Mktg. Council. Republican. Methodist. Home: 1690 Lazy River Ln Dunwoody GA 30338 Office: Buckhead Brokers 5491 Roswell Rd NE Suite 201 Atlanta GA 30342

MAJORS, SANDRA WARFIELD, investment counselor; b. Syracuse, N.Y., Apr. 23, 1947; d. Howard Chapin and Beret Sophie (Lunos) Warfield; m. Ronald Stephen Majors, May 30, 1970; 1 child, Stephen Samuel. B.A., SUNY-Binghamton, 1969; M.S., Russell Sage Coll., 1972; M.B.A., Am. U., 1978. Chartered fin. analyst. Tchr. Chenango Forks Pub. Schs., N.Y., 1969-70, Niskayuna Pub. Schs., Schenectady, 1970-73, Montgomery County Schs., Md., 1973-76; portfolio mgr. Life Ins. Co. Ga., Atlanta, 1978-82; dir. research Reiser-Builder, Inc., Atlanta, 1982—. Treas. Homeowner's Assn., Potomac, Md., 1976-78. Fellow Fin. Analysts Fedn.; mem. Fin. Mgmt. Assn., Atlanta Soc. Fin. Analysts. Republican. Club: Garden (Atlanta). Home: 174 Friar Tuck Rd NE Atlanta GA 30309 Office: Reiser-Builder Inc 7 Piedmont Ctr Suite 721 Atlanta GA 30305

MAK, STEPHEN YUCHUNG, pharmacist, administrator; b. Canton, China, Nov. 15, 1946; came to U.S., 1968, naturalized, 1985; s. Kee Y. and May (Chan) M.; m. Wanda Lane Hancock, Oct. 17, 1976; 1 child, Mamie Maeling. B.S. in Biology, U. Miss., 1970, B.S. in Pharmacy, 1975. Pharmacist intern Eastwood Hosp., Memphis, 1975-76, asst. dir. pharmacy, 1976-77, acting dir. pharmacy, 1977-78, dir. pharmacy, 1978—. Mem. Am. Soc. Hosp. Pharmacists. Roman Catholic. Avocations: gardening; raising cattle; reading; tennis. Office: Eastwood Hosp 3000 Getwell Rd Memphis TN 38118

MAKHANI, MADAN PAL SINGH, foundry exec.; b. Amritsar, India, Oct. 23, 1937; s. Gulzar Singh and Mohinder (Kaur) M.; A.T.S. (Ednl. scholar), Machine Tool Prototype Factory, Bombay, 1957; A.M.I.B.F., City and Guilds London Inst., 1958; m. Betty Jean Lowder, June 10, 1972; children—Madana Marie, Indera, Jogi Patrick. In charge pattern shop and quality control New Haven Foundry (Mich.), 1964; gen. mgr. Old South Forge, Inc., Waycross, Ga., 1965-66; pres. Am. Casting Co., Inc., Tulsa, 1966—, also Am. Investment Casting Co., Inc., Am. Alloy Casting Co. Inc., Am. Foundry Group Inc.; pres. Okla. Steel Castings Co., 1982— prof. Artisan Tng. Sch., India, 1957. Mem. Am. (dir. Tri-state 1973-75, vice chmn. Tri-state 1976-77, chmn. Tri-state 1977-78), Brit. foundryman socs., Patternmakers League N.Am. (treas. 1968-72), Soc. Mfg. Engrs., Tulsa Mfrs. Club (dir. 1980-81), Purchasing Mgmt. Assn. Tulsa. Club: Elks. Home: 3514 E 109th St S Tulsa OK 74137 Office: 14602 S Grant Bixby OK 74008

MAKI, PATRICIA CAROLINE, financial executive; b. Berwyn, Ill., July 15, 1951; d. Edward Stanley and Caroline Lillian (Zalewski) M.; B.S. in Accountancy, U. Ill., Urbana, 1973. C.P.A., Ill. Audit sr. Price Waterhouse & Co., Chgo., 1973-76; regional acctg. mgr. McDonald's Corp., Dallas, 1976-79; corp. acctg. mgr. Sangamo Weston, Atlanta, 1979-80; div. controller Cox Cable Communications, Atlanta, 1980—, dir. corp. info. services, dir. ops. fin. analysis. Mem. Am. Inst. C.P.A.s, Am. Woman's Soc. C.P.A.s, Ga. Soc. C.P.A.s. Roman Catholic. Home: 2297 Macby Ct NE Marietta GA 30066 Office: Cox Cable Communications 1400 Lake Hearn Dr Atlanta GA 30319

MAKINS, JAMES EDWARD, dental educator, educational adminstrator, dentist; b. Galveston, Tex., Feb. 22, 1923; s. James and Hazel Alberta (Morton) M.; m. Jane Hopkins, Mar. 4, 1943; children—James E. Jr., Michael William, Patrick Clarence, Scott Roger. D.D.S., U. Tex.-Houston, 1945; postdoctoral, SUNY-Buffalo, 1948-49. Lic. dentist, Tex. Practice dentistry specializing in orthodontics, Lubbock, Tex., 1949-77; dir. clinics Dallas City Dental Health Program, 1977-78; dir. continuing edn. Baylor Coll. Dentistry, Dallas, 1978—. Author: (book chpt.) Handbook of Texas, 1986. Chmn. profl. div. United Fund, Lubbock, 1958; pres. Tex. State Bd. Dental Examiners, Austin, Tex., 1968; instl. chmn. United Way, Dallas, 1983. Served to lt. comdr., USNR, 1945-47. Recipient Community Service award W. Tex. C. of C., Abilene, 1968, Clinic award Dallas County Dental Soc., 1981. Fellow Am. Coll. Dentists, Internat. Coll. Dentists; mem. Tex. Dental Assn. (v.p. 1954, Goodfellow 1973), West Tex. Dental Assn. (pres. 1955), Am. Assn. Dental Examiners, Omicron Kappa Upsilon. Methodist. Lodge: Rotary. Avocation: history. also PO Box 12689 Dallas TX 75225 Office: Baylor Coll Dentistry 3302 Gaston Ave Dallas TX 75246

MAKLER, EDWARD ALAN, optometrist, real estate broker; b. Oklahoma City, May 3, 1946; s. Max and Mary Adele (Wernick) M.; m. Lottie Clark, Aug. 10, 1969; children—Jason, Amy. B.S., U. Okla., 1968; O.D., U. Houston, 1972. Practice optometry specializing in contact lenses, Richardson, 1976—. Contbr. articles to profl. jours. Active Berkner High Sch. Boosters, Richardson, 1976—, Richardson C. of C., 1976—, Boy Scouts Am. Alumni, Dallas, 1980—. Served to capt. USAF, 1972-76. Decorated Nat. Def. Service medal, 1972, Outstanding Unit award, 1973, Presdl. Unit Citation award, 1973; Mem. Tex. Assn. Optometrists (diagnostic drug com. 1982—). Jewish. Club: First Tuesday Investments (pres. 1979—). Lodge: B'nai Brith, Temple Shalom Brotherhood. Avocations: reading; bicycling; sports. Home: 6908 Echo Bluff Dallas TX 75248 Office: 699A Richardson Sq Richardson TX 75081

MALCHON, JEANNE KELLER, state legislator, association executive; b. Newark, June 17, 1923; d. Leslie Stafford and Edith (Marcelle) Keller; m. Richard H. Malchon, Jan. 30, 1946; 1 son, Richard H. A.A. Va. Intermont Coll., 1943. State pres. Fla. chpt. LWV, 1969-71, bd. dirs. nat. orgn., 1972-74; chmn. Pinellas County Commn. (Fla.), 1975-81; mem. Fla. Senate, St. Petersburg, 1982—; communications cons. Candorcom, St. Petersburg, 1975-82. Presdl. appointee Nat. Commn. on Air Quality, Washington, 1978; past pres. Am. Lung Assn.; chmn. NCCJ, Tampa, Fla., 1983; Recipient Equal Opportunity Efforts award Pinellas County Urban League, 1980, Liberty Bell award St. Petersburg Bar Assn., 1972, Athena award Women in Communications, 1975, Women in Govt. award Soroptimist Club, 1979, numerous others; named Outstanding Citizen, City of St. Petersburg, 1963. Mem. Fla. Women's Network, LWV. Democrat. Unitarian-Universalist. Home: 2400 Pinellas Point Dr S Saint Petersburg FL 33712 Office: Suite 804 424 Central Ave Saint Petersburg FL 33701

MALDONADO, HECTOR CLEMENTE, transportation executive; b. Ciego de Avila, Cuba, Apr. 25, 1955; came to U.S., 1961; s. Abelardo Armando and Julia Silvia (Perez de Corcho) M. Grad., Charron Williams Coll., 1975. Import agt. Aerocondor Airlines, Miami, Fla., 1975-76; export agt. Intercontinental Forwarders, Miami, 1976-78; pres. USPB Corp., Miami, 1978—; v.p. Boston-Pacific Corp., Miami, 1982—; treas. Cantabria Corp., Miami, 1982—. Author: (poetry) Q-21 Antologia Poetica, 1983; Poetas de Hispano America, 1983; El Herrero, 1980; Acentos del Norte, 1981. Pres., Municipio de Ciego de Avila, Miami, 1974-75, Municipios de Camaguey, Miami, 1975-76. Republican. Roman Catholic. Club: Gala (Miami). Home: 11450 SW 40th St Miami FL 33165 Office: 3350 NW 78th Ave Miami FL 33122

MALEK, NICOLAS GEORGE, electrical, instrumentation and control company executive; b. Tripoli, Lebanon, Aug. 2, 1947; came to U.S., 1966; s. George Antoine and Yvonne (Abboud) M.; m. Marian S. Moses, July 17, 1971; children—Nicole B., George N., Sean N. B.S. in Elec. Engrng., La. State U., 1970, M.S., 1972. Registered profl. engr., La. Elec. and instrumentation engr. Barnard & Burk, Baton Rouge, La., 1969-73; sect. head engrng. and instrumentation C.F. Bean, New Orleans, 1973-75; asst. mgr. Bean/Volker, Jubail, Saudi Arabia, 1975-78; mgr. engrng. Bean Dredging, New Orleans, 1978-79; mgr. elec., instrumentation and controls div. Walk, Haydel & Assocs., New Orleans, 1979—. Mem. Instrumenta Soc. Am. (sr.), IEEE (sr.), La. Engrng. Soc., Friends of Zoo, YMCA, Nat. Law Enforcement Assn., Tau Beta Pi, Eta Kappa Nu, Phi Kappa Phi. Republican. Greek Orthodox. Home: 2101 Butternut Ave Metairie LA 70001 Office: Walk Haydel & Assocs 600 Carondelet St New Orleans LA 70130

MALEY, DONALD ROSS, communications and music educator; b. Detroit, Oct. 21, 1949; s. Rosby Roscoe and Mary Louise (Byrd) M.; m. Vickie Ann Russell, Dec. 27, 1975. B.Music Edn., Murray State U., 1971, M.Music Edn., 1973, M.S., 1974. Cert. pub. sch. tchr., Ky. Instr. Paducah Community Coll., 1975-77, asst. prof., 1977-79, assoc. prof., 1979—, chmn. dept. humanities, 1979-85; cons. S. Central Bell, Owensboro, Ky., 1983-85; faculty trustee rep. Paducah Jr. Coll., 1985—. Contbr. articles to profl. jours. Named Performer of Yr., Phi Mu Alpha, 1973, Gt. Tchr. of Yr., Paducah Community Coll., 1978, 85. Mem. Ky. State Poetry Soc., Market House Theatre, Paducah Edn. Assn., Ky. Edn. Assn., NEA, Phi Delta Kappa. Democrat. Mem. Ch. of Christ. Club: Paducah Music (pres.-elect 1985). Avocations: acting; poetry. Office: Paducah Community Coll Alben Barkley Dr PO Box 7380 Paducah KY 42004-7380

MALHOTRA, NARESH KUMAR, management educator, researcher, consultant; b. Ambala, Punjab, India, Nov. 23, 1949; came to U.S., 1975; s. Har Narian and Satya (Kakkar) M.; m. Veena Bahl, Aug. 13, 1980; 1 child, Ruth Veena. B.Tech. with honors, I.I.T., Bombay, India, 1971; M.B.A., I.I.M., Ahmedabad, India, 1973; M.S., SUNY-Buffalo, 1978, Ph.D., 1979. Mgmt. cons. ASCI, Hyderabad, India, 1971-73; asst. prof. Ga. Tech. Inst., Atlanta, 1979—, assoc. prof. mgmt., coordinator of mktg., 1982—; organizer several nat., internat. mktg. mgmt. confs. Contbr. articles to profl. jours. Fellow Acad. Mktg. Sci. (program chmn. 1984-85, 85-86); mem. Am. Mktg. Assn. (track chmn. 1983-84), Am. Inst. Decision Scis. (track chmn. 1984-85), Am. Statis. Assn. Republican. Baptist. Avocations: reading; writing; church activities; outdoor activities. Home: 1956 Lenox Rd NE Atlanta GA 30306 Office: Georgia Tech Inst Coll Mgmt Atlanta GA 30332

MALIK, THOMAS J., judge; b. Chgo., Jan. 2, 1933; s. Frank and Emily (Fanta) M.; m. Virginia Baylor, Oct. 31, 1933; children—Anne Malik Ray, Sylvia J. Malik Lofton, John Paul, Thomas A., Barbara Lynn. Ed. George Washington U., Tulane U.; J.D., Loyola U., New Orleans; diploma Nat. Coll. Trial Judges, U. Nev., 1973; grad. Am. Acad. Jud. Edn., 1983. Bar: La., N.Y., Ill., U.S. Supreme Ct., 1965. Sole practice, 1960-72; judge 29th Jud. Dist. Ct., La., 1972-85, chief judge, 1982-85; chief judge 40th Jud. Dist. Ct., La., 1985—; judge ad hoc La. Ct. Appeals (4th cir.), 1973-74; instr. legal medicine Mercy Hosp. Sch. Nursing, 1976; mem. faculty Melvin Belli Seminar, 1969-71. Founder, Roscoe Pound Found.; pres. Riverlands Civic Assn., 1963. Served with U.S. Army, 1953-56. Mem. ABA, Assn. Trial Lawyers Am., La. Bar Assn., N.Y. State Bar Assn., Ill. Bar Assn., Greater New Orleans Trial Lawyers Assn. (dir. 1963-70), Am. Judges Assn., Nat. Pilots Assn. (safe pilot award 1976), Aircraft Owners and Pilots Assn. Democrat. Roman Catholic. Club: Lions (pres. 1970) (Laplace, La.). Address: PO Box 357 Edgard LA 70049

MALIK, VIRGINIA BAYLOR, nurse; b. Carrizo Springs, Tex., Oct. 31; d. Tom Perry and Blanche Henrietta (Woods) Baylor; m. Thomas Joseph Malik, Dec. 20, 1958; children—Anne Blanche, Sylvia Jane, John Paul, Thomas Anthony, Barbara. Student Loyola U., New Orleans, 1955-56, postgrad., 1976; R.N., Hotel Dieu Sch. Nursing, 1958. Staff nurse Hotel Dieu Hosp., New Orleans, 1958-59, 1975—. Organizer, worker Drug Abuse Program, Paris of St. John the Baptist, 1972, 73, 74, Juvenile Program, 1975; formerly active local Girl Scouts U.S.A., ARC, CD, Am. Cancer Soc.; former organizer local hurricane first aid stations. Democrat. Roman Catholic. Home: 562 Welham Loop LaPlace LA 70068 Office: Hotel Dieu Hosp 2021 Pedido New Orleans LA 70112

MALIN, THOMAS ROBINSON, III, savings association executive; b. Dallas, July 20, 1942; s. Thomas R. and Elizabeth Hill Malin; student in bus. East Tex. State U., 1960-64, So. Meth. U., 1965; m. Lois Ann Brockles, Feb. 14, 1976; children—Thomas Edwin, Stephen Christopher, Angela Renee. Ins. Agt. Prudential Life Ins. Co. Am., 1963-65; area sales mgr. for North Tex., La. and Ark., Clarke Checks, Mesquite, Tex., 1965-80; v.p. Electronic Banking Systems Corp. div. Docutel Olivetti, 1980-83, First Tex. Savs. Assn., Dallas, Dallas, Money Maker EFT Services; electronic funds transfer cons. Mem. Bank Mktg. Assn. (pres. North Tex. chpt. 1980-81). Methodist. Lodge: Masons. Home: 514 Briarcliff Garland TX 75043 Office: 15400 Knoll Trail Suite 400 Dallas TX 75248

MALINAUSKAS, ANTHONY PETER, nuclear scientist; b. Ashley, Pa., Mar. 24, 1935; s. Anthony Andrew and Stella (Grzyszkewicz), m. Barbara Dorothy Derascavage, June 22, 1957; children—Anthony P. Jr., Robert, Barbara M., Richard, Brenda, Linda. B.S. in Chemistry, King's Coll., 1952-56; M.S. in Chemistry, Boston Coll., 1958; Ph.D. in Chemistry, MIT, 1962. Research staff Oak Ridge Nat. Lab., 1962-66, group leader, 1966-73, sect. head, 1973-83, program dir., 1983—; com. mem. Internat. Atomic Energy Agy., 1981—, Atomic Indsl. Forum on Three Mile Island Two Recovery, 1982; adv. group Tech. Assistance for Three Mile Island Unit Two Recovery, 1981—. Author: Gas Transport in Porous Media: The Dusty Gas Model, 1983. Mem. editorial bd. Separation Sci. and Tech., 1981—. Contbr. articles to profl. jours. Recipient E.D. Lawrence award U.S. Dept. Energy, 1985. Mem. Am. Chem. Soc., Am. Nuclear Soc. (Spl. award 1981), Sigma Xi. Republican. Roman Catholic. Avocations: fishing, boating, carpentry. Home: 107 Newton Ln Oak Ridge TN 37830 Office: Oak Ridge Nat Lab PO Box X Oak Ridge TN 37831

MALKEMES, LOIS CONSTANCE, nurse, administrator; b. Shaverton, Pa., May 1, 1940. Diploma in Nursing, Jackson Meml. Hosp., 1961; B.S. in Nursing, Fla. State U., 1964; M.S. in Nursing, U. Colo., 1966, Ph.D. in Sociology, 1972. Registered nurse. Dir. nurse practitioner program U. Ark., Little Rock, 1972-75, prof. Coll. Nursing, 1972-82; patient care adminstr. Univ. Hosp., Little Rock, 1977-82; adviser to nursing Baptist Med. Ctr., Little Rock, 1982-84, v.p. nursing, 1984—. Author: Helping Parents Who Abuse, 1984. Bd. dirs. Suspected Child Abuse and Neglect, Little Rock, 1972—, Vis. Nurses Assn., Little Rock, 1974-80. Mem. Ark. State Nurses Assn. (Ark. Nurse of Yr. 1979), Ark. Soc. for Nursing Service Adminstrs., Nat. League for Nursing, Am. Hosp. Soc. for Nursing Service Adminstrs., Am. Orgn. Nurse Execs., Sigma Theta Tau (Leadership award, 1980). Home: 12314 Timber Bend Little Rock AR 72211 Office: Bapt Med Ctr 9601 Interstate 630 Exit 7 Little Rock AR 72205

MALL, MARGARET ANN DARPHIN, sport club executive; b. Albuquerque, Aug. 13, 1943; d. Robert Douglas and Sarah Winifred (Gulley) Darphin: m. Harold Lynn Mall, Dec. 28, 1968; children: Stephen Edward, Jay Benjamin. B.A., La. State U., 1966. Pub. relations Meth. Hosp., Dallas, 1966; advt. Tracy-Locke, 1967; sec. instl. dept. Eastman Dillion Union Securities, 1968-69; office mgmt. to office mgr. White, Weld & Co., Dallas, 1969-73, retail sec., 1974-76; portfolio asst. Lionel D. Edie & Co., Dallas, 1976-77; publs. dir., v.p. Dallas Ski Club, 1983—, bd. dirs., 1982-83, v.p., 1983, pres., 1984-85, pub. relations, spl. event planning, 1985—. Corr. sec. Delta Gamma Alumnae Assn., 1970-71, social chmn., 1981-83, asst. social chmn., 1979-81, v.p., 1981-83, hospitality chmn., 1983—, heirloom appraisal clinic luncheon chmn., 1981, mem. advt. com., 1982, 83. Republican. Presbyterian. Home: 11825 Quincy Ln Dallas TX 75230 Office: PO Box 670785 Dallas TX 75267-0785

MALLETTE, JOHN MICHAEL, biology educator, research administrator; b. Houston, Aug. 6, 1932; s. Jules Loveless and Lydia (Myers) M.; m. Pazetta Veronica Berryman, Aug. 19, 1959; children—John Michael, Adelaide, Pazetta Ann. B.S., Xavier U., 1954; M.S., Tex. So. U., 1958; Ph.D., Pa. State U., 1962; cert., U. Tenn., 1977. Grad. asst. Pa. State U., University Park, 1959-62; prof. biology Tenn. State U., Nashville, 1962-70, dir. allied health professions, 1970-74, assoc. v.p. research and devel., 1979—; vice chancellor U. Tenn., Nashville, 1974-79; cons. Prof.'s of NIH, Bethesda, Md., 1965—, NSF, Washington, 1970—. Pres. bd. Catholic Charities, Nashville, 1970-72. Nashville Regional Council of Laity, 1972-73. Diocesan Ednl. Sch. Bd., Nashville, 1976; mem. U.S. Cath. Bishop's Adv. Com., Washington, 1971-74. Served with U.S. Army, 1954-56. Named Knight of St. Gregory, Pope Paul VI, 1971; recipient Tchr. of Yr. award Standard Oil Found., 1970, Martin L. King Human Relations award Nashville Met. Govt., 1982. Fellow AAAS, N.Y. Acad. Sci., Tenn. Acad. Sci.; mem. AAUP (pres. 1976—), Am. Zool. Soc. (pres. 1967-68). Avocations: jogging; walking; reading. Home: 4011 W Hamilton Rd Nashville TN 37218 Office: Tenn State U PO Box 642 3500 John A Merritt Blvd Nashville TN 37203

MALLETTE, LILA MOHLER (SRI LILANANDA), writer; b. Fort Lauderdale, Fla., June 7, 1931; d. Marvin Francis and Silvia Ione (Kenney) Mohler; student U. N.Mex., 1963-65; children—Michael F., Polly A. Mallette McPeak, Jefferson A. Founder, dir. Council for World Community, Washington, 1975—, Metamorphosis, Arlington, Va., 1982—; coordinator Arlington Visitor Ctr., 1982-85. Editor Toward Utopia! and Metamorphis newsletters. Mem. Menninger Found., NOW, World Future Soc., Assn. Humanistic Psychology, Planetary Citizens, Himalayan Inst. Yoga Sci. and Philosophy, Internat. Platform Assn. Office: Metamorphosis 2601 S Adams St Arlington VA 22206

MALLINAK, RAYMOND FRANK, dentist; b. Cleve., Jan. 25, 1947; s. Raymond Frank and Ruth Elizabeth (Sutz) M.; m. Brenda Sue Ecelberger, Aug. 11, 1973; children—Laura, Emily, Lucinda. B.S. in Chem. Engrng., Case Inst. Tech., 1968; D.D.S., Case Western Res. U., 1973. Refinery engr. Union Oil Co., Toledo, 1968-69; gen. practice dentistry, Martinsville, Va., 1975—; dir. West Piedmont Group, Inc. Treas. Piedmont Arts Assn., Martinsville, 1984—. Served to capt. Dental Corps, USAF, 1973-75. Mem. Am. Orthodontic Soc., ADA, Va. Dental Assn. (state radiation safety and environ. health com. 1984—), Patrick Henry Dental Soc. (sec.-treas. 1982-84, pres. 1984—), Alpha Chi Sigma. Republican. Methodist. Avocations: tennis; violin; golf. Home: 1006 River Forest Pl Martinsville VA 24112 Office: 604 E Church St Martinsville VA 24115

MALLINGER, BARRY LEE, psychologist, educator; b. Pitts., Oct. 16, 1943; s. Samuel and Faye (Farber) M.; m. Caroline Robertson, Nov. 17, 1964; 1 dau., Andrè Cezanne. B.A. in Psychology, U. South Fla., 1964; M.A. in Sch. Psychology, Fairfield U., 1968; Ph.D. in Ednl. Psychology, U. Conn., 1973. Lic. psychologist, Va. Research analyst, Southbury (Conn.) Tng. Sch., 1964-67; sch. psychologist pub. schs., Waterbury, Conn., 1967-70, New Haven, Conn., 1970-71; asst. prof. Radford (Va.) U., 1973-79; assoc. prof., 1979-85, prof., 1985—; cons. psychologist pub. schs., Coventry, Stonington, Manchester, Ct., 1972-73, Botetourt, Pittsylvania, Campbell County, Va., 1979-81, Va. Dept. Edn., W. Va. Dept. Edn., Project Head Start. Bd. dirs. New River Valley Agy. on Aging, 1983—. Mem. Am. Psychol. Assn., Nat. Assn. Sch. Psychologists, Va. Assn. Sch. Psychologists (past pres.), Phi Kappa Phi. Contbr. articles to profl. jours. Home: 400 Robertson St Radford VA 24141 Office: PO Box 5831 Radford U Station Radford VA 24142

MALLORY, JANICE DIANNE DAVIS, lawyer; b. Forsyth, Ga., June 9, 1957; d. Larry M. and Ann Elizabeth (Pierson) Davis; 1 dau., Pierson Davis Murphy; m. Paul S. Mallory, Jan. 5, 1985; 1 son, Paul S., Jr. B.A. magna cum laude, U. Ga., 1978, J.D., 1982. Bar: Ga. 1982. Law clk. Coweta Superior Ct. Circuit, LaGrange, Ga., 1983-84; assoc. Mattox and Baldwin, LaGrange, Ga., 1984-85. Bd. dirs. LaFayette Soc. for Performing Arts, LaGrange, 1983-85, Child Devel. Services, Grafenwohr, W.Ger., 1985-86. Mem. ABA, State Bar Ga., Troup County Bar Assn. (sec.-treas. 1984-85), Golden Key Honor Soc., Psi Chi, Alpha Omicron Pi. Republican. Baptist. Home: PO Box 1208 LaGrange GA 30240

MALLOY, DALE R., public health official; b. Marianna, Fla., May 14, 1945; s. Vernon C. and Frances A. M.; m. Marie Lyons, Nov. 17, 1967; children—Heather, Christopher. B.S., U. Fla., 1967, M.Ed., 1970, M.P.A.,

Nova U., 1978, D.P.A., 1986. Staff technologist VA hosp., Gainesville, Fla., 1967-68, Shands Teaching Hosp., Gainesville, 1968-69, chief technologist, 1969-70; exec. dir. Leon County Blood Bank, Inc., 1971—. Mem. Fla. Assn. Blood Banks (pres.), Am. Assn. Blood Banks. Club: Rotary. Contbr. articles to profl. jours. Home: Route 19 PO Box 1156 Tallahassee FL 32208 Office: 1240 Hodges Dr Tallahassee FL 32308

MALLOY, JOSEPH JOHN, JR., educational administrator; b. Phila., Feb. 16, 1940; s. Joseph John Malloy and Lydia Ellen (Bull) Malloy Bennett; m. Martha Louise Weaver, June 6, 1964; children—Elizabeth Ann Malloy Brakebill, Joseph John III. B.S., Maryville Coll., Tenn., 1968; M.A., Tenn. Technol. U., 1971; A.B.D., Middle Tenn. State U., 1972. Tchr., coach Greeneville City Schs., Tenn., 1968-69; athletic dir., curriculum coordinator Oak Ridge City Schs., 1974-77; prin. Loudon County Schs., Tenn., 1978—; cons. on Title IX, Anderson County Dist. Atty., Tenn., 1974-77; adminstr. evaluator Tenn. Dept. Edn., Nashville, 1984-85. Coordinator Spl. Olympics, Oak Ridge City Schs., 1972-77; bd. dirs. Campfire Girls, Oak Ridge, 1973-76. Served with USMC, 1958-65; to lt. comdr. USNR. Recipient letter of commendation Sec. of Navy, 1983; NSF fellow N.C. State U., 1968; doctoral fellow Middle Tenn. State U., Murfreesboro, 1972. Mem. E. Tenn. Edn. Assn., Tenn. Edn. Assn. (rep. to gen. assembly 1974), NEA, Tenn. Assn. Health Phys. Edn. and Recreation, AAHPER, Naval Res. Assn., Phi Kappa Phi. Presbyterian. Lodges: Lions (pres. local club 1982-83), Ruritan (chmn. local scholarship com. 1978-81). Avocations: golf; fishing; hunting. Home: Route 3 Box 104 Loudon TN 37774 Office: N Middle Sch Route 1 Hickory Creek Rd Lenoir City TN 37771

MALONE, DOROTHY ANN, insurance agent, marketing executive, consultant, lecturer; b. Logansport, Ind., June 19, 1931; d. Harry and Lena Estella Malone. B.B.A., McKendree Coll., Radcliff, Ky., 1981; postgrad. in humanities Webster Coll., 1981-84; M. Pub. Service Adminstrn., Western Ky. U., 1984, M. Counselling, 1985. Lic. life and health agt. Joined U.S. Army, 1952, advanced through grades to master sgt., 1972, ret., 1975; ind. life underwriter, Elizabethtown, Ky., 1977—; dir. mktg. and sales Dixie Rabbit, Inc., Ekron, Ky., 1981—; cons., lectr. minority and women's subjects. First v.p. Hardin County (Ky.) chpt. NAACP., 1975; mem. Hardin County Human Relations Com., 1977-78; chairperson Hardin County Blue Ribbon Com., 1977; trustee Embry Chapel African-Meth. Episcopal Ch., Elizabethtown, 1983—. Decorated Army Commendation medal with 5 oak leaf clusters; recipient numerous letters of commendation and appreciation and awards, including cert. of appreciation NAACP, 1976, others. Mem. Federally Employed Women (chairperson program Ft. Knox Area chpt. 1978-79, v.p. Ft. Knox Area chpt. 1978-79), Ky. Assn. Ret. Mil., Nat. Assn. Exec. Women, Ky. Central Assn. Life Underwriters, Life Investors' Pacer Club, Am. Defender Life Ins. Co., NAACP (life), Am. Soc. Profl. and Exec. Women.

MALONE, JAMES (RICHARD), manufacturing company executive; b. Cleve., Dec. 2, 1942; s. William R. and Marian (Bentley) M.; B.Sc., Ind. U., 1965; m. Linda Malone; children—Deanna Lynn, Lisa Suzanne, Zachary, Gabriel. Ops. mgr. Bendix Corp., South Bend, Ind., 1969-70; plant mgr. Western Acadia, Chgo., 1970-74; v.p. mfg. Haskell of Pitts., 1971-74; pres., chief exec. officer Mgmt. Concepts Co., Pitts., 1974-79; pres. chief exec. officer Facet Enterprises Inc., Tulsa, 1979—, also dir.; dir. Malibu Corp., Pennhurst Burial. Bd. dirs. Jefferson County Indsl. Devel. Authority, Tulsa Ballet Theatre, YMCA; bd. dirs. Jr. Achievement of Tulsa, pres., 1986. Mem. Young President's Orgn. Republican. Methodist. Clubs: Pitts. Field, Pitts. Athletic; Tulsa, Cedar Ridge Country. Office: 7030 S Yale Ave Tulsa OK 74136

MALONE, PERRILLAH (PAT) ATKINSON, planner; b. Montgomery, Ala., Mar. 17, 1922; d. Odolph Edgar and Myrtle (Fondren) Atkinson; B.S., Oglethorpe, U., 1956; M.A.T., Emory U., 1962. Asst. editor, acting editor Emory U., Atlanta, 1958-64; asst. project officer Ga. Dept. Public Health, Atlanta, 1965-68; asst. project dir. Ga. Ednl. Improvement Council, Atlanta, 1968-69, asso. dir., 1970-71; dir. career services State Scholarship Commn., Atlanta, 1971-74; rev. coordinator div. public health Ga. Dept. Human Resources, Atlanta, 1974-79; project dir. So. Regional Edn. Bd., Atlanta, 1979-81; adult services cons. div. family and children services Ga. Dept. Human Resources, Atlanta, 1982—; cons. continuing edn. in nursing Med. Coll. of Ga., 1972-73; mem. Ga. Gov.'s Commn. on Nursing Edn. and Nursing Practice, 1972-75; chmn. com. Ga.'s New Health Outlook Task Force, 1976; Mem. membership com. Southeastern Occupational Health Conf., 1978; mem. adminstrv. bd. Glenn Meml. Methodist Ch., 1978-82. Recipient Alumni award of honor, Emory U., 1962; recipient Korsell award of Ga. League for Nursing, 1974. Mem. Am. Public Health Assn. Club: Atlanta Press. Contbr. articles on health programs to profl. jours.; book reviewer Atlantic Jour.-Constn., 1962-79. Office: 878 Peachtree St NE Atlanta GA 30309

MALONE, WILLIAM GRADY, lawyer; b. Minden, La., Feb. 19, 1915; s. William Gordon and Minnie (Hortman) M.; m. Marion W. Malone, Sept. 26, 1943; children—William Grady, Jr., Gordon W., Marion E., Helen Ann, Margaret C. B.S., La. State U., 1941; LL.B., George Washington U., 1952. Bar: Va. 1952, U.S. Supreme Ct. 1971. Statis. analyst Dept. Agr., Baton Rouge, 1941; investigator VA, Washington, 1946-59, asst. gen. counsel, 1959-79; sole practice, Arlington, Va., 1980—. Pres., Aurora Hills Civic Assn., Arlington, 1948-49; chmn. Arlington County Fair, 1979-83; chmn. Com. of 100, Arlington, 1982-83. Served to lt. col. U.S. Army, 1941-46. Decorated Legion of Merit, 1945; recipient Superior Performance award VA, 1952, 72, Disting. Service award, 1979; Outstanding Alumni award George Washington U., 1978. Mem. Fed. Bar Assn. (pres. D.C. chpt. 1979-80, Superior Performance award 1980, nat. council 1980—), Arlington County Bar Assn., George Washington Law Alumni (Outstanding Alumni 1978). Episcopalian. Clubs: Nat. Lawyers (Washington) (bd. dirs. 1979—); Ft. Myer Officers (Arlington), Arlington Host Lions (pres. 1984-85). Home: 224 N Jackson St Arlington VA 22201 Office: 2060 N 14th St Suite 310 Arlington VA 22201

MALONEY, GLENN WILLIAM, educational administrator; b. Pitts., June 27, 1954; s. George C. and Rita Mary (Marcase) M. B.S., Indiana U. of Pa., 1976, M.A., 1978; postgrad. U. Tex.-Austin, 1981—. High sch. tchr. Indiana Area Sch. Dist., Pa., 1976-77; activities coordinator U. Nebr., Lincoln, 1978-80; student devel. specialist U. Tex.-Austin, 1980-85, asst. dean students, 1985—. Contbr. articles to profl. jours. Chmn., Austin Vol. Ctr., 1981-82; cons. Austin Transp. Program for Elderly, 1982. Mem. Am. Coll. Personnel Assn. (bd. dirs. 1984—), Tex. Assn. Coll. and Univ. Personnel Adminstrs. Democrat. Roman Catholic. Avocations: sports; traveling; reading. Office: Univ Texas-Austin Texas Union 4.304 Austin TX 78713-7338

MALONEY, J. C., JR., state senator; b. Washington, May 13, 1939; student Hinds Jr. Coll., Millsaps Coll.; m. Betty Ann Prisk. Mem. Miss. Senate; pres. Cowboy Maloney's Appliance Centers, C & O Investment Co. Bd. dirs. Magnolia Speech Sch. Mem. Home Builders Assn., Miss. Bldg Supply Dealers Assn., Jackson C. of C. (dir.), Better Bus. Bur. (dir.). Republican. Roman Catholic. Clubs: Sertoma, Sales and Mktg., Touchdown. Office: Miss State Senate Jackson MS 39205*

MALONEY, JOHN ANGUS, oral and maxillofacial surgeon; b. Eau Claire, Wis., Feb. 27, 1932; s. Llewellyn John and Claire Evelyn (MacDonald) M.; m. Elizabeth Margaret Maloney, Aug. 10, 1957; children—Shaun, Vince, Timothy, Kevin, Terrance, Bridget, Collin, Patrick. Student U. Ariz., 1952-54; D.D.S., Loyola U., New Orleans, 1958; postgrad. Sch. of Medicine, U. Pa., 1958-59. Practice dentistry, New Orleans, 1959; intern, resident Parkland Meml. Hosp., Dallas, 1959-61; practice dentistry specializing in oral and maxillofacial surgery, Tyler, Tex., 1961—; clin. instr. Baylor U. Sch. Dentistry, Dallas, 1959-61; cons. oral and maxillofacial surgery U. Tex. Health Sci. Ctr., Tyler, 1961—; cons. in anesthesia Tex. State Bd. Dental Examiners, 1982—; chmn. Smith County Bd. Health, Tyler, 1985—. Chmn. dental div. United Fund; mem. fund raising com. Boy Scouts Am.; mem. adv. com. Tyler Jr. Coll. Hygiene Sch.; chmn. Smith County dental div. Am. Heart Assn. Served with USAF, 1950-52. Fellow Am. Coll. Oral and Maxillofacial Surgeons, Internat. Coll. Oral Surgeons, Am. Assn. Oral and Maxillofacial Surgeons; mem. Am. Dental Soc. Anesthesia, Am. Soc. Oral Surgeons, Tex. Soc. Oral and Maxillofacial Surgeons (chmn. anesthesia and emergency procedures office), ADA, SW Soc. Oral Surgeons (bd. dirs.), AMA, Tex. State Bd. Dental Examiners (anesthesia adv. com.), Tex. Dental Soc. Anesthesia, Tex. Dental Assn. (IRC council), E. Tex. Dist. Dental Soc. (pres. 83-84), Smith County Dental Soc. Roman Catholic. Home: 2105 Parkway Pl Tyler TX 75701 Office: 1215 Doctors Dr Tyler TX 75701

MALONEY, LUCILLE TINKER, civic worker; b. Twin Falls, Idaho, Mar. 13, 1920; d. Edward Milo and Lillian (Schaefer) Tinker; tchr.'s cert. Idaho State U., 1940; student U. Wash., 1941; m. Frank E. Maloney, Feb. 20, 1943 (dec.); children—Frank E., JoAnn Maloney Smallwood, Elizabeth Maloney Hurst. Pres., U. Fla. Women's Club, 1960-61, Gainesville Women's Club, 1974-75, Friends of Five Sta. WUFT-TV, Public Broadcasting, 1976-77; chmn., organizer Gainesville Spring Pilgrimage, 1976; founder, pres. Thomas Center Assos., 1978-80; v.p. U. Fla. Art Gallery Guild, 1981, pres., 1982-84; mem. Fla. Gov.'s Challenge Program Com., 1981; trustee Fla. House, Washington; patron, organizer Hippodrome State Theatre, mem. found. bd., 1982-83; chmn. Santa Fe Regional Library Bd., 1980-81; mem. exec. com. Statue of Liberty-Ellis Island Centennial Commn., Fla., 1983—; co-chmn. Gainesville's 1st Designer Showcase House, 1983; pres. Fla. State Mus. Assocs., 1985-86; bd. dirs. Hippodrome State Theatre, 1984-85. Recipient Fla. Leadership pin Gov. LeRoy Collins, 1961; Disting. Service award Women in Communication, Inc., 1975, Appreciation plaque Sta. WUFT-TV, 1977, Community Service award Gainesville Sun, 1979, Appreciation cert. Rotary Club Gainesville, 1980, Outstanding Service award Jr. League, 1980, Bicentennial plaque Alachua County Bicentennial Com., 1976. Mem. Friends of Library, Friends of Music, Hist. Gainesville, Inc., Found. for Promotion Music, Civic Chorus, Fla. Trust for Hist. Preservation, Central Fla. League Conservation Voters (dir. 1982-83), Gainesville Women's Forum (co-organizer 1982-83). Clubs: Gainesville Garden, Heritage (bd. govs.). Home: 1823 N W 10th Ave Gainesville FL 32605

MALONEY, STEPHANIE JERNIGAN, art history educator, archaeologist; b. Jackson, Miss., Mar. 31, 1945; d. Stephen Alphonse Baginski and Lois (Matthews) Jernigan; m. Thomas Stephen Maloney, Mar. 25, 1977. A.B., Mount Holyoke Coll., 1967; M.A., U. Mo., 1971, Ph.D., 1974. Vol. Peace Corps, Piracanjuba, Brazil, 1967-69; instr. Mt. Holyoke Coll., South Hadley, Mass., 1971; asst. prof. U. Louisville, 1974-80, assoc. prof. art history, 1980—; dir. Allen R. Hite Art Inst., U. Louisville, 1981—. Mem. Jefferson County Hist. Landmark and Preservation Dists. Commn., Louisville, 1979—. Recipient Research Field Trip award Smithsonian Instn., Poland, 1975-76, archaeol. grantee, Poland, 1977-79; NEH grantee, Portugal, 1983-84. Mem. Ky. Soc. Archeol. Inst. Am., Medieval Acad. Am., Coll. Art Assn., Am. Soc. Hispanic Art Hist. Studies, Am. Assn. Field Archaeologists. Democrat. Presbyterian. Home: 1423 Goddard Ave Louisville KY 40204 Office: Allen R Hite Art Inst U Louisville Louisville KY 40292

MALOY, THOMAS, ophthalmologist; b. Panama City, Fla., Apr. 3, 1944; s. James Thomas and Catherine (Ward) M.; married; children—Ashley, Ward. B.S., Auburn U., 1967; M.D., U. Ala.-Birmingham, 1971. Diplomate Am. Bd. Ophthalmology. Gen. practice medicine specializing in ophthalmology, Wilmington, N.C., 1978—. Served to maj. U.S. Army, 1970-78. Office: 2310 Delaney Ave Wilmington NC 28403

MALTBY, ARTHUR LAUREN, III, human resources executive, consultant; b. New Orleans, Mar. 10, 1944; s. Arthur Lauren, Jr., and Savilla Jane (Jenny) M.; m. Carolyn Lowery, May 19, 1968; children—Sean Andrew, Scott Anthony, Derek James, Lauren Lee. Student Tulane U., 1962-64; B.A. in History, La. State U., 1967, M.P.A., 1978, M.S. in Mgmt., 1980. Personnel technician City-Parish Personnel, Baton Rouge, 1971-74, asst. adminstr., 1974-84; dir. of personnel Escambia County Civil Service Bd., Pensacola, Fla., 1984—; cons. Govtl. Services Inst., La. State U., Baton Rouge, 1977-78; adj. asst. prof. U. W.Fla., 1986; presenter seminars to profl. orgns., 1973-81. Vol. agy. services div. United Way, Baton Rouge, 1982-84, United Way, Pensacola, 1985. Served to capt. U.S. Army, 1967-71. Mem. Internat. Personnel Mgmt. Assn. (appreciation award 1983, pres. La. chpt. 1982-83, appreciation award 1983), Fla. Pub. Personnel Assn. (regional coordinator 1986), Am. Soc. Tng. and Devel., Am. Soc. Pub. Adminstrn., C. of C. Pensacola (assoc.). Republican. Roman Catholic. Club: Kenilworth (Baton Rouge) (bd. dirs. 1983-84). Avocations: stamp collecting; woodworking; tennis; basketball. Office: Escambia County Civil Service Bd 24 W Chase St Pensacola FL 32501

MALTBY, DEBORAH BRYAN, public relations administrator; b. Mineola, N.Y., Dec. 8, 1951; d. Herbert and Mary Eleanor (Morton) Kadison; m. Allan McKevlin Bryan, June 17, 1977 (div. 1984); 1 child, Michael Allan; m. David John Maltby, Aug. 18, 1984. B.A. in Journalism, U. S.C., 1974. Dir. pub. relations Alston Wilkes Soc., Columbia, S.C., 1976-77; asst. dir. Midlands EMS, Columbia, 1977-82; dir. pub. relations Columbia Coll., S.C., 1982—; columnist; freelance writer, consultant. Bd. dirs. Greater Columbia Literacy Council, 1978; chmn. Inter-Agy. Health Council, Columbia, 1980. Recipient Pub. Relations award United Way Midlands, 1976, 77, awards Nat. Fedn. Press Women, 1984. Mem. Pub. Relations Soc. Am. (sec. 1983-84, bd. dirs. 1984-86), Media Women S.C. (chmn. local chpt. 1983, state writing awards 1984, 85), S.C. Press Assn., Council Advancement/Support Edn. Presbyterian. Avocations: photography; travel. Home: 108 Little Hampton Dr Irmo SC 29063 Office: Columbia Coll Columbia College Dr Columbia SC 29203

MAMARCHEV, HELEN LORRAINE, college administrator; b. Houston, Oct. 28, 1949; d. James Dimitri and Marion Helen (Prewett) M. B.A., So. Meth. U., 1971; M.S. in Edn., Ind. U., 1973; Ph.D., U. Mich., 1981. Resident asst. So. Meth. U., Dallas, 1969-71; asst. coordinator Ind. U., Bloomington, 1971-73; asst. dean of women U. Kans., Lawrence, 1973-76; asst. dir. and sr. info. specialist Ednl. Resources Info. Ctr., Ann Arbor, Mich., 1976-83; assoc. v.p. for student affairs U. Fla., Gainesville, 1983—. Newsletter editor LWV, Gainesville, Fla., 1984-85; bd. dirs. Coordinated Transp. System, Inc., Gainesville, 1985. Mem. Nat. Assn. for Women Deans (cert. of merit 1980), Am. Coll. Personnel Assn., AAUW, Pi Lambda Theta, Phi Delta Kappa. Methodist. Avocations: running; reading. Office: U Fla 124 Tigert Hall Gainesville FL 32611

MANASSE, ROBERT JOHN, orthodontist, educator; b. Amsterdam, Netherlands, May 9, 1947; came to U.S., 1954, naturalized, 1961; s. Henri David and Janny Lynn (Borst) M.; m. Marylou Clapperton, May 14, 1977; children—Janny, Robbie, Michael. Student U. Ill.-Chgo., 1966-67; B.S. in Pharmacy, U. Ill., 1969; D.D.S., 1974, cert. in Orthodontics, 1976. Diplomate Am. Bd. Orthodontics. Lab instr. U. Ill. Coll. Dentistry, Chgo., 1973-76; asst. clin. prof. dept. pediatric dentistry postgrad. program U. Tex. Health Scis. Ctr., San Antonio, 1977-82, assoc. clin. prof., 1982—; assoc. prof. Pan Am. U. Dept. Communication, Edinburg, Tex., 1985—; lab technician Milton B. Engel, Orthodontist, Chgo., 1972-74; practice dentistry Glenn F. Boas, Chgo., 1974-76; practice dentistry specializing in orthodontics Louis Feldstein, 1976-77; pvt. practice dentistry specializing in orthodontics, McAllen, Tex., 1977—; mem. staff Meth. Hosp., McAllen, 1981—, Rio Grande Regional Hosp., McAllen, 1982—; dental cons. in field. Contbr. articles, papers to profl. publs. Precinct capt. election Othal Brand for mayor, McAllen, 1981, 85; bd. dirs. McAllen United, 1983—; participant Ptnrs. in Excellence Adopt a Sch. Program, 1985. Recipient Beautification award City of McAllen, 1984, Recognition plaque McAllen Independent Sch. Dist., 1985. Mem. Am. Dental Assn., Am. Assn. Orthodontics, Am. Assn. Dental Schs., Rio Grande Valley Cranial-Facial Anomolies Adv. Group (bd. dirs. 1978—, exec. sec. 1978-80, v.p. 1981—). Baptist. Lodge: Rotary. Avocations: swimming; jogging; tennis. Office: 900 Kerria McAllen TX 78501

MANAX, TERESA VICTORIA, physician; b. Belfast, Ireland, July 18, 1937; came to U.S., 1974, naturalized, 1980; d. James and Victoria (Shokry) Smith; M.A. in Archaeology, U. Dublin, 1966; M.D., Trinity Coll., Dublin, 1967; cert. emergency med. officer U. Western Ont., 1977; m. William George Manax, Feb. 13, 1975; 1 dau., Victoria Georgina. Lic. physician, Ireland, Eng., Can., N.H. Jr. house officer Baggott St. Hosp., Dublin, 1968, sr. house officer, 1969; with St. Joseph's Hosp., London, Ont., Can., 1971-74; emergency room physician Wentworth Douglass Hosp., Dover, N.H., 1975-76; physician Oak St. Med. Center, West, Tex., 1976—. Recipient Gold medal in anatomy Trinity Coll. Fellow Internat. Acad. Proctology (asso.); mem. Brit. Med. Assn., Ont. Coll. Physicians and Surgeons, World Med. Assn., AMA, N.H. Med. Soc., Am. Coll. Gen. Practice, Am. Soc. Contemporary Medicine and Surgery, Royal Soc. Medicine (affiliate), Med. Council Can. Home: 1505 N Jane Ln West TX 76691 Office: 407 W Oak St West TX 76691

MANBURG, ABBEY BART, teacher educator; b. Bklyn., Apr. 21, 1946; s. Theodore and Florence (Klein) M.; children—Jamie Daniel, Benjamin Ross. A.B., Temple U., 1967; M.S., CCNY, 1972; Ed.D., Nova U., 1981. Tchr., asst. prin. Park Slope Elem. Sch., Bklyn., 1968-77; dir. practicums in grad. tchr. edn. program Nova U., Fort Lauderdale, Fla., 1980-83, program prof. edn., 1981—, dir. M.A. program for child care adminstrs., 1983—. Mem. Psi Chi. co-author: All About Child Care, Trainee's Manual, 1981; co-editor: All About Child Care, 1981; mem. editorial bd. jour. Univ. Without Walls; contbr. numerous articles on early childhood and higher edn. to profl. jours. Office: Center Advancedment Edn Nova U 3301 College Ave Fort Lauderdale FL 33314

MANCHESTER, SUSAN JEAN HOYT, lawyer; b. Oklahoma City, July 15, 1950; d. Frederick J. and Jean F. (Ball) Hoyt; m. Robert A. Manchester, Jan. 28, 1984; 1 child, Andrea. B.A., Okla. State U., 1972; J.D., Okla. U., 1980. Bar: Okla. 1980, U.S. Dist. Ct. (we. dist.) Okla. 1981, U.S. Ct. Appeals (10th cir.) 1981. Asst. atty. gen. Okla. Atty. Gen., Oklahoma City, 1980-81, dep. chief criminal div., 1981-82, chief criminal div., 1982-83; assoc. McClelland, Collins, Bailey, Bailey & Manchester, Oklahoma City, 1983—. Mem. Okla. Bar Assn., Oklahoma County Bar Assn., Okla. Trial Atty. Assn., Assn. Trial Lawyers Am., Phi Delta Phi. Democrat. Presbyterian. Office: McClelland Collins Bailey Bailey & Manchester 15 N Robinson Colcord Bldg 11th Floor Oklahoma City OK 73102

MANCHIN, A. JAMES, state government official; b. Farmington, W.Va., Apr. 7, 1927; s. Joseph and Kathleen (Roscoe) M.; m. Stephanie Machel, June 9, 1951; children—Patricia Lee, Mark Anthony, Rosanna Stache. B.A. in Polit. Sci. and Sociology, W.Va. U., 1951, M.A., 1962; tchrs. certificate, Fairmont (W.Va.) State Coll., 1953. Tchr. citizenship, athletic coach pub. schs., W.Va.; dir. for W.Va., Farmers Home Adminstrn., spl. asst. to nat. adminstr., dir. for W.Va. REAP, 1973; mem. W.Va. Ho. of Dels. from Marion County, 1949; sec. of state State of W.Va., 1975—. Recipient Outstanding Service award Dept. Agr., 1968; Freedom Found. at Valley Forge award, 1969; Law and Order award Fairmont Police Dept., 1973; Internat. Communication Achievement award Toastmasters, 1979-80; named Mr. W.Va. Salem Coll., 1974. Office: State Capitol Charleston WV 25305*

MANCI, ELIZABETH ANN, physician, educator; b. Mobile, Ala., Aug. 3, 1946; d. Arthur and Avis Leo (McAdams) Manci; m. Lloyd Lindsey Gardner, Jan. 17, 1970; children—Julia, Todd. B.A. magna cum laude, St. Louis U., 1973; diploma Barnes Hosp. Sch. Nurse Anesthesia, 1970; diploma Providence Sch. Nursing, 1967; diploma, U. Ala.-Birmingham Sch. Medicine, 1979; M.D., Ala. State Licensing Bd. for Healing Arts, 1980. Cert. registered nurse anesthetist Am. Assn. Nurse Anesthetists, 1970. Nurse, Mobile Gen. Hosp., 1967-68, Barnes Hosp., St. Louis, 1968-70; nurse anesthetist St. Mary's Hosp., Clayton, Mo., 1970-72, Deaconess Hosp., St. Louis, 1972-73, Drs. Lane, Bryant, Eubanks and Dulany, Mobile, 1973-75; pathology resident Univ. Hosp., Birmingham, Ala., 1979-80, U. South Ala., 1980-83; instr. pathology U. South Ala. Med. Center, Mobile, 1983-84, asst. prof., 1984—; mem. staff U. South Ala. Med. Ctr.; tchr. Housestaff Council, 1980; acting asst. med. cons. ARC, Mobile, 1983. Mem. AMA, Med. Assn. State Ala., Mobile County Med. Soc., Am. Assn. Nurse Anesthetists, Nat. League for Nursing. Episcopalian. Contbr. articles to various med. publs. Office: 2451 Fillingim St Mobile AL 36617

MANCINI, ERNEST ANTHONY, geologist, educator, researcher; b. Reading, Pa., Feb. 27, 1947; s. Ernest and Marian K. (Filbert) M.; m. Marilyn E. Lee, Dec. 27, 1969; children—Lisa L., Lauren N. B.S., Albright Coll., 1969; M.S., So. Ill. U., 1972; Ph.D., Tex. A&M U., 1974. Petroleum exploration geologist Cities Service Oil Co., Denver, 1974-76; asst. prof. geology U. Ala., Tuscaloosa, 1976-79, assoc. prof., 1979-84, prof., 1984—; state geologist, oil and gas supr. State Ala., Tuscaloosa, 1982—. Recipient Nat. Council Citation, Albright Coll., 1983. Mem. Am. Assn. Petroleum Geologists (A.I. Levorsen petroleum geology Meml. award Gulf Coast assn., geol. socs. sect. 1980), Soc. Econ. Paleontologists and Mineralogists, Paleontol. Soc., N.Am. Micropaleontology Soc., Internat. Micropaleontology Soc., Ala. Geol. Soc., Sigma Xi, Phi Kappa Phi, Phi Sigma. Democrat. Presbyterian. Contbr. articles to profl. jours. Home: 1503 Briarcliff St Northport AL 35476 Office: PO Drawer O University AL 35486

MANDELBAUM, SIDNEY, ophthalmologist, researcher; b. N.Y.C., June 29, 1951; s. Murray and Rose (Finkelstein) M. B.S., Columbia U., 1972; M.D., Yale U., 1976. Intern medicine N.Y. Hosp., Cornell Med. Ctr., N.Y.C., 1976-77; resident ophthalmology Los Angeles Coll.-U. So. Calif. Med. Ctr., 1978-81; ophthalmology fellow Bascom Palmer Eye Inst., U. Miami, Fla., 1981-82, asst. prof. ophthalmology, 1982—. Contbr. articles to profl. jours. Fight for Sight postgrad. fellow, N.Y.C., 1981-82. Fellow Am. Acad. Ophthalmology. Office: Bascom Palmer Eye Inst 900 NW 17th St Miami FL 33101

MANDELSTAMM, ALLAN BERYLE, economics educator, consultant; b. Saginaw, Mich., Oct. 18, 1928; s. Jonas and Helen G. (Weinburg) M.; m. Maria T. Buhlmeyer, Sept. 1, 1967. B.A., U. Mich., 1950, M.A., 1951, Ph.D., 1962. Instr. Northwestern U., Evanston, Ill., 1957-59; asst. prof. Vanderbilt U., Nashville, 1959-63; assoc. prof. Mich. State U., East Lansing, 1963-67, prof., 1967-74; prof. econs. Va. Poly. Inst. and State U., Blacksburg, 1974—; vis. prof. Dartmouth Coll., 1970, U. Fla., 1972; cons. Dept. State, AID, U.S. Dept. Labor, others. Contbr. articles to profl. jours. and encys. Recipient Disting. Teaching award Mich. State U., 1968, Best Prof. award U. Fla., 1972, Va. Poly. Inst., 1976, 77; Rockefeller Found. grantee, 1958-62. Mem. Am. Econ. Assn., Indsl. Relations Research Assn., AAUP, Acad. Polit. Sci. Home: 600 Landsdowne Dr SE Blacksburg VA 24061 Office: Va Poly Inst 203 Sandy Hall Blacksburg VA 24061

MANDERNACH, CHARLES GLEN, composer, musician; b. Odebolt, Iowa, Jan. 7, 1937; s. Glen Albert and Alice Rebecca (Bye) M.; m. Judy Kay Ogden, Aug. 16, 1959; children—Kelly Kay, Kent Charles. B.Mus., U. No. Iowa, 1959; M.Mus., Eastman Sch. Music, 1964. Dir. instrumental music Humboldt (Iowa) Ind. Schs., 1959-63; instr. music Cornell U., 1964-65; 2d trombone Dallas Symphony Orch., 1965-68; assoc. creative dir. Internat. Recording, Dallas, 1968-70; ptnr. January Sound Studios, Inc., Dallas, 1970-80; creative dir. January Music, Dallas, 1970—; creative dir. Chuck Mandernach Music, Dallas, 1982—; adj. faculty So. Meth. U., Tex. Christian U., U. Tex.-Arlington, Mountain View Coll., Eastfield Coll., Richland Coll.; leader Them Bones. Mem. Am. Fedn. Musicians, Soc. Advt. Music Producers, Arrangers and Composers, ASCAP, Nat. Assn. Jazz Educators. Methodist. Composer ballet Texas on Point, 1982; composer Sonday Outing; You Asked For It; Tell Me It's Time; Waltz Me Around Again; Kent; The Better Half of Me; Yesterday's Rain; I Think It's Love; Razor Red; Never Love a Woman; composer, arranger, numerous nat., regional, local radio, TV commls., film scores. Home: 9324 Whitehurst Dallas TX 75243 Office: 3341 Towerwood Dr Suite 206 Dallas TX 75234

MANDOKI, PEDRO, hotel company executive; b. Budapest, Hungary, Dec. 8, 1941; came to U.S., 1964; s. Melchor and Margit (Schlesinger) M.; m. Sheila Ann Donlan, Nov. 1, 1959 (div. 1980); children—Margarita, Catalina, Marcia, Jessica; m. Miriam Louise Clark, Aug. 2, 1980; children—Allison, Jason. B.S., Universidad de Morelos, Mex., 1960. Cert. hotel adminstr. Various positions Hotel Corp. Am., Boston, 1965-69; gen. mgr. Callaway Gardens, Pine Mountain, Ga., 1969-74; regional dir. ops. Internat. Hospitality Group, Orlando, Fla., 1975-76; pres. Miracle Mile Resort, Panama City Beach, Fla., 1976-85, NESA, Inc., 1976—, Phoenix Advt., Inc., 1977-85, Anastasia Mgmt. Corp., 1981-85, Mandoki Enterprises, Inc., 1981—, Beach News, Inc., 1982-83; pres. Resort Mgmt. & Mktg., Inc., 1985—; dir. People's First Fin. Savs. & Loan; instr. Gulf Coast Community Coll.; consl Motel One Ltd., Panama City, 1981-83. Mem. Fla. Gov.'s Tourism Adv. Council, 1981—; mem. adv. council Bay Med. Ctr., 1981—; bd. dirs. Gulf Coast Community Coll. Found., 1983—, pres., 1986—; bd. dirs. Bay County United Way, 1982-84; mem. Bay County Adult and vocat. Edn. Adv. Council, 1980—; bd. dirs. Bay med. Ctr. Found., 1982-83, v.p., 1983-84, pres., 1984-85. Mem. Fla. Hotel/Motel Assn. (Hotelier of Yr. 1981; treas. 1983, pres.-elect 1984, pres. 1985), Am. Hotel/Motel Assn. (bd. dirs. 1985-86), Bay County Motel and Restaurant Assn. (pres. 1979-81), Internat. Council Hotel/Motel Mgmt. Cos., Fla. Hotel and Motel Health Benefit Trust (vice-chmn.), Nat. Restaurant Assn., Fla. Restaurant Assn., Hotel Sales Mgmt. Assn. Internat., Bay County C. of C. (dir. 1981-84, 1st v.p. 1983, pres. 1984). Democrat. Methodist. Home: 2622 Pretty Bayou Island Dr Panama City FL 32405 Office: 508 Airport Dr Suite C Panama City Beach FL 32405

MANDRY, GEORGE GILBERT, water conditioning company executive; b. San Antonio, Mar. 29, 1926; s. George Peter and Clarice Johannaa (Heubaum) M.; student Wartburg Coll., 1956, Internat. Corr. Schs., 1943-51; m. Edith Lenor Hamby, Sept. 23, 1961; children—Terry Ann, Sandra Kay, Vicki Marie, George Gilbert, Cindi Ann. Installer, Southwestern Bell Telephone Co., 1946, Western Electric Co., 1947; civil service employee, 1948-52; field engr., site mgr.

RCA, 1952-60; electronics engr. Southwest Research Inst., San Antonio, 1960-65; owner, mgr. Oasis Liquor & Sporting Goods, Leon Valley, Tex., 1962-73, Mandry Gen. Hardware & Supply, Leon Valley, 1965-73; partner, mgr. Continental Water Conditioning Co., San Antonio, 1975—; pres. Mandry Enterprises, Inc., Coastline Developers Inc.; partner, mgr. Amkon Airfilters, San Antonio, 1980—. Served with USAF, 1944-46. Mem. Tex. Water Conditiong Assn. (past pres.), San Antonio C. of C., Assn. U.S. Army, Air Force Assn. Lutheran. Club: Elks. Home: Joleta Ranch Bandera TX 78003 Office: Continental Water Systems Co 6405 El Verde Rd San Antonio TX 78238

MANESH, NANCY JOY LISA, safety engineer, researcher; b. Far Rockaway, N.Y., Oct. 6, 1953; d. Michael and Maria (Merone) Lastella; m. Hoss D. Manesh, Nov. 15, 1980. B.S. in Fine Arts, Molloy Coll., 1975; M.S. in Fin., U. Ariz., 1977, M.Ed. in Health and Biol. Scis., 1977. Cert. tchr., N.Y., Ariz.; cert. safety profl. Correspondent of edn. Nassau County Med. Ctr., East Meadow, N.Y., 1975-76; corp. safety engr. Grunman Aerospace and Aircraft Corp., Bethpage, N.Y., 1977; supr. safety engring. research and tng. Philip Morris USA, Richmond, Va., 1977—. Oil painting commissioned by N.Y. Commnr. Narcotics, 1975. Mem. advanced com. Woman for N.Y. Senate Campaign Repub. Nat. Party, Island Park, N.Y., 1976. Nat. Inst. Occupational Safety and Health grantee, 1976. Mem. Am. Soc. Safety Engrs. (program chairperson asst. 1984—), Va. Safety Assn. (gov. appointed indsl. chairperson, 1979, Am. Lung Assn., Nat. Safety Mgmt. Soc., Women in Bus. and Engring. Clubs: N.Y. French. N.Y. Honors. Avocations: yachting/sailing, dance, fine arts, theater, travel. Home: 7107 Riverside Dr Richmond VA 23261 Office: Philip Morris USA 2001 Walmsley Blvd Richmond VA 23261

MANFRA, ETHEL MCDONALD, moving and storage company executive; b. College Park, Ga., Sept. 26, 1915; d. Charles A. and Jessie Mae (Archie) McDonald; m. Adolph Manfra, Jan. 1, 1939 (dec. Mar. 1971). Degree in bus. adminstrn. U. Ga., 1936. Owner, Manfra Transfer & Storage Co., Atlanta, 1939—; pres. A & M Movers, Inc., Atlanta, 1971—; mem. nat. adv. council Nat. Fedn. Ind. Businesses, Washington, 1971. Recipient Outstanding Leadership award AAUW. Mem. Am. Bus. Women Assn. (past pres., chmn. transp. area council, diamond hand of friendship award, Woman of Yr. award 1984), Pres. Council (v.p., treas.), Women's C. of C. (outstanding leadership award 1976), Ga. Movers Assn. (sec.-treas.), Atlanta Movers (sec.-treas.). Democrat. Baptist. Clubs: Atlanta Women's, Soroptimist (past pres.; chmn. found. and devel. com.) (Atlanta). Lodges: Eastern Star (past worthy matron, sec.); Ladies White Shrine of Jerusalem (past high priestess; treas., trustee, pres. Ga. State 1983-84), Ladies Oriental Shrine N.Am. (high priestess), Order of Amaranth (past royal matron). Office: Manfra Transfer & Storage Co 116 Bennett St NW Atlanta GA 30309

MANGANIELLO, LOUIS OTTO JOSEPH, neurosurgeon; b. Waterbury, Conn., June 6, 1915; s. Angelo M. and Raimonda (Membrino) M.; m. Carol Graham Pryor, June 11, 1950; children—Carol Helen, Victoria R. A.B., Harvard U., 1937; M.D., U. Md., 1942; J.D., Augusta Law Sch., 1967. Diplomate Am. Bd. Neurol. Surgery. Intern, Univ. Hosp., Balt., 1942-43, resident in neurol. surgery, 1946-50; pvt. practice medicine specializing in neurosurgery, Augusta, Ga., 1951—; mem. staff Univ. Hosp., Doctors Hosp., St. Joseph Hosp., Augusta; mem., past pres. composite state bd. Med. Examiners Ga.; cons. VA Hosp., Augusta; dir. Blue Cross/Blue Shield; assoc. prof. neurosurgery Med. Coll. Ga., 1951—. Served with USN, 1942-46. Bd. dirs. ARC. Fellow ACS; mem. AMA, Richmond County Med. Soc., Med. Assn. Ga., Am. Assn. Neurol. Surgery, Congres Neurosurgeons, So. Neurosurg. Soc., Southeastern Surg. Congress, Am. Assn. Cancer Research, Am. Assn. Med. Colls., Internat. Assn. Lex and Sci., Ga. Neurosurg. Soc. (past pres.). Club: Country of Augusta, Pinnacal. Lodge: Rotary. Contbr. articles to profl. jours. Home: 656 Milledge Rd Augusta GA 30904 Office: 820 St Sebastian Way Suite 2E Augusta GA 30902

MANGHAM, JESSE ROGER, chemist, environmental health specialist; b. Plains, Ga., Nov. 18, 1922; s. Henry Gordon and Jessie Myrtice (Mallory) M.; m. Ethel Shealy Webster, June 6, 1943; children—Beverly, Gordon, Barry, Gloria, Dana. B.S., U. Ga., 1943; M.S., Ohio State U., 1946, Ph.D., 1948. Sect. leader organic chemistry Va. Carolina Chem. Co., Richmond, Va., 1949-54; research chemist to sr. environ. health assoc., 1954-83, sr. regulatory affairs assoc., 1983—. Contbr. articles to profl. jours. Patentee in field. Chmn. Republican Parish Exec. Com., Baton Rouge, La., 1970-72; area coordinator Rep. Election Orgn., Baton Rouge, 1964; alt. del. Rep. Nat. Conv., Miami, Fla., 1968; active in Southdowns Home Owners Assn., Baton Rouge, 1956—. Mem. Am. Chem. Soc., Sigma Xi. Republican. Unitarian. Lodge: Kiwanis, Ruritan. Avocations: photography; travel; beekeeping. Home: 2035 Glendale Ave Baton Rouge LA 70808 Office: Ethyl Corp 451 Florida St Baton Rouge LA 70801

MANGIERI, JOHN NICHOLAS, university administrator; b. New Castle, Pa., Nov. 1, 1946; s. John and Rose Marie (Audino) M.; m. Deborah Ann Hoerner, Aug. 23, 1969; children—Jeffrey, Deanna. B.S. in Edn., Slippery Rock State Coll., 1968; M. Ed., Westminster Coll., 1969; Ph.D., U. Pitts., 1972. Tchr. lang. arts New Castle Area Schs., Pa., 1968-70; grad. asst. U. Pitts., 1970-72; assoc. prof. edn. Ohio U., Athens, 1972-78; prof. edn. U. S.C., Columbia, 1978-82; dean Sch. Edn., Tex. Christian U., Fort Worth, 1982—. Co-author: Teaching Elementary Reading: A Comprehensive Approach, 1982; Teaching Language Arts: Classroom Applications, 1984; also articles. Recipient Alumni Achievement citation Westminster Coll., 1983; Outstanding Alumni award U. Pitts., 1985. Home: 4413 Willow Way Fort Worth TX 76133 Office: Tex Christian U PO Box 32925 Fort Worth TX 76129

MANGUM, TOM GIBSON, state legislator, real estate broker; b. Chesterfield, S.C., Jan. 23, 1916; s. Inglis Parks and Sara (Funderburk) M.; m. Louise Clyburn, Aug. 21, 1939. Student U. S.C., 1933-34, Wingate Jr. Coll., 1934-35. Mem. S.C. Ho. of Reps., 1955-58, 61—, chmn. ways and means com., 1977-84. Served with USAF, World War II. Democrat. *

MANI, GEORGE CHARLES, pathologist; b. N.Y.C., Feb. 7, 1928; s. Charles Z. and Anastasia (Papamichael) M.; m. Ann Lampe Crossett, June 30, 1956 (div. 1974); children—Corinne Louise, Philip Charles, Carol Lynn, Peter William; m. 2d, Sandra Lee Mitchell, Aug. 25, 1978; 1 son, Nicholas Elliot. B.A., Columbia U., 1947, M.D., 1951. Cert. anat., clin. pathologist. Intern, Bellevue Hosp., N.Y.C., 1951-52; residency in pathology St. Luke's Hosp., N.Y.C., 1952-55, Colo. Gen. Hosp., Denver, 1956-57; assoc. pathologist Santa Rosa Med. Ctr., San Antonio, Tex., 1958—; dir. SW Bio-Clin. Lab., San Antonio, 1969—. Fellow Coll. Am. Pathologists, Am. Soc. Clin. Pathologists; mem. AMA, Phi Beta Kappa. Eastern Orthodox. Home: 211 Grandview Pl San Antonio TX 78209 Office: 345 W Houston St Suite 206 San Antonio TX 78205

MANIA, ROBERT CHESTER, JR., physics educator; b. Mount Clemens, Mich., May 19, 1952; s. Robert Chester and Patricia Dawn (Jobse) M.; m. Cathy Gayheart, Oct. 17, 1980; children—Tracey, Anne. B.S., Mich. Tech. U., 1974, M.S., 1976; Ph.D., Va. Poly. Inst. and State U., 1981. Grad. teaching asst. Mich. Tech. U., Houghton, 1974-76; grad. teaching asst. Va. Poly. Inst. and State U., Blacksburg, 1976-79, grad. research asst., 1979-80; asst. prof. physics and phys. sci. Alice Lloyd Coll., Pippa Passes, Ky., 1980—. Sigma Xi grantee, 1973-74; Bendix award grantee, 1972-73. Mem. Am. Phys. Soc., Am. Nuclear Soc., Nat. Rifle Assn., Sigma Xi, Phi Kappa Phi, Sigma Pi Sigma. Democrat. Mem. Ch. Jesus Christ of Latter-day Saints. Home: PO Box 187 Pippa Passes KY 41844 Office: Alice Lloyd Coll Pippa Passes KY 41844

MANISON, THOMAS ARTHUR, camp director; b. Houston, Aug. 14, 1927; s. John Gabriel and Bernice (Sproles) M.; m. Marjorie Robinson, Nov. 24, 1961; children—Ruth Ann, Karen Sue. B.S., U. Houston, 1950, M.Ed., 1953, postgrad., 1954-60. Tchr. Galena Park (Tex.) Ind. Sch. Dist., 1950-52; prin., coach Barbers Hill Ind. Sch. Dist., 1952-55; supt. Friendswood (Tex.) Ind. Sch. Dist., 1955-60; exec. dir. South Tex. Diabetes Assn., Houston, 1967-70; owner, dir. Camp Manison, Friendswood, 1947—. Dir. Waters Davis Soil and Water Conservation Dist.; charter mem. Gov.'s Commn. for Health and Safety for Tex. Youth Camps; mem. speakers bur. Gov.'s Commn. for Phys. Fitness, 1970-76; chmn. bd. dirs. Presbyn. Cho-Yeh Camp and Conf. Ctr., Galveston County Beach and Park Bd., Houston-Galveston Area Council Govts. Paul Harris fellow. Served with U.S. Army, 1945-47. Mem. Am. Camping Assn. (life; cert. camp dir., pres. Tex. sect. 1984-86), AAHPER, Tex. Assn. Health, Phys. Edn. and Recreation, Tex. State Tchrs. Assn. (life), Phi Delta Kappa. Republican. Presbyterian. Lodges: Rotary, Masons, Shriners, Order Eastern Star. Home: 401 Parkwood St PO Box 148 Friendswood TX 77546 Office: Camp Manison Ln PO Box 148 Friendswood TX 77546

MANLEY, EDWARD HARRY, JR., hosp. food service dir., former navy officer; b. S.I., N.Y., Sept. 12, 1941; s. Edward H. and Dorothy I.; B.S., Cornell U., 1975; M.S., Rollins Coll., 1978; m. Geri G. Manley; children—Deborah, Michael E., Lisa E. Joined U.S. Navy, 1959, commd. ensign, 1970, advanced through grades to lt. comdr., 1979; food service dir. Naval Hosp., Annapolis, Md., 1972-73; asst. food service dir. Nat. Naval Med. Center, Bethesda, Md., 1971-72; food service dir. Naval Regional Med. Center, Orlando, Fla., 1975-80; ret., 1980; food service dir. North Broward Hosp., Pompano Beach, Fla., 1981—; mem. adv. bd. Mid-Fla. Tech. Food Service Program, 1978-80, Atlantic Vo-Tech. Dietetic Program, 1981—. Mem. evaluation team Hennessey award U.S. Air Force, 1982. Cert. food service exec. Ed Manley Scholarship Fund established, 1984. Mem. Internat. Food Service Execs. Assn. (pres. Orlando br. 1979-80, named mem. of yr. Orlando br. 1978, pres. South Fla. br. 1983-84, mem. of yr. South Fla. br. 1984, Disting. Service award 1984), Cornell Soc. Hotelmen (pres. Central Fla. chpt. 1976-80), Fla. Restaurant Assn. (bd. dirs. 1980), Am. Soc. Hosp. Food Service Adminstrs. (sec. South Fla. chpt.). Clubs: Cornell of Central Fla. (v.p. 1980), Cornell of South Fla., Naval Tng. Center Officers (pres. 1978-80). Home: 1055 SW 55 Way Margate FL 33063 Office: 201 Sample Rd Pompano Beach FL 33064

MANLEY, JAMES ORAN, real estate development company executive, former city official, lay-clergyman; b. Harris County, Tex., June 1, 1935; s. Marion Oran and Sallie Riley (McDonald) M.; m. Frances Elizabeth Marcontell, Sept. 5, 1959; children—Carla Kay Manley Longhofer, Marcus Leland. B.B.A., Tex. A&M U., 1961; B.D., Southwestern Bapt. Theol. Sem., 1966; postgrad. Rice U., 1974. Ordained to ministry Baptist Ch., 1963. Campus minister various schs. Bapt. Gen. Conv. Tex., 1961-71; adminstrv. asst. Office of Mayor, City of Houston, 1974-77, exec. asst., 1978-81, dir. Citizens Assistance, 1981-83; sr. v.p. Alexandrite Corp., Houston, 1983—; pres. pub. relations firm; pub. speaker. Pres., Houston chpt. Vols. of Am.; mem. adv. bd. Sheltering Arms of Houston; bd. dirs. Consumer Credit Counseling Services; former bd. mem. Houston Met. Ministries; mem. bd. cons. Tex. Bapt. Christian Life Commn.; mem. speakers com. Houston Livestock Show and Rodeo; mem. adv. bd. Houston Ctr. for Humanities; mem. Greater Houston Conv. and Visitors Council. Danforth grantee, 1971-72; Rice U. fellow, 1972-74. Mem. Pub. Relations Soc. Am., Internat. City Mgrs. Assn., Am. Soc. Pub. Adminstrn. (former council mem. Houston chpt.), Japan-Am. Soc., Houston Ctr. for Humanities, Houston C. of C. (advisory mem. econ. devel. council). Democrat. Club: Summit (Houston). Lodge: Houston Kiwanis (co-chmn. program com.). Home: 304 North St Baytown TX 77520 Office: Alexandrite Corp PO Box 680331 Houston TX 77068

MANLEY, RICHARD SHANNON, lawyer, former state legislator; b. Birmingham, Ala., June 23, 1932; s. Richard Sabine and Alice (Hughes) M.; B.S., U. Ala., 1953, LL.B., 1958; m. Lillian Grace Cardwell, Aug. 23, 1953 (div. Aug. 1975); children—Richard Shannon, Alyce Hughes; m. Rosemary Rankin Moseley, May 18, 1977. Admitted to Ala. bar, 1958, also U.S. Supreme Ct., U.S. Ct. Mil. Appeals; practiced in Demopolis, 1958—; mem. Ala. Ho. of Reps., 1967-83; speaker pro tem, 1979-82; dir. New Southland Nat. Ins. Co.; v.p. Demopolis Cable TV Co., Inc. Pres., Bd. Edn. Demopolis, 1969-70, Demopolis Jaycees, 1961-62; v.p. Ala. Jaycees, 1960-61; dir. U.S. Jaycees, 1962-63; bd. dirs. Marengo County Hist. Soc., Marengo County Mental Health Assn.; bd. advisers Ala. Hist. Commn., Gen. Holland M. Smith Meml. Served with USMCR, 1953-56; col. Res. Mem. Am., Ala. (bd. bar commrs. 1972—), 17th Jud. Circuit (past pres.) bar assns., Am. Trial Lawyers Assn., Comml. Law League Am., Am. Judicature Soc., Demopolis C. of C. (dir., past pres.), Marine Corps Res. Officers Assn., U. Ala. Nat. Alumni Assn. (v.p. 1967-68), Farrah Law Soc., Phi Delta Phi, Delta Chi. Methodist (trustee). Clubs: Rotary; Demopolis Country (past pres., dir.), Demopolis Athletic, U. Ala. Alumni (pres. Marengo County 1965-66); Indian Hills Country, North River Yacht (Tuscaloosa, Ala.); The Club (Birmingham, Ala.). Home: 1501 Country Club Dr SW PO Drawer U Demopolis AL 36732 Office: 111 S Walnut Ave Demopolis AL 36732

MANN, BARLOW TREADWELL, financial consultant, lawyer; b. Mobile, Ala., Sept. 5, 1953; s. Cameron Mann and Jane Snowden (Treadwell) Mann Martin; m. Rona Joyce Crockett, Apr. 23, 1981; 1 child, Arthur Barlow Treadwell, Jr. B.A. with honors, Tulane U., 1975; J.D., Memphis State U., 1978. Bar: Tenn. 1978, U.S. Dist. Ct. (we. dist.) Tenn. 1979. Assoc. Memphis Area Legal Clinic, Memphis State U. Clinic, 1977-78; asst. dir. devel. Memphis State U., 1978-82; dir. devel. U. Tenn., Memphis, 1982-84; v.p. Robert F. Sharpe and Co., Memphis, 1984—. Contbr. articles to profl. jours. Mem. ABA, Tenn. Bar Assn., Memphis Bar Assn., Shelby County Bar Assn., Council for Advancement and Support of Edn., Phi Alpha Delta (pres. 1977-78), Delta Kappa Epsilon (pres. 1974-75). Clubs: Memphis Country, University (Memphis). Lodge: Grand Krewe of Osiris. Home: 4581 Normandy Rd Memphis TN 38117 Office: Sharpe and Co Inc 5050 Poplar Ave Memphis TN

MANN, FRANKLIN BALCH, state senator; b. Ft. Myers, Fla., Aug. 29, 1941; s. George Theodore and Barbara (Balch) M.; m. Mary Lee Ferguson, 1961; children—Franklin Balch, Ian Ferguson. B.A., Vanderbilt U., 1964. Adjustor, Gen. Adjustment Bur., 1964-66; ins. agt. Hyde & Dinkel Ins. Agy., 1966-67; pres., gen. mgr. Mann-Webb Ins. Agy., Inc. 1967—; mem. Fla. Ho. of Reps., after 1974; now mem. Fla. Senate. Mem. Audubon Soc., Phi Kappa Psi. Democrat. Presbyterian. Lodges: Rotary, Masons, Shriners. Office: Fla Senate Senate Office Bldg Tallahassee FL 32304*

MANN, HAROLD WILSON, history educator; b. Columbus, Ga., Aug. 10, 1925; s. David Gilbert and Gertrude Leoline (Clark) M.; m. Frances Elizabeth Parks, Feb. 3, 1956; children—Harold Wilson, Martha Blair, Janet Parks. A.B., Emory U., 1949, M.A., 1950; postgrad. U. Wis., 1950-51, Biarritz Am. U. (France), 1946; Ph.D., Duke U., 1962. Instr., asst. prof. and chmn. div. social studies Emory U., Oxford, Ga., 1951-54, 56-61, 62-63; assoc. prof. Radford (Va.) U., 1963-66, prof., 1966—. Organist, choir dir. Grace Episcopal Ch., 1977—. Served with U.S. Army, 1943-46. Mem. NEA, Orgn. Am. Historians, Phi Beta Kappa, Omicron Delta Kappa, Phi Kappa Phi. Democrat. Author book in field; contbr. articles to profl. jours.

MANN, JEFF, college administrator, consultant; b. Raleigh, N.C., Feb. 16, 1950; s. Thurston and Lela (Davenport) M.; m. Johanna Young, July 25, 1980; 1 child, Sarah Elizabeth. B.A., E. Carolina U., 1972; M.P.A., N.C. State U., 1973, postgrad., 1981—. Asst. dean student devel. N.C. State U., Raleigh, 1974-77, dean student devel., 1977-79; dean students Winthrop Coll., Rock Hill, S.C., 1979-85, v.p. student life, 1985—. Council mem. Nat. Student Exchange, Ft. Wayne, Ind., 1982-84; bd. dirs. York County Council Alcohol and Drug Abuse, Rock Hill, 1984—, S.C. Marine Sci. Mus., Charleston, 1985. S.C. Council Alcohol and Drug Abuse grantee, 1984. Mem. Nat. Assn. Student Personnel Adminstrs., So. Assn. Coll. Student Affairs, S.C. Assn. Student Personnel Adminstrs., Omicron Delta Kappa (faculty sec. 1980—). Avocations: sailing; racquetball; biking. Home: 344 Grady Dr Rock Hill SC 29730 Office: Winthrop Coll Box 5010 WCS Rock Hill SC 29733

MANN, JOE ALLEN, chemical fibers, textile corporation research executive; b. Ronceverte, W.Va., June 20, 1941; s. Allen Ludington and Margie (Morgan) M.; B.S. in Chemistry, W.Va. U., 1963; Ph.D. in Chemistry, Ga. Inst. Tech., 1969; 1 dau., Mary Leigh. Chemist, Bendix Corp., 1963; chemistry instr. Ga. Inst. Tech., Atlanta, 1967-69; research chemist, project leader, group leader Dow Badische Co., Anderson, S.C., 1969-72, research mgr., 1972-77; research dir Badische Corp., Williamsburg, Va., 1977-82, also mgr. quality control and specialty fiber prodn.; corp. dir. research and devel. Burlington Industries, 1982—. Pres., Community Civic Assn., 1976-80. Recipient various scholarships and grants. Mem. Am. Chem. Soc. (pres. local chpt., 1961-63), Am. Mgmt. Assn., Man-Made Fiber Assn. (chem. com.), Williamsburg C. of C. (dir., chmn. edn. com.). Republican. Baptist. Patentee chemistry, fiber sci., fiber products; contbr. papers to profl. publs. and confs. Home: 3411 Rockingham Rd Greensboro NC 27407 Office: PO Box 21327 Burlington Industries Greensboro NC 27420

MANN, JOHN EASTON, real estate development and investment executive; b. Thomson, Ga., July 30, 1943; s. John Henry and Eula Mae (Bond) M.; m. Mary Charles Greene, June 28, 1964; children—Neil Avery, Jenny Ellen. B.B.A., Ga. State U., 1971. With Simmons Constrn. Co., Atlanta, 1961-62, Firestone Tire Co., Atlanta, 1962-63; from mechanic to fleet supt. Irvindale, Inc., Atlanta, 1967-71; from gen. mgr. to pres. Cline Land Co., Covington, Ga., 1971-85; chmn., chief exec. officer Woodfield Holding Co., Covington, 1985—; pres. Woodfield Devel. Co., Covington, 1983—, Woodfield Fin. Corp., Covington, 1983—; v.p. CLC, Inc., Covington, 1983—; sec.-treas. Brookview Mgmt. Co., Covington, 1983—. Mem. Republican Nat. Com., 1984—. Served with USAF, 1963-67, Labrador. Mem. Newton County C. of C. (bd. dirs., v.p. 1985—), Aircraft Owners and Pilots Assn. Baptist. Club: River Cove Recreation (co-founder, pres. 1980-82). Office: Woodfield Holding Co 1111 Church St Covington GA 30209

MANN, JOHN MICHAEL, financial executive; b. Macon, Ga., Mar. 16, 1946; s. Pell R. and Helen (Harris) M.; m. Sunday Roen, Jan. 13, 1979; 1 dau., Michelle Jean. B.S., Fresno State Coll., 1968. C.P.A. Fla., N.Y. Acct. Price Waterhouse, Miami, Fla., 1972-81; sr. v.p., chief fin. officer Maduro Group, Miami, 1981-84; v.p., chief fin. officer L. Luria & Son, Inc., 1984—; dir. Bywater Sales & Service Co. Inc., New Orleans, Lowlands Holding Inc., New Orleans, 1982-84, L. Luria & Son, Inc. Contbr. articles to profl. jours. Trustee, Expo 500, 1982—, Mus. of Sci., 1982—, Zool. Soc. Fla., 1986—. Mem. Am. Inst. C.P.A.s, Am. Soc. Pub. Adminstrs., N.Y. Soc. C.P.A.s, Fla. Inst. C.P.A.s, Mcpl. Fin. Officers Assn., Inst. Internal Auditors. Club: Bankers. Home: 3160 NW 114th Ln Coral Springs FL 33065

MANN, LAWRENCE, JR., industrial engineer, consultant, labor arbitrator; b. Baton Rouge, Feb. 12, 1926; s. Lawrence and Sophie (Mendelsohn) M.; m. Suzanne Alcus, Aug. 23, 1952; children—Lawrence, Nancy Lee. B.S.M.E., La. State U., 1949; M.S. in Indsl. Engring., Purdue U., 1950, Ph.D., 1965. Registered profl. engr. mech. and indsl. engring., La. Design engr. Exxon, Baton Rouge, 1950-57; sr. design engr. Lummus Co., Baton Rouge, 1957-59; prof. indsl. engring. La. State U., Baton Rouge, 1959—. Author: Maintenance Management, 1983; Applied Engineering Statistics, 1970. Served with USAAF, 1943-46; ETO. NSF sci. faculty fellow, 1962-63. Mem. Inst. Indsl. Engrs., Am. Soc. for Engring. Edn., La. Engring. Soc. Lodge: Rotary. Avocations: reading; sports cars; stamp collecting. Home: 4051 Churchill Ave Baton Rouge LA 70808 Office: Dept Indsl Engring La State Univ Baton Rouge LA 70803

MANN, OTHO KARL, JR., engineer, marketing educator; b. Hinton, W.Va., Sept. 7, 1951; s. Otho Karl and Jane Isabel (Lobban) M. B.S. in Chem. Engring., W.Va. U., 1973; M.B.A., U. Tenn., 1980; Ph.D., Va. Poly. Inst. and State U., 1985. Registered profl. engr., W.Va. Process engr. FMC Corp., South Charleston, W.Va., 1972-75; assoc. engr. Hooker Chem. Co., Columbia, Tenn., 1975-76; sr. project chem. engr. Mobil Oil Corp., Mt. Pleasant, Tenn., 1976-80; asst. prof. mktg. Concord Coll., Athens, W.Va., 1980-81; instr. mktg. Va. Poly Inst. and State U., Blacksburg, 1981-84; asst. prof. mktg. U. S.C., 1984—. Mem. Am. Mktg. Assn. (doctoral consortium fellow 1983), Inst. Mgmt. Sci., Acad. Mktg. Sci., Phi Kappa Psi, Tau Beta Pi. Democrat. Baptist. Author: Mathematical Models of Attitude Change, 1983. Home: 137 Bridgewater Circle Irmo SC 29063 Office: Dept Mktg U SC Columbia SC 29208

MANN, UZI, chemical engineering educator, consulting firm executive; b. Haifa, Israel, Dec. 9, 1940; came to U.S., 1968; s. Isaac and Rivkah Mendzicky; m. Helen Goodman, Nov. 1, 1970; children—David, Amy, Joel. B.S. in Chem. Engring., Technion-Israel Inst. Tech., 1965, M.S. in Chem. Engring., 1967; Ph.D. in Chem. Engring., U. Wis.-Madison, 1972. Registered profl. engr., Tex. With research and devel. ctr. Union Carbide Corp., Charleston, W.Va., 1973-77; prof. chem. engring. Tex. Tech U., Lubbock, 1978—; pres. Uzi Mann and Assocs., Inc., Lubbock, 1970—. Mem. Am. Inst. Chem. Engrs., Am. Chem. Soc. Contbr. articles to profl. jours. Office: Chem Engring Dept Tex Tech U Lubbock TX 79409

MANNES, EVE, art dealer, collector; b. Jan. 5, 1945; d. Robert and Elli (Goldschmidt) Bach; m. Harvey Mannes, Aug. 14, 1966; children—Peter Rathbone, Keith Derek. B.A., Douglass Coll., 1966. Tchr., Cinnaminson Schs., N.J., 1966-68, Jericho Schs., N.Y., 1968-69; studio artist, 1970-78; owner Eve Mannes Gallery, Atlanta, 1980—; guest lectr. Gibbes Art Gallery, Charleston, S.C., Atlanta Coll. Art. Patron mem. High Mus. Art; benefactor, mem. 20th Century Art Soc. of High Mus.; mem. Nexus, Arts Festival Atlanta. Avocations: travel; swimming; tennis; reading. Office: Eve Mannes Gallery 75 Bennett St Suite 2B Atlanta GA 30305

MANNING, GARY LON, theology educator, minister; b. San Antonio, Sept. 28, 1947; s. Burl William and Leona Jo (McCugh) M.; m. Paulette Cunningham, Aug. 22, 1968; children—Troy, Tami. B.S., Howard Payne U., 1969; M.R.E., Southwestern Bapt. Theol. Sem., 1972, Ed.D., 1982. Ordained to ministry Baptist Ch. Minister music, youth and edn. Emmanuel Bapt. Ch., Waco, Tex., 1972-75; minister edn. Emmanuel Bapt. Ch., Temple, Tex., 1975-76; pastor Acad. Bapt. Ch., Little River, Tex., 1976-82; prof. Wayland Bapt. U., Plainview, Tex., 1982—. Rec. artist: Part the Waters, 1976. Mem. Am. Assn. Marriage and Family Therapy (assoc.), Assn. Couples for Marriage Enrichment (retreat leader). Democrat. Avocations: golf; camping. Home: 1110 Borger St Plainview TX 79072 Office: Wayland Bapt Univ 1900 W 7th St Plainview TX 79072

MANNING, HERBERT, lawyer, consultant; b. Yoakum, Tex., Sept. 14, 1914; s. Bernard Herbert and Linda (McDonnell) M; m. Mary Elizabeth Cooke; children: Barbara Ann Manning Wood, Jean Elizabeth Manning Snelus. Ed. Tex. Christian U., So. Meth. U., U. Tex.-Arlington, Georgetown U.; LL.B., Cath. U. Am., 1939. Bar: D.C. 1939, Tex. 1946. Atty. SEC, Washington, 1939-42; asst. regional counsel USPHS-HUD, Ft. Worth, until 1971; spl. asst. atty. gen. State of La., 1972-77; ptnr. Groce, Manning & Groce, Ft. Worth; now sole practice, Ft. Worth; cons. housing fin. Recipient various certs. of appreciation. Mem. Fed. Bar Assoc. (nat. v.p. 5th jud. dist. 1961-62, pres. Ft. Worth 1959-60), State Bar Tex., Nat. Assn. Housing and Redevel. Ofcls., Fed. Bus. Assn. Home: 6100 Winifred Dr Fort Worth TX 76133 Office: 1525 Merrimac Suite 204 Fort Worth TX 76107

MANNING, OREN REID, pension and profit sharing consultant, financial adviser; b. Charlotte, N.C., Feb. 7, 1938; s. William G. and Pearl (Bresler) M.; m. Sheila Farbman, June 12, 1960 (div. Apr. 1972); children—Steven L., Melissa J.; m. Barbara Ruth Leiderman, June 9, 1979. B.S., U. N.C., 1959; B.A., Belmont Abbey Coll., 1960. Group rep. Protective Life Ins., Charlotte, N.C., 1960-65, Miami, Fla., 1965; regional mgr. Home Life Ins. Co. N.Y., Miami, 1965-80; v.p. Falick, Manning & Assocs., P.A., Coral Gables, Fla., 1980—; mem. pres.'s council Home Life Ins. Co.-N.Y., N.Y.C., 1974-80; mem. pres.'s club Nat. Life of Vt., Montpelier, 1980-84. Mem. Million Dollar Round Table, Fla. Life Underwriters Assn. (Nat. Quality award 1983, Quality Health award 1983), Miami Life Underwriters Assn. Jewish. Home: 8136 SW 87th Terr Miami FL 33143 Office: Falick Manning & Assocs PA 1320 S Dixie Hwy Coral Gables FL 33146

MANNING, V. C., state senator, school administrator; b. Edinburg, Miss., Dec. 23, 1947; s. Coy Clayton and Faye (Bennett) M.; m. Cynthia Denise Davis, June 20, 1982. B.S., U. So. Miss., 1970; M.A., Miss. State U., 1982. Cert. sch. adminstr. Constrn. worker Perry Constrn. Co., Philadelphia, Miss.; factory worker Superior Coach Corp., Kosciusko, Miss., 1970-71; sch. adminstr. Neshoba County Schs., Philadelphia, Miss., 1972-85; mem. Miss. Senate, 1984—. Author poetry. Bd. dirs. Neshoba County Mental Health Assn., Philadelphia, 1985, Neshoba County 4-H Adv. Bd., Philadelphia, 1985; vol. United Way, Philadelphia, 1984. Democrat. Baptist. Office: Office of the State Senate Jackson MS 39205

MANNING, WALTER SCOTT, accountant, former educator, consultant; b. nr. Yoakum, Tex.; B.B.A., Tex. Coll. Arts and Industries, 1932; M.B.A., U. Tex., 1940; m. Eleanor Mary Jones, Aug. 27, 1937; children—Sharon Frances, Walter Scott, Robert Kenneth. Asst. to bus. mgr. Tex. Coll. Arts and Industries, Kingsville, 1932; tchr. Sinton (Tex.) High Sch., 1933-37, Robstown (Tex.) High Sch., 1937-41; prof. Tex. A&M U., College Station, 1941-77; cons. C.P.A. C.P.A., Tex. Walter Manning Outstanding Jr. and Outstanding Sr. awards at Coll. Bus. Adminstrn., Tex. A&M U. named in his honor. Mem. AAUP, Am. Acctg. Assn., Am. Inst. C.P.A.s, Tex. Soc. C.P.A.s, College Station C. of C. (past pres.), Tex. Assn. Univ. Instrs. Acctg. (pres. 1963-64), Knights York Cross of Honor, Alpha Chi, Beta Gamma Sigma, Beta Alpha Psi. Democrat. Presbyterian (elder). Clubs: Masons, (32 deg.), Shriners, K.T., Kiwanis (past pres., past lt. gov. div. IX Tex. Okla. dist.). Home: 405 Walton Dr E College Station TX 77840

MANNING, WILLIAM SINKLER, mfg. co. exec.; b. 1925; B.S., N.C. State U., 1948; married. Plant gen. mgr. Deering Milliken, 1949-56; div. mgr.

Burlington Draper div. Burlington Industries Co., 1956-58, div. mgr., mfg. v.p. Burlington House div., 1958-69; pres., chief exec. officer Bibb Co., Macon, Ga., 1970—. Served to lt. (j.g.) USNR, 1943-45. Office: 237 Coliseum Dr Macon GA 31208*

MANOR, LEROY JOSEPH, association executive, retired Air Force officer; b. Morrisville, N.Y., Feb. 21, 1921; s. Walter and Rose Delia (Liberty) M.; m. Dolores Harriett Brookes, Nov. 21, 1940; children—Alan, Mary, Dean. Tchrs. cert., N.Y. State Normal Sch., 1940; B.S. in Edn., NYU, 1947. Commd. officer U.S. Air Force, 1943, advanced through ranks to lt. gen., 1976; dep. chief of staff plans and ops. Pentagon, Washington, 1964-68; comdr. tactical fighter wing, Vietnam, 1968-69; comdr. Spl. Ops. Force, 1970-71; dep. dir. ops. and spl. asst. counterinsurgency and spl. activities to joint chiefs of staff Pentagon, 1971-73; comdr. 13th Air Force, Philippines, 1973-76; chief of staff U.S. Pacific Command, Philippines, 1973-76; ret., 1978; mil. negotiator, advisor U.S. Ambassador to Philippines, 1978-80; pres. Ret. Officers Assn., 1980—. Decorated Disting. Service medal with 3 clusters, Legion of Merit medal with 1 cluster; D.F.C. with 1 cluster, Air medal with 25 clusters, Purple Heart; awards Govt. Korea, Philippines, Republic of Vietnam. Home: 1223 Michigan Ct Alexandria VA 22314 Office: Retired Officers Assn 201 N Washington St Alexandria VA 22314

MANOSEVITZ, MARTIN, psychology educator, psychologist; b. Mpls., June 22, 1938; s. Julius and Ethel (Cohen) M.; m. Carolyn Heather Margulius, Sept. 17, 1959; children—Bradley, Jason. B.A. cum laude, U. Minn., 1960, Ph.D., 1964. Asst. prof. Rutgers U., New Brunswick, N.J., 1964-67; asst. prof. U. Tex., Austin, 1967-69, assoc. prof., 1969-75, prof. psychology, 1975—, asst. dean Coll. Arts Scis., 1971-72, dir. grad. program in devel., 1973-76, dir. inst. human devel., 1974-76, dir. grad. program in clin. psychology, 1979-81. Author: Introduction to Theories of Personality, 1985. Editor: Behavior Genetics: Behavior and Research, 1969; Theories of Personality, 2d edit., 1973. Bd. dirs. Austin-Travis County Mental Health and Mental Retardation Assn., Austin, 1975-80. Grantee NIMH, 1969-74, 77-79, NSF, 1976-79, Inst. Human Devel., 1975-76. Fellow Am. Psychol. Assn.; mem. Soc. for Research Child Devel., Am. Orthopsychiat. Assn., Tex. Psychol. Assn., Southwestern Psychol. Assn. Home: 3703 Kennelwood Rd Austin TX 78703 Office: U Tex Dept Psychology Mezes Hall Austin TX 78712

MANSO, GILBERT, physician; b. Havana, Cuba, Dec. 16, 1942; s. Gilberto F. and Gricelda (Jimenez) M.; came to U.S., 1959, naturalized, 1968; B.A., U. Tex., Austin, 1965; M.D., U. Tex. Med. Br., Galveston, 1969; student U.S. Air Force Sch. Aerospace Medicine, 1970; m. Deborah L. Fowles, June 27, 1970 (div.); children—Wayne, Tammy. Rotating intern Meml. Bapt. Hosp., Houston, 1969-70; chief of staff Cochran Meml. Hosp., Morton, Tex., 1974-76; health officer Cochran County, Tex., 1974-76; chmn. med. care evaluation com. Tidelands Hosp., Channelview, Tex., 1976-77, vice-chief of staff, 1977-78, chief of staff, 1978—; faculty U. Tex. Med. Br., Houston; pres. G. Manso, M.D., P.A., Channelview, Tex., 1976—. Pres., Manso Airmotive. Served to maj. MC USAF, 1970-75. Decorated Air medal. Diplomate Am. Bd. Family Practice. Fellow Am. Acad. Family Practice; mem. AMA, Tex. Med. Assn., Harris County Med. Soc., Houston Acad. Family Practice, Am. Coll. Emergency Physicians. Republican. Roman Catholic. Editor, pub.: The Houston Wine Scene, 1979—. Office: 15101 E Freeway Channelview TX 77530

MANSON, MARY BARBARA, advertising accounting executive; b. Dallas, Oct. 18, 1938; d. George Raymond and Mary Suzanne (Phillips) Hammond; m. Bobby Frank Manson, Mar. 21, 1955; children—Bobby Ray, David Mark, John Richard. Student pub. schs., Dallas. Account supr. Gt. S.W. Life Ins., Dallas, 1965-66; print media checker Tracey-Locke Advt. Co., Dallas, 1966-69; acctg. supr. Bloom Advt. Agy., Dallas, 1969-77; prodn. acct. Bozell & Jacobs, Irving, Tex., 1977-79; pres. Barbara Manson Advt. Acctg. Specialist, Irving, 1979—; cons. in field. Republican. Baptist.

MANSON, ROBERT DENYS, geologist; b. Port Arthur, Tex., Mar. 26, 1952; s. Denys and Rose Vera (Fortuna) M.; m. Merriette Tarese Adamson, Aug. 2, 1980; children—Christine Rose, Blake Joseph. B.S., U. Tex., 1976. Geologist Strike Resources, Inc., Corpus Christi, Tex., 1977-78, Dinero Oil Co., Corpus Christi, 1978-80, Mormac Energy Corp., Corpus Christi, 1980-82, Nugget Oil Corp., Corpus Christi, 1982-84; v.p. exploration Crescent Petroleum Corp., Corpus Christi, 1984—. Editor: (guidebook) Sabinas Hidalgo-Mexico, 1978. Mem. Am. Assn. Petroleum Geologists, Corpus Christi Geol. Soc. (treas. 1981-82, chmn. continuing edn. 1979-82, editor guidebook 1978-79). Republican. Episcopalian. Avocation: sailboarding. Home: 450 University St Corpus Christi TX 78412 Office: Crescent Petroleum Corp 304 Guaranty Plaza Corpus Christi TX 78475

MANTEY, ELMER MARTIN, food company executive; b. Malone, Tex., July 20, 1926; s. Edward G. and Margaret H. Mantey; m. Donna May Scritsmier, Dec. 27, 1948; children—Patricia, Mrs. Carol Callis, Mrs. Cynthia Stockdale. B.S. in Chemistry with honors, Bradley U., 1949. Chemist, plant mgr. Am. Petrochem. Co., Mpls., 1949-63, v.p. ops., 1963-66; v.p. Polychem. Group, Whittaker Corp., Los Angeles, 1966-69, pres. textile div., 1969-71; pres., chief exec. officer Flavorite Labs. Inc., Memphis, 1971—; v.p. Craig-Hallum Corp. Served with USN, 1944-46. Mem. Inst. Food Techs., Pres.' Assn., Am. Mgmt. Assn. Evangelical. Clubs: Rotary (Memphis), Summit; Farmington Country. Home: 6925 Sugar Maple Cove Memphis TN 38119 Office: PO Box 1315 Memphis TN 38101

MANZELLA, RONALD ANTHONY, architectural designer, planner, developer; b. Yokohama, Japan, Dec. 26, 1957; came to U.S., 1959; s. Joseph Anthony and Machi (Murakami) M. B.Arch., La. State U., 1984, postgrad. Pres. Ronald A. Manzella & Assocs., Baton Rouge, 1980-84; ptnr., owner T.C.B. Partnership, Baton Rouge, 1984—; pres. T.C.B. Properties and Devel., Baton Rouge, 1984—; v.p. T.C.B. Plus AIA Architects/Planners, Baton Rouge, 1984—; devel. cons. Jefferson Partnership, Doris Thyssen Realty, Barrier Reef Project, Plank Rd. Civic Assn., Baton Rouge. Project mgr., designer urban study Urban Study for Fairfield Ave, 1985; project mgr., designer planning study Chandeleur Devel. Study, 1984. Assoc. fellow AIA, La. Architects Assn., AIA (Baton Rouge chpt.); mem. Nat. Council Archtl. Registration Bd. Club: Exchange. Avocations: painting; drawing; martial arts. Office: TCB Group/Gregory P Matherne Architect 10935 Perkins Rd Suite A Baton Rouge LA 70810

MANZO, SALVATORE EDWARD, university official; b. Bklyn., Oct. 23, 1917; s. Salvatore and Mary (Sireci) M.; B.S., U.S. Mil. Acad., 1939; m. Flournoy Davis, Mar. 11, 1960; children—Janeen, John, Joanne, Molly. Commd. 2d lt. USAF, 1939, advanced through grades to col., 1944, ret., 1962; v.p. C.H. Leavell & Co., El Paso, 1962-65; exec. dir. Met. Airlines Com., N.Y.C., 1965-67; dir. aviation City of Houston, 1967-69; pres. Trans-East Air Inc., Bangor, Maine, 1969-70; aviation mgmt. cons., Bangor, 1970-72, Sao Paulo, Brazil, 1972-74; exec. asst. to pres. Hidroservice, Sao Paulo, 1974-77; asso. Charter Fin. Group, Inc., Houston, 1977-79; dir. exec. devel. Jesse H. Jones Grad. Sch. Adminstrn., Rice U., Houston, 1979-85, asst. dean exec. devel., 1985—; pres., dir. TCI Venture Capital Corp., Houston; dir. Ad-Vantage Pub. Co., Houston; chmn., pres. Manzo Devel. Co., 1969—. Pres., El Paso C. of C., 1965; vestryman Christ Ch. Cathedral, Houston, 1979-81. Decorated Silver Star, Legion of Merit, D.F.C. (2), Soldier's medal, Air medal (5), Commendation medal (2); Croix de Guerre with palm (France). Mem. Houston C. of C. Republican. Episcopalian. Home: 1111 Hermann Dr 16-C Houston TX 77004 Office: Rice U PO Box 1892 Houston TX 77251

MAPHET, LEILA ERNESTINE, postmaster; b. Logan, Okla., June 17, 1927; d. Earnest Alexander and Virginia Alice (Estes) B.; m. David Bernard Maphet, Dec. 26, 1945; children—Tony Lee, Terry Don, Victor Joe. Clerk U.S. Postal Service, Gate, Okla., 1964-72, postmaster, 1972—; tchr. training confs., Okla., 1970—. Author: Gate to No Man's Land, 1976; Vigilantes, 1978. Co-author: Good Old Day's Cook Book, 1976. Contbr. songs, music, articles to various publs. Pres. Gateway to the Panhandle Mus. Assn., Gate, 1975—; active in PTA, Extension Homemakers and other community activities, Gate, 1950—; tchr., treas. and other activities in church and Sunday School, Gate and Rosston, Okla., 1944—; chmn., organizer Historical Tour and Bone Pickin' contest, Gate, 1976—; promoter Country Chapel Singers, Gate, 1974—. Recipient Service award Hist. Soc., 1976, Bicentennial award U.S. Postal Service, 1976. Mem. Nat. Assn. Postmasters (Okla. chpt.). Republican. Methodist. Avocation: playing in jamborees. Home: Route 1 Box 24 Gate OK 73844 Office: US Postal Service Main St Gate OK 73844

MAPLE, TIMOTHY MICHAEL, chemical company executive; b. Owensboro, Ky., Jan. 24, 1936; s. T.M. Maple and Lucille (Coons) Lambert; m. Wilda Jo Atherton, Apr. 20, 1957 (div. 1979); children—Timothy Michael II, Kimberly Jo, David Kyle; m. Carol Jean Hawes, July 12, 1980; children—Charles Anthony Gregory, Christopher Michael Gregory. B.L.S., U. Evansville, 1984. Truck driver PB&S Chem. Co., Henderson, Ky., 1960-63, supr. solvents, 1963-67, supr. vehicle maintenance, 1967-69, adminstv. asst. to v.p., 1969-77, corp. fleet mgr., 1977—; mem. task force com. Chlorine Inst., N.Y.C., 1979. Author: Operations Procedures, 1984. Fund raiser United Way, Henderson, 1972, YMCA, Henderson, 1968-72; bd. dirs. Hugh Edward Sandefur Tng. Ctr., 1973-74. Named Boss of Yr., Profl. Sec. Internat., 1980-81. Mem. Pvt. Truck Council Am. Democrat. Baptist. Avocations: country western dancing, landscaping, gardening, fishing. Home: Route 2 Box 473 Henderson KY 42420 Office: PB&S Chemical Co Hwy 136 Henderson KY 42420

MAPLES, DONNA ELAINE, religious educator; b. Bay City, Tex., May 20, 1953; d. John Cecil and Clara Ann (Moore) M. B.A. in English and Math., Baylor U., 1974; M.A. in English, Vanderbilt U., 1978; postgrad. U. Mo.-Columbia, 1981—. Assoc., Woman's Missionary Union, Mo. Bapt. Conv., Jefferson City, 1976-80, tng. design group mgr. Woman's Missionary Union, Birmingham, Ala., 1984—. Author: Friends Are For Helping, 1982. Mem. Am. Soc. for Tng. and Devel., Mo. Folklore Soc. Baptist. Office: Woman's Missionary Union PO Box C-10 Birmingham AL 35283

MAPP, RAMONA HARTLEY, college administrator; b. Hartley's Corners, Ala., Jan. 18; d. Smith Culp and Annie Bess (Owens) Hartley; m. Malcolm Hamby (dec. Jan. 1967); children—Gregory Stuart Hamby, Geoffrey Alan Hamby; m. Alf Johnson Mapp, Jr., Aug. 1, 1971; 1 stepson, Alf J. Mapp III. Student Ind. U., 1956-57, City Lit. Inst., London, 1959-61, Huntingdon Coll., 1961-62; B.A., Old Dominion U., 1965, M.A., 1966; Ed.D., Va. Poly. Inst. and State U., 1980. Instr. English, Old Dominion U., Norfolk, Va., 1966-69, 70-71; instr. English, Tidewater Community Coll., Portsmouth, Va., 1971-73, English coordinator, 1973-74, chairperson div. humanities and social scis., 1974—; judge internat. essay contest Nat. Assn. Tchrs. English, 1974; profl. devel. coordinator Southeastern Conf. on English, 1981, state rep., 1978-82, program chmn., 1984. Bd. dirs. Internat. Intercultural Consortium, Met. Arts Congress; chmn. Portsmouth Pub. Library Bd., 1978-80; pres. Tidewater Child Care Assn., 1975-77; v.p. Tidewater Literacy Council, 1971-72; pres. Va. Ballet Theater; mem. exec. com. of bd. Va. Opera Assn. Guild. Named Outstanding Woman of Hampton Roads, 1984; recipient (with husband) Nat. Service award Family Found. Am., 1980. Mem. S. Atlantic Modern Lang. Assn. (sec. 2-yr. coll. sect.), Poetry Soc. Va. (corr. sec. 1975-76), Cultural Alliance Hampton Roads (bd. dirs.), AAUW (v.p. Portsmouth 1983-85, state competition chmn. 1985), South Atlantic Assn. Chairmen Depts. English (exec. com. 1982—), Internat. Assn. Torch Clubs. Home: Willow Oaks 2901 Tanbark Ln Portsmouth VA 23703 Office: Tidewater Community Coll Frederick Campus Portsmouth VA 23703

MARABLE, JAMES ROSE, JR., civil engineer; b. Atlanta, Oct. 5, 1924; s. James Rose and Mary Spotswood (Glinn) M.; B.C.E., Ga. Inst. Tech., 1949; M.S., La. State U., 1950; m. Dawn Io Key, Dec. 24, 1946; children—Nancy Marable Livingston, Jane Marable Adams, Anne Marable, James Stephen. Hydraulic engr. U.S. C.E., Vicksburg Waterways Expt. Sta., 1950-51; sr. designer Ga. Power Co., Atlanta, 1951-54; structural engr. Kuhlke & Wade, architects, Augusta, Ga., 1954-56, W.Va. Pulp & Paper Co., Charleston, S.C., 1956-57; asst. chief structural sect. Union Bag-Camp Corp., Savannah, Ga., 1957-60; sr. structural engr. Robert & Co., Assos., architects and engrs., Atlanta, 1960-66; chief engr. br. office Simons-Eastern Co., cons.'s and engrs., Atlanta and Greenville, S.C., 1967-72; project mgr. Simons Eastern Co., 1972-75; v.p. Archtl. Corp. Atlanta, 1975-77; mgr. civil engring. Simons Eastern Cons., Inc., engrs., Decatur, Ga., 1977—; instr. La. State U., 1949-50. Pres., Columbia Valley Civic Assn., Decatur, 1965-66; scoutmaster Boy Scouts Am., 1952-54. Served with AUS, 1943-46; ETO. Named Engr. of Year in Pvt. Practice Met. Atlanta, Engrs. Greater Atlanta, 1974, Engr. of Year in Pvt. Practice Ga., Ga. Soc. Profl. Engrs., 1974. Registered profl. engr., Ga., Ala., Tex., Okla., Fla., S.C., N.C., Tenn., Pa., Va., Calif. Fellow ASCE; mem. Ga. Engring. Found. (life mem., v.p. 1978, pres.-elect 1979, pres. 1980), Am. Legion (comdr. 1949), Chi Epsilon. Presbyterian (deacon 1965-67, 76-79, elder 1980-83, 84—). Mason. Home: 3675 Tree Bark Trail Decatur GA 30034 Office: 1 W Court Sq Decatur GA 30030

MARBERRY, THOMAS LUTHER, college administrator, minister; b. Houston, May 3, 1949; s. Luther Fagan and Ruby Estelle (Sheffield) M.; m. Wilma Lee Ussery, July 22, 1983. B.A., Baylor U., 1971, Ph.D., 1982; M.Divinity, S.W. Baptist Theol. Sem., Ft. Worth, 1973. Ordained to ministry Baptist Ch., 1971. Pastor, United Free Will Bapt. Ch., Bryan, Tex., 1973-75, Prairie Bell Free Will Bapt. Ch., Putnam, Okla., 1976—; instr. Hillsdale Free Will Bapt. Coll., Moore, Okla., 1975-83, v.p. acad. affairs, 1983—; sec. Okla. Free Will Bapt. Minister's Conf., 1980—. Mem. Tex. Assn. Free Will Bapts. (asst. clk. 1973-75), Okla. Assn. Community and Jr. Coll. Instructional Adminstrs., Okla. Assn. Collegiate Registrars and Admissions Officers. Democrat. Lodge: Kiwanis (sec. 1984—). Avocations: reading; gardening. Home: 1512 SE 6th Moore OK 73160 Office: Hillsdale Free Will Baptist Coll PO Box 7208 Moore OK 73153

MARBUT, ROBERT GORDON, newspaper-broadcast corporation executive; b. Athens, Ga., Apr. 11, 1935; s. Robert Smith and Laura Gordon (Powers) M.; m. Vesta Brue Dauber, July 19, 1980; children—Robert Gordon, Laura Dodd, Michael Powers. B.Indsl. Engring., Ga. Inst. Tech., 1957; M.B.A. with distinction, Harvard U., 1963. Registered profl. engr., Calif. Engr. Esso Standard Oil Co., Baton Rouge, 1957; mgmt. trainee Copley Newspapers, Los Angeles, 1963; engring. services coordinator, La Jolla, Calif., 1965, corp. dir. engring. and plans, 1966-70; v.p. Harte-Hanks Newspapers, San Antonio, 1970-71, pres., chief exec. officer, 1971—, mem. exec. com., 1974—, also dir.; dir. A.P., Interfirst Corp.; instr. Armstrong Coll., 1951, Calif. State, Los Angeles, 1964, Woodbury Coll., 1964; Pres. adv. bd. U. Ga. Henry W. Grady Sch. Journalism, 1975—; mem. adv. Found. for Communications Sch. U. Tex., 1975—; mem. nat. adv. bd. Up With People, Ga. Inst. Tech.; bd. dirs. Tex. Research League, 1975—, Salzburg Seminar in Am. Studies. Author: (with Healy, Henderson and others) Creative Collective Bargaining, 1965; also articles in mags., jours.; frequent speaker. Bd. dirs. Up With People. Served with USAF, 1958-61. Recipient Isaiah Thomas award Rochester Inst. Tech. Mem. Newspaper Advt. Bur. (exec. com., dir. 1974-81), Am. Newspaper Pubs. Assn. Research Inst. (exec. com. 1973—), Am. Newspaper Publs. Assn. (chmn. task group on future, chmn. telecommunications com. 1974—, bd. dirs. 1976—, chmn. future task group), So. Newspaper Pubs. Assn. (pres. 1978-80, dir. 1975-81, treas. 1977, chmn. bus. and adminstrn. com. 1976), Am. Newspaper Pubs. Assn. Found. (trustee 1976—), Tex. Daily Newspaper Assn. (pres. 1979), Greater San Antonio C. of C. (chmn. long range planning task force, dir. 1979—, exec. com. 1981—), Delta Tau Delta, Omicron Delta Kappa, Phi Eta Sigma. Presbyterian. Club: Oaks Hills Country. Office: PO Box 269 San Antonio TX 78291*

MARCELL, CHARLES CLIFTON, pharmacist; b. Louisville, May 22, 1949; s. Clifton T. and Texie D. (Meredith) M.; m. Carrie Ann Campbell, Aug. 21, 1975; 1 dau., Sarah Melissa. B.S., St. Louis Coll. Pharmacy, 1973; M.B.A., Bellarmine Coll., 1982. Registered pharmacist, Ky., Ind., Ohio. Store mgr. Taylor Drugs, Louisville, 1973-75; store mgr. Union Prescription Ctrs., Inc., Louisville, 1975-78, dist. mgr., 1978-82; owner, pres. Preston Discount Pharmacy, Inc., Louisville, 1982—. Precinct capt. Republican party, 1981—. Mem. Ky. Pharm. Assn., Jefferson County Acad. Pharmacy, Kappa Psi. Mem. Christian Ch. Club: Senatorial. Lodge: Masons.

MARCELLINI, EDUARDO ALBERTO, insurance agent, financial consultant; b. Castelar, Buenos Aires, Argentina, Feb. 17, 1951; came to U.S., 1980; s. Alberto Pedro Antonio and Josefa (Paletta) M.; m. Gayle Alison Ramsey, Sept. 6, 1980; 1 child, Paul Anthony. A.A. in Acctg., Universidad de Buenos Aires, 1975; B.S. in Mktg., Barry U., 1982; cert. life ins. mktg. Life Underwriters Tng. Council, 1985. Mktg. mgr. Creart Publicidad, Buenos Aires, 1969-73; loan mgr., mortgage analyst Banco de la Provincia de Corrientes, Buenos Aires, 1973-76; dir. fin. Intercommerce S.A., Buenos Aires, 1976-79; ptnr. Nest Constructora, Buenos Aires, 1979-82; pres. Dolphin Plaza Restaurant, Miami, Fla., 1981-82; dist. agt., registered rep. Prudential Ins. Co., Miami, 1983—; cons. in field. Mem. Nat. Assn. Life Underwriters. Roman Catholic. Avocations: photography; wood craft. Home: 22930 SW 154th Ct Miami FL 33170 Office: Prudential Ins Co Am 10700 Caribbean Blvd Miami FL 33189

MARCHASE, RICHARD BANFIELD, cell biologist, educator; b. Sayre, Pa., Mar. 12, 1948; s. Nicholas and Vivian H. (Banfield) M.; m. Susan Elizabeth Darrow, Apr. 14, 1979; 1 son, Nicholas Darrow. B.S., Cornell U., 1970; Ph.D., Johns Hopkins U., 1976. Muscular Dystrophy Assn. postdoctoral fellow div. neurology, Duke U. Med. Ctr., 1976-77, USPHS postdoctoral fellow dept. anatomy, 1977-78, asst. prof. anatomy, 1978-86; assoc. prof. cell biology and anatomy U. Ala.-Birmingham, 1986—. Recipient Hamilton Watch award Cornell U., 1970; NSF grad. fellow, 1970-73, Presdl. Young Investigator grantee, 1982-87; Danforth Found. grad. fellow, 1973-76; Nanaline H. Duke scholar, 1982-85; USPHS grantee. Mem. AAAS, Am. Soc. Cell Biology, Am. Soc. Zoology, Internat. Soc. Devel. Neurosci., Sigma Xi. Contbr. chpts. to books, articles to profl. jours. Home: 2717 Countrywood Way Birmingham AL 35243 Office: U Ala-Birmingham Birmingham AL 35294

MARCHESE, JOSEPH IGNATIUS, advertising agency executive, musician; b. Little Rock, Sept. 30, 1948; s. Salvador Anthony and Marie Bernadette (Nicolosi) M.; m. Patricia Ann Rainey, May 25, 1975; children—Frances Antonia, Nathaniel Lee. Student U. Ark., 1966-70. Musician, 1965-75, 77—; staff musician, writer Jam Factory, rec. studio, 1976; staff musician, writer Audio Rec. Corp. of Ark., Little Rock, 1977-80; account exec., copywriter John Roberts & Ptnrs., advt. agy., 1980; dir. mktg. Andy's of Am., Little Rock, 1981—, Dixie Mgmt., Inc., Little Rock, 1982—; pres. Sandy & Assocs., advt., mktg., pub. relations, Little Rock, 1982—. Recipient cert. of excellence in advt. (8), Ark. Advt. Fedn., 1982, 83, 4 dist. conf. certs., 1983-86. Ark.-Little Rock scholar, 1966. Mem. Ark. Press Assn. (6 merit awards Advt. Creativity Competition 1984-86). Democrat. Roman Catholic. Lodge: K.C. (North Little Rock, Ark.). Co-editor Pulaski County Humane Soc. Newsletter, 1980-81. Office: 206 Louisiana St Little Rock AR 72201

MARCHMAN, DENNIS LEROY, accountant; b. White Plains, Ga., Feb. 20, 1915; s. Clarence Moore and Lillie Mae (Darnell) M. Student Oglethrope U., 1934, Southern Brothers Law Sch., 1936-37. With Miami (Fla.) Herald, 1936-38; bookkeeper Vultee Aircraft Co., Miami, 1941-42; acct. C.F. Wheeler Builder, Miami, 1946-49; controller Hardy Houses, Laurel, Md., 1949-50; v.p. Tec-Bilt Homes, Miami, 1950-55, Carl G. Fisher Corp., Nassau, Bahamas, 1955-57; controller Brook Gas Co., Miami, Fla., 1957-67; controller Auto-Marine Engrs., Inc., Miami, 1967—; v.p., dir. Aviation Marine and Auto Supply, Inc., 1975—. Served with USNR, 1942-45. Democrat. Baptist. Home: 5330 SW 62d Ave Miami FL 33155

MARCON, REBECCA ANN, psychology educator; b. Peckville, Pa., Aug. 15, 1952; d. Frank B. and Doris A. Marcon. B.A. in Psychology, Calif. State U.-Fullerton, 1974; M.A. in Edn., UCLA, 1976; Ph.D. in Psychology, La. State U., 1981. Lic. ednl. psychologist, Calif. Sch. psychologist Pomona Unified Sch. Dist., Calif., 1976-78; grad. asst., instr. La. State U., Baton Rouge, 1978-81; asst. prof. psychology Clemson U., S.C., 1981—; cons. S.C. Hemophilia Found., 1984—. Contbr. articles to profl. jours., research presentations to profl. socs. Co-ordinator Family Life Colloquium Series, Clemson, 1985—; mem. Strom Thurmond Inst., volunteerism group, Clemson, 1984—. Grantee NIH, 1981-83, S.C. chpt. Nat. Hemophilia Found., 1984-85; Clemson U. Provost research grantee, 1985-86, univ. faculty research grantee, 1981-82. Mem. Am. Psychol. Assn., Southeastern Psychol. Assn., Soc. for Research in Child Devel., Phi Kappa Phi, Sigma Kappa. Roman Catholic. Avocations: travel, spectator sports. Office: Clemson U Dept Psychology B5A Hardin Hall Clemson SC 29634

MARCUM, GARY DEAN, public health educator; b. Oneida, Tenn., Aug. 4, 1946; s. James and Annie (Keeton) M.; m. Judy Darlene Tervo, Oct. 11, 1969; children—Carissa Dawn, Deryck Heath. B.S., E. Tenn. State U., 1972. Pub. health educator Ga. Div. Pub. Health, Rome, 1972—, human relations specialist, 1978—; mgmt. cons. Served with USAF, 1966-69. Mem. Assn. for Creative Change Within Religious and Other Social Systems (recognation 1984), Ga. Pub. Health Assn., Am. Soc. Tng. and Devel. Democrat. Lutheran. Avocation: exercise. Home: 19 Trentwood Pl Rome GA 30161 Office: NW Regional Hosp Bldg 614 Rome GA 30161

MARCUM, GORDON GEORGE, II, oil company executive; b. Sherman, Tex., July 4, 1942; s. Gordon G. and Marjorie (Shelton) M.; m. Margaret Burleson, Aug. 24, 1963; children—Michal, Matthew, Jeffrey. B.B.A., U. Okla., 1964, J.D., 1967. Bar: Tex. 1973, Okla. 1967; cert. profl. landman. Landman, Amerada Petroleum Corp., Midland, Tex., 1964, Continental Oil Co., Oklahoma City, 1965-67; dir. oil, gas and minerals State of N.Mex., Santa Fe, 1969-71; v.p., gen. counsel Marcum Drilling Co., Midland, 1971-78; v.p., exploration mgr. Olix Energy Co., Midland, 1978-81; v.p. oil and gas Perry Energy Co., Midland, 1981-83; pres. Marcum Drilling Co., Midland, 1983—. Mem. City Council City of Midland, 1967—; mem. Midland Transp. Commn.; pres. Midland Health Facilities Bd.; bd. dirs. Permian Basin Regional Planning Commn., Young Life. Served to capt. AUS, 1967-69. Recipient Julian Rothbaum award as outstanding grad. U. Okla., 1964; Outstanding Service award N.Mex. State Land Office, 1971; Am. Assn. Petroleum Landmen scholar, 1963, 64. Mem. Midland County Bar Assn., Am. Assn. Petroleum Landmen, Permian Basin Assn. Petroleum Landmen, Internat. Assn. Drilling Contractors (v.p., bd. dirs.), Permian Basin Assn. Drilling Contractors (chmn.). Presbyterian (deacon, elder, treas.). Clubs: Rotary, Midland Country, Riverhill Country, Santa Fe Country. Office: 401 Wall Towers W Midland TX 79701

MARCUM, WALTER PHILLIP, oil company executive; b. Bemidji, Minn., Mar. 1, 1944; s. John Phillip and Johnnye Evelyn (Edmiston) M.; m. Barbara Lynn Maloof, Apr. 17, 1976. B.B.A., Tex. Tech U., 1967. Research analyst Collins Securities Corp., Denver, 1968-70; pres. Marcum & Spillane, 1970-76; pres., chief exec. officer MGF Oil Corp., Midland, Tex., 1976—; dir. Aristek Corp., Denver. Mem. Ind. Petroleum Assn. Republican. Presbyterian. Office: PO Box 360 Midland TX 79702

MARCUS, RICHARD S., blanket manufacturing company executive; b. Boston, Jan. 27, 1932; s. Maurice and Rose (Nettie) M.; m. Helene Marcus, Feb. 6, 1955 (div. 1975); m. Enid Marcus, Dec. 24, 1981; children—Stanton Craig, Leonard Seth, Michelle. B.S., NYU, 1954, postgrad. in bus. and law, 1955. Pres., Stanton Blanket Co., Bridgeport, Conn., 1955-64, Stanrich Mills, North Oxford, Mass., 1964-66, Am. Woolen Co., Miami, Fla., 1966—. Club: Miami Yacht. Lodge: Rotary. Avocation: sailing. Office: American Woolen Co PO Box 403007 Miami Beach FL 33140

MARCUS, STANLEY, art educator; b. N.Y.C., Nov. 17, 1926; s. Joseph S. and Jeanette (Brown) M.; m. Rebecca Seiff, Sept. 7, 1952 (div. Aug. 1984); children—Lynne E., Joel. B.A., NYU, 1949; M.A., Columbia U., 1970, Ed.D., 1972. Mem. faculty, chmn. art dept. Hawthorne Coll., 1974-75, U. Tex. Permian Basin, Odessa, 1977—; sculptor coordinator NYU, 1975-77. Author: David Smith: The Sculptor and His Work, 1983. Contbr. articles to profl. jours. One man shows include Lincoln Ctr., 1977. with U.S. Army, 1946-47. Home: 1475 Brittany Ln Apt 4 Odessa TX 79761 Office: Dept Art Univ Texas Permian Basin Odessa TX 79762

MARCUS, WALTER F., JR., state justice; b. 1927; B.A., Yale U.; J.D., Tulane U. Admitted to La. bar, 1955; now asso. justice Supreme Ct. La. Mem. ABA. Office: Supreme Ct La 301 Loyola Ave New Orleans LA 70112*

MAREK, ANNEMARIE, advertising and corporate communications executive; b. Austin, Tex., July 17, 1953; d. John Joseph and Lillian Lois (Hoyer) M. B.A. cum laude with honors in English, Georgetown U., 1975; M.A. in Creative Writing, U. Dallas, 1978; postgrad. Middlebury Coll., 1975. Communications specialist Southland Life Ins. Co., Dallas, 1977-78; pub. relations asst. Southwestern Life Ins. Co., Dallas, 1978-80, asst. v.p. corp. communications, 1980-84; dir. corp. communications Hall Fin. Group, Dallas, 1984-85; exec. v.p. mktg. Myers Group, Dallas, 1985—. Recipient Katherine Kraft medal Georgetown U., 1975; award of excellence Life Advertisers Assn., 1980. Mem. Pub. Relations Soc. Am., Dallas Advt. League, Dallas Bus. League, Life Advertisers Assn. (chmn. So. Roundtable 1984), Georgetown U. Alumni Assn. (bd. govs. 1986-89). Roman Catholic. Author: Preston Jones Chapbook, 1978. Office: PO Box 202573 Irving TX 75220

MAREK, VLADIMIR, ballet director, educator; b. Uzhorod, Czechoslovakia, Sept. 26, 1928; came to U.S., 1968; s. Jaroslav and Julia (Valkova) Sourek. Student Bus. Acad., Czechoslovakia, ballet schs., Czechoslovakia, 1945-47. Soloist Nat. Theater Ballet, Prague, Czechoslovakia, 1947-50, prin. dancer,

Bratislava, Czechoslovakia, 1950-69, ballet master, 1958-68; ballet tchr. Our Lady of Lake U., San Antonio, 1970-78; owner, tchr. V. Marek Ballet Acad., San Antonio, 1970—; founder, artistic dir. San Antonio Ballet, 1970—. Home: 800 Babcock Apt T-4 San Antonio TX 78201 Office: San Antonio Ballet 212 E Mulberry San Antonio TX 78212

MARES, MICHAEL ALLEN, ecologist, educator; b. Albuquerque, Mar. 11, 1945; s. Ernesto Gustavo and Rebecca Gabriela (Devine) M.; m. Lynn Ann Brusin, Aug. 27, 1966; children—Gabriel Andres, Daniel Alejandro. B.S. in Biology, U. N.Mex., 1967; M.S., Ft. Hays Kans. State U., 1969; Ph.D., U. Tex.-Austin, 1973. Adj. prof. U. Nacional de Cordoba, Argentina, 1971-72; adj. prof. U. Nacional de Tucuman, Argentina, 1972, vis. prof., 1974; from asst. to assoc. prof. U. Pitts., 1973-81; vis. scientist U. Ariz., Tucson, 1980-81; assoc. prof., curator mammals U. Okla., Norman, 1981-83, dir. Stovall Mus., 1983—, assoc. prof. zoology, 1983-85, prof., 1985—; NUS cons., Venezuela, 1980-81; cons. Argentine Nat. Sci. Found., Inst. Arid Zone Research, Mendoza, 1983; mem. Council Internat. Exchange of Scholars, Am. Republics Bd., Fulbright Commn., 1983—. NSF grantee, 1974-79, 82-84; Nat. Fulbright research fellow, 1976; Chicano Council on Higher Edn. research fellow, 1978; Ford Found. Minority Research fellow, 1980-81; Brazilian Nat. Acad. Sci. research award, 1975-78. Mem. AAAS, Am. Soc. Mammalogists, Am. Ecol. Soc., Interam. Assn. Advancement Sci., Am. Inst. Biol. Sci., Am. Soc. Naturalists, Soc. Study of Evolution, Southwestern Assn. Naturalists, Paleontol. Soc., Sigma Xi, Phi Kappa Phi, Beta Beta Beta. Contbr. articles to profl. jours. Home: 2632 Trenton Rd Norman OK 73069 Office: Stovall Mus U Okla Norman OK 73019

MARET, ELIZABETH GARDNER, sociology educator; b. Phila., Nov. 9, 1943; d. Raymond and Elizabeth (Clark) M.; m. Sam House, Jan. 1, 1977; 1 child, David Stanley. B.A., U. Tex., Austin, 1967, M.A., 1971, Ph.D., 1973. Asst. prof. Huston-Tillotson Coll., 1972-73, Tex. Tech U., 1973-76; assoc. prof. sociology Tex. A&M U., College Station, 1976—. Author: Women and the American Occupational Structure, 1978; Women's Career Patterns, 1983; contbr. articles to profl. jour. Mem. S.W. Sociol. Assn. (pres. 1982-83), Am. Sociol. Assn., N.Y. Acad. Scis., Tex. Council Family Relations, Internat. Platform Assn., Am. Simmental Assn. Democrat. Office: Dept Sociology Texas A&M Univ College Station TX 77843

MARGARETTEN, MICHAEL ELLIOT, pediatric optometrist; b. Bklyn., May 27, 1937; s. Elias Joseph and Frances Pearl (Kuhn) M.; m. Ellen Pliner Lapin, June 6, 1961; children—Mark, Jeffrey. Student U. Rochester, 1959; B.S., Pa. Coll. Optometry, 1960, O.D., 1961. Resident developmental vision Yale U., Gesell Inst. Child Devel., 1962; pvt. practice pediatric optometry, N.Y.C., 1961-71, North Miami Beach, Fla., 1971—; adj. prof. Pa. Coll. Optometry, 1978—, preceptor, 1978—; adj. prof. So. Coll. Optometry, Pacific U.; instr. Miami Dade Community Coll., 1971-75; Fla. state dir. Coll. Optometrists in Vision Devel., 1979—; bd. dirs. Optometric Center S. Fla., 1975—; Fla. state assoc. dir. Optometric Extension Program, 1973-77; mem. profl. adv. bd. Banyan Sch., Clin. Facility for Children with Learning Disabilities, Hollywood, Fla., 1980—; preceptor Optometric Extension Program Found., Inc., 1978—. Served with USCG, 1961-69. Recipient State of Fla., Dade County Sch. award, 1974; Dade County Pub. Sch. Bd. Disting. award, 1975; Dade County Pub. Sch. Disting. award, 1975, 76, 77; Dade County Optometric Assn. Disting. award 1975, Coll. Optometrists in Vision Devel. Disting. award, 1976. Diplomate Nat. Bd. Examiners in Optometry. Fellow Am. Acad. Optometry, Coll. Optometrists in Vision Devel., Nat. Soc. Optometrists in Vision Devel., N.Y. Acad. Optometry; mem. Am. Pub. Health Assn., Am. Health Plan Referring Com., Am. Optometric Assn., Optometric Extension Program Found., Inc. (clin. assoc.), Broader Opportunities for Learning Disabilities, So. Council Optometrists, N.Y. Acad. Scis., Fla. Optometric Assn. (trustee). Home: 17620 NE 3d Ct North Miami Beach FL 33162 Office: 951 NE 167th St North Miami Beach FL 33162

MARGER, EDWIN, lawyer; b. N.Y.C., Mar. 18, 1928; s. William and Fannie (Cohen) M.; m. Kaye Sanderson, Oct. 1, 1951; children—Shari Ann, Diane Elaine, Sandy Ben; m. 2d, L. Suzanne Smyth, July 5, 1968; 1 son, George Phinney. B.A., U. Miami, 1951, J.D. 1953. Bar: Fla. 1953, Ga. 1971, D.C. 1978. Sole practice, Miami Beach, Fla., 1953-67, Atlanta, 1971—; spl. asst. atty. gen. Fla., 1960-61; of counsel Richard Burns, Miami, 1967—. Tchr. Nat. Inst. Trial Advocacy. Mem. Miami Beach Social Service Commn., 1957; chmn. Fulton County Aviation Adv. Com., 1980—; trustee Forensic Sci. Found., 1984—; lt. col., a.d.c. Gov. Ga., 1971-74, 80—; col., a.d.c. Gov. La., 1977—. Served with USAAF, 1946-47. Fellow Am. Acad. Forensic Scis. (chmn. jurisprudence sect. 1977-78, sec. 1976-77, exec. com. 1983—); mem. ABA, Fla. Bar (aerospace com. 1971—, bd. govs. 1983—), State Bar Ga. (chmn. sect. environ. law 1974-75, aviation law sect. 1978), Ga. Trial Lawyers Assn., Nat. Assn. Criminal Def. Lawyers, Ga. Assn. Criminal Def. Lawyers, Assn. Trial Lawyers Am., Am. Judicature Soc., Am. Arbitration Assn. (comml. panel 1978—), Inter-Am. Bar Assn. (sr.), World Assn. Lawyers (founding), Advocates Club, Lawyer-Pilots Bar Assn. (founding; v.p. 1959-62), VFW. Lodge: Kiwanis (Atlanta). Contbr. articles to legal jours. Office: 6666 Powers Ferry Rd Atlanta GA 30339

MARGIANO, RAYMOND JOSEPH, business consultant, business executive; b. Derby, Conn., May 7, 1941; s. Raymond Joseph and Neda Margiano; B.B.A., U. New Haven, 1969; M.S., Rensselaer Poly. Inst., 1971; children—Kerrin, Raina. Dir. MIS, mgr. indsl. engring., mgmt. analyst Sikorsky Aircraft, Stratford, Conn., 1969-76; corp. bus. analyst Sybron, Rochester, N.Y., 1976-79; dir. mgmt. info. systems and adminstrn. Bostitch, East Greenwich, R.I., 1979-80, gen. mgr. Bostitch-Auto-Soler, Atlanta, 1980-83; pres. RJM & Assocs., bus. cons., 1983—, S.E. Mgmt. Services div. Martin Wright & Assocs., 1983—, Shoe Care Ctrs. Am., Inc., nat. instant shoe repair chair; lectr. bur. computer sci., indsl. engring. U. New Haven, 1972-76. Served with USN, 1959-63. Mem. Data Processing Mgmt. Assn., Assn. Prodn. and Inventory Control Systems. Club: Rotary. Home: 1114 Riverbend Club Dr Atlanta GA 30339 Office: PO Box 723116 Atlanta Ga 30339

MARGOLIS, GWEN LIEDMAN (MRS. ALLAN B. MARGOLIS), state legislator, realtor, appraiser, developer; b. Phila., Oct. 4, 1934; d. Joseph and Rose (Weiss) Liedman; student Temple U., 1951-54; spl. course U. Tampa; A.A. (hon.) Miami-Dade Community Coll., 1981; m. Allan Block Margolis, Sept. 12, 1953; children—Edward, Ira, Karen, Robin. Owner, broker Gwen Margolis Real Estate, North Miami Beach, Fla., 1965—; ptnr. 16990 Corp.; dir. Lincoln Savs. & Loan Assn.; mem. Fla. Ho. of Reps., 1974-80, Fla. Senate, 1980—. mem. human relations bd., vice chmn. bd. adjustments City of North Miami Beach; chmn. Dade County Legis. Del., 1978-79. Bd. dirs. Keystone Point Homeowners Assn., Dade County council Girl Scouts; adv. bd. Big Sisters Dade County. Recipient Spirit of Life Humanitarian City of Hope, 1974, 79; Legis. Friend of Arts award Fla. Gov., 1982; Numerous other awards from orgns. including Fla. Edn. Assn., Bus. and Profl. Women's Assn., Women in Communications; Margolis Cancer Research Fellowship established in her honor by City of Hope. Mem. Miami Bd. Realtors, Nat. Assn. Real Estate Bds., North Miami Beach C. of C. (Woman of Yr. award, dir.), S. Fla. Planning and Zoning Assn., Women's Council Realtors, Fla. Women's Polit. Caucus (award) North Dade Women's Polit. Caucus (former chairperson), LWV, Fla. Anti-Defamation League (dir., past v.p.). Home: 19355 Turnberry Way Apt 2J North Miami FL 33180 Office: 13899 Biscayne Blvd North Miami Beach FL 33181

MARIEL, photographer, former fabrication company executive; b. Pasadena, Calif., Aug. 5, 1938; d. Oscar Branche and Mary Lincoln (Hicks) Jackson; adopted dau. William Nathan Turner; m. Donald E. Coombes, June 13, 1957 (div. June 1972); children—William Cullen, Anna Maria, Joel Howard; 1 son by previous marriage, Scott Craig Goodwin. Co-incorporator, Mineral Harvestors Inc., Salem, Oreg., 1966-71, Ariz. Custom Mfg. Inc., Phoenix, 1971-81, bus. mgr., pres., 1972-81; pres. Ariz. Custom Steel, Phoenix, 1976-81, Eagle Erectors, Phoenix, 1979-81; now with Lazarus Enterprises; former co-owner WCS Constrn., Inc. Asst. dist. coordinator Oreg. Republican Party, 1964. Mem. Nat. Assn. Women Bus. Owners, Nat. Assn. Female Execs. Ariz. Network Profl. Women, Women Emerging, Internat. Platform Assn., Tolsum Farm Homeowners Assn., Ariz. Steel Fabricators Assn. (past pres.). Republican. Mem. Reorganized Ch. Jesus Christ of Latter-day Saints. Clubs: Intertel, Mensa.

MARINE, IRA WENDELL, hydrogeologist, researcher; b. Washington, Apr. 15, 1927; s. Ira M. and Mattie M. (McCready) M.; m. Helen R. Landsman, June 20, 1953; children—Karen, Andrew, Kenneth, Linda. B.A., St. John's Coll., Annapolis, Md., 1949; student Johns Hopkins U., 1949-51; Ph.D., U. Utah, 1960. Geologist, hydrologist U.S. Geol. Survey, Salisbury, Md., Newark, Del., 1951-54, Salt Lake City, 1954-60, Norman, Okla., 1960-61, Aiken, S.C., 1961-71, E.I. DuPont de Nemours & Co., Aiken, 1971—. Editor proceedings of meeting workshop on seismic performance of underground facilities, 1982. Contbr. articles to profl. jours. Served with USN, 1945-46. Recipient cert. of appreciation AEC, 1969. Fellow Geol. Soc. Am.; mem. Am. Geophys. Union, Am. Assn. Petroleum Geologists, Nat. Water Well Assn. Home: 1002 Hitchcock Dr Aiken SC 29801 Office: E I DuPont de Nemours & Co Savannah River Lab Aiken SC 29808

MARINO, DANIEL CONSTANTINE, football player; b. Pitts., Sept. 15, 1961. B.S., U. Pitts., 1983. Football player Miami Dolphins, 1983—. Recipient NFL Most Valuable Player award, 1984-85; elected to Pro Bowl, 1984, 85. Address: Miami Dolphins 3550 Biscayne Blvd Miami FL 33157*

MARIX, YVELYNE DE MARCELLUS, travel executive, mayor; b. Dorking, Surrey, Eng., July 13, 1925; came to U.S. 1925; d. Henri and Rose (Gordon Clark) de Marcellus; m. Nigel T. Marix, Apr. 7, 1956. B.A. in Polit. Sci., UCLA, 1945. Mng. dir. Embassy Travel Bur., Palm Beach, Fla., 1954-83; mem. council, Palm Beach, Fla., 1970-77, pres., council, 1978-79, mayor, Town of Palm Beach, 1983—. Republican. Roman Catholic. Home: 1570 N Ocean Blvd Palm Beach FL 33480 Office: Embassy Travel Bur 240 S County Rd Palm Beach FL 33480

MARK, JONATHAN GREENFIELD, political science educator, writer; b. N.Y.C., Dec. 22, 1948; s. Sidney Carl and Patricia (Greenfield) M.; B.A., U. Tex., Austin, 1971; M.A., U. Pa., 1976; Ph.D., U. Okla., 1981. Vice-pres., Stas. KAKC-KBEZ, Tulsa, 1976-80; instr. polit. sci. Tulsa Jr. Coll., 1981-84; vis. lectr. polit sci. U. Tulsa, 1977; vis. lectr. mass communications USAF Acad., 1977. Served with USAF, 1971-75, USAFR, 1975—. Decorated Meritorious Service medal, Air Force Commendation medal; recipient grad. research prize U. Okla., 1981. Mem. Res. Officers U.S., Air Force Assn. Contbr. numerous articles to profl. jours., newspapers and mags. Home and office: PO Box 3567 Tulsa OK 74101

MARKER, ROBERT SIDNEY, management consultant; b. Nashville, July 27, 1922; s. Forest Milton and Lassie W. M.; m. Bette Davis, Oct. 27, 1943; children—Christopher B., Andrew M. B.A., Emory U., 1947. Chmn., chief exec. officer McCann-Erickson, Inc., N.Y.C., 1961-74; chmn. exec. com. Needham, Harper & Steers, Inc., N.Y.C., 1975-80; pres. Robert S. Marker, Inc., N.Y.C., 1981—. N.Y. Bd. Trade. Am. Assn. Advt. Agys (past dir., chmn. Mich. and N.Y. councils), Nat. Outdoor Advt. Bur. (past dir.), Detroit Adcraft Club (past dir.). Home: 101-F Turtle Creek E Tequesta FL 33469 Office: 210 Jupiter Lakes Blvd Jupiter FL 33458

MARKERT, JOHN PAUL, JR., management consultant, researcher; b. Lancaster, Pa., Nov. 4, 1945; s. John Paul Sr. and Dorothy Mae (Yeager) M.; m. Gail Jenkins, Oct. 4, 1980. B.A. in Sociology, U. South Fla., 1972, M.A. in Sociology, 1975, M.A. in English, 1978; Ph.D. in Sociology, Vanderbilt U., 1984. Exec. dir. Alternative Human Services, St. Petersburg, Fla., 1969-73; dir. social services Medfield Med. Ctr., Largo, Fla., 1974-80; lectr. sociology Vanderbilt U., Nashville, 1985—; pres. The Markert Group, Nashville, 1985—. Contbr. articles to profl. jours. Bd. dirs. Hist. Nashville, Inc., 1985—. Served with USN, 1963-66. Recipient Research award NSF, 1984. Mem. Am. Sociol. Assn., Am. Mktg. Assn., So. Sociol. Soc., So. Mgmt. Assn., Young Assocs. Avocations: horseback riding; antique restoration; writing; painting. Office: 2119 Elliott Ave Nashville TN 37204

MARKEY, L. PAUL, chiropractor, educator; b. Ft. Wayne, Ind., Sept. 4, 1950; s. Calvin and Jean (Lotus) M.; m. Vickie Rowe, Oct. 23, 1982. Student Ind. U., 1969-73; D.C., Palmer Coll. Chiropractic, 1976; postgrad. Nat. Coll. Chiropractic, 1977—. Pvt. practice chiropractic, Atlanta, 1977—; tchr. Cox/Chiro-manis Technique, 1977—; mem. continuing edn. faculty Palmer Coll. Chiropractic, 1982—; cons., OSHA, 1981, labor studies program Ga. State U., 1981, Arden Zinn Health Studios, 1979. Mem. Palmer Coll. Chiropractic Alumni Assn. Ga. (past v.p.), Ga. Chiropractic Assn. (past chmn. com. chiropractic orthopedics, past sec. ins. peer rev. com.), Am. Chiropractic Assn. (Panel mem. council technique, cons. commn. indsl. relations), Internat. Acad. Chiropractic. Home: 8220 Habersham Waters Rd Dunwoody GA 30338 Office: 101 Marietta Tower Suite 3400 Atlanta GA 30305

MARKHAM, CHARLES BUCHANAN, lawyer; b. Durham, N.C., Sept. 15, 1926; s. Charles Blackwell and Sadie Helen (Hackney) M. A.B., Duke U., 1945; student U. N.C., 1945-46; LL.B., George Washington U., 1951. Bar: D.C. 1951, U.S. Ct. Appeals for D.C. 1955, N.Y. 1961, N.C. 1980, U.S. Ct. Appeals for 2d circuit 1961, U.S. Supreme Ct. 1964. Reporter Durham Sun, 1945; asst. state editor, editorial writer Charlotte (N.C.) News, 1947-48; dir. publicity and research Young Democratic Clubs Am., Washington, 1948-49, exec. sec., 1949-50; polit. analyst Democratic Senatorial Campaign Com., 1950-51; spl. atty. IRS, Washington, 1952-60; assoc. firm Battle, Fowler, Stokes & Kheel, N.Y.C., 1960-65; dir. research EEOC, Washington, 1965-68; dep. asst. sec. HUD, 1969-72; asst. dean Law Sch., Rutgers U.-Newark, 1974-76; assoc. prof. law N.C. Central U., Durham, 1976-81, prof., 1981-83; ptnr. Markham and Wickham, Durham, 1984—; mayor City of Durham, 1981-85. Trustee Historic Preservation Soc. Durham, 1982—. Mem. Greater Durham C. of C. (dir. 1982-86), ABA, Durham County Bar Assn., Phi Beta Kappa. Republican. Episcopalian. Clubs: Chapel Hill Country, Rotary. Editor: Jobs, Men and Machines: The Problems of Automation, 1964. Home: 204 N Dillard St Durham NC 27701 Office: 300 First Union Nat Bank Bldg Durham NC 27701 also 300 First Union Nat Bank Bldg Durham NC 27701

MARKIDES, KYRIAKOS SOCRATES, gerontology educator; b. Nicosia, Cyprus, Mar. 21, 1948, came to U.S., 1968; s. Socrates and Persoulla Markides; m. Evelyn A. Stanton, Dec. 18, 1971; 1 son, Michel. B.A., Bowling Green State U., 1972; M.A., La. State U., 1973, Ph.D., 1976. Asst. prof. U. Tex. Health Sci. Ctr., San Antonio, 1976-82; assoc. prof. U. Tex. Med. Br., Galveston, 1982—. Author: (with others) Older Mexican Americans, 1983; Ethnicity and Aging: A Bibliography, 1984; editorial bd. The Gerontologist Jour., 1984—. Nat. Inst. Aging research grantee, 1980—; Hogg Found. research grantee, 1984—. Fellow Gerontol. Soc. Am.; mem. Am. Sociol. Assn., Population Assn. Am. Office: University of Texas Medical Branch Galveston TX 77550

MARKL, EDWARD MARTIN, III, investment broker; b. Kansas City, Kans., Dec. 28, 1954; s. Edward Martin, Jr. and Pamela Sue (Newkirk) M. Student Tex. Christian U., 1976, Gen. Motors Inst., 1975. With Markl Motors Inc., Overland Park, Kans., 1971—, sales mgr., 1973-76, exec. v.p., gen. mgr., 1976—; dir. Wrenn Ins. Agy.; mem. Rolls Royce Regional Dealer Council, 1978-80; chmn. bd. Markl Enterprises Inc.; pres. Kelly-Markl Builders; chmn. bd. Bonanza of Tex. Dir. natural sci. soc. Kansas City Mus. Sci. and History, Mo. Mem. Nat. Assn. Home Builders, Nat. Assn. Frame Builders, Mercedes-Benz Star Sales Guild, Tex. Christian U. alumni Assn., Jr. League Kansas City (Kans.), Am. Trap Assn., Bacchus Found., Ducks Unltd. (state com.), Kappa Sigma. Clubs: Prospectors Breakfast (past pres.), Safari Internat., Shady Oaks Country. Home: 5525 Collinwood Fort Worth TX 76107 Office: PO Box 330242 Fort Worth TX 76162

MARKLE, SPENCER GRANVILLE, lawyer; b. Manhassett, N.Y., Jan. 14, 1955; s. James Peirce and Elizabeth F. (Longmore) M.; m. Theresa Eileen Allnock, May 26, 1979; 1 child, Jeremy Granville. Student Westminster Coll., New Wilmington, Pa., 1973-74; B.S., Duquesne U., 1978; J.D., U. Pitts., 1981. Asst. to gen. counsel 84 Lumber Co., Eighty Four, Pa., 1979-80; assoc. Mills, Shirley, McMicken & Eckel, Galveston, Tex., 1981-83, Dunn, Kacal, Adams, Livingston, Pappas & Law, Houston, 1983—. Mem. ABA, State Bar Tex., Houston Bar Assn., Tex. Assn. Def. Counsel, Beta Alpha Phi, Delta Theta Phi, Sigma Phi Epsilon. Republican. Presbyterian. Home: 462 Eastcape Ct Webster TX 77598 Office: Dunn Kacal Adams Livingston Pappas & Law 2600 America Tower Houston TX 77019

MARKLEY, MARVIN EUGENE, well log analyst; b. Springfield, Ohio, Nov. 20, 1946; s. Calvin Cook and Martha Alice (Demory) M. B.S. in Engring., U.S. Mil. Acad., 1968; M.A. in Econs., U. Okla., 1976. Field engr. Schlumberger Well Services, Laredo, Tex., 1977-81, sales engr., Natchez, Miss., 1981-84, log analyst, Shreveport, La., 1984—. Served to capt. U.S. Army, 1968-75. Mem. Soc. Petroleum Engrs., Am. Assn. Petroleum Geologists, Soc. Profl. Well Log Analysts, Natchez Geol. Soc. (past pres., founder). Republican. Presbyterian. Avocations: racquetball; slide trombone. Office: Schlumberger Well Services 1600 Beck Bldg Shreveport LA 71101

MARKOFF, ALAN STUART, dentist; b. Peekskill, N.Y., May 24, 1934; s. Benjamin Abraham and Rose (Goldfein) M.; m. Doris Pines, Aug. 24, 1958 (div. June 1972); children—Robert Samuel, Daniel Pines, Andrew Saul. B.A., Duke U., 1956; D.D.S., N.Y.U. Coll. Dentistry, 1961. Resident, VA Hosp., Houston, 1961-62; practice dentistry Houston, 1963—. Fellow Am. Acad. Gen. Dentistry; mem. Houston Acad. Gen. Dentistry (pres. 1975-76), Tex. Acad. Dental Practice Adminstrn. (bd. dirs. 1972-85, pres. 1978-79), Am. Acad. Dental Practice Adminstrn. (chmn. council sci. sessions 1982, 86), Internat. Acad. Oral Implantology, Am. Acad. Oral Implantology, Houston Dist. Dental Soc. (dir. dental asst. tng. program 1972-74), ADA, Tex. Dental Assn., Houston Symphony Soc., Mus. Fine Arts, Houston Zool. Soc., Houston Dental Study Club (pres. 1973). Avocations: jogging; tennis; reading. Home: 306 Bunker Hill Rd Houston TX 77024 Office: 4543 Post Oak Pl Houston TX 77027

MARKOVITS, ANDREW STEVEN, ophthalmologist, oculoplastic surgeon, naval officer; b. Port Arthur, Tex., Nov. 15, 1929; s. Joseph Arpad and Julia Anna (Diosy) M.; m. Martha Ann Mangan, June 3, 1953 (div. 1970); children—Martha, Amelia, Andrew, Clare; m. Michael Maynard Young, Aug. 8, 1975; children—Elizabeth, Dianya, Lara. A.B., U. Mo., B.S. in Medicine; M.D., St. Louis U. Diplomate Am. Bd. Ophthalmology. Commd. lt. (j.g.) U.S. Navy, 1953, advanced through grades to capt., 1984; intern U.S. Naval Hosp., San Diego, 1953-54; resident dept. ophthalmology U. Calif., San Francisco, 1967-70, Heed fellow in ophthalmology, 1970-71; pres. Cabrillo Eye Med. Clinic, Soquel, Calif., 1971-79; head dept. ophthalmology U.S. Naval Hosp., Pensacola, Fla., 1979-84; chief div. ophthalmology Naval Aerospace Med. Inst., Pensacola, 1984—; practice medicine specializing in consultive oculoplastic and lacrimal surgery, Pensacola, 1982. Contbr. articles to profl. jours. Mem. AMA, Am. Soc. Ophthalmic Plastic and Reconstructive Surgery, Aerospace Med. Assn., Assn. Mil. Surgeons U.S., Fla. Med. Assn., W. Fla. Ophthalmology Soc., Escambia County Med. Assn., Phi Beta Kappa, Phi Eta Sigma. Avocations: flying; scuba skiing; motorcycling. Home: 6809 Kitty Hawk Dr Pensacola FL 32508 Office: Naval Aerospace Med Inst NAS Pensacola FL 32508

MARKS, CHARLES PRESTON, software designer; b. Inglewood, Calif., May 7, 1941; s. George Harold and Dorothy Jane (Preston) M.; m. Mary Jo Evans, Jan. 18, 1964; children—Kyle, Karen. B.S. in Math., Calif. State Poly. Coll., 1963; postgrad. U. Ala.-Huntsville, 1976-81. Sr. sci. programmer Heliodyne Corp., San Bernardino, Calif., 1964-66; sr. scientist Booz-Allen Applied Research, Inc., Los Angeles, 1966-68; mem. tech. staff Gen. Research Corp., Santa Barbara, Calif., 1968-72; sr. systems analyst Jet Propulsion Labs., Pasadena, 1973-74; scientist III, Sci. Applications, Inc., Huntsville, Ala., 1974-76; mgr. computation scis. and services dept. Gen. Research Corp., Huntsville, 1976—. Calif. State scholar, 1959. Mem. Decus, Assn. Computing Machinery, IEEE. Republican. Lutheran. Home: 111 Benson Blvd Madison AL 35758 Office: 307 Wynn Dr Huntsville AL 35805

MARKS, JOHN COURTNEY, health systems engineer; b. Harrisburg, Pa., Mar. 1, 1924; s. Courtney B. and Muriel O. (Michael) M.; B.S. in Econs., Villanova U., 1950; B.S. in Mgmt. Engring., U. Scranton, 1953; m. Henrietta Horton, Sept. 25, 1975; children—Barbara, Lynn, Michael, Paul, Debbie, Courtney. Asst. chief engr. Air Pollution Control Dist., Louisville, Ky., 1953-56; chief engr. Louisville Med. Center, 1956-63; research engr. Am. Air Filter Co., Inc., Louisville, 1963-67; research engr. Kentec Labs., Louisville, 1967-69; systems engr. Humana, Inc., Louisville, 1969-73; systems engring. cons. Sts. Mary and Elizabeth Hosp., Louisville, 1974-76; adminstr. Shalomwald Hosp., LaGrange, Ky., 1976-77; mgr. support systems Ky. Health Systems Agy., Louisville, 1974-79; mgmt. engr. Bowling Green (Ky.) Med. Center, 1979; health planning cons. Greenview Hosp., Bowling Green; adminstr. Charterton Hosp., La Grange; now systems engr. Med. Ctr. at Bowling Green; instr. systems design Bellarmine Coll., Louisville, 1975; cons. USPHS, Louisville, 1955, Battelle Meml. Inst., Louisville, 1953-55. Mem. Bd. Appeals Jefferson County Bldg. Dept., Louisville, 1957-63, Met. Planning Council, Louisville, 1958. Served with U.S. Army, 1942-44. Recipient Service award Air Pollution Control Assn., 1960. Mem. Am. Soc. Engring. Edn., Nat. Assn. of Power Engrs. (pres. 1958-59), Louisville Engring. and Sci. Council (pres. 1960-61), Hosp. Mgmt. Systems Soc., Am. Assn. for Comprehensive Health Planning, Am. Meteorol. Soc. Contbr. articles on environ. health to profl. jours.; editor Hosp. Environ. Service Guide Humana, Inc., 1972, Hosp. Disaster Program Manuals, 1971-72. Home: 1730 O'Shea 1 Bowling Green KY 42101

MARKS, JUSTIN DAVIS, JR., clergyman, guidance counselor; b. Cynthiana, Ky., Oct. 17, 1940; s. Justin Davis and Mary Preston (Butler) M.; m. Lois Johnson, Sept. 9, 1965; children—Justine Lovell, Justin Davis III. Student Sch. Bible Prophecy, Atlanta, 1963; A.B., Am. Baptist Coll., 1965; M.Div., Lexington Theol. Sem., 1977; D.Th., Bernadean U., Los Angeles, 1979. Ordained to ministry Nat. Bapt. Conv. U.S.A., 1967. Pastor, Cadiz 2d Bapt. Ch., Ky., 1967-72, 1st Bapt. Ch., Nicholasville, Ky., 1973-75, Fellowship Bapt. Ch., Evansville, Ind., 1976—; guidance counselor Earle C. Clements Jr. Community Coll., Morganfield, Ky., 1978—; dean Christian Leadership Conf., 1974-75; instr. barbering West Ky. Area Vocat. Tech. Sch., 1966-72; mission State Bapt. Con., 1963. Sr. patrol leader Blue Grass council Boy Scouts Am., Lexington, Ky. Mem. Jessamine County Ministers Assn. Democrat. Lodges: Masons. Home: 421 S Evans St Evansville IN 47713 Office: Earle C Clements Job Corps Ctr Morganfield KY 42437

MARKS, MEYER BENJAMIN, pediatric allergist; b. Chgo., Feb. 16, 1907; s. Simon and Rose (Block) M.; B.S., U. Ill., 1929, M.D., 1933, M.S., 1934; m. Golda A. Nathan, Sept. 27, 1932; children—Linda, Stephen. Diplomate in pediatric allergy Am. Bd. Pediatrics, Am. Bd. Allergy and Immunology. Intern, Cook County Hosp., 1934-35, resident, 1935-36; practice medicine specializing in pediatrics, 1937-57, pediatric allergy and gen. allergy, 1957—; cons. pediatric allergist Mt. Sinai Med. Center, Miami Beach, chief dept. pediatrics, 1950-59; dir. pediatric allergy clinic Jackson Meml. Hosp., 1955-80, chief div. pediatric allergy, 1955-80; chief med. officer Asthmatic Children's Found. Residential Treatment Center of Fla., North Miami Beach, 1970-80; clin. prof. pediatrics, div. allergy and immunology U. Miami Sch. Medicine. Hon. pres. med. div., Southeastern div. Am. Friends Hebrew U. Pres. Asso. Convalescent Homes and Hosp. for Asthmatic Children, 1971; v.p., sec. Asthmatic Children's Found. of Fla., 1978—; Bela Schick Meml. lectr., Paris, France, 1974; guest essayist Am. Assn. Orthodontists, Washington, 1979; lectr. Fellow Am. Acad. Pediatrics (silver award 1975, bronze award 1977, Jerome Glaser Disting. Service award 1985), Am. Coll. Allergists (award of merit 1977, Fellow Disting. award 1979), Am. Acad. Allergy; mem. AMA (cert. of merit award 1966), Fla., Dade County med. assns., Fla., Miami (pres. 1954-55) pediatric socs., Fla. Allergy Soc. (pres. 1970), Sigma Xi. Jewish. Contbr. articles to med. books and jours. Established Golda and Meyer Marks Cobra art collection Ft. Lauderdale Mus. Arts, 1979, contemporary art collection Mayo Clinic, Rochester, Minn., 1981. Home: 105 E San Marino Dr Miami Beach FL 33139 Office: 333 Arthur Godfrey Rd Miami Beach FL 33140

MARKS, RICHARD SAMUEL, lawyer, real estate development executive; b. Milw., May 8, 1937; s. Lewis and Ruth Francis (Brindis) M.; m. Julia F. Newman, Aug. 7, 1962; children—Joseph, Richard, Steven. B.A., U. Wis.-Madison, 1960, D.Jud.Sci., 1963. Bar: Wis. 1963. Cert. property mgr. Founder, prin. Hillmark Corp., Madison, Wis., 1960—, chief exec. officer, 1979—, chmn. bd., 1979—. Trustee State Wis. Bond Bd., Madison, 1975-76; chmn. State Wis. Investment Bd., Madison, 1976-78; chmn. State Wis. Small Cities Israel Bonds., Madison, 1975-76; mem. bd. dir. Metro YMCA, Madison, 1974-76; bd. dirs. Madison Jewish Fedn., 1974-77; bd. dirs. Atlanta Civic Opera Assn., 1983, 20th Century Art Assn. of High Mus., 1983. Mem. Young Pres.'s Orgn. Clubs: Masons, Shriners, Elks. Home: 6040 Winterthur Dr Atlanta GA 30328 Office: 1820 The Exchange #550 Atlanta GA 30339

MARKS, ROBERTA BARBARA, artist, educator; b. Savannah, Ga., 1936; d. Philip W. and Eleanore (Margolis) Dilner; m. Lawrence M. Marks; children—Jeffery Allen, Steven Craig. B.F.A., U. Miami, Coral Gables, Fla., 1980; M.F.A., U.S. Fla., 1981. Instr., Lectr. of ceramics, vis. artist to numerous art schs., including U. S. Fla., Tampa, Chgo. Art Inst., Valparaiso U., Ind., Rochester Inst. Tech. Am. Sch. of Crafts, N.Y., Galerie de Koull, Murten, Switzerland, Santa Fe Community Coll., Gainesville, Brookfield Craft Ctr., Conn., Nat. Council on Edn. for Ceramic Arts; juror Riverside Avondale

Preservation Art Festival, Jacksonville, Fla., 1981, Ybor Square Art Festival, Tampa, 1980, Miami Lakes Art Festival, Fla., 1975. One woman shows include Brevard Community Coll., Melbourne, Fla., 1982, Cocoa, Fla., 1982, Coventry Galleries, Ltd., Tampa, 1983, Barbara Gillman Gallery, Miami, 1984, Tennessee Williams Fine Arts Ctr., Key West, 1985, Garth Clark Gallery, N.Y.C., 1985, Fred Gros Gallery, Key West, 1985, Key West Art and Historical Soc. East Martello Mus. and Gallery, 1985, many others; exhibited in group shows at Netsky Gallery, Miami, 1982, The Craftsman's Gallery, Scarsdale, N.Y., 1982, Garth Clark Gallery, Los Angeles, 1983, Nelson-Atkins Mus. Art, Kansas City, Mo., 1983, Am. Craft Mus., N.Y.C., 1984, N. Miami Mus. and Art Ctr., 1985, Joanne Lyon Gallery, Aspen, Colo., 1984, Key West Art and Hist. Soc. East Martello Mus. and Gallery, 1985, Garth Clark Gallery, N.Y.C. and Los Angeles, 1985, many others; represented in permanent collections Smithsonian Instn., Renwick Gallery, Rochester Inst. Tech. Fine Arts Dept., U. Utah Mus., U. South Fla. Fine Arts Dept., Galerie du Manoir, La Chaux-de-Fonds, Switzerland, Valencia Community Coll., Okum Gallery, others. Recipient numerous awards. Mem. Am. Craft Council, Fla. Craftsmen, Nat. Council on Edn. for Ceramic Arts, World Craft Council, Artists Equity Assn.

MARKUM, ROY LEE, advertising executive; b. Seattle, Sept. 26, 1944; s. Leroy Cleveland and Leatha Odell (Cunningham) M.; m. Kathleen June Patterson, Jan. 13, 1966 (div. Aug. 1970); 1 dau., June Kathleen; m. Carolyn Kay Fuquay, July 8, 1972; 1 son, Cleveland Mathew. B.B.A., U. Tex., 1969. Account exec. Glenn Advt. (now Bozell & Jacobs SW), 1969-70; head Dallas office Phillips Agy., 1970-71; dist. sales mgr. Offshore mag., 1971-76; owner AdCraft, Houston, 1977—. Mem. Bus. Profl. Advt. Assn. Republican. Presbyterian. Clubs: Fort Bend Country; Houstonian; Balboa Bay (Newport, Calif.). Contbr. articles to profl. jours. Office: 4740 Ingersoll St Suite 103 Houston TX 77027

MARKUN, FRANK O., food services executive; b. Des Moines, Oct. 22, 1947; s. Frank Oliver and Grace Ellen (Marshall) M.; m. Milagros Macuja, Dec. 29, 1971; children—Michael Allen, Jeffrey Patrick. B.S., Iowa State U., 1969; M.B.A., Eastern Mich. U., 1974. Registered dietitian. Dietitian II, South Quadrangle, U. Mich., Ann Arbor, 1969-71, food service supr. II Bursley Hall, 1971-77, food service mgr. II, Residential Coll., 1977-80, West Quadrangle Complex, 1980-81; dir. food services Cabell Huntington Hosp. (W.Va.), 1981—. Contbr. articles to profl. jours. Recipient various prizes for recipes; Statler Found. scholar, 1965; Mem. Am. Dietetic Assn., W.Va. Dietetic Assn. (pres. 1984-85; Outstanding W.Va. dietitian 1983-84), W.Va.-Ohio-Ky. Dist. Dietetic Assn. (chmn. council on practice 1981, pres. 1982-83, chmn. nominating com. 1984-85), Am. Soc. Hosp. Food Service Adminstrs. (accomplished health care foodservice adminstr., pres. W.Va. chpt. 1985-86). Republican. Roman Catholic. Home: 54 Twin View Ln Rural Route 4 Huntington WV 25704 Office: Cabell Huntington Hosp 1340 Hal Greer Blvd Huntington WV 25701

MARKUSSEN, JOHANNES OLAV TORNOE, marine consultant; b. Ruslinga, Fyn, Denmark, June 14, 1913; came to U.S., 1941, naturalized, 1948; s. Frederik Laurits Peter Tornoe and Dagmar D. (Hansen) M. Radio operator's cert., mate's cert., ship's master cert. Svenborg Nautical Coll. Served on sailing vessels, 1926-31; seaman in steamship, also diesel tanker, 1931-33; 2d mate Danish Mcht. Marine, 1939-41; chief mate Allied Mcht. Marine, 1941-42, capt., 1942-49; compass adjuster, marine surveyor, 1949-56; dockmaster, service mgr. Huckins Yacht Corp., Jacksonville, Fla., 1956-62; designer and builder marine, Ft. George, Fla., 1962-65; yacht broker, compass adjuster, Jacksonville, Fla., 1966-78, marine surveyor and cons., Jacksonville, 1976—. Chmn. transp., dial-a-ride service, past pres. Beaches Council on Aging. Served to lt. capt. Royal Danish Navy, 1936-39. Mem. U.S. Power Squadron (comdr. Jacksonville br. 1955-56, Fla. state staff capt. 1956-57), U.S. Coast Guard Aux. (past flotilla comdr.), Am. Amateur Radio League, Beaches Amateur Radio Soc. Democrat. Lutheran. Club: Kiwanis. Home and Office: 4669 Roosevelt Blvd Jacksonville FL 32210

MARKWELL, DICK R(OBERT), chemist; b. Muskogee, Okla., Feb. 20, 1925; s. Alex J. and May (Albright) M.; B.S., Wichita State U., 1948, M.S., 1950; Ph.D., U. Wis., 1956; m. Virginia Ann Gass, Aug. 28, 1949; children—Steven R., Scot L., Eric R., Cheryl F. Commd. 2d lt. U.S. Army, 1951, ret. lt. col., 1967, with Office Chief Research and Devel.; asso. prof. chemistry San Antonio Coll., 1967-74; chemist Corpus Christi Dept. Health, 1975-77; supr. chemistry sect. lab. div. San Antonio Met. Health Dist., 1977—. Served with USMC, 1942-45. Mem. Am. Chem. Soc., Sigma Xi. Home: 1406 Haskin Dr San Antonio TX 78209

MARLAR, JOHN THOMAS, sanitary engineer; b. Jackson, Ala., Sept. 24, 1939; s. John Thomas and Ada Jean (Hamilton) M.; m. Maryjo Borges, June 22, 1963 (div. 1979); children—John Thomas III, Jeannine Marie, Jennifer Joanne; m. Gwen Arnold Ashby, Jan. 8, 1982 (div. 1984); 1 son, Ronnie Merrill Ashby. Student Miss. So. Coll., 1957-58; B.C.E., Auburn U., 1963; M.S., Ga. Inst. Tech., 1967. Coop. student U.S. Army C.E., Mobile, Ala., 1958-63; staff engr. Fed. Water Pollution Control Adminstrn., Atlanta, 1967-68, Alameda, Calif., 1968-69; supervisory san. engr. Fed. Water Quality Adminstrn., San Francisco, 1969-71; chief tech. assessment unit U.S. EPA, Atlanta, 1971-73, chief tech. support br., 1973-76, chief water quality planning br., 1976-81, chief facilities performance br., 1981—. Served with USPHS, 1963-66. Recipient Bronze medal U.S. EPA, 1973, Silver medal, 1985. Alcoa scholar, 1962-63. Mem. Water Pollution Control Fedn., Sigma Xi. Home: 5319 Arrowind Rd Lilburn GA 30247 Office: EPA 345 Courtland St Atlanta GA 30365

MARLEY, DAVID ALEXANDER, insurance company official; b. Ellsworth, Maine, July 8, 1941; s. Foster Linwood and Marquerite Helen (Cochrane) Marley Bishop; m. Pauline Elaine Levesque, Nov. 24, 1962; children—David Alexander II, Kimberly Anne. B.S. in Bus. Adminstrn., Bryant Coll., 1966. C.L.U. Agt., Mass. Mut. Life Ins. Co., Providence, 1966-69, asst. gen. agt., 1969-72, gen. agt., Portland, Maine, 1972-76, gen. agt., Miami, Fla., 1976—; treas. QPS, Inc., Miami, 1979—; pres. South Fla. Ins. Agy., Miami, 1983—. Chmn. allocations com. United Way, Miami, 1978—; bd. dirs. Boys Club Found. Miami, 1982—; chmn. corp. fund raising com. Bryant Coll., Providence, 1968, trustee devel. com., 1968-69. Recipient Charles F. Moran award R.I. Jaycees, 1970-71. Mem. Internat. Assn. Fin. Planners, Fla. Assn. Gen. Agts. and Mgrs. Assn. (edn. chmn. 1983-84, sec.-treas. 1985-86), Miami Assn. Life Underwriters, Miami C.L.U. Soc., Gen. Agrs. and Mgrs. Assn. Miami (pres. 1982-83), Miami Estate Planning Council. Home: 7940 SW 172d Terr Miami FL 33157 Office: Mass Mut Life Ins Co 7200 Corporate Center Suite 206 Miami FL 33126

MARLEY, ROBERT JENNINGS, state education official; b. Ramseur, N.C., Oct. 2, 1925; s. Woosley Edwin and Beulah Mozel (Whitehead) M.; m. Sarah Alice Lockwood, Aug. 29, 1953; 2 children. A.B., High Point Coll., 1950; M.Ed. Univ. N.C., 1954. Tchr. Lee County Schs., Lemon Springs, N.C., 1950-52; prin. Wake County Sch. Willow Springs, N.C., 1952-54; with N.C. Dept. Pub. Instruction, Raleigh, 1954—, now dir. compensatory edn. Served as petty officer USN, 1943-46; PTO. Mem. Nat. Assn. State Dirs. (pres. 1983-84), Internat. Reading Assn. Democrat. Lodge: Lions (dist. gov. 1981-82). Home: 311 Wade St Fuquay-Varina NC 27526 Office: NC Dept Pub Instruction Raleigh NC 27611

MARLING, CARL, clinical ophthalmologist; b. Hamilton, Ohio, Oct. 5, 1941; s. John Bertram and Florence (Kelley) M.; m. Saundra Howard, July 11, 1964; children—Karen Howard, Timothy Stewart. B.A., U. Ky., 1963; M.D., Yale Med. Sch., 1967. Intern, U. Miami Hosp., Fla., 1967-68; resident in ophthalmology Vanderbilt U. Hosp., Nashville, 1968-71; practice medicine specializing in ophthalmology, Bedford, Tex., 1973—; chief of staff Hurst-Euless-Bedford Hosp., 1980-82. Served to maj. U.S. Army, 1971-73. Fellow Am. Acad. Ophthalmology, Tex. Med. Assn., AMA, Tarrant County Ophthalmol. Soc. Lodge: Rotary (Bedford). Avocations: golf; camping. Home: 1001 Overhill St Bedford TX 76022 Office: 1850 Central Dr Bedford TX 76021

MARLOW, DUSTON DADE, geologist, exploration executive; b. Junction City, Kans., Nov. 22, 1956; s. Darold Dean and Peggy Jane (DeBruler) M.; m. Jo Lea Tyler, Sept. 8, 1979; 1 child, Derec Dade. B.S. in Geology, Kans. State U., 1978. Hydrocarbon well log analyst Continental Labs., Inc., Billings, Mont., 1978-79; well site cons. research asst. Kans. Geol. Survey, Lawrence, 1979-80; sr. geologist Universal Resources Inc., Oklahoma City, 1980-83; exploration mgr., geologist Jico Exploration Inc., Oklahoma City, 1983—. Fellow Am. Assn. Petroleum Geologists, Okla. Geol. Soc. Republican. Methodist. Office: Jico Exploration Inc 5600 N May Suite 275 Oklahoma City OK 73112

MARLOW, HOBSON MCKINLEY, JR., lawyer; b. Cookeville, Tenn., Sept. 20, 1931; s. H.M. and Birtha (Bryant) M.; m. Dorothy Fay Teal, June 18, 1960 (dec. Dec. 1981), children—Darryl McKinley, Stephen Teal, Eric Martin. B.S., Tenn. Tech. U., 1954; J.D., Vanderbilt U., 1957. Bar: Tenn., 1957. Sole practice law, Nashville, 1957—; pres. Newsletters, Inc., Ashwood Music Co., Universal Computer Services, Inc. Mem. ABA (copyright com.), Nashville Bar Assn., Tenn. Bar Assn. Lodges: Masons, Shriners. Author: ABC's of Copyright Law for Songwriters, 1960. Home: Lynn Dr Nashville TN 37211 Office: Executive Park Nashville TN 37220

MARLOWE, ROBERT CHARLES, nursing home management company executive; b. Lakeland, Fla., Jan. 26, 1954; s. James Milton and Selma (Paterson) M.; m. Carolyn O'Connor, June 7, 1975; children—Jennifer Lynn, Steven Andrew. B.S. in Natural Scis., Fla. So. Coll., 1975; M.B.A. in Health and Hosp. Adminstrn., U. Fla., 1978. Lic. nursing home adminstr. Fla. Bd. Nursing Home Adminstrs. Vis. asst. prof. grad. program in health and hosp. adminstrn. U. Fla., Gainesville, 1978-79; dir. purchasing Health Facilities Mgmt., Inc., New Port Richey, 1979-80, mgmt. coordinator, 1981-83, exec. v.p., chief exec. officer, 1983-84, pres., chief exec. officer, 1985—, adminstr. Heather Hill Nursing Home, health facilities mgmt. facility, 1980-81; dir. Fla. Gulf Health Systems Agy., 1981-83, Pasco-Pinellas Health Council, 1983—; preceptor for health care adminstrn. interns from Western Ky. U., 1982—. Mem. Pasco County Democratic Exec. Com., 1983—; bd. dirs. Shadow Ridge Homeowners Assn., 1983—. Mem. Fla. Health Care Assn., (multi-facility com.), Sigma Phi Epsilon. Democrat. Methodist. Home: 12226 Shadow Ridge Blvd Hudson FL 33562 Office: Health Facilities Mgmt Inc 1165 E Kentucky Ave New Port Richey FL 33552

MARLOWE, THOMAS JOHNSON, animal science educator, researcher; b. Fairview, N.C., Sept. 15, 1917; s. Alonzo Garland and Nellie Ann (Bass) M.; m. Christine Odell Williamson, Mar. 3, 1945; children—Michael Thomas, Donald Ray, Ronald Jay, Melody Anne Marlowe Nickols. B.S., N.C. State U., 1940, M.S., 1949; Ph.D. in Animal Breeding and Genetics, Okla. State U., 1954. Tchr. agrl. edn., N.C., 1940-42; extension livestock specialist, Mecklenburg County, Va., 1949-50; asst. prof. animal husbandry Miss. State U., 1951-52; assoc. prof. animal husbandry Va. Poly. Inst. and State U., Blacksburg, 1954-64, prof. animal sci., 1964-84, prof. emeritus, 1984—; cons. Am. Angus Assn., 1957-61. Past pres. Blacksburg United Methodist Men, 1958-59, 65-66; pres. Blacksburg PTA, 1964-65, 71-72. Served with U.S. Army, World War II; lt. col. USAR (ret.). Recipient Superior service award Va. Beef Cattle Improvement Assn., 1978; R.C. Carter Meml. award Va. Shorthorn Breeders, 1981; Disting. Service award Va. Cattlemen's Assn., 1984. Fellow Am. Soc. Animal Sci. (hon.; pres. 1975-76; Disting. Service Award So. sect. 1978; Animal Industry Service award 1983); mem. Am. Inst. Biol. Scis. (dir. 1974-77), AAUP, Am. Genetics Assn., Council Agrl. Sci. and Tech. (bd. dirs. 1979-86), Va. Acad. Sci. (mem. council 1979-85), Beef Improvement Fedn., Officers Assn. U.S., Phi Kappa Phi, Gamma Sigma Delta. Republican. Methodist. Contbr. chpts. to books, articles to profl. jours.; developer 1st state beef cattle performance testing program in U.S., 1954-59.

MARNELL, EUGENE RICHARD, journalist; b. Wichita, Kans., Sept. 27, 1946; s. Bernie Daniel and Frances Marie (Rhodes) M.; m. Katherine Richey, Feb. 1, 1969; 1 son, Eugene Richard. B.A. in History, Columbus Coll. (Ga.), 1972; M.S. in Urban Adminstrn., Ga. State U., 1979. With Fayette County News, Fayetteville, Ga., 1969-70, Columbus Enquirer (Ga.), 1970-73, AP, Atlanta, 1973; dir. urban affairs City of Dalton (Ga.), 1973-77; editor Sports Merchandiser mag., Atlanta, 1977—. Advisor Jr. Achievement, Dalton. Methodist. Office: 1760 Peachtree Rd NW Atlanta GA 30357

MAROSCHER, BETTY JEAN, librarian; b. Ashland, Ky., Aug. 12, 1934; d. Raymond and Virginia Dell (Staten) Boggs; student Columbus Coll. (Ga.), 1963-64; B.S., Hardin-Simmons U., 1967; M.S. in L.S., Our Lady of Lake U., San Antonio, 1970; M.Ed., Trinity U., 1975; m. Albert G. Maroscher Mar. 21, 1955 (dec.). Tchr., McAllen (Tex.) Ind. Sch. Dist., 1967-68; tchr. Northside Ind. Sch. Dist., San Antonio, 1968-69, librarian, 1969-71; reference librarian ednl. media Trinity U., San Antonio, 1971-76; reference librarian St. Philip's Coll., San Antonio, 1976, audiovisual librarian, mgr. audiovisual dept., 1977—; lectr., cons. in field; chmn. subcom. programming and scheduling Univ. and Fine Arts Cable TV Com., 1980-81. Active ARC; sec., trustee Compañiá de Arte Espanol, 1982-83; sec. Univ. and Fine Arts Cable TV Com., 1984—; sec. Dist. Broadcast Media Adv. Council, 1984—. Recipient Minter/Medal Hardin-Simmons U., 1965, 66. Mem. Tex., Bexar County, library assns., Tex. Jr. Coll. Tchrs. Assn., Tex. Assn. Chicanos in Higher Edn. (sec. St. Philip's chpt. 1982-84), Audiovisual Instructional Media Services Group, Council Research and Acad. Libraries Coop. Circulation Group (sec.-treas. 1977-79), Pi Gamma Mu (sec. chpt. 1965-67), Alpha Chi (historian 1965-67), other orgns. Republican. Home: 5230 Galahad Dr San Antonio TX 78218 Office: 2111 Nevada St San Antonio TX 78203

MARQUARDT, WILLIAM GARLAND, utility company executive; b. Bartlett, Tex., 1920; married. B.S.E.E., U. Tex., 1941. With Tex. Electric Service Co., a company of Tex. Utilities Co., Ft. Worth, 1941—, former mgr. western div., v.p., mgr. div. ops., 1963-65, v.p. ops., 1965-75, pres., chief exec. officer, 1975—, also dir. Office: Tex Electric Service Co 115 W 7th St Fort Worth TX 76102*

MARQUER, CONSTANT GEORGE, JR., lawyer, pharmacy educator; b. New Orleans, Sept. 19, 1931; s. Constant George and Marion Frombling (Faust) M.; m. Mary Ann Rizzo, June 10, 1953; children—Constant George III, Michele Ann. B.S. in Pharmacy, Loyola U. of South, New Orleans, 1953, Pharm.D., 1983, J.D., 1971. Bar: La. 1972. Pharmacist, Marquer Pharmacy, Inc., New Orleans, 1955-72; sole practice law, New Orleans, 1972—; assoc. prof. pharmacy Xavier U., New Orleans, 1980—. Contbr. articles on pharmacy to profl. jours. Served to cpl. U.S. Army Med. Corps, 1953-55. Mem. La. Pharmacist Assn., La. Bar Assn., Am. Soc. Pharmacy Law. Democrat. Roman Catholic. Avocations: historic restoration of old buildings; golfing; football; basketball. Home: 6206 Canal Blvd New Orleans LA 70124 Office: 2404 St Claude Ave New Orleans LA 70117

MARQUETTE, PEGGIE ANN, public relations consultant; b. Cresview, Fla., Nov. 19, 1929; d. Henry Clifton and Harriet Evelyn (Hampton) White; m. William Frederick Marquette, June 24, 1950; children—Linda Jane Mayer, Anne Catherine Marquette McDonald. B.A. in Journalism, U. Miami, 1951. Regional women's editor Orlando (Fla.) Sentinel, 1964-73; editor Union Express, Houston, 1974-75; alumni editor, external affairs specialist U. Houston, 1975-78; dir. pub. relations Borgen Pub. Co., Houston, 1979-80; dir. pub. support Greater Houston chpt. ARC, 1980-82; ptnr. Mrok & Marquette Communications, Houston, 1982-85; lectr. Bd. dirs. Bloodonor Program, Inc., chpt. Am. Cancer Soc. former mem. bd. dirs. Melbourne Pub. Library, Hacienda Girls Ranch, Brevard County chpt. Am. Cancer Soc., Brevard County chpt. Nat. Found./March of Dimes. Named Woman of Yr., Melbourne Jr. Woman's Club, 1961. Mem. Pub. Relations Soc. Am., Jr. League Houston, Sigma Delta Chi. Republican. Presbyterian. Club: Eau Gallie Yacht (Indian Harbour Beach, Fla.). Office: 9243 Westwood Village Dr Houston TX 77036

MARR, JOHN ALBERT, real estate investor; b. Bath, Maine, May 14, 1931; s. John Hyde and Dorothy Louise (Lewis) M.; m. Marilyn Ann Govoni, June 13, 1954 (div. 1967); children—Michael Marr, Debra Kurtyka, David Marr; m. 2d, Mary Lee Holt, Oct. 21, 1967. B.S., Northeastern U., 1954. Registered profl. engr., Conn. Various positions with Shell Oil Co., 1954-74; ops. mgr. Bercon Co., Berwick, Pa., 1974-75; v.p. Pecten Arabian Services subs. Shell Oil Co., Riyadh, Saudi Arabia, 1975-78, mfg. advisor, Houston, 1978-83; pres. John Marr Investments, Inc., Houston, 1983—, Kingwood Energy Inc., Houston, 1985—. Bd. dirs. Tex. Chamber Orchestra, 1981—, pres., 1982-83; bd. dirs. Woods at Hudson Homeowners Assn., 1981-84, pres., 1981-82; bd. dirs. Support Ctr. of Houston, 1983—, pres., 1985—; pres. bd. dirs. N.W. Harris. County Mcpl. Utility Dist. 30, 1984—. Mem. Am. Symphony Orchestra League, Cultural Arts Council Houston, Forum Club Houston, Gulf Coast Council Fgn. Affairs, Mus. Fine Arts, Houston Seminar, Houston C. of C., Am. Businessmen's Group of Riyadh (founder, chmn. 1978). Republican. Patentee method of coloring thermoplastics. Home: 214 Sugarberry Circle Houston TX 77024 Office: 492 Town and Country Village Houston TX 77024

MARR, PHEBE ANN, historian, educator; b. Mt. Vernon, N.Y., Sept. 21, 1931; d. John Joseph and Lillian Victoria (Henningsen) Marr. B.A., Barnard Coll., 1953; Ph.D., Harvard U., 1967. Research assoc. ARAMCO, Dhahran, Saudi Arabia, 1960-62; dir. middle east program Fgn. Service Inst., 1963-66; research fellow Middle East Ctr., Harvard U., Cambridge, Mass., 1968-70; asst. prof. Stanislaus State Coll., Turlock, Calif., 1970-71, assoc. prof., 1971-74; assoc. prof. history U. Tenn., Knoxville, 1974-85, chmn. Asian Studies Program, 1977-79; sr. fellow Nat. Def. U., Washington, 1985—; cons. ARAMCO, 1979-83. Harvard U. traveling fellow, 1956. Mem. Middle East Inst., Middle East Studies Assn., Am. Hist. Assn. Author: The Modern History of Iraq.; contbr. articles to profl. jours.

MARRERO, ROBERTO, chemistry educator; b. N.Y.C., July 31, 1948; s. Roberto and Virginia (Corletto) M.; m. Sonia Margarita Rivera, Dec. 29, 1973; children—Margarita, Sonia, Roberto, Sonimar. Ph.D. in Chemistry, U. Idaho, 1977. Asst. prof. chemistry dept. Humacao (P.R.) U. Coll., 1977-82, assoc. prof., 1982—, chmn. chemistry dept., 1979-80, asst. to dir. acad. affairs, 1980-82. Served to lt. U.S. Army, 1968-70; with Army N.G., 1971—. Decorated Bronze Star. Mem. Am. Chem. Soc., Am. Assn. Clin. Chemists, AAAS, Sigma Xi. Republican. Episcopalian.

MARSALA, THERESA CLARK, registered nurse, administrator; b. Tulsa, Aug. 5, 1952; d. Robert Earl and Mary Louise (Pettigrew) Clark; m. Thomas A. Marsala, Aug. 17, 1974; children—Thomas, Leslie, Robert. B.S. in Nursing, Northeast La. U., 1975, postgrad. in counseling. Cert. advanced cardiac life support provider. Staff nurse St. Francis Med. Ctr., Monroe, La., 1975-78, head nurse dialysis, 1976-78, registered nurse instr., 1979-80, dir. edn. and tng., 1980-83, dir. nursing service, 1983-84, asst. adminstr. nursing service, 1984—; CPR instr. Am. Heart Assn., 1979—, trainer, 1980—, advanced cardiac life support instr. provider, 1982—. Named Outstanding Young Woman Am., 1984. Mem. Am. Heart Assn., Nat. Kidney Found., Am. Nurse Assn., Monroe Dist. Nurses Assn., La. Soc. for Nursing Service Adminstrs., Progressive Men's Club Aux. (treas. Monroe, La. 1978-79). Roman Catholic. Home: 2801 Breville Monroe LA 71201 Office: St Francis Med Ctr Nursing Adminstrn 309 Jackson Monroe LA 71201

MARSDEN, ELIZABETH HARLOW, educator; b. Nashville, Mar. 17, 1923; d. Frank Ernest and Harriet Ellsworth (Rees) Harlow; Mus.B., U. Miami, 1944; M.A., Columbia U., 1945; m. Edward Derwood Marsden, Dec. 23, 1946 (div. Jan. 1971); children—Elizabeth Rhys Marsden Marmion, Margaret Lee Marsden Brown, Catherine Harlow Marsden Mayhew, Harriet Ann Marsden Rice. Tchr., Southeastern La. Coll., 1945-47; asst. prof. music U. Miami, 1947-52; supr. music Penn Hills Sch., Pitts., 1954-59; tchr. piano, voice, Pitts., 1959-61; judge Music Educators Nat. Conf., Miami, 1953, Tampa, Fla., 1953; tchr. Dade County (Fla.) Schs., 1964, Brevard County (Fla.) Schs., 1966-72; minister of music Coral Way Presbyn. Ch., Miami, 1964-66, First Presbyn. Ch., Titusville, 1966-72; music cons. Marietta (Ga.) City Schs., 1972-82, music coordinator, 1983—; lectr. U. South Fla., 1967-72, Rollins Coll., 1971, U. Ga., 1972—; condr. workshops, music programs for profl. assns., music tchrs., also coll. events; mem. Cobb County Symphony Guild; chmn. Cobb County Artist Series, Cobb County Arts Council, Cobb County Jr. League, Cobb County Parks and Recreation Bd. Recipient Outstanding Contbn. to Arts award YWCA, 1981; Lillian Bennett Sullivan Award, Cobb County Arts Council, Marietta, 1982; Supt.'s award Marietta City Sch., 1985. Mem. AAUP, AAUW, Am. Guild Organists, Music Educators Nat. Conf., NEA, Classroom Tchrs. Assn., Fla. Elem. Tchrs. Assn., Brevard Edn. Assn., Ga. Music Educators Assn. (chmn. 12th dist., mem. study com.), Ga. Assn. Curriculum and Instrnl. Suprs., Ga. Music Edn. Adminstrs. Assn. (pres., steering com. 1977-78, v.p. 1978-79), Brevard Music Edn. Assn. (v.p.), DAR, Internat. Platform Assn., Delta Kappa Gamma, Chi Omega, Sigma Alpha Iota. Clubs: College, Tuesday Music, Mt. Lebanon Women's (Pitts.); Coral Gables Garden, Flamingo Dinner. Home: 335 Vineyard Dr Marietta GA 30064 Office: 145 Dodd St Box 1265 Marietta GA 30064

MARSEL, ROBERT STEVEN, lawyer, legal educator; b. N.Y.C., July 23, 1947; s. Bernard and Vivian (Gilbert) M. J.D., U. Calif., 1971. Bar: N.Y., D.C., U.S. Supreme Ct. Fellow Worcester Coll., Oxford, Eng.; vis. lectr. Faculty Law, U. Auckland N.Z.; spl. asst. U.S. atty., San Francisco; legal officer U.S. Supreme Ct., Washington; vis. asst. prof. law U. Miami, 1983-84; prof. South Tex. Coll. Law, Houston, 1984—; chmn. com. on privacy and confidentiality U.S. Dept. Commerce, 1973-75. U. Calif. hon. traveling fellow, 1971-72. Mem. Am. Arbitration Assn. Office: South Texas Coll of Law 1303 San Jacinto St Houston TX 77002

MARSH, CAROLYN O'NEAL, state official; b. Florence, S.C., Dec. 28, 1926; d. Charles O'Neal and Effie (Buzhardt) M. B.A., U. Richmond, 1947, M.A., 1948. Lic. profl. counselor, Va. Psychometrist U. Richmond, Va., 1948-51; employee interviewer Miller & Rhoads, Richmond, 1951-53, personnel counselor, 1953-55, employment mgr., 1955-61, personnel mgr., 1961-71; pres. Carolyn O. Marsh Personnel Mgmt. Inc., Richmond, 1971-78; dir. Dept. Employee Relations Counselors, Commonwealth of Va., Richmond, 1978—; mem. Gov.'s Personnel Adv. Com., Richmond, 1978—, chmn., 1980—. Pres. Goodwill Industries, Richmond, 1971-77; trustee U. Richmond, 1972-76; adv. bd. Bank Va., Richmond, 1974-80; v.p. Redeemer Luth. Ch., Richmond, 1981-83; nat. bd. Westhampton Coll. Alumni Assn., Richmond, 1969—. Recipient Outstanding Woman Va. award 1979; Disting. Westhampton Coll. Alumna award 1975. Mem. Am. Psychol. Assn., Am. Soc. Personnel Adminstrn., Omicron Delta Kappa. Lutheran. Clubs: Willow Oaks (bd. dirs. 1980-81), Downtown (Richmond). Avocation: golf. Home: 6407 Buckhill Rd Richmond VA 23225 Office: Dept Employee Relations Counselors 110 S 7th St Richmond VA 23219

MARSH, DONALD JAMES, communications engineer, executive; b. Jamaica, N.Y., Oct. 26, 1930; s. James and Rose (Leuschner) M.; m. Marilyn R. Miller, Dec. 8, 1951; children—David James, Margaret Rose, Andrew John. B.E.E., NYU, 1964; M.S. in Elec. Engring., U. Bridgeport, 1979. Registered profl. engr. Conn., Ga. With AT&T, 1950-62; with ITT, 1963-80, tech. dir. P.R. Telephone Co., 1965-67, tech. dir., gen. mgr. ITT Labs., Madrid, Spain, 1967-69; v.p. tech. Contel Bus. Systems Inc., 1980—. Mem. tech. adv. bd. U.S. Postal Service; chmn. U.S. Commerce Dept. Joint Industry Govt. Telecommunications adv. com., 1978-80. Served with USN, 1948-52. Sr. mem. IEEE (chmn. accoustics, speech and signal processing, Conn. chpt. 1979-80, Ga. chpt., 1981-83); mem. Nat. Soc. Profl. Engrs., Tau Beta Pi. Republican. Lutheran. Home: 3251 Hunterdon Way Marietta GA 30067 Office: 5550 Triangle Pkwy Norcross GA 30092

MARSH, DOROTHY HOBBS, national park service official; b. Greenwood, Miss., Nov. 28, 1928; d. George Godfrey and Dorothy May (Parker) Hobbs; m. William Hardin Marsh Sr., July 7, 1946; children—Mary Louise Marsh Beck, William Hardin Jr. Grad. high sch., Florence, Ala. Sec. Reynolds Metals Co., Lister Hill, Ala., 1946-47; cashier Citizens Savings & Loan, East Ridge, Tenn., 1962; billing clk. U.S. Stove Co., South Pittsburgh, Tenn., 1962-63; clk., stenographer Nat. Park Service, Bridgeport, Ala., 1963-67, adminstrv. technician, 1968-82, unit mgr., 1982-85, supt., 1985—. Author: (booklet) Life at Russell Cave, 1975. Active Bridgeport PTA, 1955-68, Bridgeport Band Boosters Club, 1957-68, United Methodist Women, 1955-78; Sunday Sch. tchr. Bridgeport Meth. Ch., 1955-68. Recipient Quality Performance award Nat. Park Service, 1977, 85, Spl. Achievement award 1973; Spl. Services award Eastern Nat. Park and Monument Assn. 1974. Mem. Ala. Parks and Recreation Soc. (sec. 1985), Jackson County C. of C. (com. chmn. 1984—), Nat. Park Service Employees and Alumni Assn. Democrat. Methodist. Club: Literary (sec. 1983—). Avocations: swimming; golfing; water skiing. Home: 17 Ruby St Bridgeport AL 35740 Office: Russell Cave Nat Monument Route 1 Box 175 Bridgeport AL 35740

MARSH, JOSEPH VIRGIL, commercial real estate and investment broker; b. Winston-Salem, N.C., Apr. 28, 1952; s. Gilliam Hughes and Dovie Elizabeth (Watson) M.; student Surrey Community Coll., 1970-72; Coop. Engring. Program, U.S. Govt. Schs., Md., S.C., Washington, 1972-74. With Joint Armed Services Tech. Liaison, Washington, 1974-75; cons. U.S. Govt., 1975-76; corr., cons. individuals, bus. on tech. matters, Ararat, N.C., 1977—. Mem. Presidential Task Force, 1980-85; White House fellow, 1982. Comml. real estate broker, N.C.; registered advisor SEC. Mem. Internat. Entrepreneurs Assn., VFW (hon.), Armed Forces Assn., Ind. Consultants Assn., Internat. Assn. Sci. Devel., Council Civilian Tech. Advisers. Republican. Address: PO Box 12 Route 1 Ararat NC 27007

MARSH, MALCOLM ROY, JR., electronic engineer; b. Bedford, Va., Oct. 12, 1932; s. Malcolm Roy and Mildred (Overstreet) M.; B.E.E., U. Va., 1956; children—Lauranne Ashton, James Overstreet. Elec. engr. Sperry Piedmont, Inc., Charlottesville, Va., 1957-58, Martin Orlando Co., Orlando, Fla., 1958-60; electronic engring. cons., Orlando, 1960-84. Served with U.S. Army, 1958. Mem. IEEE. Methodist. Home and Office: 2609 Tradewinds Trail Orlando FL 32805

MARSHALL, ALLEN WRIGHT, III, communications executive; b. Griffin, Ga., Dec. 4, 1941; s. Allen Wright, Jr. and Evelyn Louise (Halliburton) M.; m. Carole Anne Moore, Dec. 24, 1964; 1 child, Allen Wright IV. B.A. in Journalism, U. Ga., 1964; diploma Elkins Inst. Radio, Atlanta, 1964; postgrad. Ga. State U., 1968. 1st class radio telephone lic. FCC. Pres., Sta. WKEU-AM-FM, Griffin, Ga., 1954—; co-founder, v.p. Griffin Cable TV, 1971-74; co-founder, pres. Custom Services, Inc., Griffin, 1974—; co-founder, v.p. Cobbwells Marshall, Inc., Griffin, 1982—, Page One, Griffin, 1983—; sec., bd. dirs. Goals for Griffin and Spalding Counties, Inc., 1981—. Author radio programs, editorials (Ga. AP awards 1969-84); also articles; speaker in field. Mem. adv. com. Griffin Vocat.-Tech. Sch., 1982—; bd. dirs. Jr. Achievement, Griffin, 1977—; chmn. Griffin-Spalding Indsl. authority, 1984; mem. Gov.'s Adv. Com. on Area Planning and Devel. Commns., 1971-72; bd. dirs. McIntosh Trail Area Planning and Devel. Commn., Ga., 1971-73. Served to sgt. U.S. Army, 1966-68. Named Man of Yr., Exchange Club of Griffin, 1984. Mem. Ga. Assn. Broadcasters (bd. dirs. 1970-74, Radio Sta. of Yr. 1977), Griffin Area C. of C. (bd. dirs. 1980, chmn. indsl. com. 1980, 81). Episcopalian. Clubs: Country (charter mem. 1966), Running (Griffin). Lodge: Rotary (pres. 1976-77). Avocations: jogging; photography; computers. Home: 681 Brook Circle Griffin GA 30223 Office: Radio Sta WKEU-AM-FM PO Drawer Q 1000 Memorial Dr Griffin GA 30224

MARSHALL, ARTHUR, JR., bishop; b. High Point, N.C., Mar. 2, 1914; s. Arthur and Nellie (Kindle) M.; m. Mary Ann Stotts, May 3, 1952; 1 son, Arthur Clifford. A.B., Livingstone Coll., 1937, D.D., 1962; S.T.B., Boston U., 1951. Ordained deacon A.M.E. Zion Ch., 1934, elder, 1936, consecrated bishop, 1972; now bishop 7th Episcopal area, Atlanta; Mem. council Meth. World Conf.; chmn. bd. publs. A.M.E. Zion Ch.; pres. Kansas City (Mo.) Ministerial Alliance, 1956; mem. exec. com. Mo. Council Chs., 1961; mem. gen. bd. Nat. Council Chs., 1963; mem. exec. council St. Louis Interfaith Council, 1966. Chmn. bd. trustees Clinton Coll.; trustee Livingstone Coll.; mem. nat. council Minority Bus. Enterprise; v.p. bd. dirs. NAACP. Recipient Meritorious Service award Kansas City Coll., St. Louis Citizens award St. Louis Argus. Mem. Alpha Phi Alpha. Home: 3141 Pyrite Circle Atlanta GA 30331 Office: PO Box 41138 Atlanta GA 30331*

MARSHALL, BRUCE, artist, writer; b. Athens, Tex., Dec. 29, 1929; s. Litten B., and Myrtis (Hoover) M.; m. Ann Smith, Sept. 30, 1962; children—Susanne, Randolph, Cody. Student Univ. Ariz., 1950-52, So. Ariz. Sch. Art, 1952-54. Writer Jour. Commerce, N.Y.C., 1959-64, Houston Post, 1964-66; artist, Austin, Tex., 1970—. Executed mural Tex. Citizen Soldier, Nat. Infantry Mus., Ft. Benning, Ga., 1976. Vice-comdr. Mil. Order of the Stars & Bars, N.Y.C., 1962-64. Named to knighthood King Peter II of Yugoslavia, 1966; named artist of 65th Legislature, State of Tex., 1977; recipient Jefferson Davis medal United Daus. of Confederacy. 1976; Appreciation award Nat. Guard Assn. Tex., 1976; Alamo award Daus. Republic of Tex., 1979. Mem. Hood's Tex. Brigade Assn. (pres. 1967-69), Tex. State Hist. Assn., Sons Confederate Vets. (comdr. Trans-Miss. dept. 1970-72). Presbyterian. Club: Headliners. Avocation: horse training. Office: Westart PO Box 5512 Austin TX 78763

MARSHALL, CHARLES EDWARD, architect; b. Atlanta, Jan. 19, 1938; s. Charles Edward and Anna Mary (Schriener) M.; m. Gail Campbell Sauls, May 19, 1962; children—David Douglas, Angela Diane. B.S., Ga. Tech. Inst., 1959, B. Arch., 1960. Regis. architect, Ga., Fla., Ala., N.C., S.C., Va., Tenn., Tex., Ky., Calif., Mich., Ill. Vice-pres. John J. Harte Assocs., Inc., Atlanta, 1963—. Served with USAFR, 1960-66. Mem. AIA, Constrn. Specifications Inst. Baptist. Avocations: magic; music. Office: John J Harte Assocs Inc 3290 Cumberland Club Dr Atlanta GA 30339

MARSHALL, CHARLES JOSEPH, chemical company executive, pharmacist; b. Phillippi, W.Va., Nov. 1, 1947; s. Charles Edward and Ruth Elizabeth (Gerkin) M.; m. Carolyn Jean Riffee, Aug. 3, 1974; children—Sarah, Christopher. A.S. in Biology, W.Va. U., 1969, B.S. in Pharmacy, 1972. Registered pharmacist, W.Va. Store mgr. Rite Aid Corp., Charleston, W.Va., 1972-76, area supr., 1977-79; staff pharmacist Charleston Area Med. Ctr., 1980-81; account rep. PB&S Chem. Co., St. Albans, W.Va., 1982—. Vol., West Virginians for Reagan, Charleston, 1984, Moore for Gov., Charleston, 1984. Named Salesman of Yr., PB&S Corp. Hdqrs., 1984, 85. Republican. Presbyterian. Lodge: Masons. Avocations: golfing; hiking; fishing. Home: 4570 1/2 Woodrums Ln Charleston WV 25313 Office: PB&S Chem Co 319 1st St N Saint Albans WV 25177

MARSHALL, COGAN GLENN, federal agency executive; b. Castlewood, Va., Nov. 5, 1936; s. Ernest Hagg and Faye (Meade) M.; m. Iris Christine Brooks, June 21, 1957; children—Cheina Christine, Jeanene Michelle. Student Ind. Tech. Coll., 1958-59, U. Ky., 1966-67; B.S., Barry Coll., 1976. Registered profl. engr., Calif. Electronic technician FAA, Lexington, Ky., Miami, 1969-73, supervisory electronic technician, Miami, 1973-74, proficiency devel. and evaluation officer, 1974-76, asst. sector mgr., Norfolk, Va., 1976-80, chief performance standards sect., Jamaica, N.Y., 1980-82, asst. sector mgr., Norfolk, 1982—. Service with USAF, 1955-58. Recipient Spl. Achievement award FAA, 1971, Outstanding Fed. Service award Fed. Exec. Bd., 1974, Spl. Achievement award, 1976, Quality within grade award, 1978, 81, 83. Republican. Home: 936 General Hill Dr Virginia Beach VA 23454 Office: FAA Terminal Bldg Room 2525 Norfolk VA 23518

MARSHALL, ELINOR DORSK BLOOM, retail furniture company executive; b. Petersburg, Va., Aug. 13, 1936; d. Irvin Louis and Anita Flora (Lubman) Dorsk; m. Allan Selig Bloom, Dec. 23, 1956 (dec. May 1981); children—Arthur Lane Bloom, Stephen Mark Bloom, Lawrence Jay Bloom; m. George Clinton Marshall, Mar. 2, 1985. Mus.B., Women's Coll., U. N.C.-Greensboro, 1957. Sec.-treas. The Oak, Inc., Petersburg, 1967-81, pres., 1981—; ptnr. Bloom Properties; dir. Community Bank, Petersburg; alto soloist Christ and Grace Episcopal Ch.; choir dir. Temple Brith Achim, Petersburg. Past pres. Southside Va. Community Concert Assn.; vice chmn. Petersburg Archtl. Rev. Bd.; guild mem. Petersburg Symphony Orch.; mem. consumer and homemaking adv. com. Petersburg Pub. Schs.; vol. CanSurmount, program counseling cancer patients and families; mem. adv. bd. Massey Cancer Ctr. of Med. Coll. Va., 1984—; past pres. Tidewater Acad. Patrons Assn.; former mem. Fort Lee Army Adv. Com.; bd. dirs., former crusade chmn. and opera benefit chmn. Petersburg chpt. Am. Cancer Soc.; past mem. bd. Temple Brith Achim, also past pres. Sisterhood; former mem. bd. and v.p. ARC; past mem. bd. Easter Seal Soc.; bd. dirs. United Way Southside Va., C. of C. Found., Petersburg, Southside region Va. Lung Assn., Petersburg Ballet, Playmaker Fellows, Ltd., Va. Opera Assn. Guild, Norfolk; trustee Historic Petersburg Found. Mem. So. Home Furnishings Assn. (bd. dirs.). Jewish. Club: Fort Lee Officers'. Lodge: Hadassah (past pres. Petersburg chpt.). Office: The Oak Inc 400 N Sycamore St Petersburg VA 23803

MARSHALL, GERALD ROBERT, banking and investments executive; b. Oklahoma City, Mar. 4, 1934; m. Susan Sweeney, Mar. 3, 1972; children—Laura, Paul, Mindy, John Tom. B.B.A., U. Okla., 1957; student Oklahoma City U. Coll. Law, 1962, Southwestern Grad. Sch. Banking, 1965. Various positions comml. banking dept. Liberty Nat. Bank & Trust Co., Oklahoma City, 1957-73, exec. v.p., 1969-70, pres., 1970-73, dir., 1969-73; sr. v.p. First Nat. Bank Dallas, 1973-74; pres., dir. First Nat. Bank and Trust Co., Oklahoma City, 1974-75; chmn., chief exec. officer, dir. Capital Bank N.A., 1975-81; pres., chief exec. officer Goldman Enterprises, Oklahoma City, 1981-83; chmn. bd., chief exec. officer Bank of Oklahoma, Oklahoma City, N.A. (formerly Fidelity Bank, N.A.), 1984—. Trustee U. Okla. Found., 1974; mem. United Way Oklahoma City, 1975, Okla. Community Found., 1984, Bapt. Hosp. and Okla. Med. Research Found., 1984, Kerr Found., 1976; Mem. Am. Bankers Assn., Young Pres. Orgn., Oklahoma City C. of C. (chmn. 1984). Clubs: Beacon, Whitehall, Oklahoma City Golf and Country, River Oaks Country. Office: Robinson at Robert S Kerr Ave PO Box 24128 Oklahoma City OK 73124

MARSHALL, JERRY ALLYN, dentist, mayor; b. Brady, Tex., June 27, 1938; s. Floyd Leslie and Beth (Watkins) M.; m. Mary Ann Parks, Aug. 16, 1959; children—Jerilyn, Mark. A.S., Tarleton State U., 1958; student Tex. Tech U., 1958-59; D.D.S., U. Tex.-Houston, 1963. Gen. practice dentistry, Rotan, Tex., 1966—. Sec. Rotan Ind. Sch. Dist., mem. bd. trustees, 1969-80; councilman City of Rotan, 1980-84, mayor, 1985—; chmn. fin. First United Methodist Ch., Rotan, 1980—; pres. Rotan C. of C., 1970. Served to lt. Dental Corps, USN, 1963-66; Viet Nam. Recipient Vietnam Vets. Community Service award Pres. Jimmy Carter, 1979. Mem. ADA, Tex. Dental Assn. Democrat. Lodge: Lions (sec. 1975—, dist. 2T2 dep. dist. gov. 1985—). Home: 912 E Johnston St Rotan TX 79546 Office: 212 E Snyder St Rotan TX 79546

MARSHALL, JOHN HARRIS, JR., geologist, oil company executive; b. Dallas, Mar. 12, 1924; s. John Harris and Jessie Elizabeth (Mosley) M.; B.A. in Geology, U. Mo., 1949, M.A. in Geology, 1950; m. Betty Eugenia Zarecor, Aug. 9, 1947; children—John Harris, III, George Z., Jacqueline Ann Marshall Leibach. Geologist, Magnolia Oil Co., Jackson, Miss., 1950-59, asso. geologist Magnolia/Mobil Oil, Oklahoma City, 1959-63, dist. and div. geologist Mobil Oil Corp., Los Angeles and Santa Fe Springs, Calif., 1963-69, div. geologist, Los Angeles and Anchorage, 1969-71, exploration supt., Anchorage, 1971-72, western region geologist, Denver, 1972-76, geol. mgr., Dallas, 1976-78, chief geologist Mobil Oil Corp., N.Y.C., 1978-81, gen. mgr. exploration for Western Hemisphere, 1981-82; chief exec. officer Marshall Energetics, Inc., Dallas, 1982—. Councilman, City of Warr Acres (Okla.), 1962-63; various positions Meth. Ch., 1951—, Boy Scouts Am., 1960-68; Manhattan adv. bd. Salvation Army, 1980-82. Served with U.S. Army, 1943-46. Recipient U. Mo. Bd. Curators medal, ROTC Most Outstanding Student, 1949; cert. geologist, Calif. Mem. Am. Assn. Petroleum Geologists (Pacific sect.), Am. Geol. Inst., Petroleum Exploration Soc. N.Y., Dallas Geol. Soc., Rocky Mountain Assn. Geologists, Alaska Geol. Soc., Oklahoma City Geol. Soc., N.Y. Acad. Sci., Los Angeles Basin Geol. Soc. (pres.), Sigma Xi. Democrat. Club: Meth. Men. Home: 9526 Moss Haven Dr Dallas TX 75231 Office: Marshall Energetics Inc 7557 Rambler Rd Suite 652 Dallas TX 75231

MARSHALL, RAY MAXINE, business executive; b. Jay, Fla., Aug. 2, 1930; s. Albert F. and Mary H. Marshall; m. Doris Golden, July 18, 1951; 1 son, Philip Golden. Asst. supt. roads Couch Constrn. Co., Dothan, Ala., 1948; acct. Fla. Nat. Bank, 1948-49; with 1st Nat. Bank, Milton, Fla., 1949-51, mgr. bookkeeping dept., 1955-63; owner, operator Santa Rosa Realty & Ins. Agy., Inc., Milton, 1963-81, pres., 1981—; pres. Marshall Prodn. Co. Inc., Milton, 1981—; pres. Santa Rosa Realty, Inc., Milton, 1979—; dir. Liberty Bank, Cantonment, Fla. Served with USAF, 1951-55. Mem. Am. Petroleum Inst., Ind. Petroleum Assn. Am., Fla. Assn. Ins. Agts. Fla. Mut. Assn. Agts. Republican. Mem. Holiness Ch. Home: Route 1 Jay FL 32565 Office: 202 Escambia St Milton FL 32670

MARSHALL, TERRY ALLEN, pediatrician; b. Noblesville, Ind., Aug. 28, 1951; s. Max Lawrence and Constance Beyer (Barnwell) M.; m. Jane Wolfe, Apr. 27, 1977; children—Alan, David, Andrew. B.A., Vanderbilt U., 1973; M.D., U. Tenn., 1976. Diplomate Am. Bd. Pediatrics. Intern in pediatrics T.C. Thompson Childrens Hosp., Chattanooga, 1976-77, resident, 1977-78; fellow in neonatology U. Va. Med. Sch., Charlottesville, 1978-80; practice medicine specializing in pediatrics and neonatology, Columbia, S.C., 1980-84; asst. prof. U. S.C., Columbia, 1980-84; dir. nurseries Self Meml. Hosp., Greenwood, S.C., 1984—. Mem. Am. Acad. Pediatrics, So. Soc. Pediatric Research, So. Perinatal Assn., S.C. Perinatal Assn., Greenwood Med. Soc., S.C. Pediatric Soc., S.C. Med. Assn. Contbr. articles to profl. jours. Home: 102 Tall Pines Trail Greenwood SC 29646 Office: Self Memorial Hosp Greenwood SC 29646

MARSHALL, THOMAS OLIVER, JR., judge; b. Americus, Ga., June 24, 1920; s. Thomas Oliver and Mattie Louise (Hunter) M.; m. Angie Ellen Fitts, Dec. 20, 1946; children—Ellen Irwin Marshall Beard, Anne Hunter Marshall Peagler, Mary Olivia Marshall Pryor. B.S. in Engring, U.S. Naval Acad., 1941; J.D., U. Ga., 1948. Bar: Ga. bar 1947. Individual practice law, Americus, Ga., 1948-60; judge S.W. Judicial Circuit, Americus, 1960-74, Ga. Ct. Appeals, Atlanta, 1974-77; justice Ga. Supreme Ct., Atlanta, 1977—; chmn. bd. visitors U. Ga. Law Sch., 1970. Trustee Andrew Coll., So. Ga. Meth. Home for Aged, 1965-78; active ARC, 1948-60, United Givers Fund, 1948-54. Served with USN, World War II, Korean War. Decorated Bronze Star; named Young Man of Yr., Americus, 1953. Mem. ABA, Ga. Bar Assn. (bd. govs. 1958-60), Atlanta Bar Assn., State Bar Ga., Am. Judicature Soc., Jud. Coll. Ga. Democrat. Methodist. Clubs: Elks, VFW, Kiwanis, Am. Legion, Masons, Shriners. Home: 238 15th St NE Condominium 3 Atlanta GA 30309 Office: 528 State Judicial Bldg Atlanta GA 30334

MARSHALL, WILLIAM LEITCH, chemist; b. Columbia, S.C., Dec. 3, 1925; s. William Leitch and Georgia (Kittrell) M.; m. Joanne Fox, Apr. 16, 1949; children—Nancy Diane, William Fox. B.S., Clemson U., 1945; Ph.D., Ohio State U., 1949. Teaching asst. Clemson U., 1944-45, Ohio State U., 1945-46; Naval research fellow Ohio State U., 1947-49; mem. sr. research staff (chemistry) Oak Ridge Nat. Lab., 1949—, research group leader, 1957-75; Plenary lectr. congresses on oceanography, electrochemistry, geochemistry, high temperature water chemistry, high pressure fluids; mem. orgn. coms. internat. sci. congresses. Guggenheim fellow van der Waals Lab., U. Amsterdam, 1956-57. Contbr. articles to profl. jours. Patentee in field. Mem. Am. Chem. Soc. (nat. council 1968-83, nat. membership affairs com. 1980-82, nat. council com. chem. edn. 1970-80, nat. com. chem. edn. 1980-82, chmn. nat. subcom. on high sch. chem. edn. 1970-75, mem. nat. high sch. chemistry com. 1978-81, nat. congl. sci. counselor 1974-83, nat. com. tchr. tng. guidelines 1975-77, Charles Holmes Herty Gold medal 1977), AAAS, Geochem. Soc., Am. Geophys. Union, Sigma Xi (v.p. chpt. 1974-75), N.Y. Acad. Sci., Tenn. Acad. Sci. (vis. scientist program 1975), Internat. Assn. Properties of Steam (working group 1975—), Internat. Platform Assn., Phi Kappa Phi. Home: 101 Oak Ln Oak Ridge TN 37830 Office: Chemistry Div Oak Ridge Nat Lab Oak Ridge TN 37830

MARSIGLIA, MATTHEW (PAUL), vending company executive; b. Trenton, N.J., June 6, 1946; s. Sam and Mary (Smathmory) M.; m. Sally Robbius, Oct. 15, 1966 (div. 1972); 1 son, Matthew P.; m. 2d Judith L. Samberg, Sept. 18, 1975; children—Kelly, Scott, Jonathan, Anthony. B.A., U. Southwestern La., 1971; postgrad. U. Pitts., 1973-74, U. Md.-Washington, 1966. Caseworker, Pa. Dept. Pub. Welfare, Uniontown, 1971-73, tng. cons., Pitts., 1973-76, spl. asst. to dep. sec., Harrisburg, 1976-79, project dir., Harrisburg, 1979-82; pres. Keystone Distributors, Inc., Sunset, La., 1982—. Served with USN, 1965-67. Mem. Am. Pub. Welfare Assn. Democrat. Roman Catholic. Home: 118 Constitution Dr Maurice LA 70555 Office: Keystone Distbrs Inc 654 Napoleon Ave Sunset LA 70584

MARSLAND, DAVID BOYD, chemical engineering educator, consultant; b. Ft. Meade, Fla., Dec. 27, 1926; s. Walter Stanley and Helen (Boyd) M.; m. Annette Turner, Sept. 15, 1951; children—Laura, John, Paul, Anne. B.S. in Chem. Engring., Cornell U., 1951, Ph.D., 1958. Jr. research engr. Brookhaven Nat. Lab., Upton, N.Y., 1955-58; research engr. E.I. duPont, Wilmington, Del., 1958-61; Ford Found. resident Esso Engring. Co., Florham Park, N.J., 1966-67; staff cost engr. EPA, N.C., 1973-74; prof. chem. engring. N.C. State U., Raleigh, 1961—; cons. Corning Glass Works, 1973-75, EPA, 1974-76, Monsanto Co., 1976, Research Triangle Inst., 1977—. Served to lt. USN, 1951-53. Mem. Am. Inst. Chem. Engrs., Am. Assn. Cost Engrs., Air Pollution Control Assn., Sigma Xi. Office: PO Box 7905 NC State U Raleigh NC 27695

MARSTELLER, THOMAS FRANKLIN, JR., lawyer; b. Phila., Oct. 18, 1951; s. Thomas Franklin and Hannah Henrietta (Bender) M.; B.S. in Physics, Rensselaer Poly. Inst., 1973; J.D., U. Houston, 1979. Bar: Tex. 1980. Assoc., Pravel, Gambrell, Hewitt, Kirk & Kimball, Houston, 1979—; shareholder Marsteller & Assocs., P.C., 1984—; panelist Am. Arbiration Assn. Host, Houston Grand Opera. Served with USAF, 1973-77. Decorated Air Force Commendation medal; recipient Am. Jurisprudence award U. Houston, 1978. Mem. ABA, Am. Patent Law Assn., Internat. Bar Assn., Houston Engring. and Sci. Soc., Houston Young Lawyers Assn. (chmn. Bill of Rights com. 1980-81). Clubs: Masons, Shriners. Editor Houston Jour. Internat. Law, 1978-79. Home: 2456 Bering Dr Houston TX 77057 Office: Marsteller & Assocs PC 3000 Post Oak Blvd Suite 1400 Houston TX 77056

MARSTON, CLIFTON HENRY, lawyer; b. Mobile, Ala., Aug. 15, 1945; s. Joseph George Lanaux and Rose Marie (Smith) M.; m. Margaret Mary Smith, May 26, 1973; children—George Edward Smith, Robert Henry Smith. A.B., Spring Hill Coll., 1967; M.A., U. Ala., 1969, J.D., 1971. Bar: Ala. 1971. Assoc. firm Cabaniss, Johnston, Gardner, Dumas & O'Neal, Birmingham, Ala., 1971-76, ptnr., 1977—. Served to 2d lt., Med. Service Corps., U.S. Army, 1971. Mem. ABA, Ala. Bar Assn., Birmingham Bar Assn., Ala. Law Inst. (trademark adv. com. 1976-78), Orgn. Am. Historians (assoc.), Am. Hist. Assn. (assoc.), Order of Coif, Omicron Delta Kappa. Roman Catholic. Home: 4385 Mountaindale Rd Birmingham AL 35213 Office: 1900 First Nat So Natural Bldg Birmingham AL 35203

MARSTON, ROBERT QUARLES, university president; b. Toano, Va., Feb. 12, 1923; s. Warren and Helen (Smith) M.; m. Ann Carter Garnett, Dec. 21, 1946; children—Ann, Robert, Wesley. B.S., Va. Mil. Inst., 1943; M.D., Med. Coll. Va., 1947; B.Sc. (Rhodes scholar 1947-49), Oxford (Eng.) U., 1949. Intern Johns Hopkins Hosp., 1949-50; resident Vanderbilt U. Hosp., 1950-51, Med. Coll. Va., 1953-54, asst. prof. medicine, 1954; asst. prof. bacteriology and immunology U. Minn., 1958-59; asso. prof. medicine, asst. dean charge student affairs Med. Coll. Va., 1959-61; dean U. Miss. Sch. Medicine, 1961-66, dir., 1961-65, vice chancellor, 1965-66; asso. dir. div. regional med. programs NIH, 1966-68; adminstr. Fed. Health Services and Mental Health Adminstrn., 1968; dir. NIH, Bethesda, Md., 1968-73; scholar in residence U. Va., Charlottesville, 1973-74; Distinguished fellow Inst. of Medicine, Nat. Acad. Scis., 1973-74; pres. U. Fla., 1974—; dir. Johnson and Johnson. Author articles in field. Bd. visitors Charles R. Drew Postgrad. Sch.; past chmn. bd. trustees Air U.; mem. Fla. Council of 100; exec. council Assn. Am. Med. Coll., 1964-67; mem. com. on relationships between univs. and U.S. govt. Nat. Acad. Scis.; mem. exec. com. Assn. Caribbean Univs. and Research Insts., Nat. Assn. State Univs. and Land Grant Colls.; chmn. Nat. Assn. State Univs. and Land Grant Colls., 1982. Served to 1st lt. AUS, 1951-53. Markle scholar, 1954-59; hon. fellow Lincoln Coll. Oxford U. Fellow Am. Pub. Health Assn.; mem. Am. Hosp. Assn. (hon.), Nat. Med. Assn. (hon.), Assn. Am. Rhodes Scholars, AMA, Assn. Am. Physicians, AAAS, Assn. Am. Med. Colls. (disting. mem.), Am. Clin. and Climatol. Assn., Inst. Medicine of Nat. Acad. Scis., Soc. Scholars Johns Hopkins, Alpha Omega Alpha. Episcopalian. Home: 2151 W University Ave Gainesville FL 32601

MARSZALEK, JOHN FRANCIS, history educator, researcher, writer; b. Buffalo, July 5, 1939; s. John Francis and Regina Kathryn (Sierakowski) M.; m. Jeanne Ann Kozmer, Oct. 16, 1965; children—John Francis III, Christopher Hubert, James Stanley. A.B. Canisius Coll., 1961; A.M., U. Notre Dame, 1963, Ph.D., 1968. Instr. Canisius Coll., Buffalo, 1967-68; asst. prof. Gannon U., Erie, Pa., 1968-72, assoc. prof., 1972-73; assoc. prof. history Miss. State U., Mississippi State, 1973-80, prof., 1980—. Served to capt., M.I., U.S. Army, 1965-67; Vietnam. Hearst fellow, 1961-62; Schmitt fellow, 1964-65; NEH summer stipend, 1971; Am. Council Learned Socs. grantee, 1973-74; research grantee Gannon U., Miss. State U.; NEH travel grantee, 1984; U. Notre Dame travel grantee, 1984. Mem. Orgn. Am. Historians, Miss. Hist. Soc. (dir.), So. Hist. Assn. Roman Catholic. Club: Civitan (v.p.). Author: Court Martial: A Black Man in America, 1972; (with Sadye H. Wier) A Black Businessman in White Mississippi, 1977; (with Douglas Conner) A Black Physician: Bringing Hope in Mississippi, 1985; editor: Diary of Miss Emma Holmes 1861-66, 1979; Sherman's Other War: The General and the Civil War Press, 1981; contbr. articles to profl. jours. Home: 108 Grand Ridge Starkville MS 37959 Office: Dept History Miss State U Mississippi State MS 39762

MARTIN, ANTHONY EDWARD, III, accounting executive; b. Phila., Sept. 3, 1947; s. Anthony E. and Emily C. Martin; m. Francine McFarlane, Apr. 17, 1948; 1 son, Anthony E., N. B.S.E.E., U. Pa., 1970, M.B.A., 1976. C.P.A. Engr. Gen. Electric, Roanoke, Va., 1970-74; cons. Arthur Andersen, Phila., 1976-79; analyst Catalytic, Phila., 1979-81; div. acctg. mgr. Tandem Computer, Reston, Va., 1981—. Mem. U.S. Olympic rowing team, Mexico City, 1968. Mem. Am. Inst. C.P.A.s. Republican. Club: Wharton (Washington). Home: 12451 Oliver Cromwell Dr Herndon VA 22071 Office: Tandem Computers 12100 Sunrise Valley Dr Reston VA 22091

MARTIN, ARTHUR LEE, JR., lawyer; b. Montgomery, Ala., Jan. 13, 1949; s. Arthur Lee and Blanche (Bush) M.; m. Mary Lynne Ortmeyer, Sept. 29, 1973; children—Elizabeth Leah, Rachel Blanche. B.A. cum laude, Vanderbilt U., 1971; J.D. U. Chgo., 1974. Bar: U.S. Dist. Ct. (no. dist.) Ill. 1972, U.S. Ct. Appeals (7th cir.) 1972, Ill. 1975, Ala. 1979, U.S. Dist. Ct. (no. dist.) Ala. 1979, U.S. Ct. Appeals (5th cir.) 1979. Law clk. to Sr. judge U.S. Ct. Appeals (5th cir.), Montgomery, 1974-75; assoc. D'Ancona & Pflaum, Chgo., 1975-78; ptnr. Haskell, Slaughter, Young & Lewis, Birmingham, Ala., 1978—. Trustee Arlington Hist. Mus., Birmingham, 1980—; dir. Birmingham Housing Devel. Corp., Ala., 1981—. Mem. Nat. Assn. Bond Lawyers, ABA, Ala. State Bar, Birmingham Bar Assn., Phi Delta Phi. Democrat. Mem. United Ch. of Christ. Clubs: Relay House, Downtown Democratic. Home: 4501 10th Ave S Birmingham AL 35222 Office: Haskell Slaughter Young & Lewis 800 First Nat-So Nat Bldg Birmingham AL 35203

MARTIN, ARVEL GENE, petroleum engineering company executive, petroleum engineering and management consultant; b. Laurel, Miss., Nov. 24, 1947; s. Claude F. and Helen Ruth (Kyzer) M.; m. Susan Morrison Gregory, June 6, 1968; children—Anthony Jackson, Nicholas Morrison, Virginia Morrison. Student, Miss. State U., 1965-69; B.S. in Petroleum Engring., La. State U., 1970. Registered profl. engr., Calif., La., Tex. Engr., Continental Oil Co., Venture, Calif., 1970-73; chief engr. Drew Cornell, Inc., Lafayette, La., 1973-75; area engr. Husky Oil Co., Santa Maria, Calif., 1975-77; owner, pres. Arvel G. Martin Cons., Santa Maria, Calif., Houston, 1977-78; v.p. engring. Moncrief, Martin Wanamaker, Inc., Houston, 1978-82; pres., founder Geopet, Inc., Houston, 1982—. Coach ch. league baseball, St. Francis Episcopal Ch., Houston, 1982—, ch. league soccer, 1982—. Mem. Nat. Soc. Profl. Engrs., Tex. Soc. Profl. Engrs., Am. Assn. Petroleum Geologists, Houston Geol. Soc., Soc. Petroleum Engrs. of AIME, Soc. Ind. Earth Scientists, Sigma Gamma Epsilon, Pi Epsilon Tau, Tau Beta Pi. Republican. Club: Houstonian (Houston). Avocations: fishing; hunting; tennis; skiing. Home: One Blalock Woods Houston TX 77024 Office: Geopet Inc 1360 Post Oak Blvd Suite 1430 Houston TX 77056

MARTIN, B. FRANK, petroleum geologist; b. Tarboro, N.C., Nov. 15, 1945; s. Benjamin F. and Edna Pauline (Sawyer) M.; m. Anna Marie Conn, May 30, 1967; 1 son, Ben Frank III. B.S., Ga. State U., 1971; M.S., U. Ga., 1973. Cert. petroleum geologist; registered profl. geologist. Field geologist Ga. Geol. Survey, Atlanta, 1972-74; geol. engr. Shell Oil Co., New Orleans, 1974-77; petroleum geologist U.S. Geol. Survey, Reston, Va., 1977-79; area exploration geologist ARCO Oil & Gas Co., Tulsa, 1979-82; v.p. exploration Petroleum Res. Corp., Tulsa, 1982-83; cons. exploration geologist Davis Brothers Oil Prodn., Tulsa, 1983—. Mem. petroleum technology adv. com. Tulsa Jr. Coll., 1982-84. U.S. Coastal Plain Regional Commn. grantee, 1973; Lions Club scholar, 1964. Mem. Am. Assn. Petroleum Geologists, AIME (v.p. Ga. 1973-74), Soc. Profl. Well Log Analysts, Tulsa Geol. Soc., Oklahoma City Geol. Soc., Okla. Well Log Library, Phi Kappa Phi. Office: 6612 S 254th E Ave Broken Arrow OK 74014

MARTIN, BOBBY DALE, state official; b. Brady, Okla., Mar. 20, 1940; s. John Fletcher and Eva Coloe (Been) M.; m. Carolyn Sue Bloomfield, July 30, 1966. Student Okla. State U., 1959-60; B.S., East Central State U., 1963; M.Ed., Okla. U., 1964, postgrad., 1964-65. Cert. tchr., prin., Okla. Tchr., Moore pub. schs., Okla., 1965-67, coach, 1965-66; prin. Meeker pub. schs., Okla., 1967-68, supt., 1968-69; coordinator Okla. State Dept. Edn., Oklahoma City, 1969-76, adminstr. sch. plant services, 1977—; chmn., charter mem. Alliance for Arts Edn., Oklahoma City, 1975-76; exec. dir. Okla. Common Schs. Capital Improvement Co., Oklahoma City, 1983—. Lay leader United Methodist Ch., Newcastle, Okla., 1985—. Mem. Okla. Christmas Tree Growers Assn., Okla. Nurserymens Assn., Okla. Auctioneers Assn., Okla. Assn. for Service to Impacted Schs. (state advisor 1977—), Okla. Sch. Plant Mgmt. Assn., Coop. Council of Sch. Adminstrs., Phi Delta Kappa. Avocations: music; hunting; travel. Office: Okla Dept Edn 2500 N Lincoln Blvd Oklahoma City OK 73105

MARTIN, BOE WILLIS, lawyer; b. Texarkana, Ark., Oct. 6, 1940; s. E. H. and Dorothy Annette (Willis) M.; m. Carol J. Edwards, June 12, 1965; children—Stephanie Diane, Scott Andrew. B.A., Tex. A&M U., 1962; LL.B., U. Tex., 1964; LL.M., George Washington U., 1970. Bar: Tex. 1964. Law clk. Tex. Supreme Ct. 1966-67; assoc. Snakard, Brown & Gambill, Fort Worth, 1967-69; asst. counsel U.S. Senate Labor and Pub. Welfare Com., 1969; legis. asst. U.S. Senator Ralph W. Yarborough, 1969-71; assoc., ptnr. Snakard, Brown & Gambill, Fort Worth, 1971-72; assoc., ptnr. Stalcup & Johnson, Dallas, 1972-77; assoc., ptnr. Coke & Coke, Dallas, 1977-80; ptnr. Johnson & Swanson, Dallas, 1981—; vis. prof. law So. Meth. U. Sch. Law, 1972, 73, 75, U. Tex. Sch. Law, 1977, 79. Mem. Carter-Mondale Campaign staff, 1976, 1980; cons. to Vice-Pres. of U.S., 1977-80; cons. Mondale for Pres. Campaign, 1983-84. Served to capt. U.S. Army, 1964-69. Mem. ABA, Tex. Bar Assn.,

Dallas Bar Assn. Democrat. Methodist. Contbr. articles to legal jours. Home: 4435 Arcady St Dallas TX 75205 Office: Founders Sq 900 Jackson St Dallas TX 75202

MARTIN, BOYCE FICKLEN, JR., federal judge; b. Boston, Oct. 23, 1935; s. Boyce Ficklen and Helen Artt M.; m. Marvin Hamilton Brown, July 8, 1961; children—Mary V. H., Julia H.C., Boyce Ficklen III, Robert C. G. II. A.B., Davidson Coll., 1957; J.D., U. Va., 1963. Bar: Ky. 1963. Law clk. to Shackelford Miller, Jr., chief judge U.S. Ct. Appeals for 6th Circuit, Cin., 1963-64; asst. U.S. atty. Western Dist. Ky., Louisville, 1964, U.S. atty., 1965; practiced in Louisville, 1966-74; judge Jefferson Circuit Ct., Louisville, 1974-76; chief judge Ct. Appeals Ky., Louisville, 1976-79; judge U.S. Ct. Appeals 6th Circuit Ohio, Cin., 1979—; instr. constl. law and criminal procedure U. Louisville Sch. Law, So. Police Inst., 1965-69. Mem. vestry St. Francis in the Fields Ch., Harrods Creek, Ky., 1979-83; bd. visitors Davidson (N.C.) Coll., 1980—; mem. Ky. Gov.'s Council on Health Planning, 1967-71; sec. met. bd. dirs. YMCA Greater Louisville, 1968-74; sec., bd. dirs. Blue Ridge Assembly YMCA, Black Mountain, N.C., 1968-74; chmn. YMCA Com. on Urban Problems, 1970; trustee Isaac W. Bernheim Found., 1981—, Blackacre Found., Inc., Louisville, Hanover Coll. (Ind.); mem. exec. bd. Old Ky. Home council Boy Scouts Am., 1968-72; pres. Louisville Zool. Commn., 1971-74; Louisville-Jefferson County chpt. Am. Cancer Soc., 1965-67. Served with U.S. Army, 1958-66. Recipient Presdl. award Ky. Council on Crime and Delinquency, 1965. Fellow Am. Bar Found.; mem. Inst. Jud. Adminstrn., Am. Judicature Soc., Am. Bar Assn. (com. effective appellate advocacy Conf. Appellate Judges), Ky. Bar Assn., Louisville Bar Assn. Democrat. Episcopalian. Home: 5903 Jenness Ct Louisville KY 40222 Office: 244 United State Courthouse 601 W Broadway Louisville KY 40202*

MARTIN, CAROLINE SUE (SUZI), real estate acquisition and management company executive, psychologist; b. Uvalde, Tex., Mar. 27, 1946; m. Benjamin G. Martin; 6 children. B.S., Incarnate Word Coll., 1967; M.Ed., Our Lady of the Lake Coll., 1969; Ph.D., U. South Fla., 1983. Tchr. home econs., student counselor Tex. pub. schs.; chief staff psychologist Hillsborough County Dept. Children's Services, Fla.; part-time grad. asst. intern program U. South Fla., Ft. Myers; co-owner, pres. C.M.S. Properties, Ft. Myers, 1983-85. Pres. U. South Fla. Town and Gown Club, Soc. Symphony Women; chmn. steering com. for devel. U. South Fla. Pub. T.V. and Radio; charter mem., sec. regional adv. council Sta. WSFP-TV-FM; mem. adv. com., sec. Cape Coral Hosp. West Coast Health Found.; planning coordinator S.W. Fla. Million Dollar Endowed Chair Nursing; bd. dirs. Youth Shelter of S.W. Fla.; legis. coordinator pres.-elect Lee County Med. Aux.; organizer Naples Symphony Guild. Named Fla. Woman of 1985, Fla. Woman mag., one of Outstanding Women of Tampa, 1979; 1983 finalist in Gannett Found. Heart of Gold award; recipient Golden Signet award, 1983. Clubs: Periwinkle Garden (pres.), Fiddlesticks Country (Ft. Myers) (house com.). Lodges: United Daus. of the Confederacy (sec.); Zonta Internat.

MARTIN, CARTER WIDEMAN, dentist; b. New Orleans, Oct. 22, 1945; s. Fred Bryan and Hazell Frances (Wideman) M.; m. Cynthia Elaine Carter, Apr. 11, 1980; 1 child, Cali Layn. A.A., New Mex. Mil. Inst., 1965; B.S., Baylor U., 1967, D.D.S., 1970. Pvt. practice dentistry San Angelo, Tex., 1970—; rep. Dental Polit. Action Com., 1982-84. Bd. dirs. W. Tex. Boys Ranch, San Angelo, 1973-84, exec. bd. dirs., 1980-84, budget com., 1985; bd. dirs. Am. Heart Assn., Tom Green County, Tex., 1982-85, pres., 1982-83, v.p., 1983-84, devel. chmn., 1984. Fellow Am. Coll. Dentists; mem. Acad. Gen. Dentistry, ADA (alt. del. 1983-84), Tex. Dental Assn. (del. 1982, 83, dir. S.W. div. 1984, v.p. 1985), San Angelo Dist. Dental Soc. (pres. 1978-79, sec. peer rev. 1975-84), S.W. Prosthodontic Soc. Republican. Methodist. Avocations: hunting; fishing; golf; tennis; pistol shooting. Office: 515 Beauregard St San Angelo TX 76903

MARTIN, CHARLES, educational administrator. Supt. of schs. Orleans Parish, La. Office: 4100 Touro St New Orleans LA 70122*

MARTIN, CLARENCE WILLIAM, cattle feed yard executive; b. Elk City, Okla., Jan. 31, 1930; s. Calvin William and Lela Blanche (Baxter) M.; student public schs., Friona, Tex.; m. Martha Wynona Carter, June 22, 1947; children—Martha Ann, Larry, Mike, Greg, Keith, Kathy. Rancher, Colo., S.D., N.M., Tex., various dates; with Farwell Feed Lot (Tex.), 1958-63; pres., gen. mgr. Hi Plains Feed Yard, Inc., Friona, Tex., 1963—; v.p. W. Friona Grain, Inc., 1963—, Tri-County Elevator Co., Inc., 1980—. Mem. Friona C. of C. (dir. 1968-70, 78—), West Tex. C. of C. (dir. 1972—, chmn. agr. and ranching com. 1978-83), Tex. Cattle Feeders Assn., Tex. Southwestern Cattle Raisers, Nat. Cattleman's Assn. Address: Rural Route 2 Friona TX 79035

MARTIN, CORTEZ HEZEKIAH, social work educator, researcher; b. Jacksonville, Fla., July 25, 1935; d. Sam and Julius (Neals) Hezekiah; m. John Timothy Martin, Aug. 10, 1957; children—Sonijia, Latacha. B.S., Tenn. State U., 1955, M.S., 1957; M.S.W., Howard U., 1980, D.S.W., 1984. Grad. asst. Tenn. State U., Nashville, 1956-57; prof. Edward Waters Coll., Jacksonville, Fla., 1957-59; tchr. Memphis City Bd. Edn., 1959-78; grad. asst. Howard U., Washington, 1980-82; assoc. prof. social work Lemoyne-Owen Coll., Memphis, 1984—; asst. researcher U.S. Dept. Agr., Washington, 1978-82, Howard U., 1980-83. Worker, Campaign for Congressman Ford, Memphis, 1978. Recipient Disting. Service award Tenn. Edn. Assn., cert. Merit U.S. Dept. Agr., 1979; MIMH grantee, 1980-83; Howard U. trustee fellow, 1978--83. Mem. Nat. Assn. Social Work, NAACP, Alpha Kappa Alpha, Sigma Rho Sigma. Avocations: reading; knitting; cross stitching. Home: 931 Marjorie Cove Memphis TN 38106 Office: Dept Sociology and Social Work Le Moyne Owen Coll 807 Walker Ave Memphis TN 38126

MARTIN, DAVID EDWARD, educator; b. Green Bay, Wis., Oct. 1, 1939; s. Edward Henry and Lillie (Luckman) M.; B.S., U. Wis., 1961, M.S., 1963, Ph.D., 1970. Ford Found. research trainee Wis. Regional Primate Center, Madison, 1967-70; asst. prof. health scis. Ga. State U., Atlanta, 1970-74, assoc. prof., 1974-80, prof., 1980—; affiliate scientist Yerkes Primate Research Center, Emory U., Atlanta, 1970—. U.S. rep. to Internat. Olympic Acad., 1978. Recipient fed. and univ. grants for physiol. research; Disting. prof., 1975, 81, 85. Mem. AAUP, Soc. Study Reprodn., Am. Coll. Sports Medicine, Am. Physiol. Soc., Internat. Primatol. Soc. Clubs: Atlanta Coin, Atlanta Track. Author: Laboratory Experiments in Human Physiology, 4th edit., 1980; The Marathon Footrace, 1979; La Corsa Di Maratona, 1982; The High Jump Book, 1982; contbr. articles to profl. jours. Home: 510 Coventry Rd #13A Decatur GA 30030 Office: Dept Respiratory Therapy Ga State Univ Atlanta GA 30303

MARTIN, DAVID LINCOLN, political science educator; b. Los Angeles, May 6, 1947; s. Albert H. and Cornelia A. (Lincoln) M.; m. Catherine R. Perricone, June 6, 1975. B.A. magna cum laude, U. Redlands, 1968; M.A. in Govt., Claremont Grad. Sch., 1969, Ph.D. in Govt., 1973. Pub. adminstrn. analyst UCLA, 1972-73; asst. prof. Auburn U., Ala., 1973-77, assoc. prof. 1978-82, prof. polit. sci., 1983—; spl. projects officer Dept. Interior, Washington, 1979-80. Author: Alabama's State and Local Governments, 2d edit., 1985; Running City Hall: Municipal Administration in America, 1982; (with others) Capitol, Courthouse and City Hall, 6th edit., 1981. Contbr. articles to profl. jours. Served with U.S. Army, 1969-71, Vietnam. Calif. State Grad. fellow, 1968-69, Haynes Found. fellow, 1968-69, Nat. Assn. Schs. Pub. Affairs and Adminstrn. fellow, 1979-80. Mem. Am. Soc. Pub. Adminstrn. (chpt. pres. 1984-85), Am. Polit. Sci. Assn., So. Polit. Sci. Assn., Ala. Polit. Sci. Assn., Am. Acad. Polit. and Social Sci. Office: Auburn U Polit Sci Dept 7072 Haley Ctr Auburn University AL 36849

MARTIN, DAVID MICHAEL, gastroenterologist, educator; b. Des Moines, Mar. 10, 1951; s. Hirschel Arthur and Elaine (Swartz) M.; m. Joanne Louise Finegan, Nov. 4, 1979; children—Rebecca Ann, Julia Beth. A.B., Oberlin Coll., 1973; M.D., Emory U., 1977. Diplomate Am. Bd. Internal Medicine, Am. Bd. Gastroenterology. Intern in internal medicine Emory U. Hosp., Atlanta, 1977-78, resident in internal medicine, 1978-80, clin. research fellow in digestive diseases, 1980-81, fellow in digestive diseases, 1981-83; asst. prof. medicine Emory U. Sch. Medicine, 1983—; gastroenterologist Atlanta VA Med. Ctr., 1983-84. Trustee Congregation B'nai Israel, Riverdale, Ga., 1983—. Fellow Am. Coll. Gastroenterology, ACP; mem. Am. Gastroent. Assn., Am. Soc. Gastrointestinal Endoscopy, So. Med. Assn. Contbr. articles to profl. jours. Office: 2756-B Felton Dr East Point GA 30344

MARTIN, DEAN MONROE, religion and philosophy educator; b. Lebanon, Mo., Aug. 4, 1942; s. Francis V. and Monta V. (Butcher) M.; m. Delores Ann Burson, Mar. 27, 1965; children—William Todd, Aron Monroe. B.A., William Jewell Coll., 1964; B.D., Yale U., 1967; Ph.D., Baylor U., 1972; postgrad. Duke U., summer 1976, Univ. Coll. Swansea (Wales), summer, 1981. Instr. U.S. Internat. U., San Diego, 1971-72, asst. prof., 1972-74; asst. prof. religion and philosophy Campbell U., Buies Creek, N.C., 1974-78, assoc. prof., 1978—, chmn. humanities div., 1982—; interim pastor various Baptist Chs.; deacon Buies Creek 1st Bapt. Ch.; past pres. PTA; coach Little League Baseball. Mem. Am. Acad. Religion, Soc. Christian Philosophers, Assn. Bapt. Profs. of Religion, Lambda Chi Alpha, Omicron Delta Kappa. Republican.

MARTIN, ELIZABETH ANN, physical education educator, coach; b. Charleston, W.Va., Oct. 22, 1956; d. F. Duane and Charlotte Lora (Crighton) Hill; m. Terry Lee Martin, Aug. 20, 1976 (div. 1983); 1 dau., Melinda Nicole. B.S., W.Va. Tech., 1978; M.S., Marshall U., 1981. Tchr. phys. edn., coach Stonewall Jackson High Sch., Charleston, W.Va., 1978—. Mem. Kappa Delta Pi. Republican. Methodist. Home: 1562 Summit Dr Charleston WV 25302 Office: Stonewall Jackson High Sch Washington St W and Park Ave Charleston WV 25302

MARTIN, ELIZABETH DOMINICA, recreation educator, coach; b. Trieste, Italy, Sept. 13, 1948; d. Edward O. and Emmy (Boneclariti) M. B.S.E., Delta State U., 1971, M.Ed., 1972; postgrad U. So. Miss., 1972-75, Springhill Coll., 1983. Tchr., coach St. Joseph High Sch., Greenville, Miss., 1980—, Coleman Jr. High Sch., Greenville, 1974-79, Pearl River Jr. Coll., Poplarville, Miss., 1972-74. Fellow Am. Badminton Assn., Nat. Cath. Edn. Assn.; mem. NEA, Am. Alliance Phys. Edn., Recreation and Sports, Nat. Assn. Girls and Womens Sports. Roman Catholic. Office: St Joseph High Sch 700 Golf St Greenville MS 38701

MARTIN, GENE B., geologist, oil company executive; b. Amarillo, Tex., Oct. 31, 1931; s. John Claude and Lydia (Bourland) M.; m. Patsy Lynn Caldwell, Aug. 18, 1952; children—Gene B., Judy Lynn Martin Morro. B.S. in Petroleum Geology, Miss. State U., 1953, M.S. in Gen. Geology, 1954. Instr. geology Miss. U., Starkville, 1954-55; paleontologist Gulf Oil Corp. and Gulf Research, New Orleans, 1957-66; paleontologist Atlantic Richfield Co., Corpus Christi, Tex., 1966-69, sr. paleontologist Corpus Christi and Houston, 1969-76; sr. geol. assoc. Arco Oil & Gas Co., Houston, 1976-81; dir. stratigraphy and paleontology Arco Exploration Co., Houston, 1981-85, mgr. stratigraphy and paleontology, 1985—, sr. advisor geol. support group. Author tech. papers. Served as sgt. U.S. Army, 1955-57. Mem. Am. Assn. Petroleum Geologists, Soc. Econ. Paleontologists and Mineralogists (hon. Gulf Coast sect.), Houston Geol. Soc., Sigma Gamma Epsilon. Republican. Baptist. Club: University (Houston). Avocations: golf; fishing. Home: 5313 Barouche Plano TX 75023 Office: 2300 W Plano Pkwy Plano TX 75075

MARTIN, HAROLD EUGENE, publishing company executive; b. Cullman, Ala., Oct. 4, 1923; s. Rufus John and Emma (Meadows) M.; m. Jean Elizabeth Wilson, Nov. 25, 1945; children—Brian, Anita. B.A. in History with honors, Howard Coll., Birmingham, Ala., 1954; M.A. in Journalism, Syracuse U., 1957. Asst. gen. mgr. Birmingham News, Newhouse Newspapers, 1960-63, asst. prodn. mgr. St. Louis Globe-Democrat, 1958-60, asst. bus. mgr. Syracuse Herald Jour., 1957-58; pub. Montgomery Advertiser (Ala.) and Ala. Jour., Carmage Walls Newspapers, 1963-70; pres. Multimedia Newspapers, editor, pub. Montgomery Advertiser and Ala. Jour., Multimedia, Inc., 1970-78, v.p., mem. mgmt. bd. Multimedia, Inc., 1973-78, also corp. dir.; exec. v.p., chief exec. officer So. Baptist Radio and TV Commn., Ft. Worth, 1979; pres. Jefferson Pilot Publs., Inc., Beaumont, Tex., 1980-85, dir. Jefferson Pilot Corp., Greensboro, N.C.; pres., pub. Beaumont Enterprise, 1981-85; cons. Hearst Corp., N.Y.C., 1985—; former co-owner, pub. Herald-Citizen, daily newspaper, Cookeville, Tenn., News-Observer, weekly newspaper, Crossett, Ark. and Baxter Bull. (newspaper Enterprise Assn. Best Overall Weekly Newspaper 1973), Mountain Home, Ark., 1970-78; Disting. vis. prof. Sch. Journalism U. Fla., 1979-80; mem. faculty Samford U., 1961-63; juror Pulitzer Prize, 1971, 72. Contbr. articles to profl. jours. Bd. dirs. Billy Graham Evangelistic Assn., Mpls.; mem. exec. bd. Bapt. Gen. Conv. Tex., 1982-85. Recipient awards for articles: citation Howard Coll., 1965; Outstanding Merit award, Ala. Dental Assn., 1966; Community Service award AP Assn., 1969, 72, 73; Pulitzer prize, 1970; 1st pl. Newswriting award AP, 1971; Newswriting award for Best Stories of Yr. by Ala. Reporters, 1974, 75; Canon award for accurate and factual reporting of med. news Med. Assn. Ala., 1972; Ann. award for outstanding contbn. to health care Ala. State Nurses' Assn., 1972, News award, 1976; Communications award Ala. Bapt. State Conv., 1975; named Alumnus of Yr., Samford U., 1970. Mem. Am. Soc. Newspaper Editors, Am. Newspaper Pubs. Assn., So. Newspaper Pubs. Assn. (editorial com.), Alumni Assn. Samford U. (pres. 1967-71), Sigma Delta Chi (Green Eye Shade citation for reporting 1969). Baptist. Home and office: 4958 Overton Woods Ct Ft Worth TX 76109

MARTIN, HARRY CORPENING, state supreme court justice; b. Lenoir, N.C., Jan. 13, 1920; s. Hal C. Martin and Johnsie (Harshaw) Nelson; m. Nancy Dallam, Apr. 16, 1955; children—John A., J. Matthew, Mary D. A.B., U. N.C.-Chapel Hill, 1942; LL.B., Harvard U., 1948; LL.M., U. Va., 1982. Bar: N.C. 1948. Gen. practice, Asheville, N.C., 1948-62; judge Superior Ct., Asheville, 1962-78; judge Ct. of Appeals of N.C., Raleigh, 1978-82; assoc. justice Supreme Ct. of N.C., Raleigh, 1982—. Served with U.S. Army, 1942-45. Mem. N.C. Bar Assn. (v.p. 1972-73), Nat. Conf. State Trial Judges (del. 1967-78), Fourth Circuit Jud. Conf., N.C. Conf. of Superior Ct. Judges (pres. 1972-73). Democrat. Episcopalian. Office: Supreme Ct of NC 1 E Morgan St PO Box 1841 Raleigh NC 27602

MARTIN, HENRY JEROME, geologist, consultant; b. New Haven, Aug. 3, 1949; s. Henry Jerome and Eugenia Agnes (Morris) M.; m. Susan Margaret Richard, Nov. 30, 1974; children—Elizabeth, Erin Therese. B.S. in Physics, Bucknell U., 1971; M.S. in Geology, Brown U., 1973. Geophysicist ARCO, Lafayette, La., 1973-77, Gen. Crude Oil Co., Houston, 1977-80; geologist Pex Tech. Energy Co., Houston, 1980-82, CPC Exploration, Houston, 1983-84, Rockbridge Oil and Gas, Houston, 1984-85, Citation Oil & Gas, 1985—. Mem. Am. Assn. Petroleum Geologists. Home: 7907 Redding Oak Ct Houston TX 77088 Office: Citation Oil and Gas 1600 Greenspoint Park Dr Houston TX 77060

MARTIN, HOWARD NATHAN, association executive; b. Livingston, Tex., July 17, 1917; s. Jack Adams and Johnnie Richard (Jones) M.; A.A., Lon Morris Coll., 1937; B.B.A., U. Tex., 1939, M.A., 1941; m. Mavis Valerie Condrey, June 1, 1941; children: Howard, Marylin Gene, Ruth Ann. Bus. mgr. Lon Morris Coll., Jacksonville, Tex., 1941-42; dir. econ. and demographic research Houston C. of C., 1947—; lectr. in field, cons. Ch. bd. trustee Faribanks Meth. Ch., Houston, 1949-53; pres. bd. trustees Cypress-Fairbanks Ind. Sch. Dist. (Tex.), 1953-54. Served with USNR, 1942-46. Decorated Bronze Star; cert. Chamber exec; recipient C.K. Chamberlain award for best article E. Tex. Hist. Jour. Mem. Am. C. of C. Execs., So. Assn. C. of C. Execs., Tex. C. of C. Mgrs., Am. Statis. Assn. Nat. Assn. Bus. Economists, Am. Mktg. Assn., Am. C. of C. Researchers Assn. (nat. pres. 1961-63), Tex. Hist. Assn., Tex. Econ. and Demographic Assn. (pres. 1984), Tex. Folklore Soc., Delta Sigma Pi. Author: Chamber of Commerce Research Activities, 1975; Myths and Folktales of the Alabama-Coushatta Indian Tribes of Tex, 1977. (Book of Year, Tex. Folklore Soc. 1977); other books. Home: 8710 Cedarspur St Houston TX 77055 Office: 1100 Milam Bldg 25th Floor Houston TX 77002

MARTIN, JAMES GRUBBS, governor of North Carolina; b. Savannah, Ga., Dec. 11, 1935; s. Arthur Morrison and Mary Julia (Grubbs) M.; m. Dorothy Ann McAulay, June 1, 1957; children—James Grubbs, Emily Wood, Arthur Benson. B.S., Davidson Coll., 1957; Ph.D., Princeton U., 1960. Asso. prof. chemistry Davidson (N.C.) Coll., 1960-72; mem. 93d-98th Congresses from 9th Dist. N.C., 1973-85; gov. of N.C., 1985—. Mem. Mecklenburg (N.C.) Bd. County Commrs., 1966-72, chmn., 1967-68, 70-71; founder, 1st chmn. Centralina Council Govts., Charlotte, N.C., 1968-70; v.p. Nat. Assn. Regional Councils, 1970-72; pres. N.C. Assn. County Commrs., 1970-71. Del. Republican Nat. Conv., 1968. Danforth fellow, 1957-60; recipient Charles Lathrop Parsons award Am. Chem. Soc., 1983. Mem. Beta Theta Pi (v.p., trustee 1966-69, pres. 1975-78). Presbyterian (deacon). Clubs: Masons, Shriners, Scottish Rite (knight comdr. ct. of honor). Office: Office of the Governor 116 W Jones St Raleigh NC 27611*

MARTIN, JESS AARON, educator; b. Picher, Okla., May 2, 1926; s. Corbett Harrison and Sadie Mae (Plank) M.; A.B., San Diego State Coll., 1953; M.S. in L.S., U. So. Calif., 1955; m. Betty Jean Martin, June 20, 1948; children—Robert Kirk, Richard Lewis. Librarian, San Diego (Calif.) County Med. Soc., 1953, 56-57; chief tech. service Convair-Astronautics, San Diego, 1957-58; asst. med. librarian U. Ky., Lexington, 1958-60; dir. Ohio State U. Med. Sch. Library, Columbus, 1960-63; chief Library Br., NIH, Bethesda, Md., 1963-68; dir. Temple U. Med. Library, Phila., 1968-71; dir. U. Tenn. Center for Health Sci. Library, Memphis, 1971—; adj. lectr. U. Md. Library Sch., 1967-68, Memphis State U., 1979. Served with USN, 1944-46. Med. Library Assn. scholar, 1954-55. Mem. Med. Library Assn., Tenn. Library Assn., Southeastern Library Assn., AAUP, Beta Phi Mu. Contbr. articles to profl. jours. Home: 6477 Keswick Dr Memphis TN 38119 Office: 800 Madison Ave Memphis TN 38163

MARTIN, JOHN DAVID, finance educator, researcher, author; b. Ruston, La., Oct. 1, 1945; s. J. B. and Delia (Gay) M.; m. Sally Johnson; children—Marcus David, Jesse John. B.S. cum laude in Bus. Adminstrn., La. Tech. U., 1967, M.B.A. in Econs., 1968; D.B.A. in Fin., Tex. Tech U., 1973. Instr. econs., La. Tech. U., Ruston, 1968-69; instr. fin. Tex. Tech U., Lubbock, 1969-73; assoc. prof. fin. Va. Poly. Inst. and State U., Blacksburg, 1973-77; assoc. prof. fin., Tex. A&M U., College Station, 1977-79; assoc. prof. fin. U. Tex., Austin, 1980-83, prof. fin., 1984—, mem. univ. coms. including exec. com. of operating bd. of trustees of Tex. Student Publs., 1984—. Contbg. author: Study Guide and Workbook to Fundamentals of Financial Management, 3rd edit., 1977; Guide to Financial Analysis, 1979, Spanish transl., 1982; Cases in Financial Management, 1979; Readings in Financial Management, 1981; Personal Financial Management, 1982; Study Guide and Workbook to Basic Financial Management, 3rd edit., 1985; Basic Financial Management, 3rd edit., 1985; Cases in Finance, 2d edit., 1983; editor for fin. Jour. Bus. Research, 1977—; assoc. editor Advanced in Fin. Planning and Forecasting, 1982—; assoc. editor for fin. Jour. Fin. Research, 1980-81; editorial bd. Jour. Bus. Research, 1975-76; ad hoc reviewer Fin. Mgmt., Jour. Fin. Research, Jour. Econs. and Bus., Quar. Rev. of Econs. and Bus., Jour. of Fin.; contbr. articles to publs. in field, profl. confs., U.S., Netherlands. Commr.-elect Pony-Colt Baseball program, West Austin Youth Assn., Tex., 1984, player agt., 1985, coach, 1985; coach Little League, Westlake, Tex., 1982-83. Grad. fellow Tex. Tech U., summer 1970, fin. area scholar, 1970, Coll. Bus. Adminstrn. fellow, 1970-71; recipient Outstanding Research award Coll. Bus. Adminstrn., Tex. A&M U., 1979; research grantee, Tex. Electric Utilities, summer 1980; grantee Tex. Real Estate Research Ctr., 1977, SBA, 1978, Inst. of Quantitative Research in Fin., Columbia U., 1978, Coll. Bus. Research Fund, Tex. A&M U., summer 1977, U. Tex., 1980, 82, 84, 85. Mem. Am. Fin. Assn., Am. Econs. Assn., Fin. Mgmt. Assn. (dir. doctoral seminar 1983, chmn. editor selection com. Fin. Mgmt. 1984), So. Fin. Assn. (bd. dirs. 1978-80, 84—), Southwestern Fin. Assn. (pres. 1980-81), Phi Kappa Phi, Beta Gamma Sigma, Phi Kappa Alpha. Office: Dept Fin Univ Tex CBA 6.222 Austin TX 78712

MARTIN, JOSEPHINE WALKER, educator; b. Charleston, S.C., Jan. 15, 1927; d. George Archibald and Josephine Isabel (Walker) M.; A.B., U. S.C., 1946, M.Ed., 1950, Ph.D. (Stoddard fellow), Coll. Edn., 1971; M.A., Columbia U. Union Theol. Sem., 1952; postgrad. C.G. Jung Inst., Zurich, Switzerland, 1954-56. Nat. cert. counselor. Tchr., St. Andrew's Parish High Sch., Charleston, 1947-50; dir. Christian edn. Ch. of St. Edward the Martyr Episcopal, N.Y.C., 1952-54, 56-57; tchr., guidance counselor Crayton Jr. High Sch., Richland County (S.C.) Public Schs., 1957-67; instr. Coll. Edn., U. S.C., Columbia, 1968-71, asst. prof., 1971-77, asso. prof. ednl. founds., 1977-84, assoc. prof. emerita, 1984. Mem. vestry Trinity Episcopal Cathedral, Columbia, 1976-79. Mem. AAUP, AAUW, Am. Ednl. Studies Assn., S.C. Hist. Soc., South Caroliniana Soc., LWV, Common Cause, Phi Delta Kappa, Delta Kappa Gamma (pres. chpt. 1980-82). Club: Analytical Psychology of N.Y. Editor: Dear Sister Letters Written on Hilton Head Island 1867, 1977. Home: 1403 Haynsworth Rd Columbia SC 29205 Office: Coll Edn U SC Columbia SC 29208

MARTIN, LARRY KENNETH, artist; b. Anniston, Ala., June 7, 1939; s. A. Hughes and Esther (Lenora) M.; m. Yvonne P.; children—Tim Hunter, Phillip A., Darryl G. B.S. in Math. and Biology, Jacksonville State U., 1961; M.S. in Biostats., Tulane U., 1965, M.S. in Parasitology, 1965, Ph.D., 1970. Curator, Anniston Mus. Natural History, 1976-79; wildlife artist Wren's Nest Gallery, Jacksonville, Ala., 1979—; assoc. prof. Jacksonville State U., Ala., 1980-82; cons. for various orgns., Ala., 1976—. Contbr. articles to sci. jours. Served with U.S. Army, 1961-76. Recipient Meritorious Service award Nat. Audubon Soc., 1985. Avocations: log cabin restorations; primitive antiques. Home and Office: 507-B N Church Jacksonville AL 36265

MARTIN, MARY WILLIAMS, university dean; b. St. Louis County, Mo., Aug. 6, 1926; d. Edward Joseph and Bertha (Gerberding) Williams; m. Chester Robin Martin, Aug. 5, 1950; children—Mary Barone, Cheslynn Ann. B.S., Ohio State U., 1952; M.A., Memphis State U., 1965; Ed.D., U. Tenn., 1967. Lic. elem. and secondary sch. prin., Tenn.; lic. advanced adminstr., Tenn.; lic. supr. instrn., Tenn. Tchr. Borden High Sch., Ind., 1952-54, Woodruff High Sch., Peoria, Ill., 1955-57; instr. U. Tenn., Knoxville, 1967; prof. Middle Tenn. State U., Murfreesboro, 1968-81, dean Grad. Sch., 1981—; mem. vis. team Nat. Council for Accreditation of Tchr. Edn., 1978—; pres. Conf. Grad. Sch., State of Tenn., 1985—; mem. adv. bd. Citizens Central Bank, Murfreesboro. Editor The Ednl. Catalyst, 1974-76. Named Outstanding Tchr., Middle Tenn. State U. Found., 1974. Mem. Am. Assn. for Higher Edn., Assn. Tchrs. Educators, Am. Assn. Coll. Tchrs. of Edn., Phi Delta Kappa, Kappa Delta Pi. Presbyterian. Office: Middle Tenn State U Murfreesboro TN 37132

MARTIN, NORMA HERRINGTON, librarian; b. DeRidder, La., Jan. 5, 1947; d. Norman and Floye (Nichols) Herrington; m. Alan Elias Martin, June 2, 1968. B.S., McNeese State U., Lake Charles, La., 1969; M.L.S., La. State U., 1970. Gen. librarian La. State U., Baton Rouge, 1970-75, asst. librarian, 1975-79, assoc. librarian, 1979—, head catalog maintenance unit, 1982—, head automated processing unit, 1985—; chmn. Task Force Renovation Hill Meml. Library, Baton Rouge, 1977-85. Mem. ALA, La. Library Assn., Southeastern Library Assn., Beta Phi Mu. Home: 6532 Boone Dr Baton Rouge LA 70808 Office: Middleton Library La State U Baton Rouge LA 70803

MARTIN, PAUL EDWARD, architect; b. Lockport, N.Y., Nov. 16, 1944; s. Edward Cornell and Ellen Margaret (Collier) M.; m. Cassandra Diane Mize, Jan. 29, 1966; children—Todd Collier, Margaret Alexis, Christy Elizabeth. B.S., U. Houston, 1967, B.Arch., 1968. City planner City of Corpus Christi, Tex., 1968-69; assoc. S.I. Morris Assocs. (now Morris Aubrey), Houston, 1969-73; pres., founder Urban Arch. Inc., Houston, 1973—; bd. dirs. dean's adv. bd. Coll. of Architecture U. Houston, 1983—. Works include: Tex. Internat. Reservations Facility, 1978, Addison Market, 1984 (Dallas chpt. AIA exterior award 1985), Waugh on the Bayou Office Bldg., 1983. Trustee Tex. Inst. of Family Psychiatry, Houston, 1977-84; bd. mgmt. Palmer Drug Abuse Program, Houston, 1984—. Mem. AIA, Tex. Soc. Architects (Houston chpt. awards 1979). Avocation: photography. Office: Urban Architecture Inc 5858 Westheimer Suite 700 Houston TX 77057

MARTIN, PAUL E(DWARD), lawyer; b. Atchison, Kans., Feb. 5, 1928; s. Harres C. and Thelma F. (Wilson) M.; m. Betty Lou Crawford, Aug. 28, 1954; children: Cherry G., Paul A., Marylou. B.B.A., Baylor U., 1955, LL.B., 1956; LL.M., Harvard U., 1957. Bar: Tex. 1956, Pa. 1958. Assoc. Ballard, Spahr, Andrews & Ingersoll, Phila., 1957-58; ptnr. Fulbright & Jaworski, Houston, 1959-77; sr. ptnr. Chamberlain, Hrdlicka, White, Johnson & Williams, Houston, 1977—; instr. in estate planning U. Houston. Exec. com. Met. Houston March of Dimes, 1980—; chmn. deacons West Meml. Baptist Ch., 1979-80; trustee Baylor U., 1970—, Meml. Hosp. System, 1980—; pres. Baylor U. Devel. Council, 1973-74; trustee Fgn. Mission Bd., So. Bapt. Conv. Served to lt. comdr. USN, 1947-53. Fellow Am. Coll. Probate Council; mem. ABA (sect. real property, probate and trust law and sect. taxation), State Bar of Tex., Houston Bar Assn., Houston Estate and Fin. Forum (pres. 1965-66), Houston Bus. and Estate Planning Council, Phi Delta Phi. Republican. Club: Houston. Co-author: How to Live and Die with Texas Probate. Office: 1400 Citicorp Ctr 1200 Smith St Houston TX 77002

MARTIN, ROBERT EARNSHAW, advertising agency executive; b. Washington, Oct. 17, 1909; s. Robert Hamilton and Alice King (Earnshaw) M.; B.A., B.Ph. in Journalism, Emory U., 1931; m. Martha Frances Cross, June 17, 1959; children—Margie Hodges, Gray Rains, Patricia Calvert. Pres., Advt. Center, Atlanta, 1929—; account exec. James A. Greene Advt. Agy., 1931-33; advt. mgr. Muse's Retail Stores, 1934-38; pres. Robert E. Martin & Co., Advt. Agy., Atlanta, 1939—. Former pres. Child Service and Family Counseling Center, Family Service Soc.; mem. guild Atlanta Symphony Orch.; v.p. Emory U. Alumni Council. Served to lt. USNR, 1944-46. Cert. bus. communicator. Mem. Am. Advt. Fedn. (past dist. gov.), Atlanta Advt. Club (past pres.), Bus./Profl.

Advt. Assn., Internat. Yachting Fellowship of Rotarians, Scabbard and Blade, Chi Phi, Omicron Delta Kappa, Tau Kappa Alpha. Republican. Episcopalian. Clubs: University Yacht (founding commodore) (Atlanta); Rotary, Georgian. Home: 11 Pointe Terr Vinings GA 30339 Office: Emerson Center Office Park PO Box 724028 Atlanta GA 30339

MARTIN, ROBERT RICHARD, former coll. pres., state senator; b. McKinney, Ky., Dec. 27, 1910; s. Henry Franklin and Annie Frances (Peek) M.; A.B., Eastern Ky. U., 1934; M.A., U. Ky., 1940; Ed.D., Columbia U. Tchrs. Coll., 1951; m. Anne French Hoge, May 31, 1952. Tchr., prin. public schs., Mason and Lee counties, Ky., 1935-48; with Ky. Dept. Edn., 1948-59, beginning as auditor, successively dir. fin., head bur. adminstrn. and fin., 1948-55, supt. public instrn., 1955-59; commr. fin. Commonwealth Ky., 1959-60; pres. Eastern Ky. U., Richmond, 1960-76; dir. State Bank & Trust Co., Begley Drug Co.; mem. Ky. Senate. Assisted devel. found. program for financing of edn. in Ky. Bd. dirs. Pattie A. Clay Hosp., Telford Community Center. Served as tech. sgt. USAAF, 1942-46, meteorologist. Recipient Outstanding Alumnus award Eastern Ky. State Coll., 1956; named Kentuckian of Yr., Ky. Press Assn., 1964; recipient Service award Joint Alumni Council Ky., 1970; Civilian Service award Dept. Army, 1971. Danforth Found. grantee, 1971. Mem. NEA, Am. Assn. Sch. Adminstrs., English-Speaking Union, Civil War Roundtable (bd. dirs.), Ky. Hist. Soc. (pres. 1974—), Ky. Edn. Assn., Am. Assn. State Colls. and Univs. (pres. 1971-72), Phi Delta Kappa, Kappa Delta Pi. Democrat. Presbyn. (trustee, elder). Mason (Shriner), Rotarian. Club: Filson. Home: 300 Summit St Richmond KY 40475

MARTIN, RONNIE ELLIOTT, educator; b. Chickasha, Okla., June 18, 1936; s. Paul and Bernice (Elliott) M.; B.M.E., Tex. Christian U., 1958, M.E., 1961; A.B.D., N. Tex. State U., 1971; m. Carol Jean Wohler, June 25, 1978; children—Thomas Phillip, David James. Band dir. Public Schs. Burleson (Tex.), 1955, Azle (Tex.), 1956-59, Ft. Worth, 1959-66; project dir. Project Muse, Title III ESEA, N. Central Tex., 1966-69; cons. Edn. Service Center, Region XI, Ft. Worth, 1969-71, coordinator curriculum and staff devel., 1971—; pres. Dynamic Learning Systems, Inc., Ft. Worth, 1973-78. Mem. Ft. Worth Profl. Musicians Assn. (v.p. 1964-67), Assn. Supervision and Curriculum Devel., Assn. Tex. Profl. Educators, Tex. Community Schs. Assn., Tex. Assn. Supervision and Curriculum Devel. (pres. chpt. 1979-80), Phi Delta Kappa. Methodist. Club: Rotary. Author: Introduction to Individualized Instruction, 1970; Behavioral Objectives, An Introduction, 1972; Drug Education for Teachers, 1973; People, Things, Information and Creativity — The Elements of Jobs, 1975; Inservice Education Planning Guide, 1981. Home: 308 Glenn Dr Hurst TX 76053 Office: 3001 N Freeway Fort Worth TX 76106

MARTIN, ROY ALLAN, consulting electrical and safety engineer; b. Coffee County, Tenn., Mar. 8, 1920; s. Roy and Ella (Barton) M.; m. Norma Arnell Hixon, May 15, 1942 (div. 1967); children—Linda Christine, Norma Janis; m. Olivia Arlington Traywick, June 13, 1970. B.S. in Elec. Engring., Ga. Inst. Tech., 1942, M.S. in Elec. Engring., 1951. Registered profl. engr., Ga., Fla. With constrn. firm, 1935-37, Ga. Power Co., 1937-42, Western Union, 1946; mem. faculty Ga. Inst. Tech., Atlanta, 1946-68; prin. Roy A. Martin Assocs. Inc., engring. and med. consultation specializing in tech. and personal injury investigations, Atlanta, 1968—. Contbr. articles to profl. publs. Patentee adding machine, voting machine, aerosol sampler, rotary sorter, automatic saw control. Served as 1st lt. USAF, 1942-46, Panama, Ecuador. Episcopalian. Avocations: golf, fishing, amateur radio, square and round dancing. Office: 465-D 1874 Piedmont Ave NE Atlanta GA 30324

MARTIN, STEPHEN JAMES, petroleum services company executive; b. Jacksonville, N.C., Mar. 2, 1945; s. Clarence Rush and Marion Shepard (Park) M.; m. Beatrice Marshall Dunn, June 10, 1967; children—Leigh, Stephen. B.S., U. Ga., 1968; M.S., Ga. Inst. Tech., 1973. Research asst. Ga. Inst. Tech. and Skidaway Inst. Oceanography, 1971-73; research geologist Sun Oil Co., Richardson, Tex., 1973-75; dir. research div. Geochem Labs., Inc., Houston, 1975-77; v.p. Geochem Research, Inc., Houston, 1977-80; geol. assoc. internat. area Cities Service Co., Houston, 1980-81; pres. Ruska Petroleum Labs Inc., Houston, 1981—; comdr. USNR Office Naval Research/Naval Research Lab., 1971—. Served with USN, 1968-71. Mem. Am. Assn. Petroleum Geologists, Geochem. Soc., Am. Chem. Soc., U.S. Naval Inst., Houston Geol. Soc. Episcopalian. Office: Ruska Labs Inc PO Box 742668 Houston TX 77274

MARTIN, TERRELL OWEN, university dean; b. Florence, Ala., Mar. 25, 1937; s. Terrell Owen and Ruth Alice (Nowell) M. B.S. in Bus. Adminstrn., Erskine Coll., 1959; M.S. in Student Personnel, Ind. U., 1964, D.Recreation, 1972. Dir. student activities Franklin Coll., Ind., 1964-66; acad. adv. U. Akron, Ohio, 1966-68; counselor, 1972-74; resident counselor Ind. U., Bloomington, 1968-72; dir. spl. programs and orgns. Indiana U. Pa., 1974-82; dean student devel. Tex. A&I U., Kingsville, 1982—. Served to 2nd lt. U.S. Army, 1960. Mem. Am. Assn. Counseling and Devel. Am. Coll. Personnel Assn., Nat. Assn. Campus Activities, Nat. Assn. Student Personnel Adminstrs., Nat. Recreation and Park Assn., Phi Delta Theta, Order of Omega. Democrat. Methodist. Avocations: traveling; swimming; reading. Home: 1414 W Santa Gertrudis Apt 406 Kingsville TX 78363 Office: Tex A&I U Campus Box 133 Kingsville TX 78363

MARTIN, WAYNE A., clinical social worker; b. N.Y.C., Jan. 26, 1945; s. Bernard and Juliet (Aurbach) M.; m. Barbara Jo Goodman, Aug. 16, 1970; 1 son, Jason David. B.A. in Social Sci., Fla. State U., 1966; M.S., Sch. Social Work, Columbia U., 1968; postgrad. Old Dominion U., 1978—. Lic. clin. social worker, Va. Day camp dir. Jewish Community Center, Norfolk, Va., 1968-71, children's dept. dir., 1968-69, youth dept. dir., 1969-71; psychiat. social worker Psychiat. Assos., Ltd., Portsmouth, Va., 1971-77; clin. social worker Human Resource Inst., Norfolk, 1977-79; caseworker (part-time) Cath. Home Bur., Hampton, Va., 1977-78; primary therapist Charter Colonial Inst., Newport News, Va., 1980—; pvt. practice clin. social work, Virginia Beach, Norfolk and Newport News, Va., 1980—; program coordinator for adolescent psychiat. unit Peninsula Psychiat. Hosp., Hampton, Va., 1979-80; field supr. Va. Commonwealth U. Sch. Social Work, 1978-84, Norfolk State U. Sch. Social Work, 1982—; chmn. adv. com. Upjohn Health-care Services, 1979-80; oral examiner-/adviser Va. Bd. Social Work. Chmn., Crisis Center, 1977-78; 1st v.p. B'nai B'rith, Va. State Assn., 1977-78, pres., 1979-80, mem. dist. 5 bd. govs., 1978—, 3d v.p./treas. dist. 5, 1983-84, 1st v.p., 1985-86, pres.-elect 1986-87; chmn. Hillel Found. for State of Va., 1978-79; bd. dirs. Jewish Community Center, Norfolk, 1973-79; exec. bd. Temple Israel Synagogue, 1981-84, pres. Men's Club, 1981-82, temple sec., 1982-84. Named Outstanding Lodge Pres., B'nai B'rith Dist. Five, 1977, Outstanding State Pres., 1980; Man of Yr., Va. State Assn. of B'nai B'rith, 1980. Mem. Nat. Assn. Social Workers (v.p. Hampton Roads unit 1974-76, dist. chmn. 1982-83 state dir. 1977-83), Acad. Cert. Social Workers, ACLU, Kappa Delta Pi, Phi Alpha Theta, Pi Sigma Alpha. Democrat. Jewish. Club: Mogul Ski (v.p. 1970-71) (Norfolk). Home: 1827 Longdale Dr Norfolk VA 23518

MARTIN, WILLIAM ALEXANDER, JR., safety official; b. Northamptonshire, Eng., May 11, 1952; came to U.S. 1952; s. William Alexander and Florence Jessie (Windsor) M.; m. Fredrica Bratton Alley, Feb. 7, 1981; 1 child, Kathleen Randolph. B.S., Va. Commonwealth U., 1975. Phys. sci. tchr. Hanover pub. schs., Ashland, Va., 1974-77; asst. biol. technician Va. Electric & Power Co., Richmond, Va., 1977-79, safety staff asst., 1979-84, assoc. indsl. hygienist, 1984—; instr. ARC, Richmond, 1984—, Am. Heart Assn., 1984—, Medic First Aid, 1984—. Emergency med. technician, 1984. Served with USCGR, 1971-77. Mem. Am. Soc. Safety Engrs., Am. Indsl. Hygiene Assn. Episcopalian. Avocations: music composition; instrumental and voice performance. Home: 10107 Falconbridge Dr Richmond VA 23233 Office: Virginia Power 1 James River Plaza 10th Floor PO Box 26666 Richmond VA 23261

MARTIN, WILLIAM AUBERT, law association executive, lawyer, retired air force officer; b. Warren, Ark., Dec. 7, 1931; s. Aubert and Anna Christine (Joiner) M.; m. Mary Lou, Mauderly, Mar. 31, 1963; children—Kathryn G., Karen E., Michael W. J.D., U. Ark., 1955; M.B.A., Ariz. State U., 1969. Bar: Ark. 1955. Commd. 2d lt. U.S. Air Force, 1955, advanced through grades to col.; chief claims and tort litigation div., U.S. Air Force Hdqrs., Washington, 1973-77; staff judge adv. Oklahoma City Air Logistics Ctr., Tinker AFB, Okla., 1977-79, Hdqrs. 5th Air Force, Yokota AFB, Tokyo, 1979-81, Hdqrs. Air Tng. Command, Randolph AFB, Tex., 1981-83; ret., 1983; exec. dir. Ark. Bar Assn., Little Rock, 1983—. Mem. ABA, Ark. Bar Assn., Fed. Bar Assn., Pulaski County Bar Assn., Judge Advocates Assn. Methodist. Lodge: Rotary. Office: Ark Bar Assn 400 W Markham St Little Rock AR 72201

MARTIN, WILLIAM CLARENCE, architect; b. LaGrange, Ga., May 13, 1927; s. David Sanders and Lena (Walker) M.; B.Arch., Auburn U., 1950; m. Liselotte Hofman Cline, Dec. 16, 1975; children—William Sanders, Tobey Gregory, Tonia Claudia. Draftsman, Aeck Assocs., architects, Atlanta, 1950-51; assoc. mem. firm Toombs, Amisano & Wells, Architects, Atlanta, 1952-62; partner firm Martin & Bainbridge, Atlanta, 1962-70; prin. Martin Assocs., architects, Atlanta, 1970—; dir. Design Mgmt. Inc., Atlanta; cons. Elson's, Atlanta, Teledyne Continetal Motors, Mobile, Ala. Served with USNR, 1945-46. Frank Lloyd Wright Found. fellow, 1947-48. Mem. AIA (recipient awards 1964, 65, 70). Unitarian. Clubs: Sea Cabin Ocean (Hilton Head Island, S.C.); Sconti Ridge (Big Canoe, Ga.); Masons, Shriners. Architect: Stouffers Pine Isle Hotel, Lanier Islands, Ga., Troup County (Ga.) Court House, Clark-Holder Med. Center, La Grange, Ga., also libraries, schs., condominiums, shops, homes. Home: 3060 Pharr Ct NW Suite 118 Atlanta GA 30305 Office: 67 Peachtree Park Dr NE Suite 210 Atlanta GA 30309

MARTIN, WILLIAM HENRY, arts administrator; b. South Weymouth, Mass., Nov. 6, 1947; s. John Arthur and Virginia (Crosby) M. B.A. with honors, Harvard Coll., 1970; M.B.A., Wake Forest U., 1975. Days in the Arts counselor Boston Symphony, 1974; prodn. comptroller, house mgr. Santa Fe Opera, 1975-76; bus. mgr. Opera Theatre St. Louis, 1976; dir. adminstrn. Greater Miami Opera (Fla.), 1976-83; dir. mktg. Coconut Grove Playhouse, Miami, 1983-84; dir. devel. Nat. Found. Advancement in the Arts, Miami, 1984—. Dir. fundraising, chmn. Boston chpt. Operation Crossroads Africa Alumni, 1968-70; mem. adv. com. Kennedy Inst. Politics, Cambridge, Mass., 1968-70; mem. Health Crisis Network; mem. music com. Plymouth Congregational Ch. Recipient Canny award Miami Herald, 1980; Babcock scholar Wake Forest U., 1975, John Harvard Scholar, 1970. Mem. Greater Miami C. of C., Common Cause. Democrat. Home: 6791 SW 78th Terr Miami FL 33143 Office: Nat Found Advancement Arts 100 N Biscayne Blvd Miami FL 33132

MARTIN, WILLIAM NELSON, lawyer, state senator; b. Eden, N.C., May 25, 1945; s. Thomas W. and Carolyn (Henderson) M.; m. Hazel Broadnax, June 11, 1966 (div. 1975); children—Thomas W. and William N. (twins); m. 2d, Patricia A. Yancey, May 28, 1983. B.S., N.C. A&T U., Greensboro, 1966; J.D., George Washington U., 1973. Bar: D.C. 1974, N.C. 1975. Mgmt. trainee IBM, Bridgeport, Conn., 1966-68; claims adjuster Liberty Mut. Ins. Co., Bridgeport, 1968-70; assoc. Frye, Johnson, Barbee, Greensboro, N.C., 1974-76; gen. practice, Greensboro, 1976—; mem. N.C. senate. Commr. Greensboro Housing Commn., 1979-82; bd. dirs. Triad Sickle Cell Anemia Found., Greensboro, 1978—, Nat. Black Child Devel. Inst., Washington, 1980-82; co-founder, bd. dirs. One Step Further, Greensboro, 1982—, Charlotte Hawkins Brown Hist. Found., Greensboro, 1983—. Recipient Outstanding Leadership award Nat. Assn. Negro Bus. and Profl. Women's Clubs, 1983, Man of the Yr. award, 1983; Disting. Service award Rutledge Coll., 1983. Mem. N.C. Bar Assn., Zeta Phi Beta (award for community service and human relations 1978), Phi Beta Sigma (Outstanding Service award 1980). Democrat. Baptist. Club: Greensboro Men's. Office: William N Martin PO Box 21325 Greensboro NC 27420

MARTIN, WILLIAM WILLIAM, health services executive, psychologist; b. Albany, Ga., Mar. 24, 1951; s. William W. and Lynne (Durham) M.; m. Diana Susanne Place, Nov. 7, 1981; 1 son, Christopher William. A.A. in Liberal Arts, Clayton Jr. Coll., 1973; B.S. in Counseling Psychology, Ga. State U. 1975; postgrad. in clin. psychology Chapman Coll., 1978; postgrad. Calif. State U., 1978-80; M.A. in Marriage, Family and Child Counseling, Pepperdine U., 1980; Ph.D. in Clin. Psychology, Internat. Coll., Los Angeles, 1983. Cert. tchr., counselor, Calif.; lic. marriage, family and child counselor, Calif.; cert. rational emotive psychotherapist, N.Y.; cert reality therapist, Calif.; cert. sex educator, counselor, Washington; cert. alcohol and drug abuse counselor, Calif.; cert vocat. cons., Calif., Ga. Psychotherapist, group facilitator Ctr. for Dynamic Therapy, Los Alamitos, Calif., 1977-78, Cypress Counseling Ctr. (Calif.), 1978-80; rehab. bur. liaison, vocat. counselor Internat. Rehab. Assn. Inc., Anaheim, Calif., 1978-80; sr. vocat. counselor Internat. Rehab. Assn. Inc., Norcross, Ga., 1980-82; psychotherapist, group facilitator Buckhead Counseling Ctr., Atlanta, 1980-82; pres., exec. dir. Consol. health Services. Inc., Atlanta, 1982—, Huntington Beach, Calif., 1984—, Clin. Psychology Group, Los Alamitos, Calif., Assessment and Psychotherapy Ctr., Calif., Vocat. Exploration Services, Inc., Calif. Mem. Am. Psychol. Assn., Calif. Psychol. Assn., Am. Marriage, Family and Child Therapist Assn., Am. Assn. Sex Educators, Counselors and Therapists, Calif. Assn. Marriage and Family Therapists, Nat. Rehab. Assn., Calif. Assn. Rehab. Profls., Counselors of Alcohol and Addiction Related Dependencies. Democrat. Unitarian.

MARTIN, WILMA JEAN, hospital administrator; b. Logan, W.Va., July 30, 1937; d. Donald Queen and Elberta (Lucas) Queen Ellis; student So. W.Va. Community Coll., 1974; m. James P. Martin, Feb. 1, 1977; children—John F. Cook, J. Michael Cook. Med. sec. to chief of staff Guyan Valley Hosp., Logan, W.Va., 1954-60, asst. to hosp. adminstr., 1960-72, hosp. adminstr., 1972—; v.p., ptnr. Logan Park Care Center Nursing Home; pres., owner Guyan Distb. Co., Logan; v.p., ptnr. Mingo Health Care Center Nursing Home, 1981—. sec. Hosp. Corp. Active in community vol. work, including co-chmn. Cancer Soc., Logan. Lic. nursing home adminstr.; registered med. sec. Mem. Smithsonian Instn., Order Ky. Cols. Presbyterian. Home: 171 Nighbert Ave Logan WV 25601 Office: 396 Dingess St Logan WV 25601

MARTIN-CANNICI, CYNTHIA ELAINE, clinical psychologist; b. Matador, Tex., Aug. 25, 1953; d. Barney Joe and Cloria Martella (Neatherlin) Martin; m. Rick A. McCorkle, Sept. 25, 1982; 1 child, Brandt Martin Cannici. B.A. summa cum laude, North Tex. State U., 1977, M.S., 1980, Ph.D., 1984. Cert. psychologist, Ark., Tex. Asst. dir. Denton Area Crisis Ctr., Tex., 1975-77; dir. psychol. services children's inpatient unit, U. Ark. for Med. Scis., Little Rock, 1982-84; psychologist Mental Health Mental Retardation Services of Texoma, Sherman, Tex., 1984-85; ind. practice, Sherman, 1985—; cons. Grayson County Juvenile Alternatives, Sherman, 1985—, Grayson County Juvenile Probation, 1985—, Fannin County Juvenile Probation, 1985—, Grayson County Sheriff's Dept., 1985—; counselor CETA Youth Program, Denton, 1981; foster parent Survival House, Denton, 1979-81; chmn. prevention Greater Little Rock Community Mental Health Ctr. Adv. Bd., 1982-84; cons. Women's Crisis Ctr., Sherman, 1985—; cons. Sherman Boy's Club, 1985. Contbr. papers to profl. publs. and confs. Program chmn. Montesorri PTA, Little Rock, 1983; vol. Denton County Big Bros. Big Sisters, 1980; guardian ad litem Charleston Family Ct. System, S.C., 1978. Recipient Letter of Commendation U. Ark. Med. Scis., 1984. Mem. Am. Psychol. Assn. Avocations: Reading; crafts; games.

MARTINCHALK, RICHARD, safety and fire protection engineer; b. Connelsville, Pa., June 4, 1948; s. George Leo and Loretta (Watson) M.; m. Suzanne Aileen Huber; children—Richard, Elizabeth Ann. Assoc. Fire Tech., Del. Tech. and Community Coll., 1976, cert. in Safety Mgmt., 1976; B.Tech. in Fire Tech., Del. State U., 1977. Asst. fire chief, Civil Service, Pomona, N.J., 1971-72, fire fighter, Dover, Del., 1972-78; safety engr. Allied Chem., Hopewell, Va., 1978-81; safety and fire prevention coordinator Sohio Chem., Port Lavaca, Tex., 1981-85, sr. safety engr., 1985—; fire chief U.S. Air Force Res., Duluth, Minn., 1972-73; instr. Tex. A&M Indsl. Fire Sch., College Station, 1983-84. Served with USAF, 1967-73; Vietnam. Decorated 3 Air Medals. Mem. Nat. Fire Protection Assn., Am. Soc. Safety Engrs. (chmn. Victoria sect. 1983-84), Soc. Fire Protection Tech. (bd. dirs. 1979), Internat. Soc. Fire Service Instrs., VFW, Jaycees, Nat. Rifle Assn. Club: Toastmasters. Avocations: Trout fishing; fly tying; public speaking. Home: 209 Chesapeake Ave Victoria TX 77904 Office: Sohio Chem Co PO Box 659 Port Lavaca TX 77979

MARTÍNEZ, CARLOS QUEZADA, industrial engineer; b. Mexico City, Apr. 20, 1946; came to U.S., 1955; s. Isidro Martínez and Piedad Gonzáles Quezada; m. Teresa Flores García, July 9, 1973; children—Elisa, Dante, Francisco. B.S., Ga. Southwestern Coll., 1969; M.S.I.E., Tex. Tech U., 1982. Supr., dept. mgr. textiles plant Milliken & Co., Manchester, Ga., 1974-76, sr. indsl. engr., 1976-79; plant indsl. engr. Burlington Industries, Erwin, N.C., 1979-80; dir. indsl. engring. Am. Cotton Growers, Littlefield, Tex., 1981-84; indsl. engr. Avondale Mills, Sylacauga, Ala., 1985—. Pres. Parish Council, 1981—. Served to capt. U.S. Army, 1969-74. Mem. Am. Inst. Indsl. Engrs., Assn. Textile Indsl. Engrs. Roman Catholic. Club: K.C. (grand knight). Home: 1449 Fairmont Rd Sylacauga AL 35150 Office: Eva Jane Plant Sylacauga AL 35150

MARTINEZ, GUILLERMO IGNACIO, journalist; b. Havana, Cuba, July 11, 1941; came to U.S., 1960; s. Guillermo R. and Berta (Arocena) Martinez-Marquez; m. Ana Maria de la Campa, Nov. 1, 1969; children—Guillermo Ignacio, Ana Maria. Student Miami Dade Community Coll., 1962-64; B.S. in Journalism, U. Fla., 1966. Bur. chief UPI, Lima, Peru, 1970-73; Congl. writer FDC Reports, Washington, 1973-76; city editor El Miami Herald, (Fla.), 1976-79; Hispanic writer Miami Herald, 1979-82, columnist, 1981—, mem. editorial bd., 1982—. Pres.-elect Miami Dade Community Coll., 1981-82. Mem. Nat. Assn. Hispanic Journalists (founding pres. 1984—), Inter-Am. Businessmen's Assn. Democrat. Roman Catholic.

MARTÍNEZ, LUÍS OSVALDO, radiologist, educator; b. Havana, Cuba, Nov. 27, 1927; came to U.S., 1962, naturalized, 1967; s. Osvaldo and Felicitas (Farinas) M.; M.D., U. Havana, 1954; m. Norma Rodriguez, Nov. 20, 1955; children—María Elena, Luís Osvaldo, Alberto Luis. Intern, Calixto García Hosp., Havana, 1954-55; resident in radiology Jackson Meml. Hosp., Miami, Fla., 1963-65, fellow in cardiovascular radiology, 1965-67; instr. radiology U. Miami, 1965-68, asst. prof., 1968, clin. asst. prof., 1968-70, assoc. prof., 1970-76, prof., 1976—; assoc. dir. dept. radiology Mt. Sinai Med. Center, Miami Beach, Fla., 1969—, chief div. diagnostic radiology, 1970—, dir. residency program in diagnostic radiology; dir. Spanish Radiology Seminar. Pres. League Against Cancer. Mem. Internat. Soc. Lymphology, Interam. Coll. Radiology (pres.), Internat. Coll. Surgeons, Internat. Coll. Angiology, Internat. Soc. Radiology, Interam. Coll. Radiology (Gold medal 1975, pres. editor Jour.), Cuban Med. Assn. in Exile, Am. Coll. Chest Physicians (asso.), AAUP, AMA, Radiol. Soc. N. Am., Am. Coll. Radiology, Am. Roentgen Ray Soc., Am. Assn. Fgn. Med. Grads., Am. Profl. Practice Assn., Am. Thoracic Soc., Pan Am. Med. Assn., Am. Assn. Univ. Radiologists, Brit. Inst. Radiology, Am. Heart Assn. (mem. council cardiovascular radiology), Faculty Radiologists, Soc. Gastrointestinal Radiologists, Am. Geriatrics Soc., Am. Coll. Angiology, Royal Coll. Radiologists, Am. Soc. Therapeutic Radiologists, Assn. Hosp. Med. Edn., Am. Coll. Med. Imaging, Interasma, So. Med. Assn., N.Y. Acad. Scis., Fla. Thoracic Soc., Fla. Radiol. Soc., Dade County Med. Assn., Greater Miami Radiol. Soc., Cuban Radiol. Soc. (sec.), Can. Assn. Radiologists, Soc. Thoracic Radiologists (founding mem.); hon. mem. numerous med. socs. of Mex., Central and S. Am. Roman Catholic. Reviewer Am. Jour. Radiology, Radium Therapy and Nuclear Medicine, 1978; editor Revista Interamericana de Radiologia, 1975; contbr. articles in field to profl. jours. Office: 4300 Alton Rd Miami Beach FL 33140

MARTINEZ, MIGUEL E., industrial psychologist, educator; b. San German, P.R., June 20, 1957; s. Samuel Martinez and Nadia Lugo. Ph.D. in Indsl.-Orgnl. Psychology, Caribbean Ctr. for Advanced Studies, Santurce, 1983. Indsl. psychologist Lucy Lopez-Roig & Assocs., Hato Rey, P.R., 1980-83; prof. Inter-Am. U., Rio Piedras, P.R., 1980—; program coordinator Caribbean Ctr. for Advanced Studies, Santurce, P.R., 1983—. Recipient John F. Kennedy award U. P.R., Mayaguez, 1978; Indsl. Psychology award, Caribbean Ctr., 1980, 83. Mem. Am. Psychol. Assn., P.R. Psychologists Assn. award, Home: 1052 Ashford Ave Apt 2A Santurce PR 00907

MARTINEZ, RAUL L., mayor, real estate broker, publisher; b. Hialeah, Fla., Mar. 6, 1949; s. Chin and Aida M.; m. Angela Callava; children—Aida, Raul. B.A., Miami Dade Community Coll.; B.S. in Criminal Justice, Fla. Internat. U. Pub., founder El Sol de Hialeah, 1969—; pres. Martex Realty Inc., Hialeah, 1975—; councilman City of Hialeah, 1977-81, mayor, 1981—. Decorated Legion of Honor; recipient Citizen Involvement award Crime Commn. Greater Miami, 1977, Over the Top award Hialeah-Miami Springs YMCA, 1979. Mem. U.S. Conf. Mayors, Council Mayors, Fla. League Cities, Dade County League Cities. Democrat. Roman Catholic. Lodge: Kiwanis. Office: 501 Palm Ave Hialeah FL 33010

MARTINEZ, ROBERT, city government official; b. Tampa, Fla., Dec. 25, 1934; s. Serafin and Ida (Carreno) M. B.S., U. Tampa, 1957; M.A., U. Ill., 1964. Pres., Cafe Sevilla Spanish Restaurant, 1975-83; mayor of Tampa, 1979—. Mem. Fla. task force on med. malpractice U.S. Conf. Mayors; mem. Pres.'s Adv. Com. on Intergovtl. Relations. Office: City Hall 306 E Jackson St Tampa FL 33602*

MARTINEZ, SARA CANO, educator; b. Pinar-del-Rio, Cuba, July 13, 1936; came to U.S., 1960; d. Leonardo and Maria Balbina (Iglesias) Cano; m. Armando Martinez, Mar. 21, 1963; children—Sara B., Yamile M., Desiree. M.Ed., Escuela Normal, 1954; postgrad. U. Occidente, 1955; Ed.D., U. Cuba, 1960; B.Elem. Edn., U. Coral Gables, 1967; M.Ed., U. Miami, 1977. Tchr., Centro Escolar de S. Luis, P. Del Rio, Cuba, 1954; interim tchr. Pre-Comml. Sch., Cuba, 1955; tchr. Bejuqueras Elem. Sch., 1956; prin., tchr. Tres Por Ciento, Cuba, 1957; tchr. Fidel Miro Elem. Sch., Cuba, 1958-60; sch. prin. Gertrudis Gomez de Avallaneda, Cuba, 1960 Buena Visto Elem. Sch., Miami, Fla., 1967-71; ESOL reading tchr. Southside Elem. Sch., Miami, 1971-72, bilingual tchr., 1972-74, Title I tchr., 1975-79; tchr. sci. and math. Coral Way Elem. Sch., Miami, 1979; bilingual tchr. Southside Elem. Sch., 1979, 80-81, 82-83, 5th grade chpt. I tchr., 1983—. Recipient Pinar del Rio prize, 1948; award for commendable contbn. to edn. Dade County Sch. Bd., 1974. Mem. Fed. Educators Am., United Tchrs. Dade, NEA, Internat. Rescue Com., Tchrs. English Second Orgin Lang., U. Miami Alumni Assn. Republican. Roman Catholic.

MARTÍNEZ-ALFONSO, RAFAEL, civil engr.; b. Yauco, P.R., Sept. 21, 1923; s. Genaro and Carmen (Alfonzo) M.; B.S. in Civil Engring., U. P.R., 1950, M.S. in Civil Engring., 1979; m. Dessie Planell Justiniano, Dec. 1, 1951; children—Amy, Sahyly, Rafael, Maritza. Design engr. Dept. Public Works P.R., 1950-55; chief engr. Precast Tilt-up Constrn., Carolina, P.R., 1955-63; co-owner, mgr. Empresas Consolidadas del Caribe, Hato Rey, P.R., 1963-70; pvt. practice civil engring. cons., Hato Rey, P.R., 1971—. Mem. Colegio de Ingenieros de P.R., ASCE, Am. Concrete Inst., Internat. Assn. Bridge Engring., Earthquake Engring. Inst., Prestress Concrete Inst. Roman Catholic. Home: A-27 Fco Sein Urb Pinero Hato Rey PR 00919 Office: 65 Jose Marti Hato Rey PR 00919

MARTINEZ-FONTS, ALBERTO, JR., travel/hospitality firm executive; b. Vedado, Havana, Cuba, Mar. 20, 1943; s. Alberto and Florinda (Sanchez) Martinez-F.; m. Carole Sue Baker, Apr. 18, 1970; children—Susanna Catherine, Cristopher Alberto. Student Miami-Dade Jr. Coll., 1961-63, U. Miami, 1963-64. Dist. sales mgr. LACSA Airlines, Miami, Fla., 1967-69; regional dir. mktg. Brit. West Indian Airways, Ltd., Miami, 1969-79; v.p., dir. account mgmt. Robinsons Inc., Orlando, Fla., 1979-84; v.p. McKenzie Group Advt., Orlando, 1984—. Served with N.G., 1964-70. Recipient Interline award Delta Airlines, 1977. Mem. Am. Soc. Travel Agts., Caribbean Hotel Assn., Caribbean Tourism Assn., Airline Sales and Mktg. Execs. Miami (dir. 1976-78, v.p. 1978-79), Travel and Tourism Research Assn. (dir.), Hotel Sales Mktg. Assn. (dir.). Republican. Roman Catholic. Club: Rio Pinar Country (Orlando). Office: 1109 E Ridgewood St Orlando FL 32803

MARTINI, MARIO, physicist; b. Florence, Italy, Mar. 24, 1939; came to U.S., 1975; s. Renato and Miranda (Giovana) M.; m. Judith Ann Wachna, Aug. 1, 1966; children—Stephanie, Margot, Katherine. Doctorate in Physics, U. Bologna, 1962. Assoc. prof. Italian U., Bologna, 1962-70; dir. research Simtect Industries, Montreal, 1971-73; dir. research Electronic Assoc., Toronto, 1973-74; tech dir. EG&G ORTEC, Oak Ridge, 1975-83, mktg. mgr., 1983—. Author: Semiconductor Detectors, 1968. Contbr. articles to profl. jours. Mem. IEEE (sr.). Republican. Roman Catholic. Avocations: literature; music; tennis. Home: 942 W Outer Dr Oak Ridge TN 37830 Office: EG&G ORTEC 100 Midland Rd Oak Ridge TN 37830

MARVIN, HELEN RHYNE, state legislator; b. Gastonia, N.C., Nov. 30, 1917; d. Dane Samuel and Tessie Pearl (Hastings) Rhyne; B.A. magna cum laude, Furman U., Greenville, S.C., 1938; M.A., La. State U., 1939; m. Ned Irving Marvin, Nov. 21, 1941; children—Kathryn Andrea, Richard Morris, David Rhyne. Tchr. public schs., Gastonia, 1953-65; prof. polit. sci. Gaston Coll., Dallas, N.C., 1965-79, head social sci. dept., 1975-79; mem. N.C. Senate from 25th Dist., 1976—; mem. N.C. Social Services Commn., 1979-81, N.C. State Apprenticeship Council, 1978—, N.C. Women's Forum, 1977-82. Chmn. N.C. Council Status Women, 1976-81; mem. N.C. State Health Coordinating Council, 1977-79, Gov. N.C. Adv. Council Children and Youth, 1977—, N.C. Day Care Adv. Council, 1979-81, Gov.'s Commn. on Future of N.C.-Yr. 2000, 1980-81; trustee N.C. State Theater, 1980—, Sacred Heart Coll., Belmont, N.C.; bd. dirs. Gaston County United Way, 1975-82, Gaston County Family Counseling. Gaston County Mental Health Assn. R.J. Reynolds fellow econs.

edn., 1964; named Outstanding Tchr., Gaston Coll., 1974, Woman of Yr., Civitan Club, 1978; recipient Valand award for work in mental health, 1980. Mem. Am., So., N.C. (pres. 1977-78) polit. sci. assns., N.C. Community Coll. Social Scis. Assn. (chmn. 1976-78), Delta Kappa Gamma, Zeta Tau Alpha. Democrat. Presbyterian (elder). Club: Gastonia Altrusa.

MARWIL, STANLEY JACKSON, chemical engineer, consultant; b. Henderson, Tex., Aug. 13, 1921; s. Mose H. and Stella (Jackson) M.; m. Wilma Estella Cary, Nov. 6, 1949; children—Earl S., Nelson L. B.S. in Chem. Engring., Tex. A&M U., 1943, M.S. in Chem. Engring., 1948. Registered profl. engr., Tex. Sect. supr. Phillips Petroleum Co., Bartlesville, Okla., 1961-84, supr. air sensitive catalyst, 1984-85; mgr. Marco Engring., Bartlesville, 1985—. Patentee in field. Served with U.S. Army, 1943-45; PTO. Recipient Andre Wilkens Meml. award, 1984. Mem. Am. Inst. Chem. Engrs. (past chmn. Bartlesville sect.). Republican. Methodist. Lodge: Masons. Home: 5700 Baylor Pl Bartlesville OK 74006 Office: Marco Engineering 5700 Baylor Pl Bartlesville OK 74006

MARXSEN, BOURKE REYNALD, hospital administrator; b. Chgo., Dec. 27, 1933; s. Oscar Reynald and Doris Emaretta (Bourke) M.; m. Gertrude Lanell Fabian, June 13, 1964; children—John Gordon, Pamela Anne. B.S., Northwestern U., 1973. Bus. mgr. Hohf Clinic and Hosp., Victoria, Tex., 1965-66; chief acct. Passavant Meml. Hosp., Chgo., 1967; controller Highland Park Hosp., Ill., 1967-82; asst. adminstr. Titus City Meml. Hosp., Mt. Pleasant, Tex., 1982-83, adminstr., 1983—. Mem. Regional Health Care Adv. Council, Northeast Tex., 1984-85. Served to A/3C USAF, 1953-54. Mem. Health Care Fin. Mgmt. Assn., Tex. Hosp. Assn., Am. Hosp. Assn. Episcopalian. Club: Mt. Pleasant Bass. Lodges: Masons, Shriners. Avocations: fishing; hunting; music; stamps. Office: Titus County Meml Hosp 2001 N Jefferson St Mount Pleasant TX 75455

MARZIO, PETER CORT, museum dir.; b. Governor's Island, N.Y., May 8; s. Francis and Katherine (Mastroberti) M.; B.A. (Neva Miller scholar), Juniata Coll., Huntingdon, Pa., 1965; M.A., U. Chgo., 1966, Ph.D. (univ. fellow, Smithsonian Instn. fellow), 1969; m. Frances Ann Parker, July 2, 1979; children—Sara Lon, Steven Arnold. Research asst. to dir., then historian Nat. Mus. History and Tech., Smithsonian Instn., 1969-73, asso. curator prints, 1977-78, chmn. dept. cultural history, 1978; dir., chief exec. officer Corcoran Gallery Art, Washington, 1978-82; dir. Mus. Fine Arts, Houston, 1982—; instr. Roosevelt U., Chgo., 1966-68; asso. prof. U. Md., 1976-77; adv. council Anthrop. Film Center, Archives Am. Art Adv. council Jr. League Washington, Dumbarton Oaks. Sr. Fulbright fellow, Italy, 1973-74. Mem. Print Council Am., Am. Print Council, Dunlap Soc., Assn. Art Mus. Dirs., Am. Assn. Museums. Club: Cosmos (Washington). Author: Rube Goldberg: His Life and Works, 1973; The Art Crusade, 1976; The Democratic Art: An Introduction to the History of Chromolithography in America, 1979; editor: A Nation of Nations, 1976. Home: 1831 Albans Houston TX 77005 Office: Mus Fine Arts 1001 Bissonnet PO Box 6826 Houston TX 77265

MASCIOVECCHIO, LOUIS RICHARD, advertising executive, artist; b. Bklyn., May 3, 1937; s. Emilio and Olympia (Guarenello) M.; m. Emily Jane O'Brien, Mar. 19, 1960 (div. Mar. 1972); children—Elise, Richard; m. 2d, Mary Eleanor MacInnis, Feb. 17, 1979. Cert. completion, Cooper Union, N.Y.C., 1960. Art dir. Lennen & Newell, N.Y.C., 1959-65; creative dir. E.J. Scheaffer Advt., Miami, 1966-69; creative dir., v.p. Mike Sloan Advt., Miami, 1969-71; exec. v.p., creative dir. Beber, Silverstein, Miami, 1972-78; exec. art dir. McDonald & Little, Altanta, 1978-80; pres. Masciovecchio, Inc., Miami, 1980—; instr. Sch. Creative Thinking, Miami, 1982—; cons. McFarland & Drier, Miami, 1980-82, Crispin Advt., Miami, 1981—. Recipient Addy award Miami Advt. Fedn., 1975, 76, Clio award, 1980. Home: 818 Pizarro St Coral Gables FL 33134 Office: Masciovecchio Inc 818 Pizarro St Coral Gables FL 33134

MASH, JERRY L., lawyer, minister; b. Oklahoma City, July 9, 1937; s. Mary Irene Scott; m. Beverly Anne Cain, Aug. 3, 1958; children—Deborah Ruth, John Mark, James Michael; m. Cuba Deann Corbin, Feb. 14, 1977. A.B. in Philosophy, Phillips U.; student Grad. Sem., 1960-62; J.D., Oklahoma City U., 1967; postgrad. Fuller Theol. Sem., 1984—; Bar: Okla. 1968, U.S. Dist. Ct. (we. dist.) Okla. 1974, U.S. Dist. Ct. (ea. dist.) Okla. 1981. Adminstrv. asst., legal staff officer to Gov. of Okla., 1962-67; investment specialist, Okla. counsel Ling & Co., Dallas, 1967-68; atty. Mash and Dewart, P.C., Oklahoma City and Guthrie, Okla., 1969—; lic. to ministry Christian Ch., 1957—; minister Christian Ch. (Disciples of Christ), 1957—, sec. Okla. region, 1984—. Contbr. article to legal jour. Pres. Okla. County-City Community Action Program, 1970-72; Republican candidate for Gov. of Okla., 1978; Rep. state committeeman, 1979-82. Mem. Okla. Bar Assn., ABA, Okla. County Bar Assn., Logan County Bar Assn., Oklahoma City Securities Lawyers Group, Blue Key, Phi Delta Phi. Home: 18 Bramble Bush Ln Crescent OK 73028 Office: Mash and Dewart PC 910 NW 23d St Oklahoma City OK 73106 also 109 E Oklahoma Guthrie OK 73028

MASHBURN, JERRY ALLEN, hospital administrator; b. Marianna, Fla., Aug. 25, 1944; s. Charles C. and Mae (Tharpe) M.; m. Jo Ellen Moyer, June 15, 1970 (div. 1975); m. 2d, Karen A. Jones, Oct. 16, 1976. B.A., Fla. State U., 1966; M.B.A., Fla. Internat. U., 1975. C.P.A., Fla. Sr. auditor Ernst & Whinney Co., Miami, Fla., 1969-72; internal auditor Mercy Hosp., Miami, 1972-74, fin. dir., 1974-76, v.p., 1976—. Served to 1st lt. AUS, 1966-69. Healthcare Fin. Mgmt. fellow, Chgo., 1983. Mem. Am. Coll. Healthcare Adminstrs., Am. Inst. C.P.A.s, Fla. Inst. C.P.A.s, Am. Hosp. Assn., South Fla. Hosp. Assn. Democrat. Home: 8950 S W 59th St Miami FL 33173 Office: Mercy Hosp 3663 S Miami Ave Miami FL 33133

MASON, A. WANDA, business consulting and accounting company executive; b. Lexington, Ky., Oct. 22, 1950; d. Charles and Mary Lee (Stewart) M. B.A., Central State U., 1975; M.P.A., Ky. State U., 1979. Edn. counselor, adminstrv. asst. HUD Model Cities, Ohio, 1970-75; accountant Ky. Dept. Fin., Frankfort, 1977-79; bus. mgmt. and fin. cons. U.S. Dept. Commerce, Louisville, 1979—; owner AMC Bus. Services, Louisville, 1982—; pres. AMC Bus. Service Enterprises, Inc., 1983—. Vol. civic and community activities; mem. Louisville Econ. Devel. Corp. Served with USAR, 1976-77. Mem. Nat. Council for Negro Women, NAACP, Urban League, PAC-10, Louisville Jazz Soc. Democrat. Baptist. Office: 835 W Jefferson St Suite 205-A Louisville KY 40202

MASON, AIMEE HUNNICUTT ROMBERGER, educator; b. Atlanta, Nov. 3, 1918; d. Edwin William and Aimee Greenleaf (Hunnicutt) Romberger; B.A., Conn. Coll., 1940; postgrad. Emory U., 1946-48; M.A., U. Fla., 1979, Ph.D., 1980; M.A., Stetson U., 1968; m. Samuel Venable Mason, Aug. 16, 1941; children—Olivia Elizabeth Mason Butcher, Christopher Leeds. Jr. exec., merchandising G. Fox & Co., Hartford, Conn., 1940-41; air traffic controller CAA, Atlanta, 1942; partner Coronado Concrete Products, New Smyrna Beach, Fla., 1953-79; adj. faculty Valencia Jr. Coll., Orlando, Fla., 1969; instr. philosophy and humanities Seminole Community Coll., Sanford, 1969-83, honors instr., 1983-84. Area cons. ARC, 1947-50; del. Nat. Red Cross, Washington, 1949; founding mem. St. Joseph Hosp. Aux., Atlanta, 1950-53; v.p., treas. PTA, New Smyrna Beach, 1955-60. Bd. dirs. Atlanta Symphony Orch., Fla. Symphony Orch., 1954-59. Served to lt. USCGR, 1943-46. Recipient award in graphics Nat. Assn. Women Artists, 1939, 41, Golden Hatter award Stetson U., 1973, 74. Mem. Am. Philos. Assn., AAUP, AAUW (founding mem. New Smyrna Beach; scholarship chair 1985-86, exec. council 1984-85), Fla. Philos. Assn. (exec. council 1978-79), Collegium Phenomenologicum, Fla. Assn. Community Colls., Soc. Phenomenology and Existential Philosophy, Soc. Phenomenology and Human Scis. Home: 2103 Ocean Dr New Smyrna Beach FL 32069 Office: 2028 Sci Seminole Community College Sanford FL 32771

MASON, DAVID ERNEST, clergyman, religious organization official; b. Natchitoches, La., Jan. 3, 1928; s. Charles C. and Marjorie (O'Bannon) M.; m. Betty D. Oxford, Aug. 11, 1950 (div.); m. Alberta Martin, July 2, 1964; children—David Ernest, Paul Alexander; stepchildren—Hobart, Jeffrey, William, Suzanne. B.A., La. State U., 1949; B.D., M.Div., So. Bapt. Theol. Sem., 1952, M.Div., 1973; M.A., Syracuse U., 1954; D.D., U. Corpus Christi, 1958. Ordained to ministry Bapt. Ch., 1950. Asst. to pastor Ga. chs., 1952-55; pastor 1st Bapt. Ch., Jonesboro, La., 1955-60, Alice, Tex., 1960-62; exec. dir. Laubach Literacy, Inc., 1962-69; pres. Supportive Services, Inc., 1969-72, Greater New Orleans Fedn. Chs., 1972—; chmn. Religious Ecumenical Access Channel (REACH, Inc.), 1983—; mem. exec. com. Here's Life Am. Bd. dirs. Am. Council Vol. Agys. for Fgn. Service, 1967-68. Author: Now Then, 1957; The Charley Matthews Story, 1958; Eight Steps Toward Maturity, 1962; The Vacant Hearted, 1963; Apostle to the Illiterates, 1965; Frank C. Laubach, Teacher of Millions, 1967; Reaching the Silent Billion, 1967; The Compulsive Christian, 1968; Voluntary Non Profit Enterprise Management, 1985; (weekly TV program) Forward Together. Contbr. numerous articles to periodicals. Trustee, So. Bapt. Theol. Sem., 1959-60; chmn. adv. bd. overseers Dag Hammaroskold Coll., 1970—; bd. dirs. Koinonia Found., 1967-68, Inst. Human Understanding, 1973—, La. Council Music and Performing Arts, 1977—; mem. New Orleans Mayor's Human Relations Com., 1973—; state chmn. La. Renaissance-Religion and Arts, 1976-77, pres., 1977—. Mem. So. Bapt. Theol. Sem. Alumni Assn. La. (past pres.), Assn. Internat. Vol. Orgns. (chmn. 1966-69), Adult Edn. Assn., Jonesboro-Hodge Ministerial Assn. (past pres.), Bapt. Writers Assn. (past chmn.), Fellowship Religious Journalists (pres.), Soc. Internat. Devel., Religious Pub. Relations Assn., Assn. Edn. Journalism, La. World's Fair Ministries (pres. 1984), Assn. Vol. Action Scholars (bd. dirs. 1985—), Community Access Corp. (pres. 1985—). Lodge: Rotary. Home: 527 St Philip St New Orleans LA 70116 Office: 301 Camp St New Orleans LA 70130

MASON, FRANKLIN HARRELL, education consultant; musician; b. Dallas, Tex., Dec. 3, 1929; s. Harrell C. and Hazel (Wager) M.; B.A., North Tex. State U., 1952, M.A., 1957; postgrad. Stephen F. Austin State U., summer, 1972; Litterarum D. (hon.), Sussex Coll. Tech., 1973; pvt. study in harpsichord, 1956; master classes in organ, 1949-71. Instr. in French, Spanish, Latin Greek and English, Tyler (Tex.) public schs., 1956-74, chmn. div. fgn. langs., 1971-74; profl. church organist, 1946—; numerous organ recitals, Tex., Ga. and Ark., 1955—; asst. organist First Presbyterian Ch., Tyler, 1968—; organist Tex. Fedn. Bus. and Profl. Women's Clubs, 1959; cons. in edn. and langs. Served with U.S. Army, 1954-56. Recipient Amicii Latina award, 1969, Hawthorne award, 1972, various awards in religious service, 1947-68; Tyler Citizen Service award, 1982. Mem. Am. Guild of Organists (del. to southwest regional conv. 1963, historian, exec. council East Tex. chpt. 1980—), Nat. Council Tchrs. of English (del. to nat. conv. 1966), Organ Hist. Soc., Tex. Fgn. Lang. Assn., Tex. State Tchrs. Assn., East Tex. Latin Assn., Am. Legion, Am. Mensa Soc., Tyler Citizens League, Pi Delta Phi, Phi Eta Sigma, Sigma Delta Pi. Democrat. Presbyterian. Author: Curriculum Guide for Foreign Languages, 1964; Plot and Characterization in the Episodios Nacionales de Benito Perez Galdos, 1957; Historical Pipe Organs of Eastern Texas, 1981; contbr. articles to lit. and mus. jours. Address: 505 Sunnyside Dr Tyler TX 75702

MASON, GORDON LEE, ophthalmologist; b. Portsmouth, Va., Jan. 25, 1931; s. Lee Arnold and Hazel Marie (Simpson) M.; m. Betty Joyce Nuckols, May 4, 1958; 1 dau., Linda Marie. B.S., Coll. William and Mary, 1952; M.S., U. Mich., 1961; M.D. Med. Coll. Va., 1957. Intern Norfolk Gen. Hosp., Va., 1957-58; resident U. Mich., 1958-61; ptnr. Johnson City Eye Hosp., Tenn., 1961-76; practice medicine specializing in ophthalmology, Virginia Beach, Va., 1976—; asst. prof. ophthalmology Eastern Va. Med. Sch., Norfolk, 1976—. Fellow Am. Acad. Ophthalmology; mem. AMA, Va. Med. Soc., Phi Beta Kappa, Omicron Delta Kappa, Sigma Zeta. Methodist. Avocations: fishing; swimming; boating; jogging. Home: 4004 Oceanfront Unit 1901 Virginia Beach VA 23451 Office: 816 Independence Blvd Suite 2B Virginia Beach VA 23455

MASON, JOAN LEUNG, bank executive; b. Hong Kong, July 3, 1949; came to U.S., 1973; d. Ping Fat and Suk Tuen (Lam) Leung; m. Charles Joseph Mason, Jr., Nov. 8, 1975. B.A., Baptist Coll., Hong Kong, 1973; M.A., Baylor U., 1975. Tchr. Lock Tao Secondary Sch., Hong Kong, 1969-72; program coordinator, sec. Midwestern State U., Wichita Falls, Tex., 1976-78, dir. continuing edn., 1978-84; asst. v.p., dir. tng., asst. human resources dir. InterFirst Bank, Wichita Falls, 1984-85, asst. v.p., dir. mktg. and tng., 1985—. Bd. dirs., vice chmn. Small Bus. Council, Wichita Falls, 1981-85; bd. dirs. Pvt. Industry Council, 1983-85, ARC, Wichita Falls, 1985—; com. co-chmn. United Way, 1983, sect. leader, 1985; mem. Zoning Bd. of Adjustments and Appeals, Wichita Falls, 1985-86; mem. Mayor's Commn. on Status of Women, 1979-83, chmn., 1982-83; mem. Gold Coat Ambassadors; life mem. Wichita Falls chpt. Tex. Assn. Alcoholism and Drug Abuse Counselors, edn. chmn. 1980-82. Mem. Nat. Assn. Bank Women, Tex. Fedn. Bus. and Profl. Women's Clubs (state com. chmn. 1981-84, State Woman of Yr. 1980-81, Young Career Woman, Dist. X 1979-80), Am. Soc. Tng. and Devel., Tex.-Okla. Personnel Assn. Democrat. Roman Catholic. Avocations: reading; cooking; music; travel. Home: 5124 Edgecliff Dr Wichita Falls TX 76302 Office: InterFirst Bank 800 Scott St Wichita Falls TX 76301

MASON, JULIAN DEWEY, JR., English language and literature educator; b. Washington, N.C., Mar. 25, 1931; s. Julian Dewey and Lillie Mae (Spencer) M.; m. Elsie May, June 9, 1954; children—Christopher, Rebecca, Emily. A.B., U. N.C., 1953, Ph.D., 1962; M.A., George Peabody Coll., 1954. Tchr. Tennessee High Sch., Bristol, 1954-55; dir. student aid U. N.C., Chapel Hill, 1960-66, asst. prof. English, 1962-66; mem. faculty, English dept. U. N.C.-Charlotte, 1966—, asst. prof., assoc. prof., 1966-72, prof. English, 1972—, asst. to chancellor, 1967, Am. studies coordinator, 1974-77, chmn. English dept., 1977-84; specialist Library of Congress, Washington, 1968-70. Author: Search Party, 1953. Editor: The Poems of Phillis Wheatley, 1966. Contbr. articles to books and profl. jours. Served with U.S. Army, 1955-57. Carnegie fellow George Peabody Coll., 1953-54; career teaching fellow U. N.C., 1959-60. Mem. MLA, Am. Studies Assn., Southeastern Am. Studies Assn. (pres. 1976-77), South Atlantic Modern Lang. Assn. (chmn. Am. lit. sect. 1976-77), Soc. for Study of So. Lit. (mem. exec. council 1981, 83-86), Phi Beta Kappa. Avocations: writing; collecting rare books. Home: 5909 Ruth Dr Charlotte NC 28215 Office: U NC-Charlotte English Dept Charlotte NC 28223

MASON, MARILYN GELL, library administrator, writer, consultant; b. Chickasha, Okla., Aug. 23, 1944; d. Emmett D. and Dorothy (O'Bar) Killebrew; m. Carl L. Gell, Dec. 29, 1965 (div. Oct. 1978); 1 son, Charles E.; m. Robert M. Mason, July 17, 1981. B.A., U. Dallas, 1966; M.L.S., North Tex. State U., Denton, 1968; M.P.A., Harvard U., 1978; Librarian N.J. State Library, Trenton, 1968-69; head dept. Arlington (Va.) County Pub. Library, 1969-73; chief library program Metro Washington Council of Govts., 1973-77; dir. White Conf. on Libraries and Info. Services, Washington, 1979-80; exec. v.p. Metrics Research Corp., Altanta, 1981-82, v.p., 1981—; dir. Atlanta-Fulton Pub. Library, Atlanta, 1982—; Evalene Parsons Jackson lectr. div. librarianship Emory U., 1981. Author: The Federal Role in Library and Information Services, 1983; editor: Survey of Library Automation in the Washington Area, 1977; project dir.: book Information for the 1980's, 1980. Bd. vis. Sch. Info. Studies, Syracuse U., 1981—, Sch. of Library and Info. Sci., U. Tenn.-Knoxville, 1983—. Recipient Disting. Alumna award N.Tex. State U. 1979. Mem. ALA, Am. Assn. Info. Sci., Ga. Library Assn., D.C. Library Assn. (pres. 1976-77). Home: 1089 Mount Creek Trail Atlanta GA 30328 Office: Atlanta-Fulton Pub Library 1 Margaret Mitchell Sq Atlanta GA 30303*

MASON, MAX ALAN, pharmacist; b. Macon, Ga., June 28, 1947; s. Claude Thomas and Retta Lucille (Hegwood) M.; m. Donna Kay Carver, Mar. 1, 1968; 1 child, Patrick Ross. B.S. in Pharmacy, Mercer U., 1974. Registered pharmacist. Pharmacist Longley's Pharmacy, Rossville, Ga., 1974-80, 1982—; pharmacist, owner Lafayette Prescription Shop, Ga., 1980-82; pharmacist Tri County Hosp., Ft. Oglethorpe, 1980-81; pres. Landmark Pharmacies, Inc., Rossville, 1982; ptnr. Tri State IV Services, Rossville, 1983—; cons. Chattanooga Psychiat. Clinic, 1975-78. Vice pres. Mountain View Recreation Assn., Rossville, 1981; bd. dirs. Exchange Club, Rossville, 1984. Served to sgt. USMC, 1965-69; Vietnam. Mem. NW Ga. Pharmaceutical Assn. (pres. 1980-82), Ga. Pharmaceutical Assn. (2d v.p. 1982-83, 1st v.p. 1983-84, pres. elect 1984-85, pres. 1985—). Democrat. Baptist. Avocation: golf. Home: 739 Crestridge Dr Rossville GA 30741 Office: Landmark Pharmacies Inc 785 Chickamauga Ave Rossville GA 30741

MASON, OSCAR RAY, educator; b. North Zulch, Tex., Aug. 16, 1926; s. Oscar Mason and Aria Ophelia (Winborn) Rogers; m. Estelle Marie Rundell, Dec. 27, 1969. B.S., Sam Houston U., 1948, M.Ed., 1953; cert. U. Calif.-Extension U. Manchester, Eng., 1970. Spl. resource tchr. Cypress-Fairbanks Schs., Hempstead, Tex., 1953-63, Tex. Dept. Latin Am., Poteet, Tex., 1964-66; spl. edn. tchr. Lang. Ctr., Klein and Aldine Sch. Dists., Houston, 1966-76; spl. resource tchr. Windham Ind. Sch., Tex. Dept. Corrections, Huntsville, 1976—. Mem. Houston Mus. Fine Arts, Democratic Nat. Assn., Washington, Tex., Hist. Soc. Houston Heights. Served with USN, 1944-46. Mem. NEA, Tex. State Tchrs. Assn., Council Exceptional Children. Lodges: Masons, Shriners. Avocations: painting; cattle raising; antique collecting; history. Home: 102 S Panama St Madisonville TX 77864

MASON, PAUL MARK, economics educator, researcher; b. Buffalo, Aug. 30, 1955; s. Saul and Evalyn (Katz) M.; m. Julia Elizabeth Kline, Dec. 23, 1976; children—Jessica Lee, Joshua Aaron. B.A., U. Del., 1977, M.A., 1980; Ph.D., U. Tex., 1984. Math tchr. Bishop Eustace Prep. Sch., Pennsauken, N.J., 1977-80; asst. prof. econs. Southwest Tex. State U., San Marcos, 1980-84; vis. asst. prof. fin. Clemson U., S.C., 1984-85; asst. prof. econs. U. N. Fla., Jacksonville, 1985—. Bd. dir. Radnor Green Civic Assn., Claymont Del., 1978-79, v.p., 1979-80. Mem. Am. Econ. Assn., So. Econ. Assn., Southwestern Econ. Assn., Phi Mu Epsilon, Omicron Delta Epsilon. Avocations: tennis; basketball; softball. Home: 419 Holiday Hills Circle W Jacksonville FL 32216 Office: Univ North Florida St Johns Bluff Blvd Jacksonville FL 32216

MASON, RAYMOND K., diversified manufacturing company executive; b. Jacksonville, Fla., 1927. Grad., U. N.C., 1949. Chmn. bd., pres., chief exec. officer Charter Co., Jacksonville; chmn. bd. Charter Mortgage Co., Beach Fed. Savs. & Loan Assn.; dir. Fla. First Nat. Bank, Jacksonville. Office: Charter Co 21 W Church St Jacksonville FL 32202*

MASON, RICHARD CLYDE, consulting engineering firm executive; b. Omaha, Mar. 20, 1948; s. Raymond C. and Sue (Elmore) M. Student Austin Coll., 1966-70; B.B.A., So. Meth. U., 1971; postgrad. N. Tex. State U., 1971-72. Auditor, Dallas Fed. Res. Bank, 1972-73; br. office mgr. Neuhaus & Taylor, architects, 1974-76; auditor Lawhon, Thomas, Holmes & Co. (now Oppenheim, Appel, Dixon & Co.), Dallas, 1976-78; controller, dir. Mason Johnston & Assocs., Inc., Dallas, 1979—. Mem. Nat. Assn. Accts. (pres. North Dallas chpt.), Tex. State Hist. Assn., Tex. Hist. Found., Dallas Hist. Soc., Dallas Mus. Art. Republican. Methodist. Club: Engineers (Dallas). Home: 6776 Patrick Circle Dallas TX 75214 Office: 235 Morgan Ave Dallas TX 75203

MASON, RICHARD GORDON, lawn and garden tool company executive; b. Woonsocket, R.I., Dec. 5, 1930; s. Stephenson and Marion Irons (Cook) M.; m. Joan Elizabeth Morrison, June 29, 1957; children—Lydia Gordon, Jonathan Whitcomb, James Stephenson. B.S., Yale U., 1952; M.B.A., Harvard U., 1957. Various positions Stanley Works/Stanley Tools, New Britain, Conn., 1957-70, v.p. mfg. Stanley Tools, 1970-75; v.p. Ames Co., Parkersburg, W.Va., 1975-78, pres., 1978—. Chmn. Parkersburg Community Found.; Served to lt. USNR, 1952-55. Mem. Am. Hardware Mfrs. Assn. (v.p.), Parkersburg C. of C. (bd. dirs.). Republican. Episcopalian. Lodge: Rotary (Parkersburg). Avocations: golf; music. Office: Ames Co Box 1774 Parkersburg WV 26101

MASON, ROBERT LEE, statistician, researcher; b. San Antonio, July 11, 1946; s. James Taylor and Beatrice A. (Preusser) M.; m. Carmen Elizabeth Oertling, Aug. 2, 1969; children—Robert William, Brian George, Gregory Lee. B.S., St. Mary's U., 1968; Ph.D., So. Methodist U., 1971. Vis. asst. prof. Fla. State U., Tallahassee, 1971-72; asst. prof. Med. U. S.C., Charleston, 1972-75; sr. research statistician Southwest Research Inst., San Antonio, 1975-79, mgr. statis. analysis sect., 1979—; vis. assoc. prof. U. Calif., Davis, 1980; lectr. U. Tex., San Antonio, 1975—; reviewer Math. Reviews, Exec. Scis., Inc., 1976—; short course instr. SDL Internat., Inc., Boston, 1978, Dynamic Sci., Inc., Phoenix, 1979. Author: Regression Analysis and Its Application, 1980. Contbr. articles to profl. jours., papers to confs. Parish Council pres. St. Matthew's Catholic Ch., San Antonio, 1980-82, chmn. bldg. com., 1982-84. Served to capt. Arty., U.S. Army, 1971. Recipient Eugene W. Jacobson award ASME, 1985. Mem. Am. Statis. Assn. (chmn. council of chpts. 1985, Don Owen award 1983, Most Outstanding Presentation sect. Physical and Engring. Scis. ann. meetings, 1983, 84, 85, pres. San Antonio chpt. 1982-84), Am. Soc. Quality Control, Biometric Soc., St. Mary's U. Alumni Assn. (1st v.p., bd. dirs. 1980-85, chmn. Fiesta Oyster Bake 1985), Sigma Xi. Lodges: KC, Order of Alhambra. Avocations: tennis; coaching youth soccer and baseball; fishing. Office: Southwest Research Inst 6220 Culebra Rd San Antonio TX 78284

MASON, WILLIAM CORDELL, medical center executive; b. Montgomery, Ala., June 7, 1938; s. William C. and Sibyl (Evans) M.; m. Mona Holloway, Jan. 5, 1957; children—Michael C., Rebecca Malone, Stephen E., Holly M. B.S., U. Southwestern La., 1961; M.S. in Hosp. and Health Care, Trinity U., 1971. Hosp. rep. Eaton labs., Norwich, N.Y., 1962-66; fgn. service officer U.S. Dept. State, Manila and Saigon, 1966-69; chief exec. officer Baptist Hosp. East Africa, Mbeya, Tanzania, 1971-74, Bangalore, India, 1974-78, chief operating officer Baptist Med. Ctr., Jacksonville, Fla., 1978-84, pres., chief exec. officer, 1984—; adj. faculty U. North Fla., Jacksonville, 1985; cons. So. Baptist Foreign Mission Bd., Richmond, Va., 1980-85. Contbr. articles to profl. jours. Chmn. deacons Hendricks Ave. Baptist Ch., Jacksonville, 1984-85, Calvary Baptist Ch., India, 1976-77; treas. Karnatake State Bapt. Conv., India, 1975-77. Fellow Am. Coll. Hosp. Execs.; mem. Am. Hosp. Assn., Fla. Hosp. Assn. Lodge: Rotary. Avocations: golf; boating. Home: 9380 River Pine Rd Jacksonville FL 32217 Office: Baptist Med Ctr 800 Prudential Dr Jacksonville FL 32207

MASSET, ROYAL ANDREW, political lobbyist, consultant; b. Bklyn., Oct. 20, 1945; s. George Rowe and Aimee (Toner) M. A.B. cum laude, Princeton U., 1967; M.Div., Episcopal Theol. Sem. of Southwest, 1976; postgrad. U. Tex., 1973-76. Bar: Tex. 1977. Exec. dir. Austin Citizens League, 1976—, Tex. Taxpayers League, Austin, 1978-79; researcher, cons. Republican Party of Tex., Austin, 1980-85; polit. dir. Republican Party of Tex., 1985—; counsel Tex. Senate Com. on Intergovernmental Relations, Austin, 1983; exec. dir. Tex. Conservative Coalition, 1985. Contbr. articles to profl. jours. Mem. Austin Charter Revision Com., 1975-77; campaign mgr. Tom Pauken for Congress, Dallas, 1980; founder, atty. Citizens for Honest Electric Rates, Austin, 1983—; trustee Austin Community Edn. Consortium, Austin, 1981-83; bd. dirs. Citizens for Better Schs., Austin, 1978-79; various civic bds. and commns., 1975—. Named Disting. Citizen, City of Austin, 1977; named one of 1980s Most Interesting People in Austin, Austin Homes & Garden, 1980. Mem. Travis County Young Lawyers Assn., Travis County Bar Assn., Tex. Bar Assn., Austin Citizens League (v.p. 1975-76). Mormon. Club: South Austin Civic Assn. Home: 2021 Bluebonnet Austin TX 78704 Office: Republican Party Texas 1300 Guadalupe #205 Austin TX 78701

MASSEY, DONALD WAYNE, microfilm consultant; b. Durham, N.C., Mar. 7, 1938; s. Gordon Davis and Lucille Alma (Gregory) M.; student U. Hawaii, 1959, U. Ky., 1965, Piedmont Va. Community Coll., 1983; m. Violet Sue McIlvain, Nov. 2, 1958; children—Kimberly Shan (dec.), Leon Dale, Donn Krichele. Head microfilm sect. Ky. Hist. Soc., Frankfort, 1961; dir. microfilm center U. Ky., Lexington, 1962-67; dir. photog. services and graphics U. Va., Charlottesville, 1967-73; pres. Micrographics II, 1973—; pub. Micropublishing Series, 18th Century Sources for Study English Lit. and Culture; instr. U. Va. Sch. Continuing Edn., 1971-72, Central Va. Piedmont Community Coll., 1976; cons. Microform Systems and Copying Centers; owner Massland Farm, Shadwell, Va.; basketball coach Rock Hill Acad., 1975-77. Pres., Rock Hill Acad. Aux., 1975-76; pres. bd. Workshop V for handicapped, Charlottesville, Va., 1972-73. Served with USMCR, 1957-60. Named Ky. Col.; recipient Key award Workshop V. Mem. Am., Va. library assns., Soc. Reprodn. Engrs., Nat. (library relations com. 1973—), Va. (Pioneer award 1973, pres. 1971-72, v.p. 1973-74, program chmn. ann. conf. 1974), Ky. (Outstanding award 1967, pres. 1966-67) microfilm assns., Nat. Rifle Assn., Thoroughbred Owners and Breeders Assn. Mem. Christian Ch. (elder, chmn. bd.). Contbg. editor Va. Librarian, 1970-71, Micro-News Va. Microfilm Assn., 1970-71. Contbr. articles to profl. publs. Address: Route 2 Box 44 Keswick VA 22947

MASSEY, EARL D., Realtor; b. Killeen, Tex., Aug. 8, 1896; s. Harold Delone and Louise Elza (Bebout) M.; student Rice U., 1917-18, U. Tex., 1916-17, 20-22; m. Josephine Clair Rancier, Dec. 8, 1924; children—Sam Delone, Joe Earl. Owner-mgr., Tex. Theatre, Killeen, 1920-42, Massey Ins. Agy., 1924-29, Massey Appliance Co., 1929-42; postmaster U.S. Post Office Dept., Killeen-Ft. Hood-Harker Heights, 1939-66; owner Massey Real Estate Co., Killeen, 1967—; pres. Ft. Hood Area Bd. Realtors, 1971-72. Sec. civilian adv. com. to comdg. gen. Ft. Hood, 1960-66; sec.-treas. Bell County Water Control Improvement Dist. No. 6, 1968—; city councilman, Killeen, 1935-39; pres. Greater Killeen United Fund, 1962; chmn. Bell County Bd. Edn., 1966—; v.p., bd. dirs. Killeen Downtown, Inc., 1970—. Served with U.S. Army, 1918. Recipient Disting. Service award ARC, 1963, Greater Killeen United Fund, 1964; Golden Deeds award Exchange Club, 1965; Meritorious Service award Post Office Dept., 1966; Dedicated Service award Killeen USO, 1970; Friend of Edn. award Killeen Ind. Sch. Dist., 1978; Comdr.'s award medal for Pub. Service Dept. of Army, 1985; named Civilian of Yr., Nat. Armed Forces

YMCA, 1981. Mem. Nat. Assn. Realtors, Nat. Assn. Postmasters of U.S., Ft. Hood Area Bd. Realtors (Realtor Emeritus award 1975), Greater Killeen C. of C. (pres. 1947; Man of Year 1955), SAR (Good Citizenship award 1981), Nat. Assn. Ret. Fed. Employees (pres. Killeen chpt. 1977-78) (Meritorious Service award 1983), Assn. U.S. Army, Tex., Bell County (v.p.) hist. socs., Am. Legion (hon. life mem.; post comdr.), Lambda Chi Alpha. Democrat. Methodist (adminstrv. bd. 1969-75, 80—). Lodges: Masons (life), K.T., Shriners (comdr.), Order Eastern Star, Kiwanis (lt. gov. Tex.-Okla. dist., div. 23, 1961 Exceptional Leadership award Tex.-Okla. dist. 1961, Legion of Honor award 1982, life mem.), Sojourners (Patriot award 1979). Address: 707 Nolan Ave Killeen TX 76541

MASSEY, JACK TAYLOR, insurance company executive; b. Frederick, Okla., May 7, 1927; s. James A. and Viola (Taylor) M.; m. Sue Neal, Nov. 10, 1951; children—Sarena L., Cynthia S., J. Taylor, Neal E. B.B.A., U. Okla., 1951, LL.B., 1957; C.L.U., Am. Coll., Bryn Mawr, Pa., 1956. Bar: Okla. 1957. Agt. Mass. Mut. Life Ins. Co., Oklahoma City, 1951-62; pvt. practice ins. agt. and cons., Oklahoma City, 1962-64; with United Founders Life Ins. Co., Oklahoma City, 1964-86, exec. v.p., 1966-86, dir., 1967-86, sec., 1979-86; ins. cons., 1986—. Served with USNR, 1945-46. Mem. Am. Soc. C.L.U.s, Okla. Bar Assn., Okla. County Bar Assn., ABA, Am. Soc. Corp. Secs. Methodist. Clubs: Quail Creek Golf and Country, Beacon (Oklahoma City). Home: 2308 NW 58th St Oklahoma City OK 73112 Office: 5900 Mosteller Dr Oklahoma City OK 73112

MASSEY, JAMES EARL, clergyman, educator; b. Ferndale, Mich., Jan. 4, 1930; s. George Wilson and Elizabeth (Shelton) M.; m. Gwendolyn Inez Kilpatrick, Aug. 4, 1951. Student U. Detroit, 1949-50, 55-57; B.Th., B.R.E., Detroit Bible Coll., 1961; A.M., Oberlin Grad. Sch. Theology, 1964; postgrad. U. Mich., 1967-69; D.D., Asbury Theol. Sem., 1972; postgrad. Pacific Sch. Religion, 1972, Boston Coll., 1982-83. Ordained to ministry Church of God, 1951. Assoc. minister Ch. of God, Detroit, 1951-53; sr. pastor Met. Church of God, Detroit, 1954-76, pastor-at-large, 1976; speaker Christian Brotherhood Hour, 1977-82; prin. Jamaica Sch. Theology, Kingston, 1963-66; campus minister Anderson Coll., Ind., 1969-77, asst. prof. religious studies, 1969-75, assoc. prof., 1975-80, prof. N.T. and homiletics, 1981-84; dean of Chapel and Inst., prof. religion and society Tuskegee Inst., Ala., 1984—; chmn. Commn. on Higher Edn. in the Ch. of God, 1968-71; vice chmn. bd. publs. Ch. of God, 1968-78; dir. Warner Press, Inc. Author: When Thou Prayest, 1960; The Worshipping Church, 1961; Raymond S. Jackson, A Portrait, 1967; The Soul Under Siege, 1970; The Church of God and the Negro, 1971; The Hidden Disciplines, 1972; The Responsible Pulpit, 1973; Temples of the Spirit, 1974; The Sermon in Perspective, 1976; Concerning Christian Unity, 1979; gen. editor: Christian Brotherhood Hour Study Bible, 1979; Designing the Sermon, 1980; co-editor Interpreting God's Word for Today, 1982; editor Educating for Service, 1984; The Spiritual Disciplines, 1985; mem. editorial bd. The Christian Scholar's Rev. Leadership mag. Mem. Corp. Inter-Varsity Christian Fellowship. Served with AUS, 1951-53. Mem. Nat. Assn. Coll. and Univ. Chaplains, Nat. Com. Black Churchmen, Nat. Negro Evang. Assn. (bd. dirs. 1969—). Office: Dean of Chapel Tuskegee U Tuskegee AL 36088

MASSEY, JAY DAVIS, college administrator; b. Middlesex, N.C., Apr. 22, 1926; d. Jesse Montford and EJ (Nobles) Davis; m. Wilbur Kindred Massey, June 28, 1953; 1 child, Kathryn Massey Schooley. B.S. in Phys. Edn., U. N.C.-Greensboro, 1947; M.A., NYU, 1952. Cert. secondary tchr., N.C. Instr. phys. edn. and biology Chatham Hall, Va., 1947-49, Rock Mount Sr. High., N.C., 1954-56; instr. phys. edn. Ga. State Coll. for Women, Milledgeville, 1949-52, Duke U., Durham, N.C., 1952-54; head dept. health, phys. edn. and dance Meredith Coll., Raleigh, N.C., 1957—. Meredith Abroad Program grantee, 1980—, Fulbright grantee, 1985; recipient Teaching Excellence award Meredith Coll., 1981. Mem. Am. Alliance of Health, Physical, Edn., Recreation and Dance, N.C. Alliance of Health, Physical, Recreation and Dance (pres. 1969-70, mem. spl. structure com., fin. com. 1967, Honor award 1975). Democrat. Clubs: Raleigh Racquet, Faculty Bridge (Meredith Coll.). Avocations: tennis; golf; reading; travel; bridge. Office: Meredith Coll 3800 Hillsborough Raleigh NC 27611

MASSEY, KENNETH WAYNE, hospital department administrator; b. Tullahoma, Tenn., Sept. 22, 1953; s. Joe Dudley and Agnes Vera (Whittenburg) Adams M.; m. Rita Joy Whitaker, Nov. 21, 1980. B.S., U. Tenn., 1977; M.B.A., Memphis State U., 1984. Asst. mgr., pharmacist Super D Drugs, Memphis, 1977-80; dir. pharmacy Crippled Childrens Hosp., Memphis, 1980-82; pharmacist Skaggs Drugs, Memphis, 1982-83; mgr. cardiology, neurology Baptist Meml. Hosp., Memphis, 1983—. Mem. Am. Heart Assn., Beta Gamma Sigma. Republican. Methodist. Avocations: woodworking; gardening; water sports; golf. Home: 8264 Glen Way Cove Cordova TN 38018 Office: Baptist Meml Hosp 899 Madison Ave Memphis TN 38146

MASSEY, LARRY LEONARD, ops. research analyst; b. Mobile, Dec. 15, 1946; s. Oscar R. and Bertha J. (Howell) M.; B.S., Auburn (Ala.) U., 1971; M.S., U. So. Miss., Hattiesburg, 1974, Ph.D. (Nat. Wildlife Fedn. fellow 1974), 1977; m. Margaret Ann Gwin, Aug. 30, 1969; children—Michael Owen, Angela Gwin. Instr., Central Elem. Sch., Lucedale, Miss., 1968-69; grad. intern Miss. Marine Resources Council, Long Beach, Miss., 1973-74; intern cons. John R. Thompson & Assos., Hattiesburg, 1974; instr. Prentiss (Miss.) Jr. Coll., 1974-75; cons. Natchez (Miss.) Jr. Coll., 1975; ops. research analyst NOAA, Dept. Commerce, Beaufort, N.C. and Miami, Fla., 1975—. Recipient Outstanding Performance award Dept. Commerce, 1979, 80. Mem. Am. Inst. Fishery Research Biologists. Lodges: South Miami Rotary (merit award), West Kendall Optimist. Home: 7104 SW 139th Pl Miami FL 33183 Office: 75 Virginia Beach Dr Miami FL 33149

MASSEY, MARGARET GWIN, systems, programming exec.; b. Mobile, Ala., May 10, 1947; d. George Amos and Edna Laurene (Hannah) Gwin; B.S., Auburn U., 1969; postgrad. East Carolina U., 1975-77; M.Internat. Bus., Fla. Internat. U., 1983; postgrad. U. Miami, 1983—; m. Larry L. Massey, Aug. 30, 1969; children—Michael Owen, Angela Gwin. Computer programmer Auburn (Ala.) U., 1969-71; systems analyst U. So. Miss., Hattiesburg, 1971-75; data processing instr. Carteret Tech. Inst., Morehead City, N.C., 1977; project mgr. systems and programming div. Burdines Dept. Stores, Miami, Fla., 1978; systems and programming mgr. Fla. Internat. U., Miami, 1979-82; dir. computer application programming Miami-Dade Community Coll., 1982—. Recipient Gov. of Fla. award, 1980; Fla. Internat. U. ednl. grantee, 1980. Mem. Fla. Assn. Ednl. Data Systems. Baptist. Home: 7104 S W 139th Pl Miami FL 33183 Office: Miami-Dade Community College Miami FL

MASSEY, W(ILMET) ANNETTE, nurse; b. Big Chimney, W.Va., June 30, 1920; d. Robert Lee and Twila Augusta (Pringle) M.; student Morris Harvey Coll., 1938-39; R.N., Phila. Gen. Hosp., 1943; B.S. in Edn., U. Pa., 1948; M.S. in Nursing, Yale U., 1959. Nurse cadet instr. U.S. Cadet Nurse Corps, Huntington (W.Va.) Meml. Hosp., 1943-45; nurse instr. St. Mary's Sch. Nursing, Huntington, 1948-51; WHO nurse cons. Govt. Ceylon, 1951-55; staff nurse instr. VA Hosp., Ft. Thomas, Ky., 1955-57; asst. prof. nursing Brigham Young U., Provo, Utah, 1959-61; asso. prof. nursing W.Va. U., Morgantown, 1961-83, chmn. dept. psychiat. nursing, 1968-72; cons. Appalachian Regional Hosp., Beckley, W.Va., W.Va. Dept. Mental Health, Charleston, Valley Community Mental Health Center, Kingwood, W.Va.; group leader med.-nursing group to India, Expt. Internat. Living, Brattleboro, Vt., 1965. Mem. Appalachian Trail, Morgantown Hospice. NIMH grantee, 1964-75. Mem. Am. Nurses Assn., League Nursing, Am. Orthopsychiat. Assn., Internat. Transactional Analysis Assn., Am. Counseling Assn. (dir. 1981-82, v.p. 1982), Am. Soc. Profl. and Exec. Women, Tarrytown Group, Nat. Registry Psychiat. Nurse Specialists (edn. and resources com.), Internat. Acad. Cancer Counselors and Cons., Nat. Alliance Family Life, Inc. (founding), AAUP, Nat. Hist. Soc., Hastings Center, Nat. Wildlife Fedn., Smithsonian Assos., Phila. Gen. Hosp. Sch. Nursing Alumni, U. Pa., Yale U., W.Va. U. Sch. Nursing (hon.) alumni assns., Sigma Theta Tau. Republican. Methodist. Club: Alpine Lake Recreation Community (Terra Alta, W.Va.). Home: 432 Western Ave Morgantown WV 26505

MASSEY, YVONNE HARRIS, county official; b. Eutaw, Ala., Mar. 30, 1955; d. Samuel and Waffie Jean Wilder; m. Isaac Massey, May 7, 1977 (div. 1980); 1 dau., Mosena Renee. B.S., U. Ala., 1977. Sec. Vulcan Realty & Investment Co., Birmingham, Ala., 1977; credit mgr. Dial Fin. Corp., Tuscaloosa, Ala., 1977; sales clk. Raymons Ladies Wear, 1977-79; decorating cons. Home Interiors & Gifts, Inc., 1980-82; employment and tng. planner Tuscaloosa County Commn., 1979—. Mem. Am. Soc. Tng. and Devel., Southeastern Employment and Tng. Assn., Bus. and Profl. Women's Club. Baptist. Home: 1116 42d Ave Tuscaloosa AL 35401 Office: 2010 27th Ave Tuscaloosa AL 35401

MASSIN, EUGENE, art educator, artist; b. Galveston, Tex., Apr. 10, 1920; s. Sam and Gertrude (Nevelof) M.; m. Helen Levitt, Sept. 16, 1942; children—Barry, Leslie, Robin David. B.F.A., Sch. Art Inst. Chgo.; B.F.A., Loyola U., Chgo.; B.F.A., U. Chgo.; M.F.A., Escuela Universitaria de Bellas Artes, Guanajuato, Mex., Prof., Escuela Universitaria de Bellas Artes, Guanajuato, 1948-49, U. Wis.-Madison, 1950-51; prof. extension div. U. S.C., Charleston, 1951-53; artist-in-residence W.Va. U., Morgantown, 1964-65; prof. art U. Miami, Fla., 1956-85, prof. emeritus, 1985—, also lectr. exptl. program; artist-in-residence Ford Found., Morgantown, 1964, 65, Design for Opera, Miami; cons. various orgns., 1965—. Contbr. to books, TV interviews, articles on exptl. use of new techs., biog. movie for Ednl. TV. Works include mural in stainless steel and acrylic for Holiday, Carnival Cruise Line; commns. include mural, Cafritz Co., Washington, sculpture, So. Bell, Jacksonville, Fla., mural on canvas, City Nat. Bank, mural acrylic and lights, City Nat. Bank Miami Beach, painting World Book. Founder, past pres. Artist Equity in Fla.; adviser Cafritz Found. for Arts, Washington, Arts-Council, Miami. Recipient award Opera Design, Ford Found., awards in Humanities, U. Miami, Esso award in Plastics; James Nelson Raymond fellow, Art Inst. Chgo. Home and Office: 3891 Little Ave Coconut Grove Miami FL 33133

MASTEJ, J. MICHAEL, hospital administrator; b. Detroit, Mar. 19, 1949; s. Joseph Albert and Bertha A. (Toleikis) M.; m. Laura Thtatcher Wright, Dec. 28, 1975 (div. 1983); 1 child, Sarah Catherine; m. Lucy Shafer, July 28, 1984. B.B.A., U. Notre Dame, 1971. Asst. controller Emma L. Bixby Hosp., Adrian, Mich., 1973-75; reimbursement specialist Humana Inc., Atlanta and Louisville, 1975-77; assoc. exec. dir. Llano Estacado Med. Ctr., Hobbs, N.Mex., 1977-78; assoc. exec. dir. The Wellington Hosp., London, 1978-79; exec. dir. Garden State Community Hosp., Marlton, N.J., 1979-81; exec. dir. Humana Hosp., Ft. Walton Beach, Fla., 1981—; adv. bd. Okaloosa County Emergency Med., Fla., 1984—. Vice pres. Okaloosa Symphony, bd. dirs. Okaloosa chpt. Am. Heart Assn. Recipient Humana Mgmt. Club award, Louisville, 1981, 82; named King of Hearts, Am. Heart Assn., Okaloosa County, 1985. Mem. Am. Coll. Hosp. Adminstrs., Greater Ft. Walton Beach C. of C. (v.p. 1985). Republican. Episcopalian. Lodge: Rotary (program chmn. 1985). Avocations: skiing; sailing; golf. Office: Humana Hosp 1000 Mar Walt Dr Fort Walton Beach FL 32548

MASTERS, ALAN CRAIG, building products company executive; b. Detroit, Nov. 7, 1952; s. Carter I. and Hillis E. (Duke) M.; m. Linda Susan Piazza, Aug. 21, 1976; children—Heather Lynn, Casey Leigh. B.S. in Health Edn., Tenn. Tech. U., 1978, M.A. in Health and Phys. Edn., 1979, M.B.A., 1983. Sr. asst. mgr. Rose's Stores, Inc., Columbia, Tenn., 1979-81; loss prevention and involvement coordinator Champion Internat. Corp., Silverstreet, S.C., 1983—. Served with U.S. Army, 1972-75. Mem. Am. Soc. Safety Engrs., So. Pulp and Paper Assn., Beta Gamma Sigma. Democrat. Baptist. Avocations: golf; softball; reading; volleyball; skiing. Home: 206 Lanham St Greenwood SC 29646 Office: Champion Internat Corp Route 1 PO Box 10 Silverstreet SC 29145

MASTERS, BRUCE ALLEN, biostratigrapher, micropaleontologist; b. Terre Haute, Ind., Nov. 3, 1936; s. Cletus Hunter and Eva Lee (Osburn) M.; m. Shirley Ann Howard, Apr. 11, 1963. B.S., Valparaiso U., Ind., 1959; M.A., U. Calif.-Berkeley, 1962; Ph.D., U. Ill.-Urbana, 1970. Assoc. geologist Humble Oil and Refining Co., Houston, 1962-65; assoc. prof. Hartwick Coll., Oneonta, N.Y., 1969-74; research assoc. Amoco Prodn. Co., Tulsa, 1974—. Author: Oceanic Micropalaeontology, 1977. Contbr. articles to profl. jours. Mem. Am. Assn. Petroleum Geologists, Paleontol. Research Instn., Paleontol. Assn., Cushman Found., Swiss Geol. Soc. Office: Research Ctr Amoco Prodn Co PO Box 3385 Tulsa OK 74102

MASTERS, EVERETT EDISON, agricultural business executive, farmer; b. Pond Creek, Okla., July 13, 1913; s. William Newton and Fannie Lula (Mayo) M.; m. Melba Bandy, Dec. 15, 1934; children—Wesley Will, Jesse Everett; m. 2d, Florence Fisher Wilson, June 28, 1964. Chmn. emeritus Center Plains Industries, Inc.; farmer; former chmn. Hale County Sch. Bd. Pres. Hale County Farm Bur. (Tex.), 1949-50; founder Hi-Plains Community Hosp. (Tex.); Founder N.W. Tex. chpt. Myasthenia Gravis. Named Outstanding Man of Yr., Nat. Myasthenia Gravis Found. Inc., 1976, Hale County Man of Yr., 1983; recipient recognition Tex. Senate, 1983. Methodist. Lodges: Woodman of World (past camp comdr.), Masons (past master).

MASTERS, WESLEY WILL, corporation executive, cattleman; b. Plainview, Tex., Nov. 10, 1937; s. Everett Edison and Melba (Bandy) M.; m. Nancy Tate, Mar. 7, 1959; children—Toni Allison, Wesley Will, Elise. B.S. in Agronomy, Tex. Tech U., 1960, M.S. in Agronomy, 1962. Sales rep. Plains Grain Co., Abernathy, Tex., 1962-63; asst. mgr. So. Farm Supply, Amarillo, Tex., 1963-68; pres. Center Plains Industries, Inc., Amarillo, 1968—; dir. Fertilizer Inst., Washington, 1982—; mem. Council Agr., Sci. and Tech.; past chmn. West Tex. Agrl. Chem. Conf. Regent Tex. Tech U., 1983—; mem. Am. Heart Assn., Amarillo; bd. dirs. Myasthenia Gravis Nat. Found., 1980; active Amarillo Area Found. March of Dimes. Named Disting. Alumnus, Tex. Tech U. Sch. Agr., 1982, Man of Yr., March of Dimes, Amarillo, 1981, Boss of Yr., Nat. Secs. Assn., Amarillo, 1971-72; recipient Am. Farmer Degree, Future Farmers Am., Hale Center, Tex., 1958; award Outstanding Fertilizer Co., Tex. Plant Food Inst., Austin, 1981. Mem. Am. Soc. Agronomy, Rocky Mountain Plant Food Assn., Sigma Xi, Pi Kappa Alpha. Democrat. Methodist. Clubs: Red Raider, West Tex. State Cager, Amarillo (dir. 1982—). Lodges: Masons, (past master), Shrineers. Home: 3802 Deann PO Box 7988 Amarillo TX 79114 Office: Center Plains Industries Inc 10800 Canyon Dr Box 7988 Amarillo TX 79114

MATA, EDUARDO, conductor; b. Mexico City, Mexico, 1942; student Nat. Conservatory of Music, 1954-63; pupil Carlos Chavez, 1960-65; advanced conducting work Tanglewood, 1964; m. Carmen Cirici-Ventalló, Nov. 5, 1968. Resident condr. Tanglewood, 1964; guest condr. with U.S. orchs. including Boston Symphony, Chgo. Symphony, Cleve. Orch., Pitts. Orch., Detroit Symphony Orch., also orchs. in South and Central Am., Poland, Yugoslavia, Luxembourg, France, W. Ger., Sweden, Gt. Britain, Italy, Israel, Japan; music dir., condr. Orch. Philharmonic Mexico, 1966-75; prin. condr., musical adviser Phoenix Symphony, 1969-74, dir., 1975-78; also music dir. Dallas Symphony, 1977—; artistic dir. Puebla Music Festival, 1975—; artistic dir. Nat. Opera Mex., 1983—. Mem. Mexico Soc. Composers. Composer symphonies, chamber and vocal music. Address: Dallas Symphony PO Box 26207 Dallas TX 75226

MATCHETT, CLEVELAND CALVIN, educator; b. Palatka, Fla., Dec. 28, 1927; s. Calvin Joseph and Ada Bertha (Clarke) M. A.A., Hiwassee Coll., 1951; B.S., East Tenn. State Coll., 1953; postgrad. U. Chattanooga, 1962-66, Middle Tenn. State U., 1967-68. Tchr. Nathan Bachman Sch., Signal Mountain, Tenn., 1959-60; clerical staff Chattanooga YMCA, 1958-67; tchr. Oneida Baptist Inst., Ky., 1967-72, Central Christian Sch., Portsmouth, Va., 1973-75, Faith Christian Sch., Chesapeake, Va., 1975-77; clk. Portsmouth YMCA, 1981—. Author: Directory of U.S. Christian Schools, 1982. Recipient I Dare You award Washington Coll. Acad., 1946, Christian Service award Hiwassee Coll., 1951; U.S. Govt. grantee, 1978-79. Mem. Nat. Geog. Soc., Va. Diabetes Assn., Am. Assn. Retired Persons, Nat. Investigative Com. UFOs. Avocations: Writing epic poetry; acquiring personal library; piano performances; research; church choir. Home: PO Box 721 Portsmouth VA 23705 Office: Portsmouth YMCA 527 High St Portsmouth VA 23704

MATELSKI, DWAIN E(RWIN), periodontist; b. Colorado Springs, Colo., May 29, 1945; s. Erwin Ferdinand and Julia Beth (Corkill) M.; m. Sharon Gay Bondurant, Aug. 24, 1968; 1 son, Michael Todd. B.S., Tex. A&M U., 1967; D.D.S., Baylor Coll., Dallas, 1972, M.S.D., 1974; M.S., Baylor Coll., Waco, Tex., 1974. Practice dentistry specializing in periodontics, Ft. Worth, 1974—; cons. Fed. Correction Inst., Tex., 1975-85, Ft. Worth State Sch. for Children, 1978-85, John Peter Smith Hosp., 1978-85. Co-author: Periodontics In General Practice, 1976. NIH fellow, 1972-75. Mem. Am. Acad. Periodontigology, Tex. Dental Assn., Fort Worth Dental Assn., ADA, Baylor Periodontic Alumni, Ft. Worth C. of C. Republican. Methodist. Avocations: sailing; jogging; skiing. Home: 1655 Kemble Ct Fort Worth TX 76103 Office: 1124 S Lake St Suite B Fort Worth TX 76104

MATHENY, ADAM PENCE, JR., child psychologist, educator, consultant, researcher; b. Stanford, Ky., Sept. 6, 1932; s. Adam Pence and Dorotha (Steele) M.; m. Ute I. Debus, July 10, 1962 (div.); m. Mary P. Tolbert, June 24, 1967; children—Laura Steele, Jason Gaverick. B.S., Columbia U., 1958; Ph.D., Vanderbilt U., 1962. Sr. human factors engr. Martin Aerospace div., Balt., 1962-63; instr. Johns Hopkins U. Med. Sch., 1963-65; staff fellow Nat. Inst. Child Health and Human Devel., 1965-67; from asst. prof. to prof. pediatrics U. Louisville Med. Sch., 1967—, assoc. dir. Louisville Twin Study; cons. S.E. Ind. Rehab. Ctr. Bd. dirs. Community Coordinated Child Care, Old Louisville Day Care Ctr., 1982—. Served with USN, 1951-55. Fellow Internat. Soc. Twin Research; mem. Soc. Research Child Devel., Am. Psychol. Assn., AAAS, Behavior Genetics Soc., Ky. Speech and Hearing Assn. (dir.), Phi Beta Kappa, Sigma Xi. Co-author: Genetics and Counseling in Medical Practice, 1969; contbr. articles to profl. jours.

MATHENY, CHARLES WOODBURN, JR., retired army officer, retired civil engineer, former city ofcl.; b. Sarasota, Fla., Aug. 7, 1914; s. Charles Woodburn and Virginia (Yates) M.; B.S. in Civil Engring., U. Fla., 1936; grad. Army Command and Gen. Staff Coll., 1944; m. Jeanne Felkel, July 12, 1942; children—Virginia Ann, Nancy Carolina, Charles Woodburn III. San. engr. Ga. State Dept. Health, 1937-39; civil engr. Fla. East Coast Ry., 1939-41; commd. 2d lt. F.A., U.S. Army Res., 1936, 2d lt. U.S. Army, 1942, advanced through grades to col., 1955; arty. bn. comdr., Germany, 1945-47; gen. staff Dept. Army, 1948-51; qualified army aviator, 1952, aviation officer 25th Inf. Div., Korea, 1952-53; sr. aviation adviser Korean Army, 1954; dep. commdt., dir. combat devel. Army Aviation Sch., 1954-55; dep. dir. research dept. tactics Arty. Sch., 1955-57; aviation officer 7th U.S. Army, Germany, 1957-58; Munich sub area comdr. So. Area Command, Europe, 1959, qualified sr. army aviator, 1959, dep. chief staff for info. So. Area Command, 1960; Mich. sector comdr. VI Army Corps, 1961-62; ret., 1962; asst. dir. Tampa (Fla.), Dept. Public Works 1963-77, asst. to dir., 1977-81, ret., 1981. Mem. troop com. Boy Scouts Am., 1965-73; active various community and ch. activities; patron Tampa Art Mus., 1965-83, Tampa Community Concert Series, 1979-82; bd. dirs. Tampa YMCA, 1967-71, Fla. Easter Seal Soc., 1978; bd. dirs. Easter Seal Soc. Hillsborough County, 1971—, treas., 1973-76, pres., 1977. Decorated Bronze Star with oak leaf cluster, Air medal with three oak leaf clusters; named to U. Fla. Student Hall of Fame, 1936; registered profl. engr. and surveyor, Ga. Mem. ASCE (pres. West Coach br., dir. Fla. sect. 1973, Engr. of Yr. award West Coast br. Fla. sect. 1979, life mem. 1980), Am. Soc. Profl. Engrs. (sr.), Fla. Engring. Soc., Am. Public Works Assn. (pres. West Coast br. Fla. chpt. 1972, exec. com. Fla. chpt. 1972-77, v.p. 1977, pres. 1978), Ret. Officers Assn., Army Aviation Assn., SAR, Fla. Blue Key, Alpha Tau Omega. Episcopalian. Initiator tactical use of helicopters in Army, 1949, profl. sch. civil engring., 1973. Home: 4802 Beachway Dr Tampa FL 33609

MATHENY, TOM HARRELL, lawyer; b. Houston; s. Whitman and Lorene (Harrell) M.; B.A., Southeastern La. U., 1954; J.D., Tulane U., 1957; LL.D. (hon.), Centenary Coll., 1979, De Pauw U. Admitted to La. bar, 1957; partner firm Pittman & Matheny, Hammond, La., 1957—; trust counsel, chmn. bd. 1st Guaranty Bank, Hammond, gen. counsel, 1960-83; v.p. Edwards & Assos., So. Brick Supply, Inc. Faculty, Southeastern La. U., 5 years, Holy Cross Coll., New Orleans, 3 years; lectr. Union Theol. Sem., Law Sci. Acad.; mem. com. on conciliation and mediation of disputes World Peace through Law Center. Chmn. advancement com. Boy Scouts Am., Hammond, 1960-64, mem. dist. council, 1957-66, mem. exec. bd. Istrouma council, 1966—, adv. com. to dist. area council; pres. Tangipahoa Parish Mental Health Assn.; sec. Chep Morrison Scholarship Found.; mem. men's com. Japan Internat. Christian U. Found.; chmn. speakers com., mem. com. on community action and crime prevention La. Commn. on Law Enforcement and Adminstrn. Criminal Justice. Campaign mgr. for Dem. gov. La., 1959-60, 63-64. Bd. dirs. La. Moral and Civic Found., Tangipahoa Parish ARC, 1957-67, Hammond United Givers Fund, 1957-68, La. Council Chs., Southeastern Devel. Found., La. Mental Health Assn.; pres. Jud. Council United Meth. Ch., 1976—; pres. bd. trustees La. Ann. Conf. United Meth. Ch., 1984—; bd. dirs. Wesley Found., La. State U., 1965-68, 70—, chmn. bd.; trustee Centenary Coll., 1964-70, Scarritt Coll., 1975-81; hon. trustee John F. Kennedy Coll.; hon. sec. U.S. com. Audenshaw Found. Recipient Man of Year award, Hammond, 1961, 64, also La. Jaycees 1964; Layman of Yr. award La. Ann. Conf., United Meth. Ch. 1966, 73; Disting. Alumnus award Southeastern La. U., 1981. Fellow Harry S. Truman Library Inst. (hon.); mem. Am. (com. on probate), La. (past gen. chmn. com. on legal aid, com. prison reform), 21st Jud. Dist. (past sec.-treas., v.p. 1967-68, 71—) bar assns., Comml. Law League Am. (past mem. com. on ethics), La. Alumni Council (pres. 1963-65), Acad. Religion and Mental Health, La. Assn. Claimant Compensation Attys., Southeastern La. U. (dir., pres. 1961-62, dir. spl. fund 1959-62, past dir. Tangipahoa chpt.), Tulane Sch. Law alumni assns., Am. Trial Lawyers Assn., Am. Judicature Soc., Law-Sci. Inst., World Peace Through Law Acad., Acad. Polit. Sci., Am. Acad. Polit. and Social Sci., Internat. Acad. Law and Sci., Common Cause, Internat. Platform Assn., UN Assn., La. Hist. Assn., Friends of Cabildo, Gideons Internat., Nat. Assn. Conf. Lay Leaders (pres. 1966-82), Assn. Conf. Lay Leaders South Central Jurisdiction (pres.), Hammond Assn. Commerce (dir. 1960-65), Intern Soc. of Barristers, Intern Assn. of Valuers, Phi Delta Phi, Phi Alpha Delta. Democrat. Methodist (steward, adminstrv. bd., dist. lay leader 1960-64, past co-chmn. conf. bd. lay activities, lay minister, lay leader La. area conf., numerous other ch. activities). Mason, DeMolay (dist. dep. to supreme council 1964—, Legion of Honor), Kiwanian (v.p., dir., Layman of Yr. award for La., Miss. and West Tenn. 1972), Rotarian. Home: PO Box 221 Hammond LA 70404 Office: 401 E Thomas St PO Box 1598 Hammond LA 70401

MATHER, JAY B., photojournalist; b. Denver, Apr. 22, 1946; s. Bruce Coe and Gazel Irene (Allison) M.; m. Susan Bentley Molthop, Sept. 9, 1967 (div. Feb. 1984); children—Jesse Rand, Joshua Pike; m. Kathy Siebenmann, Aug. 17, 1985. B.A. in Geography, U. Colo., 1969. Staff photographer Sentinel Newspapers, Denver, 1972-77, Louisville Courier-Jour. and Louisville Times, 1977—. Recipient Pulitzer prize for internat. reporting, 1980; 1st place Robert F. Kennedy awards, 1981, citation of excellence Overseas Press Club, 1980; 2d place award Nat. Newspaper Photographer of Yr., 1976; named So. Photographer of Yr., 1978. Mem. Nat. Press Photographers Assn. Home: 308 S Birchwood Ave Louisville KY 40206 Office: 525 W Broadway Louisville KY 40202

MATHERLEE, THOMAS RAY, hospital administrator; b. Dayton, Ohio, Sept. 18, 1934; s. Dennis R. and Eleanor E. Matherlee; B.S. in Bus. Adminstrn. Findlay Coll., 1958; M.B.A., U. Chgo., 1960; m. Phyllis Simmons, July 16, 1960; children—Michael, Jennifer, Craig, Brent, Brian. Adminstrv. resident Shannon Hosp., San Angelo, Tex., 1959-60; asst. adminstr. Richland Meml. Hosp., Olney, Ill., 1960-61; adminstrv. asst., then adminstr. Forsyth Meml. Hosp., Winston-Salem, N.C., 1961-68; exec. dir. Gaston County (N.C.) Hosp., 1968-70; exec. dir. Gaston Meml. Hosp., Inc., Gastonia, 1970-80, pres., 1981-85; sr. v.p. Vol. Hosps. of Am. Inc., Washington, 1986—; cons. Sch. Pastoral Care, N.C. Bapt. Hosp., Winston-Salem, 1967-68; mem. sub-area adv. council Health Systems Agy., 1975-80. Dir. Olney Ill. CD, 1960-61; mem. fin. com. Piedmont council Boy Scouts Am., 1970; mem. adv. bd. Gastonia Wesleyan Youth Chorus, 1972; mem. joint com. nursing edn. N.C. State Bd. Edn. and Bd. Higher Edn., 1969-71; mem. adminstrv. bd. First United Meth. Ch., Gastonia, 1972-74; bd. dirs. Gaston County Heart Assn., 1968-70, Forsyth County Cancer Soc., 1964-65; trustee N.C. Hosp. Edn. and Research Found., 1966-71, pres., 1970-71; trustee N.C. Blue Cross and Blue Shield, Inc., 1971-77, Southeastern Hosp. Conf., 1971-72, 73-81, mem. edn. com., 1978—, mem. program com., 1975-76. Named Boss of Yr., Nat. Secs. Assn., 1970-71. Fellow Am. Coll. Healthcare Execs.;mem. N.C. Hosp. Assn. (trustee 1966-72, pres. 1970-71, chmn. council govt. liaison 1978-81, Disting. Service award 1985), N.C. League Nursing, Am. Hosp. Assn. (ho. of dels. 1973-78, 83-85, speaker no. of dels. 1985; trustee 1975-78, 83-85, chmn. bd. trustees 1984), Gastonia C. of C. (health affairs com. 1969-72). Lodge: Kiwanis. Contbr. articles on hosp. adminstrn. to profl. jours.

MATHEW, TOM, economics educator; b. Adoor, India, Dec. 10, 1935; came to U.S., 1959; naturalized, 1969; s. Mathen and Sosamma (Chandy) M.; m. Saramma Thomas, Aug. 5, 1963; children—Teki, Thomas, Alexander. B.Sc., Kerala U. (India), 1958; M.A., Howard U., 1967; Ph.D., U. Ga., 1976. Asst. prof. Piedmont Coll., Demorest, Ga., 1969-74; instr. U. Ga., Athens, 1974-76; asst. prof. Albany State Coll., Ga., 1976-80; assoc. prof. Wartburg Coll., Waverly, Iowa, 1980-83; assoc. prof. Troy State U., Montgomery, Ala., 1983—, dir. M.B.A. program, 1983—. Reviewer books in field. Mem. Am. Econ. Assn., So. Econ. Assn., Midwestern Econ. Assn., Mo. Valley Econ. Assn. Eastern Orthodox. Avocations: soccer; tennis; gardening; racquetball. Home: 325 Oldfield Dr Montgomery AL 36117-3950

MATHEWS, CHARLES R., mayor. Mayor of Garland, Tex. Office: PO Box 469002 Garland TX 75046*

MATHEWS, DANIEL MONROE, chemist; b. Paris, Ark., Oct. 18, 1926; s. Marion Daniel and Alice Virginia (LeRoy) M.; B.S., U. Ark., 1952, M.S., 1955, Ph.D., 1959; postgrad. Ga. Inst. Tech., 1956; m. Charlene Faye Alexander, Aug. 13, 1977; children—Judy Kay, Janice Carol. Research specialist U. Ark.-Fayetteville, 1952-55, jr. chemist, 1956-58, asst. prof. Sch. Medicine, 1958-59, assoc. prof. Grad. Inst. Tech., 1960-70, prof., 1970—; instr. Ga. Inst. Tech., Atlanta, 1955-56. Served with U.S. Army, 1945-46. Mem. Am. Chem. Soc., Chem. Soc. (London), Health Physics Soc., Ark. Acad. Sci., Sigma Xi. Contbr. articles to profl. jours. Home: 4200 Glenmere St North Little Rock AR 72116 Office: 1201 McAlmont St Little Rock AR 72203

MATHEWS, HARLAN, state official; b. Ala.; m. Patsy Jones; children—Stanley, Lester. B.A., Jacksonville State Coll., 1949; M.A. in Pub. Adminstrn., Vanderbilt U., J.D., 1962. Successively mem. budget staff, then dep. commr. fin. and adminstrn., then commr. fin. and adminstrn. State of Tenn., Nashville, 1950-71; with Amcon, Internat., Inc., Memphis, 1971-74; state treas. State of Tenn., Nashville, 1974—. Served with USN, 1944-46. Vanderbilt U. scholar. Mem. Tenn. Mcpl. Fin. Officers Assn., Nat. Mcpl. Fin. Officers Assn., Nat. Assn. State Auditors, Comptrollers and Treas., Nat. Assn. State Budget Officers, Tenn. Bar Assn. Baptist. Office: State Treas State Capitol 1st Floor Nashville TN 37219*

MATHEWS, PEGGY ANNE, nurse; b. Oakdale, La., Sept. 10, 1941; d. Howard Douglas and Huldah Mary (Hicks) Tyler; m. Ariel Joseph Mathews Jr., Aug. 28, 1958; children—Joseph, Mark, Debra. A.Nursing, La. State U., Alexandria, 1975. R.N., La. Nurse intensive care unit St. Frances Cabrini Hosp., Alexandria, 1975-76, 77-78, nurse edn. dept., 1979-80, dir. cardiology, 1980—, established cardiac rehab. program, 1982, now dir. Cardiac Catheterization Lab. Mem. Am. Assn. Critical Care Nurses, Am. Heart Assn. Democrat. Roman Catholic. Avocations: dancing; fishing; horse back riding; gardening. Home: 2904 Doe Run Alexandria LA 71301 Office: St Frances Cabrini Hosp 3330 Masonic Dr Alexandria LA 71301

MATHEWS, ROBERT AYDELOTTE, dentist; b. Schenectady, N.Y., Oct. 20, 1922; s. Raymond and Marguerite (Pine) M.; m. Emily Ann Grantham, June 30, 1951; children—Roberta Ann, Emily Marguerite, John Morton, Jennifer Pine. Student Coll. Liberal Arts, U. Mich., 1940-42, D.D.S., 1945. Instr., U. Mich. Sch. Dentistry, Ann Arbor, 1947-48; intern Bellevue Hosp., N.Y.C., 1948-50; dentist Davidson County Dept. Health, Nashville, 1950-52; mem. staff Davidson County Hosp., Nashville, 1950-65; pvt. practice dentistry, Nashville, 1950—; cons. VA Hosp. Sch. Dental Hygiene, Nashville, 1973-74, Vol. Community Coll., Gallatin, Tenn., 1978-81. Awards chmn. Cub Scouts, Nashville, 1970. Served to lt. USNR, 1945-47. Fellow Am. Coll. Dentists, Internat. Coll. Dentists; mem. Nashville Dental Soc. (pres. 1961-62), Am. Acad. Periodontology (assoc.), Pierre Fauchard Acad., Council on Internat. Relations of ADA, Fedn. Dentaire Internationale, Tenn. Dental Assn. (trustee 1958-61, adv. com. to Tenn. commr. pub. health 1975-84, cons. to VA 1982-83), Chi Phi, Delta Sigma Delta. Avocations: travel; tennis; music. Home: 4414 Howell Pl Nashville TN 37205 Office: 205 21st Plaza 21st and Hayes St Nashville TN 37203

MATHEWS, SHARON WALKER, artistic director, dance educator; b. Shreveport, La., Feb. 1, 1947; d. Arthur Delmar and Nona (Frye) Walker; m. John William Mathews, Aug. 14, 1971; children—Rebecca, Elizabeth, Anna. B.S., La. State U.-Baton Rouge, 1969, M.S., 1971. Cert. tchr. health, phys. edn., elem. edn., dance, La. Tchr., East Baton Rouge Parish, Baton Rouge, 1971-72, tchr. phys. edn., 1972-74; tchr. dance Dancer's Workshop, Baton Rouge, 1971—; dir. dance Baton Rouge Magnet High Sch., 1976—, choreographer, 1976—; artistic dir. Baton Rouge Ballet Theatre, 1976—, choreographer, 1975—; choreographer La. State U. Tigresses, 1971-74. Bd. dirs. Baton Rouge Ballet Theatre, pres. 1973-74. Mem. Southwestern Regional Ballet Assn., Kappa Delta. Republican. Baptist.

MATHIA, MARY LOYOLA, nun, educator; b. Hempstead, N.Y., Sept. 14, 1921; d. Paul John and Laura Marie (Linck) Mathia. B.A., Coll. Mt. St. Joseph, 1953; M. Pastoral Studies, Loyola U.-Chgo., 1980. Joined Sisters of Charity of Cin., Roman Catholic Ch., 1941. Tchr. various schs. Ohio and Mich., 1943-62, St. John Bapt. Sch., Chillum, Md., 1962-63; social studies tchr. and dept. chmn. Holy Name High Sch., Cleve., 1963-69; ednl. cons. Diocese of Cleve., 1970-78; dir. edn. St. Benedict Ch., Crystal River, Fla., 1979—; prin. Central Cath. Sch., 1985—. Republican. Office: St Benedict Ch 455 S Suncoast Blvd Crystal River FL 32629

MATHIAS, WALLER THOMAS, environmental, health and employee services manager, consultant engineer; b. Norfolk, Va., May 13, 1948; s. Melven Roe and Helen Virginia (Holloman) M.; m. Cluadette M. Thompson, Oct. 31, 1984; 1 child by previous marriage, Thomas P. B.A. in Chemistry, U. N.C., 1970, M.S. in Pub. Health, 1979. Engr. assoc. Western Electric, Greensboro, N.C., 1970-73, devel. engr., Richmond, Va., 1973-80; cons. engr. Digital Equipment Corp., Acton, Mass., 1980-81, mgr. environ., health and employee services, Greenville, S.C., 1981—; task force chmn. Inst. for Interconnecting and Pkg. Electronic Circuits, 1982—; trainee Nat. Inst. Occupational Safety and Health, Chapel Hill, N.C., 1978. Western Electric fellow, Richmond, Va., 1978. Mem. Am. Indsl. Hygiene Assn., Am. Soc. Safety Engrs. Republican. Presbyterian. Avocations: aerobics; weight lifting; tennis; racquetball; running. Home: 402 Piney Grove Rd Greenville SC 29607 Office: Digital Equipment Corp 500 Fairforest Way Greenville SC 29607

MATHIAS, WILLIAM JEFFERSON, JR., criminal justice educator, university administrator; b. Atlanta, Oct. 6, 1938; s. William J. Sr. and Jeanette (Hardman) M.; m. Elizabeth Fisher, May 25, 1981; children—Paige Elizabeth, William J. III. B.B.A., U. Ga., 1960, M.S., 1966, Ed.D., 1969. Dir. traffic and security U. Ga., Athens, 1960-64, police tng. coordinator Inst. Govt., 1966-67; asst. dean Coll. Urban and Pub. Affairs, Ga. State U., Atlanta, 1967-75; prof. criminal justice, dean Coll. Criminal Justice U. S.C., Columbia, 1975—; mem. commn. Criminology Criminal Justice Edn. Standards, Chgo., 1977-81; cons. in field. Author: Horse to Helicopter - First 100 Years of Atlanta Police Department, 1973; (with others) Foundations of Criminal Justice, 1980. Contbr. articles to profl. jours. NDEA fellow, 1964-67. Mem. Acad. Criminal Justice Scis. (pres. 1973-74, sec.-treas. 1970-72, mem. various coms.), Am. Soc. Criminology, So. Assn. Criminal Justice Educators (founder, pres. 1972-73, Educator of Yr., 1979), Ga. Assn. Criminal Justice Educators (founder, pres. 1967-68, v.p. 1970-71, mem. various coms.). Presbyterian. Home: 6007 Hampton Ridge Rd Columbia SC 29209 Office: Coll Criminal Justice U SC Columbia SC 29208

MATHIS, BETTY, public relations counsel; b. Atlanta, Oct. 5, 1918; d. Walter Rylander and Evelyn Battle (Epting) M.; student Agnes Scott Coll., 1934-36. Sports writer, columnist Atlanta Constitution, 1936-39; gen. news and feature writer, then editor spl. supplements, 1939-40; dir. public relations Atlanta Housing Authority, 1940; feature writer, asst. city editor, daily by-line columnist Atlanta Constitution, 1941-43; asst. regional info. exec. OPA, 1943-45; partner Mathis, Murphey & Bondurant public relations counsel, Atlanta, 1945-50; editor Sun Colony Mag., Fort Lauderdale, Fla., 1950-53; partner Mathis & Bondurant public relations, Ft. Lauderdale, 1953-83, owner, 1982—. Bd. dirs. ARC; mem. coms. United Way; sec. vestry All Saints Episcopal Ch., 1974-76, mem. vestry, 1978—, treas., 1979, sr. warden, 1980, del. Diocesan Conv., 1975, 79, 80. Nominee, Pulitzer prize, 1937. Mem. Public Relations Soc. Am., Am. Soc. Hosp. Public Relations (profl. advancement com. 1980), Public Relations Council Fla. Hosp. Assn. (dir. 1977-79, pres. 1977-78), Women in Communications (pres. county 1968, 69, Atlantic Fla. chpt. 1979, named Woman of Yr. 1979), Gold Coast Hosp. Public Relations Council (founding, pres. 1981-82), Am. Hosp. Assn. Democrat. Club: Tower. Home and office: 1628 NE 15th Ave Fort Lauderdale FL 33305

MATHIS, JAMES O., counselor educator; b. West Monroe, La., July 22, 1929; s. Dewey Otto and Dessie Lee (Williams) M.; m. Peggy Sue Miller, July 21, 1951; children—Linda Sue, Elizabeth Ann, James A. B.S., North Tex. State U., 1951, Ed.M., 1956, Ed.D., 1965. Lic. psychologist, profl. counselor. Art tchr. Victoria/Crane Jr. High Sch., Victoria, Tex., 1952-55; art tchr. Andrews Jr. High Sch., Tex., 1955-59, counselor, 1959-63; assoc. prof. psychology East Central State U., Ada, Okla., 1965-67; prof., coordinator Sam Houston State U., Huntsville, Tex., 1967—. North Tex. State U. scholar, 1963-65. Mem. Am. Assn. for Counseling and Devel. (pres. 1982-83), Tex. Assn. Counseling and Devel. (bd. dirs. 1983-84, Disting. service award 1983, 84, sec. so. region br. assembly 1984-86), Phi Delta Kappa (Service award 1985). Democrat. Baptist. Avocations: gardening; fishing. Home: 3778 Summer Ln Huntsville TX 77340 Office: Sam Houston State U Huntsville TX 77341

MATHY, MICHAEL EDWARD, petroleum geologist; b. Corpus Christi, May 6, 1958; s. Harold Edward and Janelle Gayle (Patterson) M.; B.S. in Geology, U. S.W. La., 1981. Cons. geologist H.E. Mathy/May Petroleum, Lafayette, La., also Dallas, 1981-84; geologist Mathy Petroleum, Inc. & Co., Lafayette, 1984-85, prin., geologist, 1985—. Mem. Lafayette Geol. Soc. (chmn. exhibit com. 1984-85), Am. Assn. Petroleum Geologists. Republican. Avocations: gold; photography; camping; snow skiing; scuba diving. Office: Mathy Petroleum 1116 Coolidge Complex 2 Lafayette LA 70505

MATKIN, GEORGE GARRETT, banker; b. Ennis, Tex., Jan. 21, 1898; s. George Garrett and Clemens (Loggins) M.; student pub. schs., El Paso, Tex.; m. Lucile Ross, June 22, 1929 (dec. Feb. 1976); children—Margaret (Mrs. George H. Jackson), Nancy Clemens (Mrs. Raymond Marshall). With State Nat. Bank of El Paso, 1917—, pres. 1949-67, chmn. bd., 1967-81, sr. chmn. bd., 1981-83, chmn. bd. emeritus, 1983—; chmn. El Paso Electric Co. Mem. El Paso C. of C. (hon.). Clubs: El Paso Country; Internat.; Coronado. Lodge: Masons. Home: 810 E Blanchard Ave El Paso TX 79902 Office: State Nat Bank El Paso TX 79901

MATLICK, GERALD ALLEN, artist, educator; b. Ft. Wayne, Ind., August 18, 1947; s. Roy Harrison and Loretta Mae (Rinearson) M.; m. Marla Jo Clark, Mar. 8, 1975. B.A., Western Ky. U., 1969, M.A., 1974; M.F.A., Bowling Green State U., 1980. County art supr. Crittenden County Schs., Marion, Ky., 1969-73; grad. teaching asst. Western Ky. U., Bowling Green, 1973-74, vis. instr., 1974-76; art instr. Crittenden County High Sch., Marion, 1976-79; grad. teaching asst. Bowling Green State U., 1979-80; coordinator dept. art Brescia Coll., Owensboro, Ky., 1981—. One-man shows include Swearingen Gallery, Louisville, 1984, Owensboro Area Mus., 1986; exhibited in group shows: Coll. St. Joseph, Cin., 1985; participated in over 90 regional, nat. and invitational art exhibits, 1969—. Recipient numerous awards for paintings and drawings in competitive shows including: Faculty Merit award Brescia Coll., 1983. Mem. Coll. Art Assn. Home: 127 W 17th St Owensboro KY 42301 Office: Dept Art Brescia Coll 120 W 7th St Owensboro KY 42301

MATRICK, JACOB MORTON, lawyer, insurance company executive; b. Chgo., Aug. 20, 1934; s. Bernard I. and Vera (Keys) M.; m. Melba Eady, Sept. 11, 1959; children—Jacob, Phillip, Russell. B.S., Miss. Coll., 1957, LL.B., 1963. Bar: Miss. 1964. Vice pres. Mississippi Valley Title Ins. Co., Jackson, from 1958, now exec. v.p.; ptnr. Taylor, Covington, Smith, & Matrick, Jackson, 1965—. Office: 315 Tombigbee St Jackson MS 39201

MATSON, ROGER ALLEN, economist; b. Minot, N.D., July 29, 1938; s. Walfred Gustav and Zella Katherine (Martinson) M.; B.A., Concordia Coll., Moorhead, Minn., 1960; Ph.D. (Woodrow Wilson fellow), U. Colo., 1965; m. Sandra Francis Winn, Sept. 2, 1967; children—Todd Allen, Melissa Francis. Instr., U. Mont., 1963-64; USPHS fellow U. N.C., Chapel Hill, 1964-65; chief econ. research staff TVA, Knoxville, 1965-70, chief budget and cost control staff, Chattanooga, 1974—; lectr. U. Tenn., Knoxville, 1969-70; regional economist Dept. Commerce, Washington, 1970-72; asst. prof. U. Wyo., 1972-74; adj. prof. U. Tenn., Chattanooga, 1974—. Mem. Am. Econ. Assn., Regional Sci. Assn., N.Am. Soc. Corp. Planning, Nat. Assn. Bus. Economists. Democrat. Lutheran. Contbr. articles to profl. jours. Home: 4944 Willow Lawn Dr Chattanooga TN 37416 Office: Budget and Cost Control Staff TVA Chattanooga TN 37401

MATT, LOUIS CARMINE, JR., real property and lease adminstrator, educator; b. Utica, N.Y., Mar. 1, 1953; s. Louis Carmine and Theresa (Rotundo) M.; m. Sandra Florcyzk, Nov. 1, 1980. B.A., LeMoyne Coll., 1974; J.D., Syracuse U., 1976; postgrad. Wharton Sch., U. Pa., 1985—. Legal research analyst DePerno Law Office, Utica, N.Y., 1976-81; prof. Herkimer County Community Coll., N.Y., 1977-81; ops. supr. Southland Corp., Naples, Fla., 1981-82; prof. Edison Community Coll., Naples, 1981-85; prof. adminstrv. law Nova U., Tampa, Fla., 1984—; real property/lease adminstr. Circle K., Tampa, 1982—. Bd. govs. LeMoyne Coll., 1976—. Mem. Am. Bus. Communication Assn., Am. Bus. Law Assn., Phi Delta Phi, Pi Gamma Mu. Roman Catholic. Club: Oneida Hist. (Utica, N.Y.). Office: Circle K PO Box 918 Mango FL 34262

MATTAUCH, ROBERT JOSEPH, electrical engineering educator; b. Rochester, Pa., May 30, 1940; s. Henry Paul and Anna Marie (Mlinarcik) M.; m. Frances Sabo, Dec. 29, 1962; children—Lori Ann, Thomas. B.S. in E.E., Carnegie Inst. Tech., 1962; M.S. in E.E., N.C. State U., 1963, Ph.D., 1967. Asst. prof. elec. engring. U. Va., Charlottesville, 1966-70, assoc. prof., 1970-76, prof., 1976-83, Wilson prof., 1983—, dir. Semiconductor Device Lab., 1967—; cons. U.S. Army Fgn. Sci. and Tech. Center, The Rochester Corp. Mem. IEEE (microelectronics com.), Sigma Xi, Eta Kappa Nu, Tau Beta Pi, Phi Kappa Phi, Pi Mu Epsilon. Patentee infrared detector; solid state switching capacitor; thin wire pointing method. Home: 2455 Foxpath Ct Charlottesville VA 22901 Office: Thornton Hall U Va Charlottesville VA 22901

MATTEI, JAMES STAFFORD, company executive, micrographics specialist, consultant; b. Beaumont, Tex., June 30, 1953; s. Charles Adrian and Betty (Borden) M.; m. Carol Janette Furmanski, Oct. 27, 1982. B.S. in Econs., Westminster Coll., 1976. Mktg. rep. Errwood Corp., N.Y.C., 1975-77, regional sales mgr., 1978-81; v.p. mktg. Southeastern Micrographics, Miami, Fla., 1981-83; exec. v.p. United Micrographics, Miami, 1984—; pres. United Bus. Corp., Miami, 1984—; cons. Racal Ltd., Redding, Eng., 1980-82, Security Investors Protection Corp., Washington, 1983. Pres. Spring Lakes Condominiums Assn., Miami, 1980-82; active Miami Progress Club, 1982-84. Mem. Assn. Info. and Image Mgmt. (pres. Miami 1984), Nat. Micrographics Assn. (v.p. 1982-83). Republican. Roman Catholic. Office: United Micrographics Inc 8095 NW 98th St Miami FL 33016

MATTEO, ALBERT PAUL, JR., petroleum geologist; b. Atlantic City, N.J., Apr. 11, 1957; s. Albert Paul, Sr. and Florence Beatrice (Newkirk) M.; m. Elizabeth Spradling, Jan. 9, 1982. B.S., Duke U., 1979; M.A., U. Mo., 1981; M.B.A. candidate Wharton Sch., U. Pa., 1985—. Geologist, U.S. Geol. Survey, Atlantic City, N.J., 1978, Mobil Oil Co., Denver, 1980; exploration geologist Shell Oil Co., New Orleans, 1981-85. Mem. Am. Assn. Petroleum Geologists, Soc. Econ. Paleontologists and Mineralogists, New Orleans Geol. Soc., Gulf Coast Soc. Econ. Paleontologists and Mineralogists. Republican. Roman Catholic. Avocations: golf; racketball; reading; swimming; running.

MATTESON, LEWIS WHITFORD, JR., automobile dealer, data processing company executive; b. Houston, Nov. 24, 1924; s. Lewis Whitford and Lillian (Hall) M.; B.S. in Elec. Engring., Rice U., 1949; m. Betty Irene Dykes, Dec. 16, 1954; children—Sherry Matteson Adelman, Whit, Debbie Matteson Wood, Ricky. Partner, Matteson S.W. Co., Houston, 1950-62, v.p., 1962-67, chmn. bd., 1967-71; owner, chmn. bd., pres. Matteson Transformers Inc., Houston, 1957-72; owner, mgr. Matteson Devel. Co., Houston, 1970—; v.p., sec., treas., dir. Plaza Lincoln-Mercury, Inc., Houston, 1971-79, pres., treas., chmn. bd., 1979—; chmn. bd., pres. Matteson's Motorcycles, Inc., Kerrville, Tex., 1973—. Served with Signal Corps, AUS, 1943-46. Registered profl. engr., Tex. Mem. Am. Theatre Organ Soc., Tex. Motorcycle Roadriders Assn., Phi Theta Kappa. Episcopalian. Club: Racquet (Houston). Home: 211 Paul Revere Dr Houston TX 77024 also Casa del Rio Hunt TX 78024 Office: 9255 Kirby Rd Houston TX 77098

MATTHEWS, CARY IRWIN, textile company executive; b. Lynchburg, Va., Oct. 11, 1940; s. Frank E. and Claudia Amanda (Irwin) M.; m. Mary Lucinda Clark, June 9, 1961; children—Kymeone Claudia, Kelly Anne. Student U. N.C., Chapel Hill, 1958-60, B.A., 1965; postgrad. U. N.C.-Greensboro, 1972, U. N.C.-Charlotte, 1975. Div. tng. dir. Beaunit Corp., Lowell, N.C., 1973; plant mgr. Caroline Throwing, Kingsmountain, N.C., 1973-75; supt., plant mgr. Duplan Corp., Dillon, S.C., 1975-78; exec. v.p. mfg. Dillon Yarn Corp., 1978—. Served to lt. (j.g.), USN, 1965-69. Republican. Methodist. Office: PO Box 1247 Dillon SC 29536

MATTHEWS, CHARLES SEDWICK, oil company consultant; b. Houston, Mar. 27, 1920; s. Charles James and Zadoc (Sedwick) M.; m. Miriam Ormerod, June 2, 1945; children—Joan, Wendy. B.S. in Chem. Engring., Rice U., 1941, M.S., 1943, Ph.D., 1944. Registered profl. engr., Tex. Engr. Shell Oil Co., San Francisco, 1944-48, then mgr. engring., N.Y.C., mgr. engring., Houston, 1972-73, sr. cons., 1973—; dir. research Shell Devel. Co., Houston, 1967-72; mem. adv. bd. U.S. Dept. Energy, Washington, 1975-80, cons., 1978-80; mem. adv. council Rice U., 1968-73. Author: Pressure Buildup and Flow Test in Wells, 1967; contbr. articles to profl. jours; patentee in field. Mem. Nat. Soc. Profl. Engrs., Soc. Petroleum Engrs., Nat. Acad. Engring., Nat. Petroleum Council. Clubs: Houston, Meyerland (treas. 1981—). Office: Shell Oil Co PO Box 2463 Houston TX 77001

MATTHEWS, CLARK J(IO), II, retail co. exec.; b. Arkansas City, Kans. Oct. 1, 1936; s. Clark J. and Betty Elizabeth (Stewart) M.; B.A., So. Meth. U., 1959, J.D., 1961; m. Janice Eleanor Hill, June 28, 1959; children—Patricia Eleanor, Pamela Elaine, Catherine Joy. Admitted to Tex. bar, 1961; trial atty. Ft. Worth Regional Office, SEC, 1961-63; law clk. to chief U.S. dist. judge No. Dist. Tex., Dallas, 1963-65; atty. Southland Corp., Dallas, 1965-73, v.p., gen. counsel, 1973-79, exec. v.p., chief officer, 1979-83, sr. exec. v.p., chief fin. officer, 1983—. Mem. Tex., Dallas, Am. bar assns., Am. Judicature Soc., Alpha Tau Omega, Pi Alpha Delta. Methodist. Club: DeMolay. Home: 7005 Stefani St Dallas TX 75225 Office: 2828 N Haskell Ave Dallas TX 75204

MATTHEWS, DORIS BOOZER, educator; b. Lexington, S.C., Aug. 18, 1932; d. Otto Raymond and Ruth (Sox) Boozer; B.S., Newberry Coll., 1952; M.Ed., U. S.C., 1955, specialist degree, 1971, Ph.D., 1972; m. Charles L. Matthews, Aug. 20, 1952; children—Shirley Ruth, Carles Ray, Sylvia Ann. Tchr., Brennen Sch., Columbia, S.C., 1952-64; supr. counseling S.C. State Employment Service, Columbia, 1964-66; counseling supr. and basic edn. specialist S.C. Com. Tech. Edn., Columbia, 1966-68; instr. elem. edn. U. S.C., Columbia, 1968-72; asst. prof. S.C. State Coll., Orangeburg, 1972-75, asso. prof., 1975-79, prof., 1979—. Chmn., Columbians Youth Com., 1968-72, Cayce Neighborhood Center, 1967-70. Mem. Nat., S.C. edn. assns., Nat., S.C. assns. supervision and curriculum devel., Assn. Ednl. Communication and Tech., Employment Counselors Assn., Am. Assn. Counseling and Devel., Assn. Tech. Edn., Am., S.C. personnel and guidance assns., S.C. Dept. Audio-Visual Instrn., AAUP (pres. S.C. State Coll. chpt. 1975-79, v.p. state conf. 1979-81, pres. 1981-83), Assn., Internat. Platform Assn., Internat. Stress and Tension Control Soc., S.C. Biofeedback Assn. (state rep. 1984—), Assn. Individually-Guided Edn., Nat. Middle Sch. Assn., Phi Delta Kappa (v.p. S.C. State Coll. chpt. 1978-79, pres. 1979-81). Lutheran. Clubs: Cayce Women's (pres. 1965-67), Fashion Rose Garden (pres. 1962-64). Author articles on burnout, relaxation tng. and biofeedback. Home: 101 Delieseline Rd Cayce SC 29033 Office: SC State Coll Orangeburg SC 29117

MATTHEWS, JAMES EVANS, flight research corporation executive; b. Ithaca, N.Y., May 6, 1928; s. James Evart and Eleanor Evans (Defort) M.; student U. Ky., 1949-50, Cornell U., 1950; m. Doris M. Mayo, Feb. 23, 1952; children—Susan Elizabeth, James Hamilton, Margaret Jane, Mary Lucille Matthews McKenzie. Pilot, instr. exptl. test pilot Eastern Airlines, 1951-68; pres. Don S. Colman Solar Water Heating Co., Miami, Fla., 1960-62; chmn. Cayman Petroleum, Ltd., Coral Gables, Fla., 1963-71; pres. Petroleum Environ. Labs., Inc., Coral Gables, 1970-73, Petro-ex Corp., Coral Gables, 1970-73, Seastrike Corp., Coral Gables, 1970-73; pres. Internat. Flight Research Corp., Winter Park, Fla., 1970—, World Flight Security, Winter Park, 1976—; pres., chief pilot Flight Test Internat., Inc., Winter Park, 1977—; chmn. bd., pres. Internat. Flight Research Fin. Corp., Las Vegas, Nev., 1981—; bd. trustees Fla. Inst. Tech., adv. council Sch. Aeros.; mem. nat. adv. bd. Am. Security Council. Founder, coordinator, flight comr. Op. Ducklings, 1961 (commendations City of Miami, Los Angeles, U.S. Navy). Recipient awards, Nat. Pilots Assn., 1974. Mem. AIAA, Nat. Aero. Assn., Aerospace Med. Assn., Fraternal Order Airmail Pilots, Helicopter Assn. Am., Soaring Soc. Am., Exptl. Aircraft Assn., Warbirds Assn., Pacific NW Aviation Hist. Found., Air Force Assn., Confederate Air Force, U.S. Air Race Assn., Am. Def. Preparedness Assn. (pres. 1982—, dir.), Internat. Oceanographic Found., U.S. Naval Inst., Am. Petroleum Inst., Soc. Naval Architects and Marine Engrs., Permanent Internat. Assn. Navigational Congresses, Oggin Rev., Oceanic Soc., Cousteau Soc., Internat. Civil Aviation Orgn., Aircraft Owners and Pilots Assn., Explorers Club. Republican. Episcopalian. Adv. bd. International Jour. of Ocean Science; chmn. internat. conf. on coastal engring., 1978; founder through Internat. Flight Research Corp. Revoredo Trophy, 1976, chmn. selection com. Home: 751 Palmer Ave Winter Park FL 32789 Office: PO Box 1887 Winter Park FL 32790

MATTHEWS, JAY ARLON, JR., publisher, editor; b. St. Louis, Apr. 13, 1918; s. Jay Arlon and Mary (Long) M.; student San Jose State Coll., 1939-41, U. Tex., 1946-47; m. May Clark McLemore, Jan. 16, 1944; children—Jay Arlon III, Emily Cochrane, Sally McLemore. Asst. dir. personnel Adj. Gen.'s Dept. Tex., 1947-53, dept. adj., 1957-65, mil. support plans officer, 1965-69, chief emergency operations, 1965-71; pub. Presidial Press, Mil. History Press; owner Presidial Art Gallery. Past dir. Civil Def., Austin; mem. adv. bd. Confed. Research Center, Hill Jr. Coll.; mil. historian 65th Legislature, Tex., 1977-78. Served with AGC, Tex. N.G., 1946—, brig. gen. ret., 1973. Fellow Co. Mil. Historians (gov. 1981-84); mem. Austin (state v.p. 1951-52), U.S. (chmn. nat. security com. 1952-53) jr. chambers commerce, Tex. Safety Assn. (dir. traffic safety), N.G. Assn. U.S. (chmn. publicity 81st Gen. Conf.), Instituto Internationale de Historia Militar (hon. life), Assn. U.S. Army, Mil. Order World Wars (comdr. Austin chpt. 1980). Episcopalian. Club: Exchange (pres. Austin chpt. 1982-83). Editor: Mil. History of Tex. and S.W. Quar. Home: 1807 Stamford Ln Austin TX 78703 Office: 1011 W 31st St Austin TX 78705 also PO Box 5248 Austin TX 78763

MATTHEWS, ROBERT EMIL, utility company executive; b. Elizabeth, N.J., May 1, 1925; s. Emil Charles and Mae Margaret (McLaughlin) M.; m. Jeanne Frances Corbett, Jan. 20, 1951; children—Robert Edward, Patricia, Thomas, John, Anne. B.M.E., Catholic U. Am., 1950; M.B.A., Morehead State U., 1978. Mech. engr. Am. Gas & Electric Service Corp. (now Am. Electric Power Service Corp.), N.Y.C., 1950-58, head engring. sect., 1958-64, dir. sales engring., 1964-67, dir., 1978—; comml. mgr. Ky. Power Co., Ashland, 1967-74, div. mgr., 1974-78, exec. v.p., 1978-80, pres., 1980—, also dir.; dir. First Bank and Trust, Ashland, Ky. Energy Research Bd., 1980—. Former bd. dirs. Hack Estep Home for Boys, Boyd County. Served with AC U.S. Army, 1943-46. Mem. ASHRAE, Ashland Area C. of C. (dir. 1975-78, pres. 1977), Ky. State C. of C. (dir. 1980—). Roman Catholic. Clubs: Rotary (past dir. club), Elks (Ashland). Office: 1701 Central Ave Ashland KY 41101

MATTHEWS, ROBERT LYNN, civil engineer; b. Hammond, Ind., Nov. 1, 1947; s. John L. and Gertrude Alice (Dobis) M.; B.S. in Civil Engring., U. Fla., 1970; m. Barbara L. Fennell, Mar. 9, 1973; 1 son, John Robert. Project engr., then sr. engr. Ross, Saarinen, Bolton & Wilder, Ft. Lauderdale, Fla., 1970-76; project mgr. CDM/Ross, Saarinen, Bolten & Wilder, Atlanta, 1976-78; mgr. ops. Camp Dresser & McKee Inc., Atlanta, 1978-83, br. mgr., Bradenton, Fla., 1983—. Named Met. Atlanta Young Engr. of Year, Atlanta Profl. Socs., 1981; registered profl. engr. Fla., Ga., N.C., S.C., Ala. Mem. ASCE (chmn. conv. activities com. 1979), Am. Water Works Assn., Water Pollution Control Fedn., Nat. Soc. Profl. Engrs. (pres. chpt. 1982; Engr. of Yr. in Pvt. Practice 1981-82), Ga. Soc. Profl. Engrs. (chmn. edn. and scholarship com. 1977-78, chpt. pres. 1981-82), Ga. Engring. Found. (chmn. ways and means com. 1980-81), Fla. Engring. Soc., Fla. Inst. Cons. Engrs. Republican. Roman Catholic. Clubs: Holly Springs, Atlanta Lawn Tennis Assn. Home: 3024 Palm Aire Dr Sarasota FL 33580 Office: 6221 14th St W Suite 302 Bradenton FL 33507

MATTHEWS, ROBERT ORIN, botanical gardens executive; b. Clifton Forge, Va., May 10, 1925; s. William Alford and Minnie Lee (Carter) M.; m. Dorothe Elizabeth Stinger, Aug. 21, 1944; 1 child, Leslie Beth. Landscaping cert. Nat. Landscape Inst., Los Angeles, 1951; Horticulture cert. Pa. State U., 1952; Revenue Sources Mgmt. Sch. cert. N.C. State U., 1970. With Norfolk Bot. Gardens, Va., 1949—, supt., 1953—; horticulture advisor Garden Clubs Norfolk, 1975—; mem. adv. bd. Tech. Vocat. Ctr., Norfolk, 1975-76. Bd. dirs. Tidewater dist. Girl Scouts U.S.A., 1960. Served with USN, 1943-46, PTO. Named Outstanding City Employee, Norfolk Civitan, 1977; Outstanding Horticulturist, Va. Nurserymen's Assn., 1977; Boss of Yr., Am. Bus. Women's Assn., 1983. Mem. Am. Camellia Soc. (bd. dirs. 1984—), Va. Camellia Soc. (pres. 1972-74), Tidewater Rose Soc. (bd. dirs. 1978-80), Bot. Gardens Soc. (bd. dirs. 1977—), Men's Garden Club (bd. dirs. 1977-79, Outstanding Club Mem. 1977), Bot. Gardens Found. (v.p. 1979—). Baptist. Avocations: antiques, lapidary, travel. Home and Office: Norfolk Bot Gardens Norfolk VA 23518

MATTHEWS, STUART, aircraft manufacturing company executive; b. London, May 5, 1936; came to U.S., 1974; s. Bernard De Lides and Daisy Vera (Woodcock) M.; chartered engr., Hatfield Coll. Advanced Tech., 1958; m. Kathleen Hilary Adams, Jan. 12, 1974; children—Anthony, Caroline, Joanna. Apprentice, de Havilland Aircraft Ltd., Hatfield, 1952-53; aircraft project design engr. Hawker Siddeley Aviation Ltd., Hatfield, 1953-64; with mktg. dept. Brit. Aircraft Co., Bristol, 1964-67; gen. mgr. planning Brit. Caledonian Airways, London, 1967-74; v.p. N.Am. div. Fokker-VFW Internat., Washington, 1974-80; pres., chief exec. officer Fokker Aircraft USA, Alexandria, Va., 1980—, Aircraft Fin. and Trade, Alexandria, 1984—; chmn. asso. mem. group Commuter Airlines Assn. Am., 1979-80. Bd. dirs. Flight Safety Found.; mem. adv. bd. Am. Security Bd. Fellow Royal Aero. Soc.; mem. Inst. Transp., AIAA. Clubs: Aero, Nat. Aviation (Washington); Wings (N.Y.C.); Lions (pres. Engleside, Va. 1977-78); Rotary Internat. Home: 9439 Mt Vernon Circle Alexandria VA 22309 Office: 1199 N Fairfax St Alexandria VA 22314

MATTHEWS, WILBUR LEE, lawyer; b. Big Spring, Tex., Jan. 20, 1903; s. Robert D. and Sallei (Bourland) M.; m. Mary LeNoir Kenney, June 22, 1932 (dec. Oct. 1972); children—Wilbur Lee, John Kenney; m. 2d, Helen P. Davis, May 28, 1976. LL.B. with highest honors, U. Tex., 1926. Bar: Tex. 1926, U.S. dist. ct. Tex. 1927, U.S. Ct. Appeals 1927, U.S. Supreme Ct. 1929. Ptnr. Matthews and Branscomb and predecessor firms, 1930—; mem. Tex. Fin. Adv. Commn., 1960. Trustee, chmn. San Antonio Med. Found., 1977-82. Fellow Am. Coll. Trial Lawyers; mem. Am. Law Inst., Tex. Bar, ABA. Clubs: San Antonio Country, Argyle, San Antonio. Author: San Antonio Lawyer-Memoranda of Cases and Clients, 1983; contbr. articles to legal jours. Home: 200 Patterson Apt 806 San Antonio TX 78209 Office: One Alamo Ctr San Antonio TX 78205

MATTHEWS, WILLIAM ELLIOTT, IV, natural gas company executive; b. Birmingham, Ala., Sept. 11, 1929; s. William Elliott and Julia Lovett (Murfee) M.; m. Wahwiece Coe, Feb. 17, 1962; children—Martha Wahwiece, William Elliott V, Julia Lovett, Mary Elizabeth. B.E.E., Ga. Inst. Tech., 1950; postgrad. Advanced Mgmt. Program, Harvard U., 1977. Registered profl. engr., Ala. With So. Natural Gas Co., Birmingham, 1950—, now pres. Bd. dirs. YMCA, Birmingham, Jefferson-Shelby div. Am. Heart Assn., Birmingham, 1982-85. Served to lt. USN, 1954-56. Mem. Am. Gas. Assn., Interstate Natural Gas Assn. Am., So. Gas Assn. (bd. dirs. 1979-82), Newcomen Soc. N.Am. Presbyterian. Lodge: Kiwanis. Avocations: golf; hunting. Office: So Natural Gas Co PO Box 2563 Birmingham AL 35202

MATTHIESEN, LEROY THEODORE, bishop; b. Olfen, Tex., June 11, 1921. Student Josephinum Coll., Columbus, Ohio, Cath. U. Washington., Register Sch. Journalism. Ordained priest, Roman Catholic Ch., 1946; consecrated bishop of Amarillo, 1980. Address: PO Box 5644 Amarillo TX 79107*

MATTICE, MARK DUDLEY, geophysicist; b. Denver, Mar. 3, 1953; s. Dudley Reese Mattice and Margaret Jane (Linn) Webb; m. Lois Millicent Abrams, Jan. 9, 1983. B.S., U. Hawaii, 1975, M.S., 1981. Research asst. Hawaii Inst. Geophysics, Honolulu, 1978-81; geophysicist Texaco USA, New Orleans, 1981—. Contbr. articles to profl. jours. Mem. Am. Assn. Petroleum Geologists, Soc. Exploration Geophysics. Republican. Avocations: ultra light airplanes, softball, volley ball. Home: 6039 Warwick Ct New Orleans LA 70114

MATTINGLY, CECELIA JEAN, electrical appliance manufacturing company official; b. Louisville, July 25, 1929; d. Edward Grove and Kathrine Elise (Winter) M.; B.S., Webster Coll. of St. Louis U., 1951. With Gen. Electric Co., Louisville, 1951—, beginning as layout artist product service, successively illustrator product service and appliance layouts, kitchen designer, supr. designers, specialist kitchen modernization, 1951-74, mgr. home modernization, 1974-84, mgr. Kitchen design promotion, 1984—; appeared on TV shows including Dinah Shore show; leader seminars on kitchen design; speaker civic and builder groups. Mem. Thorobreds of Ky. Derby Festival; former pres. Cath. Theater Guild; dir., choreographer, music dir. little theater groups. Recipient 100th ann. award Gen. Electric Co., 1978; Trouper award Cath. Theater Guild, 1964; 3 artistic achievement awards; cert. kitchen designer. Mem. Nat. Kitchen and Bath Assn., Nat. Assn. Home Builders, Nat. Assn. Remodeling Industry, Fedn. Ky. Women's Clubs, Ky. Cols. Republican. Roman Catholic. Club: Webster Alumni. Home: 8210 Montero Dr Prospect KY 40059 Office: Gen Electric Co Appliance Park Louisville KY 40225

MATTINGLY, MACK F, U.S. Senator; b. Anderson, Ind., Jan. 7, 1931; s. Joseph H. and Beatrice (Wayts) M.; B.S., Ind. U., 1957; m. Carolyn Longcamp, 1957; children—Jane, Anne. With IBM, 1959-79; mem. U.S. Senate from Ga., 1980—. Del. Republican Nat. Conv.; chmn. Republican Party of Ga., 1975-77. Served with USAF, 1951-55. Mem. Brunswick Golden Isle C. of C. Episcopalian. Clubs: Mason, Am. Legion. Office: Senate Office Bldg Room 320 Hart Washington DC 20510

MATTINGLY, MARY RAMONA, political science educator; b. Lima, Ohio, July 11, 1940; d. Michael G. and Verna Mae Mattingly; m. W. Ebarb; 1 child, Walter Michael. B.A., U. Dayton, 1962; M.A., St. Louis U., 1964; Ph.D., Mich. State U., 1969. Instr. U. Dayton, Ohio, 1962-63, Our Lady Lake Coll., San Antonio, Texas, 1964-66; prof. Texas A&I U., Kingsville, 1969—. Contbr. articles to profl. jours. Research grantee, Texas A&I U., 1985-86. Mem. Am. Polit. Sci. Assn., So. Polit. Sci. Assn., Southwestern Soc. Sci. Assn., Southwest Pre-Law Advs. Assn. (past program chmn, past exec. council mem.), AAUW (coll. corp. rep.), Nat. Women's Polit. Caucus, AAUP (past chpt. pres.). Home: 734 Santa Clara Kingsville TX 78363 Office: Texas A & I Univ Dept Polit Sci Kingsville TX 78363

MATTINGLY, PATTI JANE, educational administrator; b. Caddo Mills, Tex., May 21, 1936; d. Raymond Edward and Marjorie (Glass) M.; B.S., North Tex. State U., 1957, M.Ed., 1962; postgrad. Nova U., 1973-75. Elem. tchr. Richardson (Tex.) Public Schs., 1957-62, U. Tex. Lab Sch., Austin, 1962-67; cons. Tex. Edn. Agy., Austin, 1967-68; instr. edn., dir. materials-learning center Austin Coll., Sherman, Tex., 1968-70, asst. prof. edn., dir. Texoma Coop. Tchr. Center, 1971-74; asst. prof. edn. Tex. Christian U., Ft. Worth, 1970-71; asso. dir. Lamplighter Sch., Dallas, 1974-75, dir., 1975—. Delta Kappa Gamma scholar, 1973. Mem. Ind. Schs. Assn. S.W. (pres.), Nat. Assn. Ind. Schs., Assn. for Supervision and Curriculum Devel., Tex. Assn. for Supervision and Curriculum Devel., Assn. for Childhood Edn. Internat., Dallas Mus. Art Presbyterian. Office: Lamplighter Sch 11611 Inwood Rd Dallas TX 75229

MATTISON, LOUIS EMIL, chemistry educator; b. Lincoln, Nebr., Oct. 3, 1927; s. Edwin Lorenzo and Neva (Little) M.; m. Dorothy Louese Love, Apr. 12, 1949; children—Louis Emil, Lynn Mattison Rankin, Diana Mattison Sparger. B.S., La. State U., 1949; M.S., U. Del., 1950, Ph.D., 1952. Research chemist E.I. DuPont de Nemours and Co., Carothers Lab. Expt. Sta., Wilmington, Del., 1952-54; assoc. prof., then prof. Davis and Elkins Coll., Elkins, W.Va., 1956-62; research assoc. dept. chemistry U. Ariz., Tucson, 1962-63; prof. chemistry King Coll., Bristol, Tenn., 1963—. Served with U.S. Army, 1954-56. Mem. Am. Chem. Soc. (chmn. Northeast Tenn. sect. 1966-67), Am. Inst. Chemists, AAAS, AAUP, Tenn. Inst. Chemists (pres.-elect. 1983-85), Tenn. Acad. Sci., N.Y. Acad. Scis., Sigma Xi (pres. So. Appalachian club 1972-73). Democrat. Presbyterian. Lodge: Rotary. Home: 323 Poplar St Bristol TN 37620 Office: King Coll Bristol TN 37620

MATTOX, JAMES ALBON, state official; b. Dallas, Aug. 29, 1943; s. Norman and Mary Kathryn (Harrison) M. B.B.A. magna cum laude, Baylor U., 1965; J.D., So. Meth. U., 1968. Bar: Tex. 1968. Asst. dist. atty., Dallas County, 1968-70; partner firm Crowder & Mattox, Dallas, 1970-83; mem. Tex. Ho. of Reps. from 33d Dallas Dist., 1972-76, 95th-97th Congresses from 5th Tex. Dist.; chmn. nat. def. and internat. affairs task force Ho. budget com., mem. banking, fin. and urban affairs com.; now atty. gen. State of Tex. Named Outstanding Freshman Rep. Tex. Intercollegiate Students Assn., 1973; Legislator of Yr. Dallas County Women's Polit. Caucus. Baptist. Home: 1110 Valencia St Dallas TX 75223 Office: Office of the Atty Gen Supreme Ct Bldg PO 12548 Austin TX 78711*

MATURIN, THERESA POIRIER, nurse; b. St. Martinville, La., Apr. 21, 1932; d. Leopold and Emilie (Poche) Poirier; Cosmetician, Lafayette (La.) Beauty Sch., 1963; diploma Teche Area Nursing Sch., New Iberia, La., 1975; m. Joseph Newby Maturin, Aug. 23, 1953; 1 son, Roland Joseph. Staff nurse Lafayette Gen. Hosp., 1974, Oakwood Village Nursing Care Center, Lafayette, 1975-80; pvt. duty nurse, Lafayette, 1980—. Pres. La. chpt. Nat. Fedn. Democratic Women, 1979-83; mem. La. Dem. Fin. Council, 1982; pres. St. Mary's Guild, Lafayette. Mem. Lafayette Town House, Am. Bus. Women's Assn. (chmn. local membership 1964), La. Hist. Soc., Smithsonian Assos., Nat. Trust Hist. Preservation, Right to Life, Attakapas Hist. Assn., Am. Security Council, U.S. Capitol Hist. Soc., Nat. Hist. Soc., L'Heure de Musique, France Amerique de la Louisiane (v.p. 1982-83), DAR, Soc. Dames Ct. of Honor, Lafayette Ballet Assn., Soc. Confederacy, Beta Sigma Phi. Roman Catholic. Clubs: Catholic Daus. Ams. (ct. regent 1975-79), UDC (corr. sec. chpt. 1982-83). Home: 2710 Pinhook Rd Lafayette LA 70508

MATYS, LINDA GIANNASI, journalist; b. Springfield, Mass., Oct. 23, 1947; d. Ugo L. and Ruth (Kodis) Giannasi; m. Edward J. Matys, Dec. 20, 1969; 1 son, Justin. A.B., Mt. Holyoke Coll., 1969; M.A.T., Brown U., 1970. Women's editor The Evening News, Southbridge, Mass., 1970; exec. editor The Advocate Newspapers, Springfield and Hartford, Conn., 1974-80; exec. editor Figaro, New Orleans, 1980-81; editor New Orleans Bur. News Service, 1981—; editor, assoc. pub. New Orleans Mag., 1982—; cons. editor Sunbelt Exec. Mag., 1983—; corr. Adweek Mag., 1983—; stringer Time Mag., Atlanta, 1983—. Recipient 1st place for gen. news reporting Press Club New Orleans, 1981, 1st place media award Amos Tuck Sch. Bus. Adminstrn. Dartmouth Coll./Champion Corp., 1979; U.S. Office Edn. fellow, 1969. Mem. Investigative Reporters and Editors. Methodist. Club: Press (New Orleans). Contbr. articles to Boston Globe, USA Today, Savvy, Dallas Morning News, Washington Journalism Rev., Horizon, Continental Airlines, La. Life, New Orleans Mag., Sunbelt Exec. Home: 95 Fontainebleau Dr New Orleans LA 70125 Office: 6666 Morrison Rd New Orleans LA 70126

MATZ, JACK WILLIAM, JR., business executive; b. Reading, Pa., Apr. 20, 1949; s. Jack and Catherine (Lampros) M.; m. Nancy Louise Evans, Dec. 10, 1972; 1 dau., Catherine Ann. B.B.A., Tex. A&M U., 1971. Bus. mgmt. mgr. Chrysler Corp., Dallas, 1976-77, ops. mgr., 1977-79, zone sales mgr., Denver, 1979-81; v.p. corp. planning Koewell Oil and Gas Co., Dallas, 1980-81; pres. HydroCarbon Search, Dallas, 1981-82; pres., chief exec. officer Strategic Industries Inc., Dallas, 1981—; pres. El Dorado Systems, Inc., Vancouver, B.C., Can., 1982; dir. Strategic Industries Inc., Gold Medallion Corp., Mineral Leasing Corp., Strategic Securities, HCS Drilling and Ops., CM&M Enterprises. Mem. small bus. com. Plano C. of C., 1983-84; active No. Dallas C. of C., 1981-83, Dallas C. of C., 1981-83. Recipient Appreciation award Chrysler 300 Club, 1978. Mem. Nat. Assn. Security Dealers. Republican. Greek Orthodox. Office: Strategic Industries Inc 1350 E Arapaho Rd Suite 200 Richardson TX 75081

MAUCK, HENRY PAGE, JR., medical educator; b. Richmond, Va., Feb. 3, 1926; s. Henry Page and Harriet Hutcheson (Morrison) M.; B.A., U. Va., 1950, M.D., 1952; m. Janet Garrett Horsley, May 14, 1955; children—Henry Page III, John Waller. Intern, Henry Ford Hosp., Detroit, 1952-53; resident Med. Coll. Va., Richmond, 1953-56, asst. prof. medicine and pediatrics, 1961-66, assoc. prof., 1966-72, prof., 1972—. Cons. cardiology Langley Field Air Force Hosp., Hampton, Va., 1970—, McGuire's VA Hosp., Richmond, 1962—; editorial cons. Am. Heart Jour., 1971—. Contbr. articles to profl. jours. Served with AUS, 1944-46. Diplomate Am. Bd. Internal Medicine. Fellow in cardiology Am. Heart Assn., 1956-57; fellow Am. Coll. Physicians, Am. Coll. Cardiology; mem. Am. Physiol. Soc., So. Soc. Clin. Investigation, Am. Fedn. Clin. Research, So. Soc. Clin. Research. Presbyn. Contbr. chpt. to Pathophysiology, Autonomic Cotrol of Cardiovascular System, 1972. Home: 113 Oxford Circle W Richmond VA 23221 Office: Box 281 Medical Coll of Virginia Richmond VA 23298

MAUER, GEORGE J., management company executive; b. Jersey City, Aug. 15, 1936; m. Clydene Ellis, Dec. 23, 1984. B.A., Okla. State U., 1958; M.P.A., Kans. U., 1960; Ph.D., U. Okla., 1964. Prof. polit. sci. Oklahoma City U., 1964-66, Okla. State U., 1966-67, Drake U., 1967-70, U. Akron, 1970-71; pres. City Research & Devel. Co., 1971-73; vis. scholar U. Calif.-Berkeley, 1973-74; sr. policy analyst Office Exec. Mgmt., Office of Gov., Pierre, S.D., 1974-77; mgmt. cons. U. Tenn., Knoxville, 1977-82; pres. The Mgmt. Co., Longwood, Fla., 1982—. Author: Crises in Campus Management, 1976. Contbr. articles to profl. jours. City commr., Norman, Okla., 1963-65. Served with USN, 1951-55, Korea. Mem. Am. Soc. Pub. Adminstrn. (past state pres.), FEMA (exec. res.), Democrat. Club: U.S. Navy Officer's (Orlando, Fla.). Home: 351 Brassie Dr Longwood FL 32750

MAUGHAN, GEORGE PHILIP, army officer, account executive; b. Columbus, Ga., Dec. 12, 1951; s. George and Annie Margaret (Gasque) M.; m. Lisa Carolyn Williamson, Sept. 4, 1976 (div. 1981); m. Rose Marie Granger, Sept. 20, 1983. B.S. in Biology, Wofford Coll., 1974. Lic. broker. Commd. 2d lt. U.S. Army, 1974, advanced through grades to capt., 1978; platoon leader 1/325 Inf. 82nd Airborne Div., Ft. Bragg, N.C., 1974-76, platoon leader, co. exec. officer 3d U.S. Inf. (The Old Guard), Ft. Myer, Va., 1976-80, co. comdr., chief officer assignments 8th Inf. Div., Bad Kreuznach, W.Ger., 1980-84, adminstrv. officer Dep. Chief of Staff, Personnel Hdqrs., Forces Command, Ft. McPherson, Ga., 1984—; account exec. Stuart James Co., Atlanta, 1985—. Mem. Am. Soc. Personnel Adminstrn., Am. Mgmt. Assn. Republican. Baptist. Clubs: Atlanta Track, Atlanta Landmarks. Avocations: running; coin collecting. Home: 2310 Tree Mountain Pkwy Stone Mountain GA 30083 Office: Stuart James Co Inc 3483 Satellite Blvd Suite 201-6 Duluth Atlanta GA 30136

MAULDEN, JERRY L., energy company executive; b. North Little Rock, Ark., 1936; married. B.S., U. Ark.-Little Rock, 1963. Acct. Dyke & Assocs. Inc., 1959-61; sr. auditor Madigan James & Co., C.P.A.s, 1961-62; asst. controller Dillard Dept. Stores Inc., 1962-65; asst. to treas. Ark. Power & Light Co., a company of Middle South Utilities Inc., Little Rock, 1965-68, asst. controller, 1968-71, controller, asst. sec., asst. treas., and later spl. asst. to pres., 1971-73, sec., treas., 1973-75, v.p. fin. services, sec., treas., 1975-79, pres., chief exec. officer, 1979—, also dir. Office: Ark Power & Light Co First Nat Bank Bldg Little Rock AR 72203*

MAULDIN, HOWARD PAUL, physician; b. Shawnee, Okla., Dec. 9, 1926; s. Ulysses and Mary (Isom) M.; m. Minnie McDaniel, Dec. 10, 1944; children—Cheryl, Paul, Grant. M.D., Okla. U., 1953. Intern, St. Joseph's Hosp., Wichita; practice medicine, specializing in family practice, Oklahoma City, 1954—; pres. Mauldin Yates Wheeler Clinic, Oklahoma City, 1972—, MH&G Oil Co., Oklahoma City, 1983—. Bd. dirs. South Community Hosp., Oklahoma City, 1963-74. Served to cpl. U.S. Army, 1944-46. Mem. AMA, Okla. Med. Assn., Am. Acad. Family Practice (del. 1982), Okla. Acad. Family Practice (pres. 1974). Democrat. Episcopalian. Lodge: Masons. Home: 11232 Greenbriar Chase Oklahoma City OK 73170 Office: Mauldin Yates Wheeler Clinic 4901 S Pennsylvania Oklahoma City OK 73119

MAULSBY, TOMMIE LU STORM, association executive, publisher; b. Houston, Mar. 30, 1937; d. Mark Kennedy and Ferne Elizabeth (Sweeny) Storm; m. Robert Lyle Maulsby, Aug. 14, 1959 (div. 1973); children—Kenton Lyle, Evelyn Louise, Bryan Jay. B.A. in History and English, Rice U., 1959. Tchr., Houston Ind. Sch. Dist., 1959-62; law librarian Sewell & Riggs, Houston, 1975-84; exec. dir. Assn. Rice Alumni, Rice U., Houston, 1984—. Co-editor, pub.: Tex. Supreme Ct. Index, 1985. Mem. exec. com. Rice U. Fund Council, 1983-85; decade chmn. Rice U. Annual Fund, 1982. Mem. Council Advancement and Support Edn., Coll. Alumni Dirs. Tex. Club: Houston Area Law Librarians (treas. 1983-84). Avocations: art; music; sailing; horseback riding. Office: Assn Rice Alumni Rice U PO Box 1892 Houston TX 77251

MAUPIN, CAROL GRINSTEAD, food consultant; b. Pawhuska, Okla., Jan. 31, 1936; d. Randolph Henry and Mildred Asilee (Pfaff) Grinstead; B.A., U. Okla., 1958. Asst. to food dir. Neiman Marcus, Dallas, 1958-62; asst. to food dir. So. Meth. U., Dallas, 1963-64; asso. dir. food ops. Mut. of Omaha, 1964-69; dir. tearoom, parties and spl. events Denver Dry Goods, 1970-74; dir. food and party services Jr. League of Houston, 1974-81; owner Carol Maupin, Inc.; partner Jackson Catering Co.; food cons. Mus. Food Arts; cooking instr. Batterie de Cuisine Cooking Sch.; food lectr.; food and party cons. protocol office City of Houston; food service cons., bd. dirs. Alley Theatre of Houston. Mem. Am. Home Econs. Assn., Nat. Assn. Cooking Schs., Houston Culinary Guild. Republican. Episcopalian. Home: 3918 Hawthorne Dallas TX 75219 Office: Neiman Marcus Dallas TX 75201

MAURA, FRANK JESUS, loss control counselor; b. Havana, Cuba, Sept. 18, 1953; came to U.S., 1961, naturalized, 1963; s. Francisco and Zulema (Mas) M. A.A., Miami-Dade Community Jr. Coll., 1975; B.A., Fla. Internat. U., 1977; M.A., U. Cin., 1979. Adj. prof. Fla. Internat. U., Miami, 1979-80; safety supr. Anchor Hocking Co., Gurnee, Ill., 1981-82; safety dir. U.S. Foundry, Miami, 1982-84; loss control counselor FCCI, Sarasota, Fla., 1985—. Recipient Disting. Student award Fla. Internat. U., 1977; U. Cin. Scholar, 1978. Mem. Am. Soc. Safety Engrs., Nat. Safety Council, Hazard Control Mgmt. Soc., Am. Indsl. Hygiene Assn. Roman Catholic. Avocations: tennis, chess. Home: 8981 Sunset Dr Miami FL 33173

MAURER, VIRGINIA GALLAHER, legal educator; b. Shawnee, Okla., Nov. 7, 1946; d. Paul Clark Gallaher and Virginia Ruth (Watson) Abernathy; m. Ralph Gerald Maurer, July 31, 1971; children—Ralph Emmett, William Edward. B.A., Northwestern U., 1968; M.A., Stanford U., 1969, J.D., 1975. Bar: Iowa 1976. Tchr. social studies San Mateo (Calif.) High Sch. Dist., 1969-71; spl. asst. to pres. U. Iowa, Iowa City, 1976-80, adj. asst. prof. law, 1979-80; affiliate asst. prof. law U. Fla., Gainesville, 1981, asst. prof. bus. law, 1980-85, assoc. prof., 1985—; cons. Gov.'s Com. on Iowa 2000, Iowa City, 1976-77, Fla. Banker's Assn., Gainesville, 1982. Contbr. articles to profl. jours. Mem. fundraising com. Pro Arte Musica, Gainesville, 1980-84. Mem. ABA, Am. Bus. Law Assn., Southeastern Bus. Law Assn. (Proc. editor 1984—, treas. 1985-86), Iowa Bar Assn., LWV, U. Fla. Athletic Assn. (bd. dirs. 1982—; v.p., chmn. fin. com.), Kappa Alpha Theta, Delta Sigma Pi. Club: Univ. Women's (Gainesville, Fla.). Home: 2210 NW 6th Pl Gainesville FL 32603 Office: Grad Sch Bus U Fla Gainesville FL 32603

MAURICIO, LILIA D(UJUA), pathologist; b. Manila, Aug. 14, 1943; d. Fernando and Nieves (de Guzman) Dujua; children—Dino, Ditas. M.D., U. Santo Tomas, 1965. Diplomate Am. Bd. Pathology. Intern, Westmoreland Hosp., Greensburg, Pa., 1966-67; resident Bapt. Hosp., Nashville, 1967-68, pathologist, 1976-79; resident in pathology Vanderbilt U., Nashville, 1968-72, instr. pathology, 1972-73; dir. cytopathology Vanderbilt Hosp., Nashville, 1973-74, asst. prof. pathology, 1974-76, asst. clin. prof., 1976—; chief pathologist, lab. dir. Crockett Gen. Hosp., Lawrenceburg, Tenn., 1979—, Giles County Hosp., Pulaski, Tenn., 1983—; med. examiner Giles County. Fellow Am. Soc. Clin. Pathologists, Coll. Am. Pathologists, Internat. Acad. Pathology. Republican. Roman Catholic. Office: PO Box 784 Lawrenceburg TN 38464

MAURO, GARRY PAUL, state official, lawyer; b. Bryan, Tex., Feb. 21, 1948; s. Frank Paul and Louise (Herring) M. B.B.A., Tex. A&M U., 1970; J.D., U. Tex., Austin, 1974. Bar: Tex. 1974. Legis. asst. to Congressman Bob Krueger, Washington, 1974-76; dep. comptroller State of Tex., Austin, 1976-8; exec. dir. Tex. Dem. Com., Austin, 1979-80; ptnr. firm Mauro, Wendler, Sheets & Assocs., Austin, 1983—; land commr. State of Tex., Austin, 1983—. Active Boy Scouts Am., 1956—; mem. Leadership Austin, 1983—, Tex. Lyceum, 1982—; mem. Western States Land Commrs.; bd. dirs. St. Michael's Acad. Houston Sales Execs. Assn. scholar, 1969-70. Mem. State Bar Tex., Travis County Bar Assn., Austin Young Lawyers Assn. Roman Catholic. Club: University, Capital City A&M. Lodge: K.M. Home: 3507 Mt Bonnell Rd Austin TX 78731 Office: Tex Land Commn Stephen F Austin Bldg Room 835 1700 N Congress Ave Austin TX 78701

MAURO, JOHN BAPTIST, marketing research executive; b. St. Margherita Belice, Agrigento, Italy; June 20, 1923; came to U.S., 1931 (parents Am. citizens); s. Ignazio and Lucia (Morreale) M.; m. Dorothy T. Stix, July 19, 1945; children—Janet Lucille, Diane Rose, John Henry, Celeste Marie, Andrea Marie, Christopher James. B.S., NYU, 1953. Vice pres. research Branham Co., N.Y.C., 1957-68; dir. mktg. Family Weekly Mag., N.Y.C., 1968-69; dir. research The Tampa Tribune, Fla., 1969-73; dir. research Media Gen. Inc., Richmond, Va., 1973—; adj. prof. Va. Commonwealth U., Richmond, 1979-82, Syracuse U., 1981. Author: An Introduction to Boomerangs, 1983. Editor: Newspaper Research Primer, 1972, 2d edit., 1980; co-editor: Directory of Newspaper Public Service Programs, 1978. Contbr. articles to profl. jours. Chmn. Richmond C. of C. (research com. 1981-82); mem. advt. and mktg. coms., Met. Richmond Devel. Council, 1983—. Served to sgt., USMC, 1943-45, PTO. Decorated D.F.C.; recipient Sidney S. Goldfish award Internat. Newspaper Promotion Assn., 1974, Silver Shovel award, 1978. Mem. Internat. Newspaper Promotion Assn. (pres. 1976-77, treas. 1980-81), Am. Newspaper Publishers Assn. (news research com. 1974-82), Va. Press Assn. (chmn. promotion com. 1981), Newspaper Readership Council (chmn. promotion com. 1976-77), Am. Mktg. Assn. (pres. Fla. West Coast chpt. 1971-72, pres. Richmond chpt. 1975-76). Republican. Roman Catholic. Club: U.S. Boomerang Assn. (pres. 1985—, capt. U.S. Team 1984). Avocations: boomeranging; photography; computer programming; kite flying. Office: Media Gen Inc PO Box C-32333 Richmond VA 23293

MAUZY, OSCAR HOLCOMBE, lawyer, state senator; b. Houston, Nov. 9, 1926; s. Harry Lincoln and Mildred (Kincaid) M.; B.B.A., U. Tex., 1950, LL.B., 1952; m. Anne Rogers; children—Catherine Anne, Charles Fred, James Stephen. Admitted to Tex. bar, 1951; partner firm Mullinax, Wells, Mauzy & Baab, Inc., Dallas, 1952-79; pres. Oscar H. Mauzy, P.C., Dallas, 1979—; mem. Tex. Senate from 23d Dist., 1967—; pres. pro tem 63d Legislature, 1973—; acting gov. Tex., 1973—. Mem. nat. com. for Tex., Young Democrats, 1954-56; precinct chmn. Dem. party, Dallas, 1962-66; vice-chmn. Dem. Exec. Com. Dallas County, 1964-66. Served with USNR, 1944-46; PTO. Mem. Am., Dallas bar assns., State Bar Tex., Am. Trial Lawyers Assn., Am. Bd. Trial Advocates, VFW, Delta Theta Phi. Office: 1106 N Hwy 360 Suite 203 Grand Prairie TX 75050

MAWHINNEY, JOHN ALEXANDER, III, health services adminstr.; b. Richmond, Va., Apr. 10, 1943; s. John Alexander and Ellen Elizabeth (King) M.; B.A., Wheaton Coll., 1964; cert. in nursing home adminstrn. Mich. State U., 1969. Adminstr., v.p. Maccabee Gardens Extended Care Ctr., Saginaw, Mich., 1968-70; cons. N.Y. State Bd. Social Welfare, Syracuse, 1970-72; adminstrv. officer Cayuga County Community Mental Health Ctr., Auburn, N.Y., 1972-77; exec. dir. Southside Community Mental Health and Mental Retardation Services, South Boston, Va., 1977-82; adminstr., dir. Boston Commons Ltd., retirement residence, 1983—; mental health cons. NIMH; chmn. Region IV Consortium. Fellow Am. Coll. Nursing Home Adminstrs.; mem. Am. Mgmt. Assn., Assn. Mental Health Adminstrs., Nat. Council Community Mental Health Centers, Am. Acad. Med. Adminstrs., Va. Assn. Community Services Bds., Central Va. Health Systems Agy., Va. Human Services Inst., Va. Assn. Homes for Adults. Home: 650 Buena Vista Dr PO Box 508 Halifax VA 24558 Office: Boston Common 1146 N Main St South Boston VA 24592

MAWHINNEY, KING, insurance company executive; b. Richmond, Va., Sept. 13, 1947; s. John A. and Ellen E. (King) Mawhinney; m. Jeanne Dale Smothers, June 8, 1976 (div. Oct. 1984). A.B., Davidson Coll., 1971; M.A., Pacific Lutheran U., 1973. C.L.U.; chartered fin. cons. Devel. mgr. Prudential Ins. Co., Newark, 1977-80; sr. sales rep. USAA Life Ins. Co., San Antonio, 1980-81, sales tng. adminstr., 1981-82, dir. procedures and tng., 1983-85, dir. group/bus. sales, 1985—. Active United Way, Am. Heart Assn.; mem. choir Alamo Heights Presbyterian Ch., 1981-83, deacon, 1982-83. Served to capt. U.S. Army, 1972-77; Korea. Fellow Life Mgmt. Inst. (pres. South Central Tex. chpt. 1986—); mem. Davidson Coll. Alumni Assn. (chpt. pres. 1983—), San Antonio Chpt. C.L.U. (bd. dirs., v.p. programs, v.p. fin., v.p. adminstrn.), Am. Soc. Tng. and Devel., Phi Kappa Phi, Sigma Nu. Republican. Avocations: dog training and showing; stamp collecting; swimming; aerobic exercise. Home: 6010 Bloomwood Dr San Antonio TX 78249 Office: USAA Life Ins Co USAA Bldg D-3-W San Antonio TX 78288

MAWICKE, TRAN JAMES, artist; b. Chgo., Sept. 20, 1911; s. Henry John and Margaret (Mann) M.; m. Laura Elizabeth Dodge, Feb. 11, 1939; children—David F., Jane M. Thomas, Helen M. Ashley, Catherine. Student, Art Inst. Chgo., 1929-33. Artist, N.Y.C., 1935—. Illustrator numerous books. Mem. Soc. Illustrators N.Y. (pres. 1960-61), Am. Water Color Soc. (dir. 1973-74, juror 1956, 77). Republican. Roman Catholic. Club: Seabrook Island. Lodge: Rotary. Home and Office: 452 Golf Shore Villas Johns Island SC 29455

MAWYER, C. EDWARD, JR., retail executive; b. Washington, Nov. 2, 1945; s. Clarence Edward and Doris Marie (Lytton) M. Sales mgr. wholesale div. Thom McAn Shoe Co., Worcester, Mass., 1967-74; dir. mktg. Wohl Shoe Co., N.Y.C., 1975; pres., chief exec. officer Mawyer Enterprises, Inc., Houston, 1976 , Dallas Shoe Co.; chmn. MEI Wholesalers, Inc., Houston, 1981—; dir. Tex. Commerce Bank. Mem. Republican Nat. Com.; life mem. Two/Ten Nat. Found. Mem. Nat. Shoe Retailers Assn. (dir.). Club: Sweetwater Country.

Home: 206 Lombardy St Sugar Land TX 77478 also Mahogany Run Saint Thomas VI 00801 Office: 12852 Park One Dr Sugarland TX 77478

MAXEY, LOIS BRUNSON, clinical social worker; b. DeKalb County, Ind., Jan. 6, 1929; d. Tom Bennett and Clara Lodell (Bash) Brunson; student Cin. Bible Sem., 1946-49; A.B., SW Christian Sem., Phoenix, 1951; postgrad. Phoenix Coll., 1953-54, Catherine Spalding Coll., Louisville, 1963-64; M.S.S.W., U. Louisville, 1966; m. Victor L. Maxey, Sept. 14, 1949; children—Thomas, Victor L., David. Oral proof reader Am. Printing House for the Blind, Louisville, 1959-63; group worker Neighborhood House, Louisville, 1963-64; social service dir. Headstart, 4 schs., Louisville, 1966; caseworker Family and Children's Agy., Louisville, 1966-68; clin. social worker Comprehensive Care Center No. Ky., Newport, 1968-72, 75-80, team leader 5 offices, 1972-75, coordinator children's services Catchment B, 1980-83, clin. social worker in children's services, 1983—. Active No. Ky. chpt. Mental Health Assn. Named Social Worker of Yr., No. Ky., 1978; lic. clin. social worker, adminstrn. and mgmt., Ky. Mem. Nat. Assn. Social Workers (registered), Acad. Cert. Social Workers. Mem. Ch. of Christ. Home: 5119 Grossepointe Ln Cincinnati OH 45238 Office: 18 N Fort Thomas Ave Fort Thomas KY 41075

MAXFIELD, JAMES ROBERT, JR., radiologist, educator; b. Grand Saline, Tex., Nov. 11, 1910; s. James Robert and Marie (Streeter) M.; A.B., M.D., Baylor U., 1935; Dr. Aerospaceology, Air Force Systems Command, 1966; m. Kathryn Morgan Jester, Aug. 21, 1936; children—James Robert III, Morgan Jester, Jordan Henley Work Streeter (dec.), Jordan II. Intern United Hosp., Port Chester, N.Y., 1935-36; resident radiology Baylor U., 1937-39; resident roentgenology U. Calif. at San Francisco, 1939-40; dir. dept.radiology, also Mattie Fair Meml. Tumor Clinic, Parkland Hosp., Dallas, 1941-43; dir. dept. radiology, chmn. tumor clinic St. Paul's Hosp., Dallas, 1941-45; clin. asst. prof. radiology Southwestern Med. Sch., U. Tex., 1945—; sect. chief radiology br. VA. Hosp., 1945-49; cons. radioisotope unit Lisbon VA Hosp., 1949-50, Los Alamos Sci. Labs., 1949-57, Lawrence Radiation Lab., Livermore, Calif.; dir. Tex. Radiation and Tumor Inst., Dallas, 1946—; lectr. Blackford Meml. Cancer Lectures, Grayson County Med. Soc., 1957; Equen Meml. lectr. Ga. Med. Soc., 1958. Mem. regional adv. council nuclear energy So. Gov.'s Conf.; mem. Tex. Gov.'s Radiation Study Commn., AEC, past mem. adv. com. div. isotope devel.; chmn. Tex. Radiation Adv. Bd.; mem. permanent adv. com. So. Interstate Nuclear Bd.; mem. energy com. So. States Energy Bd.; mem. Tex. Hosp. Adv. Com.; dir. Tex. Law Enforcement and Youth Devel. Found.; mem. nat. adv. bd. Am. Security Council, Washington; mem. power plant Siting Com. State Tex. Bd. trustees, past pres. Dallas Health and Sci. Museum; trustee Fla. Inst. Tech., Melbourne; past trustee Episcopal Radio-TV Found.; past nat. commr. for Tex., Freedoms Found. of Valley Forge; mem. Fla. Council of 100. Recipient Antarctic Service medal. Fellow Internat. Coll. Surgeons, Am. Coll. Nuclear Medicine (sec.-treas, past pres., gold medal for outstanding service to nuclear medicine 1979); assoc. fellow AIAA; mem. Am., So. med. assns., Tex., Dallas County med. socs., Am. Coll. Radiology, Radiol. Soc. N.Am., Inter-Am. Congress Radiology, Am. Radium Soc., Brit. Inst. Radiology, Tex., Dallas-Fort Worth, Rocky Mountain radiol. socs., Soc. Nuclear Medicine (sec., treas., past pres.), Flying Physicians Assn., Airplane Owners and Pilots Assn., Soc. of South Pole, Dallas Execs. Assn., Former Tex. Rangers Assn. (life), Dallas C. of C. Rotarian (past pres. Dallas-Park cities; named Rotarian of Year, 1956). Contbr. papers to tech. lit. Home: 5920 Lomo Alto Dallas TX 75205 Office: 2711 Oak Lawn Ave Dallas TX 75219

MAXFIELD, JOHN EDWARD, college dean; b. Ruston, La.; s. Chauncey George and Rena Lucile (Cain) M.; m. Margaret Alice Waugh, Nov. 23, 1949; children—Frederick George (dec.), David Glen, Elaine Rebecca, Nancy Catherine, Daniel John. B.S., MIT, 1947; M.S., U. Wis., 1949; Ph.D., U. Oreg., 1951. Mathematician, U.S. Naval Ordnance Test Sta., China Lake, Calif., 1949-60; head dept. math. U. Fla., Gainesville, 1960-67, Kans. State U., 1967-81; dean grad. sch., univ. research La. Tech. U., Ruston, 1981—. Author: Abstract Algebra and Solutions by Radicals, 1971; Discovering Number Theory, 1972; Keys to Mathematics, 1973. Contbr. articles to profl. jours. Mem. Am. Math. Soc., Math. Assn. Am. (pres. southeast sect. 1966-67), Soc. Indsl. and Applied Math., Assn. Women in Math., Soc. Research Adminstrs., Research Soc., Sigma Xi. Republican. Home: 209 E Louisiana Ave Ruston LA 71270 Office: La Tech U Grad Sch PO Box 7923 Ruston LA 71272

MAXFIELD, WILLIAM STREETER, physician; b. Waco, Tex., May 9, 1930; s. James Robert and Marie (Streeter) M.; m. Patricia Jean Carter, Nov. 2, 1957; children—Alice Melissa, Maura Carter, Melinda Marie. B.A., So. Meth. U., 1950; M.D., Baylor U., 1954. Intern, So. Pacific Gen. Hosp., San Francisco, 1954-55; preceptor in radiology and nuclear medicine Maxfield Clinic-Hosp., Dallas 1955-56; asst. resident in radiology Johns Hopkins U. Hosp., Balt., 1959-60, NIH clin. fellow in cancer, 1960-61; practice medicine specializing in radiation therapy, Balt., 1961-64, New Orleans, 1964-72, Tampa, Fla., 1972-82, Largo, Fla., 1980—; practice nuclear medicine, Chelsea, Mass., 1956-57, Bethesda, Md., 1957-59, New Orleans, 1964-72, Bradenton, Fla., 1974-75; instr. in radiology Johns Hopkins U. Sch. Medicine, Balt., 1961, asst. prof. radiology, 1961-64, chief of radiation therapy sect. dept. radiology, 1961-64; chief of radiation therapy dept., co-chmn. nuclear medicine Ochsner Clinic and Ochsner Found. Hosp., New Orleans, 1964-68; prof., chmn. dept. radiology La. State U. Med. Sch., New Orleans, 1968-72; sr. physician Radioisotope Lab., Charity Hosp., New Orleans, 1968-70; chief of Radioisotope Lab., Earl K. Long Meml. Hosp., Baton Rouge, La., 1970-72; med. dir. Gulf South Radiation Therapy Center of Tampa, 1975-82, Gulf South Therapy Ctr., Radiation Therapy Hyperbaric Medicine and Hyperthermia, Largo, Fla., 1980—; cons. to Tumor Clinic, USPHS Hosp., Balt., 1961-64, Tumor Clinic, Balt. City Hosps., 1961-64, Tumor Clinic Lafayette Charity Hosp., La., 1969-72; clin. prof. radiology Tulane U., New Orleans, 1964-68; vis. physician dept. therapeutic radiology Charity Hosp., New Orleans, 1964-68; sr. physician, 1968-72; prof., chmn. dept. radiology La. State U. Sch. Medicine, New Orleans, 1968-72; rep. for La. to Med. Liaison Officer Network of USPHS and AEC, 1968-83; chmn. cancer com. La. Regional Med. Program, 1968-72; cons. in design and equipment of radiation therapy to various labs., hosp., 1968-72; mem. staff Med. Ctr. Hosp., Largo, chmn. tumor bd., 1980—; mem. staff Clearwater Community Hosp., Fla., Centro Asturiano Hosp., Centro Espanol Hosp., Tampa, Fla.; mem. Sci. Exhibit Sect. of U.S. Med. Delegation to 2d Internat. Atoms for Peace Chnf., Geneva, Switzerland, 1958, U.S. Delegation, Internat. AEC, Scintillation Scanning Symposium, Salzburg, Austria, 1968; mem. radiolpharm adv. com. FDA, 1970-74; chmn. Pub. Health sub-com. So. Govs. Task Force on Nuclear Power, 1970-71; cons., med. coordinator for Radiology, Preventive Health programs, Falls Church, Va., 1977. Trustee Arthritis Found., La. chpt., 1968-71, Pinellas County unit Am. Cancer Soc., 1984—. Served with M.C., USN, 1956-59. Arthritis Found. grantee, 1965-68, E.R. Squibb & Son grantee, 1964-65, Am. Cancer Soc. grantee, 1965-68; diplomate Am. Bd. Radiology, Am. Bd. Nuclear Medicine. Fellow Am. Coll. Nuclear Medicine (pres. 1974-75), Royal Soc. Health; mem. Soc. Nuclear Medicine (v.p. 1968-69, pres. Southwestern chpt. 1972-73), Am. Radium Soc., Fla. Med. Assn., Hillsborough County Med. Assn., AMA, Am. Roentgen Ray Soc., Am. Soc. Clin. Oncology, Am. Soc. Thermography, Radiol. Soc. N.Am. (sci. exhibits com. 1972-76), Underseas Med. Assn., Am. Cancer Soc. (trustee New Orleans area 1969-71, Pinellas County chpt. 1984—), Assn. Community Cancer Ctrs., Am. Coll. Radiology (sub-com. resident tng. 1971-73), Am. Soc. Therapeutic Radiologists, Multiple Sclerosis Soc. (chmn. bd. trustees Gulf Coast chpt. 1983—). Democrat. Episcopalian. Clubs: Sarasota Yacht; Calyx (Dallas). Contbr. numerous articles on nuclear medicine and radiology to profl. jours. Office: 198 14th St SW Largo FL 33540

MAXHEIM, JOHN HOWARD, utility company executive; b. Clinton, Iowa, Oct. 4, 1934; s. Vincent J. and Dorothy F. Maxheim; B.S. in Indsl. Engring., Iowa State U., 1958. Indsl. sales engr. Mobil Oil Co., Chgo., 1958-59; indsl. sales engr. and mgr. Milw. Gas Light Co., 1959-62; asst. to pres. United Cities Gas Co., Nashville, 1962-65, v.p., 1965-66, exec. v.p., 1966-70, pres., dir., 1970-78, chief exec. officer, 1970-78; pres., chief operating officer, dir. Piedmont Natural Gas Co., Inc., Charlotte, N.C., 1978-80, chief exec. officer, 1980-84, chmn. bd., pres., chief exec. officer, 1984—, dir., 1979—; mem. So. regional bd. Wachovia Bank & Trust Co., Univ. Research Park, Inc.; disting. exec. lectr. M.B.A. program Queens Coll. Mem. exec. bd. Boy Scouts Am.; gen. chmn. Goodwill Industries Capital Fund Drive, 1982; bd. dirs. United Community Services, Charlotte Arts and Sci. Council, Charlotte Chamber Found., Charlotte Sci. Mus., N.C. Engring. Found. trustee Ind. Coll. Fund N.C., Mercy Hosp., Central Piedmont Community Coll., Charlotte; bd. advisors U. N.C.-Charlotte, Johnson C. Smith U.; co-chmn. corp. fund drive Queens Coll., 1983-84. Mem. Am. Gas Assn. (dir., exec. com., nominating com.), So. Gas Assn. (past dir.), Southeastern Gas Assn. (past dir.), Tenn. Gas Assn. (past dir.), Greater Charlotte C. of C. (dir.), Alpha Tau Omega. Episcopalian. Clubs: Nashville City; Carolina Ambassadors, Charlotte Athletic; Capital City; Carmel Country; Quail Hollow Country. Home: 4100 Beresford Rd Charlotte NC 28211 Office: PO Box 33068 Charlotte NC 28233

MAXON, ROBERT MEAD, history educator; b. Oneonta, N.Y., Dec. 10, 1939; s. Malcolm Keeler and Isabelle Eunice (Mead) M.; m. Felicia Ethel Ayiro, July 6, 1968; children—Gertrude, Robert. B.A., Duke U., 1961; Ph.D., Syracuse U., 1972. Edn. officer Gov. Kenya, East Africa, 1961-64; grad. asst. Syracuse U., N.Y., 1965-68; asst. prof. U. W.Va., Morgantown, 1969-74, assoc. prof., 1974-82, prof. history, 1982—, chmn. dept. history, 1983—. Author: John Ainsworth and the Making of Kenya, 1980; (with others) Guide to Kenya National Archives, 1969. Contbr. articles to profl. jours. Shell Oil Co. Internat. fellow, 1968-69; U.S. Office Edn. grantee, 1978-79. Mem. Hist. Assn. Kenya, Phi Delta Kappa. Avocations: sports; soccer refereeing. Home: 657 Elysian Ave Morgantown WV 26505 Office: U WVa Dept History Morgantown WV 26506

MAXSON, NANCY O'NEAL, veterinarian; b. Bklyn., Dec. 15, 1954; d. George W. and Jean (Jourdan) O'Neal; divorced; 1 child, Marian A. B.S., La. State U.-Baton Rouge, 1975, D.V.M., 1980. Veterinarian, Veterans Veterinary Hosp., Metairie, La., 1980-83, Broadmoor Animal Hosp., New Orleans, 1983-84, Dale Mabry Animal Hosp., Tampa, Fla., 1984—. Recipient Outstanding Sr. award Phi Kappa Phi, 1980. Mem. AVMA.

MAXWELL, EARL LAVERNE, JR., lawyer; b. Atlanta, Dec. 1, 1942; s. Earl LaVerne and Grace (Rushing) M.; B.A., Fla. State U., 1964; J.D., U. Fla., 1967; children—Dacia Lynn, Brent Earl. Bar: Fla. 1967. Legis. aide Fla. State Legislature, Tallahassee, 1967; law clk. to atty. John A. Rudd, Tallahassee, 1967, Kline, Tilker & Lynch, Cheyenne, Wyo., 1967-68; atty. O'Connell & Cooper, West Palm Beach, Fla., 1972-73; partner Farish & Farish, West Palm Beach, Fla., 1973-76; atty. Earl L. Maxwell, Jr., West Palm Beach, 1976-81; partner Maxwell & Hill, West Palm Beach, 1981-83, Schneider Maxwell Spillias & Hill, 1984—. Pres., North County Choral Soc., Palm Beach County, Fla., 1977-78. Served with JAGC, USAF, 1968-72. Mem. Fed. Bar Assn., ABA, Assn. Trial Lawyers Am., Fla. Acad. Trial Lawyers, Fla. Bar Assn., Palm Beach County Bar Assn. Democrat. Club: Kiwanis (pres.). Home: 157 Santiago St Royal Palm Beach FL 33411 Office: 700 Fla Nat Bank Tower 1645 Palm Beach Lakes Blvd West Palm Beach FL 33401

MAXWELL, EUGENE OLIVER, manufacturing company executive; b. Ft. Worth, Apr. 22, 1941; s. Eugene Oliver and Nellie (Lockett) M.; M.E.T., U. Tex., Arlington, 1962; m. Terry Dawn Mayfield, June 12, 1972; children—Janna Lynn, Zxane Ian, Karen Jeanette, Shelbey Lynn. With Precision Mfg. Co., Ft. Worth, 1959-63, Gen. Dynamics, Ft. Worth, 1963-70; owner Comml. Wood Products, Ft. Worth, 1970-76; sales mgr. Ft. Worth S & S Distbn. Co., 1976-78; dir. mfg. Am. Optic Lite Corp., Ft. Worth, 1979-81; mgmt. info. mgr. Pengo Industries, Cleburne, Tex., 1981-82; pres. Camm-Tech Industries, 1983—; chmn. bd. Zxane Corp., Ft. Worth, 1976-79. Mem. Utilities Commn., City of Briar Oaks, 1980. Mem. Am. Prodn. and Inventory Control Soc., Am. Mgmt. Assn., Tex. Safety Assn., Johnson County Sports Boosters Assn., Tex. Assn. Bus. Patentee in field. Home: 116 S Briar Oaks Rd Burleson TX 76028 Office: 120 Coin St Fort Worth TX 76140

MAXWELL, JUDITH MARRE, linguist, anthropologist; b. Knoxville, Tenn., June 28, 1948; d. John Marion and Jacqueline Elaine (Kittrell) M. B.A., Mich. State U., 1970, M.A. in Linguistics, 1976; Ph.D. in Linguistics, Ph.D. in Anthropology, U. Chgo., 1982. Teaching asst. U. Mass., Amherst, 1972-73; instr. Projecto Linguistico Francisco. Marroquin, Antigua, Guatemala, 1973-76; editorial asst. Linguistic Atlas of North Central States and Canada, Chgo., 1976-79; editor-in-chief, prof. Universidad Centroamericana Jose' Sime'on Canas, San Salvador, El Salvador, 1979-80; asst. prof. anthropology Tulane U., New Orleans, 1983—; cons. Lansing Sch. Dist. (Mich.), 1977-78, Universidad Centroamericana, San Salvador, 1978. Author: (dictionary) Diccionario Español-Chuj, 1976; (with others) textbooks in Mayan languages. Editor, translator karate textbooks, 1982-84. Contbr. linguistic tech. articles to profl. jours. Fellow Mesoam. Research Inst., Ctr. for Latin Am. Studies; mem. Linguistic Soc. Am., Soc. for Study Indigenous Languages Am., Guatemalan Scholars Network, Tulane Linguistic Circle (pres., sec. 1984—). Club: Tulane Karate (New Orleans). Avocations: karate; running; backpacking; photography; river-running. Office: Dept Anthropology Tulane U 1021 Audubon St New Orleans LA 70118

MAXWELL, KATHERINE GANT, educational psychologist; b. El Paso, Tex., Nov. 27, 1931; d. Leslie and Lillian Martha (Beard) Gant; B.S., Abilene Christian U., 1955; M.S., Miss. State U., 1967, Ph.D., 1974; m. Fowden G. Maxwell, July 14, 1955; children—Steve, Rebecca, Randy. Teaching asst. Miss. State U., 1969-72, supr. student tchrs., 1973, adminstr. psychol. tests, 1974-75; sch. psychologist Martha Manson Acad., Gainesville, Fla., 1976-77, Community Counseling Center, Bronson, Fla., 1977-78, Gilchrist and Dixie County Schs., 1978-79, Bryan (Tex.) Ind. Sch. Dist., 1979-80; ednl. diagnostician Robertson County Spl. Services, 1980-81; research asst. dept. rural sociology Tex. A&M U., 1981—. Bd. dirs. Child Advocacy and Child Abuse Project, Ocala, Fla.; treas. Citizens' Com. for Mental Health, 1980; adv. com. Brazos County Mental Health/Mental Retardation. Cert. tchr., Tex., Miss., Ga.; cert. sch. psychologist, Fla., Tex. Mem. Am. Psychol. Assn., Mental Health Assn. Alachua County, Miss. Psychol. Assn., Tex. Psychol. Assn., Brazos Valley Psychol. Assn., Council Exceptional Children, AAUW (yearbook chmn. 1984), Mid-South Ednl. Research Assn., OPAS Guild, Bryan-College Station C. of C., Book Rev. Group, Campus Study Club. Phi Delta Kappa. Clubs: Univ. Women's, Extension Service (1st v.p. 1984). Contbr. articles to profl. jours. Address: Redmond Terr Sta PO Box 10027 College Station TX 77840

MAXWELL, LADELL, real estate company executive; b. San Angelo, Tex., Nov. 13, 1941; d. Jeff D. and Ethel (McMillan) Aldridge children—Ken, Sharon, Jo Ann, Sandra. Student East Central U., Ada, Okla., 1977-81. Lic. realtor, Okla.; cert. appraiser, Okla. Ptnr., Maxwell Real Estate Inc., Ada, 1967-77, pres., owner, 1977-85, also cons. Vol., Ada Services for Battered Women, 1980-81. Recipient appreciation award Ada Service for Battered Woman, 1980, Ada Arts and Humanities Council, 1982; President's Vol. Action award, 1983. Mem. Nat. Assn. Realtors (Realtor Active in Politics award 1982), Womens Council Realtors, Ada Bd. Realtors (pres. 1981-82, Realtor of Yr. award 1982, dir. required continuing edn. 1985—), Psi Chi, Beta Sigma Phi. Democrat. Presbyterian. Club: Oak Hills Country (sec. treas. 1982-83), Soroptimits (founder, pres. 1981-82). Office: Maxwell Real Estate Inc 1130 Arlington Blvd Ada OK 74820

MAXWELL, MARY CHRISTINE, physician; b. Harrisonburg, Va., June 24, 1955; d. Howard Jackson and Charlotte Christine (Moon) Maxwell. B.S. in Biology, U. Utah, 1976; M.D., W. Va. U., 1980. Intern W.Va. U. Med. Sch., Morgantown, 1980-81; staff emergency medicine Reynolds Meml. Hosp., Glen Dale, W.Va., 1981—, med. dir. Emergency Dept., 1983—; med. dir., physician McMechen V.F.D./EMS (W.Va.), 1983—; med. dir. field clinics World Med. Benevolence Fund L'Hosp. St. Croix, Leogane, Haiti, W.I., 1982. Mem. Am. Coll. Emergency Physicians, Am. Acad. Pediatrics, Phi Beta Kappa, Phi Kappa Phi. Presbyterian. Office: Reynolds Meml Hosp 800 Wheeling Ave Glen Dale WV 26038

MAXWELL, ROBERT EARL, federal judge; b. Elkins, W.Va., Mar. 15, 1924; s. Earl L. and Nellie E. M.; student Davis and Elkins Coll.; LL.B., W.Va. U., 1949; m. Ann Marie Grabowski, Mar. 1948; children—Mary Ann, Carol Lynn, Ellen Lindsay, Earl Wilson. Practiced in Randolph County, W.Va., 1949; pros. atty. Randolph County, 1952-61; U.S. atty. for No. Dist. of W.Va., 1961-64; judge U.S. Dist. Ct. for No. Dist.; W.Va., after 1965, now chief judge; judge Temporary Emergency Ct. Appeals, 1980. Del., Democratic Nat. Conv., 1956, 64; past chmn. budget com. Judicial Conf. U.S. Recipient award for outstanding community leadership Religious Heritage Am., 1979; Jurist award W.Va. Trial Lawyers. Mem. ABA (exec. com. Nat. Trial Judges), W.Va., Randolph County bar assns., W.Va. State Bar, Am. Legion. Democrat. Roman Catholic. Lodges: Lions, Moose. Home: Elkins WV 26241 Office: US Court House PO Box 1275 Elkins WV 26241

MAXWELL, WILLIAM JAMES, engineering and manufacturing company executive; b. New Castle, Pa., Apr. 12, 1942; s. Raymond Edward and Jean (Davis) M.; m. Joan Meryl Zeigler, Nov. 22, 1962; children—William Alan, Scott Edward. B.S., Youngstown State U., 1965; postgrad. in bus. Wayne State U., 1966-68, U. Detroit, 1965-66; cert. in exec. program Stanford U., 1977. Mng. dir. Chrysler Peru S.A., Lima, 1975-77, exec. asst. to v.p. internat. ops. Chrysler Corp., Detroit, 1977, pres. marine div., 1978-80; pres., chief exec. Tex. Marine Internat., Plano, 1980-81; v.p., div. pres. Stewart Systems, Plano, 1981-83, pres., chief exec. officer, 1983—, also dir.; dir. Allied Bank, Plano. Bd. dirs. United Way, Craig Gilbert Scholarship Fund, Plano, 1980—, Lone Star Recreation Ctr., Plano, 1982-83; bd. dirs., treas. Plano Cultural Arts Council, 1980—. Mem. Am. Mgmt. Assn., Am. Bakers Assn., Ind. Bakers Assn., Am. Soc. Bakery Engrs., Plano C. of C. (bd. dirs. 1980-83). Republican. Home: 2020 Biloxi Circle Plano TX 75075 Office: Stewart Systems 808 Stewart Ave Plano TX 75074

MAY, BELLA J., physical therapy educator; b. France, Aug. 19, 1930. B.S. in Phys. Edn., Pacific Lutheran U., 1952; cert. in phys. therapy Stanford U., 1953, M.A., 1966; Ed.D., U. Miami, 1970. Lic. phys. therapist, N.Y., Fla., Ga. Phys. therapist Inst. for Crippled and Disabled, N.Y.C., 1953-57, Jewish Chronic Disease Hosp., Bklyn., 1957; spl. edn. tchr., phys. therapist Dade County Bd. Pub. Instrn., Miami, 1957-59; phys. therapist Rehab. Ctr. for Crippled Children & Adults, Miami, 1959-60; pvt. practice phys. therapy, Miami, 1960-62; rehab. supr. Jackson Meml. Hosp., Miami, 1962-68; lectr. phys. therapist asst. program Miami-Dade Community Coll., Miami, 1967-70; prof. phys. therapy, Med. Coll. Ga., Augusta, 1970—, chmn. dept., 1970-84; rehab. cons. dept. orthopedics U. Miami, Coral Gables, 1968-70. Contbr. chpts. to books and articles to profl. jours. Grantee HEW 1965-66, 68-70, 72-79, VA, 1974-81, HEW, 1977-83. Mem. Am. Phys. Therapy Assn. (pres. chpt. 1975-77, sect. edn. 1980-82), Internat. Soc. Prosthetics and Orthotics, Am. Soc. Allied Health Professions (editorial bd. Jour. Allied Health 1973-79), Sigma Xi. Office: Med Coll Ga Dept Phys Therapy 1120 15th St Augusta GA 30912

MAY, CLAIRE BEASLEY, communications specialist, researcher; b. Atlanta, Aug. 16, 1945; d. Benjamin Taylor Beasley and Evelyn (Sanders) Lapp; m. Gordon Stevenson May; children—Anna Marie May Soper, Daniel Gordon. B.A., U. Tex., 1966; M.A., U. Ga., 1978, Ph.D., 1985. Communications specialist J.M. Tull Sch. Acctg., U. Ga., Athens, 1978—; cons., 1978—. Author: Effective Writing: A Handbook for Accountants, 1984. Contbr. articles to profl. jours. Mem. Am. Acctg. Assn., Am. Bus. Communication Assn., South Atlantic MLA, MLA. Episcopalian. Office: JM Tull Sch Acctg U Ga Brooks Hall Athens GA 30602

MAY, EUGENE PINKNEY, psychologist; b. Louisville, May 1, 1931; s. Eugene Pinkney and Amanda Miller (Baskette) M. B.A., George Peabody Coll., 1953, M.A., 1966; Ph.D., U. Ill., 1971. Lic. psychologist, Ill., Ohio. Counselor, Dade County Schs., Miami, Fla., 1966-71; psychologist VA Med. Ctr., Cleve., 1971-81, VA Outpatient Clinic, Oakland Park, Fla., 1981—; pvt. practice, Cleve., 1973-81; cons. psychologist, mem. adj. med. staff, dept. psychiatry Evening Mental Health Clinic, Cleve. Met. Gen. Hosp., 1974-81; adj. clin. asst. prof. dept. psychology Case Western Res. U., Cleve., 1978-81; adj. prof. dept. psychology Ursuline Coll., Pepper Pike, Ohio, 1980-81; adj. faculty Nova U. Sch. Profl. Psychology, Ft. Lauderdale, Fla., 1981—. Author: Laryngectomy-Orientation for Patient and Family, 1982; also papers. Recipient Outstanding Performance awards VA Dept. Medicine and Surgery, 1981, 83, 84, Merit citation DAV, 1982. Mem. Am. Psychol. Assn., Nat. Orgn. VA Psychologists (trustee 1984—), Ohio Psychol. Assn., Cleve. Acad. Cons. Psychologists, Cleve. Psychol. Assn., Assn. for Humanistic Psychology, Soc. for Psychol. Study Social Issues, U. Ill. Alumni Assn. (life), Nat. Register Health Service Providers in Psychology, Phi Delta Kappa, Kappa Delta Pi. Home: 2173 NE 63d St Fort Lauderdale FL 33308 Office: VA Outpatient Clinic 5599 N Dixie Hwy Oakland Park FL 33334

MAY, IRVIN MARION, JR., historian; b. Dallas, Tex., Mar. 20, 1939; s. Irvin M. and Mossie (Thompson) M.; A.A., Kilgore Coll., 1958; B.A., U. Tex., 1962; M.A., Baylor U., 1963; Ph.D., U. Okla., 1970; children—Emily Diane, Mary Elizabeth. Instr. history East Central State U., Okla. 1967-68; instr. history Tex. A&M U., College Station, 1968-70, asst. prof., 1970-74; research historian Tex. Agrl. Expt. Station, Tex. A&M U., 1974-81, Blinn Coll., 1982—, Vinson and Elkins, Houston, 1982—; pres. Hist. Assocs. of Tex., 1984—; cons. Sam Rayburn House, 1978; project reviewer Nat. Endowment for Humanities, 1977-82. Stated clk. S. Tex. Presbytery, 1985—. McMillan Found. grantee, 1978. Mem. Western History Assn., So. Hist. Assn., West Tex. Hist. Assn., Orgn. Am. Historians, Agrl. History Soc., Tex. State Hist. Assn. (Coral H. Tullis award 1980), East Tex. Hist. Assn. (pres. 1982-83, dir. 1977-85), Western Social Sci. Assn. (1st discipline chmn. agrl. studies 1976), Am. Soc. Legal History Phi Theta Kappa, Phi Alpha Theta. Presbyterian. Contbr. numerous essays on Am. agrl. history and Tex. history to scholarly jours.; contbr. numerous revs. to profl. jours.; assoc. editor Red River Valley Hist. Rev., 1974—; adv. editor Handbook of Texas; author: Marvin Jones: Agrarian Advocate, 1980; Overton; Agricultural Science and Education in Northeast Texas, 1980; co-editor: Southwestern Agriculture, 1982.

MAY, JANICE EVELYN CHRISTENSEN, educator; b. Mpls., May 29, 1923; d. Arnold Michael and Bernice Evelyn (Schauer) Christensen; B.A. summa cum laude, U. Minn., Mpls., 1944, M.A., 1946, Ph.D., 1952; m. Francis Barns May, June 9, 1956. Asst. instr. U. Minn., 1947-48; instr. U. Tex., 1948-53; instr., asst. prof. U. Okla., 1953-56; lectr. U. Tex., Austin, 1959, 64-65, instr., 1965-72, asst. prof., 1972-74, asso. prof. govt., 1974—; lectr. U. Minn., Mpls., 1960; researcher Office Gov., State Tex., 1966, Inst. Public Affairs, U. Tex., 1969, 71, Tex. Adv. Commn. Intergovtl. Relations, 1972, Inst. Urban Studies, U. Houston, 1974. Public mem. bd. dirs. State Bar Tex., 1979-82; mem. Austin Commn. Status of Women, 1975-80, vice-chmn., 1978-79; mem. Tex. Constl. Revision Commn., 1973-74, 67-68; mem. S.W. Regional Panel, Pres. Commn. White House Fellows, 1970; mem. Nat. Com. Rep. Govt., LWV, 1974-75. Recipient U. Tex. Pres.'s award, 1983. Mem. LWV (state bd. 1964-70), AAUW (award 1980, nat. legis. com. 1967-73), Am. Polit. Sci. Assn., Am. Acad. Polit. and Social Sci., Am. Judicature Soc., Nat. Mcpl. League, So. Polit. Sci. Assn., Southwestern Polit. Sci. Assn. (sec.-treas. 1980-84), Southwestern Social Sci. Assn., Women's Polit. Caucus, Austin World Affairs Council. Author: Amending the Texas Constitution, 1951-72, 1973; The Texas Constitutional Revision Experience in the 70's, 1975; (with Stuart A. MacCorkle and Dick Smith) Texas Government, 7th edit., 1974, 8th edit., 1980; contbr. articles to profl. jours. Home: 6504 Auburnhill Dr Austin TX 78723 Office: Dept Govt U Tex Austin TX 78712

MAY, JAY MELVIN, college dean, business educator; b. Cambridge, Ohio, Jan. 18, 1952; s. Mylburn Franklin and Mina Martha (Ebbert) M.; m. Mary Alice White, Nov. 25, 1976; 1 son, Travis. A.A., Northwest Miss. Jr. Coll., 1972; B.S., Ohio U., 1974; M.A., Central Mich. U., 1978; Ed.D., U. Tenn., 1985. Sales specialist Grants, Cambridge, 1974; quality control inspector Fed. Glass Co., Columbus, Ohio, 1974-77, manpower control supr., 1977-79; mem. faculty Tomlinson Coll., Cleveland, Tenn., 1979-84, chmn. dept. bus., 1981-84, acad. dean, 1984—, mem. curriculum planning com., 1980—. Editor The Advocate, 1980, Focus, 1981. Sponsor Dollars for Scholars program, Cambridge, 1970; fin. cons. Ch. of God of Prophecy, Cambridge, 1974-79. Republican. Mem. Ch. of God of Prophecy. Avocations: tennis; reading; debating. Home: 3105 Lilac Dr Cleveland TN 37320 Office: Tomlinson Coll North Lee Hwy Cleveland TN 37320

MAY, JUDE THOMAS, medical sociology educator, health services consultant; b. Grand Forks, N.D., June 7, 1936; s. James A. and Frances Clark (Temple) M.; m. Anita M. Rasi, May 27, 1964; children—Rose Marie, Thomas Garvey. B.A., B.S., St. Mary's U., 1958; M.A., U. Pitts., 1962; Ph.D., Tulane U., 1970. Asst. to prof. U. Okla. Health Scis. Ctr., Oklahoma City, 1968—; adj. prof. dept. sociology U. Okla., Norman, 1968—; health services cons. HEW, 1969-76, Nat. Endowment Humanities, 1973, 77—, NIMH, 1973-74, Nat. Assn. Community Health Ctrs., Inc., 1974-81, So. Assn. Community Health Ctr., Inc., 1975-81, NSF, 1981—, Ctr. for Program Evaluation State Dept. Mental Health, 1983—. Co-author: (with L.R. Judd, P.K. New, L.C. Anderson): The Neighborhood Health Ctr. Program: Its Growth and Problems, An Introduction. Contbrs. articles to profl. jours. and chpts. to books. Served to pfc. U.S. Army, 1960-61. Miner Found. scholar, 1968; grantee Macy Found., 1965-68, Am. Philos. Soc., 1971, Am. Council Learned Socs., 1974, NSF, 1981. Fellow Soc. Applied Anthropology (mem. exec. com. 1982—); mem. Am. Pub. Health Assn., Am. Sociol. Assn., Sigma Xi. Democrat. Roman Catholic. Home: 733 NE 18th St Oklahoma City OK 73105 Office: Coll Pub Health 801 NE 13th St Oklahoma City OK 73190

MAY, RAYMOND A., steel and energy products company executive; b. 1928; B.S., L.I. U., 1950. Salesman NCR Corp., 1958-61; regional mgr. Monroe Calculating Co., 1958-61; pres. U.S. ops. Xerox Corp., 1961-75; with LTV Corp., Dallas, 1975—, 1st v.p., cir., chmn. bd. Address: LTV Corp 1600 Pacific Dallas TX 75265*

MAY, ROBERT HENRY, JR., orthopedic surgeon; b. St. Louis, July 13, 1943; s. Robert Henry and Ruth Mae (Samuels) M.; m. Ilta Jean Tucker, Oct. 16, 1980; children—Robert Henry, Marshall Scott. Student Little Rock U., 1961-63, Ouachita Bapt. U., 1963-64; M.D., U. Ark.-Little Rock, 1968. Diplomate Am. Bd. Orthopedic Surgeons. Intern, Bexar County Hosp. Dist., San Antonio, 1968-69; resident John Peter Smith Hosp., Ft. Worth, Tex., 1971-72, Ft. Worth Affiliated Hosps., 1972-76; practice medicine, specializing in orthopedic surgery, Harlingen, Tex., 1976-80, Russellville, Ark., 1980—; chief of surgery St. Mary's Hosp., Russellville, 1983-84. Served to capt. U.S. Army, 1969-71. Decorated Bronze Star medals (2). Mem. AMA, Ark. Med. Soc., Am. Acad. Orthopedic Surgeons (fellow), Ark. Orthopedic Soc. (pres. 1985-86). Avocations: flying; civil war history. Address: Arkansas River Valley Bone & Joint Clinic 305 Skyline Dr Russellville AR 72801

MAY, T. GEOFFREY, pharmacist; b. Albany, Ga., Jan. 5, 1954; s. Thomas Grey and Frankie Anne (Stephens) M.; m. Jacquelyn Ann Duck, Feb. 6, 1982; 1 child, Stephen Geoffrey. Assoc. Sci. cum laude, Brunswick Jr. Coll., 1974; B.S. in Pharmacy, U. Ga., 1977. Staff pharmacist H&M Pharmacy, Brunswick, Ga., 1977-78; staff pharmacist, asst. mgr. Revco DS Inc, Brunswick, 1978-81, chief pharmacist, store mgr., 1982—. Rec. sec. Norwich St. Ch. God, Brunswick, 1983—, mem. pastors council, fin. com., 1984—, property devel. com., 1984—. Am. Nat. Bank scholar, 1972. Mem. Glynn Pharm. Assn. Republican. Avocations: tennis; real estate speculation; music. Home: 124 N Lake Dr Brunswick GA 31520 Office: Revco D S Inc Glynn Pl Mall Space C-1 Brunswick GA 31520

MAY, WAYNE KINNAIRD, educational administrator; b. Greensboro, Ala., Mar. 26, 1951; s. John Thomas and Marie Claire (Wilson) M.; m. Gail Moody, Mar. 16, 1974; children—Amy Gail, Clifford Wayne. B.S., Troy State U., 1973; M.Ed., U. Montevallo, 1977. Cert. elem. education, adminstrn., supr., Ala. Librarian, Westlawn Elementary Sch., Selma, Ala., 1973-74; tchr. Valley Grande Elem. Sch., Selma, 1974-77; asst. prin., tchr. Southside Elem. Sch., Selma, 1977-79; asst. prin. Dallas County High Sch., Plantersville, Ala., 1979-84, prin., 1984-85; adminstrv. asst. Dallas County Bd. Edn., 1985—. Team chmn. United Way, Selma. Named Outstanding Young Educator, Selma Jaycees, 1985. Mem. Ala. Assn. Secondary Sch. Prins., Ala. Council Sch. Adminstrs., So. Assn. Coll. and Schs. (mem. vis. com.), Omicron Delta Kappa, Delta Chi. Home: 519 Fleetwood Dr Selma AL 35701

MAYBARDUK, ALEXANDER P., surgeon; b. Berlin, Jan. 4, 1914; came to U.S., 1924; s. Peter K. and Maria H. Maybarduk; m. Ione L. Maybarduk, July 3, 1941; children—Gary, Linda. B.S., CCNY, 1935; M.D., NYU, 1939. Diplomate Am. Bd. Surgery. Intern, Kings County Hosp., N.Y.C., 1939-41; resident in surgery Fordham U. and Mt. Sinai Hosps., N.Y.C., 1945-48; asst. attending Fordham Hosp., 1948-50; clin. asst. Mt. Sinai Hosp., 1948-50; attending to cons. surgeon Fla. Hosp., Orlando, 1950—; asst. attending and cons. surgeon Orlando Med. Regional Center, 1950—; cons. examiner VA Outpatient Clinic, Orlando, 1978—. Bd. dirs. Civic Music Assn. Central Fla., 1954-72, Goodwill Industries, Central Fla. Ballet Co. Served to maj. M.C., U.S. Army, 1941-45. Fellow ACS, Internat. Coll. Surgeons, S.E. Surg. Congress; mem. Pan Pacific Surg. Assn., AMA, Orange County Med. Soc., Fla. Med. Soc. Address: 111 Laken Ln Orlando FL 32804

MAYBEN, SARA TRAUTSCHOLD, advertising executive; b. Waco, Tex., Dec. 1, 1953; d. Carl A. and Sara (Cocke) Trautschold; m. Patrick A. Mayben, Feb. 23, 1980 (div. 1983). B.F.A. cum laude, So. Meth. U., 1976; student Hollins Coll., 1972-73. Account supr. Bozell & Jacobs, Inc., Dallas, 1976-81; account mgr. Berry Brown Advt., Dallas, 1981—. Mem. Mensa. Republican.

MAYBIN, SARITA LYNN, college administrator; b. Chgo., Nov. 18, 1958; d. Hugo Eckner and Doris Elizabeth (Archie) M. B.A. in Psychology, U. Md., 1980, M.A. in Coll. Student Personnel, 1982. Program coordinator orientation U. Md., College Park, 1980-82, asst. internat. edn. services office, 1981, instr. career planning and decision making, 1981; resident dir. U. Calif.-Davis, 1982-84, mem. student affairs staff devel. com., 1983-84, asst. labor relations and staff devel. office, 1983-84; dir. orientation Old Dominion U., Norfolk, Va., 1984—, instr. univ. orientation, 1985—. Author: Sneak Preview: An Academic Planner, 1981. Editor: (newsletter) Parents Newsletter, 1984—. Vol., U. Md. Crisis Hotline, College Park, 1978-79. Mem. Nat. Orientation Dirs. Assn., Am. Coll. Personnel Assn., Omicron Delta Kappa. Avocations: travel, foreign language, aerobic dance, flea-marketing. Office: Office Orientation Old Dominion Univ 209 Webb Ctr Norfolk VA 23508

MAYBORN, FRANK WILLIS, newspaper editor and publisher; b. Akron, Ohio, Dec. 7, 1903; s. Ward C. and Nellie C. (Welton) M.; B.A., U. Colo., 1926; H.H.D. (hon.), Mary Hardin Baylor Coll., 1976. With Dallas News, 1926, N. Tex. Traction Co., Ft. Worth, 1927-29; bus. mgr. Temple (Tex.) Telegram, 1929-45, editor, pres., pub., 1945—; founder, pres., 1936-70, operator radio sta. KTEM, Temple; founder, pres., 1953—, operator KCEN-TV, Temple; owner, pres., Sherman (Tex.) Democrat, 1945-77; pres., owner, operator Killeen (Tex.) Herald, 1952—, Taylor (Tex.) Press, 1959-74; founder, operator radio sta. WMAK, Nashville, 1947-54; pres., dir. Temple Daily Telegram, 1945—, Bell Broadcasting Co., Temple, 1936-70, Red River Valley Pub. Co., 1945-77, Killeen (Tex.) Daily Herald, 1952—, Taylor (Tex.) Pub. Co., 1959-74, Channel 6, Inc., 1962—, County Developers, 1967—, FWM Properties, 1965-75, Community Enterprises, Inc., 1959-74, Frank Mayborn Enterprises, Inc., 1979—. Mem. Tex. Democratic Exec. Com., 1948. Dir. Temple Indsl. Found., 1955-60, 63-65, 67-69, 74-82, pres., 1963; Tex. Hist. Found., 1967-68; mem. Tex. Hist. Survey Com., 1966-69; mem. adv. council U. Tex. Journalism Found., 1964-66, Tex. A. and M. U. Dept. Journalism, 1958-59; mem. adv. and devel. bds. Tex. Indsl. Commn., 1958-64; mem. Ft. Hood Civilian Adv. Com., 1963—, Baylor U. Broadcast Council, 1964-65; mem. adv. bd. Scott and White Hosp. (charter mem.) 1956-61, Temple; bd. dirs. Temple Boys Choir, 1969, Waco Symphony Assn., 1968-69, Frank W. Mayborn Found., 1964—; life trustee Vanderbilt U.; v. chmn. Mary Hardin Baylor Coll. Ednl. Fedn., 1975-77; trustee Central Tex. Med. Found., 1970—, pres., 1972; chmn. bd. trustees Kinsolving Youth Center, 1971-72; trustee Donald W. Reynolds Fedn.; Served from pvt. to maj., AUS, 1942-45; ETO. Decorated Combat Bronze Star Medal; recipient Outstanding Citizens award, Temple, 1948, Tex. award for outstanding service V.F.W., 1956, award for contbn. to soil and water conservation Soil Conservation Service, 1959; Citizenship award Jr. C. of C., 1951, Man of Year award, 1971, 4-H award for outstanding service to 4-H Clubs, 1971, DAR medal of honor, 1980; named to hon. DeMolay Legion of Honor, 1978; Outstanding Citizenship, S.A.R., 1977; Disting. Citizen award Boy Scouts Am., 1983; Frank W. Mayborn Civic and Conv. Ctr. named in his honor, 1982. Mem. Am. Soc. Newspaper Editors (past dir.), Tex. Daily Press League (dir. Tex. Sunday comic sect.), Temple C. of C. (dir., past pres.), Retail Mchts. Assn. Temple, Tex. Daily Newspaper Assn. (past pres.; award 1946, 82), Am. (fed. laws com.), So. (pres. 1962, chmn. bd. 1963) newspaper pubs. assns., Tex. Council Higher Edn., Assn. U.S. Army (life, mem. mil. affairs com., certificate of achievement 1969, Gen. Creighton W. Abrams medal 1979), Broadcast Pioneers, King's Daus. Hosp. Assn., Phi Kappa Psi, Sigma Delta Chi. Presbyn. (elder). Mason (50 yr.), Rotarian (hon.). Clubs: Nat. Press (Washington); Advertising (past pres.) (Ft. Worth); Dallas Athletic, Lancers (Dallas); Headliners (Austin); Temple Country. Office: 10 S 3d St Temple TX 76501

MAYDA, JARO, law educator, international consultant; b. Brno, Czechoslovakia, 1918; s. Francis and Maria (Hornová) M.; came to U.S., 1949, naturalized, 1955; Dr. Juris Utriusque, Masaryk U., Brno, 1945; J.D. (Rockefeller fellow 1955-56), U. Chgo., 1957; m. Maruja del Castillo, 1967; children by previous marriage—Jaro II, Maria Raquel, Pavel. Legal counsel export div. Skodaworks, Plzen-Praha 1946-48; vis. prof. polit. sci. Denison U., Granville, Ohio, 1949-50, Ohio State U., Columbus, 1950-51; asst. prof. law and polit. sci. U. Wis., Madison, 1951-56; mem. faculty U. P.R., Rio Piedras, 1957—, prof. law and pub. policy, 1958-85, research prof., 1985—, dir. Inst. Policy Studies and Law, 1972-75, spl. asst. to pres., 1972; Fulbright research prof. Inst. Comparative Law, U. Paris, 1967-68; Bailey lectr. La. State U., 1969; lectr. Am. specialist program Dept. State, 1960; mem. com. environment policy and law Internat. Union Conservation Nature, 1972—; dep. sec. gen. 42d Conf. Internat. Law Assn., 1947; cons. on environment, mgmt. and law UNESCO, 1972—; cons. Am. Jury project U. Chgo., 1955-56, FAO, 1971—, UN Environment Program, 1977—, Govt. of Colombia, 1974, Govt. of Honduras, 1977, Govt. of St. Vincent, 1983; adv. panel on Ecosystem Data Handbook, NSF, 1976-77; mem., policy adviser Gov.'s study group P.R. and Sea, 1972; research assoc. Center Energy and Environ. Research, U. P.R., Dept. Energy, 1977—; mem. for law and instns. Country Environ. Profile, Haiti, 1985; vis. Fulbright prof. Ecole Nationale d'Economie Appliquée, Dakar, Senegal, 1980. Author: Environment and Resources: From Conservation to Ecomanagement, 1967; Introduction to Law, 1974; Francois Geny and Modern Jurisprudence, 1978; Policy Research and Development: Outline of a Methodology, 1979: also over 70 reports and articles. Translator: Geny, Method of Interpretation, 1963; also law treatises. Editorial bd. Am. Jour. Comparative Law, 1958-78. Office: Sch Law Univ PR Rio Piedras PR 00931-2518

MAYER, JACK FARLEY, consumer products manufacturing executive; b. Birmingham, Ala., Jan. 4, 1927; s. Louis A. and Mayme M. M.; m. Betty Brock, June 7, 1947; children—Dana Marie, Jack Douglas. B.S., Samford U., 1950. Shipping/billing clk. Graham Brokerage Co., Birmingham, 1946-50; salesman Borden Co., Birmingham, 1950-51; with Texize Chems. Co., Greenville, S.C., 1951—, v.p. sales/mktg., 1969-75, pres., 1975—. Served with USCG, 1944-45. Presbyterian. Home: 301 Raven Rd Greenville SC 29615 Office: Texize Div Dow Consumer Products Inc PO Box 368 Greenville SC 29602*

MAYER, JACOB MERRITT, surgeon; b. Hazel, Ky., Jan. 1905; s. Jacob James and Thoma Josephine (Colley) M.; B.A., U. Ky., 1927; M.D., Vanderbilt U., 1931; m. Belva Irene Graves, Sept. 15, 1935; 1 son, Jacob M. Intern in surgery Barnes Hosp., St. Louis, 1931-32; resident Louisville Gen. Hosp., 1932-35; resident in surgery; postgrad. Neurol. Inst., N.Y.C., Birmingham, Eng., Newcastle-on-Tyne, Eng., Brit. Postgrad. Med. Sch., London; gen. practice medicine and surgery, Mayfield, Ky., 1936-76; mem. staff Mayfield Hosp., 1936-72, Mayfield Community Hosp., 1972-76, mem. hon. staff, now ret.; mem. Graves County (Ky.) Bd. Health, 1949-61. Vol., ARC Bd.; mem. W. Ky. Purchase Dist. Devel. Bd.; bd. dirs. Graves County Sr. Citizens Com., mem. spl. adv. commn. for Ky. Legis. Research Commn., Frankfort, Ky. Served to lt. col. AUS, 1942-46. Diplomate Am. Bd. Surgery. Fellow ACS, Internat. Coll. Surgeons (diplomate), Southeastern Surg. Congress; mem. Ky. Surg. Soc., AMA, So. Med. Assn., Ky. State Med. Soc., Graves County Med. Soc. Democrat. Mem. Chs. of Christ. Contbr. articles on surgery to profl. jours. Home: 1213 W Broadway Mayfield KY 42066

MAYER, LEE SIDNEY, dentist, educator; b. Louisville, Nov. 26, 1947; s. Louis G. and Bernice Sue (Needleman) M.; m. Melody Kay Craig, Apr. 5, 1973 (div. 1979); m. 2d, Evelyn Anna Hall, Dec. 17, 1983. B.A., U. Louisville, 1969, M.S., 1973; D.M.D. with high distinction, U. Ky., 1979. Warehouseman, Evans' Furniture Co., Louisville, 1965-69; instr. U. Louisville, 1971, Jefferson Community Coll., 1971-72; asst. mgr. Pier I Imports, Louisville, 1972-73; sr. research analyst U. Ky., Lexington, 1973-75, tutor, writer Coll. Dentistry, 1976-79; dental extern for Dr. J.C. Lee, Lexington, 1978; dental dir. East Ky. Health Service Ctr., Hindman, 1979—; mem. Ky. River Dist. Bd. Health; extramural clin. instr. U. Ky.; dental cons. Knott County Health Care Ctr.; adult dental specialist Our Lady of the Way Hosp., Martin, Ky. Vice pres. Knott County Jaycees, 1983-84. NSF summer trainee, 1971. Mem. Am. Dental Assn., Ky. Dental Assn., Ky. Mountain Dental Assn., Ky. Primary Care Assn. (dir.), U. Louisville Alumni Assn., U. Ky. Alumni Assn., Alpha Epsilon Delta, Gamma Beta Phi, Omicron Kappa Upsilon. Democrat. Jewish. Author self-instructional texts. Home: Box 52 Mallie KY 41836 Office: Box 849 Hindman KY 41822

MAYER, THEODORE HART (MIKE), JR., air force officer, educator; b. Hot Springs, Ark., Oct. 28, 1942; s. Theodore Hart and Mary Virginia (Robertson) M.; divorced; 1 child, Christopher David. B. in Polit. Sci., U. Ark., 1965; postgrad. U. So. Calif., 1971, U. Va., 1977; M. in Pub. Adminstrn., Central Mich. U., 1977; grad. FBI Nat. Acad., Quantico, Va., 1977. Cert. tchr., Ariz. Dir. safety services div. ARC, Little Rock, 1961-64; commd. 2d lt. U.S. Air Force, 1967, advanced through grades to maj., 1979; chief security police 314th Security Police Squadron, Little Rock AFB, 1970-73; hdqr. staff officer Pacific Air Forces, Hickam AFB, Hawaii, 1976-78; chief security police 15th Air Base Wing, Wheeler AFB, Hawaii, 1978-79, 363d Security Police Squadron, Shaw AFB, S.C., 1979-81; chief ops. div. 1st Security Police Squadron, Langley AFB, Va., 1984-86; ret., 1986. Recipient Law Enforcement Commendation medal Nat. Soc. SAR, Tucson, 1982; named Outstanding Citizen of Tucson, 1984. Mem. Am. Soc. for Indsl. Security (treas., program chmn. 1982-84), FBI Nat. Acad. Assocs., Internat. Assn. Chiefs of Police. Episcopalian. Avocations: hunting; sailing; camping; miniature trains. Home: 6 Willowood Dr #103 Hampton VA 23666 Office: 1st Security Police Squadron Langley AFB Hampton VA 23665

MAYER, TIMOTHY AGNEW, dentist; b. Abilene, Tex., June 17, 1945; s. Tully August M. B.A., Trinity U., San Antonio, 1967; D.D.S., Baylor U., 1971. Pvt. practice dentistry, Pharr, Tex., 1973—; dir. Tex. Dental Polit. Action Com., Austin, 1985-86; dir. Central Nat. Bank. Mem. steering com. Am. Heart Assn. Served to capt. USAF, 1971-73. Fellow Am. Coll. Dentists, Internat. Coll. Dentists, Pierre Fauchard Acad.; mem. Acad. Gen. Dentistry, ADA (del. 1980-84, 86), Tex. Dental Assn. (v.p. 1983-85, council chmn. 1981-85, cert. appreciation 1984, 85, disting. service award 1985), Rio Grande Valley Dental Soc. (pres. 1977-78), Southwest Prosthetic Soc., Southwest Soc. Oral Medicine. Episcopalian. Club: Tex. Scuba Divers Rio Grande Valley (pres. 1984-85). Lodge: Rotary (pres. 1984-85, Outstanding Rotarian of Year 1984-85, area rep. 1985-86). Avocations: golf; scuba; underwater photography; softball; swimming. Home: 1700 Larkspur St McAllen TX 78501 Office: 129 E Caffery St Pharr TX 78577

MAYERSAK, JOSEPH ROBERT, government official; b. Superior, Wis., July 4, 1938; s. Joseph Walter and Libby Jean (Conroy) M.; m. Dianne G. Dyslin, Aug. 27, 1966; children—Jennifer L., Ryanne J., Jerome M. B.S. in Mech. Engring., Mich. Technol. U., 1961, M.S. in Mech. Engring., 1963; Ph.D. in Engring., Rice U., 1966. Mem. faculty Mich. Technol. U., Houghton, and Rice U., Houston, 1961-66; assoc. Applied Physics Lab., Johns Hopkins U.-Silver Springs, Md., 1961-62; mgr. advanced systems LTV Aerospace Corp., Sterling Heights, Mich., 1967-77; chief scientist precision guided and sensor fuzed munitions and tactical armament systems U.S. Air Force Armament Lab., Eglin AFB, Fla., 1977-79, tech. dir. for research, devel. and acquisition Armament div., 1979—; cons. U.S. Army Research Office, HEW, U.S. Tank Command, USAF Armament Lab. Recipient Meritorious Civilian Service award USAF, 1980. Mem. Sigma Xi, Pi Tau Sigma, Phi Epsilon Sigma. Lodge: Elks. Home: 2408 Roberts Dr Niceville FL 32578 Office: AD/CZ Eglin AFB FL 32542

MAYES, JOHN CLEVELAND, physician, surgeon, forensic medical specialist; b. St. Petersburg, Fla., May 26, 1944; s. Reuben and Carrie Lee (Eubanks) M.; m. Tracy Lynn Alexis, Oct. 15, 1979; 1 child, Karrie Crystallyn. B.A., Drake U., Des Moines, 1966; D. Osteopathic Medicine, U. Osteopathic Medicine and Health Scis., Des Moines, 1971; J.D., Atlanta Law Sch., 1978, LL.M., 1979; Spl. cert. psychiatry Med. Sch., Des Moines, 1971. Staff mem. Haight Ashberry Med. Detox Ctr., San Francisco, 1970-73, Fort Help, San Francisco, 1970-73, Atlanta West Hosp., Lithia Spring, 1973—, Southwest Community Hosp., Atlanta, 1973—; health careers cons. Atlanta U. Complex, 1979—; cons. U. Osteo. Medicine and Health Sci., Des Moines, 1979—. Med. dir., co-implementor Fulton County Alcoholism and Drug Treatment Ctr., Atlanta, 1973-75. Served to capt. U.S. Army, 1971-72; lt. USN, 1971-73. Mem. Ga. Osteo. Med. Assn., Am. Osteo. Assn. Home: 2523 12th St S Saint Petersburg FL 33712 Office: Airport Med Ctr Inc PO Box 490618 College Park GA 30349 also 2310 18th Ave S Saint Petersburg FL 33712

MAYES, JOHN WILMOT, geologist, consultant; b. Liberal, Kans., May 3, 1919; s. Robert Franklin and Bertha Ellen (Walters) M.; m. Luelle Oglel, Apr. 10, 1941 (div. Apr. 1959); children—John W. Jr., Joan, William C., Robert S.; m. Lillian A. Straughn, Oct. 16, 1959. B.S. in Geology, U. Okla., 1941, M.S. in Geology, 1947. Geologist, Texaco Corp., various locations, 1941-51, dist. geologist, Ardmore, Okla., 1951-54; div. geologist Samadan Oil Corp., Ardmore, 1954-62; cons. geologist John W. Mayes, cons geologist, 1962-84. Editor: Petroleum Geology of South Oklahoma, 1959. Served to 1st lt. USAAF, 1943-45. Decorated D.F.C., Air medal with 4 oak leaf clusters. Mem. Am. Assn. Petroleum Geologists, Ardmore Geol. Soc. Methodist. Club: Angel Fire Country. Avocations: lapidary, woodwork, golf. Office: PO Box 396 Ardmore OK 73402

MAYFIELD, IVAN GARRETT, JR., moving and storage company executive; b. Wichita Falls, Tex., Sept. 21, 1940; s. Ivan Garrett and Lorena (Rawlings) M.; m. Kay Caviness, Apr. 5, 1969; children—Melinda Dee, Kasha Linn. Student McMurry Coll., Abilene, Tex., 1958-60, Tex. Tech. U., Lubbock, 1960-62. Ops. supr. TIME Freight, Inc., Lubbock, 1961-64; pres., chief exec. officer Mayfield Van Lines & Warehouse, Inc., Lubbock, 1965—; mem. adv. bd. Atlas Van Lines, Inc., Evansville, Ind., 1968-72. Mem. Lubbock Traffic Club (pres. 1969), Delta Nu Alpha (pres. 1970). Republican. Baptist. Lodges: Lions Internat., Masons, Shriners (Lubbock). Home: 9602 Salisbury Ave Lubbock TX 79424 Office: PO Box 3860 Lubbock TX 79452

MAYFIELD, MARY KATHRYN, real estate broker; b. Waco, Tex., Aug. 25, 1948; d. Ray V., Jr. and Nita (Robbins) M. Student Shakespeare Inst., Stratford-Upon-Avon, Eng., 1970—; B.A., Houston Bapt. U., 1970; M.Ed., U. Houston, 1973, postgrad., 1973-74. Tchr. secondary English, Aldine Ind. Sch. Dist., 1970-74; dir. leasing Shindler/Cummins, Inc., Houston, 1974-81; owner, pres. Mayfield Interests, Inc., Houston, 1981—. Pres., Pres. Advisors, Houston Bapt. U., 1981-82. bd. dirs. Salvation Army, 1980-81; bd. dirs. L.T.G., 1982-83, pres., 1983-84; past bd. dirs. Theatre Under the Stars. Named Assoc. of Yr., Comml. div. Shindler/Cummins, Inc., 1978; Outstanding Alumnus, Houston Bapt. U., 1980. Mem. Am. Bus. Women's Assn., Profl. Women Execs., Nat. Assn. Women in Comml. Real Estate (past v.p., mem. adv. bd.), Houston Bd. Realtors, Houston Office Leasing Brokers Assn., Houston C. of C. (edn. com.), Houston Bapt. U. Alumni Assn. (past pres.). Club: University (past sec. women's assn.); Ladies Reading. Office: Mayfield Interests Inc 10333 Harwin Suite 201 Houston TX 77036

MAYFIELD, NEAL THOMAS, draftsman; b. Oklahoma City, Nov. 17, 1932; s. Floyd T. and Arta Mae (Barbee) M.; m. Sharon Ann Cooper, Oct. 12, 1963; children—Michelle A., Angela R., Amy J. Diploma in theology Southwestern Bapt. Theol. Sem., 1967; student Okla. Bapt. U., 1961-62. Ordained to ministry, Bapt. Ch., 1967. Draftsman, Capitol Steel Co., Oklahoma City, 1957-61; with Standard Steel Co., Oklahoma City, 1961-64; pastor chs., Tex. and Okla., 1967-75; estimator W & W Steel Co., Oklahoma City, 1968-71, 73-77; mgr. Encon Tech., Oklahoma City, 1977-78; pres. Central Tech. Service, Oklahoma City, 1978—. Served with U.S. Army, 1953-55. Mem. Nat. Inst. Steel Detailers, Okla. Pilots Assn., Aircraft Owners and Pilots Assn. Republican. Home: 721 Howard Ct Edmond OK 73034 Office: 111 NW 23d St Suite 4 Oklahoma City OK 73103

MAYFIELD, PEGGY JORDAN, psychologist; b. Atlanta, Aug. 4, 1934; d. Claude Emmett and Ruby Earnestine (Hutchison) Jordan; m. James Ronald Mayfield, June 14, 1953; children—Steven Jay, David Lee. B.A., Agnes Scott Coll., 1956; M.Ed., Ga. State U., 1971, S.Ed., 1976, Ph.D., 1978. Lic. psychologist, Ga. Tchr. music, Atlanta, 1956-70; exec. dir. Hi Hope Ctr., Lawrenceville Ga., 1971-74; devel. service chief program dir. Gwinnett Rockdale Newton Mental Health and Mental Retardation Service, Lawrenceville, 1974-78; owner, dir. Gwinnett Mental Health Assocs., Lilburn, Ga., 1978-85; ptnr., sec.-treas. So. Clinic, Inc., pvt. practice assessment, counseling, cons., 1985—; dir. Creative Enterprises, Lawrenceville, 1978—; adjudicator Nat. Guild Piano Tchrs., Austin, Tex., 1979—. Author community project reports, ednl. materials. Named to Hall of Fame, Nat. Guild Piano Tchrs., 1962-63; HEW fellow, 1969-71; recipient Community Program award Ga. Assn. Retarded Citizens, 1973. Mem. Am. Psychol. Assn., Am. Assn. Marriage and Family Therapists, Ga. Psychol. Assn. Avocations: music; writing; reading; fishing; travel. Office: The Southern Clinc Inc Gwinnett Profl Ctr 601-A Professional Dr Lawrenceville GA 30245

MAYFIELD, RONALD KEITH, endocrinologist; b. Morgantown, W.Va., July 15, 1950; s. Albert Keith and Mary Kathleen (Lemley) M.; m. Karen Elizabeth Gaspar, Dec. 27, 1970; children—Douglas Keith, Cortnie Anne. M.D., W.Va. U., 1975. Diplomate Am. Bd. Internal Medicine. Intern in internal medicine W.Va. U. Sch. Medicine, Charleston Area Med. Ctr., 1975-76, resident, 1976-78; fellow in endocrinology-metabolism and nutrition Med. U. S.C., Charleston, 1978-80, instr. medicine, 1980-81, asst. prof., 1981-86, asst. prof. lab. medicine, 1983-86, assoc. prof. medicine and lab. medicine, 1986—, staff physician, 1980—; dir. specialized diagnostic and therapeutic unit Charleston VA Med. Ctr., 1984—; cons. in endocrinology Med. U. Hosp., Charleston VA Med. Ctr., Charleston Meml. Hosp. Bd. govs. scholar W.Va. U. Sch. Medicine, 1971-75; Mosby scholar W.Va. U. Sch. Medicine, 1972; Spl. Emphasis Research Career award NIH, 1980-85. Fellow ACP; mem. Am. Diabetes Assn. (outstanding profl. service award S.C. affiliate 1983, bd. dirs. S.C. affiliate 1981—), AAAS, Am. Fedn. Clin. Research, N.Y. Acad. Scis., Alpha Epsilon Delta. Democrat. Contbr. articles to profl. jours. Home: 1534 Candlewood Dr Mount Pleasant SC 29464 Office: 171 Ashley Ave Charleston SC 29425

MAYHEW, ROBERT LEIGH, electronic engineer; b. Matewan, W.Va., Dec. 26, 1946; s. Philip Meeler and Virginia Dare (Wray) M.; m. Carolyn May Pillow, Sept. 28, 1974; 1 child, Jennifer Lynn. B.S., Capitol Inst. Tech., 1974. Sr. engr. E.I. DuPont, Richmond, Va., 1974—. Active, Jr. Achievement, Boy Scouts Am. Served with USAF, 1967-71; Vietnam. Home: 631 Lemoine Ln Richmond VA 23236 Office: PO Box 27001 Richmond VA 23261

MAYNARD, CHARLES DOUGLAS, radiologist, educator; b. Atlantic City, Sept. 11, 1934; s. Worth Jackson and Carrie Virginia Maynard; m. Mary Anne Satterwhite, Dec. 21, 1958; children—Charles Douglas Jr., Deanne, David. B.S., Wake Forest U., 1955; M.D., Bowman Gray Sch. Medicine, 1959. Diplomate Am. Bd. Radiology (guest examiner), Am. Bd. Nuclear Medicine. Intern, U.S. Army, Hosp., Honolulu, 1959-60; radiology resident N.C. Baptist Hosp., Winston-Salem, 1963-66, instr. Bowman Gray Sch. Medicine, 1966-67, asst. prof., 1967-69, assoc. prof., 1969-73, prof., 1973—, chmn. dept. radiology, 1977—, dir. Nuclear Medicine Lab., 1966-67, asst. dean admissions, 1966-71, assoc. dean student affairs, 1971-75. Served to capt. U.S. Army, 1959-60. Am. Cancer Soc. fellow, 1964-65; James Picker Found. radiol. research scholar, 1966-68. Mem. Soc. Nuclear Medicine, AMA, Forsyth County Med. Soc., Am. Coll. Radiology (N.C. chpt.), Med. Soc. State of N.C., Assn. Univ. Radiologists, Radiol. Soc. N.Am., Am. Coll. Nuclear Physicians, Am. Coll. Radiology, Soc. for Chairmen Academic Radiology, Piedmont Med. Found., Sigma Xi. Chmn. publs. com., cons. editorial bd. mem. Jour. Nuclear Medicine; mem. editorial bd. Magnetic Resonance Imaging. Office: Bowman Gray Sch of Medicine 300 S Hawthorne Rd Winston Salem NC 27103

MAYNARD, DONALD NELSON, horticulturist, educator; b. Hartford, Conn., June 22, 1932; s. Harry Ashley and Elsie Magnuson (Anderson) M.; m. Charlotte Louise Grybko, Mar. 23, 1974; 1 son, David Nelson. B.S., U. Conn., 1954; M.S., N.C. State U., 1956; Ph.D., U. Mass., 1963. Instr. plant and soil sci. U. Mass., 1956-62, asst. prof., 1962-67, assoc. prof., 1967-72, prof., 1972-79; prof. U. Fla., Gainesville, 1979—, chmn. vegetable crops dept., 1979-85. Fellow Am. Soc. for Hort. Sci. (Environ. Quality Research award 1975, Marion W. Meadows award 1977); mem. Fla. State Hort. Sci., Internat. Soc. for Hort. Sci. Republican. Episcopalian. Author: (with O.A. Lorenz) Knott's Handbook for Vegetable Growers, 1980; contbr. numerous research articles to profl. jours. Office: Gulf Coast Research and Edn Ctr 5007 60th St E Bradenton FL 34203

MAYNARD, JAMES EDMUND, librarian, educator; b. Lee County, S.C., Oct. 16, 1940; s. George Oscar and Pearl (Barrington) M.; m. Lois Jean McAllister, June 13, 1964 (div. Aug. 1972); m. 2d, Carol Ferrara Treacy, May 16, 1983; 1 stepson, Robert Emmet Treacy. B.A. in English, Berry Coll., 1963; M.S. in L.S., La. State U., 1967; M.A. in Mgmt., Central Mich. U., 1982. Tchr. English Rockmart (Ga.) High Sch., 1963-66; asst. prof. library The Citadel Library, Charleston, S.C., 1967-81, assoc. prof. library, 1981—. Mem. ALA, S.C. Library Assn., Southeastern Library Assn., Beta Phi Mu, Sigma Iota Epsilon. Republican. Presbyterian. Home: The Citadel Charleston SC 29409 Office: Daniel Library The Citadel Charleston SC 29409

MAYO, CLYDE CALVIN, organizational psychologist; b. Robstown, Tex., Feb. 2, 1940; s. Clyde Culverson and Velma (Oxford) M.; B.A., Rice U., 1961; B.S., U. Houston, 1964; M.S., Trinity U., 1966; Ph.D., U. Houston, 1972; m. Jeanne McCain, Aug. 24, 1963; children—Brady Scott, Amber Camille. Prin., LWFW, Inc., Houston, 1966-81; founder Mayo, Thompson, Bigby, 1981-83; founder Mgmt. and Personnel Systems, 1983—; guest lectr. U. St. Thomas, U. Houston at Clear Lake, U. Houston Central Campus, West Houston Inst., Woodlands Inst.; counselor Interface Counselling Center, 1976-84; dir. Diversified Devel. Services, 1976-84. Coach, So. Belles, S.W. Colt League, 1976-84. Mem. Am. Psychol. Assn., Tex. Psychol. Assn., Houston Psychol. Assn. (sec.), Houston Area Indsl. Psychologists, Harris County Mental Health Assn. (edn. com.), Bus. Execs. for National Security, Houston Area Quality Circle Soc., Bus. Execs. for Nat. Security. Club: Meyerland. Co-author: Bi/Polar Inventory of Strengths. Home: 8723 Ferris St Houston TX 77096 Office: 4545 Bissonnet Bellaire TX 77401

MAYO, MARTI, art historian, curator; b. Bluefield, W. Va., Oct. 17, 1945; d. Robert J. and Kathryn Ann (Kearns) Kirkwood; m. Edward K. Mayo, May 13, 1974 (div. 1983); 1 child, Nesta. B.A., Am. U., 1970, M.F.A., 1974. Asst. dir. Jefferson Place Gallery, Washington, 1973-74; coordinator exhbns. Corcoran Gallery Art, Washington, 1974-80; curator Contemporary Arts Mus., Houston, 1980—. Author: Robert Morris Selected Works: 1970-80, 1981; Other Realities: Installations for Performance, 1981; Arbitrary Order: Paintings by Pat Steir, 1983; (with others) Robert Rauschenberg, Work from Four Series: A Sesquicentennial Exhibition, 1985; Joseph Glasco 1948-1986: A Sesquicentennial Exhibition, 1986. Mem. Am. Assn. Museums, Coll. Art Assn. Office: 5216 Montrose Houston TX 77006

MAYO, PERRY WALTER, motel company executive; b. Dayton, Ohio; s. Walter A. and Lillie May (Lord) M.; children—Virginia, Diann, Martin, Teresa. Student pub. schs., Phillipsburg, Ohio. Distributor, Seven Up, Dayton, Ohio, 1951-58, sales counselor, 1958-64; owner, mgr. Hairdressers of Kettering (Ohio), 1961-71; owner, mgr. Red Curl Wigs, Dayton, 1968-73; pres. Perry Mayo Inc., Dayton, 1970-73; owner, mgr. Orlando Motel (Fla.), 1971—; pres. Perry Mayo Inc., Orlando, 1980—; mem. adv. bd. Marco Villa Ltd., Marco Island, Fla., 1971—. Republican. Lutheran. Home: 2812 Marquesas Ct Windermere FL 32786 Office: Orlando Motel 6510 W Colonial Orlando FL 32818

MAYORAL, GEORGE A., radio and television broadcasting executive, electrical engineer; b. Ponce, P.R., Sept. 1, 1916; s. A. and Isabel (Barnes) M.; m. Yvonne A. Viosca, June 16, 1941; children—Paul G., Nancy, Madeline. B.S.E.E., Tulane U., 1940; M.Sc., Notre Dame U., 1943. Registered profl. engr. Broadcast engr. NBC, N.Y.C., 1945-48; founder, pres. Summit Broadcasting Co., Inc., New Orleans, 1948—; dir., cons. Supreme Broadcasting of P.R., San Juan, 1952-72. Mem. numerous profl. organizations. Republican. Roman Catholic. Mem. social and country clubs. Office: Summit Broadcasting Co Inc 140 Carondelet St New Orleans LA 70130

MAYS, REBECCA ZEMP, university official, grants administrator; b. Camden, S.C., Mar. 27, 1941; d. Lee and Rebecca (Zemp) Mays. Ed. Winthrop Coll., 1959-61; Assoc. in Bus., Palmer Coll., 1962. Med. sec. dept. otorhinolaryngology Med. U. S.C., Charleston, 1962-66, office mgr., 1966-69, adminstrv. asst., 1969-71, staff asst. research office, 1971-77, grants coordinator and adminstr., dir. instl. rev. bd. for human research, 1977-85, dir. Office for Protection from Research Risks, 1985—, research assoc. dept. family medicine, 1985—. Prodn. coordinator more than 20 musicals, operas, operettas Charleston Opera Co., 1974-82, bd. dirs., 1972-82, pres., 1978-80; chmn. liaison com. Spoleto Festival U.S.A., 1978-81; mem. S.C. Arts Commn., 1978-81, chmn., 1980-81; mem. Tri County Arts Council, Charleston, 1975-82; mem. Charleston Area Arts Council, 1982—, sec.-treas., 1982, 1st v.p., 1982—, S-J & Friends at Docj St, pres. 1983—. Assembly State Art Agys., 1980-81, So. Arts Fedn., 1980-81, Footlight Players Inc., 1981-83, Robert Ivey Ballet, 1982—, S.C. Arts Fedn., 1982—. Home: Proprietor's Row 864 Colony Dr Charleston SC 29407 Office: Protection from Research Risks Med Univ South Carolina 171 Ashley Ave Charleston SC 29425

MAYSON, BETTY ANNE PEEPLES, medical consultant; b. Aiken, S.C., Dec. 23, 1943; d. Junius Black Peeples and Edna Earle (Sandifer) McKnight; m. Richard Grey Mayson, Sept. 23, 1959 (div. 1968); children—Richard Grey, Jr., Elizabeth Boatwright. Cert. Operating Room Technician, Adult Edn., Augusta, Ga., 1973; Assoc. Nursing, U. S.C., 1975, B.S. cum laude in Nursing, 1978. R.N. Ga., S.C. Ward clk. Plantation Gen. Hosp., Fla., 1970-72; staff nurse St. Joseph Hosp., Augusta, 1975-76; teaching assoc. U. S.C., Columbia, 1978; cons. O.F. Furr, Columbia, 1977-82, Law firm Solomon, Kahn, Smith & Baumil, Charleston, S.C., 1982—, Westinghouse Health System, Atlanta, 1977-80, Kirschner Assoc. Inc., Atlanta, 1979-80. Vol. Med. U. S.C., Charleston, 1985, Hospice, Charleston, 1985. Panhellenic scholar, 1975, Little Mae Whitehead Meml. scholar, 1976-78. Mem. Omicron Theta Alpha (pres. 1974-75), Sigma Theta Tau. Methodist. Home: 27 Lamboll Charleston SC 29401 Office: Solomon Kahn Smith & Baumil 39 Broad St Charleston SC 29402

MAZADE, AUGUST VICTOR, aerospace corporation executive; b. Detroit, Sept. 17, 1940; s. Auguste Louis and Verna Edith (Schwartz) M.; B.A., Valparaiso U., 1962; M.S., U. Houston, 1976; children—Margot Lynne, Marc Andre; m. Deedee Rebecca Storey, Jan. 7, 1984. With U.S. Dept. Interior, 1962-63, U.S. Dept. Def., 1963-72; with Lockheed Engring. & Mgmt. Services, Houston, 1972—, aerospace supr., project mgr., 1976-81 mgr. solar system exploration dept., 1982—. Rescue officer Clear Lake Vol. Fire Dept.; coach Bay Area Youth Sports. Served with AUS, 1963-69. Recipient Lunar Sci. Group Achievement award, 1974, Skylab Program award, 1975, U.S. Dept. Agr. Cert. of Merit, 1980. Mem. Nat. Mgmt. Assn. (Honor award 1975, V.P. award 1981; dir. 1982—), AIAA, Planetary Soc. Lutheran. Home: 15418 Pleasant Valley Houston TX 77062 Office: Lockheed Engring & Mgmt Services 2400 NASA Rd 1 Houston TX 77258

MAZAK, RICHARD ALLAN, clergyman, physicist, educator, consultant; b. Milw., Aug. 30, 1932; s. Stephan G. and Anne Olga (Rybarik) M.; m. Sandra G. Kropf, June 11, 1960; children—Lynn, Pamela, Scott. B.A., Concordia Sem., St. Louis, 1954, diploma in theology, 1958; M.A., U. Tex.-Austin, 1964, Ph.D., 1968. Ordained minister Lutheran Ch. Mo. Synod, 1960. Asst. prof. physics Concordia Coll., Milw., 1958-65; assoc. prof. Concordia Coll., River Forest, Ill., 1965-73; pastor Trinity Luth. Ch., San Angelo, Tex., 1973-79; pastor Mt. Olive Luth. Ch., Newton, N.C., 1979—; v.p. Austin Sci. Assocs. (Tex.), 1969-73; tchr. Catawba Valley Tech. Coll., Hickory, N.C., 1979-83; cons. in field. Bd. dirs. Am. Cancer Soc., San Angelo; mem. Spl. Task Force on Edn. Catawba County. NSF fellow, 1960, 61, 62, 63, 64, 66-68. Mem. Am. Phys. Soc., Am. Inst. Physics, Am. Assn. Physics Tchrs. Lodge: Lions. Contbr. articles to profl. jours. Home: 1010 E 23d St Newton NC 28658 Office: 7 Mount Olive Rd Newton NC 28658

MAZZEO, JOHN THOMAS, surgeon, educator; b. Newburgh, N.Y., Jan. 11, 1945; s. John Thomas and Nina Rose (Rao) M.; children—Christina, Jack. B.A., Fordham U., 1966; M.D., N.Y. Med. Coll., 1970. Diplomate Am. Bd. Surgery. Resident in gen. surgery N.Y. Med. Coll., N.Y.C., 1970-72, Nat. Naval Med. Ctr., Bethesda, Md., 1974-78; surgeon Surg. Assocs. No. Va., McLean, 1984—; mem. staff Potomac Hosp., Woodbridge, Va., chmn. dept. surgery, 1986—; mem. staff Fairfax Hosp., Commonwealth Hosp.; asst. clin. prof. surgery Uniformed Services U. Health Scis., Bethesda, 1978—; clin. instr. Georgetown U., Washington, 1983—; trustee No. Va. Peer Rev. Orgn., Falls Church, 1983-84. Served to comdr. USN, 1972-80. Fellow ACS; mem. Va. Surg. Soc., Med. Soc. Va., Fairfax County Med. Soc. Avocation: stone and wood sculpture. Home: 501 Slaters Ln 204 Alexandria VA 22314 Office: Surg Assocs No Va 1515 Chain Bridge Rd Suite 310 McLean VA 22101 also: 2200 Opitz Blvd Suite 240 Woodbridge VA 22191

MAZZETTI, AUGUST LAWRENCE, government agency official; b. Aliquippa, Pa., Jan. 5, 1931; s. Carlo Mazzetti and Jean Mazzetti Wilson Ciccanti; B.S. in Engring., Geneva Coll., Beaver Falls, Pa., 1961; m. Elizabeth Gladys Stasny, Oct. 23, 1952; children—Lawrence Lee, Tamara Lynn. Designer, Am. Bridge div. U.S. Steel Co., Ambridge, Pa., 1954-62; sr. facilities project/lead engr. Minuteman/Apollo Space Projects Boeing Co., Cape Canaveral, Fla., 1962-70; supr. engring. services staff TVA, Knoxville, Tenn., 1971-79, chmn. standards bd. of div. engring. design, 1974-79, adminstrv. analyst, 1980-81, chief planning reports and info., 1981—, chmn. mgmt. and planning activities of div., 1975-79, mem. TVA Speakers Bur., 1976-78, TVA strategic planning com., 1979—, TVA commercialization com., 1981—. Chmn. com. for unification of Knoxville and Knox County govts., 1978. bd. dirs. Grandview Community Assn., 1977-78, v.p., 1977-78, pres., 1978-80. Served with U.S. Army, 1952-54. Named to Apollo Saturn Honor Roll Smithsonian Instn., 1969. Mem. Knoxville Tech. Soc. (dir., 1st v.p. 1983—), TVA Nat. Mgmt. Assn. (chmn. bd. dirs. 1984), Nat. Mgmt. Assn. (public relations mgr.). Republican. Club: Toastmasters Internat. Home: 428 Brown Mountain Loop Knoxville TN 37920 Office: TVA 400 Commerce Ave Knoxville TN 37902

MAZZOLI, ROMANO LOUIS, congressman; b. Louisville, Nov. 2, 1932; B.S. magna cum laude in Bus. Adminstrn., U. Notre Dame, 1954; J.D. with honors, U. Louisville, 1960; m. Helen Dillon, Aug. 1, 1959; children—Michael, Andrea. Admitted to Ky. bar, 1960; with law dept. L.&N. R.R., Louisville, 1960-62; pvt. practice law, Louisville, 1962-70; mem. 92d-99th Congresses from 3d Ky. Dist.; lectr. bus. law Bellarmine Coll., Louisville, 1963-67. Mem. Ky. Senate, 1968-70. Named Outstanding Freshman Senator, 1968, Best Senator from a Public Standpoint, 1970 (both Capitol Press Club). Mem. Am., Ky., Louisville bar assns. Clubs: Notre Dame of Ky.; Notre Dame (Washington). Home: 939 Ardmore Dr Louisville KY 40217 Office: Rm 2246 Rayburn House Office Bldg Washington DC 20515*

MC ABEE, THOMAS ALLEN, psychologist; b. Spartanburg, S.C., Mar. 31, 1949; s. Thomas Walker and Doris Lee (Gillespie) McA.; student Ga. Inst. Tech., 1967-69; B.A., Furman U., 1971; M.A., U. S.C., 1975, Ph.D., 1979. Clin. counselor Adolescent Inpatient Service, William S. Hall Psychiat. Inst., Columbia, S.C., 1971-73; counselor children's therapeutic camp Columbia Area Mental Health Center, 1974; co-dir. community problems survey Eau Claire Community Project, Columbia, 1975; asst. aging services planner Central Midlands Regional Planning Council, Columbia, 1976; instr. U. S.C., 1976; NSF intern S.C. State Legislature, 1978; research dir. S.C. Legis. Gov.'s Com. on Mental Health and Mental Retardation, Columbia, 1979-80; co-dir. Kids' Media/"Feelings Just Are" TV Project, Columbia Area Mental Health Center, 1980—, cons., 1977-79; cons. S.C. Protection and Advocacy System for Handicapped Citizens, 1980, 81, S.C. Dept. Mental Health, 1981; psychologist, S.C. Dept. Mental Retardation, 1982—; mem. deinstitutionalization task force S.C. Developmental Disabilities Council, 1979-80; mem. subcom. State Commr.'s Ad Hoc Com. to Study and Develop Work/Lodge System for S.C., S.C. Dept. Mental Health, 1979-80; mem. Media Task Force of Gov.'s Adv. Com. on Early Childhood Devel. and Edn., 1980-81; chmn. primary prevention public media com. S.C. Dept. Mental Health, 1979-81. Recipient Palmetto Pictures Photography award, 1977; NIMH fellow, 1976-77. Mem. ACLU (bd. dir. S.C. chpt. 1979-83). Home: 100 Bailey Dr #E4 Summerville SC 29483 Office: Jamison Rd Ladson SC 29456

MCADAMS, CHARLES DEAN, JR., educator; b. Des Moines, May 28, 1937; s. Charles Dean and Maxine Emily (Huebner) McA.; m. Donna Sue Thompson, Aug. 2, 1964; 1 child, Charles Dean III (Trey). B.Mus. Edn., La. State U., 1960; M.A., Memphis State U., 1961; Ph.D., East Tex. State U., 1970. Head sch. band dir. pub. schs., Trumann, Ark., 1961-66; instr. East Tex. State U., Commerce, 1968; instr. Grayson County Coll., Sherman, Tex., 1969-72, dir. fine arts div., 1972-79; chmn. fine arts div. Brookhaven Coll., Dallas, 1979-84; free-lance musician, Dallas, 1979—. Percussionist, Baton Rouge Civic Symphony, 1957-60, Memphis Symphony Orch., 1960-62; string bass Memphis Summer Symphony, 1961; chmn. Sherman Musical Arts, 1972-73; mem. adminstrv. bd. Lovers Lane United Meth. Ch., 1983-85, mem. sanctuary choir, 1980—. Recipient Outstanding Music Alumnus award East Tex. State U., 1982. Mem. Tex. Bandmasters Assn., Tex. Orch. Dirs. Assn., Tex. Jr. Coll. Tchrs. Assn. Lodge: Rotary (chmn. youth exchange 1985-86, sec. 1986—). Office: Brookhaven Coll 3939 Valley View Ln Farmers Branch TX 75244

MCADOO, CAROL WESTBROOK, artist; b. Colonial Hgts., Va., Dec. 28, 1937; d. Jamie Claude and Lillian Mae (Claud) Westbrook; m. Donald E. McAdoo. Student William & Mary Coll., 1965, Richard Bland Coll., 1968. Speaker-lectr. schs. art groups and clubs. Exhibited in six one woman shows, 1973-83; exhibited in group shows at Gallery Contemporary Art, N.C., 1970-71, Lauren Rogers Mus., 1971, Mint Mus., N.C., 1971, El Paso Mus., Tex., 1971, Realists Invitational, San Francisco Ctr. Contemporary Art, 1972, Soc. Four Arts, Fla., 1973, Katherine Lorillard Wolfe, N.Y., 1980, others; represented in permanent collections Lauren Rogers Mus., Miss., NCNB Corp., AT&T Corp., Coca-Cola Corp. Author: Reflections of the Outer Banks, 1976. Contbr. articles to periodicals. Artist numerous cover commns. Recipient numerous awards for paintings, 1970-82. Mem. Southeast Center Contemporary Art, Nat. Soc. Painters in Casein & Acrylic, Piedmont Craftsmen. Episcopalian. Avocations: photography; music. Home and office: 5070 Sunset Trail NE Marietta GA 30067

MC AFEE, CARRIE R. HAMPTON (MRS. JOSHUA O. MC AFEE), educator; b. Galveston, Tex., Dec. 30, 1932; d. Tom and Daisy (Charlton) Hampton; B.A., Tex. So. U., 1952, M.A., 1963; postgrad. Lincoln U., 1958, Columbia, 1960, U. Calif.-Berkeley, 1964; m. Joshua O. Mc Afee, July 31, 1964; children—Rhonda Maria, Roy Bernard. Tchr., Houston Ind. Sch. Dist., 1953-65, counselor, 1965-68, vice prin., 1968-74, prin., 1974—. Counselor, Neighborhood Youth Corps, 1969—; vol. nurses aid ARC, 1964—; active YWCA; bd. dirs. San Jacinto Lung Assn., 1977—, Tex. chpt. Am. Lung Assn., 1984—. Recipient Outstanding Alumni award Tex. So. U., 1975, Disting. Alumnus award, 1983; Profl. award Houston League of Nat. Assn. Bus. and Profl. Women, 1976; Gov.'s Yellow Rose of Tex. award, 1976; Congl. Cert. of Recognition, 1983; Outstanding Educator award Alpha Phi Alpha, 1985; Excellence in Edn. award Nat. Coalition of 100 Black Women, 1986; Mayor's service award, 1986. Mem. Am. Personnel and Guidance Assn., Am. Assn. Sex Edn. and Counselors, Nat. Assn. Women Deans, Assn. Supervision and Curriculum Devel., Tex. Tchrs. Assn., Tex. Houston assns. supervision and curriculum devel., Houston Sch. Adminstrs. Assn., Am. Bridge Assn. (dir.), Am. Contract Bridge League, Nat., Tex. (adv. bd. dirs. 1976—, Distinguished Service award 1977) assns. secondary sch. prins., Nat. Assn. Female Execs., Zeta Phi Beta. Roman Catholic. Home: 3618 S MacGregor Way Houston TX 77021 Office: 13719 White Heather St Houston TX 77045

MC ALESTER, ARCIE LEE, JR., geologist, educator; b. Dallas, Feb. 3, 1933; s. Arcie Lee and Alverta (Funderburk) McA.; B.A., B.B.A., So. Methodist U., 1954; M.S., Yale, 1957, Ph.D., 1960; m. Virginia Wallace Savage; children—Kirstin Martine, Archibald Keven. Mem. faculty Yale, 1959-74, prof. geology, 1966-74, curator invertebrate paleontology Peabody Mus., 1966-74; prof. geol. scis., So. Meth. U., Dallas, 1974—, dean Sch. Humanities and Scis., 1974-77. Served to 1st lt. USAF, 1954-56. Guggenheim Found. fellow Glasgow (Scotland) U., 1965. Mem. Geol. Soc. Am., Paleontol. Soc., AAAS. Clubs: Yale (N.Y.C.); Dallas Country. Author: The History of Life, 1977; The Earth, 1973; Physical Geology, 1984; History of the Earth, 1980; (with Virginia McAlester), A Field Guide to American Houses, 1984, also articles. Assoc. editor Am. Scientist, 1970-74. Address: Dept Geol Sciences Southern Methodist U Dallas TX 75275

MCALESTER, VIRGINIA SAVAGE, preservationist, author; b. Dallas, May 13, 1943; d. Wallace Hamilton and Dorothy Savage; m. Clement M. Talkington, Nov. 25, 1965 (div. 1976); children—Clement M., Amy Virginia; m. 2d, A. Lee McAlester, July 11, 1977. A.B., Harvard U., 1965. Bd. dirs. Historic Preservation League, Inc., Dallas, 1972-81, 83—, pres., 1975-76; mem. Dallas Historic Landmark Preservation Com., 1973-76; pres. Friends of Far Park, 1984-86. Mem. Soc. Archtl. Historians. Episcopalian. Club: Jr. League. Author: (with Lyn Dunsavage) The Making of a Historic District: Swiss Avenue, 1975; (with Lee McAlester) A Field Guide to American Houses, 1984. Office: McAlester and Assocs 12700 Hillcrest Rd #201 Dallas TX 75230

MCALEXANDER, ALVIS LEMUEL, electrical company executive, fire protection consultant; b. Stuart, Va., July 24, 1922; s. Zera Catahille and Martha (Hall) McA.; m. Goldie Goad, Sept. 25, 1943; children—Gary Alvis, Dwight Allen, Johnny Ray. Automotive mechanic Fowler Motor Co., Mount Airy, N.C., 1946-50; asst. v.p. Floyd S. Pike Elec. Contractor, Inc., Mount Airy, 1950—; instr. fire service, Mount Airy, 1966—; fire chief Bannertown Fire Dept., Mount Airy, 1962-72, dir., 1972—. Sec., Democratic Party, Mount Airy, 1980—. Mem. Am. Soc. Safety Engrs., N.C. Soc. Fire Service Instrs. (chmn. membership com. 1980—), VFW. Presbyterian. Avocation: photography. Home: 2154 Westfield Rd Mount Airy NC 27030 Office: Floyd S Pike Elec Contractor Inc 351 Riverside Dr Mount Airy NC 27030

MCALISTER, MARTHA REMONDELLI (BONNIE), program associate, trainer, program designer; b. Newark, Nov. 5, 1939; d. Rapheal E. and Nancy Aileen (Carico) Remondelli; m. Daniel Kenney McAlister, Aug. 19, 1961; children—Nancy Sloan, Margaret Swain, Alexander Warren, Katherine Coeburn, James Daniel. B.S. with honors, Northwestern U., 1961; M.A., U. N.C.-Greensboro, 1981. Secondary sch. tchr. Durham County Sch. System, N.C., 1961-63, Charlotte Sch. System, N.C., 1963-65; composition lab lay reader Greensboro Pub. Schs., N.C., 1967-71; supr. student tchrs. U. N.C.-Greensboro, 1970-71; pvt. practice consulting, Greensboro, 1974-82; program assoc. Ctr. for Creative Leadership, Greensboro, 1982—; dir. N.C. Nat. Bank, Greensboro; cons. in field. Group facilitator Greensboro One Task Force, 1984—; v.p. Irving Park Sch. PTA, Greensboro, 1984—, chmn. tng. United Way of Greater Greensboro, 1984—, elder 1st Presbyterian Ch., 1984—, chmn. music com., 1985; bd. govs. Greensboro United Way, 1985. Mem. Am. Soc. Tng. and Devel., Leadership Greensboro Alumni Assn., Zeta Phi Eta. Club: Jr. League (rec. sec.). Avocations: reading, walking, sewing. Home: 2109 Medford Ln Greensboro NC 27408 Office: Ctr for Creative Leadership PO Box P 1 Greensboro NC 27402

MC ALLISTER, CHARLES KENNETH, physician; b. Covington, Ga., Sept. 19, 1944; s. Charles Prater and Christine (Hill) McA.; A.A., Oxford (Ga.) Coll., 1964; A.A., Emory U., 1966, M.D. cum laude, 1970; m. Judith Ann Wukas, June 17, 1967; children—Meredith Lee, Heather Elizabeth, Benjamin Hill. Intern, then resident in internal medicine U. Wash. Med. Center, Seattle, 1970-72, sr. fellow infectious diseases, 1972-74; asso. prof. medicine, dir. internal medicine residency U. Mo. Med. Sch., Kansas City, 1977-80; commd. officer M.C., U.S. Army, 1980—; asst. chief infectious disease service Brooke Army Med. Center, San Antonio, 1980-83, chief, 1983—; clin. asso. prof. U. Tex. Med. Sch., San Antonio, 1980—; cons. in infectious disease San Antonio State Chest Hosp.; mem. various speakers panels for infectious diseases. Mem. Wayside Chapel Evang. Free Ch., 1980—, elder, 1984—; discussion leader Bible Study Fellowship, San Antonio, 1980—; chmn. bd. trustees San Antonio Christian Schs. Served with USAF, 1974-77. Thomas Chalmers Swan III scholar, 1962-64; Lyndon B. Johnson scholar, 1964-66; NIH sr. fellow, 1972-74; grantee Eli Lilly & Co., 1979-80. Mem. Am. Soc. Microbiology, Infectious Disease Soc. Am., Am. Fedn. Clin. Research, Phi Beta Kappa, Alpha Omega Alpha. Club: Ft. Sam Houston Officers. Contbr. articles to profl. jours. Home: 15107 Sun Trail San Antonio TX 78232 Office: Brooke Army Med Center Beach Pavillion Box 563 Fort Sam Houston TX 78234

MC ALLISTER, GERALD NICHOLAS, clergyman; b. San Antonio, Feb. 23, 1923; s. Walter Williams and Leonora Elizabeth (Alexander) McA.; m. Helen Earle Black, Oct. 2, 1953; children—Michael Lee, David Alexander, Stephen Williams, Elizabeth. Student, U. Tex., 1942, Va. Theol. Sem., 1951; D.D. (hon.), Va. Theol. Sem., 1977. Rancher, 1946-48; ordained deacon Episcopal Ch., 1953, priest, 1954; deacon, priest Ch. of Epiphany, Raymondville, Ch. of Incarnation, Corpus Christi, St. Francis Ch., Victoria, all Tex., 1951-63; 1st canon Diocese of W. Tex., 1963-70; rector St. David's Ch., San Antonio, 1970-76; Episcopal bishop of Okla., Oklahoma City, 1977—; trustee Episcopal Theol. Sem. of S.W., 1961-72, adv. bd., 1974—; mem. Case Commn. Bd. for Theol. Edn., 1981—; pres. Tex. Council Chs., 1966-68, Okla. Conf. Chs., 1980—; bd. dirs. Presiding Bishop's Fund for World Relief, 1972-77, Ch. Hist. Soc., 1976—; chmn. Nat. and World Mission Program Group, 1973-76; mem. Structure of Ch. Standing Commn., 1979, mem. standing com. on Stewardship/Devel., 1979—; founder Chaplaincy Program, Bexar County Jail, 1968; mem. governing bd. nat. council Ch. of Christ, 1982—; chmn. standing commn. on stewardship Episcopal Ch., 1983—. Author: What We Learned from What You Said, 1973, This Fragile Earth Our Island Home, 1980. Bd. dirs. Econ. Opportunity Devel. Corp., San Antonio, 1968-69; mem. exec. com. United Way, 1968-70, vice-chmn., 1970. Served with U.S. Mcht. Marines, 1942; to 1st lt. USAAF, 1942-45. Recipient Agudas Achim Brotherhood award, 1968. Office: 1117 N Shartel Oklahoma City OK 73103*

MCALLISTER, PHYLLIS JASPER, counselor, educator; b. Somerset, Ky., Sept. 3, 1938; d. Philip Jerrill and Terrill Nannie Celeste (Coffey) Jasper; married; children—Joseph, James Kernen; m. Jeffrey James, June 12, 1982. Cert. counselor. Cert. marriage and family therapist, N.C. Tchr., Boyle County Schs., Danville, Ky., 1959-63, Danville City Schs., 1963-65, Beavercreek Schs., Xenia, Ohio, 1965-66; assoc. prof., counselor East Carolina U., Greenville, N.C., 1966—; bd. dirs. Pitt County Family Violence Program, Greenville, 1984—. Mem. Am. Psychol. Assn., N.C. Assn. Counseling and Devel., N.C. Coll. Personnel Assn., N.C. Vocation Guidance Assn., N.C. Assn. Clin. Hypnosis. Avocations: duplicate bridge; golf; square dancing. Home: 14 Palmetto Pl Greenville NC 27834 Office: Counseling Ctr East Carolina Univ 307 Wright Annex Greenville NC 27834

MC ANINCH, ROBERT DANFORD, educator; b. Wheeling, W.Va., May 21, 1942; s. Robert Danford and Dorothy Elizabeth (Goudy) McA.; A.B., West Liberty State Coll., 1969; M.A., W.Va. U., 1970; M.A., Morehead State U., 1975; postgrad. U. Hawaii, U. Ky.; 1 son, Robert Michael. Engring. technician Hydro-Space Research, Inc., Rockville, Md., 1965-66; assoc. prof. govt., philosophy Prestonsburg (Ky.) Community Coll., 1970—; v.p. Calico Corner, Inc. dir. Chase-Options, Inc. Bd. dirs. Big Sandy Area Community Action Program, Inc., 1973-76; chmn. Floyd County Solid Waste, Inc.; mem. War on Drug Task Force. Served with AUS, 1962-65. Recipient Great Tchr. award Prestonsburg Community Coll., 1971; named Ky. col., 1977. Mem. Am. Polit. Sci. Assn., Am. Philos. Soc., Ky. Philosophy Assn., Ky. Assn. Colls. and Jr. Colls. Home: Bert Combs Dr Prestonsburg KY 41653

MCARTOR, ROGER GILL, hospital pharmacist; b. Columbus, Ohio, Aug. 7, 1953; s. Jackson Hill and Dorothy Mae (Gill) McA.; B.S. in Pharmacy, Ferris State Coll., 1977. Registered pharmacist, Mich., N.Y., Fla. Pharmacy supr. Doctors Hosp., Detroit, 1978-79; clin. pharmacy coordinator Meml. Sloan-Kettering Cancer Ctr., N.Y.C., 1979-84; asst. dir. pharmacy Palms West Hosp., Loxahatchee, Fla., 1985—. Contbr. articles to profl. jours. Mem. Am. Soc. Hosp. Pharmacists, Fla. Soc. Hosp. Pharmacists (cons. Palm Beach County 1985—), Fla. Pharmacy Assn. Methodist. Avocations: caterer; tennis; swimming. Office: Palms West Hosp 13001 State Rd 80 Loxahatchee FL 33470

MCASHAN, ROBERT BURTON, III, banker; b. Houston, Apr. 18, 1946; s. Robert Burton, Jr. and Elinor June (Olcott) McA.; m. Jane E. Duke, Sept. 5, 1970; children—Elizabeth Hallie, David Burton, Robert Arthur. B.A. in Econs. and Acctg., Rice U., 1968; M.B.A. in Fin., U. Tex., 1972. Chartered fin. analyst. Research analyst Ranger Ins., Houston, 1971-76; trust investment officer Laredo Nat. Bank, Tex., 1976-81; sr. v.p. trust investments Cullen Ctr. Bank & Trust, Houston, 1981—. Mem. Houston Soc. Fin. Analysts (mem. scholarship com. 1983—, chmn. scholarship com. 1985). S.A.R. Republican. Episcopalian. Lodge: Masons. Avocations: singing; sailing. Office: Cullen Ctr Bank & Trust 600 Jefferson PO Box 1315 Houston TX 77251

MCAULIFFE, KEVIN MICHAEL, ophthalmologist, eye surgeon; b. Camden, Maine, Jan. 6, 1949; s. John Joseph and Helen Barbara (Hughes) McA.; m. Sandra L. Mercier, Jan. 7, 1978. B.A. in Biology, St. Frances Coll., 1971; M.D., Georgetown U., 1975. Diplomate Am. Bd. Ophthalmology. Intern, Suburban Hosp., Bethesda, Md., 1976-77; resident in ophthalmology U. Fla., Gainesville, 1977-79; practice medicine specializing in ophthalmology, Jacksonville, Fla., 1979—; mem. staffs Meml. Med. Ctr., Univ. Hosp., Bapt. Med. Ctr., St. Vincent's Hosp. Contbr. articles to Am. Jour. Ophthalmology, Ocular Therapy and Surgery. Med. advisor Soc. for Prevention of Blindness, Jacksonville, 1979—; bd. dirs. Neilsen Transplant Found., Jacksonville, 1983—. Fellow Internat. Coll. Surgeons; mem. Am. Acad. Ophthalmology (diplomate), Duval County Med. Soc. (dir. 1983—), Fla. Med. Assn. (del. 1983, 84), Am. Intraocular Implant Soc. Roman Catholic. Home: Ponte Vedra Blvd Ponte Vedra FL 32082 Office: 9925 San Jose Blvd Jacksonville FL 32217

MCBEE, FRANK WILKINS, JR., industrial executive; b. Ridley, Pa., Jan. 22, 1920; s. Frank Wilkins and Ruth (Moulton) McB; m. Sue U. Brandt, Apr. 10, 1943; children—Marilyn Moore, Robert Frank. B.S., U. Tex., 1947, M.S., 1950. Instr., later asst. prof. dept. mech. engring. U. Tex.-Austin, 1946-53, supr. mech. dept. Def. Research Lab., U. Tex., 1950-59; co-founder, treas. to sr. v.p. fiscal, contractual and adminstrv. affairs Tracor Inc., Austin, 1955-67, exec. v.p., 1967-70, pres., 1970—, chmn. bd., 1972—; v.p., dir. Littlefuse, Inc., Tracor Marine, Inc., Tracor No., Inc., Westronics of Tex., Inc., Tracor Jitco, Inc.; chmn. bd. MBank-Austin; dir. MCorp, Dallas, Data Card Corp., Mpls. Mem. adv. council U. Tex. Engring. Found.; trustee Ctr. Internat. Bus.; chmn. bd. Laguna Gloria Art Mus.; bd. dirs. S.W. Tex. Ednl. TV Council. Served to capt. USAF, 1943-46. Mem. Austin Heritage Assn. (life), Nat. Trust for Historic Preservation (sustaining mem.), Austin Area Research Orgn. (past pres.), Tex. Sci. and Tech. Council, (trustee) Austin C. of C. (dir., past v.p.), Tau Beta Pi. Clubs: Austin Yacht, Headliners Lakeway Yacht. Office: 6500 Tracor Ln Austin TX 78725

MC BRIDE, BEVERLEY BOOTH, psychologist; b. Richmond, Va., June 29, 1929; d. Edward Lee and Myrtle Grace (Woodlief) Booth; student Randolph-Macon Woman's Coll., 1949-51; B.S., Va. Commonwealth U., 1951, postgrad., 1951-53; M.S., Va. Poly. Inst. and State U., 1964; postgrad. Ohio U., 1969; m. John William McBride; children—John David, William Stephen, Philip Anthony, James Andrew. Staff psychologist Mountain Empire Guidance Clinic, Radford, Va., 1959-67, acting dir., 1963-65; cons. psychologist Greenbrier Valley Mental Health Clinic, Lewisburg, W.Va., 1964-70, chief psychologist, 1970—, clin. dir., 1976-79; dir. clin. services Seneca Mental Health/Mental Retardation Council, 1979—; pvt. practice, Parkersburg, W.Va., 1967-69; program cons. Headstart-Day Care Program, 1969-; W. Central W.Va. Community Action Assn., Parkersburg, 1967-70, dir. counseling unit Manpower Program, 1968-70; faculty Radford Coll., 1962-64, W.Va. U., Parkersburg, 1968-70; cons. psychologist Div. Vocat. Rehab., Richmond Area,

1953-58, Monroe County Bd. Edn., Union, W.Va., 1965-68, Greenbrier County Bd. Edn., Lewisburg, 1965-72, Monroe County Mental Health Clinic, Union, W.Va., 1970-73. Chmn. fine arts com. Radford Jr. Woman's Club, 1960-61, program chmn., 1961-62, v.p., 1962-63, pres., 1963-64; mem. Gov.'s Study Commn. on Youth, 1962-63, Gov.'s Study Commn. on Mental Health, 1964-65; chmn. Multicounty Interagy. Council, Radford, 1963-64; mem. Parkersburg Fine Arts Center, 1967-70; mem. adv. bd. Radford Fine Arts Council, 1963-65, Greenbrier Tng. Center, 1973-75; bd. dirs. Va. Thanksgiving Festival, Inc., 1983—. Mem. Nat. (del. 1971-73), W.Va. (pres. 1975-76) assns. sch. psychologists, W.Va. Psychol. Assn., Assn. Psychiat. Outpatient Centers Am. (sec. 1975-78), Assn. Rural Mental Health (vice-chmn. 1978-80, dir. 1977-82), Preservation Alliance of W.Va. (dir., publicity chmn. 1983—. Episcopalian. Home: 409 E Washington St Lewisburg WV 24901 Office: 100 Church St Lewisburg WV 24901

MCBRIDE, KENNETH EUGENE, lawyer, abstract company executive; b. Abilene, Tex., June 8, 1948; s. W. Eugene and I. Jean (Wright) McB.; m. Peggy Ann Waller, Aug. 7, 1969 (div. 1980); m. Katrina Lynne Small, June 1, 1985. B.A., Central State U., 1971; J.D., Oklahoma City U., 1974. Bar: Okla. 1974. Assoc. Linn, Helms & Kirk, Oklahoma City, 1974-76; city atty. City of Edmond, Okla., 1976-77; v.p., gen. counsel Am. First Land Title Ins., Oklahoma City, 1977-81; pres. Am.-First Abstract Co., Norman, Okla., 1981—. Bd. dirs. Norman Bd. Adjustment, 1982-85. Mem. ABA, Okla. Bar Assn., Cleveland County Bar Assn., Norman C. of C. (bd. dirs.). Democrat. Presbyterian. Avocation: sailing. Office: Am-First Abstract Co 111 E Comanche Norman OK 73069

MCBRIDE, WILLIAM J., mathematics educator, humorist; b. Anderson, S.C., July 31, 1946; s. William Ardy and Gertrude Lois (Smith) McB.; m. Barbara April Badders, July 31, 1982. A.A., Anderson Coll., 1974; B.S., Clemson U., 1975, M.Ed., 1976. Tchr. math. Ware Shoals High Sch., S.C., 1976-80; instr. math. Spartanburg Tech. Coll., S.C., 1980-81; prof. math. Anderson Coll., S.C., 1981—. Author poetry. Served with USN, 1966-70. Recipient Star award Ware Shoals High Sch., 1980. Mem. Math. Assn. Am., Nat. Assn. Developmental Edn., S.C. Assn. Devel. Edn., Phi Theta Kappa. Baptist. Avocations: humorist; poet. Office: Anderson Coll 316 Boulevard Anderson SC 29621

MCBURNEY, ROBERT F., insurance company executive, consultant; b. Pitts., Nov. 17, 1949; s. Robert L. and Mary (Costantino) McB.; m. Pamela A. Stobaugh; children—Robert S., Jeffrey A. Degree in Computer Sci. Elec. Computer Inst. Tech., Pitts., 1969. Mgr. Sun Life of Can., Pitts., 1969-71; dept. head Am. Life Ins. Co., Wilmington, Del., 1971-75; dir. Maccabees Mut., Southfield, Mich., 1975-83; pres., chief exec. officer Govtl. Health Mgrs., Inc., Redford, Mich., 1983-84; exec. v.p. 1st SE Risk Mgmt. of Fla., Inc., Tampa, 1984—; pres. URS Internat., Tampa, 1984—; cons. group ins. employee benefits, systems, Redford Mcpl. Govt. 1983—. Chmn. bd. Christian Edn., Farmington Hill, 1981-83; bd. dirs. Boys Brigrade Program, Christian Service Brigade, Farmington Hill, 1981-83. Fellow Life Mgmt. Inst. (bd. dirs. Mich. sect. 1983-84), Life Office Mgmt. Assn. (soc. rep. 1983). Republican. Office: 1st SE Risk Mgmt of Fla Inc PO Box 25637 Tampa FL 33622

MCCABE, GAY LOYCE EVANS, securities company executive; b. Tuscaloosa, Ala., Feb. 27, 1943; d. Walter H. and Loyce Roena (Park) Evans; m. James W. McCabe, Jr., July 7, 1977. B.A., David Lipscomb Coll., 1965; postgrad. George Peabody Coll., Vanderbilt U., 1968. Tchr., Houston Ind. Sch. Dist., 1970-71, Bolles Sch., Jacksonville, Fla., 1971-75; advt. account exec. William H. Coleman, Inc., Jacksonville, 1975-76, Bozell, Jacobs, Atlanta, 1976-77; test specialist Telemedia, Inc., Isfahan, Iran, 1977-79; with McCabe Petroleum Corp., San Antonio, 1979-81; advt. dir. San Anco Energy Corp., San Antonio, 1981-83; pres. McCabe Communications, San Antonio, 1981-83; pres. San Anco Securities Co., San Antonio, 1983—. Mem. Nashville Symphony Chorus, 1968, Jacksonville Symphony Chorus, 1972; vol. Texans War on Drugs, 1982-83; bd. dirs. Trinity U. Tennis Found., 1981-83. Mem. Am. Mktg. Assn., Am. Mgmt. Assn., Southwest Research Found. Forum, San Antonio C. of C. Republican. Mem. Ch. of Christ. Clubs: Retama Polo Ctr. (San Antonio); Dominion Country; Petroleum; Sawgrass (Ponte Vedra, Fla.). Office: 100 Sandau Ste 201 San Antonio TX 78216

MCCABE, ROBERT H., educator, college president; b. Bklyn., Dec. 23, 1929; s. Joseph A. and Kathryn (Greer) McC.; m. Bonnie Pasour, Dec. 22, 1961. B.Ed., U. Miami (Fla.), 1952; M.S., Appalachian State U., Boone, N.C., 1959; Ph.D., U. Tex.-Austin, 1963. Asst. to pres. Miami-Dade Community Coll. (Fla.), 1963-65, v.p., 1965-67, exec. v.p., 1969-80, pres., 1980—; pres. Essex County Coll., Newark, 1967-69; exec. com. So. Regional Edn. Bd., Atlanta, 1981-83. Bd. dirs. James E. Scott Community Assn., Miami, 1976-82, Bus. Assistance Ctr., Miami, 1982—, Southeastern Holocaust Meml. Ctr., Miami, 1982—, Community Relations Bd., Miami, 1978—; trustee Coll. Bd., 1984—. Recipient Disting. Service award Fla. Congl. Del., 1983; named Outstanding Grad., Coll. Edn., U. Tex., 1982; Disting. Service award, Dade County, Fla., 1983; Kellogg fellow, 1962-63. Mem. Am. Assn. Higher Edn. (dir. 1973-75), Am. Assn. for Environ. Edn. (pres. 1970-73), Am. Council on Edn., Commn. on Higher Edn. Issues, Higher Edn. Consortium, Am. Council Edn. (dir. 1982—), Southeast Fla. Edn. Consortium (chmn. bd. 1981-83), League for Innovation in Community Colls. (dir., exec. com. 1985—). Episcopalian. Club: Miami. Author: Man and Environment, 1971; contbr. articles to profl. jours.; editor Jour. Environ. Edn.; cons. editor Change Mag., 1980—. Home: 10270 SW 102 Terr Miami FL 33176 Office: Miami Dade Community Coll 300 NE 2d Ave Miami FL 33132

MCCABE, ROBERT JOSEPH, dermatologist; b. Covington, Ky., Mar. 19, 1921; s. John Edward and Marie Ann (Bruegger) McC.; m. Elizabeth Ann Grimes, Aug. 7, 1948; children—Robert Jerald, Molly Ann, Colleen, John Erin. B.S., Xavier U., Cin., 1941; M.D., U. Cin., 1944. Intern Cin. Gen. Hosp., 1944-45; resident in dermatology U. Cin. Hosp., 1954-56; practice medicine specializing in dermatology, Newport, Ky., 1956—; asst. prof. dermatology U. Cin. Gen. Hosp., 1968; mem. staff St. Luke Hosp., St. Elizabeth Hosp., Booth Hosp. Pres. Cin. chpt. Bass Club, 1983. Served to capt. M.C., AUS, 1945-47; Japan. Fellow Am. Acad. Dermatology; mem. AMA, Ky. Med. Assn., Cin. Dermatol. Soc. (pres. 1970), Kenton-Campbell County Dermatol. Soc. Republican. Roman Catholic. Home: 40 Linden Hill Dr Crescent Springs KY 41011 Office: 3d and Washington St Newport KY 41071

MCCAIN, ELIZABETH VIRGINIA REYNOLDS, newspaper editor; b. Starkville, Miss., Sept. 30, 1910; d. Archibald William and Charlie Elise (Harrison) R.; B.A., Miss. U. for Women, 1931; m. Dewey Marven McCain, June 8, 1933; children—Jane Douglas, Charles M., William H., Susan B. lifestyles editor Starkville (Miss.) News, weekly, 1931-46, Starkville Daily News, 1959-85; mem. faculty Miss. State U., 1941-44. Mem. Miss. Press Women, Nat. Fedn. Press Women, Am. Guild Organists, D.A.R. (regent chpt. 1968-71), Chi Omega. Episcopalian. Office: 316 University Dr Starkville MS 39759

MCCAIN, JUDY LEE, real estate developer and building contractor, educator; b. Tylertown, Miss., Sept. 21, 1949; d. Carlos Alford and Bertile (Smith) Ard; m. Jimmy Gail McCain, Feb. 28, 1970; 1 child, Wesley Todd. B.S., M.A., U. South Ala., Cert. real estate broker. Exec. sec. Mchts. Nat. Bank, Mobile, Ala., 1970-72; sales assoc. Duke Real Estate, Inc., Mobile, 1979-80; sales broker, pres. McCain Real Estate, Inc., Citronelle, Ala., 1980-85. Contbr. articles to profl. jours. Mem. Mobile United, 1985; pres. Mobile County Bd. Sch. Commnrs., Mobile, 1984-86; mem. governing bd. South Ala. Research Inservice Ctr.; mem. Mobile County Child Abuse Com. Recipient Outstanding Sales award Mktg. Inst., 1980, Resolution Commending Career award State of Ala. House of Reps., 1981. Mem. Mobile County Bd. Realtors (assoc.), Ala. Assn. Sch. Bds., Homebuilders Assn., Ala., Citronelle Area C. of C. (bd. dirs.). Democrat. Baptist. Avocations: reading; jogging; swimming; piano. Home: PO Box 295 Citronelle AL 36522 Office: McCain Real Estate Inc 510 N 3d St Citronelle AL 36522

MC CAIN, MAURICE EDWARD, investment firm executive, former uniform company executive; b. Denver, Feb. 14, 1909; s. Thomas C. and Fannie (Burke) McC.; grad. high sch.; m. Florence Inez Snowden, Dec. 27, 1927 (dec. April 1978); m. 2d, Ruth Barnhill Hinkle. With McCain Tailoring Co., 1927-32; mgr. uniform dept. Yielding Bros., 1932-39; with McCain Uniform Co., Inc., Birmingham, Ala., 1939-83, pres., 1954-83; pres. McCain Investment Co., Inc., 1983—; v.p., dir. Decatur (Ala.) Transit Trucklines, 1954-61; chmn. bd. dirs. Banner Uniform Co., Atlanta, Macon, 1962-78; v.p., dir. Burke Uniform Co., Houston, 1967-80. Trustee, Baptist Med. Centers, Birmingham, 1978—. Served with USAAF, 1943-45. Mem. Nat. Assn. Uniform Mfrs. and Distbrs. (dir. 1965-78), Birmingham Motor Truck Club, Pres.'s Forum of So. Bapt. Radio and TV Commn. Baptist. Clubs: City Salesmen's (pres. 1967-68, Man of Year 1977), Masons, Shriners, Jesters, Vestavia Country, The Club, Downtown, Rotary, Relay House. Home: 3756 Locksley Dr Birmingham AL 35223 Office: 2208 3d Ave N Birmingham AL 35203

MCCALL, CLYDE SAMUEL, JR., petroleum engineer; b. Memphis, May 29, 1931; s. Clyde Samuel and Marguerite (Rogers) McC.; m. Dodie McDonald, July 21, 1962; children—Clyde Samuel III, Amy Woolsey McDonald. B.S. in Commerce, Washington and Lee U., 1953; B.S. in Petroleum Engring., U. Tex.-Austin, 1959. Registered profl. engr., Tex. Engr. to sr. petroleum engr. Amoco Prodn. Co., Andrews and Midland, Tex., 1959-69; cons. petroleum engr., Midland, Tex., 1969-73; petroleum engr. James A. Lewis Engring., Dallas, 1973-81, pres., 1977-81; exec. v.p. McCord-Lewis Energy Services, Dallas, 1981-83; petroleum cons., pres. Cenesia Petroleum Corp., 1983—. Assoc. mem. Dallas Museum of Fine Arts. Served with U.S. Army, 1954-56. Mem. Soc. Petroleum Engrs., Soc. Eval. Engrs., Ind. Petroleum Assn. Am., Tex. Mid-Continent Oil and Gas Assn. Republican. Presbyterian. Clubs: Dallas Petroleum, Energy of Dallas, Brook Hollow Golf, Kappa Alpha Order, Chandlers Landing Yacht, Steeplechase, Confriere des Chevalier du Tastavin. Address: Suite 435 Two Energy Sq 4849 Greenville Ave Dallas TX 75206

MC CALL, DANIEL THOMPSON, JR., retired justice Supreme Court of Alabama; b. Butler, Ala., Mar. 12, 1909; s. Daniel Thompson and Caroline (Bush) McC.; B.A., U. Ala., 1931, LL.B., 1933, LL.D. (hon.), 1981; m. Mary Edna Montgomery, Apr. 3, 1937; children—Mary Winston (Mrs. Rogers Neilson Laseter), Daniel Thompson III, Nancy (Mrs. John Worrell Poynor). Bar: Ala. 1933, U.S. Supreme Ct. Practiced in Mobile, 1933-60; partner firm Johnston, McCall & Johnston, 1943-60; circuit judge 13th Circuit, 1960-69; asso. justice Ala. Supreme Ct., Montgomery, 1969-75, ret., 1975; mem. Ala. Bd. Bar Commrs., 1957-60. Mem. Mobile County Bd. Sch. Commrs. 1950-56, 58-60; trustee Julius T. Wright Sch. for Girls, 1953-63; trustee U. Ala., 1965-79, nat. alumni pres., 1963; mem. adv. council U. Ala. Med. Sch., Birmingham. Served to lt. USNR, World War II. Recipient Dean's award U. Ala. Law Sch., 1974, Order of Jurisprudence Cumberland Law Sch., Julius T. Wright Sch. Disting. Service award, 1979; Outstanding Alumnus award U.M.S. Prep. Sch., 1980. Mem. Am., Ala., Mobile County (past pres.) bar assns., Jr. Bar Assn. Ala. (past pres.), U. Ala. Law Sch. Found., Am. Judicature Soc., Inst. Jud. Adminstrn., Am. Trial Lawyers Assn., Farrah Law Soc., Nat. Hist. Assn., Ala. Hist. Soc., Ala. Wildlife Fedn., Navy League U.S., Am. Legion, 40 and 8, Mil. Order World Wars, SAR, Sons of Confederacy, Res. Officers Assn., St. Andrews Soc. Mid-South, U. Ala. Sch. Medicine Alumni Assn. (hon.), Sigma Nu, Phi Delta Phi, Omicron Delta Kappa. Democrat. Episcopalian. Clubs: University (Tuscaloosa); Athelstan, Hickory Hill Hunting. Home: 2253 Ashland Place Ave Mobile AL 36607

MCCALL, MORGAN WOODROW, JR., psychologist, behavioral scientist; b. Dallas, Feb. 7, 1948; s. Morgan Woodrow and Ada Bell (Rowe) McC.; 1 child, Morgan Woodrow, III. B.S., Yale U., 1970; Ph.D., Cornell U., 1974. Research psychologist, Ctr. for Creative Leadership, Greensboro, N.C., 1974-78, behavioral scientist, project mgr., 1978-83, dir. research, sr. behavioral scientist, 1983—; adj. prof. U. N.C.-Greensboro, 1975-78; prin. investigator, project mgr. Office Naval Research, Grant, 1976-78; instr. Grad. Sch. Bus., Duke U., 1977. Author: (with Lombardo, DeVries) Looking Glass, Inc., 1978; (with Lombardo) Leadership: Where Else Can We Go?, 1978; (with Kaplan) Whatever it Takes: Decision Makers at Work, 1984. Contbr. articles to profl. jours. Grad. fellow Cornell U., 1970-71; Owen D. Young fellow, 1972-73. Fellow Am. Psychol. Assn.; mem. Acad. Mgmt., (reviewer editorial bd. 1981—). Home: 2709 Lafayette Ave Greensboro NC 27408 Office: Ctr for Creative Leadership 5000 Laurinda Dr PO Box P-1 Greensboro NC 27402

MCCALLA, SANDRA ANN, principal; b. Shreveport, La., Nov. 6, 1939; d. Earl Gray and Dorothy Edna (Adams) McC. B.S., Northwestern State U., 1960; M.A., U. No. Colo., 1968. Cert. tchr. math., computer sci., supr., prin., supt. Math. tchr. Caddo Parish Sch. Bd., Shreveport, La., 1960-77, math. coordinator, 1970-77; asst. prin. Captain Shreve High Sch., Shreveport, 1977-79, prin., 1979—; grad. asst. Tex. A&M U., College Station, 1977; instr. evening div. La. State U., Shreveport, 1980-82. Task Force chmn. Shreveport Women's Commn. Mayor's Office, 1983—; mem. Altrusa Club of Shreveport, 1978—; mem. City of Shreveport Futureshape Commn., 1986—. Danforth Found. fellow, 1982-83. Mem. Nat. Assn. Secondary Sch. Prins. (La. excellence in edn. award 1985), La. Assn. Sch. Execs. (disting. service award 1983), La. Assn. Educators, La. High Sch. Athletic Assn. (dist. champions 1984-85), La. Assn. Prins., Caddo Assn. (educator of yr. tchr. div. 1966, administrv. div. 1984), Nat. Edn. Assn., PTA (hon. life mem.), Phi Delta Kappa (research chmn. 1985—). Home: 7048 Creswell Rd Shreveport LA 71106 Office: Captain Shreve High School 6115 E Kings Hwy Shreveport LA 71105

MCCALLUM, JACK EDWARD, physician, educator; b. Corsicana, Tex., Oct. 24, 1945; m. Cheryl Lynn Beaver, Apr. 16, 1970; 2 children. B.Sc., Ga. Inst. Tech., 1966; M.D., Emory U., 1970. Diplomate Am. Bd. Neurol. Surgery. Intern, Boston City Hosp., 1970-71; resident in gen. surgery Emory U. Affiliated Hosps., 1971-72; resident in neurol. surgery U. Pitts., 1972-77, teaching fellow, 1972-77; chmn. div. surgery Ft. Worth Children's Hosp., 1980-83; assoc. clin. prof. Tex. Tech. U., Lubbock, 1981—. Bd. dirs. Tarrant County Cancer Soc. (Tex.), March of Dimes (Tex.). Served to lt. USNR, 1970-77. Ga. Mental Health Inst. fellow, 1971-72. Mem. AMA, Tarrant County Med. Soc., Ft. Worth Surg. Soc., Tex. Med. Assn., Tex. Assn. Neurol. Surgeons, Congress of Neurol. Surgeons, Am. Assn. Neurol. Surgeons, ACS, So. Neurosurg. Soc. Episcopalian. Clubs: Ft. Worth, Shady Oaks Country (Ft. Worth). Contbr. chpts. to books and articles in field to profl. jours. Home: 40 Valley Ridge Westover Hills TX 76104 Office: 1522 Cooper St Fort Worth TX 76109

MCCAMMON, CURTIS PAUL, physician, university administrator; b. Knoxville, Tenn., Nov. 6, 1922; s. William Howard and Trula Lee (Reynolds) McC.; m. Doris Marie Meggs, May 22, 1954; children—Nan Marie, Stanley Paul, Janet Lee, Daniel Kevin. B.A., U. Tenn., 1946; M.D., Temple U., 1949; M.P.H., Harvard Sch. Public Health, 1958. Intern, Brooke Army Hosp., San Antonio, 1949-50; dir. venereal disease control Health Dept., Knoxville, Tenn., 1950-52; practice gen. medicine, Wartburg, Tenn., 1954-57; dir. occupational health Tenn. Dept. Pub. Health, Nashville, 1958-68; med. dir. U. Tenn. Meml. Hosp., Knoxville, 1968-84; dir. community relations Office of Health Affairs U. Tenn., Knoxville, 1984—. Served to capt. MC, USAF, 1943-46, AUS, 1949-50, 1952-54. Democrat. Methodist. Lodge: Masons. Avocation: golf. Office: U Tennessee 1912 Terrace Ave Knoxville TN 37996

MCCAMPBELL, JAMES BOYD, conservationist; b. Erick, Okla., Sept. 9, 1936; s. Harry Robert and Ruth Louise (Toon) McC.; m. Barbara Jo Lee, Feb. 10, 1963; 1 dau., Sheri Lynn. Student, Cameron Jr. Coll., Lawton, Okla., 1954-56; B.S. in Agr., Okla. State U., 1958; postgrad. Southwestern State U., Weatherford, Okla., 1961. With U.S. Dept. Agr. Soil Conservation Service, 1960—, farmer, Erick, 1951-59, conservation technician, Sayre, Okla., 1960-62, soil conservationist, Walters, Okla., 1963-66, dist. conservationist, Ada, Okla., 1966-72, Norman, Okla., 1973—; lectr. dept. environ. design U. Okla.; cons. Cities of Norman and Moore, Okla. planning depts., engring. firms and land users. Mem. Environ. Control Adv. Bd., Norman, 1979—, Community Devel. Policy Com., 1974—, Groundwater Devel. Plan Implementation Procedures Task Force, Norman, 1983. Served with N.G., 1959-65. Mem. Soil Conservation Soc. Am. (pres. Central Okla. chpt. 1976), Soc. Range Mgmt. (pres. Kans.-Okla. sect. 1977-78), Cleveland County 4-H (hon.), Nat. Rifle Assn. (life). Democrat. Methodist. Club: Tri-City Gun (Oklahoma City). Lodges: Masons, Lions (pres. 1981-82). Office: Soil Conservation Service 603 E Robinson Suite B Norman OK 73071

MC CANDLESS, CHARLES EMERY, educator; b. Dallas, July 26, 1931; s. Dewey Taylor and Clara (Askins) McC.; B.S., Tex. A&M U., 1956, M.Ed., 1958; Ed.D., North Tex. State U., 1966; m. Jeannie Wallace, May 14, 1977; children by previous marriage—Cathy, Sharon, Debra. Head coach Silsbee (Tex.) Jr. High Sch., 1956-58; counselor Silsbee High Sch., 1958-60; part-time instr. health, phys. edn., recreation North Tex. U., Denton, 1960-61; asst. prof. health and phys. edn., intramural athletics dir. Tex. A&M U., College Station, 1963-66, chmn. freshman courses dept. edn. and psychology, 1964-66, dir. adj., chmn. counselor edn., 1966-67, prof. ednl. psychology, 1977—, asso. dean liberal arts, 1966-74, coordinator univ. self study, 1971-73, dir. acad. planning and services, 1974—, dir. planning, 1977—, asso. v.p. acad. affairs, 1979-82, interim v.p. acad. affairs, 1982—. Pres., College Station Recreation Council, 1968-73, College Station United Chest, 1973-74; pres. adv. bd. Central Brazos Valley Mental Health Center; bd. dirs. Bryan Boys Club, 1977—; mem. exec. com. Brazos Valley Muscular Dystrophy Assn., 1979—. Served with USAF, 1951-53. Recipient Student-Faculty Relations award Coll. Liberal Arts, 1969. Mem. College Station Progress Assn. (dir. 1969-71), Am., Tex. personnel and guidance assns., Am. Coll. Personnel Assn., Assn. Counselor Edn. and Supervision, Tex. Psychol. Assn. Asso. dir. several profl. jours.

MCCANTS, CLYDE TAFT, clergyman; b. Anderson, S.C., Jan. 9, 1933; s. Edwin Clyde and Mary Rachel (Taft) McC. A.B., Erskine Coll., 1954; M.A., Duke U., 1956; M.Div., Erskine Theol. Sem., 1970. Ordained to ministry, 1970. English faculty Elon Coll., N.C., 1955-60, Erskine Coll., Due West, S.C., 1960-65; faculty English and dept. chmn. Gaston Coll., Gastonia, N.C., 1965-67; pastor Lauderdale Ch., Lexington, Va., 1970-73; dir. ch. extension Gen. Synod, Assoc. Ref. Presbyn. Ch., 1973-77; pastor First A.R. Presbyn. Ch., Burlington, N.C., 1977-78; asst. and assoc. prof. ministry Erskine Theol. Sem., 1978-82; pastor Greenville A.R.P. Ch., Greenville, S.C., 1982—; trustee Erskine Coll., 1973-78; moderator Gen. Synod of Assoc. Ref. Presbyn. Ch., 1978-79; chmn. Presbyn. Council on Chaplains and Mil. Personnel, Washington, 1983-84. Author: The God Who Makes History, 1976; David, King of Israel, 1978. Contbr. articles to profl. jours. Democrat. Lodge: Kiwanis. Avocations: classical vocal recordings. Home: 21 Timberlake Dr Greenville SC 29615 Office: 741 Cleveland St Greenville SC 29601

MCCARRON, ROBERT LOUIS, English educator, literary researcher and writer; b. Chgo., May 17, 1934; s. Harold Murphy and Helen Marie (McCready) McC.; m. Maureen Ann Darroch, June 28, 1958; 1 child, Pamela Ann. B.A., Wheaton Coll., 1958; M.A., Western Mich. U., 1960; M.A., Ind. U., 1976, Ph.D., 1980. Cert. secondary tchr., Mich. Tchr., Plainwell Community Schs., Mich., 1959-62; tchr., adminstr. ELWA Schs., Monrovia, Liberia, West Africa, 1962-71; instr., adviser Ind. U., Bloomington, 1972-76; prof., chmn. dept. English, Bryan Coll., Dayton, Tenn., 1976—. Editorial bd. Studies in the Humanities, Indiana, Pa., 1983—. Reviewer, contbr. articles to profl. jours. Sunday sch. dir. First Baptist Ch., Dayton, 1983—. Study grantee Nat. Endowment Humanities, 1983. Mem. South Atlantic Modern Lang. Assn., Conf. Christianity and Lit. (s.e. sec. 1983-84, chmn. 1984—). Republican. Baptist. Avocations: sports; travel. Home: Bryan Coll Box 7738 Dayton TN 37321-7000 Office: Bryan Coll Box 7000 Dayton TN 37321-7000

MCCARTER, MARGIE JOHNSON, investments and travel consultant; b. Bosqueville, Tex., Nov. 7, 1929; d. Joseph Bernard and Bettie Ruth (McNamara) Johnson; m. Jack McCarter, Dec. 13, 1952 (div. 1975); children—Jack III, Bettie M. Boyd, Parnell; m. William Richard Thompson, Sept. 1, 1982. Student Mary Baldwin Coll., 1947-48, U. Tex., 1948-51; B.A., Baylor U., 1951; postgrad. So. Meth. U., 1952. Saleswoman Viking Travel Agy., 1975, Unimark Travel, Dallas, 1976; ind. agt. T.H.E. Travel Agy., Dallas, 1977—. Mem. Highland Park PTA Sch. Bd.; active Crystal Charity, Dallas Summer Musicals, Symphony League, Les Femmes du Monde, Maureen Connally Brinker Found., Dallas Theater Center, Baptist. Clubs: Headliner's, T-BAR-M Racquet. Home: 3631 Asbury St Dallas TX 75205 Office: 11353 Emerald St Dallas TX 75229

MC CARTHY, EDWARD, JR., lawyer; b. Jacksonville, Fla., Jan. 17, 1931; s. Edward and Margaret R. (Durkee) McC.; A.B., Princeton U., 1953; LL.B., U. Colo., 1956; m. Julie Beville Fant, May 18, 1962; children—Mitchell Fant, Beville Durkee, Edward III. Bar: Colo. 1956, Fla., 1959. Ptnr. firm Strang & McCarthy, Montrose, Colo., 1956-59, McCarthy, Adams & Foote, Jacksonville, 1959-68, Freeman, Richardson, Watson, Slade, McCarthy & Kelly, P.A., Jacksonville, 1968-80; sole practice law, 1980—; dir. Five Points Guaranty Bank of Jacksonville, First Guaranty Bank & Trust Co. Jacksonville. Bd. dirs., past pres. Riverside Hosp. of Jacksonville. Mem. Am., Fla., Jacksonville bar assns. Republican. Episcopalian. Clubs: Timuquana Country, Selva Marina Country, Florida Yacht, Univ., River, Highlands Country (N.C.). Home: 4710 Apache Ave Jacksonville FL 32210 also PO Box 2257 Highlands NC 28741 Office: 1238 Frederica Pl Jacksonville FL 32205

MCCARTHY, EDWARD ANTHONY, bishop; b. Cin., Apr. 10, 1918; s. Edward E. and Catherine (Otte) McC.; M.A., Mt. St. Mary Sem. of West, Norwood, Ohio, 1944; Licentiate Canon Law, Cath. U. Am., 1946; D. Canon Law, Lateran U., Rome, Italy, 1947; S.T.D., Angelicum, Rome, 1948. Ordained priest Roman Catholic Ch., 1943; sec. to archbishop of Cin., 1944-65; aux. bishop of Cin., 1965-69; bishop of Phoenix, 1969-76; coadjutor archbishop of Miami, 1976-77; archbishop of Miami, 1977—. Office: 6301 Biscayne Blvd Miami FL 33138

MCCARTHY, HELEN FRANCES, nurse; b. Shreveport, La., Mar. 23, 1938; d. James Bernhart and Martha Elizabeth (Whitten) McC.; B.S., Northwestern State Coll., 1959; cert. U. Colo., 1963. Staff nurse Shumpert Hosp., Willis Knighton Hosp., Shreveport, La., 1959-63; head nurse Cook County Hosp., Chgo., 1963-64; cardiovascular nurse specialist Meth. Hosp., Houston, 1964-76; nurse specialist Quality Control Team, ARA Services, Houston, 1976-79, dir. quality assurance, 1979—; instr. CPR; cons. Am. Cancer Soc. Precinct del. Tex. State Republican Conv., 1974. Mem. Am. Cancer Soc., Am. Heart Assn., Nat. League Nursing, Am. Critical Care Assn., Western Gerontol. Soc. Republican. Roman Catholic. Clubs: Zonta, Chancellors Racquet. Home: 6019 Bankside St Houston TX 77096 Office: 15415 Katy Freeway Suite 800 Houston TX 77094

MCCARTHY, JOHN JOSEPH, physician, educator; b. Indpls., July 15, 1950; s. John Francis and Kathryn Joan (Kenney) McC.; m. Kathryn Ann McCarthy, June 23, 1973; children—Jessica Leigh, Sean Kane. B.S., U. Notre Dame, 1972; M.D., Baylor Coll. Medicine, 1976. Diplomate Am. Coll. Internal Medicine, Am. Bd. Hematology. Intern, Baylor Coll. Medicine, 1976-77, asst. prof. medicine, 1982—; chief resident in medicine Meth. Hosp., Houston, 1980. Co-dir. marathon com. St. Thomas More Parish, Houston, 1984. Recipient Lawrence H. Baldinger award U. Notre Dame, 1968. Mem. Am. Soc. Hematology, Gulf Coast Hematology Soc., Houston Soc. Internal Medicine, Tex. Med. Soc. Roman Catholic. Avocations: outdoor athletics; travel; music; literature. Home: 4402 Kingfisher Houston TX 77035 Office: Dept Internal Medicine Hematology Baylor Coll Medicine 6565 Fannin St Room 930 Houston TX 77030

MCCARTHY, MARY ELIZABETH, psychologist; b. N.Y.C., Feb. 22, 1937; d. Timothy and Beatrice (Hester) McC. B.A. in Polit. Sci. and Psychology, Hunter Coll., 1964; M.S. in Guidance and Counseling, Fordham U., 1965; M.A. in Philosophy, U. Santo Tomas, 1971, Ph.D. in Clin. Psychology, 1970. Tchr., dir. guidance Notre Dame Acad., N.Y.C., 1965-66; career placement counselor Bklyn. Coll., 1966-68; asst. prof. counseling and edn., Ateneo de Manila U., Quezon City, Philippines, 1968-71; dir. Epoch House, Friends Med. Sci. Research Ctr., Inc., Balt., 1971-72; lectr. U. Ife, Ile-Ife, Nigeria, 1972-73; assoc. prof. psychology Coll. of V.I., St. Thomas, 1973-80; postdoctoral fellow dept. psychology, Fla. State U., Tallahassee, 1979-80; planner, evaluator Fla. Dept. Health and Rehab. Services, 1980-81; program dir. Santa Rosa Geriatric Residential Ctr., Milton, Fla., 1981; psychologist Western Tidewater Mental Health Ctr., Suffolk, Va., 1982-83; dir. regional alcohol rehab. program Western Tidewater Community Services Bd., Suffolk, 1983; clin. services mgr. Chesapeake Community Services Bd., Va., 1983—; group therapist St. Vincent's Home for Boys, Bklyn., 1965-66; professorial lectr. psychology U. Santo Tomas, Manila, 1969-71; spl. lectr. theology, psychology, Assumption Coll., Makati, Rizal, Philippines, 1970-71; spl. rep. Catholic Children and Family Services, Walla Walla, Wash., 1970; prof. psychology Carribean Ctr. Advance Studies, Carolina, P.R., 1975-76; dir. Pastoral Guidance Ctr., St. Thomas, 1975-79; psychologist forensic unit Fla. State Hosp., Chattahoochee, 1980; cons. Peninsula Alcohol Services, Hampton and Newport News, Va., 1982-83; adj. faculty St. Leo Coll., Langley AFB, Hampton, 1983, Ft. Eustis, Newport News, 1983-85, Norfolk State U., 1983-85, Golden Gate U., Langley AFB, 1984-86; lectr., panelist, seminar participant. Contbr. articles to profl. publs. Mem. Adv. Council Community Drug Edn., Dept. Edn., St. Thomas, 1974-75, Community Mental Health Planning Com., St. Thomas, 1975, State Mental Health Alcoholism and Drug Dependency Manpower Devel. Task Force, 1978, Sr. Companion Program Adv. Council, 1985-86, Gerontology Curriculum Adv. Com. Tidewater Community Coll., 1985-86, Task Force on Refugee Resettlement, Tidewater, 1985-86; bd. dirs. V.I. Council on Alcoholism, 1975-79, v.p., 1976-78; bd. dirs. St. Dunstan's Episcopal Sch., St. Croix, V.I., 1977, Antilles Sch., St. Thomas, 1979, Alzheimer's Disease and Related

Disorders Assn., Hampton Rds., Va., 1983—; corr. sec. Headstart Policy Council, 1984-85. Grantee Consortium on Research Tng., U.S. Office Edn., 1976, V.I. Commn. on Aging, 1978; USPHS fellow, 1979-80; recipient cert. of appreciation Philippine Mental Health Assn. Mem. Am. Psychol. Assn., Am. Assn. Marriage and Family Therapy, Gerontol. Soc. Am., Am. Soc. Pub. Adminstrn. Democrat. Roman Catholic. Avocations: writing, gardening, travel, collecting cultural artifacts. Home: 5639 Picadilly Ln Portsmouth VA 23703

MC CARTIN, THOMAS RONALD, newspaper publishing company executive, hotel and resort developer; b. Jersey City, June 15, 1934; s. James A. and Margaret V. (Kelly) McC.; m. Ann Daley, Feb. 8, 1958; children—Margaret, Maureen, Michele, Michael, Matthew. Asst. dir. advt. Los Angeles Times, 1959-74; v.p. sales Washington Post, 1974-76, exec. v.p. Dallas Times Herald, 1975-80, pres., 1980-81, pub. and chief operating officer, 1981-83; founder, pres. Times Mirror Nat. Mktg., 1983-85; pres. Criswell Mktg. Co., 1985—. Trustee, Marymount Coll.; mem. exec. com. Center Mktg. and Design, North Tex. State U.; chmn. council Coll. Communication, U. Tex., mem. adv. bd. Sch. Mgmt.; mem. internat. bd. dirs. Up with People; bd. dirs. United Way, Dallas; bd. dirs. North Tex. Commn., Internat. Irish Cultural Inst., Children's Hosp., Dallas County Hist. Soc., St. Paul Hosp. Found., Dallas, Dallas Citizen Council; bd. dirs., chmn. fin. bd. dirs. Salvation Army, Dallas; mem. cultural com. Goals for Dallas; trustee Dallas Museum Fine Arts; vice chmn. TACA; bd. dirs., bd. govs. Dallas Symphony Orch.; exec. com. Dallas Opera; mem. Tex. Bus. Com. for Arts; pres. Palos Verdes Peninsula (Calif.) Adv. Council, 1971-73. Served with USN, 1951-55. Decorated Knight of Malta; recipient cert. and key of appreciation City of Los Angeles, 1973, The First Proclamation, City of Rancho Palos Verdes, 1974; Obelisk award for arts City of Dallas, 1981; named Father of Year, Dallas, 1983. Mem. Met. Sunday Newspapers (dir.), Newspaper Advt. Bur., Am. Assn. Newspaper Reps. (v.p. 1964-65), Navy League (dir. Dallas/Ft. Worth chpt.). Roman Catholic. Clubs: Congressional Country, Nat. Press (Washington); Dallas, Chaparral, City, Dallas Press, Salesmanship, Royal Oaks Country (Dallas); Headliners (Austin).

MCCARTNEY, ALAN PARKER, public safety officer, paramedic, fire protection and safety specialist; b. Newton, Mass., Mar. 17, 1956; s. Parker Gladstone and Barbara (Nelson) McC.; m. Dana Sue Floyd, May 9, 1981. A.A.S. in Fire Protection, N.H. Vocat. Tech. Coll., 1977; B.A. in Human Relations, Salem Coll., 1979, B. Social Work, 1979; B.S. in Fire Protection and Safety, Okla. State U., 1980. Cert. hazard control mgr.; cert. healthcare safety profl.; nat. registered paramedic. Fire/safety analyst Phillips Petroleum Co., Borger, Tex., 1981-84; firefighter, paramedic Fire Dept. City of Mansfield, Tex., 1984-85; pub. safety officer/paramedic Dept. Pub. Safety, City of Forest Hill, Tex., 1985—; vol. fire marshall City of Fritch, Tex., 1981-84. City councilman, Fritch, 1983-84. Mem. Nat. Fire Protection Assn., Soc. Fire Protection Engrs., Am. Soc. Safety Engrs., Internat. Assn. Fire Chiefs. Democrat. Congregationalist. Home: 1617 Edge Hill Rd Benbrook TX 76126-2901 Office: City of Forest Hill Dept Public Safety 6800 Forest Hill Ave Forest Hill TX 76140

MC CARTNEY, R(OBERT) ALLEN, county correctional official, government consultant, business executive; b. Phila., July 13, 1952; s. Daniel Joseph and Marion K. (Inman) McC. A.A. in Adminstrn., cert. in corrections, Bucks County Community Coll., 1972; B.S. in Adminstrn., Trenton State Coll., 1974; M.S. in Adminstrn., U. Louisville, 1976, postgrad. law sch., 1982—; postgrad. law sch. Oxford U. (Eng.), 1983—. Research asst. Nat. Crime Prevention Inst., U. Louisville, 1975-76, instr. Sch. Justice Adminstrn., 1982-83, Ky. Dept. Justice, Frankfort, 1976-81; advisor to Ecuador, 1985; exec. asst. to sec. for corrections Jefferson County Corrections Dept., Louisville, 1981—; v.p. Ins. Concepts, Inc., Louisville, 1983-84; govtl. cons. local, state and fed. orgns.; auditor AMA's health standards, Commn. on Accreditation for Corrections; trainer Ala. Sheriff's Assn., Montgomery, Nat. Sheriff's Assn., Washington; chmn. program com. on local adult detention 1982 Congress of Correction, Toronto, Can. Mem. ABA, Am. Correctional Assn. (com. local adult detention 1980-81). Democrat. Episcopalian. Lodge: Masons. Author: (with W.F. Osterhoff) Detention Facility Fire Safety, 1981; Fire Prevention and Life Safety Curriculum, Kentucky Bureau of Training, 1981. Editor: (with Ken Kerle) Local Jail and Detention Center Resource Handbook, 1981, Grapevine, 1979-80, Am. Jail Assn. Report, 1980—. Contbr. articles to profl. jours. Home: 11731 Nansemond Ct Louisville KY 40223 Office: 600 W Jefferson St Louisville KY 40202

MC CARTY, RAYMOND M., lawyer, poet; b. Council Bluffs, Iowa, July 27, 1908; s. Cecil and Eva Frances (Wilson) M.; student S.W. Mo. State Tchrs. Coll., 1931-33; LL.B., So. Law U., Memphis, 1948, Memphis State U., 1967; m. Margaret Esther Burton, Mar. 23, 1942. Chief clk. State Social Security Commn., Springfield, Mo., 1937-39; admitted to Tenn. bar 1948; with U.S. Army C.E., Memphis, 1939-72, chief planning and control br. Real Estate div., 1953-72; pvt. practice law, Memphis, 1972—. Served with AUS, 1942-43. Recipient Countess d'Esternaux Gold medal award for poetry, 1950. Mem. Poetry Soc. Tenn. (hon. mem., organizer, 1st pres., poet laureate 1977-78), World Poetry Soc. Intercontinental (Disting. citation for Poetry 1970, honoree Mid-South Poetry Festival 1983), Avalon World Arts Acad. (hon.), Ala. Writers Conclave, Nat. Fedn. State Poetry Socs., Acad. Am. Poets, Ala. State Poetry Soc., Am. Legion, Tenn. Bar Assn., Fed. Bar Assn. (sec. Memphis chpt. 1971-72), Nat. Assn. Ret. Fed. Employees. Baptist (deacon, chmn. deacons 1965-66). Author: Harp in a Strange Land, 1973; Trumpet in the Twilight of Time, 1981; The Wandering Jew, 1984; contbr. poems to profl. jours. and poetry mags. Home and office: 1247 Colonial Rd Memphis TN 38117

MCCASKILL, CLARENCE HARLAN, JR., college dean; b. Pinehurst, N.C., July 27, 1943; s. Clarence Harlan and Hessie (Hogan) McC. B.S., East Carolina Coll., 1965, M.A., 1972. Tchr. bus. Pinehurst City Sch., 1965-66; learning lab. coordinator Sandhills Community Coll., Carthage, N.C., 1966-68, dir. evening programs, 1968-72, dean continuing edn., 1972—. Mayor Town of Candor, N.C., 1977-81; pres. Montgomery County Cancer Soc., 1979-83; chmn. Montgomery County Democratic Party, 1981-85; bd. dirs. N.C. Cancer Soc., 1981—; mem. N.C. Dem. Exec. Com., 1981-85. Recipient Montgomery County Disting. Service award Montgomery County Jaycees, 1977. Mem. N.C. Community Coll. Adult Edn. Assn., N.C. Adult Edn. Assn., Phi Delta Kappa, Kappa Delta Pi. Democrat. Presbyterian. Avocations: travel; theater; piano and organ. Home: Box 254 Candor NC 27229 Office:: Sandhills Community Coll Route 3 Box 182-C Carthage NC 28327

MCCASLAND, BARNEY CLIFTON, JR., geologist; b. Movice Tex., July 12, 1917; s. Barney Clifton and Mabel (Smith) McC.; m. Frances Titus, June 11, 1939; children—Barney III, Pike, Scott, Gail, Ross. B.S., Tex. Tech., 1938. Roustabout, Conoco, Hobbs, N.Mex., 1938-39; surveyor Robert H. Ray Co., 1939-41; party chief Ark. Fuel Oil Co., 1941-46; geologist Cities Service Oil Co., U.S., Africa and Can., 1946-63; cons. geologist, 1963—. Mem. Am. Assn. Petroleum Geologists, Am. Inst. Profl. Geologists, Soc. Ind. Profl. Earth Scientists, Can. Soc. Petroleum Geologists. Avocations: travel, mountain climbing, hiking. Home: 2202 Sinclair Midland TX 79705 Office: PO Box 115 Midland TX 79702

MCCASLIN, JOHN CALVIN, exploration editor, geologist; b. Tulsa, June 2, 1926; s. Leigh Spires and Helen Benton (Edmundson) McC. B.S. in Geology, Okla. U., 1950. Geol. editor Oil and Gas Jour., Tulsa, 1951-64, exploration editor, 1964—, editor Internat. Petroleum Ency., 1970—. Served with USAF, 1944-46, 50-51. Recipient Disting. Service award West Tex. Geol. Soc., 1978. Mem. Am. Assn. Petroleum Geologists, Soc. Exploration Geophysicists, Tulsa Geol. Soc., Oklahoma City Geol. Soc. Republican. Episcopalian. Home: 1257 E 29th St Tulsa OK 74114

MCCAUGHAN, (JAMES) RUSSELL, lawyer; b. nr. Indianola, Iowa, June 18, 1907; s. Ralph Lee and Dorothy (Manbeck) McC.; m. Mary Louise Hyatt, Aug. 5, 1933; children—Mary Louise McCaughan Robison, Ralph Lee. A.B., U. Fla., 1932, M.A., 1935, LL.B., 1940. Bar: Fla. 1940. Practiced in Ft. Lauderdale, Fla., 1940-84; ptnr. firm English, McCaughan & O'Bryan, then of counsel, now ret.; atty. Fla. Condominium Commn., 1972-73. Mem. Broward County Bd. Pub. Instrn., 1947-48, Broward County Law Library Com., 1955-65; bd. dirs. Broward County YMCA, 1952-62, So. Scholarship and Research Found., 1964-71, Fla. Bar Found., 1971-73; trustee Fla. So. Coll., Lakeland, 1967-77. Served to lt. USNR, 1943-46. Mem. ABA, Broward County Bar Assn., Fla. Bar (gov. 1958-65), Phi Kappa Phi, Phi Alpha Delta, Phi Kappa Tau. Democrat. Methodist. Contbg. author: Florida Will Drafting and Estate Planning Manual; Florida Real Property Practice Manual; author: Florida Will and Trust Drafting. Home: 2754 Timbertrails Circle Tallahassee FL 32308

MCCAULEY, CLEYBURN LYCURGUS, lawyer; b. Houston, Feb. 8, 1929; s. Reese Stephens and Elizabeth Ann (Burleson) McC.; m. Elizabeth Kelton McKoy, June 7, 1950; children—Stephens Francis, Lillian Elizabeth, Cleyburn, Lucy Annette. B.S., U.S. Mil. Acad., 1950; M.S. in Indsl. Engring., Stanford U., 1959; J.D., Coll. William and Mary, 1970. Bar: D.C. 1971, Va. 1970, Tex. 1970, U.S. Ct. Claims 1971, U.S. Tax Ct. 1971, U.S. Supreme Ct. 1973. Commd. 2d lt. U.S. Air Force, 1950, advanced through grades to lt. col., 1971; ret., 1971; sole practice, Washington, 1975—. Mem. Fed. Bar Assn., Va. Bar Assn., D.C. Bar Assn., IEEE, AIAA, Am. Soc. Quality Control, Phi Alpha Delta. Office: 1900 S Eads St Suite 1007 Crystal House 1 Arlington VA 22202

MCCAULEY, LOUIS WILLARD, English educator; b. Arlington, Va., Oct. 20, 1951; s. Louis Willard and Tessie Ann (Strunk) McC.; m. Susan Kay Geuder, Aug. 12, 1978 (div. Dec. 1983). Cert. U. Stuttgart, 1973; B.A., George Mason U., 1974, M.A., 1978. Cert. tchr., Md., Colo., Fla. Tchr., dept. chmn. The German Sch., Potomac, Md., 1975-81; instr. English as a second lang. The Spring Inst., Denver, 1981-82, U. Colo., Boulder, 1982-83; reseacher U. Miami, 1983-84, head instr. EF Lang. Coll., Miami, 1984-85; tchr. English as a second lang. Dade County Pub. Schs., Fla., 1985—; test item writer Ednl. Testing Service, Princeton, N.J., 1983—. Mem. Linguistic Soc. Am., Tchrs. English to Speakers of Other Langs. Avocations: chess, tennis, languages. Home: 8941 SW 142d Ave #2-26 Miami FL 33186

MCCLAIN, HELEN COFER, state official, consultant; b. Norcross, Ga., Aug. 10, 1933; d. Henry Howell and Mardell (Merritt) Cofer; m. John Dozier Knight, May 28, 1955 (div. Sept. 1958); 1 child, Frank Knight (dec.); m. Charles Luke McClain, Sr., May 28, 1983. B.S. in Edn., Auburn U., 1954; M.Edn., Ga. State U., 1963, Edn. Specialist, 1965. Tchr., Gwinnett County, Norcross, Ga., 1954-66; supr. Ga. Dept. Edn., Atlanta, 1966—; cons. Ga. Bus. Edn. Assn., Atlanta, 1979—; dir. FBLA-PBL, Inc., Washington, 1984—. Editor Newsletter for Advisors, 1972-76. Named Educator of Yr., Ga. Bus. Edn. Assn., 1973. Mem. Am. Vocat. Assn., Ga. Vocat. Assn., Nat. Bus. Edn. Assn. (program chair 1976-80), Delta Pi Epsilon. Republican. Baptist. Avocations: skiing; sewing; reading. Home: 213 S Peachtree St Norcross GA 30071 Office: Ga Dept Edn 1752 Twin Towers E Atlanta GA 30334

MCCLAIN, JOHN NOWLIN, JR., lawyer; b. Chattanooga, July 28, 1949; s. John Nowlin and Alma (Forster) McC.; m. Frances Ann Norwood, Jan. 1, 1982; children—John Nowlin III, Andrew Norwood. A.B. in Polit. Sci., U. N.C., 1971; J.D., U. Tenn., 1974. Bar: N.C. 1974. Ptnr. Hatch, Little, Bunn, Jones, Few & Berry, Raleigh, N.C., 1974—. Chmn. bd. Wake County Council on Aging, Raleigh, 1979—; bd. dirs. Eastern N.C. Multiple Sclerosis Soc., Raleigh, 1983—, chmn. bd., 1985—; bd. dirs. N.C. Heart Assn., Wake County Health Adv. Bd., Raleigh. Served with U.S. Army, 1970-76. Mem. ABA, N.C. Bar Assn., Assn. Trial Lawyers Am., N.C. Acad. Trial Lawyers. Lodge: Kiwanis. Avocations: jogging; reading; making furniture. Office: Hatch Little Bunn Jones Few & Berry 327 Hillsborough St Raleigh NC 27602

MCCLAIN, NATHANIEL JEROME, police investigator, minister; b. Jacksonville, Fla., July 17, 1949; s. Mancy Jerome and Nettie (Sims) McC.; m. Kate Gwendolyn Sanders, Mar. 27, 1971; 1 son, Nathaniel Jerome. A.A., Fla. Jr. Coll., 1977. Ordained minister, Baptist Ch., 1980. Police patrolman Jacksonville (Fla.) Police Dept., 1971-74, detective, 1974-78, mem. sheriff's internal investigation unit, 1978-84, mem. aviation unit, 1984-85, fixed and rotary wing pilot, 1985—; pastor Julington Bapt. Ch., Jacksonville, Fla., 1980—; family counselor. Served with U.S. Army, 1967-70; Vietnam. Decorated Air medal. Mem. Fraternal Order of Police, Brotherhood of Black Police Officers, Goodwill Union (past v.p., pres.). Lodges: Masons, Jacksonville Eastern Star. Office: 501 E Bay St Room 213 Jacksonville FL 32202

MCCLANAHAN, KATHY LYNN, advertising agency executive; b. Dallas, Apr. 4, 1948; d. Allen William and Dorothy (Boone) McC. B.S.E., U. Ark., 1970; postgrad. UCLA, 1971-73, Pepperdine U., 1971-73. Artist, Ark. Dept. Parks and Tourism, 1971-73; art/promotion dir. Sta. KATV, Little Rock, 1973-75; artist Santa Fe Internat. Corp., Orange, Calif., 1975-77; art dir. N.Am. Creative Advt., Santa Monica, Calif., 1977-79; owner, creative dir. Art & Design Studio, Fayetteville, Ark., 1980—; speaker on advt. and TV prodn. to area high schs. Recipient Gold Addy awards, 1980, 81, 82; numerous awards for advt. design and campaigns. Mem. N.W. Ark. Advt. Fedn., Kappa Kappa Gamma. Finalist Nat. Opera Co. auditions, 1974; soloist with Los Angeles Symphony, 1974. Office: Art & Design Studio 114 S College Ave Suite C Fayetteville AR 72701

MCCLANE, JOHN WILLIAM, III, optometrist; b. Fernandina Beach, Fla., Aug. 6, 1952; s. John W. Jr. and Doris (Lynn) McC.; m. Linda Karen Smith, June 21, 1975; children—John William IV, David Thomas. B.S., U. Fla., 1975; O.D., Ill. Coll. Optometry, 1979. Optometrist, McClane & Stubits, O.D., P.A., Fernandina Beach, 1979—, v.p., 1979-85, pres., 1985—. Mem. N.E. Fla. Optometrists Soc. (sec. 1984-85, v.p. 1985-86; Outstanding Service award 1981-82, 83), Am. Optometrists Assn., Fla. Optometrists Assn., Ga. Optometrists Assn. Democrat. Methodist. Lodge: Rotary (sec. 1985-86). Avocations: boating; skiing. Home: 1410 Atlantic Ave Fernandina Beach FL 32034 Office: McClane & Stubits OD PA 6 S 14th St Fernandina Beach FL 32034

MCCLEARY, MICHAEL LEROY, auto dealer; b. Baton Rouge, Aug. 1, 1944; s. Milton Aubrey and Kathren (Whitehead) McC.; m. Peggy Ford, Aug. 15, 1964; children—Natalie Jan, Mellissa Dawn, Michael Aubrey. Student, La. State U. Gen. sales mgr. Nelson & East Ford, Zachary, La., 1969-79; gen. mgr. Capital Transp. Corp., Baton Rouge, 1980-83, cons., 1983; owner, operator McCleary-Efferson Chevrolet, St. Francisville, La., 1983—. Bd. dirs. La. Sch. Bd. Assn., Baton Rouge, 1982—; panelist Nat. Sch. Bds. Assn., 1983; mem. State Supt. Tchr. Task Force, 1983; liaison Spl. Olympics, 1983; pres. East Baton Rouge Parish Sch. Bd., 1983—; bd. dirs. Keep Am. Beautiful, 1983; past mem. Baton Rouge Planning and Zoning Commn. Served with USAR, 1963-69. Mem. Assn. La. Transit Operators, Southwest Transit Assn. Democrat. Methodist. Club: Rotary (pres. 1976-77). Office: McCleary Efferson Chevrolet 211 Commerce St PO Box 1160 Saint Francisville LA 70775

MCCLEARY, YEADON DELGAR, insurance company executive; b. Carrollton, Ga., Mar. 19, 1955; s. Yeadon Delgar and Clarice (Eubanks) McC.; m. Linda Dobbs, July 31, 1976; 1 son, Yeadon Delgar III. B.A., Hampton Inst., 1975. Sr. cons. Allstate Ins. Co., Atlanta, 1976—; exec. v.p., mktg. dir. Am. Info. Consortium, 1982—; v.p. mktg. On Campus Mag., 1983—. Mem. Kappa Alpha Psi. Democrat. Baptist. Home: 2605 Arundel Rd College Park GA 30337 Office: Allstate Ins 4549 Chamblee-Dunwoody Rd Atlanta GA 30338

MCCLELLAN, JANE MARTHA, English educator; b. Jenkins, Ky., Nov. 6, 1931; d. Jack Frank and Opal (Looney) McC.; m. Michael G. Becker, Sept. 25, 1950 (dec. 1964); children—Michael McClellan Becker, Jane Becker Self, Susan Lynn Becker Scott. B.A., U. South Fla., 1965, M.A., 1967; Ph.D., Fla. State U., 1976. Asst. prof. Hillsborough Community Coll., Tampa, Fla., 1968-73; assoc. prof. Brunswick Jr. Coll., Ga., 1975-82, South Ga. Coll., Douglas, 1982-85; tchr. Forest High Sch., Ocala, Fla., 1985—. Recipient Law Sarett award U. South Fla., 1964, 1965, Research award U., 1974. Mem. MLA Nat. Council Tchrs. English, Gold Key Soc., Phi Delta Kappa. Key Soc. Episcopalian. Avocations: plinking, writing. Home: PO Box 1683 Douglas GA 31533 Office: Forest High Sch 1416 SE Ft King Ocala FL 32670

MCCLELLAN, L. E. (RENIE), lawyer, magistrate. b. Richmond, Tex., Jan. 28, 1954; d. William C. and Patricia A. (Cole) McC. B.A., U. Tex., 1976, J.D., 1979. Bar: Tex. 1979, U.S. Dist. Ct. (no. dist.) Tex. 1982; cert. specialist in criminal law Tex. Bd. Legal Specialization. Asst. dist. atty. Dallas County, Tex., 1980-82; sole practice, Dallas, 1982-85; magistrate Dallas County Criminal Dist., Tex., 1985—. Mediator, vol. Juvenile Probation Dept., Dallas, 1983-84. Mem. Dallas Bar Assn. (criminal law sect.), Dallas County Criminal Bar Assn., Tex. Criminal Def. Lawyers Assn., Garland Bar Assn. Republican. Methodist. Home: 14 Hill Top Dr Cedar Hill TX 75104 Office: Dallas County Govt Ctr Dallas TX 75243

MCCLELLAN, SANDRA HARLEY, clinical pharmacist; b. San Antonio, Jan. 8, 1958; d. Russell Arnold and Catherine Ward (Cahill) Harley; m. Richard Jordan McClellan, Oct. 20, 1984. B.S. in Pharmacy, Med. U. of S.C., 1981, Pharm. D., 1983. Registered pharmacist, S.C. Staff pharmacist Anderson Meml. Hosp., S.C., 1983—, clin. coordinator pharmacy, 1985—; part-time clin. faulty Anderson Family Practice Ctr., 1984—. Vol. pharmacist Anderson Area Health Clinic, 1984—. Mem. S.C. Soc. Hosp. Pharmacists (newsletter editor 1984—), Am. Diabetes Assn., Am. Soc. Hosp. Pharmacists, Rho Chi. Presbyterian. Avocations: travel; water skiing; sailing; people. Home: 414 Central Ave Anderson SC 29621 Office: Pharmacy Dept Anderson Meml Hosp 800 N Fant St Anderson SC 29621

MCCLELLAND, JAMES RAY, lawyer; b. Eunice, La., June 21, 1946; s. Rufus Ray and Homer Florene (Nunn) McC.; m. Sandra Faye Tate, Feb. 6, 1971; children—Joseph Ray, Jeffrey Ross. B.S., La. State U., 1969, M.B.A., 1971, J.D., 1975. Bar: La. 1975, U.S. Ct. Appeals (5th cir.) 1976, U.S. Dist. Ct. (ea. dist.) La. 1976, U.S. Dist. Ct. (we. dist.) La. 1976. Assoc. Aycock, Horne, Caldwell, Coleman & Duncan, Franklin, La., 1975-78, ptnr., 1978—; dir. Bayou Bouillon Corp., Cotten Land Corp. Mem. exec. com. Democratic Party, St. Mary Parish, 1980—; del. La. Dem. Party, 1982, 84. Mem. La. State Bar Assn. (ho. of dels. 1982—, law reform com. 1984—), St. Mary Parish Bar Assn. (pres. 1978-79), Order of Coif. Club: Rotary (pres. 1981-82). Home: PO Box 268 Franklin LA 70538 Office: PO Box 592 Franklin LA 70538

MC CLELLAND, KENNETH CHARLES, hospital executive; b. Whittier, Calif., Dec. 9, 1953; s. Leroy Charles and Muriel Kerr (Spaulding) McC.; B.S. in Edn., Oklahoma City U., 1976; B.S. in Health Care Adminstrn., Okla. Baptist U., 1978; m. Susan Patricia Latham, May 21, 1976. Asst. minister music and youth First Bapt. Ch., Borger, Tex., 1974; admitting supr. Deaconess, Hosp., Oklahoma City, 1975-77, patient services mgr., 1977-83, mgr. info. resources, 1983—; adv. bd. Okla. Home Health, Inc. Chmn. personnel com., then fin. com. Britton Bapt. Ch., Oklahoma City, 1979—, chmn. deacons, 1981—. Mem. Hosp. Fin. Mgmt. Assn. (advanced), Okla. Soc. Hosp. Social Work Dirs., Oklahoma City Council Hosp. Social Work Dirs. Republican. Home: 11104 N Blackwelder St Oklahoma City OK 73120 Office: 5501 N Portland St Oklahoma City OK 73112

MCCLELLAND, TOMMY BENNETT, JR., marine corps officer; b. Houma, La., Apr. 4, 1956; s. Tommy Bennett and Agnes Charlotte (Krippendorff) M. B.A. in Math., The Citadel, 1976; M.A. in Human Resources Mgmt., Pepperdine U., 1981; M.A. in Internat. Politics, Monterey Inst. Internat. Studies, Calif., 1982. Commd. 2d lt. U.S. Marine Corps, 1977, advanced through grades to capt.; series comdr. Recruit Tng. Bn., Parris Island, S.C., 1978-81; fgn. area officer Def. Lang. Inst., Monterey, 1981-82, U.S. embassy, Tunis, Tunisia, 1982-83; tng. officer 2d Marine Div., Camp Lejeune, N.C., 1983-84, comdg. officer, 1985—. Contbr. articles to profl. jours. Decorated Navy Achievement medal, Armed Forces medal; recipient Superior Service award Marine Corps League, 1973, U.S. Embassy, 1984, numerous others. Mem. Nat. Rifle Assn. (disting. expert). Baptist. Club: Eastern Carolina Citadel (pres. 1984—) (Jacksonville, N.C.). Avocations: piloting; judo; languages.

MCCLEVEY, KAREN ANN, librarian; b. Albany, N.Y., July 1, 1949; d. Edward Anthony and Florence Helen (Schultz) Murphy; children—Stephanie, Matthew. B.A., Va. Poly. Inst. & State U., 1971; M.L.S., U. Md., 1974. Tchr. French and English, Friendly High Sch. (Md.), 1967-68; children's reference librarian George Mason and Sherwood Regional Libraries, Annandale, Va., 1975-78; abstractor Nat. League of Cities, Washington, 1981-82; substitute tchr., librarian Fairfax County Schs. (Va.), 1982—. Vol. Reston Regional Pub. Library, Arlington Central Pub. Library. Mem. ALA Va. Library Assn., Southeast Library Assn., D.C. Library Assn., Soc. Children's Book Writers, Phi Kappa Phi, Delta Zeta. Republican. Club: Cherry Hill Writers Group. Home: 7511 Long Pine Dr Springfield VA 22151

MCCLINTIC, GEORGE VANCE, III, petroleum engineer, real estate broker; b. Sayre, Okla., Jan. 27, 1925; s. George Vance and Myrtle Jane (Rogers) M.; m. Margaret Ruth, 1945; m. Betsy Ross, 1969 (dec. 1977); children—Kathern, Michael; m. Judy Prince, 1978 (dec. 1985). B.S., Okla. U., 1950. Warehouseman Mid Continent Supply Co., 1950-52, dist. machinery sales mgr., 1952-56; with Sabre Drilling Co., also v.p. 3 Rig Co., 1956-58; Okla. dist. mgr. Republic Supply Co., 1958-59; v.p. Chief Oil Tool Co., Oklahoma City, 1959-62; in real estate, Oklahoma City, 1962—; owner, mgr. McClintic Realty, and Engring. Cos., 1966—; with Jack Callaway Co., 1968-70; pres., engring. officer Geothermal Engring. and Operating Co., Oklahoma City and Carson City, Nev., 1972-76; petroleum engr. SW Mineral Energy Co., Oklahoma City, 1976-79; pres. Flat Tire Caddie Co., Oklahoma City, 1979—. Republican candidate for 5th Dist. Congress, 1976; mayoral candidate for Oklahoma City, 1983. Served with USAAF, 1943-45; ETO. Decorated D.F.C., Air medal with 11 clusters, ETO medal with 5 Campaign bronze stars. Clubs: Oklahoma, Petroleum. Lodge: Masons. Inventor flat tire caddie. Office: Flat Tire Caddie Co 2619 N Harrey #3 Oklahoma City OK 73103

MCCLINTOCK, KATHY, publicist, journalist, art director; b. Franklin County, Ill., July 22, 1951; d. John W. and Phyllis Jean (Bennett) McClintock; m. Larry G. Harris, Mar. 28, 1986. B.S. in Communications, So. Ill. U., 1972. Instr. Shawnee Community Coll., Ullin, Ill., 1972-73; instr. English lit. Vienna (Ill.) Correctional Center, 1972-73; promotional mgr. The Oak Ridge Boys, Inc., Hendersonville, Tenn., 1973-82, artist devel. mgr., 1983—; pvt. practice publicity and pub. relations, 1979-80. Mem. Nat. Acad. Rec. Arts and Sci., Country Music Assn., Nashville Entertainment Assn., Nat. Acad. Video Arts and Scis., Kappa Tau Alpha. qIG Home: 917 Wemberton Dr Donelson TN 37214Office: 329 Rockland Rd Hendersonville TN 37075

MC CLINTOCK, SIMMS, polit. scientist, educator; b. Lake Village, Ark., July 10, 1927; s. William Richey and Lilly (Simms) McC.; B.A., Hendrix Coll., 1951; M.A., Columbia, 1953. Coordinator social studies Crossett (Ark.) High Sch., 1953-65; asso. prof. polit. sci. U. Central Ark., Conway, 1966—, chmn. dept., 1976-77. Faculty adviser Ark. Model UN, 1966—. Faulkner County Hist. Soc. Sec., bd. dirs. Carmichael Found.; rep. Ark. Constl. Conv., 1979-80. Served with USNR, 1945-48, 51-52. Recipient Distinguished award Ark. Jr. C. of C., 1962; named Ark. Tchr. of Year, U.S. Office Edn. and Look Mag., 1963. John Hay fellow Columbia, 1965-66. Mem. Classroom Tchrs. Ark. (pres.), Ark. Edn. Assn., Faulkner County Hist. Soc. (pres.), Phi Delta Kappa. Episcopalian. Author: Guide To Teaching Citizenship, 1961; Guide To Teaching Economics, 1965; A Critical Analysis of the Constitutions of Arkansas for 1836, 1861, 1864, and 1868, 1978; A Critical Analysis of the Constitution of Arkansas for 1868 and 1874 and the Proposed Constitutions of 1918 and 1970, 1978. Home: 120 Baridon St Conway AR 72032

MCCLINTOCK, WILLIAM THOMAS, hospital administrator; b. Pittsfield, Mass., Oct. 23, 1934; s. Ernest William and Helen Elizabeth (Clum) M.; m. Wendolyn Hope Eckerman, June 22, 1963; children—Anne Elizabeth, Carol Jean, Thomas Daniel. B.A., St. Lawrence U., Canton, N.Y., 1956; M.B.A., U. Chgo., 1959, M.H.A., 1962. Prodn. planner Corning Glass Works, Corning, N.Y., 1959-60; adminstrv. asst. Univ. Hospitals of Cleve., 1962-65; asst. adminstr. Presby. Hosp., Whittier, Calif., 1965-68; asst. adminstr. Kaiser Found. Hosp., San Francisco, 1968-70; assoc. dir., exec. dir. Conn. Hosp. Planning Commn., New Haven, 1970-76; dir. continuing edn., lectr. sch. health studies U. N.H., Durham, 1976-77; regional mgr. Tex. Med. Found., Austin, 1977-81; adminstr. Schick Shadel Hosp., Fort Worth, 1981—; cons. M.Dixon, M.D., J.D., Provo, Utah, Cleve., 1977-80. Served to 1st lt. U.S. Army, 1957. Fellow Coll. Health Care Execs., Am. Coll. Addiction Treatment Adminstrs., Royal Soc. Health (Eng.); mem. Am. Hosp. Assn., Tex. Hosp. Assn., Am. Mgmt. Assn. Republican. Presbyterian. Lodge: Rotary, Unity No. 9. Avocations: reading; gardening; photography. Home: 828 Saddlebrook South Bedford TX 76021 Office: Schick Shadel Hosp 4101 Frawley Dr Fort Worth TX 76118

MCCLOSKEY, GARY NEIL, priest, religious educator; b. S.I., N.Y., Feb. 24, 1951; s. William Bannon and Julia Margaret (Dempsey) McC. B.A., Villanova U., 1973; M.A., Catholic U. Am., 1976, postgrad., 1976-77; Ph.D., U. Miami, 1984. Ordained priest Roman Catholic Ch., 1977. Dir. student activities Biscayne Coll., Miami, 1977-79, instr. religious studies, 1977-80, coordinator Title III, asst. to pres., 1979-81, asst. prof. religious studies, 1980-81; dir. religious edn., sch. minister St. John Neumann High Sch., Golden Gate, Fla., 1981-84; asst. to acad. v.p. St. Thomas U., 1984-85, asst. acad. v.p., 1985—; grant writing cons. Biscayne Coll., 1981-84; instr. pastoral ministry program Diocese of Orlando, Fla., 1982—. Mem. state coordinating com. Pax Christi Fla., 1983—; mem. Network, Catholic Social Justice Lobby, 1981. Title III grantee, 1980-83. Mem. Am. Ednl. Research Assn., Assn. Profs. and Researchers in Religious Edn., Religious Edn. Assn., Religious Research

Assn., Assocs. for Research in Pvt. Edn., Assn. Supervision and Curriculum Devel., Phi Delta Kappa. Republican. Lodge: K.C. (state chaplain Columbian Squires 1981-85). Office: 16400 NW 32nd Ave Miami FL 33054

MCCLUNG, JAMES DAVID, lawyer, business executive; b. Lamesa, Tex., July 16, 1943; s. Jack W. and Ruby H. (Brown) McC.; student Northeast La. State Coll., 1961-62; B.S. B.A. cum laude, Bethany Nazarene Coll., 1965; J.D. cum laude, Baylor U., 1973; m. Linda D. Nelson, Feb. 12, 1966; children—LeEtta, Dennis, Pammy, Jenny. Admitted to bar; asso. comml. law sect. firm Jackson, Walker, Winstead, Cantwell & Miller, Dallas, 1973-76; corporate counsel Austin Industries, Inc., Dallas, 1976-79, v.p. law, 1979-84, sr. v.p. adminstrn., 1984-85, pres., 1985—; v.p., dir. Brit. Am. Inst. Co.; dir. Austin Energy, Inc., Austin Land & Devel. Inc. Bd. dirs. Austin Industries Polit. Action Com; Austin Indsl., Coastal Indsl. Constructors, Coastal Constrn. Co. sec. bd. trustees Bethany Nazarene Coll.; mem. curriculum adv. com. Legal Asst. Program; dist. adv. bd. Ch. of the Nazarene, mem. gen. bd.; dist. Home Missions Bd., Bd. Ch. Extensions; mem. exec. bd. Richardson C. of the Nazarene, also bldg. com. chmn., fin. com., tchr. Served with USAF, 1965-71; Vietnam. Decorated Air medals (6). Recipient Am. Jurisprudence awards, Tex. Assn. Def. Council award, numerous scholarships. Mem. Am. Bar Assn., State Bar Tex., Dallas Bar Assn., Omicron Delta Kappa. Republican. Articles editor: Baylor Law Rev., 1973. Home: 21210 Atascocita Pl Atascocita TX 77346 Office: 3971 Beaumont TX 77704

MC CLUNG, JIM HILL, mfg. co. exec.; b. Buena Vista, Ga., Nov. 8, 1936; s. Jim Hill and Marjorie (Oxford) McC.; m. Jo Patrick, July 5, 1958; children—Jim Hill, Karen Mareese. B.A., Emory U., 1958; M.B.A., Harvard U., 1964. With Lithonia Lighting div. Nat. Service Industries, Inc., Conyers, Ga., 1964—, now pres. Served with USAF, 1958-62. Mem. Young Pres.'s Orgn. Methodist. Office: Lithonia Lighting Box A Conyers GA 30207

MC CLUNG, LUTHER THERMAN, oil operator, rancher; b. Kerens, Tex., Oct. 30, 1909; s. Luther T. and Carrie J. (Miller) McC.; student public schs., Dallas; m. Evelyn Louise Loe, Aug. 6, 1927; children—Lucian Louise McClung Richardson, Barbara Ann McClung Wells. Circulation mgr. Courier-Times, Tyler, Tex. and Ft. Worth Press, 1927-40; asst. bus. mgr. Longview (Tex.) News-Jour., 1927-40; gen. contractor Luther T. McClung and McClung Constrn. Co., 1940-48; pres. McClung Oil Corp., 1958—; pres. Western States Equipment Co., Midland, Tex.; owner, operator Luther T. McClung 4M Ranch, Kiowa, Okla. and Comanche County, Tex., 1948—. Mem. Am. (dir. 1950-56), Tex. (pres. 1950, dir. 1948-52) Angus assns. Home: Route 2 Box 99X Comanche TX 76442

MCCLURE, CHARLES RICHARD, supt. schs.; b. Morgantown, W.Va., Apr. 8, 1935; s. C.W. and Alta M. (Cale) McC.; B.A., W.Va. U., 1957, M.A., 1960; m. Shirley Pat Tallman, July 11, 1964; children—Marilyn, Scott, Mary, Marlin. Tchr., Preston County (W.Va.) schs., 1957-60, supr., personnel dir. fed. programs, 1960-67; program coordinator N. Central W.Va., W.Va. Dept. Edn., 1967-73; adminstrv. asst. Harrison County (W.Va.) schs., Clarksburg, 1974, supt., 1974—. Mem. exec bd. Harrison County United Way. Mem. Am. Assn. Sch. Adminstrs., Nat. Sch. Bd. Assn., Nat. Assn. Supervision and Curriculum Devel., W.Va. Assn. Sch. Adminstrs. (Service award 1979), W.Va. U. Alumni Assn., W.Va. Sch. Bd. Assn., W.Va. Assn. Supervision and Curriculum Devel., Clarksburg C. of C. (edn. com.), Phi Delta Kappa, Phi Mu Alpha Sinfonia. Methodist. Clubs: Clarksburg Lions, Kingwood Rotary, Masons, Shriners. Author papers in field. Home: 402 James St Bridgeport WV 26330 Office: 301 W Main St Clarksburg WV 26301

MCCLURE, JANET KAY, marketing executive; b. Dallas, Dec. 16, 1955; d. Colman David and Edith Bernice (Jackson) McClure; m. Ira Edward Montgomery, III, Aug. 8, 1981. Student, U. Tex.-Austin, 1977-79, Richland Jr. Coll., 1976-77, Dallas Fashion Merchandising Coll., 1974-75. Spl. coordinator Daily Texan, Austin, 1978; sales intern Dallas Morning News, 1979; prodn. specialist Leased Jewelry div. Zale Corp., Dallas, 1979-80, advt. mgr., 1980-82, mktg. dir. Mission div., 1982—. Mem. NOW. Democrat. Office: 901 W Walnut Hill Ln Irving TX 75038

MCCLURE, LESLIE ANNE LIGON, real estate company executive; b. Fort Worth, Apr. 11, 1922; d. Joseph Moses and Willie H. (Glasgow) Ligon; divorced; children—Ralston Hugh, Michele Ligon (Mrs. Everett W. Beelman), Anne Melissa (Mrs. John H. Bill). Student Brantley-Draughn, Fort Worth, 1960-61, Real Estate Inst., San Antonio, 1961-62. Salesperson Margie Burch Co., 1960, Beth Carter Realty, Fort Worth, 1962-63, Glen-Walker, Collett & Rigg (name changed to Wm. Rigg Co.), Fort Worth, 1964-65; owner, mgr. Leslie Ligon McClure Realtor, Fort Worth, 1965—. Active Tarrant County Hist. Soc. Mem. Greater Fort Worth Bd. Realtors, Tex. Assn. Realtors, Nat. Assn. Realtors, Fort Worth Jr. League, Ft. Worth Lecture Found. Clubs: Bon Soir, (treas. 1985-86), Met. Women's Republican, Ft. Worth Woman's. Home: 3716 Hamilton Fort Worth TX 76107

MC CLURE, LUCILLE WILMA, marketing researcher; b. Salem, Ill., Feb. 26, 1932; d. Leland G. and Nina Agnes (Branson) Brown; B.S., Fla. So. Coll., 1972; M.B.A., Rollins Coll., 1974; m. Theodore Eugene McClure, Dec. 21, 1948; children—Larry Ray, Theodora Eugena, Gwendolyn Lucille, Emma Jane, Michael Glen. Info. specialist Martin Marietta Aerospace, Orlando, Fla., 1957-78, mktg. specialist, 1978—; adj. prof. mktg. Fla. So. Coll., Orlando, 1977—; mem. industry adv. group Dept. Def., 1982-84. Mem. AIAA (adv. council central Fla. sect. 1974—), Central Fla. Astron. Soc. (pres. 1966-68), Am. Mktg. Assn., Am. Def. Preparedness Assn. Democrat. Lutheran. Clubs: Martin Marietta Mgmt. (historian 1977—, spl. recognition award 1981), Martin Marietta Astronomy (pres. 1966, 78). Contbr. over 200 research bibliographies to profl. publs. Home: 5620 Minaret Ct Orlando FL 32821 Office: PO Box 5837 MP 457 Orlando FL 32855

MCCLUSKEY, GAYLA JACQUE, risk management consultant; b. Enid, Okla., Apr. 5, 1955; d. Jack and S. Andrea (Matthiesen) McC. B.S. in Engring. Tech., Okla. State U., 1977; M.B.A. in Engring. Mgmt., U. Dallas, 1984. Cert. safety profl. Bd. Cert. Safety Profl. Indsl. hygienist Exxon Nuclear Co., Richland, Wash., 1978-79, OSHA, Dept. Lab., Irving, Tex., 1979-81, Mostek Corp., Carrollton, Tex., 1981-82; cons. risk mgmt. Sun Exploration and Prodn. Co., Dallas, 1982—. Chmn. Responsible Citizenship Program, Dallas Women's Coalition, Dallas, 1984—; bd. dirs. Women's Ctr. of Dallas. Mem. Am. Mgmt. Assn., Am. Soc. Safety Engrs., Am. Indsl. Hygiene Assn., Network of Career Women (officer Irving 1980—), Tau Iota Epsilon, Omicron Delta Kappa, Sigma Iota Epsilon (officer U. Dallas 1984—). Methodist. Home: 4211 Madera St CD 3-25 Irving TX 75062 Office: Sun Exploration and Prodn Co 5656 Blackwell St PO Box 2880 Dallas TX 75221

MC COLL, HUGH LEON, JR., banker; b. Bennettsville, S.C., June 18, 1935; s. Hugh Leon and Frances Pratt (Carroll) McC.; B.S. in Bus. Adminstrn., U. N.C., 1957; m. Jane Bratton Spratt, Oct. 3, 1959; children—Hugh Leon III, John Spratt, Jane Bratton. Trainee, NCNB Nat. Bank, Charlotte, 1959-61, officer, 1961-65, v.p., 1965-68, sr. v.p., 1968, div. exec., 1969, exec. v.p., 1970-73, vice chmn. bd., 1973-74, pres., 1974-83; chmn., pres., chief exec. officer NCNB Corp., 1983—; dir. Sonoco Products Inc., Hartsville, S.C., NCNB Corp., The Caroline Corp., Conway, S.C., Ruddick Corp., Charlotte. Former trustee Sacred Heart Coll., Belmont, N.C., St. Andrews Presbyn. Coll., Laurinburg, N.C.; bd. dirs. Microelectronics Center of N.C., U. S.C. Bus. Sch.; bd. mgrs. Charlotte Meml. Hosp. and Med. Center, 1975-81; trustee Heineman Found., Charlotte, 1976—, Queens Coll., Charlotte, U.N.C.-Charlotte Found., chmn. Charlotte Uptown Devel. Corp., 1978-81, 85. Served to 1st lt. USMCR, 1957-59. Mem. Robert Morris Assos., Assn. Res. City Bankers, Am. Bankers Assn., N.C. Bankers Assn. (pres. 1974—), N.C. Council Mgmt. and Devel. Democrat. Presbyterian. Office: One NCNB Plaza Charlotte NC 28255

MC COLLUM, BILL, Congressman; b. Brooksville, Fla., July 12, 1944; s. Ira William and Arline Gray (Lockhart) McC.; B.A., U. Fla., 1965, J.D., 1968; m. Ingrid Mary Seebohm, Sept. 25, 1971; children—Douglas Michael, Justin Randolph, Andrew Lockhart. Admitted to Fla. bar, 1968; partner firm Pitts, Eubanks & Ross, P.A., Orlando, Fla., 1973-80; mem. 97th-99th Congresses from Fla. 5th Dist. Chmn., Republican Exec. Com., Seminole County, Fla., 1976-80, rep. 5th dist., 1977-80. Served with U.S. Navy, 1969-72. Mem. Fla. Bar Assn., Am. Bar Assn., Orange County Bar Assn., Naval Res. Assn., Res. Officers Assn., Fla. Blue Key, Phi Delta Phi, Omicron Delta Kappa, Mil. Order World Wars, Am. Legion. Episcopalian. Club: Kiwanis. Home: 1010 Cathy Dr Altamonte Springs FL 32714 Office: 1507 Longworth House Office Bldg Washington DC 20515

MC COLLUM, BYRON EARL, architect, construction company executive; b. Grand Saline, Tex., Dec. 22, 1951; s. Raymond Earl and Marie (Stubblefield) McC.; student Angelina Coll., 1971, Abilene Christian U., 1972; B.Arch. cum laude, U. Houston, 1976; m. Ellen McCoy, Aug. 5, 1972; children—Matthew Lance, Anthony Bryce, Kristi Michelle. Draftsman, H. Kammerling, Lufkin, Tex., 1971; asso. Robert Brown, Jr., AIA, Tyler, Tex., 1972; asso. Charles Rainey AIA, Houston, 1972; drafting supr. Allied Tower Co., Inc., Houston, 1973; project mgr., estimator Ed Hilla AIA, Houston, 1973-74; project mgr./estimator Loftin Constrn. Co., Inc., Houston, 1975-76; architect, constrn. mgr. Feagin & McCollum Constrn. Co., Lubbock, Tex., 1976-82, also partner; mgr. design and constrn. Joe Feagin Investments, Lubbock, 1980-82; prin. McCollum & Assocs., Dallas, 1983—. Pres., Lubbock Christian Sch. PTA, 1981. Registered architect, Tex. Mem. AIA, Tex. Soc. Architects, Nat. Assn. Home Builders. Author: Old Brenham, 1975. Home: 707 Thompson Dr Richardson TX 75080

MCCOLLUM, JAMES FOUNTAIN, lawyer; b. Reidsville, N.C., Mar. 24, 1946; s. James F. and Dell (Frazier) McC.; m. Susan Shasek, Apr. 26, 1969; children—Audra Lynn, Amy Elizabeth. B.S., Fla. Atlantic U., 1968; J.D., Fla. State U., 1972. Bar: U.S. Ct. Appeals (5th cir.) 1973, Fla. 1972, U.S. Ct. Appeals (11th cir.) 1982. Assoc., Kennedy & McCollum, 1972-73, James F. McCollum, P.A., 1973-77, McCollum & Oberhausen, P.A., 1977-80, McCollum & Rhoades, Sebring, Fla., 1980-83; sole practice, 1983—; pres. Highlands Devel. Concepts, Inc., Sebring, 1982—; v.p. Focus Broadcast Communications, Inc., Sebring, 1982—; mng. ptnr. Highlands Investment Services. Treas., Highlands County chpt. ARC, 1973-76; vestryman St. Agnes Episcopal Ch., 1973-83, chancellor, 1978—; mem. Com. 100 of Highlands County, 1975-83, bd. dirs., 1985-86; chmn. bd., treas. Central Fla. Racing Assn., 1976-78; life mem. Fla. Jaycees Internat. Senate, 1977—, presdl. counselor Fla., 1984—; chmn. Leadership Sebring, 1984. Life mem., past pres. Highlands Little Theatre, Inc. Recipient citation ARC, 1974; Presdl. award of appreciation Fla. Jaycees, 1980-81, 82; named Jaycee of Year, Sebring Jaycees, 1981; Outstanding Local Chpt. Pres., U.S. Jaycees, 1977. Mem. ABA, Am. Trial Lawyers Assn., Comml. Law League Am., Am. Arbitration Assn. (comml. arbitration panel), Fla. Bar (Fla. Bar Jour. com.), Highlands County Bar Assn. (chmn. legal aid com.), Greater Sebring C. of C. (dir. 1983—, v.p. 1985). Republican. Episcopalian. Club: Lions (dir. 1972-73). Office: 129 S Commerce St Sebring FL 33870

MCCOMAS, JAMES DOUGLAS, univ. pres.; b. Prichard, W.Va., Dec. 23, 1928; s. Herbert and Nell (Billups) McC.; B.S., W.Va. U., 1951, M.S., 1960; Ph.D., Ohio State U., 1962; m. Francis Adele Stoltz, May 11, 1961; children—Cathleen, Patrick. High sch. tchr., 1951-54, 56-60; from asst. prof. to prof., head dept. agrl. and extension edn., prof. ednl. adminstrn. head dept. elem. and secondary edn. N.Mex. State U., 1961-67; dean Coll. Edn. Kans. State U., 1967-69; dean U. Tenn., 1969-76, also prof. continuing and higher edn.; pres. Miss. State U., 1976—. Field reader U.S. Office Edn.; chmn. Southeastern Manpower Adv. Com.; mem. exec. com. Southeastern Conf.; mem. appeals bd. Nat. Council Accreditation of Tchr. Edn.; mem. Nat. Accreditation Council for Agencies Serving the Blind; mem. exec. com. Land Grant Deans Edn.; chmn. com. on equal opportunity Nat. Assn. Land Grant Colls. and State Univs.; asso. mem. Nat. Manpower Adv. Com., Gov.'s Manpower Adv. Com.; chmn. council of presidents State Univs. Miss.; pres. So. Land Grant Colls. and Univs.; chmn. Tenn. Council Deans Edn.; mem. Miss. Jr. Coll. Commn. Pres. Belmont West Community Assn., Miss. Econ. Council, East Miss. Council; mem. Am. Council on Ednl. Community Leadership Devel. and Acad. Adminstrn.; civilian aide Sec. of Army. Served with M.C., AUS, 1954-56. Mem. Am. Sociol. Assn., Am. Higher Edn. Assn., Am. Acad. Polit. and Social Sci., Kappa Delta Pi, Gamma Sigma Delta, Alpha Zeta, Omicron Delta Kappa, Phi Kappa Phi, Beta Gamma Sigma. Home: PO Box J Mississippi State MS 39762

MCCONATHY, LARRY EUGENE, marketing executive, consultant; b. Houston, June 7, 1951; s. Clarence Eugene and Lynnette (Barlow) McC.; m. Carolyn Sue Hazel, July 16, 1977; 1 son, Thomas Eugene. B.B.A., Tex. A&M U., 1973, M.B.A., 1974, M.S., 1975. Regional sales rep. Wadsworth Pub., Houston, 1975-77; asst. to gen. mgr. Santa Fe Tech., Houston, 1977-78; bus. devel. mgr. Earl & Wright Engrs., Houston, 1978-80; v.p. mktg. Service Machine Group, Houston, 1980-83; mktg. mgr. Raymond Offshore, Houston, 1983—. Republican. Episcopalian. Home: 1040 Richelieu St Houston TX 77018

MCCONNELL, JOAN, dean school of nursing; b. Rayville, La., Aug. 15, 1930; d. Charles Emmett and Linnie (Averitt) McC. Diploma in Nursing, South Highland Infirmary, 1951; B.S. in Nursing Edn., U. Ala.-Tuscaloosa, 1955; M.S. in Psychiat. and Mental Health Nursing, Tex. Woman's U., 1972; Ed.D. in Adult Edn., U. So. Miss., 1981. Asst. dir. Sch. Nursing, Mobile Gen. Hosp., Ala., 1965-66; dir. assoc. degree nursing Jones County Jr. Coll., Ellisville, Miss., 1966-73; asst. prof. nursing U. So. Miss., Hattiesburg, 1973-75, U. S. Ala., Mobile, 1975-81; dean Sch. Nursing, William Carey Coll., Hattiesburg, 1981—. Active LWV, New Orleans. Mem. Am. Nurses Assn., Sigma Theta Tau. Home: 2522 Caswell Ln Metairie LA 70001 Office: Sch Nursing William Carey Coll 2700 Napoleon Ave New Orleans LA 70115

MCCONNELL, MICHAEL ARTHUR, judge; b. Ft. Worth, Jan. 15, 1947. B.A. in History, Loyola U. of the South, 1969; J.D., U. Tex.-Austin, 1975. Bar: Tex. 1976, U.S. Dist. Ct. (no. dist.) Tex. 1976, U.S. Dist. Ct. (ea. dist.) Tex. 1981, U.S. Dist. Ct. (we. dist.) Tex. 1982, U.S. Ct. Appeals (5th cir.) 1980, U.S. Ct. Appeals (11th cir.) 1981. Law clk. U.S. Dist. Ct. for No. Dist. Tex., Ft. Worth, 1976-77; assoc. Cantey, Hanger, Gooch, Munn & Collins, Ft. Worth, 1977-81, ptnr., 1981-83; U.S. Bankruptcy judge No. Dist. Tex., Ft. Worth, 1983—. Mem. ABA, Tex. Assn. Bank Counsel, Ft. Worth-Tarrant County Bar Assn. (adv. dir. 1980), Ft. Worth-Tarrant County Young Lawyers Assn. (bd. dirs. 1977, pres. 1980), Tex. Young Lawyers Assn. (Tarrant County dir. 1982-83, chmn. adminstn. of justice special com. 1982-83, chmn. annual mtg. com. 1982-83, chmn. adminstrn. of justice com. 1983-84). Office: 206 US Courthouse Fort Worth TX 76102

MCCONNELL, MITCH, U.S. Senator; b. Sheffield, Ala., Feb. 20, 1942; s. Addison Mitchell and Julia (Shockley) McC.; children—Eleanor Hayes, Claire Redmon, Marian Porter. B.A. with honors, U. Louisville, 1964; J.D., U. Ky.-Lexington, 1967. Chief legis. asst. to Senator Marlow Cook, Washington, 1968-70; sole practice law, Louisville, 1970-74; dep. asst. U.S. Atty. Gen., Washington, 1974-75; Jefferson County judge/exec., Louisville, 1978-85; U.S. Senator from Ky., 1985—. Contbr. articles to profl. jours. Chmn. Jefferson County Republican Party, Louisville, 1973-74; co-chmn. Nat. Child Tragedies Coalition, 1981; chmn., founder Ky. Task Force on Exploited and Missing Children, 1982; pres. Ky. Assn. County Judge/Execs., 1982; adv. bd. Nat. Inst. Justice, 1982-84; mem. The Pres.'s Partnership on Child Safety, 1985—. Served with USAR. Named Conservationist of Yr., League Ky. Sportsmen, 1983; recipient commendation Nat. Trust for Historic Preservation, 1982, Cert. of Appreciation, Am. Correctional Assn., 1985. Baptist. Avocations: fishing; cooking. Office: Suite 120 Russell Senate Office Bldg Washington DC 20510

MCCONNELL, PATRICK EDWARD, investment and ins. co. mktg. exec.; b. Mpls., Sept. 20, 1947; s. Paul Edward and Lois Mae (Hanson) McC.; student U. Minn., Duluth, 1966-67, 70-71, U. Houston, 1967-68, N. Tex. State U. Grad. Sch. Bus.; M.B.A., M.S. in Fin. Services, Am. Coll., Bryn Mawr, Pa., 1985; m. Sharon Lee Henderson, Aug. 1, 1970; children—Matthew Patrick, Mark Ryan. Ins. salesman New York Life, Duluth, 1971-76; regional mgr. bus. markets Investors Diversified Services, Ft. Worth, from 1976; with IDS/Am. Express, Inc. Sec., St. Vincent's Sch. Bd., Euless, Tex., 1981-83. Served to maj. Army N.G., 1964—, C.L.U.; chartered fin. cons. Mem. Internat. Assn. Fin. Planners, Am. Soc. C.L.U.s (chmn. membership, pres. Ft. Worth chpt.). Republican. Episcopalian. Home: 1804 Lincolnshire Dr Bedford TX 76021 Office: 807 Texas St Fort Worth TX 76102

MCCOOL, EARL CLAYTON, JR., psychology educator, radio archives curator, marriage counselor; b. Kokomo, Ind., Sept. 28, 1922; s. Earl Clayton and Helen Kathryn (Hansel) McC.; m. Rosalee Mizer, July 30, 1945; children—Duane Clayton, Clayton Allen. Student Ind. U., 1945-46; B.S., Okla. Baptist U., 1949; Ed.M., U. Okla., 1950. Life teaching cert., Okla. Tchr., Shawnee, Okla., 1950-52; spl. agt. FBI, Washington, 1952-60; instr. psychology Jacksonville State U. (Ala.), 1960—; marriage counselor; curriculum counselor. Sponsor Nat. Republican Congl. Com.; mem. Nat. Assn. Chiefs of Police. Served to 1st lt. USAAF, 1942-45. Recipient personal letters of commendation from J. Edgar Hoover, FBI, 1956, 57. Mem. NEA, Ala. Edn. Assn., Soc. Former Spl. Agts. FBI, DAV, Am. Legion, Kappa Delta Pi. Baptist. Club: Gadsden Country, Fraternal Order Police, Masons. Home: 417 Wildhaven Circle Gadsden AL 35901 Office: N Pelham Rd 4-D Jacksonville AL 36265

MCCORD, GUYTE PIERCE, JR., former judge; b. Tallahassee, Sept. 23, 1914; s. Guyte Pierce and Jean (Patterson) McC.; student Davidson Coll., 1933-34; B.A., J.D., U. Fla., 1940; m. Laura Elizabeth Mack, Dec. 16, 1939; children—Florence Elizabeth, Guyte Pierce III, Edward LeRoy. Bar: Fla. 1940. Practiced in Tallahassee, 1940-60; dep. commr. Fla. Insl. Commn., 1946-47; pros. atty. Leon County, 1947-48; asst. gen. counsel Fla. Pub. Service Commn., 1949-60; judge 2d Jud. Circuit Fla., Tallahassee, 1960-74; judge Ct. Appeal 1st Dist. Fla., 1974-83, chief judge, 1977-79. Mem. Appellate Ct. rules com. Supreme Ct. Fla., 1977-78, ct. structure commn., 1978-79. Pres., Murat House Assn., Inc., 1967-69; bd. dirs. Fla. Heritage Found., 1969-70, mem. exec. com., 1965-69; elder First Presbyterian Ch., Tallahassee, 1960—, trustee, 1981—. Served to comdr. USNR, 1942-46, 52-53. Mem. Ret. Officers Assn., ABA, Fla. Bar, Tallahassee Bar Assn., Fla. Conf. Circuit Judges (sec.-treas. 1970, chmn. 1972), Phi Delta Phi, Sigma Alpha Epsilon. Club: Kiwanis (dir. 1958-59); Andrew Jackson's staff Springtime Tallahassee, 1984—. Home: 502 S Ride Tallahassee FL 32303 Office: PO Box 4121 Tallahassee FL 32315

MCCORD, JAMES OSCAR, optometrist; b. Jackson, Tenn., June 16, 1934; s. Thomas Daniel and Katy Bell (Craven) McC.; m. Martha Sue Vaughan, June 25, 1954; children—Leigh Ann, Lisa Vaugan. Student Lambuth Coll., 1953; O.D., So. Coll. Optometry, Memphis, 1957. Ptnr., Robbins & McCord, Dyersburg, Tenn., 1959—. Commr., Dyer County, Tenn., 1978—. Served with U.S. Army, 1958-59. Fellow Tenn. Acad. Optometry (pres. 1978-79). Republican. Methodist. Lodge: Moose (gov. 1976-77). Avocation: bass fishing. Home: 1850 Lake Rd Dyersburg TN 38024 Office: Robbins & McCord 575 Tickle St Dyersburg TN 38024

MCCORD, KAREN LYNNE, counselor; b. Ames, Iowa, Aug. 18, 1954; d. Robert Allen and Hazel Irene (Courtright) McC. B.A., Wheaton Coll., Ill., 1976; M.A., Azusa Pacific U., Calif., 1984. Horsemanship instr. Honey Rock Camp, Three Lakes, Wis., 1976; youth dir. Calvin Presbyterian Ch., San Jose, 1976-78; counselor Arbutus Youth Assn., San Jose, Calif., 1978-82; adminstr. asst. Inst. for Marriage and Family Studies, San Jose, 1982-83; sec. testing technician Psychiat. Med. Group, San Jose, 1983-84; youth family counselor Kay County Youth Services, Ponca City, Okla., 1985—. Sec. Abundant Life Class, St. Paul's Methodist Ch., Ponca City, 1985. Mem. Am. Assn. Counseling and Devel., Am. Assn. for Marriage and Family Therapy (assoc. mem.), Christian Assn. Psychol. Studies, Nat. Women's Studies Assn. Democrat. Methodist. Avocations: horsemanship, bicycling, aerobic dance, camping, canoeing, sewing, cross stitch, needlework. Home: 2500 Bonnie Ponca City OK 74601 Office: Kay County Youth Services 415 W Grand Ponca City OK 74601

MC CORD, STEWART NELSON, college administrator, minister; Atlanta, July 19, 1935; s. Walter W. and Elsie M. (Moles) McC.; m. Mary Ina Miller, May 29, 1959; children—Kelly Maureen, Peter Andrew. B.A. in History, Asbury Coll., 1957; M.Div., Emory U., 1961; Ed.M., U. Fla., 1973, Ed.S. in Curriculum, 1974, Ed.D., 1976. Tchr. world geography and Am. history Headland High Sch., East Point, Ga., 1958-59; ordained to ministry United Methodist Ch., 1961; asso. pastor and dir. ednl. program City Meth. Ch., Gary, Ind., 1967-69; pastor Congregational Ch., Thawville, Ill.; tchr. social studies Onarga (Ill.) High Sch., 1969-70; pastor non-denom. Community Ch., Keystone Heights, Fla., 1970-73; asst. prin. elem. sch., Keystone Heights 1973-74; instrnl. team leader, chmn. social studies curriculum design com. Lincoln Middle Sch., Gainesville, Fla., 1974-77; prof. tchr. edn. Nova U., Ft. Lauderdale, Fla., 1976-79, dir. adj. faculty for tchr. edn., 1977-79, practicum advisor edn. leaders, 1985—; coordinator external studies Northwood Inst., 1985—; pres., chief adminstrv. officer research and tng. Palm Beach Research and Devel. Inst., Inc., West Palm Beach, Fla., 1980-85. Author: Modern Curriculum Design, 1978. Served as chaplain U.S. Army, 1961-67. U.S. Dept. Labor grantee, 1979-80. Mem. Assn. Supervision and Curriculum Devel., Am. Assn. Sch. Adminstrs., Phi Delta Kappa, Kappa Delta Pi. Democrat. Home: 4001 Shelley Rd South West Palm Beach FL 33407 Office: Northwood Inst 2600 N Military Trail West Palm Beach FL 33409

MC CORD, WILLIAM CHARLES, diversified energy company executive; b. San Antonio, Apr. 1, 1928; s. Sam Byard and Helen (Schoepfer) McC.; B.S. in Mech. Engring., Tex. A. and M. U., 1949; m. Margaret Ann Lancaster, Oct. 17, 1947; children—Kathleen (Mrs. Gary Burnett), Martha (Mrs. Steven Pennington), Billy, Helen (Mrs. Craig Curry), Elizabeth (Mrs. David Paschal), Richard, Douglas, James, Quannah, Korrin Li, Minta Ann. With Enserch Corp. (formerly Lone Star Gas Co.), 1949—, dir. bldg. mgmt., 1965-67, v.p. Dallas div., 1967, sr. v.p. operations, 1968-70, pres., prin. exec. officer, 1970-77, chmn., pres., 1977—; sr. v.p. Nipak, Inc., chem. subsidiary, Dallas, 1967—; dir. Republic Bank Dallas, Republic Bank Corp., Tex. Employers' Ins. Assn., Employers Casualty Co. Past pres., mem. exec. bd. Circle Ten council Boy Scouts Am., 1972-73, mem. nat. exec. bd.; bd. dirs. Tex. Research League, now chmn.; bd. dirs. Dallas Citizens Council, State Fair Tex., Children's Med. Center Dallas; trustee Southwestern Med. Found. Mem. Am. Petroleum Inst. (dir.), Tau Beta Pi. Baptist (deacon). Office: 300 South St Paul Dallas TX 75201

MC CORKLE, ALLAN JAMES, ins. co. exec.; b. Shreveport, La., Aug. 29, 1931; s. Adolphus James and Eugenia Jane (Johnson) McC.; B.S., Fla. State U., 1956; m. Rosemary Louise Hollander, June 15, 1957; children—Kimberly Rae, Scott Allan, Holly Jane. Safety engr., corp. sales rep. Liberty Mut. Ins. Co., Roanoke, Va., and Jacksonville, Fla., 1956-68; founder, pres. various mobile home dealerships, Fla., 1965—; pres. Mobile Am. Corp., Jacksonville, Mobile Am. Ins. Group, Inc., Jacksonville, 1968—, Mobile Am. Village, Inc., Jacksonville, 1969—, Fortune Ins. Co., Jacksonville, 1972—, Fortune Life Ins. Co., Phoenix, 1971—; dir. Fla. Ins. Guaranty Fund. bd. govs. Fla. Ins. Exchange, 1979-83. Chmn., Mass Transit, 1971; mem. adv. com. Jacksonville Planning Bd., 1971—. Bd. dirs. Jacksonville Transp. Authority. Served with AUS, 1948-52. Named to Top Producers Club Liberty Mut., 1963-71, Liberty Leaders Club for number 1 sales result in U.S., 1964. Mem. Fla. Mobile Home Assn., Fla. Assn. Domestic Ins. Cos. (v.p. 1978-80, pres. 1980-81, dir. 1978-83), Cummer Gallery (life), Jacksonville Art Mus. (life), Fla. State Alumni Assn. (pres. 1964), Jacksonville C. of C., Alpha Tau Omega, Kappa Tau Kappa. Democrat. Roman Catholic. Clubs: Big Tree Racquet; River, Ponte Vedra (Jacksonville). Contbr. articles on mobile home industry to various publs. Office: Gulf Life Tower Jacksonville FL 32207

MCCORKLE, BRANDT HALBERT, physician; b. Amarillo, Tex., Nov. 14, 1953; s. Jack Warren and Madalon Rose (Herren) McC.; m. Janell Simpson, May 11, 1973; children—Ryan, Megan, Sarah. B.S., Harding U., 1975; D.O., Tex. Coll. Osteo. Medicine, 1979. Intern, Okla. Osteo. Hosp., Tulsa, 1979-80; gen. practice osteo. medicine, Mansfield, Tex., 1980-82, Mineola, Tex., 1982—. Deacon, Ch. Christ, Mineola, 1982—, Bible Sch. tchr., 1982—. Mem. Am. Osteo. Assn., Tex. Osteo. Med. Assn., Am. Coll. Gen. Practitioners. Republican. Avocation: tennis. Home: Route 4 Box 126 Mineola TX 75773 Office: McCorkle Med Clinic Mineola TX 75773

MCCORMACK, JOHN MICHAEL, haircutting company executive; b. Queens, N.Y., Sept. 11, 1944; s. John Michael and Norah (Kissane) McC.; student N.Y. State Mil. Acad., 1965, N.Y. Inst. Fin., 1969; m. Maryanne Warren, Mar. 15, 1976. Mem. N.Y.C. Police Dept., 1966-69; with Walston & Co., mems. N.Y. Stock Exchange, 1969-72; sales mgr. Wascomat of Am., 1972-76; founder, pres., chmn. bd. Visible Changes, Inc., haircutters, Houston, 1977—, also dir., pres. Visible Changes N.W., Visible Changes of Meml., Inc., Visible Changes San Jacinto, Visible Changes Willowbrook Inc., Visible Changes Pasadena, Inc., Visible Changes Almeda, Inc., V.C. Mgmt. Service Bur., Inc., Fascination Inc., McCormack Oil Co.; mem. Intercoiffure. Visible Changes Inc. named to list of 500 fastest growing cos. in U.S., Inc. Mag.; featured in Money Mag. Mem. Houston Democratic Forum. Served to 1st lt. USAR, 1963-68. Democrat. Roman Catholic. Office: 1303 Campbell Rd Houston TX 77055

MCCORMACK, LOWELL RAY, oil producer, lecturer graphoanalyst; b. Ladonia, Tex., Oct. 26, 1925; d. Lowell and Orianna (McDonnold) Coney; student Rutherford Met. Coll., Dallas, 1962, U. Tex., Arlington and Dallas, Eastfield Coll., Dallas; M. Graphoanalyst, Internat. Graphoanalysis Soc.; m. Paul H. McCormack, June 4, 1948; children—Sharron Ann, Lowell Henry. Bookkeeper, Jot-Em-Down Gin Corp., Pecan Gap, Tex., 1947, Shedd-Bartush Foods, Dallas, 1948-52; acct., credit mgr. J.P. Ashcraft Co., Inc., Dallas, 1956-65; sec.-treas. Safari Oil Corp., Dallas, 1954—; chief fin. officer, v.p., sec.-treas. Dallas Title Co., 1965-83; instr. graphoanalysis Brookhaven Coll., 1980; acctg. cons. to atty.; lectr., leader seminars on graphoanalysis. Mem. North Tex. Oil and Gas Assn., Internat. Graphoanalysis Soc. (life, v.p. Tex. chpt. 1978, pres. 1979), Internat. Platform Assn. Baptist. Clubs: Zonta (co-chmn. fin. com. 1982, dir., 2d v.p. 1983-84), Internat. Tng. in Communication (pres. 1981, chmn. com. for internat. conv. 1984, workshop leader 1986) (Dallas). Home: 2712 Blanton St Dallas TX 75227

MCCORMICK, CHARLES HOWARD, history educator; b. Akron, June 2, 1932; s. Charles Edward and Ruth (Loew) McC.; m. Margie Lee Kepler, Nov. 4, 1962; B.A. cum laude, Kent State U., 1959; M.A., Yale U., 1960; Ph.D., Am. U., 1971. Contract specialist, contracting officer NASA, Houston, 1961-63; interpretive and research historian U.S. Nat. Park Service, Washington, 1964-68; lectr. Montgomery Coll., Md., 1969-70; mem. faculty Fairmont State Coll. (W.Va.), 1970—, assoc. prof. history, 1973-79, prof., 1979—. Served with USAF, 1952-56; Korea. Woodrow Wilson fellow, 1959; Yale U. fellow, 1960. Mem. Am. Hist. Assn., Orgn. Am. Historians, Phi Alpha Theta, Pi Gamma Mu, Assembly Yale Alumni (rep. 1977-78).

MCCORMICK, CHARLIE AUBRY, communications company executive, educator; b. Naruna, Va., Sept. 8, 1943; s. John Thomas and Ruth Mae (Harris) McC., Sr.; m. Victoria Katherine Ash, June 13, 1970; children—Jennifer Elizabeth, Juliet Elaine. Diploma in Electronics Tech., Danville Tech. Inst., Va., 1963; B.S., Va. Poly. Inst., 1970, M.A., 1972, Ph.D., 1978. Field ops. specialist Western Electric Co., Winston-Salem, N.C., 1963-66, spl. tech. asst., 1967, 68; grad. tchr., research asst. Va. Poly. Inst., Blacksburg, 1970-73; industry economist FTC, Washington, 1973-77, Dept. Energy, Washington, 1977-82, Def. Communications Agy., Arlington, Va., 1982—; adj. prof. Central Mich. U., Fairfax, Va., 1976—; mem. Telecommunications Industry Adv. Group, FCC, Washington, 1982—. Contbr. chpts. to books. Treas. East Hillwood Citizens Assn., Falls Church, Va., 1978, pres., 1979-81; mem. Fairfax County Citizens Adv. Com., 1979-81; mem. adminstrv. bd. Dulin Methodist Ch., Falls Church, 1979-81; v.p., bd. dirs. Colchester Towne Condominiums, Alexandria, Va., 1984—, pres., 1984—. Mem. Am. Econ. Assn. Avocations: swimming, volleyball, hiking, bowling. Home: 7965 Audubon Ave 103 Alexandria VA 22306 Office: Office of Chief Regulatory Counsel-Telecommunications Defense Communications Agy 8th St and S Courthouse Rd Arlington VA 22204

MCCORMICK, DONALD, architect, composer; b. Wilkes Barre, Pa., Aug. 20, 1898; s. Frederick and Emma Laura (Myers) McC.; m. Lillian Tookah Baze, June 18, 1932; 1 child, Sylvia. B.Arch., Cornell U., 1921. Pvt. practice architecture, Tulsa, 1926—. Composer ballet: Romanze Um Wien, 1978. Asst. adminstr. War Assets Adminstrn., Washington, 1944-45; chmn. bd. design Civic Ctr. Project, Tulsa, 1954-60; mem. Planning Commn., Tulsa, 1952-56; pres. Symphony Assn., Tulsa, 1939-40. Fellow AIA; mem. ASCAP (writer). Republican. Club: Summit (Tulsa). Avocation: musical composer. Home: 2735 E 34th St Tulsa OK 74105 Office: 2325 E 13th St Tulsa OK 74104

MCCORMICK, JAMES CLARENCE, business consultant; b. Kaufman County, Tex., Oct. 5, 1924; s. Clarence S. and Mabel R. McCormick; m. Barbara L. Ostling, Jan. 12, 1947; children—Richard J., Sharon L., Patricia C., Michael Shannon Wayne, Kelly Elizabeth. B.B.A. with honors, So. Meth. U., 1949. With Dun and Bradstreet, 1949-55; mem. exec. com., bd. dirs. Eppler, Guerin & Turner Inc., Dallas, 1955—; dir. Ennis Bus. Forms Inc., Leggett & Platt Inc., So. Co., Tex. Commerce Bank, Greater Tex. Fin. Corp., Back Systems Inc., Healthcare USA, Inc., J.D.C. Corp., Software Tchr. Inc., So. Savs. and Loan Assn. Bd. Advisors Southwestern Bapt. Theol. Sem.; v.p., dir. Greater Dallas Council Chs.; past pres., dir. Dallas Soc. Crippled Children; dir. Meth. Bd. Ch. Extension, Tex. Lit. Bd., Dallas Orthopaedic Found. Served to capt. USAF, 1942-46. Mem. Dallas Assn. Security Dealers, N.Y. Stock Exchange, Dallas Assn. Investment Analysts (past pres.), Nat. Fin. Analysts Fedn. (past pres., dir.), Air Force Assn., Alpha Kappa Psi, Beta Gamma Sigma. Methodist. Home: 14145 Valley Creek Dr Dallas TX 75240 Office: Eppler Guerin & Turner Inc PO Box 508 Dallas TX 75221

MCCORMICK, JOHN WILLIAM, JR., optometrist; b. Dumas, Tex., Jan. 31, 1953; s. John William and Mary Annie (Nall) McC.; m. Marilyn Jean Montgomery, June 5, 1976; children—John William, Kathryn Elizabeth, Christopher Harding. B.S., Abilene Christian Coll., 1975; M.S. in Physics, U. Houston, 1979, O.D., 1979. Practice optometry, McAllen, Tex., 1979-80, Dumas, 1980—. Tchr., 1st St. Ch. of Christ, Dumas, 1980—. Mem. Am. Optometric Assn., Tex. Optometric Assn., North Plains Investment Club. Republican. Avocations: reading, bow hunting, fishing, backpacking. Home: 629 Belmont St Dumas TX 79029 Office: PO Box 1538 Dumas TX 79029

MCCORMICK, J(OSEPH) BURKE, lawyer; b. Port Washington, N.Y., Mar. 27, 1957; s. Raymond Daniel and Miriam (Lynch) McC.; m. Sallie Trigg Graham, Oct. 8, 1983. B.S.B.A., Georgetown U., 1978; J.D., Fordham U., 1981. Bar: N.Y. 1981, Tex. 1982. Atty. Texaco Inc., Houston, 1981-85; assoc. Butler & Binion, Houston, 1985—. Mng. editor: Fordham Urban Law jour., 1980-81. Mem. ABA, State Bar of Tex., Houston Bar Assn., N.Y. State Bar Assn., Houston Young Lawyers Assn. Republican. Clubs: Georgetown Univ. Alumni of Houston (v.p. 1985-86), Texas (Houston); N.Y. Athletic. Avocations: sailing; golf. Home: 2510 Southgate Houston TX 77030 Office: Butler & Binion 1600 Allied Bank Plaza Houston TX 77002

MCCORMICK, LEN GARDNER, oil company executive; b. Eldorado, Tex., Oct. 28, 1922; s. Van and Jimmie (Ballew) McC.; m. Vera Sumner, Dec. 2, 1974; 1 son, Van B.; stepchildren—Kathryn Blanton Bettis, Charles V. Blanton, Daniel T. Blanton, Gail Blanton Navarro. B.B.A., Baylor U., 1949, J.D., 1969. Bar: Tex. 1950. City atty. City of Midland (Tex.), 1952-53; ptnr. McCormick, Branum, Cason & Jennings, Midland, Tex., 1953-57; oil operator Len G. McCormick & Assocs., Midland, 1957-60; pres., chmn. bd. Santiago Oil & Gas Co., chmn. bd. Big Bend Ranch Co., Midland, 1960-62; pres., chmn. bd. Santana Petroleum Co., Midland, 1962—; pres., chmn. bd. Gold Metals Consolidation Mining Co., Midland, 1963-67; pres. Pasto Nueva Oil Co., Midland, 1963-67; pres. Beacon Hill Farms, Inc., Houston, 1970—, chmn. bd., 1975—; pres. McCormick Interests, Houston, 1983—. Mem. NFL Alumni, Houston. Served to capt. USMC, 1943-45, 50-52; PTO. Mem. Mid-Continent Oil and Gas Assn., Ind. Petroleum Assn. Am., Am. Assn. Petroleum Landmen, Tex. Ind. Producers and Royalty Assn., Phi Alpha Delta. Methodist. Clubs: Petroleum (Houston and Midland). Office: McCormick Interests 9545 Katy Freeway Suite 490 Houston TX 77024

MC CORMICK, RALPH EUGENE, stationery engraving company executive; b. Nashville, May 11, 1948; s. Mildred Marie (Wells) McC.; A.S., King's Coll., Charlotte, N.C., 1972, acctg. cert., 1971; m. Eugenia Keitt, Aug. 24, 1974; children—Darby Eugenia, Caroline Keitt. Acct., Mercy Hosp., Charlotte, 1972-73; acct. W. A. Buening & Co., Inc., Charlotte, 1973-75, controller, 1975-77, treas., 1977-78, v.p. fin. and adminstrn., 1978—, also dir. Served with U.S. Army, 1966-69. Mem. Nat. Assn. Accts., Am. Mgmt. Assn., Nat. Notary Assn., Purchasing Mgmt. Assn. Episcopalian. Home: 245 Colville Rd Charlotte NC 28207 Office: 2518 Dunavant St Charlotte NC 28203

MCCORMICK, SAM ALLEN, petroleum geologist; b. Norfolk, Nebr., June 11, 1956; s. Kenneth Allen and Janice Lee (Owens) McC.; m. Jo Ellen Groothuis, May 19, 1978; 1 child, Nathan Samuel. B.S., U. Nebr., 1978. Field geologist NSF, McMurdo, Antarctica, 1975; exploration geologist Texaco, New Orleans, 1978-80, Tulsa, 1980-81; chief geologist Robinowitz Oil Co., Tulsa, 1981-83; ind. cons. geologist Tulsa, 1983-84; chief geologist Farmers Energy Corp., Tulsa, 1984—. Bd. dirs. Christ The Redeemer Luth. Ch., Tulsa, 1981—. U. Nebr. Regents scholar, 1974-78. Mem. Am. Assn. Petroleum Geologists, Tulsa Geol. Soc., Okla. Well Log Library, Sigma Xi. Democrat. Avocations: photography; softball; bicycling; handbell choir. Home: 1912 N Eucalyptus Ave Broken Arrow OK 74012 Office: Farmers Energy Corp One West 3d St Suite 400 Tulsa OK 74103

MC CORMICK, WILLIE MAE WARD (MRS. WALTER WITTEN MCCORMICK), city official, retired technical specialist; b. Centerville, Tex. Oct. 17, 1908; d. William Sylvester and Lucy (Marshall) Ward; B.A., Mary Hardin Baylor Coll., 1929; M.A., Hardin Simmons U., 1931; postgrad. So. Methodist U., Tex. Woman's U.; m. Walter Witten McCormick, May 29, 1929; 1 dau., Elizabeth Ward McCormick Wilcox. Tchr. chemistry and algebra Big Spring (Tex.) High Sch., 1941-44, 45-48; weather observer for Dept. Commerce, Big Spring, 1943-44; analytical chemist Dow Chem. Co., Freeport, 1944-45; calculator Chance Vought (now Ling-Temco-Vought), Dallas, 1951-55, structural engr., 1955-63, sci. programmer, 1963-67, tech. specialist, 1967-69; sr. program analyst Univ. Computing Co., Arlington, Tex., 1970-73; adv. council 1st City Savs. of Euless (Tex.); dir. M Bank of Euless, 1985—. Mem. Euless City Council, 1973-85, mayor pro tem, 1975-85; chmn. Trinity River Authority Central Wastewater System; mem. Water Resources Council N. Central Tex.; mem. planning and research council United Way; bd. dirs. Euless Library. Mem. AAAS, Am. Chem. Soc., Math. Assn. Am., Fedn. Am. Scientists, AAUW, Trainmen's Aux. (pres. 1940-41), Internat. Platform Assn., LWV (publicity chmn.), Bus. and Profl. Women, C. of C. (dir.). Democrat. Baptist (tchr. adult dept. Sunday sch.). Clubs: Order Eastern Star (past worthy matron), Oakcrest Woman's, Soroptimist (hon.), Altrusa. Home: 2300 N Main Euless TX 76039

MC COTTER, DINAH WHITE, guidance counselor; b. Windsor, N.C., July 14, 1951; d. Herman Franklin and Elva Una (Leggett) White; B.A., Wake Forest U., 1973; M.Ed., U. N.C., Greensboro, 1975; m. Richard Palmer McCotter, Nov. 25, 1972. Guidance counselor South Fork Elementary Sch., Winston-Salem, N.C., 1975—. Mem. Am. Assn. Counseling and Devel., N.C. Personnel and Guidance Assn., Beech Mountain Assn., Am. Sch. Counselors Assn., N.C. Sch. Counselors Assn. Methodist. Club: Bermuda Run Country. Home: 8559 Brook Meadow Ln Lewisville NC 27023 Office: 4332 Country Club Rd Winston-Salem NC 27104

MC COY, DELORES TOOKES, library administrator; b. Tallahassee, Jan. 25, 1932; d. James and Dorothy (Nash) Tookes; m. Elihu McCoy, June 27, 1953 (div.); children—James Nelson, Ronald Jerome, Bonita Yvonne. A.B., Fla. A&M U., 1952; M.L.S., Fla. State U., 1978. Head Librarian Jackson County Tng. Sch., Marianna, Fla., 1953-54; library asst. reference dept. Coleman Library, Fla. A&M U., Tallahassee, 1965-68; head librarian Salem Elem. Sch., Quincy, Fla., 1968-71; asst. librarian devel. research sch. Fla. State U., Tallahassee, 1971-73, acting dir. media services, 1973, asst. librarian, 1973-77, 78-79, acting dir. media services, 1979-80, dir. media services, 1980—; cons. Chairperson signs and posters com. Fla. Assn. Supervision and Curriculum Devel., 1973; com. mem. Speak Out for Black Community, 1978. Mem. Fla. Assn. Media Edn., Fla. Library Assn., ALA, Am. Assn. Sch. Librarians, Black Caucus, Fla. Assn. Dist. Instructional Materials Adminstrs. Roman Catholic. Home: 3207 Wheatley Rd Tallahassee FL 32304 Office: Devel Research Sch Library Fla State U Tallahassee FL 32304

MCCOY, ELIZABETH POWELL, insurance agent; b. Elba, Ala., Feb. 23, 1917; d. John Eley and Mary Ethel (Hines) Powell; m. Bennie A. McCoy, Apr. 3, 1938; children—Joy M., Jack P. Student pub. schs. office mgr. Manuel Knight Ins. Agy., Zachary, La., 1957-70; agt. State Nat. Life Ins. Co., Baton Rouge, 1970-81; ind. agt., Baton Rouge, 1981-84. Mem. consumer affairs and state law commn. LUPAC, Baton Rouge, 1977-80. Mem. C. of C., Nat. Assn. Ins. Women, Bus. and Profl. Women (pres. 1967-68), Ins. Women Baton Rouge, Women Life Underwriters Conf. (chpt. v.p. 1982), Nat. Assn. Life Underwriters (bd. dirs. 1976-79; mem. com. 1973-83). Democrat. Baptist. Club: Homemakers (sec. 1981—) (Baton Rouge). Home: 2606 Shadowbrook St Baton Rouge LA 70816

MCCOY, ELLEN THORNE, insurance company account representative; b. Cumberland, Md., June 21, 1942; d. Albert Monforte and Georgia Carolina (Gibson) T.; m. William Page McCoy, Nov. 24, 1967. Student U. N.C.-Greensboro, 1960-65. Registered rep. Nat. Assn. Securities Dealers. Group claim processor Aetna Life & Casualty Co., Charlotte, 1967-68, group claim processor, Atlanta, 1968-69, group unit leader, Coral Gables, Fla., 1970-74; group claim processor Provident Life & Accident Co., Greenville, S.C., 1969-70; group sales rater The Travelers Cos., Norfolk, Va., 1975-76, asst. service rep., 1976-76, service rep., 1980-81, group account rep., 1981—. Sec. Deerwood Trace Civic League, Virginia Beach, Va., 1977-79. Mem. Nat. Assn. Ins. Women (pres. 1981-83, local dir. 1983—, asst. profl. ins. woman). Republican. Presbyterian. Office: The Travelers Cos PO Box 1570 Norfolk VA 23501

MCCOY, RAYFORD LYNN, petroleum consultant, technical writer; b. Natchez, Miss., Apr. 1, 1953; s. Rayford Pellum and Ida Mae (Pritchard) McCoy; m. Mary Catherine Callanan, Aug. 21, 1976; children—James Randall, Maureen Elizabeth. B.S. in Geology, Miss. State U., 1975; M.S. in Petroleum Engring., U. of Houston, 1981. Cert. profl. geologists, Tex. Field engr. Dresser Atlas, Tyler, Tex., 1975-77; petroleum H.J. Gruy & Assocs., Houston, 1978-81; tech. writer Gulf Pub. Co., Houston, 1982—; petroleum cons. Patterson Powers & Assocs., Houston, 1981-83, ptnr., v.p., 1981-83, also dir.; petroleum cons. sole practice, 1983—; prin. R.L. McCoy, Petroleum Cons., Houston, 1983—. Author: Microcomputer Programs for Pet Engineering, 1983; Petro Calc III, 1984; Petro Calc VII, 1985. Contbr. articles to profl. jours. Mem. polit. fund raising com. Harris County Republican Party, Houston, 1981; mem. Spring Creek Forest Civic Assn. Tex., 1982; mem. Houston Mus. of Fine Art, 1984. Mem. Am. Assn. of Petroleum Geologist, Soc. of Petroleum Engrs. (nat. tech. editor 1984—), Soc. of Profl. Well Log Analysts, Houston Geol. Soc., Soc. of Exploration Geophysicists (assoc. mem.). Baptist. Avocations: flying; micromputers. Home: 17535 Pinewood Forest Spring TX 77379

MCCOY, WILLIAM, JR., pharmacist, consultant; b. Weeksbury, Ky., July 30, 1941; s. William and Elizabeth (Johnson) McC.; m. Patricia Sargent, July 19, 1963 (div. Feb. 1977); 1 child, Ann Allison. B.S. in Bus., Pikeville Coll., 1962; B.S. in Pharmacy, U. Ky., 1971. Lic. pharmacist; cert. secondary tchr. Tchr., Floyd County Bd. Edn., Prestonburg, Ky., 1962-68; pharmacist Economy Drug Co., Inc., Pikeville, Ky., 1971-74; pharmacist Meth. Hosp. of Ky., Pikeville, 1974-75; owner, pharmacist Profl. Pharmacy, Pikeville, 1975—; dir. Plaza Drug Inc.; cons. Pikeville Surg. Ctr., 1982—. Mem. East Ky. Pharmacist Assn. Democrat. Baptist. Avocations: Trap shooting; fishing; hunting. Home: Box 13 Betsy Layne KY 41605 Office: Professional Pharmacy Profl Associates Bldg Pikeville KY 41605

MC CRACKEN, JAMES BERNARD, JR., government official; b. Huntington, W.Va., Apr. 28, 1947; s. James B. and Elizabeth J. McCracken; B.S. in Mgmt. Scis., Fla. Atlantic U., 1969; M.P.A. in Human Resource Mgmt., Am. U., 1980; m. Jo Ann Wilson, Oct. 30, 1971; children—James Wilson, Joseph Robert, Jon Paul. Adminstrv. intern NOAA, 1970-72; employee devel. specialist Smithsonian Instn., 1972-76; tng. officer Bur. Public Debt, Treasury Dept., 1977-78; sr. employee devel. specialist Naval Facilities Engring. Command, Navy Dept., Alexandria, Va., 1978-84; program mgr. Naval Sea Systems Command, Shipyard Tng. Div., 1984—; chmn. Tng. Officers Conf., Washington, 1975-77. Chmn. tng. com. Alexandria dist. Boy Scouts Am., 1973-78, Weblos den leader, 1982—; chmn. Alexandria City CETA Adv. Council, 1977-78; v.p. Strawberry Hill Civic Assn., 1976-78; pres. Virginia Hills Civic Assn., 1980-83. Recipient EEO award Smithsonian Instn., 1975; various other letter commendations. Mem. Tng. Officers Conf. (Excellence in Leadership award 1977), Am. Soc. Tng. and Devel., Delta Pi Sigma (life). Home: 6501 Berkshire Dr Alexandria VA 22310 Office: Code SEA 072 CG-1 1235 Jefferson Davis Hwy Arlington VA 22202

MCCRACKEN, RICHARD JOSEPH, college administrator, English educator; b. Mineola, N.Y., Dec. 29, 1938; d. Clarence Aloysius and Margaret Elise (Dowling) McC. B.A., St. John's U., 1962, M.A., 1966; postgrad. U. Tex., 1968. Grad. asst. St. John's U., Jamaica, N.Y., 1962-64; asst. prof. English, Incarnate Word Coll., San Antonio, 1964—, dir. pub. relations, 1966-82, asst. to pres., 1982—; bd. govs. St. Peter's-St. Joseph's Children's Home, San Antonio, 1983—; task force target 90 City San Antonio, 1984. Coordinator United Way Bexar County, San Antonio, 1972-80. Recipient 20 Yr. Service medal Incarnate Word Coll., 1984. Mem. Council for Advancement and Support Edn. (past officer, competition coordinator, Appreciation award SW dist. 1983-84), Southland Corp. Pilot Scholarship Program (task force). Democrat. Roman Catholic. Avocations: gourmet cooking; gardening; art; writing. Home: 128 Harrigan Ct Apt 6 San Antonio TX 78209 Office: Incarnate Word Coll 4301 Broadway San Antonio TX 78209

MCCRARY, DOUGLAS L., utility company executive. Pres., chief exec. officer Gulf Power Co., 1983—. Office: Gulf Power Co 75 N Pace Blvd Pensacola FL 32505*

MCCRAY, CURTIS LEE, university president; b. Wheatland, Ind., Jan. 29, 1938; s. Bert and Susan McCray; m. Mary Joyce MacDonald, Sept. 10, 1960; children—Leslie, Jennifer, Meredith. B.A., Knox Coll., Galesburg, Ill., 1960; postgrad. U. Pa., 1960-61; Ph.D., U. Nebr., 1968. Chmn. dept. English, Saginaw Valley Coll., University Center, Mich., 1972-73, dean arts and scis., 1973-75, v.p. acad. affairs, 1975-77; provost, v.p. acad. affairs Govs. State U., Chgo., 1977-82; pres. U. North Fla., Jacksonville, 1982—. Bd. dirs. Jacksonville United Way, 1982—, Sta. WJCT Channel 7 and Stereo 90, Jacksonville, 1982—, Jacksonville Art Mus., 1982—, Meml. Med. Ctr., Jacksonville, 1982—; mem. Downtown Jacksonville Adv. Bd., 1982; hon. dir. Jacksonville Symphony Assn., 1983; mem. Dame Point Bridge Commn., Jacksonville, 1982; mem. Jacksonville High Tech Task Force, 1982; com. chmn. Jacksonville Community Council, 1983. Woodrow Wilson fellow, 1960; Johnson fellow, 1966; George F. Baker scholar, 1956; Ford Found. grantee, 1969; recipient Landee award for excellence in teaching Saginaw State Coll., 1972. Mem. AAUP. Clubs: Torch, River (Jacksonville). Lodge: Jacksonville Rotary. Office: University of North Florida 4567 Saint Johns Bluff Rd Jacksonville FL 32216

MC CRAY, EVELINA WILLIAMS, librarian, researcher; b. Plaquemine, La., Sept. 1, 1932; d. Turner and Beatrice (Gordon) Williams II; m. John Samuel McCray, Apr. 7, 1955; 1 dau., Johnetta McCray Russ. B.A., So. U., Baton Rouge, 1954; M.S.L.S., La. State U., 1962. Librarian, Iberville High Sch., Plaquemine, 1954-70, Plaquemine Jr. High, 1970-75; proofreader short stories, poems Associated Writers Guild, Atlanta, 1982—; library cons. Evaluation Capitol High Sch., 1964, Iberville Parish Educators Workshop, 1980, Tchrs. Core/Iberville Parish, 1980-81. Vol. service Allen J. Nadler Library, Plaquemine, 1980-82; librarian Local Day Care Ctr., Plaquemine, 1978-79. Mem. ALA, La. Library Assn., Nat. Ret. Tchrs. Assn., La Ret. Tchrs. Assn., Iberville Ret. Tchrs. Assn. (info. and protective services dir. 1981—). Democrat. Baptist. Home: PO Box Q Plaquemine LA 70765

MCCREADY, ERIC SCOTT, museum director; b. Vancouver, Wash., Mar. 14, 1941; s. S.W. and Evelyn L. (Brandley) McC.; children—Eric Scott, Alexander Read. B.S., U. Oreg., 1963, M.A., 1968; B.A., U. Pavia (Italy), also U. Oreg., 1965; Ph.D., U. Del., 1972. Vis. lectr. art history U. Victoria, B.C., 1968-69; instr. U. Del., 1970; instr., then asst. prof. art Bowling Green (Ohio) State U., 1972-75, asst. coordinator acad. program devel., 1973-74, asst. to provost, 1974-75; dir. Elvehjem Mus. Art, U. Wis., Madison, 1976-79, Huntington Art Gallery, U. Tex., Austin, 1979—; asst. prof. art history U. Wis., 1975-79; asso. prof. U. Tex., 1979—, sr. lectr. dept. art, 1979—. Author: The Nebraska State Capitol: Its Design, Background and Influence. Decorated knights cross 1st class Royal Order St. Olav, Norway, 1979; Winterthur Mus. Inst. fellow, 1977; mem. faculty, 1978. Mem. Assn. Art Mus. Dirs. (trustee, treas. 1983—), Tex. Hist. Commn. (dir.), Soc. Archtl. Historians (dir.); mem. Tex. Assn. Mus. (council 1983—), Hist. Soc. Austin (nominating com. 1983—), Ams. Soc. (visual arts network bd. 1982—). Episcopalian. Home: 3104 Skylark Austin TX 78757 Office: Huntington Art Gallery 23d and San Jacinto Sts Austin TX 78712*

MCCRELESS, PATRICK PHILLIP, music educator, organist; b. Odessa, Tex., Oct. 9, 1948; s. R. Truman and Doreen (Ferguson) McC.; m. Linda Felton, Aug. 28, 1970; children—Michael Patrick, Erin Elizabeth. B.Mus., U. Mich., 1970, M.Mus., 1973; Ph.D. in Music, Eastman Sch. Music, U. Rochester, 1981. Instr., asst. prof. music Eastman Sch. Music, U. Rochester, N.Y., 1978-83; asst. prof. music U. Tex., Austin, 1983—, div. head music theory and composition, 1985—; organist 1st Presbyterian Ch., Austin, 1984—. Author: Wagner's Siegfried: Its Drama, History, and Music, 1981. Contbr. articles to profl. jours. Summer research grantee U. Tex., Austin, 1984. Mem. Soc. Music Theory, Am. Musicol. Soc. Democrat. Office: Music Dept U Tex at Austin Austin TX 78712

MCCUEN, WILLIAM JAMES, secretary of state; b. Fort Smith, Ark., Aug. 19, 1943; s. Garland Grandville and Sarah Emma (Early) McC.; m. Nancy Sue Hyde. B.S.E., Coll. of Ozarks, 1968; M.S.E. Henderson State U., 1972. Tchr. Pomona Sch. Dist., Calif., 1968-69; tchr., prin. Hot Springs Sch., Ark., 1969-76; county judge Garland County, Ark., 1977-80; commr. of state lands State of Ark., Little Rock, 1981-84, sec. of state, 1985—; alderman Hot Springs City Council, 1973-76. Regional trustee Cystic Fibrosis Found., Ark., Okla., Kans., 1985—, bd. dirs. Ark. chpt., 1982—. Democrat. Presbyterian. Home: PO Box 269 Hot Springs AK 71902 Office: Office of Secretary of State 256 State Capitol Bldg Little Rock AK 72201

MCCULLOH, RICHARD PATRICK, geologist, researcher; b. Oklahoma City, June 6, 1951; s. Robert LeRoy and Gracelyn Elsie (Allert) McC.; m. June Hiroko Urakawa, May 22, 1984. B.S., Okla. State U., 1973; M.A., U. Tex., 1977. Teaching asst. U. Tex., Austin, 1974-76; student geologist Jerry D. Scott, Oklahoma City, 1976, Radian Corp., Austin, 1976-77; editorial asst. Erico Inc., Tulsa, 1977-78; delineation geologist Conoco Minerals, Falls City, Tex., 1978-80; geologist supr. La. Geol. Survey, Baton Rouge, 1980—; research assoc. V, La. State U., Baton Rouge, 1980-82, 1985—. Author: (with others) Louisiana Atlas of Flood Plains, 1983. Sponsor Union Concerned Scientists, 1984—. Mem. Nat. Wildlife Fedn., ACLU, Planned Parenthood, Am. Assn. Petroleum Geologists, Baton Rouge Geol. Soc., AAAS, Phi Kappa Phi, Sigma Gamma Epsilon (v.p. 1971-74). Avocations: natural history; Chinese and Japanese languages. Office: La Geol Survey Box G University Sta Baton Rouge LA 70893

MCCULLOUGH, BILLIE GIBSON, pharmacist; b. Muskogee, Okla., Oct. 25, 1924; s. Elmo Weeks and Esther (Gibson) McC.; m. Shirley Ann Hevel, Nov. 22, 1948 (dec. 1976); children—David G., Steven F. B.S. in Pharmacy, Kans. U., 1950. Registered pharmacist, Tex. Pharmacist retail drug stores, Coffeyville, Kans., 1950-52; salesman Eli Lilly & Co., Coffeyville, Waco, Tex., 1954-67; asst. dir. pharmacy Providence Hosp., Waco, 1967—. Served to LCDR, USN, 1942-45, PTO, 1952-53, Korea. Mem. Am. Soc. Hosp. Pharmacists, Tex. Soc. Hosp. Pharmacists, Heart of Tex. Soc. Hosp. Pharmacists. Republican. Episcopalian. Lodge: Masons. Avocations: classical music; study of economics. Home: 5200 Lake Charles Dr Waco TX 76710 Office: Providence Hosp Pharmacy 1700 Providence Dr Waco TX 76703

MCCULLOUGH, DARRYL JOHN, mathematician, educator; b. Columbus, Ohio, Dec. 20, 1951; s. Milton W. and Frances M. (Whiteside) McC.; m. Laurie A. Callender, May 15, 1976. B.A., Ohio State U., 1972; M.A., U. Mich., 1974, Ph.D., 1978. Teaching asst. U. Mich., Ann Arbor, 1972-78; asst. prof. math. U. Okla., Norman, 1978-84, assoc. prof. math., 1984—; vis. teaching asst. U. Tex., 1977; vis. mem. Math. Scis. Research Inst., Berkeley, Calif., 1984; reviewer NSF, referee Proc. Am. Math. Soc., Proc. Boulder Conf. on Group Actions. Contbr. writings to profl. pubis. in field; invited speaker profl. confs. U.S., W.Ger., Poland, Netherlands, Eng. Arts and Scis. summer fellow U. Okla., 1979, jr. faculty fellow, 1980; NSF grantee, 1981-83, 85—; research council grantee U. Okla., 1984. Mem. Am. Math. Soc. Office: Dept Math Univ Okla Norman OK 73019

MCCULLOUGH, JAMES D., educational administrator. Supt. of schs. Chattanooga. Office: 1161 W 40th St Chattanooga TN 37402*

MC CULLOUGH, JOHN PHILLIP, management educator; b. Lincoln, Ill., Feb. 2, 1945; s. Phillip and Lucile Ethel (Ornellas) McC.; B.S., Ill. State U., 1967, M.S., 1968; Ph.D., U. N.D., 1971; m. Barbara Elaine Carley, Nov. 29, 1968; children—Carley Jo, Ryan Phillip. Adminstrv. mgr. McCullough Ins. Agy., Atlanta, Ill., 1963-68; ops. supr. Stetson China Co., Lincoln, 1967; instr. bus. Ill. Central Coll., East Peoria, 1968-69; home and hosp. instr. Grand Forks (N.D.) pub. schs., 1969-70; research asst. U. N.D., 1970-71; asst. prof. bus. West Liberty (W.Va.) State Coll., 1971-72, assoc. prof. mgmt., 1972-74, chmn., prof. mgmt., 1974—, dir. Sch. Bus., 1982—; mgmt. cons., Triadelphia, W.Va., 1971—; adj. prof. Wheeling Coll., 1972—; vis. prof. St. Francis Xavier U., 1971; instr. Am. Inst. Banking, 1971—; lectr. W.Va. U., 1972—, W.Va. No. Community Coll., 1972—, SBA, 1974—; profl. assoc. Inst. Mgmt. and Human Behavior, 1975—; mgmt. cons. Active AFL-CIO Community Services program, Upper Ohio Valley United Fund, Am. Cancer Soc., W.Va. No. Community Coll. Community Service Edn. program. Recipient AFL-CIO community service citation, United Fund Community Service citation, Harris-Casals Found. award. Mem. Soc. Humanistic Mgmt. (exec. com., nat. chmn.), Soc. Data Educators, Cath. Bus. Edn. Assn. (mem. exec. bd. central unit), Am. Soc. Personnel Adminstrn., Adminstrv. Mgmt. Soc., Nat. Acad. Behavioral Sci., Alpha Kappa Psi, Delta Mu Delta, Delta Pi Epsilon, Delta Tau Kappa, Phi Gamma Nu, Phi Theta Pi, Pi Gamma Mu, Pi Omega Pi, Omicron Delta Epsilon. Co-author: Primer in Supervisory Management, 1973. Contbr. articles to profl. jours. Home: 68 Elm Dr Triadelphia WV 26059 Office: Dept Mgmt West Liberty State Coll West Liberty WV 26074

MCCULLOUGH, RALPH CLAYTON, II, lawyer; b. Daytona Beach, Fla., Mar. 28, 1941; s. Ralph C. and Doris (Johnson) McC.; B.A., Erskine Coll., 1962; J.D., Tulane U., 1965; m. Carolyn Rodgers Reid, Sept. 1, 1962; children—Melissa Wells, Clayton Baldwin. Bar: La. 1965, S.C. 1974. Assoc., Baldwin, Haspel, Maloney, Rainold and Meyer, New Orleans, 1965-68; of counsel Finkel et al, 1979—; asst. prof. law U. S.C., 1968-71, asso. prof., 1971-75, prof., 1975—, chair prof. advocacy, 1982—, asst. dean Sch. Law, 1970-76, instr. Med. Sch., 1970-79, adj. prof. law and medicine, 1979—; trustee S.C. Dist. U.S. Bankruptcy Ct., 1979—; exec. dir. S.C. Continuing Legal Edn. Program. Bd. visitors Erskine Coll. Mem. La. Bar Assn., S.C. Bar (sec. 1975-76, exec. dir. 1972-76, award of service 1978), ABA, New Orleans Bar Assn., Am. Trial Lawyers Assn., S.C. Trial Lawyers Assn. (bd. govs. 1982—), Am. Law Inst., Southeastern Assn. Am. Law Schs. (pres.), Phi Alpha Delta. Republican. Episcopalian. Club: Forest Lake. Author: (with J. L. Underwood) The Civil Trial Manual, 1974 supplements, 1976, 77, 78, II, 1981; (with Myers & Felix) New Directions in Legal Education, 1970; (with J.L. Underwood) The Civil Trial Manual II, 1981; (with G.M. Finkel) South Carolina Torts, 1981; co-reporter S.C. Criminal Code, 1977, S.C. Study Sentencing, 1977. Home: PO Box 1799 Columbia SC 29206 Office: U SC Sch Law Columbia SC 29201

MCCULLOUGH, ROBERT WALTER, optometrist; b. Atlanta, Oct. 19, 1951; s. Benjamin Hudson and Isabell Octavia (Booth) McC.; m. Norma Carol Craig, Aug. 7, 1976. A.S. with honors, Middle Ga. Coll., 1971; B.S., U. Ga., 1973; O.D. with honors, So. Coll. Optometry, 1977. Pvt. practice optometry, Jonesboro, Ga., 1979—; cons. Atlanta Fed. Penitentiary, 1979—; lectr. in field. Served to lt. USN, 1977-79. U.S. Navy Health Professions scholar, 1975. Mem. Am. Optometric Assn., Ga. Optometric Assn. (chmn. bd. trustees), 4th Dist. Optometric Assn. (pres. 1981-82), Beta Sigma Kappa, Sigma Alpha Sigma, Phi Theta Kappa. Methodist. Club: Jonesboro Kiwanis (pres. 1981-82). Contbr. articles to profl. jours. Home: 2762 Austin Ln Jonesboro GA 30236 Office: 7718 N Main St Suite E-1 Jonesboro GA 30236

MCCULLOUGH, THOMAS RICHARD, geologist; b. San Fernando, Calif., Feb. 18, 1931; s. Thomas John and Florence M. (Crawford) McC.; m. Marilyn Darlene Schlichenmayer, July 10, 1959; children—Patrick Thomas, Michelle Susan. B.A., Occidental Coll., 1953; M.A., UCLA, 1957. Geologist Pauley Petroleum, Westwood, Calif., 1957-65; v.p. Transam. Petroleum, Los Angeles, 1965-66; sr. geologist Core Labs., Inc., Dallas, 1966-68; v.p. Suburban Propane Gas Corp., San Antonio, 1968-77; mng. ptnr. Stringer Oil and Gas Co., San Antonio, 1977—. Served with U.S. Army, 1953-55. Mem. Am. Assn. Petroleum Geologists, So. Tex. Geol. Soc. (del. 1985—), West Tex. Geol. Soc., Corpus Christi Geol. Soc., Am. Inst. Petroleum Geologists. Republican. Clubs: Woodlake Golf, Petroleum (San Antonio). Home: 310 Arcadia Pl San Antonio TX 78209 Office: Stringer Oil and Gas Co 8961 Tesoro Dr San Antonio TX 78217

MCCUMBER, RICK WAYNE, pharmacist; b. Hinton, Okla., Jan. 26, 1951; s. Eldon Walker and Donna Mae (Stevens) McC.; m. Lizbeth Kay Clark, Nov. 19, 1983; 1 child, Andrew Walker. B.S. in Pharmacy, Southwestern Okla. State U., 1975; M.B.A., U. Tex.-Arlington, 1982. Pharmacy intern St. Anthonys Hosp., Oklahoma City, 1975; staff pharmacist All Saints Episcopal Hosp., Fort Worth, 1976-79, asst. dir. pharmacy, 1979-81, dir. pharmacy, 1981—; pharmacist in charge Duncan Meml. Hosp., Fort Worth, 1983-85; pharmacy cons. to profl. adv. com. Tarrant County Mental Health-Mental Retardation Assn., Fort Worth, 1983—. Loaned exec. United Way of Tarrant County, Fort Worth, 1983. Recipient Bristol award Bristol Labs., 1975. Mem. Am. Soc. Hosp. Pharmacists, Tex. Soc. Hosp. Pharmacists, N. Central Tex. Soc. Hosp. Pharmacists (bd. officer 1984—), Rho Chi (pres. 1974-75). Republican. Mem. Ch. of Christ. Avocations: running; coin and stamp collecting. Office: All Saints Episcopal Hosp 1400 8th Ave Fort Worth TX 76104

MCCUNE, GORDON AMOS, engineering firm executive, mechanical engineer; b. Tulsa, Aug. 20, 1925; s. Malcolm Lloyd and Elizabeth Wright (Goodjohn) McC.; m. Anne Blair Keeton, June 9, 1951; children—Margaret B. McCune Malone, Murray Davis, Kelly Ann McCune-Miller. B.S.M.E., U. Kans., 1948. Ptnr. McCune McCune & McCune, Tulsa, 1950-56; McCune McCune & Assocs., Tulsa, 1956-77; mng. ptnr., pres. McCune Ptnrs., Inc., Tulsa and Dallas, 1977—; pres. Eastpark Properties Inc. Chmn. bd. deacons First Presbyterian Ch., Tulsa, 1980-81, mem. bd. of session, 1984—; bd. dirs. Tulsa Philharm., 1975—; bd. dirs. Greater Tulsa adv. bd. Salvation Army, 1977—, 2d v.p. adv. bd., 1985—. Mem. Okla. Soc. Profl. Engrs. (pres. 1968-70, Tulsa chpt. Engr. of Yr. 1970), Nat. Soc. Profl. Engrs. (nat. bd. dirs. 1966-70). Republican. Clubs: So. Hills Country, Tulsa (Tulsa). Office: McCune Ptnrs Inc 5110 S Yale Tulsa OK 74135

MCCUNE, JOHN R., state senator; b. May 27, 1926; A.B., Princeton U.; M.A. Notre Dame U. Mem. Okla. Senate, 1969—. Republican. Home: 3301 Quail Creek Rd Oklahoma City OK 73120

MC CURDY, DAVID KEITH, lawyer, Congressman; b. Canadian, Tex., Mar. 30, 1950; s. Thomas L. and Aileen G. McC.; B.A., U. Okla., 1972, J.D., 1975; postgrad. U. Edinburgh (Scotland), 1978; m. Pamela Mary Plumb, Aug. 14, 1971; children—Josh, Cydney, Shannon. Admitted to Okla. bar; asst. atty. gen. State of Okla., 1975-77; asso. firm Luttrell, Pendarvis & Rawlison, 1978-79; individual practice law, Norman, Okla., 1979-80; mem. U.S. Congress from 4th Dist. Okla., 1980—. Served with USAFR. Okla. Bar Found. scholar, 1972, Albert G. Kulp Meml. scholar, 1973, Jerome Sullivan Meml. scholar, 1974; named outstanding young man U.S. Jaycees, 1984. Mem. Okla. Bar Assn., Norman C. of C., Jaycees, Omicron Delta Kappa. Club: Rotary. Office: 313 Cannon House Office Bldg Washington DC 20515*

MCCURDY, ROBERT CLARK, lawyer, consultant; b. Cin., Sept. 23, 1939; s. Edward Robert and Martha (Moul) McC.; m. Marjorie Ann Boehm, Oct. 7, 1967; children—Jonathan, Melinda. B.S. in Pharmacy, U. Fla., 1962; J.D., Stetson U. Coll. Law, 1973; M.S. in Hygiene, U. Pitts., 1974. Bar: Fla. 1973. House counsel Lee Meml. Hosp., Fort Myers, Fla., 1975—. Author, cons.; Hospital Law Manual, Aspen Systems, 1977-83. Served with U.S. Army, 1963-66. Mem. Am. Coll. Hosp. Adminstrs., Am. Acad. Hosp. Attys., ABA, Fla. Soc. Hosp. Attys., Fla. Soc. Hosp. Risk Mgrs. (dir. 1985—). Office: Lee Meml Hosp 2776 Cleveland Ave Fort Myers FL 33901

MCCUSKEY, ROBERT SCOTT, anatomy educator, researcher; b. Cleve., Sept. 8, 1938; s. Sidney Wilcox and Jeannette M. (Scott) M.; m. Rebecca Woodworth, July 4, 1958; (div.); m. 2d, Patricia A. Randolph Reed, June 26, 1974; children—Geofrey, Gregory, Michael. A.B., Western Res. U., 1960, Ph.D., 1965. Instr. anatomy U. Cin., 1965-67, asst. prof., 1967-71, assoc. prof., 1971-75, prof., 1975-78; prof., chmn. anatomy W.Va. U., Morgantown, 1978—. Recipient NIH Research Career Devel. award, 1969-74; Humboldt Sr. U.S. Scientist prize, W.Ger., 1982. Mem. Microcirculatory Soc. Am. Assn. Anatomists, Am. Assn. Study Liver Disease, Shock Soc., Am. Soc. Hematology. Contbr. articles to profl. jours.; mem. editorial bd. Microvascular Research, 1974—. Office: Dept Anatomy WVa U Med Ctr Morgantown WV 26506

MC CUTCHEN, JAMES NORMAN, management consultant; b. Texas City, Tex., Feb. 21, 1949; s. Norman Louis and Marian V. McCutchen; B.S. in Chem. Engring., Purdue U., 1972; postgrad. Bates Coll. Law, 1975—; m. April Allyn Blackburn, Feb. 4, 1978; children—Christopher James, Kelly Michael. Ops. engr. Union Oil Co. of Calif., Beaumont, Tex., 1972-74; mgr. econ. analysis Litwin Engring. & Constrn. Co., Houston, 1974-75; v.p. Bonner & Moore Assos., Inc., Houston, 1975—. Mem. Am. Inst. Chem. Engrs. Episcopalian. Office: 2727 Allen Pkwy Houston TX 77019

MCCUTCHEON, MARTIN, biomedical engineering educator; b. Little Rock, Dec. 23, 1941; m. Wanda Culver, Sept. 3, 1963; children—Shaun, Karen. B.S. in Elec. Engring., U. Ark., 1964, M.S. in Elec. Engring., 1965, Ph.D., 1967. Registered profl. engr., Ala. Research asst. U. Ark., Fayetteville, 1965-67; asst. prof. engring. U. Ala. at Birmingham, 1967-70, assoc. prof. engring., 1970-79, prof. biomed. engring., 1979—, prof. elec. engring., 1979—, assoc. prof. bio-communications, 1975-85; cons. Ala. Power Co., Birmingham, 1973, NIH, Madison, Wis., 1980, Zurn Air Systems, Birmingham, 1983. Contbr. articles to profl. jours. Patentee pseudopalate for diagnostic and treatment speech impairment. P.A. Lashley scholar U. Ark., 1963. Sr. mem. IEEE; mem. Acoustical Soc. Am., Engring. and Medicine Soc. of IEEE, Atlanta Photo Club, Sigma Xi, Tau Beta Pi (adv. bd. student chpt.), Eta Kappa Nu. Avocation: photography. Home: 3035 Tara Ln Birmingham AL 35216 Office: Dept of Biomed Engring Univ of Ala at Birmingham University Station Birmingham AL 35294

MCCUTCHEON, STEPHEN CHRISTIAN, college administrator; b. Atlanta, Mar. 23, 1939; s. Clyde Ray and Mattie Ophelia (Barrett) McC.; m. Cynthia Margaret Browning, Sept. 2, 1961; 1 child, Stephanie Lynn. B.A., Auburn U., 1961; M.S., Fla. State U., 1964; Ed.D., Ind. U., 1968. Asst. dean students Wofford Coll., Spartanburg, S.C., 1964-66; assoc. head counselor Ind. U., Bloomington, 1966-67, research assoc., 1967-68; asst. to pres. W. Ga. Coll., Carrollton, 1968-73, dir. div. continuing edn., 1973—; cons. long range planning, hosps., religious orgns., colls. 1979—. Mem. Ga. Title XX, Planning Council, 1974-76; treas. bd. dirs. Tech. Tng. and Edn. Consortium Ga., 1982—; dist. fund chmn. Ga. Am. Heart Assn., Northwestern Ga., 1983—; campaign chmn. Ga. Ho. of Reps. candidate, 1984. Grantee NEH, 1976, Title I Higher Edn. Act, 1977. Mem. Ga. Adult Edn. Assn. (treas. 1977-79), Nat. Univ. Continuing Edn. Assn. Baptist. Lodge: Rotary (bd. dirs. 1980-82). Avocations: golfing; camping. Home: 123 Ole Hickory Trail Carrollton GA 30117 Office: W Ga Coll Maple St Carrollton GA 30118

MCCUTCHEON, STEVEN CLIFTON, hydrologist; b. Decatur, Ala., Oct. 29, 1952; s. Bernard Clifton and Rosa May (Askenburg) McC.; m. Sherry Lynn Sharp, July 23, 1971; 1 son, Michael Ian. A.S., Calhoun Community Coll., 1973; student U. Ala., 1973-74; B.C.E. with honors, Auburn U., 1975; M.S. in Environ. Engring., Vanderbilt U., 1977, Ph.D. in Hydraulics and Water Resources Engring., 1979. Registered profl. engr., La. Lectr., research asst. Vanderbilt U., Nashville, 1976-79; hydrologist U.S. Geol. Survey, Nashville, and NSTL, Miss., 1977—; adj. asst. prof. Tulane U., New Orleans, 1984—; cons., lectr. in field. Mem. Zoning Commn. and Planning Adv. Bd., St. Tammany Parish, La., 1984—. Whirlpool Corp. fellow, 1976, U.S. Energy Research and Devel. Adminstrn. fellow, 1975; Daniels Constrn. Co. Found. fellow, 1975; U.S. Geol. Survey grantee, 1977. Mem. ASCE (Young Civil Engr. in Govt. award Zone II, 1984, br. pres., sect. dir.), Am. Geophys. Union, Am. Geomorphological Field Group, Sigma Xi (former chpt. sec.), Phi Kappa Phi, Phi Theta Kappa. Contbr. articles to profl. jours. Home: 103 Chance Circle Slidell LA 70458 Office: Building 2101 Gulf Coast Hydroscience Center NSTL MS 39529

MCDANIEL, ALLEN POLK, stock broker; b. Nashville, Feb. 22, 1943; s. Matthew Fontaine Maury and Anne (Hargraves) McD.; m. Sara Leighton Sherwood, Dec. 29, 1967; children—James Polk, Fontaine Maury. B.A., Vanderbilt U., 1965. Stockebroker Salomon Bros., Atlanta, 1966-67, N.Y.C., 1968-69, v.p., Atlanta, 1969—. Mem. Young Men's Roundtable High Mus. Art, 1981—. Roman Catholic. Clubs: Atlanta Quarterback (pres. 1980), Atlanta Track (Grand Prix award 1979, 80, 81), Phi Delta Theta Alumni (pres. 1980), Cherokee Town and Country; Capitol City (Raleigh, N.C.). Home: 2858 Mornington Dr Atlanta GA 30327 Office: 2100 Atlanta Center Atlanta GA 30365

MCDANIEL, BERT THOMAS, lawyer, mortgage company executive; b. Waco, Tex., May 31, 1923; s. Bert Carpenter and Lillian Abby (McLendon) McD.; m. Gene Dees Morgan; children—Dwight Thomas, Timothy Morgan. LL.B., Baylor U., 1948; B.B.A., 1950, J.D., 1962. Bar: Tex. 1948. Gen. counsel, sec. 1st Am. Life Ins., Houston, 1959-62; pres. Gen. Mortgage Co., Houston, 1960-63; gen. counsel, v.p. Drew Mortgage Co., Houston, 1967-83; sec., v.p. Morgan Mortgage Co. Tex., Houston, 1983—. Mem. Tex. Ho. of Reps., 1951-55. Served with U.S. Army, 1942-45. Recipient cert. of honor Tex. Legislature, 1981. Mem. Tex. Bar Assn., Houston Bar Assn., Am. Judicature Soc., McLennon Bar Assn. (sec. 1950); Amvets (vice comdr. Tex.). Democrat. Methodist (adminstrv. bd. local ch.). Clubs: Warwick, 100 of Houston. Lodge: Masons. Avocations: hunting; fishing; boating. Office: 2727 Allen Pkwy Houston TX 77019

MCDANIEL, ELIZABETH LOGAN, psychologist, educator; b. Youngstown, Ohio; d. Lawrence Adair and Henrietta (Villeneuve) Logan; m. David Cotter McDaniel (dec. Feb. 1969); children—David, Steven, Donna, William, Susan. B.A., UCLA, 1948; M.S., U. Ill., 1951; Ph.D., U. Tex., 1967. Lic. psychologist, Tex. Mem. faculty S.W. Tex. State U., San Marcos, 1969—, prof. psychology, 1969—; practice psychology, San Antonio, 1975—. NIMH fellow, 1964-67. Mem. Am. Psychol. Assn., Nat. Assn. Sch. Psychologists (state del. 1975-79, 81-85), Tex. Psychol. Assn. (pres. 1984-85). Office: 4550 NW Loop 410 Suite 101 San Antonio TX 78229

MCDANIEL, GARY ALLAN, geologist; b. Enid, Okla., Oct. 14, 1931; s. William Taylor and Golda Mae (Bell) McD.; m. Elizabeth Marie Vacin, June 15, 1951 (div. 1980); children—Mark, Gari Lynn, Dana, Lance, Lisa. B.Sc. in Geology, U. Okla., 1953, M.Sc. in Geology, 1959. Geologist, Shell Oil Co., 1959-62; advanced geologist Skelly Oil Co., 1962-66; geologist Midwest Oil Co., Oklahoma City, Okla., 1966-68; dist. geologist Champlin Petroleum Co., Oklahoma City, 1968-70; div. geologist Clarcan Petroleum Corp., Oklahoma City, 1970-74; v.p. May Petroleum Co., Dallas, 1974-75; cons., Oklahoma City, 1975—. Contbr. articles to profl. publs. Served as 1st lt. USMC, 1953-56. Mem. Am. Assn. Petroleum Geologists (chmn. publicity com. 1974-75, award of Merit 1975), Oklahoma City Geol. Soc. (pres. 1972-73, award of Recognition 1969, 73, 78, award of Appreciation 1971), Am Inst. Profl. Geologists (pres. Okla. sect. 1980, award of Recognition 1980), Sigma Xi, Sigma Gamma Epsilon (E.L. McCullough award 1959), Phi Kappa Psi. Home: 2617 Acacia Ct Norman OK 73069 Office: 1805 1st Nat Ctr W Oklahoma City OK 73102

MC DANIEL, HAYNES A, JR., pharmacist; b. Washington, Aug. 4, 1939; s. Haynes A and Edna (Knowles) McD.; B.S. in Pharmacy, George Washington U., 1961; M.B.A., Fla. Atlantic U., 1972; children by previous marriage—Haynes A III, Dana Elizabeth, Diane Lynn; m. Sarah Katherine Ward. Intern, Friendship Pharmacy, Washington, 1956-61; pharmacist Peoples Drug Store, Washington, 1961, McClure Drug Co., Vero Beach, Fla., 1962-67; chief pharmacist Indian River Meml. Hosp., Vero Beach, 1967-79, dir. pharmacy, 1979—; owner Glass Oven Bakery; cons. pharmacist to Fla. Bapt. Retirement Center Nursing Home, 1973—; asst. prof. pharmacology Indian River Community Coll., 1973; pharmacist for med. assistance team to Antigua, 1975; cert. preceptor U. Fla., 1973—; owner MAC Shops, model railroading, 1980—. Mem. Citizens Adv. Com., City of Vero Beach, 1973-75; mem. choir First Bapt. Ch., 1973—; bd. dirs. Am. Cancer Soc., Indian River County, 1968-72, chmn. edn. com., 1970-72; bd. dirs. Indian River Fed. Credit Union, 1981—, pres., 1985—. Mem. Am. Pharm. Assn., Am. Soc. Hosp. Pharmacists, Fla. Pharm. Assn. (chmn. edn. com. 1977-78, exec. com. 1974-75, 80-82, dist. pres. 1980-81, dist. v.p. 1979-80; Frank Toback Cons. Pharmacist award 1981), Fla. Soc. Hosp. Pharmacists (chmn. profl. placement 1978-79, pres. 1974, Pharmacist of the Year award 1977), Indian River Pharm. Assn., Southeastern Soc. of Hosp. Pharmacists, Vero Beach Jaycees. Club: Treasure Coast Model Railroad (pres. 1975-76). Home: 2715 52d Ave Vero Beach FL 32960 Office: 1000 36th St Vero Beach FL 32960

MCDANIEL, JOHN NOBLE, university dean; b. Washington, Jan. 30, 1941; s. Noble Ashby and Emily (Robb) McD.; m. Jean Smart, Aug. 26, 1967; children—Scott Noble, Craig Thomas. B.A., Hampden-Sydney Coll., 1963; M.A.T., Johns Hopkins U., 1964; Ph.D., Fla. State U., 1972. Asst. prof. to prof. Middle Tenn. State U., Murfreesboro, 1970-84, chmn. dept. English, 1978-84; dean liberal arts, 1984—. Author: The Fiction of Philip Roth, 1974. Translator: The History of Folklore in Europe, 1981. Contbr. articles to profl. jours. NEH scholar Harvard U., summer 1983. Mem. Tenn. Coll. English Assn. (vice pres. 1978-80, pres. 1980-81), S. Atlantic Modern Language Assn., Southeastern Conf. Linguistics, Tenn. Council Tchrs. English. Office: Dean Liberal Arts Middle Tenn State Univ Murfreesboro TN 37132

MCDANIEL, JOHN PERRY, III, sheriff; b. Bascom, Fla., Oct. 9, 1940; s. John Perry McDaniel, Jr. and Ruby Ruth (Grant) McDaniel Owens; m. Lois Phyllis Scott, Mar. 30, 1961 (div. Aug. 1977); children—Lois Machelle Hill, John P. IV. Student Chipola Jr. Coll., Marianna, Fla., 1958-59; cert. in Corrections, Fla. A&M U., 1976. Br. mgr. AVCO Fin. Services, Marianna, 1962-72; chief dep. Jackson County Sheriff's Dept., Marianna, 1973-76, sheriff, 1981—; gen. mgr. Peacock Motors, Marianna, 1977; used car mgr. Rahal Chevrolet, 1978-80. Bd. dirs. Fla. Sheriffs Boys Ranch, 1980. Recipient Good Govt. award Jackson County Jaycees, 1984. Mem. Fla. Sheriffs Assn. (bd. dirs. 1985). Democrat. Baptist. Lodges: Lions, Elks, Masons, Shriners (ambassador 1979). Home: Route 5 Box 490-28 Marianna FL 32446 Office: Jackson County Sheriffs Dept PO Box 919 Marianna FL 32446

MCDANIEL, LAWRENCE HAMMOND, university administrator; b. Atlanta, July 21, 1932; s. Lawrence Pearson and Pearl (Hammond) McD.; m. Margaret O'Gene Sinyard, May 12, 1977. B.B.A., U. Ga., 1958. Nat. Alumni sec. Phi Kappa Tau Fraternity, Oxford, Ohio, 1962-66; dir. devel. research U. Ga., Athens, 1966-75; pres. McDaniel and Assocs., Atlanta, 1975-78; regional mgr. Community Service Bur., Inc., Atlanta, 1978-84; dir. devel. and alumni affairs U. West Fla., Pensacola, 1984—; cons. Reinhardt Coll., 1983, Cowboy Artist of Am. Mus., Tex., 1982, Dallas Mus. Fine Arts, 1981, Tex. and S.W. Cattle Raisers, 1980, Birmingham So. Coll., 1979. Served to sgt. USAF, 1950-53. Mem. Nat. Soc. Fundraising Execs., Council Advancement and Support Edn. Club: Exec. (Pensacola). Lodge: Rotary. Office: U West Fla Pensacola FL 32514

MCDANIEL, MICHAEL CONWAY DIXON, bishop, theologian; b. Mt. Pleasant, N.C., Apr. 8, 1929; s. John Henry and Mildred Juanita (Barrier) McD.; m. Marjorie Ruth Schneiter, Nov. 26, 1953; 1 son, John Robert Michael. B.A., U. N.C., 1951; B.D., Wittenberg U., 1954; M.A., U. Chgo., 1969, Ph.D., 1978; D.D. (hon.), Lenoir-Rhyne Coll., 1983; L.L.D., Belmont Abbey Coll., 1984. Ordained to ministry Lutheran Ch. in America, 1954. Pastor Faith Luth. Ch., Faith, N.C., 1954-58, Ch. of the Ascension, Savannah, Ga., 1958-60; assoc. dir. evangelism United Luth. Ch. in Am., N.Y.C., 1960-62; sr. pastor Edgebrook Luth. Ch., Chgo., 1962-67; prof. Lenoir-Rhyne Coll., Hickory, N.C., 1971-82, Raymond Morris Bost disting. prof., 1982; bishop N.C., Luth. Ch. in Am., Salisbury, 1982—; cons. grant coordinator NEH, 1977-79; master tchr. Hickory Humanities Forum, 1981—; chmn. humanities div. Lenoir-Rhyne Coll., 1973-82; chmn. task force on ecumenical and interfaith relationships Commn. Forming a New Luth. Ch., 1983—; rep. Luth. Orthodox Dialogue in U.S.A., 1983—. Author: Welcome to the Lord's Table, 1972. Mem. Englewood Human Relations Council, N.J., 1959-60; pres., bd. trustees Edgebrook Symphony, Chgo., 1965-67; sec. Chgo. Astron. Soc., 1966-67; pres. Community Concerts Assn., Hickory, N.C., 1977-80. Served to sgt. U.S. Army, 1946-48; Korea. Luth. World Fedn. fellow, 1967-69; named Vol. of Yr. Western Piedmont Symphony, Hickory, N.C., 1982. Mem. AAUP, Soc. Bibl. Lit. and Exegesis, Inst. Theology in Encounter with Sci. and Tech., Am. Acad. Religion, Luth. Acad. Scholarship. Democrat. Home: Route 11 Box 301H Salisbury NC 28144 Office: NC Synod Lutheran Ch in Am 1950 Holiday Inn Dr Salisbury NC 28144

MCDANIEL, MYRA ATWELL, lawyer, state official; b. Phila., Dec. 13, 1932; d. Toronto Canada and Eva Lucinda (Yores) Atwell; m. Reuben Roosevelt McDaniel, Jr., Feb. 20, 1955; children—Diane Lorraine, Reuben. B.A., U. Pa., 1954; J.D., U. Tex.-Austin, 1975. Bar: Tex., U.S. Dist. Ct. (ea. dist.) Tex. 1979, U.S. Dist. Ct. (we. dist.) Tex. 1977, U.S. Dist. Ct. (no. dist.) Tex. 1978, U.S. Dist. Ct. (so. dist.) Tex. 1978, U.S. Ct. Appeals (5th cir.) 1978, U.S. Supreme Ct. 1978. Asst. atty. gen. State of Tex., Austin, 1975-79, chief taxation div., 1979-81, gen. counsel to gov., 1983-84; asst. gen. counsel Tex. R.R. Commn., Austin, 1981-82; gen. counsel The Wilson Cos., San Antonio and Midland, Tex., 1982; assoc. Bickerstaff, Heath & Smiley, Austin, 1984—; bd. dirs. Nat. Leadership Conf. for Exec. Women in State Govt., Washington, 1983-84; dir. Austin Cons. Group, Inc., 1983—; lectr. Bd. visitors U. Tex. Law Sch., 1983—, vice-chmn., 1983-84; bd. dirs. Friends of Ronald McDonald House Central Tex., 1983—, chmn. house ops. com., 1983-84; clk., vestry bd. St. James Episcopal Ch., 1976-79, 81-83. Recipient medal West Phila. Citizens League, 1950; honoree Serwa Yetu chpt. Mt. Olive Grant chpt. Tex. Order Eastern Star, 1979. Fellow Tex. Bar Found., Am. Bar Found.; mem. State Bar Tex. (chmn. subcom. profl. efficiency and econ. research 1978-84), Tex. Bar Assn., ABA, Travis County Bar Assn., Austin Black Lawyers Assn., Travis County Women Lawyers Assn. Democrat. Clubs: Soroptimists, Women in Mgmt. (Austin). Office: United Bank Tower 400 W 15th St Suite 1419 Austin TX 78701

MCDANIEL, VAN RICK, zoology educator; b. San Antonio, Oct. 29, 1945; s. William Carr and Patricia (Biron) McD.; m. Mary Ann O'Hara; children—Jonathan, Zachary. B.S. in Biology, Tex. A&I U., 1967, M.S. in Biology, 1969; Ph.D., in Zoology, Tex. Tech U., 1973. Asst. prof. zoology Ark. State U., Jonesboro, 1972-77, assoc. prof., 1977-84, prof., chmn. dept. zoology, 1984—. Contbr. articles to profl. publs. Recipient numerous grants. Mem. Ark. Acad. Sci. (editor jour.), Am. Soc. Mammalogists, Southwestern Assn. Naturalists, Soc. for Study of Amphibians and Reptiles, Sigma Xi. Lodge: Elks. Avocations: photography; fishing. Office: Dept Biol Sci Ark State U State University AR 72467

MC DAVID, JOEL DUNCAN, clergyman; b. Georgetown, Ala., June 10, 1916; s. Harry and Ola Elizabeth (McCaskill) McD.; B.A., Millsaps Coll., 1941, D.D., 1977; B.D., Emory U., 1944; D.D., Birmingham So. Coll., 1959, Fla. So. U., 1973, Bethune-Cookman Coll., 1973, Millsaps Coll., 1976, Emory U., 1980; m. Milah Dodd Gibson, Aug. 29, 1942; children—Ben A., Joel G., Karen Anne McDavid Beville. Ordained to ministry Meth. Ch., 1944; pastor, Grand Bay, Ala., 1944-46, Toulminville, Ala., 1946-50, Auburn, Ala., 1950-58, First Meth. Ch., Montgomery, Ala., 1958-66, Dauphin Way Ch., Mobile, Ala., 1966-72; bishop United Meth. Ch., 1972-84, Fla., 1972-80, Atlanta, 1980-84; faculty Auburn U., 1950-58. Mem. Ala. State Ethics Commn., 1966-67, Bi-racial Com. Montgomery, 1964-66, Mobile, 1970-72; v.p. United Meth. Southeastern Jurisdictional Council, 1968-72; mem. Gen. Bd. Discipleship, 1972—; pres. Southeastern Jurisdiction Council Bishops, 1977—; exec. com. Council Bishops, 1977—. Trustee Fla. So. Coll., Bethune Cookman Coll., Wesleyan Coll., Paine Coll., Young Harris Coll., Andrew Coll., Reinhardt Coll., Interdenoml. Theol. Center, Atlanta, Emory U. Named Man of Yr., Montgomery, 1965. Clubs: Masons, Kiwanis. Author: Waiting, 1969.

MCDAVID, JOHN WALTER, JR., psychologist, educator; b. Longview, Tex., May 27, 1933; s. John W. and Lue Mae (Lacey) McD.; m. Marilyn Joan Vreugde, May 30, 1956 (div. 1971); children—John Christopher, Bruce Alan. B.A., Rice U., 1953; M.A., Princeton U., 1956, Ph.D., 1957. Lic. psychologist, Ga. Asst. prof. U. Iowa, Iowa City, 1957-60; prof. U. Miami, 1960-68; chief research Head Start Program, Dept. Edn., Washington, 1968-70; prof. Ga. State U., Atlanta, 1971—; psychologist Atlanta Psychol. Ctr., Atlanta, Author: (textbooks) Individual Groups, Societies, 1968, Psychology and Social Behavior, 1974, Understanding Children, 1978. Contbr. articles to profl. jours. Mem. Am. Psychol. Assn., Ga. Psychol. Assn., Nat. Assn. Sch. Psychologists. Democrat. Episcopalian. Home: PO Box 54031 Atlanta GA 30308 Office: Ga State U Univ Plaza Atlanta GA 30303

MCDERMOND, JOSEPH WILLIAM, JR., motor carrier company administrator; b. Carlisle, Pa., Oct. 3, 1948; s. Joseph William and Bertha Florence (Barrick) M.; m. Connie Louise Vaughn, Jan. 27, 1968; children—Joseph William III (dec.), Ami Nicole. A.A., Goldey Beacom Coll., 1977. Traffic clk. C. H. Masland & Sons, Carlisle, 1968, 69-71; traffic clk. Hercules Inc., Wilmington, Del., 1971-73, sr. rate specialist, 1973-74, asst. rate analyst, 1974-75, mgr. rate div., 1975-79, mgr. rates, 1979, mgr. traffic services, 1979-81, regional traffic mgr., 1981-82; dir. traffic and adminstrn. Hemingway Transport Inc., New Bedford, Mass., 1982; dir. traffic Tex.-Okla. Express, Inc., Irving, Tex., 1982-83; dir. pricing Hall's Motor Transit Co., Mechanicsburg, Pa., 1983-85; mgr. pricing NE TNT Pilot Freight Carriers Inc., Winston-Salem, N.C., 1985—; cons. in field. Past bd. dirs. Middle Atlantic Conf., Inc. and Niagara Frontier Traffic Bur. Served with U.S. Army, 1968-69. Decorated Bronze Star. Mem. 101st Airborne Div. Assn. Republican. Lutheran. Club: Captain's Cove Golf and Yacht. Home: 725 Luxbury Rd Winston-Salem NC 27104 Office: 4103 N Cherry St Winston-Salem NC 27153

MC DEVITT, ELLEN, physician; b. Shubuta, Miss., Sept. 3, 1907; d. James Andrew and Alma (McManus) McDevitt; A.B., Miss. State Coll., 1930; M.D., U. Utah, 1949. Chief technician vascular clinic N.Y. Post Grad. Hosp., 1934-46; intern Meadowbrook Hosp., Hempstead, N.Y., 1949-50; asst. resident Hackensack (N.J.) Hosp., 1950-51, Bellevue Hosp., N.Y.C., 1953-54; research asso. medicine N.Y. Hosp.-Cornell U. Med. Coll., 1951-52; provisional asst. physician out patient dept. N.Y. Hosp., 1951-52, asso. attending, dir. vascular sect., 1968-72, courtesy staff, 1972—; mem. staff, chief 2d med. div. vascular clinic Bellevue Hosp.; instr. medicine Cornell U., 1954-56, asst. prof., 1957-63, asso. prof., 1963-72; cons. staff Watkins Meml. Hosp., Quitman, Miss. Fellow Am. Soc. Geratics; mem. AMA, Am. (fellow council on circulation, fellow council on stroke), N.Y., Miss. heart assns., Miss. Med. Assn., East Miss. Med. Soc., Altrusa Internat., Sigma Xi. Contbr. articles to profl. jours. Home: 1520 Olive St Gulfport MS 39501

MC DONALD, ANDREW J., bishop; b. Savannah, Ga., Oct. 24, 1923; s. James Bernard and Theresa (McGrael) McD. A.B., St. Mary's Sem., Balt., 1945, S.T.L., 1948; J.C.B., Catholic U. Am., 1949; J.C.D., Lateran U., Rome, 1951. Ordained priest Roman Cath. Ch., 1948; consecrated bishop, 1972, curate, Port Wentworth, Ga., 1952-57; chancellor Diocese of Savannah, 1952-68; vicar gen., 1968—, vice officialis, 1952-57, oficialis, 1957; pastor Blessed Sacrament Ch., 1963; named papal chamberlain, 1956, domestic prelate, 1959; bishop Diocese of Little Rock, 1972—. Office: 2415 N Tyler St Little Rock AR 72210*

MCDONALD, ANN GILBERT, writer, antiques dealer; b. Ithaca, N.Y., June 23, 1939; d. Perry W. and Claire (Kelly) G.; m. Bradley G. McDonald, Sept. 3, 1964; 1 child, Perry Gilbert. B.A., Nazareth Coll., 1961; M.A., Cornell U., 1962; Ph.D., George Washington U., 1969. Instr. Marymount Coll., Arlington, Va., 1962-64; asst. prof. Georgetown U., Washington, 1969-70. Author: Evolution of the Night Lamp, 1979. Contbr. articles to profl. jours. Active Com. of 100, Arlington, 1975—; mem. women's com. Arlington Symphony, 1975—. Mem. Nat. League Am. Penwomen, Victorian Soc., Rushlight Club, Nat. Early Am. Glass Club, Opera Soc. No. Va. Avocations: swimming; reading; opera. Office: Box 7321 Arlington VA 22207

MCDONALD, CLARK EDWARD, association executive; b. Greenville, Miss., Jan. 21, 1917; s. Volney Lemoyne and Jane (Posey) McD.; m. Sylvia Keen, Mar. 25, 1944; 3 children. B.A. in Econs. with distinction, Rhodes Coll., 1938; M.B.A., Harvard U., 1942. Exec. v.p. Central Atlanta Improvement Assn., 1946-48; exec. v.p. So. Sash & Door Jobbers, Memphis, 1948-50; v.p. Central Woodwork Inc., Memphis, 1950-54; v.p. S.R. Hungerford Co., Memphis, 1954-56; pres. Hardwood Plywood Mfrs. Assn., Reston, Va., 1958—; mem. nat. def. exec. res. U.S. Dept. Commerce; advisor World Conf. on Panel Products U.S. Dept. State, Rome. Contbr. articles to profl. jours. Served to maj. U.S. Army, 1942-46. Mem. Am. Soc. Assn. Execs. (Key award 1969), Nat. Bldg. Materials Distbrs. Assn., U.S. C. of C., Greater Washington Soc. Assn. Execs. (pres.), NAM (pres. Assn. Council). Republican. Presbyterian. Home 1115 Raymond Ave McLean VA 22101 Office: Hardwood Plywood Mfrs Assn PO Box 2789 1825 Michael Faraday Dr Reston VA 22090

MCDONALD, DONALD, civil engineering educator; b. Montgomery, Ala., Oct. 16, 1930; s. John Fairley and Juliet Ruth (Burke) McD.; m. Judith Ann Chaney, Dec. 31, 1960; children—John Bruce, Katheryn Ann, Emily Ferrell. B.C.E., Auburn U., 1952; M.S., U. Ill., 1957, Ph.D., 1959. Bridge design engr. Ala. Hwy. Dept., 1954-55; research asst. U. Ill., Urbana, 1955-57; sr. research engr., research specialist Lockheed Missiles and Space Co., Sunnyvale, Calif., 1959-62; asst. prof. N.C. State U., 1962-65, assoc. prof., 1965-67; mgr. structures and mechanics dept. Lockheed Missiles and Space Co., Huntsville, Ala., 1967-72; prof. civil engring. Tex. A&M U., 1973—, assoc. head dept. civil engring., 1974-79, head dept. civil engring., 1979—, interim dean engring., assoc. dep. chancellor, 1983-84; cons. various industries. Served with USAF 1952-54. Standard Oil Co. of N.J. fellow, 1957-58; U. Ill. Grad. fellow, 1958-59. Fellow ASCE (chmn. com. on electronic computation 1974-77, mem. structural div. exec. com. 1977-85, sec. 1977-81, chmn. 1983-84), AIAA (assoc.); mem. Nat. Soc. Profl. Engrs., Am. Soc. Engring. Edn., Tex. Soc. Profl. Engrs., Sigma Xi, Tau Beta Pi, Chi Epsilon, Phi Kappa Phi. Republican. Episcopalian. Contbr. articles to profl. jours. Home: 425 Chimney Hill Dr College Station TX 77840 Office: Dept Civil Engring Tex A&M U College Station TX 77843

MCDONALD, EVELYN COCKILL, computer system designer; b. Detroit, July 1, 1938; d. James Eliot and Elizabeth Morrison (Watson) Cockill; m. Robert A. McDonald, Aug. 24, 1963 (div. 1985); 1 child, Heather Lynn. B.A., U. Mich., 1960; postgrad. U. Md., 1963-66. Sr. systems analyst Computer Usage Co., Bethesda, Md., 1963-71; regional support mgr. Computer Machinery Corp., Alexandria, Va., 1971-73; computer systems adminstr. U.S. Postal Service, Washington, 1973-75; dir. govt. mktg. Paradyne Corp., Largo, Fla., 1975-81; owner McDonald Bus. Assocs., Clearwater, Fla., 1981—; chmn. Data Communications Conf., Washington, 1983. Mem. steering com., pres. Small Bus. Network; bd. dirs. Girls Clubs of Pinellas County. Mem. Assn. Computing Machinery, Am. Mgmt. Assn., Nat. Assn. Women Bus. Owners, AAUW, Clearwater C. of C., Office: 2305 E Bay Dr 312 Clearwater FL 33546

MCDONALD, F. ALAN, physics educator; b. Dallas, Jan. 11, 1937; s. Frank Cobb and Margaret (Heimbach) McD.; m. Julie-Anne Orlando, Dec. 26, 1964; children—Glenn, Melissa. B.S. in Physics, So. Meth. U., 1958, B.A. in Math., 1958; M.S. in Physics, Yale U., 1959, Ph.D. in Physics, 1964. Asst. prof. Tex. A&M U., College Station, 1964-69; assoc. prof. So. Meth. U., Dallas, 1969-81, prof., 1981—, chmn. physics dept., 1981—. Mem. Am. Phys. Soc., Am. Assn. Physics Tchrs., AAUP. Contbr. numerous articles to profl. jours.; mem. editorial bd. Jour. Photoacoustics. Home: 3212 Milton Dallas TX 75205 Office: Physics Dept So Meth U Dallas TX 75275

MCDONALD, GABRIELLE ANNE KIRK, judge; b. St. Paul, Apr. 12, 1942; d. James G. and Frances R. Kirk; m. Mark T. McDonald; children—Michael, Stacy. LL.B., Howard U., 1966. Bar: Tex. Staff atty. Legal Def. Fund, N.Y.C., 1966-69; ptnr. McDonald & McDonald, Houston, 1969-79; judge U.S. Dist. Ct., Houston, 1979—; asst. prof. Tex. So. U., Houston, 1970, adj. prof., 1975-77; lectr. U. Tex., Houston, 1977-78. Bd. dirs. Community Service Option Program, Alley Theatre, Houston, Nat. Coalition of 100 Black Women, ARC; trustee Howard U., 1983—; bd. vistors Thurgood Marshall Sch. Law, Houston. Mem. ABA, Nat. Bar Assn., Houston Bar Assn., Houston Lawyers Assn., Black Women Lawyers Assn. Democrat. Congregationalist. Office: U S Dist Ct 515 Rusk Ave Houston TX 77208*

MCDONALD, J. PAUL, lawyer; b. Clinton, Mass., June 10, 1937; s. James Paul Navin and Arlyle Elizabeth (Perkins) McD.; m. Margo B. Florimbio, May 3, 1964 (div. 1972); children—Kevin Sean, Erin Colleen; m. Mary Virginia Monroe, Sept. 3, 1976. B.S. cum laude, Am. U., 1959, M.B.A., 1960; J.D., George Mason U., 1983. Bar: Va. 1983, U.S. Dist. Ct. (ea. and we. dists.) Va. 1983, U.S. Ct. Appeals (4th cir.) 1983. Dist. mgr. Dun and Bradstreet, Washington, 1966-83; ptnr. McDonald, Johnson and Filiatreau, Leesburg, Va., 1983—. Candidate State Senate Va., 33rd Senatorial Dist., 1975, U.S. Congress, 7th Dist. Va., 1984; vice chmn. Leesburg Planning Commn., 1965-70; mem. Leesburg Bd. Archtl. Rev. 1965-70; former fin. chmn. Blue Ridge Council Boy Scouts Am.; former county chmn. Cancer Crusade; former vice chmn. Am. Heart Fund; former collector United Givers Fund, Jr. Achievement, Nat. Alliance Businessmen. Mem. Clarke and Loudoun Counties C. of C., ABA, Assn. Trial Lawyers Am., Va. Bar Assn., Va. Trial Lawyers Assn., Am. Judicature Soc., Loudoun County Bar Assn., Va. Lawyers Referral Service, Delta Theta Phi. Republican. Roman Catholic. Club: Preservation Soc. Loudoun County. Lodge: Lions. Home: Route 1 Box 158B White Post VA 22663 Office: 158-B Gun Barrel Ln White Post VA 22663

MCDONALD, JAMES THOMPSON, JR., lawyer; b. Atlanta, Nov. 13, 1939; s. James Thompson and Frances (LeBron) McD.; m. Mary Davis, Nov. 25, 1967; children—James Thompson III, Frances Avonell. B.A., Citadel, 1961; LL.B., U. Va., 1964. Bar: Va. 1964, Ga. 1967, U.S. Dist. Ct. (no. dist.) Ga. 1968. Ptnr. Swift, Currie, McGhee & Hiers, Atlanta, 1968—. Chancellor bd. trustees Holy Innocents' Sch., 1979-84. Served to capt. USAF, 1964-67. Mem. Ga. Bar Assn., ABA (vice chmn. workers compensation and employers liability com.), Def. Research Inst. (chmn. workers compensation com., speaker seminars), Ga. Bar Assn. (chmn. workers compensation sect. 1983-84), Fedn. Ins. Counsel (chmn. workers compensation com., v.p. 1984-86). Presbyterian. Club: Ansley Golf. Office: 771 Springs St NW Swift Currie et al Atlanta GA 30379

MC DONALD, MILLER BAIRD, management consultant, newspaper columnist, state commissioner; b. Huntsville, Tenn., Feb. 16, 1920; s. Melva Lawson and Bertha Clarence (Baird) McD.; student Lincoln Meml. U., 1939-40, U. Tenn., 1948-49, Cornell U., 1958, U. Wis., 1967, U. Mich., 1971 B.S., Ph.D., Pacific Western U., 1985; m. Anna Lois Fox, Nov. 30, 1941; children—Miller Baird, L. Martin, Willard E., Kathryn Lois. Adminstrv. asst. Home Owners Loan Corp., Washington, 1940-41; personnel ofcl. AEC, 1946-51, personnel tng. and security ofcl., 1953-59; policy devel. ofcl. FAA, 1959-60; chief out-service tng. IRS, Washington, 1960-66; dir. mgmt. tng. Office Sec. of Commerce, Washington, 1966-72; pres. Miller McDonald & Assos., cons. to mgmt., Arlington, Va. and La Follette, Tenn., 1972—; syndicated columnist County Line, 1980—; owner County Services Syndicate, 1981—; instr. U. Ga., 1970, La. State U., 1971. Bd. dirs. Wesleyan Found., 1978—; nat. adv. bd. Am. Security Council, 1979—; chmn. Pres. Ford Com., E. Tenn., 1976; mem. Pres.'s Task Force on Career Advancement, 1965; chmn. Campbell County Republican Com., 1976-80; mem. Tenn. Commn. Human Devel., 1979-86; del. White House Conf. on Aging, 1981—; charter mem. Statue of Liberty Found., 1983; mem. Republican Nat. Com., 1974. Served from pvt. to col., U.S. Army, 1942-46, 50-53. Recipient Superior Performance award AEC, 1960, Cert. of Recognition, IRS, 1966; medal Sec. of Army, 1971; cert. of service Dept. Commerce, 1972; Meritorious Service medal Pres. U.S., 1977; Presdl. Achievement award Rep. Nat. Com., 1982; numerous mil. medals and awards. Mem. Am. Soc. Tng. and Devel., Adult Edn. Assn., Inst. Applied Behavioral Sci., Am. Legion (Legionnaire of Yr. 1950, comdr., dist. comdr. 1948-50, state historian Reserve Officers Assn. 1946-57, chmn. fed. personnel council 1957-59), Clan Donald U.S.A. Methodist. Clubs: Rotary, Masons. Author syndicated 5-part series Our Governments, What's Wrong, 1982; also articles. Address: 109 Crestview Dr LaFollette TN 37766

MC DONALD, OWEN PETER, govt. ofcl.; b. Yankton, S.D., June 5, 1916; s. Peter Joseph and Beatrice (Cogan) McD.; teaching certificate Black Hills Tchrs. Coll., 1936; B.A., Nebr. State Coll., 1939; M.A., Am. U., 1954; m. Elinor Dawn Johnson, Sept. 24, 1942; children—Kathleen Ann, John Owen, Lawrence Edward. Tchr., adminstr. Shannon County Pub. Schs., Danby, S.D., 1939-41; personnel classification analyst WPB, 1941-42; mem. planning staff, asst. adminstr. for constrn., supply and real estate VA, Washington, 1946-48; analyst mgmt. div. Hdqrs. USAF, Washington, 1948-51, chief systems and procedures br. mgmt. div., 1951-55; specialist for analysis and rev. properties and installations Office Asst. Sec. Def., Washington, 1955—, staff asst., 1955-56, chief mgmt. div., 1957-58, realty officer Dept. Def., 1958-65, chief mgmt. and reporting div. contract support services directorate, 1965-70, contract specialist, 1970—, with directorate of maintenance policy, 1977-79; spl. asst. to adminstr. GSA, Washington, 1956; ret., 1979. Served from 2d lt. to capt., U.S. Army, 1942-46; CBI; col. USAF Res. ret. Decorated Bronze Star medal, Air Force Commendation medal. Mem. Am. Polit. Sci. Assn. Roman Catholic. K.C. Home: 9000 Linton Ln Stratford on the Potomac Alexandria VA 22308

MCDONALD, PARKER LEE, state supreme court justice; b. Sebring., Fla., May 23, 1924; s. Monroe R. and Mattie (Etheredge) McD.; B.S., B.A., LL.B., U. Fla.; m. Velma Ruth McDonald, Dec. 17, 1949; children—Martha Rebecca, Bruce Lee, Robert Reid, Ruth Ann. Sole practice law, Sebring, Fla., 1950-51, Orlando, Fla., 1951-61; judge Fla. Circuit Ct., 9th Jud. Circuit, Orlando, 1961-79; assoc. justice Fla. Supreme Ct., Tallahassee, 1979—. Methodist. Office: Supreme Ct Bldg Tallahassee FL 32304

MCDONALD, RUTH ISABEL, pediatrician; b. Valleyfield, Que., Can., Jan. 28, 1944; came to U.S., 1964; d. James Allen Emmons and Isabel Ruth (Seifert) M.; m. Gerald Chasin, May 24, 1975. B.S. with honors in Genetics, McGill U., Montreal, Que., 1964, M.D., 1978; Ph.D. in Devel. Biology, Ind. U., 1970; Lic. physician Md., D.C., Va. Postdoctoral fellow, instr. Rush Presbyn. Hosp., Chgo., 1969-73; research assoc. Iowa U., Iowa City, 1975-76; resident in pediatrics Johns Hopkins Hosp., Balt., 1978-81; pediatrician Health Maintenance Orgn., Va., 1981-84, Fairfax Pediatrics, Va., 1984—; cons. NIH, Bethesda, Md., 1982; attending physician Fairfax Hosp., Va., 1983—. Contbr. articles to profl. jours. Recipient Annie MacIntosh prize, 1962; McGill U. scholar, 1962-64; Nat. Research Council Can. scholar, 1965-68; Ind. U. Found. scholar, 1966; Eigenmann fellow, 1968-69; Nat. Research Council Can. postdoctoral fellow, 1970-72; McGill Med. Sch. scholar, 1974-75, grantee, 1975-78. Fellow Am. Acad. Pediatrics; mem. AMA. Avocations: kayaking; skiing; camping; Tae Kwon Do. Office: Fairfax Pediatrics 3545 Chain Bridge Rd Fairfax VA 22031

MCDONALD, THOMAS DENNIS, lawyer, portrait artist, author; b. Huntsville, Ala., May 18, 1916; s. James Hoffman and Ola Ozell (Dennis) McD.; m. Ethel Virginia Cranley, Nov. 27, 1943; 1 child, Mary Ethel (dec.). B.S., Peabody Coll., 1940; LL.B., U. Ala., 1948; cert. Nat. Coll. State Judiciary, 1972; cert. in photography U. Ala., 1985. Bar: Ala. 1948, U.S. Dist. Ct. Ala. 1949, U.S. Ct. Appeals (5th cir.) 1954. Tchr. city schs., Asheville, N.C., 1940-41; reporter Columbus Enquirer, Ga., 1945-46; city atty. City of Madison, Ala., 1956-61; judge Madison County Ct., Huntsville, Ala., 1962-72, Gen. Sessions Ct., Huntsville, 1973-74; sole practice, Huntsville, 1980—; mem. faculty Am. Acad. Jud. Edn., Tuscaloosa, Ala., 1970. Author: Next of Kin in Jail, 1978; (with James Record) The 1978 Code of Madison County, 1980. Editor: (with J. Record) Huntsville Sesquicentennial Album, 1956. Publicity chmn. United Giver's Fund, Huntsville, 1956; chmn. adv. bd. Salvation Army, Huntsville, 1964-66; mem. adv. bd. traffic ct. program ABA, Chgo., 1968; mem. exec. com. 8th Dist. Democratic Com., 1957-61. Served with U.S. Army, 1941-45. Recipient Good Govt. award Huntsville Jr. C. of C., 1963, Mr. Woodman award Woodmen of World, 1964, merit citation Madison County Commn., Huntsville, 1971. Mem. Nat. Assn. Criminal Def. Lawyers, Ala. Criminal Def. Lawyers Assn., Ala. Trial Lawyers Assn., Am. Portrait Soc., Huntsville C. of C. (life), Intermediate Judge's Assn. (pres. 1969), Huntsville-Madison County Bar Assn. (pres. 1971), Am. Legion (comdr. Huntsville 1955), Phi Alpha Delta. Presbyterian. Lodges: Lions (pres. Huntsville 1963), Elks. Avocation: photography. Office: 209 Randolph Ave SE PO Box 171 Huntsville AL 35804

MC DONALD, WAYMON WAYNE, mortgage banker; b. San Antonio, Sept. 16, 1938; s. Lester Lewis and Alligene Holder (Elsberry) McD.; B.S., U. Tex., 1961; m. Mary Louise Erskine, Jan. 28, 1961; children—Deborah Deann, Wayne Erskine. Profl. baseball player Milw. Braves, 1960-63; with Lumbermen's Investment Corp., Austin, Tex., 1963—, v.p. mktg. and prodn., 1968-71, exec. v.p., 1971-72, pres., chief operating officer, 1972-74, pres. chief exec. officer, 1974-78, chmn. bd., chief exec. officer, 1978-80, chmn. bd., 1980—; exec. v.p., chief operating officer Temple-Eastex, Inc., Diboll, Tex., 1979—; dir. Inland Container Corp., Bank of Southwest, Houston, Sunbelt Ins. Co.; chmn. bd. Eastex Packaging, 1980—, Loper Mortgage Co.; dir., chmn. bd. Lumbermen's Investment Corp. Gen. Agy.; ptnr. Timberline Ins. Agy., 1969—, Assoc. Ins. Agy., 1971—; dir. mgmt. com. Time Inc. mag., 1981—. Time Inc. Home Box Office, 1981—, mem. adv. com. Fed. Nat. Mortgage Assn., 1978-79. Mem. policy adv. bd. Harvard-MIT, Joint Center Urban Affairs, 1973-79; pres. U. Tex. Longhorn Hall of Honor Council, 1979. Mem. Mortgage Bankers Assn. Am., Tex. Mortgage Bankers Assn., Soc. Real Estate Appraisers. Austin Homebuilders Assn., Mass. Purchasing Group, Lufkin C. of C. (dir.). Baptist. Clubs: Onion Creek (chmn. bd. 1978—), Crown Colony Country (dir. 1980—). Office: PO Drawer N Diboll TX 75941*

MCDONALD, WILLIAM ALLEN, accountant; b. DeFuniak Springs, Fla., Nov. 1, 1943; s. Allen Peter and Beatrice (Weimorts) McD.; B.S., Fla. State U., 1968; M.B.A., Pepperdine U., 1975; J.D., Southland U., 1980; m. Beverly Havens, Nov. 6, 1976; children—Debbie, Suzie, Robbie. Tax atty., Honolulu, 1981; pvt. practice acctg., Honolulu, 1981-83, Chapel Hill, N.C., 1983—; mem. faculty U. Hawaii, 1980-81; prof. taxation and acctg., estate planning U.N.C., Chapel Hill, 1983-85. Bd. dirs. Sudden Infant Death Syndrome. Served with USMC, 1962-65. Democrat. Presbyterian. Office: PO Box 3489 Chapel Hill NC 27514

MCDONNELL, MICHAEL R. N., lawyer; b. Paterson, N.J., Sept. 24, 1940; s. Thomas Edward and Margaret (Chapline) McD.; m. Nina Carlotta Gray, Jan. 5, 1980; children—Amy Kathleen, Andrew Gray; children by previous marriage—Michael R.N., James Egan. B.S., U.S. Mil. Acad., 1962; J.D., Stetson U., 1970. Bar: Fla. 1970, U.S. Dist. Ct. (so. and mid. dists.) Fla. 1972, U.S. Dist. Ct. (no. dist.) Fla. 1976, U.S. Supreme Ct. 1974, U.S. Ct. Appeals (5th cir.) 1975, (11th cir.) 1985; cert. civil trial lawyer Fla. Bar. Hearing officer Div. Adminstrv. Hearings, State of Fla., Tallahassee, 1977-79; pres. McDonnell & Berry, Naples, Fla., 1981—; pres., dir., lectr. Am. Trial Forum, Naples, 1983-84. Contbr. articles to legal jours. Pres., Voters League of Collier County, Naples, 1982. Served to capt. U.S. Army, 1962-66. Mem. Assn. Trial Lawyers Am., Acad. Fla. Trial Lawyers. Republican. Episcopalian. Club: Naples Athletic. Office: McDonnell & Berry 720 Goodlette Rd Suite 304 Naples FL 33940

MCDOUGALL, ANGUS CRAIG, paint company official; b. Wisconsin Rapids, Wis., Oct. 27, 1944; s. Angus William and Elizabeth Alice (Jardon) McD.; m. Kathleen Black, June 21, 1974; children—Lorna Jean, Robert Brian. B.S. in Bus. Adminstrn., Mo. Valley Coll., 1972. Area sales mgr. Internat. Harvester Co., Memphis, 1973-76, instr. developer, Ottawa, Ill., 1976-79, program coordinator-mgr., 1979-81; mgr. tng. Porter Paint Co., Louisville, 1981—. Served with USAF, 1966-70, Vietnam. Decorated Air medal with 6 oak leaf clusters, D.F.C. with 2 oak leaf clusters, Silver Star with oak leaf cluster. Mem. Am. Soc. Tng. and Devel. (pres. elect. local Kentuckiana chpt. 1985), Nat. Soc. Sales Tng. Execs. Office: Porter Paint Co PO Box 1439 Louisville KY 40201

MCDOWELL, MARILYN MOOD, interior designer; b. El Campo, Tex., Oct. 3, 1950; d. Rene Lafayette and Gladys Vera (Trojack) Mood; m. Robert Todd McDowell, Apr. 8, 1978. A.A., San Jacinto Coll., 1983; B.S., U. North Ala., 1972. Adminstrv. asst. Phila. Life Ins. Co., Houston, 1978, supr., 1978-80, cons. methods, 1980-81; designer Interior Looks, Crosby, Tex., 1983-84, McDowell Interiors, Houston, 1984—. Docent Mus. Fine Art, Houston, 1984, 85. Mem. Am. Soc. Interior Designers (assoc.), Nat. Home Fashions League (v.p., mem. com.). Republican. Methodist. Office: McDowell Interiors 3768 Carlon St Houston TX 77005

MCDOWELL, MICHAEL RAY, city official; b. Jacksonville, Fla., Oct. 3, 1950; s. Donald Ray and Joyce Adelle (Rowell) McD.; m. Sherryl Ann Wilson, May 27, 1978; children—Michael Langston, Jordan Wilson, Daniel Griffin. Student U. Calif.-Berkeley, 1968, Jacksonville U., 1969-72. With City of Jacksonville, 1969—, mgr. support services, 1979—; adminstr., owner Animal Emergency Clinic, Jacksonville, 1976—. State of Fla. scholar, 1968. Mem. Nat. Audubon Soc., Wilderness Soc., World Wildlife Fund, Animal Protection Inst., Cousteau Soc., Jacksonville Suprs. Assn. Democrat. Mormon. Club: Old English Sheepdog (dir. So. region, chmn. health and research com.). Contbr. articles on purebred dogs to profl. jours.

MCDOWELL, PAT LEWIS, entrepreneur; b. Bronaugh, Mo., July 7, 1933; d. Clarence L. and Mary Bell (Pitts) Lewis; student public schs., Shreveport; La.; m. E. A. McDowell, June 4, 1954 (dec. Oct. 1983); children—David Albert. Adminstrv. asst. Cities Service Oil Co., Shreveport, 1950-54; with Riley-Beaird, Inc., Shreveport, 1956-58, Pitney & Bowes, Inc., Shreveport, 1958-70; owner Pat McDowell & Assos., Inc., Shreveport, 1970—; ptnr. The Gordian Knot, Shreveport, 1979—; owner Tapes 'n Thoughts, Inc., Shreveport, 1982—; v.p. public relations Accu-Med Corp., Shreveport, 1982—; chmn. bd. Self Devel. Inst. Inc., 1983—; lectr. in field. Pres. bd. dirs. La. Assn. for Blind, Shreveport, 1978-80, 79-80, chmn. bd., 1980-81; adv. bd. Nat. Industries for the Blind, Bloomfield, N.J., 1977-82, bd. dirs. Community Action for Corrections in La., 1975, Youth Advocates, Inc., 1976. Recipient J. Cheshire Peyton award; numerous awards Success Motivation Inst. Mem. Sales and Mktg. Execs., Am. Soc. for Training & Devel. Episcopalian. Clubs: Positive Mental Attitude Breakfast (bd. dirs., founding mem.), Toastmasters Hi-Noon. Home: 427 Pennsylvania St Shreveport LA 71105 Office: 3722 Youree Dr Shreveport LA 71105

MCEACHERN, J. ALBERT, JR., mechanical engineer, consultant; b. Ft. Leavenworth, Kans., Apr. 14, 1949; s. Joe Albert and Mary Evie (Wyckoff) McE.; m. Sharon Ann Wheeler, June 17, 1983; children—Joe Albert, III, Mary Bess. B.S. in Mech. Engring., U. Tenn., 1972. Registered profl. engr., N.J., Ala. Assoc. engr. nuclear submarine overhaul Newport News Shipbldg. & Dry Dock Co. (Va.), 1972; project engr. research and devel. rotary engines, reciprocating engines and compressors Ingersoll Rand Co., Princeton Research Ctr. (N.J.), 1972-81; sr. project engr., devel. engr. research and devel. rotary engines and turbochargers aircraft products div. Teledyne Continental Motors, Mobile, Ala., 1981—; cons. rotary engines NASA, 1983—. Ordained elder and deacon, Presbyn. Ch., 1976. Mem. ASME, Soc. Automotive Engrs., Aircraft Owners and Pilots Assn. Home: 4265 Michael Blvd Mobile AL 36609 Office: Teledyne Continental Motors PO Box 90 Mobile AL 36601

MCEACHERN, WARREN SHANKS, publishing executive; b. Memphis, Feb. 9, 1954; s. Shanks and Betty Jean (Price) McE.; m. Deborah Ann Kennington, June 18, 1977; 1 child, Laurel Brooke. Cert. in Refrigeration, Duval County Bd. Edn., 1971. Mgr. editors supply dept. Herff-Jones Co., Montgomery, Ala., 1975-80; shipping/traffic mgr. The Brown Printing Co., Montgomery, 1980—. Chmn. hist. restoration com. Am. Legion Dept. of Ala., 1975-78, hist. commn., 1978-81; mem. bd. advisors Ala. Hist. Commn., 1975-81, Ala. Hist. Soc., 1980-83; lt. col. personal mil. staff Gov. of Ala., 1977-86. Served with Army NG, USN, Ala. Def. Force. Recipient Gen. Billy Mitchell award Civil Air Patrol, 1970, Amelia Earhart award, 1970; Award of Merit, Ala. Hist. Commn., 1977; Disting. Service medal Exec. Order Gov. Ala., 1984; Nat. Def. Service medal Pres. of U.S., 1972. Mem. Am. Legion, DAV. Democrat. Baptist. Club: Montgomery of Printinghouse Craftsmen. Avocation: military history. Home: Route 5 Box 22B Prattville AL 36067 Office: The Brown Printing Co 2734 Gunter Park Dr W Montgomery AL 36109

MCELDOWNEY, GLORIA JEAN, nursing educator, nursing administrator; b. Fairview, W. Va., July 19, 1942; d. Leonard N. and Pauline E. (Lynch) Bell; m. Gary L. McEldowney, Aug. 19, 1967; children—Michael, James. B.S. in Nursing, Alderson-Broaddus Coll., 1964; M.S. in Family Resources, W. Va. U., 1979, M.S. in Nursing, 1985. Instr. nursing Shenandoah Coll., Winchester, Va., 1971-74, United Career Ctr., Clarksburg, 1981-82; asst. dir. nursing United Hosp. Ctr., Clarksburg, W. Va., 1974-76, dir. staff devel., 1976-77; asst. prof. nursing W. Va. Wesleyan Coll., Buckhannon, 1977-81; dir., adminstr. nursing Salem Coll., Salem, W.Va., 1982—; site visitor St. Bd. Nursing, Charleston, W. Va.; health cons. Compton Health Program, Salem, W. Va. Mem. Am. Nurses Assn., W. Va. Nurses Assn., Sigma Theta Tau. Baptist. Avocations: running; reading; gardening. Office: Salem Coll 307 Carlson Hall Salem WV 26426

MCELLISTREM, MARCUS T., physics educator, nuclear researcher; b. St. Paul, Apr. 19, 1926; s. Marcus T. and Loretta Camille (Simard) McE.; m. Eleanor DeMeuse, Aug. 17, 1957; children—Mary Ann, Marcus T., Rebecca, Joan, Catherine, Deborah. B.A., St. Thomas Coll., 1950; M.S., U. Wis., 1951, Ph.D., 1955. Research asst. U. Wis., Madison, 1952-55; research assoc. Ind. U., Bloomington, 1955-57; asst. prof. U. Ky., Lexington, 1957-60, assoc. prof., 1960-65, prof. physics, 1965—, Univ. Research prof., 1979-80; Collaborateur Etr., CEA, France, Bruyeres-le-Chatel, 1974, 75, 78, 81; cons. Arnold AFB, Tullahoma, Tenn., 1968-70, Wright Patterson AFB, Dayton, Ohio, 1971-74; pres. Adena Corp., Lexington, 1971-75. Contbr. articles to profl. jours. Sponsor Newman Ctr., U. Ky., 1960-70, pres., 1979-81; sec. bd. Lexington Catholic High Sch., 1983-85. Served with USNR, 1944-46; PTO. Named Disting. Prof. Coll. Arts and Sci., U. Ky., 1981-82. Fellow Am. Phys. Soc., mem. AAAS, Sigma Xi. Roman Catholic. Home: 1841 Blairmore Ct Lexington KY 40502 Office: Dept Physics and Astronomy Univ Ky Lexington KY 40506

MCELROY, CARL EDWARD, oil service company representative, evangelist; b. Beaumont, Tex., July 28, 1949; s. Lee August Sr. and Ada Mae (Ford) McE. B.B.A. in Mktg., Central Okla. State U., 1973. Service supr. Western Co. of N.Am., Yukon, Okla., 1980-81, safety and tng. supr., 1981-82, ops. supr., Clinton, Okla., 1982-84, sales and service rep., 1984—; instr. Nat. Safety Council, Yukon, 1981-82. Com. mem. YMCA, Clinton, 1984, Clinton Assn. for Rights and Equality, 1985. Republican. Baptist. Lodge: Masons (jr. warden 1984—). Avocations: reading; writing; cooking; fishing. Home: 313 S 3d St Clinton OK 73601 Office: Western Co of N Am 801 Marshall St Clinton OK 73601

MCELROY, DAVID MICHAEL, clinical psychologist; b. Bowling Green, Ky., July 24, 1945; s. Archie A. and Margeret Essie McE.; B.A., Western Ky. U., 1967; M.S.W., U. Tenn., 1969; Ph.D., U. So. Calif., 1976; diplomate Am. Bd. Biofeedback Clinicians; m. Crystal R. Durham, Dec. 28, 1984; children—Scott Michael, Samuel David Patrick. Program dir. VA Hosp., Los Angeles, 1971-75; clin. psychologist VA Hosp., Murfreesboro, Tenn., 1975—; assoc. clin. prof. Meharoy Med. Sch.; coordinator psychology edn. and tng. Murfreesboro VA Med. Ctr.; adj. prof. U. Tenn., Middle Tenn. State U., Vanderbilt U., Peabody Coll. Bd. dirs. Epilepsy Found., Vanderbilt U. Mem. Am. Psychol. Assn. Home: Route 3 Bryan Grove Rd Mt Juliet TN 37122 Office: VA Hosp Murfreesboro TN 37130

MCELROY, JUNE PATRICIA, sales consultant; b. Atlantic City, Sept. 26, 1929; d. Edmund N. and Dorothy R. (McDowell) Ricchezza; m. David Waycott Carson, Apr. 8, 1947 (div. 1954); m. 2d, Ottavio Gelmi, Dec. 16, 1954 (div. 1964); 1 dau., Alessandra; m. 3d, Robert Joseph McElroy, Oct. 16, 1970 (dec. May 1974). Student Temple U., 1947-48, Inst. Linguistics, Georgetown U., 1951-53. Mem. staff Am. consulate gen., Milan, Italy, 1954; legis. asst. U.S. Senate, Washington, 1956; social sec. to ambassador of Finland, Washington, 1958; legis. asst. to congressman, Washington, 1960-65; sr. assoc. Gillmore M. Perry Co., Washington, 1965-76; sales exec./cons. furniture industry, Hilton Head, S.C., 1981—. Mem. Georgetown U. Alumni Assn. Republican. Roman Catholic. Club: Army Navy (Washington). Home: 65 Wood Duck Rd Hilton Head SC 29928

MC EMBER, ROBERT ROLAND, airlines official, musician; b. Ludington, Mich., Feb. 26, 1919; s. Francis Roland and Lillian Laurentine (Hansen) McE.; B.A., John B. Stetson U., 1946, B.M., 1946, M.A., 1951; m. Elizabeth Anderson Futch, Dec. 15, 1942; children—Sharon Leigh, Elizabeth Anne. Critic tchr. Western Mich. U., 1950-55; asst. prof. Purdue U., 1955-63; asso. prof. U. Wis., 1964-67; mgr. flight tng. aids and tech. writing Am. Airlines, 1967-69; mgr. flight tng. program devel. Eastern Airlines, Miami, Fla., 1970—;

guest lectr.; leader workshops and seminars on instrnl. tech.; mus. dir., condr. Ludington Civic Symphony Orch., 1948-50; condr. Central Wis. Symphony Orch., 1964-67. Served with USAAF, 1942-45; col. Res., 1945-72. Recipient cert. of appreciation U.S. Air Force, 1972. Mem. Nat. Acad. Rec. Arts and Scis., Nat. Soc. Scabbard and Blade, Mil. Order World Wars, Daedalian Soc., Am. Soc. Tng. and Devel., Internat. TV Assn. (pres. 1974-75, dir. 1976-77), Res. Officers Assn. U.S., Am. Fedn. Musicians, Phi Delta Kappa. Republican Lutheran. Author: C-124 Aircraft Homestudy, 1970; (with others) Communication Security for AF Personnel, 1972, Principles and Practices of Occupational Safety and Health, 1975; editorial adv. bd. Am. Soc. Tng. and Devel. Jour., 1979-82; editor Flight Line (Flight Safety Found. Publs. award 1980), 1957-81; contbr. articles to ednl. jours.; composer: All-American Bands, 1958; several orchestral works. Home: 8310 SW 81st Terr Miami FL 33143 Office: Eastern Airlines Flight Training Center International Airport Miami FL 33148

MCENTIRE, LARRY HUGHES, state director of pupil transportation; b. Spartanburg, S.C., Aug. 14, 1950; s. Hoyt D. and Marion (Hughes) McE.; m. Patricia Ann Jenkins, May 28, 1982. B.A., Wofford Coll., 1972; M.S., Fla. State U., 1980. Tchr., coach Polk County Bd. Edn., Columbus, N.C., 1972-74, driver edn. instr., 1972-74; program specialist Fla. Dept. Edn., Tallahassee, 1975-77, program specialist III, 1977-81, state dir. pupil transp., 1981—; mem. steering com. chassis standards 10th Nat. Conf. Sch. Transp., Warrenburg, Mo., 1985—. Contbr. articles to profl. jours. Mem. Nat. Safety Council (sch. transp. sect.), Nat. Assn. State Dirs. Pupil Transp. Services. (area dir. 1983—), Southeastern States Pupil Transp. Assn. (pres. 1985-86). Democrat. Baptist. Avocations: golf; fishing; gardening. Home: 2501 Blue Bell Pl Tallahassee FL 32308 Office: Fla Dept Edn 377 Knott Bldg Tallahassee FL 32301

MCFALL, BILLY GENE, chiropractor; b. Pound, Va., Oct. 31, 1932; s. Willie Talmadge and Sarah Genera (Baker) McF.; m. Arlene Bailey, July 18, 1953; children—Ricky Lynn, Randall Mark, Vickie Lee McFall Newcomb. Jr. Acctg. Degree, Steed Coll. Tech., 1952; Dr. Chiropractic, Palmer Coll. Chiropractic, 1956. Lic. chiropractor, Tenn. Pres. Morristown Chiropractic Clinic, Inc., Tenn., 1983—. Election commr. State of Tenn., 1975-77, 1977-79; hon. sgt.-at-arms Tenn. Ho. of Reps., 1972; mem. Democratic Exec. Com., 1980. Mem. Internat. Chiropractic Assn., Morristown C. of C. (bd. dirs. for profl. mems. of U.S.A. 1982). Baptist. Home: Doc McFall Rd Morristown TN 37814 Office: 714 S Cumberland St Morristown TN 37814

MCFARLAND, JACLANEL MOORE, lawyer; b. Dawson, Tex., June 6, 1952; d. Jack Leon and Frances Junell (Linch) Moore; m. Allen Keith McFarland, Aug. 14, 1976; children—Linch Moore, Allen Keith. B.A., Baylor U., 1974, J.D., 1977; postgrad. Oxford U., 1974. Bar: Tex. 1977, U.S. Dist. Ct. (so. dist.) Tex. 1979. Atty. Tarrant Title Co., Ft. Worth, 1977-78; assoc. Gerald L. King and Assocs., Inc., Spring, Tex., 1978-79; sole practice, Houston, 1979—; prof. govt., bus. law North Harris County Coll., 1979-80. Campaign mgr. Gerald L. King for State Rep., 1982; mem. legal com. South Main Bapt. Ch., 1979-83. Mem. ABA, Tex. Bar (continuing law focused edn. com.), Houston Bar Assn., Criminal Def. Lawyers Assn., Baylor U. Alumni Assn., Baylor Law Sch. Alumni Assn. (life), Harvey M. Richey Moot Ct. Soc., Assn. Women Attys., Phi Alpha Delta, Pi Sigma Alpha. Home: 542 Pine Walk Trail Spring TX 77373 Office: 400 FM 1960 W Suite 111 Houston TX 77090

MC FARLAND, JAMES WILLIAM, real estate development company executive; b. Montgomery, Ala., Sept. 7, 1948; s. Ward Wharton and Frances Adelia (Morrow) McF.; B.S., U. Ala., 1970; m. Miriam Melinda Webster, Feb. 20, 1971; children—James William, Mimi Morrow. Dir. real estate for Ky., Ind. and Tenn., Winn-Dixie Stores, Inc., Louisville, 1970-72; v.p. Ward McFarland, Inc., Tuscaloosa, Ala., 1972—, also dir. Mem. Council for Devel. of French in La., 1976—, Friends of Library, 1975—; young churchmen adviser Episcopal Diocese Ala., 1976—; charter investor, chair of real estate U. Ala.; bd. dirs. Tuscaloosa Kidney Found.; chmn. State of Ala. Rapid Rail Transit Commn.; vice chmn. La.-Miss.-Ala. Rapid Rail Transit Commn.; Republican candidate from Ala. 7th Dist. for U.S. Ho. of Reps., 1986; sustaining mem. Rep. Nat. Com., Ala. Rep. Party; mem. mayor's staff, Mobile; mem. U.S. Congl. Adv. Bd. Named hon. citizen City of New Orleans, City of Mobile. Mem. Nat. Assn. Realtors, Tuscaloosa Bd. Realtors, Nat. Small Bus. Assn., U. Ala. Commerce Execs. Soc., U. Ala. Alumni Assn., Nat. Assn. R.R. Passengers, Ala. Assn. R.R. Passengers (pres. 1982), Delta Sigma Pi. Clubs: North River Yacht; Kiwanis of Greater Tuscaloosa. Home: 4714 7th Ct E Tuscaloosa AL 35405 Office: 325 Skyland Blvd E Tuscaloosa AL 35405

MCFARLANE, EDWARD MEANS, health and physical education educator, administrator; b. Pitts., June 19, 1940; s. Charles Carroll and Lyda Doris (Means) McF.; m. Nancy Elaine Johnston, June 16, 1962; children—Amy D., Todd E. B.S., Slippery Rock U., 1962; M.Ed., U. Pitts., 1965; M.H.L. (hon.), Davis and Elkins Coll., 1978. Grad. asst. U. Pitts., 1962-63; tchr., coach Marion Ctr. Joint High Sch., Indiana County, Pa., 1963-64, Slippery Rock State Coll., Pa., 1964-68; adminstr., coach Cuyahoga Community Coll., Cleve., 1968-70, adminstr., 1970-71; tchr., coach dept. health and phys. edn., adminstr. Davis and Elkins Coll., W.Va., 1971—. Bd. dirs. Randolph County YMCA, Elkins, 1971-73; treas. Randolph County Spl. Olympics, Elkins, 1979-82. Named Basketball All-Am., AP, 1961; inducted Hall of Fame, Slippery Rock U., 1985. Mem. Nat. Assn. Intercollegiate Athletics, Athletic Dirs. Assn., AAHPERD, W.Va. Alliance for Health, Phys. Edn. and Recreation, Nat. Assn. Coll. Dirs. Athletics, Phi Delta Kappa, Phi Epsilon Kappa. Republican. Presbyterian. Home: Route 3 Box 604 Elkins WV 26241 Office: Davis & Elkins Coll Elkins WV 26241

MCFARLANE, WALTER ALEXANDER, lawyer; b. Richlands, Va., May 4, 1940; s. James Albert and Frances Mae (Padbury) McF.; m. Judith Louise Copenhaver, Aug. 31, 1962; children—Brennan Alexander, Heather Copenhaver. B.A., Emory and Henry Coll., 1962; J.D., T.C. Williams Sch. Law, U. Richmond, 1966. Bar: Va. 1966, U.S. Supreme Ct. 1970, U.S. Ct. Appeals (4th cir.) 1973, U.S. Ct. Appeals (D.C. cir.) 1977, U.S. Dist. Ct. (ea. dist.) Va. 1973. Asst. atty. gen. Office Va. Atty. Gen., Richmond, 1969-73, dep. atty. gen., 1973—; adj. prof. U. Richmond, 1978—. Chmn. transp. law com. Transp. Research Bd., NRC-Nat. Acads. Scis. and Engring., Washington, 1977-85, chmn. legal affairs, Am. Assn. Hwy. and Transp. Ofcls., 1978-85, chmn. environ., archeol. and hist. preservation com., 1985—. Contbr. articles to profl. jours. Pres., Windsor Forest Civic Assn., Midlothian, Va., 1975-76; bd. govs. Emory and Henry Coll., 1985—; bd. dirs. Greater Midlothian Civic League, 1981—, v.p., 1980; instr. water safety ARC, 1962—; chmn. bldg. com. Mt. Pisgah United Meth. Ch., 1980-85, pres. men's club, 1980-81. Served as capt. JAGC, USAF, 1966-69. Decorated Air Force Commendation medal; recipient J.D. Buscher Disting. Atty. award Am. Assn. State Hwy. and Transp. Ofcls., 1983, John C. Vance legal writing award NRC-Nat. Acad. Scis. and Engring., 1982; 4th ann. outstanding evening lectr. award Student Body U. Richmond, 1980. Mem. Va. Trial Lawyers Assn., Richmond Bar Assn., Richmond Scottish Soc. (bd. dirs. 1980-82), Emory and Henry Coll. Alumni Assn. (chpt. pres. 1971-73, regional v.p. 1974-77, pres. 1981-83). Club: Stonehenge Country (Midlothian). Home: 11909 Deerhurst Dr Midlothian VA 23113 Office: Office Atty Gen 8th St Richmond VA 23219

MCFARLIN, DEAN LEONARD, banker; b. Toccoa, Ga., July 29, 1954; s. L.C. and Dorothy Cleo (Canady) McF.; m. Wanda Gail Collins, Aug. 29, 1983. B.B.A. in Mgmt. and Mktg., N. Ga. Coll., 1976; postgrad. U. Va. Sch. of Retail Bank Mgmt., 1985. Trainee Citizens Bank, Toccoa, 1979-82, loan officer, 1980-82, br. mgr., 1982-83; asst. v.p. 1st Nat. Bank of Habersham, Cornelia, Ga., 1983—. Profl. coordinator Cornelia United Way, 1982, treas., 1985. Served to capt. U.S. Army, 1976-78. Mem. Ga. Banker Assn., Am. Banker Assn., Bankers Adminstrv. Inst., Cornelia C. of C., Toccoa Jaycees (v.p., treas. 1981-83). Baptist. Lodges: Kiwanis, Elks. Avocations: skiing; softball; hunting; fishing; golf. Home: Route 1 Box 38A Baldwin GA 30511 Office: 1st Nat Bank of Habersham 308 Front St PO Box 310 Cornelia GA 30531

MCFATRIDGE, KEITH WILLIAM, JR., banker; b. Wichita Falls, Tex., Mar. 28, 1946; s. Keith William and Margaret (Daniel) McF.; m. Marilyn Sue McFatridge, June 16, 1979; children—Keith, Kyle, Eric, Michael, Jeffrey. B.B.A., So. Meth. U., 1968, M.B.A., 1969. Exec. v.p., chief operating officer U.S. Nat. Bank, Galveston, Tex., 1975—; credit dept. officer Citizens Nat. Bank, Austin, Tex., 1971-73; treas. Woods Tucker Leasing, Hattiesburg, Miss., 1973-75; dir., mem. exec. com. U.S. Nat. Bank, 1980—. Bd. dirs. Salvation Army, 1980—, Tex. Coastal Higher Edn. Authority, 1982—, Ronald McDonald House, 1985—, Boy Scouts Am., 1984—, Galveston Crimestoppers, Inc., 1981—. Named Family of the Yr., Boy Scouts Am., 1982; Admiral of Tex. Navy, 1983. Mem. Robert Morris Assn., Am. Bankers Assn., Tex. Bankers Assn., C. of C. (dir.). Republican. Methodist. Clubs: Bob Smith Yacht, Galveston Country, Galveston Arty. Address: PO Box 179 2201 Market St Galveston TX 77553

MCFEE, ARTHUR STORER, surgery educator; b. Portland, Maine, May 1, 1932; s. Arthur Stewart and Helen Knight (Dresser) McF.; m. Iris Goeschel, May 13, 1967. B.A. cum laude, Harvard U., 1953, M.D., 1957; M.S. in Biochemistry, U. Minn., 1965, Ph.D. in Surgery, 1967. Diplomate Am. Bd. Surgery (guest examiner 1979-81, 83-84, 86). Intern in surgery U. Minn. Hosps., 1957-58; surg. resident U. Minn., 1958-65; staff surgeon, dir. ICU, U.S. Naval Hosp. U.S.S. Repose, 1966-67, staff surgeon and asst. chief surgeon U.S. Naval Hosp., Charleston, S.C., 1967; asst. prof. dept. surgery U. Tex. Med. Sch., San Antonio, 1967-70, assoc. prof. dept. surgery U. Tex. Health Sci. Center, San Antonio, 1970-74, prof., 1974—; co-dir. surg. ICU Bexar County Teaching Hosps., 1967—; staff physician Audie L. Murphy Meml. Vets. Hosp., San Antonio, 1973—; guest lectr. Baylor U. Med. Center, 1976; spl. cons. Am. Acad. Orthopaedic Surgeons. Recipient Physicians Recognition award AMA, 1978, 79, 81, 84. Mem. Am. Assn. History of Medicine, ACS, AMA, Am. Trauma Soc., Assn. for Acad. Surgery, N.Y. Acad. Scis., Bexar County Med. Soc., Owen H. Wangensteen Found., Royal Soc. Medicine (affiliate), So. Med. Assn., Tex. Med. Assn., Tex. Surg. Soc., Western Surg. Assn., Halsted Soc., San Antonio Surg. Soc. (pres. 1983) Soc. Surgery Alimentary Tract, So. Surg. Assn. Editorial bd. for com. on injuries Am. Acad. Orthopaedic Surgeons, 1st-4th edits.; contbr. articles to profl. publs. Home: 131 Brittany Dr San Antonio TX 78212 Office: Dept Surgery Univ Tex Health Sci Center San Antonio 7703 Floyd Curl Dr San Antonio TX 78284

MCGAGHIE, WILLIAM CRAIG, medical educator; b. Chgo., June 28, 1947; s. William and Vivian Iona (Skoglund) M.; m. Pamela Wall, Mar. 13, 1976; children—Michael Craig, Kathleen Ann. B.A., Western Mich. U., 1969; M.A., Northwestern U., 1971, Ph.D., 1973. Lectr., Northwestern U., Evanston, Ill., 1973-74; asst. prof. U. Ill., Chgo., 1974-78; asst. prof. U. N.C., Chapel Hill, 1978-81, assoc. prof. sch. of medicine, 1981—. Author: Competency-Based Curriculum Development, 1978. Editor: Handbook for the Academic Physician, 1986; mem. editorial bd. Jour. Evaluation and the Health Professions, 1981—. Lic. lay reader Episcopalian Ch., Chapel Hill; bd. dirs. Vols. for Youth. USPHS grantee. Mem. Am. Psychol. Assn., Am. Ednl. Research Assn. Avocations: running; gourmet cooking. Home: 112 Village Ln Chapel Hill NC 27514 Office: U NC Sch of Medicine 322 MacNider Bldg 202H Chapel Hill NC 27514

MCGAHA, LORETTA, nurse; b. Gordo, Ala., Aug. 23, 1944; d. James Aaron and Ola Mae (Lewis) Driver; m. William Robert McGaha, Aug. 19, 1966 (div. July 1973); children—Kathryn Faline, Timothy Keith. A.D., Calhoun Community Coll., Decator, Ala. R.N., Ala. Insp. Chrysler Corp., Huntsville, Ala., 1973-80; staff nurse labor delivery room Huntsville Hosp., 1980—. Home: 3503 Flamingo Rd Huntsville AL 35805

MCGAHEE, BERNARD MONCRIEF, psychologist; b. Macon, Ga., Nov. 26, 1943; s. Bernard Bryon and Maggie Mae (Moncrief) McG.; m. Marianne Nesbitt, Sept. 28, 1969; children—Heather, Erin, Sean. A.B., Mercer U., 1965; M.Ed., U. Ga., 1967; Ph.D., Tex. Tech U., 1974. Psychologist Ga. Prison System, Jackson, 1969-70, Ga. Youth Devel., Macon, 1970-71, U.S. Army, Savannah, Ga., 1975-82, pvt. practice Psychol. Assocs., Savannah, 1982—; cons. Offender Rehab. Program, Savannah, 1983—. Mem. Ga. Psychol. Assn., Am. Psychol. Assn., Coastal Assn. Lic. Psychologists. Home: 12506 Cranwood Ln Savannah GA 31419 Office: Psychol Assocs 7370 Hodgson Meml Dr B6 Savannah GA 31406

MCGARR, CAPPY RAY, petroleum company executive; b. San Angelo, Tex., Aug. 1, 1951; s. Wilbur Ray and Bobbie Carolyn (Honea) M.; m. Jane Elizabeth Strauss, May 27, 1978; children—Elizabeth Nan, Kathryn Jane. B.A., U. Texas, 1973, B.J., 1975; M.B.A. Grad. Sch. Bus., 1977. Asst. to lt. gov. State of Tex., Austin, 1972-73; council aide Austin City Council, 1974-75; securities salesman Goldman, Sachs & Co., Dallas, 1977-80; pres. Fortune Petroleum, Inc., Dallas, 1980—; pres., dir. Nat. Capital Group, Inc.; bd. chmn. MFE Inc., Dallas; dir. Harrison & Co., United Nat. Bank, Dallas. Bd. dirs. Tex. Lyceum, Dallas; trustee Goals for Dallas; mem. Dallas Democratic Forum, Dallas. Mem. Ind. Petroleum Assn. Am., Am. Petroleum Inst., Tex. Ind. Producers, Royalty Owners Assn. Episcopalian. Clubs: Dallas, Dervish, Grad. Sch. Bus. (Dallas). Office: 2050 North Tower Plaza Americas Dallas TX 75201

MCGAUGHEY, EDGAR HOWARD, III, oil drilling company executive; b. West Columbia, Tex., Jan. 22, 1947; s. Edgar Howard and Ruth (Beal) McG.; m. Suzanne Bordner, Apr. 2, 1969; children—Melanie and Jennifer (twins). B.S., U. Houston, 1972. Mgr. employment Milchem div. Baker Oil Tools, Houston, 1972-74; dir. personnel Progress Drilling & Marine, Houston, 1974-80; dir. human resources Huthnance Corp., Houston, 1980—. Mem. Am. Compensation Assn., Am. Soc. Personnel Adminstrn., Houston Personnel Assn., Tex. State Safety Assn., Internat. Assn. Drilling Contractors (chmn. com. 1976—). Republican. Presbyterian. Club: Pecan Grove Country. Home: 1703 Cobblestone Ct Richmond TX 77469 Office: 601 Jefferson St Suite 500 Houston TX 77002

MCGAW, KENNETH ROY, furniture wholesale company executive; b. Parry Sound, Ont., Can., Aug. 25, 1926; s. Dalton Earnest and Grace (Crockford) McG. Student Denison U., 1946-48; B.A., Western Res. U., 1949. With Bigelow Carpets, N.Y. and Ohio, 1949-53; mfrs. rep. Bolender & Co., Chgo., 1953-58; home furnishing sales, Gates Mills, Ohio, 1958-74, Ft. Lauderdale, Fla., 1974-77, Dallas, 1978-79; pres. Ken McGaw, Inc., Dallas, 1979—; factory rep. for maj. furniture and furniture accessory mfrs. Bd. dirs. Big Bros. Cleve., 1963-65, Dallas Opera Co., 1981—; v.p. Nat. Council on Alcoholism, Cleve., 1972-74; chmn. fund-raising drive Wholesale div. Dallas Industry for Dallas Opera, 1982-83; ruling elder 1st Presbyterian Ch. Dallas, 1981—. Served to 2d lt. U.S. Army, 1944-46. Mem. S.W. Homefurnishings Assn., S.W. Roadrunners Assn., Internat. Homefurnish Reps. Assn. Lodge: Dallas Rotary. Home: 4621 Mockingbird Ln Dallas TX 75209 also 8360 E San Bernardo Scottsdale AZ 85258 Office: Ken McGaw Inc 9010 Dallas World Trade Ctr PO Box 58495 Dallas TX 75258

MCGEE, CAROLYN BOGAN, computer services executive; b. Pottstown, Pa., Jan. 8, 1947; d. John Joseph and Beverley Valeria McGee; B.S., Carnegie Mellon U., 1968, M.S., 1970; Ph.D., U. Ala., 1971; m. Denis J. Bogan, June 7, 1969; children—Kathleen Bogan, John Bogan. Mem. faculty Kans. State U., Manhattan, 1972-74; v.p. Am. Mgmt. Systems, Arlington, Va., 1974—. Recipient Cert. of Merit, GAO, 1979. Mem. AAUW. Contbr. articles to profl. jours. Home: 5110 Althea Dr Annandale VA 22003 Office: 1777 N Kent St Arlington VA 22209

MC GEE, DAMOUS EMANUEL, clergyman; b. Fleming, Ky., Sept. 2, 1930; s. Sebastian, Jr. and Callie (Evans) McG.; m. Shirlene Powell, June 14, 1952; 1 dau., Karen Renae. Diploma, Bible Tng. Inst., 1968; M.S., Old Dominion U., 1970; Th.M., Bible Baptist Sem., 1952; postgrad. U. Wis., 1971-72, Union Theol. Sem., Va., 1965-66. Ordained to ministry Ch. of God of Prophecy, 1952. Tchr. pub. schs., Norfolk and Virginia Beach, Va., 1956-59; internat. dir. Youth for Christ, Greenville, S.C., Ft. Worth, 1950-52; material releaseman Convair-Vultee Air Craft Co., Ft. Worth, 1950-52; pastor Ch. of God of Prophecy, Richmond, Va., 1952-56, Norfolk, 1956-61, Newport News, Va., 1962-70; pres. Calif. Holding Assn., 1972-76; v.p. West Coast Bible Tng. Inst., Fresno, Calif., 1972-76; overseer of Wis., 1970-71, of Calif. (English), 1972-76, Ill. Ch. of God of Prophecy, Bartonville, 1976-82, Okla. Ch. of God of Prophecy, Broken Arrow, 1982—. Trustee, Tomlinson Coll., 1968-74. Mem. Soc. Pentecostals. Author: Marriage Booklet, 1968. Office: 210 S Elm Pl Broken Arrow OK 74013

MC GEE, HUMPHREY GLENN, architect; b. Hartsville, S.C., June 26, 1937; s. James Gladney and Elizabeth Adams (Williams) McG.; B.Arch., Clemson U., 1960. Designer, Clark, McCall & Leach, Hartsville-Kingstree, S.C., 1961; Designer prodn. A. G. Odell & Assos., Charlotte, N.C., 1962; chief designer Clark, McCall & Leach, Hartsville-Kingstree, S.C., 1963; sr. designer LBC & W, Inc., Columbia, S.C., 1965-69, pres., 1969-76, sr. v.p. client services and design, 1976; pres. CEDA, Inc., Columbia, S.C., 1976—. Served with U.S. Army Res., 1961-67. Mem. AIA, Nat. Soc. Interior Designers (award 1972), Am. Soc. Interior Designers (chmn. S.C. chpt. com. on Found. Interior Design Edn. and Research 1976), Columbia Council Architects. Home: 415 Harden St Columbia SC 29205 Office: 1605 Blossom St Columbia SC 29201

MC GEE, JOHN FRAMPTON, communications co. exec.; b. Charleston, S.C., Jan. 9, 1923; s. Hall Thomas and Gertrude (Frampton) McG.; B.S. in Bus. and Polit. Sci., Davidson Coll., 1943; m. Ruth Bouknight Smedley, June 19, 1971; children—Beverly C. McGee Kinder, Catharine F. McGee Mebane, Charles V. Smedley. With Charleston (S.C.) Post-News and Courier, 1946-62; asst. gen. mgr. State-Record Newspapers, Columbia, S.C., 1962-64, gen. mgr., pres., co-pub., 1964-69; gen. exec. Knight Newspaper, Inc., Miami, Fla., 1969-70; pres., associated pub. Charleston (W.Va.) Daily Mail, 1970—; pres. Clay Communications, Inc., parent co. Charleston Daily Mail, Raleigh Register, Beckley Post Herald, Enquirer-Jour., Monroe, N.C., Shelby Daily Star, TV Stas.-WWAY, N.C., KFDX, Tex., KJAC, Tex., WAPT, Miss., dir. AP, N.Y.C.; Kanawha Banking & Trust Co., Charleston, W.Va.; mem. adv. bd. Sch. Journalism, W.Va. U. Trustee, Charleston Area Med. Center, Davis and Elkins Coll.; mem. gen. exec. bd. Presbyterian Ch., U.S.A., 1974-76; mem. S.C. Commn. for Higher Edn., 1966-69. Served to capt. inf. U.S. Army, 1943-45. Decorated Purple Heart (2), Bronze Star with 3 oak leaf clusters (U.S.); Croix de Guerre with palm (France and Belgium). Mem. So. Newspaper Pubs. Assn. (chmn. labor com. 1967-68, chmn. new processes com. 1966-67, dir. 1967-69), Internat. Press Inst. (bd. dirs. Am. com.), W.Va. Press Assn. (pres. 1977-78), New Eng. Soc. S.C. Clubs: Cosmos (Charleston, W.Va.); Edgewood Country of W.Va. Office: 1001 Virginia St E Charleston WV 25301

MCGEE, SEARS, state judge; b. Houston, Sept. 29, 1917; s. James Butler and Alice (Sears) McG.; m. Mary Beth Peterson, Mar. 8, 1941; children—James Sears, Mary Gray McGee Neilson, Claire Logan McGee Holmes, Alice Gray McGee Ruckman, George Sears, Erwin Smith. Student Rice U., 1934-36; LL.B., U. Tex., 1940; also continuing legal edn. Bar: Tex. 1940. Assoc. Sears, Blades, Moore & Kennerly, Houston, 1940-43, 46-48; instr. in civil law procedure U. Houston, 1950-52; ptnr. law firm, Houston, 1955-58; judge County Ct. at Law, Harris County, Tex., 1948-54, 151st Dist. Ct., Harris County, 1954-55, 55th Dist. Ct., Harris County, 1958-69; justice Supreme Ct. Tex., Austin, 1969—. Mem. nat. awards jury Freedoms Found. at Valley Forge, Pa., 1971; bd. dirs. Central Br. YMCA, Houston; mem. Houston Community Council; pres. Houston Council for Deaf Children. Recipient Cert. of Merit award Appellate Judges Conf. of Am. Bar, San Francisco, 1978, Ann. Gavel award for disting. jurist St. Mary's Sch. Law, San Antonio, 1980. Mem. State Bar Tex. (dir.), Houston Jr. Bar (sec.-treas., v.p.), Tex. Bar Found. (charter), ABA, Am. Judicature Soc., Houston Rose Soc., U. Tex. Ex-Students' Assn., Phi Delta Theta. Lodge: Sons of Hermann. Office: Supreme Ct Tex PO Box 12258 Capitol Sta Austin TX 78711

MCGEE, WILLIAM EARL, psychologist; b. Knoxville, Tenn., Oct. 30, 1948; s. George Carlton and Elinor Hope (Miller) McG.; m. Roslyn Meriwether Vanstone, June 10, 1973; children—Abigail Susan, Sara Elizabeth, William Meriwether. B.S., U. Tenn., 1970, M.A., 1976, Ed.D., 1982. Lic. psychologist, Tenn. Counselor Juvenile Ct., Knoxville, 1972-74; counselor, program coordinator Tenn. Dept. Mental Health, Knoxville, Nashville, 1974-78; coordinator residential treatment program, Ohio, 1979-80; psychologist Anderson County Schs., Clinton, Tenn., 1980-84; ptnr. Wray & McGee, Chattanooga, 1984—; cons. Tenn. Dept. Vocat. Rehab., Chattanooga, 1984—, Tenn. Dept. Human Services, 1981—; dir. Child Learning Inst., Knoxville, Riverbend Day Sch. Mem. Am. Psychol. Assn., Tenn. Psychol. Assn., Nat. Assn. Sch. Psychologists, Tenn. Assn. Sch. Psychologists (pres. 1985-86), Knoxville and Chattanooga Area Psychol. Assn. Episcopalian. Avocations: bicycling; day hiking; photography. Office: 516 Vine St Chattanooga TN 37402

MCGEHEE, ARTHUR LEE, police chief; b. Ocala, Fla., Feb. 10, 1943; s. F.L. and Agnes (Albritton) McG.; m. Abby Smallwood; children—Gay, Amy, David, Susan. B.S. in Criminology, Fla. State U., 1965; M.P.A., U. Ga., 1970. Cert. police officer, Fla. Mem. faculty St. Petersburg Jr. Coll., Fla., 1967-68, U. Ga., Athens, 1968-71; with St. Petersburg Police Dept., 1971-74; planning dir. Pinellas County Sheriff's Office, St. Petersburg, 1974; chief police Ocala Police Dept., 1974—; mem. Police Standards and Tng. Commn., Tallahassee, 1980-85. Mem. criminal justice adv. bd. Central Fla. Community Coll., 1974-85. Author: Literature on Law Enforcement: An Annotated Bibliography, 1969; also numerous articles in profl. publs. Recipient Pub. Safety Mgmt. award City of St. Petersburg, 1972; Good Govt. award Ocala Jaycees, 1976; Outstanding Law Enforcement award Fla. Council on Crime and Juvenile Delinquency, 1980. Mem. Internat. Assn. Chiefs Police, Fla. Police Chiefs Assn. (bd. dirs. 1983—). Democrat. Baptist. Lodges: Masons, Shriners, Kiwanis. Office: Ocala Police Dept 214 SE Fort King St Ocala FL 32678

MC GEHEE, CARDEN COLEMAN, banker; b. Franklin, Va., Aug. 11, 1924; s. Clopton Vivian and Laura (Coleman) McG.; student Va. Poly. Inst., 1941-43; B.S., U. Va., 1947; grad. Rutgers U. Grad. Sch. Banking, 1955-58, Harvard Advanced Mgmt. Program, 1970; m. Caroline Yarnall Casey, Apr. 21, 1951; children—Carden Coleman, Stephen Yarnall, Margaret Fox Verner. With First & Mchts. Nat. Bank, Richmond, Va., 1948-83, asst. trust officer, 1954-56, trust officer, 1956-59, v.p., 1959-62, sr. v.p., 1962, pres., chief adminstrv. officer, 1972-73, chmn. bd., chief exec. officer, 1973-83, also dir.; chmn. bd., chief exec. officer, dir. First & Mchts. Corp., 1974-84; pres., dir. Sovran Fin. Corp., 1984—; pres. Sovran Bank, 1984—, Sovran Fin. Corp., 1984—; dir. Chesapeake and Potomac Telephone Co. Va., Dan River, Inc., Sovran Bank, Sovran Fin. Corp., N.A., RF&P R.R. Co. Instr. evening div. U. Richmond, 1956-62, Va. Commonwealth U., 1958-64. Pres., United Givers Fund, 1971; bd. visitors Va. Commonwealth U., 1968-78; bd. govs. St. Christophers Sch., 1968-74; bd. sponsors Colgate Darden Grad. Sch. Bus. Adminstrn., 1980—, Sch. Bus. Adminstrn., Coll. William and Mary, 1974-80; treas. Retreat Hosp.; trustee Va. Hist. Soc. Served with AUS, 1943-46; maj. Va. N.G. Mem. C. of C., St. Andrews Soc., Beta Theta Pi, Delta Sigma Rho, Phi Alpha Delta, Beta Gamma Sigma, Omicron Delta Epsilon, Omicron Delta Kappa. Lodge: Rotary (pres. Richmond 1971-72). Clubs: Commonwealth; Country of Va.; Harvard, Board Room (N.Y.C.). Home: 6128 St Andrews Lane Richmond VA 23226 Office: Sovran Center 12th and Main Sts PO Box 27025 Richmond VA 23261

MCGEHEE, OSCAR CARRUTH, mathematics educator; b. Baton Rouge, Nov. 29, 1939; s. Oscar M. and Louise Blanche (Carruth) McG. B.A. in Math., Rice U., 1961; M.A. in Math., Yale U., 1963, Ph.D. in Math., 1966. Math. instr. U. Calif., Berkeley, 1965-67, asst. prof., 1967-71; prof. math. La. State U., Baton Rouge, 1971—, dept. chmn., 1979-84; NATO postdoctoral fellow U. Paris-South, Orsay, 1967-68; vis. assoc. prof. U. Ill., Champaign-Urbana, 1977, U. Oreg., 1978. Co-author: Essays in Commutative Harmonic Analysis, 1979; author, co-author research articles. NSF research grantee, 1972-80; recipient AMOCO Award for Teaching, La. State U., 1980. Fellow AAAS; mem. Am. Math. Soc. (council mem.-at-large 1981-83, nominating com. 1983-84), Sigma Xi (pres. La. State U. Chpt. 1981-82). Methodist. Home: 366 Magnolia Wood Ave Baton Rouge LA 70808 Office: Dept Math La State Univ Baton Rouge LA 70803

MCGEHEE, WILLIAM KENNETH, JR., alarm company executive, export trading company executive; b. Fort Smith, Ark., Dec. 20, 1942; s. William Kenneth and Virginia Anne (Creekmore) McG.; m. Janet Ann Kirby, Sept. 7, 1979; 1 child, William Kenneth III. Student U. Ark., 1960-62. Mgr. Houston div. Hickory Springs Mfg. Co., 1966-70; founder, owner, Mundo Sales Co., Fort Smith, 1971—; owner Spurling Fire & Burglar Alarm, Fort Smith, Little Rock and Fayetteville, Ark., 1978—; cons. internat. trade. Co-founder Judge Isaac C. Parker Found., Fort Smith, 1978; fin. dir., bd. dirs. Mt. Magazine council Girl Scouts U.S.A., 1978; active Westark Area council Boy Scouts Am., 1980—, v.p. fin., 1983—, pres., 1985, pres. nat. council, 1985-86; adv. trustee Sparks Regional Med. Ctr., Ft. Smith, 1981-84; mission pilot CAP, Ft. Smith, 1981—, squadron ops. officer, 1981-82; founder Life Flight, N.W. Ark., 1982; mem. Ark. Dist. Export Council, 1984—. Recipient Silver Beaver award Boy Scouts Am., 1983. 1978. Mem. Ark. Exporters Roundtable, Ft. Smith Home Builders Assn., Ft. Smith/Van Buren Advt. Fedn. (club pres. 1979-80, club bd. dirs. 1980-81), Westark Pilots Assn. (pres. Ft. Smith area 1983-84), Ark. Pilots Assn. (pres. 1984), U.S. Pilots Assn. (nat. sec. 1983-84), Ft. Smith C. of C. (N.W. Ark. polit. action com. 1979-83, Ft. Smith Aviation com. 1983), Quiet Birdmen. Methodist. Club: Fianna Hills Country. Lodge: Rotary (pres. club 1977-78, bd. dirs. club 1978—, dist. gov.'s rep. 1980-81, Paul Harris fellow 1978) (Ft. Smith). Holder aviation world speed records (2), 1985. Office: PO Box 4445 Fort Smith AR 72914

MC GILL, GARY RONALD, consulting engineer; b. Knoxville, Tenn., Apr. 5, 1947; s. Robert Bruce and Maxine (Davis) McG.; B.S. in Civil Engring., U. Tenn., 1970; cert. in Water Supply Engring., U. N.C., 1977; Design engr. Fla. Power Corp., St. Petersburg, 1970-72; head of engring. Misener Marine Constrn. Co., Inc., St. Petersburg, 1973-74; city engr. Asheville (N.C.),

1974-76; corp. partner, officer Butler/McGill Assocs., P.A., Asheville, 1976-84; dir., pres. McGill & Assocs., P.A., Asheville, 1984—. Registered profl. engr., N.C., Tenn., Va., Ky. Mem. Am. Water Works Assn., Water Pollution Control Fedn., Nat. Soc. Profl. Engrs., Nat. Rural Water Assn., Audubon Soc., Sierra Club, Cousteau Soc., Appalachian Trail Conf. Democrat. Presbyterian. Office: 216 Executive Park Asheville NC 28801 also PO Box 2269 Asheville NC 28802

MCGILL, HENRY COLEMAN, JR., physician, educator, researcher; b. Nashville, Oct. 1, 1921; s. Henry Coleman and Thursa (Lowry) McG.; m. Cloace Laurite Ferguson, Sept. 12, 1945; children—Margaret Ann, Laurilynn, Elizabeth Gail. B.A., Vanderbilt U., 1943, M.D., 1946. Intern Vanderbilt Hosp., Nashville, 1946-47; asst. prof. La. State U. Med. Ctr., New Orleans, 1950-55, assoc. prof., 1955-61, prof., chmn. pathology U. Tex. Health Sci. Ctr., San Antonio, 1961-72; sci. dir. S.W. Found. for Biomed. Research, San Antonio, 1979—. Served to capt. U.S. Army, 1948-50. Mem. Phi Beta Kappa, Sigma Xi, Alpha Omega Alpha. Contbr. numerous articles to profl. jours. Home: 4102 Fawnridge Dr San Antonio TX 78229 Office: 7703 Floyd Curl Dr San Antonio TX 78284

MCGILL, JERRY CLINTON, psychologist, educator; b. Squires, Mo., Sept. 28, 1947; s. Archie Wesley and Alta Louise (Hardcastle) McG.; m. Carolyn Fisher, July 31, 1972; 1 child, James Wesley. B.A., Hardin-Simmons U., 1969; M.A., Tex. Tech U., 1971; Ph.D., N. Tex. State U., 1979. Lic. psychologist, Tex. Staff psychologist W. Tex. Rehab. Ctr., Abilene, 1970-71, Tex. Rehab. Commn., Lubbock, 1972-76; grad. asst. N.Tex. State U., Denton, 1976-79; asst. prof. psychology Tex. Coll. Osteo. Medicine, Ft. Worth, 1979—. Contbr. articles and papers to profl. lit. Served with USAR, 1970. Faculty grantee Tex. Coll. Osteo. Medicine, 1982. Mem. Am. Psychol. Assn., Tex. Psychol. Assn., Tarrant County Psychol. Assn. (ethics com. 1985), Southwestern Psychol. Assn. Avocation: gardening. Home: Route 1 Box 8 Summer Dell Ct Roanoke TX 76262 Office: Dept of Rehab/Sports Medicine Tex Coll Osteo Medicine 1501 Merrimac Circle Fort Worth TX 76107

MC GILL, SAM PEYTON, state senator, automobile dealer, farmer; b. Lincoln County, Ga., Aug. 30, 1914; s. Adolphus Cecil and Lillian Inez (Norman) McG.; student S. Ga. State Coll.; m. Florence Clary, Sept. 22, 1935; children—Sam Clary, Kathryn McGill Lamar. Owner service sta., 1936-38; owner, pres. McGill Truck & Tractor (inc. into McGill's Inc. 1975), 1939—; owner Wilkes County Stockyard, Washington, Ga., 1950—; owner, S.P. McGill Farms, 1942—; dir. Washington Loan & Banking Co. Mem. Washington City Council, 1952-58; mem. Ga. State Senate, chmn. agr. com. Named Wilkes County Citizen of Yr., 1977; recipient Ga. County Agts. award, 1974; Disting. Service award U. Ga. Vet. Sch.; Hon. State FFA Farmer degree. Mem. Ga. Farm Equipment Assn., Ga. Stockyard Assn., Nat. Livestock Mktg. Assn. Democrat. Baptist. Clubs: Lions, Wilkes Country, Atlanta City, Atlanta Athletic. Office: 402 N By-Pass Washington GA 30673

MCGILL, WILLIAM MCPHERSON, III, electric motor repair company executive; b. Washington, Oct. 6, 1932; s. William McPherson and Alta (Cookman) McG.; m. Sally Ingraham, Sept. 12, 1952; children—Deborah, Jacqueline, Molly. B.S. in Elec. Engring., Purdue U., 1956; postgrad. Syracuse U., Va. Poly. Inst., Roanoke Coll. Reactor engr. E.I. DuPont de Nemours & Co., Inc., Aiken, S.C., 1956-57; mgr. Gen. Electric Co., Roanoke, Va., 1957-67; instr. math. U. Va., 1957-67; chief elec. engr. Tippins Machinery Co. Inc., Pitts., 1967-72; pres., chief engr. A&F Electric Motor Repair, Inc., Miami, Fla., 1972—. Mem. IEEE (sr.), Elec. Apparatus Service Assn., Am. Inst. Steel Engrs. Republican. Episcopalian. Lodge: Lions. Home: 6934 Bottle Brush Dr Miami FL 33014 Office: A&F Electric Motor Repair Inc 8148 N W 74th Ave Miami FL 33166

MCGINN, MARTY JOHNSON, advertising agency executive, writer; b. Salisbury, N.C., June 3, 1947; d. Joseph Wayne and Martha Deibert Johnson; m. Philip Duke Stukey, Dec. 15, 1969 (div. 1976); 1 son, Peter Duke McGinn; m. John Francis McGinn, Jr., July 4, 1980. B.S. in Journalism, U. Fla., 1970. Sales promotion coordinator Kirby Bldg. Systems, Houston, 1978-79; pres. Marty Johnson Advt., Ltd. Co., Rockwell, N.C., 1980—; columnist Metal Bldg. Rev. mag., 1982—. Mem. Nat. Writer's Club (profl. mem.). Club: Toastmasters.

MCGINN, RICHARD JOHN, equipment company executive; b. Ardmore, Pa.; s. Hugh and Delia (Kelly) McG.; m. Marguerite Gleason; children—Richard John, David. B.S. in Commerce and Fin., Bucknell U., 1949. Sales engr., Nelson Stud Welding div. TRW, regional mgr. Midwest area, Cleve., 1950-60; founder, pres. R.J. Mack Co., Jacksonville, Fla., 1960—. Mem. Com of 100. Served with USMC, 1942-45. Mem. Jacksonville C. of C., Phi Gamma Delta. Clubs: River, University, Ponte Vedra. Office: 9076 Cypress Green Dr Jacksonville FL 32216

MCGINNIS, DENNIS ROBERT, educational administrator, educator; b. New Albany, Ind., Apr. 20, 1941; s. Dennis Arthur and Eleanor Ann (Shyne) McG.; m. Johnna Lou Fuller, Aug. 31, 1968; children—Kelleen Anne, Kathryn Jo. A.B., Georgetown U., 1962; M.A., George Washington U., 1971; Ed.D., U. Ga.-Athens, 1980. Dir. research Western Carolina U., Cullowhee, N.C., 1971-77, dir. univ. devel., 1977-82; v.p. univ. devel. East Tenn. State U., Johnson City, 1982-85; exec. dir. East Tenn. State U. Found., 1982-85; v.p. univ. relations U. Central Fla., Orlando, 1985—, exec. dir. Found., 1985—; asst. inspector gen. U.S. Naval Res., Charleston, S.C., 1984-85, dir. plans Naval Res. Readiness Command, 1985—. Bd. dirs. United Way, Johnson City, 1983—, Vol. Johnson City, 1984—, Directions 2000-Higher Edn. Comm., Johnson City; vice chmn. Springfest '85, Johnson City, Fla. Symphony Orch., 1985—. Served with USN, 1963-71; capt. Res. Grantee U.S. Office Edn., 1975; NSF fellow, 1976; recipient Leadership award Kiwanis, 1971. Mem. Nat. Council Univ. Research Adminstrs. (conf. coordinator), Council Advancement and Support Edn., Naval Res. Assn., Naval War Coll. Found., Mountain Empire Devel. Officers Assn., Phi Delta Kappa, Phi Kappa Phi. Roman Catholic. Home: 2160 Chinook Trail Maitland FL 32751 Office: U Central Fla Box 25000 Orlando FL 32816

MCGINNIS, GLENN EDWARD, business owner; b. Abilene, Kans., July 25, 1939; s. Edward Day and Hannah Andrena (Wang) McG.; m. Crystal Ann Gandy, Dec. 19, 1964; children—Michelle Lee, Craig Alan. Student Kans. State U., 1957-61. Inside salesman Capitol Pipe and Steel Co., Houston, 1960-61, sales rep., 1962-64, dist. mgr., Los Angeles, 1964-67, asst. v.p. mktg., Phila., 1967-70, div. v.p., Houston, 1970-81; owner, operator The Dove's Nest, Kerrville, Tex., 1981—. Vice pres. U.S. Jaycees, Turnersville, N.J., 1969-70; dir. Hill Country Arts Found., Ingram, Tex., 1984—, ARC, Kerrville, 1984—. Served to petty officer USCG, 1961-69. Mem. Christian Booksellers Assn., Kerrville Area C. of C. (bd. dirs. 1982-83, 85—). Republican. Methodist. Lodge: Rotary. Avocations: golfing; jogging; reading; traveling. Home: 623 East Ln Kerrville TX 78028 Office: The Dove's Nest 214 Quinlan St Kerrville TX 78028

MCGINNIS, JAMES WESLEY, petroleum co. exec.; b. Caney, Kans., Oct. 8, 1943; s. James Riley and Reta (Clark) McG.; A.A., Coffeyville Coll., 1963; B.S., Pittsburg U., 1968; children—James Randall, Russell Brent. Analyst/programmer Phillips Petroleum Co., Bartlesville, Okla., 1968-74, mgmt. services cons., 1975-77, dir. projects info. mgmt. div., exploration and production group, 1978—; tchr. Tulsa Vo-Tech Sch., 1981-82. Mem. Assn. Systems Mgmt. Republican. Clubs: Musicians Assn., Frank Phillips Mens. Lodge: Elks. Home: 4516 Barlow Dr Bartlesville OK 74006 Office: 1 MW Bldg Bartlesville OK 74004

MCGINNIS, LYLE DAVID, geophysicist, educator, researcher; b. Appleton, Wis., Mar. 5, 1931; s. Lyle Andrew and Rose Mary (Heimmermann) McG.; m. Mary Eileen Croake, Oct. 10, 1959; children—John, Mary, Robert, Thomas, Joseph. B.Sc., St. Norbert Coll., 1954; M.Sc., St. Louis U., 1960; Ph.D., U. Ill.-Urbana, 1965. Geophysicist Carter Oil Co., Tulsa, 1954-57, Arctic Inst. N.Am., Antarctica, 1957-59, Ill. State Geol. Survey, Urbana, 1959-66, UN Devel. Program, Kabul, Afghanistan, 1966-67; prof. No. Ill. U., DeKalb, 1967-83; prof. dept. geology La. State U., Baton Rouge, 1983—, chmn., 1983-85; vis. scientist U.S. Geol. Survey, Woods Hole, Mass., 1976-77. Editor: Dry Valley Drillings Project, 1980; contbr. articles to profl. jours. Served with USN, 1949-50. Recipient Research awards U.S. Geol. Survey, 1960—, NSF, 1967—. Fellow Geol. Soc. Am.; mem. Soc. Exploration Geophysics, Am. Geophys. Union, Seismological Soc. Am., Am. Assn. Petroleum Geologists. Office: La State U Dept Geology Baton Rouge LA 70803

MCGINTY, MILTON BRADFORD, architect; b. Houston, July 6, 1946; s. Milton Bowles and Ruth Louise (Dreaper) McG.; m. Margaret Louise O'Donnel, Dec. 11, 1967; 1 son, Daniel Milton. B.A., Rice U., Houston, 1970, B.Arch., 1973; M.B.A., Fla. Atlantic U., Boca Raton, 1980. Lic. real estate broker, Tex.; registered architect, Tex. Designer, draftsman Carden L. Jenkins, Consulting Mech. Engrs., 1968-70; job capt. Welton Becket & Assocs., Architects, 1970-74; project mgr. The McGinty Partnership, Architects, Inc., Houston, 1975-76, v.p., 1976—, also dir.; pres. City Assocs., Inc., Houston; cons. and lectr. in field. Mem. AIA, Houston Bd. Realtors, Tex. Soc. Architects, Am. Mgmt. Assn. Episcopalian. Clubs: Univ., Briar (Houston). Lodge: Kiwanis (sec.). Office: 601 Sawyer St Houston TX 77007

MCGLAUCHLIN, ALAN E., geophysicist; b. Beloit, Wis., Oct. 26, 1930; s. Charles Orion and Lenore Frances (Cadman) McG.; m. Norene A. Molcan, Aug. 15, 1953; children—Carol Frances, Susan Lee, Michael Alan, Lisa Kay. Geophysical engr., Colo. Sch. Mines, 1961. Geophysicist Mobil Oil Corp., Dallas, 1961-73; v.p., dir. Profl. Geophysics Inc., Dallas, 1974-82; pres., chmn. Timeback Systems Inc., Dallas, 1982—. Mem. Soc. Exploration Geophysicists, Am. Assn. Petroleum Geologists, Dallas Geophysical Soc. (sec. 1982-83). Episcopalian. Club: Dallas Energy. Home: 4140 Hockaday Dr Dallas TX 75229 Office: Timeback Systems Inc PO Box 814208 Dallas TX 75381

MCGLINCHEY, DIANNE WATKINS, marketing executive, consultant; b. Meridian, Miss., Dec. 29, 1949; d. W. Warren and Alaine (Kynerd) Watkins; m. Bruce McGlinchey, May 27, 1979. B.S. summa cum laude, U. So. Miss., 1970. Supr. merchandising specialists Fla. Dept. Natural Resources, Miami, 1971-74; seafood consumer specialist mktg. div. Nat. Marine Fisheries Service, U.S. Dept. Commerce, Pascagoula, Miss., 1975-77; mgr. menu diversification and product devel. Red Lobster Inns of Am., Orlando, Fla., 1977-79; mktg. cons. McGlinchey Enterprises, Orlando, 1981-84, dir. mktg. Beatrice Specialty Pet, 1984—; cons. to SBA, 1981-82. Recipient citation Sec. Commerce, 1976. Mem. Orlando Advt. Fedn., Am. Mgmt. Assn. Republican. Methodist.

MC GLOHEN, PATTI JON ROSS, educator; b. Corsicana, Tex., Apr. 3, 1948; d. John Franklin and Leora (Richardson) Ross; B.S., North Tex. State U., 1970, M.Ed., 1977; postgrad. Stephen F. Austin U., 1971, So. Meth. U., 1977, U.Tex.-Arlington, 1984; m. Macon Wesly McGlohen, Apr. 7, 1969; children—John Ross, Meghan Kathleen. Tchr., Dallas Ind. Sch. Dist., 1971-73; tchr. elem. sch. Grand Prairie, Tex., 1973-79; tchr. computer literacy and sci., asst. dir. articulation project Dallas County Community Coll. Dist., 1979-80; tchr. home econs. and English, Grand Prairie Ind. Sch. Dist., 1980-85; MCLS project tng. coordinator M Bank, Dallas, 1985—; mem. adv. com. profl. devel. area Tex. Educator Initial Cert. Testing Program; cons., writer ednl. mdse. Tex. Instruments, Inc., Dallas, 1978-79. Mem. North Tex. State U. Profl. Adminstrs and Suprs. Council, Assn. Supervision and Curriculum Devel., Am. Soc. Tng. and Devel. Phi Delta Kappa. Developer ednl. games and software. Office: PO Box 610525 Dallas/Ft. Worth Airport TX 75261

MC GLOHON, LOONIS, pianist, composer, broadcasting co. exec.; b. Ayden, N.C., Sept. 29, 1921; s. Max Cromwell and Bertha (Andrews) McG.; B.S., East Carolina U., 1942; m. Nan Lovelace, June 19, 1943; children—Reeves, Fan, Laurie. With Jefferson Pilot Broadcasting Co., Charlotte, N.C., 1949—; composer numerous recorded jazz and popular works, film scores, network TV themes; co-author opera Mountain Boy; performed at Carnegie Hall, Lincoln Ctr., Davies Symphony Hall, numerous internat. performances, Organizer 1st Carolina chpt. Big Bros./Big Sisters Agy., 1972; bd. dirs. Spirit Sq., Historic Bath Commn., NCCJ, Community Sch Arts. Recipient numerous awards including Peabody award, 1977, 78. Mem. Am. Guild Authors and Composers, Broadcast Music Inc., Pub. Relations Soc. Am. Club: Charlotte Athletic. Club: Charlotte Athletic. Home: 222 Wonderwood Dr Charlotte NC 28211 Office: 1 Julian Price Pl Charlotte NC 28208

MCGLOTHLIN, MICHAEL GORDON, lawyer; b. Richlands, Va., Oct. 31, 1951; s. Woodrow Wilson and Sally Ann (Cook) McG.; m. Sandra Lee Keen, Oct. 1, 1983; 1 child, M. Alexander. B.A., U. Va., 1974; J.D., Coll. William and Mary, 1976. Bar: Va. 1977, U.S. Dist. Ct. (we. dist.) Va. 1978. Ptnr. McGlothlin, McGlothlin, Grundy, Va., 1977-79; commonwealth atty. Buchanan County, Grundy, 1980-83; ptnr. McGlothlin & Wife, Grundy, 1984—; county atty., Buchanan County, 1984—; dir. Gt. Southwest Home Commn. Mem. adv. bd. Clinch Valley Coll.; sec. Buchanan County Dem. Com., 1984—. Mem. ABA, Va. State Bar Assn., Buchanan County Bar Assn. (pres. 1984), Phi Alpha Delta. Presbyterian. Home: PO Drawer 810 Grundy VA 24614 Office: PO Drawer 810 Grundy VA 24614

MCGONIGLE, ROBERT BRIAN, university counselor; b. Boston, June 7, 1956; s. George Patrick and Ruth Claire (Cullen) McG. B.A., Wittenburg U., 1978; M.S., W. Ill. U., 1982; postgrad. U. Ga., 1984—. Hall dir. Wittenberg U., Springfield, Ohio, 1978-80; complex dir. Western Ill. U., Macomb, 1981-84; jud. officer U. Ga., Athens, 1985—; research cons. So. Tech. Inst., Marietta, Ga., 1985. Mem. Nat. Assn. Student Personnel Adminstrs., Am. Coll. Personnel Assn., Am. Assn. for Counseling and Devel., U. Ga.-Athens Student Personnel Assn. (treas. 1985), Phi Kappa Phi, Phi Kappa Delta. Democrat. Roman Catholic. Home: PO Box 2296 Athens GA 30612-0296 Office: Office U Housing Russell Hall U Ga Athens GA 30602

MCGOOKEY, DOUGLAS ALAN, geologist; b. Lewistown, Mont., Nov. 10, 1952; s. Donald Paul and Doris Jean (Masell) McG. B.A. in Geology, U. Tex.-Austin, 1977, M.S. in Geology, 1986. Geophys. technician Western Geophys., Houston, 1978; research assoc. scientist Bur. Econs., Austin, 1978-85; geologist D. M. Exploration, Midland, Tex., 1978—. Author: Regional Structural Cross Sections, Mid-Permian to Quaternary, Texas Panhandle and Eastern New Mexico, 1985. Contbr. articles on geology to profl. jours. Sponser, leader Episcopal Young Churchmen, Austin, 1975-80; active Big Bros., Austin, 1974-84; researcher Lloyd Dogget U.S. Senate campaign, Austin, 1984. Mem. Am. Assn. Petroleum Geologists, Austin Geol. Soc. Democrat. Episcopalian. Club: Canturbury Assn. (Austin). Avocations: canoeing; softball; history; science fiction. Home: 2406 Culpeper St Midland TX 79705 Office: D M Exploration 310 W Illinois St Suite 314 Midland TX 79701

MCGOUGH, LARRY JOE, educational administrator; b. Ft. Worth, Mar. 4, 1945; s. Presley Arthur and Cornelia Hazel McGough; m. Constance E. Meeks, July 12, 1970; children—Chris, Jon. B.S., Tex. A&M U., 1967; M.Ed., Tarleton State U., 1976. Tchr., coach Bonham Jr. High Sch., Amarillo, Tex., 1967-68, Castleberry High Sch., Fort Worth, 1971-74, Mansfield High Sch. (Tex.), 1974-78; prin. Mansfield Elem. Sch., 1978-79, J.L. Boren Elem. Sch., 1979-83, asst. to supt., 1983—. Life mem. PTA; mem. adminstrv. bd. First Methodist Ch., 1973-74; active Jaycees, 1978-79. Served with U.S. Army, 1968-71. Mem. Tex. Elem. Prins. Assn., Nat. Elem. Prins. Assn., Assn. Community Schs., Tex. Tchrs. Assn. Home: 106 Wisteria Mansfield TX 76063 Office: 609 E Broad St Mansfield TX 76063

MCGOUGH, MARY ANN, electronics technician; b. Boston, Sept. 28, 1948; d. Henry Howard and Eva Elizabeth (Ecklof) Groff. A.S. in Elec. and Electronic Engring., Franklin Inst. Boston, 1968; B.S. in Mgmt., Jones Coll., Jacksonville, Fla., 1983. Communications technician AT&T Communications, Jacksonville, 1974—. Served with USN, 1968-73. Episcopalian. Home: 1638 Hazelhurst Dr Jacksonville FL 32216 Office: AT&T Communications 424 Pearl St Room 300 Jacksonville FL 32202

MCGOUGH, WILLIAM MALCOLM, JR., construction executive; b. Vicksburg, Miss., Dec. 9, 1946; s. William Malcolm and Della Mae (Seawright) McG.; m. Jamie Louise Wacker, July 11, 1970; children—Traci Elizabeth, William Christopher. B.S. in Bus. Mgmt., U. Ala., 1970; B.S. in Civil Engring., Auburn U., 1973. Registered profl. engr., Ala. Engr., estimator Weaver & Morris Constrn. Co., Mobile, Ala., 1971-72; engr., estimator Laidlaw Contracting Co., Inc., Mobile, 1973-76, gen. supt., 1976-78; pres., owner McGough Constrn. Co., Inc., Mobile, Ala., 1978—; v.p. RLT Constrn. Co., Inc., Mobile, 1983—; cons. estimating and cost control. Pres., John Will Sch. PTA, Alpine Hills Swim Club. Served to capt. C.E., USAR, 1970-80. Mem. Mobile County Roadbuilders Assn. (past pres.), ASCE (past chpt. pres.), Nat. Soc. Profl. Engrs. Baptist. Home: 1556 McIntyre Dr Mobile AL 36608 Office: PO Box 8681 Mobile AL 36608

MCGOVERN, SANDRA LYNN, cable TV executive; b. Huntington, W.Va., Aug. 21, 1947; d. Tennis and Ruth (Finley) Gravely; m. Andrew Wyatt Ball, Oct. 17, 1970 (div. Oct. 1975); m. William David McGovern, May 29, 1976. B.A., Marshall U., 1969, M.A., 1972; postgrad. W.Ga. Coll., 1974-76. Counselor, tchr. public schs., W.Va., Md., Ga., 1969-75; dir. child and adolescent services Ga. Div. Mental Health, LaGrange, Ga., 1976; cons. psychologist Atlanta Back Clinic, 1977; sales exec. Xerox Corp., Atlanta, 1977-80; regional dir. S.E., Rainbow Programming Services, Atlanta, 1980-84, v.p. field ops. Rainbow Programming Services, N.Y.C., 1984—. Mem. Nat. Cable TV Assn., Women in Cable Soc., Cable TV Adminstrn. and Mktg. Assn., Phi Delta Kappa. Republican. Presbyterian.

MCGOWAN, JOHN EDWARD, JR., clinical microbiology educator, epidemiologist, infectious diseases specialist; b. Poughkeepsie, N.Y., June 30, 1942; s. John Edward and Doris Robinson (Wearne) McG.; m. Linda Kay Hudson, May 28, 1967; 1 child, Angela Kay. B.M.S., Dartmouth Coll., 1965; M.D., Harvard U., 1967. Diplomate Am. Bd. Internal Medicine, Am. Bd. Infectious Diseases, Am. Bd. Pathology, Am. Bd. Clinical Microbiology. Intern, resident Harvard Service, Boston City Hosp., 1967-69; research fellowship Thorndike Lab. Harvard Med. Sch., 1971-72; instr. Harvard Med. Sch., Boston, 1972-73; asst. prof. Emory Med. Sch., Atlanta, 1973-76, assoc. prof., 1977-81, prof. pathology and medicine, 1982—; dir. microbiology Grady Meml. Hosp., Atlanta, 1982—. Author: Outline Guide to Antimicrobial Therapy, 1983; contbr. sci. articles to profl. jours. Governing bd. Young Singers of Callanwolde, Decatur, Ga., 1981—; treas. Leafmore Creek-Park Club, Decatur, 1982-84. Served to sr. surgeon with USPHS, 1969-71. Fellow Infectious Diseases Soc. Am. (assoc. editor Infection Control jour. 1980—). So. Soc. for Clin. Investigation; mem. Am. Soc. for Microbiology (div. chmn. 1982-84, governing bd. 1984—), Soc. Hosp. Epidemiologists of Am. (pres. 1981). Home: 1763 Council Bluff Dr Atlanta GA 30345 Office: Emory Univ Sch Medicine 69 Butler St Atlanta GA 30335

MCGOWAN, JOHN EVANS, investment banker; b. Los Angeles, May 16, 1933; s. Thomas John and Miriam Ruth (Evans) McG.; m. Nora McLin, Apr. 8, 1954; 1 child, Keith. B.S. in Agrl. Engring., La. State U., 1956, M.B.A., 1958; postgrad. Harvard U., 1969. Chartered fin. analyst. Asst. v.p. securities Mana & Research, Galveston, Tex., 1968-71; v.p. securities Am. Nat. Ins., Galveston, 1958-71; v.p. Moroney Bessiner & Co., Houston, 1972-74; v.p. fin. Tex. United Corp., Houston, 1974—; pres., owner Investment & Fin. Services, Inc., Houston, 1974—, also dir.; dir. FINCO of Houston, 1968—. Mem. Inst. Chartered Fin. Analysts, Houston Grampion Assn., Houston Soc. Fin. Analysts, Nat. Assn. Securities Dealers. Home: 11 Mott Ln Houston TX 77024 Office: Investment & Fin Services Inc 2000 W Loop S Suite 800 Houston TX 77027

MCGOWAN, KATHLEEN KEER, artist; b. Newark, Mar. 8, 1918; d. Theodore F. and Florence (MacRae) Keer; B.A., Smith Coll., 1940; postgrad. Columbia U., 1943, N.J. Tchrs. Coll., 1946-49; m. B.C. Breeden, June 29, 1940 (div. 1943); 1 dau., Kathy; m. 2d, Harold F. Allenby, July 28, 1949 (div. 1977); m. 3d, John Francis McGowan, Apr. 24, 1981. Kindergarten tchr. Kimberly Sch., Montclair, N.J., 1946-49; tchr. art to handicapped Kessler Inst. Rehab., West Orange, N.J., 1961-77. Exhibited one-man shows Woman's Club Montclair, 1st Savs. & Loan Bank, Cedar Grove, N.J., Music Sch., Cedar Grove, Piggins Art Gallery, Montclair, N.J., all 1972; 2-man show 1st Nat. Bank of Palm Beach, 1978; exhibited in group shows N.J. State Fedn. Women's Clubs, Art Center of Oranges. Leader, Girl Scouts U.S.A., Little Falls, N.J., 1955-56; social dir. PTA, Great Notch, N.J., 1955-56. Recipient art awards Upper Montclair Women's Club; cert. of merit in art N.J. Fedn. Women's Clubs, 1st pl. essay award, 1973; second award for "Sea Scape," Lighthouse Gall., Jupiter, Fla., 1985. Mem. Art Center Oranges, West Essex Art Assn., N.J. State Fedn. Women's Clubs (7th dist. art chmn. 1973-74), West Palm Beach Coin Club (sec. 1978-81). Clubs: Glen Ridge Country (N.J., handicap chmn. 1970, past publicity chmn. women's golf group); Upper Montclair Women's (dir. art dept. 1971-72, garden chmn. 1976-77); Little Falls Women's (treas. 1959-61); Quill (Palm Beach) (recording sec. 1985—), Beach (Palm Beach); Smith of the Palm Beaches (treas. 1976-77). Home: Apt G331 The Waterford 603 South US Hwy 1 Juno Beach FL 33408

MCGOWAN, SEAN MICHAEL, aquaculture company executive, consultant, researcher; b. Chgo., Feb. 22, 1948; s. Donald Martell and Anna (Baran) McG. B.S., U. Wash., 1970; postgrad. in zoology student in electronics Coll. Dupage, 1976; student Acad. Real Estate, 1982-83. Oceanographer U. Wash., Seattle, 1969-73; research asst. Waterman Hydraulics, Chgo., 1974-76; med. researcher VA Hosp., Chgo., 1976-77; sales mgr. Walgreen Co., Houston, 1977-82; sales mgr. investments NPC Investments, Houston, 1982-83; exec. v.p., dir. Tex. United Fisheries, Houston, 1983—; oceanographer CREEL, Hanover, N.H., 1971. Mem. World Mariculture Soc., Ancient Order Hibernians, Alvin Aero Club. Republican. Roman Catholic. Home: 1201 Bering 98 Houston TX 77057 Office: Tex United Fisheries 2620 Fountainview 222 Houston TX 77057

MCGOWEN, GERRY F(RANK), insurance executive; b. Tulare, Calif., May 5, 1937; s. Bryant Clark and Bonnie B. (Chrisman) McG.; m. Naomi L. Hartsfield, Feb. 18, 1961; children—Shawn Lynn, Gregory Allen. B.S. in Acctg., Calif. State U.-Fresno, 1961. With U.S. Dept. Treasury, 1961-62; personnel dir. marine div. Bendix Corp., 1963-65; v.p. U.S. Computers, 1965-74; sr. v.p. John S. Dunn & Son, Inc., Houston, 1974-82; pres., chmn. bd. Foster Ins. Mgrs., Inc., Foster Ins. Services, Inc., Security Capital Lloyd's, Lloyd's Mgmt. Corp., Houston, 1982—; chmn. agt. adv. council Aetna Liability and Casualty, Houston; mem. agt. adv. council Indiana Lumbermen's. Active Nat. Republican Congl. Com., 1982-83; mem. Ronald Reagan 500 Adv. Assn., 1983. Served with Fin. Corps U.S. Army, 1956-59. Mem. Nat. Assn. Ind. Ins. Agts., Tex. Assn. Ind. Ins. Agts., Houston Assn. Ind. Ins. Agts. (chmn. law enforcement com.). Office: 1111 N Loop W Suite 400 Houston TX 77008

MCGRADY, WILLIAM FLEMING, state educational administrator; b. Lodi, Ohio, Jan. 19, 1944; s. Harold James and Cora Elizabeth (Fleming) McG.; m. Chloe Annette Crawford, Dec. 29, 1973 (div. 1976); m. Diane Marie Gerchario, July 28, 1980; children—Andrew Ryan. B.S. in Edn., Bowling Green U., 1968; M.Ed., U. Ariz., 1974. Program planner N.C. Dept. Pub. Instrn., Jacksonville, 1975-77, regional coordinator, 1977-80, staff devel. cons., Raleigh, 1980, asst. div. dir., 1980-85, dep. asst. state supt., 1985—; adj. instr. U. N.C.-Wilmington, 1979—. Project coordinator Heart Fund, Jacksonville, 1979, 80. Served to capt. USAF, 1968-73. Recipient Founders award N.C. Heart Assn., Chapel Hill, 1980. Mem. Council for Exceptional Children, Jacksonville Jaycees (dir. 1979-80). Democrat. Roman Catholic. Club: N.C. Roadrunners. Avocations: running; reading. Office: NC Dept Pub Instrn 114 Edenton St Raleigh NC 27611

MCGRATH, VALENE KAREN, vocational training center director; b. Salt Lake City, Aug. 23, 1942; d. Albert Clark and Violet (Robinson) Robison; m. Mikel Eugene McGrath, Dec. 1, 1957; children—Cynthia McGrath Buchanan, Karen McGrath Hill, Kimberlie, Mikelene, JoDell, Mathew. Student U. Idaho, 1959-60, Samaritan Sch. Nursing, Nampa, Idaho, 1961-62; L.P.N. U. Oreg., 1967-69; student U. Utah, 1978-79. Lic. practical nurse, Idaho. In various nursing positions, 1962-66; surg. floor supr., med. nurse U. Oreg. Tongue Point Job Corps, Astoria, 1966-69, residential supr., 1974-75; motel operator, Long Beach, Wash., 1972-73; coordinator student govt. and religious coordinator Thiokol Corp. Clearfield Job Corps (Utah), 1975-79, mgr. health services, 1979-80; residential dir. tng. and mgmt. resources Denison Job Corps. (Iowa), 1980; center dir. Tng. and Mgmt. Resources Inc., 1980-83, with corporate office tng. and mgmt. resources, Atlanta, 1983—. Capt., CAP, 1965—, mem. Rocky Mountain Staff, Ogden, Utah, 1976-80, mem. staff Regional Staff Coll., Portland, Oreg., 1979; franchise cons. Sav-A-Buc Internat., Jacksonville, Fla.; dir. programs Brunswick Job Corp., 1983-84; co-owner, v.p. Diamond M Enterprises, mktg. and indsl. tng., 1984—. Mem. Assn. Supervision and Curriculum Devel., Nat. Assn. Vietnamese Am. Edn. Home and Office: 21 Windsor Circle Brunswick GA 31520

MC GRAW, DARRELL VIVIAN, JR., judge; b. Wyoming County, W.Va., Nov. 8, 1936; s. Darrell Vivian and Julia (Zekany) McG. A.B., W.Va. U., 1961 LL.B., J.D., 1964, M.A., 1977. Bar: W.Va. bar 1964. Gen. atty. Fgn. Claims Settlement Commn., Dept. State, 1964; counsel to Gov., State of W.Va., 1965-68; practice law Shepherdstown, Morgantown and Charleston, 1968-76; judge W.Va. Supreme Ct. Appeals, Charleston, 1977—, chief justice, 1983—. Served with U.S. Army, 1954-57. Democrat. Office: Supreme Ct State Capitol Bldg Charleston WV 25305*

MCGRAW, RICHARD LYLE, former airline executive; b. Montgomery, W.Va., Dec. 27, 1936; s. Henry Paul McGraw and Edythe Lyle (Bagby)

Williams; m. Beverly Vaughan, Aug. 4, 1960 (div. Feb. 1964); 1 son, Patrick; m. Barbara A. Callison, May 15, 1964; 1 son, Douglas. Student W.Va., U., 1959-61; B.A., Wash. State U., 1964; M.A., Mich. State U., 1968. Exec. asst. to sec. U.S. Dept. HUD, Washington, 1973-75, dep. under sec., 1975-77; exec. dir. Alliance to Save Energy, Washington, 1977-79, bd. dirs., 1977—; v.p. G.D. Searle & Co., Skokie, Ill., 1979-83; sr. v.p. Eastern Air Lines, Inc., Miami, Fla., 1983-85. Contbr. articles to profl. jours. Bd. dirs. Skokie Valley Hosp., 1978-79, Mailman Ctr., Miami, 1984—. Served with USAF, 1964-71. Decorated Bronze Star; recipient Golden Trumpet award Publicity Club Chgo., 1982. Republican. Episcopalian. *

MCGRAW, STEPHEN SCHNEIDER, clinical psychologist; b. Ft. Worth, Jan. 12, 1953; s. Duane Darwin and Genevieve Claudia (Schneider) McG.; m. Linda Miriam Lanier, Nov. 11, 1972; 1 child, Sean Stephen. B.A., U. Miami, 1979; M.S., Fla. Inst. Tech., 1981, D.Psychology, 1983. Lic. psychologist, Fla. Intern, San Bernardino County Med. Ctr., San Bernardino, Calif., 1982-83; clin. psychologist Anneewakee, Inc., Carrabelle, Fla., 1983—; cons. psychologist Parents United, Inc., San Bernardino, 1982-83; cons. psychologist, Carrabelle and Tallahassee, 1984—. Active Spl. Olympics, Franklin County, Fla., 1984-85. Fellow Psi Chi; mem. Am. Psychol. Assn., Southeastern Psychol. Assn., Fla. Psychol. Assn., Nat. Register Health Service Providers in Psychology. Avocations: golf, tennis, scuba diving, fishing, skiing. Address: 2851-A Par Ln Tallahassee FL 32301 also Anneewakee Inc Star Route Box 73 Carrabelle FL 32322

MC GREGOR, FRANK HAMILTON, JR., physician; b. New Orleans, Mar. 19, 1938; s. Frank Hamilton and Sarah Louise (Mayo) McG.; B.S., Duke U., 1959, M.A., 1963, M.D., 1965; m. Eleanore Ruth Stone, Dec. 16, 1961 (div. 1980); children—Sarah Goodwin, Holly Jane; m. 2d, Ava Patricia Carvan, Jan. 3, 1981. Research asso. Duke U., Durham, N.C., 1959-61, fellow in cardiovascular surgery, 1965, 68-69, intern, 1965-66, resident in surgery, 1969-70; resident in surgery Tulane U., New Orleans, 1970-73; practice medicine specializing in surgery, Monroe, La., 1974—; mem. staff St. Francis Med. Center, Monroe, chief surgery, 1979-82, vice chief staff, 1980-81; mem. staff North Monroe Community Hosp., chief of staff, 1983-84, chief surgery, 1986. Served to capt. M.C., AUS, 1966-68; Vietnam. Decorated Bronze Star, Army Commendation medal; diplomate Am. Bd. Surgery. Fellow ACS, Am. Soc. Abdominal Surgeons; mem. AMA, La., Ouchita Parish (v.p. 1980-81) med. socs., Alpha Omega Alpha. Republican. Episcopalian. Club: Lions. Home: 3301 Deborah Dr Monroe LA 71201 Office: 3418 Medical Park Dr Suite 2 Monroe LA 71203

MCGREGOR, RALPH, textile chemistry educator, consultant, researcher, author; b. Leeds, Eng., Feb. 11, 1932; s. Robert and Evelyn (Hutchison) McG.; m. Maureen Mabel McGaul, Aug. 8, 1959; children—Alasdair, Ralph, Francine. B.Sc with 1st class honors, Leeds U. (Eng.), 1953, Ph.D. in Applied Chemistry, 1957, D.Sc., 1979. Chemistry tchr. Roundhay Sch., Leeds, 1956-58; Courtauld research fellow U. Manchester, 1958-59, lectr. in polymer and fiber sci., 1959-68; vis. sr. researcher Ciba A.G., Basel, Switzerland, 1965-66; sr. scientist Fibers div. Allied Corp., Petersburg, Va., 1968-70; from assoc. prof. to prof., Cone Mills Disting. prof. textile chemistry N.C. State U., Raleigh, 1970—. Recipient LeBlanc medal Leeds U., 1953; research medal Dyers Co., 1976; Perkin travel fellow, 1962; U.S.-Japan NSF Coop. Sci. Program grantee, 1981; N.C. Japan Ctr. fellow. Mem. Am. Chem. Soc., Am. Assn. Textile Chemists and Colorists, Soc. Dyers and Colorists, Fiber Soc., AAUP, Sigma Xi, Phi Kappa Phi, Phi Sigma Iota. Author: Diffusion and Sorption in Fibres and Films, 1974. Contbr. articles to profl. jours. Home: 1420 Banbury Rd Raleigh NC 27607 Office: Dept Textile Chemistry NC State U PO Box 5201 Raleigh NC 27695

MCGUCKIN, BRIAN JOSEPH, insurance agency executive; b. Phila., Feb. 6, 1940; s. Joseph John and Elizabeth Ann (Kelly) McGuckin. Assoc. in Econs., St. Joseph's Coll. Spl. agt. CNA Ins. Group, East Orange, N.J., 1962-64, state mgr., N.J., 1964-67, asst. agy. dir., Chgo., 1967-69; So. regional mgr. Am. Internat. Group, N.Y.C., 1969-72, worldwide dir. individual lines, 1972-73; with Mid-Am. Med. Services Ga., Atlanta, 1975—, now chmn. bd., chmn. bd. Ga. So. Ins. Agy., 1973—. Served with USMC. Home: 196 Rumson Rd NE Atlanta GA 30305

MCGUFFEY, CARROLL WADE, JR., lawyer; b. Decatur, Ga., June 1, 1951; s. Carroll Wade and Dorothy (Landers) McG.; m. Virginia Elizabeth Miller, Aug. 12, 1972; children—Carroll Wade, III, Michelle Elizabeth, Jennifer Lanier. B.B.A., U. Ga., 1973, J.D. cum laude, 1976. Bar: Ga. 1976, Fla. 1977. Capt., Chief Claims Tort Litigation div. U.S. Air Force, Eglin AFB, Fla., 1976-80; ptnr. Savell, Williams, Cox & Angel, Atlanta, 1980—. Ward capt. Athens Mayoral Campaign (Ga.), 1975. Mem. ABA, Atlanta Bar Assn., Decatur-DeKalb Bar Assn. Methodist. Clubs: Athens Boat (dir. 1982—); Lawyers (Atlanta).

MCGUIRE, DENNIS, clinical psychologist; b. Oakland, Calif., Aug. 29, 1937; s. Francis Joseph and Coral Amber (Parker) M. B.A., U. Calif.-Berkeley, 1969; M.A., U. Mo., 1973, Ph.D., 1979. Lic. psychologist, Tex., Okla. Predoctoral fellow U. Mo., 1969-72; postdoctoral fellow Galveston Family Inst., 1982-83; clin. psychologist Fulton State Hosp., Mo., 1975-76; research psychologist Mid-Mo. Mental Health Ctr., Columbia, 1977-79; psychologist, coordinator Woodward County Guidance Ctr., Okla., 1979-82; ptnr. Psychol. Assocs. of Lake Jackson, Tex., 1984—; program dir. Gulf Coast MHMR Ctr., 1983—. Contbr. articles to profl. jours. Served to pfc. USMC, 1956-58. Mem. Am. Psychol. Assn., Am. Soc. Clin. Hypnosis, Am. Assn. Marriage and Family Therapy, Southwestern Psychol. Assn., Tex. Psychol. Assn. Lodge: Rotary. Avocations: traveling; reading; running; backpacking; scuba diving. Home: 201 Dixie Dr Apt 1406 Clute TX 77531 Office: Gulf Coast Regional MHMR Ctr 110 Heather Ln Lake Jackson TX 77566

MCGUIRE, STEPHEN ALLEN, statistician, consultant; b. Charleston, W.Va., Oct. 13, 1946; s. Jason Carl and Mary Elizabeth (Brewer) McG.; m. Susan Diane Noble, June 2, 1972; children—Kristen Ann, Heather Lynn, Lauren Paige. B.A., W.Va. U., 1968, M.S., 1974; Ph.D., Kans. State U., 1981. Statistician Martin Marietta Energy Systems, Oak Ridge, 1979—. Contbr. articles to profl. jours. Served with U.S. Army, 1969-71, Vietnam. Mem. Am. Statis. Assn., Am. Soc. Quality Control. Baptist. Avocations: model rocketry; golf. Home: 11715 Bunting Dr Farragut TN 37922 Office: Martin Marietta Energy Systems PO Box Y Bldg 9983-61 MS-1 Oak Ridge TN 37830

MCGUIRE, STEPHEN CRAIG, physicist, educator; b. New Orleans, Sept. 17, 1948; s. Harry Stewart and Ruth (Barsock) McG.; m. Saundra Elaine Yancy, Aug. 28, 1971; children—Carla Abena, Stephanie Niyonu. B.S., So. U., 1970; M.S., U. Rochester, 1974; Ph.D., Cornell U., 1979. Research asst. U. Rochester (N.Y.), 1971-74; lectr. Stanford Linear Accelerator Ctr., Stanford, Calif., 1976; research asst. Cornell U., 1975-78; develop. assoc. Oak Ridge Nat. Lab., 1978-82, cons. chem. tech. div., 1982—; physicist Lawrence Livermore Lab., Livermore, Calif., 1983; asst. prof. physics Ala. A&M U., Normal, Ala., 1983—; cons. Los Alamos Nat. Lab., 1984—. Mem. Am. Phys. Soc., Am. Nuclear Soc., NAACP, Am. Assn. Physics Tchrs., Sigma Xi. Contbr. articles to profl. jours. Home: 6506 Green Meadow Rd Huntsville AL 35810 Office: PO Box 523 Normal AL 35762

MCGUIRE, TERRANCE EDWARD, school administrator, facility planner; b. San Antonio, Nov. 20, 1935; s. James Howard and Muriel Katherine (Drake) McG.; m. Charlene Yvonne Stuart, Aug. 27, 1957; children—Janice Lynn, Patrick Stuart. B.S. in Agriculture, Tex. A&I U., 1957; M.Edn. in Sch. Adminstrn., Southwest Tex. State U., 1961; D. Edn., Tex. A&M U., 1986. Cert. elem. tchr. Tchr., Somerset Sch. Dist., Tex., 1957-61; prin. Helotes Elem. Sch., Tex., 1961-64, John Jay High Sch., San Antonio, 1967-74; asst. prin. John Marshall High Sch., San Antonio, 1964-67; asst. supr. Northside Ind. Sch. Dist., San Antonio, 1974—; cons. Ednl. Facility Plan, San Antonio, 1980—. Life mem. San Antonio Livestock Assn., 1981—; dir. Northwest YMCA, San Antonio, 1982—; mem. Site Selection Com. San Antonio Coll., 1984. NSF fellow, 1961, Scottish Rite fellow, 1985. Mem. Nat. Facility Mgmt. Assn., Phi Delta Kappa. Republican. Methodist. Lodges: Masons, Alzafar Shrine (divan 1982—). Avocations: hunting; golf. Office: Northside Ind Sch Dist ISD Central Office 5900 Evers Rd San Antonio TX 78238

MCGUIRT, WILLIAM FRANKLIN, county sheriff; b. Monroe, N.C., June 10, 1946; s. Robert Hall and Lucille (Price) McG.; m. Jenny Lee Ratliff, June 12, 1976; children—William Sean, Jonathan Hall. A.S., Wingate Coll., 1967; B. Gen. Studies, 1984. Sheriff's lt., Union County, N.C., 1970-79, sheriff, 1979—. Bd. dirs. United Way, Charlotte, N.C., 1981—, Contact Counseling Service, Charlotte, 1985—, Union County Arts Council, Monroe, 1983—; mem. exec. com. Union County Democrats, 1972-78. Served with Army N.G., 1966-72. Named Young Law Enforcement Officer of Yr., Monroe Jaycees, 1980; Young Law Enforcement Officer of Yr., Wingate Jaycees, 1981. Mem. Nat. Sheriff's Assn., N.C. Sheriff's Assn. Baptist. Lodges: Rotary (bd. dirs. 1983-84) (Monroe-Union), Masons. Avocation: photography. Home: 113 Todd Circle Wingate NC 28174 Office: Union County Sheriff's Office 500 N Main St Monroe NC

MCGURK, FRANK CRAIG JOSEPH, psychologist, former educator; b. Phila., May 26, 1910; s. Leon A. and Eleanor (Law) McG.; m. Berenice Lockey. B.S., U. Pa., 1933, M.A., 1937; Ph.D., Catholic. U. Am., 1952. Instr. to asst. prof. psychology, Lehigh U., Bethlehem, Pa., 1950-54; cons. psychology Mil. Acad., West Point, N.Y., 1954-56; assoc. prof. psychology Villanova U., Pa., 1956-62; prof. psychology U. Montevallo, Ala., 1962-76. Contbr. articles to profl. jours. Served to 1st lt. U.S. Army, 1941-45. Mem. Am. Inst. Med. Climatology, Am. Psychol. Assn., Sigma Xi. Republican. Avocation: music. Home: 651 SW 6th St Apt 1112 CT Pompano Beach FL 33060

MCHATTON, STEPHEN RAY, dentist; b. Peoria, Ill., Dec. 30, 1949; s. Dean and Verna Jean (Mowery) McH.; m. Tina Adeane Trammell (div. 1976); m. Marsha Nacetta Liles, Sept. 29, 1984. B.S., U. Ala., 1971, D.M.D., 1976; postgrad. Birmingham Sch. of Dentistry. Practice dentistry Marshall, N.C., 1976-79, Asheville, N.C., 1979—, Waynesville, N.C., 1982-83. Designer interior of geodesic dome dental office, 1985. Founder, Buncombe County Friends of Animals, Asheville, 1985. Mem. Am. Acad. Implant Dentistry, ADA, Acad. Gen. Dentistry, Am. Acad. of Cosmetic Dentistry (founding mem.). Avocations: water skiing; snow skiing; salt water fishing. Home: 878 Old Leicester Hwy Asheville NC 28806 Office: Stephen R McHatton DMD PA 18 Johnston Blvd Asheville NC 28806

MCHUGH, ROBERT JOSEPH, JR., civil engineer, construction manager; b. Danville, Pa., Feb. 5, 1934; s. Robert Joseph and Mary (Howley) McH.; m. Nancy Lee Melson, June 27, 1959; children—Kathleen, Robert J. III, Maureen. B.S., U.S. Naval Acad., 1956; B.C.E., Rensselaer Poly. Inst., 1960; M.S. in Civil Engring., Ga. Inst. Tech., 1968. Registered profl. engr. Ala., Miss., Wis. Commd. ensign U.S. Navy, advanced through grades to capt., 1977; comdg. officer U.S. Naval Constrn. Bn. Ctr., Gulfport, Miss., 1979-81, No. Div. Naval Facilities Engring. Command, Phila., 1981-82; v.p. Booker Assocs. Inc., St. Louis, 1982-84; constrn. mgr. Sverdrup Corp., St. Louis, 1984—. Decorated Legion of Merit, Bronze Star. Mem. ASCE, Soc. Am. Mil. Engrs. (Phila. pres. 1982), U.S. Naval Inst. Republican. Roman Catholic. Lodge: K.C. Avocations: swimming; horseback riding. Home: 11008 Crown Point Dr Knoxville TN 37922 Office: Sverdrup-Gilbane PO Box 19815 Knoxville TN 37939

MCHUGH, THOMAS EDWARD, state supreme court justice; b. Charleston, W.Va., Mar. 26, 1936; s. Paul and Melba McH.; m. Judith McHugh, Mar. 14, 1959; children—Karen, Cindy, James, John. A.B., W.Va. U., 1958, LL.B., 1964. Bar: W.Va. 1964. Individual practice law, Charleston, 1964-66; law clk. to Judge Harlan Calhoun, W.Va. Supreme Ct. of Appeals, 1966-68; individual practice law, Charleston, 1969-74; chief judge W.Va. Circuit Ct., 13th Jud. Circuit, Fairmont, W.Va., 1974-80; asso. justice W.Va. Supreme Ct., Charleston, 1980—. Bd. dirs. Goodwill Industries. Served to 1st lt. U.S. Army, 1958-61. Mem. W.Va. Jud. Assn., Am. Judicature Soc., W.Va. Bar Assn., Order of the Coif. Democrat. Roman Catholic. Club: Serra (Charleston). Office: Supreme Ct Bldg Charleston WV 25305*

MCINNES, ALLEN T., diversified company executive; b. 1937. B.B.A., M.BTex, Ph.D., U. Tex. With Tenneco Inc., Houston, 1960—, budget analyst-fin. dept., until 1967, dir.-fin. evaluation and devel., 1967-73, v.p.-corp. devel. and planning, 1973-75, pres. Tenneco West Inc., 1975-81, corp. sr. v.p.-internat. devel., 1981-82, exec. v.p., 1982—. Office: Tenneco Inc 1010 Milam Houston TX 77001*

MCINNIS, HARRY ELWOOD, JR., construction executive; b. Shreveport, La., Feb. 21, 1944; s. Harry Elwood and Janie Claire (Burks) McI.; B.B.A., La. State U., 1966, J.D., 1970; m. Nancy Elizabeth Bickham, Aug. 6, 1966; children—Marshall, Katherine, Kyle. Vice-pres., McInnis Bros. Constrn., Inc., gen. contractors, Minden, La., 1969—; dir. Minden Bank and Trust Co. Chmn. bd. deacons Baptist Ch., 1980; bd. dirs. United Givers Fund South Webster Parish, 1973-76, pres., 1974-76; pres. N.W. La. Devel. Center, 1977-78, bd. dirs. Constrn. Industry Adv. Fund, 1977-82, La. Polit. Action Council; bd. dirs. Minden Econ. Devel. Corp., pres., 1984; mem. La. Bd. Commerce and Industry, 1982-84; pres. Norwella council Boy Scouts Am., 1981-83. Named Minden Jaycee of Year, 1972. Mem. La. State U. Alumni Assn. (pres. chpt. 1976-77), Associated Gen. Contractors, Minden C. of C. (pres. 1980, dir. 1980-83), Council for a Better La., Pub. Affairs Research Council La., La. Assn. Bus. and Industry (chmn.), Minden Jaycees (dir. 1970-74, pres. 1972-73) Order of Coif, Dorcheat Hist. Assn. (pres. 1976-77), Omicron Delta Kappa. Baptist. Club: Minden Lions (Lion of Yr. 1977-78; pres. 1977-78, dir. 1976-79). Mng. editor La Law Rev., 1968-69. Home: 1113 Broadway Minden LA 71055 Office: 119 Pearl St Minden LA 71055

MC INNIS, JOHN ROBERT, physician, surgeon; b. Moore County, N.C., July 15, 1908; s. James Dalton and Florence Elizabeth (Blue) McI.; student Davidson Coll., 1927-29, U. Okla., 1931; A.B., U. N.C., 1933; M.D., U. Tenn., 1956; m. Esther Alice Hurley, Dec. 26, 1941; children—John Robert, Charles Hurly, Marilyn Esther, Nancy Catherine. Vice pres., mgr. Caroline Handerchief Co., Inc., West End, N.C., 1935-42; accountant, office mgr. Sandhill Furniture Corp., 1947-51; intern, surgery resident Mercy Hosp., Oklahoma City, 1956-58; pvt. practice medicine and surgery, 1956—; mem. staffs Mercy, Bapt. Meml., South Community hosps., McInnis Clinic, Oklahoma City. Chmn. sch. bd. West End (N.C.) Pub. Schs., 1959-61. Served from pvt. to capt. AUS, 1942-47; col. M.C. Res. ret. Mem. A.M.A., Am. Acad. Family Practice, Okla., Oklahoma County med. socs., Oklahoma City Clin. Soc., Ret. Officers Assn., Am. Assn. Ret. Persons. Presbyterian (elder, trustee). Clubs: Masons (32 deg.), Shriners, Order Amaranth, White Shrine Jerusalem, Order Eastern Star (worthy grand patron Okla. 1977-78), Rotary (pres. So. Oklahoma City 1986-87). Home: 7008 S Country Club Dr Oklahoma City OK 73159 Office: 4515 S Pennsylvania St Oklahoma City OK 73119

MCINTEER, JIM BILL, minister, publishing executive, farmer; b. Franklin, Ky., June 16, 1921; s. William Thomas and Mary Edna (Rutherford) McI.; m. Betty Bergner, July 20, 1943; children—MariLynn McInteer Canterbury, Mark Martin. Cert. David Lipscomb Coll., Nashville, 1940; B.A., Harding U., 1942; LL.D. (hon.), Pepperdine U., 1980. Ordained to ministry Ch. of Christ (non-denominational). Minister, Ch. of Christ, Sheridan, Ark., 1942-46, Isabel, Kans., 1947, Locust Grove, Ky., 1948-52, Grace Ave. Ch., Nashville, 1952-56, West End Ch., Nashville, 1956—; bus. mgr., pres., publisher 20th Century Christian, Nashville, 1947—; farmer, Franklin, Ky., 1948—. Author: Tiny Tot's Bible Reader, 1956; Great Preachers of Today, 1966. Bd. dirs. Harding U., Searcy, Ark., 1950—, Potter Orphan Home and Sch., Bowling Green, Ky., 1960—, Fanning Found., Nashville, 1975—, Campbell Trust Fund, Nashville, 1978—. Named Alumnus of Yr., David Lipscomb Coll., 1985. Mem. SAR. Lodge: Civitan Interant. (dist. chaplain 1975). Avocations: photography, woodcutting, vegetable gardening. Home: 1100 Belvedere Dr Nashville TN 37204 Office: 20th Century Christian Inc 2809 Granny White Nashville TN 37204

MCINTIRE, JON WILLIAMS, psychologist; b. Barberton, Ohio, Feb. 2, 1944; s. John Frederick and Magel Madeline (Williams) McI.; m. Louise Emily Walters, June 14, 1965; children—Kevin Jon, Brian Douglas. B.S., Mich. State U., 1965; Ph.D., U. Tex., 1973. Lic. psychologist, Va. Practicum supr. U. Tex., Austin, 1968-69, research asst., 1969, intern, 1969-71; asst. prof. Madison Coll., Harrisonburg, Va., 1971-73; dir. and assoc. prof. James Madison U., Harrisonburg, 1973-81; pvt. practice psychology, Harrisonburg, 1981—. Author article. Vice chmn. Mental Health and Retardation Bd., Harrisonburg, 1980-84, chmn., 1984—; chmn. Va. Alcohol Safety Action Program, Harrisonburg, 1980-84; bd. dirs. Community Counseling Ctr., Harrisonburg, 1973-80. Mem. Am. Psychol. Assn., Va. Psychol. Assn. (chmn. bd. profl. affairs 1984, newsletter editor 1979-80), Am. Soc. Clin. Hypnosis. Lodge: Elks. Avocations: horses; radio-controlled airplanes; softball. Home: 520 S Mason St Harrisonburg VA 22801 Office: 356 S Main St Harrisonburg VA 22801

MCINTOSH, DENNIS KEITH, veterinary practitioner, consultant; b. Newark, June 12, 1941; s. Sheldon Weeks and Enid Nicholson (Casey) McI.; m. Mary Catherine Frady, Nov. 3, 1973; children—Kevin, Kim, Jamie, Steve. B.S. in Animal Sci., Tex. A&M U., 1963, B.S. in Vet. Sci., 1967, D.V.M., 1968. Asst. county agrl. agt., Cleburne, Tex., 1963-65; owner, operator Park North Animal Hosp., San Antonio, 1970-75, El Dorado Animal Hosp., San Antonio, 1973—; pres., mgr. Bexar County Emergency Animal Clinic, Inc., 1978-81; vet. mem. Tex. Bd. Health, 1984—. Team capt. Alamo Roundup Club and Pres.' Club of San Antonio C. of C., 1970-75; mem. Guadalupe County Youth Fair Bd., 1978-80; 1st v.p. No. Hills Lions Club, 1972-73. Served with Vet. Corps, USAF, 1968-70. Recipient Alumnus award Guadalupe County 4-H Club, 1979. Mem. Tex. Vet. Med. Assn. (pres., chmn. bd.), Tex. Acad. Vet. Practice (pres.), Am. Animal Hosp. Assn., AVMA, Vet. Hosp. Mgrs. Assn., San Antonio C. of C. (life), Tex. County Agrl. Agts. Assn. (4th v.p. 1964). Conservative. Methodist. Contbr. articles to profl. jours. Office: 13039 Nacogdoches St San Antonio TX 78217

MC INTOSH, JOHN MOHR, electric utility executive; b. Savannah, Ga., Jan. 18, 1924; s. Olin Talley and Jane Kirkland (Lawton) McI.; m. Barbara Ann Neff, Mar. 30, 1945; children—Angela, John Mohr, Neff, Olin, Aileen, Barbara. Student, U. Ga., 1941-42. Vice pres. sales Rock Wool Products Corp., Savannah, 1946-49; pres. McIntosh & Co., Savannah, 1949-57; v.p., gen. mgr. Neal-Blun Co., Savannah, 1956-66, pres., 1966-74; chmn. bd., chief exec. officer Savannah Electric & Power Co., 1974-86; dir. Savannah Foods & Industries, Gt. So. Fed. Savs. & Loan. Chmn. Savannah Port Authority, 1964-65; gen. chmn. United Way, Savannah, 1972. Served with USAAF, 1942-44. Mem. Southeastern Electric Exchange (dir. 1975—), Edison Electric Inst. (dir. 1981—). Episcopalian. Home: 217 E Gordon St Savannah GA 31401 Office: 600 E Bay St Savannah GA 31402*

MCINTOSH, LOUISA AICHEL, interior design firm, art gallery executive; b. Atlanta, June 1, 1925; d. Siegfried Louis and Margaret Katura (Rosser) Aichel; m. Alexander Preston McIntosh, Sept. 2, 1947 (dec. Jan. 1966); children—Alexa Louis McIntosh Selph, Preston Stuckey, Peter Aichel, Patricia Amelia. B.A., Agnes Scott Coll. Owner, Louisa McIntosh Interiors, Atlanta, 1967—; owner, dir. McIntosh Gallery, Atlanta, 1982—; design cons. Fed. Res. Bank, Atlanta, 1975-78, Sci. Atlanta, 1976-80, English Lang. Sch., Atlanta, 1980-82, Nat. Bank of Ga., 1984-85, Lantel Co., 1985. Treas., Midtown Bus. Assn., Atlanta, 1978, pres., 1979; trustee Atlanta Pub. Library, vice chmn. bd., 1981-82; trustee Atlanta Fulton Pub. Library, chmn. bd., 1983-85. Mem. Inst. Bus. Design. Episcopalian. Home: 75 Inman Circle NE Atlanta GA 30309 Office: Louisa McIntosh Interiors 1421 Peachtree St NE Atlanta GA 30309

MCINTOSH, THOMAS S., dredging company executive; b. 1937. B.S., Rice U., 1960; M.B.A., Stanford U., 1964. Mgr. supply and distbn. Tenneco Oil Co., Houston, 1964-73; with Zapata Off-Shore Co., Houston, 1973—, planning and fin. analyst, v.p. corp. devel., 1973-74, pres., 1975—, v.p. offshore mktg., 1974-77, v.p. offshore drilling, 1977-83; exec. v.p., chief operating officer, 1983—. Office: Zapata Corp PO Box 4240 Houston TX 77001*

MC INTYRE, BERNARD J., state senator; b. Muskogee, Okla., July 17, 1942; m. Carlye Jimerson, 1981. Student Tulsa Jr. Coll., U. Tulsa, U. Okla. Mem. Okla. Ho. of Reps., 1971-83; now mem. Okla. Senate, chmn. Okla. Legis. Black Caucus, vice chmn. human resources com., mem. fin., bus. and labor, standards and ethics coms. Mem. NAACP, Tulsa Urban League. Mem. Nat. Bus. League, A. Phillip Randolph Inst. Democrat. Lodge: Masons. Office: Okla Senate Room 516 Oklahoma City OK 73105*

MCINTYRE, BRYCE WHITNEY, JR., engineer; b. Washington, Oct. 19, 1949; s. Bryce Whitney and Dorothy Jo (Castle) McI.; m. Jennifer Anne Giobbi, May 27, 1978; children—Nathan, Rachel, Rebecca, Daniel. B.S., MIT, 1971; M.Div., Bibl. Theol. Sem., Pa., 1982; M.S. in Math., E. Tex. State U., 1983. Tchr., U.S. Peace Corps, Liberia, 1972-73; pvt. tchr., Liberia, 1977; tchr. Bonham High Sch., Tex., 1975-76; maintenance foreman Rosenberger's Dairies, Hatfield, Pa., 1978-82; automatic test engr. S.W. Energy Control Systems, Bonham, 1982—. Republican. Baptist. Avocations: computers; music; Bible study. Home: 301 W 10th St Bonham TX 75418 Office: Southwest Energy Control Systems 1300 Bicentennial Bonham TX 75418

MCINTYRE, JOHN ARMIN, physics educator, researcher; b. Seattle, June 2, 1920; s. Harry John and Florence (Armin) McI.; m. Madeleine Ruth Forsman, June 13, 1947; 1 child, John. B.S.E.E., U. Wash., 1943; M.A., Princeton U., 1948, Ph.D., 1950. Instr. Carnegie Inst. Tech., Pitts., 1943-44; radio engr. Westinghouse, Balt., 1944-45; research assoc. Stanford U., Calif., 1950-57; asst. prof. Yale U., New Haven, 1957-60, assoc. prof., 1960-63; prof. physics Tex. A&M U., College Station, 1963—; councilor Oak Ridge Assn., Tenn., 1964-67; panel mem. NSF, Washington, 1974-76; exec. council Am. Sci. Affiliation, Ipswich, Mass., 1967-72, pres., 1972. Contbr. articles to profl. jours. Patentee in field. Grantee Robert A. Welch Found. 1964, Am. Cancer Soc. 1980. Fellow Am. Phys. Soc. Presbyterian. Avocations: theology; history of science. Home: 2316 Bristol St Bryan TX 77802 Office: Tex A&M U Physics Dept College Station TX 77843

MCINTYRE, MICHAEL DEAN, economics educator, administrator; b. Natchez, Miss., June 6, 1947; s. James June and Georgia Helen (Perkins) McI.; m. Charlotte Diane Payne, Aug. 30, 1969; 1 child, Michael Dean. A.A., Copiah-Lincoln Jr. Coll., 1967; B.S. in Bus. Adminstrn., U. S. Miss., 1970, M.B.A., 1971. Grad. asst. U. So. Miss., Hattiesburg, 1970-71; instr. economics Copiah-Lincoln Jr. Coll., Wesson, Miss., 1971—, chmn. bus. div., 1975—, varsity tennis coach, 1978—. Author: Economic Roots (PBL Nat. award 1978), 1978; Views from San Francisco to Washington, D.C. (Most Outstanding Project award 1981), 1981. Coordinator, editor: Project Dialogue (Bus. Advocacy award 1983, 84) 1982-84, Free Enterprise (Amoco award 1982), 1982; Recipient Outstanding Instr. award Copiah-Lincoln Alumni Assn., 1982; Selected Participant award NSF, 1983. Mem. Copiah-Lincoln Edn. Assn. (pres. 1984-85), Miss. Jr. Coll. Tennis Assn. (pres. 1984—), Midsouth Acad. Economists (jr. coll. coordinator 1979-80), Miss. Jr. Coll. Faculty Assn. (legis. com.), Intercollegiate Tennis Coaches Assn. Methodist. Avocations: tennis; jogging; sports; traveling; photography.

MCIVER, PERCY LEE, chief of police; b. N.C., Feb. 20, 1940; s. John and Georgia Bell (Campbell) McIver; m. Patty Jean Burke, Jan. 7, 1961; children—LaRunda Jean, Michael Lee. Grad. high sch., Edenton, N.C., Adminstrv. specialist Dept. Army, Washington, 1958-61; police officer Fredericksburg Police Dept., Va., 1961-68; dep. Wake County Sheriff's Dept., Raleigh, N.C., 1968-70; police chief Garner Police Dept., N.C., 1970—. Mem. Garner Civitan Club, Chief of Police Assn. Baptist. Avocation: amateur radio operator. Office: Garner Police Dept PO Box 446 900 Seventh Ave Garner NC 27529

MCKAY, JIMMY LLOYD, sales executive; b. Coupland, Tex., Aug. 7, 1943; s. Chester Lloyd and Louise May (McCarty) McK.; m. Sharon Lou Herrod, Apr. 15, 1966; children—Stephanie Michelle, Jimmy Lloyd II. A.A., N.Mex. Jr. Coll., 1976; B.A., Coll. of SW, 1979; postgrad. U. Tex.-Permian Basin, 1981-82. Sales trainee NL Acme Tool, Odessa, Tex., 1979-80, dist. salesman, 1981, sr. salesman, 1981-82, account rep., 1982—. Sr. vice comdr. DAV, Roswell, N. Mex., 1970-73. Served with U.S. Army, 1968-70. Mem. Phi Theta Kappa. Republican. Club: Lee High Sch. Band Booster (treas. 1985-86). Avocations: hunting; fishing; watching football; bowling; golf. Home: 3600 Dentcrest Midland TX 79707 Office: NL Acme Tool PO Box 2432 Odessa TX 79760

MCKAY, JOHN JUDSON, JR., lawyer; b. Anderson, S.C., Aug. 13, 1939; s. John Judson and Polly (Plowden) McK.; m. Jill Hall Ryon, Aug. 3, 1961 (div. Dec. 1980); children—Julia Plowden, Katherine Henry, William Ryon, Elizabeth Hall; m. Jane Leahey, Feb. 18, 1982; 1 son, Andrew Leahey. A.B. in History, U. S.C., 1960, J.D. cum laude, 1966. Bar: S.C. 1966 U.S. Dist. Ct. S.C. 1966, U.S. Ct. Appeals (4th cir.) 1974, U.S. Supreme Ct. 1981. Assoc. Haynsworth, Perry, Bryant, Marion & Johnstone, Greenville, S.C., 1966-70; ptnr. Rainey, McKay, Britton, Gibbes & Clarkson, P.A., and predecessor, Greenville, 1970-78; sole practice, Hilton Head Island, S.C., 1978-80; ptnr. McKay & Gertz, P.A., Hilton Head Island, 1980-81; ptnr. McKay & Mullen, P.A., Hilton Head Island, 1981—; assoc. mem. S.C. Bd. Commrs. Grievances and Discipline, 1983—. Served to lt. (j.g.) USNR, 1961-64; lt. comdr. Res. (ret.). Mem. ABA, S.C. Bar Assn. (pres. young lawyers sect. 1970, exec. com. 1971-72), S.C. Bar, Beaufort County Bar Assn., Hilton Head Bar Assn., Assn. Trial Lawyers Am., S.C. Def. Attys. Assn., S.C. Trial Lawyers Assn., S.C. Bar Found. (pres. 1977) Blue Key, Wig and Robe, Phi Delta Phi. Episcopalian. Clubs: Poinsett (Greenville); Sea Pines (Hilton Head Island). Editor-in-chief: U. S.C. Law Rev., 1966; contbr. articles to legal jours. Home: 6 Rice Ln Sea Pines Plantation Hilton Head Island SC 29928 Office: PO Box 5066 Suite 203 WatersEdge Hilton Head Island SC 29938

MC KAY, SAMUEL LEROY, clergyman; b. nr. Charlotte, N.C., Oct. 15, 1913; s. Elmer Ranson and Arlena (Benfield) McK.; A.B. cum laude, Erskine Coll., 1937; B.D. cum laude, Erskine Theol. Sem., 1939; postgrad. U. Ga., 1941-42, Union Theol. Sem., 1957; m. Martha Elizabeth Caldwell, Apr. 29, 1939; children—Samuel LeRoy, Mary Louise, William Ranson. Ordained to ministry of Presbyn. Ch., 1940; pastor Prosperity Asso. Ref. Ch., Fayetteville, Tenn., 1942-46, Bethel Asso. Ref. Ch., Oak Hill, Ala., 1946-50, 1st Asso. Ref. Ch., Salisbury, N.C., 1950-53, 1st Ch. U.S., Dallas, N.C., 1953-60, First Ch., Kernersville, N.C., 1960-66, Cooleemee (N.C.) Presbyn. Ch., 1966-69, Broadway (N.C.) Presbyn. Ch., 1969-80. Stated clk. Gen. Synod Asso. Ref. Presbyn. Ch., 1950-53; commr. Gen. Assembly Presbyn. Ch. U.S., 1960, 69; permanent clk. Winston-Salem Presbytery, 1961-69, chmn. leadership edn. com., 1962-66, chmn. Christian edn. com., 1967-68; chmn. nominations com. Fayetteville Presbytery, 1977-79, mem. com. on ministers, 1984—; supr. chaplaincy program Davie County Hosp., 1968-69. Pres. Dallas PTA, 1955-56; bd. mgrs. Kernersville YMCA, 1962-66, chmn. membership com., 1963, treas., 1964, pres., 1965-66; bd. dirs. Winston-Salem-Forsyth County YMCA, 1965-66. Mem. Kernersville Area Ministers Assn. (pres. 1963-64), N.C. Poetry Soc. (dir. 1971—, chmn. poetry contests 1970-72, 84—, pres. 1972-74), Clan MacKay Soc. N.Am. (pres. 1971-75, chaplain 1976—, chmn. nominating com. 1983-84), Lion. Contbr. articles, sermons and poems to periodicals and publs. Office: 12 Knollwood Dr Broadway NC 27505

MC KAY, VICKI HIGGASON, educator; b. Haynesville, La., Dec. 29, 1948; d. Victor William and Elba Adis (Walker) Higgason; B.S. in Home Econs., Mary Hardin-Baylor Coll., 1970; tchr. cert. distributive edn. U. Houston, 1974, postgrad., 1976-77; m. Malcolm Stuart McKay, June 11, 1976; children—Laura Tiffany, Blair Alexander. With Sanger Harris Dept. Store, Dallas, 1971-72; tchr. distributive edn. Lampasas (Tex.) High Sch., 1972-76, Channelview (Tex.) High Sch., 1977-85. Bd. dirs. Capistrano Villas Homeowners Assn., 1977-79, Channelview YMCA, 1982-85; mem. pres.'s adv. council, alumni bd. dirs. U. Mary Hardin Baylor, 1983-85, chmn. Southeast Houston Alumni Club, 1983—. Elected to Distributive Edn. Tchr. Hall of Fame, 1973; Free Enterprise Tchr. award Webb Hist. Soc., 1983. Mem. Nat. Assn. Distributive Edn. Tchrs., Am. Vocat. Assn., Tex. Vocat. Tchrs. Assn., Mktg. and Distributive Edn. Tchrs. Assn. (v.p. area V 1975-76), Nat. Assn. Distributive Edn. Clubs Am., Alumni, Tex. Assn. Distributive Edn. Alumni (life mem., dir., exec. sec. 80-81, Outstanding Service award 1980-82, membership services dir. 1981-82); Tex. Profl. Educators Assn., Internat. Platform Assn. Presbyterian (elder). Contbr. articles to profl. jours. Home: 927 Sterling Green South Dr Channelview TX 77530

MCKECHNIE, GERALD DAVID, state agency official, radio communications engineer; b. Detroit, Aug. 29, 1932; s. Ian C. and Claire Marie (Custer) McK.; m. Dolores Hughes, Apr. 26, 1952 (div. 1956); children—David, Michael; m. Bessie Marie Usery, Dec. 31, 1956; children—Kathy, Taffy. Student, Chipola Jr. Coll., 1964. Instr. metal working and electronics Fla. Indsl. Sch. for Boys, 1957-59; with Mac's TV Service, Chipley, Fla., 1959-61; owner, editor Weekly Advertiser, Chipley, 1961-63; with Fla. Dept. Transp., Chipley, 1963—, dist. communications engr., 1983—; mem. guidance council Washington-Holmes Vo-Tech. Center, 1979—. Search mission coordinator Civil Air Patrol, 1980—, group comdr., All W. Fla. Squadrons, 1981—; vice chmn. Tri-County Airport Authority, 1981—, sect. emergency coordinator, 1967-72. Served with U.S. Army, 1952-54. Recipient Cert. Dept. Def., 1971. Mem. Associated Pub. Safety Communications Officers, Confederate Communications Commn., Aircraft Owners and Pilots Assn. Baptist. Home: 527 S 4th St PO Box 545 Chipley FL 32428 Office: Fla Dept Transp PO Box 607 Chipley FL 32428

MCKECHNIE, JOHN CHARLES, gastroenterologist, educator; b. Louisville, Feb. 1, 1935; s. Albert Hay and Edna Scott (Johnson) M.; m. Patricia Louise Sturgill, Dec. 28, 1956; children—Steven Keith, Kevin Stuart. B.A., U. Louisville, 1955; M.D., Baylor Coll. Medicine, 1959. Diplomate Am. Bd. Internal Medicine, Am. Bd. Gastroenterology. Intern Jefferson Davis Hosp., Houston, 1959-60; resident in internal medicine Baylor Affiliated Program, Houston, 1960-61, 65-66; gen. practice medicine, Benham, Ky., 1964; practice medicine specializing in gastroenterology, Houston, 1966—; clin. instr. Baylor Coll. Medicine, Houston, 1966-69, asst. prof., 1969-72, assoc. prof., 1972-77, prof., 1977—; mem. staff Methodist Hosp.; cons. Ben Taub Hosp., St. Luke's Episcopal Hosp., St. Joseph's Hosp. Served to capt. USMC, 1962-64. Fellow Am. Coll. Gastroenterology (gov. Tex. 1979-80, trustee 1981—), ACP; mem. AMA, So. Med. Assn., Tex. Med. Assn., Am. Gastroent. Assn., Digestive Disease Found., Am. Soc. Gastrointestinal Endoscopy, Tex. Soc. Gastrointestinal Endoscopy, Houston Gastroent. Soc. (pres. 1983), Alpha Omega Alpha. Republican. Baptist. Contbr. numerous articles to profl. jours. Office: 6560 Fannin St Suite 1630 Houston TX 77030

MCKEE, CHARLES ALLEN, state official; b. New Orleans, Apr. 18, 1944; s. Henry and Elnora (Allen) McK.; m. Sylvia Jones, Sept. 28, 1968; children—Uanessa Lien, Mark Charles. B.A. in Sociology, Dillard U., 1966. Cement mason Local Union 567, New Orleans, 1968-70; welfare visitor State of La., Orleans Parish, 1970-74, quality control investigator, Baton Rouge, 1974-76, fraud investigator, New Orleans, 1976-81; regional supr. support enforcement services La. Dept. Health and Human Resources, New Orleans, 1981—. Served with inf. U.S. Army, 1966-68, S.E. Asia. Decorated Army Commendation medal. Mem. Dist. Atty. Assn. La., Am. Pub. Welfare Assn. Democrat. Baptist. Office: La Dept Health and Human Resources Support Enforcement New Orleans LA 70119

MCKEE, JAMES BATTLE, concrete products manufacturing company executive; b. Raleigh, N.C., Mar. 31, 1916; s. James Battle and Marguerite (McPheeters) McK.; m. Lucile B. Aycock, Aug. 22, 1942; children—Marguerite McKee Moss, Lucile McKee Clarkson. Student U. N.C., 1933-36. Cashier, So. Aggregates Corp., Raleigh, 1937-39; with N.C. Products Corp., Raleigh, 1939—, pres., 1972—; dir. N.C. Nat. Bank, Raleigh. Served to capt., F.A., U.S. Army, World War II; ETO. Mem. Am. Concrete Pipe Assn. (dir. S.E. region 1969-84, chmn. govt. relations com. 1980-81, nat. dir. 1982-84), N.C. Soc. of Cincinnati (standing com. 1982-84). Episcopalian. Clubs: Caroline Country, Sphinx. Lodge: Rotary. Office: NC Products Corp PO Box 27077 Raleigh NC 27611

MCKEE, L. K., food company executive. Chmn. Fed. Co. Office: PO Box 17236 Memphis TN 38117*

MCKEE, NANCY ANN, foreign service officer; b. Tulsa, Mar. 12, 1933; d. Charles and Estelle Marie (Larrieu) McK.; student U. Tulsa, 1950-52. Sec., Jones & Laughlin Supply Div., Tulsa, 1952-63; sec. Am. Embassy, Bonn, W.Ger., 1963-66, Lagos, Nigeria, 1963-68, Dept. State, Washington, 1968-70, 71-72, Am. Embassy, Nicosia, Cyprus, 1970-71; commd. fgn. service officer Dept. State, 1972; consular officer Am. Embassy, Manila, 1972-74, Mexico City, 1975-79, Nairobi, Kenya, 1979-82; supr. visa sect., dept. prin. officer Am. Consulate Gen., Juarez, Mex., 1982—. Republican. Roman Catholic.

MCKEE, OATHER DORRIS, bakery executive; b. Dixon, Miss., Jan. 21, 1905; s. Finis E. and Sarah Ann Elizabeth (Cooper) McK.; m. Anna Ruth King, Aug. 4, 1928; children—Winifred, Ellsworth, Elizabeth, Jack. Student Southern Coll., Collegedale, Tenn. Founder, pres. McKee Baking Co., Collegedale, 1934-71, chmn. bd., 1971—; dir., mem. trust com. Pioneer Bank. Mem. Tenn. Air Pollution Control Bd., 1971-79; chmn. bd. Hewitt Research Found., 1970—. Recipient Alumnus of Yr. award So. Coll., 1978; Arthur G. Vieth Meml. award Chattanooga C. of C., 1979. Mem. Am. Soc. Bakery Engrs., Biscuit and Cracker Mfrs. Assn. (dir. 1972—), Am. Bakers Assn. (gov. 1976—), Profl. and Bus. Men's Assn. (pres. 1966—), Greater Chattanooga Area C. of C. (dir. 1978-82). Republican. Adventist. Clubs: Rotary (Chattanooga, Tenn.); Mountain City. Inventer automated bakery equipment. Home: 3901 Ooltewah Ringgold Rd Ooltewah TN 37363 Office: PO Box 750 Collegedale TN 37315

MCKEE, R. ELLSWORTH, baking company executive; b. Hendersonville, N.C., Dec. 24, 1932; s. O.D. and Anna Ruth (King) McK.; m. Sharon Sue Sisson, June 21, 1953; children—Debra, Badia McKee Huggins, Malinda, Russell. B.A. in Bus. and Econs., Collegedale, Tenn., 1954. With McKee Baking Co., Chattanooga, 1951—, v.p. prodn. and fin., 1954-62, exec. v.p., treas., Collegedale, 1962-71, pres., chief exec. officer, 1971—; dir. Pioneer Bank, Chattanooga. Bd. dirs. So. Coll. Seventh-day Adventists, Collegedale, 1971—, Andrews U., Berrien Springs, Mich., 1976—. Mem. Am. Bakers Assn., Cookie and Snack Bakers Assn., Ind. Bakers Assn. Adventist. Lodge: Rotary. Avocations: dirt cycling; spelunking; stunt flying; skiing; water skiing. Office: McKee Baking Co PO Box 750 Collegedale TN 37315

MCKEE, ROBERT BUTLER, civil engineer, landscape architect; b. Chincoteague, Va., Dec. 1, 1947; s. Robert Wilson and Mary Florence (Butler) McK.; m. Virginia Faulconer Lord, June 5, 1971; children—Molly Butler, Sarah Wilhelm. B.S. in Civil Engring., U. Va., 1970, M. Landscape Architecture, 1978. Registered profl. engr., Va., N.C. Civil engr. G.W. Stephens & Assoc., Balt., 1971; project engr. G.W. Clifford & Assoc., Fredericksburg, Va., 1971-75; cons. engr., Charlottesville, Va., 1975-78; prin. Cox McKee Okerlund, 1978-84, McKee & Assocs., Charlottesville, 1984—; lectr. Sch. Architecture U. Va., 1980—. Mem. ASCE, Am. Soc. Landscape Architects, Nat. Trust Hist. Preservation. Episcopalian. Avocations: golf; squash; tennis; gardening; designing. Office: Robert B McKee & Assocs 218 W Main St Charlottesville VA 22901

MCKEE, TIMOTHY CARLTON, lawyer, educator; b. South Bend, Ind., Mar. 9, 1944; s. Glenn Richard and Laura Louise (Niven) McK.; m. Linda Sykes Mizelle, Oct. 13, 1984. B.S. in Bus. Econs., Ind. U., 1970, M.B.A. in Fin., 1973, J.D., 1979; LL.M., DePaul U., 1980. Bar: U.S. Dist. Ct. (no. dist.) Ill. 1980, Ill. 1980. C.P.A., 1981. Procedures analyst Assocs. Corp., South Bend, 1969-71; asst. dir. fin. Ind. U., Bloomington, 1971-79; sr. tax mgr. Peat, Marwick, Mitchell, Chgo., Norfolk, Va., 1979-84; corp. counsel, K&K Toys Inc., Norfolk, 1984, asst. prof. Old Dominion U., Norfolk, 1985—; computer coordinator Peat, Marwick, Mitchell, Norfolk, 1982-84. Loaned exec. United Way, Chgo., 1981; chmn. telethon Va. Orch. Group, Norfolk, 1983. Served to cpl. USMC, 1961-62. Mem. Art Inst. Chgo., Friends Music, ABA, Sales and Mktg. Execs., Chgo. Bar Assn., Ill. C.P.A. Assn., Am. Inst. C.P.A.s. Home: 4921 Brookeway Dr Virginia Beach VA 23464 Office: Old Dominion U 2065 Hughes Hall Norfolk VA 23508

MCKEE, WENDY EUNICE, psychologist; b. Princeton, N.J., Feb. 7, 1942; d. Walter Thomas and Helen (Hoffman) McK.; m. V. Dennis Golladay, Aug. 16, 1963 (div. Apr. 1975). B.S., James Madison U., Harrisonburg, Va., 1963; M.Ed., U. Va., 1969, Ed.D., 1973. Lic. psychologist, Fla. Clin. psychologist Lakeview Ctr., Pensacola, Fla., 1972-77; adj. prof. U. West Fla., Pensacola, 1976-78; program dir. Geriatric Residence Ctr., Milton, Fla., 1981-82; pvt. practice clinical psychology, Pensacola, 1981—; cons. Family Practice Residency Program, Pensacola, 1981—, Crisis Stablzn. Unit, Milton, 1981-83. Contbr. articles to profl. jours. Mem. Am. Psychol. Assn., Fla. Psychol. Assn., N.W. Fla. Psychol. Assn. (bd. dirs. 1983—), Southeastern Psychol Assn., Gulf Coast Neurology, Psychiatry, Neuropsychiatry and Psychology Assn. Democrat. Avocations: sailing, golf, windsurfing. Home: 2810 Blackshear Ave Pensacola FL 32503 Office: Psychol Assocs 103 S Alcaniz St Pensacola FL 32501

MC KEEN, CHESTER M., JR., helicopter company executive; b. Shelby, Ohio, Mar. 18, 1923; s. Chester Mancil and Nettie Augusta (Fox) McK.; B.S. in Mil. Sci., U. Md., 1962; M.B.A., Babson Coll., Wellesley, Mass., 1962; m. Alma Virginia Pierce, Mar. 1946; children—David Richard, Karin, Thomas Kevin. Enlisted in U.S. Army, 1942, commd. 2d lt., 1943, advanced through grades to maj. gen., 1973; service in Pacific Islands, Germany, Vietnam; dir. procurement Army Materiel Command, also comdr. Tank/Automotive Command, 1975-77; ret., 1977; dir. logistics Bell Helicopter Internat., 1977-79, v.p.-procurement Bell Helicopter Textron, Ft. Worth, 1979-81, v.p. materiel, 1981—. Decorated D.S.M., Legion of Merit with 2 clusters, Commendation medal (3). Mem. Am. Assn., Am. Helicopter Soc., Am. Def. Preparedness Assn. (v.p. S.W. region), Assn. U.S. Army (pres. Ft. Worth chpt.), Sigma Pi. Clubs: Rotary, Masons, Shriners, Ridglea Country (Ft. Worth).

MC KELL, MARION ELIZABETH TERWILLIGER, artist; b. Dayton, Wash., Mar. 8, 1919; d. Lloyd Ranson and Florence Marion (Harper) Terwilliger; student Chouinard Sch. Art, Los Angeles, 1936-37; B.A., Scripps Coll., 1941; postgrad. Claremont U. Grad. Sch., 1941, Pa. Acad. Fine Arts, Phila., 1941-42; m. James Cook McKell, III, Dec. 2, 1942; children—Marion Lloyd McKell Fogler, Lynn Gaylord McKell Gazjuk, James Forrest. Staff, Alexander Film Co., Colorado Springs, 1943-44; painter portraits on commns., 1946-55; pvt. tchr. art, 1965-68; instr. youth classes in art Chester County (Pa.) Art Assn., 1968-72; art instr. Delaware County Women's Prison, Pa., 1972-75; one-person shows: Lancaster County (Pa.) Art Assn. Center, 1959, Chester County Art Assn. Center, 1960, 76, West Chester (Pa.) State Coll., 1964, Strawbridge & Clothier, Springfield, Pa., 1975, Moore County Library, Carthage, N.C., 1981, Carthage County Library (N.C.), 1982, Southern Pines Library (N.C.), 1983; group shows include: Los Angeles Art Mus., 1941, Chester County Assn. Retarded Citizens Anns., 1965-77, Pa. Acad. Fine Arts, Yellow Springs, 1977, others; represented in permanent collections; v.p. public relations Chester County Art Assn., 1979-80; lectr. in field. Exec. bd. Chester County Council on Addictive Disease, 1964-71; founding com., adv. bd. Vitae House Inc., 1969—; active women's div. Del. Valley Council on Alcoholism; bd. dirs. Del. Valley Main Line Council on Alcohol and Drug Abuse; mem. Sandhill Arts Council, Southern Pines, N.C., 1982—. Recipient awards Chester County Art Assn., 1965. Nat. League Am. Pen Women State Bienniels, 1972-78. Mem. Nat. League Am. Pen Women (pres. Chester County br. 1974-76), Internat. Platform Assn., Scripps Coll. Alumnae Assn. Republican. Episcopalian. Club: Whispers Woman's (Whispering Pines, N.C.). Home: 54A Shadow Ln Whispering Pines NC 28327

MCKELLAR, ALFRED DONALD, forester; b. Vinton, La.; s. Lauchlin Wordsworth and Maria Elizabeth (Duggan) Mc.; m. Jacqueline Phelps, Dec. 22, 1930 (dec. 1983); children—Jacqueline Ann, Judith Aileen. B.S. in Forestry, La. State U., 1930; M.S., U. Ga., 1937. With forest service USDA, 1930-36; asst. prof. U. Ga. Forestry Sch., 1936-43; with Tariff Commn., 1943-46; with lumber and wood products br. forest products div. U.S. Dept. Commerce, 1946-71, chief of br., 1963-71; chief lumber prodn. br. Nat. Prodn. Authority, 1950-53 (temporary assignment from Dept. Commerce). Author publs. and reports. Recipient Silver medal Dept. Commerce, 1963; Quality Performance awards Dept. Commerce, 1964, 65, 69, 70; Nat. Forest Products Assn. Spl. award, 1969. Mem. Soc. Am. Foresters, Phi Kappi Phi, Alpha Zeta, Alpha Xi Sigma (hon.). Democrat. Episcopalian. Avocations: art, photography, travel, writing. Home: Route 1 Box 475 Warrenton VA 22186

MCKELLIPS, TERRAL LANE, mathematics educator, university administrator; b. Terlton, Okla., Dec. 2, 1938; s. Raymond Orlando and Patrice Lillian (Fuller) McK.; m. Karen Kay Sweeney, Sept. 7, 1958; children—Marty Suzanne, Kyle Bret. B.S in Edn., S.W. Okla. State U., 1961; M.S., Okla. State U., 1963, Ed.D., 1968. Asst. prof. S.W. Okla. State U., Weatherford, 1962-66; prof., dept. chmn. Cameron U., Lawton, Okla., 1968-72, 73-83, prof., div. head math. and applied sci., 1983—; vis. prof. Okla. State U., Stillwater, 1972-73; dir. Bank of Elgin, Okla., 1983—. Contbr. articles to profl. jours. State coordinator Dept. Leadership Inst., Am. Council Edn., 1982-83. NSF Sci. Faculty fellow, 1966-68. Mem. Math. Assn. Am. (cons. bur. 1975—), Nat. Council Tchrs. Math., Pi Mu Epsilon, Phi Kappa Phi. Democrat. Club: Lawton Country (dir. 1982—). Avocations: golf; genealogy. Home: 825 NW 44th St Lawton OK 73505 Office: Cameron U Div Math and Applied Sci 2800 W Gore Blvd Lawton OK 73505

MCKELVEY, VINCENT ELLIS, geologist; b. Huntingdon, Pa., Apr. 6, 1916; s. Ellis Elmer and Eva Rupert (Faus) McK.; m. Genevieve Patricia Bowman, June 5, 1937; 1 son, Gregory Ellis. B.A. with honors, Syracuse U., 1937, D.Sc., 1975; M.A., U. Wis., 1939, Ph.D., 1947; D.Sc., S.D. Sch. Mines and Tech., 1976. Jr. geologist Soil Conservation Service, part-time, 1938-40; asst. geologist Wis. Geol. and Natural History Survey, 1938-40; geologist U.S. Geol. Survey, 1941—, chief radioactive minerals investigations, Washington, 1950-53, asst. chief geologist for econ. and fgn. geology, 1960-65, sr. research geologist, 1969-71, chief geologist, 1971, dir., 1971-78; adj. prof. Fla. Inst. Tech., 1982, 84; sr. sci. advisor to U.S. del. UN Conf. on Law of Sea, 1978-81; mem. bd. mineral resources NRC, 1980-83; U.S. rep. seabed com. UN, 1968-73; dir. Resources for Future, 1978—. Recipient Disting. Service award Interior Dept., 1963, award for sustained excellence Nat. Civil Service League, 1972, Rockefeller Pub. Service award, 1973, Alexander Winchell Disting. Alumnus award Syracuse U., 1976, Disting. Service award N.W. Mining Assn., 1977, Disting. Pub. Service award Rocky Mountain Assn. Geologists, 1977; Mt. McKelvey, Antarctica, named in his honor, 1977; named Disting. Alumnus, Lycoming Coll., 1983. Fellow AAAS, Geol. Soc. Am. (council 1969-72), Am. Geophys. Union; mem. Am. Geol. Inst. (dir. 1968-70), Soc. Econ. Geologists (council 1967-70), Econ. Geol. Pub. Co. (dir.), Am. Inst. Mining Engrs., Am. Assn. Petroleum Geologists (spl. award for meritorious service 1977, human needs award 1979), Soc. Exploration Geophysicists (hon.), Marine Tech. Soc., Soc. Econ. Paleontologists and Mineralologists, Sigma Xi. Club: Cosmos (Washington). Contbr. articles to profl. jours. Home: 510 Runnymeade Rd Saint Cloud FL 32769 Office: US Geological Survey Orlando FL 32801

MCKENNY, JERE WESLEY, oil company executive; b. Okmulgee, Okla., Feb. 14, 1929; s. Jere Claus and Juanita (Hunter) McK.; m. Anne Ross Stewart, May 4, 1957; children—Jere James, Robert Stewart. B.S. in Geol. Engring., U. Okla., 1951, M.S. in Geol. Engring., 1952. Geologist, dist. geologist Kerr-McGee Corp., Oklahoma City, 1955-59, div. exploration mgr., Amarillo, 1959-65, supt. domestic oil and gas exploration, Oklahoma City, 1965-68, mgr. oil and gas exploration, Oklahoma City, 1968-69, v.p. oil and gas exploration, Oklahoma City, 1969-74, v.p. exploration, Oklahoma City, 1974-77, vice chmn. bd., Oklahoma, 1974-77, pres., 1983-84, pres., chief operating officer, 1984—; dir. Bank of Okla.; mem. Domestic Petroleum Council. Mem. bd. visitors Sch. Engring. U. Okla.; mem. Allied Arts Found. Mem. Am. Assn. Petroleum Geologists, Am. Petroleum Inst. (dir., mem. gen. com. exploration affairs), Independent Petroleum Assn. of Am. (dir.), Oil Flights (dir.), Houston Geol. Soc., Oklahoma City Geol. Soc., Newcomen Soc. N.Am., C. of C. Clubs: Roustabout (charter mem.), 25 Year Club of Petroleum Industry, Men's Dinner, Oklahoma City Golf and Country, Petroleum of Oklahoma City) (dir.), Sirloin (Oklahoma City). Office: Kerr-McGee Corp 123 Robt S Kerr Ave Oklahoma City OK 73102

MCKENZIE, CAROLE ANN, nursing administrator; b. Uniontown, Pa., Jan. 16, 1949; d. Lawrence Wayne and Kathryn M. (Cooley) Miller; m. Roger Alan McKenzie, June 21, 1969; children—Ryan Alan, Kathryn Elizabeth Ann. B.S., Tex. Woman's U., 1970; M.S. in Nursing, Cert. Nurse Midwife, Yale U., 1973; Ph.D., Tex. A&M U., 1983. Cert. nurse midwife; R.N. Staff nurse Meth. Hosp., Houston, 1969-70; sch. nurse, tchr. Bridgeport Sch. Dist., Conn., 1970-71; instr. Tex. Woman's U., Houston, 1973-75; asst. prof. U. Tex., Houston, 1976-79; assoc. prof., chmn. dept. Med. U. S.C., Charleston, 1979-81; dean nursing, allied health Sumter Area Tech. Coll., S.C., 1983-86; adj. vis. assoc. prof. Med. U. S.C., 1982-86, assoc. prof. U. S.C., 1986—; dir. Lee Med. Practice, Bishopville, S.C., 1983—; expert witness S.C. Nurses Assn., Columbia, 1984—. Author Handbook of Clin. Nursing, 1984. Author, editor: High Risk Perinatal Nursing, 1983; Nursing Clinics of North America, 1982. Editor Health Care For Women Internat., 1977—. Mem. Jr. Welfare League, Bishopville, 1983—, Sumter Forum, 1984—. Mem. Am. Nurse's Assn. (mem. council edn. 1984-86), Am. Coll. Nurse Midwives, Nat. p Perimatal Assn., Nat. League for Nursing, S.C. Council Nurse-Midwifery, Bishopville Primary PTA (pres. 1982-83), Sigma Theta Tau, Beta Beta Beta, Tex. Nursing Leader's Corp.,Democrat. Methodist. Club: Rebecca Dennis Circle (devotion chmn. 1983-85). Home: 226 Roundup Dr Bishopville SC 29010 Office: U SC Columbia SC 29208

MCKENZIE, CHRIS ANNA, rehabilitation educator, counselor; b. Little Rock, Dec. 17, 1958; d. William Duke and Pearl Virginia (Dearman) McK. B.A., Harding Coll., 1979; Ed.M., U. Ark., 1982. Lic. assoc. counselor, Ark. Mail clk. Ark. Farm. Bur., Little Rock, 1979-80; counselor Pulaski County Ct., Little Rock, 1983; rehab. tchr. Div. Services for Blind, Dept. Human Services, Little Rock, 1983—. Pres. Disabled Students Assn., U. Ark., 1980-81; mem. women's com. Sebastian County Farm Bur., Fort Smith, Ark., 1984-85; cons. 4-H Club, Fort Smith, 1985. Mem. Am. Personnel Guidance Assn., Assn. for Edn. Rehab. of Blind Visually Impaired. Democrat. Mem. Ch. of Christ. Avocations: reading; computers. Office: Dept Human Services Div Services for Blind 616 Garrison PO Box 2002 Fort Smith AR 72902

MCKENZIE, CLIF ALLEN, Indian tribe official, accountant; b. Lawton, Okla., Sept. 29, 1942; s. Robert Allen and Rubie (Paukei) Williams; m. Michele Ann Martin, Aug. 4, 1972; children—Kasey Roberta, Kristen Marti. B.S. in Acctg., U. Okla., 1965; M.B.A., Pa. State U., 1976. Fin. analyst United Tribes of Okla., Shawnee, 1973-75; credit officer Bur. Indian Affairs, Dept. Interior, Horton, Kans., 1975-77, liaison officer, Syracuse, N.Y., 1977-80, program analyst, Denver, 1980-81; tribal adminstr. Kiowa Tribe of Okla., Carnegie, 1981-82; chief exec. officer, tribal bus. mgr. Cheyenne and Arapaho Tribe of Okla., Concho, 1982—; pres. Indian Devel. Corp., Oklahoma City, 1973—; police commr. City of Horton, 1976-77, city commr., 1976-77; dir. LECO, Inc., Tulsa. Life mem. DAV, U. Okla. Alumni Assn.; mem. Kiowa Black Legging Soc., Nat. Assn. Accts., Am. Soc. Notaries (dir. govt. affairs 1975-80), Nat. Taxpayers Investigative Fund (Whistleblower award 1982). Republican. Served to capt. U.S. Army, 1959-68. Lodges: Elks, Moose. Home: 3329 Del Aire Pl Del City OK 73115 Office: Indian Devel Corp PO Box 15613 Del City OK 73155

MC KENZIE, HILTON EUGENE, construction co. exec.; b. Berlin, Pa., Sept. 5, 1921; s. Enoch Joseph and Nellie Savilla (Colefleish) McK.; M.S.C.E. and M.E., M.I.T., 1941; B.S.C.E. and C.E., Va. Poly. Inst., 1939; m. Dorothy Elyea, May 19, 1949; children—Carol, Deborah, Cynthia, Hilton. Sr. cons. Bank Bldg. Corp., St. Louis, 1950-72; sec.-treas. Fin. Bldg. Cons., Atlanta, 1972-75; pres., chmn. Fin. Structures Inc., Atlanta, 1975—, Fin. Instn. Research, Inc., Atlanta, 1980—; instr. Cornell U., Ithaca, N.Y., 1976. Served to lt. col. U.S. Army, 1940-45. Decorated Silver Star, Bronze Star, Purple Heart. Mem. Nat. Soc. Profl. Engrs., N.C. Soc. Engrs., Soc. Am. Mil. Engrs. Protestant. Club: Elks. Home: Route 1 Mansfield GA 30255 Office: 2990 Brandywine Rd Atlanta GA 30341

MCKENZIE, LEWIS HARRIS, insurance company executive, state senator; b. Atlanta, Mar. 20, 1926; s. William Hill and Esther (Harris) McK.; student Ga. Inst. Tech., 1943-44; B.S., Washington and Lee U., 1948; m. Christy Armstrong, Nov. 13, 1948; children—Gray, Thomas Armstrong, Ione Lewis. Owner, pres., mgr. The McKenzie Ins. Agy., Montezuma, Ga., 1948—; dir. Bank of Macon County, Montezuma; mem. Ga. Senate, 1981—. Mem. city council City of Montezuma, 1967, mayor, 1968-69. Served with U.S. Navy, 1945-46. Mem. Independent Ins. Agts. of Ga. Democrat. Episcopalian. Club: Kiwanis. Home: 602 Engram St Montezuma GA 31063 Office: 122 Cherry St Montezuma GA 31063

MCKENZIE, PATRICIA MAE, nurse educator; b. Lufkin, Tex., Dec. 30, 1940; d. Norris M. Donley and Berta M. (Lilly) Hightower; divorced; 1 child, Stephanie Denise. B.S. in Nursing, Prairie View A&M U., 1963; M.P.H., U. Pitts., 1968; postgrad., Tex. A&M U., 1982-1985. Sch. nurse, health educator Wichita Fall Ind. Sch. Dist., Tex., 1963-65; peace corps volunteer, Dominican Republic, 1965-67; nursing instr. U. Pitts., 1968-69; nursing instr., asst. dir. nursing div., assoc. dir. nursing, Angelina Coll., Lufkin, Tex., 1969—; chairperson pub. responsibility com. Lufkin State Sch., 1980—. Chairperson program com. Am. Heart Assn., Lufkin, 1978—; mem. adv. council Planned Parenthood, Lufkin; mem. sch. bd., chair edn. com. St. Cyprians Episcopal Ch. Recipient Five Yr. Meritorious Service award Am. Heart Assn. Mem. NAACP, Angelina County Voters League, Dunbar Alumni Assn., Tex. Nurses Assn., Am. Nurses Assn., Tex. Jr. Coll. Tchrs. Assn., Black Nurses Assn., Tex. Assn. Vocat. Nurse Educators (program com. 1980-81), Orgn. Advancement Assoc. Degree Nursing Tex. Democrat. Methodist. Club: Top Ladies Distinction Inc. Avocations: sewing; reading; foil art. Office: Angelina Coll PO Box 1768 Lufkin TX 75901

MCKENZIE, ROBERT WILLIAM, structural engineer; b. Homer, La., June 4, 1931; s. Harry and Sallie Mae (Dawson) McK.; m. Nell Cowart, Nov. 25, 1933; children—Mary Elizabeth, Robert William, Barbara Ann. B.S., La. State U., 1952, M.S., 1954. Registered engr., La. Structural design engr. Bodman,

Murrel & Smith, Baton Rouge, 1953; jr. engr. Pyburn & Odom, 1953-54; structural engr., assoc. Alfred G. Rayner, 1958-68; ptnr. Rayner & McKenzie, Baton Rouge, 1968—. Served to lt. (j.g.) USNR, 1954-57. Mem. ASCE, Am. Cons. Engrs. Council, Cons. Engrs. Council La. (past pres.), Am. Concrete Inst., Prestressed Concrete Inst., La. Engring. Soc., Chi Epsilon. Democrat. Methodist. Home: 5647 Hyacinth Ave Baton Rouge LA 70808 Office: Rayner & McKenzie 5131 Payne Dr Baton Rouge LA 70809

MCKEON, DONNA FORILL, journalist; b. Cleve., Dec. 18, 1927; d. Paul John and Helen Ann (Winkel) Forill; m. John Vincent McKeon, Nov. 3, 1951; children—Mary Christine, Paul, Patrick. B.A., St. Mary-of-the-Woods Coll., 1949; M.A., Marquette U., 1951. Pub. relations chmn. Easter Seal Soc., Madison, Wis., 1952-56, Christmas Seal Soc., Madison, 1952-56; editor Smilin'Thru, Madison, 1952-56; society asst. Madison Capital Times, Wis. State Jour., Madison, 1953-56; advt. clk. Western Auto Supply, Cleve., 1951; gen. assignment reporter West Life, Cleve., 1967-69; asst. society editor Cleve. Press, 1969-71; freelance writer Richmond (Va.) LifeStyle, 1979-82; contbg. editor Met. Woman, Richmond, 1982—. Author: This Is Sister, 1968; contbr. articles to profl. jours. Trustee St. Mary-of-the-Woods Coll., 1971-73, mem. nat. alumnae bd., 1964-68. Recipient editing and writing award Am. Newspaper Guild, 1948; service award Wis. Easter Seal Soc., 1955; hon. mention for non-fiction Pen Women Biennial award, 1982; 3d place for non-fiction Pen Women Mid-Adminstrn. Congress award, 1985. Mem. Nat. League Am. Pen Women (pres. 1982-84), Women in Communications (pres. 1953-55), Va. Press Women. Roman Catholic. Home: 4122 Old Gun Rd E Midlothian VA 23113

MCKIM, RUTH ANN, realtor; b. Keokuk, Iowa, Nov. 26, 1932; d. Carl Edward and Ruby Irene (Martin) McK.; m. William James Ashbrook, Aug. 15, 1959 (div. 1974); children—Leslie McKim, Diane Hodges. B.S., U. Louisville, 1955, M.S. in Community Devel., 1977. Co-dir. art therapy Norton-Children's Hosps. Inc., Louisville, 1956-67; dir. art therapy Ky. Baptist Hosp., Louisville, 1955-56, NKC Hosps. Inc., 1957-59; researcher Bd. Aldermen, Louisville, 1976; pub. relations staff Dept. Consumer Affairs, Louisville, 1976-78; realtor assoc. Century 21, Louisville, 1979—; tutor Ky. Assn. Specific Perceptual-Motor Disability, Louisville, 1970-74. Author: Banking Survey, 1977. Sec., treas. ch. sch. 2nd Presbyn. Ch., Louisville, 1975-76, arts festival com., 1975-77; chmn., coordinator Louisville Food Day, 1978; canvasser Voter Registration, Louisville, 1976, 78, 82; vol., art donor Pub. Broadcasting System, Louisville, 1985. Scholar Allen R. Hite Art Inst., 1952-54, Bd. Realtors, 1979—. Mem. Louisville Craftsmans Guild (life), Ky. Artists and Craftsmen, Louisville Bd. Realtors, Ky. Realtors Assn., Nat. Assn. Realtors., Inst. Community Devel. Assn., U. Louisville Alumni Assn. Republican. Avocations: Oil and acrylic painting; jewelry design and execution; collecting prints. Home: 430 Sprite Rd Louisville KY 40207

MC KINLEY, JIMMIE JOE, business executive; b. Bertram, Tex., July 23, 1934; s. Joseph Crofford and Velma Anne (Barnett) McK.; B.J., U. Tex., 1955; M.S., U. Ky., 1964. Asst. librarian Bethel Coll., McKenzie, Tenn., 1961-63, reference librarian, 1966-70, acting head librarian, 1970-71; owner, mgr. Longview Book Co. (Tex.), 1974—. Former mem. bd. dirs. Longview-Piney Woods chpt. ARC, sec., 1983-84; trustee Bethel Coll., 1977-86. Mem. ALA, Gregg County Hist. and Geneal. Soc., Sigma Delta Chi. Presbyn. Home: PO Box 2106 Longview TX 75606

MCKINLEY, MARVIN DYAL, chemical engineering educator; b. Ocala, Fla., Mar. 3, 1937; s. Johnson Edward and May Josephine (Dyal) McK.; m. Beebe Lynn Mills, June 12, 1958; children—Kathryn, Julia, Jennifer. B.S. in Chem. Engring., U. Fla., 1959, M.S. in Engring., 1960, Ph.D., 1963. Cert. profl. engr., Ala. Engr. E.I. duPont De Nemours, Orange, Tex., 1963-65; asst. prof. U. Ala., University, 1965-68, assoc. prof., 1968-76, prof. chem. engring., 1976—, head chem., metall. engring. dept., 1980—; vis. prof. Busan Nat. U., Korea, 1972-73; mem. adv. bd. fuel sci. D. Reidel Publ. Co., Dordrecht, Holland, 1984—; assoc. dir. Metal Casting Tech. Ctr., University, 1984—. Contbr. articles to profl. jours. Grantee NSF, 1975, Dept. Energy, 1978, Dept. Agr., 1981. Mem. Am. Inst. Chem. Engrs., Am. Chem. Soc., Am. Soc. Engring. Edn. Methodist. Avocations: art; tennis. Office: Univ Ala Box G University AL 35486

MCKINNEY, BOBBY GENE, chemical company executive; b. El Dorado, Ark., Aug. 2, 1956; s. Hubert Lee and Louise (Murphy) McK.; m. Kelly Ann Matochik, Aug. 11, 1979; 1 son, Blake Joseph. B.S. in Chem. Engring., La. Tech. U., Ruston, 1979. Project engr. Monsanto, El Dorado, Ark., 1979-80, area engr., 1980-81, mfg. supr., 1981-82; mgr. mfg. El Dorado Chem. Co., 1982—. Republican. Baptist. Office: El Dorado Chem Corp PO Box 231 El Dorado AR 71730

MCKINNEY, BRUCE DALE, diagnostic clinic administrator; b. Harrisburg, Pa., Feb. 4, 1943; s. Bruce Watson and Eleanor (Wood) M.; m. Linda K. Connell, Sept. 29, 1979; 1 dau., Joy Elizabeth. B.S. in Mech. Engring., Purdue U., 1965, M.S. in Indsl. Adminstrn., 1966. Asst. to mgr. Logistics Engring., Martin Marietta Corp., Orlando, Fla., 1966-70; asst. mgr. Watson Clinic, Lakeland, Fla., 1970-77; exec. dir. Kidneycare Fla. Inc., Tampa, 1977-81; adminstr. Diagnostic Clinic, Largo, Fla., 1981—. Mem. bd. dirs., pres., treas. Central Fla. Speech & Hearing Ctr., 1972-80; pres. Orange County Young Republicans, Republican exec. com. Mem. Am. Coll. Med. Group Adminstrs., Med. Group Mgmt. Assn. (chmn. personnel com. 1972-73), Fla. Clinic Mgrs. Assn. (pres. 1976). Republican. Club: Rotary (treas., dir.). Contbr. articles to profl. jours. and papers to profl. confs. Home: 1662 Long Bow Ln Clearwater FL 33546 Office: 1551 West Bay Dr Largo FL 33540

MCKINNEY, FRANCES BAILEY, art psychotherapist; b. Newton, Mass., July 18, 1935; d. Gage and Ellen (Nealley) Bailey; m. Peter T. McKinney, June 7, 1957 (div. Nov. 1981); children—Peter, Karen, David. A.B., Vassar Coll., 1957; M.A., U. Houston-Clear Lake, 1979. Social worker State Bd. Child Welfare, Elizabeth, N.J., 1957-58; art therapist Mental Health and Mental Retardation Authority, Houston, 1979—; exec. dir. Creative Alternatives, Houston, 1982—. Bd. dirs. Citizens Alliance for Mentally Ill, Houston, 1983, 84, 85. Mem. Am. Art Therapy Assn., Nat. Art Edn. Assn., Am. Group Psychotherapy Assn., Am. Assn. Counseling and Devel. Episcopalian. Avocation: scuba diving. Home: 1206 Fountainview Houston TX 77057 Office: Creative Alternatives 1540 Sul Ross Houston TX 77006

MCKINNEY, JAMES ALTON SMITH, physician assistant, administrator; b. San Francisco, Apr. 15, 1954; s. Bryan Lloyd and Violet (Perry) McK.; m. Deborah Ann Hill, Feb. 4, 1974. A.A. summa cum laude, Tarrant County Jr. Coll., 1975; B.Sc. in Medicine, U. Tex. Health Sci. Ctr., 1978. Operating room technician John Peter Smith Hosp., Ft. Worth, 1973-77; coordinator spine unit Dallas VA Hosp., 1978-82; physician's asst. N. Tex. Orthopedic Assn., Plano, Tex., 1982-83; spine clinic mgr. Holt-Krock Clinic, Ft. Smith, Ark., 1983-84; spine clinic coordinator, asst. dir. Orthopaedic and Spinal Assocs., Ft. Smith, 1984-85, Glen Lakes Orthopedic Clinic, Dallas, 1985—; clin. instr. orthopaedics U. Tex. Health Sci. Ctr., Dallas, 1979-81; orthopaedic instr. Tex. Women's U., Dallas, 1979-82, Dallas County Paramedic Program, Dallas, 1979-81. Recipient Meritus Achievement award Dallas VA Med. Ctr., 1979, 81. Fellow Am. Acad. Physician's Assts.; mem. Okla. Acad. Physician's Assts., Tex. Acad. Physician's Assocs., Ark. Acad. Physician's Assocs. (v.p. 1985), Am. Acad. Neurol. and Orthopedic Surgeons (hon. mem.), Mensa, Phi Theta Kappa. Republican. Roman Catholic. Club: Chess (sec. 1970-73, Ft. Worth). Home: PO Box 6181 Fort Smith AR 72906 Office: 9900 N Central Expressway Suite 101 Dallas TX 75231

MCKINNEY, JAMES MARION, dentist, educator; b. Siguatepeque, Honduras, Oct. 19, 1950 (parents Am. citizens); s. Marion Barry and Helen (King) McK.; m. Jan Westbrook, Dec. 8, 1973; children—Mark Wesley, Caroline Elizabeth, Sarah Westbrook. D.D.S., U. Tenn.-Memphis, 1974. Lic. dentist, Tenn. Staff dentist VA Hosp., Asheville, Tenn., 1975-76; gen. practice dentistry, Knoxville, Tenn., 1976—; clin. instr. gen. dental residency program U. Tenn., Knoxville, 1980—. Author/presenter: research abstracts to profl. orgns. Deacon Cedar Springs Presbyterian Ch., Knoxville, 1977-80, elder, 1980—. Mem. ADA, Tenn. Dental Assn., Am. Assn. Hosp. Dentistry, Internat. Assn. Dental Research. Republican. Avocations: golf; camping.

MC KINNEY, LANDON EARL, medical sales representative; b. Nashville, May 17, 1949; s. Lawrence Vernon and Constance Joy McK.; B.S., Middle Tenn. State U., 1973, M.S., 1978; m. Lela D. Fulcomer, Dec. 17, 1982; 1 son, Eric. Grad. teaching asst. Middle Tenn. State U., 1973; profl. sales rep. Pennwalt Rx div., Nashville, 1975—. Served with USNR, 1968-70. Mem. Tenn. Acad. Sci., So. Appalachian Bot. Soc., Assn. S.E. Biologists, Ky. Acad. Sci., Tenn. Native Plant Soc. Address: 2874 Lyncrest Dr Nashville TN 37214

MC KINNEY, LOLA UTTERBACK, health care system administrator; b. Corpus Christi, Nov. 18, 1934; d. Clifford Rogers and LaJuana (Knowles) Utterback; A.A., El Centro Jr. Coll., 1980. Sec., Gt. A&P Tea Co., Dallas, 1953-62; exec. secretarial asst. Baylor U. Med. Center, Dallas, 1962-79; office mgr., exec. sec. to v.p. Hamilton Assocs., Inc., Dallas, 1979-84; mem. adv. com. Exec. Secretarial Sch.; mem. secretarial careers adv. com. Richland Jr. Coll., 1972-80; mem. office careers adv. com. El Centro Jr. Coll., 1981—. Mem. com. on adminstrn. Central Br., YWCA, Dallas, 1976—, chmn., 1978, 81; pres. adminstrv. secs. Dallas Hosp. Council, 1965. Mem. Profl. Secs. Internat. (Big D Chpt. Sec of Yr. 1972). Republican. Baptist. Office: PO Box 225999 Dallas TX 75265

MCKINNEY, MARLON E., communications company executive; b. White Pine, Tenn., Nov. 30, 1955; s. E. H. and Evelyn J. (Stepp) McK.; m. Rebecca S. Llewellyn, Mar. 15, 1975. B.S. in Acctg., Carson-Newman Coll., 1979. Asst. cashier First Tenn. Bank, Morristown, Tenn., 1973-79; sec.-treas. Pratt, Alexander, Thompson & Co., C.P.A.s, Morristown, 1979-81; account exec. industry cons. South Central Bell Telephone Co., Knoxville, Tenn., 1981—. Mem. Lakeway Tennis Assn. Republican. Baptist.

MC KINNEY, MICHAEL WHITNEY, trade association executive; b. San Angelo, Tex., Aug. 23, 1946; s. Wallace Luster and Mitzi Randolph (Broome) McK.; B.A. in Govt., U. Tex. at Austin, 1973; m. Martha LaNan Hooker, Feb. 24, 1973; children—Wallace Blake, Lauren Brooke. Adminstrv. asst. to lt. gov. State of Tex., Austin, 1968-69, adminstrv. asst. to gov., 1969-73, asst. to dir. Tex. Water Quality Bd., Austin, 1973-76; chief of staff Tex. Alcoholic Beverage Commn., 1976-83; v.p. for industry affairs Wholesale Beer Distbrs. Tex., 1984—. Bd. dirs. Tex. Alpha Ednl. Found., Inc., Austin, 1969—; mem. Travis County Zoo Task Force, 1986; mem. Senate Com. on Fees and Grants, 1982-83. Mem. Phi Kappa Psi. Democrat. Presbyterian. Club: Masons (32 deg., K.T.). Home: 3131 Honey Tree Ln Austin TX 78746 Office: 406 San Jacinto Bldg Austin TX 78701

MCKINNEY, ROY CHESTER, JR., art gallery owner; b. Rossville, Ga., July 4, 1941; s. Roy C. and Frances Lanelle (Williams) McK.; m. Mary Helen Weatherford, Aug. 20, 1962; children—Krista L., Karyn D. Student Pratt Inst., 1959; B.A. in Art, U. Chattanooga, 1963; postgrad. U. Denver, 1966; grad. U.S. Army Command and Gen. Staff Coll., 1977. Research image interpreter HRB-Singer, Inc., Rome, N.Y., 1966-69; sr. mktg. research assoc. Provident Life and Accident Ins. Co., Chattanooga, 1970-85, mgr. mktg. info. services, 1985—; owner Genesis Fine Arts, Chattanooga, 1974—; instr. U.S. Army Command and Gen. Staff Coll., Chattanooga, 1980-85. Active United Way, Cancer Drive. Served with U.S. Army, 1963-65. Recipient Crandall scholar, 1962-63; Leadership medal SAR, 1963; Gilman award Gilman Corp., 1963; Academic award Assn. U.S. Army, 1973. Mem. Am. Council Life Ins., Am. Mktg. Assn., Res. Officers Assn., C. of C. Republican. Mem. Church of Christ (deacon). Home: 1820 Old Ringgold Rd Chattanooga TN 37404 Office: Fountain Square Chattanooga TN 37402

MCKINNON, ARNOLD BORDEN, railroad company executive; b. Goldsboro, N.C., Aug. 13, 1927; s. Henry Alexander and Margaret (Borden) McK.; m. Oriana McArthur, July 19, 1950; children—Arnold Borden, Colin McArthur, Henry Alexander. A.B., Duke U., 1950, LL.B., 1951; postgrad. advanced mgmt. program Harvard U., 1972. Bar: N.C., D.C. Law asst. So. Ry. System, 1951-52, solicitor, 1952-54, asst. gen. solicitor, 1955-56, asst. gen. tax atty., 1956-61, gen. atty., 1962-64, sr. gen. solicitor, 1965-67, asst. v.p. law, 1969-70, v.p. law, 1971-75, sr. v.p. law and acctg., 1977-80, exec. v.p. law and fin., 1981-82; exec. v.p. mktg. Norfolk So. Corp., Va., 1982—; dir. Am. Security Bank, Washington. Bd. dirs. Va. Symphony, Norfolk, 1983—, Local Initiatives Support Corp., Norfolk, 1983—, Conv. and Visitors Bur., Norfolk, 1984—, Children's Health System, Inc., Norfolk, 1985; bd. visitors Old Dominion U., Norfolk, 1985. Served with U.S. Army, 1946-47. Mem. ABA, Nat. Freight Transp. Assn., 4th Cir. Jud. Conf., Greater Hampton Roads C. of C. (dir. Norfolk council 1983—). Democrat. Presbyterian. Clubs: Norfolk Yacht and Country; Chevy Chase (Md.); Metropolitan (Washington). Avocations: golf; reading. Office: Norfolk So Corp 1 Commercial Pl Norfolk VA 23514

MCKINNON, MURRAY CAMPBELL, petroleum company executive; b. Los Angeles, Sept. 14, 1930; s. Douglas David and Jean Christine (McQueen) McK.; Petroleum Engr., Colo. Sch. Mines, 1948-52; m. Janet Marilyn Brett, Jan. 23, 1954; children—Caroline, Douglas, Diane. Engr., Mobil Oil Corp., Los Angeles, 1952-62; prodn. supt., v.p. ops., exec. v.p. Pan Canadian Petroleum, Calgary, Alta., 1962-74; v.p. exploration Berry Holding Co., Houston, 1974-76; pres., chief exec. officer Trinity Resources Ltd., Houston, 1976—, also dir. Served with USNR, 1954-57. Mem. Houston C. of C., Ind. Petroleum Assn. Am., Tex. Ind. Producers and Royalty Owners, Tex. Midcontinent Oil and Gas Assn., Soc. Petroleum Engrs. Republican. Episcopalian. Clubs: Petroleum, Forest, Lochinvar, Calgary Golf and Country, Ranchmen's.

MCKINSEY, MARK HOWARD, furniture company executive; b. Ardmore, Okla., Feb. 28, 1934; s. Mark Howard and Elizabeth Anne (Abernethy) M.; m. Vanessa Cacacie, 1964; children—Scott, Stewart, Colin. B.S. in Indsl. Mgmt. Engring., U. Okla., 1956; M.B.A. in Bus. Adminstrn. & Gen. Mgmt., Harvard, 1961. Fin. Analyst Cosden Petroleum, subs. W.R. Grace & Co., Big Spring, Tex., 1961-64; treas., exec. v.p. Hamilton Cosco, Columbus, Ind., 1964-65; owner, pres. Norquist Products, Jamestown, N.Y., 1965-70; chmn., chief exec. officer Dictaphone Furniture Group, Stamford, Conn., 1970-74; group v.p. U.S. Filter, N.Y.C., 1974-77; chmn. bd., chief exec. officer DMI Furniture, Inc., Louisville, 1977—. Served to lt., USNR, 1956-59. Mem. Nat. Assn. Furniture Mfrs. (dir.), soc. Furniture Mfrs. Office: 10401 Linn Station Rd Suite 123 Louisville KY 40223

MCKITTRICK, CHARLES DENNIS, investment firm executive; b. Greenville, S.C., Sept. 5, 1949; s. Charles Victor and Betty Jo (Shadgett) McK.; m. Peggy Loraine Branyon, May 27, 1972; 1 child, Catherine Harley. B.S., Baptist Coll., 1975. First v.p. Johnson, Lane, Space, Smith and Co., Charleston, S.C., 1976—; prof. continuing edn. Bapt. Coll., Charleston, 1979-80. Author: (weekly newspaper editorial) Bears and Bulls, 1978—. Vice pres., bd. dirs. Sertoma Club, 1978-81; bd. dirs. Pinewood Sch. Bd., 1985—; mem. Summerville Exchange, 1982—. Served with USAF, 1969-73. Recipient Outstanding Sertoma Year award, 1978, Tribune award Sertoma Internat., 1979, Life Mem. award, 1980; Johnson, Lane, Space, Smith & Co. award excellence, 1977-85. Mem. N.Y. Stock Exchange, Nat. Assn. Securities Dealers. Methodist. Avocations: landscaping; writing; cooking. Office: Johnson Lane Space Smith and Co 19 Exchange St Charleston SC 29401

MCKNIGHT, MICHELYNN, librarian; b. Monmouth, Ill., May 9, 1947; d. Roger Glenn and Jane Eleanor (Morgan) Smith; m. Curtis C. McKnight, Nov. 29, 1968. B.A. in Music Edn., Western Ill. U., 1969; M. Music, U. Ill., 1971, M.S. in L.S., 1981. Cert. med. librarian. Tchr. band and music Fairmount (Ill.) Pub. Schs., 1970-72; dir. band, orch. Urbana (Ill.) Pub. Schs., 1972-75; orch. dir., tchr. music Champaign (Ill.) Pub. Schs., 1975-79; tchr. music, instrumental music Univ. High Sch., Urbana, Ill., 1979-81; adult services librarian Shawnee (Okla.) Pub. Library, 1981-83; supr. health scis. library Norman (Okla.) Mcpl. Hosp., 1983—; chmn. Greater Oklahoma City Area Health Scis. Library Consortium, 1984-85. Melinger Found. scholar, 1965-69. Mem. LWV, Med. Library Assn., Am. Soc. Info. Sci., ALA, Okla. Library Assn., Am. Fedn. Musicians, Music Educators Nat. Conf., Beta Phi Mu, Mu Phi Epsilon. Democrat. Home: 2208 Whiteoak Circle Norman OK 73071 Office: Health Scis Library Norman Regional Hosp PO Box 1308 Norman OK 73070

MC KNIGHT, PAUL JAMES, JR., hosp. corp. exec.; b. Nashville, Dec. 22, 1935; s. Paul James and Elizabeth Mayo (Cate) McK.; B.A. in Bus. Adminstrn., Emory U., 1957; cert. in hosp. adminstrn. St. Louis U., 1974; m. Ruth Evelyn McBryde, Jan. 26, 1963; children—Paul James, Margaret, Mary Ann. Corp. personnel dir. Hosp. Corp. Am., Gainesville, Fla., 1969-70, v.p., 1980—; adminstr. Epperson Hosp., 1971-72, North Fla. Regional Hosp., 1972-80; preceptor U. Fla. Sch. Health and Hosp. Adminstrn.; mem. Statewide Health Planning Council, 1982—. Bd. dirs. Athens (Tenn.) C. of C., Gainesville C. of C., Civitan Regional Blood Bank of North Fla. Served with USN, 1957-61. Paul Harris fellow, 1981. Mem. Am. Coll. Hosp. Adminstrs., Fla. League Hosps. (pres. 1976), Fla. C. of C. (dir. 1984—), Fedn. Am. Hosps. (dir.). Republican. Methodist. Club: Rotary. Home: 2356 Arendell Way Tallahassee FL 32308 Office: PO Box 1695 Tallahassee FL 32302

MCLAIN, MAURICE CLAYTON, real estate lawyer; b. Hillsboro, Tex., Sept. 22, 1929; s. Otis Ogen and Rachel Elizabeth (Estes) McL.; m. Martha Orlana Gould, Sept. 25, 1953; 1 son, William Gould. Student Hillsboro Jr. Coll., 1945-46, Tex. A&M Coll., 1946-47; B.A. in Math., N.Tex. State U., 1950; J.D., So. Meth. U., 1962. Bar: Tex. 1962, U.S. Supreme Ct. 1976, U.S. Ct. Appeals (4th, 5th, 9th, 11th cirs.). Engring. contracts coordinator Vought Aerospace Div. L.T.V. Corp., Dallas, 1961-64; assoc. firm Abney & Burleson, Dallas, 1964-66; counsel Fed. Nat. Mortgage Assn., Dallas, 1966-69; sr. v.p. and gen. counsel USLIFE Real Estate Services Corp., Dallas, 1970-84; of counsel Clark, Thomas, Winters & Newton, Austin, Tex., 1984—. Served with USNR, 1949-58. Fellow Am. Coll. Mortgage Attys.; mem. Am. Coll. Real Estate Attys., ABA, Fed. Bar Assn., State Bar Tex., Dallas Bar Assn., Tex. Bd. Legal Specialization (chmn. real estate specialization adv. commn. 1979—), Am. Judicature Soc., Real Estate Fin. Execs. Assn., Assn. Life Ins. Counsel, Nat. Mortgage Banking Legal Com., SAR, Sigma Phi Epsilon, Phi Delta Phi. Republican. Episcopalian. Clubs: Dallas Scottish Soc., English Speaking Union. Home: 3908 Royal Ln Dallas TX 75229 Office: 1200 Texas Commerce Bank Bldg Austin TX 78767

MC LALLEN, MILLARD DANIEL, coll. ofcl.; b. Fowler, Colo., Feb. 24, 1931; s. Samuel B. and Hester Frances (Jones) McL.; B.S., Wayland Bapt. Coll., 1953; M.A. in Speech, W. Tex. State U., 1957; Ph.D., U. Tex., 1975; m. Laura F. Stringer, Aug. 19, 1955; children—Deborah L., Benjamin T. Chief engr. and mgr. Sta. KHBL-FM, Wayland Bapt. Coll., Plainview, Tex., 1950-53; propr., mgr. Ben Franklin Variety Store, Hereford, Tex., 1955-57; asst. prof. speech Mary Hardin Baylor Coll., Belton, Tex., 1957-60; instr. in speech U. Denver, part-time 1960-61; chmn. dept. speech Mary Hardin Baylor Coll., 1961-64, prof. communication, 1961-64; tchr. English and math. Englewood (Colo.) High Sch., 1964-65; asso. prof. English, Met. State Coll., Denver, 1965-67, acting chmn. English dept., 1966-67; prof. English and speech So. State Coll. (name changed to U. S.D. at Springfield 1969), 1967-69, chmn. humanities div., 1968-69; edn. specialist Visual Instrn. Bur., U. Tex., Austin, 1969-70, research asso. Center for Sch. Studies, 1970, research asso. computer-assisted instructional lab., 1970-71; dean of instrn. Tarrant County Jr. Coll., Fort Worth, 1971-78, research project dir. indsl. coop. tng., 1974-76; v.p. acad. affairs Wayland Bapt. Coll., 1978—. Program chmn. Heart of Tex. council Boy Scouts Am., 1961-64; bd. dirs. Grad. Career Devel. Center, Arlington, Tex., 1973-76, Horned Frog council Boy Scouts Am., 1974—, merit badge counselor, 1973-76. Served with U.S. Army, 1953-55. NDEA fellow, 1967; NSF research grantee, 1970. Mem. Nat. Council Tchrs. English, Tex. Assn. Jr. Coll. Instructional Adminstrs., Am. Assn. Higher Edn., Am. Assn. Univ. Adminstrs., Gen. Semantics Inst., Am. Tech. Edn. Assn., Nat. Assn. Environ. Edn., Council Occupational Edn., Community Coll. Assn. Instrn. and Tech., Tex. Assn. Tchr. Educators, AAUP, Nat. Council Aging, Nat. Ret. Tchrs. Assn., Nat. Aerospace Edn. Assn., Internat. Narcotics Enforcement Officers Assn., Nat. Council Crime and Delinquency, Phi Delta Kappa, Alpha Psi Omega, Alpha Chi, Tau Kappa Alpha, Phi Theta Kappa. Democrat. Baptist. Contbr. articles on programmed learning and edn. in communications to profl. publs. Home: 1110 Ennis St Plainview TX 79072 Office: Wayland Baptist College Plainview TX 79072

MC LANE, H. ARTHUR, judge; b. Valdosta, Ga., Apr. 2, 1939; s. Carson H. and Philena (Tyson) McL.; B.A., Emory U., 1961; J.D., U. Ga., 1963; m. Jane Campbell Bennet, June 17, 1961; children—Mary Campbell, Paul Corbett. Admitted to Ga. bar, 1963, U.S. Supreme Ct. bar, 1972; practiced in Valdosta, 1963-83; county atty. Lowndes County (Ga.), 1965-73; atty. Echols County Bd. Edn., 1966-83; judge State Ct., 1977-83. Adv. bd. Valdosta Area Vocat. Tech. Sch., 1967—; bd. dirs. Valdosta Boys Club, 1966-81, pres., 1971-72; bd. dirs. Valdosta Entertainment Assn., 1968-71; chmn. show div. Valdosta-Lowndes County Bicentennial Celebration, 1975-76; exec. bd. Ga. Sheriffs Boys Ranch, 1979-83, chmn., 1982-83. Mem. State Bar Ga., Valdosta Bar Assn. (pres. 1974), Am. Judicature Soc., Valdosta-Lowndes County C. of C. (dir. 1978-80, v.p. 1983, pres. 1984-85), Blue Key, Sigma Alpha Epsilon, Phi Delta Phi, Omicron Delta Kappa, Phi Kappa Phi. Methodist. Clubs: Rotary (dir. 1973, 76-77, 78-79, 82-83, pres. 1985), Gridiron, Valdosta Country (dir., pres. 1971). Office: Lowndes County Courthouse PO Box 1349 Valdosta GA 31603

MCLAUGHLIN, ALEXANDER CHARLES JOHN, oil company executive; b. N.Y.C., June 3, 1925; s. Alexander and Margaret (Percival) McL.; B.S., Va. Poly. Inst., 1946; postgrad. Columbia, 1947-48; m. Joan Kosak, June 10, 1950; 1 dau., Jena Hilary. With Standard Vacuum Oil Co., N.Y.C., Shanghai, China, Manila, Saigon, Indochina, Hongkong, Yokohama, Japan, 1946-50; with Trans Arabian Pipeline Co., Turaif, Saudi Arabia, 1951; with Andean Nat. Corp., Cartagena, Colombia, 1952-54; practice civil engring., N.Y.C., 1954-55; chief project engr. mktg. Am. Oil Co., N.Y.C., chief engr. South, Atlanta, sr. head engr., Chgo., 1955-64; sr. process engr. mfg. and marketing dept. Amoco Internat. Oil Co., Europe, S.A., Asia, N.Y.C., Chgo., 1969-72; mgr. distbn. Singapore Petroleum Co., 1972-73; constrn. supr. Iran Pan Am. Oil Co., 1973, onshore/offshore supr., 1974-75; sr. staff engr. Amoco Internat. Oil Co., Chgo., 1975-78, Amoco Prodn. Co. Internat., Houston, 1978-85, inspection supr. offshore and overseas constrn. dept., 1985—. Vol. fireman Long Beach Fire Dept., 1955-63; tng. officer USCG Aux., 1962; Eagle scout, scoutmaster, troop com. mem. Nassau County N.Y. council Boy Scouts Am., 1946-49. Decorated Order White Cloud. Fellow ASCE; mem. Nat. Soc. Profl. Engrs., Nat. Assn. Corrosion Engrs., Internat. Platform Assn., Omicron Delta Kappa. Republican. Club: Pathfinders (London, Eng.); Columbia Country (Shanghai); Singapore Swim, Singapore Petroleum, Singapore American; Tehran American; Moose. Home: 3106 Cedar Knolls Dr Kingwood TX 77339 Office: Amoco Ctr 501 W Lake Blvd PO Box 3092 Houston TX 77253

MCLAUGHLIN, DOROTHY CLAIRE, employment program administrator, consultant; b. Kansas City, Mo.; d. Earl H. and Hazel Loucille (Allen) Klopfenstine; m. Patrick M. McLaughlin, Feb. 20, 1968; children by previous marriage—Michael L. Gant (dec.), Margaret C. Gant. B.A. in Sociology, UCLA, 1976; postgrad. Eastern Mont. Coll., 1977—. Student governance adv., coordinator Calif. State U., Los Angeles, 1974-76; dir. Am. Assn. Ret. Persons Sr. Community Service Employment Program, Billings, Mont. 1977-81, Dallas, 1981—; cons., lectr., speaker in field. Co-founder Gray Panthers Dallas. 1985; rep. pub. sector Employment Security Council, Helena, Mont., 1979-81; mem. aging com. Mental Health Aging Program, Dallas, 1981-82. Recipient Superior Achievement honors Pasadena City Coll., 1974; Pres.'s Club award Avon Products, Inc., 1973. Mem. AAUW (chmn. women's issues 1979), Assn. Bus. Profl. Women, Am. Sociol. Assn., Nat. Assn. Accts., Am. Personnel Guidance Assn., Mont. Assn. for Female Execs. (co-founder 1980). Home: PO Box 36524 Dallas TX 75235 Office: Sr Community Service Employment Program 4917 Harry Hines Blvd Dallas TX 75235

MC LAUGHLIN, (EDWARD) BRUCE, lawyer; b. Omaha, Apr. 2, 1921; s. Charles F. and Margaret (Bruce) McL.; B.S., Georgetown U., 1943; postgrad. George Washington U., 1950-51; J.D., U. Miami, 1953. Announcer, Sta. KTSM, El Paso, 1943-44; news editor KFRE, Fresno, Calif., 1944; with McKesson-Robbins, San Francisco, 1945-46; radio prodn. Sta. KOSA, Odessa, Tex., 1947-49, Sta. KPHO, Phoenix, 1949; TV prodn. Sta. WITV, Miami-Ft. Lauderdale, Fla., 1953-55; admitted to Fla. bar, 1955, practiced, Miami, until 1982. Served with Signal Corps, U.S. Army, World War II. Mem. Fla. Bar, Am., Dade County bar assns., Lawyers Club Dade County (dir. 1969-70), Screen Actors Guild (pres. Fla. br. 1965-69, mem. Fla. council 1962—, mem. nat. bd. dirs. 1968—, nat. v.p. 1983—), AFTRA (dir. Miami chpt. 1975—), Am. Legion, Gamma Eta Gamma. Democrat. Roman Catholic. Clubs: Coral Gables (Fla.) Country; Jockey (Miami, Fla.); University (Washington). Editor: Florida Screen Actor, 1974—; contbr. articles to profl. publs. Home: 45 Antilla Ave Coral Gables FL 33134 Office: PO Box 344657 Coral Gables FL 33134

MCLAUGHLIN, ELLEN WINNIE, biologist, educator; b. Roosevelt, N.Y., Aug. 17, 1937; d. Merle Emery and Winnie Matilda (Prinz) McL. B.S., SUNY-Albany, 1958; M.A., U. N.C., 1962, Ph.D., Emory U., 1967. Instr. biology Converse Coll., Spartanburg, S.C., 1960-63; asst. prof. biology Samford U., Birmingham, Ala., 1967-70, assoc. prof., 1970-75, prof., 1975—. Emory U. Fellow, 1965; Samford U. research grantee, 1968, 85. Mem. AAAS, Am. Soc. Zoologists, Ala. Acad. Sci., Assn. So. Biologists, Ala. Conservancy, Phi Kappa Phi. Mem. Christian and Missionary Alliance. Author: Laboratory Guide for General Biology, 1972; contbr. articles to profl. jours. Home: 5604 12th Ave S Birmingham AL 35222 Office: Samford U Biology Dept Birmingham AL 35229

MCLAUGHLIN, GREGORY CHARLES, metals company executive, statistical consultant; b. Phila., Mar. 25, 1953; s. Charles Joseph McLaughlin and

Eleanor May (Low) McLaughlin Rodgers. B.S. in Meteorology, Fla. State U., 1975, M.S. in Stats., 1978. Math. analyst Eastman Kodak Co., Rochester, N.Y., 1978-82; sr. statistician Baxter Travenol Labs., Round Lake, Ill., 1982-84; technology dir. Reynolds Metals Co., Richmond, Va., 1984—; mem. adj. grad. faculty Rochester Inst. Tech., N.Y., 1980-81; mem. adj. faculty U. N.C.-Asheville, 1982. Mem. Am. Soc. for Quality Control (cert. quality engr., tech. chmn. Rochester sect. 1980-81), Am. Statis. Assn. Home: 5300 Glenside Dr Apt 2101 Richmond VA 23228 Office: Reynolds Metals Co 6601 W Broad St Richmond VA 23230

MCLAUGHLIN, JOHN LARRY, economics educator; b. Atoka, Tenn., Nov. 19, 1938; s. John and Goldie (Smith) McL.; m. Rose Dathelyn Goode, July 12, 1959; children—Michael Hunter, Patrick Scott, Jon Stuart. Student U. Tenn.-Martin, 1956-59; B.S., Bethel Coll., 1960; M.A. in Edn. Adminstrn., Concordia Tchrs. Coll., 1971; postgrad. Pepperdine U., 1979-80, Memphis State U., 1981-84. Lic. tchr., Tenn. Commd. 2d lt. U.S. Marine Corps, 1960, advanced through grades to maj., 1968, ret., 1980; tchr. Brighton (Tenn.) High Sch., 1980-81; tchr./coach Kirby High Sch., Memphis, 1981—. Decorated Bronze Star. Mem. NEA, Tenn. Edn. Assn., West Tenn. Edn. Assn., Shelby County Edn. Assn., Assn. for Supervision and Curriculum Devel., Nat. Fedn. Interscholastic Coaches Assn., Tenn. Athletic Coaches Assn., Marine Corps Assn. Presbyterian. Home: Ware McLaughlin House Atoka TN 38004 Office: 4080 Kirby Pkwy Memphis TN 38115

MCLAUGHLIN, WILLIAM FOOTE, land development and property management consultant; b. Chgo., July 16, 1929; s. Frederic and Irene Castle (Foote) McL.; B.S. in Bus. Adminstrn., Hofstra U., 1951; M.B.A., U. Ark., 1957, Ph.D., 1962; diplomate Community Assocs. Inst.; m. Delores Feliu, July 29, 1950 (div. 1961); 1 dau., Irene Castle; m. 2d, Dorothy Begier, July 3, 1975; 1 son, David Lee. Vice pres., dir. W.F. McLaughlin Co., Chgo., 1957-68; mktg. adminstr. Mid-Western Instruments, Tulsa, 1964; economist, planning analyst Skelly Oil Co., Tulsa, 1968-72; exec. v.p., chief operating officer Main Place Corp., Tulsa, 1972-76; pres. Koppel Devel. Co., Bartlesville, Okla., 1977-79; mgr. corp. facilities and real estate Western Co. N.Am., Ft. Worth, 1979-81; dir. property mgmt. Kiawah Island Co. (S.C.), 1981-83; pres. RSVP Mgmt. Co., Myrtle Beach, S.C., 1983—; instr. econs. and real estate U. Ark., 1957-61, Tulsa Jr. Coll., 1974-78; real estate cons., 1971—. Mem. Mayor's Community Devel. Com., Tulsa, 1972—. Fellow Co. Mil. Historians, Sons of Confederacy, Culver Legion; mem. Bldg. Owners and Mgrs. Assn. (Man of Yr. award 1976, 77), Nat. Assn. Corp. Real Estate Execs., Am. Planning Assn., Nat. Assn. Bus. Economists, Am. Econs. Assn., Nat. Assn. Fin. Adminstrs., Nat. Assn. Rev. Appraisers (cert.), Inst. Real Estate Mgmt. (cert. property mgr.) Community Assn. Inst. (profl. community assn. mgr.; chmn. resort mgmt. com.), Sigma Chi. Episcopalian. Club: Aztec. Home: 235 Sparrow Hawk Rd Kiawah Island SC 29455

MCLAURIN, RONALD DE, political analyst, consultant, author, research analyst; b. Oakland, Calif., Oct. 8, 1944; s. Lauchlin De and Marie Annette (Friedman) McL.; m. Joan Adcock, June 11, 1966; children—Leila, Cara. B.A., U. So. Calif., 1965; student U. Tunis, Tunisia, 1964-65; A.M., Tufts U., 1966, M.A.L.D., 1967, Ph.D., 1973. Instr. Merrimack Coll., North Andover, Mass., 1966-67; mgmt. asst. Office Sec. Def., Washington, 1967-68; asst. for Africa, Office Asst. Sec. Def. for Internat. Security Affairs, 1968-69; research scientist Am. Inst. Research, Washington, 1969-75; sr. assoc. Abbott Assocs., Inc., Alexandria, Va., 1975—; v.p. Internat. Contracting and Trading, 1985—; fellow Ctr. Internat. Devel., U. Md., 1983—; internat. research assoc. Inha U., Korea, 1985—; dir. Lau-Mar, Ltd., Honolulu, 1981—, also chmn.; cons. Am. Insts. Research, 1975-76, Analytical Assessments Corp., 1977-79, Ctr. Advanced Internat. Studies, U. Miami, 1973, Ctr. Advanced Research, Inc., 1977—, Ctr. Strategic and Internat. Studies, Georgetown U., 1981, Middle East Assessments Group, 1982—, Getty Oil Co., 1982, Office of Pres., Lebanon, 1982-83, Office Crown Prince, Jordan, 1981-82, 84—, Office U.S. Sec. Def., 1973, Bus. Council for Internat. Understanding, 1984, others. Author: The Middle East in Soviet Policy, 1975; The Art and Sci of Psychological Operations, 2 vols., 1976; Foreign Policy Making in the Middle East, 1977; The Political Role of Minority Groups in the Middle East, 1979; Beyond Camp David, 1981; Military Propaganda, 1982; Middle East Foreign Policy: Issues and Processes, 1982; Lebanon and the World in the 1980s, 1983; The Emergence of a New Lebanon: Fantasy or Reality?, 1984; Jordan: The Impact of Social Change on the Tribes, 1984. Contbr. articles to profl. jours. Mem. Mil. Ops. Research Soc., Fgn. Policy Research Inst., Psychol. Ops. Soc., Internat. Studies Assn., Inter-Univ. Seminar Armed Forces and Soc., Middle East Inst. Home: 8600 Powder Horn Rd Springfield VA 22152 Office: Abbott Assocs Inc PO Box 2124 Springfield VA 22152

MCLEAN, JOHN WILLIAM, banker; b. Okmulgee, Okla., Apr. 2, 1922; s. Lawrence White and Margaret (McGill) McL.; m. Eleanor Jane Johnson, May 8, 1943; children—Margo, Lawrence William, Scott Johnson. B.S., U. Okla., 1943. Asst. cashier, v.p. First Nat. Bank Tulsa, 1948-58; pres. Tex. Nat. Bank, Houston, 1959-64; dir. mktg. Bank Am., San Francisco, 1964-67; chmn. Liberty Nat. Bank and Trust Co., Oklahoma City, 1967—, Banks of Mid-Am., Inc. Served with arty. U.S. Army, World War II. Decorated Bronze Star medal; named to Okla. Hall of Fame, 1976; recipient Disting. Service Citation, U. Okla., 1975; Disting. Service award Oklahoma City U., 1983; named Regional Banker of Yr., Fin. Mag., 1972. Mem. Bankers Assn., Assn. Res. City Bankers, Oklahoma City C. of C. (life), Okla. Heritage Assn. (pres.). Republican. Presbyterian. Clubs: Oklahoma City Golf and Country, Oak Tree Golf. Author: Fundamental Principles of Sound Bank Credit, 1961; cons. author: (with Herbert Prochnow) Commercial Banking Handbook, 1983. Home: 7150 N Country Club Dr Oklahoma City OK 73112 Office: Liberty Nat Bank and Trust Co PO Box 25848 Oklahoma City OK 73125

MCLEAN, KATHLEEN GUILFOYLE, nurse; b. Mpls., Oct. 24, 1943; d. Frederick Bertram and Lucille Margaret (Volkert) G.; m. William John McLean, III, Oct. 3, 1964. Diploma Practical Nursing, St. Joseph Hosp., St. Paul, Minn., 1964. Staff nurse Divine Redeemer Hosp., S. St. Paul, Minn., 1964-66, Obion County Gen. Hosp., Union City, Tenn., 1970, U.S. Army Hosp., Ft. Campbell, Ky., 1973-76, VA Med. Ctr., Memphis, 1976—, mem. Ambulatory Care Com. for Quality Assurance, 1982—, mem. Continuing Edn. for Lic. Practical Nurses, 1978—. Vol. March of Dimes, Memphis, 1982-84. Recipient Superior Performance award Nursing Service VA, 1978, 79, 82, Outstanding Rating award, 1983, 84. Mem. Tenn. Lic. Practical Nurses Assn. (sec. 1982—), Am. Bus. Women's Assn. Republican. Roman Catholic. Club: Releigh-Bartlett Belles (Memphis). Home: 5132 Twinmeadows Dr Memphis TN 38134

MCLEAN, ROBERT CAMERON, real estate and mortgage loan analyst; b. Birmingham, Ala., Feb. 17, 1957; s. Laughlin Chalmers and Sammye (Sturdivant) McL. B.S., U. Ala., 1978, M.A. in Fin., 1979. Acct. Liberty Nat., Birmingham, 1980-81, securities analyst, 1981-84; real estate analyst Torchmark Investment Adv., Birmingham, 1984—. Fellow Life Mgmt. Inst.; mem. Breakfast Exchange Club Birmingham, Atlanta Soc. Fin. Analysts, Mortgage Bankers Assn. Ala. Republican. Presbyterian. Club: Chace Lake Country (Birmingham). Avocations: golf, tennis, jogging. Home: 1167 H Green Springs Ave S Birmingham AL 35205 Office: Torchmark Investment Adv 2001 3d Ave S PO Box 2612 Birmingham AL 35202

MCLEAN, THOMAS RICHARD, exploration geologist; b. Portmouth, Va., Nov. 26, 1957; s. Carl Thomas and Mary Anne (Taylor) McL.; m. Suzanne Marie Bernard, Mar. 2, 1985. B.S. in Geology, U. Okla., 1980, M.S. in Geology, 1983. Teaching asst. geology U. Okla., Norman, 1980-82; geologist Union Oil Co. of Calif., Oklahoma City, 1983—. Mem. Am. Assn. Petroleum Geologists, Oklahoma City Geol. Soc. (assoc. editor 1984-85, editor 1985—). Democrat. Methodist. Avocations: golf: softball; tennis; volleyball. Office: Union Oil Co of Calif 2000 Classen Center Oklahoma City OK 73106

MCLEAN, WALTER COPLEY, JR., ophthalmologist; b. Charlottesville, Va., June 18, 1949; s. Walter Copley and Margaret Louise (Kleppinger) McL.; m. Leta Merriweather Barron. B.A., Princeton U., 1971; M.D., U. Va., 1975. Diplomate Am. Bd. Ophthalmology. Intern Roanoke Meml. Hosp., Va., 1975-76; resident in ophthalmology U. Va., Charlottesville, 1976-79; fellow St. John's Ophthalmic Hosp., Jerusalem, 1979-80, Bascom Palmer Eye Inst., Miami, Fla., 1980-81; assoc., then ptnr. Western Carolina Retina Assocs., Asheville, N.C., 1981—, v.p., 1983—. Fellow Am. Acad. Ophthalmology; mem. Western Carolina Ophthalmol. Assn., N.C. Med. Assn., AMA, Aspen Retinal Detachment Soc. Presbyterian. Avocations: sports; hiking; bee keeping. Home: 2 Westwood Rd Asheville NC 28804 Office: Western Carolina Retina Assocs 276 E Chestnut St Asheville NC 28801

MCLEES, WILLIAM ANDERSON, university hospital executive; b. Winterset, Iowa, Oct. 21, 1925; s. Ralph and Mabyl Mildred (McKenzie) McL.; m. Joan Elizabeth Lint, Jan. 18, 1958; children—Mark Andrew, Steven Alan. B.A., Drake U., 1953; M.A., U. Iowa, 1955, Ph.D., 1958. Asst. prof. grad. program hosp. adminstrn. U. Iowa, Iowa City, 1958-60; prin. investigator Assn. Rehab. Ctrs., Evanston, Ill., 1960-61; asst. adminstr. Ind. U. Med. Ctr., Indpls., 1961-65, dir. div. plans and devel., 1965-69, Ind.-Purdue U., 1969-71; exec. dir. Med. U. S.C. Hosp., Charleston, 1971—, assoc. prof. health service adminstrn. Coll. Allied Health Sci., 1982—; cons. Inst. for Neurol. Disorders, NIH, Bethesda, Md., 1970—; adj. prof. pub. health adminstrn. U. S.C., Columbia, 1982—. Served with USN, 1946-48. U. Iowa grad. fellow, 1954. Mem. Am. Hosp. Assn. (life), Am. Coll. Hosp. Adminstrs., S.C. Hosp. Assn., Assn. for Advancement Med. Instrumentation (sec. 1975-77, v.p. 1977-79). Presbyterian. Home: 1562 Inverness Dr Charleston SC 29412 Office: Med Univ SC Hosp 171 Ashley Ave Charleston SC 29425*

MCLELLAN, REX BOOKER, science educator, consultant; b. Leeds, Eng., Nov., 21, 1935; came to U.S., 1963, naturalized, 1968; s. Alexander and Ivy (Booker) McL.; m. Shirley Webster, Nov. 2, 1957; 1 child, Robert Neil. B. Metallurgy, U. Sheffield, Eng., 1957; Ph.D., U. Leeds, 1962. Research assoc. U. Ill., Champaign, 1963-64; prof. materials sci. Rice U., Houston, 1964—. Contbr. articles to profl. jours. Recipient Mappin medal U. Sheffield, Eng., 1957; Am. Sci. award, Fed. Republic Ger., 1974. Mem. Am. Soc. Metals. Republican. Avocations: squash; pistol shooting. Home: 2153 Swift Houston TX 77030 Office: Materials Sci Dept Rice Univ PO Box 1892 Houston TX 77251

MCLELLAN, ROBERT NEIL, insurance company executive, state legislator; b. San Francisco, July 27, 1924; s. Timothy Alexander and Dorothy (Ryan) McL.; m. Doris Murphree, Dec. 21, 1947; children—Carol, Bobby, Vivian, Johnny. A.B., U. S.C., 1949. Pres. Byrd-McLellan Agy., Inc., Seneca, S.C., mem. S.C. Ho. of Reps., 1977—; dir. Oconee Savs. & Loan Assn. Elder Seneca Presbyterian Ch., 1966—. Served with U.S. Army, 1943-46. Recipient Disting. award S.C. Sch. Bds. Assn., 1983, Leadership award S.C. Assn. Adult Educators, 1984. Mem. Ind. Ins. Agts. S.C. (pres. 1971-73), Ind. Ins. Agts. Am. (bd. dirs. 1973-76). Democrat. Office: Box 796 Seneca SC 29679*

MC LELLAND, CLAUDE ALLEN, otolaryngologist; b. Ennis, Tex., May 22, 1933; s. Rufus Allen and Claudia Irene (Purdue) McL.; B.A., Southwestern U., 1956; M.D., Southwestern Med. Sch., Dallas, 1960; m. Joyce Ann Allen, June 24, 1961; children—Jaye Alane, Tracy Ann. Rotating intern Methodist Hosp., Dallas, 1960-61; commd. 2d lt. U.S. Air Force, 1961, advanced through grades to lt. col., 1969; chief aerospace medicine Chenault AFB, Lake Charles, La., 1961-63; resident in otolaryngology Baylor U., Houston, 1963-67— chief otolaryngology service USAF Med. Center, Keesler AFB, Biloxi, Miss., 1967-74, ret., 1974; practice medicine specializing in otolaryngology, Corpus Christi, 1974—; mem. staff Meml. Med. Center, Spohn Hosp., Driscoll Found. Children's Hosp.; instr. Tulane U. Med. Sch., 1969; asst. prof. otolaryngology Med. Sch., Baylor U., Houston, 1974—. Bd. dirs. S. Tex. Speech, Hearing and Lang. Center, 1974—, Driscoll Found. Childrens Hosp., 1978—. Decorated Air Force Commendation medal. Diplomate Am. Bd. Otolaryngology. Fellow A.C.S.; mem. Am. Acad. Ophthalmology and Otolaryngology, AMA, Tex. Med. Assn., Tex. Otolaryn. Assn., S. Tex. Otolaryngology Study Club (pres. 1977), Tex. Soc. Ophthalmology and Otolaryngology, Centurian Club of Deafness Research Found., Nueces County Med. Soc., Phi Rho Sigma. Episcopalian. Home: 5326 River Oaks Corpus Christi TX 78413 Office: 2601 Hospital Blvd Suite 117 Corpus Christi TX 78405

MCLEMORE, DAVID BYRON, government security specialist; b. Hattiesburg, Miss., Apr. 19, 1951; s. Byron and Frances (Henderson) McL.; m. Margaret Fishel, Dec. 24, 1982; children—Brandi, Bryson. B.S. in Criminal Justice, U. So. Miss., 1980; grad. Biloxi Police Law Enforcement Acad., 1983. Camera mgr. Woolco Dept. Store, Hattiesburg, 1970-74; owner Cameras Etc., Hattiesburg, 1974-78; mgr. Telray Corp., Hattiesburg, 1978-82; U.S. Govt. Security specialist U.S. Air Force, Keesler AFB, Miss., 1982—; photo counselor U.S. Drug Enforcement Agy., Gulfport, Miss., 1985; security specialist ROTC, Harrison County, Miss., 1982—; firearms instr. Police Dept., Biloxi, 1983—. Dir./producer video film: Diamondhead 83, 1983, Air Base Defense, 1984. Res. police lt. Biloxi Police Dept., 1982—. Served with USAFR, 1977—. Recipient Air Force Achievement award, 1983; U.S. Govt. Sustained Superior Performance award, 1984, 85. Republican. Methodist. Home: 563 Baywood Circle Biloxi MS 39532 Office: 403 RWRW/WSSF Keesler AFB MS 39531

MC LEMORE, SAMUEL DALE, sociologist, educator; b. Beaumont, Tex., Oct. 12, 1928; s. Samuel Duard McLemore and Opal Dane (Hargraves) Gibney; B.S., U. Tex., 1952, M.A. (Univ. fellow 1955-56), 1956; Ph.D. (Commonwealth Fund fellow 1957-59), Yale U., 1961; m. Patsy Marie Reaves, Apr. 15, 1954; children—Jean Marie, Scott David. Social studies tchr. Austin (Tex.) Ind. Sch. Dist., 1952-55; asst. prof. U. Tex. Med. Br., Galveston, 1959-61, asst. prof. to prof. sociology U. Tex., Austin, 1961—. Served with USMC, 1946-48. USPHS grantee, 1962-65. Mem. Am. Sociol. Assn., Southwestern Social Sci. Assn., Southwestern Sociol. Soc. Author: Racial and Ethnic Relations in America, 1980, 2d edit., 1983; Sociological Measurement, 1967; A Statistical Profile of the Spanish-Surname Population of Texas, 1964; Management-Training Effectiveness, 1965. Home: 8503 Silver Ridge Dr Austin TX 78759 Office: Dept Sociology BUR 436 U Tex Austin 78712

MCLENDON, HINKLE, JR., civil engineer, purchasing agent; b. Americus, Ga., Jan. 30, 1919; s. Hinkle and Willie Estelle (Van Riper) McL.; m. Doris Irene Rogers, Dec. 31, 1942; children—Carol Jean McLendon Porter, James Hinkle. B.S. in Civil Engring., The Citadel, 1940; grad. U.S. Army Command and Gen. Staff Coll., 1963. Registered profl. engr., S.C. Concrete insp. Harza Engring. Co., Santee-Cooper hydroelec. dam and lock, S.C., 1940-41; resident engr. Vannort Engrs., Inc., Charlotte and Boone, N.C., 1945-48; structural design engr. J.E. Sirrine Engrs., Inc., Greenville, S.C., 1948-49; structural design engr. Westvaco Corp., Charleston, S.C., 1949-53, chief design engr. and project engr., 1953-62, purchasing agt., 1962—. Instl. rep. Coastal Carolina council Boy Scouts Am., 1960-63; bd. dirs. John C. Calhoun Homes, Inc. Served to maj. U.S. Army, 1941-45; PTO, ETO; to lt. col. USAR, 1949-67. Mem. ASCE (past pres. Eastern S.C. sect.), Civil Engrs. Club Charleston (past pres.), Nat. Soc. Profl. Engrs. (sec.-treas.), Res. Officers Assn. (life), S.C. Hist. Soc., Ga. Hist. Soc., N.C. Hist. Soc., N.Y. Geneal. and Biog. Soc., S.C. Geneal. Soc. (pres. chpt.), Scottish Soc. Charleston (bd. dirs.), Citadel Alumni Assn. Methodist (past chmn. bd. stewards and bd. trustees). Club: Brigadier. Lodge: Masons. Home: 7 Yeamans Rd The Crescent Charleston SC 29407 Office: Westvaco Corp Virginia Ave Charleston SC 29406

MCLEOD, BARBARA ANN, television producer; b. Chgo., Apr. 19, 1945; d. John Francis and Mignonne Elinor (Huffman) Burke; m. E. Bruce McLeod, Feb. 5, 1982. Student U. Chgo., summers 1964, 65; B.A. (Univ. scholar), Purdue U., 1967; M.A. in Journalism, U. Ga., 1980. Programmer, data processor Time, Inc., Chgo., 1967, interviewer personnel dept., 1967-69, asst. employment mgr., 1969-70, dept. head mag. subscriber relations, 1970-72, mem. adminstrv. staff, 1972-76; promotion exec. Paul Harris Stores, Inc., Indpls., 1976-77; news producer Sta. WSB-TV, Atlanta, 1979-82, Sta. WTSP-TV, St. Petersburg, Fla., 1982—; mng. dir. Ron Nielsen Photography, Nielsen Communication Team, Four Quarters, Chgo., 1973-76. Vol. worker Children's Meml. Hosp., 1969-72, Rehab. Inst. Chgo., 1973-76. Mem. Women in Communications (2d v.p. membership 1974-75, chmn. hospitality com. 1973-74), Purdue U. Alumni Assn., U. Ga. Alumni Assn., Mortar Bd., Sigma Delta Chi, Zeta Tau Alpha. Presbyterian. Club: Tampa Bay Bulldog. Address: PO Box 58143 Tierra Verde FL 33715

MCLEOD, KENNITH DOYLE, accountant; b. Hazelhurst, Ga., Oct. 1, 1946; s. James Doyle and Thelma (Simmons) M.; m. Latrelle Sellers, May 4, 1968; children—Matthew Doyle, Chesley Sellers. Student Abraham Baldwin Coll., 1964-65; B.B.A. cum laude, U. Ga., 1972. C.P.A., Ga. Sr. acct. DeLoitte, Haskins, and Sells, Savannah, Ga., 1972-75; pvt. practice acctg., Hazlehurst, 1975—; tchr. Brewton Parker Coll. Deacon, treas. 1st Baptist Ch.; bd. dirs. Jefferson Davis Hosp. Authority, 1981—. Served with USAF, 1966-69. Mem. Ga. Soc. C.P.A.s (pres. Waycross chpt. 1982-83), Am. Inst. C.P.A.s, Beta Alpha Psi, Beta Gamma Sigma, Phi Kappa Phi. Home: N Tallahassee St Hazlehurst GA 31539 Office: Kennith D McLeod CPA PO Box 870 S Tallahassee St Hazelhurst GA 31539

MCLEOD, PEDEN BROWN, lawyer state senator; b. Walterboro, S.C., Sept. 3, 1940; s. Walton James and Rhoda Lane (Brown) McL.; A.B., Wofford Coll., 1962; J.D., U. S.C., 1967; m. Mary Waite Hamrick, July 7, 1962; children—Mary Carlisle, Peden Brown, Rhoda Lane, John Reaves. Student instr. U. S.C. Law Sch., 1967; admitted to S.C. bar, 1967; law clk. to U.S. dist. judge C.E. Simons, Jr., 1967-69; practice in Walterboro, 1969—; permanent mem. 4th Circuit U.S. Jud. Conf., 1975-83; dir. First Nat. Bank in Orangeburg, Walterboro; mem. Walterboro City Council, 1970-72, S.C. Ho. of Reps., from Colleton County, 1972-79, S.C. Senate, 1979—. Sec., Colleton County Democratic party, 1967-71. Served with AUS, 1962-64. Recipient Distinguished Ser. award Walterboro Jr. C. of C., 1972. Mem. S.C. State Bar (Ho. of Dels.), Kappa Alpha. Mason, Elk, Moose. Office: Box 230 Walterboro SC 29488

MCLEOD, RODMAN AUSTIN, business executive; b. Atlanta, Sept. 27, 1943; s. Theodore B. and Sarah (Austin) McL.; m. Patricia Clift, Nov. 14, 1970; children—Anna K., Michael R. B.S.E.E., MIT, 1965; M.B.A., Harvard U., 1968. Vice-pres. mktg. Stuart McGuire Co., Salem, Va., 1968-73; dir. Sperry's div. Sperry & Hitchinson Co., Cin., 1973-79; pres., prin. Espy Lumber Co., Savannah, Ga., Hilton Head Island, S.C., 1979—, White Hardware Co., Savannah, also Hilton Head Island, 1980—; dir., officer, prin. Resort Designs, Inc., Hilton Head Island, 1982—; dir. Trust Co. Bank, Savannah, Ga. Bd. dirs. Savannah chpt. ARC, Ga. Pub. Radio. Mem. Sales Execs. Assn. (dir.), So. Indsl. Distbrs. Assn., Carolina Lumber and Bldg. Material Dealers Assn., Savannah Homebuilders Assn., Hilton Head Homebuilders Assn., Savannah Area C. of C. (dir.). Clubs: Rotary; Yacht, Oglethorpe (Savannah). Home: 315 Whitfield Ave Savannah GA 31406 Office: 15 Whitaker St PO Box 8184 Savannah GA 31412

MCLEOD, RONALD, educational administrator. Supt. of schs. El Paso, Tex. Office: Box 20100 El Paso TX 79998*

MCLEOD, WILLIAM LASATER, JR., lawyer, state legislator; b. Marks, Miss., Feb. 27, 1931; s. William Lasater and Sara Louise (Macaulay) McL.; A.B., Princeton U., 1953; J.D., La. State U., 1958; m. Marilyn Qualls, June 16, 1962; children—Sara Nelson, Martha Ellen, Ruth Elizabeth. Admitted to La. bar, 1958, U.S. Supreme Ct. bar, 1980; practiced law, Lake Charles, La., 1958—; partner firm McLeod, Little, Hopkins & Lloyd, 1976—; mem. La. Ho. of Reps., 1968-76; mem. La. Senate, 1976—. Chmn. Lake Charles Salvation Army Adv. Bd., 1965-66; pres. Calcasieu Area council Boy Scouts Am., 1978. Served with U.S. Army, 1953-55. Recipient Disting. Service award, Lake Charles Jaycees, 1963. Mem. La. Bar Assn., S.W. La. Bar Assn. (pres. 1980). Democrat. Presbyterian (elder). Club: Mason. Office: 1011 Lakeshore Dr Lake Charles LA 70601

MCLEROY, KENNETH RILEY, educator; b. Palestine, Tex., Mar. 31, 1946; s. William Barto and Eloise (Hanks) McL.; m. Nancy Dembroski, Jan. 3, 1981; 1 child, Christopher Lael. A.A., Tyler Jr. Coll., 1965; B.S. in Psychology, U. Houston, 1967; M.S. in Psychology, U. Okla., 1970; Ph.D., U. N.C., 1982. Vol. Peace Corps, Tarija, Boliva, 1968-70; sr. health analyst Research Triangle Inst., N.C., 1973-83; asst. prof. health edn. U. N.C., Greensboro, 1983—; cons. Research Triangle Inst., 1983—, Rural Health Office, Tucson, 1982-83. Contbr. articles to profl. jours. Served with U.S. Army, 1971-73. Mem. Am. Sociol. Assn., Am. Pub. Health Assn., Soc. for Pub. Health Edn., Soc. for Psychol. Study of Social Issues, Am. Acad. Polit. and Social Sci., Delta Omega, Eta Sigma Gamma. Avocations: wine collecting and tasting. Office: Univ NC Room 349 Curry Bldg Greensboro NC 27412

MC MAHAN, ROBERT CHANDLER, savings and loan association executive; b. Sevierville, Tenn., June 17, 1940; s. Homer Wright and Cathryn Alexander (Murphy) McM.; B.B.A., Ga. State U., 1972; grad. Sch. Savs. and Loan, U. Ind., 1977; m. Judith Ann Raymer, Dec. 23, 1963; children—Kellie Elizabeth, Alice Marie. Mgr., Credithrift Fin. Corp., Tenn., La., Tex. and Ga., 1961-69; with Decatur Fed. Savs. and Loan Assn. (Ga.), 1969—, sr. v.p., mgr. loan dept., 1974-75, exec. v.p., chief operating officer, 1975-84, pres., chief operating office, 1984— pres., dir. DFS Services, Inc. Bd. dirs. Decatur-DeKalb YMCA, 1974-76, 79-81, sec., 1976; bd. dirs., treas. Goals for DeKalb, 1977-80; chmn. bd. Med. Assistance State of Ga., 1982-84; chmn. DeKalb Heart Fund, 1984; bd. dirs. Callanwolde Fine Arts Ctr., 1983-85; mem. Met. Atlanta adv. bd. Salvation Army, 1985—. Served with AUS, 1962-63. Mem. Home Builders Assn. Met. Atlanta (dir.), DeKalb Bd. Realtors, DeKalb Developers Assn. Citizens for Better Govt., DeKalb C. of C. (v.p., pres. 1982), Ga. League Savs. Instn. (bd. dirs. 1985—), Sigma Phi Omega. Mem. Ch. of Christ. Lodges: Rotary (Decatur); Masons. Office: 250 E Ponce de Leon Ave Decatur GA 30031

MC MAHEN, CHARLES EDWIN, bank holding company executive; b. McKamie, Ark., May 19, 1939; s. Carl E. and Mattie L. (Nations) McM.; B.B.A. in Acctg., U. Houston, 1962; m. Patricia L. Dixon, Aug. 14, 1965; children—Craig Randall, Dixon Andrew. Auditor, Phillips, Sheffield, Hopson, Lewis & Luther, Houston, 1962-63, Haskins & Sells, C.P.A.s, Houston, 1963-66; from asst. auditor to v.p., controller Tex. Commerce Bank, Houston, 1966-70, sr. v.p., controller, 1972, exec. v.p., 1974-76; exec. v.p. Tex. Commerce Bancshares, Houston, 1975-76; exec. v.p., chief operating officer Southwest Bancshares, Inc., Houston, 1976-81, pres., chief operating officer, 1981-84; vice chmn. MCorp., 1984—. Bd. dirs. Houston chpt. ARC, CBA Alumni Ednl. Found. of U. Houston; pres., bd. dirs., mem. exec. com. Soc. Performing Arts; chmn. 1986 Mayor's Internat. Festival Ball. Served with AUS., 1963. C.P.A., Tex. Mem. Tex. Soc. C.P.A.s, Tex. Assn. Bank Holding Cos. (treas., dir.), Am., Tex. bankers assns. Presbyterian. Clubs: Ramada, Forest, Houstonian (Houston). Office: PO Box 2629 Houston TX 77252

MCMAHON, DONALD AYLWARD, business executive; b. N.Y.C., Feb. 20, 1931; s. William F. and Anne (Aylward) McM.; m. Nancy Lantz, Apr. 12, 1953; children—Gail, Brian, Lisa, Glenn, Anne, Carol, William, Douglas. M.B.A., Emory U., 1982. With Dime Savings Bank, Bklyn., 1952; salesman Monroe Calculating Machine Co., Bklyn., 1952-55, asst. br. mgr., Pitts., 1955-56, br. mgr., Phila., 1955-63, asst. gen. sales mgr., Orange, N.J., 1963-64, eastern regional sales mgr., 1964-65, v.p. mktg., 1965-66, pres., 1966-70; v.p. parent co. Litton Industries, Inc., 1967-70; pres., chief operating officer, Baker Industries, Inc., Parsippany, N.J., 1970-75; pres., chief exec. officer, dir. Royal Crown Cos., Atlanta, 1975-84; dir. Roper Corp., Kankakee, Ill., Intelligent Systems Corp., Norcross, Ga., Norell Corp., Atlanta, Kidde, Inc., Saddle Brook, N.J. Bd. visitors, mem. mgmt. conf. bd. Emory U.; bd. dirs. Metro Atlanta Area Boys Clubs, Georgetown U., Atlanta Ballet. Mem. Bus. Council Ga. Home: 1665 Winterthur Close NW Atlanta GA 30328 Office: Royal Crown Cos Inc 41 Perimeter Ctr East NE Atlanta GA 30346

MCMAHON, EDWARD FRANCIS, oil company executive; b. N.Y.C., Dec. 13, 1930; s. Edward F. and Ellen (Tully) McM.; m. Rosemary Virginia Freda, Feb. 5, 1955; children—Ned, Maryellen, Tracey, Thomas, Mark. B.C.E., Villanova U., 1954; M.B.A., CUNY, 1959; postgrad. Stanford U., 1970. Indsl. engr. Colgate Palmolive, Jersey City, 1957-59; mktg. mgr. Shell Oil Co., Chgo., 1970-74, mgr. econs., 1974-76, gen. mgr. polymers group Shell Chem. Co., 1975-81, gen. mgr. comml. sales, Houston, 1981-83, v.p. Supplies and Transp., Shell Refining and Mktg. Co., Houston, 1983-84; pres. TW Oil (Houston) Inc., 1984—; chmn. bd. Bercon Packing Co., 1975-79; chmn. Sea Bound, Inc., Houston, 1983—. Served with USN, 1949-50, 54-57. Mem. Soc. Plastics Industry, Soc. Plastics Engrs. Roman Catholic. Clubs: Houston City; Sugar Creek Country (Sugar Land, Tex.). Office: One Shell Plaza 2501 Houston TX 77001

MCMAHON, EDWARD JOSEPH, engineering company executive; b. Newark, Dec. 8, 1937; s. William Vincent and Madge Eileen (Tittel) McMahon; B.S. in Mech. Engring., N.J. Inst. Tech., 1961, postgrad., 1964; postgrad. U. Ala., 1966, George Washington U., 1967-69; m. Virginia Karen Payne, Oct. 5, 1976; 1 child, Heather Noelle. Engr., Weston Instruments, Newark, 1961-64; reliability analyst Apollo Support Dept., Gen. Electric, Cocoa Beach, Fla., 1964-66; mgr. reliability engring. Chrysler Aerospace Co., Huntsville, Ala., 1966-67; systems analyst Vitro Labs., Silver Spring, Md., 1967-68; mgr. maintainability engring. Amecom div. Litton Systems, College Park, Md., 1968-71, mgr. reliability and maintainability engring. Columbia Research Corp., Gaithersburg, Md., 1971-75; pres. Reliability Scis., Inc., Arlington, Va., 1975—, also chmn. bd.; chmn. bd. Design & Engring. Applications. Served with Army N.G., 1961. Registered profl. engr., Ala. Mem. IEEE. Roman Catholic. Co-author: Electrostatic Discharge Control: successful Methods for Microelectronics Design and Manufacturing, 1985. Also author of handbooks, manuals. Contbr. articles to profl. jours. Home: Route 1 Box 16A Middleburg VA 22117 Office: PO Box 1841 Middleburg VA 22117

MCMAHON, JAMES VINCENT, university educator German, and literature, translator; b. Buffalo, Oct. 10, 1937; s. James Vincent and Nora Marie (Cunningham), McM.; m. Elizabeth Ann Hargrove, Jan. 26, 1963; children—Christopher, Mark, Stephen. B.A., St. Bonaventure U., 1960; Ph.D., U. Tex.-Austin, 1967. Instr. Emory U., Atlanta, 1964-67, asst. prof., 1967-71, assoc. prof., 1971—. Contbr. articles to profl. jours. Mem. MLA, AAUP, Medieval Acad. Am., Am. Translators Assn., Am. Assn. Tchrs. German. Avocations: music; cooking. Office: Emory U Dept Modern Langs and Classics Atlanta GA 30322

MCMAHON, JIM TOM, marketing executive; b. Beaumont, Tex., Mar. 21, 1947; s. Tom Ball and Eula Lee (Montgomery) McM.; m. Charleye Delane Needham, Mar. 1966 (div. 1967); 1 dau., Melissa; m. 2d, Patricia Gail McMahon, Dec. 28, 1972; children—Amanda, Jim Brant. B.S., Lamar U., 1969. Ptnr. McMahon Oil Co., Newton, Tex., 1970-74, v.p., 1974-77, pres., 1977-83; pres. McMahon Mktg., Inc., Beaumont, Tex., 1983—. Commr. Sabine River Compact Adminstrn., 1983—. Mem. Tex. Oil Marketers Assn., Newton and Beaumont C. of C. Democrat. Methodist. Lodge: Lions. Office: McMahon Mktg Inc 4335 Laurel Ave Beaumont TX 77707

MC MAHON, RHETT RUSSELL, rental property company executive; b. Baton Rouge, Nov. 16, 1916; s. Rhett Gustav and Pearl F. (Fridge) McM.; student La. State U., 1934-35; B.S., Tulane U., 1939; m. Yvonne Marie Barbe, May 29, 1941; children—Rhett, Claudia Barbe, Diane Marie. Owner, mgr. rental properties, Baton Rouge, 1946—; dir. Baton Rouge Water Works Co. Served as m/sgt. M.C., AUS, 1941-45; ETO. Mem. Baton Rouge C. of C., Kappa Sigma. Kiwanian (pres. 1952). Club: Baton Rouge Country. Address: 1645 Perkins Rd Baton Rouge LA 70808

MCMAHON, WILLIAM HERBERT, health systems exec.; b. Chgo., Sept. 6, 1943; s. Ambrose James and Mary Ann (Herbert) McM.; B.A., Eastern Wash. State Coll., 1972; M.P.H., Okla. U., 1974; m. Marian J. Beaty, Aug. 23, 1967; children—Christina, William Herbert, Tracy. Health planner Spokane County (Wash.), 1972-73; asst. adminstr. Univ. Hosp., Oklahoma City, 1974-76; cons. Univ. Hosp., Ann Arbor, Mich., 1976-77; cons. Deloitte, Haskins & Sells, Detroit, 1977-79; pres. Trans-Coastal Health Systems, Terrell, Tex., 1979—; faculty field supr. Okla. U. Grad. Sch. Health, 1975; chmn. Spokane County Emergency Services Planning Com., 1972. Served with USAF, 1965-68. Mem. Hosp. Mgmt. Systems Soc. (chmn. nursing com. Mich. chpt. 1979), Am. Coll. Hosp. Adminstrs., Am. Hosp. Assn. Home: Box 304 Edgewood TX 75117

MCMANUS, EVELYN COOKE, university administrator; b. Georgetown, Tex., Sept. 30, 1921; d. Emmett Marion and Berna (Sillure) Cooke; m. Orville O. McManus, May 1944 (div.); children—Richard Irvine, David Carroll, Jeremy Cooke. B.A., Southwestern U., 1943; M.L.S., E. Tex. State U., 1966. Asst. librarian Southwestern U., Georgetown, 1943-44; asst. law librarian U. Tex., Austin, 1957-58; head librarian Tyler Jr. Coll. (Tex.), 1958-81, assoc. dean learning resources, 1981-83, dean learning resources, 1983—. Mem. ALA, Tex. Library Assn., Southwestern Library Assn., Tex. Jr. Coll. Tchrs. Assn., Delta Kappa Gamma, Zonta. Office: Tyler Jr Coll Vaughn Library and Learning Resources Ctr Box 9020 Tyler TX 75701

MCMILLAN, EDWARD LEE, college administrator, history educator; b. Blytheville, Ark., Jan. 28, 1929; s. William Ayres and Maggie Myrtie (Smith) McM.; m. Lysbeth Carnette Rackley, Dec. 23, 1951; children—David Lee, Dale Wayne. B.A., Miss. Coll., 1950; M.A., U. Miss., 1951; Ph.D., Tex. Tech U., 1960. Prof. history Wayland Baptist U., Plainview, Tex., 1951-61; dean, prof. history La. Coll., Pineville, 1961-73; v.p. for grad. studies and spl. programs, prof. history Miss. Coll., Clinton, 1973—; pres. Conf. of La. Colls. and Univs., 1966-67. Contbr. articles to hist. jours. and encys. Named Prof. of Yr., Wayland Bapt. U., 1958, La. Coll., 1968; U. Miss. fellow, 1950-51. Mem. Miss. Hist. Soc. (bd. dirs. 1980-83), So. Hist. Soc., Orgn. of Am. Historians, Am. Hist. Assn., So. Bapt. Hist. Soc., Clinton C. of C. (pres. 1984). Baptist. Lodge: Lions (pres. 1968-69). Mem. Phi Kappa Phi, Pi Sigma Alpha, Omicron Delta Kappa, Phi Alpha Theta. Avocations: gardening; fishing. Home: 1209 Dartmoor Clinton MS 39056 Office: Miss Coll Box 4185 Clinton MS 39058

MCMILLAN, JAMES BRYAN, judge; b. Goldsboro, N.C., Dec. 19, 1916; s. Robert Hunter and Louise (Outlaw) McM.; grad. Presbyn. Jr. Coll., 1934; A.B., U. N.C., 1937; LL.B., Harvard, 1940; m. Margaret Blair Miles, Feb. 27, 1944; children—James Bryan, Marjorie Miles Rodell. Admitted to N.C. bar, 1941; mem. staff N.C. atty.-gen., 1940-42; partner Helms, Mulliss, McMillan & Johnston, Charlotte, 1946-68; U.S. dist. judge Western Dist. N.C., Charlotte, 1968—; judge pro tem Charlotte City Ct., 1947-51; mem. faculty Nat. Inst. Trial Advocacy, Boulder, Colo., 1973-81; instr. trial advocacy course Harvard Law Sch., 1975-81, U. N.C. Law Sch., 1976—, U. Fla. Law Sch., 1978—; mem. N.C. Cts. Commn., 1963-71. Pres., Travelers Aid Soc., 1957-59; bd. visitors Davidson Coll. Served from apprentice seaman to lt. USNR, 1942-46; ETO. Recipient Algernon Sydney Sullivan award St. Andrews Presbyn. Coll. Fellow Internat. Acad. Trial Lawyers; mem. Am., 26th Dist. (pres. 1957-58), N.C. (pres. 1960-61) bar assns., United World Federalists, Newcomen Soc., St. Andrews Coll. Alumni Assn. (pres. 1965-66), Order of Coif, Golden Fleece, Omicron Delta Kappa. Democrat. Presbyn. Clubs: Charlotte City, Charlotte Country, Charlotte Philosophers. Home: 1930 Mecklenburg Ave Charlotte NC 28205 Office: US Dist Ct US Courthouse Room 254 Charlotte NC 28202

MCMILLAN, JOHN ALEXANDER, III, congressman; b. Charlotte, N.C., May 9, 1932; s. John Alexander and Mildred (Shepherd) McM.; m. Caroline Houston, Nov. 21, 1959; children—Elizabeth H., John Alexander IV. B.A. in History, U. N.C., 1954; M.B.A., U. Va., 1958. With dept. sales and control Carolina Paper Bd. Corp., Charlotte, 1958-60; with sales-control dept. Shepherd Lumber Co., Charlotte, 1961-63; sec., v.p. R.S. Dickson & Co., Investment Bankers, Charlotte, 1963-70; sec., v.p., v.p. fin. and treas. Ruddick Corp., Holding Co., Charlotte, 1968-78; pres., chief exec. officer, chmn. Harris-Teeter Super Markets, Inc., Charlotte, 1976-83; mem. Congress from 9th N.C. dist., 1985—; mem. com. on banking, fin. and urban affairs and small bus. com.; v.p. Republican Freshman Class. Elder, Myers Park Presbyterian Ch., 1973-79; mem. United Community Services Bd., 1973-84; mem. Mecklenburg County Bd. Commrs., 1973-75; mem. Spirit Sq. Bd., Charlotte, 1976-83, pres. 1976-77; pres. Darden Grad. Sch. Bus. Alumni Bd., U. Va., 1979-81, trustee, 1977—; trustee Woodberry Forest Sch., Orange, Va., 1978-85; trustee Union Theol. Sem., Richmond, Va., 1978—, vice-chmn., 1979—; bd. dirs. Inroads, Inc., Charlotte, N.C., 1982-83, Charlotte-Mecklenburg Arts and Scis. Council, 1974-79, Charlotte Speech & Hearing Ctr., 1974-77; mem. Mecklenburg Presbyn. Task Force on Hunger, 1975-76; mem. adv. bd. Johnson C. Smith U., Charlotte, 1981-84; bd. visitors Davidson Coll., N.C., 1983-84; chmn. Charlotte-Mecklenburg Pub. Broadcasting Authority WTVI, Charlotte, 1978-83; bd. dirs. Mecklenburg County Bd. Social Services, 1974-77, chmn., 1975-77. Mem. Greater Charlotte C. of C. (bd. dirs. 1980-82). Club: Charlotte City (bd. dirs. 1981-84). Office: US Ho of Reps 507 Cannon Bldg Washington DC 20515

MC MILLAN, MADELYN RINGUS, insurance company executive; b. Des Moines, Oct. 1, 1944; d. Tony J. and Gertrude (Zanios) Ringus; children—Cassandra Lee, Anthony Malcolm, Suzanna Lynn. Student Drake U., 1963-64; A.A., Jones Coll., 1965. Sales rep. Prudential Ins. Co., San Diego, 1970; owner, mgr. Fla. Fin. Planners, Tarpon Springs, 1972-77; sales rep. Paul Revere Companies, Tampa, 1978-80, brokerage supr., 1981-82; sales mgr. Springfield-/Monarch Life Ins. Co., 1982-85; disability income specialist Guardian Life Ins. Co., Miller & Assocs., Tampa, 1985-86; ptnr. N.Y. Life Ins. Co., Kent Moss and Assocs., 1986—. Author motivational and tng. film. Contbr. articles to profl. jours. Pres., PTA, 1972, v.p., 1973-74, state rep., 1972; fin. chmn. Tarpon Springs Police Aux., 1974-75; chmn. Sch. Adv. Com., 1974, 78; cons. bus. project Jr. Achievement. Mem. Resident Home Assn. (dir.), Am. Businesswomen's Assn. (v.p. 1972), Nat. Assn. Life Underwriters Fla. Assn. Life Underwriters (exec. com., state health ins. chmn. 1985—, pub. relations chmn. 1984-85), Tampa Assn. Life Underwriters (chmn. health ins. com. 1982-84), St. Petersburg Assn. Life Underwriters (dir.), Gen. Agts. and Mgrs. Assn. (dir., edn. chmn.), Life Underwriters Tng. Council, Women Life Underwriters Conf. (state co-chmn. Fla. 1979-82, state chmn. 1982-83), Nat. Assn. Health Underwriters, Registered Health Underwriters, Network of Exec. Women. (audit com. Tampa Bay area 1982), Nat. Assn. Female Execs. Republican. Greek Orthodox. Clubs: Sertoma (Tampa) (charter, bd. dirs. 1985—); Toastmistresses (v.p. 1971), Ins. Women West Pasco County. Office: 103 S Blvd Tampa FL 33606

MCMILLAN, MICHAEL REID, orthopedic surgeon; b. Conway, S.C., Aug. 28, 1941; s. Hoyt and Sara Best (Sherwood) McM.; B.S., The Citadel, 1963; M.D., Duke U., 1967. Intern in medicine Balt. City Hosps., 1967-68; fellow in medicine Johns Hopkins Hosp., Balt., 1967-68; resident in orthopedic surgery Greenville (S.C.) Hosp. Systems and Greenville Shriners Hosp., 1971-75; practice medicine specializing in orthopedic surgery, Conway, S.C., 1975—; mem. staff Conway Hosp., 1975—, chief of orthopedics, 1975-82. Trustee Burroughs Found., Conway, 1979—. Served to lt. comdr. MC, USN, 1968-71; Vietnam. Diplomate Nat. Bd. Med. Examiners, Am. Bd. Orthopedic Surgery; lic. physician, S.C. Mem. AMA, So. Med. Assn., S.C. Med. Assn., S.C. Orthopedic Assn., Horry County Med. Soc., Assn. of Citadel Men, Stelling Soc. Baptist. Clubs: Horry County Citadel, Georgetown County Citadel. Home and Office: 1400 9th Ave Conway SC 29526

MCMILLEN, HOWARD LAWRENCE, city ofcl.; b. Phoenix, Apr. 8, 1937; s. John Lawrence and Bessie Nora McM.; A.A. in Bus. Adminstrn., Phoenix Coll., 1957; A.A. in Fire Sci., Phoenix Coll., 1965; B.A. in Public Mgmt., St. Mary's Coll., Moraga, Calif., 1977; m. Paula Simmerman, Nov. 8, 1978; children—Linda, Karen. Fireman, Phoenix, 1959-63, fire engr., 1963-68, fire capt., 1968-70, br. chief, 1970-76, div. chief, 1976-78, dep. chief, 1978-80; fire chief, City of Ft. Worth, 1980—; vocat. instr. Ariz. Fire Sci. Curriculum; instr. Calif. Fire Officers Acad., Pacific Grove; fireground comdr., seminar instr. Okla. State U.; chmn. Ariz. Fire Tng. Com., 1974-80. Mem. Nat. Fire Protection Assn. (chmn. program com. fire service sect. 1973-80), Internat. Assn. Fire Chiefs Assn., S.W. Fire Chiefs Assn., Tex. Fire Chiefs Assn., Internat. Assn. Fire Instructors, Ariz. Fire Prevention Assn. Methodist. Club: Optimist (Ft. Worth). Office: 1000 Throckmorton St Fort Worth TX 76102

MCMILLIAN, MARTHA MARTIN, educator; b. McAlester, Okla., July 1, 1947; d. Cecil Charles and Mary (Korenowski) M.; m. Roger Lee McMillian, Sept. 27, 1969; children—Michol, Morgan. B.S., Okla. State U., 1969, M.S., 1975, Ed.D., 1981. Demographic researcher U.S. Census Bur., Silver Spring, Md., 1969; social studies tchr. Donart High Sch., Stillwater, Okla., 1969-70, Gilcrease Jr. High Sch., Tulsa, 1970-74; adminstrv. intern Pub. Sch. System Stillwater, 1979; grad. teaching asst. Okla. State U., Stillwater, 1975-81, soc. acad. counselor, 1982-85, sr. acad. counselor, coordinator advisement services Coll. Edn., 1985—; editor sociol. newsletter Okla. State U., 1982-85, Edn. Advisers' Newsletter, 1985—. Exec. bd. Payne County Human Energy Linking Program, Stillwater, 1983-85; bd. dirs. Payne County Community Resitution Com., Stillwater, 1983-85; vice chmn. Okla. State U. Wesley Found. bd. dirs., 1983-85; chmn. Commn. on Ch. and Soc., 1984-85. Named Outstanding Advisor, Coll. Arts and Scis., Okla. State U., 1985, Outstanding Teaching Asst., 1977-78. Mem. Am. Sociol. Assn., Okla. Sociol. Assn., Mid-South Sociol. Assn., Nat. Acad. Advisers Assn., LWV, Okla. Women's Polit. Caucus, Phi Kappa Phi, Delta Kappa Gamma, Chi Omega. Democrat. Methodist. Lodge: P.E.O. Home: 30 Yellow Brick Rd Stillwater OK 74074 Office: Okla State U 103 Gundersen Hall Stillwater OK 74078

MCMULLAN, JAMES FRANKLIN, insurance consultant, financial planner; b. Atlanta, Feb. 24, 1928; s. Jesse James and Ruth G. (Thomason) McM.; B.B.A., Emory U., 1949; M.S.F.S., Am. Coll., 1986; m. Jo Anne Lovern, Sept. 13, 1951; children—Anne McMullan Cox, Martha Jane (dec.), Lynn McMullan Hart, Robert L., Beth Lovern. Agt., asst. gen. agt., gen. agt. State Mut. Life Assurance Co. of Am., Atlanta, 1955-78, gen. agt. emeritus, 1979—. Elder, Word of Life Fellowship; pres. bd. dirs. The Cornerstone, 1976—; bd. dirs. Am. Vision, 1983—. Recipient Nat. Mgmt. award for Agency Building, 1973, life mem., 1977, nat. quality award, 1957-86; MDRT Qual mem.; Atlanta Agy. Man of Yr., 1981. life mem. Ga. Leaders Roundtable; named S. Fulton's Young Man of Year, 1961; chartered fin. cons.; C.L.U. Mem. Am. Soc. C.L.U.s, Atlanta Estate Planning Council, Internat. Assn. Fin. Planners (Ga. chpt.), Assn. Fin. Planners, Atlanta Life Underwriters Assn., Gen. Agts. and Mgrs. Assn. (pres. Atlanta 1976). Republican. Clubs: Jaycees (dir.), Optimists (charter pres. Tri-City, lt. gov. Ga. Clubs, life mem.). Home: 2935 Duke of Gloucester East Point GA 30344 Office: 2849 Paces Ferry Rd Suite 640 Atlanta GA 30339

MCMULLEN, GARY PAUL, advertising agency executive, marketing consultant, photographer; b. Dennison, Tex., Feb. 16, 1949; s. Donald Perry and Gloria Catherine (O'Toole) M.; m. Terry Ann Fleming, Nov. 25, 1972; children—Patrick Corey, Michael Casey. B.S. in Journalism and Mktg., U. Iowa, 1976. Account exec. O'Toole & Sons Pubs., Norwalk, Conn., 1968-73, Young & Rubicam Advt., Cedar Rapids, Iowa, 1976-78; advt. mgr. Nissen-Universal subs. Kidde, Inc., Cedar Rapids, 1978-81; v.p., creative dir. McMullens Garret & Eaves Advt., Cedar Rapids, 1979-82; advt. dir. Control Flow/Flocon, Houston, 1982-83; exec. v.p., creative dir. Graphic Ideas, Inc., Houston, 1982—. Mem. Houston Advt. Fedn., Bus. Profl. Advt. Assn., Profl. Photographers Assn. Roman Catholic. Office: 11819 Glenway Dr Houston TX 77070

MCMURRY, MARY JANE, loss control representative; b. Texas City, Tex., Mar. 5, 1949; d. Peter Henry and Virginia Mary (Daugherty) Fernandez; m. Sam James McMurry, Aug. 29, 1969; children—Eric, Amy. B.A. in English, East Tex. State U., 1970; M.S. in Safety, Central Mo. State U., 1978. Cert. hazard control mgr. Loss control rep. Aetna Life & Casualty Ins. Co., San Antonio, 1979-82, Ranger Ins. Co., Fort Worth, 1982—. Mem. Am. Soc. Safety Engrs. Democrat. Methodist. Home: 213 Timber Ridge Circle Burleson TX 76028 Office: Ranger Ins Co PO Box 2807 Houston TX 77252

MC MURTRY, EDWARD HOYSE, architect; b. Silverton, Tex., July 11, 1912; s. Edward Dawson and Ollie Mae (Smithee) McM.; m. Esther Lloyd Jones, Sept. 4, 1938; children—Kathryn McMurtry Hunt, Allan Edward, Steven Lloyd. B.A. in Arch., Tex. Tech U., 1937. Draftsman, Robert E. Merrell, architect, Clovis, N.Mex., 1938-41, Wyatt C. Hedrick, Houston, 1941-42, Atcheson & Atkinson, architects, Lubbock, Tex., 1946-51; chief draftsman O.R. Walker, Lubbock, 1951-53; partner McMurtry & Craig, architects and engrs., Lubbock, 1953-83. Pres., Friends of Tex. Libraries, 1971-73; mem. Code Study Commn., Community Devel. Adv. Com. and Bldg. Bd. Appeals, community devel. adv. com. City of Lubbock; trustee, mem. exhibits com. West Tex. Mus. Assn., Lubbock; mem. camper program com. Tex. Lions Camp for Crippled Children. Served with USAAF, 1944-46. Mem. AIA (pres. Lubbock chpt. 1966), Tex. Soc. Architects, Lubbock C. of C. (mem. edn. com.), Tau Beta Pi. Democrat. Baptist. Club: Lions (dist. gov. 1972-73), Lubbock Kife and Fork (bd. dirs.). Prin. works: Tulia (Tex.). High Sch., 1956; Evans Jr. High Sch., Lubbock, 1958; Tex. Tech. U. Mus., Lubbock, 1968, dormitory bldgs., 1957-63; George and Helen Mahon Library, Lubbock, 1973; Copper Breaks State Park, Quanah, Tex., 1974; Goddard Range and Wildlife Mgmt. Bldg., Tex. Tech. U., 1975; Swisher County Meml. Library, Mus. and Sr. Citizens Center, Tulia, 1979; Rural Telephone Coop. Hdqrs., Tulia, 1979; Hall County Jail, 1980; various chs. and schs. Home and Office: 3813 27th St Lubbock TX 79410

MCNAIR, MICHAEL STEPHEN, lawyer; b. Montgomery, Ala., Sept. 30, 1952; s. William Hooten and Norma Jean (Hickman) McN.; m. Susan Stuart, Dec. 30, 1972; children—Stuart Michael, Michael Stephen. B.S. in Fin., U. South Ala., 1975; J.D., U. Ala., 1978, LL.M., 1983. Bar: Ala. 1978, U.S. Dist. Ct. (so. dist.) Ala. 1979. Atty. Mobile Police Dept., Ala., 1978-80; ptnr. Noojin & McNair, Mobile, 1980—. Editor Jour. of Legal Profession, 1976-77. Contbr. articles to profl. jours. Pres. Exchange Club Mobile, 1980-81; v.p. Ala. Dist. Exchange Clubs, 1983-84, 84-85, dir. 1981-83; named to Selective Service Bd., 1982. Hugo L. Black scholar U. Ala. Sch. Law, 1977. Mem. Ala. State Bar, Mobile Bar Assn., ABA, Ala. Trial Lawyers Assn., Am. Trial Lawyers Assn., Bench and Bar. Baptist. Home: 224 Walshwood Ave Mobile AL 36604 Office: Noojin & McNair PO Box 6283 Mobile AL 36660

MCNALLEN, JAMES BERL, marketing specialist; b. Heber Springs, Ark., Feb. 17, 1930; s. George Berl and Sally Louise (Brown) McN.; m. Marianne Patricia Kakos, Mar. 4, 1952 (div. Dec. 1981); children—James Lawrence, Marianne Victoria, Thomas Berl, John Kennedy. A.B., Columbia U., 1951; M.B.A., NYU, 1960, Ph.D., 1975. Mktg. asst. Am. Petroleum Inst., N.Y.C., 1954-67, coordinator products mktg., 1967-69, asst. dir., div. fin. and acctg., 1969-70; corp. mgr. mktg. research Atlantic Richfield Co., N.Y.C., 1970-71; instr. bus. adminstrn. Sch. Bus. Adminstrn. U. Conn., Storrs, 1972-75, asst. prof., 1975-76; mktg. research specialist market research and mktg. div. Fed. Supply Service, GSA, Washington, 1976-78, mgr. mktg. research, 1978-82, mgr. forecasting and bus. analysis, 1982-84; mktg. specialist, tng. officer Central Procurement and Supply Mgmt. Project, U.S.-Saudi Arabian Joint Econ. Commn., Riyadh, 1984—; ptnr. McNallen Enterprises, Big Spring, Tex.; lectr. mktg. Va. Poly. Inst., Reston, 1976-77, George Mason U., 1977-84, Georgetown U., 1978-80; adj. prof. mgmt. U. D.C., 1980-84. Mem. planning bd. Twp. of South Brunswick (N.J.), 1966-67; sec., vice chmn. South Brunswick Mcpl. Utilities Authority, 1966-68; pres. South Brunswick Library Assn., 1965-69. Served with USN, 1951-54, to capt. USNR, 1975—. Recipient Gold medal N.Y.C. chpt. Am. Mktg. Assn., 1960. Mem. Naval Res. Assn. (pres. Washington chpt. 1978-79, pres. 5th dist. 1979-81, mem. nat. exec. com. 1979-81), Naval Order U.S., U.S. Naval Inst., Ancient Order Hibernians, Mil. Order World Wars, Res. Officers Assn. (exec. v.p. Navy chpt. Washington 1981-84). Roman Catholic. Clubs: Riyadh Desert Golf; Army-Navy (Washington); NYU (N.Y.C.). Home and Office: USREP/JECOR PO Box 169 APO New York NY 09038

MCNALLY, TERRENCE JAMES, business communication educator; b. Cin., Jan. 5, 1937; s. Robert Joseph and Veronica Mary (Lenahan) McN.; m. Joan Eling, Aug. 22, 1964; children—Aileen, Carolyn, Timothy. B.A. in Philosophy, Duns Scotus Coll., 1960; M.A. in English, Xavier U., 1963; Ph.D. in English, Loyola U., Chgo., 1968. Asst. prof. English, DePaul U., Chgo., 1966-68, Xavier U., Cin., 1968-70; assoc. prof., then prof. English (bus. communication) No. Ky. U., Highland Heights, 1970—; cons. various corps. and govt. agys. Author: (with Peter Schiff) Contemporary Business Writing, 1968. Vice pres. Winding Trails Civic Assn., Edgewood, Ky., 1980—. Mem. Am. Bus. Communication Assn., Assn. Tchrs. Tech. Writing, Internat. Assn. Bus. Communicators. Republican. Avocations: tennis, classical music, Revolutionary War history. Home: 789 Woodbine Ct Edgewood KY 41017 Office: Dept of Lit and Lang No Ky U Highland Heights KY 41076

MCNAMARA, A. J., U.S. district judge; b. 1936. B.S., La. State U., 1959; J.D., Loyola U., New Orleans, 1968. Bailiff, law clk. U.S. Dist. Ct., New Orleans, 1966-68; individual practice law, New Orleans, 1968-72; mem. firm Monton, Roy, Carmouche, Hailey, Bivins & McNamara, New Orleans, 1972-78, Hailey, McNamara, McNamara & Hall, 1978-82; U.S. dist. judge Eastern dist. La., New Orleans, 1982—. Mem. La. Ho. of Reps., 1976-80. Office: Chambers C-316 US Courthouse 500 Camp St New Orleans LA 70130*

MCNAMARA, NEIL ROBERT, government official, computer equipment analyst; b. Washington, June 5, 1951; s. James Desmond and Madeline Green (Scroggs) McN. B.S., U. Md., 1975. Computer programmer U.S. Census Bur., Suitland, Md., 1974-78; computer specialist EPA, Washington, 1978-79, computer systems analyst, Research Triangle Park, N.C., 1979-82; computer equipment analyst IRS, Falls Church, Va., 1982-85, supervisory computer equipment analyst, 1985—, also cadre mem. mgmt. devel. program, 1985—. Recipient Outstanding Performance award IRS Computer Services, 1984. Mem. Mensa. Republican. Roman Catholic. Club: Raleigh Astronomers. Avocations: astronomy; photography; tennis; wrestling; reading.

MCNAMARA, PATRICIA RAE, English educator, sister, consultant; b. Lima, Ohio, Oct. 24, 1936; d. Raymond Joseph and Hildreth Josephine (Kuhn) McN. A.A., St. Catharine Coll., Springfield, Ky., 1959; B.A., Siena Coll., 1966; M.A., Morehead State U., 1973; cert. devel. edn. specialist Appalachian State U., 1983. Cert. English lang. arts tchrs/instr., life-time tchr. cert., Ky. Joined Dominican Sisters of St. Catharine of Siena, Roman Cath. Ch., 1953; tchr. elem. Cath. schs., Springfield, Ky., Memphis, 1956-63; jr. high tchr. Cath. schs., Forrest City, Ark., McMechen, W.Va., 1963-67; tchr. Cath. high schs., Springfield, Louisville, 1968-79; instr. English St. Catharine Coll., Springfield, 1979—; pres. Greater Louisville High Sch. Press Assn., 1973-75. Ga. State Coll. Newspaper Fund grantee, 1970; Eastern Coll. Am. Studies grantee, 1977. Mem. Ky. Council Internat. Reading Assn. (chmn. coll. reading com. 1983-86), Internat. Reading Assn. (mem. Ky. Council 1979-86, regional leader 1984-85), Nat. Council Tchrs. of English (regional judge, ann. awards in writing 1978-86, cons. to Coll. English Edn. Commn. 1984-87), Nat. Writing Program Adminstrs. Assn., Ky. Assn. of Devel. Educators, Greater Louisville English Council (v.p. 1977-79), Ky. Council Tchrs. of English (v.p. 1981-82, pres. 1982-83, Faithful Service plaque, 1984). Democrat. Avocations: writing poetry; singing for liturgies; reading; visiting historical and literary landmarks. Home: Saint Catharine PO Saint Catharine KY 40061 Office: Saint Catharine College Bardstown Rd 150 East Springfield KY 40069

MCNEAL, BRIAN LESTER, university educator; b. Cascade, Idaho, Jan. 27, 1938; s. Robert Henry and Maude (Hall) McNeal; m. Dee Ann McKay, June 17, 1958; children—Deborah Jane, Mark Brian, Laurie Lynn, Julie Ann. B.S. in Soil Sci., Oreg. State U., 1960, M.S. in Soil Sci., 1962; Ph.D. in Soil Chemistry, U. Calif.-Riverside, 1965. Student trainee USDA/ARS, Corvallis, Oreg., 1960-61; research soil scientist U.S. Salinity Lab., Riverside, Calif., 1961-70; assoc. prof. to prof. Washington State U., Pullman, 1970-83; prof., chmn. U. Fla., Gainesville, 1983—; vis. prof. Colo. State U., Ft. Collins, 1980; vis. scientist Am. Soc. Agronomy, 1971-73; assoc. editor Soil Sci. Soc. Am. Jour., 1982-85. Co-author: Soil Chemistry, 1979, 2d ed. 1985, Saline and Sodic Soils, 1982; also scientific articles. Recipient Award of Merit Riverside County council Boy Scouts Am., Riverside, Calif., 1969. NSF fellow, 1960-61. Fellow Am. Soc. Agronomy, Soil Sci. Soc. Am. (soil chemistry div. chmn. 1977); mem. West Soc. Soil Sci. (pres. 1978), Soil and Crop Sci. Soc. Fla., Council Agri. Sci. and Tech. Democrat. Mormon. Lodge: Kiwanis. Avocations: golf; backpacking; fishing; photography. Home: 8613 SW 5th Pl Gainesville FL 32607 Office: Soil Sci Dept Univ Fla Gainesville FL 32611

MCNEEL, THOMAS EUGENE, analytical research chemist; b. Memphis, Aug. 26, 1952; s. Archie A. and Mary Elizabeth (Paschall) McN. B.S. in Chemistry, Southwestern at Memphis, 1974; Ph.D. in Analytical Chemistry, MIT, 1979. Analytical research chemist Buckman Labs., Inc., Memphis, 1979—; vol. cons. Bd. dirs. Love, Unltd. NSF grad. fellow, 1974-77. Mem. Am. Chem. Soc., Phi Beta Kappa, Sigma Xi. Republican. Methodist. Home: 3509 Amesbury Memphis TN 38134 Office: 1256 N McLean Memphis TN 38108

MCNEELY, ORLAND MURRAY, lawyer; b. Lubbock, Tex., Apr. 11, 1940; s. Orland Cecil and Cartha Jean (Fry) McN.; B.A., Tex. Tech. U., 1964; J.D., Jackson Sch. Law, 1966; m. Martha Jean Forrest, Dec. 16, 1962; children—David Forrest, Kevin Murray, Russell Lamar, Jennifer Jean, Christina Jean. Dept. tax assessor-collector Lubbock County, Tex., 1962-64; admitted to Miss. bar, 1967, Tex. bar, 1982; mgmt. trainee First Nat. Bank, Jackson, Miss., 1967-68; asso. firm Young, Young & Scanlon, Jackson, 1968-73; individual practice law, Jackson, Miss., 1973-81; ptnr. Freeman, McNeely & Smith, P.C., 1982-84, McNeely & Smith, 1984—. chmn. atty.'s div., Am. Heart Fund, 1969-72, 83; mem. exec. bd. dirs. Jackson Youth For Christ, 1973-76. Served to capt. AUS, 1964-66. Mem. ABA, Tex. Bar Assn., Lubbock County Bar Assn., Am. Judicature Soc., Kappa Alpha. Republican. Baptist. Lodge: Rotary. Home: 4906 78th Lubbock TX 79424 Office: 6400 Quaker Suite B Lubbock TX 79413

MCNEIL, HOYLE GRAHAM, JR., hospital pharmacist, administrator, pharmacy firm executive; b. Knoxville, Tenn., Jan. 29, 1950; s. Hoyle Graham Sr. and Betty Sue (Stone) McN.; m. Kathryn Kimberly Bebb, Aug. 10, 1985. Student U. Tenn., 1968-72; B.S. in Pharmacy, Mercer U., 1975, D.Pharmacy, 1977. Lic. pharmacist, Ga., Tenn. Clin. pharmacist, drug info. coordinator U. Tenn. Meml. Hosp., Knoxville, 1976-80; dir. pharmacy, purchasing and ancillary services Peninsula Hosp., Louisville, Tenn., 1980—; ptnr., pres. First Pharmacy Mgmt., Inc., Knoxville, 1985—; cons. hosps., nursing homes; bd. dirs. Knox County Bd. Health, Knoxville, 1985. Contbr. articles to Jour. Am. Pharm. Assn., Urban Health Jour., other publs. Editor newsletter: Drug Info. Update, 1977-81. Pres., 2d yr. profl. class Mercer U., 1973-74. Mem. Knoxville Soc. Hosp. Pharmacists (pres. 1983-84), Knoxville Pharm. Assn. (pres. 1984-85), Tenn. Pharm. Assn. (del. 1983-85, co-chmn. impaired pharmacists com. 1984), Tenn. Soc. Hosp. Pharmacists, Am. Pharm. Assn., Am. Soc. Hosp. Pharmacists, Knox County Mental Health Assn., Phi Lambda Sigma, Kappa Psi (pres. Gamma Psi chpt. 1974-75, Brother of Yr., 1975). Avocations: reading; gardening; traveling; spectator sports. Home: 5314 Stone Oak Ln Knoxville TN 37920 Office: Peninsula Hospital Jones Bend Rd Louisville TN 37777

MC NEIL, WALTER HARVE, sales representative; b. Harlan, Ky., Apr. 21, 1920; s. John Charles and Marie E. (McBrayer) McN.; grad. Pikeville Coll. Acad., 1937; student Pikeville Coll., 1956-59; grad. Squadron Officer Sch.,

1955, Air Command and Staff Coll., 1960; m. Nellie Dean, June 1, 1946; children—Kay Francis (Mrs. Barry Runyon), Paula Jean (Mrs. Freddy Branham). With Sycamore Coal Corp., Patterson, Va., 1937-42; enlisted pvt. USAAF, 1942, commd. 2d lt. U.S. Army, 1943, advanced through grades to capt., 1946; staff communication officer Hdqrs. ETO; trans. to USAF Res., 1946, advanced through grades to lt. col., 1967, ret., 1970; liaison officer Air Force Acad. coordinator W.Va., Ky., So. Ohio, 1961-70; with Foster Thornburg Hardware Corp., Huntington, W.Va., 1946-61; sales rep. Tidewater Supply Co., 1961-81; owner Ky. Screen Service, Pikeville, Ky., 1981—. Named Outstanding Liaison Officer Coordinator in South, USAF Acad., 1965. Charter mem. Armed Forces Communications and Electronics Assn. (life); mem. Air Force Assn. (life), Naval Res. Assn., U.S. Capitol Hist. Soc., USAF Hist. Found. (life), Met. Opera Guild, Ret. Officers Assn. (life), Res. Officers Assn. (life), Mil. Order World Wars. Democrat. Baptist (deacon). Club: Lafayette (Lexington, Ky.). Lodges: Masons, Rotary (pres. 1960-61). Weekly columnist Pike County News. Home: 508 1/2 5th St Pikeville KY 41501 Office: PO Box 2097 Pikeville KY 41501

MCNEILL, JOSEPH PEELE, librarian; b. Galveston, Tex., Feb. 27, 1947; s. Joseph Peele and Christine Adele (Evans) M.; m. Linda Ann Hartshorn, Aug. 30, 1980; 1 dau., Mary Lin. B.A., Austin Coll., Sherman, Tex., 1970; postgrad. U. Ams., Puebla, Mex., 1970-71; M.S.L.S., East Tex. State U., Commerce, 1972; M.L.S., La. State U., Baton Rouge, 1976. Catalog librarian Wiley Coll., Marshall, Tex., 1972-74; tech. services librarian Austin Coll., 1976-79; catalog librarian Midwestern State U., Wichita Falls, Tex., 1979-84; head cataloguer McNeese State U., Lake Charles, La., 1985—; cataloger personal library pastor 1st Bapt. Ch., Wichita Falls. Co-editor: Periodicals in Library and Information Sciences, prepared for Union List, 1976. Bd. dirs. Sherman Hist. Mus., Tex., 1978-79. Mem. ALA, Tex. Library Assn., Beta Phi Mu. Republican. Baptist. Home: 1045 Walters #913 Lake Charles LA 70605 Office: Frazar Meml Library McNeese State U Ryan St Lake Charles LA 70609

MC NIEL, NORBERT ARTHUR, retired farmer; b. Moody, Tex., Dec. 22, 1914; s. Arthur A. and Gertrude (Burt) McN.; B.S., Tex. A. and M. Coll., 1935, M.Ed., 1952, Ph.D., 1955; m. Jane Edith Richter, Aug. 13, 1939; children—Rebecca McNiel McAulay, Ruth McNiel Garner, Fred, Larkin. Tchr. high sch., Alvin, Tex., 1935-41; supr. McLennan County Vocat. Sch., Waco, Tex., 1946-51; adviser fgn. programs Tex. A. and M. Coll. System, Pakistan, 1955-56; mem. faculty Tex. A. and M. U., 1957-79, prof. genetics, 1972-79, prof. emeritus, 1979—; farmer-stockraiser, 1980-85. Served to lt. col. AUS, 1941-46. Decorated Bronze Star; recipient Disting. Faculty award Assn. Former Students Tex. A. and M. U., 1964. Mem. Am. Genetic Assn., Am. Legion (post comdr. 1946-50), China-Burma-India Vets. Assn. (basha comdr. 1982-83). Mem. Ch. of Christ. Club: Kiwanis (lt. gov. div. 9 T-0 dist. 1977-78). Home: 508 4th St Moody TX 76557

MC NINCH, ELEANOR NEUBERT, librarian; b. Lowell, Mass., June 8, 1906; d. Charles Neubert and Isabella Maud (Cowley) Midwood; m. Frank Trenholm Coffyn, July 13, 1930 (div. 1938); 1 dau., Julie; m. Joseph Hamilton McNinch, Mar. 1, 1949. B.S. in L.S., Simmons Coll., 1927. Asst., Clark U. Library, Worcester, Mass., 1927-29; cataloguing asst. Hispanic Soc. Am. Library, N.Y.C., 1929-30; reference librarian Boston Med. Library, 1936-38; asst. librarian City Library, Lowell, 1938-43; reference librarian Army Med. Library (U.S.), Washington, 1946-47, chief reference div., 1947-49; asst. librarian U.S. Naval Research Lab. Library, Washington, 1949-50; chief reference div. U.S. Dept. Agr. Library, Washington, 1951-52; librarian Tokyo Army Hosp. Library spl. services div., 1952, Camp Zama Regional Post Library spl. services div. U.S. Army (Japan), 1952-54; asst. librarian Weather Bur. Library Dept. Commerce, Suitland, Md., 1955-56. Contbr. articles to library jours. Bd. dirs., instr. Girls' City Club, Lowell, 1939-41; mem. Fla. Hist. Soc., St. Petersburg, 1983-84; mem., vol. Mus. Fine Arts, St. Petersburg, 1983-84. Served to lt. WAVES, 1943-46. Recipient Disting. Woman of Yr. award Lowell Bus. and Profl. Woman's Club, 1940. Mem. ALA (hon. life), Am. Hemerocallis Soc. (life; show chmn. 1966), Ikebana Internat., Am. Legion. Democrat. Episcopalian. Home: 6909 9th St S #336 Saint Petersburg FL 33705

MCNULTY, GEORGE FRANK, mathematician, educator; b. Palo Alto, Calif., June 18, 1945; s. George Ellis and Helen Dorothy (Emigh) McN.; m. Nieves Austria, Dec. 12, 1981; 1 child, Alfred. B.Sc., Harvey Mudd Coll., 1967; Ph.D., U. Calif.-Berkeley, 1972. J. Young instr. Dartmouth Coll., Hanover, N.H., 1973-75; asst. prof. math. U. S.C., Columbia, 1975-79, assoc. prof., 1979—; vis. assoc. prof. U. Hawaii, 1982, U. Calif., San Diego, 1979, U. Colo., 1985; vis. researcher Technische Hochschule, Fed. Republic Germany, 1975, U. Calif., Berkeley, 1973. Co-author: Algebras, Lattices, Varieties, 1985; also articles. Alexander von Humboldt Stiftung fellow, 1983; NRC Can. fellow, 1972-73; NSF fellow, 1967-69, 1971-72; Woodrow Wilson Found. fellow, 1967-68; Fulbright lectr. Manila, 1982-83. Mem. Am. Math. Soc. Office: Dept of Math U of South Carolina Columbia SC 29208

MCNUTT, JACK W., oil company executive; b. 1934; married. B.S., Harding Coll., 1956; M.S., Columbia U., 1957. With Murphy Oil Corp., El Dorado, Ark., 1957—, exec. v.p., 1981—, also dir. Office: Murphy Oil Corp 200 Jefferson Ave El Dorado AR 71730*

MC NUTT, KENNETH LEE, manufacturing company executive; b. College Springs, Iowa, June 24, 1930; s. Clay Everett and Gladys Fern (Pierce) McN.; A.A., San Diego City Coll., 1956; B.A., San Diego State Coll., 1958; m. Betty Jeanne Gamel, Mar. 11, 1951; children—Judy Charlene, Sandra Lee, Pamela Jeanne, Diana Lynn, Shawn Patrick, Jacqueline Renee, Janette Michelle. With Oroweat Foods Co., Hawaii, 1954—, asst. v.p., 1971, gen. mgr. Hawaii market area, 1983—. Served with U.S. Navy, 1948-54. Cert. adminstrv. mgr. Adminstrv. Mgmt. Soc. Mem. Soc. Cert. Adminstrv. Mgrs., Sales and Mktg. Execs. Club. Presbyterian. Clubs: Toastmasters Internat, Rotary. Home: 4609 Woodland Park Blvd Arlington TX 76013 Office: PO Box 45585 Dallas TX 75235

MCNUTT, WANDELLA, educator; b. Holdenville, Okla. B.S., E. Central U., 1959, M.S., 1965; Ed.D., U. Okla., 1970. Bus. tchr. pub. schs., Holdenville, Gerty, and Cromwell, Okla., 1959-66; faculty E. Central U., Ada, Okla., 1973—, prof. bus. edn., 1977—. Mem. Internat. Word Processing Assn., Nat. Bus. Edn. Assn., Okla. Bus. Edn. Assn., Mountain-Plains Bus. Edn. Assn., S.W. Adminstrv. Services Assn., Delta Pi Epsilon, Phi Delta Kappa. Club: Soroptimists Internat. Contbr. articles to profl. jours. Home: 1320 Lakehurst Ada OK 74820 Office: E Central U Sta 1 Ada OK 74820

MCPEAK, ALLAN, consultant, mediator; b. Hot Springs, Ark., Oct. 1, 1938; s. Kenneth L. and Dorothy (Whiteman) McP.; m. Judith L. Mathison, Oct. 26, 1973. B.A., U. Fla., 1960, J.D., 1965; M.S., Nova U., 1984; postgrad. Fla. State U., 1984—. Bar: Fla. 1965, U.S. Supreme Ct. 1980. Sole practice, Naples, Fla., 1965-85; cons. in human relations, Tallahassee, 1984—; pres. Lawyers Abstract Service, Naples, Fla., 1978-80; organizer Marine Savs. & Loan, Naples, 1980-81; pres. Am. Title Ins., Naples, 1982-83. Contbr. articles to profl. jours. Served with U.S. Army, 1960-63. Mem. Acad. Family Mediators, Am. Arbitration Assn., Southeastern Psychol. Assn., Assn. Family and Conciliation Cts., Fla. Bar Assn., Collier County Bar Assn. (pres. 1968-69), Blue Key, Pi Sigma Alpha. Lodges: Elks, Moose, Masons, Order Eastern Star. Home: PO Box 20732 Tallahassee FL 32316

MCPEAK, DAILEY AUSTIN, ophthalmologist; b. Fort Riley, Kans., June 21, 1943; s. Dailey Warren and Alma Ree (Herron) McP.; m. Margaret Evelyn Bennett, Sept. 3, 1966; children—Troy, Vickie. B.S., Western Ky. U., 1964; M.D., U. Louisville, 1968. Diplomate Am. Bd. Ophthalmology. Intern, Louisville Gen. Hosp., Ky., 1968-69; resident in ophthalmology Parkland Hosp., Dallas, 1972-75; practice medicine specializing in ophthalmology, Glasgow, Ky., 1975—; mem. staff T.J. Samson Community Hosp., Glasgow, The Med. Ctr., Bowling Green, Ky., Greenview Hosp., Bowling Green. Served with U.S. Army, 1969-71. Mem. Am. Acad. Ophthalmology, Ky. Acad. Eye Physicians and Surgeons, Ky. Med. Assn., Louisville Acad. Ophthalmology. Home: Route 7 N Jackson Hwy Glasgow KY 42141 Office: Bravo Blvd Glasgow KY 42141

MCPHAIL, PATRICIA DYER, real estate broker; b. Andver, Mass., Apr. 23, 1932; d. E. Dewey and Rose A. (Desjardins) Dyer; m. James H. McPhail, July 23, 1955; children—Barry, Brian, Steven, Kent. B.S., U. Lowell, 1954. Broker, owner Colonial Realty, Hattiesburg, Miss., 1976—; pres. Pat McPhail Inc., Hattiesburg, 1978—; v.p. McPhail Resorts Inc., Hattiesburg, 1985—; pres. Realtors Multiple Listing Service, Hattiesburg, 1983-84. Vice pres. N.E. Lamar Devel. Found., Hattiesburg, 1984; nat. scholarship chmn. Nat. Assn. Jr. Auxs., 1985—. Mem. Nat. Assn. Realtors, Miss. Assn. Realtors, Hattiesburg Bd. Realtors (bd. dirs. 1983-85, treas. 1984-85, sec. 1985—). Democrat. Roman Catholic. Home: 1 Shady Ln Lake Serene Hattiesburg MS 39401 Office: Lake Serene Box 602 Hwy 98 W Hattiesburg MS 39401

MCPHEETERS, EDWIN KEITH, architect, university dean; b. Stillwater, Okla., Mar. 26, 1924; s. William Henry and Eva Winona (Mitchell) McP.; B.Arch., Okla. State U., 1949; postgrad. U. Okla., 1952; M.F.A. (Univ. fellow), Princeton U., 1956; m. Patricia Ann Foster, Jan. 29, 1950 (div. 1981); children—Marc Foster, Kevin Mitchell, Michael Hunter; m. Mary Louise Marvin, 1984. Instr. dept. architecture U. Fla., 1949-51; asst. prof. architecture Auburn (Ala.) U., 1951-54, dean, prof. Sch. Architecture and Fine Arts, 1969—; asst. prof. U. Ark., Fayetteville, 1956-58, assoc. prof., 1958-65, prof., 1965-66; dean, prof. Sch. Architecture, Rensselaer Poly. Inst., 1966-69; mem. Ala. Bd. Registration for Architects, 1978—; cons. S. Central Bell Telephone Co., Ala. Power, So. Co. Services, Central Bank of South, Ala. Sch. Fine Arts. Served to 2d lt. AC, U.S. Army, 1943-45. Recipient 4th prize Carson-Pirie-Scott Planning Competition, 1954. Fellow AIA (Ala. council 1975-79, pres. council 1978, Merit award Ala. council 1976); mem. Assn. Collegiate Schs. Architecture (dir. 1970-77). Democrat. Episcopalian. Office: Sch Architecture Auburn U Auburn AL 36849

MCPHERON, ALAN BEAUMONT, lawyer; b. McAlester, Okla., July 6, 1914; s. Robert Lee and Jeannette (Kridler) McP.; m. Mary Jane Bass, Apr. 8, 1938; 1 dau., Jill McPheron Wigington. LL.B., U. Okla., 1937; grad. Nat. Coll. State Trial Judges, 1967. Bar: Okla. 1937, U.S. Dist. Ct. (no., ea. and we. dists.) Okla., U.S. Dist. Ct. (no. dist.) Tex. asst. county atty., Durant, Okla., 1939-42, county atty., 1942-43; sole practice, Durant, 1946-65, 75—; dist. judge Bryan County, Okla., 1965-75; tchr. bus. law So. Okla. State U., 1970-73. Mem. War Vets Commn. Okla., 1949-51; mem. bd. rev. Okla. Employment Security Commn., 1951-59; mem. Okla. Jud. Nominating Commn., 1983—. Served to master sgt. U.S. Army, 1943-46; ETO. Decorated Bronze Star; Croix de Guerre (France). Mem. ABA, Okla. Bar Assn., Okla. Trial Lawyers Assn., Am. Judicature Soc., Okla. Criminal Def. Lawyers Assn. (charter mem.). Am. Legion, VFW. Democrat. Presbyterian. Club: Elks. Office: 116 N 3d St Durant OK 74701

MCPHERSON, ALICE RUTH, ophthalmologist, educator; b. Regina, Sask., Can., June 30, 1926; d. Gordon and Viola McP.; m. Anthony Mierzwa. B.S., U. Wis., 1948, M.D., 1951. Intern, Santa Barbara Cottage Hosp., Calif., 1951-52; resident Hartford Hosp., 1952, Chic EENT, 1953, Univ. Hosp., Madison, Wis., 1953-55; ophthalmologist Davis & Duehr Clinic, Madison, 1956-57, Scott & White Clinic, Temple, Tex., 1958-60; practice medicine specializing in ophthalmology McPherson Assocs., Houston, 1960-62; practice medicine specializing in diseases and surgery of retina McPherson Assocs., Houston, 1962—; pres. Retina Research Found., Houston. Editor: New and Controversial Aspects of Vitreoretinal Surgery, 1977. Mem. editorial bd. Ophthalmic Surg., 1982—. Contbr. articles to profl. jours. Active Am. Diabetes Assn., Assn. for Community TV, Bay Coll. of Medicine Campaign for 80's, Houston Mus. Natural Sci., Better Bus. Bur., Friends of Eye Research, Houston Ballet, Houston Grand Opera Assn., Houston Symphony Soc., Mus. Fine Arts, Mus. Med. Sci., Physicians' Benevolent Fund, Retina Research Found., South Tex. Diabetes Assn., Inc., Tex.-Pac, Jr. League Houston. Recipient award of Appreciation Knights of Templar Eye Found., 1978; named Peter Duehr prof. ophthalmology U. Wis., 1956; named to Wisdom Hall of Fame, 1979. Mem. Med. Assn. Penido Burnier' Inst. (hon.), The Retina Soc. (pres. 1977-79), Am. Acad. Ophthalmology (sect. v.p. 1979), Am. Acad. Ophthalmology and Otolaryngology (honor award 1972), Am. Soc. Contemporary Ophthalmology (Charles L. Schepens honor award 1983), ACS (Tex. credentials com. 1977—), The Macula Soc., Am. Assn. Ophthalmology, AMA, Am. Med. Women's Assn., Assn. Research in Vision and Ophthalmology, Internat. Assn. Ocular Surgeons, Internat. Coll. Ocular Surgeons, Internat. Coll. Surgeons, Internat. Glaucoma Congress, Harris County Med. Soc., Houston Acad. Medicine, Houston Ophthalmol. Soc., Ninth Dist. Med. Soc., Pan Am. Assn. Ophthalmology, Pan Am. Med. Assn., Pan Pacific Surg. Assn., Research to Prevent Blindness, Royal Soc. Medicine, Southern Med. Soc., Tex. Med. Assn., Soc. Eye Surgeons, Wis. Alumni Assn., Wis. Med. Alumni Assn. Club: Club Jules Gonin. Home: 1323 South Blvd Houston TX 77006 Office: McPherson Assocs 6560 Fannin St Suite 2200 Houston TX 77030

MC PHERSON, FRANK ALFRED, corporation executive; b. Stilwell, Okla., Apr. 29, 1933; s. Younce B. and Maurine Francis (Strauss) McP.; m. Nadine Wall, Sept. 10, 1955; 4 children. B.S., Okla. State U., 1957. With Kerr-McGee, 1957—; gen. mgr. Gulf Coast Oil and gas ops., Morgan City, La., 1969-73; pres. Kerr-McGee Coal, 1973-76, Kerr-McGee Nuclear, 1976-77; vice chmn. Kerr-McGee Corp., 1977-80, pres., 1980—, chmn., chief exec. officer, 1983—; dir. Liberty Nat. Bank, Oklahoma City, Mem. adv. bd. Salvation Army, Oklahoma City; bd. dirs. YMCA of Oklahoma City., Okla. Bapt. Found., Bapt. Med. Ctr. of Okla., Okla. State U. Found. Served to capt. USAF, 1957-60. Mem. Soc. Mining Engrs., Am. Mining Congress (dir., exec. com., adv. council), Am. Petroleum Inst., Oklahoma City C. of C. (dir.). Republican. Baptist. Patentee in field. Office: PO Box 25861 Oklahoma City OK 73125*

MCPHERSON, MARGARET LORE, librarian; b. Balt., Feb. 19, 1951; d. Robert Grier and Margaret Hibbard (Lore) McPherson. B.A., U. Ga., 1973; M.L.S., Ind. U., 1974. Circulation asst. Athens Regional Pub. Library (Ga.), 1974-75; asst. librarian Emory U. Library, Oxford, Ga., 1975-82, head librarian, 1982—. Mem. ALA, Ga. Library Assn. Episcopalian.

MCPHERSON, ROBERT MERRILL, entomologist, researcher; b. Enid, Okla., Nov. 12, 1948; s. Norman Louis and Jean Erlene (Ziegler) McP.; m. Laura Ann Dragoo, Dec. 19, 1970; children—Michael, Matthew, Patrick. B.S., Sam Houston State U., 1971; M.S., La. State U., 1975, Ph.D., 1978. Carpenter's aide Victoria Remodeling Co. (Tex.), 1971-73; grad. research asst. La. State U., Baton Rouge, 1973-75, research assoc., 1975-78; assoc. prof. and extension entomologist Va. Tech. U., Blacksburg, 1978—; cons. Coop. Extension Service Agts. asst. coach Richmond County Little League, 1982, bd. dirs., 1984-86. Mem. Entomol. Soc. Am., Va. Acad. Sci., Va. Assn. Extension Agts., Am. Soybean Assn. (Research Tour award 1985), Va. Soybean Assn. (Meritorious Service award 1986), Sigma Xi, Epsilon Sigma Phi (Outstanding Achievement award 1983), Gamma Sigma Delta. Republican. Methodist. Club: Richmond County Ruritan (chmn. transp. com. 1980-82, treas. 1984-85). Contbr. chpts. to books, articles to profl. jours. Home: Route 2 PO Box 105 Warsaw VA 22572 Office: Eastern Va Research Sta Warsaw VA 22572

MCPHERSON, WILLIAM JOSEPH, JR., state senator; b. Pineville, La., Dec. 18, 1950; s. William Joseph and Jeffie McP.; m. Karen Saucier, Apr. 6, 1974; 1 child, William Joseph. B.A., Northwestern State U., 1975; postgrad. La. State U. Law Sch., 1975-76. Tugboat operator, 1969-72; owner, pres. Newmac Marine, Inc., Alexandria, La., 1976—; mem. La. State Senate from 29th Dist., 1984—, mem. health and human resources, transp., hwys. and pub. works com., agr. com. Mem. adv. council Alexandria Vocat.-Tech. Inst., 1984—; bd. dirs. Cenla Chem. Dependency Council, 1985—; mem. Indsl. Devel. Bd., Alexandria, La. Served with U.S. Army, 1972-76. Mem. Rapides Wildlife Assn. (v.p.), La. Marine Trade Assn. (dir.), La. Wildlife Fedn. (exec. com.), C. of C. Democrat. Baptist. Home: 2708 Maureen St Pineville LA 71360

MCQUAIL, EDWARD JOSEPH, III, business executive; b. Bluefield, W.Va., Feb. 1, 1939; s. Edward Joseph and Elinor (Ritz) McQ. B.S. in Edn., Concord Coll., 1970; M.A., Marshall U., 1975; M.S. in L.S., U. Tenn., 1981. Cert. tchr., Ky., Ohio, Tenn., W.Va., Va. Salesman McQuail's, Inc., Bluefield, W.Va., 1961-72; tchr. East Welch Sch., Welch, W.Va., 1972-74; tchr., librarian Pocahontas (Va.) High Sch., 1976-79; info. specialist TVA, Knoxville, 1981-82; assoc. ptnr. Ednor Enterprises, Bluefield, W.Va., 1982—. Bd. dirs., treas. Greater Bluefield Jr. C. of C., 1963-69. Mem. ALA. Republican. Roman Catholic. Club: Clover (Bluefield, W.Va.). Home: PO Box 146 Bluefield WV 24701 Office: Ednor Enterprises Room 220 Law and Commerce Bldg Bluefield WV 24701

MCQUEEN, SANDRA MARILYN, educator; b. Greenville, S.C., Nov. 30, 1948; d. Clement Edgar and Sara Elizabeth (Gentry) McQ.; B.A., Presbyn. Coll., Clinton, S.C., 1970; M.A., Presbyn. Sch. Christian Edn., Richmond, Va., 1972; doctoral candidate Ga. State U., 1986. Dir., Christian edn. Rock Spring Presbyn. Ch., Atlanta, 1972-74; tchr. Thomasville Heights Elem. Sch., Atlanta, 1974-80; tchr. gifted students Sutton Middle Sch., Atlanta, 1980—, chmn. dept. spl. edn., 1982—; cons. in field. Mem. chancel choir Rock Spring Presbyn. Ch., elder, 1986-88; mem. camps and confs. Presbyn. Synod S.E.; mem. Women's Advocacy Task Force, Atlanta Presbytery, 1980—, co-chmn., 1985-86, mem. div. Christian Concern, 1985—; sec. Calvin Task Force, 1974-79. Mem. Assn. Supervision and Curriculum Devel., NEA, Ga. Edn. Assn., Atlanta Assn. Educators, Ch. Sch. Tchrs., Presbyn. Coll. Alumni Assn. (pres. Atlanta club 1982-83), Sigma Kappa, Kappa Delta Pi. Office: 4360 Powers Ferry Rd NW Atlanta GA 30327

MC QUIGG, ADDISON CLARK, III, optometrist; b. Miami, Okla., Mar. 14, 1955; s. A.C. and Arbbara McQuigg; m. Jane E. Sherrod, May 13, 1979; children—Mac, Megan, Carter. A.A., Northeastern A&M, 1976; B.S., U. Houston, 1979, O.D., 1979. Practice medicine specializing in optometry, Miami, Okla., 1980—. Mem. Am. Optometric Assn., Okla. Optometric Assn. Lodge: Lions (pres. 1985). Home: 1909 Inverness Ct Miami OK 74354 Office: PO Box 1205 Miami OK 74355

MCQUIGG, JOHN DOLPH, lawyer; b. Abilene, Tex., Oct. 19, 1931; s. John Lyman and Dorothy Elinor (King) McQ.; m. Sandra Elainea Duke, Oct. 18, 1969; 1 son, John Revel. B.A., Denison U., 1953; LL.B., U. Tex., Austin, 1962. Bar: Fla. 1962, U.S. Supreme Ct. 1971. Asso., Shackleford, Farrior, Stallings & Evans, 1962-66, ptnr., Tampa, Fla., 1966-73; pres. John McQuigg, P.A., Tampa, 1973-80; shareholder Fowler, White, Gillen, Boggs, Villareal & Banker, P.A., Tampa, 1980—. Bd. dirs. Fla. Gulf Coast R.R. Mus., Inc., 1985—. Served to 1st lt. USAF, 1953-57. Mem. Fla. Bar, ABA. Republican. Episcopalian. Clubs: Tampa. Home: 10114 Lindelaan Tampa FL 33618 Office: PO Box 1438 Tampa FL 33601

MCQUISTON, JOHN WARD, II, lawyer; b. Memphis, Sept. 19, 1943; s. John Ward and Anna Vance (Hall) McQ.; m. Robbie Walker, Aug. 20, 1966; children—Anna Stewart, Katherine Walker. B.A., Rhodes Coll., Memphis, 1965; J.D., Vanderbilt U., 1968; hon. grad. U.S. Naval Justice Sch., 1969. Bar: Tenn. 1968. Ptnr., Goodman, Glazer, Greener, Schneider & McQuiston, Memphis, 1972—; instr. constrn. contract law Memphis State U., 1982. Pres., Les Passes Rehab. Center, 1982, Planned Parenthood of Memphis, 1985; pres. St. Mary's Episcopal Sch.; bd. dirs. NCCJ. Served with USCG, 1968-72. Mem. ABA, Tenn. Bar Assn. (chmn. sect. on antitrust 1983—) Memphis Bar, Shelby County Bar Assn., Forum Com. on Constrn. Law, Order of Coif. Episcopalian. Club: University (Memphis). Contbr. article to Tenn Bar Jour., 1983. Office: Suite 1500 First Tenn Bank Bldg Memphis TN 38103

MC RAE, JAMES HENDRY, physician; b. Detroit, Aug. 4, 1914; s. Claude F. and Isabelle (Hendry) McR.; B.A., Wayne State U., 1936, M.B., 1940, M.D., 1941; m. Luella R. Quick, Sept. 11, 1941; children—James Hendry, Barbara, Catherine, Sandra. Intern, W.A. Foote Meml. Hosp., Jackson, Mich., 1940-41; asst. resident Wayne County Gen. Hosp., Detroit, 1945-46, resident 1947, chief resident, 1948; practice medicine specializing in internal medicine, St. Petersburg, Fla., 1948—; mem. staff St. Anthonys Hosp., Bayfront Med. Center, Edward H. White Meml. Hosp., St. Petersburg. Bd. dirs. Rogers Heart Found., St. Petersburg, 1971-76. Served to capt. USAAF, 1941-45. Decorated Legion of Merit; recipient AMA Physicians Recognition award, 1977, 82, 86. Diplomate Am. Bd. Internal Medicine. Mem. Am. Soc. Internal Medicine, So. Med. Assn., Fla. Soc. Internal Medicine, Fla., Pinellas County med. socs., Royal Soc. Medicine (affiliate), Pi Alpha Kappa, Nu Sigma Nu. Methodist. Home: 646 17th Ave NE Saint Petersburg FL 33704 Office: 4444 Central Ave Saint Petersburg FL 33711

MCRAE, JOHN LEONIDAS, civil engineer; b. Lexington, Miss., Sept. 16, 1917; s. James Wright and Lota (O'Bryant) McR.; m. Thelma Lucile Nabors, Mar. 23, 1940; children—John Malcolm, Virginia Margaret McRae Pugh. B.S. in Civil Engring. and Geotech. Engring., Northwestern U., 1948. Chief bituminous and chem. lab. U.S. Army Engring. Waterways Exptl. Sta., Vicksburg, Miss., 1950-61, research engr. mobility and environ. div., 1961-72; pres. EDCO Inc., Vicksburg, 1960—; cons. on soil mechanics and bituminous pavements. Fellow ASCE; mem. Nat. Soc. Profl. Engr., ASTM, Assn. Asphalt Paving Technologists. Baptist (deacon). Contbr. numerous tech. papers to profl. lit. Patentee in field. Home: 416 Groome Dr Vicksburg MS 39180 Office: PO Box 1109 Vicksburg MS 39180

MC RAE, ROBERT, principal; b. Wadesboro, N.C., Feb. 25, 1928; s. Clyde and Lillian (Hinson) Mc R.; B.S., Fayetteville State U., 1955; M.S., A and T State U., Greensboro, N.C., 1965; edn. specialist East Carolina U., 1981; postgrad. U. N.C., 1968-69. Cert. in elem. edn., adminstrn., supervision, N.C. Tchr. upper grades Woodson Sch., Richlands, N.C., 1959-70, prin., 1970-72; prin. Trexler Sch., Richlands, 1972—; tchr. adult edn. Coastal Community Coll., Jacksonville, N.C., 1962-64. Leader Onslow County council Boy Scouts Am., 1959-63, active Explorer Post, 1963-70. Named Tchr. of Yr., Onslow County, 1965. Mem. N.C. Tchrs.' Assn. (pres. 1963-65), Onslow County Prins.' Assn. (pres. 1977-79), Onslow County Tchrs.' Assn. (pres. 1974-76), NEA, N.C. Assn. Educators, Onslow County Assn. Educators (del. to NEA 1964, 68, 78, 83, del. to Southeast Regional Assn. 1965, 66, past chmn. legis. com., Tchr. of Yr. 1965), Div. of Prins., Prin. and Asst. Prin.'s Assn. Democrat. Methodist. Lodge: Masons. Avocations: fishing; tennis; basketball. Office: Trexler Sch PO Box 188 Richlands NC 28574

MC RAE, ROBERT MALCOLM, JR., district judge; b. Memphis, Dec. 31, 1921; s. Robert Malcolm and Irene (Pontius) McR.; B.A., Vanderbilt U., 1943; LL.B., U. Va., 1948; m. Louise Howry, July 31, 1943; children—Susan Campbell, Robert Malcolm III, Duncan Farquhar, Thomas Alexander Todd. Admitted to Tenn. bar, 1948; practiced in Memphis, 1948-64; partner firm Apperson, Crump, Duzane & McRae, 1955-59, Larkey, Dudley, Blanchard & McRae, 1959-64; judge Tenn. Circuit Ct., 1964-66; U.S. dist. judge Western Dist. Tenn., Memphis, 1966—, chief judge, 1979—. Served to lt. USNR, 1943-46. Mem. Jud. Conf. U.S. (mem. com. on adminstrn. criminal law 1979-86), Dist. Judges Assn. 6th Circuit (pres. 1975), Phi Delta Phi, Omicron Delta Kappa. Episcopalian (pres. Episcopal Churchmen of Tenn. 1964-65). Home: 220 Baronne Pl Memphis TN 38117 Office: 167 N Main St Memphis TN 38103

MCRAE, THOMAS KENNETH, investment company executive; b. Richmond, Va., July 7, 1906; s. Christopher Duncan and Sarah Alice (Lawrence) McR.; m. Marion Lanier White, Sept. 11, 1937; children—Thomas Kenneth Jr., John Daniel. B.A., U. Richmond, 1927; postgrad. Sch. Banking, Rutgers U., 1936-38. Asst. cashier First Mchts. Nat. Bank, Richmond, 1940-46, asst. v.p., 1946-49, v.p., 1949-63, sr. v.p., 1963-71; v.p. Davenport and Co., Richmond, 1971—. Trustee Va. Supplemental Retirement System, 1964-71; active Va. Mus. Fine Arts, Va. Hist. Soc. Mem. Richmond Soc. Fin. Analysts. Republican. Baptist. Clubs: Country of Va., Downtown, Bd. of Va. Lodges: Masons, Rotary. Avocations: golf; stamp collecting. Home: 8910 Ginger Way Ct Richmond VA 23229 Office: Davenport & Co Va PO Box 1377 Richmond VA 23211

MCRAITH, JOHN JEREMIAH, bishop, Roman Catholic Church; b. Hutchinson, Minn., Dec. 6, 1934; s. Arthur Luke and Marie (Hanley) McR. B.A. cum laude, Loras Coll., Dubuque, Iowa, 1956. Ordained priest, Roman Catholic Church, 1960. Asst. pastor Sleepy Eye, Minn., 1960-64; pastor, Milroy, Minn., 1964-67, St. Leo, Minn., 1967-68; pastor St. Mary's Parish, Sleepy Eye, 1968-72, prin. high sch., 1968-72; exec. dir. Nat. Cath. Rural Life Conf., Des Moines, 1972-78; ordained bishop of Owensboro, Ky., 1982—. Pres. Minn. Cath. Edn. Assn., 1971. Address: 4005 Frederica St Owensboro KY 42301

MCSEVENEY, DENNIS ROBERT, sociology educator, university administrator; b. Cleve., Sept. 13, 1940; s. Robert Edgar and Wilma (Demjanovic) McS.; m. Jane Sidley, June 10, 1965 (div. 1972). B.S., John Carroll U., 1965; M.A., Emory U., 1971, Ph.D., 1972. Asst. prof. U. New Orleans, 1972-76, assoc. prof., 1976-82, chmn. dept. sociology, 1979-81, prof. sociology, 1982—, assoc. dean, 1981—; cons. City New Orleans, 1974-76, U.S. Congress, Washington, 1977-78, Lefkoff & Assocs., Santa Fe, 1981—. Contbr. articles to profl. jours. Mem. Am. Sociol. Assn., Mid South Sociol. Assn. (sec., treas. 1983—), So. Sociol. Soc. Southwest Sociol. Assn., Council Colls. Arts Scis. Democrat. Avocations: sociology; athletics; reading. Home: 4760 Marigny St New Orleans LA 70122 Office: U New Orleans Coll Liberal Arts New Orleans LA 70148

MCSHAN, MICHAEL WADE, physician; b. Brady, Tex., Oct. 14, 1949; s. Harold Dean and Evangeline Faye (Stapper) McS.; children—Michael Elliot, Deborah Michelle. B.S. with honors, Baylor U., 1972; M.D., U. Tex. Med. Br., 1975; M.S., Pacific Western U., 1984. Research asst. Baylor U., 1969-72; research student U. Tex. Med. Br., Galveston, 1972-73, intern in surgery, 1975-76, resident in surgery, 1976-77; practice medicine, specializing in family practice, Houston, 1977-80; family physician, Kilgore, Tex., 1980—; staff physician Longview Regional Hosp., Roy H. Laird Meml. Hosp., 1980—; staff physician East Tex. Treatment Ctr., 1980—; aviation med. examiner FAA, 1980—; sports medicine cons. Mem. Am. Acad. Family Practice, Internat. Acad. Protology, AMA, Tex. Med. Assn., Family Practice Assn., Am. Med. Soc. Vienna, Undersea Med. Soc., Tex. Soc. Sports Medicine, Am. Coll. Sports Medicine, Am. Med. Joggers Assn., Aviation Med. Soc., Am. Coll. Emergency Physicians. Episcopalian. Clubs: Lions, Rotary, Longview Running, Summit. Contbr. articles to profl. jours. Office: 316 Henderson Blvd Kilgore TX 75662

MCSHANE, JERRY MICHAEL, family medicine practitioner; b. Pasadena, Tex., Oct. 11, 1945; s. Howard James and Ollie Masy (Whiddon) McS.; m. Elaine R. Hooks, Nov. 20, 1966; children—Ricky, Mandy. A.A., San Jacinto Coll., 1966; B.S., U. Houston, 1970; M.S., Sam Houston U., 1973; D.O., Tex. Coll. Osteo. Medicine, 1979. Instr. biology, chemistry San Jacinto Coll., 1973-75; chief resident Dallas/Ft. Worth Med. Ctr., 1979-80; sec., treas. Southeast Med. Services, Pasadena, Tex., 1983—. NIH grantee, 1977. Mem. Tex. Osteo. Med. Assn., Am. Osteo. Med. Assn., AMA. Methodist. Avocations: golf; skiing; hunting; fishing. Office: PO Box 854 321 W San Augustine Deer Park TX 77536

MCSPADDEN, GEORGE ELBERT, educator; b. Albuquerque, Feb. 25, 1912; s. Elbert Leonidas and Zoe Elizabeth (Fabre) McS.; m. Natalia Jane Allen, 1941; children—Thomas Edward, Robert Allen, George David, John Steven. A.B., U. N.Mex., 1933, A.M., 1935; Ph.D., Stanford U., 1947. Teaching asst. Stanford U., 1935-39, sec. dept. Romance langs., 1937-39; instr. Spanish and Latin, U. Idaho, Pocatello, 1939-40; assoc. prof. U. B.C., 1946-54; vis. assoc. prof. U. Chgo., 1953-54, assoc. prof., 1954-57; prof. Romance langs. George Washington U., 1957-67, exec. officer dept., 1957-61; coordinator grad. studies, 1961-67, cons., 1967—; prof. Romance langs. U. N.C.-Greensboro, 1967-79, head dept., 1967-75, dir. Latin Am. Studies, 1976-79, emeritus, 1979—; prof. lang. and lit. John Wesley Coll., High Point, N.C., 1980—. Served to lt. comdr. USNR, 1941-46. Carnegie Corp. and Inst. Internat. Edn. fellow, 1938-39. Mem. Am. Assn. Tchrs. Spanish and Portuguese (pres. Ill. chpt. 1955-56, v.p. Chgo. area chpt. 1956-57, pres. elect. 1957, nat. v.p. 1964-67), MLA, South Atlantic Assn. Depts. Fgn. Langs. (chmn. 1977), So. Humanities Assn., Internat. Platform Assn., Phi Kappa Phi, Pi Delta Phi, Sigma Delta Pi. Author: Spanish Spoken in Chilili, New Mexico, 1935; An Introduction to Spanish Usage, 1956; The Spanish Prologue Before 1700, 1976; Don Quijote and the Spanish Prologues, 2 vols., 1978, 79; contbr. articles to profl. jours. Home: 3004 W Market St Greensboro NC 27403

MCSURDY, CHARLES EARL, mathematics educator; b. Washington, Sept. 28, 1939; s. Joseph Howard and Mae Delores (Burns) McS.; m. Kathryn Salmon, Sept. 9, 1961; 1 child, Michael. B.S., Va. Poly. Inst., 1964; M.S., Radford U., 1967, Ed.D., U. Va., 1975. Instr. Va. Western U., Roanoke, 1963-69, U. Va., Charlottesville, 1969-70; instr., head div., Coastal Carolina U., Jacksonville, N.C., 1970-77; div. head Nashville State Tech. Inst., 1977-80, prof., head math. and physics dept., 1980—. Served with U.S. Army, 1959-60. Mem. Math. Assn. Am., Tenn. Math. Assn. Two Year Colls. (v.p. 1984—), Am. Soc. Engring. Edn., Am. Assn. Physics Tchrs., Am. Vocat. Ann., Tenn. Vocat. Assn., Kappa Delta Pi, Kappa Mu Epsilon, Phi Delta Kappa. Lodge: K.C. Club: Fairview Community (treas. 1979). Avocation: flutist. Home: 222 Littlejohn Ln SW Fairview TN 37062 Office: Nashville Tech Inst 120 White Bridge Rd Nashville TN 37209

MCSWAIN, BYRDIE ENGLE, clin. lab. scientist, immunohematologist; b. Ethel, Ark., Oct. 13, 1939; d. James Marvin and Katherine Engle (Martin) McSwain; B.S., U. Ark., 1968; B.S. in Med. Tech., U. Ark. Sch. Medicine, 1969; M.S., U. Central Ark., 1973; Specialist in Blood Banking, U. Ark. Med. Scis., 1976. Med. technologist, Supr. blood bank, Univ. Ark. Med. Scis., Little Rock, 1970-77, clin. instr., 1977—; dir. tech. services and product mgmt. ARC Blood Services, Little Rock, 1977—. Recipient Grad. scholarship, Am. Soc. Med. Tech., 1975; named Med. Technologist of Yr. Ark. Soc. Med. Tech., 1981. Mem. Ark. Soc. Med. Tech., Am. Assn. Blood Banks, South Central Assn. Blood Banks, Am. Soc. Med. Tech., Clin. Lab. Mgmt. Assn., Am. Soc. Clin. Pathologists, Phi Theta Kappa. Home: 2800 Vancouver Dr Little Rock AR 72204 Office: PO Box 5654 Little Rock AR 72215

MCVEIGH, MIRIAM TEMPERANCE, artist; b. Wabash, Ind., July 12, 1921; d. Guy C. and Nina T. (Hill) Lenig; m. Robert W. McVeigh, Feb. 9, 1948. Cert., John Herron Art Sch., Indpls., 1933, Prunty Comml. Art, Indpls., 1940, Taflimgers Studio, Indpls., 1947; B.F.A., Calif. Coll. Arts and Crafts, Oakland, 1950; cert. Paris Am. Acad., 1972. Display artist W.H. Block & Co., Indpls., 1945-47; tchr. painting Adult Edn., Indpls., 1953-56, Clearwater, Fla., 1957-59; owner McVeigh Art Studio Gallery, St. Petersburg, Fla., 1960-62; dir. arts dept. Shorecrest Sch., St. Petersburg, 1970-83. One woman shows: St. Petersburg Jr. Coll., Fla., 1961; Galerie Internationale, N.Y.C., 1974; Ray Anthony's Gallery, St. Petersburg, 1985; group shows include: Butler Art Inst., Youngstown, Ohio, 1951; Circulating Gallery, Dayton Art Inst., Ohio, 1956; Am. Vet. Soc. of Artist, N.Y.C., 1961; Art Club of St. Petersburg, 1972. Recipient award Hoosier Salon, Indpls., 1954, award Galariers Raymond Doncan, Paris, 1973; Palmes D'or du Merite award Belgo-Hispanique, 1973; award Galerie Internat., N.Y.C., 1974; Legionde Honor Grand Prix, Humanicaire de France, 1975. Mem. Free Painters and Sculptors, Societe de Sur Independant. Democrat. Methodist. Lodge: Eastern Star. Avocations: sculpture; gardening. Home: 8200 14th St N Saint Petersburg FL 33702

MCVEY, CAROL ANDERSEN, college administrator; b. Hillside, N.J.; d. Robert C. and Amelia (Federico) Andersen; m. James Richard McVey, July 7, 1962; children—Carolann, James R. Jr. A.B. in Math., Rutgers U., 1961; M.Ed., U. S.C., 1977. Tchr. math. Hillside High Sch., N.J., 1961-63, Jewish Edn. Ctr., Elizabeth, N.J., 1965-66; instr. Florence-Darlington Tech. Coll., Florence, S.C., 1972-79, head math. dept., 1979-80, div. chmn., 1980-84, dean tech. studies, 1984—; bd. dirs. Ford Consumer Appeals Bd., Charlotte, N.C., 1983—. Leader Girl Scouts U.S.A., Florence, 1970-76, day camp dir., 1972-74; active Leadership Florence, 1984-85. Recipient Pres.'s Mgmt. Excellence award Florence-Darlington Tech. Coll., 1982. Mem. Phi Delta Kappa (newsletter editor 1984-86). Roman Catholic. Club: Florence Woman's (sec. 1981-83). Office: Florence-Darlington Tech Coll PO Drawer F-8000 Florence SC 29501

MCVEY, GEORGE JENNINGS, educational administrator; b. Richmond, Va., Feb. 8, 1939; s. Henry Hanna and Eva Lawson (Jennings) McV.; m. Nancy Harrison McLaughlin, Dec. 22, 1962; children—George Jennings Jr., James Harrison, Henry Hanna. Diploma St. Christopher's Sch., Richmond, Va., 1957; B.S. magna cum laude, Hampden-Sydney, Coll., Va., 1961, B.A. magna cum laude, 1961, LL.D., 1976; M.A., Va. Commonwealth Coll., 1973. Instr. math. and English St. Christopher's Sch., Richmond, 1961-65; asst. prin. Middle Sch., 1965-66, prin., 1966-69, dir. studies, 1969, asst. headmaster, 1971-72, acting headmaster, 1972-73, headmaster, 1973—; counselor and head counselor Camp Maxwelton, 1956-63; dir. Camp Briar Hills, 1964-68; bd. dirs. Johnston Willis Hosp., 1984—; former advisory bd. mem. River Rd Branch Colonial Savings & Loan; bd. dirs. New Va. Review, Buford Acad. 1980; former bd. dirs. Blue Cross-Blue Shield of Va., Richmond ARC, English Speaking Union, Aylett Country Day Sch., Friends of Richmond Pub. Library; former bd. mem. Va. Adv. Com. on Tchr. Edn. Active Grace & Holy Trinity Ch., Richmond. Mem. Nat. Assn. Ind. Schs. (bd. dirs., treas.), Va. Assn. Ind. Schs. (mem. exec. com., past pres.), Country Day Headmaster's Assn., Phi Beta Kappa, Chi Phi (past pres.), Omicron Delta Kappa, Eta Sigma Phi. Clubs: Country Club of Va., The Forum, The Richmond Hundred. Office: St Christopher's Sch 711 St Christopher's Rd Richmond VA 23226

MCVEY, JAMES WILLIAM, electronics company executive; b. Newark, Ohio, Sept. 14, 1953; s. William and Edith (Brown) McVey; m. Barbara Williams, June 9, 1979. Student pub. schs. Columbus, Ohio. Sales supr. J.C. Penney Co., Columbus, 1973-74; sales mgr. Vanguard Inc., Chgo., 1974-78; tech. sales rep. Am. Amixtures & Chems., Inc., Chgo., 1978-80; mgr. sales Beacon Marine Electronics, Cape Canaveral, Fla., 1980-82; v.p. sales Daytona Marine Electronics, Daytona Beach, Fla., 1982-85; owner, pres. Quality Electronics of Daytona, Port Orange, Fla., 1985—; system cons. Entré Computer Ctr. of Daytona, Daytona Beach, 1986—. Chmn. bd. Daytona Beach Boat Show Com., 1982—; adv. mem. Fla. Sea Grant com. Fla. State U., 1983—; co-chmn. Greater Daytona Beach Striking Fish Tournament, Daytona, 1982—. Vice pres. Melbourne Scuba Search and Recovery Team, Fla., 1974. Dive master Profl. Assn. Diving Instrs., 1974; recipient expert skydiver award U.S. Parachute Assn., 1980; expert parachute pilot award 1984. Mem. Volusia County Marine Dealers Assn. (pres. 1984-85). Republican. Clubs: Halifax Sport Fishing; Marina Point Yacht (Daytona). Avocations: Fishing; scuba diving; skydiving; cooking. Home: 1311 Woodward Ave Holly Hill FL 32017 Office: Quality Electronics Daytona 3961 Ridgewood Ave Port Orange FL 32019

MCVICKER, DAVID WILLIAM, operations research analyst; b. Quaker City, Ohio, Dec. 15, 1937; s. Donald Gwendolyn and Margaret Cranston (Shipley) Mc V.; B.S., in Chemistry, U. So. Calif., 1960; M.B.A., Chapman Coll., 1977; m. Susan Carole Griffin, Dec. 1, 1961; children—Paul, Edward, Michael, Susan. Commd. 2d lt. U.S. Air Force, 1961, advanced through grades to capt., 1976; ops. research analyst Tng. and Doctrine Command U.S. Army, 1976-78, U.S. Army Logistics Center, Ft. Lee, Va., 1978-82; former asso. adj. prof. St. Leo Coll. Decorated Bronze Star; recipient cert. achievement, Ft. Monroe. Mem. AAAS, Soc. Logistics Engrs. Republican. Methodist. Home: 908 E Ellerslie Ave Colonial Heights VA 23834 Office: Hdqrs USA Materiel Devel and Readiness Command Alexandria VA 22333

MCWATTERS, GARLAND CALHOUN, JR., multimedia consultant; b. Marlow, Okla., Aug. 18, 1948; s. Garland C. and Jessie Faye (Dehtan) McW.; m. Elizabeth Ann Strealy, Sept. 20, 1969; children—Jason Allen, Sabrina Ann. B.A. in Religion cum laude, Okla. Christian Coll., 1970; M.S. in Mass Communications, Okla. State U., 1978, postgrad. 1982-83. Ordained to ministry, Ch. of Christ, 1970; minister 16th and Fla. Ch. of Christ, Chickasha, Okla., 1970-72, San Jose Ch. of Christ, Jacksonville, Fla., 1972-73; account exec. KXXK-FM, Chickasha, Okla., 1973; broadcast announcer KSPI-AM/FM, Stillwater, 1973-74; program dir. KWCO-KXXK-FM, Chickasha, Okla., 1974-75; news dir. KOSU-FM, Stillwater, 1976-77; mktg. specialist Coll. Bus. Adminstrn., Okla. State U., Stillwater, 1977-79; asst. prof. communications Okla. Christian Coll., 1979-80; coordinator pub. info. Great Plains Vo-Tech., Lawton, Okla., 1980-81; dir. curriculum and media devel. Francis Tuttle Vo-Tech., Oklahoma City, 1981-83; exec. v.p. Images, Inc., Oklahoma City, 1983—; sr. cons. Leadership Devel. Inst., Oklahoma City, 1976—; leadership cons. field services div. Future Bus. Leaders of Am., Div., 1980-82; leader workshops on communication and mktg., Am. Vocat. Assn. Nat. Conf., 1981, 82, Platte County pub. schs. (Mo.), 1982; profl. devel. cons. Jobs for Am. Graduaters, Inc., Washington, 1983; leadership cons. The Gov.'s Day of Leadership, 1981, 82, 83; audiovisual cons. Audiovisual Ctr., Okla. State U., 1973-78. Recipient Brownfield Meml. award for outstanding service Chickasha (Okla.) Jaycees, 1974; Award of Excellence for sch. publ., 1983; Awards of Merit and Excellence, Nat. Assn. Vo-Tech. Edn. Communications, 1983. Mem. Am. Vocat. Assn., Okla. Vocat. Assn., Okla. Sch. Publs. Assn. (pres., awards of merit 1982, 83), Nat. Sch. Pub. Relations Assn., Nat. Audiovisual Assn., Assn. for Multi-Image, Okla. Adult and Continuing Edn. Assn., Okla. Council Local Adminstrs., Nat. Council Local Adminstrs., Phi Kappa Phi. Democrat. Clubs: Kiwanis, Lions. Contbr. articles to profl. jours. Home: 316 Clermont Dr Edmond OK 73033 Office: 4300 Highline St Suite 212-D Oklahoma City OK 73108

MCWHIRTER, J(AMES) CECIL, lawyer; b. Marion County, Ala., Apr. 28, 1937; s. Grady Jackson and Anna Florence (Roby) McW.; m. Patricia Davis, Aug. 16, 1961; children—Warren Douglas, Barry Jason, Wenda Gail. B.S., Miss. State U., 1960; J.D., Memphis State U., 1969. Bar: Tenn. 1969, U.S. Dist. Ct. (we. dist.) Tenn. 1969, U.S. Ct. Appeals (6th cir.), 1978, U.S. Supreme Ct. 1975. Assoc., Neely, Green & Fargarson, Memphis, 1969, Holt, Batchelor, Taylor & Spicer, Memphis, 1970; ptnr. Sisson, McWhirter, Lowrance & Austin, Memphis, 1971-80, Walsh, McWhirter & Wyatt, Memphis, 1980—. Pres. several civic or similar groups including PTA, 1974-75, Scenic Hills Action Com., 1975-76. Mem. ABA, Tenn. Bar Assn., Memphis and Shelby County Assn. (assoc. editor Syllabus 1981—, editor 1982—). Office: Walsh McWhirter & Wyatt Suite 3404 100 N Main Bldg Memphis TN 38103

MCWHORTER, RALPH CLAYTON, health care executive; b. Chattanooga, Sept. 27, 1933; s. Ralph and Gladys (Dover) McW.; children—Jodie, Stuart. Student U. Tenn.-Knoxville, 1951-52; B.S. in Pharmacy, Samford U., 1955. In hosp. adminstrn., until 1970; adminstr. Hosp. Corp. Am., Albany, Ga., 1970-73, div. v.p., Atlanta, 1973-76, sr. v.p. domestic ops., Nashville, 1976-80, exec. v.p. ops., 1980-85, pres., chief operating officer, 1985—, dir., 1983—; dir. Third Nat. Bank. Fellow Am. Coll. Healthcare Execs. Avocations: water sports; boating. Address: Hosp Corp of Am 1 Park Plaza Nashville TN 37202

MCWILLIAMS, JOHN LAWRENCE, III, lawyer; b. Phila., Dec. 21, 1943; s. John Lawrence and Elizabeth Dolores (Chevalier) McW., Jr.; m. Paula Ann Root, July 19, 1969; children—John Lawrence, IV, Robert Root, Anne Elizabeth, David Stanford, Peter Farrell. B.S., St. Joseph's Coll., 1965; J.D., Seton Hall U., 1969. Bar: N.J. 1969, N.Y. 1975, U.S. Supreme Ct. 1975, Fla. 1977. Trial atty. regional office SEC, N.Y.C., 1969-72; assoc. Mudge Rose Guthrie & Alexander, N.Y.C., 1972-77; mem. Freeman, Richardson, Watson & Kelly, P.A., Jacksonville, Fla., 1977—, chmn., pres., 1984—; apptd. spl. U.S. atty. Dist. of N.J., 1971. Trustee Mcpl. Service Dist. Ponte Vedra Beach, 1981—, chmn. bd. trustees, 1984—; treas. Ponte Vedra Community Assn., 1980-82; mem. Leadership Jacksonville, 1981, mem. steering com., 1982; dir. Jacksonville Country Day Sch., 1985—. Mem. ABA, Assn. Bar City N.Y., N.J. Bar Assn., Nat. Assn. Mcpl. Bond Lawyers, Fla. Bar Assn. Republican. Roman Catholic. Clubs: Ponte Vedra, Sawgrass, University, River, Seminole (Jacksonville). Home: 500 LeMaster Dr Ponte Vedra Beach FL 32082 Office: 1200 Barnett Bank Bldg Jacksonville FL 32202

MCWILLIAMS, SCOTT MURRY, oil company executive, geological consultant; b. San Angelo, Tex., Aug. 1, 1953; s. William Leland and Minnie VaRue (Kendrick) McW.; m. Robin Leigh Robinson, Mar. 8, 1980. B.S. in Geology, Univ. Tex. Permian Basin, 1980. Geologist, Post Petroleum Co., Inc., Midland, Tex., 1980-82; self-employed geologist, Midland, 1982-83; pres. Geostar Petroleum Inc., Midland, 1983—. Named to Nat. Deans Honor List, U. Tex. Permain Basin, 1980. Mem. West Tex. Geol. Soc., Am. Assn. Petroleum Geologists. Home: 4508 Brookdale Midland TX 79703 Office: Geostar Petroleum Inc 310 W Illinois Suite 324 Midland TX 79701

MCWILLIAMS, WARREN LEIGH, religion educator; b. Fort Smith, Ark., Dec. 12, 1946; s. George Leslie and Werdna Jane (Johnson) McW.; m. Patricia Kay Long, May 31, 1968; children—Amy Elizabeth, Karen Annette. B.A., Okla. Bapt. U., 1968; M. Div., So. Bapt. Theol. Sem., 1971; M.A., Vanderbilt U., 1974, Ph.D., 1974. Asst. prof. religion Stetson U., Deland, Fla., 1974-76; vis. prof. So. Bapt. Theol. Sem., Louisville, 1976; asst. prof. religion Okla. Bapt. U., Shawnee, 1976-82, Auguie Henry Assoc. prof. Bible, 1982—. Author: Free in Christ, 1984, The Passion of God, 1985; also articles. Mem. Am. Acad. Religion, Nat. Assn. Bapt. Profs. Religion, AAUP, Okla. Bapt. Hist. Soc. Democrat. Office: Okla Bapt U Shawnee OK 74801

MEAD, GEORGE FRANCIS, JR., mathematics and computing science educator and administrator; b. Arlington, Mass., July 12, 1946; s. George Francis and Mary Ann (Saccary) M.; m. Donna Mae Hartsell, Dec. 31, 1977; children—DeAnn Van Dusen, Rachel L., Thomas M. A.B., Providence Coll., 1968; M.A., U. South Fla., 1977, Ph.D., 1980. Instr. Berkeley Prep. Sch., Tampa, Fla., 1968-72, 77-81; dir. religious edn. Sacred Heart Parish, Tampa, 1972-76; part-time instr. Shorecrest Prep. Sch., St. Petersburg, Fla., 1974-77; assoc. prof. math./computing sci., statistics McNeese State U., Lake Charles, La., 1981—, dept. head, 1983—; dept. chmn. Berkeley Prep. Sch., 1977-81; coordinator religious edn. Diocese of St. Petersburg, 1972-73. Editor/author: Concepts in Elementary Algebra, 1982; College Mathematics, 1985; author: Applied Finite Math, 1985; author paper in field. Mem. Math. Assn. Am., Am. Math. Soc., Assn. for Computing Machinery, Nat. Assn. Tchrs. of Math., La. Assn. Tchrs. of Math., Phi Kappa Phi, Cum Laude. Democrat. Roman Catholic. Home: 4031 W Walton Lake Charles LA 70605 Office: Dept Math/Computing Sci/Statistics McNeese State Univ Lake Charles LA 70609

MEADE, VIOLET ARLENE, nurse; b. Pikeville, Ky., Feb. 19, 1948; d. Fred and Evelyn (Harrison) Damron; m. Joseph G. Raucci, Feb. 24, 1968 (div. 1976); 1 son, James; m. 2d. Roger Lowell Meade, Dec. 17, 1976. Grad. Mayo Vocat. Sch., 1976. Carhop Parkmoor Restaurant, Fairborn, Ohio, 1966; waitress Frisch's Restaurant, Fairborn, 1966-67; clk. Johnson's Cleaners, Colonial Heights, Va., 1972; cashier Wards Bakery, Colonial Heights, Va., 1972-73; dispatcher Pike County Detective Bur., Pikeville, Ky., 1974-75; nurse Meth. Hosp., Pikeville, 1976—. Sec. Parent Tchrs. Orgn., Robinson Creek, Ky., 1980-83. Democrat. Home: Route 4 Box 747 Pikeville KY 41501

MEADOR, LINDA, hospital association executive; b. Nashville, Feb. 10, 1943; d. Prentice Avery and Margaret Leone (Staggs) M. B.A., David Lipscomb Coll., 1965; M.A., Memphis State U., 1967; Ed.S., U. Tenn., 1974; Ph.D., Peabody Coll. of Vanderbilt U., 1978. Licensed clin. psychol. examiner. Instr. Metro-Nashville Schs., 1966-78, U. Tenn., Nashville, part-time 1968-78, Vol. State Coll., Gallatin, Tenn., part-time 1976-81; secondary sch. cons. Metro-Nashville Sch., 1978-82; edn. dir., clinician Nashville Pain and Stress Clinic, 1981-83, mgr. exec. devel., 1982-85; asst. v.p. mgmt. devel. Hosp. Corp. Am., Nashville, 1985—; lectr. and cons. various organs., schs. and workshops. Co-author: A Competency Based Manual of Career Education for Guidance Counselors, 1974; co-author booklet: Ethical Guidelines for the Use of Human Experimentation, 1980. Contbr. articles to profl. jours. Mem. Youth Services com. Red Cross, Nashville, 1980—, Allocations Panel United Way, Nashville, 1982-84; bd. dirs. Dede Wallace Mental Health Ctr., Nashville, 1979-82. Internat. scholar Delta Kappa Gamma, 1978. Mem. Am. Soc. Tng. and Devel., Am. Psychol. Assn. (ad hoc com. on psychology in secondary schs. 1978-81), Tenn. Assn. Tchrs. Psychology (pres. 1975-76, v.p. 1973-75), Delta Kappa Gamma, Pi Delta Epsilon. Republican. Mem. Ch. of Christ. Avocations: running; tennis; boating. Home: 432 Hill Rd Nashville TN 37220 Office: Hosp Corp Am One Park Plaza Nashville TN 37202

MEADORS, ALLEN COATS, health administrator, educator; b. Van Buren, Ark., May 17, 1947; s. Hal Barron and Allene Coats (Means) M. A.A., Saddleback Coll., 1981; B.B.A., U. Central Ark., 1969; M.B.A., U. No. Colo., 1974; M.P.A., U. Kans., 1975; M.A. in Psychology, Webster U., 1979; M.A. in Health Services Mgmt., So. Ill. U., 1980, Ph.D. in Adminstrn., 1980. Assoc. adminstr. Forbes Hosp., Topeka, 1971-73; asst. dir. health services devel. Blue Cross Blue Shield of Kans., Topeka, 1973-76; asst. dir. Kansas City Health Dept. (Mo.), 1976-77; program dir., asst. prof. So. Ill. U., Carbondale, and Webster U., St. Louis, 1978-82; assoc. prof., dir. div. health adminstrn. U. Tex.-Galveston, 1982-84; exec. dir. N.W. Ark. Radiation Therapy Inst., Springdale, Ark., mem. faculty Calif. State U., Long Beach, 1977-81; grad. faculty U. Ark. Sch. Bus. Adminstrn., Fayetteville, 1984—; cons. Surgeon Gen. Office and Air Force System Command. Bd. dirs. Martin Luther King Hosp., Health Care Services Adv. Bd.; mem. Orange County Health Planning Agy. Served with Med. Service Corps, USAF, 1969-73. Fellow Am. Coll. Hosp. Adminstrs., Ark. Hosp. Assn., Soc. Radiation Oncology Adminstrs., mem. Am. Hosp. Assn., Am. Pub. Health Assn., Am. Soc. Law and Medicine, Am. Assn. Health Planners. Contbr. articles to profl. jours. Home: 1513 Circle Dr Springdale AR 72764 Office: 5005 W Sunset Springdale AR 72764

MEADOWS, LEONARD PAUL, JR., linen service company executive; b. Asheville, N.C., June 14, 1927; s. Leonard Paul and Vernie Beatrice (Ingle) M.; m. Helen Lucille Hendrix, Mar. 24, 1948; children—Monte, Marilyn. B.B.A., Ga. State U., 1969. With Nat. Linen Service, Atlanta, 1941-78, v.p., 1972-78; owner, pres. Pioneer Services, Inc., Dallas, 1978-82; v.p. sales Texel Industries, Inc., Cleburne, Tex., 1979-82; dir. Marriott Textile Service Ctr., Irving, Tex., 1982—. Served with USN, 1944-46. Lodge: Masons. Home: 7108 Winterwood Ln Dallas TX 75248 Office: Marriott Textile Service Ctr 8440 Freeport Pkwy Irving TX 75063

MEADOWS, ROBERT LEE, pharmacist; b. Cynthiana, Ind., July 2, 1919; s. Joseph Hampton and Lillian Ola (Johnson) M.; m. Roberta Huddleston, Jan. 2, 1942; children—Connie Lee, John Robert. B.S. in Pharmacy with honors, Louisville Coll. 1942. Pharmacist, Countzler Pharmacy, Greenville, Ky., 1945-48; owner, pharmacist Meadows Pharmacy, Cadiz, Ky., 1948-72, ret. 1972. Mem. Civitan Club, Cadiz, Ky., 1956. Served to sgt. U.S. Army, 1942-45, ETO. Mem. Pharm. Assn. of Ky. (pres. 1st dist. West Ky. 1955), Kappa Psi. Democrat. Home: 249 E Main St PO Box 165 Cadiz KY 42211

MEADOWS, STEPHEN PARRIS, chiropractor; b. Hinton, W.Va., Nov. 26, 1938; s. Clifford Lowe and Mary Catherine (Baker) M.; m. Joan Joyce Montag, Oct. 28, 1961 (div. July 1977); children—Merry Sloan, Marcia Stuart; m. Joyce Leigh Caudle, Oct. 6, 1977 (div. Oct. 1983). Student Marshall U., 1957-61, Winston-Salem State U., 1965-67; D. Chiropractic, Logan Chiropractic Coll., St. Louis, 1964. Practice chiropractic Winston-Salem, N.C., 1964—. Mem. N.Y. Chiropractic Soc., W.Va. Chiropractic Soc., N.C. Chiropractic Assn. (com. chmn. 1977), Am. Chiropractic Assn. Served with U.S. Army, 1959-61. Libertarian. Roman Catholic. Clubs: Trout Unlimited, Mercer's Anglers. Lodge: K.C. Home: 3231 Zuider Zee Dr Apt H Winston-Salem NC 27107 Office: Forsyth Med Park Suite 208 Winston-Salem NC 27103

MEAGHER, MICHAEL ALAN, financial consultant; b. Shreveport, La., Feb. 5, 1949; s. John Paul and Thetis Elaine (Treadwell) M.; m. Marilyn Gayle Sage, Nov. 26, 1971 (div. 1983); children—Michael Alan, Jr., Kelley Elaine. B.S. in Fin., La. State U., 1971; M.B.A., U. Houston, 1975. Chartered fin. analyst; cert. compensation profl. Investment officer Am. Capital Mgmt., Houston, 1971-77; acquisition analyst Service Corp. Internat., Houston, 1977-79; sr. mgr. Peat, Marwick, Mitchell & Co., Houston, 1979-85; cons. William M. Mercer-Meidinger Inc., Houston, 1985—. Founding dir. Friends of Stehlin Found., Houston, 1980—, mem. exec. com., 1980—; trustee Stehlin Found. for Cancer Research, Houston, 1982—; fund raiser St. John's Sch., Houston, 1985; concert master Houston Symphony Orch., 1985. Mem. Am. Compensation Assn., Assn. for Corp. Growth, Inst. Chartered Fin. Analysts, Fin. Analysts Fedn., Houston Soc. Fin. Analysts. Republican. Episcopalian. Clubs: Houston City, Briar (Houston). Avocations: tennis; jogging; team sports. Home: 1824 Milford Houston TX 77098 Office: Mercer Meidinger Inc 5718 Westheimer Suite 1750 Houston TX 77057

MEALMAN, GLENN EDWARD, marketing executive; b. Prescott, Kans., June 10, 1934; s. Edgar R. and Mary E. (Holstein) M.; m. Gloria Gail Proch, June 12, 1955; children—Michael Edward, Cathy Gail. B.S. in Bus, Kans. State Coll., Emporia, 1957; postgrad., Harvard U., 1970. With Fleming Cos., Topeka, 1957—, sr. v.p. mktg., 1981-82, exec. v.p. mktg., 1982—; dir. Topeka Savs. Assn. Pres. bd. Topeka YMCA, 1981; trustee Ottawa (Kans.) U., 1980. Served with USNR, 1954-56. Baptist. Clubs: Rotary, Shangri-La Country, Quail Creek Country. Office: 6301 Waterford Blvd Oklahoma City OK 73118

MEALOR, WILLIAM THEODORE, JR., geography educator, consultant; b. Atlanta, Apr. 20, 1940; s. William Theodore and Doris (Pittman) M.; m. Jennifer Joyce Hancock, Dec. 28, 1968; children—Stephen Theodore, Augustus Everett, William Griggs. B.A., U. Fla., 1962; M.A., U. Ga., 1964, Ph.D., 1972. Instr. dept. geography U. Ga., Athens, 1970-71; asst. prof. dept. geography and area devel. U. So. Miss., Hattiesburg, 1971-75, assoc. prof., 1975-78, asst. dean Coll. Liberal Arts, 1977-78; prof., chmn. dept. geography Memphis State U., 1978-83, prof., chmn. dept. geography and planning, 1983—; cons. real estate devel. and land use analysis. Active Memphis Job Conf. Served to 1st lt. U.S. Army, 1964-66; Vietnam. Recipient Outstanding Tchr. award U. So. Miss., 1976-77; NASA Remote Sensing grantee, 1972-75; Miss. Marine Resources Council award, 1974-75; U.S. Dept. Transp. award, 1974-76, 79-80; Miss. Research and Devel. Ctr. award, 1976-77; NSF Found. award, 1981. Mem. Assn. Am. Geographers, Am. Soc. Photogrammetry, Nat. Council Geog. Edn., Am. Planning Assn., Sigma Xi, Phi Kappa Phi, Pi Gamma Mu, Gamma Theta Upsilon, Pi Tau Chi, Sigma Chi. Presbyterian. Contbr. articles to profl. jours. Office: Dept Geography and Planning Memphis State U Memphis TN 38152

MEANS, JACQUELINE ANNETTE COKE, equipment leasing company executive; b. Birmingham, Ala., Jan. 20, 1938; d. Homer D. and Irene F. (Strong) Coke; m. Max W. Starks, II, Jan. 5, 1957 (div. 1964); children—Max W., Monte H. B.S., Fla. A&M U., 1960; postgrad. U. Ala.-Birmingham, 1967-71; student Tenn. State U., 1955-57. Tchr., pub. schs., Birmingham and Orlando, Fla., 1960-72; social worker State Ga., Atlanta, 1972-73; specifications writer Parsons B.T./Bechtel, Atlanta, 1973-74; program dir. Mining Engring. Program, Atlanta, 1974-78; S.E. mktg. dir. Parametric Engring., Atlanta, Birmingham, 1978—; real estate salesman E. F. Robinson Realty, Atlanta, 1978—; partner Constrn. Service Assocs., Raleigh, 1982—; pres. JAC Corp., Birmingham, Atlanta, 1981—. Mem. Leadership Atlanta, 1984—, Resurgens Atlanta, 1984—; supporter Atlanta and Birmingham Urban League, 1984—; program coordinator Com. Enhance Cultural Horizons, Birmingham, 1984—, dir., 1982—; bd. dirs. CIMPEAT, 1973—. Recipient Disting. Service plaque CIMPEAT, Atlanta, 1978, Com. Enhance Cultural Horizons, 1983. Mem. Am. Mgmt. Assn., Empire Real Estate Bd., Alpha Kappa Alpha. Democrat. Episcopalian. Club: Law Dames.

MEARDY, WILLIAM HERMAN, association executive; b. Peoria, Ill., Feb. 28, 1925; s. Herman and Madeleine (McReynolds) M.; m. Joyce Dorothy Horn, Mar. 28, 1946; children—William Wesley, Karen Lynn. Student Bradley U., 1948-50; B.A., Calif. State U.-Los Angeles, 1952, M.A., 1958; postgrad. UCLA, 1964. Tchr., La Puente Union High Sch., Calif., 1953-56; acad., personal and job placement counselor Mt. San Antonio Coll., Walnut, Calif., 1956-63; dean student personnel services Rio Hondo Coll., Whittier, Calif., 1963-67; dean student services and activities Shasta Coll., Redding, Calif., 1967-70; exec. sec. Council of Community Coll. Bds., Evanston, Ill., 1970-72; exec. dir. Assn. Community Coll. Trustees, Washington, 1972—. Contbr. articles to profl. jours. Bd. dirs. Nat. Council for Responsible Pub. Interest Groups; chmn. West Covina council Boy Scouts Am., West Covina, Calif., 1960-61. Served with U.S. Navy, 1943-46; PTO; 2d lt. USAF Res., 1952. Mem. Am. Soc. Assn. Execs. Lodge: Masons. Home: 7700 Tremayne Pl A-204 McLean VA 22102 Office: Assn Community Coll Trustees 6928-A Little River Turnpike Annandale VA 22003

MEARS, MICHAEL JON, mathematics educator; b. St. Petersburg, Fla., Dec. 25, 1954; s. Harold Frederick and Adine Alice (Audibert) M.; m. Beatriz Sofia Pando, June 17, 1978; 1 child, Gabriel. A.A., St. Petersburg Jr. Coll., 1974; B.S. in Math., Fla. State U., 1977; M.S. in Math., U. Ky., 1979. Instr. Manatee Jr. Coll., Bradenton, Fla., 1979-81, dept. chmn., 1981-85; div. chmn. math. Manatee Community Coll., Bradenton, 1985—; projects cons. Mant City Govt., Bradenton, 1979-81. Contbr. articles to profl. jours. Spl. events chmn. Am. Cancer Soc., Bradenton, 1982—; soccer coach Manatee Area Youth Soccer Orgn., Bradenton, 1980-83. Mem. Fla. 2 Year Coll. Math. Assn. (treas. 1982—), Math. Assn. Am. (v.p. 1984—), Am. Math. Assn. 2 Year Colls. Democrat. Baptist. Club: Math. and Sci. Exchange (Bradenton) (pres. 1982-83, sec. 1982—). Avocations: sports; recreational math.; people. Home: 4811 65th St Ct E B Bradenton FL 34203 Office: Manatee Community Coll PO Box 1849 Bradenton FL 33506

MEASURES, PAMELA ANN, public relations counselor; b. Ft. Worth, Mar. 24, 1956; d. W. Winston and Dorothy Ann (Bassham) M.; m. Mark Clinton Thomasson, June 25, 1983. B.S., Baylor U., 1978; postgrad. U. Houston, 1979-81. Pub. relations specialist Hermann Hosp., Houston, 1978-81; pub. relations dir. Winius-Brandon Advt., Houston, 1981-83; pub. relations mgr. Weekley and Penny Advt., Houston, 1983-85; pres. M & M Communications, 1985—. Bd. dirs. Houston Ballet Guild, 1983—; active Baylor U. Alumni Assn. Recipient Tex. Hosp. Assn. Pub. Relations award for spl. event, 1979. Mem. Pub. Relations Soc. Am., Internat. Assn. Bus. Communicators (dist. 5 award 1979). Democrat. Baptist. Contbr. articles to profl. jours. Home: 11870 Fairpoint Dr Houston TX 77099 Office: 11870 Fairpoint Houston TX 77099

MECK, DONALD STEVEN, clinical psychologist, management consultant; b. Omaha, Aug. 8, 1949; s. Donald Herbert Meck and Blanche Robinson; m. Deborah Stevenson, May 24, 1969; children—Shawn, Aaron, Ryan. B.S., Purdue U., 1971; M.A., St. Mary's U., 1973; Ph.D., Tex. A&M U., 1977. Diplomate Am. Bd. Family Psychology, Am. Bd. Profl. Neuropsychology; lic. psychologist, Ga.; biofeedback cert. Psychol. assoc. Personnel Assessment and Devel. Corp., John D. Hezel, Ph.D., Inc., San Antonio, Tex., 1972-75 (part-time); instr. psychology evening div. San Antonio Coll., Tex., 1974-75; psychiatric clinic spl. mental health Clinical Psychology Service, Wilford Hall U.S. Air Force Med. Ctr., San Antonio, 1971-75; lectr. psychology, Tex. A&M U., College Station, 1975-77; psychol. cons. Tex. Youth Council, Brazos Valley MH-MR Ctr., Bryan, Tex., 1977, Wellston Acad. learning disabilities program, Warner Robins, Ga., 1982—, Happy Hour Sch./Worship for Mentally Handicapped, Warner Robins, 1981—; acting coordinator of edn. Chem. Abuse Program Brazos Valley MH-MR Ctr., 1977; chief clin. psychology service Dept. Mental Health Robins AFB Hosp., Warner Robins, 1978-81; clin. psychologist Psychometrics, Inc., Warner Robins, Macon, Ga., 1981-84, U.S. Air Force Reserve Robins AFB, 1982—; solo practice clin. psychology, Warner Robins, 1984—; cons. psychologist Med. Ctr. of Houston County, Warner Robins, Charter Lake Hosp., Macon, Coliseum Park Hosp., Macon. Contbr. numerous articles to profl. jours. Bd. dirs. Houston County Assn. for Exceptional Children, Inc., Hospice of Houston County, Inc., Am. Heart Assn. Served to capt. USAF, 1971-74, 77-81, USAF Reserve, 1981—. Tex. A&M U. Found. grantee, 1976, Mem. Am. Psychol. Assn., Acad. Family Psychology (editor nat. directory 1980—), Nat. Acad. Neuropsychologists, Ga. Psychol. Assn., Am. Soc. Clin. Hypnosis, Ga. Psychologists in Action (sec./treas. 1980—), Biofeedback Soc. Am., Warner Robins C. of C. Lodges: Rotary, Masons. Avocations: fishing; jogging; softball; water skiing; hunting. Home: 112 Julie Emilyn Dr Bonaire GA 31005 Office: PO Box 1864 119 Carl Vinson Parkway Warner Robins GA 31093

MEDFORD-RHYMES, NANCY ELIZABETH, pharmacist; b. Tifton, Ga., Nov. 1, 1950; d. Harmon Crum and Dorothy Eugenia (Colley) Medford; m. Thomas Lee Rhymes, Sept. 17, 1983; 1 child, Jonathan Thomas Medford. B.S. in Biology, Emory U., 1972; B.S. in Pharmacy, Auburn U., 1976. Licensed pharmacist, Ala., Ga., Fla. Pharmacy intern The Med. Ctr., Columbus, Ga., 1976; pharmacist Pic N Save Drugs, Gainesville, Fla., 1976-78, The Med. Ctr., Columbus, 1978-79; pharmacist, supr. Winter Park Meml. Hosp., Fla., 1979—. Democrat. Baptist. Avocations: personal computer; foreign travel. Home: PO Box 4686 Winter Park FL 32793

MEDICO, FRANK, state legislator; b. South Braintree, Mass., Apr. 23, 1924; s. Domenic and Christine (Regatta) M.; m. Billie Vaughnita Osborne, Feb. 9, 1947; children—Jane, Fred, Patricia. B.C.S., Benjamin Franklin U., 1950; M.F.A., Columbus U., 1952; postgrad. Advanced Mgmt. Program, Harvard U., 1962. C.P.A., Mass. Staff acct. Def. Prodn. Adminstrn. and Dept. Agr., Washington, 1950-56; supr. acctg. GAO, 1956-66, asst. dir. gen. govt. div., 1966-79; mem. Va. Gen. Assembly, 1981—. Served with USN, 1942-46, 50. Mem. Am. Mgmt. Assn., Nat. Assn. Accts., Am. Inst. C.P.A.s, Am. Soc. Pub. Adminstrn., Alexandria C. of C. Republican. Roman Catholic. Lodges: K.C., Lions, Moose.

MEDINA, RAUL JUAN, hospital executive; b. Santiago, Cuba, June 24, 1940; came to U.S., 1961; s. Raul and Maria (Sali) M.; m. Yolanda Lamarque, Apr. 30, 1962; children—Raul J., Yolanda. B.B.A., U. Miami, 1969. Acct. Ernst & Whinney C.P.A.s, Miami, Fla., 1969-72; budget dir. Mt. Sinai Med. Ctr., Miami Beach, 1972-79, asst. dir., 1983—; fin. dir. So. Fla. Group Health, Miami, 1979-82; fin. dir. Internat. Med. Ctr., 1982-83; pres. Stein, Russell & Fernandez, Miami, 1977—. Bd. dirs. Khory League, Miami, 1977. Mem. Assn. Interam. de Hombres de Empresa, Hosp. Fin. Mgmt. Assn., Nat. Accts. Assn., Family Encounter. Democrat. Roman Catholic. Office: Mount Sinai Med Ctr 4300 Alton Rd Miami Beach FL

MEDLAR, STANLEY WAYNE, retail executive; b. San Antonio, Nov. 1, 1948; s. Robert Eugene and Betty Jean (Pierce) M.; m. Linda Diane Jones, Sept. 21, 1974; 1 dau., Kristan Leigh. B.B.A., Tex. Tech. U., 1972. Personnel adminstr. Tex. Instruments, Houston, 1972-74; mgr. Medlar's N., San Antonio, 1974-81; co-owner, pres. Redback Corp., San Antonio, 1978—; co-owner, v.p. MPM, Inc., Austin, Tex., 1980—; co-owner, v.p. Medlar's N., Inc., San Antonio, 1981—. Active Greater San Antonio C. of C., N. San Antonio C. of C. Mem. Am. Numismatic Assn., Tex. Numismatic Assn., Tex. Coin Dealer Assn., Jeweler's Bd. Trade. Republican. Clubs: Petroleum, City (San Antonio). Office: Medlar's N Inc 54 North Star Mall San Antonio TX 78216

MEDLEY, DONALD MATTHIAS, educational educator, consultant; b. Faulkton, S.D., Feb. 18, 1917; s. Thomas Arnot and Cecilia Agnes (Kellen) M.; m. Betty Ann Robertsen, Aug. 23, 1948; 1 child, Timothy Laurence. B.S., Coll. St. Thomas, St. Paul, 1938; M.A., U. Minn., 1950, Ph.D., 1954. Tchr., Am. Sch. Guadalajara, Mex., 1941-42, Floodwood Pub. Schs., Minn., 1946-48; instr. English, Coll. St. Thomas, 1948-50; asst. prof. CUNY, 1954-59, assoc. prof., 1959-64, prof., 1964-65; sr. research psychologsit Ednl. Testing Service, Princeton, N.J., 1965-70; prof. U. Va., Charlottesville, 1970—; mem. exec. bd. Consortium for the Improvement of Tchr. Evaluation, Atlanta, 1985—. Author: Measurement-Based Evaluation of Teacher Performance, 1984. Contbr. articles to profl. jours. Served as staff sgt. U.S. Army, 1942-46. Fellow Am. Psychol. Assn.; mem. Am. Ednl. Research Assn. (div. sec. 1962), Nat. Council on Measurement in Edn., Assn. Tchr. Educators. Democrat. Roman Catholic. Avocations: conjuring; travel. Office: Curry Sch Edn Univ Va 405 Emmet St Charlottesville VA 22901

MEDLEY, RAYMOND H., JR., mathematics and computer science educator; b. Nashville, Aug. 10, 1932; s. Raymond H. and Mary Louise (Link) M.; m. Marion Ruth Shepherd, Mar. 28, 1952; children—R. Alan, Karen G. Medley Woods, B.S., Peabody Coll., 1957, M.A., 1959, Ph.D., 1975; postgrad. U. Evansville, Clarkson U. Tchr. Hillsboro High Sch., Nashville, 1957-64; prof. math., computer sci., chmn. dept. Belmont Coll., Nashville, 1964—; tchr. Fisk U. Pre-Coll. Ctr., Nashville, 1964-67. Author basic algebra study guide. Recipient Outstanding Prof. award Belmont Coll., 1976; NSF fellow, 1962-64. Mem. Assn. for Computing Machinery, Math. Assn. Am., Nat. Council Tchrs. Math., Nat. Hemophilia Found. (chmn. bd. dirs. Cumberland Chpt.), Nat. Geographic Soc., Tenn. Hist. Soc. Hist. Belmont Soc., Tenn. Math. Tchrs. Assn., Middle Tenn. Math. Tchrs. Assn. Democrat. Baptist. Avocations: church choir; handbells; orchestra; coin collecting; camping. Office: Belmont Coll 1900 Belmont Blvd Nashville TN 37203

MEDLEY-MOORE, BETTE JEANNE, marketing executive; b. Tulsa, Mar. 20, 1950; d. William Charles and Betty (Howell) Medley; grad. with distinction Inst. Fin. Edn., 1978; 1 dau., Tanya Ann. Teller, Hawaii Thrift & Loan, Honolulu, 1970-71; savs. supr. Am. Savs., Tucson, 1972-73; asst. br. mgr. Albuquerque Fed. Savs., 1973-78, asst. sec.; asst. v.p. Am. Savs., Albuquerque, 1978; solicitor, underwriter Van Schaack Mortgage, Albuquerque, 1978-79; real estate and fin. mgr. Nu-West, Inc., Phoenix, 1979-82; mktg. dir. Fausett Mgmt. Co., Little Rock, 1982-84; pres. Vesta Mktg. Group, Inc., 1984—; lectr. in field. Mem. Am. Bus. Women's Assn., Inst. Fin. Edn. (dir. 1973-78). Republican. Episcopalian. Club: Civitan (Duke City 1977, 78). Home: 112 Midland Little Rock AR 72205 Office: 700 E 9th St #10K Little Rock AR 72202

MEDLIN, JOHN GRIMES, JR., banker; b. Benson, N.C., Nov. 23, 1933; s. John Grimes and Mabel (Stephenson) M.; B.S. in Bus. Adminstrn., U. N.C., Chapel Hill, 1956; grad. Advanced Mgmt. Program, U. Va., 1965; m. Pauline Winston Sims, Aug. 3, 1957. With Wachovia Bank & Trust Co., Winston-Salem, N.C., 1959—, exec. v.p., 1971-74, pres., 1974-85, chief exec. officer, 1977—, also dir.; pres., chief exec. officer Wachovia Corp., 1977-85, chmn., chief exec. officer Wachovia Bank and Wachovia Corp., 1985—; pres., chief exec. officer First Wachovia Corp.; mem. fed. adv. council Fed. Res. System; dir. Carolina Power & Light Co., Summit Communications, Inc., Piedmont Aviation, Norfolk So. Corp., Inc., R.J. Reynolds Industries, Inc. Active numerous civic and service orgns. Chmn. bd. dirs. Bus. Found. of U. N.C.; trustee Salem Acad. and Coll.; chmn. N.C. Gov.'s Council Mgmt. and Devel. Served as officer USNR, 1956-59. Mem. Assn. Res. City Bankers (pres.). Am. Bankers Assn. (bd. dirs.), Order Holy Grail, Order Old Well, Phi Delta Theta. Clubs: Old Town, Rotary (pres.) (Winston-Salem). Office: Wachovia Bank & Trust Co NA PO Box 3099 Winston-Salem NC 27150

MEDLOCK, PAUL NORTON, dentist; b. Atchison, Kans., June 24, 1940; s. Charles Edward and Mary Virginia (Norton) M. Student U. Kans., 1958-60; B.S. in Biology, U. Mo.-Kansas City, 1962, D.D.S., 1965. Gen. practice dentistry, South Houston, Tex., 1965—; pres. Timberlock, Inc., South Houston, 1972—. Mem. Houston Dist. Dental Soc., Tex. Dental Assn., Am. Dental Assn. Club: Univ. Avocation: sailing. Office: 2006 Spencer St South Houston TX 77587

MEDLOCK, T. TRAVIS, attorney general, lawyer; b. Joanna, S.C., Aug. 28, 1934; s. Melvin Kelly and Mayme (DuBose) M.; m. Laura Virginia Orr, Oct. 11, 1969; children—Tom, Glenn. A.B., Wofford Coll., 1956; LL.B., U. S.C., 1959. Bar: S.C., 1960, U.S. Supreme Ct., U.S. Ct. of Appeals, (4th cir.). Asst. atty. gen. S.C. Atty's Gen. Office, Columbia, 1961-62, atty. gen., 1983—; sole practice law, Columbia, 1960-82; mem. S.C. Ho. of Reps., Columbia, 1964-72; mem. S.C. Senate, 1972-76; chmn. Gov.'s Sub-Com. on Econ. Devel. for S.C., 1975-76. Mem. S.C. State Tri-Centennial Commn., 1966-71; chmn. U.S. Pres.'s Com. on Children and Youth, S.C., 1971; mem. Wofford Coll. Alumni Bd., Spartanburg, S.C., 1972; bd. visitors Winthrop Coll., Rock Hill, S.C., 1975. Served to capt. U.S. Army, 1975. Mem. S.C. State Bar Assn. (mem. legis. com. 1979-80), Richland County Bar Assn., Assn. Trial Lawyers Am., Phi Beta Kappa, Blue Key, Phi Alpha Theta. Democrat. Methodist. Club: Civitan (Cola, S.C.). Office: Atty Gen of SC PO Box 11549 Columbia SC 29211

MEDORO, JOHN VINCENT, general contractor, construction consultant; b. Phila., Sept. 17, 1933; s. Augustine Mario and Frances Nina (DiCamillo) M.; m. Dianne Marie Sena, June 16, 1956; children—Dana, Jodi, Maria, Janean. Student U. Miami, 1951-54. Gen. contractor DiCamillo Constrn. Co., Miami, 1956-63, ptnr., 1963—; cons. Served with USMC, 1954-56. Mem. Builder's Assn. South Fla., Coral Gables C. of C. Democrat. Roman Catholic. Clubs: Lions, St. Louis Men's, Italian-Am. (dir.), Coral Gables Country; Country of Colo. (Colorado Springs). Home: 11915 SW 67th Ct Miami FL 33156 Office: DiCamillo Constrn Co 11020 SW 196th St Miami FL 33157

MEDWAY, FREDERIC JEFFREY, pediatrics and psychology educator, psychologist; b. June 4, 1947; s. Irwin and Corrine (Finkel) M.; m. Marcia Fern Lutz, Aug. 13, 1977; children—Lauren, Scott. B.A., Syracuse U., 1969; M.A., Fairleigh Dickinson U., 1970; Ph.D., U. Conn., 1975. Lic. psychologist, S.C. Asst. prof. psychology U. S.C., Columbia, 1975-80, assoc. prof., 1980—, adj. assoc. prof. pediatrics Med Sch., 1984—; pvt. practice psychology, Columbia, 1980—; cons. guidelines Press, Lake Park, Fla., 1980—, Prentice-Hall, 1984; numerous sch. dists. Editor: Psychological Services in the High School, 1982; Jour. Sch. Psychology Monograph, 1980. Contbr. articles to profl. jours. Fellow Am. Psychol. Assn. (Lightner Witmer research award 1982); mem. Nat. Assn. Sch. Psychologists, Am. Edn. Research Assn. Avocations: sailing; cooking; boxing. Home: 101 Larkspur Rd Columbia SC 29210 Office: Dept Psychology U SC Columbia SC 29208

MEECE, BERNARD CLAYTON, clergyman, church administrator; b. Somerset, Ky., Mar. 7, 1927; s. Bernard and Myrtle (Sweeney) M.; m. Georgia Ann Curry, Sept. 2, 1950; children—Judith, Jeannine, Jacquelyn. A.B., Transylvania U., 1949, D.D., 1980; B.D., Lexington Theol. Sem., 1952; D.Min., Drew U., 1981. Ordained to ministry Christian Ch. (Disciples of Christ), 1952. Pastor, 1st Christian Ch., Cadillac, Mich., 1952-57; assoc. minister N.C. Christian Soc., Wilson, 1957-62; pastor 1st Christian Ch., DeLand, Fla., 1962-69, Sarasota, Fla., 1969-81; regional minister Christian Ch. in N.C., Wilson, 1981—; dir. Ch. Fin. Council, Indpls., 1983—. Mem. screening com. Sarasota Sch. Bd., 1975-81; trustee Atlantic Christian Coll., Wilson, 1981—. Lodge: Kiwanis (pres. Sarasota club 1976-77). Home: 805 Trinity Dr Wilson NC 27893 Office: Christian Ch in NC 509 NE Lee St PO Box 1568 Wilson NC 27893

MEECE, VOLNEY, newspaper reporter, association administrator; b. Tonkawa, Okla., Jan. 23, 1925; s. Charles Walter and Maude Belle (Barclay) M.; m. Mattie Lou Barker, June 13, 1966; children—Pamela Kay, Robin Renee, Michelle Dawn. A.A., No. Jr. Coll., 1948; B.A., U. Okla., 1950. Sports reporter Daily Oklahoman & Times, Oklahoma City, 1950-52; sports columnist Oklahoma City Times, 1952-84; sports reporter Daily Oklahoman, 1984—; exec. dir. Football Writers Assn., Edmond, Okla., 1973—. Author: 13 Years of Winning Oklahoma Football Under Bud Wilkinson, 1960. Served with USAF, 1943-46: Recipient Jake Wade award, Coll. Sports Info. Dirs. Am., 1974. Mem. Football Writers Assn. (pres. 1971-72, exec. dir. 1973), U.S. Basketball Writers Assn., Coll. Sports Info. Dirs. Am., Am. Football Coaches Assn. Avocations: jazz; swimming. Home: 3025 Wanetta Edmond OK 73013

MEEK, PAUL DERALD, oil and chemical company executive; b. McAllen, Tex., Aug. 15, 1930; s. William Van and Martha Mary (Sharp) M.; B.S. in Chem. Engring., U. Tex., Austin, 1953; m. Betty Catherine Robertson, Apr. 18, 1954; children—Paula Marie Burford, Kathy Diane, Carol Ann Miller, Linda Rae. With tech. dept. Humble Oil & Refining Co., Baytown, Tex., 1953-55; process engr., then pres. Cosden Oil & Chem. Co., 1968-76; v.p., dir. parent co. Am. Petrofina, Inc., 1968-76, pres., chief operating officer, 1976-83, chief exec. officer, 1983—, chmn. bd. dirs., pres., 1984—. Chmn. Engring. Found. adv. council U. Tex., Austin, 1979-80, chmn. chem. engring. vis. com., 1975-76; mem. research com. Tex. Research League, 1979—; mem. YWCA Adv. Council, 1983—; assoc. bd. visitors Univ. Cancer Found., 1985-86; trustee Southwest Research Inst., Southwest bd. group Boys' Clubs Am. Named Disting. Engring. Grad., U. Tex., Austin, 1969; registered profl. engr., Tex. Mem. Am. Petroleum Inst. (exec., budget and awards coms. of bd. dirs.), Am. Inst. Chem. Engrs., Mfg. Chemists Assn. Office: Box 2159 Fina Plaza Dallas TX 75221

MEEK, PHILLIP JOSEPH, publisher; b. Los Angeles, Nov. 17, 1937; s. Joseph Alcinus and Clara Amy (Phillips) M.; B.A. cum laude, Ohio Wesleyan U., 1959; M.B.A., Harvard U., 1961; m. Nancy Jean LaPorte, June 25, 1960; children—Katherine Amy, Brian Joseph, Laurie Noel. Fin. analyst Ford Motor Co., 1961-63, supr. capacity planning, 1963-66, supr. domestic scheduling, 1966, controller mktg. services, 1966-68, on loan as pres. Econ. Devel. Corp. Greater Detroit, 1968-70; pres., pub. Oakland Press Co., Pontiac, Mich., 1970-77; exec. v.p., gen. mgr. Ft. Worth Star-Telegram, 1977-79, pres., editorial chmn., 1980-82, pres., pub., 1982—. Past mem. Pontiac Stadium Bldg. Authority; pres. United Way Pontiac-N. Oakland, 1977; v.p., bd. dirs. Tarrant County United Way, 1981; bd. dirs. Ft. Worth C. of C., Arts Council Ft. Worth and Tarrant County, Van Cliburn Found., Inc.; chmn. N. Tex. Commn., 1984. Mem. Am. Newspaper Pubs. Assn., So. Newspaper Pubs. Assn., Tex. Daily Newspaper Assn. (pres. 1984), Phi Beta Kappa, Omicron Delta Kappa, Sigma Delta Chi, Pi Delta Epsilon, Phi Gamma Delta. Methodist. Clubs: Orchard Lake Country (Mich.); Rivercrest (Tex.) Country; Shady Oaks (Tex.) Country; Ft. Worth, Petroleum of Ft. Worth. Office: 400 W 7th St PO Box 1870 Fort Worth TX 76101

MEEKER, JACKIE O'DELL, association administrator; b. Denton, Tex., Apr. 25, 1949; s. Harold and Elwanda (Warren) M.; m. Teresa Jean Vinson, May 29, 1971; children—Mandy Kaye, Lindee Collette, Crystal Rae. B.S., Hardin-Simmons U., 1974. Houseparent, South Tex. Children's Home, Beeville, 1975; coach Sento High Sch., Tex., 1977-79; asst adminstr. Texas Pythian Home, Weatherford, Tex., 1979-81, adminstr., 1983—; coach Millsap High Sch., Tex., 1981-83. Recipient Grand Chancellors award Knights of Pythias, 1979. Mem. Southwest Assn. Adminstrs. Baptist. Lodges: Lions, Knights of Pythias. Avocations: sports; team roping. Home: 1825 Bankhead Dr PO Box 239 Weatherford TX 76086 Office: Tex Pythian Home 300 Home Weatherford TX 76086

MEEKER, ROBERT ROY, English educator, former marine corps officer; b. Pensacola, Fla., Mar. 8, 1927; s. Robert Roy and Bernice Beatrice (Coley) M.; m. Gloria McQueen, June 6, 1947; children—Robert Roy III, Robyne Anne, Michael David. Student U. Fla., 1943-44, U. Southwestern La., 1944-45, Tulane U., 1945-46; A.B., U. Miami, Fla., 1947, M.A., 1948; postgrad. U. Md., 1963-65. Instr. N. Tex. State U., Denton, 1948-51; enlisted in U.S. Navy, 1944, commd. officer, 1946; commd. 2d lt. U.S. Marine Corps, 1951, advanced through ranks to lt. col., 1967; inf. and supply officer; ret., 1969; instr. Broward Community Coll., Coconut Creek, Fla., 1970—. Co-author: (documentary movie) Les Marines, 1958 (French Acad., Venice, Cannes Festival award 1958), A Day in Vietnam, 1968 (Freedom Found. award 1968). Contbr. articles to profl. jours. Vice-pres., dir. Unitarian Fellowship, Boca Raton, Fla., 1969-70. Decorated Bronze Star with combat V. Mem. Nat. Council Tchrs. English. Democrat. Avocations: sailing; aviculturist; carpenter. Home: Route 2 Box 9-B Pompano Beach FL 33067 Office: Broward Community Coll-N 1000 Coconut Creek Blvd Coconut Creek FL 33063

MEEKS, WILLIAM HERMAN, III, lawyer; b. Ft. Lauderdale, Fla., Dec. 30, 1939; s. Walter Herman and Elise Walker (McGuire) M.; m. Patricia Ann Rayburn, July 30, 1965 (div. 1971); 1 son, William Herman IV; m. Miriam Andrea Bedsole, Dec. 28, 1971; 1 dau., Julie Marie. A.B., Princeton U., 1961; LL.B., U. Fla., 1964; LL.M., N.Y. U., 1965. Bar: Fla. 1964. Ptnr. McCune, Hiaasen, Crum, Ferris & Gardner, Ft. Lauderdale, 1964—; dir. Attorneys Title Services, Inc. Mem. Fla. Bar, ABA, Broward County Bar Assn., Attys. Title Guaranty Fund, Ft. Lauderdale Hist. Soc., Ft. Lauderdale Mus., Phi Delta Phi. Democrat. Presbyterian. Clubs: Lauderdale Yacht, Tower. Lodge: Kiwanis. Office: McCune Hiaasen Crum Ferris & Gardner 25 S Andrews Ave PO Box 14636 Fort Lauderdale FL 33302

MEEM, JAMES LAWRENCE, JR., nuclear scientist; b. N.Y.C., Dec. 24, 1915; s. James Lawrence and Phyllis (Deaderick) M.; m. Buena Vista Speake, Sept. 5, 1940; children—James, John. B.S., Va. Mil. Inst., 1939; M.S., Ind. U., 1947, Ph.D., 1949. Aero. research sci. NACA, 1940-46; dir. bulk shielding reactor Oak Ridge Nat. Lab., 1950-53, in charge nuclear operation aircraft reactor expt., 1954-55; chief reactor sci. Alco Products, Inc., 1955-57; in charge startup and initial testing Army Package Power Reactor, 1957; prof. nuclear engring. U. Va., Charlottesville, 1957-81, dept. chmn., dir. reactor facility, 1957-77, prof. emeritus, 1981—; cons. U.S. Army Fgn. Sci. and Tech. Ctr., 1981—; vis. cons. nuclear fuel cycle programs Sandia Labs., Albuquerque, 1977-78; vis. staff mem. Los Alamos Sci. Lab., 1967-68; mem. U.S.-Japan Seminar Optimization of Nuclear Engring. Edn., Tokai-mura, 1973. Author: Two Group Reactor Theory, 1964. Fellow Am. Nuclear Soc. (sec. reactor ops. div. 1966-68, vice chmn. 1968-70, chmn. 1970-71, Exceptional Service award 1980); mem. Am. Phys. Soc., Am. Soc. Engring. Edn., SAR. Home: Mount Airy Route 12 Box 45 Charlottesville VA 22901

MEENAGHAN, GEORGE FRANCIS, college dean, chemical engineer; b. Holyoke, Mass., June 17, 1929; s. Patrick Joseph and Helen (Toher) M.; m. Mary Frances Dyer, June 6, 1953; children—Susan Lee, John David. B.S. in Chem. Engring., Va. Poly. Inst. and State U., 1952, M.S., 1954, Ph.D., 1956. Registered profl. engr., Tex. From asst. prof. to prof. chem. engring. Clemson U., S.C., 1955-68; prof., chmn. chem. dept. engring. Tex. Tech U., Lubbock, 1969-75, assoc. v.p. research, 1976-78; v.p. for acad. affairs, dean of coll. The Citadel, Charleston, S.C. 1979—; environ. cons. to numerous corps. Author: An Introduction to Chemical Engineering, 1959. Contbr. articles to profl. publs. Served to capt. U.S. Army, 1956-58. Mem. Am. Inst. Chem. Engrs., Am. Soc. Engring. Edn., Nat. Soc. Profl. Engrs., Smithsonian Assocs., Sigma Xi, Tau Beta Pi, Phi Lambda Upsilon, Phi Kappa Phi. Roman Catholic. Avocations: reading, bridge, golf. Home: 2-B Hammond Ave Charleston SC 29409 Office: Office of Vice Pres for Acad Affairs The Citadel Charleston SC 29409

MEFFERD, ROY B., JR., medical scientist, psychometrician; b. Hico, Tex., Sept. 22, 1920; s. Roy B. and Delfa (Russell) M.; m. Mary Louise Kay; children—Marsha Ellen, Roy Scott. A.S., Tarleton State U., 1937; B.S., Tex. A&M U., 1940, M.S., 1940; Ph.D., U. Tex., 1951. Research scientist bacteriology U. Tex., Austin, 1947-51; dir. metabolism lab. Southwest Found. for Research and Edn., San Antonio, 1951-54; dir. mental health research lab. Biochem. Inst. U. Tex., Austin, 1954-59; dir. psychiatric and psychosomatic research lab. Houston VA Med. Ctr., 1959-80; sr. cons. Birkman and Assocs., Inc., Houston, 1966—; prof. physiology Baylor Coll. of Medicine, Houston, 1949—; adj. prof. behavioral scis. Sch. Pub. Health, U. Tex., 1976—; adj. prof. psychology U. Houston, 1972-80. Contbr. articles to profl. jours. Served to capt. U.S. Army, 1942-47. Recipient Rosalie B. Hite cancer research fellowship, 1949-51; Damon Runyon cancer research fellow, 1952-53. Mem. Am. Psychol. Assn., Am. Physiol. Soc., Am. Chem. Soc. Avocations: painting; music. Home: 823 Longview St Sugar Land TX 77478 Office: Birkman & Assocs Inc Suite 1425 Continental Resources Bldg 3040 Post Oak Blvd Houston TX 77056

MEGARGEE, EDWIN INGLEE, psychology educator, researcher; b. Plainfield, N.J., Feb. 27, 1937; s. S. Edwin Megargee, Jr. and Jean (Inglee) Dunn; m. Ann Piemonte, Aug. 1, 1959; children—Elyn, Edwin Jr., Christopher, Stephen; m. Sara Jill Mercer, June 27, 1980; 1 stepchild, Heather Lynn Dunham. A.B. magna cum laude, Amherst Coll., 1958; Ph.D., U. Calif.-Berkeley, 1964. Licensed clin. psychologist, Fla.; Nat. Register of Health Service Providers. Asst. prof. U. Tex., Austin, 1964-67; assoc. prof. Fla. State U., Tallahassee, 1967-70, prof., 1970—; cons. U.S. Secret Service, 1980—; pres. Criminal Justice Assessment Service, Tallahassee. Author: Classifying Criminal Offenders, 1979; California Psychological Inventory Handbook, 1972; also 3 additional books. Contbr. articles to profl. jours. and chapters to books. Pres. Soc. Arts and Crafts, Tallahassee, 1978-79. Fellow Am. Psychol. Assn.; mem. Internat. Differential Treatment Assn. (vice pres. 1984-85), Am. Assn. Correctional Psychologists (pres. 1973-75, disting. achievement in correctional psychology award 1985); Am. Correctional Assn. (bd. dirs 1973-75), Capital Area Psychol. Assn. (pres. 1981), Phi Beta Kappa, Sigma Xi, Delta Sigma Rho. Club: Cosmos (Washington). Avocations: model railroading; painting; sculpting. Office: Psychology Dept Fla State Univ Tallahassee FL 32306

MEGGINSON, MARYLU, school nurse; b. Houston, Aug. 25, 1928; d. Forrest Lindsey McCormick and Ina (Ponder) Clement; m. Bill Megginson, Feb. 7, 1949; children—Arthur Wayne, David Lee, Deborah Ann. Diploma R.N. Hendrick Meml. Hosp., Abilene, Tex., 1948. Head nurse Henrick Meml. Hosp., Abilene, 1949-58, staff supr. 1958-62; school nurse Abilene Ind. Sch. Dist., 1979—; office nurse to physicians, Abilene, 1970—, part time. Nurse ARC, Abilene, 1949-84, served after tornado in Sundown, Tex., 1949. Mem. Tex. State Tchrs. Assn. (sec. school health sect. Abilene, 1982-84), Am. Nurses Assn., Tex. Nurses Assn., Nat. Assn. Sch. Nurses, Tex. Sch. Health Assn., Abilene Educators Assn., Am. Bus. Women's Assn. (pres., Woman of Yr.

award 1972). Democrat. Baptist. Home: 649 Westview Abilene TX 79603 Office: Abilene Ind Sch Dist 4250 Potomac Abilene TX 79605

MEGGS, PHILIP BAXTER, art educator, graphic designer; b. Newberry, S.C., May 30, 1942; s. Wallace N. and Sara Elizabeth (Pruitt) M.; m. Libby Phillips, Aug. 15, 1964; children—Andrew, Elizabeth. Student U. S.C.-Florence, 1960-61; B.F.A., Va. Commonwealth U., 1964, M.F.A., 1971. Sr. designer Reynolds Aluminum, Richmond, Va., 1965-66; art dir. A.H. Robins, Richmond, 1966-68; mem. faculty Va. Commonwealth U., Richmond, 1968-74, chmn. dept. comml. art and design, 1974—. Author: A History of Graphic Design, 1983; (with others) Typographic Design: Form and Communication, 1985. Contbr. articles to profl. jours. Recipient cert. excellence Assn. Am. Pubs. Office: Va Commonwealth U 325 N Harrison St Richmond VA 23227

MEGILL, ROBERT EDGAR, retired oil company executive, consultant; b. Lawrence, Kans., Nov. 26, 1923; s. David Lucian and Margaret (Caskey) M.; m. Margaret Ann Webb, Feb. 24, 1945; children—Gregory Alan, Jana Lynn Green. B.S. in Geol. Engring., U. Tulsa, 1948. Various positions Exxon Co., U.S.A., Houston, 1941-65, div. planning mgr., Corpus Christi, Tex., 1965-73, coordinator planning, Houston, 1973-76, coordinator econ. evaluation, 1976-84; cons., advisor to petroleum industry. Author: An Introduction to Exploration Economics, 2d edit., 1979; How to be a More Productive Employee, edit., 1980; May I Touch Your Life (poems), 1979; An Introduction to Risk Analysis, 2d edit., 1984; Life in the Corporate Orbit, 1981; Long Range Exploration Planning, 1985: contbr. articles to profl. jours. Served with USN, 1942-45, PTO. Mem. Am. Assn. Petroleum Geologists (assoc. editor 1983—, columnist Explorer Mag. 1984—). Republican. Methodist. Lodge: Masons. Avocations: golf; reading; writing. Home: 4314 Valley Branch Dr Kingwood TX 77339

MEGO, JOHN LORENCE, biochemistry educator; b. Pukwana, S.D.; s. Michael and Katherine (Putera) M.; m. Elizabeth Eileen Williams, Dec. 26, 1953 (div. Aug. 1975); children—Janet C., Paul A.; m. 2d, Barbara Louise Dunn, July 2, 1976. A.S., Mitchell Coll., 1953; Ph.D., Johns Hopkins U., 1960. Research assoc. Neurosurgery Research Lab., Balt. City Hosps., 1960-67; instr. Johns Hopkins Sch. Medicine, Balt., 1960-67; U.S.-Czechoslovak Nat. Acad. Sci. Exchange fellow, Bratislava, Czechoslovakia, 1967-68; mem. faculty U. Ala., University, 1968—, prof. biology and biochemistry, 1975—. Served with U.S. Navy, 1941-53. Grantee NIH, 1972-75, USPHS, 1976-79; fellow Del. Generale Researche Scientifique et Technicale, France, 1979. Mem. Am. Soc. Cell Biology, Am. Chem. Soc., Soc. Biol. Chemists, Sigma Xi. Contbr. articles to various publs. Home: Route 1 Box 272 Northport AL 35476 Office: Box 1927 University of Ala University AL 35486

MEGOWN, CHARLES FREDERICK, naval officer, health care administrator; b. Sharpsville, Pa., Aug. 2, 1945; s. Charles F. and Anna Rose (Fullerton) M.; m. Eileen B. Shields, Dec. 9, 1967; children—Cathleen Eleanor, Charles Frederick. A.A., Ariz. Western Coll., 1974; B.A., Pepperdine U., 1977; M.B.A., Boston U., 1982. Enlisted U.S. Navy, 1965, commd. and advanced through grades to lt. Med. Service Corps, 1980; with U.S. Navy Health Care Facilities, St. Alban's Hosp., N.Y., 1965-66, 1st Marine Div. Vietnam, 1966-67, facilities at Quantico, 1968-70, Yuma, Ariz., 1972-76, Camp Le Jeune Hosp., N.C., 1976-79; adminstr. Field Med. Service Sch., Camp Le Jeune, 1979-83, commanding officer Med. Co., 1983—; cons. in field; condr. seminars on small bus. mgmt.; dir. Mentor Assocs., Jacksonville, 1978—. Decorated Purple Heart; Cross of Gallantry (Vietnam). Mem. Am. Mgmt. Assn. Club: Toastmasters. Contbr. articles to profl. jours. Home: 102 Stewart Ct Jacksonville NC 28540

MEHARG, MICHAEL PATRICK, dentist, army officer; b. Troy, N.Y., Dec. 6, 1949; s. James W. and Jane (Lane) M.; m. Corinne Sullivan, Aug. 7, 1971; children—Jesse David, Erin Lane. B.S. in Biology, Lemoyne Coll., 1971; D.D.S., Georgetown U., 1975. Research asst. Smithsonian Inst., Washington, 1972-75; commd. 2d lt. U.S. Army, 1973, advanced through grades to lt. col., 1986; dental intern, Ft. Sill, Okla., 1975-76; resident in gen. practice dentistry Reynolds Army Hosp., Ft. Sill, 1975-76; chief clinician, Heidelberg, Fed. Republic Germany, 1976-80; pvt. practice dentistry, Troy, N.Y., 1980-82; mem. staff-dental activity, Ft. Bragg, N.C., 1982—. Coach YMCA, Fayetteville, N.C., 1983, 84, 85; vol. dental services Georgetown Orgn. for Latin Am. Concern, Dominican Republic, 1981, 82, 83. Recipient Essay award Block Drug Co., 1975. Decorated Army Commendation medal, 1979; Expert Field Med. Badge, 1984; Mem. ADA, Assn. U.S. Army, Psi Omega. Roman Catholic. Avocations: children's literature; sports; travel. Home: 3509 Sugarcane Circle Fayetteville NC 28303 Office: Dental Activity Fort Bragg NC 28307

MEHENDALE, HARIHARA MAHADEVA, toxicologist, educator; b. Philya, India, Jan. 12, 1942; s. Shinginakodhu Mahadeva Bhat and Narmada M. (Tahmankar) M.; m. Rekha H. Joshi, May 10, 1968; children—Roopa, Neelesh. B.Sc., Karnatak U., Dharwar, India, 1963; M.S. in Physiology, N.C. State U., 1966, Ph.D., 1969. Diplomate, Am. Bd. Toxicology (bd. dirs. 1986—), Acad. Toxicol. Scis. Postdoctoral fellow in toxicology U. Ky., Lexington, 1969-71; vis. fellow Nat. Inst. Environ. Health Sci., 1971-72, staff fellow, 1972-75; asst. prof. dept. pharmacology and toxicology, U. Miss. Med. Center, Jackson, 1975-78, assoc. prof., 1978-80, prof., 1980, dir. toxicology tng. program, 1982—; vis. prof. dept. forensic medicine, Karolinska Inst., Stockholm, 1983-84. Mem. editorial bds. Toxicology and Applied Pharmacology, 1983-86, Jour. Toxicology and Environ. Health, 1983-86. Overseas editor Indian Jour. Pharmacology, 1984—. Contbr. articles to profl. jours. Past pres. India Assn. Miss.; bd. dirs. Ctr. for Toxicology, J.J. Coll. Criminal Justice, N.Y.C. Recipient Sr. Fogarty Internat. fellowship, 1983; grantee NIH, Miss. Lung Assn., Miss., Hearth Assn., EPA. Mem. AAAS, Am. Soc. Pharmacology and Exptl. Therapeutics, Soc. Toxicology, Am. Chem. Soc., Internat. Soc. Study Xenobiotics, Am. Thoracic Soc., Internat. Union Pharmacologists, South Central Toxicology Assn., Assn. Scis. Indian Origin in Am., Indian Sci. Congress Assn., Entomol. Soc. India, Miss. Acad. Sci. (Outstanding Contbns. to Sci. award 1986), Miss Heart Assn., Sigma Xi (chpt. v.p. 1981-82, pres. 1982-83). Mem. editorial bd. Jour. Toxicology and Applied Pharmacology, 1983-86, Jour. Toxicology and Environ. Health, 1983-86. Contbr. articles to profl. jours. Home: 58 Crownpointe Dr Jackson MS 39211 Office: Dept Pharmacology/Toxicology 2500 N State St Jackson MS 39216

MEHERIN, MARGARET WILSON, accountant; b. Mobile, Ala., Jan. 5, 1955; d. Joseph Henry and Rose Patricia (McNamara) Wilson; B.S.C., Spring Hill Coll., 1975; m. Dennis Peter Meherin, May 31, 1975; 1 dau., Bridget Claire. Staff acct. L.E. Nicholas & Co., Mobile, 1975, Morrison & Smith, C.P.A.s, Mobile, 1975-77; pvt. practice public acctg., Mobile, 1977—; sec.-treas. Wilson Electric Co., Inc., Mobile, 1980—, Gulf Coast Electronics, Inc., Mobile, 1980-81. Mem. Art Patrons League Mobile, 1979—; sec.-treas. Med. Clinic Bd., Second of the City of Mobile, 1980-82. C.P.A., Ala. Mem. Am. Inst. C.P.A.s, Am. Soc. Women Accts., Am. Women's Soc. C.P.A.s, Ala. Soc. C.P.A.s. Roman Catholic. Home: 1283 Skywood Dr Mobile AL 36609 Office: 32 Tacon St Mobile AL 36607

MEHURIN, CHESTER ARTHUR, real estate development company executive; b. Staunton, Va., Aug. 29, 1894; s. Oscar Cary and Ida May (Stevens) M.; m. Evelyn Marie Grace, Dec. 21, 1944; children—Chester Arthur Jr., Julia Penn Challenger. Student Templeton Coll., 1913-14. Vice pres. Chocolate Products Co., Balt., 1919-24, Mavis Bottling Co., N.Y.C., 1925-32; sec., dir. Pepsi-Cola Co., N.Y.C., 1933-38; pres. Pepsi-Cola Bottling, New Orleans, 1939-50; pres. The Mehurin Corp., New Orleans, 1950—. Pres., Met. Crime Commn., New Orleans, 1957-58; bd. dirs. Internat. House World Commerce and Affairs, New Orleans; bd. dirs. New Orleans Opera House Assn., New Orleans Philharmonic Symphony Soc.; mem. vestry Christ Episcopal Cathedral. Served to capt. U.S. Army, 1918-1919. Recipient Presdl. award of Duty Gen. Staff, Washington. Mem. Founders and Patriots Am. (pres.), S.A.R. (pres. La.), Soc. Colonial Wars. Clubs: Knight of the Golden Circle; Army and Navy (Washington); Pickwick, Lake Shore, Stratford, New Orleans Country. Republican. Avocation: travel. Home: 1524 3d St New Orleans LA 70130 Office: The Mehurin Corp New Orleans LA 70130

MEINKE, ROY WALTER, electrical engineer; b. Cleve., Aug. 7, 1929; s. George F. and Marie (Reyer) M.; B.S., Miami U., Oxford, Ohio, 1952; postgrad. Ohio State U., 1952-53, 67-68; postgrad. in engring. Columbia Pacific U., 1985—. Asst. instr. dept. math. Ohio State U., Columbus, 1953; tchr. high sch., Edgerton, Ohio, 1953-54, Kingman, Ariz., 1954-56; aerodynamics engr. N.Am. Aviation, Los Angeles, 1956-57; instr. physics dept. Central State Coll., Edmond, Okla., 1957-58; elec. engr. Boeing Co., Seattle, 1958-62, Huntsville, Ala., 1962-74; mem. staff engring. mgmt. Lockheed Corp., Houston, 1974—. Co-pilot Mercy Flight Systems, 1973-74; treas. Houston United Campus Christian Life Com., 1983; judge Harris County Optimists Club Youth Scholarship Fund, 1983-85. Recipient Apollo Achievement award NASA, 1970, Group Achievement awards, 1979, 82, 83; recipient Phase III Pilot Proficiency Wings Dept. Transp., 1982. Mem. IEEE (sr.), AIAA (Outstanding Sect. award Houston 1979), Nat. Soc. Profl. Engrs. Mem. United Ch. of Christ (dir. S.E. conf. 1969-73). Home: 2935 Calder Dr E-8 League City TX 77573 Office: 2400 NASA Rd 1 Houston TX 77058

MEINS, VIVIAN ARLENE, nursing home administrator; b. DeWitt, Ark., Sept. 15, 1931; d. Robert Alnzo and Flora Dee (Allen) Manis; m. Wilbur Nolan Meins, June 29, 1952; 1 son; Michael Allen. Student pub. schs., DeWitt. Asst. adminstr. DeWitt City Nursing Home, 1968-76, adminstr., 1976—; consumer rep. Ark. Bd. Psychology, 1983—. Vice pres. Hosp. Aux., 1970-71. Mem. Ark. Nursing Assn. (pub. relations com. 1980-83). Democrat. Baptist.

MEISCH, BETTE JEAN, hospital nursing administrator, consultant; b. Sioux City, Iowa, July 22, 1946; d. Willie D. and Alice Joyce (Barry) Davis; m. Arthur Sterrett, June 20, 1970; 1 child, Bradley Sterrett. Grad. St. Joseph Mercy Sch. Nursing, 1967. Asst. charge nurse coronary intensive care St. Joseph Mercy Hosp./Marion Health Ctr., Sioux City, Iowa, 1967-71; staff nurse Wiskek Community Hosp., N.D., 1971-73; staff nurse Burgess Meml. Hosp., Onawa, Iowa, 1973-75, operating room supr., 1975-77, infection control nurse, 1977-79, infection control/employee health nurse, 79-82, risk mgr., 1982-84; surveillance coordinator infection control/employee health Pendleton Meml. Hosp., New Orleans, 1984-85; quality resource cons. Northshore Regional Med. Ctr., Slidell, La., 1985—. Mem. Dist. A. Practitioners in Infection Control (pres. 1980). Democrat. Roman Catholic. Home: 317 Margon Ct Slidell LA 70458 Office: Northshore Regional Med Ctr 100 Medical Center Dr Slidell LA 70461

MEISTER, JOHN DAVID, engineering company executive; b. Miami, Fla., Apr. 16, 1939; s. Clarence Raymond and Rose E. (Dasch) M.; B.S. in Elec. Engring., U. N.Mex., 1962; m. Martha Elizabeth Terwilliger, June 30, 1962; children—John David, James Christopher. Exploration geophysicist Humble Oil Co., Houston, 1962; mgr. systems engring. TRW, Inc., San Bernardino, Calif., 1965-68; program dir. Tracor, Inc., Austin, Tex., 1968-74; pres. Meister Engring. Inc., Austin, 1983—; pres., chief exec. officer Key Concepts, Inc., 1984-85, now dir. Active U. Tex. Internat. Student Host Family Program, 1969—; adult vol. Capitol Area council Boy Scouts Am., 1972—, recipient Wood Badge; Tex. instr. Nat. Hunter Safety Program. Served to 1st lt. USAF, 1962-65. Registered profl. engr., registered pub. surveyor, Tex. Mem. Armed Forces Communication Electronics Assn. (founding pres. Austin-Bergstrom chpt.), Tex. Computer Industry Council (bd. dirs.), Inventors and Entrepreneurs Assn. (bd. dirs.), Kappa Alpha. Republican. Presbyterian (elder). Research, publs. in systems engring. field. Home: 8307 High Oak Dr Austin TX 78759 Office: Echelon 4 Suite 400 9430 Research Blvd Austin TX 78759

MEITZEN, MANFRED OTTO, religious studies educator; b. Houston, Dec. 12, 1930; s. Otto Hugo and Laura Emma (Munsch) M.; m. Frederica Haden Kilmer, May 16, 1970. B.A., Rice U., 1952; M.Div., Wartburg Sem., Dubuque, Iowa, 1956; Ph.D., Harvard U., 1961. Vicar, Peace Luth. Ch., Menomonie, Wis., 1955, Sharon Luth. Ch., Pasadena, Tex., 1959, Zion Luth. Ch., Houston, 1960; assoc. prof. religious studies Rocky Mountain Coll., Billings, Mont., 1961-65; prof., chmn. dept. religious studies W.Va. U., Morgantown, 1965—. Contbr. chpts. to books, also articles to various profl. jours. Columnist Dominion-Post newspaper, Morgantown, 1975—. Pres. Oakview Homeowners Assn., Morgantown, 1979-81. Harvard Div. Sch. fellow, 1958; doctoral fellow Rockefeller Found., 1959-60; Sheldon travelling fellow Harvard U., 1961; recipient Outstanding Tchr. award W.Va. U. Coll. Arts and Scis., 1979-81. Mem. Am. Acad. Religion, Univ. Profs. for Acad. Order (pres. 1979, bd. dirs. 1980-83). Republican. Avocations: piano and organ; hunting; skiing; motorcycling. Home: 119 Forest Dr Morgantown WV 26505 Office: Dept Relgious Studies W Va U 324 Stansbury Hall Morgantown WV 26505

MEITZLER, JEAN MILLER, insurance company official; b. Laurel, Miss., Oct. 15, 1926; d. Clifton Valmer and Katie Cornelia Williams Miller; m. Charles Edward Meitzler, Aug. 22, 1948 (div. Dec. 1956); 1 child, Charles Edward. Cert. advanced casualty U. Houston, 1970, cert. fire-comml. risks, 1972; cert. Ins. Inst. Am., 1974. Cert. profl. ins. woman. Mgr., B. Whitfield, Picayune, Miss., 1946-48, 52-57, J. Ben Poteet, Houston, 1958-63; agt. Trezavant & Cochran, Houston, 1963-65; account mgr. Alexander & Alexander Inc., Houston, 1965-76, Frank B. Hall & Co., Houston, 1976-81; account exec. Howe & Jones, Houston, after 1981; now supr. property and casualty dept. Fred S. James & Co. Tex., Inc. Lector, minister eucharist St. Leo the Great Parish, Houston; founder Div. Ministry and Div.-We-Care, Houston; sec. Bd. Pastoral Care to Div., Separated and Widowed, Houston-Galveston Diocese, adv. Tribunal. Recipient plaque Houston-Galveston Diocese, 1983. Mem. Ins. Women Bellaire (charter; pres. 1972-73; cert. of Appreciation 1983), Nat. Assn. Ins. Women, Fedn. Ins. Women Tex. Democrat. Roman Catholic. Home: 12410 Ladbroke Ln Houston TX 77039

MELANCON, DONALD JAMES, computer science educator; b. Opelousas, La., Oct. 14, 1946; s. Willis Paul and Gladys (Miller) M.; m. Cindy Francine Hills, Aug. 21, 1971. B.S., Oklahoma City U., 1972; M.B.A., West Tex. State U., 1975. Cert. data processor, computer programmer Inst. Cert. Computer Profls. Pres. Bus. Software Systems, Amarillo, Tex., 1976—, Profl. Bus. Info. Systems, Inc., 1980—; instr. computer info. systems West Tex. State U., Canyon, 1977-83; instr. computer sci. U. S.W. La., Lafayette, 1983—. Mem. Data Processing Mgmt. Assn., Assn. Computing Machinery, Assn. Inst. Cert. Computer Profls. Republican. Roman Catholic. Home: 3508 Kileen St Amarillo TX 79109 Office: PO Box 7948 Amarillo TX 79114

MELANCON, MICHAEL RAY, business machines company executive; b. Beaumont, Tex., May 29, 1950; s. Joseph Whitney and Hester Dave M.; B.B.A., Lamar U., 1972; postgrad. bus. adminstrn. Tex. So. U., 1977—; m. Gradie B. Hopper, Aug. 12, 1972; children—Leah Michelle, Ray Michael. Counselor, High Sch. Equivalency Program, Beaumont, 1971-72; acct. Ernst & Whinney, Detroit, 1972-75; account rep. IBM, Houston, 1975-84, bus. programs adminstr., 1984—; v.p., chief operating officer African Expressions, Inc., 1984—. Adviser, Jr. Achievement, 1973-75. Mem. Nat. Assn. Accts., Nat. Assn. Black Accts., Delta Sigma Pi. Roman Catholic. Club: Toastmasters Internat. Home: 6859 Calle Del Paz N Boca Raton FL 33432

MELANCON, ROBERT MICHAEL, executive search firm owner; b. Biloxi, Miss., July 14, 1947; s. Andrew James and Elizabeth (Mangin) M.; m. S. Lynell Langston, July 31, 1968; children—Monique Lynell, R. Michael, Jr. B.S. in Bus. Mgmt. cum laude, Loyola U., New Orleans, 1972; A.S. in Engring. Tech., Miss. Gulf Coast Jr. Coll., 1967. Sr. personnel analyst Shell Oil Co., New Orleans, 1967-73; personnel mgr. Celanese Corp., Chatham, N.J., 1973-77; zone personnel mgr. Frito-Lay Inc., Dallas, 1977-80; mng. ptnr. McKeen Melancon & Co., Dallas, 1980—. Served with USAR, 1967-73. Mem. Dallas Personnel Assn., Am. Soc. for Tng. and Devel., Am. Compensation Assn., Am. Soc. for Personnel Adminstrn., Human Resource Planning Soc., Cross Keys. Republican. Methodist. Avocations: stock market analysis; tennis; racquetball; golf. Office: McKeen Melancon & Co 1200 S Sherman St Suite 180 Richardson TX 75081

MELCOLM, ALBERT EDWARD, JR., broadcasting company executive; b. Jacksonville, Fla., Apr. 17, 1952; s. Albert Edward Melcolm and Ruth Nell (Simpson) Dean; 1 dau., Amanda Lynn. Student Fla. Jr. Coll., 1969-71. With advt. staff WQIK-FM, Jacksonville, Fla., 1972—, sales mgr., 1981—. Founder, v.p. Jacksonville Balloon Club, 1983-84. Recipient Level IV Balloon Fedn. Am. Pilot Achievement award, 1982. Mem. Balloon Fedn. Am. Republican. Roman Catholic. Home: 14031 Inlet Dr Jacksonville FL 32225 Office: 5555 Radio Ln Jacksonville FL 32207

MELDE, CRAIG HENRY, architect; b. Dallas, May 28, 1951; s. Gus Simon and Bernice (Gersch) M.; m. Rebecca Rea Russell, Dec. 29, 1973; 1 child, Nicholas Craig. B. Arch., U. Tex.-Austin, 1974. Ptnr. JC Constrn., Dallas, 1974-75; prodn. and design architect Reavis Assoc. Architects, Dallas, 1974-76; urban planner, designer Dallas Planning Dept., 1976-78; ptnr. ArchiTexas, Dallas, 1978—; adj. prof. architecture U. Tex.-Arlington, fall 1984. Mem. Luth. Ch. Synodical Commn. on Architecture. Avocations: handball; photography; travel. Home: 5823 Prospect Dallas TX 75206 Office: ArchiTexas 1907 Marilla Dallas TX 75201

MELEAR, ERIK LAMONT, civil/environmental engineer; b. West Palm Beach, Fla., Oct. 31, 1950; s. Richard Charles and Beverly Layne (Beacham) M. A.A., Palm Beach Jr. Coll., 1970; B.S., Fla. Atlantic U., 1973, M.A., 1975; Ph.D., U. Fla., 1986. Registered profl. engr., real estate broker, Fla., lobbyist. Structural engr. Alpine Engineered Products, Pompano Beach, Fla., 1973-74; lab. instr. U. Fla., Gainesville, 1976-77, 79-82, lab. chemist, 1977-79; acad. counselor U. Fla. Athletic Assn., 1981-82; assoc. environ. engr. Boyle Engring. Corp., Orlando, Fla., 1983—. Vice chmn. bd. adjustment City of Gainesville, 1981-83; chmn. Gainesville Housing Bd., 1981-83, mem., 1980-83; bd. dirs. Conservation Planning Coalition of Alachua County, 1981-83; mem. Growth Mgmt. Adv. Com., Alachua County, 1980-83; chmn. Growth Mgmt. Citizens Adv. Com., Orange County 1985—; mem. Emergency Med. Services Bd., Alachua County, 1979-81; mem. Code Enforcement Bd., Gainesville, 1982, Orlando, 1985. Mem. Democratic exec. com., Alachua County, 1980-83, Orange County, 1983—. Mem. Am. Water Works Assn., Am. Chem. Soc., Am. Inst. Chem. Engrs., Am. Soc. Civil Engrs., Water Pollution Control Fedn., Fla. Blue Key, Sigma Xi, Omicron Delta Kappa, Tau Beta Pi. Presbyterian. Home: 1306 Shorewood Dr Orlando FL 32806 Office: Boyle Engring Corp 320 E South St Orlando FL 32801

MELECKI, SHERRY MILLER, educational administrator; b. Brownfield, Tex., Oct. 13, 1950; d. T.J. and Lois (Forrest) Miller; m. Thomas G. Melecki, May 27, 1978; 1 child, Meredith Lynn. B.A. in English, Angelo State U., 1971; M.Ed., Tex. Tech U., 1972. Cert. tchr. Residence hall dir. Ball State U., Muncie, Ind., 1973-77; coordinator residence life So. Ill. U., Carbondale, 1977-78; asst. to dir. housing and food service U. Tex.-Austin, 1978-81, coordinator women's residence halls, 1981-84, coordinator mgmt. tng. and career devel., 1984—. Active Am. Cancer Soc. Mem. Am. Soc. Tng. and Devel., Intergovtl. Tng. Council, Personnel Assn. Tex. State Colls. and Univs., AAUW, United Meth. Women. Democrat. Avocations: reading; baking. Home: 3607 Ambleside Austin TX 78759 Office: U Tex 2613 Wichita Austin TX 78713

MELGAR, JULIO, retired mechanical engineer; b. Bklyn., July 4, 1922; s. Lorenzo and Maria (Lopez) M.; B.M.E., U. Detroit, 1952. Mech. engr. Chance Vought Aircraft, Dallas, 1952-53, Wyatt C. Hedrick Architects and Engrs., Dallas, 1953, Zumwalt & Vinther, Cons. Engrs., Dallas, 1953-54, Joe Hoppe, Inc., Dallas, 1954-55, A.J. Boynton & Co., Dallas, 1956-57, Wyatt Metal and Boiler Works, Dallas, 1958, Tinker AFB, Okla., 1958-60; mech. engr. FAA, Ft. Worth, 1960-85. Mem. Metroplex Recreation Council, 1975—; mem. Tarrant County Mental Health and Mental Retardation, Ft. Worth Opera Guild, Dallas Opera Guild, Goodwill Industries; bd. dirs. Fort Worth Opera Assn., Tarrant County Humane Soc., Animal Protection Inst. Served with USMCR, 1943-45. Mem. Nat. Soc. Profl. Engrs., ASME, Am. Soc. Heating, Refrigerating and Air Conditioning Engrs., Profl. Soc. Protective Design, Fed. Bus. Assn., Amateur Athletic Union. Roman Catholic. Home: 6108 Menger Ave Dallas TX 75227

MELL, SHIRLEY ANN, physical education teacher; b. Savannah, Ga., Sept. 10, 1938; d. Charles Edwin Mell and Ida M. Dutton. B.S., Ga. State Coll. Women, 1960; M.S., U. Tenn., 1966. Tchr. Fulton County Schs., East Point, Ga., 1960-65; tchr. Va. Poly. U., Blacksburg, Va., 1966-69; tchr. Savannah-Chatham Sch. (Ga.), 1970—, dept. chmn., 1973—; cons. Programmed Instrn. Va., 1968-69. Actress, backstage worker Little Theatre of Savannah, 1969—. Recipient honor award Little Theatre of Savannah, 1973-74. Mem. Ga. Assn. Health, Phys. Edn., Recreation (pres. health div. 1980-81), Am. Alliance Health, Phys. Edn., Recreation, Dance (chmn. secondary phys. edn. council 1983-84), Ga. Assn. Health, Phys. Edn., Recreation (chmn. 1st dist. evaluation com. 1978-79), AAUW, Delta Kappa Gamma (chmn. membership 1982-84). Roman Catholic. Office: Savannah High Sch 500 Washington Ave Savannah GA 31405

MELNICK, ALICE JEAN, counselor; b. St. Louis, Dec. 25, 1931; d. Nathan and Henrietta (Hausfater) Fisher; B.J., U. Tex., Austin, 1952; M.Ed., N. Tex. State U., 1974; m. Harold Melnick, May 24, 1953; children—Susan, Vikki, Patrice. Lic. profl. counselor. Reporter, San Antonio Light, 1952-53; instr. journalism project Upward Bound, So. Meth. U., Dallas, 1967-71; instr. writing El Dallas County Community Coll., Dallas, part time 1972-74; instr. human devel. Richland Community Coll., Dallas, part-time 1974-79; tchr. English and journalism Dallas Ind. Sch. Dist., 1969-81; counselor Ursuline Acad., 1981—. Mem. Tex. Assn. Counseling and Devel., Am. Assn. Counseling and Devl., Nat. Vocat. Guidance Assn. Democrat. Jewish. Clubs: Dallas Sports Car, Dallas Camera. Home: 6730 Desco Dr Dallas TX 75225 Office: Ursuline Acad 4900 Walnut Hill Ln Dallas TX 75229

MELODY, MICHAEL EDWARD, political science educator; b. Phila., Oct. 14, 1947; s. Edward Joseph and Mary Rita (Marotta) M.; B.S., St. Joseph's U., 1969; M.A., U. Notre Dame, 1971, Ph.D., 1976. Instr., U. Notre Dame, South Bend, Ind., 1974-76, research assoc., 1976; vis. asst. prof. Kenyon Coll., Gambier, Ohio, 1977; asst. prof. St. Leo Coll., Fla., 1977-79; assoc. prof. Barry U., Miami, Fla., 1979—. Editor and coordinator: Native American Indian Policy Network, 1981—; mem. editorial bd. Policy Perspectives, 1984—. Contbr. articles to profl. jours. Mem. adv. council Dade County Inst. Govt., 1984; mem. Forum North Dade County, Fla., 1984—. Named Outstanding Faculty Mem., St. Leo Coll., 1978. Mem. Am. Polit. Sci. Assn., So. Polit. Sci. Assn., Midwest Polit. Sci. Assn., Fla. Polit. Sci. Assn., Am. Anthrop. Assn., for Polit. and Legal Anthropology, Am. Folklore Soc., Native Am. Policy Network, Am. Ethnological Soc., Western Soc. Sci. Assn. Avocation: backpacking. Home: 38 Allan Rd Hollywood FL 33023 Office: Barry Univ 11300 NE 2d Ave Miami FL 33161

MELOY, SYBIL PISKUR, lawyer; b. Chgo., Dec. 1, 1939; d. Michael M. and Laura (Stevenson) Piskur; children—William, Brad. B.S., U. Ill., 1961; J.D., Ill. Inst. Tech., 1965; postgrad. John Marshall Law Sch., 1966-72, Harvard U., 1979. Bar: Ill. 1965. Patent chemist G.D. Searle & Co., Skokie, Ill., 1961-65, patent atty., 1965-67, sr. atty., 1967-71, internat. counsel, 1971-72; regional counsel Abbott Labs., North Chicago, Ill., 1972-78; assoc. firm J.P. Biestek & Assocs., Arlington Heights, Ill., 1978-79; asst. gen. counsel Alberto Culver Co., Melrose Park, Ill., 1979-83; corp. counsel Key Pharms., Miami, Fla., 1983—; of counsel firm Palmer, Blackman, Mancini & Riebandt P.C., 1980-83; adj. prof. U. Miami Sch. Law. Recipient BNA prize, 1965. Mem. ABA, Chgo. Bar Assn., Am. Patent Law Assn., Am. Chem. Soc., Lic. Execs. Soc., Phi Beta Kappa, Phi Kappa Phi, Iota Sigma Pi. Home: 1915 Brickell Ave Apt C-1108 Miami FL 33129 Office: 4400 Biscayne Blvd Miami FL 33137

MELSON, GORDON ANTHONY, chemistry educator; b. Sheffield, Yorkshire, Eng., July 6, 1937; came to U.S., 1969, naturalized, 1977; s. John Albert and Dorothy Whiley (Nelson) M.; married; children—Michael Iain, Sharon Jane. B.S. with honors, Sheffield U., Eng., 1959, Ph.D., 1962. Research assoc. Ohio State U., 1962-64; lectr. chemistry Strathclyde U., 1964-69; asst. prof. Mich. State U., 1969-75; assoc. prof. Va. Commonwealth U., 1975-80, prof., 1980—, chmn. dept. chemistry, 1983—. Editor: Coordination Chemistry of Macrocyclic Compounds, 1979, Transition Metal Chemistry #8, 1983, Transition Metal Chemistry #9, 1985. Mem. Am. Chem. Soc. Office: Va Commonwealth Univ Box 2006 1001 W Main St Richmond VA 23284-0001

MELTON, BETH H., marketing specialist; b. New Orleans, June 26, 1943; d. Thomas N. and Lelia R. (Reilly) Morey; m. Lance E. Herrington, Apr. 19, 1964; children—Shannon, Amie; m. James M. Melton, Apr. 17, 1976. B.A., Mich. State U., 1965, M.A., 1967. Instr., Grandledge High Sch., Mich., 1965-69, Brookhaven Community Coll., Dallas, 1972-82; program dir. Am. Lung Assn., Dallas, 1974-79; curriculum specialist Dallas Ind. Sch. Dist., 1980-82; dir. mktg. Spine Edn. Ctr., Dallas, 1982—. Author articles in field. Troop leader Girl Scouts U.S.A., 1971-81; spl. events chair PTA, 1970-72. Land Grant scholar, 1961. Mem. Am. Soc. Safety Engrs. (assoc., membership com. 1984-85, newsletter editor 1985—), Am. Soc. Tng. and Devel. Office: Spine Edn Ctr 6161 Harry Hines Blvd #312 Dallas TX 75235

MELTON, HOWELL WEBSTER, judge: b. Atlanta, Dec. 15, 1923; s. Holmes and Alma (Combee) M.; m. Margaret Catherine Wolfe, Mar. 4, 1950; children—Howell Webster, Carol Anne. J.D., U. Fla. 1948. Bar: Fla. 1948. Mem. firm Upchurch, Melton & Upchurch, St. Augustine, 1948-61; judge 7th Jud. Circuit Fla., St. Augustine, 1961-77; U.S. Dist. Ct. Middle Dist. Fla., Jacksonville, 1977—. Past chmn. Fla. Conf. Circuit Judges, 1974. Trustee, Flagler Coll., St. Augustine; past chmn. bd. trustees Methodist Ch. Served with U.S. Army, 1943-46. Recipient Disting. Service award St. Augustine Jaycees, 1953. Mem. ABA, St. Johns County Bar Assn., Volsuia County Bar Assn.,

Jacksonville Bar Assn., Fed. Bar Assn., Fla. Bar Assn. (past chmn. council bar pres.'s), Am. Judicature Soc., Fla. Blue Key, Phi Delta Theta, Phi Delta Phi. Clubs: Ponce de Leon Country (St. Augustine); Sawgrass (Ponte Vedra, Fla.): Fla. Yacht (Jacksonville). Lodges: Masons, Kiwanis (past pres.). Home: 41 Carrera St Saint Augustine FL 32084 also 6208 Lake Lugano Dr Jacksonville FL 32216 Office: US Dist Ct 311 W Monroe St Jacksonville FL 32201

MELTON, KATHERINE ROSE, surgeon, gynecologist, nutritionist; b. Eatonton, Ga., Dec. 25, 1926; d. Guyton and Katharine Harwell (Denham) Melton. B.S., U. N.C., 1950; M.D., Womans Med. Coll. Pa., 1954. Diplomate Am. Bd. Surgery. Intern N.C. Meml. Hosp., Chapel Hill, 1954-55; resident in surgery Hosp. Woman's Med. Coll. Pa., Phila., 1955-59; practice medicine specializing in surgery, Matthews, N.C., 1959-70, Charlotte, N.C., 1970—; mem. staff Mercy Hosp., Charlotte; farmer, caprine culturist, 1968—. Mem. AMA, So. Med. Assn., N.C. Med. Soc., Mecklenburg County Med. Soc., Am. Dairy Goat Soc. Democrat. Rosicrucian. Home: Route 4 Box 7528 Old Dowd Rd Charlotte NC 28208 Office: 1900 Randolph Rd Suite 718 Charlotte NC 28207

MELTON, LARRY LEON, banker; b. Chickasha, Okla., July 17, 1938; s. Alfred Leon and Yvonne (Shaber) M.; m. J'Nevelyn Lee, Sept. 3, 1960; children—Julie Lee, Jeffrey Leon. B.S. in Engring., Tex. Tech U., 1961, B.A. in Math., 1961. Registered profl. engr., Tex. Staff engr. Phillips Petroleum, Odessa, Tex., 1961-69; sr. v.p. First Nat. Bank, Midland, Tex., 1969-77, InterFirst Bank, Odessa, 1983—; pres. Home Savs., Odessa, 1977-81, Tex. Nat. Bank, Odessa, 1981-83; dir. Home Savs. Assn., Odessa, 1977-81, Tex. Nat. Bank, Odessa, 1981-83. Pres. Odessa Indsl. Devel. Corp., 1982, Permian Playhouse, Odessa, 1981; chmn. United Way Odessa, 1981. Served to capt. U.S. Army, 1982-66. Mem. Odessa C. of C. (pres. 1982), Midland Jr. C. of C. (pres. 1968-72), Am. Business Women (Boss of Yr.). Democrat. Presbyterian. Home: 1508 Englewood Ln Odessa TX 79761 Office: InterFirst Bank PO Box 4798 Odessa TX 79760

MELTON, WAYNE CHARLES, finance company executive; b. Oak Ridge, Aug. 30, 1954; s. Charles Estel and Una Faye (Hull) M.; m. Carol Susan Carson, Mar. 21, 1975 (div.); 1 dau., April Suzanne; m. 2d, Terri Deal, Oct. 2, 1983. A.B. in European Intellectual History, U. Ga., 1975. Br. rep. Household Internat. Consumer Fin. Co., Athens, Ga., 1975-76, asst. mgr., Athens and Hickory, N.C., Doraville, Ga., 1976-77; mgr., Athens, 1977—; cons. Georgia Furniture; trustee Mu, Inc. Page, Ga. Ho. of Reps., 1968; chmn. Rep. Party of Madison County, 1973-74. Mem. Jaycees, Zeta Beta Tau, Republican. Presbyterian. Office: 183 Alps Rd Athens GA 30613

MELVIN, DOROTHY MAE, retired microbiologist; b. Fayetteville, N.C., Jan. 27, 1923; d. Willie James and Lillie Mae (Bain) Melvin. A.B., U. N.C.-Greensboro, 1942; M.S., U. N.C.-Chapel Hill, 1945; Ph.D., Rice U., 1951. Cert. Am. Acad. Microbiology. Microbiologist lab. tng. and cons. div. Centers for Disease Control, Altanta, 1945-49, with parasitology tng. lab., 1951-61, chief parasitology tng. sect., Atlanta, 1963-85. Mem. Am. Soc. Tropical Medicine and Hygiene, Am. Soc. Parasitologists, Sigma Xi. Author manuals; contbr. articles to sci. jours. Home: 2418 Kingscliff Dr NE Atlanta GA 30345

MELVIN, NORMAN CECIL, III, plant systematist, educator; b. Balt., July 11, 1950; s. Norman Cecil and Louise (Gillen) M.; m. B. Renee Long, Aug. 14, 1982. B.S., Presbyn. Coll., Clinton, S.C., 1973; M.S., Clemson U., 1976; Ph.D., Miami U., 1980. Asst. prof. biology St. Andrew's Presbyn. Coll., Laurinburg, N.C., 1980—, curator Herbarium, 1980—, dir. and mgr. greenhouse, 1980—, chmn. admissions com., 1982—; research for flora inventory S.C. Wildlife Dept., 1982—, dir. internship, 1980—; plant patent researcher U.S. Nat. Arboretum, 1982-83; mem. com. on preservation of Carolina bays N.C. Nature Conservancy, 1985—. Willard Sherman Turell Herbarium grantee, 1978; St. Andrew's Presbyn. Coll. faculty grantee, 1982, 83, 85. Mem. So. Appalachian Bot. Club, Soc. Econ. Botany, Assn. Southeastern Biologists, AAAS, Assn. Systematic Collections, Baileya, Sigma Xi. Contbr. articles to profl. jours. Home: Route 4 Random Wood Dr Laurinburg NC 28352 Office: Dept Biology St Andrew's Presbyn Coll Laurinburg NC 28352

MENAKER, LEWIS, dental educator; b. N.Y.C., Apr. 15, 1942; s. David and Sophie (Hochberg) M. D.M.D., Tufts U., 1965; Sc.D., MIT, 1971. Asst. prof. U. Ala. Sch. Dentistry-Birmingham, 1971-73, assoc. prof., 1973-77, asst. dean, 1975-81, sr. scientist, prof., 1977—, chmn. dept. oral biology, 1980—, assoc. dean for acad. affairs, 1981—. Author: Biologic Basis of Wound Healing, 1975; (with Morhart and Navia) Biologic Basis of Dental Caries, 1980. Translator: Biologic Basis of Dental Caries, 1982 (Japanese), 1983, (Italian), 1983 (Portuguese), 1984 (Spanish). Served to capt. USAF, 1965-67. Clin. investigator Nat. Inst. Arthritis, Metabolic and Diagestive Diseases, NIH, 1972-75; NIH fellow, 1967-71. Fellow Am. Coll. Dentists, Royal Soc. Promotion of Health; mem. Am. Dental Assn., Am. Assn. Dental Schs., Internat. Assn. Dental Research, Am. Assn. Dental Research. Republican. Jewish. Home: 1132 S 14th St Birmingham AL 35205 Office: U Ala Sch Dentistry Univ Sta Birmingham AL 35294

MENARD, DANA ANCELET, juvenile detention administrator; b. Lafayette, La., Sept. 3, 1956; d. Elmo Jean and Maude Ann (Mayers) Ancelet; m. Willert Dale Menard, Aug. 9, 1975. Assoc. degree, U. So. La., 1986. Receptionist, sec. II, exec. asst., asst. adminstr. Lafayette Juvenile Detention Home, La., 1976—. Editor La. Juvenile Detention Assn. Jour., 1982, also newletters. Mem. Am. Correctional Assn., Nat. Juvenile Detention Assn. (sec., treas. 1979—, conf. coordinator 1984, award chmn. 1982), La. Juvenile Detention Assn. (sec., treas. 1979-80, exec. bd. 1981-83, pres. 1980-81, 84-85). Home: Route 1 Box 269C Scott LA 70583 Office: Lafayette Juvenile Detention Home PO Box 2399 1613 Surrey St Lafayette LA 70502

MENDELSON, GAIL K., public relations executive; b. Cleve., Mar. 18, 1940; d. Joseph S. and Ida (Horr) Kreinberg; m. Robert Louis Mendelson, June 26, 1960; 1 child, Rebecca Ruth. B.S. Miami U., Oxford, Ohio, 1962. Cert. elem. tchr., Ohio. Tchr., Hamilton, Ohio, 1962-63, Champaign, Ill., 1963-66; talk-show host Cable TV, Wheeling, W.Va., 1978-79; anchorperson, reporter WWVA Radio, Wheeling, 1979-81; dir. pub. relations Wheeling Coll., 1982—; pub. relations adminstr. for med. groups, Wheeling, 1980—; cons. for ednl. groups. Bd. dirs. Temple Shalom, Wheeling, 1981-82; mem. consumer adv. bd. Health Plan of Upper Ohio Valley, 1980. Mem. Council for Advancement and Support of Edn., Coll. and Univ. Pub. Relations Assn. Pa. Jewish. Avocations: swimming; jogging; piano; reading; cross-country skiing; tennis. Office: Wheeling Coll 316 Washington Ave Wheeling WV 26003

MENDENHALL, GERALD VERNON, geologist; b. Lincoln, Nebr., Feb. 17, 1930; s. Vernice Nathaniel and Mayme May (Wear) M.; m. Ruth Irene Bergstraesser, Apr. 5, 1953; children—Susan Kay, John Mark. B.S., U. Nebr., 1951, M.S., 1953. Geologist Pure Oil Co., Wichita, Kans., 1957-59, Fort Worth, Chgo., 1959-62; geologist Pure Oil Co. and Union of Calif., Midland, Tex., 1962-69; dist. geologist Union Oil Co. Calif., Midland, 1969-81; mgr. region Horizon Exploration Co., Midland, 1981-84; geologist Valero Producing Co., Midland, 1984—. Contbr. articles to profl. jours. Cons. Permian Basin Grad. Ctr., Midland, 1971-73, bd. dirs., 1973-79; pres. congregation Midland Lutheran Ch., 1966. Mem. Am. Assn. Petroleum Geologists, Am. Inst. Profl. Geologists (com. 1975-78, sec. treas. sect. 1978-80). Republican. Lodge: Elks. Avocations: beekeeping; photography; geneology. Home: 1908 Sparks St Midland TX 79705 Office: Valero Producing Co 10 Desta Dr Midland TX 79705

MENDENHALL, LESLIE WARD, JR., wholesale company executive; b. Fort Worth, Sept. 20, 1920; s. Leslie Ward and Viola (Herring) M.; student Tex. Christian U., 1938-41, 45-48; m. June Helen McCord, May 5, 1942; children—Leslie Ward III, June Anne Mendenhall Jenney, Melinda Kaye Mendenhall Blair. Acct., Patterson, Leatherwood & Miller, Fort Worth, 1945-47; acct., office mgr. J.P. Bowlin Co., Fort Worth, 1947-48; head accounts payable dept., acctg. dept., mgr. budget control Montgomery Ward, Fort Worth, 1948-51; acct., Fort Worth, 1951-59; sec.-treas., controller, dir. Nationwide Advt. Splty. Co. and related cos., Arlington, Tex., 1959—; sec.-treas., dir. Newbern Corp., 1959—, SRI Publ. Co., 1968—, Texad Splty. Co., 1964—, NACO Advt. Splty. Co., 1973—, Nat. Calendar & Advt. Co., 1972—(all Arlington), Heritage Mfg. Corp., Fort Worth, 1959—. C.P.A., Tex. Episcopalian. Lodges: Elks, Rotary. Home: 1510 W Lavender Ln Arlington TX 76013 Office: 2025 S Cooper St Arlington TX 76010

MENDEZ, GLORIA ISABEL, psychologist; b. Santurce, P.R., Feb. 4, 1952; d. Hector Manuel and Gloria Maria (Caratini) M.; m. Edward Haskins Jacobs, Dec. 29, 1979; 1 child, Renee Marie. B.A. magna cum laude, U. P.R., 1974; M.A., U. Pitts., 1977, Ph.D., 1979. Teaching fellow U. Pitts., 1977-78, grad. research asst., 1978-79; prin. investigator ASPIRA-Nat. Inst. Edn. Grant, Washington, 1980-81; psychologist Ednl. Diagnostic Ctr., Christiansted, St. Croix, V.I., 1980-84; pvt. practice psychology, Christiansted, 1982—. Contbr. articles to profl. jours. Nat. Inst. Edn. fellow, 1978, assistantship, 1978, grantee, 1980. Fellow Am. Psychol. Assn. Roman Catholic. Avocations: tennis; arobic dancing. Office: Six Company St Christiansted St Croix VI 00820

MENDEZ, RICARDO, engineer; b. Havana, Cuba, Sept. 20, 1952; came to U.S., 1961, naturalized, 1974; s. Ricardo and Elena (Martinez) M.; m. Mirta Costa, Oct. 29, 1976; children—Melisa, Michael. A.A., Miami-Dade Community Coll., 1973; B.S. in C.E., U. Miami, 1975, postgrad. Fla. Internat. U., 1978-79. Project mgr. plans rev. sect. Dade County Pub. Works, Miami, Fla., 1976-78, asst. plans rev. engr., 1978-80, cons. coordinator, 1980-81, asst. chief traffic engr., 1981-82, secondary rd. project coordinator, 1982—; cons. in field. Registered profl. engr., Fla. Mem. ASCE, Fla. Engring. Soc., Nat. Soc. Profl. Engrs. Democrat. Roman Catholic. Office: 909 SE 1st Ave Miami FL 33131

MENDOZA, CHARLES JOHN, educator; b. N.Y.C., Nov. 23, 1935; s. Carlos John and Catherine (Guiets) M.; m. Jane Liddell, Dec. 19, 1959; children—Aston, Kristi. B.S. in Social Sci., Campbell Coll. (N.C.), 1966; grad. U.S. Army Command and Staff Coll., 1968; M.Ed. in Adminstrn., Ga. State U., 1970, Ed.S. in Adminstrn., 1974, Ph.D. in Adminstrn., 1978; M.B.A. in Pub. Adminstrn., George Washington U., 1973; M.C.J. in Adminstrn., Troy State U., 1980; J.D., Woodrow Wilson Coll. Law, 1983. Bar: Ga. Commd. 2d lt. U.S. Army, 1953, advanced through grades to lt. col., 1974; personnel officer U.S. Army' Inf. Sch., Ft. Benning, Ga., 1961-63; ops. officer, Fort Bragg, N.C., 1963-65; comdt. Inf. Officer Candidate Sch., Ft. Benning, 1967-69; dir. instrn. U.S. Army Inf. Sch., Fort Benning, 1969-72; project mgr. U.S. Army Concepts Analysis Agy., Bethesda, Md., 1972-74; ret., 1974; asst. prof. dept. ednl. adminstrn. Ga. State U., Ft. Benning, 1974—; chmn. bd. Nonage, Inc., Atlanta. Decorated Legion of Merit, Bronze Star, Meritorious Service medal, Air medal, Purple Heart. Mem. Assn. Trial Lawyers Am., Am. Assn. Sch. Adminstrs., Ga. Assn. Ednl. Leaders, Ret. Officers Assn. (v.p.). Lodge: East Columbus Lions. Author: A Study of Role and Decision Making of School Superintendents, 1977. Office: Grad Programs Ga State Univ PO Box 1998 Fort Benning GA 31905

MENDOZA, MANUEL, statistics educator, consultant; b. Mexico, D.F., Mex., Mar. 13, 1956; s. Manuel and Silvia (Ramirez) M.; m. Lelia Mendoza, May 2, 1981. B.S., Nat. Autonomous U. Mex., 1978, M.S., 1982. Asst. prof. Nat. Autonomous U. Mex., D.F., 1978-81, assoc. prof. statistics, 1982—; cons. Informatica y telecom., D.F., Mex. D.F., 1980-80, Conalep, D.F., Mex., 1980. Fellow Royal Statis. Soc.; mem. Am. Statis. Assn., Biometric Soc. Avocation: photography. Home: Don Manuelito 55-B108 Mexico D F Mexico 01780 Office: Dept Matematicas Fac Ciencias UNAM Cd Universitaria Mexico D F 04510 Mexico

MENGES, PAUL FILLMORE, educator; b. Abilene, Kans., July 16, 1917; s. Arthur Charles and Charlotte Mae (Frank) M.; 1 son, Richard Eric. Diploma Brown Mackie Sch. Bus., 1939; B.A., George Washington U., 1947; M.A., Columbia U., 1948; Ph.D., U. No. Colo., 1975. Head acctg. sect. Brit. Supply Mission, Washington, 1941-45; with N.Y. Dept. Labor, N.Y.C., 1949-54; editor Bur. Bus. Mgmt. U. Ill., Champaign-Urbana, 1954-56, teaching asst. U. Wash., Seattle, 1956-60; asst. prof. bus. Humboldt State Coll., Arcata, Calif., 1957-59, Eastern Mont. Coll., Billings, 1960-63; instr. U. N.D., Grand Forks, 1963-66; asst. prof. bus. Western Mich. U., Kalamazoo, 1966-67; assoc. prof. U. Wis.-Stout, Menomonie, 1967-78, Oral Roberts U., Tulsa, 1978-80; coordinator bus. U.So. Miss., Natchez, 1980-81; prof. mgmt. Delta State U., Cleveland, Miss., 1981—; mgmt. cons. Served with U.S. Army, 1941. U. Wash. scholar, 1956-60, U. N.D. scholar, 1963-66. Mem. Acad. Mgmt., Delta Sigma Pi. Mem. Christian Ch. (Disciples of Christ). Lodges: Rotary, Masons. Contbr. articles to profl. jours. Address: Delta State Univ Sch Bus Broom Hall 215 E Box 3275 Cleveland MS 38733

MENIUS, ESPIE FLYNN, JR., elec. engr.; b. New Bern, N.C., Mar. 5, 1923; s. Espie Flynn and Sudie Grey (Lyerly) M.; B.E.E., N.C. State U., 1947; M.B.A., U. S.C., 1973; adopted children—James Benfield, Ruben Hughes, James Sechler. With Carolina Power & Light Co., 1947-63, asst. to dist. mgr., Raleigh, Henderson, N.C., Sumter, S.C., 1947-50, elec. engr., Asheville, Southern Pines, Dunn, N.C., 1950-52, dist. engr. Hartsville, S.C., 1952-63; sr. elec. engr. Sonoco Products Co., Hartsville, 1963-74, engring. group leader, 1974—; instr. Florence-Darlington Tech. Ednl. Center. Mem. Hartsville Vol. Fire Dept., 1958—; Eagle Scout, Boy Scouts Am., 1938, scout troop leader New Bern, N.C., 1940-41, Raleigh, 1941-47, Henderson, 1948-49, Asheville, N.C., 1950, Southern Pines, N.C., 1951-52, Sumter, 1949-50, Hartsville, 1952-64; bd. mgrs. Nazareth Children's Home, Rockville, N.C., 1980—; chmn. bd. examiners City of Hartsville, 1980—. Served with AUS, 1943-46. Recipient Silver Beaver award Boy Scouts Am., 1959; named Hartsville's Citizen of Year, Rotary, 1960. Registered profl. engr., N.C., S.C., Tenn., Ga. Mem. IEEE, AAAS, Nat. Assn. Engrs., Knight of St. Patrick, Scabbard and Blade, Eta Kappa Nu, Pine Burr, Phi Eta Sigma, Theta Tau, Beta Gamma Sigma. Presbyn. (elder, tchr. men's Bible class). Club: Civitan (past dir.). Author articles in field. Home: 423 Richardson Circle W Hartsville SC 29550 Office: Sonoco Products Co N 2d St Hartsville SC 29550

MENSCHER, BARNET GARY, steel co. exec.; b. Laurelton, N.Y., Sept. 5, 1940; s. Samuel and Louise (Zaimont) M.; student Centenary Coll., 1958-59; B.B.A., U. Tex., 1963; m. Diane Elaine Gachman, June 12, 1966; children—Melissa Denise, Corey Lane, Scott Jay. Vice pres. mktg. Ella Gant Mfg., Shreveport, La., 1964-77; v.p., Gachman Steel Co., Fort Worth; pres. Menko Steel Service Inc., Houston, 1979—; investment cons. D & L Enterprises, 1966—. Mem. solicitation com. United Fund; mem. Nat. Alliance of Businessmen Jobs Program. Served with AUS, 1963-65. Mem. Assn. Steel Distbrs., Tex. Assn. Steel Importers, Purchasing Agts. Assn. Houston, Credit Assn. Houston, Am. Mgmt. Assn., Phi Sigma Delta, Alpha Phi Omega. Democrat. Jewish. Home: 314 Tealwood Dr Houston TX 77024 Office: 6607 Flintlock St Houston TX 77040

MENTZ, HENRY ALVAN, JR., judge; b. New Orleans, Nov. 10, 1920; s. Henry Alvan and Lulla (Bridewill) M.; m. Ann Lamantia, June 23, 1956; children—Ann Mentz Harbison, Carli Mentz Tessier, Hal, Frederick, George. B.A., Tulane U., 1941; J.D., La. State U., 1943. Bar: La. 1943. Practice, Hammond, La., 1948-62; sole practice, 1948-53; ptnr. Mentz & Ford, 1953-74, Mentz & Cashe, 1974-81, Mentz & Gorrell, 1981-82; judge U.S. Dist. Ct. (ea. dist) La., New Orleans, 1982—. Author: Combined Gospels, 1976. Pres. La. Civil Service League, 1978-81; mem. La. Bd. Election Suprs., 1980-82; bd. dirs. Southeastern La. U., 1983—; trustee WYES-TV Found., 1983—; vestryman Christ Ch. Cathedral, 1985—. Served with inf. U.S. Army, 1943-46. Decorated Bronze Star; recipient Disting. Service award AMVETS, 1950. Mem. Delta Tau Delta. Republican. Episcopalian. Clubs: Boston, Essex. Lodges: Shriners, Masons. Office: 508 US Courthouse New Orleans LA 70130

MENUT, D. CHARLES, oil and gas exploration co. exec.; b. Hanover, N.H., Mar. 19, 1933; s. D.C. and F.E. (Post) M.; B.A. in Geology, Tex. Christian U., 1956, M.A. in Geology, 1957; m. Ruth M. Krischus, 1954; children—Sandra, Daniel, Deborah. Sr. geologist Sun Oil Co., 1957-69; area offshore geologist Belco Petroleum Corp., Houston, 1969-72; cons., offshore mgr. Corpus Christi Oil & Gas Co., Houston, 1972-79; pres. Menut, Inc., Houston, 1979—, Menut/Gray & Assocs., Inc., Whaler Oil; v.p. South Hampton Mineral Corp. Cert. petroleum geologist Ill. Mem. Am. Assn. Petroleum Geologists, Houston, Lafayette and New Orleans geol. socs., Geophys. Soc. Houston, Soc. Exploration Geophysicists. Office: Citicorp Center Suite 1750 Houston TX 77002

MENUTIS, RUTH ANN, mcht.; b. Lafayette, La., Aug. 7, 1939; d. Minus and Annie (Duhon) Pellerin; ed. S.W. La. Inst., Patricia Stevens Sch. Modeling; m. Jimmie Menutis, Feb. 15, 1960; children—Jamie, Marika, Dimitri. Comml. announcer, traffic mgr. KLFY-TV, 1957-58; hostess Trans Tex./Tex. Internat. Airlines, also model Dallas Apparel Mart, 1958-68; owner, mgr. Playgril Shop of Am. and Ruth Ann Fashion, New Orleans, 1960—; owner Natural Energy Unltd., Inc. (doing bus. as Grove); acting pres. French Market Corp.; real estate investor; real estate salesman French Quarter Realty; clothing designer Miss Jane of Miami. Bd. dirs. Better Bus. Bur., Contemporary Arts Ctr.; chmn. La. del. to White House Small Bus. Conf., 1980; vice chmn. midwest U.S.A. Small Bus. Nat. Unity Council; chmn. New Orleans Mayor's, French Quar. Task Force. Mem. Vieux Carre Action Assn. (v.p.), Bourbon Mchts. Assn. (pres.), New Orleans C. of C. (dir.). Greek Orthodox. Office: 108 Royal St New Orleans LA 70130

MENZEL, ROBERT WINSTON, oceanography educator; b. James City County, Va., Jan. 29, 1920. B.S. in Botany, Coll. of William and Mary, 1940, M.A. in Aquatic Biology, 1943; postgrad. in biology, U. Va., 1945-46; Ph.D. in Biology, Tex. A&M U., 1954. Research asst. Va. Fisheries Lab., 1940-42, asst. biologist, 1942-46; biologist Tex. A&M Research Found., 1947-51; asst. prof. Tex. A&M U., 1952, instr., 1953-54, vis. prof. marine biology, 1972-73; asst. prof. Fla. State U., Tallahassee, 1954-58, assoc. prof., 1958-70, prof. dept. oceanography, 1970—; fishery biology instr. Gulf Coast Research Lab., 1957; cons. in field. Mem. ofcl. bd. John Westley United Methodist Ch., 1968-73, chmn., 1968-70. Grantee: Fla. State U. Research Council, 1954-59, 62, 64-65, U.S. Fish and Wildlife Service, 1955-57, 64-65, NIH, 1960-65, Office Naval Research, 1957-63, USPHS, 1963-65, Sport Fishing Inst., 1964-65, Fire Island Sea Clam Co., Inc., 1960-63, NSF, 1966-68, 79-83, Water Pollution Control Adminstrn., 1968-69, So. Services, 1970-71, NOAA, 1972-75, Fla. State Bd. Natural Resources, Fla. Sea Grant Coll., 1972-75; recipient Saltwater Conservation award Fla. Wildlife Fedn., 1964. Fellow Tex. Acad. Scis.; mem. Am. Soc. Limnology and Oceanography, Am. Fisheries Soc. Nat, Shellfisheries Assn. (exec. com. 1968-74, pres. 1972-73, various coms.), Estuarine Research Fedn. (governing bd. 1974-76), Gulf Estuarine Research Soc. (pres. 1974-75, archivist 1979—, exec. bd. dirs. 1973—, various coms.), Sigma Xi (sec. Fla. State U. chpt. 1955-56). Contbr. numerous articles on oceanography to profl. jours. Home: 1605 Kolopakin Tallahassee FL 32301 Office: Dept Oceanography Fla State U Tallahassee FL 32306

MENZIE, DONALD E., educator; b. DuBois, Pa., Apr. 4, 1922; s. James Freeman and Helga Josephine (Johnson) M.; B.S. in Petroleum and Natural Gas Engring., Pa. State U., 1942, M.S., 1948, Ph.D., 1962; m. Jane Cameron Redsecker, Nov. 6, 1946; children—Donald, William Lee, John Peter, Thomas Freeman. Marine engr. Phila. Navy Yard, 1943-46; research asst. air-gas dr. recovery Pa. State U., 1946-48, instr. petroleum and natural gas engring., 1948-51; asst. prof. petroleum engring. U. Okla., 1951-55, asso. prof., 1955-64, prof., 1964—, dir. Sch. Petroleum and Geol. Engring., 1963-72, petroleum engr. research info. systems program, 1979—, asso. exec. dir. Energy Resources Inst., 1979—, Halliburton disting. lectr. Coll. Engring., 1981; pres., owner Petroleum Engring. Educators, Norman, Okla., 1971—; cons. Commr., scoutmaster Last Frontier council Boy Scouts Am., Norman, 1951-81; mem. adminstrv. bd. McFarlin United Methodist Ch., Norman, also Sunday sch. tchr., pres. fellowship class; treas., pres. Jackson PTA, Norman; treas. Republican party, Cleveland County, Okla.; mem. Norman Park Commn., 1974-80. Mem. AIME, Am. Assn. Petroleum Geologists, Okla. Soc. Profl. Engrs., Nat. Soc. Profl. Engrs., Am. Soc. Engring. Edn., Soc. Petroleum Engrs., Am. Petroleum Inst., AAAS, Okla. Engring and Tech. Guidance Council, Sigma Xi, Pi Epsilon Tau, Alpha Chi Sigma, Phi Lambda Upsilon. Clubs: Sportsmen of Cleveland County, Masons, Sooner Swim (dir. 1966-78). Author: Reservoir Mechanics, 1954; Waterflooding for Engineers, 1966; Secondary Recovery for Engineers, 1968; Applied Reservoir Engineering for Geologists, 1971; New Recovery Techniques, 1973; Enhanced Recovery Techniques, 1975; contbr. articles to profl. jours. Home: 1503 Melrose Dr Norman OK 73069 Office: 601 Elm St Norman OK 73019

MERBACK, WILLIAM DENNIS, management consultant; b. Salt Lake City, Mar. 28, 1938; s. William Jacob and Gloria (Duste') M.; m. Patricia Rose Fabiano, Sept. 28, 1963; children—Jacquelyn, Jeffrey, Jennifer, Joanna. B.S.E.E., U. Utah, 1961; postgrad. UCLA, 1964. Cert. mgmt. cons. Inst. Mgmt. Cons., Inc. Indsl. engr. Litton Industries, Los Angeles, 1963-64, Eldon Industries, Los Angeles, 1964-65; mgmt. cons. Arthur Young & Co., Chgo., Sacramento, and Atlanta, 1965—, ptnr., 1978—, S.E. dir. indsl. engring., Atlanta, 1976—. Served as lt. (j.g.) USNR, 1961-63. Mem. Am. Inst. Indsl. Engrs. (sr.), Inst. Mgmt. Cons., Sigma Pi (pres. 1960-61). Club: Dunwoody Country (pres. 1982-83). Developer Resource Mgmt. System, 1970-78; contbr. articles to profl. jours. Home: 5635 Trowbridge Dr Dunwoody GA 30338 Office: Arthur Young & Co 2100 Gas Light Tower Atlanta GA 30043

MERCER, JAMES LEE, management consultant; b. Sayre, Okla., Nov. 7, 1936; s. Fred Elmo and Ora Lee (Davidson) M.; B.S., U. Nev., 1964, M.B.A., 1966; cert. in mcpl. adminstrn. U. N.C., 1971; postgrad. exec. devel. program Cornell U., 1979; m. Carolyn Lois Prince, Nov. 16, 1962; children—Tara Lee, James Lee. Methods and results supr. Pacific Tel. & Tel., Sacramento, 1965-66; prodn. control supr. Gen. Dynamics, Pomona, Calif., 1966-67; nuclear submarine project mgr. Litton Industries, Pascagoula, Miss., 1967-70; asst. city mgr. City of Raleigh (N.C.), 1970-73; nat. program dir. Pub. Tech., Inc., Washington, 1973-76; gen. mgr. Battelle So. Ops., Atlanta, 1976-79; v.p. Korn/Ferry Internat., Atlanta, 1979-81; pres. James Mercer & Assocs., mgmt. cons., Atlanta, 1981—; chief, Indsl. Extension Div., Ga. Inst. of Tech., Atlanta, 1981-83; dir. cons. services Coopers & Lybrand, 1983-84; regional v.p. Wolfe & Assocs., Inc., mgmt. cons., 1984—; ad hoc prof. N.C. State U., 1972-73. Chmn. Raleigh Mayor's Civic Center Authority Study Commn., 1971. Served with USN, 1955-59. Mem. Internat. City Mgmt. Assn., Nat. Mcpl. League; Am. Soc. Public Adminstrn., Am. Inst. Indsl. Engrs. (past pres.'s award 1970, pres. chpt. 1969-70), Tech. Transfer Soc. (dir. 1978—; treas. 1985-86), Ga. Indsl. Devel. Assn.; U. Nev. Alumni Assn. (exec. com. 1969-79); trustee U. Nev. Found., 1980—; mem. Calif. Poly. State U., (adv. council Coll. Bus. Adminstrn.) San Luis Obispo, 1980—. Active Atlanta C. of C. Republican. Clubs: Rotary, Masons, Shriners, Atlanta Commerce. Author: Public Management Systems, 1978; Public Technology, 1981; Managing Urban Government Services, 1981; contbr. articles to profl. jours. Home: 1119 Aurora Ct Dunwoody GA 30338 Office: 1100 Johnson Ferry Rd Suite 200 Atlanta GA 30342

MERCER, PATRICIA ANNE, English and foreign language educator, tennis activities director; b. Wheeling, W.Va., May 22, 1951; d. William Nelson and Mary Agnes (Kelly) M.; A.B. in Edn., West Liberty State Coll., 1973; M.S. in Safety Mgmt., W.Va. U., 1982, postgrad., 1982-85; postgrad. Western Ill. U., 1985. Permanent profl. teaching cert., W.Va. Tchr.-coach, Diocese of Wheeling-Charleston, W.Va., 1974-78; substitute tchr. Ohio County Bd. Edn., Wheeling, 1978; tchr.-coach Brooke County Bd. Edn., Wellsburg, W.Va., 1979—; adj. edn. instr. W.Va. No. Community Coll., Wheeling, 1974; dir. volleyball clinics, 1983—; tennis program dir. Wheeling Country Club, summer 1985. Advisor for lit. mag., Brooke County Bd. Edn., 1980-83; author ednl. game: German Trivia, 1984; editor Diagnostic Test of English, 1982. Chmn. volleyball com. Ohio Valley Athletic Conf., 1982—; mem. planning com. Fgn. Lang. Day, Bethany Coll., 1983; vol. worker W.Va. Open Tennis Tournament, 1979—; mem. Austrian-Am. Cultural Soc., Pitts. Mem. Nat. Council Tchrs. of English, Nat. Fedn. Interscholastic Coaches Assn., NEA, Am. Soc. Safety Engrs., Am. Assn. Tchrs. of German, Collegiate Volleyball Coaches Assn., W.Va. Edn. Assn., W.Va. Fgn. Lang. Tchrs. Assn. Roman Catholic. Club: Wheeling-Oglebay Tennis. Avocations: tennis; travel; sewing. Home: 207 Main St Wheeling WV 26003

MEREDITH, SANDY RAY, medical administrator; b. Louisville, Miss., Apr. 3, 1948; d. Samuel Theodore and Sammye Dolores (Donald) Ray. Staff technologist Univ. Med. Ctr., Jackson, Miss., 1970-71, St. Dominic Hosp., Jackson, 1971-72; dir. acute care lab. Univ. Med. Ctr., Jackson, 1972-78; cons. Miss. Crime Lab., 1979-80; cons. acute care lab. U. Tex. Med. Br., Galveston, 1977-78, dir., 1978-79, dir. research and edn. support services dept. anesthesiology, 1979-80, dir. acute care services, 1980-82, dir. med. instrumentation services, 1980—; chief exec. officer, pres. Windsor, Britton & Fairchild, Inc., Houston, 1982—; mem. faculty U. Tex. Sch. Medicine, 1980—. Contbr. articles to profl. jours. Cert. clin. lab. specialist Nat. Cert. Agy. for Med. Lab. Personnel. Mem. Miss. Alliance of Health Related Assns. (exec. com. 1977-80), Miss. State Soc. Med. Tech. (pres. 1977-78, dir., 1976-78, chmn. 1977-78), Am. Soc. Med. Tech. (del. 1976-78, 81-81), Tex. Soc. Med. Tech. (del. 1979-81, chmn. traveling seminar com. 1980-82, dir. 1981-83), Assn. Advancement of Med. Instrumentation, Am. Hosp. Assn., Am. Soc. Clin. Pathology, Gulf Coast Engring. Soc., Med. Electronics Am., Nat. Assn. Female Execs., Tex. Hosp. Assn., U. Tex. Med. Br. Faculty Womans Assn. Democrat. Baptist. Office: 8A-John Sealy Ell Univ Tex Med Br Galveston TX 77550

MEREY, DAISY, physician; b. Tangiers, Morocco, Feb. 1, 1949, came to U.S., 1961; d. Theodore and Lilly (Roth) Breuer; m. John Howard Merey, Dec. 26, 1967; children—DeAnne, Andrew. B.A., Barnard Coll., 1964; Ph.D., NYU,

1971; M.D., St. George's U., 1979. Resident Broward Gen. Med. Ctr., Ft. Lauderdale, Fla., 1979-80; practice medicine, West Palm Beach, Fla., 1981—; med. cons. Vis. Nurse Assn., 1981-83. Recipient Founder's Day award NYU, 1970. Fellow Am. Soc. Bariatric Physicians, Interam. Physicians Assn.; mem. AMA (Physicians Recognition award 1982), Internat. Acad. Bariatric Physicians (pres. 1986), Exec. Women Assn. Palm Beaches, Am. Bariatric Assn., Internat. Bariatric Assn., Am. Soc. Clin. Nutrition, Am. Soc. Contemporary Medicine and Surgery. Office: 900 N Olive Ave West Palm Beach FL 33401

MERGENHAGEN, PAULA MARIE, statistician, planning analyst; b. Buffalo, May 2, 1957; d. Stephan Edward and Marjorie Ann (Carr) M. B.S., James Madison U., 1979; M.A., Vanderbilt U., 1982, Ph.D., 1984. Instr. sociology Vanderbilt U., 1982-84; statistician, planning analyst Tenn. Dept. Health and Environ., Nashville, 1984—. Vol. counselor Rape and Sexual Abuse Ctr. of Nashville, 1982—. Univ. scholar Vanderbilt U., 1979-83; mass media sci. fellow AAAS, 1983. Mem. Population Assn. Am., Am. Pub. Health Assn., Am. Sociol. Assn., So. Sociol. Assn. Democrat. Home: 2115 Portland Ave #F1 Nashville TN 37212 Office: Tenn Dept Health and Environ Bur Health Services 100 9th Ave N Nashville TN 37219

MERHIGE, ROBERT REYNOLD, JR., U.S. judge; b. N.Y.C., Feb. 5, 1919; s. Robert Reynold and Eleanor (Donovan) M.; m. Shirley Galleher, Apr. 24, 1957; children—Robert Reynold III, Mark Reynold. LL.B., U. Richmond, 1942, LL.D., 1976; LL.M., U. Va., 1982. Bar: Va. 1942. Practice in, Richmond, 1942-67; judge U.S. Dist. Ct., Richmond, 1967—; guest lectr. trial tactics U. Va. Law Sch.; adj. prof. U. Richmond Law Sch.; appeal agt. Henrico County Draft Bd., 1954-67. Co-author: Virginia Jury Instructions. Mem. Richmond Citizens Assn.; mem. citizens adv. com. San Dist. A, Henrico County. Served with USAAF, World War II. Decorated Air medal with 4 clusters; recipient Amara Civic Club award, 1968; spl. award, jud. council Nat. Bar Assn., 1972; citation City Richmond, 1967; named Citizen of Yr. 3d dist. Omega Psi Phi, 1972, Richmond Urban League, 1977; Disting. Alumni award U. Richmond, 1979; Disting Service award Nat. Alumni Council, U. Richmond, 1979. Mem. ABA (Herbert Harley award), Va. Bar Assn., Richmond Bar Assn. (pres. 1963-64), Va. State Bar, Va. Trial Lawyers Assn. (chmn. membership com. 1964-65, distinguished service award 1977), Jud. Conf. U.S., Omicron Delta Kappa. Office: US Courthouse Richmond VA 23219*

MERIJANIAN, JEANETTE LEWIS, nurse, health educator, consultant; b. Mason City, Iowa, June 3, 1932; d. Clifford Wilson and Ruth Evelyn Lewis; m. Aris Merijanian, Dec. 26, 1953 (div. 1978); children—Randy, Lori, Greg, John. R.N., Kahler Sch. Nursing, Rochester, Minn., 1953; B.S., U. Montevallo, 1974; M.P.H., U. Ala., 1980. R.N., Minn. Head nurse eye floor Worrell Hosp., Mayo Clinic, Rochester, 1953; float nurse Mitchell County Meml. Hosp., Osage, Iowa, part-time 1953-54; obstetric and evening supr. Riley County Hosp., Manhattan, Kans., 1954; float supr. Baptist Hosp., San Antonio, 1955-56; night supr. San Marcos (Tex.) Hosp., 1957-58; obstetric supr. St. Mary's Hosp., Bryan, Tex., part-time 1958-60; evening charge nurse Tex. A&M U. Student Health Services, College Station, 1959-61; evening nurse U. Montevallo (Ala.) Student Health Services, 1968, staff nurse 1971, 72, coordinator student health services, 1975—; nursing dir. Shelby County chpt. ARC; guest lectr. high schs. and community programs; chmn. Shelby County Teenage Pregnancy Prevention Com.; mem. Ala. Regional Prenatal Com. Mem. Health Educators Assn. Ala. (charter, a founder), Shelby County Health Council (charter, a founder). Author: But Who Can I Ask About Growing Up, 1979; The Mysterious Body Jack Is Building, 1979. Home: 248 Highland Montevallo AL 35115 Office: 261 Student Health Services U Montevallo Montevallo AL 35115

MERLIN, ALVIN SIMON, urologist; b. New Orleans, June 15, 1936; s. Joseph Boris and Claire (Kamil) M.; student Tulane U., 1952-53, Sch. Elec. Engring., La. State U., Baton Rouge, 1953-55; M.D., La. State U., 1964; m. Carol R. Hochberg, May 14, 1977; children—Shel, Lisa, Kim, Max, Andrew, Ashley, David. Intern, Charity Hosp., New Orleans, 1964-65: resident Touro Infirmary, VA Hosp., New Orleans, 1965-69; practice medicine specializing in urology, Metairie, La., 1969—; chief sect. urology E. Jefferson Gen. Hosp., 1980-83; mng. ptnr. Med. Enterprises, 1982—; bd. dirs. Jo Ellen Smith Hosp., 1972-74, Doctors Hosp. of Jefferson, 1983—. Exec. com. New Orleans Area Health Systems Agency, 1978; chmn. long range fin. com. Congregation Gates of Prayer, 1976-77; mem. East Jefferson Civic and Cultural Commn.; chmn. Jefferson Parish Charter Adv. Bd., 1980. Served with USN, 1955-59. Cert. mortgage loan broker La. Commr. Securities. Diplomate Am. Bd. Urology. Mem. Am. Urol. Assn. (Southeastern sect.), New Orleans Office Bldg. Assn., La. Restaurant Assn. Jewish. Club: Masons. Home: 4525 Hessmer Ave Metairie LA 70002 Office: 4300 Houma Blvd Metairie LA 70006

MERLIN, JAMES (MERLIN J. JOHNSON), artist; b. Chokio, Minn., Sept. 23, 1906; s. Nels H.K. and Lena (Robertson) Johnson; student Okla. State U., 1930; Diploma of Merit, U.Arts, Salsamaggiore Terme Pr, Italy; m. Nola Rogers, Feb. 26, 1931; 1 son, James Roger. Statistician, Gulf Oil Corp., 1950-61; sr. analyst, 1961-68; exhibited one-man shows Galleries I and II, Houston, 1971—, Gallery Cypress, Gallery Woodway, Gallerie Atascocita, Gallerie Lewisville; group shows include Community Center, 1967, 68, 69, Dimension Houston IV, Houston Fine Arts, Gulf Fine Arts (1st prize); represented in pvt. and corp. collections. Served with AUS, World War II. Republican. Baptist. Address: 1525 Chislom Trail Lewisville TX 75067

MERLISS, WILLIAM SIDNEY, architect, engr.; b. Okmulgee, Okla., Sept. 26, 1922; s. Sidney Samuel and Bonnie Bessie (Farr) M.; B.Arch., B.Archtl. Engring., Okla. A&M U., 1950; m. Dorothy Halphen Kolb; children—Sherri Lynn Merliss Voebel, Benjamin Harrison. Architect, engr. Hudgins, Thompson & Ball, Oklahoma City, 1950; engr. Dow Chem. Co., Freeport, Tex., 1953-54; project engr. Walter P. Moore, Houston, 1954-55; cons. engr. W.S. Merliss & Assos., Houston, 1955-61; partner firm Merliss, Jones and Robinson, Houston, 1961-77, Merliss & Jones, 1977—; v.p. Aubibon Land Co.; dir. Freaky Fritters World Inc., Universal Domes Inc., Condo Domes Inc., Time Systems Inc.; chmn. bd. Bandit Messenger Service Inc., Houston, also Dallas. Adv. trustee Dorothy H. and Allison R. Kolb Ednl. Trust Found.; mgr. D. Kolb interests. Democrat precinct chmn., 1968-75. Served with USAF, 1941-45, 51-53. Decorated Purple Heart. Mem. Nat., Tex. socs. profl. engrs., Tex. Soc. Architects, AIA, Prestressed Concrete Inst., Gulf Coast Okla. State Alumni Assn. (pres. 1956-65), Kappa Kappa Psi. Republican. Jewish. Clubs: Masons, Shriners, Consistory, Artisans; Frolikers, Camelot, Baton Rouge City, Big Timers (Baton Rouge). Home: 7420 Reinzi Blvd Baton Rouge LA 70809 Office: 4669 Southwest Freeway Suite 300 Houston TX 77027

MERLO, RICHARD BARTLETT, radiologist; b. St. Louis, Nov. 30, 1935; s. William Joseph and Kathryn (Kolowrat) M.; m. Ann Hall Hornthal, Jan. 20, 1960; children—William Henry, James Bartlett. A.B., Harvard Coll., 1957; M.D., Duke U., 1961. Diplomate Am. Bd. Radiology, Am. Bd. Nuclear Medicine. Intern, de Paul Hosp., Norfolk, Va., 1961-62; resident in radiology George Washington U. Hosp., Washington, 1962-65; chief radiology U.S. Army Hosp., Fort MacArthur, San Pedro, Calif., 1965-67; radiologist Hugh Chatham Meml. Hosp., Elkin, N.C., 1965—; clin. instr. radiology Bowman Gray Sch. Medicine, Winston-Salem, N.C., 1979—. Contbr. articles to profl. jours. Served to capt. U.S. Army, 1965-67. Mem. AMA, Am. Coll. Radiology, Am. Coll. Nuclear Physicians, Am. Inst. Ultrasound Medicine. Republican. Roman Catholic. Home: 773 Brookwood Dr Elkin NC 28621 Office: 180-M Parkwood Dr Elkin NC 28621

MERO-SCHROEDER, MARY WINIFRED, nurse, health adminstr.; b. Bayshore, L.I., N.Y., May 20, 1942; d. Robert Sills and Letitia Florence (Seon) M.; B.S., Pace U., Westchester, N.Y., 1975; postgrad. Adelphi U., 1976-77; M.S. in Nursing, U. Tenn., 1979. Staff nurse Cabrini Health Care Center, Dobbs Ferry, N.Y., 1973-74, acting asst. dir., 1974-75, coordinator primary nursing care unit, 1976-76, inservice instr., 1976-80; asst. dir. nursing for supportive services, also dir. staff devel. dept. Shelby County Health Care Center, Memphis, 1978—; instr. dept. primary and long term care Sch. Nursing, U. Tenn., 1979—; supr. nursing, dir. VA nursing home care unit, Memphis, 1980—. Mem. Nat. Com. Task Force for Mental Health in Elderly, 1979—. Mem. Gerontol. Soc., Tenn. Nursing Assn., Am. Nurses Assn., AAAS, N.Y. Acad. Scis. Democrat. Roman Catholic. Home and office: 5006 Golfbrook Dr Stone Mountain GA 30088

MERRELL, DAVID BOLES, educator, university administrator; b. Akron, Ohio, June 24, 1942; s. Ralph John and Audrey Dale (Boles) M.; m. Martha Ann Page, Aug. 21, 1971; children—Jocelyn Leigh, Phylliese Ann, Flynt Page Gaines, Dezarae Gaines. B.A., Abilene Christian U., 1964; M.A., U. Ark., 1966; Ph.D., Tex. A&M U., 1979. English tchr. Abilene Christian U., Tex., 1966-69, 70-72, 75—; v.p. Cascade Fashions Akron, Ohio, 1969-70; English instr. Tex. A&M U., College Station, 1972-75; golf coach Abilene Christian U., 1976-78, chmn. English dept., 1981-85, dean Coll. Liberal and Fine Arts, 1985—; councillor Conf. Coll. Tchrs. English, Tex., 1983—. Coordinator: (book) Good Writing, 1974. Recipient Tchr. of Yr. award Abilene Christian U., 1984. Mem. North Am. Soc. for Sport Hist., Nat. Council Tchrs. English, Am. Bus. Communication Assn., Conf. on Christianity and Lit. Ch. of Christ. Avocations: photography; physical fitness; music; drama; woodworking. Home: 833 Harrison Ave Abilene TX 79601 Office: Abilene Christian U 1600 Campus Ct Abilene TX 79699

MERRELLI, F. H., oil and gas production company executive; b. 1936. B.S., Colo. Sch. Mines, 1959. With Terra Resources Inc., Tulsa, Okla., 1959—, v.p., 1976, now pres., also dir. Office: Terra Resources Inc 5416 S Yale St Tulsa OK 74135*

MERRILL, HERBERT WALKER (BARRY), JR., computer analyst; b. White Plains, N.Y., Apr. 19, 1941; s. Herbert Walker and Margatet Mary (King) M.; m. Judith Anne Spencer, June 6, 1981; children—Rachel Angela, Nathaniel Lee. Student Notre Dame U., 1958-62; Purdue U., 1964-67; B.S. with highest honors in Elec. Engring., Purdue U., 1967, M.S. with honors in Elec. Engring., 1967; Ph.D., U. Ill., 1979. Cert. data processing. Systems analyst, sr. systems analyst State Farm Mut. Auto. Ins. Co., Bloomington, Ill., 1972-76; computer resource evaluation specialist, sr. computer measurement cons., computersmith Sun Info. Services Co., Dallas, 1976-82; mgr. resource analysis Sun Co., Dallas, 1983-84; pres. Merrill Cons., Dallas, 1984—; lectr. Computer Inst. Def. Dept., SSA, Govt. Czechoslovakia. Served to lt. (j.g.) USN, 1962-72. Mem. Assn. Computing Machinery, (IEEE, Computer Measurement Group (A.A. Michelson award 1982), Computer Measurement and Evaluation Project, Share Inc., European Computer Measurement Assn., Dallas Amateur Radio Club. Mem. Unity Ch. Author: Merrill's Guide to Computer Performance Evaluation, 3d edit., 1983; contbr. articles to profl. jours. Home: 10717 Cromwell Dr Dallas TX 75229

MERRIMAN, ILAH COFFEE, financial executive; b. Amarillo, Tex., Mar. 22, 1935; d. Oran and Frances Elizabeth (Rocque) Coffee; children—Pamela, Michael. B.S. in Math., Tex. Tech U. Cert. secondary tchr., Tex. Chief exec. officer H&R Block Houston; pres. H&R Block Inc. Tex.; dir. Republic Bank of Post Oak, Houston; bd. dirs., sec. H&R Block Major Francise Assn. Trustee Tex. Tech U. Alumnae Loyalty Fund; mem. steering com. Double T Connection, Tex. Tech. Women's Athletics. Mem. Dallas Mus. Fine Art, Houston Mus. Fine Art, Shakespeare Festival, Dallas Hist. Soc., AAUW, Tex. Tech. Ex-Students Assn. (chmn. Century Club). Methodist. Office: 8609 Northwest Plaza Dr Suite 212 Dallas TX 75225

MERRITT, CAROL YVONNE, nurse, clinical specialist; b. Dehue, W.Va., Feb. 23, 1944; d. Ray and Almeda (Simpkins) M.; 1 dau., Kimberly Yvonne. B.S.N., U. South Ala., 1983; R.N., U. Tenn., 1974; L.P.N., Southwestern Mich. Coll., 1968. Charge nurse Golden Hours Villa Convalescent Ctr., Long Beach, Calif., 1968; staff nurse coronary care Maine Med. Ctr., Portland, 1969-70, Bapt. Hosp., Nashville, 1970; charge and staff nurse coronary care Meml. Hosp., Madison, Tenn., 1970-72; critical care staff nurse St. Thomas Hosp., Nashville, 1972-74; family planning practioner State Tenn. Dept. Pub. Health, Nashville, 1974-75; physician's asst., Nashville, 1975-76; regional coordinator Tenn. Found. Med. Care, Nashville, 1976-79; oncology/immunology research nurse Vanderbilt U. Coll. Medicine, Nashville, 1979; head nurse ICU and surg. ward St. Anthony's Hosp., The Pas, Man., Can., 1980, supr., 1979-80; clin. oncology coordinator Coll. Medicine, U. South Ala., Mobile, 1980-83; lectr. A.H. Robins Co., 1982—; pres. Advantages Unlimited Ednl. Opportunities, Mobile, Ala., 1980—; dir. edn. Home Health-Home Care, Mobile, 1983—; founder, past pres. Mobile Area Oncology Support Group; cons. to hosps., schs. nursing, pharm. cos. Scholar, Southwestern Mich. Coll., 1967, Ala. Bd. Nursing, 1983. Mem. Internat. Soc. Nurses in Cancer Care, Nat. Oncology Nursing Soc., Am. Assn. Critical Care Nurses, Can. Nurses Assn., Tenn. Nurses Assn., Alumni Assn. U. Tenn., Alumni Assn. U. South Ala. Methodist. Office: PO Box 160046 Mobile AL 36616

MERRITT, GILBERT STROUD, federal judge; b. Nashville, Jan. 17, 1936; s. Gilbert Stroud and Angie Fields (Cantrell) M.; B.A., Yale U., 1957; LL.B., Vanderbilt U., 1960; LL.M., Harvard U., 1962; m. Louise Clark Fort, July 10, 1964 (dec.); children—Stroud, Louise Clark, Eli. Admitted to Tenn. bar, 1960; asst. dean. instr. Vanderbilt Law Sch., 1960-61, lectr., 1962-76, assoc. prof. law, 1969-70; asso. dir. law Nashville Met. Govt., 1963-65; U.S. dist. atty. for Middle Tenn., 1966-69; partner firm Gullett, Steele, Sanford, Robinson & Merritt, Nashville, 1970-77; judge U.S. Ct. of Appeals for 6th Circuit, Nashville, 1977—. Del., Tenn. Constl. Conv., 1965. Mem. Vanderbilt Law Alumni Assn. (pres. 1979-80), Am. Law Inst., Order of Coif. Episcopalian. Mng. editor Vanderbilt Law Rev., 1959-60; contbr. articles to law jours. Office: US Ct Appeals 736 US Courthouse Nashville TN 37203

MERRITT, JAMES ALMOND, mech. contracting co. exec.; b. Magnolia, N.C., Aug. 6, 1932; s. Addie Almond and Janie Evelyn (Groves) M.; student public schs., Charleston, S.C.; m. Elizabeth Ann Lackey, Dec. 3, 1955; children—James Almond, Jamie Shayne. With W. I. Champman & Sons, Charleston, 1956-57, F. A. Bailey & Sons, Charleston, 1957-66; founder, James A. Merritt & Sons, Inc. (and predecessor co.), Charleston, S.C., 1967—, pres., chief exec. officer, 1981—. Served with S.C. N.G., 1951. Mem. Mech. Contracting Assn. S.C., ASHRAE, Mil. Engrs., Air Force Assn. Am., Asso. Gen. Contractors Am., Charleston Contractors Assn., Carolinas Constrn. Tng. Council (chmn. 1973-79), Aircraft Owners and Pilots Assn. Repbulican. Baptist. Club: Elks. Home: 1930 Capri Dr Charleston SC 29407 Office: 1929 Belgrade Ave Charleston SC 29407

MERRITT, JAMES FRANCIS, biological sciences educator, administrator; b. Raleigh, N.C., July 21, 1944; s. Clifton and Emily (Rogers) M.; m. Sue Wall, Aug. 9, 1969; children—Ashley Grant, Bradley Gene, Carey Reid. B.S., E. Carolina U., 1966, M.S., 1968; Ph.D., N.C. State U., 1973. Asst. prof. biological scis. U. N.C., Wilmington, 1973-78, assoc. prof., chmn., 1978—. Contbr. articles to profl. jours. Chmn. PTA, Wilmington, 1983, Marine Expo Com., Wilmington, 1984—. E.G. Moss fellow N.C. State U., 1972. Mem. Am. Genetic Assn., N.C. Acad. Sci. (sect. chmn. 1975-76, vice pres. 1979-80), Chi Beta Phi (Outstanding Service award 1966). Avocations: fishing; woodworking. Home: 105 Mamie Ct Wilmington NC 28403 Office: Dept Biological Scis Univ NC at Wilmington 601 S College Rd Wilmington NC 28403

MERRITT, LYNN GARNARD, company executive; b. Christianburg, Ohio, May 2, 1930; s. Earl R. and Elizabeth M. (Huddleston) M.; m. Beverly J. Grauser; children—Richard Grauser, Peter Flynn. B.S., Bowling Green U., 1952; M.A., Millikin U., 1963. Training dir. Decatur Meml. Hosp., Ill., 1957-61; training cons. State of N.J., 1961-63; mgr. LOMA, N.Y.C., 1963-65, dir., 1965-68, v.p., 1968-70, pres., Atlanta, 1970—. Mem. Atlanta C. of C. Served to lt. USAF, 1952-57. Republican. Methodist. Clubs: Capital City (Atlanta), Georgian. Lodge: Kiwanis. Office: Life Office Mgmt Assn Inc 5770 Powers Ferry Rd Atlanta GA 30361

MERRITT, MICHAEL LOUIS, petroleum geologist; b. Blackwell, Okla., Oct. 2, 1952; s. Robert Louis and J. Wynell (Johnston) M.; m. Jane Ann Tullius, Feb. 19, 1977; 1 child, James Michael. A.S. in Pre-Engring., No. Okla. Coll., 1972; B.S. in Physics, Southwestern Okla. State U., 1974; postgrad. Casper Coll., 1975; M.S. in Geology, U. Okla., 1978. Cert. geologist. Mud logging engr. N.L. Industries, Houston, 1974-75; grad. asst. U. Okla., Norman, 1975-76, Okla. Geol. Survey, Norman, 1976-77; geol. draftsman George L. Roller, Norman, 1976-78, Frank A. Melton, Norman, 1977-79; assoc. geologist SUN Prodn. Co., Longview, Tex., 1979-80; geologist Conoco Inc., Ponca City, Okla., 1980—. Author antique car mag. columnist, 1982—. Tuba player various bands, Okla.; mem. academic standards com. No. Okla. Coll., Tonkawa, 1971, student body pres., 1972; asst. scoutmaster Central Wyo. council Boy Scouts Am., 1975; mem. Toastmasters Internat., Oklahoma City, 1980-82; master ceremonies Bethany Fourth July Parade, Okla., 1982; sci. fair judge Geophys. Soc. Oklahoma City, 1982; mem. Skyline Urban Ministry Edn. Employment Com., Oklahoma City, 1983; vol. Tonkawa Pub. Library, 1984; coordinator No. Okla. Coll. Alumni Car Show, Tonkawa, 1984; participant Conoco, Inc. Speakers Program, Ponca City, Okla., 1985. Mem. Soc. Exploration Geophysicists (assoc.), Am. Assn. Petroleum Geologists (jr.), Ardmore Geol. Soc., Eastern Tex. Geol. Soc., Mustang Owners Club, Nash Car Club Am., Profl. Car Soc., Milestone Car Soc., Chrysler 300 Club, Inc., Eastern Tex. Vintage Auto Club, many others. Avocation: collector of automobile memorabilia including more than 50 vehicles. Home: Box 185 Lamont OK 74643 Office: Conoco Inc 1000 S Pine Ponca City OK 74601

MERRIWEATHER, RUSSELL DELL, college administrator; b. Birmingham, Ala., Oct. 10, 1924; s. William and Myrtle (Rhodes) M.; m. Ruby Rogers, July 2, 1955. Student Tuskegee Inst., 1942-43; A.B., Fisk U., 1950; postgrad. Am. Inst. Banking, 1957-58, Weaver Sch. Real Estate, 1962. Asst. Cashier Citizens Savs. Bank, Nashville, 1950-54, v.p., 1954-67; chief acct. Lane Coll., Jackson, Tenn., 1967-73, chief bus. officer, 1973—. Bd. dirs. Salvation Army, Jackson, 1979-82, chmn. fin. com., 1981-82; v.p. Jackson Area Council on Alcoholism and Drug Abuse, 1982; mem. exec. com. NAACP, Nashville, 1960-66; mem. visitation com. So. Assn. Colls. and Schs., Atlanta, 1981-83; bd. dirs. Consumer Credit Counseling, Nashville, 1966-68. Recipient certs. of appreciation March of Dimes Nat. Found., 1959, Fisk U., 1959-60. Mem. Jackson C. of C. (bd. dirs. 1979-81), So. Assn. Fin. Aid Counselors, So. Assn. Coll. and Univ. Bus. Officers, Nat. Assn. Coll. and Univ. Bus. Officers, Phi Beta Sigma. Mem. Christian Methodist Episcopal Ch. Lodge: Elks (sec. 1958-59). Avocations: bridge; reading; working with underprivileged boys. Home: 1603 Haynes Meade Circle Nashville TN 37207 Office: Lane Coll 501 Lane Ave Jackson TN 38301

MERRIWETHER, DUNCAN, retired manufacturer; b. Greenville, Ala., June 9, 1903; s. Jacob and Claudia (Robinson) M.; B.S., Columbia U., 1928, M.S., 1938; m. Asenath Kenyon, Feb. 9, 1929; children—Duncan Charles, Virginia Ann Merriwether Disharoon, Julia Elizabeth Merriwether Arnold, Jacob Douglass. Asst. to mgr. indsl. dept. Peat, Marwick, Mitchell & Co., C.P.A.s, N.Y.C., 1929-33; various assignments Irving Trust Co., 1933-39; chief acct. Rohm & Haas Co., Phila., 1939-41, asst. treas., 1941-43, treas., dir., mem. exec. com., 1943-48, exec. v.p., 1948, vice chmn., 1953-58, past dir., mem. exec. com. Bd. dirs. Haas Community Fund, 1943-70; trustee Mt. Holyoke Coll., 1958-68, chmn. emeritus, 1968—. Mem. Columbia U. Assos. (Disting. Alumni Service medal 1949), Am. Inst. C.P.A.s, Alpha Kappa Psi, Beta Gamma Sigma. Episcopalian. Clubs: Merion Cricket, Rittenhouse (Phila.); Marco Island (Fla.), Marco Island Yacht; Masons. Country. Home: Sunset House N Apt 611 Marco Island FL 33937

MERRY, FRIEDA ANNETTA, retired psychologist, educator; b. Dayton, Ohio, July 20, 1897; d. Charles Albert and Caroline Agnes (Schaefer) Kiefer; m. Ralph Vickers Merry, June 1, 1929 (dec. 1972). B.A., Ohio State U., 1921, Ph.D., 1927; M.A., U. Mich., 1923; postgrad., U. Wash., 1923-24. Research asst. U. Mich., Ann Arbor, 1921-23; psychol. examiner Pub. Schs., Seattle, 1923-24; asst. prof. psychology Whittenberg Coll., Springfield, Ohio, 1924-26; dir. dept. spl. studies Am. Found. For Blind, N.Y.C., 1927-32, Perkins Inst. for Blind, Watertown, Mass., 1927-32; prof. psychology, dean women Alfred Holbrook Coll., Lebanon, Ohio, 1933-34; prof. psychology Morris Harvey Coll., Charleston, W.Va., 1934-62, prof. emeritus, 1962—; cons. in field. Author: (with Ralph V. Merry) From Infancy to Adolescence, 1940; The First Two Decades of Life, 1950, rev. edit., 1958. Contbr. articles to profl. jours. and publs. Mem. editorial bd. W.Va. Single Curriculum. Chmn. W.Va. Com. on Human Growth and Devel.; mem. quality fund U. Charleston, 1981. Fellow AAAS (life), Am. Psychol. Assn. (emeritus), Nat. Council Women Psychologists (now Internat. Council Psychologists); mem. AAUP (emeritus), W.Va. Psychol. Assn. (co-founder, life, Disting. Psychologist 1983), Nat. Congl. Club. Lutheran. Avocations: reading; travel; genealogy. Home: 2108 Kanawha Ave SE Charleston WV 25304

MERSHON, WILLIAM WILBUR, geologist; b. Sentinel, Okla., July 15, 1952; s. Wilbur K. and Lillian D. (Long) M.; m. Pattie J. Martin, Apr. 9, 1957; children—Carrie A., Jillian R. B.S., U. Okla., 1979. Petroleum geologist Exploration Services, Inc., Midland, Tex., 1979-80, Arapaho Petroleum, Denver, 1981-83; 101 Energy Corp., Oklahoma City, 1983—. Served with USN, 1975-76. Democrat. Mem. Ch. of Christ. Office: 101 Energy Corp 2601 NW Hwy 508W Oklahoma City OK 73112

MERTENS, LAWRENCE EDWIN, electronics systems engineer, educator; b. N.Y.C., Mar. 6, 1929; s. John Henry and Marie (Loehr) M.; m. Margarete Anna Waider, July 8, 1975; children—Oliver Larry, Thomas John. B.S., Columbia U., 1951, M.S., 1952, D.Eng., 1955. Engr. RCA Def. Electronic Products Co., Camden, N.J., 1952-54, mgr. systems engring., 1954-58, staff engr., 1958-60, mgr. digital communications, 1960-62; chief scientist RCA Service Co., Patrick AFB, Fla., 1962-72, project mgr., 1972-80, mgr. tech. analysis, chief scientist, 1980—; pres. Photoquatics Co., 1967-72; adj. prof. ocean engring. Fla. Inst. Tech., 1968—. Recipient hon. mention award Soc. Motion Picture and TV Engrs., 1968; Samuel Willard Bridgham fellow Columbia U., 1951-52; Boese fellow Columbia U., 1952-53. Mem. IEEE, Soc. Photo-Optical Instrumentation Engrs., Marine Tech. Soc. Author: In-Water Photography, 1970. Guest editor Optical Engring., 1977. Patentee in field. Home: 690 Pebble Beach Ave NE Palm Bay FL 32905 Office: Bldg 989 MU 645 Patrick AFB FL 32925

MERWIN, WILLIAM RICHARD, lawyer, editor; b. Berwyn, Ill., Jan. 20, 1943; s. George R. and Phyllis (Schofield) M.; B.S. in Bus. Adminstrn., U. Fla., 1964, J.D., 1967. Bar: Fla. 1968. Trust asst. Fla. Nat. Bank, Jacksonville, 1967-68, trust adminstrv. asst., 1971-73; asst. counsel City of Jacksonville, 1973-84, chief legis. counsel, 1976-79, chief editorial counsel, 1980-84; v.p. Am. Legal Publ. Co., Inc., Jacksonville, 1984-85; v.p. Amalon Pub. Co., 1985—. Editor: Ordinance Code City of Jacksonville, 1984. Mem. adminstrv. bd. Lakeshore United Meth. Ch., Jacksonville, 1972-79, chief atty., trier of fact, 1972-79, pres. choir, 1973-75, 77-79; advisor Jr. Achievement, Jacksonville, 1972. Served to lt. USN, 1968-71. Recipient Book award Am. Jurisprudence, U. Fla., 1966. Mem. ABA, Phi Eta Sigma, Delta Theta Phi, Delta Sigma Pi, Phi Mu Alpha. Democrat. Home: 7524 Strato Rd Jacksonville FL 32210 Office: 4613 Phillips Hwy Suite 221 Jacksonville FL 32207

MERWITZER, WILLIAM MICHAEL, insurance agent, office time-sharing company official; b. Pitts., Oct. 9, 1940; s. Charles S. and Helen (Kramer) M.; m. Barbara Lee Stock, Aug. 12, 1962; children—Craig, Kenneth, Randi. B.S., Duquesne U., 1962. Buyer, gen. mdse. mgr. May Co. Dept. Stores, Pitts., Balt., 1962-69; pres. Wearhouse, Garden Grove, Calif., 1969-74; career agt. Mass. Mut. Ins. Co., Miami, Fla., 1974-77; pres., William M. Merwitzer & Assocs., Miami, 1977—. Contbr. articles to profl. jours. Bd. dirs. So. Dade Hebrew Acad., Miami, 1974-77. Served with USCGR, 1960-68. Mem. Nat. Assn. Life Underwriters (Nat. Quality, Nat. Sales Achievement, Health Ins. Quality awards 1983), Internat. Assn. Fin. Planners, Million Dollar Round Table. Republican. Jewish. Club: Bet Breira Temple Men's (pres. 1975 Miami). Office: William M Merwitzer Inc Suite 230 8370 W Flager St Miami FL 33144

MESCHAN, ISADORE, diagnostic radiologist; b. Cleve., May 30, 1914; s. Julius and Helen Anna (Gordon) M.; m. Rachel Farrer, Sept. 3, 1943; children—David Farrer, Eleanor Jane Meschan Foy, Rosalind Meschan Weir, Joyce Irene. B.A., Western Res. U., 1935, M.A., 1937, M.D., 1939; D.Sc. (hon.), U. Ark.-Little Rock, 1983. Lic. physician, Ohio, Ark., N.C. Intern, Cleve. City Hosp., 1939-40; resident in radiology Univ. Hosp., Cleve., 1940-42; teaching research fellow Western Res. U., 1936-37, instr. radiology, 1946-47; prof., head dept. radiology U. Ark., Little Rock, 1947-55; prof., head dept. radiology Wake Forest U., Winston-Salem, N.C., 1955-77, assoc. dept. anatomy, 1977—, dir. continuing edn. dept. radiology, 1977-84; cons. Walter Reed Army Med. Ctr., Oak Ridge Inst. Nuclear Medicine; mem. spl. med. adv. group VA; guest examiner Am. Bd. Radiology; chmn. com. radiology NRC-Nat. Acad. Scis.; bd. govs. Am. Coll. Med. Imaging; sci. adv. bd. Armed Forces Inst. Pathology. Author 20 books including: (with R.F. Meschan) Analyse der rontgenbilder: Klinische radiologie, Vol. I, 1978; (with W. Bo and W. Kruger) An Atlas of Cross-Sectional Anatomy, 1980; Synopsis of Radiologic Anatomy with Computed Tomography, rev. edit., 1980; Compendio di Diagnostica Radiologica, 1981. Contbr. articles to profl. jours., chpts. to books. Patentee in field. Served to maj., AUS, 1942-44. Recipient numerous research grants; Crile fellow Western Res. U., 1935-38, teaching research fellow, 1936-37; Bowman Gray Sch. Medicine yearbook dedicated in his honor, 1964; recipient Pro Mundi Beneficio medal Brazilian Acad. Humanities, 1975; Reeves and Rousseau Meml. Cup, N.C. Soc. Radiol. Technologists, 1980; named disting. alumnus Western Res. U. Med. Alumni, 1984; named to Glenville High Sch. Hall of Fame, 1982. Disting. fellow Am. Coll. Nuclear Medicine; mem. Am. Coll. Radiology (Gold medal 1978), AMA, Assn. Univ. Radiologists, Forsyth County Med. Soc., Med. Soc. N.C., Radiol. Soc. N.Am., Am. Roentgen Ray Soc., Soc. Chairmen Acad. Radiology Depts., Soc. Nuclear

Medicine, So. Med. Assn. (life), Am. Cancer Soc. (local pres.), Inter-Am. Coll. Radiology, N.C. Soc. Radiol. Technologists (hon.), Phi Beta Kappa, Sigma Xi, Alpha Omega Alpha. Jewish. Home: 305 Weatherfield Ln Kernersville NC 27284 Office: Bowman Gray Sch of Medicine Winston Salem NC 27103

MESHIRER, DAVID DONALD, electrical engineer; b. Flushing, N.Y., July 27, 1921; s. William and Rose (Rickel) M.; student U. Bridgeport; grad. RCA Inst., 1941; B.S. in Elec. Engring., A.R.C. Sch., Boonton, N.J., 1960; m. Joan May Hartley, Mar. 14, 1951; children—Donald William, Douglas Kit. Comml. sales mgr. Dayton Aviation Radio Equipment Corp., Troy, Ohio, 1966-68; mgr. Avionics-Mooney S.W. Inc., Midland, Tex., 1968-69; mgr. electronics systems div. Gen. Instrument Corp., Hicksville, L.I., N.Y., 1969-71; engring. mgr. Aquila Aero, Inc., Midland, 1971-80, dir. engring., 1980-83; mgr. avionics Fairchild Aircraft Corp., San Antonio, 1983—. Served with USAAF, 1943-45; maj. USNG. Recipient Outstanding Performance award Tex. State Guard, 1977; Individual Recognition award State of Tex. Adj. Gen., 1980, 83. Mem. Instrument Soc. Am. Editor: Instrumentation Newsletter, 1963-65; patentee microphone. Home: 15015 Flaming Creek San Antonio TX 78217 Office: PO Box 32486 San Antonio TX 78286

MESHRI, INDU DAYAL, geochemist, geological consultant; b. Hyderabad, Sindh, India, July 16, 1944; came to U.S., 1966; d. Arjandas Gyanchand and Pushpa (Advani) Chainani; m. Dayal T. Meshri, June 20, 1966; children—Geeta D., Sanjay D. B.Sc., U. Bombay, India, 1964, M.Sc., 1966; Ph.D., U. Tulsa, 1981. Teaching asst. Parle Coll., Bombay, 1964-65; research fellow Royal Inst. Sci., Bombay, 1965-66, U. Idaho, Moscow, 1966-67; research asst. Amoco Prodn. Co., Tulsa, 1974-77, research scientist, 1977—, sr. research scientist, 1983—. Patentee in field. Coordinator Middle Sch. Vol. Sci. Tchrs., Tulsa Pub. Schs., 1983—. Merit scholar U. Bombay, 1960-64, Royal Inst. Sci. fellow, 1965-66; earth sci. grad. fellow U. Tulsa, Bombay, 1976-77. Mem. Am. Assn. Petroleum Geologists, Soc. Econ. Mineralogists and Petrologists, Am. Chem. Soc., Tulsa Geol. Soc., Sigma Xi. Democrat. Hindu. Club: India Chemists Avocations: reading; science teaching; cooking. Office: Amoco Prodn Co Tulsa OK 74102

MESSEGUER, MANUEL (MANNY), retail business executive, consultant; b. Holquin, Oriente, Cuba, June 15, 1943; s. Manuel A. and Rosa A. (Alvarez) M.; came to U.S., 1949; m. Rita A. Valdes, Dec. 7, 1963; children—Melissa, Mark, Manuel. Student in electronics U.S. Air Force Schs., Biloxi, Miss. Owner, operator BAMA VW Co., Montgomery, Ala., 1980-82, B&K Auto Parts Co., Orlando, Fla., 1979-83, M.E. Auto Sales Co., Orlando, 1975-84, Universal Motors Co., Orlando, 1979-81; gen. mgr. Englandek Toyota Co., Orlando, 1982-83; gen. mgr. Sunstate Ford, 1983; sales trainer for motivating, organizing franchise dealers. Mem. Central Fla. Heart Assn. Served with USAF, 1963-67. Recipient Airman of Quater award U.S. Air Force, 1965. Mem. Pilots of Central Fla. Assn. Republican. Roman Catholic. Club: Aero (Orlando). Lodges: Lions, Eagles. Creator sales techniques used in numerous states for Ford Motor Co. and Gen. Motors Acceptance Corp. Home: 3000 Ardsley Dr Orlando FL 32804 Office: 3535 W Colonial Dr Orlando FL 32808

MESSERSMITH, DAVID ROSS, architect; b. Ft. Worth, Jan. 16, 1949; s. Robert Charles and Dorothy Jean (Loafman) M.; student Northwestern U., 1967-69; B. Arch., Tex. Tech. U., 1973; m. Leanne Floyd, May 25, 1974. Staff architect Campbell, Yost, Grube, Portland, 1973-76, Reddick, Brun, Moreland, Portland, 1976-77; asso. Robert Messersmith & Assos., Midland, Tex., 1977-80; partner Messersmith Whitaker Messersmith, Midland, 1980-81; prin. MWM Architects, Inc., 1981—. Mem. Midland Bldg. Bd. Appeals, 1983—. Mem. AIA (pres. West Tex. chpt. 1984), Tex. Soc. Architects, Midland C. of C., Tau Sigma Delta. Club: Lions (chmn. young men's com. 1981). Office: 30-A Village Ct Midland TX 79701

MESSICK, WILLIAM JOHN, clergyman, university official; b. Phila., July 31, 1944; s. William John and Catherine (Olish) M.: A.B., Catholic U. Am., 1968; M.A., Niagara U., 1970, St. Charles Sem., Phila., 1976; Ph.D., U. Md., 1978; Ed.D., Nova U., 1983. Ordained priest Roman Cath. Ch., 1971; tchr. Northeast Cath. High Sch., Phila., 1963-65; counselor, campus minister Georgetown U., 1969-72; dir. pupil personnel services Salesianum Sch., Wilmington, Del., 1974-77; prin. St. Joseph Central Cath. High Sch., Huntington, W.Va., 1977-80; pres. Father Lopez High Sch., Daytona Beach, Fla., 1980-83; dir. planned giving and research Barry U., Miami Shores, Fla., 1982-84, exec. asst. to pres., 1984—. Gen. Electric Co. fellow, 1975. Mem. Am. Personnel and Guidance Assn. (dir. 1978-81, chmn. pub. relations com. 1979-80, exec. com. 1979-80, awards com. 1983), Assn. Religious and Value Issues in Counseling (treas. and dir. 1975-77, Senator 1977-78, pres. 1982, profl. service award 1977), Nat. Cath. Edn. Assn. (regional adv. bd. 1978-82). Democrat. Office: Barry Univ Miami Shores FL 33161

MESSINA, JAMES JOHN, counseling psychologist; b. Niagara Falls, N.Y., Mar. 6, 1945; s. Paul Salvatore and Gilda Marie (Ruffalo) M.; B.A., Cath. U. Am., 1968; Ed.M., SUNY-Buffalo, 1970, Ph.D. in Counseling Psychology, 1973; postgrad. U. Fla., 1974; m. Constance Mayme Giovino, Aug. 4, 1973; children—Melissa Messina, Steven. Instr., counselor Bishop Timon High Sch., Buffalo, 1969; sch. counselor Hamburg (N.Y.) Jr. High Sch., 1970-72; head resident Dormitory Authority, SUNY-Buffalo, 1973, grad. asst., 1973; instr. dept. counselor edn. U. Fla., Gainesville, 1974; dir. preventive edn. services Child Devel. Center, Pensacola, Fla., 1974-77; adj. prof. dept. psychology U. West Fla., Pensacola, 1976; faculty counseling dept. Johns Hopkins U., also dir. Evening Coll., Columbia (Md.) Center, 1977-78; project dir., assoc. prof. Fla. Mental Health Inst., Tampa, 1978-80; pvt. practice psychology, Tampa, 1980—. Temple Terrace, Fla., 1980—. Pres., Advanced Devel. Systems, Inc., Tampa, 1982—; adj. faculty U. South Fla.; cons. in field; bd. dirs. Nat. Bd. Cert. Counselors, 1982—. Author skills tng. manuals and numerous articles. Bd. dirs. Fla. Ctr. Children and Youth, 1982-84, Fla. div. Mental Health Assn. 1980-81. Mem. Am. Personnel and Guidance Assn. (dir. 1978—; Profl. Devel. award 1982). Named Vol. of Yr. Mental Health Assn. Hillsborough County, 1981, Am. Psychol. Assn., Am. Mental Health Counselors Assn. (dir. 1976—, pres. 1978-79; Counselor of Yr. 1981-82), Nat. Acad. Cert. Clin. Mental Health Counselors (bd. dirs., chmn. 1979-82). Home: 10700 62d St Temple Terrace FL 33617 Office: 7405-D Temple Terrace Hwy Tampa FL 33617

MESSMER, HAROLD MAXIMILIAN, JR., holding corporation executive; b. Jackson, Miss., Feb. 20, 1946; s. Harold Maximilian and Margaret (Dee) M.; m. Marcia Elizabeth Nesmith, Apr. 5, 1973; children—Michael Christopher, Matthew Gordon. A.B. summa cum laude, Loyola U., 1967; J.D. cum laude, NYU, 1970. Ptnr. corp. law and securities O'Melveny & Myers, Los Angeles, 1970-80; sr. v.p., gen. counsel Pacific Holding Corp., Los Angeles, 1981-82, pres., dir., chief operating officer, 1982-85; pres., dir., vice chmn., chief operating officer Cannon Hills Co. (subs.), Kannapolis, N.C., 1982-85; exec. v.p., dir. Castle & Cooke, Inc., San Francisco, 1985; dir. Boothe Fin. Corp., San Francisco, NCNB of N.C., Charlotte, Flexivan Corp., N.Y.C. Trustee Davidson Coll., N.C., U. N.C.-Charlotte, 1983—. Valedictorian, Loyola U., New Orleans, 1967. Mem. ABA, Los Angeles County Bar Assn., Calif. Bar Assn., Sigma Nu (editor jour.). Address: Boothe Fin Corp 100 Bush St San Francisco CA 94104

MESTROVIC, STJEPAN GABRIEL, sociology educator; b. Zagreb, Yugoslavia, Mar. 12, 1955; came to U.S., 1963, naturalized, 1968; s. Tvrtko Mestrovic and Tea (Kosac) Dudley; m. Cathy Ann Wasson, Mar. 3, 1984. B.A. cum laude, Harvard U., 1976, Ed.M., 1977, M.T.S., 1979; Ph.D., Syracuse U., 1982. Asst. prof. sociology Lander Coll., Greenwood, S.C., 1982—. Contbr. articles to profl. jours. Fulbright fellow, 1985. Mem. Internat. Acad. Law and Mental Health, Am. Sociol. Assn., So. Sociol. Soc., Internat. Inst. Sociology, Soc. Sci. Study Religion. Democrat. Roman Catholic. Home: 1102 Florence St Greenwood SC 29646 Office: Lander Coll Sociology Dept Greenwood SC 29646

MESZAROS, JORDANKA POPOFF, architect; b. Bulgaria, May 30, 1925; came to U.S., 1961, naturalized, 1969; d. Christo Petroff and Maria Zlateva (Michailova) Popoff; student Technische Hochschule, Vienna, Austria, 1943-44; B.Arch., State Poly. Sofia (Bulgaria), 1948; m. Zoltan Meszaros Laub, May 24, 1946; 1 son, Kristian Meszaros Popoff. With Office of A. E. Konstantinoff, Architect, Rome, 1949; with Martin Engring. Co., Maracaibo, Venezuela, 1949-52, INARCO; Maracaibo, 1952; pvt. practice design and constrn. services, 1952-58; assoc. Fritz Schmidt, San Juan, PR., 1958-61, Angel Aviles, San Juan, 1961-63; with Public Bldgs. Authority P.R., San Juan, 1965—, asst. exec. dir. planning and design, 1973-77, dir. planning and programming dept., 1977—; lectr. U. P.R. Faculty of Architecture; cons. Market Devel. Co., San Juan. Active Asociacion pro Orquestra Sinfónica de P.R., San Juan. Mem. AIA (P.R. chpt. dir. 1976-78, sec. 1979), Inst. Architects P.R. (sec. 1975, 76). Greek Orthodox. Club: Metropolitano de Tiro (San Juan). Participant numerous seminars. Home: 709 Miramar Ave Santurce PR 00907 Office: Govt Center Minillas de Diego Ave Santurce PR 00940

METCALF, ROGER DALE, SR., dentist; b. Fort Worth, July 24, 1950; s. Frank Dean and Fannie Pauline (Yarbrough) M.; B.S., Baylor U., 1973, D.D.S., 1977; m. Linda Susan Cervenka, June 15, 1974; children—Roger Dale, Kelli Anne, Ryan David. Pvt. practice dentistry, Arlington, Tex., 1977-85, Prairie, Tex., 1985—; owner Medicalc, Arlington, 1980—. Pres., chmn. bd. Am. Cancer Soc., 1983, 84. Mem. ADA Tex. Dental Assn., Fort Worth Dist. Dental Soc., Acad. Gen. Dentistry, Am. Acad. Gold Foil Ops., Profl. Photographers Am., Mensa. Republican. Baptist. Lodge: Rotary Internat. Home: 5126 Bridgewater Arlington TX 76017 Office: 350 Independent Am Savs Bldg 530 S Carrier Pkwy Grand Prairie TX 75051

METTS, BROOKS CONRAD, clinical pharmacy educator, poison information specialist; b. Oxford, Miss., July 10, 1943; s. Brooks C. and Clara Lynn (Moorman) M.; m. June Inez Kilpatrick, Oct. 7, 1972; 1 child, Jonathan Patrick. B.S. in Pharmacy, U. Tenn.-Memphis, 1967, Pharm.D., 1970. Registered pharmacist, Tenn., S.C. Asst. prof. W.Va. U., Morgantown, 1970-72, dir. Drug and Poison Info. Ctr., 1971-72; asst. prof. U. S.C., Columbia, 1972-77, assoc. prof. pharmacy, 1977—, dir. Drug and Poison Info. Ctr., 1972-84, coordinator clin. pharmacy edn., 1974-79, dir. Palmetto Poison Ctr., 1980—. Co-author: A Handbook of Information for the Pharmacy Student in the Clinical Setting, 1971. Contbr. articles to profl. jours. Recipient Bristol award Bristol Labs., 1967. Mem. Am. Soc. Hosp. Pharmacists (adv. panel student membership 1976—), Am. Pharm. Assn., Am. Assn. Colls. Pharmacy (liaison rep. 1980—), Nat. Poison Ctr. Network (chmn. dept. patient info. 1982-83), Am. Assn. Poison Control Cts. Lutheran. Lodge: Optimists (pres. 1976-77, bd. dirs. 1981-83). Avocation: Photography. Office: Palmetto Poison Ctr U S C Columbia SC 29208

METWALLI, SAYED MOHAMED, mechanical engineering educator; b. Suez, Egypt, Apr. 18, 1943; came to U.S., 1968; s. Mohamed and Khadiga Sayed (Abdel-Al) M.; m. Tahani Hassan Elmamlouk, June 27, 1974; children—Nader, Tamer. B.S. with honors, Cairo U., 1965; M.S., SUNY-Buffalo, 1970, Ph.D., 1973. Instr., Cairo U., 1965-68, asst. prof., 1973-76, assoc. prof., 1978-81; teaching and research asst. SUNY-Buffalo, 1968-73; vis. asst. prof. N.C. State U., 1976-78; assoc. prof. dept. mech. engring. U. Central Fla., Orlando, 1981—; cons. in field. Grantee: Nasr Boiler and Pressure Vessels, Egypt, 1979-81, Dept. Def./Naval Research Lab., 1982-83, U. Central Fla. Div. Sponsored Research and Engring. and Indsl. Expt. Sta., 1982-83. Mem. Am. Acad. Mechanics, Fla. Acad. Scis., ASME, Am. Inst. Indsl. Engrs., Soc. Exptl. Stress Analysis, Sigma Xi, Pi Tau Sigma, Tau Beta Pi. Moslem. Editor: (with G.S.A. Shawki) Current Advances in Mechanical Design and Production, 1981; contbr. articles to profl. jours. Office: PO Box 25000 Orlando FL 32816

METZDORF, DAVID, orthodontist; b. Cleve., July 23, 1940; s. Elmer G. and Alice (Haskins) M.; m. M. Jean Fisher, Aug. 13, 1961; children—Rebecca, Deborah, David. D.D.S., Loma Linda U., 1965; M.S., Ohio State U., 1973. Gen. practice dentistry, Chatsworth, Calif., 1965-71; practice dentistry specializing in orthodontics, Vienna, Va., 1973—. Mem. ADA, Am. Assn. Orthodontists (orthodontic cert. 1973), Am. Assn. Functional Orthodontists. Republican. Home: 5 Alloway Ct Potomac MD 20854 Office: 301 Maple Ave W Vienna VA 22180

METZGER, KENT ALAN, insurance company executive, construction executive; b. Dallas, Sept. 30, 1952; s. Elmer William Metzger Jr. and Dora Margaret (Klenk) Metzger Hines; m. Genevieve Taylor, May 2, 1981; children—Taylor Kent, Genevieve Ann. B.S., U. Tex.-Arlington, 1975; student in constrn. mgmt. Richland Coll., 1980. Civil-structural designer Haguer/Hixon Inc., Dallas, 1973-74; elec.-mech. designer GMR Inc., Dallas, 1975; project architect Dales Y. Foster, Architects, Dallas, 1975-76; constrn. rep., store planner J. C. Penney Co., Inc., Dallas, 1976-84; facilities mgr. J. C. Penney Ins. Co., Plano, Tex., 1984—; owner, operator KAM Constrn., Dallas, 1982—. Judge Miss T.E.E.N. Pageant, Dallas, 1983; charter mem. Rep. Presdl. Task Force, Washington, 1980. Mem. Inst. Store Planners, Soc. Archtl. Historians. Presbyterian. Avocations: woodworking; photography; racquetball.

MEW, THOMAS JOSEPH, III, artist, educator; b. Miami, Fla., Aug. 15, 1940; s. Thomas Joseph and Maude Edith (Perry) M.; m. Mary Ann Kelley, June 17, 1966; 1 child, Thomas Joseph IV. Student U. Houston, 1958-59; B.S., Fla. State U., 1962, M.A., 1964; Ph.D., NYU, 1966. Grad. teaching asst. Fla. State U., Tallahassee, 1963-64; asst. prof. art Troy State U., Ala., 1966-68, Jacksonville U., Fla., 1968-70; prof., chmn. dept. art Berry Coll., Mount Berry, Ga., 1970—; bd. dirs. Contemporary Art/S.E., 1976. Author books of poetry, the most recent being: Some Small Deaths, 1980. One-man shows include Montgomery Mus. Fine Arts, Ala., 1970, Drawing Gallery, Poznan, Poland, 1980, Southeast Ctr. Contemporary Art, Winston-Salem, S.C., 1985; group shows include High Mus. Art, Atlanta, 1971, Liverpool Acad. Arts, Eng., 1979, Modern Realism Gallery, Dallas, 1985; represented in permanent collections Kansas City Art Inst., Middleburg Netherlands Mus., Jacksonville Art Mus., A.T.&T., Provincial Mus., Hasselt, McDonald's Corp., Macon Mus. Arts and Scis. Bd. dirs. Interface, Tulsa, 1980. Grantee Cowperthwaite, 1971, Lilly Found., 1975, Gulf Life, 1977. Mem. Southeastern Coll. Art Assn., Coll. Art Assn. Am., Am. Fedn. Arts, Nat. Art Edn. Assn. Episcopalian. Avocations: marathon running; hang gliding; surfing. Home: 100 Saddle Trail Rome GA 30161 Office: Berry Coll Dept Art PO Box 580 Mount Berry GA 30149

MEYER, C. LEE, educational administrator. Supt. of schs. Pasadena, Tex. Office: Box 1799 Pasadena TX 77501*

MEYER, DALE THOMAS, architect; b. St. Louis, Aug. 21, 1948; s. Thomas Patrick and Dorothy Ann (Bene) M. Exchange student, London, 1970; B. Arch., U. Nebr., 1971. Owner, architect Dale Meyer Assoc., Redwood City, Calif., 1976-83, Argyle, Tex., 1984—; ptnr. Meyer Stewart Assoc., San Carlos, Calif., 1983-84. Mem. Bartonville Planning Commn., Tex., 1985, Redwood City Hist. Commn., Calif., 1981-83. Curators scholar U. Nebr.; Rash scholar State of Mo. Mem. AIA (design commn., hist. commn., energy commn.), AIA (Tex. and San Francisco chpts.), Nat. Hist. Preservation Soc. Democrat. Roman Catholic. Avocations: art; photography; sports.

MEYER, DAVID ALFRED, financial development executive; b. Camp Dennison, Ohio, Sept. 10, 1912; s. Joseph Henry and Mary Ellen (Metz) M.; m. Marie Barnhart Zeisler, May 17, 1933; children—David Alfred Jr., Frank Joseph, Betty Ann Meyer Perkins. B.S., Ohio State U., 1934. Dist. exec. Toledo area council Boy Scouts Am., Ohio, 1942-48, scout exec. Tomahawk council, Coshocton, Ohio, 1948-52, dep. regional dir., Memphis, 1952-59, asst. dir. fin., 1959-72, nat. dir. fin., New Brunswick, N.J., 1972-77; prin. David A. Meyer Agy., Dallas, 1977—. Author: Four Phase Sustaining Membership Enrollment, 1972; Financing the Local Council, 1973; Developing Prospects, 1975; (pamphlets) Fund Raising Auctions, 1980; Financing in Metropolitan Areas, 1982. Pres. Faust Community Club, Fremont, Ohio, 1947; trustee Am. Humonics Found., Kansas City, Mo., 1960-70, Cranbury Hist. Soc., N.J., 1973-77. Recipient George Washington Honor medal Freedoms Found., 1967, 68, 69, 85. Republican. Presbyterian. Lodge: Lions (pres. Cranbury 1976-77, zone chmn. Dallas, 1985). Avocation: antique and art collecting. Home and Office: 7018 Duffield Dr Dallas TX 75248

MEYER, ELMER EPHRAIM, JR., university official; b. Green Bay, Wis., Jan. 4, 1928; s. Elmer E. and Irma (Heins) M.; m. Nancy S. Ramsay, June 26, 1954; children—Marc Ramsay, Megan Christina, Rene Jean. B.A., Carroll Coll., 1950; M.S., U. Wis., 1955, Ph.D., 1965; cert. Inst. Edn. Mgmt., Harvard U., 1977. Admissions counselor Carroll Coll., Waukesha, Wis., 1950, 52-54; counselor Integrated Liberal Studies, U. Wis., Madison, 1955-57; asst. to dir. tchr. placement, 1956-57, activities adviser, 1952-63, asst. dean students, 1963-66; asst. chancellor student affairs U. Wis. Ctr. System, 1966-68; dean students, asst. v.p. student affairs Cornell U., Ithaca, N.Y., 1968-72, dean students, asst. v.p. campus affairs, 1972-79; vice chancellor student life East Carolina U., Greenville, N.C., 1979—. Mem. adv. bd. CHOICE, 1977-80; chmn. parent tchr. bd. Ithaca Elem. Sch., 1971-72; trustee Ithaca Montessori Soc., 1970-75. Served with U.S. Army, 1950-52. Mem. Am. Assn. Higher Edn., Am. Coll. Personnel Assn., Am. Assn. Counseling and Devel., Assn., Nat. Assn. Student Personnel Adminstrs. (chmn. 1974-75), Council Student Personnel Adminstrn. in Higher Edn., Phi Delta Kappa, Phi Kappa Phi. Clubs: Ithaca Yacht. Contbr. articles to profl. jours. Home: 1316 Rondo Dr Greenville NC 27834 Office: 204 Whichard Bldg East Carolina U Greenville NC 27834

MEYER, FREDERICK RAY, manufacturing company executive; b. Highland Park, Ill., Dec. 30, 1927; s. Raymond Thorne and Marian Catherine (Anderson) M.; m. Barbara Spreuer, Oct. 24, 1953; children—Cheryl L., Amy Sue, Bradley A. B.S., Purdue U., 1949; M.B.A., Harvard, 1958. Registered profl. engr., Ind. Treas. Aladdin Industries, Nashville, 1958-67; pres. Crescent Dallas div. Tyler Corp., 1967-68, v.p. corporate staff, 1968-70, sr. v.p., 1970-77, exec. v.p., 1977—, dir., 1967—, mem. exec. com., 1971—; dir. Aladdin Industries, Inc., Arvin Industries, Inc. Chmn. Rep. Alan Steelman's campaigns, 1972, 74; chmn. Dallas County Rep. Com.; trustee Inst. for Aerobics Research; bd. dirs. Fund for Theol. Edn. Served with U.S. Army, 1953-55. Mem. Dallas Petroleum Club. Republican. Presbyn. (elder). Club: Mason. Home: 5830 Averill Way Dallas TX 75225 Office: 3121 Southland Center Dallas TX 75201*

MEYER, LAWRENCE JOSEPH, lawyer; b. Chgo., July 7, 1927; s. Joseph Benjamin and Sarah (Peilet) M.; student Roosevelt Coll., Chgo., 1948-50; LL.B., U. Miami, 1954; children—Sandra Leigh, Janice Beth, Pamela Sue. Admitted to Fla. bar, 1955; individual practice law, Hollywood, Fla., 1955—; small claims judge Broward County, 1963-73. Past chmn. T-Y Park Bd. Broward County; mem. Com. of 100, Hollywood. Served with USNR, 1945-48. Ky. col. Mem. Am. Bar Assn., Fla. Bar Assn., Broward Bar Assn. (past mem. exec. com.), South Broward Bar Assn. (past dir.). Mason (Shriner). Office: 2435 Hollywood Blvd Hollywood FL 33020

MEYER, LOUIS B, state supreme ct. justice; b. Marion, N.C., July 15, 1933; s. Louis B. and Beulah (Smith) M.; B.A., Wake Forest U., 1955, J.D., 1960; m. Evelyn Spradlin, Dec. 29, 1956; children—Louis B. III, Patricia Shannon, Adam Burden. Admitted to N.C. bar, 1960; research asst. N.C. Supreme Ct., 1960; spl. agt. FBI, 1961-62; practice law, Wilson, N.C., 1962-81; asso. justice Supreme Ct. N.C., Raleigh, 1981—. Served as 1st lt., U.S. Army 1955-57. Mem. N.C. Bar Assn., 7th Jud. Dist. Bar Assn., Wilson County Bar Assn. Democrat. Baptist. Office: Box 1841 Raleigh NC 27602

MEYER, PETER, college administrator, educator, consultant; b. Bremen, Germany, May 2, 1930; came to U.S., 1937; s. Hans and Marianne M. (Bach) M.; m. Ursula M. Thuemer, July 3, 1951 (div. Feb. 1972); 1 son, David; m. Linda W. Shoulberg, Dec. 31, 1980; 1 stepdau., Amy Shoulberg. B.A., Queens Coll., CUNY, 1955; M.S., Columbia U., 1957; Ph.D., NYU, 1963. Asst. dean, counseling supr. Queens Coll., Flushing, N.Y., 1959-69; program assoc. So. Regional Edn. Bd., Atlanta, 1970-72; chmn. social work, prof. Fla. Internat. U., Miami, 1972-76; cons. adult degree programming and mgmt. devel., Burnsville, N.C., 1976-81; exec. dir. Queens Inst. for Lifelong Learning, Charlotte, N.C., 1981-82; dean, prof. social work Pfeiffer Coll., Charlotte, 1982-85; assoc. dir. Ctr. Urban Affairs, assoc. prof. adult and community coll. edn. N.C. State U., Raleigh, 1986—; Served to cpl. U.S. Army, 1951-53. Recipient Founders Day award NYU, 1963; Ford Found. grantee, 1973. Mem. N.C. Adult Edn. Assn. (exec. com.), Council for the Advancement Experiential Learning, Am. Assn. Higher Edn. Author: Awarding College Credit-For Non-College Learning, 1975; contbr. numerous articles on adult edn. and counseling to profl. jours. Home: 6516 Suburban Dr #2B Raleigh NC 27609 Office: NC State U Box 7401 Raleigh NC 27695

MEYER, RANDALL, oil company executive; b. Mt. Union, Iowa, Jan. 19, 1923; s. Carl Henry and Edythe (Stuck) M.; B.S. in Mech. Engring., U. Iowa, 1948; LL.D. (hon.), Iowa Wesleyan Coll., 1977; m. Barbara Swetman, Nov. 29, 1958; children—Warren, Gretchen, Kirsten. With Exxon Co. U.S.A. (formerly Humble Oil & Refining Co.) div. Exxon Corp., 1948—, with tech. and mgmt. depts., Baton Rouge, Houston, 1948-66, exec. asst. to pres. Exxon Corp., N.Y.C., 1966-67, sr. v.p., dir. Exxon Co. U.S.A., Houston, 1967-72, pres., 1972—. Bd. dirs. Tex. Research League; trustee Exec. Service Corp., Houston; bd. dirs., mem. exec. com. Meth. Hosp.; chmn. bd. trustees Found. For Bus. Politics Econs.; chmn. bd. trustees, mem. exec. com. Kinkaid Sch.; assoc. mem. Univ. Cancer Found. Bd. Visitors; chmn. Princeton U. Parents Assn. Mem. Am. Petroleum Inst. (dir.), Tex. Assn. Taxpayers (dir., mem. exec. com., past pres.), Sigma Xi, Tau Beta Pi, Omicron Delta Kappa, Pi Tau Sigma. Methodist. Office: PO Box 2180 Houston TX 77001

MEYER, ROBERT NORFLEET, architect; b. Jefferson, Ohio, Nov. 6, 1957; s. William John and Mary Rebecca (Norfleet) M. B.Arch., Va. Polytechnic Inst. and State U., 1980; student Va. Commonwealth U., 1979. Lic. architect, Va. Draftsman Ernie Rose, Inc., Architects, Richmond, Va., 1978-79, 80-81; project capt. Freeman & Morgan Architects, P.C., Richmond, 1981-83; project mgr. Architecture Unlimited, P.C., Richmond, 1983—. Recipient Alice Lehman Sunday prize for presentation sketches, 1985. Avocations: bicycle; snow skiing; plants; swimming; painting. Office: Architecture Unlimited PC 9323 Midlothian Turnpike Richmond VA 23235

MEYER, VAUGHAN BENJAMIN, lumber company executive; b. Eagle Pass, Tex., Dec. 13, 1920; s. Otto Charles and Genevieve Curtis (Vaughan) M.; m. Courtenay Langdon Lyon, May 25, 1946 (dec.); m. 2d, Alice Gertrudis King Kleberg Reynolds, Dec. 22, 1973; children—Courtenay (dec.), Catherine H. Meyer Lange, Beverly V. B.S. in Mech. Engring., Rice U., 1941; postgrad. Calif. Inst. Tech., 1941-42. Exec. v.p. Alamo Lumber Co., San Antonio, 1948-61; pres. Eagle Lumber Co., San Antonio, 1961—, Art Homes, Inc., San Antonio, 1964—, Eagle Sand & Gravel, Inc., San Antonio, 1982—; dir. Vaughan & Sons, San Antonio, Lumbermen's Underwriters, Austin. Councilman, mayor pro tempore, City of Terrell Hills (Tex.), 1965-68; trustee Vaughan Found., Raymond Dickson Found., Alice Kleberg Reynolds Meyer Found., Southwest Found. for Research and Edn., St. Mary's Hall. Served to lt. comdr. USNR, 1942-46. Mem. SAR, Soc. Colonial Wars, Mil. Order Loyal Legion, Sigma Xi. Republican. Episcopalian. Clubs: Argyle, San Antonio Country, Tex. Cavaliers. Home: 200 Patterson St Apt 906 San Antonio TX 78209 Office: PO Box 6985 San Antonio TX 78209

MEYERS, CARL, safety engineer, educator; b. N.Y.C., Sept. 19, 1919; m. Myra Gordon, Oct. 20, 1945; children—Francine, Arthur. B.S. in Mgmt., NYU, 1958, M.A. in Indsl. Safety, 1960; postgrad. in Edn., SUNY-N.Y.C., 1962, in Labor Mgmt., Cornell U., 1965. Asst. regional adminstr. for compliance Dept. Labor, N.Y.C., 1972-73, asst. regional adminstr. for tng., 1973-76, area dir., mgr., 1976-78, supr., 1978-82, safety engr., 1972—; asst. dir. safety N.Y.C. Transit Authority, 1962-72; assoc. prof. indsl. safety NYU, N.Y.C., 1972-75, Fla. Internat. U., Miami, 1984. Author: New York City Transit Safety Rule Book, 1965; Fire Protections Systems Booklet, U.S. Dept. Labor, 1980. Instr. ARC; lt. Plainview Vol. Fire Dept., N.Y., 1960-79, mem. rescue squad, 1960-79. Served with USAAF, 1943-46, ETO. Recipient Honor award Tampa Fed. Agys., 1982. Mem. Am. Soc. Safety Engrs. (cert. safety profl., pres. 1980-84). Republican. Avocations: golf, tennis, bridge, lecturing. Home: 1430 Gulf Blvd Apt 303 Clearwater FL 33515

MEYERS, GRANT ULYSSES, foundry company executive; b. Moline, Ill., May 1, 1913; s. George C. and Lillian (Rommel) M.; B.S.C., Northwestern U., 1933; M.B.A., U. Chgo., 1955; m. Doris M. Fraser, Jan. 23, 1953 (dec. July 1977); children—Stuart, Joan, Glen, Eric, Marcia. Mgr. accounting dept. Wis. Steel Works div. Internat. Harvester Co., Chgo., 1933-55; v.p., comptroller Radiant Mfg. Corp., Morton Grove, 1955-59; sec.-treas. Security-Columbian Banknote Co., N.Y.C., 1959-60, financial v.p., sec., 1960-65; owner, chmn., pres., chief exec. officer Oil City Iron Works, Inc., div. Grandor Corp., Corsicana, Tex., 1965—. Mem. Financial Execs. Inst., Nat. Assn. Accountants (internat. pres. 1969-70), Acacia, Beta Gamma Sigma, Beta Alpha Psi. Mason. Clubs: Metropolitan (N.Y.C.); Corsicana Country; Dallas Petroleum. Home: 2514 Big Horn Ln Richardson TX 75080 Office: PO Drawer 1560 Corsicana TX 75110

MEYERS, HOWARD HARMON, university career counselor, consultant; b. Buffalo, Apr. 23, 1951; s. Samuel and Joanne (Marks) M. B.A., Alfred U., 1972; M.S., Canisius Coll., 1976. Lic. counselor, Tex.; cert. sch. counselor, N.Y. Group guidance cons. Group Guidance Program, Buffalo, 1976-80; career counselor Jewish Vocat. Counseling Services, Dallas, 1980-81; career counselor U. Tex., Arlington, 1981—. Mem. Am. Assn. Counseling Devel., Am. Coll. Personnel Assn., Tex. Assn. Counseling and Devel., Nat. Vocat. Guidance Assn. Avocations: jogging; chess; reading; tennis. Home: 2104 Count Fleet 703 Arlington TX 76011 Office: U Tex Arlington PO Box 19156 Arlington TX 76019

MEYERS, JAMES FRANK, electronics engineer; b. Binghamton, N.Y., Sept. 9, 1946; s. Edwin Fox and Louise (Okrepkie) M.; B.E.E., U. Louisville, 1969, M.E., 1972; postgrad. George Washington U. Instr. elec. engring lab. U. Louisville, 1968-69; engring coop. technician Langley Research Center, NASA, Hampton, Va., 1966-69, aerospace technologist, 1969—. Mem. IEEE (sect. chmn. 1975), Turnberry Two Owners Assn. (pres., dir. 1979-82), Sports Car Club Am. (div. rallye exec. 1982—), Eta Kappa Nu, Tau Beta Pi, Sigma Tau. Author articles, papers in field. Office: M/S 235A Langley Research Center NASA Hampton VA 23665

MEYERS, WILLIAM CADY, geologist; b. Vicksburg, Miss., Apr. 3, 1931; s. William Baller and Mary (Cady) M.; children—Scott, Marianne, Leslie. B.A., So. Ill. U., 1956; M.S., Tulsa U., 1963, Ph.D., 1977. Research geologist Sinclair Research, Tulsa, 1956-69; sr. research geologist Cities Service Oil Co., Tulsa, 1970-79, assoc. geologist, Houston, 1979-83; staff geoscientist Murphy Oil Co., El Dorado, Ark., 1983—. Contbr. articles to profl. jours. Adviser, tchr. Boy Scouts Am., Tulsa, 1969-74. Served to 1st lt. USAF, 1952-54. Mem. Am. Assn. Stratigraphic Palynologists, Am. Assn. Petroleum Geologists. Soc. Organic Petrography, Alaska Geol. Soc. Shreveport Geol. Soc. Club: El Dorado Racquet. Avocations: tennis, fishing, boating, photography. Home: 2300 Calion Rd El Dorado AR 71730 Office: Murphy Oil Co 200 Peach St El Dorado AR 71730

MEYERSON, MORTON HERBERT, computer service company executive; b. Ft. Worth, June 3, 1938; s. Maurice Brudus and Bernice Estell (Gressman) M.; B.A. in Philosophy and Econs., U. Tex., Austin, 1960; m. Marlene Nathan, Apr. 26, 1964; children—David Nathan, Marti Ann. Vice pres., dir. Electronic Data Systems Corp., Dallas, 1966-71, pres. E.D.S. Fed. Corp. subs. Electronic Data Systems Corp., Dallas, 1975-79, pres., dir. Electronic Data Systems Corp., Dallas, 1979—; pres., dir. duPont Glore Forgan Inc., N.Y.C., 1971-75; pres. Nat. Heritage Ins. Co., Dallas, subs. E.D.S., 1976—. Bd. govs. Dallas Symphony Orchestra, chmn. concert hall com., 1980—. Served with U.S. Army, 1961-63. Jewish. Office: 7171 Forest Ln Dallas TX 75230

MEYERSON, STANLEY PHILLIP, lawyer; b. Spartanburg, S.C., Apr. 13, 1916; s. Louis A. and Ella Meyerson; m. Marion Legg, Feb. 6, 1941; children—Marianne Martin, Camilla Jurskis, Margot Ellis, Stanley P. A.B., Duke U., 1937, J.D., 1939. Bar: S.C. 1939, N.Y. 1940, Ga. 1945. Assoc. Edward L. Coffey, 1939-41; ptnr. Johnson Hatcher & Meyerson, Atlanta, 1945-55, Hatcher, Meyerson, Oxford & Irvin, Atlanta, 1955-78, Westmoreland, Hall, McGee, Oxford & Meyerson, Atlanta, 1978—; dir., officer various corps; former chmn. tax coms. Ga. Bar, Atlanta Bar Assn. Past pres. Atlanta chpt. Duke U. Alumni Assn. Mem. Am. Coll. Mortgage Attys., Atlanta Estate Planning Council. Served to lt. cmdr. USNR, 1941-45.

MEYNIER, MAURICE JOSEPH, JR., obstetrician-gynecologist, educator; b. New Orleans, Oct. 16, 1904; s. Maurice Joseph and Louise Julie (Charpantier) M.; m. Charlotte Dorothee Mosle, May 3, 1934; children—Margaret Louise, Maurice Joseph. B.A., Rice U., 1927; M.D., U. Tex.-Galveston, 1931. Diplomate Am. Bd. Ob-Gyn. Intern and resident Grad. Hosp. U. Pa., Phila., 1931-33; resident in ob-gyn King's County Hosp., Bklyn., 1933-35; practice medicine specializing in ob-gyn, Houston, 1935-77; past mem. staff Jefferson Davis Hosp., Hermann Hosp., Meth. Hosp.; past pres. St. Joseph Hosp., 1968 (all in Houston); assoc. clin. prof. ob-gyn Baylor Coll. Medicine, Houston, 1946-77, now emeritus prof.; assoc. clin. prof. ob-gyn U. Tex. Health Scis. Ctr., Houston, 1975-77, emeritus prof. Served to maj. USAAF, 1942-46. Contbr. numerous articles to med. jours.; patentee nipple shield for breast nursing, vaginal tampon, pivoting boat motor device unit. Fellow ACS; mem. AMA, Am. Coll. Ob-Gyn, So. Med. Assn., Tex. Med. Assn., Houston Surg. Soc., Tex. Assn. Ob-Gyn (past pres. 1960), Houston Ob-Gyn Soc. (pres. 1964), Harris County Med. Soc. (pres. 1969), Alpha Kappa Kappa. Republican. Clubs: Houston, Doctors. Home: 5672 Cedar Creek Houston TX 77056

MEZACK, MICHAEL, III, university administrator; b. Friedens, Pa., May 31, 1935, s. Michael and Anna Marie (Strelko) M.; m. Barbara Jeanne Myers, Dec. 27, 1958; children—Michael IV, Janienne Renee, Melissa Marie, Rebeccah Ann. B.S., Lock Haven State Coll., 1958; M.S., Bucknell U., 1968; Ed.D., Pa. State U., 1974. Area and asst. dir. continuing edn. Pa. State U., University Park, 1963-70, research assoc. in continuing edn., 1971-75; assoc. dean continuing edn., asst. prof. higher edn. Tex. Tech U., Lubbock, 1975-77, dir. continuing edn., assoc. prof., 1977—, assoc. chmn. higher edn. dept. Coll. of Edn., 1980—; mem. adv. com. instructional TV, Tex. Edn. Agy., 1977—; mem. Tex. Gov's Com. on Aging, Tex., 1976-77. Bd. dirs. Multiservice Ctr. for Older Persons, Lubbock, 1979-80; mem. research and steering com. Southwest Gerontol. Inst., Lubbock, 1980; active Lubbock Cultural Affairs Council, 1982—; vice chmn. bd. dirs. Lubbock Visitors and Conv. Bus., 1982—. Served with Med. Service Corps, U.S. Army, 1958-62. Recipient Alumni Achievement award Lock Haven State Coll., 1980; Pa. Dept. Edn. grantee, 1973. Mem. Nat. Univ. Continuing Edn. Assn. (nat. bd. dirs. 1981-83, chmn. numerous coms.), South Central Assn. for Lifelong Learning, Nat. Ret. Tchrs. Assn., Nat. Assn. State Univs. and Land Grant Colls. (council extension and continuing edn.), Tex. Assn. for Community Service and Continuing Edn. (bd. dirs. 1980-83, 1st v.p. 1981, pres. 1982, various coms.), Assn. Pub. Broadcasting (bd. dels.), West Tex. Council for Higher Edn. (coordinating bd.), Tex. Coll. and Univ. System (chmn. 1977-78), Kappa Delta Pi, Kappa Delta Rho (v.p. 1957-58). Democrat. Presbyterian. Avocations: trout fishing; skiing; scuba diving; gardening; cooking. Home: 3214 41st St Lubbock TX 79413 Office: Tex Tech U McClellan Hall Lubbock TX 79409

MEZER, ROBERT ROSS, physician; b. Boston, Feb. 2, 1923; s. Joseph Henry and Evelyn (Cabitt) M.; A.B., Harvard U., 1942; M.D., Tufts U., 1945; m. Lois Sternlieb, Apr. 10, 1949; 1 son, Harry Cabitt. Intern, Boston City Hosp., 1945-46; psychiat. resident Bedford and Cushing VA hosps., 1946-48, Boston Psychopathic Hosp., 1948-49; practice medicine specializing in psychiatry, Boston, 1949-79, Hollywood, Fla., 1979—; sr. staff psychiatrist Southard and Community Clinics, Mass. Mental Health Center, 1949-56; instr. Harvard Med. Sch., 1949-59, Mass. Gen. Hosp. Sch. Nursing, 1951-59; clin. dir. Parole Clinic, 1956-59; asst. prof. Boston U. Schs. Medicine and Law, 1959-60; sr. psychiatrist S. Fla. State Forensic Hosp., 1979-82; dir. day treatment program Oakland Park (Fla.) VA Clinic, 1982—. Mem. Nat. Council on Crime and Delinquency, 1959—. Served to capt., M.C., AUS, 1946-48. Diplomate Am. Bd. Psychiatry and Neurology. Fellow Am. Psychiat. Assn. (com. law and psychiatry 1960-61), Mass. Med. Soc. (councillor 1960-79); mem. AMA, Norfolk Dist. Med. Soc. (chmn. com. on mental health 1960-76, pres. 1977-79), Phi Delta Epsilon. Author: Dynamic Psychiatry in Simple Terms, 4th edit., 1970; Elements of Psychiatry for Nurses, 1965. Home: 2375 N 37th Ave Hollywood FL 33021 Office: Mental Hygiene Clinic VA Outpatient Clinic Oakland Park FL 33334

MIAZGA, JOHN JOSEPH, JR., counselor educator; b. North Hampton, Mass., Nov. 21, 1946; s. John Joseph and Agnes L. (Neis) M.; m. Karen Lee Butler, Aug. 12, 1978; children—Andrew R., Brenna L. B.A., Colo. Coll., 1968; M.S., Emporia State U., 1975; Ed.D., East Tex. State U., 1980. Tchr., counselor Hamilton Ind. Sch. Dist., Kans., 1975-76; asst. prof. Angelo State U., San Angelo, Tex., 1980—, coordinator counselor edn., 1982—, dir. field experiences, 1985—. Vol. Peace Corps, Ghana, 1968-73, Tchr. Corps., Hamilton, Kans., 1973-75; bd. dirs. In Home Respite Care Program, 1982—, Pleasure and Leisure for Autistic Youth, 1984—, Pub. Responsibility Com., 1981—. Truax scholar East Tex. State U., 1977. Mem. Am. Assn. Counseling and Devel., Tex. Assn. Counseling and Devel., Council Exceptional Children, Tex. Assn. Humanistic Edn. and Devel., Am Coll. Personnel Assn., Assn. Counselor Edn. and Supervision, Nat. Vocat. Guidance Assn., Assn. Humanistic Edn. Devel., Am. Sch. Counselors Assn., Assn. Measurement and Evaluation in Guidance, Assn. Religious Values in Counseling, Assn. Specialist Group Work, numerous others. Office: Dept Edn Angelo State U San Angelo TX 76909

MICA, DANIEL ANDREW, congressman; b. Binghamton, N.Y., Feb. 4, 1944; s. Adeline Mica; B.A. in Edn., Fla. Atlantic U., 1966; m. Martha Fry; children—Christine, Daniel Andrew, Caroline, Paul. Tchr. schs. in Palm Beach County (Fla.) and Montgomery County (Md.), 1966-67; staff aide Congressman Paul Rogers, 1967-78; mem. 96th-97th Congresses from 11th Dist. Fla., pres. Democratic freshman group, 1979; mem. 98th Congress from 14th Dist. Fla. Founder, sec. Forum Club Palm Beaches, 1975; bd. dirs. Community Mental Health Center Palm Beach, 1976, Goodwill Industries Palm Beach, 1977. Mem. Palm Beach Jaycees. Roman Catholic. Office: 131 Cannon House Office Bldg Washington DC 20515

MICHAEL, DAVID HOWARD, retail store executive; b. Lawrence, Kans., July 30, 1948; s. Vernon Dwight and Hazel (Miller) M.; m. Roxine Rae Lindula, Jan. 26, 1985; children—J. Michael, Bryan Michael. B.A., Baker U., 1970. Free lance photographer, Baldwin City, Kans., 1971-76; salesman Baldwin Lumber Co., Baldwin City, 1976-78; salesman Payless Cashways Inc., Kansas City, Kans., 1978-79, store supr., 1979-81, corp. trainer, 1981-84, regional trainer, 1984—. Mem. Am. Soc. Tng. and Devel. Avocations: photography, bicycling, cooking, woodworking. Home: 1200 Dallas Dr Apt 713 Denton TX 76205 Office: Payless Cashways Inc 500 N Stemmons Lake Dallas TX 75065

MICHAEL, JAMES HARRY, JR., judge; b. Charlottesville, Va., Oct. 17, 1918; s. James Harry and Reuben (Shelton) M.; m. Barbara E. Puryear, Dec. 18, 1946; children—Jarrett Michael Stephens, Victoria. B.S., U. Va., 1940, LL.B., 1942. Bar: Va. bar 1942. Since practiced in, Charlottesville; mem. firm Michael and Musselman, 1946-54, J.H. Michael, Jr., 1954-59, Michael and Dent, 1959-72, Michael, Dent & Brooks Ltd., 1972-74, Michael and Dent, Ltd., 1974-80; asso. judge Juvenile and Domestic Relations Ct., Charlottesville, 1954-68; judge U.S. Dist. Ct., Charlottesville, 1980—; mem. Va. Senate, 1968-80; Exec. dir. Inst. Public Affairs, U. Va., 1952; chmn. Council State Govts., 1975-76; also mem. exec. com.; chmn. So. Legis. Conf., 1974-75. Mem. Charlottesville Sch. Bd., 1951-62; bd. govs. St. Anne-Belfield Sch., 1952-76; sec. Charlottesville Com. Fgn. Relations, 1950-75. Served with USNR, 1942-46; comdr. Res. ret. Wilton Park fellow Wilton Park Conf., Sussex, Eng., 1971. Mem. Am. Bar Assn., Va. Bar Assn. (v.p. 1956-57), Charlottesville-Albemarle Bar Assn. (pres. 1966-67), C. of C., Am. Judicature Soc., Nat. Consumer Fin. Assn., 4th Jud. Conf., Va. Trial Lawyers Assn., Am. Trial Lawyers Assn., Raven Soc., Sigma Nu Phi, Omicron Delta Kappa. Episcopalian (lay reader). Office: US District Ct Room 340 255 W Main St Charlottesville VA 22901

MICHAEL, MAX, III, physician; b. Atlanta, Mar. 14, 1946; s. Max, Jr., and Barbara Elizabeth (Seigel) M.; m. Marilyn Anne Losco, June 22, 1970; children—David Max, Sara Adrienne. B.A. cum laude with honors in Biology, Vanderbilt U., 1968; M.D., Harvard U., 1972. Diplomate Am. Bd. Internal Medicine. Med. resident Med. Ctr., U. Ala., Birmingham, 1972-74; Robert Wood Johnson clin. scholar, Chapel Hill, N.C., 1974-76; staff physician Cooper Green Hosp., Birmingham, 1977—, dir. outpatient services, 1977—, chief staff, 1982—, chmn. dept. medicine, 1983—; surveyor ambulatory health sect. Joint Commn. for Accreditation of Hosps. Mem. adv. com. Avondale Community Sch. Fellow ACP; mem. AMA, Am. Soc. Internal Medicine, Am. Pub. Health Assn., Jefferson County Med. Soc., Physicians for Social Responsibility. Democrat. Jewish. Contbr. articles to sci. jours. Home: 1012 42nd St S Birmingham AL 35222 Office: 1515 6th Ave S Birmingham AL 35233

MICHAEL, STEPHEN WILLIAM, electrical engineer; b. El Centro, Calif., Sept. 22, 1946; s. William Eugene and Anna Mae (Lunceford) M.; m. Joanne Francis Frings, June 10, 1978. A.A., Napa Coll., 1971; B.S., U. Calif.-Davis, 1973. Product engr. Nat. Semiconductor Corp., Santa Clara, Calif., 1973-76, supervising product engr., 1976-79; mgr. div. engring. Fairchild Camera and Instrument, Mountain View, Calif., 1979-83; v.p. research and devel. engring. GE Intersil, Cupertino, Calif., 1983-84; gen. mgr., custom integrated circuit dept. General Electric, Research Triangle Park, N.C., 1984—. Lt., Alameda County Underwater Recovery Unit, 1976-81; chmn. San Jose Young Reps., 1976-83; active Calif. Rep. Assembly, 1976-84, treas. Los Gatos-Saratoga chpt., 1978; assoc. mem. Rep. State Central Com. Calif., 1977-80; airport commr. San Jose Mcpl. Airport, 1978-84, vice chmn. commn., 1981-82, chmn., 1982-83; bd. dirs. Happy Hollow Park and Baby Zoo, 1978-84; treas., v.p., 1979, pres., 1982-84; vice chmn. Santa Clara County Young Reps., 1978-79; mem. Rep. State Central Com. Calif., 1980-83; bd. dirs. Santa Clara and Santa Cruz Counties of Campfire, 1978-81; bd. assocs. N.C. Child Advocacy Inst., 1986—. Served with USCG, 1966-70. Mem. Soc. Automotive Engrs., IEEE, San Jose Jaycees (pres. 1979, internat. senator 1982), Aero Club of No. Calif., Internat. Platform Assn. Mormon. Lodge: Rotary. Home: 8520 Valley Brook Dr Raleigh NC 27612 Office: General Electric One Micron Dr Research Triangle Park NC 27709

MICHAELS, JOHN PATRICK, JR., investment banker, broker; b. Orlando, Fla., May 28, 1944; s. John Patrick and BettyElizabeth (Jackson) M.; m. Ingeborg D. Theimer, May 2, 1970; 1 dau., Kimberly Lynn. grad. Jamaica Coll., Kingston, 1961; B.A. magna cum laude, Tulane U., 1966; M.S. in Communications (ABC fellow), U. Pa., 1968; student London Sch. Econs., 1964; m. Ingeborg D. Theimer, May 2, 1970; 1 dau., Kimberly Lynn. With Times Mirror Co., 1968-72, v.p. mktg. and devel. TM Communications Co., 1968-72; v.p. Cable Funding, N.Y.C., 1973; founder, chmn. Communications Equity Assocs. 1973—; chmn. Gulfstream Cablevision, 1985—; bd. dirs. Sonic Cable TV, 1985—; pres. Silver King Broadcasting Inc., 1982—, CEA Properties Inc., 1982—, Atlantic Am. Properties Inc., 1982—; mem. FCC Adv. Com. (local, state, fed.), Fla. Victory Com. bd. dirs. Berkely prep. Sch. Fellow Inst. Dirs. (London); mem. Nat. Cable TV Assn., Nat. Assn. Broadcasters, Broadcast Fin. Mgmt. Assn., Internat. Radio and TV Soc. Community Antenna TV Assn., Am. Mktg. Assn., Royal TV Soc., Phi Beta Kappa, Phi Eta Sigma. Clubs: Univ., Tampa Yacht, City Centre, Jockey (Miami). Contbr. numerous articles on cable TV investment to trade jours. Home: 3024 Villa Rosa Park Tampa FL 33611 Office: 851 Lincoln Center 5401 W Kennedy Blvd Tampa FL 33609

MICHAELS, KAYE R., advertising executive; b. Evansville, Ind., June 6, 1949; d. Guy and Nancy Alice (Jackson) Johnston; m. Stuart Tyler Smith, Jan. 24, 1973; 1 son, Michael Tyler. Student U. Evansville, 1968, Ind. State U., 1969-72. Prodn. coordinator Keller Crescent Co., Evansville, 1969-78; advt. mgr. H & R Devel. Co., 1978-81; owner, pres. Kaye Michaels, Inc., Casselberry, Fla., 1981—; cons. in field. Recipient Outstanding Mktg. awards Bank Systems and Equipment Assn., 1982; Am. Banking Assn. award, 1982. Mem. Orlando Advt. Fedn., Orlando Tourist and Trade Assn., Fla. C. of C. Republican. Home: 407 Wekiva Springs Rd Longwood FL 32779 Office: 316 Live Oaks Blvd Casselberry FL 32707

MICHAELS, W. E., diversified company executive; b. 1921. With Venable Tobacco Co., 1941-65, pres., to 1965; with Dibrell Bros. Inc., Danville, Va., 1965—; now pres., chief operating officer, dir. Dibrell Bros., Inc. Address: Dibrell Bros Inc 512 Bridge St Danville VA 24541*

MICHALEK, JOEL EDMUND, mathematical statistician, investigator; b. Detroit, Aug. 30, 1944; s. Edmund Frank and Hester Louise (Glunt) M.; m. Anne Marie Milenovic, Dec. 28, 1953; children—Andrew David, Nicole Louise. B.S., Wayne State U., 1966, M.A., 1968, Ph.D., 1973. Asst. prof. Syracuse U., N.Y., 1973-76; math. statistician U.S. Dept. of Transp., Boston, 1976-77, U.S. Air Force Sch. Aerospace Medicine, San Antonio, 1977—. Mem. Am. Statis. Assn., Inst. Math. Stats. Roman Catholic. Home: 2634 Pebble Valley San Antonio TX 78232 Office: USAFSAM/EKB Brooks AFB TX 78235

MICHELS, KENNETH MILFRED, university administrator, psychologist, educator; b. Chgo., Sept. 17, 1922; s. Milfred and Alice (Richter) M.; m. Esther Eloise Baker, Feb. 1, 1945; children—Kenneth Michels, Jeanne Ann. B.A., Emory U., 1949, M.A., 1950; Ph.D., U. Wis., 1953. Asst. prof. Purdue U., West Lafayette, Ind., 1953-56, assoc. prof., 1956-60, prof., 1960-64, coordinator Off-Campus Grad. Programs, 1960-62, asst. dean Univ. Extension Adminstrn., 1962-64; chmn., prof. psychology Fla. Atlantic U., Boca Raton, Fla., 1964-67, dean Coll. Social Sci., 1967-68, dean Coll. Sci., 1968-71, v.p. acad. and student affairs, 1971—, dir. Inst. for Epidemiol. Studies Health Care Delivery, 1985—; vis. prof. U. Calif.-Berkeley, summer 1964; summer vis. investigator Roscoe B. Jackson Meml. Labs., 1962; research scientist Mil. Ops. Research Div., Lockheed Aircraft Corp., Marietta, Ga., 1957; summer dir. Primate Research Lab., Emory U., 1955. Contbr. articles to profl. jours. Mem. Citizens adv. com. Boca Raton Downtown Redevel. Agy., chmn., 1983; bd. advisors Sci. Mus. and Planetarium of Palm Beach County, Fla., 1968-72; mem. Fla. Statewide Health Coordinating Council, 1978-82; mem. City of Boca Raton Civil Service Bd., 1965-71, chmn., 1969; bd. dirs. Health Planning Council, Inc., 1971-83, pres., 1977. Served with USAAF, 1941-45. Decorated D.F.C., Air medal with 6 oak leaf clusters; recipient Health Planning Council Outstanding Service award; NSF grantee. Fellow AAAS; mem. Am. Psychol. Assn., N.Y. Acad. Sci., Ind. Acad. Sci., Brit. Soc. Study of Animal Behavior, Blue Key, Sigma Xi, Phi Beta Kappa, Phi Kappa Phi. Club: Exchange. Home: 800 Forsyth St Boca Raton FL 33431 Office: Fla Atlantic U Boca Raton FL 33431

MICHELSON, DONALD DAVID, historian; b. Balt., Dec. 31, 1913; s. Aaron Adolph and Amalia Mary (Sussman) M.; A.B., Eastern Ky. U., 1936; M.A., George Peabody Coll., 1937; Ph.D., Peabody-Vanderbilt U., 1940; m. Dorothy Murchison, July 2, 1941; children—Jan Deborah, David Nathaniel, Joseph Darryl. Asst. prof. history George Peabody Coll., Nashville, 1940-46; chmn. div. social sci., prof. history Austin Peay State U., Clarksville, Tenn., 1946-48; adj. prof. U. Miami (Fla.), 1948-67; dir. B'nai B'rith Hillel Found., U. Miami, 1948-68; asso. dean div. humanities Miami Dade Community Coll., 1967-69, prof. history, 1969—, chmn. dept., 1980—. Dir. religious edn. Temple Israel, Miami, 1951-52, Congregation Beth David, Miami, 1972-73; discussion leader White House Conf. on Youth, 1960; dir. research Dade County Council Community Relations, 1952-56. Served with USCG, 1942-46; ETO, MTO, PTO; to comdr. Res., 1942-73. Mem. Am. Hist. Assn., Am. Acad. Polit. and Social Sci., Nat. Council Social Studies, Jewish War Vets, Am. Zionist Assn., Phi Delta Kappa, Kappa Delta Pi. Democrat. Author: Biography of William Franklin Phelps, 1941; Images of America; others. Office: 11011 SW 104th St Miami FL 33176

MICHIE, LUCILE EASTHAM, school psychologist, consultant; b. Charlottesville, Va., Jan. 22, 1907; d. Rosser Jackson Eastham and Helen Hodges (George) Eastham; m. James Tevis Michie, Aug. 6, 1929 (dec. Aug. 1977); children—Robert Kinloch, Martha Tevis. B.S. in Edn., U. Va., 1928, M.Ed., 1960; postgrad. U. Va., 1963-80. Lic. sch. psychologist, Va. Tchr. Latin, history Wakefield High Sch., Va., 1928-30; tchr. Latin, English Lane High Sch., Charlottesville, 1931-45; sec., treas. Helen G. Eastham Sch., Charlottesville, 1940-60; chief sch. psychologist Charlottesville Pub. Schs., 1960-72, Fluvanno County Pub. Schs., Palmyra, Va., 1972-84; mem. Va. Bd. Psychology, Richmond, 1976—, chairperson, 1980-84. Contbr. articles to profl. jours. Pres. Charlottesville Bus. and Profl. Women's Club, 1938-40, Va. Fedn. Bus. and Profl. Women's Club, Richmond, 1944-46. Recipient Scribaner-Garnett award C & A Mental Health Assn., 1976. Mem. Am. Psychol. Assn., Va. Assn. Sch. Psychologists (chmn. profl. affairs com. 1974-76), Va. Psychol. Assn., NEA, Phi Delta Kappa (Disting. Service award 1979), Kappa Delta Pi (Disting. Service award Eta Kappa chpt. 1976, treas. 1963-69). Republican. Episcopalian. Club: 2300. Avocations: doll collecting, crocheting. Home and Office: PO Box 3445 Charlottesville VA 22903

MICHIE, THOMAS JOHNSON, JR., state senator; b. Pitts., June 12, 1931; s. Thomas Johnson and Cordelia (Ruffin) M.; A.B., Trinity Coll. (Conn.), 1953; LL.B., U. Va., 1956; m. Molly Ingle, 1955 (dec. 1979); children—Thomas Johnson, John Ingle, Edmund Ruffin, George Rust Bedinger; m. 2d, Janet Johnson, 1982. Bar: Va. Mem. sch. bd. Charlottesville (Va.), 1965-70; chmn. planning bd. Charlottesville-Albemarle Vocat. Tech. Coll. Edn. Center, 1969-70; mem. Va. Ho. of Dels., 1970-80; mem. Va. Senate, 1980—. Served to lt. USN, 1956-59; to comdr. USNR. Pres. Albemarle Hist. Soc.; dir. Charlottesville Housing Found.; active Civic League of Charlottesville. Named man of yr., recipient disting. service award Jaycees, 1963. Mem. Am. Bar Assn., Charlottesville-Albemarle Bar Assn. (pres.), Delta Psi, Phi Alpha Delta. Unitarian. Office: Va State Senate Richmond VA 23219

MICKEL, BUCK, construction company executive; b. Elberton, Ga., Dec. 17, 1925; s. James Clark and Reba (Vaughn) M.; B.S., Ga. Inst. Tech., 1947; m. Minor Herndon, May 2, 1946: children—Minor Mickel Shaw, Buck Alston, Charles Clark. With Daniel Constrn. Co., Greenville, S.C., 1947—, exec. v.p., 1960-65, pres., 1965-74, chmn., from 1974; chmn. Daniel Internat. Corp.; dir. Citizens & So. Nat. Bank S.C., Duke Power Co., Monsanto Co., Fluor Corp., Liberty Corp., Nat. Intergroup, Inc., J.P. Stevens & Co., So. Net; dir., vice-chmn. R.S.I. Corp., U.S. Shelter Corp. Past pres. Greenville YMCA; past dir. United Fund; life trustee Clemson U.; mem. adv. bd. U. S.C. Bus. Sch., S.C. Found. Ind. Colls. Served to 1st lt. C.E., AUS, World War II. Mem. Ga. Tech. Alumni Assn., Bus. Council Alpha Epsilon. Clubs: Green Valley Country (past dir.), Greenville Country, Poinsett (past dir.), Cotillion Commerce (Greenville); Linthead Assocs. (Spartanburg); Capital City; Links (N.Y.C.); Palmetto (Columbia); Collins Creek Gun; Pawleys Island Yacht; Augusta (Ga.) Nat. Golf; Pacific (Newport Beach, Calif.). Lodge: Masons. Office: Daniel Internat Corp Daniel Bldg Greenville SC 29602*

MICKOLUS, EDWARD FRANCIS, writer; b. Cin., Dec. 28, 1950; s. Edward Francis and Catherine Teresa (Lawlor) M.; m. Susan Schjelderup, Jan. 15, 1983. A.B., Georgetown U., 1973; M.A., Yale U., 1974, M.Phil., 1975, Ph.D., 1981. Bd. chmn. NCCA, Inc., 1972-73; tchr. Georgetown U., Yale U., 1972-75; polit. analyst U.S. Govt., 1975—; TV producer, 1983—; pres. Vinyard Software, Inc., 1984—; vis. scholar Georgetown U., 1977-78. Ford Motor Co. scholar, 1969-73; recipient Conn. Alumni medal Dept. Govt., Georgetown U., 1973; NSF grad. fellow, 1973-76; Univ. Concilium for World Order Studies fellow, 1976-77. Mem. Acad. Polit. Sci., Am. Acad. Polit. and Social Sci., Am. Polit. Sci. Assn., Am. Soc. Internat. Law, Internat. Studies Assn., Jour. Conflict Resolution Referee Group, Soc. Basic Irreproducible Research, Mensa, Phi Beta Kappa, Delta Tau Kappa, Pi Sigma Alpha. Roman Catholic. Polit. sci. editor Jour. Irreproducible Results, 1979; contbr. articles to profl. jours.; author books on terrorism and politics; co-author numerous computer games.

MIDDLETON, CLYDE WILLIAM, state senator; b. Cleve., Jan. 30, 1928; s. Edward George and Eleanor Genevieve (Mertz) M.; B.S., U.S. Naval Acad., 1951; M.B.A., Xavier U., 1962; J.D., No. Ky. State Coll., 1974; m. Mary Ann Janke, Aug. 14, 1954; children—Ann Eleanor, David Edward, Richard Carl, John Clyde. Mfg. dept. mgr. Procter & Gamble Co., Cin., 1955-57, buyer, 1957-64; field underwriter N.Y. Life Ins. Co., Covington, Ky., 1964-74; mem. firm Theissen, Middleton & Wohlwender, and predecessor, 1974—; mem. Ky. Senate from 24th Dist., 1967—, minority whip, 1978-82. Dist. chmn. Young Republicans, 1962-63; chmn. Kenton County Rep. party, 1961, Ky. State Rep. party, 1975-76; candidate for U.S. Ho. of Reps., 1962, 64. Mem. No. Ky. Mental Health Bd., 1968-70; chmn. Ky. Comprehensive Health Planning Council, 1968-72. Served from ensign to lt. (j.g.) USN, 1951-55, now capt. Res. Recipient Pub. Ser. awards Ky. Pub. Health Assn., 1969, Newport Elks Club, 1970, No. Ky. Tchrs. Assn., 1972, 75, Ky. Comprehensive Health Planning Council, 1973. Mem. Ky. Circuit Ct. Judges Assn., No. Ky. C. of C. (dir. 1969-72). Lutheran. Optimist (pres. Covington 1969-70). Address: PO Box 546 Covington KY 41012

MIDDLETON, ELWYN LINTON, lawyer; b. Pomona, Fla., Oct. 16, 1914; s. William Spencer and Lizzie A. (Williams) M.; LL.B., Stetson U., 1939; m. Annie L. Fielding, Dec. 7, 1942; children—Elwyn Linton, Mary Ann, John David, Phillip Fielding. Admitted to Fla. bar, 1939, since practiced in Palm Beach; asso. E. Harris Drew, 1939-42; mem. firm Steel, Hector, Davis, Burns & Middleton, (formerly Burns, Middleton, Farrell & Faust); town atty., Palm Beach, 1953-81. Dir. Bank of Palm Beach & Trust Co., Palm Beach. Trustee Eckerd Coll. Served from ensign to lt. USNR, 1942-46. Mem. Am., Palm Beach County (pres. 1951) bar assns., Fla. Bar (gov. 1954-56), Phi Alpha Delta. Democrat. Presbyterian. Home: 242 Dunbar Rd Palm Beach FL 33480 Office: 205 Worth Ave Palm Beach FL 33480

MIDDLETON, HARRY JOSEPH, library administrator; b. Centerville, Iowa, Oct. 24, 1921; s. Harry Joseph and Florence Genevieve (Beauvais) M.; m. Miriam Miller, Oct. 29, 1949; children—Susan, Deborah, James Miller, Jennifer. Student Washburn U., 1941-43; B.A., La. State U., 1947. Reporter, AP, 1948-49; editor Archtl. Forum Mag., 1949-53; writer March of Time, 1953-55; free lance writer, 1955-66; staff asst. to Pres. Lyndon B. Johnson, Washington, 1966-69, spl. asst., 1969-70; dir. Lyndon B. Johnson Library, Austin, Tex., 1970—. Served with Armed Forces, 1943-46, 50-52. Author: Compact History of the Korean War. Decorated Bronze Star. Mem. Sigma Delta Chi. Home: 2201 Exposition Blvd Austin TX 78703 Office: LBJ Library Austin TX 78705

MIDDLETON, HERMAN DAVID, educator; b. Sanford, Fla., Mar. 24, 1925; s. Arthur Herman and Ruby Elmerry (Hart) M.; B.S., Columbia, 1948, M.A., 1949; Ph.D., U. Fla., 1964; postgrad. N.Y. U., summer 1950, Northwestern U., summer 1951; m. Amelia Mary Eggart, Dec. 1, 1945 (dec. 1976); children—Herman David, Kathleen Hart. Instr., dir. drama and speech Maryville (Tenn.) Coll., 1949-50; instr., designer-tech. dir. theatre U. Del., 1951-55; stage mgr. Unto These Hills, Cherokee (N.C.) Hist. Assn., summers 1952-56; asst. prof., head dept. drama U. N.C., Greensboro, 1956-59, asso. prof., head dept. drama and speech, 1959-65, prof., head dept., 1965-74, prof., 1974—, Excellence Fund prof. communication and theatre, 1979—; designer Chucky Jack, Great Smokey Mountains Hist. Soc., Gatlinburg, Tenn., 1956, designer, dir., 1957; tech. dir. The Confederacy, Tide Water Hist. Assn.,

Virginia Beach, Va., summer 1958. Communications cons. N.C. Nat. Bank, 1968, Jefferson Standard Life Ins. Co., Greensboro, 1969, Gilbarco, Inc., Greensboro, 1969-70, 73; dir. region X (S.E.) and mem. central com. Am. Coll. Theatre Festival, 1977-79. Mem. N.C. Arts Council Commn., 1964-66, Guilford County Bi-Centennial Celebration Commn., 1969-70. Pres., Shanks Village Players, Orangeburg, N.Y. 1947-48, Univ. Drama Group, Newark, Del., 1954-55; bd. dirs. Broadway Theatre League of Greensboro, 1958-60, Community Theatre of Greensboro, 1983-86; bd. dirs. Southeastern Theatre Conf., 1963-68, pres., 1965, pres. pro-tem, 1966; bd. dirs. Greensboro Community Arts Council, 1964-67, 69-72. Recipient O. Henry award for distinguished artistic contbns. to Greensboro, 1966, Gold medallion Am. Oil Co., 1973, Suzanne M. Davis award Southeastern Theatre Conf., 1975. Mem. Del. (dir. 1950-55), Carolina 1958-59) dramatic assns., Am. Nat. Theatre Acad. (exec. v.p. Piedmont chpt. 1957-60), N.C. Drama and Speech Assn. (pres. 1966-67), Am. Theatre Assn. (chmn. bd. nominations 1971-72), Am., So. speech communication assns., N.C. Theatre Conf. (co. founder 1970, bd. dirs. 1983-85), Nat. Collegiate Players, Phi Delta Kappa, Phi Kappa Phi, Theta Alpha Phi, Alpha Psi Omega. Democrat. Methodist. Drama critic, columnist The Sunday Star, Wilmington, Del., 1952. Theatre editor Players mag., 1959-61. Theatre columnist Sunday edits. Greensboro Daily News, 1959-62. Home: 203-A Village Ln Greensboro NC 27409

MIDDLETON, MAX EVERETT, safety engineer; b. Greenville, Ala., Dec. 31, 1947; s. James R. and Melba (Holley) M.; m. Mary Alice Powell, Aug. 18, 1973. B.Chem. Engring., Auburn U., 1970. Registered profl. engr., S.C.; cert. safety profl., S.C. Loss prevention engr. Factory Mut. Engring., Atlanta, 1971-74, Charlotte, N.C., 1974-76; sr. chem. engr. Carolina Eastman Co., Columbia, S.C., 1976—; dir. treas. S.C. Occupational Safety Co.; ind. fire protection rep. adv. com. S.C. Fire Acad., Columbia, 1978—. Mem. Am. Soc. Safety Engrs. (pres. 1979-80, Safety Profl. of Yr. 1983), Am. Inst. Chem. Engrs. Club: S.C. Mil. Minatures (pres. 1985—). Lodge: Kiwanis (pres. 1978-79). Avocations: collecting, casting and painting military minatures and toy soldiers. Home: 1724 Quail Valley E Columbia SC 29210 Office: Carolina Eastman Co PO Box 1728 Columbia SC 29202

MIDDLETON, MORRIS HITT, psychologist; b. Eupora, Miss., Dec. 1, 1941; s. Morris Fuller and Lucy Catherine (Hitt) M.; m. Margaret Katherine Suesse, Aug. 18, 1968; 1 child, Sharon Amanda. B.S., Memphis State U., 1963; M.A., U. Ark., 1966, Ph.D., 1969. Lic. psychologist, Ark. Asst. prof. psychology Memphis State U., 1968-72; dir. research and tng. East Ark. Regional Mental Health Clinic, Helena, 1972-74; dir. research and evaluation Ark. Mental Health Services, Little Rock, 1975-81; pvt. cons., Little Rock, 1981-83; dir. planning and devel. Ozark Counseling Services, Mountain Home, Ark., 1983—, program dir., 1983-84; mem. Ark. Bd. Examiners in Psychology, 1985—. Contbr. articles to profl. jours. NIMH grantee, 1975; recipient awards Ark. Mental Health Services, 1981, Ozark Counseling Services, 1984. Mem. Am. Psychol. Assn., Ark. Psychol. Assn. Avocations: chess, amateur radio, swimming. Home: Route 1 Box 87 Lakeview AR 72642 Office: Ozark Counseling Services PO Box 487 Mountain Home AR 72653

MIDDLETON, NORMAN GRAHAM, social worker, counselor; b. Jacksonville, Fla., Jan. 21, 1935; s. Norman Graham and Betty (Quina) M.; B.A., U. Miami (Fla.), 1960; M.S.W., Fla. State U., 1962; m. Judy Stephens, Aug. 1, 1968; stepchildren—Monty Stokes, Toni Stokes. Casework counselor Family Service, Miami, 1962-64; psychiat. social worker asso. firm Drs. Warson, Steele, Wiener, Sarasota, Fla., 1964-66; marriage, family counselor, Sarasota, 1966—. Instr. Manatee Jr. Coll., Bradenton, Fla., 1973-76; psychiat. social work cons. Sarasota Meml. Hosp. Author: The Caverns of My Mind, 1985. Pres. Council on Epilepsy, Sarasota, 1969-70. Served with USAF, 1954-58. Fellow Fla. Soc. Clin. Social Work (pres. 1978-80); mem. Nat. Assn. Social Workers, Am. Assn. Marriage and Family Therapists, Am. Group Psychotherapy Assn., Am. Assn. Sex Educators and Counselors (cert. sex educator), Acad. Cert. Social Workers. Democrat. Episcopalian. Home: 16626 Winburn Dr Sarasota FL 33540 Office: 1857 Floyd St Sarasota FL 33579

MIDDLETON, PAUL BEADLE, software development company executive, consultant; b. Jackson, Miss., Mar. 8, 1944; s. Richard Temple and Johnie (Beadle) M.; m. Juliette Floyd, June 18, 1967; children—Crystan, Kara. B.S. in Math., Lincoln U., 1964; M.S. in Applied Math. and Stats., U. Mo.-Rolla, 1967; postgrad. in stats. George Washington U., 1977. With Def. and Space Systems, TRW, 1969-71, Tetra Tech., Inc., Arlington, Va., 1971-78, Automated Scis. Group, Silver Spring, Md., 1978-84; pres. Statcom, Inc., Herndon, Va., 1984—. Lay reader St. Timothy's Episcopal Ch., Herndon, 1984—. Served to capt. U.S. Army, 1967-69. Mem. Am. Statis. Assn., Am. Def. Preparedness Assn., Alpha Phi Alpha. Avocations: swimming; painting; tennis. Home: 2503 Arnsley Dr Herndon VA 22071 Office: Statcom Inc 2503 Arnsley Dr Herndon VA 22071

MIDKIFF, JOHN L., JR., health care administrator, retired army officer; b. Hamlin, W.Va., Oct. 26, 1932; s. John L. and Mary E. (Marcum) M.; m. Shirley L. Hedrick, Mar. 3, 1956; children—Cathy A. Martin, Karla J. Arndt. B.A. in Psychology, Marshall U., 1955; M.H.A., Baylor U., 1966; grad. U.S. Army Command and Gen. Staff Coll., Fort Leavenworth, Kans., 1970. Enlisted U.S. Army, 1953, advanced through grades to col., 1976; adminstrv. officer U.S. Army Dispensary, Pentagon, Washington, 1954-56; adminstrv. asst. Dental Surgeon, 5th U.S. Army, Chgo., 1957-59; comdr. 556th Med. Co., Ulm, Karlsruhe, Fed. Republic Germany, 1960-61; ops. officer 67th Med. Group, Republic Vietnam, 1970-71; ret., 1978; health care adminstr. Healthsouth Rehab. Corp., Birmingham, Ala., 1984—, v.p. ops., 1985—; asst. dir. gen. services U. Md., Balt., 1978-79, assoc. dir. hosp. ops., 1979-83; dir. hosp. acquisition Lifemark Corp., Houston, 1983-84; cons. in field. Contbr. articles to profl. jours. Decorated Legion of Merit, Bronze Star, Meritorious Service medal with oak leaf cluster, Commendation medals, Nat. Def. Service medal, Republic of Vietnam Gallantry Cross, Civil Actions medal. Fellow Am. Coll. Hosp. Adminstrs.; mem. Am. Hosp. Assn., Ret. Officers Assn., Res. Officers Assn., Ala. Hosp. Assn. Lutheran. Lodge: Masons. Home: 3633 Cumberland Trace Birmingham AL 35243 Office: Healthsouth Rehab Corp 2 Perimeter Park South Birmingham AL 35243

MIELE, ANTHONY WILLIAM, state librarian; b. Williamsport, Pa., Feb. 12, 1926; s. Harry John and Louise Casale (Troyano) M.; B.S., Marquette U., 1951; M.L.S., U. Pitts., 1966; m. Ruth Cassidy, Jan. 29, 1955; children—Terri Ann, Anthony, Robert John, Elizabeth Ann. Partner, mgr. restaurant, Williamsport, 1960-66; dir. Elmwood Park (Ill.) Pub. Library, 1967-68; asst. dir. Oak Park (Ill.) Pub. Library, 1968-70; asst. dir. for tech. services Ill. State Library, Springfield, 1970-75; dir. Ala. Pub. Library Service, Montgomery, 1975—; mem. library of Congress Network Adv. Com., 1983-84; mem. SOLINET/OCLC Users' Council, 1984—. Mem. Pub. Printers Adv. Council for Depository Libraries, 1973-76, vice chmn., 1975-76. Mayor, Arrowhead Community, 1984. Served with USNR, 1944-46. Mem. ALA (mem. com. Nat. Library Week 1971-74, chmn. Govt. Documents Round Table 1973-75), Ill., Ala. library assns., Internat. Fedn. Libraries, Nat. Microfilm Assn., Chief Officers State Library Agencies (chmn. network com.), Beta Phi Mu. Roman Catholic. Club: Rotary. Assoc. editor Govt. Publs. Review, 1974. Home: 500 Eastdale Rd Townhouse D-4 Montgomery AL 36117 Office: 6030 Monticello Dr Montgomery AL 36130

MIELZAREK, ROLF HERBERT, psychologist; b. Elizabeth, N.J., July 2, 1932; s. Wilhelm and Julie Pauline (Laur) M.; B.A., Wagner Coll., 1954; B.D., Luth. Sem., Gettysburg, Pa., 1957; Ph.D., U. Md., 1976; m. Lee Anna Hammond, May 29, 1969; children—Lori Kristine, Erik Paul, Kara Lynn. Exec. dir. Montgomery Workshop, sheltered workshop for handicapped, Kensington, Md., 1965-68; asso. dir. Commn. Govtl. Efficiency and Economy, Balt., 1968-69; dir., owner Camp Shenandoah, residential camp for mentally retarded, Winchester, Va., 1969—; psychologist Hope Center, Temple Hills, Md., 1971-73; psychologist Great Oaks Center, state inst. for mentally retarded, Silver Spring, Md., 1974-75; psychologist, dir., owner Concord, residential community for mentally retarded, Yellow Spring, W.Va., 1974—. Chief cons. Cons. on Programs for Mentally Retarded Persons, Yellow Spring, 1974—; operator Shenandoah Adventures, travel programs for mentally retarded, Yellow Spring, 1974—; instr. psychology Shenandoah Coll., Winchester. Named Man of Year, Silver Spring Jaycees, 1968. Mem. Council for Exceptional Children, Am. Assn. Mental Deficiency, Am. Camping Assn. (pres. sect. 1972-74, dir. region, chmn. conv. 1975), Nat. Assn. Pvt. Residential Facilities for Mentally Retarded (dir. 1977—). Home: Concord Yellow Spring WV 26865 Office: Camp Shenandoah Mountain Falls Route Winchester VA 22601 also Concord Yellow Spring WV 26865

MIERAU, MICHAEL DENIS, army officer, organization development consultant; b. Akron, Ohio, Aug. 10, 1936; s. Henry and Mary Geraldine (Sullivan) M.; children—Lisa Ann, Debra Lynn, Michael Denis. B.S., U.S. Mil. Acad., 1960; M.S. in Bus. Adminstrn., Boston U., 1973; M.A., M.Ed., George Washington U., 1979, postgrad., 1979—. Commd. 2d. lt. U.S. Army, 1960, advanced through grades to lt. col., 1975; aide-de camp to chief of staff U.S. Army, Washington, 1968-69; air-ground ops. officer U.S. Army, Europe and Korea, 1970-73, 76-77; project officer U.S. Army Tng. and Doctrine Command, Fort Monroe, Va., 1973-76; prof. leadership Armed Forces Staff Coll., Norfolk, Va., 1977-81; orgn. devel. cons. U.S. Army Transp. Sch., Fort Eustis, Va., 1981-82; chief orgn. devel. U.S. Army Materiel Command, Alexandria, Va., 1982—; pres. Performance Alternatives, Springfield, Va., 1978—; mem. U.S. Army Materiel Command Speakers Bur., Alexandria, 1982—. Contbg. author: Transforming Work, 1984. Decorated Silver Star. Mem. Am. Soc. Tng. and Devel. (nat. research com. 1984—), Washington Consortium of Human Resource Devel. Cons., Phi Kappa Phi. Republican. Episcopalian. Avocations: running; skiing; cooking; photography. Home: 8580 Gwynedd Way Springfield VA 22153

MIERSWA, CAROLYNE GRIMM, consultant, psychology educator, counselor; b. Rochester, Pa., Aug. 16, 1926; d. Charles Karl and Grace (Graham) G.; m. Myles Herbert Mierswa, Sr., Sept. 12, 1950 (div. Sept. 1972); children—Kathleen Grace, Myles Herbert Jr. (dec.), Michael Graham, Mary Katherine. B.A. in Psychology and Sociology, U. Central Fla., 1975, M.S. in Indsl. Psychology, 1978, postgrad., 1979-81. Adj. prof. psychology Valencia Community Coll., Orlando, Fla., 1980—; field supr., interviewer John Hopkins U., Baltimore, Md., 1977-78, U. Mich., 1977-84, U. Chgo., 1978—, West Fla. Naval Tng. Ctr., Orlando, 1979-81; counselor Cath. Social Services, Orlando, 1981—; owner, mgr. RCM Research Assocs., Winter Park, Fla., 1975—. Author: Employability Skills Training, 1978. Contbr. articles to profl. jours. Bd. dirs. Village Ctr. Student Activity U. Central Fla., 1974-75; bd. dirs. Mich. Youth Services, Orlando, 1975. Recipient Outstanding Contbn. award Mich. Youth Services, 1974; Beth Johnson Meml. scholar, 1974. Mem. Am. Psychol. Assn. (assoc.), Women's Network, Women's Purchasing Council, Fla. Assn. Counseling Devel., Diocese Orlando (pastoral minister), Toastmasters Internat., Delta Tau Kappa (pres.). Republican. Roman Catholic. Club: Internat. Women Conf. (Germany) (sec. 1960-61). Avocations: golf; swimming; horseback riding; jogging, piano. Home: 817 Chipley Ct Winter Park FL 32792 Office: Cath Social Services 3191 Maguire Blvd Orlando FL 32803

MIESCH, DAVID CHEATHAM, physician; b. Clarksville, Tex., July 6, 1928; s. Raymond John and Mamie (Cheatham) M.; M.D., U. Tex. at Galveston, 1951; m. Jo Peevey, Mar. 22, 1956; children—Margaret Louise, Mary Gail. Intern, Hosp. of U. Pa., Phila., 1951-52; resident in internal medicine Parkland Hosp., Dallas, 1952-53, John Sealy Hosp., Galveston, Tex., 1953-55; pvt. practice internal medicine, Paris, Tex., 1973—; mem. staff McCuiston Regional Med. Center. Mem. devel. bd. U. Tex. Med. Sch. at Galveston, 1973—; mem. Chancellor's Council U. Tex., 1975—. Diplomate Am. Bd. Internal Medicine. Fellow A.C.P.; mem. Am., Tex. med. assns., Tex. Soc. Internal Medicine, Alpha Tau Omega. Episcopalian. Home: 665 31st St SE Paris TX 75460 Office: 2850 Lewis Ln Paris TX 75460

MIESSE, MARY ELIZABETH (BETH), educator; b. Amarillo, Tex.; M.Ed. in Guidance and Counseling, M.A., W. Tex. State U., Canyon, 1952, M.B.A., 1960; M.Personnel Service, U. Colo., Boulder, 1954. With various bus. firms and radio stas., 1940-47; prof. Amarillo (Tex.) Coll., 1947-63; tchr. pvt. and pub. schs., also TV work, 1963-78; spl. edn. cons., writer, 1978—. Mem. NEA, Tex. State Tchrs. Assn., Am. Psychol. Assn., North Plains Assn. for Children with Learning Disabilities, AAUP Pioneered in ednl. TV in West Tex.; recipient awards in typewriting and ednl. TV; elected to Top Ten Women of Yr., Am. Bus. Women's Assn., 1962. Certified in spl. edn. supr., spl. edn. counselor, ednl. diagnostician, spl. edn. (lang. and/or learning disabled, mentally retarded) tchr., profl. counselor, profl. tchr., supt., prin., Tex. Editor, Tex. Jr. Coll. Tchrs. Assn. publ., 7 yrs. Office: Box 3133 Valle de Oro Boys Ranch TX 79010

MIGNEREY, RICHARD EUGENE, university administrator; b. Stryker, Ohio, Feb. 6, 1932; s. James Emmett and Mabel Leanna (Wolf) M.; m. Joan McCartney, Aug. 28, 1955; 1 child, Roberta Jami. B.S.Ed., Defiance Coll., 1959; M.Ed., U. Toledo, 1969, Ed.D., 1971. Cert. Inst. Cert. Profl. Mgrs., 1979. Tchr. pub. schs., Ottawa, Ohio, 1956-59; mem. faculty Tri State Coll., Angola, Ind., 1959-61; asst. to technologist quality control Campbell Soup Co., Napoleon, Ohio, 1962-64; mem. faculty U. Toledo, 1965-67; research assoc. Pinellas County Schs., Clearwater, Fla., 1967-68, dir. faculty planning, 1969-71; math. specialist Mich. Dept. Edn., Lansing, 1972-74; v.p. REI, Inc., Clearwater, 1975-79; v.p. Nat. Mgmt. Assn., Dayton, Ohio, 1978-84; exec. dir. Inst. Cert. Profl. Mgrs., Dayton, 1979-84; dir. mktg. Nova U., Lauderdale, Fla., 1984—; adj. prof. Hillsborough Community Coll., 1973-75; adj. dir. Nova U., 1975-77. Author: Solar Distillation of Fuel Grade Ethanol, 1978; Group Discussion for Learning, 1981; editor: Minimal Performance Objectives for Mathematics in Michigan, 1973; Minimal Performances Objectives for Mathematics in Migrant Education, 1974. Mem. Pinellas County Republican Com. Recipient Arthur Healey Citizenship award 1966; named Ky. Col. NSF grantee, 1961-62. Mem. Nat. Mgmt. Assn., MENSA, NEA, Am. Soc. Tng. and Devel., Phi Delta Kappa. Office: Nova U 3301 College Ave Fort Lauderdale FL 33314

MIKA, JOSEPH JOHN, library educator, administrator; b. McKees Rocks, Pa., Mar. 1, 1948; s. George Joseph and Sophie Ann (Stec) M.; m. Karen Ann Wingertszahn, Apr. 4, 1970; children—Jason-Paul Joseph, Matthew Douglas, Meghan Leigh. B.A. in English, U. Pitts., 1969, M.L.S., 1971, Ph.D. in L.S., 1980. Asst. librarian, instr. Ohio State U., Mansfield, 1971-73; asst. librarian, asst. prof. Johnson State Coll. (Vt.), 1973-75; grad. asst., teaching fellow Sch. Library and Info. Sci. U. Pitts., 1975-77; asst. dean, assoc. prof. library service U. So. Miss., Hattiesburg, 1977—; cons. to libraries. Served to maj. USAR. Decorated Army Commendation medal. Mem. ALA (councilor 1983—, chmn. constn. and bylaws com. 1985—), Assn. Library and Info. Sci. Edn., (chmn. membership com. 1982-83, chmn. nominating com. 1982, exec. bd. 1986), Miss. Library Assn. (pres.-elect 1985), Assn. Coll. and Research Libraries (chmn. 1982-83, chmn. budget com. 1982-83), Soc. Miss. Archivists (treas., exec. bd. 1981-83), Beta Phi Mu, Phi Delta Kappa. Lodge: Kiwanis (Hattiesburg). Contbr. articles to profl. jours. Home: 355 Emerson Dr Hattiesburg MS 39401 Office: Sch of Library Service U So Miss Southern Station PO Box 5146 Hattiesburg MS 39406

MIKELL, ALAN GLEN, exploration company executive; b. Prentiss, Miss., Dec. 31, 1951; s. Luther Glen and Mildred (McPhail) M.; m. Virginia Lee Martin, June 2, 1973; children—Chad, Courtney, Jennifer. B.S. in Petroleum Engring., La. State U., 1973. Staff engr. Getty Oil Co., 1973-77, dist. fin. planning coordinator, New Orleans, 1977-78; mgr. evaluations and gas contracts Southport Exploration, Tulsa, 1978-81; pres. Tidemark Exploration, Inc., Tulsa, 1981—. Chmn. fund drive La. State U. Alumni Fedn., Northeast Okla., 1984-85; active mem. Fellowship of Christian Athletes, Tulsa, 1982—. Named Outstanding Young Men of Am., 1983. Mem. Am. Assn. Petroleum Geologists, La. Engring. Soc., Independent Petroleum Assn. Am., Okla. Independent Petroleum Assn., Soc. Petroleum Engrs., Petroleum Club, Pi Epsilon Tau, Tau Beta Pi. Republican. Roman Catholic. Avocations: fishing; flying; racquetball; golf. Home: 6716 E 105th St Tulsa OK 74133 Office: Tidemark Exploration Inc PO Box 702675 2250 E 73rd St Tulsa OK 74170

MIKULAS, JOSEPH FRANK, graphic design executive, educator; b. Jacksonville, Fla., Sept. 15, 1926; s. Joseph and Marina (Zeman) M.; m. Joyce Gregory Haddock, Sept. 29, 1946; children—Joyce Marina Mikulas Abney, Juliana Claire Mikulas Catlin. Student Harold Hilton Studios, 1942-50. Art dir. Peeples Displays, Inc., 1945-50, 53-56, Douglas Printing Co. Inc., 1950-53, 56-59; ptnr., graphic design exec. Benton & Mikulas Assocs., Inc., Jacksonville, 1960-67; pres. Mikulas Assocs., Inc., Jacksonville, 1968—, exec. graphic designer, dir. communications, adj. prof. advt. design Jacksonville U. Chmn. Youth Resources Bur.; chmn. Mayor's Medal Com. Served with USAAF, 1945. Recipient Gold medal Am. Advt. Fedn., 4th dist., 1971; numerous other awards, 1960-81. Mem. Advt. Fedn. of Jacksonville (past pres. 1970). Democrat. Episcopalian. Clubs: San Jose Country, River, Art Dirs. of Jacksonville (past pres.). Lodges: Masons, Rotary (past pres. S. Jacksonville 1970, Paul Harris fellow), Torch of Jacksonville (past pres. 1977). Creator over 30 trademarks for local, regional, nat. and internat. use by corps. based in Jacksonville. Home: 2014 River Rd Jacksonville FL 32207 Office: 3886 Atlantic Blvd Jacksonville FL 32207

MIKULENKA, EDWARD JOHN, JR., office equipment company executive, consultant; b. El Campo, Tex., Apr. 18, 1936; s. Edward John and Bertha May (Eilert) M.; m. Myra Louise Henon, Feb. 8, 1963; children—Susan Marie, Edward John. B.S., Tex. A&M U., College Station, 1967. Sales rep. Med. Publisher, N.Y.C., 1962-64; sales mgr. Xerox Corp., Tucson, Ariz., 1964-68; v.p. Uni-Copy Corp., Tucson, 1968-74, pres., Houston, 1974—; dir. Tex. Nat. Leasing Inc., San Antonio, Uni-Copy Distbn. Corp., New Orleans. Recipient Commendation Xerox Corp., 1967; Achievement award Savin Corp., 1978. Mem. Nat. Office Machine Dealer Assn. Clubs: Century Tex. A&M U., Raveneaux; Los Rois (Dallas). Home: 16203 Chasemore St Spring TX 77373 Office: Unico Corp 11231 Richmond St Suite 104 Houston TX 77082

MILAM, MARY JUSTINA GRATTAN, sociologist, writer; b. Kansas City, Kans., May 10, 1930; d. Francis Patrick and Catherine Mary Lyonsgrattan (Byrnes) G.; Grattan; student U. Mo., Kansas City, 1947-49; B.A. with honors, N. Tex. State U., 1969, M.A., (fellow), 1971; Ph.D. in Sociology and Liguistics (fellow), Tex. Woman's U., 1977; postgrad. London Sch. Econs. and Polit. Sci., 1983-84; m. David Leake Milam, Sr., Nov. 23, 1950 (div. 1979); children—Melinda Sue, David Leake, Barnaby Walker (Twins). Freelance writer and stringer Kansas City Star, Kansas City Kansan, Prom mag.; radio continuity Sta. KCMO; author short stories, articles and interviews for various mags. and jours.; instr. sociology N. Tex. State U. and Laredo State U.; sociolinguistic researcher, cons. Active Girl Scouts Am., Cub Scouts. Mem. Internat. Sociol. Assn., Am. Social. Assn., S.W. Sociol. Assn., Mid-South Sociol. Assn., Soc. Study of Social Problems, Internat. Sociolinguistics Research Com., Alpha Kappa Delta. Roman Catholic. Author: An Axiomatic Theory of Adolescence. Papers collected at Kinsey Inst., Ind. and Lockwood Meml. Library, Buffalo. Address: 6222 Malcolm Dr Dallas TX 75214

MILAN, THOMAS LAWRENCE, accountant, financial consultant; b. Catonsville, Md., Nov. 23, 1941; s. Lawrence Francis and Mary Elizabeth (Feely) M.; m. Mary Agnes Lacoste, Oct. 3, 1965; children—Thomas Brian, Kathrine Mary. B.S., U. Balt., 1965. C.P.A., Md., Va. Staff acct. Ernst & Ernst, Balt., 1965-70, supr., mgr., 1970-76, ptnr., 1976-80, Ernst & Whinney, Richmond, Va., 1980—. Mem. acctg. adv. bd. Va. Commonwealth U., Richmond, 1981-85; mem. adv. com. Balt. Mus. Art, 1978-80. Mem. Inst. Internal Auditors (pres. 1973-74), Md. Assn. C.P.A.s (chmn. acctg. and auditing com. 1974-76), Am. Inst. C.P.A.s (mem. com. on ICC matters 1982—), Beta Alpha. Republican. Roman Catholic. Clubs: Annapolis Yacht; Commonwealth (Richmond). Avocations: sailing; waterfowling; tennis. Home: 500 Welwyn Rd Richmond VA 23229 Office: Ernst & Whinney 901 E Cary St Richmond VA 23219

MILANES, MIGUEL ANGEL, educational administrator, educator; b. Niquero, Oriente, Cuba, Sept. 29, 1951; came to U.S., 1963; s. Justino Ramon and Teresa (Cardella) M. B.A. in Secondary Edn., Oklahoma City U., 1974. Instr. T. Day Sch., Miami, Fla., 1974-76; asst. dir. Okla. Hispanic Ctr., Oklahoma City, 1976—. Developer Spanish course Spanish for Law Enforcement, 1980; developer learning ctr. Bilingual Resource Ctr., 1981. Vice chmn. Olde Capitol Hill Council, Oklahoma City, 1980—; bd. dirs. Neighborhood Housing Services, Oklahoma City, 1980-84; mem. EEO com. Oklahoma City Pub. Schs., 1984-85; commr. Mayor's Arts Commn., Oklahoma City, 1982—; mem. Mayor's Hunger/Shelter Task Force, Oklahoma City, 1984—; pres. Capitol Hill Neighborhood Assn., Oklahoma City, 1983—. E.K. Gaylord scholar, 1973. Mem. So. Oklahoma City C. of C. Methodist. Avocations: stamp collecting, bodybuilding. Home: 3520 NW 24th St Oklahoma City OK 73107 Office: Okla Hispanic Ctr 228 SW 25th St Oklahoma City OK 73109

MILANICH, JERALD THOMAS, archaeologist, museum curator, educator; b. Painesville, Ohio, Oct. 13, 1945; s. John Joseph and Jean Marie (Bales) M.; m. Maxine L. Margolis, Dec. 20, 1970; children—Nara Bales. B.A, U. Fla., 1967, M.A., 1968, Ph.D., 1971. Cert. Soc. Profl. Archaeologists, 1975. Post doctoral fellow Smithsonian Inst., Washington, 1971-72; asst. prof. anthropology U. Fla., Gainesville, 1972-75; asst. curator Fla. State Museum, 1975-77; assoc. curator, 1977-81, chmn. dept. anthropology, 1981-83, curator, 1981—. Author: (with Samuel Proctor): Tacachale—Essays on the Indians of Flordia and Southeastern Georgia during the Historic Period, 1978; (with Charles Fairbanks): Florida Archaeology, 1980; McKeithen Weeden Island, 1984. Recipient Ripley P. Bullen award, 1980; grantee NSF, 1970-71, 73-75, 77-81, 82, Wentworth Found., 1976-77, 81-82, 83, 84. Mem. Am. Anthrop. Assn., Soc. Am. Archaeology, Soc. Profl. Archeologists (pres. 1981-82), So. Anthrop. Soc., S.E. Archeol. Conf. (pres. 1986—). Office: Fla State Museum Gainesville FL 32611

MILANO, PAMELA CREESE, systems and software company executive; b. Ensenada, P.R., Sept. 28, 1947; d. Philip Guy and Jean Craig (Cooper) Creese; exec. sec. degree, Bixby Bus. Coll., 1965; student St. Petersburg Jr. Coll., 1965-72, Tampa Coll., 1976-78; spl. courses; m. Richard Nicholas Milano, May 26, 1973; children—Saria Pattan, Richard Creese. Platform sec. Barnett Bank, St. Petersburg, Fla., 1967-73; asst. cashier Ellis N.E. Nat. Bank, St. Petersburg, 1967-73; corp. officer Cheezem Devel. Corp., St. Petersburg, 1973-74; legal sec. Marlow, Shofi, Ortmayer, Smith & Spangler, Tampa, Fla., 1974-76; office mgr./acct. SHS Assos., Inc., St. Petersburg, 1977-81; group v.p. loans and v.p., dir. mortgage loans Fla. Software Services, Inc., Orlando, 1979-82; dir. edn. services Digital Systems, Inc., Pensacola, Fla., 1982—, also dir. software design, devel. edn. and support; condr. banking seminars for students; cons. seminars on lending instruments. Formerly active League to Aid Retarded Children, Young Republicans; vol. United Way. Lic. real estate asso., Fla.; cert. profl. sec. Mem. Am. Inst. Banking, Am. Bus. Women's Assn., Nat. Assn. Female Execs., Fla. Soc. Cert. Profl. Secs., Pensacola Arts Council, North Hills Preservation Dist. (bd. dirs.). Episcopalian. Home: 110 W Strong St Pensacola FL 32501 Office: 114 E Gregory St Pensacola FL 32501

MILAZZO, BARBARA ANNE, rehabilitation counselor; b. Evergreen Park, Ill., Sept. 9, 1954; d. Samuel Anthony and Irene (Szymanski) M. B.S., U. Ill., 1975; M. Rehab. Counseling, Wright State U., 1985. Rehab. counselor, Beverly Hills, Fla. Contbr. poems. to jours. and anthologies. Mem. Am. Assn. Counseling and Devel., Am. Rehab. Counseling Assn., Nat. Head Injury Found. Avocations: reading; writing; listening and recording classical music. Home: 36 S Lucille St Beverly Hills FL 32665

MILES, LEROY FRANCIS, sociology educator; b. Meyers, Ark., July 7, 1923; s. Ed Leroy and Effie (Hendon) M.; m. Marcia Langford, Nov. 26, 1952; 1 child, John Edward. B.S. in Edn., Henderson State Tchrs. Coll., 1951; M.S. in Edn., E. Tex. State U., 1955, Ed.D., 1973. Cert. tchr. social studies, Ark., Tex. Tchr. pub. schs., Ark., 1943-55, Tex., 1955-62; instr. Henderson State U., Arkadelphia, Ark., 1962-64, asst. prof., 1964-69, assoc. prof., 1969-73, prof. sociology, 1973-79, chmn. dept., prof., 1979—; cons. programs for aged, Ark., 1975—; lectr. in field. Presenter papers profl. confs. Mem. NEA, Am. Sociol. Assn., Southwestern Social Sci. Assn., Mid-South Sociol. Assn., Ark. Edn. Assn., Ark. Sociol. Assn., Phi Delta Kappa, Alpha Kappa Delta. Democrat. Baptist. Lodge: Masons. Home: 1554 Pine Manor Dr Arkadelphia AR 71923 Office: Henderson State U PO Box 7573 Arkadelphia AR 71923

MILES, MICHAEL VAN, clinical pharmacy educator, researcher, consultant; b. Springfield, Mo., Oct. 5, 1944; s. Benny Leroy and Betty Jean (White) M.; m. Kena Elizabeth Stierwalt, May 27, 1967; children—Michelle, Melanie, Matthew, Mark. B.S., U. Okla., 1976; Dr. Pharmacy, U. Tex., 1979. Registered pharmacist. Asst. prof. Samford U., Birmingham, Ala., 1979, U.N.C.-Chapel Hill, 1985—; asst. pharmacy dir. Children's Hosp., Birmingham, 1979-85; cons. Comprehensive Epilepsy Ctr. for Children, Birmingham, 1983-85. Contbr. author: Applied Clinical Pharmacokinetics, 1984, also articles. Speaker Am. Lung Assn. chpt. Birmingham, 1985. Coach Am. Soccer League, Pelham, Ala., 1985. Served to lt. USN, 1968-72. Mem. Am. Coll. Clin. Pharmacy, Am. Assn. Colls. Pharmacy, Am. Soc. Clin. Pharmacology and Therapeutics, Am. Soc. Parenteral and Enteral Nutrition. Avocations: computer programming, running. Office: Sch Pharmacy Beard Hall 200 H UNC Chapel Hill NC 27514

MILES, MINNIE MARIANNE, artist; b. Austin, Tex., Aug. 18, 1941; d. John Jordan and Gladys Katherine (Brewer) M. A.B. in Art, Fisk U., 1963; M.A. in Art, NYU, 1968. Instr. art Met. Pub. Schs., Nashville, 1963-65, Fisk U., Nashville, 1966-68, Tenn. State U., Nashville, 1971-72, Austin Community Coll., 1981—; art cons. curriculum developer, English coordinator Fisk U., Nashville, 1969-71; personal mgmt. vocalists Golden Horn Prodns., Nashville, 1971-76; curator Heritage Collection Huston-Tillotson Coll., Austin, 1976-77; dir. coll. relations, 1977-80; pub. info. specialist Austin Ind., 1980-81. One woman shows include Huston-Tillotson Coll., Austin, 1956, Marketplace,

Nashville, 1967, The Partham, Nashville, 1970, Univ. Club, Nashville, 1970, East Tex. State U., Commerce, 1970, Tenn. State U., Nashville, 1971, Carver Gallery, San Antonio, 1978, Westwood Country Club, Austin, 1981, others; exhibited in numerous group shows; represented in permanent collections First Am. Nat. Bank, Nashville, Fisk U., Nashville. Bd. dirs. Nashville Film Soc., 1969; mem. Austin Pub. Service Communications, 1980-81; mem. Austin Arts Commn., 1984. Recipient Honorable Mention for Painting Atlanta U., 1957. Mem. Tex. Jr. Coll. Tchrs. Assn., Phi Delta Kappa. Episcopalian. Avocations: photography; reading; mosaic structure.

MILES, RICHARD MICHAEL, telephone company executive; b. Indpls., Jan. 26, 1946; s. Albert Richard and Martha Jane (Foerderer) M. B.A. in Journalism and English, U. Ala., 1968; postgrad. U. Tex., 1968. Reporter, Birmingham Post-Herald, 1966-68; corr. Newsweek, 1966-68; assoc. editor for English lang. publs. Turkish Ministry of Tourism, Ankara, 1968-69; reporter, drama editor Atlanta Constitution, 1969-71; with So. Bell Telephone Co., Atlanta, 1971—, successively pub. relations mgr., dist. mgr. pub. relations, ops. mgr., pub. relations and advt. for Ga. Bd. dirs. Atlanta Ballet, 1979—, chmn. mktg. com., 1980—; mem. communications adv. bd. Brenau Coll., Gainesville, Ga., 1980—. Mem. Soc. Profl. Journalists (sec., past pres.), Nat. Acac. TV Arts and Scis., Ga. Assn. Broadcasters, Ga. Press Assn. Roman Catholic. Clubs: Atlanta Press, Ansley Golf. Home: 6280 River Overlook Dr NW Atlanta GA 30328 Office: 125 Perimeter Center W Atlanta GA 30348

MILES, TRAVIS ANTHONY, state senator; b. Eagle City, Okla., Dec. 6, 1937; s. Paul McDill and Stella (McCrary) M.; student Phillips U., 1954-59; 1 dau., Laura Lynne. Mem. Ark. Senate, 1981—; exec. v.p., gen. mgr., dir., partner Beals Advt. Agy., Inc., Ft. Smith, Ark., 1961—. Served with U.S. Army, 1953-64. Pres. council Boy Scouts Am., 1977-78; pres. Ft. Smith Girls' Club, 1979-81, hon. girl, 1979. Named outstanding young man, Jaycees, 1967; recipient Silver Beaver award Boy Scouts, 1968; disting. service award, 1979; recipient outstanding service award St. Edward Med. Center, 1979. Mem. Van Buren Advt. Fedn. (pres. 1972-73), Old Ft. Christian Bus. Men (chmn. com. 1976-78). Mem. Christian Ch. (Disciples of Christ). Club: Kiwanis (past pres.). Office: Ark State Senate Little Rock AR 72201 also 220 N Greenwood Ft Smith AR 72901

MILGRAM, ABRAHAM SAMUEL, construction executive; b. Tel-Aviv, Sept. 25, 1936; s. Jaime and Esther (Reich) M.; came to U.S., 1952; B.S., U. Tex., 1958; postgrad. Central U. Venezuela, 1958-59, Northwestern U., 1958; m. Zelma K. Milgram; children—Andrew Scott, Katherine Cecilia. Field engr. Atlantic Refining Co., Port Arthur, Tex., 1958; design engr. Orinoco Mining Co., Port Ordaz, Venezuela, 1958-63; gen. mgr. Bella Co., Beaumont, Tex., 1963-66, exec. v.p., 1966—, also dir.; exec. v.p., dir. Hurco, Inc., Beaumont, 1967—; mem. S.W. adv. bd. Liberty Mut. Ins. Co. dir. Tex. Bank Beaumont. Trustee, Sabine Area Laborers Tng. Trust, Sabine area Carpenters Apprenticeship Tng. Fund. Mem. ASTM, Am. Concrete Inst., ASCE. Home: 680 Heritage Ln Beaumont TX 77706 Office: PO Box 5421 Beaumont TX 77702

MILKEREIT, JOHN EUGENE, public relations executive, consultant; b. Dayton, Ohio, May 23, 1937; s. Richard David and Clara Rowena (Fellers) M.; m. Martha Joanne Benham, June 17, 1961; children—John Richard, David Allen, William Fellers. B.S., Purdue U., 1960; M.A., U. Chgo., 1977. Univ. editor U. Akron, 1965-67, dir. News Bur., 1967-70; assoc. dir. pub. info. U. Chgo., 1970-72; dir. med. ctr. pub. affairs U. Chgo. Med. Ctr., 1972-80; dir. pub. relations Med. U. S.C., Charleston, 1980—; cons. health care pub. relations. Bd. dirs. Charleston Symphony, 1984—. Served to capt. USAR, 1961-69. Mem. Pub. Relations Soc. Am. (pres. S.C. chpt. 1982-83), Am. Hosp. Pub. Relations and Mktg. Soc., Assn. Am. Med. Colls. (group on pub. affairs southeast dist.). Office: 171 Ashley Ave Charleston SC 29425

MILKO, ROBERT JOHN, association information and public relations official; b. Alexandria, Va., Oct. 5, 1955; s. Robert Raymond and Ruth Ann (Gratz) M.; m. Julie Ann Donovan, Aug. 23, 1980; 1 son, Robert Joseph. B.A., Old Dominion U., 1977; postgrad. U. Va.-Richmond, 1978. Dir. devel. and communications Am. Lung Assn., Fairfax, Va., 1980-83, cons. No. Va., 1983; mgr. info. and pub. relations Nat. Audio Visual Assn., Internat. Communications Industries Assn., Fairfax, 1983—. Editor: Potomac News, 1980-83, NAVA News newsletter, 1983. Mem. Old Dominion U. Alumni Assn. (pres. D.C. Area chpt. 1979-83), Pub. Relations Soc. Am., Internat. Assn. Bus. Communicators, Meeting Planners Internat., Nat. Assn. Expn. Mgrs., Am. Soc. Assn. Execs., Profl. Photographers Am., No. Va. Press Club, Sigma Nu. Roman Catholic. Office: NAVA Internat Communications Industries Assn 3150 Spring St Fairfax VA 22031

MILLAR, ROBERT KNOWLES, chemical engineer; b. Berkeley, Calif., Dec. 15, 1923; s. Russell W. and Belle (Stewart) M.; m. Sue Pittman, Apr. 5, 1952; children—William R., Lisa S. B.S. in Chem. Engring., U. Calif.-Berkeley, 1949. Engr., Shell Chem. Co., Deer Park, Tex., 1949-54, Shell Devel. Co., Emeryville, Calif., 1954-56; engr. Shell Chem. Co., N.Y.C., 1956-60, sr. engr., La., 1960-70; sr. tng. rep. Shell Oil Co., Norco, La., 1970-81, mgr. tng., 1981—. Served with U.S. Army, 1943-46, ETO. Mem. Am. Petroleum Inst., Am. Soc. Tng. and Devel., U. Calif. Alumni Assn. Republican. Presbyterian. Club: Pelican Squares (Metairie, La.). Avocations: tennis; golf; swimming; square dancing; woodworking. Home: 5320 Cocos Plumosas Dr Kenner LA 70065 Office: PO Box 10 Norco LA 70079

MILLARD, HAROLD RAY, mortgage banker, management consultant; b. Chattanooga, May 4, 1931; s. William M. and Mable D. Millard; m. Betty Ann Letz, Apr. 8, 1955; children—Stephen. B.B.A., Memphis State U., 1958. C.P.A., Tex. Ptnr., Peat, Marwick, Mitchell & Co., Houston, 1958-80; pres. Larmar Fin. Corp., Austin, 1981; owner, pres. LFS Financial Services, Houston, 1982—. Served with USAF, 1950-54. Mem. Tex. Soc. C.P.A.s, Tex. Savs. and Loan League, Am. Inst. C.P.A.s. Episcopalian. Clubs: Houston, Golfcrest Country. Contbr. articles to profl. jours. Office: 17629 El Camino Real Suite 201 Houston TX 77058

MILLARD, JAMES KEMPER, marketing executive, consultant; b. Lexington, Ky., Oct. 28, 1948; s. Lyman Clifford and Cora Spence (Carrick) M., Jr.; children—Lyman Clifford III, Sean Duffy, James Kemper Jr.; m. Linda Madelyn Hooper, Nov. 26, 1983. B.A. in Polit. Sci., Transylvania U., 1971. Corr. AP, 1970-71; prodn. asst. sta. WLEX-TV, Lexington, Ky., 1970; floor dir., asst. news dir., 1971-73, producer, reporter, 1974-76; producer, dir. Ky. Dept. Pub. Info., Lexington, 1973; successively admissions counselor, dir. promotional services, dir. univ. relations, assoc. dir. devel. Transylvania U., Lexington, 1973-79; field mktg. mgr. Abbott Advt. Agy., Inc., Lexington, 1979-80, account exec., 1980-81, account supr., 1981-85; dir. mktg. Steak 'n Shake Inc., Indpls., 1985; field mktg. mgr. Eastern U.S., Nutri/System Inc., Phila., 1985-86, dir. field mktg., 1986—; bd. dirs., mem. advt. com., chmn. Bluegrass chpt. Ky. Restaurant Assn.; mem. acad. adv. com. mass communications Eastern Ky. U., also guest lectr. Events chmn. Nat. Kidney Found. of Ind.; deacon Central Christian Ch., Lexington. Recipient Addy (Bronze) award Lexington Advt. Club, 1976, Addy (Best of Show, Gold, Silver, Bronze, Merit) award, 1982; Addy (Silver, Bronze, Merit) award Am. Advt. Fedn., 1981, 83; Gt. Menu. Gold award Nat. Restaurant Assn., 1982; Louie (Merit) award Louisville Advt. Club, 1976; named Key Man of 1981, Jerrico, Inc.; Best Children's Menu, Fla. Restaurant Assn., 1982. Mem. Delta Sigma Phi. Democrat. Club: Columbia (Indpls.). Home: 5311 N Central Ave Indianapolis IN 46220 Office: Nutri/System Inc Willow Grove PA 19046

MILLARD, MAX, pathologist; b. London, Apr. 8, 1921; came to U.S., 1952; s. Morris and Annie (Zlotover) M.; m. Heather Millard, Apr. 4, 1951; children—Lesley Ann, Gillian Linda. M.D., U. Dublin, 1944, M.A. (hon.), 1952. Diplomate Am. Bds. Clin. Anat. Pathology. Resident, Jackson Meml. Hosp., Miami, Fla., 1952-55; assoc. prof. U. Miami Sch. Medicine, 1960-72; asst. pathologist Jackson Meml. Hosp., 1955-64, dir. surg. pathology, 1964-72; cons. pathologist Bromley & Farnborough Hosps., London, 1972-76; dir. dept. pathology South Miami Hosp., 1976—. Served to capt. M.C., Royal Army, 1948-49. Fellow Royal Soc. Medicine, Royal Coll. Pathologists, Royal Coll. Physicians Ireland; mem. Internat. Acad. Pathology. Author: Autopsy Pathology, 1953; contbr. chpts. to books. Office: South Miami Hosp 7400 SW 62d Ave South Miami FL 33143

MILLER, ALFREDA REED, retired educator; b. Monticello, Iowa, Mar. 6, 1907; d. Ervin E. and Gwendolen (Doxsee) Reed; B.A., Cornell Coll., Mt. Vernon, Iowa, 1927; M.A., U. Iowa, 1932; m. Nathan A. Miller, July 5, 1949; children—Gwenna Leu, Thomas Reed. Tchr. pub. schs., Toledo, Iowa, 1927-28, Shenandoah, Iowa, 1928-31, U. Iowa Demonstration Sch., 1931-32, Knoxville, 1933-37, Wapello, 1937-38, Dade County, Fla., 1938-72, Ada Merritt Jr. High Sch., 1941-54, Hialeah High Sch., 1954-72. Mem. Women in Communications (chmn. scholarship com. 1957-77), P.E.O. (pres. 1976-79). Baptist. Home: 570 Hunting Lodge Dr Miami Springs FL 33166

MILLER, ARCHIE RANDOLPH, church official; b. Monroe, La., July 22, 1955; s. Archie Preston and Willie Von (Jennings) M.; m. Cynthia Rene Thornhill, Nov. 27, 1982. B.A., Fla. State U., 1977; M.Ch. Music, New Orleans Bapt. Theol. Sem., 1981. Youth minister First Bapt. Ch., McComb, Miss., 1978-79; minister music and youth Woodlawn Bapt. Ch., Rayville, La., 1979-80; minister music Red Bluff Bapt. Ch., Greensburg, La., 1980-81; minister mus. and youth First Bapt. Ch., Jonesboro, La., 1981-83; asst. dir. Continental Singers, Thousand Oaks, Calif., 1981; minister mus., youth First Bapt. Ch., Cape Coral, Fla., 1983—; instrumental music cons. Royal Palm Assn. Fla. Bapt. Conv., 1985-86; adminstr. Cape Coral Christian Sch., 1986. Bd. dirs. Nehemiah Prodns., Fort Myers, Fla., 1984—, S.W. Fla. Handbell Festival, 1985—; assn. youth dir. Royal Palm Bapt. Assn., 1984—. Mem. Am. Guild English Handbell Ringers, S.W. Fla. Bapt. Singing Men. Republican. Avocations: sport fishing; hunting; scuba diving. Home: 1521 SE 41st St Cape Coral FL 33904 Office: First Bapt Ch 4117 Coronado Pkwy Cape Coral FL

MILLER, BARRY M., educational administrator; b. Balt., Sept. 14, 1952; s. Charles M. and Sonia F. (Weiner) M.; B.A. in Sociology, U. Md., 1975; M.S., W.Va. U., 1978; m. Lynn D. Sears, Aug. 23, 1975. With Am. Research Bur., Beltsville, Md., 1973-77; dir. child devel. Scotts Run Settlement House, Osage, W.Va., 1978-84; child devel. specialist Early Childhood Devel. Assn., 1985—; cons. in field. Mem. Nat. Assn. Edn. of Young Children, So. Assn. Children Under Six, Broward Assn. for Edn. Young Children, Phi Upsilon Omicron. Democrat. Jewish. Home: 11180 Royal Palm Blvd Coral Springs FL 33065 Office: 1800 Cathedral Dr Margate FL 33063

MILLER, BETTY LOUISE, mathematics educator; b. Morgantown, W.Va., May 3, 1926; d. Claud Eakin and Mary (McGuffie) M. B.S. in Chem. Engring., W.Va. U., 1947, M.S., 1957. Chemist, Celanese Corp., Cumberland, Md., 1947-48, supr., Rock Hill, S.C., 1948-53, gen. supr., 1953-55; grad. asst. W.Va. U., Morgantown, 1956-57, instr., 1957-70, asst. prof., 1970-76, assoc. prof., 1976—. Recipient Teaching award of Merit, Gamma Sigma Delta, 1975; Outstanding Tchr. award W.Va. U., 1978. Mem. Math. Assn. Am., Nat. Council Tchrs. Math., Pi Mu Epsilon, Tau Beta Pi, Alpha Delta Pi (nat. chmn. scholarship 1975—; Meritorious Service award 1979). Methodist. Home: 241 Kingwood St Morgantown WV 26505 Office: WVa U Dept Math Morgantown WV 26506

MILLER, BILLIE RUTH, guidance counselor; b. Abilene, Tex., July 9, 1924; d. George Bruce and Cordelia (Chaffin) Darnell; m. Lloyd Nathaniel Hawkins, Sept. 6, 1942 (dec. June 1962); children—Billy Loyd, Garry Lynn, Bruce Russell; m. J. Robert Miller, Mar. 27, 1969. B.A., McMurry Coll., 1966; M.Ed., Hardin Simmons U., 1971; postgrad. U. Tex.-Arlington, 1972, No. Ariz. U., 1973, Abilene Christian U., 1977. Cert. counselor, Tex.; nat. cert. counselor. Cons. Cogdell News Co., Abilene, 1945-47, sec., acct., 1942-45; tchr., counselor Kayenta Boarding Sch., Ariz., 1966-67; head guidance dept. Crownpoint Boarding Sch., N.Mex., 1967-71; edn. service officer 96 CSG/DPE, Dyess AFB, Tex., 1973-75, guidance counselor, 1971-73, 75—, edn. lectr., 1971—; pvt. practice counseling, Abilene, 1971—; guest appearances TV stas., Abilene. Vice pres. Abilene Art Forum, 1954; pres., historian N.A.T.I.O.N.S Club, Abilene, 1960, 61. Recipient Superior Performance award Civilian Personnel Dyess AFB, Tex., 1984, achievement award Dir. Personnel Dyess AFB, 1983; Ora Negra Am. Bus. Women Assn. ednl. scholar, 1967. Mem. Am. Assn. Counselor Devel. (nat. cert. 1983), Nat. Vocat. Counselor Devel., Tex. Assn. Counseling Devel. (cert. 1983), Mil. Edn. Counselor Assn. (treas. 1981-82), Western Horizon Am. Bus. Women Edn. Assn. (chmn. 1983, Woman of Yr. 1979), Mensa (sec. Abilene chpt. 1963-64), United Daus. Confederacy (sec. 1947-48). Republican. Baptist. Lodge: Order of Eastern Star (worthy matron 1957-58, dep. grand matron 1960). Avocations: amateur archaeology; astronomy; camping and rafting; painting; knitting. Home: 1857 Sycamore Abilene TX 79602 Office: 96 CSG/DPE Dyess AFB Abilene TX 79607

MILLER, BRUCE A., engineering company executive; b. N.Y.C., Aug. 3, 1930; s. William A. and Martha B. Miller; m. Joan Constance Carl, Dec. 16, 1957; children—Dawn, Susan, Bruce, Laura. B.S.M.E., U.S. Naval Acad., 1952. Various positions L.I. Lighting Co., Miacola, N.Y., 1957-64; v.p. bus. devel. Sanderson & Porter, Inc., N.Y.C., 1964-77; v.p. ops. Sid Harvey Industries, Garden City, N.Y., 1977-78; sr. v.p., gen. mgr. Tampa (Fla.) office Badger Engrs. Inc. subs. Raytheon Corp., 1978—; mem. several corporate bds. Bd. advisors The King's Coll., Briarcliff Manor, N.Y.; bd. fellows U. Tampa. Served with USN, 1952-57. Recipient award for disting. service to constrn. industry Engring. News Record, 1976. Mem. ASME. Clubs: University, Carrollwood Village Golf and Tennis (Tampa); Army Navy (Washington). Home: 3902 Northampton Way Tampa FL 33624 Office: 1401 N Westshore Blvd Tampa FL 33622

MILLER, BRUCE RICHARD, employee benefit executive; b. Hazleton, Pa., Mar. 16, 1944; s. Robert Joseph and Marguerite Marie (Fritz) M.; B.A. in Polit. Sci., Pa. State U., 1971. Supr. salary adminstrn. Govt. Employees Ins. Co., Chevy Chase, Md., 1971-73; asst. to personnel dir. MCI Telecommunications, Inc., Washington, 1973-74; wage and salary adminstr. Kay Jewelers, Inc., Alexandria, Va., 1974, dir. personnel, 1974-84, div. v.p. personnel, 1981-85; founder, pres., chief exec. officer Employee Benefit Corp. Am., Alexandria, 1984—. Pa. State U. Presdl. asso.; mem. Old Town Civic Assn., Alexandria, 1978-84; mem. Alexandria Human Rights Commn., 1982-85, chmn., 1984-85. Served with U.S. Army, 1966-70. Mem. Am. Soc. Personnel Adminstrn., Met. Washington Bd. Trade, Alexandria C. of C., Pa. State U. Alumni Assn. Clubs: Pa. State U. Nittany Lion, Pa. State U. of Greater Washington (dir.), Nat. Capital Area Nittany Lion (dir.), Back The Lions. Contbr. articles to profl. jours. Home: 400 Madison St Apt 2103 Alexandria VA 22314 Office: 400 Madison St Suite 2103 Alexandria VA 22314

MILLER, BRUCE ROGERS, television executive, advertising and marketing consultant; b. Columbia, S.C., Mar. 1, 1949; s. James and Leonina (Bell) M.; m. Jacque Lee Reaves, Mar. 11, 1971; 1 dau., Michele Elaine. Student, Spartanburg Jr. Coll., 1969; cert. Sterling Inst. Announcer sta. WABV, Abbeville, S.C., 1966-68; TV prodn. specialist sta. WSPA-TV, Spartanburg, S.C., 1968-69; sales mgr. sta. WNMB, North Myrtle Beach, S.C., 1972-73; account exec. sta. WSPA-FM, 1973-74, dir. sales, sta. WSPA-TV, 1976-84; gen. mgr. WBTW-TV, Florence, S.C., 1984—; broadcast cons. William B. Tanner Co., Memphis, 1974-76; spl. cons. in advt. and mktg. various orgns.; guest lectr. various colls., univs. and clubs. Assoc. dir. North Myrtle Beach Sun Fun Festival, 1973; mem. Panama Am. Council, 1970-71, Myrtle Beach AFB Human Relations Council, 1971-73, Greater Myrtle Beach Heart Assn., 1971-73; charter mem. bd. dirs. Grand Strand Press and Advt. Assn., 1973; pres. Horry County Heart Fund, 1974; pub. relations dir. Greenville Power Squadron; mem. Leadership Spartanburg Alumni; mem. adv. bd. Salvation Army; mem. exec. com. March of Dimes; div. chair United Way, 1985; active Florence Forward Progress. Served with USAF, 1969-72. Mem. Greenville Advt. Fedn., Columbia Advt. Fedn., Florence C. of C. (bd. dirs.). Clubs: Sertoma (Spartanburg), Columbia Ad, U. S.C. Gamecock, Lodge: Rotary. Home: 3826 Lake Dr Florence SC 29501 Office: 3430 TV Rd Florence SC 29501

MILLER, CAREY BRENT, oil company executive, geologist; b. Chickasha, Okla., Aug. 23, 1949; s. Roy Lee and Willma LaVelle (Smith) M.; m. Margie Jean Broaddus, June 7, 1969; 1 child, Derrik Brent. B.S. in Geology, U. Okla., 1978; B.S. in Math., Okla. Coll. Liberal Arts, 1970. Dist. sales rep. United Foam Corp., Shawnee, Okla., 1975-76; researcher Environ. Research Devel. Assn., U. Okla., Norman, 1976-77; dist. geologist Grace Petroleum Corp., Oklahoma City, 1977-80, Western Pacific Petroleum, Oklahoma City, 1980-82; pres., dir. BriCar Resources, Inc., Oklahoma City, 1980—; pres. Hold Exploration Co., Oklahoma City, 1982—; dir. Blue Pine Pottery Corp., Oklahoma City, Roy-Al Corp., Oklahoma City, 1983—. Served to 1st lt. U.S. Army, 1971-74. Mem. Am. Assn. Petroleum Geologists, Soc. Exploration Geophysicists, Oklahoma City Geol. Soc., Geophys. Soc. Oklahoma City, Oklahoma City C. of C., Phi Gamma Lambda (pres. 1969-70), Sigma Gamma Epsilon. Home: 2910 Meadow Ave Norman OK 73069 Office: Hold Exploration Co 1207 Sovereign Row Oklahoma City OK 73108

MILLER, CECIL ARDEN, physician, educator; b. Shelby, Ohio, Sept. 19, 1924; s. Harley H. and Mary (Thuma) M.; m. Helen Lloyd Meihack, June 26, 1948; children—John Lewis, Thomas Meihack, Helen Lewis, Benjamin Lewis. Student Oberlin Coll., 1942-44; M.D. cum laude, Yale U., 1948. Intern and resident in pediatrics, Yale U., 1948-51; mem. faculty Sch. Medicine, U. Kans., 1951-66, dean, 1961-66; vice chancellor health sci. U. N.C., Chapel Hill, 1966-71, mem. faculty Sch. Pub. Health, 1971—, prof., chmn. dept. maternal and child health, 1977—; exec. bd. Planned Parenthood Fedn. Am.; chmn. bd. Alan Guttmacher Inst. Recipient Robert Felix award in community medicine, 1977. Mem. Inst. Medicine of Nat. Acad. Scis., Am. Pub. Health Assn., Sigma Xi, Alpha Omega Alpha. Democrat. Unitarian. Contbr. articles to profl. publs.

MILLER, CHARLES, investment management executive; b. Galveston, Tex., Feb. 13, 1934; s. Samuel and Rose M.; B.A. in Math., U. Tex., 1959; m. Beth Birdwell. Investment officer Tchr. Retirement System, Austin, Tex., 1961-66; v.p., portfolio mgr. Criterion Funds, Inc., Houston, 1966-71; pres., chief exec. officer Criterion Investment Mgmt. Co., Criterion Group, Houston, 1971—; dir. Tex. Commerce Bank; bd. dirs. State Pension Review Bd. of Tex., 1979-84. Mem. Fin. Analysts Fedn., Am. Statis. Assn., Nat. Assn. Bus. Economists, Houston C. of C. (bd. dirs.). Episcopalian. Clubs: Petroleum (Houston); Headliners (Austin); Argyle (San Antonio); Ponte Vedra (Jacksonville, Fla.). Office: 333 Clay St Houston TX 77002

MILLER, CHARLES EDWARD, JR., accountant, auditor, financial executive; b. Birmingham, Ala., Oct. 16, 1953; s. Charles Edward and Sarah Nell (Fortner) M.; m. Cecilia Ann Crim, Sept. 16, 1978. B.S. in Acctg., U. Ala.-Birmingham, 1977. C.P.A., Ala. Auditor H.L. Raburn & Co., Birmingham, 1977-79, Cherry, Bekaert & Holland, Birmingham, 1979-81; v.p., controller U.S. Home Corp., Phoenix, 1981-84; auditor Coopers & Lybrand, Atlanta, 1985—. Vol. Democratic party, Birmingham, 1981. Mem. Am. Inst. C.P.A.s, Ala. Soc. C.P.A.s, Phoenix C. of C., Cobb C. of C. Methodist. Avocations: travel; jogging; theatre. Office: Coopers & Lybrand 1200 Equitable Bldg Atlanta GA 30043

MILLER, CHARLES LEO, accountant; b. Lambert, Miss., May 28, 1931; s. Louis David and Sybil (Claussen) M.; B.S., Memphis State Coll., 1953; cert. Memphis Coll. Accountancy, 1956; m. Wanda Lee Trudel, Feb. 14, 1963; 1 dau., Crystal Ann. Staff acct. Minor & Moore, Memphis, 1955-57, Edward C. Wirotious & Co., Memphis, 1957-58; office mgr. Standard Welders Supply Co., Memphis, 1959-63; staff acct. Speer, Chavez, Ruggenberg & Wright, Bakersfield, Calif., 1963-65; pvt. practice acctg. C. Leo Miller, Columbia, Tenn., 1965-76; ptnr. Miller & York, Columbia, 1977-79, Miller Stutts & York, 1979-81, Miller & Stutts, 1981—. Sec., Recreation Enterprises Inc., Columbia, 1973-85; sec. Murray Theatres, Inc., 1974—; sec., dir. Freestone, Inc., 1974-85; pres. Crystal Clear Water Co., Columbia, 1977-81; sec., treas., Funway Products Inc., Columbia, 1977-79; pres. Funamation, Inc., 1980-84; v.p. Leaplex, Inc., 1979-82, Taper Tec, Inc., 1982-84; dir. Morgan Bros. Electric Co. Inc. Adviser Jr. Achievement Columbia, 1970-72, bd. dirs., 1972-74; scoutmaster Boy Scouts Am., 1966-74, asst. dist. commr., 1972-73, chmn. Duck River dist., 1977-79, tng. chmn., 1980, area commr., 1985—; treas., adviser, also bd. dirs. Maury County Creative Arts Guild, 1972-74; founder, pres. Duck River Humane Soc., 1973-75, 77-79, bd. dirs., 1973-79; bd. dirs. Big Bros. Columbia, 1978-81. Served with U.S. Army, 1953-55. C.P.A. Mem. Am. Inst. C.P.A.s, Nat. Assn. Accts., Tenn. Soc. C.P.A.s, Am. Legion, Nat. Assn. Accts., Internat Platform Assn., Nat. Rifle Assn., Delta Sigma Pi. Methodist. Clubs: Shriners, Elks, Masons. Author: Campfire Ghost Stories (And How to Tell Them), 1975; Ghost of Crazy Horse Hollow, 1978; Tax Tips, 1981. Office: 305 W 8th St Columbia TN 38401

MILLER, CHARLES RICHARD, retired college administrator; b. Elmira, N.Y., May 1, 1924; s. Charles Hooker and Florence Rena (Brand) M.; m. Gwendolyn Virginia Davis, June 29, 1946; children—Charles Edward, Carol Ann Miller Carlin. B.A., Hobart Coll., 1949; M.Ed., St. Lawrence U., 1952; postgrad. (Esso Safety Found. fellow), NYU, 1954-58. Tchr., Elmira Free Acad., also Southside High Sch., Elmira, 1949-56; vice prin. Southside High Sch., Elmira, 1956-58; supr. N.Y. State Dept. Edn., Albany, 1958-60; prin. Maine-Endwell Sr. High Sch., Endwell, N.Y., 1960-65, asst. supt. Maine-Endwell Central Schs., 1965-67; supt. Schs. Sodus Central Sch. Dist. (N.Y.), 1967-68, Carol Morgan Schs., Santo Domingo, Dominican Republic, 1968-69; dean admissions Elmira Coll., 1969-79, asst. to pres., 1979-81, mem. continuing edn. faculty, criminal justice program, 1976-79, coordinator criminal justice program, 1979-81; founder, 1st pres. Sun City Center Security Patrol, Inc. (Fla.), 1982-84. Pres. Chemung County Safety Council, 1954-56; organizer, dir. Traffic Violators Sch., Elmira, 1956-58; v.p. Chemung County PTA, Elmira, 1957-58; chmn. Elmira Traffic Safety Bd., 1954-58; mem. Gov.'s Traffic Safety Com., 1958-60; chmn. Chemung County Disaster Preparedness Com., 1975-79, Chemung County Traffic Safety Bd., 1976-81; v.p. N.Y. Assn. County Traffic Bds.; mem. Chemung County Legislature, 1975-76; bd. dirs. So. Tier Econ. Growth Capabilities, 1979-80; gen. chmn. 50th Anniversary of Soaring, 1980; trustee Home Owners Assn., Sun City Center, 1981-84, pres., 1984; chmn. community coordinating council Sun City Ctr., 1984-85; bd. dirs. S.E. Fla. Blood Bank, 1984-86; mem. community devel. com. Sun City Ctr., 1985; pres. Good Samaritan Fund, 1985—. Served with USAAF, 1942-45; P.O.W., Ger.; with USAFR. Decorated Air medal, Purple Heart; named Young Man of Yr., Elmira, 1957; Outstanding Man of Yr., Sun City Ctr., Fla., 1984. Mem. NEA, N.Y. Edn. Assn., N.Y. Sch. Adminstrs. Assn., Nat. Assn. Coll. Admissions Counselors, N.Y. State Assn. Coll. Admissions Counselors, Am. Assn. Collegiate Registrars and Admissions Officers, European Council Internat. Schs., Internat. Council Acad. Instns., N.Y. State Deps. Assn., Chemung County Deps. Assn., N.Y. State Sheriffs Assn., C. of C. Elmira (dir. 1972-74), Sun City Ctr. C. of C., Am. Assn. Ex-Prisoners of War, Am. Legion. Republican. Congregationalist. Club: Caloosa Golf and Country (Sun City Center). Lodges: Rotary (pres. 1986); Masons (Elmira); Shriners (1st v.p. 1986). Home: 2005 East View Dr Sun City Center FL 33570

MILLER, DONALD ANGUS, physician assistant; b. Buffalo, Nov. 12, 1941; s. Ralph Harold and Catherine (Montgomery) M.; B.A. in English/Psychology, So. Ill. U., 1972; B.S. in Health Scis., SUNY, Stony Brook, 1974, Profl. Cert. Physician Asso., 1974; m. Shirley A. Swanson, Mar. 14, 1970; children—Breyana G., Erik S. Physician asst. Algoma (Wis.) Clinic, 1974-75, Alyeska Pipeline Co., Fairbanks, Alaska, 1975-76; physician asst. Nat. Health Service Corps, Aledo/Keithsburg, Ill., 1976-78, Uptown Peoples Health Center, Chgo., 1978-80; commd. capt. USAF, 1979; staff physician asst., family practice residency program, Eglin Regional Hosp., Eglin AFB, Fla., 1980—. Served with USAF, 1959-63; with Army N.G., 1976-80. Decorated Army Commendation medal; recipient Humanitarian Service award, 1980. Mem. Am. Acad. Physician Assts., Assn. Mil. Surgeons of U.S., Acad. Public Health Service Physician Assts. (founder, pres. 1979-80, editor newsletter), Air Force Soc. Physician Assts., Air Force Assn. Am. Home: 563 Chinquapin Dr Eglin AFB FL 32542

MILLER, DONALD DEAN, nursing educator; b. Hay Springs, Nebr., Mar. 10, 1933; s. Harry Allen and Frances LaVerne (Braley) M. Diploma, Mercy Hosp. Sch. Nursing, 1958; B.S., Loretto Heights Coll., 1974; M.S., U. Okla., 1979, doctoral candidate, 1985-86. R.N., Colo., Okla. Nurse, then supr. Mercy Hosp., Denver, 1963-68; dir. nursing service North Shore Manor, Loveland, Colo., 1968-69, Galaxie Nursing Ctr., Denver, 1969-70; evening supr. Davis Nursing Home, Denver, 1970-71; instr. nursing Community Coll. Denver, 1971-74, East Central U., Ada, Okla., 1974—; cons. geriatric, long-term care nursing; participant ARC nursing programs. Mem. adv. council Okla. Health Systems Agy. Served with U.S. Army, 1953-55. Recipient Disting. Service recognition ARC, 1982, 83. Fellow Am. Coll. Nursing Home Adminstrs. (past vice chmn.); mem. Am. Nurses Assn., Okla. Nurses Assn., Mercy Hosp. Alumni Assn., Loretto Heights Alumni Assn., Sigma Theta Tau. Roman Catholic. Club: Appaloosa Horse (Moscow, Idaho). Home: Route 1 PO Box 222 Holdenville OK 74848 Office: Div of Nursing East Central U Ada OK 74820

MILLER, DONALD JAMES, wholesaler, manufacturing executive; b. N.Y.C., Oct. 8, 1947; s. Edward and Alice (Freeman) M.; divorced; 1 son, Robert Neil; m. 2d Judith Lynn Petty, Dec. 11, 1982. B.S. in Bus. Adminstrn., U. Fla., 1969, postgrad. Coll. of Law, 1970. Sales mgr. PM Devel., Gainesville, Fla., 1969; div. sales mgr. Skyline Corp., Ocala, Fla., 1970-71; gen. mgr. T.S. Adams, Inc., Tampa, Fla., 1971-73; v.p. Reliatex, Inc., Tampa, 1974—; pres. Fla. Fibre, Inc., 1978—. Mem. Auto Service Industry Assn., Fla. Pest Control Assn., Tex. Pest Control Assn., Aircraft Owners and Pilots Assn. Democrat.

Home: 7820 Bullara Dr Tampa FL 33617 Office: 6004 Bonacker Dr Tampa FL 33610

MILLER, EDWARD MCCARTHY, economics educator; b. Richmond, Va., Sept. 2, 1944; s. Edward M. B.S. in Econs. and Mech. Engring., MIT, 1965, Ph.D. in Econs., 1970. Staff mem. White House, Washington, 1973-74, various govt. positions, 1974-79; staff v.p. Am. Productivity Ctr., Houston, 1979-80; Tranoff prof. pub. affairs Rice U., Houston, 1981-84; prof. econs. U. New Orleans, 1984—. Contbr. articles to profl. jours. Presbyterian. Home: 3000 Gentilly 129 New Orleans LA 70122 Office: Dept Econs and Fin U New Orleans New Orleans LA 70148

MILLER, EUGENE FERRELL, political science educator; b. Atlanta, Oct. 1, 1935; s. James Douglas and Mary Lou (Ferrell) M.; m. Eva Jean Fix, June 14, 1958; children—David, Cynthia, Gary, Gregory. B.A., Emory U., 1957, M.A., 1962; Ph.D., U. Chgo., 1965. Instr., Davidson Coll., N.C., 1962-63; asst. prof. Furman U., Greenville, S.C., 1963-67; asst. prof. U. Ga., Athens, 1967-72, assoc. prof., 1972-81, prof. polit. sci., 1981—; co.-dir. conf. series Liberty Fund, Inc., Indpls., 1982—. Editor: Hume's Essays, 1985. Contbr. articles to profl. jours. and chpts. to books. Recipient Outstanding Tchr. award U. Ga., 1974, 79, 80, 81, 83; fellow Danforth Found., 1957-62, NEH, 1972-73. Mem. Am. Polit. Sci. Assn. Methodist. Home: 380 Greencrest Dr Athens GA 30605 Office: Dept Polit Sci U Ga Athens GA 30602

MILLER, FANNIE CAROLYN ROLL (MRS. WILLIAM PEOPLES MILLER), educator; b. Kansas City, Mo.; d. Edward Francis and Louisa Caroline (Chambers) Roll; B.A., U. Buffalo, 1927; postgrad. SUNY, State Tchr. Coll., Buffalo, Canisius Coll., Buffalo, Beaver Coll., Jenkintown, Pa.; Temple U.; m. William Peoples Miller, Nov. 24, 1937 (dec. May 1961); children—Frances Roll (Mrs. Robert Alan Barnett), Janet Peoples (Mrs. Harold Robert Crooks). Tchr. Pub. Schs., Clarence, N.Y., 1927-28; tchr. English and social studies, librarian Lewiston High Sch., Lewiston, N.Y., 1928-32, Buffalo Sch. System, 1932-38; tchr., English and social studies St. Basil Acad., Phila., 1959-70, chmn. social studies dept., 1965-70. Mem. Nat. League Am. Pen Women, Internat. Platform Assn. Republican. Roman Catholic. Contbr. Verses and poems to childrens publications, also original radio plays for amateur childs productions. Home: 7719 Jansen Dr Springfield VA 22152

MILLER, FRANK GEORGE, data systems company executive; b. Harlingen, Tex., Apr. 8, 1930; s. Oscar Rudolph and Lydia Hermenia (Driska) M.; B.B.A., U. Tex., 1958; M.B.A., Pace Coll., 1972; m. Diane Marie Grimm, Feb. 7, 1959 (dec. Sept. 3, 1979); children—Michael Frank, Janet Marie, Susan Anne; m. Minnie B. Hafertepe, Oct. 1983. With Western Union Telegraph Co., Dallas, 1953-85, mgr. applications software, 1981-85; mgr. applications software EDS, Dallas, 1985—. Served with AUS, 1951-53. Mem. Assn. for Systems Mgmt. Republican. Roman Catholic. Clubs: K.C., Order of Alhambra. Home: 9415 Shady Valley Dr Dallas TX 75238 Office: 7171 Forest Ln Dallas TX 75230

MILLER, FREDERICK WARREN, executive; b. Pitts., Nov. 19, 1935; s. Warren Jennings and Grace Elizabeth (Sawhill) M.; B.S. in Chem. Engring. (H.H. Geist scholar, Pa. Senatorial scholar), Pa. State U., 1957; Ph.D. (fellow), Rice U., 1965; m. Ann Louise Sutton, Jan. 30, 1960; children—Karinne Adele, David Sutton, Diane Elizabeth. With E.I. du Pont de Nemours & Co., Inc., 1957-81; research supr., Old Hickory, Tenn., 1970-81; pres., co-owner Wine Celler, Inc., Hendersonville, Tenn., 1973-83, Meml. Bus. Systems, Inc., Nashville; v.p., co-owner Pensacola Meml. Gardens (Fla.), Hillcrest Meml. Gardens, Orange, Tex. Mem. exec. com. Sumner County (Tenn.) Republican Exec. Com., 1969-78, county chmn., 1972-78; regional dir. Henderson Rep. Party, 1970-78; vice chmn. Tenn. 4th Congl. Dist., 1972-76; mem. Capitol Club Tenn., 1973-76. Mem. Clubs: Nashville Aquatic (pres. 1976-78, chmn. 1979-81); Toastmasters (pres. Wilmington, Del. 1967, Disting. Achievement award 1967); Hendersonville Seroma (sec. 1970-71). Author, patentee in field. Home and Office: 313 Appomattox Dr Brentwood TN 37027

MILLER, FREIDA LAJUAN, nurse; b. Sumrall, Miss., Sept. 8, 1947; d. Fred B. and Laura Jane (Deen) Gilbert; m. Carey L. Miller, June 30, 1963; children—Robert Laurns, Paul Brian. A.S., Pearl River Jr. Coll., 1976. R.N., Miss. Med. surg. nurse Meth. Hosp., New Orleans, 1976; Emergency room and ICU relief supr. L.O. Grosby Meml. Hosp., Picayune, Miss., 1976-78; ICU/CCU nurse Slidell (La.) Meml. Hosp., 1978—. Acad. scholar U. Miss., 1976. Mem. Am. Assn. Critical Care Nurses, Planetary Soc., Phi Theta Kappa.

MILLER, GARY SCOTT, endodontist; b. N.Y.C., Dec. 31, 1949; s. Julian Soloman and Roslyn (Fogelman) M.; m. Beth Susanne Klein, Aug. 5, 1972; children—Evan Craig, Dana Lauren, Aron Blake. B.A., Harpur Coll., 1970; D.D.S., NYU, 1974, cert. in endodontics, 1977. Intern Fla. State Hosp., Chattahoochee 1974-75; endodontist Mautner, Miller, and Oppenheimer, D.D.S., P.A., North Miami Beach and Miami Beach, Fla., 1977—; mem. staff Sinai Hosp., Miami Beach, 1978—. Contbr. articles to profl. jours. Mem. Am. Assn. Endodontics, ADA, Fla. Dental Assn., South Fla. Endodontic Study Club, North Dade Dental Soc., Miami Beach Dental Soc., Alpha Omega. Jewish. Avocations: jogging; guitar; video; tennis; reading; gardening. Office: Mautner Miller and Oppenheimer DDS PA 951 NE 167th St North Miami Beach FL 33162

MILLER, GARY WOODROW, wholesale lumber company executive; b. High Point, N.C., Jan. 4, 1951; s. Dempsey Woodrow and Mary Ellen (Silman) M.; m. Susan Kathy Scott, June 9, 1973; children—Meredith Suzonne, Britainy Colleen, Andrea Elizabeth. B.S., U.S. Naval Acad., Annapolis, Md., 1973; M.B.A., Babcock Sch. Mgmt., Wake Forest U., Winston-Salem, N.C., 1983. Commd. ensign U.S. Navy, 1973, advanced through grades to lt., 1976, resigned, 1978; lt. comdr. Res., 1978—; adminstrv. mgr. Blackwelder Furniture Co., Statesville, N.C., 1978-80; dir. fin., adminstrn. and planning Epperson Lumber Sales, Inc., Statesville, N.C., 1980—; cons. system design and software devel. to wholesale lumber industry, personal devel. and motivation. Pres. Statesville Noon Exchange Club; bd. dirs. Jr. Achievement; mem. Iredell County Child Abuse Prevention Council. Baptist. Home: 1139 Lakeside Dr Statesville NC 28677 Office: PO Box 1559 Statesville NC 28677

MILLER, GRACE TAYLOR, pharmacist; b. New Orleans, Mar. 26, 1908; d. Thomas Alexander and Margaret (Burke) Taylor; m. Peter E. Miller Sr., Aug. 14, 1937 (dec. Oct. 1982); children—Peter E. Jr., Eugene P., Thomas T. Pharm.D., Loyola U.-New Orleans, 1927. Registered pharmacist, La. Chief pharmacist K & B Drugs, New Orleans; pharmacist Napoleon Med. Drugs, Krown Pharmacy #11, Krown #2, 1983—. Gold cert. La. State Bd. Pharmacy, 1977. Republican. Roman Catholic. Home: 30 Schill Ave Kenner LA 70065

MILLER, HELEN LOUISE, city commissioner; b. Pottstown, Pa., Apr. 23, 1925; d. James E. and Frances Morse; m. Walker Miller (div. 1973); children—Regina Miller, Cotez Rivers, Gail Miller, Alvin, Alvina, Walker (dec.), Dwight (dec.). Commr., City of Opa-Locka (Fla.), 1980-82, 84—, mayor, 1982-84. Mem. Community Devel. Corp., Opa-Locka, 1982—; bd. dirs. Dade League Cities, 1982. Recipient Citizen of Yr. award Zeta Phi Beta; named Outstanding Citizen, Community Action Agy., Miami; Outstanding Black Woman, Miami-Dade Pub. Library; Recognition award as black female mayor Booker T. Found., 1983. Mem. NAACP, Women in Mcpl. Govt., Nat. Conf. Black Mayors, Nat. Orgn. Black Law Enforcement Execs., North Dade Citizens Council, Black Elected Ofcls. of Dade County, Com. 100 Women of Dade County, Com. 100 Women of Fla. Meml. Coll. Democrat. Methodist. Club: Civic (past pres.) (Opa-Locka). Home: 14235 NW 22d Pl Opa-Locka FL 33054 Office: City of Opa-Locka 777 Sharazad Blvd Opa-Locka FL 33054

MILLER, HERBERT DELL, petroleum engr.; b. Oklahoma City, Sept. 29, 1919; s. Merrill Dell and Susan (Green) M.; B.S. in Petroleum Engring., Okla. U., 1941; m. Rosalind Rebecca Moore, Nov. 23, 1947; children—Rebecca Miller Friedman, Robert Rexford. Field engr. Amerada Petroleum Corp., Houston, 1948-49, Hobbs, N.Mex., 1947-48, dist. engr., Longview, Tex., 1949-57, sr. engr., Tulsa, 1957-62; petroleum engr. Moore & Miller Oil Co., Oklahoma City, 1962-78; owner Herbert D. Miller Co., Oklahoma City, 1978—. Served to maj., F.A., AUS, 1941-47; ETO. Decorated Bronze Star with oak leaf cluster, Purple Heart (U.S.); Croix de Guerre (France). Registered profl. engr., Okla., Tex. Mem. AIME, Petroleum Club. Republican. Episcopalian (pres. Men's Club 1973). Clubs: Oklahoma City Golf, Country. Home: 6708 NW Grand Blvd Oklahoma City OK 73116 Office: 1236 First Nat Ctr West Oklahoma City OK 73102

MILLER, ISABEL MOUNT, architect; b. Denton County, Tex., Mar. 27, 1916; d. Jess Wallace and Ellen Nancy (Donald) Mount; m. Tom Polk Miller, Aug. 10, 1947; children—Crispin Mount, Abigail Mount. B.A. with distinction, Rice Inst., 1936, B.S. in Architecture, 1937. Registered architect, Tex., Calif. Draftsman for various firms, 1937-49; pvt. practice as architect, Calif., 1952-53; architect Mount-Miller, Denton, Tex., 1953—; mem. Tex. Solar Adv. Commn., Austin, 1980. Mem. editorial bd. The Voice, jour., 1971-73; advt. mgr., contbg. author Arkwork Rev., 1979-83; publs. designer LWV of Tex. Hdqrs. designer Denton County Democrats, 1956, 60, 64; pres. Denton Unitarian Fellowship, 1966-67. Recipient Community Arts Recognition award Greater Denton Arts Council, 1982; Mary Alice Elliott travel grantee Rice Archtl. Faculty, 1940. Mem. Tex. Solar Energy Soc. (bd. dirs. 1981-85), Am. Solar Energy Soc., Soc. Archtl. Historians, Nat. Trust for Hist. Preservation, ACLU, Denton LWV (pres. 1975-76), Fellowship of Reconciliation. Democrat. Avocations: crafts; gardening. Home and Office: 711 W Sycamore St Denton TX 76201

MILLER, J. RICHARD, oil producer; b. Kansas City, Mo., July 18, 1931; s. Sanderson Staley and Bertha Amelia (Hoeger) M.; B.S. in Econs., U. Pa., 1952; 1 dau., Jill Elizabeth. Co-founder, pres. Miller Martin & Co., Dallas, 1960—; dir. Realex Corp., Kansas City, 1st Nat. Bank of Euless (Tex.), Waples Platter Corp., Fort Worth. Mem. corp. com. Dallas Mus. Fine Arts; bd. dirs., mem. exec. bd. Circle Ten council Boy Scouts Am. Served as officer Transp. Corps, U.S. Army, 1952-55. Mem. Nat. Comml. Fin. Conf. (dir.), Sigma Chi. Clubs: City, Phoenix (Dallas); Fort Wort, Rivercrest Country (Fort Worth); Steeplechase. Home: The Beverly 3621 Turtle Creek Blvd Dallas TX 75219 Office: Suite 590 Saint Paul Tower 750 N Saint Paul St Dallas TX 75201

MILLER, JACK ORMAND, oil and gas consultant; b. San Antonio, Sept. 18, 1922; s. Theodore Iris and Florence Golden (Ormand) M.; m. Glenna Lea Couch, Dec. 15, 1947; children—Michael Ormand, Mimi Ormand, Merrilynn Ormand, Melanie Ormand. B.A., U. Tex., 1947. Cert. profl. geologist. Proration engr. R.R. Commn. of Tex., Austin, 1947-50, 1952-54, field engr., Pampa, Tex., 1954-57, dist. engr., 1957-60, dist. dir., 1960-70; ind. oil and gas cons., Pampa, 1970—. Chmn., City Traffic Commn., Pampa, 1957-60, Gray County Nat. Found. Bd., Tex., 1960-63; del. county Democratic Conv., Gray County, 1960; bd. dirs. Quivira council Girl Scouts U.S., 1962-66; active Pampa Indsl. Found., 1960—. Served to lt. commdr. USN, 1943-46, PTO, 1950-52, Korea. Mem. Am. Inst. Profl. Geologists (cert.), Am. Assn. Petroleum Geologists (cert.), AAAS, Am. Anthrop. Assn., Current Anthropology, Soc. Applied Anthropology. Democrat. Episcopalian. Club: Engineers (Austin, Tex.). Lodges: Rotary, Masons (32d degree), Shriners. Avocations: restoring classic cars; golf; fishing; hunting; gun and coin collecting. Home and Office: 1615 Grape St Pampa TX 79065

MILLER, JAMES BRUCE, lawyer; b. Louisville, Oct. 7, 1940; s. J.R. and Marceline S. M.; m. Norma Carter, Feb. 14, 1983; children—James Bruce, Alexandra Jayne, Sarah Maxwell; stepchildren—Gavin Osborne, Carter Osborne, Mitchell Osborne. B.A. cum laude in Polit. Sci., Vanderbilt U., 1962, LL.B. cum laude, 1965. Bar: Ky. 1965, U.S. Dist. Ct. (we. dist.) Ky. 1966, U.S. Court Appeals (6th cir.) 1967, U.S. Supreme Court, 1972. Asst. dean of men undergrad. student body Vanderbilt U., Nashville, 1962-63, 1963-64, mem. regional moot court, 1963; owner, prin. Vanderbilt U. Laundry and Linen Agy., 1962-63, 1963-64; law clk. Middleton, Seelbach, Wolford, Willis & Cochran, Louisville, summer 1964; assoc. Carroll & Carroll, Carroll & Miller, Carroll, Miller & Conliffe, 1973-78, Carroll, Chauvin, Miller & Conliffe, 1978-81; Miller, Conliffe, Sandmann, Gorman & Sullivan, 1981—; county atty. Jefferson County, Ky., 1969-85; legal counsel Democratic State Exec. Com., 1976-83. Jefferson County campaign chmn. John Y. Brown Jr. for Gov., 1979. Mem. Louisville Mental Health Assn., 1974-77; bd. dirs. Ky. Leukemia Soc., 1977-83; mem. Gov.'s Task Force of Young Kentuckians, 1966; mem. So. Growth Policies Bd., 1980-83; bd. govs. Continental Basketball Assn., 1983. Ford Found. scholar, 1960; Univ. scholar, 1962-64; recipient Founders medal in oratory Vanderbilt U., 1961. Mem. ABA (com. on sports and entertainment 1983—), Ky. Bar Assn. (jour. com. 1968-71), Louisville Bar Assn., Jefferson County Bar Assn., Nat. Assn. Def. Lawyers in Criminal Cases, Ky. County Attys. Assn. (treas. 1973-75, sec. 1975-77, v.p. 1977-78, pres. 1978-80), Ky. Prosecutors Adv. Council, Nat. Dist. Attys. Assn. Office: 621 W Main St Louisville KY 40202

MILLER, JAMES EDWARD, computer science educator, consultant; b. Hodgenville, Ky., Oct. 22, 1937; s. Charles L. and Alta (Miller) M.; m. Betty Jane Ruble, June 4, 1960; children—Karen, Kim, Kell. B.A., Western Ky. U., 1959; M.A., U. Ky., 1964, Ph.D., 1967. Instr., Murray State U., Ky., 1961-63; asst. prof. computer sci. Transylvania U., Lexington, Ky., 1966-70, assoc. prof., 1970-79, prof., 1979—; cons. Author research articles. Mem. Assn. Computing Machinery, Am. Math. Soc., Soc. Math. and Its Applications, Phi Delta Kappa, Sigma Xi, Pi Xmu Epsilon. Home: 314 Jesselin Dr Lexington KY 40503 Office: Transylvania U Lexington KY 40508

MILLER, JAMES EDWARD, computer science educator; b. Lafayette, La., Mar. 21, 1940; s. Edward Gustave and Orpha Marie (DeVilbis) M.; m. Diane Moon, June 6, 1964; children—Deborah Elaine, Michael Edward. B.S., U. Southwestern La., 1961, Ph.D., 1972; M.S., Auburn U., 1964. Systems engr. IBM, Birmingham, Ala., 1965-68; asst. prof. U. West Fla., Pensacola, 1968-70, chmn. systems sci., 1972—; grad. researcher U. Southwestern La., Lafayette, 1970-72; computer systems analyst EPA, Washington, 1979; gen. cons. on computer related topics; lectr. on computer crime. Contbr. articles to profl. jours. Mem. Assn. for Computing Machinery (editor Spl. Interest Group on Computer Sci. Edn. bull. 1982—, dir. edn. spl. interest group 1986—), Data Processing Mgmt. Assn. Democrat. Methodist.

MILLER, JANE ANDREWS, accountant; b. Nashville, Aug. 14, 1952; d. Joseph Raymond Andrews and Allison (Bartlett) Fang; m. Thomas C. Heselton, June 22, 1970 (div. 1978); 1 child, Elizabeth Lyn; m. Keith Evan Miller, Apr. 14, 1984. Degree in Bus. Typing and Computers, Fairfax Bus. Sch., Va., 1974. Adminstrv. asst. T.J. Fannon & Sons, Alexandria, Va., 1973-79; distbn. clk., adminstrv. asst. U.S. Post Office, Merrifield, Va., 1980-83; acct., sec., treas. Aux. Electric Power Co., Fairfax, Va., 1983—; self-employed acct., investment counselor, Fairfax. Mem. Smithsonian Inst., Wolftrap Found., Am. Horticulture Soc. Republican. Avocations: gardening; music; interior design; drama.

MILLER, JEFFREY HAROLD, designer; b. Wilkes-Barre, Pa., Aug. 27, 1942; s. Milton and Irma (Ganz) M.; B.A., Pa. State U., 1964, postgrad., 1964-65; children—Erin Fitzpatrick, Jacob Milton, Benjamin David Ganz, Jonathan Peter Desmond. Pres., Jeff Miller Assos., 1964-65, MG Assos., Alexandria, Va., 1969-71, Hunter/Miller & Assos., Design Cons., Alexandria, 1971—; mem. fed. portfolio rev. panel U.S. CSC; cons. Nat. Endowment for Arts; mem. Fed. Hwy. Adminstrn. Task Force on Transp. Graphics and Communications; mem. adv. panel Interior Design Mag. Served to lt. USNR, 1965-69. Decorated Navy Achievement medal; recipient Achievement award Va. Travel Council, 1973, Design Rev. award Indsl. Design Mag., 1970. Mem. Fed. Design Council, Constrn. Specifications Inst., Washington Bd. Trade, Am. Craftsmen's Council. Club: Belle Haven Country. Home: 117 Prince St Alexandria VA 22314 Office: 225 N Fairfax St Alexandria VA 22314

MILLER, JIM ALAN, land development company executive; b. Orange, Tex., July 22, 1949; s. Charles Elan and Jo-Ann (Guidry) M.; m. Shirle Jean Pursley, Sept. 23, 1971; children—Erika, Alana. Student Southwest Tex. State U., 1968, 69, Tex. A&M U., 1970, 71. Supt., Milner Constrn. subsidiary Kickerillo Co., Houston, 1967-69, v.p., Kickerillo Co., Houston, 1973-75, sr. v.p., 1975-77, exec. v.p., 1977—; dir. United Bank Houston, United Bank 1-10 West, United Bank-Metro, all Houston. Mem. Greater Houston Home Builders Assn., W. Houston Assn. Republican. Baptist. Club: West Lake. Office: 1300 Texas St Suite 201 Houston TX 77002

MILLER, JO CAROLYN, marriage and family counselor, educator; b. Gorman, Tex., Sept. 16, 1942; d. Leonard Lee and Vera Vertie (Robison) Dendy; m. Douglas Terry Barnes, June 1, 1963 (div. June 1975); children—Douglas Alan, Bradley Jason; m. Walton Sansom Miller, Sept. 19, 1982. B.A., Tarleton State U., 1964; M.Ed., N. Tex. State U., 1977. Tchr. Mineral Wells High Sch., Tex., 1964-65, Weatherford Middle Sch., Tex., 1969-74; counselor, psychology instr. Tarrant County Jr. Coll., Hurst, Tex., 1977-82; marriage and family counselor, Dallas, 1982—. Author: (with others) Becoming: A Human Relations Workbook, 1981. Mem. Tex. State Bd. Examiners Profl. Counselors, Tex. Assn. Counseling and Devel., Am. Mental Health Counselors Assn., Am. Assn. Counseling and Devel., N. Central Tex. Assn. Counseling and Devel. Methodist. Avocations: miniature dolls; tennis. Home: 3556 Binkley Ave Dallas TX 75205 Office: 5956 Sherry Ln Suite 1000 Dallas TX 75225

MILLER, JOHN BROUGH, artist, educator, sculptor; b. Emerson Twp., Mich., Apr. 4, 1933; s. Henry Arthur and Mildred Marie (Walter) M.; m. Janet Marlene Pabst, June 10, 1959; children—Heidi Lynn, Maija Grotell, MacIan Brough. B.S., Central Mich. U., 1960; M.F.A., Cranbrook Acad. Art, 1964; indsl. cert. Indsl. Welding Trade Sch., 1971. Tchr. Brandon Sch., Ortonville, Mich., 1959-63; prof. art Tex. Woman's U., Denton, 1964—, chmn. dept. art, 1975-76, 79-82; instr. Mus. Sch., Dallas Mus. Fine Art, 1968-69. One man shows include Selwyn Sch., Denton, Tex., 1973, Central State U., Edmond, Okla., 1973, North Tex. State U., Denton, 1976, Richland Coll., Tex., 1977, U. Dallas, 1977, Tyler Mus. Art, Tex., 1984; exhibited in group shows at Julius Schmidt Invitational, Cameron U., Okla., 1980, Great Plains Outdoor Sculpture Exhbn., Lincoln, Nebr., 1981-82, U. Dallas, Irving, 1976; represented in permanent collections Fla. State U. Law Library, U. Mo.-Columbia, Tyler Mus. Art, Amarillo Art Ctr., Tex. Woman's U., Selwyn Sch., Richland Coll., Tex. Woman's U. Inwood Campus, Lakewood br. Dallas Pub. Library, others. Recipient Solo Exhbn. award Tyler Mus. Art, 1984, Purchase award North Lake Coll., 1984; Connemara Conservancy Found. grantee, 1984. Mem. AAUP. Lutheran. Home: Box 289 Route 1 Argyle TX 76226 Office: Dept Art Box 3656 Tex Woman's U Denton TX 76204

MILLER, JOHN DAVID, agronomist; b. Todd, N.C., Aug. 9, 1923; s. Reuben Patterson and Chessie (Graham) M.; B.S., N.C. State U., 1948, M.S., 1950; Ph.D., U. Minn., 1953; m. Frances McCollum, June 9, 1946 (dec.); children—John David, Glenn, Mary; m. 2d Jimmie Heard, Mar. 24, 1984. Research fellow U. Minn., 1953; asst. prof. Kans. State Coll., 1953-57; research agronomist Agrl. Research Service, U.S. Dept. Agr., Blacksburg, Va. and Tifton, Ga., 1957-75, research leader, 1972-79, sr. agronomist, 1975—. Dist. commr. Boy Scouts Am., 1971-74. Served with AUS, 1943-46. Decorated Bronze Star medal. Mem. Am. Soc. Agronomy, Phi Kappa Phi, Gamma Sigma Delta, Sigma Xi. Clubs: Toastmasters, Lions. Home: 801 E 12th St Tifton GA 31794 Office: Agrl Research Service USDA Coastal Plain Sta Tifton GA 31793

MILLER, JOHN HENRY, clergyman; b. Ridgeway, S.C., Dec. 3, 1917; s. Fletcher and Frances Helo (Turner) M.; B.A., Livingstone Coll., 1941; M. Div., Hood Theol. Sem., 1945; postgrad. Hartford Theol. Sem. Found., 1954; m. Bernice Frances Dillard, June 27, 1945; children—George Frederick, John Henry. Ordained to ministry, AME Zion Ch., 1940, ordained bishop, 1972; bishop, 10th Dist., 1972-80, 8th Dist., Dallas, 1980—; chmn. bd. home and ch. sect. Christian Edn. Dept., AME Zion Ch. Trustee Livingstone Coll.; chmn. bd. Lomax-Hannon Jr. Coll. Mem. NAACP, World Meth. Council, Alpha Phi Alpha. Republican. Clubs: Masons, Elks. Address: 8605 Caswell Ct Springdale Estates Raleigh NC 27612

MILLER, JOHN MICHAEL, market research company executive, consultant; b. Washington, Nov. 27, 1941; s. Ray and Katherine SinClair (Matthews) M.; m. Mary Linda Nord, Aug. 1, 1964 (div. 1981); children—Jennifer Lynn, Kristen; m. Sandra Jean Johnson, Mar. 13, 1981; children—Joell, Grant, Jennifer Lee. B.A., U. Chgo., 1963, M.S., 1965. Chief statistician Marplan Research Co., N.Y.C., 1965-69, research dir., Houston, 1969-79; ptnr. CDS Research, Houston, 1979-83; pres., owner BenchMark Research Co., The Woodlands, Tex., 1983—; adj. staff CUNY, 1966-67, No. Harris County Coll., Houston, 1984. Bd. dirs. Performing Arts Ctr., Houston, 1981-85; mem. Census Statis. Areas Com., Houston, 1984—; chmn. 1990 Census Planning Conf., Houston, 1985. Mem. Tex. Econ. Demographic Assn. (founding mem., pres. 1984—), Am. Mktg. Assn. (pres. 1980-81, pres.-elect 1979-80, treas. 1978-79), Am. Statis. Assn., Am. Assn. for Public Opinion Research, Houston C. of C., Research Roundtable (founding). Democrat. Home: 11925 S Red Cedar Circle The Woodlands TX 77380 Office: BenchMark Research PO Box 9006 The Woodlands TX 77387

MILLER, JOHN PHILLIP, real estate developer; b. Logan, Ohio, Jan. 30, 1946; s. Charles E. and Marcia J. (McKiddie) M.; B.S. in Mgmt., U. Nebr., 1968; M.B.A. in Fin., U. Nev., 1970; m. Diana Lynn Fuchs, Apr. 18, 1974; children—Mike, Vicki, Randy, Douglas. Sales mgr. Ryland Homes, Houston; v.p. U.S. Home Corp., Houston; v.p. Homecraft Corp., Houston; pres. Showcase Builders, Inc., Houston; now pres. Miller Internat., Inc., Houston; dir. Union Savs. Assn., Stylecraft Homes, Inc., Cambridge Homes Inc. Served to 1st lt. U.S. Army, 1970-72. Mem. Houston Builders Assn. (sales and mktg. council), Am. Mktg. Assn., Am. Mgmt. Assn., Nev. Acctg. Assn. Republican. Methodist. Clubs: Rotary, Elks. Home: 17422 Cedar Pl Houston TX 77068 Office: 4715 Strack Rd Suite 125 Houston TX 77069

MILLER, JOHN STEWART, III, sociology educator, college administrator; b. Eugene, Oreg., June 21, 1946; s. John Stewart Jr. and F. Sue (Cardwell) M.; m. Linda Mary Bussell, June 19, 1971; children—Michael J., Kevin P. B.A., U. Oreg., 1968, M.A., 1972, Ph.D., 1977. Asst. prof. sociology U. Ark., Little Rock, 1977-81, assoc. prof., 1981—, chmn. dept., 1981-83, assoc. dean Coll. Liberal Arts, 1983—. Author: Sociological Concepts Issues, 1983. Served with U.S. Army, 1968-70, Vietnam. Recipient Urban Mission award U. Ark., 1981; NSF grantee, 1980-82; Winthrop Rockefeller Found. grantee, 1984-85. Mem. Am. Sociol. Assn., Soc. for Study Social Problems, S.W. Sociol. Assn., Pacific Sociol. Assn., Ark. Sociol. Assn. (pres. 1984-85). Democrat. Methodist. Lodge: Rotary. Avocations: golf; tennis. Home: 10007 Lemoncrest Little Rock AR 72209 Office: Coll Liberal Arts U Ark 33rd University Little Rock AR 72204

MILLER, JOSEPH ALFRED, corporation executive; b. Richmond, Va., Feb. 23, 1907; s. Ernest Hutchinson and Caroline (Lipscombe) M.; m. Berenice K. Moss, Sept. 5, 1929; 1 child, James Alfred. Student, U. N.C.-Chapel Hill, 1953-54. Pres., Miller Printing Co., Asheville, N.C., 1930-71, Millco, Inc., Asheville, 1972—; dir. First Union Nat. Bank, Asheville. Trustee, U. N.C., Asheville, 1958-63, Montreat-Anderson Coll., Montreat, N.C., 1961-65; chmn. Asheville Redevel. Commn., 1961-70; chmn. bd. deacons Presbyterian Ch., 1954. Recipient Spl. award City of Asheville, 1970. Mem. Printing Industry of the Carolinas (pres. 1955, hon.), Blue Ridge Pkwy. Assn. (pres. 1963-64), Asheville C. of C. (dir. 1957-62, spl. award 1959). Democrat. Clubs: Am. Bus. (pres. Asheville 1938), Rotary, Country Club of Asheville (pres. 1949-50). Home: 55 Windsor Rd Asheville NC 28804 Office: Millco Inc PO Box 18507 Asheville NC 28814

MILLER, JUDY E., author, bookseller; b. Denver, July 20, 1950; d. Benjamin K. Miller and Marianne (Winter) Miller Cohn. B.A., Loretto Heights Coll., U. Without Walls, Denver, 1974; M.A., U. Denver, 1977; M.S.W., La. State U., 1985. Owner, operator Books (& Other Things)-In-A-Bag, Baton Rouge, 1979—, First Light Profl. Services, Alexandria, La., 1985—. Author: Dove Over the Edge, 1972. Bd. dirs. Found. for Health Edn. New Orleans, 1984—; research writer Sun King catalog La. State Mus., New Orleans, 1984. Librarian, vol. New Orleans Mus. Art, 1981-83. Mem. Nat. Assn. for Social Workers. Office: PO Box 12657 Alexandria LA 71315

MILLER, LOUIS O., JR., association executive. Pres. Peninsula C. of C., Hampton, Va. Office: Peninsula C of C 1800 W Mercury Blvd PO Box 7269 Hampton VA 23666*

MILLER, LYNN HARVEY, banker; b. Mpls., Mar. 4, 1927; s. Lynn Harvey and Mary (Johnson) M.; student Yale, 1944-48; m. Anne Carter Jeffris, Sept. 4, 1948; children—Marion, Roys, Lynn Harvey, Rufus, Jacqueline. Sr. v.p., head banking dept. No. Trust Co., Chgo., 1948—; exec. v.p. Merc. Trust Co., N.A., St. Louis, 1974-76, pres., 1977-78; vice chmn., adv. dir. MBank Houston, 1978—. Bd. dirs. Boy Scouts Am., Met. YMCA. Served with USMCR, 1945. Mem. Assn. Res. City Bankers. Clubs: Chicago, Houston, Houston Racquet, Houston Yacht. Office: MBank 910 Travis PO Box 2629 Houston TX 77252

MILLER, MARY RUTH, educator; b. Bartow, Fla., Dec. 22, 1926; d. Willie Boyd and Ruth (Anderson) Miller; A.B. in Edn., Fla. State U., 1948; M.A., George Peabody Coll., 1951; Ph.D., Duke, 1966; postgrad. Columbia, summer 1953, U. So. Calif., summer 1954, Shakespeare Inst., Stratford-on-Avon, Eng., summer 1955, U. Edinburgh (Scotland), summer 1969, Oxford U., summer 1984. Tchr. elementary sch., Palatka, Fla., 1948-49; tchr. high schs., Bell, Fla., 1949-50, Brandon, Fla., 1950-51, Webster, Fla., 1951-53; tchr. English, dir.

pub. relations Reinhardt Coll., 1953-59; asst. prof. English, Fla. So. Coll., 1962-67; prof. English and chmn. dept. Tenn. Wesleyan Coll., Athens, 1967-76; prof. English, head dept. N. Ga. Coll., Dahlonega, 1976—, dir. Ga. Mountains Writing Project, 1979—. Recipient Lewis State Tchr.'s Scholarship, Fla. State U., 1945-48; Danforth Tchrs. Summer Scholarship, U. So. Calif., 1954; Cokesbury award in Coll. Teaching, Duke U., 59-60, 61-62, grad. research assistantship, 1960-61. Mem. South Atlantic Modern Lang. Assn., Coll. English Assn., Modern Lang. Assn., Nat. Council Tchrs. English, Research Soc. Victorian Periodicals, S.E. Renaissance Conf., Ga.-S.C. Coll. English Assn. Democrat. Methodist. Author: Thomas Campbell. Home: 605 N Hall Rd Dahlonega GA 30533

MILLER, MARY TOMPKINS, trust company investment officer; b. Richmond, Va., June 17, 1950; d. Christopher Robinson and Mary (Jerman) Tompkins; m. James Gregory Miller, July 5, 1980. B.A., Mary Baldwin Coll., 1972. Chartered fin. analyst. Trust investment officer Bank Va. Trust Co., Richmond, 1980-84, sr. trust investment officer, 1984—. Mem. Richmond Jr. League, 1975—. Mem. Fin. Analysts Fedn., Richmond Soc. Fin. Analysts. Episcopalian. Clubs: Country of Va., Brandermill Country, Richmond Ski. Avocations: tennis; skiing. Office: Bank of Va Trust Co 7 N 8th St Richmond VA 23219

MILLER, MAURICE HUGH, JR., petroleum geophysicist; b. Birmingham, Ala., Jan. 27, 1950; s. Maurice Hugh and Bernice Inez (Cooper) M.; m. Catherine Jane Pope, June 12, 1976. B.S. in Math., U. Ala., 1971, M.A. in Math., 1972, Ph.D. in Math., 1974. asst. prof. math., U. Miss., Oxford, 1974-75; researcher, advanced interpreter Texaco, Houston and Tulsa, 1975-80; sr. geophysicist Natomas Oil Co., Tulsa, 1980-81; staff geophysicist Tenneco Oil Co., Houston, 1981-82, project mgr. Integrated Exploration and Prodn. System, 1982-84, div. geophysicist, 1984—. Contbr. articles to profl. jours. Sunday sch. tchr. Tallowood Baptist Ch., Houston, 1977-79, So. Hills Bapt. Ch., Tulsa, 1980-81, Champion Forest Bapt. Ch., Houston, 1982—. Mem. Soc. Exploration Geophysicists, Am. Assn. Petroleum Geologists, Nat. Honor Soc., Am. Math. Soc. (hon.). Democrat. Avocations: swimming; spectator sports; camping; hiking; snow skiing. Home: 17910 Canyon Creek Houston TX 77090 Office: Tenneco Oil Co PO Box 2888 Houston TX 77001

MILLER, MELBA JEAN, guidance counselor; b. Grantsville, W.V.; d. Sullie A. and Carrie (Parsons) M. A.B., Glenville State Coll., 1964; M.A., Marshall U., 1966, postgrad., 1979. Cert. counselor (nat.); cert. counselor, W.Va. Tchr. Edison Jr. High Sch., Parkersburg, W.Va., 1964-65; counselor Calhoun County High Sch., Grantsville, 1966—; mem. task force for devel. of supervised entry level counseling program W.Va. State Dept. Edn., Charleston, 1978-79, task force for selection of career info. software for computer network, 1984, task force for devel. of content area exam in counseling, 1984. Editor newspaper: UPDATE, 1979, 84—; The Challenger, 1983-84 (1st place award). Mem. Am. Assn. Counseling and Devel., Nat. Career Devel. Assn., Am. Sch. Counselors Assn. (research com. 1984—), W.Va. Assn. for Counseling and Devel. (membership chairperson 1982—, pres.-elect 1985, Outstanding Service award 1985), W.Va. Edn. Assn. Lodge: Order of Eastern Star. Avocations: short stories and related writing; sketching. Home: PO Box 18 Grantsville WV 26147 Office: Calhoun County High Sch PO Box 898 Grantsville WV 26147

MILLER, MICHAEL CONRAD, nurse anesthetist; b. Taylorsville, N.C., Oct. 12, 1951; s. Conrad Massey and Elinor Elizabeth (Stine) M. Diploma in Respiratory Therapy, N.C. Baptist Hosp., 1971; A.Applied Sci., Forsyth Tech. Inst., 1974; diploma in Nurse Anesthesia, Charlotte Meml. Hosp., 1978; B.S. in Health Arts, Coll. St. Francis, Joliet, Ill., 1985. Mem. staff respiratory therapy, Med. Park Hosp., Winston-Salem, N.C., 1971-73; nurse recovery room Ga. Bapt. Hosp., Atlanta, 1974-76; nurse anesthetist Broward Gen. Hosp., Fort Lauderdale, Fla., 1978-80, W. Paces Ferry Hosp., Atlanta, 1980—. Mem. Am. Assn. Nurse Anesthetists, Fla. Assn. Nurse Anesthetists, Ga. Assn. Nurse Anesthetists. Republican. Lutheran. Home: 1748 Helen Dr NE Atlanta GA 30306

MILLER, NATHAN ANDERSON, educator; b. Dandridge, Tenn., May 24, 1914; s. Thomas Norman and Leutitia (Davis) M.; A.B. magna cum laude, Carson-Newman Coll., 1936; M.S., U. Tenn., 1944; m. Alfreda Rowena Reed, July 5, 1949; children—Gwenna, Thomas. Tchr. grammar sch., Jefferson City, Tenn., 1936-38, prin. high sch., 1943-44; tchr. O'Keefe High Sch., Atlanta, 1938-43; dir. tchr. internes Carson-Newman Coll., 1944; dean Little River Sch., Miami, Fla., 1945-55; dean of boys Madison Jr. High Sch., 1955-56; cons. Reader's Digest, Pleasantville, N.Y., 1956-58; tchr. North Miami (Fla.) High Sch., 1958-65; asst. prin. North Dade High Sch., 1965-67, Miami Springs (Fla.) Jr. High Sch., 1967-81; owner, dir. Camp Sky-Top, Rosman, N.C., 1950—; cons. Ednl. Testing Service, Princeton, N.J., 1955—; chmn. interviewing com. for Exchange Tchrs., U.S. Office Edn., 1952—. Chmn., Jefferson County A.R.C. Fund, 1943-44; v.p. Little River Youth Center Found.; bd. dirs. Fla. Youth Found. Mem. Nat. Council Tchrs. English (dir., chmn. audio visual aids com. 1942-50, co-editor Speak-Look-Listen 1943), Dade County Classroom Tchrs. Assn. (hon. life; pres. 1948-49), Nat. Soc. for Study Communication (charter mem.), Jefferson County Bapt. Assn. (Sunday sch. supt.), Phi Kappa Phi, Phi Delta Kappa. Rotarian. Editor: Atlanta Teacher, 1941-43; co-founder, editor: Dade County, Fla. Teacher, 1946-48; editorial collaborator Reading Skill Builders, 1957-58. Home: 570 Hunting Lodge Dr Miami Springs FL 33166

MILLER, NEWTON EDD, communications educator; b. Houston, Mar. 13, 1920; s. Newton Edd and Anastasia (Johnston) M.; m. Edwina Whitaker, Aug. 30, 1942; children—Cathy, Kenneth. B.S., U. Tex., 1939, M.A., 1940; Ph.D., U. Mich., 1952; LL.D. (hon.), U. Nev., 1974. Asst. prof. U. Tex.-Austin, 1940-47; from asst. prof. to prof. U. Mich., Ann Arbor, 1947-65; chancellor U. Nev.-Reno, 1965-68; pres., 1968-73; pres. U. Maine Portland Gorham, Portland, 1973-78; chmn. communications dept. No. Ky. U., Highland Heights, 1978—. Author: (with others) Discussion and Conference, 1952, 1968; The First Course in Speech, 1947; Discussion and Debate, 1956-66; Public Speaking: A Pratical Handbook, 1985; also articles. Pres. Ann Arbor Bd. Edn., 1959-65. Mem. Speech Communication Assn. (fin. bd. 1983-85), Central States Speech Assn. (pres. 1957), So. Speech Assn., Internat. Communication Assn. Home: 1058 Emerson Rd Park Hills KY 41011 Office: No Ky U Highland Heights KY 41076

MILLER, NORMAN C., JR., food science educator; b. Fort Pierce, Fla., July 2, 1925; s. Norman C. and Nelle Mae (Morely) M.; m. Luella Mae Sweger, June 28, 1946; children—Tamea Ann, Norman C. III, Charles A. B.Sc., Pa. State U., 1950, M.Sc., 1959 Asst. mgr. Knouse Foods, Peach Glen, Pa., 1953-57; canneries mgr. N.C. Prison Enterprises, Raleigh, 1959-62; asst. prof. food sci. N.C. State U., Raleigh, 1962-67, assoc. prof., 1967-74, prof., 1974—, specialist-in-charge food sci. extension, 1980—; mem. better process com. Nat. Canners Assn.-FDA, 1969-79; mem. processing sch. com. Pickle Packers Internat., 1979—; mem. community cannery adv. com. N.C. Dept. Agr., 1975—. Served with U.S. Army, 1943-46; ETO. Decorated Purple Heart; recipient Disting. Service award N.C. Yam Commn., 1978; award of merit Yadkin Valley Econ. Devel. Dist., 1972; Cert. of Appreciation, N.C. Apple Growers, 1978, Engring. Found., 1978. Mem. Inst. Food Technologists (profl.; councilor, past sect. chmn. award 1972), Soc. Thermal Processing Specialists (charter), Inst. Nutrition, Nat. Geog. Soc., Sweet Potato Collaborators Conf., S.E. Peach Workers Conf. (past chmn., processing chmn.), N.C. Assn. Coop. Extension Specialists, N.C. Council Nutrition, DAV (life), Sixth Armored Div. Assn., Sigma Xi, Gamma Sigma Delta, Phi Tau Sigma (charter mem. N.C. chpt.), Epsilon Sigma Phi (20 yr. service award 1980). Democrat. Methodist. Club: MacGregor Downs Country (Cary, N.C.). Lodges: Masons, Shriners. Contbr. articles to profl. jours. Home: 439 Kevin Way Cary NC 27511 Office: 129 Schaub Hall Food Sci Dept Box 7624 NC State U Raleigh NC 27650

MILLER, PATRICK DANA, investment banker; b. El Dorado, Ark., Feb. 3, 1948; s. Roy Dale and Margaret H. Miller; m. Cynthia Coates, Jan. 24, 1977; children—Mathews Mitchell, Marian Margaret. B.S.B.A., U. Ark., 1970. Registered options prin., security prin. Account exec. Merrill Lynch Pierce Fenner & Smith, Little Rock, 1974-80; exec. v.p., dir. T.J. Raney & Sons, Inc., Little Rock, 1980—. Chmn. bd. dirs. Pulaski County chpt. Am. Heart Assn., 1981-83. Served to capt., USAF, 1970-74. Mem. Nat. Assn. Security Dealers, Security Industry Assn., U.S. Golf Assn., Ark. Golf Assn., U. Ark. Alumni Assn., Ducks Unltd., Sigma Chi. Democrat. Episcopalian. Clubs: Country (Little Rock); Flat Acres Hunting Lodge. Lodge: Rotary. Home: 5200 Country Club Blvd Little Rock AR 72207 Office: T J Raney & Sons Inc 3600 Cantrell Rd Little Rock AR 72202

MILLER, PAUL DANIEL, management educator, consultant, clergyman; b. Oakton, Va., Aug. 25, 1919; s. Ray Daniel and Marjorie Madeline (Saunders) M.; m. Marjorie Jane Caskey, 1955 (div. 1965); children—Eugenia, Robert, Karen, Faith; m. 2d, Mary Dolores Lehner, Nov. 3, 1968; stepchildren—Robert, Kenneth. B.S. in Bus. Adminstrn., U. Fla., 1943, B.A., 1946; B.D., Columbia Sem., Decatur, Ga., 1949; M.B.A., U. Miami, 1966. Ordained to ministry Presbyn. Ch., 1948. Asst. prof. bus. adminstrn. Iowa Wesleyan Coll., Mt. Pleasant, 1960-66; asst. dean U. Miami, 1966-68, assoc. prof. mgmt., Coral Gables, 1968—, dir. Small Bus. Inst. 1981—; pres. Creative Mgmt. Cons., Inc., Miami, 1972—; Ford Found. fellow, 1964. Mem. Acad. Mgmt., Small Bus. Inst. Dirs. Assn., Purchasing Mgr. Assn., USCG Aux. Republican. Lodges: Rotary, Masons. Contbr. in field. Home: 14801 SW 89th Ave Miami FL 33176 Office: 414 Jenkins Bldg Univ of Miami Coral Gables FL 33124

MILLER, RHOETA BETH, nurse; b. Plainfield, N.J., Aug. 14, 1927; d. Reginald Bazil and Ruth Naugle; B.R.E., Arlington Bapt. Coll., 1971; A.D. in Nursing, El Centro Coll., 1974; postgrad. Northwestern State U., 1981, La. Inst. Tech.; m. Harold Stanley Miller, Oct. 31, 1980; children—Dawn H. Butler, W. David Butler, Paul D. Butler, Clay D. Butler, Dwight A Broach, Gregg M. Miller. Staff nurse Brookhaven Hosp., Dallas, 1974-75; charge nurse Bossier Med. Center, Bossier City, La., 1975-77; public health nurse Shreveport, La., 1977-79; dir. nursing Midway Manor Nursing Home, Shreveport, 1979-80; sch. nurse Caddo Parish Sch. Bd., Shreveport, 1980—. Vol., ARC, 1974—; mem. Substance Abuse Team for Prevention by Edn., 1981-82; active PTA, 1953-82. Sue Armstrong Nursing scholar, 1972, 73, 74; recipient Service award B.T. Washington High Sch., Shreveport, 1981. Mem. Am. Nurses Assn., La. Sch. Nurses Assn., Nat. Sch. Nurses Assn., Am. Sch. Health Assn., Internat. Platform Assn. (sec. 1983-84) Democrat. Baptist. Contbr. articles to profl. jours. Home: 1810 Pollyanna St Bossier City LA 71112 Office: 4150 Linwood Shreveport LA 71109

MILLER, RICHARD ANDERSON, librarian; b. Bowling Green, Va., Oct. 31, 1941; s. Richard Allen and Lillian Annette (Wenrich) M.; m. Carmen Marian O'Rork, May 1, 1965 (div.); 1 dau., Heather Katherine; m. 2d, Joanne Victoria Skarbek, Sept. 18, 1976. A.A., Orlando Jr. Coll., 1962; B.A., Fla. State U., 1963, M.L.S., 1965. Cert. librarian, med. librarian, Emory U., 1968. Asst. librarian Med. Coll. Va., Richmond, 1965-70, librarian, 1970-73; library dir. Handley Library, Winchester, Va., 1973—. Merit badge counselor Shenandoah Area council Boy Scouts Am., Winchester, 1973—; fireman Reynolds Store Vol. Fire Dept., Cross Junction, Va., 1982—; med. technician Winchester Vol. Rescue Squad, 1983—; dir. Vol. Action Ctr., Winchester, 1983—. Mem. ALA, Va. Library Assn. (intellectual freedom com. 1977-79, legis. com. 1979-82, joint projects com. 1984—), Spl. Library Assn. (pres. Va. chpt. 1971-72). Mormon. Home: HC I Box 360 Cross Junction VA 22625 Office: Handley Library 100 W Piccadilly St PO Box 58 Winchester VA 22601

MILLER, RICHARD BRUCE, purchasing executive; b. N.Y.C., Aug. 8, 1938; s. Milton and Naomi E. Miller; m. Sandra E. Rosenblum, Dec. 19, 1965; children—David Craig, Michael Alan, Daniel Bryan. B.S., Lehigh U., 1962. C.P.A., N.Y. Staff acct. Price Waterhouse & Co., C.P.A.s, N.Y.C., 1962-64; internal auditor United Parcel Service, N.Y.C., 1964-65; sr. acct. Kohlerlter & Spandoff, C.P.A.s, Melville, N.Y., 1965-67; controller Herbert Rose, Inc., Long Island City, N.Y., 1967-68; pvt. practice acctg., Bklyn., 1968-73; with Lisa Enterprises, Inc., 1974—, asst. controller S.E. Toyota Distbrs., Inc., Pompano Beach, Fla., 1974-77; v.p., controller Joyserv Co., Ltd., Jacksonville, Fla., 1977-78, v.p. fin. and adminstrn., 1978-83, dir. corporate purchasing, 1983—; treas., mgr. J. M. Assocs. Fed. Credit Union, Jacksonville, 1980-83; dir. Progressive Credit Union, Jacksonville, 1982—. Served with U.S. Army, 1958-60. Mem. Nat. Assn. Accts. (assoc. mem. of yr. N.Y. chpt. 1964), Am. Inst. C.P.A.s, N.Y. State Soc. C.P.A.s, Fla. Inst. C.P.A.s, Beta Alpha Psi. Democrat. Jewish. Club: University (Jacksonville). Lodge: B'nai B'rith (pres.). Home: 3760 Rubin Rd Jacksonville FL 32217 Office: 7849 Bayberry Rd Jacksonville FL 32217

MILLER, ROBERT ELMER, management consultant; b. Kansas City, Mo., Sept. 4, 1920; s. Harold Elmer and Henrietta Mary (Mersch) Miller; student Am. U., 1949-50, Kans. U., 1951-52, U. N.Mex., 1953-54; grad. U.S. Army Command and Gen. Staff Coll.; m. Louise Isabelle Hartman, Nov. 3, 1940; children—Sharron Louise Miller Hughes, Antoinette Lynn, Theresa Beth Miller Maun. Enlisted as pvt. U.S. Army, 1940, commd., 1942, advanced through grades to col., 1964; ret. 1968; with AEC, Las Vegas, Nev., 1952-57, test planner ops., dep. mgr., 1957-69, mgr. nuclear test ops., 1969-72, mem. AEC On-Off Continent Test Planning Bd., 1962-69; v.p. plans Resource Scis. Corp., Tulsa, 1972-73, v.p. ops., 1973-74, exec. v.p., 1974-79; former vice chmn. bd. Alaskan Resource Scis. Corp.; pres. REM Mgmt. Corp., 1977—; exec. v.p. Williams Bros. Engring. Co., 1979; v.p. U.S. Filter Corp., 1980-81; dir. ADVR. Pres., Indian Springs Homeowners Assn., 1974-75. Decorated Bronze Star, Purple Heart. Mem. Am. Nuclear Soc., Assn. Ret. Officers Assn. Republican. Clubs: Tulsa, Indian Springs Country, Cherokee Yacht, Army-Navy. Home: 841 Millwood Rd Broken Arrow OK 74012 Office: PO Box 192 Broken Arrow OK 74013

MILLER, ROBERT JAMES, architect; b. Hamilton, Ohio, Mar. 12, 1954; s. Robert James and Jerri (Burran) M.; m. Patricia MacLeish, May 27, 1977 (div. 1981). B.A., Clemson U., 1976, M. Architecture, Rice U., 1979. Registered architect, Ga. Staff assoc. Rice Ctr., Houston, 1978-79; designer Thompson, Ventulett, Stainback & Assocs., Architects, Atlanta, 1979-81; assoc. RHPMHR Architects, Atlanta, 1981-85; lectr., critic Clemson U., S.C., 1982; propr. Rob Miller, Architect, Atlanta, 1985—. Rice U. scholar, 1976. Mem. AIA, Nat. Council Archtl. Registration Bds., Tiger Brotherhood, Phi Kappa Phi, Tau Sigma Delta, Roman Catholic. Home and Office: 101 Ardmore Place NW Apt 7 Atlanta GA 30309

MILLER, ROBERT JAMES, lawyer; b. Dunn, NC., Jan. 14, 1933; s. Robert James and Edith Irene (Crockett) M.; m. Patricia L. Shaw; children—Patricia, Susan, Nancy. B.S., N.C. State U., 1956; M.F., Yale U., 1962, M.S., 1965, Ph.D., 1967; J.D. N.C. Central U., 1985. Registered land surveyor. Forester, Westvaco Pulp & Paper Co., 1956-59; chief forester Tilghman Lumber Co., 1959-61; prof. biology Radford Coll. (Va.), 1965-73, v.p. acad. affairs, 1970-73; prof. law, dean coll., St. Mary's Coll., Raleigh, N.C., 1973-85; sole practice, Raleigh, N.C., 1985—. Hill Family Found. fellow, 1963-65; Danforth Found. awardee, 1952. Mem. ABA, N.C. Acad. Trial Lawyers, N.C. Bar Assn., Sigma Xi, Xi Sigma Pi, Phi Kappa Phi. Democrat. Episcopalian. Clubs: Yale of Central N.C., Lodges: Masons, Shriners. Author: Assimilat on of Nitrogen by Tree Seedling, 1967; A Guide to the Woody Vegetation of Radford and Vicinity, 1967; Liberal Arts and the Individual, 1973; Liberal Arts: An educational Philosophy, 1973; Educational Malpractice, 1984; Prenuptial Agreements: Romance and Reality, 1986. Office: PO Box 366 Raleigh NC 27602

MILLER, ROBERT LOUIS, university dean, chemistry educator; b. Chgo., Jan. 26, 1926; s. Samuel P. and Ida (Reich) M.; m. Virginia Southard, Oct. 28, 1947 (dec. 1973); children—Ruth, Stephen, Martin, Andrew; m. Bonnie Seay, Nov. 28, 1975; children—Edouard, John Derek. Ph.B., U. Chgo., 1947, B.S., 1949, M.S., 1951; Ph.D., Ill. Inst. Tech., 1963. Mem. prodn. staff NBC-TV, Chgo., 1951-52; from instr. to assoc. prof. chemistry U. Ill.-Chgo., 1952-67, asst. dean, then assoc. dean, 1952-67; dean, prof. chemistry U. N.C.-Greensboro, 1968—; accreditation mem. Middle States Assn., Pa., 1972. Contbr. articles to profl. jours. Bd. dirs. Weatherspoon Art Gallery, Greensboro, 1976—; mem. Bd. Edn., Oak Park, Ill., 1966-67; mem. task force on energy City of Greensboro, 1978-82; pres. Hospice at Greensboro, 1982-84. Fellow NSF, 1961-62, 64, Am. Council on Edn., 1967-68. Mem. AAAS, AAUP, Sigma Xi. Avocations: tennis, chess, music. Office: U NC 1000 Spring Garden Greensboro NC 27412

MILLER, ROBERT REXFORD, oil company executive, geologist; b. Oklahoma City, Feb. 8, 1953; s. Herbert Dell and Rosalind Rebecca M.; m. Sally Ann Sneed, Aug. 8, 1975; children—Robert Dell, John Dustin. Student Oklahoma City U., 1974-75, Univ. Ill., England, Scotland, Wales, 1974. B.S. in Geology, So. Meth. U., 1975. Cert. geologist, Tex. Geologist, DeGolyer & MacNaughton, Dallas, 1974-76, Bright & Schiff, Dallas, 1976-83, H.G. Schiff & Co., Dallas, 1983—; oil finder Haskell County, Tex., 1978, Stonewall County, Tex., 1980, 82. Mem. Geological Info. Library of Dallas, contbr., 1975-85, Petroleum Info. Library, Dallas, Abilene, Tex.; Geomap Library; bd. dirs. 500 Inc. Mem. Am. Assn. Petroleum Geologists, Energy Minerals div. of Am. Assn. Petroleum Geologists (founding), Soc. Petroleum Engrs. Petroleum Engrs. Club, Dallas Geol. Soc., North Tex. Geol. Soc., West Tex. Geol. Soc., Energy Club (charter). Office: HG Schiff & Co 5307 E Mockingbird #1001 Dallas TX 75206

MILLER, ROBERT T., political science educator; b. Ogburn, Tex., Feb. 17, 1920; s. Francis James and Edna Jeannette (Stokes) M.; m. Ann Vardaman, Dec. 22, 1949; children—Robert T., Laurie Anne Smith. B.A., Baylor U., 1941, M.A., 1941; Ph.D., U. Tex., 1954. Adminstrv. asst. Congressman W.R. Poage, Washington, 1961-62; from asst. prof. to prof. polit. sci. Baylor U., Waco, Tex., 1946—, chmn. dept., 1962, vice provost instructional programs, 1984—. Co-author: Church and State in Scripture, History and Constitutional Law, 1958; Toward Benevolent Neutrality: Church, State and the Supreme Court, 1977, rev. edit., 1982. Mem. McLennan County com. Democratic Party, Tex., 1965-85; mem. dist. com. Grievance Com., Tex. State Bar, Waco, 1980-85. Served to lt. comdr. USNR, 1942-46. Mem. Am. Polit. Sci. Assn., AAUP, So. Polit. Sci. Assn., Southwestern Social Sci. Assn., Omicron Delta Kappa. Democrat. Baptist. Home: 4908 Ridgeview Dr Waco TX 76710 Office: Chmn Dept Polit Sci Baylor U Waco TX 76798

MILLER, RONALD IRVIN, JR., oral and maxillofacial surgeon, air force officer; b. Hartford, Conn., Apr. 6, 1946; s. Ronald Irvin and Jennie Beatrice (Smith) M.; m. Joan Marie Kucala, Nov. 25, 1980; children—Christine Louise, Maxwell Stephen. B.A., Earlham Coll., 1968; D.D.S., Ind. U., 1972. Diplomate Am. Bd. Oral and Maxillofacial Surgery. Resident Albert Einstein Coll. of Medicine, Lincoln Hosp., 1972-75; commd. capt. U.S. Air Force, 1975, advanced through grades to lt. col., 1981; chief oral and maxillofacial surgery McGuire AFB, N.J., 1975-77; mem. staff oral and maxillofacial surgery Wilford Hall Med. Ctr., San Antonio, 1977-80; chief oral and maxillofacial surgery U.S. Air Force Hosp., Seymour Johnson AFB, N.C., 1980-82, staff mem. oral and maxillofacial surgery, Yokota Air Base, Japan, 1982-84; chmn. oral and maxillofacial surgery Keesler U.S. Air Force Med. Ctr., Miss., 1984—; cons. in field. Author teaching manuals, 1977-79. Contbr. articles to profl. jours. Fellow Am. Assn. Oral and Maxillofacial Surgery, Internat. Assn. Oral Surgery, Am. Dental Soc. Anesthesiology, ADA, Soc. Air Force Clin. Surgeons. Republican. Home: 102 Timothy Ln Ocean Springs MS 39564 Office: Dept Oral and Maxillofacial Surgery US Air Force Med Ctr Keesler Kessler Air Force Base MS 39534

MILLER, ROSE MARIE, counselor, therapist; b. Leesville, La., Nov. 4, 1929; d. Houston Homer and Nettie (Perkins) Tibbits; m. Clarence Olen Miller, Sept. 17, 1948; children—Judith Lynn Miller Meeks, Steven Gary. B.A., McNeese State U., 1980, M.A., 1982; cert. in family therapy Family Therapy Ctr., Shreveport, La., 1983; postgrad. Walden U., 1985. Lic. profl. counselor, Tex. Tchr. Calcasieu Parish Schs., Lake Charles, La., 1980; counselor, therapist Profl. Counseling Service, Lake Charles, 1983-84, Individual and Family Counseling Service, Lake Charles, 1985—; counselor trainer Human Service Orgn., Lake Charles, 1978-83; conductor edn. program Meml. Hosp., Lake Charles, 1984-85; counselor area coordinator La. Assn. Mental Health, 1985; coordinator baby sitter edn. programs; speaker, lectr. in field. Mem. Am. Assn. Marriage and Family Therapy (mediators cert. 1986), La. Assn. Marriage and Family Therapy, Am. Assn. Counseling and Devel., La. Assn. Counseling and Devel. (counselor area coordinator Lake Charles 1985), Am. Assn. Bus. Women. Lodge: Eastern Star. Avocations: needle work; art; theater; jogging. Home: 700 Mathilda Dr Sulphur LA 70663 Office: Individual and Family Counseling Service Suite L 751 Bayou Pines St E Lake Charles LA 70663

MILLER, ROWLAND SPENCE, social psychologist, psychology educator; b. San Diego, Dec. 31, 1951; s. Donald Wesley and Charlotte Warden (Williams) M.; m. Gale Annette Lewis, Dec. 18, 1982; 1 child, Christopher Rowland. B.A., Cornell U., 1973; M.A., U. Fla., 1976. Ph.D., 1978. Asst. prof. Sam Houston State U., Huntsville, Tex., 1978-84, assoc. prof. psychology, 1984—, coordinator grad. studies, 1984—; vis. assoc. prof. Cornell U., Ithaca, N.Y., 1985. Co-author: Social Psychology and Dysfunctional Behavior, 1986. Assoc. editor Jour. Ednl. Studies, 1982—. Recipient Edwin Newman award Psi Chi/Am. Psychol. Assn., 1980. Mem. Am. Psychol. Assn., Soc. Personality and Social Psychology, Southwestern Psychol. Assn., Soc. Southwestern Social Psychologists (coordinator 1983-84), Sigma Xi. Office: Psychology Dept Sam Houston State U Huntsville TX 77341

MILLER, TANFIELD CHARLES, accountant; b. Phila., Jan. 25, 1947; s. Richard and Wylma Jane Miller; B.A. in History, N.D. State U., 1967; M.B.A., U. Pa., 1974; m. Helen Adams McClennen, Aug. 14, 1977; children—Sophia Adams, Peter Alexander Adams. Vice pres. fin. Nat. Student Mktg. Corp., N.Y.C., 1967-70; pres. Strider Ocenic Corp., N.Y.C., 1970-73; acct. Price, Waterhouse & Co., C.P.A.s, N.Y.C., 1973-77; sr. ptnr. T.C. Miller & Co., C.P.A.s, Ft. Lauderdale, Fla., 1977—; chmn. Brazil Safari & Tours Ltda., 1980-81, Rio de Janeiro; dir. Pleasant Bay Group, Inc.; treas. Gold Coast Savs. & Loan; vice chmn. Kornhauser & Calene Advt. Inc., N.Y.C. Bd. dirs. Youth for Humphrey, 1968, N.D. State U. Devel. Found., 1969—; trustee Ft. Lauderdale Mental Health Assn., 1979-81, Fla. Oaks Sch., 1981-84. Named Outstanding Young Person, Hearst Press, 1969; C.P.A., N.J., Fla. Mem. Am. Inst. C.P.A.s, N.J. Soc. C.P.A.s, Fla. Inst. C.P.A.s. Clubs: Chatham Yacht, Pleasant Bay Beach and Tennis (Chatham, Mass.). Contbg. editor Practical Acct., 1975-79. Office: 1012 E Broward Blvd Fort Lauderdale FL 33301

MILLER, THOMAS BURK, state justice; b. Buffalo, May 4, 1929; s. Clarence Edwin and Helen Elizabeth (Burk) M.; m. Vaughn-Carol Nolte, Apr. 17, 1954; children—Kenneth L. Goudy, George H. Goudy, Brian D. Miller, Bradley R. Miller. A.B., U. Va., 1950; LL.B., W.Va. U., 1956. Bar: W.Va. bar 1956. Sr. partner firm Schrader, Miller, Stamp & Recht, Wheeling, 1959-76; justice W.Va. Supreme Ct. Appeals, 1977—. Served with USNR, 1950-53. Mem. Am., W.Va. bar assns., Assn. Trial Lawyers Am., W.Va. Trial Lawyers Assn. Democrat. Methodist. Office: Room E301 State Capitol Charleston WV 25305*

MILLER, THOMAS WAINWRIGHT, JR., consulting engineer, state official; b. Clearwater, Fla., Nov. 28, 1927; s. Thomas Wainwright and Grace Ellen (Gilbert) M.; B.C.E., Ga. Inst. Tech., 1952; m. Mavis Stinson, Dec. 25, 1952; 1 son, Thomas Wainwright III. Registered engr. Fla. State Bd. Health, 1952-56; dir. Lee County Mosquito Control Dist., Ft. Myers, Fla., 1956—; engr.-in-charge Lee County Hyacinth Control Dist., 1961—; pres. T.W. Miller & Assos., Inc., 1962—; dir. First Fed. Savs. & Loan Assn. Ft. Myers. Trustee, pres., chief exec. officer Price Found.; trustee Bapt. Found., Palm Beach Atlantic Coll., U. South Fla. Found., Edison Community Coll. Endowment Corp.; bd. dirs. Lee Meml. Hosp.; treas. First Bapt. Ch. of Ft. Myers. Served with AUS, 1946-47. Registered profl. engr., Fla., La., Mass. Fellow Fla. Engring. Soc., Met. Ft. Myers C. of C. (pres. 1983, dir.). Clubs: Fort Myers Rod and Gun (pres. 1969, now dir.); Royal Palm Yacht. Lodges: Masons, Shriners, Rotary (pres. 1975). Contbr. articles to profl. jours. Office: Lee County Mosquito Control Dist PO Box 06005 Fort Myers FL 33906

MILLER, TODD NEIL, industrial hygienist; b. Borger, Tex., Mar. 1, 1955; s. Neil Clement and Velma (King) M.; m. Brenda Lea Browning, Aug. 11, 1979. A.S., No. Okla. Coll., 1975; B.S., Southwestern Okla. State U., 1977; M.S., U. Okla., 1980. Chem. technician II, Phillips Petroleum Co., Bartlesville, Okla., 1978-79; safety and health adminstr. Weber Aircraft div. Kidde, Inc., Gainesville, Tex., 1981—. Asst. scoutmaster, safety merit badge counselor Longhorn council Boy Scouts Am., 1984—, Cooke County Roundtable commr. Frontier Trails dist., 1985—. Recipient Eagle Scout and God and Country award Kaw council and Presbyterian Ch., 1970. Mem. Am. Indsl. Hygiene Assn., Weber Aircraft Mgmt. and Profl. Assn., U. Okla. Alumni Assn. (life), Nat. Eagle Scout Assn. Republican. Presbyterian. Avocations: camping; scouting; hunting; canoeing; football. Home: 313 Circle Dr PO Box 227 Lindsay TX 76250 Office: Weber Aircraft Div Kidde Inc 2000 Weber Dr Gainesville TX 76240

MILLER, TOM WILLIAM, engineering consultant; b. Revloc, Penn., May 23, 1933; s. Luther Carl and Margaret M. (Grime) M.; m. Marilyn Beth Presley; children by previous marriage—Michele Marie, Timothy Ivan. B.S. in Indsl. Engring., U. Balt., 1959. Registered profl. engr. Calif., 1977. Supr. quality control, mfg. Bendix Corp., Md., then Pa., 1954-64; quality and reliability engring. mgr. AMP, Inc., Harrisburg, Pa., 1964-70, Darling Anchor Valve Co., Williamsport, Pa.; quality assurance-quality control mgr. Unitec Industries, York, Pa., 1970-72; mgr. nuclear div. Value Engring. Co., Alexandria, Va., 1972-77; owner mgr. TWM Inc., cons., 1977—; owner, pres. Profl. Cons. Services, 1977—; cons. UN, IAEA, bus., govt. agys. and industry throughout U.S. Served with USN, 1950-54. Recipient Regional award, GAO. 1978, GAO Dirs. award for excellence; Nat. award Philippine Atomic Energy Commn.

Mem. Nat. Soc. Profl. Engrs., Ky. Soc. Profl. Engrs., Va. Soc. Profl. Engrs., Calif. Soc. Profl. Engrs., Pa. Soc. Profl. Engrs., ASME, Profl. Engrs. in Pvt. Practice, Am. Nuclear Soc., Am. Soc. Quality Control, Hon. Order Ky. Cols. Contbr. numerous articles to profl. jours. Home and Office: 1126 Franelm Rd Louisville KY 40214

MILLER, TONY LEE, college dean, minister; b. Amarillo, Tex., Aug. 23, 1948; s. Henry Ezekiel and Edna Ruth (Garrison) M.; m. Jeanette Linda Wick, June 8, 1974; children—Marjean Ruth, Michael Anthony. B.A., M.A., Bob Jones U. Hall supr. Bob Jones U., Greenville, S.C., 1969-72, dorm. supr., 1972-74, student counsellor, 1974-80, dean of men, 1980—, bd. dirs., 1980—, advising bd. vintage staff, 1981—, dir. mission team west, 1980-85, adviser mission prayer band. Pastor Welcome Bapt. Ch., Centrall, S.C., 1977-80. Contbr. articles to profl. jours. Bd. dirs. Voice of Hope Radio, Pickens, S.C., 1981—. Recipient Bob Jones Sr. Meml. award Bob Jones U. 1972. Republican. Baptist. Avocations: gardening; racquetball; basketball; fishing. Home: 6 Seminar Dr Greenville SC 29609 Office: Bob Jones U 1906 Wade Hampton Greenville SC 29614

MILLER, WILLIAM JACK, dairy science and animal nutrition educator, reseacher; b. Nathan's Creek, Feb. 7, 1927; s. William Thomas and Virginia Juanita (Bledsoe) M.; m. Marianna Morris, Dec. 21, 1950; children—Virginia, Nancy, Barbara, William. B.S., N.C. State U., 1948, M.S., 1950; Ph.D., U. Wis., 1952. Research assoc. U. Ill., Urbana, 1952-53; asst. prof. U. Ga., Athens, 1953-58, assoc. prof., 1958-64, prof., 1964-73, disting. prof. dairy sci. and animal nutrition, 1973—. Author: Dairy Cattle Feeding and Nutrition, 1979; co-author of two books, 1970, 79. Contbr. papers, articles to profl. and popular lit., also chpts. to books. Served with USN, 1945-46. Named Ga. Scientist of Yr., Ga. Sci. and Tech. Commn., 1969, Alumni Found. disting. prof. U. Ga., 1973; Trace Mineral travel fellow Nat. Feed Ingredient Assn., 1969. Fellow Am. Soc. Animal Sci. (Morrison award 1980, Gustav Bohstedt award 1971); mem. Am. Council on Sci. and Health, Am. Dairy Sci. Assn. (So. honors award 1984, Bordon award 1971, Am. Feed Mfr. Assn. Research award 1963), Am. Inst. Nutrition, Soc. for Environ. Geochemistry and Health, Sigma Xi, Phi Kappa Phi, Gamma Sigma Delta (Internat. award 1970). Office: Dept Animal and Dairy Sci U Ga 313 L-P Bldg Athens GA 30602

MILLER, ZELL BRYAN, state official; b. Young Harris, Ga., Feb. 24, 1932; s. Stephen Grady and Birdie (Bryan) M.; student Young Harris Jr. Coll., 1951; A.B., U. Ga., 1957, M.A., 1958, also postgrad.; m. Shirley Ann Carver; children—Murphy Carver, Matthew Stephen. Mayor, Young Harris, 1960; mem. Ga. State Senate, 1961-64; mem. State Bd. Children and Youth, 1965; personnel officer Ga. Dept. Corrections, 1968; exec. sec. to Gov. of Ga., 1969, to Lt. Gov. of Ga., 1971; mem. Bd. Pardons and Paroles, 1973; lt. gov. of Ga., 1975—. Del., Democratic Nat. Conv., 1972, 76; exec. dir. Dem. Party Ga., 1971-73. Served with USMC, 1953-56. Methodist. Mason. Author: The Administration of E.D. Rivers as Governor of Georgia; The Mountains Within Me; The Legend of Hiawassee; Great Georgians; They Heard Georgia Singing. Home: Young Harris GA 30582 Office: 240 State Capitol Atlanta GA 30334

MILLER-LUSSIER, BARBARA, architectural services company executive; b. Phila., June 21, 1956; d. Ronald E. and Barbara (Brennan) Miller; m. Grant P. Lussier, Aug. 8, 1981. B.S., Sch. Mgmt., Boston Coll., 1978. Asst. buyer designer sportswear Lord & Taylor, N.Y.C., 1978-81; v.p. mktg., co-owner 3XM Inc., Houston, 1981—. Mem. Urban Land Inst (assoc.), Houston C. of C., Boston Coll. Alumni Club. Home: 5210 Wesleyan Suite 309 Houston TX 77005 Office: 3XM Inc 1210 N Post Oak Houston TX 77005

MILLERO, FRANK JOSEPH, JR., marine and physical chemistry educator; b. Greenville, Pa., Mar. 16, 1939; s. Frank Joseph and Jennie Elizabeth (Marta) M.; m. Judith Ann Busang, Oct. 2, 1965; children—Marta, Frank, Anthony. B.S., Ohio State U., 1961; M.S., Carnegie-Mellon U., 1964, Ph.D., 1965. Chemist, Nat. Bur. Standards, 1961; teaching and research asst. Carnegie-Tech., 1961-65; research chemist ESSO Research and Engring. Co., Linden, N.J., 1965-66; chemist Research Sci. U. Miami, 1966-68, asst. prof., 1968-69, prof. marine and phys. chemistry, 1969—; vis. prof. U. Kiel, W.Ger., 1975, Water Research Inst., Rome, 1979-80; mem. UNESCO Panel for Ocean Standards, 1976—, NSF Panel, 1973-75, 82, Ocean Sci. Bd., 1981-83; chmn. Gordon Conf., 1983; cons. in field. Coach Little League, Miami, Fla. Mem. AAAS, Am. Chem. Soc., N.Y. Acad. Sci., Geochem. Soc., Sigma Xi. Democrat. Roman Catholic. Lodge: K.C. Contbr. numerous articles to profl. jours. Home: 7720 SW 90th Ave Miami FL 33173 Office: RSMAS U Miami Miami FL 33149

MILLIGAN, J(OSEPH) BRYCE, literary critic, free-lance book columnist, poet, novelist, editor, bibliographer; b. Dallas, Jan. 18, 1953; s. Joseph Bryce and Mettie Maxine (Carey) M.; m. Mary Frances Guerrero, May 24, 1975; children—Michael Bryce, Brigid Aileen. B.A., North Tex. State U., 1976; M.A., U. Tex., 1980. Rare books cataloger On Paper Bookstore, San Antonio, 1978-79; asst. mgr. Half Price Books, San Antonio, 1979-80; owner, operator Gutenberg's Folly: Rare & Scholarly Books and Writing Services, San Antonio, 1979—; mgr. Rosengren's Books, San Antonio, 1980-81; free-lance researcher Inst. Texan Cultures, San Antonio, 1982; book columnist San Antonio Express News, 1983—; founder (with Isabeth Hardy), editor Pax: A Journal for Peace through Culture, 1982—; founder, editor Vortex: A Critical Rev. Jour., 1985, writer-in-residence Tex. Commn. on the Arts, 1985; dir. lit. program Guadalupe Cultural Arts Ctr., 1985—. Author: Daysleepers & Other Poems, 1984; (novel) With the Wind, Kevin Dolan, 1986. Editor: The History of the Air Force Military Training Center, Lackland AFB, 1982, 83, 84; contbr. book revs. to Dallas Morning News, San Antonio Express News, Tex. Observer, other newspapers, small mags. Founder, organizer Ann. Tex. Small Press Bookfair, San Antonio, 1984—. Recipient award for scholarly excellence Ancient Order of Hibernians, 1982, 83; named Noted Local Author, Friends of San Antonio Pub. Library, 1984. Mem. Coordinating Com. of Literary Mags., Com. of Small Mag. Editors and Pubs., Tex. Pubs. Assn. Democrat. Roman Catholic. Avocations: folk music; luthier; carpentry. Home and Office: Gutenberg's Folly Writing Editing & Research 627 E Guenther St San Antonio TX 78210

MILLIKAN, LARRY EDWARD, dermatologist; b. Sterling, Ill., May 12, 1936; s. Daniel Franklin and Harriet Adeline (Parmenter) M.; B.A., Monmouth Coll., 1958; M.D., U. Mo., 1962; m. Jeanine Dorothy Johnson, Aug. 27, 1960; children—Marshall, Rebecca. Intern, Great Lakes (Ill.) Naval Hosp., 1962-63; housestaff in tng. U. Mich., Ann Arbor, 1967-69, chief resident, 1969-70; asst. prof. U. Mo., Columbia, 1970-74, asso. prof., 1974-77; prof., chmn. dept. dermatology Tulane U., New Orleans, 1981—; staff Tulane U. Hosp., St. Tammany Hosp., St. Jude Hosp.; cons. physician Charity Hosp., New Orleans, Lallie Kemp Charity Hosp., Huey P. Long Charity Hosp., Alexandria VA Hosp. (La.), New Orleans VA Hosp., Student Health Service, Gunn Clinic. Served with USN, 1960-67. Nat. Cancer Inst. grantee, 1976—. Fellow A.C.P.; mem. Am. Acad. Dermatology, Am. Dermatol. Assn., Am. Dermatol. Soc. for Allergy and Immunology (past pres.), Soc. for Investigative Dermatology, South Central Dermatol. Congress (sec. gen.), Coll. Physicians Phila., AMA, Orleans Parish Med. Soc., La. Med. Soc., AAAS, Mo. Allergy Assn. (past pres.), Mo. Dermatol. Assn. (past pres.), Internat. Soc. for Tropical Dermatology, Nat. Bd. Med. Examiners, Sigma Xi, Alpha Omega Alpha, Alpha Tau Omega. Assoc. editor Internat. Jour. of Dermatology, 1980—; mem. editorial bd. Current Concepts in Skin Disorders, Am. Jour. Med. Scis.; contbr. articles to med. jours. Home: Lacombe LA Office: Dept Dermatology Tulane U New Orleans LA

MILLIKEN, RUTH LONGHENRY, librarian; b. Bklyn., Jan. 19, 1920; d. Ernest Albert and Rose Catherine (Martina) Longhenry; m. Trent Simon Milliken, June 6, 1975. Student SUNY-New Paltz, 1937-40; B.S., State U. N.Y.-Geneses, 1941, Columbia U., 1949; M.S., Shippensbrg, State U., 1972. Librarian U.S. Army 2d Service Command, Governors Island, N.Y., 1941-48, Armed Forces Staff Coll., Norfolk, Va., 1948-51, Army War Coll., Carlisle Barracks, Pa., 1951-74, Cocoa Beach (Fla.) Pub. Library, 1975—1975-85. Citizens' League, Cocoa Beach, 1980. Recipient Meritorious Civilian Service award U.S. Army War Coll., 1974. Mem. ALA, Spl. Libraries Assn. (div. sec., treas. 1967-68), Fla. Library Assn., AAUW, Library Assn. Brevard (chmn. com. 1983). Clubs: Women's (sec., v.p. 1980-83), Power Squadron (Cocoa Beach). Home: 1605 Minutemen Causeway Apt 217 Cocoa Beach FL 32931

MILLIKIN, PATRICIA SUE, psychotherapist, columnist; b. Pine Bluff, Ark., Mar. 14, 1945; d. Thomas Steele and Nell Celeste (Calkins) Ingram; m. Robert H. Millikin, June 30, 1967; children—Patrick David, Crandall Bronwyn. B.A., Ark. Coll., 1966; M.Ed., Memphis State U., 1978, Ed.D. in Counseling, 1982. Tchr. pub. schs., Ariz., 1966-67, Tenn., 1968-69; social worker, Tenn., 1968-70, tchr. Tenn. Pub. Schs., 1971-79; grad. asst. Memphis State U., 1979-81; individual practice marital and family psychotherapy, Memphis, 1981—; columnist Germantown News (Tenn.), 1981—, Collierville Herald (Tenn.), 1981—; co-host Coping, Channel 7, Cable TV, Memphis, 1982. Mem. coll. bd. Mademoiselle, 1966. Mem. Am. Assn. Marriage and Family Therapists (clin. mem. 1982—), Am. Personnel and Guidance Assn., Am. Mental Health Counselors Assn. Unitarian. Office: 5050 Poplar St Suite 2432 Memphis TN 38157

MILLING, FRANCIS WILLIAM, psychologist; b. Laurel, Miss., Nov. 25, 1940; s. William Franklin and Sue Delores (Watts) M.; m. Irmgard Kreszenzia Pfahler, Feb. 10, 1966; children—Justin Garrett, Wendy Francette. B.S., U. So. Miss., 1962, M.A., 1973, Ph.D., 1976. Staff psychologist VA Med. Ctr., Tuskegee, Ala., 1976-77, chief psychologist VA Domiciliary, White City, Oreg., 1977-83; staff psychologist VA Med. Ctr., Murfreesboro, Tenn., 1983—; adj. instr. psychology Meharry Med. Coll., Nashville, 1985—. Served to capt. USMC, 1962-68, Vietnam; col. Res. Decorated various mil. medals. Mem. Am. Soc. Clin. Hypnosis, Am. Psychol. Assn., Marine Corps Res. Officers Assn., Mensa. Avocations: genealogical research; jogging; flying. Home: 2602 Regency Park Dr Murfreesboro TN 37130 Office: Psychology Service VA Med Ctr Murfreesboro TN 37130

MILLING, ROBERT NICHOLSON, psychiatrist; b. Greenwood, S.C., July 5, 1933; s. Robert Lyon and Sarah Elizabeth (Marbert) M.; B.S., U. S.C., 1954; M.D., M.U.S.C. 1958; m. Marjorie Jean Snell, Sept. 30, 1961; children—Julia Pearson, Melanie Torrance, Marjorie Jean Van Brunt, Deborah Marie Milling, Mary Alexander, Elizabeth Gallo, Melissa Brooks Milling. Intern Ga. Baptist Hosp., Atlanta, 1958-59; fellow in cardiology Sch. Medicine, U. Tenn., Memphis City Hosps., 1959-61; resident in psychiatry William S. Hall Psychiat. Inst., Columbia, S.C., 1961-64; dir. Sumter-Clarendon-Kershaw (S.C.) Mental Health Center, 1964-66; practice medicine specializing in psychiatry, Columbia (S.C.) Psychiat. Assos., 1966—; clin. asso. prof. psychiatry, William S. Hall Psychiat. Inst., Sch. Medicine, U. S.C., Columbia, 1977—; cons. in psychiatry, Columbia VA Hosp., 1974—; bd. trustees, Columbia Area Mental Health Center, 1972—, vice chmn., chmn. bd. Served with USPHS, 1959-61, med. dir. USPHS Res. Recipient Ravenel award in Pub. Health, Med. U. S.C., 1958. Diplomate Am. Bd. Psychiatry. Fellow Am. Psychiat. Assn. (pres. S.C. Dist. Br., 1977), Southeastern Group Psychotherapy Assn. (pres., 1975-76), Carolinas Soc. Adolescent Psychiatry (pres. 1976-77), AMA, S.C. Med. Assn., Columbia Med. Soc. (pres. 1982-84). Episcopalian. Club: Columbia Rotary. Editorial bd. Medical Audit Review; contbr. articles on psychophysiologic mechanisms epidemiology of various cardiovascular diseases to profl. pubs. Home: 1627 Woodlake Dr Columbia SC 29206 Office: 1401 Laurel St Columbia SC 29201

MILLNER, WALLACE B., III, banker; b. Charlotte, N.C., Aug. 1, 1939; s. Wallace B., Jr. and Virginia (Reed) M.; m. Nancy Jean Bost, Aug. 25, 1961; children—Wallace Michael, Christopher Bost. A.B., Davidson Coll., 1961; M.B.A., U. N.C., 1962. Chartered fin. analyst. Asst. v.p., dir. investment research Bank of Va. Co., Richmond, 1971-72, treas., 1973-74, v.p., treas., 1974-76, sr. v.p., treas., 1976-80, chief fin. officer, 1980—, exec. v.p., 1985—. Chmn. bd. Family and Children's Services, Richmond, 1984—. Served to 1st lt. U.S. Army, 1962-64. Mem. Richmond Soc. Fin. Analysts (pres. 1984-85), Inst. Chartered Fin. Analysts. Republican. Presbyterian. Club: Westwood Racquet (bd. dirs. 1985—) (Richmond). Avocations: tennis; woodworking. Office: Bank of Va Co 7 N 8th St Richmond VA 23260

MILLS, ALFRED PRESTON, chemist; b. Fallon, Nev., Jan. 8, 1922; s. Percy Edward and Ruth (Candee) M.; B.S. in Chemistry, U. Nev., 1943; Ph.D., Tulane U., 1949; m. Josephine Elizabeth Sullivan, Aug. 6, 1946; children—James Everett, Nancy Louise. Instr. chemistry U. Miami, 1949-51, asst. prof., 1951-56, asso. prof., 1956—, acting asst. dean Grad. Sch., 1964-65, adj. asst. dean for curricula Grad. Sch., 1973—, chmn. div. natural sci. and math., 1960-61, dir. Radioisotopes Lab., 1954-62, pres. U. Miami Credit Union, 1965-68; SE regional dir. Univ. Profs. for Acad. Order, 1971-72; dir. South Fla. Regional Sci. Fair, 1954-58; mem. sci. edn. panel NSF. Bd. dirs. Fla. Found. Future Scientists, 1960-63, Men's Supersenior Tennis, 1983—, Fla. State Sci. Talent Search, 1967. Served to lt. comdr. USNR, 1943-46, 52-53, now capt. Res., ret.; comdg. officer Naval Res. Officers Sch., 1965-68; S. Fla. coordinator Naval Acad. Info. Program, 1970-75. Referee, Jr. Orange Bowl, 1961-81. Mem. Am. Chem. Soc. (nat. council 1956-58, 61-70, 72-74, 78—, sec. membership affairs com. 1983—, chmn. Southeast Regional Councilors Caucus 1982—, chmn. personnel com., chmn. S. Fla. subsect., chmn. phys. chemistry exams. com. 1963-74, chmn. Fla. sect. 1971), Am. Phys. Soc., Am. Inst. Chemists (orgn. and rules com. 1982—), AAAS, Fla. Acad. Sci. (pres. 1962), U.S. Tennis Assn. (sanction and schedule com. 1978-84), sr. tennis council 1984—, chmn. men's 55 ranking com. 1985—), Fla. Tennis Assn. (pres. 1964-65, jr. ranking chmn. 1967, jr. tournament chmn. 1968—, sanction and schedule com. 1973—, Jr. Tennis Council 1981—, adult tournament chmn., adult tennis council 1985—, named to Hall of Fame), South Fla. Men's Tennis League (dir. 1966—), Naval Res. Assn. (chpt. pres. 1966-67), Res. Officers' Assn. (chpt. pres. 1959-60), Ret. Officers Assn., AAUP, Sigma Xi (pres. U. Miami chpt. 1973-74, sec. 1979-83, treas. 1983—), Phi Kappa Phi (pres. U. Miami chpt. 1965-66). Club: Royal Palm Tennis (pres. 1968; sec. 1971, 72, tennis chmn. 1966, 67, 76-78). Author: Laboratory Manual in Physical Chemistry, 1953. Abstractor, Chem. Abstracts, 1953-74. Editor, Fla. Acad. Scis. Newsletter; Fla. regional editor Tennis, USA. Home: 7540 SW 28th St Miami FL 33155 Office: Dept Chemistry U Miami Coral Gables FL 33124

MILLS, BOBBIE Y., insurance executive; b. Toccoa, Ga., Dec. 4, 1925; d. Andrew J. and Jessie (Sosebee) Yearwood; m. Luther G. Mills, Jr., Feb. 5, 1944; children—Rosalyn Mills Vaughn, Luther G. III. Student Piedmont Coll. Supr., Travelers Ins. Co., Atlanta, 1969-75; mgr. personal lines Worley & Schilling, Inc., Marietta, Ga., 1975-83, Phoenix Assocs., Marietta, 1983—. Pres., PTA, Marietta, 1954-55, treas., 1956-57, chmn. membership com., 1958-59. Mem. Am. Bus. Women's Assn., Ins. Women Cobb County. Democrat. Methodist. Home: 155 Charles Ave SE Marietta GA 30067 Office: Phoenix Assocs Marietta GA

MILLS, EDWARD WARREN, lawyer, precision bearings and machine parts manufacturing company executive; b. N.Y.C., Apr. 7, 1941; s. Foy Fitzhugh and Isabelle Marie (Vega) M.; B.S. in Commerce, Washington and Lee U., 1962; M.B.A., Hofstra U., 1974, J.D., N.Y. Law Sch., 1977; m. Maria Parascandolo, Sept. 19, 1971; children—Edward Warren, Foy Fitzhugh. Acct., Wasserman & Taten, N.Y.C., 1962-69; exec. v.p. L.H. Keller Co., Inc., N.Y.C., 1969-73, Hugo P. Keller, Inc., 1969-73; pres. Gen. Ruby & Sapphire Corp., New Port Richey, Fla., 1973—, Qualistar Corp., New Port Richey, 1973—; admitted to N.Y. State bar, 1978, D.C. bar, 1981. C.P.A., N.Y. Mem. Am., N.Y. State, D.C. bar assns., N.Y. County Lawyers Assn., Am. Inst. C.P.A.s, N.Y. State Soc. C.P.A.s, Sigma Phi Epsilon, Phi Delta Phi. Contbr. to Suburban Econ. Network, 1977. Home: 1913 Ingersol Pl New Port Richey FL 33552 Office: 101 Massachusetts Ave New Port Richey FL 33552

MILLS, ERIC ROLAND, college dean; b. Conner, Fla., Mar. 16, 1920; s. Eric Roland and Cora (Welhoner) M.; m. Nell Newton, July 11, 1947; 1 child, Judith Ann. B.S.A. in Agronomy, U. Fla., 1942, Ed.S. in Higher Edn., 1967, Ed.D. in Higher Edn., 1968; M.B.A. in Prodn., U. Miss., 1959. Cert. community coll. educator, Fla. Asst. county agt. Agr. Extension Service, Madison, Fla., 1946-47; commd. 2d lt. U.S. Army, 1942, advanced through grades to maj., 1946, served U.S. and Pacific, commd. maj., 1947, advanced through grades to col., 1963, served, U.S., Korea, Guam, Turkey, ret., 1966; dean occupational and adult edn. Fla. Jr. Coll., Jacksonville, 1969—; adj. prof. U. N. Fla., Jacksonville, 1975-79; cons. on community coll. ops., 1972—; mem. accreditation teams So. Assn. Colls. and Schs., 1971—. Editor U. Miss. S.A.M. Newsletter, 1957-59; contbr. articles to pubs. Scholar, Fla. Bankers Assn., 1942, Sears Roebuck Co., 1942; fellow Fla. Bd. Regents, 1967-68. Mem. Fla. Adult Edn. (bd. dirs. 1983—), Fla. Vocat. Assn. (Outstanding Vocat. Educator 1974, com. chmn. 1984), Fla. Adult Edn. Com. for Community Colls. (chmn. 1983-84, plaque award 1984), Am. Assn. Tng. Dirs. (com. chmn. N.E. Fla. chpt. 1977-78), Fla. Assn. Community Colls. (com. mem. 1983-84), Jacksonville C. of C. (Com. of 100 1982—). Democrat. Baptist. Club: Officers (Jacksonville Navy Base). Lodges: Masons, Scottish Rite, Shriners. Avocations: fishing; travel. Home: 5007 Dian Wood Dr E Jacksonville FL 32210 Office: Fla Jr College Jacksonville 501 W State St Jacksonville FL 32202

MILLS, FRANCES JONES, state government official; b. Gray, Ky.; d. William Harrison and Bertie (Steely) Jones; grad. Cumberland Coll., Williamsburg, Ky. Public sch. tchr.; mem. Ky. Ho. of Reps., 1961-62, asst. to speaker, 1963-65; dir. women's activities Ky. Civil Def., 1965-72; clk. Ky. Ct. Appeals, 1972-76; treas. Commonwealth of Ky., Frankfort, 1976-79, 84-88, sec. of state, 1979-84; mem. Ky. Personal Service Contract Rev. Commn., 1976—, Ky. Tchrs. Retirement Bd., 1976—; pres. Nat. Conf. Appellate Ct. Clks., 1975-76. Del. Democratic Nat. Conv., 1964, 68, 76, alt., 1972. Named Southeastern Ky. Outstanding Woman, 1973, Bus. and Profl. Women's Club Woman of Achievement, 1976, Outstanding Alumna, Cumberland Coll., 1978; Pub. Service award Ky. Fedn. Bus. and Profl. Womens Club, 1983. Mem. AMA Aux., Whitley County Med. Aux. Baptist. Clubs: Order Eastern Star, Bus. and Profl. Women's. Author: What Would You Do? (Civil Def. booklet). Office: Office State Treasury Capitol Annex Frankfort KY 40601

MILLS, GEORGE FRANKLIN, JR., architect; b. Durant, Okla., Apr. 30, 1945; s. George Franklin and Martha Lucille (Freeze) M.; m. Monica Jay Fox, May 23, 1970; children—David, Patrick. B.Arch., U. Tex.-Austin, 1970. Registered Architect, Tex. Draftsman, V. E. Emory, Inc., Garland, Tex., 1970-72; architect-in-tng. Harwood K. Smith & Ptnr., Dallas, 1972-74; dir. facilities and planning Baylor Coll. Dentistry, Dallas, 1974-78; v.p. Mills & Mills, Inc., Dallas, 1978—. Mem. Urban Rehab. Standards Bd., City of Dallas, 1981—, chmn., 1983—. Mem. AIA, Constrn. Specifications Inst., Am. Hosp. Assn., Nat. Fire Protection Assn., Am. Inst. Hosp. Planners, E. Dallas C. of C. (dir. 1982—), Tex. Execs. Club (pres. 1984). Mem. Ch. of Christ. Office: 801 N Peak St Dallas TX 75246

MILLS, HARRY LEE, JR., psychologist, consultant; b. Huntsville, Ala., Sept. 17, 1944; s. Harry L. and Florence (Barnette) M.; m. Joyce Reynolds, May 20, 1972; children—Candice Michelle, Courney Sullivan. Student U. Miss. Med. Sch., 1970-71; Ph.D., U. So. Miss., 1973. Lic. clin. psychologist, Tenn., Ala. Clin. psychologist Mobile Mental Health Ctr., Ala., 1974-75; dir. adult services Huntsville Mental Health Ctr., Ala., 1975-79; assoc. exec. dir. Dede Wallace Ctr., Nashville, 1979—; dir. tng. Cumberland Consortium, Nashville, 1979—; adj. assoc. prof. psychology Vanderbilt U., 1979—. Contbr. chpts. to books and articles to profl. jours. NDEA fellow, 1968; NIMH grantee, 1975-79. Mem. Am. Psychol. Assn., Tenn. Psychol. Assn., Assn. Advancement of Behavior Therapy. Democrat. Methodist. Avocations: distance running; classical music; fiction writing.

MILLS, HELEN LUCILLE, librarian; b. Guerneville, Calif., Jan. 1, 1926; d. Sidney Shepherd and Louise (Proschold) Davis; m. Harold L. Dunning, July 1, 1943 (div. 1965); children—Claudia Lively, Carol Castellou, Chester Dunning; m. 2d John E. Mills, Sept. 1, 1965; 1 dau., Alicia. B.A., U. Calif.-Humboldt, 1961; M.L.S., U. Hawaii, 1971; M.F.A., U. Guanajuato (Mexico), 1978. Tchr, Toddy Thomas Sch., Fortuna, Calif., 1957-60, Santa Rosa City Schs. (Calif.), 1961-62; tchr. Cotati Schs. (Calif.), 1962-70; library dir. Am. Sch., Monterrey, Mexico, 1971; adult service librarian Petaluma Pub. Library (Calif.), 1972; reference library asst. Jackson County Library, Medford, Oreg., 1974-77; dist. sch. librarian Susanville Schs. (Calif.), 1979-80; dir. LaSalle Parish Library, Jena, La., 1982—. Author, illustrator: Edible Plants of No. Calif., 1959. Mem. ALA, La. Library Assn., Southeastern Library Assn., Cotati Tchrs. Assn. (pres. 1965-66), LaSalle Parish Art and Museums Assn. Democrat. Unitarian. Club: Pilot. Address: LaSalle Parish Library PO Drawer P Jena LA 71342

MILLS, JEAN EMILE, data processing educator; b. Joliet, Ill., June 20, 1941; s. Jack W. and Elizabeth (Kerr) M. B.S. in Math., Fla. State U., 1963; M.Ed., U. Ga., 1970; postgrad. Ga. State U., 1976. Tchr., DeKalb County Bd. Edn., Druid Hills High Sch., Decatur, Ga., 1964-66, DeKalb County Bd. Edn., Lakeside High Sch., Atlanta, 1968-82; data coordinating analyst Econ. Opportunity Assn., Atlanta, 1966-68; data processing instr. Sperry Corp., Atlanta, 1982—. Bd. dirs. Meadow Wood Homeowners Assn., Chamblee, Ga., 1974-79. Mem. Ga. Assn. Edn., DeKalb Assn. Edn., Nat. Council Tchrs. Math., C. of C. Republican. Presbyterian. Home: 3192 Bolero Way Atlanta GA 30341 Office: Sperry Corp Suite 200 880 Johnson Ferry Rd Atlanta GA 30341

MILLS, RICHARD JOSEPH, police chief; b. Gallup, N.Mex., Mar. 30, 1939; s. A.W. and Francis D. (Dolan) M.; m. Theta Katherine May, Jan. 27, 1978. A.A.S., Tarrant County Coll., 1972; B.S., Tex. Christian U., 1976. Cert. police instr., Tex., Okla. Police officer Grand Prairie Police Dept., Tex., 1965-72; police chief Lake Worth Police Dept., Tex., 1972-75, Pampa Police Dept., Tex., 1975-79, Sherman Police Dept., Tex., 1979-81, Moore Police Dept., Okla., 1982—; patrol mgr. Network Security, Dallas, 1981-82. Named Officer of Yr., Grand Prairie Police, 1970, Lake Worth Police, 1975. Mem. Internat. Assn. Chiefs Police, Okla. Assn. Chiefs Police, Tex. Police Chief Assn. (bd. dirs. 1977-79, v.p. 1980-81). Roman Catholic. Lodges: Elks (trustee 1983-84), Lions (bd. dirs. 1983-85). Avocations: military reserves. Home: PO Box 7638 Moore OK 73153 Office: PO Box 7248 117 E Main St Moore OK 73153

MILLS, ROYAL B., educational administrator; b. Los Angeles, June 14, 1928. B.S., Black Hills State Coll., 1963; M.A. in Edn., Tex. A&I U., 1969; A.E.D., Houston U., 1975. Cert. tchr., Tex. Tchr. sci. Corpus Christi Ind. Sch. Dist., Tex., 1964-69, asst. prin. King High Sch., 1969-76, prin. Cullen Jr. High Sch., 1976—, co-chmn. text book selection for dist., 1985. Mem. Corpus Christi Sister City Selection Com., 1983-85. Served to maj. U.S. Army, 1945-50. Mem. Nat. Prins. Assn., Tex. Prins. Assn., Tex. N.G. Assn., Nat. Assn. Secondary Sch. Prins., Tex. Assn. Secondary Sch. Prins., Corpus Christi Prins. Assn., Sigma Tau Gamma. Republican. Methodist. Avocations: woodworking; dancing; fishing; hunting. Home: Route I Box 111-D Corpus Christi TX 78415 Office: Cullen Place Jr High 5225 Greely Corpus Christi TX 78412

MILLS, SHARON SISK, mortgage banker; b. Columbia, S.C., Sept. 7, 1958; d. Felton and Louise (Bouknight) S.; m. Richard Ernest Mills, Aug. 7, 1982. A.S., Miami-Dade Community Coll., 1978; B.S., Palm Beach Atlantic Coll., 1980. With comml. loan dept. Atlantic Nat. Co., West Palm Beach, Fla., 1980-81; with loan servicing dept. Standard Fed. Co., Columbia, S.C., 1981-82; escrow rep. S.E. Mortgage Co., Miami, 1982-83, mgmt. trainee, 1983-84, head tng. dept., 1984—. Mem. Am. Soc. for Tng. and Devel., Mortgage Bankers Assn., Nat. Soc. Female Execs. Avocations: swimming; water skiing; photography; reading. Office: SE Mortgage Co 2500 79th Ave Miami FL 33122

MILLS, WILLIAM HAROLD, JR., construction company executive; b. St. Petersburg, Fla., July 24, 1939; s. William Harold and Caroline (Bonfoey) M.; m. Kimberly Keyes, May 4, 1985; m. Sylvia Ludwig, Jan. 4, 1962 (div. Dec. 1975); children—William Harold III, Robert Michael, Leslie Anne. B.S. in C.E., U. Fla., 1961. Vice pres. bus. devel. Mills & Jones Constrn. Co., St. Petersburg, 1964-68, exec. v.p., 1971-79; v.p. Wellington Corp., Atlanta, 1968-71; pres., chmn. Fed. Constrn. Co., St. Petersburg, 1979—; dir. Landmark Union Trust Bank. Chmn., Pinellas Marine Inst., St. Petersburg; mem. pres.'s council U. Fla., Gainesville; past chmn. blue ribbon zoning com. City of St. Petersburg; former mem. Pinellas County Constrn. Licensing Bd., Fla., Tampa Bay Aviation Adv. Com.; former bd. dirs. United Fund Pinellas County. Hon. liaison officer Brit. Royal Navy, 1984—. Mem. ASCE, Nat. Soc. Profl. Engrs., Am. Mgmt. Assn., St. Petersburg Area C. of C. (bd. govs. 1983—), Mensa, Sigma Alpha Epsilon. Democrat. Episcopalian. Clubs: St. Petersburg Yacht, Presidents (bd. dirs.); Les Ambassadeurs, Annabel's (London); University (Tampa); Useppa Island (Pineland, Fla.). Avocations: golf, fishing. Office: Federal Constrn Co 800 2d Ave S Saint Petersburg FL 33701

MILLS, WILLIAM HOWARD, guidance and control mechanics engr.; b. Clarinda, Iowa, Apr. 6, 1954; s. Austin Carl and Florence Renata (Kalthoff) M.; m. Margaret Dora Schulz, June 18, 1983. B.S., Wichita State U., 1978. Tech. aide Gates Learjet Corp., Wichita, Kans., 1977-78; assoc. engr. command and control software McDonnell Douglas Tech. Services Co., Houston, 1978-79, engr. guidance and control mechanics, 1982—; design engr. Mooney Aircraft Corp., Kerrville, Tex., 1979-82. Mem. Exptl. Aircraft Assn. (past sec. chpt. 747), Aircraft Owners and Pilots Assn. Republican. Lutheran. Home: 14127 Lorne Dr Houston TX 77049 Office: 16441 Space Center Blvd Houston TX 77058

MILLSAP, MARGARET ISRAEL, nursing educator; b. Pensacola, Fla., Feb. 4, 1923; d. James Buchanan and Ludia Ann Israel; m. William A. Millsap Jr.; children—Cynthia Ann Boykin, Susan Jane. B.S.N., U. Ala., 1956, M.S.N., 1958, Ed.D., 1974. Instr. nursing Bapt. Med. Ctr., Birmingham, 1947-73; prof. nursing Sanford U., Birmingham, 1973-75; dir. nursing U. Ala.-Birmingham, 1975-81; chmn. nursing dept. Birmingham So. Coll., 1981—. Author: National

League for Nursing, 1976; Community Health Nursing, 1984. Bd. dirs. Children's Aid Soc., Birmingham, 1983—, Assn. Retarded Citizens, Birmingham, 1982—; mem. State Com. Pub. Health, Montgomery, Ala., 1980-83. Recipient Cert. of Recognition, Ala. Commn. Nursing, 1985, Resolution of Honor, Ala. Bd. Nursing, 1983. Mem. Ala. State Nurses Assn. (pres. 1975-76), Ala. League Nurses (pres. 1961-63), Am. Assn. Mental Deficiency, Sigma Theta Tau (pres. 1958). Republican. Baptist. Lodge: Order Eastern Star. Avocations: flower gardening; travel. Home: 2500 Old Rocky Ridge Rd Birmingham AL 35216 Office: Birmingham So Coll 800 8th Ave W Birmingham AL 35254

MILLSAPS, SHELBY J., nurse, college administrator; b. Coalfield, Tenn., Oct. 24, 1940; d. Oscar W. and Lois Kathleen (East) Justice; m. Charles H. Millsaps, Oct. 27, 1961. Diploma Erlanger Hosp., Chattanooga, 1961; B.S., U. Chattanooga, 1968; M.S.N., Med. Coll. Ga., 1976. Staff nurse Victory Meml. Hosp., Bklyn., 1961-63; instr. Erlanger Hosp., Chattanooga, 1963-74; instr. Cleveland State Community Coll., Tenn., 1974-77, dir., 1977—. Mem. Tenn. Nurses Assn. (chmn. practice 1984—), Chattanooga Nurses Assn., Chattanooga League Nursing, Cleveland Diabetic Assn. (sec. 1983—), Deans and Dirs. (chmn. 1984-85), Sigma Theta Tau. Republican. Baptist. Office: Cleveland State Community Coll Cleveland TN 37411

MILOJKOVIC-DJURIC, JELENA, art historian, researcher, piano teacher; b. Belgrade, Yugoslavia, Dec. 2, 1931; came to U.S., 1965; d. Borislav A. and Zora (Vujovic) Milojkovic; m. Dusan Djuric, Sept. 24, 1955; children—Zora, Mara. Absolvent, U. Belgrade, 1955; filosofie kandidat, U. Stockholm-U. Uppsala, Sweden, 1958; M.A., U. Belgrade, 1963, Ph.D., 1981. Lectr. U. Belgrade, Yugoslavia, 1963-65; research assoc. Musicol. Inst., Yugoslavia, 1963-65; lectr. Slavic langs. U. Colo., Boulder, 1968; lectr. German & Russian, Tex. A&M U., College Station, 1972-74; freelance writer, 1974—; research contbr. Office Edn., HEW, 1974-76. Author: Tradition and Avant-garde, 1984; The Music of Eastern Europe, 1978. Contbr. articles to profl. jours. Vice pres. citizens' adv. bd. appearance com. City of College Station, 1984—. Grantee Tex. A&M U., 1974, Serbian Acad. of Scis. and Arts 1978-79. Mem. Am. Assn. Advancement Slavic Studies, Am. Musicol. Soc., Western Social Sci. Assn., Rocky Mountains Assn. Slavic Studies, Gesellschaft für Musikforschung, Bryan-College Station Music Tchrs. Assn. (pres. 1978-79). Serbian Orthodox. Avocation: gardening.

MILSTEAD, CHARLES CLIFTON, JR., school administrator; b. Natchitoches, La., July 5, 1946; s. Charles Clifton and Eva Joyce (Hare) M.; m. Marilynn Joanne Hamner, June 17, 1971; children—Jonathan Mark, Karen Elizabeth, Jeffrey Ryan, Timothy Alan. B.S. in Edn., La. Tech. U., 1968, M.S. in Edn., 1973. Tchr. Bienville Parish Sch., Castor, La., 1968-71; prin. Cherry Ridge Christian Sch., Bastrop, La., 1971-73; tchr. Jackson Parish Sch., Chatham, La., 1973-80, prin. elem. sch., 1980-82, prin. secondary sch., 1982—. Sustaining mem. Republican Nat. Com., Washington, 1984, 85. Mem. La. Assn. Prins., Jackson Assn. Prins. Baptist. Avocations: photography; hunting. Home: Route 1 Box 196 Jonesboro LA 71251 Office: Chatham High Sch Corner Pine and Chatham Chatham LA 71226

MILSTEIN, BERNARD ALLEN, ophthalmologist; b. Newark, N.J., June 11, 1941; s. J. Edwin and Helen (Seisholtz) M.; m. Phyllis Ruth Schwartz, June 21, 1964; children—Andria Michelle, Julie Marlene. B.A., Lafayette Coll., 1963; M.D., Univ. Tex., 1967. Diplomate Am. Bd. Ophthalmology. Intern, D.C. Gen. Hosp., Washington, 1967-68; resident ophthalmology U. Tex., Galveston, 1968-71, clin. assoc. prof. ophthalmology, 1972—; chief of ophthalmology USPHS, Galveston, 1971-72; pres. The Eye Clinic of Galveston, 1974—; pres. med. staff St. Mary's Hosp., 1986—; sec., treas. U. Tex. Med. staff, 1981-82; mem. staff Mainland Ctr. Hosp., 1973—; cons. USPHS, 1972-80; v.p. Ophthalmic Cons., Lufkin, Tex., 1985—; founding dir. Galveston Savings & Loan Assn., 1976-84; vice-chmn. Galveston Emergency Med. Service Commn., 1974-79. Contbr. articles to profl. jours. Chmn. Galveston County United Bd. Health, 1978—; chmn. bd. trustees Galveston Wharves, 1980—; co-chmn. Anti-Oil Drilling Campaign, Galveston, 1976; co-chmn. JOBS Campaign-Pro Oil Terminal, Galveston, 1980; county chmn. Lt. Gov. Billy Hobby Campaign, Galveston, 1976—; pres. Congregation Beth Jacob, 1976-77; founding dir. Galveston Racquet Club, 1974-79; bd. visitors Tex. A&M U., Galveston, 1984—. Fellow Am. Acad. Ophthalmology; mem. Galveston County Med. Soc. (sec. treas. 1978-80), AMA, Tex. Med. Assn., Tex. Ophthal. Assn., So. Med. Assn., Am. Intra-Ocular Implant Soc., Intraocular Lens Soc., Galveston C. of C. Democrat. Jewish. Club: Galveston Yacht. Home: 59 Adler Circle Galveston TX 77550 Office: The Eye Clinic 2302 Avenue P Galveston TX 77550

MILSTEIN, RICHARD CRAIG, lawyer; b. N.Y.C., July 16, 1946; s. Max Milstein and Hattie (Jacobson) Milstein Worchel; m. SuAnn Leiken; children—Brian Matthew, Rachel Helaine. A.B. cum laude, U. Miami, 1968, J.D., 1973. Bar: Fla. 1974, U.S. Ct. Appeals (5th cir.) 1974, U.S. Dist. Ct. (so. dist.) Fla. 1974, U.S. Supreme Ct. 1977, U.S. Ct. Appeals (11th cir.) 1983. Assoc. August, Nimkoff & Pohlig, Miami, 1974-76; mng. ptnr. firm Jepeway, August, Gassen & Pohlig, Miami, 1977-78, August, Gassen, Pohlig & Milstein, Miami, 1978-80, August, Pohlig & Milstein, Miami, 1980-83; ptnr. Milstein & Wayne, Coral Gables, Fla., 1983—. Co-founder Dade County Vol. Lawyers for Arts; former mediator Citizens Dispute Settlement Ctr. Met. Dade County; former chmn. Legal Info. Ctrs., 1979-81; mem. Met. Dade County Ind. Rev. Panel, 1984—; bd. dirs. South Fla. Mediation Ctr., 1982—, chmn. bd., 1985—; bd. dirs. Ptnrs. for Youth; bd. dirs. Beth David Congregation, 1980—, asst. treas., 1982-85; pres. Bet Shira Congregation, 1985—; treas. South Fla. Inter-Profl. Council, Inc., 1983-84, sec., 1984-85, v.p., 1985—. Mem. ABA, Dade County Bar Assn. (dir. 1980-83, treas. 1983, sec. 1984-85, v.p. 1985—), Coral Gables Bar Assn., Fla. Bar (Tobias Simon award 11th jud. circuit 1986), Acad. Am. Trial Lawyers, Acad. Fla. Trial Lawyers, Phi Theta Kappa, Delta Theta Mu, Omicron Delta Kappa, Phi Alpha Theta, Kappa Delta Pi, Phi Kappa Phi, Alpha Kappa, Zeta Epsilon Nu. Home: 12225 SW 97th Ct Miami FL 33176 Office: Milstein and Wayne 250 Catalonia Ave Suite 400 Coral Gables FL 33134

MILTON, JOSEPH PAYNE, lawyer; b. Richmond, Va., Oct. 24, 1943; s. Hubert E. and Grace C. M.; m. Ann King, Apr. 22, 1967; children—Michael Payne, Amy Barrett, David King. B.S. in Bus. Adminstrn., U. Fla., 1967, J.D., 1969. Bar: Fla. 1969, U.S. Ct. Appeals (5th cir.) 1971, U.S. Supreme Ct. 1972, U.S. Ct. Appeals (11th cir.) 1981. Assoc. Toole, Taylor, Moseley & Gabel, Jacksonville, 1969-70; ptnr. Toole, Taylor, Moseley, Gobel & Milton, Jacksonville, 1971-78, Howell, Liles, Braddock & Milton, Jacksonville, 1978—. Mem. Mayor's Blue Ribbon Task Force; pres. Civic Round Table of Jacksonville, 1980-81; campaign chmn. NE Fla. chpt. March of Dimes, 1973-74, v.p., 1974-75; pres. Willing Hands, 1974-75; chmn. attys.' div. United Way, 1977; mem. exec. com. Jacksonville Area Legal Aid, Inc., 1982-83; mem. Law Center Council, U. Fla. Coll. Law, 1972-78; chmn. pvt. bar involvement com. Legal Aid Bd. dirs., 1982-83. Recipient Outstanding Service award for Individual Contbns. in Support of Legal Services for the Poor, 1981. Mem. Jacksonville Bar Assn. (pres. 1980-81, pres. young lawyers sect. 1974-75), Fla. Bar (4th jud. cir. nominating commn. 1980-82, grievance com. 1975-77, chmn. 1976, mem. exec. council for trial sect. 1982—, chmn. voluntary bar liaison com. 1982-83), Jacksonville Assn. Def. Counsel (pres. 1981-82, lectr. CLE programs, guest lectr. U. Fla., Jones Coll.), ABA, Fed. Bar Assn., Fla. Council Bar Assn. Pres. (exec. com. 1982—, v.p. 1984-85, pres. 1985-86), Nat. Assn. R.R. Trial Counsel (exec. com. 1983—, S.E. region v.p. 1984—), Maritime Law Assn. U.S., Acad. Fla. Trial Lawyers, Assn. Trial Lawyers Am., Am. Judicature Soc. Democrat. Clubs: San Jose Country (Jacksonville), University, Gulf Life Tower (Jacksonville). Home: 1129 Mapleton Rd Jacksonville FL 32207 Office: 901 Blackstone Bldg Jacksonville FL 32202

MILTON, ROBERT C., diversified company executive; b. 1923; married. B.A., U. Mt. Allison, 1949. With Johns-Mansville Corp., 1950-59; pres. Sandair Corp., 1960—; with Tidewater Marine Service Inc., 1968—, v.p., 1970-78, sr. v.p., 1978-79, exec. v.p., 1979—; exec. v.p. Tidewater Inc., New Orleans; pres. Tidewater Compression Inc. Office: Tidewater Inc 1440 Canal St New Orleans LA 70112*

MILWARD, HENDREE BRINTON, JR., management and public administration educator; b. Lexington, Ky., Nov. 14, 1945; s. Hendree Brinton and Jane (Baynham) M.; children—Hendree Brinton, Andrew Malan; m. Mary Anne Ellis, Dec. 3, 1983. Student U. of South, 1964-66; B.A., U. Ky., 1968, M.A., 1973; Ph.D., Ohio State U., 1978. Asst. prof. polit. sci. U. Kans., 1975-79; asst. prof. mgmt. and pub. adminstrn. U. Ky., Lexington, 1979-81, assoc. prof., 1981—, dir. Ctr. for Bus. and Econ. Research, 1984—; cons. in field. Mem. Gov.'s Commn. on Effective Mgmt., State of Kans., 1976-77. Served with Peace Corps, 1968-70. HEW grantee, 1979-82; Ashland Oil Co. research grantee, 1982. Mem. Acad. Mgmt., Am. Soc. Pub. Adminstrn. (pres. Ky. chpt.), Am. Polit. Sci. Assn. Democrat. Episcopalian. Mem. editorial bd. Pub. Adminstrn. Rev., Policy Studies Jour., Am. Jour. Pub. Adminstrn. Contbr. numerous articles on mgmt., pub. policy and pub. adminstrn. to profl. jours. Office: Ctr Bus and Econ Research 301 Mathews Bldg Lexington KY 40506

MIMS, LAMBERT CARTER, mayor; b. Uriah, Ala., Apr. 20, 1930; s. Jeff and Carrie (Lambert) M.; grad. high sch.; m. Reecie Philips, Aug. 17, 1946; children—Dale, Danny. Engaged in retail and wholesale food bus., 1949-65; owner Mims Brokerage Co., Mobile, Ala., 1958-70; public works commr. City of Mobile, 1965—, mayor, 1968-69, 72—; former mem. exec. com. Ala. League Municipalities, 1966-68; mem. human resources com. Nat. League Cities; former mem. com. transp. U.S. Conf. Mayors; past pres. Mobile County Mcpl. Assn.; lectr. in field. Former trustee Judson Coll., Marion, Ala.; bd. dirs. Keep Am. Beautiful. Named Mobile's Most Outstanding Young Man, 1965. Mem. Ala. (pres. 1969-70, 72—), Am. (dir., pres. 1979-80) public works assns., Mobile C. of C. (mil. affairs com.), Baptist (deacon; chmn. bd. 1950-65; 1st v.p. Ala. Bapt. State Conv. 1969-70, pres. 1970-71; mem. Mobile Camp Gideons, pres. 1962-65; mem. Christian businessmen's com. internat. 1965-70; bd. dirs. Mobile rescue mission; past pres., now dir. Mobile Bapt. Brotherhood). Clubs: Masons (32 deg.), Shriners, Kiwanis. Author: For Christ and Country, 1969. Address: PO Box 1827 Mobile AL 36633

MIMS, THOMAS JEROME, insurance company executive; b. Sumter, S.C., Dec. 12, 1899; s. Lazarus and Sarah Rebecca (White) M.; A.B., Furman U., 1921; m. Valma Gillespie, Dec. 14, 1926; children—Thomas Jerome, George Franklin. Apprentice, Rec. & Statis. Corp. of N.Y., Detroit, 1921, N.Y.C., 1921-22, asst. mgr., Phila., 1922-25, mgr., Indpls., 1925-27, Boston, 1927-29; salesman Burroughs Adding Machine Co., Detroit, Boston, 1929-31; ins. spl. agt. State N.J., Morley Gen. Agy., Camden, 1931-32; mgr. William R. Timmons Agy., Greenville, S.C., 1933—; v.p., sec. Canal Ins. Co., Greenville, 1942-48, pres., treas., dir., 1948—; dir., pres. Canal Indemnity Co.; dir., mem. bd. mgmt., bd. govs., chmn. nominating com. Internat. Ins. Seminar; bd. electors Ins. Hall of Fame. Bus. mgr. Greenville Little Theater, 1951-53, 64-66, council, 1951—, v.p., 1956-57, pres., 1957-58, 72-75; pres. Rotary Charities, Inc., 1964-65; mem. adv. bd. S.C. Safety Council, 1969-70, pres., 1970-75, 81-84; past dir. Met. Arts Council; bd. dirs. United Way Greenville, 1970-81, hon., 1981—, chmn. bd., 1979, campaign chmn., 1976, v.p., 1977-78, pres., 1978; bd. dirs. United Way S.C., 1981-82; vice chmn. Found. Modern Liquor Regulations and Control; adv. council Furman U. Named Boss of Year Greenville Jr. C. of C., 1964, Greenville Assn. Ins. Women, 1966; Spl. award S.C. Assn. Ins. Women, 1977; S.C. Vol. of Year, United Way, 1979. Mem. Nat., S.C., Greenville (past pres.) assns. ins. agts., S.C. Motor Transp. Assn. (chmn. ins. com. 1951-63, dir. 1973-75), S.C., U.S. (ins. com. 1959-61, 64-68), Greenville (chmn. community relations com. 1964-69, dir. 1969-74, pres.-elect 1972, pres. 1973, pres. found. 1973) chambers commerce, Am. Mgmt. Assn. (pres.'s assn.), AIM (fellow pres.'s council), Truck and Heavy Equipment Claims Council (charter mem., chmn. membership com.), Assn. S.C. Property and Casualty Ins. Cos. (pres. 1962-63, 72-73, mem. exec. com. 1963-68), Internat. Platform Assn., Pres.'s Assn. Baptist (past pres. men's Bible class, mem. fin. com.). Clubs: Elks, Rotary (pres. Rotary Charities, Inc. 1964-65; dir. Greenville 1957-58, pres. 1963-64, v.p. 1964-65), Touchdown (charter mem.; pres. 1963-64), Greenville City (dir. 1964, pres. 1965, chmn. bd. dirs. 1966-67), Poinsett, VIP (Greenville); Palmetto, Summit (Columbia, S.C.); World Trade (Atlanta). Home: Knollwood Dr Route 6 Greenville SC 29607 Office: 417 E North St Greenville SC 29602

MINARIK, JON, direct marketing company executive; b. Cleve., Mar. 9, 1947; s. Paul Francis and Alice Mary (Mann) M.; m. Terri Sue Butler, June 30, 1973; children—Anne, Michael. B.A. in Communications, Ohio U., 1973; postgrad. No. Va. Sch. Law, 1978-80. Dir. congl. affairs Pub. Service Research Council, Vienna, Va., 1976-78; account exec. The Viguerie Co., Falls Church, Va., 1978-79; dir. direct mail Connally for Pres., Arlington, Va., 1979-80; pres. Jon Minarik & Assocs., Oakton, Va., 1980—. Served with U.S. Army, 1966-68. Mem. Direct Mktg. Assn. Republican. Roman Catholic. Home: 3212 Miller Heights Rd Oakton VA 22124 Office: PO Box 423 Oakton VA 22124

MINASI, MARK JEROME, economist, microcomputer consultant; b. White Plains, N.Y., Oct. 14, 1957; s. Jerome John and Virginia Marie (Hartley) M. B.A. in Econs., SUNY-Stony Brook, 1978, M.S. in Policy Analysis, 1980; M.Ph., George Washington U., 1985. Cons. ICF, Inc., Washington, 1980-82; econs. assoc. Brookhaven Nat. Lab., Washington, 1982—; ptnr. Moulton & Co., Columbia, Md., 1984—; v.p. Triad Research Inc., 1984—. Contbr. articles to profl. jours. Mem. Am. Econs. Assn., Ops. Research Soc. Am. Avocations: sailing; cooking. Home and Office: 5400 Wilson Blvd Arlington VA 22205

MINCH, VIRGIL ADELBERT, civil and sanitary engineer; b. Cleve., Dec. 24, 1924; s. Henry Joseph and Mary (Terlaak) M.; B.S., N.D. State U., 1946; S.M. in San. Engring., Mass. Inst. Tech., 1948; m. Elma Queen, Jan. 6, 1947; children—David, Philip. Research asso. Mass. Inst. Tech., 1948-49; sr. asst. san. engr. USPHS, Cin., 1949-53; staff engr. Mead Corp., Chillicothe, Ohio, 1953-55, group leader, 1956-59, mgr. pollution control activities, 1960-65, asso. dir. tech. services, 1966-68, coordinator environmental resources, 1969-73; v.p., dir. Asso. Water and Air Resources Engrs., Nashville, 1972-74; project mgr. Stanley Cons., Muscatine, Iowa, 1974, v.p., 1974-77; v.p. John J. Harte Assos., Inc., Atlanta, 1977-78; S.E. regional mktg. mgr. Environ. Research and Tech., Atlanta, 1978-80; engr., design mgr. Daniel Constrn. Co., Greenville, S.C., 1980-83, project mgr., 1983—; engr. dir. USPHS Res., 1980—. Recipient Indsl. liaison service award Ohio River Valley Water Sanitation Commn., 1959. Registered profl. engr. Ga., N.J. Mem. Scioto Conservancy dist. (v.p., dir. 1959—), Am. Meteorol. Soc., Am. Water Works Assn., Water Pollution Control Fedn., Air Pollution Control Assn., TAPPI, Ga. Pulp and Paper Assn. (sec. 1955-65), Nat. Council Air and Stream Improvement (chmn. S. Central region 1963-69), Nat. Rivers and Harbors Congress (chmn. S.E. Ohio sect. 1968-72), Sigma Xi, Tau Beta Pi, Sigma Phi Delta. Contbr. articles profl. jours. Patentee plastic film trickling filter. Home: 3146 Smokecreek Ct Atlanta GA 36345 Office: Daniel Bldg Greenville SC 29602

MINCHEFF, EDISON ELAINE, construction company executive; b. Winnett, Mont., July 20, 1920; s. Peter and Lota (Hooker) M.; B.S. in Mech. Engring., U. Kans., 1949; m. Evelyn Lee Moore, Nov. 4, 1943; children—Sharon Lee, Claudia Anne, Cristine Marie, Marc Edison. Engr., Bendix Aviation Co., Kansas City, Mo., 1949-51; asst. chief engr. Great Lakes Pipeline Co., Kansas City, 1951-57; engr., v.p. Williams Bros. Co., Tulsa, 1957-75; v.p. Williams Internat. Group, Inc., Tulsa, 1976-84; project mgr. Willbros Butler Engrs., Inc., 1984—; pvt. cons. to oil and gas pipeline industry. Served with USNR, 1942-45. Registered profl. engr., Ill., Fla., Mo., Okla. Mem. ASME, Am. Petroleum Inst., Internat. Pipeline Assn., Pipeline Industries Guild (Eng.), Soc. Am. Mil. Engrs. Club: Masons. Contbr. articles to tech. jours. Home: 3244 S Evanston St Tulsa OK 74105 Office: 2087 E 71st St Tulsa OK 74145

MINER, JOHN BURNHAM, business administration educator; b. N.Y.C., July 20, 1926; s. John Lynn and Bess (Burnham) M.; A.B., Princeton U., 1950, Ph.D., 1955; M.A., Clark U., Worcester, Mass., 1952; m. Barbara Allen Williams, June 1, 1979; children—Barbara, John, Cynthia, Frances, Jennifer, Heather. Mgr. psychol. services Atlantic Refining Co., Phila., 1957-60; prof. bus. adminstrn. U. Oreg., Eugene, 1960-68; prof. bus. adminstrn., chmn. dept. U. Md., 1968-73; research prof., program chmn. doctoral studies bus. adminstrn. Ga. State U., Atlanta, 1973—; pres. Orgnl. Measurement Systems Press, 1976—. Author: Intelligence in the United States, 1957; Studies in Management Education, 1965; Personnel and Industrial Relations, 1969, 73, 77, 85; The Management Process, 1973, 78; The Human Constraint, 1974; The Challenge of Managing, 1975; (with George Steiner) Management Policy and Strategy, 1977, 82, 86; Motivation To Manage, 1977; Theories of Organizational Behavior, 1980; Theories of Organizational Structure and Process, 1982; Introduction to Management, 1985; People Problems: The Executive Answer Book, 1985. Served with AUS, 1944-46. Decorated Combat Inf. badge, Bronze Star. Recipient James A. Hamilton Hosp. Adminstrs. Book award, 1979. Fellow Acad. Mgmt. (pres. 1978, editor jour. 1973-75), Am. Psychol. Assn., Soc. Personality Assessment; mem. Indsl. Relations Research Assn., Am. Soc. Personnel Adminstrn. Club: Princeton (N.Y.C.). Home: 651 Peachtree Battle Ave NW Atlanta GA 30327 Office: Dept Mgmt Ga State U Univ Plaza Atlanta GA 30303

MINER, TERRY LEE, exploration geologist; b. Lawrence, Kans., Aug. 28, 1953; s. Herbert Milton and Helen (Rinck) M.; m. Deana Louise Felkner, Sept. 17, 1983. B.S., Emporia State U., 1976. Registered profl. geologist. Jr. geologist Wilshire Oil Co., Oklahoma City, 1977-78; staff geologist Arkla Exploration, Oklahoma City, 1978-80; sr. geologist Forest Oil Co., Oklahoma City, 1980-81; exec. v.p. Deep Gas Exploration, Oklahoma City, 1981-82; geol. cons. Oklahoma City, 1982-85; sr. area geologist Reading and Bates, Tulsa, 1985—. Chmn. del. Republican County Conv., 1980. Mem. Am. Assn. Petroleum Geologists, Oklahoma City Geol. Soc., Oklahoma City Geol. Library. Republican. Methodist. Home: 908 Garden Grove Yukon OK 73099

MINES, LINDA SUE MOSS, human resources professional, employee development consultant; b. Cookeville, Tenn., Sept. 10, 1952; d. Marvin A. and Louise (Apple) Moss; m. Eras Anthony Mines, Mar. 28, 1979; 1 child, Jessica Eras. B.S., Tenn. Tech. U., 1972, M.A., 1975; postgrad. in edn. U. Tenn.-Knoxville, 1976-78. Cert. tchr., ednl. adminstr., prin., supt. Chmn. social scis. White County Jr. High Sch., Sparta, Tenn., 1972-75; indsl. relations coordinator Motlow State Community Coll., Tullahoma, Tenn., 1975-76; research asst. U. Tenn., Knoxville, 1976-78; spl. projects adminstr. Chattanooga State Community Coll., 1978-81, indsl. relations coordinator, 1981-82; mgr. employee devel. McKee Baking Co., Collegedale, Tenn., 1982—; cons. Profl. Picture Framers Assocs., Richmond, Va., 1985. Contbr. articles to profl. jours. Bd. dirs. Hamilton County Bd. Edn., Chattanooga, 1984—, Tri-Community Vol. Fire Dept., 1983—; chmn. Chattanooga Energy Bd., 1979-82; mem. state bd. Tenn. Energy Authority, 1979-82; vice chmn. Chattanooga Total County Census, 1980; bd. dirs., pub. relations dir. Chattanooga Audubon Soc., 1984—. Recipient Civic Leadership citation, Gov. Alexander, 1980. Mem. Am. Soc. Tng. and Devel. (pres. 1984, bd. dirs. 1985, nat. chmn. food industries div. 1984-85), Southeast Hamilton County C. of C. (chmn. Collegedale 1985—), Tri-State Chamber Fed. and State Affairs (bd. dirs.), Kappa Delta Pi, Phi Delta Kappa, Phi Lambda Theta. Republican. Presbyterian. Avocations: art; music; landscape gardening. Home: 2401 Haven Cove Ln Chattanooga TN 37421 Office: McKee Baking Co 1000 McKee Rd Collegedale TN 37315

MINETTE, DENNIS JEROME, financial computing consultant; b. Columbus, Nebr., May 18, 1937; s. Lawrence Edward and Angela Ellen (Kelley) M.; B.S.E.E., U. Nebr., 1970; M.B.A., Babson Coll., 1978; m. Virginia Rae Jordan, Oct. 27, 1961; children—Jordan Edward, Lawrence Edward II. Brokerage systems designer Honeywell Info. Systems, Mpls. and Wellesly, Mass., 1970-75; devel. mgr. Investment Info., Inc., Cambridge, Mass., 1975-77; product support mgr. Small Bus. Systems div. Data Gen. Corp., Westboro, Mass., 1977-81; pres. Minette Data Systems, Inc., Sarasota, Fla., 1981—. Capital improvement programs committeeman Town of Medway (Mass.), 1978-79, mem. town fin. com., 1979-80. Served with USN, 1956-60, 61-67. Mem. IEEE, IEEE Computer Soc., Data Processing Mgmt. Assn. (cert.), Naval Res. Assn. (life), Res. Officers Assn., Am. Legion, U. Nebr. Alumni Assn. (life), Eta Kappa Nu, Sigma Tau. Republican. Roman Catholic. Home: 3377 Bee Ridge Rd Suite 2C Sarasota FL 33579 Office: PO Box 15435 Sarasota FL 33579

MINGEE, JAMES CLYDE, III, lawyer; b. Natchez, Miss., Oct. 10, 1943; s. James Clyde and Vivian Annette (Gunning) M., Jr.; m. Donna Jean Jezek, Dec. 28, 1964; children—Timothy Shawn, Shae Lin. B.P.A., U. Miss., 1965, J.D., 1968. Bar: Miss. 1968, D.C. 1974, U.S. Supreme Ct. 1978. Atty., CIA, Washington, 1968-73; legal asst. to chancellor U. Md.-College Park, 1973-77; assoc. gen. counsel, asst. sec. Carling Nat. Breweries, Inc., Balt., 1977-78; assoc. gen. counsel Stokely-Van Camp, Inc., Indpls., 1978-80; pvt. practice, Jackson, Miss., 1980—; instr. bus. law U. Md., 1970-72; dir. Republic Bank for Savs., VOLARE, Ltd., J&M Trading Co.; cons. counsel com. intelligence U.S. Ho. of Reps., 1975-76; legal bus. cons. U.S., fgn. corps., 1973—. Mem. ABA, Miss. State Bar Assn., Am. Arbitration Assn., Fed. Bar Assn., U.S. Trademark Assn. Roman Catholic. Co-author: Miss. Construction Law Seminar Coursebook, 1980. Home: 102 Coker Rd Jackson MS 39213 Office: PO Box 1291 Jackson MS 39205

MINK, ELLEN BRITZ, psychologist; b. Huntington, W.Va., Oct. 8, 1941; d. Norman Charles and Dorothy Harriet (Kuttendrier) Britz; m. Oscar Gorton Mink, Feb. 14, 1966 (div. 1974); children—Jeffrey, Lisa. B.A., Marshall U., 1963; M.A., W.Va. U., 1969; Ph.D., U. Miss., 1979. Lic. psychologist, Tex., Ark. Psychologist VA Med. Ctr., Waco, Tex., 1980—. Mem. properties com. Bluebonnet council Girl Scouts U.S., 1983—; sec. Jefferson-Moore High Sch. PTA, Waco, 1984—. Mem. Am. Psychol. Assn. Mormon. Home: 6412 May Dr Waco TX 76710 Office: VA Med Ctr Memorial Dr Waco TX 76703

MINK, WILLIAM RALPH, pharmacist; b. New Tazewell, Tenn., Oct. 23, 1938; s. Isaac Buford and Addie Lee (Watson) M.; m. Peggy Lynette Trent, June 4, 1960; children—Sandra Gail, Regina Ann, William Ralph. B.S. in Pharmacy, U. Tenn., 1964. Staff pharmacist East Tenn. Bapt. Hosp., Knoxville, 1964-66, Cole Drug Co., Knoxville, 1966-67; chief pharmacist Appalachian Regional Hosp., Middlesboro, Ky., 1967—; vol. faculty U. Ky., Lexington, 1975—, Med. Coll. Va., Richmond, 1975—. Chmn. Mountain Trail Health Plan Bd., Harlan, Ky., 1983, Appalachian Regional Hosp. Employees Fed. Credit Union, 1984, chmn. bd. Mem. Am. Soc. Hosp. Pharmacists, Ky. Pharmacists Assn. Republican. Methodist. Avocations: tennis; flying; bicycling. Home: 3306 W Cumberland Ave Middlesboro KY 40965 Office: Appalachian Regional Hosp 3600 W Cumberland Ave Middlesboro KY 40965

MINKLEY, SUZANNE SAWYER (MRS. CARL H. MINKLEY), educator; b. Middletown, Ohio, May 15, 1915; d. Clifford Louis and Harriett May (Logan) Sawyer; m. Carl Henry Minkley, Apr. 3, 1943; children—Elizabeth Suzanne Minkley Jarrard, Philip Carl. A.B., John B. Stetson U., 1937, M.A., 1942; B.L.S., George Peabody Coll. Tchrs. Vanderbilt U., 1940; postgrad. Manatee Jr. Coll., 1960, Fla. So. Coll., 1966, U. South Fla., 1966-67. Tchr., librarian Mt. Dora High Sch., 1937-41, Leesburg High Sch., 1941-43, Delray Beach High Sch., 1943-45, Samsula Elementary Sch., 1955-56; tchr. Spanish, Sarasota High Sch., 1956-57; reading specialist, chmn. lang. arts Bayshore Jr. High Sch., 1963-74; tchr. social studies Bradenton Middle Sch., 1974-85; cons. tchr. tng. program Edn. Professions Devel. Act of U.S. Dept. Edn., 1970-71; parliamentarian Manatee County Edn. Assn., 1968-72, Bradenton Middle Sch. PTA, 1976—. Author: (booklet) Parliamentary Procedure for Teen-Agers. Chmn. bd. Deland (Fla.) Children's Mus., 1954-56, Volusia County Continuing Council on Edn., 1954-56; state bd. dirs. Am. Cancer Soc., 1954-61, v.p., crusade chmn. Volusia County unit, 1952-55. Recipient citation Am. Cancer Soc., 1952-55; various radio and newspaper awards; certificate of profl. acceptance NEA, 1966-67. Mem. Volusia County Fedn. Women's Clubs (legis. chmn. 1952-54), Fla. Fedn. Women's Clubs (chmn. radio and TV 1962-66), DAR, NEA, Nat. Council Tchr. of English, AAUW (chmn. edn. com. 1943-45, 60-62), Am. Inst. Parliamentarians (cert., parliamentarian Bradenton unit 1982-83), Gulfcoast Parliamentarians (pres. 1985-86), Nat. Assn. Parliamentarians (pres. Sarasota unit 1973-77, 79-82), Fla. Edn. Assn., Manatee County Edn. Assn., Fla. Assn. Parliamentarians, Gen. Fedn. Women's Clubs, DAR, Joan Ortiz Soc. (sr. pres. 1961-63), Leonardy Gaveliers (pres. 1972-73), Mu Omega Xi, Sigma Kappa. Democrat. So. Baptist. Clubs: Primrose Garden (founder, pres. 1953-55), Orange Blossom Garden (pres. 1962-63), DeLand Women's (pres. 1951-53), Woman's of Sarasota (pres. 1960-61), Fla. Fedn. Women's Clubs (dist. dir. 1960-63, parliamentarian dist. 1963-65). Coordinator Have Gavel, Will Travel panels for civic and social orgns., 1959-65. Home: 2540 Hibiscus St Sarasota FL 33579

MINNERATH, JANET EARNSHAW, librarian; b. South Gate, Calif., Nov. 24, 1938; s. Spencer Arnold Earnshaw and Helen Scott (Douglas) E.; m. Gary Ray Minnerath, June 5, 1965; B.A., UCLA, 1959, M.L.S., 1963. Acquisitions librarian Calif. State U.-Los Angeles, 1963-64; librarian, Rancho Los Amigos, Downey, Calif., 1964-69, Med. Coll. Va., Va. Commonwealth U., 1969-80, Alton Ochsner Med. Found., New Orleans, 1980-82; head librarian Tulsa Med. Coll., U. Okla., 1982—. Mem. Med. Library Assn., Okla. Library Assn., South Central Regional Group Med. Library Assn., Internat. Women Pilots Assn. Club: 99s. Home: 12941 E 28th Pl Tulsa OK 74134 Office: 2808 S Sheridan Rd Tulsa OK 74129

MINOR, WALTER NATHAN, physician; b. Port Huron, Mich., Sept. 19, 1931; s. Earl Nathaniel and Dorothy Marion (Westrick) M.; m. Virginia Belanger, July 14, 1951; children—Michelle, Michael, Dwight, David, Karen. B.S., Central Mich. U., 1963; M.D., U. Mich., 1973. Intern, Blodgett Meml. Hosp., Grand Rapids, Mich., 1973-74; gen. practice medicine, Fuquay Varina, N.C., 1974—; mem. staff Wake Hosp. System, Raleigh Community Hosp. Commr., City of Fuquay Varina, N.C., 1982—. Served to maj. U.S. Army,

1951-54. Mem. AMA. Roman Catholic. Home: 303 Pineburr St Fuquay Varina NC 27526 Office: 320 W Ransom St Fuquay Varina NC 27526

MINSHALL, DREXEL DAVID, retired manufacturing company executive; b. Bridgeport, Nebr., Nov. 1, 1917; s. Charles D. and Minnie C. (Nordell) M.; m. Betty Jane Tesdell, Feb. 12, 1938 (dec. June 1971); children—Drexel David, Carol J. Minshall Preston; m. Roylynn Hurlburt McAllister, Apr. 19, 1974. Student, Colo. U., 1934-38. Sales mgr. Gates Rubber Co., Denver, 1939-61; v.p. mktg. Perfect Circle Corp., Hagerstown, Ind., 1961-65; pres. Dana Parts Co. div. Dana Corp., Toledo, Ohio, 1965-67, group v.p., 1967-73, sr. group v.p., 1973-79; pres. Service Parts Worldwide, 1979-81; chmn. bd. Dana Western Hemisphere Trade Corp., Toledo, 1970-81; dir. Dana World Trade Corp., Ludwig Motors Corp., Corp. HZ, Caracas, Venezuela, Arcamsa, Rosario, Argentina, Brown Bros. Ltd., London, Eng.; pres. Double D Mktg. Corp. Bd. dirs. Community Chest, 1972-75; trustee Toledo Boys Club, 1967-82. Mem. Automotive Service Industries Assn. (past pres.), Automotive Hall of Fame (past chmn.), Automotive Acad., Nat. Inst. Automotive Service Excellence (bd. dirs. 1972-86, past chmn.), Nat. Automotive Parts Assn. (bd. dirs. mfrs. council 1971-81, past chmn.), Motor and Equipment Mfrs. Assn. (product v.p. 1972-75), Alpha Tau Omega. Clubs: Toledo, Inverness; Atlantis Golf (Fla.). Lodges: Masons, Shriners. Contbr. articles to profl. jours. Home: 620 Estates Way Atlantis FL 33462 Office: PO Box 3503 Lantana FL 33415

MINTICH, MARY ELLEN RINGELBERG, sculptor, art educator; b. Detroit; d. Clayton Harris and Mary Inez (Barber) Ringelberg; m. George Mintich; children—Barbara, Mark. A.B., Ind. U.; M.F.A., U. N.C.-Greensboro, 1971. Art tchr. Charlotte-Mecklenburg Schs., Charlotte, N.C., 1961-67; asst. prof. art Sacred Heart Coll., Belmont, N.C., 1967-73; prof. Winthrop Coll., Rock Hill, S.C., 1973—; juror Nat. Scholastic Art Awards, N.Y.C., 1973, Gt. Gulf Coast Festivals, Pensacola, Fla., 1977, 80, Nat. Endowment for Arts/Southeastern Ctr. for Contemporary Art Southeastern grant competition, Winston-Salem, N.C., 1982; mem. artist adv. com. Mint Mus. Art, Charlotte, 1977—. Spirit Sq. Art Ctr., Charlotte, 1977—; artist-in-residence, studies abroad program U. Ga., Italy, 1978. One-woman shows N.C. Dept. Cultural Resources, Raleigh, 1982, Southeastern Ctr. Contemporary Art, Winston-Salem, 1983, Sculpture Garden Waterworks Gallery, Salisbury, N.C., 1983, St. John's Mus., Wilmington, N.C., 1984, Converse Coll., Spartanburg, S.C., 1985, also numerous other one to three person shows; group shows include numerous colls., pub. bldgs. and corps.; represented in permanent collections: Everson Mus., Mint Mus. Art, N.C. Nat. Bank, N.C. Nat. Bank Radisson Plaza, Charlotte, St. John's Mus., R.J. Reynolds World Hdqrs., Waterworks Gallery, Winthrop Coll. Recipient Purchase award Mint Mus. Art, 1972, N.C. Artists Competition-R.J. Reynolds Industries, 1977, 1st place award Waterworks Gallery Sculpture Commn. Competition, Salisbury, 1984. Mem. Piedmont Craftsmen Inc. (bd. standards 1970-78, trustee 1973-79), Visual Arts Coalition (steering com. 1980-83), Tri-State Sculptors, Coll. Art Assn., Internat. Sculpture Ctr., Alpha Chi Omega. Methodist. Home: 515 Dogwood Ln PO Box 913 Belmont NC 28012 Office: Winthrop Coll Dept Art Oakland Ave Rock Hill SC 29733

MINTON, JERRY DAVIS, lawyer; b. Ft. Worth, Aug. 13, 1928; s. Robert Bruch and Anna Elizabeth (Davis) M.; m. Martha Drew Fields, Nov. 28, 1975; children—Marianne, Martha, John Morgan. B.B.A., U. Tex., Austin, 1949, J.D., 1960; grad. cert., Northwestern U., 1960. Bar: Tex. 1960. Vice pres., trust officer InterFirst Bank Ft. Worth, 1965-69, v.p., exec. trust officer, 1969-70, sr. v.p., exec. trust officer, 1970-80, exec. v.p., mgr. trust investment mgmt. group, 1980-82, vice chmn. bd., 1982—. Trustee All Saints Hosp.; trustee City of Ft. Worth Community Trust; mem. Ft. Worth Air Power Council; mem. exec. bd. Longhorn council Boy Scouts Am.; trustee Ft. C. of C. Found.; bd. dirs. Child Study Ctr. Served to capt. USAF, 1951-55, Tex. N.G., 1955-57. Decorated D.F.C., Air medal with three oak leaf clusters. Mem. State Bar Tex., Tarrant County Bar Assn., Tex. Bankers Assn. (chmn. trust div. 1975-76, Disting. Service award to Trust Industry in Tex. 1985), ABA, Newcomen Soc. N.Am., U.S. Yacht Racing Union, Sigma Iota Epsilon, Phi Delta Phi. Episcopalian. Clubs: River Crest Country (Ft. Worth); Ft. Worth, Ft. Worth Boat; Eagle Mountain Yacht; Breakfast (Ft. Worth). Lodges: Masons, Shriners. Home: 5404 El Dorado Dr Fort Worth TX 76107 Office: 2100 InterFirst Tower Fort Worth TX 76102

MINTON, PAUL DIXON, statistics educator, consultant; b. Dallas, Aug. 4, 1918; s. William M. and Evelyn (Croft) M.; m. Mary Frances Hickman, June 5, 1943; children—George R., Roland B. B.S., So. Meth. U., 1941, M.S., 1948; Ph.D., N.C. State U., 1957. Assoc. prof. math., dir. computing lab. So. Meth. U., Dallas, 1952-61, prof., chmn. dept. stats., 1961-72; dean Sch. Arts and Scis., Va. Commonwealth U., Richmond, 1972-79, dir. Inst. of Stats., 1979—; cons. stats. Author: (with R.J. Freund) Regression Methods: A Tool for Data Analysis, 1980. Fellow Am. Statis. Assn., Am. Soc. for Quality Control (cert. quality engr.), Tex. Acad. Scis.; mem. Inst. Math. Stats., Biometric Soc., Math. Assn. Am., Va. Acad. Sci. Democrat. Episcopalian. Avocations: classical music; voice. Home: 2626 Stratford Rd Richmond VA 23225 Office: Inst Statistics Va Commonwealth U 901 W Franklin St Richmond VA 23284

MINTZ, MORRIS FRED, plastic manufacturing company executive; b. New Orleans, Aug. 15, 1954; s. Saul Aron and Jean (Strauss) M.; m. Melinda Fleisher, June 12, 1977; children—Mark Alan, Clifford Strauss. B.S. in Commerce and Bus., U. Ala.-Tuscaloosa, 1976, M.A. in Fin., 1977. With F. Strauss & Son, Inc., New Orleans, 1978-79; chmn. bd., owner Fiberseal of South La., Inc., New Orleans, 1979; purchasing and personnel mgr. Sunbelt Mfg., Inc., Monroe, La., 1979-80, v.p., treas., 1980—. Mem. Citizens Review Com. of United Way, Monroe, 1981-82; bd. dirs. Monroe Symphony, 1983—; pres. United Jewish Charities of N.E. La., Monroe, 1982-83, Temple B'nai Israel, 1985-86; mem. United Jewish Appeal Nat. Young Leadership Cabinet, 1984—. Mem. Omicron Delta Epsilon, Zeta Beta Tau. Club: Bayou DeSiard Country. Lodge: Rotary. Avocations: golf; skiing. Office: Sunbelt Mfg Inc PO Box 7400 4611 Central Ave Monroe LA 71211

MINYARD, JAMES PATRICK, JR., chemist, educator; b. Greenwood, Miss., May 11, 1929; s. James Patrick and Mary Lou (Duke) M.; m. Mary Louise Whitesell, Aug. 11, 1956; children—Mary Susan, Thomas James, Barbara Lynn, Carol Ann, William Patrick. B.S. in Chemistry, Miss. State U., 1951, Ph.D., 1967; postgrad. Calif. Inst. Tech. (Gen. Edn. Bd. scholar), 1951-52. Field engr. Minyard Well Co., Belzoni, Miss., 1954-58; asst. chemist Miss. State Chem. Lab., 1958-59, chemist, 1959-64, state chemist, 1967—; research chemist Boll Weevil Research Lab., Agrl. Research Service, Dept. Agr., 1964-67; faculty Miss. State U., 1961—, prof. chemistry, 1967—; cons. legal firms, govtl. agys., FDA, EPA, TVA, pvt. industry. Editorial advisory com. Jour. Agrl. and Food Chemistry, 1977-83; editorial adv. bd. Environ. Toxicology and Chemisty 1981—. Contbr. to profl. jours. Served with U.S. Army, 1952-54. Fellow Assn. Ofcl. Analytical Chemists (chmn. editorial bd., dir. 1977-83, pres. 1982); mem. Am. Chem. Soc. (chmn. 1977; fellow div. agrochems. councilor, com. for environ. improvement 1983—), AAAS, Miss. Acad. Scis., Newcomen Soc. Am., Am. Oil Chemists Soc., Am. Assn. Feed Control Ofcls. (pres. 1975-76), Assn. Am. Fertilizer Control Ofcls., (bd. dirs. 1984—), ASTM, Assn. Am. Pesticide Control Ofcls., Assn. Food and Drug Ofcls., Soc. Environ. Toxicology and Chemistry, Sigma Xi, Phi Lambda Upsilon, Phi Kappa Phi. Democrat. Methodist. Home: Box 2198 Mississippi State MS 39762 Office: Miss State Chem Lab Box CR Mississippi State MS 39762

MIRABELLA, FRANK A., state education official; b. Tampa, Fla., Sept. 7, 1950; s. Charles Carmen and Jenny (Boromei) M.; m. Susan Gail Sutton, Mar. 16, 1974 (div. 1984); children—Kate Frances, Laura Ann. A.A., Hillborough Community Coll., 1971; B.A., Fla. State U., 1973. Administrv. asst. Fla. Dept. Edn., Tallahassee, 1974-75, exec. asst., 1975-79, chief cabinet aide, 1979—, pub. info. dir., 1983—. Mem. Fla. Pub. Relations Assn., Nat. Sch. Pub. Relations Assn., Sunshine State Sch. Pub. Relations Assn., Centurion Council. Democrat. Roman Catholic. Club: Governors (Tallahassee). Home: 111 Dawn Lauren Ln Tallahassee FL 32301-3435 Office: Fla Dept Edn PL08 The Capitol Tallahassee FL 32301

MIRABILE, THOMAS KEITH, lawyer; b. Lancaster, Ohio, May 11, 1948; s. Joseph Anthony and Marie Johanna (Reynolds) M.; m. Margaret Sue Hughes, Feb. 14, 1981; children—Michael, Adrian. B.A., No. Ill. U., 1972; M.A., Northeastern Ill. U., 1974; J.D., Oklahoma City U., 1975. Bar: Okla. 1976, Ill. 1977, U.S. Dist. Ct. (we. dist.) Okla. 1976, U.S. Ct. Appeals (10th cir.) 1980, U.S. Tax Ct. 1977, U.S. Supreme Ct. 1983, U.S. Ct. of Claims 1985. Prof. sociology Oklahoma City U., 1976-77; prof. bus. Central State U., Edmond, Okla., 1977-82; ptnr. firm Mirabile and Assocs. P.C., Oklahoma City, 1977—; bd. dirs. New World Sch., 1983—, Oklahoma City Counseling Ctr., 1977-81. Mem. Ill. Bar Assn., Okla. Trial Lawyers Assn., Okla. Bar Assn., Oklahoma County Bar Assn. Republican. Baptist. Home: 5912 N Billen St Oklahoma City OK 73112 Office: Mirabile and Assocs PC 5100 N Brookline Oklahoma City OK 73112

MIRACLE, HERBERT GARON, oil company executive; b. Shreveport, La., Jan. 16, 1928; s. John Herbert and Bernice Viva (Elza) M.; m. Ovie Kolkijkovind, Nov. 30, 1956; children—Lee Ann, John Garon. B.S., Centenary Coll. La., 1949. Various positions Mobil Oil Corp., Los Angeles, N.Y., Fairfax, Va., 1958-83, mgr. planning and tech. U.S. mktg. and refining div. Systems & Computer Services, 1983—. Served as sgt. USMC, 1950-52, Korea. Baptist. Home: 1726 Asoleado Ln Vienna VA 22180 Office: Mobil Oil Corp 3225 Gallows Rd Fairfax VA 22037

MIRACLE, WILLIAM DUNAVENT, college dean; b. Harlan, Ky., June 14, 1947; s. Andrew Wilbur Sr. and Theda (Dunavent) M.; m. Andrea Poletis, Aug. 26, 1972; children—Molly Dunavent, Andrew Ellington. A.B., Newberry Coll., S.C., 1969; M.Ed., U. Ga., 1970, Ed.D., 1977. Admissions counselor U. Ga.-Athens, 1970-71, alumni field rep., 1973-75; dir. alumni affairs Newberry Coll., S.C., 1975-77; dean of students Suomi Coll., Hancock, Mich., 1977-80; dean student devel. Bridgewater Coll., Va., 1980—. Dep. clk. City of Hancock, 1978-79. Recipient Cert. of Recognition, Family Ctr. Edn., 1978. Mem. Assn. Coll. and Univ. Housing Officers, Southeastern Assn. Housing Officers, Am. Personnel and Guidance Assn. Democrat. Mem. Ch. of Brethern. Home: Route 1 Box 15 Bridgewater VA 22812 Office: Bridgewater Coll Bridgewater VA 22812

MIRANDA, OSMUNDO AFONSO, educator; b. Araguary, Minas Gerais, Brazil, Dec. 23, 1926; came to U.S., 1956, naturalized, 1977; s. Olympio Afonso Miranda de and Laurinda Ferreira Nascimento; M.Div., Campinas Theol. Sem., Campinas S.P., Brazil, 1954; Th.M., Princeton Theol. Sem., 1957, Ph.D., 1962; children—Laurinisa, Georgeolimpio A., Cheyenne A. Ordained to ministry Presbyterian Ch., 1956; pastor Presbyn. chs., Brazil, U.S. 1955; prof. Bibl. criticism, dean Sem. Campinas (Brazil), 1962-65; instr. modern langs. Midwestern Coll., Denison, Iowa, 1966-68; prof. religion and philosophy Stillman Coll., Tuscaloosa, Ala., 1968—. Mem. Am. Acad. Religion, Soc. Bibl. Lit., So. Conf. Humanities, Am. Assn. for Advancement of Humanities, Soc. for Sci. Study of Religion, AAUP. Contbr. articles and book revs. to theol. jours. Home: 80 E Lake St Tuscaloosa AL 35405

MIRE, JOHN MORRIS, educational administrator; b. Slidell, La., Oct. 24, 1946; s. Julius Andrew and Ethel (Robert) M.; m. Kathleen Marie Minnaert, Nov. 19, 1966; children—Laura Ann, John Andrew. B.S., Southea. La. U., 1974, M.Ed., 1979. Cert. tchr., La. Tchr. sci. St. Tammany Parish Sch. Bd., La., 1974-79, 80, asst. prin., 1980-83, prin., 1983—. Exec. dir. Northlake Marriage Encounter, Slidell, 1976-77; supr. Fed. Youth Conservation Corps, Slidell, summer 1979. Served with USN, 1969-72. Recipient cert. of merit City of Slidell, 1979, Prin.'s award Boyet Jr. High Sch., Slidell, 1980-81. Mem. La. Assn. Educators, La. Assn. Sch. Execs., St. Tammany Parish Assn. Sch. Adminstrs., NEA. Democrat. Roman Catholic. Avocations: duck hunting; fishing; travel. Home: 103 Rooks Dr Slidell LA 70458 Office: St Tammany Parish Sch Bd 212 W 17th Ave Covington LA 70434

MIRKIN, GEORGE, petroleum geologist; b. Leningrad, USSR, Mar. 21, 1936; came to U.S., 1978, naturalized, 1985; s. Rakhmuel and Goda (Kunin) M.; m. Inessa Berlin, Mar. 14, 1958; children—Marina, Daniel. M.S., Mining Inst., Leningrad, 1959; Ph.D., Nat. Exploration Petroleum Research Inst., Leningrad, 1967; cert. Nat. Inst. Patent Law, Leningrad, 1977. Cert. geologist. Geologist Nat. Exploration Petroleum Research Inst., 1959-67, research assoc., 1967-70, research adv., 1970-78; research specilist Exxon Prodn. Research Co., Houston, 1979—; cons. U. Moscow, 1976-78, Northwest Regional Dept. Mingeo, USSR, Leningrad, 1976-78, Sci. Dept. Mingeo USSR, Moscow, 1973. Author: Morphostructural Methods of Studying Oil-Bearing Regions, 1968; Instruction of Optical Processing of Geological Data, 1977. Contbr. articles to profl. jours. Patentee in field. Pres.'s Assn. Immigrants from USSR, Houston, 1979-80; vice chmn. com. Houstonian for Free Emigration from Soviet Union, 1983—. Recipient honor rank Inventor of USSR, State Com. Inventions and Discovering USSR, 1975; honor diploma All Union Exhbn. Achievements in Sci. and Tehcnique, 1974. Mem. Am. Assn. Petroleum Geologists. Avocations: painting; sports. Home: 5514 Yarwell Houston TX 77096 Office: Exxon Prodn Research Co PO Box 2189 Houston TX 77001

MIRO-MONTILLA, ANTONIO RAFAEL, architect, educator; b. San Juan, P.R., Dec. 18, 1937; s. Rafael Miro-Sojo and Enriqueta Montilla; B.Arch., U. Notre Dame, 1961; m. Sonia Acevedo Morales, Dec. 16, 1984; children—Mercedes, Antonio, Laura. Architect, P.R. Bldg. Authority, 1961-64; assoc. Amaral & Morales, Architects, San Juan, 1964-69; exec. dir. P.R. Bldgs. Authority, San Juan, 1969-71; prof. architecture U. P.R., Rio Piedras, 1968—, dean Sch. Architecture, 1971-78, chancellor Rio Piedras campus, 1978-85. Mem. Colegio de Arquitectos de P.R. (Gold medal 1979); hon. mem. Instituto de Arquitectos de Brasil, Sociedad de Arquitectos Mexicanos, Sociedad Bolivariana de Arquitectos. Roman Catholic. Various archtl. works in edn., office bldgs., recreation and residential architecture, including: Miro residence, Rio Piedras (Urke Gold Medal). Office: Sch Architecture U PR Rio Piedras Campus San Juan PR 00931

MISCHER, WALTER M., diversified company executive, bank holding company executive; b. 1923; m. With Stone & Webster, 1943-46; chmn. bd. Allied Bancshares Inc.; chmn. bd., chief exec. officer Mischer Corp., Houston, 19—. Office: Mischer Corp 2727 N Loop West Houston TX 77008*

MISH, ANNE EVERETT, health, physical education and horsemanship educator; college adminstrator; b. Newsoms, Va., Apr. 22, 1926; d. Caleb Roy and Thelma Lee (Eley) Everett; m. Robert Warren Howe Mish, Aug. 9, 1952; children—Robert Warren Howe III, Everett Hall. B.S., Mary Washington Coll., 1947; M.Ed., U. Va., 1968. Div. chmn. health, phys. edn. and horsemanship So. Sem. Jr. Coll., Buena Vista, Va., 1947—. Advisor, mem. steering com. Va. Horse Ctr., Lexington, 1984-85. Mem. Va. Horse Show Assn. (bd. dirs.), Am. Assn. Health, Phys. Edn., Recreation and Dance, Va. Assn. Health, Phys. Edn., Recreation and Dance (chmn. riding com.). Republican. Presbyterian. Club: Rockbridge Hunt; Farmington Hunt. Avocations: riding; showing; training and breeding horses. Home: PO Box 887 Route 5 Lexington VA 24450 Office: So Sem Jr Coll Burna Vista VA 24416

MISKOVSKY, GEORGE, lawyer, former state senator; b. Oklahoma City, Feb. 13, 1910; s. Frank and Mary (Bourek) M.; J.D., U. Okla., 1936; m. Nelly Oleta Donahue, Dec. 30, 1932; children—George, Gary, Grover, Gail Marie. Admitted to Okla. bar, 1936, since practiced in Oklahoma City; sr. mem., head firm Miskovsky, Sullivan & Taylor, Oklahoma City; pub. defender Oklahoma City, 1936; county atty. Oklahoma County, 1943-44; mem. Okla. Ho. of Reps., 1939-42; mem. Okla. Senate, 1950-60. Pres. Economy Square, Inc. and Penn 74 Mall Inc. Shopping Centers. Mem. ABA, Okla. Bar Assn., Oklahoma City Bar Assn., Am. Judicature Soc., C. of C., Am., Okla. trial lawyers assns., U. Okla. Law Assn., Order of Coif, Pi Kappa Alpha, Phi Alpha Delta. Democrat. Episcopalian. Clubs: Lions, Oklahoma City Golf and Country, Oklahoma City Press, Bailli Okla. Confrerie de la Chaine des Rotisseurs, Masons, Shriners. Home: 1511 Drury Ln Oklahoma City OK 73116 Office: 302 Hightower Bldg Oklahoma City OK 73102

MISSIMER, THOMAS MICHAEL, geologist; b. Lancaster, Pa., Mar. 10, 1950; s. Jacob M. and Lorraine L. (Bilodeau) M.; A.B. in Geology, Franklin and Marshall Coll., 1972; M.S. in Geology, Fla. State U., 1973. Hydrologist, U.S. Geol. Survey, Ft. Myers, Fla., 1973-75; research asso. sedimentology U. Miami, Coral Cables, Fla., 1975-76; pres. Missimer & Assocs., Inc., Cape Coral, Fla., 1976—. Mem. citizens planning adv. com. Bd. Lee County (Fla.), 1981-82, chmn., 1982-83. Registered profl. geologist, Ga., Ind. Mem. Geol. Soc. Am., Am. Inst. Profl. Geologists (cert. profl. geol. scientist), Am. Water Resources Assn., Am. Water Works Assn., AAAS, Am. Inst. Hydrology (cert. profl. hydrologist), Fla. Acad. Scis. (chmn. earth and planetary sci. sect. 1973-74), Southeastern Geol. Soc. Republican. Contbr. hydrogeol. studies of Southeastern U.S. to sci. jours. Home: 4919 SW 8th Place Cape Coral FL 33914 Office: 428 Pine Island Rd Rt 8 Box 625-D Cape Coral FL 33909

MITCHAM, BOB ANDERSON, lawyer; b. Atlanta, July 16, 1933; s. George Anderson and Pearl (Bing) M.; m. Lupe M. Vazquez, Dec. 6, 1969; children—Robert Anderson, Tamara Lynn, Matthew Vazquez. B.S., Fla. So. Coll., Lakeland, 1959; J.D., Stetson U., 1962. Bar: Fla. 1963, U.S. Dist. Ct. (mid. dist.) Fla. 1963, U.S. Ct. Apls. (5th cir.) 1965, U.S. Ct. Apls. (11th cir.) 1983. Ptnr., Mitcham & Honig, Tampa, Fla., 1963-66, Mitcham. Leon & Guito, Tampa, 1966-68; sole practice, Tampa, 1968-82; ptnr. Mitcham, Weed & Barbas, Tampa, 1982—; lectr. Oxford U., Eng., 1981. Contbr. articles to profl. jours. Pres. Young Democrats of Fla., Tampa, 1968. Served with USAF, 1952-59. Perry Nicholas Trial scholar, 1961. Mem. Criminal Def. Lawyers of Hillsborough County (pres. 1981-82), Hillsborough County Bar Assn. (dir. 1981-85), Ybor City C. of C. (dir. 1981-84, chmn. Super Bowl XVIII). Democrat. Mem. Ch. of God. Office: Mitcham Weed Barbas Allen & Morgan 1509 E 8th Ave Tampa FL 33605

MITCHELHILL, JAMES MOFFAT, engineering consultant; b. St. Joseph, Mo., Aug. 11, 1912; s. William and Jeannette (Ambrose) M.; B.S., Northwestern U., 1934, C.E., 1935; m. Maurine Hutchason, Jan. 9, 1937 (div. 1962); children—Janis Maurine Mitchelhill Johnson, Jeri Ann Mitchelhill Riney; m. 2d, Alicia Beuchat, 1982; Engring. dept. C., M., St. P. & P.R.R. Co., Chgo. and Miles City, Mont., 1935-45; asst. mgr. Ponce & Guayama R.R. Co., Aguirre, P.R., 1945-51, v.p., gen. mgr., 1969-70; mgr. Central Cortada, Santa Isabel, P.R., 1951-54; r.r. supt. Braden Copper Co., Rancagua, Chile, 1954-63; staff engr. Coverdale & Colpitts, N.Y.C., 1963-64; asst. to exec. v.p. Central Aguirre Sugar Co., 1964-67; v.p., gen. mgr. Coddea, Inc., Dominican Republicn, 1967-68; asst. to gen. mgr. Land Adminstrn. of P.R., La Nueva Central Aguirre, 1970-71, for Centrals Aguirre Lafayette and Mercedita, 1971-72; asst. to gen. mgr. Corporacion Azucarera de P.R., 1973-76, asst. to exec. dir., 1977-79, asst. exec. dir. for environ., 1979-82; engring. cons., 1982—; Kendall County engr., 1985—. Registered profl. engr., Mont., P.R., Tex. Fellow ASCE; mem. Nat. Soc. Profl. Engrs., Am. Ry. Engring. Assn., Colegio de Ingenieros y Agrimensores de P.R., Sigma Xi, Tau Beta Pi, Explorers Club. Clubs: Explorers, Travellers Century. Lodge: Rotary. Home: PO Box 506 Boerne TX 78006 Office: 840 E Adler Boerne TX 78006

MITCHELL, ANITA KAY, public relations executive; b. Alliance, Ohio, July 25, 1941; d. William Edward and Maxine Anita (Salisbury) Orr; m. Edgar D. Mitchell, Nov. 23, 1973; children by previous marriage—Kimberly Anne, Paul, Mary Beth. Student U. N.C., 1959. Promotions dir., on-air anchor Gannett Radio, Cocoa Fla., 1966-67; continuity dir. Cox Broadcasting Co., Orlando, Fla., 1968-69; co-campaign mgr. Congressman Lou Frey, 1968; conv. coordinator Walt Disney World, 1969-71; dir. pub. relations Am. Film Inst., Beverly Hills, Calif., 1971-72; founder, dir. Inst. Noetic Scis., Menlo Park, Calif., 1972-75; prin. Anita Mitchell Assocs., West Palm Beach, Fla., 1975—. Recipient 10 Addy awards Advt. Fedn. Palm Beaches. Mem. Exec. Women of Palm Beaches, C. of C. of Palm Beaches, Home Builders and Contractors Assn., Forum of Palm Beaches (v.p.). Republican. Presbyterian. Clubs: Citrus (Orlando); Poinciana, Palm Beach Yacht, Charter of Palm Beach County (founding).

MITCHELL, BURLEY BAYARD, JR., state supreme court justice; b. Oxford, N.C., Dec. 15, 1940; s. Burley Bayard and Dorothy Ford (Champion) M.; m. Mary Lou Willett, Aug. 3, 1962; children—David Bayard, Catherine Morris. B.A., N.C. State U.-Raleigh, 1966; J.D., U. N.C.-Chapel Hill, 1969. Bar: N.C. 1969, U.S. Supreme Ct. 1972. Asst. atty. gen. State of N.C., Raleigh, 1969-73, dist. atty., 1973-77, judge Ct. Appeals, 1977-79, sec. of crime control and pub. safety, 1979-82; justice N.C. Supreme Ct., 1982—; mem. N.C. Cts. Commn., Raleigh, 1983—; adj. prof. N.C. State U., 1966—. Chmn. United Fund Drive, Raleigh, 1979. Served with U.S. Navy, 1958-62. Recipient Freedom Guard award, 1975; Citizen's Commendation award N.C. N.G., 1982. Mem. Delta Theta Phi. Democrat. Methodist. Lodge: Kiwanis (Raleigh). Office: Supreme Ct NC PO Box 1841 Raleigh NC 27602

MITCHELL, CYNTHIA ANN, nurse; b. Pitts., Nov. 2, 1941; d. Albert Joseph and Gertrude Genieve (Clarke) Ladesic; m. Joseph Neal Mitchell, May 7, 1971; (div. 1979). Diploma, St. Francis Sch. Nursing, Pitts., 1962; B.S. in Nursing, U. Central Ark., Conway, 1981; M.S. in Nursing, U. Tex., 1983. Staff nurse surg. unit VA Hosp., Spokane, Wash., 1971-72; charge nurse obstetrics Loring (Maine) AFB Hosp., 1974-76; staff nurse ICU, Baptist Med. System, Little Rock, 1979-80; inservice dir. Jackson County Meml. Hosp., Aitus, Okla., 1981; teaching asst. U. Tex., Austin, 1983; staff devel. coordinator Girling Health Care Inc., Austin, 1984—. Vol. ARC, Zaragosa AFB Spain, 1977. Served to 1st lt. USAF, 1965-67. Mem. Am. Nurses Assn., Tex. Nurses Assn., Sigma Theta Tau.

MITCHELL, DAVID BARRY, psychology educator; b. Ft. Worth, Apr. 27, 1952; s. Howard Barry and Laura Ethel (Tollison) M.; m. Nancy Elaine Rosenwald, May 27, 1973 (div. Dec. 1980); m. 2d, Deborah Gail Garfin, July 5, 1982; 1 dau., Lillian Garfin. B.A., Furman U., 1976; M.A., Wake Forest U., 1978; Ph.D., U. Minn., 1982. Lectr. psychology Macalester Coll., 1980-82; postdoctoral fellow Duke U. Med. Ctr., Durham, N.C., 1982-83; asst. prof. psychology So. Meth. U., Dallas, 1983—. Contbr. articles to profl. jours. Gordon Allport scholar Furman U., 1975-76; NIMH grantee, 1978-80, 81-82. Mem. Am. Psychol. Assn., Gerontol. Soc. Am., Southeastern Psychol. Assn., Behavioral and Brain Scis. (assoc.), The Psychonomic Soc. (assoc.). Democrat. Jewish. Avocations: music, carpentry, cycling. Office: So Meth Univ Dept Psychology Dallas TX 75275

MITCHELL, GARY EARL, physicist, educator; b. Louisville, July 5, 1935; s. Earl Raymond and Delma Kathlene (Lockard) M.; m. Carolyn Fey Stutz, Aug. 4, 1957; children—Scott Frederick, Karen Lee. B.S., U. Louisville, 1956; M.A., Duke U., 1958; Ph.D., Fla. State U., 1962. Research assoc. Columbia U., N.Y.C., 1962-64, asst. prof., 1964-68; assoc. prof. N.C. State U., Raleigh, 1968-74, prof. physics, 1974—, assoc. head physics dept., 1982—. Contbr. numerous articles to sci. publs. Sr. scientist Alexander Von Humboldt Found., Bonn, Fed. Republic Germany, 1975. Fellow Am. Phys. Soc.; mem. numerous sci. assns. Avocation: history. Home: 2913 Harriman Ave Durham NC 27705 Office: Dept of Physics NC State U Box 8202 Raleigh NC 27695

MITCHELL, HAROLD DEE, architect; b. Floydada, Tex., July 9, 1924; s. A.J. and Lena May (Stagner) M.; B.Arch., Tex. Tech. U., Lubbock, 1952; m. Dorothy Jane Lucas, May 1, 1954; children—Steven Craig, Kelly Diane. Owner, prin. Harold Mitchell & Assos., Amarillo, Tex., 1959-85; ptnr. Mitchell/Sims, Architects, Amarillo, 1985—. Chmn. Amarillo Planning and Zoning Commn., 1968, Community Devel. Amarillo, 1974; mem. Amarillo Bldg. Bd. Appeal, Amarillo Airport Zoning Bd. Served with USN, 1942-46. Mem. AIA (pres. Amarillo chpt. 1972), Constrn. Specification Inst. (pres. Amarillo chpt. 1975), Am. Bus. Club (pres. elect Amarillo chpt. 1979), Amarillo Exec. Assn. (pres. 1978-79). Home: 1502 S Alabama St Amarillo TX 79102 Office: 1408 S Jefferson St Amarillo TX 79101

MITCHELL, HAROLD ELBERT, technical college administrator; b. Ahoskie, N.C., Sept. 15, 1938; s. Wayland Junius and Cleatrice (Dickerson) M.; m. Doretha Winston, Apr. 23, 1963; children—Glenn JaVonne, Darrin Craig. B.S., N.C. Agrl. and Tech. State U., 1959; M.S., Ph.D., N.C. State U., 1978. Cert. tchr., N.C. Tchr., Hartford County Schs., Winton, N.C., 1959-71; instr., asst. dean gen. studies Roanoke-Chowan Tech. Coll., Ahoskie, N.C., 1971—. Ford Found. fellow, 1974-75; recipient Acad. Yr. Inst. award NSF, 1966-67. Mem. AAUP. Democrat. Baptist. Club: Kappa Alpha Psi. Avocations: instrumental music; choral music. Home: Rt 3 Box 1250 Ahoskie NC 27910 Office: Dept Gen Edn Roanoke Chowan Tech Coll Rt 2 Box 46A Ahoskie NC 27910

MITCHELL, HENRY HEYWOOD, clergyman; b. Columbus, Ohio, Sept. 10, 1919; s. Orlando Washington and Bertha (Estis) M.; m. Ella Muriel Pearson, Aug. 12, 1944; children—Henry Heywood IV (dec. Apr. 1972), Muriel M., Elizabeth Ann, Kenneth R. B.A. cum laude, Lincoln U., 1941; B.D., Union Theol. Sem., 1944; M.A., Calif. State U.-Fresno, 1966; Th.D., Sch. Theology at Claremont, 1973. Ordained to ministry Baptist Ch., 1944. Asst. minister Concord Ch., Bklyn., 1942-44; dir. religions activities, instr. English, N.C. Central U., Durham, 1944-45; exec. staff No. Calif. Bapt. Conv., Oakland, 1945-59; pastor Second Ch., Fresno, 1959-66, Calvary Bapt. Ch., Santa Monica, Calif., 1966-69; Martin Luther King Meml. prof. black ch. studies Colgate Rochester Div. Sch., N.Y., 1969-74; dir. Ecumenical Ctr. for Black Ch. Studies, Los Angeles, 1974-82; adj. prof. Sch. Theology at Claremont, Calif., 1974-82, Fuller Theol. Sem., Pasadena, Calif., 1974-82; adj. prof. Am. Bapt. Sem. of West, Berkeley, Calif., 1974-82, U. LaVerne, Calif., 1974-82; prof.

religion and pan-African studies Calif. State U.-Northridge, 1981-82; mem. spl. pastoral ministries staff 2d Bapt. Ch., Los Angeles, 1978-82; dean, prof. history and homiletics Sch. Theology, Va. Union U., 1982—; Lyman Beecher lectr. Div. Sch., Yale U., New Haven, 1974; cons. to World Council Chs., London, 1969; ind. cons. on human relations and theol. edn. for blacks, 1968—. Author: Black Preaching, 1970, 2d edit., 1979; Black Belief, 1975; The Recovery of Preaching, 1977. Contbr. articles to profl. jours. Trustee U. Redlands. Mem. Soc. for Study Black Religion, Nat. Com. for Black Churchmen, Martin Luther King Fellows, Inc., Phi Kappa Epsilon, Phi Kappa Phi. Office: Sch Theology Va Union U 1601 W Leigh St Richmond VA 23220

MITCHELL, JAMES ROBERT, accountant, investment advisor; b. Shreveport, La., Sept. 30, 1942; s. Robert A. and Frances Helen (McCarty) M.; m. Anne Marguerite Krison, Mar. 15, 1969; children—James Barrett, Marguerite Ladell. B.S. magna cum laude, Centenary Coll. La., 1964; M.B.A., U. Ala.-Tuscaloosa, 1967. C.P.A., La. Traffic mgr. So. Bell Telephone Co., Shreveport, 1965-66; account exec. Merrill Lynch, Pierce, Fenner & Smith, Shreveport, 1968-71; sr. mgmt. cons. Peat, Marwick, Mitchell & Co., Houston, 1971-73, ptnr.-in-charge tax dept., Shreveport, 1975—; asst. v.p. Querbest & Bourquin, Inc., Shreveport, 1973-75; part-time instr. acctg. La. State U.-Shreveport; speaker on tax related topics. Guest columnist series of articles Shreveport Jour., 1981. Advisor Jr. Achievement, 1966; del. Leadership Shreveport, 1979; trustee Centenary Coll., 1979, 80; mem. adv. bd. Vols. of Am., pres., 1981; mem. Holiday-in-Dixie Ambassadors, 1979—; mem. budget com. United Way, 1981; bd. dirs. Downtown Shreveport Unltd., 1981-83, Goodwill Industries, 1982—; mem. Assn. Children with Learning Disabilities, 1982—. Served with USAR, 1964-70. Grad. sch. scholar U. Ala., 1966. Mem. Am. Inst. C.P.A.s, La. Soc. C.P.A.s, Ark-La-Tex. Tax Inst. (dir. 1980-83), Alumni Assn. Centenary Coll. (pres. 1979-80), Shreveport C. of C. (legis. affairs task force 1981), Omicron Delta Kappa, Beta Gamma Sigma, Kappa Sigma Alumni. Democrat. Episcopalian. Clubs: Shreveport Country, Petroleum, Cambridge, Cotillion (Shreveport). Home: 4827 Crescent Dr Shreveport LA 71106 Office: 1400 American Tower Shreveport LA 71101

MITCHELL, JAN EHART, children's librarian; b. Miami, Fla., Sept. 3, 1945; d. William McMein Ehart and Rosalie (Boswell) Dorrn; m. James Stephen Mitchell, Dec. 30, 1964; children—Sara Kate, Alisa Jan, Andrew John McMein. A.A., Manatee Jr. Coll., Bradenton, Fla., 1981; B.A. in English Lit., U. South Fla., Sarasota, 1984, M.A. in Library Sci., 1986. Tchr. Julie Rohr Acad., Sarasota, 1979-81, librarian, 1981—. Women's Exchange Sarasota scholar, 1982. Mem. ALA, Fla. Library Assn., Fla. Assn. Media Educators, Honor Soc. Coll. Arts and Letters, Phi Kappa Phi. Roman Catholic. Home: 3326 Spainwood Dr Sarasota FL 33582 Office: Julie Rohr Acad 4466 Fruitville Rd Sarasota FL 33582

MITCHELL, JERE HOLLOWAY, physiologist, medical educator, researcher, and administrator; b. Longview, Tex., Oct. 17, 1928; s. William Holloway and Dorothea (Turner) M.; m. Pamela Battey, Oct. 1, 1960; children—Wendy Keener, Laurie Clemens, Amy Dewing. B.S., Va. Mil. Inst., 1950; M.D., Southwestern Med. Sch., 1954. Intern Parkland Meml. Hosp., Dallas, 1954-55, resident in internal medicine, 1955-56; asst. prof. medicine and physiology U. Tex. Health Sci. Ctr., Dallas, 1962-66, dir. Weinberger Lab. for Cardiopulmonary Research, 1966—, assoc. prof., 1966-69, prof., 1969—, dir. Harry S. Moss Heart Ctr., 1976—, holder Frank M. Ryburn Jr. chair in heart research, 1982—. Pres. Tex. affiliate Am. Heart Assn., 1983-84, established investigator, 1962-67. Recipient Career Devel. award USPHS, 1968-73; recipient Citation award Am. Coll. Sports Medicine, 1983. Fellow Am. Coll. Cardiology (young investigator award 1961, Donald W. Seldin research award 1978); mem. Assn. Am. Physicians, Am. Soc. Clin. Investigation (emeritus), Am. Physiol. Soc., Am. Fed. Clin. Research (emeritus). Office: U Tex Health Sci Center at Dallas Southwestern Med Sch 5323 Harry Hines Blvd Dallas TX 75235

MITCHELL, JERRY DON, psychologist; b. Coleman, Tex., Dec. 24, 1940; s. Wilbur Robert and Mary Lena (Moore) M.; m. Margaret Cloeane Walker, May 15, 1971; children—Melissa Lynn, John Brent. B.A., Howard Payne Coll., 1963; M.Ed., Sul Ross State U., 1970, M.B.A., 1979; Ed.D., East Tex. State U., 1974. Lic. psychologist, Tex. Psychologist, Big Spring State Hosp., Tex., 1975-76; clin. dir. Davis Mountain Achievement Ctr., Tex., 1976-78; adj. asst. prof. Sul Ross State U., 1978-81; dir. psychology Rusk State Hosp., Tex., 1981—; cons. in field. Bd. dirs. High Frontier Ctr., Ft. Davis, Tex., 1981—. Served to capt. U.S. Army, 1966-69, Vietnam. Mem. Am. Assn. Counseling and Devel., Am. Psychol. Assn., Nat. Acad. Neuropsychologists. Democrat. Baptist. Lodges: Masons, Kiwanis. Home: Rt 4 Box 345A Rusk TX 75785 Office: Rusk State Hosp Box 318 Rusk TX 75785

MITCHELL, JOHN GERALD, educational administrator; b. Cadiz, Ky., Oct. 8, 1936; s. John Carter and Mary Cicero (Terrell) M.; m. Barbara Jane Hayes, Dec. 18, 1960; children—David Terrell, Angela Carol. A.A., Bethel Coll., Hopkinsville, Ky., 1960; B.A. in English Edn., Western Ky. U., 1962; B.D., So. Bapt. Theol. Sem., 1966, Ph.D. in Bibl. Lang., 1970; Ph.D. in Edn. Leadership, Vanderbilt U., 1984. Cert. secondary sch. tchr., Ky. Dir. admissions Bethel Coll., 1963; vocat. guidance cons. Bapt. Sunday Sch. Bd., Nashville, 1970-72; pres., exec. dir. Edn. Corp. Am., Nashville, 1972-76; acad. dean Truett McConnell Coll., Cleve., 1976-80; asst. acad. v.p. Wayland Bapt. U., Plainview, Tex., 1982—; seminar leader U. Geneva, 1975, 76; workshop leader Harris Tchrs. Coll., St. Louis, 1975; cons. U. Calif.-Riverside, 1975. Co-author: The Church Covenant, 1971. Contbr. articles to profl. publs. Mem. exec. com. Ga. Mountain Program on Aging, Cleveland, Ga., 1977-78; mem. edml. adv. com. U.S. Congressman Edward Jenkins, Ga., 1978-79; mem. careers com. N.Ga. Tech. Sch., Clarkesville, 1979. Served with U.S. Army, 1956-58. Mem. Plainview C. of C. (gov. affairs com. 1985), World Future Soc., Am. Conf. Acad. Deans, Am. Assn. Sch. Adminstrs., Tex. Edn. Assn., Am. Assn. for Higher Edn. Democrat. Baptist. Clubs: Internat. Relations Bethel Coll. (pres. 1958-59), Grad. So. Bapt. Theol. Sem. (v.p. 1968-69). Avocations: flying; fishing; camping; gardening. Home: 1407 Aramillo St Plainview TX 79072 Office: Wayland Bapt U 1900 W 7th St Plainview TX 79072

MITCHELL, JOSEPH BRADY, mil. historian, author; b. Ft. Leavenworth, Kans., Sept. 25, 1915; s. William A. and Margery (Brady) M.; B.S., U.S. Mil. Acad., 1937; m. Vivienne French Brown, Aug. 20, 1938; children—Sherwood N., J. Bradford. Mem. ops. div. War Dept. Gen. Staff, 1945-49; chief historian Am. Battle Monuments Commn., 1950-61, hist. cons., 1969—; curator Ft. Ward Mus. and Park, Alexandria, Va., 1964-77. Served from 2d lt. to lt. col., 5th inf. div., AUS, 1937-45; ETO. Decorated Bronze Star; recipient Am. Revolutionary Round Table prize for best book in field, 1962. Mem. Alexandria Hist. Soc. (pres. 1981-83), Soc. of Cin., Civil War Round Table Alexandria (past pres., Joseph B. Mitchell award named in honor of biographee), Civil War Round Table D.C. (past pres., Bruce Catton award), Am. Revolution Round Table D.C. (past pres.), SCV (comdr.-in-chief 1980-82, chmn. nat. affairs com. 1982—). Episcopalian. Author: Decisive Battles of the Civil War, 1955; Decisive Battles of the American Revolution, 1962; Twenty Decisive Battles of the World, 1964; Discipline and Bayonets, 1967; The Badge of Gallantry, 1968; Military Leaders in the Civil War, 1972; contbr. articles to encys. and mags. Home: 625 Pommander Walk Alexandria VA 22314

MITCHELL, LARRY DELL, mechanical engineering educator, consultant; b. Royal Oak, Mich., Aug. 7, 1938; s. Basil Burton and Lucille (Brown) M.; m. Leanne Avis Dyke, Nov. 18, 1967; children—Scott Alan, Kirk Dana. B.S. in Mech. Engring., U. Mich., 1961, M.S., 1962, Ph.D., 1965. Registered profl. engr., Del. Sr. research engr. DuPont Co., Wilmington, Del., 1965-71; assoc. prof. mech. engring. Va. Poly. Inst. and State U., Blacksburg, 1971-78, prof., 1978—; cons. IBM, Am. Electric Power, Allied Chem. Co. Recipient Sporn award for Teaching Excellence Va. Poly. Inst. & State U., 1972. Mem. ASME, Soc. Automotive Engrs. (recipient Colwell award 1983), Nat. Soc. Profl. Engrs., Acoustical Soc. Am., Soc. Exptl. Mechanics. Presbyterian. Club: Square Dance (Blacksburg). Author: (with J.E. Shigley) Mechanical Engineering Design, 1983; contbr. articles to profl. jours. Office: Dept Mech Engring Va Poly Inst & State U Randolph Hall Blacksburg VA 24061

MITCHELL, MARK W., chemist, microbiologist; b. Ringgold, La., Nov. 22, 1952; s. Robert, Jr. and Ruth (Woodard) M.; m. Virginia L. Mitchell, June 12, 1982; 1 child, Meghan Marie. B.S. in Microbiology, Zoology and Chemistry, Northwestern State U., 1976. Quality control supr. Aeropres Corp., Shreveport, La., 1976-78, dir. mfg. and quality control, 1978-82, ops. mgr., 1982—; mem. Hazardous Material Adv. Council. Mem. Am. Chem. Soc., ASTM. Democrat. Methodist. Home: PO Box 297 Hwy 7 S Sibley LA 71033 Office: Aeropres Corp PO Box 198 Hwy 7 S Sibley LA 71073

MITCHELL, MARLYS MARIE, occupational therapy educator; b. Hamburg, Minn., Feb. 6, 1931; d. Ernst Fredrick and Lydia Martha (Weller) Panning; m. Earl Nelson Mitchell, July 23, 1955. B.S. in Occupational Therapy, U. Minn., 1955; M.S. in Elem. and Spl. Edn., U. N.D., 1964; Ph.D. in Special Edn., U. N.C., 1968. Tchr. St. John's Luth. Sch., Glencoe, Minn., 1949-51; occupational therapist St. John's Hosp., St. Paul, 1955-58; tchr. spl. edn. Grand Forks Schs., N.D., 1959-62, Chapel Hill Schs., N.C., 1963-66; asst. prof., then prof. occupational therapy U. N.C., Chapel Hill, 1968—, dir. 1976-84; cons. in field. Contbr. articles to profl. jours. Chmn. bldg. com. Grace Luth. Ch., Durham, N.C., 1984—. Recipient Sanford award State of N.C., 1967; Peabody award U. N.C. Sch. Edn., 1972. Fellow Am. Occupational Therapy Assn., 1982. Mem. Council for Exceptional Children, Am. Occupational Therapy Assn. (chmn. communications com. 1981-83, chmn. program adv. com. 1985—), AAUP, Pi Lambda Theta, AAUW (chmn. pub. relations com. 1963-66). Lutheran. Avocations: hiking; sewing; vineyard. Home: 220 Glenhill Ln Chapel Hill NC 27514 Office: U NC Occupational Therapy Div Med Sch Wing E 222 H Chapel Hill NC 27514

MITCHELL, MARY CONNELL, department store executive; b. Cherry Ridge, La., July 25, 1934; d. W.C. and Ora Mae (Henderson) Webb; student St. Louis Bus. Coll., 1961; m. Bill H. Mitchell, May 15, 1966. Women's dir., hostess Noon Show, Sta. KTHV-TV, Little Rock, 1964-73; v.p. account service Holland & Assos., advt. agy., Little Rock, 1973-76; dir. corp. broadcast advt. Dillard Dept. Stores, Inc., Little Rock, 1973—. Active United Fund, Ark. Heart Assn.; bd. dirs. Better Bus. Bur. Ark. Mem. Nat. Sales and Mktg. Execs. Assn., Little Rock Sales and Mktg. Execs. Assn., Ark. Advt. Assn., Internat. Platform Assn. Office: Dillard Dept Stores Inc 900 W Capitol St Room 214 Little Rock AR 72203

MITCHELL, MARY HAMILTON, artist; b. Clovis, N.Mex., July 7, 1918; d. Carl and Margueriete Mildred (Morrison) Hamilton; student Amarillo Coll., 1937-38; m. John Zinn Mitchell, Feb. 24, 1940; 1 dau., Kayla Jo Mitchell Palmer. With Bur. of Reclamation, Amarillo, Tex., 1962-65; founder, exec. officer Artists Studio, Inc., Amarillo, 1965—; co-owner The Gallery, 1969-75; one man shows: Gallery III, Dosowood Gallery, Ruidoso, N.Mex., XIT Mus., Dalhart, Tex., Lee Babb Gallery, Tulsa, 1965, House of Pictures, Lubbock, Tex., 1966-69, No-Mans Land Hist. Mus., Panhandle State Coll., Goodwell, Okla., 1978; group shows include: Finley Cultural Center, Sherman, Tex., Hill County Found. Center, Ingram, Tex., St. Mary's Univ. Center, San Antonio, U. Corpus Christi, U. Tex., Dallas, McMurray Coll., Ryan Fine Arts Center, Abilene; represented in permanent collections: St. Anthonys Hosp., High Plains Baptist Hosp., Amarillo Psychiat. Hosp., Whitlow Lee Bldg., Happy, Tex., Union County News, Clayton, N.Mex. Mem. Internat. Soc. Artists, Internat. Platform Assn., Nat. League Am. Pen Women, Tex. Fine Arts Assn., Panhandle Art Assn., Amarillo C. of C., Epsilon Sigma Alpha. Democrat. Baptist. Home and office: 1813 Mustang St Amarillo TX 79102

MITCHELL, MARY LEE CLACK, media coordinator; b. Henderson, N.C., Apr. 12 1930; d. James and Carrie Etta (Blackwell) Clack; m. James Melvin Mitchell, June 4, 1949; children—James Melvin, Karla Maria, Evangeline Rosetta. B.S., Winston-Salem State U., 1952; M.E., N.C. Central U., 1959, M.L.S., 1962. Sec., Colored PTA, Central Dist., N.C., 1960-62, v.p., after 1963; historian Rollins F.O.R., Henderson, N.C., 1972-73, pres., 1973-74; mem. vis. team So. Assn. Secondary Schs., 1984; dir. Vance Tech. Child Care, Henderson, BLGB Apts., Henderson. Leader, 4-H Club, Henderson, 1954—; sec. Williamsboro Community Devel. Club, 1957-69; bd. dirs. H. Leslie Perry Meml. Library, Vance County Group; active Big Ruin Creek Baptist Ch. Fellow N.C. Tchrs. Assn., Classroom Tchrs. Vance County, NEA; mem. Home Extension Club, Alumni Club (Henderson), Zeta Phi Beta (pres. 1976). Democrat. Lodge: Eastern Star, Golden Circle, Daus. of Isis. Office: Media Coordinator Vance County Schs 1000 Chestnut St Henderson NC 27536

MITCHELL, MARY LOU, department store executive; b. Cherry Ridge, La., July 25, 1934; d. W.C. and Ora Mae (Henderson) Webb; student St. Louis Bus. Coll., 1961; m. Bill H. Mitchell, May 15, 1966. Women's dir., hostess Noon Show, Sta. KTHV-TV, Little Rock, 1964-73; v.p. account service Holland & Assos., advt. agy., Little Rock, 1973-76; dir. corp. broadcast advt. Dillard Dept. Stores, Inc., Little Rock, 1973—. Active United Fund, Ark. Heart Assn.; bd. dirs. Better Bus. Bur. Ark. Mem. Nat. Sales and Mktg. Execs. Assn., Little Rock Sales and Mktg. Execs. Assn., Ark. Advt. Assn. Office: Dillard Dept Stores Inc 900 W Capitol St Room 214 Little Rock AR 72203

MITCHELL, MAURICE MCCLELLAN, JR., chemist; b. Lansdowne, Pa., Nov. 27, 1929; s. Maurice McClellan and Agnes Stewart (Kerr) M.; m. Marilyn M. Badger, June 14, 1952. B.S. in Chemistry, Carnegie-Mellon U., 1951, M.S. in Chemistry, 1957, Ph.D. in Phys. Chemistry, 1960. Group leader research and devel. U.S. Steel Corp., Pitts., 1951-61; br. head phys. chemistry research and devel. Melpar Inc., Falls Church, Va., 1961-64; group leader research and devel. Atlantic Richfield Co., Phila., 1964-73; dir. research and devel. Houdry div. Air Products and Chems., Inc., 1973-81; dir. research and devel. Ashland Oil Inc. (Ky.), 1981—. Fellow Am. Inst. Chemists; mem. Am. Chem. Soc., Assn. Research Dirs., Catalysis Soc. N.Am. (pres. 1985-89), AAAS. Republican. Presbyterian. Lodge: Kiwanis. contbr. articles to profl. jours.; patentee in field. Home: 2380 Hickory Ridge Dr Ashland KY 41101 Office: Ashland Petroleum Research and Devel PO Box 391 Ashland KY 41114

MITCHELL, MORRIS, art educator, consultant, artist; b. Highland Park, Ill., June 30, 1935; s. Claude Ernest and Lillian M.; m. Fran Ann Schroeder, Aug. 29, 1964 (div.); m. Pia Kerr, 1979 (div. 1982); children—Justice Wilford, Andra Vinetta. M.A. U. Tulsa, 1974. Display artist Marshall Fields, Evanston, Ill., 1955-58; instr. art Ringling Sch. Art, Sarasota, Fla., 1959—, chmn. dept. fine art, 1974-83; asst. U. Tulsa, 1974. Exhibited in group shows including Miami Met. Mus. Art (Best of Show award), 1977, Polk County Mus., 1980, Daytona Painter Mus., Fla., 1980, Tampa Mus., 1982; represented in permanent collections Eckerd Coll., St. Petersburg, Fla., U. Tulsa, Okla., Ruth Sherman Gallery, N.Y.C. Art cons. King Neptune Civic Orgn., 1985; mem. ecumenical bd. for campus ministries Ringling Sch. Art, 1976-79. Ringling Sch. Art Faculty grantee, Eng., Italy, 1985. Mem. Fla. Arti's Group (v.p. 1978-80, ednl. cons. 1980-85), Coll. Art Assn. Republican. Methodist. Avocations: nautilus training; travel; listening to music. Home: 2624 Hawthorne St Sarasota FL 33579 Office: Ringling Sch Art 1111 27th St Sarasota FL 33580

MITCHELL, PATRICIA BRUCE, educational association administrator, consultant; b. Atlanta, Sept. 27, 1950; d. Delmar Ellis and Nellie Louise (Herndon) Bruce; m. Philip James Mitchell, Nov. 27, 1977; 1 child, Lauren Elizabeth. B.A. magna cum laude, U. Ga., 1972; M.S., Pa. State U., 1975. Traffic mgr. So. Bell Telephone Co., Macon, Ga., 1972-73; tchr. Sch. Contemporary Edn., Ellicott City, Md., 1975-76; info. specialist Council Exceptional Children, Reston, Va., 1976-77; program dir. Nat. Assn. State Bds. Edn., Alexandria, Va., 1977—; cons. in field. Editor: A Policymaker's Guide to Education Gifted and Talented Children, 1981; An Advocate's Guide to Building Support for Gifted and Talented Children, 1981. Guest editor Jour. Edn. of the Gifted, 1984. Mem. adv. com. Presdl. Acad. Fitness Awards Program, Washington, 1983-84. Inst. for Ednl. Leadership fellow, 1976-77. Mem. Assn. for Gifted (pres. 1984-85), Council Exceptional Children (bd. govs. 1981-83), Nat. Assn. Gifted Children, Va. Assn. Edn. Gifted, Phi Beta Kappa. Presbyterian. Home: 6708 Holford Ln Springfield VA 22152 Office: Nat Assn State Bds Edn 701 N Fairfax St Alexandria VA 22314

MITCHELL, PRINCE, college administrator; b. Ridgeland, S.C., Aug. 28, 1926; s. Cain and Mattie (Miller) M.; m. Mary Amy McRae, Dec. 20, 1959; children—Gary, Gale. B.B.A., Savannah State Coll., 1957. Asst. comptroller Savannah State Coll., Ga., 1957-70, comptroller, 1972-78, v.p. bus. and fin., 1978—; comptroller Wilberforce U., Ohio, 1970-72, Central State U., Wilberforce, 1972. Bd. dirs. Hodge Meml. Nursing Home, Savannah, 1968. Served with USAF, 1951-55. Mem. Nat. Assn. Coll. and Univ. Bus. Officers (com. mem. 1980-82). Democrat. Home: 4812 Jasmine Ave Savannah GA 31404 Office: Savannah State Coll Savannah GA 31404

MITCHELL, RICHARD FRANK, retail company executive; b. Columbus, Ga., Sept. 22, 1931; s. Harry Frank and Esther (Davis) M.; B.S., Auburn U., 1955; grad. exec. program U. Va., 1968; m. Iris Faye Tarvin, Aug. 7, 1955; children—Alison, Bradley. Chief accountant Vulcan Materials Co., Birmingham, Ala., 1958-62, treas., 1965-70; gen. accounting mgr. Bigelow-Sanford Inc., Greenville, S.C., 1962-63; asst. controller Blount Bros. Corp., Montgomery, Ala., 1963-65; exec. v.p. Waddell & Reed, Kansas City, Mo., 1970-74; v.p. fin., treas. Rich's, Inc., Atlanta, 1974—; v.p. fin., treas. Zale Corp., 1976-80, exec. v.p., 1980-84, vice chmn., 1984—; dir. InterFirst Bank Las Colinas. Past mem. fund raising com. Pembroke County Day Sch., Kansas City, Mo.; mem. bus. adv. council So. Meth. U., Auburn U.; mem. fin. com. Dallas Symphony Assn.; mem adv. bd. Grad. Bus. Sch., U. Tex., Dallas. Served with AUS, 1957. Mem. Fin. Execs. Inst. (sec. Birmingham 1969, past dir. Kansas City chpt., program chmn.), Nat. Assn. Accountants (v.p. Birmingham 1970), Birmingham, Kansas City chambers commerce. Presbyterian. Club: Las Colinas Sports (Dallas). Office: Zale Corp 901 W Walnut Hill Ln Irving TX 75038

MITCHELL, RONNIE MONROE, lawyer; b. Clinton, N.C., Nov. 10, 1952; s. Ondus Cornelius and Margaret Ronie (Johnson) M.; m. Martha Cheryl Coble, May 25, 1975; children—Grant Stephen, Mitchell, Meredith Elizabeth Mitchell. B.A., Wake Forest U., 1975, J.D., 1978. Bar: N.C. 1978, U.S. Dist. Ct. (ea. dist.) N.C. 1978, U.S. Ct. Appeals (4th cir.) 1983, U.S. Supreme Ct. 1984. Assoc. atty. Brown, Fox & Deaver, Fayetteville, N.C., 1978-81; ptnr. Harris, Sweeny & Mitchell, Fayetteville, 1981—. Contbr.: chpts. to books. Bd. dirs. Cumberland County Rescue Squad, Fayetteville, 1983—. Recipient U.S. Law Week award Bur. Nat. Affairs, 1978. Mem. N.C. Bar Assn. (councillor Young Lawyers div. 1982-85), Cumberland County Bar Assn., N.C. Acad. Trial Lawyers, Am. Trial Lawyers Assn. Democrat. Club: Fayetteville Ind. Light Infantry. Lodges: Moose, Masons. Home: Route 5 Box 8C Fayetteville NC 28301 Office: Harris Sweeny & Mitchell 308 Person St Fayetteville NC 28302-0186

MITCHELL, ROY DEVOY, mgmt. engr., govt. ofcl.; b. Hot Springs, Ark., Sept. 11, 1922; s. Watson W. and Marie (Stewart) M.; B.S., Okla. State U., 1948, M.S., 1950; B.Indsl. Mgmt., Auburn U., 1960; m. Jane Caroline Gibson, Feb. 14, 1958; children—Michael, Marilyn, Martha, Stewart, Nancy. Instr., Odessa (Tex.) Coll., 1953-56; prof. engring. graphics Auburn (Ala.) U., 1956-63; field engr. HHFA, Community Facilities Adminstrn., Atlanta, Jackson, Miss., 1963-71; area engr. Met. Devel. Office, HUD, 1971-72, chief architecture and engring., 1972-75, chief program planning and support br., 1975, dir. archtl. br., Jackson, 1975—; cons. Army Ballistic Missile Agy., Huntsville, Ala., 1957-58, Auburn Research Found., NASA, 1963; mem. state tech. action panel Coop. Area Manpower Planning System. Mem. Central Miss. Fed. Personnel Adv. Council; mem. House and Home mag. adv. panel, 1977. Served USNR, 1943-46. Commended by Sec. HUD, Outstanding Achievement award HUD; registered profl. engr., Ala., Miss. Mem. Nat. Soc. Profl. Engrs., Am. Soc. for Engring. Edn., Miss. Soc. Profl. Engrs., Nat. Assn. Govt. Engrs. (charter mem.), Jackson Fed. Execs. Assn., Central Miss. Safety Council, Am. Water Works Assn., Iota Lambda Sigma. Methodist (trustee, mem. bd. 1959-60). Clubs: River Hills, University (Jackson). Home: 706 Forest Point Dr Brandon MS 39042 Office: HUD 100 W Capitol St Jackson MS 39201

MITCHELL, RUSSELL HARRY, dermatologist; b. Erie, N.D., Oct. 19, 1925; s. William John and Anna Lillian (Sögge) M.; B.S., B.A., U. Minn., Mpls., 1947, B.M., M.D., 1951; postgrad. U. Pa. Med. Sch., 1968-69; m. Judith Lawes Douvarjo, May 24, 1968; children—Kathy Ellen, Gregory Alan, Jill Elaine, Crystal Anne. Intern, Gorgas Hosp., C.Z., 1951-52; resident in dermatology U.S. Naval Hosp., Phila., 1967-70; asst. chief out-patient dept. Gorgas Hosp., 1955-64; chief med. and surg. wards Ariz. State Hosp., Phoenix, 1965; commd. lt. (j.g.) M.C., U.S. Navy, 1953, advanced through grades to capt., 1968; service in Vietnam; ret., 1981; practice medicine specializing in dermatology, Leesburg, Va., 1978—; mem. staff Loudoun Meml. Hosp., 1975—; dermatologist Nat. Naval Med. Center, Bethesda, Md., 1973-80; asst. prof. Georgetown U. Med. Sch., 1975—. Pres. Archaeol. Soc. Panama, 1962-64. Decorated Bronze Star with combat V; Vietnam Gallantry Cross with palm and clasp; caballero Orden de Vasco Nñez de Balboa (Panama); diplomate Am. Bd. Dermatology. Fellow Am. Acad. Dermatology, Am. Acad. Physicians, Explorers Club; mem. AMA, Assn. Mil. Surgeons, Assn. Mil. Dermatologists (life), Naval Inst., Soc. Am. Archaeology, Explorers Club, Pan Am. Med. Assn., Loudoun County Med. Soc., Dermatology Found., Royal Soc. Medicine, Marine's Meml. Club (asso.), Phi Chi. Contbr. articles to med. and archeol. publs. Home: Rural Route 2 Box 99 Leesburg VA 22075 Office: 821-D S King St Leesburg VA 22075

MITCHELL, RUTH ELLEN (BUNNY), sales director; b. Mpls., Jan. 2, 1940; d. Burt and Helen (Bolnick) Horwitz; children—Cathy Ann, Thomas Charles, Andrew Robert. Student UCLA, 1957, U. Minn., 1957-60. Substitute tchr. Holy Innocents' Sch., Atlanta, 1972-76; office mgr. Atlanta Area Family Psychiatry Clinic, 1976-79; account exec. Am. Advt. Distbrs., Atlanta, 1979-81, Brown's Guide to Ga. mag., Atlanta, 1981-82; account mgr. So. Hosps. mag. Billian Pub., Atlanta, after 1982; now Southeastern regional sales dir. Am. Hosp. Pub., Inc., Atlanta; active IBM Med. Seminars, 1979; cons. G.C.C. Inc., 1982—. Formerly active Walker Art Ctr., Mpls., Mpls. Art Inst., Tyrone Guthrie Theatre, Mpls.; former mem. Temple Israel Edn. Bd., Temple Israel Sisterhood Bd., Temple Israel Couples Club, Minn. Symphony Bd., St. Louis Park Recreation and Park Commn.; former fundraiser Sta. KTCA (pub. broadcasting system); past troop leader Mpls. area Girl Scouts U.S.A.; mem. Northside Hosp. Aux., Atlanta, 1971-77; active High Mus. Art, Atlanta, 1971—, Arts Festival Atlanta, 1972-80, Temple Sisterhood Bd., 1972-77, Holy Innocents Sch. Bd., 1973-77, Holy Innocents' Ch. summer program, 1974-76, Buckhead Mental Health Clinic, 1975-77, Encore, Atlanta Ballet; fundraiser Sta. WETV (pub. broadcasting system), 1976-80; Ga. pres. Preference Primary Ballot, 1980; active Carter-Mondale nat. campaign, 1976, Mondale nat. campaign, 1984. Mem. Atlanta Advt. Club, Met. Atlanta Media Assn. (steering com.), Mag. Advt. Reps. of the South (v.p. 1983-84). Home: 255 Blackwater Cove NW Atlanta GA 30328 Office: Am Hosp Pub Inc 5th Floor East 1117 Perimeter Ctr W Atlanta GA 30338

MITCHELL, RUTH URSULA, physical therapy educator, consultant; b. Cleve., Feb. 17, 1932; d. Vincas Stasys and Ursula (Cyzauskas) Maciulis. B.S. in Phys. Therapy magna cum laude, St. Louis U., 1954; M.A. in Edn., Western Res. U., 1961; Ph.D. in Sociology, Case Western Res. U., 1970. Staff phys. therapist Highland View Hosp., Cleve., 1954, sr. phys. therapist, 1958, asst. chief phys. therapist, 1959, 62, acting chief phys. therapist, 1961-62, instr. and phys. therapy cons. to nursing edn., 1962, 63-64; clin. instr. phys. therapy curriculum Western Res. U., Cleve., 1962, lectr. sociology, 1965; clin. assoc. div. phys. therapy Sargent Coll., Boston U., 1962; research asst. Vocat. Guidance and Rehab. Services, Cleve., 1965-67; regional coordinator Region II, Bur. Vocat. Rehab., Cleve., 1967-68; assoc. prof. phys. therapy div. allied health Ind. U. Sch. Medicine, Indpls., 1969-75; prof. and dir. div. phys. therapy, dept. med. allied health professions Sch. Medicine, U. N.C., Chapel Hill, 1975-80, prof., 1980—, resource specialist in phys. therapy N.C. Area Health Edn. Ctrs. Program, 1980, phys. therapy grad. edn. cons., div. phys. therapy, 1971, mem. chmn.'s adv. com., 1975-80, mem. ad hoc adv. com. for phys. therapy, gen. adminstrn., 1976-80, mem. rehab. com. Sch. Medicine, 1976-77, mem. curriculum adv. com. div. occupational therapy, 1976-78, mem. promotions and tenure com., 1976—, com. on undergrad. programs in health affairs, 1978-80; mem. com. on M.A. in Coll. Teaching, Sch. Edn., 1978; planning and chpt. mem. Region V Continuing Edn. Priorities Com. on Phys. Therapy, Northwestern U. and Rehab. Inst. Chgo., 1973-75; med. sociology cons., mem. steering com. sociology dept. Ind. U.-Purdue U.-Indpls., 1974-75; grad. edn. cons. phys. therapy Northwestern U., 1975; mem. N.C. Dept. Human Resources Phys. Therapy Roundtable, 1975-76; cons., external reviewer phys. therapy program Marquette U., 1979; geriatric cons. depts. medicine and phys. therapy Cleve. Met. Gen. and Highland View Hosps., 1981; external examiner phys. therapy program Kuwait U., 1984, 85; dir. therapeutics com. Home Health Agy. of Chapel Hill, 1981-83, chmn. bd. dirs. 1985—, mem.-at-large exec. com., 1982-85, mem., chmn. coms. Mem. editorial bd. Phys. Therapy in Health Care, 1983—; editorial cons. sect. Theoretical Issues in Professional Nursing, 1971; manuscript cons. Rehabilitation of the Disabled and the Hospital, 1982; contbr. articles to profl. jours., papers to profl. confs., U.S., Japan. Active Ackland Meml. Art Ctr., 1977—, Eno River Assn., 1981—. Recipient Alumni Merit award St. Louis U., 1977. Mem. Am. Phys. Therapy Assn. (chmn. Northeastern Ohio Dist. 1959-61, pres. Ind. chpt. 1973-75, dir. N.C. chpt. 1976-78, del. 1976-81, mem. community health sect. 1982—, geriatrics sect., 1980—, manuscript reviewer Jour. Am. Phys. Therapy Assn. 1977—), Am. Sociol. Assn., Soc. for Behavioral Kinesiology (founding, dir. 1981-83), AAUP, Am. Acad. Polit. and Social Scis., Am. Pub. Health Assn., Inst. of Society, Ethics and Life Scis., Assn. for Women Faculty U. N.C., Am. Heart Assn. (stroke work group N.C. affiliate 1981-84), Alpha Kappa Delta. Democrat. Roman Catholic. Club: Zonta. Avocations: fishing; camping; stamp collecting; photography. Home: Route 3 Box 233-A Apex NC 27502 Office: Univ NC Div Phys Therapy Med Sch Wing E 222H Chapel Hill NC 27514

MITCHELL, WALTER IRVIN, JR., marketing executive; b. Tuscaloosa, Ala., Jan. 18, 1943; s. Walter Irvin Mitchell and Edna Ann (Huff) Mitchell Montgomery; m. Jo Anne Mary Alger, June 3, 1972; children—Amanda Rose, Kathryn JoAnna. B.S. in Edn., Henderson State U., 1966; cert. in internat. bus. Ga. State U., 1972. Mktg. mgr. govt. services Seatrain Lines, Inc., N.Y.C., 1970-72, area mktg. mgr., Atlanta, 1972-75; dist. mgr. Norton, Lilly & Co., Inc., Atlanta, 1975-79; pres. Consol. Cargo Carriers, Atlanta, 1979-81; gen. sales mgr. Carolina Shipping Co., Charleston, S.C., 1981-83; mgr. Zim-Am. Israeli Shipping Co., Inc., Atlanta, 1983—. Served as capt. U.S. Army, 1966-70, Vietnam. Decorated Bronze Star. Mem. Ga. Internat. Trade Assn., Atlanta Maritime Assn. (past dir.). Republican. Roman Catholic. Club: Mountain Creek Recreational Assn. (Roswell, Ga.) (past dir.). Lodge: Mason. Avocations: tennis; salt-water fishing; golf. Home: 4895 McPherson Dr Roswell GA 30075 Office: Zim-Am Israeli Shipping Co Inc 1584 Tullie Circle Suite 113 Atlanta GA 30329

MITCHELL, WILEY FRANCIS, JR., railway company counsel; b. Franklin County, N.C., July 23, 1932; s. Wiley Francis and Nancy Irene (Edwards) M.; B.A., Wake Forest U., 1953, J.D., 1954; m. Marshale Moody, May 31, 1953; children—Katherine, Frances. Bar: N.C. 1954, D.C. 1962. Assoc. firm Joyner & Howison, Raleigh, N.C., 1954-60; ptnr. firm. Joyner, Howison & Mitchell, Raleigh, 1960-62; gen. atty. So. R.R. Co., Washington, 1962-68, gen. solicitor, 1968-83; sr. gen. solicitor Norfolk-So. Corp., 1983—. Mem. city council, Alexandria, Va., 1967-76, vice mayor, 1970-76; mem. Va. Senate, 1976—, asst. minority leader, 1978—. Served with USAR, 1948-70. Mem. ABA, N.C. Bar Assn., D.C. Bar Assn., Va. Bar Assn. (hon. life), Alexandria C. of C. (George Washington Leadership award 1984). Republican. Baptist. Club: Rotary. Home: 511 Canterbury Ln Alexandria VA 22314 Office: 1050 Connecticut Ave NW Suite 740 Washington DC 20036

MITCHELL, WILLIAM DEWEY, JR., educational adminstrator; b. Greenville, S.C., June 15, 1933; s. William Dewey and Victoria Louise (Rickenbacker) M.; m. Peggy P. Atkins, Feb. 13, 1954; children—Vicki Mitchell Smith, Lisa Mitchell Cheek. B.S. in Indsl. Edn., Clemson U., 1955; M.A., Converse Coll., 1970. Cert. tchr., S.C., Tchr. Beaufort High Sch., S.C., 1957-61, Jenkins Jr. High Sch., Spartanburg, S.C., 1961-67; dean evening services Spartanburg Tech. Coll., 1967—. Pres. Beaufort Civitan Club, S.C., 1960, Sunrise Civitan Club, 1968; sec. Beaufort County Fair Assn., 1960; lt. gov. zone B, S.C. Dist. Civitan Internat., Spartanburg, 1969. Served with U.S. Army, 1955-57. Republican. Baptist. Club: Shirts and Skirts (pres. 1983-84) (Boiling Springs, S.C.). Avocation: western style square dancing. Home: 105 Stribling Circle Spartanburg SC 29301 Office: Spartanburg Tech Coll Drawer 4386 Spartanburg SC 29305

MITCHELL-GRUBB, YVONNE EVLYN, systems analyst; b. Birmingham, Ala., Aug. 30, 1952; d. Cleophus Homer and Doris (Robinson) Mitchell; B.A., cert. secondary edn. (Nat. Achievement scholar), Macalester Coll., 1973; m. Broderick Carl Grubb, Aug. 21, 1971; children—David, Adrian, Alicia. Jr. high sch. math. tchr. Lubbock (Tex.) Public Schs., 1973-74; research analyst Wayne County Dept. Substance Abuse Services, Detroit, 1975-76, systems supr., 1976-78; programmer analyst Volkswagen of Am., Warren, Mich., 1978-79; sr. programmer analyst Hibernia Nat. Bank, New Orleans, 1979-80; sr. systems analyst McDermott, Inc., New Orleans, 1980—; ind. cons. in data processing, 1975—. Mem. Assn. for Systems Mgmt., Assn. for Gifted and Talented Students, NOW. Presbyterian. Home: 2625 Holiday Dr New Orleans LA 70114 Office: McDermott Inc 1010 Common St New Orleans LA 70160

MITCHIM, CHARLES FRANCIS, optometrist; b. DeSoto, Mo., July 29, 1911; s. Charles Cloude and Leathe Lillian (Word) M.; B.S., U.S. Mil. Acad., West Point, 1937; M.S., U. Calif., Berkeley, 1939; O.D., So. Calif. Coll. Optometry, Los Angeles, 1965; m. Eleanor Lucyle Outlaw, Aug. 3, 1937; 1 son, Charles Amos. Commd. 2d lt. U.S. Army, 1937, advanced through grades to col., 1962; service in France, Germany, South Pacific; ret., 1962; pvt. practice optometry, Winona, Miss., 1975—. Bd. dirs. Montgomery County Econ. Council. Decorated Legion of Merit, Army Commendation medal (3). Mem. Am. Optometric Assn., Assn. Grads. U.S. Mil. Acad., Miss. Optometric Assn., N.W. Optometric Soc. Republican. Presbyterian. Club: Winona Rotary (dir. 1980). Office: 614A Tyler Homes Dr Winona MS 38967

MITRA, AMITAVA, management science and applied statistics educator, researcher, consultant; b. Darbhanga, Bihar, India, Nov. 26, 1948; came to U.S., 1970; s. Debendra Nath and Sephalika (Raha) M.; m. Sujata Biswas, Sept. 10, 1980; 1 child, Arnab. B.Tech. with honors, Indian Inst. Tech., Kharagpur, 1964-69, DIIT, 1970; M.S., U. Ky., 1972; Ph.D., Clemson U., 1977. Cert. prodn. and inventory mgr. Grad. teaching/research asst. U. Ky., Lexington, 1970-72, Clemson U., S.C., 1972-77; asst. prof. U. So. Calif., Los Angeles, 1977-79; asst. prof. Auburn U., Ala., 1979-84, acting asst. dean Sch. Bus., 1984-85, assoc. prof. dept. mgmt., 1984—; cons. RBI Corp., Dalton, Ga., 1980; paper reviewer Internat. Jour. Prodn. Research, Leicestershire, U.K., 1984, 86, Psychometrika, Copenhagen, 1981, Am. Inst. Decision Sci., Atlanta, 1979—; workshop lectr. Sch. Bus. Continuing Edn. Services Auburn U., 1980—; discussant So. Mgmt. Assn., New Orleans, 1982; book reviewer John T. Wiley & Sons, Inc., N.Y.C., 1984, Random House, Inc., N.Y.C., 1985-86. Contbr. articles to profl. jours. Grad. fellow Clemson U., S.C., 1973; recipient Outstanding Grad. Prof. award Auburn U. Sch. Bus. Adminstrn., 1983-84. Mem. Am. Statis. Assn., Am. Inst. Decision Scis. (session chmn. 1981). Home: 1116 Elkins Dr Auburn AL 36830 Office: Auburn U Dept Mgmt Auburn AL 36849

MITTEL, JOHN J., economist, business executive, consultant; b. L.I., N.Y.; s. John and Mary (Leidolf) M.; 1 child, James C.; B.B.A., CUNY. Researcher econs. dept. McGraw Hill & Co., N.Y.C.; mgr., asst. to pres. Indsl. Commodity Corp., J. Carvel Lange Inc. and J. Carvel Lange Internat., Inc., 1956—, corp. sec., 1958—, v.p., 1964-80, exec. v.p., 1980—; pres. I.C. Investors Corp., 1972—, I.C. Pension Adv., Inc., 1977—; dir. several corps.; plan adminstr., trustee Combined Indsl. Commodity Corp. and J. Carvel Lange Inc. Pension Plan, 1962—, J. Carvel Lange Internat. Inc. Profit Sharing Trust, 1969—, Combined Indsl. Commodity Corp. and J. Carvel Lange Inc. Employees Profit Sharing Plan, 1977—. Mem. grad. adv. bd. Bernard M. Baruch Coll., CUNY, 1971-72. Mem. Conf. Bd., Am. Statis. Assn., Newcomen Soc. N.Am. Club: Union League (N.Y.C.). Co-author: How Good A Sales Profit Are You, 1961; The Role of the Economic Consulting Firm; also numerous market surveys. Office: PO Box 817 Palm Harbor FL 33563

MITTELSTET, STEPHEN KEITH, college president; b. Enid, Okla., Sept. 18, 1943; s. Reinhold Albert and Mary Ellen (Thomas) M.; m. Sandra Jane Pirtle, Apr. 8, 1966; children—Mary Amelia, Amanda Claire. B.A. summa cum laude, McMurry Coll., 1967, D.Hum., 1980; Ph.D., U. Tex., 1973. Asst. dean instrn. and community service Richland Coll., Dallas, 1973-74, assoc. dean instrn., 1974-75, dean community and instructional services, 1975-76; dist. dir. instructional TV, Dallas County Community Coll. Dist., 1976-77, asst. chancellor, 1977-79; pres. Richland Coll., Dallas, 1979—; v.p., dir. Borger Gas Engine and Machine Co. (Tex.), 1977—; adj. prof. North Tex. State U., Denton, 1976-77; dir. Tex. Am. Bank, Richardson. Exec. producer ednl. TV series American Government, 1978, The American Story, 1977, Communicating Through Literature, 1977. Pres. Richardson YMCA, 1983-84. Recipient award for excellence in film and TV, Ohio Nat. Film Festival, 1980; N.Y. Internat. Film and TV Silver award, 1978; cert. of merit for instrnl. TV Freedoms Found., 1979. Mem. Dallas C. of C., Richardson C. of C. (dir. 1981—), Tex. Assn. Community Service and Continuing Edn. (sec. 1976-77), Assn. Higher Edn., Phi Delta Kappa, Phi Kappa Phi. Methodist. Lodge: Rotary (dir. service 1983—, pres.-elect 1984).

MITTENDORF, THEODOR HENRY, paper manufacturing consultant; b. Clay Center, Kans., Jan. 14, 1895; s. Theodor Henry and Antonie (Carls) M.; B.S., Okla. State University, 1917; m. Dorothy E. Solger, May 18, 1919 (dec. Mar. 1979); 1 dau., Laone M. Mittendorf Hoerl; m. 2d, Margueritte E. McLean, Oct. 3, 1980. Lectr. extension div. Okla. State U., 1917; lectr., free lance writer, 1919-20; dept. supt. Armour & Co., Chgo., 1920-22; sec., dir. sales and advt. Mid-States Gummed Paper Co., Chgo., 1922-38; v.p. charge sales Industrial Training Inst., 1938-39, v.p., gen. mgr. The Gummed Products Co., Troy, Ohio, 1940-48; v.p. charge sales Hudson Pulp and Paper Corp., N.Y.C., 1948-56, exec. v.p., 1956-58, cons., 1958—; pres. Mitt Industries, Inc., Mount Dora, Fla., 1972—; dir. 5 East 71st St. Corp. Bd. dirs. Waterman Meml. Hosp., Eustis, Fla., Muscular Dystrophy Assn.; life mem. Okla. State U. President's Club. Served from 2d lt. F.A. to 1st lt. AS, U.S. Army, World War I, AEF. Named to Okla. State U. Alumni Hall of Fame, 1961. Mem. Kraft Paper Assn. (dir., mem. exec. com. 1951-58), Gummed Industries Assn. (pres. 1955-56). Paper Bag Inst. (pres. 1955-56), Paper Club N.Y., Am. Legion, Okla. State U. Henry G. Bennett Soc. (life), Symposiarchs, Kappa Sigma, Alpha Zeta, Pi Kappa Delta. Republican. Methodist. Clubs: Mt. Dora (Fla.) Golf, Mt. Dora Yacht; Ponte Vedra (Fla.); African Safari of Fla. Lodges: Masons, Order Eastern Star. Home: Box 1138 Mount Dora FL 32757 Office: PO Box 1138 Mount Dora FL 32757

MITTLEBEELER, EMMET VAUGHN, political science educator, lawyer; b. Louisville, Aug. 8, 1915; s. Jacob J. and Katherine (Moorman) M. B.A. with honors, U. Louisville, 1936, LL.B., 1939, J.D., 1970; M.A., U. Chgo., 1950, Ph.D., 1951. Bar: Ky. 1939, D.C. 1965, U.S. Supreme Ct. 1954. Asst. atty. gen. State of Ky., Frankfort, 1945-48; congl. asst. Ho. of Reps., Washington, 1953-54, cons. com. on govt. ops., 1956; cons. Adminstrv. Office of U.S. Cts., Washington, 1964; prof. govt. and pub. adminstrn. Am. U., Washington, now emeritus; prof. adminstrn. Troy State U., overseas with U.S. Air Force, 1984, African univs., 1962-63, 69-70, 76-78; bd. dirs. Assn. for Acad. Travel Abroad, Washington, 1969—; Author: African Custom and Western Law, 1976. Bur. Fgn. Scholarships and Com. for Exchange of Persons lectr., So. Rhodesia, Nigeria, 1976-78. Contbr. articles to profl. jours. Served with USAAF, 1942-45, ETO. Mem. Am. Polit. Sci. Assn., Fulbright Assn., Ky. Bar Assn., N.Am. Vexillological Assn. (founder). Republican. Baptist.

MIX, CLARENCE REX, speech communication educator, minister, consultant; b. Greenville, Tex., Jan. 14, 1935; s. Wilbur Myers and Lula Ruth (McSpadden) M.; m. Susan Shank, Aug. 24, 1961; children—Helen Michelle, Meredith. B.A., Tex. Christian U., 1957, M. Div., 1961; Ph.D., U. Denver, 1972. Ordained to ministry Christian Church (Disciples of Christ), 1960. Minister Central Christian Ch., Rosenberg, Tex., 1961-62; dir. Christian edn. youth Tex. Assn. Christian Chs., Ft. Worth, 1962-67; assoc. prof. SUNY, Fredonia, 1970-75; dir. Value of Life Project, Tex. Conf. Chs., Austin, 1975-78; assoc. prof. speech communication Lynchburg Coll., Va., 1978—; cons. Gaf Corp., N.Y.C., 1971-72, Digital Equipment, Maynard, Mass., 1973-75, Babcock & Wilcox, Lynchburg, 1979-83. Author: Toward Effective Teaching, 1970; Life and Death Issues, 1977. Contbr. articles to profl. jours. Bd. dirs. Lynchburg Fine Arts Ctr. Performing Arts Div. 1984—, mem. personnel com., 1982-83, bd. dirs. Theatre Div., 1981-84, co-founder and chmn. Fine Arts Ctr. Technicians, 1982-84; mem. sexual assault task force Family Services, Central Va., 1982-83; elder First Christian Ch., Lynchburg, 1981—, Pecan Springs Christian Ch., Austin, Tex., 1976-78, First Christian Ch., Boulder, Colo., 1968-70; chmn. program com. Nat. Men's Gathering, 1979, The Christian Ch. (Disciples of Christ), 1977-79. Mem. Speech Communication Assn., Internat. Communication Assn., AAUP, Alpha Psi Omega, Phi Eta Sigma. Lodge: Masons. Avocations: travel; theatre; photography; music. Office: Lynchburg Coll Lynchburg VA 24501

MIXON, ALVIN, farmer, merchant, cattleman; b. Georgiana, Ala., Dec. 19, 1908; s. Samuel Henderson and Lela (Cook) M.; grad. Massey Bus. Sch., Birmingham, Ala., 1930; m. Frances Brassell, May 15, 1936; 1 son, Alvin. Salesman, interior decorator Morgan Bros. Dept. Stores, Birmingham, Georgiana and Evergreen, Ala., 1930; founder, owner S. H. Mixon's Store, Gin & Milling Co., Georgiana, Alvin Mixon Merc., Harper Merc. Co., Belleville; cattleman, Georgiana, 1952—; dir. Georgiana Bank; organizer So. Pine Electric Co-op, Brewton, Ala., 1938; pres. So. Electric Co-op, Brewton, 1957—, So. Pine Electric Coop., Brewton; dir. Ala. Electric Power Generation Plants and High Voltage Transmission Lines, Andalusia; mem. Ala. Energy Adv. Council; bd. dirs. Ala. Rural Electric Assn., 1981. Asso. dir. SSS, Conecuh County, 1938-42; organizer Conecuh County United Fund; organizer Conecuh County Hosp., 1954, bd. dirs., 1954—. Recipient Father of Yr. award Conecuh County Cattlemen's Cow Bells, 1980; Cert. of Achievement award Nat. Rural Electric Coop. Assn., 1983; Leadership Appreciation award So. Pine Elec. Coop., 1984; permanent marker erected in his honor near hdqrs. So. Pine Elec. Coop. Mem. Ala. Forest Products Assn., Am. Angus Assn. (Historic award 1983), Ala. Angus Assn., Ala., Conecuh County cattlemens assns., Conecuh County Hist. Soc., Conecuh Farm Bur. (dir.), Georgiana, Evergreen chambers commerce, Internat. Platform Assn., Woodmen of World, SAR. Methodist (steward, layman). Clubs: Masons, Shriners, Rotary, Kiwanis (Service award 1981), Quarterback (Georgiana). Address: Route 1 Georgiana AL 36033

MIXON, ELIZABETH ANN, librarian; b. Hickman, Ky., Jan. 14, 1945; d. Zack Elizah and Annie Helen (Hurst) Curlin Spillers; m. Edgar Allen Mixon, Jr., July 25, 1975 (div. Oct. 1983); 1 son, John Anthony. B.S., U. So. Miss., 1977, M.L.S., 1980. Cert. librarian, media specialist. Head librarian, media specialist Bayou View Elem. Sch., Gulfport, Miss., 1977—. Co-author: Selection Policy for Schools, 1982. Campaign worker for re-election Miss. state rep., 1983. U. So. Miss. Pulley, Pulley and Gough scholar, 1976. Mem. ALA, Phi Delta Kappa, Delta Phi Mu. Democrat. Methodist. Home: 307 Shady Ln Biloxi MS 39531

MIXON, VIKKI WILLIAMSON, geologist; b. Bastrop, La., Dec. 14, 1957; s. Albert Virgil and Jimmie Nell (Derrick) W.; m. Donnie Wayne Mixon, Aug. 20, 1983. B.S. in Merchandising/Mktg., Northeastern La. U., 1978, B.S. in Geology, 1985. With Savs./trust dept. Am. Bank, Monroe, La., 1978-82; sec. computer services Mixon Bros. Drilling, Monroe, 1984—; geologist, pres. Acadian Exploration, Monroe, 1984—. Mem. Am. Petroleum Inst., Am. Assn. Petroleum Geologists, La. Real Estate Assn. Republican. Avocations: racquetball; snow skiing. Home: 1702 Ridgemar Dr Monroe LA 71201 Office: Mixon Bros Drilling Inc 506 Jonesboro Rd West Monroe LA 71291

MIXSON, JOHN WAYNE, lt. gov. Fla., cattleman; b. Coffee County, Ala., June 16, 1922; s. Cecil Marion and Mineola (Moseley) M.; m. Margie Grace, Dec. 27, 1947. Student, Columbia U., 1944, U. Pa., 1945; B.S. in Bus. Adminstrn, U. Fla., 1947. Acct. So. Bell Telephone Co., Jacksonville, 1947-48; farmer, cattleman, Jackson County, Fla., 1948—; dir. orgn. Fla. Farm Bur., Gainesville, 1954-59; dir. field services So. region Am. Farm Bur., 1959-61; mem. Fla. Ho. of Reps., Tallahassee, 1967-78; lt. gov., Fla., 1979—. Served with USNR, 1942-46. Named Legislator of Yr. Fla. Assn. Community Colls., 1975, Man of Yr. in Fla. Agr. Progressive Farmer mag., 1976; recipient awards from numerous So. agrl. groups. Mem. Fla. Farm Bur., Fla. Cattlemen's Assn. Democrat. Methodist. Club: Rotary. Office: Lt Gov's Office The Capitol Tallahassee FL 32304

MIYAGAWA, ICHIRO, physicist, educator; b. Hiratsuka, Japan, Mar. 5, 1922; s. Shigejiro and Tsuma (Itoh) M.; B.S., Nagoya U., 1945; D.Sc., U. Tokyo, 1954, postgrad., 1954-56; postgrad. Duke U., 1956-59; m. Mitsuko Yamada, Feb. 10, 1950; children—Shigeru, Haruyo, Mari. Came to U.S., 1962. Asst. prof. chem. physics U. Tokyo, 1959-62; vis. asst. prof. Duke U., 1963-65; asst. prof. U. Ala., University, 1965-66, asso. prof., 1966-70, prof. physics, 1971-80, Univ. research prof., 1980—. Cons. to Redstone Arsenal, 1966-72. Chmn. Southeastern Magnetic Resonance conf., 1973. USPHS grantee, 1967. Fellow Am. Phys. Soc.; mem. AAAS, Sigma Xi. Contbr. articles on magnetic resonance to sci. jours. Home: 4905 10th Ct E Tuscaloosa AL 35405 Office: Box 1921 University AL 35486

MIZE, DAVID GRANT, college bookstore manager educator; b. Bokchito, Okla., Oct. 17, 1937; s. John Paul and Anna D. M.; m. Barbara J. Proffer, Aug. 31, 1956; children—Michael, Gloria, Joan. M.Ed., Southeastern Okla. State U., 1972. Chief dep. Bryan County Clk., Durant, Okla., 1960-65; v.p. Midcontinent Map, Tulsa, Okla., 1965-70; instr. bus. adminstrn.-mgmt. Southeastern Okla. State U., Durant, 1972—, mgr. Campus Book Exchange, 1972—; cons., appraiser Bryan County Tax Assessor, Durant, 1970—; sec., co-owner White's R-T-W, Inc., Durant, 1972—. Bd. dirs. Bryan County United Way, Durant, 1981-82. Mem. Nat. Assn. Coll. Stores (nominating com., merchandising com.), Southwest Bookstore Assn. (v.p. 1985—), Okla. Bookstore Assn. Democrat. Baptist. Lodge: Kiwanis (pres. elect 1985). Avocation: reading. Home: 2206 Gershwin Dr Durant OK 74701 Office: Campus Book Exchange Southeastern Okla State Univ Durant OK 74701

MIZEL, MARK STUART, orthopedic surgeon; b. N.Y.C., May 23, 1945; s. Harold Henry and Irene (Adelman) M. B.S., Columbia U., 1966, M.S., 1968; M.D., Tufts U., 1977. Diplomate Am. Bd. Orthopedic Surgery. Intern, George Washington U. Hosp., 1977-78, resident in surgery, 1978-79; resident Mass. Gen. Hosp., Boston, 1979-82; fellow in foot and ankle surgery U. Calif.-San Francisco, 1983; practice medicine specializing in orthopedic surgery Brandon Assocs., West Palm Beach, Fla., 1983—. Served with U.S. Navy, 1969-72; Vietnam. Mem. AMA, Palm Beach County Med. Soc. Home: 3701 S Flagler Dr #403 West Palm Beach FL 33405 Office: Orthopedic Center 4801 S Congress Ave Lake Worth FL 33461

MIZELL, AL PHILIP, university official, consultant in microcomputer literacy, applications and telecommunications; b. Atlanta, Dec. 23, 1934; s. Kathryn M. (Grimshaw) M.; m. Mary Lou Vickery, June 11, 1960; children—Michael B., Laureen B. Mizell Gambill, Susan K. B.Ed. in Sci. and Math., U. Miami, 1956; M.S. in Sci. Edn., Fla. State U., 1964; Ed.S. in Audiovisual Prodn., Ind. U., 1969, Ed.D. in Instructional Systems Tech., 1970. Cert. tchr., Fla. Tchr. high sch., Dade County, Fla., 1956-68; adj. prof. Miami (Fla.)-Dade Jr. Coll., 1964-68; assoc. dean instrn. Howard Community Coll., Columbia, Md., 1970-78; dir. curriculum Nova U., Ft. Lauderdale, Fla., 1978-82, dir. Office Computer Studies, 1982-84; dir. Ed.D. in Computer edn., 1984—; dir. cons. hosp. and nursing sch. tng. programs; condr. workshops on microcomputers. Served with U.S. Army, 1957-59; capt. Res. Named Community Leader of Week, Sta. WJOY and Eastern Airlines, 1982; State of Fla. scholar, 1953-56; Sloan fellow Purdue U., 1976-77. Mem. NEA (life), Am. Soc. Tng. and Devel., Assn. Ednl. Communications and Tech. (chmn. microcomputer com.), Fla. Assn. Media in Edn., Scabbard and Blade, Phi Delta Kappa. Democrat. Methodist (lay leader, past chmn. edn. commn.). Author: (with Beebe) Computer Education: Book of Readings, 1982; co-editor Exploring Teaching Alternatives, 1977; contbr. articles to profl. jours. Home: 4524 Monroe St Hollywood FL 33021 Office: Office Computer Edn Nova U 3301 College Ave Fort Lauderdale FL 33314

MLOTT, SYLVESTER ROMAN, clinical psychologist, researcher; b. Chgo., Dec. 17, 1925; s. Roman and Mary Margaret (Haber) M.; m. Yvonne Dunaway, Jan. 25, 1964; children—Brent Allan, Bruce Wayne. B.S. in Psychology, Roosevelt U., Chgo., 1950, M.A. in Psychology, 1953; postgrad. Mich. State U., 1958-59; Ph.D. in Psychology, U. Miss., 1963. Psychologist Oak Park Neuropsychiat. Clinic, Ill., 1953-55, 55-57; pvt. practice psychology, Oak Park, 1957-58; chief clin. psychologist S.E. Psychiat. Clinic, Lincoln, Nebr., 1964-65; assoc. in clin. psychology, asst. dir. adolescent unit Med. U. S.C., Charleston, 1965-71; asst. prof., 1971-76, assoc. prof. clin. psychology, 1976—; cert. examiner Probate Ct., Charleston, S.C., 1979—; cons. Dialysis Clinic of Charleston, 1979—. Contbr. articles to profl. jours. Served with USAF, 1944-46. Mem. Am. Psychol. Assn., Nat. Assn. Vocat. Rehab., S.C. Psychol. Assn., Southeastern Psychol. Assn., S.C. Acad. Profl. Psychologists, Charleston Area Psychol. Assn. (treas. 1972, pres. 1973-74). Roman Catholic. Avocations: fishing; boating; stamp collecting; swimming. Home: 745 Creekside Dr Mount Pleasant SC 29464 Office: Med U SC 171 Ashley Ave Charleston SC 29425

MMAHAT, JOHN ANTHONY, lawyer; b. New Orleans, Sept. 5, 1931; s. Joseph and Mary (Bertucci) M.; B.A., Tulane U., 1956, J.D., 1958; m. Arlene Cecile Montgomery, Aug. 12, 1967; children—Arlene Cecile, Amy Montgomery, John Anthony. Admitted to La. bar, 1958, since practiced in Metairie; sr. ptnr. Mmahat, Duffy & Richards, 1958—; chmn. bd. Medallion Mgmt., Inc.; chmn. bd. Gulf Fed. Savs. Bank, Exec. Office Center, Inc. Vice chmn. New Orleans Aviation Bd., 1964-69. Served with USAF, 1951-53. Recipient Glendy Burke medal for oratory Tulane U., 1956. Mem. Am., La., New Orleans (chmn. pub. relations com.) bar assns., La. Landmarks Soc., New Orleans Mus. Art. Club: K.C. Home: 1239 1st St New Orleans LA 70130 Office: 5500 Veterans Memorial Blvd Metairie LA 70003

MOBLEY, CLEON MARION (CHIP), JR., physics educator, real estate executive; b. Reidsville, Ga., July 14, 1942; s. Cleon M. and Lucile (Anderson) M.; m. Martha Hewlett, 1962 (div. 1970); children—Lisa Anne, Arthur Marion. A.S., So. Tech. Inst., 1961; B.S., Oglethorpe U., 1963; M.S., U. Mo., 1966. Lic. pilot. Faculty research assoc. Ga. Inst. Tech., Atlanta, 1963-65; instr. So. Tech. Inst., Marietta, Ga., 1965-67; faculty fellow NASA, 1967-68; asst. prof. physics Ga. So. Coll., Statesboro, 1968—, dir. planetarium; pres. Assoc. Income Properties, Inc. Statesboro, 1982—; dir. Savannah Properties Mgmt., Inc., 1983—; cons. in field. AEC fellow, 1965. Mem. Statesboro Home Builders Assn., Am. Inst. Physics, Sigma Phi Epsilon. Methodist. Club: Optimist. Lodge: Elks. Office: PO Box 8023 Statesboro GA 30460

MOCHARLA, RAMAN, microbiologist, researcher, educator; b. Mattigiri, Karnataka, India, Sept. 19, 1953; came to U.S. 1981; s. V. Krishnarao and Savithramma Mocharla; m. Hanna Tialowska, Jan. 15, 1983; 1 child, Robert Michael. B.S. in Biology, U. Agra, 1972; M.S. in Microbiology, G.B.P. U., India, 1976; Ph.D. in Microbiology, U. Kurukshetra, India, 1980. Scientist S-1 Indian Council Agr. Research, New Delhi, 1977-80; UNESCO/WHO fellow Czechoslovak Acad. Sci., Prague, 1980-81; postdoctoral fellow U. Okla., Norman, 1981-83; assoc. research scientist Okla. Med. Research Found., Oklahoma City, 1983-84, S.R. Noble Found., Ardmore, Okla., 1984—. Contbr. articles to profl. jours. Fellow Dayalbagh U., 1970-72, Council Sci. and Indsl. Research New Delhi, 1974-77, Nat. Inst. Gen. Med. Sci., 1981-83. Mem. Am. Soc. Microbiology, Am. Assn. Immunologists, Inst. Biology London, N.Y. Acad. Scis., Sigma Xi (assoc.), Phi Lambda Upsilon (life). Avocations: music; travel; outdoor games. Home: Route One Box 9 Ardmore OK 73401 Office: SR Noble Found Inc PO Box 2180 Ardmore OK 73402

MODLIN, DAVID MICHAEL, dentist; b. Lincolnton, N.C., Nov. 3, 1948; s. Eugene Dellinger and Rosalyn (Francis) M.; m. Jane Leigh Kiser, Dec. 27, 1970; children—Candace Jane, David Michael Jr. D.D.S., U. N.C., 1975, M.P.H., 1982. Gen. dentist, Gastonia, N.C., 1975-77, Lincolnton, 1977-81, Mebane, N.C., 1982—; part-time faulty U.N.C.-Chapel Hill Sch. Denistry. Fellow Acad. Gen. Dentistry; mem. ADA, N.C. Dental Soc. Democrat. Methodist. Home: 105 Ledge Ln Chapel Hill NC 27514 Office: 200 S 5th St Mebane NC 27302

MODLIN, TERRY ARTHUR, restaurateur; b. Biloxi, Miss., Mar. 3, 1944; s. Herbert Charles and Mildred (Thornton) M. Student DePauw U., 1963; B.A. in Psychology, Kans. U., 1967, postgrad. Law Sch., 1967. Stockbroker, Paine, Webber, Topeka, Kans., 1967-70; asst. to med. dir. Highland Hosp., Asheville, N.C., 1970-73; personnel dir. St. Joseph's Hosp., Asheville, 1973-76; asst. dir. Western N.C. Splty. Hosp., Black Mountain, N.C., 1976; pres. Poncho's La Casita Restaurants, Inc., Asheville, 1976—. Pres. Asheville Tourist Assn., 1979, Buncombe County Mental Health Assn., 1972; v.p. N.C. Mental Health Assn., 1973. Mem. N.C. Restaurant Assn. (bd. dirs. 1982—, exec. com. 1986), Nat. Restaurant Assn., Western N.C. Culinary Assn., N.C. Hosp. Personnel Assn. (bd. dirs. 1975). Republican. Home: 112 Leisure Mountain Rd Asheville NC 28804 Office: Poncho's La Casita Restaurants 505 Tunnel Rd Asheville NC 28805

MOE, PALMER, gas company executive; b. 1944. B.S. in Bus. Adminstrn., U. Denver, 1966. Mem. audit staff to mng. ptnr. Arthur Anderson Co., 1965-83; chief operating officer Valero Energy Corp., San Antonio, 1983—; dir. Valero Natural Gas Co., Valero Storage, Valero Transmission Co., also vice chmn. bd.; dir. Valero Offshore Inc., Valero Offshore Properties Inc., Valero Producing Co. Served with USAR, 1963-69. Office: Valero Energy Corp 350 McCullough St San Antonio TX 78292

MOEHLMAN, ROBERT STEVENS, independent consultant; b. Rochester, N.Y., Feb. 23, 1910; s. Conrad Henry and Berth Anna (Young) M.; m. Lillian Johnson, Sept. 17, 1934; children—Karen M, Linda. B.A., U. Rochester, 1931; M.A., Harvard U., 1932, Ph.D., 1935. Mining geologist Anaconda Co., Butte, Mont. and Reno, Nev., 1935-45; chief geologist S.Am. Mines, N.Y.C., 1946-50; exec. v.p. Austral Oil Co., Houston, 1951-62; pres., dir. Newmont Oil Co., Houston, 1962-77; dir. Newmont Oil Co., Houston, 1978-84; ind. cons., 1985—. Mem. AIME, Am. Assn. Petroleum Geologists, Soc. Econ. Geologists, Soc. Petroleum Engrs., Ind. Petroleum Producers Am. Clubs: Met., Harvard (N.Y.); Petroleum of Houston. Home: 242 Maple Valley Rd Houston TX 77056 Office: Suite 1017 600 Jefferson Houston TX 77002

MOELLER, JEROME FREDERICK, pharmacist; b. Bastrop, La., Feb. 8, 1939; s. Jerome Harry and Faye (Holloway) M.; m. Elizabeth Amy Leavell, July 21, 1962; children—Jerome Frederick, Mary Elizabeth Amy, Susan Hadley. B.S., N.E. La. U., 1962. Registered pharmacist. Pharmacist, Fuller Drug Co., Arkadelphia, Ark., 1962-63; pharmacist, co-owner Moeller Pharmacy, Bastrop, La., 1964-66, Moeller's Inc., Honda and Yamaha Dealership; dir. pharmacy Morehouse Gen. Hosp., Bastrop, 1964—; pres. Abner Wimberly Meml. Fed. Credit Union, Bastrop, 1982-83; chmn. bd. 1st Nat. Bank La., Bastrop, 1984—. Mem. Am. Soc. Hosp. Pharmacists, La. Soc. Hosp. Pharmacists, La. Pharmacists Assn., 5th Dist. Phar. Assn., N.La. Soc. Hosp.

Pharmacists. Methodist. Home: 3014 Capella Dr Bastrop LA 71220 Office: Morehouse Gen Hosp 323 W Walnut St Bastrop LA 71221

MOELY, BARBARA E., psychology educator; b. Prairie du Sac, Wis., July 17, 1940; d. John Arthur and Loretta Ruth (Giese) M.; m. Gerald Wiener, May 21, 1974; children—John Jacob, David Andrew. B.A., U. Wis., 1962, M.A., 1964; Ph.D., U. Minn., 1968. Asst. prof. U. Hawaii, Honolulu, 1967-71; research psychologist UCLA, 1971-72; asst. prof. Tulane U., New Orleans, 1972-75, assoc. prof., 1975-85, prof., 1985—; cons. New Orleans Public Schs., 1973-75. Contbr. numerous articles to profl. jours. Grantee La. Commn. Extension and Continuing Edn., 1973, U.S. Office Edn., 1977, 1978, 1979, Tulane U., 1978, 1975, 1977, 1983, Inst. Mental Hygiene New Orleans, 1983, Nat. Inst. Edn., 1983. Mem. S.W. Soc. Research and Human Devel. (pres. 1984-86), Soc. Research Child Devel., Am. Psychol. Assn., Am. Ednl. Research Assn., Phi Beta Kappa (pres. chpt. 1981-82).

MOEN, MATTHEW CURTIS, political science educator, researcher; b. Sioux Falls, S.D., June 19, 1958; s. Kenneth Marion and Verona Clarice (Anderson) M.; B.A. with honors, Augustana Coll., 1980; M.A., U. Okla., 1983. Polit. scientist Carl Albert Ctr., Norman, Okla., 1980—; participant Inter-U Consortium Polit. and Social Research, Ann Arbor, Mich., 1982, U.S.-Canadian Legis. Exchange Program, Washington, 1984; legis. asst. Congressman Phil Sharp, Washington, 1984. Contbr. articles to profl. jours. Participant White House Conf. Small Bus., Sioux Falls, S.D., 1980. Carl Albert fellow, 1980; Am. Polit. Sci. Assn. congl. fellow 1983-84. Recipient Doug Brown leadership award YMCA, 1976. Mem. Am. Polit. Sci. Assn., Southwest Polit. Sci. Assn., Legis. Studies Group, Soc. Sci. Study Religion. Democrat. Lutheran. Avocations: athletics; reading. Office: Carl Albert Ctr 630 Parrington Oval 106 Norman OK 73019

MOERINGS, BERT JOSEPH, stockbroker; b. Lobith, Holland, Oct. 11, 1945; came to U.S., 1950, naturalized, 1957; s. Nicolaas A. and Betty J. M.; B.S. in Econs., Spring Hill Coll., 1980; m. Marsha Rinker, Mar. 15, 1980; children—Nicholas, Lauren. Stockbroker, E. F. Hutton, Vero Beach, Fla., 1972-73, Merrill Lynch, Palm Beach, Fla., 1973-79; v.p. sales Alan Bush Brokerage Co., Palm Beach, 1979-86; pres. CMC Services, Inc., 1986—. Served to Capt. U.S. Army, 1968-71. Decorated Bronze Star. Republican. Home: 2329 Prosperity Bay Ct Palm Beach Gardens FL 33410 Office: 1220 US Hwy 1-North Palm Beach FL 33408

MOESEL, BRUCE A., building materials distributor; b. Pauls Valley, Okla., July 8, 1957; s. Richard H. and Marjorie A. (Ball) M. B.S. in Bus. Mgmt., Okla. State U., 1979. Constrn. mgr. Moesel's Hort-Haven, Oklahoma City, 1976-78, bus. mgr., 1979-82, cons., 1982—; gen. mgr. Collegiate Products, Inc., Stillwater, Okla., 1978-79; pres. Glasshouses by Moesel's Inc., Okla. City, 1982—. Chmn. City Univ. Task Force, Stillwater, 1979; adminstrv. v.p. Residence Halls Assn., Stillwater, 1978; senator Student Senate, Stillwater, 1979; chmn. precinct Rep. Party, Oklahoma City, 1983. Mem. Nat. Glass Dealer's Assn., Nat. Jr. Horticulture Assn. (dir.), Oklahoma City C. of C., Okla. Hort. Soc. Contbr. articles to profl. jours. Office: Glasshouses by Moesel's Inc 350 S Vermont Suite 321 Oklahoma City OK 73108

MOESER, JOHN VICTOR, urban studies and planning educator, researcher; b. Colorado City, Tex., Nov. 3, 1942; s. Charles Victor and Virginia Alice (James) M.; m. Sharon Ann Gary, June 11, 1966; children—Jeremy Mark, Charles David. B.A. in Polit. Sci., Tex. Tech U., 1965; M.A. in Polit. Sci., U. Colo., 1967; Ph.D. in Polit. Sci., George Washington U., 1975. Asst. prof. urban studies and planning Va. Commonwealth U., Richmond, 1971-77, assoc. prof., 1977-85, prof., 1985—. Author: (with others) The Politics of Annexation, 1982. Editor: A Virginia Profile, 1981. Chmn. Richmond Human Relations Commn., 1981-83; vice chmn. Downtown Coop. Ministry, Richmond, 1984—; mem. Va. Interfaith Ctr. for Pub. Policy, Richmond, 1983—. Recipient Disting. Faculty award Va. Commonwealth U., 1983, Outstanding Leadership as Chmn. award Richmond Human Relations Commn., 1983. Mem. Am. Polit. Sci. Assn. Democrat. Presbyterian. Home: 4800 E Seminary Ave Richmond VA 23227 Office: Dept Urban Studies Planning Va Commonwealth U 812 W Franklin St Richmond VA 23284

MOFFETT, KENNETH MCKEE, architect; b. Alma, Mich., Mar. 26, 1944; s. Samuel McKee and Janet (Holt) M.; m. Marian Scott, May 21, 1971; 1 child, Alison Elizabeth. Student Coll. of Wooster, Ohio, 1962-64; B.Arch. with high honors, N.C. State U., 1969. Registered architect, Mass., Tenn. Architect, facilities planning div. N.C. State U., 1970-71; architect The Architect Collaborative, Cambridge, Mass., 1971-75; assoc. McCarty Bullock Holsaple, Knoxville, Tenn., 1975-84; dir. design Bullock, Smith & Ptnrs., Knoxville, 1984—. Contbr. articles to profl. jours. Bd. dirs. Community Design Ctr., Knoxville, 1985—, project dir., 1984. Recipient award of excellence Tenn. Soc. Architects, 1984; Assn. Collegiate Schs. Architecture fellow, 1968; recipient Paris prize, 1969. Mem. AIA, Nat. Trust Historic Preservation, Soc. Arch. Historians. Unitarian. Avocations: painting; classical music. Home: 5508 Riverbend Dr Knoxville TN 37919 Office: Bullock Smith & Ptnrs Suite 424 2 Northshore Ctr 1111 Northshore Dr Knoxville TN 37919

MOFFETT, T(ERRILL) K(AY), lawyer; b. Becker, Miss., July 11, 1949; s. Elmer C. and Mary Ethel (Meek) M.; m. Rita C. Millsaps, Mar. 11, 1972; 1 child, Tara Leigh. B.S., U.S. Mil. Acad., 1971; M.A. in Polit. Sci., U. Hawaii, 1974; J.D., U. Miss., 1979. Bar: Miss. 1979. Grad. tchr. Am. govt. U. Miss., Oxford, 1977-80; ptnr. Moffett and Thorne, Tupelo, Miss., 1980—. Republican candidate for U.S. Congress 1st Miss. Dist., 1978, 80; 1st dist. coordinator Reagan for Pres., 1980; mem. Lee County Rep. Exec. Com., 1980—; deacon 1st Baptist Ch., Tupelo; bd. dirs. Sav-A-Life Tupelo, Inc. Served to capt. U.S. Army, 1971-76. Mem. Miss. State Bar Assn., Lee County Bar Assn., Phi Sigma Alpha. Lodges: Civitan, Masons, Corinth. Avocations: music; hunting; tennis; travel. Home: PO Box 711 136 Pyle Dr Saltillo MS 38866 Office: Moffett and Thorne Attys at Law 210 W Main St Tupelo MS 38801

MOFIELD, WILLIAM RAY, communications educator; b. Hardin, Ky., July 3, 1921; s. Kelzie E. and Zela (Irvan) M.; A.B., Murray State Coll., 1943; M.A., Columbia, 1958; Ph.D., So. Ill. U., 1964; LL.D., Idaho Christian Coll., 1962; m. Janie Belle Bloomingburg, July 24, 1953; 1 dau., Ruth Ann. Tchr., Vienna (Ill.) High Sch., 1944-45; with WPAD-AM-FM, Paducah, Ky., 1945-59, mgr., 1959; mgr. WCBL-AM-FM, Benton, 1959; dir. acad. affairs radio-TV dept. So. Ill. U., 1959-64, v.p., 1982—; exec. pres. Murray (Ky.) State U., 1964-68, chmn. dept. communications, 1968—; stringer CBS News, 1945-64; sportscaster Ashland Oil Network, 1946-59; radio-tv mgmt. cons., 1945—; alt. mem. Ky. Commn. Higher Edn., 1965—; mem. nat. alumni bd. So. Ill. U., 1980—. Bd. dirs. to Assn., Paducah, Ky., 1956-59; commr. Boy Scouts Am., 1965, 66—, bd. dirs., 1965—; bd. dirs. Benton (Ky.) Hosp., Ky. State Penitentiary, Eddyville. Served with USNR, 1942-43. Recipient Duke of Paducah Civic award Mayor Paducah, 1956; named Ky. Communication Tchr. of Year, 1977; Disting. Alumni award Murray State U., 1981; Regent's prize as best tchr. Murray State U. Coll. Communications, 1985; Ky. Col.; CBS Found. News fellow, 1958. Mem. Nat. Assn. Broadcasters, Am. Soc. Disk Jockey Newscasters and Sportscasters, Ky. Broadcasters Assn., Internat. Radio and TV Soc., Ky. Edn. Assn., So. Ill. U. Alumni Assn. (nat. pres. 1983-84), Alpha Phi Omega, Alpha Phi Gamma, Sigma Delta Chi, Tau Kappa Alpha, Sigma Beta Gamma. Democrat. Mem. Ch. of Christ. Club: Rotary (pres. local club). Home: RFD 1 Hardin KY 42048 Office: Murray State U Murray KY 42071

MOGABGAB, WILLIAM JOSEPH, physician, educator; b. Durant, Okla., Nov. 2, 1921; s. Anees and Maude (Jopes) M.; m. Joy Roddy, Dec. 24, 1948; children—Robert (dec.), Ann, Kay, Edward R., Jean, Robert M. Berryman, William J.M. Berryman. B.S., Tulane U., 1942, M.D., 1944. Diplomate Am. Bd. Internal Medicine, Am. Bd. Microbiology. Intern Charity Hosp. La., New Orleans, 1944-45, resident, 1946-49, vis. physician, 1949-51, sr. vis. physician, 1971-75; cons. 1976—; mem. faculty Tulane U. Med. Sch., 1948—, prof. medicine, 1962—; vis. investigator, asst. physician Hosp. Rockefeller Inst. Med. Research, N.Y.C., 1951-52; chief infectious disease VA Hosp., Houston, 1952-53; asst. prof. medicine Baylor U. Coll. Medicine, 1952-53; head virology div. NAMRU 4, USNTC, Gt. Lakes, Ill., 1953-55; cons. infectious disease VA Hosp. New Orleans, 1956—; assoc. mem. Commn. on Influenza, Armed Forces Epidemiological Bd., 1959-71. Mem. mayor's health adv. com. New Orleans Health Dept. Fellow Nat. Found Infantile Paralysis, 1951-52, ACP, Am. Acad. Microbiology, Infectious Disease Soc. Am., Am. Coll. Epidemiology; mem. Soc. Exptl. Biology and Medicine, So. Soc. Clin. Research, Central Soc. Clin. Research, Am. Fedn. Clin. Research, Am. Soc. Cell Biology, Am. Soc. Microbiology, Am. Soc. Clin. Investigation, Tissue Culture Assn., Am. Pub. Health Assn., Am. Soc. Internal Medicine, Am. Soc. Clin. Pharmacology and Therapeutics, So. Med. Soc., AMA, Southwestern Assn. Clin. Microbiology, AAAS, Soc. for Epidemiologic Research, Am. Soc. for Virology. Research and publs. on agts. of and vaccines for respiratory infections, viruses, mycoplasma, new antibiotics. Home: 39 Lark St New Orleans LA 70124 Office: Sect Infectious Disease Dept Medicine Tulane U Sch Medicine 1430 Tulane Ave New Orleans LA 70112

MOGAVERO, JOANNA CARLA, therapist, educator; b. Bklyn., Nov. 10, 1959; d. Carl Thomas and Josephine (Milone) M. A.A., Indian River Community Coll., 1978; B.A., Eckerd Coll., 1981; M.Ed., Ga. State U., 1985. Counselor Eckerd Coll., St. Petersburg, Fla., 1980-82; shelter supr. Runaway-/Youth Crisis Ctr., St. Petersburg, 1981; tchr. Happy Workers Kindergarten, St. Petersburg, 1982-83; assoc. coordinator rape crisis Clayton Gen. Hosp., Riverdale, Ga., 1983-85; sexual assault therapist Family Service Ctr., Clearwater, Fla., 1985—. Active Mobilization for Animals, Ga., 1984-85. Mem. Am. Assn. Sex Educators, Counselors and Therapists, Am. Assn. Counseling and Devel., Ga. Abortion Rights Action League. Democrat. Roman Catholic. Avocations: jogging; swimming; journal writing; basketball. Home: 271 Alexander St Marietta GA 30060 Office: Family Service Ctrs 2960 Roosevelt Blvd Clearwater FL 33520

MOGGE, HARRIET MORGAN, educational association executive; b. Cleve., Jan. 2, 1928; d. Russell VanDyke and Grace (Wells) Morgan; B.M.E., Northwestern U., 1959; postgrad. Ill. State U., 1969; m. Robert Arthur Mogge, Aug. 17, 1948 (div. 1977); 1 dau., Linda Jean. Instr. piano, Evanston, Ill., 1954-58; instr. elem. music pub. schs., Evanston, 1959; editorial asst. archivist Summy-Birchard Co., Evanston, 1964-66, asst. to editor-in-chief, 1966-67, cons., 1968-69, ednl. dir., 1969-74, also historian, 1973-74; supr. vocal music jr. high sch., Watseka, Ill., 1967-68; asst. dir. profl. programs Music Educators Nat. Conf., Reston, Va., 1974-84, dir. meetings and convs., 1984—, mgr. direct mktg. service, 1981—. Active various community drives. Mem. Music Educators Nat. Conf., Am. Choral Dirs. Assn., In and About Chgo., Music Educators Assn. (dir.), Suzuki Assn. Ams. (exec. sec. 1972-74), Nat. Assn. Exposition Mgrs. (cert. exhbn. mgr.; edn. com. 1979—, chmn. edn. com. 1985—, bd. dirs. Washington chpt. 1983-85, nat. bd. dirs. 1986—), Mu Phi Epsilon, Kappa Delta (province pres. 1960-66, 72-76, regional chpts. dir. 1976-78, nat. dir. scholarship 1981-84), Republican. Presbyterian. Clubs: Bus. and Profl. Women's (dir. 1968-70) (Watseka); Antique Automobile Club, Model T Ford Internat. (v.p. 1971-72, 76, 77, pres. 1981, treas. 1983—, dir. 1971—). Mng. editor Am. Suzuki Jour., 1972-74; display advt. mgr. Model T Times, 1971—. Home: 1919A VillaRidge Dr Reston VA 22091 Office: 1902 Association Dr Reston VA 22091

MOHAJIR, NASIR AHMED, geologist, reservoir engineer; b. Karachi, Sind, Pakistan, Nov. 1, 1956; came to U.S., 1974, naturalized, 1982; s. Abdur Rasheed and Tayaba M.; m. Tasneem Nasir, Aug. 3, 1984. Assoc. of Sci., Seward County Community Coll., Liberal, Kansas, 1976; B.S. of Gen., U. Kans., 1979, B.S. in Geology, 1981. Draftsman, Trunkline Gas Co., Houston, 1979-80, assoc. geologist, 1981-84, geologist, 1985—. Mem. Am. Assoc. Petroleum Geologists, Houston Geol. Soc. Republican. Muslim. Club: Trunkline Employees (chmn. social com. 1985—) (Houston). Avocations: painting; photography; reading; tennis; bowling. Office: Trunkline Gas Co 3000 Bissonet St Houston TX 77005

MOHAPATRA, MANINDRA KUMAR, public affairs educator; b. Bhadrak, Orissa, India, Aug. 1, 1935; came to U.S., 1966, naturalized, 1977; s. Baishnab and Indumati Mohapatra; m. Urmila Mohanty; children—Simani, Sangram. M.P.A., U. Mich., 1967; Ph.D., U. Ky., 1971. From instr. to assoc. prof. Old Dominion U., 1969-80; prof. pub. affairs Ky. State U., Frankfort, 1980—. Author: A Study of Affluent Asian Indians in the United States, 1984. Contbr. articles to profl. jours. Mem. Am. Soc. Pub. Adminstrn., Am. Polit. Sci. Assn., Indian Inst. Pub. Adminstrn., Ky. Polit. Sci. Assn. (v.p. 1982-83, exec. sec. 1983-86). Democrat. Hindu. Home: 673 Montclair Rd Frankfort KY 40601 Office: Sch Pub Affairs Ky State U Frankfort KY 40601

MOHEREK, ANTHONY JOSEPH, oil company executive; b. Passaic, N.J., Oct. 31, 1952; s. Emil Anthony Sr. and Anna Catherine (Birish) M.; m. Virginia Lozano, May 12, 1984; 1 child, Adrienne Joy. B.S. in Geology, Rutgers U., 1974; M.S. in Oceanography, Tex. A&M U., 1976. Geologist, Tenneco Oil, Houston, 1976-80; regional exploration geologist Gulfstream Petroleum Corp., Houston, 1980-83, chief geologist, 1983—. Contbr. articles to profl. jours. Vol., Ctr. for Retarded, Inc., Houston, 1984; bd dirs. Greenspoint Log Library, Houston, 1985—. U.S. Army C.E. research grantee, 1975-76. Mem Am. Assn. Profl. Geologists, Houston Geol. Soc. Roman Catholic. Avocations: fishing; hunting; golfing; photography. Home: 2902 Crystal Falls Dr Kingwood TX 77345 Office: Gulfstream Petroleum Corp 350 N Belt St Suite 101 Houston TX 77060

MOHLER, JUNE FOSTER, college administrator, textiles educator; b. Brunswick, Md.; d. John Stanley and Edna (Deaner-Foster) Everline; m. Robert D. Mohler (div.); 1 child, R. Douglas, Jr. B.S., U. Md.; M.A., NYU; Ph.D., U. N.C.-Greensboro. Vice pres. Lee Ballard Assocs., N.Y.C.; exec. dir. Sales Tng. Inst., N.Y.C.; asst. to pres. Fin. Planning Corp.; fashion dir. Fieldcrest Mills, N.Y.C.; v.p. Design Research Internat., Cambridge, Mass.; assoc. prof., acting chmn. NYU; dean, prof. textiles Winthrop Coll., Rock Hill, S.C., 1979. Author: (with others) Textile Fabrics and Their Selection, 1984. Named Burdine's Woman of Distinction, 1973; Disting. Citizen of Brunswick, Md., 1983. Mem. Am. Home Econs. Assn. (several offices), Assn. Adminstrs. Home Econs. (sec.-treas. So. Region 1981-84), Assn. Coll. Profs. of Textiles and Clothing (exec. council, treas. 1982-85), Fashion Group of Charlotte (N.C.) (exec. bd. dirs. program chmn. 1982-86, regional dir.-elect 1986), N.C. Home Econs. Assn. (v.p. 1976-77). Democrat. Episcopalian. Office: Sch Consumer Sci Winthrop Coll Rock Hill SC 29733

MOHLER, ROBERT RICHARD JOHN, earth scientist, remote sensing specialist; Moab, Utah, Mar. 26, 1953; s. Robert Edison and Agnes Elizabeth (Schafer) M.; m. Amy Louise Szumigala, June 11, 1977; 1 son, Jeremy. B.S., U. Toledo, 1975, M.A. in Geography, 1977; M.S. in Agr./Climatology, U. Nev., 1979; postgrad. U. Houston. Adminstrv. technician Tex. Dept. Hwys., Houston, 1980; sr. scientist Lockheed-EMSCO, Houston, 1980—. Contbr. articles to profl. jours. Recipient New Tech. award NASA; also several co. and govt. research commendations. Mem. Assn. Am. Geographers, Am. Assn. Photogrammetry, Am Assn. Petroleum Geologists, Sigma Xi, Phi Kappa Phi, Gamma Sigma Delta. Roman Catholic. Avocation: photography. Office: Lockheed EMSCO 2400 NASA Rd 1/C09 Houston TX 77258

MOHR, CHARLES, music educator, consultant, arts administrator; b. Clinton, Okla., Sept. 30, 1939; s. Olin L. and Alta (Smith) M.; divorced; children—Patrick Shawn, Jenny Reynolds. B.S., Southwestern State U., 1960; M., 1965, North Tex. State U., 1963, Okla. State U., 1967. Elem. music tchr. Lawton Pub. Schs., Okla., 1960-63, jr. high choral dir., 1963-65, high sch. choral dir., 1965-70; music specialist Okla. State Dept. Edn., Oklahoma City, 1970-80, adminstr. arts in edn., 1980-85; choir dir. Western Oaks Christian Ch., Oklahoma City, 1975-85; edn. cons. state and private schs., 1970—; regional chmn. Alliance for Arts Edn., 1985. Author (with others): New Wind Blowing, 1978; The Arts-A Process, 1980. Advisor, Frontier council Boy Scouts Am., 1975-85; bd. dirs. Harlweldin Inst., Tulsa, 1984-85; rev. panel State Arts Council Okla., 1983-85. Recipient Gov.'s arts award, Oklahoma City, 1984. Mem. Music Educators Nat. Conf. (chmn. 1978), Okla. Music Educators, Nat. Council Music Suprs., Assn. Supervision and Curriculum Devel., Am. Choral Dirs. Democrat. Christian Ch. Avocations: reading; arts; neurolinguistic programming. Office: Okla State Dept Edn 2500 N Lincoln Oklahoma City OK 73105

MOHR, ROBERT JAMES, aeronautics company executive; b. Tiffin, Ohio, May 1, 1932; s. Glenn Orland and Catherine Francis (Crist) M.; m. Roberta Joyce Tank, May 1, 1955; children—Scott Aaron, Todd Darren, Lynne Annette. B.S. in Aero. Engring., Calif. Poly. State U., 1959; cert. bus. UCLA, 1972. Project engr. McDonnell Douglas Astronautics Co., Sacramento, Calif. and Huntington Beach, Calif., 1959-70, configuration mgr., Huntington Beach, 1970-72, program integration mgr., 1972-83, test mgr., Alexandria, Va., 1983-85, program mgr., 1985, CBS TV network Apollo 11 MDAC rep., Los Angeles, 1969, tech. team dir., Huntsville, Ala., 1969, 70. Vice chmn., then chmn. Inst. Acro. Scis., San Luis Obispo, Calif., 1957-59; coordinator, coach Youth Basketball League, Mission Viejo, Calif., 1970-76; pres., v.p. Little League Baseball, Mission Viejo, 1970-71. Mem. Naval Inst. Republican. Presbyterian. Avocations: golf; tennis; jogging; civil war literature; aircraft. Home: 8703 Sheridan Farms Ct Springfield VA 22152 Office: McDonnell Douglas Astronautics Co PO Box 19109 Alexandria VA 22320

MOI, STEVEN JOSEPH, advertising executive; b. St. Louis, Mar. 11, 1946; s. Joseph O. and Dorothy Lillian (Houston) M.; m. Joanie Marie Luckett, Feb. 19, 1964; children—Joseph Steven, Lisa Marie. Student Stephen F. Austin Coll., Nacogdoches, Tex., 1964-66. Radio, TV personality, Nacogdoches, 1964-66; exec. Wyatt & Williams Advt. Agy. and Lennen & Newell, Dallas and N.Y.C., 1966-72; exec. Glenn Advt. Agy., Dallas, 1972-73; exec. v.p., dir. Internat. Town Homes, Inc., Dallas, 1973; prin. Steve Moi & Assocs., Inc., Pres. Associated Corp., Dallas, 1973—; pres. SM&A Records Inpro Inc., McVett Custom Builders Co., Dallas, 1977—; dir. Custom Home Builders; cons. Greater Dallas Housing Opportunity Ctr., 1978; instr. advt. U. Tex., Dallas, 1975-76, Recipient Houston Art Dirs. Bronze Medal for best newspaper ad, 1974. Mem. Dallas Advt. League (gold medal best corp. brochure, image campaign 1977, 78), Dallas Soc. Visual Communications (best corp. brochure 1976), Home, Apt. Builders Assn., Sales and Mktg. Council (Dallas bd. dirs. 1983, maximum creativity award 1982). Republican. Roman Catholic. Club: Oakridge Country (Garland, Tex.) Office: 7515 Greenville Ave Suite 601 Dallas TX 75231

MOLANO, CELIA, health care administrator; b. Maiquetia, Venezuela, Oct. 9, 1935; d. Felipe and Isabel de Molano (Cardenas) M.; B.S., U. Panama, 1957, postgrad., 1959-61; masters degree U. P.R., 1976; 1 child, Otilda I. Pinilla. Med. technologist Gorgas Meml. Lab., Panama, 1957-62; asst. prof. natural scis. and Pharmacy Sch., U. Panama, 1960-61, asst. prof. microbiology Med. Scis. Sch., 1960-62, asst. prof. microbiology Med. Tech. Sch., 1961-62; microbiologist FDA, Panama, 1961-62; dir. Pavia Hosp. Lab., P.R., 1962-68; owner, dir. San Martin Hosp. Lab., Rio Piedras, P.R., 1968-84; asst. adminstr. San Martin Hosp., 1975-80, personnel dir., 1977—; pres. Lab. Services Group, Hato Rey, P.R., 1980—, Celia Molano & Assos., Rio Piedras, 1982—; assoc. adminstr., mktg. dir. Our Lady of Guadalupe Community Hosp., 1984—. Trustee I. Gonzalez Martinez Oncological Hosp., 1970—, Blue Cross P.R., 1984—. Recipient Pres.'s award Health Service Adminstrn., 1976, 77, 78; various recognition awards. Mem. P.R. Hosp. Adminstrs. Assn. (pres. 1981), Hosp. Fin. Mgmt. Assn., P.R. Hosps. Assn. (trustee, sec. 1983), Am. Soc. Clin. Pathologists, Am. Soc. Med. Technologists, P.R. Coll. Med. Technologists, P.R. Labs. Owners Assn. (pres. 1982—), P.R. Profls. Assn. Roman Catholic. Office: PO Box 29689/65 Inf Sta Rio Piedras PR 00929

MOLDOFF, TERRY BETH, lawyer; b. Miami, Fla., May 27, 1959; d. David and Jean Deborah (Polillo) Moldoff. B.A., U. South Fla., 1980; postgrad. U. Tulsa, 1980-81; J.D., Fla. State U., 1983. Bar: Fla. 1984. Assoc. Esler & Kirschbaum, Ft. Lauderdale, Fla., 1984-85; Parrillo, Weiss & Moss P.A., North Miami, Fla., 1985—. Mem. Fla. Audubon, Fla. Nat. Wild Life Fedn., Nat. Wildlife Fedn. Animal Protection Inst. Am., Broward County Bar Assn., Am. Trial Lawyers Assn., Assn. Fla. Trial Lawyers, Phi Delta Phi. Democrat. Jewish. Home: 1101 River Reach Dr #519 Fort Lauderdale FL 33315 Office: Parrillo Weiss & Moss 2925 Aventura Blvd #308 North Miami FL 33180

MOLINARI, JOSEPH FRANCIS, optometrist; b. Worcester, Mass.; s. Wallace F. and Anntoinette M. (Tortora) M. A.A., Central New Eng. Coll., 1972; B.S., New Eng. Coll., 1973, O.D., 1974; M.Ed., Mercer U., 1979. Staff optometrist Lahey Clin. Med. Ctr., 1977-79; asst. prof. U. Ala., 1979-82; gen. practice optometry, Panama City Beach, Fla., 1982—; cons. U.S. Air Force, Tyndall AFB, 1980—. Contbr. articles to profl. jours. Item writer Nat. Bd. Optometry, Washington, 1980-83. Pres., Studio Villas Assn., Inc., 1985, Gulf of Mex. Optics Inc., Panama City Beach, 1984-85; chmn. Bay Point Anterior Segment Symposium Inc., 1984-85. Served to capt. USAFR, 1974—. Recipient Spurgeon Eure award Am. Optometric Found., 1978, 81, 82, Dallos Contact Lens Research award Brit. Contact Lens Assn., 1984. Fellow Am. Acad. Optometry, Am. Coll. Optometric Physicians; mem. Fla. Optometric Assn. (del. 1984, 85), Neuro-optometry Soc. (chmn. 1985), Am. Coll. Optometry Physicians; Lodges: Lions, K.C. Office: 10010 Middle Beach Rd Panama City Beach FL 32407

MOLLISON, RICHARD DEVOL, mining executive; b. Faribault, Minn., June 7, 1916; s. Allan Edwin and Edna (Devol) M.; B.Mining Engring., U. Minn., 1941; m. Elizabeth Ellen Cobb, June 7, 1941; children—Steven Cobb, Ann Elizabeth Mollison Waters, Mark Richard. Mining engr. various locations, 1941-47; with Texasgulf Inc., 1947—, v.p., mgr. exploration, 1962-64, v.p. metals div., 1964-72, sr. v.p., 1972-73, pres., 1973-79, vice chmn., 1979-81, chmn., 1981-82, ret., 1982, dir., 1973—; dir. Kidd Creek Mines Ltd., 1981—, chmn., 1983—; dir. Callahan Mining Corp. Mem. Tau Beta Pi, Theta Xi. Republican. Clubs: Sky, Mining (N.Y.C.); Royal Canadian Yacht (Toronto, Ont., Can.); Riverside Yacht (Conn.); Greenwich Country; Marco Island Country. Home: 1777 Inlet Dr Marco Island FL 33937

MOLLOHAN, ALAN B., congressman, lawyer; b. Fairmont, W.Va., May 14, 1943; s. Robert H. and Helen (Holt) M.; m. Barbara Whiting, Aug. 7, 1976; children—Alan, Robert, Andrew, Karl. A.B. in Polit. Sci., Coll. William and Mary, 1966; J.D., W.Va. U., 1970. Bar: W.Va. Assoc. Furbee, Amos, Webb & Critchfield, Fairmont, 1970-73, Rose, Schmit, Dixon, Pitts. and Washington, 1973-81, Parker & Parker, Fairmont, 1981-83; mem. 98th Congress from W.Va. 1st dist. Chmn. Marion County Democratic Exec. Com., 1971-74; del. Dem. Nat. Conv., 1968, 72, 76. Mem. ABA, W.Va. Bar Assn., D.C. Bar Assn. Baptist. Lodge: Moose. Home: 812 Benoni Ave Fairmont WV 26554 Office: 516 Cannon House Office Bldg Washington DC 20515

MOLNAR, JOHN EDGAR, higher education administrator; b. Cin., Sept. 12, 1942; s. John William and Bonnie (Hannaford) M. A.B. in History with high honors, Coll. of William and Mary, 1964; A.M.L.S., U. Mich., 1965, Ph.D., 1978; M.Hum., U. Richmond, 1968. Librarian, Kelsey Mus., Ann Arbor, Mich., 1965; asst. librarian Longwood Coll., Farmville, Va., 1965-70; librarian Cleary Coll., Ysilanti, Mich., 1973-75; coordinator library planning Council of Higher Edn., Richmond, Va., 1975—; co-chmn. Va. Task Force on Computer Sci. Programs, 1982-83; adviser on licensure of fgn. med. sch. grads. Va. Bd. Medicine, 1983—; co-chmn. Va. Task Force on Fgn. Langs., 1983-85, Va. Fgn. Lang. Council, 1986—. Author: Author-/Title Index to Sabin, 1974. Editor: Assessment of Computer Science Degree Programs in Virginia, 1983; Assessment of the Foreign Language Discipline in Virginia's State-Supported Institutions of Higher Education, 1985. Mem. Am. Philatelic Soc., SAR, Persons Responsible for Oversight and Approval Nonpub. Degree-granting Instns. Beta Phi Mu. Republican. Anglican. Home: 900 High St Farmville VA 23901 Office: Council Higher Edn 101 N 14th St Richmond VA 23219

MOLONEY, LOUIS CAREY, retired librarian; b. Trenton, N.J., Nov. 26, 1920; s. Louis Carey and Florence (Smith) M.; B.S. in Edn., Trenton State Coll., 1942, B.L.S., 1948; postgrad. U. Chgo., 1950-51; M.S., Tex. A. and I. U., 1958; D.L.S., Columbia U., 1970; m. Doris Lee Pettit, Nov. 30, 1944; children—Doris Lee, Evelyn Estabrook, Louis Carey III. Head librarian Bishop Meml. Library, Toms River, N.J., 1947-50, Trenton Jr. Coll., 1951-52; asst. librarian Tex. A. and I. U., Kingsville, 1952-64; Cons. Welder Wildlife Found. Library, Sinton, Tex., 1958-64; asso. librarian Southwest Tex. State U., San Marcos, 1964-65, head librarian, 1965-75, dir. Learning Resources Center, 1975-82, univ. librarian, 1982-86, ret., 1986. Bd. dirs., chmn., sec. Southside Community Center, 1973-79. Served with USAAF, 1942-43, USNR, 1943-45. Mem. ALA, Tex. Library Assn. (past publicity chmn., Dist. III past chmn.), Tex. Council State U. Librarians (past chmn.), Council Research and Acad. Libraries (past pres.), Phi Delta Kappa (treas.). Democrat. Methodist. Club: Lions (pres. 1976-77). Author articles. Home: 604 Dale St San Marcos TX 78666

MOLONY, MICHAEL JANSSENS, JR., lawyer; b. New Orleans, Sept. 2, 1922; s. Michael Janssens and Marie (Perret) M.; J.D., Tulane U., 1950; m. Jane Leslie Waguespack, Oct. 21, 1951; children—Jane Leslie, Michael Janssens III, Megan, Kevin, Sara, Brian, Ian, Duncan. Admitted to La. bar, 1950, since practiced in New Orleans; partner firm Molony & Baldwin, 1950; asso., partner firm Jones, Flanders, Waechter & Walker, 1951-56; partner firm Jones, Walker, Waechter, Poitevent, Carrere & Denegre, 1956-75; partner firm Milling, Benson, Woodward, Hillyer, Pierson & Miller, 1975—. Instr., lectr. Med. Sch. and Univ. Coll., Tulane U., 1953-59. Mem. Eisenhower Legal Com., 1952. Mem. Corporate bd. Boys' Clubs Greater New Orleans, 1969-71; mem. Goals Found. Council and ex-officio mem. Goals Found., Met. New Orleans Goals Program, 1969-72; vice chmn. Ad Hoc Planning Com. Goals Met. New Orleans, 1969-73; vice-chmn. Port of New Orleans Operation Impact, 1969-70; mem. Met. Area Com., New Orleans, 1970-84; chmn. La. Gov.'s Task Force on Space Industry, 1971-73; chmn. La. Gov.'s Adv. Com. Met. New Orleans Transp. and Planning Program, 1971-77; mem. La. Gov.'s Task Force Natural Gas Requirements, 1971-72, Mayor's Council on Internat. Trade and Econ. Devel., 1978. Bd. dirs., exec. com. New Orleans Tourist and Conv. Com., 1973-74, 78, chmn. Family Attractions Com., 1973-75; bd. dirs. Internat. Trade Mart, 1982, chmn. internat. banking task force, chmn. internat. bus. com., 1983-85; trustee Loyola U., New Orleans, Pub. Affairs Research Council La., 1970-73, Acad. Sacred Heart, 1975-77; bd. commrs. Port of New Orleans, 1975-85, pres., 1978; vice chmn. Past Presidents Council, 1985—; trustee, mem. exec. com. So. States Legal Ctr., 1983—. Served with AUS, USAAF, 1942-46; PTO. Mem. Fed., Am. (mgmt. co-chmn. Com. Devel. Law Union Adminstrn. and Procedures 1969), La. (past sec.-treas., gov. 1959-60; editor jour. 1957-59, sec. spl. supreme ct. com. on drafting code jud. ethics), New Orleans (dir. legal aid bur. 1954, vice chmn. standing com. pub. relations 1970-71) bar assns., Am. Judicature Soc., La. Law Inst. (asst. sec.-treas. 1958-70), Internat. House, So. (founder), Am. insts mgmt. U.S. (urban and regional affairs com. 1970-72), La. (dir. 1963-66), New Orleans C. of C. (v.p. met. devel. and urban affairs 1969, past chmn. council, dir. 1970-78, pres.-elect 1970, pres. 1971, exec. com. 1972) Sigma Chi (pres. alumni chpt. 1956). Roman Catholic. Clubs: Pickwick, Southern Yacht, Serra, Plimsoll, Bienville, Lakewood Country, City (New Orleans). Home: 3039 Hudson Pl New Orleans LA 70114 Office: 1100 Whitney Bldg New Orleans LA 70130

MOLPUS, CHESTER MANLY, association executive; b. Louisville, Aug. 9, 1941; s. C.A. and Helen R. Molpus; student U. Miss., 1961-62; B.S., Miss. Coll., 1964; m. Penny Nichols, July 11, 1964; children—Mary, Maggie. Dir. public relations Miss. Retail Mchts. Assn., Jackson, 1965; exec. mgr. Canton (Miss.) C. of C., 1966-67, mgr. govt. relations The Kroger Co., Cin., 1967-69, dir. public affairs, 1969-73, v.p. public affairs, 1973-78, v.p. corp. affairs, 1979; pres. Am. Meat Inst., Arlington, Va., 1979—, bd. dirs. U.S. Meat Export Fedn., Nat. Livestock and Meat Bd. Served with U.S. Army, 1959. Mem. U.S. C. of C. (mem. regulatory affairs com.). Office: Am Meat Inst 1700 N Moore St Arlington VA 22209 also PO Box 3556 Washington DC 20007*

MOLPUS, DICK, state official; b. Philadelphia, Miss., Sept. 7, 1949; s. Richard and Frances (Blount) M.; m. Sally Nash, May 27, 1971; children—Helen Nash, Richard Gregory. B.B.A., U. Miss., 1971. Vice pres. mfg. Molpus Co., Philadelphia, Miss., 1971-80; exec. dir. Gov.'s Office Fed.-State Programs, Jackson, Miss., 1980-83; sec. of state State of Miss., Jackson, 1984—. Vice pres. Miss. Agr. and Forestry Mus., 1979; campaign dir., chmn. bd. United Givers Fund, Neshoba County, Miss., 1979-80; bd. dirs. Miss. PTA, 1984—, Miss. Forestry Assn., 1980—. Named Friend of Children, Miss. Assn. Elem. Sch. Adminstrs., 1984, Pub. Ofcl. of Yr., Miss. chpt. Am. Soc. Pub. Adminstrn., 1985. Mem. Sigma Chi. Democrat. Episcopalian. Office: Sec of State's Office 401 Mississippi St Jackson MS 39201

MOLTZAN, JANET ROZDIL, librarian; b. Bridgeport, Conn., Jan. 6, 1945; d. Andrew Peter and Helen (Botsko) Rozdil; m. Herbert John Moltzan, July 30, 1976. B.S.L.S., Tex. Woman's U., 1967, M.L.S. (scholar), 1973. Spl. counselor Tex. Woman's U., Denton, 1967-68; children's librarian Dallas Pub. Library, 1968-74, asst. library mgr., 1974-76, library mgr., 1976-85, asst. dir. pub. services, 1985—; cons. Lamplighter Sch., Dallas, 1971; mem. Caldecott Award jury, 1982-84. Contbr. articles to profl. jours. Cons. to author Reminiscences: A Glimpse of Old East Dallas, 1983. Bd. dirs. Lakewood Library Friends, Lakewood-Skillman Bus. and Profl. Assn., Dallas. Mem. ALA (conf. chmn. 1978-79), Tex. Library Assn. (legis. coordinator 1976-78, recognition award 1980), Pub. Library Assn. (chmn. services to children com. 1976-77), Assn. for Library Services to Children (nominating com. 1980, publs. com. 1984—), Tex. Library Assn. (children's roundtable, v.p. 1975-76, pres. 1976-77). Mem. Eastern Orthodox Ch. Home: 6935 Northaven Rd Dallas TX 75230 Office: Lakewood Community Library Dallas Pub Library System 1515 Young St Dallas TX 75201

MONACELLI, WALTER JOSEPH, patent lawyer; b. Albion, N.Y., Jan. 16, 1914; s. Horace and Hyacinth (Lombard) M.; m. Miriam E. Johnson, Sept. 7, 1947 (div.); children—Linda, Janet; m. Phyllis E. Fuhrman, 1973. B.S.C.E., U. Notre Dame, 1938, Ph.D. in Organic Chemistry, 1941; J.D., DePaul U., 1945. Bar: Ohio 1946, Ill. 1946, U.S. Supreme Ct. 1953. Research chemist Atlantic Refining Co., Phila., 1941-42, Sinclair Oil Co., East Chicago, Ind., 1942-43, Sherwin-Williams Co., Chgo., 1943-45; patent atty. Indsl. Rayon Corp., Cleve., 1946-47; mgr. patent dept. Koppers Co., Inc., Pitts., 1947-57; sole practice patent law, Cleve., 1957-72, St. Petersburg, Fla., 1972—; pres. Interlock Corp., Cleve., 1965—; v.p. Deltronix Corp., 1963—; Patentee in field. Mem. ABA, Intellectual Property Assn., Cleve. Patent Law Assn., Bar Assn. Greater Cleve., Phi Alpha Delta. Republican. Roman Catholic. Club: St. Petersburg Yacht. Home and Office: 720 36th Ave N Saint Petersburg FL 33704

MONAGHAN, MARVIN DANIEL, optometrist; b. Wichita Falls, Tex., Mar. 14, 1926; s. Marvin Gaines and Lillian Frances (Adair) M.; m. Ruth Carolyn Rice, June 15, 1952. B.A. in Physics, U. Tex., 1948; O.D., No. Ill. Coll. Optometry, 1950. Lic. optometrist, Tex. Assoc. James L. Crawford, Sulphur Springs, Tex., 1950-52; gen. practice optometry, Garland, Tex., 1952—; curator: Southwest R.R. Hist. Soc. Mus., 1965—. Editor Clearance Card Jour., 1974—. Mem. Landmark Mus. Soc., Garland, 1983—; mem. North Central Expressway Task Force Citizens adv. com., Dallas, 1984, 85; Dallas Area Rapid Transit Citizens adv. com., 1984—. Served with USNR, 1944-46. Recipient Southwest R.R. Hist. Soc. award, 1974. Mem. Am. Optometric Assn., North Tex. Optometric Soc. (pres. 1955-56), Tex. Optometric Assn. Methodist. Lodge: Rotary. Avocations: railroad museum restoration; photography; model building; antique automobiles; amateur radio. Home: 2920 Old Orchard Rd Garland TX 75041 Office: 808 W Avenue A Garland TX 75040

MONAHAN, THOMAS PAUL, accountant; b. Pitts., Feb. 27, 1951; s. Thomas Andrew and Patricia (Tompkins) M.; m. Ellen McKeithan Easterby, Aug. 2, 1975; children—Kelley Kathleen, Thomas Patrick. B.S. in Acctg., U. S.C., 1973. C.P.A., S.C. Staff acct. Rogers, Brigman, Peterson & Co., Columbia, S.C., 1972-75, ptnr., 1975-82; treas., prin. GMK Assocs., Columbia, 1982—; lectr., cons. Mem. Com. of 100. Mem. S.C. Assn. C.P.A.s, Am. Inst. C.P.A.s. Democrat. Club: Spring Valley Country, Faculty House (Columbia, S.C.). Home: 1117 Adger Rd Columbia SC 29205 Office: GMK Assoc 1331 Elmwood Ave Suite 101 Columbia SC 29201

MONCIBAIS, FERNANDO (MONTY), police officer, security consultant; b. San Antonio, Dec. 15, 1950; s. Herbert and Matilda (Soto) M.; m. Deborah Ann Hulsey (div.); children—Jayson Eduardo, Angela Robyn; m. 2d, Terri Annette Brooks; 1 child, Monica Marie. A.A., Dallas County Community Coll., Dallas, 1971. Lic. polygraph operator, Tex.; cert. criminal hypnotist, Tex. Patrolman Dallas Police Dept., 1971-76, criminal investigator, 1976-78, polygraph examiner, 1978-84, corporal investigator, 1984—; security dir. to police Trailways, Inc., Dallas, 1971—; ptnr., owner Tex. Polygraph Investigation, Dallas, 1980-83; v.p., Polygraph Assocs., Dallas, 1983—. Recipient Expert Markmanship award Dallas Police Dept., 1977, Cert. of Merit, Dallas Police Dept., 1983. Mem. Tex. Assn. Polygraph Examiners, Tex. Assn. for Investigative Hypnosis (bd. dirs. North Tex.), Soc. Investigation and Forensic Hypnosis, Dallas Police Assn., Am. Assn. Police Polygraphists. Democrat. Roman Catholic. Avocations: racquetball; jogging; basketball; music. Office: Dallas Police Dept 106 S Harwood St Dallas TX 75201

MONCK, JOHN WILLIAM, engineering services corporation executive, management consultant; b. Homestead, Pa., Nov. 8, 1933; s. Matthew Lawrence and Mary Mathilda (Schibley) M.; m. Joan Blount, Aug. 23, 1958; children—John William II, Joann Annette, Jennifer Marie. A.A., St. Petersburg Jr. Coll., 1956; B.A., U. South Fla., 1972. Engr., Honeywell Co. Aerospace Div., St. Petersburg, 1960-68; utilities dir. City of St. Petersburg, 1969-77; pres., dir. Engring. Services Inc., Brooksville, Fla., 1977—, Gulf Coast Services, Inc., Floral City, Fla., 1978—; sr. cons. R.J. Hansen, Inc., Sacramento, 1984—; dir. Airrication Engring. Co. Inc., Carmel, Calif., 1982—; faculty mem. Am. Pub. Works Assn., Chgo., 1976—; tech. advisor Nat. Assn. Sewer Services Co., Winter Park, Fla., 1978—. Deacon, New Testament Baptist Ch., Floral City, Fla. Served with USN, 1956-58. Mem. ASCE, Fla. Assn. Realtors, Am. Soc. Safety Engrs., Fla. Inst. Parks Personnel. Lodge: Masons. Home: 12713 S Old Jones Rd Floral City FL 32636 Office: Engineering Services Inc Route 2 Box 613 Brooksville FL 33512

MONCRIEF, JAMES ELBERT, geologist, oil company executive; b. Vivian, La., Dec. 22, 1930; s. Joseph Miller and Edna (Barnett) M.; m. Barbara Jim Lawton, Sept. 10, 1950; children—Jo Lynn, Jane Lawton, James Robert, Janice Michelle, Jefferson Miller. B.S., La. State U., 1952, M.S., 1954. Cert. profl. geologist, La. subsurface geologist Tidewater div. Getty Oil Co., Lafayette, La., 1954-55; dist. geologist Austral Oil Co., 1955-59; pres. Monrich Oil & Gas, Inc., Lafayette, 1959—, Cyclops Oil & Gas, Inc., 1969—; cons. geology, Lafayette, 1962—. Mem. Geol. and Mining Soc. (pres. 1949-50), Lafayette Geol. Soc., Am. Assn. Petroleum Geologists, AIME, La. Assn. Independent Producers and Royalty Owners. Club: Nat. Republican. Avocations: woodworking; gardening. Home: 401 Alonda Dr Lafayette LA 70503 Office: PO Box 52062 103 Bayou St Lafayette LA 70505

MONCRIEF, JOHN WILLIAM, college dean, chemistry educator; b. Brunswick, Ga., Jan. 23, 1941; s. Millard Snow and Sadie Cleo (Drummond) M.; m. Barbara Ann Land, July 20, 1963; children—Michael Sean, Marel Lynne, Heather Marie. B.S. with highest honors, Emory U., Atlanta, 1963; Ph.D., Harvard U., 1966. Teachng asst. Harvard U., Cambridge, Mass., 1963-66; asst. prof. Amherst Coll., Mass., 1966-68; asst. prof. Emory U., Atlanta, 1968-71, assoc. prof., 1971-76, prof. chemistry, 1976—, dean and div. exec. Oxford Coll., Ga., 1976-85, dean, chief exec. officer, 1985—. Author: Elements of Physical Chemistry, 1976; also articles. Mem. dist. com. Atlanta area council Boy Scouts Am., 1984—; elder First Presbyn. Ch., Covington, Ga., 1981—; trustee George Walton Acad., Monroe, Ga., 1980-84. Named lt. col. aide de campe of gov.'s staff, Gov. of Ga., 1985; Woodrow Wilson nat. fellow Harvard U., 1963-64; Danforth fellow Harvard U., 1963-66; NSF fellow Harvard U., 1963-66; Sloan research fellow, 1968-71; Danforth assoc., 1976—. Mem. Nat. Assn. Schs. and Colls. of United Meth. Ch., Assn. Pvt. Colls. and Univs. Ga. (bd. dirs. 1984—, v.p. 1985-86), Covington C. of C. (bd. dirs. 1981—, pres. 1986), Phi Beta Kappa, Sigma Xi, Omicron Delta Kappa. Avocations: jogging; photography; amateur naturalist. Home: 1145 River Cove Rd Social Circle GA 30279 Office: Oxford Coll of Emory U Oxford GA 30267

MONCRIEF, MICHAEL JOSEPH, county judge, independent oil producer; b. Houston, Sept. 5, 1943; s. Richard Barto Sr. and Mary Daisy (Wiley) M.; m. Rosemary Brewer, Dec. 31, 1980; children—Troy L., Mitchell K. B.S., Tarleton State U., 1968. Ind. oil producer, Fort Worth, 1969—; mem. Tex. Ho. of Reps., mem. appropriations com., 1970-72; judge Tarrant County, Tex., 1974-78, 1978—; past mem. Tarrant County Drug Abuse Bd., Lone Star Transp. Authority, N. Central Tex. Council of Govts.; mem. Gov.'s Blue Ribbon Commn. on Criminal Justice, many other groups. Bd. dirs. Assn. Retarded Citizens (hon. chmn.), chmn. Neighborhood Resources Devel. Council, Tarrant County Med., Edn. and Research Found., Tarrant County Mental Health Assn., Drug Treatment Ctr., Tarrant County Juvenile Bd., Fort Worth State Sch., Inst. of Public Service Tarleton State U.; pres. Neighborhood Health Horizons. Past bd. dirs. Gill Children Services, Inc., Fort Worth Library Bd., Longhorn Council Boy Scouts Am., Tex. Soc. for Prevention of Blindness, North Tex., many others. Named Outstanding Community Leader Am., 1970; Outstanding Young Man Am., 1971; Newsmaker of Yr., 1974, 78; Freshman Legislator of Yr. Tex. Legislature, 1971; many other honors. Mem. Tarleton Alumni Assn. (Disting. Alumni 1977), Ind. Petroleum Assn. Am., Am. Judicature Soc., Nat. Coll. Probate Judges, Fort Worth Res. Police Officers, other profl. orgns. Avocations: skiing; tennis; golf; hunting rattlesnakes and alligators. Office: Mike Moncrief Investments Inc Ft Worth Club Tower Suite 1200 Fort Worth TX 76102

MONCURE, ALBERT F., county administrator; b. Lancaster, Pa., Apr. 19, 1924; s. Fletcher Alexander Moncur and Irene (Murray) Wilson; m. Edna Mae Abramson, June 18, 1944 (div. 1985); children—Sheila Ann Moncure Belfon, Albert F., Alexandria Marie; m. Benni Sue Morrison, Aug. 31, 1985. Student Lincoln U., 1942; B.S. in Acctg., L.I. U., 1950; M.B.A., NYU, 1956, postgrad. Grad. Sch. Edn., 1958-59. Asst. mgr. ops. Port Authority, N.Y.-N.J., N.Y.C., 1963-67, asst. personnel dir., 1970, dir. gen. services, 1971-83; dep. commr. Dept. Social Services, N.Y.C., 1967-70; adminstrv. services div. chief Dept. Human Services, Arlington, Va., 1984—; chmn. N.Y.-N.J. Minority Purchasing Council, 1975; chmn. ethics bd. Port Authority, 1980-83, mem. equal opportunity council, 1979-83. Weekly radio show host, sta. WNYC, 1968; mem. N.Y.C. Council Against Poverty, 1967-70; v.p. Community Council Greater N.Y., 1975-82; bd. dirs. United Way of Tri-State, N.Y.C., 1978-81; chmn. health sect. Citizens Com. for Children, N.Y.C., 1983. Recipient Black Achievers award Harlem YMCA, 1973; named Most Active Vis. Prof., Nat. Urban League Black Exec. Exchange Program, 1979; Disting. Pub. Leader, Peoples Alliance, Bklyn., 1983. Mem. Am. Soc. Pub. Adminstrn. (life; N. Va. chpt. council 1980-85), Nat. Assn. Purchasing Mgmt. (pres. N.Y. chpt. 1979-80). Avocations: skiing; golf. Home: 909 Hillwood Ave Falls Church VA 22042 Office: Arlington Dept Human Services 1800 N Edison St Arlington VA 22207

MONES, MANUEL, JR., speech pathologist, educator, public relations executive; b. Tampa, Fla., Nov. 5, 1945; s. Manuel and Lydia (Sanchez) M.; m. Yolanda Solis Sandoval, June 29, 1968; children—Melinda Ann, Karen Arlene, Conrad Jason. M.S., U. South Fla., 1973. Speech and lang. pathologist, diagnostician St. Luke's Hosp., 1974-76, Tex. Children's Hosp., 1974-76, Tex. Heart Inst., 1974-76; clin. instr. Baylor Coll. Medicine, 1974-76, clin. asst. instr., 1980—; v.p. Speech and Lang. Remediation Ctr., Houston, 1976-78; coordinator community relations Speech and Hearing Inst., U. Tex. Health Sci. Ctr., Houston, 1978-80; dir. community relations and devel. Houston Sch. for Deaf Children, 1980—; cons. Houston Mental Health and Mental Retardation Ctr., 1976, Monterey (Calif.) Learning Systems, 1976, Cerebral Palsy Treatment Ctr., 1980. Bd. dirs. Parish Sch.; mem. adv. bd. Children's Mus., Houston. Served with USAF, 1967-71. Recipient Best of Tex. award Tex. Pub. Relations Assn., 1982; Outstanding Performance Campaign award United Way of Tex. Gulf Coast, 1982, 1st and 3d pl. awards excellence for outstanding achievement in communications. Mem. Pub. Relations Soc. Am., Am. Speech Lang. and Hearing Assn. (chmn. media prodn. task force), Houston Area Assn. Communication Disorders (adv. bd.). Democrat. Roman Catholic. Club: Southwest Greenway Exchange. Office: 3636 W Dallas Houston TX 77019

MONGAN, SANDRA JEAN, retail company executive; b. Roanoke, Va., July 15, 1937; d. James Lilburn and Dorothy Ellen (Newman) Blankenship; m. Brenton Sylvester Mongan, July 3, 1974 (div. 1982); 1 child, Michael. Student Va. So. U., 1957. Med. sec. Lewis Gale Hosp., Roanoke, 1961-67; owner, operator Mystic Sea Hotel, Myrtle Beach, S.C., 1974-77, Pindexter Hotel, Myrtle Beach, 1974-77, Sheraton by-the-Sea, Jekyll Island, Ga., 1978-80; owner, pres. Cassandra's Ltd, Roanoke, 1978—, Cassandra's Carousel, Roanoke, 1983—. Bd. dirs. Recreation Dept., Roanoke, 1971-72; pres. Va.'s Jr. Miss Pageant, 1961-76. Recipient Am.'s Jr. Miss State Pageant award 1973. Mem. Bus. Women of Am. (bd. dirs. 1982-83). Republican. Baptist. Club: Roanoke Jr. Woman's (v.p. 1968-73). Home: 2110 Stephenson Ave SW Roanoke VA 24014 Office: Cassandra's Ltd 2121 Colonial Ave SW Roanoke VA 24015

MONK, JAMES FRANCIS, chiropractor; b. Emmetsburg, Iowa, June 19, 1952; s. W.E. and Izetta Charlotte (Corley) M.; m. Karen Kay Morgan, Dec. 29, 1979; 1 son, Joshua James. A.A., Iowa Lakes Community Coll., 1972; B.S., U. Iowa, 1974; D.Chiropractic, Palmer Coll. Chiropractic, 1977. Dir., treating physician Monk Chiropractic Clinic, Chickasha, Okla., 1978—; research asst. Inst. Chiropractic Mgmt. Mem. Am. Chiropractic Assn., Chiropractic Assn. Am., Chickasha Jaycees. Republican. Roman Catholic. Lodge: Elks. Home: PO Box 1538 Chickasha OK 73023 Office: 816 Choctaw Ave Chickasha OK 73023

MONK, SAMUEL HOLT, II, circuit court judge; b. Anniston, Ala., July 14, 1946; s. Richard Hunley and Marjorie Louise (Schneider) M.; m. Mary Lou Gibbins, June 11, 1971; children—Carolyn Elizabeth, William Gibbins. B.A., Jacksonville State U., 1969; J.D., U. Ala., 1975. Bar: Ala. 1975, U.S. Dist. Ct. (no. dist.) Ala. 1976, U.S. Tax Ct. 1978. Sole practice, Anniston, 1975-78; asst. dist. atty. 7th Jud. Cir., Anniston, 1977-78, circuit ct. judge, 1979—; dist. ct. judge Calhoun-Cleburne Counties, Anniston, 1978-79. Bd. dirs. YMCA, Anniston, 1979—, Choccolocco council Boy Scouts Am., 1980—, Am. Cancer Soc., Calhoun County, 1984—; bd. dirs., pres. Vol. and Info. Ctr., 1981—. Served to capt. USAR, 1969-72, Vietnam. Mem. ABA, Ala. Bar Assn., Calhoun County Bar Assn., Ala. Circuit Judges Assn., Ala. Jud. Coll. Faculty Assn., Order of Coif. Democrat. Episcopalian (vestryman 1983-86, jr. warden 1984, sr. warden 1985). Clubs: Rotary, Exchange (Anniston and Jacksonville). Lodge: Masons. Home: 614 Ayers Dr Anniston AL 36201 Office: Cir Ct 7th Jud Circuit Ala PO Box 636 Anniston AL 36202

MONK, WILLIAM HOOVER, clergyman; b. Washington, May 17, 1930; s. Jeemes Henry and Jannie (Allen) M.; m. Shirley Louise Smith, June 1954 (div. 1968); children—Wayne William, Daryl Louis, Karen Renay, Owen Lamont; m. Sarah Irving, June 13, 1976; children—Tiara Charrise, Jairon Paul. Student Fordham U., 1975-76; B.A., Oakwood Coll., 1985; postgrad. Lincoln Meml. U., 1986. Ordained to ministry Seventh-day Adventist Ch., 1983. Lit. evangelist Ch. Conf., N.Y.C., 1956-59; fund raiser Oakwood Coll., Huntsville, Ala., 1978-79; minister Seventh-day Adventist Ch., Nashville, 1979—. Composer, Be My Wife (song), 1958. Served with U.S. Army, 1954-55. Mem. Morristown Ministerial Assn., Morristown C. of C. Democrat.

MONNIG, REGINA LOUISE, nurse educator; b. Ironton, Ohio, Dec. 3, 1932; d. Otto Stephen and Mary Agnes (Boll) M. B.S.N., Coll. St. Teresa, 1957; M.S.N., Cath. U., 1965; Ph.D., U. Minn., 1975. Chmn., Coll. St. Teresa, Winona, Minn., 1974-78; assoc. prof. Wichita State U., Kans., 1978-80; assoc. dean, acting dean U. Louisville, 1980-81; assoc. dean Sch. Nursing, Med. Coll. Ga., Augusta, 1981-85; dean Sch. Nursing, Tenn. State U., Nashville, 1985—; Italian-Am. clin. study U. Rome, 1984; chmn. East Coach Forum, 1983; cons. to hosps., 1976—. Contbr. chpts. to books. Judge, Central Savannah River Area, Sci. Fair Bd., Augusta, 1983; dir. Hospitality House, Augusta, 1985; with disaster nursing ARC, Augusta, 1985; with chaplains program Univ. Hosp., Augusta, 1985. HHS grantee, 1980-85. Mem. Am. Nurses Assn., Nat. League Nursing, Ga. League Nursing (v.p. 1984). Home: Knollwood Apt D-2 865 Bellevue Rd Nashville TN 37221 Office: Tenn State U Nashville TN 37203

MONNINGER, ELIZABETH, college administrator, family nurse practitioner; b. Martinsville, Ind., Oct. 26, 1927; d. Walter Austin and Mae Alice (Brown) H.; divorced; children—Mark, Kurt, Deborah, Pamela. B.S., Duquesne U., 1967; M.S., U. Calif., San Francisco, 1969; postgrad. U. Tex.-Austin, 1980—. Family nurse practitioner Kaiser Permanente, Los Angeles, 1976-77; assoc. prof. Boise State U., Idaho, 1977-79; dir., assoc. clin. prof. U. Calif., San Diego, 1979-82; asst. dean, assoc. prof. U. Tex., El Paso, 1984—. Mem. Am. Nurses Assn., Am. Pub. Health Assn. (governing bd., 1984—), Nat. Assn. Nurse Practitioner Faculty, Phi Kappa Phi. Democrat. Avocations: jogging; hiking; travel. Home: 728 Tepic El Paso TX 79912

MONROE, BURT LEAVELLE, biology educator; b. Louisville, Aug. 25, 1930; s. Burt L. and Ethelmae (Tuell) M.; m. Rose Louise Sawyer, Dec. 27, 1960; children—Burt Leavelle III, Mark Sawyer. B.S., U. Louisville, 1963; Ph.D., La. State U., 1965. Mem. faculty dept. biology U. Louisville, 1965—, prof., chmn., 1970—. Pres., Louisville Zoo Found., Inc.; pres. Louisville Zool. Commn.; bd. trustees past pres. Bernheim Forest Found.; advisor Ky. Nature Preserves Commn. Served to lt. USN, 1953-59. Dept. Interior grantee, 1977-82. Fellow Am. Ornithologists Union (past treas., v.p. 1983-84), AAAS; mem. Cooper Ornithol. Soc., Wilson Ornithol. Soc., Lepidopterists Soc., Herpetologists League, Soc. Study Amphibians and Reptiles. Republican. Presbyterian. Author: The Birds of Honduras, 1968; editorial coordinator Check-List of North American Birds, 1983; contbr. articles to profl. jours. Home: 12204 Ridge Rd Anchorage KY 40223 Office: Dept Biology U Louisville Louisville KY 40292

MONROE, CHARLES MCCANTLAS, JR., insurance company executive; b. Norfolk, Va., Apr. 5, 1940; s. Charles McCantlas and Mary Hortense (Love) M.; m. Donna Charlean Anthony, Dec. 27, 1962; children—Charles McCantlas, Karen, Stephen. B.S. in Marine Engring., U.S. Mcht. Marine Acad., 1961. Sr. loss control rep. The Travelers Ins. Co., Charlotte, N.C., Richmond, Va., Norfolk, Va., 1964-74, Allstate Ins. Co., Houston, Norfolk, 1974-80; casualty loss control cons. Johnson & Higgins, Houston, 1980-85, asst. v.p., 1985—. Mem. Westlake Vol. Fire Dept., Houston, 1978-83. Mem. Am. Soc. Safety Engrs., Jaycees (dir. Norfolk 1972-77). Republican. Avocations: tennis; swimming. Home: 19422 Leafwood Ln Houston TX 77084 Office: Johnson & Higgins 1400 Capital Bank Plaza Houston TX 77002

MONROE, DORIS DRIGGERS, editor, author; b. Mt. Pleasant, Tex., July 11, 1916; d. Samuel Wyatt and Leola (Harris) Driggers; student Mary-Hardin Baylor Coll., 1934-35, William Jewell Coll., 1935-37, Southwestern Bapt. Theol. Sem., 1937-38, So. Bapt. Theol. Sem., 1938-39, 44-45, George Peabody Coll., 1947-50; m. Edwin Ulys Monroe, Aug. 6, 1937; children—Leola Fran (Mrs. Dudley B. Burton), Billie Barbara (Mrs. William F. Hardy, Jr.). Music dir., pastor's asst. Bethany Bapt. Ch., Kansas City, Mo., 1945-47; asso. editor Story Hour Leader, Bapt. Sunday Sch. Bd., Nashville, 1947-50, editor Primary Leader, Every Day with Primaries, 1950-68, cons. Work with Exceptional Persons, 1968—. Mem. Sunday sch. bd. So. Bapt. Conv. Mem. Nat. Assn. for Retarded Children, Am. Camping Assn., Am. Pen Women, Beta Lit. Soc. Author: When Marcia Goes to Church, 1966; The Come-and-Go Village, 1967; A Church Ministry to Retarded Persons, 1971; Reaching and Teaching the Mentally Retarded through the Sunday School, 1980; co-author: The Primary Leadership Manual, 1957; co-author, co-editor Adventures in Christian Living and Learning, Exploring Life Curriculum Series, 1968-72. Home: 2308 Donna Hill Ct Nashville TN 37214 Office: 127 9th Ave N Nashville TN 37203

MONROE, FREDERICK LEROY, chemist; b. Redmond, Oreg., Oct. 13, 1942; s. Herman Sylvan and Mary Roberta (Grant) M.; B.S., Oreg. State U., 1964; M.S., Wash. State U., 1974. Control specialist Air Pollution Authority, Centralia, Wash., 1969-70; asst. chemist Wash. State U., 1970-74; environ. engr. Ore-Ida Foods, Inc., Idaho, 1974-77; cons., Idaho, 1977-78; applications engr. AFL Industries, Riviera Beach, Fla., 1979-80; mgr. chem. control PCA Internat., Matthews, N.C., 1980—. Pres. Unity Ch. Served with USAF, 1964-68, maj. Res. ret.; served with N.G., 1973-78. Decorated Air Force Commendation medal. Mem. Am. Chem. Soc., Water Pollution Control Assn. Republican. Club: Kiwanis. Office: 801 Crestdale Ave Matthews NC 28105

MONROE, HASKELL M., JR., university president; b. Dallas, Mar. 18, 1931; s. Haskell M. and Myrtle Marie (Jackson) M.; B.A., Austin Coll., 1952, M.A., 1954, D.H.L. (hon.), 1984; Ph.D., Rice U., 1961; m. Margaret Joan Phillips, June 15, 1957; children—Stephen, Melanie, Mark, John. Instr., Tex. A&M U., 1959-62, asst. prof., 1962-65, assoc. prof., 1965-70, prof., 1970-80; pres. U. Tex., El Paso, 1980—; instr. Schreiner Inst., Kerrville, Tex., summer 1959; vis. lectr. Emory U., 1967-72; Alumni lectr. Austin Coll., 1980; dir. Security Southwest Life Ins. Co., Southwestern Bell Corp. Chmn. humanities com. 125th Anniversary Commn., Austin Coll., 1974-75; chmn. Tex. A&M United Fund Drive, 1975; trustee Bryan Hosp., 1976-79, chmn., 1979; mem. project steering com. Mus. and Community, Tex. Assn. Mus., 1978; bd. ch. visitors Austin Coll., 1977-78; bd. dirs. Brazos Valley Rehab. Center, 1975-77; Crime Stoppers of El Paso, 1980-84; chmn. pres.'s council Western Athletic Conf., 1980—; mem. Gov.'s Task Force on Higher Edn., 1980-81, Gov.'s Task Force on Undocumented Workers, 1981-82. Served with USNR, 1954-56. Recipient Disting. Teaching award Tex. A&M U., 1964; Cert. of Merit, Ill. Civil War Centennial Com., 1965; Centennial medallion U.S. Civil War Centennial Com., 1965; Founders award Mus. of Confederacy, Richmond, Va., 1972; Disting. Alumnus award Austin Coll., 1980; Social Sci. Research Council fellow, 1961; Henry E. Huntington Library and Art Gallery summer research fellow, 1971. Mem. Am. Hist. Assn., Orgn. Am. Historians, So. Hist. Assn., Hist. Found. Presbyn. and Reformed Chs. (exec. com. 1964-72, chmn. 1970-72), So. Conf. Deans of Faculties and Acad. Vice Pres. (pres. 1978), South Caroliniana Soc. (hon. life), Phi Kappa Phi, Alpha Chi, Phi Alpha Theta, Alpha Epsilon Delta (hon.), Kappa Delta Pi. Presbyterian. (deacon 1961-62, elder 1965-67, 69-71, 73-74, 82-85, clk. session 1973-74, mem. Presbytery's council 1969-71, chmn. pulpit nominating com. 1971-72, resources for '80's steering com. 1978-80). Club: El Paso (dir. 1980—). Contbr. articles to profl. jours. Editor, The Papers of Jefferson Davis, 1964-69; adv. editor Texana, 1964—; mem. bd. editorial advs. The Booker T. Washington Papers, 1965—. Home: 711 Cincinnati St El Paso TX 79902 Office: U Tex El Paso TX 79968

MONROE, LESLIE DAVID, ophthalmologist; b. N.Y.C., Jan. 20, 1952; s. Leonard and Jeanette (Glassman) M.; m. Lori Gilman, June 10, 1973; 1 child, Britt. B.A. cum laude, NYU, 1973; M.D., U. Miami, 1976. Diplomate Am. Bd. Ophthalmology. Resident ophthalmology La. State U. Eye Ctr., New Orleans, 1979; practice medicine specializing in ophthalmology, Ft. Lauderdale, Fla., 1979—; mem. surg. staff Fla. Med. Ctr., Ft. Lauderdale, 1979—, Plantation Gen. Hosp., Fla., 1980—. Fellow Am. Acad. Ophthalmology; mem. Broward County Ophthal. Soc. Republican. Avocations: guitar; drums; music appreciation; sports. Office: 2951 NW 49th Ave Fort Lauderdale FL 33313

MONROE, RICKY DALE, retail store executive; b. White Hall Ill., Nov. 3, 1953; s. Herman Louis and Mary Ann (Little) M.; m. Diana Sue Branson, Dec. 27, 1982; children—Lisa Marie Bieber, Michelle Kathleen. B.A., Ind. U.-South Bend, 1980, M.A., Bloomington, 1981. Delivery driver South Bend Drug Co., South Bend, Ind., 1979; research asst. Larry Griffin Ind. U., Bloomington,

1980; computer programmer Agy. Instructional TV, Bloomington, 1980-81; research asst. Diane Felmle Ind. U., Bloomington, 1980-81; store mgr. P.N. Hirsch & Co., Austin, Ind., 1981-83; asst. store mgr. Wal-Mart Stores, Inc., Glasgow, Ky., 1983-84, Danville, Ky., 1984—. Mem. Am. Sociol. Assn. Avocations: playing guitar; amateur astronomy; reading; golf. Home: 1043 Butler Dr Danville KY 40422 Office: Wal-mart 692 Danville Sq Danville KY 40422

MONROE, STUART BENTON, chemistry educator; b. Manassas, Va., Oct. 26, 1934; s. Robert Stuart and Beulah Margaret (Sowers) M.; m. Beverly Anne Duncan, Dec. 17, 1960 (div. 1982); children—S. Gavin, Kathryn A., Shannon E. Student Va. Mil. Inst., 1952-54; B.S., Randolph-Macon Coll., 1956; Ph.D., U. Fla., 1962. Research chemist Hercules, Inc., Wilmington, Del., 1961-65; assoc. prof., then prof. chemistry Randolph-Macon Coll., Ashland, Va., 1965—, chmn. dept. chemistry, 1974-78, 84—; research assoc. chemistry dept. Duke U., Durham, N.C., 1972; research chemist A.H. Robins, Richmond, Va., 1982-83. Patentee in field. Pres. Henry Clay PTA, Ashland, 1970-71. Du Pont teaching fellow U. Fla., 1960-61, Koppers research fellow U. Fla., 1961; Eli Lilly scholar Duke U., 1977. Mem. Am. Chem. Soc., Va. Acad. Sci. Avocations: sports; reading; dancing; music; drama. Office: Randolph-Macon Coll Ashland VA 23005

MONTANARI, MARION GOODRUM, treatment center administrator; b. McKeesport, Pa., Apr. 20, 1935; d. John Thomas and Edith (Lutz) Goodrum; B.A. in Psychology, Carlow Coll., Pitts., 1962; M.Ed. in Counseling, Duquesne U., Pitts., 1969; m. Adelio J. Montanari, Dec. 20, 1971; stepchildren—Gary, Adele. Tchr., then prin. pvt. elem. and jr. high sch., Pitts.; child care counselor, Pitts.; assoc. dir. Montanari Residential Treatment Center, Hialeah, Fla., 1970—, also inservice staff tng. dir.; co-owner Marion Hills Thoroughbred Farm, Ocala, Fla.; cons. Troubled Children's Found., 1971—. Trustee Greater Miami Opera Assn. Mem. Fla. Group Child Care Assn., Am. Orthopsychiat. Assn., Inc., Am. Assn. Counseling and Devel. Roman Catholic. Office: 291 E 2d St Hialeah FL 33010

MONTEIRO, MARILYN JEAN, psychologist; b. St. Paul, July 25, 1954; d. Manuel James and Madelyn Jean (Wilcox) M.; m. Timothy Laster Allen, July 30, 1983. B.A. in Psychology/Edn., Grinnell Coll., 1975; M.A. in Exptl. Psychology, Drake U., 1977; Ph.D. in Psychology/Behavior Analysis, Western Mich. U., 1980; cert. of completion S.W. Family Inst., Dallas, 1983. Lic. psychologist. Program dir. tutoring service Western Mich. U., Kalamazoo, Mich., 1976-80; coordinator Title I reading project Dallas Pub. Schs., 1980-83; coordinator behavioral services Irving Pub. Schs., Tex., 1983-84; coordinator for family services Dallas Autism Program, Dallas Pub. Schs., 1984—; coordinator regional family services U. Tex. Health Sci. Ctr. Psychology, 1985—; ednl. cons. SRA, Dallas, Mount Pleasant, San Antonio, 1980-83. Recipient Cert. of Appreciation, Nat. Soc. Children and Adults with Autism, 1984. Mem. Am. Psychol. Assn., S.W. Family Inst. Alumni Assn., Dallas Psychol. Assn. Office: Dallas Autism Program 3801 Herschel St Dallas TX 75219

MONTERO, ARMANDO MIGUEL, architect, educator; b. Havana, Cuba, Sept. 29, 1954; came to U.S., 1962; s. Armando Angel and Cary (Perdomo) M.; m. Lourdes C. Gonzalez, July 5, 1974; children—Brandy Christie, Kevin Bradley. B.Arch., U. Miami, 1979. Draftsman Architectonica, Coral Gables, Fla., 1977-79; prin., ptnr. Aragon Assoc. Architects Inc., Coral Gables, 1979-83; instr. architecture Miami Dade Community Coll., 1982—, Recipient award of excellence for renovation Coral Gables C. of C., 1983, award of excellence AIA, 1983; co-winner internat. competition Ft. Lauderdale Riverfront Plaza, 1982. Mem. Archtl. Club Miami. Roman Catholic. Office: Miami Dade Community Coll 11011 SW 104th St Miami FL 33176

MONTFORD, JOHN THOMAS, lawyer, state legislator; b. Ft. Worth, June 28, 1943; s. Thomas L. and Jewell F. (Coursey) M.; m. Pamela Jacobs, June 3, 1966 (div.); 1 dau., Melinda; m. 2d, Debra Kay Mears, Dec. 24, 1975; children—Melonie, John Ross. B.A., U. Tex.-Austin, 1965, J.D., 1968. Bar: Tex. 1968. Sole practice, Lubbock, Tex., 1971-78; criminal dist. atty. Lubbock County, Tex., 1979-82; state senator Dist. 28, Lubbock, 1983—. Trustee S. Park Hosp., Lubbock, 1981-82; bd. dirs., trustee Tex. Boys Ranch, Lubbock, 1982—; chmn. profl. div. United Way, Lubbock, 1980; energy com. So. Legis. Conf., 1983; senate appointee So. Growth Policies Bd., 1983. Served to maj. USMC, 1968-71. Recipient Outstanding Young Man of Lubbock award Jaycees, 1973; Headliner of Yr. award Greater Lubbock Press Club, 1979; Man of Yr./Law Enforcement award Lubbock Optimist Club, 1979; Boss of Yr. award Legal Secs. Assn., 1980; Exec of Yr., Lubbock Sales Exec. Assn., 1981; named Finest Freshman, Tex. Bus. Mag., 1983; Best New Legislator Tex. Monthly mag., 1983. Mem. State Bar Tex. (com. admissions), Tex. Criminal Def. Lawyers Assn., Tex. Dist. and County Attys. Assn. (legis. com.), Western States Water Council, Omicron Delta Kappa, Delta Theta Phi. Club: Jaycees (v.p. 1974). Home: 4424 79th St Lubbock TX 79424 Office: PO Box 1709 Lubbock TX 79408

MONTGOMERY, CHARLES RAYMOND, firechief; b. Irondale, Ala., Aug. 15, 1940; s. John Raymond Montgomery and Carol Mildred (Jones) Montgomery Neely; m. Connie Sue Lindsey; children—Teresa, James, Frank, Vance. Student Jefferson State Jr. Coll., 1970-72, U. Montevallo, 1972-73, U. Ala., 1973-74. Fire fighter Columbus Fire Dept. (Miss.), 1962-66; lt., paramedic Birmingham Fire Dept., Ala., 1966-78, chief Riverside Police Dept., Ala., 1979-84; chief Oneonta Fire Dept., Ala., 1984—; bd. dirs. Blount County Project, Smoke and Fire Edn., Oneonta, 1985; mem. Blount County Emergency Med. Services Council. First v.p. Crestwood Youth Athletic Assn., Birmingham, 1973-75; athletic dir. Southside Boys' Baseball Assn., Birmingham, 1973-76; mem. bd. Avondale Community Sch., Birmingham, 1975. Served with USAF, 1958-62. Mem. Internat. Assn. Fire Chiefs, Nat. Fire Prevention Assn., Ala. State Firefighters Assn., (2d dist. v.p.), Blount County Fire Protection Assn. (pres.). Baptist. Home: Route 1 Box 3330 Oneonta AL 35121

MONTGOMERY, DANIEL ALAN, architect, planner, educator, researcher; b. Toledo, Mar. 16, 1942; s. James Grant and Virginia Helen (Baker) M.; m. Alison Fry, Oct. 8, 1966; children—Leah Horton, Anna Bird. B.S. in Arch., U. Cin., 1966; M.Regional Planning, U. Mich., 1973. Vol., Peace Corps, Malaysia, 1966-68; urban planner SSOE, Toledo, 1969-70; land devel. coordinator, City of Ann Arbor, Mich., 1971-76; asst. prof. landscape arch. Pa. State U., 1977-83; facilities planner U. Va., Charlottesville, 1984—; dir. Environ. Bur. City of Ann Arbor, 1973-76, Lab. for Environ. Design and Planning, Pa. State U., State College, 1979-83; solar architect and resdl. cons., 1976—. Contbr. articles to profl. jours. Chmn. Mcpl. Traffic Commn., State College, 1979-83. Grantee Ford Found., 1978, Inst. for Arts and Humanities Studies, 1979, Lab. for Environ. Design, 1981, U.S. Dept. Energy, 1982. Mem. Nat. Council Archtl. Registration Bds. (registered architect), Am. Inst. Cert. Planners (charter, cert. planner), Environ. Design Research Assn., Am. Solar Energy Soc. Home: 2400 Fox Path Court Charlottesville VA 22901 Office: 575 Alderman Rd Charlottesville VA 22903

MONTGOMERY, ELIZABETH FLANAGAN (MRS. STEWART MAGRUDER MONTGOMERY), ch. and civic worker; b. Cary, Miss., July 25, 1898; d. Robert Edward Lee and Annie May (Purdy) Flanagan; grad. Northwestern Sch. Speech, 1918; A.B., Miss. State Coll. for Women, 1924; summer study Peabody Coll., U. Cal., Columbia; m. Stewart Magruder Montgomery, Jan. 5, 1935. Instr. elementary grades, high sch. English and dramatics, Cary, 1924-51. Mem. King's Daus. and Sons, state pres. 1949-51, 55-56, dir. Indian work, speaker internat. conv.; state pres. Miss. Women's Cabinet, 1954-55; mem. adv. council Miss. Children's Code Commn.; edn. com. Miss. Assn. Mental Health, 1958—, dir., exec. com., nominating com., 1963-66, dir., 1966—, sec., 1973—; chmn. Miss. Mental Health Conv., 1964; county commr. Fifth Region Mental Health Center, 1967—; commr. Delta Mental Health Service; del. Nat. Mental Health Conv., 1963, meeting, N.Y.C.; dir. State Mental Health Bd.; sec. Miss. Mental Health Assn., 1971-73; county campaign chmn. A.R.C., 1962. Mem. pub. relations com. Miss. Women's Cabinet, 1961—, now also recreation chmn.; mem. Gov.'s Ladies Staff, Miss., 1960-64; sec. Miss. Mental Health, 1969—; mem. Sharkey County Mental Health Commn., 1967—. Trustee King's Daus. Home, Natchez, Miss., 1948-52, pres. gov.'s bd., 1956—, gov.'s bd. trustees, 1965—; pres. gov.'s bd. Recipient Woman of Achievement award Rolling Fork Bus. and Profl. Women, 1965; named Outstanding Civic leader Am., 1967. Mem. Miss. King's Daus. and Sons (historian 1969—, parliamentarian), Internat. Platform Assn., Daus. Am. Colonists, Order of Washington, Daus. of 1812, Colonial Dames of XVII Century (chpt. pres. 1971-73, state 1st v.p. 1971-73, state pres. 1973—), Dames of Court Honor, Daus. Confederacy, Soc. Magna Charta Dames, Ams. Royal Descent, Nat. Soc. New Eng. Women, Zeta Phi Eta. Episcopalian (state pres., women's orgn., 1952-55; pres. IV province Episcopal Ch. 1957-60). Clubs: Sharkey County Home Makers (sec.), Highland (pres. aux. 1963-64), Delta Debutante (patron 1961—). Home: Route 2 Rolling Fork MS 39159

MONTGOMERY, GILLESPIE V., congressman; b. Meridian, Miss.; s. Gillespie M. and Emily (Jones) M.; B.S., Miss. State U. Mem. Miss. Senate, 1956-66; mem. 90th-99th congresses from 3d Dist. Miss.; chmn. select com. on missing persons in S.E. Asia, 94th Congress; mem. Presdl. Commn. on MIA's, 1977; chmn. House Vets. Affairs Com.; mem. House Armed Services Com.; leader ho. del. to observe presdl. elections, El Salvador, 1984; leader ho. group 40th anniversary D-Day invasion, Normandy, 1984. Pres. Miss. N.G. Assn., 1959; pres. Miss. Heart Assn., 1967-68. Served with AUS, World War II, Korean War. Decorated Bronze Star, Combat Inf. Badge; recipient Miss. Magnolia award, 1966; certificate of merit for saving a life ARC, 1947. Mem. VFW, Am. Legion, 40 and 8, Miss. Farm Bur., Congressional Prayer Breakfast Group (pres. 1970), Miss. State U. Alumni Assn. (past pres.), Kappa Alpha. Episcopalian. Clubs: Masons, Shriners, Moose. Home: PO Box 5618 Meridian MS 39301 also 1200 N Nash St Apt 1135 Arlington VA 22209 Office: 2184 Rayburn House Office Bldg Washington DC 20515

MONTGOMERY, JAMES HARVEY, geologist, oil company executive; b. Monroe, La., Apr. 16, 1926; s. Mitchell Wallace and Ruth Inez-(Barron) M.; m. Dorothy James Warner, June 30, 1944; 1 child, Fabienne Cardinal. Student La. State U., 1942-44; B.S., Centenary Coll., 1948; M.S., U. Tulsa, 1950. Registered profl. engr., Tex., Okla.; registered profl. geologist, 12 states. Div. mgr. Magnolia Petroleum Co., Mobil, Midland, Tex., 1950-56; v.p. Wessely Energy Corp., Dallas, 1970-75; sr. v.p. Saxon Oil Co., Dallas, 1976-80; pres. Warmont Corp., Dallas, 1980—; dir. Sabine Royalty Co., Dallas, Petro-Tieg, Inc., La Jolla, Calif. Contbr. articles to profl. jours. Served to 1st lt. USMC, 1944-46, PTO. Mem. Am. Assn. Petroleum Geologists, Am. Inst. Profl. Geologists, Soc. Petroleum Engrs. of AIME, Soc. Econ. Paleontologist and Mineralogist, Dallas Geol. Soc. (pres. 1964-65), Theta Xi. Club: Dallas Engineers (v.p. 1974). Office: Warmont Corp 17311 Dallas Pkwy Suite 230 Dallas TX 75248

MONTGOMERY, JOHN RICHARD, pediatrician, educator; b. Burnsville, Miss., Oct. 24, 1934; s. Guy Austin and Harriet Pauline (Owens) M.; m. Dottye Ann Newell, June 26, 1965; children—John Newell, Michelle Elizabeth. B.S., U. Ala., 1955, M.D., 1958. Intern U. Miss., Jackson, 1958-59, resident in pediatrics, 1959-60; resident in pediatrics Baylor Coll. Medicine, Houston, 1960-61, 63-64, fellow in pediatric infectious diseases and immunology, 1965, asst. prof. pediatrics, 1966-70, assoc. prof. pediatrics, 1970-75; chief pediatric programs U. Ala. Sch. Medicine, Huntsville, 1975—. Served with AUS, 1961-62; Korea. Mem. Soc. Pediatric Research, Am. Assn. Immunologists, Infectious Diseases Soc. Am., N.Y. Acad. Scis., Am. Acad. Pediatrics, Sigma Xi, Phi Beta Kappa. Contbr. articles to profl. jours.; assisted in devel. of germ-free environ. bubble to protect patient with no natural immunity (patient later subject of movie The Boy in The Bubble).

MONTGOMERY, JOSEPH WILLIAM, investment broker; b. Wytheville, Va., Dec. 23, 1951; s. Ivan Martin and Evelyn Powell (Delp) M.; m. Linda Gail Winebarger, Aug. 30, 1980. B.B.A., Coll. William and Mary, 1974. Cert. fin. planner. Account exec. Wheat, First Securities, Inc., Lynchburg, Va., 1975-79, Williamsburg, Va., 1979-81, v.p., investment officer, 1981-82, sr. v.p., investment officer, 1982—; dir. Williamsburg Landing, Inc., 1985—. Contbr. article to Va. Cattleman. Pres. William and Mary Athletic Ednl. Found., 1985—; com. mem. Future of Hampton Roads, Norfolk, Va., 1984—; mem. personnel com. Williamsburg Community Hosp.; mem. long range fin. planning com. Williamsburg United Methodist Ch., 1985—; mem. planning com. Kingsmill Community Services Assn., Williamsburg, 1981-82; mem. Peninsula White Sox Adv. Bd.; team capt. YMCA Fund Drive, Lynchburg, 1979; solicitor United Way, Lynchburg, 1978, Salvation Army Bldg. Fund, Lynchburg, 1977. Named Outstanding Broker of 1984, Registered Rep. mag.; mem. chmn.'s group Wheat, First Securities, Inc., 1983, 84, 85, pres.'s club, 1983, Century Club, 1981; hon. mention Football All Am., AP, 1973, All East, 1973. Mem. Internat. Assn. Fin. Planning, Inst. Cert. Fin. Planners, Pro-Trac Survey Fin. Profl. Adb. Panel. Home: 32 Ensigne Spence Williamsburg VA 23185 Office: Wheat First Securities Inc PO Drawer W Williamsburg VA 23187

MONTGOMERY, JULIAN STANLEY, JR., insurance, financial adviser; b. Atlanta, Apr. 24, 1945; s. Julian Stanley Sr. and Mary Jayne (Blackmon) M.; m. Gail McClurkin, Oct. 1965 (div. 1976); 1 child, Mary Patricia; m. Ann Colquitt Head, Aug. 7, 1976; 1 child, Joshua Head. Student Auburn U., 1963-65. C.L.U., Am. Coll., 1982. Registered health underwriter. Broker, agt. Prudential Ins. Co., Jacksonville, Fla., Montgomery, Ala., 1971—; speaker, lectr. in field. Chmn. planned giving com. Episcopal Diocese Ala., Birmingham, 1984-86; dist. rep. Tukabatchee council Boy Scouts Am., Montgomery, 1979-85; mem. Life Underwriters Polit. Action Com., Washington, 1985-86; vestry Holy Comforter Episcopal Ch., del. Diocesan Conv., 1986. Served with USANG, 1965-71. Mem. Million Dollar Round Table (Knight 1977-865), Am. Soc. C.L.U. (ethics com. Central Ala. chpt. 1984-85), Montgomery Health Underwriters Assn. (pres. 1986), Montgomery Life Underwriters Assn., Nat. Assn. Life Underwriters, Nat. Assn. Health Underwriters, Montgomery Estate Planning Council, Golden Key Soc. Avocations: swimming; hand engravings. Office: 2368 Fairlane Dr Bldg E Suite 38 Montgomery AL 36116

MONTGOMERY, KATHERINE MARSH, college adminstrator, art educator; b. High Point, N.C., Sept. 23, 1936; d. Howard Darnaby and Katherine (Hardin) Marsh; m. Joseph Raymond Montgomery, Jr.; children—Joseph Raymond III, Stewart Marsh. B.F.A., U. N.C., 1958, M.F.A., 1971; postgrad. Penland Sch. Crafts, Spruce Pine, N.C., 1974, 75, Bryn Mawr Summer Inst., Pa., 1984. Classroom tchr. Colonial Dr. Sch., Thomasville, N.C., 1958-59; instr. art Ferndale Jr. High Sch., High Point, N.C., 1959-60, High Point Coll., 1969-70, Guilford Coll., Greensboro, N.C., 1970-72; art instr. Davidson Community Coll., Lexington, N.C., 1972-83, chmn. fine arts and humanities, 1983—. One woman shows include High Point Coll., Guilford Coll., Greensboro Coll., Weatherspoon Art Gallery at U. N.C., Greensboro, Garden Studio, Rockingham Community Coll.; exhibited in group shows at Southeastern Ctr. for Contemporary Art, N.C. Mus. Art., Butler Inst., Hickory Mus. Art, Davidson County Art Gallery, High Point Theater Art Galleries. Sec. Dem. Precinct, Davidson County, 1981-85; mem. Assn. Jr. Leagues, High Point, 1959-85, bd. dirs. 1963, 64, 66, 72; exhibiting craftsman Davidson County, World's Fair, Knoxville, 1982; mem. Banner Commn., N.C. Bicentennial Com., Raleigh, 1976. Grantee N.C. Humanities Com., Davidson County, 1983. Mem. Nat. Council Adminstrs., N.C. Mus. Art, N.C. Watercolor Soc. (original bd. dirs.), N.C. Fiber Arts Assn. (original bd. dirs.), High Point Fine Art Guild (pres. 1979-80), High Point Arts Council (bd. dirs. 1968, 69). Democrat. Episcopalian. Club: Emerywood Country (High Point). Office: Davidson County Community Coll PO Box 1287 Lexington NC 27293

MONTGOMERY, LUCILLE STEPHENSON, book store executive; b. Baskin, La., Mar. 25, 1925; d. Jeffrey Strickland and Jennie M. (Weeks) Stephenson; m. Raymond Lee Montgomery, June 24, 1945; children—Gloria M. Ritchie, James R. Cert. Draughans Bus. Coll., 1964. Sec. Baptist Ch., Baton Rouge, La., 1958-63; founder, mgr. Christian Book Store, Baton Rouge, 1966—; cons. Christian Book Store, Baton Rouge, 1968—, bd. dirs., 1967—. Mem. Better Bus. Bur., Christian Booksellers Assn., Retail Assn., C. of C., Baptist. Office: Christian Book Store Inc 8312 Florida Blvd Baton Rouge LA 70806

MONTGOMERY, PORTER ATHREL, JR., geologist, stratigrapher, consultant; b. Dalhart, Tex., Sept. 9, 1916; s. Porter A. and Vera Mae (Burkhead) M.; m. Louise George, June 3, 1939 (div. 1967); children—Porter A., III, Nancy, Susan. B.S. in Geology, Tex. Tech. U., 1942. Registered profl. geologist, Kans., Tex. Geologist, Stanolind Oil & Gas, Tex., N.Mex., Colo., Kans., 1942-58; owner Montgomery's Stratigraphic Service, San Antonio, 1958—. Mem. Am. Assn. Petroleum Geologists, Geol. Soc. of Am., Soc. Econ. Paleontologists and Mineralogists, S. Tex. Geol. Soc. (v.p.), Am. Inst. Profl. Geologists. Unitarian. Club: Numismatic Study Group (San Antonio). Office: Montgomery's Stratigraphic Service 1134 Milam Bldg San Antonio TX 78205

MONTGOMERY, ROBERT LOUIS, chem. engr.; b. San Francisco, Nov. 20, 1935; s. Louis Clyde and Fay Elythe (Myers) M.; B.S., U. Calif., Berkeley, 1956; Ph.D., Okla. State U., Stillwater, 1975; m. Patricia Helen Cook, Mar. 17, 1962; children—Cynthia E., Jeanette L., Cecelia I., Howard E. Phys. chemist U.S. Bur. Mines, Reno, 1956-62; sr. engr. Boeing Co., Wichita, 1966-75; data engr. M.W. Kellogg Co., Houston, 1977-82; sr. research assoc. Rice U., Houston, 1982—. Petroleum Research Fund fellow, 1962-63; NSF fellow, 1963-66; Robert A. Welch Found. postdoctoral fellow, 1975-77. Mem. Tex. Soc. Profl. Engrs., Am. Chem. Soc., Am. Inst. Chem. Engrs., Am. Soc. Metals, AAAS, Houston Engring. and Sci. Soc., Sigma Xi. Club: Moose. Office: Chemistry Dept Rice U PO Box 1892 Houston TX 77251

MONTGOMERY, SHERRY SHANNON, business management educator, consultant; b. Navasota, Tex., Jan. 23, 1943; d. Roy Arthur and Dottie LaRue (Dyess) Shannon; m. James Michal Montgomery, Jan. 30, 1966 (div. 1981); children—James Michael, III, Adriane. B.A. in Modern Langs., N.Mex. State U., 1965; M.A. in Mgmt. and Supervision, Central Mich. U., 1978. Cert. tchr., Tex. Market developer W. Lan Assocs., Inc., Houston, 1978-79; instr. San Antonio Coll., 1981-83, St. Philip's Coll., San Antonio, 1984—; cons. in field; instr. Sheriff's Dept., San Antonio, 1984; market researcher St. Philip's Coll., 1985. Pres. Central Oahu Com. Mental Health Ctr. Adv. Bd., Pearl City, Hawaii, 1977-78; organizer Hawaii's Boarding Care Home Operators, Oahu, 1977-78, Health Coalition, Hawaii, 1976-78; vol. various campaigns, Tex., 1981-85. Recipient Gov.'s award State of Hawaii, 1978, Senate Health Com. award, 1977, Dept Mental Health award, 1978, Vol. Citizen Advocacy award, 1978. Republican. Roman Catholic. Avocations: gardening; swimming. Home: 4211 Bunker Hill San Antonio TX 78230 Office: St Philip's Coll 2111 Nevada St San Antonio TX 78203

MONTGOMERY, SUZANNE HOWARD, psychologist, business executive; b. Atlanta, Apr. 19, 1949; d. Douglas Legate and Patricia Jean (Younkins) Howard; m. David C. Montgomery, Nov. 24, 1974 (div. 1980); m. William M. Copley, III, June 14, 1985. B.A., U. Fla., 1971, Ph.D., 1982; M.S.W., Mich. State U., 1973. Lic. psychologist, Fla. Psychotherapist, Univ. Hosp., Jacksonville, Fla., 1973-77, dir. aftercare services, 1976-77, dir. mental health cons. and edn., 1977-80, dir. tng. and devel., 1980-85; cons. psychologist, owner Montgomery, Copley & Assocs., Jacksonville, 1985—. Author tng. manual: Decisions, 1982; contbr. chpt. to book. Sec., com. chmn. Vol. Jacksonville Bd., 1980-85; mem. Leadership Jacksonville, 1981—; mem. Jacksonville Women's Network, 1983-85; pres. Mental Health Assn., Jacksonville, 1985—. NIMH research grantee, 1980; State Foster Care Edn. grantee, 1979, research grantee, 1977; named Mental Health Profl. of Yr., 1984; recipient Mental Health Merit Edn. award, 1976. Mem. Am. Psychol. Assn., Fla. Psychol. Assn., Fla. Hosp. Assn. Club: Jr. League Jacksonville. Avocations: reading; swimming; tennis. Home: 1759 Emory Circle S Jacksonville FL 32207 Office: Montgomery Copley & Assocs Inc 6621 Southpoint Dr N 390 Jacksonville FL 32216

MONTGOMERY, THOMAS, foreign language educator; b. Seattle, May 19, 1925; s. Earl F. Montgomery and Elaine (MacCuaig) Easton; m. Shaula Jacobs, Oct. 8, 1983. B.A., Wash. State U., 1949; M.A., U. Wis., 1950, Ph.D., 1955. Asst. prof. Elmira Coll., N.Y., 1955-58; asst. prof. Spanish, Tulane U., New Orleans, 1958-61, assoc. prof., 1961-70, prof., 1970—, chmn. dept. Spanish and Portuguese, 1978-81. Editor: El Evangelio de San Mateo, 1962; co-editor: El Nuevo Testamento, 1970; Simply A Man of Letters, 1980. Contbr. articles to profl. jours. Served with U.S. Army, 1943-45, ETO. Inst. Internat. Edn. fellow, Spain, 1953-54. Mem. Phi Beta Kappa. Home: 7709 Burthe St New Orleans LA 70118 Office: Tulane U Dept Spanish and Portuguese New Orleans LA 70118

MONTGOMERY, THOMAS PENN, JR., cotton merchant, farmer; b. Fort Sill, Okla., Jan. 6, 1945; s. Thomas Penn and Martha Cordelia (Smith) M.; m. Constance Kirk, June 22, 1968; children—Anna Shealy, Martha Kirk, James Middleton. Degree in bus. Auburn U., 1967. Farmer, 1968—; cotton mcht. Montgomery Co., Inc., Opelika, Ala., 1973—; dir. 1st Nat. Bank, Opelika, Toys' Plus, Montgomery, Ala.; bd. mgrs. N.Y. Cotton Exchange, N.Y.C., 1984—. Bd. dirs. Sheriff's Girls Ranch, Opelika. Mem. Am. Cotton Shippers Assn., Atlantic Cotton Assn. Methodist. Clubs: Saugahatchee Country (Auburn, Ala.); Ponte Vedra Country (Fla.). Avocations: golf; horses. Office: Montgomery Co Inc PO Box 707 Opelika AL 36801

MONTGOMERY, WAYNE SWOPE, orthopedic surgeon, county commissioner; b. Battle Creek, Mich., Apr. 21, 1925; s. Frank Swope and Mildred (Schroder) M.; m. Elizabeth Jeschke, Oct. 19, 1946; children—Swope, Woody, Ann, Jane, Mary. A.B., DePauw U., 1946; M.D., Wayne U., 1948; M.S., U. Tenn.-Memphis, 1955. Diplomate Am. Bd. Orthopedic Surgery. Intern, Harper Hosp., Detroit, 1948-49, resident, 1949-50; orthopedic surgeon Asheville Bone and Joint Clinic, N.C., 1955—. Mayor City of Asheville, 1969-71; commr. Buncombe County, N.C., 1984—; trustee Davidson Coll., 1973-85; chmn. Buncombe County Republican Party, 1966-69; bd. dirs. U. N.C. Asheville Found., 1968—; 3rd clarinet U. N.C. Asheville Community Band. Served to lt. (s.g.) USN, 1952-54; Japan. Fellow Am. Acad. Orthopedic Surgery, Am. Acad. Cerebral Palsy; mem. Am. Orthopedic Soc. for Sports Medicine, Buncombe County Med. Soc. (pres. 1973). Presbyterian. Avocations: Tennis; swimming (master). Home: 55 Sunset Pkwy Asheville NC 28801 Office: Doctors Dr Asheville NC 28801

MONTORO, RAFAEL DE LA TORRE, physician; b. Havana, Cuba, Oct. 14, 1918; came to U.S., 1959, naturalized, 1964; s. Octavio Eliseo and Elisa Isabel (De La Torre y Soublette) M.; M.D., Havana U., 1946; m. Katherine Caragol Sanabria, Mar. 16, 1960; children—Victoria Montoro Zamorano, Rafael, Maria Therese Montoro Gross. Gen. practice medicine, Havana, 1946-52; mem. staff Hijas de Galicia Hosp., 1948-52; mem. Cuban del. WHO, 1952; E.E. and M.P. to Portugal, 1953-56; ambassador to Netherlands, 1956-59; minister to Iceland, 1957-59; adminstr. Profl. Registry Medicaid, N.Y.C., 1966-69; acting dir., physician Psychiat. Hosp., Ponce, P.R., 1970-73; practice gen. medicine, Coral Gables, Fla., 1973—; pres. Delray Med. Group Inc.; med. dir. Cooper Med. Group; mem. staff South Shore Hosp., Miami Beach, Fla. Bd. dirs. Cuban Mus. Arts and Culture, Inst. of Ophthalmology Horacio Ferrer. Decorated grand cross Order Orange Nassau (Netherlands), Order Carlos Manuel de Cespedes (Cuba); grand officer Order Red Cross (Cuba), Order Merit (Chile); comdr. Order Finlay (Cuba); named Marquis de Montoro (Spain). Mem. Fla. Med. Assn., Dade County Med. Assn. Republican. Roman Catholic. Club: Coral Gables Country. Home: 446 Majorca Ave Coral Gables FL 33134 Office: 158 Almeria St Coral Gables FL 33134

MONTZ, S(IDNEY) DAN, JR., university administrator; b. St. Rose, La., Aug. 2, 1930; s. Sidney Daniel and Stella Marie (Daigle) M., Sr.; m. Angele Barkate, Dec. 28, 1958; children—Don Sidney, Kim Angele. B.S., La. State U., 1952, M.Ed., 1955; Ed.S., Nicholls State U., Thibodaux, La., 1970. Instr. Flint Community Coll., Mich., 1955-57; asst. registrar McNeese State Coll., Lake Charles, La., 1957-63; asst. registrar Nicholls State U., Thibodaux, 1963-72, dean admissions, registrar, 1972—. Editor: How To Book for All Students, 1975; International Students Handbook, 1977. Served to sgt. U.S. Army, 1951-53, Korea. Mem. La. Tchrs. Assn., Am. Assn. Adminstrs., La. Assn. Mentally Retarded, Nicholls Honor Soc., La. Assn. Collegiate Registrars and Admissions Officers (pres. 1968), So. Assn. Collegiate Registrars and Admissions officers (awards), Am. Assn. Collegiate Registrars and Admissions Officers, So. Assn. Admissions Counselors, Nat. Assn. Fgn. Students Affairs, Am. Inst. Biol. Scis., Red Red Rose, Phi Delta Kappa, Kappa Phi Kappa, Phi Delta Theta. Democrat. Roman Catholic. Lodges: Civitan, K.C. Home: 606 Country Club Blvd Thibodaux LA 70301 Office: Nicholls State U Office Dean Admissions and Registrar PO Box 2004 Univ Sta Thibodaux LA 70310

MOODY, BOBBY DANIEL, chief of police; b. Atlanta, Feb. 28, 1947; s. Charles Lamb and Mary Beulah (Morris) M.; m. Brenda Sue Meadows, June 26, 1966; children—Robert D., Robin D. A.A. in Criminal Justice, DeKalb Community Coll., 1981; B.S. in Criminal Justice, Ga. State U., 1985. Accredited Commn. on Law Enforcement Accreditation. Police officer City of Covington, Ga., 1975-77, police capt., 1977-78, chief of police, 1978—; chmn. Clayton County Police Acad. Adminstrn. Bd., 1980—; sec. Peace Officers Standards and Tng. Council, Atlanta, 1983-84; mem. State Bd. Pub. Safety, Atlanta, 1984—, Organized Crime Council, Atlanta, 1984—. Mem. Ga. Assn. of Chiefs of Police (pres. 1983-84, Outstanding Chief 1984). Baptist. Club: Newton County Touchdown (Covington) (pres. 1983-84). Lodge: Rotary. Avocations: running; golf; speaking. Office: Covington Police Dept 2111 Conyers St SE Covington GA 30209

MOODY, HOWARD MAXWELL, optometrist; b. Gainesville, Fla., July 21, 1943; s. Isaac I. and Freida (Maxwell) M.; m. Kathryn LaBarbera, Nov. 24, 1976; children—Melissa Kathryn, Michael Howard. B.S., Fla. State U., 1966; O.D., So. Coll. Optometry, 1969. Pvt. practice optometry, Tallahassee, 1972—. Mem. Am. Optometric Assn., Fla. Optometric Assn., Tallahassee C. of C.

Democrat. Presbyterian. Clubs: Tiger Bay, Springtime Tallahassee, Seminole Boosters, Tallahassee Quarterback (pres. 1979), Fla. Econs., Killearn Golf and Country. Lodges: Lions, Elks.

MOODY, JAMES W(ILLIAM), JR., historic preservationist, museum administrator; b. Oak Park, Ill., July 20, 1920; s. James William and Bessie Jean (Hanna) M.; m. Elizabeth Yawn, Dec. 15, 1942; B.A., U. of South, 1942. Agt. N.E. Mut. Life Ins. Co., Nashville, 1955-63; exec. sec. Tenn. Hist. Commn., Nashville, 1963-67; exec. dir. Va. Hist. Landmarks Commn., Richmond, 1967-72; exec. dir. Historic Pensacola Preservation Bd., Fla., 1972—; dir. Gulf Coast History and Humanities Conf., Pensacola, 1972—; resident coordinator Seminar for Hist. Adminstrn., Williamsburg, Va., 1977-81; bd. dirs. Hist. Richmond Found., 1967-72. Served to lt. USNR, 1942-46; PTO. Mem. Am. Assn. for State and Local History (awards com. 1969-82, mem. council 1971-75), Fla. Hist. Soc. Democrat. Episcopalian. Avocations: boating; gardening. Home: 1417 E Lakeview Ave Pensacola FL 32503 Office: Historic Pensacola Preservation Bd 205 E Zaragoza St Pensacola FL 32501

MOODY, LAMON LAMAR, JR., consulting engineer; b. Bogalusa, La., Nov. 8, 1924; s. Lamar Lamon and Vida (Seal) M.; B.C.E., U. Southwestern La., 1951; m. Eve Thibodeaux, Sept. 22, 1954; children—Lamon Lamar, Jennifer Eve, Jeffrey Matthew. Engr., Tex. Co., N.Y.C., 1951-52; project engr. African Petroleum Terminals, West Africa, 1952-56; chief engr. Kaiser Aluminum & Chem. Corp., Baton Rouge, 1956-63; pres., owner Dyer & Moody, Inc., Cons. Engrs., Baker, La., 1963—, also chmn. bd., dir. Chmn., Baker Planning Commn., 1961-63; trustee Pub. Affairs Research Council of La., 1982-86; mem. exec. Com. La. Good Roads and Transp. Assn., 1983—. Served with USMCR, 1943-46. Decorated Purple Heart; registered profl. engr., La., Ark., Miss., Tex. Fellow ASCE; mem. La. Engring. Soc. (dir., pres.-elect 1981-82, pres. 1982-83, Charles M. Kerr award for pub. relations 1971, ann. award Engr.-in-Mgmt. 1981, Leo Odom award for disting. services to engring. profession 1985), Profl. Engrs. in Pvt. Practice (state chmn. 1969-70), Am. Congress Surveying and Mapping (award for excellency 1972), La. Land Surveyors Assn. (pres. 1968-69, Land Surveyor of Yr. 1976), Cons. Engrs. Council, Engrs. Joint Council, Nat. Soc. Profl. Engrs., Greater Baker Assn. Commerce (dir. 1974, chmn. indsl. devel. com. 1974-75), Baker C. of C. (v.p. 1976, pres. 1977, Outstanding Bus. Leader of Year award 1975), Blue Key. Democrat. Baptist. Clubs: Masons (32 deg., KCCH), Kiwanis (dir. 1964-65). Home: 3811 Charry Dr Baker LA 70714 Office: 2845 Ray Weiland Dr Baker LA 70714

MOODY, PATRICIA JANE ROWELL, nurse; b. Atlanta, Apr. 18, 1953; d. Elbert Jackson and Hilda Jane (Boyce) Rowell; m. Melvin Wayne Moody, July 14, 1972; children—Daniel, Erin. R.N., Grady Meml. Hosp., 1974. R.N., Ga. Sales staff Rich's Dept. Store, Atlanta, 1969-71; nurse Crawford W. Long Hosp., Atlanta, 1974-75; supr., emergency room nurse R.T. Jones Hosp., Canton, Ga., 1975—, obstet., operating room nurse, supr., 1983—. Asst. blood drives ARC, Canton, 1975-80. Fulton-Dekalb County Authority scholar, 1971. Mem. Assn. Operating Room Nurses. Baptist. Lodge: Order Eastern Star. Avocations: camping; reading; gardening. Home: Route 9 Tall Oaks Estates Canton GA 30114 Office: R T Jones Meml Hosp Box 906 Canton GA 30114

MOODY, SARAH TUTTLE, guidance counselor; b. Summerville, S.C., Mar. 24, 1948; d. Edgar Argurant and Queen Esther (White) T.; m. Randy Huggins, Apr. 14, 1974; 1 child, Everett Randall. B.S., Baptist Coll., 1970; M.A.T., The Citadel, 1976. Tchr., lang. arts chmn. Boulder Bluff Elem. Sch., Goose Creek, S.C., 1973-75; guidance dir. Sedgefield Middle Sch., Goose Creek, 1975-76; guidance staff Alston Jr. High Sch., Summerville, S.C., 1976-78; guidance counselor Summerville Intermediate High Sch., 1978—, career edn. coordinator, parent vol. coordinator, sec. adv. com., 1985. Cons. PTA; program chmn. Low Country Epilepsy Assn., Charleston, S.C., 1984—; dir. 6th grade Summerville Baptist Ch. Sunday Sch., 1979, dir. 11th grade, 1983, tchr. married couples, 1985. Mem. Nat. Bd. Cert. Counselors, Am. Assn. Counseling Devel., Am. Sch. Counselors Assn., S.C. Assn. Counselor Devel., S.C. Assn. Sch. Counselors (treas. 1981-82), AAUW, NEA, S.C. Edn. Assn. Club: Democratic (Summerville). Avocations: reading; writing; poetry. Home: 209 Harter Dr Quail Arbor I Summerville SC 29483 Office: Summerville Intermediate High Sch 500 Greenwave Blvd Summerville SC 29483

MOODY, WILLIS ELVIS, JR., engineer, lawyer, educator; b. Raleigh, N.C., Mar. 30, 1924; s. Willis Elvis and Inez Marie (McDade) M.; B.S. in Ceramic Engring., N.C. State U. at Raleigh, 1948, M.S., 1949, Ph.D., 1956; postgrad. in nuclear metallurgy Iowa State U., 1957; J.D., Woodrow Wilson Coll. Law, 1979; m. Mary Susan McAfee, Mar. 22, 1947 (div. June 1967); children—Susan E., Michael T., Peggy A., Willis Elvis, III, William S. Ceramic engr. Spark Plug div. Electric Auto Lite Co., Fostoria, Ohio, 1949-50; ceramic engr. Lab. Equipment Corp., St. Joseph, Mich., 1950-51; instr. ceramic engring. and metallurgy N.C. State U. at Raleigh, 1951-56; faculty Ga. Inst. Tech., Atlanta, 1956—, prof. ceramic engring., 1960—; research participant Oak Ridge Nat. Lab., summers 1954, 55; cons. to clay and ceramic industries, 1951—. Served with AAC, 1943-46; ETO. Decorated Air medal with two oak leaf clusters; registered profl. engr., Ga. Fellow Orton Ceramic Found., Am. Ceramic Soc. (trustee 1965-68, dir. Southeastern sect. 1962); mem. State Bar Ga., Am. Bar Assn., Ceramic Ednl. Council (pres. 1963), Am. Soc. Engring. Edn. (chmn. materials div. 1971), Am. Phys. Soc., AAAS, Assn. Applied Solar Energy, Nat. Inst. Ceramic Engrs. (pres. 1980), Clay Minerals Soc. (councillor 1969-71), Am. Assn. Engring. Socs. (bd. govs. 1980-82), Keramos, Sigma Xi, Sigma Pi Sigma, Tau Beta Pi. Contbr. articles to tech. jours. Patentee in field. Home: 4545 Northside Pkwy Apt 13K Atlanta GA 30339 Office: Sch Materials Engring Ga Inst Tech Atlanta GA 30332

MOOHAN, JAMES JOSEPH, packaging company executive, consultant; b. N.Y.C., Apr. 29, 1934; s. Patrick J. and Easter Alice (Gallogley) M.; m. Rita L. Wilson, Nov. 10, 1962 (dec. Oct. 1972); children—Theresa Louise, James Joseph. B.B.A. cum laude, CCNY, 1955; postgrad. Fla. Atlantic U., 1972-73, U. Tampa, 1982-83. Sales rep. Continental Can Co., N.Y.C., Tampa, Fla., 1957-71, Cain & Bultman, Miami, Fla., 1971-72, Fed. Paper Bd., Seffner, Fla., 1972-76; pres. Moohan Packaging Co., Seffner, 1976—; dir. Action Orthopedics, Tampa, 1975-82; v.p. Thermotemp, Inc., Tampa, 1982-85, also dir. Chmn. Tampa-St. Petersburg Marathon, 1984, dir., 1985; dir. Brandon Balloon Rally, Fla., 1983, 84, 85; Served to sgt. U.S. Army, 1955-57. Recipient Cert. of Appreciation, Fla. Spl. Olympics, 1984, Outstanding Service award Hillsborough County Spl. Olympics, 1984-85, Am. Cancer Soc., 1984, Key Vol. award Tampa Bay Brit. Am. Marathon, 1984, Brandon Balloon Rally, 1983-85. Mem. Brandon Balloon Chase (bd. dirs.), Brandon Running Assn. (pres. 1982-85), Tampa Bay Running Council (life, chmn. 1984-85). Club: Ybor City Rotary (dir.). Avocations: running; promoting running as healthful and life enriching especially to young. Home: 415 Cactus Circle Seffner FL 33584

MOOK, BARBARA HEER HELD, civic worker; b. Akron, June 9, 1919; d. Harold Edward and Helen Wilhelm (Heer) Held; student Coll. Wooster, 1937-39; diploma Actual Business Coll., 1941; m. Conrad Payne Mook, Sept. 6, 1941; children—Patricia Ann Mook Harris, Mary Ann Mook Barnum. Tchr., lectr. DAR Museum, Washington, 1973-79; sr. nat. asst. organizing sec. Children of the Am. Revolution, Washington, 1974-76, hon. sr. nat. v.p., 1977-83. Troop leader Girl Scouts U.S.A., Arlington, Va., 1951-53, neighborhood chmn., 1953-55, mem. program com. Arlington County council, 1955-56; rec. sec. Thomas Nelson chpt. DAR, Arlington, 1963-65, 73-75, librarian, 1967-69, regent, 1965-67. Recipient medal of appreciation SAR, 1981, Martha Washington medal, 1984. Mem. Va. Hist. Soc., Ohio Geneal. Soc., First Families Ohio, Soc. Descs. of Washington's Army at Valley Forge (charter v.p. 1976-78), Daus. of Union Vets. of Civil War 1861-65 (sr. v.p. 1978-80, pres. 1981-82), Children of Am. Revolution (sr. nat. officers club), Potomac Regents Club DAR (treas. 1974-75, librarian historian 1983-84), Aux. Sons Union Vets. of Civil War (patriotic instr. 1981—). Home: 5222 26th Rd N Arlington VA 22207

MOOK, BRYANT MASON, petroleum geologist; b. Dayton, Ohio, Apr. 10, 1953; s. Emerson Hadley and Elise Marie (Mason) M.; m. Shelly Jean Porsch, July 10, 1982. B.S., So. Meth. U., 1975; postgrad. U. Tex.-Dallas, 1975-78. Assoc. geologist Enserch Corp., Dallas, 1976-77; geologist Mitchell Energy, Dallas, 1977-80, Tesoro Petroleum, San Antonio, 1980-81; dist. geologist Am. Trading and Prodn., Midland, Tex., 1981-82; prin. Bryant M. Mook Oil Exploration, Dallas, 1982—. Bd. dirs. Am. Heart Assn., Midland, 1982-83, Big Bros. Am., San Antonio, 1980-81; advisor Internat. Jr. Achievement, San Antonio, 1980-81; fundamental in establishing Midland-Odessa chpt. Mothers Against Drunk Driving, 1983; 1st bass Midland-Odessa Symphony Chorale, 1982-83; mem. Dallas County Democratic Exec. Com., 1978-80, State Senate Resolution Com., Dallas, 1980, Republican Nat. Com., Dallas, 1982—; del. Rep. State Conv., Corpus Christi, 1984; mem. Zion Luth. Ch. Bd. Missions, Dallas, 1984—. Recipient Gold medal U.S. Figure Skating Assn., 1965; Outstanding Achievement award Gov. of Tex., 1981. Mem. Am. Assn. Petroleum Geologists, Dallas Geol. Soc., Tex. Gun Ranges, Inc., Pi Kappa Alpha. Avocations: small arms collector; pistol and skeet shooting.

MOOK, CONRAD PAYNE, meteorologist, former government official; b. Titusville, Pa., May 2, 1914; s. Raymond L. and Ella (Payne) M.; A.B., Coll. of Wooster, 1939; M.S., N.Y. U., 1943; m. Barbara Heer Held, Sept. 6, 1941; children—Patricia Ann Mook Harris, Mary Ann Mook Barnum. Instr., N.Y. U., 1941-43; meteorologist U.S. Weather Bur., Washington, 1943-57; geophysicist Harry Diamond Labs., Washington, 1957-61; hurricane forecaster U.S. Weather Bur., Washington, 1961-62; program mgr., space vehicle thermal control and vacuum tech. NASA Hdqrs., Washington, 1962-70; del. 11th gen. assembly Internat. Union Geodesy and Geophysics, Toronto, 1957; mem. commn. IV, U.S. nat. com. Internat. Sci. Radio Union, 1958-65; chmn. Govt.-Industry Com. on High Powered Light Source Devel., 1969-70. Mem. Am. Meteorol. Soc. (chmn. D.C. br. 1953-54); Am. Geophys. Union, AIAA (thermo-physics com. 1965-70), Order Founders and Patriots Am. (treas. D.C. Soc. 1977-86), Soc. Mayflower Descs. in D.C. (editor Pilgrim News 1976-80, dep. gov. 1983-84, gov. 1984-86), SAR (pres. George Mason chpt. 1979-81, Va. SAR-Children Am. Revolution coordinator 1980-81, 3d v.p. 1981-82, 1st v.p. 1982-83, pres. 1983-84, trustee 1984-85, chmn. U.S. stamps com. 1984—), Valley Forge Hist. Soc., Sons Union Vets. Civil War (comdr. Lincoln-Cushing Camp 1984-85), Ohio Geneal. Soc., Explorers Club. Presbyterian (fin. Sec. 1977-78, trustee 1977-80). Club: N.Y. University. Lodge: Lions (pres. Arlington Sunrise chpt. 1985-86). Editor Meteorology Trans., Am. Geophys. Union, 1956-58; assoc. editor Jour. Geophys. Research, 1959-65; contbr. articles to profl. and patriotic publs. Home: 5222 26th Rd N Arlington VA 22207

MOOMAW, WILLIAM HUGH, school administrator; b. London, June 8, 1925; came to U.S., 1940; s. Samuel Bowman and May Blackham (Downs) M.; m. Lee Anne Bowman, Aug. 26, 1950; children—William Hugh, Jr., Susan Downs. B.A., Washington and Lee U., 1949; M.A., U. Va., 1953, Ph.D., 1955. Instr. to full prof. Randolph-Macon Coll., Ashland, Va., 1954-61; exec. dir. U.S. Ednl. Commn. in U.K., London, 1961-63; pres. Stratford Coll., Danville, Va., 1963-74; headmaster Cape Henry Collegiate Sch., Virginia Beach, 1974—. Nat. judge Miss Am. Pageant, Atlantic City, N.J., 1971, 72. Served to 1st lt. U.S. Army inf., 1944-46, ETO. Mem. Phi Beta Kappa, Omicron Delta Kappa. Lodge: Rotary. Home: 1113 Ditchley Rd Virginia Beach VA 23451 Office: Cape Henry Collegiate Sch 1320 Mill Dam Rd Virginia Beach VA 23454

MOON, JAMES E., hospital administrator; b. Apr. 4, 1929; B.A. in Indsl. Arts, Iowa State Tchrs. Coll., 1951; postgrad. U. Houston, 1957-58; M.A. in Hosp. and Health Adminstrn., State U. Iowa, 1960; M.B.A., Samford U., 1976; Ph.D., U. Ala., 1980. Adminstrv. resident Washington Hosp. Center, D.C. Gen. Hosp., 1959-60; asst. adminstr. Washington Hosp. Center, 1961-69; asso. adminstr. U. Ala. Hosps. and Clinics, Birmingham, 1969-71, adminstr., 1971—; asst. prof. Sch. Health Services Adminstrn., U. Ala., 1969—. Served with USAF, 1951-56. Fellow Am. Coll. Hosp. Adminstrs.; mem. Am. Hosp. Assn. (com. on edn. 1983-85, com. on governing council sect. for met. hosps. 1985—), Southeastern, Ala. (fiscal devel. com. 1971, trustee 1976-78, sec.-treas. 1979, chmn. 1981) hosp. assns., Assn. Am. Med. Colls. (council teaching hosps.), Birmingham Regional Hosp. Council (dir. 1971, pres. elect 1972, bd. dirs. 1984), Birmingham Community Service Council (community health planning commn. 1972). Contbr. articles profl. jours. Home: 2457 Dolly Ridge Trail Birmingham AL 35243 Office: 619 S 19th St Birmingham AL 35233

MOON, JAMES MONROE (JIM), artist; b. Graham, N.C., June 7, 1928; s. James Monroe and Lurlene (Moore) M. B.F.A., William and Mary Coll., 1957. Tchr. fine arts Hofstra U., Hempstead, N.Y., 1960-61; chmn. dept. visual arts Barber Scotia Coll., Concord, N.C., 1965-66, N.C. Sch. Arts, Winston Salem, 1967-71. Works displayed Mus. Modern Art, N.Y.C., N.C. Mus. Art, Northwood Inst., Midland, Mich., Peggy Guggenheim Mus., Venice, Italy, Winston Salem Pub. Library. Served to cpl. U.S. Army, 1950-53. Home and Office: Route 3 Box 410A Lexington NC 27292

MOON, JOHN HENRY, SR., banker; b. Van Buren, Ark., Aug. 19, 1937; s. B.R. and Alma (Witte) M.; A.A., Delmar Coll., Corpus Christi, 1956; B.B.A. cum laude, Tex. A. and I. Coll., 1958; m. Agnes Rose Dickens, Aug. 16, 1958; children—John Henry, Randall Allen. Sr. acct. Tex. Eastern Transp. Co. and subsidiaries, 1958-63; exec. v.p., dir. Houston Research Inst., 1963-68; sr. v.p., asst. to chmn. bd., dir. Main Bank, 1968; vice chmn. bd., dir. N.E. Bank, 1969; chief exec. officer, chmn. bd., dir. Pasadena (Tex.) Nat. Bank, 1970-81; gen. partner Moon and Assos., Ltd. 1977—; chmn. bd., pres. Interservice Life Ins. Corp., Phoenix, Community Ins. Co., Tex., 1975-81; adv. dir., adv. chmn. bd. Community Bank, Houston, 1975-81, Interstate Bank, Houston, 1977-81; chmn. bd., pres. Community Capital Corp., Houston, 1975—, Ellington Bank Commerce, Houston, 1983—; chmn. bd. Community Nat. Bank, Friendswood, Tex., 1983—; chmn. bd., Peoples Nat. Bank, Pasadena, Tex., 1983—. Past bd. dirs. Pasadena Heart Assn., Salvation Army, Tex. Assn. Prevention of Blindness; past chmn. City of Pasadena Bd. Devel.; past chmn. adv. bd. Pasadena Civic Center. Named Outstanding Young Man of Year, Pasadena Jr. C. of C., 1973. Mem. Pasadena C. of C. (dir.), Am. Inst. C.P.A.s, Tex. Soc. C.P.A.s, Tex., Ind. bankers assns. Club: Rotary. Home: 3914 Peru Circle Pasadena TX 77504 Office: PO Box 34278 Houston TX 77234

MOON, MARY MARGARET, school of nursing administrator; b. Jasper, Ind., Nov. 17, 1927; d. Paul Raymond and Delia R. (Doane) Smiley; m. Jon Alva Coman, Sept. 8, 1953 (dec. Apr. 1976); m. Paul Edward Moon, Nov. 20, 1982. Diploma of grad. nurse John Sealy Coll., 1948; B.S., U. Tenn., Knoxville, 1961; M.Ed., U. Tenn.-Chattanooga, 1970. R.N., Tenn., Tex., Fla. In various nursing positions, 1948-59; instr. med. and surg. nursing U. Tenn. Research Ctr. and Hosp., Knoxville, 1959-62; instr. Baroness Erlanger Hosp. Sch. Nursing, Chattanooga, 1962-65, asst. dir. nursing edn., chmn. dept. med. and surg. nursing, 1965-72, dir. nursing edn., 1972—. Helen Fuld Health Trust grantee, 1974, 76, 80, 84. Mem. Nat. League Nursing, Tenn. League Nursing (sec. 1975-77), Chattanooga League Nursing (vice chmn. 1984-86), Fedn. for Accessible Nursing Edn. and Licensure, Tenn. Assn. for Diploma Nurse Edn. (v.p. 1982-84). Democrat. Roman Catholic. Avocations: golf; swimming; reading. Home: 5600 Lake Resort Terr Apt 204-E Chattanooga TN 37415 Office: Erlanger Hosp Sch Nursing 975 E 3d St Chattanooga TN 37403

MOON, WILLIAM BYRD, psychologist; b. Athens, Ga., July 7, 1943; s. Paul Sanders and Betty (Winn) M.; married; children—M. Michelle, William M.; m. Frances Lynn Richards, Nov. 19, 1983; 1 child, Whitney Anne. A.B., Armstrong State Coll., Savannah, Ga., 1970; M.S.W., U. Ga., 1972; Ph.D., Fla. Inst. Tech., 1984. Asst. dir. Chatham County Day Ctr., Savannah, 1972-73; dir. social services Anneewakee Hosp., Douglasville, Ga., 1973-75; dir. child and adolescent service Pineland MH/MR Programs, Statesboro, Ga., 1975-78, dir. M.H. services, 1978-81; exec. dir. Youth Estate, Inc., Brunswick, Ga., 1981-84; staff psychologist Anneewakee Hosp., Douglasville, Ga., 1984—; cons. Bulloch Meml. Hosp., Statesboro, 1977-79; instr. St. Leo Coll., Hinesville, Ga., 1979, Ga. So. Coll., Statesboro, 1980, Armstrong State Coll., Savannah, Ga., 1972-73, Tift Coll., Annewakee Ctr., Douglasville, 1984—. Served to E-5 U.S. Army, Vietnam. Mem. Am. Psychol. Assn., Ga. Psychol. Assn., Soc. Personality Assessment. Episcopalian. Lodge: Optimist. Home: 2515 NE Expressway Apt D-10 Atlanta GA 30345 Office: 4771 Anneewakee Rd Douglasville GA 30135

MOONAN, JEFFREY KEITH, cardiologist, consultant, educator; b. New Orleans, Aug. 10, 1945; s. John Simms and Virginia (Ellison) M.; m. Marcia Stevens, June 19, 1967 (div. 1970); 1 dau., Lauren Keathe; m. Linda Louise Himel, Dec. 12, 1981. B.S., La. State U., 1967; M.D., U. Va., 1971. Diplomate Am. Bd. Internal Medicine. Intern, La. State U., 1972, resident, La. State U. and Georgetown U., 1972-75, staff physician, Georgetown U., 1973-74; mem. staff Baton Rouge Gen. Hosp., Our Lady of the Lake Hosp., Doctors' Hosp., Earl K. Long Hosp., La. State U., East Ascension Hosp., Dixon Meml. Hosp.; ptnr. La. Cardiology Assocs., Baton Rouge, 1977—; mem. cardiovascular diagnostic coms. Our Lady of the Lake Hosp., Baton Rouge Gen. Hosp. Ochsner Found. fellow, 1975-77. Assoc. fellow Am. Coll. Chest Physicians; mem. AMA, La. State Med. Soc., Am. Heart Assn., East Baton Rouge Med. Soc., Alpha Epsilon Delta. Presbyterian. Office: 5228 Dijon Dr Baton Rouge LA 70809

MOONEY, ALFONSO JOHN, III, family physician, hospital administrator; b. Statesboro, Ga., Sept. 28, 1948; s. Alfonso John and Dorothy Carolyn (Riggs) M.; m. Jane Roberts, Mar. 25, 1972; children—Alfonso John IV, Rachel Deneen. B.S. in Biology, Emory U., 1970; M.D., 1974. Diplomate Am. Bd. Family Practice, Nat. Bd. Med. Examiners. Cert. alcoholism counselor. Lic. physician, Ga., Ky., N.C. Intern, U. Louisville Afiliated Hosps., Ky., 1974-75; resident in family medicine, U. N.C., Chapel Hill, 1977-79, postdoctoral fellow, 1979-80; staff physician Jefferson Alcohol and Drug Abuse Ctr., Louisville, 1975-76; med. dir. Shalomwald Hosp., La Grange, Ky., 1976; clin. instr. dept. family medicine U. N.C., Chapel Hill, 1979-81, clin. asst. prof., 1982—; asst. med. dir. Willingway Hosp., Statesboro, Ga., 1981-82, med. dir., 1982—, dir., 1982—; med. dir. Vista Hall Alcohol and Drug Ctr., Statesboro, 1982—; assoc. clin. prof. family medicine Med. Coll. Ga., 1985—; lectr. in field. Mem. Alcohol and Drug Profl. Devel. Council, 1982—, State Adv. Council for Mental Health and Mental Retardation, 1983—, Am. Acad. Addictionology, study com., 1982—; physician rep. Bulloch County Bd. of Health, 1983—; chmn. Bullock Alcohol and Drug Abuse Council, Inc.; bd. dirs. United Way, 1983—. Fellow Am. Acad. Family Physicians; mem. Soc. Tchrs. Family Medicine, Am. Med. Soc. on Alcoholism (chmn. state chpt.), C. of C. (bd. dirs.), Sigma Chi. Methodist. Lodge: Rotary. Home: 318 Savannah Ave Statesboro GA 30458 Office: Willingway Hosp 311 Jones Mill Rd Statesboro GA 30458

MOONEY, MAUREEN EVE, oil company executive; b. Batavia, N.Y., June 8, 1948; d. Paul F. and Eva (George) M. B.A., Niagara U., 1970; M.S., So. Ill. U., 1972; M.B.A., U. Conn., 1984. Asst. dean Rider Coll., Trenton, N.J., 1972-75; dean of students Manhattanville Coll., Purchase, N.Y., 1975-79; mgr. employee relations Playtex, Inc., Stamford, Conn., 1980-81; compensation supr. Mobil Oil Corp., N.Y.C., 1981-84, supr. human resources, New Orleans, 1984—. Regional coordinator Common Cause, Trenton, 1973; v.p. Big Bros., Big Sisters, Fairfield County, Conn., 1983-85; mem. citizens adv. bd. U. New Orleans, 1985. Mem. Am. Soc. Tng. and Devel. (bd. dirs.), Women in Mgmt., Nat. Assn. Student Personnel Adminstrn. (adv. bd. 1972-79). Home: 46 Avant Garde Circle Kenner LA 70065

MOORE, ARCH A., JR., governor; b. Moundsville, W.Va., Apr. 16, 1923; s. Arch. A. and Genevieve (Jones) M.; m. Shelley S. Riley, 1949; children—Shelley Capito, Lucy Durbin, Arch III. Student Lafayette Coll., 1943; A.B., W.Va. U., 1948, LL.B., 1951. State del. W.Va., 1952; U.S. rep. 1st dist., W.Va., 1956-69; gov. W.Va., 1969-77; Rep. candidate U.S. Senate, 1978; Rep. candidate gov., 1980; gov. of W.Va., 1985—. Mem. ABA, W.Va. Bar Assn., Am. Judicature Soc. Address: State Capitol Office of Gov Charleston WV 25305*

MOORE, ARCHIE BRADFORD, JR., educator, university administrator; b. Montgomery, Ala., Jan. 8, 1933; s. Archie Bradford and Annie Ruth (Jeter) M.; m. Dorothy Ann Flowers, Jan. 21, 1957; children—Angelo Juan, Kimmerly DeAnna. B.S., Ala. State U., 1959, Ed.M., 1961; Ph.D., Kans. State U., 1974. Instr. Russell County Pub. Sch. System, Ala., 1959-61, Montgomery County Pub. Sch. System, 1961-69; wholesale cosmetic distbr. Koscot Interplanetary, Inc., Orlando, Fla., 1969-70; asst. prof. social sci., Clark Coll., Atlanta, 1970-75; dir. Thirteen Coll. Curriculum Program, Ala. State U., Montgomery, 1975-77, coordinator continuing edn., 1977-78, dean evening, weekend coll. pub. services, 1978-83, assoc. prof. edn., spl. asst. to dean grad. studies and continuing edn., 1983—; cons. in field. Author articles in field of desegregation and education. Chmn. Catholic Charity Dr.; chmn. bd. dirs. Resurrection Cath. Sch. System Bd. Edn. Served with USN, 1952-56. Recipient Tchr. Recognition State award Ala. Social Studies Fair, 1968; NSF grantee, 1965; fellow Nat. Def. Edn. Act, 1967, 68, 69, Edn. Profl. Devel. Act, 1972-74. Mem. NEA, Assn. for Continuing Higher Edn., Nat. Community Edn. Assn., Phi Delta Kappa, Phi Beta Sigma. Democrat. Avocations: reading; playing musical instruments; fishing; walking. Home: 2966 Vandy Dr Montgomery AL 36110 Office: Ala State U 915 S Jackson St Montgomery AL 36195

MOORE, BEVERLY ANN, nurse; b. Sullivan, Ind., June 25, 1935; d. Elza Wayne and Eunice Marie (Hixon) McBride; m. Dean James Pennock, Feb. 7, 1953 (div. 1958); children—Jane, Dean James; m. 2d James Curtis Moore, Dec. 23, 1960; children—John, Jackie. A.A., Ind. U.-Gary, 1970. Dir. in-service edn. for surgery Meth. Hosp., Gary, 1970-75; nursing instr. IVY Tech, Gary, 1972-75; staff RN, in-service trainer Hopkins County Hosp., Ky., 1975-76; dir. surgery Muhlenberg Community Hosp., Greenville, Ky., 1976-85, patient educator, 1985—; examiner Operating Room Technicians, Gary, Ind. and Madisonville, Ky., 1974-77. Mem. Assn. Operating Room Nurses, Ind. U. Alumni Assn. Democrat. Avocations: reading; sewing; walking. Home: 317 N 3rd St Central City KY 42330 Office: Muhlenberg Community Hosp 440 Hopkinsville St Greenville KY 42345

MOORE, CARL R., business executive, state senator; b. Appalachia, Va., Feb. 26, 1930; B.S. in Bus. Adminstrn., U. Ala.; 4 children. Owner Lee Garden Apts., Bristol, Va.; developer Deer Run Apts., Bristol, Tenn.; mng. partner Best Western-Capitol Park Inn; mem. Tenn. Senate. Bd. dirs. Va. Travel Council, Tenn. Performing Arts Found.; charter mem. East Tenn. State U. Found. Recipient Outstanding Young Man of Yr. award Jr. C. of C., 1957, Exec. of Yr. award Tri-Cities chpt. Nat. Secs. Assn. Mem. Nat. Conf. State Legislatures (chmn. arts, tourism and cultural resources com.), Internat. Hot Rod Assn. (chmn.), Tenn. Hotel and Motel Assn. (dir.), U.S. Navy League, Am. Legion, U. Ala. Alumni Assn. Democrat. Episcopalian. Office: Room 309 War Memorial Bldg Nashville TN 37219

MOORE, CARRIE KIRK, counselor; b. Tampa, Fla., Aug. 28, 1931; d. Walter Kirk and Inez (Farmer) Kirk Franklin; m. McDonald Moore, Aug. 13, 1955; children—McDonald Moore, Karon L., Patricia Ann. B.A., Talladega Coll., 1953; M.Ed., Fla. A&M U., 1960. Social studies instr. Luthersville High Sch., Ga., 1953-56; counselor Hampton Jr. Coll., Ocala, Fla., 1960-65, Central Fla. Jr. Coll., Ocala, 1966-67, Bishop State Jr. Coll., Mobile, Ala., 1967—; adj. faculty U. Ala., Birmingham, 1975—. Recipient cert. of appreciation Regional Tech. Inst., U. Ala., 1975. Mem. Ala. Assn. Counseling and Devel., Ala. Assn. Non-White Concerns, Am. Assn. Counseling and Devel., NEA, Ala. Edn. Assn., Assn. Handicapped Student Services and Programs in Higher Edn., Talladega Coll. Alumni Assn. (v.p. chpt. 1983-85). Methodist. Avocations: sewing; needlework; interior decorating; bowling. Office: Bishop State Jr Coll 351 N Broad St Mobile AL 36690

MOORE, CHARLES RAY, government administrator, psychotherapist, consultant; b. Paris, Tex., Nov. 25, 1938; S.N.H. and Genevieve Mildred (Mazy) M.; m. Juanita Marie Range, Sept. 2, 1962; children—Linda Diane, Michael David, Elizabeth Gene. B.B.A., Tex. Tech U., 1962; M.Div., Southwestern Sem., 1966; M.S., East Tex. State U., 1968, Ed.D., 1971. Cert. profl. mental health counselor, Tex. Asst. prof. St. Mary's U., San Antonio, 1971-72, assoc. dir. report, alcohol/drug program, 1975-77; instr., class adviser Acad. Health Sci., Fort Sam Houston, Tex., 1972-77; adminstr. drug and alcohol program Hdqrs., Forces Command, U.S. Army, Fort McPherson, Ga., 1977-85; adminstr. corps staff, dir. program integration U.S. Army, Fort Hood, Tex., 1985—; cons., bd. dirs. Bus. Growth Inst., Belton, Tex., 1972—; psychotherapist, bd. dirs. Psychophys. Health Inst., Belton, 1985—. Author: Alcoholism in the Military, 1978; Stopsmoking Program, 1981; Alcoholism in Workforce, 1982; Commanders Handbook—Marijuana Abuse, 1983. Tchr. Bapt. Ch., Marietta, Ga., 1977-81. Recipient Employee Supr. of Yr. award Fed. Exec. Bd., 1979; ofcl. commendation, Exceptional Performance award FORSCOM, 1985; ofcl. commendation, Exceptional Performance award U.S. Army, Fort Hood, 1985. Mem. Am. Assn. Counseling and Devel., Am. Mental Health Counselors Assn. (cert. 1985), Assn. Labor-Mgmt.-Adminstrs. and Cons. on Alcoholism, Phi Kappa Psi, Kappa Delta Pi, Phi Delta Kappa. Avocations: sports; music; running.

MOORE, CLARENCE, physical education educator, writer, consultant; b. St. Louis, Apr. 17, 1928; s. Clarence Joseph and Hannah (Linn) M.; m. Sharon E. Selk, 1973; children—Penny, Patti, Peggy. A.B., Tarkio Coll., 1952; M.A., U. Ala., 1953, Ph.D., 1964. Cert. tchr. secondary, phys. edn. Coach high sch., Fowler, Mich., 1953-54; instr., asst. prof. U. Ala., 1954-66; prof., chmn. dept. phys. edn., Bloomsburg State Coll., Pa., 1966-71; prof., chmn. dept. phys. edn. U. Fla., Gainesville, 1971—; editor Hunter Textbooks, Inc., Winston-Salem, N.C. Author: Tennis Everyone, 1979; Weight Training Everyone, 1980; Jogging Everyone, 1981; Fitness-The New Wave, 1979. Served with USN, 1946-48. Fellow AAHPER (life). Democrat. Avocations: writing; sports. Home: Box 41 Turkey Creek Alachua FL 32615 Office: Dept Phys Edn U Fla Gainesville FL 32611

MOORE, CLARK WILLIAM, park ranger; b. N.Y.C., Apr. 20, 1955; s. Jessie and Margarite (Richardson) M.; m. Shasta U. Henderson, Mar. 23, 1978; 1 child, Chasidy Unee. A.A. Morristown Coll., 1975; B.A., Rust Coll., 1978. Park technician Nat. Park Service, Tupelo, Miss., 1976-77; Park ranger Nat. Park Service, Ninety-six S.C., 1978-80, chief park ranger Tuskegee Inst., Ala., 1980-85, Martin L. King, Jr. N.H.S., Atlanta, 1985—; guest lectr. Auburn U., Ala., 1985. Vice-pres. Tuskegee Jaycees, 1984; treas. Twin Cities Project, Tuskegee, 1985. Recipient Nat. Park Service Spl. Achievement award, 1983. Mem. Phi Theta Kappa, Alpha Kappa Mu, Phi Alpha Theta. Democrat. Methodist. Lodge: Masons. Avocations: tennis; track; coin collecting. Office: Martin Luther King NHS 522 Auburn Ave NE Atlanta GA 30312

MOORE, CONARD DEA, ophthalmologist; b. Okmulgee, Okla., July 8, 1928; s. Conard Milton and Mildred Ezelle (Fenno) M.; B.A., Baylor U., 1950, M.D., 1955; m. Kitzia Poniatowska, Dec. 20, 1975; children—Pablo, Alex, Jeff, Santiago, Constance, Diego, Kitzia, Marc, Sean, Kevin. Intern, Meth. Hosp., Houston, 1956; resident in ophthalmology Baylor Coll. Medicine, 1960, asst. prof. ophthalmology, 1957-72; practice medicine, specializing in ophthalmology, Houston, 1980—; chief dept. ophthalmology Center del Oro Hosp., Houston, 1980—, chief med. staff, 1980—. Served with U.S. Navy, 1948-53; col. USAR, 1960-862. Diplomate Am. Bd. Ophthalmology. Fellow A.C.S., Internat. Coll. Surgeons; mem. Soc. Eye Surgeons, Mil. Ophthalmol. Soc. Republican. Roman Catholic. Club: River Oaks Country. Office: 7000 Fannin Blvd Houston TX 77030

MOORE, DALTON, JR., petroleum engr.; b. Snyder, Tex., Mar. 25, 1918; s. Dalton and Anne (Yonge) M.; diploma Tarleton State U., 1938; B.S., Tex. A. and M. U., 1942; diploma U.S. Army Command and Gen. Staff Sch., 1945. Field engr. Gulf Oil Corp., 1946; dist. engr. Chgo. Corp., 1947-48, chief reservoir engr., 1949; mgr. Burdell Oil Corp., N.Y.C. and Snyder, Tex., 1950-52; mgr. Wimberly Field Unit, 1953-55; profl. petroleum cons., Abilene, Tex., 1956—; pres. Dalton Moore Engring. Co., 1957-67, First Oil Co., 1960-67, Second Oil Co., 1960-72, Petroleum Engrs. Operating Co., 1967—, Evaluation Engr. for Investment Bankers Corp., 1968—, Investment Bankers Oil Co., Inc., 1968—. Pres., Sweetwater (Tex.) Jr. C. of C., 1938; precinct chmn. Taylor County Democratic Com., 1956-76; bd. Bd. dirs. Taylor County chpt. ARC, 1956-62, Preini Log Library. Served from 2d lt. to maj., AUS, 1940-46. Eagle Scout, Boy Scouts Am. Mem. AIME (chmn. W. Central Tex. sect. 1954), Abilene Geol. Soc., VFW. Address: 4065 Waldemar Dr Abilene TX 79605

MOORE, DAVID LLOYD, marketing educator, marketing researcher; b. Cambridge, Mass., Aug. 26, 1948; s. Lloyd Holly and Maxine Anne (Saunders) M.; m. Regina Karen Sulenski, Aug. 17, 1968; children—Stacy Erin, Kristofer Kelly. B.S.B.A., Old Dominion U., 1976; M.S.B.A., U. Mass., 1979, Ph.D., 1985. Mktg. rep. Brown & Williamson Tobacco Corp., Louisville, 1972-74; savs. and loan examiner Fed. Home Loan Bank Bd., Boston, 1976-77; placement dir. U. Mass. Bus. Sch., Amherst, 1977-79; teaching assoc. U. Mass., Amherst, 1979-83; asst. prof. mktg. Coll. William and Mary Williamsburg, Va., 1983—. Bd. dirs. Williamsburg unit ARC, 1984—. Served with USN, 1969-72. Direct Mktg. Edn. Found. fellow, 1984. Named Outstanding Mktg. Tchr. of Yr., U. Mass., 1981, 82. Mem. Am. Mktg. Assn. (fellow doctoral consortium 1981), Assn. Consumer Research, Am. Psychol. Assn. (div. 23), Bus. and Profl. Advt. Assn., Alpha Mu Alpha, Omicron Delta Epsilon. Avocations: raquet sports; swimming; photography. Home: 285-4 Merrimac Trail Williamsburg VA 23185 Office: Coll William and Mary Sch Bus Adminstrn Williamsburg VA 23185

MOORE, DAVID MICHAEL, nurse; b. Memphis, Aug. 19, 1945; s. Russell Miller and Myrtle (Griffis) M.; m. Donna Marie Deans, July 27, 1968; 1 child, David Brent. B.S., Lee Coll., 1973; R.N., Central Piedmont Community Coll., 1976. Operating room attendant Bradley Meml. Hosp. Cleve., Tenn., 1973-74, emergency dept. supr., 1978—; shift change nurse Charlotte Meml. Hosp., Charlotte, N.C., 1976-78; instr. advanced cardiac life support Am. Heart Assn., Chattanooga, 1984—. Served to sgt. USAF, 1964-68. Mem. Tenn. Hosp. Assn. Club: Liasons (Cleve.) (pres. 1982-84). Avocations: fishing; camping; music; electronics. Office: Bradley County Meml Hosp PO Box 3060 Cleveland TN 37311

MOORE, DENNIS JAMES, veterinarian; b. Canton, Ohio, Feb. 8, 1949; s. Emery Glenn and Ruth Evelyn (Knowlton) M.; m. Constance Snyder, May 16, 1970; children—Lisa Ann, Christopher James, Scott William Glenn. B.S. summa cum laude, W.Va. U., 1971; D.V.M., Ohio State U., 1975. Veterinarian, Cross Lanes Vet. Hosp., Nitro, W.Va., 1975-79; veterinarian, owner Fairmont Vet. Hosp. (W.Va.), 1979—. Bd. dirs. W.Va. Christian Youth Camp. Mem. AVMA (W.Va. rep. Ho. of Dels. 1981-83, pres. W.Va. chpt. 1981-83). Democrat. Mem. Ch. of Christ. Club: Rotary. Address: 1313 Fairmont Ave Fairmont WV 26554

MOORE, DONALD LEE, JR., construction company executive, land developer; b. Brevard, N.C., July 6, 1944; s. Donald Lee and Cornelia (Ratchford) M.; m. Roselyn Chandler, July 29, 1967; children—Natalie, Jennifer, Katie, Jaime, Lee. B.S., N.C. State U., 1967. Sales engr. Gen. Electric Co., Hendersonville, N.C., Tampa, 1967-73; pres. Intercoastal Assocs., Savannah, Ga., 1973-78; v.p. Lattinore Land Corp., Savannah, 1973-78; pres. Ratchford & Moore, Inc., Savannah, 1978—. Vice pres. Blue Ridge, Black Mountain, N.C., 1980-86; pres. YMCA of Savannah, 1981-85; bd. dirs. Savannah Christian Prep. Sch., 1983—, Parent and Child Devel. Services, Savannah, 1983—; active Leadership Savannah Program. Named Vol. of Yr., YMCA Savannah, 1985. Presbyterian. Club: Savannah Yacht (bd. stewards 1983-86). Avocations: scuba diving; snow skiing; tennis; golf; raquetball. Home: 6 Anchor Ct Savannah GA 31410 Office: Ratchford & Moore Inc PO Box 30039 Savannah GA 31410

MOORE, DONALD RICHARD, cardiovascular clinical nurse specialist; b. Greensboro, N.C., June 25, 1946; s. Aubrey D. and Wilma I. (Bowman) Winslow M. B.S. in Nursing, U. N.C.-Greensboro, 1974; M.S. in Nursing, U. Ala.-Birmingham, 1979. Head nurse Keesler USAF Med. Ctr., Kessler AFB, Miss., 1974-76; flight nurse 9th Aeromed. Evac Sq, Clark Ab, Philippines, 1976-78; clin. specialist cardiovascular nursing Wilford Hall USAF Med. Ctr., Lackland AFB, Tex., 1979-82; chief nurse cardiovascular Sch. Aerospace Medicine, Brooks AFB, Tex., 1982-83; nursing supr. critical care UCLA Hosp. and Clinics, Los Angeles, 1983; dir. nursing critical care Meml. Med. Ctr., Jacksonville, Fla., 1983-85; clin. specialist Cobb Cardiac Rehab., Austell, Ga., 1985—; nursing cons. USAF, Lackland AFB, Tex., 1980-82; flight nurse USAF Res., 31st Aeromed. Evac Sq, Charleston AFB, S.C., 1984—. Mem., speaker Am. Heart Assn. Task Force, San Antonio, 1980-82; senator U. N.C. Student Govt., Greensboro, 1973-74. Served to capt. USAF, 1974-82. Mem. Am. Assn. Critical Care Nurses (pres. elect 1984-85), Am. Soc. Nursing Service Adminstrs., Am. Nurses Assn., ARC Nurses, Sigma Theta Tau. Republican. Avocation: water skiing. Home: 1475-A Willow Lake Dr Atlanta GA 30329 Office: Cobb Cardiac Rehab 1793 Mulkey Rd Austell GA 30001

MOORE, DWIGHT MCCLINTOCK, petroleum geologist; b. Detroit, Sept. 9, 1956; s. Alfred Cleon and Clara Childs (Nicol) M. B.A. in Geology cum laude, So. Meth. U., 1978, B.B.A. in Fin. cum laude, 1978. Jr. geologist Diamond Shamrock Exploration Co., Houston, 1978-79, geologist, 1979-82, sr. geologist, 1982—. Univ. scholar So. Meth. U.; Sabine scholar Dallas Geol. Soc., 1977-78. Mem. Am. Assn. Petroleum Geologists, Geol. Soc. Am., Soc. Petroleum Engrs., Soc. Profl. Well Log Analysts (hydrocarbon well logging com. 1980—), Soc. Exploration Geophysicists (assoc.), So. Meth. U. Alumni Assn. (dir. 1984—, v.p. admissions 1985—, pres.-elect 1985). Republican. Episcopalian. Office: Diamond Shamrock Exploration Co 3040 Post Oak Blvd Suite 2200 Houston TX 77056

MOORE, EDWARD LEON, JR., surgeon, banker, real estate broker; b. Uniontown, Pa., Aug. 14, 1914; s. Edward and Mildred (Boyle) M.; m. Rita Marie McGrady, May 9, 1942; children—Rita Marie Fork, Darleen K. Potts, Karen Lee Harris, Jan Patrice Brown. A.B., W.Va. U., 1935; M.D., St. Louis U., 1939. Diplomate Am. Bd. Surgery. Intern, St. Frances Hosp., Pitts., 1939-40, resident in surgery, 1940-42, 46-47; surgeon Mayo Clinic, 1944; chief of staff St. Francis Hosp.; chief of surgery St. John's Hosp., Tulsa, 1947-78, now hon. staff, mem. adv. bd., 5 yrs.; hon. staff St. Francis Hosp., Hillcrest Meml. Hosp.; dir. Am. Bank & Trust Co. Tulsa; real estate broker, Okla. Med. chmn. Red Feather campaign, Tulsa. Served to maj. USAAF, 1942-46. Fellow ACS; mem. Southwestern Surg. Congress (founder), Internat. Coll. Surgeons, Tulsa Surg. Soc. (founder, 1st pres. 1948), Okla. Med. Soc. (chmn. com. on peer rev., gen. chmn. meeting). Republican. Roman Catholic. Club: So. Hill Country (Tulsa). Contbr. articles to profl. jours. Home: 1818 E 42d St Tulsa OK 74105

MOORE, EDWARD LYNN, safety engineer; b. Roanoke, Va., June 13, 1949; s. Clarence Edward and Sarah Arlene (Beatty) M. B.S. in Indsl. Engring. and Ops. Research, Va. Poly. Inst. and State U., 1971. Cert. safety profl. Safety rep. U.S. Fidelity & Guaranty Co., Richmond, Va., 1972-74; sr. safety engr. Carolina Power & Light Co., Raleigh, N.C., 1974—. Basketball coach Cary Recreation Dept., N.C., 1978-84. Mem. Am. Soc. Safety Engrs. (chmn. pub. relations N.C. chpt. 1983-84), ASTM (membership sec. for com F-18, 1982—), Engrs. Club of Raleigh, Va. Tech. Alumni Assn. (v.p. Research Triangle chpt. 1982—), Theta Delta Chi Alumni Assn. (pres. 1982-84). Mem. Ch. of the Brethren. Clubs: Jaycees, Raleigh Sports. Avocations: tennis; basketball; fraternity advisor; reading; working on beach house. Office: Carolina Power & Light Co PO Box 1551 411 Fayetteville St Raleigh NC 27602

MOORE, ELISE LYNETTE, residence education administrator; b. Cin.; d. Kent Harry and Helen Elizabeth (Bowman) M. B.S., James Madison U., 1980; Ed.M., U. Va., 1982. Coordinator residence edn. Longwood Coll., Farmville, Va., 1980-82; dir. residence edn. Va. Commonwealth U., Richmond, 1982—; adv. in field. Adv., organizer Campus-wide Fast for African Relief Fund, 1985; organizer week non-violence issues Longwood Coll., 1984; big sister Big Bros. Big Sisters Program, Charlottesville, Va., 1982. Recipient Outstanding Young Woman Am. award, 1984, Fed. Internship award, 1979. Mem. Am. Assn. Coll. Deans, Nat. Assn. Student Personnel Adminstrs., Am. Personnel Guidance Assn. Va. Assn. Student Personnel Adminstrs., Va. Counselor's Assn., Psi Chi. Democrat. Mem. Brethern Ch. Avocations: tennis; running; basketball. Office: PO Box 265 MCV Sta Housing Office Richmond VA 23294

MOORE, G(EORGE) PAUL, educator, speech pathologist, consultant, researcher; b. Everson, W. Va., Nov. 2, 1907; s. George B. and Emma (Ayers) M.; m. Gertrude H. Conley, June 10, 1929 (dec.); children—Anne Gertrude Moore Dooley, Paul David; m. 2d, Grace MacLellan Murphey, Mar. 1, 1981. A.B., W. Va. U., 1929, D.Sc. (hon.), 1974; M.A., Northwestern U., 1930, Ph.D., 1936. Faculty dept. communicative disorders, Sch. Speech, Northwestern U., 1930-62, dir. voice research lab., 1940-62, dir. voice clinic, 1950-62; lectr. in otolaryngology Northwestern Med. Sch., 1953-62, dir. research lab. Inst. Laryngology and Voice Disorders, Chgo., 1957-62; prof. speech U. Fla., Gainesville, 1962-77, chmn. dept. speech, 1962-73, dir. communicative scis. lab., 1962-68, disting. service prof., 1977, acting chmn. dept. speech, 1977-78, disting. service prof. emeritus, 1980, adj. prof. elec. engring., 1981—; vis. faculty U. Colo., summer 1948, 51, 67, U. Minn., 1963, U. Witwatersrand, Johannesburg, S.Africa, summer 1971; co-chmn. Internat. Voice Conf., 1957; mem. communicative scis. study sect. NIH, 1959-63; mem. speech pathology and audiology adv. panel, Vocat. Rehab. Adminstrn., HEW, 1962, 64; mem. rev. panel speech and hearing, Neurol. and Sensory Disease Service Program, Bur. State Services, HEW, 1963-66, adv. com., 1964-67; mem. communicative disorders research tng. com. Nat. Inst. Neurol. Diseases and Blindness, NIH, 1964-68; mem. communicative disorders program project rev. com. Nat. Inst. Neurol. diseases and Stroke, 1969-73, chmn. 1971-72, mem. nat. adv. neurol. and communicative disorders and stroke council, 1973-77; mem. Am. Bd. Examiners in Speech Pathology and Audiology, 1965-67. Served with USAF, 1944-45. Recipient merit award Am. Acad. Ophthalmology and Otolaryngology, 1962; Gould award William and Harriet Gould Found., 1962; Barraquer Meml. award Smith, Miller and Patch, 1969; Disting. Faculty award Fla. Blue Key, 1975; Tchr. Scholar award U. Fla., 1976; honors Ill. Speech, Lang. and Hearing Assn., 1979; Fellow Am. Speech-Lang.-Hearing Assn. (pres. 1961; Honors of Assn. award 1966); mem. Fla. Speech and Hearing Assn. (honor award 1977), So. Speech Assn., Speech Communication Assn. (Golden Anniversary award for scholarship 1969), Internat. Coll. Exptl. Phonology, Internat. Assn. Logopedics and Phoniatrics, Am. Assn. Phonetic Scis., AMA (spl. affiliate), Sigma Xi. Republican. Presbyterian. Club: Kiwanis. Author: Organic Voice Disorders, 1971; patentee laryngoscope, 1975; contbr. chpts. to books, articles to profl. jours. Home: 2234 NW 6th Pl Gainesville FL 32603 Office: U Fla 16 ASB Gainesville FL 32611

MOORE, GLOVER, educator; b. Birmingham, Ala., Sept. 22, 1911; s. Glover and Maud (Mims) M.; B.A., Birmingham-So. Coll., 1932; M.A., Vanderbilt U., 1933, Ph.D., 1936. Teaching fellow Vanderbilt U., 1935-36; instr. history Miss. State U., 1936-38, asst. prof., 1938-46, asso. prof., 1946-53, prof., 1953-77, prof. emeritus, 1977—. Pres. Miss. Hist. Soc., 1970-71. Served with Adj. Gen.'s Dept., AUS, 1942-46. Mem. Am., So. hist. assns., Orgn. Am. Historians. Episcopalian. Author: The Missouri Controversy, 1819-1821, 1953; William Jemison Mims, Soldier and Squire, 1966; editor: A Calhoun County, Alabama, Boy in the 1860s, 1978. Home: 404 Myrtle St Starkville MS 39759 Office: Box 5326 Mississippi State MS 39762

MOORE, GREGORY FRANK, geophysics educator, researcher; b. Bismarck, N.D., Sept. 25, 1951; s. Walter Edgar and Mildred F. (Lang) M.; m. Susan K. Heller, Aug. 11, 1974. B.A., U. Calif.-Santa Barbara, 1973; M.A., Johns Hopkins U., 1974; Ph.D., Cornell U., 1977. Postdoctoral assoc. Cornell U., Ithaca, N.Y., 1977; postgrad. research geologist Scripps Inst. Oceanography, La Jolla, Calif., 1978-79, asst. research geologist, 1979-82; research geologist Cities Service Oil Co., Tulsa, 1982-83, cons., 1984-85; assoc. prof. U. Tulsa, 1983—; cons. Marathon Oil Co., Houston, 1984. Contbr. articles to profl. jours. Grantee NSF, 1978-85. Fellow Geol. Soc. Am.; mem. Am. Geophys. Union, Am. Assn. Petroleum Geologists, Soc. Exploration Geophysicists, Soc. Econ. Paleontologists and Mineralogists. Democrat. Presbyterian. Office: Dept Geosciences U Tulsa 600 S College Tulsa OK 74104

MOORE, HUGH JACOB, JR., lawyer; b. Norfolk, Va., June 29, 1944; s. Hugh Jacob and Ina Ruth (Hall) M.; B.A., Vanderbilt U., 1966; LL.B., Yale, 1969; m. Jean Garnett, June 10, 1972; children—Lela Miller, Sarah Garnett. Admitted to Tenn. bar, 1970, U.S. Supreme Ct. bar, 1973, U.S. Ct. Appeals (6th circuit), 1973. Law clk. U.S. Dist. Court, Middle Dist. of Tenn., Nashville, 1969-70; asst. U.S. atty., Eastern Dist. of Tenn., Chattanooga, 1973-76; assoc. Witt, Gaither & Whitaker, Chattanooga, 1976-77, partner, 1977—. Mem. bd. dirs. Adult Edn. Council, Chattanooga, 1976-81, pres., 1977-79; bd. dirs. Chattanooga Opera Assn., 1981—, Riverbend Festival, 1983—. Mem. alumni council McCallie Sch. Mem. Am., Tenn., Chattanooga, bar assns. Methodist. Bd. editors ABA Litigation News, 1983—. Home: 101 Ridgeside Rd Chattanooga TN 37411 Office: 1100 American National Bank Bldg Chattanooga TN 37402

MOORE, JAMES LINTON, III, sales training specialist; b. Little Rock, Nov. 5, 1941; s. James Linton and Frances I. (Cromer) M.; m. Jean Lee Chapel, Sept. 20, 1966; children—Andrew L., Matthew C. B.A., U. Ga., 1964; M.Div., Princeton Theol. Sem., 1972. Commd. 2d lt. U.S. Air Force, 1964, advanced through grades to capt., 1967; resigned, 1969; pastor Presbyn. chs., Ohio and N.D., 1972-77; sales mgr. trainer Hanes Knitwear, Ohio, Tex. and Mo., 1978—, nat. sales tng. mgr., Winston-Salem, N.C., 1980—; cons., speaker in field; instr. jr. colls. Editor, Nat. Industry Sales Newsletter, 1984, 85. Contbr. articles to trade jours. Cons., adv. Local Minority Vendors' Council, 1984—. Mem. Nat. Soc. Sales Tng. Execs. Democrat. Avocations: reading; camping; hiking; travel. Home: 102 Brentwood Advance NC 27006 Office: Hanes Knitwear PO Box 3019 Winston-Salem NC 27102

MOORE, JAMES OTIS, chemical company executive; b. Fayetteville, Tenn., Aug. 29, 1935; s. Harry Freeman and Nell (Commons) M.; m. Sara Pauline Powel, Aug. 8, 1959; children—Christopher, Lauren. Student U. Tenn., 1953-54; B.S. in Math., Middle Tenn. State U., 1957, M.A. in Physics, 1967. Supt. E.I. DuPont, Nashville, 1966-76, Chattanooga, 1976-80, Clinton, Iowa, 1980-82, Louisville, 1982—. Bd. dirs. Iowa Safety Council, Des Moines, 1980-82. Served to capt. U.S. Army, 1954-66. Mem. Am. Soc. Safety Engrs., Nat. Fire Protection Assn. Republican. Presbyterian. Avocations: treasure hunting, radio. Home: 5311 Barkwood Dr LaGrange KY 40031 Office: E I DuPont Co 4200 Camp Ground Rd Louisville KY 40216

MOORE, JAMES RICHARD, podiatrist; b. Columbus, Miss., Dec. 24, 1915; s. Henry Lee and Emma Eugenia (Reeves) M.; student Paris (Tex.) Jr. Coll., 1939, A.A. (hon.), 1984; student U. Ala., 1946-47; D.Podiatric Medicine, Temple U., Phila., 1951; m. Mary Jayne Hunter, Nov. 23, 1940; children—James Richard, Cynthia Jayne, Matthew Hunter. Pvt. practice podiatry, Paris, 1951—; mem. med.-surg. staff McCuistion Regional Med. Center, Paris, 1952-83, emeritus staff, 1983—. Mem. Paris City Council, 1965-69, mayor pro-tem, 1968, mayor, 1969; bd. regents Paris Jr. Coll., 1972-84, v.p., 1978, pres., 1979-84, chmn., 1982-83; commr. Housing Authority, Paris, 1967-83; trustee David Graham Hall Trust, 1974—; formerly mem. vestry Brotherhood of St. Andrew's, Holy Cross Episcopal Ch. Served with AUS, 1940-42; to capt. USAAF, 1942-45. Mem. Am. Podiatry Assn., Tex. Podiatry Assn., Tex. Assn. Jr. Colls., Am. Public Health Assn., Assn. Tex. Colls. and Univs., U. Ala. Alumni Assn., Temple U. Alumni Assn. (life), Paris C. of C., Am. Legion, Former Students Paris Jr. Coll. (life), Paris Community Theatre, Paris Community Concert Assn., Dallas Mus. Arts, Smithsonian Assocs., Theta Kappa Omega (past. nat. pres.), Kappa Alpha Order, Pi Epsilon Delta (past nat. pres.). Office: 2850 Lewis Ln Paris TX 75460

MOORE, JOHN HENRY, II, federal district judge; b. Atlantic City, Aug. 5, 1929; s. Harry Cordery and Gertrude (Wasleski) M.; m. Joan Claire Kraft, Dec. 29, 1951; children—Deborah Joan, Katherine Louise. Student, Cornell U., 1947; B.S., Syracuse U., 1952; J.D., U. Fla., 1961. Bar: Fla. 1961. Assoc. Fisher & Phillips, Atlanta, 1960-61; ptnr. Fleming, O'Bryan & Fleming, Ft. Lauderdale, Fla., 1961-67, Turner, Shaw & Moore, Ft. Lauderdale, 1967; judge 17th Circuit Ct. of Fla., Ft. Lauderdale, 1967-77; appellate judge 4th Dist. Ct. Appeals, West Palm Beach, Fla., 1977-81; U.S. dist. judge Middle Dist. of Fla., Jacksonville, 1981—; asst. sch. bd. atty. Broward County Bd. Pub. Instrn., Ft. Lauderdale, 1967. Pres., Broward Assn. for Retarded Children, 1964; bd. dirs. Community Service Council, Ft. Lauderdale, 1970-75; mem. Fla. Jud. Qualifications Commn., Ft. Tallahassee, 1979-81, chmn., 1980-81; mem. Fla. Constn. Revision Commn., Tallahassee, 1977-78. Served to lt. (j.g.) USNR, 1952-56; Korea. Recipient Good Govt. cert. Gov. Fla., 1967; Outstanding Service award South Broward Bar Assn., 1973, 74. Mem. ABA, Fla. Bar Assn., Jacksonville Bar Assn., Fla. Conf. Circuit Judges (chmn. elect 1976-77). Clubs: Timuquana Country (Jacksonville); Lauderdale Yacht (sec. 1973-77). Office: US Dist Ct Middle Dist Fla 311 Monroe St Jacksonville FL 32201

MOORE, JOHN IVAN, tire company executive; retired air force officer; b. Salem, Va., Jan. 7, 1936; s. Ivan Hoy Moore and Jean Brown (Hogston) Moore Palermo; m. Dolores Elizabeth Mulcahy, Mar. 25, 1958 (div. 1963); children—Lisa Pamella, Holly Michele; m. Mary Eloise Glaizer, July 11, 1964; 1 child, John Ivan. B. Gen. Edn., U. Omaha, 1965; M.S. in Edn., U. So. Calif., 1971; grad. Air Command and Staff Coll., Air U., Maxwell AFB, 1974, Armed Forces Intelligence Sch., 1966. Commd. U.S. Air Force, 1955, advanced through grades to maj., 1969, retired, 1975; squadron control officer Tan Son Nhut Air Base, Vietnam, 1966-67, chief systems and resources div., dep. chief staff Lindsey, Fed. Republic Germany, 1967-72, combat crew commdr. Davis Montman AFB, Ariz., 1972-73, chief plans div., 1973, controller, 1974-75; v.p., sec. Moore Tire Co., Inc., Roanoke, Va., 1975—. Mem. City of Salem Sch. Bd., 1980-81, vice chmn., 1981-82, chmn., 1982—; mem. Salem Edn. Found. Decorated Bronze Star, Air Force Commendation medal, Republic of Vietnam Commendation medal. Mem. Roanoke Valley Alliance for Progress, Nat. Tire Dealers and Retreaders Assn., Am. Retreaders Assn. (speaker conv. 1983), Va. Tire Dealers and Retreaders Assn., Roanoke Valley C. of C., Ret. Officers Assn. Republican. Episcopalian. Club: Salam Sports Found. Avocations: golf; handball; skiing; swimming; jogging; racquetball. Home: 700 Beech Rd Salem VA 24153 Office: Moore Tire Co Inc 1860 S Jefferson St Roanoke VA 24016

MOORE, LEONARD VANARD, geologist; b. Fort Wayne, Ind., Mar. 23, 1949; s. Maurice Gene and Betty Jane (Ferree) M.; m. Gail Ann Gerdes, Aug. 21, 1971; children—Alexander Ferree, Benjamin David, Andrew Arthur, Katherine DeVries. B.S., U. Conn., 1971; M.S., So. Meth. U., 1974; postgrad. U. Tex., 1973-74. Cert. petroleum geologist. Exploration geologist Phillips Petroleum Co., Bartlesville, Okla., London, Singapore, Bangkok, 1974-85; sr. geologist Europe/Africa div. Esso Exploration, Houston, 1985—. Contbr. articles to profl. jours. Mem. Am. Assn. Petroleum Geologists, Soc. Petroleum Engrs., S.E. Asia Petroleum Exploration Soc. (co-editor SEAPEX Procs. 1981-82), Geol. Soc. Thailand, Houston Geol. Soc. Republican. Avocations: Orchid growing, stamp collecting, fishing, hunting. Office: Esso Exploration PO Box 146 Houston TX 77001

MOORE, LESSLIE GAIL, dentist; b. Gloucester, Mass., Oct. 13, 1945; d. Arthur Leonard and Dorothy Elizabeth (Marshall) Hage; m. Lawrence Lee Moore, May 19, 1968; 1 child, Kimberly Dawn. B.A. in Biology and Chemistry magna cum laude, Pacific Lutheran U., 1967; D.D.S., Baylor Coll. Dentistry, 1980. Human genetics research technician Rainier State Sch., Buckley, Wash., 1967-69; dental technician pvt. dentists, Denison, Tex., 1969-76; owner, mgr. dental lab., Denison, 1976-77; instr. Baylor Coll. Dentistry, Dallas, 1980-81; dentist pvt. practice, Dallas, Plano and Leonard, Tex., 1980—. Dir., treas. Leonard Emergency Med. Service, Tex., 1981-84; bd. dirs. Fannin County Ambulance Rev. com., Bonham, Tex., 1983-84. Recipient award Southwest Acad. Restorative Dentistry, 1980, Gold Medal Baylor Coll. Dentistry, 1980, cert. of Honor for Outstanding Scholarship, Baylor Coll. Dentistry, 1980, award for Excellence, Alpha Omega, 1980, award Outstanding Achievement Denture Prothesis Southwest Soc. Denture Prothesis, 1980, Hon. Sci. award Bausch & Lomb Co., 1963. Fellow Acad. Internat. Dental Studies; mem. Acad. Internat. Med. Studies, ADA, Tex. Dental Assn., Dallas County Dental Assn., Acad. Gen. Dentistry, Tex. Acad. Gen. Dentistry, Clin. Found. Orthopedics and Orthodontics, Am. Soc. Clin. Hypnosis, Internat. Soc. Hypnosis, Leonard C. of C., Plano C. of C., Omicron Kappa Upsilon. Club: Greater Plano Dental Study.

MOORE, LOIS BAILEY (MRS. JAMES L. MOORE), village official; b. Little Rock, Oct. 23, 1929; d. Joseph Samuel and Lelah (Wyatt) Bailey; m. James Leon Moore, Jr., May 11, 1952; children—James Leon III, Vance Bailey, Mark Brian. B.S. in Edn., U. Ark., 1951. Founder, dir. Pioneer Village, Rison, Ark., 1975, founder Pioneer Craft Festival, 1971—; commr. Ark. Dept. of Parks and Tourism, Little Rock, 1982-87. Chmn. Cleve. County Parks Commn., Rison, 1975—, Cleveland County Bicentennial Com., Rison, 1976, Cleveland County Centennial Com., Rison, 1973; charter mem. Historic Preservation Alliance of Ark., Little Rock, 1982; bd. dirs. Ark. Tourism Devel. Found. Mem. Ark. Hist. Assn., Pi Beta Phi (Little Rock). Democrat. Episcopalian. Avocation: historic preservation. Home: Box 426 Rison AR 71665

MOORE, LOIS MARIE, oil and gas company personnel trainer; b. Clarendon, Tex., Mar. 14, 1933; d. Frank Johnson and Gladys Irene (Johnson) Hommel; m. James Andrew Moore, Apr. 23, 1950; children—Danny Lynn, Jacquelynn McDuffee, James Hayden, Mark Tremaine. B.S. in Bus. Mgmt., Wayland Baptist U., 1985. Cert. instr. Interaction Mgmt.; cert. program dir. Devel. Dimensions Internat. Personnel technician City of Amarillo, Tex., 1961-70; employment interviewer and DOE program coordinator Mason & Hanger, Amarillo, 1970-78; staffing and tng. mgr. Diamond Shamrock Corp. Exploration Co., Amarillo, 1978—. Bd. dirs. Music Festival, Amarillo, 1979-83, Guidance and Counseling Ctr., Amarillo, 1980-83, United Way Employee Assistance, Amarillo, 1979-82; adv. Amarillo Coll. and West Tex. State U., Amarillo, Canyon, Tex., 1976—; mem. personnel com. Young Women's Christian Organ., Amarillo, 1981-82. Mem. Am. Soc. Tng. and Devel. (pres.-elect 1982-84, pres. 1984, bd. dirs. 1985—, outstanding pres. award 1984), Panhandle Personnel Assn. (nominating com. 1982, tng. and devel. adv. com. 1985). Republican. Baptist. Avocations: reading, music, listening to motivational and inspirational tapes. Office: Diamond Shamrock Exploration Co 8th and Tyler Sts Amarillo TX 79101

MOORE, MICHAEL RANDOLPH, legislative assistant; b. Tallahassee, Fla., Nov. 10, 1953; s. Richard Lee and Janie Belle (Ash) M.; m. Juanita Y. Payne, Dec. 18, 1976; 1 dau., Crystal. Y. Cert. exchange program U. Fla., 1974; B.S. in Polit. Sci./Pub. Adminstrn., Fla. A&M U., 1976; J.D., John Marshall Law Sch., 1985. Labor arbitrator Fla. Dept. Commerce, 1975-76; dist. asst. to Congressman Don Fuqua, Tallahassee, 1976-83, exec. asst., 1985—; exec. dir. Fla. A&M U. Boosters Club, 1980; paralegal specialist U.S. Dept. Transp., 1983-84; dir. Starlight Realty Co. Mem. Tallahassee Mayor's Adv. Council; bd. dirs. Tallahassee Jaycees, 1979-80, Frenchtown Area Devel. Authority; pres. C.K. Steele Jaycees, Tallahassee, 1981-82; v.p. Tallahassee NAACP, 1980; team leader Suwannee River Area council Boy Scouts Am., 1981-82. Recipient Outstanding Service plaque Tallahassee NAACP, 1981, St. James Royal Arch Masons, 1980; Disting. Service award Fla. A&M U., 1983; Carnegie fellow, 1974. Mem. Am. Mgmt. Assn., N.Y. Acad. Sci., Fla. Roster Arbitrators for Labor Disputes, Fla. Assn. Polit. Scientists, Kappa Alpha Psi (chpt. Outstanding Service plaque 1980, bd. dirs. chpt. housing found.), Alpha Phi Omega (Fla. chpt. Outstanding Service plaque 1982). Democrat. Mem. Ch. of God in Christ. Club: Toastmasters (past pres.). Lodges: Masons, Shriners, KP. Home: 2901 Tyron Circle Tallahassee FL 32308 Office: PO Box 562 Tallahassee FL 32302

MOORE, NATHAN, English educator; b. Mayaro, Trinidad and Tobago, June 26, 1931; came to U.S., 1961, naturalized, 1975; s. William Bartholomew and Eugenie (Samuel) M.; m. Mary Lisbeth Simmons, July 2, 1967; children—Christina Melissa, Serena Louise. B.A., Rockford Coll., 1963; M.A., Carleton U., 1965; Ph.D., U. B.C., Vancouver, 1972. Teaching fellow Carleton U., Ottawa, Ont., Can., 1963-65, sessional lectr., summer 1964, 65; high sch. tchr. Caribbean Union Coll., Maracas, Trinidad, 1956-58, Barbados SDA Secondary Sch., Bridgetown, 1958-61, Barrier Sch. Dist., B.C., 1966-67; tchr. Walla Walla Coll., College Place, Wash., 1967-79; prof. English, chmn. dept. Ala. State U., Montgomery, 1980—. Scholar Rockford Coll., 1961, Reader's Digest, 1962; Carleton U. fellow, 1963-64. Mem. Am. Soc. for 18th Century Studies, MLA, S. Atlantic MLA. Democrat. Adventist. Avocations: gardening; real estate investing; reading. Home: 2928 Moorcroft Dr Montgomery AL 36116 Office: Ala State U Dept English Jackson St Montgomery AL 36195

MOORE, PATRICK DAVID, ophthalmologist; b. New Kensington, Pa., Oct. 7, 1940; s. David Benjamin and Ruth Catherine (Vonderheid) M.; m. Pamela Jane Cox, Dec. 22, 1962; children—Tracy Lynne, David Ellis, Kelly Jane. B.A., Washington and Jefferson Coll., 1962; M.D., Temple U., Phila., 1966. Diplomate Am. Bd. Ophthalmology. Intern, Allentown Gen. Hosp., Pa., 1966-67; resident in ophthalmology Wills Eye Hosp., Phila., 1969-72; practice medicine specializing in ophthalmology, Newport News, Va., 1972—; clin. instr. ophthalmology dept. Eastern Va. Med. Sch., Norfolk, Va., 1978—. Fellow Am. Acad. Ophthalmology; mem. Va. Soc. Ophthalmology, AMA, Contact Lens Assn. Ophthalmologists. Republican. Episcopalian. Club: James River Country. Lodge: Lions. Avocations: photography; antique collecting. Home: 49 Hertzler Rd Newport News VA 23602 Office: Eye Physicians & Surgeons Inc 318 Main St Newport News VA 23601

MOORE, RAYBURN SABATZKY, literature educator; b. Helena, Ark., May 26, 1920; s. Max Sabatzky and Sammie Lou (Rayburn) M.; A.B., Vanderbilt U., 1942, M.A., 1947; Ph.D., Duke U., 1956; m. Margaret Elizabeth Bear, Aug. 30, 1947; children—Margaret Elizabeth, Robert Rayburn. Vice pres. Interstate Grocer Co., Helena, 1947-50; research asst. Duke U., 1952, grad. asst., 1952-54; asst. prof. English, Hendrix Coll., Conway, Ark., 1954-55, assoc. prof., 1955-58, prof., 1958-59; assoc. prof. English, U. Ga., Athens, 1959-65, prof., 1965—, dir. grad. studies in English, 1964-69, chmn. Am. studies program, 1968—, chmn. div. lang. and lit., 1975—; vis. scholar Duke U., 1958, 64. Mem. troop com. Boy Scouts Am., Athens, 1973-75. Served to capt. AUS, 1942-46. Mem. Soc. for Study So. Lit. (exec. com. 1968, 74-80, v.p. 1981-82, pres. 1983—), MLA (exec. com. Gen. Topics VI 1972-75), South Atlantic Grad. English Coop. Group (exec. com. 1969-79, chmn. 1971-72), S. Atlantic MLA (exec. com. 1975-77), Blue Key, Phi Beta Kappa, Sigma Chi. Presbyterian (deacon, elder 1962—). Author: Constance Fenimore Woolson, 1963; For the Major and Selected Short Stories of Constance Fenimore Woolson, 1967; Paul Hamilton Hayne, 1972; A Man of Letters in the Nineteenth-Century South: Selected Letters of Paul Hamilton Hayne, 1982; contbr. articles to profl. jours.; editorial bd. U. Ga. Press, 1972-74; editorial bd. Ga. Rev., 1974-82, chmn., 1980-82. Office: 130 Park Hall U Ga Athens GA 30602

MOORE, REBECCA PHILLIPS, English educator; b. Henrietta, Okla., June 22, 1949; d. Robert Sills and Anna Lee (Bowdon) Phillips; m. Russell Ivan Moore, Aug. 30, 1969; children—Rebecca Susan, James Bradford. Student Tex. Tech U., 1967, U. Tex.-El Paso, 1968-69; B.S., West Tex. State U., 1974, M.Ed., 1976; postgrad George Washington U., 1984-85. Instr. Eastwood High Sch., El Paso, 1977-81, El Paso Community Coll., 1981-84, George Washington U., Washington, 1984-85; instr. English, El Paso Community Coll., 1985—, mem. sophomore English supervisory com., 1981-84, mem. exit exam com., 1983-84, participant team teaching pilot, 1982-83, chmn. devel. composition skills com., 1983. Mem. Nat. Council Tchrs. English, S.W. Regional Council English, Tex. Jr. Coll. Tchrs. English, Paso del Norte Council Tchrs. English, Sigma Tau Delta, Chi Omega. Club: Fort Bliss Officer's Wives (El Paso). Avocations: theaters; computers; crewel embroidery; counted beadery. Home: 10537 Brian Mooney St El Paso TX 79935 Office: El Paso Community Coll PO Box 20500 El Paso TX 79998

MOORE, RICHTER HERMANN, JR., lawyer, polit. scientist, criminal justice cons.; b. Mayo, S.C., Aug. 19, 1928; s. Richter Hermann and Hettie Greene (Jackson) M.; B.S., U. S.C., 1949, LL.B., 1951; M.A., U. Ky., 1956, Ph.D., 1964; postgrad. Va. Poly. Inst., 1966, U. Wis., 1967; grad. Indsl. Coll. Armed Forces, 1969, Air War Coll., 1976; m. Carolyn McBride Dabbs, Dec. 30, 1950; children—Cassandra, Diana, Susan. Instr. polit. sci. East Tenn. State U., Johnson City, 1955-56, asst. prof., 1956-60, asso. prof., 1960-64, prof., 1964-70, chmn. dept. polit. sci., 1964-70; research dir. Com. on Office Atty. Gen., Nat. Assn. Attys. Gen., 1969-70; prof. dept. polit. sci./criminal justice Appalachian State U., Boone, N.C., 1970—, chmn. dept., 1970-83, dir. summer study in Gt. Britain, 1976—; cons. law enforcement tng., 1969—; dir. Appalachian Regional Bur. Govt., 1972-83, Planning and Land Use Edn. for Western N.C., 1971-74, Rural Govt. Tng. and Assistance Program, 1974-76; chmn. criminal justice adv. com. N.W. N.C. Council Govts., 1975-81; chmn. exec. com. and policy bd. N.W. Planning Council Crime Deterrence, 1972-75; N.C. rep. to Nat. Conf. Criminal Justice Standards and Goals, 1973; mem. Nat. Joint Commn. on Criminology and Criminal Justice Edn. and Standards, 1977-82. Mem. County Democratic Exec. Com., 1958-72; mem. staff Tenn. del. Dem. Nat. Convs., 1964, 68, 80, State Convs., 1956-72; elder Jonesboro Presbyn. Ch. Served with USAF, 1951-53; col. Res. Ret., 1985. Recipient Outstanding Res. Judge Adv. award Tactical Air Force, 1976, 9th Air Force, 1976, 84; Outstanding Criminal Justice Educator award So. Assn. Criminal Justice Educators, 1980; Founders award Acad. Criminal Justice Scis., 1983. Fellow Acad. Criminal Justice Scis. (sec.-treas. 1975-77, 1st v.p. 1977-78, pres. 1978-79, exec. council 1979-80); mem. N.C. (pres. 1971-73, Outstanding Criminal Justice Educator award 1982), So. (pres. 1974-75, 1st v.p. 1973-74, 2d v.p. 1972-73, exec. council 1975-76) assns. criminal justice educators, Am., Internat., Midwest, N.C. (pres. 1971-72), Tenn. (v.p. 1968-69), So. (exec. council 1974-77) polit. sci. assns., Assn. Social and Behavioral Scientists (treas. 1969-77, 2d v.p. 1977-78, exec. council 1978-82), S.C. Bar, Law and Soc. Assn., Res. Officers Assn. (v.p. for air N.C. dept. 1981-84, pres. 1985-86; pres. Catawba Valley chpt. 1981-85), Pi Sigma Alpha, Phi Gamma Mu (gov. N.C. province 1974-76, vice chancellor Atlantic region 1976-78, chancellor 1978—). Democrat. Editor: So. Jour. Criminal Justice, 1974-77; asso. editor Jour. Social and Behavioral Scis., 1970—; cons. editor: World Affairs, 1975-79, Readings in Criminal Justice, 1976; contbr. articles to profl. jours. Home: Ski Mountain Route 1 Box 110 Blowing Rock NC 28605 also 725 Depot St Jonesboro TN 37659 Office: Dept Political Science/Criminal Justice Appalachian State University Boone NC 28608

MOORE, ROBERT FRANKLIN, correctional psychologist; b. Jacksonville, Fla., Oct. 18, 1945; s. Glenn Dalton and Dorothy Elizabeth (Messenger) M.; m. Paula Jean Robbins, Apr. 26, 1974; children—Jennifer Kristen, John Robert. B.S. in Psychology, Fla. State U., 1967; M.S. in Psychology, Auburn U., 1970. Cert. clin. mental health counselor; lic. mental health counselor. Psychologist, Reception and Med. Ctr., Lake Butler, Fla., 1970-74; psychology instr. Lake City Community Coll., Fla., 1971-83; drug abuse counselor Fla. State Prison, Starke, 1974-77, psychologist, 1977-85; psychologist Union Correctional Inst., Raiford, Fla., 1985—. Contbr. articles to profl. jours. Served with USAR, 1968-74. Recipient Programs award Fla. State prison, 1982. Mem. Am. Psychol. Assn., Am. Correctional Assn., Am. Assn. Counseling and Devel., Am. Mental Health Counselors Assn., Fla. Mental Health Counselors Assn., Fla. Assn. for Counseling and Devel., Acad. Cert. Clin. Mental Health Counselors. Democrat. Home: Route 2 Box 1663 Starke FL 32091 Office: Union Correctional Instn PO Box 221 Raiford FL 32083

MOORE, ROBERT STUART, furniture company executive; b. Filbert, W.Va., Mar. 28, 1924; s. Robert Harless and Anna Ethel (Fowler) M. Student Va. Poly. Inst., 1942-43; B.B.A., So. Meth. U., 1948; M.B.A., Harvard U., 1950. Trainee, The Lane Co., Inc., Altavista, Va., 1953-54, asst. to v.p. and gen. mgr., 1955-58, sec., dir., 1959—, exec. v.p., 1969-81, pres., 1981—; dir. United Va. Bank, 1st Nat. Bank of Lynchburg (Va.), So. Furniture Market Ctr., High Point, N.C.; mem. furniture bd. govs. Dallas Market Center, Atlanta Market Ctr., Western Mdse. Mart. Pres. Piedmont Area council Boy Scouts Am., 1965-67; trustee Ferrum Coll., 1970-73, 82—. Served to sgt. C.E., AUS, 1943-46, to 2d lt. USAF, 1951-52. Mem. Phi Delta Theta, Delta Sigma Pi. Republican. Methodist. Club: James River (Lynchburg). Home: Avondale Ave Altavista VA 24517 Office: The Lane Co Inc Altavista VA 24517

MOORE, ROLAND LEE, retail/wholesale computer hardware co. exec.; b. Atlanta, July 12, 1933; s. Edgar Wilkes and Willie Mae (Zachary) M.; B.S., Ga. State U., 1959; 1 son, Robert Ray. Dir. mktg., sales, adminstrn. TLW Computer Industries, Atlanta, 1967-77; v.p. sales CLE Leasing, Atlanta, 1977-78; pres., chmn., chief exec. officer Computer Hardware Sales, Inc., Atlanta, 1978—. Pres., North Fork Homeowners Assn., 1975-78. Served with USAF, 1951-55; Korea. Mem. Data Processing Mgmt. Assn. (dir. 1959-81), Computer Dealers/Leasors Assn., Sales and Mktg. Execs. Club (membership com. 1982), Dekalb C. of C. (Pres.'s Club). Republican. Baptist. Clubs: City (Atlanta); Optimist, Ansley Country. Home: 3824 Savannah Sq W Atlanta GA 30340 Office: 2700 NE Expressway Suite C-1000 Atlanta GA 30345

MOORE, SARA FRANCES, exploration geologist; b. Midland, Tex., Feb. 2, 1957; d. Wilbur Ross and Martha Frances (Hurt) Moore. B.A. in Geology, U. Tex., 1979. Devel. geologist Tex. Pacific Oil Co., Oklahoma City, 1979-80, Sun Tex. Co., Oklahoma City, 1980-81; geologist Sun Prodn. Co., Oklahoma City, 1981; geologist Wessely Energy, Dallas, 1981-85, dist. geologist, 1985—. Mem. Dallas Energy Forum, 1983—. Mem. Am. Assn. Petroleum Geologists, Soc. Profl. Well Log Analysts (sec., treas. 1980-81), Assn. Women Geoscientists, Dallas Geol. Soc. Republican. Presbyterian. Avocations: raising black labrador retrievers; water skiing. Home: 6503 E Lovers Ln Dallas TX 75214 Office: Wessely Energy Co 2001 Bryan Tower Suite 953 Dallas TX 75201

MOORE, STEPHEN CHARLES, accountant; b. Louisville, Aug. 8, 1954; s. Charles Calvin and Anna Lois (Davis) M.; m. Laurali Susan Baird, Aug. 28, 1976. B.S. in Bus. Adminstrn. with honors, Samford U., 1976. C.P.A., Ala. With Ernst & Whinney, C.P.A.s, Huntsville, Ala., 1976-78; acct. McGriff, Dowdy & Assocs., P.A., C.P.A.s, Huntsville, 1978—, also supr. Past bd. dir. Huntsville Jaycees. Served to capt. USAFR, 1976—. Mem. Am. Inst. C.P.A.s, Ala. Soc. C.P.A.s (state taxation com., vice chmn. Huntsville-Decatur chpt. 1983—), Nat. Assn. Accts. (pres. N. Ala. chpt. 1982-83, mem. nat. com.). Baptist. Club: Valley Hills Country (Huntsville). Home: 1201 Aldridge Dr SE Huntsville AL 35803 Office: McGriff Dowdy Assocs PA Central Bank Bldg Suite 900 Huntsville AL 35801

MOORE, T. PATRICK, geophysicist; b. Chattanooga, Sept. 4, 1947; s. Ishmael Dudley and Beatric Mabel (Rogers) M.; m. Carole Lane Coleman, Dec. 31, 1974; children—Michael Patrick, Jennifer Lane. A.A., Brewton-Parker Jr. Coll., 1975; B.S., Ga. Southwestern Coll., 1977; M.S. in Geophysics, Va. Poly. Inst. and State U., 1979. Geophysicist Exxon Co. USA, New Orleans, 1979-82; sr. geophysicist Forest Oil Corp., Midland, Tex., 1982-83, Michel T. Halbouty Energy Co., Houston, 1983—. Contbr. papers to profl. lit. Served with USMC, 1965-69. Vietnam. Mem. Soc. Exploration Geophysicists, Am. Assn. Petroleum Geologists, Houston Geol. Soc., Order of Gown, Alpha Lambda Delta. Republican. Episcopalian. Avocations: hunting; fishing. Home: 2907 Skypark Dr Houston TX 77082 Office: Michel T Halbouty Energy Co 5100 Westheimer St Suite 500 Houston TX 77056

MOORE, THERESA THROWER, marriage and family therapist; b. Lafayette, Ind., Mar. 26, 1953; d. Jack Elwyn and Barbra (Burke) Thrower; m. Kevin Howell Moore, Mar. 25, 1983. B.A., U. Minn., 1976; M.S.W., Our Lady of the Lake Coll., 1979. Lic. profl. counselor, Tex. Sr. staff counselor John DeFoore Ctr. for Pastoral Care & Counseling, Boerne, Tex., 1978-84; pvt. practice, Boerne, 1984—. Mem. Internat. Transactional Analysis Assn., Am. Assn. Marriage and Family Therapists. Republican. Episcopalian. Avocations: snow skiing; water sports; pottery. Office: Counseling Services 29190 Fair Oaks Pkwy #212 Boerne TX 78006

MOORE, THOMAS RYAN, sedimentologist, researcher; b. Waynesburg, Pa., Apr. 4, 1954; s. Ira Orville and Rose Marie (Hogue) M.; m. Karen Lou Mertz, July 31, 1976; children—Duane Padraic, Ruth Aileen. B.S. in Geology, Ind. U. Pa., 1976; M.S. in Geology, U. Mo., 1981. Environ. geologist Penn Environ. Cons., Pitts., 1976-77; asst. foreman milling Lone Star Steel Co., Tex., 1977-78; devel. geologist Phillips Petroleum, Oklahoma City, 1981-84, staff sedimentologist, Bartlesville, Okla., 1984—. Contbr. articles to profl. jours. Recipient Best Paper award, Tech. Sessions 2d Ann. Geosci. Day, Ind. U. Pa., 1976. Mem. Soc. Econ. Paleontol. and Mineralogists, Am. Assn. Petroleum Geologists, Sigma Gamma Epsilon. Democrat. Mem. Christian and Missionary Alliance. Club: Phillips 66 Fencing (Bartlesville, Okla.). Avocations: hunting; fishing; hiking; fencing. Office: Phillips Petroleum 254 GB PRC Bartlesville OK 74004

MOORE, VIRGINIA VANCE, educational administrator, consultant; b. Atlanta, Mar. 12, 1938; d. Hugh Lewis and Beatrice (Watts) Vance; m. Roland Lee Moore, Aug. 9, 1973 (div. Oct. 1980). B.S., U. Ga., 1960; M.Ed., Ga. State U., 1973, Ed.S., 1977. Teller C & S Bank, Atlanta, 1960, Bank N.Y., N.Y.C., 1961; tchr. 1st grade DeKalb County Bd. Edn., Atlanta, 1961-62, tchr. 1st grade and kindergarten, 1970-76; tchr. kindergarten Atlanta City Bd. Edn., 1962-66; tchr. English grades 9-12, pub. schs., Sydney, Australia, 1966-68; service rep. Liberty Mut. Ins. Co., Atlanta, 1968-70; instructional lead tchr. Gwinnett County Bd. Edn., Ga., 1976-80, coordinator remedial and primary programs, 1980-84, prin. Lawrenceville Elem. Sch., 1984—; mem. faculty Mercer U., Atlanta, 1979; cons. to bds. edn.; cons. for exemplary math. program Ga. Dept. Edn., Atlanta, 1982. Tchr. adults Smoke Rise Baptist Ch., Stone Mountain, Ga., 1977—; active Young Republicans, Atlanta, 1962-64. Mem. Assn. Supervision and Curriculum Devel., Elem. Sch. Prins., Alpha Delta Pi. Avocations: clogging; playing piano; bridge; reading; cooking. Office: Lawrenceville Elem Sch 122 Gwinnett Dr Lawrenceville GA 30245

MOORE, W. HENSON, III, congressman; b. Lake Charles, La., Oct. 4, 1939; s. William Henson Moore Jr.; m. Carolyn Ann Cherry; children—William Henson IV, Jennifer Lee, Cherry Ann. B.A. in Polit. Sci., La. State U., 1961, J.D., 1965, M.A. in Polit. Sci., 1973. Bar: La. 1966. Asso. firm Dale, Woen, Richardson, Taylor & Mathews, 1967-69, mem. firm, 1969-74; mem. 94th-99th Congresses from 6th La. Dist., mem. ways and means com., budget com., Rep. exec. com. Served to capt. M.P., AUS, 1965-67. Mem. Fed., Am., La., Baton Rouge bar assns., Am. Legion, SAR, Phi Alpha Delta, Sigma Chi. Episcopalian. Clubs: Rotary, Masons. Office: Rm 2183 Rayburn House Office Bldg Washington DC 20515

MOORE, WALTER D., JR., physician; b. Houston, Sept. 29, 1924; s. Walter D. and Mary Nellie (Kincaid) M.; m. Barbara Jane Farrar; children—Diane Elizabeth, Michelle Louise, Michael Andrew. Student U. Tex., 1946-48; M.D., Baylor Coll., 1952. Diplomate Am. Bd. Pathology, Am. Bd. Nuclear Medicine. Intern, Cleve. City Hosp., 1952-53; resident VA Hosp., Houston, 1953-54; Albany Hosp., N.Y., 1954-55, U. Tex. Med. Br.-Galveston, 1955-59; pathologist Wilson N. Jones Hosp., Sherman, Tex., 1959-65, Fox Hosp., Onfonza, N.Y., 1965-76, St. Mary's Hosp., Galveston, 1976—. Served with U.S. Army, 1943-46. Fellow Coll. Am. Pathologists, Am. Soc. Clin. Pathology; mem. Am. Coll. Nuclear Physicians, Am. Coll. Radiology, Soc. Nuclear Medicine, Alpha Epsilon Delta, Phi Sigma Kappa, Alpha Kappa Kappa. Episcopalian. Avocation: jogging. Office: Walter D Moore Jr PO Box 730 League City TX 77573

MOORE, WILLIAM BLACK, JR., retired aluminum company executive; b. Jackson, Miss., Sept. 18, 1924; s. William Black and May Isom (Whitten) M.; m. Lillian Wells, Sept. 14, 1946; children—Kathryn Ramsey Moore Dannels, William Black III, Bethany Moore Richmond. B.S. in Chem. Engring., U. Louisville, 1945, M.S. in Chem. Engring., 1947. Registered profl. engr., Ky. Chem. engr. U. Louisville Research Inst., 1947-49; mktg. mgr. Reynolds Metals, Louisville, 1949-58, dir. mktg., Richmond, Va., 1958-61, regional gen. mgr., St. Louis, 1961-69, v.p., Richmond, 1969-80, ret. Contbr. articles to profl. jours. Served to lt. USNR, 1943-47. Mem. Ky. Soc. Profl. Engrs., AIA (hon.). Baptist. Club: Indian Creek (Kilmarnock, Va.); Country of Va. (Richmond). Avocations: fishing; farming. Home: PO Box 1300 Kilmarnock VA 22482

MOORE, WILLIAM GROVER, JR., consultant, former air freight executive, former air force officer; b. Waco, Tex., May 18; s. William Grover and Annie Elizabeth (Pickens) M.; student Kilgore (Tex.) Coll., 1937-39, Sacramento State Coll., 1951, George Washington U., 1962; grad. Air War Coll., Air U., 1957, Nat. War Coll., 1962; m. Marjorie Y. Gardella, Jan. 18, 1943; 1 dau., Allyson. Enlisted U.S. Army Air Force, 1940, commd. 2d lt., 1941, advanced through grades to gen., 1977; comdr. 777th Squadron, 15th AF, Italy, 1944-45, 3535th Maintenance and Supply Group, Mather AFB, Calif., 1951, 3d Bomb Group, Korea, 1952; chief bases and units div. Hdqrs. USAF, 1952-56; asst. dep. chief of staff ops. Hdqrs. USAF Europe, 1957-61; comdr. 314th Troop Carrier Wing, Stewart AFB, Tenn., 1962-63, 839th Air Div., 1963-65; asst. J3 U.S. Strike Command, 1965-66; comdr. 834th Air Div., Vietnam, 1966-67; dir. operational requirements Hdqrs, USAF, 1967-70; comdr. 22d AF, 1970-73, 13th AF, 1973; chief of staff Pacific Command, 1973-76; asst. vice chief of staff Hdqrs. USAF, 1976-77; comdr. in chief Mil. Air Lift Command, 1977-79; ret., 1979; pres., chief operating officer Emery Air Freight Corp., Wilton, Conn., 1981-83; bus. cons., 1983—; exec. dir. Met. Nashville Airport Authority, 1984—. Decorated Def. D.S.M., Air Force D.S.M. with 2 oak leaf clusters, Legion of Merit with 4 oak leaf clusters, Silver Star, D.F.C. with oak leaf cluster, Air medal with 9 oak leaf clusters, AF Commendation medal with 10 oak leaf clusters (U.S.); Croix de Guerre with palm (France); Armed Forces Honor medal 1st class (Vietnam); Republic of China Cloud and Banner; Legion of Honor (Republic of Philippines); recipient L. Mendel Rivers award of excellence; Jimmy Doolittle fellow in aerospace edn., 1978; named to Minuteman Hall of Fame, 1979. Mem. Air Force Assn., Nat. Def. Transp. Assn., Am. Ordnance Assn. Home: 932 W Main St Franklin TN 37064

MOORE, WILLIAM JASON, museum director; b. Asheboro, N.C., Aug. 4, 1938; s. Lonnie James and Pauline (Hamilton) M.; m. Jane Beane, Dec. 16, 1962; 1 son, William David. B.B.A., High Point Coll., 1960. Asst. to archeologist Town Creek Indian Mound, Mt. Gilead, N.C., 1959; dir. Greensboro Mus., (N.C.), 1963—; assessor Am. Assn. Mus., Washington, 1976—. Mem. N.C. Mus. Council (award 1976; pres. 1973-74), Am. Assn. Mus., Am. Assn. State and Local History. Episcopalian. Lodge: Rotary.

MOORE, WILLIAM JOSEPH, physician; b. Barboursville, W.Va., June 12, 1938; s. Joseph P. and Gertrude (Michael) M.; m. Sue Harney, Aug. 26, 1961; children—Tarenna Sue, Deborah Lynn, William Joseph II. B.A., U. Ky., 1958, M.D., 1965. Rotating intern Keesler AFB Hosp., Biloxi, Miss., 1965-66; resident Dermatology U. Ala. Med. Ctr., Birmingham, 1969-72, chief resident, 1971-72; practice medicine specializing in dermatology Dermatology Clinic, P.A., Anderson, S.C., 1972—; mem. adv. bd. S.C. chpt. Nat. Psoriasis Found. S.C., 1973-74. Bd. mem. Heart Assn., Anderson, S.C., 1981-84; bd. trustees Anderson Acad., 1976-79, 80-83; family coordinator/adminstrv. bd. St. John's Methodist Ch., Anderson, 1974-76, adminstrv. bd., 1978-80. Served to capt. USAF, 1964-69. Haggin scholar U. Ky., 1959-60. Mem. Internat. Soc. Pediatric Dermatology, Am. Acad. Dermatology (Physician Recognition award 1984), AMA (Physician Recognition award 1972, 84). Soc. Investigative Dermatology, So. Med. Assn., S.C. Med. Assn., S.C. Dermatologic Assn. (v.p. 1977), Anderson County Med. Assn., Piedmont Dermatologic Assn. (sec.-treas. 1984, pres. 1985-86), Alpha Chi Sigma, Alpha Epsilon Delta. Methodist. Office: Dermatology Clinic PA 801 E Greenville St Anderson SC 29621

MOOREHEAD, RODERICK EMMANUEL, educational administrator; b. St. Croix, V.I., Apr. 22, 1950; s. Hugo L. and Marilyn D. (Rogers) M.; m. Maureen E. Wynter, Apr. 15, 1983; children—Lisa, Ronni, Kimberly. B.A., Coll. V.I., 1971, M.A., 1976; C.A.G.S., U. Conn., 1977, Ph.D., 1979. Elem. sch. tchr., V.I., 1971-74; asst. dir. Project Upward Bound, Coll. V.I., St. Croix, 1974-76; spl. asst. to v.p. student affairs U. Conn., Storrs, 1977-78, research asst., 1978-79; assoc. dir. continuing edn. Coll. V.I., 1979—; pres. St. Thomas Reading Council, 1975-76; rep. Am. Fedn. Tchrs., 1972-74. Author: Faculty Job Satisfaction, 1979. Bd. dirs. Island Ctr. for Performing Arts, St. Croix, 1984—, St. Joseph's Cath. High Sch., St. Croix, 1984—, Statewide Job Coordinating Council, 1985—. Recipient award Nat. Fellowships Fund, 1978. Mem. St. Croix C. of C. (v.p. comml. devel. 1985—), Am. Assn. Counseling and Devel., Am. Assn. Higher Edn., Am. Coll. Personnel Assn. (commn.). Roman Catholic. Avocations: softball; crossword puzzles; dominoes; cards; reading. Home: Plot 1X Little Princesse PO Box 5622 Sunny Isle Saint Croix VI 00820 Office: College Virgin Islands PO Box 84 Kingshill Saint Croix VI 00850

MOORER, DOUGLASS CHARLES, educator; b. Birmingham, Ala., May 5, 1951; s. Charles and Lou Ethel (Thornton) M.; B.S., Ala. State U., 1975. Instr., Lawson (Ala.) State Community Coll., 1974-76; Tchr. Corps Project community coordinator Miles Coll., Fairfield, Ala., 1976-77; elem. sch. tchr. Birmingham Bd. Edn., 1977—; athletic trainer Summer Youth Sports Program, Miles Coll., 1977-82, Carver High Sch., Birmingham, 1979—. Vol. water safety instr. ARC, 1969-82; Boys' Club worker, 1969-73, 78-81. Recipient Vol. Service award ARC, 1980, 81, Service award Upward Bound Program, 1979. Mem. Assn. for Secondary Curriculum Devel., Assn. Supervision and Curriculum Devel., Am. Swimming Coaches Assn., AAHPER. Democrat. Roman Catholic. Lodge: Ind. Order Foresters. Home: 3140 Spaulding Ave SW Birmingham AL 35221 Office: Birmingham Bd Edn 4311 Court J Birmingham AL 35207

MOORES, EUGENE ALBERT, oil company executive; b. Waterville, Maine, Oct. 27, 1931; s. Pitt Harold and Velma Idela (Briggs) M.; m. Lolisa Ann Waddell; 1 child, Gregory Lee. B.S., U. Alaska, 1961, M.S., 1962; Ph.D., Iowa State U., 1966. Mgr. exploration research Sun Co., 1963-69, dir. research, 1975-76; mgr. geology Sun Exploration Co., Dallas, 1976-79, earth sci. cons., 1979-83; mgr. regulatory affairs Sun Exploration & Prodn. Co., Dallas, 1983-84, mgr. applications devel., 1984—. Bd. dirs. Dallas Council on World Affairs. Served with USN, 1950-52; lt. comdr. USCG, 1955-59. NSF Field Inst. grantee, 1960, 61. Mem. Am. Assn. Petroleum Geologists, Soc. Econ. Paleontologists and Mineralogists, Am. Petroleum Inst., Nat. Ocean Industries Assn., Nat. Security Indsl. Assn. (chmn. petroleum panel). Republican. Unitarian. Home: 163 Moonlight Dr Plano TX 75074 Office: Box 2880 Dallas TX 75221

MOORHEAD, GERALD LEE, architect; b. Davenport, Iowa, Feb. 18, 1947; s. Wayne Lee and Marilou (George) M.; B.A., Rice U., 1969, B. Arch., 1971. Architect, Middleton & Statton, El Paso, Tex., 1967, M.A. Floyd Assos., Houston, 1968, CRS Design Inc., Houston, 1969-70, Phillips & Peterson AIA, Houston, 1969-73; architect, v.p. Charles Tapley Assos., Houston, 1973-83; propr. Gerald Moorhead, Architect, 1983—; photog. group exhbns: Galveston Arts Council, Tex., 1976, Jewish Community Center, Houston, 1977, Cronin Gallery, Houston, 1977; one-man photographic exhbns.: Autry House Gallery, Houston, 1979. Recipient Spl. award Houston AIA/Houston Home & Garden, 1979; Honor award Houston AIA, 1979. Mem. Soc. Archtl. Historians, Nat. Trust for Historic Preservation, AIA, Tex. Soc. Architects (1st Honor award 1976), Rice Design Alliance. Contbr. articles on architecture to profl. publs. Home: 1842 Marshall St Houston TX 77098 Office: 2138-A Welch St Houston TX 77019

MOORHEAD, WILLIAM DAVID, III, lawyer, corporate executive; b. Knoxville, Tenn., Aug. 13, 1952; s. William David and Virginia (Wood) M.; m. Thelma Rogena Murray, Sept. 4, 1976; children—John Murray, Virginia Salima. B.B.A. summa cum laude, U. Ga., 1973, J.D. cum laude, 1976. Bar: Tenn. 1976, Ga. 1977, U.S. Tax Ct. 1977, U.S. Claims Ct. 1985, U.S. Supreme Ct. 1985. Assoc. Stophel, Caldwell & Heggie, Chattanooga, 1976-77; ptnr. Murray & Moorhead, Americus, Ga., 1977-80, Vansant, Corriere & Moorhead, Albany, Ga., 1981-85; pres. Continental Consol. Corp., Albany, 1983—. Del. Ga. Democratic Conv., 1978. Vassar Wooley scholar, 1973-76. Mem. ABA, Tenn. Bar Assn., Ga. Bar Assn., Dougherty Circuit Bar Assn., Albany Estate Planning Council (v.p. 1982-83). Baptist. Home: 1305 Baker Ave Albany GA 31707 Office: Continental Consol Corp PO Box 3406 611 N Jefferson St Albany GA 31706

MOORHOUSE, MARGARET DALTHORP, geologist; b. Denver, June 21, 1959; d. James Arthur and Maureen (Neylon) Dalthorp; m. Burton Liles Moorhouse, Dec. 29, 1985. B.S. in Geol. Scis., U. Tex., 1980; M.B.A., Corpus Christi State U., 1985. Clk., Tax Collector's Office, Houston, 1978; hydrologic field asst. U.S. Geol. Survey, Houston, 1979; jr. engr. Lower Colorado River Authority, Austin, Tex., 1980-81; sr. geologist Exxon Co., USA, Corpus Christi, Tex., 1981-86, sr. petroleum geologist, 1986—. Com. mem. Young Life, Corpus Christi, 1985; mem. Corpus Christi City Charter Revision Commn.; chmn. pub. relations LWV, Corpus Christi, 1984. Mem. Am. Assn. Petroleum Geologists, Corpus Christi Geol. Soc., Soc. Profl. Well Log Analysts, Exxon Club, (v.p. 1981-82), Corpus Christi C. of C. (energy resources com.), Kappa Kappa Gamma (pres. 1984—). Lodge: Inner Wheel Rotary. Avocations: jogging; tennis; reading. Office: Exxon Co USA PO Box 2528 Corpus Christi TX 78403

MOOSE, TALMADGE BOWERS, artist, illustrator, portrait artist; b. Albemarle, N.C., June 4, 1933; s. Cecil Hahn and Flora (Bowers) M.; m. Miriam Ruth Morris, June 17, 1956; children—Lyle Morris, Barry Neal. B.F.A., Va. Commonwealth U., 1955. Staff artist Porter, Hargis, Inc., Winston-Salem, N.C., 1958-59; art dir. Arts Engraving Co., Inc., Charlotte, N.C., 1959-64; pvt. practice artist, designer, illustrator, Charlotte, 1964-72; art instr. Stanly Tech. Coll., Albemarle, N.C., 1972-77; pvt. practice artist, tchr., Albemarle, 1977—; project dir. Artists/Writers Dialogue, Albemarle, 1975; bd.

mem. Stanly County Arts Council, 1974-76, N.C., Cultural Adv. Com., Raleigh, 1980-84. Works include drawing: Rain, 1970 (1st prize 1971), paintings and drawings; illustrator: Exploring the Piedmont, 1985. Named Artist of Month, sta. WBTV, Charlotte, 1978; recipient Cert. of Recognition, Stanly County C. of C., 1976; winner over 30 awards for works. Mem. N.C. Watercolor Soc. (advisor 1978), Uwharrie Artists (pres. Albemarle 1974-76). Republican. Presbyterian. Home: Route 2 Box 469 Stony Mountain Rd Albemarle NC 28001

MORA, RALPH, psychologist, consultant, psychology educator; b. N.Y.C., Jan. 25, 1947; s. Raphael Baudilio and Theresa (De Jesus) M.; m. Monica Veronica Julian, Aug. 10, 1973; children—Devin Michael, Raquel Angelique; m. Peggy Lee Dickens. A.A., Hostos City Coll., 1974; B.A. cum laude, CCNY, 1976; M.A. Inst. Advanced Psychology, 1978; Ph.D., Adelphi U., 1983. Cert. sch. psychologist, Ariz., Conn.; lic. clin. psychologist, Tenn. Acting dir., clin. supv. So. Bronx CMHC-Alcoholism OPD, N.Y., 1980-81; adj. instr. Hostos City Coll., Bronx, 1981-83; psychol. cons. Puerto Rican Family Inst., N.Y.C., 1981-83; intern supv. Child & Family Services, Hartford, Conn., 1983-84; treatment team leader Mid-South Hosp., Memphis, 1984—; agy. liaison Wilderness Program, Hartford, 1983-84; cons. in field. Author: Delineating Two Borderline Subgroups, 1983. Contbr. articles to profl. jours. Chairperson Hispanic Caucus Inst. Advanced Psychol. Studies, Garden City, N.Y., 1976-79, sch. health Adv. com., Hartford, 1983-84; mem. Hartford Coalition for Adolescents, 1983-84, Bronx Betterment Com. for Alcoholism, 1980-82. Served with U.S. Army, Vietnam. Recipient Service award Hartford Bd. of Edn., 1984, Humanitarian award S. Bronx Mental Health Council, 1982; fellow NIMH. Mem. Am. Psychol. Assn., Am. Orthopsychiat. Assn., N.Y. Acad. Scis., Soc. Personality Assessment, Nat. Hispanic Psychol. Assn. Republican. Avocations: sculpting stone; martial arts; drawing; photography. Home: 6080 Forrest View Sq Memphis TN 38115 Office: Mid-South Hosp 135 N Pauline Memphis TN 38105

MORADI-ARAGHI, AHMAD, research chemist; b. Tehran, Iran, Mar. 23, 1943; came to U.S., 1968, naturalized, 1985; s. Rajabali and Kobra (Bakhtiari) M.; m. Anita Mendoza, Feb. 2, 1974; children—Kevin, David, Michael. B.S., U. Tehran, 1965; M.S., Tenn. Tech. U., 1971; Ph.D., N. Tex. State U., 1976. Postdoctoral fellow N. Tex. State U., Denton, 1976-77; asst. prof. Jundi Shapur U., Ahwaz, Iran, 1977-78; postdoctoral fellow Tex. Christian U., Fort Worth, 1978-80; research chemist Phillips Petroleum Co., Bartlesville, Okla., 1980—. Contbr. articles to profl. jours. Patentee in field. Served to 2d lt. Iranian Army, 1965-67. Robert A. Welch Found. fellow, 1973-76, 76-77, 78-80. Mem. Am. Chem. Soc., Soc. Petroleum Engrs., Alpha Xi Sigma. Democrat. Islam. Club: Tulsa Zoo Friends. Avocations: photography; gardening; woodworking. Home: 1925 Limestone Ct Bartlesville OK 74006 Office: Phillips Petroleum Co 229 GB PRC Bartlesville OK 74004

MORALES-BEST, MARIA TERESA, architect, executive; b. Laredo, Tex., Oct. 2, 1956; d. Amador P. and Carmen (Santos) Morales; m. Herbert Best, Jr., July 21, 1984. B.Arch. with high honors, U. Tex., 1980. Registered architect, Tex. Draftsperson MGR Designs, Laredo, 1976, 77; archtl. designer T.R.B. & Assocs., Corpus Christi, Tex., 1980-81; intern architect Turner, Hickey & Assocs., Laredo, 1979, archtl. designer, 1981-83; architect-in-charge Turner, Morales & Assocs., McAllen, Tex., 1983—. Prin. works include orthopedic clinic, cottages for Laredo Human Devel., Webb County Jail and Law Enforcement Ctr., also several homes in Laredo. Mem. com. women of yr. Laredo Bus. Profl. Women's Assn., 1983. Scholar Achievement U. Tex., 1975-79, D.D. Hacitars Found., 1975-80, Lulac Found., 1979. Mem. AIA, Tex. Soc. Architects, Laredo C. of C. (small bus. com. 1981-83, spl. activities com. 1982-83, Extra Mile award 1982), Ex-Student Assn., McAllen C. of C., Bus. Profl. Women's Assn. Roman Catholic. Home: 6109 N 14th St McAllen TX 78504 Office: Turner Morales & Assocs 1418 Beech Suite 111 Mc Allen TX 78501

MORAN, ALTON TRACY, lawyer; b. Pascagoula, Miss., Dec. 8, 1942; s. Alton Joseph and Rachel Annabell (Green) M.; m. Margaret Alexander, Aug. 28, 1965; children—Joel David, Amy Elizabeth. B.A., La. State U., 1963, J.D., 1966; diploma Office Spl. Investigations, USAF, Washington, 1967; diploma in nat. security mgmt. Nat. Colls. Armed Forces, Ft. Holobird, Md., 1968. Bar: La. 1966, U.S. Dist. Ct. Md. 1970, U.S. Dist. Ct. La. 1970. Spl. agt. Def. Intelligence Agy., Arlington, Va., 1966-67; asst. dist. atty. East Baton Rouge Parish (La.), 1967-76, dir. Office Pub. Defender, 1976-80; magistrate U.S. Dist. (mid. dist.) La., Baton Rouge, 1980-84; instr. La. State U., 1973, So. U., 1983; owner Moran-Greco Art Gallery. Pres. La. State U. Track and Field Ofcls. Assn. Mem. S.C. Geneal. Soc., Huxford Geneal. Soc., Phi Eta Sigma. Roman Catholic. Club: Southwood. Contbr. articles to Huxford Geneal. Mag. Office: 305 France St Baton Rouge LA 70802

MORAN, CHRISTA ILSE MERKEL, investor, linquist; b. Leipzig, Saxony, Germany, Jan. 5, 1946; came to U.S., 1968; d. Erich Harry and Ilse Dora (Waehnert) Merkel; m. William Joseph Moran, May 5, 1967 (dec. Mar. 4, 1979); children—Leslie Paige, Linda Christa. B.A., U. Tuebingen, 1968; postgrad. U. Alaska, 1968-69. Cert. in German linquistics. Clerk Anchorage Westward Hotel, 1969-71; sales mgr. Windsor Park Hotel, Washington, 1971-75; linquist, instr. Def. Lang. Inst., Dept. Def., Washington, 1975-79; investor in real estate, sports cars, Atlanta, 1979—; cons. Dept. Def., 1976-79. Author: Die Mille Miglia, 1969; Der Neurburgring, 1975; German Culture, 1977. Chmn. For a United Germany Com., Washington and Atlanta; fundraiser UNICEF. Named Sportswriter of Yr., ADAC of Germany, 1977. Democrat. Home: 2684 Brookwood Dr Atlanta GA 30305 Office: Christa Moran Investments PO Box 20084 Atlanta GA 30358

MORAN, JAMES D., III, child development educator; b. Bklyn., Mar. 2, 1951; s. James D. and Monica (Scherzinger) M.; m. Laurette Virginia Miller, Aug. 11, 1973; 1 child, Ryan. B.A. magna cum laude, Duke U., 1973; M.S., U. Okla., 1975; Ph.D., Okla. State U., 1978. Asst. prof. U. Okla., Norman, 1978-80; asst. prof. Va. Poly. Inst. and State U., Blacksburg, 1980-83, assoc. prof., asst. head dept. family and child devel., 1983-85; prof., head dept. family relations and child devel. Okla. State U., Stillwater, 1985—. Editorial bd. Home Econs. Research Jour., 1983—. Recipient Outstanding Research award Va. Home Econs. Assn., 1982. Mem. Am. Home Econs. Assn. (vice chmn. family relations and child devel. sect. 1985—, named among New Faces to Watch 1984), Nat. Assn. for Edn. Young Children, Soc. for Research in Child Devel., Am. Psychol. Assn. Democrat. Roman Catholic. Avocation: golf. Home: 1008 Woodbury Dr Edmond OK 73034 Office: Dept Family Relations and Child Devel Okla State U Stillwater OK 74078

MORAN, JAMES PATRICK, mayor; b. Buffalo, May 16, 1945; s. James Patrick and Dorothy (Dwyer) M.; m. Mary Craig, Dec. 27, 1967 (div. June 1974); children—Jimmy, Mary. B.A., Coll. of Holy Cross, 1967; M.P.A., U. Pitts., 1970. Budget analyst U.S. Govt., Washington, 1968-74; specialist budget and fiscal policy Library of Congress, Washington, 1974-76; staff U.S. Senate Appropriations Com., Washington, 1976-79; investment broker A.G. Edwards & Sons, Alexandria, Va., 1979—; mem. Alexandria City Council, 1979-82; vice mayor City of Alexandria, 1982-84, mayor, 1985—. Chmn. United Way, Alexandria, 1980-82, Mental Health Bd., 1982-83; bd. dirs. No. Va. Transp. Commn., 1985—, Council of Govts., Washington, 1985—. Recipient Outstanding Citizenship award YMCA, 1983. Mem. Alexandria C. of C. (bd. dirs. 1985). Democrat. Roman Catholic. Home: 205 W Uhler Terr Alexandria VA 22301 Office: 301 King St Alexandria VA 22314

MORAN, WALTER BRIAN, oil production firm executive, electrical engineer; b. Lima, Ohio, Nov. 9, 1901; s. Martin and Helen (Cusack) M.; m. Catherine Jackie Crosbie, Feb. 8, 1928; children—Patricia Moran Henthorne, Walter Brian. E.E., U. Notre Dame, 1924. Elec. engr. Texas Co., 1924-25; field engr. O G & E Co., Sapulpa, Okla., 1925-27; v.p. J. E. Crosbie, Inc., Tulsa, 1927-37, pres., 1937-52; pres. E.F. Moran, Inc., Tulsa, 1952—. Republican. Roman Catholic. Clubs: So. Hill Country (Tulsa), Tulsa. Home: 1712 E 29th St Tulsa OK 74114 Office: EF Moran Inc Suite 1212 320 S Boston St Tulsa OK 74103

MORAN, WILLIAM EDWARD, university administrator; b. White Plains, N.Y., May 28, 1932; s. Frank Joseph and Margaret Mary (Farrell) M.; A.B., Princeton, 1954; M.B.A., Harvard, 1959; Ph.D., U. Mich., 1967; m. Barbara Carol Baillet, Apr. 20, 1963; children Kathryn, Kevin, Colin, Christian. Mgmt. cons. Booz, Allen & Hamilton, N.Y.C., 1959-61; mem. adminstrv. staff Harvard U., Boston, 1961-63; asst. exec. v.p. State U. N.Y., Stony Brook, 1966-71; chancellor Flint Campus U. Mich., 1971-79, U. N.C., Greensboro, 1979—; dir. Jefferson-Pilot Growth Fund, Greensboro, N.C., Connors Investor Services, Reading, Pa. Served with USN, 1954-57. Rotarian. Contbr. articles to profl. jours. Home: 1102 Spring Garden St Greensboro NC 27403 Office: U North Carolina Greensboro NC 27403

MORD, IRVING CONRAD, II, lawyer; b. Kentwood, La., Mar. 22, 1950; s. Irving Conrad and Lillie Viva (Chapman) M.; m. Julia Ann Russell, Aug. 22, 1970 (div. Apr. 22, 1980); children—Russell Conrad, Emily Ann. B.S., Miss. State U., 1972; J.D., U. Miss., 1974. Bar: Miss. 1974, U.S. Dist. Ct. (no. dist.) Miss. 1974, U.S. Dist. Ct. (so. dist.) Miss. 1984. Counsel to bd. suprs. Noxubee County, Miss., 1976-80, Walthall County, Miss. 1980—, Bd. Educ., Walthall County, 1980—. Trustee, Walthall County Gen. Hosp., 1982—; county pros. atty. Noxubee County, Miss., Macon, 1974-80, Walthall County, Tylertown, 1982—. Bd. dirs. East Miss. Council, Meridian, 1978-80; v.p. Macon council Boy Scouts Am., 1978, mem. council, 1979; county crusade chmn. Am. Cancer Soc., Macon, 1976-78, county pres., 1979; chmn. fund drive Miss. State U. Fine Arts Complex, Macon, 1979. Recipient Youth Leadership award Miss. Econ. Council, 1976. Mem. Miss. Prosecutors Assn., Miss. Assn. Board Attys., Miss. State Bar, Am. Judicature Soc. (Torts award 1972), Miss. Assn. Trial Lawyers, Assn. Trial Lawyers Am., Miss. Criminal Justice Planning Commn., Nat. Fed. Ind. Bus., Miss. State U. Alumni Assn., Macon-Noxubee County C. of C., Phi Kappa Tau (bd. govs. 1976-80, grad. council, 1972—, pres. grad. council 1977-80, pres. house corp. 1977-80, alumnus of yr. Alpha Chi chpt. 1979), Phi Delta Phi. Republican. Methodist. Lodge: Rotary (sec. treas. 1977, v.p. 1978, pres. Macon 1979) Office: 816 Morse St Tylertown MS 39667

MORE, PHILIP JEROME, archeologist, engineer, arts and antiquities company executive; b. Chgo., Dec. 11, 1911; s. Louis Eli and Anna Leah (Kahn) M.; B.S., Heidelberg (Germany) U., 1933; postgrad. Ill. Inst. Tech., 1936; LL.D. (hon.), Roosevelt U., 1967; M.B.A., Columbia Pacific U., 1980, Ph.D. in Archeology, 1981; m. Sylvia Sally Bernstein, Oct. 16, 1937 (div. 1977); children—Andrea More Williams, Michael E., William M. Owner, pres. Feris Flying Service, Chgo., 1936-38; metallurgist Standard Dental Labs., Chgo., 1938-39; project design engr. Birtman Electric Co., Chgo., 1939-41; sr. design engr. Hotpoint div. Gen. Electric Co., Cicero, Ill., 1950-68; dir. purchasing Modern Maid, McGraw Edison, Chattanooga, 1968-76; pres. Choo-Choo Indsls. Inc., 1976-79; pres. Things of Beauty, 1979—; mem. indsl. and sci. conf. Appliance Design and Mfg. Adv. Council; cons. primitive monies, museums and univs.; sponsor numismatic studies Roosevelt U., Chgo., 1966-67, chmn. Numismatic Library Project; Presdl. appointee Assay Commn., 1965. Chmn., Engrs. for Senator Baker, 1972—, Engrs. for Sasser for Senator, 1976, Engrs. for Carter for Pres., 1976. Served to comdr. USNR, 1950-58. Decorated Navy Cross; recipient Gen. Electric citation for cost saving, 1966. Mem. Gas Appliance Engring. Soc. (pres. 1970-71), Am. Soc. Gas Engrs. (nat. pres. 1975—), Am. Assn. Ret. Persons (pres. chpt. 1986). Clubs: North Shore Coin (founder, pres. 1950-58), Chgo. Coin (pres. 1964-65) (Chgo.); Central States Numismatic Soc. (pres. 1965-66). Author: The Lure of Primitive Money, 1960; Odd and Curious Monies of the World, 1963; Primitive Money of the World: Fact and Fantasy, 1982; purchasing editorial adv. bd. Appliance mag.; contbr. articles on monies and engring. design to profl. jours. Patentee in field. Home: 1414 Continental Dr #804 Chattanooga TN 37405 Office: PO Box 4864 Chattanooga TN 37405

MORECOCK, ROBERT CLIFTON, psychology educator, counselor; b. Portsmouth, Va., July 21, 1946; s. Albert Clifton Jr. and Beulah Marie (Rockliff) M. B.A., Randolph-Macon Coll., 1969; M.A., U. Houston, 1980. Lic. counselor, Tex. Stockbroker Merrill Lynch, Houston, 1974; realtor, Vista Homes, Houston, 1975-81; adj. prof. psychology Houston Community Coll., 1981—; psychology intern N. Tex. State U., Denton, 1984. Served with U.S. Army, 1971-74, Vietnam. Mem. Am. Assn. for Counseling Devel., Houston Behavior Therapy Assn. Methodist. Home: 12415 Garden Estate Houston TX 77072

MORELAN, PAULA KAY, ballet company director; b. Lafayette, Ind., Nov. 24, 1949; d. Dickie Booth and Marian Maxine (Fetterhoff) M.; m. Kerim Sayan, Aug. 10, 1974. Student U. Utah, 1968-69; B.F.A., Tex. Christian U., 1972; student El Centro Coll., 1969-70. Tchr., Rosello Sch. Ballet, Dallas, 1972-74; mgr., tchr. Ballet Arts Center, Dallas, 1974-76; owner, tchr. Ballet Classique, Garland, Tex., 1976—; asst. to Mythra Rosello, Tex. Civic Ballet, Dallas, 1972-74; assoc. artistic dir. Dance Repertory Theatre Dallas, 1974-75; artistic dir. Dance Repertory Theatre Dallas, 1975-76, Garland (Tex.) Ballet Assn., 1977—. Home: 4230 Cedar Creek Dr Garland TX 75043 Office: Garland Ballet Assn 3704 Dividend St Garland TX 75042

MORELLI, HENRY ERNEST, JR., electronic service company executive; b. N.Y.C., Jan. 14, 1944; s. Henry E. and Grace R. (Cinelli) M.; A.A.S., Pace U., 1965, B.B.A., 1967, M.B.A., 1970; m. Cynthia Ann Chisholm, Feb. 18, 1984; 1 child, Brian Michael; children by previous marriage—John, Paul, Christine, Henry Ernest III, Timothy. Dir., Hudson River Mus. and Planetarium, Yonkers, N.Y., 1966-67; systems specialist IBM, White Plains, N.Y., 1967-71; corp. staff cons. Burndy Corp., Norwalk, Conn., 1971-72; cons. Informatics, Inc., communications systems div., River Edge, N.J., 1972-75; dir. mgmt. info. systems Racal-Milgo, Inc., Miami, 1975-83; v.p. Datapoint Corp., San Antonio, 1983-85, v.p., corp. officer Intelogic Trace, Inc., San Antonio, 1985—; v.p. USE, Inc., Univac Computers Users Group, 1980—. Mem. Assn. Computing Machinery, Data Processing Mgmt. Assn. Republican. Roman Catholic. Club: Ariel House (San Antonio). Office: 8415 Datapoint Dr PO Box 400044 San Antonio TX 78229-8440

MORELOCK, JAMES CRUTCHFIELD, mathematician; b. Martin, Tenn., Feb. 7, 1920; s. Joseph Fletcher and Lura Martha (Crutchfield) M.; student Bethel Coll., McKenzie, Tenn., 1937-39; B.S., Memphis State Coll., 1941; M.A., U. Mo., 1948; Ph.D. (fellow), U. Fla., 1952; m. Eugenia Scott Browne, Apr. 29, 1945 (dec.); children—Elinor Morelock Smith, Constance Morelock Grear (dec.), Diana Morelock Brown. Instr. astronomy and math. U. Fla., Gainesville, 1949-52; asst. prof. math. Auburn (Ala.) U., 1952-56; head math. dept. King Coll., Bristol, Tenn., 1956-60; mathematician U.S. Naval Computation Lab., Dahlgren, Va., 1960-61; mem. staff Computation Center Gen. Electric, Huntsville, Ala., 1961-63; mathematician computation lab. Marshall Space Flight Center, Huntsville, Ala., 1963-78, ret., 1978. Instl. rep. to Boy Scouts, Civitan Club, Auburn, 1952-56; v.p. Huntsville Concert Band, 1963—. Served with USAAF, 1941-45; PTO. Manning scholar, 1940-41; recipient U.S. Treasury award, 1968, NASA 10 year Achievement award, 1969, NASA Apollo Achievement award, 1969. Mem. Am. Math. Soc., Math. Assn. Am., Assn. Computing Machinery, Bristol Astronomy Soc. (pres. 1956-60). Methodist. Club: Pistol. Home: 2917 Garth Rd SE Huntsville AL 35801

MORENO, FERNANDO, legal educator; b. Santurce, P.R., Oct. 17, 1934; s. Esteban and Maria (Salas) M.; m. Rosario Gonzalez, Dec. 21, 1957; children—Rosario, Esteban, Marie, Fernando. B.A., U. P.R., 1955, postgrad. in pub. adminstrn., 1955-56, J.D. magna cum laude, 1973; LL.M. in Ocean and Coastal Law, U. Miami, 1982. Bar: P.R. 1974, U.S. Dist. Ct. P.R., 1974, U.S. Ct. Appeals (1st cir.) 1974. Teaching asst. U. P.R. Sch. Law, 1972-73; office mgr., personnel dir., in-house counselor at law, dir. Gonzalez Rodriguez Investment Corp., Catalan Gonzalez & Co., Inc., Indsl. Gonzalez, Inc., Santurce, 1958-79; lectr. Sch. Law, U. P.R., 1973-79; law lectr. marine sci. program U. Miami (Fla.), 1982—; treas. Gonzalez R. Investment Corp., P.R., 1958-79, dir., 1958-83. Recipient Civil and Comparative Law award, 1973. Mem. U. P.R. Law Rev., 1971-73. Chmn. San Juan Mail Users Council, 1968. Mem. ABA, P.R. Bar Assn., P.R. Philatelic Soc. (founder 1952, pres. 1967-68). Home: 1811 SW 99th Pl Miami FL 33165

MORENO, JOSE LUIS, safety company executive; b. Ponce, P.R., July 17, 1943; s. Isidro and Agripina (Montalvo) M.; m. Yolanda Lagares, Dec. 20, 1970; children—Jose Luis, Alexis, Nestor Luis. B.S. in Math., P.R. Coll. Agrl. and Mech. Arts, Mayaguez, 1970; B.B.A., World U., San Juan, P.R., 1976. Safety supr. P.R. Hwy. Authority, Ponce, 1971-78, C.O.R.C.O., 1978-82; safety and security prof. Medtronic P.R., Inc., Villalba, 1982—. Editor mag. El Cable, 1984. Com. mem. Ponce council Boy Scouts Am., 1984-85. Served with U.S. Army, 1967-69, Vietnam. Decorated Purple Heart, recipient Pres.'s award P.R. Manufacturer's Assn., 1983. Mem. Am. Soc. Safety Engrs., Am. Indsl. Hygienists Assn., Am. Soc. Indsl. Security. Methodist. Avocations: basketball; swimming; camping. Office: Medtronic P R Inc Box M Villalba Puerto Rico 00766

MORETTO, JANE ANN, nurse; b. Belgium, Ill., Apr. 9, 1934; d. Bernard James and Mildred Bertha (Sutton) Moretto; R.N., Mercy Hosp. Sch. Nursing, Urbana, Ill., 1955; B.S. in Nursing, St. Joseph Coll., Emmitsburg, Md., 1969. Relief head nurse, staff nurse Mercy Hosp., Urbana, Ill., 1955-57; staff nurse in psychiatry VA Hosp., Danville, Ill., 1957-59; staff nurse pulmonary disease VA Hosp., Long Beach, Calif., 1959-60, staff nurse surg. unit, Los Angeles, 1960-61, staff nurse operating room, 1961-64; staff nurse USPHS Hosp., Galveston, Tex., 1964-66, staff nurse tumor ICU, Balt., 1967, asst. operating room supr., New Orleans, 1969-71, operating room supr., Brighton, Mass., 1971-78, dep. dir. nursing, dir. inservice edn. Carville, La., 1978-80, dir. nurses Nat. Hansen's Disease Center, 1980—; cons. in field; lectr. in field. Commd. lt. comdr., USPHS, 1969, advanced through grades to capt., 1975—. Recipient Superior Performance award, USPHS Hosp., Galveston, 1966; named hon. citizen Town of White Castle, 1983. Mem. Am. Nurses Assn., La. Nurses Assn., La. Hosp. Assn., La. Soc. Nursing Service Adminstrs., Nat. Assn. for Uniformed Services, Assn. Mil. Surgeons of U.S., Assn. Operating Room Nurses, Mary Knoll Missionary Assn. of Mary Immaculate, St. Elizabeth Ann Seton Assn., Alumnae Assn. of Schlarman High Sch., Alumnae Assn. of St. Joseph Coll., Commd. Officers Assn. USPHS. Roman Catholic. Home: 303 Bridgett St Westville IL 61883 Office: Nat Hansen's Disease Center Carville LA 70721

MORFORD, WILLIAM JACOB, service company executive; b. Phila., Mar. 18, 1931; s. Herbert Northrup and Laura Bertha (Neef) M.; B.A., Hobart Coll., 1953; postgrad. in Hosp. Adminstrn., U. Minn., 1953-55; m. Jean Carter, May 4, 1956; children—Carter, Scott, Margo. Adminstrv. resident San Jose (Calif.) Hosp., 1954-55; mgmt. analysis supt. Parks AFB Hosp. (Calif.), 1955-56; salesman, dist. sales mgr. Vestal Labs. div. W.R. Grace, Calif., N.C., Fla., Md., 1958-71; dir. hosp. services Bldg. Services div. Macke Co., Cheverly, Md., 1971-72; dir. contract services Marriott Corp., Bethesda, Md., 1972-74; pres., prin. stockholder Health Environs, Inc., Lexington, S.C., 1974—, JIL Corp.; cons. in field. Bd. dirs. Coastal Evangelism, Missionary Outreach, El Shaddai Ministries. Served wtih U.S. Army, 1956-58. Mem. Bldg. Service Contractors Assn., Internat. Fabricare Inst., Textile Rental Services Assn. Mem. Assembly of God Clubs: Lexington County Saddle (past pres.), Lexington Toastmasters (past pres.). Home: Route 11 Box 285-A Lexington SC 29072 Office: 125 Parker St Lexington SC 29072

MORGAN, BETTIE RAE, therapist, consultant; b. Tampa, Fla., Feb. 27, 1928; d. Webster Edward and Marcella (Helveston) Bridges; m. Robert Leon Morgan, Nov. 25, 1950; children—Deborah Elaine, Donna Lynne, Elizabeth Annette. B.A., U. South Fla., 1964, Ed.S., 1986; M.A., U. Central Fla., 1976. Tchr. county schs., St. Petersburg, Fla., 1965-67; adminstr. U. Central Fla., Orlando, 1974-76; continuing edn. coordinator St. Petersburg Jr. Coll., 1976-79; pres. Athenian Enterprises, Inc., St. Petersburg, 1979-83; founding dean Internat. Acad. Merchandising and Design, Tampa, 1984; therapist, cons. East Tampa Ctr. for Individual and Family Therapy, 1985—; cons. for businesses in pre-retirement planning, stress, time mgmt., 1985—. Mem. Fla. Symphony Guild, St. Petersburg, 1964—, Pinellas County Sci. Ctr. Guild, St. Petersburg, 1977-84; adv. council Coop. Extension Service, St. Petersburg, 1979—; vol. counselor Suicide and Crises Ctr., Tampa, 1985-86; vol. reader Radio Reading Services for Visually Impaired, Tampa, 1985-86. Fulbright scholar, 1976. Mem. AAUW, Am. Assn. Counseling and Devel., Fla. Mental Health Counselors Assn., Fla. Career Devel. Assn., Bus. and Profl. Women's Assn. Republican. Avocations: sculpting; fashion design; reading; travel. Office: East Tampa Ctr for Individual and Family Therapy 21st St at 4th Ave Tampa FL 33605

MORGAN, BRYANT TIMOTHY, experimental psychologist; b. Seattle, June 8, 1954; s. Wesley Bryant and Nellie Darlene (Borgeson) M.; m. Joanna Marie Duke, Aug. 18, 1976; children—Emerson Albert, Raleigh Bryant, Charlotte Rene. Student U. Ala.-Huntsville, 1972-73; B.S. in Psychology, Brigham Young U., 1980; M.A. in Exptl. Psychology, Hollins Coll., 1982. Research asst. Hollins Communications Research Inst., Roanoke, Va., 1981-82, staff researcher, 1982—, grad. intern supr., 1983-84; program mgr. Satellite Program Services, Roanoke, 1983. Contbr. articles to profl. jours. Mem. Am. Psychol. Assn. (assoc.), Eastern Psychol. Assn. Mormon. Avocations: photography; skiing; softball. Home: PO Box 9721 Roanoke VA 24020 Office: Hollins Communications Research Inst PO Box 9737 Roanoke VA 24020

MORGAN, CATHERINE MARIE, psychologist; writer; b. Duluth, Minn., Mar. 27, 1947; d. George Anthony and Charlotte Ruth (Hicken) Nothhelfer; m. Ralph Rexford Morgan, Aug. 28, 1967; 1 son, Andrew. B.S., U. Nebr., 1968; M.Ed., U. Okla., 1973; Ph.D. candidate Okla. State U. Child devel. specialist Southwest Guidance Ctr., Wheatland, Okla., 1973-74; pvt. practice Family Counseling Assocs., San Antonio, 1974-75; psychol. asst. Edmond Guidance Ctr., Okla., 1975-82; psychol. asst. supr. Southeast Guidance Ctr., Del City, Okla., 1982—; v.p. Behavior Mgmt. Specialists, Oklahoma City, 1983—. Mem. Okla. Psychol. Assn., Southwestern Psychol. Assn., Am. Personnel and Guidance Assn., AAUW, Am. Bus. Women's Assn., P.E.O., Kappa Delta Pi. Avocations: writing; reading; knitting; racquetball. Office: Southeast Guidance Ctr 3945 SE 15th St Suite 204 Del City OK 73115

MORGAN, CECIL, JR., urologist; b. Shreveport, La., Mar. 13, 1933; s. Cecil and Margaret Harriet (Geddes) M.; B.A., Tulane U., 1954, M.D., 1959; m. Jane Headly, Aug. 11, 1965; children—Philippa, Cecil, Delia, Alison Lockridge (stepdau.). Intern, Touro Infirmary, New Orleans; resident urology Ochsner Found. Hosp., New Orleans, 1959-63; asst. prof. urology U. Ala. Med. Sch., Birmingham, 1963-68; staff urologist Lloyd Noland Clinic, Birmingham, 1967-70; pvt. practice urology, Birmingham, 1970—; mem. staff Baptist Med. Center, St. Vincent's, Brookwood, U. Ala. hosps.; pres. surg. staff Children's Hosp., 1974, pres. gen. staff, 1976-77, asst. chief pediatric urology, 1977—; cons. Social Security Adminstrn.; asst. clin. prof. U. Ala. Med. Center, 1967-85, assoc. clin. prof., 1985—. Fellow ACS; assoc. fellow urology Am. Acad. Pediatrics; mem. AMA, Am. Urol. Assn., Ala. Urology Soc. (past pres.), Soc. Pediatric Urology, Jefferson County Med. Soc. (trustee 1974-76, censor 1978-80, pres. 1985-86); Newcomen Soc. N.Am., Delta Kappa Epsilon, Nu Sigma Nu. Clubs: Birmingham Country; Boston (New Orleans). Contbr. articles to med. jours. Chmn. bd. Ala. Med. Rev., 1974-78. Home: 4308 Corinth Dr Birmingham AL 35213 Office: 2660 10th Ave S Birmingham AL 35205

MORGAN, CELIA ANN, economics educator; b. Midland, Tex., Jan. 6, 1932; d. Thurman Glenn and Cecil Elizabeth (Hill) M. A.A., Lamar U., 1951; B.B.A., U. Tex., 1953; M.A. in Econs., U. Houston, 1967, Ph.D. in Econs., 1971. Asst. prof. SW Tex. State U., San Marcos, 1971-76, assoc. prof., 1976-81, prof. econs., 1981—, chairperson dept. fin. and econs., 1984—; cons. to sec. state Tex., Austin, 1982—. Contbr. articles to profl. jours. Mem. Am. Econ. Assn., So. Econ. Assn., Western Social Sci. Assn., Southwestern Soc. Economists (pres. 1978-79), Southwestern Econ. Assn., LWV (bd. dirs. San Marcos 1983-85). Democrat. Presbyterian. Avocations: hiking; classical music. Home: 819 A Hazelton St San Marcos TX 78666 Office: Southwest Tex State U San Marcos TX 78666

MORGAN, EVELYN BUCK, nursing educator; b. Phila., Nov. 3, 1931; d. Kenneth Edward and Evelyn Louise (Rhineberg) Buck; m. John Allen McGeary, Aug. 15, 1958 (div. 1964); children—John Andrew, Jacquelyn Ann McGeary Keplinger; m. Kenneth Dean Morgan, June 26, 1965 (dec. 1975). R.N., Muhlenberg Hosp. Sch. Nursing, 1955; B.S. in Nursing summa cum laude, Ohio State U., 1972, M.S., 1973; Ed.D., Nova U., 1978. R.N., N.J., Ohio, Fla., Calif.; cert. specialist Am. Nurses Assn. Psychiat.-Mental Health Clin. Specialists; advanced R.N. practitioner Fla. Bd. Nursing. Staff nurse Muhlenberg Hosp., Plainfield, N.J., 1955-57; indsl. nurse Western Electric Co., Columbus, Ohio, 1957-59; supr. Mt. Carmel Hosp., Columbus, 1960-65; instr. Grant Hosp. Sch. Nursing, 1965-72; cons. Ohio Dept. Health, 1972-74; prof. nursing Miami (Fla.)-Dade Community Coll., 1974—; family therapist Hollywood Pavilion Hosp., 1977-82; pvt. practice family therapy, Ft. Lauderdale, Fla., 1982—. Sustaining mem. Democratic Nat. Com., 1975—. Mem. Am. Nurses Assn., Fla. Council Psychiat.-Mental Health Clin. Specialists, Am. Nurses Found., Am. Holistic Nurses Assn., Sigma Theta Tau. Democrat. Roman Catholic.

MORGAN, FRED MORRIS, electrical test engineer, consultant; b. San Francisco, Aug. 12, 1948; s. Donald Bernard and Evelyn Mae Morgan; m. Patricia Ann Chaler, May 15, 1968; children—Kerry D., Kelly D., Matthew Donald. Student Centenary Coll., Shreveport, 1966-68, Internat. Corr. Sch., Scranton, Pa., 1970-74. Journeyman electrician Southwestern Electric Power Co., Longview, Tex., 1968-75; nuclear power plant instrument technician Southport, N.C., Middletown, Pa. and Port Gibson, Miss., 1975-82; elec. test engr. Multi-Amp Corp., Underwood, N.D. and Brownsville, Tex., 1978-79; elec. test engr., v.p. Elec. Testing Specialist, Inc., Longview, Tex., 1979—. Republican. Baptist. Office: 301 Enterprize St Suite E Longview TX 75604

MORGAN, GEORGE MARK, JR., dentist; b. Quincy, Fla., June 17, 1937; s. George Mark and Mamie Lou (Sapp) M.; m. Elizabeth Shelfer, Feb. 4, 1958; children—Amy Elizabeth, George Cass, Alison Stacy, Charles Howard. D.D.S., Emory U., 1962. Gen. practice dentistry, Tallahassee. Fellow Acad. Gen. Dentistry; ADA, Fla. Dental Assn. Methodist. Lodge: Elks. Avocations: hunting; fishing. Home: 150 Bellac Rd Tallahassee FL 32303 Office: 510 N Adams St Tallahassee FL 32301

MORGAN, GEORGE MICHAEL, development geologist; b. Long Beach, Calif., May 8, 1953; s. George Frank and Doris Vivian (Hawsey) M.; m. Sharon' Botts, May 23, 1975; children—Jason, Kristin. B.S. in Geology, U. Tex., 1975. Devel. geologist Gulf Oil Co., Kilgore, Tex., 1975-77, Columbia, Miss., 1977-78; sr. geol. engr. Tenneco Oil Rocky Mountain div., Denver, 1978-80, div. geol. engr. Gulf Coast div., Houston, 1980-84, Internat. div., Houston, 1984—. Mem. Am. Assn. Petroleum Geologists (cert.). Home: 3322 Wildcandle Spring TX 77388 Office: Tenneco Oil 1100 Louisiana St Houston TX 77208

MORGAN, HARCOURT ALEXANDER, JR., physician; b. Knoxville, Tenn., Aug. 20, 1909; s. Harcourt Alexander and Sara Elizabeth (Fay) M.; B.A., U. Tenn., 1931, M.D., 1933; M.P.H., Johns Hopkins U., 1941; m. Sarah Lanier Stone, Aug. 9, 1934; children—Harcourt Alexander III, Sarah Lanier Morgan Davis, Lucy-Fay Morgan Hinds. Intern, Memphis Gen. Hosp., 1933-35; commd. officer, staff U.S. Marine Hosp., Balt., 1936-37, Detroit, 1937; gen. practice medicine, Sparta, Tenn., 1937-39; pub. health physician Tenn. Dept. Pub. Health, 1939-78; pvt. practice medicine, Lewisburg, Tenn., 1978—; mem. staff Lewisburg Community Hosp.; dir. Bank of Belfast, Tenn., Middle Tenn. Heart Assn., Nashville, 1970-74; med. adviser Selective Service, Lewisburg, 1948—; dir. Marshall County Farm Bur., Lewisburg, 1955-72; magistrate Marshall County, Tenn., 1951-67. Bd. dirs. League for Hearing Impaired, Nashville, 1978-82. Served to 1st lt. AUS, 1935-36; served with USPHS, 1936-37. Diplomate Am. Bd. Preventive Medicine. Fellow Am. Pub. Health Assn.; mem. Am. Assn. Pub. Health Physicians (charter), Marshall County Med. Soc. (charter), Tenn. Med. Assn., AMA, Delta Omega. Methodist (ofcl. bd. 1948-72). Clubs: Elks, Lions (pres. 1956-57). Home: 1525 White Dr Lewisburg TN 37091 Office: 1525 White Dr Lewisburg TN 37091

MORGAN, HARRY HAMILTON, entrepreneur, consultant; b. Petersburg, Va., Nov. 28, 1930; s. Ernest Maxie and Evelyn Jean (Batts) M. Student Va. State Coll., 1948, Los Angeles City Coll., 1954. Owner, pres. Twin Globe Fin. Service, Petersburg, 1981—; owner, pres. New Dir. Assn., Petersburg, 1983—; owner, pres. Circle M Distbg. Co., Petersburg, 1983—. Served to sgt. U.S. Army, 1949-54. Mem. DAV (Liberty Lobby). Democrat. Home and office: 617 Fort Lee Rd Petersburg VA 23803

MORGAN, HUGH JACKSON, JR., natural gas company executive, lawyer; b. Nashville, Aug. 10, 1928; s. Hugh Jackson and Robert (Porter) M.; m. Ann Moulton Ward, Aug. 28, 1954; children—Ann, Grace, Carolina, Hugh. Bar: Tenn. 1956. Assoc., Miller and Martin, Chattanooga, 1956-60; with So. Natural Gas Co., Birmingham, Ala., 1960—, v.p., 1971-77, sr. v.p., 1978-81, pres., 1982—, dir., 1982—; gen. atty. Sonant, Inc., Birmingham, 1973-79, sr. v.p., 1979; dir. ADUSCO Industries, Mobile, Inst. Gas Tech., Chgo. Bd. dirs. Nat. Ocean Industries Assn., 1983—; trustee, mem. exec. com. Children's Hosp. Ala., Birmingham; trustee Brooke Hill Sch., Birmingham, ARC, Birmingham. Served to lt. (j.g.) USN, 1950-53. Recipient Bennett Douglas Bell Meml. award Vanderbilt Law Sch., 1956. Mem. ABA, Tenn. Bar Assn., Am. Gas Assn., So. Gas Assn., Order of Coif. Episcopalian. Clubs: Mountain Brook, Redstone, Downtown (Birmingham); Boston (New Orleans); Army-Navy (Washington); Linville (N.C.) Golf; University Cottage (Princeton, N.J.). Home: 3121 Brookwood Rd Birmingham AL 35223 Office: PO Box 2563 Birmingham AL 35202

MORGAN, JAMES FRANKLIN, real estate broker; b. Gainesville, Fla., Nov. 23, 1946; s. James W. and Mae (Hudson) M.; m. Mary Nelson, Feb. 26, 1983; 1 son, James Douglas. B.S.B.A., U. Fla., 1968; postgrad. U. Fla., 1971-72, U. N. Fla., 1977-78. Registered real estate broker, mortgage broker, Fla. Asst. and acting dir. Alumni Assn., Alumni Affairs Office, U. Fla., Gainesville, 1971-73; sales exec. Amelia Island Plantation, 1973-74; v.p. Plantec Realty, sales mgr. Sun'N Green Condos, River Bend Resort, 1975-76; pres. Plantec Realty Corp., Jacksonville, 1977—; mng. dir. Bardoon Properties, 1982—. Realtor polit. action chmn., 1983, polit. affairs chmn., 1984; mem. Jacksonville Com. 100; mem. Travel Ambassadors Task Force. Served to lt. U.S. Army, 1969-70. Decorated Army Commendation Medal. Mem. Jacksonville Bd. Realtors, Nat. Assn. Realtors, Fla. Assn. Realtors, Farm and Land Inst., Real Estate Security and Syndication Inst. Democrat. Methodist. Clubs: University, Amelia Island Plantation. Office: 6767 Southpoint Dr S Jacksonville FL 32216

MORGAN, JAMES HERBERT, sales executive; b. St. Paul, Mar. 3, 1932; s. David Jay and Beryl LaVern (Harrington) M. Student Macalester Coll., 1955-57. With 3M Co., 1957—, sales rep. Retail Tape div., Tex., 1957-67, mktg. coordinator, St. Paul, 1967-68, internat. market devel. mgr., St. Paul, 1968-75, sr. account rep. Occupational Health and Safety Products div., Boston, 1975-77, account exec. Occupational Health and Safety Products div., Atlanta, 1977-86; account exec. Filtration Products, Atlanta, 1986—. Served with USAF, 1950-55. Mem. Am. Soc. Safety Engrs., Am. Indsl. Hygiene Assn. Republican. Home: PO Box 430 Alpharetta GA 30201 Office: 1706 Chantilly Dr NE Atlanta GA 30324

MORGAN, JAMES IRA, psychologist, educator; b. Havana, Ill., Oct. 17, 1940; s. Cornelius and Olive Adeline (Horner) M.; m. Dorothy Estella Weaver, July 10, 1965; children—Mary Kathryn Blake, Michael Owen Blaich, James Ira, Jr., Meredith Caprice. B.S., Bradley U., 1962, M.A., 1964; Ed.D., U. Fla., 1967. Lic. psychologist, Fla.; diplomate in profl. psychotherapy; registered profl. hypnotherapist. Counseling psychologist U. Fla. Counseling Ctr., Gainesville, Fla., 1967-80, acting dir., 1980-81, counseling psychologist and research coordinator, 1981—; mem. accrediting bd. Internat. Assn. of Counseling Services, Inc., Arlington, Va., 1982-85; cons. in psychology, 1973—. Author book chpts. Editor Psychol. and Vocat. Center monograph, Series Vol. I-III, 1973-79. Contbr. articles to profl. jours. Vice-pres., mem. steering com. Citizens for Equal Opportunity in Licensing of Psychologists, Gainesville, 1973-78; chmn. evaluation com. Stephen Foster Elem. Sch. citizens adv. com., Gainesville, 1973-75; class agt., co-chairperson Bradley U. Alumni Assn. Ann. Fund, Peoria, Ill., 1972-74. Ill. State Merit scholar, 1958-62. Mem. Am. Psychol. Assn., Am. Assn. Counseling and Devel., Am. Coll. Personnel Assn. (mem. directorate body coms. VI, VII, cert. of appreciation 1980), Am. Soc. Clin. Hypnosis, Fla. Soc. Clin. Hypnosis (pres. elect 1985—, 1st v.p., 1984-85, 2d v.p. 1983-84, mem. various coms.). Democrat. Avocation: private pilot. Home: Rt 1 Box 707 Newberry FL 32669 Office: University Counseling Ctr 311 Little Hall U Fla Gainesville FL 32611

MORGAN, JIMMY DALE, electronic engineer; b. Dallas, July 28, 1944; s. James Middleton and Bennie Frances (Holman) M.; B.S.E.E., U. Tex., 1969; A.S. in Aviation Adminstrn., Mountain View Coll., 1974; M.E., U. Houston, 1978; D.D., S.W. Theol. Sem.; m. Mary Ellen Turner, May 23, 1964; children—La Dawn Babette, Brigitte Monique. Lic. minister Assembly of God. Ch.; lic. FCC. With Tex. Instrument Co., Dallas, 1965-67, LTV Corp., Dallas, 1967-76; elec. project engr. DFW Regional Airport Bd., DFW Airport, Tex., 1976—. Editor Tex. Polit. Jour. Contbr. articles to profl. jours. Precinct chmn. Democratic Party, 1968; Republican precinct chmn.; notary public; del. Rep. State Conv., 1980; mem. Dist. 23 Rep. Club; mem. Dallas County Rep. Assembly, chmn. 23d Senatorial Dist. Conv.; mem. Tex. Rep. Exec. Com., 1984-86, mem. auxs. com., 1985, chmn. coalitions com., 1985; state chmn. Conservative Caucus; Congl. dist. coordinator Freedom Council. Named Mr. Conservative of Dallas County, 1985. Mem. ASME, Nat. Soc. Profl. Engrs., Tex. Soc. Profl. Engrs., Soc. Logistics Engrs., Internat. Platform Assn., Am. Soc. Notaries, Bibl. Archeology Soc., SAR, SCV (chmn. dist. conv. 1984), Mil. Order Stars and Bars. Home: 217 SW 6th St Grand Prairie TX 75051 Office: PO Box 61204 DFW Airport TX 75261

MORGAN, JOE LEE, educator, innkeeper, writer; b. nr. Marshall, N.C., May 14, 1931; s. Frank Woodard and Effie Mae (McDaris) M.; A.B. in History and Polit. Sci., Berea Coll, 1954; postgrad. No. Ill. U., 1955, U. Hawaii, 1956, U. Colo., 1957, 58, U. N.C., 1957-58, Asian Affairs Inst., Duke, summer 1959; M.A. (Title II-B grantee), East Tenn., State U., 1975; J.D., Woodrow Wilson Law Sch., 1978; diploma hotel-motel tng. LaSalle Extension U.; diploma Atlanta Sch. Apt. Mgrs., 1976. Farmer, Marshall, 1945-75; tchr. pub. schs., Mendota, Ill., 1954-55, Charlotte, N.C., 1957-59; tchr.-librarian Madison County (N.C.) Schs., 1959-65; librarian Truett-McConnell Coll., Cleveland, Ga., 1965-67; tchr. history Capt. Riverside Mil. Acad., Gainesville, Ga., 1967-69; librarian Vardell Hall Girls' Prep. Sch., Red Springs, N.C., 1969-72; mgr. Cavalier Motel, Asheville, N.C., 1972-73; librarian Cloverleaf Sch., Cartersville, Ga., 1973-78. Owner, Circle A Motel, Cedartown, Ga., 1976-79, Bakersville (N.C.) Motel and Restaurant, 1979-81; instr., librarian Blanton's Jr. Coll., Asheville, 1981—; mediator Dispute Settlement Ctr., Asheville, 1984—; chmn. meal site com. Sr. Opportunity Ctr., Asheville, 1985—; mem. adv. com. Buncombe County Nursing Home, 1985—. Regional rep. N.C. Sch. Performing Arts; mem. library council, chmn. adult lit. program French Broad Bapt. Assn., 1964-67, clk., 1965-69, contbr. minutes, 1965-69; Sunday Sch. sec., tchr., supt., librarian Peek's Chapel Bapt. Ch., Marshall, 1946-66; mem. Arts and Humanities Commn., Council So. Mountains, 1966-69, edn. commn., 1970-73; mem. Citizens Com. for Free Cuba; bd. policy of Liberty Lobby; mem. Am. Friends Vietnam, Inc.; mem. Civic Arts Council, Inc. Asheville, N.C., 1964-67; active A.R.C. Broadcasting bd. sponsors Radio Free Asia. Precinct chmn., mem. Mecklenburg County Republican Exec. Com., 1958-59; temporary chmn. White County (Ga.) Rep. Conv., 1966; 1st vice chmn. White County Rep. party, 1966-67; del. Ga. congl. and state convs., 1966, 75, N.C., 1958, 62, 64, 70, 71, 73, 74, 75, 79, 81, 82, 83, 85; mem. United Reps. Am.; chmn. Robeson County Young Reps., 1970-71; chmn. community services com. N.C. Fedn. Young Reps., 1971, also mem. exec. bd.; del. Young Reps. Fedn. nat. conv., Phoenix, 1971; chmn. Madison County Rep. Com., 1971-73; mem. 11th Dist. N.C. Rep. exec. com., 1971-73; del So. Rep. Conf., 1973; mem. sec. Madison County Bd. Elections, 1974-77; mem. Toe River Dist. Bd. Health, 1980-82; parliamentarian project rev. com. Western N.C. Health Systems Agy.; nat. adv. council Nat. Right to Work Found. Served with AUS, 1955-57. Recipient certificate appreciation N.C. Rep. party, founding supporter's certificate Radio Free Asia; named Young Am. of Day radio sta. WWNC, Asheville, N.C.; commd. Ky. col. Mem. N.E.A. (del. assembly), N.C. Edn. Assn., N.C. Librarians Assn., Ga. Assn. Educators (del. rep. assembly 1973, del. state conv. 1975), Korean Cultural and Freedom Found., Young Ams. for Freedom, N.C. Literary and Hist. Assn., RCA Victor Soc. Great Music (founding mem.), N.C. Farm Bur., Nat. Congress Parents and Tchrs., Western N.C. Hist. Assn. (chmn. awards com. 1973-76), Roanoke Island Hist. Assn. (chmn. Madison County 1971-72), Madison County Classroom Tchrs. Assn. (sec.-treas. 1959-63), N.C. Soc. Preservation Antiquities, UN Assn. Western N.C., Asheville (N.C.) Community Concerts Assn., Am.'s Future, Inc., Am. Econ. Found., Internat. Platform Assn., Common Cause, United Taxpayers Am. Author: A Librarian's Handbook, 1964; Reflection on the Scopes Evolution Trial, 1965; North Carolina and the Admission of Kansas, 1966; Jeter Conley Pritchard, Senator and Jurist, 1975; weekly column Profiles and Flashbacks, Tri-County News, Spruce Pine, N.C., 1980-82. Contbr. to profl. publs. Home: 100 Morgan Branch (East Fork) Marshall NC 28801

MORGAN, JOHN AUGUSTINE, university executive, consultant; b. Medford, Mass., Feb. 4, 1934; s. John Augustine and Mary Frances (Maley) M.; m. Jean Marie Doyle, Jan. 8, 1959 (div. 1980); 1 child, John Patrick. B.S., Boston U., 1954; M.S., U. Colo., 1963; diploma War Coll., 1967; Ed.D., Nova U., 1980. Commd. 2d lt. U.S. Air Force, 1954, advanced through grades to col., 1976; served various Air Force ops., combat, world-wide, 1954-72; dir. planning Def. Indsl. Ctr., Phila., 1970-73, dir. ops., 1973-74; dir. weapon system U.S. Air Force, Belleville, Ill., 1974-76; v.p. Piedmont Tech. Coll., Greenwood, S.C., 1976-84, exec. v.p., 1984—; pvt. practice as cons., Greenwood, 1976—; doctoral adv. Nova U., Ft. Lauderdale, Fla., 1983—. Author: Retrenchment in the 80s, 1981 (Nat. Practicum of Yr. award 1981). Contbr. articles to profl. jours. Chmn. Piedmont Found. Fund Dr., Greenwood, 1985. Decorated Legion of Merit, Silver Star, Bronze Star; named Educator of Yr. S.C. Tech. Assn., 1981. Mem. Am. Assn. Community Jr. Colls., S.C. Assn. Govt. Purchasing Ofcls., S.C. Assn. State Planning Ofcls., C. of C., Greenwood Running Club, Greenwood Riding Hunt Club, Am. Legion. Lodges: Kiwanis, Elks. Home: Gatewood A-64 Route 5 Greenwood SC 29646 Office: Piedmont Tech Coll Box 1467 Greenwood SC 29648

MORGAN, JOHN ELMORE, JR., economic educator, antitrust consultant; b. Knoxville, Tenn., Sept. 22, 1930; s. John Elmore and Emma LeBerta (Huston) M.; m. Archie Ann Hatchell, Feb. 1, 1962 (div. 1973); children—Merry Gayle, John E., III; m. Margaret Ivonne Whichard, Dec. 31, 1982. B.S. in Physics, William and Mary U., 1951; M.S. in Indsl. Mgmt., Ga. Inst. Tech., 1955; Ph.D. in Econs., U. Ga., 1981. Market research mgr. bleached board div. W.Va. Pulp & Paper Co., Covington, Va., 1959-62; cons. solid waste, mktg., econs., material handling equipment mfrs. agent, 1962-76; chmn. bus. adminstrn. dept. Williamsburg Tech. Coll., Kingstree, S.C., 1976-78; asst. prof. econs. U. of N.C., Wilmington, 1981—; cons. in field. Author: (with others) Economic Opportunity in Mexico, 1979, Test Bank for Dolan's Economics, 1983. Contbr. articles to profl. jours. Chmn. Cerebral Palsy Walkathon, Florence, S.C., 1973-76; bd. dirs. Food Bank Lower Cape Fear, Wilmington, 1982—, Cape Fear Literacy Council, Wilmington, 1983—. Served to capt. U.S. Army, 1951-53. Grantee DuPont, 1982, 84, U. of N.C., 1984. Mem. Am. Econ. Assn., Eastern Econ. Assn., Atlantic Internat. Econ. Assn., Western Econ. Assn., So. Econ. Assn., Southwestern Econ. Assn. Republican. Episcopalian. Avocations: deep sea fishing; tennis. Home: 754 George Trask Dr Wilmington NC 28405 Office: Dept Econs and Fin U of NC 601 S College Rd Wilmington NC 28403-3297

MORGAN, KATHRYN NEWSOM, librarian; b. Fargo, N.D., Mar. 31, 1947; d. Donald Wilson and Luella Mae (McNally) Newsom; m. James Davis Morgan, Jan. 20, 1968; children—Amanda Kathryn, James Wilson. B.A., La. State U., 1977, M.L.S., 1979. Librarian E.A. McIlhenny natural history collection and rare book collection La. State U., Baton Rouge, 1980—. Contbr. articles to library publs. Mem. Baton Rouge Arts and Humanities Council, Friends of Library, Old State Capitol Assocs., Baton Rouge. La. State U. Marguerite B. Hanchey scholar, 1978. Mem. ALA, La. Library Assn. (sec. subject specialists sect. 1983-84), Soc. for History of Natural History, Hunt Inst. Bot. Documentation. Lutheran. Clubs: Baton Rouge Area Library, La. State U. Women's Faculty. Home: 330 Magnolia Wood Ave Baton Rouge LA 70808 Office: Special Collections Hill Meml Library Louisiana State U Baton Rouge LA 70803

MORGAN, MICHAEL BURNETT, geophysicist; b. Birmingham, Ala., Apr. 28, 1950; s. Grover A. Morgan and Ann Carolyn (Cowart) Schleder; m. Robin Loraine Knox, Jan. 7, 1978; 1 child, Eric Christopher. B.S. in Geophysics, U. Utah, 1984, B.S. in Geology, 1984. Flight instr. McClellan Aero, Inc., Sacramento, Calif., 1973-74; air traffic controller Dept. Transp. FAA, Salt Lake City, 1973-81; geophysicist Arco Exploration Co., Plano, Tex., 1984—. Served with USAF, 1969-73. Mem. Soc. Exploration Geophysicists, Am. Assn. Petroleum Geologists, Phi Kappa Phi. Lutheran. Avocations: competition aerobatics, photography. Home: 6028 Frontier Ln Plano TX 75023 Office: Arco Exploration Co PO Box 2819 PPC1045 Dallas TX 75221

MORGAN, PATRICK MICHAEL, construction company executive; b. Buffalo, Sept. 2, 1944; s. John A. and Mary R. (Hoffmann) M.; B.A. in Anthropology and Modern Langs. (N.Y. State Regents scholar 1962), U. Buffalo, 1966; M.S. in Mgmt., U. Ark., 1972; m. Linda Joanne Howard, June 26, 1976; children—Michael John, Thomas Howard. Sr. benefits analyst Evans Products Co., Portland, Oreg., 1977-78; systems coordinator Daniel Constrn. Co., Greenville, S.C., 1979-80, quality assurance mgr., 1984—; mktg. coordinator, 1980-82; logistics mgr. on loan to Saudi Arabian Presidency of Civil Aviation, 1982-84. Served to capt. USAF, 1966-77, now Res. Decorated Air Force Commendation medal with oak leaf cluster. Mem. Am. Mktg. Assn., Assn. Systems Mgmt., Air Force Assn., Internat. Lefthanders, Res. Officers Assn. Republican. Lutheran. Office: Daniel Power Services PO Box 5415 Tyler TX 75712

MORGAN, PAUL EDWARD, management consultant; b. Mountain Lakes, N.J., Jan. 21, 1917; s. James Jay and Adele May (Duhme) M.; B.S., Harvard U., 1939; diploma exec. program, U. So. Calif., 1968; m. Nancy Louise Hill, Apr. 2, 1941; 1 son, James J. Program mgr. OWI, Washington, 1942-43; account exec. Cunningham & Walsh, advt., N.Y.C., 1946-48; partner Stephen, Fitzgerald & Co., N.Y.C., 1948-56; with Exxon Corp., 1957-80, Sr. public affairs adviser 1979-80; pres. Paul Morgan Assos., Ft. Lauderdale, Fla., 1980—. Chmn. World Press Inst., St. Paul, 1975-83; chmn. public relations com. Nat. Fgn. Trade Council, 1975-82; bd. dirs. N.Y. chpt. Nat. Council Alcoholism, 1977-82. Served with USAAF, 1943-46, USAF, 1949-51. Mem. Center Inter-Am. Relations (hon.), Public Relations Soc. Am., Inter-Am. Press Assn. Republican. Episcopalian. Clubs: Overseas Press, Harvard (N.Y.C.); Nat. Press (Washington); Sleepy Hollow Country, Coral Ridge Country. Author articles in field. Home: 3430 Galt Ocean Dr Fort Lauderdale FL 33308 Office: 3213 N Ocean Blvd Fort Lauderdale FL 33308

MORGAN, RAYMOND VICTOR, JR., university administrator, mathematics educator; b. Brownwood, Tex., May 10, 1942; s. Raymond Victor and Lovey Lucille (Tate) M.; m. Mary Jane Folks, Aug. 13, 1967; children—Jason Wesley, Jeremy Victor. B.A., Howard Payne U., 1965; M.A., Vanderbilt U., 1966; Ph.D., U. Mo., 1969. Asst. prof. So. Meth. U., Dallas, 1969-75; assoc. prof. Sul Ross State U., Alpine, Tex., 1975-82, math. dept. chmn., 1976-85, prof., 1982—, dean of scis., 1979-86, exec. asst. pres., 1985—. Author textbook: Agricultural Mathematics, 1978; author articles. Founder, regional commr. Alpine Soccer League, 1984; v.p., coach Alpine Baseball League, 1983; pres. Alpine PTA, 1982-83; founder, pres. So. Meth. U. Faculty Club, 1973-75. NSF grantee, 1979. Mem. Am. Math. Soc., Nat. Council Tchrs. of Math., Tex. Assn. Coll. Tchrs. (chpt. v.p. 1978-79), Math. Assn. Am. (chmn. Tex. sect. 1985—). Republican. Mem. Ch. of Christ. Clubs: Lions (pres. 1979-80, Lion of Yr. 1980, 83), Alpine Country. Avocations: motorcycling; golf; shooting. Home: PO Box 1341 Alpine TX 79831 Office: Sul Ross State U Box C-20 Alpine TX 79832

MORGAN, RICHARD PAUL, marketing executive; b. Marlin, Tex., July 12, 1941; s. Samuel Travis and Elsie Marie (Huseby) M.; m. Doris Irene Talbert, Aug. 21, 1960; children—Deborah Irene, Valerie Renee. A.A. in Engring., Fullerton Coll. (Calif.), 1962; B.S. in Bus. Adminstrn. with honors, Calif. State Poly. U.-Pomona, 1963. Comml. mktg. rep. West Coast div. Mobil Oil Corp., 1963-67, div. aviation rep., 1967-69, spl. rep. gen. aviation N.Y. hdqrs., 1969-71, comml. dist. mgr. New England div., 1971-74; dir. mktg. Long Mile Rubber Co., Dallas, 1974-76, v.p. mktg., 1976—. Mem. Am. Retreaders Assn., Nat. Tire Dealers and Retreaders Assn., Am. Chem. Soc. (mem. Energy Rubber Group), Tire Retread Info. Bur. (dir.). Republican. Methodist. Lodge: Masons. Home: 16814 Park Hill Dr Dallas TX 75248 Office: 5550 LBJ Freeway Suite 200 Dallas TX 75240

MORGAN, ROBERT GEORGE, accounting educator, researcher; b. Sanford, Maine, Feb. 20, 1941; s. George Andrew and Katherine (Gray) M.; m. Jacqueline Buhl, Jan. 2, 1965; children—Robert George, Katherine Neva. B.A., Piedmont Coll., Demorest, Ga., 1969; M.Acctg., U. Ga., 1971, Ph.D., 1974. C.P.A., N.C. Asst. prof. acctg. U. Wyo., Laramie, 1974-76, Drexel U., Phila., 1976-80; assoc. prof. acctg. U. N.C.-Greensboro, 1980-83; prof. acctg. Loyola Coll., Balt., 1983-85; chmn. dept. acctg. East Tenn. State U., Johnson City, 1985—. Editor Jour. The Mgmt. Rev., 1983-85. Contbr. articles to profl. jours. Treas., Running Brook PTA, Columbia, Md., 1984-85. Mem. Am. Inst. C.P.A.s, Nat. Assn. Accts., Am. Acctg. Assn., Acad. Acctg. Historians, Beta Gamma Sigma, Beta Alpha Psi. Methodist. Avocation: golf. Home: 1 Townview Dr Johnson City TN 37601 Office: E Tenn State Univ Dept Acct PO Box 23800-A Johnson City TN 37614

MORGAN, ROBERT JAMES, political science educator; b. Port Jervis, N.Y., July 25, 1918; s. Gideon Liege and Florence Zita (Dailey) M.; m. Naomie Pegues, Aug. 4, 1943; children—Sara Jacquelyn Morgan Padfield, Charles Richard. B.S., Iowa State Coll., 1940; Ph.D., U. Va., 1951. Asst. prof. U. Nebr., Lincoln, 1951-56, assoc. prof., 1956-57; instr. U. Va., Charlottesville, 1948-51, assoc. prof., 1957-64, prof. govt. and fgn. affairs, 1964—. Served to lt. col. AUS, 1940-46; ETO. U. Va. Sesquicentennial fellow, 1972, 80. Mem. So. Polit. Sci. Assn., Am. Polit. Sci. Assn., Raven Soc. of U. Va., Phi Beta Kappa. Club: Colonnade (Charlottesville). Author: A Whig Embattled, 1954, 2d edit., 1974; Governing Soil Conservation, 1966. Contbr. articles on polit. sci. to profl. jours. Home: 1811 Meadowbrook Heights Rd Charlottesville VA 22901 Office: 232 Cabell Hall U Va Charlottesville VA 22903

MORGAN, WALTER HUGH, physician; b. Augusta, Ga., Nov. 15, 1951; s. Claude Calhoun and Mary Elizabeth (Smith) M.; m. Maryedith Clarkson Butler. Student U. S.C., 1970-73; M.D., Med. U. S.C., 1977. Diplomate Am. Acad. Family Practice, Nat. Bd. Med. Examiners. Intern Greenville (S.C.) Hosp. System, 1977-78, resident, 1977-80, chief resident, 1980; staff physician Edgefield (S.C.) Med. Clinic, 1977-80; emergency room physician Allen Bennett Meml. Hosp., Greer, S.C., 1977-79, Cannon Meml. Hosp., Pickens, S.C., 1978-80; physician, Trenton (S.C.) Family Practice Ctr., 1980—; asst. instr. Greenwood Family Practice Residency Program, 1980-81; pres. med. staff Edgefield County Hosp.; instr. family medicine U. S.C. and U. S.C. Med. Sch., 1980—. Bd. dirs. Beckman Mental Health Ctr., Edgefield Vocat. Health Careers Ctr., Am. Cancer Soc.; Sunday sch. tchr., deacon Edgefield 1st Bapt. Ch. Mem. Am. Acad. Family Practice (outstanding resident award 1980), S.C. Med. Soc., Ridge Med. Soc., Phi Beta Kappa, Phi Eta Sigma, Alpha Epsilon Delta. Baptist. Clubs: Tradewinds Yacht, Pine Ridge Country (Edgefield). Home: 214 Highland Ave Edgefield SC 29824 Office: 219 Railroad Ave Trenton SC 29847

MORGAN, WILLIAM ANDREW, oil company geologist; b. Madison, Wis., Jan. 24, 1953; s. James Robert and Evonne Marie (Kellerman) M. B.S., U. Wis., 1975, M.S., 1977. Assoc. geologist Conoco, Inc., Casper, Wyo., 1977-78, geologist, Oklahoma City, 1978-79, petroleum geologist, 1980-81, project supr., 1981-83, sr. research scientist, Ponca City, Okla., 1983-85, research assoc., 1985—. Contbr. articles to profl. jours. Mem. Am. Assn. Petroleum Geologists, Soc. Econ. Paleontologists and Mineralogists (v.p. mid-continent sect. 1984-85), Oklahoma City Geol. Soc. (v.p.), Internat. Assn. Sedimentologists. Avocations: Scuba diving; travel; oenology. Home: PO Box 20067 Oklahoma City OK 73156 Office: Conoco Inc 1000 S Pine St Ponca City OK 74603

MORGAN, WILLIAM JAMES, psychologist; b. Rochester, N.Y., Apr. 30, 1910; A.B., U. Rochester, 1933; Ph.D., Yale U., 1937; m. Antonia Mary Farquharson Bell, Nov. 2, 1944; children—William James, Jean Elizabeth, Robert Macnair. Chief clinician Vineland (N.J.) Tng. Sch., 1936-38; psychologist Bd. Edn. Rochester, 1939-41; dir. Psychol. Test Bur., Rochester, 1941-42; dep. chief tng., chief psychol. assessment CIA, 1947-52; mem. Psychol. Strategy Bd., White House, 1952-53; pres. Aptitude Assos., Merrifield, Va., 1953—; dir. Strategic Power Analysis Corp.; mem. Army Research Com.; cons. Dept. Justice, Dept. Def., other agys.; mem. Va. Bd. Cert. Clin. Psychologists. Trustee, Va. Psychol. Found. Served from pvt. to lt. col. AUS, 1942-47; OSS, ETO. Diplomate in clin. psychology Am. Bd. Examiners Profl. Psychology. Mem. Va. Psychol. Assn. (pres. 1957-58), Sigma Xi. Author: Spies and Saboteurs (Gollancs-London), 1955; The O.S.S. and I, 1957; numerous articles and tests. Home: 2816 Gallows Rd Vienna VA 22180

MORGANELLI, DANIEL, exploration geologist; b. Bklyn., July 26, 1950; s. Donato Eugene and Anne Carmela (Palmieri) M.; m. Catherine Lynn Brunner, May 18, 1975; children—Christopher David, Casey Ryan. B.A. in Earth and Space Scis., SUNY-Stony Brook, 1972; M.S. in Geology, Okla. State U., 1975. Geologist, Sun Oil Co., Dallas, 1976-82; dist. geologist AmQuest Corp., Dallas, 1982-83; mgr. exploration upper Tex. coast Moseley Petroleum Corp., Dallas, 1984—; cons. in field. Mem. Am. Assn. Petroleum Geologists, Dallas Geol. Soc., Am. Inst. Profl. Geologists. Republican. Methodist. Avocations: bridge, fishing, photography, guitar. Home: 3234 Potomac Dr Garland TX 75042 Office: Moseley Petroleum Corp Suite 406E 13601 Preston Rd Dallas TX 75040

MORGRET, ANDREW JACOB, educational administrator, accountant; b. Napoleon, Ohio, Aug. 1, 1941; s. Frank Clay and Ruth Shepard (Love) M.; m. Jane Gay Hoskins, Nov. 22, 1967; children—Ann Marie, Mimi Gay, John Andrew. B.S. in Edn., Memphis State U., 1968, M.Ed., 1971. Quality control mgr. Header Products Inc., Romulus, Mich., 1968-70; grad. research asst. Memphis State U., 1970-71, asst. dir., 1975-78, assoc. dean, 1978—; guidance counselor West Memphis Pub. Schs., Ark., 1971-75; com. mem. ESEA Needs Assessment, West Memphis, 1974. Contbr. articles to profl. jours. Pres. Down's Parents Memphis, 1974-75, 1979-81, treas., 1975-78, 81-82. Served with USMC, 1961-63, Japan. Recipient Outstanding Service award Down's Parents Memphis, 1979. Memphis State U. grant 1981. Mem. Am. Assn. Counseling and Devel., Am. Coll. Personnel Assn., Nat. Assn. Accts., Phi Delta Kappa, Kappa Delta Pi. Episcopalian. Avocation: timpanist. Home: 4301 Powell Ave Memphis TN 38122 Office: Memphis State U Memphis TN 38152

MORIARTY, HERBERT BERNARD, JR., lawyer; b. Memphis, June 5, 1929; s. Herbert Bernard and Kathleen (Prindaville) M.; 6 children. B.A., Vanderbilt, U., 1950, J.D., 1952. Bar: Tenn. 1952, U.S. Supreme Ct. 1956, U.S. Ct. Mil. Appeals 1956. Magistrate Shelby County Quar. Ct., 1960-66; mem. firm Moriarty & Smith, Memphis; mem. Tenn. State Legislature, 1959-60, Democratic exec. com., 1959-62; lectr. ABA, Am. Law Inst., 1980. Pres., Muscular Dystrophy Assn., 1957-62; dir. Goodwill Industries, 1960-66; life bd. dirs. NCCJ, Memphis, 1963—. Served to capt. JAGC USAF, 1952-54. Recipient Disting. Service award, U.S. Jaycees, Memphis, 1963, Disting. Merit Citation, NCCJ, 1968. Mem. ABA, Tenn. Bar Assn., Shelby County Bar Assn., Memphis Bar Assn., Young Lawyers Assn. Memphis (v.p. 1957-58), Am. Legion (adj. Memphis Post 1 1959), Sigma Chi, Delta Theta Phi. Democrat. Roman Catholic. Clubs: University, Racquet (Memphis). Home: 222 Meadowgrove Ln Memphis TN 38119 Office: Moriarty & Smith 14210 White Station Tower Memphis TN 38157

MORISSEAU, DOLORES SCHANNÉ, psychologist, government agency official; b. N.Y.C., Dec. 1, 1936; d. Lawrence Charles and Anne Lucy (Jelincic) Schanné; B.A. summa cum laude, George Mason U., 1978, M.A. in Psychology, 1980; M. Kenneth Clay Morisseau, May 3, 1958; children—Anne Lavita, Kenneth Clay. Stewardship editor Luth. Woman's Quarterly, St. Louis, 1969-75; mng. editor patient newsletter Georgetown U. Center for Continuing Health Edn., Washington, 1975, faculty moderator, 1974-75; instr. activated patient skills Nat. Public Broadcasting, 1975; fed. intern, personnel psychologist, U.S. Office Personnel Mgmt., Washington, 1979; lectr. psychology No. Va. Community Coll., Loudoun, 1981—; tng. and assessment specialist U.S. Nuclear Regulatory Commn., Washington, 1981—. Mem. Fairfax (Va.) Hosp., Aux., 1969-78, coordinator library service for patients, publicity dir., 1974-76. Mem. Am. Psychol. Assn., Human Factors Soc., AAUW, Alpha Chi, Psi Chi. Contbr. articles in field to profl. jours. Home: 11800 Breton Ct 32B Reston VA 22091

MORISSETTE, DIANE MACHON, bank official; b. Providence, Feb. 12, 1941; d. Charles Stephen and Helen (Wilks) M.; m. William Lee Morissette, Feb. 10, 1961; children—William Scott, Sheree Diane, Alan Glenn, Danielle Cynthia. Student Brevard Community Coll., 1962—, U. Gainesville, 1980-82; Banking Cert., U. Okla., 1981, Am. Inst. Banking, 1970. Asst. cashier Flagship Bank Melbourne (Fla.), 1969-77; asst. v.p., v.p. Atlantic Nat. Bank of Fla., Melbourne, 1977-84; asst. ops. officer Am. Bank of Merritt Island, Melbourne, 1984—. Trustee Brevard County Dist. Mental Health. Mem. Nat. Assn. Banking Women Republican. Methodist (trustee). Club: Pilot. Home: 356 Ash St West Melbourne FL 32901 Office: 440 S Babcock St Melbourne FL 32901

MORK, KNUT ANTON, economist, management educator; b. Meldal, Norway, May 24, 1946; came to U.S., 1974; s. Olav and Borghild (Angelskar) M.; m. Laila Tregde, July 18, 1970; children—Erling, Knut. B.A. in Bus. Adminstrn., Norwegian Sch. Econs. and Bus. Adminstrn., Bergen, 1972, M.A. in Econs., 1974; Ph.D. in Econs., MIT, 1977. Research assoc. Energy Lab. MIT, Cambridge, 1977-81; vis. asst. prof. U. Ariz., Tucson, 1981-83; assoc. prof. Owen Grad. Sch. Mgmt. Vanderbilt U., Nashville, 1983—. Author, editor: Energy Prices, Inflation, and Economic Activity, 1981; contbr. articles to profl. jours. Served with Norwegian Army, 1968-69. NSF grantee, 1979. Mem. Am. Econ. Assn., Internat. Assn. Energy Economists. Lutheran. Office: Owen Grad Sch Mgmt Vanderbilt U Nashville TN 37203

MORKRID, LORETTA VIRGINIA, nurse, home care company executive; b. Spurgeon, Mo., Sept. 3, 1933; d. Luther Adolphis Harris and Alta Irene (Coon) Harris Lett; m. Oct. 22, 1960 (div. June 1982); 1 dau., Michelle Lea. R.N. diploma St. John's Hosp., Joplin, Mo., 1954; student St. Rose Coll., Gt. Bend, Kans., 1955-58, U. Ark., 1972-78. R.N., Mo. Staff nurse St. John's Hosp., Joplin, 1954-55, St. Rose Hosp., Gt. Bend, 1955; joined Sisters of St. Dominic, Roman Catholic Ch., 1955-58; staff nurse various hosps., 1958-61, VA hosps., Livermore, Calif., 1962-68, Omaha, 1971, Fayetteville, Ark., 1971-81; nursing care coordinator Cura Services Inc., Fayetteville, 1982—; 1st v.p. DCCW, Little Rock, 1981—; hospice coordinator N.W. Hospice Orgn., Fayetteville, 1982—. Pres. Greenland Sch. PTA, Greenland, Ark., 1979. Democrat. Clubs: Extension (Greenland); Altar Rosary Soc. (v.p. 1975) Fayetteville. Home: PO Box 87 4041 Wedington Fayetteville AR 72702 Office: Cura Services Inc 129 W Lafayette Fayetteville AR 72701

MORLAND, JESSIE PARRISH, educator; b. Parrish, Fla., Dec. 3, 1924; d. Jonah and May (Lowry) Parrish; B.A., Fla. Southern Coll., 1947; m. Richard B. Morland, Mar. 17, 1949; 1 dau., Laura. Dir. publicity Fla. Southern Coll., 1948-50; editor Dun's Bulletin, Dun and Bradstreet, N.Y.C., 1950-52; feature writer Deland Sun News, Daytona Beach (Fla.) News Jour., 1952-65; tchr. English, journalism Deland (Fla.) Jr. High Sch., 1967-83, tchr. gifted students, 1983—. Bd. dirs. Deland Mus., 1957-62, Democratic Women's Club, 1952-65; pres. DeLand Cultural Com., 1980-82. Mem. AAUW (dir. 1955-62), Nat. League Am. Pen Women, Alpha Delta Pi. Democrat. Methodist. Club: DeLand Country. Home: 524 McDonald Ave N Deland FL 32724 Office: Aquarius Ave Deland FL 32724

MORLAND, RICHARD BOYD, educator; b. Huntsville, Ala., June 27, 1919; s. Howard Cannon and Ethel May (Cowan) M.; A.B., Birmingham-So. Coll., 1940; M.Ed., Springfield Coll., 1947; Ph.D. (So. Fellowships Fund fellow 1957-58), N.Y. U. 1958; m. Jessie May Parrish, Mar. 17, 1949; 1 dau., Laura. Phys. dir. YMCA, Frankfort, Ky., 1940-41; dir. athletics, head basketball coach Fla. So. Coll., 1947-50; lectr. in edn., N.Y. U., 1950-51; chmn. dept. phy. edn., Stetson U., Deland, Fla., 1952-60, head basketball coach, 1952-57, asso. prof., 1956-63, prof., 1963—, J. Ollie Edmunds prof., 1982—, chmn. grad. council, 1962-69, chmn. dept. edn., 1969-75. Served to lt. USNR, 1941-45. Decorated 11 battle stars, USS Lexington. Named to Stetson U. Sports Hall of Fame; recipient McEniry award for Excellence in teaching, 1983. Mem. Philosophy of Edn. Soc. (pres. region 1963-64), Fla. Council Deans and Dirs. Tchr. Edn. (pres. 1974-75), Am. Ednl. Research Assn., Am. Edn. Studies Assn., Soc. Profs. Edn., Univ. Profs. for Acad. Order, Omicron Delta Kappa, Phi Alpha Theta, Kappa Delta Pi, Phi Delta Kappa (pres. region 1977-78, editorial bd. Phi Delta Kappan 1978-83), Kappa Alpha. Democrat. Methodist. Club: DeLand Country. Contbr. articles to profl. jours. Home: 524 N McDonald St DeLand FL 32724

MORONEY, ROBERT EMMET, retired stock and bond broker, investment banker, securities appraiser; b. Dallas, Feb. 15, 1903; s. William Joseph and Lelia (Rodgers) M.; student U. Dallas, Georgetown U., 1920-21; A.B., U. Wis., 1923; m. Jessie Dew Robinson Coolidge, Mar. 31, 1940; children—Linda, June. With Texpolite, Bldg. & Loan Assn., Dallas, Anchor Savings Bank, Madison, Wis., 1923-25; with Guaranty Co. of N.Y., 1925-27; with Moroney, Beissner & Co. and predecessors, Houston, 1927-62, pres., 1930-62; bus. mgr. St. John The Divine Episcopal Ch., 1963-64; v.p. Capital Nat. Bank, Houston, 1965-67; ind. fin. cons., 1966-68; salesman Moroney, Beissner & Co., Inc., Houston, 1968-74; v.p. Rotan Mosle Inc., Houston, 1974—. Bd. dirs. Houston Found. for Ballet, Houston Grand Opera Assn., Assn. Community TV, Soc. for Performing Arts; dir. Diocesan Devel. Bd., Ch. Found. Rice U., 1963-65; bd. dirs. Sheltering Arms, Intercontinental Airport Interfaith Chapel, ARC, Christian Community Service Ctr., Houston Metro. Meals-on-Wheels (disting. driver award, 1984, sr. award, 1985); trustee Retina Research Found., Houston. Fellow Fin. Analysts Fedn.; mem. Houston Soc. Fin. Analysts, Nat. Security Traders Assn., Investment Bankers of Am. Tex. group, Investment Bankers Assn. Am., Houston Stock and Bond Club. Episcopalian. Served USNR, 1943-45. Clubs: Houston, River Oaks Country. Home: 3730 Overbrook Ln Houston TX 77027

MORR, CHARLES VERNON, food science educator; b. Ashland, Ohio, Oct. 7, 1927; s. Perry Allen and Helen Lucile (Hoag) M.; m. Dorothy Dela Bowers, Sept. 8, 1951; children—Douglas Charles, Debra Jean. B.S., Ohio State U., 1952, M.S., 1955, Ph.D., 1959. Asst. prof. Ohio State U., Columbus, 1961-64; prof. U. Minn., St. Paul, 1964-73; research dir. Ralston Purina Co., 1973-76; prof., chmn. dept. Tex. Tech U., Lubbock, 1976-78; Stender prof. food sci. Clemson U., S.C., 1978—. Contbr. chpts. to books, articles to profl. jours. Served with USN, 1945-47. Recipient Dairy Research Found. award Am. Dairy Sci. Assn., 1973. Fellow Inst. Food Technologists; mem. Am. Dairy Sci. Assn. (bd. dirs. 1981-84), Am. Chem. Soc. (coordinator agr. food chemistry div. S.E. sect. 1984—), Am. Oil Chemists Soc. Republican. Lutheran. Home: 390 Ridgecrest Clemson SC 29631 Office: Dept Food Sci Clemson U Clemson SC 29631

MORRAN, DONALD WAYNE, industrial engineer; b. Dallas, Nov. 24, 1946; s. Louis Thomas and Lois (Weber) M.; m. Douglass Ann Strouhal, June 8, 1968; 1 child, Daryn Blaine. B.S., U. Tex., 1970. Registered profl. engr., Tex. Field engr. Employers Ins. Co., Abilene, Tex., 1970-80; staff engr. Abco Industries Inc., Abilene, 1980-82, chief engr., 1982—. Pres. Big Country Safety Assn., Abilene, 1979. Mem. Am. Soc. Safety Engrs., Tex. Soc. Profl. Engrs. (pres. 1980-81, Outstanding Service award 1981), Aircraft Owners and Pilots Assn., S.W. Ofcls. Assn. (bd. dirs. 1978-80). Avocations: football officiating; model railroading. Home: 2902 Nonesuch Rd Abilene TX 79606 Office: Abco Industries Inc 2675 E Hwy 80 Abilene TX 79601

MORRELL, GENE PAUL, pipeline company executive; b. Ardmore, Okla., Oct. 4, 1932; s. Paul T. and Etta L. (Weaver) M.; B.S. in Geology, U. Okla., 1954, LL.B., 1962; m. Jan A. Foster, Aug. 20, 1954; children—Jeffrey T., Kelly Ann, Rob Redman. Geologist, Gilmer Oil Co., Ardmore, Okla., 1957-59, atty.-geologist, 1962-63; admitted to Okla. bar, 1962, D.C. bar, 1973; practiced law, Ardmore, 1963-69; ofcl. Dept. Interior, Washington, 1969-72; v.p. Lone Star Gas Co., Washington, 1972-76; sr. v.p. United Energy Resources, Inc., Houston, 1976—; chmn. bd. UER Internat. Ltd., 1978—, PetroUnited Inc., 1981—. City commr. Ardmore, 1967-69, vice-mayor, 1968. Mem. Am. Okla., D.C., bar assns., Am. Assn. Petroleum Geologists, Am. Soc. Internat. Law, Council Fgn. Relations, European Mgmt. Forum. Phi Alpha Delta, Sigma Alpha Epsilon. Episcopalian. Club: City Tavern (Washington). Contbr. articles to profl. jours. Office: 1 Texas Commerce Tower PO Box 1478 Houston TX 77001

MORRIS, AARON MYLES, retail/wholesale executive; b. Miami, Oct. 15, 1952; s. Abram Melvin and Rita (Platt) M.; student U. Miami, 1970-73; m. Barbara Swan, Mar. 20, 1977 (div. Dec. 1985); children—Lonny, Lisa. Exec. v.p. Rex Art Co., Coral Gables, 1970—, Myles Unlimited, Coral Gables, 1970—, DMR Internat., Miami, 1981—, Blackmoor Co., 1977—, Upper Gallery, Coral Gables, 1977—; ptnr. Morris Investment Partnership, 1975—, North Miami Beach Framing, Inc., 1983. Vice pres. Film Soc. Miami, pres. 1986—; bd. dirs. Miami Film Festival, 1983—, mem. exec. com., exec. v.p., 1984; bd. dirs. Players Theatre, 1971-77, 77-79; bd. dirs., mem. steering com. Miami Book Fair Internat., 1984—. Mem. Am. Inst. Graphic Arts, Nat. Art Material Trade Assn., Profl. Picture Framers Assn., Fine Arts Trade Guild London, Am. Booksellers Assn. Jewish. Author: Random Feelings, 1974. Office: 2263 SW 37th Ave Miami FL 33145

MORRIS, ALPHA LOCKHART, sociology educator, researcher; b. Taylor, Miss., Mar. 17, 1932; d. Odeal William and Ruby (Smith) Lockhart; m. Jesse Anderson Morris Sr., Dec. 25, 1952 (dec. 1980); children—Jesse Anderson Jr., Patricia Alpha. B.S., Alcorn State U., 1952; M.A., Mich. State U., 1955; Ph.D., Miss. State U., 1978. Cert. secondary tchr., Miss. Tchr. home econs. Union County Schs., New Albany, Miss., 1952-53, Clairborne County, Port Gibson, Miss., 1964-70; instr. social sci. Alcorn State U., Lorman, Miss., 1970-78, asst. prof. sociology, 1978—; dir. Lilly Endowment Project, Lorman, 1984—; cons. Miss. Council on Aging, McComb, 1984—; guest speaker Claiborne County Schs., Port Gibson, 1981—. Contbr. articles to profl. jours. Mem. exec. com. Miss. Cultural Crossroads, Port Gibson, 1980—, Clairborne County Democratic Party, Port Gibson, 1984—. Recipient People to People Internat. award U. Neb., 1982; Fulbright-Hays scholar, 1984. Mem. Am. Sociol. Assn., Mid-South Sociol. Assn. (nominations com. 1984), Claiborne County Ushers Assn.; Sociologists for Women in Soc. (area reporter 1981), So. Sociol. Soc. (minorities com. 1983—), Phi Delta Kappa, Delta Sigma Theta (pres. 1981—), Alpha Kappa Delta. Baptist. Home: Route 2 Box 30 Lorman MS 39096

MORRIS, BENJAMIN HUME, lawyer; b. Louisville, Sept. 25, 1917; s. Benjamin and Mary (Hume) M.; m. Lacy Abell, July 7, 1942 (div.); children—Benjamin Hume II, Lacy Wayne Morris Matzner; m. 2d, Mary Frances Fowler Gatlin, Nov. 9, 1968; J.D., U. Louisville, 1941. Bar: Ky. 1940. Assoc. Doolan, Helm, Stites & Wood, Louisville, 1941-50; atty. Brown-Forman Distillers Corp., Louisville, 1950-56, resident counsel, 1956-74, v.p., 1964-81, gen. counsel, 1974-81, corporate sec., 1981, retired, 1981; dir. and pres. Can. Mist Distillers, Ltd., Collingwood, Ont., 1971-81; trustee and sec. W.L. Lyons Brown Found., Louisville, 1964—. Chmn. Jefferson County Social Service adv. com., 1961-64; dir. Ky. C. of C., 1969-71; dir. Better Bus. Bur. Louisville, 1969-72; trustee City of Riverwood, Ky., 1977-81; trustee and sec. Ky. Alcoholism Council, 1976—; active Sons of Am. Revolution, pres. Louisville Thruston chpt., 1965-66, pres. Ky. soc., 1978, v.p. gen. nat. soc., 1981, chancellor gen., 1982-83, sec. gen., 1984, pres. gen., 1985; active Soc. Colonial Wars, Soc. War of 1812, Sons and Daus. Pilgrims. Served to col. USAFR, 1941-77. Decorated Air medal and Oak Leaf Cluster. Recipient Disting. Alumni award U. Louisville, 1981; Patriot medal Ky. Soc. SAR, 1985; 1979, Minuteman award Nat. Soc. SAR., 1984. Mem. Ky. Bar Assn., Louisville Bar Assn., Bar Supreme Ct. U.S., Ky. Distillers Assn. (dir. 1966-81, chmn. 1969), Distilled Spirits Inst. (pres. 1969, chmn. 1970, dir. 1966-72), Distilled Spirits Council U.S. (dir. 1973-81), pres. and chmn. 1973, chmn. 1974, elected chmn. emeritus 1982, Assn. Can. Distillers (dir. 1971-81). Republican. Presbyterian (elder). Clubs: Louisville Boat, Midland Trail Golf, Filson (Louisville); Army and Navy (Washington). Home: 2005 High Ridge Rd Louisville KY 40207 Office: 850 Dixie Hwy Louisville KY 40210

MORRIS, CAROL ANN, nursing educator; b. Quapaw, Okla., July 31, 1935; d. Grover Cleveland and Sylvia Veota (McBee) Bingham; m. Ernest Guye Morris, Nov. 21, 1955; children—Kimberly Diane Jacobs, Timothy Duane Morris. Diploma Nursing, St. John's Sch., Joplin, Mo., 1956; B.S. Nursing, Pittsburg State U., Kans., 1973, M.S., 1975; M.Nursing, U. Kans., 1982; Ed.D., Okla. State U., 1985. Head nurse Bapt. Regional Health Ctr., Miami, Okla., 1956-67; nursing instr. Northeastern Okla. A&M Coll., Miami, 1967-82, dir. dept. nursing, 1983—. Contbr. articles to profl. publs. Mem. Am. Nurses Assn., Okla. Tech. Soc., Midwest Nursing Research Soc., N.Am. Nursing Diagnosis Assn., DAR (vice regent local chpt.). Republican. Mem. Disciple of Christ Ch. Avocations: reading; needlework.

MORRIS, EMMA WARD, marketing executive; b. Lafayette, Ind., Sept. 6, 1952; d. Curtis Howard and Charlotte Berkley (Reed) Ward; m. John Harry Morris, Jr., Sept. 12, 1975; B.A. cum laude, Emory U., 1974; M.B.A., U. S.C. Columbia, 1976. Tchr. Ashley Hall Sch., Charleston, S.C., 1975-76; systems engr. IBM, Columbia and Charleston, 1976-78, mktg. rep., Charleston, 1979-81; v.p. mktg. Cambar Bus. Systems, Inc., Charleston, 1981-83; sr. mgr. Ernst & Whinney Cons., Atlanta, 1983-85; dir. industry mktg. Mgmt. Sci Am., Inc., Atlanta, 1985—; mem. mgmt. info. services adv. bd. U. Ga., 1983, mem. vocat. edn. adv. bd. Charleston County, S.C., 1981-83. Leader Congaree council Girl Scouts U.S.A., 1975-81. Mem. Assn. Systems Mgrs., Assn. Computer Users of Atlanta, Assn. Data Processing Service Orgns., Bus. and Profl. Women (pres. 1982-83), Atlanta C. of C., Phi Sigma Iota. Republican. Baptist (Sunday sch. tchr.). Home: 3791 Ridge Rd Atlanta GA 30080 Office: 3445 Peachtree Rd NE Atlanta GA 30326

MORRIS, EVA MAY, dance educator; b. Laurinburg, N.C., Feb. 17, 1920; d. Cecil Farwell and Eva (Gilbert) Morris; m. Cameron Gregory, Jan. 3, 1942; 1 child, Cam G. Williams. Grad. high sch., Norfolk, Va. Tchr. Mabel Swift Dance Sch., Norfolk, 1936-37; owner, tchr. Eva May Morris Dance Sch., Norfolk, 1938—. Producer shows and benefits for armed services, many civic and charitable causes. Recipient citations Norfolk chpt. DAV, 1949, Norfolk unit Am. Legion Aux., 1970. Mem. Chgo. Nat. Assn. Dance Masters, Theta Kappa Sigma. Methodist. Avocations: reading, photography. Home: 1037 S Lexan Crescent Norfolk VA 23508 Office: Eva May Morris Sch of Dancing 1408 Lafayette Blvd Norfolk VA 23509

MORRIS, FRANCES JEANETTE, college dean; b. Cary, Miss., Nov. 28, 1943; s. Sidney Brevard and Mary Elizabeth (Rodman) M. B.S. in Biology, U. Ala., 1965; M.S. in Health Care Edn., Central Mich. U., 1977; M.P.A. in Pub. Adminstrn., U. Ky., 1980, Ph.D., 1985. Med. technologist Father Fox Hosp., Tai Nan, Taiwan, Republic China, 1969-71, Harlan ARH Regional Hosp., Ky., 1971-72; assoc. prof. U. Ky. Southeastern Community Coll., Cumberland, 1972-78; higher edn. specialist Ky. Council Higher Edn., Frankfort, 1979-82; acad. dean Louisville Coll., 1983—; cons. in field. Contbr. articles to profl. jours. Chmn., Harlan County Diabetics Soc. Program, 1973-78, All-Ky. City Com., 1976; bd. dirs. ARC, Louisville, 1985—. Named Outstanding Young Women of Am., 1972. Mem. Am. Soc. Med. Tech., Am. Edn. Research Assn., Am. Soc. Allied Health Professions, Am. Assn. Higher Edn., Alpha Mu Tau, Pi Alpha Alpha, Omicron Sigma. Republican. Roman Catholic. Avocations: reading; fishing; camping. Home: 2017 Player Pl New Albany IN 47150 Office: Louisville Coll 1512 Crums Ln Louisville KY 40216

MORRIS, GORDON EARL, sheriff; b. Fort Davis, Tex., May 9, 1947; s. Ewing Boyd and Lillian (Clark) Thorpe; m. Cynthia Kay Evartt, May 14, 1970; children—Sue Ann, Dexter Duane. Student Howard County Coll., 1966-68, Sul Ross U., 1965-66, Tex. A&M U., 1981. Cert. advanced instr. law enforcement. Chief dep. sheriff Lampasas County, Tex., 1974-79, sheriff, 1980—; judge Lampasas County Justice Ct., 1978-80. Chmn. The Chem. People, 1982—; bd. govs. Organized Crime Commn., Austin, Tex., 1980—; bd. dirs. Alcohol Adv. Com., 1983—, ARC, 1984—. Recipient Great Achievements award Big Spring C. of C., Tex., 1985, Outstanding Service Recognition award Lampasas County Justice Ct., 1982. Mem. Nat. Sheriff's Assn., Tex. Sheriffs Assn., Central Tex. Peace Officers, Nat. Rifle Assn., Lampasas VFW (Outstanding Judge 1979, Officer of Yr. 1983). Democrat. Mem. Ch. Christ. Lodges: Lions, Masons. Avocations: hunting; fishing. Home: #1 Castleberry St Lampasas TX 76550 Office: Lampasas County Sheriffs Dept PO Box 465 Lampasas TX 76550

MORRIS, GORDON JAMES, diversified company executive, financial consultant; b. Mount Vernon, Ohio, Oct. 6, 1942; s. R. Hugh and Betty Jane (Roberts) M.; m. Janet Ann Swanson, Aug. 28, 1965 (div. 1971); m. Nancy Joan Meyfarth, July 26, 1975; 1 child, Lawrence Hugh. Student Ohio State U., 1960-61; B.A., Otterbein Coll., 1966; postgrad. Law Sch., Capital U., Bexley, Ohio, 1967-68, Coll. Fin. Planning, Denver, 1983—. Registered investment adviser SEC. Asst. to pres. Jaeger Machine Co., Columbus, Ohio, 1968-73; rep. Equitable Fin. Services, Sarasota, Fla., 1974-81; pres. Morris & Assocs. P.A., Sarasota, 1981—; chmn. bd. MAP Fin. Group, Inc., Sarasota, 1985—; chmn. bd. MAP Property & Casualty Ins. Co., Sarasota, 1985—; v.p. AMPKO Devel. Co., Sarasota, 1985—; ptnr. MAP Realty Co., Sarasota, 1985—. Chmn. West Coast chpt. March of Dimes, Bradenton, Fla., 1983-84; v.p. Council on Epilepsy, Inc., Sarasota, 1984-85, pres.-elect, 1986-87. Mem. Internat. Assn. Fin. Planning, Nat. Assn. Life Underwriters, Million Dollar Roundtable, Nat. Assn. Realtors, Nat. Inst. Fin. Planning. Republican. Methodist. Lodge: Sertoma (pres. local club 1979-80). Office: MAP Fin Group Inc 1950 Landings Blvd Suite 202 Sarasota FL 33581

MORRIS, HORTON HAROLD, pigment company executive; b. Post, Tex., May 26, 1922; s. Max Lindsay and Ida (Nelson) M.; B.S. in Chemistry, Tex. Technol. U., 1949; M.S. in Chemistry, U. Maine, 1953; m. Jean Burke, Aug. 21, 1982; children—Karen, Lindsay, Larry. Tchr. sci. Lockney (Tex.) High Sch., 1949-50; asso. prof. chemistry U. Maine, Orono, 1953-57; research dir. So. Clays, Inc., Gordon, Ga., 1957-62; v.p. research and devel. Freeport Kaolin Co., Gordon, 1963-74, 79-84; pres. SSI Consultants, Macon, Ga., 1977-79, 84—. Served with U.S. Army, 1943-45. Mem. Am. Chem. Soc., Clay Minerals Soc., ASTM, Am. Inst. Chemists, Am. Ceramic Soc., N.Y. Acad. Sci., AAAS, TAPPI, Sigma Xi. Contbr. articles to profl. jours. Home and office: 1715 Waverland Dr Macon GA 31211

MORRIS, JAMES BRUCE, physician; b. Rochester, N.Y., May 13, 1943; s. Max G. and Beatrice Ruth (Becker) M.; B.A., U. Rochester, 1964; M.D., Yale U., 1968; m. Susan Carol Shencup, July 31, 1966; children—Carrie, Douglas, Deborah, Rebecca. Intern, SUNY, Buffalo, 1968-69, resident, 1969-70, 72-73, chief resident, 1973; fellow U. Miami, 1974; practice medicine specializing in internal medicine and infectious diseases, Plantation, Fla., 1974—; chmn. infection control com. Lauderdale Lakes Gen. Hosp., 1974-76; chmn. infection control com. Plantation Gen. Hosp., 1976-80, 83-85, chmn. pharmacy com., 1980-81, chmn. tissue com., 1982; sec., program chmn. dept. medicine Bennett Community Hosp., 1978-80, chmn. dept. medicine, 1980-81, vice chief staff, 1981-83; chmn. infection control com. Fla. Med. Center, 1980-82; chief staff Humana Hosp. Bennett, 1983-85, trustee, 1983-86, chmn. infection control com., 1985—; clin. asst. prof. U. Miami Med. Sch., 1975—. Served with USAR, 1970-72. Diplomate Am. Bd. Internal Medicine, Am. Bd. Infectious Diseases. Mem. ACP, Am. Soc. Microbiology, AMA, Am. Soc. Internal Medicine, Fla. Med. Assn., Broward County Med. Assn. Office: 7353 NW 4th St Plantation FL 33317

MORRIS, JAMES GRAHAM, engineering educator, consultant; b. Parkersburg, W. Va., Mar. 20, 1928; s. Harold Watson and La Rue Esther (Graham) M.; m. Virginia Lee Barrett, Sept. 26, 1953; 1 son, James Richard. Student Marietta Coll., 1946-48; B.S. in Metall. Engring., Purdue U., 1951, Ph.D., 1956. Research engr. Dow Chem. Co., Midland, Mich., 1956-57; project engr. Kaiser Aluminum and Chem. Corp., Spokane, Wash., 1957-58; sr. research scientist Olin Corp., New Haven, 1958-59; prof. dept. metall. engring., U. Ky., Lexington, 1959—, dir. light metals research labs., dept. metall. engring., Coll. Engring.; research cons. Nat. adv. bd. Am. Security Council. Recipient W.A. Tarr award, 1951; NSF Faculty Participating awards, 1975, 76. Mem. AIME, Am. Soc. Engring. Edn., AAAS, Metals Soc., N.Y. Acad. Scis., Am. Soc. Metals, Sigma Xi, Tau Beta Pi. Republican. Methodist. Patentee (5); contbr. articles to profl. jours. Home: 741 Glendover Dr Lexington KY 40502 Office: Dept Metall Engring Anderson Hall U Ky Lexington KY 40506

MORRIS, JAMES REECE, educator, accountant; b. Englewood, Tenn., Mar. 12, 1946; s. Johnnie Linton and Bessie Lee (Davis) M.; m. Roma Sue Barr, Oct. 12, 1968; 1 child, Sara Rebecca. B.S. in Acctg., U. Tenn., 1968; M.B.A., E. Tenn. State U., 1972. Auditor Price Waterhouse & Co., Nashville, 1968-69; bus. mgr. Cleveland State Community Coll., Tenn., 1972—; cons. So. Assn. Colls., Atlanta, 1974—, Tenn. State Bd. Regents Computer Evaluation Team, Nashville, 1985; pres. N. Bradley Utility, Cleveland, 1976—. Elder Cleveland Christian Ch., 1976-84; v.p. Cleveland-Bradley County Fed. Credit Union, 1978-84; pres. Tri-County Men's Fellowship, Athens, Tenn., 1978-79; pres. Rotary Club, Cleveland, 1979-80. Served with U.S. Army, 1969-70. Mem. Tenn. State Bd. Accountancy (C.P.A. award 1972), So. Assn. Coll. and Univ. Bus. Officers, Nat. Assn. Edn. Buyers, Tenn. State Bd. Regents Bus. Council. Republican. Home: Route 12 Box 99 Cleveland TN 37311 Office: Cleveland State Community Coll PO Box 3570 Cleveland TN 37311

MORRIS, JAMES WILLIAM, JR., oil company executive; b. Augusta, Ga., Feb. 7, 1940; s. James William and Juanita (Mitchell) M.; m. Deborah Waddell, Apr. 24, 1981. B.A., Augusta Coll., 1964. With Citizens and So. Nat. Bank, Augusta, 1960-62; pres. Boardman Petroleum, Inc., Augusta, 1975—; dir. Smile Gas, Inc. Served with AF N.G., 1961-64. Mem. Augusta Jaycees (v.p. 1970). Clubs: Augusta Country, Kiwanis, Augusta Golf Assn. (v.p.). Home: 2320 Overton Rd Augusta GA 30904 Office: PO Box 3366 Augusta GA 30904

MORRIS, JOHN BURNETT, clergyman; b. Brunswick, Ga., Feb. 10, 1930; s. Hervey Clark and Anne (Burnett) M.; m. Harriet Barnes Pratt, Aug. 25, 1952; children—Anne, Christopher, John Burnett, Ellen. B.A., Columbia U., 1951; B.D., Va. Theol. Sem., 1954. Ordained priest, Episcopal Ch., 1955. Vicar St. Barnabas' Ch., Dillon, S.C., 1954-58; founder, exec. dir. Episcopal Soc. for Cultural and Racial Unity, Atlanta, 1958-67; spl. asst. So. Regional Council, Atlanta, 1968-71, U.S. Office for Civil Rights, 1971-80; proprietor Julian Burnett, Books, Atlanta, 1980—. Del. Democratic Nat. Conv., 1968. Recipient Bishop Lichtenberger Human Rights award Episcopal Diocese of Chgo., 1968. Editor: South Carolinians Speak, 1957; contbr. articles to periodicals. Address: 4655 Jett Rd NW Atlanta GA 30327

MORRIS, JOHN THOMAS, physician; b. Ashland, Ala., May 15, 1918; s. John Thomas and Ida Dora (Brown) M.; m. Sylvia June Burbank, Jan. 1, 1948 (div. 1971); children—Thomas Dean, Richard Lee, John Douglas; m. 2d, Miriam Anna Wenhold, Feb. 4, 1972. B.S., Birmingham-So. Coll., 1941; postgrad., U. Ala., 1941-43; M.D., Johns Hopkins U., 1945. Intern in internal medicine Balt. City Hosp., 1945-46, U. Ala. Hosp., Birmingham, 1948-49; practice medicine specializing in internal medicine, Cullman, Ala., 1949-85; med. dir. Cullman Health Care Ctr., 1971—; chief med. service Cullman Hosp., 1950-70; past guest lectr. physiology St. Bernard Coll., Cullman. Served as capt., M.C., USAAF, 1946-48; ETO. Decorated Bronze Star medal. Mem. AMA (Physician's Recognition award), Am. Heart Assn. Lutheran. Contbr. articles to med. jours.

MORRIS, NANCY MITCHELL, research chemist; b. Griffin, Ga., Jan. 9, 1940; d. Roy Eugene and Winifred Florence (Puckett) Mitchell; m. Cletus Eugene Morris, June 5, 1962; 1 child, Kendall Eugene. A.B. in Chemistry, LaGrange Coll., Ga., 1960; M.S., Auburn U., Ala., 1964. Chemist, West Point-Pepperell, Shawmut, Ala., 1964-65; chemist So. Regional Research Ctr., USDA, New Orleans, 1966-72, research chemist, 1972—. Contbr. articles to profl. publs, chpt. to book. Mem. Am. Chem. Soc., Am. Assn. Textile Chemist and Colorists (sec. gulf coast sect. 1978-79), Soc. Applied Spectroscopy (sec. La. sect. 1984-86), Orgn. Profl. Employees of Dept. Agrl. (v.p. 1983, pres.

1984), Sigma Xi. Methodist. Office: So Regional Research Ctr U S Dept Agrl PO Box 19687 New Orleans LA 70179

MORRIS, PAUL ROBERT, energy company executive; b. Sykesville, Pa., June 30, 1924; s. John J. and Mary (Skovran) M.; student Ohio State U., 1943-44; B.S.I.E., Pa. State U., 1950; postgrad. Syracuse U., 1964-65, Cornell U., 1965-67; m. Alberta N. Stinson, June 30, 1951; children—Paul Kyler, Barry, Philip Grant. Indsl. engr. Electronic Tube div. Sylvania Corp., Emporium, Pa., Reynoldsville, Pa., Huntington, W. Va., Burlington, Iowa, 1950-53, mfg. dept. mgr., Burlington, 1953-58, indsl. relations supr., Burlington and Seneca Falls, N.Y., 1958-59; mgr. personnel and mfg. services W.M. Chace Co., Detroit, 1969-70; v.p., gen. mgr. Chace Internat. Corp., San Juan, P.R., 1970-75; v.p. new bus. and new facilities devel. GTE Sylvania, Reidsville, N.C., 1975-80; exec. v.p. Reidsville C. of C., 1980-81; sr. project coordinator N.C. Alternative Energy Corp., Research Triangle Park, N.C., 1981-84, waste-to-energy coordinator, Mecklenburg County, 1984—; dir. Chace Internat. Corp., Chace Precision Materials Corp. Mem. Selective Service bd., 1962-63; bd. dirs. Girl Scouts U.S.A., 1950-62; chmn. Boy Scouts Am., 1967-69; bd. dirs. Salvation Army, 1958-64; pres., bd. dirs. U.N.C. Dental Parents Assn. Served with AUS, 1943-46. ETO. Recipient SSS award 1963. Mem. Nat. Foreman's Assn. (pres. 1953), Pa. State U. Alumni Assn., Triangle. Republican. Lutheran. Lodges: Rotary, Mason. Home: 1601 Country Club Rd Reidsville NC 27320 Office: Suite 212 Pamlico Bldg Research Triangle Park NC 27709

MORRIS, RICHARD SCOTT, lawyer, energy co. exec.; b. Oklahoma City, July 28, 1932; s. Winfield Scott and Mary Loine (Holmes) M.; student Rice U., Houston, 1949-51; J.D., U. N.Mex., 1960; m. Mary Frances Smith, Feb. 1, 1960; children—Daniel, Edward, Joseph, Maria. Bar: N.Mex. 1961, Tex. 1984. Asst. atty. gen. State of N.Mex., 1960-62; ptnr. Montgomery, Federici, Andrews, Hannahs & Morris, Santa Fe, N.Mex., 1962-73; v.p., asso. gen. counsel The El Paso Co., Houston, 1973-80, exec. v.p., gen. counsel, 1980-83; pres. El Paso Natural Gas Co., 1983—. Served as officer USAF, 1951-56. Address: PO Box 1492 El Paso TX 79978

MORRIS, ROBERT ARTHUR, JR., architect, developer; b. Cleve., Sept. 7, 1942; s. Robert Arthur and Betty Irene (Rice) M.; m. Judith Lynn Roth, Dec. 16, 1968 (div. 1978); 1 child, Robert Arthur III; m. Pamela Joy Windt, Oct. 12, 1982; 1 child, Randall Arthur. B.Arch., U. Fla., 1965, M.A., 1966, postgrad., 1966-68. Cons. econ. feasibility of real estate projects, Gainesville, Fla., 1966-68; instr. U. Fla. Coll. Architecture and Fine Arts, Gainesville, 1966-68; exec. trainee, francise acquisition specialist Micanopy Group Cos., Alachua, Fla., 1968; dir. devel. Barco R.D.C., Gainesville, 1968-70; dist.-wide campaign mgr. Joe Z. Lovingtood Congl. campaign, Fla. S.W. Coast, 1970, 74, 76; chmn. bd. Ramar Group Co., Inc., Sarasota, Fla., 1973—, First Presdl. Savs. & Loan Assn., Sarasota, 1980—, Equity Properties Group, Sarasota, 1980—, Fla. Incredibles, Inc., Sarasota, 1982—; mem. info. industry council U.S. Office Govt. Printing, Washington, 1980—. Mem. adv. bd. U. Fla., 1981—; mem. Fla. Council 100, Tampa, 1982—; trustee Eckerd Coll. Found., St. Petersburg, Fla., Out-of-door Acad., Sarasota; bd. govs. Sarasota County Hist. Soc.; pres. Gulf Coast Heritage Assn., Sarasota. Mem. AIA (pres. chpt. 1972-74), Fla. Planning and Zoning Assn. (founding mem. bd. dirs. and pres. 1978-80), Gargoyle Soc., Tau Sigma Delta. Republican. Clubs: University, Field (Sarasota). Office: Ramar Group Cos Inc PO Box 5979 5255 S Tamiami Trail Sarasota FL 33579

MORRIS, ROBERT CLARENCE, geology educator, researcher; b. Electra, Tex., Feb. 19, 1928; s. William W. and Maude B. (Layton) M.; m. Barbara Scott, Aug. 7, 1954 (div. 1984); children—William, Michael, Craig, Robert; m. Ellen Mullen, June 30, 1984. B.S. in Geology, Tex. Tech. U., 1952; M.S. in Geology, U. Wis.-Madison, 1962, Ph.D. in Geology, 1965. Petroleum geologist Internat. Petroleum, Lima, Peru, 1952-61; from asst. prof. to prof. No. Ill. U., DeKalb, 1964-79; prof., chmn. dept. geology Eastern Ky. U., Richmond, 1979-80; prof., chmn. dept. U. Ark., Fayetteville, 1980-84, prof., 1984—. Contbr. articles to profl. jours. Served with U.S. Army, 1946-49. Recipient Student Merit award W. Tex. Geol. Soc., 1952; grantee NSF, 1966, 74, 76, 77, 79. Fellow Geol. Soc. Am.; mem. Am. Assn. Petroleum Geologists, Soc. Econ. Mineralogists and Paleontologists, Internat. Assn. Sedimentologists, Peruvian Geol. Soc. Home: 405 Mashburn Fayetteville AR 72701 Office: U Ark Dept Geology 118 Ozark Hall Fayetteville AR 72701

MORRIS, SAMUEL SOLOMON, JR., bishop; b. Norfolk, Va., Nov. 1, 1916; s. Samuel Solomon and Mayme (Lawson) M.; B.S., Wilberforce U., 1937; M.Div., Yale U., 1940; D.D. (Hon.), Payne Sem., 1964; LL.D., Kittrell Coll., 1963; m. Ermine Smith, Nov. 30, 1942; children—Joyce Green, Ermine, Samuel Solomon, III. Ordained to ministry African Meth. Episcopal Ch., 1940; pastor St. Luke A.M.E. Ch., Gallatin, Tenn. and St. John A.M.E. Ch., Springfield, Tenn., 1940-41, St. Paul A.M.E. Ch., Nashville, 1943-46, 1st A.M.E. Ch., Gary, Ind., 1949-56, Coppin A.M.E. Ch., Chgo., 1956-72; prof. Payne Sem. and Wilberforce U., 1941-43; pres. Shorter Coll., 1946-48, chmn. bd. trustees, 1972-76; bishop A.M.E. Ch., Little Rock, 1972-76, 11th dist., Jacksonville, Fla., 1976—. Pres. Chgo. br. NAACP, 1960-62; trustee Nat. Urban League. Recipient Silver Beaver award Boy Scouts Am., 1966. Mem. Alpha Phi Alpha. Author: An African Methodist Primer, 1962.

MORRIS, TERI HENRY, consulting geologist; b. San Angelo, Tex., Sept. 7, 1956; d. Wayne Benjamin and Beatrice (Garner) H.; m. Thomas Elmore Morris III, Nov. 12, 1983; 1 child, Thomas Elmore IV. Student Balliol Coll., Oxford, Eng., summer 1974; B.A. in Geology, Trinity U., San Antonio, 1978. Lab. analyst Core Labs., Midland, Tex., 1978-79; geologist Nucorp Energy Co., San Antonio, 1979-80, Earle M. Craig Jr. Corp., Midland, Tex., 1980-85; cons. geologist, Odessa, Tex., 1985—. Mem. Am. Assn. Petroleum Geologists, Soc. Petroleum Engrs., Soc. Econ. Paleontologists and Mineralologists, W. Tex. Geol. Soc. Republican. Presbyterian. Avocations: piano; voice; snow skiing; water skiing; flying. Home: 1603 Patton St Odessa TX 79761

MORRIS, TERRY LEE, human factors/industrial engineer, research consultant; b. Eastland, Tex., July 20, 1947; s. Melvin Gene and Billie Faye (Mitchell) M.; m. Sarah Elizabeth Hetherly, July 17, 1965. A.A., SUNY-Albany, 1975; B.S. in Psychology, Tex. A&M U., 1977, M.S., 1979, Ph.D. in Indsl. Engring., 1984. Lectr. dept. psychology Tex. A&M U., College Station, 1977-79, dept. indsl. engring., 1979-83; research psychologist U.S. Air Force Sch. of Aerospace medicine, Brooks AFB, Tex., 1983-84; engring. cons. OAO Corp., San Antonio, 1984; research assoc. Nat. Research Council, Washington and Brooks Air Force Base, 1984—; data communication specialist Data Processing Ctr., Tex. A&M U., 1979-81. Contbr. articles to profl. jours. Served with USN, 1967-76. Recipient Amoco Found. award Amoco Oil Co. and Tex. A&M Research Found., 1982. Mem. Am. Psychol. Assn., Human Factors Soc. (sec. Alamo chpt.), Am. Inst. Indsl. Engrs., Aerospace Med. Assn., Nat. Oceanic Edn. Found. Club: Assn. Former Students, Tex. A&M. Avocations: camping, photography, travel. Office: USAF SAM/VN Brooks Air Force Base TX 78235

MORRIS, THOMAS ROBBINS, political science educator; b. Roanoke, Va., July 28, 1944; s. Robert Vaughan and Ethel (Robbins) M.; m. Barbara-Lyn Belcher, July 23, 1966; children—Sheila Dawn, Tabbitha Lyn, Sharon Robbins, Rosa-lyn Vaughan. B.A. in History, Va. Mil. Inst., 1966; M.A., U. Va., 1969, Ph.D. in Govt., 1973; postgrad. Princeton Theol. Sem., 1966-67. Asst. prof. U. Richmond, Va., 1971-78, assoc. prof. polit. sci., 1978—, chair dept., 1981-84; polit. analyst WTVR-Channel 6 TV, Richmond, 1981—. Author: The Virginia Supreme Court: An Institutional and Political Analysis, 1975, Virginia Government and Politics: Readings and Comments, 2d edit., 1984. Bd. dirs. Housing Opportunities Made Equal, Richmond, Va., 1982—. Liberal arts fellow Harvard Law Sch., Cambridge, Mass., 1976-77, NEH fellow U. Wis.-Madison, 1979-80; named Disting. Educator, U. Richmond, Va., 1982. Mem. Am. Polit. Sci. Assn., Omicron Delta Kappa. Methodist. Home: 3216 Noble Ave Richmond VA 23222 Office: Dept Polit Sci U Richmond Richmond VA 23173

MORRIS, WILLIAM COOK, international marketing executive; b. Olanta, S.C., Feb. 15, 1948; s. William Ellison and Janie Lou (Cook) M.; m. Kaye Petit, June 15, 1969 (div. 1971); 1 dau., Meredith Shannon; m. Debbie Edwards, Feb. 12, 1977. B.S., Baptist Coll., Charleston, S.C., 1970. Athletic dir. Hannah/-Pamplico Sch. (S.C.), 1971-75; sales dir. Gem Marine, Inc., Lake City, S.C., 1975-78; pres. Nat. Marine, Inc., Lake City, 1978-79, Flightmaster Corp., Lake City, 1979-82; pres., chief exec. officer Morris Internat. Corp., Lake City, 1982—. Served with Ark. N.G., 1970-76. Republican. Baptist. Club: Lake City Country (v.p. 1982-83, pres. 1983-84). Lodge: Rotary. Home: 307 Scotland Rd Lake City SC 29560 Office: Morris Internat Corp 263 Kelly St Lake City SC 29560

MORRIS, WILLIAM RONALD, accounting educator; b. Birmingham, Ala., Feb. 12, 1926; s. John B. Morris and Allie Rollings Morris Burke; m. Virginia Elizabeth West, July 3, 1949; children—William Ronald, Jr., Scott West. B.S. in Commerce and Bus., U. Ala., 1949; M.B.A., Memphis State U., 1967. C.P.A., Tenn., W. Va., N.C., S.C. Claims supr. Liberty Mut. Ins., Memphis, 1949-68; asst. prof. acctg. Western Carolina U., Cullowhee, N.C., 1968-76; assoc. prof. acctg. Marshall U., Huntington, W.Va., 1977-79, U. S.C.-Aiken, 1979—; pvt. practice acctg., Cullowhee, N.C., 1970-75, Huntington, W.Va., 1977-79; ptnr. Lindsey & Morris, C.P.A.s, Cullowhee, 1973-74. Bd. dirs. United Way, Aiken, 1983—. Served with U.S. Army, 1944-45. Mem. Am. Acctg. Assn., Am. Inst. of C.P.A.s, S.C. Assn. C.P.A.s. Republican. Methodist. Club: Houndslake Country (Aiken). Avocations: tennis; gardening. Home: 1732 Huntsman Aiken SC 29801 Office: U SC at Aiken 171 U Parkway Aiken SC 29801

MORRIS, WILLIAM SHIVERS, III, newspaper executive; b. Augusta, Ga., Oct. 3, 1934; s. William Shivers Jr. and Florence (Hill) M.; A.B. in Journalism, U. Ga., 1956; m. Mary Sue Ellis, Jan. 18, 1958; children—William Shivers IV, John Tyler, Susie Blackmar. Asst. to pres., pub. Southeastern Newspapers and Augusta Newspapers, 1956-60; v.p., dir. Savannah Newspapers, Inc. and Savannah News-Press, Inc. (Ga.), 1960-63; v.p., dir. Southeastern Newspapers Corp., 1963-65; pres. Banner-Herald Pub. Co., Athens, Ga., 1965; pres. Southeastern Newspaper Corp., Morris Communications Corp., Southwestern Newspapers Corp., N. Am. Publs., Inc.; pub. Augusta Chronicle and Augusta Herald, 1966—, Juneau (Alaska) Empire; chmn. bd., chief exec. officer all newspaper divs. Fla. Pub. Co., pubs. Fla. Times-Union & Jacksonville Jour., 1983 dir. Ga. Power Co., Atlanta, So. Co., Atlanta, A.P. Trustee Augusta Coll. Found.; bd. regents Univ. System Ga., 1967-73. Served to capt. USAF, 1956-58. Named Outstanding Alumnus, U. Ga. Sch. Journalism and Mass Communications, 1983. Mem. Am. Newspaper Pubs. Assn., Southeastern Newspaper Pubs. Assn. (dir. 1966—), So. Newspaper Pubs. Assn., Internat. Press Inst., Golden Quill Soc. (hon.). Presbyterian (elder). Clubs: Pinnacle (past pres.) (Augusta); University (N.Y.C.); Oglethorpe (Savannah); Commerce (Atlanta); Timuquana Country (Jacksonville). Office: PO Box 1988 725-31 Broad St Augusta GA 30902

MORRIS, WINSTON CREIGHTON, steel company worker, former city commissioner; b. Ashland, Ky., June 23, 1932; s. Alva Wayland and Georgia (McNeal) M.; student Ashland Jr. Coll., 1954-55, U. Louisville, 1956-57; m. Frances Coleman, Feb. 11, 1961; children—Lisa Lynn, Scott Alan, Lori Jane. Adminstrv. asst. Ky. N.G., 1952-56; lab. technician Nitrogen div. Allied Chem. Co., 1957-58; with Armco Steel, Inc., Ashland, 1958—, in heating and rolling ops., 1959—; commr. City of Ashland, 1980-83. Pres., Boyd County Citizens Caucus, 1978; active Ashland Performing Arts Guild. Republican. Mem. Ch. of God. Clubs: Ashland Toastmasters (pres. 1977); Ashland Armco Vets. (pres. 1984). Home: 1406 Maxwell St Ashland KY 41101 Office: HS Office Armco Inc Ashland KY 41101

MORRISON, BILLY HAROLD, oil company executive, geologist; b. McAdoo, Tex., Jan. 9, 1928; s. James Morris and Opal Mae (Holt) M.; m. Donna Sue Raybon; children—Kim, Virginia Lee. B.S., U. Tex.-El Paso. Cert. profl. geologist. Geologist, U. of the Lands, Midland, Tex., 1952-56; dist. geologist Cabot Corp., Midland, Calgary, Alta., Can., 1956-68, Diamond Shamrock Corp., Calgary, Amarillo, Tex., Houston, 1968-72, 72-76, 76-80; dist. mgr. Nortex Gas & Oil Internat., Midland, 1980-81; v.p. exploration and prodn. Nortex Gas & Oil, Houston, 1981-84; v.p., gen. mgr. Belnorth Petroleum, Midland, 1984-86, HNG/Internorth Exploration, Midland, 1986—. Served with USN, 1946-48. Mem. Am. Assn. Petroleum Geologists, Am. Inst. Profl. Geologists, Can. Soc. Petroleum Geologists, Houston Geol. Soc., West Tex. Geol. Soc. Clubs: Plaza, Green Tree Country (Midland). Lodge: Masons. Avocations: Western art; first edition Texana; golf. Home: 2506 Dartmouth St Midland TX 79705 Office: HNG/Internorth PO Box 2267 Midland TX 79702

MORRISON, DARREL GENE, environmental design educator; b. Orient, Iowa, June 20, 1937; s. Raymond Delbert and Rosy Christina (Mensing) M.; m. Dawna Lee Hauptman, June 29, 1963; children—Jon David, Scott Darrel. B.S. in Landscape Architecture, Iowa State U., 1959; M.S. in Landscape Architecture, U. Wis., 1969. Landscape architect Md.-Nat. Capitol Park & Plan Commn., Silver Spring, 1962-64, T.D. Donovan & Assocs., Silver Spring, 1964-66, D.C. Dept. Hwys., 1966-67; faculty mem., chmn. dept. land architecture U. Wis., Madison, 1969-83; dean sch. environ. design U. Ga., Athens, 1983—. Editor Landscape Jour., 1981— (Am. Soc. Landscape Architecture award of merit 1983). Served with U.S. Army, 1960-62. Named Outstanding Educator Council of Educators in Landscape Architecture, 1977; recipient Excellence in Teaching award Coll. Agr., U. Wis.-Madison, 1973, Disting. Teaching award U. Wis., 1975, Bascom Professorship title bd. regents U. Wis., 1976. Fellow Am. Soc. Landscape Architects. Methodist. Lodge: Rotary. Office: 609 Caldwell Hall Sch Environ Design U Ga Athens GA 30602

MORRISON, DUDLEY BUTLER, JR., insurance company executive; b. Miami, Fla., Nov. 30, 1937; s. Dudley Butler and Ina Ingelow (Holmes) M.; m. Elise Heydecker Morris, Feb. 3, 1962 (div. 1973); m. Elizabeth Victoria Boyd, Oct. 2, 1982. B.A., Brown U., 1959. Sr. underwriter Travelers Ins. Co., N.Y.C., 1962-69; sr. systems analyst Allstate Ins. Co., Northbrook, Ill., 1969-76; v.p. Am. Mut. Reins. Co., Chgo., 1976-84; mgr. Pollution Liability Ins. Assn., Chgo., 1982-84; cons. mgmt. State Capital Ins. Co., Raleigh, N.C., 1985—. Bd. dirs. Chase House, Inc., Chgo., 1970-84; pres. Willow Green Condominium Assn., Northfield, Ill., 1979-84. Republican. Episcopalian. Club: Packard Automobile Classics, Inc. (regent 1980—). Home: 2913 Meadowview Ct Apex NC 27502 Office: State Capital Ins Co 2700 Wycliff Rd Raleigh NC 27611

MORRISON, GLEN WARREN, accountant; b. Montgomery, Ala., Sept. 20, 1934; s. Marcus and Gladys (Deavers) M.; m. Joyce Lannom, July 12, 1958; 1 son, Gregg. B.S., U. Ala., 1961; J.D., Jones Law Sch., 1972. C.P.A., Ala., Ga., Miss. Staff acct. J. Bradley Haynes & Co., Rome, Ga., 1961-64; sr. acct. Dudley, Hopton-Jones, Sims & Freeman, Birmingham, Ala., 1964-68, ptnr., 1968—, mem. exec. com., 1982—. Mem. Am. Inst. C.P.A.s, Ala. Soc. C.P.A.s (audit com. 1975—), Assoc. Acctg. Firms Internat. (audit com. 1973—), Commerce Exec. Soc. Club: Tip-Off (Birmingham, Ala.). Lodges: Masons, Vestavia Hills Lions (past pres.). Home: 1804 Laurel Rd Birmingham AL 35216 Office: Dudley Hopton Jones Sims & Freeman 3d Floor 2101 Magnolia Ave South Birmingham AL 35205

MORRISON, JOHN EGAN, research psychologist; b. Greenville, S.C., July 5, 1950; s. Ralph Edgar and Florence Rose (Egan) M.; m. Claire Denise Dinnen, Oct. 20, 1979; children—Catherine Egan, William Dinnen. B.S., Va. Poly. Inst., 1972; M.A., Wake Forest U., 1974; Ph.D., Tulane U., 1979. Research psychologist U.S. Army Research Inst., Fort Knox, Ky., 1979-84; sr. scientist Human Resources Research Orgn., Ft. Knox, 1984—; instr. U. Ky., Ft. Knox, 1980—. Contbr. articles to profl. jours. Bd. dirs. Iroquois Child Care, Inc., Louisville, 1984-85. Mem. Am. Psychol. Assn. (co-editor newsletter 1985—), Assn. for Devel. Computer-Based Instructional Systems. Democrat. Roman Catholic. Avocation: photography. Home: 4508 Southcrest Dr Louisville KY 40215 Office: Human Resources Research Orgn Box 293 Fort Knox KY 40121

MORRISON, JUNIUS DAVIS, college administrator, educator; b. Atlanta, Oct. 3, 1942; s. Junius Davis and Lil Kirk (Huggins) M.; m. Lorena Ann Prosser, June 15, 1968; children—Anna Elizabeth, Nathan Robert. A.B. in Social Sci., Wheaton Coll., 1964; M.B.A. in Bus., Northwestern U., 1966. Bus. mgr. Miami Christian Sch., Fla., 1966-78; purchasing officer Miami Elevator Co., 1978-80; student service dir., asst. to pres. Miami Christian Coll., 1980—. Recipient Alumnus of Yr. award Miami Christian Sch., 1979. Mem. Greater Miami Urban Coalition, S. Fla. Under God, Assn. Christians in Student Devel., Am. Assn. Bible Colls. (accreditation evaluator). Republican. Presbyterian. Avocations: orchid growing; boating. Home: 201 S Biscayne River Dr Miami FL 33169 Office: Miami Christian Coll 2300 NW 135 St Miami FL 33167

MORRISON, MORRIS ROBERT, poetry therapist, psychology educator; b. Bklyn., Nov. 1, 1908; s. Jacob and Sarah (Swerdlov) M.; m. Theresa Gillman, June 6, 1936; children—Nadine Markova, Felicia, Chet. B.A., CCNY, 1931; B.A. in English, U. Tex., 1933; M.A. in English, U. for Humanistic Studies, 1980, Ph.D. in Counselling Psychology. Tchr. spl. edn. N.Y.C. Bd. Edn., 1933-60; mem. faculty English dept. CCNY, 1960-70; mem. faculty psychology dept. New Sch. for Social Research, 1970-76; adj. prof. psychology St. Edwards U., Austin, Tex., 1980—. Fellow Am. Assn. for Social Psychiatry; sci. assoc. Am. Acad. Psychoanalysis; mem. Nat. Assn. Poetry Therapy (founder, pres. emeritus), Am. Acad. Poetry Therapy (pres. 1976—), Am. Acad. Psychoanalysis (sci. assoc.), Nat. Ednl. Council for Creative Arts Therapies (dir. 1980—). Democrat. Author: (poetry) Prologue and Performances 1972; editor: The Use of Poetry and the Other Creative Arts to Healing, Poetry as Therapy. Contbr. poetry to profl. jours., also Ency. Psychiatry, Psychology, Psychoanalysis and Neurology.

MORRISON, RANDALL GENE, personnel and industrial relations executive; b. Peoria, Ill., Dec. 4, 1954; s. William L.D. and Ola Mae (Ackerman) M.; m. Susan Nanette Henson, Jan. 3, 1976; children—Jennifer Leigh, William Ross, Erin Suzanne. B.A., U. S.C., 1978. Photographer, dir. WYFF-TV, Greenville, S.C., 1975-78; writer/producer Goudelock Advt. Agy., Inc., Greenville, S.C., 1979-80; supr. employee relations Yeargin Constrn. Co., Inc., Greenville, S.C., 1980—; also mktg. cons. Am. Advt. Fedn./AD2 div. edn. adviser, 1983—, Eastern region chmn., 1982-83. Recipient P-R-I-D-E in Workmanship award Yeargin Constrn. Co., Inc., 1981. Mem. AD2 Greenville (pres. 1981-82), Advt. Fedn. Greenville. Republican. Baptist. Home: 3 Branch Court Taylors SC 29687 Office: 105 Edinburgh Ct Greenville SC 29606

MORRISON, RAYMOND EARL, JR., high technology advisory council executive, consultant; b. Latham, N.Y., Dec. 3, 1941; s. Raymond Earl, Sr., and Mary Ellen (Doran) M.; m. Christine Marie Owocki, Oct. 22, 1982; children—Arianne, Michael, Janine. A.A.S., Hudson Valley Community Coll., 1967; B.S., SUNY-Oswego, 1964; M.S., Syracuse U., 1970; Ph.D., U. Mo., 1975. Tng. mgr. Los Alamos Nat. Lab., N.Mex., 1975-80, sr. budget, fiscal analyst, 1980-83; exec. dir. High Tech. Adv. Council, Atlanta, 1983—; cons. Morrison & Assocs., Los Alamos, 1975-80, State Dept. Edn., Atlanta, 1983-84; internal cons. U. Calif., Los Alamos, 1980-83, Los Alamos Tech. Assn., 1979-81. Contbr. articles to profl. jours. Mem. bd. reviewers Los Alamos Schs. Credit Union, 1979-81; mem. exec. com. Private Industry Council, Santa Fe, N.M., 1980-82. Mem. Soc. Automotive Engrs. (sec. 1968-69), Am. Soc. Engring. Edn. (dir. 1979-82, S.I.G. chmn. 1980), Am. Psychol. Assn., AAAS. Home: 2692 Shadow Bluff Dr Marietta GA 30062 Office: High Tech Adv Council 660 Omni International S Atlanta GA 30335

MORRISON, ROBERT EDWIN, songwriter, song publisher; b. Biloxi, Miss., Aug. 6, 1942; s. Charles Hewitt and Myrtis Harriet (Marshall) M.; m. Barbara Lethbridge O'Malley, July 6, 1967; children—Wendy Leigh, Andrea Lyn. B.S. in Nuclear Engring., Miss. State U. Staff songwriter Music City Music, Nashville, 1973-84; pub., songwriter Bob Morrison Music, Nashville, 1984—; actor Screen-Gems TV, Hollywood, Calif., 1968-70. Films include: Iron Horse, The Outcase, various commls.; appearance Merv Griffin Show, 1981; performing artist Columbia Records, 1966—. Songs include: You Decorated My Life (Grammy award 1979), Love the World Away, Lookin' for Love (Nat. Music Pubs. Assn. country song of yr. 1980, nominated Grammy best country song), The River's Too Wide, You're The One, Up to Heaven, Born to Love Me, Gravel on the Ground, Make Believe It's Your First Time, The Love She Found in Me, Shine On, We'll Be Together; co-writer songs for films Urban Cowboy and Grease II; writer of logo song for ABC-TV; We're the One, 1979. Named ASCAP Nashville Songwriter of Yr., 1978, 80, 81, 82. Songwriter of Yr., 1980. Mem. ASCAP, Nashville Songwriters Assn. (Songwriter of Yr. 1980), Screen Actors Guild, AFTRA, Am. Fedn. Musicians. Methodist.

MORRISON, ROBERT RIGBY, hospital administrator, psychologist; b. Joliet, Ill., Nov. 5, 1946; s. Raymond Kier and Janet Rae (Rigby) M.; m. Mary Margaret Carroll, Aug. 28, 1968 (div. Dec. 1976); 1 child, Jennifer Rigby; m. Mary Elizabeth Fanning, Nov. 26, 1977. B.A., Lawrence U., Appleton, Wis., 1968; M.A., Tex. Christian U., 1969; Ph.D., U. Pa., 1976. Lic. psychologist, N.C. Clin. psychologist Fed. Bur. Prisons, Marion, Ill., 1976-78; research units psychologist Fed. Bur. Prisons, Butner, N.C., 1978-80; staff psychologist Meml. Hosp. of Alamance, Burlington, N.C., 1980-84, clin. services dir. psychiatry, 1984—. Vol. Orange County 4-H, N.C., 1981—. Served with U.S. Army, 1969-72. Dissertation Yr. fellow U. Pa., 1975. Mem. Am. Psychol. Assn. Democrat. Presbyterian. Avocation: traditional american music. Home: PO Box 191 Efland NC 27243 Office: Meml Hosp of Alamance 730 Hermitage Rd Burlington NC 27215

MORRISON, WALTON S., lawyer; b. Big Spring, Tex., June 16, 1907; s. M. H. and Ethel (Jackson) M.; student Texas A. and M. Coll., 1926-28; J.D., U. Tex., 1932; m. Mary Bell, Dec. 19, 1932. Admitted to Tex. bar, 1932: asso. Morrison & Morrison, Big Spring, 1932-37; county atty. Howard County, Tex., 1937-39; county judge Howard County, 1941-42, 47-48; pvt. practice, 1946-47; partner Morrison & Morrison, 1949-53; pvt. practice, 1953—; city atty. Big Spring, 1949-58. Pres., Tex. City Attys., 1955-56. Served with USAF, 1942-46; lt. col. Res. ret. Fellow Am. Coll. Probate Counsel; mem. Am., Tex. (mem. taxation council 1967-76), local bar assns. Rotarian; Mason (Shriner). Home: 1501 E 11th Pl Big Spring TX 79720 Office: 113 E 2d St Big Spring TX 79720

MORRISON, WILLIAM FOWLER, JR., hospital administrator; b. Wilmington, N.C., June 26, 1928; s. William Fowler and Gladys (Polvogt) M.; A.B. in Biology, Johns Hopkins, 1949; hosp. adminstrv. residency, Rex Hosp., Raleigh, N.C., 1949-51; m. Patricia Biggs; children—William Stephen, Janet Elizabeth, Nancy Elise. Asst. dir. Ch. Home and Hosp., Balt., 1953-55, dir., 1955-65; dir. coll. hosps. Med. Coll. Va., 1965-69, New Hanover Meml. Hosp., Wilmington, N.C., 1969—; mem. faculty Sch. Hosp. Adminstrn., Med. Coll. Va., 1965—. Bd. dirs. Blue Cross Va., 1968-69, Va. Hosp. Assn., 1968-69, Md., D.C., Del. Hosp. Assn., 1964-65, N.C. Hosp. Assn., 1975-77, 79-82, Health Scis. Found., 1975—; mem. N.C. State Health Coordinating Council, 1979—. Served with USAF, 1951-53. Mem. Am. Coll. Hosp. Adminstrs., Sigma Phi Epsilon. Episcopalian. Author articles. Office: New Hanover Meml Hosp S 17th St Wilmington NC 28401

MORRISS, MARY RACHEL, art educator, painter; b. Memphis; d. William Dale and Lizzie Henrie (Woodward) M. B.S., Memphis State U., 1927; postgrad. U. Colo., 1931, 34, 37, 40; various art workshops Maxine Masterfield, 1983, 84. Cert. high sch. tchr., Tenn. Tchr., Bellevue Sch., Memphis, 1936-66; ret.; pvt. art classes, Memphis, 1966—; represented by Art Gallery East, Memphis. Exhibited in group juried shows Central South Parthenon, Nashville, Hunter Annual Show, Delta Annual, Little Rock, Mid-Am., Owensboro, Ky., 1979, Mid-South Memphis Brooks Gallery, So. Watercolor Soc., 1983, Patrons' Watercolor Gala, Oklahoma City, 1983, 84, Tenn. Watercolor Soc. Annual Traveling Show, Ga. Watercolor Soc., 1986, and many others; represented in numerous pub. and pvt. collections. Recipient Best Cotton Design award Brooks Art Gallery; Purchase prize Mid-South Fair, 1971, Best in Show and 1st in watercolors, 1985; Doochin of Madison award Central South, 1984, and many other awards. Mem. Tenn. Watercolor Soc., So. Watercolor Soc., Friends of Dixon Gallery, Memphis Watercolor Soc. Presbyterian. Home: 4819 Parkside Ave Memphis TN 38117

MORROW, BRUCE W., business executive; b. Rochester, Minn., May 20, 1946; s. J. Robert and Frances P. Morrow; B.A., U. Notre Dame, 1968, M.B.A. with honors in Mgmt., 1974, M.A. in Comparative Lit., 1975; grad. U.S. Army Command and Gen. Staff Coll., 1979. Adminstrn. mgr. Eastern States Devel. Corp., Richmond, Va., 1977; v.p. JDB Assos., Inc., Alexandria, Va., 1976-78; owner Aardvark Prodns., Alexandria, 1978-80, Servital Foods, Alexandria, Va., 1980-82; sr. cons. Data Base Mgmt., Inc., Springfield, Va., 1979-81; systems analyst/staff officer Hdqrs., Dept. Army, Washington, 1980-84; pres. Commonwealth Dominion Corp., Alexandria, 1982—; cons. advt. writer The Miracle of Birth, Arlington, Va., 1979. Active Boy Scouts Am., 1960-69; chmn. elem. German, U. Notre Dame, 1973-75. Served to maj. U.S. Army. Decorated Bronze Star, Army Commendation medal, Parachutist's badge. Mem. Nat. Eagle Scout Assn., Internat. Entrepreneurs Assn., songwriters Assn. Washington (dir.), Nat. Writers Club, Alexandria C. of C. VFW (life), Am. Legion, Beta Gamma Sigma, Delta Phi Alpha. Clubs: Friends Internat. (Am. v.p. 1969-71) (Boeblingen, Germany); Order of DeMolay. Contbg. columnist Notre Dame Mag., 1974—; composer songs. Office: 708A W Glebe Rd Alexandria VA 22305

MORROW, JC DUNCAN, electronics manufacturing company executive, engineer; b. Monticello, Ky., Dec. 17, 1941; s. Raymond Leonard and Gussie (Correll) M.; m. Alice Faye Adkins, Dec. 20, 1964; children—JC Duncan, Jr.,

Susan Jenine. B.S., Eastern Ky. U., 1964, M.A., 1970; Electronics, Murray U., Ky., 1967. Indsl. arts tchr. Sch. Bd., Winchester, Ky., 1964-69; chief engr. Sta. WWKY, Winchester, 1965-70; instr. Vocat. Sch., Lexington, Ky., 1968-69; indsl. relations, Trane Co., Lexington, 1969-70, mgr. safety and tng., Clarksville, Tenn., 1970—; chief engr. Sta. WDXN, Clarksville, 1972—; adj. faculty electronics Austin Peay State U., 1978; cons. in field. Mem., Civitan, Clarksville, 1973; chmn. Band Booster N.E. High Sch., 1985 (Band Dirs. award 1985), treas. Jaycees, Winchester, 1967; mem. Presdl. Task Force, Washington, 1985. Recipient Highest award for achievement Dale Carnegie Course, 1976. Mem. Am. Soc. Safety Engrs. (vice chmn. 1982-83), Am. Mgmt. Assn., Soc. Broadcast Engrs. Republican. Baptist. Avocations: electronics, crafts, numismatics, hobbies. Home: 1788 Auburn Dr Clarksville TN 37043 Office: Trane Co PO Box 1008 Clarksville TN 37043

MORROW, JOHN CHARLES, III, chemistry educator, university administrator; b. Hendersonville, N.C., Sept. 20, 1924; s. John Charles and Marguerite (Jenkins) M.; m. Mary Frances Nunn, Dec. 20, 1950; children—Marguerite, William, Charles. Mem. faculty U.N.C., Chapel Hill, 1949—, prof. chemistry, 1959—, dean arts and sis., 1966-68, provost, 1968-84. Served to lt. (j.g.) USNR, 1944-46. Mem. Am. Chem. Soc., Am. Phys. Soc., Am. Crystallographic Assn., Phi Beta Kappa, Sigma Xi. Home: 420 Brookside Dr Chapel Hill NC 27514 Office: 263 Venable Hall 045A U NC Chapel Hill NC 27514

MORROW, MATTHEW EDWARD, pharmacist; b. Jacksonville, Fla., Nov. 20, 1952; s. Matthew Edward, Jr. and Sara Marion (Watson) M.; m. Elizabeth Ann Wohlberg, Aug. 30, 1975 (div. Dec. 1983); m. Karron Faye Watkins, Mar. 1, 1985. Registered pharmacist, Fla. Intern pharmacist VA Med. Ctr., Gainesville, Fla., 1978-80, research drug coordinator, 1979-80; intern pharmacist Alachua Gen. Hosp., Inc., Gainesville, 1980-81, asst. pharmacy dir., 1980—; cons. in field; pres., bd. dirs. Santa Fe Health Care Credit Union, 1984—. CPR instr. ARC, Am. Heart Assn., 1980—. Recipient Merck award, 1981; Lilly Sr. Achievement award, 1981; Fla. Soc. Hosp. Pharmacists scholar, 1979. Mem. Am. Soc. Hosp. Pharmacists, Fla. Soc. Hosp. Pharmacists, Phi Kappa Phi, Rho Chi (pres. 1980). Democrat. Presbyterian. Avocations: tennis; fishing; auto mechanics. Home: 5010 NE Waldo Rd 55 Gainesville FL 32609 Office: Alachua Gen Hosp Inc 801 SW 2d Ave Gainesville FL 32601

MORSE, EUGENIA MAUDE, architect, educator; b. Houston, Feb. 23, 1920; d. Robert Emmett and Eugenia Elizabeth (Maddox) Morse; B.A. in Architecture, Rice U., 1942, B.S. in Architecture, 1944. Practicing architect, 1949—; asso. prof. U. SW La., 1954-59; prof. architecture Tex. Tech. U., Lubbock, 1959—. Pres. bd. dirs. Storm Def. Club, 1970-73. Mem. Am. Forestry Assn. (life), West Tex. Watercolor Assn. (treas., dir. 1971-72), Nat. Geog. Soc., Mus. Natural History, Smithsonian Instn. Prin. works include Seitter Photography Bldg., Corpus Christi, Tex., Miles Ramagosa Clinic, Lafayette, La., Haltom Optical Co. Office and Lab., Corpus Christi, Buccaneer Gardens Housing Project, Corpus Christi, others, also residences. Office: Div Architecture 1008 F Architecture Bldg Tex Tech U Lubbock TX 79409

MORSE, F. D., JR., dentist; b. Glen Lyn, Va., Apr. 5, 1928; s. Frank D. and Ida Estell (Davis) M.; B.S., Concord Coll., 1951; D.D.S., Med. Coll. Va., 1955; m. Patsy Lee Apple, Feb. 4, 1967; children—Fortis Davis, Pamela Marie. Free lance photographer, 1950-56; practice dentistry, Pearisburg, Va., 1958—; mem. staff Giles Hosp., Pearisburg, 1958—. Served from asst. dental surgeon to sr. asst. dental surgeon USPHS, 1955-57; assigned to USCG, 1957-58. Mem. Am., S.W. Va. dental assns., Assn. Mil. Surgeons, AAAS, Nat. Assn. Advancement Sci., Fedn. Dentaire Internat., Internat. Platform Assn., W.Va. Collegiate Acad. Sci., Beta Phi. Kiwanian. Home: Bicuspid Acres Pearisburg VA 24134 Office: Giles Profl Bldg Pearisburg VA 24134

MORSE, FRANCIS FREDERICK EDGAR, E, dentist; b. N.Y.C., Dec. 23, 1921; s. Robert John and Frances Elizabeth (Moulton) M.; m. Dorothea Marie Hespe, Mar. 16, 1946 (div.); children—Francis Frederick Edward, Marianne Elizabeth, Robert John, Christopher George; m. Margaret Amelia Livengood, May, 1975. Student Hobart Coll., 1939-42; D.O.S., U. Pa., 1945. Practice dentistry, Durham, N.C., 1977—; guest lectr. Columbia U., N.Y.C., 1960-70, U. Pa., Phila., 1965-68, Seton Hall U., Jersey City, 1962-65. Alumni exec. com. mem. U. Pa. Sch. Dental Medicine, 1962-67. Served to lt. USNR, 1945-47, China. Recipient Alumni award of Merit, U. Pa., 1971. Fellow N.Y. Acad. Dentistry, Greater N.Y. Acad. Prosthodontics (life), Am. Acad. Restorative Dentistry; mem. ADA, Durham-Orange County Dental Soc. Republican. Episcopalian. Club: Hope Valley Country. Avocations: architecture; boating; skiing. Home: 3822 Regent Rd Durham NC 27707 Office: 3001 Academy Rd Durham NC 27707

MORSE, FREDERICK WHITTON, writer; b. Gordonsville, Va., Sept. 10, 1915; s. Frederick Anderson and Rosa Belle (Yancey) M.; A.B., Hampden-Sydney Coll., 1940; m. Linda Firestone, 1977; children by previous marriage—Frederick Anderson, Ann Dabney. Reporter, sports editor, city editor Daily Progress, Charlottesville, Va., 1935-36; publicity dir. Hampden-Sydney (Va.) Coll., 1936-40; reporter, feature writer Richmond (Va.) Times-Dispatch, 1940-42; news specialist, dir. radio and TV for VA, office covering five states and Washington, 1946-49; public relations dir. Richmond Area Community Chest and Council, 1949-51; dir. public relations, account exec. Cabell Eanes Advt. Agy., Richmond, 1951-55, sec., 1955-57, exec. v.p., 1957-66, pres., 1966-79; pres. Communications Assos., Inc., Richmond, 1979-80, chmn. bd., 1980-81, sec.-treas., 1981-85; sec. Bill Muller, The Toymaker, Inc., Oak Hall, Va., 1978-85; author: (with Linda Firestone) Virginia's Favorite Islands, Chincoteague and Assateague, 1976, Florida's Enchanting Islands, Sanibel and Captiva, 1976, Jefferson's Country, Charlottesville and Albemarle County, 1977; contbr. articles to trade mags. Served with USN, 1942-46; to lt. comdr. USNR, 1946-63; lt. comdr. Res. ret. Office: 14100 Nash Rd Chesterfield VA 23832

MORSE, FREDRICH GUENTHER, engineering and construction company executive, engineer; b. Gauting, West Germany, Apr. 14, 1947; came to U.S., 1953, naturalized, 1960; s. Norman Charles and Suzanne Sophie (Zoeller) M.; m. Camille Ann Puca, July 3, 1971 (div. 1985). B.S., U.S. Mcht. Marine Acad., 1971; M.S., Northwestern U., 1975; J.D., U. Fla., 1978. Registered profl. engr., Fla. Project engr. Craven Thompson, Inc., Fort Lauderdale, Fla., 1973-74, dir. engring., 1974-76; tax specialist Coopers & Lybrand, N.Y.C., 1978-79; pres. Craven Thompson & Assocs., Inc., West Punta Gorda, Fla., 1979-80; chief exec. officer Morse Engring., Inc., Morse Constrn. Inc., Englewood, Fla., 1980—. Chmn., Charlotte County Code Enforcement Bd., Fla., 1983. Served to lt. USNR, 1971-79. Mem. Fla. Engring. Soc., Water Pollution Control Fedn., ASCE, Nat. Soc. Profl. Engrs. Democrat. Avocations: sculpture; sailboat racing; motor racing, golf. Home: 210 Cerromar Way S Venice FL 33595 Office: Morse & Co Inc 3070 S McCall Rd Englewood FL 33533

MORSE, LINDA ARKELL, school counselor; b. Feb. 25, 1943; 2 children. B.S. in Social Studies Edn., Oreg. State U., 1964; M.S. in Elem. Counseling, Purdue U., 1970; postgrad. Gestalt Inst. Ky., 1980; Ed.S., U. Ky., 1986. Counselor, Russell Elem. Sch., Lexington, Ky., 1974-79, Central Alternative Sch., Lexington, 1979-80, Millcreek Elem. Sch., Lexington, 1980—; cons. Ky. Sch. Social Workers Conf., Ohio Sch. Counselor Assn. Conf., Oakland Intermediate Schs., Mich., 1980, 84, Austin, Pub. Schs., Tex., 1978, N.Y. Sch. Counselors Assn., 1978. Mem. editorial bd. Elem. Sch. Guidance and Counseling, 1984—. Contbr. articles to profl. jours. Tchr. Crestwood Ch., 1979; co-leader adult divorce support groups, 1984; counselor Spouse Abuse Shelter, 1985. Recipient Outstanding Elem. Guidance Program award Ky. Assn. Counselor Edn. and Supervision, 1983, Elem. Counselor of Yr. award Am. Sch. Counselor Assn., 1984; Linda A. Morse Leadership award established Ky. Sch. Counselor Assn., 1981. Mem. Am. Sch. Counselor Assn. (governing bd. 1981-83, co-chmn. leadership devel. conf. 1979-81, workshop presenter). Home: 3086 Pimlico Pkwy Lexington KY 40502 Office: Millcreek Sch 3066 Appian Way Lexington KY 40502

MORSE, MICHAEL LEO, health care administrator; b. Jefferson, Iowa, Dec 26, 1946; s. Forrest Francis and Nedra Josephine (DeWitt) McDonald; m. Tommie Karen Jackson, Mar. 23, 1979 (div. May 1983); 1 son, Thomas Issac; m. 2d, Leticia Angela Christina, Nov. 19, 1983. B.S., Park Coll., 1980; M.S., Trinity U., San Antonio. Lic. nurse, emergency med. technician. Enlisted U.S. Army, 1969; sr. clin. instr., Ft. Sam Houston, San Antonio, 1971-81, resigned, 1981; dir. ops., Santa Rosa Med. Center, San Antonio, 1981-83; dir. materials mgmt. Humana Corp., San Antonio, 1983-84; dir. support services Clearview (a facility of Midland Camelback Samaritan Inc.), Midland, Tex., 1985—; cons. Morse Med., San Antonio, 1981-84. Active Young Democrats, Jefferson, 1962. Named Soldier of Year, U.S. Army, Brooke Med. Center, 1973. Mem. Am. Acad. Med. Adminstrs., Am. Coll. Hosp. Adminstrs. (nominee, mem. program com. 1982—). Presbyterian. Club: Alamo Hosp. Assn. (San Antonio). Office: Clearview Hosp PO Box 4757 Midland TX 79707

MORTON, CAROLINE JULIA, devel. co. exec.; b. N.Y.C.; B.S. in Edn., U. Pa.; M.B.A., N.Y. U.; grad. cert. in profl. writing and effective communication, CCNY. Vice pres. mktg. mgmt. V-TEC Corp., Hopewell, Va.; pres. CMR Co., Hopewell; past cons. Advt. Women of N.Y. Mem. Am. Mktg. Assn. (past dir.), Advt. Women of N.Y., Fedn. Profl. Bus. Women, Am. Mgmt. Assn., AAUW. Contbr. articles to profl. jours. Address: PO Box 841 Hopewell VA 23860

MORTON, FLORENCE HORTENSE BRASHEAR, educational administrator; b. Cleburne, Tex., Apr. 18, 1926; d. Alpheus Webb and Eula Hortense (Burnett) Brashear; B.A., Fisk U., 1947; M.A., Murray State U., 1971, cert. in adminstrn. and supervision, 1979; m. Andrew White Morton, Dec. 29. 1946; children—Lucia Diane Morton Moorman, Clifford Harrison, Tchr. lang. arts and social studies Paducah (Ky.) Public Schs., 1956-64; tchr. adult basic. edn., 1964-79; tchr. exceptional children Paducah Tilghman High Sch., 1965-74; dean students, 1974—; tchr., counselor Project Upward Bound, Murray State U., 1965-71. Mem. Paducah Mayor's Bi-Centennial Commn., 1975-76; counselor Bear Creek and West Ky. councils Girl Scouts U.S.A., 1959-62; facilitator Paducah Youth Leadership Council, 1981. Recipient Woman of Achievement award River City Bus. and Profl. Women's Club, 1982; Duchess of Paducah award, 1985. Mem. NEA, Paducah Edn. Assn., First Dist. Edn. Assn., Ky. Edn. Assn., Ky. Dental Assn. Aux., Western Ky. Dental Assn. Aux., Nat. Dental Assn. Aux., Alpha Kappa Alpha, Phi Delta Kappa, Delta Kappa Gamma. Club: Order Eastern Star, The Links, Inc. (pres. Paducah chpt. 1985—). Home: 1329 Rudy Ave Paducah KY 42001 Office: 2400 Washington St Paducah KY 42001

MORTON, FRED J., lawyer; b. El Paso, Tex., Nov. 13, 1935; s. R.A.D. and Julianne (More) M.; m. Anne Adele Reynolds, July 19, 1960; children—Chris, Anne, John, Robert, Peter, Mary Virginia, Thomas, Mary Katherine. B.A., U. Tex.-El Paso, 1957; LL.B., U. Tex.-Austin, 1958. Bar: Tex. 1958. Asst. U.S. atty., El Paso, 1961-65; U.S. commnr. cts., El Paso, 1966-71; sole practice, El Paso, 1966-71; ptnr. Calhoun, Morton & Villa, El Paso, 1971—. Trustee, Southwestern Children's Home Trust, El Paso, 1983—; pres. El Paso County Hist. Soc., 1967. Mem. Tex. Bar Assn., El Paso Trial Lawyers Assn. (pres. 1972), El Paso Bar Assn. (pres. 1985), Sigma Alpha Epsilon, Phi Delta Phi. Democrat. Roman Catholic. Avocation: artist. Home: 211 Lombardy El Paso TX 79922 Office: Calhoun Morton & Villa 210 N Campbell El Paso TX 79901

MORTON, JEROME HOLDREN, school psychologist; b. Duluth, Minn., July 30, 1942; s. Jerome Raefield and Svea (Holdren) M.; B.A., Centre Coll., 1964; M.S., Miami U., Oxford, Ohio, 1966; Ph.D., U. Tenn., 1973; m. Anna Mary Moore, June 9, 1964; children—Scot, Jeanette. Psychologist Pinellas County Sch. System, Clearwater, Fla., 1969-71; dir. psychol. and spl. edn. services Little Tenn. Valley Ednl. Cooperative, Lenoir City, Tenn., 1973-76, exec. dir., 1977—; due process hearing officer State of Tenn. Dept. Edn., Nashville, 1974-86; dir. Alternative Ctr. for Learning, Knoxville, 1985—; hon. asst. prof. psychology dept. U. Tenn., Knoxville, 1978—; cons. S.W. Va. Consortium for a Coop. Services Orgn., Bristol, 1983—; ptnr. Psychol. and Ednl. Cons., Knoxville, Tenn., 1985—. Co-chmn. East Tenn. Coalition for Children, 1983-84, chmn., 1984-85. Served with U.S. Army, 1966-69. Mem. Tenn. Assn. Psychology in Schs. (pres. 1976-77), Tenn. Psychol. Assn. (v.p. 1976-77), Nat. Assn. Sch. Psychology, Am. Psychol. Assn. Home: 7309 Bonny Kate Dr Knoxville TN 37920 Office: Route 9 Box 316 Lenoir City TN 37771

MORTON, LELAND CLURE, judge; b. Knoxville, Tenn., Feb. 20, 1916; s. George W. and Birdie (Myers) M.; B.A., U. Tenn., 1934, J.D., 1936; m. Marjorie J. Hernandez, Sept. 13, 1945. Admitted to Tenn. bar, 1937; practiced in Knoxville, 1937-41, 46-70; spl. agt. FBI, U.S., 1941-42, Central and S.Am., 1942-46; U.S. dist. judge Middle Dist. Tenn., Nashville, 1970-77, chief judge, 1977—; instr., U. Tenn.; co-founder Vol. State Bank, Knoxville, dir., 1964-70. Counselor East Tenn. council Boy Scouts Am., 1937-40. Bd. dirs. Cerebral Palsy Found., Boys Club, Boys of Tenn. Mem. Tenn., Nashville bar assns., S.R., Phi Kappa Phi. Republican. Methodist. Office: A-845 US Courthouse Nashville TN 37203*

MORTON, MICHAEL JOE, research and development statistician; b. Dallas, Mar. 5, 1954; s. Charles Buddy Morton and Mary Frances (Perdue) Payton; m. Nancy Parmelee, June 12, 1982; 1 child, Julia Catherine. B.A., U. Tex., 1976, M.A., 1978; Ph.D., So. Meth. U., 1981. Teaching asst. math. dept. U. Tex., Austin, 1976-78, stats. dept. So. Meth. U., Dallas, 1978-81; systems engr. Bell Telephone Labs., Holmdel, N.J., 1981-84; statistician Transp. Test Ctr., Pueblo, Colo., summer 1980, R.J. Reynolds Inc., Winston-Salem, N.C., 1984—. Mem. Am. Statis. Assn., Phi Beta Kappa, Phi Kappa Phi. Avocations: tennis; racquetball; running.

MORYL, WALTER JOHN, textile company executive; b. Newark, May 13, 1937; s. Walter and Cathrine (Hozempa) M.; m. Selma H. Mandel; children—Jeffrey Scott, Kathi Lynn. B.B.A., Upsala Coll., 1955; M.B.A., Rutgers U., 1960; student, Inst. Human Engring., Chgo., 1962. Budget analyst Curtiss Wright Corp., Woodridge, N.J., 1955-58; mgr. fin. reporting Electronic Computation div. RCA Corp., Harrison, N.J., 1958-73; div. v.p. fin. and adminstrn. Coronet Carpets, Dalton, Ga., 1973-76; v.p., treas. fin. Coronet Industries, Inc., Dalton, 1976-80, exec. v.p. fin., 1980—. Bd. dirs. Whitfield County United Way, Ga., 1980-82; dir. Hamilton Med. Ctr., Dalton, 1980—; trustee Dalton Jr. Coll., 1982—, Creative Arts Guild, 1981—; mem. pres.' council Upsala Coll., East Orange, N.J., 1980—. Served with USNG, 1950-53. Mem. Nat. Assn. Accts., Am. Mgmt. Assn., Dalton C. of C. (dir.). Roman Catholic Club: Dalton Golf and Country. Lodge: Elks. Home: 2246 Rocky Face Circle Dalton GA 30720 Office: Coronet Industries Inc Coronet Dr Dalton GA 30720*

MOSBY, CAROLYN LEWIS, college administrator; b. Lynchburg, Va., Mar. 6, 1937; d. William Thomas and Nannie (Jackson) Lewis; m. Alexander Lipscomb Mosby, Jr., Aug. 17, 1963. B.S., Va. Union U., 1958; M.A., Morgan State U., 1970; D.Edn., Coll. William and Mary, 1983. Spl. edn. educator Buffalo Pub. Schs., 1959-61; math. educator Richmond Pub. Schs., Va., 1961-74; dir. learning skills Va. Union U., Richmond, 1974-76; div. chmn. John Tyler Community Coll., Chester, Va., 1978—. Mem. budget com. United Givers' Fund, Richmond, Va., 1972-74; bd. dirs. Southside Resources Council, Richmond, 1980-82, Health Regulatory Bds., State Va., 1978-82, Adv. Bd., Dept. Pub. Welfare, Richmond, 1984-85. Mem. Va. Community Coll. Assn. Baptist. Clubs: The Links, Inc., Nat. Epicureans Inc. (nat. pres. 1984-86), Girlfriends, Inc. (Richmond). Home: 3524 Bathgate Rd Richmond VA 23234 Office: John Tyler Community Coll Chester VA 23831

MOSBY, EMMA GRACE, educator; b. Elgin, Tex., Dec. 9, 1948; d. Otha and Annie Lee Haywood; B.A., Huston-Tillotson Coll., 1969; M.Ed., U. Tex., El Paso, 1971; Ph.D., Tex. A&M U., 1982; m. Richard Allen Mosby, Dec. 21, 1969; 2 sons, Richard Allen, Haywood Edward Elem. tchr. Elgin (Tex.) Ind. Sch. Dist., 1969-74; reading tchr. Copperas Cove (Tex.) Ind. Sch. Dist., 1974, 77-78; elem. tchr. NE Ind. Sch. Dist., San Antonio, 1974-77; reading specialist Spring Branch (Tex.) Ind. Sch. Dist., 1978-81; grad. asst. Tex. A&M U., 1980—; adminstr. Medcare Clinic and Roentgen Services, 1982—. Active, Assocs. of Mus. Fine Arts. Named Camelot Tchr. of Yr, 1975. Mem. NEA (conv. del. 1976, 79), Tex. State Tchrs. Assn. (conv. del. 1976, 79), Internat. Reading Assn., Tex. Assn. Reading, Greater Houston Reading Assn., Assn. Supervision and Curriculum Devel., Phi Delta Kappa. Roman Catholic. Clubs: Baylor Coll. Medicine Wives, VFW Aux., Aux. to Houston Med. Forum, Aux. to San Antonio Doctors, Alpha Kappa Alpha. Condr. research in field. Home: 3622 S Braeswood Houston TX 77025 Office: PO Box 20554 Houston TX 77225

MOSBY, JOHN OLIVER, retired civil service official; b. Trenton, N.J., Mar. 6, 1917; s. John Oliver and Florence (Stewart) M., Sr.; A.A., St. Philips Coll., 1949; B.B.A., St. Mary's U., 1956, M.A., 1966; m. Sylvia Ann Harris McKane, Feb. 16, 1980. Civilian staff U.S. Army, Fort Sam Houston, 1952-66, inventory mgmt. specialist Fifth Army, 1966-82; instr. St. Philips Coll., San Antonio, 1968—. Vice pres. parish council Holy Redeemer Cath. Ch., 1982-83, pres., 1983-84. Served with AUS, 1942-46, USAF, 1950-52; ETO; PTO. Recipient Fifth Army Comdr.'s award, 1982. Mem. Am. Acctg. Assn., Am. Econ. Assn., Assn. Social Econs., San Antonio Bus. and Econs. Soc., Alamo City C. of C., Assn., Holy Name Soc., Knights of St. Peter Claver, Omicron Delta Epsilon, Omega Psi Phi (Basileus 1977—, past Basileus award 1978; outstanding achievement award 1985). Clubs: Serra, Optimist (charter mem., pres., membership award 1973-74). Home: 4922 Stoneleigh Dr San Antonio TX 78220

MOSCOVICH, ELIZABETH ANN, graphics company executive; b. Pleasant Hill, Mo., Feb. 18, 1950; d. Dennis Vernon and Mary Esther (Edmondson) Reeves; m. Edgard J. Moscovich, Nov. 21, 1976; 1 dau., Dawn Marie. Student pub. schs., Lee's Summit, Mo. Cert. real estate salesperson, lic. real estate sales broker, Fla. Sec., Fordick Corp., Kansas City, Mo., 1970-72; office mgr. Dackus Tile & Marble Co., Fort Lauderdale, Fla., 1972-75; exec. v.p. Am. Graphics Corp., Fort Lauderdale, 1975—, prodn. dir. reference book, 1980. Hon. mem. Friends of Ft. Lauderdale Library, 1981—, Friends for Life of U. Miami Sch. Medicine, 1984—. Mem. Bd. Realtors (communications com. 1985), Phi Theta Kappa (Omega Phi chpt.).

MOSCRIP, ANDREW LOOMIS, savings and loan exec.; b. Norwalk, Ohio, June 3, 1950; s. George Alexander and Phyllis (Wilson) M. B.S., Ga. So. Coll., 1972. Tchr. Tattnal City Bd. of Edn., Collins, Ga., 1972-73; credit mgr. Cert. Fin. Service, Savannah, Ga., 1973-75; sr. v.p. Biscayne Fed. Savs. & Loan Assn., Miami, Fla., 1975—; tchr. Inst. Fin. Edn. Mem. Progress Club Miami, Arabian Horse Assn. Fla., Am. Mgmt. Assn., Am. Soc. Personnel Adminstrn., Savs. Insts. Mktg. Soc. Am., Sigma Nu. Republican. Episcopalian. Home: 8090 SW 72d Ave Apt J-4 Miami FL 33143 Office: Biscayne Fed Savs & Loan Assn 1790 Biscayne Blvd Miami FL 33132

MOSELEY, GEORGE KINLOCK, pharmacist; b. N.Y.C., Dec. 8, 1931; s. George K. and Dorothy Scianimanico (Heinbockel) M.; m. Betty Jean Broussard, Nov. 28, 1952; children—George Keith, Karen Moseley Seals. B.S. in Pharmacy, Purdue U., 1955. Registered pharmacist, Tex. Mgr. Woods Drugs, Evansville, Ind., 1955-59, Armstrong Pharmacy, Pasadena, Tex., 1959-63; mgr. Green Pharmacy, Pasadena, 1963—, owner, 1969—. Served with U.S. Army, 1950-52. Mem. Harris County Pharm. Orgn., Tex. Pharm. Assn., Nat. Rifle Assn. Republican. Baptist. Lodge: Elks. Avocations: hunting; fishing; boating. Home: 1504 Lavonia Ln Pasadena TX 77502 Office: Greens Pharmacy 1009 E Thomas St Pasadena TX 77506

MOSELEY, JAMES FRANCIS, lawyer; b. Charleston, S.C., Dec. 6, 1936; s. John Olin and Kathyrn (Moran) M.; A.B., The Citadel, 1958; J.D., U. Fla., 1961; m. Anne McGehee, June 10, 1961; children—James Francis, John McGehee. Admitted to Fla. bar, 1961, U.S. Supreme Ct. bar, 1970; partner firm Taylor, Moseley & Joyner, Jacksonville, Fla., 1963—; chmn. Fourth Jud. Circuit Nominating Commn., 1980-82. Pres. Civic Round Table, Jacksonville, 1974; pres. United Way, Jacksonville, 1979; chmn. Southeastern Admiralty Law Inst., 1980; chmn. bd. trustees Jacksonville Libraries, 1981. Fellow Am. Coll. Trial Lawyers; mem. Jacksonville Bar Assn. (pres. 1975), Fla. Bar, Fla. Counsel Bar Pres.' (counsel 1979), Maritime Law Assn. (exec. com. 1978-81), Fedn. Ins. Counsel, Internat. Assn. Ins. Counsel, R.R. Trial Lawyers Assn. Clubs: Deerwood, River. Contbr. articles on admiralty law to legal jours. Home: 7780 Hollyridge Rd Jacksonville FL 32217 Office: Taylor Moseley & Joyner 501 West Bay St Jacksonville FL 32202

MOSELEY, LAURICE CULP, piano sales and service company executive; b. Chilton County, Ala., Feb. 15, 1927; d. John Curtis and Alma Roma (Hand) Foshee; student Air U. Extension Course Inst., 1951-57; m. Charles W. Culp, Oct. 23, 1946; children—Randall D., Robert C.; m. 2d, Ernest B. Moseley, Jr. May 21, 1966. Auditor, personnel clk. fed. govt., 1949-55; owner, pres., treas. Culp Piano Co. (doing bus. as Fairview Piano Co., Inc., Electronics Organ Service Co., Moseley Piano Co., Crown Gems Internat., Culp Internat. Inc.), Montgomery, Ala., 1955—, also dir.; dir. Dimensions Inc., Montgomery. Mem. Nat. Assn. Music Mchts., Am. Music Conf., Nat. Assn. Female Execs. Republican. Club: Soroptimist. Author: (with A.T. Thomas) 6 Lessons Toward Keyboard Mastery, 1978. Home: 2543 Wildwood Dr Montgomery AL 36111 Office: Care Culp Piano & Organ Co 634 E Patton Ave Montgomery AL 36111

MOSELEY, WILLIAM WARD, architect; b. Lawrenceville, Va., Mar. 26, 1930; s. William Stuart and Annie Gray (Duke) M.; m. Jewel Mason Moncure, Aug. 22, 1959 (div. 1981); children—William Ward, II, Robert Moncure; m. Patricia Ann Salmon, Sept. 3, 1982. B.S. Va. Poly. Inst. and State U., 1952; postgrad., 1953. Registered architect, Va., N.C., Md., Ohio, Washington D.C. Ptnr. Marcellus Wright & Ptnrs., Richmond, 1965-69; pvt. practice as architect, Richmond, 1969-72; pres. Moseley-Hening Assocs., Inc., Richmond, 1972—; mem. faculty Va. Commonwealth U., Richmond, 1970. Contbr. articles to profl. jours. Pres. Highland Hills Community Assn., 1964-65; bd. stewards Bon Air Meth. Ch., 1967; chmn., charter mem. Southport Property Owners Assn., 1980—; chmn. econ. progress billboard com. Central Richmond, 1983-84; charter mem. Businesses Who Care, Richmond, 1982—, Brandermill Archtl. Review Bd., 1975-76, Brandermill Community Assn., 1975; acct. exec. United Way Campaign, 1981-83, sect. chmn. for architects, 1985; mem. Chesterfield Bus. Council, 1981—. Served to 2d lt. USAFR, 1952-56. Recipient Merit award for excellence in design, 1966, Honor award for excellence in design, 1974, Design award for excellence in masonry construction, 1978, Energy Design award, 1979, Honor award for excellence in design, 1980, Excellence in masonry construction hon. mention, 1982, Small Bus. Person of Yr., Richmond Metro C. of C., 1982, Small Bus. Assn., 1983, Disting. Service Presdl. award, 1965, and many others. Mem. AIA, Soc. Am. Mil. Engrs., Va. Assn. Professions, Bronze Hokie Club Va. Tech Student Aid Assn., Metro Richmond C. of C., Va. Tech. Alumni Assn., Va. State C. of C. (mem. small bus. council 1982—), U.S. C. of C., St. Paul's Coll. Capital Campaign, Exchange Club Va., Better Bus. Bur., Omicron Delta Kappa (charter mem. Richmond chpt.). Lodge: Rotary. Home: 9313 Groundhog Dr Richmond VA 23235 Office: Moseley-Hening Assocs Inc 601 Southlake Blvd Richmond VA 23236

MOSELY, LINDA HAYS, surgeon; b. New Orleans, Feb. 20, 1941; d. Charles Hodge Mosely and Florence (Morley) Mosely Williams. Student Emory U., 1959-61; B.S., La. State U., 1963, M.D., 1967. Diplomate Am. Bd. Surgery, Am. Bd. Plastic Surgery; lic. physician, Va., D.C., La. Rotating intern Charity Hosp., New Orleans, 1967-68, med. resident, 1968-69, gen. surgery resident, 1970-72; surgery resident Mt. Sinai Hosp., N.Y.C., 1969-70; hand surgery fellow Dr. Harold Kleinert, Louisville, 1972, 74; clin. surg. fellow U. Louisville Med. Ctr., 1972, gen. surgery resident, 1973; research fellow Yale Med. Ctr., New Haven, 1975, plastic surgery resident, 1975-77; tour specialist Middlemore Hosp., Auckland, N.Z., 1977-78; practice aesthetic surgery Clinica Planas, Barcelona, Spain, 1978-79; cons. plastic surgery John Fitzgerald Kennedy Hosp., Monrovia, Liberia, 1979; clin. and research fellow Toronto Gen. Hosp., Ont., Can., 1979-80; practice medicine specializing in gen. and plastic surgery, Alexandria, Va., 1980—. Contbr. articles to med. jours. Mem. A.C.S., Am. Soc. for Plastic and Reconstructive Surgeons, Met. Washington D.C. Soc. for Surgery of Hand, D.C. Met. Plastic Surgery Soc., Med. Soc. Va., Alexandria Med. Soc., Arlington County Med. Soc. Home: 5318 Echols Ave Alexandria VA 22311 Office: 2500 N Van Dorn St Suite 128 Alexandria VA 22302

MOSELY, RALPH ELLINGTON, III, employee and environmental safety executive; b. Chattanooga, Tenn., Aug. 2, 1944; s. Ralph Ellington and Sara Ester (Smith) M.; m. Karen Lee Whittemore, May 15, 1965; children—Sara Michelle, Jennie Lee. B.S., Tenn. Tech. U., 1966; M.B.A., U. Tenn., 1978. Cert. safety profl. Sr. loss prevention cons. Liberty Mut. Ins. Co., Atlanta, Birmingham, Ala. and Memphis, 1968-74; gen. mgr. Pacific Eastern Corp., Nashville, 1974-76; sr. cons. safety services Resource Cons., Inc., Brentwood, Tenn., 1976-77; corp. dir. employee and environ. safety Genesco, Inc., Nashville, 1977—; assoc. prof. Tenn. State U., Nashville, 1977—; cons. safety engring. Alley, Young & Baumgartner, Brentwood, Tenn., 1983—; cons. indsl. hygiene Barcon, Inc., LaVergne, Tenn., 1984—. Editor: Noise Control-A Guide for Workers and Employers, 1984; Refresher Guide for the Safety Professional, 1985; cons. editor: Readings in Noise Control and Hearing Conservation, 1985. Contbr. articles to profl. jours. Vice-chmn. Metro Nashville Safety Adv. Bd., 1981-85; mem. ergonomics com. Meharry Med. Ctr., Nashville, 1984-85; mem. environ. com. Tenn. Mfrs. Assn., Nashville, 1983-85. Served to capt. U.S. Army, 1966-68. Recipient awards of appreciation Mayor of Nashville, 1981, 83, Gov. of Tenn., 1983, Resolution of Appreciation, Tenn. Ho. of Reps., 1983, Superior Achievement Recognition award Genesco, Inc., 1984. Mem. Am. Soc. Safety Engrs. (chpt. pres. 1978-79, most outstanding mem. 1979), Nat. Safety Council (gen. chmn. meat and leather sect. 1983-85, award of appreciation 1984-85), program chmn. ergonomics com. 1984-85), Am. Indsl. Hygiene Assn., Southeastern Occupational Health Conf., Inc. (bd. dirs. 1981-85), Tenn. Safety Congress (treas. 1980—). Republican. Avocations: long distance running; tennis; golf; auto repair. Home: 156

Haverford Dr Nashville TN 37205 Office: Genesco Inc 430 Genesco Park Nashville TN 37202

MOSER, PAUL WAYNE, optometrist; b. Raleigh, N.C., July 14, 1951; s. Paul Becham and Doris Ruth (Rollins) M.; m. Jane Louise Bunch, Aug. 16, 1975; 1 child, Susan Rollins, A.A., Mt. Olive Coll., 1971; B.A. in Biology, E. Carolina U., 1974; D.Optometry, So. Coll. Optometry, 1980. Practice optometry, Raleigh, N.C. Mem. Am. Optometric Assn., N.C. Optometric Assn. (trustee). Democrat. Episcopalian. Club: Crabtree Rotary (pres. 1984-85). Avocations: dogs; fishing; skeet, trap shooting. Home: 6401 Margate Ct Raleigh NC 27612 Office: 5105 Bur Oak Circle Raleigh NC 27612

MOSES, JOHN HERRICK, JR., state official; b. N.Y.C., Mar. 15, 1939; s. John Herrick and Katharine Dieterich M.; B.A., Bowdoin Coll., 1960; M.Ed., Va. Commonwealth U., 1976; m. Sara Ann Woolford, Oct. 12, 1978; children—Dawn Sophia, Christopher John Herrick. With Dept. State, Washington, 1961-62; tchr. Waldorf Schs., Germany, N.Y. and Washington, 1962-69, trustee Waldorf Schs. Fund Inc., 1965-69; tchr. St. Christopher's Sch., Richmond, Va., 1971-72; purchase officer Commonwealth of Va., Richmond, 1973—. Sec.-treas., dir. De' Vine Ltd., 1974—. Bd. dirs. Richmond Community Action Program, 1976—, treas., 1979-81, pres., 1982-84; bd. dirs. Ctr. for Am. Studies, Concord, Mass., 1985—. Mem. Va. Assn. Govtl. Purchasing, Alpha Delta Phi. Episcopalian. Club: Richmond First. Home: 4813 Morrison Rd Richmond VA 23230

MOSLEHY, FAISSAL ABDEL-HALEEM, mechanical engineering educator; b. Sharkia, Egypt, Dec. 4, 1950. B.S. in Mech. Engring., Cairo U., 1973, M.S., 1976; Ph.D., U. S.C., 1980. Registerd profl. engr., Fla. Instr. dept. mech. engring. Cairo U., 1973-76; teaching, research asst. dept. mech. engring. Auburn U. (Ala.), 1976-78; teaching and research asst. U. S.C., Columbia, 1978-80, instr., 1980; asst. prof. U. Central Fla., Orlando, 1980-85, assoc. prof., 1985—. Naval Research Lab. grantee, 1982. Mem. ASME, Soc. for Exptl. Mechanics, Nat. Soc. Profl. Engrs., Fla. Engring. Soc., Fla. Acad. Sci., Egyptian Soc. Engrs., Tau Beta Pi, Pi Tau Sigma. Contbr. articles to profl. jours. Home: 4405 Bridgewater Dr Orlando FL 32817

MOSLEY, MADISON MCNEIL, JR., librarian; b. Leesburg, Fla., Jan. 17, 1950; s. Madison McNeil Mosley and Reatha Mae Mosley-Crummer; B.A., Fla. State U., 1971, Ph.D. (Univ. fellow 1978-79), 1980; M.L.S., U. N.C., Greensboro, 1974. Librarian, Lake Placid (Fla.) High Sch., 1971-73; coordinator tech. services Cape Fear Tech. Inst., Wilmington, N.C., 1974-77; crime intelligence technician Fla. Dept. Law Enforcement, Tallahassee, 1980-81; mgr. manual searching Fla. Educators' Info. Service, Center for Studies in Vocat. Edn., Tallahassee, 1981-82; dir. library services South Fla. Community Coll., Avon Park, Fla., 1982—. Bd. dirs. ARC/Ridge Area, 1984—, Avon Park Hist. Soc., 1985—; commr. Avon Park Housing Authority; mem. Fla. Devel. Disabilities Council, 1985—; pres. Avon Park chpt. NAACP, 1986—. Mem. ALA, Nat. Soc. Study of Edn., Southeastern Library Assn., Fla. Library Assn. Lodge: United Order of Salem. Home: 1015 W Bell Apt 19 Avon Park FL 33825 Office: 600 W College Dr Avon Park FL 33825

MOSLEY, ZACK TERRELL, cartoonist; b. Hiclory, Okla., Dec. 12, 1906; s. Zack Taylor and Irah Corrina (Aycock) M.; m. Bety Sue Adcock, May 31, 1945; 1 child, Jill Mosley Sandow. Student Chgo. Acad. Fine Arts, 1926-27, Chgo. Art Inst. Sch., 1927-28. Asst. artist Buck Rodgers and Skyroads comics, Chgo., 1929-33; creator Smilin' Jack, Chgo. Tibune, N.Y. News syndication, N.Y.C., 1933-73; artist/writer Tribune Media Service, Orlando, 1973—; author, artist: Smilin' Jacks Brave Coward Zack, 1976, Hot Rock Glide, 1979, De-Icers Galore, 1980. Served to col. CAP, 1941-46. Decorated Air medal. Mem. Aircraft, Owners and Pilots Assn., Quiet Birdmen, Nat. Cartoonists Soc. Lodges: Elks. Address: 262 SE Edgewood Dr Stuart FL 33494

MOSS, CHARLES ALBERT, JR., architect; b. Spartanburg, S.C., Sept. 16, 1929; s. Charles A. and Jessie Louise (Muckenfuss) M.; B.Arch., N.C. State U., 1956; m. Frances Adele Hicks, June 21, 1957; children—Charles Albert III, Torrey Amanda, Jordan Harrison. Draftsman, Edwards, McKimmon & Ethridge, Architects and Engrs., Raleigh, N.C., 1956-57, Caldwell & Harmon, Architects, Birmingham, Ala., 1957-58, Carroll C. Harmon Architect, Birmingham, 1958-62; partner Harmon & Moss Architects, Birmingham, 1962-72; pres. Moss, Garikes & Assos. Architects, Inc., Birmingham, 1971-82; sec.-treas. Health Facilities Planning, Inc., Birmingham, 1973-82; pres. Moss & Assocs., Architects, Inc., 1982—. Bd. dirs. Ala. Adv. Council on Libraries; v.p. Ala. Symphony Assn.; bd. mem. Birmingham Festival Arts; pres. men's com. Ala. Symphony Assn.; mem. Ala. Gov's. Conf. on Library and Info. Services, 1979; mem. archtl. review bd. Morris Ave. Served with U.S. Army, 1952-55. Recipient citation of merit Ala. Library Assn., 1980. Mem. AIA (pres. Birmingham chpt. 1969, Ala. council 1974, chmn. Gulf states regional conv. 1977), Constrn. Specifications Inst., Council Ednl. Facility Planners, Ala. Library Assn. Presbyterian. Club: Rotary (Birmingham). Home: 3749 Jackson Blvd Birmingham AL 35213 Office: 415 N 21st St Birmingham AL 35203

MOSS, DEWEY LEE, carpet company executive; b. Dalton, Ga., July 1, 1943; s. Denver D. and Lois (Wilson) M.; m. Charlotte A. Adams, May 22, 1968; children—Angela, Amy, Michael, Amanda. B.S. in Indsl. Mgmt., Ga. Inst. Tech., 1965. Staff cons. Kurt Salmon Assocs., Atlanta, 1968-72; assoc. v.p. mfg. Male Jeans, Atlanta, 1972-75; dir. ops. London Fog Sportswear, Atlanta, 1975-76; pres. D.L.M. & Assocs., Dalton, Ga., 1976-79, Gold Label Carpets, Dalton, 1979—. Served with U.S. Army, 1974-76. Lodges: KC (grand knight 1984-85), Elks. Home: 2217 Rocky Face Circle Dalton GA 30720 Office: Gold Label Carpets PO Box 3876 Dalton GA 30721

MOSS, DWAYNE, pharmacist; b. Paducah, Ky., Oct. 16, 1948; s. Thomas and Marion M.; m. Cynthia Carol Pierce, Jan. 7, 1981; children—Rodney Dale, Allison Nichole. B.S. in Pharmacy, Med. U. S.C., 1972; postgrad. Murray State U., 1985. Registered pharmacist. Staff pharmacist Fountain Inn Drug Co., S.C., 1972-74; staff pharmacist Lourdes Hosp., Paducah, Ky., 1974-79, asst. dir. pharmacy, 1979-85, dir. pharmacy, 1985—, mem. pharmacy and therapeutic com., 1979-85, mem. infection disease, safety and standards coms., 1985. Mem. Ky. Soc. Hosp. Pharmacists, Am. Soc. Hosp. Pharmacists, Ky. State Pharm. Assn., S.C. State Pharm. Assn., Western Ky. Soc. Hosp. Pharmacists. Avocations: water skiing; outdoor activities; reading. Home: Route 8 Box 47 Paducah KY 42001

MOSS, EDWARD ASHLEY, lawyer; b. Kosciusko, Miss., Sept. 5, 1953; s. Claude E. and Eleanor Grace (Lucas) M.; m. Donna Kay Phillips, Mar. 2, 1972; children—Ashley S., Mary Grace. B.A., U. Colo., 1978; J.D., U. Miss., 1981. Bar: Miss. 1981, U.S. Dist. Ct. (no. dist.) Miss. 1981, U.S. Dist. Ct. (so. dist.) Miss. 1983, U.S. Ct. Appeals (5th and 6th cirs.) 1983. Assoc. Holcomb, Dunbar, Connell Chaffin & Willard, Clarksdale and Oxford, Miss., 1981-84, ptnr., 1984—. Served with USAF, 1972-79. Decorated Air Force Commendation medal; recipient Am. Jurisprudence award U. Miss., 1980. Mem. Assn. Trial Lawyers Am., Miss. Trial Lawyers Assn., ABA, Miss. Bar Assn., Def. Research Inst., Lafayette County Bar Assn., Coahoma County Bar Assn., Am. Inn. of Ct. III. Methodist. Home: 405 Lakeview Ct Oxford MS 38655 Office: Holcomb Dunbar Connell Chaffin & Willard PO Drawer 707 Oxford MS 38655

MOSS, JOHN RICHARD, psychology educator, psychologist; b. Earlsboro, Okla., Nov. 6, 1928; s. John R. and Hazel (Matlock) M.; m. Nancy McCauley, May 25, 1950 (div. May 1954); m. Betty Jane Coppedge, July 23, 1963; children—Kevin Brian Cowley (stepson), Monette Denise. B.S. in Edn., Central State U., Edmond, Okla., 1950; M.Ed., So. Meth. U., Dallas, 1954; Ed.D., U. Tulsa, 1960. Lic. psychologist, Tex. Tchr., counselor, prin. Tulsa Pub. Schs., Okla., 1954-60; asst. prof. Northwestern State U., Alva, Okla., 1960-61; sch. psychologist Littleton Pub. Schs., Colo., 1961-67; prof. No. State Coll., Aberdeen, S.D., 1967-70, East Tex. State U., Commerce, Tex., 1970—; dir. Launch, Inc., Commerce, Called, Inc., Commerce. Editor newsletter Launcher (Pres.'s award 1980, Nat. Network award 1982). Pres. Hunt Rockwall Health Council, Greenville, Tex., 1984—, Sabine Valley Area Council, Greenville, 1980—. Served to 1st lt. U.S. Army, 1952-54. Mem. Am. Psychol. Assn., Assn. for Children and Adults with Learning Disabilities. Democrat. Baptist. Lodge: Kiwanis (pres. 1981-82). Home: Route 1 Campbell TX 75422 Office: East Tex State U East Tex Station Commerce TX 75428

MOSS, KENNETH EUGENE, oil company executive; b. Hollis, Okla., Nov. 9, 1936; s. Kenneth L. and Norma E. (Bledsoe) M.; m. Jerelyn Davis, Aug. 25, 1956; children—Kenneth G., Kristi. B.A., Oklahoma City U., 1959; student W. Tex. State U., 1975-76. Logging engr. Baroid, Oklahoma City, 1959-63; prodn. foreman Union Oil Co. of Calif., Perryton, Tex., 1963-74; dist. prodn. supr. Pioneer Prodn. Corp., Amarillo, Tex., 1974—. Contbr. articles to profl. jours. Patentee solar powered pump. Served with U.S. Army, 1960-62. Chmn., Community Devel. Adv. Com., Amarillo, 1980-85. Mem. Soc. Petroleum Engrs. (chmn. Amarillo sect. 1981-82), Am. Assn. Petroleum Geologists, Panhandle Geol. Soc. Republican. Club: Lambda Chi Alpha. Avocations: hunting; fishing. Home: 3807 Teckla St Amarillo TX 79109 Office: Pioneer Prodn Corp PO Box 2542 Amarillo TX 79189

MOSS, RAYMOND GENE, II, lawyer; b. Duncan, Okla., Apr. 11, 1945; s. Raymond Gene and Jimmie Orene (Boyles) M.; m. Grenda Falene Penhollow, Mar. 29, 1969; children—Travis Penhollow, Clayton Boyles. B.A., U. Okla., 1967; postgrad. George Washington U., 1967-68; J.D., U. Okla., 1970. Bar: Okla. 1970, U.S. Dist. Ct. (we., no., ea. dists.) Okla. 1970, U.S. Ct. Appeals (10th cir.) 1970. Law clk. Pierce, Couch, Hendrickson, Johnston & Baysinger, 1968-69; legal intern Walker & Watson, 1969-70; assoc. McAffee & Taft, 1970-75, mem. firm, 1975-84; ptnr. DeSpain & Moss, 1984, Ames, Dougherty, Asabranner, Fowler, Taylor, Lawrence & Moss, 1985, Daogherty, Bradford, Fowler & Moss, 1986—. Bd. dirs. Okla. div. Am. Cancer Soc., 1975-85. Served to capt. USAF, 1969-75. Mem. ABA, Okla. Bar Assn., Oklahoma County Bar Assn., Oklahoma City C. of C. (facilities com., Bicentennial com.), Phi Gamma Delta (pres. chpt. 1974-81). Democrat. Episcopalian. Club: Kiwanis. Address: 900 First City Pl 204 N Robinson Oklahoma City OK 73102

MOSS, SANDRA HUGHES, legal administrator; b. Atlanta, Dec. 24, 1945; d. Harold Melvin and Velma Aileen (Norton) H.; m. Marshall L. Moss, May 1, 1965; children—Tara Celise, Justin Hughes. Student W. Ga. Coll., 1964-65. Legal sec. Smith, Cohen, Ringel, Kohler & Martin, Atlanta, 1965-78; real estate salesman Century 21-Phoenix, College Park, Ga., 1978-80; office mgr./personnel dir. Smith, Cohen, Ringel, Kohler & Martin, Atlanta, 1980-85; dir. adminstrn. Smith Gambrell & Russell, 1985—. Bd. dirs., sec. N. Clayton Athletic Assn., Riverdale, Ga., 1981-83; sec. E.W. Oliver PTA, Riverdale, 1981; exec. com. E.W. Oliver and N. Clayton Jr. PTA, Riverdale, 1980, 81, 82; den leader Cub Scouts, Pack 959, Riverdale, 1984. Mem. Am. Soc. Personnel Adminstrs., Assn. Legal Adminstrs. Home: 1627 Lauranceae Way Riverdale GA 30296 Office: Smith Gambrell & Russell 2400 First Atlanta Tower 2 Peachtree St Atlanta GA 30383

MOSSER, DENNIS MCHENERY, SR., fire protection technician, consultant; b. Martinsburg, W.Va., June 30, 1945; s. Samuel Ralph and Gertrude Edith (McHenery) M.; m. Marianna Arms, May 29, 1970; children—Dennis M., Jr., Stephen M., Tricia L. B.S. in Occupational Edn., So. Ill. U., 1983; A.A.S. in Fire and Safety Engring., Rowan Tech. Coll., 1973. Fed. fire fighter Dept. Defense U.S. Army, Fort Indiatown Gap Mil. Reservation, 1971; sr. fire fighter Prince William Co. Fire Service, Manassas, Va., 1973-74; faculty instr. Midlands Tech. Coll., Columbia, S.C., 1974-76; tng. specialist S.C. Fire Acad., West Columbia, 1976-82; loss control cons. Fireman's Fund Ins. Co., Columbia, 1983-84; fire protection technician Carolina Power & Light Co., Hartsville, S.C., 1984-85; program chmn. St. Petersburg Jr. Coll., Clearwater, Fla., 1985—; adj. faculty Internat. City Mgmt. Assn., Washington, 1982—; tech. adv. S.C. Gov.'s Office, Columbia, 1978. Asst. chief Paxtang Vol. Fire Dept., Harrisburg, Pa., 1971, tng. officer, 1968-71, lt., 1967-71. Served with USN, 1963-66. Recipient Fireman of Yr. award Dauphin County Firemen's Assn., 1970, Outstanding Service award Paxtang Fire Dept., 1971, Disting. Service award Paxtang Fire Dept., 1968, Appreciation award Charleston Fire Dept., 1978. Mem. Nat. Fire Protection Assn., Am. Soc. Safety Engrs., Paxtang Pa. Fire Dept. (life). Republican. Mem. Christian Missionary Alliance Ch. Avocations: organic gardening; mechanical repair; painting. Home: 1389 Chesterfield Dr Clearwater FL 33516 Office: St Petersburg Jr Coll Clearwater Campus 2465 Drew St Clearwater FL 33575

MOSTOWYCH, LEONIDAS, radiologist; b. Ukraine, Oct. 4, 1919; came to U.S., 1957, naturalized, 1962; s. Gregory and Maria (Luchynska) M.; M.D., U. Innsbruck (Austria), 1951; m. Oksana Martha Iwanochko, Mar. 12, 1948; children—Irene, Mark. Resident in internal medicine and radiology Univ. Clinics, Innsbruck, 1952-57; intern St. Mary and St. Elizabeth Hosps., Louisville, 1958-61; resident in chest diseases Tb Hosp., Waverly Hills, Ky., 1961-64; resident in radiology U. Louisville Hosp., 1964-66; instr. radiology U. Ky., Lexington, 1964-66, asst. prof., 1966-70, asso. prof., 1970-78, prof. 1978—; dept. chmn. VA Med. Center, Lexington, 1964—. Contbr. articles to profl. jours. Recipient award for outstanding contbn. for nat. and state health care services Bd. Fed. Exec. Assn., 1975; cert. commendation VA, 1983. Fellow Am. Coll. Radiology; mem. AMA, Ky. Med. Assn., Fayette County Med. Soc., Bluegrass Radiologic Soc., Radiol. Soc. N.Am., Ukrainian Am. Med. Assn. Greek Orthodox. Office: Radiology Dept University of Kentucky Medical Center Lexington KY 40511

MOSTROM, LLOYD CLERMONT, management analyst, consultant; b. Hawlay, Minn., July 12, 1909; s. Ludvig J. and Jerone (Reierson) M.; m. Jean Sherman Thompson, Sept. 1, 1945; children—Elizabeth, James, Anne, Susie, Alison, Ingrid. B.A., Concordia Coll., 1933; postgrad. U. Minn., 1935, Mich. State Coll., 1938; M.A., U. Okla., 1940. Commd. officer U.S. Navy, 1942, advanced through grades to capt.; statistician, mgmt. analyst Naval Shipyard, Charleston, S.C., 1947-51, head budget br., 1945-47; mgmt. analyst field mgmt. div. Bur. Ships, Washington, 1951-55; head fin. mgmt. br. Field Mgmt. div. NAVSEA, Arlington, Va., 1955-73, dept. comptroller, 1973-81; ret., 1965; cons. in field. Inventor bomb demolition device, detection device. Asst. scoutmaster local council Boy Scouts Am., 1967-86; pres. Yorktown High Sch. PTA, Arlington, 1971-73, 76-78; dist. dir. Potomac dist. Va. Congress PTAs, 1982-86; pres. Arlington County Scholarship Fund Tchrs., 1983-85, treas., 1985-86; vol. Washington Area Legis. Services, 1983-86. Recipient Outstanding Citizen award Arlington County Sch. Bd., Scouter of Yr. award Boy Scout Troop 162, 1966. Lutheran. Home: 910 N Montana St Arlington VA 22205

MOTA, GUILLERMO HUMBERTO, radio station executive; b. Havana, Cuba, Dec. 12, 1924; came to U.S., 1961, naturalized, 1969; s. Jose and Carmen (Castro) M.; m. Yolanda U. Ugalde, Aug. 30, 1953; children—Yolanda, Carmen. LL.B., Havana Inst., 1942; J.D., U. Havana, 1951. Registered real estate broker, Fla. Sales mgr. WCMQ Broadcasting Co., Havana, 1960-61; ptnr. Permod Importers, San Juan, P.R., 1961-63; account exec. San Juan Broadcasting Corp., 1963-68; account exec. Susquehanna Broadcasting Co., Miami, Fla., 1969-82, sales mgr., 1982—. Mem. Asociacion Interamericana de Hombres de Empresa. Republican. Roman Catholic. Clubs: Casino Espanol, American. Home: 5900 SW 89th Ave Miami FL 33173 Office: Sta WQBA 701 SW 27th Ave Miami FL 33135

MOTT, JANE ADELE, physical education educator; b. Fresno, Calif., Aug. 28, 1919; d. Edwin Leland and Margaret Ross (Derby) M. B.A., Fresno State Coll., 1941; M.S., U. Wis.-Madison, 1944; Ph.D., U. So. Calif., 1954. Lectr. and teaching asst. phys. edn. U. So. Calif., Los Angeles, 1949-52; asst. prof. phys. edn. dept. San Jose State Coll., Calif., 1953-54; prof. Smith Coll., Northampton, Mass., 1954-76, dir. phys. edn. dept., 1960-76; chmn. dept. dance Tex. Woman's U., Denton, 1976—, instr. U. Nebr., 1944-49. Author: Conditioning and Basic Movement Concepts, 1977; Soccer and Speedball for Women, 1973; assoc. editor research quar., Exercise and Sport, 1964-78; evaluation editor Wm. C. Brown Sports Activities Series, 1966—. Recipient Amy Morris Womans Research award, Wellesley Coll., 1962; postdoctoral fellow U. So. Calif., 1963, 70. Fellow Am. Acad. Phys. Edn., (sec.-treas. 1971-1978), Am. Coll. Sports Medicine; mem. Am. Alliance for Health, Physical Edn., Recreation and Dance (v.p. 1958). Republican. Episcopalian. Lodge: Eastern Star. Home: 610 Northridge Dr Denton TX 76201

MOTTA, JOHN RICHARD, professional basketball coach; b. Salt Lake City, Sept. 3, 1931; s. Ambrose and Zelda (Squires) M.; m. Janice Fraser, June 4, 1954; children—Kip A., Jodi, Kirt Glen. B.S., Utah State U., 1953, M.A., 1960. Jr. high sch. basketball coach, Grace, Idaho, 1953, high sch. basketball coach, Grace, 1956-59; basketball coach Weber State Coll., Ogden, Utah, 1961-68; basketball coach Chgo. Bulls, 1969-76, gen. mgr., dir. player personnel, 1973-76; coach Washington Bullets, 1976-80, Dallas Mavericks, 1980—. Served with USAF, 1954-56. Named Coach of Yr., Nat. Basketball Assn., 1970-71. Address: Dallas Mavericks Club 777 Sports St Dallas TX 75207*

MOTTO, ANNA LYDIA, classicist, educator; b. N.Y.C.; d. Michael Angelo and Molly (Gross) Motto; m. John R. Clark, Nov. 7, 1959; children—Valerie Molly, Bradford Russell. B.A., Queens Coll., CUNY, 1946; M.A., N.Y. U., 1948; Ph.D., U. N.C., 1953. Asst. prof. Washington Coll., Chestertown, Md., 1953-57; asst. prof., chmn. classics Alfred U., 1958-65; assoc. prof., chmn. classics Muhlenberg Coll., Allentown, Pa., 1965-66, assoc. prof. St. John's U., Jamaica, N.Y., 1966-68; prof., chmn. classics Drew U., Madison, N.J., 1968-73; vis. prof. U. Mich., summer 1969; prof. classics U. South Fla., Tampa, 1973—, chmn. fgn. langs., 1974-78, dir. classics, 1982-85, chmn. dept., 1985—; resident Inst. for Advanced Study, Princeton, N.J., summers 1979-80. U. N.C. Fellowship awardee, 1950-51; Fulbright grantee, 1956. Mem. Modern Lang. Assn., Am. Classical League, Classical Soc. Am., Vergilian Soc., N.Y. Class. Club, Classical Assn. Middlewest and South (pres. 1983), Classical Assn. Atlanta States (v.p. 1972), South Atlantic Modern Lang. Assn. Author: Seneca Sourcebook: Guide to the Thought of Lucius Annaeus Seneca, 1970; Seneca, 1973; Senecan Tragedy, 1986; editor: Satire—That Blasted Art, 1973; Seneca: Moral Epistles, 1985; contbr. numerous articles to scholarly jours. Office: Classics Dept U South Fla Tampa FL 33620

MOTYL, GARY PAUL, investment company executive; b. Reading, Pa., Mar. 29, 1952; s. Paul and Marie (Volk) M. B.S. in Fin., Lehigh U., 1974; M.B.A. in Fin., Pace U., 1977. Security analyst Standard & Poor's Corp., N.Y.C., 1974-79; trust investment officer Landmark First Nat. Bank, Ft. Lauderdale, Fla., 1979-81; v.p. portfolio mgr. Templeton Investment Counsel Inc., Ft. Lauderdale, 1981—. Mem. Inst. Chartered Fin. Analysts (cert.), Fin. Analysts Fedn. Republican. Avocations: bridge, golf. Home: 2260 NE 53d St Fort Lauderdale FL 33308 Office: Templeton Investment Counsel Inc One Financial Plaza #2202 Fort Lauderdale FL 33394

MOULTON, JAMES COGSWELL, JR., educational administrator; b. Washington, June 13, 1944; s. Charles Spann and Elizabeth Orilee (Miller) Baumann; m. Ruth Irene Swart, June 17, 1967 (div. 1979); children—Jeffrey Charles, Stacy James; m. Donna Sue McCubbin, Dec. 18, 1982. B.A., U.Va., 1966, M. Ed., 1968. Tchr., intern U. Va. Fairfax County Schs., Edison High Sch., 1966-67; tchr. history Fairfax County Schs., Oakton High Sch., 1967-70; adminstrv. aide Oakton, Marshall High Sch., 1970-72; sub. sch. prin., Robinson Secondary Sch., 1972-84; prin. Joyce Kilmer Intermediate Sch., Vienna, Va., 1984—. Mem. Nat. Assn. Secondary Sch. Prins., No. Va. Secondary Sch. Adminstrv. Assn., Assn. Supervision and Curriculum Devel., Tau Kappa Epsilon, Phi Delta Kappa. Methodist. Avocations: handbell ringer; travel; camping; photography. Home: 5322 Windsor Hills Dr Fairfax VA 22032 Office: Joyce Kilmer Intermediate Sch 8100 Wolftrap Rd Vienna VA 22180

MOUNTS, JERRY, dentist, pharmacist; b. Williamson, W. Va., June 9, 1955; s. Herbert and Norma Jean (Davis) M. B.S., W.Va. U., 1978; D.D.S., 1983. Pharmacist intern Revco Drugs, Huntington, W. Va., 1979, pharmacist mgr., Beckley, W.Va., 1979; relief pharmacist various locations, 1979-84; pvt. dentist, Matewan, W.Va., 1984—. Mem. ADA, W.Va. State Dental Assn., Am. Soc. Dentistry for Children, Huntington Dental Soc., W.Va. Pharmacists Assn., W.Va. U. Alumni Assn., W.Va. U. Dental Alumni Assn., W.Va. U. Pharmacy Alumni Assn., Psi Omega. Democrat. Mem. Ch. of Christ. Lodge: Masons. Avocations: basketball; tennis; swimming; bicycling; fishing. Home: 1004 E 4th Ave Williamson WV 35661 Office: PO Box 537 Matewan WV 35667

MOURSUND, ALBERT WADEL, III, lawyer, rancher; b. Johnson City, Tex., May 23, 1919; s. Albert W. and Mary Frances (Stribling) M.; LL.B., U. Tex., 1941; m. Mary Allen Moore, May 8, 1941; children—Will S., Mary M. Admitted to Tex. bar, 1941; practice in Johnson City, 1946—; mem. firm Moursund & Moursund, 1963-80, Moursund, Moursund, DesChamps & Moursund, 1980—; chmn., dir. First Bank, Llano, 1963—, also dir.; pres., dir. Arrowhead Co., Lakeland Investment Corp., Ranchlander Corp., pres., dir. Cattleman's Nat. Bank, Round Mountain, Tex.; pres., dir. Tex. Am. Moursund Corp., Southwest Moursund Corp., Arrowhead West, Inc.; dir. Scott Corp., Scott Plaza, Inc., Las Vegas. Mem. Tex. Parks and Wildlife Commn., 1963-67; Tex. Ho. of Reps. 1948-52. Served with USAAF, 1942-46. Mem. Am., Tex., Hill County (past pres.) bar assns., Blanco County Hist. Soc. (charter), Sons of Hermann. Democrat. Clubs: Masons, Woodman of World. Home: Johnson City TX 78636

MOURSUND, KENNETH CARROLL, grocery chain executive; b. Austin, Tex., Oct. 21, 1937; s. Leif Erickson and Ethel Alberta (Aiken) M.; B.A., U. Tex., Austin, 1963; m. Claudia Frances Reifel, Dec. 21, 1963; 1 son, Kenneth Carroll. Mgmt. trainee Am. Warehouses, Inc., 1963-64; with Kroger Co., Houston, 1964—, transp. supr., 1964, distbn. mgr. charge all warehousing and transp. Houston div., 1969-83, dir. distbn. Houston, S. Tex. and S. La., 1983—; profl. baseball player N.Y. Yankees and Detroit Tigers, 1957-61. Life mem., chmn. group ticket com. Houston Livestock and Rodeo Assn.; vestryman Trinity Episcopal Ch., 1977-79, jr. warden, 1978, sr. warden 1979, mem. endowment bd., 1980-82; bd. dirs. Am. Diabetes Assn. Served with USAR, 1960-66. Mem. Houston C. of C., Houston Symphony Soc., Delta Nu Alpha; life mem. Ex-Student Assn. U. Tex., Nat. Rifle Assn. Club: Pine Forest Country. Office: PO Box 1309 Houston TX 77001

MOUSSATOS, MARTHA ANN TYREE, librarian; b. Parris Island, S.C., Sept. 18, 1936; d. Frank La Prade and Vireen Florrie (Varn) Tyree; m. Apostolos Harilaos Moussatos, June 27, 1959; children—Vasiliana Vireen, Harilaos Apostolos. B.A., Columbia Coll., 1958; M.L.S., U. Ariz., 1974. Asst. reference librarian U. S.C., Columbia, 1958-59; librarian Fulton High Sch., Atlanta, 1962; substitute tchr. pub. schs., Sierra Vista, Ariz., 1967-68; librarian Naco Elem. Sch. (Ariz.), 1968-70, Benson High Sch. (Ariz.), 1970-75; head librarian Depot Library, Parris Island, S.C., 1975—. Author: Hagar (play), 1980; Young Eliza (play), 1958; Marshgrass and Muscadines (poetry), 1980; Scuppernong Wine at Room Temperature (poetry), 1984; contbr. articles to profl. jours. and popular mags. Mem. Historic Port Royal Found. (S.C.), 1976—, bd. dirs., 1981—. Recipient award as head of outstanding single parent family Beaufort County Homebuilders Assn. (S.C.), 1980. Mem. ALA, Library Assn. Beaufort County, S.C. Library Assn. (editorial com. 1979—), Poetry Soc. S.C. (bd. dirs. 1980-83). Greek Orthodox. Home: 3011 Hickory St Burton SC 29902 Office: Depot Library PO Drawer 5-055 Parris Island SC 29905

MOUTON, JANE SRYGLEY, industrial psychologist; b. Port Arthur, Tex., Apr. 15, 1930; d. Theodore and Grace (Stumpe) Srygley; B.S. in Edn., U. Tex., 1950, Ph.D. in Psychology (Univ. fellow 1954-55), 1957; M.S. (Lewis fellow) U. Fla., 1951; m. Jackson C. Mouton, Jr., Dec. 22, 1953; children—Jane, Jacquelyn. Research asst. U. Tex., Austin, 1953-57, social sci. research asst., 1957-59, instr. in psychology, 1957-59, asst. prof. psychology, 1959-62; v.p. Scientific Methods, Inc., Austin, 1961—. Diplomate Am. Psychol. Assn. Licensed, certified Tex. State Bd. Examiners of Psychologists. Mem. Internat. Assn. Applied Social Scientists, N.Y. Acad. Scis., Southwestern Psychol. Assn., Interam. Soc. Psychology. Author: The Marriage Grid, 1971; The Grid for Sales Excellence, 1970; Corporate Excellence through Grid Organization Development, 1968; How to Assess the Strengths and Weaknesses of a Business Enterprise, 1972; Corporate Darwinism, 1966; Managing Intergroup Conflict, 1964; The Managerial Grid, 1964; Consultation, 1976; Instrumented Team Learning, 1975; The Supervisory Grid, 1975; The New Managerial Grid, 1978; The Social Worker Grid, 1979; The Real Estate Grid, 1980, others contbr. articles to profl. jours. Home: 2305 Hartford Rd Austin TX 78703 Office: PO Box 195 Austin TX 78767

MOUTRAY, DENNIS ROBERT, oil company safety representative; b. Oklahoma City, Okla., July 6, 1949; s. George Ballard and Goldie Loretta (Pilgreen) M.; m. Dena Jean Mallow, May 23, 1974. B.B.A., Central State U., 1972. Ins. adjuster Crawford and Co., Oklahoma City, 1973-81; safety rep. Helmerich & Payne, Inc., Oklahoma City, 1981—. Vice chmn. booklet: How to Keep Drugs Off Your Rigs, 1984. First aid instr. ARC, Oklahoma City, 1984. Mem. Petroleum Safety Profls. Okla., Am. Soc. Safety Engrs., Internat. Assn. Drilling Contractors (co. rep., vice chmn. narcotics awareness task group), Okla. Claims Assn., Central State Alumni Assn. Republican. Baptist. Avocations: waterskiing; golf; camping; softball; photography. Office: Helmerich & Payne Inc 5401 S Hattie Oklahoma City OK 73143

MOVASSAGHI, KAM KAMBIZ, civil engineer, educator; b. Mashad, Iran, May 20, 1940; came to U.S., 1960; s. Abbas and Fatemeh (Tabatabaei) M.; m. Mazie Sonia Bodden, Dec. 24, 1966; children—Eric A., Jennifer L. B.S., U. Southwestern La., 1963; M.S., La. State U., 1965, Ph.D., 1971. Cert. profl. engr., La., Miss. Structural engr. Fromherz Engrs., New Orleans, 1965-69; asst., assoc. researcher La. State U., Baton Rouge, 1969-71, asst. prof., 1972-75; pres. Arithma Engring Co., Tehran, Iran, 1975-79; assoc. prof. U. Southwestern La., Lafayette, 1980—, also dir. engring mgmt. program. Active local Boy Scouts Am. Grantee La. Dept. Natural Resources, 1980-81. Mem. ASCE, Am.

Soc. Engring. Edn., Nat. Soc. Profl. Engrs., La. Engring Soc., Miss. Engring Soc., Sigma Xi, Phi Kappa Phi, Chi Epsilon. Democrat. Contbr. articles and papers to profl. publs. Dept Civil Engring U Southwestern La USL Box 42291 Lafayette LA 70504

MOWAD, JULIE ANN, coach, educator, sports commentator; b. Alexandria, La., Dec. 31, 1954; d. Anthony Peter and Mary Ann (Rush) M. B.S., U. New Orleans, 1979. Coach, Jefferson Parish Recreation Dept., Metairie, La., 1975-79; tchr., coach Oakdale (La.) High Sch., 1979—; sports commentator Sta. KGBM-FM, Oakdale, 1981—; owner, mgr. Julie's Place, restaurant, 1981-83; sales rep. Anthony's Sport Shop, 1979—. Mem. La. Democratic Com., 1982; advisor Catholic Youth Orgn., 1979—; v.p. Oakdale Dixie Girls Softball Assn., 1980; pres. Oakdale Band Boosters Club, 1982-84. Mem. La. High Sch. Athletic Assn., La. Assn. Educators, Oakdale Athletic Assn., AAPEHRD, Allen Parish Assn. Educators, Oakdale Bus and Profl. Womens Club (young careerist award 1982). Office: Oakdale High Sch 101 13th St Oakdale LA 71463

MOWBRAY, RALEIGH THOMAS, III, pharmaceutical company executive; b. Richmond, Va., Aug. 3, 1948; s. Raleigh Thomas and Alice Ann (Meador) M.; m. Frances Roberta Bourne Mowbray, Apr. 15, 1978; 1 son, Mark T. B.A. in Polit. Sci., N.C. Wesleyan Coll., 1978. Cert. emergency med. technician, N.C.; cert. law enforcement officer, N.C. Attendant, sec., treas. Stony Creek Rescue Squad, Rocky Mount, N.C., 1970-71; foreman R.T. Mowbray & Son, Richmond and Greenville, S.C., 1971-73; attendant Momeyer Rescue Squad (N.C.), 1973; with Abbott Labs., Rocky Mount, 1973—, maintenance planner-scheduler, 1973-74, supr. shop, 1974-75, supr. engring. services, 1976, systems engr., 1976, certification engr., 1976-78, documentation sect. mgr., 1978-79, documentation mgr., 1979-83, documentation and tng. mgr., 1983—. Bd. dirs. East Carolina Emergency Med. Services Systems, Inc., 1980-84; capt. Nash County Sheriff's Dept. Aux., 1976-78; pres. Stony Creek Fire Dept. and Rescue Squad, 1979—, fire chief, 1977—. Recipient Buck Overton Service award Stony Creek Fire Dept. and Rescue Squad, 1979, named Rescue Man of Yr., 1969, 74. Mem. Nash County Fire-Rescue Assn. (bd. dirs.), Edgecombe County Fire-Rescue Assn., N.C. Firemen's Assn., N.C. State Assn. Rescue Squads, N.C. Fire Chief's Assn., Nat. Fire Protection Assn., Internat. Assn. Fire Chiefs. Democrat. Methodist. Club: Northgreen Country (Rocky Mount, N.C.); Fairfield Harbour Country (New Bern, N.C.). Home: 1333 Mc Duffers Rd Rocky Mount NC 27804 Office: PO Box 2226 Rocky Mount NC 27802

MOXLEY, ROY ANTHONY, early childhood educator; b. Grosse Pointe Farms, Mich., Jan. 30, 1934; s. Roy Anthony and Anetta May (Van Alstyne) M. B.S. in Sci., U. Detroit, 1958; M.A. in English, Wayne State U., 1962; Ph.D. in Edn., U. Mich., 1972. Instr. U. Mich., Ann Arbor, 1970-71; asst. prof. edn. Ind. U., 1971-72; prof. edn. W.Va. U., Morgantown, 1972—. Mem. Am. Edn. Research Assn., Assn. for Behavior Analysis, Internat. Reading Assn., Nat. Assn. for Edn. of Young Children. Author: (with Mary Fitch) Changing Patient Behavior: A Behavior Modification Manual for Dental Professionals, 1978, 2d edit., 1984; Writing and Reading in Early Childhood, 1982; contbr. articles to profl. jours. Home: 884 E Everly #15 Morgantown WV 26505 Office: 604 Allen Hall W Va U Morgantown WV 26506

MOYE, CHARLES ALLEN, JR., federal judge; b. Atlanta, July 13, 1918; s. Charles Allen and Annie Luther (Williamson) M.; A.B., Emory U., 1939, J.D., 1943; m. Sarah Ellen Johnston, Mar. 9, 1945; children—Henry Allen, Lucy Ellen. Admitted to Ga. bar, 1943; practice in Atlanta, 1943-70; partner firm Gambrell, Russell, Moye & Killorin, and predecessors, 1955-70; judge U.S. Dist. Ct. for No. Dist. Ga., Atlanta, 1970—, chief judge, 1979—. Chmn. DeKalb County Republican Exec. Com., 1952-56, Rep. Exec. Com. 5th Congl. Dist. Ga., 1956-64; mem. Ga. Rep. Central Com., 1952-64; Rep. candidate for Congress, 1954; del. Rep. Nat. Conv., 1956, 60, 64; chmn. Rep. Exec. Com. 4th Congl. Dist. Ga., 1964; Rep. presdl. elector, 1964. Mem. Fed. Bar Assn., ABA, Atlanta Bar Assn., State Bar Ga., Lawyers Club Atlanta, Am. Law Inst., Am. Judicature Soc., Delta Tau Delta. Congregationalist. Clubs: Atlanta Athletic, Atlanta City; Nat. Lawyers (Washington). Contbr. articles to legal jours. Home: 1317 Council Bluff Dr NE Atlanta GA 30345 Office: US Dist Courthouse 75 Spring St SW Atlanta GA 30303

MOYER, JERRY MILLS, financial services company executive; b. Oklahoma City, Mar. 19, 1940; s. Charles and Dorothy Moyer; B.S., Okla. State U., 1962; m. Cecilia L. Clark, Aug. 28, 1960; children—Jerry, James. Salesman, Jamco, Inc., 1965, Procter & Gamble, 1966; from salesman to credit mgr. B.F. Goodrich Co., 1967-71; with UCC-Communications Systems, Inc., Dallas, 1971-73; mgr. funds control Dr. Pepper Co., Dallas, 1973-80; pres. Cash Cons., Inc., Dallas, 1980-81; v.p. InterFirst Services Corp., Houston, 1981—; cash mgmt. cons. Active United Fund, InterFirst Polit. Action Com., Served with U.S. Army, 1962-65. Decorated Air medal (26), Purple Heart; various profl. awards. Mem. Tex. Cash Mgmt. Assn. (founder, past pres.), Nat. Corp. Cash Mgmt. Assn. (co-founder). Baptist. Lodges: Masons, Shriners, Lions. Contbr. articles to profl. jours. Office: Po Box 2555 Houston TX 77001

MOYERS, SYLVIA DEAN, med. record librarian; b. Independence, W.Va., Oct. 22, 1936; d. Wilkie Russell and Ina Laura (Watkins) Collins; student Am. Med. Record Assn., 1977-79; m. Paul Franklin Moyers, June 29, 1957; children—Tammy Jeanne, Thomas Paul, Tara Sue. Sec., Teets Lumber Co., Terra Alta, W.Va., 1954-58, Preston County News, Terra Alta, 1958-60; med. record clk. med. record dept. Hopemont (W.Va.) Hosp., 1960-75, dir., 1975—. Charter mem., past mother advisor Terra Alta Assembly No. 26, Order of Rainbow for Girls, past grand editor Mountain Echoes. Mem. Am. Med. Record Assn., W.Va. Med. Record Assn. Republican. Methodist. Club: Women of Moose. Home: 304 Ringer Ave Terra Alta WV 26764 Office: Hopemont Hosp Hopemont WV 26764

MOYES, CHRISTOPHER PETER, petroleum engineer; b. Winchester, Eng., Dec. 22, 1946; came to U.S., 1976; s. Peter Morton and Judith Mary (Knight) M.; m. Francoise Carnal, Feb. 10, 1984. B.Sc., U. Western Australia, 1968; Geologist, Royal Sch. Mines, London, 1973. Geologist, Wapet, Perth, Western Australia, 1968-72; petroleum engr. Gaffney Cline & Assocs., London, 1972-73, mng. dir., Singapore, 1973-77, mgr., Dallas, 1977-83, pres., 1983-84; ptnr. Moyes McGee Inc., Dallas, 1980—. Contbr. articles to profl. jours. Mem. Soc. Petroleum Engrs. (pres. Singapore 1976), Am. Assn. Petroleum Geologists, Soc. Exploration Geophysicists, Nat. Assn. Petroleum Investment Analysts. Avocations: sailing; skiing; opera. Home: 6444 Mimosa St Dallas TX 75230 Office: Moyes McGee Inc 400 N Saint Paul St Dallas TX 75201

MROCZEK, WILLIAM JOSEPH, research physician; b. N.Y.C., Aug. 9, 1940; s. William and Helena (Federowicz) M.; B.A., Seton Hall U., 1962; M.D., N.J. Coll. Medicine, 1966; m. Christine Landegger, Apr. 7, 1979; 1 child, Phoebe Victoria; children by previous marriage—Michelle Anne, Melissa Lynn, Ashley Elizabeth, Natasha Elene. Intern, St. Michael Hosp., Newark, 1966-67; resident Georgetown U. med. div. D.C. Gen. Hosp., 1967-69; fellow in cardiovascular disease Georgetown U. Sch. Medicine, 1969-70, asst. prof. medicine, 1972-77; chief dept. hosp. clinics Ft. Campbell, Ky., 1970-72; assoc. prof. medicine Howard U., Washington, 1977-82; dir. hypertension and hemodynamics lab. D.C. Gen. Hosp., 1972-82. Pres. No. Va. chpt. Am. Heart Assn., 1983-84; dir. Cardiovascular Ctr. No. Va., 1983—. Served to maj. U.S. Army, 1970-72. Diplomate Am. Bd. Internal Medicine. Fellow Am. Coll. Cardiology, Am. Coll. Clin. Pharmacology, Am. Coll. Angiology, Am. Coll. Geriatrics, Am. Coll. Clin. Pharmacology; mem. Am. Fedn. Clin. Research, Am. Soc. Nephrology, Am. Soc. Clin. Pharmacology and Therapeutics, Nat. Kidney Found., N.Y. Acad. Scis., AMA. Contbr. numerous articles to med. jours. Office: 6043-6045 Arlington Blvd Falls Church VA 22044

MSEZANE, ALFRED ZAKELE, physics educator; b. Springs, Transvaal, South Africa, Dec. 31, 1938; s. Albert and Esther (Mbuli) M.; m. Gail Patrick, Nov. 30, 1969; children—Temba, Lambda. B.Sc. with honors, U. South Africa, 1962, 1964; M.Sc., U. Sask., 1967; Ph.D., Western Ont. U., 1973. Research assoc. Witwatersrand U., Johannesburg, 1968-69, Ga. State U., Atlanta, 1974-76; instr. U. N.B. (Can.), Fredericton, 1976-78; vis. prof. La. State U., Baton Rouge, 1978-80; assoc. prof. Morehouse Coll., Atlanta, 1980-83; prof. physics Atlanta U., 1983—; chmn. physics and astronomy group Univ. Ctr. in Ga., 1983-84. Contbr. articles to profl. jours. Soccer coach YMCA, Decatur, Ga., 1980—, Baton Rouge, 1978-80; treas. East Lake Community Club. Grantee NSF, 1981-83, Dept. Energy, 1983-84, Acad. Applied Sci., 1981—; recipient Sir Oppenheimer Meml. bursary Anglo Am. Corp., 1965-69; World Univ. Service scholar, 1965-67; Witwatersrand U. scholar, 1968-69; bursary Rotary Club, 1962, City Council Springs, 1960-62. Mem. Am. Phys. Soc., AAAS, Sigma Pi Sigma. Office: Atlanta U Dept Physics 223 Chestnut St Atlanta GA 30314

MUDAHAR, MOHINDER SINGH, economist; b. Ludhiana, Punjab, India, Apr. 10, 1943; came to U.S., 1967, naturalized, 1982; s. Kartar Singh and Dalip Kaur (Gill) M.; m. Bhajan Kaur Sangha, Jan. 14, 1974; children—Baljinder Kaur, Rupinderpal Singh. B.Sc. with distinction, Punjab Agrl. U., 1965, M.Sc. with honors, 1967; M.S., U. Wis., Madison, 1970, Ph.D., 1972. Research assoc. Cornell U., Ithaca, N.Y., 1972-76; economist Internat. Fertilizer Devel. Ctr., 1976—. Contbr. numerous articles, research papers to profl. publs. Indian Council of Agrl. Research fellow, 1965-67; Ford Found. fellow 1969-71. Mem. Am. Econ. Assn., Am. Agrl. Econs. Assn. (travel fellow 1973), Internat. Assn. Agrl. Economists, Indian Soc. Agrl. Econs., U. Wis. Grad. Club (v.p. 1970-71). Avocations: reading; gardening; travel. Office: Internat Fertilizer Devel Ctr PO Box 2040 Muscle Shoals AL 35662

MUELLER, BILLY DON, geologist; b. Ranger, Tex., Sept. 7, 1953; s. Bobby D. and Dorothy (White) M.; m. Pamela Rae McCarty, July 31, 1982; 1 child, Meaghan Elissa. B.S. in Geology, Sul Ross State U., 1977, M.S., 1984. Geologist Kerr McGee, Grants, N.Mex., 1977-78, Core Labs., Midland, Tex., 1978-80; instr. lab. Sul Ross State U., 1978-80; geology cons., Post, Tex., 1980—. Recipient Outstanding Faculty award Sul Ross State U., 1977. Mem. Am. Assn. Petroleum Geologists (jr.) Avocations: paleontology; photography; hunting; golf. Office: PO Box 573 Post TX 79356

MUELLER, KEITH LEATON, insurance company executive; b. Mankato, Minn., Dec. 23, 1939; s. Kenneth Lockerbie and Harriet Lucille (McQueen) M.; m. Bobbie Joyce Crow, Nov. 24, 1983; 1 child, Joann. Grad. Pillsbury Mil. Acad., 1957. Salesman, Hunt-Wesson Co., Green Bay, Wis., 1967-70, Armour-Dial, Green Bay, 1970-74; nat. sales trainer Double Day Pub. Co., Green Bay, 1974-78; salesman Am. Family Life, Green Bay, 1978-81; owner brockerage company, Houston, 1981—. Served with U.S. Army, 1957-65. Recipient Salesman of Yr. award Canada Dry Corp., 1963, 64, Am. Family Ins., 1977, 78; Top Grad. award Dale Carnegie Sales Course, 1964. Lodges: Shriners (32 deg.), Scottish Rite (Legion of Honor). Avocations: racquetball; tennis; chess; travel. Home: 18423 Walden Forest Dr Humble TX 77346

MUELLER, MARK CHRISTOPHER, lawyer, accountant; b. Dallas, June 19, 1945; s. Herman August and Hazel Deane (Hatzenbuehler) M.; B.A. in Econs., So. Meth. U., 1967, M.B.A. in Accounting, 1969, J.D., 1971; m. Linda Jane Reed. Bar: Tex. 1971. Practiced in Dallas, 1971—; accountant A.E. Krutilek, Dallas, 1968-71, Arthur Young & Co., Dallas, 1967-68; assoc. L. Vance Stanton, Dallas, 1971-72; instr. legal writing and research So. Meth. U., 1970-71, instr. legal accounting, 1975. C.P.A., Tex. Mem. Am., Tex. bar assns., Tex. Soc. C.P.A.s, Nat. Rifle Assn., Order of Coif, Beta Alpha Psi, Phi Delta Phi, Sigma Chi. Clubs: Masons (32 deg.), Shriners. Home: 7310 Brennans St Dallas TX 75214 Office: 9854 Plano Rd Suite 100 Dallas TX 75238

MUELLER, ROY CLEMENT, graphic arts company executive; b. Weehawken, N.J., Aug. 15, 1930; s. Adam and Bertha Mueller; student Rochester Inst. Tech., 1976; m. Patricia Robinson, Sept. 3, 1970; children—Eric, Janet, Debra, Gregory. Mgr. estimating/billing dept. Editors Press, Hyattsville, Md., 1962-66; v.p., gen. mgr. Peninsula Press div. A.S. Abell Corp., Salisbury, Md., 1968-70; owner, mgr. Crown Decal & Display Co., Bristol, Tenn., 1972—; pres. Bristol Screen Inc. (Tenn.), 1977—. Recipient Ad award Tri City Advt. Fedn., 1975; internat. exhbn. award Screen Printing Assn., 1977. Mem. Screen Printing Assn., Am. Philatelic Soc.. Republican. Lutheran. Office: 1608 Edgemont Ave Bristol TN 37620

MUELLER, TRUDE, sculptress; b. Bielsko, Poland, Jan. 2, 1913; came to U.S., 1941; d. Igo and Irene (Kreiger) Werbel; m. Paul Mueller, May 21, 1957 (dec. Apr. 1976); m. George Piccardi, Jan. 2, 1979; children—Alice, Carol. Student, New Sch., 1969-70, Greenwich House, 1961-68, Norton Sch. Art, 1977-84 Tchr. Child Sch., N.Y.C., 1968; pvt. instr., Larchmont, N.Y., 1976-77. Prin. works include sculptures Palm Desert Mus., Ben Gurion U., Israel, Joseph Hirshhorn Collection, other pvt. collections. Home: 1200 S Flagler Dr Apt 1806 West Palm Beach FL 33401

MUFSON, DAVID ETHAN, real estate company executive; b. Miami Beach, Fla., Jan. 20, 1951; s. Julius and Rhoda Loretta (Jacobs) M. B.A., Syracuse U., 1973. Real estate salesman Arthur Shandloff, Realtor, Miami, Fla., 1975; writer sports articles for Miami Rev. newspaper, Daily Record, 1977; asst. to TV advt. dir. Jefferson Stores, Miami, 1977-78; real estate salesman Allen Fuller Co., Realtors, Miami Beach, Fla., 1979—. Mem. Fla. Assn. Realtors, Miami Beach Bd. Realtors. Democrat. Jewish. Club: Westview Country (Miami). Lodge: B'nai B'rith.

MUFWENE, SALIKOKO SANGOL, linguist, semanticist; b. Mbaya-Lareme, Bandundu, Zaire, Nov. 1, 1947; came to U.S., 1974; s. Tienebwe Mufwene and Nzaam Embu; m. Patricia Ann Hill, June 2, 1979. Candidature en Philo. et Lettres, Lovanium U., Kinshasa, Zaire, 1970; Agregation d'enseignement, Nat. U. Zaire, 1973, Licence en Philosophie et Lettres, 1973; Ph.D. in Linguistics, U. Chgo., 1979. Translator, interpreter USAID, Kinshasa, Zaire, 1971; teaching asst. Nat. U. Zaire, 1973-74; lectr. U. of W.I., Kingston, Jamaica, 1979-81; asst. prof. linguistics U. Ga., Athens, 1981—; mem. exec. com. Chgo. Linguistic Soc., 1975-76. Author: (with others) Papers from CLS 12, 1976; (with others) CLS Parasession on Diachronic Syntax, 1976. Contbr. chpts. to books and articles to profl. jours. Mem. editorial bd. Am. Jour. Lexicography, 1984, Jour. of Pidgin and Creole Langs., 1985. Mem. Linguistic Soc. Am., Am. Dialect Soc., Dictionary Soc. N.Am., Soc. for Caribbean Linguistics, S.E. Conf. Linguistics. Avocations: sports; travel; dancing. Office: Dept Anthropology U Ga Baldwin Hall Athens GA 30602

MUGITS, MICHAEL JAMES, school administrator, educator; b. Schenectady, N.Y., Jan. 14, 1953; s. James Arthur and Betty (Hartingstall) M.; m. Brenda Kathleen Pierce, May 25, 1975; children—Justin Caleb, Misha Monique. B.S. in Elem. Edn., U. Maine-Machias, 1975; M.Ed. in Adminstrn., U. N.H., 1978; postgrad. Harvard U., 1979, 80. Elem. tchr., prin. Stonington (Maine) pub. schs., 1975-77; elem. prin. Litchfield (Maine) pub. schs., 1977-79, Franklin (Mass.) pub. schs., 1979-82; elem. prin. Forest Hill Sch., Amarillo, Tex., 1982—; instr. W. Tex. State U., 1983. Coach, Kids Inc. of Amarillo sports program; bd. dirs. Amarillo YMCA; big brother Amarillo Big Bros. and Big Sisters Orgn.; treas. Amarillo Area PTA. Mem. Assn. Supervision and Curriculum Devel., Tex. Elem. Prins. Assn. Home: 4903 Goodnight Trail Amarillo TX 79109 Office: 3601 Amarillo Blvd E Amarillo TX 79107

MUHLHAUSEN, JOHN PRAQUE, design consultant; b. Norwalk, Conn., Jan. 29, 1940; s. Edward Conrad and Alice (Scofield) M.; student Coll. of William and Mary, 1958-60; B.F.A., R.I. Sch. Design, 1963; m. Kitza Them, Apr. 13, 1968; 1 son, David Prague. With Union Camp Corp., N.Y.C., 1963-64, Cambridge Seven Assocs., Cambridge, Mass., 1964-66, Visual Kommunication, Copenhagen, 1966-67, Hauser Assocs., Atlanta, 1967-72, Jova/Daniels, Busby, Atlanta, 1972-74; pres. John Muhlhausen Design & Assocs., Inc., Atlanta, 1975—. Bd. dirs. Sculptural Arts Mus., Atlanta, 1980-82. Recipient DESI Ann. award, 1979, 80; Soc. Environ. Graphic Designers award, 1978; Indsl. Design Rev., 1969, 71; Graphis Ann., 1970-72; Print Casebooks, 1976-79; many others. Mem. Am. Inst. Graphic Arts, Soc. Environ. Graphic Designers (dir. 1984-86, nat. chmn. 1986—), Soc. Typographic Arts, Snipe Class Internat. Racing Assn. (dir. 1981-84). Club: Atlanta Yacht (bd. dirs. 1977-79). Author: Wind and Sail, 1971; contbr. articles to profl. jours. Home: 3453 Winter Hill Dr Marietta GA 30062 Office: 1146 Green St Roswell GA 30075

MUIR, HELEN, author; b. Yonkers, N.Y., Feb. 9, 1911; d. Emmet A. and Helen T. (Flaherty) Lennehan; student Yonkers pub. schools; m. William Whalley Muir, Jan. 23, 1936; children—Mary Muir Burrell, William Torbert. With Yonkers Herald Statesman, 1929-30, 31-33, N.Y. Eve. Post, 1930-31, N.Y. Evening Jour., 1933-34, Carl Byoir & Assos., 1934-35; syndicated columnist Universal Service, 1935-38, Miami Daily News, 1935-39; broadcaster stas. WIOD, WQAM, 1935, 42; columnist Miami Herald, 1941-42; woman's editor Miami Daily News, 1943-44; free lance mag. writer, Sat. Evening Post, This Week, Nation's Bus., Woman's Day, 1944—; children's book editor Miami Herald, 1949-56; drama critic Miami News, 1960-65. Trustee Coconut Grove Library Assn., Friends U. Miami Library, Met. Dade County Library Bd., State Library Adv. Council; mem. vis. com. for libraries U. Miami. Recipient award Delta Kappa Gamma, 1960; Trustees and Friends award Fla. Library Assn., 1973; award Dade County Library Assn., 1977; trustee citation ALA, 1984; named to Fla. Women's Hall of Fame, 1985. Mem. Soc. Women Geographers, Women in Communications (Community Headliner award 1973). Clubs: Fla. Women's Press (award 1963); Biscayne Bay Yacht (flag mem.); Cosmopolitan (N.Y.C.). Author: Miami, U.S.A., 1954. Home: 3855 Stewart Ave Miami FL 33133

MUKAMAL, DAVID SAMIER, sign manufacturing company executive; b. Baghdad, Iraq, Oct. 6, 1944; came to U.S., 1950; s. Abraham Sassoon and Mary (Murad) M.; m. Anitamarie Costa, July 31, 1970; children—Adam Scott, Rebecca Kate. B.B.A. in Econs. with honors, Bryant Coll., 1970; M.B.A. in Fin. Mgmt., Iona Coll., 1975. Budget analyst USV Pharm./Revlon, Inc., Tuckahoe, N.Y., 1970-72; sr. budget officer Met. Transp. Authority, N.Y.C., 1972-74; sr. fin. analyst Am. Airlines, Inc., Dallas, 1974-82; pres. All State Signs, Richardson, Tex., 1982—. Served with USN, 1965-66. Recipient Jeremiah Clarke Barber award Bryant Coll., 1970. Mem. Dallas Apt. Assn., Tex. Sign Mfrs. Assn., Omicron Delta Epsilon. Republican. Jewish.

MUKENGE, IDA FAYE ROUSSEAU, sociology educator, social science researcher; b. Troup, Tex., Mar. 16, 1941; d. Gentry Charles Burnett and Jessie (Andrews) Rousseau; m. Tsilemalema Leonard, Nov. 1, 1975; children—Ndaya, Muadi, Tshimpolepole, Malongo. B.A. in French, U. Calif.-Berkeley, 1962, M.A. in Edn., 1966; M.A. in Sociology, 1971, Ph.D. in Sociology, 1980. French instr. Harford Sch., Moyamba, Sierra Leone, 1962-64; project dir. Neighborhood House, Richmond, Calif., 1964-66; asst. cultural attache U.S. Inf. Service Kinshasa, Zaire, 1966-69; fulbright prof. Nat. U. Zaire, Lubumbashi, 1974-75; prof. sociology Morehouse Coll., Atlanta, 1971—; escort, interpreter U.S. Dept. State, 1980—; research dir. Atlanta U. Ctr. Summer Study Abroad, Haiti, Guadeloupe, 1979-82; research evaluator U.S. AID, Kenya, Ivory Coast, Senegal, 1977; program. Cons. New Careers, Contra Costa Coll., Calif., 1969-71 Author: The Black Church in Urban America, 1984; also articles Bd. dirs. Alzheimer's and Related Diseases Assn., Atlanta Area, 1984—, Women's Inst. Southeast, Atlanta, 1981-84; program chmn. Woodland High Sch. Parent Tchr. Student Assn., East Point, Ga., 1983—; community organizer and troop leader Northwest Ga. council Girl Scouts U.S.A., East Point, 1976-82. Fellow Rockefeller Found., 1984—, United Negro Coll. Fund, 1979-80, HHS, 1983-84. Mem. Am. Sociol. Assn., Sociologists for Women in Soc.-South (book rev. editor 1985—), So. Sociol. Soc. (state membership chmn. 1984—, com. on minorities 1985—), Fulbright Alumni Assn. (prof. 1974-75), Phi Beta Kappa, Delta Sigma Theta (charter pres. 1961-62). Avocations: reading, sewing, interior decoration. Home: 2907 Blossom Ln East Point GA 30344 Office: Morehouse Coll Sociology Box 32 830 Westview Dr SW Atlanta GA 30344

MULDER, JOHN MARK, theology educator, clergyman; b. Chgo., Mar. 20, 1946; m. Mary Margaret Hakken, June 29, 1968; children—Aaron Martin, Anna Cornelia. A.B., Hope Coll., 1967; M.Div., Princeton U., 1970, Ph.D. in History, 1974; LL.D., Centre Coll., 1984; D.D., Southwestern at Memphis, 1984. Ordained to ministry United Presbyn. Ch., 1970. Instr. in Am. ch. history Princeton Theol. Sem., N.J., 1974-75, asst. prof., 1975-80, assoc. prof., 1980-81; pres., prof. hist. theology Louisville Presbyn. Theol. Sem., Ky., 1981—; pastor Rensselaerville Presbyn. Ch., N.Y., summer 1977. Chmn. com. to develop seal for reunited Presbyn. Ch. (U.S.A.), 1983-85. Author: Woodrow Wilson: The Years of Preparation, 1978. Editor books, essay and paper collections. Contbr. articles and essays to profl. publs. Grantee Am. Philos. Soc., 1976, Nat. Hist. Publs. and Records Commn., 1978. Recipient Francis Makemie award, Hist. Found., 1978. Mem. Presbyn. Hist. Soc. (dir.), Am. Soc. Ch. History, Cath. Hist. Assn., Am. Acad. Religion, Orgn. Am. Historians, Am. Hist. Assn., Ky. Humanities Council, Acad. Parish Clergy. Office: Louisville Presbyn Theol Sem 1044 Alta Vista Rd Louisville KY 40205

MULFORD, RAND PERRY, business executive; b. Denver, Sept. 30, 1943; s. Roger Wayne and Ann Louise (Perry) M.; m. Constance A. Powell, Mar. 22, 1981; 1 son, Conrad Perry. B.S.E. cum laude, Princeton U., 1965; M.B.A. with highest distinction (Baker scholar), Harvard U., 1972. Mgmt. cons. McKinsey & Co., Chgo., 1972-78, dir. adminstrn., 1979; v.p. planning and control Plastics and Chem. Spltys. Group, Occidental Chem. Co./Occidental Petroleum Inc., Houston, 1980-81; pres. Technivest Inc., 1982-83, 85—; pres. Home-Med Services, Inc., 1983-84; dir. Quest Med. Inc., Carrollton, Tex., Sea Trailer Co., Inc., Houston, OMI Internat., Detroit; adv. bd. L. Karp & Sons, Elk Grove Village, Ill. Served with USN, 1965-70. Clubs: Harvard Bus. Sch. of Houston. Home: 2118 Nantucket Dr Apt 3 Houston TX 77057 Office: 2500 E TC Jester Blvd Suite 510 Houston TX 77008

MULGREW, JOHN, human development and psychology educator, psychotherapist; b. N.Y.C., Jan. 12, 1936; s. James Francis and Stella Elizabeth (Deserosurs) M.; m., Aug. 10, 1963; children—Catherine, John. B.S., Fordham U., 1963; M.S., St. John's U., 1967; Ph.D., Fla. State U., 1971. Asst. dir. counseling ctr. Appalachian State U., Boone, N.C., 1971-73, dir. counseling ctr., 1973-82, prof. human devel. and psychology counseling dept., 1982—; dir. Gestalt Tng. Ctr., Boone, 1974—. Mem. Am. Acad. Psychotherapists, Am. Group Psychotherapy Assn. Republican. Home: 204 Hillandale Dr Boone NC 28607 Office: Human Relations and Psychol Counseling Appalachian State Univ Boone NC 28607

MULHOLLEN, DAN BYRON, consulting engineer; b. Doniphan, Mo., Sept. 14, 1942; s. Robert W. and Lena (Crafton) M.; m. Rebecca Jane O'Neal, Jan. 2, 1967 (div. 1975); children—Melissa Gayle, Kristi Jane; m. Catherine Jean Spence, Dec. 8, 1975. B.S.C.E., U. Ark., 1965. Registered profl. engr.; registered land surveyor, Ark. Mo. Asst. resident engr. Ark. Hwy. Dept., Nashville, 1968-70; assoc. Crafton-Tull Engrs., Rogers, Ark., 1970-75; owner, pres. Mulhollen and Assocs. Inc., Jonesboro, Ark., 1975—; pres. Am. Cons. Engrs. Council of Ark., Little Rock, 1984-85. Pres. Exchange Club, Jonesboro, 1983, Fine Arts Council, Jonesboro, 1980-82, Jonesboro Band Boosters Club, 1984-85; chmn. Streets and Hwy. Com. Jonesboro, 1985. Recipient Volunteerism award Exchange Club 1982; named Exchangite of Yr., Exchange Club 1982. Mem. Ark. Soc. Profl. Engrs. (chapt. pres. 1980), Ark. Assn. Land Surveyors, ASCE (area dir. 1984). Lodge: Elks. Avocations: sports; banjo. Home: 1809 Kenwood St Jonesboro AR 72401 Office: Mulhollen and Assocs Inc 1825 E Nettleton Suite I Jonesboro AR 72403-0009

MULKEY, JACK CLARENDON, library director; b. Shreveport, La., Oct. 31, 1939; s. Jack Youmans and Hilda Lillian (Beatty) M.; m. Mary Lynn Shepherd, Jan. 30, 1971; 1 dau., Mary Clarendon. B.A., Centenary Coll., 1961; postgrad. (Rotary scholar), U. Dijon, France, 1961-62, Duke U. Law Sch., 1962 63; M.S., La. State U., 1969, Jr. exec. Lykes Bros. S.S. Co., 1964-66; asst. dir. admissions Centenary Coll. of La., 1966-67; head reference services and acquisitions Sheveport Pub. Library, 1968-71; dir. Green Gold Library System of N.W. La., 1971-73; mgmt. cons. Miss. Library Commn., 1973-74, asst. dir., 1974-76, dir., 1976-78, Jackson Met. Library System, 1978—; adj. prof. U. So. Miss. Grad. Sch. Library Sci., 1979—; cons. in field. Chmn. Miss. Govs. Conf. on Libraries, 1979; chmn. Miss. delegation White House Conf. on Libraries, 1979. Served with USAF, 1963-64. Mem. ALA, Southeastern Library Assn., Miss. Library Assn. (pres. 1981—), Chief Officers of State Library Agys., Phi Alpha Delta, Beta Phi Mu, Omicron Delta Kappa, Phi Kappa Phi. Episcopalian. Home: 6467 Richwood Dr Jackson MS 39213 Office: 301 N State St Jackson MS 39201*

MULLAN, PAUL HOWARD, chewing gum company executive; b. Keyser, W.Va., Oct. 2, 1945; s. Paul Kempton and Betty Lee (Reeves) M.; m. Jean Carol Almond, July 20, 1968; children—Jeffrey, David. B.S., U. Md.-College Park, 1968, M.B.A., 1970. Vice-pres. mktg. Donruss Co., Memphis, 1979-83, pres., 1983—. Mem. Sales and Mktg. Execs., Nat. Assn. Chewing Gum Mfrs. Republican. Roman Catholic. Home: 2300 Wickersham Ave Germantown TN 38138 Office: The Donruss Co PO Box 2038 Memphis TN 38101

MULLE, GEORGE ERNEST, petroleum geologist; b. Collingswood, N.J., Dec. 21, 1919; s. George Melvin and Eleanor (Matilda) (Clevenger) M.; m. Molly Elizabeth Jones, Nov. 17, 1950; children—Alan Russell, David George, William Ernest. Student Rutgers U., 1942-44; A.B. in Earth Scis., U. Pa., 1948. Cert. petroleum geologist, Tex. Geologist, Tide Water Oil Co., Houston and Corpus Christi, 1948-51; dist. geologist La Gloria Oil & Gas Co., Corpus Christi, Tex., 1952-60; ptnr. Santa Rosa Gas Co., 1960-62; pvt. practice geology, Corpus Christi, 1962-73, 75-80, 83—; v.p. Corpus Christi Mgmt. Co., 1973-75; exploration mgr. So. Tex., Mormac Energy Corp., 1980-82. Pres. Palm Harbor Property Owners Assn., Rockport, Tex., 1984, Bahia Log Library, Corpus Christi, Santa Fe Log Library, Corpus Christi, 1981; sec.-treas. The

Villas of Harbor Oaks Owners Assn., 1985—; del. People-to-People Petroleum Tech., People's Republic China, 1983. Served with USN, 1944-46. Mem. Corpus Christi Geol. Soc. (author book 1967), Am. Assn. Petroleum Geologist (author book and editor 1968), Am. Inst. Profl. Geologists, Soc. Ind. Profl. Earth Scientists. Republican. Baptist. Avocation: photography. Home: 121 Ocean Dr Rockport TX 78382 Office: Suite 404 Guaranty Plaza Corpus Christi TX 78475

MULLEN, ANDREW JUDSON, physician; b. Selma, Ala., June 23, 1923; s. Andrew J. and Helen (Johnson) M.; A.B., Vanderbilt U., 1948; M.D., Jefferson Med. Coll., 1952; children—J. Thomas, Debbie, Gail, Andrea, Shawn, Connie, Beth. Intern, U.S. Marine Hosp., Galveston, Tex., 1952-53; resident Tex. Med. Center, Houston, 1954-57; chief neurology and psychiatry service VA Hosp., Jackson, Miss., 1957; dir. Mobile (Ala.) Mental Health Center, 1957-58; practice medicine, specializing in psychiatry and neurology, Shreveport, La., 1958—; chief female service Confederate Meml. Med. Center, 1959-63, bd. dirs., chmn. pub. relations com., 1964-72; med. dir. Shreveport Child Guidance Center, 1961-64; mem. med. adv. bd. Humana Corp.; cons. psychiatry and neurology Barksdale AFB, VA Hosp.; chief staff Brentwood Neuro-Psychiat. Hosp., Shreveport, 1970-73; clin. prof. psychiatry La. State U. Sch. Medicine, 1975—. Dep. coroner, cons., Caddo Parish, La., 1964; chmn. mental health com. Community Council, 1964—; chmn. bd. dirs. Brentwood Hosp., Shreveport, 1982-84, chief med. staff, 1985-86; bd. dirs. Humana, Brentwood hosps., 1986—. Served with RCAF, 1941-42, AUS, 1942-45. Decorated Purple Heart with oak leaf cluster, Bronze Star. Diplomate Am. Bd. Psychiatry and Neurology (asso. examiner). Fellow Am., So. psychiat. assns., Am. Coll. Psychiatrists; mem. AMA, So. Med. Assn., Shreveport Med. Soc. (dir. 1971-72), Flying Physicians Assn., Alpha Tau Omega, Nu Sigma Nu. Episcopalian. Home: 333 Berkshire Pl Shreveport LA 71101 Office: 745 Olive St Suite 203 Shreveport LA 71104

MULLEN, DAVID EDWARD, clergyman, psychologist; b. Omaha, Sept. 6, 1938; s. Edward Francis and Gretchen Louise (Schultz) M.; B.A., Davidson Coll., 1960; M.Div., Union Sem., 1963; M.A. in Psychology, W.Ga. Coll., 1974; doctoral candidate Fielding Inst., 1981—; m. Sandra Little, June 26, 1961; children—Lynn, Michael. Ordained to ministry Presbyn. Ch., 1963; pastor Faith Presbyn. Co., Greensboro, N.C., 1965-68; dir. Carroll County Alcoholism Clinic, Carrollton, Ga., 1973-74; staff psychologist Marian-Citrus Mental Health Center, Ocala, Fla., 1974-76; dir. Episcopal Pastoral Counseling Center, Sarasota, Fla., 1976—. Adj. instr. psychology Eckerd Coll. Bd. dirs. Career and Counseling Center, Eckerd Coll., 1976. Mem. Am. Assn. Marriage and Family Counselors, Am. Assn. Sex Educators and Therapists, Am. Personnel and Guidance Assn., Am. Psychol. Assn., Am. Soc. Clin. Hypnosis, Fla. Soc. Clin. Hypnosis, Am. Orthopsychiat. Assn. Home: 2108 41st St W Bradenton FL 33505 Office: 222 S Palm Ave Sarasota FL 33577

MULLEN, JOHN DANIEL, JR., oil company executive, lawyer; b. Galveston, Tex., Jan. 31, 1951; s. John Daniel and Maxine Janet (Ray) M.; m. Susan Leslie Smith, Dec. 9, 1972; children—Kristen, Leslie. B.B.A., U. Okla., 1973; J.D., 1976. Bar: Tex. 1977, U.S. Dist. Ct. (so. dist.) Tex. 1977, U.S. Supreme Ct. 1980. Assoc. Vickery Law Corp., Houston, 1976-78; sr. counsel Mitchell Energy & Devel. Corp., Houston, 1978-80; gen. counsel, v.p., corp. sec., dir. Wes-Tex Drilling Co., Abilene, Tex., 1980—; dir. Toltek Exploration Co., Denver, Tex-Mex Drilling Co., Roswell, N.Mex., Crescent Supply Co., Abilene. Mem. Internat. Assn. Drilling Contractors, West Central Tex. Oil and Gas Assn., Taylor County Bar Assn., Okla. U. Pres. Ptnrs., Okla. U. Alumni Assn., State Bar Tex., Young Producers Forum, Tex. Young Lawyers Assn., Republican. Episcopalian. Clubs: Abilene Petroleum, Midland Petroleum, Fairway Oaks Golf and Racquet, (Abilene), Okla. U. Letterman's (Norman). Home: 1725 Woodridge Abilene TX 79605 Office: Wes-Tex Drilling Co 519 First Nat Bank Bldg Abilene TX 79601

MULLEN, SANFORD ALLEN, physician; b. Tampa, Fla., Jan. 16, 1925; s. Earl and Edith (Allen) M.; student Mercer U., 1943-45; M.D., Columbia U., 1949; m. Minnie Lucille Woodall, Dec. 23, 1945 (dec.); children—Sanford Allen, Henry Woodall, Michael Hill; m. 2d, Mrs. V.P. Crowe, Mar. 1, 1984. Intern, Grady Meml. Hosp., Atlanta, 1949-50, resident anatomic pathology, 1950, 53-54; fellow clin. pathology U. Minn. Hosps., Mpls., 1954-56; clin. assoc. prof. U. Fla., 1977-80, clin. prof., 1980—; practice medicine specializing in pathology, Jacksonville, Fla., 1958—; mem. staff, co-chief dept. pathology U. Hosp. of Jacksonville; mem. staff Bapt. Med. Center, St. Vincent's Med. Center, Nemours Children's Hosp., Meml. Hosp.; chief med. staff Cathedral Health and Rehab. Center (all Jacksonville), Putnam Community Hosp., Palatka, Fla., Lake Shore Hosp., Lake City, Fla., St. Augustine (Fla.) Gen. Hosp.; mem. adv. council Nat. Heart, Lung and Blood Inst., 1983-86. Nat. bd. govs. Arthritis Found., 1963-64, pres. Duval County div., 1960-61, pres. Fla. chpt., 1963-64; chmn. Jacksonville Mayor's Citizens Adv. Com. on Water Pollution Control, 1965-66, United Fund Campaign; vice chmn. Jacksonville Water Quality Control Bd., 1971-73; mem. Health Planning Council N.E. Fla., 1976-77; exec. v.p., med. dir. Jacksonville Blood Bank, 1970-81, pres., med. dir., 1982—; mem. various adv. coms. Fla. Bd. Health, Fla. Dept. Edn., Fla. Jr. Coll., Jacksonville; mem. adv. bd. Fla. div. Salvation Army, 1971-76; pres. Civic Round Table, 1967-69; mem. Fla. Council 100, 1983—; rep. Greater Jacksonville Econ. Opportunity, Inc., 1966-68. Bd. dirs. Jacksonville Symphony Assn., 1970-77, v.p., 1971-73, sec., 1976-77; bd. dirs. Northeast Fla. region Kidney Found., Inc., 1972-74; bd. dirs. Jacksonville Area chpt. ARC, 1972-77, 83—, treas., 1974-75, vice chmn., 1975-77; bd. dirs. Cathedral Found., 1972-76, exec. vice chmn., 1972-76; bd. dirs. Jacksonville Exptl. Health Delivery System, Inc., 1973-76, pres., 1973-76; trustee Jacksonville Hosps. Ednl. Program, 1971-76; organizing com. Am. Blood Commn., 1973-75, bd. dirs., 1975-79. Served with M.C., USNR, 1950-52; on loan to AUS in Korea; comdr. Res. Ret. Recipient Disting. Service award Arthritis Found., 1961; Service to Mankind award West Jacksonville Sertoma Club, 1974; Sanford Mullen Pub. Service award established by Fla. Soc. Pathologists, 1981. Diplomate Am. Bd. Pathology (clin. pathology, anatomic pathology, blood banking), Am. Bd. Dermatopathology/Pathology (dermatopathology). Fellow Coll. Am. Pathologists (gov. 1966-69, 70-73, chmn. state legis. com. 1969-72); mem. AMA, AAAS, Jacksonville Acad. Medicine (pres. 1963, dir. 1966-68, 72-77), Fla. Soc. Pathologists (pres. 1964-66, 72-73, v.p. 1966-67, 73-74), Am. Soc. Clin. Pathologists (councilor Fla. 1962-66), Duval County Med. Soc. (chmn. legis. council 1967, 70-72, dir. 1972—, pres. 1974), Fla. Med. Assn. (ho. of dels. 1964—, chmn. com. state legis. 1969-75, vice speaker ho. of dels. 1976-78, speaker 1978-80, pres.-elect 1980-81, pres. 1981-82, del. to AMA 1983—, com. on programs and priorities 1985, A.H. Robins award 1973), Fla. Med. Assn. Com. on Programs and Priorities 1985, So. Med. Assn. (vice-chmn. sect. pathology 1967-68), N.E. Fla. Heart Assn. (dir. 1967-69), Fla. (dir. 1968-76, pres. 1973-74), Am. (state rep. for Fla. 1971-72) Assns. Blood Banks, Am. Blood Com. (organizing com. 1973-75, bd. dirs. 1975-79), Am. Cancer Soc., Fla. Med. Polit. Action Com. (dir. 1964-65), Jacksonville Zool. Soc. (dir. 1971-77), Jacksonville Area C. of C. (gov. 1966-68, 72-74, chmn. pub. health com. 1965-66, v.p. membership affairs, membership devel. award 1969), Jacksonville Art Mus., Cummer Gallery Art, Ye Mystic Revellers, Blue Key, Sigma Mu, Gamma Sigma Epsilon, Phi Eta Sigma, Alpha Tau Omega (pres. Jacksonville alumni 1958-59). Episcopalian (vestryman 1967-69, sr. warden 1969). Clubs: Fla. Yacht, Timuquana Country, River, St. Johns Dinner (dir. 1967-70, pres. 1969-70), Torch (dir. 1968-72, pres. 1971-72). Lodge: Rotary (pres. Jacksonville 1970-71). Home: 505 Lancaster St Jacksonville FL 32204 Office: Box 2921 Jacksonville FL 32203

MULLENDORE, RICHARD HARVEY, university administrator; b. Charlottesville, Va., June 22, 1948; s. James Myers and Elaine (Gregg) M.; m. Jane Wand, Aug. 15, 1981; 1 child, Jenna Beth. Student U. Fla., 1966-68; B.A., Bradley U., 1970; M.S., So. Ill. U., 1975; Ph.D., Mich. State U., 1980. Head resident advisor Mich. State U., East Lansing, 1975-77; asst. dean students Tusculum Coll., Greeneville, Tenn., 1977-78, acting dean students, 1978-79; researcher, cons. Strengthening Institutions Through Improving Retention, Princeton, N.J., 1979-81; dir. student services, athletics U. Charleston, W.Va., 1981-84; dean students U. NC-Wilmington, 1984—. Bd. dirs. Charleston Sternwheel Regatta Festival, Charleston, 1982-84; mem. exec. steering com. Kanawha Alcohol Safety Action Program, Charleston, 1984. Mem. Am. Assn. Counseling and Devel., Am. Coll. Personnel Assn., Nat. Orientation Dirs. Assn., So. Assn. Coll. Student Affairs. Republican. Avocations: jogging, tennis, golf, swimming, camping. Office: U NC-Wilmington 601 S College Rd Wilmington NC 28403

MÜLLER, GENE ALAN, historian; b. Grand Island, Nebr., Jan. 10, 1943; s. Ludwig Frederick and Erma Gertrude (Gorin) M.; m. Diana June Currey; children—Michelle Nicole, Alyssa Katherine. B.A. cum laude, Midland Lutheran Coll., Fremont, Nebr., 1965; NYU in Spain scholar, U. Madrid, 1963-64; Fulbright-Hays scholar, U. Nacional Tucuman, Argentina, 1965-66; M.A., U. Kans., Lawrence, 1969, Ph.D., 1982. Asst. instr. U. Kans., 1967-73; asst. prof. history Ft. Hays State U., Kans., 1973-74; bilingual historian El Paso Community Coll., Tex., 1974—; project reviewer Nat. Endowment Humanities, 1978—. Author: The Church in Poverty: Bishops, Bourbons, and Tithes in Spanish Honduras, 1700-1821; A Select Bibliography on the Catholic Church in Latin America, also articles, book revs., chpts. in books. Mem. council Good Shepherd Luth. Ch. Am., El Paso, 1974-78, St. Timothy's Luth. Ch., El Paso, 1980—; v.p. El Paso Council Internat. Visitors, 1982-83, pres., 1983-85; pres. So. N.Mex./El Paso br.; bd. dirs. Nat. Council for Internat. Visitors, Leadership El Paso. Luth. Brotherhood Am. Field Service scholar, N.Z., 1960; NDFL Title VI fellow U. Kans., 1969; Ford Found. grantee, Nicaragua, 1969, Central Am., 1970; OAS fellow to Guatemala, 1973; Fulbright summer grantee, Brazil, 1982, Netherlands, 1983. Mem. Am. Hist. Assn., Am. Cath. Hist. Assn., Latin Am. Studies Assn., Conf. Latin Am. Studies, Tex. Cath. Hist. Assn., Rocky Mountain Council Latin Am. Studies, Midwest Assn. Latin Am. Studies, AAUP. Democrat. Home: 10708 Vista Lomas El Paso TX 79935-3611 Office: El Paso Community Coll PO Box 20500 El Paso TX 79998

MULLER, MICHAEL JOSEPH, counseling psychologist; b. San Antonio, Nov. 17, 1945; s. Charles John and Mary Elizabeth (FitzGerald) M. B.A., St. Mary's U., 1968; M.A., U. Tex.-Austin, 1973, M.Ed., 1975, Ph.D., 1983. Lic. psychologist, Tex. Staff psychologist U. Tex-Austin, 1977-78; counseling psychologist VA, San Antonio, 1981-84; counselor A. Phillip Gerard Assocs., San Antonio, 1984; counseling psychologist in pvt. practice, San Antonio, 1984—. Served to 1st lt. U.S. Army, 1968-71. Mem. Am. Psychol. Assn., Bexar County Psychol. Assn. Home: 101 Arcadia Pl Apt #106 San Antonio TX 78209 Office: 8500 Village Dr Suite 102 San Antonio TX 78217

MULLER, PATRICIA ANN, nurse educator; b. N.Y.C., July 22, 1943; d. Joseph H. and Rosanne (Bautz) Felter; m. Frank Mair Muller, Aug. 28, 1965; children—Frank M. III, Kimberly Michele. B.S. in Nursing, Georgetown U., 1965; M.A., Tulsa U., 1978, Ed.D., 1983. Staff devel. coordinator St. Francis Hosp., Tulsa, 1978-79, asst. dir. nursing service, nursing edn., 1979-82, dir. ednl. resources, 1982—; faculty U. Okla. Sch. Nursing, Northeastern State Sch. Nursing. Contbr. articles to profl. jours. Mem. Am. Nurses Assn., Am. Soc. Nursing Service Adminstrs., Am. Soc. Health Manpower Edn. Training, Nat. League Nursing, Okla. Soc. Nursing Service Adminstrs., Okla. Nurses Assn., Sigma Theta Tau. Roman Catholic. Home: 6632 S Harvard Tulsa OK 74136 Office: St Francis Hosp 6161 S Yale Tulsa OK 74136

MULLET, DARLENE MARILYN, rehabilitation teacher; b. Butte, Mont., Oct. 16, 1935; d. Ernest John Onnela and Iva Eleanor Onnela Sullivan; B.S., Western Mich. U., 1960; m. Stanley Mullet, Feb. 24, 1961 (dec. 1973); 1 son, Kevin. Rehab. tchr. Ohio Commn. for Blind, Columbus, 1960-61, 62-63; occupational therapist Goodwill Industries, Denver, 1966-70; rehab. tchr. for adults Tex. Commn. for Blind, Galveston, 1973—. Recipient service pin and cert. Tex. Commn. for Blind, 1978, 84. Mem. Assn. for Edn. and Rehab. of Blind and Visually Impaired, Nat. Assn. Female Execs., Mus. Fine Arts (Houston). Devised, conducted functional testing program for disability determination for social security, 1966-70. Home: PO Box 428 Friendswood TX 77546

MULLET, GARY MICHAEL, statistical consultant, lecturer, educator; b. Gladwin, Mich., June 18, 1937; s. Stanley L. and Elizabeth (Callihan) M.; m. J.A. Nowak, Oct. 22, 1960 (div. 1978); children—Michael, Susan, Mark; m. Sandra G. McGrew, Aug. 18, 1978; 1 child, Jenny. B.S., Central Mich. U., 1964; M.E.S., N.C. State U., 1966; Ph.D., U. Mich., 1973. Asst., then assoc. prof. Ga. Inst. Tech., Atlanta, 1970-77; dir. statis. analysis Burke Mktg. Research, Cin., 1977-78; assoc. prof. U. Cin., 1978-80; dept. head Berry Coll., Rome, Ga., 1980-82; dir. statis. services SDR, Inc., Atlanta, 1982—; cons. Grady Hosp., Atlanta, 1976, Monsanto Co., St. Louis, 1981-82, So. Co., Atlanta, 1981-82, U.S. Fish Wildlife. Atlanta, 1975-80, also others. Author: (with others) Handbook Compositions, 1965. Contbr. articles to profl. jours. Served with U.S. Army, 1957-59. U. Mich. scholar, 1967-69. Mem. Am. Inst. for Decision Scis., Am. Mktg. Assn., Acad. Mktg. Sci., Am. Statis. Assn., Atlanta Zool. Soc., Phi Kappa Phi, Beta Gamma Sigma, Kappa Mu Epsilon. Lodge: Masons. Avocations: horseback riding; reading; tennis; roller skating. Office: SDR Inc 2251 Perimeter Park Dr Atlanta GA 30071

MULLIGAN, DONALD JAMES, banker; b. Lowell, Mass., July 13, 1948; s. Donald Peter and Kathleen Mae (Moran) M.; m. Tina Linley Southard, Jan. 28, 1972; children—Kyle Andrew, Mackenzie Devon. B.S., Fla. State U., 1970; banking cert. Northwestern U., 1978. Residential loan specialist Chase Fed. Savs. & Loan Assn., Miami, Fla., 1972-77, regional v.p., 1977-81, sr. v.p., 1981—. Trustee Dade County Zool. Soc., 1983—; mem. Found. Friends Bapt. Hosp., 1979—; mem. So. Fla. Coordinating Council. Served with USAR, 1971-77. Mem. Fla. Savs. and Loan League. Democrat. Roman Catholic. Home: 10820 SW 127th St Miami FL 33176 Office: Chase Fed Savs & Loan Assn 7300 N Kendall Dr Miami FL 33156

MULLIGAN, F. BARRY, computer consultant; b. S.I., N.Y., May 25, 1942; s. Frank E. and Marjorie (English) M. B.S. in Elec. Engring., Lehigh U., 1970. Cert. data processor. Sr. programmer/analyst City N.Y. Dept. Fin. Adminstrn., 1971-75; systems programmer Atlanta Jour. and Constn., 1976-78; cons. microcomputer systems, Atlanta, 1978—; instr. micro-processor programming, 1979-81. Served with USAF, 1962-66. Mem. Assn. Computing Machinery, IEEE/Computer Soc. Republican. Roman Catholic. Author: The Basic Toolkit, 1979, Terminal Control Program, 1980. Office: 300 W Peachtree St NW Suite 12 M Atlanta GA 30308

MULLINIX, BENJAMIN GRAYSON, JR., agriculture research statistician, computer systems executive; b. Manhattan, Kans., Aug. 8, 1942; s. Benjamin Grayson, Sr. and Eleanor Brunhilda (Blockcolsky) M.; m. Kathryn Elaine Kelley, Dec. 29, 1985. A.S., Okla. State U., 1972, B.S., 1973, M.S., 1975. Inventory clk. Evans Home Furnishings, Oklahoma City, 1965-68, 68-73; delivery swamper Stouts Delivery, Oklahoma City, 1968; grad. asst. Okla. State U., Stillwater, 1973-75; agr. research statistician Ga. Coastal Plain Expt. Station, Tifton, 1975—; owner BM Cons., Tifton, 1981—. Contbr. articles to profl. jours. Mem. Am. Statis. Assn., Phi Kappa Phi. Republican. Mem. Ch. of Christ. Club: Toastmasters (Tifton) (pres. 1980, area gov. 1981). Avocations: ancient history; reading; computers. Office: Ga Coastal Plain Expt Station Moore Hwy Tifton GA 31793

MULLINS, CHARLES BROWN, physician, university chancellor; b. Rochester, Ind., July 29, 1934; s. Charles E. and Mary Ruth B. (Bamberger) M.; B.A., N. Tex. State U., 1954; M.D., U. Tex., 1958; m. Stella Churchill, Dec. 27, 1955; children—Holly, David. Intern, U. Colo. Med. Center, Denver, 1958-59; resident medicine Parkland Meml. Hosp., Dallas, 1962-64; USPHS research fellow U. Tex. Southwestern Med. Sch., Dallas, 1964-65; chief resident medicine Parkland Meml. Hosp., 1965-66; USPHS spl. research fellow cardiology br. Nat. Heart Inst., Bethesda, Md., 1967-68; practice medicine specializing in cardiology, Dallas, 1966—; mem. sr. attending staff Parkland Meml. Hosp., dir. med. affairs, 1977-79; mem. cons. staff Presbyn. Hosp., VA Hosp.; asst. prof. medicine U. Tex. Southwestern Med. Sch., Dallas, 1968-71, asso. prof., 1971-75, dir. clin. cardiology, 1971-77, prof., 1975-79, clin. prof. medicine, 1979-81, prof., 1981—; prof. medicine U. Tex. Health Sci. Center, Dallas, 1979-81; exec. vice-chancellor health affairs U. Tex. System, 1981—; chief exec. officer Dallas County Hosp. Dist., 1979-81. Served with M.C., USAF, 1959-62. Diplomate Am. Bd. Internal Medicine. Fellow ACP, Am. Coll. Cardiology (Tex. gov. 1974-77, chmn. bd. govs. 1976), Am. Heart Assn. Council on Clin. Cardiology; mem. Am. Fedn. Clin. Research, Assn. Acad. Health Ctrs., Assn. Univ. Cardiologists, Laennec Soc., AMA, Alpha Omega Alpha. Contbr. articles on cardiology to med. jours. Office: 601 Colorado St Austin TX 78701

MULLINS, CLYDE W., lawyer; b. Meadville, Miss., Oct. 27, 1914; s. William Rutledge and Sula L. (Sullivan) M.; m. Vergie Case, May 21, 1940; children—Wendell P., Max R. B.A., State Tchrs. Coll., 1937; M.A., La. State U., 1939. Bar: Miss. 1950, U.S. Dist. Cts. 1953, U.S. Supreme Ct. 1971. Tchr. public schs., 1937-43; ptnr. Mullins and Walden, 1953-54; ptnr. Mullins and Brown, 1960-61; ptnr. Mullins and Smith, 1969-72; sole practice, Natchez, Miss., 1946-50, 61-69, 72—; spl. chancellor 17th Jud. Dist., 1979; mem. State Bar Commn., 1984—. Served to sgt. USNG, 1930-40. Menninger Found. fellow. Mem. ABA (chmn. Miss. Criminal Sect. 1965), Miss. State Bar, Am. Judicature Soc., Assn. Trial Lawyers Am., Miss. Trial Lawyers Assn., Alton Oschner's Med. Found. Soc., Planetary Soc. Democrat. Methodist. Clubs: Tarrytown Group, Masons, Shriners, KT. Home: 107 Concord St Natchez MS 39120 Office: 404 Main St Natchez MS 39120

MULLINS, LARRY CHESTER, gerontology educator; b. Montgomery, Ala., Dec. 25, 1948; s. Irie Chester and Ruth Elizabeth (Booth) M.; m. Ginger Edgar; children—Geoffrey Sean, Lesley Elida; m. Mary Lou Whitaker, June 28, 1980; 1 child, Benjamin Chester. B.A., U. Ala., 1971, M.A., 1972; M. Philosophy, Yale U., 1975, Ph.D., 1978. Instr. sociology Va. Poly. Inst., Blacksburg, 1976-78, asst. prof., 1978-80; asst. prof. gerontology U. So. Fla., Tampa, 1980-83, assoc. prof., 1983—; program coordinator Internat. Exchange Ctr. on Gerontology, Tampa, 1981—. Contbr. articles to profl. jours. Bd. dirs. Sr. Companionship Program, Radford, Va., 1977-78; lectr. numerous civic groups. Pub. Health Services fellow, 1972-76; Retirement Research Found. grantee, 1983-84. Mem. Gerontol. Soc. Am., Am. Sociol. Assn., So. Sociol. Soc., So. Gerontol. Soc., Yale Alumni Assn. Avocations: woodworking; reading; sports. Office: Dept Gerontology U South Fla Tampa FL 33620

MULLIS, KENNETH ELLISON, construction company executive; b. Winston-Salem, N.C., Mar. 25, 1946; s. Ellison Dewey and Edith (Johnson) M.; m. Jerri Sue Russell, Aug. 23, 1970; 1 son, Russell Stockton. A.A.S., Forsyth Tech. Coll., 1972; grad. Builders Inst., N.C. State U., 1980. Design draftsman Brenner Steel, Winston-Salem, 1969-73, Triad Steel, High-Point, N.C., 1973-74; pres. K.E. Mullis Constrn. Co., Inc., Winston-Salem, 1974—; dir. Home Owners Warranty Corp. of N.C., Raleigh. Mem. Red Cross Pherisis Com., Winston-Salem, 1983—. Served with USN, 1966-69, Vietnam. Mem. Winston-Salem Home Builders Assn. (pres. 1983, Builder of Yr. 1984), N.C. Home Builders Assn., Nat. Home Builders Assn. Republican. Moravian. Lodge: Stratford Sertoma (v.p. 1984, centurion 1984, tribune 1985). Avocations: golf; reading; antique furniture restoration. Home: Route 12 Box 353-A Winston-Salem NC 27107 Office: KE Mullis Constrn Co Inc 2200 Silas Creek Pkwy Suite 5A Winston-Salem NC 27103

MULLIS, SARAH RUTH, pharmacist; b. Columbia, S.C., Sept. 20, 1941; d. James Marvin, Sr. and Jimmy (Wilson) M. B.S. in Pharmacy, U. S.C., 1965. Lic. pharmacist, Ga. Staff pharmacist Piedmont Hosp., Atlanta, 1965-67, asst. dir., 1967-71, dir., 1971—; adj. prof. Mercer Sch. Pharmacy, Atlanta, 1979—. Contbr. articles to profl. jours. Pres., U. S.C. Sch. Pharmacy Partnership Bd., 1984-85; prof. edn. com. Am. Cancer Soc., Atlanta, 1985—. Named Woman Pharmacist of Yr., Kappa Epsilon, 1979-80. Mem. Ga. Soc. Hosp. Pharmacists (pres. 1984-85), Atlanta Acad. Instnl. Pharmacists (pres. 1982-83, Pharmacist of Yr. award 1983), Am. Soc. Hosp. Pharmacists, Pi Beta Phi (nat. dir. 1985—). Republican. Presbyterian. Club: Arrowmont Sch. Gatlinburg (chmn. bd. govs. 1977-79). Avocations: snow skiing; jogging. Home: 10 Kings Tavern Pl Atlanta GA 30318 Office: Pharmacy Dept 1986 Peachtree Rd NW Atlanta GA 30309

MUMFORD, ANDER MORGAN, physician, otolaryngologist; b. Ayden, N.C., Jan. 13, 1916; s. Heber Gardner and Emma Lyde (Roberson) M.; m. Bedie A. Price, Dec. 21, 1941; 1 child, Emma Mumford Roberts. B.S. in Chemistry, Wake Forest U., 1937, B.S. in Medicine, 1939; M.D., Jefferson Med. Sch., 1941. Intern Meth. Hosp., Phila., 1941-42; practice gen. medicine, Winterville, N.C., 1946-59; mem. staff gen. practice, obstetrics Pitt County Meml. Hosp., Greenville, N.C., 1946-59, chief obstet. sect., 1954-58, organizer dept. otolaryngology, 1962, chief otolaryngology sect., 1962-81; resident in otolaryngology Duke U. Med. Ctr., Durham, N.C., 1959-62; practice medicine specializing in otolaryngology, Greenville, 1962-70; pres., co-owner Pitt Otolaryngologists, 1970-81; established Speech and Hearing Clinic, East Carolina U. Missionary, deacon Baptist Ch. Served to capt. M.C., AUS, 1942-46. Mem. Pitt County Med. Soc. (pres. 1950, 58). Clubs: Greenville Golf and Country, Brook Valley Country. Lodge: Kiwanis. Home: 311 Middleton Pl Greenville NC 27834 Office: Pitt Otorhinolaryngologist Inc 8 Doctors Park Greenville NC 27834

MUMFORD, FRANK ALAN, aviation company executive; b. Crawfordsville, Ind., June 26, 1949; s. Pearl E. and Eleanor M. (Funk) M.; m. Marla Sue Burnett, July 4, 1970; children—Zane, Amanda. B.S. in Bus. Adminstrn., Eastern Ill. U., 1976. Acct. Larsson, Woodyard & Henson, Charleston, Ill., 1976-78; bursar Eastern Ill. U., Charleston, 1978-80; controller Presbyn. Coll., Clinton, S.C., 1980-81, treas., 1981-83; treas. Ky. Wesleyan Coll., Owensboro, 1983-85; v.p. ops. Bullfrog Aviation, Owensboro, 1985—. Served with USAF, 1970-74. Mem. Nat. Assn. Accts., Nat. Assn. Coll. and Univ. Bus. Officers, So. Assn. Coll. and Univ. Bus. Officers. Baptist. Lodge: Rotary. Avocations: bowling; swimming; water skiing. Office: Bullfrog Inc PO Box 1949 Owensboro KY 42301

MUMPHREY, ANTHONY JOSEPH, JR., consulting urban planner, educator; b. New Orleans, May 15, 1942; s. Anthony J. and Josephine (Trumbaturi) M.; B.S. in Civil Engring., Tulane U., 1963, M.S., 1964; postgrad. La. State U., New Orleans, 1968-69; M.A. in Regional Sci., U. Pa., 1971, Ph.D., 1973; m. Kathleen M. McCahill, Jan. 6, 1968; children—Kathleen A., Anthony J. III, Benjamin L., Christina M. Civil engr. Boh Bros. Constrn. Co., Inc., New Orleans, 1968-69; instr. and research coordinator div. bus. and econ. research La. State U., New Orleans, 1969-70; research asst. regional sci. dept. U. Pa., Phila., 1970-73; prof. urban and regional planning Sch. Urban and Regional Studies, U. New Orleans, 1973—, assoc. dir. Urban Studies Inst., 1976-78; mayor's exec. asst. for planning and devel. City of New Orleans, 1978-84; pres. Anthony Mumphrey & Assocs., Inc., New Orleans, 1984—; cons. energy and transp. planning Tex. So. U., 1973-78; bd. dirs., mem. mgmt. and exec. coms. 1984 La. World Expn., 1980-84. Served to lt. USNR, 1964-69. NSF research fellow, 1973; registered profl. engr., La. Mem. Regional Sci. Assn., Am. Pub. Works Assn., Am. Planning Assn. (pres. La. chpt. 1976-78), Am. Inst. Cert. Planners, Regional Sci. Assn. (treas. 1973-78), Omicron Delta Kappa. Democrat. Roman Catholic. Contbr. articles on urban devel. and planning to profl. jours. Home: 2237 Oriole St New Orleans LA 70122 Office: 442 Canal St Suite 400 New Orleans LA 70130

MUNCY, THOMAS PHIPPS, JR., educator; b. Mullens, W.Va., Aug. 15, 1941; s. Thomas Phipps and Beatrice (Akers) M.; m. Virginia Jervis, Aug. 16, 1964; children—Michele Leigh, Clint Thomas. B.S. in Biology and Physics, Concord Coll., Athens, W.Va., 1963; M.Ed., U. Va., 1969. Cert. tchr., sch. adminstr., Va. Tchr. Richlands High Sch., Va., 1963-65; tchr. Waynesboro High Sch., Va., 1965-72, asst. prin., 1972-74, prin., 1974—. Author curriculum guide in phys. sci. Co-founder drug edn. program Sch. Orgn. Developing Attitudes, 1971; chmn. Waynesboro-East Augusta Drug Edn. Com., 1971-72; mem. Waynesboro Police Res., 1975—, comdr., 1983—; trustee Waynesboro Community Hosp., 1979. Recipient cert. of honor Westinghouse Ednl. Found., 1969-70; meritorious service cert. NASA-Nat. Sci. Tchrs. Assn., 1970. Mem. NEA (life), Waynesboro Edn. Assn. (pres. 1969-70), Va. High Sch. League, Va. Assn. Secondary Sch. Prins., Nat. Assn. Secondary Sch. Prins., So. Assn. Colls and Schs., Assn. Supervision and Curriculum Devel., Fraternal Order Police Aux., Phi Delta Kappa. Lodge: Rotary. Avocation: karate. Home: 2016 Mt Vernon St Waynesboro VA 22900 Office: Waynesboro High Sch 1200 W Main St Waynesboro VA 22980

MUNDAY, JOHN CLINGMAN, JR., science policy educator, remote sensing researcher; b. Plainfield, N.J., June 10, 1940; s. John Clingman and Anna (Fegley) M.; m. Judith Berrien, Jan. 29, 1965; children—Brandon, Sarah, Sherrod. A.B., Cornell U., 1962; Ph.D., U. Ill., 1968. Postdoctoral fellow Holloman AFB, Alamogordo, N.Mex., 1968-69; asst. prof. geography U. Toronto, Can., 1971-75; assoc. prof., prof. marine sci. Coll. William and Mary, Gloucester Point, Va., 1975-84, mem. assoc. faculty, 1984—; prof. natural scis. Sch. Pub. Policy, CBN U., Virginia Beach, Va., 1983—; cons. Commonwealth Data Base, Commonwealth of Va., 1978—. Contbr. articles to profl. jours. and chpt. to tech. book Va. edn. coordinator Freedom Council, 1984—. Mem. AAAS, Am. Soc. Photogrammetry (chmn. hydrospheric scis. com. 1981), Am. Sci. Affiliation, Assn. Am. Geographers, Internat. Assn. Energy Economists, Sigma Xi. Republican. Avocations: music performance and composition, ragtime piano; folk music. Home: 1512 Waterway Circle Chesapeake VA 23320 Office: CBN U Virginia Beach VA 23463

MUNDT, PHILIP AMOS, oil company executive; b. Sioux Falls, S.D., Oct. 2, 1927; s. John Carl and Marie Dorothy (Jacobson) M.; m. Lorraine Jean Blom, Dec. 27, 1951; children—Alan Philip, Sheryl Ann, Larry Bruce. B.S. in Geol. Engring., S.D. Sch. Mines, 1951; M.A. in Geology, Washington U., 1953; Ph.D. in Geology, Stanford U., 1955. Registered geologist, Calif. Geologist, supr. Mobil Oil Corp., world-wide, 1955-69, mgr. geol. geochem. research, Dallas, 1972-77, exploration mgr., Lagos, Nigeria, Medan, Indonesia, 1977-82, mgr. regional geology, Dallas, 1982—; exploration mgr. U.S. Natural Resources, Menlo Park, Calif., 1969-72. Served with U.S. Army, 1946-48. Standard Oil Calif. fellow, 1954. Mem. Am. Assn. Petroleum Geologists (cert., sec. 1964-65, v.p. 1965), Dallas Geol. Soc., Sigma Xi, Sigma Tau. Club: Lago Vista Country. Avocations: golf; sailing. Home: 1221 Rock Springs Rd Duncanville TX 75137

MUNDY, KAREN CARROLL, sociology educator; b. Chattanooga, Tenn., Apr. 23, 1950; d. James L. and Dorothy (Pullen) Carroll; m. James Daniel Mundy, Dec. 29, 1971; children—James Matthew, Ryan Daniel. B.A., Lee Coll., 1972; M.A., U. Tenn., 1975, Ph.D. in Sociology, 1985. Instr. sociology Lee Coll., Cleveland, Tenn., 1979—; prenatal lectr. Bradley Meml. Hosp., 1984-85; cons. Children's Home, 1984-85. Contbr. articles to profl. jours. Mem. adult edn. com. North Cleveland Ch. of God, 1984, team tchr., 1984-85. Recipient Woman of Achievement award U. Tenn., 1984, Excellence in Teaching, Lee Coll., 1983. Mem. Am. Sociol. Assn., So. Sociol. Assn., Christian Sociol. Soc., Sociologists for Women in Society, South (book rev. chairperson 1984-85, sec. 1985-87). Republican. Avocations: jogging; art; reading; politics. Office: Lee Coll Dept Behavioral Sci Ocoee St Cleveland TN 37311

MUNFORD, DILLARD, specialty retailing company executive; b. Cartersville, Ga., May 13, 1918; s. Robert Sims and Katherine (Aubrey) M.; B.S. in Mech. Engring., Ga. Inst. Tech., 1939; m. Danné Brokaw Shaw, 1980; children—Dillard, Page Shepherd, Mary Aubrey, Robert Davis, Henry Allan. Founder, 1946, since pres., chief exec. officer Munford Inc., Atlanta; founder, 1952, since pres. Munford-Do-It-Yourself Stores, Atlanta; chmn. bd., chief exec. officer Atlantic Co., Atlanta, 1962-68, Munford, Inc., 1968—; dir. Bill Publs., N.Y.C., Blount Inc., Am. Bus. Products, Inc., Redfern Foods, Provident Life Ins. Co., Chatta Tem, Asso. Distbrs. Trustee Ida Cason Callaway Found., Atlanta, Morris Brown Coll., LaGrange Coll., Southeastern Legal Found.; mem. Republican Nat. Finance Com. Served to capt. AUS, 1942-46. Mem. Young Pres.'s Orgn. (past pres.), Chief Execs. Forum (past dir.), NAM (past v.p., dir., mem. exec. com.), Atlanta C. of C. (past dir.), Sigma Alpha Epsilon. Methodist. Clubs: Rotary, Piedmont Driving, Capital City; Commerce; Racket; River (N.Y.C.); Peachtree Golf; Annabels (London); Cartersville Country; Wildcat Cliffs (Highlands, N.C.). Office: PO Box 7701 Sta C Atlanta GA 30357

MUNGER, RICHARD LEHR, child psychologist; b. Ann Arbor, Mich., July 20, 1951; s. George Walter and Mary Elizabeth (Lehr) M. B.Ed., U. Mich., 1973, Ph.D., 1979; M.A., Goddard Coll., 1976. Lic. psychologist, S.C. Sch. cons. Washtenaw County Community Mental Health Ctr., Ann Arbor, 1973-78; coordinator of consultation and edn. Zepf Community Mental Health Ctr., Toledo, Ohio, 1979-80; research assoc. Community Effectiveness Inst., Ann Arbor, 1980-81; coordinator of child and adolescent services Coastal Empire Mental Health Ctr., Walterboro, S.C., 1981-84, staff psychologist, Hilton Head Island, S.C., 1985—; clin. asst. prof. psychiatry and behavioral scis. Med. U. S.C., Charleston, 1983—; contract cons. Nat. Cancer Inst., Bethesda, Md., 1984—; dir. Child Psychology Cons., Hilton Head Island, 1984—. Author: How to be Boss: A Parent's Guide to Changing Children's Behavior Quickly, 1985. Chmn., Beaufort-Jasper Community Child Devel. Adv. Com., S.C., 1985—; profl. advisor Parents Without Ptnrs., Hilton Head Island, 1984—; vice chmn. Children and Youth Council, S.C. Dept. Mental Health, Columbia, 1982-83. Named Outstanding Young Man Am., OYM Assn., 1984. Fellow Am. Orthopsychiat. Assn.; mem. Assn. for Advancement of Behavior Therapy, S.C. Psychol. Assn., Am. Psychol. Assn. Episcopalian. Club: Island Running. Avocations: Triathlon, sculling. Home: PO Box 1584 Broad Creek Marina Hilton Head Island SC 29925 Office: Coastal Empire Mental Health Center 509 Pineland Mall Office Center Hilton Head Island SC 29928

MUNIR, RAMSEY MICHAEL, architect, builder, restaurateur, retailer; b. Austin, Tex., June 10, 1950; s. Isam Abdul Razzak and Frances Christine (Anderson) M.; m. Michele Hensahw, May 26, 1973; children—Michael Kinan. B.Arch. cum laude, U. Tex., Austin, 1973. Registered profl. builder. Supr. food and beverages Six Flags over Texas, 1967-71; architect/ptnr. ANPH, Inc., Architects, Dallas, 1973-78; pres. Sharif Munir, Inc., Builders, Dallas, 1978—; exec. v.p. Al Vera's Mexican Restaurants, Plano, Tex., 1980—, Garland, Tex., 1982—, Dallas, 1983—, R.K. Davidson Co. Builders, Richardson, Tex., 1980—, Zaks Splty. Stores, Inc., Dallas, 1982—, Irving, Tex., 1984—, Baja Louies Restaurant, Dallas, 1983—, Al Veras of Lewisville, 1984— pres. Munir Interiors, Inc., Dallas, 1981—; dir. Premier Nat. Bank. Six Flags over Tex. scholar, 1969. Mem. AIA, Tex. Soc. Architects, Nat. Assn. Home Builders, Home and Apt. Builders, Sales and Mktg. Council. Episcopalian. Home: 6223 Raintree Ct Dallas TX 75240 Office: 1011 Hampshire Ln Richardson TX 75080

MUNK, ZEV MOSHE, physician; b. Stockholm, July 14, 1950; m. Susan Deitcher; 3 children. B.Sc., McGill U., 1972; M.D., C.M., 1974. Licentiate Med. Council Can.; diplomate Am. Bd. Internal Medicine, Am. Bd. Allergy and Clin. Immunology. Intern Royal Victoria Hosp., Montreal, 1974-75, resident, 1975-76; resident in clin. immunology and allergy Montreal Gen. Hosp., 1976-78; practice medicine specializing in allergy and clin. immunology, Houston, 1978—; mem. staff Meml. City Gen., Meml. S.W., Meth., Spring Branch Meml., Sam Houston Meml., Ben Taub Gen., Alief Gen., Cy-Fair hosps. (all Houston); clin. instr. allergy and clin. immunology Baylor Coll. Medicine, 1979—, U. Tex.-Houston, 1979—. Vice pres. Hebrew Acad. Houston, 1982—. McGill U. scholar, 1968-74. Fellow Am. Acad. Allergy, Am. Soc. for Allergy and Clin. Immunology, Royal Coll. Physicians (Can.); mem. Tex. Med. Assn., Que. Med. Assn., ACP, Am. Fedn. Clin. Research, Am. Acad. Allergy, Harris County Med. Soc., Can. Soc. Allergy and Clin. Immunology, Am. Assn. Clin. Immunology and Allergy, Contbr. articles to med. jours. Office: 902 Frostwood St #189 Houston TX 77024

MUNOZ, GERMAN, social science educator; b. Santiago de Cuba, Cuba, July 13, 1950; came to U.S., 1962, naturalized, 1976; s. German and Noelia (Fajardo) M.; m. Piedad Eugenia Del Pino, Aug. 31, 1973; children—German Daniel, Patricia Cristina. B.S. in Psychology, Spring Hill Coll., 1972; M.A. in Internat. Affairs, U. Miami, 1975, Ph.D. in History, 1981. Instr., asst. prof. Miami Dade Community Coll., Fla., 1976-82, assoc. prof.-chairperson, Dept. Social Sci., 1983—; cons. Ctr. for Bus. and Industry, Miami, 1983—, and numerous other internat. bus. and societies. Author (with others) The Torrijos Legacy, 1985; producer Edn. Video Tape Cassettes, Social Science Series, 1983—; publisher-editor-writer mag. Collegium Magazine, 1983—; contbr. articles to profl. jours. Bd. dirs. The Faculty Forum, Miami, 1983—; producer-panelist, pub. affairs program WAQI Radio, Miami, 1985. Recipient John Barrett prize for Best Dissertation on Hispanic and Latin Am. Affairs, U. Miami, Coral Gables, Fla., 1981. Clubs: Ciudamar; Yacht (Miami). Avocations: reading; swimming, Shuri-Ryu Karate. Office: Miami Dade Community Coll 300 NE 2nd Ave Miami FL 33132

MUNRO, (HARRIET) BERNICE, mathematician, former educator; b. Detroit, June 17, 1916; d. George Thomas and Viola Banghart (McCormick) Proctor; B.A., Mich. State U., 1938; M.Ed., Wayne State U., Detroit, 1961; m. Donald McAlpine Munro, Oct. 23, 1942 (dec. Sept. 1980); children—Douglas Roy, David McAlpine. Tchr. public schs., Detroit, Clare, Mich., 1940-63; NSF aide, instr. Applied Mgmt. Tech. Center, Wayne State U., 1960-68; tchr. Ann Arbor (Mich.) public schs., 1963-71, math. coordinator, 1971-78; cons. in field. Mem. Nat., Mich. (past pres.), Detroit (past pres.) councils tchrs. math., Math. Assn. Am., Nat. Council Suprs. Math., Kappa Delta, Delta Kappa Gamma, Alpha Delta Kappa. Club: Order Eastern Star. Editor: Math Mots, 1971-78. Home: 163 Saunders Rd Franklin NC 28734

MUNS, NEDOM CONWAY, III, industrial technology educator, consultant; b. Corsicana, Tex., May 11, 1939; s. Nedom Conway II and Lillian Allene (Rogers) M.; m. Sandra Lee Small, July 21, 1962; children—Amanda Kay, Mary Allene, Kelly LeAnn. B.S., Abilene Christian Coll., 1961; M.Ed., Sam Houston State U., 1966; Ed.D., North Tex. State U., 1969. Tchr. Pasadena Ind. Sch. System, Tex., 1961-66; grad. teaching fellow North Tex. State U., Denton, 1968-69; dept. chmn. Northwestern State U., Natchitoches, La., 1969-78, Sam Houston State U., Huntsville, Tex., 1978—; regional v.p. A.L. Williams Co., Conroe, Tex., 1985—; cons. Nat. Accreditation Com., Washington, 1980—; lectr. in field. Commr. Huntsville Youth Orgn., 1978—. Recipient Outstanding Service award La. Vocat. Assn., 1973, La. Indsl. Arts Assn., 1974, Outstanding Educator award La. Assn. Cosmetology Sch., 1977; named Outstanding Indsl. Edn. Grad., Abilene Christian U., 1984. Mem. Am. Indsl. Arts Assn. (mem. affiliation com. 1980—), Am. Vocat. Assn. (awards com. 1977-83). Mem. Ch. of Christ. Avocation: golf. Home: 3701 Spring Dr Huntsville TX 77340 Office: Sam Houston State U PO Box 2266 Huntsville TX 77341

MUNYON, WILLIAM HARRY, JR., architect; b. Panama City, Panama, Feb. 20, 1945; s. William Harry and Ruth (Hyde) M.; (parents Am. citizens); B.A., Tulane U., 1967; postgrad. U. Hawaii, 1972-73; B.Arch. with high distinction, U. Ariz., 1978; student U.S. Naval War Coll., 1984. Elec. designer Ohlsen-Mitchell, Inc., New Orleans, 1966-67; research cons. historic preservation U. Ariz., Tucson, 1974-75; cons. historic preservation State of Ariz., Phoenix, 1974-75; archtl. designer, interior designer, graphic designer, archtl. programmer, mktg. dir. Architecture One, Ltd., Tucson, 1975-78; dir. Mktg. Hansen Lind Meyer, P.C., Iowa City and Chgo., 1978-79; v.p. John F. Steffen Assocs. subs. Turner Constrn., St. Louis and Houston, 1979-80; sr. assoc., dir. corp. devel. Rees Assocs., Inc., Oklahoma City, 1980-82; dir. planning, asst. to pres. SHWC, Inc., Dallas, 1982-84; dir. justice facilities program Henningson, Durham & Richardson, Inc., Dallas, 1984—; mng. prin. Artistic License II, graphics and design, Irving, Tex., 1975—; mktg. cons., 1979—; mem. adv. panel Interior Design mag., 1978-79; mem. adv. panel on building energy performance standards, 1979-81; founder ann. archtl. history prize U. Ariz. Coll. Architecture, 1979. Scoutmaster, council adminstr. Aloha council Boy Scouts Am., 1970-73; adv. Okla., State Senate Com. on Corrections, 1981. Served with USN, 1967-73, to comdr. USNR, 1973—. Decorated Legion of Merit, Bronze Star, D.S.C., D.S.M., Cross of Gallantry, others; founder Joe E. Allen Meml. award to outstanding midshipmen Tulane U. NROTC, 1985. Mem. Nat. Trust for Historic Preservation, AIA (assoc., com. on architecture for justice 1978—, Henry Adams award 1978, others), Soc. Archtl. Historians, Soc. Mktg. Profl. Services (1st pl. cert. of excellence 1981), Profl. Services Mgmt. Assn., Am. Correctional Assn., Res. Officers Assn., Naval Res. Assn., Naval Inst., Lionel Collectors Club Am., Brit. Model Soldier Soc., U. Ariz. Alumni Assn., Tulane U. Alumni Assn., Assn. Former Intelligence Officers, Navy League, Dallas Mus. Fine Art, Am. Planning Assn., Naval War Coll. Found., Nat. Rifle Assn., 65 Roses Club, Scabbard and Blade, Dallas 500, Inc., Blue Key, Mensa, Sigma Chi (life), Phi Kappa Phi (life). Republican. Roman Catholic. Club: LaCima. Home: 4140 Hackmore Loop Irving TX 75061 Office: 9847 Buxhill Dallas TX 75238

MURCHISON, HENRY DILLON, II, lawyer; b. Alexandria, La. Feb. 27, 1947; s. Julian Truett and Annie Laurie (Liddell) M.; m. Darla Aymond, Sept. 29, 1984. B.S., La. Tech. U., 1969; J.D., La. State U., 1974. Bar: Texas 1974, La. 1974, U.S. Dist. Ct. (we. dist.) Tex. 1974, U.S. Ct. Appeals (5th cir.) 1974, U.S. Dist. Ct. (we., cen., and ea. dist.) La. 1977, U.S. Tax Ct. 1977, U.S. Supreme Ct. 1977. Assoc. Baer, Cryon, Keen & Kelley, Houston, 1974-76; gen. counsel Jetero Corp. Houston, 1976-77; ptnr. Stafford, Randow et al, Alexandria, 1977-78, Craven, Scott & Murchison, Alexandria, 1978-79, Davis & Murchison, Alexandria, 1979-84, Broadhurst, Brook, Mangham & Hardy, New Orleans, 1984—; dir. Security 1st Nat. Bank, Alexandria, First Nat. Bancshares of La. Dist. chmn. La. Republican Com., 1982. Mem. La. Bar Assn., New Orleans Bar Assn., Alexandria-Pineville C. of C. (dir. 1982-83), New Orleans River Region C. of C. Presbyterian. Lodge: Kiwanis (program chmn. 1982). Office: Broadhurst Brook Mangham & Hardy 400 Poydras Suite 2600 New Orleans LA 70130

MURDOCK, ALVIN EDWIN, counselor; b. Sand Springs, Tex., Jan. 3, 1918; married, 5 children. M.S. in Agr., Sam Houston State U., Huntsville, Tex., 1947, M.A. in Agr., 1949. Counselor, Victoria (Tex.) Ind. Sch. Dist., 1960-61, Tyler (Tex.) Ind. Sch. Dist., 1961-64, Llano (Tex.) Ind. Sch. Dist., 1964-66, Anderson County Coop., Palestine, Tex., 1966-86; ret., 1986; supr-counselor Night Adult Basic Edn., 1974-76. Scout master Boy Scouts Am., 1953-55; sustaining mem. Republican Nat. Com., 1980-81. Served with USMC, 1943-45. Mem. Tex. Small Schs. Assn., Tex. Personnel and Guidance Assn., Am. Security Council (adv. bd. 1980-81). Baptist. Club: U.S. Senatorial. Test cons. for Tex. Edn. Agy.; coop. coordinator for crime prevention and drug edn. Tex. Edn. Assn.

MURFIN, ALLEN EUGENE, association executive; b. Kirksville, Mo., Sept. 29, 1938; s. John Larkin and Lois Pauline (Epperson) M.; m. Evelyn Marie Rottinghaus, May 25, 1963; children—Christina Marie, Jo Ann Renee, Marcie Lynn. Student Rockhurst Coll., Kansas City, Mo., 1964-67. Cert. assn. exec. Am. Soc. Assn. Execs. With Davis Paint Co., Kansas City, 1956-58; various positions Massey Ferguson, Inc., Kansas City, Kans., 1962-68; office mgr. real estate co., 1968-70; pres. Mo. Jr. C. of C., Sedalia, 1970-71; v.p. U.S. Jr. C. of C., Tulsa, 1971-72, dir. regional office, Marlboro, Mass., 1972-74; tng. officer U.S. Jaycees, Tulsa, 1974-75; exec. v.p. Columbia C. of C., Mo., 1975-81; v.p. Food and Energy Council, Inc., 1981-82; assoc. dir. S.W. Hardware and Implement Assn., Ft. Worth, 1982—. Mem. City Planning Commn., Gladstone, Mo., 1966-70; mem. City Zoning Bd. of Adjustments, Gladstone, 1970-72; bd. dirs. Wonder Land Camp Found., 1969-71, 77-82, Spl. Bus. Dist., Columbia, 1979-81, Columbia Conv. and Visitors Bur., 1979-81, bd. dirs., pres. Anderson Hayes Child Care Ctr., 1975-78, Vol. Action Ctr., 1981-82; bd. dirs., v.p. Show-Me Community Devel. Credit Union, 1980-82; mem. Boon County Indsl. Revenue Bond Authority, 1981-82; dist. commr. Boy Scouts Am. Served with USAR, 1956, USMC, 1958-62. Club: Cosmopolitan. Lodges: Kiwanis, Elks. Home: 6524 Woodcreek Ln Fort Worth TX 76118 Office: SW Hardware and Implement Assn 4629 Mark IV Pkwy Fort Worth TX 76106

MURPHEY, BOB WYNNE, humorist, lawyer, rancher; b. Nacogdoches, Tex., July 31, 1921; s. French L. and Reba (Wright) M.; m. Nada Evans, June 27, 1953; children—Brenda Gayle, Reba Jane. B.S., Stephen F. Austin State U., Nacogdoches, 1942; J.D., U. Tex., 1947. Bar: Tex. 1947, U.S. Dist. Ct. (ea. dist.) Tex. 1960. Sgt.-at-arms Tex. Ho. of Reps., 1949-52; county atty. Nacogdoches County, Tex., 1953-54; dist. atty. 2d Jud. Ct., Tex., 1954-61; sole practice, Nacogdoches, 1961—; also profl. humorist, rancher; dir. Fredonia State Bank, Nacogdoches. Rec. artist (comedy albums) Delta Records, 1972-84, (humor album) Executive Humor, 1984. Pres. East Tex. Fireman's Assn., 1955, State Firemen's and Fire Marshall's Assn. of Tex., 1969, Jaycees, Nacogdoches, 1953. Served to ensign Med. Service Corps, USMS, 1943-46, ETO, PTO. Recipient Silver Beaver award Boy Scouts Am., 1968; named Disting. Alumnus, Stephen F. Austin State U. Tex., 1972. Mem. State Bar Tex., Nacogdoches County Bar Assn. (pres. 1967-69), Nat. Speakers Assn. (Citizen of Yr. Nacogdoches County 1983), Coon and Cat Hunters Assn., Chili Appreciation Soc. Internat. Club: Nacogdoches County. Avocations: hunting, volunteer fire service. Home: Route 14 Box 4067 Nacogdoches TX 75961 Office: Law Office PO Box 854 Nacogdoches TX 75963

MURPHREE, THOMAS EUGENE, paper manufacturing company executive; b. Troy Ala., Sept. 9, 1923; s. Joel Dyer and Minnie Marie (Wilson) M.; m. Janet Sterling, June 7, 1947; children—Theodore Sterling, Thomas Eugene, Timothy Michael. B.S., U.S. Naval Acad., 1947; M.S., Rensselaer Poly. Inst., 1963. Enlisted USMC, 1942, advanced through grades to col., 1974; mgr. Xerox Corp., Phila., 1974-77; v.p. Garden State Paper Co., Richmond, Va., 1977—; pres. Gt. Eastern Paper Stock Co., 1978—; pres. consumer div. Nat. Assn. Recycling Ind., N.Y.C., 1978—; chmn. govt. affairs subcom. Am. Paper Inst., N.Y.C., also mem. transp. com. Mem. adv. com. Va. Opera Assn., Richmond. Decorated Legion of Merit (3), D.F.C., Air medal (9), Army Commendation medal. Purple Heart. Mem. Am. Mgmt. Assn., Marine Corps Assn., Marine Corps Aviation Assn. Episcopalian. Clubs: Westchester Country; Willow Oaks; Army Navy. Office: Garden State Paper Co Inc 600 E Broad St 10th Floor Richmond VA 23219

MURPHY, ANN CARTER, pharmacist; b. Princeton, Ky., June 20, 1958; d. Charles Lindy and Mildred Lucille (Carter) M. A.S., Hopkinsville Community Coll., 1978; B.S. in Pharmacy, U. Ky., 1981. Registered pharmacist, Ky. Staff pharmacist Muhlenberg Community Hosp., Greenville, Ky., 1981—; ptnr. Murphy Prints, Princeton, 1981—. Sec. council on ministries Ogden Meml. United Meth. Ch., Princeton, 1984—, mem. adminstrv. bd., 1984—. Mem. Ky. Pharmacists Assn., Ky. Soc. Hosp. Pharmacists, First Dist. Ky. Pharmacists Assn., Lambda Kappa Sigma. Democrat. Avocations: music, art, bicycling, walking. Office: Muhlenberg Community Hosp 440 Hopkinsville St Box 387 Greenville KY 42345

MURPHY, BRIAN MICHAEL, political science educator; b. Cleve., Feb. 13, 1952; s. William Patrick and Helen Marie (Durma) M. B.A., U. Dayton, 1974; M.A., Miami U., Oxford, Ohio, 1976, Ph.D., 1980. Teaching fellow Miami U., 1978-80; vis. lectr. Ind. U.-Richmond, 1980; instr. North Ga. Coll., Dahlonega, 1981-82, asst. prof., 1982—. Contbr. articles to profl. jours. Mem. Clergy and Laity Concerned, Atlanta, 1985. Recipient faculty research and devel. grants North Ga. Coll., 1983, 84. Mem. Am. Polit. Sci. Assn., So. Polit. Sci. Assn., Midwest Polit. Sci. Assn., Ga. Polit. Sci. Assn. (exec. council, ACLU, Nat. Pub. Radio, Pi Sigma Alpha. Democrat. Home: 3200 Riverwood Ln Apt A Roswell GA 30076 Office: North Ga Coll Social Scis Dept Dahlonega GA 30597

MURPHY, CHARLES HAYWOOD, petroleum company executive; b. El Dorado, Ark., Mar. 6, 1920; s. Charles Haywood and Bertie (Wilson) M.; ed. pub. schs., Ark., pvt. tutors; LL.D., U. Ark., 1966; m. Johnie Walker, Oct. 14, 1939; children—Michael Walker, Martha, Charles Haywood, III, Robert Madison. Ind. oil producer, 1939-50; pres. Murphy Oil Corp., 1950-72, chmn., dir., 1972—. Mem. Ark. Bd. Higher Edn., 17 yrs.; bd. govs. Oschner Med. Found.; trustee Hendrix Coll.; bd. adminstrs. Tulane U. Served as infantryman World War II. Recipient citation for outstanding individual service in natural resource mgmt. Nat. Wildlife Fedn. Mem. Am. Petroleum Inst. (past mem. exec. com.), Nat. Petroleum Council (past chmn.), 25 Yr. Club Petroleum Industry (past pres.). Home: 200 Peach St El Dorado AR 71730 Office: Murphy Bldg El Dorado AR 71730

MURPHY, CHARLES THOMAS, accountant; b. Shannon, Ga., Aug. 10, 1931; s. Joseph Samuel and Sallie Francis (Bennett) M.; m. Norma Jean Sadler, Sept. 21, 1952. B.B.A., Marshall U., 1963. P.A., W.Va. Acct. trainee VA Hosp., Lexington, 1963-64; supervisory acct. VA Hosp., Ann Arbor, Mich., 1964-66; budget analyst VA Hosp., Dayton, Ohio, 1966; internal revenue agt. U.S. Dept. Treasury, Logan, W.Va., 1966—; dist. dirs. rep. IRS, Logan, 1968—, safety officer, 1968—. Contbr. articles on gospel music to newspapers. Gospel concert promoter VMS Ann. Labor Day Outdoors Sing, Wilkinson, W.Va., 1979—, River Regatta Days, Logan, 1983, 84, 85, Logan's County Arts and Crafts Fair, 1982, 83, 84, 85, Coal Digger Days, Hardy, Ky., 1984, 85. Served with USAF, 1951-55. Recipient Spl. Service award IRS, 1972, Appreciation award ARC, 1977, Am. Cancer Soc., 1983, 85; named W.Va. Ambassador of Good Will Among All People, Sec. State W.Va., 1983. Democrat. Lodges: Kiwanis, Odd Fellows. Avocations: tennis; badminton. Home: PO Box 1946 Logan WV 25601 Office: VMS Production PO Box 1946 Logan WV 25601

MURPHY, CLEVELAND LOUIS, architect; b. Miami, Fla., May 29, 1950; s. Grover Cleveland and Rosemary Jean (Braxton) M.; m. Joanne TerWaarbeek, May 29, 1971; children—Beth Miriam, Timothy Stephen. B.A., Va. Wesleyan U., 1979; Th.M., Drew U., 1981. Registered architect, Va., Nat. Council Archtl. Registration Bds. Project mgr. Design Collaborative, Virginia Beach, Va., 1976-77, Walsh, Ashe & Dills, 1977-79; sr. designer Rancorn, Wildman & Krause, York County, Va., 1981-83; pres., Alts. in Architecture, P.C., Hampton, Va., 1983—. Served as sgt. USMC, 1968-72. Recipient award House Designs, 1966, 67. Mem. AIA (Va. soc., Tidewater chpt.). Methodist. Avocation: painting. Office: Alternatives in Architecture PC PO Box 6 Hampton VA 23669

MURPHY, DALE BRYAN, professional baseball player; b. Portland, Oreg., Mar. 12, 1956; s. Charles and Betty M.; m. Nancy Thomas; children—Chad, Travis, Shawn. Student, Portland Community Coll., Brigham Young U. Outfielder Atlanta Braves, Nat. League, 1974—. Named Nat. League Most Valuable Player, 1982; recipient Gold Glove award, 1982. Address: care Atlanta Braves PO Box 4064 Atlanta GA 30302*

MURPHY, DOROTHY EASTERWOOD, educator, football coach; b. Jackson, Miss., Sept. 20, 1952; d. Thad E. and Virginia Faye (Hamilton) Easterwood; m. Thomas Eugene Murphy, Dec. 19, 1976; children—Kelly Everette, Jennifer Rae. B.S. in Edn., Miss. U. Women, 1974; M.Ed., Miss. State U., 1977. Women's basketball coach, instr. phys. edn. U. Tenn., Martin, 1975-76, Itawamba Jr. Coll., Fulton, Miss., 1976-77, Miss. U. for Women, Columbus, 1977-82; asst. football coach Hinds Jr. Coll., Raymond, Miss., 1984—; instr./counselor Miss. Sports Camp, Jackson, 1968-76; counselor Patsy Neal's Basketball Sch., Brevard, N.C., 1972; women's athletic trainer Miss. State U., 1975; instr. Miss. U. Women Sports Camp, Columbus, 1974-76, dir., 1977-81. Recipient Gov.'s Outstanding Ms. award State of Miss., 1973. Baptist. Address: PO Box 403 HJC Raymond MS 39134

MURPHY, EWELL EDWARD, JR., lawyer; b. Washington, Feb. 21, 1928; s. Ewell Edward and Lou (Phillips) M.; m. Patricia Bredell Purnell, June 26, 1954 (dec. 1964); children—Michaela, Megan Patricia, Harlan Ewell. Student San Angelo Coll., 1943-45; B.A., U. Tex., 1946, LL.B., 1948; D.Philosophy, Oxford U. (England), 1951. Bar: Tex. 1948. With Baker & Botts, Houston, 1954—, assoc., 1954-63, ptnr., 1964—, chmn. internat. dept., 1971—, sr. ptnr., 1980—. Pres. Houston World Trade Assn., 1972-74; pres. Houston Philos. Soc., 1976-77; chmn. Houston com. on fgn. relations, 1984-85. Served to lt. USAF, 1952-54. Rhodes Scholar, 1948-51; recipient Carl H. Fulda award Univ. Tex. Internat. Law Jour., 1980. Mem. ABA (chmn. sect. internat. law and practice 1970-71), Southwestern Legal Found. (trustee 1978—, chmn. inst. transnational arbitration 1985—), Inter-Am. Bar Assn., State Bar of Tex., Houston Bar Assn., Houston C. of C. (chmn. internat. bus. com. 1964, 65). Presbyterian. Club: Plaza (Houston). Contbr. articles on internat. bus law and legal philosophy to profl. jours. Home: 17 West Oak Dr Houston TX 77056 Office: 3200 One Shell Plaza Houston TX 77002

MURPHY, GRETA WERWATH, educator; b. Milw., Aug. 24, 1910; d. Oscar and Johanna (Seelhorst) Werwath; m. John Heery Murphy, Sept. 18, 1941. Student U. Wis., summer 1929, Ohio State U., 1943-45. With Milw. Sch. Engring., 1928-79, v.p. pub. relations and devel., 1966-79, regent, 1974-83, emeritus, 1983—. Mem. Milwaukee County Planning Commn., 1966, vice chmn., 1974-75, chmn., 1976-77. Mem. Pub. Relations Soc. Am. (chpt. pres. 1957, dir. 1952-53; Spl. Service citation 1980, Presdl. citation 1955), Am. Coll. Pub. Relations Assn. (dir. 1953-55, trustee 1960-61), Council for Advancement of Edn. Republican. Lutheran. Club: Woman's of Wis. Lodge: Zonta Internat. (dir. regional govt. 1961-62, pres. 1959-60). Home: 1032 Malaga Ave Coral Gables FL 33134 also 5562 S Cedar Beach Rd Belgium WI 53004

MURPHY, HAROLD LOYD, judge; b. Haralson County, Ga., Mar. 31, 1927; s. James Loyd and Georgia Gladys (McBrayer) M.; m. Jacqueline Marie Ferri, Dec. 20, 1958; children—Mark Harold, Paul Bailey. Student, West Ga. Coll., 1944-45, U. Miss., 1945-46; LL.B., U. Ga., 1949. Bar: Ga. 1949. Practice law, Buchanan, Ga., from 1949; partner firm Howe and Murphy, Buchanan, Tallapoosa, Ga., 1958-71; judge Superior Cts., Tallapoosa Circuit, 1971-77; U.S. dist. judge No. Dist. of Ga., Rome, 1977—; rep. Gen. Assembly of Ga., 1951-61; asst. solicitor gen. Tallapoosa Jud. Circuit, 1956; mem. Jud. Qualifications Commn., State of Ga., 1977. Served with USNR, 1945-46. Mem. Am. Bar Assn., Ga. Bar Assn., Dist. Judges Assn. for 11th Circuit, Am. Judicature Soc., Tallapoosa Circuit Bar Assn. Democrat. Methodist. Clubs: Lions, Gridiron Secret Soc., Masons. Home: Buchanan Rd Tallapoosa GA 30176 Office: 600 E 1st St Fed Bldg Rome GA 30161

MURPHY, HENRY JOSEPH, accountant; b. Chgo., July 25, 1935; s. Henry J. and Alice (Foley) M.; m. Marilyn, June 25, 1960; children—Laura, Gina, Todd, Henry. B.S., St. Joseph Coll., 1960. C.P.A. Ptnr. Arthur Andersen and Co., Atlanta, 1960—, ptnr. in charge real estate practice. Served with U.S. Army, 1954-56. Mem. Am. Inst. C.P.A.s, Urban Land Inst., Nat. Assn. Real Estate Investment Trusts, Ga. Soc. C.P.A.s. Clubs: Commerce, Atlanta Country. Office: 133 Peachtree St Suite 2700 Atlanta GA 30303

MURPHY, J. NEIL, construction company executive; b. Harlingen, Tex., Apr. 7, 1934; s. Dan Walter and Elizabeth (Regent) M.; B.S. with honors in Civil Engring., U. Tex., 1957; m. Gerri Merrick, Dec. 29, 1971; children—John Neil II, Brian Stuart, Erick Hiecke, Kyle Ashley. Field engr. Chgo. Bridge & Iron, 1956; office engr. Stone & Webster, 1957-59; with Coastal Engring., Inc., San Benito, Tex., 1959—, chmn. bd., pres. 1978—; chmn. bd., pres. Solar Shield Sunscreen Inc., JNM Inc., JNK Concrete Inc.; chmn. bd. Rejoice, Inc.; partner Coastal Enterprises; officer Climas y Servicios, Viajes Aeromex; mem. dist. adv. council SBA. Mem. county exec. bd., precinct chmn. Republican Party; active Boy Scouts Am.; nat. lay leader Episcopal Ch.; chmn. bd. Compadre Beach Ministry; minister of reconciliation Full Gospel Chs.; mem. adv. council State Fire Marshal Served to capt. USAR, 1957-67. Registered profl. engr., Tex. Mem. Nat. Soc. Profl. Engrs., Fellowship Cos. for Christ, ASHRAE, Tex. Fire Sprinkler Contractors Assn. (pres.), U.S. Power Squadron (adv. pilot), Oceanic Soc., Order of St. Luke's Chi Epsilon, Sigma Chi. Club: Laguna Madre Yacht (vice commodore). Lodge: Rotary (sec.) Contbr. numerous articles to profl. jours. Office: PO Drawer 893 San Benito TX 78586

MURPHY, JAMES BRYSON, JR., banker; b. Columbia, S.C., June 16, 1932; s. James Bryson and Katherine Elizabeth (Zemp) M.; m. Marian Louise Meyers, Apr. 4, 1959; children—James Bryson III, Louise Madden, Harry Meyers. B.S. in Commerce, The Citadel, 1954; grad. La. State U. Sch. Banking of South, 1966; grad. Advanced Mgmt. Program, Harvard U., 1975. Mgr. Kimbrell's Inc., Statesville, N.C., 1957-61; with S.C. Nat. Bank, Columbia, 1961—, presently sr. v.p., sec.; sr. v.p., sec. S.C. Nat. Corp.; dir. Furniture Distbrs. Inc. Served to lt. AUS, 1954-56. Mem. Am. Soc. Corp. Secs., Greater Columbia C. of C. (pres.), Soc. of Cincinnati. Episcopalian. Clubs: Sertoma (former pres.), Greater Columbia Citadel (former pres.), Palmetto, Forest Lake. Home: 5007 Hillside Rd Columbia SC 29206 Office: 1426 Main St Columbia SC 29226

MURPHY, JAMES LAWSON, music educator; b. Greenville, S.C., Jan. 30, 1951; s. Marion Wales and Clyde (Morgan) M.; m. Karen Joyce Antolick, May 29, 1973; 1 child, Bethany. Mus.B., Stetson U., 1973; Mus.M., Southwestern Sem., 1976; Ph.D., Tex. Tech U., 1980. Entertainer Walt Disney World, Orlando, Fla., 1973; choral dir. DeLand High Sch., Fla., 1973; asst. prof. music Wayland Bapt. U., Plainview, Tex., 1976-81; chmn. dept. music Temple Jr. Coll., Tex., 1981—, v.p. faculty council, 1985-86; choral clinician, various sch. choirs, Tex., 1981—. Author: The Choral Music of Halsey Stevens, 1980. Composer various works for miscellaneous media, 1971—. Choir dir., various chs., S.E. U.S., 1970—; bd. dirs. Plainview Civic Theater, 1980, Central Tex. Orchestral Soc., Temple, 1981-83, Community Concert Assn., Temple, 1983-85. Named to Outstanding Young Men Am., U.S. jaycees, 1980; named Best Actor 1980-81, Plainview Civic Theater, 1981; Tex. Gen. Bapt. Conv. fellow Tex. Tech U., 1977. Mem. Coll. Music Soc., Nat. Assn. Tchrs. Singing, Nat. Assn. Schs. Music, Am. Choral Dirs. Assn. (state chmn. com. for music in jr. colls.), Tex. Music Educators Assn., Tex. Choral Dirs. Assn., Tex. Assn. Music Schs. (acad. standards commn. 1982-85, dir. 2-yr. schs. 1985-88), Phi Mu Alpha Sinfonia, Omicron Delta Kappa. Presbyterian. Avocations: travel; photography; tennis; golf. Home: 212 Tanglewood Rd Temple TX 76502 Office: Temple Jr Coll Dept Music 2600 S First St Temple TX 76501

MURPHY, JAMES WOODYARD, management consultant, minister; b. Pennsboro, W.Va., May 24, 1932; s. Donald C. and Ruth E. (Emrick) M.; m. Lisa Godfrey, Nov. 29, 1985; children by previous marriage—Steven, Kevin, Cheryl, Robb. B.A., Glenville State U., W.Va., 1970; LL.D. (hon.), Clarksville Sch. Theology, Tenn., 1974. Ordained to ministry American Bapt. Conv., 1979. Orgnl. devel. dir. E.I. Dupont deNemours & Co., Parkersburg, W.Va., 1975-85; pres. J.W. Murphy and Assocs. Inc., bus. cons., Florence, S.C., 1985—. Mem. Am. Soc. Tng. and Devel. (bd. dirs. 1979-85). Avocation: travel. Home and Office: 412 S Burris Rd Apt 2 Florence SC 29501

MURPHY, JOHN JOSEPH, manufacturing company executive; b. Olean, N.Y., Nov. 24, 1931; s. John Joseph and Mary M.; m. Louise John; children—Kathleen A., Karen L. Murphy Rochelli, Patricia L. Murphy Smith, Michael J. Asso. Applied Sci. in Mech. Engring., Rochester Inst. Tech., 1952; M.B.A., So. Meth. U. Engr. Clark div. Dresser Industries, Olean, 1952-67, gen. mgr., Connersville, Ind., 1967-69, pres., Muskegon, Mich., 1969-70; pres. machinery group Dresser Industries, Houston, 1970-75, sr. v.p. ops., Dallas, 1975-80, exec. v.p., 1980—, now chmn., dir. 1st Nat. Bank Dallas. Trustee St. Bonaventure (N.Y.) U.; bd. dirs. Tex. Research League; vice chmn. Ctr. for Internat. Bus. Served with U.S. Army, 1954-56. Mem. Am. Council for Capital Formation (bd. dirs.), Machinery and Allied Products Inst. (exec. com.). Office: PO Box 718 Dallas TX 75221*

MURPHY, JOSEPH FRANCIS, clergyman, retired educator; b. Chattanooga, Dec. 1, 1910; B.A., St. John's U., Collegeville, Minn., 1932; M.A., U. Okla., 1942, Ph.D., 1961. Joined Benedictine order Roman Catholic Church, 1930, ordained priest, 1936; mem. faculty St. Gregory's Coll., Shawnee, Okla., 1936-86, instr. in history and govt., 1936-86, treas., 1939-42, chmn. dept. social scis., 1960-77, headmaster St. Gregory Coll. and High Sch., 1942-49, v.p., 1949-54; civilian chaplain Ft. Sill, Okla., 1941—. Recipient Archival award D.A.R., Okla., 1961, cert. of achievement, commanding gen. Ft. Sill, 1966; service award Okla. Cath. Edn. Assn., 1975; named Tchr. of Yr. (5), St. Gregory's Coll., hon. Potawatomi, 1985; Kellog Found. grantee to UCLA, 1962; Ford Found. grantee to U. Tex., Austin, 1964. Mem. Am. Cath. Hist. Soc. Democrat. Author: Tenacious Monks, 1975; contbr. articles to New Catholic Ency. Home and office: St Gregory's College 1900 MacArthur St Shawnee OK 74801

MURPHY, KEITH EDWARD, marketing executive; b. Peru, Ind., Nov. 9, 1944; s. Edward W. and Vivian Marcella (Martin) M.; m. Brenda Darlene Rock, June 17, 1967; children—Michelle Paige, Monica Lynn. B.A., Marion Coll., 1968; M.B.A., Ind. U., 1976. Vocalist, composer, rec. artist Stacy Records and King Record Co., Chgo. and Cin., 1962-69; customer service coordinator, asst. plant mgr. Central Soya Co., Ft. Wayne, Ind., 1969-72; sr. mktg. research analyst Peter Eckrich & Sons div. Beatrice, Ft. Wayne, 1972-79; dir. mktg. intelligence Wilson Foods Corp., Oklahoma City, 1979-84; dir. mktg. research M&M/Mars, Inc., Waco, Tex., 1984—. Mem. Am. Mktg. Assn., Am. Mgmt. Assn., Oklahoma City C. of C., Am. Meat Inst. (consumer survey com.). Club: New Eng. MG-T Register Ltd. (pres. 1983-84). Songwriter: Cindy Lou, 1963; Little Loved One, 1963; Karate, 1963; I Don't Like It, 1963; Slightly Reminiscent of Her, 1967; Dirty Ol Sam, 1967. Home: 302 Hidden Oaks Waco TX 76710 Office: 1001 Texas Central Pkwy Waco TX 76710

MURPHY, MARGARET ANN HENRY, English language educator; b. Guntersville, Ala., Dec. 27, 1938; d. Marshall Cochran and Ruth Judson (Parnell) Henry; student Judson Coll., 1956-57; B.S. with honors, Auburn U., 1960; M.Ed., Livingston U., 1968; Ed.D., U. So. Miss., 1980; m. Cecil L. Murphy, Aug. 22, 1957 (div. Feb. 1983); children—Lee Ann Murphy Wasden, Sherry Lynn Murphy Gregson, Tammy Cecile, Cecil L., Margaret Ann. Instr. English, Livingston U., 1968-70, William Carey Coll., 1970-71; chmn. lang. and fine arts div. So. Union State Jr. Coll., 1972-74; chmn. lang. and fine arts div., instr. English, Patrick Henry State Jr. Coll., Monroeville, Ala., 1974—; instr. English, Troy State U., part-time, 1975-81. Mem. steering com., mem. exec. com. Com. of 100; chmn. Sumter County Cancer Crusade, 1970. Named Favorite Tchr., Patrick Henry State Jr. Coll., 1981. Mem. Nat. Council Tchrs. English (life), Southeastern Conf. English in the Two-Yr. Colls., NEA, Ala. Edn. Assn., Ala. Coll. English Tchrs. Assn., Patrick Henry State Jr. Coll. Tchrs. Assn. (pres. 1983-84). Phi Kappa Phi, Lambda Iota Tau. Democrat. Baptist. Home: PO Box 386 Monroeville AL 36461 Office: PO Box 2000 Monroeville AL 36461

MURPHY, MARY KATHLEEN CONNORS (MRS. MICHAEL C. MURPHY), fundraiser, educational administrator; writer; b. Pueblo, Colo.; d. Joseph Charles and Eileen E. (McDermott) Connors; A.B., Loretto Heights Coll., 1960; M.Ed., Emory U., 1968; Ph.D., Ga. State U., 1980; m. Michael C. Murphy, June 6, 1959; children—Holly Ann, Emily Louise, Patricia Marie. Tchr. of English, pub. schs. of Moultrie, Ga., 1959, Sacramento, 1960, Marietta, Ga., 1960-65, DeKalb County, 1966; tech. writer Ga. Dept. Edn., 1966-69; editorial asst. So. Regional Edn. Bd., Atlanta, 1969-71; dir. alumni affairs The Lovett Sch., Atlanta, 1972-75, dir. publs. and info. services, 1975-77; free lance edn. writer, 1968—; contbr. and contbg. editor numerous articles on teaching, secondary and higher edn. to profl. publs.; columnist Marietta Daily Jour., 1963-67, The Atlanta Constn., 1963-68; cons. Ga. Postsecondary Edn. Commn., 1977; coordinator summer series in aging Ga. State U., 1979; dir. for devel./found. relations Ga. Inst. Tech., 1980—. Bd. dirs. The Bridge Family Center, 1981—, Cathedral of Christ the King Bd. Edn., 1980-85, Northside Sch. Arts, 1981, Ga. State U. Gerontology Center, 1981; bd. dirs. Met. Atlanta Fulton County ARC, 1982; mem. allocations com. United Way Met. Atlanta, 1982; v.p. Atlanta Women's Network, 1983-84; mem. council Atlanta Symphony Assocs., 1984—; mem. Leadership Atlanta, 1983-85. NDEA fellow, 1965-66, Adminstrn. of Aging fellow, 1977-79. Mem. Council for Advancement and Support of Edn. (publs. com., bd. dirs. Southeastern sect. 1981—, editor dist. newsletter 1981-84, co-dir. Southeastern dist. conf. 1986), Am. Council Edn., (Nat. Identification Program for Women in Higher Adminstrn.), Edn. Writers Assn., Nat. Assn. Ind. Schs. (publs. com.), Nat. Soc. Fund Raising Execs. (co-chmn. Southeast multistate Conf. 1984; v.p. Ga. chpt. 1985-86; mem. at large nat. bd. 1985-87; chmn. pub. relations com. 1985-87), Phoenix Soc. (publicity chmn. 1981—), Phi Delta Kappa, Kappa Delta Pi (pres. 1980-81). Co-author: Fitting in as a New Service Wife, 1966. Home: 2903 Rivermeade Dr NW Atlanta GA 30327

MURPHY, MELINDA BROWN, banker, personnel administrator; b. Denver, May 25, 1950; d. Clarence Arch and Mary (Taylor) Brown; m. Richard Hardy Murphy, Sept. 26, 1981; 1 child, Taylor Murphy. B.A., U. Mich., 1972. Corr. sec. to chmn. Tex. Commerce Bank Houston, 1975-79, tng. specialist, 1979-82, v.p., tng. dir., 1982—. Named Coordinator of Yr., Inroads of Houston, 1984. Mem. Am. Soc. Tng. and Devel. Republican. Home: 6118 Hurst St Houston TX 77008 Office: Tex Commerce Bank-Houston 711 Travis St Houston TX 77002

MURPHY, RANDALL KENT, consulting company executive; b. Laramie, Wyo., Nov. 8, 1943; s. Robert Joseph and Sally (McConnell) M.; student U. Wyo., 1961-65; M.B.A., So. Meth. U., 1983; m. Cynthia Laura Hillhouse, Dec. 29, 1978; children—Caroline, Scott. Dir. mktg. Wycoa, Inc., Denver, 1967-70; dir. Communications Resource Inst., Dallas, 1971-72; account exec. Xerox Learning Systems, Dallas, 1973-74; regional mgr. Systema Corp., Dallas, 1975-76; pres. Performance Assos., also pres., dir. Acclivus Corp., Dallas, 1976—. Served with AUS, 1966. Mem. Soc. Applied Learning Tech., Nat. Soc. Performance and Instrn., Nat. Soc. Sales Tng. Execs., Am. Mktg. Assn., Am. Soc. Tng. and Devel., Sales and Mktg. Execs. Internat., Assn. Mgmt. Cons., U. Wyo. Alumni Assn., Dallas Hist. Soc., Dallas Symphony Assn., Dallas Mus. Fine Arts. Roman Catholic. Author: Performance Management of the Selling Process, 1979; Coaching and Counseling for Performance, 1980; Communication/Motivation and Performance, 1981; (with others) BASE for Sales Performance, 1983; co-author: Acclivus Sales Negotiation, 1985. Co-inventor The Randy-Band, multi-purpose apparel accessory, 1968. Home: 15702 Nedra Way Dallas TX 75248 Office: 13601 Preston Rd Dallas TX 75240

MURPHY, RICHARD VANDERBURGH, lawyer, consultant; b. Syracuse, N.Y., May 9, 1951; s. Robert Drown and Reta Rose (Vanderburgh) M.; m. Patricia Lynn Eades, May 18, 1973. A.B., Dartmouth Coll., 1973; J.D., U. Ky., 1976. Bar: Ky. 1976, U.S. Supreme Ct. 1980. Corp. counsel Lexington-Fayette Urban County Govt. (Ky.), 1976-82, acting asst. commr. law, 1980-82; assoc. H. Foster Pettit, Lexington, 1982-83; asst. county atty., Fayette County, Ky., 1982-84; ptnr. Pettit & Murphy, Lexington, 1983-84; sr. atty. Wyatt, Tarrant & Combs, Lexington, 1984—. Vice chmn. bd., elder South Elkhorn Christian Ch., Lexington. Mem. ABA, Ky. Bar Assn. (continuing edn. recognition award 1982, 83), Am. Planning Assn., Fayette County Bar Assn., Louisville Bar Assn. Democrat. Mem. Christian Ch. Home: 3313 Otter Creek Dr Lexington KY 40502 Office: 1100 Kincaid Towers Lexington KY 40507

MURPHY, TERENCE JOSEPH, television station executive; b. St. Louis, Sept. 10, 1956; s. John Thomas and Shirley (Pollnow) M. B.S. in Radio-TV-Film, U. Tex.-Austin, 1979. Promotion asst. KPLR-TV, St. Louis, 1980-81; promotion mgr. KRBK-TV, Sacramento, 1981-83, WEVU-TV, Naples, Ft. Myers, Fla., dir. creative services, 1983. Recipient 1st Place Addy award, Advt. Fedn. S.W. Fla., 1983, 84. Mem. Broadcast Promotion and Mktg. Execs. Roman Catholic. Office: WEVU-TV 28950 Old 41 Rd SE Bonita Springs FL 33923

MURRAH, JEFFREY DIXON, psychotherapist, consultant; b. El Paso, Tex., Dec. 15, 1958; s. Ernest Dixon Murrah and Patricia Louise (Gravell) Murrah Dolgner. B.S., U. Houston, 1981, M.A., 1984. Cons., CMA, Inc., Pasadena, Tex., 1979—; psychotherapist Deer Park Hosp., Tex., 1981—; psychotherapist, Baytown, Tex., 1984; researcher U. Houston-Clear Lake, 1980-82; cons., researcher Beltway Clin. Assocs., Pasadena, 1984—. Contbr. poetry to publs. Mem. Am. Psychol. Assn. (assoc.), Southwestern Psychol. Assn., Biofeedback Soc. Tex., Biofeedback Soc. Harris County. Baptist.

MURRAH, WILLIAM FITZHUGH, III, ophthalmologist; b. Memphis, Jan. 14, 1945; s. William Fitzhugh Jr. and Ester (Gavin) M.; m. Ann Dickey, Mar. 21, 1970. B.A., Rhodes Coll., 1967; M.D., U. Tenn., 1970. Diplomate Am. Bd. Ophthalmology. Rotating intern Meth. Hosp., Memphis, 1971, USPHS Hosp., New Orleans, 1971; resident in ophthalmology U. Tenn.-Memphis, 1974-77; fellow in ophthalmology James H. Little, M.D. and U. Okla., Oklahoma City, 1977-78; practice medicine specializing in ophthalmology Murrah Eye Clinic, Fairhope, Ala., 1978—. Served as surgeon USPHS, 1971-73. Mem. Ala. Acad. Ophthalmology, Am. Acad. Ophthalmology, Am. Intraocular Implant Soc., AMA, Med. Assn. State Ala., Soc. Geriatric Ophthalmology. Roman Catholic. Avocations: sailing, hunting. Office: Murrah Eye Clinic 150 S Ingleside Fairhope AL 36532

MURRAY, ANNE COOP, university administrator, educator, consultant; b. Danville, Ky., Dec. 8, 1942; d. Paul Jones and Sara Adaline (Barger) Coop; m. Lee Murray, Sept. 5, 1964; children—Lee Anne, Susan. B.A. in Psychology, Western Ky. U., 1964, M.A. in Guidance and Counseling, 1972, M.A. in Speech Communication, 1986. Social worker Ky. Dept. of Child Welfare, Louisville, 1964-69; staff asst. Western Ky. U., Bowling Green, 1969-72, asst. dean of student affairs, 1972—. Deacon, First Christian Ch., Bowling Green, 1978-80; team chair Leadership Bowling Green, 1985; mem. nat. identification program Women in Higher Edn. Adminstrn. Mem. Ky. Assn. Women Deans Adminstrs. and Counselors (pres. 1972-74), Coll. Personnel Assn. Ky. (pres.-elect 1985-86), Nat. Assn. Student Personnel Adminstrs. (chair profl. devel. Ky. chpt. 1982-83). Avocation: tournament tennis. Office: Office of Student Affairs 111 Potter Hall Western Ky U Bowling Green KY 42101

MURRAY, BRIAN SHERLOCK, petroleum geologist; b. Monroeville, Ala., Feb. 26, 1958; s. John Monroe and Suzanne (Sherlock) M.; m. Donna Louise Worley, Nov. 27, 1981; 1 child, Joshua. B.S., U. South Ala., 1981. Geologist, Transco Exploration Co., New Orleans, 1981—. Mem. Am. Assn. of Petroleum Geologists, Soc. Profl. Well Log Analysts (jr. mem.), Soc. of Econ. Paleontologists and Mineralogists. Roman Catholic. Avocations: photography; woodworking; scuba diving. Office: Transco Exploration Co 24th Floor 1250 Poydras St New Orleans LA 70112

MURRAY, CHARLES ANDREW, chemical company executive; b. Franklin County, Ind., Oct. 9, 1911; s. Archibald K. and Maude M. (Stafford) M.; m. Marguerite Jensen (dec.), Sept. 3, 1938; children—Bonnie Christine, Lance Kerr, Robin Elo, Jamie Andrew; m. 2d, Eleanor Chapman Laughridge, June 10, 1979; 1 stepdau., Linda. B.S. in Chem. Engring, Purdue U., 1934; M.S., U. Mich., 1936, Ph.D., 1940. Chemist E.I. du Pont de Nemours & Co., Deepwater, N.J., 1934-35, Central Soya Co., Decatur, Ind., 1940-42; pilot plant supr. Reichold Chems. Co., Inc., Ferndale, Mich., 1942-46, plant mgr., Tuscaloosa, Ala., 1946-48, dist. sales mgr., New Orleans, 1948-55; mgr. paint and varnish dept. Crosby Forest Products Co., Picayune, Miss., 1955-60; dir. research Cordo Chem. Corp., Mobile, Ala., 1960-63; pres. M&W Enterprises, Inc., Savannah, Ga., 1963-67; product devel. mgr. Cordo div. Ferro Corp., Mobile, 1967; tech. dir. Mobile Rosin Oil Co., Mobile, 1968—, dir., v.p., 1968—; del. conf. on coatings Argentina Bur. Standards, 1959. Active CAP, Boy Scouts Am. Mem. Am. Chem. Soc., Fedn. Soc. Coatings Tech. (gulf coast sect.), Aircraft Owners and Pilots Assn., Sigma Xi, Phi Lambda Upsilon, Alpha Chi Sigma. Presbyterian. Club: Lake Forest Yacht and Country (Daphne, Ala.). Contbr. numerous articles to profl. jours. Home: PO Box 635 Spanish Fort AL 36527 Office: Mobile Rosin Oil Co PO Drawer 70107 Mobile AL 36607

MURRAY, ELIZABETH DAVIS REID, writer, lectr.; b. Wadesboro, N.C., June 10, 1925; d. James Matheson and Mary Kennedy (Little) Davis; A.B. cum laude, Meredith Coll., Raleigh, N.C., 1946; postgrad. N.C. State U., 1957-58, 74-75; m. James William Reid, Feb. 7, 1948 (dec. June 1972); children—Michael Ernest, Nancy Kennedy, James William; m. Raymond L. Murray, May 12, 1979; stepchildren—Stephen, Ilah Garton, Marshall. Continuity writer Sta. WPTF, Raleigh, 1946-47; program mgr., women's commentator Sta. WADE, Wadesboro, 1947-48; dir. news bur. Meredith Coll., 1948-51; state woman's news editor, columnist Raleigh News and Observer, 1951-52; exec. sec. Gov.'s Coordinating Com. on Aging, 1959-61; research asst. to Dr. Clarence Poe, Raleigh, 1963-64; contbg. editor Raleigh Mag., 1969-72; local history corr. Raleigh Times, News and Observer, Spectator of Raleigh; lectr. art and local history; tchr. Wake history Wake Tech. Coll., Wake pub. schs. and libraries; research cons. Wake County Pub. Libraries, Mordecai Historic Park, State Visitor Center, Exec. Mansion; resource person Wake Public Schs.; dir. Capital County Pub. Co.; writer; books include: From Raleigh's Past (cert. of commendation Am. Assn. State and Local History), 1965; Wake: North Carolina's Capital County, vol. 1, 1983 (W.P. Peace award for best book on N.C. history 1983); editor, compiler: North Carolina's Older Population: Opportunities and Challenges, 1960; editor, contbr. Wake County Hist. Soc. newsletter, 1965-69; History of Raleigh Fire Dept., 1970; guest editor Raleigh Mag. Wake County Bicentennial Issue, 1971; author, photographer filmstrip for Wake Pub. Schs., 1971; author sect. Windows of the Way, 1964; Am. arts slide lectures for pub. library; author instructional materials State Exec. Mansion and Mordecai Hist. Park docents; author monthly history page Raleigh Mag., 1969-72; contbr. biog. sketches Dictionary of North Carolina Biography, 1979; contbr. to newspapers and mags. Mem. Raleigh City Council, 1973; pres. Jr. Woman's Club, 1956-57; organizing pres. Arts Council Raleigh, 1965; exec. com. N.C. Humanities Found., 1974-76; dir., officer North Carolinians for Better Libraries, 1965-69; mem. Meredith Bd. Assos., 1976-79; trustee Pub. Libraries, 1956-67, Meredith Coll., 1966-69; pres. Wake Meml. Hosp. Aux., 1962-63; mem. Raleigh Hist. Sites Commn., 1969-73; trustee Pullen Meml. Bapt. Ch., 1975-78, chmn., 1977-78, also deacon; chmn. Mayor's Com. to Preserve Hist. Objects, 1965—; mem. Tryon Palace Commn., 1967-78; adv. council WUNC-FM, 1976-80, N.C. Art Soc.; vis. lectr. N.C. Mus. History Assos., 1980; docent, lectr. N.C. Exec. Mansion, Mordecai Hist. Park, N.C. Mus. Art; bd. dirs. Raleigh-Wake County Symphony Orch. Devel. Assn., 1979-83, Estey Hall Found., 1980—, Friends of Meredith Library, 1980-83. Recipient Outstanding Community Service award, 1952, best all-round Jr. Woman's Club mem., 1955, Disting. Alumna award Meredith Coll., 1970, recognition for service award Raleigh Hist. Sites Commn., 1973, Raleigh City Council, 1973; Community Service award Raleigh Bd. Realtors, 1983. Mem. N.C. Soc. County and Local Historians (life), N.C. Lit. and Hist. Assn., N.C. Art Soc. (Disting. Service citation 1979), Docents N.C. Mus. Art (pres. 1980-81), Friends of N.C. State U. Library, Friends of Carlyle Campbell Library (charter, life), Kappa Nu Sigma. Democrat. Clubs: Carolina Country, Capital City (charter mem.). Home: 10801 Strickland Rd Raleigh NC 27609 Mailing Address: PO Box 26064 Raleigh NC 27611

MURRAY, ERIN VADEAN (VICKI), consultant, company executive; b. Tupelo, Miss., June 7, 1935; d. Charles Cecil and Byvirl Louise (Mackey) Smith; m. Thomas A. White, Aug. 1, 1957 (dec. 1976); children—David Anthony, Tamara Elizabeth; m. John Joseph Murray, Aug. 18, 1983. Student N.Y. Inst. Design, 1975. Office mgr. Dr. T.A. White, Kingston, N.Y., 1957-64; owner Vicki White Interiors, Slidell, La., 1977-80; co-owner Jack Murray Field Service Co., Slidell, 1983—. Active Mother's March of Dimes, 1974-83, Easter Seal, 1974-83; membership chmn. Slidell High Sch. Band Boosters, 1977-84. Republican. Club: Profl. Women. Home: Whisperwood Estates Slidell LA 70458

MURRAY, FREDERICK FRANKLIN, lawyer; b. Corpus Christi, Tex., Aug. 1, 1950; s. Marvin Frank and Suzanne Louise M.; m. Susan McKeen; B.A., Rice U., 1972; J.D., U.Tex., 1974. C.P.A., Tex., 1977; bar: Tex. 1975, U.S. Ct. Appeals (5th Cir.) 1976, U.S. Ct. Appeals (D.C.) 1976, U.S. Tax Ct. 1976, U.S. Ct. Claims 1976, U.S. Supreme Ct. 1978, U.S. Dist. Ct. (so. dist.) Tex. 1976, U.S. Dist. Ct. (no. dist.) Tex. 1985, U.S. Ct. Internat. Trade 1983. Sr. assoc. Chamberlain, Hrdlicka, White, Johnson & Williams, Houston, 1984-85, ptnr., 1985—. Mem. Tax Law Adv. Commn., Tex. Bd. Legal Specialization, 1984—; adj. prof. U. Houston Law Ctr., 1984—. Mem. adv. bd., co-chmn. deferred giving com. Houston Symphony Soc., 1984—; chmn. parish council Sacred Heart Cathedral, Galveston, Houston Diocese, 1979-81; del. Bishop's Diocesan Pastoral Council, 1979-80. Author, speaker on taxation, business and property law. Mem. Am. Arbitration Assn., ABA (chmn. subcom. community property issues 1981—), internat. Bar Assn., Houston Bar Assn., Am. Inst. C.P.A.s, Tex. Soc. C.P.A.s (vice chmn. taxation com. Houston 1982-83), Internt. Tax Forum Houston (pres. 1984—), Houston Estate and Fin. Forum, Internt. Bar Assn., Internat. Fiscal Assn., Am. Soc. Internat. Law, Am. Fgn. Law Assn., Union Internationale des Avocats.

MURRAY, HAROLD DIXON, biological educator, malacologist; b. Neodesha, Kans., May 25, 1931; s. Claude Allen and Beulah Augusta (Dixon) M.; m. Beverly Frances Martindale, Oct. 3, 1954; 1 child, Stephen Weston. B.S., Ottawa U., 1952; M.Sc., Kans. State Coll., 1953; Ph.D., U. Kans., 1960. Instr. U. Kans., Lawrence, 1960-61; asst. prof. Trinity U., San Antonio, 1961-66, assoc. prof., 1966-73, chmn. biology, 1975-84, acting dean, 1979-80, prof. biology, 1973—. Author: Unionid Mussels in Kansas, 1962. Author booklet Premedical Advising in Texas, 1981. Served to cpl. U.S. Army, 1953-54. Fellow Tex. Acad. Sci.; mem. Am. Malacological Union (pres. 1974-75), Am. Soc. Parasitologists, AAAS, Sigma Xi. Home: 247 Pinewood Ln San Antonio TX 78216 Office: Trinity U 715 Stadium Dr San Antonio TX 78284

MURRAY, JEANNE MORRIS, scientist, educator, consultant; b. Fresno., Calif., July 6, 1925; d. Edward W. and Augusta R. (French) Morris; m. Thomas Harold Murray, June 19, 1964; children—Jeanne, Margaret, Barbara, Thomas, William. B.S. in Math., Morris Harvey Coll., 1957; M.S. in Info. and Computer Sci., Ga. Inst. Tech., 1966; Ph.D., in Pub. Adminstrn., Tech. Mgmt., Am. U., 1981. Research scientist Ga. Inst. Tech., Atlanta, 1959-68; adj. prof. Am. U., Washington, 1968-73; computer scientist U.S. Dept. Def., Washington, 1968-69; staff scientist Delex Systems, Inc., Arlington, Va., 1969-70; mgmt. analyst GSA, Washington, 1971-74; assoc. prof. No. Va. Community Coll., 1975-76, U. Va., 1976—; cons., TechDyn Systems, ABA Corp., OrKand Corp., 1978-80; pres. Sequoia Assocs., Arlington, Va., 1981—; mem. Carter transition team, 1976-77. Mem. Arlington (Va.) Civil Def. Com., 1983—; mem. Washington Met. Area Emergency Assistance Com.; mem. Arlington County Com. on Sci. and Tech. Mem. IEEE (sr. mem., vice chmn. Washington), N.Y. Acad. Scis., Assn. Computing Machinery, Soc. Gen. Research, Am. Soc. Pub. Adminstrn., World Future Soc., Better World Soc., Acad. Polit. Sci., AAAS. Episcopalian. Author: Cybernetics and the Management of the Research and Development Function in Society, 1971; Cybernetics as a Tool in the Control of Drug Abuse, 1972; Development of a General Computerized Forecasting Model, 1971; Political Humankind and the Future of Governance, 1974; The Doctrine of Management Planning, 1973; Policy Design, 1980; Computer Futures, 1982. Home and Office: 2915 N 27th St Arlington VA 22207

MURRAY, ROBERT JOHN, economist; b. Gouverneur, N.Y., Apr. 15, 1947; s. Maurice Grovenor and Julia Maude (Baker) M.; m. Martha Lillian Gipson, Mar. 2, 1968; 1 child, Christine Gipson. Student U. Montevallo, 1965-68, B.S. in Econs., 1974. Labor market analyst State of Ala., Alexander City, 1976-81; economist U.S. Army C.E., Mobile, Ala., 1981—. Analyst labor market info., county newsletters, affirmative action, county packets, 1976-81. Served with USAF, 1968-72, Eng. Hon. Lt. Col. Aide-de-Camp to Gov. Ala., 1967. Mem. Am. Econs. Assn., Jaycees. Presbyterian. Clubs: Mobile Doubloon Club. Avocations: chess; coin collecting; fishing. Home: 2705 Appian Way Mobile AL 36609 Office: US Army Corps Engrs PO Box 2288 Mobile AL 36628

MURRAY, SONIA BENNETT, real estate executive; b. Norfolk, Eng., May 15, 1936; came to U.S., 1956, naturalized, 1961; d. Marcus Warburton and Ruth Lillian (Clarke) B.; m. Gilbert Lafayette Murray, Jr., June 25, 1955; children—Gilbert L. III, Keith David, Kathryn Sonia. Student U. Miss., 1958-61, U. Ala., 1983—. Mgr. Airway Apts., Biloxi, Miss., 1958-65; owner Airway Apts. and other properties, 1965—. Pres. Friends of Biloxi Libraries, 1979-81. Republican. Humanist. Author: Shell Life and Shell Collecting, 1969; Shell Collectors' Handbook and Identifier, 1974. Address: 1609 Oaklawn Pl Biloxi MS 39530

MURRELL, ROBERT GEORGE, lawyer; b. Atlanta, Jan. 27, 1932; s. Samuel Edwin and Myrtle Josephine (Hailey) M.; m. Bonnie Bird Robinson, Nov. 11, 1961; children—Robert George, Michele Grace, Bonnie Melissa. B.A., U. Fla., 1952, J.D., 1953. Bar: Fla. 1953, U.S. Dist. Ct. (so. dist.) Fla. 1953, U.S. Ct. Appeals (5th cir.) 1953, U.S. Ct. Mil. Appeals 1958, U.S. Supreme Ct. 1958, U.S. Ct. Claims 1975, U.S. Tax Ct. 1975, U.S. Ct. Customs and Patent Appeals 1975, D.C. 1976, U.S. Ct. Internat. Trade 1980, U.S. Dist. Ct. (mid. dist.) Fla. 1980, N.Y. 1981, Pa. 1982, U.S. Ct. Appeals (11th cir.) 1982. Ptnr. Sam E. Murrell & Sons, Orlando, Fla., 1953—; mem. Citrus Assocs. of N.Y. Stock Exchange; pres. Colonial Mortgage Co. Fla., Inc.; dir. Weiss Realty Corp., Lake Margaret Co., We Care, Inc.; owner, Vista Travel, Inc.; arbitrator Am. Arbitration Assn. Served to sgt. U.S. Army, 1953-55. Mem. ABA, Fla. Bar, Orange County Bar Assn., Attys. Title Services, Inc. Republican. Baptist. Clubs: Univ. of Winter Park (Fla.); Masons, Shriners, Elks (Orlando). Home: 415 Raintree Ct Winter Park FL 32789 Office: One N Rosalind Ave Orlando FL 32801

MURRELL, STRATTON CHADWICK, optometrist; b. Jacksonville, N.C., Jan. 11, 1928; s. Zachariah Enniss and Louise (Chadwick) M.; m. Billie Jean Smith, July 24, 1954; 1 child, Mark Steven. B.S., Wake Forest Coll., 1949; O.D., Pa. Coll. Optometry, 1954. Practice optometry, Jacksonville, N.C., 1954—. Author: The Somatic Eye Chart, 1977; contbr. articles to popular mags., profl. jours. Recipient Disting. Service award Jacksonville Jaycees, 1963, Order of Arrow award Boy Scouts Am., 1947, Silver Beaver award, 1961; only optometrist lic. to use systemic medications. Mem. Coastal Optometric Dist., N.C. State Optometric Soc., Am. Optometric Assn., Eye Research Found., Sociedad Americana de Oftalmologia y Optometria, Internat. Found. Preventive Medicine, Royal Soc. Health, AAAS, Am. Sci. Affiliation. Democrat. Baptist. Club: Lions Internat. Office: Northwoods Profl Plaza Suite 2 Jacksonville NC 28540

MURRILL, PAUL WHITFIELD, utility company executive; b. St. Louis, July 10, 1934; s. Horace William and Grace Virginia (Whitfield) M.; m. Nancy Hoover Williams, May 17, 1959; children—Whit, John, Britt. B.S., U. Miss., 1956; M.S., La. State U., 1962, Ph.D., 1963. Sr. v.p. research and devel., dir. Ethyl Corp.; Successively spl. lectr. La. State U., Baton Rouge, asst. prof., assoc. prof., prof., head chem. engring. dept., provost, vice-chancellor acad. affairs, then chancellor; chmn. bd., chief exec. officer Gulf States Utilities Co., Beaumont, Tex., 1982—; dir. The Foxboro Co., First Miss. Corp., Tidewater Inc., First City Bancorp. Tex., First Security Bank of Beaumont; cons. editor Instrument Soc. Am. Trustee, Gulf South Research Inst., John E. Gray Found. Recipient Halliburton award La. State U., 1967; Faculty Service award Nat. U. Extension Assn., 1968; La. Engring. Soc. Tech. medal, 1970; Coates award, 1975; Nat. Donald Eckman award Instrument Soc. Am., 1976; Andrew Lockett award La. Engring. Soc. 1978. Contbr. articles to tech. and profl. jours. Office: Gulf Utilities Co Beaumont TX

MURSTEN, HARRY, construction company executive; b. Buffalo, Nov. 11, 1930; s. Sidney and Ruth (Lunenfeld) M.; m. Linda Fenton (div.); children—David, Pamela, Amy, Michael; m. 2d, Margaret Brown Feldman, Sept. 24, 1967; children—Jacqueline, Scott. B.S. in Bus. Adminstrn., U. Buffalo, 1953. Cert. gen. contractor, Fla. Chief exec. officer Retail Store, Buffalo, 1953-59; pres. Barlin Constrn. Co., Miami, Fla., 1960-70; pres., chief exec. officer Mursten Constrn., Miami, 1971—; faculty mem. Nova U., Ft. Lauderdale, Fla., 1984, 85; tech. presenter People's Republic China, 1982. Chmn. Com. 100, Hialeah, Fla., 1983-84; pres. NW Dade Regional YMCA, Miami, 1983-84, metro bd., 1985; pres. Learning Disabilities Found., Miami, 1978-79. Recipient Community Service award Dade County Pub. Schs., 1977. Mem. Am. Inst. Constructors, Constrn. Specifications Inst., Associated Builders & Contractors (nat. asst. sec. 1984, pres. Fla. chpt. 1982-83, Member of Year award Washington, 1982, Member of Year award Boca Raton, 1982, 79 (nat. 3rd v.p. 1985, nat. 2d v.p. 1986), NW Dade C. of C. (dir. 1982-84). Lodges: United Craft, Scottish Rite, Ismalia Temple.

MURTAUGH, GORDON MATTHEW, consultant; b. N.Y.C., Mar. 20, 1924; s. George Edward and Rose Mary (Meeske) M.; m. Lois Betty Koch, Sept. 6, 1952; children—Gordon, Joan Murtaugh Borstell, Kathryn Murtaugh Ross, Thomas, Patricia. M.E., Stevens Inst. Tech., 1945; M.B.A., NYU, 1954. Process engr. M. W. Kellogg, Jersey City, 1946-51; prodn. supt., plant controller AMF, Long Island, N.Y., 1951-66; corp. staff mem. ITT, N.Y.C., 1966-69, asst. to exec. v.p., 1969-71; product line mgr. Levitt & Sons, Long Island, 1971-73, sr. v.p., 1973-75; pres. Palm Cable, Palm Coast, Fla., 1975-84, also dir.; pres. Palm Coast Utility, 1975-84, also dir.; v.p. Admiral Corp., Palm Coast, 1975-84, also dir. Mem. sch. system adv. bd. Flagler County Sch. Curriculum Com., Fla., 1979-81. Served with USAAF, 1945-46. Democrat. Presbyterian. Home and Office: 4595 Dudley Ln NW Atlanta GA 30327

MUSACCHIA, X. J., physiology educator, university dean; b. Bklyn., Feb. 11, 1923; s. Castrense and Orsolina (Mazzola) M.; m. Betty Cook, Nov. 23, 1950; children—Joseph, Mary, Thomas, Laura Ann. B.S., St. Francis Coll., 1943; M.S., Fordham U., 1947, Ph.D., 1949. Instr. biology Marymount Coll., N.Y.C., 1948-49; instr., asst. prof., then assoc. prof. biology St. Louis U., 1949-61, prof., 1961-65; prof. physiology U. Mo., Columbia, 1965-78; prof. physiology and biophysics, dean grad. programs and research U. Louisville, 1978—, also assoc. provost for research; mem. corp. Marine Biol. Lab., Woodshole, Mass. Bd. govs. Louisville Regional Cancer Ctr. Served with AUS, 1943-45. NIH, NASA research grantee. Fellow AAAS; mem. Am. Physiol. Soc., Am. Soc. Zoologists, Soc. Exptl. Biology and Medicine, Sigma Xi (chpt. pres.). Contbr. numerous articles to profl. pubs. Office: Grad Programs and Research U Louisville Jouett Hall Louisville KY 40292

MUSE, PATRICIA ALICE, writer, educator; b. South Bend, Ind., Nov. 27, 1923; d. Walter L. and Enid (Cockerham) Ashdown; B.A., Principia Coll., 1947; student Columbia U., 1946, Seminole Community Coll., 1977, U. Central Fla., 1978-83; m. Kenneth F. Muse, Dec. 2, 1950; children—Patience Eleanor, Walter Scott. Substitute tchr. pub. schs., Key West, Fla., also Brunswick, Ga., 1962-68; free lance writer, Casselberry, Fla., 1968—; tutor Adult Literacy League, 1983—; novels: Sound of Rain, 1971, The Belle Claudine, 1971, paperback, 1973, Eight Candles Glowing, 1976; creative writing instr., Valencia Community Coll., 1974-75; instr. various writers confs. Community resource vol. Orange County (Fla.) Sch. Bd. (recipient certs. of appreciation 1975, 76, 77). Mem. AAUW.

MUSE, VONCEIL FOWLER, school librarian, educator; b. Tyler, Tex., July 12, 1915; d. Dennis Cleveland and Elva Mary (Wallace) Fowler; m. Bert Cromwell Muse, Dec. 28, 1938 (dec. Jan. 1983). B.A., Tex. Coll., 1936; M.S.L.S., U. So. Calif., 1953; postgrad. NDEA seminars (grantee) Tex. Women's U., 1965. Cert. profl. all levels, Tex. Elem. tchr. Jasper (Tex.) Schs., 1936-37, Trinidad (Tex.) Schs., 1937-39; tchr.-librarian Stanton Rural High Sch., Whitehouse, Tex., 1940-46; co-owner, pub. Tyler (Tex.) Tribune, 1946-49; tchr.-librarian Tyler Schs., 1949-52; sch. librarian Dallas Pub. Schs., 1952-78; past dir. Women's Southwest Fed. Credit Union, Dallas, 1975-80; yearbook chmn. Dallas Sch. Librarians, 1976; mem. social com. Dallas Ret. Tchrs., 1979. Founder, Glenview Neighbors Assn., Dallas, 1980; mem. Mental Health Assn. Dallas County, 1978, Community Connection, Dallas, 1983, South Central Dallas Civic Group, 1984. Tex. State scholar, 1950. Mem. Dallas Classroom Tchrs. (bldg. rep. 1969-78), Dallas Ret. Tchrs. Assn., Am. Assn. Ret. Persons, United Tchrs. Tex. State Tchrs. Assn. (life), NEA (life), Tex. Library Assn., ALA, Tex. and Southwestern Cattle Raisers Assn. (assoc.), Southwestern Cattle Raisers Assn. (assoc.), Tex. Coll. Nat. Alumni, Alpha Kappa Alpha (nat. officer; life). Democrat. Mem. Christian Methodist Episcopal Ch. Lodge: Court of Calanthe.

MUSGRAVE, MARY ANNESE, public relations executive; b. Huntington, W.Va., June 3, 1937; d. Clarence Wilson and Anagene Calhoun (Plymale) Bartram; m. Robert Stewart Musgrave, Feb. 25, 1961; children—Robert Stewart III, Anne Clare. B.S., Fla. State U., 1959; M.F.A., So. Meth. U., 1982. Tchr. West Palm Beach Elem. Sch. (Fla.), 1959-60, Ceredo Elem. Sch. (W.Va.), 1960-62; dir. community relations 1st Nat. Bank, Ceredo, 1971-77; with consumer relations dept. Tradewell Supermarkets, Kenova, W.Va., 1977-78; dir. communications Cox Bus. Sch., So. Meth. U., Dallas, 1981-82; pres. Marsecomm Assocs., Dallas, 1982—. Mem. Pub. Relations Soc. Am., Sigma Delta Chi. Republican. Mem. Christian Ch. Club: Las Colinas Country, Women of Rotary. Home and Office: 4325 Cedarbrush Dallas TX 75229

MUSGROVE, JUDY AUTRY, advertising company executive; b. San Antonio, Tex., Aug. 5, 1946; d. Monte L. and Mary E. (Hohner) Autry; m. Joe F. Musgrove, May 24, 1969 (div. 1974). Student U. Tex., 1964-68. Bus. mgr. Emergency Med. Services, P.A., Houston, 1974-81; mgr. bus. affairs Eisaman Johns & Laws Advt., Houston, 1981-83, v.p. bus. affairs, 1983—; guest lectr. women's profl. orgn., U. Houston. Mem. Friends of Houston Library; vol. Bellaire Hosp. Cardiac Care Program, 1979-80; chmn. com. Greater Hartford Open Golf Tournament, 1970-71; mem. Nashville Symphony Women's Guild, 1972-73. Mem. Am. Bus. Women's Assn. (dir. 1980-84, v.p. 1981, Woman of Yr. 1984), Fedn. Houston Profl. Women (organizing chmn. 1981, pres. 1982, exec. bd. 1983), Nat. Assn. Female Execs. Republican. Methodist. Home: 7022 Jetty Ln Houston TX 77072 Office: 2121 Sage Rd Suite 145 Houston TX 77056

MUSLIN, HARVEY PAUL, lawyer; b. Chgo., Jan. 5, 1945; s. Isidore Sam and Margie (Axelrod) M.; m. Adrienne Marilyn Berg, Sept. 5, 1966; children—Ivan Scott, Erica Beth, David Oliver. B.S.B.A., Roosevelt U., 1967; J.D., John Marshall Law Sch., 1971. Bar: Ill. 1971, Fla. 1980, U.S. Dist. Ct. (mid. dist.) Fla. 1981, U.S. Dist. Ct. (no. dist.) Ill. 1971, U.S. Supreme Ct. 1979. Asst. state atty. Cook County, Ill., 1971-74; sole practice, Chgo., 1974-80, Tampa, Fla., 1981—. Mem. Decalogue League Lawyers, Ill. Bar Assn., Fla. Bar Assn., Hillsborough County Bar Assn. Democrat. Jewish. Club: B'nai B'rith (v.p. 1982-83). Office: 1905 W Kennedy Blvd Tampa FL 33606-1530

MUSSAT, GEORGE ROBERT, safety professional; b. Frontenac, Kans., Mar. 27, 1943; s. George A. and Alice Mae (Pichlemier) M.; m. Nancy J. Sheets, Apr. 4, 1964; children—Robert Joseph, Brenda Joann, Becky Jo. B.A. in Chemistry, Kans. State Coll., 1966. Shift supr. E.I. duPont de Nemours & Co., S.C. and Tenn., 1968-77, day supr., Charleston, S.C., 1977-79, sect. supr., 1979-81, area maintenance supr., 1981, safety supr., 1981—; mem. S.C. Fire Adv. Bd., 1981—; mem. TEC adv. bd. Trident Tech. Coll., 1981-83. Bd. dirs. Trident United Way, 1981-84. Mem. Am. Soc. Safety Engrs. (sect. chair 1982-83, chpt. charter pres. 1983-84), Vets. of Safety, Nat. Safety Council, Internat. Soc. Fire Service Instrs. Democrat. Roman Catholic. Lodge: K.C. (state sec. 1984—; charter navigator 1983-84; Sir Knight of Yr. 1984). Avocations: bowling; fishing; softball. Home: 107 Inwood Dr Summerville SC 29483 Office: DuPont Co PO Box 10228 Charleston SC 29411

MUSSENDEN, GEORG ANTONIO, electronics engineer; b. San Juan, P.R., Aug. 25, 1959; s. Gustavo Adolfo and Christa-Maria (Gotsch) M. Student U. P.R.-Rio Piedras, 1977-79; B.S. in E.E. with honors, U. Fla.-Gainesville, 1982. Electronics technician Radiotelephone Communicators of P.R. (Motorola), 1976; computer systems programmer and operator U. P.R., Rio Piedras, 1978-79, research asst. dept. physics, 1978-79; computer programmer Regional Electrocardiogram Analysis Ctr., J. Hillis Miller Health Ctr., U. Fla., Gainesville, 1981; pre-profl. engr. IBM Corp. Devel. Lab., Endicott, N.Y., 1981, assoc. engr. systems products div., design and devel. lab. IBM, Boca Raton, Fla., 1982—. Scholar San Jose Alumni, 1973-77, Fonalledas Found., 1977-79, Procter and Gamble, 1980, U.F. Sr. Honors scholar, 1980, Nat. Fund Minority Engring., 1980, Du Pont, 1981; Nat. Consortium for Grad. Degrees for Minorities in Engring. fellow, 1981. Mem. N.Y. Acad. Scis., IEEE, Golden Key, Eta Kappa Nu, Tau Beta Pi, Phi Kappa Phi. Roman Catholic. Clubs: Audio-Visual, Amateur Radio. Office: IBM Corp Systems Products Div 1000 NW 51st St Dept 27Q Bldg 223-1 Boca Raton FL 33432

MUSSER, JOHN HERR, lawyer; b. Yazoo City, Miss., Sept. 4, 1944; s. John Herr and Wilma Childress (Bradley) M.; m. Margaret Helen Norman, June 6, 1966 (div. 1981); children—Susan Bradley, John H., Christopher Couret, David Norman. B.A., Tulane U., 1966, J.D., 1969. Bar: La. 1969, Miss. 1969, U.S. Supreme Ct. 1975. Assoc., Montgomery, Barnett, Braun & Rand, New Orleans, 1969-73; asst. U.S. atty., New Orleans, 1973-76; assoc. Francis Emmett, New Orleans, 1977; mng. trial atty. CNA Ins. Co., New Orleans, 1978-83; ptnr. Longenecker & Musser, New Orleans, 1983—. Mem. exec. com. Orleans Parish Republican Exec. Com., 1980—; mem. Alliance for Good Govt., 1975—. Inst. Politics fellow, 1970-71. Mem. ABA, La. Bar Assn., Miss. State Bar Assn., Maritime Law Assn., La. Assn. Def. Counsel. Republican. Episcopalian. Home: 2333 Chestnut St New Orleans LA 70130 Office: 2404 ITM Bldg New Orleans LA 70130

MUSTAFA, SHAMS, chemist, consultant; b. Karachi, Pakistan, Oct. 8, 1952; came to U.S., 1977; s. Mustafa Hasan Zuberi and Shaista Shakri Mustafa; m. Naheed Shams Mustafa, Apr. 23, 1982; 1 child, Sharjeel. B.S., Punjab U., Lahore, Pakistan, 1969, honors, 1970, M.S., 1971. Sr. chemist Ace Labs., Karachi, 1972-77, cons., 1972-77; chemist Am. Standards Testing Bur., N.Y.C., 1977-79; scientist Caleb Brett (USA), New Orleans, 1979—. Author: Carbohydrate Chemistry, 1971. Mem. Am. Oil Chemists Soc. (referee), Am. Inst. Chemists, Assn. Ofcl. Analytical Chemists, ASTM, AAAS, N.Y. Acad. Scis., Nat. Soybean Porcessors Assn. Republican. Islam. Home: 1417 Meeker Loop Laplace LA 70068 Office: Caleb Brett (USA) Inc 4927 Jefferson Hwy Jefferson LA 70121

MUSTIAN, MIDDLETON TRUETT, hosp. adminstr.; b. Texarkana, Tex., Mar. 27, 1921; s. Thomas William and Hattie (Cornelius) M.; B.B.A., Baylor U., 1949; m. Jackie Cain, Dec. 3, 1955; children—Mark Thomas, John Perry, Janet Louise. Asst. adminstr. Bapt. Hosp., Alexandria, La., 1950-54; asst. adminstr. Miss. Bapt. Hosp., Jackson, 1954-55; adminstr. Meml. Hosp., Panama City, Fla., 1955-60, Alachua Gen. Hosp., Gainesville, Fla., 1960-64; adminstr. Meml. Bapt. Hosp., Central unit, also asst. dir. Meml. Bapt. Hosp. System, Houston, 1964; pres., chief exec. officer Tallahassee Meml. Regional Med. Center Hosp., 1964—; clin. instr. dept. health adminstrn. U. Gainesville; bd. dirs. Blue Cross of Fla.; mem. Fla. Statewide Health Coordinating Council. Served to capt. Med. Adminstrv. Corps, U.S. Army, 1940-45. Decorated Purple Heart. Fellow Am. Coll. Hosp. Adminstrs. (regent); mem. Am., Fla. (past pres.) hosp. assns. Democrat. Baptist. Clubs: Kiwanis, Masons. Contbr. articles to hosp. jours. Home: 1302 Leewood Dr Tallahassee FL 32303 Office: Tallahassee Meml Hosp Magnolia Dr and Miccosukee Rd Tallahassee FL 32303

MYCUE, DAVID JOHN, historian, librarian, archivist; b. Niagara Falls, N.Y., Oct. 4, 1935; s. John Powers and Ruth Agnes (Delehant) M.; B.A., North Tex. State U., 1964; M.A. (Fellow), U. Ill., Champaign, 1973, M.S., 1976; m. Elena De Los Santos, June 13, 1964; children—Alfredo, Victoria, Marcelo. Instr. history N. Tex. State U., Denton, 1966-67; tchr. high schs., Irving, Tex., 1964-65, San Antonio, 1967-68; historian, mil. airlift command Office of Chief Staff USAF, Scott AFB, Ill., 1968-71; instr. history U. Ill., Champaign, 1972-75; sr. archivist Ill. State Archives, Office of Sec. State, Springfield, 1976-80; asst. dir. budget and tech. services McAllen Meml. Library, Tex., 1980-85; reference librarian Pan Am. U., Edinburg, Tex., 1985—. Treas., Hidalgo County Hist. Commn., 1985—. Served with Security Agy. U.S. Army, 1958-61. Recipient Donald G. Wing award Sch. Library Sci. U. Ill., 1976. Mem. Am. Hist. Assn., ALA, Valley Library Assn. (historian 1982-84), Hidalgo County Hist. Soc. (treas. 1984—). Contbr. articles to archival, hist. and library jours. Home: 1212 Highland St McAllen TX 78501 Office: Learning Resource Center Pan Am U Edinburg TX 78539

MYERS, ALBERT DEAN, vocational educator, consultant; b. Crescent, Okla., Aug. 28, 1943; s. John W. and Velma Marie (Wilson) M.; m. Cheryl Reece, Mar. 19, 1966; children—Deidre Dawn, Aric Dean. B.S. in Trade and Indsl. Edn., Okla. State U., 1977, M.S. in Trade and Indsl. Edn., 1979. Farmer, rancher, 1959—; supr. Kerr McGee Nuclear Facility, Crescent, Okla., 1968-73; owner Myers Haus Interiors, Inc., Edmond, Okla., 1973-78; welding instr. Oklahoma City Skill Ctr., 1974-76; dist. supr. trade-indsl. edn. State Dept. Vocat.-Tech. Edn., Stillwater, Okla., 1976—; ranch cons., industry cons. Mem. adv. com. Job Corps; mem. Logan County Indsl. Authority Bd. Served with USAR, 1965-67. Recipient Service award Central State U. Interior Design Club, 1983. Mem. Okla. Council Local Adminstrs., Am. Vocat. Assn., Am. Welding Soc., Okla. Adult Continuing Edn. Assn., Exptl. Aircraft Assn., Phi Delta Kappa, Iota Lambda Sigma. Home: Route 2 Box 457 Crescent OK 73028 Office: 1500 W 7th St Stillwater OK 74074

MYERS, ALTA MAE, collection agency executive; b. Mutual, Okla., May 4, 1933; d. Fisher and Ruby M. (Manning) Williamson; m. Warren G. Myers, July 4, 1950; children—Ronald Eugene, Randy Warren. Student Woodward Beauty Coll. Operator, Dons, Woodward, Okla., 1977-79; mgr. Alta's House of Beauty, Woodward, 1969-77; debt. collector Collection Service, Woodward, 1981; credit mgr. Woodward Meml. Hosp., 1981-83, cons.; pres., mgr. Capital Recovery Cons., Inc., Woodward, 1983—. Mem. Healthcare Fin. Mgmt. Assn., Am. Collectors Assn., Okla. Collectors Assn., Delta Alpha Beta Sigma Phi. Democrat. Episcopalian. Home: 2200 2d St Woodward OK 73801

MYERS, CHARLES BENNETT, social studies educator; b. June 8, 1939, Columbia, Pa.; s. John Charles and Bernice (Sieple) M.; m. Lynn Knisely, Sept. 12, 1959; children—Jeffrey A., Mark D., Brian L. B.S., Pa. State U., 1961; M.S., George Peabody Coll., 1963, Ph.D., 1968. Asst. prof. edn. and history Rider Coll., Trenton, N.J., 1965-69; social sci. specialist Speedier Project, Palmyra, Pa., 1968-70; from asst. prof. to prof. social studies edn. George Peabody Coll., Nashville, 1970-79, dir. program for educators of youth, 1974-79, asst. dir. Peabody Ctr. Econ. and Social Studies Edn., 1979-82, dept. chmn. and prof. social studies edn., Vanderbilt U., 1979—. Author: (with others) The Environmental Crisis, 1970, 2d edit., 1976, Teaching Stratatgy for Developing Children's Thinking, 1970—; People, Time and Change, 1983; author, gen. editor: The Taba Program in Social Science, 1975. Mem. commn. on teaching Office of the Ch., Tenn. Cath. Sch., Nashville, 1984—. Mem. Nat. Council for Social Studies (bd. dirs. 1979-81), Tenn. Council for Social Studies (pres. 1974-76, exec. com. 1976-80), Assn. of Pvt. Enterprise Edn. (pres. 1980-81, v.p. 1979-80, sec. treas. 1978-79), Council for Advancement of Citizenship (orgn. com. 1980-81, adv. com. 1982-83), Consortium for Improvement of Instrn. in Middle Tenn. (bd. dirs. 1977-83). Democrat. Roman Catholic. Club: Pa. State U. of Middle Tenn. (founder 1978) (Nashville). Office: Peabody Coll Vanderbilt U Dept Teaching and Learning Nashville TN 37203

MYERS, CHARLES HENRY, real estate executive; b. Hamlin, Tex., July 8, 1931; s. Charles Henry and Juanita (McClaren) M.; m. Beverly E. Butler, June 3, 1959; children—Robyn Lynn. B.B.A., U. Tex., Austin, 1953; M.B.A., So. Meth. U., 1962. Registered investment advisor SEC. Exec. v.p. Townhome Properties, Inc., Dallas, 1974, now dir.; regional mgr. IBM, Dallas, 1974-81, cons., 1982—; chief exec. officer Designer Townhomes, Inc., 1982, now chmn. bd.; v.p. Heidrick & Struggles, 1982; exec. v.p. Paragon Properties, Austin, 1983—. Office: 2030 American Bank Tower Austin TX 78701

MYERS, DONNY PAUL, hospital administrator; b. Greenville, Ky., June 22, 1943; s. David Paul and Dora Mae (Harris) M.; 1 child, David; m. Grace E. Hamilton, Feb. 1, 1985. Student So. Acad. Clin. Tech., 1961, U. Ala.-Birmingham, 1976. Lab., x-ray tech. Clay County Hosp., Ft. Gaines, Ga., 1964-76; health adminstr. Abernethy Meml. Hosp., Flomaton, Ala., 1976—. Chmn. Flomaton Planning Commn., 1980—, Southwest Ala. Emergency Med. Service, Grove Hill, 1983-85; mem. Flomaton Indsl. Devel., 1982—; sec. Gulf Coast Health Coop., Pensacola, Fla., 1984—; pres. Escambia County Emergency Med. Service, Flomaton, 1985. Lodge: Lions. Avocation: Spectator sports. Home: PO Box 346 Flomaton AL 36441 Office: Abernethy Meml Hosp Drawer A Flomaton AL 36441

MYERS, EUGENE EKANDER, art consultant; b. Grand Forks, N.D., May 5, 1914; s. John Q. and Hattye Jane (Ekander) M.; B.S. in Edn., U. N.D., 1936, M.S. in Edn., 1938; postgrad. U. Oreg., summer 1937; M.A., Northwestern U., 1940; M.A., Columbia U., 1947; grad. Advanced Mgmt. Program, Harvard, 1953; cert. Cambridge (Eng.) U., 1958; postgrad. U. Md., 1958-61, Oxford (Eng.) U., 1964; diploma various mil. schs.; m. Florence Hutchinson Ritchie, Sept. 9, 1974. Student asst. U. N.D., 1935-36, instr. summer sessions, 1936, 37, asst., 1936-37; prof., head dept. N.D. Tchrs. Coll., 1938-40; instr. Columbia Tchrs. Coll., 1940-41; prof. U. Vt., summers, 1941, 42; commd. 1st lt. USAAF, 1942, advanced through grades to col., 1951; dir. personnel plans and tng. Hdqrs. Air Force Systems Command, Washington, 1959-60, dir. personnel research and long-range plans, 1960-62; head dept. internat. relations Air War Coll., Air U., Maxwell AFB, Ala., 1962-63, dir. curriculum, dean, 1963-65; dir. res. affairs Hdqrs. Air Res. Personnel Center, Denver, 1965-66; ret., 1966; dean Corcoran Sch. Art, Washington, 1966-70, founder Corocon Sch. Art Abroad, Leeds, Eng., 1967, v.p. mgmt. Corcoran Gallery Art, 1970-72; art cons., 1972—; vis. art dir., Palm Beach, Fla. and Washington. Adviser Washington chpt. Nat. Soc. Arts and Letters. Bd. assos. Artists Equity; bd. dirs. Columbia (Md.) Inst. Art, World Arts Found., N.Y., Court Art Center, Montgomery, Ala. and Palm Beach, Order of Lafayette, Boston, English-Speaking Union, Palm Beach. Recipient Sioux award U. N.D., 1978. Mem. Internat. Communication Assn. (hon.), U. N.D. Alumni Assn. (pres. Washington chpt. 1959), Mil. Classics Soc., Titanic Soc., Mil. Order Carabao, Co. Mil. Historians, Mil. Order World Wars, Ancient Order United Workmen, Sovereign Order St. John of Jerusalem, Knightly Assn. St. George the Martyr, Saint Andrews Soc., Clan Donnachaidh (Perthshire, Scotland), Soc. Friends St. Andrews (Scotland) U., Delta Omicron Epsilon, Lambda Chi Alpha, Delta Phi Delta, Phi Delta Kappa, Phi Alpha Theta. Presbyterian. Clubs: Union (hon.) (Manchester, Eng.); Royal Overseas (London); New (asso.) (Edinburgh, Scotland); Royal Scottish Automobile (Glasgow); Army and Navy, Nat. Aviation, City Tavern (Washington); Army and Navy Country (Arlington, Va.); Metropolitan, Wings, Explorers (fellow), Harvard (N.Y.C.); Minneapolis; Everglades, Beach, Sailfish of Fla. (Palm Beach, Fla.); Fairmont (W.Va.) Field Country; Hamilton St. Vol. Fire Dept. and Literary Soc. (Balt.); Lions. Author: with Paul E. Barr Creative Lettering, 1938; (with others) The Subject Fields in General Education, 1939; Applied Psychology, 1940. Contbr. articles, reports to mags. and profl. pubs. Home: One Royal Palm Way Palm Beach FL 33480 also 3320 Volta Pl NW Washington DC 20007

MYERS, FRED ARTHUR, museum executive; b. Lancaster, Pa., Dec. 21, 1937; s. Joseph A. and Mary C. (Leaman) M.; B.A., Harvard U., 1959, M.A., 1962; m. Mary Frances McGrann, May 6, 1961; children—Elizabeth, Benjamin, Margaret. Asst. to dir. Mus. Art, Carnegie Inst., Pitts., 1962-70; dir. Grand Rapids (Mich.) Art Mus., 1970-78, Thomas Gilcrease Inst. Am. History and Art, Tulsa, 1978—. Served with U.S. Army, 1959-60. Mem. Am. Assn. Museums, Assn. Art Mus. Dirs., Okla. Mus. Assn. (pres.) Clubs: Tulsa Country, Summit. Home: 1212 N 27th West Ave Tulsa OK 74127 Office: Thomas Gilcrease Institute American History and Art 1400 N 25th West Ave Tulsa OK 74127

MYERS, GEORGE HENRY, manufacturing company executive; b. Mount Vernon, Ill., Jan. 22, 1943; s. William Henry and Carol (Hughes) M.; m. Gloria M. Heginbotham, June 6, 1963; children—John Henry, Michael Todd. B.S., Drury Coll., 1965. Sales and mktg. mgr. sales promotion Sears, Dallas and El Paso, Tex., 1965-77; v.p. Paragon Market, El Paso, 1977-79; pres., owner Frame Industry Suppliers, El Paso, 1979—; owner Phototec, El Paso, 1979—, Fast Hour Foto, El Paso, 1981—; dir. Ad Council El Paso, 1979-81. Bd. dirs. Goodwill Industry, El Paso, 1978-81, United Way El Paso, 1979-81; deacon Bethany Christian Ch., El Paso, 1983. Mem. C. of C. (dir. 1981-82). Republican. Club: Ad (v.p. 1980-81) (El Paso). Home: 10535 Janway Dr El Paso TX 79925 Office: Frame Industry Suppliers Inc 11130 Rojas Dr El Paso TX 79935

MYERS, GERRY LYNN, public relations, marketing and advertising consulting firm executive; b. Dallas, July 23, 1943; d. Saul H. and Helen Frances (Hafter) Golden; m. Randolph P. Myers, Aug. 30, 1964; children—Richard Scott, Deborah Ruth, Kenneth Andrew. B.S. cum laude, U. Tex., 1964; M.B.A., North Tex. State U., 1980. Account supr. Dykeman & Assocs., Dallas, 1978-81; account exec. Teich Communications Co., Dallas, 1981; exec. v.p., ptnr. Shiroma & Myers, Inc., Dallas, 1981—. Mem. Pub. Relations Soc. Am., Women in Communications, Addison Bus. Assn., North Dallas Fin. Forum, Metrocrest C. of C., Richardson C. of C. Mem. Republican Forum. Jewish. Clubs: B'nai Brith Women (past pres. Starlight chpt., Best Communications award 1972), Architects Wives. Home: 6812 St Anne St Dallas TX 75248 Office: Shiroma & Myers Inc 14901 Quorum Dr Suite 210 Dallas TX 75240

MYERS, GOVAN THOMPSON, JR., textile manufacturing corporation executive; b. Gadsden, Ala., Nov. 24, 1943; s. Goven Thompson and Robbie (Blackmon) M.; m. Harriett Evann McDavid, Oct. 23, 1971; children—Govan Thompson III, Claire Evann. B.A., Wofford Coll., 1966; M.S. in Bus. Adminstrn., Winthrop Coll., 1978. With Springs Industries, 1966—, corp. compensation analyst, Ft. Mill, S.C., 1972-75, personnel dir. knit div., Ft. Mill, 1975-77, dir. personnel apparel div., Ft. Mill, 1977—. Mem. fin. com. First United Meth. Ch., Lancaster, S.C., 1973-83. Served to lt. U.S. Army, 1966-68. Mem. Am. Soc. Personnel Adminstrn. Methodist. Home: Route 4 West Manor Lancaster SC 29720 Office: PO Box 70 Fort Mill SC 29715

MYERS, JEFFREY LEE, lawyer; b. Ft. Benning, Ga., Aug. 23, 1944; s. Clifford Lawrence and Florence Margaret (Barnes) M.; m. Linda Gail Bazemore, Dec. 20, 1975; children—Christopher Lee, Justin Lee, Michael Lee. A.A., Chgo. Jr. Coll., 1964; B.A., Tulane U., 1966, J.D., 1969. Bar: Fla. 1969, U.S. Dist. Ct. (mid. dist.) Fla. 1972, U.S. Ct. Appeals (5th cir.) 1972, U.S. Supreme Ct. 1974, U.S. Ct. Appeals (11th cir.) 1983. Asst. pub. defender State of Fla., Clearwater, 1971-74; sole practice, Largo, Fla., 1975—; city atty. Pinellas Park, Fla., 1975-78, Indian Rocks Beach, Fla., 1978—; atty. Pinellas-Pasco Dist. Mental Health Bd., 1978—; chmn. bd. Prepaid Health Care, Inc., Clearwater, 1975-81; spl. asst. pub. defender State of Fla., Clearwater, 1981-82, apptd. fed. arbitrator U.S. Dist. Ct. (mid. dist.) Fla., 1984. Bd. dirs. Seminole Jr. Warhawks Athletic Assn., 1984—. Recipient Outstanding Service award Office of Pub. Defender, 1974; named Health Care Pioneer, INA Healthplan of Fla., 1981. Mem. Criminal Def. Lawyers Assn. (pres. 1975-76, dist. service award 1976, chmn. juvenile reform com. 1980), Nat. Criminal Def. Lawyers Assn., Nat. Health Lawyers Assn., Fla. Trial Lawyers Assn., Fla. Mcpl. Attys. Assn., Nat. Pub. Defenders Assn. (legis. com. 1972), Clearwater Bar Assn. (criminal law sect., chmn. pub. relations com. 1984). Democrat. Roman Catholic. Lodge: Kiwanis (Seminole, Fla.). Home: 13576 101st Terr N Seminole FL 33542 Office: Jeffrey L Myers PA 1101 Beecher Rd Largo FL 33544

MYERS, JUDIANN ALLEN, pharmacist; b. Charlotte, N.C., Feb. 5, 1953; d. John Watson and Doris C. (Leggette) Allen; m. H. William Myers, Feb. 5, 1981. B.S., U. S.C., 1977. Registered pharmacist. Pharmacist Eckerd Drug Co., Charlotte, N.C., 1977-80; asst. mgr. MediSave Pharm., Charlotte, 1980-84, cons., 1984—; cons. pharmacist Nursing Home Cons., Easley, S.C., 1984—. Mem. S.C. Pharm. Soc., Oconee Humane Soc. Republican. Episcopalian. Clubs: Pine Lake Country (Charlotte, N.C.); Spindle Tree (Seneca, S.C.). Avocations: tennis; snow and water skiing; horseback riding. Home: 108 Sunnyview Dr Seneca SC 29678

MYERS, MARILYN, cooking school owner, writer; b. Michigan City, Ind., July 25, 1943; d. Budd Arthur and Agnes Helen (Orzech) Myers; A.B., Ind. U., 1965; postgrad. Inst. for Ednl. Mgmt., Harvard U., 1974; diploma

L'Academie de Cuisine, 1978. Program asst. OEO, Washington, 1965-67; legis. asst., select subcom. on labor Com. on Edn. and Labor, U.S. Ho. of Reps., Washington, 1967-68; mng. editor Poverty and Human Resources, Inst. Labor and Indsl. Relations, U. Mich., Ann Arbor, 1968-71; free-lance writing, editing and pub. relations work, 1971-72; legis. specialist Mass. Econ. Opportunity Office, Boston, 1972-73; spl. asst. to pres. Hood Coll., Frederick, Md., 1973-75; coordinator equal opportunity and affirmative action Ark. State U., State University, 1975-78; propr., tchr. cooking sch. Marilyn Myers Kitchen, Little Rock, 1978—; food writer Ark. Gazette, 1984; dir. Acad. Travel Abroad, Inc. Chairperson adv. com. Capital Zoning Dist. Commn. Mem. Am. Assn. Cooking Schs., Nat. Food Editors and Writers Assn. Author: Fresh Monthly: Menus from Marilyn Myers' Kitchen, 1981; also pamphlets in field. Home and Office: 115 S Victory St Little Rock AR 72201

MYERS, ROBERT ERROL, oil company executive; b. Noblesville, Ind., Sept. 8, 1931; s. Errol Goodwin and Lucille (Johnson) M.; m. Glenda Sandifer, Oct. 9, 1959; children—Susan Eileen, Mary Lynn, Kenneth Goodwin. B.S., DePauw U., 1953; M.S., U. Ill., 1955. Geologist, Pan Am. Prodn. Co., Lafayette, La., 1955-58; geologist Columbia Gas Devel. Co., Lafayette, 1958-72, chief geologist, Houston, 1972-79, exploration mgr., 1979-84, dir. res. devel., 1985—. Served with U.S. Army, 1958-59. Mem. Am. Assn. Petroleum Geologists, Houston Geol. Soc. Republican. Baptist. Home: 12502 Briar Forest Dr Houston TX 77077 Office: Columbia Gas Devel Corp PO Box 1350 Houston TX 77001

MYERS, THOMAS ANDREW, marketing educator; b. Richmond, Va., May 24, 1951; s. James C. and Sally Anne (Morris) M.; m. Carolyn Mann, Oct. 10, 1976; children—Bret Rothschild, Jessica Burk. B.A., Va. Commonwealth U., 1974, M.S., 1977; postgrad. U. Md., 1981—. Adj. prof. mktg. Va. Commonwealth U., Richmond, 1977—; asst. prof. mktg. and bus. mgmt. Piedmont Va. Community Coll., Charlottesville, 1979-84, assoc. prof., 1984—; adj. prof. mktg. and bus. Mary Baldwin Coll., Staunton, Va., 1981—; bd. dirs. Va. Assn. Coop. Edn., 1983—; mktg./tng. cons. ARC, United Way, U.S. Action, U. Va., Va. Dept. Health, Home Mut. Life Ins. Co., CETA, Va. Div. Children, others. U.S. Dept. Edn. Title III/Ednl. grantee, summer 1981. Mem. Am. Mktg. Assn., Am. Soc. Tng. and Devel., Va. Community Colls. Assn., Va. Assn. Coop. Edn. Club: Hermitage Country. Contbr. articles to profl. jours. Office: Piedmont Va Community Coll Route 6 Box 1A Charlottesville VA 22901

MYERS, VAN E., corporate executive; b. Norfolk, Va., July 29, 1917; s. Sylvan Edward and Lucile (Stern) M.; m. Jane F. Friedman, Aug. 11, 1940; children—Cathy L., Bruce H. B.A. cum laude, Harvard U., 1939. Div. head Wometco Enterprises, Miami, Fla., 1946-50, v.p., 1950-59, sr. v.p., 1959-79, exec. v.p., 1979-83, pres., chief exec. officer, 1983—, dir., 1961-83. Served to lt. USN, 1942-46; PTO. Mem. Nat. Automatic Merchandising Assn. (dir. 1975-81), Nat. Assn. Concessionaires (v.p., dir. 1950-83), Nat. Coin Inst. (pres. 1982-83), Miami-Dade C. of C. Democrat. Jewish. Club: Coral Gables Country. Home: 2530 Columbus Blvd Coral Gables FL 33134 Office: Wometco Enterprises Inc 316 N Miami Ave Miami FL 33128*

MYERS, WILLIAM EARL, educational administrator, musician; b. Greenville, N.C., Dec. 27, 1932; s. William Moses and Olga (Battle) M.; m. Diana Davis, Aug. 4, 1963; children—Michael Earl, Michelle Earlisa. B.S., Va. State U., 1955; M. Mus., East Carolina U., 1972, M. Arts Edn., 1977. Music tchr. Frederick Douglass High Sch., Elm City, N.C., 1958-69, Elm City High Sch., 1970-76; prin. Elm City Middle Sch., 1976—; band camp staff East Carolina, Greenville, summer 1972, 73; dir. adult edn. Wilson Tech. Sch., Elm City, 1978—; guest condr. North East Dist. All State Band, East Carolina U., 1973, Band Day, U. N.C., Chapel Hill, 1972. Composer of music. Program chmn. Men's Civic Club, Wilson, N.C., 1982-84; bd. dirs. Arts Council, Wilson, 1978-82, United Way, Wilson, 1982—, Wilson Theater of Performing Arts, 19. Served to 1st lt. U.S. Army, 1955-58, Korea. Recipient Terry Sanford award N.C. Assn. Educators; named Outstanding N.C. Citizen WNCT-TV 1974. Mem. N.C. Prins. Assn., Wilson County Prins. Assn. (pres. 1981-83), Omega Psi Phi. Clubs: Bachelor-Benedict. Avocation: music. Home: 1301 Fikewood Dr Wilson NC 27893 Office: Elm City Middle Sch PO Box 729 Elm City NC 27822

MYERS, WILLIAM GEORGE, physician, state senator; b. Kittanning, Pa., Sept. 28, 1930; s. William George and Emma Adeline (Webb) Roberts; m. Carol Anne Edgar, June 15, 1954; children—Jacqueline Jolane, William George, Bradley Stephen, Brian Jeffry, Barry Douglas, Jennifer Sue. B.S., U. Pitts., 1952, M.D., 1956. Intern, Southside Hosp., Pitts., 1956-57, resident in internal medicine, 1957-58; practice medicine, Pitts., Bethel Park and Whitehall, Pa., 1958-61, Hobe Sound, Fla., 1962—; dir. Palm Beach/Martin County Med. Ctr., 1973-76; columnist Permission to Speak, 1973-83; mem. Fla. Ho. of Reps., 1978-82; mem. Fla. Senate, 1982—, also Republican floor leader. Mem. Republican State Exec. Com., 1968-72, dist. vice chmn., 1964; county commr. Martin County, Stuart, Fla., 1968-72; chmn. Martin County Republican Exec. Com., 1964-68. Recipient Disting. Service award Fla. State Soc. Ophthalmology, Fla. Emergency Technicians and Paramedics, Fla. Assn. Bldg. and Contractors, Fla. Heart Assn., Stuart C. of C., 1983; named Senator of Yr. Fla. Hosp. Assn., 1983. Mem. AMA, So. Med. Assn., Fla. Med. Assn., Martin County Med. Assn., Hobe Sound C. of C. (pres. 1963-65). Home: 8563 SE Seagrape Way Hobe Sound FL 33455 Office: Dist 27 Senate Office 308 Tequesta Dr Suite 10 Tequesta FL 33458

MYINT, HLA, psychiatrist, educator; b. Mandalay, Burma, Sept. 14, 1921; s. U San Kyu and Daw Ma Ma Lay; M.D., U. Rangoon, 1942; I.Sc., Rangoon Med. Coll., 1945; M.B., B.S., Grant Med. Coll., Bombay, India, 1947; m. Sofie Noronha, May 18, 1947; children—Fleur, David, Cherie, Dean, Desmond, Anne, Christina. Intern, Rangoon (Burma) Gen. Hosp., 1947-49; resident, postgrad. trainee in gen. surgery J.J. Hosp., Bombay, 1949-54; gen. practice medicine, Mandalay, Burma, 1954-72; resident in psychiatry Terrell (Tex.) State Hosp., 1972-73, staff psychiatrist, 1975-78, unit dir., unit A, 1978-82; resident in psychiatry Southwestern Med. Sch.-Parkland Hosp., Dallas, 1973-75, mem. staff, 1975—; clin. asst. instr. dept. psychiatry Southwestern Med. Sch., U. Tex., Dallas, 1975-80, clin. asst. prof., 1980-83, asst. prof., 1983—; chmn. mental health quality assurance com. Tex. Dept. Mental Health and Retardation, Austin, 1980-81; staff psychiatrist Routh St. Dallas County Mental Health and Mental Retardation Clinic, 1982-83; cons. liaison service, univ. staff Presbyn. Hosp. of Dallas, dir. psychiat. emergency room service Presbyn. Hosp. of Dallas, 1984—. Served as capt. Burmese Army Med. Corps, 1963-66. Diplomate Am. Bd. Psychiatry and Neurology. Mem. Am. Psychiat. Assn., Tex. Med. Assn. Buddhist. Home: 7130 Winedale St Dallas TX 75231 Office: 3525 Routh St Dallas TX 75219

MYRBERG, ARTHUR AUGUST, JR., marine biology educator; b. Chicago Heights, Ill., June 28, 1933; s. Arthur August and Helen Katherine (Stelle) M.; children—Arthur August III, Beverly Priscilla. A.B., Ripon Coll., 1954; M.S., U. Ill., 1958; Ph.D., UCLA, 1961. Research asst. Ill. Natural History Survey, Champaign-Urbana, 1957; NIH predoctoral fellow UCLA, 1960-61; mem. faculty U. Miami (Fla.). 1964—, a assoc. prof. Sch. Marine and Atmospheric Sci., 1967-72, prof., 1972—. Mem. Khoury League, 1967-75. Served to 1st lt. AUS, 1954-57. NIH postdoctoral fellow Max Planck Inst. Behavioral Physiology, Seewiesen, W.Ger., 1961-64. Fellow Animal Behavior Soc., Inst. Biol. Scis., Am. Inst. Fishery Research Biologists; mem. Am. Soc. Ichthyologists and Herpetologists, Am. Soc. Zoologists, Am. Elasmobranch Soc. (bd. dirs.), Internat. Assn. Fish Ethologists, Sigma Xi (nat. lectr. 1980-82, pres. U. Miami chpt. 1985-86). Contbr. articles to profl. jours., chpts. to books. Home: 6001 SW 65th Ave Miami FL 33143 Office: Rosenstiel Sch Marine and Atmospheric Sci U Miami Sci 4600 Rickenbacker Causeway Miami FL 33149

MYRICK, DONAL RICHARD, computer scientist; b. Lubbock, Tex., Dec. 21, 1938; s. Russell and Bernice A. (Wolffarth) M.; m. Rachel Jean Black; children—Richard, Rachel, Lynn, Amanda. B.S. in Math., Tex. Tech U., 1960, M.S., 1962. Instr., Tex. Tech U., 1960-63; research engr. N.Am. Aviation, Los Angeles, 1963-65, Teledyne Brown Engring., Huntsville, Ala., 1965-74; div. mgr. Science Applications, Fort Walton Beach, Fla., 1974-82; pres. Spectrum Sciences, Fort Walton Beach, 1982—. Author: Fern Cave, 1971; also sci. articles. Tex. Tech U. grad. fellow, 1960-62. Mem. Armed Forces Communications and Electronics Assn. (officer chpt. 1983), AAAS, Am. Soc. Safety Engrs., Nat. Speleological Soc. (fellow 1973), Nat. Audubon Soc., Fort Walton Beach C. of C., Emerald Coast Computer Soc. (librarian). Avocations: skiing; caving; mountain climbing; scuba diving; canoeing. Home: 511 Circle Dr Fort Walton Beach FL 32548 Office: 11 Racetrck Rd NE Suite E-1 Fort Walton Beach FL 32548

MYRICK, HENRY NUGENT, waste management company executive, environmental scientist; b. Cisco, Tex., Apr. 30, 1935; s. Elbert Porter and Lila Faye (Hill) P.; m. Mary Francis Ross, June 15, 1968. B.S. in Biology and Chemistry, Lamar U., 1957; M.S. in Environ. Sci. and Engring., Rice U., 1959; Sc.D. in Environ. Sci. and Engring., Washington U., St. Louis, 1962. Instr., fellow chem. engring. dept. Rice U., Houston, 1962-63; instr. san. engring. dept. Harvard U., Cambridge, Mass., 1963-65; asst. prof., then assoc. prof. U. Houston, 1965-74; pres. Process Co., Inc., Houston, 1970—. Pub., editor Tex. Solid Waste Mgmt. Newsletter, 1973—. Mem. Water Pollution Control Fedn. (Harrison P. Eddy award Water Pollution Control Fedn. 1962), Air Pollution Control Assn., ASCE, Am. Inst. Chem. Engrs., Am. Water Works Assn. Republican. Presbyterian. Lodge: Rotary. Home and Office: 2123 Winrock Blvd Houston TX 77057

MYRICK, REBECCA SAUNDERS, nurse, educator; b. Pinehurst, N.C., Feb. 15, 1935; d. Ervin Ray and Locia Ann (Shields) Saunders; m. Vernon Russell Myrick, Sept. 6, 1958; children—Michael, Scott. Diploma, Meml. Sch. Nursing, Charlotte, N.C., 1956; B.S.N., U. N.C.-Greensboro, 1976. Head nurse Moore Meml. Hosp., Pinehurst, 1962-72; instr., 1972—; cons. Manor Care Nursing Home, 1984, St. Joseph's Hosp., 1984; coordinator Basic Leadership Skills Workshops, 1984—, CPR tng. in community, 1984—. Speaker, Rotary Club, Southern Pines, N.C., 1981, Moore County Career Days, Pinehurst, 1983; sec.-treas. Woman's Missionary Union, Eagle Springs, N.C., 1982-83. Mem. Am. Soc. Tng. and Devel., Carolina Soc. Health Care Edn. and Tng. Republican. Baptist. Avocations: gardening, walking, reading. Home: Box 246 Robbins NC 27325

MYTTON-MILLS, RICHARD DAVID, international banker; b. Cheltenham, Eng., Nov. 18, 1950; came to U.S., 1982; s. Richard and Julia Marguerita (Dean) M-M. B.A. with honors, Trinity Coll., Cambridge (Eng.) U., 1971, M.A., 1976. Asst. mgr. Samuel Montagu & Co. Ltd., London, 1972-76, mgr., 1976-80, asst. dir., 1980-82; chief credit officer, v.p. First Palm Beach Internat. Bank, Coral Gables, Fla., 1982—; dir. Surinvest Casa Bancaria S.A., Montevideo, Uruguay, 1980-82. Mem. Church of England. Office: First Palm Beach Internat Bank 2655 Le Jeune Rd Coral Gables FL 33134

NABUTOVSKY, FRED DANIEL, accountant; b. Trenton, N.J., July 18, 1944; s. Albert and Elizabeth Nabutovsky; A.A., Miami-Dade Jr. Coll., 1966; B.A., U. W.Fla., 1970; m. Dorothy Jean Coursen; 1 son, Daniel Anton. Auditor, Naval Audit Service, Pensacola, Fla., 1969-70; sr. auditor Ernst & Ernst (now Ernst & Whinney), Orlando, Fla., 1970-75; with Fletcher and Johns, C.P.A.s, Stuart, Fla., 1975-78, acct., dir. Fletcher, Johns, Nabutovsky & Co., Chartered C.P.A.s, Stuart, 1978-81; pres. Fred D. Nabutovsky, Chartered C.P.A., 1981—; instr. acctg. prins. Indian River Community Coll. Treas., Arts Found. Martin County, Inc., 1980-81; cons. Performing Arts Soc. of Stuart, Inc., 1980—; mem. fin. com., adminstrv. bd., chmn. pre-sch. bd. First United Meth. Ch., Stuart. Served with USMC, 1964-65. C.P.A., Fla. Mem. Am. Inst. C.P.A.s, Fla. Inst. C.P.A.s, Mcpl. Fin. Officers Assn. (asso.). Republican. Lodge: Kiwanis (sec., Stuart-Sunrise 1976-78, del. internat. conv. 1977). Home: 8799 SW Tropical Ave Stuart FL 33497 Office: 430 Colorado Ave Stuart FL 33497

NACHWALTER, MICHAEL, lawyer; b. N.Y.C., Aug. 31, 1940; s. Samuel J. Nachwalter; m. Irene Nachwalter, Aug. 15, 1965; children—Helynn, Robert. B.S., Bucknell U., 1962; M.S., L.I.U., 1967; J.D. cum laude, U. Miami, 1967; LL.M., Yale U., 1968. Bar: Fla. 1967, D.C. 1979, U.S. Dist. Ct. (so. dist.) Fla., U.S. Ct. Apls. (5th cir.), U.S. Ct. Appeals (11th cir.), U.S. Supreme Ct. Law clk. U.S. Dist. Ct. (so. dist.) Fla.; ptnr. Kelly, Black, Black & Kenny; now ptnr. Kenny Nachwalter & Seymour, Miami; lectr. Law Sch. U. Miami. Mem. Fla. Bar (bd. govs.), Fla. Bar Assn., ABA, Fed. Bar Assn., Dade County Bar Assn., Omicron Delta Kappa, Phi Kappa Phi, Phi Delta Phi, Iron Arrow, Soc. Wig and Robe. Democrat. Jewish. Editor in chief U. Miami Law Rev., 1966-67. Office: 400 Edward Ball Bldg 100 Chopin Plaza Miami Ctr Miami FL 33131

NACOL, MAE, lawyer; b. Beaumont, Tex., June 15, 1944; d. William Samual and Ethel (Bowman) N.; children—Shawn Alexander, Catherine Regina. B.A., Rice U., 1965; J.D., S. Tex. Coll. Law, 1969. Bar: Tex. 1969. Diamond buyer, appraisor Nacol's Jewelry, Houston, 1961; diamond cons., Houston, 1961—; mem. firm Mae Nacol & Assocs., Houston, 1969—; dep. constable Precinct One, Harris County, Tex., 1980—; chmn. bd. HBO Med. Ctr. Houston, 1981—; nat. dir. Arms of Am., 1984—. Recipient Mayor's Recognition award Houston, 1972; Ford Found. fellow, 1965. Mem. ABA, Tex. Bar Assn., Internat. Bar Assn., Fed. Bar Assn., Houston Bar Assn., Tex. Trial Lawyers Assn., Nat. Assn. Women Lawyers, Am. Judicature Soc. Club: Pres's. Rice U. Office: 1801 Main St Suite 901 Houston TX 77002

NADAL, HARRY, civil engineer; b. Mayaguez, P.R., Feb. 21, 1927; s. Juan M. and Ana (Fremaint) N.; B.S. in Civil Engring., U. P.R., 1950, B.S. in Mech. Engring., 1955; postgrad. in civil engring. W.Va. U., 1967; m. Herlinda E. Noboa, July 30, 1964; children—Harry, Carlos E., Mary E., Kenneth J., Doreen J. Mgr. engring. indsl. and residential mech. systems installations Westinghouse Electric Co., San Juan, P.R., 1956-58; div. engr. design and constrn. supervision Esso Standard Oil Co., San Juan, 1958-62; pres. Comml. & Indsl. Builders Corp., San Juan, 1962-64; public health engr. Nassau County (N.Y.) Dept. Health, 1964-65; chief sanitary engr. Health Dept., State of N.Y., 1967-69; dir. natural resources dept. P.R. Public Works Dept., San Juan, 1968-69; dir. engring. dept. Housing Bank of P.R., San Juan, 1969-71; dep. dir. Dept. Public Works, City of San Juan, 1971-73; pres. Systems Techniques Corp., San Juan, 1973-74; chief planning engr. Roe & Assos., San Juan, 1974-76, project dir., 1976-80, mgr. engring. ops., 1980-81; dir. maintenance mgmt. program Savannah River Plant, U.S. Dept. Energy, 1981—. Served with U.S. Army, 1950-52; Korea. USPHS grantee, 1965; registered profl. engr., Conn., P.R. Mem. ASCE, ASME, ASTM, Inst. Engrs. and Surveyors, Am. Water Works Assn., Am. Soc. Sanitary Engring., Brazilian Assn. Sanitary Engring., Nat. Soc. Prof. Engrs., Inst. of Engrs., Architects and Surveyors of P.R., Air Pollution Control Fedn., P.R. Profls. Assn., Inst. Engrs. and Architects of El Salvador, Alpha Beta Chi. Roman Catholic. Clubs: Lions; Santa Tecla. Research on pollution free internal combustion engine. Home: 102 Recreation Dr Gem Lakes Aiken SC 29801 Office: Savannah River Plant Aiken SC 29801

NADLER, SYLVIA FAYE, physical education and athletics educator; b. Carrollton, Mo., Feb. 14, 1949; d. Omar William and Margaret Cornelia (Sehrt) N. B.S., Wayland Baptist U., 1971; M. Edn., W. Tex. State U., 1974; D. in Edn., E. Tex. State U., 1980. Instr. health, phys. edn. and recreation Wayland Bapt. U., Plainview, Tex., 1971-74, asst. prof. health, phys. edn. and recreation, 1974-81, assoc. prof., 1981-83, prof. 1983—, div. chmn., 1978—, athletic dir., 1983—, dir. Nichols Health Fitness Ctr., 1983—. Bd. dirs. Plainview chpt. Am. Heart Assn., 1985, YMCA, 1985; instr. Hale County chpt. ARC, 1985. Mem. AAHPERD (life), Tex. Assn. Health, Phys. Edn., Recreation and Dance, Nat. Assn. Intercoll. Athletics, Athletic Dirs. Assn. (nat. officer), Alpha Chi. Republican. Baptist. Home: 1404 W 7th St Plainview TX 79072 Office: Wayland Bapt U 1900 W 7th St Plainview TX 79072

NADREAU, RONALD CHARLES, development company executive; b. Nashua, N.H., Oct. 18, 1928; s. Clifford E. and Rose (Cadieux) N.; m. Doris Hudon, Aug. 14, 1949 (div. Apr. 1972); children—Kenneth, Karen, Karolyn; m. Trudy Kimball Felling, Dec. 15, 1974; stepchildren—Michael Felling, Teresa Felling, Cynthia Felling. Student Lowell Tech. Inst., 1946-48, Internat. Corr. Schs., 1952-56; LL.B., LaSalle U., 1958. Supt. Boston div. Internat. Corr. Schs., 1957-60; Conn. sales mgr. Gulf Am. Land Corp., 1960-63; owner, mgr. Hartford Placement Inc., employment and exec. search co., Hartford and Simsbury, Conn., 1963-74; pres., chmn. Unimed, Inc., Simsbury, 1970-72, Highland Acres Extend-a-care Ctr., Hilldale Extend-a-Care Ctr., Torrington Extend-a-care Ctr., Ronad Extend-a-care Ctr. (Conn.), 1969-74; v.p. Royak Enterprises, Simsbury, 1971-74, Universal Devel., Simsbury, 1970-74, So. Farms, Inc., Ft. Lauderdale, Fla., 1976-77; pres. United Art Corp., Coral Springs, Fla., 1978-81, Tan Devel. Corp., Coral Springs, 1974—; sec., cons. DeMarco & Sons Realty Inc., Delray Beach, Fla., 1976—; v.p., cons. Camelot Prodns., Inc., Ft. Lauderdale, 1982-83; pres. Camelot Mktg. Assocs., Inc., Coral Springs, Fla., 1983-84; pres. Benchmark Internat. Devel. Corp., Coral Springs, 1984—. Chmn. bldg. fund Our Lady's Cath. Ch., Waltham, Mass., 1960-63. Republican. Designer, builder nursing homes, Torrington, Winsted and Marlborough, Conn.; designer, developer, operator Life Care Community Retirement Ctrs.; co-patentee auto hat and coat hanger. Home: 8524 NW 27th Dr Coral Springs FL 33065 Office: 7914 Wiles Rd PO Box 8463 Coral Springs FL 33075

NAGAO, DENNIS HIROSHI, business educator, consultant; b. Chgo., Oct. 14, 1953; s. Hiroshi and Mary Machiko (Murakami) N. A.B. with high distinction, U. Ill., 1975, A.M., 1980, Ph.D., 1984. Asst. prof. psychology So. Meth. U., Dallas, 1981-83; vis. lectr. bus. Ga. Inst. Tech, Atlanta, 1983-84; asst. prof. bus., 1984—; cons. Airmics U.S. Army, Atlanta, 1984—. Contbr. chpts. to books, profl. publs. Ill. State scholar, 1971. Mem. Acad. of Mgmt., Am. Psychol. Assn., Soc. Personality and Social Psychology, Midwestern Psychol. Assn., Southeastern Psychol. Assn., Sigma Xi. Club: Atlanta Ski. Avocations: skiing; tennis; computers; dance. Home: 3211 H Post Woods Dr Atlanta GA 30339 Office: Coll of Mgmt Ga Inst Tech Atlanta GA 30332

NAGEL, PAUL CHESTER, historian; b. Independence, Mo., Aug. 14, 1926; s. Paul Conrad and Freda (Sabrowsky) N.; B.A., U. Minn., 1948, M.A., 1949, Ph.D., 1952; m. Joann Peterson, Mar. 19, 1948; children—Eric John, Jefferson, Steven Paul. Historian, SAC, USAF, Omaha, 1951-53; asst. prof. Augustana Coll., Sioux Falls, S.D., 1953-54; asst. prof., then asso. prof. Eastern Ky. U., Richmond, 1954-61; mem. faculty U. Ky., 1961-69, prof. history, 1965-69, dean Coll. Arts and Scis., 1965-69; spl. asst. to pres. for acad. affairs, prof. history U. Mo., 1969-71, v.p. acad. affairs, 1971-74, prof. history, 1974-78; prof., head dept. history U. Ga., 1978-80; dir. Va. Hist. Soc., Richmond, 1981-85; Disting. Lee scholar Robert E. Lee Meml. Assn., 1986—; vis. prof. Amherst Coll., 1957-58, Vanderbilt U., 1959, U. Minn., 1964. Mem. Council Colls. Arts and Scis., 1965-69. Mem. Ky. Arts Commn., 1966-69. Vice chmn. bd. dirs. Center for Research Libraries, Chgo., 1973-74; trustee Colonial Williamsburg Found., 1984—; adv. bd. Am. Heritage, 1984—. Fellow Soc. Am. Historians; mem. Va. Writers Club, So. Hist. Assn. (pres. 1985), Mass. Hist. Soc. Episcopalian. Author: One Nation Indivisible, 1964, 2d edit., 1980; This Sacred Trust, American Nationality 1798-1898, 1971, 2d edit., 1980; Missouri: A History, 1977 (named Best Book pub. in history for 1977, Soc. Midland Authors); Descent from Glory: Four Generations of the John Adams Family, 1983; co-author: Extraordinary Lives, 1986; bd. editors Group for Study of Nationalism, 1976—, contbr. articles profl. jours. Home: 612 W Franklin St Apt 8-B Richmond VA 23220

NAGIN, STEPHEN E., lawyer, educator; b. Phila., Nov. 7, 1946; s. Harry S. and Dorothy R. (Pearlman) N.; m. Marjorie. B.B.A., U. Miami, 1969, J.D., 1974. Bar: Fla. 1974, D.C. 1976, U.S. Supreme Ct. 1978. Asst. atty. gen. State of Fla., Miami, 1974-75; atty., FTC, 1975-80; spl. asst. U.S. atty. D.C., 1980-81; ptnr. firm Ginsburg, Nagin, Rosin & Ginsburg, PA, 1981-84; adj. prof. St. Thomas Sch. Law, 1984—. Mem. ABA, Fed., Fla., D.C. bar assns., Assn. Trial Lawyers Am., Acad. Fla. Trial Lawyers, Coral Gables Bar Assn. (bd. dirs. 1983—), Fla. Bar (editor, trial lawyers sect. 1983-84; mem. spl. antitrust task force 1983—, chmn. editorial bd., 1982-83), Am. Arbitration Assn. Home: Miami FL Office: Penthouse 1570 Madruga Ave Coral Gables FL 33146

NAGLE, RICHARD KENT, mathematics educator; b. Detroit, Feb. 19, 1947; s. Glenn Monroe and Geneva Molden (Whelchel) N.; m. Sandra Edith Westgate, Aug. 9, 1969; 1 child, Kevin Glenn. B.S., U. Mich., 1968, M.A., 1969, Ph.D., 1975. Asst. prof. U. Mich., Dearborn, 1975-76; asst. prof. U. South Fla., Tampa, 1976-80, assoc. prof., 1980—; dir. Ctr. Math. Ser., Tampa, 1984—. Contbr. articles to profl. jours. Served with U.S. Army, 1969-71. Recipient Disting. Tchr. award Coll. Natural Scis., U. South Fla., 1985, Outstanding Asst. Prof. award, 1980. Mem. Am. Math. Soc., Math. Assn. Am., Soc. Ind. and Applied Math., Sigma Xi. Methodist. Office: Ctr Math Ser Univ South Florida 4202 E Fowler Ave Tampa FL 33620

NAGY, STEVEN, biochemist; b. Fords, N.J., Apr. 7, 1936; s. Steven and Martha (Moberg) N.; m. Suzanne McQuagge, May, 1980; 2 children. B.S. in Chemistry, La. State U., 1960; M.S. in Physiology and Biochemistry, Rutgers U., 1962, Ph.D. in Biochemistry, 1965; M.Engring. in Indsl. Engring., U. South Fla., 1977. Analytical chemist USPHS, Metuchen, N.J., 1962-65; research asso. Lever Bros., Edgewater, N.J., 1965-67; research chemist Dept. Agr., Winter Haven, Fla., 1968-79; processing research coordinator Fla. Dept. Citrus, Lake Alfred, 1979—; adj. prof. U. Fla., 1979—. Mem. Am. Chem. Soc. (chmn. div. agrl. and food chemistry 1983), Phytochem. Soc. N. Am., Inst. Food Technologists, Am. Soc. for Hort. Sci., Internat. Soc. Citriculture, Fla. Hort. Soc., Sigma Xi. Republican. Author: Citrus Science and Technology, 2 vols., 1977; Tropical and Subtropical Fruits, 1980; Citrus Nutrition and Quality, 1980; Fresh Citrus Fruits, 1986; contbr. articles to profl. jours. Home: 103 Arietta Shores Dr Auburndale FL 33823 Office: 700 Experiment Station Rd Lake Alfred FL 33850

NAIL, B. A., educational administrator. Supt. of schs. Columbus, Ga. Office: 1200 Bradley Dr Columbus GA 31906*

NAIL, BILLY RAY, academic administrator; b. Roby, Tex., Jan. 19, 1933; s. Radney Harmon Nail and Helen Juanita (Parker) Nail Moore; m. Glenda Fern Campbell, July 12, 1952; children—Marsha Anderson, Vicky Holbrook, Penny Kelley. B.A., Hardin-Simmons U., 1956; M.A., U. Ill., 1962, Ph.D., 1967. Cert. elem. and secondary tchr., Tex. Tchr., coach Merkel High Sch., Tex., 1957-61; instr. math. Wayland Baptist Coll., Plainview, Tex., 1962-64; head dept. math. Morehead State U., Ky., 1967-72; dean of coll. Clayton Jr. Coll., Morrow, Ga., 1972—. Pres. Ga. div. Am. Cancer Soc., 1985-86. Mem. Math. Assn. Am. Baptist. Avocations: computers, photography. Home: 2201 Carmen Ct Morrow GA 30260 Office: Clayton Jr Coll 5900 Lee St Morrow GA 30260

NAINI, BHOOPAL REDDY, geophysicist; b. Hyderabad, India, Mar. 30, 1944; came to U.S., 1969, naturalized, 1977; s. Prathap Reddy and Laxmi Devi (Thummalapalli) N.; m. Krystyna Teresa Kaczmarek, Aug. 15, 1975; children—Devdat J., Anjali N. B.Sc., Osmania U., Hyderabad, 1963, M.Sc., 1966, M.Sc. Tech., 1967; M.A., CCNY, 1972; M.Phil., Columbia U., 1978, Ph.D., 1980. Grad. fellow Osmania U., 1964-67; asst. geophysicist UN Devel. Program, Madras, India, 1968-69; faculty fellow Columbia U., N.Y.C., 1972-80; research geophysicist Gulf Sci. and Tech. Co., Pitts., 1980-82; area geophysicist Sohio Petroleum Co., Dallas, 1982—. Contbr. articles to profl. publs. Vetlesen fellow, 1974. Mem. Am. Geophys. Union, Soc. Exploration Geophysicists, Am. Assn. Petroleum Geologists, Sigma Xi. Avocation: photography. Home: 2403 Seedling Ln Dallas TX 75252

NAISMITH, LAURIE, state official; b. Norfolk, Va., Apr. 21, 1952; d. George and Mary Helen (Campbell) N. B.A. in Polit. Sci., Old Dominion U., 1975. Legis. staff Nat. Student Lobby, Washington, 1973; legis. asst. Del. Robert E. Washington, Norfolk, 1974-76; cons. Va. Internship Program, Richmond, 1975; field dir. Elmo Zumwalt U.S. Senate Campaign, Richmond, 1976; dir. pub. affairs and programs Lt. Gov. Charles Robb, Richmond, 1978-81, scheduler, 1981, mem. transition team, 1981-82; sec. of state Commonwealth of Va., Richmond, 1982—; mem. State Agy. Group, Richmond, 1982—. Hon. sec. Va. Young Democrats, 1983; del. Dem. Convs., 1972, 76, 77, 78, 80, 81; bd. dirs. Central Va. council Girl Scouts U.S.A., 1984. Recipient Fast Track Favorite award Commonwealth Mag., 1983; Exec. Dir.'s award Nat. Black Assn. Speech, Lang. and Hearing, 1983. Mem. Richmond C. of C. (leadership metro Richmond 1983), Women Execs. in State Govt. (conf. program chair 1984), Nat. Assn. Secs. State (chmn. fin. com. 1982, mem. voter edn. com.), Nat. Assn. Extradition Ofcls., Commn. Intergovt. Coop., Richmond Bicentennial Commn. (bd. dirs. 1982), Pi Sigma Alpha. Democrat. Presbyterian. Office: State Capitol Richmond VA 23219

NAKAMURA, EUGENE LEROY, fishery biologist; b. San Diego, June 8, 1926. B.S. with high honors in Zoology, U. Ill., 1950, M.S., 1951. Research asst. zoology U. Hawaii, Honolulu, 1951-56; fishery biologist U.S. Bur of Comml. Fisheries, Honolulu, 1956-70; dir. Eastern Gulf Marine Lab., Panama City, Fla., 1970-72; dir. Panama City Lab., Southeast Fisheries Ctr., Nat. Marine Fisheries Service, 1972—. Served with U.S. Army, 1945-46. Mem. Am. Inst. Fishery Research Biologists (pres. 1979-80), Am. Fisheries Soc., Am. Soc. Ichthyologists and Herpetologists, Am. Soc. Limnology and Oceanography, Am. Inst. Biol. Scis., AAAS, Sigma Xi. Author pubs. in field. Office: Panama City Lab Southeast Fisheries Ctr Nat Marine Fisheries Service 3500 Delwood Beach Rd Panama City FL 32407

NAKARAI, CHARLES FREDERICK TOYOZO, musicologist; b. Indpls., Apr. 25, 1936; s. Toyozo Wada and Frances Aileen N.; B.A. cum laude, Butler U., 1958, Mus.M., 1967; postgrad. U. N.C., 1967-70. Organist, dir. choirs Northwood Christian ch., Indpls., 1954-57; minister music Broad Ripple Christian Ch., Indpls., 1957-58; asst. prof. music Milligan Coll., Tenn., 1970-72; pvt. instrn. organ, piano, Durham, 1972—. Served with USAF, 1958-64. Mem. Am. Musicol. Soc., Coll. Music Soc., Am. Guild Organists, Music Tchrs. Nat. Assn., Music Library Assn., Durham Music Tchrs. Assn.

(festival chmn.). Composer: Three Movements for Chorus, 1971, Bluesy, 1979. Address: 3520 Mayfair St Apt 205 Durham NC 27707

NAKARAI, TOYOZO WADA, educator; b. Kyoto, Japan, May 16, 1898; s. Tosui and Wakae (Harada) N.; A.B., Kokugakuin U., Tokyo, 1920; A.B., Butler U., 1924, A.M., 1925; Ph.D. (fellow Sch. Religion), U. Mich., 1930, also post-doctorate studies; grad. student Nippon U., Tokyo, U. Chgo., Hebrew Union Coll., N.Y. U.; m. Frances Aileen Yorn, June 22, 1933; children—Charles Frederick Toyozo, Frederick Leroy. Came to U.S., 1923, naturalized, 1953. Instr. Tokyo Fourth High Sch., Sei Gakuin Mission Sch., Matsumiya Lang. Sch., Tokyo, 1920-23; instr. Coll. of Missions, Indpls., 1923-25; instr. Semitics, Butler U., Indpls., 1927-28, asst. prof., 1928-29, asso. prof., 1929-31, prof., head dept. Semitics, 1931-65, prof. emeritus, 1965—; prof., head dept. Semitics, Emmanuel Sch. Religion, 1965-71, Disting. prof. Old Testament, 1971-83, sr. prof., 1983—; profl. appointee Am. Sch. Oriental Research, Jerusalem, 1947-48, hon. asso., 1962-63; alumni lectureship Ky. Christian Coll., 1956, T. H. Johnson Meml. lectr. Manhattan Bible Coll., 1957; lectr. Sch. Ministry, Milligan Coll., 1957, 66; vis. prof. Tainan Theol. Coll., Formosa, 1963; faculty lectr. Christian Theol. Sem., 1964; lectr. Ashland Theol. Sem., 1974, Westwood Christian Consortium, 1976, Lincoln Christian Sem., 1977. Mem. Gov.'s Abraham Lincoln Commn. to Orient, 1960. Recipient Baxter Found. award, medal and scroll Internat. Order B'rith Abraham, Nat. Assn. Profs. Hebrew, also citation for scholarship and merit, also Hebrew Tchr. award; J.I. Holcomb prize Butler U.; citation and scroll Histadrut Ivrit; named Ch. Statesman of Day, N. Am. Christian Conv. Mem. AAUP, Am. Oriental Soc., Am. Sch. Oriental Research (chmn. cast investigation com. 1941-42), Am. Acad. Religion, Soc. Sci. Study Religion, Soc. Bibl. Lit. (v.p. Midwest br. 1949-51, pres. 1951-52), Nat. Assn. Profs. Hebrew (pres. 1956-58, editor Iggeret, 1974-77, asso. editor Hebrew Studies 1974-77, nat. adv. council 1981—), Israel Exploration Soc., Nippon Kyuyaku Gakkai, Israel Soc. for Bibl. Research, Internat. Inst. for Study Religions, Eta Beta Rho, Phi Kappa Phi, Theta Phi. Author: A Study of the Kokinshu, 1931, Biblical Hebrew, 1951, rev. edit., 1976; (with others) To Do and To Teach, 1953; Shin Tosa Nikki, 1962; An Elder's Public Prayers, 1968, rev. enlarged edit., 1979; (with others) The Mind of a Faculty, 1973; (with others) Essays on New Testament Christianity, 1978; The Dead Sea Scrolls and Biblical Faith, 1980. Home: Route 4 PO Box 240 Elizabethton TN 37643 Office: PO Box 369 Milligan College TN 37682

NALL, DANIEL HUGH, building energy consultant, architect, engineer; b. Pine Bluff, Ark., Aug. 12, 1948; s. Daniel Max and Aileen Hazel (Byrn) N.; m. Juliana Fuerbringer, Aug. 26, 1972 (div. 1978); m. 2d, Sheila Gail Spriggs, May 22, 1982. A.B., Princeton U., 1970; postgrad. Boston Archtl. Ctr., 1971-72; B.Arch., Cornell U., 1975. Research specialist Cornell U. Program for Computer Graphics, 1975-77; research architect U.S. Nat. Bur. Standards, 1977-78; lectr. Princeton U. Sch. Architecture and Urban Planning, 1978-79, cons. Sch. Architecture and Urban Planning, 1979; project mgr. Berkeley Solar Group, 1979-80; sr. cons. Heery Energy Cons., Atlanta, 1980-82, assoc. dir., 1982-84; prin. Jones, Nall & Davis, Inc., Cons. Engrs., Atlanta, 1984—; chmn. energy jury Ga. Energy Design Awards, 1983; bd. dirs. Bldg. Thermal Envelope Coordinating Council, 1985; mem. expert tech. rev. program U.S. Dept. Energy, 1983; seminar instr. profl. devel. program AIA, 1981; mem. planning com. Nat. Conf. Climate and Architecture, AIA Research Found., 1979. Served with USNR, 1970-71. Energy Info. Adminstrn. grantee, 1979. Mem. AIA (chmn. energy data base com. Ga. Assn. mem. nat. energy com.), ASHRAE (sec. subcom. on natural heating, cooling and lighting). Contbr. articles in field to profl. jours. Office: 84 Peachtree St NW Suite 900 Atlanta GA 30303

NALL, JOSEPH TRIPPE, lawyer; b. Atlanta, May 16, 1942; s. Robert Glenn and Annie Geraldine (Trippe) N.; m. Carolyn Elizabeth Baker, Aug. 17, 1963; children—Molly Elizabeth, Anna Kate. B.A. in History, Furman U., 1964; M.Div., Southeastern Bapt. Theol. Sem., Wake Forest, N.C., 1968; J.D., Wake Forest U., 1973. Bar: N.C. 1973, U.S. Dist. Ct. (ea. dist.) N.C. 1973, U.S. Ct. Appeals (4th cir.) 1974; ordained to ministry, Baptist Ch., 1968. Asst. Minister 1st Bapt. Ch., Smithfield, N.C., 1965-69; minister Beth Car Bapt. Ch., Halifax, Va., 1969-70; ptnr. Mast, Tew & Nall, P.A., Smithfield, 1973-81; sole practice, Smithfield, 1981—. Pres., United Way of Johnston County; founder, sec. Day by Day Home Johnston County. Recipient Atlanta Jour. cup, 1960; Algernon Sydney Sullivan award Furman U., 1964; Nanny Bruce Nelson award Southeastern Bapt. Theol. Sem., 1968. Mem. Johnston County Bar Assn., N.C. Bar Assn., N.C. Acad. Trial Lawyers, ABA, Smithfield-Selma C. of C. (past pres., Pres.'s Plaque 1979), Wake Forest Law Sch. Alumni Assn. (past pres.). Democrat. Contbr. articles to Wake Forest Law Rev., 1973, Pvt. Pilot mag., Aero Mag. Home: 1107 Chestnut Dr Smithfield NC 27577 Office: Suite 211 201 Market St Smithfield Savs and Loan Bldg PO Box 179 Smithfield NC 27577

NANCE, BETTY LOVE, librarian; b. Nashville, Oct. 29, 1923; d. Granville Scott and Clara (Mills) Nance. B.A. magna cum laude in English, Trinity U., 1957; A.M. in Library Sci., U. Mich., 1958. Head dept. acquisitions Stephen F. Austin U. Library, Nacogdoches, Tex., 1958-59; librarian 1st Nat. Bank, Ft. Worth, 1959-61; head catalog dept. Trinity U., San Antonio, 1961-63; head tech. processes U. Tex. Law Library, Austin, 1963-66; head catalog dept. Tex. A&M U. Library, College Station, 1966-69; chief bibliog. services Washington U. Library, St. Louis, 1970; head dept. acquisitions Va. Commonwealth U. Library, Richmond, 1971-73; head tech. processes Howard Payne U. Library, Brownwood, Tex., 1974-79; library dir. Edinburg Pub. Library (Tex.), 1980—. Mem. ALA, Pub. Library Assn., Tex. Library Assn., Hidalgo County Library Assn. (v.p. 1980-81, pres. 1981-82), Pan Am. Round Table of Edinburg (corr. sec. 1986-87), Alpha Lambda Delta, Alpha Chi. Methodist. Club: Zonta of West Hidalgo County. Home: 1602 John St Apt 4 Edinburg TX 78539 Office: Edinburg Pub Library 401 E Cano St Edinburg TX 78539

NANCE, CHARLES WAYNE, oil company executive; b. Thornton, Tex., Nov. 28, 1931; s. Louie D. and Bertha (Walker) N.; m. Jane Ann Watson, Sept. 3, 1954; children—Steven Wayne, Scott Edward. B.S., U. Tex.-Austin, 1952, M.D.P., Grad. Sch. Bus., 1970; postgrad. Harvard U., 1981, 82. Petroleum engr. Amoco Prodn. Co., Henderson, Ft. Worth, Midland, Tex., 1952-58; petroleum engr. Tenneco Oil Co., Odessa, Midland, Denver, 1958-79, v.p., Lafayette, 1979-81, sr. v.p., Lafayette, Houston, 1981-82, exec. v.p. exploration and prodn., Houston, 1982—. Mem. adv. council Coll. Engring. Found., U. Tex., Austin, 1984—. Mem. Nat. Ocean Industries Assn., Am. Petroleum Inst., Soc. Petroleum Engrs. of AIME. Republican. Mem. Church of Christ. Clubs: Houston, Raveneaux Country. Avocations: tennis; fishing. Office: Tenneco Oil Exploration and Prodn 1100 Milam Bldg 15th Fl 1100 Milam St Houston TX 77002

NANCE, DENNIS ARNOLD, welding technology educator, consultant, welding inspector; b. Clarinda, Iowa, Nov. 25, 1944; s. John Wesley and Edna May (Welch) N.; m. Susan MacDonald, Sept. 18, 1966; children—Denise, Dennis, Patrick. A.A.S., Ferris State Coll., 1975; B.A., Southwestern U., 1982. Tchr. welding tech. Nebr. Dept. Edn., Lincoln, 1968-73, Ferris State Coll., Big Rapids, Mich., 1973-75, Joliet Jr. Coll., Ill., 1975-82, Tex. State Tech. Inst.-Harlingen, 1982—. Contbr. articles to tech. jours. Served as sgt. USAR, 1962-70. Mem. Am. Welding Soc. (cert., chmn. 1981-82, Meritorious Tchr. award 1980). Methodist. Lodges: Masons, Lions. Home: 2002 Ellie Ln Harlingen TX 78552 Office: Dept Welding Tech Tex State Tech Inst Rio Grande Harlingen Indsl Harlingen TX 78550

NANCE, FRANK LEON, financial and construction company executive; b. Beaufort, N.C., July 17, 1924; s. Alva L. and Effie Alice (Willis) N.; student Cornell U., 1945; B.S., Murray State U., 1948; m. Mary Lou Babcock, Apr. 1, 1971; children—David L., Dace, Dianne Nance Marrs. Pres., F. L. Nance & Assocs., Fin. Services, Investments, Tulsa, 1952—; pres. SpeedSpace, Inc., Aero-Bilt Portable Bldg. Co., Service Bldg. Systems, 1982-83; v.p. Prefabrication Inc., Tulsa, 1974—, Habitat Devel., Inc., 1983—; industrialized bldg. cons. Served with USMCR, 1942-45. Mem. Am. Legion (comdr. 1950), Am. Mgmt. Assn., Am. Soc. Profl. Cons., Constrn. Specifications Inst. Office: Drawer 6666 Tulsa OK 74156

NANCE, GEORGE LAWRENCE, JR., dental educator; b. Fredericksburg, Va., May 15, 1947; s. George Lawrence and Sarah Margaret (Posey) N.; m. Christine Taylor, June 27, 1970; children—George Oliver, Megan Ann. B.S., Coll. William and Mary, 1969; D.D.S., Med. Coll. Va., 1975; M.S. in Dentistry, Mayo Clinic, 1983. Lic. dentist, Va., Wis., Minn. Intern. U.S. Army, Fort Belvoir, Va., 1976; prosthodontic resident Mayo Clinic, Rochester, Minn., 1980-83; asst. prof. dentistry Med. Coll. Va., Richmond, 1983—; cons. Children's Hosp., Richmond, 1984—. Vol. PTA, Richmond, 1983—, St. Paul's Episcopal Ch., Richmond, 1984—. Served to maj. U.S. Army, 1975-80. Decorated Army Commendation medal. Mem. ADA, Am. Coll. Prosthodontists, Am. Cleft Palate Assn., Southeastern Acad. Prosthodontists, Va. Dental Assn., Am. Assn. Dental Schs., Am. Assn. Dental Research, Internat. Assn. Dental Research. Democrat. Episcopalian. Avocation: photography. Office: Box 566 MCV Sta 521 N 11th St Richmond VA 23298

NANCE, MARY JOE, educator; b. Carthage, Tex., Aug. 7, 1921; d. F. F. and Mary Elizabeth (Knight) Born; B.B.A., North Tex. State U., 1953; postgrad. Northwestern State U. La., 1974; M.E., Antioch U., 1978; m. Earl C. Nance, July 12, 1946; 1 child, David Earl. Tchr., Port Isabel (Tex.) Integrated Sch. Dist., to 1979; tchr. English, Splendora (Tex.) High Sch., 1979-80, McLeod, Tex., 1980-81, Bremond, Tex., 1981—. Served with USAAF, 1942-45. Recipient Image Maker award Carthage C. of C., 1984; cert. bus. educator. Mem. Nat. Bus. Edn. Assn., NEA, Tex. Tchrs. Assn., Tex. Bus. Tchrs. Assn., Nat. Women's Army Corps Vets. Assn., Air Force Assn. (life), Assn. Supervision and Curriculum Devel., Council for Basic Edn., Nat. Hist. Soc., Tex. Council English Tchrs. Baptist.

NANCE, MURRAY HENDERSON, lawyer; b. Waco, Tex., Mar. 14, 1916; s. Murray Henderson and Bertha Maybelle (Haltom) N.; m. Pauline Carey Johnson, June 28, 1941; children—Brenda Wright, Marsha Young. B.A., Baylor U., 1938, J.D., 1940. Bar: Tex. 1941, U.S. Dist. Ct. (ea. dist.) Tex. 1946, U.S. Dist. Ct. (no. dist.) Tex. 1950, U.S. Supreme Ct. 1967. Spl. agent FBI, 1940-46; city atty. Sherman, Tex., 1949-51; county atty. Grayson (Tex.) County, 1951-57; practice, Sherman, 1957—, ptnr. Nance, Caston and predecessors Nance, Caston & Nall, Caston, Duncan, Green & Stagner; dir. Grayson County (Tex.) State Bank. Bd. dirs. Camp Fire Girls, Sherman, former bd. dirs. United Way, Boy Scouts Am.; former pres. Board Grayson County Child Welfare Soc.; past trustee Dallas Bapt. Coll.; past mem. and pres. bd. trustees Sherman Ind. Sch. Dist. Recipient Luther Gulick award Camp Fire Girls, Sherman. Mem. ABA, Tex. State Bar Assn., North Tex. Bar Assn., Grayson County Bar Assn., C. of C. (former dir., Sherman), Ex-Students Assn. Baylor U. (past trustee), Pi Gamma Mu (former pres.) Lodges: Lions (former pres.), Masons. Home: 604 N McKown St Sherman TX 75090 Office: 421 N Crockett St Sherman TX 75090

NANNEY, SCOTT CURTIS, technical services consultant; b. Forest City, N.C., Nov. 24, 1956; s. Boyd Coolidge and Lillian (Briscoe) N. B.S. in Health Edn., Appalachian State U., 1979. Indsl. hygiene technician Elb Assocs., Chapel Hill, N.C., 1979-81, safety and health specialist, 1981-82; tech. service cons., sales rep. ELB Monitor, Inc., Gastonia, N.C., 1982—. Mem. Am. Soc. Safety Engrs. Democrat. Baptist. Avocations: baseball card collecting; weightlifting; tennis.

NAPIER, DOUGLAS WILLIAM, lawyer, county attorney; b. Alexandria, Va., Sept. 11, 1951; s. William Wilson and Leo Elizabeth (Moore) N.; m. Kathy Gwen Talbert, Aug. 24, 1974; children—Brian Douglas, Adam Scott. B.S., Va. Poly. Inst. and State U., 1973; J.D., Wake Forest U., 1976. Bar: Va. 1976, U.S. Ct. (ea. and we. dist.) Va. 1978, U.S. Ct. Appeals (4th cir.) 1983. Assoc., Ambrogi, Mote & Ritter, Winchester, Va., 1976-77; ptnr. Napier & Napier, Front Royal, Va., 1977—; county atty. Warren County (Va.), 1978—; atty. Chem. Abuse Task Force, 1983—. Author: The Cross, 1982. Mem. staff, contbr. Wake Forest Law Rev., 1976. Bd. dirs. United Way, Front Royal, 1978; parliamentarian Warren County Republican Com., 1981; cons. Council Domestic Violence, 1984. Mem. Warren County Bar Assn. (v.p.), Va. Bar Assn., Va. Trial Lawyers Assn., ABA. Baptist. Clubs: Optimist Internat. (sec. 1980-81, Achievement award 1980), Isaac Walton League. Home: 119 W Stonewall Dr Front Royal VA 22630 Office: Napier & Napier 10 Court House Sq Front Royal VA 22630

NAPIER, JOHN HAWKINS, III, historian; b. Berkeley, Calif., Feb. 6, 1925; s. John Hawkins and Lena Mae (Tate) N.; B.A., U. Miss., 1949; M.A., Auburn U., 1967; postgrad. Georgetown U., 1971; m. Harriet Elizabeth McGehee (dec.) m. Cameron Mayson Freeman, Sept. 11, 1964. Journalist, tchr. Picayune (Miss.) High Sch., 1946; commd. 2d lt. U.S. Air Force, 1949, advanced through grades to lt. col., 1966, ret., 1977; staff dir. Congressional Com. on S.E. Asia, 1970; faculty Air War Coll., 1971-74; Air U. Command historian, 1974-77; asst. to exec. dir. Ala. Commn. on Higher Edn., Montgomery, 1977-78; adj. history faculty Auburn U., Montgomery, 1980-85; columnist Montgomery Advertiser, 1980—; lectr. in field. Pres., Montgomery Opera Guild, 1974-75, Montgomery Community Concert Assn., 1974-76, Old S. Hist. Soc., 1977-78. Served with USMC, 1943-46. Decorated Legion of Merit, also others; recipient award of Merit, Ala. Hist. Commn., 1976; Merit award English Speaking Union U.S., 1983; Taylor Medal and grad. fellow U. Miss., 1949; Storrs scholar Pomona Coll., 1942-43. Mem. English-Speaking Union (pres. 1978—, nat. dir. 1980-86), Newcomen Soc., Ala. Hist. Assn. (pres. 1979-80), Soc. Pioneers Montgomery (pres. 1980-81), Soc. Colonial Wars, SCV (vice comdr. Ala. 1979-80), Soc. War of 1812 (pres. Ala. 1980-82), St. Andrews Soc., S.R., SAR (pres. 1974-75), Clan Napier in N.Am. (lt. to chief 1985—), Order 1st Families Va., Jamestowne Soc., Sigma Chi, Phi Kappa Phi, Omicron Delta Kappa, Phi Alpha Theta, Pi Sigma Alpha, Scabbard and Blade. Democrat. Episcopalian. Clubs: Montgomery Country, Aztec 1847, Mil. Order Carabao: Victory Services (London). Author: Lower Pearl Rivers Piney Woods: Its Land and People, 1985; The Air Force Officers Guide, 27th edit., 1986. Contbr. articles to profl. jours. Home: Kilmahew Box 614 Route 2 Ramer AL 36069

NAPIER, JOHN LIGHT, lawyer, former congressman; b. Blenheim, S.C., May 16, 1947; s. John Light and Miriam Keys (Keys) N.; A.B., Davidson (N.C.) Coll., 1969; J.D., U. S.C., 1972; m. Pamela Ann Caughman, June 12, 1971; 1 dau., Mary Katerine Page. Bar: S.C. 1972, U.S. Dist. Ct. 1972, U.S. Ct. Appeals 1975, U.S. Tax Ct. 1975, U.S. Supreme Ct. 1978. U.S. senatorial counsel and asst., 1972-78; atty. firm Goldberg, Cottingham & Easterling, P.A., Bennettsville, S.C., 1978-80; mem. 97th Congress from 6th Dist. S.C., mem. agr. com., vets. affairs com., asst. whip; mem. firm Goldberg, Cottingham, Easterling and Napier, P.A., Bennettsville, 1983-84; ptnr. Napier & Jennings, 1984—. Active local United Way, Boy Scouts Am.; pres. Marlborough Hist. Soc., 1978-80. Served as officer USAR, 1969-77. Recipient Disting. Service award Marlboro County Jaycees, 1980. Mem. Am. Bar Assn., D.C. Bar, S.C. Bar (mem. commn. on grievances and discipline 1984—), Marlboro County Bar Assn. Republican. Presbyterian. Club: Capitol Hill, Caroliniana Ball. Office: 114 N Liberty St Bennettsville SC 29512

NAPOLITANO, PAT, former union official; b. N.Y.C., Feb. 1, 1916; s. Giuseppe and Anna (Liquori) N.; adult edn. courses Fordham U., 1944-47; m. Beatrice G. Gagliardo, Apr. 25, 1959. With tech. facilities dept. Western Union, 1943-80; mem. exec. bd. Local 14, Comml. Telegraphers Union, 1945-60; sec.-treas. local 1177 Communications Workers Am., AFL-CIO, 1966-69, del. L.I. Fedn. Labor, AFL-CIO, 1966-76; freelance writer. Mem. N.Y. Police Coordinating Councils, 1940-55, N.Y. CD, 1943-55; sch. visitor N.Y. Adult Edn. Council, Inc., 1945-55; active Boy Scouts Am., 1938-55. Mem. Nassau County (N.Y.) Democratic Com., 1960-72; pres. New Hyde Park Dem. Club, 1969-70; trustee Ch. Most Precious Blood, 1942-59. Named Citizen of Month, Beverly Hills (Fla.), 1984. Mem. Assn. Catholic Trade Unionists, Sons of Italy (charter lodge), Ams. of Italian Descent, Father Drumgoole Alumni Assn. (pres. 1965-73, chmn. bd. officers 1974-79), Nat. Council Catholic Men, Holy Name Soc., Third Order St. Francis. Democrat. Roman Catholic (lector, usher, extraordinary minister of eucharist). Clubs: KC (grand knight Abbot Francis Sadlier Council 1983-85), Italian-Am. Social (pres. 1981-83). Home: 221 S Harrison St Beverly Hills FL 32665

NAQUIN, DAVID ADAMS, police chief; b. Franklin, La., Mar. 20, 1953; s. Edmund and Marian (Adams) N.; divorced; 1 child, Chad Edmund. B.S., NE La. U., 1976. Jailer, Monroe Police Dept., La., 1974, patrolman, 1974-78, detective, 1978-82; chief of police Franklin Police Dept., 1982—, organizer city-wide Neighborhood Watch program, 1983—. Named Law Enforcement Officer of Yr., Franklin Jaycees, 1982. Mem. La. Assn. Chiefs Police, La. Forgery Investigators, La. Peace Officers Assn., Mcpl. Police Officers Assn., Internat. Assn. Chiefs Police, Internat. Assn. Non-Lethal Weapons, La. Juvenile Officers Assn., Nat. Assn. Chiefs Police. Clubs: Optimist, Rotary (Franklin). Home: PO Box 191 Franklin LA 70538 Office: Franklin Police Dept 508 2d St PO Box 257 Franklin LA 70538

NARANJO, JENNINGS NEAL, marketing and management consulting executive; b. Lufkin, Tex., July 1, 1948; s. J. Neal and Stella Frances (Jennings) N.; m. Mary Ann Platz, Aug. 18, 1979. B.A. with honors, U. Tex.-Austin, 1971; M.A., U. So. Calif., 1977; Ph.D., 1978. Lic. counselor, Tex. Mem. faculty dept. psychology Brooklyn Coll. City U. N.Y., 1971-74; mem. faculty dept. mgmt. U. So. Calif., Los Angeles, 1975-78, dept. mktg., 1978; asst. neuroanatomist McLean Hosp., Belmont, Mass., 1979-81; instr. Harvard Med. Sch., Boston, 1980-81; dir. mktg. and mgmt. cons. Narjen Internat., Lufkin, 1982—. Author: Organizational Behavior, 1977; contbr. articles to profl. jours. Mem. Leadership Lufkin, Angelina County C. of C., 1982-83; production dir. Angelina County Christmas Carolers, Lufkin, 1983; mem. Cultural Arts Council Angelina County C. of C., 1983—; Bd. dirs. St. Cyprians Episcopal Sch., Lufkin, 1983—. Harvard Med. Sch. fellow, 1979. Mem. Am. Psychol. Assn., Am. Mktg. Assn., Am. Soc. Metals, Phi Beta Kappa, Sigma Xi, Psi Chi, Kappa Delta Pi, Omicron Delta Kappa, Alpha Kappa Psi. Clubs: U. Tex. Ex-Students Assn. Club, Austin, 1984—; Harvard (N.Y.C.); Jonathan, Magic Castle (Los Angeles); Crown Colony Country (Lufkin). Lodges: Masons, Order Eastern Star, Sons of Am. Revolution. Episcopalian. Office: Narjen Internat PO Box 1745 Lufkin TX 75901

NARINS, CHARLES SEYMOUR, lawyer, instrument company executive, hospital official; b. Bklyn., Mar. 12, 1909; s. Joshua and Sarah E. (Levy) N.; LL.B., Yale U., 1932; B.S., N.Y. U., 1929; m. Frances D. Kross; children—Lyn Ross, Joyce Hedda. Admitted to N.Y. bar, 1933, Mass. bar, 1955; atty. Curtin & Glynn, N.Y.C., 1932-34, Glynn, Smith & Narins, 1934-37, Probst & Probst, 1937-47; pres., dir., counsel C. L. Berger & Sons, Inc., 1947-68; div. chmn. Berger Instruments div. High Voltage Engring. Corp., Boston, 1968-74; dir., chmn. med. planning New Eng. Sinai Hosp., Stoughton, Mass., 1974—. Trustee Boston Ballet Co., Boston Opera; bd. dirs. Boston Civic Symphony, 1975-76; bd. dirs., 1st v.p. Greater Palm Beach Symphony. Mem. corp. Norfolk House, Boston. Mem. Am., N.Y., Mass., Boston bar assns., Assn. Bar City N.Y., N.Y. County Lawyers Assn., Am. Congress Surveying and Mapping, Am. Judicature Soc., Boston C. of C., Assn. Yale Alumni (law sch. rep.), Internat. Cultural Soc., Pi Lambda Phi. Clubs: Univ., Yale (Boston); Yale, Poinciana (Palm Beach); Yale, N.Y. U. (N.Y.C.); Kernwood Country (Salem, Mass.); Palm Beach (Fla.) Country (bd. govs., sec.). Home: 150 Bradley Pl Palm Beach FL 33480

NASCA, PETER ANTHONY, public relations executive; b. Oceanside, N.Y., June 12, 1948; s. Salvatore M. and June M. (Achille) N.; m. Nancy Randsman, July 29, 1973; children—Christian Pierce, Jarrett Ryan, Lindsey Rose. B.A., U. Bridgeport, 1970. News dir. WKQW Radio, Spring Valley, N.Y., 1971-73; gen. assignment reporter WBRE-TV, NBC, Wilkes Barre, Scranton, Pa., 1973-77; v.p. advt. and pub. relations Nasca Compound, Inc., Island Park, N.Y., 1977-79; dir. pub. relations Fidelity Electronics, Miami, Fla., 1979-80; ptnr., v.p. Bruce Rubin Assocs., Inc., Miami, 1980-84; pres. Peter Nasca Assocs., Inc., Miami, 1984—. Mem. housing com. Rockland County Human Rights Commn. Accredited mem. Pub. Relations Soc. Am. (pres. Miami chpt., judge silver anvil awards ceremony). Home: 8216 NW 8th Pl Plantation FL 33324 Office: Peter Nasca Assocs Inc 9781 NW 91st Ct Miami FL 33166

NASEEF, JAMES RICHARD, linens company executive; b. Bloomington, Ill., Sept. 17, 1908; s. Richard Rasheed and Jessie Jasmine (Rashid) N.; m. Marguerite Mary Tadross, Oct. 22, 1938; 1 dau., Carolyn Marguerite Naseef Nelson. B.S., U. Ill., 1935. Owner, James Lingerie & Linens, Dallas, 1950-70; pres. James Lingerie and Linens, Inc., Dallas, 1966—. Mem. Pi Kappa Alpha. Republican. Presbyterian. Club: Royal Oaks Country. Lodges: Rotary, Masons. Home: 7209 Eudora Dr Dallas TX 75230 Office: 4017 Villanova Dallas TX 75225

NASH, MARY HARRIET, artist; lecturer; b. Washington, May 8, 1951; d. Richard Harvey and Janet Rose (Nivinski) N. B.A., George Washington U., 1973; M.F.A., Washington State U., 1976. Guest lectr. Mus. Art, Wash. State U., Pullman., 1976, 2d St. Gallery, Charlottesville, Va., 1980, U. Ala., Tuscaloosa, 1981, SEWSA Conf., Charlottesville, 1983; artist-in-residence Va. Mus. Fine Arts, Richmond, 1984—; guest juror Twinbrook Art Show, Fairfax, Va., 1978; teaching asst. Wash. State U., 1975-76. Author art show catalogue: Personal Paintings, 1978. Recipient Cert. Outstanding Achievement, Women in Design Internat., 1983; MacDowell Colony fellow, 1977. Mem. Coll. Art Assn., Southeastern Ctr. for Contemporary Art (hon. mention 1979), Phi Kappa Phi. Office: 8536 Aponi Rd Vienna VA 22180

NASSER, MOES ROSHANALI, optometrist; b. Sumve, Mwanza, Tanzania, Jan. 20, 1956; came to U.S., 1976; s. Roshanali Hassanali and Rehmat (Kara) N.; m. Anar Hemnani, Dec. 20, 1979; 1 child, Faria M. B.S. in Optometry, U. Houston, 1980; D. Optometry, 1982. Cons., mgr. optometric practice, Houston, 1984—, Beaumont, Tex., 1985—; cons. in field. Vol. Agakhan Ch., Tanzania, 1966-71; sec. Agakhan Ch. health com., 1976-82, mem. ch. council, Houston, 1981-82. Agakhan Found. Scholar Switzerland, 1976-82. Mem. Harris County Optometric Soc., Tex. Optometric Assn., Tex. Assn. for Optometrists, Am. Optometric Assn., Alta. Optometric Assn., Can. Assn. Optometrists. Avocations: tennis; volleyball; reading. Home: 3134 Redcliff Dr Sugar Land TX 77479 Office: 2416-A University Blvd Houston TX 77005

NASTOFF, ROBERT DEAN, engineer; b. Gary, Ind., May 25, 1943; s. Boris Nicholas and Esther Marie (St. Germain) N.; m. Janice Elizabeth Wesley, Oct. 13, 1973; 1 child, Jorie Marie. B.S. in Indsl. Engring., Purdue U., 1966; M.S. in Bus. Adminstrn., Ind. U.-Gary, 1977. Mfg. engr. United Tech. Corp., Windsor Lakes, Conn., 1966-70; product engr. Anderson Co., Gary, Ind., 1970-72, indsl. engr., 1972-78, safety dir., 1978-84; plant engr. Am. Transp., Conway, Ark., 1984—. Mem. Am. Soc. Safety Engrs. (sec. 1980-81, treas. 1981-82, v.p. 1982-84, pres. 1983-84). Lutheran. Avocations: golf; swimming. Home: 137 Davis St Conway AR 72032

NATAUPSKY, MARK, air force officer, psychologist; b. Everett, Mass., Sept. 12, 1942; s. George Herbert and Marian (Sandler) N.; m. Marilyn Joy Greene, Mar. 8, 1969; children—Deborah, Glenda. B.S., U. Mass., 1964; M.S., Purdue U., 1966; M. Aerospace Ops. Mgmt., U. So. Calif., 1970; Ph.D., U. Hawaii, 1974. Commd. 2d lt. U.S. Air Force, 1967, advanced through grades to lt. col., 1983; assoc. prof. dept. behavioral scis. and leadership, dir. How to Study program U.S. Air Force Acad., Colo., 1978-82; chief tng. devel. br. Tactical Air Command, Langley AFB, Va., 1982-84, chief tng. research br., 1984-85; program coordinator, human factors researcher NASA Langley Research Ctr., 1985—. Contbr. articles to profl. jours. Co-chairperson Newport News Soviet Jewry Com., Va., 1984—. Decorated Meritorious Service medal. Mem. Assn. Aviation Psychologists (pres. 1981-83), Human Factors Soc. (sec. Rocky Mt. chpt. 1980-81), Am. Ednl. Research Assn., Am. Coll. Personnel Assn., Sigma Xi. Avocations: photography, coin collecting, shooting, hunting. Home: 317 Lynchburg Dr Newport News VA 23606 Office: NASA Langley Research Ctr Mail Stop 152E Hampton VA 23665

NATCHER, WILLIAM HUSTON, congressman; b. Bowling Green, Ky., Sept. 11, 1909; s. J. M. and Blanche (Hays) N.; A.B., Western Ky. State Coll., Bowling Green, 1930; LL.B., Ohio State U., 1933; m. Virginia Reardon, June 17, 1937; children—Celeste, Louise. Admitted to Ky. bar, 1934, pvt. practice, Bowling Green, 1934—. Fed. conciliation commr. Western Dist. Ky., 1936-37; atty. Warren Co., 1937-49; commonwealth atty., 8th Jud. Dist., 1952-53; elected to 83d Congress (to fill unexpired term of Garrett L. Withers), 1953; mem. 84th to 98th Congresses, 2d Ky. Dist. Served as lt. USNR, 1942-45. Mem. Bowling Green Bar Assn. (pres.), Am. Legion, 40 and 8. Democrat. Odd Fellow, Kiwanian. Home: 638 E Main St Bowling Green KY 42101 Office: 414 E 10th St Bowling Green KY 42101

NATELSON, STEPHEN ELLIS, neurosurgeon; b. N.Y.C., Dec. 23, 1937; s. Samuel R. and Ethel D. (Nathan) N.; B.A. magna cum laude, Carleton Coll., 1958; Fulbright scholar in Math., Westfälische-Wilhelms U., Germany, 1958-59; M.D., U. Rochester, 1963; children—Lea Jane, Jamie Ann, Jessica Ilana, Benjamin Henry, Marissa Claire. Intern, USAF Hosp., Wright-Patterson AFB, 1963-64; resident in neurosurgery Ohio State U., 1967-71; chief resident in neurology U. N.Mex., 1971-72; pvt. practice specializing in neurosurgery, Knoxville, Tenn., 1972—; clin. assoc. prof. U. Tenn. Served with USAF, 1962-67. Decorated Air Force Commendation medal; diplomate Am. Bd. Neurol. Surgery. Fellow ACS; mem. Am. Assn. Neurol. Surgeons, Congress Neurol. Surgeons, AMA, Knoxville Acad. Medicine, Am. Physicians Fellowship, Undersea Med. Soc., Phi Beta Kappa, Sigma Xi, Alpha Omega Alpha. Republican. Jewish. Contbr. articles to profl. jours. Office: 103 Newland Professional Bldg Knoxville TN 37916

NATH, JOGINDER, genetics educator; b. Joginder Nagar, India, May 12, 1932; s. Moti and Vira Wali (Khorana) Ram; came to U.S., 1957, naturalized, 1966; m. Charlotte Lynn Reese, Apr. 5, 1969; children—Pravene, Brian. B.S.

with honors Panjab U., 1953, M.S. with honors, 1955; Ph.D., U. Wis., 1960. Research assoc. Inst. Cryobiol. Research, Madison, Wis., 1960-63; asst. prof. physiology So. Ill. U., Carbondale, 1964-66; assoc. prof. genetics W.Va. U., Morgantown, 1966-72, prof. genetics, 1972—, chmn. genetics and devel. biology 1975—. NSF grantee, 1967. Mem. Internat. Soc. Cryobiology, Sigma Xi. Contbr. articles to profl. jours. Home: 43 Linnwood Rd Morgantown WV 26505 Office: 1120 Coll of Agr W Va Univ Morgantown WV 26506

NATH, RAVINDER, management educator; b. Hashiarpur, Panjab, India, Aug. 16, 1952; came to U.S., 1974, naturalized, 1981. B.A. with honors, Panjab U., 1972, M.A., 1974; M.S., Wichita State U., Kans., 1975; Ph.D., Tex. Tech U., 1980. Teaching asst. Tex. Tech U., Lubbock, 1975-80; assoc. prof. quantitative analysis, dept. mgmt. Fogelman Coll. Bus. and Econs., Memphis State U., 1980—. Contbr. articles to profl. lit. Mem. Am. Inst. Decision Scis., Am. Statis. Assn., Inst. Mgmt. Sci. Avocations: racquetball; photography; camping. Office: Dept of Mgmt Memphis State U Memphis TN 38152

NATH, SUNIL BARAN, planner, researcher, state agency administrator; b. Silchar, Assam, India, Mar. 31, 1937; s. Sarat Chandra and Sarada (Devi) N.; came to U.S., 1968, naturalized, 1977; B.A., Visva-Bharati Internat. U., Sriniketan, India, 1960; M.A. in Sociology, Agra (India) U., 1964, Ph.D. candidate in Sociology, 1967; M.A. candidate in Pub. Adminstrn., Fla. State U., 1978, Ph.D. candidate in Criminology, 1978—, student in Bus. Law, 1978—, grad. cert. in pub. adminstrn., 1978; M.B.A. and Ph.D. candidate Calif. Coast U., 1983—; m. Abha Rani Barua, Dec. 3, 1967; children—Subrata (Bobby), Sunita, Lipika. Asst. prof. sociology B.V. Rural Higher Inst., Agra, 1964-67; instr., field dir. Survey Data Center, Polit. Research Inst., Fla. State U., Tallahassee, 1969-70, research asso., field dir., 1970-71; statistician Fla. Parole and Probation Commn., Tallahassee, 1971, project dir. Fla. intensive probation and parole projects, 1971-73, dir. research planning and statistics, 1973-74, dir. planning and evaluation, 1974-76; planner, evaluator Dept. Offender Rehab., Tallahassee, 1976-79; civil rights adminstr. Fla. Dept. Transp., Tallahassee, 1978-81, supr. budget and planning, 1981-83, ops. and mgmt. cons. II, asst. bur. chief minority programs, 1983—; co-dir. Fla. Conf. on Evaluation Research; owner Nath Auto Super Mktg. Services, Tallahassee, 1977—; cons. Human Research & Devel. Services, Inc., Univ. Research Corp., Inc., Washington; a founding mem. Good Life Gen. Store, Tallahassee, 1979—; sub-agt. A Tour Travel Agy., Chgo. and Travel Connection, Inc., Miami, 1978—. Cubmaster Cub Scouts, 1979-80; active Boy Scouts Am., 1976—; mem. Gov.'s Adult Reform Plan, 1972-73; project dir. L.E.E.A. grant, 1972-74; 4-H Club community leader, 1979—. Mem. Am., Fla., So. States correctional assns., Am., So. sociol. assns., Am. Judicature Soc., Am. Acad. Polit. and Social Scis., Internat. Platform Assn., Nat., Fla. councils on crime and delinquency, Assn. for Correctional Research and Statistics, Internat. Howard League for Penal Reform (Eng.), Am. Soc. Pub. Adminstrn., Conf. Minority Pub. Adminstrs., Nat. Assn. Ams. of Asian Indian Descent (nat. exec. bd. 1980—), India Assn. Tallahassee pres. 1983-84), Delta Tau Kappa, Alpha Kappa Delta. Democrat. Hindu. Club: Toastmasters (pres. 1979-80, gov. Suwannee div. 1985—) (Tallahassee). Lodge: Kiwanis. Contbr. articles to profl. jours. Home: 431 Victory Garden Dr Tallahassee FL 32301 Office: 605 Suwannee St Tallahassee FL 32301

NATHAN, RONALD GENE, medical educator, writer, researcher, consultant; b. Paterson, N.J., Feb. 22, 1951; s. Kurt Caesar and Hinda (Kremer) N.; m. Myra Helen Malmed, June 30, 1974; children—Jennifer Rose, William Miles. B.A. with distinction, Cornell U., 1973; M.A., U. Houston, 1975, Ph.D., 1978. Diplomate Am. Acad. Behavioral Medicine; lic. psychologist, La. Teaching fellow U. Houston, 1974-76, teaching asst., 1976, 78, instr. child devel., 1977-78; part time psychometrician, U. Tex., Houston, 1978; intern Tex. Research Inst. of Mental Scis., Tex. Med. Ctr., Houston, 1977-78; clin. asst. prof. dept. psychology, U. N.C., Chapel Hill, 1978-79, asst. prof. depts. psychiatry and family medicine, La. State U. Sch. Medicine, Shreveport, 1979-83, assoc. prof., dir. med. psychology, 1983—, assoc. prof., dir. behavioral scis., 1986—; mem. adv. bd. for mental health/psychiat. nursing, Coll. Nursing Northwestern State U. La., 1983—; cons. Merrill Lynch Pierce Fenner & Smith, Ruston and Shreveport, 1983, Libbey Glass, Shreveport, 1983-84, AT&T, Shreveport, 1985, Blue Cross/Blue Shield, Baton Rouge, 1985, behavioral sci. curriculum com. Med. Sch. U. Mo., Kansas City. Co-author: Stress Management: A Conceptual and Procedural Guide, 1980; Stress Management: A Comprehensive Guide to Wellness, 1982, 84 (alt. selection Book-of-the-Month Club, also in paperback); contbr. chpts., monographs, articles to profl. publs. in field, papers to profl. confs.; guest reviewer Focus on Critical Care, 1984, Am. Psychologist, 1984. Prin. investigator NIH research grant, 1981-83. Fellow Am. Inst. of Stress; mem. Am. Psychol. Assn. (divs. 1, 2, 12, 29, 38, 42, pub. info. rep. 1980—), La. Psychol. Assn., NW La. Psychol. Assn., Biofeedback Soc. Am., Soc. Behavioral Medicine, Psychologists in Family Medicine and Primary Care, Nat. Ctr. for Health Edn. (charter assoc), Phi Beta Kappa, Phi Kappa Phi. Home: 8467 Indian Hills Blvd Shreveport LA 71107 Office: Dept Psychiatry La State U Med Ctr 1501 Kings Hwy PO Box 33932 Shreveport LA 71130

NATION, HORACE HENDRIX, III, circuit judge; b. Birmingham, Ala., Oct. 8, 1948; s. Horace Hendrix, Jr. and Lucy Faye (Diesker) Nation Bearden; m. Jean Marie Lawley, Dec. 30, 1970; children—Horace H. IV, James Leighton. B.S. in Bus. Adminstrn., U. Ala., 1971; J.D., Cumberland Sch. Law, 1974. Bar: Ala. 1974. Asst. dist. atty., Jasper, Ala., 1975-77, dist. judge, 1977-80; circuit judge, Jasper, 1980-83, presiding circuit judge, 1983—; instr. Walker Coll., Jasper, 1980—; mem. law enforcement planning agy. adv. bd. State of Ala., 1981. Mem. Ala. State Bar, Ala. Assn. Circuit Judges, ABA, Walker County Bar Assn., Phi Delta Phi. Democrat. Mem. Disciple of Christ. Lodge: Rotary. Office: PO Box 1442 Jasper AL 35502

NATRELLA, VITO, economic consultant; b. Bklyn., Dec. 2, 1916; s. Michael and Mary (Orobello) N.; m. Elinor Entrekin, Jan. 14, 1950; children—Michael, Steven. B.A., Bklyn. Coll., 1937; M.A., Am. U., 1962. Fin. statistician SEC, Washington, 1939-60, asst. dir. trading div., 1960-64; dir. stats. div. IRS, Washington, 1964-80; econ. cons., Arlington, Va., 1980—. Author (with others) Volume and Composition of Individual Saving, 1954. Editor: The Flow of Funds Approach to Social Accounting, 1962. Contbr. articles to profl. jours. Fellow Am. Statis. Assn.; mem. Am. Econ. Assn., Nat. Economists Club. Club: Cosmos (Washington). Home and Office: 1718 N Hartford St Arlington VA 22201

NATZKE, ROGER PAUL, dairy scientist, educator; b. Wis., June 15, 1939; children—Cindy, Brent. B.S., U. Wis.-Madison, 1962, M.S., 1963, Ph.D., 1966. Asst. prof. Cornell U., Ithaca, N.Y., 1966-71, assoc. prof., 1971-79, assoc. dir. instrn., 1979-81, prof., 1980; chmn. dept., prof. dairy sci. U. Fla., Gainesville, 1981—. Recipient W. Agro-Chem. award Am. Dairy Sci. Assn., 1982. Home: 425 SW 83d Terr Gainesville FL 32601 Office: Dairy Sci Dept U Fla Shealy Dr and Richey Rd Gainesville FL 32611

NAU, JAMES MICHAEL, civil engineering educator; b. Hickory, N.C., Dec. 26, 1951; s. Walter Theodore and Elizabeth Anne (Esch) N.; m. Mary Benjamin Hester, July 31, 1977. B.S., N.C. State U., 1974, M.S., 1977; Ph.D., U. Ill., 1982. Registered profl. engr., N.C. Grad. teaching asst. dept. mech. and aerospace engring. N.C. State U., Raleigh, 1974-76; mech. engr. Corporate Cons. and Devel. Co., Ltd., Raleigh, 1974-76, sr. engr., 1976-77; grad. research and teaching asst. dept. civil engring. U. Ill., Urbana-Champaign, 1977-82; asst. prof. dept. civil engring. N.C. State U., Raleigh, 1982—. Recipient C. P. Siess award dept. civil engring. U. Ill., 1982; Outstanding Tchr. award student sect. ASCE, N.C. State U., 1984, 85; Kimley-Horn Faculty award dept. civil engring. N.C. State U., 1984; U. Ill. fellow, 1977-79. Mem. ASCE (assoc.); mem. Earthquake Engring. Research Inst., Am. Acad. Mechanics, Am. Soc. Engring. Edn., Sigma Xi, Tau Beta Pi, Phi Kappa Phi, Pi Tau Sigma, N.C. State U. Alumni Assn., U. Ill. Alumni Assn. Club: Wolfpack. Contbr. articles in field to profl. jours. Home: 2111 Reaves Dr Raleigh NC 27608 Office: Dept Civil Engring PO Box 7908 NC State U Raleigh NC 27695

NAUGLE, MARGARET VANCE, community relations official; b. West Point, Miss., Nov. 17, 1946; d. James O'Neil and Allie Laura (Stevens) Vance; B.S., Miss. State Coll. for Women, 1970; M.Ed., Miss. State U., 1977, Ed.D., 1980; m. Andrew Kincannon Naugle, III, Jan. 4, 1979; 1 dau., Laura Natalie Pickens. With admissions office Miss. State Coll. for Women, 1970; tchr. Lowndes County (Miss.) Schs., 1970-73, Hendry County (Fla.) Schs., 1973-74, Pickens County (Ala.) Schs., 1974-76; dir. adult edn. Miss. Band of Choctaw Indians, 1976-80; tng. specialist Daniel Constrn.-Weyerhauser Columbus Project, 1980-82; dir. community relations Golden Triangle Regional Med. Ctr., 1982—; adj. prof. U. Ala., Tuscaloosa, 1980-81; tech. advisor Fermodyl Labs., Inc.; tchr. Seminole Tribe of Fla., Golden Triangle Vo-Tech Miss. Mem. Am. Soc. Tng. and Devel., Assn. for Supervision and Curriculum Devel., Miss. Assn. for Supervision and Curriculum Devel., Nat. Assn. Public Continuing and Adult Edn. (nat. award for program 1976), Adult Basic Edn. Commn., Miss. Assn. for Public Continuing and Adult Edn., Adult Edn. Assn. U.S.A., Am. Hosp. Assn., Am. Soc. Hosp. Pub. Relations, Pub. Relations Assn. Miss., Am. Advt. Assn., Golden Triangle Advt. Fedn. (bd. dirs.), Am. Diabetes Assn. (bd. dirs. Miss. chpt.), So. Pub. Relations Fedn. (Lantern award of merit). Mem. Christian Church (Disciples of Christ). Club: Investment, Health Club Am., Toastmasters (sec.-treas.). Author: A Comparison of the EDL Learning 100 Program and the Workbook Method of Teaching Reading to Choctaw Adults, 1980; Mill Economics, Parts I and II, 1981; contbr. articles to Indian and profl. publs., 1976-79. Home: PO Box 1152 202 Court St West Point MS 39773

NAUMER, HELMUTH JACOB, museum administrator, consultant; b. Santa Fe, May 7, 1934; s. Helmuth and Tomee (Reuter) N.; m. Mary Ann Singleton, Sept. 3, 1957 (div. Feb. 1966); children—Karina Anne, Helmuth Karl; m. Carolyn Palmer, Oct. 9, 1966; children—Kirsten Anne, Tanya Elizabeth. B.A., U. N. Mex., 1957; postgrad. U. Minn., 1958. Mgr., Taos Ski Valley, N.Mex., 1958-59; archaeologist in charge Town Creek Indian Mound, Mt. Gilead, N.C., 1959-60; dir. Charlotte Nature Mus., N.C., 1960-62; exec. dir. Ft. Worth Mus. of Sci. and History, Tex., 1962-76, Pacific Sci. Ctr., Seattle, 1976-79, San Antonio Mus. Assn., 1979—; mem. Smithsonian/Kellogg Project, Smithsonian Instn., Washington, 1983-85; bd. dirs. Art Mus. Assn., San Francisco, 1979-82; panel mem. Nat. Endowment for Arts Mus. Programs, 1973-76, Nat. Endowment Humanities Mus. Programs, 1971-72; pres. Am. Assn. of Youth Museums, 1967, 71; organizer Tex. Inst. of Small Museums, 1965-69; mem. ICOM Edn. Com., 1969-70, 73; mem. Smithsonian Conf. on Mus. Edn., 1970; mem. Tex. Arts & Humanities Commn., 1972-76; nat., internat. speaker in field. Mem. White House Conf. on Children, 1970-71. Author: Of Mutual Respect and Other Things, 1977; contbr. articles on museum related subjects to profl. publs. Bd. dirs. Invisible U., Fort Worth, 1973-77, High Frontier, Fort Davis, Tex., 1978-85; mem. exec. bd. Dallas/Fort Worth Council of Sci. and Engring. Socs., 1971-73; gov. Tex. Sesquicentennial Mus. Bd., Austin, 1983-89. Recipient Elsie M.B. Naumberg award Natural Sci. for Youth Found.; named to Turkish Nat. Mus. of Sci. and Tech. Bd., 1984. Mem. Am. Assn. Museums (council mem. 1972-78, mem. exec. com. 1975-76, mem. nominating com. 1977, 83, nat. program and site conf. chmn. 1974, mem. commn. on museums for a new century 1981-83), Mt. Plains Mus. Assn. (regional rep. 1982-85), Tex. Assn. Museums (pres. 1969, 71, chmn. by-laws com. 1985, councellor). Republican. Club: Argyle (San Antonio). Lodge: Rotary. Office: San Antonio Museum Assn PO Box 2601 San Antonio TX 78299

NAVARRO, ANDREW JESUS, educator; b. Havana, Cuba, Sept. 11, 1946; came to U.S. 1951, naturalized 1968; s. Andrew Jesus and Carmen Caridad (Torres) N.; m. Deborah Anne Goodman, Aug. 3, 1968 (div. July, 1985); children—Andrew Robert, Laurie Lee. Student Fla. State U., 1964-67; B.Ed, U. Miami, 1968; M.Ed., Fla. Atlantic U., 1971, postgrad., 1972-78. Cert. tchr., Fla. Varsity debate coach Miami Norland High Sch., Fla., 1973-82, varsity tennis coach, 1976-83, asst. prin., 1978-79, dept. chmn., 1980—; instr. Miami-Dade Community Coll., 1984; supervising tchr. Dade County Schs., Miami, 1982, 85, directing tchr., 1972-73, 76. Author: (jour.) Notes From the Lecturn, 1977. Editor jours. Perspectives, 1976, Reflections, 1977, Charles Merrill Pub. Co. Chmn. Dade County Instructional Materials Council, Miami, 1985—; mem. Dade County Exam. Rev. Panel, 1986; coordinator Close-Up Found., Washington, 1979, 82-83; mem. Young Americans for Freedom, Miami, 1965-66, Lakes Homeowners Assn., Pembroke Pines, Fla., 1976-85, Broward County Bi-Centennial Com., Fla., 1975-76. Recipient Outstanding Spokesman for Freedom award VFW, 1976, 79, 81, Diamond Key award Nat. Forensic League, 1977, Barkley Forum Membership award Emory U., 1976, Voice of Democracy award VFW, 1977. Mem. Nat. Council Social Studies, Nat. Forensic League, Am. Anthropol. Assn., Dade County Debate Coaches Assn. (pres. 1975, 77), Sigma Phi Epsilon. Republican. Lodge: Optomists. Avocations: tennis; gardening; camping; various animal welfare orgns. Home: 450 NW 214th St #205 Miami FL 33169 Office: Miami Norland Sr High Sch 1050 NW 195th St Miami FL 33169

NAVARRO, CESAR OSWALDO, personnel, safety and insurance administrator; b. Lima, Peru, Feb. 3, 1943; came to U.S., 1964, naturalized, 1970; s. Saturnino and Sara (Gallegos) N.; m. Maricela Ramirez, Apr. 1, 1985. B.S. in Indsl. Engring., NYU, 1968; postgrad. in labor law Antioch Sch. Law, 1982. Personnel supr. Western Electric Co., Kearny, N.J., 1978-81; personnel mgr. K-Mart, Northbergen, N.J., 1981-83, PetroPeru, Lima, 1973-77, Proler Internat., Houston, 1977—. Mem. Houston Hispanic Forum, 1984. Mem. Am. Soc. Personnel Adminstrn. (sr. mem.), Am. Soc. Safety Engrs., Interam. C. of C. (v.p. 1978-85). Republican. Roman Catholic. Club: Toastmasters Internat. (Houston). Home: 16802 Pastoria Dr Houston TX 77083

NAVIAUX, LAREE DEVEE, psychologist; b. Lewellen, Nebr., Aug. 18, 1937; d. Prosper Leo and Dorothy DeVee (Walters) N.; m. Frank Anthony D'Abreo, June 16, 1973. B.S., U. Nebr., 1959; M.S., Iowa State U., 1963; Ph.D., Duquesne U., 1973. Instr. Iowa State U., Ames, 1963-65; asst. prof. Kans. State U., Manhattan, 1965-66; grad. faculty Carnegie-Mellon U., Pitts., 1966-69; asst. prof. West Ga. Coll., Carrollton, 1969-72; regional dir. Children's Mental Health, Charleston, W.Va., 1973-80; therapist, educator Community Mental Health Center, Charleston, 1980-82; pvt. practice, 1982—; asst. clin. prof. W.Va. U., 1977—. Active Family and Children Together Speaker's Bur., 1980-83; bd. dirs. Creative Arts Clinic, 1981-83, Parents Anonymous of W.Va., 1979-82. Humanities Found. W.Va. grantee, 1978, 79, 81, 82. Fellow Menninger Found.; mem. U. Nebr. Alumni (life), Iowa State U. Alumni (life), Am. Psychol. Assn., Assn. for Humanistic Psychology, Mental Health Assn. (life), Inst. Noetic Scis. Democrat. Roman Catholic. Clubs: Kanawha Players, Gourmet, Friendship Force, Indian Assn. Contbr. articles to profl. jours. and books. Home: 1603 Longridge Rd Charleston WV 25314

NAYLOR, DEBORAH ANNE, financial analyst; b. Euclid, Ohio, Oct. 6, 1956; d. Douglas and Eleanor Ruth (Pavlik) Naylor. B.A. in Life Scis. and Econs., U. Pitts., 1978. Advt. mgr. The Pitt News, U. Pitts., 1975-78; jr. exec. Barium and Chems., Inc., Steubenville, Ohio, 1978-82; spl. projects exec. Well Control, Inc., Houston, 1982; fin. analyst, tax planner Hughes Offshore div. Hughes Tool Co., Houston, 1982—. Mem. fin. bd. Martha Manor Home for Aged Women. Mem. Nat. Assn. Accts., AAUW (chpt. publicity dir. 1979-80), Big Red Booster Club, Antique Collectors Club, Cambridge Glass Club, Am. Fox Terrier Club, Female Exec. Nat. Assn., Delta Delta Delta, Beta Sigma Phi. Republican. Office: PO Box 40901 Houston TX 77240

NEAL, CLIFTON TRUBY, JR., college administrator, bookstore executive; b. Bluefield, W.Va., Nov. 13, 1942; s. Clifton T. and Lora Edith (Witt) N.; m. Vera Carol Billips, Apr. 4, 1964; children—Clifton Lee, Mary Ellen, Lora Ann. B.S., Bluefield State Coll., 1974; M.S., Radford U., 1978. Asst. equipment supt. W.Va. State Rd. Commn., Princeton, 1961-69; bookstore mgr., asst. budget dir. Bluefield State Coll., 1969—; chmn. Bd. Regents Adv. Council Classified Employees, Charleston, W.Va., 1982—; mem. W.Va. Bd. Regents, Charleston, 1983—. Home: 405 Union St Bluefield WV 24701 Office: Bluefield State Coll 9W Pulaski St Bluefield WV 24701

NEAL, CONSTANCE ANN TRILLICH, lawyer, librarian; b. Chgo., Apr. 16, 1949; d. Lee and Ruth (Goodhue) Trillich; m. Robert Dale Neal, Dec. 25, 1972; 1 son, Adam Danforth. B.A. in French, U. Tenn., 1971, cert. Sorbonne, 1970; M.Ln., Emory U., 1979; J.D., Mercer Law Sch., 1982. Bar: Ga. 1982. Reservationist AAA, Tampa, Fla., 1971-72; library tech. asst. I, Mercer U., Macon, Ga., 1973-74, library tech. asst. II, 1974-78; teaching asst. Mercer Law Sch., Macon, 1981; cataloger Mercer Med. Sch., Macon, 1980-82; sole practice, Macon, 1982-85; cons. info. sci., 1985—; research asst. Ctr. Constl. Studies, Macon, 1983; instr. bus. Wesleyan Coll., Macon, 1982; Amway distbrs., 1985—. Bd. dirs. Macon Council World Affairs, 1981-82; mem. Friends Emory Libraries, Atlanta, 1980—; mem. Friends Eckerd Coll. Library, St. Petersburg, Fla., 1980—. Mem. ABA, Am. Soc. Law and Medicine, Am. Judicature Soc., Nat. Assn. Female Execs. (network dir. 1985—), Phi Alpha Delta. Republican. Presbyterian.

NEAL, DAVID LINDSAY, construction company executive; b. Eden, N.C., Jan. 21, 1947; s. Latimer Briggs Jr. and Lois (Martin) N.; m. Katherine Milner, June 14, 1969; children—Stephanie, Lindsay, Sarah, Matthew. B.A., Principia Coll., 1969. Tchr. Daycroft Sch., Greenwich, Conn., 1969-71; mgr. Colony IV Motel, Kill Devil Hills, N.C., 1971-72; sales rep. Equity Investments, Richmond, Va., 1972-73; office mgr. D.B. Weeson Co., Monson, Mass., 1973-74; loan officer Planters Nat. Bank, Manteo, N.C., 1974-77; owner, pres. L.B. Neal Constrn., David Neal Constrn., Kitty Hawk, N.C., 1978—. Treas. Outer Banks Toastmasters, Kitty Hawk, 1975; advisor Raoul Wallenberg Com. of U.S., 1981—. Mem. N.C. Lic. Contractors, Jaycees. Christian Scientist. Avocations: guitar; piano; travel. Home: Twiford St PO Box 277 Kitty Hawk NC 27949 Office: David Neal Design 103 Clarke St Kill Devil Hills NC 27948

NEAL, DAVID SCOTT, business planning consultant; b. Somerset, Ky., Apr. 27, 1952; s. Cecil Adrian and Wilma Laura (Anderson) M. B.B.A., Eastern Ky. U., 1974, M.B.A., 1975. C.P.A., Ky. Staff acct. James F. Scott, C.P.A., Madison, Ind., 1975; cons. Deloitte Haskins & Sells, Cin. and Lexington, Ky., 1980-82; ptnr. S.E. DeRossett & Assocs., bus. planners, Lexington, 1982-84; mgr. Carpenter & Co., C.P.A.s, Lexington, 1985—. Bd. dirs. Vol. Action Center, Lexington; deacon Calvary Bapt. Ch., Lexington. Served to capt. AUS, 1975-79. Mem. Am. Inst. C.P.A.s, Ky. (Soc. C.P.A.s, Internat. Assn. for Fin. Planners). Republican. Baptist. Home: 3410 Merrick Dr Lexington KY 40502 Office: 366 S Broadway Lexington KY 40508

NEAL, GEORGE DAVID, oil company executive, lawyer; b. Dallas, May 20, 1933; s. A. D. and Ida Mae (Pace) N.; m. Carolyn Louise Fleming, Mar. 16, 1957; children—Janet Carol, David Patrick. B.B.A., So. Meth. U., 1954, J.D., 1959. Bar: Tex. 1959, U.S. Dist. Ct. (no. dist.) Tex. 1975, U.S. Supreme Ct. 1977. Gen. atty., sec. Sun Prodn. Co. div. Sun Exploration and Prodn. Co., Dallas, 1977-80, v.p., gen. atty., 1980-81, v.p. res. expansion, 1981-83, mgr. res. expansion, 1983-84, mgr. acquisitions, 1984—. Sun Prodn. Co. chmn. United Way, Met. Dallas, 1980-81. Served to capt. USAF, 1954-57. Mem. Am. Petroleum Inst., Am. Assn. Petroleum Geologists, ABA, Tex. Bar Assn., Dallas Bar Assn., others. Republican. Methodist. Club: Petroleum (Dallas). Lodge: Masons. Avocations: photography; fishing; skiing. Home: 8946 Bretshire Dr Dallas TX 75228 Office: Sun Exploration and Prodn Co 5656 Blackwell St Dallas TX 75231

NEAL, JAMES AUSTIN, architect; b. Greenville, S.C., Nov. 23, 1935; s. Charles Albert Neal and Jane (Anderson) Cole; m. Leonette Dedmond, Apr. 13, 1963; 1 child, Heather Anderson. B. Arch., Clemson U., 1959. Registered architect, S.C. Designer McMillan Architects, Greenville, S.C., 1960-62; project mgr. W.E. Freeman Architects, Greenville, 1963-64; project architect J.E. Sirrine Co., Greenville, 1964-68; pres., prin. Neal, Prince & Browning, Greenville, 1969—; vis. prof. Clemson U. Coll. Architecture, 1974-75; mem. bd. advisors S.C. Nat. Bank. Pres. Leslie Meyer Devel. Ctr., Greenville, 1980-82. Recipient Leadership award Greenville C. of C., 1983. Mem. AIA (Merit Design award 1978), Greenville Council Architects (past pres.). Baptist. Club: Poinsett (pres. 1985—). Avocations: jogging; flying. Office: Neal Prince Browning Architects Inc 11 Cleveland Ct Greenville SC 29607

NEAL, JERRY HAROLD, police chief; b. Wanette, Okla., Mar. 10, 1943; s. William Odus and Anna (Way) N.; divorced; children—Jamee Lynn, Jerry Harold Jr.; m. Ellen Teresa Robertson, Aug. 12, 1983; 1 child, Jordan Kent. A.A., Okla. State U., 1972, B.S., 1973, M.S., 1977. Patrolman, sgt., lt., capt. Norman Police Dept., Okla., 1968-78, maj. of police, 1978-81; chief of police Amarillo Police Dept., Tex., 1981—; bd. mem. State Police Pension System, Okla., 1980-81; regional dir. Tex. Police Chiefs Assn., 1981-83; tng. adv. bd. Tex. Commn. Law Enforcement, Austin, 1982-84. Bd. dirs. Maverick Boys Club, Amarillo, 1985, Rape Crisis, Domestic Crisis Violence, Amarillo, 1981-84, Amarillo Council Alcoholism, 1981-84; exec. bd. Llayno council Boy Scouts Am., 1985. Served to Sgt. E-5 U.S. Army, 1965-68. Mem. Tex. Police Chiefs Assn. (regional dir. 1981-83), Tex. Police Assn., Fed. Bur. Investigation Nat. Assocs. Democrat. Lodge: Rotary. Avocations: golf; softball. Home: 4321 Omaha Amarillo TX 79106 Office: Amarillo Police Dept 609 S Pierce Amarillo TX 79101

NEAL, ROBERT LEE, lawyer, former army officer; b. Dalton, Ga., Apr. 27, 1933; s. Arvil and Jessie Mae (Robinson) N.; m. Ruth Rose Kain; children—Donna Gail, Connie Lynn. B.S. cum laude, Troy State U., 1972; J.D., Woodrow Wilson Coll. of Law, 1980. Bar: Ga. 1982, U.S. Dist. Ct. (no. dist.) Ga. 1982. Commd. capt. U.S. Army, 1963, advanced through grades to lt. col., 1981; served as aviator in Vietnam, 1965-66, 68-69, Iran, 1967-68; forces command, Atlanta, 1977-81, ret., 1981; sole practice, Jonesboro, Ga., 1982—; lectr. aviation safety. Decorated Bronze Star, Cross of Galantry with Silver Star. Home: 1596 Cyprus Ct Riverdale GA 30296 Office: Robert L Neal 165 N Main St Jonesboro GA 30236

NEAL, STEPHEN LYBROOK, congressman; b. Winston-Salem, N.C., Nov. 7, 1934; s. Charles H. and Mary Martha (Lybrook) N.; student U. Calif., Santa Barbara; B.A. in Psychology, U. Hawaii, 1959; m. Rachel Landis Miller, June 13, 1964; children—Mary Piper, Stephen Lybrook. Mortgage banker, hotel mgr., until 1966; pres. Community Press, Inc., Winston-Salem, 1966-75; mem. 94th-98th Congresses from N.C. 5th Dist.; chmn. subcom. internat. trade, investment and monetary policy, former chmn. and ranking majority mem. subcom. on domestic monetary policy. Democrat. Presbyterian. Office: 2463 Rayburn House Office Bldg Washington DC 20515

NEALIS, JAMES GARRY THOMAS, III, pediatric neurologist, educator, author; b. N.Y.C., Mar. 7, 1945; s. James and Catherine N.; m. Arlene Dee Kramer, Feb. 6, 1981; children—Douglas Andrew, Gregory Haynes, James Garry Thomas IV, Patrick Ryan. B.A., Fordham U., 1966; M.D., U. Miami, 1971. Diplomate Am. Bd. Psychiatry and Neurology, Am. Bd. Electroencephalography. Intern in pediatrics Babies Hosp., Columbia Presbyn. Med. Ctr., Columbia U. Sch. Medicine, N.Y.C., 1971-72, resident, 1972-73; resident in neurology Boston U. Sch. Medicine, 1973-74, 75-76, resident in neurology Harvard U. Sch. Medicine, Boston, 1975-76, instr. pediatric neurology, 1976-78; chief resident Boston City Hosp., 1975-76; asst. in neurophysiology Boston Children's Hosp., 1976-78; founder Neuro-Ednl. Evaluation Clinic, 1977-78; asst. prof. clin. neurology U. Fla., Jacksonville; chief pediatric neurology Jacksonville Children's Hosp., 1979—; clin. instr. neurology; lectr. U. North Fla.; cons. Naval Regional Med. Ctr., Jacksonville, 1979—; adviser Pres.'s Com. Med. Ethics, Washington, 1980; sec. Fla. Neurol. Inst., 1985; lectr. in field; numerous TV appearances; host TV show To Your Health, Sta. WJXT, 1983. Contbg. author: Physical Disabilities and Health Impairments. Contbr. chpts. to med. books, articles to med. jours. Inventor pediatric nasopharyngeal electrode. Trustee Epilepsy Found.; bd. dirs. Speech and Hearing Clinic; founder, bd. dirs. Northeast Fla. League Against Reye's Syndrome; founder, bd. dirs. Jacksonville Parents Assn. Against Gilles de la Tourette Syndrome; mem. Jacksonville Police Council, 1981—; founder Jacksonville Alzheimer's Ctr.; profl. adviser Parents in Action Against Drugs and Substance Abuse, 1983—. Recipient citation Yearbook Neurology and Neurosurgery, 1977; named Outstanding Young Man of Yr., Bold City Jr. C. of C., 1980. Mem. Am. Acad. Neurology, Eastern Assn. EEG, Am. Med. Electroencephalographic Assn. (pres. elect 1983), Boston Soc. Psychiatry and Neurology, Jacksonville Assn. Children with Learning Disabilities (bd. advisers), Am. Epilepsy Soc., Duval County Med. Soc., (trustee) Child Neurology Soc. (mem. nat. com. med. ethics 84-85, advisor 1985-86, nat. adv. pediatric brain death 1985, mem. practice com. 1986), Fla. Soc. Neurology (sec. 1980, v.p. 1981, pres. 1983), Fla. Med. Assn. (del. 1983-84), Council Exceptional Children, Jacksonville C. of C. Club: Harvard (Jacksonville). Office: 836 Prudential Dr Suite 313 Jacksonville FL 32207

NEAS, JOHN THEODORE, petroleum company executive; b. Tulsa, May 1, 1940; s. George and Lillian J. (Kasper) N.; B.S., Okla. State U., 1967, M.S., 1968; m. Sally Jane McPherson, June 10, 1966; children—Stephen, Gregory, Matthew. With acctg. dept. Rockwell Internat., 1965; with controller's dept. Amoco Prodn. Co., 1966-67; mem. audit and tax staff Haskins & Sells, 1968-75; pres. Nat. Petroleum Sales, Inc., Tulsa, 1975—, Port City Bulk Terminals, Inc., Tulsa, 1976—; owner John Neas Tank Lines; asst. instr. U. Tulsa, 1974. C.P.A., Okla. Mem. Nat. Assn. Accountants (v.p. membership 1976-77), Am. Inst. C.P.A.'s, Okla. Soc. C.P.A.'s, Port of Catoosa C. of C. Republican. Lutheran. Clubs: Petroleum, Oil Marketers, Transportation (Tulsa); Propeller; Oaks Country, Golf of Okla., Oaks Country. Home: 2943 E 69th St Tulsa OK 74136 Office: 5401 S Harvard Suite 200 Tulsa OK 74135

NEAT, JAMES RODNEY, pharmacist; b. Liberty, Ky., Jan. 15, 1953; s. James Albert and Mildred (Rodgers) N.; m. Paula Rush, Aug. 19, 1978; 1 child, James (Jamie) Christopher. A.S., Jefferson Community Coll., 1973; B.A. in Biology, U. Louisville, 1975; B.S. in Pharmacy, Samford U., 1979. Pharmacist

Wesley Drug Store, Liberty, Ky., 1980-81; staff pharmacist Baptist Hosp. East, Louisville, 1981—. Asst. scoutmaster Boy Scouts Am., Liberty, 1979-81, unit commr., 1980-81, chpt. mem. Eagle Scouts Assn., 1973—. Recipient Eagle Scout award Boy Scouts Am., 1967, Order of Arrow award, 1968, God and Country award, 1968; Outstanding Young Men of Am. award U.S. Jaycees, 1983; Ky. Col. award, 1977. Mem. Ky. Pharmacist Assn., Ky. Soc. Hosp. Pharmacists, Jefferson County Acad. Pharmacists, Kappa Psi, Phi Kappa Tau. Republican. Mem. Christian Ch. Club: Cola Clan (chpt. historian 1983, v.p. 1986). Avocations: coins; pharmacy and coca-cola memorabilia; travel; basketball; softball. Home: 3527 Hanover Rd Louisville KY 40207 Office: Bapt Hosp E 4000 Kresge Way Louisville KY 40207

NEATHERY, ALICIA, artist; b. Bogota, Columbia, Nov. 22, 1915; d. Ramon and Isabel (Reyes) Serrano; came to U.S., 1935, naturalized, 1939; ed. Academia de Bellas Artes, Argentina, 1950-52, Corcoran Sch. Art, Academie de Beaux Arts, Meuron, Switzerland, 1962-64; m. Jack B. Neathery, Apr. 24, 1935; 1 dau., Elizabeth. Owner, dir. Art Sch. and Atelier, Washington, 1956-58; tchr. sculpture and ceramics, Potomac/Darnestown, Md., 1969-70; founder, dir., restorer Centro Internat. de Cultura y Arte Spain, 1972-74; commd. work in sculpture, ceramics, potter's wheel, portraiture, Houston, 1974—; one woman shows: Smithsonian Instn., Washington, 1955, Gallery Chatel, Washington, 1958, Jung Center, Houston, 1976; group shows include: (Mus. Natural History, Washington, 1955-56, Balt. Mus., 1960-61, Mus. Art, Neuchatel, Switzerland, 1963; represented in permanent collections: Smithsonian Instn., also pvt. collections; judge Internat. Biennial Exhibit Balt. Mus. Art, 1964, Am. Artists League, 1968. Club: Contemporary Art (Montgomery County, Tex.). Office: PO Box 553 Conroe TX 77301

NEAVES, C.L., gas company executive. Pres., chief operating officer Lone Star Gas Co. Office: 301 S Harwood St Dallas TX 75201*

NEBEL, REYNOLD, business executive; b. Perth Amboy, N.J., May 3, 1928; s. G.F. and Ruth (Pedersen) N.; m. Joan D. Smith, Apr. 18, 1951; children—Laur, Leslie, Reynold, Peter. B.S. in Math. and Physics, Rutgers U.; M.S. in Applied Sci, Harvard U. V.p., gen. mgr. Johns-Manville, Denver, 1951-77, Guardian Industries, 1977-79; chief exec. officer Ibstock-Johnson Marion Brick Subs., 1979-80; pres., chief exec. officer Kusan, Inc., Brentwood, Tenn., 1981—; sr. v.p., corp. exec. Bethlehem Steel Corp., 1985—. Mem. NAM (dir. 1982—), Am. Mgmt. Assn. Clubs: Belle Meade Country (Nashville); Cherry Hills Country (Englewood, Colo.). Office: Kusan Inc Seven Maryland Farms Brentwood TN 37027

NEBIL, CORINNE ELIZABETH, artist; b. Varmland, Sweden, Apr. 30, 1918; came to U.S., 1920, naturalized, 1942; d. Eric and Elisabet (Tillstrom) Erickson; student NAD, 1954, Traphagen Sch. Fashion, 1955-56, Art Students League, N.Y.C., 1949-52, Whitney Sch. Art, 1948, U. Bridgeport, 1955; m. Roland Nebil; 1 dau., Ninette. Co-owner The Little Gallery, Bridgeport, Conn., 1954-60; art dir. Kid Stuff mag., 1964; freelance fashion illustrator, 1966-81; one-woman shows: Westport Country Playhouse, 1955, Chappalier Gallery, N.Y.C., 1958, Radio City Music Hall, N.Y.C., 1955, others; group shows: Art-U.S.A., Madison Sq. Garden, N.Y.C., 1948, Pastel Soc. Am., N.Y.C., 1982, Smithsonian Instn., Washington, 1965, others; represented in numerous pvt. collections; instr. art Famous Artists Schs. Internat., Westport, Conn., 1975-76, Central Fla. Jr. Coll., 1981—, Silvermine Sch. Art, Norwalk, Conn., 1980, Bridgeport Art League and Conn. Classic Arts Workshop, 1981-82. Mem. Nat. League Am. Penwomen, Conn. Classic Arts, Pastel Soc. Am., Am. Portrait Soc. Designer, painter ceiling mural St. Joseph's Ch., Bridgeport, Conn., 1958. Home: 853 NE 10th Ave Ocala FL 32670

NECESSARY, GWENDOLYN SMOOT, pharmacist; b. Man, W.Va., June 3, 1958; d. Ivory and Hazel M. (Gilliam) Smoot; m. Robert Clark Necessary, July 25, 1982. B.S., W.Va. U., 1980. Pharmacist, mgr. Rite Aid Pharmacy, Man, 1980—; relief pharmacist Adkins Pharmacy, Gilbert, W.Va., 1984—. Sec., v.p. Hemlock Hills Garden, Man, 1983—; historian Triadelphia Woman's Club, Man, 1983—. Mem. W.Va. Pharmacists Assn., Am. Pharm. Assn., W.Va. U. Alumni Assn., W. Va., Nat. assn. parliamentarians. Democrat. Methodist. Avocations: travel; cooking; playing piano; volunteer work. Home: PO Box 47 Lorado WV 25630 Office: Rite Aid Pharmacy PO Box 576 Mountain Mart Village Man WV 25635

NEDDERMAN, WENDELL HERMAN, college president; b. Lovilia, Iowa, Oct. 31, 1921; s. Walter Herman and Fern (Gray) N.; m. Betty Ann Vezey, Dec. 20, 1947; children—Howard, John, Jeff, Eric. B.S., Iowa State Coll., 1943; M. Engring., Tex. A&M U., 1949; Ph.D., Iowa State U., 1951. Registered profl. engr., La., Tex. Instr. civil engring. Tex. A&M U., 1947-49, asst. prof., 1951-52, asso. prof., 1952-57, prof., 1957-59; dean engring. U. Tex.-Arlington, 1959-69, prof. civil engring., v.p. acad. affairs, 1968-72, pres., 1972—; pres. N. Tex. Higher Edn. Authority, 1978—; cons. structural engr. in coastal and offshore structures in petroleum industry; dir. Arlington Bank of Commerce, 1970-74. Mem. Arlington Pub. Sch. System Bd. Edn., 1970-72; bd. dirs. Arlington Meml. Hosp., Metro Tarrant County United Way, 1974—; gen. campaign chmn. Metro Tarrant County United Way, 1977, pres., 1978, chmn. bd., 1979. Served with AUS, 1943-46. Recipient Faculty Disting. Teaching award Tex. A&M U., 1959, Profl. Achievement citation Iowa State U., 1976; Silver Beaver award Boy Scouts Am., 1980. Mem. Arlington C. of C. (dir. 1972—), ASCE, Tex. Soc. Profl. Engrs., Sigma Xi, Phi Kappa Phi, Tau Beta Pi, Chi Epsilon. Republican. Home: 4165 Shady Valley Arlington TX 76013*

NEDELCOVYCH, SAVA MIODRAG, surgeon; b. Yugoslavia; came to U.S., 1962, naturalized, 1968; married. M.D., U. Belgrade, Yugoslavia, 1952; postgrad. Harvard Med. Sch., 1965. Lic. surgeon, Md., Va., Ohio, N.Y., Washington. Surg. resident Belgrade, Yugoslavia and Lausanne, Switzerland, 1952-54, 1954-57; pvt. physician to Emporor Haile Selassie, Addis Ababa, Ethiopia, 1954-57; dir., surgeon Imperial Palace Force Hosp., Addis Ababa, 1957-62; rotating intern Barberton Citizens Hosp., Ohio, 1962-63, resident in ob-gyn, 1963-65; surg. fellow, 1965; practice medicine specializing in surgery, Falls Church, Va., 1966—; staff surgeon Jefferson Meml. Hosp., Alexandria, Va., 1981—. Fellow Royal Soc. Health; mem. Internat. Coll. Surgeons, Gynecol. Soc. Breast Disease, Am. Soc. Abdominal Surgery, Assn. Am. Physicians and Surgeons, AMA, Med. Soc. Va., Fairfax County Med. Soc., Am. Assn. Fgn. Med. Grads., Internat. Club, Capitol Hill Club (Republican life). Home: 6204 Waterway Dr Falls Church VA 22044 Office: Jefferson Meml Hosp 4600 King St Alexandria VA 22302

NEEDHAM, THOMAS ARCHIE, JR., artist, corporation art director; b. Providence, Feb. 19, 1947; s. Thomas Archie and Margaret Jean (Yager) N. A.A., El Camino Coll., 1968; B.F.A., Art Ctr. Coll. of Design, 1972. Asst. art dir. Metro Media TV, Washington, 1974-75; art dir. Benchmark Advt., Herndon, Va., 1975-76, Systems Internat. div., Computer Scis. Corp., Herndon, Va., 1976—; pres. Southpaw Studios, Fairfax, 1982—. One-man shows, 1981, 83, 72, two-man exhbn., 1976; works appeared sports publs., exhbns., Nat. Mus. Sport; sports paintings displayed Pentagon, murals Mus. Sci. and Industry, Chgo.; rep. pub. and pvt. collections U.S. Served with U.S. Army, 1972-74. Recipient best of show watercolor awards Carson Art Assn. (Calif.), 1973, City of Manhattan Beach (Calif.), 1972; semi-finalist Am. Artist mag., 1978. Fellow Internat. Graphics Inc. (award of merit 1979, art and design chmn. 1978). Republican. Club: Washington Landscape (sec. 1978-83). Office: Systems Internat Div Computer Scis Corp 555 Herndon Pkwy Herndon VA

NEEDLE, SUSAN JUDITH, image consultant; b. Newark, June 18, 1941; d. Joseph J. and Betty (Levinson) N.; m. Robert J. Henderson. B.Ed., U. Miami (Fla.), 1962; M.A. in Human Resources and Psychology, U. Houston, 1980. Tchr. public schs., Fla., 1963-72, Houston, 1973-77; part-time profl. model, 1974-79; sales mgr. ADF Services, Houston, 1975-80; event mgr. Summit Arena, Houston, 1980-83; pres., chmn. bd. Colorific, Inc., Houston, 1976—, Can-Am Energy Corp., 1984—; corp. sec. Fin. Resources and Services Corp., N.J., 1983—; assoc. prof. Coll. of Mainland, Texas City, Tex., 1983—; beauty and fashion editor Clear Lake Voice, 1986—; guest lectr. cruise ships. Named Outstanding Educator in Fla., 1968. Mem. Nat. Assn. Female Execs. (dir.), Am. Bus. Women's Assn. (Woman of Yr. 1985-86), Internat. Platform Assn., Assn. Fashion and Image Cons. (Charter), Profl. Image Cons. Assn. (charter) Exec. Link, Am. Inst. Esthetics, Hotel Sales Mgmt. Assn., Performax, Alpha Epsilon Phi, Alpha Delta Kappa, Alpha Kappa Alpha. Democrat. Jewish. Address: 15302 Pleasant Valley Rd Houston TX 77062

NEEL, SAMUEL NICHOLAS, physician; b. Geiger, Ala., May 15, 1928; s. Malcolm Mooney and Martha Mae (Dillard) N.; m. Jacqueline Hunnicutt, June 7, 1952; children—Margaret, Samuel, Anthony, Patricia, Suzanne, James. B.S., U. Ga., 1952; M.D., Med. Coll. Ga., 1958; M.P.H., Tulane U., 1979. Commd. ensign U.S. Navy, advanced through grades to comdr.; intern Naval Hosp., Jacksonville, Fla., 1958-59; resident in ob-gyn Naval Hosp., San Diego, 1962-65; flight surgeon Helicopter Antisubmarine Squadron 2, San Diego, 1960-61, Air Group 57, 1961-62; chief dependents service Naval Hosp., Key West, Fla., 1965-70; chief obstetrics Naval Hosp., Beaufort, S.C., 1970-71; assigned Marine Corps Command and Staff Coll., Quantico, Va., 1971-72; ednl. officer Naval Hosp., Quantico, 1972-73; force surgeon Fleet Marine Force, Atlantic, Norfolk, Va., 1973-75; flight surgeon and staff med. officer for Chief of Naval Res. Naval Air Station New Orleans, 1975-78, ret., 1978; med. dir. family planning program Office of Health Services and Environ. Quality, Dept. Health and Human Resources, New Orleans, 1979-80, dir. div. local health services, 1980-85. Mem. La. Pub. Health Assn. (pres. 1983-84), Am. Coll. Preventive Medicine, Am. Acad. Med. Dirs., Am. Pub. Health Assn., Am. Assn. Pub. Health Physicians, Assn. Mil. Surgeons U.S., World Med. Assn., Blue Key, Delta Omega. Clubs: New Orleans Roundtable, Model A Ford of Am. Lodges: Masons, Shriners.

NEELY, CHARLES LEA, JR., physician, educator; b. Memphis, Aug. 3, 1927; s. Charles Lea and Ruby Perry (Mayes) N.; m. Mary Louise Buckingham, Mar. 30, 1957; children—Louise Mayes, Charles Buckingham. B.A., Princeton U., 1950; M.D., Washington, U., St. Louis, 1954. Intern, Cornell Med. Service, Bellevue Hosp., N.Y.C., 1954-55; resident in medicine Barnes Hosp., St. Louis, 1955-57; fellow in medicine and hematology Washington U. Sch. Medicine, St. Louis, 1957-58; chief div. med. oncology U. Tenn. Ctr. for Health Scis., Memphis, 1973-79, chief div. hematology, oncology, 1979-84, prof. pathology, 1977—, prof. medicine, hematology, 1971—; acting dir. Memphis Regional Cancer Ctr., 1979-84, U. Tenn. Cancer Program, Memphis, 1979-84; dir. U. Tenn. Cancer Clinic, Memphis, 1979—; practice medicine specializing in oncology and hematology, Memphis, 1958—; mem. staff U. Tenn. Hosp., Regional Med. Ctr.; cons. staff Bapt. Meml. Hosp., Meth. Hosp., St. Joseph Hosp., VA Hosp., all Memphis; prin. investigator Southeastern Cancer Study Group, U. Tenn. Ctr. Health Scis., 1977-84; dir. Hematology Spl. Function Lab., 1979-84; dir. B'nai B'rith Lab., Memphis, 1976-86; mem. profl. edn. com. Am. Cancer Soc., Memphis and Shelby County Unit, 1979—; chmn. patient qualification rev. bd. State of Tenn., 1981-84. Contbr. articles to profl. jours. Served with USNR, 1945-47. Fellow ACP; mem. Am. Soc. Clin. Oncology, Am. Fedn. Clin. Research, Am. Soc. Hematology, Internat. Soc. Hematology, Memphis Acad. Internal Medicine, Memphis Med. Assn., Shelby County Med. Assn., Tenn. Med. Assn., Alpha Omega Alpha, Sigma Xi. Clubs: Memphis Country; Princeton (N.Y.C.); Hatchie Coon Hunting and Fishing (Tulot, Ark.). Home: 440 Goodwyn St Memphis TN 38111 Office: 3 N Dunlap St Room N202 Memphis TN 38163

NEELY, PAUL, newspaper editor; b. San Francisco, July 30, 1946; s. Ralph and Virginia (Gaylord) N.; m. Linda Borsch, Oct. 6, 1977; children—David King, Michael Paul. B.A., Williams Coll., 1968; M.S. in Journalism, Columbia U., 1970, M.B.A., 1970. Reporter, editorial writer Press Enterprise, Riverside, Calif., 1970-73; copy editor, asst. mng. editor Courier Jour., Louisville, 1973-79; news features editor St. Petersburg Times (Fla.), 1980-83; mng. editor Chattanooga Times, 1983—. Mem. Am. Assn. Sunday and Feature Editors (pres. 1981-82), AP Mng. Editors, Am. Soc. Newspaper Editors, Sigma Delta Chi. Home: 111 Augusta Dr Lookout Mountain TN 37350 Office: Chattanooga Times 117 E 10th St Chattanooga TN 37402

NEELY, RICHARD, state supreme court justice; b. Aug. 2, 1941; s. John Champ and Elinore (Forlani) N.; A.B., Dartmouth, 1964; LL.B., Yale, 1967; m. Carolyn Elmore; 1 son, John Champ II. Admitted to W.Va. bar, 1967; practiced in Fairmont, W.Va., 1969-73; chmn. Marion County Bd. Pub. Health, 1971-72; mem. W.Va. Ho. of Dels., 1971-72; justice W.Va. Supreme Ct. of Appeals, Charleston, 1973—, chief justice, 1980; prof. econs. U. Charleston; Frederick William Atherton lectr. Harvard U., 1982-83; chmn. bd. Kane & Keyser Co., Belington, W.Va. Served from 1st lt. to capt., U.S. Army, 1967-69. Decorated Bronze Star medal, Vietnam Honor medal 1st Class. Mem. W.Va. Bar Assn., Am. Econ. Assn., V.F.W., Am. Legion, Phi Delta Phi, Phi Sigma Kappa. Episcopalian. Moose. Author: How Courts Govern America, 1981; Why Courts Don't Work, 1983. Home: Pinelea Country Club Rd Fairmont WV 26554 Office: E-306 State Capitol Bldg Supreme Ct of Appeals Charleston WV 25305

NEELY, ROBERT ALLEN, physician; b. Temple, Tex., Mar. 1, 1921; s. Jubal A. and Almeida (Fordtran) N.; B.A., U. Tex., 1942, M.D., 1944; postgrad. Washington U., 1951-52; m. Eleanor V. Stein, June 29, 1944; children—Byron D., Warren F. Intern, also resident Hermann Hosp., Houston, 1944-45, 55-57; gen. practice medicine, 1946-51, specializing in ophthalmology, Bellville, Tex., 1955—; trustee, staff mem. Bellville Hosp., Inc.; dir. 1st Nat. Bank of Bellville. Mem. Bellville Ind. Sch. Dist. Sch. Bd., 1948-53; past pres. Bellville Area United Fund; adv. bd. mem. Sam Houston Area council Boy Scouts Am., past mem. nat. council; mem. chancellor's Council U. Tex. System. Served with USNR, 1943-46, 53-55. Recipient Silver Beaver award Boy Scouts Am. Fellow Am. Acad. Ophthalmology; mem. AMA, Austin-Grimes-Waller Counties (past pres.), Ninth Dist. (past pres.) med. soc., Tex. Med. Assn., Tex. Ophthal. Assn., Houston Ophthal. Soc., Tex. Soc. Opthalmology and Otolaryngology, Bellville C. of C., VFW (life). Republican. Lutheran. Clubs: Bellville Golf (past pres.), Champions Golf, Doctors, Lions (past pres.). Home: 105 E Hacienda Ln Bellville TX 77418 Office: Bellville Clinic Bldg Bellville TX 77418

NEESE, C. G., judge; b. Paris, Tenn., Oct. 3, 1916; s. Charles Gentry and Sarah Anna (Nunn) N.; student U. Tenn., 1936; LL.B., Cumberland U., 1937; m. Althea Debord; children—Charles Gelbert III, Gerry Jan. Admitted to Tenn. bar, 1938, practiced in Paris and Nashville, 1938-61; exec. asst. to gov. Tenn., 1944; adminstrv. asst. to Senator Kefauver, 1949-51; U.S. dist. judge Eastern Dist. Tenn., 1961-82, sr. judge, 1982—. Past sec., gen. counsel Capitol Life Ins. Co. Tenn. Dir. primary campaigns Senator Kefauver, 1948, 54. A founder, original trustee, 1st pres. Family Clinic, Nashville; former trustee Tusculum Coll. Mem. Fed. Bar Assn., Phi Delta Phi. Democrat. Mason. Home: 6666 (501) Brookmont Terr Nashville TN 37205 Office: A-820 US Courthouse Nashville TN 37203

NEFF, EDWIN FARNSWORTH, educational administrator, government official; b. Vandergrift, Pa., Jan. 27, 1939; s. Fred Farnsworth and Muriel Adelaid (Males) N.; m. Sue Elaine Young, Jan. 22, 1960; children—Kimberly Sue, Beth Anne. B.S., Indiana U. (Pa.), 1960; M.Ed., Coll. William and Mary, 1969, advanced grad. cert., 1971. Instr., Quartermaster Sch., U.S. Army, Fort Lee, Va., 1960-63, instr., course dir., program mgr. intern tng. Army Logistics Mgmt. Ctr., 1963-72, dir. spl. tng. Def. Civil Preparedness Agy. Statt Coll., Battle Creek, Mich., 1972-75, dir. continuing edn. U.S. Army, Europe, 1979-82, dep. dir. edn. U.S. Army Hdqrs., Alexandria, Va., 1982-84; Army edn. advisor, 1984-85; dep. dir. tng. and edn. logistics ctr., 1985—. asst. chief tng. and edn. Hdqrs. U.S. Coast Guard, Washington, 1975-79. Served with U.S. Army, 1960-62. Decorated Army Commendation medal. Mem. Am. Soc. Tng. and Devel., Mil. Testing Assn., Res. Officers Assn., Assn. U.S. Army, Kappa Delta Pi. Mem. United Ch. Christ. Lodge: Odd Fellows. Home: 908 Germar Ct Colonial Heights VA 23834 Office: US Army Logistics Ctr Fort Lee VA 23801-6000

NEGRON, NAYDA MILAGROS, psychologist; b. Ponce, P.R., July 24, 1952; s. Bernardo Negron and Rafaela Montalvo de Negron. M.A. with distinction, Caribbean Ctr. Grad. Studies, Carolina, P.R., 1975, Ph.D., 1981. Intern, Boston City Hosp., 1977-79; prof. Cath. U. P.R., Ponce, 1975-76; mental health cons. Project Headstart, Boston, 1979, Veterans Ctr., Boston, 1980-81; staff psychologist Whittier St. Health Ctr., Roxbury, Mass., 1980-81, 82-83; clin. dir. Concilio Human Services, Boston, 1980-81; staff psychologist Mass. Correctional Insts., Goldberg Med. Assocs., Boston, 1982-83, unit coordinator, 1983-84; unit dir., 1984. Editor (videotape) Alcoholism and Drug Abuse in the Latin Women, 1983. Mem. Am. Psychol. Assn., P.R. Psychol. Assn., Mujeres Unidas en la Jornada de Educacion y Rehabilitacion. Roman Catholic. Avocation: stamp collecting. Home: Munoz Rivera 29 Villalba PR 00766

NEHER, DAVID DANIEL, soil scientist, educator; b. McCune, Kans., July 12, 1923; s. Eli Edwin and Myra Sybil (Lange) N.; m. Joyce Patricia Adams, July 23, 1950; children—Prudence, George, Edwin. B.S., Kans. State U., 1946, M.S., 1948; Ph.D., Utah State U., 1959. Cert. profl. soil scientist. Instr. soils Kans. State U., Manhattan, 1948-49; asst. prof. soils Tex. A&I U., Kingsville, 1949-59, assoc. prof., 1959-65, prof. soils, 1965—, acting dean Coll. Agr. and Home Econs., 1984—. Author: Laboratory Manual for Principles of Soil Science, 1982. Recipient Tchr. of Yr. award Tex. A&I U. Coll. Agr., 1982, Dist. Teaching award Tex. A&I U. and Alumni Assn., 1982; Minnie Steven Piper Prof. award, 1985. Mem. Soil Sci. Soc. Am., Crop Sci. Soc. Am., Am. Soc. Agronomy, Soil Conservation Soc. Am. Club: Noon Lions (past pres.) (Kingsville). Avocations: fishing, gardening, woodwork. Home: 526 West Ave A Kingsville TX 78363 Office: Coll Agr and Home Econs Tex A&I U West Santa Gertrudes Kingsville TX 78363

NEIGHBORS, RONALD JOE, municipal manager; b. Hominy, Okla., Jan. 4, 1937; s. Joseph Andrew and Ruth Mae (Jordan) N.; student Hardin-Simmons U., 1954-55; B.B.A., Tex. Tech. U., 1958; m. Glenda Cherie Smith, May 18, 1972; children from previous marriage—Norman Bradley, Bryan Devin, Brooks Daron; stepchildren—Krista d'Ann, Mindy Gay. Budget officer City of Lubbock, Tex., 1956-58; asst. city mgr. Snyder, Tex., 1958-60; dir. of finance City of Arlington, Tex., 1960-63; asst. city mgr. Wichita Falls, Tex., 1963-66; city mgr. Carrollton, Tex., 1966-68, Odessa, Tex., 1968-77; gen. mgr. Harris-Galveston Coastal Subsidence Dist., 1977—. Bd. dirs. Odessa United Fund, 1968-74, v.p., 1975-77. Mem. Odessa C. of C. (dir. 1968-77), Tex., West Tex. (pres. 1972), Internat. city mgmt. assns, Tex. Indsl. Devel. Council, Texas City Mgmt. Assn., Groundwater Dists. Mgmt. Assn. (dir., v.p. 1978, pres. 1979), Tex. Water Conservation Assn. (dir. 1979—, pres.-elect 1983, pres. 1984). Baptist (deacon 1968-71). Club: Space Center Rotary. Home: 1314 Crawford Friendswood TX 77546 Office: 1660 W Bay Area Blvd Friendswood TX 77546

NEILD, WILLIAM, mayor. Mayor City of Beaumont, Tex. Office: PO Box 3827 Beaumont TX 77704*

NEILL, ROLFE, newspaperman; b. Mount Airy, N.C., Dec. 4, 1932; s. Kenneth A. and Carmen (Goforth) N.; A.B. in History, U. N.C., 1954; m. Rosemary Clifford Boney, July 20, 1952 (div. 1982); children—Clifford Randolph, Sabrina Ashley, Dana Catlin, Jessica Rosemary Ingrid, Quentin Roark Robinson. Reporter, Franklin (N.C.) Press, 1956-57; reporter Charlotte (N.C.) Observer, 1957-58, bus. editor, 1958-61; editor, pub. Coral Gables (Fla.) Times and The Guide, 1961-63, Miami Beach (Fla.) Daily Sun, 1963-65; asst. to pub. N.Y. Daily News, 1965-67, suburban editor, 1967-68, asst. mng. editor, 1968-70; editor Phila. Daily News, 1970-75; v.p., dir. Phila. Newspapers Inc., 1970-75; chmn., pub. Charlotte (N.C.) Observer, 1975—. Served with AUS, 1954-56. Home: Box 32188 Charlotte NC 28232

NELLI, ELIZABETH ROLFE, educational administrator; b. Toronto, Ont., Can., Feb. 14, 1935; came to U.S., 1956; d. George Millar and Anne Noela (Seaborne) Thomson; B.A., U. Chgo., 1959; M.A., U. Ky., 1974, Ed.D., 1980; m. Bert S. Nelli, Dec. 28, 1961; children—Steven, Christopher, William. Elem. sch. tchr., Toronto, 1955-56, Chgo., 1956-59, Vancouver, B.C., Can., 1959-61; nursery sch. tchr. U. Chgo., 1964-65; kindergarten tchr. Inner City Vol. Programs, Lexington, Ky., 1969-72; research asst./assoc. U. Ky., Lexington, 1974-79, asst. to dean, 1979-80, asst. dean Coll. Edn., 1980-84; with Ky. Dept. Edn., 1984—; Nat. Assn. Edn. Young Children, Am. Assn. Colls. Tchr. Edn. (instl. rep. 1979—), Bluegrass Assn. Children under Six, Ky. Citizens for Child Devel., Women's Neighborly Orgn., Phi Delta Kappa. Author: (with G. Denemark) Emerging Patterns of Initial Preparation for Teachers Generic Teaching, 1980; Program Redesign in Teacher Preparation, 1981; Five Myths in Need of Reality, 1982; A Research-Based Response to Changes that Teacher Education Students are Inferior, 1984, and other works. Office: Div Tchr Edn and Art 1823 Capital Plaza Tower Frankfort KY 40601

NELSEN, HART MICHAEL, sociologist, educator; b. Pipestone, Minn., Aug. 3, 1938; s. Noah I. and Nova (Ziegler) N.; m. Anne Kusener, June 13, 1964; 1 dau., Jennifer. B.A., U. No. Iowa, 1959, M.A., 1963; M.Div., Princeton Theol. Sem., 1963; Ph.D. (NSF faculty fellow), Vanderbilt U., 1972. Asst. prof. sociology Western Ky. U., Bowling Green, 1965-70, assoc. prof., 1970-73; assoc. prof. Catholic U. Am., 1973-74, prof., 1974-81, chmn. dpet. sociology, 1974-77, mem. Boys Town Ct. for Study Youth Devel., 1974-81; prof., chmn. dept. sociology, head dept. rural sociology La. State U., Baton Rouge, 1981—; cons. Alban Inst., Washington, 1979-81. Co-rec. sec. Capitol Hill Restoration Soc., 1979-80, v.p., 1980-81. Presbyn. Chs. grantee, 1966-69; NIMH co-grantee, 1969-72; Russell Sage Found. co-grantee, 1972-73. Mem. Assn. Sociology Religion (exec. council 1974-76, 78—, v.p. 1978-79, pres. 1980-81), Religious Research Assn. (dir. 1978), Soc. Sci. Study Religion (council 1981-84, exec. sec. 1984—), Am. Sociol. Assn., So. Sociol. Soc., Brit. Sociol. Assn. Presbyterian. Author: (with Anne K. Nelsen) Black Church in the Sixites, 1975; contbr. articles to profl. jours.; editor: (with others) The Black Church in America, 1971; adv. editor Sociol. Quar., 1976-81; assoc. editor Sociol. Analysis, 1977-80; assoc. editor Rev. Religious Research, 1977-80, editor, 1980—. Office: Dept Sociology La State Univ Baton Rouge LA 70803

NELSON, ANTHONY RAY, medical group administrator; b. Hartselle, Ala., Apr. 20, 1948; s. Buron Ray and Hilda (Powell) N.; 1 son, Jeremy Ray. B.S. in Bus. Adminstrn., Athens Coll., 1970; M.B.A., Samford U., 1976. Merchandise mgr. W.T. Grant Co., Birmingham, 1970-72; asst. dir. Univ. Hosp., Birmingham, 1972-78; bus. mgr. Jefferson County Dept. Health, Birmingham, 1978-81, Radiology Assocs. Birmingham, 1981—. Mem. Med. Group Mgmt. Assn., Radiologists Bus. Mgrs. Assn. Home: 1200 W Ridge Ln Birmingham AL 35235 Office: Radiology Assocs of Birmingham PC 1920 Huntington Rd Birmingham AL 35209

NELSON, BILL, congressman; b. Miami, Fla., Sept. 29, 1942; B.A., Yale U., 1965; J.D., U. Va., 1968; m. Grace H. Cavert, 1972; children—C. William, Nan Ellen. Admitted to Fla. bar, 1968; practiced law; mem. Fla. Ho. of Reps., 1972-78; mem. 96th and 97th Congresses from 9th Dist. Fla.; mem. 98th-99th Congresses from 11th Dist., chmn. space subcom.; vol. asst. to gov. Fla., 1971. Served to capt. U.S. Army, 1968-70. Named One of 5 Outstanding Young Men in Fla., 1975, Fla. Democrat of 1975. Mem. Fla. Bar Assn., D.C. Bar Assn. Democrat. Mem. Christian Ch. Crew Mem. Space Shuttle Columbia, Jan. 12-18, 1986. Office: Room 307 Cannon House Office Bldg Washington DC 20515

NELSON, DAVID ARTHUR, lawyer; b. Corpus Christi, Jan. 26, 1948; s. Arthur Emanuel and Bert Mae (Dunlap) N.; B.A., Baylor U., 1969; M.Computing Scis., Tex. A&M U., 1970; J.D., Baylor U., 1978; m. Joy Elaine Edwards, Apr. 12, 1969; children—Carol Christine, Harlan Claire. Systems engr. Omnis Corp., Dallas, 1971-72; data processing mgr. Republic Nat. Bank Dallas, 1972-76, trust officer, 1978-79, v.p. corp. banking, 1979-83; v.p., corp. counsel Richardson Energy Corp., 1983-84. Asst. dist. commr. Boy Scouts Am., 1981-83, asst. scoutmaster, 1978-81; Long House officer YMCA, 1981; major chmn. The 500, Inc., 1981; deacon Park Cities Bapt. Ch.; dist. chmn. Baptist In-Reach, Bapt. Assn. for Scouting, 1981; mem. Leadership Dallas, 1982-83, STEP, 1983-84; bd. dirs. Girls Club of Dallas, 1984—. Leon Jaworski scholar, 1977. Mem. Tex. Bar Assn., Dallas Bar Assn., Dallas Mus. Fine Arts, Dallas Heritage Soc., Phi Delta Phi (Grad. of Yr. 1978). Club: Rotary (officer). Home: 3424 Princeton St Dallas TX 75205

NELSON, EILEEN SCHMITT, psychology educator, counselor; b. New Haven, Dec. 10, 1933; d. Edward John and Lydia (Petocchi) Schmitt; m. William Richard Nelson, May 8, 1976; children—R. Ryan, Pamela S., Edward R. Farnen. A.B., Syracuse U., 1960; M.A., George Peabody Coll., 1970; Ed.D., U. Va., 1980. Spl. edn. tchr. Kennedy Ctr., Nashville, 1969-70; devel. specialist Vanderbilt U. Hosp., Nashville, 1970-72; instr. James Madison U., Harrisonburg, Va., 1973-80, asst. prof., 1980-85, assoc. prof. psychology, 1985—; counselor in pvt. practice, Harrisonburg, 1976—. Contbr. articles to profl. jours. Mem. Am. Assn. Counseling and Devel., Assn. Counselor Edn. and Supervision, Va. Counselors Assn., So. Assn. Counselor Edn. and Supervision. Avocations: travel; poetry writing. Home: 1217 Windsor Rd Harrisonburg VA 22801 Office: James Madison U Dept Psychology Harrisonburg VA 22807

NELSON, JAMES ALBERT, librarian, state official; b. Grand Junction, Colo., June 13, 1941; s. Gerhardt Melvin and Lettie Louise (Sanders) N.; m. Judith Ann Brown, Sept. 5, 1965 (div. July 1972); children—Colm Corbett, Rebekah Sanders; m. Carol Stern, Aug. 8, 1982; 1 son, Michael Leland. B.A. in English, U. Colo., 1965; M.S. in L.S., U. Ky., 1969. Head librarian Hardin County Pub. Library, Elizabethtown, Ky., 1969-70; dir. interlibrary coop. Ky. Dept. Libraries and Archives, Frankfort, 1970-72, state librarian, commr., 1980—; speech writer Gov. Ky., Frankfort, 1972-73; dir. continuing edn. Coll. Library Sci. U. Ky., Lexington, 1973-77; asst. prof. library sci. U. Wis.-Madison, 1977-80; vol. U.S. Peace Corps, Bulan, Sorsogon, Philippines, 1965-66. Editor column, Jour. Edn. for Librarianship, 1976-79; contbr. articles to jours.

Pres. Increase Lapham Community Edn., Madison, 1979. Mem. Assn. Coop. and Specialized Library Assn., ALA (chmn. continuing edn. com. 1976-78, pres. elect 1983-84), Continuing Library Edn. Network and Exchange (pres. 1979-80), Beta Phi Mu (chpt. pres. 1969). Democrat. Home: 624 Alfa Dr Frankfort KY 40601 Office: KY Dept Libraries and Archives 300 Coffee Tree Rd Frankfort KY 40602

NELSON, JIMMIE JACK, engineer, former Air Force officer; b. McLoud, Okla., Feb. 1, 1928; s. Clifton Edward and Thyra Irene (Miller) N.; B.S. in Chem. Engring., U. Okla., 1949; B.S. in Aero. Engring., Air Force Inst. Tech., 1957, M.S. in Aero. Engring., 1962; m. Beth C. Carlsson, July 14, 1956; children—Paul C., Amy E. Commd. 2d lt. U.S. Air Force, 1949, advanced through grades to lt. col., 1971; sta. in Korea, 1953-54; with SAC, Biggs AFB, 1954-56, Air Force Inst. Tech., 1956-57, 60-62, 5th Air Force, Tokyo, 1957-60, Hdqrs. Systems Command, 1962-66, Pentagon, 1966-70, Da Nang, S. Vietnam, 1970-71; ret., 1971; engr. Fairfax County (Va.), 1972-79, developer, designer Air Monitoring Network, 1979; engr., mgr. research and devel. Am. Petroleum Inst., Washington, 1979-83, environ. cons., 1983—; staff engr. Eagle Tech., Inc., 1984—; cons. U.S. State Dept., 1973-74. Decorated D.F.C. Mem. AIAA, Am. Chem. Soc., Air Pollution Control Assn. Republican. Baptist. Club: Masons. Contbr. articles to profl. publs. Home: 4308 Adrienne Dr Alexandria VA 22309

NELSON, JOHN ROBERT, surgeon; b. Humbolt, Tenn., June 6, 1933; s. Thomas Hubert and Ina May (Hudson) N.; m. Janice Carole Lovelace, July 13, 1958; children—Sharon Elizabeth, John Craig, David Brian, Leigh Anne, Catherine Lovelace. M.D., U. Tenn., 1956. Diplomate Am. Bd. Surgery. Straight intern in surgery Grady Meml. Hosp., Atlanta, 1956-58; gen. practice of medicine and surgery Jacksonville, Fla., 1960-66; resident in surgery Mayo Grad. Sch. Medicine, Rochester, Minn., 1966-70; practice medicine, specializing in gen. and oncologic surgery, Jacksonville, 1970—; active surg. staff St. Vincent's Med. Center, Jacksonville, 1970—, Riverside Hosp., Jacksonville, 1970—; vis., teaching surg. staff Univ. Hosp., Jacksonville, 1970—; courtesy staff Bapt. Med. Center, Jacksonville, 1970—, Meml. Hosp., Jacksonville, 1970—; mem. ad hoc com. for hospice unit Meth. Hosp., Jacksonville, 1979—. Chmn. smoking withdrawl clinic St. Vincent's Med. Center, Jacksonville, 1972-76; trustee Fla. Lung Assn., 1974-78; trustee Assn. of Community Cancer Centers, 1972, pres., 1978-79, laison to Nat. Cancer Adv. Bd., 1978—; trustee N.E. Fla. Cancer Program, Inc., 1978; organizer 1st Assn. of Community Cancer Centers Regional Southeastern Meeting on Hospice, Orlando, 1979; mem. Fla. Cancer Control and Research adv. bd., 1979—, chmn., mem. exec. com., 1985—. Served with USN, 1958-60. Fellow Am. Soc. Abdominal Surgeons; mem. Mayo Alumni Assn., Priestey Surg. Soc., Fla. Physicians Assn., Duval Med. Soc., Found. for Med. Care in Duval County (Ind.), Fla. Med. Assn., AMA, So. Med. Assn., Jacksonville Area C. of C. (com. of 100), Alpha Omega Alpha. Address: 2105 Riverside Ave Jacksonville FL 32204

NELSON, KAY LOUISE, financial analyst; b. Lafayette, La., Aug. 28, 1954; d. Joseph Madison and Peggy (McIntire) N. B.A., U. Del., 1976; M.B.A., Tulane U., 1978. Fin. analyst Trust Co. Ga., Atlanta, 1978-82, Howard Weil, New Orleans, 1982—. Mem. Fin. Analysts Soc. New Orleans. Republican. Roman Catholic. Avocations: tennis; sailing. Office: Howard Weil Inc Energy Centre Suite 900 New Orleans LA 70163

NELSON, KNOX, state senator. Mem. Ark. Senate, chmn. pub. health, welfare and labor com. and select com. on rules, resolutions and mems., 1981—, co-chmn. joint com. on energy, 1981—. Democrat. Office: Ark Senate State Capitol Little Rock AR 72201*

NELSON, LEONARD C., university president; b. Albia, Iowa, Aug. 26, 1920; s. John and Faye (Coulson) N.; m. Barbara L. Parcher, June 29, 1946; children—Randall, David, Laurel, Sheryl. B.S., Iowa State U., 1943; M.S., Mo. Sch. Mines and Metallurgy, 1949; Ph.D., Northwestern U., 1953. Registered mech. engr., W.Va. Project engr. Fisher Body div. Gen. Motors, 1945-47; asst. prof. Mo. Sch. Mines, 1947-50; assoc. prof. mech. engring. N.C. State Coll., 1954-56; dean engring. West Va. Inst. Tech., 1956-61, pres., 1961—; Mem. Montgomery Park Commn.; regional chmn. W.Va. Centennial Commn. Bd. dirs. W.Va. Boy Scouts Am., Urban Renewal Authority, Kanawha Valley Mining Inst. Served to lt. (s.g.) USNR, 1943-46. Mem. Montgomery C. of C. (bd. dirs.), W.Va. Council State Coll. and U. Presidents (pres.), W.Va. Assn. Coll. and U. Presidents (pres.), ASME, Am. Soc. Engring. Edn., Sigma Xi. *

NELSON, LEONARD JOHN, III, law educator; b. Spokane, Wash., July 31, 1949; s. Leonard John, Jr. and Lois Marian (McCuaig) N.; m. Janice Helen Linebarger, Aug. 15, 1970; children—Leonard John IV, Mary Beth, Monica Teresa. Student, Whitman Coll., 1967-68; B.A. magna cum laude, U. Wash., 1970; J.D. cum laude, Gonzaga U., 1974; LL.M., Yale U., 1984. Bar: Wash. 1974, Okla. 1979. Asst. prof. Gonzaga U. Law Sch., 1974; law clk. Wash. Supreme Ct., Olympia, 1975-76; ct. clk. Wash. Ct. Appeals, Spokane, 1976-78; from asst. to assoc. prof. O.W. Coburn Sch. Law, Tulsa, 1979-83; assoc. prof. Cumberland Sch. Law, Birmingham, Ala., 1984—. Contbg. editor: The Death Decision, 1984; contbr. articles to law revs. Reporter Wash. Pattern Jury Instrn. Com., Seattle, 1975-76; precinct coordinator Reagan for Pres., Tulsa, 1980; bd. dirs. Western Neighbors, Inc., 1981, Handicapped Opportunity Workshop, 1983; advisor, bd. dirs. Oklahomans for Life, 1982-83; mem. instl. rev. Oral Roberts U., 1982-83; pres. Sunny Meadows Neighborhood Assn., Birmingham, 1984; mem. institutional rev. bd. Samford U., 1985—. Named an Outstanding Young Man of Am., U.S. Jaycees, 1982; recipient Nat. Chmn.'s award Nat. Coll. Republican League, 1980. Mem. Am. Soc. Law and Medicine, Federalist Soc., Catholic League Religious and Civil Rights, Phi Beta Kappa. Roman Catholic. Home: 3140 Sunny Meadows Ln Birmingham AL 35243 Office: Cumberland Sch of Law 800 Lakeshore Dr Birmingham AL 35229

NELSON, LYLE ENGNAR, soil science educator; b. Donnybrook, N.D., Jan. 6, 1921; s. John Emanuel and Elsie Marie (Anderson) N. B.S., N.D. State U., 1948; M.S., Cornell U., 1950, Ph.D., 1952. Cert. profl. soil scientist. Soil scientist, Soil Conservation Service, U.S. Dept. Agr., Minot, N.D., 1948; asst. prof., asst. agronomist Miss. State U., 1952-55, assoc. prof. and agronomist, 1957-60, prof. and agronomist, 1960-86, prof. emeritus, 1986—; vis. assoc. prof. U. Philippines, Los Banos, 1955-57; vis. prof. N.C. State U., 1965; vol. worker Rothamsted Exptl. Sta., Harpenden, Eng., 1971-72; vis. scientist Internat. Rice Research Inst., Los Banos, 1979. Served with U.S. Army, 1942-45. Named Alpha Zeta Agr. Prof. of Yr., 1970; recipient Miss. State U. Alumni Assn. Faculty Achievement award for teaching-research, 1973, award for Outstanding Accomplishments in Soil and Water Conservation, Internat. Paper Co., 1980, Agronomy Dept. Grad. Student Citation for Outstanding Guidance Miss. State U., 1982. Fellow AAAS; mem. Am. Soc. Agronomy, Soil Sci. Soc. Am., Internat. Soil Sci. Soc., Am. Inst. Biol. Sci., Soil Conservation Soc. Am., Alpha Gamma Rho. Republican. Methodist. Contbr. chpts. to books, papers to profl. jours. and sci. confs. Home: 213 N Montgomery Starkville MS 39759 Office: Agronomy Dept Box 5248 Miss State U Mississippi State MS 39762

NELSON, PHYLLIS JANE, sales representative; b. Johnson City, Tenn., May 20, 1952; d. Ivan Jerome and Vivian Margarette (Houser) Dempsey; 1 child, Ronald Samuel. Student East Tenn. State U.; Cert. in Acctg., Kraft Comprehensive Sales Tng. Program, 1984. Acct. J.C. Housing Authority, Johnson City, Tenn., 1972-77; sales rep. Kraft, Inc., Knoxville, Tenn., 1984—. Recipient Top Sales award Knoxville Market, 1984-85, Vice Presdl. Sales award Kraft, Inc., 1985, Advt.-Merchandising award Knoxville Market, 1984, 85. Club: Jr. Monday. Avocations: tennis; house minatures. Home: 1607 Idlewilde Dr Johnson City TN 37601 Office: Kraft Inc PO Box 10788 W Knoxville Sta Knoxville TN 37919

NELSON, RALPH ERWIN, landscape architect; b. Chgo., July 30, 1946; s. Vernon Leslie and Astrid Lorraine (Seagren) N.; B.S., McPherson Coll., 1971; M.B.A., U. Sarasota, 1980, M.F.M., 1981, M.H.S., 1983; Ph.D., Columbia Pacific U., 1984; m. Elarie Marie Fletcher, Oct. 14, 1967; 1 dau., Anne Marie. Chief planning dept. Roberts & Zoller Inc., Bradenton, Fla., 1971-76; v.p., supr. planning div. Dan Zoller Engring. Inc., Bradenton, 1976-78; pres. Nelson, Hall & Assocs., Landscape Architects, Planners, and Engrs., Inc., Bradenton, 1978—. Mem. Fla. Planning and Zoning Assn., Am. Soc. Cert. Engring. Technicians, Am. Soc. Landscape Architects, Am. Forestry Assn. Republican. Baptist. Home: PO Box 11255 Bradenton FL 34282 Office: PO Box 11255 4630 5th St W Bradenton FL 34282

NELSON, RALPH LOUIS, petroleum geologist, consultant; b. Belton, Tex., Nov. 1, 1952; s. Robert Richard and Mary Frances (Shell) N.; m. Dale Kay Kimble, Aug. 2, 1975; children—Stephanie, Scott, Robert. B.S. in Geology, U. Tex.-Arlington, 1975, M.S. in Geology, 1978. Cert. petroleum geologist. Geologist Sun Oil Co., Dallas, 1975-80, Julian Ard Co., Fort Worth, 1980-81, Quanah Petroleum, Dallas, 1981-82, geologist, 1982-83, exploration mgr., Dallas, 1983—; cons. Petrostar Energy, Dallas, 1984—, Lyco Energy, Dallas, 1984—, Stroube Energy, Dallas, 1983—. Mem. Am. Assn. Petroleum Geologists, Dallas Geol. Soc., W. Tex. Geol. Soc. Republican. Methodist. Avocations: hunting, fishing. Office: Ralph L Nelson 16475 Dallas North Pkwy Suite 570 Dallas TX 75248

NELSON, RICHARD WALTER, sales executive; b. New Castle, Pa., July 19, 1949; s. V. Walter and Martha Helen (Kleimo) N.; m. Lynn Troian, Aug. 12, 1972; children—Jennifer Courtney, Richard Walter II. B.S., U. Central Fla., 1971. Territory rep. Burroughs Corp., Miami, 1972-73, comml. named account rep., 1973-74, fin. acct. mgr., 1974-78, zone mgr., 1978-81, br. mgr., 1981-83, dist. mgr., 1983—. Recipient Legion of Honor, Burroughs Corp., 1973, 75, 77, 78, 80, 81, Pres. Honor Roll., 1972, 73, 75, 76, 77. Republican. Lutheran. Home: 12350 SW 106th St Miami FL 33186 Office: Burroughs Corp 8600 NW 53d Terr Miami FL 33166

NELSON, ROBERT FORD, economic analyst; b. St. Clair, Mich., Aug. 16, 1946; s. Harry Jacob and Ruth Jenny (Middleton) N.; m. Carol Evelyn Corriere, June 20, 1970; children—Thomas Ford, Felicity Ruth, Harry Jacob II, Catherine Elizabeth, Nicholas Robert, George Joseph, Mary Grace, Blaise Corrriere. B.A. in Math., Mich. State U., 1970; M.S. in Elec. Engring., George Washington U., 1977. Inventor Trice V, Arlington, Va., 1972-73; logistics engr. Logistics Mgmt. Engring., Inc., Severna Park, Md., 1973-76; econ. analyst Ga. Power Co., Atlanta, Ga., 1977—. Contbr. article to profl. jour. Served with U.S. Army, 1970-72. Mem. IEEE, Woodworkers' Guild of Ga. Republican. Roman Catholic. Club: 1st Friday (Atlanta; past pres.). Developer of scenarios forecasting models used to forecast electrical sales. Home: 3348 E Hwy 5 Carrollton GA 30117 Office: 333 Piedmont Ave Atlanta GA 30308

NELSON, SHIRLEY ANGEL, college administrator; b. Jellico, Tenn., Feb. 26, 1949; d. Glenore Chester and Ruth (Perry) Angel; m. John Philip Nelson, May 26, 1974. B.A., Cumberland Coll., 1973; M.A., Eastern Ky. U., 1976; Ed.D., Vanderbilt U., 1985. Tchrs. aide Campbell County Bd. Edn., Newcomb, Tenn., summer 1971-72, reading tchr., 1973-74; instr. reading Cumberland Coll., Williamsburg, Ky., 1974-77, dir. learning skills ctr., 1977—. Andrew W. Mellon grantee, 1980-83. Mem. Nat. Assn. Remedial and Developmental Post-Secondary Educators, Coll. Reading Assn., Ky. Assn. Developmental Educators. Republican. Home: Box 7 Skylark Dr Corbin KY 40701 Office: Cumberland College Williamsburg KY 40769

NELSON, STUART OWEN, agricultural engineer, researcher, educator; b. Pilger, Nebr., Jan. 23, 1927; s. Irvin Andrew and Agnes Emilie (Nissen) N.; m. Carolyn Joye Fricke, Dec. 27, 1953 (dec. Nov. 1975); children—Richard Lynn, Jane Sue; m. 2d, Martha Ellen White Fuller, Apr. 8, 1979. B.S. in Agrl. Engring., U. Nebr., 1950, M.Sc. in Agrl. Engring., 1952, M.A. in Physics, 1954; Ph.D. in Engring., Iowa State U., 1972. Grad. asst. U. Nebr., Lincoln, 1952-54, research assoc., 1954-60, assoc. prof., 1960-72, prof., 1972-76; project leader Farm Electrification Research, Agrl. Research Service, U.S. Dept. Agr., Lincoln, 1954-59, research investigations leader, 1959-72, research leader, 1972-76, research agrl. engr. Russell Research Ctr., Athens, Ga., 1976—; adj. prof. U. Ga., 1976—; sci. adv. council Am. Seed Research Found.; mem. CAST Task Force on Irradiation for Food Preservation and Pest Control; adv. com. grain moisture measurement Nat. Council Weights and Measures. Served with USN, 1946-48. Recipient HM Crops and Soils award Am. Soc. Agronomy, 1966; recipient Founders Gold medal and named Fed. Engr. of Yr., Nat. Soc. Profl. Engrs., 1985; Superior Service award U.S. Dept. Agr., 1986. fellow Am. Soc. Agrl. Engrs. (sr., Tech. Paper award 1965); mem. IEEE (sr.), Internat. Microwave Power Inst. (Decade award 1981), AAAS, Orgn. Profl. Employees of Dept. of Agr. (pres. Athens area chpt. 1984-86), Sigma Xi, Sigma Tau, Gamma Sigma Delta, Tau Beta Pi. Methodist. Club: Athens Optimist (pres. 1980-81, lt. gov. Ga. dist. 1983-84, Optimist of Yr. award 1982, disting. and outstanding lt. gov. Ga. dist. 1985), Assoc. editor Jour. Microwave Power, 1975-76; contbr. numerous articles to sci. and tech. jours. Home: 270 Idylwood Dr Athens GA 30605 Office: Box 5677 Athens GA 30613

NELSON, SYDNEY B., lawyer, state senator; b. Mar. 12, 1935; B.B.A., U. Okla.; LL.B., La. State U.; m. Gail Anderson. Law clk. U.S. Dist. Ct., 1963-64; pvt. practice law, Shreveport, La., 1964—; Mem. La. Senate, 1980—. Mem. adminstrv. bd. 1st Methodist Ch., Shreveport; mem. exec. bd. Norwella council Boy Scouts Am.; bd. dirs. ARC. Served as officer USN, 1957-60. Mem. La. Bar Assn. Democrat. Office: 705 Milam St Shreveport LA 71101

NELSON, TED LONG, distributor; b. Independence, La., Jan. 22, 1927; s. Henry L. and Johnnie (Warren) N.; m. Lula Mae Robertson, Dec. 26, 1957 (div.); children—Cynthia Dianne, Pamela Sue, John Christian, Hyacinth Fern, Ted Barry. Student Southeastern La. U., 1947-49. Factory rep. Mac's Super Gloss Co., Inc., 1954-56; owner, operator Nelson Distbg. Co., Bunkie, La., 1957—. Developer, vol. distbr. cucuzzi seeds. Mem. La. Ho. Reps., 1956-60. Served with USN, 1943-45. Democrat. Baptist. Lodges: Masons, Lions. Office: Nelson Distbg Co 100 Walnut St Bunkie LA 71322

NELSON, WILLIAM JOSEPH, JR., neurosurgeon; b. Marfa, Tex., Oct. 4, 1928; s. William Joseph and Chelsea May (Vinyard) N.; m. Ellen Kate Cox, June 9, 1951; children—Mary Grace, Ellen Kate, Nancy Jane. B.A. in Biology, East Tex. State U., Commerce, 1948; M.D., U. Tex.-Galveston, 1953; M.S. in Neurophysiology, U. Louisville, 1951; postgrad. (fellow), U. London, 1966-67. Diplomate Am. Bd. Neurol. Surgery. Intern, Harris Hosp., Ft. Worth, Tex., 1953-54; resident U. Tex. Med. Br. Hosps., 1962-66; gen. practice medicine, Yuma, Ariz., 1957-62; practice medicine specializing in neurosurgery, El Paso, Tex., 1967—; pres. El Paso Neurol. Inst., 1972-84; assoc. clin. prof. Tex. Tech U., 1974—, assoc. chmn. med. and surg. neurology, 1985—. Served to lt. comdr. M.C., USN, 1955-57. Fellow ACS; mem. Am. Assn. Neurol. Surgeons, Tex. Assn. Neurol. Surgeons (pres. 1978-79), Rocky Mountain Neurosurg. Soc., Yuma County Med. Soc. (pres. 1960). Contbr. articles to profl. jours. Office: S 307 1810 Murchison St El Paso TX 79902

NELSON, WILLIAM NEAL, academic librarian, Latin American specialist; b. Bastrop, La., Dec. 26, 1941; s. Noble William and Nova Helen (Jenkins) N.; m. Julia Elizabeth Carden, Jan. 28, 1968; children—Beth Ann, Christopher William. B.A. in English, Centenary Coll., Shreveport, La., 1963, B.A. in History, 1964; M.A., La. State U.-Baton Rouge, 1973, M.L.S., 1974, Ph.D., 1981. Vol., U.S. Peace Corps, Caarapo, Brazil, 1964-66; library trainee La. State U., 1973-74; library dir. Mobile Coll. (Ala.), 1974-82; library dir. Carson-Newman Coll., Jefferson City, Tenn., 1982-85; Univ. librarian Samford U., Birmingham, Ala., 1985—. Author: Status and Prestige as a Factor in Brazilian Foreign Policy 1905-1908, 1981; contbr. articles to profl. jours. Deacon, So. Baptist Conv., 1973. Served to lt. U.S. Navy, 1966-71; comdr. USNR, 1983. Recipient Robertson/Farmer scholarship So. Bapt. Conv., 1978. Mem. ALA, Southeastern Library Assn., Tenn. Library Assn. (speaker 1984), Ala. Library Assn., Conf. Latin Am. History, South Eastern Council on Latin Am. Studies, Phi Alpha Theta, Beta Phi Mu. Independent. Office: Box 2210 Samford U Birmingham AL 35229

NELSON-HUMPHRIES, TESSA (UNTHANK), English language educator, writer, lecturer; b. Yorkshire, Eng.; came to U.S., 1955; m. Kenneth Nelson Brown, June 1, 1957 (dec. 1962); m. 2d, Cecil H. Unthank, Sept. 26, 1963 (dec. 1979). B.A., U. London, 1953; M.A., U. N.C., 1965; Ph.D. in English, U. Liverpool (Eng.), 1973. Head English dept. Richard Thomas Girls Sch., Elmore Green Sch., Walsall, England, 1956-58; dir. English studies Windsor Coll., Buenos Aires, Argentina, 1958-59; prof. English, Cumberland Coll., Williamsburg, Ky., 1964—. Best Actress award Carlsbad (N.Mex.) Little Theatre, 1962, Cumberland Coll., 1979; Fulbright fellow, 1955-56; Danforth fellow, 1971; James Still fellow, 1983; Mellon travel/study grantee, China, 1981. Fellow AAUW; mem. Soc. Women Writers and Journalists (Short Story prize 1975, Article prize, London, 1986. Julia Cairns Silver trophy for Poetry, 1978, article prize, London, 1986), Nat. Council Tchrs. English, Soc. Children's Book Writers, Vegetarian Soc. (life), Mensa. Episcopalian. Contbr. articles to Cats Mag., Let's Live, The Lookout, Child Life, Vegetarian Times, Alive!, The Dalesman, Mich. Quar. Rev., Bull. of Soc. Children's Book Writers, Bull. Soc. Women Writers and Journalists, others.

NEMEROFF, CHARLES BARNET, neurobiology and psychiatry educator; b. Bronx, N.Y., Sept. 7, 1949; s. Philip Peace and Sarah (Greenberg) N.; m. Melissa Ann Pilkington, May 24, 1980; 1 son, Matthew Pilkington. B.S., CCNY, 1970; M.S., Northeastern U., 1973; Ph.D., U. N.C., 1976, M.D., 1981. Lic. physician, N.C. Research asst. ichthyology Am. Mus. Natural History, N.Y.C., 1968-71, neurochemistry lab. McLean Hosp., Belmont, Mass., 1971-72; research assoc. surgery Beth Israel Hosp., Boston, 1972-73; teaching asst. biology Northeastern U., 1972-73; postdoctoral fellow Biol. Scis. Research Ctr., U. N.C., Chapel Hill, 1976-77, research fellow, 1977-83, clin. instr. psychiatry, 1983; resident in psychiatry N.C. Meml. Hosp., Chapel Hill, 1981-83; asst. prof. dept. psychiatry and pharmacology Duke U., Durham, N.C., 1983-85, assoc. prof. psychiatry, 1985—; vis. prof. physiology Cath. U., Santiago, Chile, 1978. Predoctoral fellow Schizophrenia Research Found., Soc. Scottish Rite, Lexington, Mass., 1975-76; postdoctoral fellow Nat. Inst. Neurol., Communicative Disorders and Stroke, 1977; recipient Michiko Kuno award U. N.C., 1978, 79; Merck award for acad. excellence, 1981; grantee Nat. Inst. Aging, 1982-83, NIMH, 1983—; Merck award for young investigators Am. Geriatrics Soc., 1985; Nanaline Duke fellow Duke U. Med. Ctr., 1985-87. Mem. Soc. Neurosci., AAAS, N.Y. Acad. Scis., Internat. Soc. Psychoneuroendocrinology (Curt P. Richter award 1985), Internat. Soc. Neurochemistry, Am. Soc. Neurochemistry, Endocrine Soc., Internat. Soc. Neuroendocrinology, Soc. Biol. Psychiatry (A.E. Bennett award 1979), Am. Fedn. Clin. Research, AMA, Am. Pain Soc., Am. Psychiat. Assn., N.C. Neuropsychiat. Assn., Am. Coll. Neuropsychopharmacology (Mead Johnson travel award 1982), Argentine Assn. Psychoneuroendocrinology (sci. council), Sigma Xi. Democrat. Jewish. Editor: (with A.J. Prange, Jr.) Neurotensin, a Brain and Gastrointestinal Peptide, 1982; (with A.J. Dunn) Peptides, Hormones and Behavior, 1984; contbr. numerous articles and abstracts to profl. jours., chpts. in books. Home: 101 Overland Passage Chapel Hill NC 27514 Office: Dept Psychiatry Duke U Med Center Box 3859 Durham NC 27710

NESBITT, LENORE CARRERO, U.S. district judge; b. 1932; m. Joseph Nesbitt; children—Sara, Thomas. A.A., Stephens Coll., 1952; B.S., Northwestern U., 1954; postgrad. U. Fla., 1954-55; LL.B., U. Miami, 1957. Bar: Fla. 1957. Research asst. Dist. Ct. Appeal 1st Dist., 1957-59; mem. Nesbitt & Nesbitt, 1960-63; spl. asst. to Fla. atty. gen., 1961-63; research asst. Dade County Circuit Ct., 1963-65; lawyer Office of John Robert Terry, 1969-73; counsel Fla. Bd. Med. Examiners, 1970-71; mem. Petersen McGowan & Feder, 1973-75; judge criminal div. Circuit Ct., 1975-80, gen. div., 1980-82; judge U.S. Dist. Ct. for So. Fla., Miami, 1983—. Mem. ABA, Fla. Bar Assn. Office: PO Box 010669 Flagler Sta Miami FL 33101*

NESBITT, MARGOT LORD (MRS. CHARLES R. NESBITT), fine arts appraiser; b. Tonbridge, Kent, Eng., Feb. 13, 1927; d. Douglas G.R. and Octave (Waghorne) Lord; came to U.S., 1930, naturalized, 1937; B.A. in English Lit., U. Okla., 1950, B.F.A. in Art History, 1970, M.A., 1975; m. Charles R. Nesbitt, June 6, 1948; children—Nancy Margot, Douglas Charles, Carolyn Jane. Appraiser fine arts, Oklahoma City, 1968—; treas. Apollo Oil Corp., 1974—. Mem. Okla. Arts and Humanities Council, 1971-76; mem. women's com. Oklahoma City Symphony, 1964—; life mem. Okla. Art Center, women's bd., 1962-63; chmn. art collection State of Okla., 1975-76; bd. dirs. Okla. Found. for Disabled, 1972-75; bd. advisers Nat. Trust Historic Preservation, 1976-81. Mem. English Speaking Union, Okla. Hist. Soc. (dir. 1975—), Hist. Preservation Oklahoma City (treas. 1977-80), Am. Soc. Appraisers (sr. mem.; pres. Okla. chpt. 1978-79), Appraisers' Assn. Am., Kappa Alpha Theta (pres. alumni chpt. 1962-64, Okla. chmn. Theta Link 1965-66, treas. corp. bd. 1976-77). Democrat. Episcopalian (treas. assemblies 1971-72, mem. women's bd. 1971-72, treas. altar guild 1972-73, treas. cathedral 1976-78, mem. vestry 1978-82, 84—, jr. warden 1978-82). Clubs: Connoisseur (pres. 1956-57); Early American Glass (treas. 1973-75). Address: 1703 N Hudson St Oklahoma City OK 73103

NESBITT, NANCY ANNE, utility company executive; b. Ft. Worth, Aug. 19, 1937; d. Charles Keith and Naomi Lucille (Robbins) N. Student North Tex. State U., 1954-57. With Gulf States Utility, Beaumont, Tex., 1957—, sect. head invoice processing and materials mgmt., 1979-81, supr. procurement control and materials mgmt., 1981-82, supr. purchasing services and materials mgmt., 1982—. Youth dir. Pine Burr Baptist Ch. Beaumont, 1969-72. Mem. Nat. Assn. Female Execs., Am. Mgmt. Assn., Research Inst. Am., Sabine Neches Purchasing Assn., R.R. Indsl. Clearance Assn., Beaumont C. of C. (transp. com. 1983), Bus. and Profl. Men's Club Beaumont, North Tex. State U. Alumni Assn., Beaumont Assn. Mental Health. Clubs: Emerald Century, Live Wires (Beaumont). Lodge: Order Eastern Star.

NESS, ALBERT KENNETH, artist; b. St. Ignace, Mich., June 21, 1903; s. Albert Klingberg and Violet Matilda (Sutherland); m. Lenore Consuelo Chrisman, Aug. 4, 1926; children—Peter, James Kenneth, Jane Lenore. Student U. Detroit, 1923-24, Detroit Sch. of Applied Art, 1924-26, Wicker Sch. of Fine Art, 1926-28; Diploma, Sch. of Art Inst., 1932. Show-card writer, window display man S.S. Kresge Co., Detroit, 1923-24; artist poster and advt. Cunningham Drugs, Detroit, 1924-26; artist layout lettering and design W.L. Flemming Studios, Detroit, 1926-28, McAleer Displays, Chgo., 1929-32; artist, design asst. Layman-Whitney Assocs., 1933 World's Fair, Chgo.; layout artist, poster designer Elevated Advt. Co., Chgo., 1934-37; instr., art dir. Sch. of Applied Art, Chgo., 1938-40; Carnegie resident artist U. N.C., Chapel Hill, 1941-43, dir. War Art Ctr., 1942-43, resident artist, assoc. prof. art, 1943-49, acting head, dept. art, acting dir. Person Hall Art Gallery, 1944-45, resident artist, prof. art, 1949-73, acting head dept. of art, acting dir. Person Hall Art Gallery, 1955, 57-58, resident artist, prof. emeritus, 1973—. One man shows include: Chester Johnson Galleries, Chgo., 1932, Evanston Art Ctr., Ill., 1940, Person Hall Art Gallery, 1941, N.C. Art Soc. Gallery, Raleigh, 1942, Duke U. Art Gallery, Durham, N.C., 1955, Louisburg Coll. Gallery, N.C., 1964, Ackland Art Mus., U.N.C. Chapel Hill, 1973; Internat. Water Color Exhbn. Chgo. Art Inst., 1934-39; Golden Gate Internat. Exposition, San Francisco, 1939, exhibited in group shows: Whitney Mus., N.Y.C., 1933, U. Chattanooga, Tenn., 1946, Centennial Exhbn. U. Fla., Gainesville, 1953, Jacksonville Art Mus, Fla., 1960; exhibited nationally Am. Artists' Anns., Chgo. Art Inst., 1935-37, Butler Art Inst., Youngstown, Ohio, 1951, Pa. Acad. Am. Annuals, Phila., 1953-54, others; works in pub. collections include: N.C. Mus., Raleigh, Ackland Art Mus., Reynolds Found., Winston Salem, Duke U. Art Mus., Durham. Contbr. to local and state newspapers. Editor, designer, photographer: A brochure on art study, 1964. Recipient Jenkins Meml. prize 38th Ann. Chgo. Artists' Exhbn., 1934, Purchase award N.C. Artists' Ann., Raleigh, 1953; 2-Star award Movie Maker Competition, London, 1970, N.C. award in Fine Arts, 1973, Purchase award Reynolds Competition, Winston Salem, 1977. Home: Farrington Mill Rd PO Box 14 Chapel Hill NC 27514

NESS, JULIUS B., state supreme court justice; b. Manning, S.C., Feb. 27, 1916; s. Morris P. and Raye (Levy) N.; m. Katherine Rhoad, Jan. 25, 1946; children—Gail Ness Richardson, Richard B. B.S., U. S.C., 1938, LL.B., 1940. Bar: S.C. 1940. Practice of law, Bamberg, S.C., 1940-58; judge S.C. Circuit Ct., 1958-74; assoc. justice S.C. Supreme Ct., 1974—; mem. S.C. State Senate, 1957-58; instr. Nat. Coll. State Judiciary, 1971; chmn. S.C. Jud. Continuing Legal Edn. Com., 1979—. Mem. S.C. Hwy. Commn., 1954-56, chmn., 1956. Served to capt. U.S. Army, 1941-45. Named S.C. Judge of Yr., Assn. Trial Lawyers Am. and S.C. Trail Lawyers Assn., 1973, 79. Mem. S.C. Bar Assn., ABA. Democrat. Office: County Courthouse Bamberg SC 29003

NETHERCUT, WILLIAM ROBERT, educator, baritone; b. Rockford, Ill., Jan. 11, 1936; s. Robert C. and Constance E. (Stanley) N.; A.B. magna cum laude, Harvard, 1958; M.A. (Henry Drisler fellow, Pres.'s fellow), Columbia U., 1961, Ph.D., 1963; student New Eng. Conservatory of Music, 1959-60; m. Jane Lillian Swann, July 27, 1977; children—William Andrew, Amanda Jane, Robert Christopher, Jason Scott. Instr. Greek and Latin, Columbia, 1961-66, asst. prof., 1966-67, Lawrence H. Chamberlain fellow, 1967; asso. prof. Classics U. Ga., Athens, 1967-72, prof., 1972-75; prof. Classics U. Tex., Austin, 1975—; vis. prof. Brigham Young U., 1986; lectr. NEH Seminar, 1986. Announcer radio sta. WROK, Rockford, 1957-58; soloist New Eng. Opera Theatre, Boston, 1958-59, debut as Figaro in Barber of Seville, 1958; soloist recital Carnegie Hall, N.Y.C., 1966; soloist Atlanta Opera Co., 1968; appearance ednl. program TV sta. WGTV, Athens, Ga., 1970-72. Lectr. 1st Internat. Conf. on Ovid, Constanta, Rumania, 1972, Internat. Soc. Homeric Studies, Athens, Greece, 1973, 74, 2d Internat. Congress Cypriot Studies, Nicosia, 1974, 3d Internat. Congress Southeast European Studies, Bucharest, 1974, Conf. on Ancient Novel, Bangor, Wales, 1976; vis. research fellow U. New Eng., Armidale, Australia, 1985. Am. Council Learned Socs. grantee, 1972; recipient Tex. Excellence in Teaching award, 1982. Mem. Am. Classical League (conv. coordinator 1986), Am. Philol. Assn., Classical Assn. Middle West and South, Classical Assn. S.W. U.S., Archaeol. Inst. Am. (pres. Athens chpt. 1972-74), Vergilian Soc. Am. (trustee 1974-78, pres. 1983-84), Tex. Classical Assn. (pres. 1980-81). Clubs: Harvard, University, Explorers of New York City. Translator: De Praestigiis Daemonum (Johan Weyer), 1964, Almanach Perpetuum Celestium Motuum (Rabbi Abraham Zacuto), 1973. Editor: The World and Its Peoples, Italy, 1964; asso. editor Latina et Graeca, 1974-75; Texas Classics in Action, 1976-82. Contbr. articles on classic lit. and antiquity to profl. jours. Home: 1003 High Rd Austin TX 78746

NETTERVILLE, GEORGE BRONSON, clergyman; b. McComb, Miss., Dec. 31, 1929; s. George Irving and Eula Hazel (Bronson) N.; m. Mary Elbridge Bogie, Mar. 15, 1957. B.A. with honors, Southeastern La. U., 1951; B.D., Lexington Theol. Sem., 1957, Th.M., 1958; Ph.D., Sussex Coll. (Eng.), 1971. Ordained to ministry Christian Ch. (Disciples of Christ), 1952. Minister various chs. in Miss. and Ky., 1953-59; minister 1st Christian Ch., Clarksdale, Miss., 1959-64, Univ. Christian Ch., Starkville, Miss., 1964-68; assoc. regional minister Christian Ch. in Tenn., Nashville, 1968-80; regional minister, pres., 1980—; bd. dirs. Christmount Christian Assembly, Black Mountain, N.C., 1975—; mem. gen. bd. Christian Ch., Indpls., 1980—; pres. Tenn. Assn. Chs., Nashville, 1982-84; bd. dirs. Ch. Fin. Council, Indpls., 1986—; treas. So. Christian Services, Macon, Ga., 1986—. Served as cpl. U.S. Army, 1951-53; Korea. Mem. Conf. Regional Ministers, Am. Acad. Religion, Soc. Bibl. Lit., Am. Schs. of Oriental Research, Council of Ministers of Christian Ch. Lodge: Masons. Office: Christian Ch in Tenn 3700 Richland Ave Nasvhille TN 37205

NETTLES, ANN CRENSHAW, English educator; b. Dallas, Feb. 8, 1934; d. Troy Clay and N. Maurine Crenshaw; m. Albert E. Burgin, Jr., May 17, 1950 (div. Apr. 1981); children—John Knox, Cynthia Burgin Peltier, Kimberly Burgin Graham; m. William Douglass Nettles, Jan. 1, 1983. B.A., Tex. Christian U., 1955, M.A., 1966; postgrad. U. Tex.-Austin, 1972-74. Tchr., Fort Worth Ind. Sch. Dist., 1955, Hinesville Pub. Schs. (Ga.), 1955, Long Beach Sch. Dist. (Calif.), 1956-57, Lompoc Unified Sch. Dist. (Calif.), 1957-58, Fort Worth Pub. Schs. (Tex.), 1960-65; instr. English, U. Tex., Arlington, 1966-67; instr. Tarrant County Jr. Coll., Ft. Worth, Tex., 1968-72; asst. to dean San Antonio Coll., spring 1973; tchr. Dilley Ind. Schs. (Tex.), 1974-76; instr. English, Southwest Jr. Coll., Uvalde, 1976—; part-time instr. Upward Bound Program. Mem. Gov.'s Council on War Against Drug Abuse, 1981. NDEA grantee, 1965-66. Mem. Tex. Jr. Coll. Tchrs. Assn., MLA, Southwest Regional Conf. English Tchrs., Coll. Classroom Tchrs. English, Southwest Tex. Jr. Coll. Tchrs. Assn., Tex. Assn. Creative Writers, Uvalde Arts Council, Uvalde Garden Club, AAUW, Delta Kappa Gamma. Episcopalian. Home: PO Box 286 Uvalde TX 78801 Office: Dept English Southwest Tex Jr Coll Uvalde TX 78801

NETTLES, JOHN BARNWELL, physician, educator; b. Dover, N.C., May 19, 1922; s. Stephen A. and Estelle (Hendrix) N.; B.S., U. S.C., 1941; M.D., Med. Coll. S.C., 1944; m. Eunice Anita Saugstad, Apr. 28, 1956; children—Eric, Robert, John Barnwell. Intern Garfield Meml. Hosp., Washington, 1944-45; research fellow in pathology Med. Coll. Ga., Augusta 1946-47; resident in obstetrics and gynecology U. Ill. Research and Ednl. Hosps., Chgo., 1947-51; instr. to asst. prof. obstetrics and gynecology U. Ill. Coll. Medicine, Chgo., 1951-57; asst. prof., asso. prof., prof. obstetrics and gynecology U. Ark. Med. Center, Little Rock, 1957-69; dir. grad. edn. Hillcrest Med. Center, Tulsa, 1969-73; prof. U. Okla. Coll. Medicine, Oklahoma City, 1969—; prof., chmn. dept. gynecology and obstetrics U. Okla. Coll. Medicine, Tulsa, 1975-81, prof., 1981—, mem. council on residency edn. in obstetrics and gynecology, 1974-80; dir. Tulsa Obs. and Gynecol. Edn. Found., 1969-81. Coordinator med. edn. for Nat. Def., Ark., 1961-69; mem. S.W. regional med. adv. com. Planned Parenthood Fedn. Am. Served as lt. (j.g.) M.C., USNR, 1945-46, as lt., 1953-54. Diplomate Am. Bd. Obstetrics and Gynecology. Fellow Am. Coll. Obstetricians and Gynecologists (dist. sec.-treas., dist. chmn. exec. bd. 1970-73, v.p. 1977-78), A.C.S. (bd. govs. 1969-71), Royal Soc. Health, Royal Soc. Medicine; mem. Ark. Obstet. and Gynecol. Soc. (exec. sec. 1959-69), Central Assn. Obstetrics and Gynecology (exec. com. 1966-69, pres. 1978-79), Internat. Soc. Advancement Humanistic Studies in Gynecology, Assn. Mil. Surgeons U.S., Am. (sect. council on obstetrics and gynecology 1975—), So. (chmn. obstetrics 1973-74) med. assns., Okla., Tulsa County, Chgo. med. socs., Am. Assn. for Maternal and Infant Health, Assn. Am. Med. Colls., Am. Pub. Health Assn., Assn. Hosp. Med. Edn., Assn. Planned Parenthood Physicians, Am. Assn. Sex Edn. Counselors and Therapists (SW regional bd. 1976—), N.Y. Acad. Sci., Soc. for Gynecol. Investigation, A.A.A.S., Am. Soc. for Study Fertility and Sterility, Internat. Soc. Gen. Semantics, Aerospace Med. Assn., Am. Cancer Soc. (pres. div. 1978—), So. Gynecol. and Obstet. Soc. (pres. 1981-82), Sigma Xi, Phi Rho Sigma. Lutheran. Research and main publs. on uterine malignancy, kidney biopsy in pregnancy, perinatal morbidity and mortality, sch. age pregnancy. Home: 5601 S Evanston Tulsa OK 74105 Office: U Okla Tulsa Med Coll Dept Gynecology and Obstetrics 2808 S Sheridan Rd Tulsa OK 74129

NETTLES, LARRY THOMAS, farmer, wholesale business executive; b. Sumter, S.C., July 7, 1947; s. James P. and Marjorie B. (Blackburn) N., Sr.; m. Garland M. Gulledge, Sept. 6, 1970; children—Larry, Edmund, Jackson James. Student Sumter Tech. Inst., 1966-68. Pres., Nettles Farms, Sumter, 1968—; pres. Gamecock Trucking Co., Sumter, 1977—, Sumter Coal Co., 1977—, Carolina Coal Dist., Sumter, 1980—; v.p. Mid-State Investment Co., Sumter, 1979—. Zone chmn. Duck Unltd., Sumter; local chmn., bd. dirs. S.C. Duck Calling Assn., Sumter. Mem. Nat. Hay Assn., S.C. Farm Bur., Aircraft Owners and Pilots Assn., Nat. Beeflo Assn. Democrat. Baptist. Club: Sunset Country. Home: 562 Pringle St Sumter SC 29150 Office: Nettles Farms 1200 Pocalla Rd Sumter SC 29150

NEUBERT, RHYNE E., accountant; b. Okolona, Miss., Apr. 21, 1933; s. Rhynehardt Eugene and Sara Edwards (Stevens) N.; m. Cecelia Pigott, June 3, 1961; children—Lisa, David. B.S., Miss. State U., 1956, M.P.A., 1957. C.P.A., Miss., La. Acct., Dick D. Quin & Co., Jackson, Miss., 1958-61; acct. Peat, Marwick, Mitchell & Co., Jackson, Miss., 1961—, ptnr., 1967—; lectr. Miss. State U., Millsaps Coll. Bd. dirs. Miss. Econ. Council, 1979-80, Miss. State U. Devel. Found., 1983—. Named Patron of Excellence, Miss. State U., 1981. Mem. Am. Inst. C.P.A.s (past council mem.), Miss. Soc. C.P.A.s (past pres.), Miss. Tax Inst. (past chmn.), Miss. Soc. C.P.A.s Found. (trustee). Mem. First Baptist Ch. (Deacon, past chmn. fin. com.). Clubs: Country of Jackson, Univ., Kiwanis. Home: 735 Lenox Dr Jackson MS 39211 Office: 1600 Deposit Guaranty Plaza Jackson MS 39201

NEUMAN, SUSAN CATHERINE, public relations and marketing consultant; b. Detroit, Jan. 29, 1942; d. Paul Edmund and Elise (Goetz) N.; A.B., U. Miami (Fla.), 1964; M.B.A., Barry U., Miami Shores, Fla. Journalist, writer The Miami Herald (Fla.), 1962-65; editor Miamian Mag., 1965-69; pres. Susan Neuman Inc., Miami, 1969—. Mem. Fla. Gov.'s Pub. Relations Adv. Council, 1978—. Mem. Pub. Relations Soc. Am. (accredited, past officer, bd. dirs. Miami chpt.), Ins. Exchange of Ams. (founding mem.), Econ. Soc. South Fla. (past officer, bd. dirs.), Miami C. of C., Counselor's Acad. Democrat. Roman Catholic. Clubs: Surf (Surfside, Fla.) (com. chmn. 1980-82); Palm Bay Club, City (Miami). Home: 13540 NE Miami Ct Miami FL 33161 Office: Susan Neuman Inc Plaza Venetia 25th Floor 555 NE 15th St Suite 25K Miami FL 33132

NEUMANN, DONALD LESTER, computer systems executive; b. Highland, Ill., Jan. 14, 1931; s. Lester H. and Cornelia R. (Wiedner) N.; B.S.C.E., U. Ill., 1953; postgrad. U.S. Air Force Communications Sch., 1953-54, Washington U., 1957, Miss. Coll., 1960-61, Miss. State U., 1965-66; m. Marjorie Ann Stelbrink, Sept. 3, 1955; children—Mark, Heidi. Mgr. Automatic Data Processing Center, U.S. Corps Engrs., Vicksburg, Miss., 1957-82; tech. dir. Datapak, Inc., 1982-84, pres., 1985—; owner Mardon Tech.; cons. on computer systems to govt., bus. and industry. Served to maj. USAF Res.; Korea, 1953-54. Registered profl. engr., Miss. Mem. Data Processing Mgmt. Assn., Aircraft Owners and Pilots Assn., ASCE, CAP. Clubs: Vicksburg Engrs., Lions (pres. local club 1969) (Vicksburg). Contbr. articles on computers to profl. jours. Home: 5 Bugle Ridge Dr Vicksburg MS 39180 Office: 1023 Walnut St Vicksburg MS 39180

NEUMANN, EDWARD SCHREIBER, transportation engineering educator; b. Harvey, Ill., Mar. 6, 1942; s. Arthur Edward Schreiber and Adeline Ruth (Spenks) N.; m. Carole Ann Dunkelberger, Apr. 19, 1969; children—Edward Schreiber, Jonathan David. B.S., Mich. Technol. U., 1964; M.S., Northwestern U., 1967, Ph.D., 1969. Registered profl. engr., W.Va. Mem. faculty W.Va. U., Morgantown, 1970—, prof. transp. engring., 1980—, interim dir. Harley O. Staggers Nat. Transp. Ctr., 1982-85, dir., 1985—. Bd. dirs. Mason Dixon Hist. Park Assn., 1978—. Served to capt., C.E., AUS, 1969-70. Resources for Future fellow, 1969. Mem. ASCE (chmn. com. on automated people movers chmn. com. on alsthetics and visual desing), Nat. Soc. Profl. Engrs., Am. Soc. Engring. Edn., Inst. Transp. Engrs., OITAF-NACS Advanced Transit Assn. (bd. dirs.), Sigma Xi, Tau Beta Pi, Phi Kappa Phi, Phi Eta Sigma, Chi Epsilon. Methodist. Editor numerous conf. proc. Contbr. numerous articles and research reports to profl. lit. Home: 1481 Dogwood Ave Morgantown WV 26505 Office: Dept Civil Engring WVA U Morgantown WV 26506

NEUMANN, JOACHIM PETER, metallurgical engineer; b. Berlin, Germany, June 15, 1931; naturalized, 1964. Diplom-Ingenieur, Technische Universitat Berlin, 1956; Ph.D., U. Calif.-Berkeley, 1965; m. Freya del Carmen Ortiz, Sept. 13, 1962; children—Veronica Carmen, Christine Irma. Metall. engr. Sherritt Gordon Mines, Can., 1956-57; metall. engr. Aluminum Co. Can., 1957-58; asst. prof. metallurgy UCLA, 1963-69; tech. adv. UNESCO, Spain and Venezuela, 1969-74; sr. scientist U. Wis., Milw., 1974-78; metallurgist U.S. Bur. Mines, Albany, Oreg., 1978-80; assoc. prof. metall. engring. U. Ala., Tuscaloosa, 1980—. Mem. Am. Soc. Metals, Metall. Soc. AIME, Am. Soc. Engring. Edn. Contbr. articles to profl. jours. Home: 12109 Northwood Lake Northport AL 35476 Office: PO Box G Dept Metall Engring U Ala University AL 35486

NEUNDORF, NORMAN, drafting and design educator; b. Homestead, Pa., Mar. 10, 1924; s. Adolph Carl and Christine (McCafferty) N.; m. Louise Hegdus, Apr. 1, 1953; 1 child, Mark. B.S., Calif. State Tchrs. Coll., 1952; M. Ed., Tex. A&M U., 1953. Assoc. prof. San Antonio Coll., Tex., 1963—. Author: Computer Aided Drawing Using the Tektronix Graphic System, 1976. Del., Republican State Conv., Dallas, 1984. Served with USN, 1942-47. Mem. Tex. Jr. Coll. Tchrs. Assn., Am. Tech. Edn. Assn. Lutheran. Lodge: Mason (master 1964). Office: San Antonio Coll 1300 San Pedro San Antonio TX 78284

NEUSTADT, BRUCE BAKER, insurance company official; b. Ardmore, Okla., Sept. 8, 1952; s. Jean and Patsy Louise (Baker) N. B.B.A., Southwestern U., Georgetown, Tex., 1974. Salesman Prudential Ins. Co., Dallas, 1976—. Chmn. and mem. coms. Jewish Fedn. Greater Dallas, 1983—. Republican. Jewish. Home: 7124 Meadow Rd Dallas TX 75230 Office: Prudential Ins Co 5728 LBJ Freeway Suite 230 Dallas TX 75240

NEVEU, WILMA BARBRE, librarian; b. Rayne, La., Feb. 25, 1926; d. John Wilmer and Sylvia (Campbell) Barbre; m. Durwood Herbert Neveu, Apr. 4, 1948; children—Margaret N. Lambert, Kathryn N. Bruno. B.A., U. Southwestern La., 1946; B.L.S., La. State U., 1947, M.L.S., 1974. Cert. Med. Librarian. Cataloger, Lafayette (La.) Parish Library, 1947-48; asst. head circulation librarian N.E. La. U., 1960-64; br. librarian New Orleans Pub. Library, 1964-66; head circulation and res. library Tulane Med. Library, 1966-69; asst. regional br. librarian, New Orleans, 1969-71; chief library service VA Med. Ctr., New Orleans, 1971—. Mem. Med. Library Assn., La. Library Assn., New Orleans Health Scis. Library Assn. Home: 508 Elsie Ln River Ridge LA 70123 Office: 1601 Perdido St New Orleans LA 70146

NEVILLE, RHEA TERESA, utility official, research analyst; b. Los Angeles, June 10, 1952; d. Anthony Garside and Rhea Elaine (Buras) Neville; m. Edwin Reed Hall, Mar. 6, 1976; children—Patrick Eamonn, Hilary Eileen. B.A., U. So. Calif., 1974; M.L.S., U. Okla., 1975. Cert. med. librarian. Med. librarian East Tex. Chest Hosp., Tyler, 1975-76; supr. res. area Okla. State U., Stillwater, 1976-77; 1st asst. interlibrary loans Houston Pub. Library, 1981-82; supr. litigation support Houston Lighting & Power Co., 1982-84, supr. corp. planning, 1984—. State of Calif. scholar, 1970-74. Mem. Spl. Libraries Assn., Am. Soc. Info Sci., Assn. Record Mgrs. and Adminstrs. Home: 13410 Chipman Glen Dr Houston TX 77082 Office: PO Box 1700 611 Walker St Houston TX 77001

NEWBERN, (WILLIAM) DAVID, justice Arkansas Supreme Court; b. Oklahoma City, Okla., May 28, 1937; s. Charles Banks and Mary Frances (Harding) N.; m. Barbara Lee Rigsby, Aug. 19, 1961 (div. Jan. 1968); 1 child, Laura Harding; m. Carolyn Lewis, July 31, 1970. B.A., U. Ark., 1959, J.D., 1961; LL.M., George Washington U., 1963; M.A., Fletcher Sch. Law and Diplomacy, Tufts U., 1967. Bar: Ark. 1961. Prof., U. Ark. Sch. Law, Fayetteville, 1970-85; adminstr. Ozark Folk Ctr., Mountain View, Ark., 1973; judge Ark. Ct. Appeals, Little Rock, 1979-80; justice Ark. Supreme Court, Little Rock, 1985—. Author: Arkansas Practice and Procedure, 1985. Editor-in-chief Ark. Law Rev., 1961. Served to maj. JAGC, U.S. Army, 1961-70. Recipient Moot Court trophy Vanderbilt Law Sch., 1960; Ferguson award Jim Ferguson Trust, 1961; Lawyers' Title Ins. award, 1961. Mem. Ark. Bar Assn., Am. Judicature Soc. Democrat. Avocation: string band music. Office: Arkansas Supreme Court Justice Bldg Little Rock AR 72201

NEWBERRY, JOSEPH ORION, fund raising executive; b. New Orleans, Jan. 19, 1913; s. Joseph Orion and Stella Eola (Smith) N.; B.S., Stephen F. Austin Coll., 1934; m. Harriette Rachel Baldion, Nov. 28, 1948; children—Joseph Orion, Patricia Ann, Linda Chell. With J.J. Collins Law Firm, Lufkin, Tex., 1938-39; asst. mgr. Lufkin C. of C., 1939-40; mgr. Gladewater (Tex.) C. of C., 1940-42, Texarkana (Tex.) C. of C., 1942-43; founder, chmn. bd. Community Service Bur., Inc., 1946—; lectr. seminars on fund raising. Bd. dirs. Dallas Health and Sci. Mus., Dallas County Community Coll. Dist. Found.; chmn. City Planning Commn. Served with U.S. Army, 1943-46. Mem. Am. Assn. Fund-Raising Counsel (pres. 1971-72), Press Club of Dallas, Am. Assn. C. of C. Execs., So. Assn. C. of C. Execs., Tex. C. of C. Mgrs., Nat. S.W. Socs. Fund Raisers, Coalition of Nat. Voluntary Orgns., Sigma Delta Chi. Democrat. Methodist. Clubs: Brookhaven Country, City, Lancers, 2001, Cipango 21. Lodge: Rotary. Contbr. articles to publs. in philanthropic field. Home: 11349 Crest Brook St Dallas TX 75230 Office: 3500 Oak Lawn Suite 180 Dallas TX 75219

NEWBERRY, MARTHA JANE, physical education educator, coach; b. Parkersburg, W.Va., Sept. 10, 1957; d. Robert E. and Doris Virginia (Tice) N. B.A., Morehead State U., 1979. Internat. cert. volleyball coach. Tchr., coach Wetzel County Bd. Edn., New Martinsville, W.Va., 1979—, asst. coach Magnolia girls' track team, 1979-81, coach Magnolia volleyball team, 1979-84; advisor Girls' Athletic Assn., New Martinsville, 1979-81; coach trip to Europe, W.Va. Basketball Stars, 1980-81. Instr. CPR, fund-raiser Am. Heart Assn.; chaperone/coach Spl. Olympics, Parkersburg, W.Va., 1975; hostess to Miss America, Morehead State U., 1978. Named Athlete of Yr., Womens Sport Mag., 1975; coach state championship, W.Va. Sports Writers Assn., 1983; athletic scholar, 1975-79. Mem. U.S. Volleyball Assn. (cert. coach), Sigma Sigma Sigma. Republican. Mem. Church of Christ. Home: 2000 Newberry Dr Parkersburg WV 26101 Office: Magnolia High Sch Maple Ave New Martinsville WV 26155

NEWBOLD, JAMES LAWRENCE, corporate pilot, flight instructor; b. Flint, Mich., Mar. 1, 1944; s. James Clay and Berthinue Bell (Talbert) N.; m. Emell Jean Ingram, July 15, 1966 (div. Oct. 15, 1974); children—Tonya Patrice, Lisa Dawn; m. 2d, Kathy Haynes, Mar. 15, 1977 (div. Nov. 1981); 1 son, James L.; m. 3d, Linda Carol Ward, Jan. 29, 1982. Student Coll. Albermarle, 1962-63, Ariz. State U., 1963-64; B.S. in Bus. Adminstrn., Guilford Coll., 1970. Chief flight instr. H.A.L. Aviation, Kennett, Mo., 1977-78, Atlantic Aero, Inc., Greensboro, N.C., 1979-80; dir. flight ops., chief pilot Indiana Aiomotive, Huntingberg, Ind., 1978-79; chief pilot Roche Biomed. Labs., Burlington, N.C., 1980—. Served with USAF, 1963-64. Mem. Aircraft Owners and Pilots Assn. Republican. Baptist. Home and office: 730 Westbrook Dr Burlington NC 27215

NEWBOLD, KENNETH, educational administrator. Supt. of schs. Greensboro, N.C. Office: 712 N Eugene St PO Drawer V Greensboro NC 27402*

NEWBY, HI EASTLAND, physician; b. Del Rio, Tex., Dec. 8, 1929; s. Byron Elvel and Amanda (Eastland) N.; student Schreiner Inst., 1947-48; B.A., Baylor U., 1951, M.D., 1957; postgrad. Sul Ross State U., 1948, 51-52; m. Ona Darlene Northcutt, Apr. 25, 1959; children—Byron Edgar, Hi Eastland. Intern, Bexar County Hosp., Dist., San Antonio, 1957-58; practice family medicine, Del Rio, 1958-77; chief staff Val Verde Meml. Hosp., Del Rio, 1968-69; med. cons. Tex. Rehab. Agy., San Antonio area, 1966-73; examining physician So. Pacific Co., 1959-77; assoc. chief med. officer Burlington No. R.R.; 1984—. Clin. prof. dept. family practice U. Tex. Med. Sch., San Antonio, 1974—, asst. clin. prof. dept. family practice U. Tex. Med. Sch., Houston, 1979-84. Mem. charter commn., City of Del Rio, 1966-67. Mem. Del. Rio Ind. Sch. Dist. Bd., 1968-71, pres., 1969-71; pres. San Felipe Del Rio Consol. Ind. Sch. Dist., 1971-72; mem. Val Verde County Sch. Bd., 1972-77; v.p. Cypress Creek Utility Dist., Houston, 1979-80, pres., 1980-84. Diplomate Am. Bd. Family Practice. Fellow Am. Acad. Occupational Medicine; AMA, Tex. Med. Assn., Tex. Acad. Gen. Practice (dir. 1966-70), mem. Am. Occupational Med. Assn., Tex. Acad. Family Physicians (chmn. membership and credential com. 1971-72, mem. edn. com. 1977-81). Lodges: Masons, Shriners. Home: 2114 Coolidge Dr Arlington TX 76011 Office: 3000 Continental Plaza 777 Main St Fort Worth TX 76011

NEWELL, DAVID ROBERT, real estate developer-owner; b. Ft. Worth, June 1, 1940; s. Jack and Delle (Shofner) N.; m. Delane Ray, Dec. 25, 1977; children—Dayna Rachelle, Dawn Regan. B.B.A., U. Tex.-Arlington, 1966; M.B.A. in Fin., U. Houston, 1968, M.A., 1969. Asst. prof. fin. U. Mo., Columbia, 1969-71; controller Jack P. DeBoer, Inc., Wichita, Kans., 1971-72; pres. Plan-Tec, Jacksonville, Fla., 1972-74; ptnr. Newell & Newell, Ft. Worth, 1974—. Mem. adv. bd. Bus. Sch., U. Tex., Arlington, 1985—. Served with USN, 1960-63. Recipient Disting. Alumni award U. Tex., Arlington, 1985; fin. analyst fellow U. Houston, 1967. Fellow Nat. Assn. Indsl. and Office Parks (co-founder Ft. Worth chpt. 1985), Am. Fin. Assn.; mem. Am. Econ. Assn., Tarrant County Pvt. Industry Council (chmn. 1983—), Ft. Worth C. of C. (bd. dirs. 1982—), East Ft. Worth C. of C. (past chmn.). Republican. Mem. Ch. of Christ. Clubs: Colonial Country, Woodhaven Country (Ft. Worth). Avocation: sports. Home: 508 Havenwood Ln N Fort Worth TX 76112 Office: Newell & Newell 2501 Gravel Dr Fort Worth TX 76118

NEWELL, JAMES THAXTON, engineer; b. Vernon, Ala., Dec. 31, 1939; s. Ernest Clovis and Welthey (Younghance) N.; A.A.S. with honors, DeVry Tech. Inst., 1960; B.S. in Engring. summa cum laude, U. Central Fla., 1975, M.S. in Engring., 1979; m. Sylvia Ellen Thomas, Mar. 9, 1963; children—Karen Lynn, James Thomas, Kelly Elizabeth, Jonathan Michael; m. Susan Gail Malone, Oct. 9, 1973; 1 son, Jason Roy. Reliability engr. McDonnell Douglas Aircraft Co., St. Louis, 1960-66; reliability program mgr. Emerson Electric Co., St. Louis, 1966-67; engring mgr. Naval Plant Rep. Office, St. Louis, 1967-68; ILS mgr., also reliability and maintainability engr. Naval Tng. Equipment Center, Orlando, Fla., 1968-77, ops. research analyst, 1977-82; gen. engr. U.S. Army Missile Command, Redstone Arsenal, Ala., 1982-84; supr. ops. research U.S. Army Missile and Munitions Ctr. and Sch., Redstone Arsenal, 1984—. Founder, dir. AstroCel Research Inst., Inc.; instr. Seminole Community Coll., 1974-79. Registered profl. engr., Mo., Fla. Mem. Am. Fedn. Astrologers, Alpha Pi Mu. Baptist (Sunday sch. tchr. 1962-63). Home: Rt 1 Box 170A Grant AL 35747 Office: US Army Missile and Munitions Center and School (ATSK-CT) Redstone Arsenal AL 35897

NEWMAN, BERNARD, chemical engineering educator; b. N.Y.C., Sept. 17, 1913; s. Samuel and Hannah (Lissman) N.; m. Belle Herrlich, Sept. 10, 1935 (div. 1945); m. Edna Albert, Sept. 7, 1946; children—Paul, David, Jonathan, Brian. B.S. in Engring., CCNY, 1935, M.S., 1943; Ph.D., NYU, 1956. Registered profl. engr. N.Y., Fla. Assoc. prof. NYU, N.Y.C., 1957-63; dir. Newing Lab. Inc., Islip, N.Y., 1957-80; dir. Suffolk County police Lab., Hauppauge, N.Y., 1960-74; prof. environ. sci. C.W. Post Coll., L.I. U., 1968-78; prof. chemistry SUNY-Stony Brook, 1978-80; cons. USPHS, Raritan, N.J., 1958-64. Contbr. articles to profl. jours. Mem. Planning Commn., City of Tamarac, Fla., 1980—; dir. Islip Town Library, 1965-82. Served to maj. U.S. Army, 1942-46, ETO. Fellow Am. Pub. Health Assn., Am. Acad. Forensic Sci.; mem. Am. Chem. Soc. Republican. Avocations: Photomicrography; astronomy. Home: 6307 NW 74th Ave Tamarac FL 33319

NEWMAN, CHARLES FORREST, lawyer; b. Grenada, Miss., Jan. 15, 1937; s. Wiley Clifford and Lurene (Westbrook) N.; B.A. magna cum laude, Yale, 1959, J.D., 1963; postgrad. (Adenauer fellow) U. Bonn (Germany), 1959-60; m. Jeannette Kay Bailey, May 26, 1973. Admitted to Tenn. bar, 1964; law clk. U.S. Dist. Judge Bailey Brown, Western Dist. Tenn., 1963-64; mem. firm Burch Porter & Johnson, Attys., Memphis, 1965—, partner, 1966—; commr. Memphis Landmarks Commn.; assoc. Environ. Law Inst. Past bd. dirs. Tenn. Environ. Council, Environ. Action Fund, Inc., Tenn. Conservation League; bd. dirs. LeMoyne-Owen Coll., Memphis Acad. Arts, Wolb River Conservancy Inc.; mem. exec. com. Yale Law Sch. Assn., 1984—, Pres.'s Council Southwestern Coll.; Memphis-Shelby County chmn. Gary Hart Presdl. Campaign, 1984, Mondale Presdl. Campaign, 1984; mem. class council Class of '59, Yale Coll.; mem. ABA, Tenn., (corp. law revision com.) Memphis and Shelby County, (co-chmn. jud. recommendations com. 1983—, continuing legal edn. com. 1984—) Bar Assns., Am. Judicature Soc., Am. Assn. Trial Lawyers, Memphis C. of C. (state legis. liaison com., econ. develop. council) Commitment Memphis, Wilderness Soc., Soaring Soc. Am., Airplane Owners and Pilots Assn., L.Q.C. Lamar Soc., Tenn. Environmental Council, Sierra Club, Phi Beta Kappa. Clubs: Tennessee, Economic, Yale of Memphis (past pres.), Yale of N.Y. Home: 3880 Poplar Ave Memphis TN 38112 Office: 130 N Court Memphis TN 38103

NEWMAN, JAMES, educational administrator. Supt. of schs. Knoxville, Tenn. Office: 101 E 5th Ave Knoxville TN 37917*

NEWMAN, JERRY OKEY, research engineer; b. New Martinsville, W.Va., May 9, 1936; s. James Okey and Hazel Edna (Howell) N.; m. Patricia Grace Devericks, May 25, 1958; children—Tamrah M., Lucetta R., Symantha C., Onika M. B.S., W.Va. U., 1958, M.S., 1960; Ph.D., U. Md., 1972. Registered profl. engr., W.Va. Grad. asst. W.Va. U., Morgantown, 1958-60; engr. VA, Clarksburg, W.Va., 1960-62; research engr. U.S. Dept. Agr., Beltsville, Md., 1962-73, research engr. rural housing and solar energy, S.C., 1973-80, research leader, 1980-85; engring. cons., 1985—. Pres. Pickens County Retarded Citizens Assn., 1975-78. Recipient Superior Performance award VA, 1960-61; Danforth summer fellow, 1957. Mem. Am. Soc. Agrl. Engrs., Nat. Inst. Bldg. Sci., Internat. Solar Energy Soc., Profl. Engrs. Soc. Underground Space Inst., Sigma Xi, Tau Beta Pi. Democrat. Clubs: Red Necks (Clemson); 4-H All Stars (Clarksburg). Contbr. articles to profl. jours. Home: 474 Route 1 Central SC 29630

NEWMAN, LEROY GREGORY, adult education counselor/coordinator b. Las Vegas, N.Mex., Feb. 4, 1935; m. Carolyn Ann Baker, Apr. 4, 1964; children—Gregory, Kristin, Garrett, Gavin. Student So. Methodist U., 1954-55; B.A., N.Mex. Highlands U., 1958, M.A., 1960. Lic. pvt. profl. counselor, cert. tchr., Va. Elem. sch. sci. specialist Fairfax County Pub. Schs., Va., 1969-71, intermediate sch. counselor, 1971-73, adminstrv. intern, sch. census mgr., 1973-74, research asst., 1974-78, vocat. counselor/coordinator, 1978-85, adult edn. counselor/coordinator, 1985—; sec./treas. Internat. Leadership Learning Inst.; pres., dir. CRI, Woodbridge, Va., 1984—; dir. C.E.S., Woodbridge. Author: program publs. Pres., commr. Prince William Soccer, Inc., Dale City, Va., 1976-78; pres. Woodbridge Our Lady of Angels Ch. Credit Union, Woodbridge, 1978-79; v.p. Bel Air Elem. Sch. PTA, Dale City, 1979. Served with USN, 1953-54; Korea. Recipient Coe Fellowship Edn. History Writing award, 1967; fellow/designee U. Ariz., Tucson, 1971, U. Colo., Boulder, 1971; NDEA fellow, 1977. Mem. NEA (life), Am. Soc. Tng. and Devel., Am. Assn. Counseling and Devel., Am. Mental Health Counselors Assn., Assn. Part Time Profls., Roman Catholic. Club: Dale City Sports (treas., then v.p. 1982-84). Lodges: Elks, Kiwanis, K.C. Avocations: music; development and assessment of programs; reading; sports. Home: 14250 N Forge Ct Woodbridge VA 22193

NEWMAN, RICHARD OAKLEY, utilities exec.; b. Enid, Okla., Aug. 30, 1920; s. O.B. and Grace E. N.; B.S. in Mech. Engring., Okla. State U., 1942; m. Betty Lou Bennett, Mar. 13, 1940; children—Linda Lou Newman Weathers, Richard Oakley, Mark B. With Pub. Service Co. of Okla., Tulsa, 1946—, exec. v.p., 1968-70, exec. v.p., dir., 1970-72, pres., chief exec. officer, dir., 1972—; chmn. bd., chief exec. officer, dir. Transok Pipe Line Co., Ash Creek Mining Co.; dir. 1st Nat. Bank & Trust Co., Williams Cos.; chmn. S.W. Power Pool; past chmn. S.W. Underground Distbn. Exchange; dir. Central & S.W. Corp., Conf. Bd.; trustee Nat. Electric Reliability Council. Past chmn. ofcl. bd., deacon, elder, trustee, Sunday Sch. supt. East Side Christian Ch.; dir. Tulsa Christian Found.; past pres. Tulsa Area Christian Missionary Soc.; mem. Gov.'s Energy Advisory Council, 1973—; bd. dirs., chmn. Industries for Tulsa, Inc.; bd. dirs., past pres. Goodwill Industries of Tulsa; bd. dirs. Indian Nations council Boy Scouts Am., Goodwill Industries Am., Inc., Okla. State U. Found.; trustee St. Francis Hosp., Phillips U.; mem. advisory bd. Downtown Tulsa Unlimited, Inc.; mem. advisory bd. Coll. Engring. and Phys. Scis., chmn. bd. trustees Deans Advisory Council Bus. Adminstrn., U. Tulsa. Served with AUS, 1942-46. Mem. IEEE, Am. Nuclear Soc., ASME, Nat., Okla. socs. profl. engrs., Okla. Petroleum Council, Mid-Continent Oil and Gas Assn., Tulsa C. of C.

(pres., bd. dirs., exec. com.), Nat. Alliance Businessmen (past met. chmn.), Edison Electric Inst. (dir.), Mo. Valley Electric Assn. (exec. com., past pres.). Clubs: Masons (32 deg.), Shriners, Royal Order Jesters, So. Hills Country, Tulsa, Utica 21, Tulsa Press. Home: PO Box 129 Tulsa OK 74101 Office: PO Box 201 Tulsa OK 74102

NEWMAN, SLATER EDMUND, psychologist, educator; b. Boston, Sept. 8, 1924; s. Max and Gertrude (Raphael) N.; m. Corrine Lois Silfen, June 18, 1950 (div. Dec., 1968); children—Kurt Douglas, Jonathan Mark, Eric Bruce; m. Patricia Ellen Christopher Thomas, July 2, 1969; 1 stepson, Arthur C. Thomas III. B.S., U. Pa., 1947; M.A., Boston U., 1948; Ph.D., Northwestern U., 1951. Research psychologist U.S. Air Force, 1951-57; mem. faculty N.C. State U., Raleigh, 1957—, now prof. psychology; vis. fgn. mem. Exptl. Psychology Soc. U.K., 1973-74, 82-83. Pres. N.C. Civil Liberties Union, 1980-82; mem. Amnesty Internat.; coordinator Com. To Reverse Arms Race. Served with USAAF, 1943-46; to 2d lt. USAF, 1952-53. USPHS spl. research fellow U. Calif.-Berkeley, 1965-66; U. London hon. research fellow, 1973-74, 82-83. Fellow AAAS, Am. Psychol. Assn.; mem. Psychonomic Soc. Contbr. articles to profl. publs. Home: 315 Shepherd St Raleigh NC 27607 Office: Dept Psychology North Carolina State U Raleigh NC 27695-7801

NEWMAN, TILLMAN EUGENE, JR., food company executive; b. Greenwood, Ark., Feb. 13, 1938; s. Tillman Eugene and Theresa Christine (Simmons) N.; m. Linda Gail Childers, Feb. 13, 1983; children—James Barton Langley, Robert, John, Michael, Kristen Newman. B.S. in Chem. Engring., U. Ark., 1963. Registered profl. engr., Ark., Iowa, Mo. Plant mgr. Ralston Purina, St. Louis, 1963-67, project mgr., 1967-71; v.p. Huxtable-Hammond, Kansas City, Mo., 1971-79; dir. engring. Tyson Foods, Russellville, Ark., 1979—; bd. dirs. Mech. Controllers of Iowa, 1976-78; mem. Ark. Allied Industries, Little Rock, 1980—. Bd. dirs. Ark. Fedn. Water and Air, 1984—. Served to sgt. USNG, 1956-65. Mem. Nat. Soc. Profl. Engrs., Am. Inst. Chem. Engrs., Am. Soc. Mech. Engrs., Russellville C. of C. Baptist. Avocations: fishing; boating. Office: Tyson Foods PO Box 847 Russellville AR 72801

NEWMARK, BERNICE ELLEN, business and public awareness consultant; b. Reading, Pa., Apr. 15, 1923; d. Joseph Michael and Dorothy (Wood) N.; children—Susan Lee, Douglas Jeffrey. B.Sc., NYU, 1941; postgrad. New Sch. Social Research, 1953-60; M.Sc., 1977. With Aides to Mgmt., Inc., West Palm Beach, Fla., 1969—, pres., 1984—; pres. New Directions Publs., 1984—. Mem. Am. Soc. Assn. Execs., Fla. Chess Assn. Clubs: Zonta, Gold Coast Chess (exec. dir., 1964-84). Exec. editor Fin. Planning Today, 1977-84.

NEWSOM, DOUGLAS ANN JOHNSON, journalist; b. Dallas, Jan. 16, 1934; d. J. Douglas and R. Grace (Dickson) Johnson; B.J. cum laude, U. Tex., 1954, B.F.A. summa cum laude, 1955, M.J., 1956, Ph.D., 1978; m. L. Mack Newsom, Jr., Oct. 27, 1956 (div.); children—Michael Douglas, Kevin Jackson, Nancy Elizabeth, William Macklemore. Gen. publicity State Fair Tex., 1955; advt. and promotion Newsom's Women's Wear, 1956-57; publicity Auto Market Show, 1961; lab. instr. radio-tv news-writing course U. Tex., 1961-62; local publicist Tex. Boys Choir, 1964-69, nat. publicist, 1967-69; public relations dir. Gt. S.W. Boat Show Dallas, 1966-72, Family Fun Show, 1970-71, Horace Ainsworth Co., Dallas, 1966-76; pres. Profl. Devel. Cons.'s, Inc., non-profit seminar prodn., 1979-81; prof. prof. dept. journalism, chmn. dept., Tex. Christian U., Ft. Worth, 1970-78; dir. Oneok Inc., diversified energy co. Sec.-treas., Public Relations Found. Tex., 1979-80, also trustee; trustee Found. Pub. Relations Research and Edn., 1985—; mem. journalism awards William R. Hearst Found., 1981—; public relations chmn. local Am. Heart Assn., 1973-76, state public relations com. 1974-82, chmn., 1980-82. Mem. Assn. Edn. in Journalism (pres. public relations div. 1974-75, pres. elect 1983-84, pres. 1985—), Women in Communications (nat. conv. treas. 1967, nat. public relations chmn. 1969-71), Public Relations Soc. Am. (nat. edn. com. 1975, chmn. 1978, nat. faculty adv.), Tex. Public Relations Assn. (dir. 1976—, v.p. 1980-82, pres. 1982-83), Am. Women in Radio and TV, Delta Delta Delta, Mortar Bd. Alumnae (adviser Tex. Christian U. 1974-75). Episcopalian. Author: (with Alan Scott) This is PR, 1976, 2d edit., 1981; (with Tom Siegfried) Writing for Public Relations Practice, 1981 (with Bob Cawell) Public Relations Writing: Form and Style; editorial bd. Public Relations Rev., 1978-82. Home: 4237 Shannon Dr Fort Worth TX 76116

NEWSOM, MAX, geologist; b. Teague, Tex., June 11, 1924; s. Joel Thomas and Willie (Sammon) N.; m. Dorothy Marketell, July 3, 1954. B.S. in Geol. Engring., Tex. A&M U., 1949. Geologist, Gulf Oil Corp., Houston, New Orleans, Jackson, Miss. and Casper, Wyo., 1949—. Served to cpl. USMC, 1941-45, PTO. Mem. Am. Assn. Petroleum Geologists, New Orleans Geol. Soc., Soc. Exploration Geophysicists. Southeastern Geophys. Soc., Am. Petroleum Inst. Republican. Home: 6111 Duplessis St New Orleans LA 70122

NEWSOM, MICKEY BRUNSON, business executive; b. Columbia, Miss., July 26, 1941; s. James Hezzie and Opal Eugenia (Prescott) N.; A.A., Hartnell Coll., 1961; B.B.A., Golden Gate U., 1964, M.B.A., 1976; m. Rose Marie Christensen, May 25, 1963. Mgr., Roy's Restaurants, Salinas, Calif., 1964-67; prin. Humboldt County Schs., Redcrest, Calif., 1967-69; educator Bur. Indian Affairs, Wide Ruins, Ariz., 1969-71; owner Hardware Auto Store, Columbus, Miss., 1971-80, Newsom & Co., 1971—; mgmt. cons. Div. Adminstrn., State of La., 1981—. Polit. cons. various state and nat. candidates; mem. Mcpl. Democratic Exec. Com., 1977-80; bd. dirs. County Assn. Retarded Citizens, 1979-80. Mem. East Miss. Council (dir. 1977-80), Mid-Continent Oil and Gas Assn., Marion County C. of C., Forest Farmers' Assn., Nat. Assn. Suggestion Systems, Golden Gate U. Alumni Assn. Tower Club. Democrat. Lutheran. Lodge: Kiwanis. Clubs: Civitan (pres. 1977-78, lt. gov. Miss. North dist. 1978-79); Commonwealth of Calif.; Kiwanis. Office: PO Box 44413 State Capitol Baton Rouge LA 70804

NEWSOM, NEIL EDWARD, lawyer; b. Fort Worth, Nov. 24, 1945; s. Raymond E. and Alice Ruth (Daniel) N.; m. Jan Lynn Reimann, Apr. 15, 1972; children—Kelly Ann, Loren Elizabeth. B.B.A., Tex. Christian U., 1967; J.D., U. Tex.-Austin, 1970. Bar: Tex. 1970, U.S. Dist. Ct. (no. dist.) Tex. 1971. Assoc., Coke & Coke, Dallas, 1971-76; assoc. Hughes Luce Hennessy Smith & Castle, Dallas, 1977-78; assoc. Gardere Porter & Dehay, Dallas, 1978-79; ptnr. Gardere & Wynne, Dallas, 1979-84, Freytag Là Force Rubinstein & Teofan, Dallas, 1984—. Served with USAR, 1970-78. Mem. State Bar Tex., ABA (com. on governmentally assisted housing programs 1985—), Dallas Bar Assn., Tex. Assn. Bank Counsel, Tex. Law Rev. Assn., Tex. Christian U. Alumni Assn. (nat. dir. 1981—, pres. Dallas chpt. 1980-81, recipient Pres. Service award 1981). Clubs: Exchange (Dallas). Office: Suite 2000 Lincoln Plaza 500 N Akard Dallas TX 75201

NEWTON, DON A., association executive. Pres., Birmingham C. of C., Ala. Office: Birmingham C of C 202 71st Ave N PO Box 10127 Birmingham AL 35202*

NEWTON, ELIZABETH PURCELL, counselor, consultant, author; b. Madison, N.C., June 3, 1925; d. Charles Augustus and Anna Meta (Buchanan) P.; m. William Edward Newton, June 11, 1949; children—James Purcell, Betsy Newton Hein, Christian Newton Harwood. A.A., Peace Coll., 1944; B.A., U. N.C., 1946; M.Ed., Ga. State U., 1969; Ed.S., West Ga. Coll., 1981. Tchr., counselors Cobb High Sch., Austell, Ga., 1965-69; counselor, dept. head Wheeler High Sch., Marietta, Ga., 1969-76; counselor, div. head guidance services Walton High Sch., Marietta, Ga., 1976—; sch. rep. Coll. Bd., Princeton, N.J., 1981—, panelist, presenter S.E. region, Atlanta, 1983-85; presenter Ga. Sch. Counselors Assn., Atlanta, 1980—; cons. Panhandle Area Edn. Coop., Chipley, Fla., 1985. Author: Steps to College Admissions, 1978; Student's Guide to College Admissions, 1981; Student's Guide to Career Preparation, 1982. Sch. rep. Citizens Adv. Council, Marietta, 1981, 82, 85. Ga. Dept. Edn. grantee, 1981; named Outstanding Woman in Edn., Atlanta Jour., 1985. Mem. Cobb Counselor Assn. (organizer, chmn. nominations com. 1985), Ga. Sch. Counselors Assn. (Secondary Counselor of Yr. 1983), Am. Sch. Counselors Assn. (Nat. Secondary Counselor of Yr. 1984), Phi Delta Kappa. Presbyterian. Office: George Walton Comprehensive High Sch 1590 Bill Murdock Rd Marietta GA 30062

NEY, JUDY LARSON, lawyer; b. St. Louis, Mar. 4, 1951; d. Robert and Annette (Palan) Larson; B.A. (scholar), Bradley U., 1973; M.A., U. Mo., St. Louis, 1975; J.D., South Tex. Coll. Law, 1982; bar: Tex. 1983; m. Leo Edwin Ney, Jr., May 25, 1975; 1 child, Leo Edwin IV. Teaching asst., lectr. Bradley U., Peoria, Ill., 1972-73; grad. teaching and research asst. U. Mo. St. Louis, 1973-74; sr. scheduler/supr. Brown & Root Inc., Houston, 1974-83; gen. civil law practice, Houston, 1983—; lectr. on alcohol/drug recovery programs and the law; advocate Houston Area Women's Ctr. Mem. ABA, Tex. Bar Assn., Houston Bar Assn., Assn. Trial Lawyers Am., Tex. Young Lawyers Assn., Houston Young Lawyers Assn., Alumni Assn. South Tex. Coll. Law, Bradley U. Alumni Assn. (Tex. rep.), U. Mo. St. Louis Alumni Assn., Chimes, Phi Alpha Delta, Gamma Sigma Phi. Jewish. Home: 12242 Brookvalley Houston TX 77071 Office: 3100 Weslayan Suite 450 Houston TX 77027

NG, KAI TIM, trust company executive; b. Kwangtung, China, Jan. 19, 1942; came to U.S., 1963, naturalized, 1971; s. Tse Hong and Hang Sun (Lee) N.; m. Eleanor Wu, Oct. 23, 1971; children—Kevin, Emily. B.B.A., Pace U., 1967, M.B.A., 1970. Chartered fin. analyst. Fin. analyst Shell Pension Trust, N.Y.C., 1967-72, investment specialist, Houston, 1973-78, sr. investment specialist, 1978-80, mgr. equities, 1981—; dir. K&N Investments Inc., Houston. Mem. Houston Soc. Fin. Analysts, Fin. Analysts Fedn. Avocations: swimming, stamp collecting. Home: 11715 Cherryknoll Dr Houston TX 77077 Office: Shell Pension Trust PO Box 1438 Houston TX 77001

NGUYEN, BINH NGOC, management consultant; b. Hanoi, Vietnam, Sept. 17, 1942, came to U.S., 1973; s. Quynh and Thin Thi(Bui) N.; m. Minh-Chau Thi Hoang, Nov. 11, 1970; children—An Ngoc, Bao-Hanh Ngoc. B.S. in Pharmacy, U. Saigon, 1967; M.P.H., U. Tenn., 1975. Chief, Bur. Health Planning and Promotion, Nat. Health Edn. Service Ministry of Health, Saigon, Vietnam, 1972-73; pub. health educator Miss. Band of Choctaw Indians, Philadelphia, Miss., 1975-78, exec. dir. Health Dept., 1978-83; pres. Wynn Inc., Philadelphia, 1983—. Mem. Am. Pub. Health Assn., Nat. Assn. Vietnamese Am. Edn. Home: 2309 Mary's Creek Ct Pearland TX 77581 Office: Route 7 Box 21 Philadelphia MS 39350

NICASTRI, HELEN JEANNE, real estate company executive; b. Pittston, Pa., Dec. 11, 1948; d. Frank Julio and Mary (Menik) Meehan; m. Joseph Nicastri (div. 1985); children—Astrid Justine, Joseph Alexander. M.A. in Latin Am. Relations, NYU, 1971. Dir. internat. div. Cousins Assocs., Miami, Fla., 1979-81; sales mgr. Grove Towers Condominium, Miami, 1979-84; dir. sales Merrill Lynch Realty Internat. Div., Miami, 1981—. Chmn. patrons com. ARC, Miami, 1982—; mem. Viscaya com. 100 Viscaya Found., Coconut Grove, Fla., 1983—; mem. gala com. March of Dimes, Miami, 1984—; patron Met. Mus., Coral Gables, Fla., 1980—. Club: Oriental Art Soc. Avocations: art collecting; sailing; swimming; travel; literature. Home: 3765 Carmen Ct Coconut Grove FL 33133 Office: Merrill Lynch 5830 SW 73rd St Miami FL 33143

NICEWARNER, MARTHA DIANE, bank executive; b. Front Royal, Va., Feb. 5, 1958; d. Thomas Landis and Annie Myrtle (Dodson) N. A.A.S. in Bus. Adminstrn. cum laude, Lord Fairfax Community Coll., 1978; B.B.A., North Ga. Coll., 1980; M.B.A., Shenandoah Coll., 1985; cert. Inst. Fin. Edn., Chgo., 1985. Assoc. Jewel Box, Front Royal, 1976-81; acctg. clk. Front Royal Savs. and Loan Assn., 1980, asst. treas. (named changed to Va. Savs. Bank), 1980—; instr. Inst. Fin. Edn., Front Royal, 1982. Instr. Aerobic Dance Co., Front Royal, 1983. Mem. Nat. Assn. Bank Women, Nat. Assn. Female Execs., Inst. Fin. Edn. (pres.), Phi Theta Kappa, Phi Beta Lambda, Phi Mu (Rose Carnation Queen 1980). Mem. Ch. of the Brethren. Home: 500 Happy Creek Rd Front Royal VA 22630 Office: Va Savs Bank PO Box 1238 Front Royal VA 22630

NICHOLAS, CHARLES THOMAS, commercial and industrial roofing manufacturing company executive; b. Indpls., Mar. 31, 1949; s. Charles and Marcella (Hadjieff) N.; m. Marsha Lynne Stephens, June 23, 1973; children—Tara Lynne, Todd Stephen. B.S. in Bus. Mgmt. and Adminstrn., Ind. U., 1972. Real estate broker F.C. Tucker Co., Indpls., 1971-72; state trooper State of Ind., Charlestown, 1972-76; sales rep. Gifford-Hill & Co., Louisville, 1976-78, gen. mgr., Jefferson, Ohio, 1978-81; gen. mgr. Metal Sales Mfg. Corp., Jacksonville, Fla., 1981-85, v.p., regional gen. mgr. Southeast region, 1985—. Republican. Presbyterian. Home: 11682 Wellington Way Jacksonville FL 32223 Office: 6600 Suemac Pl Jacksonville FL 32205

NICHOLAS, JACK DANIEL, accountant; b. Rockingham County, Va., June 24, 1944; s. Joseph Daniel and Lillie Ellen (Donovan) N.; m. Carolyn Sue Roach, July 6, 1963; children—Melissa Renee, Mark Duane; m. Barbara Jean Hamilton, July 29, 1978; stepchildren—Donald Lee Huntley, Todd Hamilton Huntley. B.S. in Bus. Adminstrn., James Madison U., 1968. C.P.A., Va. Tchr. bus. Turner Ashby High Sch., Dayton, Va., 1968-70; staff acct. Keeler, Phibbs & Co., Harrisonburg, Va., 1970-72, audit mgr., 1972-73; ptnr. Young, Nicholas, Mills & Co., Harrisonburg, 1973-77, ptnr.-in-charge Culpeper Office, 1977—; mem. faculty James Madison U., 1973-74. Treas. Harrisonburg Halfway House, 1974-76; pres. Farmington Elem. Sch. PTO, 1982-83; mem., pres. Blue Devil Athletic Boosters, 1982-85; bd. dirs., crusade chmn. Culpeper unit Am. Cancer Soc., 1984-85. Mem. Am. Inst. C.P.A.s, Va. Soc. C.P.A.s, Blue Ridge C.P.A.s, Culpeper C. of C. (dir. 1982-85). Methodist. Club: Exchange (dir., sec. 1969-76). Lodge: Lions (pres. 1985—). Home: 553 Woodlawn Pl Culpeper VA 22701 Office: 301 S West St PO Box 49 Culpeper VA 22701

NICHOLAS, LAWRENCE BRUCE, import company executive; b. Dallas, Nov. 9, 1945; s. J. W. and Helen Elouise (Whiteacre) N.; B.B.A., So. Meth. U., 1968; m. Virginia Pearl Farmer, Aug. 5, 1967; children—Helen Brooke, John Lawrence, Alexis Bradlee. Mem. sales staff Nicholas Machinery Co., Dallas, 1963-69; sales mgr. Indsl. and Comml. Research Corp., Dallas, 1969-74; v.p. Precision Concepts Corp., Dallas, 1974-76, gen. mgr., 1976-78, pres., Addison, Tex., 1978—, dir., 1974—; pres. INCOR Inc., Addison, 1974—, dir., 1972—; pres., dir. INCOR Internat., Inc., Dallas, 1981—; dir. Multiple Axis Machines Corp., Dallas. Served as officer Ordnance Corps, U.S. Army, 1968, N.G., 1968-74. Mem. Woodworking Machinery Distbrs Assn. (dir.), Nat. Archtl. Woodwork Inst., Nat. Sporting Goods Assn., Nat. Assn. Furniture Mfrs., Internat. Trade Assn. Tex., Nat. Rifle Assn., Nat. Shooting Sports Found., Safari Club Internat, Game Conservation Internat., Dallas Council World Affairs (dir.). Club: Bent Tree Country. Office: 4200 Westgrove Dr Addison TX 75001

NICHOLAS, NICKIE LEE, industrial hygienist; b. Lake Charles, La., Jan. 19, 1938; d. Clyde Lee and Jessie Mae (Lyons) Nicholas; B.S., U. Houston, 1960, M.S., 1966. Tchr. sci. Pasadena (Tex.) Ind. Sch. Dist., 1960-61; chemist FDA, Dallas, 1961-62, VA Hosp., Houston, 1962-66; chief biochemist Baylor U. Coll. Medicine, 1966-68; chemist NASA, Johnson Spacecraft Center, 1968-73; analytical chemist TVA, Muscle Shoals, Ala., 1973-75; indsl. hygienist, compliance officer Occupational Safety and Health Adminstrn., Dept. Labor, Houston, 1975-79, Tulsa area dir., 1979-82, Austin area dir., 1982—; mem. faculty VA Sch. Med. Tech., Houston, 1963-66. Recipient award for outstanding achievement German Embassy, 1958, Suggestion award VA, 1963, Group Achievement award Skylab Med. Team, NASA, 1974, cert. of appreciation Dept. Labor, 1977, personal achievement award Fed. Women's Program, 1984. Mem. Am. Chem. Soc. (dir. analytical group Southeastern Tex. and Brazosport sects. 1971, chmn. elect 1973), Am. Assn. Clin. Chemists, Am. Harp Soc., Kappa Epsilon. Office: 611 E 6th St Room 303 Austin TX 78701

NICHOLAS, SAMUEL JOHN, JR., lawyer, arbitrator; b. Yazoo City, Miss., July 4, 1937; s. Samuel J. and Mildred Lucille (Jefferies) N.; children—Samuel John III, Christopher Walter, Patrick Peterson, John Thomas. B.A., U. Miss., 1959, M.B.A., 1962; J.D., Miss. Coll., 1966. Bar: Miss. 1966. Asst. prof. econs. Millsaps Coll., 1963-70; arbitrator, 1970—; adj. prof. law U. Miss., Miss. Coll. Labor. Home: Box 22512 Jackson MS 39205

NICHOLLS, RICHARD AURELIUS, obstetrician, gynecologist; b. Norfolk, Va., Aug. 12, 1941; s. Richard Beddoe and Aurelia (Gill) N.; m. Geri Bowden, Feb. 24, 1986. B.S. in Biology, Stetson U., 1963; M.D., Med. Coll. Va., 1967. Diplomate Am. Bd. Ob-Gyn. Intern, Charity Hosp., Tulane div., New Orleans, 1967-68, resident in ob-gyn, 1968-71; asst. prof. ob-gyn Tulane Med. Sch., New Orleans, 1973-74, clin. asst. prof., 1974-83; practice medicine specializing in ob-gyn, Pascagoula, Miss., 1974—; mem. staff Singing River Hosp., chmn. surg. and ob-gyn depts., 1979-80. Bd. dirs. Miss. Racing Assn. Served to maj. US. Army, 1971-73. Fellow Am. Coll. Ob-Gyn, ACS; mem. Miss. State Med. Soc., Singing River Med. Soc., Am. Fertility Soc., Am. Assn. Gynecol. Laparoscopists, Am. Med. Soc., So. Med. Soc., New Orleans Grad. Med. Assembly, New Orleans Ob-Gyn Soc., Gulf Coast Ob-Gyn Soc., Conrad Collins Ob-Gyn Soc., Am. Venereal Disease Soc. Contbr. articles to med. jours.

NICHOLS, ALPHA LEE, school counselor; b. Richmond, Va., June 8, 1937; d. Chappell George and Beatrice (Scott) Lee; m. Walter Leroy Nichols, Sept. 27, 1958; children—Wanda Nichols Glover, Sherry Lerone. B.A., Va. Union U., 1960; M.Ed., Va. Commonwealth U., 1977. Vol. tchr. Richmond Pub. Schs., 1958-59, long range substitute, 1960, itinerant French tchr., 1960-73, middle sch. French tchr., 1973-77, elem. sch. counselor, 1977—; workshop leader religious and profl. orgns.; participant Supt.'s Roundtable for Leadership Devel., 1985. Mem. North Chamberlayne Civic League, Va., 1974—; mem. Henrico County Civic League, Va., 1983—. Mem. Am. Assn. Counseling and Devel. (also mem. divs.), Central Va. Assn. Pupil Personnel Workers, Am. Mental Health Assn., NEA, Assn. Supervision and Curriculum Devel., Alpha Kappa Alpha. Clubs: Tots and Teens, Met. Bus. Lodge: Odd Fellows. Avocations: sewing; reading; collecting dolls. Home: 517 Ironington Rd Richmond VA 23227 Office: Overby-Sheppard Elem Sch 2300 1st Ave Richmond VA 23222

NICHOLS, IRBY COGHILL, JR., historian, educator; b. Baton Rouge, Apr. 10, 1926; s. Irby Coghill and Pauline (Wright) N.; B.A., La. State U., 1947; M.A., U. N.C., 1949; Ph.D., U. Mich., 1955; m. Margaret Sunshine Irby, Apr. 18, 1953; children—Nina Keith, Irby Coghill, III. Instr., Catawba Coll., 1949; teaching fellow U. Mich., 1949-52; instr. N.Mex. Mil. Inst., 1952-55; asst. prof. European history North Tex. State U., 1955-57, asso. prof., 1957-67, prof., 1967—, also dept. grad. adv.; vis. asso. prof. La. State U., summer 1962. Served with USMC, 1944-46. Recipient Louis Knott Koontz award Pacific Hist. Assn., 1968, First Ann. Jo Houston Shelton award North Tex. State U., 1976; 15 N. Tex. State U. Faculty Research Grants, 1956—. Mem. Am. Acad. Arts, Scis., So. Hist. Assn., Soc. French Hist. Studies, Southwestern Soc. Sci. Assn. (chmn. sessions 1971—, chmn. history sect. 1969-70), Smithsonian Instn., World Future Soc., Phi Kappa Phi, Phi Alpha Theta. Democrat. Episcopalian. Author: The European Pentarchy and the Congress of Verona, 1822, 1971; (with Paul Smith and Dwane Kingery) North Texas State University A Self-Study, 1962; history asso. editor Social Sci. Quar. (formerly Southwestern Social Sci. Quar.), 1961-64; contbr. articles to profl. publs. Home: 2514 Royal Ln Denton TX 76201 Office: Box 6212 North Tex Sta Denton TX 76203

NICHOLS, JACK BRITT, lawyer; b. Tampa, Fla., Mar. 14, 1936; s. Robert Jack and Dora Virginia (Knight) N.; B.S. in Bus. Adminstrn., U. Fla., 1958, J.D., 1965; m. Janice Magill, Apr. 4, 1958; children—Sara Lynn, Douglas Britt. Bar: Fla. 1966. Assoc. firm Gurney & Skolfield, Winter Park, Fla., 1966-68, Gurney, Skolfield & Frey, 1968-69, officer Skolfield, Gilman, Cooper, Nichols, Tatich & Adams, 1969-71, v.p. Skolfield, Nichols & Tatich, 1971-73, pres. Nichols & Tatich, 1973-75, Jack B. Nichols, P.A., Orlando, Fla., 1975—. Chmn., Maitland (Fla.) Arts Festival, 1979; mem. Pres.'s Council, U. Fla., 1973—. Served to maj. AUS, 1958-63. Decorated Army Commendation medal; recipient Disting. Service award Winter Park Jaycees, 1972. Diplomate Acad. Fla. Trial Lawyers; cert. civil trial adv. Nat. Bd. Trial Advocacy; cert. civil trial lawyer, Fla. mem. Assn. Trial Lawyers Am. (sustaining), ABA, Fla. Bar, Orange County Bar Assn. (exec. council 1973-75), Fla. Blue Key, Delta Tau Delta. Methodist. Lodges: Rotary (pres. Maitland 1978; Paul Harris fellow); Masons (32 deg.), Scottish Rite. Home: 20 Maitland Groves Rd Maitland FL 32751 Office: PO Box 33 Orlando FL 32802

NICHOLS, JACK EDWARD, JR., ednl. adminstr.; b. Huntington, W.Va., Feb. 3, 1948; s. Jack Edward and Elizabeth A. (Arrington) N.; B.A., Marshall U., 1970, M.A., 1972; Ph.D., Ohio U., 1980; m. Sue Ellen Ferguson, Dec. 22, 1973. Tchr. Cox's Landing Elem. Sch., Cabell County, W.Va., 1970-76; prin. Greenbottom Elem. Sch., Cabell County, 1977; asst. prin. Milton Elem. Sch., Cabell County, 1978; prin. Harveytown Elem. Sch., Huntington, W.Va., 1979-81, Jefferson Elem. Sch., Huntington, 1981-83, Culloden Elem. Sch., 1983—. Active Big Bros. Am.; coach Boys' Club. Hershel C. Price Ednl. Found. scholar, 1976-79. Mem. NEA, Cabell County Elem. Prins. Assn., Phi Delta Kappa. Republican. Methodist. Club: Esquire Country. Home: 826 Big Bend Rd Barboursville WV 25504

NICHOLS, JAMES RICHARD, civil engineer; b. Amarillo, Tex., June 29, 1923; s. Marvin Curtis and Ethel N.; B.S. in Civil Engring., Tex. A&M U., 1949, M.S. in C.E., 1950; m. Billie Louise Smith, Dec. 24, 1944; children—Judith Ann, James R., Jr., John M. Pres., Freese and Nichols, Inc., Ft. Worth, 1977—; dir. Ft. Worth Corp.; dir. M/Bank Fort Worth. Bd. dirs. North Tex. Commn., Fort Worth, 1969—; chmn. bd. trustees All Saints Episcopal Hosp., Ft. Worth; trustee Tex. A&M U. Research Found.; chmn. bd. trustees Tex. Wesleyan Coll., Ft. Worth; chmn. United Way Campaign, 1983; past pres. United Way of Tarrant County. Served with AUS, 1943-46. Registered profl. engr., Tex., Okla., N.Mex. Mem. Cons. Engrs. Council, ASCE, Nat. Soc. Profl. Engrs., Newcomen Soc. Methodist. Club: Ft. Worth. Lodges: Masons, Rotary. Home: 4821 Overton Woods Dr Fort Worth TX 76109 Office: 811 Lamar St Fort Worth TX 76102

NICHOLS, JOYCE HILLEY, nurse; b. Calhoun Falls, S.C., Sept. 4, 1931; d. Weaver Donald and Julia Mazelle (Adams) Hilley; m. Harold Penrod Simmons, Apr. 1, 1952 (div. 1975); children—Carolyn Simmons Griffith, Eugene Penrod; m. 2d James Victor Nichols, Feb. 22, 1980. R.N., Med. U. S.C., 1952; E.M.T., North Trident Tech. Coll., 1981; student Coll. Charleston, 1979. Cert. occupational health nurse. Head nurse surgery Roper Hosp., Charleston, S.C., 1966-69; mgr. Community Blood and Plasma Services, Inc., 1969-75; occupational health nurse Mobay Chem. Corp., Charleston, 1975-78, supr. med. dept., 1978—; CPR/first aid instr. Active Charleston County Civil Def., ARC. Mem. Am. Assn. Occupational Health Nurses, S.C. Assn. Occupational Health Nurses, Southeastern Occupational Health Nurses, Alumni Assn. Med. U. S.C., Am. Contract Bridge League (life master), Nat. Trust Historic Preservation, Preservation Soc. of Charleston (vol. home tours), Historic Ansonborough Assn. Episcopalian. Contbr. articles to profl. jours. Home: 27 1/2 Wentworth St Charleston SC 29401 Office: PO Box 10288 Charleston SC 29411

NICHOLS, LYNN DAVID, choral-band educator; b. Hawkins County, Tenn., Sept. 11, 1933; s. Charles Seviere and Ruby (Carter) N.; B.S., M.E., Carson Newman Coll., 1955; dip. Wurzburg Conservatory, 1957-58; D.Higher Edn. (hon.), Memphis State U., 1956. Band dir. McNairy County, Tenn. Bd. Edn., 1955-56; music dir. Morristown (Tenn.) City Schs., 1958-60, Knoxville (Tenn.) City Schs., 1960-62; entertainment dir. U.S. Army Spl. Services, Stuttgart and Augsburg, Ger., 1962-68; band and music supr. Greene County Bd. Edn., Mosheim, Tenn., 1969—; dir. music Christ Ch., Greeneville, Tenn.; choir dir., soloist Church St. Meth. Ch., Knoxville, 1960-62. Served with U.S. Army, 1956-58. Tenn. Bur. Transp. scholar, 1978-79. Mem. Music Educators Nat. Conf., NEA, Tenn. Edn. Assn., Tenn. Choral Soc., Tenn. Band Assn., Am. Guild Organists. Democrat. Methodist. Club: Exchange (bd. dirs. 1978-79, pres.-elect 1979-80), European Recreation Soc. Home: 135 Woodbine Ave Bulls Gap TN 37711 Office: Union at Charles St Greenville TN 37743

NICHOLS, MYRNA BULLOCK, commercial real estate broker; b. Dallas, May 7, 1937; d. Ollie O. and Patty Lou (Sutherland) Bulloch; children—Susan Janice Nichols Walton, Jere Blake Nichols. Student McMurry Coll., 1955-56, U. Tex.-Arlington, 1957, Stephen F. Austin State U., 1958. Licensed real estate broker, Tex. Documentation engr. Sci. Control Corp., Carrollton, Tex., 1967-69; asst. to v.p. Electronic Data Systems, Dallas, 1969-73; mktg./leasing agt. Vantage Companies, Dallas, 1973-76; comml. broker Cushman & Wakefield of Texas, Inc., Dallas, 1979—. Named 1984 Broker of the Year, Cushman & Wakefield; recipient 1984 Outstanding Achievement award, Comml. Real Estate Women. Mem. Tex. Assn. Realtors, Nat. Assn. Realtors, Women in Indsl. Real Estate, Comml. Real Estate Women (pres. 1985, treas. 1984), Greater Dallas Bd. Realtors (comml. investment div.). Methodist. Republican. Home: 3226 San Sebastian Dr Carrollton TX 75006 Office: Cushman & Wakefield of Texas Inc Three Lincoln Centre Dallas TX 75240

NICHOLS, PETER BALDWIN, college administrator; b. Mt. Kisco, N.Y., Apr. 14, 1949; s. Charles Eaton and Barbara Ann (Baldwin) N.; A.A., Strayer Coll., 1969; B.S., Fort Lauderdale U., 1971; M.Ed., Nova U., 1974, Ed.D., 1983; m. Elda Margot Marth, June 20, 1970; 1 son, Matthew David. Supt. schs. All Saints Ch., Ft. Lauderdale, Fla., 1970-72; tchr., coach, supt. schs. St. Ambrose Sch., Ft. Lauderdale, 1972-74; tchr., coach Am. Heritage Sch., Plantation, Fla., 1974-78, vice prin., 1978-82; dir. ednl. services Prospect Hall Coll., Hollywood, Fla., 1982-86, v.p., 1986—. Asst. cubmaster Cub Scouts Am.; bd. dirs. Pine Island Ridge Condominium Assn. Mem. Nat. Assn. Secondary Sch. Prins., Assn. Supervision and Curriculum Devel. Republican. Episcopalian. Office: 1725 Monroe St Hollywood FL 33021

NICHOLS, WARD HAMPTON, artist; b. Welch, W.Va., July 5, 1930; s. Hugh Hampton and Frances (Logan) N.; m. Ethel Marsh, June 6, 1953; children—David, Stephen, Michael. Artist in residence U. Ind., Terre Haute, 1972, The Greenbrier, White Sulphur Springs, W. Va., 1971, West Liberty Coll., W.Va., 1980. One man shows: The Gutenberg Collection, Gutenberg Mus., Mainz, Fed. Republic Germany. Recipient several major awards. Home: 318 Elm St Beaumont North Wilkesboro NC 28659

NICHOLS, WILLIAM, congressman; b. Amory, Miss., Oct. 16, 1918; B.S. in Agr., Auburn U., 1939, M.A., 1941; m. Carolyn Funderburk; children—Memorie Nichols Mitchell, Margaret, Flynt. Vice pres. Parker Fertilizer Co., Sylacauga, Ala., 1947-66; pres. Parker Gin Co., Sylacauga, 1947-60; mem. Ala. Senate, 1963-66, chmn. mil. affairs com., also fin. and taxation com.; mem. 90-92d congresses from 4th Ala. Dist., mem. armed services com., chmn. subcom. on mil. compensation, 1978-82, agr. com., chmn. house flag day com., 1971-76; mem. 93d-98th Congresses from 3d Ala. Dist., chmn. armed services investigations subcom., 1983—. Mem. Sylacauga Bd. Edn.; bd. govs. Nat. hall of Fame; trustee Auburn U. Served to capt. AUS, 1942-47. Decorated Bronze Star, Purple Heart. Named Outstanding Mem. Ala. Senate, Capitol Press Corps, 1965, Man of Year in Agr., Progressive Farmer mag., 1965; named to Ala. Acad. Honor, 1983. Mem. Ala. Cattlemens Assn., U. Auburn Alumni Assn., Ala. Farm Bur., VFW, DAV, Am. Legion, Blue Key, Scabbard and Blade, Gamma Sigma Delta. Democrat. Methodist. Office: 2407 Rayburn House Office Bldg Washington DC 20515

NICHOLSON, ADELE JACQUELINE, nurse, cosmetic company executive; b. Newark, May 14, 1948; d. Francis and Terry (Scailla) La Morte; m. Robert E. Nicholson Jr., Apr. 29, 1978. Nursing diploma Elizabeth (N.J.) Gen. Sch. Nursing; A.A., Miami Dade Community Coll., 1976; B.S. in Mgmt., Fla. Internat. U., 1981; postgrad., U. Miami, 1982-85. R.N. Obstet. nurse South Miami (Fla.) Hosp., 1976-80; asst. mgr. Saks Fifth Avenue, Bal Harbour, Fla., 1980-81; clin. educator Victoria Hosp., Miami, Fla., 1981-83; pub. relations asst. Neiman-Marcus, Bal Harbour, 1983-85; pub. relations dir. Clientele Cosmetics Inc., 1985—. Author, instr. Time Mgmt., 1982. Mem. West Orange Republican Com., 1968-72. Merit scholar Fla. Internat. U., 1978-80; Am. Inst. Abroad scholar, France. Mem. So. Fla. Health Care Educators, Patient Edn. Assn., Phi Theta Kappa. Roman Catholic. Clubs: FASHA (v.p. 1980-81), Internat. Relations (Miami). Office: Clientele Cosmetics 5205 NW 163d St Miami FL 33014

NICHOLSON, GRACE MARIA, therapist, counselor; b. Tucson, May 2, 1952; d. Rocco Joseph and Eloise Annette (Krebs) Cambareri; m. Kenneth Morgan Nicholson, Dec. 21, 1974. A.A., Broward Community Coll., 1972; B.S., Fla. State U., 1974, Ed.S., 1980; M.A., U. West Fla., 1978; Contract specialist Eglin AFB, Fla., 1974; ednl. aide, Korat RTAFB, Thailand, 1975; youth counselor Children and Youth Services, Fort Walton Beach, Fla., 1976-81; rehab. counselor Vocat. Rehab., Fort Walton Beach, 1981-82; staff psychologist Eastern State Hosp., Williamsburg, Va., 1982-83; family therapist 8th Dist. Ct. Services Unit, Hampton, Va., 1983-85. Chmn. Family Counseling Adv. Com., Suffolk Region, Va., 1984-85. Mem. Howe Farms Archlt. Control Com., Hampton, 1985; block capt. Neighborhood Watch, 1983-85. Mem. Nat. Acad. Cert. Clin. Mental Health Counselors, Am. Assn. Counseling and Devel., Am. Mental Health Counselors Assn., Phi Kappa Phi. Club: Peninsula Tennis Patrons Assn. Avocations: tennis; skiing; sailing; running; photography. Office: 435 CSG/FS APO New York NY 090570

NICHOLSON, LUTHER BEAL, accountant; b. Sulphur Springs, Tex., Dec. 15, 1921; s. Stephen Edward and Elma (McCracken) N.; B.B.A., So. Meth. U., 1942, postgrad., 1946-47, Tex. U., 1947-48; diploma Southwestern Grad. Sch. Banking, 1967; m. Ruth Wimbish, May 29, 1952; children—Penelope Elizabeth, Stephen David. Controller, Varo, Inc., Garland, Tex., 1946-55, dir., 1947-72, v.p. fin., 1955-66, sr. v.p., 1966-67, exec. v.p., 1967-70, pres., 1970-71, chmn. bd., 1971-72, cons. to bd. dirs., 1972-75. Gen. mgr. Challenger Lock Co., Los Angeles, 1956-58; dir. Varo Inc. Electrokinetics div., Varo Optical, Inc., Biometrics Instrument Corp., Varo Atlas GmbH, Micropac Industries, Inc., Gt. No. Corp., Mercantile Bank Garland, Garland Enterprises, Inc., Newan Oil Co., Inc. Bd. dirs., exec. v.p. Harriett Stanton-Edna Murray Found. Served with AUS, 1942-46. Mem. Financial Execs. Inst. (past pres.), Am. Inst. C.P.A.s, A.I.M., Am. Mgmt. Assn., N.A.M. Home: 1917 Melody Ln Garland TX 75042 Office: 610 W Garland Ave Garland TX 75040

NICHOLSON, MYREEN MOORE, researcher, artist; b. Norfolk, Va., June 2, 1940; d. William Chester and Illeen (Fox) Moore; m. Roland Quarles Nicholson, Jan. 9, 1964 (div. 1978); 1 dau., Andrea Joy; m. 2d Harold Wellington McKinney, II, Jan. 18, 1981; 1 dau., Clara Isadora. B.A., William and Mary Coll., 1962; M.S.L.S., U. N.C., 1971; postgrad. Old Dominion U., 1964-68, 75—, The Citadel, 1968-69. Tech. writer City Planning/Art Commn., Norfolk, 1964-65; art tchr. Norfolk pub. schs., 1965-67; prof. lit., art Palmer Jr. Coll., Charleston, S.C., 1968; librarian Charleston Schs., 1968-69; asst. to dir. City Library Norfolk, 1970-72, research librarian, 1972—; dir. W. Ghent Arts Alliance, Norfolk, 1978—. Book reviewer Art Book Revs., Library Jour., 1973-76; editor, illustrator Acquisitions Bibliographies, 1970—. Mem. Virginia Beach Arts Ctr., 1978—, Peninsula Art Ctr., 1983—; bd. dirs. W. Ghent Art/Lit. Festival, 1979. Coll. William and Mary art scholar, 1958; Nat. Endowment Arts grantee, 1975. Mem. ALA, Southeastern Library Assn., Poetry Soc. Va., Art Libraries Soc. N.Am., Tidewater Artists Assn., Acad. Am. Poets. Home: 1404 Gates Ave Norfolk VA 23507 Office: Norfolk Pub Library 301 E City Hall Ave Norfolk VA 23507

NICKLE, DENNIS EDWIN, computer scientist; b. Sioux City, Iowa, Jan. 30, 1936; s. Harold Bateman and Helen Cecilia (Killackey) N.; B.S. in Math., Fla. State U., 1961. Reliability mathematician Pratt & Whitney Aircraft Co., W. Palm Beach, Fla., 1961-63; br. supr. Melpar Inc., Falls Church, Va., 1963-66; prin. mem. tech. staff Xerox Data Systems, Rockville, Md., 1966-70; sr. tech. officer WHO, Washington, 1970-76; software quality assurance mgr. Melpar div. E-Systems Corp., Falls Church, 1976—; ordained deacon Roman Catholic Ch., 1979. Chief judge for math. and computers Fairfax County Regional Sci. Fair, 1964-82; scoutmaster, commr. Boy Scouts Am., 1957—; youth custodian Fairfax County Juvenile Ct., 1973—; chaplain No. Va. Regional Juvenile Detention Home, 1978—; moderator Nocturnal Adoration Soc. Served with arty. U.S. Army, 1958-60. Recipient Eagle award, Silver award, Silver Beaver award, other awards Boy Scouts Am.; Ad-Altare Dei St. George Emblem, Diocese of Richmond. Mem. Assn. Computing Machinery, Old Crows Assn., Rolm Mil-Spec Computer Users Group (internat. pres.), IEEE (sr.), Nat. Rifle Assn. (life), Alpha Phi Omega (life), Sigma Phi Epsilon. Club: KC (4 deg.). Home: 4925 Van Walbeek Pl Annandale VA 22003 Office: 7700 Arlington Blvd Falls Church VA 22046

NICKLES, DON, U.S. senator; b. Ponca City, Okla., Dec. 6, 1948; s. Robert C. and Coeweene (Bryan) N.; B.B.A., Okla. State U., 1971; m. Linda L. Morrison, Sept. 5, 1968; children—Donald Lee, Jennifer Lynn, Kim Elizabeth, Robyn Lee. Propr., Don Nickles Profl. Cleaning Service, Stillwater, Okla., 1968-71, Nickles Machine Corp., Ponca City, 1972-80; mem. Okla. State Senate, 1979-80; mem. U.S. Senate from Okla., 1981—, mem. com. labor and human resources, energy and natural resources, small bus., chmn. subcom. labor, subcom. govtl. procurement, subcom. on water and power. Bd. dirs. Ponca City United Way; mem. Kay Council Retarded Children, St. Mary's Parish Council; mem. adv. bd. Salvation Army. Served with Kans. N.G., 1970-76. Named Outstanding State Legislator by conference of conservative groups, 1979. Mem. Ponca City C. of C., Fellowship Christian Athletes. Republican. Roman Catholic. Club: Rotary. Office: US Senate Washington DC 20510

NICKLES, JAMES ALLEN, accountant; b. Ponca City, Okla., Dec. 9, 1946; s. Robert Clair and Coeweene B. (Bryan) N.; m. Janie Faye Hutchison, Aug. 3, 1968; children—James Allen II, Denae Leanne, Lindsey Noel. B.B.A., Okla. State U., 1970. C.P.A., Okla. Staff acct. Peat, Marwick, Mitchell & Co., Tulsa, 1970-73, supr., mgr., 1973-80; pvt. practice acctg., Tulsa, 1980—. Bd. dirs., treas. PTA, 1979-80, Okla. Mu Alumni Corp., 1978—; active Leadership Tulsa. Served with Okla. N.G., 1968; with USAR, 1969-73. Mem. Am. Inst. C.P.A.s, Okla. Soc. C.P.A.s. Republican. Roman Catholic. Home: 7509 S 70th East Ave Tulsa OK 74133 Office: 4853 S Sheridan Suite 603 Tulsa OK 74145

NICKS, ROY SULLIVAN, university president; b. Chapel Hill, Tenn., June 30, 1933; s. Richard D. and Cora (Sullivan) N.; m. Barbara Jean Love, Jan. 22, 1960; children—Beverly Jean, Richard Matthew. Student, Martin Coll., 1952-53; B.S., Middle Tenn. State U., 1955; M.A., U. Tenn., 1957; Ed.D., Memphis State U., 1969. Personnel trainee State of Ala., 1955; instr., tng. officer Bur. Pub. Adminstrn., U. Tenn., 1956-57; sr. budget analyst dept. fin. and adminstrn. State of Tenn., 1959-60, chief of budget, 1961-63, dep. commr., 1963-65, commr. dept. welfare, 1963-65, asst. to gov., 1965-67; asst. to pres. Memphis State U., 1967-69; chancellor U. Tenn-Nashville, 1970-75; chancellor State Univ. and Community Coll. System of Tenn., Nashville, 1975—; v.p. urban and pub. affairs U. Tenn. System, 1973-75. Pres., Tenn. Conf. Social Welfare, 1964-65; trustee United Givers Fund; bd. dirs. Frank G. Clement Found. Inc., Better Bus. Bur. Nashville and Middle Tenn. Served with AUS, 1957-58. Mem. Nashville Area C. of C. (edn. com. 1970—, bd. govs. 1974—), Am. Pub. Welfare Assn. (pres. 1969-70), Kappa Delta Pi. Democrat. Methodist. Contbr. articles to profl. jours. Office: State University and Community College System of Tenn 1161 Murfreesboro Rd Nashville TN 37217

NICOL, WILLIAM KENNEDY, ins. co. exec.; b. Hamilton, Ont., Can., July 20, 1922; s. William R. and Mae (Kennedy) N.; B.A., U. Toronto, 1949; m. Phyllis Bowie, Feb. 7, 1946 (dec. 1969); children—Frances Mae (Mrs. Ben H. Teague), Christine (Mrs. Recy L. Dunn), Catherine (Mrs. Joe Meyer); m. 2d, Jessie Helms, Jan. 18, 1974. Came to U.S., 1952. Asso. actuary Tchrs. Ins. and Annuity Assn., 1952-55; controller, actuary Commonwealth Life Ins. Co., Louisville, 1955-61; v.p., actuary Am. Nat. Ins. Co., Galveston, Tex., 1961-69, exec. v.p. ins. services, 1969-74, exec. v.p. research, 1974—; v.p., dir. Am. Nat. Life Ins. Co. Tex., Standard Life and Accident Ins. Co. Okla.; dir. Commonwealth Life & Accident Ins. Co., St. Louis, Am. Nat. Credit Ins. Co., Dallas, Am. Nat. Gen. Ins. Co., Am. Nat. Property and Casualty Co., Mo. Enrolled actuary. Fellow Soc. Actuaries; mem. Am. Acad. Actuaries, Actuaries Club S.W.; corr. mem. Canadian Inst. Actuaries. Home: 7009 N Holiday Dr Galveston TX 77550 Office: Am Nat Ins Co One Moody Plaza Galveston TX 77550

NICOLADIS, FRANK, engineering company executive; b. Gulfport, Miss., Oct. 23, 1935; s. Michael P. and Maria T. Nicoladis; m. Pagona Gemelos, Feb. 15, 1959; children—Micahel, Dean, Maria. B.S. in Civil Engring., Miss. State U., 1957. Engr., Fromherz Engrs., New Orleans, 1957-61; assoc., br. office mgr. Albert Switzer & Assocs., Baton Rouge, 1961-65; asst. chief engr. Howkratt Constrn. Co., New Orleans, 1965; project engr. Burk & Assocs. Inc., New Orleans, 1965-69; pres. N-Y Assocs. Inc., Metairie, La., 1969—; Served with USAR, 1957-65. Mem. ASCE, Water Pollution Control Fedn., Am. Waterworks Assn., Am. Pub. Works Assn., La. Engring. Soc., Miss. Engring. Soc., Nat. Soc. Profl. Engrs., Am. Planning Assn., Am. Soc. Cons. Planners, Soc. Am. Mil. Engrs. Home: 5924 Wheeler Dr Metairie LA 70003 Office: 2700 Lake Villa Dr Metairie LA 70002

NICOLETTI, PAUL LEE, veterinarian, educator; b. Goodman, Mo., Oct. 26, 1932; s. Felix and Clarice Nicoletti; m. Earlene Blackburn, June 6, 1954; children—Diana, Julie, Nancy. B.S. in Agr., U. Mo., 1956, D.V.M., 1956; M.S., U. Wis., 1962. Veterinarian, U.S. Dept. Agr., Mo., Wis., N.Y., 1956-68, UN Food and Agr. Orgn., Teheran, Iran, 1968-72, U.S. Dept. Agr., Jackson, Miss., 1972-75, Gainesville, Fla., 1973-78; prof. veterinarian medicine U. Fla., Gainesville, 1978—. Recipient awards from Fla. Cattleman's Assn., 1978, Dairy Farmers, Inc., 1978, Borden's award, 1979; Gold Star award Fla. Veterinary Medicine Assoc., 1981; Universidad Austral de Chile, 1981, Puerto Rico Dairy Assn., 1978. Mem. Am. Veterinary Medicine Assn., Am. Coll. Veterinary Preventive Medicine, Am. Assn. Bovine Practice. Contbr. numerous articles to profl. jours. Home: 2552 SW 14th Dr Gainesville FL 32608 Office: College of Veterinary Medicine Box J 136 U Fla Gainesville FL 32610

NICOLITZ, ERNST, ophthalmologist, educator; b. Surabaja, Java, Indonesia, Jan. 7, 1947; came to U.S., 1956; naturalized, 1961; s. Alexander Renauld and Augustine Adeline (Godschalk) N.; m. Elizabeth Ann Perkins, July 30, 1971; children—Ryan, Marlana, Jennifer. B.S. in Chemistry, N.Mex. State U., 1969; grad. UCLA, 1969-70; M.D., U. N.Mex., 1974. Diplomate Am. Bd. Ophthalmology, Nat. Bd. Med. Examiners. Resident in eye surgery U. Ala., Birmingham, 1974-77; oculoplastic fellow Wills Eye Hosp., Phila., 1977-78; practice medicine specializing in ophthalmology, Jacksonville, Fla., 1978—; chief ophthalmology Baptist Med. Ctr., Jacksonville, 1984—; asst. clin. prof. U. Fla., Gainesville, 1979—. Contbr. articles to profl. jours. Med. advisor Prevent Blindness, Jacksonville, 1978—. Recipient Physician Recognition award AMA, 1984. Fellow ACS, Am. Soc. Ophthalmic Plastic Surgery, Am. Acad. Ophthalmology. Republican. Presbyterian. Avocations: fishing; travel; photography; tennis. Office: 820 Prudential Dr #107 Jacksonville FL 32207

NIEDERGESES, JAMES D., bishop; b. Lawrenceburg, Tenn., Feb. 2, 1917. Student, St. Bernard Coll., St. Ambrose Coll., Mt. St. Mary Sem. of West, Athenaeum of Ohio. Ordained priest Roman Catholic Ch., 1944; pastor Our Lady of Perpetual Help, Chattanooga, 1962-73, Sts. Peter and Paul Parish, 1973-75; bishop of, Nashville, 1975—; mem. personnel bd. Diocese of Nashville. Office: 2400 21st Ave S Nashville TN 37219*

NIEDERMEIER, WILLIAM, biochemistry educator; b. Evansville, Ind., Apr. 1, 1923; s. Christian Henry and Emma Margaret (Sailer) N.; m. Jane Eleanor Bacon, June 26, 1945 (div. 1973); children—Nancy, Wayne, Michael, Craig; m. 2d, Beverly Joan Ward, June 8, 1974. Student, Evansville (Ind.) Coll., 1941-42; B.S., Purdue U., 1946; M.S., U. Ala.-Birmingham, 1953, Ph.D., 1960. Chemist, Mead Johnson & Co., Evansville, Ind., 1946-49; instr. nutrition and metabolism Northwestern U., 1950-60; asst. prof. biochemistry in medicine U. Ala.-Birmingham, 1960-69, assoc. prof., 1969—. Mem. Am. Chem. Soc. (chmn. Ala. sect. 1967, mem. exec. com. Ala. sect. 1975—), Soc. Applied Spectroscopy, AAAS, Am. Soc. Biochemists, Am. Assn. Immunologists. Contbr. 100 articles to nat. and internat. sci. jours. Served with USN, 1943-46. Office: Med Ctr Dept Medicine U Ala Birmingham AL 35294

NIELSEN, PENNY JO, education educator, consultant; b. Redfield, S.D., July 14, 1949; d. Vernon Leon and Joree Marley N. B.S., So. Coll., 1971; M.Ed., Memphis State U., 1973, Ed.D., 1976. Elementary tchr., Winter Haven, Fla., 1971-72, Memphis, 1972-73; reading improvement tchr., Memphis, 1973-75; asst. prof. edn. Nicholls State U., Thibodaux, La., 1976-78; assoc. prof. edn. Jacksonville (Ala.) State U., 1978-83; cons. La. Assisted Program, Houma, 1978-79; profl. growth cons. Anniston (Ala.) City Schs., 1982-83; pvt. reading tutor, Anniston, 1979-83; pres. Leadership Dynamics, Anniston, 1985—; assoc. prof. edn. Talladega Coll., Ala., 1984-85; adj. prof. Gadsden Community Coll., Anniston, 1985—. Mem. Internat. Reading Assn., Nat. Reading Conf., Coll. Reading Assn., NEA, Internat. Platform Assn., Ala. Reading Assn., Post Secondary Reading Council Ala., Cheaha Area Reading Assn., Phi Delta Kappa, Kappa Delta Pi. Contbr. articles to profl. jours. Home: 900 Parker Blvd Weaver AL 36277

NIEMANN, KURT MAX WALTER, orthopaedic surgeon, educator; b. Bklyn., July 31, 1932; s. Walter and Walburg V. S. N.; m. Violet Theresa Humenik, Feb. 14, 1956; children—Susan, Kurt Max Walter, Rebecca, Eric. B.S., Trinity Coll., 1954; M.D., Med. Coll. Ala., 1960. Diplomate Am. Bd. Orthopaedic Surgery. Intern, Med. Coll. Va. Hosp., Richmond, 1961; resident U. Pitts., 1962-65, asst. prof. orthopaedic surgery, 1967-69; assoc. prof. orthopaedic surgery U. Ala., Birmingham, 1969-74, prof. and dir. div. orthopaedic surgery, 1974—. Served to 2d lt. USAF, 1954-56. Mem. Am. Acad. Orthopaedic Surgery, Am. Orthopaedic Soc. for Sports Medicine, Clin. Orthopaedic Soc., So. Orthopaedic Assn. Lutheran. Contbr. chpts. to books, articles in field to publs. Office: 619 S 19th St Birmingham AL 35233

NIETO-CARDOSO, EZEQUIEL, counseling educator, consultant; b. Valle, Guanajuato, Mex., Oct. 28, 1933; s. Ezequiel José and María (Cardoso) N. B.S., U. Coahuila, Saltillo, 1960; M. Theology, U. Letran, Rome, 1959; M.Ed., Loyola U., 1971, Ph.D., 1975; M. Orgn. Devel., U. Monterrey, Nuevo León, Mex., 1976. Prof., U. Monterrey, 1975-78, dean, 1980-82, dean emeritus, 1982—, cons., 1984—, cons. researcher, 1985—; prof. U. Iberoamericana, Mexico City, 1978-80, now cons.; researcher Centro Interdisciplinario de Investigación y Docencia en Educación Técnica, Querétaro, Mex., 1982-84; pres. Nat. Council of Psychology, Mexico City, 1975-77. Editor several orgn. devel. books, 1979—. Translator several psychology books, 1976-82. Contbr. articles to profl. jours. Mem. Peace World Movement, Mex., 1977, Ecumenical Movement, Rome, 1970. Named Disting. Mem., Nat. Council Psychology, 1975; Christian Brothers fellow, 1968. Mem. Am. Psychol. Assn., Am. Assn. Counseling and Devel., Assn. Humanistic Psychology, Mex. Assn. Psychology. Roman Catholic. Clubs: La Hacienda, Serra Internat. Avocations: archeology, swimming, reading, creative writing, traveling. Home: Hacienda Balvanera 45 Mansiones 76180 Querétaro México 76180 Office: U Monterrey San Pedro 102 Sur/Col del Valle Garza Garcia Nuevo León México 66220

NIEVES-RODRIGUEZ, MIGUEL ANGEL, mercantile executive; b. Penuelas, P.R., May 8, 1913; s. Vicente Cosme Nieves and Gertrudis Rodriguez; m. Ana Maria Rodriguez, Dec. 10, 1934; children—Maria del Rosario, Miguel Angel, Ana Teresa, Carmen Luisa, Jose Randolph. Student U. P.R., 1967. Office mgr. Bosch Bros., Ponce, P.R., 1930; corr. El Imparcial newspaper, P.R., 1933; columnist various local newspapers, P.R., 1932-74; announcer, script writer Sta. WPRP, Ponce, 1934-47; founder Federacion Deportiva, Mercedita-Ponce, P.R., 1933-41; sales mgr. Colgate-Palmolive Co., San Juan, P.R., 1964; gen. mgr. and asst. v.p. Spanish Am. Trading, San Juan, 1966; exec. dir. Bd. Trade of P.R., San Juan, 1967—; 1st v.p. Inst. Psicopedagogico of P.R., 1957. P.R. del. Internat. Symposium on Mental Retardation, Bombay, India, 1979; apptd. personal escort to rep. of Pope Paul VI, Mariologic Congress, Santo Domingo, Dominican Republic, 1964; bd. dirs. P.R. council Boy Scouts Am., 1963. Served with N.G., 1940. Recipient cross medal Pro Ecclesia et Pontifice, 1983, spl. diploma for Golden Wedding Anniversary, 1984, Merit award Bd. Trade of P.R., 1975, Merit award Broadcasters Associates of P.R., 1978, spl. award Camara Comerciantes Mayoristas P.R., 1986, other merit awards from K.C., Lions Club, Penuelas Mcpl. Govt., P.R. Ho. of Reps. Mem. Hist. Assn. P.R., Am. Assn. of Mental Deficiency. Roman Catholic. Clubs: Peñolano (past navigator), K.C. (hon. life, 4th degree, bd. dirs.).

NIGH, GEORGE, governor of Oklahoma; b. McAlester, Okla., June 9, 1927; s. Wilber and Irene (Crockett) N.; m. Donna Mashburn, 1963; children—Mike, Georgeann. Student, Eastern A&M Coll., 1946-47, 47-48; B.A., E. Central State Coll., 1950. Partner Nigh Grocery, McAlester, 1956-60; mem. Okla. Legislature, 1950-58; lt. gov., Okla., 1958-63, 67-79, gov., 1963, 79—; Chmn. Nat. Conf. Lt. Govs., 1970-71. Mem. Okla. Young Democrats (pres.), Okla. Jr. C. of C. (sec.), Am. Legion, V.F.W., Am. Vets. Baptist. Club: Mason (32 deg., Shriner). Office: Office of Governor Oklahoma City OK 73105*

NISTAL, GERARD ELMER, business educator; b. Corona, N.Y., July 6, 1920; s. Sixto P. and Adalaide K. (Keene) N.; m. Rose Lee Grace, Aug. 27, 1960; 1 dau., Mary Grace Kathleen. B.S. in Engring. Mgmt., NYU, 1954, M.B.A., 1958; Ed.D. in Higher Edn. Adminstrn., U. So. Miss., 1981; postgrad. USAF Command and Staff Coll., 1974, NYU Law Sch., La. State U. Grad. Sch. Bus. Cert. hearing examiner, La. With RCA, N.Y.C., 1950-55, Philco-Ford, Phila., 1955-60; mktg. dir., gen. mgr. ATP and WatchMaster divs. Bulova Watch Co., N.Y.C., 1960-67, mgr. tech. sales and service co.; v.p. mktg. MOWBOT Inc., Buffalo, 1967-69, exec. v.p., 1969-71; asst. prof. bus. Erie County Community Coll., Buffalo, 1971-74, Southeast La. U., Hammond, 1974-76; assoc. prof., div. chmn. Holy Cross Coll. Sch. Bus., 1976-82, prof., dean, 1982—; litigation cons., expert witness Nat. Forensic Ctr. Bus. and econs. sect. chmn. La. Conf. Colls. and Univs. Mem. New Orleans Met. Bus. Task Force on Edn.; mem. Jefferson Parish steering com. on edn.; pres., bd. dirs. N. Shore Republican club, mem. Queens County Rep. com., 1952-67; candidate N.Y. Legislature, 1962, 64; mem. Jefferson Parish Rep. com., 1978—; bd. dirs. N. Shore Boys Club, N. Shore chpt. ARC, N.Y.C.; mem. Terrytown Civic Assn., 1976—. Served with USAF, 1937-52; CAP/USAF, 1962-82, lt. col. ret. Mem. Assn. La. Bus. Deans, West Bank Council Greater New Orleans, C. of C., Nat. Assn. Bus. Economists, Am. Mktg. Assn., AAUP, AIAA, IEEE, Acad. Mgmt., So. Bus. Adminstrn. Assn., Mensa, Air Force Assn. (pres. New Orleans chpt. 1984—), Phi Kappa Phi. Roman Catholic. Contbr. numerous articles to profl. publs. Home: 721 Mystic Ave Gretna LA 70053 Office: 4123 Woodland Dr New Orleans LA 70114

NIVEN, KURT NEUBAUER, art appraiser; b. Vienna, Austria, July 19, 1922; s. Salmon and Julia (Waldmann) Neubauer; ed. Austria; m. Helen Wexler Niven; 1 dau., Dorit. Came to U.S., 1958, naturalized, 1963. Certified appraiser Albert Einstein Coll. Medicine, Bronx, N.Y., 1959-61, buyer constrn. dept., 1959-61; pres. Visual Art and Gallery, Inc., Dallas, 1964-77; pres. K. Niven Sales Corp., Dallas, 1974—; appraiser of art World Trade Center, 1974—; collector graphic art. Served with Brit. Army, 1939-45, Israeli Army, 1948-49. Mem. Am. Soc. Appraisers, Tex. Art Assn., New Eng. Appraisers Assn. Odd Fellow. Office: WTC 338-1 World Trade Center Dallas TX 75258 also 1444 Oak Lawn Pl Suite 525 Dallas TX 75207

NIX, HARVARD KEITH, retail executive, commercial real estate broker; b. Monroe, La., Dec. 31, 1942; s. Harvard S. and Elaine G. (Grayson) N.; m. Judith Kadane, Jan. 16, 1971; 1 son, Kevin Kadane. B.B.A. in Acctg. and Mktg., U. Tex.-Austin, 1964. Cert. property mgr. With Trammell Crow Co., Dallas and St. Louis, 1964-69; v.p. bldgs. div. Henry S. Miller Co., Dallas, 1969-71, sr. v.p. office bldgs. div., 1972-76; v.p. office bldgs. div. Southwestern Dynamics, Inc., Dallas, Tampa, Fla. and Phoenix, 1971-72; with Neiman-Marcus, Dallas, 1976—, asst. buyer gift galleries, 1976, spl. trainee stationery, 1976, dir. pub. relations, 1976-80, v.p., dir. pub. relations, 1980—; dir. Chow Gourmet Caterers. Bd. dirs. Dallas Theater Ctr., exec. com., v.p. pub. relations and city liaison; dir. TACA; bd. dirs. Lambert's, Friends of Dallas Arts Dist.; mem. adv. council Arts Magnet High Sch.; sponsor, past pres. The 500; mem. N.Tex. Commn. on Arts and Humanities, Dallas Mus. of Art, KERA/Channel 13; past trustee Dallas Symphony Orch.; past bd. dirs. Theater Three. Mem. Dallas Real Estate Bd., Dallas Bldg. Owners and Mgrs. Assn., Tex. Real Estate Bd., Nat. Inst. Real Estate Mgmt., Pub. Relations Soc., Dallas Hist. Soc. (bd. dirs.). Am. Home: 5311 Edlen Rd Dallas TX 75220 Office: Main and Ervay Sts Dallas TX 75201

NIX, SHARON LOUISE, educator; b. Houston, July 21, 1946; d. E. Marion and Dorothy (Oakes) Fendley; m. Richard Barm Nix, June 26, 1946. B.A., U. Houston, 1969, M.Ed., 1983. Cert. secondary tchr., Tex. Staff, Devel. Office, U. Houston Central Campus, 1974, in charge of undergrad. edn. student records, Coll. Edn., 1977, asst. dir. continuing optometric edn., University Park campus, 1981—, calligraphist, 1983—. Mem. Health Planners of Houston (continuing health edn. network 1982—), Am. Mgmt. Assn., Nat. Assn. Female Execs., Splendora Network (dir.), NOW, AAUW. Republican. Club: Houston Calligraphy Guild. Office: Univ Houston Optometry 4901 Calhoun Houston TX 77004

NIXON, ARLIE JAMES, gas and oil company executive; b. Ralston, Okla., May 22, 1914; s. James Gordon and Wella May (Platt) N.; B.S., Okla. State U., 1935; m. Wylie Elizabeth Jones, Apr. 21, 1938 (div. May 1950); children—Cole Jay, Kathleen (Mrs. S. Brent Joyce); m. 2d, Lisa Marie Grant, Dec. 7, 1981. Airline capt. Trans World Airlines, N.Y.C., 1939-73; pres. Crystal Gas Co., Jennings, Okla., 1960—, Blackburn Gas Co., Jennings, 1964—, Blackberry Oil Co., Jennings, 1969—; represented U.S. in several ofcl. dels. to internat. aviation tech. meetings, also represented Internat. Fedn. Air Line Pilots Assns. at internat. confs. Served to lt. (j.g.) USNR, 1935-39. Mem. Internat. Fedn. Air Line Pilots Assn. (regional v.p. 1972), Internat. Platform Assn. Democrat. Clubs: Wings (N.Y.C.); Cushing (Okla.) Country. Home: RFD 2 Jennings OK 74038 Office: PO Box 68 Jennings OK 74038

NIXON, JAMES DAWSON, college administrator, sociology educator; b. Jonesville, Mich., Nov. 21, 1922; s. Lloyd H. and Pearl (Dawson) N.; m. Evelyn Ruby Newhouse, Dec. 20, 1967; children—Thomas L., Pamela Jo. A.B., U. Mich., 1954; B.D., Garrett Theol. Sem., 1957; M.A., U. Mich., 1968, Ph.D., 1971. Pastor Meth. Ch., Tecumseh, Grosse Pointe, and Saginaw, Mich., 1957-67; asst. prof. sociology Austin Peay State U., Clarksville, Tenn., 1972-73, chmn. dept. sociology, assoc. prof., 1973-76, prof., 1977—, dean coll. arts and scis., 1976—. Contbr. articles to profl. jours. Served with USN, 1942-45. Mem. Am. Sociol. Assn., Mid-South Sociol. Assn., So. Sociol. Soc., Council Colls. Arts and Scis. Avocations: camping; birding; carving. Home: 3 Canterbury Rd Clarksville TN 37043 Office: Austin Peay State U Coll Arts and Scis College Ave Clarksville TN 37044

NIXON, JOHN TRICE, federal judge; b. New Orleans, Jan. 9, 1933; s. H. C. and Anne (Trice) N.; A.B. cum laude, Harvard Coll., 1955; LL.B., Vanderbilt U., 1960; m. Betty Chiles, Aug. 5, 1960; children—Mignon Elizabeth, Anne Trice. Admitted to Ala. bar, 1960, Tenn. bar, 1972; individual practice law,

Anniston, Ala., 1960-62; city atty., Anniston, 1962-64; trial atty. Civil Rights Div., Dept. Justice, Washington, 1964-69; staff atty., comptroller of Treasury, State of Tenn., 1971-76; individual practice law, Nashville, 1976-77; circuit judge, 1977-78, gen. sessions judge, 1978-80; U.S. dist. judge, Middle Dist. Tenn., Nashville, 1980—. Served with U.S. Army, 1958. Mem. Am. Bar Assn., Tenn. Bar Assn., Nashville Bar Assn., Ala. State Bar. Democrat. Methodist. Clubs: D.U. (Cambridge); Harvard-Radcliffe (Nashville). Home: 1607 18th Ave N Nashville TN 37212 Office: 825 US Courthouse Nashville TN 37203

NIXON, TAMARA FRIEDMAN, economist; b. Cleve., June 3, 1938; d. Victor and Eva J. (Osteryoung) Friedman; B.A. with honors in econs. (Wellesley scholar), Wellesley Coll., 1959; M.B.A. (fellow), U. Pitts., 1961; m. Daniel D. Nixon, June 14, 1959; children—Asa Joel, Naomi Devorah, Victoria Eve. Asst. economist Fed. Res. Bank, N.Y.C., 1959-60, 61-62; economist R.P. Wolff Econ. Research, Miami, Fla., 1972-75; econ. cons., Miami, 1975-79; sr. v.p. Washington Savs. & Loan Assn., Miami Beach, Fla., 1979-81; pres. T.F. Nixon Econ. Cons. Inc., 1982—; sr. v.p. Cen Trust Savs. Bank, 1984—; real estate feasibility cons.; investment adminstr. Land use chmn. Dade County chpt. LWV, 1975-76. Mem. Econ. Soc. S. Fla. (v.p. programs, dir.), Am. Econ. Assn. Office: 4646 North Bay Rd Miami Beach FL 33140

NOBLE, DOUGLAS ROSS, museum administrator; b. Sturgis, Ky., Jan. 19, 1945; s. Roscoe and Robbie Rae (Martin) N.; m. Catherine Ann Richardson, Nov. 3, 1973; children—Kate Faxon, Jennifer Martin. B.S., Okla. State U., 1967; M.S.A., Ga. Coll., 1978; postgrad. U. Ga., 1979-81. Asst. to dir. Savannah Sci. Mus., Ga., 1971-73; exec. dir. Mus. of Arts and Scis., Macon, Ga., 1973-80; dir. of museums Memphis Mus. System, 1980—; mem. mus. assessment program Inst. of Mus. Services, Washington, 1982—, grant reviewer, 1983—; cons. Mus. Mgmt. Program, Sarasota, Fla., 1985. Contbr. articles to profl. jours. Grad. Leadership Memphis, 1984. Served to 1st lt. U.S. Army, 1968-70; Vietnam. Decorated Bronze Star. Mem. Natural Sci. for Youth Found. (trustee 1980—, Naumburg award 1978), Am. Assn. Museums (S.E. rep. 1984—, chmn. nature ctr. accreditation com. 1985), Southeastern Museums Conf. (pres. 1982-84), Memphis Museums Roundtable (co-founder), Ga. Assn. Museums and Galleries (co-founder), Tenn. Assn. Museums (chmn. tax reform com. 1984-85). Episcopalian. Office: Memphis Pink Palace Mus and Planetarium 3050 Central Ave Memphis TN 38111

NOBLE, FRANCES ELIZABETH, educator, author; b. Chgo., Sept. 3, 1903; d. George William and Clara Louise (Lane) N.; B.A. cum laude, Northwestern U., 1924, M.A., 1926, Ph.D., 1945. Mem. faculty Western Mich. U., Kalamazoo, 1931—, prof. French, head dept., 1955-73, prof. emerita, 1973—; French tchr. Fort Lauderdale (Fla.) Public Library, 1978—. Pres., Crippled Children's Guild Broward County, Inc. Decorated palmes academiques, 1945. Mem. Alliance Francaise (past pres.), Am. Assn. Tchrs. of French, Phi Beta Kappa. Republican. Author: (novel) Destiny's Daughter, 1980; The Political Ideas of Alfred de Musset, 1945; also articles. Home: 2915 NE Center Ave Fort Lauderdale FL 33308

NOBLES, WILLIAM LEWIS, college president; b. Meridian, Miss., Sept. 11, 1925; s. J. S. and Ruby (Roper) N.; m. Joy Ford, Aug. 29, 1948; children—Sandra Nobles Nash, Suzanne (dec.). B.S., U. Miss., 1948, M.S., 1949; Ph.D., U. Kans., 1952. Assoc. prof. U. Miss., University, 1954-55, prof., 1955-68, dean Grad. Sch., 1960-68, coordinator univ. research, 1964-68; pres. Miss. Coll., Clinton, 1968—. Lectr. drug abuse Dept. Edn. State Miss. Served to lt. (j.g.) USN, 1944-46. Recipient award Am. Pharm. Assn. Found., 1966. Mem. Am. Pharm. Assn., Am. Chem. Soc., AAAS, Chem. Soc. Gt. Britain, Nat. Assn. Ind. Colls. and Univs. (bd. dirs. 1983, 85-87), N.Y. Acad. Sci., Sigma Xi, Kappa Psi, Rho Chi. Baptist. Club: Rotary. Author: (with Burbage and Autian) Physical and Technical Pharmacy, 1961. Home and Office: PO Box 4186 Clinton MS 39058

NOBLITT, JAMES RANDALL, air force officer, psychologist; b. Houston, Dec. 7, 1948; s. James Reuben and Joanne Marion (Lynch) N.; m. Pamela Sue Perkins, Oct. 30, 1970; children—Danielle, Randy. B.S. cum laude, N. Tex. State U., 1971, M.S., 1973, Ph.D., 1970. Behavioral scientist Human Resources Lab., Lowry AFB, Colo., 1973; commd. 2d lt. U.S. Air Force, 1971, advanced through grades to capt., 1975; clin. psychologist USAF Hosp., Sheppard AFB, Tex., 1973-74, clin. psychologist, 1978-79, 82-83; dir. RAF Lakenheath Overweight Rehab. Ctr. (Eng.), 1979-82, chief psychol. services, 1982; lectr. U. Md., 1978-82; adj. prof. Vanderbilt U., 1980-81. Air Force scholar, 1968-71. Mem. Am. Psychol. Assn., Brit. Psychol. Soc., Internat. Council Psychologists, Mensa. Office: 375 Municipal Dr Richardson TX 75080

NOE, RANDOLPH, lawyer; b. Indpls., Nov. 2, 1939; s. John H. and Bernice (Baker) Reiley; student Franklin Coll., 1957-60; B.S., Ind. State U., 1964; J.D., Ind. U., 1967; m. Anne Will, Mar. 2, 1968; children—John Henry Reiley, Anne Will, Randolph, Jr., Jonathan Baker. Bar: Ind. 1968, Ky. 1970. Trust officer Citizens Fidelity Bank and Trust Co., Louisville, 1969-71; sole practice law, Louisville, 1971-83; ptnr. Greenebaum, Young, Treitz & Maggiolo, Louisville, 1983—; asst. Jefferson County (Ky.) atty., 1979-84. Mem. exec. bd. Louisville Area Muscular Dystrophy Assn., 1971-73; bd. dirs. Holy Rosary Acad., 1978-82; chmn. Eagle Scout Assn. Old Ky. Home council Boy Scouts Am., 1975-77; football coach St. Stephen Martyr Sch., 1978—. Mem. Am., Ky. (probate and trust law com.), Ind., Louisville bar assns. Democrat. Clubs: Pendennis, Wranglers. Author: Kentucky Probate Methods, 1975, Supplement, 1985. Editor: Kentucky Law Summary, 1985—. Home: 3222 Crossbill Rd Louisville KY 40213 Office: 25th Floor First Nat Tower Louisville KY 40202

NOEL, JAMES LATANÉ, III, steel company executive; b. Houston, Oct. 15, 1948; s. James L. and Virginia G. Noel; B.A., Williams Coll., 1971; M.B.A., U. Pa., 1972. Vice pres. First City Nat. Bank, Houston, 1973-80; pres. Tex. Steel Conversion, Inc., 1980—; dir. First Mgmt. Corp. Mem. Am. Bankers Assn., Tubular Finishers and Processors Assn. (bd. dirs.), Houston Mus. Fine Arts, Houston Symphony Soc. Republican. Methodist. Clubs: Williams of Houston (treas.); Williams (N.Y.C.). Home: 1915 Hazard Houston TX 77019 Office: 3101 Holmes Rd Houston TX 77051

NOER, HAROLD ROLF, surgeon; b. Madison, Wis., Apr. 3, 1927; s. Harold R. and Blanche K. (Field) N.; m. Betty Schlegelmilch, Sept. 16, 1950; children—Harold Rolf III, Karen Marie, Carol Ann. B.A., U. Wis., 1946, M.D., 1948. Diplomate Am. Bd. Surgery. Intern, Augustana Hosp., Chgo., 1948-49; fellow in anatomy Wayne U. Med. Coll., Detroit, 1949-50; fellow in surgery Detroit Receiving Hosp., 1949-50; resident Grace Hosp., Detroit, 1953-55; practice medicine specializing in orthopedic surgery Alexandria and Arlington, Va.; commd. lt. (j.g.) M.C., U.S. Navy, 1950, advanced through grades to comdr., 1961; flight surgeon USMC Air Sta., Cherry Point, N.C., 1952-53; resident orthopedic surgeon U.S. Naval Hosp., Oakland, Calif., 1955-57; asst. then acting chief orthopedics U.S. Naval Hosp., Camp Lejeune, N.C., 1958-61, U.S. Naval Hosp., St. Albans, N.Y., 1961-63; chief neurosurgery U.S. Naval Hosp., Camp Lejeune, 1958-61; sr. med. officer U.S. 6th fleet Mediterranean, 1962-65; orthopedic basic sci. dir. U.S. Armed Forces Inst. Pathology, Washington, 1965-67; ret., 1967; cons. orthopedics U.S. Naval Hosp. Bethesda, Md., 1965-68, U.S. Dept. Transp., 1969—; attending surgeon Crippled Children's Program, Arlington, Va., 1967-83; mem. staff Nat. Orthopedic and Rehab. Hosp., Arlington, 1967—, Alexandria (Va.) Hosp., 1967—, also Circle Terrance Hosp., Alexandria Hosp. Decorated Purple Heart. Fellow ACS, Internat. Coll. Surgeons, Am. Acad. Orthopedic Surgery; mem. Va. Med. Soc., Alexandria Med. Soc., Soc. Mil. Orthopedic Surgeons, Washington Orthopedic Soc. (past pres.), Va. Orthopedic Soc. Club: West River Sailing. Episcopalian. Author: Navigator's Pocket Calculator Handbook, 1983; contbr. articles to profl. jours. Office: 2465 Army Navy Dr Arlington VA 22206

NOETZEL, GROVER ARCHIBALD JOSEPH, economics educator emeritus; b. Greenwood, Wis., June 14, 1908; s. August Herman and Coralie Marie (Van Den Bossche) N.; A.B., U. Wis., 1929, Ph.D., 1934; certificate in econs., U. London, 1930, U. Geneva, 1936; D.Aviation Edn. (hon.), Embry Riddle U., 1975; fellow Social Sci. Research Council, 1935-36; m. Anna B. Dobbins, June 11, 1953. Instr. econ. U. S.D., 1930-32; instr. econ. U. Wis., 1934-35; economist Nat. Bur. Econ. Research, 1936-37; asst. prof. Temple U., 1937-40, asso. prof., 1940-46; pvt. cons. econ. and investment counselor, Phila. and N.Y.C., 1939-46; prof. econs. U. Miami, 1946-48, dean Sch. Bus. Adminstrn., 1948-61, prof. econs., 1961-72, dean emeritus and prof., 1972—, cons. economist, 1961—; cons. South Miami Galleries. Bd. dirs. Med. Service Bur. Miami. Mem. Econ. Soc. South Fla. (dir., pres. 1956), Phi Kappa Phi, Alpha Phi Omega, Alpha Delta Sigma, Delta Sigma Pi, Artus, Beta Gamma Sigma. Clubs: Rotary (Miami, Fla.); Coral Gables Country, Rivieria Country, Century (Coral Gables). Author: Recent Theories of Foreign Exchange, 1934; Cooperation Entre L'Universite et Les Milieux Economiques, 1956; Objectives of a Management Center, 1956; Decisions That Affect Profits, 1957; Today's Economy, 1974; Housing: How Sick is the Patient, 1975; also articles in field. Home and office: 2845 Granada Blvd Apt 1A Coral Gables FL 33134

NOFFSINGER, JAMES PHILIP, archtl. historian; b. Union City, Ind., May 30, 1925; s. Forrest Ruby and Martha (Earl) N.; m. Anne-Russell Lillis, July 1, 1964; children—Ward Pell, Gretchen, Hansel. B.Arch., Catholic U. Am., 1952, M.Arch., 1953, D.Arch., 1955; student U. Ill.-Urbana, 1954. Asst. prof. arch. U. Minn., 1955-56, U. Kans., 1956-58, Institut Teknologie Bandung, Java, Indonesia, 1958-59; assoc. prof. U. Ky., 1960-67, prof., 1967—, acting dean, 1968-69; architect Nat. Park Service, 1956, 57, 58, 61; U.S. Commn. of Fine Arts, 1966, 71. Mem. edn. com. Ecuador, Ky. Ptnrs. Alliance for Progress, 1968. Served with AUS 1945-46. Recipient King Olav V award Am.-Scandinavian Found., 1983. Fulbright Lectr., Japan, 1968, Eng., 1976; group leader Expt. in Internat. Living, Japan, 1962. Mem. Soc. Archtl. Historians (past nat. dir.), AIA, Alpha Rho Chi, Scarab, Omicron Delta Kappa. Republican. Presbyterian. Club: Spindletop. Home: 206 Shady Ln Lexington KY 40503 Office: Pence Hall U Ky Lexington KY 40506

NOFTLE, RONALD EDWARD, chemistry educator; b. Springfield, Mass., Mar. 10, 1939; s. Harold E. and Edith L. (Johnson) N.; m. K. Alayne Johnson, Mar. 21, 1964; 1 son, Erik E. B.S., U. N.H., 1961; Ph.D., U. Wash., 1966. Instr. dept. chemistry U. Wash., Seattle, 1966; postdoctoral fellow dept. chemistry U. Idaho, Moscow, 1966-67; asst. prof. chemistry Wake Forest U., Winston-Salem, N.C., 1967-73, assoc. prof., 1973-79, prof., 1979—, chmn. dept., 1980—; vis. scientist U.S. Naval Research Lab., Washington, 1975-76. Allied Chem. Co. fellow U. Wash., 1965-66. Fellow Am. Inst. Chemists; mem. AAUP, Am. Chem. Soc. (officer div. fluorine chemistry 1984-85), Sigma Xi, Phi Kappa Phi. Contbr. articles to profl. jours. Office: Dept Chemistry Wake Forest U Box 7486 Reynolda Sta Winston-Salem NC 27109

NOKES, GLORIA A. THOMAS, state official, nurse; b. Albertsville, Ala., Dec. 13, 1948; d. Lelon Edward and Geneva (Springfield) Thomas; children—Heather, Jessica, Stephanie; m. 2d, Zacky Blaine Nokes, Sept. 5, 1981. A.S., Thornton Community Coll., South Holland, Ill., 1975; B.S., Gov.'s State U., 1979; postgrad. in edn. Ga. State U., 1982—. R.N., Ill., Ga. Obstetric staff nurse Ingalls Meml. Hosp., Harvey, Ill., 1975-77, South Suburban Hosp., Hazel Crest, Ill., 1977, Olympia Fields (Ill.) Osteo. Med. Ctr., 1977-79; psychiat. supr. Parkway Regional Hosp., Lithia Springs, Ga., 1980-81, psychiat. staff nurse, 1982—; dir. patient edn. Paulding Meml. Hosp., Dallas, Ga., 1981, cons. on edn., 1981—; dir. nursing edn. State of Ga., Paulding County, 1982—; pub. health educator, hosps., 1976-81. Dir. youth edn. Faith Baptist Ch., Harvey, 1970-72. Mem. Am. Nurses Assn., Ga. Vocat. Assn., Am. Vocat. Assn., Phi Theta Kappa. Office: Paulding Meml Hosp 600 W Memorial Dr Dallas GA 30132

NOLAN, CARSON YOUNG, printing co. exec.; b. Indpls., Oct. 21, 1925; s. Clarence Herman and Margaret (Odessa) N.; m. Bess Gravitt, Dec. 19, 1946; children—Thomas, Sarah, Jeffrey, Christopher. B.S., U. Ky., 1950, M.A., 1950; Ph.D., Washington U., St. Louis, 1953. Chief Field Unit 1, Air Force Personnel and Tng. Research Center, Forbes AFB, Kans., 1953-56; research scientist Human Resources Research Office, Ft. Knox, Ky., 1957; dir. dept. ednl. research Am. Printing House for the Blind, Louisville, 1958-76, pres., 1976—; asso. prof. U. Louisville, 1962-72. Contbr. chpts. to books, articles to profl. jours.; author monographs. Served with USAAF, 1943-46. Mem. Council for Exceptional Children, Assn. for Edn. Visually Handicapped. Office: Am Printing House for the Blind 1839 Frankfort Ave Louisville KY 40206

NOLAN, DONNY RAY, petroleum geologist, consultant; b. Monroe, La., Dec. 12, 1939; s. Robert and Floy Cristine (Smith) N.; m. Betsy Ann Bayles, Nov. 22, 1960; children—Richard M., Pamela Dawn. B.S., Northeast La. U., Monroe, 1962, M.S., 1967. Exploration geologist Texaco, Inc., New Orleans, 1967-72; dist. geologist Koch Exploration, New Orleans, 1972-73; dist. geologist Damson Oil, Houston, 1973-75; div. geologist Southport Exploration, Houston, 1975-77; cons. petroleum geologist, Houston, 1977—. Mem. adv. bd. Geology Found. Northeast La. U., Monroe. Served to 1st lt. U.S. Army, 1962-65. Mem. Am. Assn. Petroleum Geologists (cert. petroleum geologist), Am. Inst. Profl. Geologists (cert.), Houston. Geol. Soc., New Orleans Geol. Soc., Humble Area C. of C. Republican. Baptist. Club: Kingwood Country (Tex.). Office: 2 Kingwood Pl Suite 260 Kingwood TX 77339

NOLAN, ROBERT LEROY, electrical manufacturing executive; b. Soddy, Tenn., Dec. 1, 1947; s. Lawrence Alton and Virginia (Morgan) N.; B.S. in Mech. Engring., U. Tenn., Knoxville, 1970; M.B.A., Murray State U., 1978; M.S., U. Ky., 1979; m. Nedra Ann Burge, June 2, 1978; 1 son, David Henry. Sr. asso. devel. engr. IBM Corp., Lexington, Ky., 1970-74; franchise dealer Townecraft Sales of Ky., Paducah, 1974; mgr. cost and mfg. enging. Ingersoll Rand Co., Mayfield, Ky., 1974-82; mgr. mfg. enging. Westinghouse Electric Co., Charlotte, N.C., 1982-83, mgr. Quality assurance, 1983—. Democrat. Baptist. Contbr. articles to profl. jours. Home: 3126 Rock Springs Rd Charlotte NC 28226 Office: Westinghouse Electric Co Box 7002 Charlotte NC 28217

NOLAND, PATRICIA HAMPTON, writer; b. New Orleans; d. Leon Maxwell and Clara Hampton (Whittle) Noland; B.A. in English, U. Houston, 1981; Dr. Leadership in Poetry (hon.), Internat. Acad. Leadership, Philippines, 1969; D.L.H. (hon.) Free U. Asia, 1973. Founder, pres. Internat. Poetry Inst., Houston, 1969—. Chmn. music com. First Ch. of Christ, Scientist, Houston, 1983-86. Named Hon. Internat. Poet Laureate, United Poets Laureate Internat., Manila, Philippines, 1969. Mem. Internat. Platform Assn., Am. Hort. Soc., Mus. Fin Arts Houston, Mus. Art of Am. West, English-Speaking Union, Met. Opera Guild, Am. Film Inst., L'Alliance Française, Planetary Soc., Poetry Soc. of Tex., Costeau Soc., Nat. Trust Historic Preservation, Mus. Women in Art, Isabella Stewart Gardner Mus., Boston Mus. Fine Arts, Met. Mus., New Orleans Mus. Art, Norton Gallery and Sch. Art, Colonial Williamsburg Found. Democrat. Christian Scientist. Author: Poems, 1960; editor: Whoever Heard a Birdie Cry?, 1970; editor monthly newsletter of Internat. Poetry Inst., 1969-78. Club: Jr. League Luncheon. Home: 2400 Westheimer Rd Apt 215W Houston TX 77098 Office: PO Box 53087 Houston TX 77052

NOLDE, JACK EDWARD, geologist; b. Elmhurst, Ill., Jan. 27, 1951; s. Donald Arthur and Shirlene Eleanor (Lindquist) N. B.S. in Geology, Tenn. Tech. U., 1975; M.S. in Geology, U. Ill.-Chgo., 1981. Hydrogeologist Post, Buckley, Schuh & Jernigan, Inc., Fort Myers, Fla., 1975-79; lab instr. U. Ill.-Chgo., 1979-81; geologist Va. Div. Mineral Resources, Abingdon, 1981—. Contbr. articles to profl. jours. Mem. Am. Assn. Petroleum Geologists, Paleontological Soc., Paleontol. Research Inst., Internat. Assn. Math. Geology, Am. Statis. Assn. Methodist. Home: 155 W Valley St Abingdon VA 24210 Office: Va Div Mineral Resources 468 E Main St Room 100 Abingdon VA 24210

NOLEN, FRANK WILLIAM, state senator, engineer, farmer; b. Macon County, N.C., Dec. 26, 1939; m. Nancy Paige Weese; children—John, Will, Amber. B.E.E., Va. Poly. Inst. and State U. Mem. Va. Senate, 1974, 79—. Elder, Presbyterian Ch. Mem. Va. Soc. Profl. Engrs., IEEE, Augusta County Farm Bur., Shenandoah Valley Feeder Calf Assn. (dir.), Eta Kappa Nu, Tau Beta Pi. Democrat. Club: Ruritan (New Hope, Va.). Office: Va Senate Gen Assembly Bldg 9th and Broad Sts Richmond VA 23219*

NONDORF, JAMES LEO, oil and gas company executive; b. Alva, Okla., Nov. 3, 1947; s. Leo Charles and Marjorie Ann (Leitner) N.; m. Sandra Lynn, Aug. 17, 1968; children—Erik Lance, Kyle Stuart, Darin Lee. B.S., U. Okla., 1969. Geologist, Texaco, Inc., Houston, 1968-69, G.H.K. Co., Oklahoma City, 1969-73; chief geologist Payne, Inc., Oklahoma City, 1973-76; pres. L & N Exploration, Inc., Oklahoma City, 1976-80, Nondorf Oil & Gas, Inc., Oklahoma City, 1980—; sec.-treas., owner, S.W. Prodn. Equipment Co., Oklahoma City, 1976—; dir. Giant Rig No. 1 Ltd., Oklahoma City, 1981—, Orlando Oilfield Services, Crescent, Okla., 1981—; organizer, dir. North Bank, Oklahoma City; chmn. profl. conv., 1974. Contbr. articles to profl. publs. Mem. Am. Assn. Petroleum Geologists, Oklahoma City Geol. Soc., Oklahoma City C. of C. Republican. Mem. Christian Ch. (Disciples of Christ). Club: Summerfield (dir. 1982—) (Oklahoma City). Home: 12201 Quail Creek Rd Oklahoma City OK 73120 Office: Nondorf Oil & Gas Inc 101 Park Ave Suite 410 Oklahoma City OK 73102

NONOYAMA, MEIHAN, biomedical research institute executive; b. Tokyo, Feb. 25, 1938; came to U.S., 1966; s. Hayakichi and Kie (Kasagi) N.; m. Keiko Sakaguchi, Jan. 19, 1969; 1 son, Akihisa. B.S., U. Tokyo, 1961, M.S., 1963, Ph.D., 1966. Research assoc. U. Ill.-Urbana, 1966-68; vis. scientist Wistar Inst., Phila., 1968-70; asst. prof. U. N.C.-Chapel Hill, 1970-73; assoc. prof. Rush Presbyn. St. Luke's Hosp. and U. Ill.-Chgo., 1973-76; dir. molecular virology Life Scis., Inc., St. Petersburg, Fla., 1976-81; pres. Showa U. Research Inst. for Biomedicine, 1981—; prof. U. South Fla., 1981—. Fulbright fellow, 1966; NIH grantee, 1973—; Am. Cancer Soc. grantee, 1975, 85; Leukemia Found. grantee, 1976. Mem. Am. Soc. Microbiology, Am. Soc. Virology, Am. Assn. Cancer Research, Soc. Exptl. Biology, Japanese Soc. Cancer. Contbr. articles to profl. jours. Office: 10900 Roosevelt Blvd N Saint Petersburg FL 33702

NOONAN, THOMAS ADDIS, JR., surgeon; b. San Antonio, Sept. 30, 1950; s. Thomas A. and Vivian (Hicks) N.; m. Lori Leigh Mayles, May 25, 1973; 1 child, Rayne. B.S. in Biology, Tarleton State Coll., 1973; D.O., Tex. Coll. Osteo. Medicine, 1977. Intern, Phoenix Gen. Hosp., 1977-78; resident Okla. Osteo. Hosp., Tulsa, 1978-81, resident thoracic and cardiovascular surgery, 1981-82, chief resident gen. surgery, 1980-81, chief resident thoracic and cardiovascular surgery, 1981-82; practice medicine specializing in surgery, Colorado City, Tex., 1982-84, Groves, Tex., 1984—; chief surgery Root Meml. Hosp., Colorado City, 1983-84; asst. prof. surgery Okla. Coll. Osteo. Medicine and Surgery, Tulsa, 1978-82. Recipient Achievement award Upjohn Co., 1977. Mem. Am. Osteo. Assn., Tex. Soc. Gastrointestinal Endoscopy, Tex. Osteo. Med. Assn. (sec. dist. IV 1984-85). Republican. Roman Catholic. Avocation: raising horses and cattle. Home: 4131 75th St Apt 132 Port Arthur TX 77642 Office: 5502 39th St Suite 104 Groves TX 77619

NOOR, AHMED KHAIRY, engineering educator, researcher; b. Cairo, Egypt, Aug. 11, 1938; s. Mohamed Sayed and Fatma Mohamed (El-Zeini) N.; m. Zakia Mahmoud Taha, Aug. 18, 1966; 1 son, Mohamed. B.S. with honors, Cairo (Egypt) U., 1958; M.S., U. Ill., Urbana, 1961, Ph.D., 1963. Asst. prof. aeros. and astronautics Stanford U., 1963-64; sr. lectr. structural mechanics, Cairo (Egypt) U., 1964-67; vis. sr. lectr. structural mechanics U. Baghdad, Iraq, 1967-68; sr. lectr. structural mechanics U. New South Wales, Australia, 1968-71; prof. engring. and applied sci. George Washington U., Hampton, Va., 1971—; mem. coms. computational mechanics and large space systems Nat. Acad. Engring. Assoc. fellow AIAA; mem. ASME, ASCE, Am. Acad. Mechanics, Internat. Assn. for Computational Mechanics (founder mem.), Sigma Xi. Editor books on structures and solids and computational mechanics; contbr. articles to profl. jours. Home: 31 Towler Dr Hampton VA 23666 Office: George Washington U-NASA Langley Research Ctr MS-269 Hampton VA 23665

NORAN, WILLIAM HAROLD, neurologist; b. Mpls., June 22, 1943; s. Harold Hans and Kathryn Mae (Anderson) N.; B.S., U. Minn., 1965, M.D., 1968; m. Sally Ann Blackburn, Mar. 14, 1969; children—Nicole Yvette, Suzanne Noelle. Diplomate Am. Bd. Psychiatry and Neurology. Intern, Los Angeles County Gen. Hosp., 1968-69; resident U. Minn., Mpls., 1969-72; neurologist Jacksonville (Fla.) Neurol. Clinic, 1974—. Served with M.C., USAF, 1972-74. Mem. AMA, Fla. Med. Assn., Am. Acad. Neurology. Office: Suite 601 3599 University Blvd S Jacksonville FL 32216

NORDQVIST, STAFFAN ROLF BJÖRNSON, gynecologic oncologist, educator b. Lund, Sweden, July 16, 1936; s. Bjorn R.B. and Liv (Wicksell) N.; M.D., U. Lund, 1963, Ph.D., 1969; m. Rebeca Llave-Vaccaro; children by previous marriage—Joakim, Jesper, Jonas. Intern, U. Lund, 1963-64, resident in ob-gyn, 1964-67, assoc. prof. ob-gyn, 1970-71; assoc. prof. ob-gyn Cornell U. Med. Sch., N.Y.C., 1972-74; assoc. prof. U. Miami (Fla.) Med. Sch., 1974-77, prof. ob-gyn and oncology, 1977-80; pres. med. staff Cedars Med. Ctr., Miami, 1985-86; assoc. Meml. Sloan Kettering Cancer Center, N.Y.C., 1972-74; pres., chief staff Cedars Med. Ctr., Miami, 1985-86. Bd. dirs. Am. Cancer Soc., Dade County, 1978—. Served with Swedish Army, 1955-71. Mem. Fla. Med. Assn., Dade County Med. Assn., Fla. Ob-Gyn Soc., Am. Coll. Ob-Gyn, Miami Ob-Gyn Soc., Soc. Gynec. Oncologists, Meml. Soc. Gynec. Oncologists, Internat. Soc. Gynec. Pathologists, Continental Gynec. Soc. Lutheran. Club: Coral Reef Yacht. Contbr. articles to profl. jours. Home: 40 Island Dr Key Biscayne FL 33149 Office: 1295 NW 14th St Suite H Miami FL 33125

NORFLEET, FRANK M., automotive parts executive; b. Memphis, Nov. 27, 1918; s. Cecil M. and Esther (Cook) Norfleet Abston. Chmn. bd. Parts Industries Corp., Memphis; mng. dir. GKN Autoparts Internat. U.K.; dir. CSX Corp., Richmond, Va., Fed. Co., C.H. Bailey, PLC, U.K., First Tenn. Nat. Corp., KSH, Inc., St. Louis, Choctaw, Inc., Memphis. Bd. dirs. Memphis State U. Pres.'s Council; past chmn. bd., pres. Memphis Area C. of C.; chmn. U. Tenn. Devel. Council; past pres. Future Memphis, Inc.; chmn. adv. bd. Bapt. Meml. Hosp., Memphis; past chmn. bd. govs. Memphis Plough Community Found. Served from pvt. to maj. U.S. Army, 1941-45. Decorated Bronze Star with oak leaf cluster, Silver Star; Croix de Guerre, France; named Memphis Cotton Carnival King, 1960, Automotive Man of Yr., 1972; recipient Outstanding Citizen award Civitan Club, 1972; Jerome M. Comar Meml. award Inst. Human Relations, Am. Jewish Com., 1976; Brotherhood award NCCJ, 1976. Mem. Assn. Automotive Aftermarket Distbrs. (past pres.), Automotive Warehouse Distbrs. Assn. (past pres., dir.), Automotive Engine Rebuilders Assn. (past pres., dir.). Republican. Presbyterian. Clubs: Memphis Country, Memphis Hunt and Polo, University, Summit, Century, U. Tenn., 100 of Memphis, H.K. Jones Hunting, Old River Hunting, Chancellor's Roundtable U. Tenn., Pres.'s of U. Tenn., Greater Memphis State; Rolling Rock (Ligonier, Pa.); Bayou DeView Farm and Hunting (Fair Oaks, Ark.); Flyfishers (London); Anglers (N.Y.C.). Home: 90 S Perkins Rd Memphis TN 38117 Office: 4729 Spottswood Memphis TN 38117*

NORIEGA, ARTHUR, IV, management consultant; b. Tampa, Fla., July 8, 1941; s. Arthur, and Obdulia (Nunez) N.; B.S., U. Tampa, 1963; M.A. (univ. fellow), U. Miss., 1964; M.B.A., Ph.D., Calif. Western U., 1985; m. Santa Mendez, Jan. 7, 1978; children—Arthur, V, Stephanie Ann. Project mgr. Roy Jorgensen Assocs., Inc., Gaithersburg, Md., 1965-76, v.p., 1978-80; dir. manpower mgmt. and devel. Medfield Corp., St. Petersburg, Fla., 1976-78; dir. mgmt. cons. services Post, Buckley, Schuh & Jernigan, Inc., Tampa, 1980-83; v.p. Diaz, Seckinger & Assocs., Tampa, 1983-85; pres. Noriega & Assocs., Wesley Chapel, Fla., 1986—; tchr. exptl. psychology U. Miss. Mem. Am. Soc. Tng. and Devel., Internat. Fedn. Tng. and Devel. Orgn., Psi Chi. Democrat. Roman Catholic. Author papers in field. Office: 100 Quail Hollow Plaza Wesley Chapel FL 34249

NORIEGA, RUDY JORGE, hospital administrator; b. Havana, Cuba, Apr. 23, 1937; s. Rodolfo and Iris (Santini) N.; came to U.S., 1961; naturalized, 1966; B.S., Masonic U., 1960; m. Rosa E. Del Castillo, Jan. 2, 1960; children—Rudy A., George. Accountant, Continental Can Co., Havana, Cuba, 1961, Am. Fgn. Ins. Assn., N.Y.C., 1961-62, North Miami Gen. Hosp., Miami, Fla., 1962-64; asst. controller Jackson Meml. Hosp., Miami, 1964-65; asst. adminstr. Plantation (Fla.) Gen. Hosp., 1965-72, adminstr., trustee, 1972-80; v.p., trustee Internat. Hosp., Miami, 1980-83; exec. v.p., chief operating officer Am. Hosp., Miami, 1983—. Mem. Am. Coll. Hosp. Adminstrs., So. Fla. Hosp. Assn. (pres. 1979-80), Broward County Hosp. Assn. (pres. 1978-79), Fla. League Hosps. (pres. 1974-75), Fedn. Am. Hosps. (dir. 1973-74), Hosp. Fin. Mgmt. Assn. (dir. 1971-72), Plantation C. of C. (pres. 1978-79). Club: Kiwanis (v.p. 1978-79) (Plantation). Office: Am Hosp Miami FL

NORMAN, ALBERT GEORGE, JR., lawyer; b. Birmingham, Ala., May 29, 1929; s. Albert G. and Ila Mae (Carroll) N.; B.A., Auburn U., 1953; LL.B., Emory U., 1958; M.A., U. N.C., 1960; m. Catherine Marshall DeShazo, Sept. 3, 1955; children—Catherine Marshall, Albert George III. Admitted to Ga. bar, 1957; asso. firm Moise, Post & Gardner, Atlanta, 1958-60, partner, 1960-62; partner firm Hansell & Post, Atlanta, 1962—; dir. Atlanta Gas Light Co. Served with USAF, 1946-49. Mem. Am., Ga., Atlanta bar assns., Lawyers Club Atlanta (pres. 1973-74), Am. Law Inst., Am. Judicature Soc. (dir. 1975-78). Club: Cherokee Town and Country. Home: 3381 Valley Circle NW Atlanta GA 30305 Office: 3300 First Atlanta Tower Atlanta GA 30383

NORMAN, DONALD HAMILTON, lawyer; b. Bergen County, N.J., Mar. 6, 1930; s. William H. and Nellie S. Norman; m. Joan R. Blackledge, Aug. 28, 1954; 1 dau., Carol L. B.A. summa cum laude, Rutgers U., 1952; J.D. magna cum laude, U. Miami, 1955, LL.M. in Taxation, 1968. Bar: Fla. 1955. Asst. atty. City of Ft. Lauderdale (Fla.), 1955-59; ptnr. Ross, Norman & Cory, P.A., Ft. Lauderdale, 1959—; adj. lectr. taxation U. Miami, 1970-74; adj. prof. law Nova U., 1975-77. Named One of Five Outstanding Young Men of Ft. Lauderdale, Jr. C. of C., 1965. Mem. ABA, Fla. Bar (gov. 1974-78), Broward County Bar Assn. (pres. 1964-65), Phi Beta Kappa, Phi Alpha Theta, Phi Kappa Phi. Democrat. Presbyterian. Clubs: Lauderdale Yacht (Ft. Lauderdale); Tamarac Country (Oakland Park, Fla.). Office: 2720 E Oakland Park Blvd Fort Lauderdale FL 33306

NORMAN, EDWARD COBB, psychiatrist, educator; b. Prince George, B.C., Can., Oct. 5, 1913; s. Arthur J. and Lilla E. (Cobb) N.; m. June Marie Morris, Sept. 24, 1949; children—Donald, Cornelia, Sharon. B.S., U. Wash., 1935; M.D., U. Pa., 1940; M.P.H., Tulane U., 1965. Intern, Phila. Gen. Hosp., 1940-42; resident, Pa. Hosp., 1942-43; resident Michael Reese Hosp., 1946-49; asst. surgeon, USPHS, 1943-46; pvt. practice psychiatry, Chgo., 1949-53, New Orleans, 1953—; clin. instr. psychiatry U. Ill., Chgo., 1949-53; asst. prof. clin. psychiatry Tulane U., New Orleans, 1953-60, assoc. prof., 1960-64, prof., 1964-79; emeritus, 1979—; dir. community mental health sect. Tulane U. Sch. Pub. Health Tropical medicine, 1967-79; assoc. dir. Pain Rehab. Unit Hotel Dieu Hosp., 1978—; adminstr. Learning Procedures, Inc., New Orleans, 1977-78, v.p., 1978—; cons. to govt. agys. Fellow Am. Psychiat. Assn. (life), Am. Acad. Psychoanalysis Am. Pub. Health Assn.; mem. N.Y. Acad. Sci., Forum for Improvement of Quality of Life (sec.); Delta Omega (pres. Eta chpt.). Contbr. numerous articles to profl. jours. Home: 439 Pine St New Orleans LA 70118 Office: 2714 Canal St Suite 302 New Orleans LA 70119

NORMAN, HERBERT PENNELL, town official, volunteer fire chief; b. Farmville, N.C., June 10, 1926; s. Bobby Amous and Sarah (Wooten) N.; m. Nannie Lee Corbett, June 3, 1946; 1 child, Pennell. Grad. high sch., Farmville. Fireman, Farmville Fire Dept., 1951-62, line officer, 1962-68, chief, 1968—; insp. Town of Farmville, 1972-76, code dir., 1976—. Chmn. bd., Sunday Sch. tchr. Kings X Roads Free Will Bapt. Ch. Served with U.S. Army, 1944-46. Named Fireman of Year, Farmville Fire Dept. 1983, Fireman of Year, Pitt County Firemans Assn., 1983. Mem. N.C. State Fireman Assn., N.C. Bldg. Insp. Assn., N.C. Zoning Ofcl. Assn., N.C. Mech. Insps. Assn., N.C. Elec. Insps. Assn. Democrat. Club: Pitt County Safety Council (pres. 1981-82). Avocations: gardening; wood working. Home: 506 Bynum Dr PO Box 1123 Farmville NC 27828-1123 Office: Town of Farmville 121 N Main St Farmville NC 27828

NORMAN, MOSES CONRAD, sr., superintendent schools; b. Haddock, Ga., Jan. 3, 1935; s. Walter Raleigh and Rosa Lee (Macon) N.; m. Gertrude Clark, Nov. 29, 1963; children—Moses Conrad, Christopher Kent, Jeffrey Brenton. B.A., Clark Coll., 1957; M.A., U. Mich., 1963; Ph.D., Ga. State U., 1978. Tchr. English, Atlanta Pub. Schs., 1957-68, dept. head, 1968-70, instructional supr., 1970-71, program coordinator, 1971-72, program planner, 1972-73, area I supt., 1973—; dir. Nat. Merit Corp. Evanston, Ill., 1977-80. Contbr. articles to profl. jours. Mem. exec. com. Boy Scouts Am., Atlanta. Mem. Assn. Supervision and Curriculum Devel., Atlanta C. of C. (dir.), Atlanta Partnership of Bus. and Edn. (dir.), Omega Psi Phi. Democrat. Baptist. Home: 1837 Austin RD SW Atlanta GA 30331 Office: Atlanta Pub Schs 711 Catherine St SW Atlanta GA 30310

NORMAN, PATRICIA CHAMBERLAND, insurance broker; b. Dallas, May 26, 1942; d. Buddie Henry and Bernice (Fortune) Chamberland; m. Freddie Burl Hill, Sept. 17, 1960 (div. 1974); children—Freddie Michael, Mark Edward; m. Robert Merril Norman, Sept. 14, 1978. Student Amarillo Jr. Coll., 1960. Lic. ins. broker, notary pub., La. Sr. sec. Tenneco Oil Co., Lafayette, La., 1972-76; v.p. GEM Agy., Lafayette, 1977-78; chmn., pres. P.C. Hill & Assocs., Inc., Lafayette, 1978—. Mem. U.S. Def. Com., Nat. Republican Senatorial Com., Nat. Rep. Congl. Com. Mem. Lafayette C. of C. Clubs: Oakbourne Country, City (Lafayette); Emerald Bay (Tex.). Avocations: golf; music; travel. Office: PC Hill & Assocs Inc 3008 Pinhook Rd Lafayette LA 70501

NORMAN, STELLA LYBRAND, substance abuse counselor, consultant; b. Pine Bluff, Ark., Sept. 1, 1934; d. John Vance and Myrtle Marie (Taylor) Lybrand; m. William Lloyd Norman, Apr. 12, 1955 (div. June 1984); children—Russell Alan, Michael Blain, Janice Lee, Elizabeth Faye. B.S., U. Md.-Heidelberg, 1975; M.Ed., Boston U., 1977, cert., 1978. Cert. tchr., reality therapist. Trainer Girl Scouts U.S.A., U.S.A. and Fed. Republic Germany, 1974-79; tchr. math. Dept. Army, Ludwigsburg, Fed. Republic Germany, 1976; teaching asst. Boston U., Fed. Republic Germany, 1977-78; mental health counselor Dept. Army, Fed. Republic Germany, 1976-77, edn. counselor, 1977-78; counselor Alternative House, Vienna, Va., 1978-79; substance abuse counselor Crossroads Therapeutic Community, Alexandria, Va., 1979-80; sr. counselor Crossroads-South County, Alexandria, 1980-82, sr. counselor, Farifax, 1983—; practicum supr. Inst. of Reality Therapeutics, Canega Park, Calif., 1983—; mem. dual diagnosed task force Fairfax-Falls Church Community Services Bd., 1983—, substance abuse awareness week task force, 1983—. Contbr. articles to profl. jours. Recipient Thanks Badge Girl Scouts U.S.A., 1976; fellow Inter-Univ. Seminar on Armed Forces and Soc. Mem. Reality Therapy Assn. of Va. (pres. 1983—, workshop leader 1982—), Assn. for Specialists in Group Work, Inst. Reality Therapy, Am. Mental Health Counselor Assn., Am. Assn. Counseling and Devel., Parents Without Ptnrs. Home: 10194 Bessmer Ln Fairfax VA 22032 Office: Crossroads Drug Abuse Program 10331 Democracy Ln Fairfax VA 22030

NORMAN, WALLACE, pipe co. exec.; b. Houlka, Miss., Feb. 5, 1926; s. Leland Fleming and Alma Lucile (Brown) N.; student East Central Jr. Coll. 1942, U. Miss., 1946, Millsaps Coll., 1946; B.S., Oklahoma City U., 1948; m. Maurene Collums, Dec. 26, 1950; children—Wallace, Karen Jean, Emily June, Lauren Beth, John Crocker. Owner, operator Wallace Norman Ins. Agy., Houston, Miss., 1949—; pres. Norman Oil Co., Houston, 1956—, Nat. Leasing Co., Houston, 1969—, U.S. Plastics, Inc., Houston, 1969—, Calhoun Nat. Co., 1974—, Norman Trucking Co., 1975—. Chmn. Running Bear dist. Boy Scouts Am., 1971-73. Served with USNR, World War II. Mem. Miss. Assn. Ins. Agts., Miss. Mfrs. Assn., Am. Waterworks Assn., DAV, VFW, Am. Legion. Methodist. Clubs: Gideons, Exchange. Address: PO Box 208 Houston MS 38851

NORRID, HENRY GAIL, osteopathic physician and surgeon, biomedical researcher; b. Amarillo, Tex., June 4, 1940; s. Henry Horatio and Johnnie Belle (Combs, Cummins) N.; m. Andreia Maybeth Hudson, Jan. 29, 1966; children—Joshua Andrew, Noah Adam. A.A., Amarillo Coll., 1963; B.A., U. Tex., 1966; M.S., West Tex. State U., 1967; D.O., Kirksville Coll. Osteo. Medicine, 1973. Diplomate Bd. Osteo. Physicians and Surgeons, Nat. Bd. Examiners Osteo. Physicians and Surgeons. Intern Interboro Gen. Hosp., Bklyn., 1973-74; gen. practice medicine specializing in osteo., lectr. in biomechanics, N.Y.C., 1974-77, Amarillo, Tex., 1978—; attending physician Osteo. Hosp. and Clinic N.Y., N.Y.C., 1974-77; emergency room physician Amarillo Emergency Receiving Ctr., 1978-79; mem. exec. com. Southwest Osteo. Hosp., Amarillo, 1983-84, chief of staff, 1984-85; mem. credentials com. Northwest Tex. Hosp., Amarillo, 1984—; mem. Amarillo Hosp. Dist. Dept. Family Practice.; mem. organizing com. dept. osteo. prins., chmn. Manhattan group N.Y. Coll. Osteo. Med., 1977. Contbr. articles to Tex. Jour. Sci., other publs. Scout physician Llano Estecato council Boy Scouts Am., Texas, 1978-85; Vice pres. Class of 1973, Kirksville Coll. Osteo. Medicine, 1969. Served to E-4 U.S. Army, 1956-63. Mem. Am. Coll. Gen. Practitioners Osteo. Physicians and Surgeons (Tex. Soc.), Tex. Osteo. Med. Assn., Tex. Soc. Sons of Am. Revolution, The Sons of Republic of Tex., Am. Osteo. Acad. of Sports Medicine, Sigma Sigma Phi (pres. 1972), Alpha Phi Omega, Psi Sigma Alpha, Theta Psi, Theta Psi Clowns (1969-73), 11th Armored Cavalry Assn. Lodge: Masons. Avocations: astronomy; short wave listening; camping; fishing. Office: 819 Martin Rd PO Box 5733 Amarillo TX 79117

NORRIS, FRANKLIN GRAY, surgeon; b. Washington, June 30, 1923; s. Franklin Gray and Ellie Narcissus (Story) N.; B.S., Duke U., 1947; M.D., Harvard U., 1951; m. Sara Kathryn Green, Aug. 12, 1945; children—Gloria Norris Sales, F. Gray III. Resident, Peter Bent Brigham Hosp., Boston, 1951-54, Bowman Gray Sch. Medicine, 1954-57; practice medicine, specializing in thoracic and cardiovascular surgery, Orlando, Fla., 1957—; mem. staff Brevard Meml. Hosp., Melbourne, Fla., Waterman Meml. Hosp., Eustis, Fla., West Orange Meml. Hosp., Winter Garden, Fla.; Orange Meml. Hosp., Fla. Hosp., Lucerne Hosp., Holiday Hosp., Mercy Hosp. (all Orlando). Bd. dirs. Orange County Cancer Soc., 1958-64, Central Fla. Respiratory Disease Assn., 1958-65. Served to capt. USAAF, 1943-45. Decorated Air medal with 3 oak leaf clusters. Diplomate Am. Bd. Surgery, Am. Bd. Thoracic and Cardiovascular Surgery, Am. Bd. Gen. Vascular Surgery. Mem. Fla. Heart Assn. (dir. 1958—), Orange County Med. Soc. (exec. com. 1964-75, pres. 1971-75), A.C.S., Soc. Thoracic Surgeons, So. Thoracic Surg. Assn., Am. Coll. Chest Physicians, Fla. Soc. Thoracic Surgeons (pres. 1981-82), So. Assn. Vascular Surgeons, Phi Kappa Psi. Presbyterian (elder). Clubs: Citrus, Orlando Country. Home: 1801 Bimini Dr Orlando FL 32806 Office: 55 W Columbia St Orlando FL 32806

NORRIS, HORACE LEON, JR., city official; b. Washington, Ga., Aug. 22, 1939; s. Horace Leon and Hazel (Burden) N.; student various water works and wastewater specialized courses; diploma pastoral ministries, So. Baptist Conv., 1973, cert. in pastoral tng., 1973; diploma Berean Sch. Bible, 1980; m. Anna Mae Hadden; children—Theresa Margene, Deborah Ann. With engring. sect. Ga. Hwy. Dept., 1957-72; with water dept. City of Thomson (Ga.), 1972—, plant supt., 1973—, chief operator, 1973—; ordained to ministry Full Gospel Ch., 1980; asst. pastor Dearing Full Gospel Ch., 1981—; asst. gen. supt. Free Gospel Holiness Ch., 1981—; mem. clergy staff Univ. Hosp. Mem. Christians United for Israel Inc., Creation Sci. Internat., Am. Waterworks Assn., Ga. Water and Pollution Control Assn., Augusta Geneal. Soc. Home: PO Box 593 Thomson GA 30824 Office: PO Box 1017 Thomson GA 30824

NORRIS, PHILLIP ERIC, university administrator, psychologist; b. Montgomery, Ala., Nov. 21, 1948; s. Dave and Kathryn (Alsobrook) N.; m. Carol Pope Alexander, Sept. 14, 1974. B.A., U. Ala., 1971, M. Social Work, 1973; Ed.M., U. Mass., 1976, Ed.D., 1979. Postdoctoral fellow Harvard U., Cambridge, Mass., 1982-83, research assoc. Law Sch., 1982-83; pres. Nat. Job Search Tng. Lab., Cambridge, 1982-84, So. Ala. Inst., Mobile, 1981-84; chairperson U. So. Ala., Mobile, 1977-81, asst. prof. behavioral studies, 1981—; dir. U. So. Ala. Baldwin County, Bay Minette, 1984—; cons. strategic planning Ala. Commn. Higher Edn., Montgomery, 1982—, cons. legis. affairs, 1984—. Author: (video-tape) The Interview, 1983; (manual) The Achievement Card, 1974; (syndicated series) How to Find a Job, 1985. Editor newsletter, 1984-85. Chmn. econ. devel. commn. Baldwin County United, 1985—; mem. human resource com. Corp Engrs., Mobile, 1982-85; vice chmn. Small Bus. Com., Mobile, 1982; bd. dirs. Pvt. Industry Council, Mobile, 1982-84. Recipient Recognition citation Mass. State Legis., 1985, Rush Silver medal Am. Psychiat. Assn., 1974. Mem. Am. Psychol. Assn., World Future Soc., Am. Soc. for Tng. Devel. Home: 612 Cillege Ave Daphne AL 36526 Office: U So Ala Baldwin County Hwy 31 S Bay Minette AL 36507

NORRIS, ROBERT PETER, geologist; b. Bridgeport, Conn., Mar. 12, 1926; s. Michael John and Anne P. (Hein) N.; m. Mary E. Fagan, Apr. 12, 1950; children—Margaret, Robert, Elizabeth, Mary. B.S., Yale U., 1948; M.S., Kans. U., 1951. Geologist Shell Oil Co., various locations, 1951-79, Mich.-Wis. Pipeline Co., Houston, 1979-80, Champlin Petroleum Co., Houston, 1980—. Editor: Field Studies, 1957. Mem. Am. Assn. Petroleum Geologists, Soc. Petroleum Engrs. Republican. Episcopalian. Home: 5926 Green Springs Dr Houston TX 77066 Office: Champlin Petroleum Co 1400 Smith Suite 1500 Houston TX 77002

NORRIS, ROBERT REYNOLDS, newspaper executive; b. Columbus, Ga., Nov. 11, 1926; s. G. Rudolph and Eva Roberta (Reynolds) N.; B.S., Auburn (Ala.) U., 1957; m. Nita Adams, Aug. 8, 1947; children—Christopher Reynolds, Ann Allison. Formerly mech. supr. Columbus (Ga.) Enquirer, Oreg. Jour., St. Petersburg (Fla.) Times; formerly bus. mgr., gen. mgr. Augusta (Ga.) Chronicle-Herald; now v.p., gen. mgr. Lubbock (Tex.) Avalanche-Jour. Trustee, Meth. Hosp., Lubbock, W. Tex. Museum Assn.; bd. dirs. Tex. Tech. Found., Red Raider Club, S. Plains Fair; exec. bd. Ranch Hdqrs.; mem. pres.'s bd. Lubbock Christian Coll.; fin. chmn. Goodfellows Club: co-chmn. Water, Inc.; adv. council Lubbock YWCA; past v.p. Lubbock Arthritis Found.; past pres., dir. Lubbock Symphony. Served with USNR, 1943-46. Mem. Newspaper Enterprise Assn., Newspaper Advt. Bur., Tex. Daily Press Assn., Am. Press Inst. UPI Editors Assn., So. Newspapers Pubs. Assn., Am. Newspaper Pubs. Assn., Ducks Unlimited (past chpt. pres.). Presbyterian. Clubs: Lubbock, Lubbock Country. University City. Office: 710 Ave J Lubbock TX 79408

NORRIS, SHIRLEY GAY, geologist; b. El Paso, Tex., July 8, 1950; d. Samuel Byron and Nona Kathleen (Denman) N. B.S., U. Tex., El Paso, 1980. Geologist, BB & H Operating Co., Shreveport, La., 1980-82; geologist McMoRan Exploration Co., Longview, Tex., 1982—. Mem. Am. Assn. Petroleum Geologists, E. Tex. Geol. Soc., Zeta Tau Alpha. Republican. Episcopalian. Avocations: breeding, training and showing Australian Shepherds; snow skiing. Home: 10 Finch St Longview TX 75601 Office: McMoRan Exploration Co PO Box 2909 Longview TX 75606

NORRIS, THOMAS ROBERT, school principal; b. Neodesha, Kans., Mar. 13, 1956; s. Henry T. and Patricia J. (Main) N.; m. Ruth Ann Wilson, Aug. 9, 1980. B.A., Columbia Coll., 1976; M.S., Baylor U., 1978, Ed.D., 1981. Tchr. Milford Ind. Sch. Dist., Tex., 1977-78, Midway Ind. Sch. Dist., Waco, Tex., 1979-80; asst. prin. Temple Ind. Sch. Dist., Tex., 1980-82; prin. La Marque Jr. High Sch., Tex., 1982-85, La Marque High Sch., 1985—; lectr. U. Houston, Clear Lake, Tex., 1985. Mem. Tex. Assn. Secondary Sch. Prins., Tex. Assn. Supervision and Curriculum Devel., Nat. Assn. Supervision and Curriculum Devel., Phi Delta Kappa. Baptist. Lodge: Kiwanis (sec. 1984-85, v.p. 1985—). Avocation: refinishing antique furniture. Home: 1114 N Noble Rd Texas City TX 77591

NORSWORTHY, LAMAR, petroleum company executive; b. 1946. With Holly Corp., Dallas, 1967—, pres., 1971—, treas., from 1975, now chmn. bd., chief exec. officer. Office: Holly Corp 2600 Diamond Shamrock Tower Dallas TX 75201*

NORTH, ALEXA BRYANS, business educator; b. Dublin, Ga., Sept. 15, 1949; d. William B. and Trabue (Daley) Bryans; m. John Adna North, Jr., Mar. 20, 1976. B.S. in Edn., U. Ga., 1971, M.Ed., 1973; Ph.D., Ga. State U., 1981. Tchr. McDuffie High Sch., Anderson, S.C., 1971-72; grad. research asst. U. Ga., Athens, 1972-73; instr. Gordon Jr. Coll., Barnesville, Ga., 1973-76; adj. instr. DeKalb Community Coll., Ga., 1976-83; grad. teaching asst. Ga. State U., Atlanta, 1979-84, asst. prof. bus. edn., 1984—; book reviewer Dryden Press, 1984—; mem. bus. communication adv. bd. Random House, 1985—. Sec. Ruth Mitchell Dance Adv. Bd., Atlanta, 1979—. Mem. Assn. for Bus. Communication, Nat. Bus. Edn. Assn., So. Bus. Edn. Assn., Ga. Bus. Edn. Assn., Delta Pi Epsilon (pres. 1980-81), Phi Chi Theta, Kappa Delta. Presbyterian. Office: Ga State U VCD Dept Urban Life Plaza Atlanta GA 30303

NORTHCRAFT, LARRY PHILLIP, industrial and systems engineer; b. Bens Run, W.Va., Sept. 14, 1944; s. Glen Alvarious and Grace Louise (Jones) N.; m. Pamela Jean Ray, Oct. 28, 1976. B.S. in Indsl. Engring., W. Va. U., 1966; M.S., Ariz. State U., 1968, Ph.D., 1975. Engring. cons. Ariz. State Tb San., Phoenix, 1967; statis. quality control engr. AT&T Techs. (formerly Western Electric Co.), Phoenix, 1969-71, resource planning engr., Norcross, Ga., 1971-75, product and inventory control engr., Atlanta, 1975-81, sr. lightguide engr., Norcross, Ga., 1981-82, lightguide mfg. and engring. systems designer, 1982—. NDEA fellow Ariz. State U., 1966. Mem. Am. Soc. Quality Control, Ops. Research Soc. Am., Am. Inst. Indsl. Engrs., Norcross Citizens Council, Alpha Pi Mu. Republican. Methodist. Contbr. articles to profl. jours. Home: 946 Williamsburg Ln Norcross GA 30093 Office: 2000 Northeast Expressway Norcross GA 30071

NORTHEN, CHARLES SWIFT, III, banker; b. Birmingham, Ala., Jan. 25, 1937; s. Charles Swift and Jennie Hood (Hunt) S.; m. Margaret Carson Robinson, Dec. 27, 1959 (div. 1972); children—Margaret Allen, Charles Swift IV, Bryce Robinson,; m. Betty Jean Taylor, Oct. 3, 1981. B.A. cum laude, Vanderbilt U., 1959, M.A., 1961. Chartered fin. analyst. Mem. staff trust dept. Birmingham Trust Nat. Bank, 1960-64; with First Ala. Bank Birmingham, 1964-80, sr. v.p., trust officer, 1975-80; sr. v.p., trust officer Central Bank of South, Birmingham, 1981-85; sr. v.p. 1st Ala. Bancshares, 1985—; lectr. So. Trust Sch., Birmingham So. Coll., 1975—; dir. Hubbard Press, Findlay, Ohio. Bd. dirs. United Presbyn. Found, N.Y.C., 1977—; mem. Birmingham Com. Fgn. Relations, 1970—. Mem. Ala. Security Dealers Assn. (pres.), Atlanta Soc. Fin. Analysts, Inst. Chartered Fin. Analysts, Newcomen Soc. Presbyterian. Clubs: Mountain Brook, The Club. Lodge: Kiwanis. Home: 3024 N Woodridge Rd Birmingham AL 35223 Office: PO Box 10566 Birmingham AL 35296

NORTHRUP, JAN ELAINE, management consultant; b. Ottumwa, Iowa, June 25, 1949; d. Floyd E. and Mary Marcine (Hurley) Harrington; m. John B. Alexander, Dec. 27, 1981. A.A., Ottumwa Heights Coll., 1971; B.A., Parsons Coll., 1972; M.A., NE Mo. State Coll., 1976; Ph.D., Walden U., 1978. Cert. tchr., Iowa. Instr. Ottumwa Community Sch. Dist., 1972-80, dir. gifted edn., 1980; instr. George Washington U., Washington, 1982; pres. Mgmt. Tng. Systems, Inc., Springfield, Va., 1980—; trainer, cons. Morrow Inst. Applied Sci., Nellysford, Va., 1983—; facilitator, instr. Project TEACH, various cities, Iowa, 1978-80, Personal Dynamics Inst., 1976—. Creator, co-author video workshop. Vol. Children's Hospice Internat., Alexandria, Va., 1983—, Internat. Assn. Near-Death Studies, U. Conn., 1983—. Mem. Nat. Assn. Female Execs., AAUW (grantee 1978), Soc. Accelerated Learning Teaching (treas. 1984-85), Bus. Profl. Women's Club (Iowa Young Career Woman award 1979-80), Exec. Club. Avocations: equestrian-related sports; ceramics. Office: Mgmt Tng Systems Inc 5594 Backlick Rd Springfield VA 22151

NORTHUP, TERRY ELMER, educator; b. Chgo., Jan. 13, 1941; s. Clifford Elmer and Verna Juanita (Rahm) N.; m. Mary Jacque Sloter, Apr. 6, 1968; children—Michael Andrew, Derek Scott. B.A. in Edn., U. Miss., 1963, M.Ed., 1966; Ph.D., Purdue U., 1971. Tchr. Dist. 168, Sauk Village, Ill., 1963-67, Pekin High Sch., Ill., 1967-68; grad. instr. Purdue U., Lafayette, Ind., 1968-71; from asst. prof. to assoc. prof. Ga. State U., Atlanta, 1971-76; assoc. prof. edn. Wayland Baptist U., Plainview, Tex., 1976-81, prof., 1981—, chmn. div. edn., 1976—. Co-author: Using Computers to Teach Social Studies, 1986. Co-editor: Crackers and Red Suspenders, 1976; sect. editor Social Edn., 1976. Pres. bd. dirs. YMCA, Plainview, Tex., 1979-81; chmn. Tex. Tech Wesley Found., Lubbock, 1982-84; v.p. Hale County Tchrs. Credit Union, Plainview, 1984, pres., 1985. Danforth assoc. fellow, 1979—. Mem. Nat. Council Social Studies, Assn. Supervision and Curriculum Devel., Tex. Computer Edn. Assn. (bd. dirs. 1984—), Tex. Council Social Studies (bd. dirs. and chmn. tchr. standards 1985—), Assn. Liberal Arts Colls for Tchr. Edn. (chmn. tech. task force 1984—), Kappa Phi Kappa. Lodge: Rotary (sec. local club 1980-81, pres. local club 1983-84). Avocations: leather work; golf. Home: 1307 Wayland St Plainview TX 79072 Office: Wayland Bapt U 1900 W 7th St Plainview TX 79072

NORTON, CARMEL CORINNE, educational administrator; b. Orange, Tex., Apr. 9, 1922; d. Arthur Louis and Mathilde (Hotard) Boudreaux; B.S., Sam Houston State U., 1944; M.Ed., U. Houston, 1947; postgrad. Tex. Tech. U.; m. William Stancil Norton, Dec. 17, 1949; children—Therese, Michael, Alexine. Health and phys. edn. tchr., dir. Lee Brigadiers Drum and Bugle Corps, Robert E. Lee High Sch., Goose Creek Consol. Ind. Sch. Dist., Baytown, Tex., 1944-53, 61-65, phys. edn. tchr. Horace Mann Jr. High Sch., 1956-58, phys. edn. tchr. Ross Sterling High Sch., 1965, coordinator health and phys. edn. for girls, 1967-77, coordinator health and phys. edn., 1977—; mem. schs. and colls. com. Am. Cancer Soc., 1974—; mem. vis. coms. So. Assn. Colls. and Schs. Mem. AAHPER and Dance (alliance rep.), NEA (conv. del. 1970), Tex. Found. Intercollegiate Athletics for Women (bd. govs. 1975—, exec. treas. 1979—), Tex. Assn. Health, Phys. Edn. and Recreation (pres. 1974-75, honor award com., chmn. 1978—, honor award 1976, PEPT award 1980), Tex. State Tchrs. Assn. (mem. dist. ho. of dels.), Baytown Edn. Assn. (1st v.p. 1970-71), Delta Kappa Gamma. Roman Catholic. Club: Goose Creek Country. Home: 5004 Fairway Dr Baytown TX 77521 Office: Goose Creek Consol Ind Sch Dist PO Box 30 Baytown TX 77520

NORTON, DANIEL THOMAS, marine engineer; b. N.Y.C., Sept. 20, 1955; s. Thomas and Norma (Harrington) N.; m. Betsey Jane Pyatt, Oct. 27, 1979; children—John, Kathleen. B.S. in Marine Engring., Maine Maritime Acad., 1977. Cert. 1st asst. engr. steam vessels, U.S. Coast Guard. Third asst. engr. motor vessels U.S.A. Marine Dept Exxon Corp. (now Exxon Shipping Co.), Baytown, Tex., 1977-79, 2d asst. engr., 1979-81, 1st asst. engr. oceangoing oil tankers, 1981—. Home: 1301 Eagle Ave Virginia Beach VA 23456 Office: Exxon Shipping Co Box 3251 Baytown TX 77520

NORTON, LINDA ECK, forensic pathologist, medical-legal consultant; b. Balt., Apr. 26, 1945; d. William Albert and Frances Anita (Stallings) Eck; m. Charles Bryan Norton, Jr., Jan. 16, 1969 (div. 1974); children—Carol Beth, Jennifer Lee. A.B. in Chemistry, Duke U., 1967, M.D., 1971. Diplomate Am. Bd. Pathology. Intern in pathology Duke U. Med. Ctr., Durham, N.C., 1971-72, resident in pathology, 1972-74; resident in pathology N.C. Meml. Hosp., Chapel Hill, 1975-76; fellow in forensic pathology Office of Chief Med. Examiner N.C., Chapel Hill, 1974-75, assoc. chief med. examiner, 1976; instr. pathology U. N.C., Chapel Hill, 1976; med. examiner Dallas County Med. Examiner's Office, Dallas, 1976-81; instr. pathology Southwestern U., Dallas, 1976-78, asst. prof. pathology, 1978-81; assoc. chief med. examiner Jefferson County Coroner/Med. Examiner's Office, Birmingham, Ala., 1981-82; assoc. prof. U. Ala.-Birmingham, 1981-82; med. examiner Bexar County Med. Examiner's Office, San Antonio, 1982-83; cons. forensic pathology, Dallas, 1983—; head med./dental team for exhumation and identification Lee Harvey Oswald, 1981—; expert on child abuse/neglect. Fellow Am. Soc. Clin. Pathologists, Am. Acad. Forensic Scis.; mem. Nat. Assn. Med. Examiners. Contbr. articles to profl. publs. Office: 701 Commerce St Suite 200 Dallas TX 75202

NORTON, MIKE KELLY, petroleum geologist; b. Houston, Aug. 4, 1956; s. Ben Kelly and Billie Jean (Simpson) N.; m. Jana Leigh Hunter, Sept. 10, 1983. B.S. in Geology, Tex. A&M U., 1978. With Moore McCormack Energy, Dallas, 1978-81, Soltex Oil and Gas, Dallas, 1981-82, Tracy Engring., Dallas, 1982-84; ind. petroleum geologist, Norton Geol. Services, Dallas, 1984—. Mem. Am. Assn. Petroleum Geologists, Dallas Geol. Soc. Republican. Presbyterian. Home: 7757 Goforth Circle Dallas TX 75238 Office: Norton Geol Services 7757 Goforth Circle Dallas TX 75238

NORTON, RONALD RAY, lawyer; b. Bennettsville, S.C., Mar. 21, 1952; s. Lucian Carlisle and Myra Dean (Knight) N.; m. Sarah Lane Dowling, Aug. 18, 1973; children—Matthew Collins, Lucia Elizabeth. B.A., U. S.C., 1974, J.D., 1977. Bar: S.C. 1977, U.S. Dist. Ct. S.C. 1978, U.S. Ct. Appeals (4th cir.) 1979, U.S. Supreme Ct. 1985. Ptnr. Barber & Norton, Garden City, S.C.; trustee Beaufort County Pub. Defender Corp., S.C., 1982—. Active Hilton Head Island Jaycees, 1977-79; trustee St. Andrew United Meth. Ch., Hilton Head Island, S.C. Mem. Hilton Head Island Bar Assn., Beaufort County Bar Assn., Point Comfort Plantation Property Owners Assn. (bd. dirs.). Presbyterian. Office: Barber & Norton PO Box 330 Murrells Inlet SC 29576

NORWINE, ROBERT JACKSON, real estate broker; b. St. Louis, Mar. 31, 1924; s. Olin Dale and Lucille Alter (Kingsland) N.; m. Peggy Sue Sayers, 1949 (div. 1960); children—Kerry Norwine Dunning, Kyle; m. Betty Lou Straub, Sept. 14, 1962; 1 son, Dale; stepchildren—Theresa, Gregory. B.A., Westminster Coll., 1949. Dir. admissions, coach Westminster (Mo.) Coll., 1949-53; dir. admissions Wesleyan U., Middletown, Conn., 1953-63; dean admissions, dean students, v.p. New Coll., Sarasota, Fla., 1964-74; real estate broker Aid Realty, Sarasota, 1971-75, R.J. Norwine Real Estate, Sarasota, 1975-77; exec. v.p. Singer Weiss Realty, Sarasota, 1977-79; exec. v.p. Taylor & Saunders, Inc., Sarasota, 1979-84; pres. Fred J. Gibson & Assocs., Sarasota, 1985—. Chmn. charter rev. com. City of Sarasota, 1984-85; chmn. Parks and Recreation Adv. Bd. Sarasota, 1977-82; coach Babe Ruth Baseball Team, 1965-83; pres. Research Bur. Sarasota County Civic League, 1973-74; bd. dirs., v.p. United Appeal Sarasota County, 1974-78; bd. dirs. pres. Bird Key Improvement Assn., 1965-69, Boys Club Sarasota County, 1972-73; dir. Indsl. Devel. Council Sarasota County. Served with USN, 1943-46; PTO. Recipient Disting. Alumnus award Westminster Coll., 1966. Mem. Nat. Assn. Realtors, Fla. Assn. Relators, Sarasota Bd. Realtors, Nat. Assn. Coll. Admissions Counselors (dir., v.p., 1951-55), Beta Theta Pi. Club: Bird Key Yacht (commodore 1974). Home: 405 Pheasant Way Sarasota FL 33577 Office: 3100 S Tamiami Trail Sarasota FL 33577

NORWOOD, SAMUEL WILKINS, III, corporate planning and development executive; b. Chgo., Apr. 6, 1941; s. Samuel Wilkins and Miriam Lois (Cary) N.; m. Julianne P. Jones, June 15, 1962 (div. 1981); children—S. Parker, Elizabeth C. m. 2d, Lesley M. Eason, Feb. 5, 1983. Student, Vanderbilt U., 1959-61; B.A., Tulane U., 1964; M.B.A., U. Chgo., 1965. Supr. appropriations and spl. studies Fabricated Products div. Allied Corp., N.Y.C., 1965-67; mgr. fin. analysis Semicondr. div. ITT, Palm Beach, Fla., 1967-69; dir. fin. planning Fuqua Industries, Inc., Atlanta, 1969-70, group controller, 1970-71, asst. corp. controller, 1971-75, dir. planning, 1976-77, v.p. planning, 1977-79, v.p. corp. devel., 1979—. Mem. Planning Execs. Inst. (dir., chmn. 1984-85), Planning Forum (bd. dirs. 1985—). Presbyterian. Club: Atlanta Yacht (dir.). Contbr.

chpts. to books. Home: 1851 Walthall Dr NW Atlanta GA 30318 Office: 4900 GA Pacific Bldg Atlanta GA 30303

NOTH, NANCY CLAIRE, university official; b. Indpls., Mar. 24, 1950; d. John F. and Mary Jane (Heinen) N. B.A., Purdue U., 1972; M.A., U. Mont., 1975; Ph.D., Wash. State U., Pullman, 1983. Sch. psychologist pub. schs., Mont., 1975-78; asst. dir. career services Wash. State U., Pullman, 1981-83; dir. career planning and placement U. Ark., Fayetteville, 1983—; cons. in field. Mem. SW Placement Assn., Western Coll. Placement Assn., Am. Coll. Personnel Assn., Am. Assn. Counseling and Devel., Nat. Assn. Student Personnel Adminstrs. Office: U Ark 747 W Dickson Fayetteville AR 72701

NOTTAY, BALDEV KAUR, microbiologist; b. Nairobi, Kenya, East Africa, Jan. 15, 1936; d. Santa Singh and Swaran (Kaur) N. B.S. with honors, U. Bombay, 1960; M.Sc., U. Bombay, 1964. Research student Polio Research Unit, Haffkine Inst., Bombay, India, 1962-63; assoc. head poliovirus research Virology Dept., Med. Research Lab., Nairobi, 1964-71; vis. assoc. viral reagents CDC Ctrs. Disease Control, Atlanta, 1972-74, vis. assoc. enteric virology br., 1974-78, research microbiologist molecular virology br., div. viral diseases, 1978—. Contbr. articles to profl. jours. Home: 5574 Wylstream St Norcross GA 30093 Office: 1600 Clifton Rd Atlanta GA 30333

NOVAK, JONATHAN BLANDING, executive development and consulting executive; b. Pitts., Aug. 11, 1944; s. John and Violet Emelia (Dicey) N.; m. Betty Jane DeMoss, July 2, 1966; children—Kimberly Layne, Christopher Taylor, Tiffany Beth. B.A. in Sociology and Psychology, Eckerd Coll., 1968; M.B.A., Brenau Coll., 1984. Tech. cons., computer and teleprocessing services group leader Sears Roebuck & Co., Atlanta, 1968-81; ops. support mgr., mgmt. info. systems Ga. Power Co., Atlanta, 1981-83, devel. mgr., 1983-85; info. services mgr. product research, 1985-86; sr. teaching assoc. Inst. Systems Sci., Nat. U. Singapore, Kent Ridge, 1986—; cons.; adj. faculty Brenau Coll., Atlanta, 1984—; instr. Am. Mgmt. Assn., Oglethorpe U., Atlanta, 1985. Edison Electric Inst. Computer Com. Adult Sunday sch. tchr. Highlands Presbyn. Ch., 1970-71, 81—; founding vice chmn. Stone Mountain Civic Assn., 1972; pres. Redan Hills Civic Assn., 1976; coordinator Dekalb (Ga.) Police Target Hardening Opportunity Reduction, 1980-86; asst. emergency flight ops. officer CAP, 1985; active campaign Sam Nunn for U.S. Senate, 1984. Mem. Mensa, Soc. for Info. Mgmt. (nat. exec. bd. 1986, pres. Atlanta chpt. 1985-86), Edison Electric Inst., Am. Mgmt. Assn., Aircraft Owners and Pilots Assn., CAP. Home: 8 Cairnhill Rise 12-02 Singapore 0922 Singapore

NOVELL, EARL KENYON, ins. corp. exec.; b. Bridgeport, Conn., Sept. 13, 1925; s. Michael and Allegra Nancy (Kenyon) N.; student Marysville Coll., 1944-45, U. Conn., 1947-48; m. Stephanie T. Coleman, June 21, 1959; children—Michael K. and Paula W. (twins), Stephen J. Photographer, USN Underwater Sound Lab., New London, Conn., 1949-51; asst. mgr. Retail Credit Co., Boston, 1951-61; rep. Employers Ins. of Wasau, Brockton, Mass., 1961-66; dir. ins. and safety Perini Corp., Framingham, Mass., 1966-72; mng. dir. Marta Ins. Mgrs., Atlanta, 1972-77; dir. risk mgmt. Met. Atlanta Rapid Transit, 1977-78; sr. v.p. internat. brokerage services div. Molton, Allen & Williams Ins. Corp., Birmingham, Ala., 1979-81, sr. v.p. parent co., 1981—; v.p. nat. accounts McGriff, Seibels & Williams, Birmingham, 1981—; cons. risk mgmt. U.S. Dept. Transp., Urban Mass Transit Adminstrn. studies, 1976-78; cons. constrn. rapid transit, 1976-78; mem. safety adv. bd. Transit Devel. Corp., Washington, 1973—; Served with USAAF, 1943-46. Registered profl. engr., Calif.; cert. hazard control mgr. Mem. Nat. Safety Council (exec. com. transit sect. 1977—), Am. Soc. Safety Engrs., Am. Soc. Ins. Mgmt., Am. Passenger Transit Assn., Nat. Fire Protection Assn., Inst. Rapid Transit (patron safety com. 1974-76). Office: McGriff Seibels & Williams PO Box 10265 Birmingham AL 35202

NOVO, ADOLFO (TONY), JR., consulting engineer; b. Havana, Cuba, June 13, 1939; came to U.S., 1950; naturalized, 1956; s. Adolfo and Helvia (Queral) N.; m. Consuelo Arias, Jan. 28, 1961 (div. 1978); children—Yvonne, Michael, Christine; m. Miriam Fernandez, Nov. 17, 1978. B.S.E.E., U. Miami, 1967. Registered profl. engr., D.C., N.J., Md., La., Tex., Ala., Ga., Fla. Dir. engring. Harris, Anson, Grove & Haack Architects and Engrs., Inc., Fort Lauderdale, Fla. and N.Y.C., 1970-71; sales engr. Emerson Electric Co., Miami, Fla. and St. Louis, 1971-72; assoc. A.A. Hertz and Assocs. Cons. Engrs., Miami, 1972-74; pres. Pace, Inc. Cons. Engrs. Coral Gables, Fla., 1974—. Mem. minority contracting com. Dade County Sch. Bd., Fla. Mem. Nat. Soc. Profl. Engrs., Fla. Engring. Soc., Fla. Soc. Cons. Engrs., Constrn. Specifications Inst. (numerous offices and coms.), ASHRAE (com.), Latin Builders Assn. (contbr. to newsletter), Illuminating Engring. Soc. (various offices and coms.; disting. service award), Miami C. of C., U. Miami Alumni Assn., Internat. Businessmens Assn., Iron Arrow Soc. Clubs: Founders (Miami); Key Biscayne Yacht; Ensign Bitters (Coconut Grove). Avocations: painting; travel. Office: Pace Inc 207 Santillane Ave Coral Gables FL 33134

NOWFEL, RONALD CAMILLE, management consulting firm executive; b. Beirut, July 10, 1949; s. Camille Shrick and Dixie Lee (Webb) N. B.S. in Communications, So. Union Coll., 1971. Recruitment advertisor Nowfel, Edwards and Nunley, Orlando, Fla., 1972-76; mgr. personnel Harris Corp., Melbourne, Fla., 1976-82; pres. human resource cons. Nowfel and Assocs., Melbourne, 1982—; exec. locator Recruiters, Inc., Melbourne, 1982—. Vice pres. Toastmasters, Melbourne, 1981-82. Mem. Am. Soc. Tng. Devel. (v.p. 1981-82), Am. Soc. Personnel Adminstrs. (v.p. 1982-83). Home: 1411 S Riverside Dr Indialantic FL 32903 Office: Nowfel and Assocs PO Box 2385 Melbourne FL 32901

NOWICKI, STEPHEN, psychologist, educator, consultant; b. Milw., June 19, 1941; s. Stephen John and Frances (Padovano) N.; m. Kaaren Andersen, Aug. 28, 1965; 1 child, Stephen Andersen. B.A., Carroll Coll., 1963; M.S., Marquette U., 1965; Ph.D., Purdue U., 1969. Diplomate in clin. psychology. Asst. prof. psychology Emory U., Atlanta, 1969-74, assoc. prof., 1974-79, prof., 1979—, head counseling ctr., 1979-83. Author: (textbook) Abnormal Psychology, 1978, 2d edit., 1984; also articles, papers. Fulbright fellow, 1976; recipient Von Humboldt Internat. Research award, 1977. Fellow Am. Psychol. Assn. Roman Catholic. Avocations: running; tennis. Home: 1410 Drayton Woods Dr Tucker GA 30084

NOY, FAUSTO RAUL, anesthesiologist; b. Oriente, Cuba, Mar. 27, 1915; s. Jose M. and Gertrudis E. (Oliva) N.; m. Teresa Maria Anchia, Feb. 24, 1945; children—Raul de Jesus, Teresa Margarita, Ada Georgina. B.S., U. Havana, 1935, M.D., 1941. Lic. anesthesiologist, P.R. Rotating intern Hosp. Provincial de Santa Clara, Cuba, 1941-42, mem. anesthesiology staff, 1944-60, chief anesthesiology, 1960-64; chief anesthesiology Arecibo (P.R.) Dist. Charity Hosp., 1965-79; chief anesthesiology Buen Pastor, Hosp. Susoni, Arecibo, 1979—; prof. Provincial Hosp., Cuba. Named hon. med. capt. Cuban Police, 1948-52. Mem. AMA, P.R. Med. Assn., P.R. County Med. Soc., Med. Assn. in Exile, Miami, P.R. Soc. Anesthesiologists, Anesthesia Research Soc. U.S., Am. Soc. Anesthesiologists. Republican (nat. com.). Club: Liceo de Villaclara (Cuba.). Contbr. articles to profl. jours. Home: B-25 1 Marques Arecibo PR 00612

NOYA, RAMON ARGUDIN, electrical engineer, lighting designer, consultant; b. Havana, Cuba, July 24, 1940; came to U.S., 1959, naturalized, 1968; s. Ramon Freyre and Visitacion (Argudin) N. B.E.E., Ga. Inst. Tech., 1964. Registered profl. engr., Ga. Sr. elec. engr. Newcomb & Boyd, Atlanta, 1962-70; sr. elec. engr., project mgr. Morris Harrison & Assocs., Atlanta, 1970-72; pres., owner Ramon Luminance Design, Atlanta, 1972—. Designer lighting Boardwalk Restaurant 1982, (merit award 1982), Atlanta U. Library 1983, (merit award 1983), Rich's Magnolia Room 1983, (good practice award 1983), Stadium Hotel Renovations 1983; (good practice award 1983). Trustee Prosperos religious-ednl. orgn. Republican. Avocations: building hi fi gear; cooking; theater and symphony. Office: Ramon Luminance Design 3110 Maple Dr #409 Atlanta GA 30305

NOYES, CLAUDIA MARGARET, chemist; b. Haverhill, N.H., Apr. 30, 1940; d. Claude Edmund and Margaret Alice (Smith) N. B.S. in Chemistry, U. Vt., 1961; Ph.D., U. Colo., 1966. Research chemist Armour Grocery Products Co., Chgo., 1965-67; research technologist/research assoc. U. Chgo., 1968-75; research assoc. U. N.C., Chapel Hill, 1975-85, research asst. prof., 1985—. Mem. Am. Chem. Soc., AAAS, Am. Soc. Biol. Chemists, Sigma Xi. Author: (with R.L. Lundblad) Chemical Reagents for Protein Modification, 1984; contbr. articles to profl. jours. Office: Hematology 229H U NC Chapel Hill NC 27514

NUCKELS, MARK GORDON, geologist; b. Covington, Ky., Jan. 21, 1955; s. Clarence Edward and Ruth Laverne (Hall) N.; m. Carol Ann Jacobs, Apr. 21, 1984. B.A., U. S. Fla., 1976; M.S., 1981. Ops. trainee Geophys. Services, Inc., Saudi Arabia, 1977-79; geologist Mobil Oil Corp., Dallas, 1981-83, New Orleans, 1983-84, exploration geologist, 1984—. Contbr. articles to profl. jours. Mem. Am. Assn. Petroleum Geologists, Sigma Xi, Phi Kappa Phi. Avocations: gardening; racketball; jogging. Home: 511 Elmwood Dr Lafayette LA 70503

NUESCH, FREDERICK CHARLES, sports information administrator; b. Malvern, Ark., July 10, 1938; s. James Charles and Charlene (Hudson) N.; m. Joan Isabel Howe, Dec. 27, 1969. B.A. in English, Henderson State U., 1960; M.A. in Journalism, U. Mo., 1962. Sports editor Malvern Daily, Ark., 1962; sports writer Ark. Democrat, Little Rock, 1962-63; sports editor Paris News, Tex., 1963-68; sports info. dir. Tex. A&I U., Kingsville, 1968—; Editor athletic brochures, programs 1968—. Chmn. parish St. Gertrude Roman Catholic Ch., Kingsville, 1979—; publicity chmn. Kleberg County Cancer Soc, Kingsville, 1982—. Served as sgt. USAF, 1963-69. Recipient Main Press Ctr. Mgr. award Los Angeles Olympic Organizing Com., 1984. Mem. Coll. Sports Info. Dirs. Am. (sec. 1979—, named to Hall of Fame 1983), Nat. Assn. Intercollegiate Athletics (named to Hall of Fame 1979, Sports Info. Dir. of Yr. 1982), Sports Info. Dirs. Assn. of Nat. Assn. Intercollegiate Athletics (pres. 1972-74). Club: Corpus Christi Press. Lodge: Rotary (pres. 1984—). Home: 1601 Santa Cecelia Kingsville TX 78363 Office: Coll Sports Info Dirs Am Tex A&I U Campus Box 114 Kingsville TX 78363

NUESSEL, FRANK HENRY, linguistics educator; b. Evergreen Park, Ill., Jan. 22, 1943; s. Frank Henry and Rita Elizabeth (Aspell) N. A.B., Ind. U., 1965; M.A., Mich. State U., 1967; Ph.D., U. Ill., 1973. Instr. No. Ill. U., DeKalb, 1967-70; asst. prof. Ind. State U., Terre Haute, 1973-75; prof. linguistics U. Louisville, 1975—, dir. program linguistics, 1980—; mem. editorial bd. Hispanic Linguistics U. Pitts., 1983—; assoc. editor Lang. Problems and Lang. Planning, U. Tex., 1983—. Editor: Linguistic Approaches to the Romance Lexicon, 1978; Contemporary Studies in Romance Languages, 1980; Current Issues in Hispanic Phonology and Morphology, 1985. Contbr. articles to profl. jours. Mem. exec. bd. Understanding Aging Inc., Acton, Mass., 1984—. Mem. Linguistic Soc. Am., MLA, Gerontological Soc. Am., Am. Assn. Tchrs. Spanish and Portuguese. Home: 912 Pennwood Dr New Albany IN 47150 Office: U Louisville Dept Modern Languages Louisville KY 40292

NUGENT, RAY EDWARD, retail bookstore company executive, educator; b. Detroit, Nov. 18, 1932; s. Rayford Edward and Gladys Fancher (Allen) N.; m. Shirley Elizabeth Spires, June 4, 1955 (div. 1976); children—Kathleen, Lori, Carolyn, Susan, Ray; m. Zena A. Archilla, Dec. 28, 1976. B.A. in Commerce, The Citadel, 1955. With Philco-Ford, 1957-76; dir. distbn. Aeroneutronic-Ford, Phila., 1971-73, gen. mktg. mgr., 1973-75, gen. sales mgr., 1975-76; pres. Nugent & Assocs., Inc., Naples, Fla., 1976—; cons. Hospice, Inc., Naples, 1984—; lectr., lit. agt., book and author program dir. Editor: Rotary Internat. Bull., 1984-85. Pres. Horsham Youth Orgn., Pa., 1974-75; pres. St. Williams Secular Activities, Naples, 1984—; bd. dirs. Collier County Friends of Library, 1980—. Recipient Honor award Collier County Friends of Library, 1984. Mem. Am. Soc. Appraisers (keynote speaker internat. conf.), Am. Booksellers Assn., Fla. Council Libraries (bd. dirs. 1982—). Republican. Roman Catholic. Lodges: Rotary Internat. (sec. 1985—), Optimist (coach 1983-84). Avocations: boating, golf. Home: 4548 Genoa Ave Naples FL 33940 Office: The Book Trader 170 10th St N Naples FL 33940

NUGENT, ROBERT CHARLES, geologist, geophysicist; b. Jersey City; Sept. 22, 1936; s. James Francis and Alice Elizabeth (Wagner) N.; m. Marie Rutigliano, Dec. 21, 1958; children—Wendy Anne, William Robert, Anne Marie. B.A., Hofstra U., 1958; M.S., U. Rochester, 1960; Ph.D., Northwestern U., 1967. Devel. geologist Chevron Oil Co., New Orleans, 1965-68; assoc. prof. SUNY-Oswego, 1968-80, chmn. dept. earth scis., 1970-76; sr. reseach specialist Exxon Prodn. Research Co., Houston, 1980—. Served to capt. U.S. Army, 1963-65. Mem. Geol. Soc. Am., Am. Assn. Petroleum Geologists, Soc. Exploration Geophysicists. Republican. Roman Catholic. Avocation: jogging. Office: Exxon Prodn Research Co PO Box 2189 Houston TX 77001

NUGTEREN, ARIE, trading corporation executive; b. 1927; married. With Internat. Rotterdam, until 1963; v.p. Holco Trading Co., 1963-68, ACLI Internat. Inc., 1968-72; exec. v.p., dir. Kay Corp., Alexandria, Va. 1972—. Office: Kay Corp 320 King St Alexandria VA 22314*

NUNAN, ADRIENNE NICHOLA, geophysicist, geologist; b. Cork, Ireland, Nov. 9, 1956; came to U.S., 1958, naturalized, 1963; d. Timothy Raymond and Bridget Carmel (Cotter) N. B.S. in Geology, U. Ala., 1979; M.S. in Geology, U. N.C., 1983. Geologist, Law Engring. Testing Co., Atlanta, 1979-80, Miami, Fla., 1980; sr. geophysicist Exxon Co., U.S.A., Houston, 1983—; research and teaching asst. geology dept. U. Ala., Birmingham, 1976-79, U. N.C., Chapel Hill, 1980-83. Martin fellow U. N.C., 1981. Mem. Geol. Soc. Am., Am. Assn. Petroleum Geologists, Soc. Exploration Geophysicists, Houston Bicycle Club, Phi Kappa Phi. Avocations: bicycling; racquetball; golf. Home: 620-B Woodland St Houston TX 77009 Office: Exxon Co USA A/P Div 440 Benmar St Houston TX 77060

NUNEZ, OCTAVIO JOSE LUIS, aircraft company executive; b. Lima, Peru, Apr. 11, 1951; s. Octavio Inocencio and Belgica Eulalia (Miranda) N.; m. Blanca Rose Echevarria (div.); children—Anicia Isabel, Jonathan Octavio Nunez; m. 2d, Teresa De Jesus Verastegui, Feb. 9, 1983. Student Miami Dade Community Coll., 1970-75. Supr. Jerry's Aircraft Service, Miami, Fla., 1970-75; mgr. Tech. Indsl. Corp., Miami, 1979-80; pres. Comml. & Gen. Aviation Corp., Miami, 1980—; cons. on aircraft tech. Served with U.S. Army, 1973-79. Mem. Am. Legion. Democrat. Mem. Ch. of God. Office: 1670 W 39th Pl Suite 1304 Hialiah FL 33012

NUNEZ-PORTUONDO, RICARDO, investment company executive; b. N.Y.C., June 9, 1933; s. Emilio and Maria (Garcia) N.-P.; LL.D., U. Havana, 1958; postgrad. in law U. Fla., 1975; m. Dolores Maldonado, Sept. 7, 1963; children—Ricardo José, Emilio Manuel, Eduardo Javier. Press attache Cuban embassy, Madrid, 1958-59; writer, editor news dept. Latin Am. div. USIA, Miami and Washington, 1961-71; pres. Internat. Mktg. Realty, 1977—; Chmn. bd. Interstate Bank Commerce, Miami, 1985—; dir. Miami Nat. Bank; nat. dir. Cuban Refugee Program, Washington and Coral Gables, Fla., 1975-77; pres. Central Investment Trust Corp., 1977—. Trustee, mem. founders council Fla. Internat. U.; mem. Fla. Elections Commn., 1981-84; mem. Gov.'s Council Econ. Affairs, Tallahassee; pres. Mercy Hosp. Found.; mem. citizens bd. U. Miami Latin Am. Adv. Bd.; mem. planning com. City of Coral Gables. Clubs: Met. (N.Y.C.); Lyford Cay (Nassau); Ocean Reef (Key Largo); Key Biscayne Yacht; 200 of Greater Miami, Big Five (Miami). Home: 675 Solano Prado Coral Gables FL 33156 Office: PO Box 141720 Coral Gables FL 33114

NUNLEY, WILLIAM TERRELL, insurance agency executive; b. Salt Lake City, May 27, 1948; s. William Timothy and Virginia Ella (Hart) N. Student Pacific Lutheran U., 1966-68, C.W. Post Coll., 1969-71; B.A. in Communications, U. Central Fla., 1975. Ins. agt., 1972-76; dep. ins. commr., Melbourne, Fla., 1977-79; chief bur. field ops. Fla. Dept. Ins., Tallahassee, 1979-81; v.p. Associated Ins. Brokers, Inc., Coral Gables, Fla., 1981-83; sr. v.p. Interstate Underwriting Agys., Inc., Coral Gables, 1983—; mem. gen. line agts. adv. com. Fla. Dept. Ins. Active Democratic party Fla.; del. Fla. Dem. Conv., 1981, 83. Mem. Fla. Assn. Ins. Agts. Office: Interstate Underwriting Agys Inc 999 Ponce de Leon Blvd Coral Gables FL 33134

NUNN, ROGER DAVID, ophthalmologist; b. Sacramento, Sept. 27, 1941; s. Harvey Cecil and Othni Leona (Hilgenfeld) N.; m. Gail Ann McAllister, June 13, 1964; children—Lesie Lynne, Kristin Michelle. A.B., Asbury Coll., 1963; M.D., Ohio State U., 1967. Diplomat Am. Bd. Ophthalmology. Resident in ophthalmology Ohio State U. Hosp., Columbus, 1968-72; practice medicine specializing in ophthalmology, Denton, Tex., 1972—; chief of staff Flow Meml. Hosp., Denton, 1982—. Served to capt. U.S. Army NG, 1967-73. Fellow ACS, Am. Acad. Ophthalmology; mem. Kerato-Refractive Soc., Am. Soc. Cataract and Refractive Surgery, Out-Patient Ophthalmolic Surgery Soc., Tex. Med. Assn., Denton County Med. Soc. (sec. 1979), Tex. Ophthal. Assn. Republican. Mem. Bible Ch. Avocations: skiing; tennis; travel. Office: 525 A Bryan Denton TX 76201

NUNN, SAM, U.S. senator; b. Perry, Ga., Sept. 8, 1938; s. Samuel Augustus and Elizabeth (Cannon) N.; m. Colleen O'Brien, Sept. 25, 1965; children—Michelle, Brian. Student, Ga. Tech. Coll., 1956-59; LL.B., Emory U., 1962. Bar: Ga. 1962. Legal counsel armed services com. U.S. Ho. Reps., 1963; mem. firm Nunn, Geiger & Rampey, Perry, Ga., 1964-73; mem. Ga. Ho. Reps., 1968-72; U.S. senator from Ga., 1973—; ranking minority mem. Armed Services Com.; mem. Govtl. Affairs Com., Small Bus. Com., Intelligence Com.; farmer, Perry, 1964—. Named One of Five Outstanding Young Men in Ga. by Ga. Jaycees, 1971; recipient Most Effective Legislator award Dist. Attys. Assn., 1972. Mem. Perry C. of C. (pres. 1964), Ga. Planning Assn. (dir. 1966, pres. 1971). Office: 303 Dirksen Senate Office Bldg Washington DC 20510

NUNN, WALTER MELROSE, JR., electrical engineering educator, research scientist; b. New Orleans, Sept. 16, 1925; s. Walter M. and Leah (Hennessey) N.; m. Hortense Hillery, Sept. 14, 1949. B.S.E.E., Tulane U., 1950; M.S.E.E., Okla. State U., 1952; Ph.D., U. Mich., 1960; M.S. in Physics, U. Ill., 1969. Registered profl. engr., Fla. Research engr. Hughes Aircraft Co., Fullerton, Calif., 1954-56, sr. staff engr., 1985—; asst. prof. elec. engring. U. Minn., Mpls., 1960-63; prof. elec. engring. Tulane U., New Orleans, 1963-67; research scientist D.B.A. Systems, Inc., Melbourne, Fla., 1983-85; prof. elec. engring. Fla. Inst. Tech., Melbourne, 1969—; cons. U.S. Navy Dept., 1966-67, Harris Corp., Melbourne, 1973, NASA, 1981-82, U.S. Army Missile Command, Redstone, Ala., 1978-79. Contbr. articles to profl. jours. Served as sgt. USMC, 1943-46. Mem. Am. Phys. Soc., Tau Beta Pi, Sigma Pi Sigma. Office: Dept Elec Engring Fla Inst Tech Melbourne FL 32901

NUNNERY, LOUIS WALLACE, ballet master; b. Fort Lawn, S.C., Mar. 8, 1919; s. Charles Henry and Mary Emma (Gibson) N. B.A., U. S.C., 1939; postgrad. Corcoran Art Sch., 1939-41, Sch. Dance Arts, 1945-50, Lubor Egorova Ballet Sch., Paris, 1950-51. Prin. Classical Ballet Sch., Hickory, N.C., 1952—; dir., dancer Charlotte Ballet Co., N.C., 1952-56; founder, dir. New South Dance Theatre, Hickory, 1957-60; dir. Tarheel Ballet Co., Hickory, 1965—; Lead dancer Unto These Hills, Cherokee, N.C., 1956-62, actor, choreographer, 1968-75. Served with USN, 1940-43. Methodist. Avocations: antique automobiles; raising Russian wolfhounds; writing; painting. Home: Villa del Buffone Triste Country Club Dr Route 1 Newton NC 28658 Office: Louis Nunnery Sch Classical Ballet 254 1st Ave NW Hickory NC 28601

NUSYNOWITZ, MARTIN LAWRENCE, nuclear medicine physician; b. N.Y.C., July 21, 1933; s. Morris Nusynowitz and Esther Clara (Rechtschaffen) Pober; m. Harriet Rubinstein, Aug. 28, 1955; children—Murray Mark, Russell Neil, Leah Rachel. Student Fordham U. Coll. Pharmacy, 1951-53; B.A., NYU, 1954; M.D. cum laude, SUNY-Syracuse, 1958. Cert. Nat. Bd. Med. Examiners; diplomate Am. Bd. Internal Medicine (Endocrinology and Metabolism), Am. Bd. Internal Medicine, Am. Bd. Nuclear Medicine. Intern Letterman Army Med. Ctr., San Francisco, 1958-59; resident in internal medicine Tripler Army Med. Ctr., Honolulu, 1959-62; commd. 2d lt. U.S. Army, advanced through grades to col., 1977; various med. assignments, 1962-65; chief med. research & devel., nuclear medicine, endocrine services William Beaumont Army Med. Ctr., El Paso, Tex., 1965-77; ret., 1977; assoc. clin. prof. radiology George Washington U., Washington, 1974; clin. prof. medicine Tex. Tech U., Lubbock, 1974; chief nuclear medicine Bexar County Hosp., San Antonio, 1977-82; prof., head nuclear medicine U. Tex. Health Sci. Ctr., San Antonio, 1977-82, U. Tex. Med. Br., Galveston, 1982—; cons. clin. nuclear medicine Surgeon Gen., U.S. Army, Washington, 1972-77, Audie Murphy Meml. VA Hosp., San Antonio, 1977-82; cons. in endocrinology and nuclear medicine Brooke Army Med. Ctr., San Antonio, 1978—. Contbr. articles to profl. jours., chpts. to textbooks. Bd. dirs., pres. El Paso Diabetes Assn., 1970-72; bd. dirs., mem. steering com. Gulf Coast Council on Fgn. Affairs, Galveston, 1982—. Decorated Legion of Merit; recipient Boss of Yr. award Am. Bus. Women's Assn., 1975. Fellow ACP, Am. Coll. Nuclear Physicians; mem. Am. Fedn. for Clin. Research, AMA, Soc. Nuclear Medicine (pres. Southwestern chpt. 1977-78, Silver Medal award 1972, 76), Endocrine Soc., Southwestern Clin. Ligand Assay Soc. (pres. 1984-85). Jewish. Avocations: horseback riding; jogging; sailing. Home: 15726 Brook Forest Dr Houston TX 77059 Office: U Tex Med Br Div Nuclear Medicine Galveston TX 77550

NUTT, REX LYNN, physical therapist; b. Tipton, Okla., June 30, 1933; s. Lacy Brackston and Nell (Smith) N.; children—Robert Lynn, Ronald Lee. B.S., Abilene Christian U., 1956; postgrad. Tex. Woman's U. Lic. phys. therapist. Staff phys. therapist Gonzales Warm Springs Found., Tex., 1955-57, 59; asst. edn. adminstr. Hermann Sch. Phys. Therapy, Houston, 1959-61, edn. adminstr., 1962-65; dir. phys. therapy dept. Spring Br. Meml. Hosp., Houston, 1964-84; pres. Houston Phys. Therapy Service, 1969—; mem. Tex. State Bd. Phys. Therapy Examiners, 1979-85. Contbr. articles to Clin. Mgmt. Mag. Bd. dirs. Herod Sch. PTO, Houston, 1967-69; mem. edn. of schs. and orgns. subcom. Am. Heart Assn., Houston, 1972; mem. adv. com. spl. services Houston Ind. Sch. Dist., 1975-78; elder Southwest Central Ch. of Christ, Houston, 1969—. Mem. Abilene Christian U. Alumni Assn. (Citation award 1976), Tex. Phys. Therapy Assn., Am. Coll. Sports Medicine. Avocations: photography.

NUTTER, CHARLES WILLIAM, city official; b. Kansas City, Mo., Sept. 17, 1937; s. Charles Perry and Eleanor (Haldeman) N.; student Rice U., 1956-58; B.B.A., Tulane U., 1961; m. Dawna Beth Eukel, Oct. 18, 1974; children—Andrew David, Christy Anne. Dist. exec. New Orleans council Boy Scouts Am., 1962-67; classification analyst New Orleans Civil Service Commn., 1967-69; asst. ops. adminstr. New Orleans Adminstrv. Office, 1969-71; dir. recreation City New Orleans, 1971-78, supt. Parkway and Parks Commn., 1978-82; asst. dir. Tulsa Park and Recreation Dept., 1982—. Troop scoutmaster New Orleans council Boy Scouts Am., 1963-74, v.p. exec. bd., 1977-82. Bd. dirs. Greater New Orleans Fedn. Chs., 1970-72, La. Nature Center, Episcopal Community Services. Served to 2d lt. AUS, 1961-62. Recipient Silver Beaver award Boy Scouts Am., 1971; Nat. Disting. Community Service award Nat. Recreation and Park Assn., 1979; Monte M. Lemann award La. Civil Service League, 1979; Pres.'s citation Okla. Recreation and Park Soc. Mem. SAR, Urban Park and Recreation Alliance, Audubon Soc., Am. Forestry Assn., Am. Hort. Soc. Episcopalian (vestryman). Club: Rotary (New Orleans). Home: 7010 S Richmond Ave Tulsa OK 74136 Office: 200 Civic Ctr Room 642 Tulsa OK 74136

NUTTER, ROGER VICTOR, aerospace engineer; b. Taft, Calif., June 12, 1939; s. Paul Andrew and Frances Elizabeth (Krause) N.; m. Bonnie Linda Huffman, July 6, 1963; 1 son, Scott Allen. B.S. in Aerospace Engring., U. Va., 1963; postgrad. in ops. research Fla. State U., 1966-67. Project engr. Naval Tng. Equipment Ctr., Orlando, Fla., 1967-72; project dir. tng. analysis and evaluation group Dept. Navy, Orlando, 1972—; mem. Tech. Adv. Group for Advanced Devel. Program for Aviation Wide Angle Visual Systems. Vol., Bicentennial Celebration, Orlando, United Fund, Orlando, Boy Scouts Am., Little League, Orlando; keyman U.S. Savs. Bond Campaign, Orlando; program rep. Comml./Indsl. Activities Program, Orlando. Served to capt. USAF, 1963-67. Recipient 10 Sustained Superior Performance awards and outstanding ratings Dept. Navy, 1967-83. Mem. Human Factors Soc. (treas. Central Fla. chpt.), Sigma Xi. Republican. Methodist. Clubs: Citrus, U. Va. Alumni (exec. bd.) (Orlando). Author: Management System Concept, 1982; author tech. reports Dept. Navy. Home: 608 Lake Orienta Dr Altamonte Springs FL 32701 Office: Tng Analysis and Evaluation Group Dept Navy Orlando FL 32813

NUTZHORN, CARL ROBBINS, lawyer; b. Rockville Centre, N.Y., Sept. 13, 1927; s. Carl William and Lorena Waite (Robbins) N.; m. Marta RoseMarie Larsson, Feb. 1965 (div. 1966). B.A. cum laude, Woodrow Wilson Sch. Pub. and Internat. Affairs, Princeton U., 1951; J.D., Columbia U., 1955. Bar: N.Y. 1957, U.S. Dist. Ct. (so. and ea. dist.) N.Y. 1957, U.S. Ct. Appeals (2d cir.) 1962, U.S. Dist. Ct. (we. dist.) Okla. 1968, U.S. Ct. Appeals (10th cir.) 1971, U.S. Dist. Ct. Colo. 1972, U.S. Supreme Ct. 1961. Assoc. Carter, Ledyard & Milburn, N.Y.C., 1955-57; assoc. atty. to gen. counsel Am. Fore Loyalty Ins. Group, N.Y.C., 1959-60; assoc. Smith & Auslander, N.Y.C., 1960-61, Smith, Steibel & Alexander, N.Y.C., 1962-63; sole practice, Aspen, Colo., 1972-81; semi-retired, Ft. Lauderdale, Fla., 1983—. Author: Wage-Price Spiral and the Presidential Tariff Power, 1958; Hydrogen-Oxygen Energy Systems, 1964;

Considerations Whose Time Has Come, 1985. Mem. Pitikin County Bd. Adjustment, Aspen, 1972-80; auditor Summer Arms Control Workshops of Aspen Inst., 1976-82. Served with USMCR, 1945-46. Mem. U.S. Tenth Cir. Jud. Conf., Colo. Bar Assn., Am. Arbitration Assn. (panel of arbitrators), Navy League U.S. (Ft. Lauderdale council), Ft. Lauderdale Beach Environ. Assn., Phi Delta Phi. Democrat. Lutheran. Home: 1900 S Ocean Dr No 1101 Ft Lauderdale FL 33316

NUWER, JOHN EDWARD, electrical engineer; b. El Paso, Tex., June 30, 1949; s. John Edward and Jane (Whitten) N.; m. Carol Joyce Reynolds, Dec. 28, 1971; 1 child, Jennifer Danielle. B.S.E.E., U. Tex.-El Paso, 1971, M.S.E., 1973. Instr. U. Tex., 1972-73; mem. tech. staff Bell Telephone Labs., Holmdel, N.J., 1973-74; supr. data transmission Atlantic Richfield Co., Dallas, 1974-78; mgr., engr. West region Sun Info. Services, Dallas, 1978-79; mgr. planning and evaluation, electronics and telecommunications Atlantic Richfield Co., Los Angeles, 1979-83; dir. teleconf. devel. Isacomm, Inc., Atlanta, 1983-85; exec. v.p. Environ. and System Integration, Inc., Atlanta, 1985—; planner 1st pvt., nat. video conferencing network; speaker, cons. on digital data, satellite communications, videoconferencing and network/tech. control. Spencer fellow Tau Beta Pi, 1972-73. Mem. Nat. Soc. Profl. Engrs., IEEE, Am. Mgmt. Assn., Tau Beta Pi (pres. chpt. 1971-72), Eta Kappa Nu (treas. chpt. 1971-72). Republican. Contbr. articles to Data Communications. Project engr. first pvt., digital very high speed data system in U.S. Office: Isacomm 1815 Century Blvd Suite 500 Atlanta GA 30345

NWADIKE, EMMANUEL VICTOR, engineering educator; b. Port Harcourt, Nigeria, May 2, 1948; came to U.S., 1977; s. Michael Anowai and Eunice Adaku (Emetoh) N.; m. Naomi Adassa Gray, Aug. 7, 1978. B.Engring., Ahmadu Bello U., 1970; M.S., U. Surrey (Eng.), 1971; M.Phil., U. London, 1975; Ph.D., U. Miami, 1980. Registered profl. engr., Fla. Asst. prof. mech. engring. U. Miami (Fla.), 1978-82, assoc. prof., 1982—, dept. chmn., 1982—; v.p. Pawa Complex Internat., Inc., 1982—. Mem. steering com. Congress of Black Scholars, 1983—. Mem. ASME, AIAA, British Instn. Mech. Engrs., Sigma Xi, Omicron Delta Kappa, Tau Beta Pi, Pi Tau Sigma, Phi Kappa Phi. Contbr. articles to profl. jours. Home: 16610 SW 103d Pl Miami FL 33157 Office: Fla Internat U Miami FL 33199

NYCE, JOHN DANIEL, lawyer; b. York, Pa., Sept. 7, 1947; s. Harry Lincoln and Dorothy (Wagner) N.; m. Karen Martzolf, Dec. 28, 1974; children—Joshua David, Laura Kimberly. B.A., SUNY-Buffalo, 1970; J.D., U. Miami, 1973. Bar: Fla. 1973, U.S. Dist. Ct. (so. dist.) Fla. 1973, U.S. Dist. Ct. (middle dist.) Fla. 1973, U.S. Ct. Appeals (5th cir.) 1973, U.S. Supreme Ct. 1984. Assoc. Ralph P. Douglas, Pompano Beach, Fla., 1974, Coleman, Leonard & Morrison, Ft. Lauderdale, Fla., 1975-78; ptnr. Nyce and Smith, Ft. Lauderdale, 1979; sole practice, Ft. Lauderdale, 1980—. Bd. dirs. Alliance for Responsible Growth, Inc., Habitat for Humanity of Broward County, Inc.; bd. dirs., co-founder Fla. Family Adoption, Inc.; mem. Broward County Right to Life; mem. exec. com. Broward County Republican Party; bd. dirs. Shepherd Care Ministries, Inc.; cert. trainer Evangelism Explosion III Internat., Inc. Mem. ABA, Christian Lawyer's Assn. (founder, past pres., bd. dirs.), Atty's. Title Ins. Fund, Conservative Caucus of Broward County, Fla. Tennis Assn., The Gideons, Delta Theta Phi. Republican. Presbyterian. Home: 5910 NE 21st Ln Fort Lauderdale FL 33308 Office: 4367 N Federal Hwy Fort Lauderdale FL 33308

NYDORF, ROY HERMAN, artist, educator; b. Port Washington, N.Y., Oct. 1, 1952; s. Seymour and Elsi (Rosenberg) N.; m. Theresa Nadine Hammond, May 12, 1984. B.A., SUNY-Brockport, 1974; M.F.A., Yale U., 1976. Teaching asst. Yale U., 1975-76; instr. U. New Haven, 1977-78; asst. prof. art Guilford Coll., Greensboro, N.C., 1978—, chmn. art dept., 1983-85. Exhibited in group shows at Nat. Acad. Design, N.Y.C., Pratt Graphics Ctr., N.Y.C., Weatherspoon Art Gallery, U. N.C., Greensboro, N.C. Mus. Art, Raleigh, SECCA, Winston-Salem, N.C. Recipient 1st prize Port Washington Arts Council, 1974, Purchase award Honolulu Acad. Arts, 1983. Mem. Green Hill Ctr. N.C. Art, Greensboro Artists League (bd. dirs. 1983-84). Democrat. Jewish. Avocations: American history; archaeology; architecture; music. Office: Guilford Coll Art Dept 5800 W Friendly Ave Greensboro NC 27410

NYE, ARNOLD COY, JR., technical center executive; b. Salem, Ohio, Feb. 23, 1936; s. Arnold Coy and Martha Jean (Young) N.; m. Margarethe Birk, Dec. 29, 1962; children—Eva Maria, Robert Edmund. B.S. in Mgmt. summa cum laude, Hampton Inst., 1973; M.S. in Mgmt., U. Ark., 1975. Joined U.S. Air Force, 1954, advanced through grades to master sgt., 1970, ret. 1976; asst. for fin. and personnel Peninsula Vo-Tech., Hampton, Va., 1976-85; asst. dir. New Horizons Tech. Ctr., Hampton, 1985—. Decorated Air Force Commendation medal, Meritorious Service award. Mem. Am. Vocat. Assn., Assn. Sch. Bus. Ofcls., Am. Assn. Sch. Personnel Adminstrs., Va. Assn. Sch. Personnel Adminstrs. Home: 424 Dare Rd Grafton VA 23692 Office: 2102 Mercedes Dr Hampton VA 23661

NYE, ERLE ALLEN, utility executive, lawyer; b. Ft. Worth, June 23, 1937; s. I.B. Nye; m. Alice Ann Grove, June 5, 1959; children—Elizabeth Nye Kirkham, Palema K., Erle Allen, Edward Kyle, Johnson Scott. B.S. in E.E., Tex. A&M U., 1959; J.D., So. Methodist U., 1965. Bar: Tex. 1965. Vice-pres., Dallas Power & Light Co., 1975-79; exec. v.p., chief fin. officer Tex. Utilities Co., Dallas, 1979—. Bd. dirs. INROADS/Dallas Inc. Served with U.S. Army, 1959-60. Mem. ABA, Tex. Bar Assn., Dallas Bar Assn., Fin. Execs. Inst., Soc. Rate of Return Analysts, Edison Electric Inst., Dallas Economists Club, Dallas Bar Found. (past trustee). Methodist. Club: Northwood. Lodge: Rotary (Dallas). Office: 2001 Bryan Tower Dallas TX 75201

NYE, JOHN ROBERT, furniture company executive, transportation consultant; b. Phila., Apr. 18, 1947; s. William E. and Mary B. (Brick) N.; m. Judy Burris, May 31, 1969 (div. Dec. 1977); children—Keith, Lanny, John; m. 2d, Grace M. Adams, Feb. 28, 1981; children—Annette, Mark. B.A., N.C. State U.-Raleigh, 1969. Prodn. mgr. Highland House, Hickory, N.C., 1969-79; distbn. mgr. Hickory Chair Co., 1979—. Mem. Catawba Valley Traffic Club. Republican. Lutheran. Home: PO Box 3136 Hickory NC 28603 Office: Hickory Chair Co 37 9th St Pl SE Hickory NC 28601

NYERGES, ALEXANDER LEE, museum director; b. Rochester, N.Y., Feb. 27, 1957; s. Sandor Elek and Lena (Angeline) N.; m. Helena Marie Strauch, June 6, 1981. B.A., George Washington U., 1979, M.A., 1981. Intern The Octagon, Washington, 1976-79; archeol. asst. Smithsonian Instn., Washington, 1977, curatorial intern Nat. Mus. Am. History, 1978-79; adminstrv. asst. George Washington U., Washington, 1979-81; exec. dir. DeLand Mus. Art, Fla., 1981-85, Miss. Mus. Art, Jackson, 1985—; field surveyor Inst. Mus. Services, Washington, 1985-86; treas., bd. dirs. Volusia County Arts Council, Daytona Beach, Fla., 1983-85. Contbr. articles to profl. jours. Bd. dirs. West Volusia Hist. Soc., 1984-85; trustee Cultural Arts Ctr., DeLand, 1984-85. U.S. Dept. Edn. scholar, 1973. Mem. DeLand Area C. of C. (bd. dirs., tourist adv. com. 1984-85), Am. Art Mus. Assn. (Miss. regional rep.), Am. Assn. Mus. (SE regional rep. to non-print media com. 1983-85), Miss. Museums Assn., Southeastern Mus. Conf., Fla. Mus. Assn., Fla. Art Mus. Dirs. Assn., Phi Beta Kappa. Republican. Presbyterian. Avocations: restoring old houses; gardening; music; writing; sports. Home: 4351 Forest Park Dr Jackson MS 39211 Office: Miss Mus Art Lamar at Pascagoula St Jackson MS 39201

NYIRI, JACK PHILLIP, hospital administrator; b. Cleve., Sept. 3, 1951; s. Frank Andrew and Lottie (Wagner) N.; m. Cheryl Jane Parker, Mar. 23, 1985. B.A. in Bus. Adminstrn., Wittenberg U., 1973; M.H.A., George Washington U., 1975. Adminstrv. asst. Montgomery Gen. Hosp., Olney, Md., 1975-79; asst. adminstr. Kings Dau. Meml., Frankfort, Ky., 1979-82; adminstr. Edgefield Hosp., Nashville, 1982—. Mem. admissions panel United Way, Frankfort, Ky., 1980-82, Nashville, 1982—. Nominee Am. Coll. Hosp. Adminstrs. Avocations: tennis; amateur radio. Home: 804 Creek Valley Ct Nashville TN 37221 Office: Edgefield Hosp 610 Gallatin Rd Nashville TN 37206

OAKES, JOHN WARREN, artist, educator; b. Bowling Green, Ky., Feb. 26, 1941; s. John Edward and Marian Frances (Connor) O.; m. Elizabeth Ann Thompson, Apr. 16, 1956; children—Christopher Warren, Kathryn Marya, Antonia Elizabeth. A.B., Western Ky. U., 1964; M.A., U. Iowa, 1966, M.F.A., 1973. Composite artist Graham Studios, Bowling Green, Ky., 1961-66; artist news dept., film editor Sta. WLTV-TV, Bowling Green, 1965; instr. art Western Ky. U., Bowling Green, 1966-71, asst. prof. art, 1971-76, staff asst., gallery dir., 1966; curator Collector's Gallery, Woodstock, N.Y., 1967; curator, instr. Genesis Gallery and Art Ctr., Bowling Green, 1968; staff asst. Potter Coll. Arts and Humanities, Bowling Green, 1973-75, asst. dean for adminstrn., 1975—, assoc. prof. art, 1976—, acting dean, 1977, 1980, acting head dept. journalism, 1984. One man shows include Owensboro Area Mus., Ky., 1980, Lens Unltd. Gallery, Ky., 1980, Western Ky. U. Gallery, 1980, WKU Gallery, Bowling Green, 1980, Houchens Ctr., Ky., 1978; exhibited in group shows at Gov.'s Exhbn. of Ky. Art, 1961, High Mus. Art, Ga., 1965, Collector's Gallery, N.Y., 1967, Insel Gallery, N.Y., 1972, Arnot Art Mus., N.Y., 1976; represented in numerous pub. and pvt. collections. Juror numerous art exhibits, Ky.; project dir. numerous theatre groups. Recipient numerous prizes for painting, drawing, and photography. Mem. Acad. of Italy (Gold medal), Am. Council for Arts, Assn. Coll., Univ., and Community Arts Adminstrs., Exhibiting Artists Fedn., Ky. Alliance Arts Edn., Ky. Art Edn. Assn., Ky. Arts Adminstrs. (pres. 1982), Ky-Ecuador Ptnrs., Kappa Pi. Office: Wester Ky U Ivan Wilson Ctr Bowling Green KY 42101

OAKEY, DANIEL GILBERT, management consultant; b. Roanoke, Va., Jan. 21, 1957; s. Clarence Milton and Dorothea Clopton (Cheves) O.; m. Sherie Marie Potter, Aug. 8, 1981; 1 dau., Ellen Dale. Student Kennesaw Coll., 1976-78. Welding foreman Thrall Car Mfg. Co., Chicago Heights, Ill., 1978-79; fabrication foreman Evans Products at So. Iron and Equipment Co., Atlanta, 1979-80; field engr., materials coordinator Equitable Shipyards, New Orleans, 1981-82; engring. liaison/planner, Bergeron Industries, St. Bernard, La., 1982; mgmt. cons., New Orleans, 1982-83; corp. pavilion mgr. La. World Exposition, Inc. (1984 World's Fair), New Orleans, 1983-84; mgmt. cons. Chrysler Corp., Union Pacific Systems, Gentilly Dodge, New Orleans, 1984-85; prin. Gillespie Oakey & Assocs., mktg. co., New Orleans, 1985—. Dist. A coordinator New Orleans chpt. Alliance for Good Govt. Mem. Soc. Naval Architects and Marine Engrs., Am. Welding Soc. Republican. Episcopalian. Home: 5214 Pratt Dr New Orleans LA 70122

OAKLEY, JOHN DANIEL, bookstore executive, educator; b. Statesville, N.C., July 29, 1951; s. John Silas and Ola Bell (Stevenson) O.; m. Lori Ann Bussard, Oct. 17, 1981. A.A., Wilkes Community Coll., 1971; B.A., Appalachian State U., 1973. Cert. tchr., N.C. Tchr. Davidson County Schs., Lexington, N.C., 1973-85; owner Oakley's Books & Gifts, Lexington, 1974—, Thomasville, N.C., 1979—. Treas., John Wesley Camp, High Point, N.C. Mem. Christian Booksellers Assn., Thomasville C. of C. Democrat. Methodist. Home: 307 A Welborn St Thomasville NC 27360 Office: Oakley's Books & Gifts 809 Winston Rd Lexington NC 27292

OAKLEY, WILLIAM EDWIN, chemical company executive; b. Tampa, Fla., Oct. 22, 1939; s. Llewellyn Cardiff and Mary Agnes (Herring) O.; B.E. in Chem. Engring., Vanderbilt U., 1961; M.B.A., Baruch Coll., 1974; m. Mary Jo Peck, Sept. 19, 1970; children—Mary Alysia, William Edwin. Asst. supt. phosphoric acid plant Armour Agrl. Chem. Co., Ft. Meade, Fla., 1964-65; process engr., 1965-66; with Mobil Chem. Co., 1966-78, tech. services mgr., N.Y.C., 1973-75, planning asso., Richmond, Va., 1975-78; exec. v.p. Wright Chem. Corp., Riegelwood, N.C., 1978-84, pres., 1984—, also dir. Mem. commn. on ministry East Caroline Diocese, Episcopal Ch.; vestryman St. James Ch.; mem. bd. visitors Kanuga. Served to 1st lt. Air Def. Arty., U.S. Army, 1962-64. Mem. Am. Inst. Chem. Engrs. (chmn. Coastal Carolina sect.), Beta Gamma Sigma, Kappa Sigma. Republican. Home: 514 Wayne Dr Wilmington NC 28403 Office: Wright Chem Corp Acme Sta Riegelwood NC 28456

OAKS, BRENDA INSCO, insurance executive; b. Union City, Tenn., Apr. 18, 1949; d. Elbert B. and Lou (Bell) Insco; m. Edward T. Oaks, June 5, 1967; children—Lori Paige, Alisha Dawn. Student pub. schs., Memphis. Cert. ins. counselor, profl. ins. woman. Sales asst. E.H. Crump & Co., Memphis, 1967-76; v.p. Phillipy Co., Inc., Memphis, 1976-83; owner, mgr. Oaks Ins. Agy., Southaven, Miss., 1983—; comml. ins. instr. Ins. Women of Memphis, 1979-83. Bd. dirs. Women in Polit. Process, Memphis, 1983. Mem. Ins. Women Memphis (Ins. Women of Yr. award 1982; 1st v.p. 1983-84), Ind. Ins. Agts. Am., Bus. and Profl. Womens Club. Baptist. Home: 7526 Millbridge St Southaven MS 38671

OAKS, EARLENE AGNES, nurse; b. Falmouth, Ky., Sept. 2, 1943; d. Earl Ray and Stella May (Smith) Oaks; m. Robert Oaks, Jan. 2, 1970; children—Donald, Ruby, Bobbie. Assoc. Degree Nursing, No. Ky. U., 1983. Seamstress Palm Beach County, Erlanger, Ky., 1970-80; staff nurse St. Luke Care Unit, Falmouth, 1981-82; instr. No. Ky. Childbirth Edn. Assn., Covington, 1981—; med. surg. nurse Booth Hosp., Florence, Ky., 1982—. Mem. Salvation Army Nurses Fellowship, Am. Nursing Assn. Democrat. Mem. Assembly of God. Lodge: Eastern Star. Home: 314 Totten Ln Florence KY 41042 Office: Booth Hosp Turfwax Rd Florence KY 41042

OAKS, FLOYD LAWERENCE, historical association executive; b. Birmingham, Ala., May 16, 1943; s. Walter H. and Dorothy L. Oaks; m. Susan Kaye Wiley, Aug. 21, 1965; 1 child, Brian Wiley. B.A., U. Ala., 1965, M.A., 1968; postgrad. in govt. Georgetown U., 1968-71; postgrad. in adminstrn. and edn. U. Va., 1971-73. Program dir. Ala. Student Union, U. Ala., Tuscaloosa, 1965-68; tchr. Va. Pub. Schs., Fairfax, 1968-77, adminstrv. asst., 1977-80; exec. dir. Ala. Hist. Commn., Montgomery, 1980—, state hist. preservation officer, 1981—. Mem. Nat. Trust Hist. Preservation, Nat. Conf. State Hist. Preservation Officers (bd. dirs.), Ala. Assn. Historians, Ala. Archaeol. Soc. (bd. dirs.). Presbyterian. Avocations: architectural history, design, antiques; restoration of houses; blacksmithing. Home: 1471 S Perry St Montgomery AL 36104 Office: Ala Hist Commn 725 Monroe St Montgomery AL 36130

OATES, CARL EVERETTE, lawyer; b. Harlingen, Tex., Apr. 8, 1931; s. Joseph William and Grace (Watson) O.; student Schreiner Inst., 1948-49, Tex. A. and I. Coll., 1949-50; B.S., U.S. Naval Acad., 1955; LL.B., So. Meth. U., 1962; m. Nadine Bosley McCreary, Mar. 3, 1984; children by previous marriage—Lisa M. Morris, Carl William, Patricia Grace. Admitted to Tex. bar, 1962; mem. firm Akin, Gump, Strauss, Hauer & Feld (and predecessor firm), Dallas, 1962—; chmn. Met. Bancshares, Inc. Bd. dirs. Park Cities YMCA, 1973; pres. Wesley Dental Found.; chmn. S.W. Mus. Sci. and Tech.; v.p. S.W. Sci. Mus. Found., 1982—; chmn. adv. council Dallas Health and Sci. Mus., 1972-75, trustee, 1975—. Served as pilot USN, 1955-59. Mem. Am., D.C., Nebr., Tex., Dallas bar assns., Barristers, N. Dallas C. of C. (dir., exec. com. 1973), Sons of Republic of Tex., Delta Theta Phi. Presbyterian (deacon). Clubs: Northwood, Dallas Country, Dallas, Engineers, Plaza (Tyler, Tex.). Lodges: Masons (32 degree), Kiwanis. Home: 6924 Stefani Dr Dallas TX 75225 Office: 1700 Pacific Ave 4100 First City Ctr Dallas TX 75201

OBEAR, FREDERICK WOODS, university administrator; b. Malden, Mass., June 9, 1935; s. William Fred and Dorothea Louise (Woods) O.; B.S. with high honors, U. Lowell, 1956; Ph.D., U. N.H., 1961; m. Patricia A. Draper, Aug. 30, 1959; children—Jeffrey Allan, Deborah Anne, James Frederick. Mem. faculty dept. chemistry Oakland U., Rochester, Mich., 1960-81, prof., 1979-81, v.p. for acad. affairs, provost, 1970-81; chancellor U. Tenn., Chattanooga, 1981—. Bd. trustees Marygrove Coll., 1973-79; mem. nat. adv. panel Nat. Commn. on Higher Edn. Issues, 1981—. Am. Council Edn. fellow, 1967-68. Mem. Am. Chem. Soc., AAAS, Am. Assn. Higher Edn., Sigma Xi. Roman Catholic. Office: Univ of Tenn Office of Chancellor Chattanooga TN 37403

OBERDIER, RONALD RAY, lawyer; b. Norwood, Mo., Nov. 11, 1945; s. Albert Jr. and Edith Louise (Vaughn) O.; m. Frances Marie Moniz, Aug. 23, 1969; children—James Myron, Steven Michael. Student, Ohio State U., 1963-64; A.A., SUNY-Albany, 1975; B.A., Mary Hardin-Baylor U., 1978; J.D., U. Tex., 1980. Bar: Fla. 1981, U.S. Dist. Ct. (no., so. and mid. dists.) Fla. 1981, U.S. Ct. Appeals (5th and 11th cir.) 1981. Enlisted U.S. Army, 1965, served as electronic intelligence specialist, 1965-77; assoc. Mahoney, Hadlow, Jacksonville, Fla., 1981-82, Coker, Myers & Schickel, Jacksonville, 1982—. Mem. Fed. Bar Assn., Jacksonville Claims Assn., Jacksonville Bar Assn., Am. Trial Lawyers Assn. (assoc.). Republican. Club: Tex.-Exes (Austin). Office: Coker Myers & Schickel 10 S Newnan St Jacksonville FL 32201

OBERLANDER, HERBERT, insect physiologist, educator; b. Manchester, N.H., Oct. 2, 1939 s. Solomon and Minnie (Shapiro) O.; m. Barbara Judith Marks, June 12, 1962; children—Jonathan, Beth. B.A. cum laude in Zoology, U. Conn., 1961; Ph.D. in Biology, Western Res. U., 1965. Postdoctoral fellow U. Zurich (Switzerland), 1965-66; asst. prof. Brandeis U., Waltham, Mass., 1966-71; research physiologist U.S. Dept. Agr., Agrl. Research Service, Gainesville, Fla., 1971-76, research leader, physiology unit, insect attractants lab., 1976-84, lab. dir. insect attractants, behavior and basic biology research lab., Gainesville, 1984—; adj. prof. entomology U. Fla., Gainesville, 1979—. NSF fellow, 1961-65; NIH fellow, 1965-66; NSF Research grantee, 1966-71, 83. Mem. Internat. Soc. Devel. Biology, Tissue Culture Assn., Entomol. Soc. Am., Am. Soc. Zoologists, Soc. Devel. Biology, Phi Beta Kappa, Sigma Xi, Phi Kappa Phi. Contbr. chpts. to books, articles to profl. jours. Office: USDA ARS PO Box 14565 Gainesville FL 32604

OBERLE, M(ARY) ANN WILSON, nursing educator; b. Hodge, La., Aug. 1, 1939; d. Albert Glen and Eminora (Robison) Wilson; m. Arnold D. Oberle, Aug. 15, 1964; children—Karen, Mark, Lauren. B.S.N., Northwestern State U., 1961; M.Nursing, Emory U., 1963. Staff nurse U. Fla., Gainesville, 1961-62; instr. nursing U. Ark., Little Rock, 1963-64, Northwestern State U., Natchitoches, La., 1964-66, asst. prof. nursing, 1966-70, 76—; cons., research participant Sch. Pharmacy, U. Ark., Little Rock, 1963-64; course coordinator Coll. Nursing, Northwestern State U., 1977-79, faculty curriculum rep., 1977-79, 83—; cons. nursing care plan com. La. State U. Med. Ctr., Shreveport, 1983—. Author: (with others) RN to BSN Outreach Satellite in Underserved Rural and Urban Areas, 1984. Active PTA, Bossier City, La., 1979—, Airline Band Booster Club, Bossier City, 1981—, Airline Athletic Booster Club, 1983—. Named Outstanding Freshman Woman, Northwestern State U., 1958. Mem. Shreveport Dist. Nurses Assn., La. Nurses Assn., Sigma Theta Tau, Beth Chi chpt. Democrat. Clubs: Women of the Church, Bossier Racquet. Home: 2408 Ashdown Dr Bossier City LA 71111 Office: Coll of Nursing Northwestern State Univ 1800 Warrington St Shreveport LA 71102

OBERMAYER, HERMAN JOSEPH, editor, publisher; b. Phila., Sept. 19, 1924; s. Leon J. and Julia (Sinsheimer) O.; student U. Geneva (Switzerland), 1946; A.B. cum laude, Dartmouth Coll., 1948; m. Betty Nan Levy, June 28, 1955; children—Helen Julia, Veronica Atnipp, Adele Beatrice, Elizabeth Rose. Reporter, L.I. Daily Press, Jamaica, N.Y., 1950-53; classified advt. mgr. New Orleans Item, 1953-55; promotion dir. New Bedford (Mass.) Standard-Times, 1955-57; editor, pub. Long Branch (N.J.) Daily Record, 1957-71, No. Va. Sun, Arlington, 1963—; dir. Moleculon Research Corp., Cambridge, Mass. Bd. dirs., mem. exec. council Boy Scouts Am., Monmouth (N.J.) council, 1958-71, Nat. Capital Council, 1971-79, 1st v.p., 1974-77; bd. dirs. Long Branch Community Adult Sch., 1958-71, Arlington (Va.) Bicentennial Commn., Arlington chpt. ARC, 1975-78, No. Va. Heart Assn., 1976-81; mem. Anti-Defamation League N.J. Regional Adv. Council, 1963-71, Am. Jewish Com., 1984—; mem. adv. bd. Service League of No. Va., 1980—; trustee Nat. Capital Council March of Dimes, 1982-85; mem. Va. Legis. Alcoholic Beverage Control Study Commn., 1972-74; bd. dirs., v.p. Monmouth (N.J.) Med. Center, 1958-71; Pulitzer prize judge, 1983-84. Served with AUS, 1943-46; ETO. Recipient Friends of Scouting award, 1966, Silver Beaver award, 1977. Mem. Am. Soc. Newspaper Editors (program com.), Am. Newspaper Pubs. Assn., So. Newspaper Pubs. Assn. (dir. 1981-84), White House Corrs. Assn., Sigma Chi, Sigma Delta Chi. Jewish. Clubs: Nat. Press (Washington); Dartmouth (N.Y.C.); Washington Golf and Country, Rotary (Arlington). Contbr. column Editor's Viewpoint to No. Va. Sun, articles to popular, trade mags. Home: 4114 N Ridgeview Rd Arlington VA 22207 Office: 1227 N Ivy St Arlington VA 22201

OBERST, PAUL, retired legal educator; b. Owensboro, Ky., Apr. 22, 1914; s. Albert B. and Marie E. (Wittgen) O.; m. Elizabeth Durfee, June 11, 1946; children—Paul, James, George, Mary, John. A.B., U. Evansville, 1936; J.D., U. Ky., 1939; LL.M., U. Mich., 1941. Bar: Ky. 1938, Mo. 1942. Assoc. Ryland, Stinson, Mag & Thomson, Kansas City, Mo., 1941-42; prof. law U. Ky., Lexington, 1946-82, prof. emeritus, 1982—; prof. law NYU, 1959-61, dir. civil liberties program, 1959-61. Contbr. articles to profl. jours. Mem. Ky. Com. on Corrections, 1961-65, Ky. Commn. on Human Rights, 1962-76, 80—; mem. Ky. adv. com. U.S. Civil Rights Commn., 1980—, chmn., 1980-82; faculty trustee U. Ky., 1963-69, 72-75. Served to lt. USNR, 1942-46. Mem. Assn. Am. Law Schs. (exec. com. 1970-72), ABA, Ky. Bar Assn., Am. Law Inst., AAUP (nat. council 1963-66), Order of Coif. Democrat. Roman Catholic. Home: 829 Sherwood Dr Lexington KY 40502 Office: U Ky Coll Law Lexington KY 40506

O'BRIEN, CORNELIUS GERALD, JR., clinical psychologist; b. Louisville, Mar. 10, 1948; s. Cornelius Gerald and Mary Estelle (Garner) O'B.; B.A., U. Ky., 1971; M.A., U. Louisville, 1974, Ph.D., 1976; m. Sue Ann Meng, May 20, 1978; 1 child, Cornelius Gerald III. Research asso., corp. partner Kemper & Assos., Inc., Louisville, 1973-75; instr. psychology U. Louisville, 1974-75, U. Ky., Louisville, 1975; research asso. Riddick Flynn & Assos., 1975; clin. psychology intern U. Miss., Jackson, 1975-76, clin. asst. prof. psychiatry (psychology) Sch. Medicine, 1986—; supervising psychologist Jackson Mental Health Center, St. Dominic-Jackson Meml. Hosp., 1976-79; pvt. practice clin. psychology, Jackson, 1977—. Mem. Am. Psychol. Assn., Miss. Psychol. Assn. (past pres.), Southeastern Psychol. Assn., Assn. for Advancement Behavior Therapy, Assn. Advancement Psychology. Contbr. articles to profl. jours. Office: Suite 204 Highland Village Jackson MS 39211

O'BRIEN, DAVID MICHAEL, political science educator, researcher; b. Rock Springs, Wyo., Aug. 8, 1951; s. Ralph Rockwell and Lucile (Resel) O'B.; m. Claudine Mendelovitz, Dec. 19, 1983; 1 child, Benjamin Michael. B.A., U. Calif.-Santa Barbara, 1973, M.A., 1974, Ph.D., 1977. Lectr. U. Calif.-Santa Barbara, 1976-77; asst. prof. U. Puget Sound, Tacoma, Wash., 1977-79; chmn. polit. sci. dept., 1978-79; assoc. prof. polit. sci., grad. advisor U. Va., Charlottesville, 1983—; research assoc. U.S. Supreme Ct., Washington, 1983-84; cons. Nat. Acad. Pub. Adminstrn., 1985. Author: Privacy, Law and Public Policy, 1977 (Outstanding Book in Polit. Sci. award 1979); The Public's Right to Know, 1981 (Outstanding Book in Polit. Sci. award 1981); Storm Center: The Supreme Court in American Politics, 1986. Editor: (with others) Views from the Bench, 1985. Fellow Russell Sage Found., 1981-82, U.S. Supreme Ct., 1982-83, Tom C. Clark Jud. Fellows Commn., 1983. Mem. Am. Polit. Sci. Assn., Am. Soc. for Pub. Adminstrs., Internat. Polit. Sci. Assn., Supreme Ct. Hist. Soc., Pub. Adminstrn. Rev. (editorial bd. 1984—). Avocations: oil painting; surfing. Office: U Va 232 Cabell Charlottesville VA 22901

O'BRIEN, GREGORY MICHAEL ST. LAWRENCE, university administrator; b. N.Y.C., Oct. 7, 1944; m. Mary K. McLaughlin; children—Jennifer Jane, Meredith Kathleen. A.B. in Social Relations, Lehigh U., 1966; A.M. in Psychology, Ph.D. in Social Psychology, Boston U., 1968. Asst. prof., dir. human services design lab. Case Western Res. U., Cleve., 1970-71, assoc. prof., dir., 1971-74; prof., dean Sch. Social Welfare, U. Wis.-Milw., 1974-78; provost, prof. psychology U. Mich.-Flint, 1978-80; prof. social work and psychology v.p. for acad. affairs, U. S. Fla., Tampa, 1980—, provost, 1983—. Assoc. editor Jour. Asian-Pacific World Perspectives. Bd. dirs. Northside Community Health Ctr., 1981-84; mem. Tampa bd. dirs. Fla. Orch., 1981-84; trustee Berkeley Prep. Sch., 1984—. Mem. Am. Coll. Mental Health Adminstrn. (pres. 1984—), Greater Tampa C. of C. (edn. com. 1982—). Home: 4314 Northpark Dr Tampa FL 33624 Office: U S Fla 4202 Fowler Ave Tampa FL 33620

O'BRIEN, INGE FRANCES RAPSTINE, geological and geophysical consultant; b. Amarillo, Tex., Jan. 10, 1952; d. B. Frank and Frances Louise (Schulze) Rapstine; m. Michael Edwin O'Brien, Sept. 21, 1979; children—Bonnie Lou, Abbey Gayle. B.S. in Geology, W. Tex. State U., 1976, M.S., 1980. Geophys. technician Oil Devel. Co., Amarillo, 1975-76, jr. geophysicist, 1976-78; geophysicist Santa Fe Energy Co., Amarillo, 1979-81, sr. geophysicist, 1981-83; cons. geol., Amarillo, 1983—; v.p. Lufrank Corp., Amarillo, 1979—, v.p., dir., LF Prodn., Inc., 1985—; dir. Inland Prodn. Corp., Edmond, Okla. Mem. Am. Assn. Petroleum Geologists, Panhandle Geol. Soc. (editor, sec., treas. 1980-83), Am. Inst. Profl. Geologists (cert.), Mensa, Sigma Gamma Epsilon, Chi Omega. Roman Catholic. Avocations: skiing; bowling; mineral collecting. Home and Office: 6416 Hurst St Amarillo TX 79109

O'BRIEN, JOHN EDWARD, mktg. exec.; b. St. Louis, May 30, 1929; s. Edward Joseph and Norma Mary (Yaw) O'B.; A.B., Notre Dame U., 1952; m. Marilyn Jean O'Brien, Aug. 15, 1953; children—Mary Pat, Cathryn Jean, Lynn Marie. Asso. advt. mgr. paper div. Procter & Gamble, 1954-67; v.p., dir.

Campbell-Muthun Advt. Agy., Chgo., 1967-72; v.p. mktg., dir. Calgon Consumer Products, Pitts., 1972-77; pres. NoNonsense Fashions, Inc., Greensboro, N.C., 1977—. Served with USNR, 1952-54. Republican. Roman Catholic. Home: 3023 Lake Forest Dr Greensboro NC 27408 Office: PO Box 77057 Greensboro NC 27407

O'BRIEN, WILLIAM FRANCIS, psychologist; b. Westfield, Mass., Aug. 9, 1948; s. George Edward and Mary Agnes (Lynch) O'B.; B.A., LeMoyne Coll., Syracuse, N.Y., 1970; M.A., Ohio State U., 1972, Ph.D., 1975; m. Julia M. Crimmings, Aug. 14, 1971; 1 dau., Erin Elizabeth. Staff psychologist VA Med. Center, Battle Creek, Mich., 1975-79; coordinator alcohol rehab. unit, family therapist Mental Hygiene Clinic, VA Med. Center, Hampton, Va., 1979—; adj. asst. prof. St. Leo Coll., Langley AFB; dir. Kecoughtan Fed. Credit Union. Mem. Am. Psychol. Assn. Roman Catholic. Author articles in field. Home: 143 Moline Dr Newport News VA 23606 Office: Bldg 70 VA Med Center Hampton VA 23667

OBST, EMILY VIRGINIA, architect, planner; b. Norfolk, Va., Dec. 18, 1918; d. Morris Stettiner and Diana Valentine (Umstadter) Turk; m. Harold Anthony Obst, Nov. 8, 1943; children—Anthony, Mary Diana, James Hagen. B.A., Barnard Coll., 1939; M.Arch., Columbia U., 1944. Registered architect, Fla. Draftsman N.Y. dist. U.S. Corps. Engrs., 1942-43; archtl. designer U.S. Navy, Key West, Fla., 1944; prin. Obst Assocs., Palm Beach, Fla., 1950-78; pres., chief exec. officer Obst. Assocs., Architects/Planners, Inc., West Palm Beach, Fla., 1979—; chmn. Palm Beach County Land Use Adv. Bd., 1980-81. Works include: Country Squire Inn, Lake Worth, Fla., 1974, Heller Office Bldg., Miami, 1975 (award 1975), Gemini Club, North Palm Beach, 1975, Southgate, Palm Beach, 1975. Chmn. adv. bd. So. Fla. Pub. Telecommunications, Boynton Beach, Fla., 1983-84; bd. dirs. Civic Music Assn. of Palm Beaches, West Palm Beach; chmn. planning bd. Town of Lake Clarke Shores, Fla., 1973. Mem. AIA (pres. Palm Beach chpt. 1975-76). Avocations: music; horticulture. Office: Smith-Obst Assocs Architects/Planners Inc 2326 S Congress Ave West Palm Beach FL 33406

O'BURKE, JOHN EMMETT, corporate risk manager, consultant; b. Port Arthur, Tex., June 13, 1947; s. Jack Emmett and Janice (Brown) O'B.; m. Ann Carol Daleo, May 30, 1968; children—Willard Sam, Daniel Patrick. A.A.S., Lee Coll., 1975; D.M.S., Commonwealth Coll. Sci., 1978; postgrad. U. Tex. Sch. Pub. Health, 1985. Cert. quality assurance profl., hazard control mgr.; lic. funeral dir., Tex. Safety engr. H.B. Zachry, San Antonio, 1977-81; corp. risk mgr. SCH Healthcare System, Houston, 1981—; safety cons. La. Workers Compensation Bd., 1984—. Served with U.S. Navy/USCG, 1964-72. Named Service Man of Yr., U.S. Coast Guard, 1969. Mem. Am. Soc. Safety Engrs., Risk Ins. Mgmt. Soc., Nat. Assn. Quality Assurance Profls. (chmn. fin. com. 1984-85). Republican. Roman Catholic. Avocations: chess; golf. Office: SCH Healthcare System Corp Offices 2002 S Wayside Suite 209 Houston TX 77023

O'CALLAGHAN, DENNIS JOHN, microbiology educator, researcher; b. New Orleans, July 26, 1940; s. John J. and O'Deal Dora (Fitzpatrick) O'C.; m. Helen Frances Briscoe, June 24, 1967; 1 son, Brady. B.S. in Biology, Loyola U., New Orleans, 1962; Ph.D. in microbiology, U. Miss. Med. Ctr., 1968; postdoctoral fellow U. Alta. Med. Ctr., 1968-70. Asst. prof. biochemistry U. Alta. Med. Ctr., Edmonton, 1970-71; asst. prof. microbiology U. Miss. Med. Ctr., Jackson, 1971-74, assoc. prof. microbiology, 1974-77, prof. microbiology, 1977—, also chmn. dept. microbiology and immunology; tumor virology tchr. and researcher; mem. virology study sect. NIH. NIH research grantee; Grayson Found. research grantee, 1982—. Mem. Am. Soc. Microbiology, Am. Soc. Virology, Am. Assn. Cancer Research, Am. Soc. Biol. Chemists, Am. Soc. Exptl. Pathologists, Soc. Gen. Microbiology, AAAS. Assoc. editor Virus Research, Virology; contbr. chpts. to books, articles to profl. jours. Office: Dept Microbiology & Immunology Louisiana State Univ Med Ctr 1501 Kings Hwy Shreveport LA 71130

O'CARROLL, LLOYD THOMAS, economist; b. Washington, N.C., May 21, 1947; s. Joseph Daniel and Juanita Pearl (Moore) O'C.; m. Nancy Grey Mitchiner, June 8, 1969. B.A., N.C. State U., 1969, M.Econs., 1978. Account exec. Merrill Lynch, Raleigh, N.C., 1972-74; economist Bur. Labor Stats., Washington, 1969-72; economist N.C. Gen. Assembly, Raleigh, 1974-76, N.C. Office of State Budget, Raleigh, 1977-78; economist Reynolds Metals Co., Richmond, Va., 1978-82, chief economist, 1982—; statis. com. Internat. Primary Aluminum Inst., London, 1982—. Staff economist transition staff Office of Gov. N.C., 1976. Mem. Aluminum Assn., Nat. Assn. Bus. Economists, Am. Econs. Assn., Econometric Soc., Richmond Assn. Bus. Economists (pres. 1982-83), Richmond Metro C. of C. (vice chmn. research com. 1982-83). Club: Richmond Toastmasters. Office: Reynolds Metals Co 6603 W Broad St Richmond VA 23261

OCHSE, DANIEL ROGER, health care exec.; b. Newark, July 27, 1941; s. Daniel C. and Mildred Elizabeth (Shoemaker) O.; B.A., Dickinson Coll., 1963; M.A., U. Rochester, 1966; m. L. Ann Estes, Jan. 24, 1973; children—Weston, Ingrid, Karl, J. Daniel. Instr. English, Ripon (Wis.) Coll., 1967-70; asst. prof. English, Sioux Falls (S.D.) Coll., 1970-72; adminstrv. intern House of the Good Shepherd, Hackettstown, N.J., 1972-73, asst. dir., 1973-76; adminstr. Alexian Bros. Rest Home, Signal Mountain, Tenn., 1976-78; v.p. Health Futures Investment Corp., Cleveland, 1978-79; pres. Seniorcenters of Am., Chattanooga, Tenn., 1979—, Walden Corp. U. Rochester grad. fellow, 1966-67. Fellow Am. Coll. Nursing Home Adminstrs.; mem. Tenn. Health Care Assn. (dir. 1979-80), Gerontol. Soc., Chattanooga Health Care Assn. (pres. 1979-80), Am. Assn. of Homes for the Aging. Episcopalian. Club: Masons. Home: 4916 Lake Haven Dr Chattanooga TN 37416 Office: 7602 Lee Hwy Chattanooga TN 37421

OCHSNER, JEFFREY KARL, architect, urban designer, educator; b. Milw., Sept. 25, 1950; s. Richard Stanley and Mary Anne (Zaccardi) O.; m. Sandra Lynn Perkins, Aug. 5, 1979. Student Calif. Inst. Tech., 1968-69; B.A., Rice U., 1973, M.Arch., 1976. Registered architect, Tex., Wis. Designer Gunnar Birkerts & Assocs., Architects, Birmingham, Mich., 1973-74, Ray B. Bailey, Architects, Houston, 1975-76, Kahler Slater & Fitzhugh Scott, Architects, Milw., 1977; assoc. William T. Cannady & Assocs., Architects, Houston, 1977-78; architect Flad & Assocs., Inc., Madison, Wis., 1978-79, Denny, Ray & Wines, Architects, Houston, 1980-81; coordinator planning Houston Transit Cons., 1981-82, coordinator archtl. design, 1982-83; sr. planner Met. Transit Authority, Harris County, Tex., 1983-84; lectr. architecture Rice U., Houston, 1981—; prin. Jeffrey Karl Ochsner Assocs., Architecture/Urban Design/Planning, Houston, 1984—. Author: H.H. Richardson: Complete Architectural Works, 1982. Curator exhibit H.H. Richardson: Late Houses, Rice U., 1982. Contbr. articles to profl. jours. Mem. Downtown Houston Assn., South Main Ctr. Assn.; bd. dirs. Citizens Environ. Coalition, Houston, 1984—; Bayou Preservation Assn., Houston, 1985—. Mem. AIA (Design award Houston chpt. 1984), Soc. Archtl. Historians, Nat. Trust for Hist. Preservation, Rice Design Alliance, Houston C. of C., Phi Beta Kappa. Office: Jeffrey Karl Ochsner Assocs 2472 Bolsover St #376 Houston TX 77005

O'CONNER, AUDREY NEAMS, educator; b. New Orleans, Jan. 23, 1939; s. Walter Scott and Mary Lee (Robinson) Carter. B.S. in Social studies, So. U., 1961, M.Guidance, 1965. Tchr., coach volleyball for girls, East Baton Glen Oaks High Sch., Baton Rouge 1962—, dep. chmn. social studies, 1975—. Mem. East Baton Rouge Parish Sch. Bd., Recipient Glen Oaks High Sch. Favorite Tchr. award, 1974, 75. Mem. NEA Black Caucus (sec. 1975-77), So. U. Alumni Assn., La. Edn. Assn., East Baton Rouge Edn. Assn. (chaplain, sec. 1965-79), J.K. Haynes Found., Nat. Council for Social Studies (citizenship com. 1975, 78), Baton Rouge Women's Bowling Assn. (pres.'s com.). Democrat. Baptist. Clubs: 600 of Nat. Bowling Assn. Home: 5360 Astoria Dr Baton Rouge LA 70812 Office: Glen Oaks High Sch 6650 Cedar Grove Dr Baton Rouge LA 70812

O'CONNOR, JOHN REGIS, speech communication educator, administrator; b. Louisville, Jan. 17, 1941; s. John Regis and Elise Mary (Grenough) O'C.; m. Patricia Jean Doyle, Oct. 21, 1971; children—Jennifer, Kimberly. B.A., Bellarmine Coll., Louisville, 1965; M.A., Ind. U., 1966, Ph.D., 1971. Prof. speech communication Western Ky. U., Bowling Green, 1969—, forensics dir., 1969-71, staff asst. to dean, 1974, acting dept. head speech/theatre, 1979-80, head, 1980—. Author: Speech: Exploring Communication, 1981, 84. Contbr. articles to profl. jours. Mem. Com. on Free Enterprise Fair, Bowling Green, Ky., 1983. Mem. Speech Communications Assn., So. Speech Communication Assn., Phi Delta Kappa (pres. 1974-75). Lodge: Rotary.

O'CONNOR, KAREN, political science educator, researcher; b. Buffalo, Feb. 15, 1952; s. Robert J. and Norma (Wilton) O'C.; m. F. Allen McDonogh, June 7, 1974 (div. 1986). 1 child, Meghan. B.A., SUNY-Buffalo, 1973, J.D., 1977, Ph.D., 1979. Bar: Ga. 1978. Instr. polit. sci. Emory U., 1977-78, asst. prof., 1978-83, assoc. prof., 1983—, adj. prof. law, 1980—. Author: Women's Organization's Use of the Courts, 1980; (with N.E. McGlen) Women's Rights, 1983. Mem. editorial bd. Women & Politics, 1980—, Law & Policy, 1982—, Jour. of Politics, 1984—. Contbr. articles to profl. jours. Mem. Am. Polit. Sci. Assn. (exec. council 1985—), So. Polit. Sci. Assn. Home: 100 Palisades Rd Atlanta GA 30309 Office: Dept Polit Sci Emory U Atlanta GA 30322

O'CONNOR, PETER DAVID, college administrator; b. Yonkers, N.Y., Mar. 20, 1936; s. Eugene A. and Mary C. (Donoghue) O'C.; m. Patricia T. Nichols, May 28, 1960; children—Jeanne Marie, Judith, Alison, Peter Jr., David, Seán. B.S. in Edn., Fordham U., 1958; M.A. in English, Lehigh U., 1962, Ph.D. in English, 1969. English tchr. Hicksville High Sch., N.Y., 1958-59; mem. English faculty SUNY-Oswego, 1962-77, U. P.R., Cayey, 1970-71; v.p. for acad. affairs, acad. dean Incarnate Word Coll., San Antonio, 1977—; facilitator, nat. inst. Council for Advancement of Small Colls., Washington, 1981, mem. task force, 1980-81; coordinator Assn. Tex. Colls. and Univs., San Antonio, 1980. Author: Major American Books, 1967; also articles. Mem. Project Equality—The Coll. Bd., 1981—; mem. edn. com. United San Antonio, 1980—; adv. mem. bd. trustees San Antonio Art Inst., 1979-80. Alumni Fund fellow Lehigh U., 1964. Mem. Assn. Tex. Acad. Deans and Vice Presidents (pres.-elect 1985—), Acad. Council United Colls. of San Antonio (chmn. 1983-84), Joseph Conrad Soc. (v.p. 1975-77). Democrat. Roman Catholic.

O'DANIEL, CAROLYN, respiratory therapy educator, administrator; b. Somerset, Ky., May 27, 1947; d. Harold Raymond Hancock and Helen Faye (Wilson) Snyder; m. Paul Joseph O'Daniel, Dec. 22, 1972; 1 child, Jennifer Lori. A.A., Somerset Community Coll., 1967; B.A. in English, U. Ky., 1972, M.S. in Edn., 1980, postgrad. 1982—; A.A.S. in Respiratory Therapy, Lexington Tech. Inst., 1975. Registered respiratory therapist; cert. respiratory therapy technician. Respiratory therapy technician Chandler Med. Ctr., Lexington, Ky., 1969-73; staff technician Jewish Hosp., Louisville, 1973, day shift supr., 1973, acting dir. respiratory therapy, 1973-74; respiratory therapy tech. dir. Somerset City Hosp. and Lake Cumberland Med. Ctr., Somerset, Ky., 1975-76; instr. respiratory therapy Lexington Tech. Inst., 1976-78; asst. prof. respiratory therapy, dir. clin. edn. Lexington Tech. Inst., 1978-80; acad. program coordinator respiratory therapy program Jefferson Community Coll., Louisville, 1980—, assoc. prof., 1982—, allied health div. chairperson, 1983—; presentation of papers and lectures to workshops and confs. Recipient Appreciation Plaque for chairing bd. Region II for respiratory therapy Ky., Ohio, Ind., 1981, 84. Mem. Am. Assn. Respiratory Therapy (nom. com. 1985, edn. sect. program com. 1985, Ky. del. 1982-84, region II com. chairperson elect. 1979, region II long range planning sub-com. 1979), Ky. Soc. Respiration Therapy (long range planning com. chairperson 1985, legis. com. 1985, chairperson procedure manual com. 19821, pub. relations com., chairperson and program moderator respiratory therapy review seminar com. 1980, exec. com. 1979, pres. 1978, sec. 1976, mem. numerous coms., president's award 1978, 80, 82), Ky. Thoracic Soc., Council for Occupational Edn. Avocations: camping; aerobic dance; card playing; reading; writing. Office: Jefferson Community College 109 E Broadway Louisville KY 40202

O'DAY, BUCKLEY EARL, JR., oil company executive; b. Victoria, Tex., Dec. 15, 1942; s. Buckley Earl and Hilda (Vyvial) O'D.; student Southwestern U., 1960-61, Alvin Jr. Coll., 1963, U. Md., 1967; B.A., U. Tex., 1974; m. Katie Belle Shirey, Oct. 26, 1965; children—Hilda, Anna, Buckley Earl III, Julia. Asst. to cost engr. Bechtel Corp., San Francisco, 1961-63; lab. technician U. Tex. Med. Br., Galveston, 1964, Clayton Found., Austin, Tex., 1968; lab., x-ray technician Austin (Tex.) State Sch., 1969-71; air pollution research div. Tex. Air Control Bd., Austin, 1971-73; tchr. Houston Ind. Sch. Dist., 1974; drilling fluids engr. Dresser Industries, Houston, 1975-77; offshore supr. drilling dept. Union Oil Co. of Calif., Houston, 1977-81; drilling engr. Midlands Energy Corp., 1981-85; ind. cons., 1985—. Served with U.S. Army, 1965-68. Mem AIME, Spl. Forces Assn., V.F.W. Home: PO Box 776 Van TX 75790 Office: Excelsior Oil Corp Longview TX 75606

O'DAY, JOHN PATRICK, social worker; b. Flint, Mich., Nov. 24, 1942; s. John Hopkins and Bernice (Peterson) O'D. B.A., Minot State Coll., 1965; M.S.W., U. Houston, 1979. Cert. social worker, Tex. Caseworker Mo. Dept. Pub. Health and Welfare, St. Louis, 1965-68; asst. mg. trainee F.W. Woodworth Co., St. Louis, 1968-69; tenant relations coordinator Fletcher-Emerson Mgmt. Co., Houston, 1970; stockbroker asst. Rotan, Mosele-Dallas-Union, Inc., Houston, 1971; with Martin Surg. Supply Co., Houston, 1971; caseworker I, II, III, Tex. Dept. Human Resources, Houston, 1972-77; with Am. Automobile Assn., also Southwestern Security Systems, Houston, part-time 1973-76; with J.H. Thompson & Assocs., Houston, 1978-79; supr. Sheltering Arms Agy., Houston, 1979-82; social worker Tex. Dept. Human Resources, Liberty, 1982—. Chmn. Inter-Agy. Social Service Bd., Liberty, 1983-84. Title XX HEW grantee, 1978; NIMH grantee, 1979. Mem. Am. Pub. Welfare Assn., Nat. Assn. Social Workers, Internat. Transactional Analysis Assn., Nat. Coalition for Children and Youth, Nat. Assn. Marriage and Family Counselors, Civic War Roundtable. Republican. Roman Catholic. Home: 2203 Woodhead St Houston TX 77019 Office: Tex Dept Human Resources 2720 N Main St Liberty TX 77575

ODDO, JACQUELINE MARIA, occupational therapist, early intervention specialist; b. Birmingham, Ala., Jan. 11, 1955; d. Jack Joseph and Rosemary Theresa (Traina) O. B.S. in Occupational Therapy, U. Ala.-Birmingham, 1977; M.S. in Early Intervention, Wheelock Coll., 1985. Registered occupational therapist; lic. occupational therapist, Ga. Staff therapist Primary Care Service, Winnebago Mental Health Inst. (Wis.), 1978-80; chief therapist adult service Mendota Mental Health Inst., Madison, Wis., 1980; sr. staff therapist Developmental Disabilities, Baton Rouge Gen. Hosp., 1981-84; pediatric occupational therapist Scottish Rite Children's Hosp., Atlanta, 1985; contract therapist East Baton Rouge Parish, 1982-83. Mem. Am. Occupational Therapy Assn. (La. sensory integration spl. interest sect. liaison 1982-84), La. Occupational Therapy Assn., Baton Rouge Occupational Therapy Assn. (pub. relations chmn. 1982-84). Roman Catholic. Office: SRCH 1001 Johnson Ferry Rd Atlanta GA 30342

ODE, JAMES AUSTIN, musician, educator; b. Brandon, S.D., Dec. 9, 1934; s. Paul Edgar and Sally Christine (Pearson) O.; m. Edna Gilbertson, June 7, 1957; children—Karen, Elizabeth, Kathryn. B.A., Augustana Coll., Sioux Falls, S.D., 1957; Mus.M., Eastman Sch. Music, 1961, D.Musical Arts, performers cert. in trumpet, 1965. Band dir. Lyons High Sch., S.D., 1956-57; asst. band dir. Augustana Coll., 1961-63; prof. trumpet and music lit. Ithaca Coll., N.Y., 1965-81; chmn. dept. music Trinity U., San Antonio, 1981-86; chmn. div. music So. Meth. U., Dallas, 1986—; prin. trumpet 9th Div. Band, Fort Carson, Colo., 1957-59, Sioux Falls Symphony, 1961-63, Cayuga Chamber Orch., Ithaca, 1978-81; founder, prin. trumpet Ithaca Brass Quintet, 1965-81, Trinity Chamber Players, 1984—. Author: Brass Instruments in Church Services, 1970. Editor: Handel Arias for Trumpet and Voice, 1974. Co-composer: Hymns, Descants and Fantasias for Brass Ensemble, 1971. Served with U.S. Army, 1957-59. Grad. fellow Danforth Found., 1957-65; HEW fellow, 1969. Mem. Am. Fedn. Musicians (local bd. dirs. 1967-81), Tex. Assn. Music Schs. (bd. dirs. 1983—), Music Educators Nat. Conf., Music Tchrs. Nat. Assn. Republican. Lutheran. Avocations: photography; reading. Office: Div Music So Meth U Dallas TX 75275

ODEH, AZIZ SALIM, oil company scientist, researcher; b. Nazareth, Palestine, Dec. 10, 1925; came to U.S., 1947, naturalized 1953; s. Salim N. and Kamela M (Audeh) O.; m. Bonnie Willis, Apr. 21, 1956; children—Susan L., Linda G. B.S., U. Calif.-Berkeley, 1951; M.S., UCLA, 1953, Ph.D., 1959. Registered profl. engr., Tex. Research technologist Mobil Research and Devel., Dallas, 1953-56, sr. research technologist, 1959-64, research assoc., 1964-73, sr. research assoc., 1973-80, sr. scientist, 1980—. Contbr. articles to profl. jours. Bd. dirs. Abu Dhabi Nat. Reservoir Research Found., 1980—. Recipient John Franklin Carll award Soc. Petroleum Engrs., 1984. Mem. Research Soc. Am. Club: Good Fellowship (pres. 1984) (Dallas). Avocations: tennis; jogging. Home: 5840 Gallant Fox Ln Plano TX 75075

ODELL, DANIEL KEITH, biologist, consultant; b. Auburn, N.Y., Nov. 16, 1945; s. Dewitt Thornton and Lucy Mary (Kozol) O.; m. Terry Lee Carter, Aug. 24, 1967; children—Jason Paul, Jessica Lynne, Nicole Elyse. B.S. with distinction, Cornell U., 1967; M.A., UCLA, 1970, Ph.D., 1972. Lectr. biology UCLA, 1972-73; asst. prof. U. Miami, Fla., 1973-79, assoc. prof., 1979—; cons. Govt. of Papua, New Guinea, 1978. Asst. scoutmaster S. Fla. council Boy Scouts of Am., Miami, 1984, 85. Research grantee U.S. Fish and Wildlife Service, 1978—, State of Fla., 1982-83, Minerals Mgmt. Service, 1983—. Mem. Soc. Marine Mammalogy (charter), Am. Soc. Mammalogists, Wildlife Soc. Avocations: gardening; canoeing; birding. Office: BLR-RSMAS U Miami 4600 Rickenbacker Miami FL 33149-1098

ODELL, SHIRLEY HARTMANN, nurse, administrator, consultant; b. Chillicothe, Ohio, May 22, 1936; d. John Walter and Kathryn (Lofty) Hartmann; m. John Browning Odell, Nov. 28, 1959 (dec. 1971); children—John, Sherrill Elizabeth, Scott Andrew. B.S. in Nursing, Med. Coll. Va., 1958, M.S., 1978. Registered nurse, Va. Staff nurse, head nurse Med. Coll. Va. Hosp., Richmond, 1958-60; staff nurse Sutter Meml. Hosp., Sacramento, 1961-63; nursing instr. Riverside Sch. Nursing, Newport News, Va., 1973-76; patient, community edn. coordinator Riverside Hosp., Newport News, 1978-79; dir. Riverside Sch. Nursing, 1979—; adj. faculty Christopher Newport Coll., Newport News, 1984—. Mem. editorial bd. Riverside Nurse publ., 1982—. Contbr. articles to profl. jours. Edn. cons., bd. dirs. Hampton Roads chpt. ARC, Newport News, 1981—; trustee Med. Coll. Va. Alumni Assn., Richmond, 1986-89; Y-Teen bd. dirs. YWCA, Hampton, Va., 1967-76, Newport News Day Care Ctr., 1970-73; mem. budget com. United Way, Newport News, 1971-73; vol., lectr. Peninsula Nature Sci. Ctr., Newport News, 1969-72. Mem. Am. Nurses Assn., Nat. League for Nursing, Century Club of Am. Nurses Found. Democrat. Baptist. Avocations: basket making; needlework; reading; crafts; herb gardening. Home: 108 Villa Rd Newport News VA 23601 Office: Riverside Hosp Sch Nursing J Clyde Morris Blvd Newport News VA 23601

ODEN, KENNETH, lawyer; b. Yoakum, Tex., Sept. 5, 1923; s. J.D. and Lena (Upchurch) O.; student Kilgore Jr. Coll., 1941-42, U. Tulsa, 1943, Navarra Coll., 1946; A.B., LL.B., Baylor U., 1950; m. Frances Walker, May 29, 1948; children—Kenneth, Theresa Lynne, Patricia Marie. Admitted to Tex. bar, 1950, since practiced in Alice, Tex.; mem. firm Perkins, Oden, Warburton, McNeill & Adami, 1950—. Sec.-treas., dir., mem. John G. and Marie Stella Kennedy Meml. Found., 1963-85. Served to maj. USAAF, 1944-46; ETO. Decorated Air medal with 5 oak leaf clusters. Mem. Am., Coastal Bend (past pres.) bar assns., State Bar Tex. (past mem. prosecuting grievance com.), Tex. Assn. Def. Counsel. Baptist. Home: 1821 Walker St Alice TX 78332 Office: 601 E Main St Alice TX 78332

ODOM, MARJORIE MILDRED MORGAN, librarian; b. Lavernia, Tex., July 22, 1924; d. Andrew Jackson and Estella Fledia (Phillips) Morgan; cert. in cosmetology C.J. Walker Beauty Coll., 1943; B.A. in L.S., Our Lady of Lake U., San Antonio, 1964, M.A. in Edn., 1979; m. Steven Odom, Jr., June 25, 1944 (dec.). Mgr., Mme. C.J. Walker Beauty Salon, San Antonio, 1944-52; propr. Ross Hotel Beauty Salon, San Antonio, 1952-63; asst. supr. children's dept. San Antonio Main Public Library, 1964-65; secondary sch. librarian San Antonio Ind. Sch. Dist., 1965—; sponsor Library Reading Club. Mem. Tex. Senator's adv. council on legis. affairs; chmn. evangelism com. Corinth Bapt. Ch., San Antonio, 1983—. Recipient outstanding award analysis and design Kappa Pi Sigma, 1978, appreciation plaque PTA, 1981; cert. Internat. Center Learning, 1982, 83. Mem. NEA (life), Tex. Tchrs. Assn., Tex. Classroom Tchrs. Assn., San Antonio Ind. Sch. Dist. Librarians Assn., Bexar Library Assn., PTA, San Antonio Tchrs. Council. Democrat. Home: PO Box 8374 San Antonio TX 78208

O'DONNELL, MARY MURPHY, nurse epidemiologist, consultant; b. Lincoln, Ill., Feb. 21, 1918; d. Thomas Edward and Frances Ward (Hayes) Murphy; m. Maurice A. O'Donnell, Jan. 29, 1942. Diploma St. John's Sch. Nursing, Springfield, Ill., 1939. Registered nurse, Ill., Fla. Asst. to ear, nose and throat specialist, 1939-42; nurse U.S. Govt. Hosp., 1942-43; asst. to gen. practitioner, Springfield, 1943-55; staff nurse City Health Dept., Springfield, 1955-65; dir. tng. and edn. Springfield and Sangamon County Civil Def. Agy., 1965-66; exec., cons. in charge med. self-help Ill. Dept. Pub. Health, 1966-74; nurse epidemiologist St. Joseph Hosp., Port Charlotte, Fla., 1975—. Vice pres. S. Central area Ill. Women's Civil Def. Council; mem. Ill. Civil Def. Council; chmn. civil def. activities ARC; v.p., mem. health services adv. com. U.S. Civil Defense Council; ofcl. vol. rep. Am. Social Health Assn. Recipient Spl. award State Dept. of Am. Legion Aux., 1954, Cert. of Honor, hon. life membership U.S. Air Force Air Def. Team, 1959, Silver Wing Bracelet, Ground Observer Corps, 1959, Cert. of Honor, Mayor of City of Springfield, 1966, Pfizer award of merit U.S. Civil Def. Council, 1969, Presidential citation U.S. Civil Def. Council, 1972. Mem. Assn. for Practitioners in Infection Control, SW Regional Infection Control. Republican. Roman Catholic. Avocations: boating; swimming; clog dancing; golf; horse racing. Home: 819 Napoli Ln Punta Gorda FL 33950

OEHLER, RICHARD D., architect; b. Hannibal, Mo., Aug. 19, 1950; s. Patrick and Helen (Newberry) O.; B.Arch., Kent State U., 1975; m. Cynthia Syvertsen, Aug. 24, 1974; children—Carlene, Joshua. Job capt., designer Mastran & Assos., Tallmadge, Ohio, 1976-78; asst. v.p. R.B. Williams & Assos., Yuma, Ariz., 1978-81; owner, architect R.D. Oehler, Yuma, 1981—; v.p. design div. Environ. Coordination Assos., Inc., architects, planners, developers, also dir.; prin. works include Marquis Pool Complex, City of Yuma (Ariz.), Holy Redeemer Ch., Odessa, Tex., Marklyn Control Office Bldg., Odessa, San Mateo Square, Odessa; renovation of New Orleans pub. sch.; McMain High Sch.; Gayarre Elem. Sch.; designer ednl., ecclesiastical, recreational, govtl., residential facilities, comml. master planning; architect New Orleans Sch. Bd. Active VISTA, summer 1972. Served with USN, 1969-71; Vietnam. Registered profl. architect, Ohio, Tex., Ariz. Mem. AIA, Nat. Trust for Historic Preservation. Author: Urban Renewal Social and Cultural Ills, 1974. Home: PO Box 57468 New Orleans LA 70115

OELBERG, DAVID GEORGE, neonatologist, educator; b. Waukon, Iowa, May 26, 1952; s. George Robert and Elizabeth Abigail (Kepler) O.; m. Debra Penuel, Aug. 4, 1979. B.S. with highest honors, Coll. William and Mary, 1974; M.D., U. Md., 1978. Diplomte Am. Bd. Pediatrics. Intern U. Tex. Med. Br., Galveston, 1978-79, resident, 1979-81, pediatric house staff, 1978-81; postdoctoral fellow in neonatal medicine U. Tex. Med. Sch., Houston, 1981-84, asst. prof. dept. pediatrics, 1984—; mem. hosp. staff Hermann Hosp., Houston, 1983—; physician Crippled Children's Services Program, Houston, 1985—. Contbr. articles to profl. jours. Physician cons. Parents of Victims of Sudden Infant Death Syndrome, Houston, 1984. Recipient award in analytical chemistry Am. Chem. Soc., 1974. Fellow Am. Acad. Pediatrics; mem. AMA, So. Soc. Pediatric Research, Tex. Med. Assn., Houston Pediatric Soc. Avocations: sailing; gardening. Home: 3502 Bellaire Blvd Houston TX 77025 Office: U Tex Med Sch Dept Pediatrics 6431 Fannin St Houston TX 77030

OERTLI, KARRIE ANN, material company executive, marketing executive; b. Austin, Tex., June 2, 1957; d. Freddie Ray Oertli and Betty Lou (Hornsby) Warren. B.A., Tex. A & M U., 1978. Communication specialist Litwin Constructors, Houston, 1979; tech. writer I and II, sr. editor, pub., corp. liaison for users group Datapoint Corp., San Antonio, 1979-84; v.p. mktg. Grizzly Material Handling, San Antonio, 1984-86, sec. bd., San Antonio, 1984-86; mktg. cons. Castle Hills 1st Baptist Ch., San Antonio, 1984—. Editor: Source Data Mag., 1981-84. Pub. relations staff Republican Party, San Antonio, 1984, Phil Gramm for Senate, College Station, Tex., 1978. Mem. Am. Mktg. Assn., Soc. Tech. Communication (v.p. 1982-84), San Antonio C. of C. (com. mem.), Beta Sigma Phi (v.p. 1981-82, Women of Yr. award 1981). Baptist. Club: San Antonio A&M (bd. dirs. 1983—). Avocations: Skiing; softball; reading; travel; singing. Home: 11711 Braesview # 3605 San Antonio TX 78213

O'FARRILL, HILDA AVILA CAMACHO Y CASAZZA, journalist; b. Xalapa, Veracruz, Mex., Nov. 19, 1922; d. Maximino Avila Camacho and Feliza Casazza; m. Romulo O'Farrill, Jr., May 9, 1942; children—Victor Hugo, Jose Antonio, Hilda Gloria, Roberto. Student Colegio Helen Herlihy Hall, Mexico City, Colegios Cruz y Celis y Aleman, Academia Moderna Comercial and Verbo Encarnado in Puebla. Founder Hosp. Maximino Avila Camacho, Mex., 1950—; pres. Sch. Nurses Emmanuele, 1950; founder, sec. Voluntaries Hosp. Pediatrico del Centro Medico Nacional del IMSS; dir. youth's page Novedades Newspaper, Mex., 1964; pres. Patronage El Mexicanito, A.C., Pub. Relations Patronage Caridad Lomas, 1966-72; v.p. Acapulco Festival (Red Cross), 1972—; mem. Mex. Inst. Assistance to Children, 1973; v.p. Patronage Pro-Feast 50 deg. Found. Symphonic Orchestra Xalapa, 1979; bd. dirs. Interam. Press Assn. San Diego, 1980, Rio Janeiro, 1981; hon. v.p. Pro-Universidad Veracruzana, A.C., 1981; global counsellor Inst. de Asuntos Culturales Internacionales, 1983; pres. Patronage Pro-Universidad Veracruzana, A.C.,

1984—. Decorated Cross of Malta, Sovereign and Mil. Order of Malta, 1971; recipient diploma Salvation Army Social Work, 1970, awards of merit, Publicaciones Herrerias, S.A., World Press Congress, 1973, Nat. Fed. Animals Benefactors Assns., 1978, Liric Art Co., 1978, Voluntaries of the Hosp. Pediatrico del Centro Medico, 1965, Com. of Social and Cultural Service, A.C., 1970. Clubs: Marco Polo, Metro. (N.Y.C.); Club Internat. Des Anciens (Monte Carlo); Losagne D'or Yacht (Monaco); Yacht (Acapulco); Mex. Country. Office: 87 Balderas St 06040 Mexico D F

O'FLANNERY, DENNIS COLLINS, hotel and resort executive; b. Balt., Apr. 13, 1940; s. Francis Xavier and Wilhelmina Clare (Heavey) O.; m. Sharon Elizabeth Stone, Apr. 15, 1961 (div. 1977); children—Dawn, Sean; m. 2d, Gloria Jean Slechta, May 16, 1980. B.S., Pacific Western U., 1976, M.B.A., 1978. Cert. hotel adminstr. Am. Hotel and Motel Assn. Mgmt. positions with various hotels and motels, 1964-70; v.p. Sea Pines Co. (S.C.), 1969-72; pres. Sandestin Corp. div. Evans & Mitchell Industries, Destin, Fla., 1972-75; v.p., gen. mgr. John's Island, Vero Beach, Fla., 1975-76; sr. v.p. mktg. and sales Golf Hosts Internat., Tarpon Springs, Fla., 1976-79; dir. mktg. The Mariner Corp., Fort Myers, Fla., 1979-83; exec. v.p., gen. mgr. Saddle-brook Resort, St. Lucie, Fla., 1983—. Served with U.S. Army, 1958-62. Mem. Hotel Sales Mgmt. Assn. (cert. hotel sales exec.), SKAL Club, Am. Soc. Assn. Execs., Fla. Soc. Assn. Execs., Hotel Sales Mgmt. Assn. Internat. (dir.), Meeting Planners Internat., Fla. Real Estate Assn. Republican. Roman Catholic. Club: Athletic (N.Y.). Contbr. articles to profl. jours. Office: Sandpiper Bay Resort Saint Lucie FL 33452

OGDEN, ALAN WILLIAM, food vending company executive; b. Endwell, N.Y., Nov. 4, 1947; s. William Curtis and Grace Elizabeth (Coyle) O.; m. Kay Ellen Pedigo, Nov., 1969 (div. July 1979); children—Jefferson Scott, Jonathan Andrew; m. 2d, Etta Louise Riggan, Sept. 28, 1980; 1 dau., Adrianne Leigh Malone. A.A., Broome Community Coll., Binghamton, N.Y., 1971; B.A., Plattsburg State Coll. (N.Y.), 1973. Cert. air traffic controller. Territory mgr. Burroughs Corp., Utica, N.Y., 1973-76; sales engr. Exide Corp., Rochester, N.Y., 1976-78, dist. mgr., Charlotte, 1978-81; sales mgr. Treat Am., Charlotte, 1981-82, v.p., sale mgr., 1982—. Recipient Salesmanship award Exide Electro Energy, 1977, Dist. Mgr. award, 1979. Republican. Lodge: Toastmasters. Home: 735 Riverwood Rd Matthews NC 28105 Office: Treat Am 8041 E Arrowridge Rd Charlotte NC 28210

OGDEN, HOWARD ALBERT, librarian; b. N.Y.C., Oct. 20, 1928; s. Howard Albert and Ellen Cecilia (Rogers) O.; m. Patricia Spang, Sept. 2, 1961; children—Carol, Janet, Patricia. A.B., U. Pa., 1952; M.S. in Library Sci., U. N.C., 1973; M.Pub. Adminstrn., Golden Gate U., 1979. Joined U.S. Navy as seaman, 1946, advanced through grades to comdr., 1965; engr. officer U.S.S. Strive, 1952-53; explosive ordnance disposal officer, U.S. and Far East, 1954-58; gunfire control officer U.S.S. Lake Champlain, 1958-59; served on U.S.S. Hale and The Sullivans, 1959-61; weapons officer, staff comdr. fleet activities Mediterranean, 1962-64; exec. officer U.S.S. Norris, 1964-65; comptroller 5th Naval Dist., Norfolk, Va., 1965-68; exec. officer U.S.S. Sierra, 1968-70; comdg. officer Naval Ordnance Facility, Japan, 1970-72, ret., 1972; dir. Hampton Pub. Library, Va., 1973—; Mem. Library Services Constrn. Act Title I adv. com. for continuing edn. Va. State Library, 1977-80, 82-84, also Title III, 1980-85. Mem. City of Hampton Tng. Bd., 1980-84. Mem. ALA, Va. Library Assn., Hampton Roads Hort. Soc. Roman Catholic. Club: Va. Masters Swim. Lodge: Hampton Rotary. Home: 2 Kanawha Ct Hampton VA 23669 Office: Hampton Pub Library 4207 Victoria Blvd Hampton VA 23669

OGDEN, LANE GORDON, JR., psychologist; b. Brownwood, Tex., May 5, 1954; s. Lane Gordon and Louise (Wood) O.; m. Lisa Jean Bailey, Aug. 7, 1976. B.S., Howard Payne U., 1976; M.A., Tex. Tech U., 1977, Ph.D., 1983. Lic. psychologist, Tex. Instr. career planning Richland Community Coll., Dallas, 1978-80; dir. manpower planning Rhodes & Assocs., Inc., Dallas, 1983-84; pvt. practice psychology, Dallas, 1984—; instr. Am. Inst. Banking, Dallas, 1984—; resident in VA psychology, San Antonio, 1982-83; teaching asst. Tex. Tech U., Lubbock, 1981-82; program evaluator DEBT-Lubbock Ind. Sch. Dist., 1981-82. Contbr. articles to profl. jours. Mem. Am. Psychol. Assn., Tex. Psychol. Assn., Dallas Psychol. Assn. Republican. Baptist. Avocations: reading; gardening; fishing; softball; scuba. Office: 11551 Forest Central Suite 315 Dallas TX 75243

OGDEN, SCHUBERT MILES, theologian, educator; b. Cin., Mar. 2, 1928; s. Edgar Carson and Neva Louetta (Glancy) O.; A.B., Ohio Wesleyan U., 1950, awarded Litt.D. (hon.), 1965; fellow Am. Council Learned Socs., Johns Hopkins U., 1950-51; D.B., U. Chgo., 1954, Ph.D., 1958, D.H.L. (hon.), 1983; m. Joyce Ellen Schwettman, Aug. 26, 1950; children—Alan Scott, Andrew Merrick. Ordained to ministry United Methodist Ch., 1958; mem. faculty Perkins Sch. Theology, So. Meth. U., 1956-69, assoc. prof. theology, 1961-64, prof., 1964-69; univ. prof. theology Div. Sch., U. Chgo., 1969-72; prof. theology Perkins Sch. Theology, So. Meth. U., Dallas, 1972-83, Univ. Disting. prof. theology, 1983—, dir. grad. program in religious studies, 1974—; Merrick lectr. Ohio Wesleyan U., 1965; vis. fellow Council of Humanities, Princeton U., 1977-78; Sarum lectr. U. Oxford, 1980-81; Fulbright research prof., also Guggenheim fellow Marburg (Germany) U., 1962-63. Mem. Am. Acad. Religion (pres. 1976-77), Am. Acad. Arts and Scis., Soc. Values in Higher Edn., Am. Philos. Assn., Am. Theol. Soc., Phi Beta Kappa, Omicron Delta Kappa, Phi Mu Alpha. Author: Christ Without Myth, 1961, 2d edit., 1979; The Reality of God, 1966, 2d edit., 1977; Faith and Freedom, 1979; The Point of Christology, 1982; Editor, translator: Existence and Faith; Shorter Writings of Rudolf Bultmann, 1960; New Testament and Mythology and other Basic Writings (Rudolf Bultmann), 1984. Editorial bd. Jour. Religion, 1972—, Modern Theology, 1984—, Jour. Am. Acad. Religion, 1985—. Office: Perkins School of Theology Southern Methodist U Dallas TX 75275

O'GEARY, DENNIS TRAYLOR, contracting and engineering company executive; b. Waverly, Va., Feb. 20, 1925; s. King William and Mary Virginia (Traylor) O'G.; surveying degree Tri-State U., 1943; B.S. in Civil Engring., Ill. Inst. of Tech., 1947; m. Alice Stuart Baum, Aug. 3, 1947; children—Dennis Patrick, Mary Alice, Elizabeth Christina. Resident engring. trainee Va. Hwy. Dept., Richmond, 1947-50; civil engring. supt. Wiley Jackson Co., Roanoke, Va., 1950-57; engr., asst. estimator, project mgr., v.p. and asst. to area mgr. S.J. Groves & Sons Co., Mpls. and Springfield, Ill., 1957-77, v.p., area mgr., 1978-82, v.p., asst. div. mgr., Atlanta, 1982-84; pres. Peabody Southwest, Inc., 1984—. Served with USNR, 1943-46. Mem. ASCE, Am. Concrete Inst., Soc. Am. Mil. Engrs., Internat. Oceanographic Found., Cousteau Soc. Methodist. Home: 15402 Cresent Oaks Ct Houston TX 77068 Office: 5500 Northwest Central Dr Suite 190 Houston TX 77092

OGILVIE, MARGARET PRUETT, counselor; b. McKinney, Tex., Jan. 8, 1922; d. William Walter and Ida Mae (Houk) Pruett; B.A., Baylor U., 1943; M.Ed., Hardin Simmons U., 1968; m. Frederick Henry Ogilvie, May 13, 1943; children—Ida Margaret, James William. Tchr. pub. and pvt. schs., Tex., Calif., Alaska, W.Ger., 1944, 53-65; guidance counselor Dentsville High Sch., Columbia, S.C., 1968-69, Northwest H.S., Clarksville, Tenn., 1970-72; personal and marital counselor, Fairfield Glade, Tenn., 1972—; co-owner F & M Gems & Jewelry. Treas. Officers' Wives Club, Ft. Irwin, Calif.; chmn. vols. ARC, Ft. Irwin, 1965; pres. Women's Golf Assn., Ft. Irwin, 1965-66; v.p. Ch. Women United, Crossville, Tenn., 1972-74; bd. dirs. Cumberland County Mental Health Assn., 1975—; mem. legis. com. and pub. affairs com. Tenn. Mental Health Assn., 1976—, mem. exec. bd., 1977—; mem. Middle Tenn. com. Internat. Women's Yr., 1975; bd. dirs. Battered Women, Inc., Crossville, 1984—. Mem. Am. Personnel and Guidance Assn., Nat. Ret. Tchrs. Assn., Bus. and Profl. Women's Club (chmn. 1973-75), DAR (parliamentarian Crab Orchard chpt. 1981), Pi Gamma Mu. Democrat. Baptist (choir dir., organist 1972—). Clubs: Fairfield Glade Women's (parliamentarian 1974-77), Fairfield Glade Women's Golf Assn. (pres. 1973), Fairfield Glade Sq. Dance; Order Eastern Star (Amanda chpt. IV). Home: 240 Snead Dr PO Box 1522 Fairfield Glade TN 38555

OGLE, SHARON RUTH, physical education educator; b. Dearborn, Mich., May 20, 1950; d. Oliver Leslie and Marion Elizabeth (Adams) Ogle. B.S., Eastern Mich. U., 1972; M.S., Central Mo. State U., 1976. Substitute tchr. South Lyon Pub. Schs. (Mich.), 1972; tchr., coach Owendale-Gagetown Jr.-Sr. High Sch. (Mich.), 1972-73, Centreville Jr.-Sr. High Sch. (Mich.), 1973-75; grad. asst. Central Mo. State U., Warrensburg, 1975-76; instr., coach U. Ark., Fayetteville, 1976-78; asst. prof. phys. edn. Brevard Community Coll., Cocoa, Fla., 1978—, mem. student activities council, 1982—. Contbr. articles to profl. jours. Eastern Mich. U. scholar, 1968, Cert. for Outstanding Scholarship, 1972. Mem. AAHPERD, Nat. Assn. Sport and Phys. Edn., Nat. Assn. Girls and Women's Sports, Mortar Bd., Lit. Guild. Delta Psi Kappa, Phi Kappa Phi, Phi Delta Kappa. Republican. Baptist. Club: Space Coast Runners. Office: Brevard Community Coll 1519 Clearlake Rd Cocoa FL 32922

OGLESBEE, RONALD MARTIN, engineering company executive; b. Carrollton, Mo., Oct. 22, 1940; s. Wyatt Irvin and Helen Ilene (Wallis) O.; A.S., Kansas City Jr. Coll., 1962; B.S. in Physics (Kansas City Engrs. Club fellow, NSF fellow), Mo. Sch. Mines, 1964; M.S. in Metallurgy (NSF fellow), U. Mo., Rolla, 1965; m. Margaret Grace Burch, Nov. 18, 1960; children—Robert Karl, Renee Suzanne. Inventory and costs engr. Southwestern Bell Telephone Co., St. Louis, 1965-68; subsea engr. Shell Oil Co., New Orleans, 1968-75, prodn. engr., 1968-70, subsea devel. engr., 1970-75; sales mgr. subsea systems Wellhead div. FMC Corp., Houston, 1975-77, sr. applications engr. Lockheed Petroleum Services, Houston, 1977-79; v.p. sales Single Buoy Moorings Am., Houston, 1979-82; v.p. spl. tech. Neptune Prodn. Systems, Houston, 1982-83; pres., sr. ptnr. Sea Troll Engring. Inc., 1983—; owner Petroleum Tngs. (engring. extension tng. service); engring. extension course coordinator in subsea prodn. systems for UCLA, 1979-80, Continuing Edn. Inst., 1981; rep. to Am. Petroleum Inst. task group, 1974-75. Asso. post adviser Boy Scouts Am., St. Louis, 1964-68, post adviser, New Orleans, 1970-72, asst. scoutmaster, 1974-75. Mem. AIME, Sigma Xi, Phi Kappa Phi, Alpha Sigma Mu, Kappa Mu Epsilon, Sigma Pi Sigma, Phi Theta Kappa. Club: YMCA Fencing. Office: 11601 N Galayda Houston TX 77086

OGLESBY, DANIEL KIRKLAND, JR., hospital administrator; b. Gastonia, N.C., Sept. 15, 1930; s. Daniel K. and Bettie Amelia (Smith) O.; m. Bobbie Jean Owen, Apr. 4, 1953; children—Debra Lynn, Kathie Owen, Bettie Lee. B.S., Davidson Coll., 1952; certificate in hosp. adminstrn., Duke U., 1954. Asst. adminstr. Blount Meml. Hosp., Maryville, Tenn., 1954-55; adminstr. Union Meml. Hosp., Monroe, N.C., 1955-59, Scotland Meml. Hosp., Laurinburg, N.C., 1959-67, Anderson (S.C.) Meml. Hosp., 1967-77, pres., 1977—. Mem. Anderson adv. bd., S.C. Nat. Bank, 1982—. Bd. dirs. Anderson County Health Planning Council.; Bd. dirs. Anderson County United Fund.; bd. dirs. Sun Alliance, vice chmn., 1983-84; bd. dirs. Sun Health, Inc., chmn., 1983-84. Recipient Community Achievement certificate Laurinburg C. of C. Fellow Am. Coll. Healthcare Execs. (council regents 1971-77, bd. govs. 1981-85, chmn. officer 1985-87); trustee Am. Hosp. Assn., S.C. Hosp. Assn. (dir., past pres.), Southeastern Hosp. Conf. (dir., chmn.), Carolinas Hosp. and Health Services Inc. (dir., past pres.), Hosp. Data Center S.C. (dir.), Anderson Area C. of C. (v.p. 1976-77). Methodist. Club: Rotary (past chpts. pres.). Home: 1202 Melbourne Dr Anderson SC 29621 Office: 800 N Fant St Anderson SC 29621

OGLESBY, JOHN NORMAN, distribution and oil exploration development company executive; b. Dublin, Ga., Aug. 29, 1948; s. Theodore Nathaniel and Ruth (Moncrief) O.; B.Aerospace Engring., Ga. Inst. Tech., 1971, M.Indsl. Mgmt. (research and teaching fellow), 1973; m. Jansie Marie Bennett, June 4, 1966; children—John Norman, Julia Elizabeth. Data processing cons. First Computer Services Trust, Charlotte, N.C., 1973-76; securities analyst First Union Nat. Bank, Charlotte, 1977-79; pres. Oglesby Assocs., wholesale and retail distbr. Amway products and motivational books and cassettes, Charlotte, 1978-82, Memphis, 1983—; pres. Hercules Investor Services, oil exploration and devel., 1983-84; pres. Am. Petroleum Devel., 1985—, Info. Processing Assocs., 1985—; gen. ptnr. Diamond Oil Co.; cons. data processing, bus. and fin.; internat. lectr. Active Republican Nat. Com., sponsor victory fund, 1981; mem. Citizens Choice. Acad. scholar Ga. Inst. Tech., 1966-71. Mem. AIAA (v.p. 1970), Ambassador's Internat., Amway Distbrs. Assn. Mem. Assembly of God. Designer, author Q.E.S. System, 1977, QESVAL, 1977, APT (productivity tool), 1983, CGS (county govt. system), 1984. Home and office: 7927 Woodleaf Germantown TN 38138

OGLESBY, SABERT, JR., research company executive; b. Birmingham, Ala., May 14, 1921; s. Sabert and Myrtle (Dunn) O.; m. Carolyn Vance, Mar. 4, 1944; 1 child, Donald T. B.S.E.E., Auburn U., 1943, B.E.E., 1948; M.S.E.E., Purdue U., 1951. Research engr. So. Research Inst., Birmingham, 1951-60, div. head, 1960-65, dept. head, 1965-78, v.p., 1976-81, pres., 1981—. Author: Heat Pump Applications, 1952; Electrostatic Precipitation, 1978. Bd. dirs. Birmingham Music Club, 1983-85. Served to 1st lt. U.S. Army, 1943-46. Mem. Air Pollution Control Assn. Lodge: Kiwanis (bd. dirs. 1977, 85—). Office: So Research Inst 2000 9th Ave S Birmingham AL 35255

OGLIARUSO, MICHAEL ANTHONY, chemistry educator, consultant, researcher; b. Bklyn, Aug. 10, 1938; s. Andrea and Anna (Bianco) O.; m. Basila Elizabeth Gallo, Apr. 2, 1961; 1 son, Michael Dana. B.A., Poly. Inst. Bklyn., 1960, Ph.D., 1965. Lectr. UCLA, 1965-67; asst. prof. chemistry Va. Poly. Inst. and State U., Blacksburg, 1967-72, assoc. prof., 1972-78, prof., 1978—, assoc. dean Coll. Arts and Scis., 1984—; chemistry cons., researcher, tchr. Contbr. numerous publs. relating to original chem. research and teaching to profl. jours. Served to 2d lt. C.E., U.S. Army, 1960-62. Awarded membership Va. Tech Acad. of Teaching Excellence, 1978—. Mem. Am. Chem. Soc., Va. Acad. Scis. (chmn. chemistry sect.), Sigma Xi, Phi Lambda Upsilon. Office: Va Poly Inst and State U Coll Arts and Scis 126 Williams Hall Blacksburg VA 24061

O'GRADY, TOM JOSEPH, poet, translater, winemaker; b. Balt. Aug. 26, 1943; s. Thomas Joseph Grady and Sallie Mapp (Dennis) Geady Loren; m. Frances Ann Griesser, June 15, 1966 (div. 1971); m. Bronwyn Southworth, July 17, 1971; children—Ethan, Ryan. B.A., U. Balt., 1966; M.A. in Creative Writing, Johns Hopkins U., 1967; postgrad. in English lit. U. Del., 1972-74. Instr. English, Catensville Community Coll., Md., 1969-71; Gilman fellow, teaching asst. Johns Hopkins U., Balt., 1966-69; teaching asst. U. Del., Newark, 1972-74; owner, winemaker Rose Bower Vineyard and Winery, Hampden-Sydney, Va., 1974—; poet-in-residence Hampden-Sydney Coll., 1974—, dir. vis. writers program, 1974—; mem. adv. bd. State of Va. Wine Growers, 1985—. Author: Establishing a Vineyard, 1977; The Farmville Elegies, 1980 (Impact Book award 1980); translater several books. Editor, founder Hampden-Sydney Poetry Rev., 1974— (NEA Editor's prize 1975). Served with U.S. Army, 1967-69. Recipient Leache prize Chrysler Mus., 1978. Democrat. Episcopalian. Home: PO Box 126 Hampden-Sydney VA 23943 Office: Rosebower Winery Hampden-Sydney Coll Hampden-Sydney VA 23943

O'HAIR, MADALYN MAYS, lawyer, author; b. Pitts., Apr. 13, 1919; d. John Irvin and Lena (Scholle) Mays; m. Richard Franklin O'Hair, Oct. 18, 1965; children—William J. Murray III, Jon Garth Murray, Robin Eileen Murray O'Hair. B.A., Ashland Coll., 1948; postgrad. Western Res. U., 1948-49, Ohio No. U., 1949-51; LL.B., South Tex. Coll. Law, 1953, J.D., 1975; M.P.S.W., Howard U., 1954; Ph.D., Minn. Inst. Philosophy, 1971. Psychiat. social worker, supr. family and children's agys., probation dept., psychiat. insts., welfare depts., 1948-46, 59-64; atty. NEW, Washington, 1956-59. Founder Soc. Separationists, Inc., Charles E. Stevens Am. Atheist Library and Archives, Inc., Austin, Tex., 1970; founder United World Atheists, 1976; dir. Am. Atheist Ctr., 1965-79. Served to 2d lt. WAAC, WAC, World War II. Author: Why I Am An Atheist, 1965; What on Earth Is an Atheist, 1966; The American Atheist, 1967; An Atheist Epic, 1968; The Atheist World, 1969; An Atheist Speaks, 1970; Atheist Heroes, 1971; Let us Prey, an Atheist Looks at Church Wealth, 1970; Freedom From Religion; The Atheist Plea, 1973; An Atheist Believes, 1973; Atheism, Its Viewpoint, 1973; Freedom Under Siege, 1974; Atheism in the United States, 1976; The Religious Factors in the War in Vietnam, 1976; An Original Theory in Respect to the Origin of Religion, 1977; adv. editor The Atheist Viewpoint, 25 vols., 1972; originated Am. Atheist mag., 1965; dir. Am. Atheist Radio Series, 1968-79. Prin. U.S. Supreme Ct. case which removed Bible reading and prayer recitation in pub. schs., 1963. Office: 2210 Hancock Dr Austin TX 78756

O'HAIRE, BETTY NEWELL, lawyer; b. Laurenburg, N.C., Feb. 21, 1936; d. Ernest F. Newell and Laura E. (McCraney) Newell Culver; m. James P. Cash, June 12, 1964 (dec. Oct. 1969); m. 2d Joseph W. O'Haire, June 19, 1970. Student U. Ga., 1967-69, U. Fla., Daytona Beach, 1970-72; J.D. magna cum laude, John Marshall Law Sch., Atlanta, 1979. Bar: Ga. 1979. Mgr., Credit Bur. Thomasville (Ga.), 1960-61; owner-mgr. Credit Bur. Jesup (Ga.), 1961-68; owner-mgr. Ga. So. Credit, Inc., Jesup, 1973-83, legal cons., 1983—; sec.-treas. Atlantic American, Inc., Jesup, 1970—; sole practice law, Jesup, 1979—; mem. nat. com. Assoc. Credit Burs., Inc., Houston, 1979—; dir. Assoc. Credit Burs. Ga., Inc., 1960-67, 73—, 2d v.p., 1984-85; chmn. Assoc. Credit Burs. Ga., CSD, 1984-85. Recipient Ednl. award Assn. Credit Burs. S.E., 1964; Credit Reporting award Assn. Credit Burs. Am., 1964. Mem. Jesup Bar Assn. (sec.-treas. 1980-81, pres. 1982-83), Wayne County C. of C. (ednl. chmn. 1978-79, pres. 1981-82). Episcopalian. Address: PO Box 431 Jesup GA 31545

O'HARA, ALFRED PECK, lawyer; b. Patterson, N.Y., Apr. 27, 1919; s. Peter and Anna L. (Peck) O'H.; m. Muriel A. Sandberg, Aug. 30, 1940 (dec.); children—Jane Ann O'Hara Toth, Margaret Kathleen O'Hara Duff, Peter James, John Edward. B.A., Syracuse U., 1940; LL.B., Fordham U., 1942. Bar: N.Y. bar 1942, U.S. Supreme Ct 1956. Sec. to U.S. Dist. Ct., 1942-43; partner firm McLaughlin & Stickles, 1946-52; asst. U.S. atty., chief civil div. So. Dist. N.Y., 1953-56; cons. to atty. gen., N.Y. State, 1956; sr. partner firm Rogers Hoge & Hills, N.Y.C., 1958—; counsel U.S. Trademark Assn., 1967-70; chmn., dir. Bacardi Corp., 1976-82, chmn. bd., 1982—; pres. Castleton Beverage Corp.; dir. Sogrape U.S.A. Mem. Assn. Bar City of N.Y., N.Y. State Bar Assn., Am. Bar Assn., NAM (bd. dirs. 1978—), Fed. Bar Council, Am. Law Inst. (life), Internat. Patent and Trademark Assn. Clubs: Williams, Pinnacle, Bankers of P.R., Quaker Hill., Lyford Cay. Home: Birch Hill Rd Patterson NY 12563 Office: Rogers Hoge & Hills 90 Park Ave New York NY 10016 also Bacardi Corp PO Box G3549 San Juan PR 00936*

O'HARA, PAUL STEPHEN, exploration geophysicist; b. Warren, Ohio, Apr. 17, 1955; s. Paul F. and Carolyn A. (Reynolds) O'H.; m. Cynthia Loral, Sept. 6, 1980; children—Loral Ashley, Caroline Anne. B.A., U. S. Fla., 1978, postgrad., 1978-79. Geohydrologic technologist U.S. Geol. Survey, Tampa, Fla., 1978-79; seismic processor Chevron Geophys., Houston, 1979-80; geophysicist Arco Exploration, Plano, Tex., 1980-81; exploration geophysicist Phillips Petroleum Co., Houston, 1981—. Mem. Soc. Exploration Geophysicists, Am. Assn. Petroleum Geologists, Houston Geol. Soc. Republican. Presbyterian. Clubs: Toastmasters Internat. (social com. chmn. 1982) (Houston). Home: 3114 Greenridge Dr Missouri City TX 77459 Office: Phillips Petroleum Co PO Box 1967 Houston TX 77001

O'HARE, ANDREW TIMOTHY, petroleum geologist; b. N.Y.C., Sept. 29, 1958; s. Thomas Edward and Claire Marie (Hunt) O'H. B.S. in Chemistry, U. Ky., 1980, M.S. in Geology, 1982. Petroleum geologist Union Oil Co. of Calif., Midland, Tex., 1982-85, TXO Prodn. Corp., Midland, 1985—. Fitness instr. YMCA, Midland, 1983-85; active Young Democrats, Midland, 1983—, Nat. Ski Patrol Sierra Blanca Ski Resort, N.Mex., 1984—; CPR instr. ARC, Midland, 1984—; vol. Midland Community Theatre. Mem. Am. Assn. Petroleum Geologists. Roman Catholic. Avocations: skiing; cooking; running; sailboarding; reading. Home: 4301 Raleigh Ct #1110 Midland TX 79707 Office: TXO Prodn Corp 900 Wilco Bldg Midland TX 79701

OHRSTROM, RICARD RIGGS, financial executive; b. Tarrytown, N.Y., Aug. 1, 1922; s. George Lewis and Emma (Riggs) O.; A.B. cum laude in Public Affairs, Princeton U., 1944; LL.B., U. Va., 1949; m. Mary Elizabeth Murchison, Mar. 16, 1949 (div. Mar. 1966); m. Elizabeth Rinehart, Dec. 26, 1968; m. Jane Hoyt, May 19, 1978; children—Ricard Riggs, Kenneth, George L. II, Christopher, Barnaby, Mark. Asso., G.L. Ohrstrom & Co., N.Y.C., 1949-50; admitted to Va. bar, 1949; atty. civil div. Chief Counsel's Office, Bur. Internal Revenue, Washington, 1950-52; with W.C. Norris, Tulsa, 1952-54; partner G.L. Ohrstrom & Co., N.Y.C., 1954-55, mng. partner, 1955-69, semi-active gen. partner, 1970—; dir. Carlisle Corp., 1955—, Dover Corp. 1955—, Leach Corp., Los Angeles, 1953-55, chmn. bd., 1955-74; dir. Leigh Corp., 1962-79, Round Hill Devels., Ltd., 1968—, chmn. bd., 1977-84, others. Bd. dirs. Middleburg (Va.) Community Center, 1956—, chmn. bd. 1972-77; bd. dirs. Hill Sch., 1971-76; pres. The Catesby Found.; del. Va. State Rep. Conv., 1980. Served with USMC, 1943-46. Home: Old Whitewood The Plains VA 22171 Office: PO Box 325 Middleburg VA 22117

O'KANE, JANICE MONTALBANO, banker; b. Wheeling, W.Va., Dec. 5, 1951; d. August Joseph and Helen (Stan) Montalbano; m. Michael Vogler O'Kane, Jan. 13, 1973. Student West Liberty State Coll., 1969-70, W.Va. Sch. Banking, 1979, Nat. Personnel Sch., 1980. Proof operator First Nat. Bank of Wheeling, 1970-73, installment loan clk., 1973-75, reconcilement clk., 1975-78, asst. mgr. ops., 1978-80, personnel asst., 1980-81, asst. cashier bank support, 1981-82, asst. v.p. bank support div., 1983—. Mem. Wheeling Hosp. Aux. Mem. Am. Inst. Banking (chpt. dir.), Ohio Valley Women's Forum. Republican. Roman Catholic. Home: 69 Heiskell Ave Wheeling WV 26003 Office: 2207 National Rd Wheeling WV 26003

O'KEEFE, LAWRENCE PATRICK, mechanical engineer, consultant; b. Queens, N.Y., Mar. 4, 1937; s. Vincent F. and Frances A. (O'Melia) O'Keefe; m. Helen R. Lavelle, Nov. 4, 1959; children—Lawrence, Heather, Daniel. B.A. in Econs., Queens Coll., 1959; B.S. in Mech. Engring., N.Mex. State U., 1967; M.S. in Mech. Engring., Cooper Union, 1970. Registered profl. engr., Ga., Fla., Va., N.Y. Project engr. Lunar Module Program, Grumman Aerospace Corp., Bethpage, N.Y. and Las Cruces, N.Mex., 1962-72; ptnr. Cashin Bahrenburg McDowell & O'Keefe Arch-Engrs., Mineola, N.Y., 1972-74; tech. agt. NSF Urban Tech. System, Henrico City, Va., 1974-78; project mgr. Battell So. Ops., Atlanta, 1978-81; v.p., dir. ops. Communications/Electronics Co., Atlanta, 1981; owner Applied Energing. Concepts, Atlanta, 1982—; instr. tech. forecasting Golden Gate U., Hampton, Va., 1977-78. Served to 2d. lt. U.S. Army N.G., 1959-64. Mem. Cons. Engrs. Council, Aircrafts Owners and Pilots Assn. Home and office: 5042 Post Rd Trail Stone Mountain GA 30088

O'KEEFE, MARTHA ALLEN PINNIX, bank executive; b. Greensboro, N.C., Jan. 10, 1949; d. R. Allen and Rossa E. (Smith) Pinnix; m. Thomas P. O'Keefe, Nov. 14, 1971; children—Shawn Kelly, Cathleen Michelle. A.B. in Sociology, Lenoir Rhyne Coll., 1971. Br. mgr. Central Fidelity Bank, Richmond, Va., 1971-78; auditor and monitoring unit supr. Henrico-Chesterfield-Hanover CETA Consortium, Richmond, 1979-81; consumer sales support officer Bank of Va., Richmond, 1981—. Co-founder, Richmond Profl. Women's Network, 1980, pres., 1980—. Mem. Am. Soc. Tng. and Devel. Vice-chair sch. bd. St. Patrick Sch., Richmond, 1982-84. Roman Catholic. Avocations: golf; needlework. Office: Bank of Va PO Box 25339 Richmond VA 23260

OKELL, JOBYNA LOUISE, public health administrator, accountant; b. Miami, Fla., Nov. 21, 1937; d. George Shaffer and Evelyn Maude (Pottmyer) O. B.B.A., U. Miami-Fla., 1961; postgrad. U. Miami, 1962, Nova U., 1976—. Acct. Crippled Children's Soc., Miami, Fla., 1964-65, Am. Coll. Found., Miami, 1965-66; owner Jobyna's Miniatures, Coral Gables, Fla., 1978—; exec. dir./adminstr., corp. dir. Fla. Health Profl. Services, Inc., Coral Gables, 1967—. Dist. chmn. Young Democrats Dade County and Fla., 1956-68; vice regent DAR, Coral Gables chpt., 1968-84, active Irish Georgian Soc., English Speaking Union; treas., dir. Merrick Manor Found., 1974-75; active Friends of Library, U. Miami, 1974-83; adv. bd. channeling project Miami Jewish Home and Hosp. for Aged, 1982-83. Recipient Outstanding County Young Democrat award Young Dems. Fla., 1964; Truman award Outstanding Young Dem. Young Dems. Dade County, 1965; Outstanding Jr. DAR, 1972. Mem. Am. Pub. Health Assn., Nat. League Nursing, Am. Soc. Pub. Adminstrn., Dade/Monroe Assn. Home Health Agys. (pres./dir. 1974-76), Health Planning Council South Fla., Health Systems Agy. South Fla., Fla. Assn. Home Health Agys., South Fla. In-Home Services (pres. 1985), Red-Sunset Merchants Assn., Nat. Assn. Miniature Enthusiasts, Internat. Guild Miniature Artisans, Ltd., Geneal. Soc. Greater Miami, Gamma Alpha Chi, Alpha Delta Pi. Republican. Episcopalian. Home: 715 Palermo Ave Coral Gables FL 33134 Office: Fla Health Profl Services Inc 1559 San Remo Ave Coral Gables FL 33146

O'KELLEY, WILLIAM CLARK, judge; b. Atlanta, Jan. 2, 1930; s. Ezra Clark and Theo (Johnson) O'K.; A.B., Emory U., 1951, LL.B., 1953; m. Ernestine Allen, Mar. 28, 1953; children—Virginia Leigh O'Kelley Wood, William Clark. Bar: Ga. 1952. Practiced in Atlanta, 1957-59; asst. U.S. atty. No. Dist. Ga., 1959-61; partner O'Kelley, Hopkins & Van Gerpen, Atlanta, 1961-70; U.S. dist. judge No. Dist. Ga., Atlanta, 1970—. Mem. com. on adminstrn. of criminal law Jud. Conf. U.S., 1979—; mem. Fgn. Intelligence Surveillance Ct., 1980—; corp. sec., dir. Gwinnett Bank & Trust Co., Norcross, Ga., 1968-70. Mem. exec. com., gen. counsel Ga. Republican Com., 1968-70. Served as 1st lt. USAF, 1953-57; capt. Res. Mem. Am., Atlanta bar assns., Ga. State Bar, Am. Judicature Soc., Dist. Judges Assn. 5th Circuit (pres. 1979-80), Sigma Chi, Phi Delta Phi, Omicron Delta Kappa. Baptist. Kiwanian (past pres.). Clubs: Atlanta Athletic, Lawyers of Atlanta. Home: 550 Ridgecrest Dr Norcross GA 30071 Office: US District Court 1942 US Courthouse 75 Spring St SW Atlanta GA 30303

OKES, DUKE WAYNE, quality engineer, consultant; b. Beckley, W.Va., Feb. 25, 1949; s. Karl J. and Virginia K. (Rawn) O.; m. Nancy L. Elliott, Feb. 2, 1974. A.E. in Indsl. Tech. and Electronics Tech., Tri Cities State Tech. Inst., 1976; B.S. in Bus. Adminstrn., Tusculum Coll., 1986. Quality technician TRW, Rogersville, Tenn., 1976-80, quality engr., 1980-84, mem. corp. electronics tech. transfer team, Cleve., 1983-85; project coordinator, 1984-85; owner, mgr., cons. APLOMET, Church Hill, Tenn., 1985—. Served with U.S. Army, 1970-72. Mem. Am. Soc. for Quality Control (cert., treas. 1981-82), Inst. Indsl. Engrs., Soc. Mfg. Engrs. Lodge: Moose. Avocations: reading; photography; financial analysis and investment. Office: APLOMET PO Box 116 Church Hill TN 37642

O'KON, WALTER JAMES, architect, consultant; b. Port Huron, Mich., Sept. 27, 1949; s. Walter W. and Lorraine (Trampf) O'K.; m. Christine Hutson Bryce; 1 dau., Erin Bryce. A.A., Miami Dade Jr. Coll., 1969; B.A. in Design with honors, U. Fla., 1971, M.A. in Architecture, 1973. Registered architect, Fla. Grad. architect, acoustical specialist Barrett, Daffin & Figg, Inc., Tallahassee, 1973-75; adj. asst. prof. bldg. tech. Sch. Architecture, Fla. A&M U., Tallahassee, 1975-76; asst. prof., acting head dept. bldg. tech. King Faisal U., Dammam, Saudi Arabia, 1976-78; assoc. Fitch, Holdredge, Bisone & Holcomb, Houston, 1979-80; prin. Walter J. O'Kon, Architect, Saint Augustine, Fla., 1980—. Vol., St. Johns County chpt. Am. Cancer Soc. Mem. Acoustical Soc. Am., Constrn. Specifications Inst., NW Fla. Builders Assn. Democrat. Lodges: Masons, Shriners. Avocations: reading; social activities; water sports. Home: 13 Madeira Dr Saint Augustine FL 32084 Office: 93 1/2 King St Suite 2 Saint Augustine FL 32084

OKPALOBI, MARTIS JONES, executive development consultant; b. Dayton, Ohio; d. Henry and Martha Rosetta (Fields) Jones; children—Ucheamaka, Chukwuemeka. B.S., Miami U., Oxford, Ohio, 1969; M.A., SUNY-Albany, 1971; Ph.D., Vanderbilt U., 1977. Sr. planner N.Y. State Dept. Edn., Albany, N.Y., 1971-74; research specialist Tenn. Dept. Edn., Nashville, 1974-77; pres. Results Unltd., Assocs., Dallas, 1977—; cons., lectr. mgmt. devel. Trustee Goals for Dallas, OIC's of Am. program chmn.; active March of Dimes; 1st v.p. Republican Council of Dallas County, 1980-82. Recipient Leon H. Sullivan award for outstanding leadership, 1981; Businesswoman of Yr., Iota Phi Lambda, 1979. Mem. Am. Psychol. Assn., Am. Soc. Tng. and Devel., Leadership Dallas, Opportunity Dallas, Exec. Women of Dallas, Leadership Tex., Bus. and Profl. Women. Republican. Club: Toastmasters. Contbr. articles to profl. jours. Office: PO Box 64900 Dallas TX 75206

OKULSKI, ELIZABETH IRENE GRANGE, pathologist, educator; b. Evanston, Ill., Apr. 2, 1949; d. Cecil William and Elizabeth Frances (Pearson) Grange; m. Thomas Alexander Okulski, June 14, 1969; children—Alexander Harry, Juliana Elizabeth. Student, Moore Coll. Art, 1967-70, Rutgers U., 1970-71; M.D. with honors, Temple U., 1977. Diplomate Nat. Bd. Med. Examiners, Am. Bd. Pathology. Pathology intern, resident in pathology U. South Fla. Coll. Medicine, Tampa, 1977-81; staff pathologist Patterson-Coleman P.A., Tampa, 1981-82; pathologist Centro Asturiano Hosp., Tampa, 1982; staff pathologist Smith Kline Clin. Labs., Tampa, 1983—; clin. asst. prof. pathology U. South Fla., 1981—, lectr. lab. medicine, 1982—. Recipient Lange book award Temple U. Coll. Medicine, 1977, award Am. Med. Women's Assn., Temple U. Sch. Medicine, 1977. Fellow Coll. Am. Pathologists, Am. Soc. Clin. Pathologists; mem. Internat. Acad. Pathology, Fla. Med. Assn., Fla. Soc. Pathology, Fla. West Coast Assn. Pathologists (pres. 1986-87), Hillsborough County Med. Assn., Alpha Omega Alpha. Office: Smith Kline Lab PO Box 22707 Tampa FL 33630

OKUN, JACK H., orthodontist; b. N.Y.C., Jan. 30, 1932; s. Louis and Rachel (Ziperstein) O.; m. Rosalind Yagman, Nov. 18, 1967; children—Louis Brian, Michael Scott. B.S., NYU, 1953, D.D.S., 1956; M.S., Northwestern U., 1961. Trombone player, N.Y.C., 1948-56; practice dentistry specializing in orthodontics, North Palm Beach, Fla., 1961—; guest lectr. Palm Beach County Dental Research Clinic, West Palm Beach, 1968-69, chmn. practice mgmt. sect., 1973-82; mem. U.S. Congressman's Community Relations Council, West Palm Beach, 1985. Contbr. articles to profl. jours. Vice pres. North Palm Beach Community Band. Served as capt. USAF, 1956-58. Recipient Founders Day award NYU, 1956. Mem. ADA, Am. Assn. Orthodontists, Fla. Dental Assn. (dental edn. com. 1968-70), Palm Beach County Dental Soc. (budget and audit com. 1964-69, sch. edn. com. 1967-70), North Palm Beach County Dental Soc. (treas. 1972, sch. edn. com. 1984-85), Phi Beta Kappa, Omicron Kappa Upsilon. Jewish. Avocation: playing trombone. Home: 110 Dory Rd N North Palm Beach FL 33408 Office: 849 Park Ave Lake Park FL 33403

O'LAUGHLIN, FRANCIS MICHAEL, III, engineering administrator; b. Norfolk, Va., Sept. 9, 1946; s. Francis Michael and Margaret Mae (White) O'L.; m. Marilyn Ann Huggins, July 3, 1968; children—Michelle Yvonne, Francis Michael. B.S. in Chemistry, Tex. A&I U., 1969; A.A. in Quality Control, De Anza Coll., 1977; M.S. in Systems Mgmt., U. So. Calif., 1979; M.B.A. in Internat. Bus., U. Houston, 1984. Document control supr. Nat. Semie conductor, Santa Clara, Calif., 1973-75; quality engring. mgr. Memorex Corp., Santa Clara, 1975-79; quality/reliability mgr. Basic Four Corp., Houston, 1979-80; quality assurance mgr. Dresser Magcobar Data, Houston, 1980-82; engring. standards mgr. N.L. McCullough, Houston, 1982—; instr. DeAnza Coll., Cupertino, Calif., 1977-79; seminar lectr. Calif. Inst. Quality Tech., Cupertino, 1979-83; cons., Houston, 1979—. Editorial rev. bd. Quality Mag., 1979-83. Served to comdr. USNR, 1969—. Mem. Am. Soc. Quality Control, Am. Mgmt. Assn., Naval Res. Assn. Democrat. Roman Catholic. Home: 3106 Indian Wells Ct Missouri City TX 77459 Office: NL McCullough 3000 Northbelt Houston TX 77205

OLBRICH, WILLIAM LAWRENCE, JR., librarian; b. Houston, Oct. 23, 1946; s. William Lawrence and Florine Anna (Folschinsky) O.; m. Patricia Anne Fuentes Roach, Dec. 31, 1974 (div.); children—Gregory Todd, Amy Luisa; m. Lynn Frances Lindgren, Jan. 18, 1980. B.A., Southwestern U., 1969; M.A., U. Iowa, 1974; M.L.S., U. Tex.-Austin, 1973. Pub. services librarian Ga. So. Coll., Statesboro, 1973-74; social scis. librarian Tufts U., Medford, Mass., 1975-78; reference librarian U. N.Mex., Albuquerque, 1978-79; documents librarian Baylor U., Waco, Tex., 1979—; cons. Tex. Dept. Aging, Austin, 1983, Tex. Supreme Ct., Austin, 1983, NASA, Albuquerque, 1979. Author abstracts: America: History and Life, 1974—; contbr. articles to profl. jours. Mem. McLennan County Bd. Pub. Library Commrs., Waco, 1983—. Recipient cert. of achievement U.S. Army Aviation Systems Command, Corpus Christi, Tex., 1971. Mem. ALA, Tex. Library Assn., Assn. Can. Studies U.S., Assn. Gerontology Higher Edn., Kappa Alpha. Methodist. Home: 701 Kimberly St Waco TX 76643 Office: Moody Library Baylor U PO Box 6307 Waco TX 76706

OLBRICHT, THOMAS HENRY, college administrator, Biblical theology educator; b. Thayer, Mo., Nov. 3, 1929; s. Benjamin Joseph and Agnes Martha (Taylor) O.; m. Dorothy Jetta Kiel, June 8, 1951; children—Suzanne M., Eloise J., Joel C., Adele L. Olbricht Foster, Erica M. B.S., No. Ill. U., 1951; M.A., U. Iowa, 1953, Ph.D., 1959; S.T.B., Harvard U., 1962. Asst. prof., dir. forensics Harding Coll., Searcy, Ark., 1954-55; asst. prof., chmn. dept. U. Dubuque, Iowa, 1955-59; from instr. to assoc. prof. Pa. State U., University Park, 1962-67; assoc. prof. Bibl. theology Abilene Christian U., Tex., 1967-69, prof., 1969—, dean Coll. Liberal and Fine Arts, 1981-85, chmn. grad. studies Coll. Bibl. Studies, 1985—. Author: Informative Speaking, 1968; Power To Be, 1979; He Loves Forever, 1980; The Message of Ephesians and Colossians, 1983. Pres. 2d Century Bd., 1981. Mem. Am. Acad. Religion (pres. SW chpt. 1976-77). SW Com. on Religious Studies (pres. 1978-79, sec.-treas. 1982—). Mem. Ch. of Christ. Lodge: Kiwanis (pres. local club 1972-73, chmn. Tex.-Okla. conv. 1981). Office: Abilene Christian U ACU Sta Box 8227 Abilene TX 79699

OLDER, JAY JUSTIN, ophthalmic plastic surgeon; b. Jersey City, Feb. 7, 1940; s. Lester Bernard and Gertrude Cohen O.; m. Lois Rosner, Feb. 7, 1968; children—Benjamin, Jessica. A.B., Rutgers U., 1961; M.D., Stanford U., 1966. Diplomate Am. Bd. Ophthalmology. Intern, Cornell U., Bellevue Meml. Hosps., N.Y.C., 1967, resident, 1968; resident in ophthalmology Stanford U., 1970-73; oculoplastic fellow U. Calif.-San Francisco, 1973-74; assoc. prof. ophthalmology, dir. oculoplastic service, dept. ophthalmology U. South Fla. Sch. Medicine, Tampa, 1974—; adj. prof. clin. pharmacy Sch. Pharmacy, U. Pacific, Stockton, 1972-73; lectr. anatomy Stanford U., Palo Alto, Calif., 1975, 76, 78, 80; vis. prof. ophthalmology U. Tenn., Memphis, 1981, U. Leicester (Eng.), 1981; mem. staff, chmn. outpatient surgery com. Univ. Community Hosp., Tampa; mem. staff St. Joseph's Hosp., Tampa, Tampa Gen. Hosp., VA Hosp., Tampa, Ambulatory Care Ctr., Tampa, All Children's Hosp., St. Petersburg, Fla., Women's Hosp. Bd. dirs., exec. com. Tampa Jewish Social Service, 1979-85; mem. Pres.'s Council U. South Fla. Fellow Am. Acad. Ophthalmology (honor award 1982), ACS, Am. Soc. Ophthalmic Plastic and Reconstructive Surgery (publs. chmn. 1979-81, sec. 1983-84, pres. elect. 1986); mem. AMA, Am. Eye Study Club, European Soc. Ophthalmic Plastic and Reconstructive Surgery, Quickert-Beard Study Club, Fla. Soc. Ophthalmology, Fla. Med. Assn., Hillsborough County Med. Assn. (mem. legis. com. and key contact physician). Jewish. Contbr. articles to profl. jours.

OLDFIELD, ROBERT HARRISON, geologist; b. Boston, Jan. 17, 1944; s. Homer R. and Sofia (Stavchuck) O.; m. Mary Loretta Watson, Aug. 25, 1972; 1 son, Daniel N. A.B., Mass. State Coll., Boston, 1967; M.S.T., Boston Coll., 1973. Cert. profl. geologist. Tchr. sci., pub. shs., Mass. and Ky., 1967-77; dist. geologist Manti-LaSal Nat. Forest, U.S. Forest Service, U.S. Dept. Agr., Monticello, Utah, 1977-79, Price, Utah, 1979-80; dist. zone geologist Daniel Boone Nat. Forest, Somerset, Ky., 1980-84, forest geologist, Winchester, Ky., 1984—. Served to capt. Ky. Army N.G., 1968—. Named Outstanding Young Educator, Oldham County Jaycees, 1975. Mem. Am. Inst. Profl. Geologists, Am. Assn. Petroleum Geologists, Am. Inst. Mining Engrs. Roman Catholic. Avocations: traval; photography; swimming; ice skating; volleyball. Home: 3201 Aqueduct Dr Lexington KY 40502 Office: Daniel Boone Nat Forest 100 Vaught Rd Winchester KY 40391

OLDHAM, HENRY NEVEL, weapon system analyst; b. Athens, Ga., Apr. 29, 1943; s. Arthur S. and Florrie M. (Phillips) O.; B.S., U. Ga., 1965; B.Aerospace Engring., Ga. Tech., 1965; M.Aerospace Engring., U. Va., 1968; m. Frances Wynn Hamilton, May 27, 1978; children—John Nevel, Michael Alexander, Laura Nance. Rocket propulsion design engr. Pratt & Whitney div. United Aircraft, W. Palm Beach, Fla., 1965; research asso. U. Va. Research Labs., Charlottesville, 1966-68; aerospace engr. systems engring. directorate U.S. Army Missile Command, Redstone Arsenal, Ala., 1971-76; aerospace engr. Multiple launch rocket system project office Redstone Arsenal, Ala., 1977-82; tech. mgr. CAS, Inc., Huntsville, Ala., 1982—; mem. community adv. com. Solar Energy Research Inst., 1975-76. Mem. Civic Club Council, 1975—, pres., 1977-79; bd. dirs. N.Ala. Kidney Found., 1975—, pres. 1982; bd. dirs. Madison County Heart Assn., 1979-80, fund drive chmn., 1980. Served with Ordnance Corps, U.S. Army, 1968-71; Res. 1971—. Recipient cert. of achievement U.S. Army, 1975, 77, 78, 80. Mem. AIAA, Assn. of U.S. Army (dir. 1982—), Res. Officers Assn., Aircraft Owners and Pilots Assn., Madison County C. of C. (chmn. armed forces com. 1983—), Jaycees (pres. Huntsville 1975-76, internat. senator 1977), Phi Mu Alpha Sinfonia. Methodist. Composer instrumental music for Punch and Judy Puppet Show, Fantasy Playhouse Children's Theatre, 1977. Home: 228 Teakwood Dr Huntsville AL 35801 Office: 555 Sparkman Dr Suite 1022 Huntsville AL 35816

OLDHAM, HOWARD TOWNSEND, printer; b. Camden, N.J., Dec. 25, 1943; s. Andrew Wesley and Josephine (Gandy) O.; student pub. schs.; m. Eve Stephana Stelly, Aug. 24, 1968; children—Dawn Alexis, Stephen Wesley. Salesman, Palmer Paper Co., Houston, 1970-72; mgr. Fannin Bus. Forms, Houston, 1972-74; pres. Gulf Coast Graphics Co., Houston, 1974-75; owner Patton Printing Co., Liberty, Tex., 1975—; tchr. printing San Jacinto Coll., Pasadena, Tex., 1973-74, mem. adv. com. printing tech. dept., 1975. Mem. Tex. Gov.'s Commn. Human Resources, 1975; del. Tex. Democratic Conv., 1972; bd. dirs. 1st United Meth. Ch., Liberty, 1979-81, mem. fin. com., family coordinator, 1983-84; pres. Liberty County Heart Assn., 1981-82. Served with USMCR, 1961-66. Mem. Houston Litho Club (pres. 1975; Ednl. Programs award 1973; Man of Yr. award 1972), Printing Industries Gulf Coast, Nat. Assn. Printers and Lithographers, Graphic Communications Council (v.p. 1974), Ducks Unltd. Methodist. Clubs: Rotary (dir., treas. 1984), Lions, Elks. Home: 5016 Briar Grove Liberty TX 77575 Office: 1308 N Main St PO Box 1026 Liberty TX 77575

OLDS, MILO LEO, electrical engineer; b. Glasgow, Mont., June 26, 1917; s. Arthur Ray and Petranella Pauline (Jacobs) O.; m. Mary Madaline Haley, Nov. 24, 1948; 1 dau., Milamari Antoinella Olds Cunningham. B.S. in Elec. Engring., Mont. State Coll., 1944; M.S. in Engring. Mgmt., George Washington U., 1975. With Mont.-Dakota Utilities, Williston, N.D., 1937-44; elec. engr. Bur. Reclamation, Billings, Mont., 1947-57; supr., elec. engr. engine generator set design and procurement U.S. Army, Ft. Belvoir, Va., 1957-81. Served to lt. col. USAR, 1934-77. Mem. IEEE, Friendship Vets. Fire Engine Assn., SAR (1st v.p. Fairfax Resolves), Sigma Xi. Roman Catholic. Club: Toastmasters (div. lt. gov. dist. 36). Home: 10629 Greene Dr Lorton VA 22079

O'LEARY, THOMAS MICHAEL, lawyer, army officer; b. N.Y.C., Aug. 16, 1948; s. James and Julia Ann (Conolly) O'L.; m. Luise Ann Williams, Jan. 13, 1978; 1 child, Richard Meridith. B.A., CUNY, 1974; J.D., U. Puget Sound., 1977. Bar: Wash. 1977, U.S. Ct. Mil. Appeals 1978, U.S. Supreme Ct. 1983. Dep. pros. atty. Pierce County Pros. Atty.'s Office, Tacoma, 1978; commd. 1st lt. U.S. Army, 1978, advanced through grades to capt., 1978; chief trial counsel Office of Staff Judge Adv., Fort Polk, La., 1978-79, trial def. counsel trial def. service, 1979-81; chief legal advisor Office Insp. Gen., Heidelberg, W.Ger., 1981-82; sr. def. counsel Trial Def. Service, Giessen, W.Ger., 1982-84; asst. chief adminstrv. law U.S. Army Armor Ctr., Fort Knox, Ky., 1984-85, chief adminstrv. law, 1985; chief legal assistance br. Office of Staff Judge Adv., Fort Knox, 1985—. Decorated Purple Heart; Cross of Gallantry (Vietnam). Mem. ABA, Assn. Trial Lawyers Am., Judge Advs. Assn., Wash. State Bar Assn., Pierce County Bar Assn. Home: 1019 S Woodland Dr Radcliff KY 40160 Office: Office Staff Judge Advocate US Army Armor Ctr Fort Knox KY 40121-5000

OLEJAR, PAUL DUNCAN, former information science administrator; b. Hazelton, Pa., Sept. 13, 1906; s. George and Anna (Danco) O.; A.B., Dickinson Coll., 1928; m. Ann Ruth Dillard, Jan. 6, 1933 (dec. Oct. 1978); 1 son, Peter; m. 2d, Martha S. Ross, Sept. 8, 1979. Dir. edn. W.Va. Conservation Commn., 1936-41; coordinator U.S. Fish and Wildlife Service, 1941-42; chief press and radio Bur. Reclamation, Dept. Interior, 1946-47; editor Plant Industry Sta. AGRI, 1948-51; chmn. spl. reports Agrl. Research Adminstrn., 1951-56; dir. tech. info. Edgewood Arsenal, Md., 1959-63; chief, tech. info. plans and programs Army Research Office, Washington, 1963-64; chmn. chem. info. unit NSF, Washington, 1965-70; dir. drug info. program Sch. Pharmacy, U. N.C., Chapel Hill, 1970-73, ret.; newspaper columnist, editor AP, Pa. and W.Va.; editor Hanover Record-Herald, Pa. Served with AUS, 1942-46. Decorated Army Commendation medal. Mem. Am. Soc. Info. Sci., Drug Info. Assn., Ravens Claw, Theta Chi, Omicron Delta Kappa. Author: (novel) A Taste of Red Onion, 1981. Home: 724 Port Malabar Blvd NE Palm Bay FL 32905

OLEJNIK, STEPHEN, applied statistics/research design educator; b. Detroit, Feb. 7, 1950; s. Harry Peter and Ann (Balon) O. B.S., Mich. State U., 1972, M.A., 1975, Ph.D., 1977. Research asst. Nat. Inst. Edn., Washington, 1975-76; research assoc. U. Pa., Phila., 1977-78; asst. prof. U. Fla., Gainesville, 1978-83, assoc. prof., 1983-85; assoc. prof. U. Ga., Athens, 1985—. Named Tchr. of Yr., Coll. of Edn. U. Fla., 1984. Mem. Am. Edn. Research Assn., Am. Statis. Assn., Fla. Ednl. Research Assn. (sec.-treas. 1982-83), Nat. Council on Measurements in Edn. Democrat. Roman Catholic. Office: U Ga 325 Aderhold Hall Athens GA 30602

OLEM, HARVEY, environmental engineer; b. Boston, Aug. 23, 1951; s. Louis and Bella Olem. B.S. in Civil Engring., Tufts U., 1973; M.S. in Environ. Pollution Control Pa. State U., 1975, Ph.D. in Civil Engring., 1978. Registered profl. engr., Pa. Grad. research asst. dept. civil engring. Pa. State U., 1973-76, lab. researcher, small industries research, 1976-77, research asst. Inst. for Research on Land and Water Resources, 1977-78; environ. engr. TVA, Chattanooga, 1978—; instr. Pa. Dept. Community Affairs, 1976-77. EPA trainee, 1976; Needham Social Club scholar, 1969. Mem. Water Pollution Control Fedn., Am. Water Works Assn., N. Am. Lake Mgmt. Soc. (fed. interagy. task force on acid precipitation), Sigma Xi, Phi Kappa Phi. Contbr. articles to profl. jours. Home: 9620 Pine St Ooltewah TN 37363 Office: 248 401 Bldg Chattanooga TN 37401

OLESON, NORMAN LEE, physics educator, researcher; b. Detroit, Aug. 19, 1912; s. Christian Gad and Mathilde (Halversen) O.; m. Gabrielle Dorothy Sauve, June 18, 1939; children—Karen, Norman Lee, Richard. B.S., U. Mich., 1935, M.S., 1937, Ph.D., 1940. Research physicist Gen. Electric, Cleve., 1946-48; prof. physics Naval Postgrad. Sch., Monterey, Calif., 1948-69; chmn. dept. physics U. South Fla., Tampa, 1969-78, prof., 1978—; vis. prof. Queen's U., Belfast, Ireland, 1955-56, MIT, 1967-68; cons. plasma physics Lawrence Radiation Lab., Livermore, Calif., 1958-69. Served as lt. comdr. USCG, 1940-46. Fellow Am. Phys. Soc.; mem. AAAS, Sigma Xi. Contbr. articles to profl. jours. Office: Department of Physics University of South Florida 4202 Fowler Ave Tampa FL 33620

OLIN, JAMES R., congressman; b. Chgo., Feb. 28, 1920; m. Phyllis Avery; children—Richard Davis, Thomas Avery, Katherine Price Milliken, James Randolph, Kristina Baker. Grad., Deep Springs Coll., (Calif.), 1941; B.E.E., Cornell U., 1943. With Gen. Electric Co., 1946-82, served as corp. v.p., gen. mgr. Indsl. Electronics div.; mem. 98th-99th Congresses from 6th Dist. Va. Supr. Town of Rotherdam (N.Y.); mem. Schenectady County (N.Y.) Bd. Suprs., 1953; bd. dirs. Burrell Hosp.; active Mental Health Assn., United Way, United Negro College Fund. Served as officer Signal Corps. U.S. Army, 1943-46. Mem. C. of C., Va. Mfrs. Assn., Nat. Alliance Businessman, Roanoke Symphony Soc. Democrat. Unitarian. Office: 1207 Longworth House Office Bldg Washington DC 20515

OLIPHINT, ROBERT ERSKINE, technology co. exec.; b. Austin, Tex., June 1, 1941; s. Joseph and Helen (Rhodes) O.; B.B.A., U. Tex., 1964; children—Joseph, Patricia. Jr. engr. White Instrument Labs., Austin, 1961-63; successively cost acct., materials mgr., sales mgr., ops. mgr., gen. mgr., div. v.p. Tracor, Inc., Austin, 1963-75, corp. v.p., gen. mgr., 1975—; pres. Westronics, Inc., Ft. Worth, 1971—, also dir.; pres. Tracer Atlas, Inc., Houston, 1984—, also dir. Active Austin United Way, Austin Heritage Soc.; chmn. bd. dirs. Austin Crime Stoppers, Inc. Mem. Instrument Soc. Am. (sr.), Austin C. of C. (dir. diplomat), IEEE, Austin Amateur Radio Club, Longhorn Corvette Club. Republican. Episcopalian. Contbr. articles to profl. jours. Home: 8503 Appalachian Austin TX 78759 Office: 6500 Tracor Ln Austin TX 78725

OLIVA, VIVIEN ALICE, bilingual, bicultural counselor; b. Tampa, Fla., Mar. 1, 1946; d. Martin Ernest and Alice Amparo (Rivero) Oliva. B.A., Fla. State U., 1967, M.A., 1969; M.Ed. in Guidance and Counseling, Loyola U., New Orleans, 1976; postgrad. U. New Orleans, 1982—. Tchr. Spanish, Riverdale High Sch. and Grace King High Sch., Metairie, La., 1967, 69-78; guidance counselor West Jefferson High Sch. and Bonnabel High Sch., Harvey and Metairie, La., 1978-79, 80-83; bilingual, bicultural counselor, 1984—. Recipient Outstanding Counselor award Loyola U., 1986. Mem. Am. Personnel and Guidance Assn., Am. Assn. Multicultural Counseling and Devel. Jefferson Parish Guidance Assn. (pres. 1982-83). Democrat. Roman Catholic. Office: 501 Manhattan Blvd Harvey LA 70058

OLIVER, CLIFTON, JR., educator; b. Amarillo, Tex., Dec. 3, 1915; s. Clifton and Laura Pearl (Hudson) O.; B.A., Tex. Tech U., 1935, M.A., 1936; postgrad. La. State U., 1937-38, U. Wis., 1938-39. Prof. mgmt. Tex. Christian U., Ft. Worth, 1939-43; prof. U. Fla., Gainesville, 1946-83, prof. emeritus, 1983—, dir. Mgmt. Center, 1959-71; pres. Mgmt. Assocs. Gainesville, 1969-86; cons. in field. Named track ofcl. U.S.A. Olympic Trials and Los Angeles Olympics, 1984, Pan-Am Track Meet, Orlando, Fla., 1986. Track ofcl. 1984 Olympics. Served to lt., AUS, 1943-46. Recipient service award U. Fla. Athletic Assn., 1977; President's Service award U. Fla. elected to Fla. Track and Field Hall of Fame, 1979. Mem. Acad. Mgmt., Am. Personnel Assn., Am. Soc. Tng. Dirs., Am. Arbitration Assn. (nat. panel), Nat. Police Assn., Fla. Purchasing Assn. (life), Fla. Blue Key, Alpha Kappa Psi (Service award 1968), Alpha Tau Omega (trustee, Service award 1971), Alpha Chi, Pi Sigma Alpha, Pi Gamma Mu. Elk, Kiwanian. Home: PO Box 14505 Gainesville FL 32604

OLIVER, CONSTANCE MARIE, psychologist, marriage and family therapist; b. Warren, Ohio, May 27, 1953; d. Richard Peter and Elsie Irene (Trott) Viola; 1 child, Sarah. B.A. cum laude, Kent State U., 1977, M.A., 1978, Ph.D., 1981. Lic. psychologist, Fla.; lic. marriage and family therapist, Fla. Therapist, psychotherapist Oakwood Profl. Ctr., Cuyahoga Falls, Ohio, 1978-80; psychology intern E. Stark County Mental Health Ctr., Alliance, Ohio, 1978-80, Cuyahoga Valley Community Mental Health Ctr., Cuyahoga Falls, 1980-81; psychology cons. Akron City Hosp., Ohio, 1979-81; psychologist Lee Mental Health Ctr., Fort Myers, Fla., 1981-83, Psychology Assocs. SW Fla., Cape Coral and Naples, Fla., 1983—; cons. Cape Coral Hosp., 1983—; co-host Sta. WBBH-TV Fort Myers, 1984-85; lectr. various civic groups. Contbr. articles to profl. jours., chpt. to book. Speaker Celebration of Women, Fort Myers, 1984—; mem. Cape Coral Ednl. Adv. Bd., 1984—; bd. dirs. Mental Health Assn. Lee County, Fla., 1984—. Mem. Am. Psychol. Assn., Fla. Psychol. Assn., Calusa Psychol. Assn. (sec.-treas. 1981—), Assn. Advancement Psychology. Republican. Club: Zonta. Home: 5340 SW 11th Pl Cape Coral FL 33914 Office: Psychology Assocs SW Fla 708 Del Prado Blvd Cape Coral FL 33904 also 801 Laurel Oak Dr Naples FL 33963

OLIVER, DURRETTE LAMAR, III, electrical engineer; b. Shreveport, La., Feb. 10, 1943; s. Durrette Lamar, Jr. and Laura Frances (Lawler) O.; B.S. in Elec. Engring., La. Tech. U., 1966; m. Janet Inez Moores, Nov. 17, 1967; children—Carolyn Frances, Lamar Clay. Elec. engr. PPG Industries, Lake Charles, La., 1966, 70-74, maintenance elec. engr., 1974-81, sr. maintenance engr., 1981-82, sr. project engr., 1982-85, staff engr. glass engring., Pitts., 1986—. Mem. adminstrv. bd. 1st Methodist Ch., Lake Charles, also cert. lay speaker, lay del. to ann. conf., chmn. electronics and ins. coms.; mem. fin. com. Calcasieu-Cameron Assn. Crippled Children and Adults, 1981-82; bd. dirs., 1983-85; bd. dirs. Pendleton Harbor Property Owners Assn., 1982-83, v.p., 1983-84; cub master Boy Scouts Am., 1983-86; co-chm. Parents' Guild, Episc. Day Sch., 1981-84, treas., 1981-86. Served with USAF, 1966-70. Registered profl. engr., La. Mem. Am. Arbitration Assn., Better Bus. Bur., Nat. Soc. Profl. Engrs., La. Engring. Soc. (chmn. state legis. com. 1982-83). Profl. Engrs. in Industry Practice Group (sec. 1982-83, chmn. 1984-85), S.W. Investors (treas. 1977-78). Home: 4842 Ponderosa Dr Lake Charles LA 70605 Office: PPG Industries Inc PO Box 1000 Lake Charles LA 70602

OLIVER, ELIZABETH JEANNE, nurse, educator; b. Rahway, N.J., Mar. 11, 1940; d. George James and Marguerite Elizabeth (Perkins) Schaeffer; m. Gerald William Oliver, Sept. 29, 1960; children—Christopher William, David James. A.S., Rutgers U.-Newark, 1959, B.S., 1961; M.S.N., Tex. Woman's U., 1975. Registered nurse, N.J., Md., Tex., Maine. Staff nurse Morristown Meml. Hosp., N.J., 1959-62, Johns Hopkins Hosp., Balt., 1962-66; staff nurse Galveston County Meml. Hosp., Texas City, Tex., 1970-71; mem. faculty Alvin Community Coll., Tex., 1971-79, program dir. nursing, 1979—. Mem. adv. com. Houston ARC, 1978-81; bd. dirs. Brazoria County ARC, Tex., 1985—. Mem. Am. Nurses Assn., Nat. League Nursing, Tex. Jr. Coll. Tchrs. Assn., Southern Council on Collegiate Edn. in Nursing, Sigma Theta Tau. Republican. Presbyterian. Avocations: camping; furniture refinishing; reading. Home: 1626 Seagate Ln Houston TX 77062 Office: Alvin Community Coll 3110 Mustang Rd Alvin TX 77511

OLIVER, G(EORGE) BENJAMIN, educational administrator, philosophy educator; b. Mpls., Sept. 17, 1938; s. Clarence P. and Cecile (Worley) O.; m. Paula Rae Foust, Sept. 15, 1963; children—Paul Benjamin, Rebecca Lee. B.A., U. Tex., 1960; M.Div., Union Theol. Sem., N.Y.C., 1963; M.A., Northwestern U., 1966, Ph.D., 1967. Lectr. Northwestern U., Evanston, Ill., 1966-67; asst. prof. Hobart & William Smith Coll., Geneva, N.Y., 1967-71, assoc. prof., 1971-77; prof., 1977; dean Southwestern U., Georgetown, Tex., 1977—. Contbr. articles to profl. jours. Mem. Bishop's com. Grace Ch., Georgetown, 1978-80, warden, jr. warden, 1983-85. Rockefellows fellow, 1960-61, Internat. fellow Columbia U., 1962-63; research grantee NEH, 1973-74. Mem. Am. Philos. Assn., Royal Inst. Philosophy (Eng.), Soc. for Values in Higher Edn., Am. Assn. Higher Edn., AAUP. Episcopalian. Office: Southwestern Univ Georgetown TX 78626

OLIVER, GERALD CLIFFORD, hospital administrator; b. Decatur, Ala., May 20, 1940; s. Melvin Roland and Odessa (Creel) O.; m. Betty Lou Harland, Dec. 20, 1960; children—Phillip, Nicole. B.S., U. N. Ala., 1962; M.S. in Hosp. Adminstrn., Baylor U., 1973. Exec. officer 58th Med. Battalion, U.S. Army, Vietnam, 1970-71; assoc. adminstr. U.S. Army Med. Dept., Fort Campbell, Ky., 1973-76, health facilities project officer, Fort Knox, Ky., 1976-79; exec. officer Health Facilities Planning Agy., Washington, 1979-81; dir. med. activities adminstrn. Walter Reed Med. Ctr., Washington, 1981-82; hosp. adminstr. U.S. Army Med. Dept., Fort Campbell, Ky., 1982—; preceptor George Washington U., Dept. Health Services Adminstrn., Washington, 1981-82, U. Ala., Birmingham, 1982-83, Austin Peay State U., Clarksville, Tenn., 1982—, U.S. Army-Baylor U. Health Care Adminstrn., Fort Sam Houston, Tex., 1982—. Mem. Fort Campbell Community Civilian Awards Council, 1982—, Community Health Care Consumer Com., Fort Campbell, 1982—, Med., Dental Equal Opportunity Council, Fort Campbell, 1982—. Decorated Order Mil. Med. Merit award U.S. Army Health Services Command, 1984. Fellow Am. Coll. Hosp. Adminstrs.; mem. Am. Hosp. Assn., Assn. Mil. Surgeons U.S., Assn. U.S. Army, Fed. Health Care Exec. Inst., Tenn. Hosp. Assn. (com. 1982—), Hopkinsville-Clarksville Area Hosp. Adminstrs. Assn., Pennyrile Pilots Assn. (pres. 1984-85). Mem. Ch. Christ.

Home: 108 Leslie Ct Hopkinsville KY 42240 Office: US Army Med Dept Activity Fort Campbell KY 42223-1498

OLIVER, PATSY YVONNE KEMP, vocational educator and special needs coordinator, psychometrist, business educator; b. Caldwell County, Ky., Jan. 20, 1943; d. Delmar G. and Martha Imogene (Blackburn) Kemp; m. Leroy G. Oliver, Oct. 21, 1960; children—Troy Lee, Kevin Brent. A.A., Hopkinsville Community Coll., 1969; B.S. in Bus. Edn., Murray State U., 1971, M.A., 1976, postgrad. in Guidance and Counseling, 1981. Legal sec., Princeton, Ky., 1962-68; tchr. bus. edn. Caldwell County Sch. System, 1971-80; coordinator vocat. spl. needs program Caldwell County Area Vocat. Ctr., Princeton, Ky., 1981—; part time instr. Hopkinsville Community Coll., 1979—. Mem. adv. council Hopkinsville Community Coll. Named Outstanding Secretarial Student Murray State U., 1971; recipient Secretarial award McGraw-Hill, 1971, Outstanding Alumni Recognition Hopkinsville Community Coll., 1976, Pres.' Scroll of Achievement award Ky. Fedn. Bus. and Profl. Women, 1978; Ky. col.; Delta Kappa Gamma scholar, 1970. Mem. NEA, Ky. Edn. Assn., Caldwell County Edn. Assn., West Ky. Profl. Guidance Assn., Ky. Vocat. Guidance Assn., Ky. Assn. Vocat. Spl. Needs Personnel, Ky. Assn. Gifted Edn., Profl. Secs. Internat., Bus. and Profl. Women's Club Princeton (past pres.), Council Exceptional Children and Ednl. Diagnostic Services, Phi Theta Kappa. Democrat. Baptist. Home: 906 W Main Princeton KY 42445 Office: Caldwell County Area Vocat Ctr PO Box 350 Princeton KY 42445

OLIVER, WILLIAM HUNTLEY, orthodontist; b. Nashville, Aug. 4, 1920; s. Oren Austin and Floy (Huntley) O.; m. Gray Moore, Nov. 27, 1943; children—William Huntley, Jr., Douglass M., Gray A., Floy A. D.M.D., U. Louisville, 1943. Diplomate Am. Bd. Orthodontics. Vis. instr. Meharry Dental Sch., Nashville, Washington U. Orthodontic Dept., St. Louis, U. Mo.-Kansas City, U. N.C., Chapel Hill. Editor, pub. Orthodontic Directory of the World; also articles. Served to lt. USN, 1943-46, P.T.O. Fellow Am. Coll. Dentists, Internat. Coll. Dentists; mem. Am. Assn. Orthodontists (Spl. Service award 1984), So. Soc. Orthodontists (sec., treas., pres.), Tenn. Dental Assn., Nashville Dental Soc. (sec., treas., pres.). Presbyterian. Club: Belle Meade Country (bd. dirs. 1976-79). Lodges: Masons, Shriners. Avocations: golf; tennis; snow skiing; travel. Home: 229 Deer Park Dr Nashville TN 37205 Office: Oliver and Oliver PC 1915 Broadway Nashville TN 37203

OLKINETZKY, SAM, former museum director, artist, educator; b. N.Y.C., Nov. 22, 1919; s. Isidor and Jennie O.; B.A., Bklyn. Coll., 1942; postgrad. Inst. Fine Arts, N.Y. U., 1946-47; m. Sammie Lee Sturdevant, Dec. 20, 1959; children—Joy Shan, Tova Shana. Asst. prof. art and humanities Okla. A&M U., Stillwater, 1947-57; vis. asst. prof. art U. Okla., Norman, 1957-58, assoc. prof. art, dir. Mus. of Art, 1959-84, now dir. and prof. emeritus; vis. prof. art and humanities U. Ark., Fayetteville, 1962-63, 67-68, Langston (Okla.) U., 1969-70; art cons. Kerr-McGee Industries, Inc.; advisor State of Okla. Visual Arts; mem. State Art Collection Com. Mem. Norman Arts and Humanities Council; one man exhibitions include: Arts Place II, Okla. Art Center, Kirkpatrick Art Gallery represented in permanent collections: Philbrook Art Center, Tulsa, Okla. Art Center, Mus. Art. U. Okla. Served with USAAF, 1942-45. Mem. Okla. Museums Assn. (pres. 1978-79), Internat. Council Museums, Mountain-Plains Museums Assn., Am. Assn. Museums, Western Assn. Art Museums. Route 1 Box 151-A Norman OK 73072

OLLING, EDWARD HENRY, aerospace engineer, consulting company executive; b. Zion, Ill., Feb. 18, 1922; s. Edward and Lydia Ester (Amstudz) O.; children—Linda L. Olling Taylor, Charles R., Carole Olling Forrest. B.S.M.E., Purdue U., 1949; postgrad. UCLA, 1952-54, U. Houston, 1963-66. Registered profl. engr., Tex. Sr. thermodynamics engr. Lockheed Aircraft Corp., Burbank, Calif., 1954-56; project mgr. NASA Project Mercury, Garrett Airesearch Corp., Los Angeles, 1956-60; dep. asst. mgr. Apollo Project, chief future projects (originator Apollo Soyuz, Skylab, Spacelab, Space Shuttle, Space Sta. concepts), chief Advanced Earth Orbital Missions Office and Space Sta. Office, NASA, Houston, 1960-70; dir. Galaxy Engring. Inc., Captiva Island, Fla., 1971—; cons. in oceanography, energy, environ., conservation. Pres. Captiva Island Wildlife Sci. Research Found.; bd. dirs. Captiva Seaside Flora and Fauna Research Found. Ctr., Concerned Captiva Citizens; mem. Lee County Democratic Exec. Com.; del. Dem. State Polit. Conv. and Nat. Conv., 1983-84; chmn. and commr. Captiva Erosion Prevention Dist.; pres. Satellite-TV Communications Enterprises (including LPTV Sta.); nat. campaign worker John Glenn for Pres. including Fla. steering com., 1984; pres. Theodore Roosevelt chpt. and Meml. Gardens Captiva Audubon Soc. Served with USAAF, 1942-46. Recipient sustained superior performance award NASA, Inventions and Contbn. award. Mem. Nat. Space Inst., Nat. Energy Inst., Nat. Audubon Soc., Sanibel Captiva Conservation Assn., Captiva Civic Assn., Am. Stamp Dealers Assn., Fla. Stamp Dealers Assn., Am. Topical Assn., Rocket Mail Soc., Tex. Profl. Engring. Soc., Am. Legion, Support Nuclear Energy Soc. (pres.), Strengthen Am. Def. Assn., LBJ Space Ctr. Stamp Club, Jack Knight Aerospace Philatelic Assn. Club: Purdue of S.W. Fla. Contbg. author Enciclopedia Mondadori, Italy; contbr. articles to profl. jours.; inventor in field; concept originator, others. Home: PO Box 278 Captiva Island FL 33924

OLM, LEE ELMER, history educator; b. Appleton, Wis., July 17, 1928; s. Fred John and Ada B. (Grebe) O.; m. Elizabeth B. Schofer, Feb. 6, 1954; 1 child, Anthony Lee. B.A. cum laude, Western Mich. U., 1952; M.A., Cornell U., 1953; Ph.D., U. Mich., 1960. History tchr. St. Johns High Sch., Mich., 1953-55; grad. asst. and teaching fellow in history U. Mich., Ann Arbor, 1955-59; asst. prof. Sam Houston State U., Huntsville, Tex., 1959-60, assoc. prof. then prof. history, 1960—, chmn. history dept., 1976—. Contbr. articles and revs. to profl. jours. Served with U.S. Army, 1946-48. Named Disting. Univ. Prof., Sam Houston State U., 1968. Hon. fellow Anglo-Am. Acad.; mem. Am. Hist. Assn., Orgn. Am. Historians. Office: History Dept Sam Houston State U Huntsville TX 77341

OLMSTEAD, GEORGE TRACY, executive search consultant; b. Savannah, Ga., Apr. 30, 1944; s. George Tracy Olmstead and Julie Ross (Beckett) Olmstead Drew; m. Lilla Calhoun, Jan. 26, 1966; children—Drew, George Tracy, Jonathan; m. 2d, Amanda Brown, Aug. 25, 1978; children—Vanessa, Blake. B.A., U. Ga., 1967; postgrad. Ga. State U., 1977-78. Comml. lending officer C & S Nat. Bank, Atlanta, 1968-72; ptnr. Lane-Olmstead Co., Savannah, 1972-74; mgr. Carswell of Fla., Amelia Island, 1974-76; account exec. Johnson & Higgins, Inc., Atlanta, 1977-79; ptnr. Blackshaw & Olmstead, Inc., Atlanta, 1979—. Treas., bd. dirs. Savannah (Ga.) Symphony Soc., 1972-73, Armstrong State Coll. Athletic Assn., Savannah, 1973-74; mem. adv. com. Bo Ginn for Gov., Atlanta, 1982; capt. Atlanta Arts Alliance Dr., 1981; treas. Young Mens Roundtable, Atlanta, 1983; div. chmn. Atlanta Arts Alliance Drive, 1982, 83; mem. missions com. All Saints Episcopal Ch., Atlanta. Recipient Outstanding Service award Savannah C. of C., 1973. Clubs: Oglethorpe (Savannah, Ga.); Capital City (Atlanta). Home: 36 Wakefield Dr NE Atlanta GA 30303 Office: Blackshaw & Olmstead Inc 134 Peachtree St Suite 400 Atlanta GA 30303

OLMSTEAD, PAUL SMITH, engineering statistician; b. Wilton, Conn., Aug. 10, 1897; s. Alfred Smith and Susan Ball (Downes) O.; m. Ethelwynn Walker, June 5, 1923 (dec. 1985); children—Blair Eugene, Jean Olmstead Witherington. B.S., Princeton U., 1919, Ph.D., 1923. Physicist Western Elec. Co., N.Y.C., 1920, 1922-24; engring. statistician Bell Telephone Labs., N.Y.C., Murray Hill, N.J., Whippany, N.J., 1925-62, head statis. studies dept., 1961-62; sr. cons. engr. Lockheed Electronics Co., Clark, N.J., Sunnyvale, Calif., 1962-63; cons. engring. stats. Little Silver, N.J., Winter Park, Fla., 1963—. Contbr. articles to profl. jours. Fellow Am. Phys. Soc., AAAS, Am. Statis. Assn., Am. Soc. for Quality Control (Shewhart medal 1959), ASTM, Bernoulli Soc., Biometric Soc., Ops. Research Soc. Am., Inst. Math. Stats., Am. Math. Soc., Sigma Xi. Republican. Presbyterian. Club: Univ. Avocations: applications of statistics to science, economics; stock market.

OLNEY, JOHN CRAIG, geologist; b. Houston, Apr. 24, 1954; s. John C. and Dortha (Baxter) O.; m. Kay Underbrink, Aug. 1, 1975; children—Jimmy, Ryan. B.A., U. Tex., 1977. With Oil & Gas Reserves, Inc., Corpus Christi, Tex., 1977-78; ind. geologist, Corpus Christi, 1978-80, 81—; South Tex. div. geologist Paragon Resources, 1980-81. Mem. Am. Assn. Petroleum Geologists, Corpus Christi Geol. Soc., Houston Geol. Soc., Houston Producers Forum. Republican. Clubs: Pharoh Country, Nueces. Home: 4602 Jarvis Corpus Christi TX 78412 Office: PO Box 2572 Corpus Christi TX 78403

O'LOUGHLIN, ROBERT HENRY, marine surveyor; b. Bklyn., Apr. 26, 1940; s. Bermard Thomas and Dorothea (Mitchell) O'L. B.S., SUNY, 1964. Commd. ensign U.S. Navy, 1964, advanced through grades to lt., 1967; lic. deck officer Isthmian Steamship Co., Moore McCormack Steamship Co., N.Y.C., 1964-68; info. specialist U.S. Naval Hydrographic Office, Suitland, Md., 1968-69; ops. mgr. N.E. Columbus, Lines, Inc., N.Y.C., 1969-73; prin. surveyor Hull & Cargo Surveyors, Inc., Balt., 1973-83; marine specialist CIGNA LCS Marine, Inc., Tampa, 1983—. Author: Notice to Mariners, 1968-69. Mem. The Conservative Caucus, Falls Church, Va., 1985. Mem. Soc. Naval Architects and Marine Engrs., Nat. Assn. Marine Surveyors, Am. Boat and Yacht Council. Republican. Episcopalian. Clubs: U.S. Propeller (St. Petersburg, Fla.); Tampa Bay Mariners (Fla.). Avocations: photography; model bldg.; golf; tennis. Home: 1716 Joshua Ct Palm Harbor FL 33563 Office: CIGNA Loss Control Services Inc 2505 Rocky Point Dr Tampa FL 33607

OLSEN, CARL EDWIN, retired manufacturer; b. Clifton, Tex., Aug. 3, 1902; s. Petter and Helene (Fjaestad) O.; B.S., Tex. A. and M. U., 1923; m. Elsie Duncan, Oct. 3, 1923; 1 son, Carl Edwin. Profl. baseball player, 1923-26; pres., gen. mgr., dir. Gearench Mfg. Co., Clifton, 1927-78, ret., 1978; pres. Mgmt. Info. Systems Inc., 1973—. Recipient award of honor Am. Assn. Coll. Baseball Coaches, cert. of appreciation Am. Legion Baseball; mem. Hall of Fame, Tex. A&M U., Tex. Baseball Hall of Fame; Ky. col.; registered profl. engr., Tex. Tex. A. & M. U. Baseball Field named in his honor. Mem. ASME, Am. Soc. Tool Engrs. Clubs: Houston Petroleum, Nomad. Masons, Lions, Yankee Alumni. Patentee in field. Home and Office: PO Box 10051 College Station TX 77840

OLSEN, DAVID, author, patent agent, lecturer; b. Floral Park, N.Y., Dec. 31, 1928; s. Sverre Emanuel and Hilda Marion (Edwards) O.; m. Maria Margareta Frentz, Jan. 15, 1955 (div. 1964); children—Ted, Diane Astrid, Michael David; m. Penelope Popy Karra, Sept. 2, 1965; stepchildren—Estathios Spinos, Maria Spinos. B.S. magna cum laude, Fla. So. Coll., 1978; J.D., Blackstone Sch. Law, 1970. Registered to practice before U.S. Patent and Trademark Office, 1981. Enlisted U.S. Army, 1946, advanced through ranks to sr. master sgt. USAF, 1949, ret., 1971; sr. tech. writer Northrop/Page, Tehran, Iran, 1973-74; sr. publs. engr. Internat. Laser Systems, Orlando, Fla., 1977-78; mgr., writer tech. publs. dept. Litton Laser Systems div. Litton Systems Inc., Orlando, 1978—; cons., guest lectr. U. Central Fla., Orlando, 1981—, advisor dept. English. Mem. IEEE, Soc. Logistic Engrs.; assoc. mem. Patent Office Soc. Republican. Home: 3602 Country Lakes Dr Orlando FL 32812 Office: Litton Laser Systems Div Litton Systems Inc PO Box 7300 Orlando FL 32854

OLSEN, EDGAR OLIVER, economics educator; b. New Orleans, Mar. 13, 1942; s. Edgar Oliver and Georgie Walker (Thompson) O.; m. Barbara Elliott Beasley, June 4, 1966; children—Robert Buckner, Melanie Guerry. B.A., Tulane U., 1963; Ph.D., Rice U., 1968. Postdoctoral fellow Ind. U.-Bloomington, 1967-68; vis. assoc. prof. econs. U. Wis., Madison, 1975-76, vis. prof., 1982-84; prof., U. Va., Charlottesville, 1970—; economist Rand Corp., Santa Monica, Calif., 1968-70; vis. scholar HUD, Washington, 1978-79; cons., 1973-81; dir. Thomas Jefferson Ctr. for Polit. Economy, Charlottesville, 1984—; bd. editors Am. Econ. Review, Princeton, N.J., 1985—. Contbr. articles to profl. publs. Ford Found. fellow, 1967; NIH fellow, 1983; Sesquicentennial assoc. Ctr. for Advanced Studies, 1975; recipient Cert. Spl. Achievement, HUD, 1979. Mem. Econometric Soc., Am. Econ. Assn., Pub. Choice Soc., Assn. Pub. Policy Analysis and Mgmt., So. Econ. Assn. Home: 1606 Jamestown Dr Charlottesville VA 22901 Office: U Va Dept Econs Charlottesville VA 22901

OLSEN, JOHN CALLAWAY, engineer, administrator; b. Roanoke, Va., June 28, 1938; s. Charles Henry and Alice (Callaway) O.; m. Frances Louise Rowe; children—John Callaway, Katherine Page. B.S.C.E., Va. Mil. Inst., 1960; M.B.A., U. Richmond, 1970. Mgr. tech. ops. support Fibers div. Tech. Ctr., Allied Corp., Petersburg, Va., 1976-81, mgr. cost, budgets and adminstrn. engring. dept., 1981—. Served to capt. U.S. Army, 1960-64. Mem. ASCE., Izaac Walton League (corr. sec. 1980-82). Republican. Episcopalian. Avocations: skeet, rifle, pistol competition; photography; bicycling. Home: 2221 Ermavedo Dr Richmond VA 23235 Office: Fibers Div Engr Allied Corp PO Box 31 Petersburg VA 23804

OLSEN, ROBERT JON, banker; b. Port Chester, N.Y., Jan. 25, 1943; s. Clarence O. and Grace Louise (Sofield) O.; m. Bobbet King Cross, 1979; stepchildren—Warren Cross III, Melissa Cross. B.S., in Chem. Engring., Lehigh U., 1964; M.S. in Mgmt. Sci., 1965. Vice pres., dir. Summit Ins. Co. N.Y., Houston, 1971-75; chmn. bd. Sunshine Energy Systems, Inc., Houston, 1976-77; mgmt. cons. Gulf Oil Corp., Houston, 1976-86; v.p. MBank-Houston, 1986—; founder Chicago Pizza Corp., Houston, 1976, dir., 1976—, pres., 1977—; founder, pres., dir. Am. Café Corp., Houston, 1983—. Mem. Am. Inst. Chem. Engrs., Inst. Mgmt. Sci., Tex. Ski Council (pres. 1976-77, nat. rep. 1982—), U.S. Recreational Ski Assn. (dir. 1985) Rocky Mountain Ski Assn. (dir. 1976-87). Club: Space City Ski (pres. 1975-76, dir. 1974-80). Office: MBank-Houston PO Box 2629 Houston TX 77252

OLSON, CHARLES J., advertising agency executive, educational media consultant; b. Ardmore, Okla., June 7, 1945; s. Raymond Kermit and Herbertine (Cummings) O.; m. Karen Lynn Kersey, Aug. 15, 1970; children—Katrina Lynn, Trevor Charles. B.A., Midwestern U., 1966, M.A., 1969; student N.D. State U., 1966-67; Ph.D., U. N.Mex., 1975. Instr., English and communications Lamar U., Beaumont, Tex., 1969-71; lectr. English and communications U. N.Mex., Albuquerque, 1971-76; prof. communications Damavand Coll., Tehran, Iran, 1976-77; writer, producer, narrator Air Tng. Command, U.S. Air Force, Sheppard AFB, Tex., 1977-82, ednl. media cons., 1983—; owner, operator Media Cons., Wichita Falls, Tex., 1979—; pres., gen. mgr. Media Masters Inc., Wichita Falls, 1982—; ednl. media cons. Region IX Edn. Service Ctr., Wichita Falls, 1982—, Vernon Regional Jr. Coll., Tex., 1982; tng. media cons. First Wichita Nat. Bank, Wichita Falls, 1981-82; audio-visual cons. United Way of Greater Wichita Falls, 1982—. Writer, producer, narrator numerous films, tape/slide shows, and TV and radio spot commls. Gold Coat ambassador Bd. Commerce and Industry, Wichita Falls, 1982—. Recipient Best Tape/Slide Show award Tex. Library Assn., 1979; Addy for TV spot comml., 1984; 3 Addys and 3 Silver Microphone awards for radio spot commls., mag. ad, audio-visual presentation, 1985, 86; named Outstanding Vocat. Advisor, Wichita Falls Ind. Sch. Dist., 1982-83, 85. Mem. Assn. for Ednl. Communications and Tech., Nat. Audio-Visual Assn., Am. Film Inst., Wichita Falls Ad Club (v.p. 1985-86), Vocat. Edn. Adv. Com., U.S. Air Force Assn., Phi Delta Kappa. Lodges: Masons, Rotary. Home: 2500 9th St Wichita Falls TX 76301 Office: Media Masters Inc PO Box 547 Wichita Falls TX 76307

OLSON, DOUGLAS JOHN, art educator; b. Wausau, Wis., Aug. 26, 1934; s. Marvin H. and Lucile E. (Mayer) O.; m. Myra E. Fischong, Aug. 3, 1963; children—Dione, Renee. B.F.A., Layton Sch. of Milw., 1962; M.F.A., U. Cin., 1968. Art tchr. Purdy Jr. High Sch., Marshfield, Wis., 1965-66; instr. U. Cin., 1967-68; prof. art Auburn U., Ala., 1968—. Exhibited in group shows at Lagrange Nat. X, 1985 (Best of Show), Statewide Photo Show, Auburn U., 1983 (1st prize), Auburn U. Photo Competition, 1982 (2d prize). Served to staff sgt. USAF, 1954-58. Auburn research grantee, 1982—.

OLSON, HERBERT THEODORE, trade association executive; b. Bridgeport, Conn., Feb. 9, 1929; s. Herbert Theodore and Inez Evelyn (Lindahl) O.; student Heidelberg Coll., 1947-49; A.B., Ohio U., 1951, postgrad., 1951-52; m. Ethel Victoria Cross, Oct. 29, 1960 (dec. 1983); 1 dau., Christina Victoria. Asst. to dean of men Ohio U., 1951-52; with Union Carbide Corp., 1952-71, mgr. employee relations, coordinator public affairs, Chgo., 1967-69, corp. mgr. public affairs, N.Y.C., 1969-71; exec. v.p. Am. Assn. for Aging, Washington, 1971-75; dir. spl. projects Am. Health Care Assn., Washington, 1975-79; pres. Splty. Advt. Assn. Internat., Irving, Tex., 1979—; mem. long-term care for elderly research rev. and adv. com. Dept. Health, 1972-77; mem. Longterm Care grant rev. com. HEW, 1972-77; adv. bd. Allied Bank. Mem. planning commn. City of Torrance (Calif.), 1962-64, city councilman, 1964-67; mem. nat. Exploring com., past vice chmn. nat. events com., ann. meetings com., mem.-at-large nat. council Boy Scouts Am.; chmn. Gov.'s Operation Leegit; adv. bd. Irving Hosp.; bd. dirs. Irving Cancer Soc. Served with USAR. Recipient Disting. Eagle award Boy Scouts Am., 1974, Silver Beaver award, 1968. Mem. Meeting Planners Internat. (charter), Am. Soc. Assn. Execs., U.S. C. of C., Washington Soc. Assn. Execs., Nat. Assn. Exhibit Mgrs., Irving C. of C. (past dir.), Am. Advt. Fedn., Tex. Soc. Assn. Execs., Dallas Soc. Assn. Execs. (v.p. 1985—, vice chmn. bd. Small bus. legis. council 1985—). Lutheran. Clubs: Rotary (past dir.), Las Colinas Country, Las Colinas Sports, Kiwanis (lt. gov. 1967), Masons, Shriners. Office: 1404 Walnut Hill Ln Irving TX 75062

OLSON, JAMES ROBERT, naval officer; b. Columbus, Nebr., Nov. 23, 1940; s. Robert August and Jean Elizabeth Olson; student U.S. Naval Acad.; B.A., U. Nebr., Lincoln, 1965; M.A., Central Mich. U.; diploma Nat. Def. U., 1981; 1 son, Eric Robert. Commd. ensign U.S. Navy, 1965, advanced through grades to comdr., 1980; service in S.W. Pacific, Philippines and Vietnam; operational intelligence mgr. Task Force #168, Alexandria, Va., 1977-80; intelligence program officer Naval Air Facility, Washington, 1980-82; intelligence officer Rapid Deployment Joint Task Force, MacDill AFB, Fla., 1982—; mem. faculty Def. Intelligence Sch., 1970-71; mem. Naval Insp. for Gen. Staff, 1982. Decorated Bronze Star with combat V, Air medal (5), Vietnam Service medal, Republic of Vietnam Cross of Gallantry, numerous others. Mem. Naval Res. Assn. (dir. chpt.), Naval Res. Assn. (dir. chpt.), Ry. and Locomotive Hist. Soc., Am. Assn. Pvt. R.R. Car Owners, Naval Order U.S., Nat. Ry. Hist. Soc., U.S. Naval Acad. Alumni Assn., Nat. Rifle Assn. (life), Colo. R.R. Hist. Found. (life), Internat. Platform Assn., Phi Alpha Theta. Methodist. Clubs: Army-Navy Country; Nat. Office: Rapid Deployment Joint Task Force J-2 MacDill AFB Tampa FL

OLSON, JIM L., psychologist; b. Great Bend, Kans., Jan. 3, 1941; s. Carl Arthur and Zola Aileen (Arndt) O.; m. Eva Marie Marcinkowski, May 7, 1977. B.A., San Jose State U., 1963, M.A., 1964; Ph.D., U. Kans., 1968. Clin. intern Winter VA Med. Ctr. and Menninger Found., Topeka, 1967; pvt. practice psychology, Milw., 1971-78; adminstrv. officer, supervising psychologist Milw. County Mental Health Ctr., 1971-78; dir. psychol. services Health Care Corp., Chattanooga, 1978-81; dir. psychiat. unit Hutcheson Meml. Tri-County Hosp., Fort Oglethorpe, Ga., 1978-81; dir. ops. Psychiat. Units, Health Care Corp., Chattanooga, 1980-81; dir. psychiat. unit ops. Hosp. Corp. Am.-Psychiat. Co., Nashville, 1981-82, dir. clin. programs, 1982-85; dir. splty. units ops., 1985—; asst. prof. psychiatry Med. Coll. Wis., Milw., 1973-78; mem. Milw. Mental Health Planning Council, 1973-78; resource mem. Ga.-Tenn. Regional Health Commn., 1981—. Mem. editorial bd. Neuropsychology Jour., 1978-81. Contbr. articles to profl. jours. Bd. dirs. St. Vincent Girls' Home, Milw., 1973-76. Served with M.C., U.S. Army, 1968-71. Decorated Bronze Star. Mem. Am. Psychol. Assn., Tenn. Psychol. Assn., Nashville Area Psychol. Assn., Sigma Xi, Sigma Phi Epsilon, Phi Kappa Phi. Republican. Methodist. Home: 3904 Trimble Rd Nashville TN 37215 Office: Hosp Corp Am Psychiat Co One Park Plaza Nashville TN 37202

OLSON, ROBERT KENNETH, organic geochemist, researcher; b. Chgo., July 2, 1949; s. Kenneth Gunnar and Madeline Josephine (Ernst) Olson; m. Deborah Irene Coates, May 7, 1981. B.S., No. Ill. U., 1972, M.S., 1974; Ph.D., U. Tulsa, 1981. Seismologist, Seismograph Service Corp., Tulsa, 1974-76; cons. Mapco, Tulsa, 1978-79; research scientist Amoco Prodn. Co., Tulsa, 1980—. Mem. Am. Assn. Petroleum Geologists, Soc. of Econ. Paleontol. and Mineral., Tulsa Geol. Soc., Geochem. Soc., Internat. Geochem. Soc. Republican. Lutheran. Avocations: skiing; chess. Home: 1514 E 17th Pl Tulsa OK 74120 Office: Amoco Prodn Co 4502 E 41st St Tulsa OK 74102

OLSON-WRIGHT, EVELYN JEAN, insurance company executive; b. Lima, Ohio, Feb. 13, 1951; d. Warren Gail and Bertha Eleanor (Neeper) W.; m. Gregory D. Olson. B.A., B.S., Ohio State U., 1973. With WOSU Radio-TV, Columbus, Ohio, 1973; sales rep. Am. Bankers Ins. Co., Lima, 1977; customer service rep. Blue Cross, Lima, 1977-79; with Crown Life Ins. Co., Columbus, 1979, corp. ins. group. rep. Broward and Dade Counties, Hollywood, Fla., 1980-83; mgr. spl. accident and health div. Lexington Ins. Co. affiliate Am. Internat. Group, 1983-84; sales cons. Blue Cross-Blue Shield, Miami, 1984—. Mem. Bus. and Profl. Women, Ohio State Alumni Assn. Republican. Roman Catholic. Home: 3702 NE 171st St Apt 16 North Miami Beach FL 33160

OLSSON, STURE GORDON, manufacturing executive; b. Richmond, Va., July 1, 1920; s. Elis and Signe (Granberg) O.; B.S., U. Va., 1942; m. Anne Shirley Carter, June 8, 1957; children—Lisa Maria, Anne Carter, Inga Maja, Charles Elis. Service engr. Sperry Gyroscope Co., Inc., 1943-44; plant engr. Chesapeake Corp. Va., 1946-51, v.p. charge mfg., 1952, exec. v.p., gen. mgr., 1952, pres., dir., 1952-68, chmn. bd., 1968—; dir. United Va. Bankshares, Citizens & Farmers Bank. Mem. Business-Industry Polit. Action Com.; dir. Am. Paper Inst. Bd. dirs. Va. Forests Ednl. Fund; trustee Chesapeake Bay Found.; sponsor Ducks Unlimited. Served as lt. (j.g.), USNR, 1944-46. Decorated Swedish Royal Order North Star. Mem. Va. Mfrs. Assn. (past pres.), Am. Legion, Am. Horse Council, Raven Soc. of U. Va. Clubs: Capitol Hill (Washington); West Point Country. Country of Virginia, Commonwealth. Home: Romancoke West Point VA 23181 Office: Chesapeake Corp West Point VA 23181

OLSTOWSKI, FRANCISZEK, chem. engr.; b. N.Y.C., Apr. 23, 1927; s. Franciszek and Marguerite (Stewart) O.; A.A., Monmouth Coll., 1950; B.S. in Chem. Engring., Tex. A. and I. U., 1954; m. Rosemary Sole, May 19, 1952; children—Marguerita Antonina, Anna Rosa, Franciszek, Anton, Henryk Alexander. Research and devel. engr. Dow Chem. Co., Freeport, Tex., 1954-56, project leader, 1956-65, sr. research engr., 1965-72, research specialist, 1972-79, research leader, 1979—. Lectr. phys. scis. elementary and intermediate schs., Freeport, 1961—. Vice chmn. Freeport Traffic Commn., 1974-76, chmn., 1976-79. Served with USNR, 1944-46. Fellow Am. Inst. Chemist; mem. Electrochem. Soc. (sec. treas. South Tex. sect. 1963-64, vice chmn. 1964-65, chmn. 1965-67, councillor 1967-70), AAAS, Am. Chem. Soc., N.Y. Acad. Sci. Patentee in synthesis of fluorocarbons, natural graphite products, electrolytic prodn. magnesium metal and polyurethane tech. Home: 912 N Ave A Freeport TX 77541 Office: Dow Chemical Co U S A Bldg B 4810 Freeport TX 77541

OLTMAN, DEBRA ANN, statistics/mathematics educator; b. Aberdeen, S.D., Dec. 13, 1948; d. Stanley John and Margaret Jane (Baxter) Olson; m. Robert Eugene Oltman, Feb. 20, 1971; 1 child, Elizabeth Jane. B.A., U. S.D., 1971; M.A.T., U. Nebr., 1975. Teaching asst. U. Nebr., Lincoln, 1974-75, instr. Extension Div., 1974-75; adj. instr. dept. math. U. Tulsa, 1975-76; instr. stats., math. Oral Roberts U., Tulsa, 1976—. Author: (with G.H. Weinberg, J.A. Schumaker) Statistics-An Intuitive Approach, 1962, 4th edit., 1981, Study Guide for Statistics-An Intuitive Approach, 1981. Campaign leader U. S.D. Century 2, 1982-83. Maude Hammond Fling fellow U. Nebr., 1974-75. Mem. Phi Beta Kappa. Mem. United Ch. of Christ. Club: P.E.O. Home: 4731 S 67th E Ave Tulsa OK 74145 Office: Dept Math Oral Roberts U Tulsa OK 74102

OLTMAN, JOHN HAROLD, patent lawyer; b. Grand Rapids, Mich., Nov. 18, 1929; s. Peter Harold and Hazel Evelyn (Kelly) O.; B.S. in Chem. Engring., U. Mich., 1952, J.D., 1957; m. Lita Marilyn Hagen, Aug. 16, 1952; children—David K., Laura G., John K. Admitted to Ill. bar, 1957, Ariz. bar, 1964, Mich. bar, 1965, Fla. bar, 1968; mem. firms Mueller & Aichele (Attys.), Chgo., and Phoenix, 1957-64, Barnes, Kisselle, Raisch & Choate (Attys.), Detroit, 1964-65, Settle, Batchelder & Oltman (Attys.), Detroit, 1965-67, Settle & Oltman (Attys.), Detroit and Ft. Lauderdale, Fla., 1967-72, Oltman and Flynn (Attys.), Ft. Lauderdale, 1972—. Trustee for pvt. trust. Served with USMCR, 1952-54. Mem. Am., Fla., Broward County bar assns., Am. Patent Law Assn., Am. Judicature Soc., Fla. Engring. Soc., IEEE, Phi Eta Sigma, Tau Beta Pi. Kiwanian (dir. Ft. Lauderdale Club 1972-74, 77-78, pres. 1983—chmn. Key Club com. 1970-78). Home: 2130 NE 55th St Fort Lauderdale FL 33308 Office: 915 Middle River Dr Fort Lauderdale FL 33304

O'MALLEY, KAREN RAE, pharmaceutical services administrator, consultant; b. Charlotte, N.C., May 21, 1956; d. Charles William and Loretta Lee (Powell) O'M. B.S. in Pharmacy, U.N.C.-Chapel Hill, 1979. Registered pharmacist. Staff pharmacist HPI Health Care Services, Inc., Cleveland, Tenn., 1979, traveling pharmacist, Atlanta, 1979-80, dir. pharmacy, Cheraw, S.C., 1980-83, regional mgr. home health care, Charlotte, N.C., 1983-84, dir. pharmacy, Lake Village, Ark., 1984—, asst. area dir., Cheraw, 1980-83, cons. for specialized pharmacy services, Lake Village, 1984—, clin. services reviewer, 1979—. Recipient Merck award U.N.C.-Chapel Hill Sch. Pharmacy, 1979. Mem. Am. Soc. Hosp. Pharmacists, Ark. Pharmacists Assn. (com. mem. 1984-85), Miss. Pharmacists Assn., (profl. affairs com. 1984—), N.C. Soc. Hosp. Pharmacists (membership com.). Democrat. Methodist. Avocations: running; travel; needlework. Home: PO Box 175 Lake Village AR 71653

O'MALLEY, NANCY, archaeologist. B.A. in Archaeol. Studies, U. Tex., Austin, 1974; M.A. in Anthropology, U. Kans., 1979. Research archaeologist Tex. Hist. Commn., Austin, 1972-77; researcher Mus. Natural History, U. Kans., Lawrence, 1977, research asst. dept. geography, 1977-78, research asst. Mus. Anthropology, 1978; project supr. dept. anthropology, U. Ky., Lexington, 1979-80, staff archaeologist program for cultural resource assessment, 1981-84, research assoc. Ky. Anthrop. Research Facility, 1985—, prin. investigator, co-prin. investigator, project supr. various projects; condr. spl. tng. projects, 1982—. Advisor W.S. Webb Archaeol. Soc., 1982-83; active Big

Bros./Big Sisters, Inc., 1982-83. Grantee Ky. Humanities Council, 1983, Ky. Heritage Council, 1983. U. Ky. Research Found., 1982-83. Mem. Am. Anthropol. Assn., Soc. Am. Archaeology, Smithsonian Instn., Nat. Geog. Soc., Soc. Hist. Archaeology, S.E. Archaeol. Conf. Democrat. Contbr. papers to profl. confs., writings to publs. Home: 115 12th St Paris KY 40361 Office: Dept Anthropology 211 Lafferty Hall Univ Ky Lexington KY 40506

O'MALLEY, WILLIAM CHARLES, oil drilling company executive; b. Scranton, Pa., Mar. 4, 1937; s. Russell J. and Helen B. O'Malley; m. Jane L. Lyons, June 20, 1959; children—Catherine, Jennifer, William Charles, Burke. B.S., Scranton U., 1959; postgrad. Advanced Mgmt. program Harvard U., 1976. Ptnr., Arthur Young & Co., 1970-72, mng. ptnr., Newark, N.J., 1973-75, Washington, 1975-81; with Sonat Offshore Drilling Inc., Houston, 1982—, now pres., also dir.; sr. v.p. Sonat, Inc.; dir. 1st City Bank Westheimer; prof. taxation Upsala Coll. Served to lt. U.S. Army, 1959-60. Mem. Internat. Assn. Drilling Contractors (dir.). Roman Catholic. Clubs: Baltusrol Golf, Congressional Country, Champions, Houston, University, Petroleum. Office: PO Box 2765 Houston TX 77252

OMAN, PAUL RICHARD, geologist; b. Manchester, N.H., Sept. 5, 1956. B.S. in Geology and Oceanography, Calif. State U.-Humboldt, 1977; M.B.A., U. Houston, 1984, postgrad. in geology, 1984—. Cons. geologist, Houston, 1978—. Author, organizer: Petrometrics, 1984. Contbr. articles to profl. publs. Mem. Houston Geol. Soc., Am. Assn. Petroleum Geologists. Avocations: sailing; swimming; bicycling. Home: PO Box 590011 Houston TX 77259

O'MEALLIE, KITTY, artist; b. Bennettsville, S.C., Oct. 24, 1916; d. Earle and Rosa Estelle (Bethea) Chamness; m. John Ryan O'Meallie, June 27, 1939 (dec. Apr. 26, 1974); children—Sue Ryan, Kathryn Bethea; Lee Harnie Johnson, Aug. 21, 1976. B.F.A., Newcomb Coll., 1937; postgrad., 1954-59. One-woman shows include Masur Mus., Monroe, La., 1979, Marlboro County Mus. of S.C., 1975, Meridian Mus. Art, Miss., 1981, 85; exhibited in group shows at New Orleans Mus. Art, Contemporary Art Ctr., Meadows Mus., Cushing Gallery, Southeast Ctr. of Contemporary Art, Art 80, Art Expo West, Art Expo 81. Represented in permanent collections New Orleans Mus. Art, Tulane U. Pan-Am. Life Ctr., Masur Mus. Art, Meridian Mus. Art. Nat. officer Newcomb Coll. Alumnae Assn., 1964-66; lectr. exhibitor for many charitable orgns. Recipient WYES-TV award, 1979, numerous awards and prizes in competitive exhibitions. Mem. Artists Equity Assn., Womens Caucus for Art, New Orleans Womens Caucus for Art, Chi Omega. Mothers Club (pres. 1964), Town and Country Garden Guild (pres. 1970). Avocations: bird-watching; bridge; ballroom dancing. Home and Office: 211 Fairway Dr New Orleans LA 70124

O'MORE, ELOISE PITTS, designer; b. Fayetteville, Tenn., June 7, 1911; d. William Woodruff and Josephine Martin (Diemer) Pitts; student Ward-Conley Art Sch., 1928-30, Ward-Belmont Coll., 1930-32; Baccalaureat d'Art Decoratif, Le College Feminin, Paris, 1937; m. James Robert Muratta, Oct. 4, 1929; 1 dau., Donna Maria; m. 2d, Rory O'More, IV, Dec. 26, 1940; 1 son, Rory V. Self-employed designer and muralist, 1938-60; dir. design Stoddards Office Designs, Nashville, 1960-66; partner Mitchell & O'More, designers, Nashville, 1966-69; founder, dir. O'More Sch. of Design, Franklin, Tenn., 1970—; executed historic murals 3d Nat. Bank, Nashville, 1963, First Franklin Fed., 1964, First Nat. Bank, Centerville, 1972, United Am. Bank, Nashville, 1972, Harpeth Nat. Bank, Franklin; lectr. design and decoration for various schs., clubs and bus. orgns. Mem. Heritage Found. Franklin; mem. Cheekwood Fine Arts Center, Nashville; mem. Nashville Hist. Commn. Mem. Interior Design Educators Council, Am. Soc. Interior Designers, Nat. Trust Historic Preservation, Williamson County Hist. Soc., Societe des Arts, Alliance Francaise. Roman Catholic. Office: 423 S Margin St Franklin TN 37064

ONA-SARINO, MILAGROS FELIX, pathologist; b. Manila, May 8, 1940; came to U.S., 1965; d. Venancio Vale Ona and Fidela Torres Felix; m. Edgardo Formantes Sarino, June 11, 1966; children—Edith Melanie, Edgar Michael, Edenn Michele. A.A., U. St. Tomas, Manila, 1959, M.D., 1964. Diplomate Am. Bd. Pathology. Rotating intern N.Y. Infirmary, 1965-66; resident in anatomic and clin. pathology Lenox Hill Hosp., N.Y.C., 1966-71; asst. adj. pathologist, 1972-74; assoc. pathologist St. Francis Med. Ctr., Trenton, N.J., 1974-84, Hamilton Hosp., N.J., 1974-84; pathologist, chief lab. service Louis A. Johnson VA Med. Ctr., Clarksburg, W.Va., 1984—; clin. instr. pathology Columbia U. Coll. Physicians and Surgeons, N.Y.C., 1973-85. Fellow Am. Soc. Clin. Pathologists; mem. Internat. Acad. Pathology, N.Y. Acad. Scis., AMA. Office: Louis A Johnson VA Med Ctr Clarksburg WV 26301

ONDREJCIN, ROBERT STEVE, corrosion chemist; b. Chgo., Nov. 19, 1928; s. John and Susan (Danko) O.; m. Jacqueline Lois Rawlings, Oct. 15, 1955; 1 dau., Ellen. B.S., U. Ill., 1951. Analytical chemist Argonne Nat. Labs. (Ill.), 1951-52; acad. lab. supr. Savannah River Plant, E.I. duPont de Nemours, Aiken, S.C., 1952-60, analytical chemist, 1960-65, sr. chemist, 1965-69, research chemist, 1969-73, staff chemist, 1973-83, research staff chemist, 1983—. Mem. Am. Chem. Soc., Nat. Assn. Corrosion Engrs., Sigma Xi. Lutheran. Home: 111 Burkwood Pl Aiken SC 29801 Office: Savannah River Lab Aiken SC 29808

ONDRIAS, ERNEST CLINTON, engineer; b. Wharton, Tex., May 24, 1946; s. Ernest A. and Edith (Sklar) O.; m. Jan D. Wendel, Sept. 6, 1969; children—Gavin Lee, Bryan Edward. Student Wharton County Jr. Coll., 1964-65. Operator Western Co., Wharton, 1972-75, supr., 1976-79, salesman 1979-80, dist. engr., 1980-85. Contbr. poetry to profl. jours. Served to sgt. USMC, 1964-68. Mem. Soc. Petroleum Engrs., Mensa (bd. dirs. Gulf Coast chpt. 1985—, chpt. v.p. 1986), Intertel, NOW, ACLU. Avocations: literature; running; contemporary music; cooking. Home: Box 1124 Wharton TX 77488

O'NEAL, MICHAEL SHEARER, school principal; b. Quitman, Ga., Aug. 21, 1946; s. Cyril Glynn and Agnes Cornelia (Shearer) O'N.; m. Donna Lynne Hardy, Mar. 29, 1984; children—Christy, Cassie, Matt. B.S. in Math., U. Ga., 1968, M.Ed. in Supervision, 1977, Ed.S. in Edn. Adminstrn., 1981, Ed.D. in Edn. Adminstrn., 1983. Cert. in ednl. adminstrn. and supervision, Ga. Math. tchr. Gwinnett County Bd. Edn., Lawrenceville, Ga., 1968-80, coordinator Program of Edn. and Career Exploration, 1980-81, asst. prin. high sch., 1981-84, prin. middle sch., 1984—; mem. adminstrn. com. Gwinnett County Retirement System, 1982—; mem. classified personnel evaluation com., 1984-85; mem. Gwinnett County calendar com., 1984-85; mem. steering com. 5 yr. plan for Middle Sch., 1985—. Author: The Relationship of School District Size and Property Wealth to Expenditure Patterns for Georgia's School Districts in the Decade of the 1970's, 1983. Bd. dirs. Am. Cancer Soc.; mem. Gwinnett County Leadership Devel. Steering Com., 1985—. Mem. Ga. Assn. Edn. Leaders, Assn. for Supervision and Curriculum Deve., Nat. Assn. Secondary Sch. Prins., Gwinnett County Prins. Assn., Gwinnett County Prins. Exec. Com. (treas. 1985—), Ninth Dist. Prins. Assn. (treas. 1982-85, pres.-elect 1985—), Phi Beta Kappa, Phi Kappa Phi, Phi Mu Epsilon, Phi Delta Kappa, Kappa Delta Pi. Baptist. Avocations: sports; traveling; yard work; woodworking. Home: 3167 Aycliff Ct Lithonia GA 30058 Office: Five Forks Middle Sch 3250 River Rd Lawrenceville GA 30245

O'NEAL, PEGGY ANN, lawyer; b. Houston, Aug. 31, 1952; d. J.W. and Mary Beth (Garnett) O. Student, So. Meth. U., 1970-71; B.A., U. Ark., 1974, J.D., 1976. Bar: Ark. 1976, U.S. Dist. Ct. (we. dist.) Ark. 1976. Asst. atty. gen. State of Ark., Little Rock, 1977-79, state purchasing dir., Little Rock, 1979-81; sole practice, Fort Smith, Ark., 1981-83; assoc. Dorsey Ryan, Atty., Fort Smith, 1983-85, Hardin and Grace, Little Rock, 1985—. Vice pres., sec. Community Band of Western Ark., Fort Smith, 1981-84; pres. Crossover Sch., Fort Smith, 1981, Comprehensive Juvenile Services, Fort Smith, Sebastian County Young Democrats, Fort Smith; vol. United Way, Fort Smith, 1984; mem. Jr. League of Little Rock, Jr. Civic League, Fort Smith, Ark. Regional Minority Purchasing Council, Sebastian County Democratic Com., Ark. Dem. Com.; mem. adv. bd. trustees Sparks Regional Med. Ctr., Fort Smith; nat. committeewoman Ark. Young Dems. named Outstanding Young Woman of Am., 1984. Mem. ABA (chmn. Ark. pub. contract law sect. 1981-84), Sebastian County Bar Assn. (sec.-treas. 1982-83), Ark., Pulaski County bar assns., Nat. Assn. State Purchasing Officials, Fort Smith Assn. Petroleum Landmen, Phi Alpha Delta (vice justice 1974-75), Alpha Delta Pi. Methodist. Lodge: Zonta (corresponding sec. 1983-84). Home: 1315 Kavanaugh Apt #1 Little Rock AR 72205 Office: Hardin and Grace Suite 200 Union Station Sq Markham and Victory Sts Little Rock AR 72201

O'NEAL, RUTH, pediatrician, educator; b. Dunn, N.C., June 7, 1915; d. Joseph Bryan and Jane (Wilson) O'N. A.B., Transylvania U., 1939; M.D., Med. Coll. Va., 1943; M.S. in Pediatrics, U. Minn., 1948; D.Sc. (hon.), Atlantic Christian Coll., 1983. Diplomate Am. Bd. Pediatrics. Intern Med. Coll. Va., Richmond, 1943-44; Mayo Found. fellow Mayo Clinic Rochester, Minn., 1944-48; practice medicine specializing in pediatrics, Winston-Salem, N.C., 1948-69; asst. in clin. pediatrics Bowman Gray Sch. Medicine, Wake Forest U., Winston-Salem, 1948-51, instr., 1951-59, asst. prof., 1969-72, assoc. prof., 1972—; assoc. dir. pediatrics Reynolds Meml. Hosp., Winston-Salem, 1969-72, dir., 1972-77; mem. staff N.C. Bapt. Hosp., Forsyth Meml. Hosp.; lectr. in field. Contbr. articles to med. jours. Co-leader Triad council Girl Scouts U.S.A., 1954-56, bd. dirs., 1957-60, 61-64, active various coms., 1957—; mem. numerous coms. 1st Christian Ch., Winston-Salem, 1958—, elder, 1974-79; chmn. camp com. local YWCA, 1967-69, bd. dirs., 1967-69; mem. Citizens Planning Com., Winston-Salem, 1963-64; bd. dirs. Forsyth Heart Assn., 1957-80, Polio Found., 1962-65, Day Care Assn. Task Group, 1970, Urban Coalition Day Care Assn., 1970, Forsyth unit Am. Cancer Soc., 1970-80, March of Dimes, 1972—, N.W. Childhood Devel. Bd., Planned Parenthood, 1978-85, Santree Retirement Home, 1978—, Disciples Christ Nat. Benevolent Bd., 1980-86, Battered Women's Services, Inc., 1982-85, Childrens Ctr. for Physically Handicapped, 1982—. Mem. AMA, Mayo Found. Alumni Assn., Minn. U. Alumni Assn., Med. Coll. Va. Alumni Assn., Transylvania U. Alumni Assn., Atlantic Christian Coll. Alumni Assn., Soc. for Research in Child Devel., Forsyth County Med. Soc. (sch. com. rep. 1976-80), Forsyth County Cystic Fibrosis Assn., Med. Soc. N.C., N.C. Pediatric Soc., N.C. Mental Hygiene Soc., So. Med. Assn., Am. Acad. Pediatrics, Ambulatory Pediatric Assn., So. Soc. for Pediatric Research, Internat. Coll. Pediatrics, Am. Womens Med. Assn., Nat. Assn. Child Abuse and/or Neglect, Internat. Soc. for Prevention of Child Abuse and Neglect, So. Med. Soc., Bus. and Profl. Women's Club, N.C. Art Soc., N.C. Soc. for Preservation Antiquities, Photog. Soc. Am., Piedmont Craftsmen. Democrat. Club: Soroptimist (life). Lodge: Order of Eastern Star. Home: 445 Springdale Ave Winston-Salem NC 27104 Office: Dept Pediatrics Bowman Gray Sch Medicine Wake Forest U 300 S Hawthorne Rd Winston-Salem NC 27103

O'NEAL, STEPHEN MICHAEL, software consultant, realtor; b. Denver, Oct. 4, 1955; s. Eldon Ellsworth and Ruth (Law) O'N.; m. Rebecca Susan Miller, Oct. 26, 1985. B.S. in Bus. Adminstrn., U. Colo., 1977. Software salesman Burroughs Corp., Denver, 1977-79; systems analyst ESCOM, Denver, 1979-80; sr. systems analyst Gathers Software, Inc., Denver, 1980-84, computer data ctr. mgr., Dallas, 1984-86, oil and gas trust product mngr., 1986; prime-info. cons., Dallas, 1986—. Asst. master Mile High Council Boy Scouts Am., Denver, 1981-84. Republican. Mem. Religious Sci. Ch. Home and office: 1400 Wisteria Way Richardson TX 75080

O'NEIL, CHERIE JEANNE, accounting educator; b. Denver, June 21, 1945; d. Robert A. and Eugenia G. (Kogel) Thompson; children—Brian Casey, Jennifer Jeanne. B.S., U. Colo., 1968, M.B.A., 1975, D.B.A., 1980. C.P.A., Colo. Revenue agt. IRS, Denver, 1968-73; grad. research asst. U. Colo., Boulder, 1973, part-time instr., 1974-78, 80; asst. prof. Met. State Coll., Denver, 1979; asst. prof. acctg. Va. Poly. Inst. and State U., Blacksburg, 1980-84, assoc. prof., 1984—. Treas. S.W. Va. Soccer Assn., 1982—. Recipient cert. of teaching excellence Va. Poly. Inst. and State U., 1981. Mem. Va. Soc. C.P.A.s, Am. Women's Soc. C.P.A.s. Republican. Episcopalian. Contbr. articles to profl. jours. Home: 1501 Nelson Blacksburg VA 24060 Office: Dept Acctg Va Polytechnic Inst and State Univ Blacksburg VA 24061

O'NEIL, EDWARD HERRING, university dean; b. Johnson City, Tenn., Nov. 5, 1952; s. Edward Herring and Inez (Cate) O'N.; m. Patricia Lynn Black, July 1, 1977; 1 child, Emily Ross Black O'Neil. B.A., U. Ala., 1974, M.A., 1975; M.P.A., Syracuse U., 1981, Ph.D., 1984. Asst. to pres. Birmingham-So. Coll., 1976-77; program officer W.K. Kellogg Found., Battle Creek, Mich., 1981-83; asst. dean U. N.C. Sch. Dentistry, Chapel Hill, 1983—. Mem. Am. Assn. Dental Schs., Am. Soc. Pub. Adminstrn.

O'NEIL, JOHN FRANCIS, art educator, artist; b. Kansas City, Mo., June 16, 1915; s. Michael Edward and Emma Josephine (Harms) O'N. B.F.A., U. Okla., 1936, M.F.A., 1939. Dir. sch. art U. Okla., 1951-65; chmn. art dept. Rice U., Houston, 1965-70, dir. Sewall Art Gallery, 1971-77, prof. art, 1978-80, emeritus, 1980—; adv. bd. Houston Art League, 1983—. Served to sgt. U.S. Army, 1943-46. Rice U. grantee 1976, 77, 78; fellow Huntington Hartford Found., 1962; Montalvo Assn., 1963. Home: 2224 Wroxton Rd Houston TX 77005 Office: Rice U Art and Art History Dept 6100 Main St Houston TX 77001

O'NEILL, BRIAN EDWARD, lawyer, oil and gas company executive; b. San Diego, Sept. 10, 1935; s. Edward J. and Susan (Ellis) O'N.; m. Kathryn T. Luongo, May 5, 1962; children—Kelley, Sean. B.S., U.S. Naval Acad., 1957; LL.B., U. Tex., 1965. Bar: Tex. Partner firm Andrews, Kurth, Campbell & Jones, Houston, 1965-75; sr. v.p., gen. counsel Transco Energy Co., Houston, 1975-82; pres. Transcontinental Gas Pipe Line Corp., Houston, 1982—. Served to lt. USNR, 1957-62. Mem. Am., Tex. State, Houston bar assns., Fed. Energy Bar Assn., Am. Gas Assn. (dir.), Interstate Natural Gas Assn. Am., Southeastern Gas Assn. Roman Catholic. Clubs: Univ., Houston Country. Home: 6118 Riverview Way Houston TX 77057 Office: PO Box 1396 Houston TX 77251

O'NEILL, GEORGE JOSEPH, English language educator; b. Youngstown, Ohio, July 17, 1942; s. George Joseph and Bernadette (Kramer) O'N.; m. Carole Diane Gradski, Aug. 20, 1966; children—George Joseph, Christopher Brendan. B.A. cum laude, Youngstown State U., 1965; M.A., U. So. Calif., 1967, Ph.D., 1972. Teaching asst. U. So. Calif., Los Angeles, 1967-68, lectr., 1968-69; asst. research linguist Speech Communications Research Lab., Santa Barbara, Calif., 1969-71; instr. Youngstown State U. (Ohio), 1971-72; asst. prof. Savannah State Coll. (Ga.), 1972-76, assoc. prof., 1976-83, prof. English, dir. Title III programs, 1983—, asst. v.p. for acad. affairs, 1985—. Vice chmn. allocations panel Coastal Empire United Way, 1982—. NDEA Title IV fellow, 1965-67; Speech Communications Research Lab. predoctoral research grantee, 1969-71. Mem. Nat. Council Tchrs. English, Conf. Coll. Composition and Communication, Soc. for Preservation and Encouragement of Barbershop Quartet Singing in Am. Roman Catholic. Office: PO Box 20432 Savannah State Coll Savannah GA 31404

O'NEILL, JOHN JOSEPH, JR., chemical company executive, consultant; b. N.Y.C., Sept. 13, 1919; s. John J. and Margaret (Patterson) O'N.; m. Irene Ray, Apr. 18, 1940; children—Anne, Mary Schuler. B.S. Chem. Engring., U. Mo., 1940. Corp. v.p., mgr. plastics Olin Corp., Stamford, Conn., 1967-71, corp. v.p. devel., 1971-72; exec. v.p. Kleer-Vu Ind., N.Y.C., 1972-76; pres. chief exec. officer Vertac Chem. Corp., Memphis, 1977-80, vice chmn., 1981, cons., 1981—; bus. cons. John J. O'Neill, Pinehurst, N.C., 1982—. Patentee in field. Emeritus trustee St. Mary of the Woods Coll., Ind., 1982—. Fellow Am. Inst. Chemists; mem. Am. Inst. Chem. Engrs. Roman Catholic. Club: Chemist (N.Y.C.). Home: PO Box 429 Pinehurst NC 28374

ONEL, AYDIN, physician; b. Burdur, Turkey, June 1, 1936; s. Emin and Fahriye (Demir) O.; m. Rengin Alptunaer, Sept. 9, 1968; children—Emin Kaan, Fatih Aydin. M.D., Ankara U., 1961; M.P.H., Tulane U., 1969, D.P.H., 1973. Diplomate Am. Bd. Internal Medicine. Resident in surgery Hacettepe Med. Ctr., Ankara, Turkey, 1963-65; resident in pathology E.J. Meyer Meml. Hosp., Buffalo, 1966-67; project dir. Family Health Found., New Orleans, 1971-74; resident in internal medicine Charity Hosp.-Tulane U., New Orleans, 1976-79; practice medicine specializing in internal medicine, Slidell, La., 1979—; pres. Emin Investment Corp.; dir. Nat. Affiliated Corp. Served as lt. physician Turkish Army, 1961-63. Turkish Govt. scholar, 1968-73; Population Council fellow, 1970-71. Mem. La. Med. Soc., St. Tammany Parish Med. Soc. Office: 105 Smart Pl Slidell LA 70458

ONKEN, ARTHUR BLAKE, soil chemist, researcher, educator; b. Alice, Tex., Aug. 13, 1935; s. Arthur Robert and Iley Belle (Dean) O.; m. Cara Fae Morgen, May 27, 1956; children—Blake Morgen, Denise Fae. Student Tex. A&M U., 1953-55; B.S. in Agrl. Engring., Tex. A&I U., 1959; M.S. in Soil Chemistry, Okla. State U., 1963, Ph.D. in Soil Chemistry, 1964. Cert. profl. agronomist, profl. soil scientist. Research asst. Okla. State U., Stillwater, 1959-64; asst. prof. Tex. Agrl. Exptl. Sta., Lubbock, 1964-69, assoc. prof., 1969-77, prof., 1977—; bd. dirs. Sorghum Improvement Conf. N.Am., 1981-85. Contbr. articles to jours. Bd. dirs. Presby. Med. Ctr., Lubbock, 1966-68; scoutmaster troop 404 South Plains council Boy Scouts Am., Lubbock, 1969-74, asst. scoutmaster, 1974—. NDEA fellow, 1960-63; recipient Outstanding Contbns. award, Agrl. Chem. Inst., Lubbock, 1979; named Agrl. Research Scientist of Yr., High Plains Research Found., Plainview, Tex., 1984. Mem. Am. Soc. Agronomy, Soil Sci. Soc. Am., Internat. Soil Sci. Soc., AAAS. Presbyterian. Lodge: Masons. Avocations: hunting; fishing. Home: 2206 58th St Lubbock TX 79412 Office: Tex Agrl Exptl Sta Route 3 Lubbock TX 79401

ONKS, JERRY MCKINLEY, veterinarian; b. Maryville, Tenn., Apr. 23, 1954; s. Ernest Calvin and Barbara Raye (Lambert) O.; m. Jane Lauren Wyatt, July 24, 1976; children—Mary Elizabeth, Katharine Raye. Student U. Tenn., 1972-75; D.V.M., Auburn U., 1979. With Harry B. Prince, D.V.M., Winchester, Tenn., 1979-81; practice vet. medicine, Smyrna, Tenn., 1981—; owner, operator So. Vet. Hosp., Smyrna. Mem. Middle Tenn. Vet. Med. Assn. (sec./treas. 1983, pres. 1984), AVMA, Am. Assn. Bovine Practitioners, Omega Tau Sigma Zeta. Methodist. Club: Smyrna-LaVerghe Rotary. Office: So Vet Hosp 122 Front St Smyrna TN 37167

OOSTING, KENNETH WAYNE, college dean; b. Muskegon, Mich., Nov. 15, 1936; s. Adrian J. and Marguerite F. (Van Westenburg) O.; m. Jacklyn K. Bennett, June 14, 1958; children—Wendy K., Kenneth Wayne II, Jeffrey, Jennifer. Grad. Muskegon Community Coll., 1957; A.B., U. Mich., 1959; M.A., Central Mich. U., 1963; postgrad. Mich. State U., 1963-65; Ph.D., U. Minn., 1968. Cert. tchr., Tenn., Fla. Asst. prof. history Harrisburg Area Community Coll., Pa., 1965-66; adminstrv. asst. to chancellor Minn. Jr. Coll. System, St. Paul, 1967-68; dean curriculum Santa Fe Jr. Coll., Gainesville, Fla., 1968-72; pres. Harford Community Coll., Bel Air, Md., 1972-76; acad. dean Milligan Coll., Tenn., 1976—. Author profl. publs. Past chmn. elders Downtown Christian Ch., Johnson City, Tenn., mem. choir, 1976—; active Young Life, Johnson City, 1978—, past chmn. Kellogg fellow, 1963-64; Gen. Foods fellow, 1961. Mem. Orgn. Am. Historians, So. Assn. Colls. and Schs. (chmn. and mem. vis. coms.), Nat. R.R. Hist. Soc. (Watauga Valley chpt.), Carter County C. of C. (health services council 1983—). Republican. Avocations: railroads; hiking; camping. Home: Route 2 Box 401 Johnson City TN 37601 Office: Milligan Coll PO Box 129 Milligan College TN 37682

OPALA, MARIAN PETER, justice Supreme Court Oklahoma; b. Lodz, Poland, Jan. 20, 1921; s. Antoni and Antonia (Chrobot) O.; came to U.S., 1947, naturalized, 1953; J.D., Oklahoma City U., 1953, B.S. in Econs., 1957, LL.D. (hon.), 1981; LL.M., N.Y. U., 1968; divorced; 1 son, Joseph Anthony. Admitted to Okla. bar, 1953, U.S. Supreme Ct. bar, 1970; asst. county atty. Okla. County, 1953-56; pvt. practice, Oklahoma City, 1956-60, 65-69; referee Supreme Ct. Okla., 1960-65; prof. law Oklahoma City U. Sch. Law, 1965-69; prof. law U. Okla., 1969—, adj. prof., 1980—; jud. asst. to Justice McInerney, Okla. Supreme Ct., 1967-68; adminstrv. dir. Cts. of Okla., 1968-77; presiding judge Okla. State Indsl. Ct., 1977-78; judge Workers' Compensation Ct., 1978; justice Okla. Supreme Ct., Oklahoma City, 1978—; chmn. Nat. Conf. State Ct. Adminstrs., 1976-77. Mem. NYU Inst. Jud. Adminstrn.; mem. permanent faculty Am. Acad. Jud. Edn.; commr. Conf. Commrs. Uniform State Laws, 1982. Recipient NSDAR Americanism medal, 1984; Herbert Harley award Am. Judicature Soc., 1977; Disting. Alumni award Oklahoma City U., 1979; named Outstanding Okla. Pub. Adminstr., 1979. Mem. Am., Okla., Oklahoma County bar assns., Am. Soc. Legal History, Oklahoma City Title Lawyers Assn., Order of Coif, Phi Delta Phi. Co-author: Oklahoma Court Rules for Perfecting a Civil Appeal, 1969. Contbr. articles to legal jours. Home: 5709 NW 64th St Oklahoma City OK 73132 Office: 202 State Capitol Oklahoma City OK 73105

OPELLA, JANICE LORRAINE, psychologist; b. Parks AFB, Calif., Aug. 16, 1956; s. Julius Frank and Viola Rhobeana (Long) O. B.S. in Edn., Southwestern Tex. State U., 1981, M.Ed., 1982. Cert. psychological assoc., Tex. Teaching asst. Southwestern Tex. State U., 1978-80, cons., 1982-83; editor Central Tex. Rev., 1981; psychologist Brown Sch., San Marcos, Tex., 1981-83, Travis State Sch., Austin, Tex., 1983—. Contbr. articles to profl. jours. Psi Chi scholar, 1980. Mem. Tex. Psychol. Assn., Southwestern Psychol. Assn., Am. Psychol. Assn. (assoc.) Democrat. Roman Catholic. Club: Psychology Assn. (pres. 1980-81). Avocations: baseball; photography; fishing. Home: 5905A Harwill Circle Austin TX 78723 Office: Travis State Sch Unit III PO Box 430 Austin TX 78767

OPPENHEIM, MARTHA KUNKEL, pianist; b. Port Arthur, Tex., June 25, 1935; d. Samuel Adam and Grace (Moncure) Kunkel; m. Russell Edward Oppenheim, June 18, 1960; children—Lauren Susan, Kristin Lee Oppenheim Mortenson. B.Mus. with honors, U. Tex., 1957; M.Mus., U. Tex., 1959; diploma in piano Juilliard Sch. Music, 1960; student Am. Conservatory, Fontainebleau, France, 1956, 58. Soloist with Amarillo Symphony, Austin Symphony, U. Tex. Orch., San Antonio Symphony, Dallas Symphony, Heilbronner Kammer Orch., Heilbron, Germany; solo and chamber music recitals in Tex., N.Y., France; mem. Halcyon Trio, 1974-77; teaching asst. U. Tex., 1957-59, 68-69; pvt. piano tchr., San Antonio, 1962—. Recipient First Place award Internat. Piano Recording Festival, Nat. Guild Piano Tchrs., 1956, 57; First Place award Tuesday Mus. Club Young Artist Competition, 1956; First Place award Young Artist Competition, Amarillo Symphony, 1959; First Place award G. B. Dealey Competition, Dallas Symphony and Dallas Morning News, 1959; Scholarships, U. Tex. and Juilliard Sch. Music. Mem. Music Tchrs. Nat. Assn., Tex. Music Tchrs. Assn., San Antonio Music Tchrs. Assn., Sigma Alpha Iota, Pi Kappa Lambda. Presbyterian. Club: Tuesday Musical (bd. dirs.) (San Antonio). Home: 9118 E Valley View Ln San Antonio TX 78217

OPPENHEIMER, JESSE HALFF, lawyer; b. San Antonio, Jan. 4, 1919; s. Jesse D. and Lillie (Halff) O.; m. Susan R. Rosenthal, July 31, 1946; children—David, Jean, Barbara. Student U. Tex., 1935-37; B.A. with honors in Econs., U. Ariz., 1939; J.D. cum laude, Harvard U., 1942, postgrad., 1946. Bar: Tex. 1946. Ptnr. firm Oppenheimer, Rosenberg, Kelleher & Wheatley, Inc., San Antonio, 1970—; former instr. taxation St. Mary's Law Sch.; lectr. taxation; dir., organizer Southwest Tex. Nat. Bank; dir. Standard Electric Co. Former mem. adv. council and UTSA Assocs., U. Tex.-San Antonio, v.p., 1977-78; bd. dirs., mem. exec. com. Symphony Soc. San Antonio, former pres., chmn. bd.; former trustee Robert B. Green Hosp., San Antonio, St. Mary's Hall girls' sch.; former bd. dirs. Santa Rosa Children's Hosp., United Fund, Children's Service Bur., Bexar County Mental Health Assn.; former mem. planning com. U. Tex. Law Sch. Ann. Tax Inst.; former mem. steering com. Met. San Antonio Urban Coalition; former adv. bd. trustees Southwest Found. for Research and Edn.; former mem. Adv. Hosp. Council, State of Tex.; former mem. adv. bd. Coll.-Community Creative Arts Ctr., Our Lady of the Lake Coll., San Antonio; former mem. Centro-21, San Antonio, 1975-77; former mem. nat. com. Harvard U. Ctr. for Jewish Studies; mem. economy study group Adv. Council Elected Ofcls., Democratic Nat. Com., 1975-76; mem. chancellor's council, Centennial Commn., U. Tex.; trustee, pres. Marion Koogler McNay Mus., San Antonio; former mem. adv. bd. Ursuline Acad., San Antonio; mem. Kenwood Neighborhood Council; trustee The Woodrow Wilson Internat. Ctr. for Scholars, Washington, 1979—. Served to lt. col. U.S. Army; World War II; ETO, PTO. Mem. ABA (former mem. taxation com.). Clubs: Argyle (organizing bd., bd. dirs.), San Antonio Country. Office: Oppenheimer Rosenberg Kelleher Wheatley Inc 620 San Antonio Bank and Trust Bldg 711 Navarro St San Antonio TX 78205

OPPER, JOHN HERBERT, JR., student affairs educator; b. Savannah, Ga., July 13, 1955; s. John Herbert and Sadie (Martin) O.; m. Nancy Elizabeth Newsome, Apr. 16, 1983. B.S. in Criminal Justice, Armstrong State Coll., 1979; M.Ed. in Student Personnel U. Ga., 1984. Grad. asst. U. Ga., Athens, 1980-81, advisor student affairs, 1981—; advisor Province 10, Order Omega Leadership Hon., Athens, 1981, Pegasus Newspaper, Athens, 1981, U. Ga. Interfrat. Council, 1981—; area councillor Pi Kappa Phi, 1982—; chmn. bd. Athens Univ. Coop., 1982—; advisor Southeastern Inter-frat. Conf., Atlanta, 1982-83, 85-86. Recipient Chancellors award Bd. Regents Ga., 1979; named Outstanding Young Man Am., Jaycees, 1980. Mem. Assn. Frat. Advisors, Am. Coll. Personnel Assn., So. Assn. Coll. Student Affairs. Republican. Presbyterian. Home: 175 Baxter Dr Apt I-2 Athens GA 30606 Office: Dept Student Activities U Ga 342 Tate Student Ctr Athens GA 30602

OPPERMANN, GUS JOHN CHARLES, IV, hospital administrator; b. Galveston, Tex., Dec. 18, 1931; s. Gus John III and Katherine Lillie (Shuberg) O.; m. Corrine Mary Guiberteau, June 11, 1960; children—Gus V, Suzanne, Paul. B.S., St. Edwards U., 1953; diploma, So. Meth. U., 1966; postgrad., Grad. Sch. Biomed. Sci., 1980—. Asst. v.p. Hutching Sealy Bank, Galveston, 1958-67; v.p., cashier U. Nat. Bank, Galveston, 1967-78; asst. to v.p. Univ. Hosp., U. Tex. Med. Br., Galveston, 1978-81, exec. dir. bus. affairs, 1981—; faculty assoc. sch. medicine, 1984—, faculty assoc. sch. allied health sci., 1983—, faculty advisor Phi Beta Pi Med. fraternity, 1983—, faculty advisor counciling and adv., 1979—. Budget com. United Way, Galveston, 1958—; treas. Am. Red Cross, Galveston, 1965—; v.p. Am. Heart Assn., Galveston, 1968-73; chmn. Boy Scouts Am., Galveston, 1975-79. Served with U.S. Army, 1953-55. Mem. Am. Hosp. Assn., Tex. Hosp. Assn., Tex. Pub. Employees (pres. 1980-82). Roman Catholic. Lodges: Lions (pres. 1971-72), K.C. Avocations: hunting; fishing; building. Home: 57 Cedar Lawn Circle Galveston TX 77550 Office: U Tex Med Br 8th and Mechanic Galveston TX 77550

O'QUINN, LOUISE REED, nurse; b. Jay, Maine, Dec. 16, 1934; d. James Kenneth and Grace Rose (Berube) Reed; m. Charles Stokes O'Quinn, Nov. 5, 1956; children—Michael Charles, Sandra Louise. R.N. Diploma, St. Louis Sch. Nursing, 1956. Lic. nurse, S.C. Office nurse Raymond Clinic, Republic Panama, 1956-58; surgical staff nurse Crawford W. Long, Atlanta, 1958-59; with Self Meml. Hosp., Greenwood, S.C., 1959—, critical care supr., 1971-84, spl. services coordinator, 1984—. Vice-chmn. Emergency Med. Service Bd., Greenwood County, 1974—. Recipient Employer of Yr. award Self Meml. Hosp., 1971; Spl. Recognition cert. Self Meml. Hosp., 1982. Mem. S.C. Heart Assn. (affiliate faculty). Republican. Roman Catholic. Avocations: weight lifting; reading mysteries; teaching CPR courses. Home: Rt 4 Box 115A Greenwood SC 29646 Office: Self Meml Hosp 1325 Spring St Greenwood SC 29646

ORAEFO, JOHNNY NDUBUISI, geologist, corporation executive, consultant; b. Jos, Plateau, Nigeria, June 26, 1945; s. George Madubike and Comfort O. (Onwuamaegbu) O.; m. Comfort Chinwe Onyekaba, July 9, 1976; children—Adaora, Ebeleann, Oge, Obi, Amy. A.B., U. N.C., 1982; Cert. profl. geologist, N.C. Dir. Flamingo Imports Exports, Inc., Raleigh, N.C., 1984—; cons. Internat. Trades, Raleigh, 1984—. Pres. Nigerian Student Assn. of U.S.A., Raleigh, 1981. Recipient cert. Merit Internat. Traders Assn., 1982. Mem. Am. Assn. Petroleum Geologists, Soc. Econ. Paleontologists Mineralogists, Travel Internat. Club. Mem. Christian Ch. Avocations: tennis; travel; singing; ping-pong; reading. Home: 1802 Cantwell Court Raleigh NC 27610

ORCUTT, BEN AVIS, social work educator; b. Falco, Ala., Oct. 17, 1914; d. Benjamin A. and Emily Olive Adams; A.B., U. Ala., 1936; M.A., Tulane U., 1939, M.S.W., 1942; D.S.W., Columbia U., 1962. Social worker, acting field dir. ARC, LaGarde Gen. Hosp., New Orleans, Fort Benning (Ga.) Regional Hosp., 1942-46; chief social work service VA regional office, Phoenix, 1946-51, chief social work service unit outpatient office, Birmingham, Ala., 1954-57, 58; research asst. Research Center Sch. Social Work, Columbia U., N.Y.C., 1960-62, field adv. social work, 1962, asso. prof. social work, 1965-76; asso. prof. social work La. State U., Baton Rouge, 1962-65; prof. social work, dir. doctoral program U. Ala., University, 1976-84; research cons. Tavistock Centre, London, 1972. NIMH fellow, 1957-60. Mem. Council Social Work Edn., Nat. Assn. Social Workers, Am. Assn. Orthopsychiatry, Found. Thanatology, Arts and Humanities Council (exec. bd.), Ala. Conf. Social Welfare, Group for Advancement Doctoral Edn. (steering com., editor newsletter). Episcopalian. Club: Zonta (mem. exec. bd., 2d v.p.). Author: (with Harry P. Orcutt) America's Riding Horses, 1958; (with Elizabeth R. Prichard, Jean Collard, Austin H. Kutscher, Irene Seeland, Nathan Lefkowitz) Social Work with the Dying Patient and the Family, 1977; (with others) Social Work and Thanatology, 1980; editor: Poverty and Social Casework Services, 1974; editorial bd. Jour. Social Work, 1982-84; contbr. articles to profl. books and jours. Home: 222 Fox Run Tuscaloosa AL 35406 Office: PO Box 1935 University AL 35486

ORDONEZ, ALBERTO J., lawyer; b. Havana, Cuba, Feb. 6, 1952; came to U.S., 1960; s. Antonio Rafael and Lucila (Castellvi) O.; m. Sally Martinez, Aug. 8, 1970; children—Jennifer Ann, Christopher Albert. B.S. Bus., Eastern Ill. U., 1975; J.D., U. Miami, 1979. Bar: Ill. 1979, Fla. 1982, U.S. Dist. Ct. Ill. 1980. Assoc. Conklin & Adler, Ltd., Chgo., 1979-81; assoc. Lapidus & Stettin, Miami, Fla., 1981-83; owner Alberto J. Ordonez, P.A., Miami, 1983—; dir. Monyn & Monyn, Inc., Miami; instr. Fla. Internat. U., Miami, 1983—. Named All Am. Athlete NCAA, 1973, 74, 75; Outstanding Athlete Eastern Ill. U., Charleston, 1975. Mem. ABA, Ill. Bar Assn., Chgo. Bar Assn., Fla. Bar Assn., Cuban Am. Bar Assn., Latin Am. C. of C., Inter-Am. C. of C.

O'REILLY, JAMES EMIL, chemistry educator; b. Cleve., Jan. 14, 1945; s. James Emmitt and Nella (DelCol) O'R.; m. Carol Anne Doehner, Aug. 12, 1968; children—J. Kevin, M. Shannon. B.S., U. Notre Dame, 1967; Ph.D., U. Mich., 1971. Research assoc. U. Ill., Urbana, 1971-73; vis. scientist FDA, Washington, 1980-81; asst. prof. U. Ky., Lexington, 1973-79, assoc. prof. chemistry, 1979—. Nat. Merit scholar, 1963-67; NDEA fellow, 1967-70; NSF fellow, 1970-71. Mem. Am. Chem. Soc., Soc. Applied Spectroscopy, Ky. Acad. Sci., U.S. Soccer Fedn., Central Ky. Soccer Ofcls. Assn., Sigma Xi. Roman Catholic. Editor: (with H.H. Bauer and G.D. Christian) Instrumental Analysis, 1978, 2d edit., 1986; contbr. articles to profl. jours. Home: 369 Henry Clay Blvd Lexington KY 40502 Office: Dept Chemistry Univ Ky Lexington KY 40506

O'REILLY, PATRICK ARTHUR, vocational industrial educator; b. Newport News, Va., Nov. 24, 1944; s. George Christopher and Myrtle Lucille (Mott) O'R.; m. Thresa Annette Vinardi, Aug. 19, 1966 (div. 1982); m. Brenda Ann Hines, June 26, 1982; children—Christopher Sean, Shannon Arthur. B.S., Pitts. State U., 1967, M.S., 1970; Ph.D., Pa. State U., 1973. Welder, Spicer Welding Service, Pittsburg, Kans., 1964-67, 1969-70, research asst., research assoc. dept. vocat. edn. Pa. State U., State College, 1970-73; asst. prof. indsl. edn. Alcorn State U., Lorman, Miss., 1973-74; research assoc. No. Ariz. U., Flagstaff, 1974-75; research assoc., asst. to dir. Va. Poly. Inst. and State U., Blacksburg, 1975-78, asst. prof. vocat.-indsl. edn. 1978-81, assoc. prof., 1981—. Served to 1st lt. U.S. Army, 1967-69. Mem. Nat. Assn. Trade and Indsl. Edn., Nat. Assn. Indsl. and Tech. Tchr. Educators, Nat. Employment and Tng. Assn., Am. Vocat. Assn., Am. Vocat. Edn. Research Assn., Am. Vocat. Info. Assn., Va. Assn. Trade and Indsl. Edn., Va. Employment and Tng. Assn., Vocat. Indsl. Clubs of Am., Va. Vocat. Assn., Phi Delta Kappa, Iota Lambda Sigma. Democrat. Baptist. Editor, contbr. articles to profl. jours.

O'REILLY, PHILLIP ANDREW, mfg. co. exec.; b. Chgo., Dec. 21, 1926; s. Martin and Phyllis (O'Donnell) O'R.; B.S. in Mech. Engring., Purdue U., 1949, B.Naval Sci. and Tactics, 1949; m. Patricia Ann Considine, June 28, 1952; children—M. Gordon, Phillip A., Ann, Robert S., S. Regan. Research and devel. engr. Am. Brake Shoe Co., Chgo., 1949-50, salesman, dist. sales mgr., Rochester, N.Y., 1951-60; with Houdaille Industries, Inc., various locations, 1960—, v.p. mfg. ops., Buffalo, 1972-76, exec. v.p., Buffalo, then Fort Lauderdale, Fla., 1976-79, pres., chief exec. officer, 1979—, also dir.; dir. P.T. Components. Served with USN, 1945-46. Mem. Nat. Machine Tool Builders Assn. (dir.). Office: Houdaille Industries Inc One Financial Plaza 12th Floor Fort Lauderdale FL 33394

O'REILLY, ROGER PAUL, engineering company executive; b. N.Y.C., Feb. 5, 1923; s. John James and Helen Margaret (Reno) O.; m. Dorothy Catherine Hernan, Apr. 16, 1950; children—Richard Paul, Jeffrey John, Diane Margaret, Susan Diane. B.S. in Civil Engring., U. Notre Dame, 1948. Sr. draftsman, field designer, resident engr., constrn. supt., chief estimating engr., utility cons. Ebasco Services Inc., various locations, 1948-71; v.p. Burns & Roe Inc., Jacksonville, Fla., 1971-84; v.p. Ebasco Services Inc., Jacksonville, 1984-85. Mem. Jacksonville (Fla.) Com. 100. Served with U.S. Army, 1943-46. Registered profl. engr. N.J., N.Y., Okla., Oreg., S.C., Alaska, Calif., Fla., Iowa, Kans., Ky., La., Maine, Mich., N.H. Fellow ASCE; mem. ASME, Nat. Soc. Profl. Engrs., Fla. Engring. Soc., Am. Soc. Mil. Engrs., U.S. Com. on Large Dams, Fla. C. of C., Jacksonville C. of C. Clubs: Univ., Univ. Country; Ponte Vedra, Tournament Players (Jacksonville, Fla.); Disabled Am. Vets. Lodges: Kiwanis, K.C. Home: The Fountains Unit 35 Ponte Verda Beach FL 32082

ORGLER, GORDON KENT, physician; b. Neptune, N.J., Dec. 8, 1946; s. S. Fred and Rosemary (Van Dyke) O.; B.S., Wagner Coll., S.I., N.Y., 1969; M.S. in Occupational Medicine, U. Cin., 1976; M.D., Creighton U., 1973; m. Mary E. Hart, May 12, 1973. Resident in occupational medicine U. Cin., 1974-76, AT&T, Basking Ridge, N.J., 1976-77; corp. med. dir. Torrington Co. (Conn.), 1977-78; dir. corp. health and safety M. Lowenstein Corp., Lyman, S.C., 1978—; cons. staff Spartanburg Gen. Hosp. Bd. dirs. Council on Accreditation of Occupational Hearing Conservation. Diplomate Am. Bd. Preventive Medicine. Mem. Am. Occupational Medicine Assn., Am. Acad. Occupational Medicine, AMA, Am. Coll. Preventive Medicine, Carolina Occupational Med. Assn., Spartanburg County Med. Assn., Am. Textile Mfrs. Inst. (med. subcom.). Author: Mercury Intoxication, 1976. Office: M Lowenstein Corp Lyman SC 29365

O'RIORDAN, JOAN PATRICIA, architect, educator; b. N.Y.C., July 14, 1952; d. Jeremiah J. and Helen (Haas) O'R.; m. Joseph C. Migani, Aug. 23, 1975; children—Pia O'Riordan Migani, Michael O'Riordan Migani. B. Arch., Syracuse U., 1975, B.A. in Urban Studies, 1975; M. Arch. in Urban Design, Harvard U., 1977. Registered architect, Mass. Project architect Harvard U., Cambridge, Mass., 1977-80; prin. O'Riordan Migani Architects, Derby, Conn., 1980—, asst. prof. architecture U. N.C., Charlotte, 1982—. Contbr. articles to profl. jours. Recipient Henry Adams prize AIA, 1975, Design Competition Winner, HUD, Dept. Edn., 1979; U. N.C. Urban Inst. grantee, 1983. Mem. Inst. Urban Design, Phi Beta Kappa. Roman Catholic. Home and Office: 8200 Knollwood Circle Charlotte NC 28213

ORLANDO, JACQUELINE BROWER, psychologist; b. Sioux Falls, S.D., June 11, 1937; d. John Thomas Zurcher and Sarah Elizabeth (Sigler) Brower; m. F.A. Orlando, Aug. 3, 1957 (div. Jan. 1974); children—Michael James, Kristine Marie. B.A., Barry Coll., 1959; M.R.C., U. Fla., 1963, Ph.D., 1974. Lic. psychologist, Fla. Asst. prof. psychology U. Fla., Gainesville, 1976-83; pvt. practice psychologist, Gainesville, 1983—. Mem. Am. Psychol. Assn., Southeastern Psychol. Assn., Alachua County Psychol. Assn. (pres. 1985—), Fla. Soc. of Clin. Hypnosis, Soc. Tchrs. in Family Medicine. Republican. Episcopalian. Club: Gainesville Golf and Country. Avocations: scuba diving; ballet; hunting; pottery; figure skating. Home: 1636 NW 51st Terr Gainesville FL 32601 Office: 6717 NW 11th Pl Gainesville FL 32601

ORLOFF, CURTIS BRUINS, geologist; b. Hammond, Ind., Oct. 24, 1950; s. Leo E. and Lydia Ruth (Bruins) O.; B.A., U. Houston, 1972; B.S., Ind. U., 1980. Geologist, computer operator Exploration Logging, Houston, 1980—. Author: Forever Young, 1976; Competition, 1980; Into the Wind, 1973; Scorn of Man, 1974; Thunder in the Wind, 1979. Investigator, Ind. Pub. Interest Research Group, Bloomington, 1978-79. Served to lt. U.S. Army, 1972-74. Mem. Am. Assn. Petroleum Geologists (jr.). Avocations: running; mountain climbing; skydiving; weightlifting; golfing. Office: Exploration Logging 10627 Kinghurst Houston TX 77099

ORLOSKY, DONALD EUGENE, educator; b. Mishawaka, Ind., July 21, 1929; s. Julius Edward and Ella Rebekah Orlosky; m. Diane Blackburn, Apr. 26, 1952 (dec. Dec. 1982); children—Michael J., Scott D., Jon L., Janet S., T. Dean; m. 2d Marian Mitchell, Dec. 10, 1983. B.A., Franklin Coll., 1951; M.S., Ind. U., 1957, Ph.D., 1959. From asst. prof. to prof., head dept. edn. DePauw U., Greencastle, Ind., 1959-69; prof. edn. U. South Fla., Tampa, 1969—; vis. lectr. Ind. U., Bloomington, summers 1959-67; dir. Nat. Leadership Tng. Inst. for Ednl. Personnel Devel., 1971-76; cons. editor Charles E. Merrill, Columbus, Ohio, 1967-80; speaker, project dir. tng. programs U.S. and abroad. Served to lt., arty. AUS, 1951-53. Decorated Air medal; grantee U.S. Office Edn., 1970-77, Sears Ednl. Found., 1971-75, Am. Council Life Ins., 1975-79, Lang Engring. Co., 1973-77. Mem. Am. Ednl. Research Assn., Assn. Tchr. Educators, Assn. Supervision and Curriculum Devel., Phi Delta Kappa. Author: (with B.O. Smith) Socialization and Schooling: The Basics of Reform, 1976, Curriculum Development, 1978; Introduction to Education; Educational Administration Today; contbr. articles to profl. publs.; producer tng. films. Home: 14223 Cypress Circle Tampa FL 33624 Office: FAO 151 4200 E Fowler Ave Tampa FL 33620

ORLOVSKY, DONALD ALBERT, lawyer; b. East Orange, N.J., May 15, 1951; s. M.M. and Eleanor Marie (Karr) O.; m. Susan Denise Coleman, July 12, 1980 (div. 1984). B.A., Cornell U., 1973; J.D., Rutgers U., 1976. Bar: Fla. 1976, N.J. 1977, U.S. Ct. Appeals (5th, 11th cirs.), U.S. Tax Ct., U.S. Ct. Claims, U.S. Supreme Ct. 1980. Mem. Smathers & Thompson, Miami, Fla., 1976-77; ptnr. McCune, Hiaasen, Crum, Ferris & Gardner, Ft. Lauderdale, Fla., 1978—. Mem. ABA, Comml. Law League Am., Assn. Trial Lawyers Am., Fla. Fedn. Young Republicans. Club: Tower (Ft. Lauderdale). Home: 1509 NE 28th Dr Fort Lauderdale FL 33334 Office: McCune Hiaasen Crum Ferris & Gardner 25 S Andrews Ave Fort Lauderdale FL 33301

ORLOWITZ, ELLIS KENT, foreign trade company executive; b. Phila., Jan. 12, 1919; s. Louis Brad and Ida (Katz) O.; m. Gertrude Greenstein, June 9, 1940 (div. 1947); children—Frances Carol Orlowitz Abrams, Marjorie Lynn Orlowitz Shankin; m. 2d June Felix, June 19, 1952; 1 dau., Sheri-Lee. B.A., Pa. State Coll., 1940. Embassy attache, Mexico, 1942-45; founder Swan Products Export Corp., Phila., 1946-58; pres. Camarge Trading, Phila., 1947-48; regional advisor U.S. German Council for Econ. Advancement, N.Y.C., 1948-49; U.S. rep. Swedish Ferrous Inst., 1949-50; distbr. Allied Iron Founders of Britain, 1950-52; U.S. rep. Corp. de Cobre Chileana, Santiago, Chile, 1951-52; pres. Quaker Metals, Miami Beach, Fla., 1952—. Mem. Am. Bus. Delegation to Japan, 1947; chmn. Columbian Am. Economic Growth Council, 1947; mem. Chilean-Am. Universal Council, 1954-56; mem. President's Adv. Council, 1956-61. Club: 22 Karat, Excelsior Consistory. Lodges: Masons, Knights of Red Cross. Home: King Cole Apts Miami Beach FL 33141 Office: 900 Bay Dr PH2 Miami Beach FL 33141

ORLOWSKY, MARTIN L., tobacco company executive; b. N.Y.C., Dec. 7, 1941; s. Solomon and Sylvia (Levine) O.; m. Carolyn Louise Brady, Mar. 25, 1973; children—Daniel, Keith, Matthew. B.A., L.I. U., 1963. Vol. Peace Corps, Bolivia, 1963-65; media planner Compton Advt., N.Y.C., 1968-69, Young & Rubicam, Inc., N.Y.C., 1969-71; v.p. media Grey Advt., N.Y.C., 1971-76; sr. v.p. media and mktg. services Needham, Harper & Steers, N.Y.C., 1976-77; media dir. R.J. Reynolds Tobacco Co., Winston-Salem, N.C., 1977-80, dir. mktg. services, 1980-82, v.p. brand mktg., 1982-84, sr. v.p. mktg., 1984—. Served with U.S. Army, 1966-68. Avocations: fishing; tennis. Office: RJ Reynolds Tobacco Co 401 N Main St Winston-Salem NC 27102

ORME, PAULA, interior designer; b. Stamford, Conn., Feb. 8, 1943; d. Richard Corley and Caroline Frances (Oberle) Tollefson; m. Keith Martel Orme, June 5, 1976 (div. 1984); 1 child, Sherie Lenore Hueter. B.S. in Interior Design, U. Tex., 1965. Designer trainee Tex. Office Supply, Houston, 1965-69; interior designer Litton Office Products, San Antonio, 1971-73, Stowers Furniture, San Antonio, 1973-77, David Collum, Inc., San Antonio, 1977-84; owner, pres. Paula Orme Interiors, Inc., San Antonio, 1979-84, Fabrics & Fanfare, Inc., San Antonio, 1984—; interior designer Glastron/Conroy LTD, New Braunfels, Tex., 1981—. Pres. Darmstadt Childcare Ctr., W.Ger., 1970-71; pres., mem. architecture com. Mission Trace Homeowner's Assn., San Antonio, 1980, 81, 82; active mem. Clarke High Sch. Boosters Club, San Antonio, 1981-83. Named runner-up Model Home Competition Homecraft, 1975; Student Design Competition finalist Interior Design mag., 1965; recipient honorable mention Halo Lighting Co. competition, 1977. Mem. Am. Soc. Interior Designers, (pres. San Antonio chpt. 1979-80, treas. 1978-79, bd. dirs. Tex. chpt. 1979-80). Republican. Baptist. Avocations: skiing; snorkeling; gardening; cooking; reading; traveling; boating. Office: Fabrics and Fanfare Inc 332 W Sunset Rd Suite 2 San Antonio TX 78209

ORMSBY, CHARLES WAYNE, advertising agency executive; b. Indpls., Jan. 28, 1932; s. Charles Frederick and Olive Katherine (Burchfield) O.; m. Carol Ann Watson, Sept. 6, 1952 (div. 1961); children—Cathy Lynne, Christie Lee, Lisa Ann; m. 2d, Patricia Carolyn Moss Andrews, Apr. 22, 1965; 1 son, James Elliott Andrews. Student Butler U., 1950-51. Account exec. Sta. WATI, Indpls., 1967-70, Sta. WISH-TV, Indpls., 1970-75; owner/operator Ormsby Advt., Inc., Indpls., 1975-80, Ormsby Ad Group, Inc., Ft. Myers, Fla., 1980—. Served with USMC, 1951-54. Home: 1033 Longwood Dr Fort Myers FL 33907

ORNER, MARC M(ARKOE), psychotherapist, educator; b. Phila., July 19, 1943; s. George and Rose (Markoe) O.; m. Karen J. Chanow, Dec. 18, 1966 (div. June 1976). B.A., Temple U., 1965, M.Ed., 1968; Ph.D., U. N.Mex., 1971. Diplomate Am. Bd. Psychotherapy. Dir. aftercare unit Coney Island Hosp., Bklyn., 1972-74; dir. psychol. services Dept. of Corrections, Santa Fe, 1974-81; psychologist stress ctr. Hendrick Med. Ctr., Abilene, Tex., 1982-83; pvt. practice psychotherapy, Abilene, 1982—; prof. psychology Pepperdine U., 1979-82; tchr. U. Alburquerque, 1976-81; adj. lectr. McMurry Coll., Abilene, 1982-84. Albert Einstein Med. Coll. fellow, 1971. Mem. Am. Psychol. Assn., Am. Group Psychotherapy, Western Correctional Assn. (pres. 1980-81), Tex. Psychol. Assn., Assn. Counseling Devel. Jewish. Avocations: reading, racquetball, softball, music, hiking. Home: 3198 Chimney Circle Abilene TX 79606 Office: Southwest Profl Ctr 1302 Petroleum Dr Abilene TX 79602

ORNISH, EDWIN PAUL, dentist, medical educator; b. Dallas, Jan. 17, 1925; s. Louis and Hannah (Hoffman) O.; m. Natalie Gene Moskowitz, Nov. 6, 1948; children—Laurel Ann, Dean Michael, Steven Andrew, Kathy April. B.S., So. Meth. U., 1943; D.D.S., Baylor Coll. Dentistry, 1946. Prof. oral diagnosis Baylor Coll. Dentistry, Dallas, 1974—; pres. Natwin Co., Sherry Lane Investments, Inc. Contbr. articles to profl. jours. Served to capt. USAF, 1946-48. Fellow Am. Acad. Gen. Dentistry; mem. Am. Dental Assn., Tex. Dental Assn., Dallas County Dental Assn., Tex. Acad. Gen. Dentistry, Alpha Omega Fraternity. Jewish. Lodge: Masons. Home: 7146 Curtin Dr Dallas TX 75230 Office: 6033 Sherry Ln Dallas TX 75225

OROSZ, JUDY INEZ, pediatrician; b. Woodbury, Ga., July 16, 1945; d. Joseph Michael and Ruby Inez (Brown) D. Student U. Ga., 1963-64; B.S. in Biology, Ga. State U., 1967; M.D., Med. Coll. Ga., 1971. Extern, Gracewood State Sch. Hosp. (Ga.), 1971, staff physician, 1979-80; intern Baroness Erlanger Hosp., Chattanooga, 1971-72; resident T.C. Thompson Childrens Hosp., Chattanooga, 1972-74; practice medicine specializing in pediatrics, Cartersville, Ga., 1974-79; asst. prof. pediatrics Med. Coll. Ga., Augusta, 1980—; asst. pediatric coordinator Univ. Hosp., Augusta, 1980—. Contbr. articles to So. Med. Jour. Fin. chmn. Baptist Med. Dental Fellowship, Memphis, 1983-85, v.p. Ga. chpt., 1985—; v.p., bd. dirs. Augusta Child Advocacy Ctr., 1986—; treas. Women Physicians' Council Med. Coll. Ga. Alumni, 1983-84. Recipient Ann. Appreciation award dept. social work Univ. Hosp., 1985. Mem. AMA (physicians recognition 1981, 84), Med. Assn. Ga., Richmond County Med. Soc., Ga. Chpt. Am. Acad. Pediatrics, Nat. Perinatal Assn. Republican. Baptist. Office: Univ Hosp 1350 Walton Way Augusta GA 30910

OROSZ, VIRGINIA ROSE, consulting firm executive, nutrition consultant, pilot, real estate agent; b. Detroit, Jan. 22, 1944; d. William James Beuthien and Mary Geraldine (Berger) Beuthien; m. Louis Orosz, Aug. 26, 1967; children—Peter, Lisel. B.S. in Food and Nutrition, Mich. State U., 1965; postgrad. in bus. adminstrn. Nova U., 1983. Lic. real estate agent, Fla. Adminstrv. dietitian Henry Ford Hosp., Detroit, 1965-67; therapeutic dietitian So. Baptist Hosp., Atlanta, 1967-68, St. Joseph Hosp., Atlanta, 1968-70; cons. nutrition, Miami, Fla., 1970-78; adminstrv. v.p., corp. sec. and treas. Research Fla., Inc., Ft. Lauderdale, 1978—; v.p. Sales Market Average Rate Trend, Inc.; dir. Permit Mgmt., Inc., Growth Mgmt., Inc.; tax preparer H & R Block, 1981—. Mem. Am. Dietetic Assn., Aircraft Owners and Pilots Assn., Fla. Dietetic Assn., Am. Dietetic Assn. Practice Group Cons. Nutritionists, Council of Pres. Lutheran. Clubs: Ninety-Nines Internat., Inc., Fla. Gulfstream Ninety-Nines, Inc. (chmn.), Fla. Grasshoppers. Home: 311 N 70 Ave Hollywood FL 33024 Office: Research Fla Inc PO Box 290298 Fort Lauderdale FL 33329

O'ROURKE, DOREEN MARY, legal administrator; b. Hartford, Conn., Oct. 16, 1945; d. Leonard Girard and Helen S. (Scanlon) O'Rourke. Student Elizabeth Seton Coll., 1963-64, Hartford Bus. Sch., 1964-65, Miami-Dade Community Coll., 1973, 74, 75. Legal sec. Tarlow, Poulos, Barry & Bernstein, Hartford, 1964-67; legal sec., asst. Gersten, Butler & Gersten, Hartford, Conn., 1970-72, Batchelor, Brodnax, Guthrie & Primm, Miami, 1973-75; legal adminstr. Vernis & Bowling, P.A., Ft. Lauderdale, Fla., 1976—; justice of peace, West Hartford, Conn., 1967. Pres. Young Democrats, West Hartford, 1966; mem. Hubert Humphrey for Pres. Campaign; mem. Daddario for Gov. Conn. Campaign Staff; mem. Ft. Lauderdale Boat Parade Com., 1983. Democrat. Roman Catholic. Office: Vernis & Bowling PA 301 SE 10th Ct Fort Lauderdale FL 33316

ORR, CARL ROBERT, banker; b. Memphis, Oct. 7, 1954; s. Robert Wardlaw Orr and Helen Carol (Heyer) Orr Smith; B.B.A., U. Miss., 1976; postgrad. Nat. Comml. Lending Sch., U. Okla. Norman, 1980, Stonier Grad. Sch. Banking, Rutgers U., 1983. Credit analyst Bank of New Orleans and Trust Co., 1976-77, credit officer, 1977-78, asst. v.p., 1978-82, br. comml. loan officer, 1978, adminstrv. asst. to sr. exec. v.p., 1978-79, comml. loan officer, 1979-82; asst. v.p., exec. and profl. loan specialist Hibernia Nat. Bank, New Orleans, 82-85, v.p., sect. mgr. exec. and profl. dept., 1985—. Bd. dirs. Cancer Assn. Greater New Orleans, 1984-85; mem. gifts-in-kind com. Contemporary Arts Ctr., New Orleans, bd. dirs., 1984-86. Mem. SAR. Republican. Episcopalian. Clubs: New Orleans Country, Pendennis (bd. govs. 1984-86) (New Orleans). Office: 313 Carondelet St New Orleans LA 70130

ORR, ELLIOT, artist, painter; b. Flushing, N.Y., June 26, 1904; s. William Elliot and Helene Courtenay (Couser) O.; m. Elizabeth N. Davidson, Aug. 4, 1933; 1 child, Peter C. Student Storm King Sch., 1919-23, Grand Central Art Sch., 1925-27; studied with Charles W. Hawthorne, 1928, George Luks, 1929. Head drafting dept. Woods Hole Oceanographic Inst., Mass., 1942-45; free-lance artist. Represented in permanent collections Bklyn. Mus. of Art, N.Y., Phillips Meml. Gallery, Washington, Whitney Mus. Am. Art, N.Y.C., Addison Gallery, Andover, Mass., Detroit Inst. Arts, Mich., Springfield Mus. Fine Arts, Mass., Community Fine Arts Ctr., Rock Springs, Wyo., Ill. State Mus., Springfield, Chrysler Mus., Norfolk, Va., Canton Art Inst., Ohio, Heritage Plantation, Sandwich, Mass. Recipient J.L. Weyrich Meml. award Balt. Mus. Art, 1930, Crossett First prize Cape Cod Art Assn., 1948. Home: 442 Broad Ave S Naples FL 33940 Office: Harmon-Meek Gallery 1258 3rd St S Naples FL 33940

ORR, JAMES ROBERT, feature film producer, consultant, author; b. Ann Arbor, Mich., June 28, 1952; s. Robert Frank and Marjorie (McDonnel) O.; m. Bambi Lynne Billac, Dec. 29, 1984. B.S., Bowling Green State U., 1975; M.A. in Film Prodn., U. Houston, 1983. Electronics engr. Phares Electronics, LaSalle, Mich., 1970-71; mgr. Print Shop, Zoreck's Stamp Shop, Toledo, 1970-75; tchr. high sch. Clear Creek Ind. Sch. Dist., League City, Tex., 1975-79; self-employed gen. contractor, Webster, Tex., 1979-81; pres. Panda Movie Corp., Webster, 1979—; seminar speaker Advt. Counsel Toledo, 1984-85; mng. gen. ptnr. Sonnet Prodns., Webster, 1984-85; participant Cannes Film Festival, France, 1985. Co-author screenplay and novel: The Norsemen, 1982, A Sonnet for the Hunter, 1983. Motion picture producer Garbagemen Stole My Clothes, 1980, If They Die, 1981, Witchfire, 1985; producer, dir. They Still Call Me Bruce, 1986. Recipient Key to City, City of Roanoke, Va., 1984; Motion Picture Council Houston scholar, 1982. Mem. Producers Guild Am., Am. Film Inst., Nat. Wildlife Fedn., U.S.A. Film Festival, Producers Assn. Houston, Motion Picture Council Houston (bd. dirs. 1982-83). Unitarian. Club: Toledo Truckers (pres. 1970-73). Avocations: water skiing; woodworking; model building; electronic design; robots. Office: Panda Movie Corp PO Box 57457 Webster TX 77598

ORR, MARSHALL HUGH, geophysicist; b. Providence, Dec. 7, 1942; s. Ernest M. and Elsie W. (Hawk) O.; m. Marjorie B. Yeatts, Aug. 22, 1964; children—Marshall, Jr., Michael S., Matthew W. B.S., U. R.I., 1965; M.S., U. Maine, 1967; Ph.D., Pa. State U., 1972. Asst. prof. of physics Pa. State U., State College, 1972-73, research assoc., 1973-74; asst. scientist Woods Hole Oceanographic Inst., Woods Hole, Mass., 1974-78, assoc. scientist, 1978-81; sr. research geophysicist Gulf Oil Co., Harmarville, Pa., 1981-83; staff geophysicist Sohio Petroleum Co., Dallas, 1983—. Contbr. articles to profl. jours. Mem. Am. Assn. Petroleum Geologists, Soc. for Exploration Geophysicists, Am. Geophys. Union, Sigma Pi Sigma. Avocations: photography; ham radio; sports. Home: 1713 Casa Loma Ct Plano TX 75074 Office: Sohio Petroleum Co Two Lincoln Ctr 5420 LBJ Freeway Dallas TX 75240

ORR, MORRIS LEE, real estate broker; b. Dallas, Oct. 7, 1939; s. Lee Caswell and Juanita Carl (England) O.; m. Catherine Elizabeth Bondies, June 26, 1965; children—Morris Lee, Lindsay Marie. B.A., U. Okla., 1961. Real estate salesman, sales mgr. Empire Properties Realtors, Dallas, 1962-67; pres. Orr, Luedtke, Hightower & Aldridge Co., Realtors, Dallas, 1968-75; pres. Morris Orr Inc., Dallas, 1975—. Bd. dirs., chmn. real estate investment com. Catholic Found. Mem. Greater Dallas Bd. Realtors (bd. dirs. comml. investment div.), Nat. Assn. Realtors, Tex. Assn. Realtors. Republican. Roman Catholic. Home: 3509 Crescent Ave Dallas TX 75205 Office: 12700 Hillcrest Rd Suite 100 Dallas TX 75230

ORR, STEVEN DEREK, health agency executive; b. Joplin, Mo., Feb. 11, 1940; s. Charles Thomas and Janice Laura (MacKinnon) O.; m. Maureen Jane Dumm, May 25, 1968; children—Sean Christopher, Brendan Huan. B.A., U. Ariz., 1972. Vol. Peace Corps, Panama, 1964-66; fgn. service officer Dept. State, Vietnam, 1966-68; mgr. Am. Express, N.Y.C., 1969-70; dir. edn. Planned Parenthood, Tucson, 1972-76; adminstr. Ariz. Med. Assn., Phoenix, 1976-78; regional adminstr. Family Planning Internat. Assistance, Bogotá, Colombia and Miami, Fla., 1978-84; v.p. mktg. MD Resources, Inc., Miami, 1986—; cons. Mgmt. Scis. for Health and the Futures Group, U.S. Aid, 1985-86; mem. Orange State Cons., 1985—; cons. Ariz. Dept. Pub. Health, 1975-78. Pres. Ariz. Pub. Health Assn., Phoenix, 1978. Served with USAF, 1957-60. Mem. Nat. Council Internat. Health, Med. Group Mgmt. Assn.

ORRILL, R. RAY, JR., lawyer, bank executive; b. Port Arthur, Tex., June 17, 1944; s. R. Ray and Jo Ella (LaCaze-Iles) O.; m. Gwendolyn Kay Dartez, Aug. 26, 1967; 1 child, R. Ray; m. Teresa Elizabeth Zeringue, Sept. 24, 1977. B.S., Lamar U., 1966; J.D., Loyola U., New Orleans, 1972. Bar: La. 1972, U.S. Dist. Ct. (ea. dist.) La. 1972, U.S. Ct. Appeals (5th cir.) 1977, U.S. Supreme Ct. 1981; diplomate Nat. Bd. Trial Advocacy. Grad. fellow La. State U. Med. Sch., 1966-69; asst. trial practice Loyola Law Sch., 1971; assoc. Fred J. Gisevius, Jr., New Orleans, 1972-73; ptnr. Orrill & Hecker, New Orleans, 1975-79, Orrill & Avery, New Orleans, 1982-85; vice-chmn. bd. dirs. First Eastern Bank & Trust, New Orleans, 1983—; dir. Real Records, Inc.; mem. adv. bd. dirs. Clin. Mgmt. Assocs., Inc. Author videotape lectr. series: Federal and State Trial Procedure: A Comparison, Inst. Audio Video Ct. Reporting, Inc., 1974. Mem. Am. Trial Lawyers Assn., La. Bar Assn., La. Trial Lawyers Assn., New Orleans Acad. Trial Lawyers, La. Real Estate Lawyers Assn., Fed. Bar Assn., La. Bank Counsel Assn. Methodist. Home: 9956 E Wheaton Circle New Orleans LA 70127 Office: 7240 Crowder Blvd Suite 300 New Orleans LA 70127

ORSBON, RICHARD ANTHONY, lawyer; b. North Wilkesboro, N.C., Sept. 23, 1947; s. Richard Chapman and Ruby Estelle (Wyatt) O.; m. Susan Cowan Shivers, June 13, 1970; children—Sarah Hollingsworth, Wyatt Benjamin, David Allison. B.A. (Disting. Mil. grad. ROTC), Davidson Coll., 1969; J.D., Vanderbilt U., 1972; honor grad. Officers Basic Course, U.S. Army, 1972. Bar: N.C. 1972, U.S. Dist. Ct. (we. dist.) N.C., 1972. Assoc. Kennedy, Covington, Lobdell & Hickman, Charlotte, N.C., 1972-74; assoc. Parker, Poe et. al., Charlotte, 1975-77, ptnr. 1978—. Assoc. editor, contbr. Vanderbilt Law Review, 1971-72. Pres. bd. dirs. ECO, Inc., Charlotte, 1982—; bd. dirs. Charlotte United Way, 1983—, Shepherd's Ctr. Charlotte, 1980-85; mem. planning bd. Queens Coll. Estate Planning Day, 1978—; active Myers Park United Methodist Ch.; mem. YMCA basketball com., Democrat precinct chmn., 1980-85; mem. Dem. state exec. com., 1980; bd. dirs. law explorer program Boy Scouts Am., Charlotte, 1976-78; mem. bd. visitors Johnson C. Smith U., 1985—. Served to 1st lt. U.S. Army, 1972-73. Named Outstanding Vol., Charlotte Observer/United Way, 1984; recipient Bennett Douglas Bell Meml. prize Vanderbilt U. Sch. Law, 1972; Patrick Wilson Merit scholar Vanderbilt U. Law Sch., 1969-72. Mem. N.C. Bar Assn. (probate and fiduciary law sect.), N.C. Bar Assn. Coll. of Advocacy, Mecklenburg County Bar Assn. (law day com., pro bono steering com.), ABA (real property probate sect.), Deans Assn. of Vanderbilt U. Law Sch. (bd. dirs.), Davidson Coll. Alumni Assn. (bd. dirs. 1983), Charlotte Estate Planning Council, Omicron Delta Kappa. Club: Foxcroft Swim and Racquet (pres. 1986). Home: 2819 Rothwood Dr Charlotte NC 28211 Office: Parker Poe Thompson et al 2600 Charlotte Plaza Charlotte NC 28244

ORSINO, ROBERT JOSEPH, electronic company executive; b. N.Y.C., Mar. 25, 1930; s. Joseph Anthony and Marie (Romanelli) O.; m. Toby Aurbach, Aug. 17, 1957; children—Robert K., Stephen T., Richard B. B.S. in Physics, Bklyn. Coll., 1958; M.S.E.E., U. Md., 1967. Engr., mgr. Naval Research Lab., Washington, 1958-85; v.p. Locus Inc., Alexandria, Va., 1985—; chmn. C.O.R.E., Washington, 1977-82; mem. NATO Sub-Group Q, 1984-85. Contbr. articles to profl. jours.; developer high speed signal sorter (HSSS), tactical electronic warfare environment simulator (TEWES). Served with USAF, 1951-55. Mem. IEEE, Assn. Old Crows. Roman Catholic. Avocations: gardening; home projects; computer programming. Home: 12108 Metcalf Circle Fairfax VA 22030 Office: Locus Inc 2560 Huntington Ave Alexandria VA 22303

ORTEGA, BLANCA ROSA, accounting educator, accountant; b. Havana, Cuba, Oct. 4, 1948; came to U.S., 1961; d. Carlos and Ubaldina (Fernandez) Perez; m. Jorge Luis Ortega, Sept. 9, 1967; children—Jorge Luis, Cristina Maria. A.A., Miami-Dade Community Coll., 1969; B.B.A., U. Miami, 1971; M.S. in Mgmt., Fla. Internat. U., 1979. C.P.A., Fla. Acct. RCA Service Co., Miami, Fla., 1967-70; staff acct. Herris & Rosen, Miami, 1971-72, Alexander Grant & Co., Miami, 1972-73; acct. II, Fla. Internat. U., Miami, 1973-75, budget analyst, 1975-77; assoc. prof. acctg. Miami-Dade Community Coll., 1977—; cons. Finkelstein, Mendive, Gonzalez & Co., Coral Gables, Fla., 1982—. Active fund raiser Carrollton Sch., Miami. Mem. Am. Inst. C.P.A.s, Fla. Inst. C.P.A.s. Republican. Roman Catholic. Office: Miami-Dade Community Coll 11011 SW 104th St Miami FL 33176

ORTH, DONALD A., nuclear chemist; b. San Francisco, Oct. 24, 1923; s. Richard Louis and Helen Lillian (Wilson) O.; m. Bertha Jean Ledgerwood, Oct. 11, 1952; children—Claudia Ann, Donna Jean. B.S., U. Calif.-Berkeley, 1948, Ph.D., 1951. With E.I. duPont de Nemours & Co., 1951—, assigned to Savannah River Plant, Aiken, S.C., 1953-71, 74-79, assigned to Savannah River Lab, 1971-73, 79—, departmental fellow, 1985—. Served with AUS, 1943-46. Mem. Am. Chem. Soc., Am. Nuclear Soc., Sigma Xi. Democrat. Methodist. Club: Torch. Contbr. articles to profl. jours. Home: 124 Vivion Dr Aiken SC 29801 Office: Savannah River Lab Aiken SC 29808

ORTH, JOHN VICTOR, legal educator; b. Lancaster, Pa., Feb. 7, 1947; s. John and Mildred (Spalding) O.; m. Noreen Nolan, May 20, 1972; children—Katherine E., Zachary J. A.B. magna cum laude, Oberlin Coll., 1969; J.D., Harvard U., 1974, M.A., 1975, Ph.D. in History, 1977. Bar: Mass. 1974, U.S. Ct. Appeals for 3d circuit 1978. Law clk. to Judge John J. Gibbons, U.S. Ct. Appeals for 3d circuit, 1977-78; asst. prof. law U. N.C., Chapel Hill, 1978-81, assoc. prof. law, 1981-84, prof., assoc. dean, 1984—. Recipient award for excellence in teaching, 1985. Mem. Am. Soc. Legal History (bd. dirs. 1984—), Selden Soc., Soc. for Values in Higher Edn., AAUP, Order of Coif, Phi Beta Kappa. Author: Combination and Conspiracy: The Legal Status of English Trade Unions, 1799-1871, 1977; contbr. articles to profl. jours. Home: 2449 Wayfarer Ct Chapel Hill NC 27514 Office: Van Hecke-Wettach Hall 064A Univ NC Sch Law Chapel Hill NC 27514

ORTH, RICHARD HARALD, psychologist; b. Stuttgart, Germany, July 14, 1942; came to U.S., 1951, naturalized, 1960; s. Harald and Elsa Anna (Mueller) O.; B.A., Stanford U., 1965, Ph.D. (Nat. Inst. Child Health and Human Devel. fellow), 1969; m. Lesley Miriam Swords, Aug. 14, 1965; children—Janet Corinne, Jared David. Sr. research scientist Center Research in Social Systems, Washington, 1968-70, Am. Inst. Research, Washington, 1971-75; cons. Dept. Army, Washington, 1975-78; prin. Richard Orth Assos., Research and Tng. Cons., Vienna, Va., 1978—; instr. Marymount (Va.) Coll., 1972-74. Bd. dirs. Reston Youth Football, 1970-72, Forest Edge Elem. Sch. PTA, 1979-81, Reston Little League, 1970-72; commr. Reston Little League Baseball, 1971; bd. dirs. Reston Children's Center, Inc.; chmn. Christian edn. bd. Good Shepherd Luth. Ch., Reston, 1980. Mem. AAAS, Potomac Human Factors Soc., Am. Psychol. Assn., Va. Psychol. Assn., Soc. Internat. Devel. Republican. Home: 1310 Deep Run Ln Reston VA 22090 Office: 513 W Maple Ave Vienna VA 22180

ORTH, WALTER HERBERT, JR., manufacturing company official; b. Belleville, N.J., May 2, 1944; s. Walter Herbert and Grace Gertrude O.; m. Roberta Ann Letts, July 26, 1945; children—Chelsea Elizabeth, David Erik. B.A., Rutgers U., 1966; postgrad. Centenary Coll., 1980-81. Methods analyst Mut. Benefit Life Ins. Co., 1966-67; with AT&T Technologies, Inc., Harrisburg, Pa., Balt., Phila. and Shreveport, La., 1969—, now mfg. mgr. prodn. control and bus. telephones. Bd. dirs. Salvation Army; mem. Shreveport Leadership Council; Cubscout master Boy Scouts Am.; pres. Emberwood Home Owners; v.p. E. Ridge Swim Team. Served to 1st lt. U.S. Army, 1967-71. Mem. Internat. Comanche Soc., Airplane Owners and Pilots Assn., Soaring Soc. Am., Shreveport C. of C. Republican. Methodist. Lodge: Masons, Shriners. Home: 731 Coachlight Rd Shreveport LA 71106 Office: 9595 Mansfield Rd Shreveport LA 71130

ORTIZ, ADAM JOSEPH, musician, educator; b. Abilene, Tex., Sept. 2, 1934; s. Adam Longoria and Luisa (Gonzalez) O.; B.Mus. Edn., U. So. Miss., also M.Mus.; m. Margaret Lynne Perkins, July 4, 1973; children—Margo, Mark, Daniel. Choral condr. male chorus Keesler AFB, Miss., 1956-58, condr. ann. Messiah presentations, 1977—; choral music coordinator CBS, New Orleans, 1956-58; prof. music, vocal therapist Miss. Gulf Coast Jr. Coll., Jefferson Davis Campus, Gulfport, 1969—. Singer leading roles operas and musical prodns.; condr. community chorus, Gulfport; choral master Community Opera Assn., Gulfport; music dir. First United Meth. Ch., Gulfport; guest condr. New Orleans Symphony, 1956. Served with USAF, 1955-58. Named hon. citizen, awarded key to city New Orleans, 1956. Mem. Choral Condrs. Nat. Assn. Methodist. Author workbook: Fundamentals of Writing/Reading Music, 1977. Office: Dept Music Miss Gulf Coast Jr College Gulfport MS 39501

ORTIZ, SOLOMON P., congressman; b. Robstown, Tex., June 3, 1937; children—Yvette, Solomon P. Student, Del Mar Coll., Corpus Christi, Tex.; cert., Inst. Applied Sci., Chgo.; student, Nat. Sheriff's Tng. Inst., Los Angeles. Constable, Neuces County, Tex., 1965-68, county commr., Nueces County, 1969-76, sheriff, Neuces County, 1977-82; mem. 98th Congress from 27th Dist., Tex., 1982—. Served with U.S. Army, 1960-62. Named Man of Yr. Internat. Order Foresters, 1981. Mem. Sheriffs Assn. Tex., Nat. Sheriffs Assn. Home: 4515 Carlow Dr Corpus Christi TX 78413

ORUM, ANTHONY MENDL, sociology educator; b. Milw., Nov. 20, 1939; s. Maurice Donald and Alma Clara (Osterman) O.; divorced; 1 son, Nicholas. B.A. Antioch Coll., 1962; M.A., U. Chgo., 1965, Ph.D., 1967. Asst. prof. Emory U., Atlanta, 1966-69, U. Ill., Urbana, 1969-72; assoc. then prof., U. Tex., Austin, 1972—; cons. Recipient numerous fellowships and grants. Mem. Am. Sociol. Assn. Jewish. Author: Black Students in Protest, 1972; Introduction to Political Sociology, 1978, 2d edition 1983. Contbr. articles to profl. jours. Office: Dept Sociology U Tex Austin TX 78712

ORWIG, GARY WALTER, instructional technology educator, consultant; b. Kankakee, Ill., Nov. 30, 1945; s. Franklin Werner and Mildred Kathryn (Yeates) O.; m. Joyce Amanda Schultz, Jan. 29, 1967; 1 child, Jennifer Dawn. B.S., Ill. State U., 1967; M.S. in Edn., 1972; Ed.D., Ind. U., 1977. Tchr. Chenoa High Sch., Ill., 1967-73; grad. asst. Ind. U., Bloomington, 1973-75; asst. prof. Towson State U., Md., 1975-77; assoc. prof. instructional tech. U. Central Fla., Orlando, 1977—; cons. Westinghouse Corp., Orlando, 1983-85, Harcourt Brace, Orlando, 1984-85, Digital Video Corp., Orlando, 1983-85. Author: Creating Computer Programs for Learning, 1983; (video disc) Styles of Interactivity, 1985; co-author: The Computor Tutor, 1984. Contbr. articles to profl. jours. U. Central Fla. research grantee, 1984-85. Mem. Am. Soc. Tng. and Devel., Assn. Ednl. Communications and Tech., Fla. Assn. for Media in Edn., Phi Delta Kappa, Kappa Delta Pi. Avocations: electronics; fishing; canoeing. Home: 2216 Conifer Ave Winter Park FL 32792 Office: U Central Fla PO Box 25000 Orlando FL 32816

ORY, CHARLES NATHAN, lawyer; b. Atlanta, Mar. 25, 1946; s. Marvin Gilbert and Esther Rose (Levine) O.; m. Carolyn Suzan Pruett, June 21, 1976; children—Jebidiah Marlowe, Brett Elizabeth. B.A. in Econs., George Washington U., 1968; J.D., U. Tex., Austin, 1972. Bar: Tex. 1972, U.S. Dist. Ct. (ea. dist.) Wash. 1981, U.S. Dist. Ct. (no. dist.) Tex. 1982, U.S. Ct. Appeals (5th cir.) 1982. Trial atty. civil rights div. Dept. Justice, Washington, 1973-82; spl. asst. U.S. atty. Eastern dist. Wash., 1981; asst. U.S. atty. No. dist. Tex., Dallas, 1982—. Served with USAR, 1968-69. Recipient Spl. Achievement award Civil Rights div. Dept Justice, 1979, Horney Gen.'s Spl. Achievement award Dept. Justice, 1986. Mem. Munger Place Hist. Homeowners Assn. (bd. dirs.). Co-founder, mng. editor Am. Jour. Criminal Law, 1971-72. Home: 5020 Junius St Dallas TX 75214 Office: 1100 Commerce St Suite 16G28 Dallas TX 75214

ORZE, JOSEPH JOHN, university president; b. Exeter, Pa., Dec. 11, 1932; s. John Paul and Veronica Marie (Kolcun) Orzehowski; m. Carol Mary Schiferle, Jan. 14, 1956; children—Mark Joseph, Craig Aaron, Noelle Marie. B.F.A. magna cum laude, Syracuse U., 1955, M.S., 1956; Ed.D. with honors, George Peabody Coll., 1970; D.P.A. with honors, Mass. Maritime Acad., 1983. Art specialist Syracuse Pub. Schs., 1955; grad. asst. art edn. Syracuse U., 1955-56, dual instr. art and edn., 1956-59; assoc. prof. art edn. and sculpture State Univ. Coll., New Paltz, 1959-61; assoc. prof., head art dept. Middle Tenn. State U., Murfreesboro, 1961-66; prof., chmn. art dept. So. Conn. State Coll., New Haven, 1966-69; dean Coll. Fine and Applied Arts Southeastern Mass. U., North Dartmouth, 1969-75, acting dean faculty, 1970-71, interim treas., 1971; pres. Worcester State Coll. (Mass.), 1975-82, Northwestern State U., Natchitoches, La., 1982—; sculptor; judge or jury mem. for regional and nat. art competitions and exhbns. NDEA fellow, 1967; recipient Letterman of Distinction award Syracuse U., 1983. Mem. Am. Arbitration Assn. (mem. nat. labor panel), Am. Assn. State Colls. and Univs. (dir. 1978-82, chmn. bd. dirs. 1983-84), Kappa Phi Kappa, Sigma Chi Alpha, Kappa Delta Pi, Phi Delta Kappa. Originator and host TV series Art and Ideas; contbr. articles to profl. jours.

OSAGHAE, MOSES O., political scientist, educator; b. Benin City, Nigeria, Apr. 17, 1949; came to U.S., 1975; s. Geoffrey Omoghan and Agnes Esengbe (Isibor) O.; m. Esther A. Osakue, Sept. 2, 1972; children—Osariemen Joy, Igbovomwan Timothy. B.B.A., Ft. Valley State Coll., Ga., 1978; M.A., Tex. Tech. U., 1981, Ph.D., 1985. Civil servant Dept. Edn., Benin City, Nigeria, 1967-75; actor Midwest TV, Benin City, 1973-75; instr. Tex. Tech. U., Lubbock, 1981—; dir. Internat. Inst. for Nigerian Devel., Lubbock, 1983—. Recipient Billy Ross award Dept. Mass Communications, Tex. Tech. U., 1980-81; Best Mgr. award Internat. Ctr. for Arid and Semi-Arid Land Studies, Tex. Tech. U., 1983-84; Lubbock Rotary award, 1984. Mem. Nat. Advt. Assn., Am. Polit. Sci. Assn., Acad. of Polit. Sci. Assn., Pi Sigma Alpha. Democrat. Roman Catholic. Home: 59 Nekpen St Benin City Nigeria Office: Box 4222 Tex Tech U Lubbock TX 79409

OSBORN, DAVID HANSFORD, pharmacist; b. Bangor, Maine, Oct. 9, 1959; s. Archie Bell and Margaret Ann (Patenotte) O.; m. Susan Jane Losa, Feb. 26, 1983. BS., Northeast U., La., 1982. Registered pharmacist, La., Tex. Staff pharmacist K&B Drugs, Opelousas, La., 1983—. Recipient Disting. Service award Pi Kappa Alpha, 1982. Mem. La. Pharmacists Assn., Pi Kappa Alpha Alumni Assn. Republican. Baptist. Avocations: golf, gardening. Home: 153 Greenfield Dr Carencro LA 70520 Office: K&B Drugs Heather Dr Opelousas LA

OSBORN, GLENN RICHARD, audio engr.; b. Los Angeles, Oct. 25, 1928; s. Glenn Litz and Nellie (Hoffman) O.; B.S. in Audio Engring., U. Hollywood, 1949; m. Joye Elise Hughes, Feb. 15, 1963; children—Eric William, John Howard. Head transmission engr., 1352 Motion Picture Squadron, Hollywood, 1953-60; head sound dept. Sandia Corp., Albuquerque, 1960-65; supr. sound dept. A-V Service Corp., Seabrook, Tex., 1965—; owner G.R. Osborn & Co., Audio Engrs., Seabrook, 1975—. Served with AUS, 1950-52. Mem. Audio Engring. Soc., Acoustical Soc. Am., Soc. Motion Picture and TV Engrs. Home: 2117 Willow Wisp Dr Seabrook TX 77586 Office: LBJ Space Center Bldg 2 Room 145 Houston TX 77058

OSBORN, JANIE DYSON, early childhood education educator; b. Huntsville, Ala., July 25, 1946; d. Coy Wayne and Alice Caledonia (Hill) Dyson; m. D. Keith Osborn, June 21, 1974; 1 dau., Michelle. B.S., U. Ala.-Tuscaloosa, 1967, M.A., 1969, Ed.D., 1973. Tchr. Bessemer City (Ala.) Schs., 1967-70; adminstr. Jefferson County Head Start, Birmingham, Ala., 1967; reading specialist Hale County Pub. Schs., Akron, Ala., 1971; assoc. dir. Belser-Parton Reading Ctr., Tuscaloosa, 1972-73; coordinator early childhood edn. Columbus (Ga.) Coll., 1973-75; prof., coordinator early childhood edn. North Ga. Coll., Dahlonega, 1975—; cons. World-Book-Childcraft, Inc., Chgo., U.S. Dept. Edn. Child Devel. Assoc. Program, Washington, Ga. Dept. Edn. Author: (with D. Keith Osborn) Cognitive Tasks, 1974, Discipline and Classroom Management, 1981, Cognition in Early Childhood, 1983; contbr. numerous articles to profl. jours. Cons., Kids on the Block Jr. Service League, Gainesville, Ga., 1983. Recipient Outstanding New Prof. award Columbus Coll., 1974; fellow NDEA, 1971-73, Edn. Testing Service, 1973. Mem. NEA (del. 1971), Lower Chattahoochee Assn. for Young Children (pres. 1973-74), Ga. Assn. Young Children (pres. 1975-76), So. Assn. Children Under Six (exec. bd. 1975-76), Internat. Reading Assn. Home: 2719 Northlake Rd Gainesville GA 30506 Office: North Georgia College Dahlonega GA 30533

OSBORN, STEPHEN M., clinical psychologist; b. Odessa, Tex., Nov. 20, 1950; s. D. T. and Marie (Gianetto) O.; m. Deborah Gray, June 21, 1975; children—Stephanie, Kendel. B.A., Tex. Tech U., 1973, M.A., 1974; Ph.D., Tex. A&M U., 1980. Part-time counseling intern Tex. A&M U., College Station, 1977-78, grad. asst., 1978-79; intern Central La. State Hosp., Pineville, 1979-80; coordinator, dir. Human Service Ctr., West Central Ark., 1980-81; dir. youth services Abilene Mental Health Mental Retardation Ctr., Tex., 1983-84; pvt. practice clin. psychology, Abilene, 1984—; cons. stress unit and care unit Hendrick Med. Ctr., Abilene, 1983—. Contbr. articles to jours.; workshops in field. Mem. Am. Psychol. Assn., Tex. Psychol. Assn., Am. Assn. Marriage and Family Therapy (clin.), Nat. Register Health Service Providers in Psychology (council), Psi Chi. Office: 210 Country Pl S Abilene TX 79605 Office: 2449 S Willis St Suite 107 Abilene TX 79605

OSBORNE, HAROLD WAYNE, sociology educator, consultant; b. Eldorado, Ark., Sept. 5, 1930; s. Carl Clinton and Mary Eunice (Peace) O.; m. Alice June Williams, Feb. 15, 1953; children—Michael, Van, Samuel. B.A. in History, Ouachita Baptist Coll., 1952; M.A. in Sociology, La. State U., 1956, Ph.D. Sociology, 1959. Research assoc. dept. rural sociology La. State U., 1954-56; social sci. analyst La. Dept. Agr., Baton Rouge, 1956-58; asst. prof. sociology Baylor U., 1958-60, assoc. prof., 1960-63, prof., 1963—, dir. grad. studies dept. sociology, 1963—; cons. in field; dir. workshops on crime and delinquency. Bd. dirs. Mclennan County Mental Health Assn. (Tex.), 1970-80. Served with inf. U.S. Army, 1952-54. Named Most Outstanding Baylor Prof., Baylor U., 1976. Mem. Am. Sociol. Assn., Southwestern Sociol. Assn., Southwestern Social Sci. Assn., Population Assn. Am., Population Reference Bur., Am. Social Health Assn. (Southwestern regional bd. dirs.). Democrat. Baptist. Co-editor: Research Methods: Issues and Insights, 1971; assoc. editor for sociology Social Sci. Quar., 1965-75. Home: 2717 Braemar Waco TX 76710 Office: Dept Sociology Baylor U Waco TX 76798

OSBORNE, JAMES O., petroleum operator; b. Pauls Valley, Okla., Mar. 5, 1927; s. Oder Ezikeil and Ira (Dunn) O.; m. Margie Faye McElroy, Feb. 22, 1953; children—Kevin James, Lana Elaine. Student pub. schs., Frederick, Okla. Policeman/sgt. City of Levelland, Tex., 1957-78; with Verna Drilling Co., Levelland, 1978-79, safety dir., 1981-83; justice of the peace Hockley, Levelland, 1979-81; pumper Texland Petroleum, Fort Worth, 1983—. Served with USN, 1944-45. Recipient 5 Yr. Safety award Safety Council Police Dept., Levelland, 1962, 10 Yr. Safety award, 1967. Democrat. Methodist. Lodges: Masons, Order Eastern Star. Avocations: golf; baseball; football; fishing; gardening. Home: 316 Cherry St Levelland TX 79336

OSBORNE, JOHN ARTHUR, accountant, university business officer; b. Denver, Feb. 7, 1931; s. Harold Humphrey and Erma (Allison) O.; A.A., Coffeyville (Kans.) Jr. Coll., 1954; B.S. with honors, U. Tulsa, 1956, law student, 1956-58; short course (scholarship student) U. Omaha, 1962. Acct., Pan. Am. Petroleum Corp., 1956-57; sr. acct. Frazer & Torbet, C.P.A., Tulsa, 1957-61; asst. sec.-treas. U. Tulsa, 1961—, comptroller, 1968—, assoc. v.p., 1985—. Gen. chmn. Southwest Bus. Equipment Show of Tulsa, 1965; mem. planning com. Tulsa Conf. Accts., 1965—, mayor's system study com., Tulsa, 1967; asst. treas. St. John's Episcopal Ch., 1977-79; mem. Epis. Ch. Council of Tulsa, 1980-82. Served with USAF, 1951-52. C.P.A., Okla., 1959. Recipient Scholarship key Delta Sigma Pi, 1956; Gold medal award Okla. Soc. C.P.A.s, 1956; cert. of merit Coll. Bus. Administrn., U. Tulsa, 1956, Merit award, Tulsa chapter Systems and Procedures Assn., 1967; named One of Outstanding Young Men in Am., 1966. Mem. Central Assn. Coll. and Univ. Bus. Officers (exec. com. 1963-64, 75-76, treas. 1979-81), Okla. Assn. Coll. and Univ. Bus. Officers (sec. treas. 1973-74, v.p. 1974-75, pres. 1975-76), Assn. Coll. and Univ. Auditors, Am. Inst. C.P.A.s, Okla., Tulsa socs. C.P.A.s, U. Tulsa Alumni Assn. (treas. 1960-70), Systems and Procedures Assn. (treas. Tulsa chpt. 1962-64, pres. 1965-66), Nat. Assn. Accts. (chpt. dir. 1971-76, chpt. v.p. 1973-74, chpt. pres. 1974-75, nat. membership com. 1975-76), Fin. Execs. Inst. (nat. com. on employee benefits), Assn. Coll. and Univ. Research Adminstrs., Coll. and U. Personnel Assn., Photog. Soc. Am. (area rep.), Tulsa Camera Club (treas. 1976-80, 84—, pres. 1982-84), Tulsa Council Camera Clubs (chmn. 1979), Tulsa Photog. Soc., Phi Gamma Kappa (treas. 1962-76, 83—), Alpha Kappa Psi (charter mem. U. Tulsa chpt.). Club: University (incorporator, sec.-treas. 1963-69). Home: 2934 E 26th St PO Box 4614 Tulsa OK 74159 Office: 600 S College St Tulsa OK 74104

OSBORNE, LAWRENCE FREDERICK, fire department captain; b. N.Y.C., July 18, 1947; s. John and Lillian Margaret (Fink) O.; m. Karen Lane, Aug. 19, 1972; children—Stephen, Jessica, Fritz. A.A., Fla. Jr. Coll., 1982, A.Sci., 1983; student Fla. Internat. U. Salesman, Sears, Roebuck & Co., Jacksonville, Fla., 1968-69; lt. Southside Estates Fire Dept., Jacksonville, 1965-69; capt. Jacksonville Fire Dept., 1969—; lt.-advisor Southside Estates Vol. Fire Dept., 1977-85; mem. State of Fla. Adv. council on Emergency Med. Services, 1984-85. Contbr. articles to profl. jours. Bd. dirs. N.E. Fla. Heart Assn., 1970-73; deacon Southside Estates Presbyn. Ch., 1976-79; trustee Peace Presbyn. Ch., 1981, elder, 1986—; chmn. Jacksonville City Employees Heart Fund Dr., 1981—. Internat. Assn. Fire Chiefs scholar, 1983; recipient Disting. Service award, Kiwanis, 1972; named Fireman of the Year, Southside Estates Vol. Fire Dept., 1977. Mem. Fla. State Fireman's Assn., Fellowship of Christian Firefighters, Jacksonville Assn. Firefighters (v.p. 1977-79), Internat. Assn. Firefighters, Profl. Fire Fighters of Fla., 1986—. Democrat. Presbyterian. Clubs: Firefighter's Shrine. Lodge: Masons. Avocations: collecting toy trains; photography; boating.

OSBORNE, THOMAS LEWIS, association executive; b. Independence, Kans., July 7, 1948; s. Lloyd Perry and Marvel Geral (Lewis) O. B.A., George Washington U., 1970. Dir. membership services Inst. Traffic Engrs., Washington, 1971-72; dist. mgr. Jr. Achievement, Atlanta, Ga., 1973-74; exec. dir. Jr. Achievement, Dalton, Ga., 1974-76; field service mgr., dir. publs. Va. Restaurant Assn., Richmond, 1976-79; exec. v.p. Va. Soc. AIA, Richmond, 1980-85; exec. dir. Southeastern Ind. Oil Marketers Assn., Atlanta, 1985—; treas. Foodservice Industry Va. Polit. Action com., Richmond, 1979; sec., treas. Architects Legis. Electoral Response Team, Richmond, 1981-85. Contbr. articles to profl. jours. Chmn. various coms. Richmond City Dem. Com., 1980-83; del. Va. Dem. Conv., 1980-84; treas. Mann-Netherwood Homeowners Assn., Richmond, 1979-83; deacon Second Presbyn. Ch., Richmond, 1979-83. Mem. Va. Soc. Assn. Execs., (pres. 1984), Am. Soc. Assn. Execs., Ga. Soc. Assn. Execs. Home: 1112 St Louis Pl NE Atlanta GA 30306 Office: Southeastern Ind Oil Marketers Assn 6045 Barfield Rd NE Suite 104 Atlanta GA 30328

OSBORNE, VICKIE LEIGH, nurse; b. Winston-Salem, Dec. 7, 1955; d. Mason Lee and Maude Jane (Brown) Osborne. R.N., Forsyth Tech. Inst., 1979; B.S.N. in Women's Health U. N.C.-Charlotte, 1982. Ob-gyn and relief charge staff nurse Forsyth Meml. Hosp., Winston-Salem, 1979-83; nursery, labor, delivery and gynecology relief charge staff nurse Grand Strand Gen. Hosp., Myrtle Beach, S.C., 1983—, mgmt. trainee, 1983—. Active Am. Heart Assn., Am. Cancer Soc. VFW scholar, 1978, 83. Mem. Women in Charge of Their Health. Republican. Baptist. Home: Route 2 PO Box 246 Boonville NC 27011 Office: Grand Strand Gen Hosp 82nd Ave N Myrtle Beach SC 27955

OSBORNE, WALTER WYATT, agricultural consultant, retired educator; b. Halifax County, Va., Oct. 31, 1925; s. Garnett Elmer and Maggie Elvira (Anderson) O.; m. Flora Drewry Bethell, Sept. 2, 1950; children—Walter, Jr., Bethell Anne, Alease Drewry, Anders Wright Osborne Gonzalez. B.S. in Agronomy, Va. Poly. Inst. and State U., 1951, M.S. in Plant Pathology, 1958; Ph.D. in Plant Pathology, Rutgers U., 1962. Area tobacco specialist Va. Poly. Inst. and State U., Boydton, 1953-55; asst. prof. Va. Poly. Inst. and State U., Blacksburg, 1955-58, assoc. prof., 1958-67, prof., 1967-77; pres. Internat. Agrl. Ins., Inc., Tampa, 1980—. Served with U.S. Army, 1943-45. Decorated Croix de Guerre (France); named Man of Yr. in Agr., Colombia, 1972. Mem. So. Soybean Disease Workers Council (1st pres.; Award of excellence 1975, Leadership award 1980), Tobacco Disease Council, Soc. Nematologists (co-chmn. ad hoc com.), European Soc. Nematologists, Orgn. Tropical Nematologists, Am. Phytopathol. Soc., Am. Soc. Agronomy, Extension-Industry Peanut Disease Workers Council (past pres., dir., chmn. regional projects), Tobacco Workers Council (chmn. disease council, nematode control agts., com. for disease loss esitmates), ASTM (chmn. nematology, terminology com.), Va. Acad. Sci., Va. Pesticide Assn., Va. Plant Protection Conf. (organizational chmn.), AAAS, Sigma Xi. Episcopalian. Clubs: Rotary, Lions. Contbr. articles to profl. jours. Address: 4209 Saltwater Blvd Tampa FL 33615

OSBORNE, WILLIAM LARRY, counselor educator; b. Wapakoneta, Ohio; m. Susan Angela Williams, July 29, 1967; children—Eric William, Jack Edward. B.S. in Edn., Ohio State U., 1963; M.Ed., Ohio U., 1966; Ed.D., Western Mich. U., 1970. Cert. counselor, registered practicing counselor. Tchr., Herricks High Sch., N.Y., 1963-64; tchr. Hillside Jr. High Sch., Parma, Ohio, 1964-65; counselor Bd. Coop. Ednl. Services, Bedford Hills, N.Y., 1966-68; instr. Western Mich. U., Kalamazoo, 1969-70; assoc. prof. counselor edn. U. N.C.-Greensboro, 1970—; adj. program assoc. Ctr. for Creative Leadership, Greensboro, 1975—. Author: (with B. Goldman) Directory of Unpublished Experimental Mental Measures, Vol. 5, 1985. Contbr. articles to profl. jours. Named Profl. of Yr., N.C. Rehab. Assn., 1984. Mem. N.C. Assn. for Counseling and Devel. (pres. 1982-83), Assn. for Counselor Edn. and Supervision (newsletter editor 1982-83); N.C. Assn. for Counselor Edn. and Supervision (Counselor Educator of Yr. 1982), Am. Assn. for Counseling and Devel., Am. Psychol. Assn., Nat. Vocat. Guidance Assn. Avocations: music; reading; golf; tennis; automobile racing. Office: U NC-Greensboro Sch of Edn Greensboro NC 27412

OSCAR, KENNETH JOHN, laboratory director, biophysicist, consultant; b. Stamford, Conn., Dec. 26, 1946; s. John M. and Stella G. (Rauch) O.; m. Barbara Betty Davies, Jan. 27, 1968; children—Susan Hope, Kristin Anne. B.S. in Physics, Clarkson Coll. Tech., 1968; M.S. in Physics, Am. U., 1973, Ph.D. in Physics, 1980. Physicist, Barrier Warfare Div., Mobility Equipment Research and Devel. Command, U.S. Army, Ft. Belvoir, Va., 1968-74, chief methodology and devel. br., 1974-80, chief Systems and Engring. Div., 1980-82, assoc. tech. dir., 1982-83, dir. Engring. Support Lab., 1983—; cons. biophysics. Active Cardinal Forest PTA, 1976—; bd. dirs. Va. Ballet Co. and Sch., Fairfax, 1983—; soccer coach Springfield Youth Club, 1976—. Recipient Sci. Achievement award, U.S. Army Mobility Equipment Research and Devel. Command, 1978; guest scientist Naval Med. Research Inst., Bethesda, Md., 1977-79. Mem. AAAS, N.Y. Acad. Scis., Am. Phys. Soc., Bioelectromagnetics Soc., Va. Acad. Sci., Sigma Xi (Sci. Achievement award Belvoir chpt. 1970). Methodist. Club: Lions. Contbg. author articles to sci. publs. Home: 6031 Sherborn Ln Springfield VA 22152 Office: US Army Belvoir Research and Devel Ctr Engr Support Lab Fort Belvoir VA 22060

OSENTOWSKI, MARY JEAN, college administrator; b. Omaha, May 16, 1943; d. Merlin A. and Myrna (Townsend) Noble; m. Francis E. Osentowski, June 5, 1965; children—Tagni, Christopher. B.A. in Edn., Kearney State Coll., 1965; M.S., North Tex. State U., 1972. Instr. Stockton Sch. Dist., Calif., 1965-66, Herman Pub. Schs., Nebr., 1968-69; instr. English Denton Ind. Sch. Dist., Tex., 1966-67, 69-70; instr. speech Richland Coll., Dallas, 1972-81, div. chair communications, 1981—, acting v.p. students, 1984; staff career devel. and renewal program Dallas County Community Coll. Dist., 1979-80, 84-85. Contbr. chpt. to book. Active St. Joseph Lector Group, Richardson, Tex., 1978—, Greater Dallas Youth Orchestra Parent Club, 1982—. Mem. Am. Assn. Higher Edn., Tex. Jr. Coll. Tchrs. Assn., Am. Assn. Women in Community and Jr. Colls., Phi Delta Kappa. Democrat. Roman Catholic. Office: Richland Coll 12800 Abrams Rd Dallas TX 75243

OSGOOD, NANCY JEAN, college educator, author; b. Winner, S.D., July 6, 1951; d. Jack Kent and Lois Emma (Stober) Luttrell; m. Raymond Clifford Jordan, Jr., Oct. 13, 1984. B.A. in Sociology and Spanish, Yankton Coll., 1972; M.A. in Sociology, Drake U., 1974; cert. in Gerontology, Syracuse U., 1979; Ph.D. in Sociology, 1979. Research assoc. Syracuse Research Corp., N.Y., 1975-78; asst. prof. SUNY-Cortland, 1979-80; asst. prof. Med. Coll. Va., Richmond, 1980—; mem. Nat. Com. Vital and Health Statistics, Washington, 1982-84. Editor: Life after Work: Retirement, Leisure, Recreation and the Elderly, 1982; author: Senior Settlers: Social Integration in Retirement Communities, 1982, Suicide in the Elderly: A Practitioner's Guide to Diagnosis and Mental Health Intervention, 1985; co-author: Seniors on Stage: The Impact of Applied Theatre on the Elderly, 1985; contbr. articles to profl. jours. Active Va. State Rehab. Bd., Am. Cancer Soc., selection com. King William High Sch. (Va.), 1985; coordinator sr.'s group Colosse Bapt. Ch., West Point, Va., 1985. Recipient Acad. scholarship Yankton Coll., 1969-72; N.Y. State Dept. Mental Hygiene Research fellow, 1974-75; Nat. Inst. Edn. award, 1975-78; NIMH award, 1977-79; Va. Commonwealth U. grantee, 1981-82; Presdl. Invitation to White House, 1984. Mem. Am. Pub. Health Assn., So. Sociol. Soc., Am. Sociol. Assn. Gerontol. Soc. Am., So. Gerontol. Soc., Internat. Platform Assn. Avocations: playing piano and clarinet; gourmet cooking. Home: PO Box 245 Manquin VA 23106 Office: Med Coll Va Gerontology Dept Box 228 MCV Sta Richmond VA 23298

O'SHEA, HELEN SPUSTEK, nursing educator, administrator; b. Martins Ferry, Ohio, Mar. 5, 1937; d. Stanislaw and Susan Marie (Saliga) Spustek; m. Donald Charles O'Shea, Oct. 20, 1962; children—Kathleen, Sean, Sheila, Patrick. Diploma nursing Martins Ferry Hosp., 1958; B.S. in Nursing, Ohio State U., 1961, M.S., 1962; Ph.D., Ga. State U., 1980. Staff nurse Ohio State U. Hosp., Columbus, 1958-61, instr. nursing, 1961-62; asst. prof. nursing Community Coll. Balt., 1965-68; staff nurse Mass. Gen. Hosp., Boston, 1969-70; assoc. prof. nursing Emory U., Atlanta, 1971—, asst. dean sch. nursing, 1985—. Contbr. articles to profl. jours. Mem. Am. Nurses Assn., Nat. League for Nursing (accreditation site visitor 1984—), Ga. Bd. Nursing (adv. council rules com. 1984—), Sigma Theta Tau (chmn. nominations 1984-85, research award 1984), Alpha Tau Delta. Democrat. Roman Catholic. Avocations: gardening; reading; gourmet cooking. Home: 1146 Lullwter Rd NE Atlanta GA 30307 Office: Emory Univ Sch Nursing Atlanta GA 30322

O'SHIELDS, RICHARD LEE, natural gas company executive; b. Ozark, Ark., Aug. 12, 1926; s. Fay and Anna Mae (Johnson) O'S.; B.M.E., U. Okla., 1949; M.S., La. State U., 1951; m. Shirley Isabelle Washington, Nov. 8, 1947; children—Sharon Isabelle, O'Shields Boles, Carolyn Jean O'Shields Tansey, Richard Lee. Instr. petroleum engring. La. State U., 1949-51; prodn. engr. Pure Oil Co., Fort Worth, 1951-53; sales engr. Salt Water Control, Inc., Ft. Worth, 1953-54, chief engr., 1955-59, v.p., 1956-59; cons. engr. Ralph H. Cummins Co., Ft. Worth, 1959-60; with Anadarko Prodn. Co. and parent co. Panhandle Eastern Pipe Line Co., Houston, 1960—, pres. Anadarko Prodn. Co., 1966-68, dir., 1966—, exec. v.p., Panhandle Eastern Pipe Line Co., 1968-70, pres., chief exec. officer, 1970-79, chmn., chief exec. officer, 1979—; pres., chief exec. officer Trunkline Gas Co., Houston, 1970-79, chmn. chief exec. officer, 1979—; dir. 1st City Bancorp. of Tex., Daniel Industries, Inc. Bd. dirs. Tex. Research League. Served with USAAF, 1945. Registered profl. engr., Kans., Tex. Mem. Am. Petroleum Inst. (dir. 1972—), Mid Continent Oil and Gas Assn. (dir. 1968—), Soc. Petroleum Engrs., Interstate Natural Gas Assn. (dir. 1970—, chmn. 1976-77), Am. Gas Assn. (dir. 1974-79), Ind. Petroleum Assn. Am. (dir. 1971—), So. Gas Assn., Nat. Petroleum Council (dir. 1971—), Gas Research Inst. (dir., chmn. 1985-86). Republican. Baptist. Clubs: Houston, Ramada, River Oaks Country. Lodge: Masons. Office: PO Box 1642 Houston TX 77001

OSIAS, RICHARD ALLEN, international financier, investment, finance and real estate and agriculture executive, city official; b. N.Y.C., Nov. 13, 1936; s. Harry L. and Leah (Schenk) O.; student Columbia U., 1951-63; m. Judy Bradford; children—Alexandra Kimberly, Alexandra Elizabeth. Founder, Osias Orgn., Inc., N.Y.C., also Ft. Lauderdale, Fla., St. Clair, Mich., San Juan, P.R., 1953, chmn. bd., chief exec. officer, 1953—; also mus. record producer. Mem. North Lauderdale (Fla.) City Council, 1967—; mayor and police commr. North Lauderdale, 1967—. Active Ft. Lauderdale Mus. Art, Ft. Lauderdale Symphony Soc., Tower Council of Pine Crest Prep. Sch., Ft. Lauderdale, Boys Clubs Broward County; mem. U. Miami Founders Soc.; a founder Ft. Lauderdale Civic Ballet; benefactor Atlanta Ballet, Atlanta Symphony Soc.; bd. dirs., trustee Smyrna Hosp., Atlanta. Served with USAF, 1953. Recipient Am. House award Am. Home Mag., 1962, Westinghouse award, 1968; named Builder of Year, Sunshine State Info. Bur. and Sunshine State Sr. Citizen, 1967-69. Mem. Ft. Lauderdale Better Bus. Bur., Offshore Power Boat Racing Assn., Lauderhill (Fla.) Fraternal Order Police Assn. (pres.), Fla., Margate, Ft. Lauderdale chambers commerce. Clubs: Tower, Bankers Top of First (San Juan); Quarter Deck (Galveston, Tex.); Boca Raton (Fla.) Yacht and Country; Monte Carlo Yacht; Lima Yacht; Canary Islands Yacht; Tower (Ft. Lauderdale); Tryall Golf and Country (Montego Bay, Jamaica). Prin. works include city devel., residential and apt. units, residential housing communities, shopping centers, country clubs, golf courses, hotel chains, comprehensive housing communities, grain farming. Featured in news profile on CBS, 1982. Home: 3900 Randall Ridge Rd NW Atlanta GA 30327 also Honolulu HI Office: PO Box 725047 Atlanta GA 30339

OSIER, WILLIAM RICHARD, school administrator; b. Randolph, Vt., July 23, 1938; s. Seward E. and Corolyn (Wood) O.; m. Catherine Stone, June 19, 1976; children—Hannah, William. B.A., U. Md., 1961; M.A., St. John's Coll., 1972. Tchr. Rumsey Hall Sch., Washington, Conn., 1965-67; English tchr. Moses Brown Sch., Providence, 1967-69, Thacher Sch., Ojai, Calif., 1969-79; chmn. dept. English, Marin County Day Sch., Corte Madera, Calif., 1970-72; tchr. English, dir. students Dexter Sch., Brookline, Mass., 1972-78; headmaster Lower Sch., Cin. Country Day Sch., 1978-82; headmaster Highland Sch., Warrenton, Va., 1982—. Vestryman, Leeds Episcopal Ch., Markham, Va., 1984. Mem. Elem. Sch. Heads Assn. Republican. Episcopalian. Club: Prouts Neck Country (Maine). Avocations: running; tennis. Office: Highland Sch 597 Broadview Ave Warrenton VA 22186

OSILESI, ODUTOLA, nutritionist, educator, researcher, nutritional biochemist and pharmacologist; b. Sagamu-Remo, Nigeria, Jan. 18, 1948; came to U.S., 1970; s. Ezekiel Taiku and Christiana (Oyebowale) O.; m. Elizabeth Olugbenga Awoseyi, June 14, 1973; children—Oluyemisi, Olusola, Ayodele, Omotunde. B.S. in Chemistry, Howard U., 1973, Ph.D. in Human Nutrition and Food, 1981. Lab. analyst Nigerian Breweries Ltd., Lagos, Nigeria, 1967-68; research asst. chief med. examiners office D.C. Gen. Hosp., 1977-78; research assoc. Human Nutrition Inst., Agrl. Research Service, Dept. Agr., Beltsville, Md., 1979-81; research and grad. asst. Howard U., Washington, 1975-79; asst. prof. home econs., research project leader Alcorn State U., Lorman, Miss., 1981—; cons. nutrition to health ctr.; adviser on nutrition to low income groups, S.W. Miss., 1981—. Author numerous articles on fiber, edible gums and their effect on hepatic lipogenic responses, diabetes, lipoprotein status in animals and man. Recipient Best Research Paper award Health and Home Econs. Assn. of Land Grant Colls. and State Instns. Am., 1982. Mem. Am Inst Nutrition, Soc. Nutrition Edn., Am. Home Econs. Assn., Miss. Home Econs. Assn., AAAS, N.Y. Acad. Sci. Baptist. Lodge: Rotary. Home: B-3 Faculty Gardens Apt Lorman MS 39096 Office: Alcorn State U Dept Home Econs Lorman MS 39096

OSLUND, JEFFREY SCOTT, geophysicist, geologist; b. Mpls., Oct. 14, 1954; s. Richard Robert and Roberta Lorraine (Truax) O.; m. Raelene Annette Church, Aug. 20, 1977; children—Ashley Lenora, Heather Nicole. B.A. in Chemistry, Albion Coll., 1976; M. in Geology, Ind. U., 1979. Assoc. geophysicist to geophysicist Texaco, U.S.A., New Orleans, 1979—, geophys. interpreter, 1982; advanced geophysicist Getty Oil Co., New Orleans, 1982-84; sr. geophysicist Enserch Exploration, Inc., Dallas, 1984—. Mem. Am. Assn. Petroleum Geologists, Soc. Exploration Geophysicists, Southeastern Geophys. Soc., New Orleans Geol. Soc., Dallas Geol. and Geophys. Soc., Shreveport Geol. Soc., East Tex. Geol. Soc. Avocations: golf; photography; running; snow skiing; backpacking. Office: Enserch Exploration Inc 2 Energy Square Suite 1200 4849 Greenville Ave Dallas TX 75206

OSTEEN, CARL EDWARD, computer consultant; b. Hattiesburg, Miss., Sept. 2, 1915; s. Samuel Furman and Winona Pauline (Witherspoon) O.; diploma in acctg. Northwestern U., 1951; B.S., N.Y. U., 1953, M.B.A., 1954; m. Mary Stuart Arbuckle, Sept. 12, 1942; children—Carol Ann, Edward Stuart, James Furman. With Diamond Match Co., 1946-56, corp. systems mgr., N.Y.C., 1950-56; mgr. systems and data processing N.Y. Times, 1956-69; dir. mgmt. info. services Pitney Bowes Inc., Stamford, Conn., 1969-78, spl. asst. v.p., 1978-80; pres. Osteen Info. Systems, Cape Coral, Fla., 1980—; lectr., cons. computer systems analysis, 1980—; asso. prof. N.Y. U., 1970-80. Served to 1st lt. AUS, 1942-46. Recipient Outstanding Teaching citation N.Y. U., 1975. Mem. Assn. Systems Mgmt. (Achievement award 1976), Beta Gamma Sigma. Baptist. Author: An Attack on Paperwork, 1965; Forms Analysis, 1969; also articles; mem. editorial rev. bd. Jour. Systems Mgmt. Address: 4109 Palm Tree Blvd Cape Coral FL 33904

OSTEEN, ROBERT WILLIAM, dentist; b. Memphis, Mar. 14, 1949; s. Robert Wilbert and Beulah Thelma (Bell) O.; m. Theresa Dagastino, July 1, 1966; children—Robert Kevin, Robin Kelley, Rheagan Kathryn. B.S., Memphis State U., 1971; cert. in med. tech., St. Joseph Hosp. Sch. Med. Tech., 1974; M.S., Memphis State U., 1975; D.D.S., U. Tenn., 1979. Instr., head of sci. dept., Evangelical Christian Sch., Memphis, 1971-73; med. technologist St. Joseph Hosp., 1974-76, Meth. Hosp., Memphis, 1976-79; instr. U. Tenn., Memphis, 1979-81; program dir., instr. Memphis Area Vocat. Tech. Sch., Memphis, 1982-84; pvt. practice, Memphis, 1979—; adv. com. mem. Memphis Area Vocat. Tech. Sch., 1982—. CPR instr. ARC, Memphis; Advanced Cardiac Life Support instr. Am. Heart Assn., Memphis. Recipient Annual Student award Am. Acad. Periodontology, U. Tenn., 1979; Richard and Marguerite Dean Hon. Odontological Soc. award U. Tenn., 1978. Mem. ADA, Tenn. Dental Assn., Am. Orthodontic Soc., Am. Soc. Clin. Pathologists. Republican. Avocations: running; tennis; boating; fishing; reading. Home: 1431 Treehaven Cove Cordova TN 38018

OSTERLOH, WELLINGTON FREDERICK, oil and gas company executive, public relations consultant; b. N.Y.C., Oct. 22, 1936; s. Wellington D. and Mary (Bokar) O.; m. Clauriece Ruth Eby, Jan. 21, 1960; children—Debbie, Judy, Eric. Student Bernard Baruch Sch. Bus., CUNY, 1954-56. Pub. relations mgr. Post div. Gen. Foods Corp., White Plains, N.Y., 1962-69; corp. dir. editorial services Martin Marietta Corp., N.Y.C., 1969-72; corp. dir. pub. relations Union Pacific Corp., N.Y.C., 1972-75, The Coastal Corp., Houston, 1975—. Past v.p., bd. dirs. Oak Creek Village Civic Assn. Served with U.S. Army, 1960-62. Recipient Kodak EPCOT photography award. Mem. Pub. Relations Soc. Am. (past mem. bd. dirs.), Profl. Photographers Am., Nat. Coal Assn. (pub. relations com.), Nat. Investor Relations Inst., Tex. Pub. Relations Assn. (pres.-elect, dir., Best of Tex. awards 1980), Houston Corp. Relations Roundtable (co-founder). Republican. Methodist. Clubs: Houston City, Houston Press. Office: 9 Greenway Plaza Houston TX 77046

OSTROTH, DONN DAVID, university administrator; b. Aurora, Ill., May 29, 1946; s. Donald Delbert and Marian Doris (Beyler) O.; 1 child, Amy; m. Valerie Anne Jones, Jan. 1, 1986. A.B., Allegheny Coll., Meadville, 1968; M. Counseling, Ariz. State U., 1974; Ph.D., Mich. State U., 1979. Counselor for student programs Va. Tech. U., Blacksburg, 1974-77; assoc. dir., dir. student devel. Va. Poly. Inst. & State U., Blacksburg, 1979-82, spl. asst. to v.p. student affairs, 1982-83, dir. student activities, 1983—. Mem. editorial bd: Jour. of Coll. Student Personnel, 1979-85. Contbr. articles to profl. jours. Vice chmn. Montgomery County Community Sentencing Program Adv. Bd., Christiansburg, Va., 1980-83; deacon Northside Presby. Ch., Blacksburg, Va., 1980-83, chmn. bd. deacons, 1981-82. Served to capt. USAF, 1968-73. Mem. Am. Coll. Personnel Assn., Nat. Assn. Student Personnel Adminstrs., Phi Delta Kappa, Phi Kappa Phi, Omicron Delta Kappa, Phi Kappa Psi. Republican. Avocations: water sports; gardening. Home: 31 F Terrace View Blacksburg VA 24060 Office: Va Poly Inst and State Univ Squires Student Ctr Blacksburg VA 24061

OSTTEEN, BOBBY CLAUDE, architect, planner; b. Winnfield, La., Dec. 28, 1945; s. Claude and Evestine (Bullock) O.; m. Barbara DuBose, Sept. 2, 1967; children—Erin, Owen. B.Arch., U. Southwestern La., 1970; M.Arch., M.C.P., Ga. Inst. Tech., 1972. Registered architect, La., Ga., Ark. Architect and planner II, City of Atlanta Planning Dept., 1971-72; architect, urban designer Robert & Co. Assocs., Atlanta, 1972-75; architect, planner Perkins Guidry Young Architects, Inc., Lafayette, La., 1975-85, prin., 1979-85; ptnr. Perkins-Guidry-Beazley-Ostteen, P.C., 1985—; project architect Coll. Oaks Office Bldg. (honor award La. Architects Assn. 1982). Mem. AIA, La. Architects Assn., South La. chpt. AIA, Nat. Council Archtl. Registration Bds. Democrat. Methodist. Clubs: Krewe of Zeus, Ga. Tech. Alumni Assn., U. Southwestern La. Alumni Assn., Lafayette Jaycees (past dir.). Office: PO Box 51877 Lafayette LA 70503

OSUEKE, SAMUEL O., health educator; b. Lowa Etiti, Nigeria, Sept. 19, 1948; s. Michael O. and Virginia N. (Orji) O.; m. Jane C. Ire, May 15, 1979; children—Uchenna, Anayochukwu, Oluchi, Chidozie. B.Sc. (hons.), U. Ife (Nigeria); M.Sc., Tex. So. U.; D.P.H., U. Tex.-Houston, 1980. Asst. prof. health Tex. So. U., Houston, 1979—. Coordinator health edn. program, 1985—; adj. prof. Houston Community Coll., 1982—; researcher; judge Sci. Engring. Fair, Houston. Asst. chmn. bd. dirs. Nigerian Found., Houston; bd. dirs. AFRAAM Wholistic Health Inst., Houston; patron Tex. So. U. chpt. Nigerian Student Union. Recipient Nigerian Nat. Chmn.'s award Nat. Youth Service Corps, 1974-75, Adolph Coors Co. Black History Month award, 1983. Mem. Am. Pub. Health Assn., Tex. Soc. Coll. Tchrs. Edn. Office: Dept of Health Education Tex So U Houston TX 77004

OTHMER, MURRAY EADE, consulting chemical engineer; b. Muscatine, Iowa, Aug. 6, 1907; s. Harry Rodger and Mary Louise (Eade) O.; m. Mary Magdaline Artman, Sept. 30, 1937; 1 child, David Artman. B.S., Grinnell Coll., 1929; postgrad. U. Rochester, 1930-32; M.S. in Engring., U. Mich., 1933. Registered profl. engr., Mass. Prodn. supr. Eastman Kodak Co., Rochester, N.Y., 1929-32; chem. engr. Am. Cyanamid, Bound Brook, N.J., 1932-35; prof. chem. engring. Tufts U. and U. P.R., Medford, Mass. and Mayaguez, P.R., 1940-47, 47-48, 57-59; S.Am. prodn. supr. Sterling Drug Co., S.Am., 1953-57; dir. C.A.I. Productora de Grasas, Caracas, Vanezuela, 1936-40, 59-75; cons. chem. engr., Chapel Hill, N.C., 1975—; hon. dir. C.A.I. Productora de Grasas, Caracas, Venezuela, 1976—. Contbr. articles to tech. jours. Recipient Service to Country award Internat. Exec. Service Corps, Malaysia, 1982. Fellow AAAS; mem. Am. Chem. Soc. (50 yr. mem. award 1985), Am. Inst. Chem. Engrs., Nat. Inst. Oilseed Processors (quality control com.), Sigma Xi. Clubs: Kaighn Conversation, Chapel Hill Country (N.C.). Avocations: history; travel; golf.

OTJEN, ROBERT PARK, gas pipeline company executive; b. Milw., Mar. 6, 1950; s. Theo Putnam and Jean (Leesley) O.; m. Darcy Jeanne Stiles, June 1, 1974; children—Jeffrey, Robin. B.S. in Geology, U. Wis., Madison, 1972, M.S. in Oceanography, 1975. With Tenn. Gas Pipeline, 1976-82; supt. construction State Gas Pipeline, Houston, 1982-84; supt. engring. and Constrn. Tennagasco Corp., Houston, 1984—. Bd. dirs. Maplewood West Civic Assn., Houston, 1984—. Mem. Marine Tech. Soc. (pres.), Am. Assn. Petroleum Geologists, Nat. Gas Men Houston, Pipeliners Club. Office: Tenngasco Corp PO Box 2511 Houston TX 77001

O'TOOLE, LAURENCE JOSEPH, political scientist; b. Syracuse, N.Y., Dec. 7, 1948; s. Laurence J. Sr. and Marjorie R. (Weinheimer) O'T.; m. Mary Irene Gilroy, June 26, 1971; 1 child, Conor Gilroy. B.S. with gt. distinction, Clarkson U., 1970; M.P.A., Syracuse U., 1972, Ph.D., 1975. Asst. prof. U. Va., Charlottesville, 1975-79; assoc. prof. polit. sci. Auburn U., Ala., 1979—. Author: (with others) American Government, 1984; Regulatory Decision Making, 1984. Editor: American Intergovernmental Relations, 1985. Contbr. articles to profl. jours. and chpts. to books. Mem. editorial bd. Jour. Politics, 1985—, State and Local Govt. Rev., 1985—. Recipient Teaching award Auburn U., 1985; Internat. Inst. Mgmt. fellow, 1978. Mem. Am. Soc. for Pub. Adminstrn. (Burchfield award 1979), Am. Polit. Sci. Assn. (chmn. pub. adminstrn. sect. 1985-86), Southern Polit. Sci. Assn. Democrat. Home: 1230 Juniper Dr Auburn AL 36830 Office: Dept Polit Sci 7080 Haley Ctr Auburn U Auburn AL 36849

OTT, STANLEY JOSEPH, bishop; b. Gretna, La., June 29, 1927; s. Manuel Peter and Lucille (Berthelot) O. S.T.D., Pontifical Gregorian U., Rome, 1954. Ordained priest Roman Catholic Ch. Bishop Roman Catholic Ch., 1976; assoc. pastor St. Francis Cabrini Parish, New Orleans, 1954-57; chaplain La. State U., Baton Rouge, 1957-61; officialis Marriage Tribunal, Diocese of Baton Rouge, 1961—; chancellor rector St. Joseph Cathedral, Baton Rouge, 1968-76; aux. bishop of New Orleans, 1976-83, bishop of Baton Rouge (La.), 1983; adviser Nat. Assn. Cath. Chaplains. Bd. dirs. United Way, Baton Rouge, YMCA, Baton Rouge, ARC, Boy Scouts Am. Mem. Nat. Conf. Cath. Bishops, U.S. Cath. Conf. Democrat. Club: K.C. Home: 3330 Hundred Oaks Ave Baton Rouge LA 70808 Office: 1800 S Acadian Thruway PO Box 2028 Baton Rouge LA 70821

OTTINGER, DENISE CATHERINE, university administrator; b. Wyandotte, Mich., Dec. 28, 1952; d. William D. and M. Catherine (Franks) O. B.S., Bowling Green State U., 1975, M.A., 1976. Dir. residence hall staff and programming, Ashland Coll., Ohio, 1976-78; complex dir. Western Mich. U., Kalamazoo, 1978-80; coordinator residential life Saginaw Valley State Coll., Mich., 1980-83; dir. student life, Austin Peay State U., Clarksville, Tenn., 1983-85, assoc. dean of students, 1985—; sect. coordinator Mortar Bd. Nat., Tenn. and Ky., 1984—. Vol. Spl. Olympics, 1984. Recipient Outstanding Service award Mich. Coll. Personnel Assn., 1983. Mem. Assn. Coll. and Univ. Housing Officers, Southeastern Housing Officers Assn. (newsletter editor 1984-85), Am. Coll. Personnel Assn. (chmn. task force 1984—), Am. Assn. Counseling and Devel., Alpha Lambda Delta (hon.), Kappa Delta Alumnae Assn. Democrat. Methodist. Avocations: clogging; buckdancing; aerobics. Home: N103 1834 Madison Clarksville TN 37043 Office: Austin Peay State Univ PO Box 4757 Clarksville TN 37044

OTTINGER, ROBERT STANLEY, diversified industry executive; b. San Mateo, Calif., Feb. 24, 1940; s. George Stanley and Catherine Alexandria (McKendrick) O.; m. Barbara Ann Magoon, June 10, 1961; children—Deborah Ann, Gregory Scott. B.S., Oreg. State U., 1961, Ph.D., 1965. Chemist, U.S. Navy, San Francisco, 1961; sect. head TRW Systems, Redondo Beach, Calif., 1965-74, ops. mgr. TRW Energy Devel. Group, McLean, Va., 1975-82, dir. environment TRW, Inc., McLean and Cleve., 1983—; adviser to chmn. Calif. Solid Waste Mgmt. and Resource Recovery Adv. Council, 1973-75; cons. NRC, 1975-76, task group cons., 1979-81. Contbr. tech. reports, papers to profl. lit.; patentee disposal of waste plastic, recovery of products therefrom. Shell Oil Co fellow, 1963. Mem. Soc. Petroleum Engrs., AAAS. Democrat. Methodist. Home: 11323 Myrtle Ln Reston VA 22091 Office: TRW Inc 23555 Euclid Ave Cleveland OH 44117 also 8301 Greensboro Dr McLean VA 22102

OTTO, DONALD RAY, museum director; b. N.Loup, Nebr., Oct. 7, 1943; s. Leonard R. and Lorraine E. (Lindsay) O.; B.A., Hastings (Nebr.) Coll., 1967; m. Sylvia D. Cook, Aug. 7, 1965; 1 dau., Allison Lindsay. With Kans.-Nebr. Natural Gas Co., Hastings, 1967-68; exhibits dir. Hastings Museum, 1968-72; asst. dir. Kans. State Hist. Soc., 1972-75; program dir. Ft. Worth Mus. Sci. and History, 1975-77, exec. dir., 1977—; pres. Kans. Mus. Assn., 1974, 75; officer Mountain Plains Mus. Conf., 1976-79, pres., 1977-78; spl. cons. mus. curriculum planning Coll. Liberal Studies, U. Okla., 1980. Mem. adminstrv. bd. 1st Meth. Ch., 1978, 80. Mem. Am. Assn. Mus. (accreditation on site com. 1974—), Am. Assn. State and Local History, Tex. Mus. Assn., Am. Assn. Sci. and Tech. Centers, Assn. Sci. Mus. Dirs. Methodist. Clubs: Masons, Ridglea Country, Rotary (Ft. Worth). Office: 1501 Montgomery St Fort Worth TX 76107

OTTO, INGOLF HELGI ELFRIED, institute fellow; b. Duesseldorf, Fed. Republic of Germany, May 7, 1920; s. Frederick C. and Josephine (Zisenis) O.; m. Carlyle Miller, 1943 (div. 1960); children—George Vincent Edward, Richard Arthur Frederick. A.B., U. Cin., 1941; M.A., George Washington U., 1950, Ph.D., 1959. CPCU. Assoc. prof. fin. NYU, N.Y.C., 1960-62; prof. fin. U. Nuevo Leon, Monterrey, Mexico, 1962-65, U. So. Miss., Hattiesburg, 1965-67, U. So. Ala., Mobile, 1967-81; sr. fellow Inst. Banking and Fin., Mexico City, 1981—. Contbr. articles on fin. to profl. jours. Served to col. U.S. Army, 1941-46. Decorated Legion of Merit, Meritorious Service medal, Purple Heart. Mem. Am. Econ. Assn., N.Am. Econ. and Fin. Assn.

OTTO, KENNETH LEE, diversified industry executive; b. Sheboygan Falls, Wis., July 27, 1930; s. Lester William and Edith M. (Daane) O.; student Hope Coll., 1949-52; B.S.C., State U. Iowa, 1956; m. Cherrie Ann Cartland, Dec. 20, 1952; children—Scott Cartland, Stacy Lee. Dir. personnel and orgn. planning Ford Motor Co. and Philco-Ford, Dearborn, Mich., 1956-69; v.p. orgn. devel./bldg. products Am. Standard Inc., N.Y.C., 1969-72; corp. v.p. personnel and orgn. devel. Bendix Corp., Southfield, Mich., 1972-75; corp. v.p. orgn. and personnel resources United Techs., Hartford, Conn., 1975-77; sr. v.p. employee relations Tenneco Inc., Houston, 1977—; lectr., cons. in field; mem. bus. and industry adv. council OECD. Served with Adj. Gen.'s Corps, U.S. Army, 1953-54. Mem. Conf. Bd. (adv. council on mgmt. and personnel), Personnel Roundtable, Employee Relations Com., Bus. Roundtable, Sr. Personnel Execs. Forum, Human Resources Roundtable, Labor Policy Assn., Assn. Internal Mgmt. Cons. Republican. Office: 1010 Milam St Houston TX 77002

OUALLINE, VIOLA JACKSON, psychologist; b. Edna, Tex., Oct. 17, 1927; d. S.R. Jackson and Myrtle Mae Wood; m. Charles M. Oualline Jr., Sept. 3, 1949; children—Stephen, Susan, Shari. B.S., U. Houston, 1949; M.S., North Tex. State U., 1962, Ph.D., 1975. Phys. therapist Hermann Hosp., Houston, 1948-49, pvt. practice, Austin, Tex., 1949-54, Miller Orthopedic Clinic, Charlotte, N.C., 1956-57; psychologist Dallas Soc. Crippled Children, 1963-81, dir. psychology dept., 1981—; psychol. cons. Mesquite Independent Sch. Dist., Tex., 1974—, Duncanville Sch. Dist., Tex., 1974-76, Grand Prarie Ind. Sch. Dist., Tex., 1976-79. Mem. Am. Psychol. Assn., Tex. Psychol. Assn., Dallas Psychol. Assn., Am. Assn. Counseling Devel., Council for Exceptional Children, Chi Omega Mother's Club. Baptist. Avocations: reading; bicycle riding. Office: Dallas Soc Crippled Children 5701 Maple St Dallas TX 75229

OUBARI, ADEL A., aeronautics company executive; b. Jaffa, Palestine, Dec. 8, 1932; s. Akef and Nadidah (Moufti) O.; m. Frances Jean Lewis, Feb. 13, 1961; children—Hesham D., Dalal. B.S. in Aero. Engring., Calif. Poly. Coll.-San Luis Obispo, 1956. Regional sales mgr. Internat. Cessna Aircraft Co., Wichita, Kans., 1964-71; dir. internat. sales Grumman Am. Aviation and Gulfstream Am. Aviation, Savannah, Ga., 1971-75; v.p. sales Middle East Canadair Inc., Westport, Conn., and TAG Aeros. Ltd., Geneva, 1975—; pres. TAG Aeros. (USA) Inc.; v.p. TAG Aviation (USA), TAG Flight (USA), TAG Aeros. (Saudi Arabia) Ltd., TAG Aeros. Ltd., Geneva, TAG Equity (USA),

TAG Equity Cayman Islands. Served with USAF, 1957-64. Mem. Am. Mgmt. Assn., Swiss-Arab C. of C. (Geneva), Quiet Birdmen, Wichita Hangar Club, Nat. Rifle Assn., Tex. Rifle Assn. Republican. Moslem. Clubs: American (Geneva). Home: 3805 Tapestry Ct Plano TX 75075 Office: 17400 Dallas Pkwy Suite 112 Dallas TX 75252

OUBRE, HAYWARD LOUIS, artist, art educator, consultant; b. New Orleans s. Hayward Louis and Amelie Marie (Keys) O.; m. Juanita Bernice Hurel, 1945 (dec. 1976); 1 child, Amelie Geneva. B.A., Dillard U., 1939; M.F.A., U. Iowa, 1948. Assoc. prof. art Fla. A&M U., Tallassee, 1949-50; prof. art, chmn. Ala. State U., Montgomery, 1950-65, Winston-Salem State U., 1965-81, curator Selma Burke Art Gallery, 1983-84, 85—. Exhibited in numerous group shows. Served to sgt. U.S. Army, 1941-44, Alaska. Mem. Internat. Biographical Assn. (Cambridge, Eng.) Congregationalist. Avocations: jogging; body building. Home: 2422 Pickford Ct Winston Salem NC 27101

OUDIN, CHARLES FOLGER, III, oil company geophysical specialist; b. Cooperstown, N.Y., July 4, 1958; s. Charles Folger Jr. and Jean Jennings (Godwin) O.; m. Julie Sue Peipert, Aug. 22, 1981; 1 child, Jessica Sarah. B.A. in Geology, Williams Coll., 1980. Geophys. asst. Pennzoil Co., Houston, 1980-81, assoc. geologist, 1981-82, geophysicist, 1982-84, geophys. specialist, 1984—. Mem. Am. Assn. Petroleum Geologists, Houston Geol. Soc. Presbyterian. Avocations: golf; gardening. Home: 8623 McAvoy Houston TX 77074 Office: Pennzoil Co PO Box 2967 Houston TX 77001

OUSLEY, JULIA LEE, architect; b. Corpus Christi, Tex., Feb. 23, 1942; d. James Lee and Eleanor Louise (Enfield) Herron; m. Jon Sergei Ousley, Sept. 2, 1966; children—Jon Dalton, Jodie Leigh, James Barrett. Cert. dental hygiene Baylor U., 1964, B.S., 1974; M.Arch., U. Tex.-Arlington, 1981. Pvt. practice as dental hygienist, Dallas, 1965-73; clin. instr. U. Tex. Health Sci. Ctr., Houston, 1973-75; adminstrv. asst. Omniplan, Dallas, 1979; project mgr. ArchiTexas, Dallas, 1981-83; prin. Lassiter, Ousley & Assocs., Arlington, 1983—; mem. adv. council sch. architecture and environmental design U. Tex.-Arlington, 1984—, exec. bd. Alumni, 1982—. Mem. allocations com. United Way, Fort Worth, 1985; mem. Leadership Arlington, 1984; mem. Accent Arlington, 1985. Mem. AIA (assoc.), League Women Voters. Democrat. Disciple of Christ. Clubs: Winston Parents (Dallas); Oakridge Parents, Country Day Parents (Fort Worth). Office: Lassiter Ousley & Assocs 1306 W Abram St Arlington TX 76013

OUZTS, JAMES WESLEY, bio-communications educator; b. Indianola, Miss., Apr. 21, 1937; s. Felix D. and Geneva (Hodges) O.; m. Florence Louise Uguccioni, Dec. 30, 1967; children—James Wesley, Jr., Katherine, Ruth, Mary. B.S., Delta State U., 1960; M.A., U. Miss., 1963; Ph.D., Ohio State U., 1967; D.D. (hon.), Ch. of Gospel Ministry, Calif., 1982. Diplomate Cleve. Inst. Electronics, 1972. Post-doctoral, Ohio State U., 1980; instr. U. Miss., University, 1960-63, Delta State U., Cleveland, Miss., 1962-63, Appalachian State U., Boone, N.C., 1963-65, Ohio State U., Columbus, 1965-67; asst. prof. Auburn U., Ala., 1967-70; prof. audiology-speech pathology Delta State U., Cleveland, 1970—; cons. Ala. Inst. Deaf and Blind, Talladega, 1967-70, Sunflower Co. Progress, Indianola, Miss., 1970-78; pvt. practice clin. and indsl. audiology, 1967—. Author: (play) Banjo Man, 1960, Tharp's Button, 1961. Mem. Am. Speech and Hearing Assn., Miss. Speech and Hearing Assn., Northwestern Miss. Speech and Hearing Assn. Democrat. Home: 811 S Court St Cleveland MS 38732 Office: Dept Audiology-Speech Pathology Delta State U Cleveland MS 38733

OVERALL, MARY EDITH, nurse, nursing educator and administrator; b. Oklahoma City, Dec. 2, 1940; d. Warren Harding and Malinda (Flowers) Hudspeth; m. Billy J. Overall, May 28, 1960; children—Michael D., Alesia G., James W., Edie J. Diploma in nursing Mercy Hosp. Sch. Nursing, 1961; B.S. in Health Edn., Oklahoma City U., 1974; M.S. in Nursing, 1975. Staff nurse, team leader Mercy Hosp., Oklahoma City, 1961-64; staff nurse VA Med. Ctr., Oklahoma City, 1965-69, head nurse, 1969-72; instr. Oklahoma State U., 1973-74, grad. teaching asst. nursing, 1975, asst. prof. grad. program, 1977-79, clin. asst. prof., 1979—; asst. chief nursing service VA Med. Ctr., 1979-82; dir. nursing State of Okla. Teaching Hosps., Oklahoma City, 1982—; vol. instr. Regional Med. Program, Oklahoma City, 1971-74; adj. prof. health scis. Rose State Coll., Midwest City, Okla., 1984—; served as chmn., adv. to numerous coms. Contbr. articles to profl. jours. Mem. Am. Assn. Critical Care Nurses (pres. 1982-84), Am. Nurses Assn. (dist. 1 2d v.p. 1978-79), Am. Heart Assn. (Service Citation 1983, bd. dirs. 1979—, exec. com. sec. 1979-80), Nat. League Nursing, Am. Hosp. Assn., Nat. Soc. Nursing Service Adminstrs., Nat. Black Nurses Assn. (pres. 1975-77), Okla. Nursing Network, Okla. Assn. Nursing Edn. and Service Adminstrs., Health Scis. Ctr. Nursing Adminstrs. Council, Midwest Alliance in Nursing (gov. bd. 1985—). Democrat. Baptist. Avocations: gardening; swimming; reading. Home: 1111 NE 64th Oklahoma City OK 73111 Office: State of Okla Teaching Hosps PO Box 26307 Oklahoma City OK 73126

OVERBEY, BEASLEY TURMAN, state art education consultant; b. Nashville, July 14, 1938; s. Beasley Turman and Aleda Wells O.; m. Carol Tilley, Aug. 12, 1972. B.S.B.A., Middle Tenn. State U., 1960; M.A., U. No. Colo., 1967. Tchr. arts Metro-Davidson pub. schs., Nashville, 1960-72; chief art edn. Tenn. Dept. Edn., Nashville, 1972—; cons. in field; chief exec. officer Beasley Overbey Farms, Beasley Overbey Enterprises Inc. Contbr. articles to profl. jours. Mem. Tenn. Alliance for Arts in Edn. (vice chmn.), Tenn. Performing Art Ctr., Tenn. Art Edn. Assn., Nat. Art Edn. Assn., Tenn. Assn. Curriculum Devel., Nat. Assn. Curriculum Devel., Franklin and Williamson County Hist. Assn. Lodge: Elks. Home: Rural Route 2 Lewisburg Pike Franklin TN 37064 Office: Tenn Dept Edn Suite 214 Cordell Hull Bldg Nashville TN 37219

OVERBEY, RICHARD WALKER, advertising agency executive; b. Mobile, Ala., Apr. 20, 1934; s. James Thomas and Frances (Bowden) W.; m. Marion Mitchiner, Mar. 21, 1959; 3 children. B.A., Vanderbilt U., 1956. Tchr., advisor Julius T. Wright Sch., Mobile, 1958-59; prodn. mgr. Howard Barney and Co., Mobile, 1959-62; pub. relations rep. Internat. Paper Co., Mobile, 1962-69; asst. cashier, asst. mgr. travel dept. Amsouth/The Am. Nat. Bank & Trust Co., Mobile, 1969-71, asst. v.p., advt. dir., 1971-75, v.p., asst. mktg. dir., 1975-77, v.p., mgr. internat. dept., 1977-79, v.p., sr. mktg. officer, 1979-81; pres., chief exec. officer Colonial Bank N.A., Mobile, 1981-82; sr. v.p. Barney & Patrick Advt., Inc., Mobile, 1982—. Vice chmn. U.S. Olympic Com. Ala., 1982, mem. ho. of dels., 1982-84; mem. Am. Jr. Miss Judges Com., 1982; chmn. Heart Assn., 1982; Christmas Seal chmn. Am. Lung Assn., 1981; pres. Sr. Citizens Services, 1979-81; pres. Port City Pacer, 1980; sec. YMCA, 1978; pres. Mobile Opera Guild, 1978-79; rep. Ala. U.S. Olympic Torch Relay Team, XIII Olympic Winter Games, Lake Placid, 1980. Served with U.S. Army, 1956-58. Recipient M.O. Beale Scroll of Merit, Mobile Opera, 1978. Mem. Pub. Relations Soc. Am., Pub. Relations Council Ala., Ala. World Trade Assn., Ala. C. of C., Mobile Area C. of C. (chmn. world trade com. 1982), U.M.S. Prep. Sch. Alumni Assn. (pres. 1982).

OVERMAN, HAROLD SPEIGHT, III, marketing development executive; b. Washington, Feb. 23, 1948; s. Harold Speight and Ilma Angell (Meade) O.; m. Trudee Hale Ebeling, July 28, 1973; children—Harold Speight, Laura Meade. B.S.M.E., N.C. State U., 1970, M.S.M.E., 1971; M.B.A., U. Va., 1973. Specialist strategy analysis G.E. Mobile Communications Div., Lynchburg, Va., 1973-75, regional operation adminstr., Palo Alto, Calif., 1976-77, mgr. metro sales operation, 1977-79, mgr. strategy analysis, Fairfield, Conn., 1980-82, mgr. bus. devel. G.E. Lighting Bus. Group, Cleve., 1982-83, v.p. mktg. G.E. Ceramics, Inc., Chattanooga, Tenn., 1983—. Mem. Pi Tau Sigma, Tau Beta Pi. Republican. Methodist. Club: Walden. Office: General Electric Ceramics Inc 511 Manufacturers Rd Chattanooga TN 37405

OVERSTREET, ROBIN MILES, parasitologist, researcher, educator; b. Eugene, Oreg., June 1, 1939; s. Robin M. and Laura (McGinty) O.; m. Kim Bunton, Mar. 31, 1964; children—Brian, Eric. B.A. in Gen. Biology, U. Oreg., 1963; M.S. in Marine Biology, U. Miami, 1966, Ph.D., in Marine Biology, 1968. NIH postdoctoral fellow in parasitology Tulane U. Med. Sch., New Orleans, 1968-69; head sect. parasitology Gulf Coast Research Lab., Ocean Springs, Miss., 1969—; adj. prof. U. So. Miss., U. Miss., La. State U., also others. Served with USN, 1956-62. Nat. Marine Fisheries Service grantee, 1969—; Miss.-Ala. Sea grantee, 1973-78; U.S.-Israel Binat. Sci. Found. grantee, 1974-75; Nat. Cancer Inst. grantee, 1982—. Mem. Am. Soc. Parasitologists (editoral bd. 1980—), Helminthological Soc. Washington, Am. Micros. Soc., Soc. Invertebrate Pathology, also others. Author: Marine Maladies: Worms, Germs and Other Symbionts from the Northern Gulf of Mexico, 1978; contbr. numerous articles to profl. jours. Home: 14 Paraiso Rd Ocean Springs MS 39564 Office: Gulf Coast Research Lab Ocean Springs MS 39564

OVERTON, BENJAMIN FREDERICK, state justice; b. Green Bay, Wis., Dec. 15, 1926; s. Banjamin H. and Esther M. (Wiese) O.; B.S. in Bus. Adminstrn., U. Fla., 1951, J.D., 1952; LL.D. (hon.), Stetson U., 1975, Nova U., 1977; LL.M., U. Va., 1984; m. Marilyn Louise Smith, June 9, 1951; children—William Hunter, Robert Murray, Catherine Louise. Bar: Fla. 1952. With Office Fla. Atty. Gen., 1952; with firms in St. Petersburg, 1953-64; circuit judge 6th Jud. Circuit Fla., 1964-74, chief judge, 1968-71, chmn. Fla. Conf. Circuit Judges, 1973; justice Supreme Ct. Fla., Tallahassee, 1974—, chief justice, 1976-78; chmn. Supreme Ct. Matrimonial Law Commn., Supreme Ct. Article V Rev. Commn., 1983-84, Jud. Council Fla.; mem. exec. council Conf. of Chief Justices, 1977-78; mem. exec. com. Appellate Judges Conf.; past mem. faculty Stetson U. Coll. Law, Nat. Jud. Coll.; also mem. bd. dirs.; mem. Fla. Bar Continuing Legal Edn. Com., 1963-74, chmn., 1971-74; 1st chmn. Fla. Inst. Judiciary, 1972; chmn. Fla. Ct. Ednl. Council, 1978—. Contbr. articles to legal publs. Past reader, vestryman, sr. warden St. Albans Episcopal Ch., St. Petersburg, Fla. Served as officer U.S. Army, 1945-47, USAR, 1950-74, active duty, 1961-62. Fellow Am. Bar Found.; mem. Am., Fla. bar assn., Am. Judicature Soc. (dir., past sec.). Democrat. Lodge: Rotary. Office: Supreme Ct Bldg Tallahassee FL 32301

OVERTON, KENNETH, human resources consultant; b. Port Arthur, Tex., Nov. 15, 1908; s. Ellis Andrew and Myrtle Amelia (Morgan) O.; Asso. Sci. in Economics, U. Houston, 1946; student U. Mo., Peabody Coll., Baylor U., Sam Houston U., U. Tex.; m. Mary Lou Johnson, July 17, 1932; 1 dau., Carey O. Randall. Tchr. phys. edn. Port Arthur (Tex.) Pub. Schs., 1928-32; supr. indsl. relations mgmt. and oil ops. Texaco Inc., Port Arthur, 1933-50; supt. Central/Western Arabia mgmt. Arabian Am. Oil Co. (Aramco), Saudi Arabia, 1951-63; exec. cons. to Jean Paul Getty, Getty Oil Co., Kuwait, 1963-65; sr. cost engr. Pipeline Technologists, Inc., Houston/Alaska, 1967-75; resources cons., Saudi Arabia, Houston, 1977, EG&G, Saudi Arabia and Far East, Houston, Rockville, Arlington, Caribbean area, 1976—; condr. econs. and agrl. Middle East seminars for doctoral graduates at Tex. A&M U., 1968; round-table participant Middle East-Far East forums to sr. high sch. classes in Tex., La., Va., Md., Saudi Arabia, 1960, 81-85; preparer mgmt. and project procedure manuals for corp. ops. and maintenance and on-job-tng. under active top security mil. clearance, 1943-85. Mem. Am. Petroleum Inst. Clubs: Port Arthur Country, USAF Officers (hon.), Press. Home: care DA Randall 5131 N 15th St Arlington VA 22205

OVERTON, WILLIAM RAY, federal judge; b. Malvern, Ark., Sept. 19, 1939; s. Odis Ray and Martha Elizabeth (Ford) O.; m. Susan Linebarger, Jan. 25, 1964; children—William Ford, Warren Webster. B.S. in Bus. Adminstrn, U. Ark., 1962, LL.B., 1964. Bar: Ark. 1964. Assoc., then partner firm Wright, Lindsey & Jennings, Little Rock, 1966-79; U.S. dist. judge Eastern Dist. Ark., Little Rock, 1979—; mem. Ark. Constl. Revision Study Commn., 1967. Hon. fellow Internat. Acad. Trial Lawyers. Mem. Am. Bar Assn., Ark. Bar Assn., Pulaski County Bar Assn. Democrat. Methodist. Club: U. Ark. Alumni. Home: 5300 Hawthorne Rd Little Rock AR 72207 Office: PO Box 1540 US Courthouse Little Rock AR 72203*

OWEN, DANIEL THOMAS, communications executive; b. Rutherford, N.J., Dec. 6, 1947; s. Jesse Taylor and Loretta (Kirchner) O.; B.A. in Communications, U. Dayton, 1969; m. Margaret Anne Wynne Chilton, Jan. 12, 1980; children—Margaret Anne Worsham, Joseph Irion Worsham II. Dir. communications Roman Cath. Diocese, Wheeling, W.Va., 1970-72; dir. mktg. and fundraising Sta. KERA-TV, Dallas, 1972-75, founder Sta. KERA-FM, Dallas, 1973; v.p. mktg., programming Spectradyne, Inc., Dallas, 1975—; dir. Spectradyne, Inc., Creative Council, Breakaway Techs., Inc., San Francisco. Bd. dirs. U.S.A. Film Festival, 1982—, pres., 1986—; assoc. Dallas Mus. Art, 1981—. Mem. Nat. Cable TV Assn., Am. Mgmt. Assn. Home: 3925 Potomac Ave Dallas TX 75205 Office: 1501 N Plano Rd Richardson TX 75080

OWEN, DAVID A(RTHUR), lawyer, accountant; b. Gulfport, Miss., July 14, 1949; s. Earl A. and Gertrude F. Owen; m. Polly Fife, Oct. 23, 1977; children—Rene, David A.; m. Shannon White, Oct. 16, 1982. B.B.A., U. Miss.; 1971, J.D., 1974. Bar: Miss. 1974; C.P.A., Miss., La. Acct., Deloitte, Haskins & Sells, C.P.A.s, New Orleans, 1971-72; prin. David Owen Law Firm, specializing in taxation, Gulfport, 1974—; dir. Gulf-Certco, Gt. So. Mercantile Corp. Active Spl. Olympics Com. Mem. ABA, Miss. Bar Assn., Miss. Bar Found., Am. Inst. C.P.A.s, Miss. Soc. C.P.A.s. Club: Kiwanis. Office: David Owen Law Firm Box 777 Gulfport MS 39501

OWEN, DAVID JOHN, retired beverage company executive; b. Chgo., May 5, 1925; s. Warren David and Ruth Elizabeth (Thompson) O.; student M.I.T., 1942-43; B.S. mech. engring., Northwestern U., 1945; m. Jean Frances Malcomson, July 3, 1948; children—Frances Thompson, Ruth MacKinlay, David John. Commissary prodn. supr. John R. Thompson Restaurant Co., Chgo., 1947-51, 53-54; prodn. supr., warehouse mgr. Procter & Gamble Co., Chgo., 1954-58, sect. head Ivorydale Tech. Center, Cin., 1958-69; chief engr. Indsl. Engring. Inst., Milw., 1970-73; exec. v.p. Indsl. Engring. Cons. Inc., 1973, plant mgr. Pepsi-Cola, Milw., 1974-77; v.p. ops. Nat. Beverages, Inc., Orlando, 1977-81; cons. GCC Beverages, 1982-84. Served with USN, 1943-46, 51-53. Registered profl. engr., Wis. Mem. Am. Inst. Plant Engrs., Nat. Soc. Profl. Engrs. Republican. Episcopalian. Clubs: University, Winter Park Racquet. Home: 860 Park Ave N Winter Park FL 32789

OWEN, JANET SUE, educational administrator; b. Lebanon, Ind., Aug. 13, 1940; d. Marion William and Mary Margaret Johnson; B.S., Ind. State U., 1961; M.A. in Edn., East Carolina U., 1970, M.A. in Ednl. Adminstrn., 1980; m. Jerry Don Owen, June 3, 1961. Elem. tchr. Swansboro, N.C., 1961-62; jr. high sch. tchr., Hawaii, 1963-66; tchr. Camp Lejeune, N.C., 1966-70, Fayetteville, N.C., 1970-71; elem. sci., math. tchr. Lumberton, N.C., 1971-80; prin. Tanglewood Elem. Sch., Lumberton, 1981—; condr. workshops nat. and state math. and sci. confs. Named Lumberton City Tchr. of Yr., 1975, Luberton Jr. High Tchr. of Yr., 1975, 80; recipient Terry Sanford award Lumberton City, 1976. Mem. Nat. Sci. Tchrs. Assn., Nat. Assn. Elem. Sch. Prins., N.C. Assn. Sch. Adminstrs., Assn. for Supervision and Curriculum Devel., Phi Delta Kappa, Delta Kappa Gamma. Republican. Baptist. Club: Order Eastern Star (past matron). Home: PO Box 787 Lumberton NC 28383 Office: W 29th St Lumberton NC 28358

OWEN, JOHN WILLIAM, pharmacist, consultant; b. Fort Payne, Ala., May 24, 1944; s. Oscar Eugene and Pauline Agnes (Henry) O.; m. Lynda Alyce Trotter, June 1, 1968; children—John William Tara, Richard. B.S. in Pharmacy, U. S.C., 1973. Lic. pharmacist, S.C. Pharmacy intern, Parkman's Pharmacy, Saluda, S.C., 1974-75; pharmacy unit mgr. Scottie Discount Drug, West Columbia, S.C., 1975-77; owner, pharmacist Hampton St. Pharmacy, Columbia, 1977-79, Middleburg Pharmacy, Columbia, 1979—; cons. pharmacist Lexington/Richland Alcohol and Drug Abuse Council, Columbia, 1981—. Chmn. drug edn. program U. S.C. Coll. Pharmacy, Columbia, 1973; deacon Capitol View Baptist Ch., Columbia, 1981, Kilbourne Park Bapt. Ch., Columbia, 1984; bd. dirs. Planned Parenthood of Central S.C., 1985-86. Recipient Community Service award Coll. Pharmacy, 1973. Mem. Am. Pharm. Assn., Acad. Pharmacy Practice, S.C. Pharm. Assn., 5th Dist. Pharm. Assn. (v.p. 1980-81), Am. Diabetes Assn., Am. Diabetes Assn. (S.C. affiliate) (dir. 1981-83), Nat. Assn. Retail Druggists, Naval Res. Assn. (v.p. chpt. 13 1983—), S.C. Jaycees (treas. Saluda chpt. 1975, Jaycee of Yr. 1975). Republican. Club: Scouts on Stamps Soc. (dir. 1967-68). Avocations: stamp collecting; volunteer work. Office: Middleburg Pharmacy 1701 Saint Julian Place Columbia SC

OWEN, KARL ABRAHIM, educator, architectural interior design consultant b. Baghdad, Iraq, Sept. 24, 1929; s. Abrahim Haney and Facrea J. (Quaraghooly) O.; m. Gwenivere O. Owen, Aug. 18, 1957; chidlren—Pamela Jody, Bradford Haney. M.A.T., Assumption Coll., 1966. Environ. coordinator Coll. of DuPage, Glen Ellyn, Ill., 1970-73; pres. United Interiors and Contract Designers, Inc., Wheaton, Ill., 1973-79; asst. prof. Bowing Green State U. (Ohio), 1979-82, Winthrop Coll. Sch. Consumer Sci., Rock Hill, S.C., 1982—; design cons. Am. United Interiors and Design, Rock Hill; judge interior design competition, Detroit, 1979, ann. art. exhbn., Downers Grove, Ill., 1974-77; vis. historian Republic of Iraq, 1979. Recipient Nat. Painting award Ministry Edn., Baghdad, 1950; Blue Ribbon award for analytical painting Longmeadow (Mass.) Art League, 1974; Mem. Am. Assn. Textile Chemists and Colorists, Am. Soc. Interior Designers, Interior Design Educators Council, Nat. Assn. Home Economists. Republican. Researcher, developer chromology and allotropy. Home: 4218 Wood Fores Dr Rock Hill SC 29730 Office: Am United Interiors and Design PO Box 2564 Rock Hill SC 29731

OWEN, KENNETH DALE, orthodontist; b. Charlotte, N.C., May 9, 1938; s. Olin Watson and Ruth (Watlington) O.; B.S., Davidson Coll., 1959; D.D.S., U. N.C., 1963, M.Sc. in Orthodontics, 1967; m. Lura Aven Carnes, Feb. 14, 1958; children—Kenneth Dale, Aven Anna. Individual practice orthodontics, Charlotte, 1966—. Asst. clin. prof. U. N.C. Sch. Dentistry, 1969-72. Bd. dirs. N.C. Dental Found., 1973-81, exec. com., 1974-80, v.p. 1976-77, pres., 1978-79. Served with Dental Corps, AUS, 1963-65. Diplomate Am. Bd. Orthodontics. Fellow Internat. Coll. Dentists (dep. regent N.C. 1986), Am. Coll. Dentists; mem. ADA (ho. of dels. 1981—), Am. Assn. Orthodontists (ho. of dels. 1980—) So. Soc. Orthodontists (trustee 1983-85), N.C. Orthodontic Soc. (bd. dirs. 1976—, sec.-treas. 1976-78, pres. 1979-80), N.C. (ho. dels. 1969-77, 81—, trustee 1980—), 2d Dist. (editor 1967-69, sec.-treas. 1971-74, pres. 1975-76, exec. council 1971-77, 80—), Charlotte (chmn. various coms., dir. 1978-79, v.p. 1980-81), Stanly County dental socs., Acad. Gen. Dentistry, Coll. Diplomates Am. Bd. Orthodontics, U. N.C. Orthodontic Alumni Assn. (life; sec.-treas. 1971, v.p. 1972-73, pres. 1974-75, exec. com. 1971-76), Orthovista Orthodontic Study Group, Delta Sigma Delta (life; pres. N.C. grad. chpt. 1970-71), Omicron Kappa Upsilon, Kappa Sigma, Alpha Epsilon Delta. Methodist (steward 1968-69, adminstrn. bd. 1969-71, 74-75, 77-80). Clubs: Charlotte Country, Olde Providence. Home: 3724 Pomfret Ln Charlotte NC 28211 Office: 497 W Wendover Rd Charlotte NC 28204 also 119 Yadkin St Albemarle NC 28001

OWEN, LARRY GENE, university educator, electronic consultant; b. Pine Bluff, Ark., Oct. 2, 1932; s. Cecil Earl and Helen Marie (Jacks) O.; m. Ruth Myra Newton, Sept. 3, 1953; children—Deborah, Patricia, Larry Jr., Shea. B.S. in Physics and Math., U. So. Miss., 1967. Enlisted in U.S. Air Force, 1951, advanced through ranks to m. sgt., 1968; electronic technician, 1951-61; communications supt., 1961-71, retired, 1971; tchr. math. and physics Southwestern Tech. Inst., Camden, Ark., 1971-72, tchr. electronics, 1972-75; dean tech. engring. So. Ark. U. Tech., Camden, 1975—. Sr. mem. Instrumentation Soc. Am.; mem. Am. Assn. Physics Tchrs., Am. Tech. Edn. Assn. Baptist. Home: 306 Lakeside Ave Camden AR 71701 Office: So Ark U Tech Camden AR 71701

OWEN, LINDA CARRUTH (LIN), society administrator, museum administrator; b. Laurel, Miss., Dec. 16, 1937; d. Joseph Enoch and Mary Marguerite (Bean) Carruth; m. Benjamin Lloyd Owen, Nov. 27, 1958; children—Lauren Ashley, Erin Adair. B.A., Millsaps Coll., 1958; postgrad. La. State U., 1963. Social worker La. Dept. Child Welfare, Baton Rouge and Lake Charles, 1960-68; supr. Kans. Dept. Child Welfare, Wichita, 1971-72; cons. Christian Child Help Found., Houston, 1981-84; dir. Beaumont Heritage Soc., Tex., 1984—; pres., dir. Wichita Youth Home, 1976-78. Pres. League Women Voters, Beaumont, 1983-85; bd. dirs. Beaumont Conv. and Visitors Bur., 1984—, Beaumont Plan, 1985; pres.-elect Symphony Women's League, Beaumont, 1983-84; active Mayor's Com., Beaumont, 1984-85; charter mem. Women's Commn. of Southeastern Tex., 1985 mem. block grant com. Beaumont Community Devel., 1985—. Mem. Tex. Assn. Mus., Am. Assn. Mus., Tex. Hist. Found. Democrat. Methodist.

OWEN, VICKI MARIE, physical education educator, coach; b. Lake Charles, La., Oct. 17, 1953; d. Arthur Blake and Janet (James) O. B.S., Centenary Coll., 1975; M.Ed., La. State U., 1982. Tchr. phys. edn., coach Booker T. Washington High Sch., Shreveport, La., 1975-81, Caddo Parish Magnet High Sch., Shreveport, 1982—. Mem. NEA, AAHPERD, Womens Sports Found., NOW. Democrat. Methodist. Home: 3020 Colquitt Rd Apt 1007 Shreveport LA 71118 Office: Caddo Magnet High Sch 1601 Viking St Shreveport LA 71101

OWEN, WARREN HERBERT, utility executive; b. Rock Hill, S.C., Jan. 8, 1927; s. Warren Herbert and Margaret Elizabeth (White) O.; B.M.E., Clemson (S.C.) U., 1947; m. Virginia Lea Boulware, Oct. 22, 49; children—Virginia Ann, Carol Elizabeth, Susan Laine. With Duke Power Co., 1948—, prin. mech. engr., design engring. dept., Charlotte, 1966-71, v.p. design engring., 1971-78, sr. v.p. engring. and constrn., 1978-82, exec. v.p. engring. and constrn., 1982-84, exec. v.p. engring., constrn. and prodn. group, 1984—, also dir.; dir. Systems Assocs., Inc. Bd. dirs. Jr. Achievement Charlotte, 1978—. Recipient Robinson award Duke Power Co., 1965, Philip T. Sprague award Instrument Soc. Am., 1970, Clyde A. Lilly, Jr., award Atomic Indsl. Forum, 1981. Fellow ASME; mem. Am. Nuclear Soc., Nat. Acad. Engring., N.C. Soc. Engrs. (Outstanding Engring. Achievement award 1984), Profl. Engrs. N.C., Charlotte Engrs. (Disting. Service award 1981). Club. Episcopalian. Club: Charlotte Rotary. Home: 2131 Valencia Terr Charlotte NC 28226 Office: PO Box 33189 Charlotte NC 28242

OWENS, DORIS JERKINS, insurance underwriter; b. Range, Ala., June 16, 1940; d. Arthur Charles and Jennie (Lee) Jerkins; m. Gilbert Landers Owens, Jan. 29, 1959; 1 child, Alan Dale. Student Massey Draughon Bus. Coll., 1958-59, Auburn U., 1980, 81, 82. Cert. profl. ins. woman. Exec. sec. Henry C. Barnet, Gen. Agt., Montgomery, Ala., 1959-66; underwriter So. Guaranty Ins. Co., Montgomery, 1966—. Author: Bike Safety, 1976. Instr. Coop. State Dept. Defensive Driver Instr., 1975, 78; v.p. Montgomery Citizens Fire Safety, 1981; panelist Gov.'s Safety Conf., Montgomery, 1975—; mem., panelist Women Annual Hwy. Safety Leaders, Montgomery, 1976, 78, 80. Recipient Able Toastmaster award Dist. 48 Toastmasters, 1979, Outstanding Lt. Gov. award, 1981, Outstanding Area Gov. award, 1980; named Ins. Woman of Year, 1979. Mem. Ins. Women Montgomery (pres. safety 1961, pres. 1985-86). Home: 4504 Cleveland Ave Montgomery AL 36105 Office: So Guaranty Ins Co 88 W Southern Blvd Montgomery AL 36105

OWENS, LARRY MACMURPHY, civic association executive; b. Winter Haven, Fla., Oct. 5, 1946; s. Billie MacMurphy and Anita Pauline (Taylor) O.; m. Beverly Hardy, Feb. 22, 1974; 1 son, Scott. B.S., Auburn U., 1968. Jr. acct. McWane Iron Co., Mobile, Ala., 1969-70; jr. acct. Litton Industries, Pascagoula, Miss., 1970-72; budget analyst Teledyne Continental Motors, Mobile, 1972-74; acctg. supr. Univ. Med. Ctr., Mobile, 1974-80; comptroller ARC, Mobile, 1980—. Campaign auditor United Way, 1981-83. Mem. Health Care Fin. Mgmt. Assn., Mobile Regional Cash Mgmt. Assn. Baptist. Home: 8155 Healy Dr Mobile AL 36609

OWENS, LEWIS E., newspaper executive; b. Knoxville, Tenn., Mar. 11, 1934; m. Janetta Owens. B.S., Gainesville Coll. Retail advt. salesman Fort Worth Press, 1956-59; advt. dir. Gainesville Daily Register, 1959-62; asst. retail advt. mgr. Charlotte Observer and News, N.C., 1962-66; retail advt. mgr. Tallahassee Democrat, Fla., 1966-68, Charlotte Observer and News, 1968-75; advt. dir. Lexington Herald-Leader, Ky., 1975-78, v.p. sales and mktg., 1978-82, v.p. and gen. mgr., 1982—. Sec. bd. dirs. Lexington Arts Council; v.p. Central Ky. Blood Ctr.; pres. United Way of the Bluegrass, 1978, 79, campaign chmn., 1977. Mem. Greater Lexington Area C. of C. (pres.-elect), Ky. Press Assn. (v.p.). Avocations: golf; racquetball; travel; sports. Home: 624 Teakwood Dr Lexington KY 40502

OWENS, MONROE LEE, electronics company executive; b. Bluefield, W.Va., July 24, 1947; s. William Franklin and Henrietta Roberta (Burge) O.; m. Pamela Bea, Aug. 27, 1965; children—Monroe Lee, Heather Celene. Quality inspector Atlantic Research Corp., Alexandria, Va., 1966-69; quality analyst Fairchild Hiller Corp., Franconia, Va., 1969-70; quality technician IBM Corp., Manassas, Va., 1970-75, quality engr., 1975-80; quality assurance mgr., mfg. engring. mgr. ITT Corp., Culpeper, Va., 1980-81, Interarms, Midland, Va., 1981-82; quality assurance mgr. Scope Inc., Reston, Va., 1982-85; v.p. Manufacturing Services Inc., Manassas, 1985—. Home: 1041 Sperryville Pike

Culpeper VA 22701 Office: Manufacturing Services Inc 8492 Signal Hill Rd Manassas VA 22110

OWENS, PATRICIA ANN, public relations executive; b. Newport News, Va., Sept. 18, 1957; d. Deames Clemitson and Ruth Evelyn (Jones) Owens Parker; stepdau. John T. Parker. B.A. in Profl. English, N.C. Agrl. and Tech. State U., 1978; M.S. in Journalism, Iowa State U., 1980. Program asst. English dept. N.C. Agrl. and Tech. State U., Greensboro, 1975-77; publs. intern Learning Inst. of N.C., Greensboro, 1978; teaching, research and testing asst. Iowa State U., Ames, 1978-80; asst. dir. pub. relations Hampton (Va.) Inst., 1981—. Mem. 2434-A Neighborhood Council. W.E. Kellogg scholar, 1978. Mem. Internat. Assn. Bus. Communicators (best in Va. award 1982), Pub. Relations Soc. Am., Career Guild, Am. Scholastic Press Assn. (1982 Yearbook award), Alpha Kappa Alpha, N.C. Agrl. and State U. Alumni Assn. Baptist. Home: 1228 32d St Newport News VA 23607 Office: Hampton Inst Office Pub Relations PO Box 6446 Hampton VA 23668

OWENS, PHILLIP JAY, fire department officer; b. Owensboro, Ky., Nov. 28, 1950; s. Hubert McVardiman Owens and Agnes Viola (Boyle) Freeman; m. Barbara June Goetz, May 20, 1972; 1 child, Lauren Paige. B.S., Murray State U., 1975; postgrad. in Fire Prevention, Nat. Fire Acad., Emmitsburg, Md., 1981. Cert. profl. fire fighter, Ky.; cert. fire protection instr., Ky. Chief technician emergency med. technician Mercy Ambulance, Murray, Ky., 1972-74; evidence technician Murray Police Dept., 1974-78; fire marshall Murray Fire Dept., 1978—; adj. instr. fire sci. Murray State U., 1979—. Author manual: Municipal Employees Safety, 1983. Served to lt. U.S. Army, 1969-71. Recipient Disting. Service Cross, Murray Fire Dept., 1981, Meritorious Service medal Murray Fire Dept., 1984, Outstanding Fire Officer of Yr. award Murray Fire Dept., 1984. Mem. Soc. Fire Protection Engrs. (technologist), Jackson Purchase Fire Fighters Assn. (bd. dirs. 1984—), Am. Soc. Safety Engrs., Fire Marshal's Assn. North Am., Internat. Assn. Arson Investigators, Code Adminstrs. Assn. Ky., Co. of Mil. Historians, Orders and Medals Soc. Democrat. Baptist. Avocations: study of Am. military history; collecting military medals. Home: 1507 Danbury Rd Murray KY 42071 Office: Office of Fire Marshall City Hall Bldg Murray KY 42071

OWENS, WALLACE, JR., art educator; b. Muskogee, Okla., Dec. 28, 1932; s. Wallace Arthur and Sarah (Evans) O. B.A. in Art Edn., Langston U., 1959; M. in Teaching Art, Central State U., Edmond, Okla., 1965; M.F.A., Instituto Allende, San Miguel de Allende, Mex., 1966; postgrad. North Tex. State U., 1970-71. Chmn. art dept. Langston U., Okla., 1966-80; asst. prof. art Central State U., Edmond, 1980—. One-man shows include: Langston U., 1980; Okla. Territorial Mus., 1983; Art Assn., Oklahoma City, 1985; exhibited paintings and sculpture in group shows throughout Midwest; represented in State of Okla. Collection. Served with U.S. Army, 1953-55, Fed. Republic Germany. Fulbright scholar U. Rome, summer 1970; study tour grantee African Am. Inst., 1973. Mem. Higher Edn. Alumni Council, Okla. Edn. Assn. Democrat. Baptist. Club: Lions. Home: 1223 E Vilas St Guthrie OK 73044 Office: Art Dept Central State U Edmond OK 73034

OWENS, WILBUR DAWSON, JR., judge; b. Albany, Ga., Feb. 1, 1930; s. Wilbur Dawson and Estelle (McKenzie) O.; student Emory U., 1947-48; J.D., U. Ga., 1952; m. Mary Elizabeth Glenn, June 21, 1958; children—Lindsey, Wilbur Dawson III, Estelle, John. Admitted to Ga. bar, 1952; mem. firm Smith, Gardner & Owens, Albany, 1954-55; v.p., trust officer Bank of Albany, 1955-59; sec.-treas. Southeastern Mortgage Co., Albany, 1959-62; asst. U.S. atty. Middle Dist. Ga., Macon, 1962-64; asso., then partner Bloch, Hall, Hawkins & Owens, Macon, 1965-72; U.S. dist. judge Middle Dist. Ga., Macon, 1972—, now chief judge. Served to 1st lt., JAG, USAF, 1952-54. Mem. Am. Bar Assn., State Bar Ga., Am. Judicature Soc., Phi Delta Theta, Phi Delta Phi. Republican. Presbyterian. Rotarian. Club: Idle Hour Golf and Country. Home: 4288 Old Club Rd E Macon GA 31210 Office: PO Box 65 Macon GA 31202

OWENS, WILLIAM EMMONS, citrus grower; b. Palm Beach, Fla., Oct. 7, 1925; s. James Marion, Jr., and Willa Lester (Bazemore) O.; m. Ronda W. Stephens, June 16, 1949; children—Jaima Owens Scott, William Emmons, Jr., Heather. B.S. in Bus. Adminstrn., U. Fla., 1950. Citrus grower, Indiantown, Fla., 1951—; dir. 1st Fed. Savs. & Loan Assn., 1956—, chmn. bd., 1975-83, merged with 1st Fidelity Savs. & Loan of Winter Park (Fla.), 1983, vice chmn. bd., 1983—; dir., past pres. Martin County chpt. Fla. Farm Bur.; mem. Fla. Citrus Mut., Minute Man. Mem. Fla. Ho. of Reps., 1962-66; mem. Martin County Commn., 1968-72; v.p. Palm Beach chpt. Am. Heart Assn., 1983. Served with USAAF, 1944-46. Named Farm Family of Yr., South Fla. Fair, 1965. Democrat. Presbyterian (elder). Clubs: Indianwood (Indiantown), Mariner Sands (Stuart, Fla.). Lodges: Masons, Kiwanis (past lt. gov.). Home: 67 N River Rd Stuart FL 33494 Office: PO Box 306 Indiantown FL 33456

OWINGS, ADDISON DAVIS, agronomy educator; b. Hattiesburg, Miss., Feb. 8, 1936; s. A.D. and Elizabeth Lynn (Steadman) O.; m. Kay Grace; children—Allen Davis, Don Frazier. Student Hinds Jr. Coll., 1953-55; B.S. in Agronomy-Crops, Miss. State Coll., 1957; M.S. in Agronomy-Crops, Miss. State U., 1962, Ph.D. in Agronomy-Crops, 1966. Asst. agronomist, cotton, Delta Br. of Miss. Agrl. Experiment Sta., Stoneville, 1957-59; instr. agr. Southeastern La. U., Hammond, 1963-64, asst. prof. agr., 1964-67, assoc. prof. agr., dept. head, 1967-70, prof. agr., 1970—, head dept., 1970-83; mem. agrl. adv. com. La. Bankers Assn., 1968-80, agr. adv. com. U.S. Rep. W. Henson Moore, 6th Dist. La., 1975-80. Elder First Presbyn. Ch., Ponchatoula, La., 1973—, deacon, 1968-73, sec., 1969-73, clk. of session, 1973—, trustee, 1971-73, 82-84, Sunday Sch. tchr., 1967—, Sunday Sch. supt., 1969-83, sec. bldg. com., 1973; NDEA fellow, 1959-63; recipient Congress of Freedom Liberty award, 1973; named Hon. State Farmer, La. Assn. Future Farmers Am., 1969. Mem. Am. Soc. Agronomy, La. Assn. Agronomists, Am. Farm Bur. Fedn., Council for Agrl. Sci. and Tech. (state liaison rep. 1981—), Am. Quarter Horse Assn., Southeast La. Dairy Festival, Alpha Zeta, Delta Tau Alpha (hon.). Mem. vocat. agr. textbook adoption com. State of La., 1979; contbg. author circulars, info. sheets, bulls., articles in field. Office: Southeastern La U Box 708 Hammond LA 70402

OWINGS, FRANCIS BARRE, surgeon; b. McColl, S.C., Mar. 9, 1941; s. Ralph Seer and Antoinette (Moore) O.; B.S., U. Miss., 1963, M.D., 1966; m. Judith Myers, Feb. 14, 1976; children—F. Patterson, Caroline C. Intern, San Francisco Gen. Hosp., 1966-67; resident in surgery U. Calif., San Francisco, 1969-74; surg. registrar Norfolk and Norwich Hosp., Norwich, Eng., 1971-72; practice medicine specializing in surgery, Atlanta, 1974—; mem. staff Crawford Long Hosp., pres. med. staff, 1981-82; mem. staff St. Joseph Hosp.; clin. instr. surgery Emory U. Served to capt. USAF, 1967-69. Diplomate Am. Bd. Surgery. Fellow ACS, Southeastern Surg. Congress; mem. Med. Assn. Atlanta, Med. Assn. Ga., So. Med. Assn., Naffziger Surg. Soc., Alpha Epsilon Delta, Sigma Chi, Phi Chi. Republican. Methodist. Home: 365 Brentwood Terr Atlanta GA 30305 Office: 478 Peachtree NE Atlanta GA 30308

OWINS, REBECCA ELIZABETH, nurse; b. Norfolk, Va., Feb. 11, 1940; d. Charles Joseph and Nellie Blanche (Dobbins) O. Diploma Louise Obici Sch. Nursing, Suffolk, Va., 1961; cert. Baylor Med. Ctr., Dallas, 1963. R.N., N.C., Va. Staff nurse Louise Obici Meml. Hosp., Suffolk, 1961-63, head nurse, 1963-64; staff nurse Duke U. Med. Ctr., Durham, N.C., 1964, head nurse neurology, 1964-66, asst. dir. operating room nursing services, 1966-67, dir. operating room nursing services, 1967—. Mem. Am. Heart Assn., Assn. Operating Room Nurses, Southeastern Surg. Nurses Assn. (state counciller 1984-85), N.C. Assn. for Central Service Personnel. Home: 1412 Imperial Dr Durham NC 27712 Office: Duke U Med Ctr PO Box 3237 Durham NC 27710

OWSLEY, WILLIAM CLINTON, JR., radiologist; b. Austin, Tex., Oct. 6, 1923; s. William Clinton and Lois (Lamar) O.; B.A., U. Tex., 1944; M.D., U. Pa., 1946; m. Betty Pinckard, 1949; 2 children. Intern, Hermann Hosp., Houston, 1946-47; resident Hosp. of U. Pa., Phila., 1949-52; instr. radiology U. Pa., 1950-52; practice medicine specializing in radiology, Houston, 1952—; mem. staff Hermann Hosp., Twelve Oaks Hosp., Bellville Hosp., Meml. Hosp. of Waller County, Brazos Valley Hosp.; assoc. clin. prof. radiology U. Tex. Served with USNR, 1947-48. Diplomate Am. Bd. Radiology. Fellow Am. Coll. Radiology, Am. Roentgen Ray Soc., Radiol. Soc. N.Am., AMA. Republican. Baptist. Office: 214 Hermann Profl Bldg Houston TX 77030

OXENREITER, ROBERT ANTHONY, energy company executive; b. Pitts., June 2, 1936; s. Maurice F. and Helen (Miller) O.; m. Beverly A. Axmacher, Jan. 31, 1959; children—Cheryl Lynn, Allan Robert, Denise Doreen, Rhonda Gail, Rodney Dale. B.S. in Petroleum Engring., U. Pitts., 1960; M.B.A., So. Meth. U., 1969. Registered profl. engr., Tex. Engr., analyst Panhandle Eastern Pipeline, Liberal, Kans., 1960-65; sr. petroleum engr. H.J. Gruy & Assocs., Dallas, 1965-69; asst. dir. property acquisitions Earth Resources Co., Dallas, 1969-71; v.p. Transcontinental Energy Corp., Shreveport, La., 1971-73, exec. v.p., dir., chief operating officer, 1973-80, pres., chief exec. officer, dir., 1980-83, vice chmn. bd., 1983-84; pres., chief exec. officer Nu-Era Corp., Shreveport, 1984—; dir. Bank of Commerce, Shreveport. Bd. dirs. Jr. Achievement, Shreveport/Bossier City. Mem. Ind. Petroleum Assn. Am. (dir.), Nat. Assn. Bus. Economists, AIME, Oil Investors Inst. (dir.), Internat. Assn. Drilling Contractors (dir.). Democrat. Roman Catholic. Clubs: East Ridge Country, University, Petroleum (Shreveport); Petroleum (Dallas and Houston). Office: PO Box 49 300 American Tower Shreveport LA 71161

OXFORD, HUBERT, III, lawyer; b. Beaumont, Tex., Sept. 25, 1938; s. Hubert Burton and Virginia Mary (Cunningham) O.; m. Mary Francelia Crittenden, Feb. 25, 1967; children—Mary Francelia, Hubert IV, Mary Cunningham, Virginia Barrett. B.S.M.E., Tex. A&M U., 1960; LL.B., U. Tex., 1963. Bar: Tex., 1963, U.S. Ct. Appeals (5th cir.), 1967, U.S. Supreme Ct., 1975. Briefing clk. to U.S. dist. judge Eastern Dist. Tex., Beaumont, 1966; asst. dist. atty. Jefferson County, Tex., 1967; city atty. City of Nome (Tex.), 1970—, City of China (Tex.), 1971—, City of Sour Lake (Tex.), 1972—; ptnr. firm Benckenstein, McNicholas, Oxford, Radford & Johnson, Beaumont, 19—. Bd. dirs. Ducks Unltd., 1978—, Gulf Coast Conservation Assn., 1978—; sec. bd. regents Lamar U., 1978-84; mem. Tex. Air Control Bd., 1984—; chmn. Tex. Clean Air Study. Served to capt. JAGC, USAF, 1963-66. Mem. Tex. Bar Assn., Tex. Assn. Def. Lawyers, Maritime Law Assn., Beaumont C. of C. (dir. 1978-84), Phi Delta Theta, Tau Beta Pi, Phi Kappa Phi, Phi Delta Phi. Democrat. Roman Catholic. Office: PO Box 150 3535 Calder Ave Allied Bank Bldg Beaumont TX 77704

OXLEY, PHILIP, oil company executive; b. Utica, N.Y., Feb. 1, 1922; s. Chester Jay and Beatrice (Heller) O.; m. Dafna Ronn, Dec. 19, 1981; children by previous marriage—Christopher, Jonathan, Timothy, Philip, Patricia. B.A., Denison U., 1943; M.A., Columbia U., 1948, Ph.D., 1952; Instr., asst. prof., chmn. dept. geology Hamilton Coll., Clinton, N.Y., 1948-53; geologist Calif. Co., 1953-57; dist. and div. exploration mgr. Tenn. Gas Transmission Co., 1957-61; div. exploration mgr., v.p. exploration, dir. Signal Oil & Gas Co., 1961-69; exec. v.p. Tex. Crude Oil, 1969-71; mgr. geology, v.p. Tenneco Oil Co., Houston, 1971-74, sr. v.p., 1974-79, exec. v.p. oil exploration and prodn., 1980-81, pres., 1981—; mem. adv. bd. dept. geology U. Tex., Austin. Trustee Denison U.; chmn. So. regional bd. Inst. Internat. Edn. Served with USNR, 1943-46. Fellow Geol. Soc. Am.; mem. Am. Assn. Petroleum Geologists, Sigma Xi. Presbyterian.

OZARK, DAMIAN MICHAEL, lawyer, consultant; b. Lackawanna, N.Y., Sept. 3, 1954; s. Norwood Wallace and Theresa Rita (Powers) O.; B.A., U. Miss., 1976; J.D., Miss. Coll., 1980. Bar: Miss. 1981. Atty. Chevron U.S.A., Inc., New Orleans, 1981—. Precinct capt. Republican Party, New Orleans, 1984; active Rep. Nat. Com., 1984, Nat. Rep. Congl. Com., 1984. Recipient Am. Jurisprudence award, 1980. Mem. ABA, Miss. Bar Assn., Am. Assn. Petroleum Landmen, Petroleum Landmen Assn. New Orleans, Denver Assn. Petroleum Landmen, Assn. Trial Lawyers Am., Am. Judicature Soc., Mid-Continental Oil and Gas Assn., Nat. Ocean Industries Assn., New Orleans Bar Assn. (assoc.). Roman Catholic. Home: 184 Sandra Del Mar Mandeville LA 70448 Office: Chevron USA Inc 935 Gravier St Suite 882 New Orleans LA 70112

PAANANEN, ELOISE ENGLE, writer, editor; b. Seattle, Apr. 12, 1923; d. Floyd C. and Lois Best Hopper; m. Paul R. Engle, July 7, 1943 (div. 1967); children—David, Margaret; m. Lauri A. Paananen, Oct. 1, 1973. Student George Washington U., 1944-47. Freelance writer, editor, publicist. Decorated Order of White Rose 1st class (Finland); recipient best book awards. Mem. Am. Soc. Journalists and Authors (dir.-at-large), Authors Guild, Soc. Woman Geographers. Republican. Author: Countdown for Cindy, 1962; Sea Challenge, 1962; Dawn Mission, 1962; Princess of Paradise, 1962; Sea of the Bear, 1964; Pararescue, 1964; Escape, 1965; Medic, 1966; Parachutes-How They Work, 1972; The Winter War-The Russo Finnish Conflict of 1939-40, 1973; America's Maritime Heritage, 1975; Finns in North America, 1975; Man in Flight-Achievements in Aerospace, 1979; Tremor-Earthquake Technology in the Space Age, 1982; Of Cabbages and the King, 1984; The Baltimore One-Day Trip Book, 1985; others. Home: 6348 Cross Woods Dr Falls Church VA 22044

PAARFUS, BARBARA DIANELEIDHOLDT, psychologist; b. Hartford, Conn., Apr. 29, 1936; d. Louis Frederick and Helen Gladys Christine (Christensen) Leidholdt. B.A., Gettysburg Coll., 1957; M.A., Temple U., 1959. Lic. psychologist, Va. Tchr., Overbrook Sch. for the Blind, Phila., 1958-60; guidance counselor Henrico County Sch. Bd., Richmond, Va., 1960-61; psychologist, instr. psychiatry dept. Med. Coll. Va., Richmond, 1961-74; psychologist Richmond Pub. Schs., 1975-79, Westbrook Psychiat. Hosp., Richmond, 1982-83, Mecklenburg County Pub. Schs., Boydton, Va., 1984—; cons. Fredericksburg Mental Health Clinic (Va.), 1974. Recipient REACT Sch. Cert. of Appreciation award, Richmond, Va., 1976. Mem. Am. Psychol. Assn., Va. Psychol. Assn., Nat. Assn. Sch. Psychologists, Va. Assn. Sch. Psychologists, Gettysburg Coll. Alumni Assn., Chi Omega. Clubs: Parents Without Ptnrs., Off Broad St. Players Drama. Home: 803 West St Clarksville VA 23927 Office: PO Box 190 Boydton VA 23917

PACE, CAROLINA JOLLIFF, educational communications executive; b. Dallas, Apr. 12, 1938; d. Lindsay Gafford and Carolina (Juden) Jolliff; student Holton-Arms Jr. Coll., 1956-57; B.A. in Comparative Lit., So. Meth. U., 1960; m. John McIver Pace, Oct. 7, 1961. Fashion cons., lectr. Nancy Taylor Sch., Dallas, 1959-61; promotional adv., dir. found. funding Dallas Theatre Center, 1960-61; exec. sec. Dallas Book and Author Luncheon, 1959-63; promotional and instnl. cons. Henry Regnery-Reilly & Lee Pub. Co., Chgo., 1962-65; pub. trade rep. various cos., institutional rep. Don R. Phillips Co., Southeastern area, 1965-67; Southwestern rep. Ednl. Reading Service, Inc.-Troll Assos., Mahwah, N.J., 1967-72; v.p., dir. multimedia div. Melton Book Co., Dallas, 1972-79; dir. mktg. Webster's Internat., Inc., Nashville, 1980, v.p. mktg., 1981-82; pres. Carolina Pace, Inc., 1982—; proposal and project reviewer Health and Human Services, Washington, 19823, 834, 845; mem. nat. adv. bd. Nat. Info. Center Spl. Edn. Materials; speaker seminar Nat. Media Center for Severely and Profoundly Handicapped, 1980, adv. panel, 1981—; mem. rev. panel Linc, Columbus, Ohio, 1981—. Adviser Tex. Gov.'s Com. on Employment of Handicapped, 1983—. Mem. Women's Nat. Book Assn., Internat. Communications Industries Assn., (speaker 1979 conf.), Assn. Ednl. and Communications Tech., Council Exceptional Children (chmn. publicity and public relations com. 1979 conf.), ALA (AASL arrangements coordinator 1979 conf.), Pub. Relations Soc. Am., Tex. Library Assn., Internat. Communications Industry Assn. Women in Communications, Assn. Spl. Edn. Tech. (nat. dir., v.p.), DAR, Dallas Central Bus. Assn., Dallas Civic Opera Assn., Friends of Dallas Public Library, Dallas Art Assn., Dallas Press Club, Alpha Delta Pi. Presbyterian. Contbr. articles to profl. publs. Home: 4524 Lorraine Ave Dallas TX 75205

PACE, CATHERINE CRAIG, pharmacy administrator; b. Greenwood, Miss., June 12, 1954; d. Raymond Lee, Jr. and Helen Keyes (Brewer) Craig; m. Clifford Earl Pace, Aug. 23, 1975; children—Jonathan Craig, Jennifer Allen. Student Miss. State U., 1972-74; B.S. in Pharmacy, U. Miss., 1977. Registered pharmacist, Miss. Sr. staff pharmacist Golden Triangle Regional Med. Ctr., Columbus, Miss., 1977-79; dir. pharmacy Columbus Hosp. Inc., Miss., 1979—; clin. instr. clin. pharmacy practice U. Miss., 1985—. Mem. Miss. Soc. Hosp. Pharmacists, Rho Chi (v.p. 1976). Baptist. Clubs: Lattice and Lace Garden (Columbus) (sec. 1985-86), Moonlighters Homemaker (Columbus). Avocations: cross-stitching; smocking; swimming. Office: Columbus Hosp Inc 525 Willowbrook Rd Columbus MS 39701

PACE, CHARLES MILLS, lawyer; b. Spartanburg, S.C., May 19, 1911; s. Otis Leroy and Amanda (Blackwood) P.; B.S., Clemson U., 1932; LL.B., U. S.C., 1935, J.D., 1969, Ph.D., 1970; m. June Cannington, July 23, 1966. Admitted to S.C. bar, 1935, practiced in Spartanburg, 1935-36, 71—; probate judge, Spartanburg, 1939-42; judge Superior County Ct., Spartanburg County, 1947-71. Mem. S.C. Ho. of Reps., 1937-38; mem. citizens com. Spartanburg County Council, 1963-66; mem. Brotherhood of St. Andrew, Ch. of Advent Episcopal Ch. Served from 2d lt. to maj. AUS, 1942-46; col. Res. ret. Mem. S.C. Bar Assn. (pres. county judges assn. div. 1969-70), Pace Soc. Am. (1st v.p. 1963-68), Burns Hist. Soc. (pres. 1977-79, chmn. bd. trustees 1979-80), SAR (v.p. Daniel Morgan chpt. 1979-80, pres. 1980-81, state pres. 1981-82), Phi Delta Phi, Omicron Delta Kappa, Pi Kappa Alpha. Clubs: Spartanburg Country, Piedmont. Home: 1166 Woodburn Rd Spartanburg SC 29302 Office: 248 N Church St PO Box 2413 Spartanburg SC 29304

PACE, MARSHALL OSTEEN, electrical engineering educator, researcher; b. Greenville, S.C., Sept. 10, 1941; s. Samuel Marshall and Margaret (Osteen) P.; m. Phyllis Cooper, Apr. 19, 1968; children—Whitney, Kimberly. B.S., U. S.C., 1963; M.S., MIT, 1965; Ph.D., Ga. Inst. Tech., 1970. Registered profl. engr., Tenn. Prof. elec. engring. U. Tenn., Knoxville, 1970—; cons. Oak Ridge Nat. Lab., 1973—; faculty fellow NASA, Huntsville, Ala., 1974; prin. investigator, NSF, Carborundum, Carrier, Union Carbide, Martin Marietta. Editor: Gaseous Dielectrics IV, 1984; author tech. articles; patentee gas insulation. Named Tenn. Tomorrow prof. U. Tenn., 1980, Engring. Disting. Faculty Mem., 1984. Mem. IEEE, Phi Beta Kappa, Tau Beta Pi, Eta Kappa Nu. Lutheran. Home: 5408 Lance Dr Knoxville TN 37919 Office: Elec Engring Ferris Hall Univ Tenn Knoxville TN 37996-2100

PACETTI, RICHARD MERLIN, architect; b. Miami, Fla., Nov. 8, 1943; s. William Augustine and Eddie Lee (Young) P.; m. Kathryn Wurth, Apr. 18, 1964; children—Mark Alan, Robert Matthew, Christopher Michael. Student Miami-Dade Jr. Coll., 1963, U. Miami, 1965. Registered architect, Fla., Ind. Draftsman Howard Johnson Inc., Miami, 1963-68; project mgr. O.K. Houstoun, Coral Gables, Fla., 1968-70; designer-project mgr. Rentscher & Assocs., Coral Gables, 1970-71; assoc. Diego Saez & Assocs., Miami, 1971-73; pres. Saez/Pacetti, Architects, South Miami, Fla., 1974—, Tectonics Architecture, Evansville, Ind., 1981—; v.p. Index Corp., South Miami, 1976—. Prin. works include Gloria Floyd Elem. Sch., Miami (Am. Assn. Sch. Adminstrs. and AIA Shirley Cooper award 1978, Southeastern Elec. Exchange 1st Pl. for energy conservation 1978, Owens-Corning Fiberglas energy conservation hon. mention 1979). Served with Army N.G., 1965-71. Mem. Nat. Council Archtl. Registration Bds., Greater Miami C. of C. Republican. Roman Catholic. Home: 7981 SW 36th Terr Miami FL 33155 Office: Saez/Pacetti Architects/-Planners 7206 SW 59th Ave South Miami FL 33143

PACHT, JORY ALLEN, research geologist; b. Madison, Wis., Oct. 23, 1951; s. Asher Roger and Perle (Landau) P. B.S., Ohio U., 1973; M.S., U. Wyo., 1976; Ph.D., Ohio State U., 1979. Cert. flight instr., competition and airshow aerobatic pilot. Well site geologist Sentry Engring., 1973-74; teaching asst. U. Wyo., 1975-76, Ohio State U., 1976-78; asst. prof. geology Kent State U., 1979; research geologist ARCO Oil & Gas Co., Dallas, 1980, sr. research geologist, 1980—; instr. geology U. Tex.-Dallas, 1982—; owner Pacum Aerobatics. Hill fellow U. Wyo., 1975. Mem. Am. Assn. Petroleum Geologists, Soc. Econ. Paleontologists and Minerologists, Geol. Soc. Am., Internat. Assn. Sedimentologists, Dallas Geol. Soc., Gulf Coast Soc. Econ. Paleontologists and Mineralogists (research conf. com., Disting. Service cert. 1982). Contbr. articles to profl. jours. Office: PO Box 2819 Dallas TX 75221

PACILIO, JOHN, JR., management and wine educator; b. Garfield, N.J., Dec. 8, 1935; s. John George and Sue J. (Venere) P.; B.A., Kans. State U., 1960; M.A. (Regents scholar), Colo. U., 1964; Ph.D. (Motorola fellow), Purdue U., 1972; m. Annette Sue Maxwell, June 1, 1958; children—Robert Maxwell, Richard Alyn, Catherine Sue. Asst. prof. Ariz. State U. ,1964-67, U. Ariz., 1969-72; grad. instr. Purdue U., 1967-69; asso. prof. Kent (Ohio) State U., 1972-77, dir. Bur. Mgmt. Devel. and Research, 1976-77; mgr. mgmt. devel. Factory Mut. Engring. & Research Co., Norwood, Mass., 1977-80; mgr. human resource planning and devel. Inst. Nuclear Power Ops., Atlanta, 1980-84; grad. lectr. U. Md., 1984-85; v.p., dir. studies Wine and Spirit Edn. Ctrs. Am., Inc., 1983—; cons. in field, 1964—. Served with AUS, 1954-56. Ariz. State U. faculty research grantee. Mem. Acad. Mgmt., Am. Psychol. Assn., Internat. Communication Assn., Am. Soc. Tng. and Devel., Human Resources Planning Soc., Orgnl. Devel. Inst., Soc. Wine Educators, Am. Wine Soc., Brotherhood of the Knight of the Vine, Les Amis du Vin, German Wine Soc., Pi Kappa Delta. Address: 4011 Oak Forest Circle Marietta GA 30066

PACK, ALLEN SCOTT, coal company executive; b. Bramwell, W.Va., Dec. 11, 1930; s. Paul Meador and Mable Blanche (Hale) P.; m. Glenna Rae Christian, June 21, 1952; children—Allen Scott Jr., David Christian, Mark Frederick, Andrew Ray. B.S., W.Va. U., 1952. Gen. mgr. Island Creek div. Island Coal Co., Holden, W.Va., 1969-70, Island Creek Coal Co., 1969-70; pres. Island Creek div. Island Creek Coal Co., Holden, W.Va., 1970-73, v.p. adminstrn., Lexington, Ky., 1973-75; exec. v.p. Cannelton Industries, Inc., Charleston, W.Va., 1975-77, pres., chief ops. officer, 1977-80, pres., chief exec. officer, 1980—; dir. Tilden Iron Ore Co., Cleve, 1980—, Algoma Tube Corp., Houston, 1977—, Maple Meadow Mining Co., Charleston, 1976—. Bd. dirs. Buchskin council Boy Scouts Am., Charleston, 1976—, pres. Buckskin council, Charleston, 1980; bd. dirs. W.Va. Univ. Found., Morgantown, 1978—; trustee Davis and Elkins Coll., 1981. Served to capt. USMC, 1952-54. Recipient Silver Beaver award Boy Scouts Am., 1981. Mem. W.Va. Coal Assn. (dir., past chmn.), Nat. Coal Assn. (dir.), Bituminous Coal Operations Assn. (dir.), Kanawha Coal Operations Assn. (dir.). Presbyterian. Office: Cannelton Industries 1250 One Valley Square Charleston WV 25301

PACKARD, WALTER JOHN, college administrator; b. Detroit, Aug. 21, 1947; s. Stanley William and Martha Regina (Hagman) P.; m. Nancy Lee Bass, Dec. 27, 1968; children—Bryn Woodson. A.A., Manatee Jr. Coll., 1968; B.A., U. South Fla., 1970; M.A. in Anthropology, Wayne State U., 1977; postgrad. U. Tex., since 1985—. Instr. Wayne State U., Detroit, 1973-76; assoc. prof. Manatee Community Coll., Venice, Fla., 1978-84, chmn. div. bus., social sci. and phys. edn., 1984—; adj. instr. Wayne State Community Coll., Detroit, 1972-73; lectr. U. Mich., Dearborn, 1972-74; cons. Dist. 8, Area Agy. on Aging, Ft. Myers, Fla., 1978-80; Editor: Exploring Sociology, 1981; Topics in Sociology, 1984. Bd. dirs. Sarasota County Com. of 100, 1981-83. NDEA Title IV fellow Wayne State U., 1970-73; Selby Found. scholar, 1970; named Educator of Yr., U. South Fla. Alumni Assn., 1984. Mem. Am. Anthrop. Assn., Soc. for Applied Anthropology, Council on Anthropology in Edn. (program chmn. 1984-85), Soc. for Anthropology in Community Colls. (SE region rep. 1982—), Venice Area C. of C. (bd. dirs. 1979-82, v.p. 1982-84). Democrat. Methodist. Avocations: travel; boating; reading. Home: 1605 E Pine St Nokomis FL 33555 Office: Manatee Community Coll 8000 S Tamiami Trail Venice FL 34284

PACKER, ANNE ASHBY, lawyer; b. Dallas, Feb. 17, 1953; d. Joe Ben and Betty Ann (Zapp) Ashby; m. Jodi Timothy Packer, Sept. 29, 1979. Student West Tex. State U., 1971-74; B.B.S., U. Tex., 1975; J.D., South Tex. Coll. Law, 1979. Bar: Tex. 1979. Dir., acct. Ashby AAA Auto Supply, Inc., 1968-76; adminstrv. asst. Probate Ct. 3, Houston, 1978-79; sole practice, Dallas, 1979-80; asst. dist. atty., Dallas, 1980-82; master-referee 304th Dist. Ct., Dallas, 1982—. Adviser Drug Edn. Adv. Com., 1982—; adviser to bd. dirs. Dallas County Child Welfare, 1982—, Dallas County Youth Village, 1982—, Foster Child Adv. Services, 1982—; pres., sec. 4-H Assn., 1966-67; pres., charter mem. Trinity Jr. Quarter Horse Assn., 1970-71, Tex. Jr. Quarter Horse Assn., 1971-72; charter mem., scholarship chmn. Leather & Lace, 1972-73. Mem. ABA, State Bar Tex., Tex. Criminal and County Attys.' Assn., Dallas Bar Assn., Dallas Young Lawyers Assn., Dallas Women Lawyers, Mental Health Assn., Delta Theta Phi, Zeta Tau Alpha. Office: 4711 Harry Hines Blvd Dallas TX 75235

PADDEN, ANTHONY ALOYSIUS, JR., government official, court administrator; b. Kearny, N.J., Apr. 3, 1949; s. Anthony Aloysius and Harriet Margaret (Dolan) P. B.A., Fairleigh Dickinson U., 1970; postgrad. U. Tenn. Sch. Law, 1970; M.A. in Pub. Adminstrn., Fairleigh Dickinson U., 1980. Employment interviewer N.J. Dept. Labor, Trenton, 1970-76, prin. procedure analyst, 1976-79; nat. procedure coordinator Interstate Compendium Employment Service Activities Project, Trenton, 1979-80; mgmt. analyst Dept. Justice, Washington, 1980-83, chief ops. U.S. Immigration Ct., Falls Church, Va., 1983—; cons., Dumfries, Va., 1978—. Author Dept. Labor tech. report, 1980. Contbr. and editor for other profl. studies. Alumni rep. to bd. trustees Fairleigh Dickinson Pub. Adminstrn. Inst. Presdl. Mgmt. intern, 1980; Logan Chambers grantee Internat. Assn. Personnel in Employment Security, 1979. Democrat. Roman Catholic. Home: 152727 Larkspur Ln Dumfries VA 22026 Office: US Dept Justice Exec Office for Immigration Rev 5201 Leesburg Pike Suite 1501 Falls Church VA 22041

PADGETT, CLAUDE EVERETT, dental educator; b. Sherman, Tex., July 22, 1939; s. Claude Everett, Jr. and LaVerne (Shotwell) Padgett Cervenka; m.

Janice Friedman (div. May 1975); children—Brad Nathan, Camille Kaye; m. Marilyn Patterson, Oct. 11, 1975. A.A., Del Mar Coll., 1963; D.D.S., U. Tex., 1967; M.A. in Higher Edn., U. Tex., San Antonio, 1980; M.B.A., Our Lady of the Lake, San Antonio, 1985. Gen. practice dentistry, Corpus Christi, Tex., 1967-75; dir. dental services Corpus Christi State Sch., 1975-76; assoc. prof. U. Tex. Dental Sch., Houston, 1976-77, San Antonio, 1977—; pres. Cons. Group San Antonio, 1982—. Contbr. articles to profl. jours. Am. Coll. Dentist fellow, 1985, Robert Wood Johnson Found. fellow Harvard Sch. Dental Medicine, 1985-87. Mem. ADA, Tex. Dental Assn., San Antonio Dist. Dental Soc., Orgn. Tchrs. Dental Practice Adminstrn. (v.p. 1983—), Am. Assn. Dental Schs., Psi Omega, Phi Theta Kappa, Delta Mu Delta. Avocations: fishing; reading; golfing. Home: 7939 Rugged Ridge St San Antonio TX 78250 Office: UT Health Sci Ctr 7703 Floyd Curl Dr San Antonio TX 78284

PADILLA, ARTHUR, educational administrator, economics educator; b. Havana, Cuba, Aug. 12, 1947 (parents Am. citizens); s. N.S. and M. Padilla; m. Stephanie Smith, Jan. 23, 1969; children—Jenifer, Valerie. B.S., N.C. State U., 1969, M.A., 1971; Ph.D., U.N.C., 1978. Sr. economist gen. adminstrn. U.N.C. system, Chapel Hill, 1971-75, asst. v.p. acad. affairs, 1978-80, assoc. v.p., 1981—; prof. econs. U.N.C., Chapel Hill, 1981—. Contbr. articles to profl. jours. and newspapers. Fellow The Brookings Inst., Washington, 1980-81; Young Nat. scholar U.S. Dept. Labor, 1979. Mem. Am. Econ. Assn., So. Econ. Assn., Omicron Delta Epsilon. Democrat. Clubs: Gold, U.S. Handball Assn. Avocation: tournament handball player. Home: 605 Long Leaf Dr Chapel Hill NC 27514 Office: Univ NC PO Box 2688 Chapel Hill NC 27514

PADON, MILDRED LEONA, museum curator; b. Hood County, Tex., Sept. 21, 1920; d. J.D. and Ophelia Mae (Masters) Armstrong; m. William Padon, Dec. 21, 1952 (div. Mar. 1982); children—Robert Diar Moser, William Jesse. B.S., Tex. Christian U., 1951; cert. hist. archives, U. Tex., 1985. Tchr. elem. schs. Fort Worth, 1951-53; curator Layland Mus., Cleburne, Tex., 1978—. Author: (with others) Of A Creek And A People, 1979. Hon. mem. Downtown Merchants Assn., Cleburne, 1983—. Mem. Cleburne C. of C. (ambassador, Woman of the Yr. award 1980), Delta Kappa Gamma (hon.), Zonta Internat. Democrat. Methodist. Avocations: art; writing; hiking. Home: 1502 Cobblestone Ln Cleburne TX 76031 Office: Layland Mus 201 N Caddo Cleburne TX 76031

PAGAN, GARY RICHARD, geological engineer; b. N.Y.C., June 14, 1954; s. Joseph F. and Muriel (Lepow) P.; m. Laura Jane Ison, Jan. 3, 1981. B.S. in Geology, CUNY, 1977; postgrad. Miami U., Oxford, Ohio, 1977-79. Geophysicist Exxon Co. U.S.A., Houston, 1979-81; sr. geol. engr. Tenneco Oil Exploration and Prodn., Houston, 1981—. Mem. Am. Assn. Petroleum Geologists, Houston Geol. Soc. Avocations: computers; tennis; racquetball; music. Office: Tenneco Oil Co Exploration and Prodn PO Box 2888 Houston TX 77001

PAGAN, JAMES FRANK, computer company executive; b. Little Rock, Jan. 24, 1955; s. John Frank and Betty (Hardin) P. B.S. in Psychobiology, Rhodes Coll., 1977; Ph.D. in Instructional Systems Tech., Ind. U., 1984. Juvenile probation officer Pulaski County Juvenile Ct., Little Rock, 1977-80; systems and procedures analyst Tex. Instruments, Dallas, 1984-85; computer based tng. coordinator Systematics, Inc.; Little Rock, 1985—. Named to Outstanding Young Men of Am., Jaycees of Am., 1983. Mem. Am. Soc. Tng. and Devel., Phi Delta Kappa. Avocations: musician; sports; backpacking; canoeing. Home: 46 Flag Rd Little Rock AR 72205

PAGE, GEORGE KEITH, financial executive; b. Rolling Prairie, Ind., July 7, 1917; s. Glenn Keith and Ruth (Mansfield) P.; m. Carmen Elizabeth Bailey, Aug. 4, 1979; children—Kay, Page Sullivan, Susan Page Mitchell, John Michael. Student U. Ala. Coll. Commerce and Bus. Adminstrn., 1939. Asst. cashier Baldwin County Bank, Bay Minette, Ala., 1938-43; pres., dir. Baldwin County Savs. and Loan Assn., Robertsdale and Fairhope, Ala., 1943-58; chmn. bd., chief exec. officer United 1st Fed. Savs. and Loan Assn., Sarasota, Fla., 1958—; dir. Indsl. Devel. Corp. Fla., 1973—. Chmn., Sarasota Housing Authority, 1967-71; gen. chmn. capital funds campaign Sarasota YMCA, 1969; treas., bd. dirs. Sarasota County Library Bldg. Fund, 1972-76; past pres., gen. campaign chmn., dir., mem. adv. council Sarasota United Way. Served with USN, World War II. Recipient Silver Beaver award Mobile council Boy Scouts Am., 1949; Cert. of Honor, City Commn. and C. of C., Fairhope, Ala., 1958; Outstanding Citizen award Sarasota Jaycees, 1978; Brotherhood award NCCJ, 1979; Disting. Eagle Scout award Nat. Ct. Honor, Boy Scouts Am., 1982. Mem. U.S. League Savs. Assn. (pres. Southeastern Conf. 1967-68, legis. com. 1979—), Fla. Savs. and Loan League (pres. 1970-71, mem. fed. legis. com. 1981—), Inst. Fin. Edn. (founder-tchr. Greater Mobile Bay and Sarasota-Manatee chpts.), Sarasota County C. of C. (exec. com. 1981—, past treas., dir.). Presbyterian. Clubs: Field (bd. dirs. 1968-71), University (bd. govs. 1969—, pres. 1976), Sara Bay Country (Sarasota). Lodges: Masons (32 degree), Shriners. Address: PO Box 1478 Sarasota FL 33578 Office: 1390 Main St Sarasota FL 33577

PAGE, JEANETTE GENEVIEVE, nursing administrator; b. Pottsville, Pa., Aug. 11, 1941; d. F.C. and G.V. Smith. Registered nurse Harrisburg Polyclinic Hosp. Sch. Nursing, 1962; B.A. in Human Resources, Pacific Western U., 1975, M.A. in Human Resources, 1977. Cert. registered nurse anesthetist, cert. nurse adminstr. Asst. dir. nursing Oxnard Community Hosp., Calif., 1975-78; dir. nursing service Belair Convalasarium, Balt., 1979; office nurse Dr. M. Diamond, D.D.S., Pottsville, Pa., 1979-80; dir. nursing service Tigua Gen. Hosp., El Paso, Tex., 1982-84, Parkview Hosp., Midland, Tex., 1984-85; dir. patient care services Physicians & Surgeons Hosp., Midland, 1985—; mem. adv. bd. El Paso Community Coll. R.N./L.V.N. Program, El Paso, 1982-84; com. chmn. Transcultural Council, El Paso, 1984, bd. dirs., 1985; guest lectr. U. Tex.-El Paso Coll. Nursing, 1983; mem. speakers forum Hospice of El Paso, 1982-84; mem. adv. bd. RN program Midland Coll., Tex., 1984-86. Mem. Am. Assn. Nurse Anesthetists, Am. Hosp. Assn. (Nursing Service Adminstrs. Soc.), Tex. Hosp. Assn. (com. chmn. Soc. Nursing Adminstrs. 1983-84, bd. dirs. 1985-87), West Tex. Dir. Nurses' Council, Polyclinic Sch. Nursing Alumni Assn. Lodge: Order Eastern Star. Avocations: play bagpipe; traveling; needlecrafts; collecting MI Hummel figurines.

PAGE, LINDA ANNE, land developing company manager, consultant; b. Wilmington, Del., Jan. 10, 1949; d. Roscoe Hadley and Gertrude Anne (Rogers) Platts; m. Robert H. Page, Mar. 19, 1971 (div.); children—Kevin Joseph, Kimberly Jean, Robert Christopher. Student Manteee Coll., 1973; grad. Bert Rodgers Real Estate, 1977, Interval Coll., 1983. Lic. real estate agt., Fla. Co-owner Page Internat. Airlines, 1970-72; in airport ops.-communications Orlando Jetport, 1972-74; dispatch and desk officer Sarasota Police Dept., 1974-76; sales rep. Pepper Mills, Dalton, Ga., 1976-78; with Ryan Homes, 1978-79; with Limetree Beach Resort subs. TRECO, Inc., Jacksonville, Fla., 1979-84, mgr. sales and sales tng., sales cons.; sr. v.p. MTC Devel. Inc., real estate devel., 1984—. Developed policy and procedure for timesharing and planned presentations, also video presentation In The Public Interest, Is Resort Timesharing for You?, 1983. Recipient top sales awards, 1980, 81, 82. Mem. Nat. Assn. Female Execs., Sarasota Bd. Realtors, Women's Council Realtors, Women's Network Sarasota, Am. Land Developers Assn., Nat. Timeshare Council. Democrat. Roman Catholic. Club: Internat. Toastmasters (Sarasota). Home 4001 Beneva Rd Apt 329 Sarasota FL 33583 Office: 5710 Clark Rd Sarasota FL 33583

PAGE, MARY MICHAEL, geochemist, research administrator; b. Tulsa, Mar. 8, 1946; d. Reavis Matthew and Patricia Ann (Thompson) P. B.S. in Chemistry, UCLA, 1969; M.S. in Geology, U. So. Calif., 1972; Ph.D., U. Tulsa, 1979. Geochemist, cons. AMOCO, Tulsa, 1977-78; geochemist Williams Bros. Labs., Tulsa, 1978-79; geochemist Robertson Research (U.S.), Inc., Houston, 1979-82, research coordinator, 1982-83, dir. project devel., 1983-84, coordinator new ventures assessment, 1984—; tech. Russian lang. translator, 1968—. Contbr. articles in field of geochemistry to profl. jours. Mem. lab. tng. steering com. Houston Community Coll., 1982—. Grantee U. Tulsa, 1973; Amoco scholar, 1974. Mem. Geochemical Soc., Am. Assn. Petroleum Geologists, Houston Geol. Soc., Sigma Xi. Clubs: Tex. Running, Woodlands Toastmasters. Office: Robertson Research (US) Inc 16730 Hedgecroft St Suite 306 Houston TX 77060

PAGE, OSCAR C., college administrator; b. Bowling Green, Ky., Dec. 22, 1939; s. Oscar H. and Elizabeth (Dearing) P.; m. Anna Laura Hood, June 12, 1965; children—Laura Kristen, Matthew Dearing. B.S. in Social Science Edn., Western Ky. U., 1963; M.A. in History, U. Ky., 1963, Ph.D., 1967. Asst. prof. U. Ga., Athens, 1967-71; acad. dean Wesleyan Coll., Macon, Ga., 1971-78; v.p. acad. affairs Lander Coll., Greenwood, S.C., 1978—. Mem. Greenwood C. of C. (pres. 1984). Baptist. Lodge: Rotary (bd. mem. 1983—). Home: 108 Burnham Ct Greenwood SC 29646 Office: Lander Coll Stanley Ave Greenwood SC 29646

PAGE, RICHARD COLLIN, counseling and human development educator; b. N.Y.C., June 28, 1943; s. Harry Collin and Edith (Moyer) P.; m. Anne McLaughlin, Aug. 10, 1968; children—Richard Harry, Robert Bryce. B.A., Denison U., 1966; M.A.T., U.N.C., 1968; M.R.C., U. Fla., 1971, Ph.D., 1976. Nat. cert. counselor Adv. Council of Internat. Acad. Profl. Counseling and Psychotherapy. Tchr. Cochrane Jr. High Sch., Charlotte, N.C., 1967-69; rehab. counselor Ga. Rehab. Ctr., Warm Springs, 1971-73; supr. drug counselors Fla. Correctional Inst., Lowell, 1973-76; asst. to assoc. prof. U. Ga., Athens, 1976—; counseling psychologist Andromeda House, Atlanta, 1977-80. Editor: Jour. of Offender Counseling, 1984, newletter Internationally Speaking, 1982. Contbr. articles to profl. jours. Mem. Am. Psychol. Assn. (internat. chmn. div. 22 1983-84), Am. Assn. Counseling and Devel. (internat. relations com. chmn. 1982-84), Nat. Rehab. Assn. Democrat. Presbyterian. Avocation: tennis. Home: 136 Stafford Dr Athens GA 30605 Office: Univ Ga 4123 Adcrhold St Athens GA 30602

PAGE, ROBERT HENRY, engring. educator; b. Phila., Nov. 5, 1927; s. Ernest Fraser and Marguerite (MacFarland) P.; B.S. in Mech. Engring., Ohio U., 1949; M.S., U. Ill., 1951, Ph.D., 1955; m. Lola Marie Griffin, Nov. 12, 1948; children—Lola Linda, Patricia Jean, William Ernest, Nancy Lee, Martin Fraser. Instr., research asso. U. Ill., 1949-55; research engr. fluid dynamics Esso Research & Engring. Co., 1955-57; vis. lectr. Stevens Inst. Tech., 1956-57, dir. fluid dynamics lab., prof. mech. engring., 1957-61; prof. mech. engring., chmn. dept. mech., indsl. and aerospace engring. Rutgers-The State U., 1961-76, prof., research cons., 1976-79; dean engring. Tex. A&M U., 1979-83, Forsyth prof., 1983—; spl. research base pressure and heat transfer, wake flow and flow separation. Served with AUS, 1945-47; PTO. Recipient Western Electric Fund award for excellence in engring. edn. Am. Soc. Engring Edn., 1968; Lindback Found. award for disting. teaching, 1969; Disting. Alumnus award U. Ill., 1971, Disting. Service award, 1973; Life Quality Engring. award, 1974. Fellow ASME, AIAA (assoc.), Am. Astronautical Soc. (chmn. Nat. Space Engring. Com., 1969-70, 72-76); mem. AAUP, Am. Soc. Engring. Edn., Am. Phys. Soc. Author papers in field. Home: 1905 Comal Circle College Station TX 77840

PAGE, ROBERT WESLEY, engineering company executive; b. Dallas, Jan. 22, 1927; s. Arch C. and Zelma M. (Tyler) P.; B.S., Tex. A&M U., 1950; m. Nancy Eaton, Sept. 17, 1952; children—Wes, David, Mark, Meg. Asst. prof. engring. Am. U. Beirut, 1952-55; constrn. mgr. Arabian Am. Oil Co., 1955-58; with Southeast Drilling Co., Dallas, 1958-61; asst. gen. mgr. Bechtel Corp., N.Y.C., 1961-66; pres., chief exec. officer George A. Fuller Co., 1972-76; v.p. Northrup Corp., 1976; pres. Rust Engring. Co., Birmingham, Ala., 1976-81; pres., chief exec. officer M.W. Kellogg Co., Houston, 1981-84; chmn., chief exec. officer Kellogg Rust, Inc., Houston, 1981—; sr. v.p. Wheelabrator Frye Inc., 1977—; chmn., dir. Metro Bank, Birmingham; dir. Republic Nat. Bank, Houston. Trustee Internat. Coll., Beirut, Lebanon; mem. pres.'s bd. U. Ala., Birmingham; mem. pres.'s council Tex. A & M U.; bd. dirs. Houston C. of C.; mem. Pres.'s Export Council. Served with USNR, World War II. Mem. Am. Concrete Inst., ASCE, Am. Soc. Mil. Engrs., Tau Beta Pi. Clubs: Apawamis (Rye, N.Y.); Birmingham Country; Ramada, Petroleum (Houston). Lodge: Rotary. Home: 1419 Kirby Dr Houston TX 77019 Office: 3 Greenway Plaza E Houston TX 77046

PAGE, SETONA BARBARA, health information specialist and educator, registered record consultant; b. Dickinson, N.D., Mar. 25, 1950; d. Ralph John and Beatrice Mary (Elkin) Messer; m. Joseph Hollic Page, Feb. 17, 1979. Student, Dickinson State Coll., 1968-70; B.S., Med. Coll. Ga., 1978; M.S., Armstrong State Coll., 1983. Record technician, med. staff coordinator med. care eval. studies, mgr. dept. Candler Gen. Hosp., Savannah, 1972-78; dir. health info. mgmt. program Armstrong State Coll., Savannah, Ga., 1979—; condr. workshops and seminars in health, statis. and regulatory agy.-related topics. Program youth chmn. in edn. Am. Cancer Soc. Mem. Am. Med. Record Assn., S.E. Med. Record Assn. (disting. past pres.), Ga. Med. Record Assn. Republican. Roman Catholic. Lodge: Elks Women's Aux.

PAGE, THORNTON LEIGH, astrophysicist, space scientist; b. New Haven, Conn., Aug. 13, 1913; s. Leigh and Mary (Thornton) P.; m. Helen Ashbee, Aug. 28, 1938 (div. 1944); 1 child, Tanya; m. Lou Williams, Aug. 28, 1948; children—Mary Anne, Leigh Page, II. B.S. Yale U., 1934; Ph.D., Oxford U., 1938; D.Sc. (hon.), Cordoba U., 1968. Astronomy asst. Oxford U., Oxford, Eng., 1937-38; instr., asst. prof. U. Chgo., 1938-50; dep. dir. Ops. Research Office, Chevy Chase, Md., 1950-58; prof. astronomy Wesleyan U., Middletown, Conn., 1958-70; research astrophysicist NASA Johnson Space Ctr., Houston, 1970—; research assoc. Smithsonian Astrophys. Obs., Cambridge, Mass., 1964-68; prof. Yale U., New Haven, Conn., 1968-69, U. Houston, 1981—. Served to comdr. USNR, 1942-46. Fellow Royal Astron. Soc., Am. Astron. Soc., AAAS (v.p. 1969-78), Astron. Soc. of the Pacific, Internat. Astron. Union. Clubs: Cosmos (Washington), Explorers (N.Y.C.). Home: 18639 Point Lookout Dr Houston TX 77058 Office: NASA Johnson Space Ctr Code SN Houston TX 77058

PAGETT, DON L., social services agency administrator; b. Detroit, July 26, 1944; s. Lester Huston and Marie (Dameron) P.; m. Laurie Cahill, June 26, 1970 (div. 1975); m. Marilyn Babula, Nov. 27, 1980; 1 child, Lydia. B.A., Olivet Coll., 1966; M.S. in Pub. Health, U. N.C., 1979. Cert. youth officer and gen. criminal justice instr. N.C. Criminal Justice Tng. and Standards Council. Tchr., Taylor (Mich.) Sch. System, 1966-68; vol. to Nepal, U.S. Peace Corps, 1968-70; counselor N.C. Div. Youth Services, Butner, 1970-71, project dir., 1971-72, juvenile eval. supr., 1972-74, chief of staff devel., 1975-77, facility dir. Juvenile Eval. Ctr., 1977-84; dir. black Mountain Regional Mental Retardation Ctr., 1984-85; superintendent West Tex. Children's Home, 1985—. mem. N.C. Juvenile Law Study Commn., 1980-85. Bd. dirs. Buncombe County Assn. Retarded Citizens,1985. Mem. Am. Correctional Assn. (Outstanding Profl. Service award Western region N.C. chpt. 1982), N.C. Juvenile Services Assn., So. Assn. Tng. Schs. (past sec.-treas.), Congress Advs. for Retarded, Am. Assn. Mental Deficiency, Nat. Assn. Supts. Pub. Residential Facilities for the Mentally Retarded. Home: PO Box 438 Pyote TX 79777 Office: W TX Children's Home PO Box 415 Pyote TX 79777

PAGNI, RICHARD MARTIN, chemistry educator, researcher; b. Chgo., Dec. 14, 1941; s. Martin J. and Hortense L. (Vath) P.; m. Patricia Greeba Sperling, Sept. 1, 1974; children—Lisa Anne, Sarah Ellen. B.A., Northwestern U., 1963; Ph.D., U. Wis., 1968. NIH postdoctoral fellow Columbia U., N.Y.C., 1968-69; prof. chemistry U. Tenn., Knoxville, 1969—. Mem. Am. Chem. Soc., The Chem. Soc., AAAS, Sigma Xi. Episcopalian. Contbr. articles to profl. jours. Office: Dept Chemistry U Tenn Knoxville TN 37996

PAINE, JAMES CARRIGER, federal judge; b. Valdosta, Ga., May 20, 1924; s. Leon Alexander and Josie Carriger (Jones) P.; B.S., Columbia U., 1947; LL.B., U. Va. 1950, J.D., 1970; m. Ruth Ellen Bailey, Sept. 8, 1950; children—James Carriger, Jonathan Jones, JoEllen. Admitted to Fla. bar, 1950; mem. firm Earnest, Lewis, Smith & Jones, West Palm Beach, Fla., 1950-54, Jones Adams Paine & Foster, 1954-60, Jones Paine & Foster, 1960-79; U.S. dist. judge, West Palm Beach, 1979—. Bd. dirs. pres. Children's Home Soc. Fla. 1978-80; mem. bd. Episcopal Diocese S.E. Fla. Served to lt. USNR, 1943-47. Mem. Greater West Palm Beach C. of C. (pres. 1973-74), Am. Bar Assn., Fla. Bar Assn., Palm Beach County Bar Assn. Democrat. Clubs: Mayacoo Country, Lake Toxaway Country. Office: 701 Clematis St West Palm Beach FL 33401*

PAINTER, DAVID SCOT, entrepreneur, real estate consultant; b. Erie, Pa., Apr. 30, 1955; s. Douglas Parker and Joann Ellen (Daubenspeck) P. B.A., Pa. State U., 1977. Founder, pres. Painter & Co., Hilton Head Island, S.C., 1979—, Visual Proof Ltd., Dixie Rowing Works, Ltd., Hilton Head Island, 1982—; cons. Dunes Mktg. Co., Hilton Head Island, 1980—. Inventor uni-ski, 1977. Mem. Aircraft Owners and Pilots Assn., Profl. Ski Instrs. Assn. Republican. Presbyterian. Clubs: Erie Yacht, Swiss Mountain. Home: 24 Haulaway Rd Village Villas Hilton Head Island SC 29928 Office: Painter & Co PO Box 6294 Hilton Head Island SC 29938

PAINTER, JAMES MORGAN, lawyer; b. Huntington, W.Va., Aug. 29, 1952; s. Frederick and Rosalie (Farrow) P.; m. Elizabeth Ann Griffitts, Aug. 19, 1974 (div. 1985); children—Emily Ann, Kathryn Farrow, B.B.A., cum laude, Marshall U., 1976; postgrad. U. Southampton, Eng., 1977-78; J.D., Nova U., 1980. Law clk. to Levy, Plisco, Perry, Shapiro, Kneen & Kindcade, Palm Beach, Fla., 1978-80; assoc. Levy, Shapiro, Kneen & Kingcade, 1980-81, Marchbanks, Bell & Eisen, Boca Raton, Fla., 1981-82, Marchbanks & Eisen, 1982-83; sole practice, Boca Raton, 1983—. Dir. Boca Raton-Delray Beach chpt. Am. Diabetes Assn., 1985. Rotary Internat. fellow, 1977-78. Mem. Fla. Bar Assn., ABA, Palm Beach County Bar Assn., South Palm Beach County Bar Assn., Acad. Trial Lawyers, Nat. Attys. Title Ins. Fund, Attys. Title Ins. Fund. Republican. Presbyterian. Avocations: camping; cabinetry; photography. Home: 1100 SW 4th Ave Delray Beach FL 33444

PAIR, BRENDA BENNETT, insurance executive; b. Aug. 26, 1940; d. Robert Joseph and Clarissa M. (Weekes) Bennett; m. James H. Pair Jr., Apr. 4, 1969; children—Richard Steven, Randall Joseph, Ronald Gregory. Student DeKalb Coll., 1971. Lic. property and casualty agt., surplus lines agt. Ga. Underwriter W.K. Stringer Co., Atlanta, 1961-65, Tharpe & Assocs., Atlanta, 1965-68; sr. v.p. Alexander & Howden, Atlanta, 1968-82; pres., ptnr. Pair Underwriting Mgrs., Inc., Atlanta, 1982—; v.p. Paramount Claims Services Inc., 1984—; dir. Chandler Ins. Co. Ltd., 1985—, v.p., 1986—. Mem. Atlanta Assn. Ins. Women (exec. bd. 1977-80, Davisons adv. bd. 1978-79, pres. 1978-79, Ins. Woman of Yr. 1979-80). Republican. Episcopalian. Office: Pair Underwriting Mgrs Inc 1155 Hammond Dr Atlanta GA 30328

PAJON, EDUARDO RODRIGUEZ, lawyer; b. Ciego de Avila, Camaquey, Cuba, Nov. 22, 1917; Came to U.S., 1959, naturalized, 1965; s. Francisco Rodriguez Ubals and Maria Luisa Pajon; J.D., U. Havana (Cuba), 1941, U. Miami, 1964; m. Olga M. Fernandez, Jan. 31, 1942 (div. Apr. 1973); children—Olga (Mrs. Ignacio G. del Valle), Eduardo R.; m. 2d, Maribel Maxwell, Dec. 1973 (div. Jan. 1977); m. 3d, Leah Munoz, Sept. 1977; 1 dau., Marta M. Munoz. Admitted to Fla. bar, 1965; partner firm Helio R. Ecay, Havana, 1941-59, Salley, Barns, Pajon & Immer (now Salley, Barns, Pajon Guttman & Del Valle), Miami, 1967—; head legal dept., sec. Cuban subsidiaries The Cuban Am. Sugar Co. (named changed to N. Am. Sugar Industries, Inc. 1960), N.Y.C., 1952-60; sec., counsel Talisman Sugar Corp., Miami, 1965-72; v.p., dir. Fla. Sugar Corp., Belle Glade, 1960-62, Sunshine Farms, Inc., South Bay, Fla., 1960-72; dir. Intercontinental Bank Miami, Fla. Mem. adv. bd. Fla. Meml. Coll., Miami, 1970—, endowment com. U. Miami, 1969—. Mem. Am., InterAm., Fla., Dade County bar assns. Republican. Roman Catholic. Clubs: Miami, LaGorce Country (Miami Beach); American, Bankers (Miami). Office: Suite 700 100 Biscayne Blvd Miami FL 33132

PAKALNIS, VYTAUTAS ALFONSAS, educator, vitreo-retinal surgeon; b. Augsburg, Germany, Jan. 17, 1949; came to U.S., 1951, naturalized, 1969; s. Alfonsas Antanas and Irena (Staniulis) P. B.A., Yale U., 1972; M.D., Ohio State U., 1976. Diplomate Am. Bd. Ophthalmology. Resident in ophthalmology Med. Coll. Wis., Milw., 1978-81; clin. assoc. ophthalmology Duke U., Durham, N.C., 1982-83, postdoctoral fellow, 1982-83, clin. fellow, 1981-82; asst. prof. Med. Coll. Ga., Augusta, 1983—; surg. service VA Hosp., Durham, 1981-82; surg. attending physician VA Med. Ctr., Augusta, 1983—; retinavitreous cons. Dwight David Eisenhower Army Med. Ctr., Fort Gordon, Augusta, 1983—. Contbr. articles to profl. jours. Active CSRA Assn. for Blind, Augusta, 1982-83. Recipient Individual Nat. Research Service award NIH, 1981-83. Fellow Am. Acad. Ophthalmology; mem. AMA, Internat. Soc. Ocular Transport to Tissue, Internat. Soc. Ocular Fluorophotometry, Assn. Research in Vision and Ophthalmology, AAAS. Avocations: books; science; horticulture. Home: 4423 Deer Run Evans GA 30809 Office: Med Coll GA Dept Ophthalmology Augusta GA 30912

PAKCHAR, PAUL LEWIS, consulting company executive; b. White Plains, N.Y., Sept. 13, 1951; s. Hymen and Ece (Goldman) P. B.A., SUNY, 1974, M.B.A., 1980. Instr. SUNY, Buffalo, 1978-80; dir. Criterion Inc., Dallas, 1980-84, v.p., 1985—. Mem. Human Resource Systems Profl., Am. Statis. Assn. Avocations: scuba diving; raquetball; motorcycling. Office: Criterion Inc 13140 Coit Rd Dallas TX 75240

PAKRUDA, LEONARD, gas board administrator; b. Bklyn., Aug. 28, 1938; s. Michael and Anna (Launitis) P.; m. Jeanette Louise Williams, May 31, 1958; children—Michael Ray, Leonard John. Student Community Coll., 1974-75, George Wallace Coll., 1979-80. Cert. peace officer, Ala. Aircraft maintenance tech. USAF, 1955-65, aircraft maintenance supr., 1966-75; service rep. Kershaw Mfg. Co., Montgomery, Ala., 1975-76; liquefied petroleum gas inspector Ala. LP Gas Bd., Montgomery, 1976-78, liquefied petroleum gas bd. adminstr., 1978—; adv. tech. and standards com. Nat. Liquefied Petroleum Gas Assn., Chgo., 1984—, state law and regularion com., 1982—. Served to sgt. USAF, 1955-75. Mem. Ala. Propane Gas Safety Com. Baptist. Lodge: Masons (32 degree). Avocations: boating; fishing; auto repair; citizen's band radio; cooking. Home: 141 Beth Manor Dr Prattville AL 36067 Office: Liquefied Petroleum Gas Bd 452 Clay St Montgomery AL 36104

PALADINO, TONY CHRISTOPHER, architect, residential designer; b. Kansas City, Mo., Apr. 23, 1949; s. Tony John and Flora Bell (Peeks) P.; m. Brenda Gail Brown, Sept. 5, 1972; children—Anthony Christopher, Brandon Michael. B. of Architecture, Ga. Inst. Tech., 1972. Registered architect, Ga. Designer, Smith-Jones Architects, Atlanta, 1970-71, Simons-Eastern Engrs. and Architects, Decatur, Ga., 1971-73; firm assoc. Diedrich Architects and Assocs., Inc., Atlanta, 1973—. Designer: All Saints Cath. Ch., 1979, Sugar Creek Golf Club, 1984, Atlanta Bus. Park, 1984, Northridge Shopping Ctr., 1984, Syncroflo Corp. Headquarters, 1985. Mem. Hidden Hills Civic Assn., Stone Mountain, 1976—. Mem. Tau Sigma Delta. Club: Atlanta Mutual Investment (pres. 1984—). Home: 1847 Quailwood Dr Stone Mountain GA 30088 Office: Diedrich Architects and Assocs Inc 1101 Gas Light Tower Atlanta GA 30303

PALAHACH, MICHAEL, lawyer; b. N.Y.C., Jan. 30, 1948; s. Michael and Mary Palahach; m. Miriam Ann Boghos, May 10, 1980; 1 child, Michael IV. B.S. in Bus. Adminstrn., U. Fla., 1970, J.D., 1973. Bar: Fla. 1973, U.S. Dist. Ct. (so. dist.) Fla. 1973, U.S. Ct. Appeals (5th cir.) 1973, U.S. Dist. Ct. (mid. dist.) Fla. 1979; cert. trial lawyer, Fla. Ptnr. High, Stack, Lazenby, Palahach & Lacasa, Coral Gables, Fla., 1973—; mediator 11th Jud. Circuit. Mem. Fla. Bar Assn., Dade County Bar Assn., Coral Gables Bar Assn., Fla. Acad. Trial Lawyers, Am. Acad. Trial Lawyers, Am. Arbitration Assn. (panel mem.). Home: 6934 Sunrise Pl Coral Gables FL 33134 Office: High Stack Lazenby Palahach & Lacasa 3929 Ponce de Leon Blvd Coral Gables FL 33134

PALANIAPPAN, ELLAPPALAYAM ANNAMALAI CHETTIAR, civil engineer; b. Karingarayan Palayam, India, May 24, 1942; came to U.S., 1970; s. Annamalai Chettiar and Lakshmi (Chettiar) P.; m. Jayalakshmi P. Palaniappan, Aug. 9, 1967; children—Kaushalya, Annamalai, Chokkalingam. B.S. in Civil Engring., U. Madras, 1966, M.S. in Civil Engring., 1969; Ph.D. in Geotech. Engring., Ga. Inst. Tech., 1976. Registered profl. engr., Tex. Soils technician, soils engr. Law Engring. Testing Co., Atlanta, 1970-76; staff geotech. engr., project engr. Raba-Kistner Cons., Inc., San Antonio, 1976-83, sr. geotech. engr., 1983—. Mem. exec. com. India-Asia Assn. San Antonio, 1978, 79, 82. Govt. India scholar, 1960-66; Govt. India sr. fellow, 1966-69. Mem. ASCE (treas. San Antonio br. 1979-80), Tex. Soc. Profl. Engrs. (chmn. audit com. Bexar chpt. 1978, 80), Nat. Soc. Profl. Engrs. Hindu. Home: 3334 Sackville St San Antonio TX 78247 Office: 10526 Gulfdale St San Antonio TX 78247

PALEN, J. JOHN, educator; b. Dubuque, Iowa, Feb. 24, 1939; s. Joseph John and Mary (Rowan) Toner; m. Karen Ann Doody, June 9, 1962; children—Joseph John, Elizabeth Ann, Ellen Marye. B.A., U. Notre Dame, 1961; M.S., U. Wis.-Madison, 1963, Ph.D., 1967. Demographer, UN, Addis Ababa, Ethiopia, 1971-72; assoc. prof. U. Wis., Milw., 1972-77, prof., 1977-80; vis. prof. Nat. U. Singapore, 1983-84; prof. sociology Va. Commonwealth U., Richmond, 1980—; cons., writer UN, 1983—. Author: Gentrification, Displacement and Revitalization, 1984; Urban World, 2d edit. 1981; City Scenes, 2d edit. 1981; Social Problems, 1979. Leader Boy Scouts Am., Wis., 1973-80; active Big Bros. Served to capt. U.S. Army, 1967-69. Rockefeller Found. grantee, 1985; NIH grantee, 1980-82; Ford Found. grantee, 1979; NIMH grantee, 1976; NSF grantee, 1985. Fellow Am. Sociol. Assn. (sec.-treas. community sect. 1981-84), So. Sociol. Soc.; mem. Urban Affairs Assn. Club: Civil War Roundtable. Avocations: hiking; canoeing. Home: 500 Gardiner Rd Richmond VA 23229 Office: Dept Sociology Anthropology Va Commonwealth Univ Richmond VA 23284

PALKO, STEFFEN ERICH, oil company executive, petroleum engineer; b. Backnang, Baden-Wurttenburg, W.Ger., May 19, 1950; came to U.S., 1952; s. Stephen P. Palko and Gerda (Barth) L'Heureux; m. Mary Graham, Dec. 27, 1969; children—Steffen Erich, Andrea Kristine. B.S. in E.E., U. Tex.-El Paso, 1971. Sr. engr. Exxon Corp., Houston, 1971-76; project mgr. Shenandoah Oil Corp., Ft. Worth, 1976-79; chief engr. Energy Reserves Group Inc., Wichita, Kans., 1979-81; v.p. Southland Royalty Co, Ft. Worth, 1981—. Mem. exec. com. Paschal High Sch.-Fort Worth Ind. Sch. Dist., 1985—. Served as sgt. N.G. USAR, 1971-77. Farah Corp. scholar, 1968. Mem. Am. Assn. Petroleum Geologists, Soc. Petroleum Engrs., Soc. Profl. Well Log analysts, Tau Beta Pi, Eta Kappa Nu. Roman Catholic. Clubs: Fort Worth, Fort Worth Petroleum. Avocations: boating, skiing, tennis, musical instrument. Home: 2409 Winton Terr W Fort Worth TX 76109 Office: Southland Royalty Co 801 Cherry St Fort Worth TX 76102

PALMA, WALTER, JR., glass company official; b. Detroit, Apr. 11, 1944; s. Walter and Janette Sabina (Skrzypczyk) P.; m. Margaret Mary Latas, Feb. 4, 1967; children—Mark, Matthew, Kevin. B.S. in M.E., Gen. Motors Inst., Flint, Mich., 1967. Plant engring. coordinator Fisher Body div. Gen. Motors, Detroit, 1967-70; plant engr. Guardian Industries Corp., Carleton, 1970-80, plant mgr., Corsicana, Tex., 1980-82, gen. mgr., 1982—. Author indsl. book. Mem. Glass Tempering Assn., Sealed Insulated Glass Mfrs. Assn., Flat Glass Mfrs. Assn., East Tex. C. of C., Corsicana C. of C. (chmn. transp. com. 1985, dir. 1982—, 2d v.p. 1986), Delta Tau Delta. Republican. Roman Catholic. Lodge: Rotary. Home: 1700 Jennifer Circle Corsicana TX 75110 Office: Guardian Industries Corp 3801 Hwy 287 Corsicana TX 75110

PALMER, ALVIN ANTHONY (TONY), JR., hospital pharmacy management company executive; b. Duncan, Okla., Sept. 1, 1950; s. Alvin Anthony and Evelyn Ann (Kofmehl) P.; m. Bonita Mae Geist, Sept. 27, 1975. B.S. in Pharmacy, U. Okla., 1973. Staff pharmacist St. Mary's Hosp., Galveston, Tex., 1973-75; dir. pharmacy Owen Co., Brownsville, Bonham and Dallas, Tex., 1975-79, corp. traveling pharmacist, Houston, 1979-82, asst. dir. recruitment and devel., 1982—; adj. prof. hosp. pharmacy U. Houston, 1982—. Mem. Am. Soc. Hosp. Pharmacists, Tex. Soc. Hosp. Pharmacists, Houston Galveston Soc. Hosp. Pharmacists, Phi Delta Chi Alumni Assn. Democrat. Roman Catholic. Avocations: triathletics; hunting; fishing; snow skiing. Office: Owen Co 9800 Centre Pkwy Suite 1100 Houston TX 77237

PALMER, CHRISTINE, vocal instructor, coach; b. Hartford, Conn., Apr. 2; d. John Marion and Immacolata (Morcaldo) Venditti; m. Raymond Smith, Oct. 5, 1949 (div. June 1950); m. 2d, Arthur James Whitlock, Feb. 25, 1953. Student Mt. Holyoke Coll., 1937; R.N. with honors, Hartford Hosp. Sch. Nursing, 1941; student New Eng. Conservatory Music, 1942; pvt. study music, N.Y.C., Florence and Naples, Italy. Operatic soprano N.Y.C. Opera, Chgo., San Francisco, San Carlo, other cities, 1944-62; presented concert N.Y. Town Hall, 1951; soloist with symphony orchs. maj. U.S. cities, 1948-62; soloist Marble Collegiate Ch., Holy Trinity Ch.; coast-to-coast concert tour, 1948; numerous appearances including St. Louis Mcpl. Opera, Indpls. Starlight Theatre, Lambertville Music Circus; soloist Holiday on Ice, 1949-50; rec. artist; TV performer; performer at various supper clubs, N.Y.C., Atlanta, Bermuda, Catskills, others; artist-in-residence El Centro Coll., Dallas, 1966-71; pvt. vocal instr.-coach, specializing in vocal technique for opera, mus. comedy, supper club acts, auditions, Dallas, 1962—; voice adjudicator San Francisco Opera Co., 1969-72, Tex. Music Tchrs. Assn., 1964-75, others; mem. women's bd. Dallas Opera Assn.; mem. adv. bd. Tex. Opera News; mem. Tex. Music Tchrs. Certification Bd. Recipient Phi Xi Delta prize in Italian, 1937; named Victor Herbert Girl, ASCAP; Oliver Ditson scholar, 1942. Mem. Nat. Assn. Tchrs. of Singing (pres. Dallas chpt. 1972-74), Nat. Fedn. Music Clubs, Tex. Fedn. Music Clubs, Dallas Fedn. Music Clubs (pres. 1972-74), Dallas Symphony League, Dallas Music Tchrs. Assn. (pres. 1971-72). Republican. Presbyterian. Clubs: Altrusa (2d v.p. 1972) (Dallas); Thesaurus, Wednesday Morning Choral (assoc., dir. 1974-76). Home and Studio: 6232 Pemberton Dr Dallas TX 75230

PALMER, EDWARD L., social psychology educator, children's television researcher, writer; b. Hagerstown, Md., Aug. 11, 1938; s. Ralph Leon and Eva Irene (Brandenburg) P.; m. Ruth Ann Pugh, June 2, 1962; children—Edward Lee, Jennifer Lynn. B.A., Gettysburg Coll., 1960; B.D., Luth. Theol. Sem., Gettysburg, 1964; M.S., Ohio U., 1967, Ph.D., 1970. Asst. prof. Western Md. Coll., Westminster, 1968-70; asst. prof. Davidson Coll., N.C., 1970-77, assoc. prof., 1977—, chair, 1985—; guest researcher Harvard U., Cambridge, Mass., 1977; vis. scholar UCLA, 1984; cons. Council on Children, Media, Merchandising, 1978-79, 1st Union Bank Corp., Charlotte, N.C., 1975-79; NSF proposal reviewer, 1978—. Editorial reviewer Jour. Broadcasting and Electronic Media, 1978—; editor: Children and the Faces of TV, 1980; contbr. to Wiley Ency. of Psychology, 1984; author jour. articles. Sec. A. Mecklenburg Child Devel. Assn., Davidson and Cornelius, N.C., 1974-78; bd. mem. pub. radio sta. WDAV, 1970—. Telecommunications task force Rutgers U., 1981. Mem. Am. Psychol. Assn., Internat. Communication Assn., Southeastern Psychol. Assn., Southeastern Soc. Social Psychologists, So. Assn. Pub. Opinion Research, Phi Beta Kappa (pres. elect Davidson chpt. 1984-85). Avocations: sunrise and sunset walks; writing poetry; music composition and performance. Office: Davidson Coll Davidson NC 28036

PALMER, EULA WEST, physician, administrator; b. Selma, La., Aug. 6, 1918; d. William Howard and Gertrude (Daughtry) West; m. Jack Norman Rogers, June 14, 1952; 1 dau., Anne Rogers. M.D., La. State U., 1947. Lic. physician, La. Intern, Charity Hosp., New Orleans, 1947-48; staff physician East La. State Hosp., Jackson, La., 1948-49; staff physician La. State U. Student Health Service, Baton Rouge, 1949-55, dir., 1955-74; adminstr. Cancer, Radiation and Research Found., Baton Rouge, 1975—; sec.-treas., adminstr. Baton Rouge Regional Tumor Registry, Inc.; vice chmn. Cancer and Tumor Registry Com. East Baton Rouge Parish Med. Soc. Chmn., La. Cancer and Lung Trust Fund Bd., 1983—. Mem. AMA (ret. status), La. State Med. Soc. (ret. status), East Baton Rouge Parish Med. (ret. status). Republican. Methodist. Club: Krewe of Romany (Baton Rouge). Author: FACTS, 1969. Home: 1213 Knollwood Dr Baton Rouge LA 70808 Office: 9042 Airline Hwy Baton Rouge LA 70815

PALMER, HUBERT BERNARD, dentist, retired air force officer; b. San Antonio, Sept. 6, 1912; s. Hubert Victor and Rosemary (Garvey) P.; student St. Mary's U., 1931-34; D.D.S., Baylor U., 1938; postgrad. George Washington U., 1946-47, U. Md., 1950-53; m. Elizabeth Harriet McAlary, Aug. 16, 1945; children—Hubert Bernard II, Robert Leldon. Commd. 1st lt. USAAF, 1938, advanced through grades to col. USAF, 1971; chief dept. dental research U.S. Army, 1946-50; chief dept. exptl. dentistry, USAF, 1953-54, chief research dentistry div. 1954-56; command dental surgeon, 1958-59, 63-65, 65-68; dental staff officer, 1959-62, dir. dental services, 1968-71; dir. Eastside Dental Clinic San Antonio Met. Health Dist., 1972-81; dir. Mirasol Dental Clinic, 1982-83; clin. asst. prof. U. Tex. Dental Sch., San Antonio, 1973-76. Decorated Legion of Merit, Commendation medal First Oak Leaf Cluster, Meritorious Service medal. Fellow AAAS; mem. Am. Dental Assn., Internat. Assn. Dental Research, Soc. Gen. Microbiology, Am. Soc. Microbiology, Omicron Kappa Upsilon. Contbr. articles to profl. jours. Research reduction decalcification tooth enamel. Home: 6115 Forest Timber San Antonio TX 78240

PALMER, JANET JOYCE, business educator, author, consultant; b. Providence, R.I., Feb. 26, 1941; d. John Frank and Esther Blanche (Nietupski) Anisewski; m. John Bergin Palmer, Oct. 9, 1964; 1 child, April Jayne. B.S., Bryant Coll., 1962; M.A., Tchrs. Coll. Columbia U., 1963; Ed.D., Ariz. State U., 1982. Instr., Bryant Coll., North Smithfield, R.I., 1963-67; psychology instr. Cape Cod Community Coll., West Barnstable, Mass., 1969-71; bus. tchr., chmn. Nauset Regional High Sch., North Eastham, Mass., 1970-78; grad. teaching asst. Ariz. State U., Tempe, 1978-82; asst. prof. Western Ky. U., Bowling Green, 1982—; freelance speaker, 1982; cons. Author: Office Automation: A Systems Approach, 1987; contbr. articles to profl. jours. Chmn., Devel. Ky.-Ecuador Ptnrs., Lexington, 1984—. Mem. Data Processing Mgmt. Assn. (Outstanding Service Bd. Mem. award 1984—, v.p. 1984, pres. 1984), Office Systems Research Assn. (nat. sec. 1984), Am. Soc. for Tng. and Devel., Assn. of Info. Systems Profls., Nat. Bus. Edn. Assn., So. Bus. Edn. Assn., Ky. Bus. Edn. Assn., Delta Pi Epsilon (faculty sponsor 1983—). Roman Catholic. Avocations: reading; travel; tennis; cross-country skiing. Home: 2713 Carriage Hill Dr Bowling Green KY 42101 Office: Western KY Univ Adminstrv Office Systems Dept 508 Grise Hall Bowling Green KY 42101

PALMER, JOHN ALBERT, parapsychologist; b. Phila., Oct. 30, 1944; s. John Albert and Katherine (Royer) P. B.A., Duke U., 1966; Ph.D., U. Tex., 1969. Asst. prof. McGill U., Montreal, Que., Can., 1969-71; research assoc. U. Va. Med. Sch., 1971-75, U. Calif.-Davis, 1975-77, U. Utrecht, Netherlands, 1981-84; assoc. prof. John F. Kennedy U., Orinda, Calif., 1977-81; sr. research assoc. Found. for Research on the Nature of Man, Durham, N.C., 1984—. Co-author: Foundations of Parapsychology, 1985. Editorial cons. Jour. Am. Soc. Psychical Research, 1978—. Contbr. articles to profl. jours. and chpts. to books. Recipient Weiss award Am. Soc. Psychical Research, 1977. Mem. Am. Psychol. Assn., Parapsychol. Assn. (pres. 1979). Home: 501 Dupont Circle Apt 10 Durham NC 27705 Office: Found Research on The Nature of Man Box 6847 College Station Durham NC 27708

PALMER, MARILYN JOAN, English educator; b. Mahoning County, Ohio, Mar. 3, 1933; d. Rudolph George and Marian Eleanor Wynn; phys. therapy cert. UCLA, 1954, B.S., 1955; M.A. in Philosophy, Ohio State U., 1969; postgrad. U. Okla., 1981—; m. Richard Palmer, Nov. 10, 1956 (div. 1972); children—Ricky, Larry, Kevin. Phys. therapist Neil Ave. Sch. for Handicapped, Columbus, Ohio, 1968-69; instr. philosophy Ohio State U., Columbus, 1969; instr. English, Youngstown (Ohio) State U., 1970-71; writer, editor The Economy Co., ednl. publs., Oklahoma City, 1977-81; grad. asst. in English, U. Okla., Norman, 1981—; free-lance editing and cons. Fund-raiser Easter Seal Soc., 1965-68; den mother coordinator Boy Scouts Am., 1966, 67, Dept. Energy grantee, 1976. Mem. AAUP, Am. Phys. Therapy Assn., Soc. for Women in Philosophy, Alpha Xi Delta. Editor: Kindergarten Keys Teacher's Guidebook, 1982, author parochial supplement, 1982. Office: 760 Van Fleet Oval Norman OK 73069

PALMER, MILDRED EUNICE, botanical gardens director, nurseryman; b. Kansas City, Mo., Sept. 9, 1911; d. George Lee and Georgia Marie (Murer) Sevedge; m. George Kenneth Palmer, Aug. 24, 1940. Student Kansas City Jr. Coll., 1929-30; cert. horticulture St. Petersburg Vocat., 1948. Licensed nurseryman, landscaper. Co-owner Palmers' Garden and Nursery, St. Petersburg, Fla., 1945—; garden writer St. Petersburg Times, 1967-69; founder, pres. Suncoast Bot. Garden, Inc., Largo, Fla., 1962—, designer, dir., 1962—; lectr. horticulture, flower arranging, landscape, St. Petersburg, 1951—; dir. horticulture shows, tours, St. Petersburg, 1947—. Author: Hibiscus Unlimited, 1954. Editor The Buds, 1952—. Mem. Am. Assn. Bot. Gardens and Arboretums, Garden Writers Assn. Am. (2d place award garden writer 1968), Fla. Fedn. Garden Clubs (life, life judge 1958—, outstanding service award 1977), Floralia Flower Arrangers (pres.). Democrat. Baptist. Clubs: Woodside Garden (St. Petersburg); Floralia Flower Arranging. Avocations: photography; botanical painting; wild flowers, plant collecting; sewing; knitting. Home and Office: 5063 Dartmouth Ave N Saint Petersburg FL 33710

PALMER, OWEN THACKARA, JR., lawyer; b. Gulfport, Miss., July 15, 1920; s. Owen Thackara and Lula (Barksdale) P.; B.A., U. Miss., 1942, LL.B., 1947; m. Joanne Melton, Apr. 5, 1947; children—Jan Barksdale Palmer Noll, Wawice Eugenia. Admitted to Miss. bar, 1947; with firm Eaton & Cottrell, Gulfport, Miss., 1947-48; individual practice law, Gulfport, 1948-64; sr. partner, Palmer & Stewart, Gulfport, 1965-73, Palmer, Stewart & Gaines, 1973-79, Palmer & Gaines, 1980—. Instr. Am. history U. Miss., 1947. Disaster chmn., Gulfport chpt. A.R.C., 1949-51; coach Gulfport Recreation Dept., 1954-68. City pros. atty., asst. city atty. Gulfport, 1953-69; atty. Gulfport Mcpl. Separate Sch. Dist., 1957—. Dir., past pres. Gulfport-Harrison County Library, 1954-68; bd. dirs., 1st v.p., mem. exec. com. Miss. Safety Council, 1971—, pres., 1972-73; past pres. Gulfport Little Theatre; atty., mem. exec. com. Greater Gulf Coast Arts Council, 1972-82; mem. Gov.'s Commn. on Tchr. and Adminstr. Edn., Certification, and Devel., 1983-85. Served with USNR. Mem. Miss. State Bar (chmn. traffic ct. com. 1962-68), Am. (rep. State Miss. on adv. com. to traffic ct. com. 1966—), Harrison County (past pres.) bar assns., Am. Trial Lawyers Assn., Am. Judicature Assn., Navy League U.S. (pres. Southwest Miss. council 1984-85), Miss. Council Sch. Bd. Attys. (v.p., pres.-elect 1985-86), Delta Kappa Epsilon, Phi Delta Phi. Episcopalian. Rotarian. Club: Gulfport Yacht (past commodore). Home: 1308 E Beach St Gulfport MS 39501 Office: 2209 14th St Gulfport MS 39501

PALMER, RALPH THOMAS, college administrator, clergyman; b. San Diego, Mar. 18, 1926; s. Olaf Gideon and Dorothy Louetta (Decker) P.; m. Mary Maxine Jones, Aug. 30, 1948; children—Angella Marie, Carol Celeste. B.A., Tex. Christian U., 1948, M. Div., 1950; M.S.P.H., Yale U., 1952; postgrad. Duke U., 1956-57; D.Min., Phillips U., Enid, Okla., 1973. Ordained to ministry Christian Ch. (Disciples of Christ), 1947. Missionary div. overseas ministries Christian Ch. (Disciples of Christ), Honjo, Japan, 1952-57, exec. dep. selection and tng., dean Coll. Missions, Indpls., 1957-70; sr. minister First Christian Ch., Pampa, Tex., 1970-78; chmn. div. sci. and math. Jarvis Christian Coll., Hawkins, Tex., 1978—; cons., lectr. Akita Prefecture Pub. Health Dept., Honshu, Japan, 1953-56; cons., speaker to chs., nationally, 1957—; cons. recruiting minorities to various colls., bus., 1970—. Author: Egonomous Traits in Post World War II Japanese Youth, 1957; chpt. The Minister's Own Mental Health; articles on sci., religion, 1950—. Active, founding mem. Suicide Prevention and Crisis Intervention, Pampa, 1972-78; bd. dirs. Bd. Higher Edn., Indpls., 1957-70, Pampa unit Am. Heart Assn., 1971-78, Pampa unit Am. Cancer Soc., 1971-78. Served with USNR, 1944-45. Mem. Tex. Acad. Sci., Tex. Assn. Tchr. Educators, Tex. Assn. Advisers to Health Professions, Am. Space Found. Avocations: writing fiction and non-fiction; painting and crafts; fishing. Home: 1820 Sequoia Dr Tyler TX 75703 Office: Jarvis Christian Coll Div Sci and Math Hawkins TX 75765

PALMER, RICHARD ALAN, chemistry educator; b. Austin, Tex., Nov. 13, 1935; s. Ernest Austin and Eugenia Rosalie (Robey) P.; m. Janice Leah Boyce, June 30, 1962; children—William D., Leah D., Sarah L., Benjamin C. B.S., U. Tex., 1957; M.S., U. Ill., 1962, Ph.D., 1965. NIH postdoctoral fellow U. Copenhagen, 1965-66; asst. prof. chemistry Duke U., Durham, N.C., 1966-71, assoc. prof., 1971-79, prof. chemistry, 1979—; cons. in field of transition metal coordination chemistry and spectroscopy, photoacoustic and surface spectroscopy. Served with U.S. Navy, 1957-60. Mem. Am. Chem. Soc., Sigma Xi. Author: (with W.E. Hatfield) Problems in Structural Inorganic Chemistry, 1970.

PALMER, RICHARD BRADBURY, business educator; b. Zurich, Switzerland, Jan. 17, 1922 (parents Am. citizens); s. Philip Mason and Anne Marie (Bauer) P.; m. Ruth Darlington, Sept. 20, 1943; children—Linda Palmer Greenwald, Richard I., Steven C. A.B., Lehigh U., 1943; D.Sc. (hon.), 1979; Ph.D., Johns Hopkins U., 1949. Registered petroleum geologist. Commd. 2d lt. U.S. Army, 1943, advanced through grades to maj., 1957; gen. mgr. Texaco, Inc., N.Y.C., 1969-71, v.p., 1971-73, sr. v.p., 1973-80; pres. Texaco Can., Inc., Toronto, 1980-81; exec.-in-residence Duke U., Durham, N.C., 1981—. Mem. Geol. Soc. Am., Am. Assn. Petroleum Geologists (cert.), Sigma Xi. Republican. Methodist. Club: Chapel Hill Country. Lodge: Kiwanis. Home: 1730 Allard Rd Chapel Hill NC 27514 Office: Fuqua Sch Bus Duke Univ Durham NC 27706

PALMER, RICHARD HUDSON, theatre educator, arts administrator; b. Richmond, Va., Aug. 16, 1940; s. Walter Upshur and Evelyn May (Cosby) P.; m. Rebecca Leigh Lewis, June 7, 1961; children—Virginia, Zachary, Katherine. A.B., Princeton U., 1961; M.A., U. Iowa, 1963, Ph.D., 1965. From instr. to prof. Washington U., St. Louis, 1964-80; prof. theatre and speech Coll. William and Mary, Williamsburg, Va., 1980—, chmn. dept. theatre and speech, 1982—; gen. mgr. Va. Shakespeare Festival, Williamsburg, 1982—. Author: The Lighting Art, 1985; also numerous articles. Dir., designer numerous stage prodns. Bd. dirs. University City sch. bd., Mo., 1970-74, pres., 1974-76. Mem. Va. Theatre Conf. (pres. 1984-86), Southea. Theatre Conf. (bd. dirs. 1980-85), Omicron Delta Kappa. Republican. Avocations: cabinetmaking; woodcarving. Home: 143 W Queens Dr Williamsburg VA 23185 Office: Coll William and Mary Dept Theatre and Speech Williamsburg VA 23185

PALMER, ROGER FARLEY, educator; b. Albany, N.Y. Sept. 23, 1931. B.S. in Chemistry, St. Louis U., 1953; postgrad. Fla. State U., 1955-56, Woods Hole Marine Biology Lab., 1956; M.D., U. Fla., 1960. Intern, Johns Hopkins Hosp., 1960-61, resident in medicine, 1961-62; asst. dept. biochemistry U. Fla. Gainesville, 1957; asst. medicine Osler Med. Service, 1960-62; instr. pharmacology and therapeutics U. Fla., 1962, asst. prof. pharmacology and therapeutics and in medicine, 1964-67, assoc. prof. pharmacology and medicine, 1967-69, prof. medicine, chief div. clin. pharmacology, 1970-81; prof., chmn. dept. pharmacology, prof. medicine U. Miami (Fla.), 1970-81, clin. prof. medicine, 1982—; chmn. pharmacology sect. Nat. Bd. Med. Examiners, 1977-81. cons. Nat. Acad. Scis.; chmn. pharmacology sect. Nat. Bd. Med. Examiners, 1977-81. Served with USAR. Mosby scholar, 1956-60; Markle scholar in Acad. Medicine, 1965-70; recipient Basic Sci. Teaching award U. Miami, 1975-76; Meritorious Service medal Am. Heart Assn., 1972; citation for meritorious service So. Region Am. Heart Assn., 1979; Visitante Distinguido award, Costa Rica, 1979; Outstanding Tchr. award U. Miami, 1982. Mem. Am. Coll. Clin. Pharmacology, Am. Fedn. Clin. Research, Am. Therapeutic Soc. (prize essay award 1970), Am. Soc. Pharmacology and Exptl. Therapeutics, N.Y. Acad. Sci., AAAS, So. Soc. Clin. Investigation, U.S. Pharmacopeia Revision Com., Internat. Study Group Research Cardiac Metabolism, Royal Soc. Health, Aesculapian Soc., Sigma Xi. Editorial bd. Pharmacol. Revs.; assoc. editor Advances in Molecular Pharmacology; ad hoc editor Am. Heart Jour.; editor Horizons in Clinical Pharmacology, 1976; author abstracts; contbr. articles to profl. jours. Office: 24 W Enid Dr Key Biscayne FL 33149

PALMER, THOMAS ALFRED, political science educator, researcher; b. Richmond, Va., Oct. 14, 1925; s. Frank Conrad and Daisy Belle (Jones) P.; m. Marguerite Bessie Davis, Jan. 2, 1954; children—Thomas Alfred, William Scott, Brian Conrad. B.A. in History, Coll. William and Mary, 1950; M.A. in Internat. Studies, Am. U., 1965; Ph.D., U. S.C., 1970. Commd. cpl. USMC, 1942, advanced through grades to lt. col., 1967, ret. 1967; various assignments abroad; prof. polit. sci. U. S.C.-Beaufort, 1965-67, teaching assoc., Columbia, 1968-70; speaker of faculty, 1978-80, dean continuing edn., 1975-77, prof., dean Coll. Charleston, S.C., 1970—, dir. internat. studies, 1984—. Author: (with others) Technology in Western Civilization, 1967; The Military in Am., 1975. Contbr. articles to profl. jours. Bd. dirs. Historic Charleston Found, 1982—, S.C. Hist. Soc., Charleston, 1980—; mem. Regan-Bush Scholars Com., Washington, 1984. Decorated Bronze Star; recipient Order of Nat. Def. award Republic of Korea, 1983; Earhart Found. fellow, 1968-69; Global Issues grantee S.C. Com. for Humanities, 1983-84. Fellow Inter-Univ. Seminar on Armed Forces and Soc.; mem. S.C. Polit. Sci. Assn. (pres. 1979-80), Am. Polit. Sci. Assn., Internat. Studies Assn., So. Polit. Sci. Assn., SCV (v.p.), Hibernian Soc.. Republican. Episcopalian. Club: Carolina Yacht. Home: 90 Ashley Ave Charleston SC 29401 Office: College of Charleston 66 George St Charleston SC 29424

PALMER LÓPEZ, JOSE NICOLAS, civil engineer, realtor; b. San German, P.R., July 13, 1913; s. Nicolas and Carmen Rita (Lopez) P.; m. Adela Rodriguez Barreto, Nov. 23, 1971; children by previous marriage—Tary, Milton, Tita, Marie, Jose Nicolas. Comml. cert. Arce Lugo Bus. Coll., 1932; Civil Engr., Coll. Agrl. and Mech. Arts, 1938; postgrad. U. P.R., 1967. Resident engr. Municipality of Guayama, 1938; contractor, 1939; with War Emergency Program, 1945, Dept. Pub. Works, 1947; sub-dir. and dir. Housing Authority, Municipality of Ponce, 1957; with Dept. Pub. Works, 1953; supr. Housing Authority, 1959; mem. P.R. Planning Bd., 1960, Dept. Pub. Works, 1963; with P.R. Hwy. Authority, 1968-79; dir. Office Constrn. Autopistas, Hato Rey, P.R., 1974-79; cons. in field; evaluator; realtor. Mem. Olympic Com. of P.R., 1969-72; commr. Area del Caribe Softball, 1954-55; pres. Recreation Assn. E.L.A. of P.R., 1962-65; pres. Fedn. of Volleyball of P.R., Fedn. of Baloncesto para Mayores, others. Served with U.S. Army, 1940-42. Mem. Colegio Ingenieros y Agrimensores of P.R., Soc. Civil Engrs., Soc. Profl. Engrs. in Constrn., Am. Assn. Retired Persons, Employees Assn. Commonwealth of P.R. (exec. com.), Am. Legion (comdr. P.R. and V.I.). Popular Dem. Party. Roman Catholic. Lodges: Masons (past master), Shriners, Lions, Elks. Address: PO Box 1561 Hato Rey PR 00919

PALMISANO, PAUL ANTHONY, pediatrician, educator; b. Cin., Dec. 30, 1929; s. William Robert and Lillian Rita (Schwarz) P. B.S., Xavier U., 1952; M.D., U. Cin., 1956; M.P.H., U. Calif.-Berkeley, 1979. Diplomate Am. Bd. Pediatrics, 1962. Intern, resident Children's Hosp., Cin., 1956-59; dep. dir. Bur. Medicine, FDA, 1963-66; mem. faculty U. Ala. Sch. Medicine, Birmingham, 1966—, prof. pediatrics, 1973—, asst. dean, 1975-79, assoc. dean, 1979—; dir. Jefferson County Poison Control Ctr., 1968-83; Ala. del. U.S. Pharmacopeial Conv. Served to capt. AUS, 1959-61. Mem. Am. Acad. Pediatrics (chmn. com. accidental poisoning), Am. Soc. Pharmacology and Exptl. Therapeutics, So. Soc. Pediatric Research, Med. Assn. Ala., AMA. Author numerous articles on toxicology, pharmacology and pub. health. Office: 1600 8th Ave S Birmingham AL 35294

PALMOUR, HAYNE, III, ceramic engineering educator, researcher, consultant; b. Gainesville, Ga., Feb. 27, 1925; s. Hayne Jr. and Lilly (Simmons) P.; m. Barbara Joyce Grace, Oct. 4, 1952; children—June Terry, Hayne, IV, John Williams. B. Ceramic Engring., Ga. Sch. Tech., 1948; M.S. in Ceramic Engring., Ga. Inst. Tech., 1950; Ph.D. in Ceramic Engring., N.C. State U., 1961. St. research engr. Am. Lava Corp., Chattanooga, Tenn., 1953-57; instr. mineral industries N.C. State U., Raleigh, 1957-58, research engr. dept. engring. research, 1958-61, research assoc. prof., 1961-65, research prof. engring. research services div., 1965-81, prof. ceramic engring. dept. materials engring., 1981—, assoc. head, 1985—; cons., indsl., govt., legal, archtl. cos., 1960—; adv. bd. Oak Ridge Nat. Lab., Nat. Materials Adv. Bd. Editor: (with others) Emergent Process Methods for HiTech Ceramics, 1984; Processing of Crystalline Ceramics, 1978. Contbr. articles to profl. jours. Patentee in field. Commodore Hobie Cat Fleet 97 Inc., Raleigh, 1974-77; pres. Wake County Soc. Prevention Cruelty Animals Inc., Raleigh, 1977-80. Served with USN, 1944-46, PTO. Recipient Research Achievement award Alcoa, 1981. Fellow Am. Ceramic Soc.; mem. Internat. Inst. Sci. Sintering, Ceramic Edn. Council (chmn. rules com. 1973-75), Nat. Inst. Ceramic Engrs., Keramos. Episcopalian. Home: 2707 Mayview Rd Raleigh NC 27607 Office: Dept Materials Engring NC State Univ Raleigh NC 27695

PALUCH, WALTER PETER, state official, management consultant; b. Chgo., Apr. 20, 1927; s. Walter Peter and Marie Violet (Krolczyk) P.; m. Florence Louise Creatura, Oct. 8, 1949; children—Karen Ann, Walter Peter III, Glenn Paul. Student U. Wis., 1944-45, Nat. War Coll., 1967-68; B.B.A. in Acctg., St. Edwards U., 1977, M.B.A., 1978. Lic. comml. pilot, FAA. Auditor automation div. Tex. Dept. Hwys., Austin, 1978, adminstr. tech. programs, 1979, dir. mgmt. info., policy and research, 1980—; chmn. State MBO Staff Coordinators Group. Mem. Austin exec. council USO, 1975-77, Scouting U.S.A., 1975-80. Served to brig. gen. USAF, 1944-75. Decorated D.S.M., D.F.C., Legion of Merit, Air medal, Meritorious Service medal, Air Force Commendation medal. Mem. Am. Mgmt. Assn., MBO Inst., Tex. State Bus. Adminstrs. Assn., Tex. Assn. State Supported Computer Ctrs., Tex. State MBO Task Force. Roman Catholic. Author: SDHPT Five Year Automation Development Plan, 1979; SDHPT Operational Planning Document, 1982; SDHPT Management-By-Objectives Training Program Workbook, 1980; SDHPT MBO Objective Setting Workbook, 1981. Office: Tex State Dept Hwys and Pub Trans 11th & Brazos Austin TX 78701

PALUMBO, MARIO JOSEPH, state senator; b. N.Y.C., Apr. 13, 1933; s. Jack and Nancy (Alfonso) P.; A.B., Morris Harvey Coll., Charleston, W.Va., 1954; LL.B., W.Va. U., 1957; m. Louise Corey, May 10, 1969; children—Christopher, Corey Lee. Admitted to W.Va. bar, 1957; partner firm Love, Wise & Woodroe; mem. W.Va Senate, 1969—. Served to lt. col. W.Va. Air N.G., ret. Mem. Am., W.Va. bar assns., Order of Coif. Clubs: Exchange (pres. 1969), Tennis (Charleston). Office: 1200 Charleston Nat Plaza Charleston WV 25301

PALYS, AGNES LORRAINE, optometrist; b. Manchester, N.H., Apr. 18, 1952; d. Joseph Frank and Claire Beatrice (Soucy) P.; m. George McLean II, Aug. 21, 1976; 1 child, Thomas George. Student Rivier Coll., 1970-72; O.D., New Eng. Coll. Optometry, 1976. Staff optometrist Walter Reed Army Med. Ctr., Washington, 1976-80, dir. contact lens program, 1978-80; gen. practice optometry, San Antonio, 1981—. Contbr. articles to GECU Mag. Provider vision care for underprivileged Lions Club, San Antonio, 1984—. Served to capt. U.S. Army, 1976-80. Recipient Cert. Appreciation, Optometric Council Nat. Capitol Region, Washington, 1980, Lions Club, San Antonio, 1985; honored in congl. record article by N.Y. congressman Donald Mitchell, 1979. Fellow Am. Acad. Optometry; mem. Armed Forces Optometric Soc. (pres. 1980), Tex. Optometric Assn., San Antonio Greater C. of C., Beta Sigma Kappa (sec.-treas. 1983—, Noteworthy Practitioner award 1978). Roman Catholic. Clubs: Women in Bus., Thousand Oaks Women's (San Antonio). Avocations: running; gardening; traveling. Home: 2903 Burnt Oak St San Antonio TX 78222 Office: 1628 Bandera Rd San Antonio TX 78228

PAMBOOKIAN, HAGOP SARKIS, psychology educator; b. Kerek-Khan, Turkey, Dec. 18, 1932; came to U.S., 1961, naturalized, 1971; s. Sarkis and Tamom (Karageuzian) P.; B.A., Am. U. Beirut, 1957; M.A., Columbia U., 1963; Ph.D., U. Mich., 1972; Instr. psychology Adirondack Community Coll., Hudson Falls, N.Y., 1964-66; asst. prof. SUNY, Potsdam, 1966-70; teaching fellow U. Mich., Ann Arbor, 1971-72, research asso., 1974; asst. prof. ednl.

psychology Marquette U., Milw., 1974-78; sr. Fulbright lectr. Yerevan State U., Yerevan, Armenian S.S.R., 1978-79; asso. prof. Elizabeth City (N.C.) State U., 1980—. Mem. Am. Psychol. Assn., Interam. Soc. Psychologists, Nat. Assn. Edn. of Young Children, Soc. Cross-Cultural Research, Southeastern Psychol. Assn., Internat. Council Psychologists, Nat. Assn. Armenian Studies and Research, U. Mich. Alumni Assn., Fulbright Alumni Assn., Phi Delta Kappa (organizer, pres. club 1982-83). Contbr. articles to profl. jours. Home: PO Box 2113 Elizabeth City NC 27909 Office: Elizabeth City State U Dept Psychology Elizabeth City NC 27909

PAMPE, WILLIAM RILEY, geology educator, petroleum geologist consultant; b. Parkersburg, Ill., Dec. 5, 1923; s. Carl Ernst and Zella Marie (Carrico) P.; m. Jewell Doris Pruitt, Apr. 15, 1949; children—Allen James, Eugene David. A.B., U. Ill., 1947, M.S., 1948; Ph.D., U. Neb., 1966. Exploration geologist The Pure Oil Co., Ardmore, Okla., 1948-61; prof. geology Lamar U., Beaumont, Tex., 1966—. Author: Petroleum-How It Is Found and Used, 1984. Served with U.S. Army, 1943-46, ETO. Named Prof. of the Yr., Lamar U., 1977-78, Regents' Prof., 1982; recipient Blue Key award Lamar U., 1977. Fellow Tex. Acad. of Sci.; mem. Am. Assn. Petroleum Geologists, Paleontol. Soc. Methodist. Lodge: Mason. Avocations: fly fishing; golf. Home: 1020 Howell Beaumont TX 77706 Office: Lamar Univ Box 10031 Beaumont TX 77710

PAN, POH HSI, geophysicist, mechanical engineer; b. Hangzhou, Zhejiang, China, July 15, 1922; came to U.S., 1957, naturalized, 1972; s. Mien and Lin-Shu (Ling) P.; m. Yi-Yin Pao, Oct. 30, 1955; children—Wanda, Golden. B.S., Chekiang U., Zhejiang, China, 1944; M.S., Colo. Sch. Mines, 1963; Ph.D. in Geophysics, Rice U., 1969. Chief geophysicist Chinese Petroleum Corp., Taiwan, China, 1958-60; geophys. supr. Mobil Oil Corp., Houston, 1976-81, geophys. mgr., Dallas, 1982—; adj. prof. Chengkung U., Taiwan, 1958-59; adj. lectr. Rice U., Houston, 1976. Mem. Soc. Exploration Geophysicists, Sigma Xi. Office: Mobil Oil Corp PO Box 900 Dallas TX 75221

PANCAKE, CHERRI MENY, computer software engineer, publishing executive; b. San Antonio, Oct. 9, 1949; d. John Joseph and Margaret Ann (Scott) Meny; m. Dale C. Pancake, Jr., Feb. 14, 1970 (div. 1986). B.S. with distinction, Cornell U., 1971; Ph.D., Auburn U., 1986. Editorial asst. The So. Review, Baton Rouge, 1971-73; curator Ixchel Mus., Guatemala, 1975-81; software engring. cons., Auburn, Ala., 1982—; publs. dir. Ctr. for Mesoam. Regional Studies, Guatemala/South Woodstock, Vt., 1980—; research assoc. Auburn U., 1984—. Jonathan Logan scholar, 1967-71. Mem. IEEE, Assn. Computing Machinery, Internat. Council Museums, UNESCO, Am. Assn. Museums, Am. Ethnological Soc., Internat. Com. Costume, Internat. Com. on Museums of Ethnography, Phi Kappa Phi. Office: Dept Computer Sci Dunstan Hall Auburn U Auburn AL 36849

PANDER, FRED THOMAS, psychologist; b. Coosa County, Ala., Mar. 6, 1940; s. Ruben Thomas and Gladys Elfreda (Guy) P.; m. Sara Edwina Brown, Dec. 15, 1961 (div. July, 1965); 1 child, Thomas Eric; m. Virginia Ruth Brady, July 3, 1982. B.A., U. Ala., 1967, M.A., 1968, Ed.S., 1971; postgrad. Miss. State U., 1972-74. Program dir. St. Mary's Sq., Galesburg, Ill., 1979-80; psychologist Galesburg Mental Health Ctr., Ill., 1980-81; dir Clarendon Family Service Ctr., Tex., 1981-82; pvt. practice psychology, Canyon, Tex., 1982-84; clin. psychologist Denton State Sch., Tex., 1984—; cons. Lewisville Sch. Dist., Tex., 1984—. Served to A2C USAF, 1961-63. Mem. Am. Psychol. Assn. Democrat. Unitarian Universalist. Lodge: Lions. Avocations: flying; camping; woodwork. Office: Denton State Sch PPO Box 368 Denton TX 76202-0368

PANKEY, GEORGE EDWARD, educator; b. Charlotte Court House, Va., Dec. 2, 1903; s. John Wesley and Cora Smith (Daniel) P.; B.A., U. Richmond, 1926; M.A., U. N.C., 1927; m. Annabel Atkinson, Mar. 6, 1931; 1 son, George Atkinson. Mem. faculty Ogden Coll. and Western Ky. State Tchrs. Coll., 1927-28, La. Poly. Inst., 1928-43; with land dept. Gulf Oil Corp., 1944-46; currently in research work. Former editor La. Tech. Digest. Mem. Huguenot Soc., S.A.R., Sons Am. Colonists, Sigma Tau Delta. Baptist. Mason. Author: John Pankey of Manakin Town, Virginia, and His Descendants, Vol. I, 1969, Vol. II, 1972, Vol. III, 1981; co-author: Five Thousand Useful Words, 1936. Address: PO Box 84 Ruston LA 71270

PANKEY, GEORGE STEPHEN, dentist; b. Durham, N.C., Dec. 3, 1922; s. Edwin Wilburn and Julia (Bender) P.; A.B., U. N.C., 1948; D.D.S., Emory U., 1954; m. Christina R. Curry, Jan. 17, 1959 (div. Feb. 1967); children—Julia Gay, Crista Merry; m. 2d, Diane Joy Flaim, Oct. 14, 1967 (dec. Sept. 1982); adopted children—Laura Jean, Julia Ann, George Stephen. Practice dentistry, Winter Garden, Fla., 1954-58, North Miami Beach, Fla., 1958-59, St. Cloud, Fla., 1959—; dir. Fla. United Investment, Inc. Served with U.S. Army, 1943-46; ETO. Mem. Am. Dental Assn., Fla. State, Central Dist. dental socs., V.F.W., St. Cloud C. of C. (pres. 1961-62), Sigma Chi. Republican. Episcopalian. Mason (worshipful master 1965, Shriner), Rotarian (pres. 1962-63). Home: Reflections on the River Sebastian FL 32958 Office: 4301 Neptune Rd Saint Cloud FL 32769

PANKRATZ, RONALD ELRICK, oil company executive; b. St. Louis, Dec. 13, 1945; s. Ronald Ernest and Marjorie Irene (Smith) P.; m. Linda Jean Pankratz, Feb. 17, 1967; 1 dau., Pamela. B.A., Simpson Coll., 1967; M.B.A., U. Tulsa, 1981. Quality analyst Deere & Co., Moline, Ill., 1967-71; quality mgr. Hesston Corp. (Kans.), 1971-78, Claremore, Okla., 1978-80; quality mgr. Oil Dynamics, Inc., Tulsa, 1980—. Mem. Am. Soc. Quality Control. Republican. Methodist. Lodges: Toastmasters. Home: 1006 E 12th St Claremore OK 74017 Office: Oil Dynamics Inc 7655 E 46th St Tulsa OK 74147

PANNELL, CLIFTON WYNDHAM, geography educator, writer; b. Tuscaloosa, Ala., Mar. 24, 1939; s. Henry Clifton and Anne Thomas (Gary) P.; m. Laurie Preston deBuys, Feb. 14, 1964; children—Alexander, Richard, Charles, Thomas. A.B., U. N.C., 1961; A.M., U. Va., 1962; postgrad. Inter-Univ. Ctr. Chinese Lang. Studies, Taipei, 1968-69; Ph.D., U. Chgo., 1971. Lectr. U. Md. Far East Div., Taiwan, 1970-71; asst. prof. geography U. Ga., Athens, 1971-75, assoc. prof., 1975-80, prof., 1980—; vis. prof. U.S. Mil. Acad., 1984; adv. bd. Dean Rusk Ctr. Study of Comparative and Internat. Law, 1978—, Ga. Rev., 1982—, Ga. China Council, 1981—. Served to lt. USNR, 1962-66. NSF research grantee, 1979-82; recipient medal for creative research U. Ga. Research Found., 1981. Mem. Nat. Council Geog. Edn., Assn. Am. Geographers, Am. Geog. Soc., Assn. Asian Studies, Am. Soc. Photogrammetry, Can. Assn. Geographers, Sigma Xi. Author: China: The Geography of Development and Modernization, 1983; East Asia: Geographical and Historical Approaches to Foreign Area Studies, 1983; contbr. articles and revs. to profl. jours. and mags., chpts. in textbooks.

PANNILL, WILLIAM PRESLEY, lawyer; b. Houston, Mar. 5, 1940; s. Fitzhugh Hastings and Mary Ellen (Goodrum) P.; B.A., Rice U., Houston, 1962; M.S. in Journalism, Columbia U., 1963; J.D., U. Tex., 1970; m. Deborah Inez Detering, May 9, 1966; children—Shelley, Katherine, Elizabeth. Reporter, Houston Chronicle, 1963-64; reporter, editor Houston Post, 1965-66, Detroit Free Press, 1966-68; producer Sta. WTVS-TV, Detroit, 1967-68; admitted to Tex. bar, 1970; assoc. Vinson, Elkins, Searls, Connally & Smith, Houston, 1970-71, 72-75; staff asst. to sec. of treasury, 1971-72; ind. practice, Houston, 1975-76; ptnr. Pannill and Hooper, 1977-80; dir. Reynolds, Allen, Cook, Pannill & Hooper, Inc., Houston, 1980-82, Pannill and Reynolds, 1982—; sole practice, 1985—. Served with USMCR, 1963-64. Mem. ABA, Fed. Energy Bar Assn., State Bar Tex., Houston Bar Assn. Episcopalian. Clubs: Houston, Forest. Asso. editor Litigation Jour., 1979-81, exec. editor, 1981-82, editor-in-chief, 1982-84. Home: 4715 Shetland St Houston TX 77027 Office: Two Houston Ctr Suite 1600 909 Fannin St Houston TX 77010

PANOSIAN, EDWARD MIRAN, history educator; b. Elmira, N.Y., Aug. 19, 1930; s. Nazar and Sara (Momjian) P.; m. Betty Jean Snyder, June 12, 1954; children—Mark, Lisa, Matthew. B.A., Bob Jones U., 1952, M.A., 1954, Ph.D., 1959. Grad. asst. Bob Jones U., Greenville, S.C., 1952-59, from asst. prof. to prof. history, 1959—, from asst. prof. to prof. church history, 1959—, chmn. dept. social sci., 1972—. Author: The World Council of Churches, 1983; also articles. Subject of yearbook dedication Bob Jones U. student body, 1983. Mem. Am. Soc. Ch. History, Conf. Faith and History, So. Hist. Assn. Baptist. Home: 109 Stadium View Dr Greenville SC 29609 Office: Bob Jones Univ Wade Hampton Blvd Greenville SC 29614

PANTIN, LESLIE PEDRO, insurance company executive; b. Havana, Cuba, May 10, 1922; came to U.S., 1960, naturalized, 1966; s. Leslie V. and Ondina I. (De Armas) P.; m. Rosario Kindelan, Nov. 20, 1947 (div. 1979); children—Leslie V., Victor M., Maria del Rosario; m. Maria Elena Diaz Rousselot Torano, Sept. 28, 1980. LL.D., U. Havana, 1946. C.P.C.U. Vice pres. Leslie Pantin & Sons, S.A., Havana, 1950-60; pres. LaGarantia, Compania de Seguros, S.A., Havana, 1957-60, Internat. Underwriting Agy., Inc., Miami, Fla., 1983—; chmn. bd. AmerInsurance (formerly Pantin Ins. Agy.), Miami, 1965—, Internat. Ins. Brokers, Inc., Miami, 1983—, First Alliance Ins. Co.; dir. Bank of Miami. Chmn. Little Havana Devel. Authority, Miami, 1979, Fla. State Commn. for Hispanic Affairs, Tallahassee, 1980, Fla. 1992 Columbus Exposition, Inc., Miami, 1980-82; chmn. City Miami Parking Authority. Mem. Soc. Property and Casualty Underwriters, Greater Miami C. of C. (vice chmn. 1976), InterAm. Businessmen's Assn. (pres. 1968-70). Democrat. Roman Catholic. Clubs: Miami, Big Five, City Club. Avocations: non-elective political activities. Home: 150 SE 25 Rd #14-M Miami FL 33129 Office: AmerInsurance 2620 SW 27th Ave Miami FL 33133

PANTON, RONALD LEE, engineering educator, consultant; b. Neodesha, Kans., Feb. 14, 1933; s. Charles Wilson and Catheryne (McDowall) P.; m. Ruth Elane Gulbrandsen, Feb. 6, 1960; children—William R., Thedore C., Henry M. A.B. in Math., Wichita State U., 1956, B.S. in Mech. Engring., 1956; M.S. in Mech. Engring., U. Wis.-Madison, 1962; Ph.D. in Mech. Engring., U. Calif.-Berkeley, 1965. Registered profl. engr. Tex. Assoc. prof. Okla. State U., Stillwater, Okla., 1965-71; prof. U. Tex., Austin, 1971—. Author: Incorpressible Flow, 1984; contbr. articles to profl. jours. Served to lt. U.S. Air Force, 1958-60. AIAA assoc. fellow; mem. ASME, Am. Physical Soc., Am. Assn. Univ. Profs. Office: Univ TX Mech Engring Dept Austin TX 78712

PANUSKA, JERRI LEE WILKERSON, government official; b. St. Louis, Oct. 21, 1950; d. Robert Norman and Frances Rhoden (Shafer) Wilkerson; B.S., U. Ill., 1972; postgrad. Northeastern Ill. U., Chgo., 1974; M.S., U. Ark., Fayetteville, 1983; m. Jerry Panuska, Oct. 7, 1983. Employment interviewer Gen. Electric Co., Bloomington, Ill., 1972; with Imperial Eastman Corp., Niles, Ill., 1972-73; with OSHA, U.S. Dept. Labor, 1973-78, compliance officer, Little Rock, 1974-78; community planning and devel. rep. HUD, Little Rock, 1978-83. Presbyterian. Home: 7 Piedmont Ln Little Rock AR 72212

PAO, CARI WILSON, pharmacist, pharmaceutical salesman; b. Racine, Wis., Jan. 20, 1955; d. Rayland and Carmen (Goulet) Wilson; m. Philip Pao, Aug. 12, 1978. B.S. in Pharmacy, Howard U. Coll. Pharmacy, 1979. Pharmacist Nat. Inst. Health, Bethesda, Md., 1978-80; pharmacist mgr. Safeway Stores, Inc., Alexandria Va., 1980-84; pharmaceutical sales Merck Sharp & Dohme, West Point, Pa., 1984-85. Editor: Washington Pharm. Jour. Served in PHS, USN, 1979-80. Vice Pres.'s Club awardee Merck Sharp & Dohme, 1985. Mem. Am. Pharmaceutical Assn, Washington Pharm. Assn.

PAPACHRISTOU, PATRICIA TOWNE, economics educator; b. Hartford, Conn., Oct. 16, 1946; d. George Robert and Lois Katherine (Stretch) Towne; m. Gerald Christopher Papachristou, Aug. 23, 1969; children—Mark Andrew, Angela Marie. B.A. in Polit. Sci. cum laude, Trinity Coll., Washington, 1968; M.A. in Polit. Sci., Duke U., 1970; M.A. in Econs., Memphis State U., 1975, M.B.A., 1979; postgrad. U. Miss., 1979—. Tchr., chairperson social studies dept. Immaculate Conception High Sch., Memphis, 1971-78; instr. Christian Bros. Coll., Memphis, 1980-84, asst. prof. econs., 1984—; intern Kaiser-Permanente Health Services Research Ctr., Portland, Oreg., summer 1984. Contbr. articles to profl. jours. Non-service fellow U. Miss., 1979-80; Jane Cassels Record scholar Kaiser Health Research Ctr., 1983. Mem. Am. Econ. Assn., So. Econ. Assn., Nat. Assn. Bus. Economists, Acad. MidSouth Economists, Missouri Valley Econ. Assn., Omicron Delta Epsilon, Pi Gamma Mu. Roman Catholic. Avocations: bridge, camping. Home: 2858 Shelley Cove Memphis TN 38115 Office: Christian Bros Coll Bus Div 650 E Parkway S Memphis TN 38104

PAPADAKIS, MARI, rental company executive; b. Houston, June 15, 1942; d. George Paul and Sophia (Kestikides) Panagos; children—Thomas James, Lainie. Student U. Houston, 1960-62. Exec. com. Alley Theatre, Houston, 1982-83, adv. com., 1985-86; bd. dirs. Juvenile Diabetes, Houston, 1979; pres. March Dimes, Houston, 1983-84, exec. com., 1985-86; pres. Unique Rentals Inc., Houston, 1985—; v.p., dir. Pro Houston, 1985—. Co-chmn. Sesquicentennial Celebration, Houston, 1986. Republican. Greek Orthodox. Avocations: tennis; dancing; modeling; reading; decorating.

PAPADOULOS, JUAN, hotel company executive; b. San Carlos, Chile, Aug. 8, 1937; s. Esteban and Susana (Escobar) P.; m. Patricia Cadieux, Feb. 7, 1965; children—Juan E., Constantino A., Daphne Patricia. Lawyer, U. Chile, 1956; student Tourism Sch., Santiago, Chile, 1957-63. Mgr., Empresa Hotelera Athens, Santiago, Chile, 1958-75; gen. mgr. Athens Hotel, Inc., Miami, Fla., 1975—; pub. relations exec. Hotel Claridge, Lima, Peru, 1975—. Clubs: de La Union, Hilico. Office: Athens Hotels Inc 131 SE 1st St Miami FL 33131

PAPAGIANNIS, GEORGE JOHN, educator, consultant; b. Chgo., July 1, 1937; s. John George and Kai (Bisbi) P.; m. Meredith Elise Nash, Aug. 23, 1971; children—Katherine, John. B.A., U. Chgo., 1961; Ph.D., Stanford U., 1977. Regional Peace Corps dir., Thailand, 1966-68; dep. dir. Ctr. Cross-Cultural Tng. and Research, Hilo, Hawaii, 1968-70; assoc. prof. Fla. State U., Tallahassee, 1976-85, prof., 1985—, assoc. dean for grad. studies and research, 1985—; cons. Aga Khan Found., Switzerland, Ministry of Edn., Thailand, Inst. Internat. Research, Ford Found., World Bank. Co-author, editor: Nonformal Education and National Development, 1983; also articles. Grantee Internat. Devel. Research Ctr., Can., 1985; Council Instrnl. Improvement, Fla. State U., 1985; Nat. Inst. Edn. 1985. Mem. Am. Ednl. Research Assn., Fla. Ednl. Research Assn., Am. Sociol. Assn., Comparative Internat. Edn. Assn. (bd. dir. 1981-83). Avocations: microcomputing; world travel. Home: 1109 Lothian Dr Tallahassee FL 32312 Office: Assoc Dean for Grad Studies and Research Coll Edn Fla State U Tallahassee FL 32306

PAPPAS, TED PHILLIP, architect; b. Jacksonville, Fla., Mar. 3, 1934; s. Phillip E. and Fifika Sophia (Katsevelos) P.; B.A. in Architecture, Clemson U., 1952; m. Mary Lee Bone, July 14, 1962; children—Mary Katherine, Christina Lynn, Mark Phillip. Intern architect Robert Broward, Architect, Jacksonville, 1960-62; intern, staff architect Reynolds, Smith & Hills, Architects and Engrs., Jacksonville, 1962; asso. Harry Burns & Assos., Jacksonville, 1962-67; pvt. practice architecture, Jacksonville, 1967; pres. Pappas Assos., Architects, Inc., Jacksonville, 1967—; works include office bldgs., sr. citizens recreation bldg., residences, Greek Orthodox Ch. Chmn., Duval County March of Dimes, 1973, Capitol Center Planning Comm., 1977—; bd. dirs. Willing Hands, 1973, Gateway Girl Scouts U.S.A., 1978—; bd. mgmt. YMCA, 1978—; mem. Gov.'s Com. Minimum Standards for Ct. Facilities, 1979; chmn. Jacksonville Community Council com. recreation, 1978; mem. Jacksonville Com. of 100, Downtown Devel. Council, Leadership Class of 1979. Served to lt. U.S. Army, 1958-60, to capt. M.P., USAR, 1960-67. Recipient Fla. Gold medal award, 1984, John W. Dyal meml. award 1984, Anthony L. Pullara meml. award 1982. Fellow AIA (award for design excellence 1980, v.p. 1985); mem. Fla. AIA (pres. 1981), Fla./Caribbean AIA (dir. 1982), Jacksonville AIA (pres. 1976), Jacksonville C. of C. (design recognition award 1980). Democrat. Greek Orthodox. Clubs: Fla. Yacht, River, Seminole, Meninak. Home: 1807 Elizabeth Pl Jacksonville FL 32205 Office: 100 Riverside Ave Jacksonville FL 32202

PAPPENHAGEN, JAMES DAVID, college administrator; b. Columbus, Ohio, July 10, 1956; s. James Meredith and Susanne (Davidson) P.; m. Nancy Carol Andrews, Dec. 29, 1983. B.A., Mt. Union Coll., 1978; M.A., Ohio State U., 1982. Tchr. Centerburg Pub. Schs., Ohio, 1979; residence edn. coordinator Longwood Coll., Farmville, Va., 1982-85; jud. affairs coordinator, 1984-85; asst. dir. residential ops. Loyola U., New Orleans, 1985—, dir. summer conf., 1985—; grad. adminstrv. asst. student personnel program Ohio State U., Columbus, Ohio, 1981-82. Co-developer coll. student handbook. Mem. Am. Assn. for Counseling Devel., Am. Coll. Personnel Assn., Nat. Assn. for Student Personnel Adminstrs., Nat. Acad. Advising Assn., Phi Gamma Mu (pres. 1977-78). Republican. Methodist. Avocations: World War II, Civil War, Vietnam War history buff; travel; swimming; camping. Home: 6363 St Charles Ave New Orleans LA 70118 Office: Loyola U Box 126 6363 St Charles Ave New Orleans LA 70118

PAPPER, EMANUEL MARTIN, anesthesiology educator; b. N.Y.C., July 12, 1915; m. Patricia Meyer, Nov. 30, 1975. A.B., Columbia U., 1935; M.D., NYU, 1938; M.D. (hon.), U. Uppsala (Sweden), 1964, U. Turin (Italy), 1969, U. Vienna (Austria), 1977. Diplomate Am. Bd. Anesthesiology. Intern Bellevue Hosp., N.Y.C., 1939, resident in anesthesiology, 1940-42; fellow in medicine NYU, 1938, fellow in physiology, 1940, instr. anesthesiology, 1942, asst. prof., 1946-49, assoc. prof., 1949; prof., chmn. dept. anesthesiology Columbia U., 1949-69; dir. anesthesiology service Presbyn. Hosp., 1949-69; prof. anesthesiology U. Miami (Fla.), 1969—, prof. pharmacology, 1974—, v.p., dean med. affairs, 1969-81. Served to maj. M.C., U.S. Army, 1942-46. Decorated Army Commendation medal. Fellow ACP, Am. Surg. Assn., Royal Coll. Surgeons (Eng.) (hon.); mem. AAAS, Am. Assn. Thoracic Surgery, Am. Coll. Anesthesiologists, Am. Heart Assn., AMA, Am. Pain Soc., Am. Soc. Anesthesiologists, Am. Soc. for Clin. Investigation, Am. Soc. for Pharmacology and Exptl. Therapeutics, Am. Thoracic Soc., Am. Trudeau Soc., Assn. for Academic Health Ctrs., Assn. Am. Med. Colls., Assn. Univ. Anesthetists, Australian Soc. Anesthetists (hon.), European Acad. Anesthesiology (hon.), Fla. Med. Assn., Fla. Soc. Anesthesiologists, Fla. Thoracic Soc., Halstead Soc., Harvey Soc., Internat. Assn. for Study of Pain, Israel Soc. Anesthesiologists (hon.), Md.-D.C. Soc. Anesthesiologists (hon.), Venezuelan Soc. Anesthesiology (hon.), World Fedn. Socs. Anesthesiologists, Clubs: Century (N.Y.C.), Cosmos (Washington), Grove Isle, Miami, Palm Bay, Standard. Lodge: Rotary. Author: (with others) Manual of Anesthesiology for Residents and Medical Students, 1956, rev. edit. 1962; Uptake and Distribution of Anesthetic Agents, 1963; (with R.J. Kitz) Advances in Anesthesiology: Muscle Relaxants, 1967; (with S.H. Ngai and L.C. Mark) Anesthesiology-Progress Since 1940, 1973; contbr. articles to profl. jours. Office: Dept Anesthesiology U Miami PO Box 016370 R-370 Ave Miami FL 33101

PAQUETTE, DEAN RICHARD, computer co. exec.; b. Detroit, July 15, 1930; s. William Roy and Neta Norine (Hadder) P.; B.A., U. Md., 1970; M.S., George Washington U., 1971; m. Emma Shirley Jones, July 2, 1952; children—Neta E., Diane R., Kingsley W. Commd. 2d lt. U.S. Army, 1946, advanced through grades to col., 1972; dep. dir. facilities engring. Chief of Engrs., 1975-76; div. chief, support requirements, 1973-75; sr. Army rep. in Australia, 1971-73; sr. Army liasion Internat. Civil Aviation Orgn., FAA, 1965-68; chief, research and devel. facilities constrn., 1969-71; chief of ops., mem. faculty Army Engr. Sch., 1958-61; ret., 1976; mgr. def. and space planning Control Data Corp., Alexandria, Va., 1977—. Vice pres. Waynewood (Va.) PTA, 1967. Decorated D.F.C., Purple Heart, Legion of Merit with 2 oak leaf clusters. Mem. Soc. Am. Mil. Engrs., Order of Purple Heart, Daedalions, Order of Carabao, Assn. U.S. Army, Am. Def. Preparedness Assn., Army Aviation Assn. Club: Bolling AFB. Home: 1117 Priscilla Ln Alexandria VA 22308 Office: 1800 N Beauregard St Alexandria VA 22311

PARATE, NATH SONBAJI, engineer, consultant; b. Nagbhir, Maharashtra, India, Oct. 17, 1936; came to U.S., 1977; s. Sonbaji Fagoji and Bijabai; m. Pushpa N. Parate (Patekar-Nagpur), Aug. 7, 1969; children—Sachin, Sanjay, Milind. B.Engring., Saugar U., Raipur, India, 1961; M. Engring., Sheffield U., 1965; Ph.D., Paris (Sorbonne-Ecole Polytechnique) U., 1968. Registered profl. engr., Can.; chartered Engr., cert mine mgr., Britain. Zonal inspector Railway Bd. & Ballarpur Co., India, 1961-62; mgmt. trainee, engr. Nat. Coal Bd., Britain, 1964-66; research engr. Ecole Poly. Lab., Paris, 1966-69; resident dir. instr. Nat. Materials Testing Lab., Govt. of Niger, Niamey, 1971-73; pvt. practice consulting engr. LaSalle, Que., Can., 1972-75; vis. prof., advisor grad. research and studies, geomechanics enging. Fed. U. Paraiba, Cambina Grande Brazil, as Can. (CIDA) advisor Waterloo U., Can., 1975-77; mgmt. research assoc. energy Pa. Pub. Utility Commn., Harrisburg, 1977-79; cons. UN Indsl. Devel. Orgn.; Austria for Govt. of Guinea, West Africa, 1979-80; utilities engr. N.C. Dept. Commerce Pub. Utility Commn., 1980-81; assoc. prof. engring. Tenn. State U., 1982—; cons. UN; guest scientist geomechanics/energy/geotech./geomaterials constrn. mgmt./orgn. Oak Ridge Nat. Lab., Tenn.; lectr. in field; expert witness on geomechanics/valuation, forensic, nuclear-waste storage engring., rock mechanics, rock fracture. Contbr. articles to profl. jours. TVA grantee, 1983-84, DOE grantee, 1985. Mem. Am. Soc. Civil Engrs., Internat. Soc. Rock Mechanics, Assn. Geoscientist for Internat. Devel. Hindu. Avocations: philosophy; dancing; writing; traveling; foreign languages. Home: 111 Old Hickory Rd #E170 Nashville TN 37221

PARCHER, JAMES VERNON, civil engineering educator, geotechnical consultant; b. Drumright, Okla., July 21, 1920; s. James Augustus and Pearl Lillian (Sharp) P.; m. Martha Hoff Ruckman, Aug. 7, 1943; children—Carol Susan, James Robert, David, Dee Ellen, Kay Elaine. B.S., Okla. State U., 1941, M.S., 1948; M.A., Harvard U., 1967; Ph.D., U. Ark., 1968. Registered profl. engr., Okla., Colo., Ark., Kans. Engr., Remington Arms Co., Kings Mills, Ohio, 1941-42; instr. civil engring. Okla. State U., Stillwater, 1947-48, asst. prof., 1948-53, assoc. prof., 1953-67, prof., 1967-85, prof. emeritus, 1985—, head dept., 1968-83; cons. in field of geotechnical engring. Mem. Stillwater Bd. Adjustment, 1971-73, 76—, chmn., 1980-82. Served to capt. U.S. Army, 1942-46, 50-52, to col. USAR, 1970-75. Mem. Nat. Soc. Profl. Engrs., Okla. Soc. Profl. Engrs. (named Engr. of Yr. 1976), ASCE, Am. Soc. Engring. Edn., Phi Kappa Phi, Chi Epsilon, Sigma Tau. Methodist. Author: (with R.E. Means) Physical Properties of Soils, 1963, Soil Mechanics and Foundation, 1968. Home: 1024 W Knapp St Stillwater OK 74075 Office: Sch Civil Engring Okla State U Stillwater OK 74078

PARDO, JORGE JAVIER, architect, artist; b. Havana, La Habana, Cuba, Dec. 13, 1951; came to U.S., 1960, naturalized, 1965; s. Jess Joaquin and Eneida (Lombard) P.; m. Milena Delgado, June 15, 1975; 1 child, Sebastian Bernal. B.F.A., Universidad de las Americas, Cholula, Puebla, Mex., 1973; M.F.A., Fla. State U., 1976; M.A., U. Tex., 1979. Registered architect, Tex. Intern architect Eugene George A.I.A., Austin, Tex., 1979-80; project mgr. Nutt, Wolters & Assocs., Austin, 1980-83; prin. Barbee & Pardo Architects, Austin, 1983—. One man shows include INTAR Gallery, N.Y.C., 1985, Frances Wolfson Art Gallery, 1985, U. Tex.-Austin, 1984, Trinity House Gallery, Austin, 1977, Galeria Macondo-Vittorio, Guatemala City, Guatemala, 1974; exhibited in group shows at Eloise Pickard Smith Gallery, 1985, San Antonio Art Inst., 1983, Laguna Gloria Art Mus., 1982, 81, 78, Trinity House Gallery, 1977, and many others. Cintas Found. Fellow, 1982-83. Home: 8012 Greenslope Dr Austin TX 78759 Office: Barbee Pardo Architects 2202 Nueces St Austin TX 78705

PARDUE, DWIGHT EDWARD, building supply company executive; b. North Wilkesboro, N.C., Aug. 3, 1928; s. Gilbert F. and Nina (Glass) P.; cert. Clevenger Bus. Coll., Wilkesboro; m. Annie Eller, Mar. 24, 1951; children—Richard S., Dwight Edward. Dir. warehousing Lowe's Cos., Inc., North Wilkesboro, 1956-57; store mgr. Lowe's Co., Inc., Sparta, N.C., 1957-59, Richmond, Va., 1959-70, regional v.p., North Wilkesboro, 1970-75, sr. v.p., store ops., 1975-78, exec. v.p./store ops., 1978—, mem. ops. sub-com. profit sharing plan and trust. Served with U.S. Army, 1950-52. Mem. Wilkes C. of C. (dir. 1979-81), Nat. Assn. Home Builders, N.C. Assn. Home Builders. Club: Oakwoods Country (Wilkesboro). Lodge: Masons. Office: PO Box 1111 North Wilkesboro NC 29656

PARFAIT, JOHN DOUGLAS, JR., businessman, quality consultant, writer; b. Beaumont, Tex., Mar. 9, 1942; s. John Douglas and Virginia (Crowell) P.; m. Bonnie Gayle, Dec. 13, 1963 (dec. Nov. 1972); children—Rebecca L., John Douglas III; m. 2d, Judy Amanda Marcotte, Jan. 14, 1975; children—Dylan V., Haven A. B.S. in Chemistry, U. Tex.-Arlington, 1968. Chemist, Frito-Lay, Irving, Tex., 1967-72; research scientist, 1972-74; quality mgr. Liquid Paper Corp., Dallas, 1975-80; v.p., then pres. Emanon Industries, Wylie, Tex., 1980—. Inventor cardrac, 1982, fold-a-plane, 1983. Served with U.S. Army, 1960-63. Mem. Am. Chem. Soc.

PARGH, ANDREW LEE, sales/marketing company executive; b. Nashville, Apr. 15, 1954; s. Eugene Donald and Madeline (Lipschutz) P.; B.A., U. Miami, 1975. News and pub. affairs dir. Sta. WVUM-FM, Coral Gables, Fla., 1974-75; sales mgr. advanced consumer electronic products B.A. Pargh Co., Nashville, 1975-77; sales mgr. consumer electronic products Tex. Instruments, Inc., Houston, 1977-79, with test mktg. facility, 1979-80; telecommunications mgr. Panasonic, Miami, Fla., 1980-81; pres., chief exec. officer Consumer Electronics Supply, Nashville, 1981; nat. product sales mgr. Sanyo Electric, Little Ferry, N.J., 1981-82; S.W. regional mgr. telecommunications div. Uniden Corp. Am., Dallas, 1982-83; regional mgr. Quasar Microsystems, Dallas, 1983-84; nat. sales mgr. Visual Technologies, New Canaan, Conn., 1984—. Mem. Radio & TV News Dirs. Assn., Zeta Beta Tau. Jewish. Office: Visual Technologies 125 Elm St New Canaan CT 06840

PARHAM, DAVID RENE, computer programming cons.; b. Knox City, Tex., Mar. 24, 1951; s. Albert Crow and Alyne Janelle (Ward) P.; diploma in exec.

automation, Draughon's Bus. Coll., Wichita Falls, Tex., 1971; student Midwestern U., Wichita Falls, 1972-76; m. Denise Wright, Dec. 10, 1971; children—Cory David, Heather Denise. Computer programmer, then data processing mgr. Wichita Gen. Hosp., Wichita Falls, 1971-80; propr. David Parham and Assocs., and predecessor, Iowa Park, Tex., 1980—. Mem. Data Processing Mgmt. Assn. (chpt. v.p. 1979). Republican. Baptist.

PARHAM, DONALD ALBERT, college educator, administrator; b. Atoka, Okla., Apr. 3, 1930; s. Carl Albert Parham and Louella (Mason) Parham Prosper; m. Kay M. Baker, Dec. 26, 1954; children—David William, Brent Donald, Warren Gene. Student Eastern Okla. State Coll., 1948-50; B.S. in Edn., Southeastern Okla. State U., 1952; M.S. in Ednl. Adminstrn., Okla. State U., 1955; Ed.D., George Peabody Coll., 1959. Asst. prof. So. Ark. U., Magnolia, 1956-59; prof. phys. edn., dir. athletics, chmn. health, phys. edn. and recreation dept. Southeastern Okla. State U., Durant, 1959—. Served with U.S. Army, 1952-54. Named Athletic Hall of Fame, Southeastern Okla. State U., 1984. Fellow Am. Alliance Health, Phys. Edn., Recreation and Dance; mem. Nat. Assn. Intercollegiate Athletics. Avocations: fishing; hunting. Home: 1221 Dixon St Durant OK 74701 Office: Southeastern Okla State Univ Sta A Box 4122 Durant OK 74701

PARHAM, IRIS ANN, gerontology educator; b. Orange, Tex., Nov. 14, 1948; d. George Kevlin and Nina Mabel Parham; m. Edward Swarbrick, Aug. 9, 1975; 1 child, Erin Elsbeth. B.A., U. Tex., 1970; M.S., W. Va. U., 1973; Ph.D., U. So. Calif., 1976. Asst. prof. gerontology Va. Commonwealth U., Richmond, 1976-81, assoc., 1981—. Co-editor: Modular Gerontology Curriculum, 1982, vol. II, 1984; Jour. Social Issues, 1980; spl. editor: Jour. Minority Aging, 1984. Grantee Adminstrn. on Aging, 1978-79, 79-82, 85—, Adjusting to Widowhood Va., 1978-79, Temple U., 1983-84; Health Resources and Services Adminstrn. grantee. Mem. Am. Psychol. Assn., So. Gerontol. Soc. (treas. 1984—), Assn. Gerontology in Higher Edn., Sigma Xi. Avocation: photography. Office: Gerontology Dept Med Coll VA VA Commonwealth Univ MCV Box 228 Richmond VA 23298

PARIS, KATHERINE WALLACE, museum administrator; b. Kansas City, Mo., Feb. 6, 1930; d. Julian Lee and Eva Katherine (Wright) Wallace; m. John Lyn Paris, Dec. 29, 1950; children—Nicole, Christopher, Deirdre. A.A., Stephens Coll., 1948; B.A., Carnegie-Mellon U., 1949, M.A., 1950. Adminstr. tour and docent programs Nelson-Atkin Mus., Kansas City, Mo., 1962-69; curator, registrar Columbia Mus. Art, Ohio, 1970-78; guest curator Philbrook Art Ctr., Tulsa, 1978-79; exec. dir. Beaumont Art Mus., Tex., 1980—; assessment program founding mem. Vis. Accreditation Com., Washington, 1976—; chmn. Tex. Commn. on Arts, Austin, 1984—, Visual Arts and Architecture Panel, Austin, 1982—. Author, editor exhbn. catalogues, 1976-79. Bd. dirs. Players Theater, Columbus, 1972. Mem. Am. Assn. Mus. (founding mem. curators standing profl. com. 1976—, registrars standing profl. com. 1976-78), Beaumont C. of C. (mem. community appearance com. 1980—). Clubs: Metropolitan (Columbus); Tower (Beaumont). Office: Beaumont Art Mus 1111 9th St Beaumont TX 77702

PARIS, RANDY MAX, oil company executive, exploration manager; b. Howell, Mich., Nov. 28, 1950; s. Max and Elizabeth Lois (Harrison) P.; m. Nancy L. Schuch, Feb. 14, 1975; children—Richard, Christopher. B.S., Mich. State U., 1975, M.S., 1977. Jr. geologist Hunt Energy Corp., Lansing, Mich., 1975-77; geologist Union Oil Co. of Calif., Casper, Wyo., 1977-80; geologist, sr. geologist Cotton Petroleum Corp., Tulsa, Okla., 1980-84; dist. geologist Samson Resources Co., Tulsa, 1984; chief geologist Hadson Petroleum Corp., Oklahoma City, 1984-85, exploration mgr., 1985—. Coach Edmond Soccer League, Okla., 1985. McGuire scholar, 1968-70. Mem. Am. Assn. Petroleum Geologists, Tulsa Geol. Soc., Soc. Petroleum Engrs. Republican. Roman Catholic. Avocations: aviation; camping. Office: Hadson Petroleum Corp PO Box 26770 101 Park Ave Suite 1400 Oklahoma City OK 73126

PARISH, HAVNER HURD, JR., urologist; b. New London, Mo., July 29, 1928; s. Havner H. and Mary Conn (Sayre) P.; m. Isabel Grayson, July 9, 1976; children—Robert, Grayson, Courtland, Douglas, Allen. A.B., U. Mo., 1951; M.D., Washington U., St. Louis, 1956. Diplomate Am. Bd. Urology. Intern Duke U. Med. Ctr., Durham, N.C., 1956-57, resident, 1961; assoc. Hicks, Howard and Parish, Sioux City, Iowa, 1961-70, Central Ala. Urologic, Selma, 1970-75; practice medicine, specializing in urology, Albany, Ga., 1976—; mem. staff Palmyra Park Hosp.; vice chief med. staff, chief surgery, and mem. hosp. authority Phoebe Putney Meml. Hosp.; sr. med. examiner FAA; mem. med. adv. com. Ga. Med. Care Found. Prin. bassoonist Albany Symphony Orch.; pres. Albany Symphony Orch. Assn. Served with U.S. Army, 1946-48. Fellow ACS; mem. Am. Urol. Assn., AMA (Physician's Recognition award), Flying Physicians Assn. (nat. dir.), Med. Assn. Ga., Dougherty County Med. Soc. (chmn. pub. relations com.), Am. Med. Tennis Assn., Albany C. of C. (dir.), Air Force Assn., Am. Enterprise Assn. (assoc.), Internat. Inst. Strategic Studies, Am. Def. Preparedness Assn. (life), Confederate Air Force, Aircraft Owners and Pilots Assn., Air Force Mus. Found., Inc., First Flight Soc., Am. Aviation Hist. Soc., William Greenleaf Eliot Soc. Washington U., Astron. League, Planetary Soc., Nat. Space Inst., Am. Security Council (nat. speakers bur.). Episcopalian. Club: Sertoma (life). Office: 802 N Jefferson St Albany GA 31708

PARISH, SYDNEY SIMON, accountant, govt. ofcl.; b. Bayonne, N.J., Aug. 15, 1909; s. William and Ida (Lazarus) P.; certificate in accountancy, bus. adminstrn. Pace Inst., 1935, asso. Applied Sci., 1961; m. Ruth Eleanore Kapiloff, May 27, 1934; children—David Monroe, Fern, William, Daniel, Donna, Paula, Steven, David Edward. Accountant, Sol & Orans, C.P.A.'s, N.Y.C., 1937-42; C.P.A., Bayonne, N.J., 1972—; internal revenue agt. treasury dept. Internal Revenue Service, Newark, 1942-72; tax accountant, N.Y.C., 1973-77. Bd. dirs. Hebrew Youth Acad., Newark. C.P.A., N.Y., N.J. Recipient Albert Gallatin award Sec. Treasury, 1972. Mem. Am. Inst. C.P.A.'s, N.Y., N.J. socs. C.P.A.'s, Internat. Platform Assn., Religious Zionists Am., Zionist Orgn. Am., Internat. Biog. Assn., Knights of Khorassan. Jewish religion (trustee, v.p. treas., lay cantor congregation). Mason (32 deg., Shriner), K.P. Address: Ramblewood East 4129 NW 88th Ave Coral Springs FL 33065

PARISI, BONNIE LEE, clinical social worker; b. Columbia, S.C., July 1, 1946; d. Dominick George and Barbara Pauline Parisi; B.A. in Psychology, Sacred Heart Coll., Belmont, N.C., 1970; M.S.W., U. S.C., 1978. Social worker Guilford County Mental Health Center, Greensboro, N.C., 1970-74; clin. social worker Upper Savannah Health Dept., Greenwood, S.C., 1978-79; clin. social worker, coordinator living skills program and quality assurance audits Tri-County Mental Health Center, Dillon, S.C., 1979—; trainer, group facilitator Partners-In-Parenting, Greenwood, 1978-79; mem. steering com., conf. group facilitator White House Conf. on Families, 1980; advisor Dillon County Mental Health Assn., 1983. Registered social worker. Mem. Nat. Assn. Social Workers (com. on inquiry), Acad. Cert. Social Workers, S.C. Assn. Social Workers, S.C. Social Welfare Forum. Club: Dillon Pilot (chaplain 1981-82, v.p. 1982-83). Home: PO Box 350 Dillon SC 29536 Office: PO Box 929 Dillon SC 29536

PARK, JAMES HENRY, wholesale petroleum distributing company executive; b. West, Tex., June 14, 1942; s. James Brock and Violet (Groppe) P.; m. Alison Gregg, Dec. 10, 1966; 1 dau., Lorri Alison. B.B.A., Baylor U., 1966. Lic. real estate broker, Tex. Wholesale commn. agt. Exxon Co. U.S.A., West, 1970-82; pres., owner J.H. Park Petroleum, Inc., West, 1982—. Mem. Tex. Oil Marketers Assn., West C. of C. (v.p. 1967; dir. 1981-84), Waco Bd. Realtors, Tex. Assn. Realtors. Methodist. Lodges: Kiwanis (pres. 1966-67; dir. 1967-70), Masons (worshipful master). Home: Route 2 Box 303B West TX 76691 Office: JH Park Petroleum Inc PO Box 455 201 W Oak St West TX 76691

PARK, JAMES WALLACE, economics educator; b. Forest, Miss., May 1, 1934; s. Ulric Z. and Estelle P.; m. Martha A. Mayes, June 5, 1958; children—Julia C., Mary J. B.S., U. Miss., 1958, M.Bus.Edn., 1959; Ph.D., U. Ala., 1974. Asst. prof. bus. U. N.Mex., Albuquerque, 1959-68; asst. prof. econs. Miss. U. for Women, Columbus, 1968-70; prof. bus. Jackson State U., Miss., 1974-77; prof. econs. Belhaven Coll., Jackson, 1977—. Contbr. articles to profl. jours. Mem. Gov.'s Task Force on Miss. Economy, 1981; pres. Men of Central Miss. Presbytery, 1981-84. Recipient Trustees' award for Teaching Excellence, Belhaven Coll., 1982. Mem. Am. Econ. Assn., So. Econ. Assn. Democrat. Presbyterian. Avocation: writing. Office: Belhaven Coll 1500 Peachtree St Jackson MS 39202

PARK, LELAND MADISON, college librarian; b. Alexandria, La., Oct. 21, 1941; s. Arthur Harris and Jane Rebecca (Leland) P.; student McCallie Sch., 1957-59; A.B., Davidson Coll., 1963; M.L.S., Emory U., 1964; postgrad. Simmons Coll., 1968; Adv. M. in L.S., Fla. State U., 1973, Ph.D., 1974. Reference librarian Pub. Library of Charlotte and Mecklenburg County (N.C.), 1964-65; head of reference and student personnel Davidson (N.C.) Coll. Library, 1967-70, asst. dir., 1970-75, dir., 1975—; vis. lectr. Emory U., summer 1972; temporary instr. Fla. State U., 1973; library cons.; bd. dirs. Southeastern Library Network, 1978-81; conf. speaker; chmn. state adv. com. Library Services and Constrn. Act. Mem. Wake County (N.C.) Citizens for Better Libraries, 1965-67; sec. com. library affairs Piedmont U. Center, 1969-70, chmn., 1970-72; mem. nat. bd. consultants Nat. Endowment Humanities, 1976—; mem. N.C. State Library Commn., 1983-85. Served to capt. AUS, 1965-67. Recipient H.W. Wilson library periodical award, 1979. Mem. Am., Southeastern (chmn. coll. and univ. sect. 1976-78, exec. bd. 1976-78), N.C. (2d v.p. 1975-77, 1st v.p./pres.-elect 1981-83, pres. 1983-85, exec. bd. 1981-87), Metrolina (pres. 1969-71), Mecklenburg County (treas. 1969-70) library assns., Soc. of Cin. (2d v.p. Ga. Soc. 1982-84), SAR, Davidson Coll., McCallie Sch. alumni assns., Mil. Order World Wars, Raleigh Jaycees (chmn. library com. 1965-67), Res. Officers Assn., SCV, AAUP, Soc. Colonial Wars, S.C. Huguenot Soc., Beta Phi Mu, Sigma Nu (chpt. alumni comdr. 1967—), Omicron Delta Kappa. Democrat. Episcopalian (treas. 1975-86). Editor, Southeastern Librarian, 1976-78; acad. sect. editor N.C. Libraries, 1972-77; contbr. articles to profl. jours. Home: 235 Ney Circle PO Box 777 Davidson NC 28036

PARK, WON CHOON, geologist; b. Korea, Oct. 6, 1937; came to U.S., 1960, naturalized, 1976; m. Grace Myunghee Chung, May 10, 1966; children—John, Helen. B.S., Seoul Nat. U. (Korea), 1960; M.S., U. Mo., 1962; Ph.D., U. Heidelberg (Fed. Republic Germany), 1968. Asst. to assoc. prof. Boston U., 1969-75; sr. scientist Kennecott Copper Corp., Lexington, Mass., 1975-77; prin. research scientist Occidental Petroleum, Irvine, Calif., 1977-83; research assoc. Cities Service Oil and Gas, Tulsa, 1984—; adj. prof. U. Calif., Riverside, 1978-83, Boston U., 1975-77; program chmn. Internat. Congress Applied Mineralogy, Los Angeles, 1984. Author: (with others) Glossary of Mining Geology, 1970. Editor: Process Mineralogy, 1981, Applied Mineralogy, 1985. Grantee Swiss Nat. Found., 1971. Mem. Soc. Econ. Geologists, Soc. Mining Engrs., Am. Assn. Petroleum Geologists, Soc. Petroleum Engrs., Soc. Econ. Paleontologists and Mineralogists, Metallurgical Soc. (com. chmn. 1980). Lodge: Lions (sec., v.p. 1980-83). Office: Tech Ctr Cities Service Oil/Gas POB 3908 Tulsa OK 74102

PARK (KIM), KYUNG SUK, child psychiatrist; b. Seoul, Korea, Sept. 21, 1946; came to U.S., 1973; s. Ki Eun and Bok Nam (Huh) Kim. B.S., Korea U., 1967, M.D., 1971. Resident in adult psychiatry U. Md. Hosp., Balt., 1977-80, jr. fellow child psychiatry, 1980-81; sr. fellow child psychiatry Children's Hosp., Nat. Med. Ctr., Washington, 1981-82; med. officer, child psychiatrist Saint Elizabeth Hosp., 1985—; jr. fellow-cons. emotionally disturbed children Children's Guild, Balt., 1980; cons. delinquent adolescent Balt. City Ct., 1981. Mem. Am. Acad. Child Psychiatry., Am. Psychiatry Assn., Washington Psychiatry Soc. Home: 1301 S Scott St # 134 Arlington VA 22204

PÁRKÁNYI, CYRIL, chemistry educator, research scientist; b. Prague, Czechoslovakia, Sept. 11, 1933; came to U.S., 1965; s. Ivan and Olga (Petrik) P.; m. Marie Hrebicek, Jan. 16, 1960; 1 child, Michael Peter. B.S. equivalent Charles U., Prague, 1954, M.S. with honors, 1956, Dr. rerum natur., 1966; Ph.D., Czechoslovak Acad. Scis., Prague, 1962. Phys. and analytical chemist Research and Control Inst. Food Industry, Prague, 1955-56; research scientist Inst. Phys. Chemistry, Czechoslovak Acad. Scis., Prague, 1960-65, sr. research scientist, 1967-68; assoc. prof. chemistry U. Tex.-El Paso, 1969-71, prof., 1971—, chmn. dept., 1982—; vis. prof. Rijksuniversiteit te Leiden, Netherlands, 1965, Calif. Inst. Tech., Pasadena, 1965-67, 68-69, U. d'Aix-Marseille, France, 1974, 77, 86, U. Kuwait, 1976, Rijksuniversiteit te Groningen, Netherlands, 1978, Univ. des Scis. et Techniques de Lille 1, Villeneuve d'Ascq, France, 1980, 81, 82; lectr. in field. Contbr. articles to profl. jours. Recipient Faculty Research award U. Tex.-El Paso, 1980, Disting. Achievement award, 1982; Outstanding Tchr. award Amoco Found., 1982, Acad. Excellence award, 1985. Fellow AAAS, N.Y. Acad. Scis.; mem. Am. Chem. Soc., Fedn. Am. Scientists, Intern-Am. Photochem. Soc., Internat. Soc. Quantum Biology, Am. Soc. Photobiology, European Acad. Scis., Arts and Humanities (corr.), Sigma Xi, Phi Kappa Phi. Catholic (Byzantine rite). Avocations: piano, hiking, travel, stamp collecting. Home: 6601 Mariposa Dr El Paso TX 79912 Office: Dept Chemistry Univ Tex El Paso TX 79968-0513

PARKER, ALFONSO, manufacturing company executive; b. Cleve., Oct. 5, 1947; s. James Mitchell and Madeline (Redding) P.; m. Dianne Lewis, Aug. 4, 1973; 1 son, Mitchell Ellis. A.A. in Electronic Tech., Cuyahoga Community Coll., 1969; B.S. in Electronic Tech., Cleve. State U., 1973; M.A. in Mgmt., Webster Coll., 1979. Engring. asst. Gen. Electric Co., Cleve., 1969-73, quality control engr., 1973-74, St. Louis, 1974-79, mgr. materials, Lexington, Ky., 1979—. Vice pres. Montessori House Sch., 1983—. Mem. Am. Prodn. and Inventory Control Soc. (v.p. membership Bluegrass chpt.), Omega Psi Phi (civic chmn. 1983—). Office: Gen Electric Co PO Box 1519 Lexington KY 40591

PARKER, ARCHIE DAVID, JR., state ofcl.; b. West Monroe, La., Aug. 23, 1929; s. Archie David and Ethel (Crowell) P.; B.A., Northeast La. U., 1956, M.A., 1969; student U. Ark., 1951-53; certificate social work La. State U., 1959, M.S.W., 1974; children—Daniel, Mark, Barbara. Probation officer, Monroe, La., 1959-62; dist. supr. probation Monroe dist. State of La., 1962-70, correctional instn. supt., Baker, La., 1970-75; asst. dir. for adult corrections La. Dept. Corrections, 1975-76, asst. sec. corrections, 1976—. Pres. Parker-Bergeron Distbg. Co., Monroe, 1963-66. Northeast La. U. dir. Students for Morrison, Barnham for Gov., 1955. Served to lt. col. AUS, 1945-48, 53-58. Recipient Northeast La. Alumni Assn. President's Service award, 1969; named Optimist of Yr., Greater Monroe chpt., 1970. Mem. Nat. Assn. Social Workers, Nat. Council on Crime and Delinquency, Nat. Assn. Correctional Supts., Am. Soc. Criminology, La. Council Criminal Justice (pres. 1979), Northeast La. U. Alumni Assn. (1st v.p. 1967-68). Episcopalian. Mason (Shriner). Optimist (state bldg. chmn. 1972, pres. Tigertown chpt. 1973). Home: 3030 Congress Blvd Baton Rouge LA 70808 Office: PO Box 44304 State Capitol Baton Rouge LA 70804

PARKER, BOOTS FARTHING, management consultant, public relations executive; b. Boone, N.C., Dec. 25, 1929; d. Joseph Edward and Polly Ida (Harmon) Farthing; student Ohio State U., 1948; m. Paul Hixson, Dec. 31, 1949 (dec. 1968); m. W. Dale Parker, Sept. 13, 1968; 1 adopted child, Jacquelyn Susan. With Greenpark Hotel, Blowing Rock, N.C., and Sea Ranch Hotel, Ft. Lauderdale, Fla., 1947-48, O'Neil Co., Akron, Ohio, 1948-67; chief Firestone's United Trading Co., also ofcl. hostess, chief of protocol Firestone Internat., Monrovia, Liberia, 1958-61; with Holiday Inns. Am., F.W. Woolworth, Fla., 1967-72; pres. Multiple Services, Titusville, Fla., 1972—; art collector. Former mem. Democratic Exec. Com. Recipient Internat. Humanitarian award, London, 1972, Disting. Service award Fla. Sheriff's Assn., 1976; hon. col. Ala. State Militia; named hon. navy recruiter U.S. Navy Dept., 1977. Mem. N.Y. Vets. Police Assn., Va. Sheriffs Assn. Clubs: Royal Oak Golf and Country, Order of Does, Fla. Fraternal Order Police. Home: 1111-F Adams Ave Homestead FL 33034 Office: PO Box 1441 Titusville FL 32781

PARKER, BRENT ALLEN, architect; b. Niles, Mich., Aug. 1, 1950; s. L. Burton and Rolleen Nadeen (Betts) P.; m. Brenda Kay Youngs, Aug. 8, 1971. B.Arch., U. Fla., 1973. Registered architect, Fla., Ga., S.C. With Draeger-Ramarker, Sarasota, Fla., 1973-76, project architect, 1976-79; ptnr. Palermo-Parker Architects, Sarasota, 1980-83; prin. Brent A. Parker Architect P.A., Sarasota, 1983—. Mem. Nat. Council Architects Registration Bd., Sarasota Emergency Radio Assn. (pres.). Office: Brent A Parker Architect PA 1491 2d St Suite B Sarasota FL 33577

PARKER, CARL, state senator; b. Port Arthur, Tex., Aug. 6, 1934; B.A., U. Tex., 1955, LL.B., 1958; m. Beverly Steigler Parker; children—Valerie Lynn, Christian Ann, Carl Allen. Admitted to Tex. bar, 1958; partner firm Long & Parker, Doyle, Port Arthur; mem. Tex. Ho. of Reps., 1963-77; mem. Tex. State Senate, 1977—; speaker pro tempore Tex. Ho. Reps., 1973. Served with USNR. Mem. Port Arthur C. of C. Club: Lions. Home: 3939 Chandelle St Port Arthur TX 77642 Office: One Plaza Sq Port Arthur TX 77640

PARKER, DANIEL LOUIS, insurance company executive; b. Smithfield, N.C., Sept. 2, 1924; s. James Daniel and Agnes Augusta (Toussaint) P.; A.B., U. N.C., 1947, LL.B., 1950; m. Mae Comer Osborne, Aug. 2, 1958. Bar: N.C. 1950. With escrow sect., mortgage loan dept. Pilot Life Ins. Co., Greensboro, N.C., 1950-53; with trust dept., then trust officer N.C. Nat. Bank, Greensboro, and predecessor, 1953-62; investment counsel Pilot Life Ins. Co., 1962-71, counsel, 1971-77, 2d v.p., 1977-84 2d v.p., asst. gen. counsel Jefferson Standard Life Ins. Co. Served with AUS, 1944-46. Mem. Assn. Life Ins. Counsel, N.C. State Bar, N.C. Bar Assn., Greensboro Bar Assn., Greensboro Jr. C. of C. (bd. dirs. 1954-55), Phi Beta Kappa. Republican. Roman Catholic. Author articles in field. Home: 308 W Greenway S Greensboro NC 27403 Office: 101 N Elm St Greensboro NC 27401

PARKER, DOROTHY ELLEN, nurse educator; b. Cleve., Mar. 22, 1934; d. Maurice Clifford and Alethea L. (Chappell) Archer; m. Billy Young Parker, July 23, 1954; children—Timothy Maurice, Daniel Thomas, Elisa Joy. B.S. in Nursing, Tex. Christian U., 1967; M.S. in Nursing, Tex. Women's U., 1979. R.N., Tex. Operating room nurse, Ft. Worth, 1969-70; clin. instr. nursing Tarrant County Jr. Coll., Ft. Worth, 1973-76, asst. prof., 1977-81, assoc. prof., 1982—; guest faculty W.A. Moncrief Radiation Ctr., 1976-82. Organizing mem. nurses' profl. edn. com. Nat. Kidney Found. Tex., 1980—, mem. chpt. relations com., 1981—, pres. Ft. Worth chpt., 1984-85; tchr., deacon Univ. Baptist Ch.; active Am. Heart Assn. Recipient Outstanding Service award Nat. Kidney Found. Tex., 1979; 2d place award Media Festival Am. Jour. Nursing, 1980. Mem. Am. Nurses Assn. (presenter poster session 1980), Tex. Nursing Assn., Nat. League for Nursing, Tex. League for Nursing, DAR, Woman's Aux. AVMA, Sigma Theta Tau (charter mem. Beta Alpha chpt.), Kappa Delta Pi. Home: 6157 Walla St Fort Worth TX 76133 Office: Tarrant County Jr Coll 5301 Campus Dr Fort Worth TX 76119

PARKER, FRANCES CARR, child nutrition dietitian, publishing company executive; b. Durham, N.C., July 18, 1925; d. Henry Calhoun and Maru Lucinda (Williams) Carr; m. Samuel Lester Parker, Jr., Dec. 28, 1949; children—Nancy Lucinda, Henry Samuel, Frances Carr, Holly Eleanor. B.S. in Foods and Nutrition, Salem Coll., 1947; postgrad., Watts Hosp. Sch. Dietetics, 1948. Registered dietitian. Therapeutic dietitian Watts Hosp., Durham, 1948; adminstrv. and therapeutic dietitian Duke Hosp., Durham, 1949, Mass. Gen. Hosp., Boston, 1950; dir. child nutrition programs Kinston (N.C.) City Schs., 1966—; instr. nutrition edn.; writer; lectr.; pres. TarPar, Ltd. Pubg. Co. Named Woman of Year Lenior Meml. Hosp., 1961; recipient award Austin Hansen Assn., 1983. Mem. Am. Sch. Food Service Assn. (Outstanding Service award 1979), N.C. Sch. Food Service Assn. (life), Am. Dietetic Assn., N.C. Dietetic Assn., Nutrition Edn. Soc., Nutrition Today Assn., Assn. Sch. Adminstrs., Alliance Allied Health Profls. (pres. and founder 1981—), Am. Med. Aux. Democrat. Presbyterian. Clubs: Kinston Country, Washington Yacht & Country. Author: Mushrooms, Turnip Greens and Pickled Eggs, 1969; Ponderings, 1976; Listen, 1983; Half Baked, 1975; Instant Gourmet, 1975; Instant Party, 1976; Alone With a Skillet, 1976; What Do You Do With It?, 1978, also newspaper articles. Home: 1202 Harding Ave Kinston NC 28501

PARKER, FRANK LEON, environmental engineering educator, consultant; b. Somerville, Mass., Mar. 23, 1926; s. Benjamin James and Bertha (Cohen) P.; m. Elaine Marilyn Goldman, Aug. 22, 1954; children—Nina Madeline, Aaron Bennet, Stephan Alexander, David Seth. B.S., MIT, 1948; M.S., Harvard U., 1950, Ph.D., 1955. Registered profl. engr., N.Y. Engr. U.S. Bur. Reclamation, Riverton, Wyo., 1948; field engr. Rockland Light & Power Co., Nyack, N.Y., 1949, Howard M. Turner, Boston, 1955; sect. chief IAEA, Vienna, Austria, 1960-61; chief radioactive waste disposal research sect. Oak Ridge Nat. Lab., 1956-66; prof. environ. and water resources engring. Vanderbilt U., Nashville; cons. Adv. Com. on Reactor Safeguards, 1970—, sci. adv. bd. EPA, 1982-83, U.S. Dept. Energy, Hanford, Wash., 1970—, Office Nuclear Waste Isolation, Battelle, 1975—, bd. radioactive waste mgmt. Nat. Acad. Sci., 1978. Mem. Port Authority Nashville, 1979—; chmn. appeals bd. Sewer Authority Nashville, 1979—. Served with U.S. Army, 1943-46. Mem. AAAS, Am. Nuclear Soc., Am. Geophys. Union, Health Physics Soc., ASCE, Water Pollution Control Fedn., Nat. Council Radiation Protection and Measurements. Jewish. Co-author: Physical and Engineering Aspects of Thermal Pollution, 1970; Engineering Aspects of Thermal Pollution, 1969; Biological Aspects of Thermal Pollution, 1969. Home: 4400 Iroquois Ave Nashville TN 37205 Office: PO Box 1596 Sta B Nashville TN 37235

PARKER, FRANK PEYTON, educator; b. Fort Worth, Nov. 28, 1946; s. Frank Peyton and Dorothy Elizabeth (Cummings) P.; m. Charlotte Carroll, June 17, 1969 (div. Dec. 1983). B.A., U. Houston, 1971; M.A., Purdue U., 1973, Ph.D., 1976. Asst. prof. U. B.C., Can., 1977-79; assoc. prof. La. State U., Baton Rouge, 1979-84, prof., 1984—. Author: Linguistics for Nonlinguists, 1986. Contbr. articles to profl. jours. Mem. MLA (exec. com. lang. theory div. 1984—), Linguistic Soc. Am., Acoustical Soc. Am., Am. Dialect Soc. Home: 2205 Myrtle Ave Baton Rouge LA 70806 Office: La State U English Dept Baton Rouge LA 70803

PARKER, FREDERICK L., state senator; b. Jan. 31, 1939; s. O.R. and Julia Oxley P.; m. Christine Best; children—Jeff, Jill, Mary Beth Parker Mustair. B.S., Concord Coll. Former tchr. and farmer; mem. W.Va. Senate, 1982—, chmn. agr. com. Chmn. Monroe County Democratic Exec. Com. (W.Va.). Mem. W.Va. Edn. Assn. Lodge: Lions. Office: W Va Senate Charleston WV 25305*

PARKER, FREDERICK WILLIAM, III, physician; b. Scranton, Pa., Jan. 10, 1947; s. Frederick William Jr. and Rena Adele (Arcangeletti) P.; m. Susan Linda Perrin, June 17, 1972; children—Kelly, Aimee. B.S., U. Scranton, 1968; M.D., George Washington U., 1972. Diplomate Nat. Bd. Med. Examiners. Intern George Washington U., Washington, 1972-73, resident in surgery, 1973-74; resident in surgery Ohio State U. Hosp., Columbus, 1976-77; emergency dept. physician Bethesda Hosp., Zanesville, Ohio, 1977-78; family physician Manassas Med. Ctr., Va., 1978-80; practice medicine specializing in family medicine, Manassas, 1980—; flight surgeon, chief aerospace medicine 459th Tactical Hosp., Andrews AFB, Md., 1983—; chmn. dept. medicine Prince William Hosp., Manassas, 1982-84, dir. med. edn., 1982—; staff physician Fauquier Hosp., Warrenton, Va., 1983—; team physician Osbourn Sr. High Sch., Manassas, 1983—. Served to maj. USAF, 1974-76. Mem. Prince William County Med. Soc., Med. Soc. Va., AMA (Physicians Recognition award 1982, 85), Am. Acad. Family Physicians. Republican. Roman Catholic. Avocations: golf; landscape architecture. Home: 9619 Gladstone St Manassas VA 22110 Office: 10696 B Crestwood Dr Manassas VA 22110

PARKER, GARRIS DUDLEY, JR., health physicist; b. Brevard, N.C., Jan. 11, 1953; s. Garris Dudley Parker and Betty Jeanette (Harrison) Ford; m. Barbara Lynn Stone, May 29, 1979; 1 child, Jonathan. B.S. in Nuclear Engring., N.C. State U., 1976; M.Sc. in Radiol. Health, Emory U., 1977. Co-op student Duke Power Co., Charlotte, N.C., 1973-75; radiation safety officer Chem. Industry Inst. Toxicology, Research Triangle Park, N.C., 1977-83, mgr. lab. compliance, 1983—. Contbr. articles to profl. publs. Mem. Gov.'s Ad Hoc Com. to Site a Radioactive Waste Disposal Facility, N.C., 1979-80. Mem. Am. Biol. Safety Assn., Am. Soc. Safety Engrs., Health Physics Soc. (pres. N.C. chpt. 1984—). Democrat. United Methodist. Avocations: sailing, automobiles, fishing. Home: 31 Old Sturbridge Dr Apex NC 27502 Office: Chem Industry Inst Toxicology 6 Davis Dr Research Triangle Park NC 27709

PARKER, GERALD M., physician, researcher; b. Olean, N.Y., Nov. 20, 1943; s. Richard and Kathleen (Manwaring) P.; m. Linda Kay Stuart, Dec. 28, 1968; children—Kimberly, Gerald, Cassandra, Kevin. B.A., Western Wash. U., 1965; D.O., Kirksville Coll. Osteopathy & Surgery, 1969. Intern, Art Centre Hosp., Detroit, 1969-70; ptnr. Doctor's Clinic, Amarillo, Tex., 1969—; dir. Southwest Inst. Preventive Medicine, Amarillo, 1978—, Hyperbaric Oxygen Ctr., Amarillo, 1979—. Contbr. articles to profl. jours. Appeared on That's Incredible TV show, 1982. Pres., Southwest Amarillo Little Dribblers Assn., 1979—; coach Girls Nat. Champion Basketball Teams, 1981, 83, 84. Fellow Am. Acad. Med. Preventics; mem. Southwest Acad. Preventive Medicine (pres. 1980—), Am. Osteopathic Assn. Methodist. Avocation: athletics. Office: Doctors Clinic 4714 S Western St Amarillo TX 79109

PARKER, HARRY J., educator, psychologist; b. Sioux City, Iowa, Jan. 18, 1923; A.B., Elmhurst Coll., 1947; M.A., Northwestern U., 1953, Ph.D., 1956, postgrad., 1958; postgrad. Roosevelt U., 1957-58. Counselor, Northwestern U. Counseling Center, Chgo., 1952-56, counseling psychologist, 1956-59, asst. dir., 1957-58, dir., 1958-59; pvt. practice counseling psychologist, Chgo., 1956-59, Okla., 1959-69, Tex., 1969—; prof. edn. U. Okla., 1959-69; dir. manpower planning, regional med. program and Sch. Health Related Professions U. Okla. Med. Center, Oklahoma City, 1967-69, prof. preventive medicine and public health, 1966-69, prof. human ecology, 1969; assoc. dean Sch. Allied Health Scis., U. Tex. Health Sci. Center, Dallas, 1969-74, prof. phys. medicine and rehab., 1969, prof. psychiatry, 1969—, prof. rehab. sci., 1972. Served with AUS, 1943-46. Lic. psychologist, Okla., Tex. Mem. Am., Southwestern, Dallas, Tex. psychol. assns., Sigma Xi, Phi Delta Phi. Contbr. articles to prof. jours. Office: Phys Medicine and Rehab Dept U Tex Health Sci Center 5323 Harry Hines Blvd Dallas TX 75235-9088

PARKER, HARRY S., III, museum director; b. St. Petersburg, Fla., Dec. 23, 1939; s. Harry S. and Catherine (Baillie) P.; B.A., Harvard, 1961; postgrad. U. Utrecht (Netherlands); M.A., N.Y. U., 1966; m. Ellen Margaret McCance, May 23, 1964; children—Elizabeth Day, Thomas Baillie, Samuel Ferguson, Catherine Allan. With Met. Mus. Art, N.Y.C., 1963-74, chmn. edn. dept., 1967-69, vice dir. edn., 1970-74; dir. Dallas Mus. Fine Arts, 1974—. Trustee Am. Fedn. Arts, N.Y.C., Corning (N.Y.) Mus., Museum Collaborative, N.Y.C. Fulbright fellow, 1961-62. Mem. Am. Assn. Museums (trustee, accreditation com.). Office: Dallas Mus Art 1717 N Harwood Dallas TX 75201

PARKER, HERBERT GERALD, state official; b. Fayetteville, Ark., May 13, 1929; s. Otis James and Anna Berthina (Fisher) P.; B.S., U. Nebr., Omaha, 1962; M.S., N.C. A&T State U., Greensboro, 1971; Ph.D., Fla. State U., Tallahassee, 1982; m. Florida Lucylle Fisher, June 27, 1959; 1 dau., Christie Lynne. Commd. 2d. lt. U.S. Army, 1947, advanced through grades to col., 1969; served advisor mil. assistance advisory group Republic of China, Taiwan, 1962-65; prof. mil. sci. N.C. A&T State U., Greensboro, 1965-68; comdr. all U.S. Spl. Forces units the Delta, S. Vietnam, 1968-69; dir. non-resident instrn. U.S. Army Civil Affairs Sch., Ft. Gordon, Ga., 1969-71, commandant and dir., Ft. Bragg, N.C., 1971-73; prof. mil. sci., dept. head Fla. A&M U., Tallahassee, 1973-77; ret., 1977; chief Crimes Compensation Bur., State of Fla., 1979—. Bd. dirs. Opportunities Industrialization Centers, Leon County United Way, 1977-81, Fla. Victim/Witness Network, 1985—; bd. dirs. Nat. Assn. Crime Victims Compensation Bds., 1981—, pres., 1984—; mem. Nat. Urban League, pres. Tallahassee Urban League, 1985—. pres. Fla. A&M U Boosters Club, 1983-85. Decorated Silver Star, Legion of Merit (2), Bronze Star (3), Purple Heart, Air Medal (3). Recipient distinguished service award Boy Scouts Am., 1969. Mem. Nat. Assn. Social Scientists, Res. Officers Assn., U.S. Army Civil Affairs Assn. (Disting. Service award, 1973), Assn. Parents and Teachers, Tallahassee C. of C., Sigma Pi Phi, Phi Kappa Phi. Democrat. Methodist. Clubs: Jack and Jill of Am., Am. Bowling Congress, Univ. Men's League (pres.), Fla. A&M Credit Union Bowling League (pres.), Bass Anglers Sportsman Soc., Winewood Men's Golf Assn. (v.p.), Toastmasters Internat. (pres., 1971-73), Nat. Geog. Soc. Co-author article in Internat. Jour. of Social and Behavioral Scientists. Home: 3510 Tullamore Ln Tallahassee FL 32308 Office: Fla Crimes Compensation Bur 2551 Executive Center Circle W Lafayette Bldg Suite 202 Tallahassee FL 32301

PARKER, HERMAN BRUCE, engineer; b. Hemingway, S.C., Apr. 9, 1946; s. Mack Cloe and Lillie Belle (Langley) B.; m. Linda Dianne Cooke, Feb. 15, 1969; children—Kevin Bruce, Kyle Brandon. B.S. in Electronic Engring. Math., Francis Marion Coll., 1974. Research technician Gen. Electric Co., Columbia, S.C., 1968-70, U.S. Dept. Agr., Florence, S.C., 1970-74; maintenance supt. Lockart Power Co. (S.C.), 1974—. Chmn. Parents Active As Leaders, 1981—; mem. adminstrv. bd. Grace Methodist Ch., 1978-80; pres. Johnny Jeter Sunday Sch. class, 1977-78; coach Dixie Youth Baseball, 1981—. Served with USMC, 1966-68; with N.G., 1972-73. Republican. Home: Route 2 Fairwood Estates Union SC 29379 Office: Lockhart Power Co PO Box 10 Lockhart SC 29364

PARKER, I. RUTH, dentist, nurse; b. McKinnon, Tenn., Apr. 20, 1945; d. John Ross and Mannie E. (Fisher) P. Diploma Bapt. Meml. Hosp., 1965; B.A. cum laude, Memphis State U., 1971; D.D.S., U. Tenn., 1981. Registered nurse, Staff nurse, charge nurse St. Joseph Hosp., Memphis, 1969-72; staff nurse Bapt. Hosp., Memphis, 1965-66, 75-78; gen. practice dentistry, Memphis, 1982—; cons. U.S. Surgical Corp., Stanford, Conn., 1972-74. Served to 1st lt. USAF, Nurses Corps, 1967-68. Mem. Am. Acad. Gen. Dentistry, ADA. Avocations: gardening; reading; needlepoint; world travel. Office: 1203 Poplar Memphis TN 38104

PARKER, JAKE ELZA, school counselor; b. Groveton, Tex., Oct. 1, 1939; s. Jake and Mary Mozelle (McClendon) P.; m. M. Annette Cruce, June 12, 1962; children—Robert, Kimberly. B.S., U. Houston, 1963; Ed.M., Sam Houston State U., 1976. Cert. tchr., vocat./spl. edn. counselor, Tex. Personnel mgr. Camco, Inc., Houston, 1967-69; personnel asst. Meth. Hosp., Houston, 1969-70; career edn. cons. Houston Ind. Sch. Dist., 1970-72; cons. Region IV Edn. Service Ctr., Houston, 1972-82, project dir., 1976-82; counselor Bleyl Jr. High Sch., Houston, 1982—. Editor, dir.: Career Oriented Chemistry, 1976. Project dir.: (film) Reading in Physical Science, 1980. Served with USNR, 1963-65. Mem. Am. Assn. for Counseling and Devel., Tex. Assn. for Counseling and Devel., Spring Creek Assn. for Counseling and Devel. Avocations: woodworking; jogging. Home: 15718 Cascade Point Houston TX 77084 Office: Bleyl Jr High Sch 10800 Mills Rd Houston TX 77070

PARKER, JAMES WILLIAM, food manufacturing company executive, distribution executive; b. Dallas, Apr. 5, 1938; s. W.B. and Irma (Shettlesworth) P.; m. Linda Creech, June 7, 1963; children—Laura, Kari. B.B.A., North Tex. State U., 1963. Cons. PMD Inc., Barrington, Ill., 1969-70; div. mgr. The Southland Corp., Dallas, 1974-80, v.p. dairy group, 1980-82, exec. v.p., 1982—. Bd. dirs. Milk Industry Found., Washington, 1978-84. Served with U.S. Army, 1959-61. Mem. So. Assn. Food and Dairy Mfrs. (pres. 1980-81). Republican. Methodist. Avocations: golf; swimming. Office: Southland Corp 2828 N Haskell Ave Dallas TX 75221

PARKER, JIMMIE CHOATE, army officer, social worker, businessman; b. Alpine, Tex., Mar. 18, 1933; s. Frank and Effie (Choate) P.; B.A. in Govt., U. Tex., Austin, 1957, M.S. in Social Work, 1973; children—Judith Ann, John Franklin. Commd. 2d lt. U.S. Army, 1959, advanced through grades to maj., 1969, served platoon leader, exec. officer 1st Battle Group 13th Inf., 1st Inf. Div., Ft. Riley, Kans., 1959-61, transp. career officer course, Ft. Eustis, Va., 1962, platoon leader, hdqrs. comdt. 55th Aviation Maintenance Battalion, 1962, ops. officer Mobile Tng. Team, Colombia, 1964, co. comdr. 71st Korea, 1963, exec. officer Mobile Tng. Team, Colombia, 1964, co. comdr. 71st Aviation Co. Air Mobile, Ft. Amador, C.Z., 1965-66, exec. officer 56th Aviation Recovery and Maintenance Co., Vietnam, 1967-68, div. aviation officer 2d Armored Div., Ft. Hood, Tex., 1968-69; public welfare worker Austin (Tex.) State Hosp., 1970; social and fin. service unit supr. Tex. Dept. Public Welfare Regional Office, Austin, 1971, program cons. services to aged blind and disabled, social services br., Austin, 1973-74; state program mgr. alt. care services to aged, blind and disabled Tex. Dept. Human Resources, Austin, 1975-80; human resources cons., 1980—; pres. Parker Cons. Inc., 1981—; ptnr. Anderson-Parker, Inc., Home Health Care Agy., 1981—; planner, organizer Tex., White House Conf. on Aging, 1980-81. Bd. dirs. Community Devel. Corp. Austin, 1971-73. Decorated Bronze Star, Air medal with 5 oak leaf clusters. Mem. Nat. Assn. Social Workers, Acad. Cert. Social Workers, Am. Public Welfare Assn. (nat. policy com. on long-term care 1978) Mensa. Methodist. Clubs: Masons, Scottish Rite, Lions. Hon. pilot Colombian Air Force. Office: 205 East Ave D Alpine TX 79830

PARKER, JOHN VICTOR, judge; b. Baton Rouge, Oct. 14, 1928; s. Fred Charles and LaVerne (Sessions) P.; m. Mary Elizabeth Fridge, Sept. 3, 1949; children—John Michael, Robert Fridge, Linda Anne. B.A., La. State U., 1949, J.D., 1952. Bar: La. 1952. Atty. Parker & Parker, Baton Rouge, 1954-66; asst. parish atty. City of Baton Rouge, Parish of East Baton Rouge, 1956-66; atty. Sanders, Downing, Kean & Cazedessus, Baton Rouge, 1966-79; chief judge U.S. Dist. Ct., Middle Dist. La., Baton Rouge, 1979—; vis. lectr. law La. State U. Law Sch. Served with Judge Adv. Gen.'s Corps U.S. Army, 1952-54. Mem. ABA, Am. Judicature Soc., Am. Arbitration Assn., La. State Bar Assn. (past mem. bd. govs.), Baton Rouge Bar Assn. (past pres.), Order of Coif, Phi Delta Phi. Democrat. Club: Baton Rouge Country. Lodges: Masons (32 deg.); Kiwanis (past pres.). Home: 5721 Hyacinth Ave Baton Rouge LA 70808 Office: Room 228 US Courthouse 707 Florida St Baton Rouge LA 70801*

PARKER, JOSEPHUS DERWARD, limestone company executive; b. Elm City, N.C., Nov. 16, 1906; s. Josephus and Elizabeth (Edwards) P.; A.B., U. South, 1928; postgrad. Tulane U., 1928-29, U. N.C., 1929-30, Wake Forest Med. Coll., 1930-31; m. Mary Wright, Jan. 15, 1934 (dec. Dec. 1937); children—Mary Wright (Mrs. Mallory A. Pittman, Jr.), Josephus Derward; m. 2d, Helen Hodges Hackney, Jan. 24, 1940; children—Thomas Hackney, Alton Person, Derward Hodges, Sarah Helen (Mrs. Michael R. Smith). Founder, chmn. bd. J. D. Parker & Sons, Inc., Elm City, N.C., 1955—, Parker Tree Farms, Inc., 1956—; founder, pres. Invader, Inc., 1961-63; pres., dir. Brady Lumber Co., Inc., 1957-62; v.p., dir. Atlantic Limestone, Inc., Elm City, 1970—; owner, operator Parker Airport, Eagle Springs, N.C., 1940-62. Served to capt. USAAF, 1944-47. Episcopalian. Moose, Lion. Club: Wilson (N.C.) Country. Address: PO Box 905 Elm City NC 27822

PARKER, MARY EVELYN, state treas.; b. Fullerton, La., Nov. 8, 1920; d. Racia E. and Addie (Graham) Dickerson; m. W. Bryant Parker, Oct. 31, 1954; children—Mary Bryant, Ann Graham. B.A., Northwestern State Coll., La., 1941; diploma in social welfare, La. State U., 1943. Social worker, Allen Parish, La., 1941-42; personnel adminstr. War Dept., Camp Claiborne, La., 1943-47; editor, Oakdale, La., 1947-48; exec. dir. La. Dept. Commerce and Industry, Baton Rouge, 1948-52; with Mut. of N.Y., Baton Rouge, 1952-56; chmn. La. Bd. Public Welfare, Baton Rouge, 1950-51; commr. La. Dept. Public Welfare, 1956-63, La. Div. Adminstrn., 1964-67; treas., State of La., 1968—. Chmn. White House Conf. on Children and Youth, 1960; pres. La. Conf. on Social Welfare, 1959-61; mem. Democratic Nat. Com., 1948-52; bd. dirs. Woman's Hosp., Baton Rouge; trustee Episcopal High Sch., Baton Rouge, Baton Rouge Gen. Hosp. Found.; mem. adv. council Coll. Bus., Tulane U., New Orleans. Named Baton Rouge Woman of Yr., 1976. Baptist. Home: 9309 Hill Trace Ave Baton Rouge LA 70809 Office: PO Box 44154 Baton Rouge LA 70804

PARKER, MICHAEL RAY, optometrist; b. Fort Payne, Ala., Aug. 21, 1956; s. Bobby Ray and Jo Nell (Jennings) P.; m. Laura Jane Sauls, May 30, 1976; children—Amelia, Adam. B.S. in Natural Scis., U. Ala.-Birmingham, 1977, B.S. in Physiol. Optics, 1978, O.D., 1980. Lic. optometrist, Ala. Practice optometry, Fort Payne, Ala., 1980—. Vice chmn. Zoning Bd., City of Ft. Payne, 1985. Merit scholar U. Ala.-Birmingham, 1974-76. Mem. Am. Optometric Assn., (contact lens section), Ala. Optometric Assn. (bd. dirs. 1985—), So. Council of Optometrists. Methodist. Lodge: Rotary. Avocations: golf; tennis. Home: PO Box 595 Fort Payne AL 35967 Office: PO Box 595 900 A Gault Ave S Fort Payne AL 35967

PARKER, MILTON HEROD, oil well drilling company executive; b. Grapeland, Tex., Aug. 1, 1927; s. Pinkney Herod and Mattie Ruth (Bridges) P.; m. Page Ryland, Oct. 31, 1953; children—Anne Parker Mannis, John R., Julia Parker Stevens. B.S. in Indsl. Edn., Tex. A&M U., 1951. Engr. Aetna Casualty Co., New Orleans, Tulsa, 1951-56; safety engr. Williams & Morgan, Tulsa, 1956-60, safety cons. SW Safety Co., Tulsa, 1960-66; mgr. safety Flint Steel Corp., Tulsa, 1966-72; mgr. safety, drilling Parker Drilling Co., Tulsa, 1972—. Contbr. articles to profl. jours. Chmn. Mayors Safety Com., Tulsa, 1971-75; com. chmn. Tulsa Area Safety Council, 1966-72; mem. com. Tulsa Jr. Coll., 1973-75. Served with USN, 1945-47, PTO. Mem. Am. Soc. Safety Engrs. (Safety Profl. of Yr. award 1983-84), Tulsa Chpt. of Am. Soc. Safety Engrs. (pres. 1965-66), Internat. Assn. Drilling Contractors (mem. safety com., named to Accident Prevention Hall Fame 1981), Nat. Safety Council (gen. chmn. petroleum sect. 1983-84). Republican. Methodist. Club: Oaks Country. Avocation: golf; quail hunting. Office: Parker Drilling Co 8 East 3rd St Tulsa OK 74103

PARKER, NERY FELICITA, college president, consultant; b. Havana, Cuba, July 10, 1942; came to U.S., 1963; d. Justo and Nery (Martin) Garcia; m. Osualdo Pino, June 25, 1960 (div. Jan. 1966); 1 dau., Nery M.; m. 2d James W. Parker, July 10, 1967; children—James W. III, Helen E. B.S. in Psychology summa cum laude, Mercy Coll., Westchester County, N.Y., 1979. Cert. tchr., Fla. Elem. sch. tchr. Pub. Sch. 17, Havana, 1960-62; tchr. asst. Emerson Elem. Sch., Miami, Fla., 1975-79; mem. English faculty Fla. Career Coll., Miami, 1979-80, dir., 1980-82; pres. Martin Tech. Coll., Miami, 1982—, dept. head ESL curriculum, 1979—; cons. sch. licensing and curriculum, Miami, 1980—; dept. head ESL curriculum Fla. Career Coll., Martin Tech. Coll., 1979—. Chmn. various campaigns Emerson Elem. Sch. PTA, Miami, 1978-80. Mem. Coalision, Smithsonian Assocs., Latin C. of C. Republican. Episcopalian. Home: 706 SW 99th Court Circle Miami FL 33174 Office: Martin Tech Coll 1901 NW 7th St Miami FL 33125

PARKER, OSCAR WADE, engineering associate; b. Florence, Ala., Sept. 7, 1955; s. William Burtis and Martha Ann (Hamilton) P.; m. Rebecca Ann Hale, July 13, 1973; children—Bradly Wade, Nicholas Ryan. Student, U. North Ala., 1975-76, Center for Degree Studies, Scranton, Pa., 1978-79. Draftsman, Willis Engring., Florence, Ala., 1973-77; designer/supr. Willis Engring., Florence, 1978-79; engring. assoc. TVA, Muscle Shoals, Ala., 1980—; residential design cons. Mem. TVA Engring. Assn. (rep. 1982-83), Am. Inst. Bldg. Design (registered profl. Ala.). Home: Route 1 PO Box 80 Montclair Dr Killen AL 35645 Office: 600 First Fed Bldg Florence AL 35630

PARKER, PATRICIA KAYE, nurse, medical center administrator; b. Donalsonville, Ga., Nov. 6, 1939; d. Frank Park and Audrey Louise (Mock) Williams; m. Willie Byron Parker, Aug. 7, 1960; children—Warren Byron, William Daniel. R.N., Ga. Bapt. Hosp., 1960; postgrad. Med. Coll. of Ga., 1973-74. R.N., Ga., Ala. Staff nurse Meml. Hosp., Bainbridge, Ga., 1960-61; staff nurse Eugene Talmadge Meml. Hosp. of the Med. Coll. of Ga., Augusta, 1961-65, head nurse, 1965-68, nursing instr., 1968-73, nursing supr., 1973-75; nursing supr., infection control coordinator Southeast Ala. Med. Ctr., Dothan, 1975—; cons., facilitator community service Southeast Ala. Med. Ctr., Dothan and surrounding area, 1980—. Editor, contbr., developer Infection Control Program, 1979—. Scriptwriter, originator, dir. Instructional video tape, Infection Control Orientation Program, 1981. Recipient Quality Assurance award Hosp. Affiliates Internat., 1980; Course Cert. award Ctrs. for Disease Control, 1983-84, Mem. Assn. Practitioners in Infection Control. Democrat. Baptist. Avocations: reading, walking, gift cooking, family travel. Office: Southeast Ala Med Ctr Quality Assurance Dept PO Drawer 6987 Dothan AL 36302

PARKER, RADHA JANIS, counselor educator; b. Hampton, Va., Mar. 4, 1952; d. Simon Payne and Kathryn (Ironmonger) P. B.A., Christopher Newport Coll., 1974; M.Ed., U. Va., 1982, M.A., 1978, Ed.S., 1983, Ph.D., 1986. Alternative edn. tchr. Greene County Schs., Stanardsville, Va., 1980-82; youth supr. Monticello Area Community Action Agy., Charlottesville, Va., 1983; placement counselor Workshop V, Charlottesville, 1983-84; sr. social worker Albemarle County Social Services, Charlottesville, 1983—; coordinator Ctr. for Personal and Career Devel., U. Va., Charlottesville, 1984—. U. Va. Gov.'s fellow, 1984-86. Mem. Am. Assn. Counseling and Devel., Assn. for Counselor Edn. and Supervision, Assn. for Humanistic Edn. and Devel., Am. Mental Health Counselors Assn., Va. Counselors Assn. Home: Star Route 1 PO Box 76-A Free Union VA 22940

PARKER, RICHARD WILSON, lawyer; b. Cleve., June 14, 1943; s. Edgar Gael and Pauline (Wilson) P.; m. Carolyn Edith Kratt, Aug. 9, 1969; children—Brian Jeffrey, Lauren Michelle, Lisa Christine. B.A. cum laude in Econs., U. Redlands, 1965; J.D. cum laude, Northwestern U., 1968. Bar: Ohio 1968, Va. 1974. Assoc. Arter & Hadden, Cleve., 1968-71; asst. gen. atty. Norfolk & Western Ry. Co., Cleve. and Roanoke, Va., 1971-74, asst. gen. solicitor, Roanoke, 1974-78, gen. atty., 1978-84; sr. gen. atty. Norfolk So. Corp., 1984—. Mem. ABA, Ohio Bar Assn., Va. State Bar, Va. Bar Assn., Roanoke Bar Assn. Presbyterian. Office: 8 N Jefferson St Roanoke VA 24042

PARKER, ROBERT ALAN, statistician; b. Boston, Apr. 28, 1949; s. Joseph and Eleanor Corinne (Faber) P.; m. Laurie Catherine Allen, May 6, 1977. B.S., MIT, 1970; M.S., London Sch. Hygiene and Tropical Medicine, London, 1976; D.Sc., Harvard, 1983. Statistician, Malan, Chiang Mai, Thailand, 1973-75, WHO, Geneva, 1977-80, Ctrs. for Disease Control, Atlanta, Ga., 1983—. Contbr. articles to profl. jours. Mem. Am. Statis. Assn., Biometric Soc., Royal Statis. Soc., Sigma Xi. Home: 1431 LaChona Ct Atlanta GA 30329 Office: Ctrs for Disease Control 1600 Clifton Rd Atlanta GA 30333

PARKER, ROBERT LEE, petroleum engineer, drilling company executive; b. Tulsa, July 16, 1923; s. Gifford Cleveland and Gladys Carolyn (Baker) P.; B.S., U. Tex., 1944; LL.D. (hon.), John Brown U., 1967, Oral Roberts U., 1977; m. Catherine Mae McDaniel, Dec. 16, 1944; children—Robert L., Carolyn Louise, Debra Ann. With Parker Drilling Co., 1947—, owner mgr., 1953—, pres., from 1954, chmn. bd., 1967—; also chief exec. officer; dir. Bank Okla., Facet Enterprises. Chmn. St. Francis Hosp., Tulsa, U. Tex. Engring. Found trustee U. Tulsa, 1st Methodist Ch., Tulsa; bd. dirs. Tulsa YMCA, Jr. Achievement, active Boy Scouts Am. Served with U.S. Army, 1945-47. Named Distinguished Engring. Grad. U. Tex., 1969. Mem. Am. Petroleum Inst., Internat. Assn. Drilling Contractors, Okla. Inc. Petroleum Assn., Soc. Profl. Engrs. Republican. Clubs: So. Hills Country, Tulsa, Houston, Odessa Country. Office: 8 E 3d St Tulsa OK 74103*

PARKER, ROBERT LEE, SR., transportation company official; b. Tarpon Springs, Fla., Feb. 29, 1932; s. Thomas Lester and Elizabeth (Whatley) P.; m. Barbara Craft, Nov. 4, 1951; children—Deborah Denise, Robert Lee, Clifford Thomas. B.A., Columbia of Pacific U., 1983, M.A., 1984. Police officer Hialeah Police Dept. (Fla.), 1954-58; metals buyer United Metals, Miami, Fla., 1958-62; bus operator Dade Transit, Miami, 1962-66, schedule maker, 1966-71, sr. schedule maker, 1971-79, supt. schedules, 1979—; instr. Miami Dade Community Coll. Author: Scheduling Practices, 1980. Served with N.G., 1947-50, USMC, 1950-54. Democrat. Presbyterian. Lodges: Masons, Shriners. Home: 2871 SW 108th Way Davie FL 33328 Office: Met Dade Transp Agy PO Box 520887 Miami FL 33152

PARKER, ROBERT LEE, JR., drilling company executive; b. Midland, Tex., Nov. 9, 1948; s. Robert Lee and Catherine Mae (McDaniel) P.; m. Carolyn Diane Daniel, June 1971 (div. 1974); 1 dau., Christy Diane; m. 2d, Patricia Ann Dollarhite, Oct. 21, 1977 (div. 1984); children—Robert Lee III, Austin Leeann. Student Okla. State U., 1967-68; M.B.A., U. Tex., 1972. Contract rep. Parker Drilling Co., Tulsa, 1972-73, mgr. U.S. ops., 1973-74, v.p., 1974-76, exec. v.p., 1976-77, pres., chief operating officer, 1977—, also dir.; dir. Baker Drilling Equipment, Alaska Airlines Inc., Bank of Okla. Bd. dirs. United Way, Tulsa, 1983—. Recipient 3d place award Tex. Trophy Hunters Assn., 1983. Republican. Methodist. Office: Parker Drilling Co 8 E 3d St Tulsa OK 74105

PARKER, ROBERT M., U.S. district judge; b. 1937. B.B.A., U. Tex., 1961, J.D., 1964. Adminstrv. asst. to Tex. Congressman Ray Roberts, 1956-66; assoc. Parish & Parker, Gilmer, Tex., 1964-65, Kenley & Boyland, Longview, Tex., 1965, Roberts, Smith & Parker, Longview, 1966-71, Rutledge & Parker, Fort Worth, 1971-72, Nichols & Parker, Longview, 1972-79; judge U.S. Dist. Ct. for Eastern Tex., Beaumont, 1979—. Mem. ABA, Tex. Bar Assn. Address: PO Box 3684 Beaumont TX 77704*

PARKER, ROBIN ZACHARY, architect, solar energy company executive; b. Miami, Fla., Mar. 28, 1946; s. Alfred Browning and Martha (Gifford) P.; student U. Fla., 1966-69, U. Toronto, 1969-71, U. Miami, 1972-75; m. Lydia Leach, June 25, 1977; children—Britt Zachary, Melahn Lyle. Dir., Alfred Browning Parker, Architects, P.C., Miami, 1974-83; individual practice architecture, Miami, 1975—; investment cons. Terra Investment & Trading, Honduras, 1978-83 founding dir., v.p. Solar Reactor Engines, Inc., Titusville, Fla., 1981-83; founding dir., v.p. Solar Reactor Corp., Miami, 1978-81, pres., 1983-85 founder, pres. Solar Reactor Space and Def. Techs. Inc., 1985—; community coll. instr., 1983-85; cons. Mem. AIA (corp.), Internat. Explorers Soc. Author: Indigenous Architecture, 1982; Home of the Future, 1983.

PARKER, SHASTA NAN, needlework design company executive; b. Gadsden, Ala., Jan. 1, 1957; d. Archie Lackey and Glenda Ernestine (Stephens) P. B.S. in Bus. Adminstrn., Samford U., 1980. Dept. mgr. Parisian Inc., Birmingham, Ala., 1980-85; area sales mgr. Pizitz, Birmingham, 1985-86; owner, mgr. Keep 'em in Stitches, Birmingham, 1985—; dir. mktg. and spl. projects Just Cross Stitch mag., 1986—. Vice pres. ann. fund Jr. Women com. Ala. Symphony, Birmingham, 1985—, mem. hospitality com., 1984-85; mem. Pointe Soc., Birmingham, 1985—. Republican. Home: 11 Ransom Rd Birmingham AL 35210

PARKER, TOM VERNON, highway safety executive; b. Mt. Home, Ark., Dec. 24, 1948; s. Vernon Robert and Sibyl Edwina (Narramore) P.; m. Brenda Sue Groce, Aug. 10, 1973; children—Erin Elizabeth, Matthew Thomas. B.B.A., U. Central Ark. Dir. safety Glenn Bros. Trucking Co., Little Rock, 1981-83; program mgr. Ark. Highway Safety Program, Little Rock, 1973-77, dir., 1977-83, 83—. Co-author Ark. DWI Curriculum manual, 1979. Bd. dirs. Pulaski Activity Ctr., Little Rock, 1985. Served with USNG, 1970-76. Recipient Cert. Appreciation, Ark. State Police, 1981. Mem. Nat. Assn. Govs. Highway Safety Reps. (mem. exec. bd. 1977-81, 83—, vice chmn. 1980-81, sec. 1979-80, treas. 1983-84), Transp. Research Com. (adv. bd. 1983—), Ark. Alcohol Drug Abuse Prevention (adv. bd. 1983—). Democrat. Methodist. Clubs: Optimist (Little Rock), Razorback (Jacksonville, Ark.). Avocations: snow skiing; fishing; camping. Home: 602 Devon St Sherwood AR 72116 Office: Ark Highway Safety Program 1 Capitol Mall 4B-215 Little Rock AR 72201

PARKER, WHILDEN SESSIONS, lawyer; b. Baton Rouge, La., Jan. 27, 1936; s. Fred C. and Laverne S. Parker; B.S., La. State U., 1960; J.D., George Washington U., 1970; m. Joyce Nowak; children—Pamela, Elaine, Vance. Bar: to Va. 1970, D.C. 1971, Fla. 1979. Law clk. U.S. Ct. Claims, Washington, 1970-71; assoc. law firm Sellers, Conner & Cuneo and Pettit & Martin, Washington, 1971-75; adminstrv. judge Armed Services Bd. Contract Appeals, Alexandria, Va., 1975-76; v.p., counsel Pratt & Whitney Aircraft Group, Govt. Products div. United Technologies Corp., West Palm Beach, Fla., 1976—. Served with USMC, 1960-67. Decorated Air medal. Mem. ABA, Va. State Bar, D.C. Bar, Fla. Bar. Office: 4761 Holly Dr Palm Beach Gardens FL 33410

PARKER, WILLIAM DALE, business executive, political adviser; b. Portsmouth, Va., Apr. 13, 1925; s. Otis Durie and Eva Estelle (Dempsey) P.; m. Frances Ross Jennings, Feb. 2, 1946 (dec.); children—Frances Lea, Elizabeth Dale, Kim Carolyn Jane, Penny Jo Ann, Jacquelyn Susan; m. Boots Lee Farthing, 1968. Student Coll. William and Mary, 1946; grad. indsl. engring. Internat. Corr. Schs., 1956; student U. Del., 1959-60, Calif. Western U., 1961-62, U. Calif., 1964, Stetson U., 1969; D.Sc., James Balmes U., Saltillio, Mex., 1968; Ph.D. in Edn., Fla. Inst., 1970; D.D., U. of Life, 1971. Layout, process and prodn. engr. Gen. Motors Corp., Wilmington, Del., 1949-59, asst. dir. salaried personnel pub. relations, 1959-61; mfg. engr., lectr. Gen. Dynamics/Astronautic, San Diego, 1961-64; dir. Internat. Inst. Human Relations, LaJolla, Calif., 1964—; aerospace scientist, mgmt. specialist Gemini and Expts. Program Office, NASA, Houston, 1964-67, Cape Kennedy, Fla., 1967-69; family and marriage counselor, Titusville, Fla., 1967-71; mgmt. cons., v.p. Multiple Services, Inc., Titusville and Boone, N.C., 1969—; dir., v.p. in charge franchising Am. and Internat. Model Festivals, Spangler TV, N.Y.C., 1969-73; chmn. bd. Travel Internat., Inc., Titusville, 1971-74. Author: Philosophy of Genius: American Values, Solutions to Family and Marriage Problems; Gutless America, 1973. Columnist Sentinal Newspapers, 1963-64; asst. editor Campers Illus. Mag., 1964-65, Star Adv., 1968. INSIGHT, 1969-72, Challenge, 1970—, Mountain Times, 1981-84. Hon. mem. editorial adv. bd. Am. Biog. Inst., 1975—. Patentee Amy peanut dolls. Mem. Nat. Democratic Com., 1980—; ind. candidate for Gov. Fla., 1976; founder Monroe Park CD, 1951; mem. Wilmington council Boy Scouts Am., 1953-55; chmn. Varions Agy. Fund, 1954-60; co-chmn. Del. Dept. DC TV Shows, 1956-57; mem. Middle Atlantic States Conf. Correction, 1956-60; chmn., pres. Del. Md. Pa. Tri State Hosp. Com., 1957-59; mem. Wilmington Inner City Study Comm., 1957-60; chmn. Del. DC Evacuation Commn., 1958-59, Del. Hwy. Safety Campaign, 1959-60; active PTA; faculty adviser Mensa Coll.; mem. Democratic Exec. Com., 1975-77; polit. advisor Congress, U.S. Pres., 1974—; bd. dirs. Boys and Girls Aid Soc. San Diego, 1962-64; bd. advisers Salvation Army. Served with USCGR, USN, World War II. Named Del. Outstanding Young Man of Yr., Wilmington/U.S. Jr. C. of C. 1957; recipient Silver award Del. Vol. Bur., 1957, ann. awards Va. Jr. Achievement, Inc., 1959; speech award U.S. Jr. C. of C., 1960, Gemini award NASA, 1967, Internat. Disting. Service to Humanity award 1969, Internat. Humanitarian award, 1971, Keys to City, Wilmington, 1959, 61, 72, Titusville, 1970, Miami, 1973; named Hon. Sheriff, Portsmouth, Va., 1973. Mem. Am. Legion (life), DAV (life), VFW (life), Wilmington Indsl. Mgmt. Club, Mensa (life), Monroe Park Civic Assn. (pres. 1952-53), Nat. Space Inst. (charter, life), vols. Speakers Bur. (San Diego), Coll. William and Mary Alumni Soc., S.A.R., Authors Guild, Authors League Am. Clubs: Royal Oak Golf and Country; Mexican Turf; S. Am. Turf (life). Lodges: Masons (32 degree), Elks (life), Moose (life).

PARKER, WILLIAM THOMAS, state senator; b. Chesapeake, Va., Aug. 29, 1928; m. Vivian Old. Student, Norfolk Naval Shipyard Apprentice Sch. Pres., owner Mid-Eastern Airways Inc.; mem. Va. Ho. of Reps., 1976-80; mem. Va. Senate, 1980—. Served with USAF, 1950-52. Democrat. Methodist. Lodge: Masons. Office: VA Senate Gen Assembly Bldg 9th and Broad Sts Richmond VA 23219*

PARKER, WILMER, III, lawyer, educator; b. Ozark, Ala., Oct. 3, 1951; s. Wilmer and Anne Laura (Ragsdale) P.; m. Rebecca Joy Skillern, Aug. 25, 1984;

m. Beverly Laura Barnard, Dec. 23, 1972 (div. Dec. 1977). B.S. in Commerce, U. Ala., 1972, M.B.A., 1975; J.D., 1975; LL.M., Emory U., 1976. Bar: Ala. 1975, Ga. 1976, Fla. 1976, U.S. Dist. Ct. (no. dist.) Ga. 1976, U.S. Tax Ct. 1976, U.S. Ct. Appeals (11th cir.) 1985. Assoc. Nall, Miller & Cadenhead, Atlanta, 1975-78; trial atty. tax div. U.S. Dept. Justice, Washington, 1978-83, asst. U.S. atty. Organized Crime Drug Enforcement Task Force, Atlanta, 1983—; lectr. trial advocacy Emory U. Law Sch., Atlanta, 1984—. Named Outstanding Trial Atty., Tax Div., U.S. Dept. Justice, Washington, 1979. Mem. ABA (com. on civil and criminal tax penalties of taxation com.). Presbyterian. Office: Southeastern Drug Task Force Box 523 75 Spring St Atlanta GA 30303

PARKEY, ROBERT WAYNE, radiology and nuclear medicine educator, research radiologist; b. Dallas, July 17, 1938; s. Jack and Gloria Alfreda (Perry) P.; m. Nancy June Knox, Aug. 9, 1960; children—Wendell Wade, Robert Todd, Amy Elizabeth. B.S. in Physics, U. Tex., Austin, 1960; M.D., S.W. Med. Sch., U. Tex.-Dallas, 1965. Diplomate Am. Bd. Radiology, Am. Bd. Nuclear Medicine. Intern St. Paul Hosp., Dallas, 1965-66; resident in radiology U. Tex. Health Sci. Ctr.-Dallas, 1966-69, asst. prof. radiology, 1970-74, assoc. prof., 1974-77, prof., 1977—, chmn. dept. radiology, 1977—; NIH fellow Nat. Inst. Gen. Med. Sci., U. Mo., Columbia, 1969-70; chief nuclear medicine Parkland Meml. Hosp., Dallas, 1974-79, chief dept. radiology, 1977—. Contbr. numerous chpts., articles, abstracts to profl. publs. Served as capt. M.C., Army N.G., 1965-72. Nat. Acad. Scis.-NRC scholar in radiol. research James Picker Found., 1971-74. Fellow Am. Coll. Cardiology, Am. Coll. Radiology; mem. Am. Coll. Nuclear Physicians (charter, ho. of dels. 1974—), Council on Cardiovascular Radiology of Am. Heart Assn., AMA, Assn. Univ. Radiologists, Dallas County Med. Assn., Dallas Ft. Worth Radiol. Soc., Radiol. Soc. N.Am., Soc. Chairmen of Acad. Radiology Depts., Soc. Nuclear Medicine (acad. council, rep. to Inter-Soc. Com. on Heart Diseases 1975—, trustee S.W. chpt. 1975-78), Tex. Assn. Physicians in Nuclear Medicine (charter, sec.-treas. 1973-74), Tex. Med. Assn., Tex. Radiol. Soc., Sigma Xi, Alpha Omega Alpha. Avocations: gardening; golf; tennis. Office: U Tex Health Sci Ctr Dept Radiology 5323 Harry Hines Blvd Dallas TX 75235

PARKINS, FREDERICK MILTON, university dean; b. Princeton, N.J., Sept. 8, 1935; s. William Milton and Phyllis Virginia (Plyler) P.; m. Carolyn Rude-Parkins; children—Bradford, Christopher, Eric. D.D.S., U. Pa., 1960; Ph.D., M.S.D., U. N.C., 1969. Dir. continuing edn. U. Iowa, Iowa City, 1975-77; assoc. dean, 1975-79; Robert Wood Johnson fellow Nat. Acad. Scis., Washington, 1977-78; dean Sch. Dentistry, U. Louisville, 1979—. Mem. project rev. com. Falls Region Subarea Council, 1982, exec. council, 1982; v.p. Youth Performing Arts Council, 1982, exec. com. AAAS fellow, 1980; Am. Acad. Pedodontics fellow, 1969; recipient Ann. Research award Am. Acad. Pedodontics, 1968. Mem. Ky. Dental Assn., ADA, Am. Fund for Dental Health (trustee), Am. Assn. Dental Schs., Internat. Assn. Dental Research. Unitarian. Clubs: Jefferson, Glendale Flying (Louisville).

PARKINS, JOHN HEWLETT, III, textile co. mgr.; b. Greenville, S.C., Sept. 12, 1933; s. John Hewlett and Ellen Lucille (Freeman) P.; B.S., Clemson U., 1957. Prodn. supr. and mgr. The Singer Co., Pickens, S.C., 1957-58, production mgr., Finderne, N.J., 1959; gen. mgr. Deering Milliken, Inc., La Grange, Ga., 1971—, gen. mgr., Laurens, S.C., 1969-71, White Stone, S.C., 1964-69, sales mgr., 1963-64, product mgr., Marietta, S.C., 1961-63; bd. chmn. ROBO of W. Ga., Inc.; gen. partner Glen-Mar Enterprises. Delegate Republican Convention, S.C. Served with U.S. Army, 1953-55. Mem. Am. Textile Mfrs. Inst., Ga. Textile Mfrs. Assn., Inst. Indsl. Launderers, KEX Nat. Assn. Clubs: Highland Country (LaGrange); Green Island Country (Columbus, Ga.); N.Y. Athletic (N.Y.C.), Lions. Office: 1 Dallis St La Grange GA 30240

PARKINSON, THOMAS FRANKLIN, nuclear engineering educator, consultant; b. Tampa, Fla., Feb. 22, 1925; s. William Walker and Martha Wylie (Moffatt) P.; m. Helen Fay Chapman, Apr. 3, 1948; 1 child, Martha Parkinson Craddock. B.S. in Engring. Physics, Auburn U., 1946; Ph.D. in Physics, U. Va., 1953. Research physicist E.I. duPont de Nemours, Aiken, S.C., 1952-60; prof. nuclear engring. U. Fla., Gainesville, 1960-68; prof., chmn. nuclear engring. U. Mo., Columbia, 1968-75; prof., chmn. nuclear engring. Va. Poly. Inst., Blacksburg, 1975—, dir. nuclear reactor lab., 1975-84; cons. Va. Power Co., Richmond, 1985—, also many others. Served with USNR, 1943-45. Fulbright-Hays fellow, 1967-68; recipient Internat. Atomic Energy Agy. cons. awards 1975-81, Orgn. Am. States cons. award 1978. Mem. Am. Nuclear Soc. (chmn. Va. chpt. 1983-84), AAAS, Omicron Delta Kappa, Tau Beta Pi. Republican. Presbyterian. Avocations: commercial pilot; soaring. Club: Soaring Soc. Am. Office: Va Poly Inst & State Univ Dept Mech Engring Blacksburg VA 24061

PARKS, DAVID HALL, systems consultant; b. Talladega, Ala., Nov. 25, 1918; s. Lee Otis and Kate Moss (Freeze) P.; student Jacksonville State U., 1953-55; B.B.A., Auburn U., 1956; m. Minnie Lou Henley, May 31, 1941. Adminstrv. asst. Ala. Mil. Dept., Talladega, 1949-51; cost analyst Am. Cast Iron Pipe Co., Birmingham, Ala., 1956-63; systems analyst, 1963-67, mgr. systems and procedures, 1967-84; systems cons., 1984—. Served with USAAF, 1940-46, U.S. Army, 1951-53, lt. col. ret. Recipient certificate of appreciation Goodwill Industries, 1964. Mem. Nat. Mgmt. Assn., Birmingham Mus. Art, Nat. Assn. Accountants, Ret. Officers Assn., Phi Kappa Phi. Democrat. Baptist. Lodges: Masons (32 deg.), Shriners. Home: 2220 Gay Way Birmingham AL 35216

PARKS, MARY IRENE, bookseller, antiques dealer; b. Asheboro, N.C., Apr. 19, 1919; d. Carl Clifton and Revella Rose (Strickland) Rollins; m. Albert Lee Parks, July 3, 1938; children—Albert Lee, Jr. (dec.), Rachel Yvonne White, Teresa Diana Cooper, Candace Susan Kirk, James Michael, Cynthia Revella Whitley. Bookseller Grandpa's House, Troy, N.C., 1963—. Baptist. Office: Grandpa's House Hwy 27 Route 3 Box 292 Troy NC 27371

PARKS, NORMAN HOUSTON, lawyer; b. Columbia, Tenn., May 27, 1949; s. Joe Houston and Cloa Elizabeth (Frakes) P.; m. Suzanne Cox, Oct. 1, 1976; children—Alexander Fisher. B.A. with distinction, Southwestern at Memphis, 1971; postgrad. U. N.C., 1972-73; J.D., U. Tenn., 1975. Bar: Tenn. 1975, U.S. Ct. Appeals (6th cir.) 1982. Instr. English, Maury County Schs., Santa Fe, Tenn., 1971-72; law clk. U.S. Dist. Judge, Memphis, 1975-76; pvt. practice, Columbia, Tenn., 1976—; ptnr. Trabue, Sturdivant & DeWitt, Columbia, 1982—. Mem. Maury County Bd. Edn., 1980—, chmn., 1984—; bd. dirs. Neighbors Concerned, Inc., 1982; Maury County chmn. Com. to Re-elect Senator Jim Sasser, 1982; chmn. lay tng. com. First United Meth. Ch., Columbia, 1983-84, chmn. wills and estates com., 1984—. Recipient Am. Jurisprudence award Lawyers Coop. Pub. Co., Knoxville, Tenn., 1975, Disting. Service award Columbia Jaycees, 1984. Mem. ABA, Tenn. Bar Assn., Maury County Bar Assn. (v.p. 1985), Maury County C. of C. (edn. com. 1985), Maury County Hist. Soc., Tenn. Hist. Soc., Nat. Wildlife Fedn., Phi Beta Kappa, Alpha Tau Omega, Phi Alpha Delta. Democrat. Methodist. Lodge: Kiwanis (bd. dirs., v.p., pres.). Avocations: reading; creative writing. Home: 919 Myers Ave Columbia TN 38401 Office: Trabue Sturdivant & DeWitt 13 Public Square PO Box 1004 Columbia TN 38402

PARKS, VICTOR LEE, computer electronics engineer, pilot; b. Camden, N.J., Mar. 31, 1956; s. Victor III and Gracelyn (Moore) P.; m. Ursula Ann Foster, May 3, 1986. B.E.E., Ga. Inst. Tech., 1979. Electro-optics research technician Ga. Tech. Engring. Expt. Sta., Atlanta, 1977-79; custom semicondr. test devel. engr. Datapoint Corp., San Antonio, 1979-84; lead mfg. test engr. Harris Semicondr., Melbourne, Fla., 1984—. Vol., AirLifeLine of Tex., Inc., blood bank. Mem. Aircraft Owners and Pilots Assn. Episcopalian. Home: 871 Douglas St SE Palm Bay FL 32907 Office: Harris Semicondr PO Box 883 Mail Stop 51-065 Melbourne FL 32901

PARLANTIERI, ANDREW JOSEPH, office equipment company executive; b. Salem, Ohio, June 19, 1929; s. Dominic and Mary (Guappone) P.; m. Martha Ann Warren, June 20, 1953; children—Catherine Ann, Cynthia Lou Parlantieri Bostic, Andrew Joseph Jr. B.S. in Bus. Adminstrn., Duquesne U., 1951. With Deming Plumbing Corp., Salem, 1954-55; account exec. Remington Rand div. Sperry-Rand Corp., Newport News, Va., 1955-65, sales mgr., Richmond, Va., 1965-71, dist. sales mgr., Newport News, 1971-75; founder, pres. Parlantieri-Remco, Inc., Newport News, 1975—. Commr., Va. Peninsula Port Authority, 1981—; treas. Sister City Commn., 1983—; chmn. bd. advisors Va. Penninsula Alcohol Safety action Program, 1975-82; v.p. Va. Peninsula United Way, 1983—. Named Bus. Man of Yr., Christopher Newport Coll. Bus. Fraternity, 1977; recipient Outstanding Leadership award Va. Peninsula Alcohol Safety Action Program; Appreciation resolution City Council of Newport News. Episcopalian. Lodge: Kiwanis (sec. 1959-64, v.p. 1977, pres. 1978, Outstanding Leadership award 1978). Office: Parlantieri-Remco Inc 700 Middle Ground Blvd Newport News VA 23606

PARMALEE, PAUL WOODBURN, museum director, educator; b. Mansfield, Ohio, Oct. 17, 1926; s. Max Woodburn and Marion Isabel (Fox) P.; B.S., Ohio U., Athens, 1948; M.S., U. Ill., Urbana, 1949; Ph.D., Tex. A&M U., 1952; m. Barbara J. Griswold, Aug. 28, 1949; children—John David, Patrice Ellen. Asst. prof. biology Stephen F. Austin State U., Nacogdoches, Tex., 1952-53; curator zoology, asst. museum dir. Ill. State Mus., Springfield, 1953-73; prof. zooarchaeology, dir. univ. mus. U. Tenn., Knoxville, 1973—. Served with AUS, 1944-46. Grantee NSF, Ill. State Mus. Soc. Mem. Am. Soc. Mammalogists, Am. Ornithologists Union, Wilson Ornithol. Soc., Am. Quarternary Assn., Soc. Am. Archaeology, Soc. Veterbrate Paleontology, Am. Malacological Union, Ill. Acad. Sci., Tenn. Adad. Sci., Sigma Xi. Co-author: Decoys and Decoy Carvers of Illinois, 1969; contbr. articles profl. jours. Home: 6925 Riverwood Dr Knoxville TN 37920 Office: Univ Tenn Knoxville TN 37996

PARMER, HUGH Q., state senator, marketing company executive; b. Aug. 3, 1939. B.A., Yale U. Mem. Tex. Ho. of Reps., 1962-64, mem. adminstrn., health and human resources, and intergovtl. relations coms.; now mem. Tex. Senate. Democrat. Office: Tex Senate PO Box 12068 Austin TX 78711*

PARNABY, GARY REDELLE, banker; b. Jacksonville, Fla., Nov. 15, 1945; s. Frank Ernest and Doris (Darden) P.; B.A., Fla. State U., 1969; postgrad. U. N. Fla., Grad. Sch. Bank Investments U. Ill., 1979; m. Janice Creamer, June 14, 1969; children—Gary Redelle, Laura. Mgmt. trainee Atlantic Nat. Bank of Jacksonville, 1972, bond officer, 1973-74, asst. v.p., 1974-76; dir. bond portfolio mgmt. div. Fla. Nat. Banks of Fla., Jacksonville, 1976, v.p. div., funds mgmt., 1976-83; sr. v.p. funds mgmt. div., 1983—. Mem. ad hoc adv. com. Jacksonville Housing Authority, 1978—. Served with U.S. Army, 1969-72. Decorated Bronze Star medal. Mem. Am. Bankers Assn., Nat. Assn. Bus. Economists, Fla. Bankers Assn., Dealer Bank Assn., Fla. Bankers Investment Com. Republican. Baptist. Clubs: University, Seminole, Jacksonville Racquetball, PGA Tournament Players. Office: Fla Nat Banks PO Box 689 Jacksonville FL 32201

PARNES, EDMUND IRA, oral and maxillofacial surgeon; b. Pitts., Apr. 16, 1936; s. David E. and Sara (Engelberg) P.; m. Elizabeth Cameron, Nov. 27, 1977; children—Dana, Mara, Lauren. Student Vanderbilt U., 1954-55, U. Miami, 1955-56; D.D.S., U. Pitts., 1960, Diplomate Am. Bd. Oral and Maxillofacial Surgery. Oral surgery intern Jackson Meml. Hosp., 1960-61; resident, teaching fellow anesthesiology Presbyn. Univ. Hosp., Pitts., 1963-64; sr. resident oral surgery Ben Taub Gen. Hosp., Houston, 1964-65; practice oral and maxillofacial surgery, Miami, Fla., 1965—; interim assoc. chief oral surgery Jackson Meml. Hosp., Miami, 1970-72; clin. assoc. prof. U. Miami, 1975—; lectr. in field. Served as capt. U.S. Army, 1961-63. Fellow Am. Assn. Oral and Maxillofacial Surgeons (mem. com. legislation 1972-73, com. sci. sessions 1979—); mem. ADA, Fla. Soc. Oral and Maxillofacial Surgeons (pres. 1974-75), Fla. Dental Assn. (ho. of dels., trustee 1982—), S.E. Soc. Oral Surgeons, East Coast Dist. Dental Soc. (chmn. coms. 1980-84, pres. 1981-82), North Dade Dental Soc. (pres. 1971-72), Am. Soc. Dental Anesthesiology (pres. Fla. chpt. 1970), Alpha Omega (pres. 1977-78, regent 1983). Jewish. Office: South Fla Oral and Maxillofacial Surgery Assocs 9185 SW 97th Ave Miami FL 33176

PARNES, JEFFREY MICHAEL, computer scientist; b. N.Y.C., June 11, 1950; s. Abraham and Marion (Pflaster) P.; m. Daria Ann Makowski, Oct. 26, 1974; children—Adam Jacob, Sarah Elaine. B.A. in Math., Syracuse U., 1974; student SUNY-Syracuse Coll. Forestry, 1968-72, Queens Coll., 1973; postgrad. George Mason U., 1985—. Retirement benefits examiner NYC Employees Retirement System, 1973-74; quality assurance specialist Def. Contract Adminstrn., N.Y.C., 1974-75, Atlanta, 1975-80, Def. Logistics Agy., Alexandria, Va., 1980-85; mgr. Perce Shield project Computer Scis. Corp., Herndon, Va., 1985—. Chmn. land use com. Greenbriar Civic Assn., 1981-86; mem. adv. com. Fairfax County Agrl. and Forestry Dist., 1983—. Named Citizen of Yr., Greenbrier Civic Assn., 1982. Mem. Am. Soc. Quality Control, Alpha Phi Omega (Disting. Service Key award, 1972). Office: Computer Scis Corp 555 Herndon Pkwy PO Box 745 Herndon VA 22070

PARR, EUGENE QUINCY, orthopaedic surgeon; b. Erlanger, Ky., Aug. 4, 1925; s. Benjamin Franklin and Sallie Frances (Wright) P.; m. Joan Lykins, June 9, 1951; children—Eugene Quincy Jr., Jeffrey Wright, Valerie. Student Berea Coll., Ky., 1944-45, 46-48; M.D., U. Louisville, 1952; fellow Mayo Grad. Sch. Medicine, 1956-60. Diplomate Am. Bd. Orthopaedic Surgery. Intern Baroness Erlanger Hosp., Chattanooga, 1952-53; resident in orthopaedic surgery Mayo Clinic, Rochester, Minn., 1956-60; practice medicine specializing in orthopaedic surgery, Lexington, Ky., since 1960—; adminstrv. trustee Central Baptist Hosp., Lexington, 1975-84. Trustee Berea Coll., 1966-72. Fellow Am. Acad. Orthopaedic Surgeons; mem. Doctors Mayo Soc. (founding), Orthopaedic Research and Ednl. Found., Lexington Orthopaedic Soc. (pres. 1964-66), Ky. Orthopaedic Soc. (pres. 1986), Phi Kappa Phi. Avocation: thoroughbred horse breeding and development. Home: Foxtale Farm 1825 Keene Rd Nicholasville KY 40356 Office: 2368 Nicholasville Rd Lexington KY 40503

PARR, JACK RAMSEY, judge; b. Dallas, May 10, 1926; s. Richard Arnold and Mary Lillian (Ramsey) P.; m. Martha Suttle, July 2, 1955; children—Richard Arnold II, Beverly Ann, Geoffrey Alan. B.A., U. Okla., 1949, LL'B., 1950, J.D., 1970; grad. Nat. Jud. Coll., 1966, Am. Acad. Jud. Edn., 1979, JAG Sch., U.S. Army, 1981. Cert. mil. judge. Bar: Okla. 1950, U.S. Ct. Mil. Appeals 1955, U.S. Supreme Ct. 1955. Sole practice, Edmond, Okla., 1953-58; asst. U.S. atty. Western Dist. Okla., 1958-65; judge 7th Jud. Dist. Okla., 1965—, presiding judge, 1980; vice presiding judge appellate div. Court on the Judiciary; chmn. Okla. Supreme Ct. Commn. Uniform Civil Jury Instrns.; asso. prof. law Oklahoma City U., 1966-67. Served to capt. JAGC, USNR, 1944-46, 51-53; Korea; mem. Naval Res. Trial Judiciary Unit 107, 1980—. Mem. Okla. Bar Assn. (Outstanding Com. Service award 1969, Oklahoma County Bar Assn. (cert. of merit 1971, Outstanding Service award 1977-78), ABA, Jud. Conf. Okla., Am. Judicature Soc., Navy-Marine Res. Lawyers Assn., Judge Advs. Assn. U.S., Am. Legion, Mil. Order World Wars, Res. Officers Assn. U.S., Delta Theta Phi. Clubs: Masons, Elks. Home: 2601 NW 55th Pl Oklahoma City OK 73112 Office: 706 County Courthouse 321 Park Ave Oklahoma City OK 73102

PARRIS, STANFORD E., congressman; b. Champaign, Ill., Sept. 9, 1929; s. Verne E. and Edna (Kendall) P. B.S., U. Ill., 1950; J.D., George Washington U., 1958. Bar: Va. bar 1958, D.C. bar 1976. Pres. Woodbridge Lincoln Mercury Corp., Va., 1965-79; mem. Va. Ho. of Dels., 1969-72; mem. fin. com., cts. of justice com., inter-state cooperation com., counties, cities and towns com., chmn. Joint Senate-House Republican Caucus; sec. of state Commonwealth of Va., 1978; mem. 97th Congress from 8th Va. Dist., mem. banking, fin. and urban affairs com., D.C.; com., chmn. Republican Task Force Econ. Policy. Mem. Fairfax County (Va.) Bd. Suprs., 1964-67; bd. dirs. Fairfax County YMCA; trustee George Mason U., Fairfax. Served with USAF, 1950-54; Korea. Decorated D.F.C., Air medal, Purple Heart; recipient Watchdog of the Treasury award, 1973-74. Mem. Am. Bar Assn., Va. Bar Assn., D.C. Bar Assn., Fairfax County C. of C., Am. Legion, Delta Theta Phi. Episcopalian. Clubs: Alexandria (Va.); Rotary. Office: 230 Cannon House Office Bldg Washington DC 20515

PARRISH, HENRY HOWARD, JR., electrical engineer; b. Gainesville, Fla., Feb. 6, 1944; s. Henry Howard Parrish and Margaret (Adkins) Parrish Blodgett; student U. Fla., 1961-62, 66-67. With Racal-Milgo, Sunrise, Fla., 1968—, Fellow-Modem devel., 1980—. Served with USN, 1962-66. Mem. IEEE (asso.), Assn. for Computing Machinery. Home: 3890 NW 106 Dr Coral Springs FL 33065 Office: 1601 N Harrison Pkwy Sunrise FL 33323

PARRISH, RICHARD HENRY, II, pharmacist; b. Parkersburg, W.Va., Dec. 13, 1957; s. Richard Henry and Mary Elizabeth (Johnston) P.; m. Mary Kay Mohr, Mar. 21, 1981; 1 child, Richard Henry III. M.S., Auburn U., 1985; B.S. in Pharmacy, Ohio State U., 1980. Registered pharmacist, Ohio, W.Va. Staff pharmacist Health Mgmt. Services, Columbus, Ohio, 1980, dir. pharmacy, 1980-82; staff clin. pharmacist, 1982-83; pharmacist, cons. Auburn U., Ala., 1983-85; pharmacist, adminstr. Fruth Pharmacy, Huntington, W.Va., 1985—; cons. Hocking-Logan Dist. Health, Logan, Ohio, 1980-82. Contbr. articles to profl. jours. Bd. dirs. Tri-State Montessori, Inc., Huntington, 1985—. Recipient Stephen F. Lewis Meml. award Ohio Assn. Pub. Sch. Employment, 1975; Bausch & Lomb Sci. award, 1975. Mem. Am. Pharm. Assn., Am. Pub. Health Assn., Kappa Psi, Rho Chi. Avocations: volleyball; reading; writing; camping. Home: 5271 W Pea Ridge Rd #7 Huntington WV 25705 Office: S&F Pharmacy Inc DBA Fruth Pharmacy 101-6th Ave Huntington WV 25701

PARRISH, ROBERT ALAN, dentist; b. Knoxville, Tenn., Jan. 27, 1948; s. Joseph Raymond and Virginia May (Wilkerson) P.; m. Bobbie I. Cromer, Oct. 1, 1977; children—Robert Alan II, Clayton Alan. B.S., Memphis State U., 1970; D.D.S., U. Tenn., 1974. Pvt. practice family dentistry, Albany, Ga., 1974—. Mem. ADA, Acad. Gen. Dentistry, SW Ga. Dental Assn., Albany Area Dental Soc., Ga. Dental Assn. Republican. Avocations: travel; outdoor recreation. Home: 2715 Westmeade Rd Albany GA 31707 Office: 1401 Dawson Rd Albany GA 31707

PARROTTE, WENDY ANN, meeting planner; b. Seattle, Wash., Feb. 19, 1957; d. Edwin Roscoe and Lucille Munsell (Freeman) Conklin; m. Ronald Arthur Parrotte, Oct. 24, 1982. A.A., Union Coll., Cranford, N.J., 1977; B.A., U. Conn., 1979; postgrad. in Bus. Adminstrn., U. Miami, 1981—. Mktg. rep. Snow Valley Ski Area, Golden Triangle, Vt., 1979-80; personnel counselor David Wood Personnel, North Miami, Fla., 1980-81; meeting planner U. Miami Med. Sch./Profl. Seminars, Inc., 1981—. Community coordinator The Hunger Project, 1978-80, regional program dir., 1980-82. Presbyterian.

PARSLEY, BRANTLEY HAMILTON, librarian; b. Balt., Oct. 15, 1927; s. Clarence Elroy and Florence Sally (Barnes) P.; A.A., Balt. Jr. Coll., 1950; B.A., U. Md., 1952; B.D., New Orleans Bapt. Theol. Sem., 1955, M.R.E., 1958; M.Librarianship, Emory U., 1965; m. Loyce Marie Franklin, Apr. 18, 1951; children—Linda Marie, Brantley Hamilton. Ordained to ministry Baptist Ch., 1956; pastor Calvary Bapt. Ch., Albany, Oreg., 1955-57; library asst. New Orleans Pub. Library, 1958-61; supt. night circulation and stacks Theology Library, Emory U., 1961-65; dir. library Campbellsville (Ky.) Coll., 1965-82; dir. Genealogy Workshop, Ch. History Writing Workshop. Bd. dirs. Taylor County Community Concerts, Mobile (Ala.) Coll., 1982—; pres. Central Ky. Arts Series, 1975-78; dir. Sch. Merger Workshop, 1976; sec. ACTS of Mobile, bd. dirs., 1985—. Recipient Sch. award Am. Legion, 1947. Mem. Am., Southeastern, Ky. (chmn. coll. and research sect. 1970-71, sec. treas. edn. sect. 1972-73) library assns., Ala. Library Assn. (chmn. project com. coll., univ. and spl. library div.), Bay Area Library Assn. (pres. elect 1984), Council Ind. Ky. Colls. (chmn. 1970-75), Taylor County Hist. Soc. (dir. 1970), Taylor County Bapt. Assn. (dir. tng. 1968-70), Taylor County Bapt. Sunday Sch. Assn. (supt. 1968-70). Dir. radio broadcast series: Ky. Authors, 1976; Study of Black Lit., 1978; editor Ala. Librarian, 1985—; coll. page editor Ala. Librarian, 1985—. Home: 32 Craig Dr Saraland AL 36571

PARSON, CONNIE WALTER, lawyer; b. Birmingham, Ala., Dec. 5, 1946; d. Matthew and Lorene (Ross) P.; m. Linda Jean Robinson, May 31, 1969. B.A., U. Ala., Birmingham, 1978; J.D., Miles Sch. Law, Fairfield, Ala., 1982. Bar: Ala. 1984. Ctr. mgr. United Parcel Service, Birmingham, 1970-76; auditor Days Inn Motel, Bessemer, Ala., 1976-79; terminal mgr. Express Transport, Chattanooga, 1979-81; dist. mgr. Mercury Motor Express, Tampa, Fla., 1981—; cons. TSI, Birmingham, 1981—. Vol., ARC, Birmingham, 1979—. Served with U.S. Army, 1967-70. Mem. ABA, Nat. Bar Assn., Ala. Bar Assn., Assn. Trial Lawyers Am., NAACP, Delta Theta Phi. Baptist. Lodge: Masons. Office: 517 Tuscaloosa Ave SW Birmingham AL 35211

PARSONS, A. LYNETTE, librarian; b. Loogootee, Ind., Dec. 4, 1951; d. James A. and Wilma Jane (Jones) P.; m. Raybourne R. Gupton, 1985. B.A., Ind. U., 1973, M.L.S., 1973. Extension librarian, cataloger Charlotte Glades Library System, Port Charlotte, Fla., 1974-78, head librarian Port Charlotte Library, 1976-83, adminstr. support services, 1983-84; asst. city librarian Sterling Mcpl. Library, Baytown, Tex., 1984—; library cons. Environ. Quality Lab., Port Charlotte, 1976-78. Sec., Charlotte County 4-H Adv. Council, 1981-82; pres. bd. Charlotte Chamber Music Soc., 1982, 83; bd. dirs. Baytown Symphony Orch., 1984-86. Mem. NOW (pres. Charlotte County chpt. 1978), Nat. Library Assn., Fla. Library Assn., Tex. Library Assn., LWV (bd. dirs. Baytown chpt. 1985-86); Baytown C. of C. Roman Catholic. Club: Zonta (bd. dirs. 1983) (Punta Gorda-Port Charlotte, Fla.). Home: 1601 Garth Rd Apt 203 Baytown TX 77520 Office: Sterling Mcpl Library Mary Elizabeth Wilbanks Ave Baytown TX 77520

PARSONS, ALBERT L., television executive; b. Wheeling, W.Va., June 5, 1939; s. Albert L. and Marie Damron (Balderson) P.; student public schs.; children—Scott, Jill. Store mgr. F.W. Woolworth Co., Phila., 1960-62, mdsg. mgr., Tom's River, N.J., 1962-65; promotion mgr. Montgomery Ward & Co., Oklahoma City, 1965-68; salesman, then v.p., gen. sales mgr. Sta. KOCO-TV, Oklahoma City, 1968-76, pres., gen. mgr., 1976—. Bd. dirs. Okla. Theatre Center, Cerebral Palsy Assn. Oklahoma City. Mem. Nat. Assn. TV Programming Execs., Nat. Assn. Broadcasters, Okla. Broadcasters Assn., Oklahoma City C. of C., Okla. Heritage Assn. Republican. Methodist. Clubs: Sirloin, Quail Creek Golf and Country, Oak Tree Golf and Country. Home: 9111 Autumn Rd Oklahoma City OK 73151 Office: PO Box 14555 Oklahoma City OK 73113

PARSONS, CAROLYN TAPP, bank executive; b. Somerville, Tenn., July 22, 1946; d. James Vincent and Chrystine (Hatfield) Tapp; m. Jerry Montgomery Parsons, Dec. 18, 1966; children—Teresa Carol, Alicia Jean. B.S. in Family Fin. Kans. State U., 1973; postgrad. Miss. Women's U., 1964-65, U. Tenn.-Martin, 1966-68. Mem. staff Dean's office and consumer relations bd. Kans. State U., 1973-74; tchr. pub. schs., San Antonio, 1974-77; tchr. St. Georges Episcopal Ch., 1977-79; asst. v.p. Govt. Employees Credit Union, San Antonio, 1979-84, N.W. regional br. mgr., 1983-84; asst. v.p. Leon Valley State Bank, San Antonio, 1984—. Republican precinct chmn., 1982—; bd. dirs. Forest Hills Presbyn. Sch., 1983—, Braun Sta. West, 1982—, Trinity Sch., 1976-77; fin. bd. Trinity Ch., 1976-77. Mem. Nat. Assn. Female Execs., Leon Valley Bus. and Profl. Orgn. (dir.), Am. Mgmt. Assn., C. of C. (consumer relations bd. 1972-73). Presbyterian. Home: 8415 Crooked Stream San Antonio TX 78250 Office: 7666 Bandera Rd San Antonio TX 78228

PARSONS, DON ROBERT, JR., oil corporation executive, geological, geophysical consultant; b. Richmond, Va., Jan. 30, 1950; s. Don Robert and Mary Lenora (Brown) P.; m. Cynthia Ingraham, July 27, 1974 (div. 1982) 1 child, Holly Nicole; m. Carol Kaye Edwards, Aug. 25, 1984. B.S. in Geology, U. Tex.-El Paso, 1973. Registered profl. geologist. Geophysicist Geophys. Services, Inc., Dallas, 1973-77; geologist Windsor Energy, Inc., Dallas, 1977-79; dist. geologist Delhi Oil Corp., Dallas, 1979-80; pres. Nautilus Royalty Corp., Dallas, 1980— Destiny Exploration, Inc., Dallas, 1984—, Nautilus Petroleum, Inc., Dallas, 1982—; cons. various cos., 1980—; dir. Santana Petroleum Corp., Vancouver, B.C., Can., 1982—. Discovered Peach Creek Oil and Gas Field, Gonzales County, Tex., 1980. Mem. Am. Assn. Petroleum geologists (cert.). Republican. Methodist. Avocations: sailing; scuba diving. Home: 5910 Brushy Creek Trail Dallas TX 75252 Office: Nautilus Petroleum Inc 17120 Dallas Pkwy Suite 220 Dallas TX 75248

PARSONS, DONALD HOLCOMBE, investment company executive, lawyer; b. Detroit, June 17, 1930; s. George Holcombe and Katherine (Babst) P.; m. Sarah Caswell Angell, Dec. 18, 1954 (div. 1974); children—James Angell, Sarah Babst, Donald Holcombe; m. 2d, Louise Garner Price, Aug. 31, 1974; 1 son, Patrick Adam. B.A., Yale U., 1952; LL.B., U. Mich., 1955, M.B.A., 1956. Bar: Mich., 1956. Assoc. firm Miller, Canfield, Paddock & Stone, Detroit, 1956-59; sr. ptnr. firm Emery, Parsons, Bahr, Tennent & Hogan, Detroit, 1959-65, Parsons, Tennent, Hammond, Hardig & Ziegelman, Detroit, 1965-70; chmn., pres. Resources Planning Corp., West Palm Beach, Fla., 1971—. Mem. ABA, Mich. Bar Assn., Oakland County Bar Assn., Wayne County Bar Assn. Clubs: Bath and Tennis, Beach (Palm Beach, Fla.); River (N.Y.C.), Birmingham Athletic (Mich.), Chgo. (Charlevoix, Mich.). Home: 246 Tangier Ave Palm Beach FL 33480 Office: 215 5th St West Palm Beach FL 33401

PARSONS, ERVIN IVY, JR., petroleum company executive; b. Moran, Tex., June 26, 1928; s. Ervin Ivy and Eva Lena (Childers) P.; m. LaVerne Good, Nov. 3, 1951; children—Robert Sherrell, Eva Louise. B.B.A., U. Houston, 1957. With Continental Oil Co., 1963-74, asst. treas., 1970-72, treas., 1972-74, fin. exec. various subsidiaries, 1963-70; sr. v.p. finance Tex. Oil & Gas Corp., Dallas, 1974-76, also dir., pres., dir. Holly Corp., Holly Energy Inc., 1976—. Served with USAF, 1951-53. Mem. Financial Execs. Inst., Dallas, Petroleum Club of Dallas. Home: 5421 Pebblebrook Dr Dallas TX 75229 Office: 2600 Diamond Shamrock Tower Dallas TX 75201*

PARSONS, FRANK RAYMOND, JR., hospital administrator; b. Salisbury, Md., Jan. 25, 1928; s. Frank Raymond and Ruth (Hearne) P.; B.S., U. Md., 1950; M.B.A., George Washington U., 1966; m. Barbara Hughes, June 9, 1951; children—David, Diane, Mary, Nancy. Commd. officer USAF, advanced through grades to col.; assigned Hdqrs. USAF, Washington, 1966-71, Pacific Air Forces, 1971-73, ret., 1973; asst. adminstr. Gen. Hosp., Charleston, W.Va., 1973-75, adminstr., 1975—. Bd. dirs. Am. Cancer Soc., Kanawha County, 1977—, Salvation Army, W.Va. Kidney Found., W.Va. Hosp. Assn., Shawnee Hills Community Health Ctr.; trustee Christ United Meth. Ch. mem. exec. com. Buckskin council Boy Scouts Am., Charleston, 1977—. Mem. W.Va. Hosp. Assn., Am. Hosp. Assn., Am. Coll. Hosp. Adminstrs., W.Va. Health Systems Agy. Methodist. Club: Optimist (v.p. 1975-76, pres. 1976-77, lt. gov. Ky.-W.Va. dist. 1977-78). Home: 1418 Mount Vernon Rd Charleston WV 25314 Office: PO Box 1393 Charleston WV 25325

PARSONS, LEONA MAE, hospital administrator; b. Newark, Ohio, Sept. 13, 1932; d. Enos Andrew and Emma Mae (Simmers) Chew; R.N., Andrews U., 1960; B.S. in Nursing, So. Missionary Coll., 1980; M.B.A., Rollins Coll., 1986; m. David J. Parsons, June 14, 1953; children—Davona Joy, Cynthia Carol, David J. Operating room supr. Bongo Hosp., Angola, Africa, 1961-68; dir. nurses Bongo Mission Hosp., Angola, 1968-75; nurse in charge refugee camps S. African Govt., Windhoek, S.W. Africa, 1975-76; matron, dir. nurses Windhoek (S.W. Africa) State Hosp., 1976-79; asst. v.p. Fla. Hosp., Orlando, 1980—; asst. adminstr. Fla. Hosp., Altamonte, 1980—. Mem. adv. bd. Seminole Community Coll., 1981—; mem. Child Abuse Task Force for Seminole County. Mem. Assn. Seventh-day Adventist Nurses (bd. dirs. 1981—), Nat. League Nurses, Am. Nurses Assn., Fla. Nurses Assn., Am. Med. Soc. Aux., Loma Linda Med. Soc. Aux., Fla. Med. Soc. Aux., Orange County Med. Soc. Aux. (bd. dirs.), Coalition Fla. Childbirth Educators (bd. dirs.), Greater Seminole C. of C., Fla. Perinatal Assn., Am. Soc. Psychoprophylaxis in Obstetrics, Fla. Soc. Hosp. Nursing Service Adminstrs., Nat. Assn. Female Execs., S. African Nurses Assn., Orange County Med. Soc. Aux., Am. Med. Assn. Aux.

PARTIN, WINFRED, clergyman; b. Whitley County, Ky., Oct. 19, 1946; s. Orville and Mary (Partin) P.; student Am. Sch., Chgo., Buford Ellington Vocat. Sch., Morristown, Tenn.; m. Lucille Davis, Sept. 28, 1966; children—Patsy Gail, Pamela Kaye, Paul Timothy. Ordained to ministry So. Bapt. Ch., 1966; pastor chs. in S.E. Ky. and N.E. Tenn., 1966-77; pastor Anthras Bapt. Ch., Duff, Tenn., 1977-79, King's Settlement Bapt. Ch., Clairfield, Tenn., 1981—; coin collector, 1960—; owner Partin's Coins and Stamps, Morristown, 1970—. Mem. Campbell County Bapt. Assn. Democrat. Writer for various hobby publs.; contbr. publs. including Rural Kentuckian, Scott's Stamp Jour., Stamp World, Pulpit Helps, Farm Life News, Linn's Stamp News, Danville Times-Examiner (Ky.). author poetry, fiction and non-fiction. Address: 414 Oak St Morristown TN 37814

PARTRIDGE, WILLIAM FRANKLIN, JR., lawyer; b. Newberry, S.C., July 16, 1945; s. William Franklin and Clara (Eskridge) P.; B.A., The Citadel, 1967; J.D., U. S.C., 1970; m. Ilene Stewart, Aug. 16, 1969; children—Allison Langford, William Franklin, III. Admitted to S.C. bar, 1970, since practiced in Newberry; partner firm Pope and Hudgens, 1970-84; sole practice, Newberry, 1984—; mcpl. judge City of Newberry; tchr. internat. law Chapman Coll., Riverside, Calif., 1973. Bd. dirs. Newberry Acad., 1980-83. Served as officer USAF, 1971-74. Mem. Am. Bar Assn., S.C. Bar Assn., Newberry County Bar Assn. (pres. 1980-81), Assn. Citidel Men (past dir.), Phi Delta Phi. Democrat. Methodist. Clubs: Lions (dir. Newberry 1980-82), Palmetto, Newberry Cotillion, Masons. Home: 2029 Harrington St Newberry SC 29108 Office: 1201 Boyce St Newberry SC 29108

PARUNGAO, ROMULO LAURETA, surgeon; b. Rizal, Neuva Ecija, Philippines, Dec. 11, 1943; came to U.S., 1969; s. Cirilo Matias and Emilia (Laureta) P.; m. Josefina Lopez Padiernos, June 23, 1969; children—Raymond, Ronald, Roland, Jodi. M.D., U. of East, Philippines, 1968. Diplomate Am. Bd. Abdominal Surgery. Chief resident St. Joseph's Hosp., Atlanta, 1973-74; practice medicine specializing in gen. and abdominal surgery, Rockdale and Conyers, Ga., 1974—; pres. Romulo L. Parungao, M.D., P.C., Conyers, 1979—; mem. teaching staff gen. surg. residency tng. St. Joseph's Hosp., 1974-76, courtesy staff, 1976—; courtesy staff Newton County Hosp., Covington, Ga., 1974—; active staff Rockdale County Hosp., Conyers, 1974—, chmn. emergency room com., 1978, vice chief staff, 1979. Pres., Filipino-Am. Assn. Greater Atlanta, 1979-80; hon. mem. Ga. Sheriff's Assn., 1983. Fellow Am. Soc. Abdominal Surgeons; mem. AMA (Physicians Recognition award 1974-77), So. Med. Assn., Med. Assn. Ga., Philippine Am. Med. Assn. Ga. (pres. 1982-84), Newton-Rockdale County Med. Soc., Soc. Philippine Surgeons in Am. Republican. Roman Catholic. Lodge: Kiwanis (Disting. Club Pres. award 1982). Home: 2073 Honeycreek Rd Conyers GA 30208 Office: 1315 Milstead Rd Conyers GA 30207

PARZYCK, DENNIS COS, health scientist, administrator; b. Mpls., July 10, 1946; s. Constantine Walter and Muriel Helen (Peterson) P.; m. Penelope Ann Froehlich, June 8, 1968. B.A., St. Mary's Coll., 1968; M.S., Purdue U., 1972, Ph.D., 1974. Mem. staff environ. scis. div. Oak Ridge Nat. Lab., 1974-76, mgr. regional studies program, 1976-77, leader methodology devel. and evaluations group, health and safety research div., 1977-78, mgr. policy analysis office, 1979-81, head health studies sect., 1978-83, dir. environ. and occupational safety div., 1983—. Served to lt. (j.g.) USN, 1969-70. AEC fellow, 1968; USPHS radiol. health fellow, 1973. Mem. AAAS, Am. Rural Health Assn., Health Physics Soc., Risk Analysis Soc., Sigma Xi, Phi Kappa Phi, Rho Chi, Sigma Pi Sigma. Author numerous papers, articles, book chpts., presentations in field; editor Health Physics Jour. Office: PO Box X Oak Ridge Nat Lab Oak Ridge TN 37830

PASCHAL, ANNE BALES, educator; b. Runnels County, Tex., Oct. 10, 1929; d. Wirt Samuel and Lora Louise (Corum) Bales; B.S. Angelo State U., 1970, M. Sch. Adminstrn., 1983; m. Bill Paschal, Dec. 16, 1946; children—William Douglas, Susan Louise Paschal Spates, Paul Neal. Tchr. math. Central High Sch., San Angelo, Tex., 1970—; workshop presenter; dir. Concho Educators Fed. Credit Union, 1975-80, pres. bd., 1979-80. Receipient Leadership and Scholarship award Angelo State U., 1970. Acad Excellence awards, 1968, 69, Leadership and Achievement award Angelo U., 1969, 70; named Outstanding Tchr., Central High Sch., 1977, Tchr. of Yr., 1978. Mem. Nat. Council Tchrs. of Math., San Angelo Council Tchrs. of Math (v.p. 1975), NEA, Tex. Tchrs. Assn., (local treas. 1978-79), Tex. State Classroom Tchrs. Assn. (treas. 1978-79), Kappa Delta Pi, Delta Kappa Gamma (treas. 1985—), Pi Mu Epsilon, Sigma Tau Delta, Phi Delta Kappa, Alpha Chi. Republican. Club: Execs. Dinner (v.p. 1985-86). Home: 801 W Ave D San Angelo TX 76901 Office: 100 Cottonwood St San Angelo TX 76901

PASCOE, SUSAN MARIONNEAUX, home health care administrator, nurse; b. San Antonio, Tex., Aug. 12, 1943; d. Rodney Paul and Mary Susan (Hickman) Marionneaux; m. Neil Peter Pascoe, Nov. 24, 1979; children—Paige, Venisa, Kara. Diploma in Nursing, Hotel Dieu Sch. Nursing, 1964; B.S., La. State U., 1980; M.S. in Nursing, U. Tex., 1981. Registered nurse. Clin. nurse MacGregor Clin., Houston, 1965-66; charge nurse Lake Charles Meml. Hosp., Lake Charles, La., 1967-71, staff nurse, 1973-75, head nurse, 1975-77; home care nurse Girling Health Care, Austin, Tex., 1980-81; program dir. Holy Cross Home Care, Austin, 1981—; cons. Holy Cross Home Care, Austin, 1981—. Pres., PTO, New Orleans, 1979-80. Mem. Tex. Nurses Assn., Am. Nurses Assn., Nat. League for Nursing, Nat. Assn. Home Care, Dist. Nurses Assn. (pres. 1975-77), Sigma Theta Tau, Epsilon Theta (v.p. 1985—). Democrat. Roman Catholic. Avocations: gourmet cooking; travel. Home: 9100 Texas Oaks Dr Austin TX 78748 Office: Holy Cross Hosp Home Health Care 2600 E Martin Luther King Blvd Austin TX 78702

PASCOLI, SWIFT THOMAS, sales executive; b. Pitts., Jan. 17, 1944; s. Joseph Edward and Estelle Doris (Dees) P.; m. Ansley Hurst, Jan. 24, 1976; children—Cale, Lawson. B.S. in Indsl. Engring., La. State U., 1966; postgrad. U. Houston, 1968, So. Meth. U., 1970. Salesman, Manville Corp., Dallas, 1966-73, mfg. prodn. mgr., Richmond, Ind., 1973-75, asst. sales mgr., Atlanta, 1975-76, product mgr., Denver, 1976-78, market mgr., 1978-80, dist. sales mgr., Atlanta, 1980—. Mem. Thermal Insulation Mfrs. Assn., ASHRAE. Republican. Roman Catholic. Home: 160 Zeblin Rd Atlanta GA 30342 Office: Manville Corp 3300 Holcomb Bridge Rd Norcross GA 30092

PASEWARK, WILLIAM ROBERT, emeritus educator, author, consultant; b. Mt. Vernon, N.Y., Sept. 9, 1924; s. William and Barbara (Hermann) P.; m. Marion Jean McHarg, Mar. 17, 1956; children—William Robert, Lisabeth Jean, Jan Alison, Carolyn Ann, Scott Graham, Susan Gayle. B.S., NYU, 1949, M.A., 1950, Ph.D., 1956. Instr. NYU, 1948-51; assoc. prof. Mich. State U., 1952-56; prof. Tex. Tech. U., Lubbock, 1956-82, prof. emeritus, 1982—; mem. commn. to revise curicula Tex. Edn. Agy., 1974—; cons., lectr. in field, 1955—; owner Office Mgmt. Cons., 1974; field reader research div. U.S. Office Edn., 1966—; mem. Lubbock Vocat. Office Edn. Adv. Com.; regional bd. exeminers Am. Assn. Bus. Colls.; vis. prof. Calif. State U., Fresno, 1959, No. Ariz. State U., 1969, Central Conn. State Coll., 1974. Advisor Lubbock Opportunities Industrialization Ctr.; mem. Tex. Bus. Tchrs. Edn. Council; pres. Lubbock Econ. Council; pres. Lubbock Area Presbyn. Council, 1969; chmn. Lubbock City-County Child Welfare Bd., 1973-74; active Boy Scouts Am., United Fund. Served with USMCR, 1943-46. Recipient Founders Day award NYU, 1956; Outstanding Educator of Am. award, 1970; citation Tex. Ho. of Reps., 1973; Tex. Bus. Tchr. of Yr. award, 1973. Mem. Nat. Bus. Edn. Assn., Nat. Assn. Bus. Tchr. Edn., Mountain-Plains Bus. Edn. Assn., Tex. Bus. Edn. Assn. (chmn. legis. com. 1973-80), Nat. Assn. Tchr. Edn. for Bus. and Office Edn., Edn. for Bus. Coordinating Council, Bus. Edn. State Suprs. and Tchr. Educators (nat. planning com.), W. Tex. Bus. Edn. Assn. (pres. 1958), Better Bus. Bur. (edn. com.), Am. Vocat. Assn. (pres. bus. div. 1976-77, dir. 1976-77, nat. adv. council, award of merit 1978 Outstanding Service award 1983), Lubbock Execs. Assn. (bd. dirs.), Lubbock C. of C., Office Systems Research Assn., Internat. Platform Assn., PTA (local pres. 1972), Delta Pi Epsilon, Phi Delta Kappa, Kappa Phi Kappa, Pi Omega Pi, Alpha Kappa Psi, Kappa Delta Pi. Clubs: Lions (past dir.); Lubbock Country. Author: Clerical Office Procedures, 1967, 73, 78; Rotary Calculator Course, 1962; Secretarial Office Procedures, 1972, 77, 82; Duplicating Machine Processes, 1971, 75; Office Machine Course, 1971, 79 Curso de Maquinas de Oficina, 1977; Tecnicas Secretariales y Procedimientos de Oficina, 1978; Machine Transcription Word Processing, 1979; Electronic Printing Calculator Course, 1980; Calculating Machines Simulation, 1983; Procedures for the Modern Office, 1983; Electronic Display-Printing Calculator, 1983; Electronic Printing Calculator, 1983; Reprographics, 1984; editor: Individualized Instruction in Business and Office Education, 1973; Electronic and Mechanical Printing Calculator Course, 1974; Electronic Display Calculator Course, 1984; SuperCalc 3: Learning, Using and Mastering, 1986; assoc. editor: Am. Bus. Edn. Yearbook, 1953; Contbr. articles to profl. jours.; research in office administrn. and ednl. systems. Home: 4403 W 11th St Lubbock TX 79416 Office: 1901 University Ave Lubbock TX 79408

PASKAY, ALEXANDER LESLIE, bankruptcy judge; b. Mohacs, Hungary, Nov. 5, 1922; came to U.S., 1949; s. Ferenc Paskay and Julianna Zupka; m. Rose Margaret Mazzaglia, June 10, 1950; children—Richard Lawrence, Steven Robert. Bachelor degree, Pope Pius XII, Pecs, Hungary, 1938; D. Jurisprudence, U. Budapest, Hungary, 1944; J.D., U. Miami, Fla., 1958. Bar: Fla. Research asst. U.S. Dist. Court, Miami, Fla., 1958-61, Tampa, Fla., 1961-63; bankruptcy judge U.S. Bankruptcy Court, Tampa, 1961-78, chief judge, 1978—; adj. prof. U. of Stetson Coll. of Law. Author: Handbook for Trustees and Receivers, 1968; author numerous articles. Mem. ABA, Fla. Bar Assn., Nat. Assn. of Referees in Bankruptcy (bd. dirs. 1967), Am. Bankruptcy Inst. (dir. 1985). Avocations: travel; tennis. Office: US Bankruptcy Court 700 Twiggs St Tampa FL 33602

PASSANISI, FRANK MARTIN, consultant, accountant; b. Cleve., Mar. 8, 1948; s. Joseph S. and Mary R. (Grande) P.; student John Carroll U., 1966-70; m. Diane Mary Dragolich, May 16, 1970; children—Joseph, Catherine, Matthew. Customer service mgr. W.S. Tyler Co., Inc., Cleve., 1966-68; br. mgr. Ency. Brit., Inc., Cleve., 1968-70; sales mgr. Programmed Tax Systems, Inc., Chgo., 1970-72; dir. adminstrn. CCH-Computax, Inc., Grand Prairie, Tex., 1972-78; chmn., chief exec. officer The Prairie, Ravenna, Tex., 1977—; chmn. bd. Resume House, Ravenna, 1977—. Trustee, First Ch. of Religious Science, Arlington, Tex., 1976-78; trustee Inst. Knowledge of God Almighty, Bonham, 1981—; treas. North Fannin County Vol. Fire Dept. Mem. Splty. Advt. Assn. Internat., Nat. Soc. Pub. Accts., Advt. Splty. Inst., Tex. Assn. Pub. Accts., Grand Prairie C. of C. (dir. 1979-81), Bonham C. of C. Home: Rt 1 Box 158 Ravenna TX 75476 Office: The Prairie Rt 1 Box 158 Ravenna TX 75476

PASSARELLO, NANCY HURST, media specialist; b. Braddock, Pa., Jan. 27, 1938; d. E. Ross and Stella (Hill) Hurst; m. Ralph J. Passarello, Dec. 25, 1959; children—Emily R., Alex R. B.S., California (Pa.) State Coll., 1959; M.A., No. Ky. U., 1977; M.S.L.S., U. Ky., 1981. Tchr. English, Gateway Union Schs., Monroeville, Pa., 1959-62; instr. English and drama Cin. Bible Coll., 1971-75; tchr. gifted and talented Grant County Schs., Dry Ridge, Ky., 1977-80; asst. librarian Cin. Bible Sem., 1980-83; audio visual librarian Covington (Ky.) Schs., 1981-83; media specialist Pinellas County (Fla.) Schs., 1983—; mem. curriculum com. Grant County Schs., Dry Ridge, 1979-80. Recipient Arion Found. Music award Kiwanis Internat., 1955. Mem. ALA, NEA, Pinellas County Tchrs. Assn., Phi Delta Kappa. Home: 2324 Harn Blvd Clearwater FL 33546 Office: Curlew Creek Sch 3030 Curlew Rd Palm Harbor FL 33563

PASSARIELLO, VINCENZO, construction company executive, car rental executive; b. Caserta, Italy, Nov. 8, 1949; came to U.S., 1970; s. Pompilio Mortone and Domenica (Pascarella) P.; m. Irais Josefina Labrador, Apr. 6, 1978; children—Aileen Irais, Catherine Laura. B.S.E.E., Mich. Technol. U., 1973, M.S.E.E., 1974; M.B.A., U. Miami, 1982. Asst. prof. Simon Bolivar U., Caracas, Venezuela, 1974-76, dir. coop program., 1976-77; chief engr. Mapare Corp., Caracas, 1977-78; pres. gen. mgr. Kingdom Homes Inc., Miami, Fla., 1978-83; exec. v.p. Pass Rent-a-Car, Miami, 1983—; asst. prof., cons. Venezuelan Air Force, Caracas, 1977-78. Mem. IEEE, Am. Mgmt. Assn., Colegio de Ingeniero Venezuela. Republican. Roman Catholic. Lodge: Rotary (Caracas). Inventor EKG Digital Memory Loop, 1974. Office: Pass Rent-a-Car 1000 NW 42nd Ave Miami FL 33126

PATCH, STEVEN CURTIS, mathematics educator, consultant; b. Middlebury, Vt., Nov. 15, 1953; s. Harold Noyes and Mary Alberta (Van Wyck) P.; m. Rebecca Willis, June 10, 1979; 1 child, Laura Jane. B.A., U. Conn., 1975; M.S., Clemson U., 1982, Ph.D., 1984. Canoe instr. Keewaydin Camps, Salisbury, Vt., 1971—; instr. Clemson U., S.C., 1983-84; asst. prof. math. U. N.C.-Asheville, 1984—; cons. in field. Mem. Am. Statis. Assn., Am. Canoe Assn. Methodist. Home: 2 Birchwood Ln Asheville NC 28805 Office: Univ NC Math Dept One University Hts Asheville NC 28804

PATE, JACQUELINE HAIL, equipment company manager; b. Amarillo, Tex., Apr. 7, 1930; d. Ewen and Virginia Smith (Crosland) Hail; student Southwestern U., Georgetown, Tex., 1947-48; children—Charles (dec.), John Durst, Virginia Pate Edgecomb, Christopher. Exec. sec. Western Gear Corp., Houston, 1974-76; adminstr., treas., dir. Aberrant Behavior Center, Personality Profiles, Inc., Corp. Procedures, Inc., Dallas, 1976-79; br. facilities mgr. Digital Equipment Corp., Dallas, 1979—. Active PTA, Dallas, 1958-73. Methodist. Home: 3519 Casa Verde #268 Dallas TX 75234 Office: 12100 Ford St Suite 200 Dallas TX 75234

PATE, JOHNNY RAY, engineer; b. Memphis, July 17, 1942; s. Stoy and Edith (Sawyer) P.; B.E., Vanderbilt U., 1966; B.S., David Lipscomb Coll., 1965; m. Sandra Snell, Dec. 16, 1961; children—Phil, Eric. Engr. Trane Co., LaCrosse, Wis., 1966-73; pres. Environ. Enterprises, Inc., Little Rock, 1973—, Pate Energy Systems, 1980—; contract trainer of energy auditors Ark. Energy Office. Bd. dirs. Ark. Engring. Found.; mem. Ark. State Energy Task Force; mem. adv. bd. U. Ark. Sch. Engring., Little Rock; gen. chmn. Gov.'s Prayer Breakfast. Mem. ASHRAE (chpt. pres. 1971-72, nat. membership com., Ernest N. Pettit award 1973, Lincoln Boullioun award 1973), Assn. Energy Engrs., Little Rock Engrs. Club, Little Rock C. of C. (indsl. devel. com.), Ark. Council Engring. and Related Socs. (chmn. 1979), Christian Businessmen's Com. Home: 4115 Cooper Orbit Rd Little Rock AR 72210 Office: 10802 Executive Center Dr Suite 109 Little Rock AR 72211

PATE, SAMUEL RALPH, engineering corporation executive; b. Thorsby, Ala., Oct. 27, 1937; s. Ralph Elvin and Frances Roberta (Marcus) P.; m. Tommye Caldwell, Aug. 31, 1959; children—Lisa, Sherri, Frances. B.S. in Aero. Engring., Auburn U., 1960; M.S. in Mech. Engring., U. Tenn., 1965, Ph.D., 1977. Registered profl. engr., Tenn. With Sverdrup Tech., Inc., 1960—, project engr. Arnold engring. Devel. Ctr., U.S. Air Force, Arnold Air Sta., Tenn., 1960-64, research engr., 1964-69, supr. research, engring., and testing sect., 1969-74, mgr. research, engring., and testing projects br., 1975-78, dep. dir., Propulsion Wind Tunnel Facility, 1978-79, dir., 1979-80, v.p. and gen. mgr. Tech. Group, Tullahoma, Tenn., 1980-83, sr. v.p. Tech. and Operational Groups, 1983—; cons. NASA, Australian Dept. Def.; tech. adviser U.S.-German Aero. Data Exchange; guest lectr., U. Tenn. Served with N.G., 1955-59. Recipient Arch T. Colwell Merit award Soc. Automotive Engrs., 1983. Fellow AIAA (assoc., chmn. nat. ground testing com., Gen. H.H. Arnold award Tenn. sect. 1969); mem. Nat. Mgmt. Assn., Air Force Assn., Supersonic Tunnel Assn. (chmn.), Sigma Xi. Contbr. articles, reports to profl. publs. Office: PO Box 884 600 William Northern Blvd Tullahoma TN 37388

PATE, WILLIAM AUGUST, lawyer; b. Selma, Ala., Dec. 9, 1942; s. William Herbert and Shirley Rosemary (DeMattie) P.; m. Wanda Arlene Whaley, Feb. 2, 1973. B.A. in Polit. Sci., Citadel, 1964; J.D., U. Miss., 1972. Bar: Miss. 1972, U.S. Dist. Ct. (no. dist.) Miss. 1972, U.S. Dist. Ct. (so. dist.) Miss. 1973. Sole practice, Gulfport, Miss., 1972—. Pres., Saucier (Miss.) Vol. Fire Dept.; chmn. Harrison County Park Commn. Served to capt. USAF, 1965-69. Mem. Miss. State Bar, Harrison County Bar Assn., ABA, Miss. Trial Lawyers Assn. Club: Gulfport Yacht. Home: Rt 3 Box 219 Saucier-Lizana Rd Saucier MS 39574 Office: 2017 20th Ave PO Box 1976 Gulfport MS 39501

PATEL, BIPIN MOTIBHAI, internist; b. Kericho, Kenya, Apr. 10, 1951; came to U.S., 1977; s. Motibhai M. and Maniben M. Patel; m. Dharmistha Bipin, Dec. 20, 1976. M.B.B.S., Bombay U., 1976. Diplomate Am. Bd. Internal Medicine, Am. Bd. Pulmonary Disease. Intern LaGuardia Hosp., N.Y.C., 1977-78; resident in internal medicine Cath. Med. Ctr., Wyckoff Heights Hosp., N.Y.C., 1978-80; fellow in pulmonary medicine U. Louisville, 1981-83; practice medicine specializing in pulmonary medicine, Columbus, Ga., 1983—. Mem. AMA, Am. Thoracic Soc., Am. Coll. Chest Physicians. Office: St Francis Med Park Suite C-1 2300 Manchester Expressway Columbus GA 31904

PATEL, REKHA RAVJI, geologist; b. Nairobi, Kenya, Oct. 21, 1954; came to U.S., 1976; d. Ravji Arjan and Santok (Amba) P. B.S. in Geology, N. Wadia Coll., Pune, Maharashtra, 1975. Asst. geologist Borg & Lawrence, Tulsa, 1977; cons. geologist Wilson & Assocs., Tulsa, 1978-80; exploration geologist World Exploration, Tulsa, 1980-81, Adams Petroleum, Tulsa, 1981-82; ind. exploration geologist, cons., Tulsa, 1982—; owner, mgr. Santok Energies, Inc. Fellow Tulsa Geol. Soc., Am. Assn. Petroleum Geologists, India Assn. Tulsa. Hindu. Avocations: reading; stamp and coin collecting; indoor exercise. Address: 8261 S Louisville St Tulsa OK 74137

PATILLO, LEONARD SYLVESTA, association executive; b. Paducah, Ky., Jan. 25, 1923; s. Prentice Sylvester and Mallie Louise (Hill) P.; certificate Paducah Jr. Coll., 1942; m. Mary Kathryn Kindred, Jan. 15, 1943; children—Patricia (Mrs. Robert Estes), Dennis Lynn. Reporter, photographer Paducah Sun Democrat, 1942-43, 45-46; editor, publicity dir. Houston C. of C., 1946-52, mgr. publs. dept., 1954-59, bus. mgr., 1959-70, gen. mgr., 1970-72, exec. v.p., gen. mgr., 1972—; dir. pub. relations Tex. Mfrs. Assn., 1952-54. Instr. Inst. Orgn. Mgmt., 1973-75. Exec. v.p. Greater Houston Community Found., 1971—; dir. Houston Port Bur., 1969-82, Houston World Trade Assn., 1980—. Bd. dirs. Tex. Soc. Prevention Blindness, 1963-70, v.p., 1980-81. Served to 1st lt. USAAF, 1942-45. Decorated Purple Heart with oak leaf cluster. Mem. Am. C. of C. Execs. (chmn. bd. 1975-76), Am. Assn. Commerce Publs. (pres. 1965-66), C. of C. U.S. (mem. community and urban affairs com. 1973-77, internat. trade subcom. 1977—, Houston Jr. C. of C. (hon.), So. Assn. C. of C. Execs. (pres. 1978-79), Inst. Dirs. (London), Japan-Am. Soc. Houston (dir. 1976—). Clubs: Houston, Rotary. Contbr. articles to profl. jours. Home: 5402 Rutherglenn St Houston TX 77096 Office: 1100 Milam Bldg 25th Floor Houston TX 77002

PATISAUL, WILTON, health care administrator, minister; b. Cadwell, Ga., Oct. 18, 1932; s. Homer and Annie Mae (Woodward) P.; m. Ruth Wood, Feb. 9, 1952 (dec. 1976); children—Robert Earl, Charles Edward, Gary Philip; m. Ruth Lee Swymer, Apr. 13, 1977. A.A., Brewton-Parker U., 1976. Enlisted in U.S. Army, 1953, advanced through ranks to sgt. 1st class, 1969; retired, 1973; mgr. Caldwell Opticians, Macon, Ga., 1973-74; pastor Mount Zion Bapt. Ch., Rentz, Ga., 1974-76; optician Murphy-Robinson, Augusta, Ga., 1976-80; mgr. Lee Optical, Macon, 1980-81; dir. central services Baldwin County Hosp., Milledgeville, Ga., 1981—. Bd. dirs. Baldwin County Employment Credit Union, Milledgeville, 1983—. Mem. Am. Hosp. Assn. Republican. Avocations: fishing; boating; golfing. Home: Route 4 12 Chicasaw Trail N Sparta GA 31087 Office: Baldwin County Hosp 1957 N Cobb St Milledgeville GA 31061

PATMAN, PHILIP FRANKLIN, lawyer; b. Atlanta, Tex., Nov. 1, 1937; s. Elmer Franklin and Helen Lee (Miller) P.; m. Katherine Sellers, July 1, 1967; children—Philip Franklin, Katherine Lee. B.A., U. Tex., 1959, LL.B., 1964; M.A., Princeton U., 1962. Bar: Tex. 1964, U.S. dist. ct. (we. dist.) Tex. 1975, U.S. dist. ct. (so. dist.) Tex. 1971, U.S. Supreme Ct. 1970. Atty. office of the legal adviser Dept. of State, Washington, 1964-67; dep. dir. office internat. affairs Dept. Housing and Urban Devel., Washington, 1967-69; sole practice, Austin, Tex., 1969—. Ofcl. rep. of Gov. Tex. to Interstate Oil Compact Commn., 1973-83. Pres. Heritage Soc. of Austin, 1975-77; trustee St. Andrew's Episcopal Sch., 1983—. Woodrow Wilson fellow 1959. Mem. ABA, Tex. Bar Assn., Tex. Ind. Producers and Royalty Owners Assn., Tex. Law Review Assn., Phi Beta Kappa, Phi Delta Phi. Democrat. Episcopalian. Clubs: Austin. Citadel, Westwood Country, Princeton (N.Y.C.). Contbr. articles to legal jours. Office: Perry-Brooks Bldg Suite 312 Austin TX 78701

PATNAIK, PRASANT KUMAR, razor company executive; b. Chatrapur, India, Oct. 7, 1942; s. Bonobasi and Pramila (Mahanty) P.; m. Monjula Patnaik, Jan. 16, 1971; 1 son, Amar. B.S. in Metall. Engring., Indian Inst. Tech., 1964; M.S., Frostburg State Coll., 1976. Warranty adminstr. Copperweld Steel Co., Warren, Ohio, 1967-73; plant metallurgist Mack Trucks, Inc., Hagerstown, Md., 1973-78; mgr. quality engring. Clark Equipment Co., Jackson, Mich., 1978-82; mgr. quality assurance Am. Safety Razor Co., Staunton, Va., 1983—. Served with U.S. Army, 1968-70; Vietnam. Decorated Bronze Star. Mem. Am. Soc. Quality Control (speaker confs.), Am. Soc. Metals (speaker confs.). Republican. Hindu. Office: Am Safety Razor Co PO Box 500 Staunton VA 24401

PATRICK, KENNETH ALAN, business computer executive; b. Phila., Apr. 5, 1947; s. Kenneth Nelson and Lillian Jackson (Halleck) P.; m. Rita Elaine Phillips, Sept. 16, 1967; children—Joan Elaine, Leslie Ellen. B.S. in Mktg. So. Ill. U., 1969. Mgmt. analyst, tech. specialist So. Ill. U., Carbondale, 1969-75; systems programmer Southwestern Bell, St. Louis, 1976-78; sr. systems cons. Informatics, Inc., Dallas, 1978-80; owner, operator Texmatics, ind. cons., Dallas, 1980-82; owner Tex-Matics Micro Systems, Plano, Tex., 1983—. Mem. Plano C. of C., Aircraft Owners and Pilots Assn., Dallas-Ft. Worth/Heath Users Group (dir.), Metroplex CP/M Interest Group (dir.). Baptist. Contbr. software articles to Sextant mag. Office: Tex-Matics Micro Systems 3059 W 15th St Suite 100 Plano TX 75075

PATRICK, MARTY, lawyer; b. N.Y.C., May 10, 1949; s. Harry and Evelyn (Beroza) P.; B.S., L.I. U., 1971; Cert. Inst. for Leadership Devel., Jerusalem, 1974; J.D., Nova U., 1981. Exec. dir. Zionist Orgn. Am., Miami Beach, Fla., 1975-78; pres. Enigma Enterprises, Inc., Miami, Fla., 1978-82; ptnr. firm Martin Howard Patrick, P.A. Miami, 1982—; pres. Patrick Law Ctr., Miami, 1983—; pres. First Fla. Title & Abstract Co., Miami, 1983—. Horovitz scholar, 1980. Mem. ABA, Ga. Bar Assn., Fla. Bar Assn. Lodges: Rotary, Lions. Contbr. articles to profl. jours. Home: PO Box 6715 Hollywood Hills FL 33021 Office: 444 Brickell Ave Suite 650 Miami FL 33131

PATRICK, STEPHEN ALLAN, librarian, art documents specialist, bibliographer, educator; b. Memphis, Feb. 20, 1951; s. Henry Houston and Christine (Cashion) P. B.A., Rhodes Coll., 1973; M.S. in Library Sci., U. Tenn., 1976. Tchr. Ellis-Munford Jr. High Sch., (Tenn.), 1973-75; art-audio visual-film reference librarian Greenville County Library, Greenville, S.C., 1976-78, govt. documents reference librarian, 1978-82; asst. prof. librarianship, govt. documents, law and maps librarian East Ten. State U., Johnson City, 1982—. Contbr. art book revs. to Library Jour., 1980—; co-editor: Directory of Federal and State Depository Libraries in Tennessee, 1983; co-editor Item No. newsletter, 1982-86; column editor ARLIS/NA Newsletter, 1981—, Art Documentation, 1982—. Mem. Greenville Civic Chorale, 1976-82, Johnson City Civic Chorale, 1982-83. Named to Outstanding Young Men in Am., U.S. Jr. C. of C., 1982. ALA, Assn. Coll. and Research Libraries (chmn. ad hoc com. on missions and goals art sect.), Govt. Documents Round Table, Mem. Art Libraries Soc. N.Am. (sec.-treas. S.E. chpt. 1978-79, vice chmn. chpt. 1980, chmn. chpt. 1981), Southeastern Library Assn. (exec. bd. 1984-86), Govt. Documents Roundtable (chmn. 1984-86), Tenn. Library Assn. (chmn. adv. com. on state documents 1984-86, exec. bd. 1983-86, long-range planning com. 1985-87), Govt. Documents Orgn. Tenn. (vice chmn. 1982-83, chmn. 1983-84, chmn. ad hoc com. on state documents 1983). Presbyterian. Home: 604 W Pine

St Apt 2 Johnson City TN 37601 Office: PO Box 24492 East Tenn State U Johnson City TN 37614

PATTEE, HAROLD EDWARD, research chemist; b. Phoenix, June 27, 1934; s. Earnest Harold and Ina Mae (Hamblin) P.; m. Phyllis Adams, June 8, 1956; children—Floyd Lee, Phyllis Ann, Linda, Deborah, Sherri Kae, Sheila Marie, Yvonne Rae. B.S., Brigham Young U., 1958; M.S., Utah State U., 1960; Ph.D., Purdue U., 1962. Research chemist Agrl. Research Service, U.S. Dept. Agr., Raleigh, N.C., 1963—. Mem. exec. bd., chmn. outdoor com. Occoneechee council Boy Scouts Am., 1980-83, v.p. programs, 1984—, Area 7 program chmn., 1975—. Served with U.S. Army, 1954-56. Recipient Silver Beaver award Boy Scouts Am., 1976; Golden Peanut Research award Nat. Peanut Council, 1977. Fellow Am. Peanut Research and Edn. Soc. (publisher jour.); mem. Am. Chem. Soc., Council Biology Editors, Inst. Food Technologists. Republican. Mormon. Editor: Peanut Sci. and Tech., 1982; Peanut Sci., 1976—; Evaluation of Quality of Fruits and Vegetables, 1985; contbr. articles to profl. jours. Home: 6201 Winthrop Dr Raleigh NC 27612 Office: PO Box 7626 NC State U Raleigh NC 27695

PATTEN, BERNARD CLARENCE, ecologist, zoology educator, researcher; b. N.Y.C., Jan. 28, 1931; s. Bernard Clarence and Margaret Juliana (Paller) P.; m. Marie Anne DeLattre, Sept. 5, 1953; 1 child, Karen Marie. A.B. in Zoology, Cornell U., 1952; M.S. in Botany, Rutgers U., 1954, Ph.D. in Botany, 1959; M.A. in Zoology, U. Mich., 1957. Assoc. marine scientist Va. Inst. Marine Sci., Gloucester Point, 1959-63; assoc. prof. marine sci. Coll. William and Mary, Williamsburg, Va., 1959-63; ecologist Oak Ridge Nat. Lab., 1963-68; assoc. prof. botany U. Tenn., Knoxville, 1963-68; prof. zoology U. Ga., Athens, 1968-85, Regents' prof. zoology, 1985—; mem. sci. adv. bd. EPA, Washington, 1978—; chmn. SCOPE sci. adv. com. Wetlands, Paris, 1980—; vis. disting. prof. SUNY-Plattsburgh, 1981. Editor: Systems Analysis and Simulation in Ecology, 1971-72, 1975-76. Contbr. articles to profl. jours. Served with U.S. Army, 1954-56. NSF research grantee, 1975—. Fellow AAAS, Ecol. Soc. Am., Internat. Soc. for Ecol. Modelling (pres. N.Am. sect. 1982—), Am. Soc. Naturalists, Am. Soc. Limnology and Oceanography, Am. Inst. Biol. Sci., Soc. for Gen. Systems Research, Sigma Xi. Home: 177 Chinquapin Way Athens GA 30605 Office: Dept Zoology U Ga Athens GA 30602

PATTERSON, BARBARA FRANTZ, portfolio manager; b. N.Y.C., Aug. 25, 1953; d. Kenneth Emerson and Martha Ann (McCray) F.; m. Thomas Robert Patterson, May 28, 1977 (div. 1981). A.B., Middlebury Coll., 1975; M.B.A., U. Va., 1977. Jr. fin. analyst Provident Life and Accident Ins. Co., Chattanooga, 1978-79, assoc. fin. analyst, 1979, fin. analyst, 1979-80, investment officer equities, 1980-82; asst. v.p. Provident Nat. Assurance Co., Chattanooga, 1982—; dir. Dental One, Inc., Atlanta, 1983—. Advisor St. Paul's Episc. Young Churchmen, Chattanooga, 1981—, Chattanooga Dist. Episcopal Young Churchmen, 1984—; treas. Provident Employees Credit Union, 1982-83, pres., 1983-84. Mem. Fin. Analysts Fedn.-Atlanta Soc., Inst. Chartered Fin. Analysts, Chattanooga Investment Assn. (treas. 1979-80, program chmn. 1980-81, pres. 1981-82). Avocations: youth work; reading. Home: 1012 Signal Rd Signal Mountain TN 37377 Office: Provident Nat Assurance Co Fountain Sq Chattanooga TN 37402

PATTERSON, CECIL HOLDEN, educator, writer; b. Lynn, Mass., June 22, 1912; s. Cecil Edwin and Emma Mabel (Banks) P.; m. Frances L. Spano, July 4, 1942; children—Joseph, Francine, Jenifer, Christopher, Thomas, Charles, Mary. A.B., U. Chgo., 1938; M.A., U. Minn., 1945, Ph.D., 1955. Research asst. Fels Research Inst., Yellow Springs, Ohio, 1939-41; psychol. asst. USAAF, San Antonio, 1942-45; clin. psychologist U.S. Army, Philippines, 1945-46; counseling psychologist U.S. VA, St. Paul, 1946-55; prof. ednl. psychology U. Ill., Urbana, 1955-77; adj. disting. prof. U. N.C.-Greensboro, 1984—. Author: Counseling and Psychotherapy, 1959; Theories of Counseling and Psychotherapy, 4th edit. 1986; The Therapeutic Relationship, 1985, others. Served with U.S. Army, 1942-46. Fulbright Hays sr. lectr., 1972-73, 76-77. Fellow Am. Psychol. Assn. (past pres. div. counseling psychology). Address: 272 Lakewood Dr Asheville NC 28803

PATTERSON, DAVID CHARLES, health, wellness and safety promotion administrator; b. Glasgow, Mont., Mar. 11, 1949; s. Harvill Hamilton and Lillyan Mae (Blair) P; m. Barbara Ann Gibbs, Dec. 20, 1969. B.S. in Biology and Chemistry, Belmont Coll., 1971; safety engring. cert. U. Tenn., 1982; M.S. in Safety Mgmt., Middle Tenn. State U. Cert. Am. Coll. Sports Medicine, YMCA's Way to Fitness, Aerobics Inst., Dallas. Tchr., Castle Heights, Lebanon, Tenn., 1971-76; environmentalist Metro Govt. of Nashville, 1976-80, safety engr., 1980-82; loss control cons. Hosp. Corp. of Am., Nashville, 1982-84; health and safety promotion mgr. TryUMPH for Health, The United Meth. Pub. House, Nashville, 1984—; cons. on wellness Bridgestone Tire Co., Nashville, 1985—, City of Clarksville, Tenn., 1985—. Lectr. in field. Mem. Mayor's Task Force on Wellness, Nashville 1984, Gov.'s Council on Health and Fitness, Tenn., 1985, Mayor's Safety Adv. Bd., Nashville; mem. corp. steering com. Am. Red Cross "Healthy Lifestyles" Program, Nashville, 1985. Recipient Outstanding Coach, 1973, Century award YMCA, 1982. Mem. Am. Soc. of Safety Engrs. (pres. 1985—), Tenn. Health and Safety Assn. (treas. 1982), Am. Coll. of Sports Medicine, Assn. Fitness in Bus. (nominated Achievement award 1985, Tenn. state rep. 1985-86). Baptist. Clubs: Nashville Triathlon (race dir. 1984), YMCA-Nashville Striders Running (race dir. 1982), Music City Bikers (Nashville). Lodge: Masonic (3rd degree). Avocations: running; biking; swimming; marathons; triathlons.

PATTERSON, DOUGLAS MACLENNAN, financial educator; b. Tallahassee, Jan. 16, 1945; s. Thomas and Ruth (MacLennan) P.; m. Sara Louise Lucas; children—Cara Beth, John Douglas. B.S.E.E., U. Wis., 1968, M.B.A., 1972, Ph.D., 1978. Elec. engr. Westinghouse Electric, Balt., 1968-71; asst. prof. U. Mich., Ann Arbor, 1976-80, Va. Tech., Blacksburg, 1980—. Contbr. articles to profl. jours. Mem. ad hoc com. Detroit Area Hosp. Assn., 1978-79. Recipient Tchng. Excellence award Va. Tech., 1983; U. Mich. fellow, 1979; U.S. Navy grantee, 1984, 85. Mem. Am. Finance Assn., Am. Economic Assn., Fin. Mgmt. Assn., Beta Gamma Sigma. Presbyterian. Home: 211 Primrose Dr Blacksburg VA 24060 Office: Va Poly Inst Dept Finance Blacksburg VA 24061

PATTERSON, ELIZABETH JOHNSTON, state ofcl.; b. Columbia, S.C., Nov. 18, 1939; d. Olin DeWitt and Gladys (Atkinson) Johnston; B.A., Columbia Coll., 1961; postgrad. U. S.C., 1961-62, 64; m. Dwight Fleming Patterson, Jr., Apr. 15, 1967; children—Dwight Fleming, Olin, Catherine. Public affairs officer Peace Corps, Washington, 1962-64; recruiter Vista, Office Econ. Opportunity, Washington, 1965-66, state coordinator, head start, Columbia, S.C., 1966-67; tri-county dir. Head Start, Piedmont Community Actions, Spartanburg, S.C., 1967-68; adminstrv. asst. Congressman James R. Mann, Spartanburg, 1969-70; mem. S.C. Senate, 1979—, Spartanburg County Council, 1975-76. Vice-pres., Spartanburg County Democratic Party, 1968-70, sec., 1970-75; trustee Wofford Coll., 1978—. Mem. Bus. and Profl. Women's Club. Methodist. Home: 1275 Partridge Rd Spartanburg SC 29302 Office: 508 Gressette Bldg Columbia SC 29202

PATTERSON, EUGENE CORBETT, editor; b. Valdosta, Ga., Oct. 15, 1923; s. William C. and Annabel (Corbett) P.; m. Mary Sue Carter, Aug. 19, 1950; 1 dau., Mary Patterson Fausch. Student, N. Ga. Coll., Dahlonega, 1940-42; A.B. in Journalism, U. Ga., 1943; LL.D., Tusculum Coll., 1965, Harvard U., 1969, Duke U., 1978, Stetson U., 1985; Litt.D., Emory U., 1966, Oglethorpe Coll., 1966, Tuskegee Inst., 1966, Roanoke Coll., 1968, Mercer U., 1968, Eckerd Coll., 1977. Reporter Temple (Tex.) Daily Telegram and Macon (Ga.) Telegraph, 1947-48; mgr. for S.C. United Press, 1948-49, night bur. mgr., N.Y.C., 1949-53, mgr., also chief corr., U.K., 1953-56; v.p., exec. editor Atlanta Jour. and Constn., 1956-60; editor Atlanta Constn., 1960-68; mng. editor Washington Post, 1968-71; prof. practice of polit. sci. Duke, 1971-72; editor, pres. St. Petersburg (Fla.) Times, 1972-84, chmn., chief exec. officer, 1984—; editor, pres. Congl. Quar., Washington, 1972-86, chmn., chief exec. officer, 1986—; chmn. bd. Fla. Trend mag., 1980—, Modern Graphic Arts, Inc., 1978—, Modern Media Inst. (now Poynter Inst. Media Studies), 1978—, Poynter Fund, 1978—. Vice chmn. U.S. Civil Rights Commn., 1964-68; mem. Pulitzer Prize Bd., 1973-85; trustee ASNE Found., 1981-85, U. Ga. Found., 1982—. Served from pvt. to capt. U.S. Army, 1943-47. Decorated Silver Star, Bronze Star with oak leaf cluster; recipient Pulitzer prize for editorial writing, 1966; William Allen White nat. citation, 1980. Fellow Soc. Profl. Journalists; mem. Am. Soc. Newspaper Editors (pres. 1977-78), Am. Newspaper Publishers Assn. Clubs: St. Petersburg Pres., St. Petersburg Yacht, Nat. Press, Federal City. Home: 1967 Brightwaters Snell Isle Saint Petersburg FL 33704

PATTERSON, GARY ALLEN, state official; b. Gadsden, Ala., Aug. 7, 1943; s. Joseph Morrow and Willie Mae (Thrasher) P.; B.S., U. Ala., 1969, M.A. in Psychology, 1972; m. Kathleen Ann Schoppet, July 4, 1977; children—Brett Joseph, Brian Allen. Research asst. Center Developmental and Learning Disorders, U. Ala., Tuscaloosa, 1969-72; coordinator research/evaluation Office of Child Devel., Office Gov. Tenn., Nashville, 1972-75; dir. research and evaluation Interagy. Council for Child Devel. Services, W.Va. Gov.'s Office of Econ. and Community Devel., Charleston, 1975-78; project adminstr. evaluation and planning in children's services S.C. Gov.'s Office of Health and Social Devel., Columbia, 1978-80, adminstr. Office Children's Affairs, Div. Health and Human Services, 1980-84, adminstr. info. tech. services, 1984—; cons. Edn. Commn. States, 1976-77, La. Dept. Edn., 1976-77, W.Va. Schoolage Parents, 1977-78. Mem. Nashville Public TV, 1974-75, Tenn. Senate Com. on Child Neglect, Dependency and Abuse, 1974-75; Tenn. Gov.'s rep. Developmental Disability Council, 1973-75; ex-officio mem. bd. S.C. Children's Bur., 1980-81; staff Interagy. Council for Early Childhood Devel. and Edn. and interagy. adv. com. for early childhood devel. and edn., 1979—; liaison S.C. Child Protection Adv. Com., 1979-84; staff Gov.'s Task Force on Child Abuse and Neglect, 1980-84, Children's Coordinating Cabinet, 1980-84. Recipient cert. Recognition, Regional Child Devel., Tenn., 1974; citation Early Childhood Cons. Directory, 1976. Mem. Soc. Research in Child Devel., Am. Ednl. Research Assn., Day Care and Child Devel. Council Am., W.Va. Assn. Children Under Six, Tenn. Assn. Young Children. Presbyterian. Contbr. articles to profl. jours.; author: An Introduction to State Capacity Building: Planning, Management and Delivery of Child and Family Services, 1977; Child Development Management Information Systems, 1976; others. Office: 1205 Pendleton St 4th Floor Columbia SC 29201

PATTERSON, GEORGE ANTHONY, lawyer; b. Claremont, N.H., July 15, 1933; s. George Anthony and Irene Katherine (Quigley) P.; m. Miriam Bledsoe, July 3, 1965; children—Stephen, John, Brian. A.B. in Polit. Sci., Citadel, 1955; J.D., Notre Dame U., 1958. Bar: Fla. 1958, U.S. Dist. Ct. (no. dist.) Fla. 1961, U.S. Ct. Mil. Appeals 1962, U.S. Ct. Appeals (5th cir.) 1962, U.S. Supreme Ct. 1962, U.S. Dist. Ct. (so. dist.) Fla. 1963. Law clk. U.S. Dist. Ct. D.C., 1961-62; city atty. Coral Springs (Fla.), 1965-66; asst. mcpl. judge Deerfield Beach (Fla.), 1969-71; town prosecutor Hillsboro Beach (Fla.), 1969-72; ptnr., pres. George A. Patterson, P.A., Deerfield Beach, 1972—. Chmn. Deerfield Beach Charter Revision Com., 1973-74; pres. Notre Dame Alumni Club of Fort Lauderdale, Fla., 1964-65. Served with USAF, 1958-61. Mem. Broward County Bar Assn. (chmn. grievance com. 1969-70, pres. 1975-76), Deerfield Beach C. of C. (pres. 1972-73). Roman Catholic. Club: Deerfield Beach Rotary (pres. 1970-71). Home: 1528 SE 12th Ct Deerfield Beach FL 33441 Office: 665 SE 10th St Deerfield Beach FL 33441

PATTERSON, GILLETTE VANCE, manufacturing company executive; b. Oklahoma City, Mar. 18, 1922; s. Howard V. and Neva (Gillette) P.; m. Martha Martin, Jan. 16, 1944; children—Marty, Vance, Janette. B.S. in Econs., U. Mo., 1948. Mfr.'s agt. Patterson Co., Kansas City, Mo., 1949-51; sales mgr. Jenn Air Products, Indpls., 1952-57; gen. mgr. Swartwout Co., Cleve., 1958, v.p., 1959; pres., treas. Swartwout Fabricators, Kokomo, Ind., 1959-70; pres. Swartwout Plastics Inc., Sharpsville, Ind., 1963-70, Swartwout-Pacific Inc., 1970; v.p. Zurn Internat. div., Erie, Pa., 1969-73; pres. Mar-Van Inc., Kokomo, 1974-77, Solar Shield Inc., Columbia, S.C., 1978—, Mobil-Mist Inc., Columbia, 1980—. Served to lt. USAAF, 1942-46. Mem. Young Pres. Orgn. Lodges: Masons, Shriners, Rotary. Developer of devices in field. Home: 6153 Crabtree Rd Columbia SC 29206 Office: Windsor Lake Landing 1 Windsor Point Rd Columbia SC 29206

PATTERSON, GRADY LESLIE, JR., state treasurer; b. Abbeville County, S.C., Jan. 13, 1924; s. Grady Leslie and Claudia (McClain) P., Sr.; m. Marjorie Harrison Faucett, 1951; children—Grady Leslie III, Steven G., Marjorie Lynne, Laura Anne, Amy Susan, Mary Beth. Student Clemson U., 1942-43, U. Ala., 1943; B.S., LL.B., LL.D., U. S.C. County service officer Abbeville County, 1950; asst. atty. gen. S.C., 1959-66; state treas. S.C., 1967—. Served to lt. USAAF, 1943-46, PTO; USAFR, 1950-52, Korea, Berlin Call Up, 1961-62; to maj. gen. Air N.G., 1947—, ops. officer, 1952-58. Decorated Air medal with two oak leaf clusters, D.S.M. Mem. S.C. Bar Assn., Nat. Assn. State Auditors, Comptrollers and Treass. (pres. 1976—), Mcpl. Fin. Officers Assn., Am. Legion, Mil. Order of World Wars, Kappa Sigma. Democrat. Presbyterian. Office: Office of Treasurer PO Box 11778 Columbia SC 29211

PATTERSON, HAROLD E., mayor. Mayor City of Arlington, Tex. Office: PO Box 231 Arlington TX 76010*

PATTERSON, HUGH BASKIN, JR., publisher; b. Cotton Plant, Miss., Feb. 8, 1915; s. Hugh Baskin and Martha (Wilson) P.; student Henderson State Tchrs. Coll., 1933; m. Louise Caroline Heiskell, Mar. 29, 1944; children—Carrick Heiskell, Ralph Baskin. Sales dept. Smith Printing Co., Pine Bluff, Ark., 1933-36; asst. to sales mgr. Democrat Printing & Lithographing Co., Little Rock, 1936-38, promotion mgr., 1940-42; sales dept. Art Metal Constrn. Co., N.Y.C., 1938-39; planning and prodn. mgr. Rufus H. Darby Co., printers and pubs., Washington, 1939-40; with Ark. Gazette, 1946—, successively nat. advt. mgr., advt. dir. and asst. bus. mgr., pub., 1948—; pres., treas. Ark. Gazette Co.; pres. Ark. Bldg. Co. Bd. dirs. Fgn. Policy Assn., Inc.; bd. visitors U. Ark. at Little Rock. Served to maj. USAAC, 1942-46. Gazette recipient Pulitzer gold medal for pub. service, 1957, Freedom award Freedom House, 1958. Mem. Am., So. (pres. 1959-60) newspaper publs. assns., Inter Am. Press Assn. (dir.), Council Fgn. Relations, Internat. Press Inst., Sigma Delta Chi. Democrat. Presbyterian. Clubs: Overseas Press; Nat. Press; Little Rock Country. Address: Arkansas Gazette Co 112 W 3d St Little Rock AR 72203*

PATTERSON, J. O., bishop. Presiding bishop Ch. of God in Christ, Memphis. Address: Ch of God in Christ PO Box 320 Memphis TN 38101*

PATTERSON, JAMES THURSTON, marketing executive, consultant; b. El Paso, July 19, 1944; s. James Stephens and Lorraine (Gentry) P. B.A., Abilene Christian U., 1966. Youth minister Ch. of Christ, Nashville, 1968-71; account exec. Sta. WTVF-TV, Nashville, 1971-78; v.p. mktg. and mgmt. MPII, Inc., Dallas, 1978-80; mktg. engr. Texas Instrument, Dallas, 1980-83; sales/mktg. mgr. Am. Salvage Recovery, Houston, 1983—; mem. bd. Nashville Advt. Fedn., 1973-78. Youth editor Nashville Christian Jour., 1970; chmn. Com. Against Pornography, Nashville, 1971; chmn. pub. relations Am. Hearth Assn., Nashville, 1976; exec. bd. Lamb and Lion Ministries, Plano, Tex., 1980-84. Named best speaker Toastmasters Internat., 1972; Outstanding Young Man Am., Jaycees Internat., 1979, 80, Tenn. Squire, Tenn. Squires Assn., 1980, Adm. Tex. Navy, 1982, Ky. col., 1984. Republican. Baptist. Office: 42 Lakeview Galveston TX 77551

PATTERSON, JANA NELSON, psychologist; b. Montgomery, Ala., Sept. 4, 1954; d. Gustav Arthur and Jeanne Carolyn (Massey) N.; m. Randall Gerald Patterson, May 17, 1975. B.A., Belhaven Coll., 1976; M.A., U. Miss., 1979, Ph.D., 1982. Lic. psychologist, Miss. Head div. psychologist, dir. adolescent services East Miss. State Hosp., Meridian, 1982-85; coordinator clin. services Miss. Children's Home Soc., Jackson, 1985—; dir. Time Out and Co.; cons. Delta Community Mental Health Ctr., Greenville, Miss., 1985—; pvt. practice psychology, Meridian, 1985—; presentations in field. Contbr. articles to profl. publs. Mem. Commn. for Children and Youth Mental Health Task Force, 1983—, Gov.'s Council on Handicapped Services, 1984. Danforth assoc., 1979—. Mem. Am. Psychol. Assn., Assn. for Advancement of Behavior Therapy, Southeastern Psychol. Assn., Miss. Psychol. Assn., Menninger Found. Presbyterian. Avocations: tennis; cycling; skiing. Office: Miss Children's Home Soc PO Box 1078 Jackson MS 39205

PATTERSON, JOE WHEELER, sheriff; b. Apr. 17, 1929; s. Richard Washington and Effie (Owen) P.; m. Willa Jo Counts, Nov. 15, 1953 (div. June 1967); m. Jane McKee, Sept. 16, 1968; children—Brent, Jason. Student spl. law enforcement classes Huntsville Police Acad., 1961, 63, FBI schs., 1966, 71, 73, 74, Ams. for Effective Law Enforcement, 1979, U. Ala., 1979, Houston Police Civil Liability, 1979. Sheriff Madison County, Ala., 1978—; bd. dirs. Ala. Peace Officers Minimum Standards and Tng. Commn.; mem. U.S. atty.'s law enforcement coordinating com. North Dist. Ala.; coordinator tng. div. Madison County Sheriff's Res. Officers Div., 1985—; founder ednl. program Madison County Schs., finger printing program, pub. schs., Huntington, Ala. and Madison County. Active Boys Club Am., mem. state bd., adv. bd. Ala. Sheriffs' Boys and Girls Ranches, 1978—, dir. North Ranch project, 1978—; founder Operation Needy; active in fundraising. Recipient award of Merit, Cahaba Temple, 1981, Good Govt. award Madison County Jaycees, 1982, also numerous awards and recognition from other community, profl. groups; ranch home named in his honor Ala. Sheriff's Boys and Girls Ranches, 1978. Mem. Ala. Sheriffs' Assn. (pres. 1982-83), VFW Club, Am. Legion (Law Enforcement Officer of Yr. 1981), Huntsville Heritage Club. Baptist. Lodge: Elks. Avocations: working with youth; gardening. Home: 200 Colonial Dr Toney AL 35773 Office: Madison County Sheriff's Dept Madison County Courthouse Huntsville AL 35801

PATTERSON, MARGARET ANN TUCKER, architect; b. Amherst County, Va., June 11, 1927; d. Cornelius Page and Katharine Jewel (Bryant) Tucker; m. Gerald Raymond Patterson, June 19, 1954; children—Suzann Frances Patterson Ankrom, Scot Mace, Sarah Kathryn Patterson Harvey, Patricia Ann. Student Mary Washington Coll., 1944-45; B. Arch., Cath. U. Am., 1949. Lic. architect, Va., D.C. Assoc. architect J.R. Mims & Assocs., Arlington, Va., 1949-54, jr. ptnr., 1954-67; prin. architect M.A. Patterson, Annandale, Va., 1967-68; cons. architect Olivola and Assocs., Alexandria, Va., 1968-70; prin. Humphrey-Patterson, Assocs., Annandale, 1970-75, M.A. Patterson, Annandale, 1975—. Bd. dirs. First Christian Ch., Falls Church, Va., 1978-84, chmn. bd., 1984—; vol. cons. Fairfax County Schs. Career Guidance, 1979—; active Architect Control Commn. Civic Assn., Annandale, 1975—. Democrat. Avocations: gardening; reading; tennis; cooking; painting.

PATTERSON, MARY ANNE, nurse; b. Andalusia, Ala., Mar. 6, 1952; d. Howell Mason and Karma Lou (Rhodes) McInnish; m. James Elliott Patterson, July 18, 1980; children—Alicia, Emilia, Janifer. Student, Auburn U., 1970, Lurleen B. Wallace Jr. Coll., 1971, 1973-74; B.S., Troy State U., 1977. R.N., Ala. Asst. supr. Andalusia Hosp. (Ala.), 1977-78; staff nurse neonatal intensive care unit Bapt. Med. Ctr., Montgomery, Ala., 1978-79, charge nurse neonatal intensive care unit, 1979-82, asst. head nurse regional neonatal ICU, 1982—. Mem. Mothers of Twins Club, La Leche League, Gamma Beta Phi. Baptist. Home: 3341 Woodpark Ct Montgomery AL 36116 Office: Bapt Med Ctr 2105 E South Blvd Montgomery AL 36198

PATTERSON, NEVILLE, chief justice Mississippi Supreme Court; b. Monticello, Miss., Feb. 16, 1916; s. E.B. Patterson; LL.B., U. Miss., 1939; m. Catherine Sough; 3 children. Admitted to Miss. bar, 1939; practiced with father, Monticello, 1939-41; with legal dept. Fed. Land Bank, New Orleans, 1941; chancellor 15th Chancery Ct. Dist., 1947-63; asst. atty. gen. State of Miss., 1963; justice Supreme Ct. of So. Dist. Miss., 1964—, now chief justice. Prof., Jackson Sch. Law, 1966—. Chmn., Miss. Jud. Council; past chmn. Miss. Adv. Council on Rule Changes. Served to capt. inf. AUS, 1941-45. Decorated Bronze Star. Mem. Am. Legion, Miss. Bar Assn., V.F.W., 40 and & Democrat. Methodist. Clubs: Country of Jackson, Patio. Home: 4235 Old Orchard Pl Jackson MS 39206 Office: Supreme Court of Mississippi Carroll Gartin Justice Bldg Jackson MS 39205*

PATTERSON, ORUS FUQUAY, III, geologist; b. Lee County, N.C., June 15, 1945; s. Orus Fuquay and Sarah Christine (Wicker) P.; m. Sara Kathryn Campbell, Aug. 15, 1971; children—Orus Fuquay, Joshua Campbell. B.Sc. in Geology, Campbell U., 1968; M.Sc., N.C. State U., 1969. Cert. profl. geologist, 1975. Chief geologist Explo Assocs., Sanford, N.C., 1970-74; geologist, chief exec. officer Patterson Exploration Services, Sanford, 1975—; commr. (notary) State of W.Va., 1976-86. Mem. Soc. Mining Engrs. of AIME (sec.-treas. Carolinas sect. 1982-83, dir. 1979—, chmn. 1985), Am. Inst. Profl. Geologists, Sigma Xi. Republican. Baptist. Contbr. articles to profl. jours. Office: PO Box 1473 Sanford NC 27330

PATTERSON, PEGGY LOU, army officer; b. Weleetka, Okla., June 21, 1944; d. Walter and Cinderella (Johnson) P.; B.A., Golden Gate U., 1979; 1 dau., Kiila Michelle. Englisted U.S. Army, 1965, commd. 2d lt. 1971; served in Vietnam; comdr. 9th Inf. Div. Mil. Police Co., 1976-77; asst. prof. mil. sci. La. State U.; provost marshall U.S. Mil. Community Activity, Zweibrucken, W.Ger., dep. comdr. U.S. Army Confinement Facility, Mannheim, Ger., 1983-85. Decorated Bronze Star, Army Commendation medal, Meritorious Service medal. Mem. Assn. U.S. Army. Baptist. Home: PO Box 572 Weleetka OK 74880 Office: Adj Gen's Office Alexandria VA 33221

PATTERSON, P(ICKENS) ANDREW, lawyer; b. Cotton Plant, Ark., Aug. 1, 1944; s. Pickens Andrew and Willie Mae (Miller) P.; m. Gloria Neltine Peebles, Nov. 25, 1967; children—Pickens Andrew, Staci Elizabeth. B.A., Fisk U., 1965; J.D., Harvard U., 1968. Bar: Ga. 1969, N.C. 1978, U.S. Dist. Ct. (no. dist.) Ga. 1969, U.S. Dist. Ct. (mid. dist.) N.C. 1978, U.S. Ct. Appeals (11th cir.) 1983. Vice pres. Urban East Housing Consl. Atlanta, 1968-69; mng. atty. Atlanta Legal Aid, 1968-70; sr. ptnr. Patterson, Parks, Jackson & Howell, Atlanta, 1970-77; atty. adviser HUD, Greensboro, N.C., 1977-81; exec. v.p. Arrington, Patterson & Thomas, P.C., Atlanta, 1982—; of Counsel Thomas, Kennedy, Sampson & Edwards, P.C.; dir. Gladden Devel. Corp., Atlanta; Davis-Hudson Assocs., Inc., Atlanta, Creance Internat., Inc., Atlanta; Pres. Atlanta Legal Aid Soc., 1976, Central Carolina Legal Services, Greensboro, 1980; Co-author pamphlet. Mem. Atlanta Charter Study Commn., 1972; bd. dirs. Louisville Presbyn. Theol. Sem., 1983—. Recipient Key to City Atlanta, 1972, plaque awards Atlanta Legal Aid Soc., 1977, Central Carolina Legal Services, 1981, Cert. of Spl. Achievement, Office of Gen. Counsel, HUD, 1980. Mem. Nat. Bar Assn., State Bar Ga., N.C. Bar Assn., Atlanta Bar Assn., Gate City Bar Assn. (pres. 1986), Alpha Phi Alpha. Democrat. Presbyterian. Home: 3905 Somerled Trail College Park GA 30349 Office: Suite 1200 First Federal Bldg 40 Marietta St NW Atlanta GA 30303

PATTERSON, RICKEY LEE, clergyman; b. Indpls., Sept. 24, 1952; s. William Irving and Wanda Lou (Calbert) P.; B.A., Ind. U., 1976; M.B.A., U. Miami, 1980; M.Theology, Internat. Bible Inst. and Sem., 1983; m. Sharon Rose Leonard, May 4, 1974. Sales mgr. Spartan Security, Miami, Fla., 1977-79; pres. Pat-Cat Enterprises, Inc., Miami, 1977—; pastor, 1972—; founder, pres. Jesus Students Fellowship, Inc., 1973—, pastor, 1979—, radio broadcast speaker, 1978—, dir. J.S.F. Cassette Ministries, 1978—; pres. Jesus Fellowship, Inc., 1981—; ordained to ministry Internat. Conv. Faith Chs. and Ministers, Inc., 1980; coll. unit dir. Northwestern Mut. Life Ins. Co., Milw., 1980-83; founder, supt. Jesus Fellowship Christian Sch., 1983—; pres. Dade County Pvt. Sch. Systems, Inc., 1983—; instr. Bible, Ind. U., 1973-76; instr. Bible, U. Miami, 1976—, also guest lectr. dept. religion; pres. Miami Bible Inst., 1984—; guest lectr. Miami North Community Correctional Center, Dade County Correctional Inst., Fed. Inst. Corrections; adv. Miami chpt. Women Aglow, 1980-82; campus minister Ind. U., U. Miami, Fla. Internat. U., Miami-Dade Community Coll., U. P.R. Charter mem. Rep. Presdl. Task Force; sustaining mem. Rep. Nat. Com.; bd. govs. Am. Coalition Traditional Values, 1984—. Mem. Bur. Bus. Practice, Nat. Audubon Soc., Am. Entrepreneurs Assn., Inst. Cert. Fin. Planners., Am. Security Council, U.S. Senatorial Club, Zool. Soc. Fla., Christian Booksellers Assn., Nat. Assn. Life Underwriters, Miami Assn. Life Underwriters, Am. Mktg. Assn., Full Gospel Businessmen's Fellowship Internat., Ind. U. Alumni Assn., Sigma Pi. Republican. Editor: Spirit of Life Mag., 1980—; chief editor Miami Jour., 1984—. Home and Office: 9775 SW 87th Ave Miami FL 33176

PATTERSON, ROBERT WALKER PALMER, Army officer; b. Oxford, Miss., Feb. 11, 1940; s. Claude R. and Vera (Cupit) P.; m. Arlene Stokes, May 8, 1965; children—Robert Stokes, Christopher Lee. Student Marion Mil. Inst., 1959; B.S. in Profl. Aviation, La. Tech. U., 1974. Commd. 2d lt. U.S. Army, 1967, advanced through grades to lt. col. 1983; asst. div. br. chief Multi-Engine Br., Ft. Rucker, Ala., 1969-71; ops. officer 147th Aviation Command, 1968-69, 213th Aviation Command, Vietnam, 1971-72; bn. signal officer 2d. Bn. 4th Inf., Germany, 1975-78; aviation advisor U.S. Army Advisor Group, North Little Rock, 1978-81; asst. div. signal officer 2d. Inf. Div., Korea, 1981-82; chief Air Traffic Control Laision Office, Army Air Traffic Control Combat Support Activity, Ft. McPherson, Ga., 1982—; adv. SR Army Adv. Group, Miss., 1985—. Author: S.A.R.A. Tng. 1983; contbr. articles to jours. Mem. Republican Presdl. Task Force, Washington, 1981. Decorated Bronze Star with one oak leaf cluster, Meritorious Service medal with 2 oak leaf clusters, Air medal with 16 awards. Mem. Soc. Amateur Radio Astromers, Am. Radio Relay League, Army Aviation Assn., Quarter Century Wireless Assn. Republican. Mem. Assembly of God. Home: 410 Mill Run Rd Brandon MS 39042

PATTERSON, ROBERT WILLIAM, exploration administrator, geophysicist; b. Vine Grove, Ky., July 25, 1927; s. Thomas Henry and Lottie Mae (Davis) P.; m. Helen Jane Holland, June 12, 1954; children—Thomas Holland, Richard Douglas. B.S. in Civil Engring. U. Ky., 1953. Supr., ptnr. Seismic Engring. Co., 1967-72; mgr. fgn. ops. Seismic Explorations Co.,

Houston, 1973-74; supr., cons. Rogers Explorations Co., Midland, Tex. and Houston, 1974-75; regional geophysicist Tex. Pacific Oil Co., Abilene, 1976-81; central mgr. Sun Exploration & Prodn. Co., Dallas, 1981—. Served as sgt. USAF, 1945-49. Mem. Soc. Exploration Geophysicists, Am. Assn. Petroleum Geologists, Dallas Geophys. Soc., Abilene Geol. Soc., Permian Basin Geophys. Soc. Republican. Avocations: rocks, minerals, jewelry design and fabrication. Home: 1713 Oxford Pl Mesquite TX 75149 Office: Sun Exploration & Prodn Co Box 2880 Dallas TX 75221

PATTERSON, RON, architect, land planning company executive; b. Killeen, Tex., Aug. 23, 1951; s. Carl Lee and Ruth (Sell) P.; m. Becky E. Espinosa June 9, 1973; children—Melissa Marie, Christopher Patrick. B.Arch., U. Houston-University Park, 1977; cert. in site planning Grad. Sch. Design, Harvard U., 1985. Registered architect, Tex. Graphic designer Caudill Rowlett Scott, Houston, 1973; staff planner Lockwood Andrews & Newnam, Inc., Houston, 1973-80, head planning dept., 1980-82, mktg. dept., 1982-83; pres. Urban Planning Inc. (formerly Patterson & Assocs.), Austin, Tex., 1983—. Chmn. task force Clean Houston, 1976-78. Mem. AIA, Am. Planning Assn., Urban Land Inst., Tex. Soc. Architects, Austin C. of C., Austin-San Antonio Corridor Assn., Metro Austin. Republican. Baptist. Avocations: geneology; photography. Office: Urban Planning Inc 9111 Jollyville Rd Suite 108 Austin TX 78759

PATTERSON, ROSALYN VICTORIA MITCHELL, biologist, educator; b. Madison, Ga., Mar. 25, 1939; d. Walter Melvin and Hazeltine Virginia (Jones) Mitchell; B.A., Spelman Coll., 1958; M.S., Atlanta U., 1960; Ph.D. Univ. fellow, Emory U., 1967; m. Joseph William Patterson, June 1, 1961; children—Hazelyn Mamette, Joseph William II, Rosman Victor Melvin. Instr. to prof. biology Spelman Coll., 1960-70; So. Fellowship Funds postdoctoral fellow Ga. Inst. Tech., 1969-70; staff specialist to commr., cons. Bur. Reclamation, Dept. of Interior, Washington, 1970-71; coordinator nat. environ. edn. devel. program Nat. Park Service, Dept. of Interior, 1971-72; NIH postdoctoral fellow expt. cytology br. NIH and Bur. Biologics, FDA, Bethesda, Md., 1972-73; assoc. prof. biology Ga. State U., 1974-76; prof., chmn. dept. biology Atlanta U., 1977—; cons. Dept. Interior, 1970-71. NRC postdoctoral fellow Ctrs. for Disease Control, Atlanta, 1983-84, NIH postdoctoral fellow, 1984-85. Mem. AAAS, Am. Soc. Cell Biology, Soc. Devel. Biology, Tissue Culture, Assn., Sigma Xi, Phi Sigma, Baptist. Research on mammalian chromosomes in cell culture. Home: 109 Burre Ln SW Atlanta GA 30331 Office: 223 JP Brawley Dr Atlanta GA 30314

PATTERSON, SOLON PETE, investment counselor; b. Atlanta, Nov. 11, 1935; s. Pete George and Frances Marinos P.; m. Marianna Reynolds, Oct. 29, 1960; children—John Solon, Joseph Peter. B.B.A., Emory U., 1957, M.B.A., 1958. Security analyst, portfolio mgr. Piedmont Adv. Corp., N.Y.C., 1958-62; chmn. bd., chief exec. officer Montag & Caldwell, Inc., Atlanta, 1962—; chmn. bd. Alpha Fund, Inc., Atlanta, 1968—; Trustee, chmn. fin. com. Gammon Theol. Sem.; mem. Leadership Atlanta Alumni Assn., mem. regional bd. NCCJ; bd. visitors Emory U., mem. Bus. Sch. Mgmt. Conf. Bd.; bd. dirs. Atlanta Coll. Art; bd. govs. Bus. Council Ga. Named Atlanta's Outstanding Young Man of Yr., Atlanta Jr. C. of C., 1968. Mem. Fin. Analysts Fedn. (past nat. chmn.), Nat. Assn. Bus. Economists, Atlanta Soc. Fin. Analysts (past pres.), Inst. Chartered Fin. Analysts, Atlanta Econs. Club (past pres.), Atlanta C. of C. Greek Orthodox. Clubs: Rotary; Commerce, Piedmont Driving (Atlanta). Office: 2 Piedmont Center Suite 500 Atlanta GA 30363

PATTERSON, TRUDY JENKINS, librarian; b. Eunice, La., Feb. 2, 1951; d. Jack Gordon and Bettie (Brunson) Jenkins; m. Donald Ray Patterson, Feb. 9, 1979; children—Daniel Alan, Abby Elizabeth. B.A. in English Edn., U. Southwestern La., 1972; M.L.S., La. State U., 1974. Adminstrv. librarian Richland Parish Library, Rayville, La., 1974-77, Webster Parish Library, Minden, La., 1978-79; head reference dept. Lafayette (La.) Pub. Library, 1979-80; tech. services librarian Calcasieu Parish Pub. Library, Lake Charles, La., 1981-82; adminstrv. librarian Jefferson Davis Parish Library, Jennings, La., 1982—. Mem. ALA, La. Library Assn., Southeastern Library Assn., Bus. and Profl. Women's Assn. Democrat. Methodist. Home: PO Box 127 Elton LA 70532 Office: Jefferson Davis Parish Library 118 W Plaquemine St Jennings LA 70546

PATTERSON, ZELLA JUSTINA BLACK, home economist, historian, poet; b. Coyle, Okla., May 20, 1909; d. Thomas and Mary Elizabeth (Horst) Black; B.S. in Home Econs. Edn., Langston (Okla.) U., 1937; M.S., Colo. State U., Ft. Collins, 1941; postgrad. U. Calif., Berkeley, Okla. State U.; m. George W. Patterson, Dec. 24, 1946 (dec.). Elem. sch. tchr., 1931-34; extension worker, 1934-36; vocat. home econs. tchr., supervising tchr., 1937-60; mem. faculty Langston U., 1937-46, 60-72, prof. home econs. and home econs. edn., 1965-72, chmn. dept., 1965-72; vocat. home econs. tchr., supervising tchr. Langston City High Sch., 1946-60 family living specialist coop. extension Okla. State U.-U.S. Dept. Agr., 1972-74; mem. Langston Community Edn. Adv. Com.; bd. dirs. Logan County Hist. Soc.; govs. appointee to bd. dirs. Okla. Hist. Soc., 1983—, also chmn. Black heritage com., 1983—; mem. Diamond Jubilee Commn. Okla.; mem. Okla. Hist. Soc. Black Heritage adv. com. to exec. com.; author: Langston University: A History, 1979, A Garden of Poems, 1978; also family histories. Recipient Honor Alumna award Colo. State U., 1976, Outstanding Woman award Langston U., 1979; named to Okla. Women's Hall of Fame, 1984. Mem. Okla. Edn. Assn. (Outstanding Educator Recognition award 1973), Am. Home Econs. Assn., Okla. Home Econs. Assn., Okla. Ret. Soc., Nat. Ret. Tchrs. Assn., Alpha Kappa Alpha. Republican. Baptist. Clubs: Langston Beautiful, Langston Coyle Bus. and Profl. Women's, Order Eastern Star. Author: History of Churches of Langston, 1983. Address: PO Box 96 Langston OK 73050

PATTESON, ROY KINNEER, JR., educational administrator, clergyman; b. Richmond, Va., Oct. 27, 1928; s. Roy Kinneer and Mary Elizabeth (Anderson) P.; m. Pauline Cox, Apr. 15, 1950; children—Stephen Kinneer, David Blair. B.A., U. Richmond, 1957; B.D., Union Theol. Sem., 1961; Th.M., Duke U., 1964, Ph.D. (univ. scholar), 1967. Postdoctoral fellow Inst. of Medieval Studies, Duke U., Durham, N.C., 1968; ordained to ministry Presbyterian Ch., 1961; pres. So. Sem. Jr. Coll., Buena Vista, Va., 1970-72; v.p. Mary Baldwin Coll., Staunton, Va., 1972-77; pres. King Coll., Bristol, Tenn., 1977-79; v.p., prof. history and philosophy Va. Wesleyan Coll., Norfolk, Va., 1979-85; v.p., Westminster-Canterbury of Hampton Roads, Inc., 1985—; cons. in coll. devel., Council of Ind. Colls. Mem. Career Edn. Adv. Com., Norfolk (Va.) Sch. Bd. Served with U.S. Army, 1948-49; served in N.G., 1950-55. Mem. Council for Advancement and Support of Edn. Club: Rotary (Norfolk). Contbr. articles to profl. jours. Office: Westminster-Canterbury of Hampton Roads Inc 3100 Shore Dr Virginia Beach VA 23451

PATTHOFF, DONALD EDWARD, dentist; b. Delphos, Ohio, May 30, 1946; s. Donald Edward and Joann Marie (Karst) P.; m. Deborah Kay Ruf, Aug. 3, 1974; children—Erica, Alex, Adria. D.D.D., U. Detroit, 1974; B.S. in Zoology, Ohio State U., 1968. Research assoc. Kettering Found., Yellow Springs, Ohio, 1968; gen. practice VA Hosp. Martinsburg, W.Va., 1974-75, staff dentist, 1975-82, prin. investigator, 1975-82; pvt. practice, Martinsburg, W.Va., 1978—. Contbr. articles to profl. jours. Pres., co-founder, Panhandle Life Awareness, Eastern Panhandle, W.Va., 1984; bd. dirs. Inter-County Health, Inc., 1976-84. Served in U.S. Army, 1969-71, Vietnam, Germany. Health Services Research grantee, VA, Washington, 1979. Fellow: Acad. Gen. Dentistry (bd. dirs. 1981); mem. ADA (alt. del. 1974-85), W.Va. Dental Assn. (pres. elect 1984-85). Roman Catholic. Avocations: tennis; canoeing; back packing; golf; music. Home: Rt 1 Box 162 Martinsburg WV 25401 Office: Donald E Patthoff DDS 300 Foxcroft Ave Martinsburg WV 25401

PATTISON, EDWARD MANSELL, psychiatrist; b. Portland, Oreg., June 23, 1933; s. Horace Evans and Alice (Mohr) P.; m. Myrna Loy Mischke, June 22, 1956; children—Stefanie, Stewart, Benno. B.A., Reed Coll., 1956; M.D., U. Oreg., 1958. Intern, U. Oreg. Med. Sch. Hosp., Portland, 1959; resident in psychiatry U. Cin., 1961-64; forensic psychiatrist U.S. Med. Ctr., Springfield, Mo., 1959-61; fellow in psychiatry U. Cin., 1961-64; sr. psychiatrist NIMH, Washington, 1964-65; asst. prof. psychiatry U. Wash., Seattle, 1965-70; prof. psychiatry Social Sci., Social Ecology U. Calif.-Irvine, 1970-79; prof. and chmn. dept. psychiatry Med. Coll. Ga., Augusta, 1979—; nat. cons. NIMH, Nat. Inst. Drug Abuse, Nat. Heart and Lung Inst.; internat. health cons. WHO. Served with USPHS, 1959-65. NIMH Career Devel. fellow, 1961-65; recipient Man of Yr. in Pastoral Psychology, 1969; VA Superior Performance award, 1982. Fellow Am. Psychiat. Assn. (Significant Achievement award 1977), Am. Group Psychotherapy Assn., Am. Acad. Psychiat. and Law, Am. Assn. Social Psychiatrists, Am. Anthropol. Assn. and others. Author: History of American Group Psychotherapy, 1969; Clinical Psychiatry and Religion, 1969; Pastor and Parish-A-Systems Approach, 1977; Emerging Concepts of Alcohol Dependence, 1977; Clinical Applications of Social Network Theory, 1981; Encyclopedic Handbook of Alcoholism. 1982; contbr. numerous articles to profl. jours. Home: 2150 Battle Row Augusta GA 30904 Office: Dept Psychiatry Med Coll Ga Augusta GA 30912

PATTON, ARTHUR GORDON, lawyer, consultant; b. Herndon, Va., Sept. 19, 1922; s. Arthur Jennings and Lena Ann (Cox) P.; m. Nellie Estelle Shafer, Dec. 25, 1945; children—Arthur Gordon, James Scott. B.A., Yale U., 1946; J.D. with honors, George Washington U., 1950, LL.M., 1954. Bar: D.C. 1951, Fla. 1970, U.S. Dist. Ct. D.C. 1951, U.S. Dist. Ct. (mid. dist.) Fla. 1973, U.S. Tax Ct., U.S. Ct. Mil. Appeals 1957, U.S. Ct. Appeals (D.C. cir.) 1951, U.S. Supreme Ct. 1957. Intelligence analyst Chief Naval Ops., U.S. Navy, 1948-49, spl. agt. Office Naval Intelligence, 1949, counterintelligence analyst, 1949-51, security policy and control officer, 1951-54, security policy officer, 1954-55; asst. chief for indsl. security Office of Insp. Gen. U.S. Air Force, 1955-62, asst. to insp. gen., 1962, mem. procurement rev. com., 1963, chief AFETR base procurment office, 1965-66, chief adminstrv. and logistics br. Air Force Range Measurments Lab., 1966-69; sole practice, Melbourne, Fla., 1970-74; assoc. dir. continuing legal edn. The Fla. Bar, Tallahassee, 1974-75; v.p. DBA Systems, Melbourne, 1976-78; sole practice, Indian Harbour Beach, Fla., 1978—; pvt. practice legal and mgmt. consulting, 1970—. Contbr. articles to profl. jours. Served to lt. USMC, 1942-47. Mem. Fed. Bar Assn., Nat. Indsl. Security Assn. (hon.), Delta Theta Phi. Republican. Episcopalian. Home: 690 Anderson Ct Satellite Beach FL 32937

PATTON, CELESTEL HIGHTOWER, educator; b. Nacogdoches, Tex., July 14; d. Felix and Martha Jane (Turner) Hightower; D.H., Meharry Med. Coll., 1947; B.S., Tenn. A. and I. State U., 1952; M.A., Columbia U., 1954; M.A. in Spanish, Interam. U., Saltillo, Mex.; m. Ural L. Patton, Feb. 1, 1930. Dental hygienist pub. schs., Tex., 1947-52; dean women and tchr. health Bishop Coll., Marshall and Dallas, 1954-60; dir. phys. edn. for women Wilberforce (Ohio) U., 1960-62; asso. prof. health edn. So. U., Baton Rouge, 1962—. Active Community Chest, Dallas, 1950-58. Recipient Meharry Pres.'s award, 1967, Alumni's Award for Outstanding Achievement in the Area of Dental Hygiene, 1972. Mem. Dental Hygienists Soc., Meharry Coll. Alumni Assn. (pres. 1952), AAUP, AAUW, Am. Dental Hygienists Assn., Tex. Dental Hygienist Assn., Am. Pub. Health Assn., AAHPER. Democrat. Christian Ch. Contbr. articles to profl. jours.

PATTY, CHARLES EDGAR, JR., physicist, educator; b. Anniston, Ala., Aug. 29, 1946; s. Charles Edgar and Velma Doris (Roper) P.; m. Stephanie Ruth Carter, May 8, 1971; children—Kira Dawne, Charles Edgar III, B.S., Jacksonville State U., 1969; M.S., U. Ala., 1977, Ph.D., 1983. Research/teaching asst. U. Ala., Huntsville, 1974-79; dir. Redstone Arsenal Br., Columbia Coll. Extended Studies Div., Restone Arsenal, Ala., 1979-82; electronics engr. U.S. Army Missile Lab., Redstone Arsenal, Ala., 1982-84; sr. systems analyst Teledyne Brown Engring., 1984—; mem. adj. faculty Columbia Coll., Redstone br., 1978—. Chmn. bd. dirs. Bingham Mountain Landowners Assn., 1984-85; block capt. Neighborhood Watch, 1982-83; chmn., founding mem. Council Sci. Students, U. Ala., Huntsville, 1976. Served as officer SAC, USAF, 1969-74. Mem. Am. Phys. Soc., Sigma Xi, Sigma Pi Sigma. Baptist. Author: Introduction to Experimental Physics, 1975; Experiment and Knowledge, 1986. Home: 3202 Reynolds Dr NW Huntsville AL 35810 Office: Teledyne Brown Engring Cummings Research Park Huntsville AL 35805

PATURIS, E(MMANUEL) MICHAEL, lawyer; b. Akron, Ohio, July 12, 1933; s. Michael George and Sophia (Manos) P.; m. Mary Ann Toompas, Feb. 28, 1965; 1 child, Sophia Elena. B.S. with honors, U. N.C., 1954, J.D. with honors (Block award 1959, staff law rev. 1957-59), 1959, postgrad. in acctg., 1959-60; Admitted to N.C. bar, 1959, D.C. bar, 1969, Va. bar, 1973; C.P.A., N.C. With acctg. firms, Charlotte and Wilmington, N.C., 1960-63; assoc. Poyner, Geraghty, Hartsfield & Townsend, Raleigh, N.C., 1963-64; tax atty. Chief Counsel's Office, IRS, Washington, 1964-66, sr. tax trial atty. Regional Counsel's Office, Richmond, Va., 1966-69; partner firm Reasoner, Davis & Vinson, Washington, 1969-78; practice law, Alexandria, Va., 1978—; instr. bus. law, econs. and acctg. Served with U.S. Army, 1954-56. Mem. Am. Assn. Atty.-CPAs (pres. Potomac chpt. 1977-79), D.C. Inst. CPAs, Va. Soc. CPAs, Am. Bar Assn., N.C. Bar Assn., Va. Bar Assn., D.C. Bar Assn., Phi Beta Kappa, Beta Gamma Sigma. Republican. Greek Orthodox. Club: Washington Golf and Country. Lodge: Rotary (Tyson's Corner, Va.). Home: 2732 N Radford St Arlington VA 22207 Office: Lee St Square 431 N Lee St Alexandria VA 22314

PAUL, ALIDA RUTH, educator; b. San Antonio, May 30, 1953; d. Richard Irving and Anne Louise (Holman) P. B.S. in Edn., Southwest Tex. State U., 1975; M.Ed., U. Houston, 1984. Cert. elem. and secondary tchr., Tex. Tchr. arts and crafts Houston Ind. Sch. Dist., 1975—. Mem. Am. Assn. for Counseling and Devel., Tex. Assn. for Counseling and Devel., Nat. Art Edn. Assn. Republican. Episcopalian. Avocations: drawing; painting; bicycling; volunteer work. Home: 17727 Wolfhollow St Houston TX 77084

PAUL, CHRIS WESLEY, II, economics educator; b. Malden, Mo., Oct. 7, 1949; s. Chris Wesley and Elsie Mae (Clark) P.; m. Linda Joyce McElroy, June 15, 1979. B.S. in Econs., S.W. Mo. State U., 1972; Ph.D. in Econs., Tex. A&M U., 1979. Research asst. Tex. A&M U., College Station, 1973-74, teaching asst., 1975-76, research asst. Tex. Transp. Inst., College Station, 1974-75; asst. prof. U. Ga., Athens, 1976-82; assoc. prof. econs. U. Ala., Huntsville, 1982—; prof. econs. Kenneshaw Coll., Marietta, Ga., 1984—; asst. research economist Fed. Energy Adminstrn., Washington, 1975; cons. FTC, Washington, 1978-79; cons., expert witness Aciation Consumer Action Project, Washington, 1979-80. Contbr. articles to profl. publs. Recipient Outstanding Undergrad. Teaching award Dept. Econs., U. Ga., 1980, Swift Teaching award, 1981. Mem. Am. Econ. Assn., Atlantic Econ. Assn., Midsouth Acad. Economists, Western Econ. Assn., So. Fin. Assn., Southwestern Fin. Assn., Omicron Delta Epsilon, Alpha Kappa Delta. Avocations: art, music, reading. Home: 3230 Hickory Crest Dr Marietta GA 30064 Office: Kennesaw Coll Frey Rd Marietta GA 30061

PAUL, GABRIEL GABE, profl. baseball club exec.; b. Rochester, N.Y., Jan. 4, 1910; s. Morris and Celia (Snyder) P.; ed. public schs., Rochester; m. Mary Frances Copps, Apr. 17, 1939; children—Gabriel, Warren, Michael, Jennie Lou, Henry. Reporter, Rochester Democrat and Chronicle, 1926-28; publicity mgr., ticket mgr. Rochester Baseball Club, 1928-34, traveling sec., dir., 1934-36; publicity dir. Cin. Baseball Club, 1937, traveling sec., 1938-48, asst. to pres., 1948-49, gen. mgr., 1951-60, v.p., 1949-60; v.p., gen. mgr. Houston Baseball Club, 1960-61; gen. mgr. Cleve. Baseball Club (Cleve. Indians), 1961-63, pres., treas., 1963-72, v.p., gen. mgr., 1972-73; pres. N.Y. Yankees, 1973-77; pres., chief exec. officer Cleve. Indians, 1978-84. Dir. or trustee various charitable instns. Served with inf. AUS, 1943-45. Named Major League Exec. of Yr., Sporting News, 1956, 74, Milw. chpt. Baseball Writers Assn., 1976, Sports Exec. of Yr., Gen. Sports Time, 1956, Baseball Exec. of Yr., Boston chpt. Baseball Writers Assn., 1974, 76, Maj. League Exec. of Yr., United Press, 1976; recipient J. Lewis Comiskey Meml. award Chgo. chpt. Baseball Writers Assn. Am., 1961, Judge Emil Fuchs Meml. award Boston chpt., 1967, Bill Slocum Meml. award N.Y. chpt. Baseball Writers Assn. Am., 1975, Sports Torch of Learning award, 1976. Clubs: Palma Ceia Country (Tampa); Shaker Heights (Ohio) Country. Home: 5115 S Nichol St Crescent Pl Tampa FL 33611 Office: 3601 Swann Ave Tampa FL 33609

PAUL, GORDON LEE, psychologist, educator; b. Marshalltown, Iowa, Sept. 2, 1935; s. Leon Dale and Ione Hickman (Perry) P.; m. Joan Marie Wyatt, Dec. 24, 1954; children—Dennis Leon, Dana Lee, Joni Lynn. Student, Marshalltown Community Coll., 1953-54, San Diego City Coll., 1955-57; B.A., U. Iowa, 1960; M.A., U. Ill., 1962, Ph.D., 1964. Social sci. analyst VA Hosp., Danville, Ill., 1962; counseling psychologist U. Ill., Urbana, 1963; clin. psychologist VA Hosp., Palo Alto, Calif., 1964-65; gen. practice clin. psychology, 1964-65; asst. prof. psychology U. Ill., Urbana, 1965-67, assoc. prof., 1967-70, prof., 1970-80; Cullen disting. prof. psychology U. Houston, 1980—; pvt. practice, Champaign, Ill., 1965-80, Houston, 1980—; psychotherapy research cons. Palo Alto, 1964-65; cons. Ill. Dept. Mental Health, 1965-73, 78-84, NIMH, 1968-78; adviser Ont. Mental Health Found., Can., 1968-69, NSF, 1968-69, Can. Council, 1969-75, VA, 1972-80, Am. Psychol. Assn., 1970—. Author: Insight vs. Desensitization in Psychotherapy: An Experiment in Anxiety Reduction, 1966, Anxiety and Clinical Problems, 1973, Psychosocial Treatment of Chronic Mental Patients, 1977; editorial bd. Behavior Therapy, 1969-75, Jour. Abnormal Psychology 1972-76, Jour. Behavior Therapy and Explt. Psychiatry, 1969—, Jour. Behavioral Assessment, 1979-85, Jour. Behavioral Residential Treatment, 1983—, Jour. Psychopathology and Behavioral Assessment, 1985—, Schizophrenia Bull., 1971—; cons. editor Jour. Applied Behavior Analysis, 1966-77, 81—, Psychol. Bull., 1967—, Jour. Abnormal Psychology, 1970-72, 76—, Psychosomatic Medicine, 1971-77, Psychophysiology, 1971-77, Jour. Clin. and Cons. Psychology, 1972—, Archives Gen. Psychiatry, 1973-74, Behavior Therapy, 1976—, Profl. Psychologist, 1977-79, Hops. Community Psychiatry, 1980—, Biobehavioral Revs, 1980-84; Jour. Community Psychology, 1985, Am. Psychologist, 1983—, Brit. Jour. Clin. Psychology, 1985; contbr. articles to profl. jours. Served with USN, 1954-58. Recipient Creative Talent award Am. Inst. Research, 1964, Teaching award U. Ill., 1968, 75; NIMH fellow, 1963-64; research award Mental Health Assn., 1985. Fellow Am. Psychol. Assn. (corr. com. 1965-70, pres. sect. ill. div. 12, 1972-73, exec. com. div. 12, 1974-77, Disting. Scientist award sect. ill. div. 12, 1977); mem. Midwestern Psychol. Assn., Tex. Psychol. Assn., Houston Psychol. Assn., Assn. Advancement Psychology, Phi Beta Kappa, Chi Gamma Iota. Subject of NIMH science report monograph, 1981: Treating and Assessing the Chronically Mentally Ill: The Pioneering Research of Gordon L. Paul. Office: Dept Psychology Univ Houston University Park Houston TX 77004

PAUL, JAMES LARRY, teacher educator; b. Columbia, Tenn., Aug. 8, 1938; s. James Arthur and Margaret Elizabeth (Holloway) P.; children—Larry Scott, Margaret Gail. B.A., Scarritt Coll., 1960, M.A., 1961; M.A., Peabody Coll., 1962; Ed.D., Syracuse U., 1967. Lic. psychologist, N.C. Assoc. prof. U. N.C., Chapel Hill, 1969-75, chmn. spl. edn., 1977-82, acting dean edn., 1982-83, prof. edn., 1976—, vis. scholar Harvard U., 1984; cons. to univs. and fed. agys. on programs and tng. for profls. for working with handicapped. Author: (with Betty Epanchin) Educating Emotionally Disturbed Children, 1982; numerous others. Recipient Spl. Service award N.C. Council for Children with Behavior Disorders, 1981—. Mem. Internat. Acad. for Research in Learning Disabilities (v.p. 1981—), Council for Exceptional Children, N.C. Assn. for Emotionally Troubled (pres.), Phi Delta Kappa. Democrat. Methodist. Avocation: music. Home: 60 Hamilton Rd Chapel Hill NC 27514 Office: Sch of Edn Univ of NC 016 Peabody Hall 037A Chapel Hill NC 27514

PAUL, MAURICE M., U.S. district judge; b. 1932. B.A., U. Fla., 1954, LL.B., 1960. Instr. U. Fla. Coll. Law, 1960; assoc. Sanders, McEwan, Mims & MacDonald, Orlando, Fla., 1960-64; ptnr. Akerman, Senterfitt, Eidson, Mesmer & Robinson, Orlando, 1965-66; atty., Orlando, 1967; ptnr. Pitts, Eubanks, Ross & Paul, Orlando, 1968-69; atty., 1970-72; judge 9th Fla. Circuit Ct., 1973-82; judge U.S. Dist. Ct. for No. Fla., Tallahassee, 1982—. Address: 110 E Park Ave Tallahassee FL 32301*

PAUL, ROBERT, lawyer; b. N.Y.C., Nov. 22, 1931; s. Gregory and Sonia (Rijock) P.; B.A., N.Y. U., 1953; J.D., Columbia, 1958; m. Christa Holz, Apr. 6, 1975; 1 dau., Gina. Admitted to Fla. bar, 1958, N.Y. bar, 1959; ptnr. Paul, Landy Beiley, Harper & Morrison, P.A., Miami, 1964—; counsel Republic Nat. Bank Miami, 1967—. Past pres. Fla. Philharm., Inc., 1978—; trustee U. Miami. Mem. Am., N.Y., Fla., Inter-Am. bar assns., Greater Miami C. of C. (vice chmn.), French-Am. C. of C. of Miami (pres. 1986—). Home: 700 Alhambra Circle Coral Gables FL 33134 Office: 200 SE 1st St Miami FL 33131

PAUL, WALTER H. (WALT), JR., community college administrator; b. Shiner, Tex., Jan. 30, 1938; s. Walter H. and Harriet Edith (Phillips) P.; m. Margaret Ann Reeves, Feb. 6, 1965; children—Toni Michelle, Misty Rochelle, Sunny Janelle. B.S., Lamar U., 1960; M.Mus. Edn., VanderCook Coll. Music, 1965; Ed.D., East Tex. State U., 1974. Cert. tchr., Tex. Band dir. Bloomington High Sch., Tex., 1960-64, Brenham High Sch., Tex., 1964-67; band dir., instr. music theory and applied instruments, chmn. music dept., chmn. fine arts dept. Hill Jr. Coll., Hillsboro, Tex., 1967-72; asst. instr. East Tex. State U., Commerce, 1972-74; dean student services Temple Jr. Coll., Tex., 1974-81, v.p. instructional services, 1981—, chmn. various coms.; cons. student services div. Cooke County Community Coll., Gainesville, Tex., 1978; mem. reaffirmation com. So. Assn. Colls. and Schs., South Fla. Jr. Coll., Avon Park, 1981, Internat. Fine Arts Coll., Miami, Fla., 1983, mem. candidacy for accreditation com., Phillips Coll., Gulfport, Miss., 1985. Editor manual: Administration by Objectives, 1975-81; contbr. book rev. to publs.; speaker, panelist, moderator profl. confs., coordinator workshops. Bd. dirs. Central Tex. Orchestral Soc.; adv. com. Central Tex. Council Govts. Regional Alcoholism and Drug Abuse; bd. dirs. United Way, Temple, 1977, 78, 79, 80; exec. com. Temple Centennial Commn., 1980-82. Mem. North Central Tex. Coll. Student Personnel Assn., Tex. Jr. Coll. Tchrs. Assn. (state chmn. instrumental div. music sect. 1970-71, state chmn. music sect. 1971-72, state chmn. student affairs adminstrs. sect. 1977-78, 78-79), Tex. Assn. Community Coll. Chief Student Affairs Adminstrs. (founding pres. 1978-79), Tex. Assn. Coll. and Univ. Student Personnel Adminstrs. (legis. task force 1978-80, chmn. research commn. 1976-77), Jr. Coll. Student Personnel Assn. Tex. (bd. dirs. 1979-81), Nat. Council Student Devel. for Community and Jr. Colls., Southwest Assn. Student Personnel Adminstrs., Tex. Assn. Jr. and Community Coll. Instructional Adminstrs. (coms.), Tex. Jr. Coll. Athletic Conf. (pres. 1984—), Assn. Tex. Jr. Coll. Bd. Mems. and Adminstrs., Nat. Council Instructional Adminstrs., Phi Delta Kappa, Phi Mu Alpha Sinfonia, Kappa Kappa Psi, Temple C. of C. Clubs: Kiwanis (past pres.), Rotary. Avocations: music; tennis; golf; reading. Home: 3702 Cole Porter Dr Temple TX 76502 Office: Temple Jr Coll 2600 S First St Temple TX 76501

PAULETTE, MARY FLORENCE, oil company merchandiser; b. Levelland, Tex., Jan. 8, 1947; d. Willard Jerome and Mary Lucy (Shannon) P.; m. Allen Henry Scott, June 6, 1977 (div. 1982). B.A., U. Tex., 1969; postgrad. Tex. A&M U., 1979; grad. Mgmt. Inst., U. Ala., 1980. Supr. Tex. Dept. Human Resources, Houston, 1972-75, mgmt. tng. specialist, 1975-80; tng. specialist Pennzoil Co., Houston, 1980-83, retail merchandiser, 1983—; sales tng. cons. Mem. ops. com. YMCA, Houston, 1982—. Office: Pennzoil Company 700 Milam St Houston TX 77002

PAULEY, STANLEY FRANK, manufacturing company executive; b. Winnipeg, Man., Can., Sept. 19, 1927; s. Daniel and Anna (Tache) P.; came to U.S., 1954, naturalized, 1961; B.E.E., U. Man., 1949; m. Dorothy Ann Ruppel, Aug. 21, 1949; children—Katharine Ann, Lorna Jane. With Canadian Industries Ltd., Kingston, Ont., 1949-53, sr. engring. asst., 1952-53; controls designer Standard Machine and Tool Co. Ltd., Windsor, Ont., 1953-54; prodn. supt. E.R. Carpenter Co., Richmond, Va., 1954-57, pres., 1957-83, chmn. bd., chief exec. officer, 1983—, also dir.; dir. Carpenter Chem. Co., Carpenter Oil & Gas Co., Carpenter Insulation & Coatings Co., Carpenter-Jackson Ltd., Carpenter Insulation Co., Carpenter Packaging Co., Internat. Packaging Systems Inc., E.R. Carpenter Co. of Can. Ltd., Camino Réal Travel, Inc., Sovran Fin. Corp., Sovran Bank, Am. Filtrona Corp.; adv. dir. Allendale Ins. Co., Southeastern Growth Fund. Trustee, U. Richmond, Westminister-Canterbury Found., Va. Mus. Found. Republican. Presbyterian. Clubs: Country of Va., Commonwealth. Home: 314 St David's Ln Richmond VA 23221 Office: 5016 Monument Ave Richmond VA 23261

PAULIN, ANNE MEREDITH, medical supply company executive; b. Richmond, Va., Dec. 15, 1954; d. Lehan Bernard and Thelma Monroe (Sutton) Paulin. B.A. in Polit. Sci., Agnes Scott Coll., 1977. Ter. mgr. Kendall Co./Colgate Palmolive, Atlanta, 1979-81; cardiopulmonary systems specialist Baxter Travenol Labs., Atlanta, 1981-83; ter. mgr. Deseret/Warner Lambert, Atlanta, 1983—; pres., owner Hermelon, Atlanta, 1981—; cons. in field. Team leader Atlanta Ballet Guild, 1982—; mem. jr. com. Atlanta Symphony Orch., 1980—; bd. dirs. City Ctr. Dance Theatre, v.p., 1981-82; mem. High Mus. Art, 1973—, charter mem., 1982—, mem. young careers com., 1983—; mem. jr. com. Shepherd Spinal Ctr., 1983—; bd. dirs. Terpsichore, v.p., 1982. Charles A. Dana scholar, 1976. Mem. Nat. Assn. Female Execs., King and Queen Hist. Soc., Atlanta Ballet Assocs., Atlanta Ballet Soc., Alpha Sigma Beta (pres. 1976—). Roman Catholic. Contbr. articles to med. jours.

PAULSON, ALLEN EUGENE, aircraft manufacturing executive; b. Clinton, Ohio, Apr. 22, 1922; s. Harry Godfrey and Lillian (Rothert) P.; m. Irene Eddy Kastner (div.); children—Robert (dec.), Richard Allen, James Douglas, John Michael; m. Mary Lou Paulson (div.). Student, U. W.Va., 1941, Iowa State Tchrs. Coll., 1943; LL.D., Lynchburg Coll., 1983. Comml. pilot, FAA. Flight engr. Transworld Airlines, various locations, 1945-53; chmn., chief exec. officer, pres. Calif. Airmotive Corp., Burbank, 1951-70, Am. Jet Industries, Van Nuys, Calif., 1970-78, Gulfstream Aerospace Corp., Savannah, Ga., 1978—; dir. Trust Co. Bank of Savannah, Wheeling-Pitts. Steel Corp., Murray Chris-Craft, Inc., Ft. Lauderdale, Fla. Bd. dirs. Savannah Symphony Soc., 1981—, Telfair

Acad. Arts and Sci., Savannah, 1982—, Air Force Acad. Found., 1982—. Served with USAAF, 1943-45. Mem. Gen. Aircraft Mfg. Assn. (bd. dirs. 1978—), Soc. Exptl. Test Pilots (Doolittle Trophy 1982), Air Force Assn. (bd. dirs. 1981—), Nat. Aero. Assn. (bd. dirs. 1980—). Club: Quail Creek Country (Oklahoma City). Office: Gulfstream Aerospace Corp PO Box 2206 Savannah GA 31402*

PAULSON, MICHAEL ALBERT, petroleum geologist; b. Dallas, Feb. 6, 1950; s. John Albert and Jeanne Elizabeth (Kincaid) Tillery P.; m. Martha Louise Longmire, Feb. 8, 1985. B.A. in History, Tulane U., 1972; B.S. in Geosci., U. Tex.-Dallas, Richardson, 1982. Performer, mgr. The Bee's Knees, Dallas, 1975-80; geotech H & S Prodn., Inc., Dallas, 1980-82; geologist H & S Operating, Inc., Dallas, 1982-83; self-employed cons. geologist, Dallas, 1983—. Singer, producer, composer The Bee's Knees. Mem. Am. Assn. Petroleum Geologists (jr.). Avocations: running; reading; skiing. Home: 6427 Lontos St Dallas TX 75214 Office: 6440 N Central Expressway Suite 619 Dallas TX 75206

PAULY, JOHN EDWARD, anatomist, university official, biomedical scientist, chronobiologist, editor; b. Elgin, Ill., Sept. 17, 1927; s. Edward John and Gladys Bell (Myhre) P.; m. Margaret M. Oberle, Sept. 3, 1949; children—Stephen John, Susan Elizabeth, Kathleen Ann, Mark Edward. B.S., Northwestern U., Evanston, Ill., 1950; M.S., Loyola U., Chgo., 1952, Ph.D. in Anatomy, 1955. Research asst. dept. anatomy Chgo. Med. Sch., 1952-54, research instr., 1954-55, instr. gross anatomy, 1955-57, assoc., 1957-59, asst. prof., 1959-63, asst. to pres., 1960-62; assoc. prof. anatomy Tulane U. Sch. Medicine, New Orleans, 1963-67; prof. and chmn. dept. anatomy U. Ark. for Med. Scis., Little Rock, 1967-83, prof., chmn. dept. physiology and biophysics, 1978-80, vice chancellor acad. affairs and sponsored research, assoc. dean grad. sch., 1983—. Served with USN, 1945-47. Decorated Meritorious Citation; recipient Bronze award Ill. State Med. Soc., 1959; Cert. of Merit AMA, 1953, 59; Lederle Med. Faculty award, 1966. Fellow AAAS; hon. mem. Consejo Nacional de Profesores de Ciencias Morphologicas; mem. Am. Assn. Anatomists (sec.-treas. 1972-80, pres. 1982-83), So. Soc. Anatomists (pres. 1971-72), Assn. Anatomy Chmn. (sec.-treas. 1969-71), Internat. Soc. Chronobiology, Internat. Soc. Electrophysiol. Kinesiology, Am. Physiol. Soc., Internat. Soc. Steriology. Roman Catholic. Author: (with Elias) Human Microanatomy, 1960, 62; (with Elias and Burns) Histology and Human Microanatomy, 1978; editor: (with Scheving and Halberg) Chronobiology, 1974; (with von Mayersbach and Scheving) Biological Rhythms in Structure and Function, 1981; Anatonical News, 1972-80; Proceedings of the American Association of Anatomists, 1972-80; Directory of Departments of Anatomy in the United States and Canada, 1975, 79; Am. Jour. Anatomy, 1980—; co-mng. editor: Advances in Anatomy, Embryology and Cell Biology, 1980—; adv. editorial bd. Internat. Jour. Chronobiology, 1973-83; contbr. articles to profl. jours. Home: 11 Hearthside Dr Little Rock AR 72207 Office: Office of Vice Chancellor U Ark Med Scis 4301 W Markham St Little Rock AR 72205

PAVIA-VILLAMIL, ANTONIO, physician, medical educator; b. Santurce, P.R., Oct. 22, 1927; s. Manuel Pavia-Fernandez and Josefina Villamil de Pavia; B.S., Georgetown U., 1949; M.D., Loyola U., Chgo., 1954; m. Dec. 21, 1953; children—Antonio, Priscilla, Gerardo, Ricardo. Intern, Mercy Hosp., Chgo., 1954-55; resident Mercy Hosp. and Boston City Hosp., 1955-58; med. dir., chief of medicine Hospital Pavia, Santurce, P.R., 1964-83, pres. bd. dirs., 1964-85; bd. dirs. Escuela de Medicina del Caribe de Cayey, 1976-81; mem. faculty Escuela de Medicina del Caribe; dir. Casino de P.R., First Fed. Savs. Bank of P.R. Mem. ACP, Am. Coll. Cardiology, Am. Geriatric Soc., Internat. Coll. Law and Sci., AMA, P.R. Med. Assn. (pres. La Fundación Médica de P.R. 1981). Roman Catholic. Club: Dorado Beach Golf. Contbr. article to profl. jour. Home: 2407 Granada St Punta Las Marias Santurce PR 00913 Office: Hospital Pavia Box 11137 Santurce PR 00910

PAVON, VICTOR MANUEL, consulting structural engineer; b. P. Negras, Coahuila, Mexico, June 12, 1932; s. Victor Manuel and Julia (Rodriguez) Pavon Abreu; m. Maya Alfaro, Mar. 5, 1960; children—Victor Manuel, Mauricio, Maria-del Mar. Civil Engr., U. Mexico, 1959, M.Enging., 1970. Dir., PAR, Engrs. & Architects, Mexico City, 1960-74; assoc. prof. U. Mexico, Mexico City, 1968-71; prof. U. Anahuac, Mexico City, 1978, Inst. Tech. de Monterrey Atizapan, 1978-81; prin. VM Pavon, Cons. Engrs. Cd. Satelite, Edo. de Mexico, 1974—; cons. Mexican Inst. Cement and Concrete, 1972—, Mexico City Subway Design, ISTME, 1984. Author: (with Horacio Ramirez) Design Criteria for Concrete Structures, 1975; Structural Design of Concrete Building, 1977. Contbr. articles to profl. jours. Mem. ASCE, Am. Concrete Inst., Earthquake Enging. Research Inst., Mexican Soc. Seismic Enging., Nat. Acad. Enging. Mexico. Home: Bosque de Arces 59 Mexico City DF Mexico 05120 Office: VM Pavon Cons Engrs PO Box 74A Ciudad Satelite Estado de Mexico Mexico 53100

PAWLOWSKI, ROBERT STANLEY, educator literature; b. Perham, Minn., June 26, 1930; s. Joseph Bernard and Victoria Martha (Ceynowa) P.; m. Margaret Elaine Changos, Aug. 13, 1960; children—Robert Stanley Jr., Vincent Roderick. B.A., B.S., Moorhead State U., 1953; M.A., U. Iowa, 1964; Ph.D., U. Denver, 1968. Dir. writing, prof. English U. Denver, 1968-77; chmn. dept., prof. English U. So. Miss., Hattiesburg, 1977-80; provost grad. sch. Tex. Woman's U., Denton, 1980-83; chmn. dept. English, prof. English U. South Fla., Tampa, 1983—. Author: Versheets II, 1971, Ceremonies for Today, 1972, University of Denver Prize Poems, 1973, Seven Sacraments, 1982. Served with AUS, 1954-56. Home: 1711 Woodhaven Dr Brandon FL 33511 Office: Univ South Fla Dept English 4202 Fowler Ave Tampa FL 33620

PAXSON, CHARLES STANLEY, III, dentist; b. Bryn Mawr, Pa., May 25, 1945; s. Charles S. and Katherine T. (Thompson) P.; m. Sibyl Woosley, Dec. 5, 1970; 1 child, Brian S. B.S., U. Va., Fredericksburg, 1977; D.D.S., Temple U., 1981. Pvt. practice dentistry, Gaffney, S.C., 1981—; mem. staff Cherokee County Meml. Hosp., Gaffney, 1981—. Contbr. articles on dentistry for children to profl. jours. Regional rep. Am. Cancer Soc., Columbia, S.C., 1984—; bd. dirs. Boys' Club Cherokee County, 1982—, Cherokee council Boy Scouts Am., 1983—. Served with U.S. Army, 1966-69. Am. Cancer Soc. fellow Sloan Kettering Cancer Ctr., 1980. Mem. Acad. Gen. Dentistry, ADA, Acad. Reconstructive Dentistry, Am. Soc. Dentistry for Children, Acad. Implant Dentistry, Xi Xsi Phi. Avocations: cooking; music; magic. Home: 114 Hillcrest Dr Gaffney SC 29340 Office: 909 N Limestone St Gaffney SC 29340

PAXTON, JOHN WESLEY, electronics company executive; b. Camden, N.J., Jan. 9, 1937; s. John Irving and Francis Rose (Jones) P.; m. Janet Rose Croteau, Nov. 4, 1975; children—David R., William A., John Wesley, Jacqueline R., Thomas W., Scott A. B.S., NYU, 1970; postgrad. in mfg. tech. U. Mich., 1976; postgrad. Rivier Coll., 1979, Calif. Western U., 1980. Registered profl. engr., Calif. With RCA, Camden, Hightstown, N.J. and Burlington, Mass., 1959-75, mgr. quality assurance, 1972-75; dir. mfg. Kollsman Instrument Co. div. Sun Chem. Corp., Merrimack, N.H., 1975-80; dir., plant mgr. Ocala ops. Martin Marietta Corp. (Fla.), 1980-83, dir. product ops., Orlando, Fla., 1983—. Served with USN, 1955-59. Mem. Nat. Soc. Profl. Engrs., Am. Soc. Quality Control, Am. Soc. Mfg. Engrs. Republican. Presbyterian. Lodges: Lions, Masons.

PAYNE, ARNOLD PERSHING J., educator; b. Williamsburg, Ky.; s. Joseph S. McGuire and Sallie Kidd (Wilder) P.; B.S. in Phys. Edn., Math., U. Tex., Austin, 1948, M.Ed. in Phys. Edn., Ednl. Adminstrn., 1950; Ph.D. in Ednl. Adminstrn., Ednl. Psychology, Curriculum, Tex. A and M U., 1973; m. Beverly Donahoe Greer. Prin., Aldine Jr. High Sch., Houston, 1954-65; grad. asst. Tex. Agrl. and Mech. U., Coll. Sta., 1969-70; curriculum coordinator Windham (Tex.) Schs., 1970-71; asst. supt., 1976-83, adminstrv. asst., curriculum Gonzales (Tex.) Ind. Sch. Dist., 1973—; ednl. cons., 1983—; lectr. Stephen F. Austin State U., Nacogdoches, Tex., 1984—. Chmn. edn. com. Don Yarborough campaign for gov., 1967-68; chmn. Cystic Fibrosis Bike-A-Thon, 1981. Mem. Gonzales Tchrs. Assn. (pres. 1978-79), Tex. Assn. Sch. Adminstrs., Tex. State Tchrs. Assn., NEA, PTA, Phi Delta Kappa. Cert. in gen. elementary, secondary edn., supervision, sch. adminstrn., Tex. Contbr. articles to profl. jours. Author: Education is an Intrinsic Process, 1980; co-author: Student Involvement in Policy Making, 1974. Home: 1616 Glenbrook Dr Nacogdoches TX 75961 Office: PO Box 2764 Nacogdoches TX 75963

PAYNE, BARBARA PITTARD, sociologist, educator; b. Atlanta, Dec. 25, 1919; d. Thomas Pierce and Elizabeth Myrick (Edmondson) Brinsfield; m. Marion Carter Pittard, June 14, 1967 (div. Nov. 1967); children—Barbara Pittard Styles, Marion Tarlton Pittard; m. Raymond Payne, July 30, 1970 (dec.). B.A., Oglethorpe U., 1952; M.A., Emory U., 1955, Ph.D., 1963. From asst. prof. to assoc. prof. Ga. State U., Atlanta, 1963-71, prof. sociology, dir. Gerontology Ctr., 1972—; mem. Ga. Council on Aging, 1978—. Contbr. articles, chpts. to profl. publs. Mem. stroke subcom. Am. Heart Assn.; trustee St. Paul's Sem., Kansas City, Mo.; bd. dirs. Wesley Homes, Inc., Dunwoody United Methodist Ch.; dir. adult edn. North Ga. Conf. United Meth. Ch., 1953-59. Fellow Gerontol. Soc. Am.; mem. Assn. for Gerontology in Higher Edn. (pres. 1985-86), So. Gerontol. Soc. (first pres. 1980-82), Am. Sociol. Assn., So. Sociol. Soc., World Future Soc., Am. Assn. Ret. Persons, Western Gerontol. Soc., Soc. for Sci. Study Religion. Office: Ga State U Gerontology Ctr University Plaza Atlanta GA 30303

PAYNE, DAVID SETH, clergyman, accountant; b. Stowe Twp., Pa., Apr. 3, 1934; s. Seth Harry and Eva Retta (Over) P.; m. Nancy Judith Worsnop, July 18, 1959; children—David Seth II, Cynthia E. Payne Van Pelt, Donald J. Student Robert Morris Bus. Sch., 1954-56, 59-60; A.A., Nazarene Bible Coll., 1973; B.A., Mid-Am. Nazarene Coll., 1975; M.A.R., Asbury Theol. Sem., 1978; postgrad. Denver Sem., 1979—. C.P.A., Pa., Colo.; ordained to ministry Nazarene Ch., 1979. Staff acct. various pub. acctg. cos., Pitts. and Pensacola, Fla., 1961-66; mgr. budgets and measurements Escambia Chem. Corp., Pensacola, 1966-68, parent co. Ebasco Industries, N.Y.C., 1968-69; internal auditor Air Products & Chem. Corp., Allentown, Pa., 1969; pub. acct., Pensacola, 1969-70, Lexington, Ky., 1976-78; sr. acct. Nygren Sears and Co., C.P.A.s, Colorado Springs, Colo., 1970-73, 80-82, Fred Marting, C.P.A., Colorado Springs, 1979; instr. acctg. Lexington Tech. Inst., 1974-75; bus. office mgr. Mid-Am. Nazarene Coll., Olathe, Kans., 1973-74; pastor First Ch. of Nazarene, Nicholasville, Ky., 1976-78, Black Forest Ch. of Nazarene, Colorado Springs, 1978-82, Forestdale Ch. of Nazarene, Birmingham, Ala., 1982—; acct. Nazarene Bible Coll., Colorado Springs, 1978-79, instr. Bible, fall 1979-80; aux. chaplain U. Ala. Hosps., Birmingham, 1982-83; sec. standing ways and means com. Ala. North dist. Ch. of Nazarene, 1982-83, chmn., 1983—, mem. Ala. North dist. bd. orders and relations, 1983-84, mem. Ala. North Dist. Bd. Ministerial Studies, 1983-84. Bd. dirs. Ala. Citizens Action Program, 1983—; mem. textbook com., Jefferson County, Ala., 1983. Served with USN, 1956-59. Mem. Am. Inst. C.P.A.s, Am. Sch. Oriental Research, Bibl. Archaeology Soc., Wesleyan Theol. Soc., Hon. Order Ky. Cols. Republican. Office: 361 Foust Ct Birmingham AL 35214

PAYNE, EUGENE EDGAR, university administrator; b. San Antonio, Aug. 9, 1942; s. Eugene Edgar and Louise (Speer) P.; m. Karen S. James, June 10, 1978; children—Kelly Lynn, Katherine Louise, Mary Patricia, Kerry Erin, Kimberley Ann, Thomas Julius. B.S., Tex. A&M U., 1964, M.S., 1965; Ph.D. (research fellow 1968-70), U. Okla., 1970. Mgmt. cons. E.I. DuPont de Nemours Co., Del., 1965-68; dir. mgmt. info. systems, spl. cons. Electronic Data Systems Corp., Dallas, 1970-71; dir. planning and mgmt. systems U. Tex., Dallas, 1971-74; v.p. fin. and mgmt. S.W. Tex. State U., San Marcos, 1974-81; v.p. fin. and adminstrn. Tex. Tech. U., Tex. Tech. Health Ctr., Lubbock, 1981-85; treas. Tex. Tech. U. Found.; cons. in field. Contbr. articles to profl. jours. Active vestry, fin. com. St. Christopher's Episc. Ch.; trustee All Saints Episc. Sch., Lubbock, Episc. Sem. of Southwest, Austin, Tex. NDEA fellow, 1969. Mem. Am. Inst. Indsl. Engrs., Inst. Mgmt. Scis., Ops. Research Soc. Am., Assn. Computing Machinery, Assn. Instl. Research, Soc. Coll. and Univ. Planning, Nat. Assn. Coll. and Univ. Bus. Officers. Club: Rotary. Home: 2309 56th Lubbock TX 79412 Office: Tex Tech U PO Box 4469 Lubbock TX 79409

PAYNE, FRED J., physician; b. Grand Forks, N.D., Oct. 14, 1922; s. Fred J. and Olive (Johnson) P.; student U. N.D., 1940-42; B.S., U. Pitts., 1948, M.D., 1949; M.P.H., U. Calif., Berkeley, 1958; m. Dorothy J. Peck, Dec. 20, 1948; children—Chris Ann Payne Graebner, Roy S., William F., Thomas A. Intern, St. Joseph's Hosp., Pitts., 1949-50; resident Charity Hosp., New Orleans, 1952-53; med. epidemiologist Center Disease Control, Atlanta, 1953-60; prof. tropical medicine La. State U. Med. Center, New Orleans, 1961-66; dir. La. State U. Internat. Ctr. Med. Research and Tng., San Jose, Costa Rica, 1963-66; epidemiologist Nat. Nutrition Survey (10 state) Bethesda, Md., 1967-68; chief public health professions br. NIH, Bethesda, 1971-74, med. officer, sr. research epidemiologist Nat. Inst. Allergy and Infectious Diseases, 1974-78; asst. health dir. Fairfax County (Va.) Health Dept., 1978—; clin. prof. La. State U., 1966-80; cons. NIH, 1979-81; leader WHO diarrheal disease adv. team, 1960. Served with AUS, 1942-46, 49-52. Decorated Combat Medic Badge. Diplomate Am. Bd. Preventive Medicine. Fellow Am. Coll. Preventive Medicine, Am. Coll. Epidemiology; mem. Am. Public Health Assn., AMA, Am. Soc. Microbiology, AAAS, Internat. Epidemiology Assn., Soc. Epidemiologic Research, USPHS Commd. Officers Assn., Sigma Xi. Contbr. articles to profl. jours. Home: 2945 Fort Lee St Herndon VA 22070 Office: 4080 Chain Bridge Rd Fairfax VA 22030

PAYNE, GENE-PAUL, nursing administrator, nurse, consultant; b. Charleston, W.Va., Apr. 11, 1942; s. Donald Simpson and Mollie Rae (Lohman) P.; m. Nancy Faye Pittman, Jan. 15, 1966; children—Joseph Edward, Marthae Gayle. A.S. in Biology, Beckley Coll., 1967; A.S. in Nursing, Salem Coll., 1972; B.S. in Nursing, SUNY-Albany, 1985; Ph.D. cand., Columbia Pacific U., 1985. Staff nurse United Hosp. Ctr., Clarksburg, W.Va., 1975-77; nurse practitioner, pvt. practice, contract services Harrison County Health Dept., Clarksburg, 1977-79; adminstrv. supr. Centro Asturiano Hosp., Tampa, Fla., 1979-81, supr. critical care dept., 1981-84; dir. nursing services, 1984—; owner, pres. Critical Care Emergency Dept. Edn. Services, Tampa, 1981—; paramedic instr. Dept. Health, Clarksburg, 1978; instr. PRN Inc., Tampa, 1981; cons. Tampa Heart Inst., 1981—; lectr. in field, 1981-85. Mem. Am. Assn. Critical Care Nurses (founder, pres. Suncoast chpt. 1981-84). Emergency Nurses Assn., Am. Nurses Assn., Soc. Critical Care Medicine, Am. Assn. Nurse Execs. Lodges: York and Scottish Rite, Shriner, Masons. Office: Centro Asturiano Hosp 1302 21st Ave Tampa FL 33605

PAYNE, G(EORGE) FREDERICK, college development officer; b. Summerville, S.C., Jan. 29, 1941; s. Fred N. and Lota (Griffith) P.; m. Kay Martin, June 23, 1963; children—John F., Mark C., Janet E. Student Ga. Inst. Tech., 1959-60, U.S. Naval Acad., 1960-62; B.S., U. S.C., 1963, M.A., 1966; M.R.E., Luth. Theol. Sem., 1968; postgrad. U. Ga., 1969-71. From instr. to asst. prof. Ga. So. Coll., Statesboro, 1966-78; dir. admission Brewton-Parker Coll., Mt. Vernon, Ga., 1978-80; v.p. for devel. North Greenville Coll., Tigerville, S.C., 1980—; dir. various grants. Author: An Introduction to the Principles of Geography: Facts, Skills, Concepts, and Models, 1973; also articles. Active Leadership Greer, S.C., 1980-81, regent, 1982-84; active AACTion Consortium, 1980-82, Leadership Greenville, S.C., 1982-83; bd. dirs. Greenville County unit Am. Cancer Soc., 1985—. Served with USN, 1960-62. Recipient Disting. Service award Brewton-Parker Coll., 1980. Mem. Council for Advancement and Support Edn., Greater Greer C. of C. (bd. dirs. 1981-84). Baptist. Club: Commerce (Greenville). Avocation: reading. Home: Route 1 Box 274 Blackwell Rd Travelers Rest SC 29690 Office: North Greenville Coll Hwy 253 and 414 Tigerville SC 29688

PAYNE, JAMES FRANKLIN, educator biology, university administrator; b. Athens, Ala., Mar. 27, 1941; s. Spafford O. and Mildred (Younger) P.; m. Marcella Ruth Ryan, June 2, 1963; children—Christopher R., Polly A. B.S., U. Tenn.-Martin, 1962; M.S., Memphis State U., 1965; Ph.D., Miss. State U., 1968. Asst. prof. biology Memphis State U., 1968-72, assoc. prof. biology, 1972-77, assoc. dean, 1977-80, acting dean, 1980-81, prof., chmn. dept. biology, 1981—. Author: Zoology Lab Studies also articles. Scoutmaster Boy Scouts Am., Memphis, 1975; ruling elder Presby. Ch., Memphis, 1978-81. Recipient Nat. Sci. Found. Traineeship award Miss. State U., 1967; Disting. Teaching award Memphis State U., 1972. Mem. Assn. Southeastern Biologists, Am. Soc. Zoologists, AAAS, Internat. Assn. Astacologists (sec./treas. 1981-84, pres.-elect 1984-86), Crustacian Soc. Avocations: reading; gardening. Office: Memphis State Univ Dept Biology Memphis TN 38152

PAYNE, JUANITA BRINKLEY, astrologer, psychic; b. Shady Valley, Tenn., Jan. 12, 1939; d. Floyd Cletis and Thelma Ruth (Farris) Brinkley; B.A., U. Tenn., 1960; M.S., U. Tenn., Knoxville, 1964; postgrad. Middle Tenn. State U., 1978—; m. Barnett Payne, Sept. 3, 1960; children—Michael, Rachael, Elizabeth, Valerie. Sec. to chmn. Dept. English, Middle Tenn. State U., Murfreesboro, 1971-75, exec. sec. Sch. Bus., 1975-78; astrologer, co-dir. Tenn. Life Counseling Services, Murfreesboro, 1980—; astrological cons. for area corps.; parapsychology instr., area schs.; lectr. in field. Pres., Middle Tenn. State U. Adminstrv. Staff Orgn., 1978, chmn. campus gubnatorial campaign for adminstrv. staff personnel, 1978-79. Cert. profl. Sec., 1978; certified profl. astrologer, 1975; Nat. Merit scholar, 1957-58. Mem. AAUW, Nat. Assn. Female Execs., Am. Astrological Assn., Internat. Assn. Entrepreneurs, Exec. Women Internat., Assn. for Research and Enlightment, Nat. Assn. Secs. Internat. Home: 413 Double Springs Rd Murfreesboro TN 37130 Office: Nissan Motor Mfg Corp USA Smyrna TN 37167

PAYNE, MARTHA LEE HARVEY, interior designer; b. Oakland, Calif., Sept. 29, 1944; d. Ira Omar and Dorothy (Page) Harvey; children—Gregory Thomas, Alysha Carol, David Lee Harvey. B.A., So. Meth. U., 1966; postgrad. UCLA, 1975. Retail trianee Neiman-Marcus, Dallas, 1964-65; interior designer Jan Grierson, Austin, Tex., 1970; owner, operator Inside-Out Interior Design, Pacific Palisades, Calif., 1974-81; fabric buyer, furniture designer Elite Upholstery Co., City of Industry, Calif., 1975; West Coast area mgr. decorative fabrics Milliken & Co., Los Angeles, 1976-78; mgr. Calif. ter. Design Resources, Los Angeles, 1978-80; account exec. Pindler & Pindler, Los Angeles, 1980-81; nat. account mgr. Coral of Chgo., 1981-82; western regional mgr. Computer Roomers, Dallas, 1982-84; owner Contract Connection, Dallas, 1984—. Mem. fund-raising com. YMCA, 1975-76, football coach YMCA, 1975-79, bd. dirs., 1981. Mem. Am. Soc. Interior Designers (West Coast student nat. v.p. 1976), S.W. Furniture Mfrs. Assn., Fabric Club So. Calif., So. Meth. U. Alumni Assn. Republican. Home: 10 Heritage Ct Roanoke TX 76262

PAYNE, MICHAEL LEWIS, pharmacist, computer and business consultant; b. Florence, S.C., May 11, 1953; s. John Alford Payne and Dorothy Brunson (Lewis) Payne Owen; m. Kathy Sue Youngblood, June 26, 1976; 1 child, Michael Chase. B.S. in Chemistry, Francis Marion Coll., 1974; B.S. in Pharmacy, U. S.C., 1976; M.B.A., 1985. Registered pharmacist, S.C. Congl. intern, Washington, 1967-70; pharmacy researcher U. S.C., Columbia, 1974-76; pharmacist Revco Drug stores, Florence, 1976-83; owner, operator Advanced Software Products, Florence, 1983-84; pharmacist Rite Aid, Darlington, S.C., 1984-85; prin. Advanced Software, Florence, 1980—; mem. bd. dirs., auditor Ocean Bridge Cond. Assn., Myrtle Beach, S.C., 1985-87. Co-author computer inventory program; author payroll program. Mem. S.C. Pharm. Assn., Pee Dee Pharm. Assn., Nat. Assn. Retail Druggist, U. S.C. M.B.A. Assn. Republican. Baptist. Club: Country (Florence). Avocations: golf; sailing; fishing; hunting. Home: 3658 Breckridge Circle N Florence SC 29501 Office: Rite Aid Pearl St Darlington SC 29532

PAYNE, PAMELA SUE, safety executive; b. Clarksburg, W.Va., Aug. 23, 1944; d. Louis Joseph and Pauline Ramona (Gerard) P. B.S. in Dental Hygiene, West Liberty State U., 1967; B.S. in Occupational Safety and Health, Salem Coll., 1982; M.S. in Safety Mgmt., W.Va. U., 1986. Dental hygienist, Clarksburg, W.Va., 1967-80; draftsman Alamco, Inc., Clarksburg, 1978-80, 80-83, draftsman safety trainer, 1982-83, safety rep., 1983; head safety dept., 1983-85; safety dir. Louie Glass Co., Inc., Weston, W.Va., 1985-86; with Consol. Gas Tranmission Corp., Clarksburg, 1986—. Bd. dirs. W.Va. Safety Council, Charleston, 1984—, v.p. pub. relations, 1984—, 1st v.p., 1985—, pres. elect, 1986. Co-chmn. Gov.'s Conf. Com., 1985, chmn., 1986. Mem. Am. Soc. Safety Engrs. (treas. 1984—, sec. 1985-86), Ind. Oil and Gas Assn. (safety com. 1983—), Chi Omega. Democrat. Roman Catholic. Avocations: golf; tennis; music; water and snow skiing. Office: Consol Gas Tranmission Corp 445 W Main St Clarksburg WV 26301

PAYNE, PATRICIA HOLMES, early childhood educator, consultant; b. Jacksonville, Fla., Oct. 31, 1946; d. Ancel Dudley and Katherine B. (Lee) Holmes; m. Michael Finley Payne, Feb. 24, 1980; 1 son by previous marriage, Joshua Carl. B.S., Jacksonville U., 1968; M.A., Appalachian State U., 1972; Ed.D., U. Ga., 1975. Asst. tchr. Learning to Learn Sch., Jacksonville, 1967-68, tchr., 1968-69; elem. sch. tchr. Jacksonville Country Day Sch., 1969-72; research asst. U. Ga., Athens, 1972-74; faculty mem. Tex. Woman's U., Denton, 1974—, assoc. prof. early childhood edn., 1981—, mem. funding council, 1978-83; cons. Peppermint Pl., WFAA-TV, Dallas, 1975-78; ednl. cons. Tex. Instruments, Inc., Dallas, 1979; mem. Denton Tchr. Ctr., 1981—; mem. adv. com. on early childhood edn. Edn. Service Ctr., Fort Worth, 1977-78. Author: Principles and Practices of Teaching Young Children, 1977; On Teaching Children, Vol. 1, 1977, Vol. 2, 1981; Young Children: Their Growth and Education, 1983; contbr. sects. to books, ency., articles in field to profl. jours. Active N.Tex. Area Art League, 1982-84. Instl. research grantee Tex. Women's U., 1974-77, 78-80. Mem. Fedn. N. Tex. Area Univs. (early childhood adv. council 1974—, co-chmn. symposia on early childhood adv. com. 1981-82), Assn. for Childhood Edn. Internat. (faculty advisor univ. student br. 1975—, mem. internat. com. on infancy 1977-80), Tex. Assn. for Childhood Edn. (co-dir. 1977 study conf., state student branch coordinator 1977-79), Denton Assn. for Edn. Young Children (membership chmn. 1975-76, constrn. chmn. 1976-79, treas. 1979-80), Nat. Assn. for Edn. Young Children, So. Assn. on Children Under Six, Tex. Assn. for Edn. Young Children, Tex. Assn. Coll. Tchrs., Tex. Computer Edn. Assn., Phi Delta Kappa. Presbyterian. Home: 3704 Cooper Branch W Denton TX 76201 Office: Dept Curriculum and Instrn Tex Woman's U PO Box 23029 Denton TX 76204

PAYNE, TYSON ELLIOTT, JR., insurance company executive; b. Dallas, May 25, 1927; s. Tyson Elliott and Winnie Claris (Denman) P.; B.J., U. Tex., 1949; m. Billie Jane Spears, Aug. 28, 1948; children—David Tyson, Sally Jane. C.L.U.; chartered fin. cons., Sports editor Lufkin (Tex.) News, 1949-51; sports editor Tyler (Tex.) Courier Times, 1951-53; with Am. Nat. Ins. Co., Galveston, Tex., 1953—, v.p. health ins. ops., St. Louis, 1965-70, v.p. mktg., Galveston, 1970—. Pres. Galveston Bay C.L.U.s. (pres. 1983-84), Lufkin Jr. C. of C., 1950, Jr. C. of C., Tyler, 1954. Served with USNR, 1945-46. Presbyterian (elder). Home: 2318 Carriage Lane La Marque TX 77568 Office: 1 Moody Plaza Galveston TX 77550

PAYNE, VIRON ERNEST, SR., computer service company executive; b. Corsicanna, Tex., Aug. 14, 1918; s. William Rufus and Aletha (Hocker) P.; B.S., Tex. A&M U., 1941; postgrad. U. Ala., 1962-63; m. Willodean Davis, Aug. 11, 1957; children—William E., Barry D., Viron Ernest. TV technician RCA, Hollywood, Calif., 1948-49; self-employed mfr. TV antennas, Los Angeles, 1949-50; field engr. with USAF, Philco Corp., Guam, Korea and U.S.A., 1950-54; project engr. John I. Thompson & Co., Key West, Fla., 1954-55; project engr. Naval Ordnance Unit, Key West, 1955-56, chief analysis div., 1956-62; electronic engr. Future Missile Systems div., Redstone Arsenal, Ala., 1962-63; aerospace mgr., tech. staff to dir. tech. support Kennedy Space Center, Fla., 1963-69; pres. Viron E. Payne & Co., Inc., Merritt Island, Fla., 1955—; dir. Spaceport Flyers, Inc., Merritt Island, 1964-69. Bd. dirs. N. Merritt Island Little League, 1973-74, sec., 1974. Served to 1st lt. USAF, 1941-48. Registered investment adviser. Mem. SAR, Mensa, Brevard Geneal. Soc. (pres. 1976-78). Republican. Mem. Ch. of Christ. Contbr. articles to profl. publs.; author/pub.: Genealogies of the Hocker-Hawker Families of the U.S., 1984. Patentee in field. Address: 200 Juniper Ave Merritt Island FL 32953

PAYNE, WILLIAM EDWARD, exploration geophysicist; b. Kansas City, Mo., Aug. 6, 1932; s. Reed and LaVena (Wilson) P.; m. George Ann Everline, Dec. 7, 1952; children—Deborah Ann, Michael Reed. B.A. in Geology, Tex. Tech U., 1954. Sr. exploration geophysicist Exxon Co. U.S.A., Midland, Tex., 1954-81; dir. geophysics, no. region Kerr-McGee Corp., Oklahoma City, 1981—. Mem. Soc. Exploration Geophysicists, Am. Assn. Petroleum Geologists. Republican. Avocations: golf; travel. Home: 11208 Leaning Elm Oklahoma City OK 73120 Office: Kerr-McGee Corp PO Box 25861 Oklahoma City OK 73125

PAYNTER, VESTA LUCAS, pharmacist; b. Aiken County, S.C., May 29, 1922; d. James Redmond and Annie Lurline (Stroman) Lucas; m. Maurice Alden Paynter, Dec. 23, 1945 (dec. 1971); children—Sharon Lucinda, Maurice A. Jr., Doyle Gregg. B.S. in Pharmacy, U. S.C., 1943. Lic. pharmacist. Owner, pharmacist Cayce Drug Store, S.C., 1944-52, Dutch Fork Drug Store, Columbia, S.C., 1955-60, The Drug Ctr., Cayce, 1963-81; pharmacist Lane-Rexall, Columbia, 1952-55; dist. pharmacist S.C. Dept. Health and Environ. Control, Columbia, 1983—. Named Preceptor of Yr., Syntex Co., student body U. S.C., 1981. Fellow, 5th Dist. Pharm. Assn., S.C. Pharm. Assn., S.C. Pub. Health Assn., Alpha Epsilon Delta; mem. China, India, Burma VA Assn., 14th Air Force Assn. Baptist. Lodges: Order of Eastern Star, Order of Amaranth Sinclair, White Shrine of Jerusalem, Palmetto Shrine. Avocations: travel; tennis; golf; art. Home: 2351 Vine St Cayce SC 29033 Office: East Midlands Health Dept 1221 Gregg St Columbia SC 29201

PAYTON, BENJAMIN FRANKLIN, college president; b. Orangeburg, S.C., Dec. 27, 1932; s. Leroy Ralph and Sarah (Mack) P.; B.A., S.C. State Coll., 1955; B.D. (Danforth grad. fellow 1955-63), Harvard, 1958; M.A., Columbia, 1960; Ph.D., Yale, 1963; LL.D., Eastern Mich. U., 1972; L.H.D., Benedict Coll., 1972; Litt.D., Morgan State U., 1974; m. Thelma Louise Plane, Nov. 28, 1959;

children—Mark Steven, Deborah Elizabeth. Asst. prof. sociology of religion and social ethics Howard U., Washington, also dir. Community Research-Service Project, 1963-65; dir. Office of Ch. and Race, Protestant Council, N.Y.C., 1965-66; exec. dir. dept. social justice and Commn. on Religion and Race, Nat. Council Chs. of Christ in U.S.A., 1966-67; pres. Benedict Coll., Columbia, S.C., 1967-72; program officer higher edn. and research Ford Found., 1972-81; pres. Tuskegee (Ala.) Inst., 1981—. Mem. vis. com. bd. overseers Harvard; mem. nat. rev. bd. Center for Cultural and Tech. Exchange between U.S. and Asia. Bd. dirs. United Negro Coll. Fund, Liberty Corp. Recipient Billings prize Harvard, 1957; named South Carolinian of Year by statewide TV-Radio, 1972. Mem. Am. Soc. Scholars, Am. Sociol. Assn., Soc. for Religion in Higher Edn. (dir.), N.A.A.C.P., Alpha Phi Alpha, Alpha Kappa Mu. Author: (with Dr. Seymour Melman) A Strategy for the Next Stage in Civil Rights: Metropolitan-Rural Development for Equal Opportunity, 1966. Office: Office of Pres Tuskegee Inst Tuskegee AL 36088*

PAYTON, CALVIN WORTH, ophthalmologist; b. Lethbridge, Alta., Can., Sept. 28, 1919; came to U.S., 1925; s. Franklin Smith and Lona Odessa (Still) P.; m. Bessie Joyce Ross, Aug. 26, 1950; children—Charlotte, Rene, Sandra, Susan, Sheryl, Calvin. A.B., U. Kans., 1940; M.D., 1943; postgrad. U. Pa., 1947-48, U. Tex.-Galveston, 1949-50. Diplomate Am. Bd. Ophthalmology. Intern, Grasslands Hosp., Valhalla, N.Y.; resident in ophthalmology U. Tex. Med. Branch, Galveston, 1949-54; clin. assoc. prof. ophthalmology U. Tex., Galveston, 1953—; pvt. practice ophthalmology, Longview, Tex., 1953-84. Served to capt. U.S. Army, 1944-46. Fellow ACS; mem. Gregg County Med. Soc., Tex. Med. Soc., Am. Med. Soc. Republican. Methodist. Lodge: Rotary. Home: Route 5 Box 37A Longview TX 75601 Office: Box 406 Longview TX 75606

PAYTON, NEAL IRA, architect, architectural educator; b. Balt., July 24, 1956; s. Moses and Freda (Lessans) P. B.A. in Architecture, Carnegie-Mellon U., 1978; M.A. in Architecture, Syracuse U., 1981. Designer Skidmore, Owings & Merrill, N.Y.C., 1980; asst. prof. architecture U. Va., Charlottesville, Va., 1980—; vis. asst. prof. Cath. U., Washington, 1984; urban design cons. Shockoe Slip Found., Richmond, Va., 1983—. Prin. work arch. competition entry for hist. Savannah Found., Victorian Dist. Residential Design Competition, Ga., 1981 (winning entry); contbr. articles to profl. jours. Asst. campaign coordinator John Anderson for Pres., Bklyn., 1980. U. Va. Summer Research fellow, 1984. Mem. Am. Inst. Architects. Democratic. Jewish. Office: The Architecture Office 100 Court Sq Annex Suite E Charlottesville VA 22901

PEACE, MIRIAM SISKIN, cytotechnologist, lawyer; b. Winnipeg, Man., Can., Feb. 13, 1931; d. David L. and Rissa (Ghitter) Siskin; children—Brian Smiley, Carl Smiley, Janice Smiley Hazlehurst, Vickie Smiley Sholes, Rissa Peace. Cert., Sch. Cytology, Med. Coll. of Ga., Augusta, 1951; LL.B., John Marshall Sch. Law, 1972. Cytologist, Med. Coll. Ga., Augusta, 1951-52, Grady Hosp., Atlanta, 1956-57; supr. St. Joseph's Infirmary, Atlanta, 1957-62, Peace Labs., Atlanta, 1962-69; cytotechnologist Peachtree Lab., Atlanta, 1969—; supr. Piedmont Hosp., Atlanta, 1979—; admitted to Ga. bar, 1973; sole practice law, Atlanta, 1974-75. Precinct co-chmn. Andrew Young campaign for Congress, 1970, 72. Mem. Am. Soc. Clin. Pathologists (registered cytotechnologist, charter mem.), Am. Soc. Cytotechnology, State Bar of Ga. Democrat. Jewish. Home: 4717 Roswell Rd NE Apt D7 Atlanta GA 30342 Office: 1968 Peachtree Rd NW Atlanta GA 30309

PEACE, WILLIAM KITTRELL, librarian; b. Rusk, Tex., Mar. 25, 1925; s. George Wesley and LaVada May (Meltabarger) P.; B.A., Tex. Christian U., 1950; M.Ed., U. Tex., 1960; M.S. in Library Sci. (grad. fellow 1966-67), La. State U., 1964; cert. county and regional librarianship Rutgers U., 1954. Library asst. Fort Worth Pub. Library, 1948-49, U. Tex. Library, Austin, 1950-52; asst. legis. ref. librarian Tex. State Library, Austin, 1952-53, extension librarian, 1953-55, asst. state librarian, 1955-60, 1962-66, acting state librarian, 1960-62; librarian Lee Coll., Baytown, Tex., 1967-—. Cons. Pub. Library Insts., Tex. State Library, 1954-66, library services Tex. Dept. Corrections for coll. programs, 1969-71, So. Assn. Colls. and Schs., 1972-—. Served with USNR, 1943-46. Mem. Baytown C. of C., ALA, Brit. Library Assn., Tex. Library Assn. (dist. chmn. 1969), AAUP (chpt. pres. 1968-69), Tex. Jr. Coll. Tchrs. Assn. (chpt. pres. 1969-71 sect. chmn. 1970), Assn. Ednl. Tech. Communications. Author: History of the Texas State Library With Emphasis on the Period, 1930-59, 1959. Home: 611 N Whiting St Baytown TX 77520 Office: Box 818 Lee Dr Baytown TX 77520

PEACOCK, JAMES HARRY, gear company and remanufactured truck and auto parts executive; b. Del Rio, Tex., Sept. 16, 1928; s. Joseph Willis and Lois Jewell (Shipman) P.; m. Sarah Jane Redmond, July 5, 1980; children by previous marriage—Ellen, James Jr., Niccole, Joshua. Student Eastern Mich. U., 1950-52. Gen. plant mgr. materials handling parts div. Eaton Corp., Flemington, N.J., 1972-76, div. mgr. hydrostatic transmission div., 1977-81; gen. mgr. Perfection Hy-Test Co., Darlington, S.C., 1981—. Home: 3132 Beechwood Rd Florence SC 29501 Office: Perfection Hy-Test Co Route 5 Dovesville Hwy Darlington SC 29532

PEAGLER, TERRY C., insurance company official, loss prevention consultant; b. Morton, Miss., Aug. 13, 1949; s. Troy C. and Exo N. (Easom) P.; m. Brenda C. Butts, Mar. 17, 1973; children—Shane, Seth. B. Engring. Tech.-Arch., So. Tech. Inst. div. Ga. Inst. Tech.), 1978; Assoc. in Risk Mgmt., Ins. Inst. Am., 1982. Cert. safety profl. in comprehensive practice. Loss prevention service rep. Comml. Union Ins., Atlanta, 1976-77, loss prevention cons., 1977-78, Charlotte, N.C., 1978-79, risk control mgr., Charlotte, 1979-84; regional loss prevention mgr. Amerisure-Mich. Mut., Charlotte, 1984—. Various coms. South Charlotte Bapt. Ch., Pineville, N.C., 1984-85. Served with USN, 1969-71. Recipient Naval Res. Meritorious Service medal USN, 1979, Nat. Def. Service medal, 1981. Mem. Am. Soc. Safety Engrs. Republican. Avocations: sports; gardening. Home: 5901 Cherrycrest Ln Charlotte NC 28210 Office: Amerisure-Mich Mut Ins PO Box 25908 Charlotte NC 28229

PEAK, JAMES MATTHEW, university administrator, fund raising consultant; b. Canton, Ill., Feb. 21, 1936; s. Merle Harry and Hilda (Sepich) P.; m. Julia Lord, Nov. 22, 1962; children—Cynthia, Matthew, Mark, Katherine. B.A., U. Tex.-El Paso, 1958. Agent, trainer Penn Mut. Life Ins., El Paso, Tex., 1965-70, gen. agt., Albuquerque 1970-73; gen. agent Mass. Mut. Life Ins., El Paso, 1973-76; dir. devel. U. Tex.-El Paso, 1977—; dist. relations Case, Tex., 1984—; fund raising cons., S.W. Dist. S.W. IV Case, Tex., 1977—, conf. dir., 1985—. Contbr., A Handbook of Proven Strategies and Techniques, 1982. Bd. dirs. Am. Cancer Soc., El Paso, 1958-83, El Paso Arts Alliance, 1984—; mem. El Paso Estate Planning Council, 1984—. Served with U.S. Army, 1958-61. Recipient Outstanding Service to Students award U. Tex.-El Paso, 1980, Disting. Service award, 1982. Mem. Council for Advancement and support of Edn. (conf. chmn. 1985), El Paso Assn. Life Underwriters (v.p. 1973-76). Roman Catholic. Lodges: K.C. (dir. 1973-75), Lions (v.p. 1984—). Avocations: fishing; sports. Home: 4832 Costa De Oro El Paso TX 79922 Office: Devel Office U Tex El Paso El Paso TX 79968

PEAKE, LUISE EITEL, musicologist, educator; b. Konigsberg, Federal Republic Germany, Jan. 11, 1925; came to U.S., 1948, naturalized, 1960; d. Wilhelm and Annemarie (Engelien) Eitel; m. Joseph S. Peake, June 1, 1962 (dec.); children—William Alexander, Thomas Christian (dec.); m. Allen B. Dickerman, July 23, 1985. B.A., U. Tenn., 1950; Mus.M., Chgo. Mus. Coll., 1952; Ph.D., Columbia U., 1968. Cert. music tchr., Berlin, Fed. Republic Germany. Instr. music U. S.C., Columbia, 1967-69, asst. prof., 1969-78, assoc. prof., 1978—; vis. prof. SUNY-Buffalo, 1974-75. Assoc. editor Piano Quar. Columbia U. fellow, 1958-60. Mem. Am. Musicol. Soc. (chmn. S.E. chpt. 1972-74); Coll. Music Soc. (pres. mid-Atlantic chpt. 1984-85). Home: 4828 Citadel Ave Columbia SC 29206 Office: U SC Sch Music Columbia SC 29208

PEARCE, BETTY MCMURRAY, manufacturing company executive; b. Hastings, Nebr., Oct. 11, 1926; d. Frank Madry and Scereta (Mudd) McMurray; B.S. in Aerospace, U. Tex., Austin, 1949; 1 dau., Karen A. Harsley. Draftsman, Koch & Fowler, Civil Engrs., Dallas, 1945-47; with Vought Corp., Dallas, 1949—, project engr., 1955-77, engring. project mgr., 1977-83, dir. engring., 1983—, dir. LTV Fed. Credit Union, v.p. LTV Mgmt. Club; cons. Pres., St. Andrews Catholic Ch. Council, Fort Worth, 1977-78; mem. Bishop's Adv. Council Fort Worth Diocese, 1980—, pres., 1981-82, 84. Mem. AIAA, Tech. Mktg. Soc. Am., St. Joseph's Hosp. Aux. Home: 4205 Galway Ave Fort Worth TX 76109 Office: PO Box 225907 Dallas TX 75265

PEARCE, CHARLES WELLINGTON, surgeon; b. Ballinger, Tex., Nov. 2, 1927; s. Francis Marion and Fannie (Brown) P.; student Rice U., 1945-46, 48-49, U. Tex., 1948; M.D., Cornell U., 1953; m. Dorothy Andree DeLorenzo, Apr. 2, 1955; children—Charles Wellington, Andrew F., Margaret E., John Y., III; m. Patricia Mary Flannery, Dec. 28, 1983; 1 child, Leslie E. Intern, resident N.Y. Hosp.-Cornell U. Med. Center, N.Y.C., 1953-55, 56-60; resident Baylor U. Affiliated Hosps., 1955-56, Charity Hosp., New Orleans, 1960-61; practice medicine specializing in cardiovascular and thoracic surgery, New Orleans, 1961—; mem. staff Touro Infirmary, So. Bapt. Hosp., Hotel Dieu, Mercy Hosp., East Jefferson Hosp. (all New Orleans); mem. faculty Tulane U., New Orleans, 1960-83, asso. prof. surgery, 1966-69, head sect. cardiovascular and thoracic surgery, 1967-69, asso. prof. clin. surgery, 1969-83; head cardiothoracic surgery, clin. prof. surgery La. State U., 1983—; vis. surgeon Charity Hosp., New Orleans, 1961—; cons. surgery Huey P. Long Charity Hosp., Pineville, La., 1961-70, Lallie Kemp Charity Hosp., Independence, La., 1961-70, VA Hosp., Alexandria, La., 1961—, Keesler Air Force Hosp., Biloxi, Miss., 1967-70; cons. cardiac sect. crippled children program La. Dept. Health. Served with AUS, 1946-48. La. Heart Assn. grantee, 1961-62. Diplomate Am. Bd. Surgery, Bd. Thoracic Surgery. Fellow A.C.S., Am. Coll. Chest Physicians, Am. Coll. Cardiology; mem. Am. Assn. Thoracic Surgery, Soc. for Vascular Surgery, Am. Heart Assn. (established investigator 1962-65), Soc. Thoracic Surgeons, Internat. Cardiovascular Soc., Internat. Surg. Soc., So. Med. Assn., Orleans Parish, La. med. socs., La., New Orleans surg. socs., La. Heart Assn., New Orleans Postgrad. Med. Assembly, Soc. Mayflower Descs. (La. gov. 1975—), SAR, New Orleans Opera House Assn. (dir. 1976—), New Orleans Spring Fiesta Assn., New Orleans Opera Club, Fgn. Relations Assn., La. Landmark Soc., New Orleans Mus. Art, New Orleans Area C. of C., Internat. Platform Assn., R Assn. Rice U., Phi Chi, Alpha Omega Alpha. Republican. Presbyn. Contbr. articles to profl. jours. Office: 1524 7th St New Orleans LA 70115 Home: 1662 State St New Orleans LA 70118

PEARCE, DOROTHY ANDREE DE LORENZO, civic worker; b. N.Y.C., Mar. 22, 1927; d. Andrew John and Margaret (Robilotti) De Lorenzo; m. Charles W. Pearce, Apr. 2, 1955; children—Charles W., Andrew Francis, Margaret Elizabeth, John Y. B.A., Barnard Coll., 1947. Research asst. cardiac catherization lab. Bellevue Hosp., 1948-50; research asst. to Dr. George Papamicolasu, Cornell Med. Coll., 1950-55; exec. research librarian Shell Chem. Co., 1955-57. Rep. thrift shop Soc. N.Y. Hosp. Women's Aux., 1959-60; bd. govs. New Orleans Opera House Assn. Women's Guild, 1965-73, social hostess, 1966-71, historian, 1969—, chmn. uptown subscription com., 1967-69, mem. children's concerts com., 1964-66; mem. tour com. New Orleans Springs Fiesta Assn., 1966-67; mem. opera orientation com. New Orleans Opera House Assn., 1964-72, registrar, hostess, 1965; active New Orleans Symphony Previews, 1968—; mem. fund raising com. De Paul Hosp. Women's Aux., 1968—; vol. Crippled Children's Hosp. Guild, 1965-66; mem. La. Council for Performing Arts, 1967—; mem. Gallier Hall Women's Com., 1967; mem. bd. Community Concerts Assn., New Orleans; mem. fund raising com. Hotel Dieu Women's Aux., 1968—; bd. dirs. Mercy Hosp. Women's Aux., 1965-72, pres., 1970; bd. dirs. Sara Mayo Hosp. Guild, 1964—, chmn. hospitality com., 1967-72; bd. dirs. Orleans Paris Med. Soc. Women's Aux., 1969-71, chmn. AMA edn. and research fund com., 1969-71; bd. dirs. Vis. Nurses Assn. Mem. New Orleans Garden Soc. (chmn. Christmas decorations 1969-70), Fgn. Relations Assn., AAUW, La. Landmark Soc. Republican. Roman Catholic. Club: New Orleans Country. Home: 1750 Saint Charles Ave New Orleans LA 70130

PEARCE, MARY MCCALLUM, artist; b. Hesperia, Mich., Feb. 17, 1906; d. Archibald and Mabel (McNeil) McCallum; m. Clarence A. Pearce, June 30, 1928; children—Mary Martha Pearce Robinson, Thomas McCallum. A.B., Oberlin Coll., 1927; student John Huntington Inst., 1929-34, Cleve. Inst. Art, 1935-37, 54, Dayton Art Inst., 1946-49. One-woman shows at Cleve. Women's City Club, 1959, 69, Cleve. Orch., 1967, Cleve. Playhouse Gallery, 1968, 71, 76, Van Wezel Hall, 1979, Sarasota Library (Fla.), 1979, Hilton Leach Gallery, Sarasota, 1979, 80, 81, 85, Fed. Bank, Sarasota, 1980, 86; exhibited in group shows at Oberlin Art Mus., Akron Art Inst., Grand Rapids Art Gallery (Mich.), Dayton Art Inst. (Ohio), Smithsonian Inst., Birmingham Mus. of Art, Am. Watercolor Soc., Cleve. Mus. Art, Longboat Key Parade of Fla. West Coast Prize Winners, 1979, 80, 81, 82, 83; exhibited nat. shows Butler Inst. Am. Art, Youngstown, Ohio, Knickerbocker Artists, N.Y.C., Watercolor, U.S.A., Springfield, Mo., many others: represented in pvt. collections: tchr. art, supr. pub. schs., Mayfield Heights, Ohio, 1927-28, Maple Heights, Ohio, 1928-30, Chagrin Falls, Ohio, 1938-39. Named best woman artist Ohio Watercolor Soc., 1955; recipient Bush Meml. award Columbus Gallery Fine Arts, 1962; nat. 1st prize for drawing Nat. League Am. Penwomen, 1966, 68; Littlehouse award Ala. Watercolor Soc., 1967; Wolfe award Columbus Gallery Fine Arts, 1971; 2d prize Longboat Key Art Ctr., 1973, 75-80, West Coast prize winner 1979-85, 4-person show, 1984, award Southeastern Art Soc., 1975; 2d prize Art League Manatee County, 1977, 78; 3d prize Sarasota Art Assn., 1977, 78, Merit award, 1981; 1st prize Venice Art League (Fla.), 1979, 2d prize 1979, 80, 81, 3d prize, 1978; 1st prize Hilton Leach Gallery, 1981, 85; 1st prize Venice Watercolor Exhbn., 1982; 1st prize Venice Spring All Media Exhbn., 1983; 1st prize Venice Winner's Showcase Equal award Longboat Key Art Ctr., 1983, numerous others. Mem. Nat. League Am. Pen Women (treas. 1962), Am. Watercolor Soc., Ala. Watercolor Soc., Fla. Watercolor Soc. Republican. Congregationalist. Home: 5400 Ocean Blvd Apt 1401 Sarasota FL 34242

PEARCE, WILLARD CAIL, JR., optometrist; b. Champaign, Ill., July 19, 1947; s. Willard Cail and June Ruth (Lotz) P.; m. Deborah Jane Murray, Dec. 23, 1971; children—Will, Ben, Christopher. B.A., U. South Fla., 1971; B.S., U. Ala., 1974; O.D., 1976. Assoc., Dr. Carroll P. Ezell, Lake Wales, Fla., 1976-77; ptnr. Drs. Ezell and Pearce, Optometrists, Lake Wales, 1977—. Pres., Found. for Christian Growth. Served with USNR, 1970-76. Recipient Bausch and Lomb award U. Ala., 1976, Irvin Borish award, 1976; athletic scholar U. South Fla., 1968-70. Fellow Am. Acad. Optometry; mem. Am. Optometric Assn., Fla. Optometric Assn., Lake Region Optometric Assn. (pres. 1981—), Gold Key, Omicron Delta Kappa, Sigma Chi. Republican. Presbyterian. Clubs: Booster, Lake Wales Country. Lodge: Kiwanis. Home: 834 Campbell Ave Lake Wales FL 33853 Office: 125 E Central Ave Box 632 Lake Wales FL 33853

PEARL, PATRICIA DOLE, librarian, writer; b. Detroit, Oct. 6, 1927; d. Harry Alden and Dorothy Frances (Smith) Dole; m. James Marshall Pearl, Aug. 8, 1953; children—Peter, Deirdre. B.A. cum laude, Conn. Coll., 1948; M.L.S., U. N.C.-Greensboro, 1980. Editorial asst. Time Inc., N.Y.C., 1950-54; librarian First Presbyterian Ch., Martinsville, Va., 1966—; cons. children's religious lit. Author religious books for children; contbr. articles, book revs. to profl. jours., 1980—. Mary Frances Kennon Johnson scholar, 1980. Mem. Ch. and Synagoguge Library Assn., Children's Lit. Assn., N.C. Library Assn., Va. Library Assn., Women's Nat. Book Assn. Presbyterian. Home: 1106 Mulberry Rd Martinsville VA 24112 Office: First Presbyn Ch Patrick Henry Ave Martinsville VA 24112

PEARLE, STANLEY CHARLES, optometrist, consultant; b. Pitts., Oct. 12, 1918; s. Goodman and Dorothy Ruth (Goldberg) P.; m. Elsie Cohen, Sept. 10, 1940; children—David L., Linda M., Gary, Roberta. O.D., No. Ill. Coll. Optometry, 1940. Pres., Opticks, Inc., Dallas, 1958-76; chmn. Searle Optical Group, Dallas, 1976-80; cons. Pearle Health Service, Dallas, 1980—. Pres., Jewish Fedn. Greater Dallas, 1974-75, United Way of Dallas, 1982; bd. dirs. Temple Emanu-El, Dallas, 1978-80, NCCJ, Dallas, 1980—. Honoree Optical div. United Jewish Appeal, N.Y., 1975. Mem. Tex. Assn. Optometrists, Nat. Assn. Optometrists and Opticians (pres. 1973-75, treas. 1980-85), Tex. Optometry Bd., Opticians Assn. Am. (bd. dirs. 1975-80). Club: Columbian Country of Dallas (Carrollton). Avocation: tennis. Home: 9929 Strait Ln Dallas TX 75220 Office: Pearle Health Services Inc 2534 Royal Ln Dallas TX 75229

PEARMAN, ALLEN LEE, economist; b. Alliance, Nebr., July 24, 1942; s. Jean Richardson P. B.A. in Econs., No. Mich. U., 1964; M.A. in Econs., Mich. State U., 1968; M.S. in Planning, Fla. State U., 1974. Asst. prof. econs. U. Tenn., Knoxville, 1968-72; research assoc. Fla. State U., Tallahassee, 1974-77; research and planning specialist Fla. Dept. Community Affairs, Tallahassee, 1978-79, local govt. assistance specialist, 1979-80; econ. analyst Hosp. Cost Containment Bd., Tallahassee, 1980-84, dep. dir. research, 1984—. Woodrow Wilson fellow, 1964-65. Mem. Am. Econ. Assn., Assn. for Evolutionary Econs., Omicron Delta Epsilon, Pi Kappa Pi. Democrat. Office: Hospital Cost Containment Bd Tallahassee FL 32301

PEARSON, DONALD EMANUAL, chemistry research investigator, consultant; b. Madison, Wis., June 21, 1914; s. Gustav Emanual and Clara (Bjeldr) P.; m. Gwen Smiseth, June 6, 1950; children—Don T., Jeanah Pearson McClure, Sam S. B.S., U. Wis., 1936; Ph.D., U. Ill., 1940. Chemist Pitts. Plate Glass, Milw., 1940-42; tech. aide U.S. Govt. Office Sci. Research and Devel., Washington, 1942-46; asst. prof. Vanderbilt U., Nashville, 1946-49, assoc. prof., 1949-52, prof., 1952-79, prof. emeritus, 1979—; cons., researcher; pres. Pearson Research Corp., Nashville, 1980—; v.p. Viking Corp., Murfreesboro, Tenn., 1985—. Patentee; author: Survey of Organic Synthesis, 1970; also articles. Tech. cons. Tenn. Environ. Soc., 1983. Mem. Am. Chem. Soc. Lutheran. Home: 112 Clydelan Ct Nashville TN 37205 Office: Vanderbilt U Box 1539 Nashville TN 37235

PEARSON, ELIZABETH MARIA, religious leader; b. Wauchula, Fla., Apr. 22, 1953; d. Walter Morgan and Naomi (Marsh) P. B.S., Carson-Newman Coll., 1975; M.Religious Edn., So. Bapt. Sem., 1979. Youth minister Stock Creek Baptist Ch., Knoxville, Tenn., 1975, First Bapt. Ch., Bartow, Fla., 1976; cons. Woman's Missionary Union, Ga. Bapt. Conv., Atlanta, 1979—; intern Bapt. Goodwill Ctr., Knoxville, 1972-73; conf. leader N.Y. Bapt. Conv., 1980, Ridgecrest Bapt. Ctr. (N.C.), 1983; dir. Camp Pinnacle, Clayton, Ga.; vol. Briarcliff Bapt. Ch., Atlanta; pianist chapel services Ga. Mental Health, Atlanta. Named Carson-Newman Coll. Miss Tenn. Jenkins, 1975; So. Bapt. Sem. Joyce scholar, 1978. Mem. Ky. Bapt. Religious Edn. Assn. Democrat. Office: Georgia Baptist Convention 2930 Flowers Rd S Atlanta GA 30341

PEARSON, GEORGE BERNARD, business executive; b. Mercedes, Tex., Feb. 19, 1938; s. Bernard and Agatha (Peterson) P.; B.A., U. Tex., 1959, M.B.A., 1961; m. Margaret Jean Royall, May 1, 1965. Statistician, Bur. Bus. Research, U. Tex., Austin, 1959-60; sales engr. IBM Corp., Endicott, N.Y., also Dallas, 1959; lead engr. Ling-Temco-Vought, Inc., Dallas, 1961-65, engring. specialist, 1965-67; mgr. finance Pan Am. World Airways, Inc., N.Y.C., 1967-69, mgr. operations research and system planning, 1969-72, dir. system planning, 1972, dir. operating plans and system devel., 1972-74, dir. planning systems and administrn., 1974-75; v.p. planning and research Beneficial Mgmt. Corp., 1975-81; gen. mgr. Geotronics Corp., Austin, Tex., 1982-84; chmn., pres. Royson, Inc., Auston, 1985—; dir. corps. Mem. U. Tex. Alumni Assn. Lutheran. Contbr. articles to profl. jours. Home: 3618 Doe Trail Austin TX 78746 Office: 3636 Executive Center Dr Austin TX 78731

PEARSON, GEORGE WILLIAM, safety engineer; b. Bronx, N.Y., Feb. 8, 1946; s. John A. and Margaret E. (Jeffrey) P.; m. Helen Carole Svenson, Nov. 1, 1969; 1 child, Kari Elizabeth. B.A., Fordham U., 1973; M.A., NYU, 1976. Cert. safety profl., 1976. Loss control cons. Hartford Ins. Group, Bklyn., 1969-72; safety supr. Seatrain Shipbldg. Corp., Bklyn., 1972-74; safety adminstr. Consol. Edison N.Y., Bklyn., 1974-77; program mgr. Safety Sci. Applications, Inc., McLean, Va., 1977-82; nat. safety dir. Waite Hill Services, Inc. subs. Figgie Internat., Inc., Richmond, Va., 1982—. Mem. Am. Soc. Safety Engrs. (chpt. dir. 1984-85). Republican. Lutheran. Avocations: golf; sailboat racing. Home: 10701 Baypines Ln Richmond VA 23233 Office: Waite Hill Inc 1000 Virginia Center Pkwy Richmond VA 23295

PEARSON, H(ENRY) CLYDE, U.S. bankruptcy judge; b. Ocoonita, Lee County, Va., Mar. 12, 1925; s. Henry James and Nancy Elizabeth (Seals) P.; m. Jean Calton, July 26, 1956; children—Elizabeth F., Timothy Clyde. Student Union Coll, Ky., 1947-49; LL.B., U. Richmond, 1952. Bar: Va. 1952. Sole practice, Pennington Gap, Jonesville, Va., 1952-56; asst. U.S. atty. Dept. Justice, Roanoke, Va., 1956-61; sole practice law, then mem. firm Hopkins, Pearson & Engleby, Roanoke, 1961-70; bankruptcy judge U.S. Bankruptcy Ct., Western Dist. Va., 1970—. Contbg. editor Ann. Survey. of Bankruptcy Law, 1983, 84. Exec. sec. Republican Party, Va., 1954-56; mem. Va. Ho. of Dels., 1954-56; Republican nominee for gov. of Va., 1961; mem. Va. Senate, 1967-70. Served with USN, 1943-46; ETO, PTO. Mem. Nat. Conf. Bankruptcy Judges, Va. State Bar, ABA, Va. Trial Lawyers, Am. Assn. Trial Lawyers, Am. Judicature Soc., Fed. Bar Assn., Am. Judges Assn., Am. Legion, VFW, 40-8. Republican. Methodist. Lodges: Masons (32 degree), Shriners. Office: Federal Bldg Box 2389 Roanoke VA

PEARSON, MARION WILLIAM, JR., college administrator; b. Tuscaloosa, Ala., Jan. 7, 1945; s. Marion William and Amy Jean (Barksdale) P. A.B., U. Ala., 1967, M.A., 1975. Mem. faculty Christ Sch., Arden, N.C., 1972-75; research project dir. alumni affairs U. Ala., Tuscaloosa, 1976-77; mem. Faculty, dept. chmn. Tuscaloosa Acad., 1977-78; assoc. dir. admissions Dalton Jr. Coll., Ga., 1978—, assoc. registrar, 1978—. Bd. dirs. English Speaking Union, Chattanooga, 1980—, treas., 1980-83, pres., 1983—; mem. Atlanta Symphony Orch. League. Served to 1st lt. U.S. Army, 1969-71. Mem. Ga. Assn. Collegiate Registrars and Admissions Officers, Am. Assn. Collegiate Registrars and Admissions Officers, So. Assn. Collegiate Registrars and Admissions Officers, So. Polit. Sci. Assn., S.C., Hist. Soc. Episcopalian. Avocations: music; tennis. Office: Dalton Jr Coll 213 N College Dr Dalton GA 30720

PEARSON, MARY ANN, nursing educator; b. Tuscaloosa, Ala., Dec. 30, 1940; d. Clyde Sommerkamp and Willow Dean (Sims) Martin; m. John Allen Pearson, Aug. 25, 1962; children—June, Dena. B.S. in Nursing, U. Ala., 1962, M.A. in Curriculum Devel., 1981. R.N., Ala. Supt., State Psychiat. Hosp., Tuscaloosa, 1962-63; asst. dir. nursing Hale Meml. Hosp., Tuscaloosa, 1964; instr. practical nursing Shelton State Community Coll., Tuscaloosa, 1965-66, coordinator practical nursing, 1970-80, chmn. dept. nursing, 1980—, developer curriculum assoc. degree nursing program, 1982; developer curriculum Sch. Practical Nursing, Bessemer State Tech. Inst. (Ala.), 1966, head instr., 1966-70; curriculum cons. to practical nursing programs; mem. State Curriculum Com. for Practical Nursing; mem. accreditation team So. Assn. Colls. and Schs.; mem. Nursing Task Force for W. Ala. Vol. worker ARC; mem. nominating and fin. coms. Ridgecrest Baptist Ch. Recipient Outstanding Service award Postsecondary div. Ala. State Dept. Edn., 1980. Mem. NEA, Am. Nurses Assn. (Nurse Day com. for Ala.), Ala. Edn. Assn., Nat. League for Nursing, Ala. League for Nursing, Deans and Dirs. Assn., Assn. Acad. Suprs., Ala. Assn. women Deans, Adminstrs. and Counselors, Bus. and Profl. Women's Assn., Ala. Vocat. Assn. (dir. local chpt., Disting. Service award Health Occupations sect. 1979), Kappa Delta Pi, Sigma Theta Tau (treas. local chpt.). Clubs: Univ. Women's, Lynn Haven. Home: 1463 50th Ave E Tuscaloosa AL 35404 Office: Shelton State Community College 202 Skyland Blvd Tuscaloosa AL 35405

PEARSON, ROBERT EDWIN, psychiatrist; b. Toledo, Apr. 29, 1923; s. Albin L. and Elizabeth (Christ) Pearson; m. Karen S. Kamerschen, June 18, 1983; m. Katherine L. Gerrie, Oct. 15, 1955 (dec. 1981); children—Robert A., Michael A., Barbara A., Eric J., Brian S., Katherine E. B.S., Wayne U., 1949, M.D., 1952. Diplomate Am. Bd. Psychiatry and Neurology. Intern, Highland Park Gen. Hosp., Mich., 1952-53; gen. practice medicine Boyne City, Mich., 1953-66; resident in psychiatry Traverse City State Hosp., Mich., 1966-69, dir. adult services, 1969-83; practice psychiatry, Houston, 1983—. Contbr. articles to profl. jours. Served to capt. AUS, 1941-46; ETO. Fellow Am. Soc. Clin. Hypnosis (pres. 1969-70, chmn. Edn. and Research Found. 1972-73), Soc. Clin. and Exptl. Hypnosis, AAAS; mem. Am. Psychiat. Assn. Roman Catholic. Home: 10044 Lynbrook Dr Houston TX 77042 Office: 7887 San Felipe St 248 Houston TX 77063

PEARSON, WILLIAM DEAN, biology educator, consultant; b. Moline, Ill., Dec. 6, 1941; s. Paul C. and Virginia F. (Conlon) P.; m. B. Juanelle Lozano, July 19, 1977; children—Leslie, Eric. B.S., Iowa State U., 1964; M.S., Utah State U., 1967, Ph.D., 1970. Fishery Aid U.S. Fish & Wildlife Service, Yankton, S.D., 1962-63, fishery biologist, Logan, Utah, 1964-66; research asst. Utah State U., Logan, 1967-70; asst. prof. North Tex. State U., Denton, Tex., 1970-75; prof. biology U. Louisville, Ky., 1975—; cons. Upper Miss. River Commn., LaCrosse, Wis., 1981. Author: Status of Ohio River Fishes, 1984; contbr. articles to profl. jours. Mem. AAAS, Ecol. Soc. Am., North Am. Benthological Soc., Am. Assn. Ichthyologists and Herpetologists, Am. Fisheries Soc. Avocations: fishing; woodcarving; reading; gardening. Office: Water Resources Lab U Louisville Louisville KY 40292

PEAVY, DAN CORNELIUS, orthodontist; b. San Antonio, Jan. 26, 1939; s. Dan C. and Mary (Terrell) P.; m. Harriet Williams, Nov. 9, 1941; children—Daniel, Gardner. B.S., So. Meth. U., 1962; D.D.S., Baylor U., 1962, M.S.D. Orthodontics, 1964. Diplomate Am. Bd. Orthodontics. Pvt. practice orthodontics, San Antonio, 1966—; clin. prof. dept. orthodontics, U. Tex. Dental Sch. San Antonio, 1972—; dir. Nat. Bank Fort Sam Houston. Mem. devel. bd. Inst. Texan Cultures, Health Careers High Sch.; trustee Baylor Coll. Dentistry 1972-83, San Antonio Med. Found. Served to capt. USAF, 1964-66, Japan

Fellow Am. Coll. Dentistry, Internat. Coll. Dentistry, Acad. Gen. Dentistry; mem. Am. Assn. Orthodontists, ADA, Southwestern Soc. Orthodontists (del., dir. 1985), San Antonio Dist. Dental Soc. (pres. 1984), Tex. Assn. Orthodontists (pres. 1984), Baylor Orthodontic Alumni Assn. (pres. 1975), Baylor Alumni Assn., Omicron Kappa, Upsilon. Republican. Presbyterian. Clubs: Conopus (pres. 1972), German, San Antonio Country, Cavaliers, Order of Alamo (pres. 1974), Argyle, Gireau. Lodge: Rotary. Home: 627 Lamont St San Antonio TX 78209 Office: 110 Melrose Pl San Antonio TX 78212

PEAVY, DON EZZARD, SR., lawyer; b. Ft. Worth, Dec. 2, 1950; s. Dan Aubrey, Sr. and Roxie Mae (Dawson) P.; A.A. with honors, Tarrant County Jr. Coll., 1974; B.A., Tex. Christian U., 1976; J.D., U. Tex., 1982. m. Pattie Jo Clark, Aug. 31, 1974; children—Cheryl Lynn, Don Ezzard. Dir., Vets. Upward Bound Project, Tarrant County Jr. Coll., Ft. Worth, 1974-76; pres. Donepe Co., Ft. Worth, 1976-82; editor Tex. Vets. News, Ft. Worth, 1974-82; treas., mgr. Tex. Vets. Fed. Credit Union, Ft. Worth, 1977-82, treas. bd. dirs.; with Law Offices of Huey Mitchell, Ft. Worth, 1982—. cons. AMVETS. Pres. Maddox Neighborhood Council, 1979; exec. v.p., asso. editor A Galaxy of Verse Lit. Found., 1977-79; bd. dirs. 12th Dist. Conservative Caucus, 1978-79. Served with U.S. Army, 1970-72. Mem. ABA, Tarrant County Bar Assn., Tex. Young Lawyers Assn., Press Club Ft. Worth, Nat. Writers Club, Tex. Press Assn., Tex. Credit Union League, Regular Vets. Assn. Tex. (dept. comdr.), AMVETS. Baptist. Author: Brotherhood of the Battlefield, 1976; Without Humor or Grief, 1979. Home: 4820 El Rancho Rd Fort Worth TX 76119 Office: 210 W 6th St Suite 1206 Fort Worth TX 76102

PEAVY, JOHN WESLEY, III, finance educator, consultant; b. Dallas, July 3, 1944; s. John Wesley Jr. and Ermine Palmer (Arnold) P.; m. Deanna Jeannine Bond, Sept. 29, 1979. B.B.A., Southern Methodist U., 1966; M.B.A., U. Pa., 1968; Ph.D., U. Tex.-Arlington, 1978. Chartered fin. analyst. Securities salesman Goldman, Sachs & Co., N.Y.C., Dallas, 1970-75; instr. U. Tex., Arlington, 1976-77, Tex. Christian U., Fort Worth, 1977-78; asst. prof. Ariz. State U., Tempe, 1978-79; assoc. prof. finance Southern Meth. U., Dallas, 1979—; cons. First Nat. Bank, Kerrville, Tex., 1979—; pres. Peavy Fin. Services, Inc., Dallas, 1982—. Author: Hyperprofits, 1985. Editor: Takeovers and Shareholders: The Mounting Controversy, 1985. Contbr. articles to profl. jours. Recipient Disting. Prof. award Southern Meth. U., 1982, Rotunda award, 1980, Research Excellence award, 1985; fellow Columbia U., 1983, 85, Southern Meth. U., 1981-84. Mem. Fin. Mgmt. Assn. (pres. honor soc. 1985), Southwestern Fin. Assn. (bd. dirs. 1985), Inst. for Chartered Fin. Analysts (bd. examiners 1984-85), Western Risk Ins. Assn. (treas. 1980-81). Home: 10102 Woodlake Dr Dallas TX 75243 Office: So Meth U Cox Sch Bus Dallas TX 75275

PEAVY, THOMAS OSTINE, hospital educator/counselor; b. Milledgeville, Ga., July 4, 1946; s. Ostine and Mammie Annell (Newsome) P.; m. Rita Hazel Long, Feb. 8, 1969; children—Thomas Ostine, Erin Nicole. A.A., Ga. Mil. Coll., 1970; B.S., Ga. Coll., 1972; Ed.M., Ga. So. Coll., 1976; M.S., Troy State U., 1984; Edn. Specialist, U. Ga., 1978. Cert. tchr., Ga. Tchr., chmn. dept. Baldwin High Sch., Milledgeville, 1973-77; edn. specialist Ga. Diagnostic and Classification Ctr., Jackson, 1979-80; tchr., dir. adult edn. service W. Central Ga. Regional Hosp., Columbus, 1980—. Author: Directory of Adult Education Services-Milledgeville, Baldwin County, Ga., 1978. Chmn., Muscogee Area Literacy Assn., Columbus, 1984—; mem. Laubach Literacy Action; adv. com. Muscogee-Multi Adult Edn. Program, Columbus, 1985—; Served with USN, 1963-67. Mem. Am. Assn. Counseling and Devel., Am. Mental Health Counselors Assn., NEA, Ga. Assn. Counseling and Devel., Ga. Assn. Educators, Columbus Youth Soccer Assn. Republican. Presbyterian. Avocations: antique bottle collecting; fly fishing. Home: 4806 Fairview Dr Columbus GA 31907 Office: West Central Ga Regional Hosp 3000 Shatulga Rd PO Box 12435 Columbus GA 31995

PECK, GLADYS CASE, physical education educator, consultant; b. Rock Hill, N.Y., Jan. 4, 1914; d. Blake Marvin (dec.) and Lena (Smith) Case; m. Earl Travis Peck, June 28, 1938; 1 dau., Nancy Elin. Diploma in Teaching, Potsdam Coll. (N.Y.), 1933; B.S. in Edn., Oglethorpe U., 1954; M.Ed., Emory U., 1959, Diploma for Advanced Study in Teaching, 1964. Cert. in instructional supervision, Ga. Tchr. rural sch. Dist. 18, Hurleyville, N.Y., 1933-38, pub. schs., Atlanta, 1951-56; tchr. dance pub. schs., Atlanta, 1962-67; tchr. phys. edn. on Ednl. TV, WETV Channel 30, Atlanta, 1962-74; coordinator elem. phys. edn. through 12th grade, pub. schs., Atlanta, 1975-79; instr. fitness for sr. citizens Mary Branan Ch., Atlanta; cons. Tenn. Assn. Health Phys. Edn. Recreation and Dance, So. Assn. Phys. Edn. Colls. for Women, Nat. Assn. Educators Young Children, Assn. Childhood Edn. Internat., Assn. Elem. and Kindergarten Educators, Ga. Assn. Health Phys. Edn. Recreation and Dance, AAHPERD. Author: Jump for the Health of It, 1980; contbr. articles to profl. jours. Vol., Ga. Phys. Edn. Pub. Info Project, 1970-75; Am. Cancer Soc., 1976-79; first aid vol. ARC, Atlanta, 1976-78; active Jump Rope-a-Thon, Am. Heart Assn., 1980. Recipient Honor award Ga. Assn. Health Phys. Edn. Recreation and Dance, 1970; Certs. of Merit, Am. Cancer Soc., 1974-79; So. Dist. award Southern Dist. Health Phys. Edn. Recreation and Dance, 1977; Minerva award Potsdam Coll., 1977; named Leady Lady of Atlanta, 1974. Mem. AAHPERD (elem. sect. chmn. So. dist. 1963-64), Ga. Assn. Health Phys. Edn. Recreation and Dance (v.p. for health 1968, pres. 1972-73). Democrat. Methodist. Home: 810 Casplan Ct SW Atlanta GA 30310

PECK, RICHARD HYDE, hospital administrator; b. Ft. McClelland, Ala., Aug. 30, 1941; s. Robert H. and Elizabeth M. P.; m. Barbara Mansfield, Dec. 27, 1964; children—Catherine, Nancy, Joanne. A.B. in Econs, U. N.C., 1963; M.S. in Health Adminstrn, Duke U., 1966. Adminstrv. asst. U. Hosps., Cleve., 1966-67, asst. adminstr., 1967-69; asst. dir. Duke U. Hosp., 1969-71, asso. dir., 1971-73, adminstrv. dir., 1973-81; asso. prof. health adminstrn. program Duke U.; chief exec. officer Eliza Coffee Meml. Hosp., Florence, Ala., 1981—. Mem. exec. com., Durham, N.C. chpt. ARC, 1976-79, Duke U. Children's Classic, 1979. Mem. Am. Coll. Hosp. Adminstrs., N.C. Hosp. Assn. Democrat. Presbyterian. Office: PO Box 818 Florence AL 35630*

PEDDY, JOE MURRAY, bank executive; b. Clovis, N. Mex., Mar. 27, 1940; s. Otis Leonard and Murray Loyce (Hefner) P.; m. Sally Park, Sept. 12, 1970; children—Joseph Brent, Marcus Todd. B.B.A. in Fin., Tex. Tech U., 1963; grad. Southwestern Grad. Sch. Banking, 1973; grad. bank seminars Harvard U. Bank examiner U.S. Dept. Treasury, Dallas, 1964-72; sr. v.p. Long Point Nat. Bank, Houston, 1973-75; exec. v.p. Post Oak Bank, Houston, 1975-81; pres. Houston Bank Commerce, 1981—, also dir.; regional credit adminstr. RepublicBank Corp., 1984-86; chmn. bd. dirs. United Nat. Bank, Houston, 1986—. Adv. bd. dirs. Houston Community Coll., 1981-82; committeeman, life mem. Houston Livestock Show and Rodeo; membership com. Houston Mus. Fine Arts, 1979; chmn. Tex. Tech U. Speakers Assn., 1980, bd. dirs. Red Raiders Club, 1983. Served with U.S. Army, 1963-64. Mem. Robert Morris Assocs., Am. Mgmt. Assn., Kappa Sigma. Clubs: Touchdown of Houston, Forum. Home: 3562 Ashfield Dr Houston TX 77082

PEDEN, ROBERT F., JR., lawyer; b. Ft. Worth, July 26, 1911; s. Robert F. and Laura (Phillips) P.; LL.B., Cumberland U., 1933; m. Virginia LeTulle, May 25, 1939. Admitted to Tex. bar, 1934; practice law, Bay City, 1934—; city atty., Bay City, 1935-38, 65-79; atty. Matagorda County, Tex., 1939-46, 50-54. Bd. dirs. Bay City Library Assn. Mem. State Bar Tex., Am., Matagorda (pres. 1961-62, v.p. 1967-68) bar assns., Am. Judicature Soc., Lambda Chi Alpha. Presbyterian (clk. session 1969-71). Rotarian (v.p. 1968-69, pres. 1969-70). Club: Knife and Fork (dir. 1968-69, pres. 1970-71). Home: 1916 Austin St Bay City TX 77414 Office: 1212 7th St PO Box 1245 Bay City TX 77414

PEDERSEN, GEORGE CHRISTIAN, industrial executive, chemical engineer; b. Miami, Fla., Dec. 9, 1940; s. George Christian and Pasqualina T. (Trombetta) P.; m. Pauline June Theresa D'Abbraccio, June 10, 1962; children—George Christian, Mary, Kimberly, Rachelle. B.S., MIT, 1962, M.S., 1963, degree in Chem. Engring., 1966. Sr. devel. engr., mgr. research and devel., cons. Albany Internat. Corp., N.Y., 1967-74; pres. Kimre, Inc., Perrine, Fla., 1973—. Contbr. articles to profl. jours. Patentee hydrazine, mist eliminator, tower packing. Mem. MIT Club South Fla. (treas. 1981-84), AIChe Club South Fla., Profl. Engring. Soc., Fla. Engring. Soc. Republican. Roman Catholic. Club: South Dade Anglers (Miami, Fla.) (treas. 1983-84). Avocation: fishing. Office: PO Box 570846 17420 S Dixie Hwy Perrine FL 33257

PEDERSON, WILLIAM DAVID, political scientist, educator; b. Eugene, Oreg., Mar. 17, 1946; s. Jon Moritz and Rose Marie (Ryan) P. B.S. in Polit. Sci., U. Oreg., 1967, M.A. in Polit. Sci., 1972, Ph.D. in Polit. Sci., 1979. Teaching asst. polit. sci. dept. U. Oreg., Eugene, 1975-77; instr. govt. dept. Lamar U., Beaumont, Tex., 1977-79; asst. prof. polit. sci. dept. Westminster Coll., Fulton, Mo., 1979-80; asst. prof., head polit. sci. and pre law Yankton Coll. U. S.D., 1980-81; assoc. prof., dir. Am. studies polit. sci. dept. La. State U., Shreveport, 1981—; program analyst NIH, Bethesda, Md., summer 1973; assoc. prof. jr. state program Am. U., Washington, summer 1984; research assoc. Russian and East European Ctr. U. Ill., Urbana, summers 1982, 83, 84. Contbr. articles to profl. jours. Friend Shreveport Symphony, 1984; patron Shreveport Little Theater, 1984; active Barnwell Ctr., Shreveport, 1984, Am. Rose Soc., Shreveport, 1982. Served with U.S. Army, 1968-70. Recipient training award NIH 1973; Outstanding Prof. award Westminster Coll. 1980, La. State U., 1984; La. State U. grantee 1982. Fellow Am. Polit. Sci. Assn., Am. Judicature Soc.; mem. Ctr. Study Presidency, Internat. Soc. Polit. Psychology, Am. Studies Assn. Home: 142 Atkins Shreveport LA 71104 Office: La State U 8515 Youree Dr Shreveport LA 71115

PEDLEY, ELLEN MACK, lawyer; b. N.Y.C., Mar. 8, 1934; d. Harry Ranger and Minnie Mack; m. Lawrence Lindsay Pedley, Oct. 9, 1957 (div.); children—Lawrence Lindsay, David Mack, Joan Elizabeth. B.A., Newcomb Coll., 1955; J.D., Yale U., 1958; Bar: Ky. 1959, Fla. 1979. C.P.A., Ky. With Ky. Legis. Research Commn., Frankfort, 1959-60; clk. Ky. Ct. of Appeals, Frankfort, 1960; C.P.A., Eskew & Gresham, Louisville, 1960-70 assoc. firm Greenebaum, Doll & McDonald, Louisville, 1970-72, ptnr., 1972—. Mem. ABA, Ky. Bar Assn., Fla. Bar Assn., Louisville Bar Assn., Jefferson County, Women's Bar Assn., Am. Inst. C.P.A.s., Ky. Soc. C.P.A.s. Home: 5200 Indian Woods Ct Louisville KY 40207 Office: Greenebaum Doll McDonald 1st National Tower Suite 3300 Louisville KY 40202

PEEBLES, ROBERT W., educational administrator. Supt. of schs. Alexandria, Va. Office: 3801 W Braddock Rd Alexandria VA 22302*

PEELER, RAY DOSS, JR., lawyer; b. Bonham, Tex., May 4, 1929; s. Ray Doss and Opal (Porter) P.; B.A. with high honors, U. Tex., 1948, LL.B., 1951; children—William Bryan, Maribel Porter. Admitted to Tex. bar, 1951; practiced law, Bonham, 1953—, dist. and county atty., Fannin County, 1960-61; pres. Fannin Nat. Bank, Windom, Tex., 1963-70, chmn. bd., 1970—; chmn. bd. 1st Nat. Bank, Bonham, 1972—. Del. Democratic Nat. Conv., 1960; trustee S.B. Allen Meml. Hosp., Bonham, 1962—; chmn. Bonham United Fund, 1959; pres. Bonham Indsl. Found., 1965-75. Served to capt. USAF, 1951-53. Mem. State Bar Tex., Am. Bar Assn., State Jr. Bar Tex. (v.p. 1959-60), Tex. Horticulture Soc. (pres. 1974-76), Tex. Pecan Growers Assn. (pres. 1974-76), Bonham C. of C. (pres. 1958), Fannin County Hist. Soc. (hon. life, sponsor 1954-60), Phi Beta Kappa, Phi Gamma Delta, Phi Alpha Delta. Mem. Christian Ch. Clubs: Bonham Rotary (pres. 1957), Bonham Golf (dir. 1958-61), Quail Hollow Country. Home: 1912 Nancy Lea Dr Bonham TX 75418 Office: 302 Peeler Bldg Bonham TX 75418

PEELER, WILLIAM JAMES, lawyer; b. Highland Park, Mich., Nov. 27, 1927; s. Herb and Beulah (Wells) P.; m. Nancy Jean Bradley, Dec. 26, 1949; children—Nannette Peeler Goddard, Jeana Peeler Hosch, Jacqueline Peeler Fuqua. LL.B., Cumberland U., 1952. Bar: Tenn. 1952. Ptnr. Porch, Peeler, Williams, Thomason & Bradley, Waverly, Tenn., 1952—; gen. counsel, dir. Commerce Union Bank, Waverly, 1968—, New Life Found., Burns, Tenn., 1983—. Mem. Tenn. Ho. of Reps., 1959-63; majority leader Tenn. Senate, 1967-75; trustee Cumberland U., Lebanon, Tenn., 1985—. Fellow Am. Coll. Trial Lawyers, Tenn. Bar Found.; mem. Am. Judicature Soc., ABA, Tenn. Bar Assn., Humphreys County Bar Assn. Democrat. Mem. Ch. of Christ. Clubs: Cumberland, City, Capitol (Nashville); Jefferson (Louisville). Lodges: Elks (1st exalted ruler), Masons. Home: Little Richland Creek Rd Waverly TN 37185 Office: Porch Peeler Williams Thomason & Bradley 102 S Court Sq Waverly TN 37185

PEELLE, ELIZABETH BROWN, environmental sociologist, researcher; b. Milw., June 3, 1932; s. Irwin Cuyler and Flora (Keller) Brown; m. Robert W. Peelle, Sept. 24, 1955; children—Evelyn, Annette. B.A. in Chemistry, Western Coll. Women, Oxford, Ohio, 1954; M.A. in Sociology, U. Tenn., 1964. Interviewer, Ford Found. Appalachia Survey, Ky., 1958; pres. or bd. dirs. Planned Parenthood of So. Mountains, Oak Ridge, Tenn., 1968-72; mem. research staff Oak Ridge Nat. Lab., 1975—. Contbr. articles to profl. jours. Pres. Oak Ridge Community Relations Council, 1958-60; pres. Oak Ridge Unitarian Ch., 1955-56. Mem. Am. Sociol. Assn. (sec. environ. soc. sect. 1980-82), So. Sociol. Soc., Internat. Assn. for Impact Assessment, East Tenn. Soc. for Risk Analysis (sec. 1984-85). Democrat. Home: 130 Oklahoma Ave Oak Ridge TN 37830 Office: Oak Ridge Nat Lab PO Box X Integrated Assessments Sect Oak Ridge TN 37830

PEEPLES, KATHLEEN GAY, project manager; b. Morgantown, W.Va., Feb. 25, 1944; d. Carl Bertram and Kathleen (Callahan) Osborne; B.A., U. Okla., 1966; M.A.E., Inter Am. U., 1969; M.A., Goddard Coll., 1975; M.B.A., M.S.M., Houston Baptist U., 1984; postgrad. U. Calif., 1979, NYU, 1979-80; m. Gerald T. Peeples, Dec. 27, 1966. Instr. composition Inter Am. U., P.R., 1968-70; tchr. Ramey Base Schs. and Antilles Consol. Sch. System, P.R., 1970-78, coordinator elem. edn. Antilles Consol. Sch. System, 1978-80, dir. instrn., asst. supt., 1980-81; sr. tng. evaluation specialist Brown & Root, Houston, 1981-82; tng./devel. mgr. Igloo Corp., 1982-84, new products project mgr., 1984—. Vice pres., editor Informa, LWV, P.R., 1980; mem. cons. Options Career Coop., 1981. Cert. tchr., Tenn., Calif., N.Y.; cert. adminstr., N.Y., Calif. Mem. Assn. Supervision and Curriculum Devel. (curriculum com.), Am. Soc. Tng. and Devel., Orgn. Devel. Network, Career Devel. Network, Ednl. Leadership Council Am., Project Mgmt. Inst., Assn. Ednl. Communication and Tech., Learning Styles Network. Contbr. articles to profl. jours. Home: 110 Stratford Houston TX 77006

PEEPLES, VERNON MCCOY, oil company executive, geologist; b. Clarksdale, Miss., Sept. 4, 1952; s. Lewis Terry and Frances (McCoy) P.; m. Beverly Kaye Owens, May 15, 1976; 1 child, Matthew Allen. B.S. in Geology, Miss. State U., 1974; M.S. in Geology, U. S.C., 1976. Registered profl. geologist. Area ops. geologist Amoco, New Orleans, 1976-80, asst. to v.p., Chgo., 1980, div. geologist, Houston, 1980-84, regional geologic mgr., New Orleans, 1984—. Contbr. articles to profl. jours. Bd. dirs. Dramedy, Inc., Chgo., 1980; counselor Jr. Achievement, New Orleans, 1977; youth dir. First Baptist Ch., Katy, Tex., 1982. Amoco Found. fellow, 1975-76. Mem. Am. Assn. Petroleum geologists (cert.), Sigma Gamma Epsilon (pres. 1973-74, W.A. Tarr award 1974). Republican. Club: Bass Angler Sportsman Soc. Avocations: fishing; music; water skiing. Office: Amoco Prodn Co PO Box 50879 New Orleans LA 70150

PEFKAROU, ATHENA (CHRISTODOULOU), pediatric hematologist and oncologist; b. Nicosia, Cyprus, July 30, 1948; came to U.S., 1974; d. Miltiades and Loula (Demetriadou) Christodoulou; m. Kyriacos C. Pefkaros, Jan. 14, 1973; children—Chryso, Soula. Resident in pediatrics, Mercy Hosp., Balt., 1974-77; fellow in pediatric hematology and oncology Children's Hosp., Miami, Fla., 1977-80, attending in pediatric hematology and oncology, 1980—. Fellow Am. Acad. Pediatrics; mem. AMA, Fla. Med. Assn., Fla. Pediatric Soc. Greek Orthodox. Home: 14405 SW 84th Ct Miami FL 33158 Office: Miami Children's Hosp 6125 SW 31st St Miami FL 33155

PEGG, PHILLIP OLIVER, data processor, government official; ofcl.; b. Bayard, Nebr., Aug. 24, 1929; s. Harley Thomas and Gretna Lois (Gray) P.; B.S., Am. U., 1956, M.B.A., 1958; student U. Nebr., 1947-49; m. Ursula Anna M. Frank, July 26, 1954; children—Linda Marie, Phillip Oliver. With U.S. Steel Corp., Fairless, Pa., 1957-61, cost analyst, 1960, methods analyst, 1961; systems cons. CBS, N.Y.C., 1961-63; systems cons. Fawcett Publs., Louisville, 1963-66, mgr. systems design and data processing Fawcett Printing, 1966-69; asst. v.p. data processing Life of Ky. Ins. Co., Louisville, 1969-70; mgr. data processing Dairymen Inc., Louisville, 1970-75; computer specialist fed. order no. 4 Middle Atlantic milk mktg. area dairy div. Agrl. Mktg. Service, USDA, Alexandria, Va., 1975—. Served to 1st lt. USMCR, 1950-54. Mem. Assn. Systems Mgmt. (pres., dir. 1966-67). Home: 8617 Old Mount Vernon Rd Alexandria VA 22309 Office: 1199 N Fairfax Alexandria VA 22314

PEGRAM, GEORGE WORTHY, JR., optometrist; b. Chesapeake, Va., Apr. 26, 1926; s. George Worthy Sr. and Fannie Elizabeth (Holloman); m. Bernice Lambert, May 26, 1956; children—Jan Sheree, Jill Nannette, Joan Lynn, George W. III. B.A., Bridgewater Coll., Va., 1950; B.S., O.D., So. Coll. Optometry, Tenn., 1953. Gen. practice optometry, Chesapeake, Va. Commn. mem. Chesapeake Fine Arts Commn., 1983—; bd. dirs. Chesapeake Sch. Bd. Dist., 1975-82; bd. dirs. Tidewater council Girls Club, Inc., 1978—, pres., 1982-84; bd. dirs. Virginia Beach Family Ctr., 1978—. Fellow Va. Acad. Optometry (pres. 1978-79); mem. Tidewater Optometry Assn. (pres. 1965-66), Va. Optometric Assn. (bd. dirs. 1970-77), So. Council Optometry, Am. Optometric Assn. Methodist (lay leader 1982—). Lodge: Lions (pres. 1972-73). Avocation: golfing. Home: 1120 Virginia Ave Chesapeake VA 23324 Office: 1109 Poindexter St Chesapeake VA 23324

PEHL, GLEN EUGENE, risk and insurance consultant; b. Woodford, Wis., Aug. 10, 1932; s. Henry Earnest and Ella Viola Pehl; m. Mazie Lee McCrackin, July 9, 1960; children—Keith, Tracey. B.S. in Bus. Adminstrn., Ala. Poly. Inst., 1958. Indsl. account rep. Am. Mut. Liability Ins. Co., Charlotte, N.C., 1958-60, br. sales mgr., 1960-64, dist. sales mgr., 1964-66; chmn., pres., treas. Indsl. Ins. Mgmt. Corp. and Corp. Life Cons., Inc., Charlotte, 1966—; dir. N.C. Self-Insurers Assn., 1976-80; lectr. Trustee Alexander Children's Home, Charlotte, 1982—. Served with USAF, 1951-55. Decorated Nat. Def. medal. Mem. N.C. Citizens Assn. Republican. Presbyterian. Clubs: Charlotte City, Cedarwood Country. Lodge: Masons. Home: 4516 Randolph Rd Apt #110 Charlotte NC 28211 Office: Indsl Ins Mgmt Corp 5222 Monroe Rd PO Box 18308 Charlotte NC 28218

PEIFFER, ARTHUR LEROY, health care professional, hospital corporation executive, behavioral scientist; b. Borger, Tex., July 30, 1942; s. Clifton Lee and Eloise Mae (Brown) P.; m. Susan Jean Munn, Apr. 7, 1969 (div. 1973); children—Gregory Lloyd, Rochelle Jean. B.S. in Psychology and Sociology, Eastern N.Mex. U., 1965; M.A. in Counseling Psychology, U. N.Mex., 1968, postgrad., 1969-77; Ph.D. in Behavioral Sci., Clayton U., 1978; grad. Sarus Inst. Biofeedback Tech. Cert. alcoholism counselor, Tex.; profl. hypnotist; cert. biofeedback practitioner. Psychol. counselor, div. vocat. rehab. N.Mex. Dept. Edn., Albuquerque, 1965-66; dir. counseling and testing Home Edn. Livelihood Program, OEO Project, N.Mex. Council of Chs., Albuquerque, 1966-67; instr. Western State Coll., Gunnison, Colo., summer 1968; doctoral intern, Nazareth Psychiat. Hosp., Albuquerque and U. N.Mex., 1968-69; psychometrist, U. N.Mex., Albuquerque, 1967-69; cons. psychologist, div. vocat. rehab., Inmate Program, N.Mex. State Penitentiary, Santa Fe, 1969-70, dir. placement, instr. psychology, Coll. of Santa Fe, 1969-70; cons. psychologist, div. vocat. rehab. Patient Program, Alcoholism Treatment Program, Albuquerque, 1970-71, chief clin. psychologist, 1971-72; program psychologist, adminstr. Alcohol Safety Action Program, Albuquerque, 1970-71; adj. prof. for internship programs, Eastern N.Mex. U., Portales, 1971-72; dir. clin. services La Hacienda Alcoholism Rehab. Facility (br. Nat. Living Ctrs., Inc.), Hunt, Tex., 1972-74, exec. dir. La Hacienda Alcoholism Treatment Ctr., Inc., Hunt, 1974-75; instr. psychology Schreiner Coll., Kerrville, Tex., 1972-75; founder-clin. dir. Stress, Tension, & Anxiety Tng. Clinic, Inc., Houston, 1975-77; dir. clin. services program for alcoholisms, addictions, stress and anxiety Houston Internat. Hosp. and Med. Ctr. Del Oro Hosp., East Dallas Hosp., Shoal Creek Hosp., Austin, 1975-77; v.p. Positive Alternatives to Anxiety, Stress, and Addictions, Inc., Houston, 1977-78; corp. staff specialist Hosp. Affiliates Internat., Inc., Gulf Coast Region, Houston, 1977-78; exec. v.p., full ptnr. Contemporary Health, Inc., nat. hdqrs., Houston, 1978-82; founder, exec. dir. Stress Mgmt. Research Assocs., Inc., Houston, 1978—; pres. Vista Health, Inc. of Calif., San Diego, 1981—; pres. Med. Programs, Inc., nat. hdqrs., Houston, 1982—; pres. Vista Health Programs, Inc., nat. hdqrs., Houston, 1982—. Charter mem. Republican presdl. task force; mem. Nat. Rep. Congl. Com.; campaign mem. Rep. Nat. Com., 1982. Mem. Tex. Assn. Alcoholism Counselors, Nat. Assn. Alcoholism Counselors and Trainers, Biofeedback Soc. Am., Am. Assn. Biofeedback Clinicians, Biofeedback Soc. Tex., Nat. Rehab. Counselors Assn., Council for Exceptional Children, Am. Personnel and Guidance Assn., Am. Group Psychotherapy Assn., World Congress Profl. Hypnotists, Am. Assn. Marriage and Family Therapy, Sigma Alpha Epsilon (founder mem. N.Mex.). Author: Alcohol, The Individual and the Automobile, 1972, cassette tape series: Stress Management Tng. Program, 1980; contbr. papers to profl. publs. and confs. Home: 2719 Olympia Missouri City TX 77459 Office: 3401 Louisiana Suite 230 Houston TX 77002

PEIXOTO, JULIO LEON, statistician, educator; b. Montevideo, Uruguay, Feb. 14, 1950; came to U.S. 1977, permanent resident, 1984; s. Julio Francisco Peixoto and Margarita Magdalena (Schwab) de Maldonado; m. Elbia Raquel Scarone, Jan. 14, 1976; children—Marcos, Magdalena. Economista, U. de la Republica, Montevideo, 1976; M.S. in Stats., Iowa State U., 1979, Ph.D. in Stats., 1982. Tchg. asst. U. de la Republica, Montevideo, 1971-76; cons. Ministry of the Economy, Montevideo, 1976, Centro de Investigaciones Económicas, Montevideo, 1979; tchg. asst. Iowa State U., Ames, 1980-82; asst. prof. U. Houston, 1982—; referee Jour. of Am. Statis. Assn., 1984—. Contbr. articles to profl. jours. Mem. Am. Statis. Assn., Biometric Soc., Inst. Math. Stats., Colegio de Doctores en Ciencias Economicas del Uruguay, Phi Kappa Phi, Mu Sigma Rho. Avocation: soccer. Home: 11654 Corkwood Dr Houston TX 77089 Office: Dept Quantitative Mgmt Sci U Houston Univ Park 4800 Calhoun Houston TX 77004

PELLEGRIN, LLOYD MICHAEL, corporation human resources manager, oil drilling contractor; b. Houma, La., Oct. 24, 1947; s. Gilmore Joseph and Gloria Geraldine (Gomes) P.; m. Martha Jane Duplantis, Jan. 20, 1968 (div. 1979); children—Keith James, Brian Anthony. B.S., Nicholls State Coll., 1969. Mgr. safety Atlantic Pacific Marine Corp., Houma, La., 1979-81, mgr. safety, tng., 1981, mgr. bus. adminstrn., 1981-83, mgr. human resources, 1983—. Served with USN, 1970-74. Democrat. Roman Catholic. Lodge: Lions (pres. 1979). Home: 377 Westside Blvd Apt 240 Houma LA 70364 Office: Atlantic Pacific Marine Corp 821 Saadi St Houma LA 70361

PELLEGRINI, ANTHONY DAVID, psychology educator; b. Providence, Feb. 17, 1949; s. Antonio and Anne (Algeni) P.; m. Lee Galda, Jan. 22, 1983; 1 child, Anna. B.A., Nasson Coll., 1971; M.A., Ohio State U., 1976, Ph.D., 1979. Asst. prof. U. R.I., Kingston, 1978-79; assoc. prof. psychology U. Ga., Athens, 1979—. Editor: Social Context of Language, 1984; Play, 1984. Sarah Moss fellow, 1984. Mem. Am. Psychol. Assn., Am. Ednl. Research Assn., Soc. Research Child Devel. Home: 1695 Morton Rd Athens GA 30605

PELLENZ, EDWARD JAMES, civil engineer, mining engineer; b. Cheboygan, Mich., Feb. 21, 1949; s. Edward and Eleanor Marie (Faggion) P.; children—Edward James, Adrian Matthew, Patricia Jo. B.S. in Civil Engring., Mich. Technol. U., 1973. Registered profl. engr., Ky., Mich., Fla. Civil engr., mining div. Agrico Chem. Co., Pierce, Fla., 1973-77; chief engr. Three Rivers Rock Co., Smithland, Ky., 1977-79; div. ops. mgr. Ottawa Silica Co., Rockwood, Mich., 1979-80; project engr. Badger Engrs., Inc., Tampa, Fla., 1980—; prin. Pellenz & Assocs., Brandon, Fla. State of Mich. scholar, 1967. Mem. ASCE, AIME. Club: Brandon Amateur Radio Soc. Roman Catholic. Home: PO Box 222 Brandon FL 34299 Office: 1401 N Westshore Blvd Tampa FL 33622

PELOSI, LORRAINE MARY, educational administrator; b. N.Y.C., Apr. 8, 1941; d. Joshua and Elizabeth Orgel (Deming) Esposito; B.S., Pace Coll., 1971; m. William Demarest, Jan. 13, 1962 (dec. 1969); children—William, Susan, Robert; m. 2d, Andrew Pelosi, Apr. 7, 1971; children—Gina, Nicole. Pvt. tutor, Thornwood, N.Y., 1969; nursery sch. asst. Pace Little Sch./Pace Cottage, Pleasantville, N.Y., 1970; tchr. emotionally disturbed Pleasantville (N.Y.) Cottage Sch., 1970-73; founder, dir., tchr. Gingerbread Nursery Sch., St. Petersburg, Fla., 1972—; founder, dir. Wellington Sch., St. Petersburg, 1974; founder, pres. Gingerbread Nursery Sch., Seminole, Fla., 1978—; pres. Gingerbread-Wellington Schs., St. Petersburg, 1975—; founder Gingerbread Nursery Sch. Azalea, St. Petersburg, 1982; pres. Gingerbread Sch. NE, Inc.; founder Gingerbread-Wellington Sch.-Bardmoor, Seminole, 1983. Lectr., cons. Mem. So. Assn. Children Under Six Pinellas Assn. Children Under Six, Pinellas Assn. Acad. Non-Public Schs., Women's Forum. Lutheran. Home: 931 79 St S Saint Petersburg FL 33707 Office: 4355 Central Ave Saint Petersburg FL 33713

PELS, LAURA KRALICKE, optometrist; b. Crowell, Tex., Oct. 5, 1956; d. Martin M. and Mary Elizabeth (Gravelle) K.; m. Kevin H. Pels, Dec. 29, 1979. B.S., U. Houston, 1980, D.Optometry, 1982. Optometrist dept. ophthalmology U. Tex. Health Sci. Ctr., Dallas, 1982—, dir. contact lenses, 1982—, dir. low vision, 1982—. CCD instr. St. Ann's Catholic Mission, Coppell, Tex., 1984-85. Bausch & Lomb softlens scholar, Houston, 1980, 82; recipient Tex. Optometric Aux. award Edith Greene, Houston, 1981, award Beta Sigma Kappa, 1982. Mem. Am. Optometric Assn., Tex. Optometric Assn., North Tex. Optometric Soc. Roman Catholic. Home: 237 Park Meadow Coppell TX 75019 Office: U Tex Health Sci Ctr Dept Ophthalmology 5303 Harry Hines Dallas TX 75235

PELTON, JAMES RODGER, librarian; b. St. Louis, Mar. 21, 1945; s. Norman C. and Leona V. (Schulte) P.; m. Sandra Lee Birdsell, Mar. 29, 1969; 2 daus., Joni Lee, Vicki Sue. B.A., U. Mo., 1967, M.L.S., 1969. Br. librarian Scenic Regional Library, Union, Mo., 1968-71; adminstr. Daniel Boone Regional Library - Columbia Center, Columbia, Mo., 1971-78; cons. La. State Library, Baton Rouge, 1978-80; dir. Shreve Meml. Library, Shreveport, La., 1980—. Mem. ALA, La. Library Assn. Home: 907 Booth St Shreveport LA 71107 Office: 424 Texas St Shreveport LA 71101*

PEMBERTON, CHARLES EDWARD, JR., educator; b. Covington, Ky., Dec. 28, 1942; s. Charles Edward and Marjorie Evelyn (Smallwood) P.; m. Cassandra Marie Underhill, Apr. 3, 1965 (div. 1970); children—Charles Edward, Jonathan Robert; m. Nancy Young, Aug. 13, 1977. B.S. in Math. and Phys. Edn., Eastern Ky. U., 1965; M.S. in Phys. Edn., U. Ky., 1969. Aquatics dir. U. N.C.-Charlotte, 1970-73; advt. mgr. Dacor Corp., 1973-76; dist. mgr. 3M Co., Bloomington, Ill., 1976-77; tchr. aquatics Clinton (Tenn.) City Schs., 1977—; dir. handicapped swimming U. Tenn., Knoxville, 1977-78; cons., tchr. Pediatric Assocs., Knoxville, 1981—. Served to 1st lt., U.S. Army, 1965-67. Decorated Bronze Star, Army Commendation medal with V. Mem. Undersea Med. Soc., Profl. Assn. Diving Instrs. (master instr., course dir., dist. dir. for Tenn), Tenn. Assn. Health, Phys. Edn. and Recreation and Dance (aquatics chmn. 1980-82). Republican. Baptist. Contbr. articles to profl. jours. Address: 1332 Scotsbury Circle Knoxville TN 37919

PEMBERTON, LEWIS SANFORD, oilfield supply company executive; b. Ardmore, Okla., May 31, 1948; s. Lewis Sanford and Rose Gloria (Hammons) Wilson P.; m. Peggy J. Snow, Aug. 2, 1974 (div. 1985); children—Kristy Michelle, Holli Elizabeth. Student, Southeast State U., 1966-68, Okla. State U., 1972. Sales rep. Am. Tobacco, Dallas, 1974-79, mgr. dist. sales, 1979-82; mgr. sales Tussing Resources, Oklahoma City, 1982-83; v.p. Peacock Mining Inc., Oklahoma City, 1983—; co-chmn. Okla. Tubular Inst., 1984-85; mem. Okla. Oil Producers Ind. Service Co., 1984—; cons. Consol. Pipe Suppliers, 1985. Served with USAF, 1968-72. Republican. Avocations: snow and water skiing; history; geography. Home: 4706 Hemlock Ln Oklahoma City OK 73132 Office: Peacock Mining Inc 205 NW 63d St 160 Oklahoma City OK 73116

PENA, AMADO MAURILIO, JR., artist, curator, lecturer; b. Laredo, Tex., Oct. 1, 1943; s. Amado Maurilio and Maria Baldomera (Arambula) P.; children—Marcos, Jose Luis, Amado Maurilio III. B.A., Tex. A&I U., 1965, M.A. in Art, 1971. Tchr. Laredo Ind. Sch. Dist., 1965-70, Tex. A&I U., Kingsville, 1970-72, Crystal City Ind. Sch. Dist., Tex., 1972-74, Austin Ind. Sch. Dist., Tex., 1974-80; resident artist El Taller, Inc., Austin, 1985—. One man shows include Squash Blossom, Denver, 1985, Lincoln Sq. Gallery, Arlington, Tex., 1985, Galeria Capistrano, San Juan Capistrano, Calif., 1985, Andrews Gallery, Albuquerque, N.Mex., 1985, Joy Tash Gallery, Scottsdale, Ariz., 1985, Byrne-Getz Gallery, Aspen, Colo., 1985, Parke Gallery, Vail, Colo., 1985, Am. West Gallery, Chgo., 1985, Adagio Gallery, Palm Springs, Calif., 1985, Houshang's Gallery, Dallas, 1985, Mus. Native Am. Art, Spokane, Wash., 1985, El Taller, Taos, N.Mex., 1985, Austin, 1985, Kauffman Gallery, Houston, 1985, others; represented in permanent collection: Palacio del Gobernador, Baja California, Mex., Hist. Creative Arts Ctr., Lufkin, Tex., Mus. Nuevo Santander, Laredo, Smithsonian Inst., Washington, Whitney Mus., San Antonio, Tex., also corp., univs., and pvt. collections. Commd. by civic and arts orgns. for fund-raising events and spl. presentations. Avocations: purchasing quarter horses; horseback riding. Office: El Taller Inc 510 E Ave Austin TX 78701

PEÑA, LUCILO ANDRÉS, architect; b. Havana, Cuba, Jan. 4, 1957; came to U.S. 1974, naturalized 1980; s. Lucilo Andrés and Maria Elena (Morales) P. B.A. in Design, U. Fla., 1978; B.Arch., Cornell U., 1980, M.Arch., 1982. Instr. Boston Archtl. Ctr., 1981; archtl. designer W.Z.M.H. Group, Inc., Dallas, 1982-84; archtl. project mgr. Trammell Crow Design and Constrn., Dallas, 1984, Dallas Mkt. Ctr. Co., Dallas, 1985—. Editor: Harvard U. Meml. Chapel, 1981. Contbr. to book and exhbn. The Urban Garden, Berlin, 1978. Grantee Cornell U., 1981; recipient Eschweiler prize Cornell U., 1980. Mem. Phi Kappa Phi, Phi Eta Sigma. Roman Catholic. Office: Dallas Mkt Ctr Co 2100 Stemmons Freeway Dallas TX 75207.

PENA, MODESTA CELEDONIA, educator; b. San Diego, Tex., Mar. 3, 1929; d. Encarnacion E. and Teofila (Garcia) P.; B.A., Tex. State Coll. for Women, 1950, M.A., 1953, cert. supr., 1979; cert. prin. Tex. A&I U., 1961, cert. supt., 1981. Tchr. English, San Diego (Tex.) High Sch., 1950-76; asst. supt. curriculum and instrn. San Diego Ind. Sch. Dist., 1976-80; gifted edn. resource tchr. William Adams Jr. High Sch., Alice, Tex., 1980-83, asst. prin. for instrn., 1983—; faculty Bee County Coll., 1975-76. Vice-pres., San Diego PTA, 1963; mem. Duval County Hist. Commn., 1979—. Newspaper Fund Inc. fellow, 1964. Mem. Tex. State Tchrs. Assn. (rec. sec. 1952-53, 63-64, 1st v.p. 1957-58, 66-67 pres. 1961), Nat. Council Tchrs. English, Tex. Council Tchrs. English, Delta Kappa Gamma (rec. sec. chpt. 1972-74, first v.p. 1974-76, pres. 1976-78; Achievement award 1986), Phi Delta Kappa (treas. chpt. 1978-79, sec. chpt. 1983-84). Home: PO Box 353 306 W Gravis Ave San Diego TX 78384 Office: 901 E 3d Ave Alice TX 78332

PENA, RAYMUNDO JOSEPH, bishop; b. Corpus Christi, Tex., Feb. 19, 1934; s. Cosme A. and Elisa (Ramon) P.; grad. St. John's Sem., San Antonio; D.D., Assumption Sem., San Antonio, 1957. Ordained priest Roman Catholic Church, 1957; asst. pastor St. Peter's, Laredo, Tex., 1957-60, St. Joseph's/Our Lady of Fatima, Alamo, Tex., 1960-63, Sacred Heart, Mathis, Tex., 1963-66, Christ the King and Our Lady of Pillar Parishes, Corpus Christi, 1966-69; founding pastor Our Lady of Guadalupe Parish, Corpus Christi, 1969-76; diocesan positions in Diocese of Corpus Christi include diocesan youth dir., 1967-70, asso. editor, editor Tex. Gulf Coast Cath., 1970-75, diocesan consultor, 1968-76, dir. dept. Mexican Am. Affairs, 1971-76, prosynodal judge, 1971-76, mem. liturgical commn., 1973-76, mem. Corpus Christi Sem. Clergy Bd., 1973-76, v.p. Corpus Christi Diocesan Senate of Priests, 1970-76; named titular bishop of Trisipa and aux. to archbishop of San Antonio, 1976; ordained bishop, 1976; appointments in Archdiocese of San Antonio include: aux. bishop, 1976, exec. dir. Office for Laity, 1977, vicar gen., 1977, diocesan consultor, 1977, adminstr. Sede Vacante, 1979; bd. dirs. Ecumenical Council of Chs., Archdiocese of San Antonio, 1977, vice chmn., 1977, chmn., 1978, bd. dirs. Region X Office for Hispanic Affairs, v.p., Tex. Conf. Chs., 1979; appointed bishop of El Paso, Tex., 1980—. Mem. nat. com. Campaign for Human Devel., 1974-76; active civic positions, Corpus Christi, including founding pres. Mathis Community Action Agy., v.p. Nueces County Child Welfare Bd., mem. 1969-72, Corpus Christi Econ. Devel. Corp. Bd., 1968-74, mem. Goals for Corpus Christi Com., 1972, bd. dirs. Nueces County Mental Health-Mental Retardation Community Center, 1974-76; civic positions, San Antonio, include: charter mem. adv. council Family Life Center, St. Mary's U., 1977, charter mem. adv. council Villa Rosa Hosp., 1977; mem. ad hoc com. on evangelization Nat. Conf. Cath. Bishops, 1979-84, com. on parish, 1980-83, com. on vocations, bd. dirs. Nat. Shrine of Immaculate Conception, 1981-84. Mem. Nat. Conf. Cath. Bishops, U.S. Cath. Conf. (com. on communications). Clubs: KC, Padres Asociados para Derechos Religiosos Educativos y Sociales. Office: 499 St Matthews El Paso TX 79907

PENALOZA, CHARLES AARON, jeweler, appraiser; b. San Antonio, Jan. 17, 1948; s. Charles G. and Marie Grace (Patino) P.; m. Mary Holm, July 17, 1971; children—Charles Anthony, Catherine Adele. Student U. Tex., 1966-72. Mgr., Penaloza & Sons, Inc., San Antonio, 1973-75, corp. sec., 1975-83, pres., 1983—; mem. steering com. jewelry program San Antonio Coll., 1983. Bd. dirs. Paseo Del Rio Assn., San Antonio, 1982—. Mem. Nat. Assn. Gem and Jewelry Appraisers (cert. appraiser, sr.), Jewelers Am. Internat. Soc. Appraisers (pres. San Antonio chpt.), Jewelers Bd. Trade, Retail Jewelers Am., San Antonio Mus. Assn., San Antonio Zool. Assn., Gallery of McNay Art Mus. Club: San Antonio Gun, St. Anthony (San Antonio). Office: Penaloza & Sons Inc 214 W Crockett St San Antonio TX 78205

PENBERTHY, ANN ROWLEY, clinical psychologist; b. Idaho Falls, Idaho, Feb. 10, 1941; s. Coy Brooks and Zelma J. (Waller) Rowley; m. John Albert Penberthy, Sept. 5, 1963; children—John Scott, David Rowley. B.A. in Psychology with honors, U. Mo., 1963; M.A., U. Richmond, 1977; Ph.D., Va. Commonwealth U., 1982. Lic. clin. psychologist, Va. Intern predoctoral clin. psychology dept. child psychiatry Med. Coll. Va., Richmond, 1980-81, postdoctoral fellow clin. neuropsychology dept. rehab., 1981-82, asst. clin. prof. gerontology, 1983—; clin. psychologist Hunter Holmes McGuire VA Med. Ctr., Richmond, 1982—; asst. affiliate prof. psychology Va. Commonwealth U., 1983—. Recipient Research Design award Va. Ctr. Aging, 1979. Mem. Am. Psychol. Assn., Va. Psychol. Assn. (com. 1982—), Va. Acad. Clin. Psychologists, So. Gerontol. Soc., Va. Acad. Sci. (chmn. sect. 1985—, sec. 1983—) Soc. Behavioral Medicine. Psi Chi, Sigma Phi Omega, Pi Beta Phi. Republican. Baptist. Office: Hunter Holmes McGuire VA Med Ctr 1201 Broad Rock Rd Richmond VA

PENDERGAST, RICHARD JOSEPH, ins. co. exec.; b. Newburg, W.Va., June 12, 1933; s. Thomas Leo and Edith (Gibson) P.; A.A., Potomac State Coll., 1953; B.S. in Journalism, W.Va. U., 1959; children by previous marriage—Mary Elizabeth, Jennifer Ann, Kathryn Lesley. Newsman, AP, New Orleans, 1959; editor Pan-Am. Life Ins. Co., New Orleans, 1959-65, asst. dir. pub. relations, 1965-73, dir. pub. relations, 1973—; mem. pub. relations com. United Way, New Orleans; communications adviser New Orleans Pub. Schs. Served with USMC, 1953-57. Recipient Distinguished Service award Internat. Council Indsl. Editors, 1968; named Communicator of Year Indsl. Editors La., 1964. Mem. Pub. Relations Soc. Am. (accredited, pres. New Orleans chpt. 1975-76), Life Advertisers Assn. (exec. com.), La. Press Assn., New Orleans C. of C., Marine Corps Combat Corr. Assn. Club: New Orleans Press. Editor Life Advertiser, 1976-77. Home: 2020 Dartmouth St Gretna LA 70053 Office: Pan-Am Life Center New Orleans LA 70130

PENDERGRASS, EWELL DEAN, communications executive; b. Houston, Dec. 24, 1945; s. Ewell Burl and Mary LaVerne (Sharp) P.; A.A.S., Westark Community Coll., 1979; m. Linda Jo Williams, 1973; children—William Dean, Douglas Aaron, Nagaya Jo. Communication technician Murdock Communication, Ft. Smith, Ark., 1966-73; electronics technician City of Ft. Smith, 1973—; now electronics supr.; co-owner LED Communications, 1975—; broadcast engr. Sta. KWHN, 1972-73, Sta. KFSA, 1975-76. Mem. Am. Water Works Assn., Ark. Water Works and Pollution Control Assn. (chmn. Western dist. 1985). Democrat. Methodist. Club: Border Amateur Radio (pres. 1974-75). Home: 119 Martin Circle Fort Smith AR 72903 Office: Box 1908 13 North P St Fort Smith AR 72901

PENDERGRASS, ROSE HELEN, nursing administrator, consultant; b. Pittstown, N.J., Apr. 30, 1926; d. John Peter and Elizabeth (Jacob) Hahola; m. Jack Hoyt Pendergrass, June 26, 1953; children—Elizabeth, Gregory, John. Staff nurse Somerset Hosp., Somerville, N.J., 1946-49; asst. head nurse NYU Hosp., 1950-52; pediatric instr. Duke U. Sch. Nursing, Durham, N.C., 1952-54; nursing supr. Duke Hosp., Durham, 1955-63; inservice edn. dir. McPherson Hosp., Durham, 1969-73, dir. nursing, 1973—. Mem. N.C. Nursing Adminstrn. Soc., Nat. League Nursing, Am. Nurses Assn., N.C. Hosp. Assn., N.C. Nurses Assn. Democrat. Roman Catholic. Club: Catholic Daus. (sentry). Avocations: helping elderly and needy families; music; dancing; art; sewing. Home: 226 Argonne Dr Durham NC 27704 Office: McPherson Hosp 1110 W Main St Durham NC 27701

PENDLETON, WILLIAM HARRY, trucking company executive; b. Seminole, Okla., Sept. 4, 1938; s. William Ordell and Clara Nadine (Herndon) P.; student U. Md., 1957-60; B.B.A., Washburn U., 1965; m. Joan C. Francis, Feb. 21, 1958; children—Terry L., William D., Laura L. Ops. mgr. Roadway Express Inc., Chgo., 1965-68; asst. to v.p. Spector Freight System, Chgo., 1969; terminal mgr. Spector Freight, Nashville, 1970; gen. mgr. Lewisburg Transfer Co. (Tenn.), 1971; pres., owner Dyersburg Express Inc. 1972—, Delta Drayage & Distbn. Co., Dyersburg, 1977—, Sartain Truck Line, 1977—; owner Pendleton Industries, Inc., Roadmasters, 1979—; pres. Motor Carrier Corp., 1981—. Chmn., Dyer County Election Commn., 1975—; vice chmn. bd. dirs. Parkview Hosp.; mem. Conservative Caucus; col., a.d.c. staff gov. Tenn.; mem. consumer adv. council Tenn. Public Service Commn., 1978. Served with USAF, 1956-64. Mem. Am. Trucking Assn. (bd. govs.), Irregular Route Conf. (dir.), Regional and Distbn. Carriers Conf. (dir.), Tenn. Motor Transport Assn. (chmn. bd.), Dyersburg C. of C. (v.p. legis. affairs), Nat. Small Bus. Assn. (action council), Delta Sigma Pi. Baptist. Clubs: Lions, Rotary, Masons, West Tenn. Traffic. Home: Route 3 Dyersburg TN 38024 Office: PO Box 1298 Dyersburg TN 38024

PENFIELD, HENRY IRVIN, JR., political science educator, consultant, survey researcher; b. Birmingham, Ala., Feb. 15, 1940; s. Henry Irvin and Lois Iwilda (Ellis) P.; m. Elise McWilliams, June 9, 1939; children—Russell Ellis, Matthew Irvin. B.A., U. Ala., 1962, M.A., 1965, Ph.D., 1970; postgrad. U. Mich., 1976, U. Wis., 1979. Asst. prof. polit. sci. Birmingham-So. Coll. (Ala.), 1967, prof., 1978—, head grad. program mgmt., 1982-83, chmn. div. behavioral and social scis., 1972—; also cons. Bd. dirs. Birmingham Housing Service, 1977-79; sec. Ala. State Commn. Ethics in Judiciary, 1973; mem. Birmingham Com. Fgn. Relations. Recipient Omicron Delta Kappa award Danforth Assn. Mem. So. Polit. Sci. Assn., Am. Polit. Sci. Assn., Western Polit. Sci. Assn., Mid-West Polit. Sci. Assn., Ala. Polit. Sci. Assn., Ga. Polit. Sci. Assn., Southwestern Polit. Sci. Assn. Methodist. Author numerous profl. papers. Home: 1204 Greensboro Rd Birmingham AL 35208 Office: Birmingham-Southern College 800 8th Ave W Birmingham AL 35254

PENFIELD, MARJORIE PORTER, food scientist, educator; b. Mt. Pleasant, Pa., May 28, 1942; d. Harry Percy and Frieda L. (Wood) Porter; m. Rogers C. Penfield, July 29, 1972. B.S., Pa. State U., 1964, M.S., 1966; Ph.D., U. Tenn., 1973. Instr., extension specialist Va. Poly. Inst. and State U., Blacksburg, 1966-71; asst. prof. U. Ky., Lexington, 1974; asst. prof. U. Tenn., Knoxville, 1974-78, assoc. prof., 1978-86, prof. nutrition and food scis., 1986—, prof. food tech. and sci., 1986—. Recipient U. Tenn. Coll. Home Econs. Faculty Excellence award, 1982. Mem. Am. Home Econs. Assn., Am. Dietetic Assn., Inst. Food Technologists, Am. Meat Sci. Assn., Am. Assn. Cereal Chemists, Soc. Nutrition Edn., Pa. State Alumni Assn., Sigma Xi, Phi Kappa Phi, Omicron Nu, Phi Upsilon Omicron, Sigma Delta Epsilon, Phi Tau Sigma, Gamma Sigma Delta, Alpha Omicron Pi. Presbyterian. Author textbook in food sci.; co-author The Experimental Study of Food, 1979; contbr. numerous articles to profl. jours. Office: U Tenn Dept Food Tech and Sci Knoxville TN 37996

PENG, LIANG-CHUAN, mech. engr.; b. Taiwan, Feb. 6, 1936; came to U.S., 1965, naturalized, 1973; s. Mu-Sui and Wang-Su (Yang) P.; diploma Taipei Inst. Tech., 1960; M.S., Kans. State U., 1967; m. Wen-Fong Kao, Nov. 18, 1962; children—Tsen-Loong, Tsen-Hsin, Lina, Linda. Project engr. Taiwan Power Co., 1960-65; asst. engr. Carlson & Sweatt, N.Y.C., 1966-67; asst. engr. Pioneer Engrs., Chgo., 1967-68; mech. engr. Bechtel, San Francisco, 1969-71; sr. specialist Nuclear Services Co., San Jose, Calif., 1971-75; sr. engr. Brown & Root, Houston, 1975; stress engr. Foster Wheeler, Houston, 1976; staff engr. AAA Technologists, Houston, 1977; prin. engr. M.W. Kellogg, Houston, 1978-82; pres., owner Peng Engring., Houston, 1982—; instr. U. Houston. Chmn., South Bay Area Formosan Assn., 1974, No. Calif. Formosan Fedn., 1975. Registered profl. engr., Tex., Calif. Mem. ASME, Nat. Soc. Profl. Engrs., Confucian. Home: 3010 Manila Ln Houston TX 77043

PENICK, MICHAEL HAYES, construction company executive; b. Martin, Tenn., Mar. 2, 1944; s. William Tommie and Myrtle (Jackson) P.; m. Mary Elizabeth Penick, July 15, 1967; children—Michael Hayes, Carolyn Elizabeth. B.S.C.E., U. Tenn.-Knoxville, 1967. Estimator Blount Bros. Corp., Montgomery, Ala., 1967-69, project engr., Cin., 1970-72; project engr. Mercury Constrn. Corp., Lakeland, Fla., 1973-74, chief estimator, Montgomery, 1975-79; dir. estimating Blount Internat. Ltd., Montgomery, 1980-82; v.p. Blount Bros. Corp., Dallas, 1983—. Chmn. bd. East YMCA, Montgomery, 1979-81. Mem. Assoc. Gen. Contractors, North Tex. Contractors Assn., Dallas C. of C. Republican. Methodist. Clubs: 2001, Prestonwood Country. Home: 3109 Citadel Plano TX 75023 Office: Blount Bros Corp 14901 Quorum Dr Suite 420 Dallas TX 75240

PENLAND, JOHN ERWIN, JR., extermination company executive; b. Waycross, Ga., Aug. 31, 1926; s. Nell Glenn (Bates) P.; m. Amy Elizabeth, Apr. 11, 1981; children—Sandra Penland Blease, David; stepchildren—Susan, Johnny, David, Jerry. A.B. in Biology, Emory U., 1950; postgrad. Citadel U. Salesman, mgr. Orkin Co., several states, 1953-59; termite cons., 1959-79; owner, pres. Pied Piper Inc., Charleston, S.C., 1979—; pub. speaker, seminar trainer in field; v.p. Nebr. Pest Control Assn., 1957; pres. Kans. Pest Control Assn., 1958. Served with USN, 1944-46. Mem. S.C. Pest Control Assn., Home Builders Assn. (bd. dirs.), MENSA, Phi Sigma, Pi Chi Omega. Republican. Episcopalian. Clubs: James Island Yacht (treas.), Toastmasters (pres. S.C.). Lodges: Sertoma, Elks. Home: 694 Clearview Dr Charleston SC 29412 Office: Pied Piper Inc PO Box 12859 Charleston SC 29412

PENLEY, ALYCE BROOKE, principal; b. Roanoke, Va., May 4, 1939; d. Charles Cornelius and Thelma Mae (Fringer) Rodeniser; m. Dean Fuller Penley, Oct. 28, 1960; 1 child, Kristie Adora. B.S., Roanoke Coll., 1960; M.A., Hollins Coll., 1978; M.A., Va. Tech and State U., 1979, postgrad. in sch. adminstrn. Cert. secondary prin., Va. Tchr., Roanoke City Pub. Schs., 1962-69, 73-80, asst. prin., 1980-83, prin., 1983—; tchr. Kingsport City Pub. Schs., Tenn., 1969-73. Cons. Williamson Rd. Action Forum, 1983—, ARC, 1984—. Recipient U.S. Dept. Edn. Nat. Secondary Sch. award, 1984, 85, Bus. Woman of Yr. award Am. Bus. Women's Assn., 1984. Mem. NEA, Va. Edn. Assn., Roanoke Edn. Assn., Nat. Assn. Secondary Prins., Phi Kappa Phi, Phi Delta Kappa. Republican. Methodist. Avocations: antiques; painting; biking; writing; piano. Home: 1713 Windsor Ave SW Roanoke VA 24015

PENN, BERNARD MICHAEL, special education educator, administrator, coach; b. Alexandria, Va., Aug. 15, 1952; s. Bernard Arthur, Jr. and Barbara Ernestine (McGowan) P. B.S., Appalachian State U., 1974; M.A., George Washington U., 1985. Tchr. mentally disabled Alexandria Schs., Va., 1974-83, chmn. spl. edn. dept., 1975-80, tchr. emotionally disturbed, 1983-85, work experience coordinator, 1985—; rowing coach T.C. Williams High Sch., Alexandria, 1975—, basketball coach, 1976—, football equipment cons., 1985—; site coordinator Alexandria Recreation Dept. Mem. Council Exceptional Children, U.S. Rowing Assn., Nat. Rowing Fedn., Phi Delta Kappa. Presbyterian. Clubs; Alexandria Sportsman, Alexandria Crew Boosters. Avocations: rowing; photography. Office: TC Williams High Sch 3330 King St Alexandria VA 22302

PENN, HUGH FRANKLIN, postmaster, restaurant owner; b. Morgan County, Ala., Aug. 15, 1917; s. Charles Franklin and Bessie Melinda (Praytor) P.; student U. Ala., 1936-37; m. Marynelle Walter, Nov. 12, 1939; children—Hugh Franklin, Charles Phillip, Beverly Ann. Asst. purchasing agt. for contractors constructing Huntsville Arsenal and Redstone Arsenal, Ala., 1941-43; purchasing agt. U.S. Army Air Force, Courtland Army Air Field, Ala., 1943-46; owner, mgr. Hugh Penn Lumber Co., Hartselle, Ala., 1946-60; owner, mgr. C.F. Penn Hamburgers, Hartselle, 1958-81, chmn. bd., 1981—; postmaster Hartselle, 1957-81; office mgr., realtor assoc. Charlie Penn Realty, 1981-85. Chmn., Hartselle Bd. Zoning Adjustment, 1956-76; founder, bd. dirs. Hartselle Downtown Action Com., 1971—; dir. Morgan County Combined Fed. Campaign, 1971-81. Mem. Nat. Assn. Post Masters U.S., Hartselle C. of C. (pres. 1976-77). Republican. Baptist. Club: Kiwanis (Legion of Honor award 1977). Home: 204 Short St Hartselle AL 35640 Office: PO Box 8 Hartselle AL 35640

PENNINGTON, GERALD L., private investor; b. Ashland, Ky., Mar. 6, 1933; s. William Lewis and Carrie Elma (Davis) P.; m. Margaret Angela Handler; children—Amy Lou Pennington Virgen, Abby Lee. Student schs., Ashland. With Ashland Lumber Co., 1954-56, dir., 1959—; sales mgr. Pennco, Inc., Ashland, 1956-69, exec. v.p., 1959-79, cons., 1979—; pres. Storage Ctrs., Ashland, 1979—, Ponderosa Golf Club, Inc., Ashland, 1979—, Penn Products, Venice, Fla., 1982—, Shannsongs, Inc., Nashville, 1985—; chmn. bd. 1st Venice Savs. and Loan Assn., Venice, Fla., 1985—; dir. Suncoast Communications, Inc., Sarasota, Fla., 1983—, Rich, Swartz & Joseph, Nashville, 1975—, United Window Co., Inc., Columbus, Ohio, 1972—. Served with U.S. Merchant Marines, 1951-53, U.S. Army, 1953-54. Mem. Aircraft Owners and Pilots Assn. Baptist. Address: 2207 Casey Key Rd Nokomis FL 33555

PENNINGTON, KENNETH CARLTON, dentist; b. Woodville, Tex., Mar. 21, 1929; s. Robert Earl and Gladys Otelia (Young) P.; m. Margaret Delauris Best, July 6, 1950; children—Peggy Elizabeth Pennington Whitlow, Jerry Stephen. D.D.S., U. Tex.-Houston, 1952. Gen. practice dentistry, Lake Jackson, Tex., 1955—; chmn. bd. Chem. Nat. Bank, Clute, Tex. Pres., Brazosport Jr. Achievement Assn., Lake Jackson, His Love Christian Services, Lake Jackson, 1981. Served to 1st lt. Dental Corp, U.S. Army, 1952-54. Fellow Acad. Gen. Dentistry; mem. 9th Dist. Dental Soc., Southwest Prosthodontic Soc. (pres. 1975), Brazosport C. of C. (pres. 1965, Outstanding Citizen award 1966). Republican. Methodist. Avocation: tennis. Home: 101 Ligustrum St Lake Jackson TX 77566 Office: 102 Flag Lake Rd Lake Jackson TX 77566

PENNINGTON, MARY ANNE, art museum administrator, educator; b. Franklin, Va., Apr. 12, 1943; d. James Clifton and Martha Julia (Futrell) P. Student East Carolina U., 1960-62, U. Md., 1962; B.F.A., Va. Commonwealth U., 1965, M.F.A., 1966; postgrad. Cameron U., 1970, East Carolina U., 1970-72, U. N.C., 1980. Instr. fine arts Presbyn. Coll., Clinton, S.C., 1966-69, Greenville City and Pitt County Schs., N.C., 1970-73, Pitt Community Coll., Greenville, 1971-73; humanities program coordinator Ludwigsberg, West Germany, 1974-76; asst. prof. U. N.C.-Pembroke, 1976-80; dir. Greenville Mus. Art, 1980—. Author: Application of Industrial Sand Casting to Sculpture, 1966; also articles. Dir., cons. Pitt-Greenville Arts Council, 1980-82; program speaker N.C. Dept. Corrections, 1980—; programs coordinator Pitt-Greenville Leadership Inst., 1982—; art competition judge. Recipient Artist-in-Residence award Salt Pond Art Ctr., Blacksburg, Va., summer 1978; Gov.'s Vol. award N.C. Gov.'s Office, 1981. Mem. Am. Assn. Mus., Southeastern Mus. Conf., N.C. Mus. Council (del. 1984-86). Avocations: drawing; reading; travel. Office: Greenville Mus of Art 802 S Evans St Greenville NC 27834

PENNINGTON, RANDY GLEN, human resource management consultant; b. Greenville, Tex., Feb. 16, 1953; s. Claude G. and Pauline (Alexander) P.; m. Susan Rene Adams, July 31, 1977 (div. Dec. 1982). B.S., E. Tex. State U., 1975, M.S., 1978; postgrad. Tarleton State U., 1980. Recreation dir. Terrell (Tex.) State Hosp., 1976-78, asst. personnel dir., 1978-79; dir. aux. services Waco (Tex.) Ctr. for Youth, 1979-84; sr. cons. Performance Systems Corp., Dallas, 1984—; mem. faculty McLennan Community Coll., Waco, 1980-84; cons. organizational devel. Mem. planning com. United Way of McLennan County, 1980-81; pres. McLennan chpt. Am. Heart Assn., 1981-83. Mem. Am. Soc. Pub. Adminstrs., Tex. Pub. Employees Assn. (dir. 1981-84), Waco Personnel and Mgmt. Assn. Democrat. Home: 1414 Walnut St Greenville TX Office: 2925 LBJ Freeway Suite 281 Dallas TX 75234

PENNINGTON, THOMAS KENNY, insurance company executive; b. Bklyn., June 2, 1936; s. Dale Kelsey and Helene Josephine (Kenny) P.; m. Mary Jane Lane, Sept. 7, 1957; children—Thomas Kenny, Mary Jane, Dale K., Mary Helene, Patrick J. B.S., Fordham Coll., 1958; postgrad. Okla. U., 1958-59. Cons. actuary George V. Stennes & Assocs., Mpls., 1961-68; v.p., actuary Coll. Life Ins. Co., Indpls., 1968-70; exec. v.p. Protective Life Ins. Co., Birmingham, Ala., 1970—; exec. v.p., dir. Protective Life Corp., Birmingham, 1982—; dir. United Founders Life Ins. Co., Oklahoma City, Am. Found. Life Ins. Co., Columbus Nat. Life Ins. Co., Ohio. Fellow Soc. Actuaries; mem. Am. Acad. Actuaries, Southeastern Actuaries Club. Republican. Roman Catholic. Lodge: KC. Home: 3717 Locksley Dr Birmingham AL 35223 Office: PO Box 2606 Birmingham AL 35202

PENNINGTON, WILLIAM DAVID, college dean, educator; b. Anadarka, Okla., Nov. 15, 1943; s. Royce Weldon and Marian Elizabeth (Sherrard) P.; m. Margaret Ann Gowans, July 2, 1966; children—Mallory, Mary Martha, David Beatty. B.S., U. Tulsa, 1966, M.A., 1967; Ph.D., U. Okla., 1972. Asst. to pres., dir. devel. William Woods Coll., Fulton, Mo., 1970-73; dir. community schs. Tulsa Pub. Schs., 1973-74; tchr., coach Will Rogers High Sch., Tulsa, 1974-76; dir. student activities Tulsa Jr. Coll., 1976-82, dean student services, 1982—; coordinator 2-yr. schs. Assn. Coll. Unions Internat., 1981-82; chmn. nat. com. on non-resident students Nat. Assn. for Campus Activities, 1982-83; mem.-at-large area III planning council Tulsa Pub. Schs., 1984-85. Contbr. articles to profl. jours. Mem. Am. History Assn., Nat. Assn. Student Personnel Adminstrs., Okla. Coll. Personnel Assn. (v.p., pres.-elect 1984—), Am. Coll. Personnel Assn. (directorate commn. XVII 1983-85), Phi Delta Kappa (pres., del. Tulsa chpt. 1981-83). Democrat. Methodist. Lodge: Kiwanis (sec. 1973). Avocation: jogging. Home: 4150 E 37th St Tulsa OK 74135 Office: Tulsa Jr Coll Northeast Campus 3727 E Apache Tulsa OK 74115

PENNINGTON, WILLIAM LUTHER, geologist; b. Erick, Okla., Apr. 2, 1923; s. William Luther and Ona Izora (McClinton) P.; m. Georgia Armstrong, Dec. 23, 1942 (div. July 1971); m. Camille Pendleton, Dec. 11, 1973; children—Paula, Patricia, James, Denise, Liz, Robby. B.S., U. Okla., 1950. Chief geologist Frank Wood Assocs., Wichita Falls, Tex., 1949-55, sr. geologist Texaco Inc., Wichita Falls, 1955-57, pres. W.L. Pennington Inc., Wichita Falls, 1957—; cons. in field. Served as spl. agent CIC, U.S. Army, 1944-47; ETO. Mem. Am. Assn. Petroleum Geologist, Ind. Producers Assn. Am., Am. Inst. Petroleum Geologists, N. Tex. Oil and Gas Assn., Tex. Ind. Producers and

Royalty Owners. Republican. Clubs: Wichita Falls Country, Wichita Falls. Home: 2013 Hampstead St Wichita Falls TX 76308 Office: 920 Oil and Gas Bldg Wichita Falls TX 76301

PENROSE, GILBERT QUAY, financial planning company executive; b. Robinson, Pa., Sept. 8, 1938; s. Albert Snyder and Olive Jeanette (Boring) P.; B.S. in Chem. Engring., Pa. State U., 1960; m. Anna Mae Riffle, Aug. 22, 1959; children—Kim Denise, Kevin Lee, Kara Lynn. Registered rep. Investors Diversified Services, 1969-70, div. mgr., Huntington, W.Va., 1972-73, Miami, 1973-76; regional mgr. S. Fla., Westamerica Fin. Corp., Miami Lakes, 1976—; pres. Gilbert Penrose & Assocs., Inc., Cert. Fin. Planners, Miami, 1976—, South Pitts. Mgmt. Co., So. Fla. Mgmt. Co., Inc.; pres., chmn. bd. Three K Investments, Inc., B.P.R., Inc., Five Star Concepts, Inc., Columbus Mgmt. Co. Inc., Pitts. Mgmt. Co. Inc., Penrose Internat., Inc., West Fla. Mgmt. Co. Inc.; chmn. bd. Exec. Investments & Ins. Group, Inc. Bd. dirs. Miami Lakes Civic Assn., 1975-76. Cert. fin. planner; registered investment adviser SEC. Mem. Internat. Assn. Fin. Planners, Assn. Cert. Fin. Planners. Home: 17531 SW 68th Ct Fort Lauderdale FL 33331 Office: 6120 SW 173d Way Fort Lauderdale FL 33331

PENROSE, JOHN MORGAN, business communications educator; b. Tulsa, June 16, 1942; s. John Morgan and Garnet (Hasten) P.; m. Margaret Iwanaga, June 15, 1983. B.S. in Journalism, Ohio U., 1964, M.S., 1966; Ph.D., U. Tex., 1978. Dir. ann. giving Ohio U., Athens, 1966-69; asst. to dean So. Ill. U., Edwardsville, 1969-72; sr. lectr. gen. bus. dept. Grad. Sch. Bus., U. Tex., Austin, 1972—; cons. to regional bus. firms, 1978—. Author: Business Communication Applications, 1981; Business Communication Readings and Applications, 1985; (with others) Business Communication Strategies and Skills, 1985; also articles. Mem. Assn. for Bus. Communications (v.p. Southwest region 1981-85, chmn. grad. studies com. 1981-85, mem. editorial bd. jour. 1984—). Home: 2678 Crazyhorse Pass Austin TX 78734 Office: U Tex Gen Bus Dept Grad Sch Bus CBA 5202 Austin TX 78712

PENTECOST, JOSEPH LUTHER, ceramics engineering educator, consultant; b. Winder, Ga., Apr. 23, 1930; s. Joseph Edwin and Vera (Sims) P.; m. Joanne Jackson, July 30, 1949 (dec. 1967); m. Maxene Meyer, Jan. 3, 1969; children—David E., Steven J., Richard J., Brian A., Madge A. B.S. in Ceramic Engring., Ga. Inst. Tech., 1951; M.S., U. Ill., 1954, Ph.D., 1956. Sr. engr. Melpar, Inc., Falls Church, Va., 1956-59, dir. research, 1961-68; sr. research engr. Aeronca Mfg. Corp., Middletown, Ohio, 1959-60; assoc. prof. ceramic engring. Miss. State U., Starkville, 1960-61; asst. to v.p., W.R. Grace, Columbia, Md., 1968-72; prof., dir. Sch. Ceramic Engring., Ga. Inst. Tech., Atlanta, 1972-85; chief engr. Matcos Co., Marietta, Ga., 1960—. Contbr. articles to profl. jours. Patentee in field. Served to capt. USMCR, 1951-53. Recipient Profl. Achievement in Ceramic Engring. award Nat. Inst. Ceramic Engring., 1967. Fellow Am. Ceramic Soc. (treas. 1984-85, pres. 1986—, trustee 1980-83, v.p. 1983-84). Republican. Presbyterian. Avocations: hunting; amateur radio; computers. Home: 3605 Clubwood Trail Marietta GA 30067 Office: Materials Engring GA Inst Tech 778 Atlantic Dr Atlanta GA 30332

PENTES, JACK MICHAEL, design company executive, dimensional designer; b. Dothan, Ala., Aug. 23, 1931; s. Jack Michael and Emma Lucile (Johnson) P.; m. Ruth E. Jones, July 21, 1957; children—Dorne Michael, Danna Barnes. Student U. N.C. Pres. Pentes Design, Inc., Charlotte, N.C., 1949—; chmn. adv. com. Central Piedmont Community Coll. Sch. Design, 1972-74; co-founder Carolina Clowns, 1956-65. Designer theme park Land of Oz (Washington Star award), Beech Mountain, N.C., 1971; modular play system Playport (Attraction of Yr. award, Edward L. Scholl trophy Internat. Assn. Amusement Parks and Attractions 1983); patentee Graphisphere (projection system). Bd. dirs. Community Sch. of Arts, Charlotte, 1983, Central Charlotte Assn., 1973; chmn. Mayor's Com. Blue Heaven, Charlotte, 1969. Served with N.G., 1951-57; Korea. Recipient 1st place for sign design Signs of Times mag., 1983; 1st place package design award N.Y. Art Dirs. Club, 1969. Mem. Art Dirs. Club Charlotte (co-founder). Home: 6510 Sharon Hills Rd Charlotte NC 28210 Office: Pentes Design Inc 1346 Hill Rd Charlotte NC 28210

PENTLAND, LADY SUE-BYRD, ballerina; b. Sioux City, Iowa, Mar. 25, 1928; d. Edgar O. and Mabel (French) Hill; student Ark. U., 1943; m. Ernest Edward Roberts, June 10, 1944 (dec. Sept. 1960); 1 son, William-Hill; m. 2d Sir Robert Pentland, Jr., Jan. 25, 1963 (dec. July 1979). Formerly prima ballerina Miami Ballet; tchr. acad. classical ballet technique St. Stephen's Episcopal Day Sch., Coconut Grove, Fla., 1959-62. Active USO; prin. dancer, soloist The Iham Follies for crippled children, 1953-61; mem. Debutante Com., Opera Guild Greater Miami; patron life mem. Variety Internat. Club. Founder Miami Children's Hosp. Found., 1984. Recipient gold medal U.S.O.; Queen of Hearts award Variety Internat. Club, 1971, Great Gal award, 1972, 1st Golden Harvest Queen, 1984; lady of justice Order St. John Jerusalem, Knights Malta. Mem. U.D.C., Dance Masters Am., Internat. Platform Assn., Soc. Univ. Founders, Navy League. Democrat. Episcopalian. Clubs: Miami Woman's (perpetual mem.; chmn. ballet, drama and music div. fine arts dept., 1958-60, 61-62), Hibiscus Garden; U. Miami Woman's; Indian Creek Country, Surf (Miami Beach); Golden Hills Turf and Golf Country (Ocala, Fla.); Brookfield West, Country (Roswell, Ga.). Home: Quarter-Mile Farms South Box 609 Fairfield FL 32634 also Ballynahinch 12173 Mountain Laurel Dr Brookfield West Roswell GA 30075 also Pentland-Court 2813 N Surf Rd Hollywood Beach FL 33019

PENWELL, GARY WILLIAM, air force officer, hospital administrator; b. Columbus, Ohio, Oct. 20, 1945; s. Edgar William Penwell and Mary Josephine (Reaver) Penwell Dilley; m. Margaret Jane Batdorf, July 22, 1967; children—Amy Suzanne, Lori Jane. B.S. in Fin., Ohio State U., 1967; M.B.A., U. Utah, 1973. Commd. 2d lt. U.S. Air Force, 1968, advanced through grades to lt. col., 1984; asst. adminstr. USAF Hosp., Perrin AFB, Tex., 1968-69; med. advisor U.S. AID, Vietnam, 1969-70; dir. resource mgmt. USAF Clinic, Rhein-Main, Germany, 1970-74; health services staff officer Hdqrs. USAF, Washington, 1974-78; assoc. adminstr. USAF Hosp., Mather AFB, Calif., 1978-81; hosp. adminstr. USAF Hosp., Seymour Johnson AFB, N.C., 1981—; dir. USAF Resource Mgmt. Symposium, Sheppard AFB, 1974; mem. cost mgmt. tng. subcom. Dept. Def., Washington, 1976-78; mem. Mil. Med. Region 8 Tri-Service Regional Rev. Com., Norfolk, Va., 1981—. Decorated Bronze Star, Air Force Commendation medal, Meritorious Service medal (3). Mem. Am. Coll. Hosp. Adminstrs., Air Force Assn., Assn. Mil. Surgeons U.S. Home: 17 Lakeview Dr Poquoson VA 23662 Office: HQ TAC/SGAF Langley AFB VA 23665

PEOPLES, JOHN ARTHUR, JR., university president; b. Starkville, Miss., Aug. 26, 1926; s. John Arthur and Maggie Rose (Peoples) P.; B.S., Jackson State U., 1950; M.A., U. Chgo., 1951, Ph.D., 1961; m. Mary E. Galloway, July 13, 1951; children Kathleen, Mark Adam. Tchr. math. Froebel Sch., Gary, Ind., 1951-58; asst. prin. Lincoln Sch., Gary, 1958-62; prin. Banneker Sch., Gary, 1962-64; asst. to pres. Jackson (Miss.) State U., 1964-66, v.p., 1966-67, pres., 1967—; asst. to pres. State U. N.Y., Binghamton, 1965-66; lectr. summers U. Mich., 1964, Tex. A. and M. U., 1967. Active Boy Scouts Am.; bd. govs. So. Regional Edn. Bd.; bd. visitors Air U.; adv. com. U.S. Army Command and Gen. Staff Coll.; bd. commrs. Jackson Airport Authority. Recipient Distinguished Am. award Nat. Football Found.; citation for service with Nat. Alliance for Bus., Pres. of U.S., 1983. Served with USMCR, 1944-47. Mem. Am. Council Edn. (chmn. dir. 1975), Am. Assn. Higher Edn. (dir. 1971-74), NEA, Miss. Tchrs. Assn., Jackson C. of C. (econ. council), NAACP (life), Alpha Kappa Mu, Phi Kappa Phi, Phi Delta Kappa, Omega Psi Phi (Man of Year, Sigma Omega chpt. 1966). Club: Masons (33 deg.) Contbr. articles to profl. jours. Home: 386 Heritage Pl Jackson MS 39212

PEPPARD, FELIX PRUNTY, surgeon; b. Wichita, Kans., Feb. 6, 1934; s. Richard Kenneth and Bonnie Helen (Prunty) P.; B.S., U. Tex., 1958; M.D., Southwestern Med. Sch., 1962; children—Richard Mark, Kelton Denise, William Felix. Intern, John Peter Smith Hosp., Fort Worth, 1962-63; resident in surgery Baylor U. Med. Center, Dallas, 1963-67; practice medicine specializing in surgery, pres. Peppard, Halloran & Small, Assos., Dallas, 1967—; chief div. trauma, asso. dir. surg. edn. Med. Center, Baylor U., 1968—, dir. div. trauma, 1985—; clin. asso. prof. surgery Southwestern Med. Sch., 1969—; med. dir. Buckner Bapt. Benevolences, 1967—; chmn. bd., chief exec. officer Health Econs. Corp., 1984—. Served with AUS, 1954-56. Diplomate Am. Bd. Surgery. Mem. ACS, Southwestern Surg. Congress, Royal Soc. Medicine Eng., Tex. Surg. Soc., So. Med. Assn. Democrat. Roman Catholic. Office: 401 Baylor Med Plaza 3600 Gaston Ave Dallas TX 75246

PEPPER, CLAUDE DENSON, congressman; b. Dudleyville, Ala., Sept. 8, 1900; s. Joseph Wheeler and Lena (Talbot) P.; m. Irene Mildred Webster, Dec. 29, 1936 (dec. 1979). A.B., U. Ala., 1921; J.D., Harvard U., 1924; LL.D., McMaster U., 1941, Toronto U., U. Ala., 1942, Rollins Coll., 1944; D.Sc., U. Miami, 1974; Baylor U., 1983; D. Humane Letters, Mt. Sinai. Med. Ctr., N.Y.C., 1982, U. So. Fla., 1982, Fla. State U., 1985; D. Humanities, Barry U., 1983, U. Miami, 1984. Bar: Ala. bar 1924, Fla. bar 1925. Instr. law U. Ark., 1924-25; practiced law, Perry, Fla.; mem. Fla. Ho. Reps., 1929; practiced law, Tallahassee, 1930-37; mem. Fla. Bd. Public Welfare, 1931-32, Fla. Bd. Law Examiners, 1933, U.S. Senate from Fla., 1936-51; mem. coms. on Fgn. Relations, on mil. affairs, on small bus., on edn. and labor, chmn. subcom. on wartime health and edn., 78th congressional reorgn. of Congress; chmn. com. on inter-oceanic canals, Middle East sub-com. of Senate Fgn. Relations Com.; mem. 88th-99th congresses from 3d, 11th, 18th Fla. dists.; chmn. com. on crime; chmn. Fla. delegation Dem. Nat. Conv., 1940-44, del., 1948, 52-56, 60-64, 68, 72, 76, 80, 84. Contbr. articles to periodicals. Vice chmn. nat. bd. dirs. Nat. Parkinson Found. Recipient Mary and Albert Lasker public service award, 1967; Eleanor Roosevelt Humanities award, 1968; Ballington and Maud Booth award Vols. of Am., 1978; Hubert H. Humphrey Statesmanship award Fla. Dem. Party, 1979; Andrus award Nat. Ret. Tchrs. Assn., 1980; Ze'ev Jabotinsky Centennial award, 1980; Man of Year award Fla. Gold Coast C. of C., 1981, Golden State award Am. Acad. Achievement, 1983; Hall of Fame award Fla. Council on Aging, 1983; Hugo Black award U. Ala., 1984; Murray-Green-Meany award AFL-CIO, 1984; others. Mem. Internat. Bar Assn., Inter-Am. Bar Assn., ABA, Fla. Bar Assn. (exec. com.), Tallahassee Bar Assn., Miami Beach Bar Assn., Coral Gables Bar Assn., Dade County Bar Assn., Bar City of N.Y., Western C. of C. of the Americas, Fla. State U. Alumni Assn., Fla. State Soc., Am. Legion, Jasons, Fla. Blue Key, Phi Beta Kappa, Omicron Delta Kappa, Phi Alpha Delta (outstanding alumnus award U. Fla. chpt. 1975), Sigma Upsilon, Kappa Alpha. Baptist. Clubs: Masons, Shriners, Elks, Optimists, Moose, Kiwanis, Woodman of World, Harvard (Washington, Miami, Fla.); Jefferson Island, Army and Navy (Washington); Coral Gables' Country, Miami Shores Country, Miami, Jockey, Bankers, Palm Bay (Miami); La Gorce Country (Miami Beach, Fla.); Columbia Country (Chevy Chase, Md.); Burning Tree (Bethesda, Md.). Home: 2121 N Bayshore Dr Miami FL 33137 also 4201 Cathedral Ave NW Washington DC 20016 Office: 2239 Rayburn House Office Bldg Washington DC 20515 and Rm 904 Federal Bldg 51 SW First Ave Miami FL 33130

PEPPER, DARRELL WELDON, mechanical engineer; b. Kirksville, Mo., May 14, 1946; s. Weldon Edward and Marjorie Louise (Dove) P.; m. Jeanne Evelyn Limbacher, Aug. 16, 1969; 1 child, Erik Weldon. B.S., U. Mo.-Rolla, 1968, M.S., 1970, Ph.D., 1973. Postdoctoral U. Mo., Rolla, 1973-74; research engr. E.I. duPont, Aiken, S.C., 1974-78, research supr., 1978-84, research staff engr., 1984—; pres. Softcrunch Inc., Aiken, 1984—. Author: (with others) Introduction to Solving Transport Equations with Finite Elements on the IBM Personal Computer, 1985. Contbr. articles to profl. jours. Bd. dirs. Aiken United Way, 1983—, Aiken Community Playhouse, 1977-78; adminstrv. bd. St. Johns United Methodist Ch., Aiken, 1976-77. Served to capt. USAR, 1968-76. NSF fellow 1969-73; U. Mo. scholar 1964. Named one of Outstanding Young Men Am., 1975. Mem. ASME, Sigma Xi, Pi Tau Sigma. Republican. Congregationalist. Club: Houndslake Country (Aiken). Avocations: golf; white water rafting; woodworking; personal computing. Home: 1227 Evans Rd Aiken SC 29801

PEPPER, WILLIAM DONALD, forest biometrician; b. Dadeville, Ala., Apr. 29, 1935; s. Herman William and Jessie Florence (McGhee) P.; m. Carol Lynn Jones, June 29, 1968; 1 child, Joanna McGee. B.S. in Forestry, Auburn U., 1959; M.F., N.C. State U., 1965, Ph.D. in Forestry, 1975. Forester, Ga. Kraft Co., Rome, 1959-63; forest biometrician Forest Service Research, U.S. Dept. Agr., Research Triangle Park, N.C., 1968-77, New Orleans, 1977-84, Athens, Ga., 1984—. Contbr. articles to profl. jours. Mem. Am. Statis. Assn., Biometrics Soc. Republican. Methodist. Avocations: jogging; public speaking. Home: 285 Gentry Dr Athens GA 30605 Office: US Forest Service Carlton St Athens GA 30602

PEPPERMAN, ARMAND BENNETT, JR., chemist; b. New Orleans, May 30, 1941; s. Armand Bennett Sr. and Alice Marie (Fernandez) P.; m. Elaine Mae Kramer, May 13, 1961 (div. Oct. 1984); children—Karl Joseph, Kim Marie, Scott Gerard. B.S. in Chemistry, U. New Orleans, 1963, Ph.D. in Organic Chemistry, 1973. Chemist, Oil Seed Crops Lab., U.S. Dept. Agr., New Orleans, 1963-68, research chemist Cotton Finishes Lab., 1968-70, Cotton Textile Lab., 1970-82, Crop Protection Research, 1982—; instr. U. New Orleans, 1968-70, 82, 84-86. Contbr. articles to profl. jours., chpt. to books. Patentee flame retardants for cotton cellulose. Mem. Am. Chem. Soc. (pres. sect. 1983), Weed Sci. Soc. Am., U. New Orleans Alumni Assn. (bd. dirs.), Sigma Xi (treas. sect. 1980-81). Republican. Roman Catholic. Club: Centurion Carnival (Harahan). Avocations: fishing; jogging; bridge. Office: So Regional Research Ctr 1100 Robert E Lee Blvd New Orleans LA 70119

PEPPLER, RICHARD DOUGLAS, reproductive physiologist, educator, anatomist; b. Trenton, N.J., Sept. 24, 1943; s. Norman T. and Elizabeth C. (Wilson) P.; m. Patricia A. Grisnik, Jan. 27, 1968. B.A., Gettysburg Coll., 1965; Ph.D., U. Kans. Med. Ctr., 1969. Asst. chief clin. research Fitzsimons Gen. Hosp., Denver, 1968-70; asst. prof. dept. anatomy and ob-gyn. La. State U. Med. Ctr., New Orleans, 1970-74, assoc. prof., 1974-78; assoc. prof. dept. anatomy and ob-gyn. East Tenn. State U. Quillen-Dishner Coll. Medicine, Johnson City, 1978-80, prof., 1980-85, assoc. chmn. anatomy dept., 1980-85; assoc. dean acad. affairs Coll. Medicine, U. Tenn., Memphis, 1985—, prof. anatomy, 1985—. Served to lt. col. USAR, 1965—. Mem. Am. Assn. Anatomy, Soc. Study Reprodn., Soc. for Study Fertility, Endocrine Soc., Soc. Exptl. Biol. Medicine, AAAS, Tenn. Acad. Sci., Sigma Xi. Lodge: Masons. Contbr. writings to profl. publs. Office: Coll Medicine U Tenn Memphis 3 N Dunlap Memphis TN 38163

PERALES, MARGARET ROSE, petroleum geologist; b. San Antonio, Aug. 20, 1958; d. Robert Edward and Kathryn Rose (Guerra) P. B.A., Trinity U., 1979. Geol. technician Gulf Energy Devel. Corp., San Antonio, 1979-80; staff geologist Tesoro Petroleum Co., San Antonio, 1980-83; cons. geologist Durst Energy Corp., San Antonio, 1983—; ind. cons. geologist, San Antonio, 1983—; founder MPG Petroleum, Inc., Von Ormy, Tex., 1985. Mem. Am. Assn. Petroleum Geologists, South Tex. Geol. Soc. Republican. Roman Catholic. Avocations: music; golf; tennis; painting; photography. Home: 343 Eastley St San Antonio TX 78217 Office: MPG Petroleum 20905 Hwy 16 S Von Ormy TX 78073

PERCHIK, BENJAMIN IVAN, operations research analyst; b. Passaic, N.J., May 3, 1941; s. Morris and Frances (Antman) P.; m. Ellen Mae Colwell, Aug. 25, 1963; children—Joel, Dawn. B.A., Rutgers U., 1964; postgrad. N.Y. Inst. Tech., 1964-65. Quality control E.R. Squibb Corp., New Brunswick, N.J., 1964-67; edn. specialist Signal Sch., Ft. Monmouth, N.J., 1967-74; edn. specialist Armor Sch., Ft. Knox, Ky., 1974-75, ops. research analyst, 1975-78; ops. research analyst HQ TRADOC, Ft. Monroe, Va., 1978-80, HQ DARCOM, Alexandria, Va., 1980—; cons. Delta Force, Carlisle Barracks, Pa., 1982-84, Internat. Policy Inst., 1983-85, World Future Soc., 1982—; nat. coordinator MENSA Investment SIG, 1983—. Mem. Ops. Research Soc. Am., Internat. Platform Assn., Mensa (speaker's bur.). Clubs: Old Dominion Boat, Watergate at Landmark (chmn. safety, sec. com.). Chmn., DARCOM Credit Union, Alexandria, 1982—. Author: ADP Program and Repair, 1972; writer, pub. newsletter Speculation and Investments, 1983. Home: 203 Yoakum Pkwy Apt 1624 Alexandria VA 22304 Office: HQ DARCOM (DRCDP-IM) 5001 Eisenhower Ave Alexandria VA 22333

PERCIVAL, LAWRENCE GERALD, account executive, consultant; b. Bangor, Maine, Aug. 1, 1950; s. Clifton Merrill and Mildred (Danzig) P. B.E., U. Miami (Fla.), 1973, M.E., 1976; postgrad. in health edn. and adminstrn. mgmt. Fla. Internat. U., 1979. Cert. tchr., Fla. Adminstrv. officer Dept. Youth and Family Devel., Met. Dade County Govt., Miami, Fla., 1979-82, adminstrn. div. Program Productivity Analysis Unit, 1982-83; account exec. Consortium Group, Miami, 1983—; pres. Dynamic Creative Achievement, Inc., Miami, 1976—. Vice pres. Kiwanis Youthland, chmn. gymnastics and judo/karate ops. coms.; bd. dirs., chmn. speaker's bur. Project Sci. Outreach, Inc.; v.p., chmn. fund raising com. Community Advocates for Mentally Ill; bd. dirs. Boystown Fla. Served with U.S. Army, 1973-78. Recipient Outstanding Com. Chmn. award So. Miami Kiwanis Clubs, 1982. Mem. U. Miami Sch. Edn. and Allied Professions Alumni Assn. (dir.), Athletic Fedn. Booster Club. Democrat. Presbyterian. Home: 5500 SW 77th Ct Apt 105 Miami FL 33155 Office: 8585 Sunset Dr Suite 15 Miami FL 33143

PERCIVAL, STEPHEN FRANCIS, JR., micropaleontologist; b. Camden, N.J., Aug. 27, 1932; s. Stephen Francis and Clara (Caskey) P.; m. Jeannette Kennedy, June 16, 1957; children—George Donald, Linda Percival Staab. B.A. in Geology, U. Pa., 1956; M.S. in Geology, Pa. State U., 1959; Ph.D. in Geology, Princeton U., 1972. Micropaleontologist Mobil Oil de Venezuela, Anaco, 1958-60, Mobil Oil Can., Tripoli, Libya, 1960-61, Mobil Field Research Lab., Dallas, 1962-72, Mobil E&P Services Inc., Dallas, 1972—. Author: (with others) Leg 3 South Atlantic DSDP, 1970; Leg 42B Black Sea DSDP, 1978; Leg 73 South Atlantic DSDP, 1984. Served to cpl. US Army, 1952-54. Mem. Geol. Soc. Am., Am. Assn. Petroleum Geologists, AAAS. Avocations: photography, tropical fish. Home: 326 Suddith Ln Midlothian TX 76065 Office: Mobil Exploration and Producing Services Inc PO Box 900 Dallas TX 75221

PERDUE, GARLAND DAY, surgeon, educator, hospital director; b. Clermont, Ga., Mar. 19, 1926; s. Garland Day and Nina (Keith) P. B.A., Emory U., 1948, M.D., 1952. Ptnr., Emory Clinic, Atlanta, 1957, clinic dir., 1984—; mem. faculty Emory U. Sch. Medicine, Atlanta, 1955—, prof. surgery, 1971—, dean clin. affairs, 1983—; med. dir. Emory U. Hosp., Atlanta, 1983—. Mem. Specialty Surg. Socs., Am. Surg. Assn., So. Surg. Assn., Soc. Vascular Surgery, Internat. Soc. Cardiovascular Surgery, Internat. Soc. Surgery. Contbr. articles to profl. jours. Home: 1594 Rainier Falls Dr Atlanta GA 30329 Office: 1365 Clifton Rd NE Atlanta GA 30322

PEREBOOM, MARGARET GAMBLE, psychologist; b. Lusk, Wyo., May 30, 1928; d. George D. and Cecile (Durst) Gamble; m. Andrew Clinton Pereboom, Feb. 11, 1952; children—Joanne, Drew. B.A., UCLA, 1950; M.A., Tex. Tech U., 1963; Ph.D., U. Tex., 1972. Lic. psychologist, La. Psychologist C.P. Ctr., Baton Rouge, 1962-72; asst. prof. La. State U. Spl. Edn., Baton Rouge, 1973; psychologist M. Dumas Mental Health Ctr., Baton Rouge, 1974-78; pres. Edn. and Psychol. Services, Inc., Baton Rouge, 1977—; owner Assoc. Psychol. Services, Baton Rouge, 1980—; guest lectr. Win With Women, La., 1982-85. Pres. Baton Rouge Youth; chmn. Govs. Commn. Children and Youth, Baton Rouge, 1984-85; bd. dirs. YWCA, Friends Pub. Edn., East Baton Rouge Sch. Bd., 1979-82; legis. lobbyist La. Women's Polit. Caucus, Older Women's League. Fellow Am. Acad. Clin. Psychology and Devel. Medicine; mem. Am. Psychol. Assn., Soc. Pediatric Psychology, Council for Exceptional Children, LWV, Sigma Pi Sigma, Psy Chi. Democrat. Mem. Unitarian Ch. Home: 719 Carriage Way Baton Rouge LA 70808 Office: Assoc Psychol Services 4256 Perkins Rd Baton Rouge LA 70808

PEREIRA, RONALD MANUEL, retail executive; b. Sandusky, Ohio, Sept. 20, 1938; s. Antonio and Helen (Miller) P.; grad. Howe Mil. Sch., 1956; B.A., Cornell U., 1960; M.B.A., Columbia U., 1965; B.S. in Acctg., U. Miami (Fla.), 1976; m. Karin Devan Harasz; children—Charles Manuel, William Wyatt, Michelle Louise, Ronald Andrew. Corp. internal auditor The Singer Co., N.Y.C., 1965, cost acctg. mgr. Power Tool Div., Pickens, S.C., 1966; sr. fin. analyst hdqrs. Esso InterAm., Coral Gables, Fla., 1967-69; v.p., dir., fin. mgr. Esso Paraguay, Asunción, 1970-72; mgr. credit, internal audit and systems functions Esso Caribbean, Coral Gables, 1973-81; controller Am. Express Regional Ops. Ctr., Mex., dir. Mex. and Grand Cayman Island corps.; 1982-84; pres. The Mountain Store, Somerset, Va., 1984—; fin. mgr. Smithsonian Instn. Mail Order Div., 1985—; pres. Game box. Served with USN, 1960-63; to lt. comdr., USNR, 1977-79. Recipient Danforth Found. award, 1956; Delta Upsilon Leadership award, 1960; Navy ROTC scholar, 1956-60; C.P.A., Md., Fla. Mem. Coconut Grove C. of C., Nat. Assn. Accts., Fla. Soc. C.P.A.s, Am. Inst. C.P.A.s, Naval Res. Assn., Fla. Hort. Soc., Cornell U. Alumni Assn. (v.p.), Delta Upsilon. Republican. Episcopalian. Lodge: Rotary. Address: 11799 Antietam Rd Woodbridge VA 22192

PEREZ, ALICIA SALINAS, psychology educator, college dean; b. Rio Hondo, Tex., June 31, 1931; d. Valentin and Candelaria (Garcia) Salinas; m. Antonio Perez, Dec. 26, 1954; children—Antonio Eduardo, Zonia Nela, Zelda Melissa. B.A., Tex. Women's U., 1953, B.S., 1953; M.A., Tex. A&I U., 1956, postgrad., 1957—. Tchr. Raymondville Ind. Sch. Dist., Tex., 1953-64, T.G. Allen Elem. Sch., Corpus Christi, Tex., 1964-66; counselor Roy Miller High Sch., Foy Moody High Sch., W.B. Ray High Sch., Corpus Christi Ind. Sch. Dist., 1966-72; tchr. psychology Del Mar Coll., Corpus Christi, 1971-72, asst. prof. psychology dept., 1972-79, assoc. prof., 1980, chmn. dept. psychology, 1981-83, asst. dean East Campus Evening Sch., 1984—. Del. Democratic Nat. Conv., N.Y.C., 1976; mental health trainer Psychiat. Vols., Corpus Christi, 1980; exec. bd. YWCA, Corpus Christi, Amigos Orgn., Corpus Christi. Recipient Master Tchr. award Del Mar Coll., Portland, 1983, 84. Mem. Nat. Orgn. Women Deans, Adminstrs. and Counselors, Tex. State Tchrs. Assn. (life), Del Mar Faculty Orgn., Am. Coll. Personnel Assn., Phi Delta Kappa. Democrat. Roman Catholic. Clubs: United Married Couple, Sembradores de Amistad, Damas y Caballeros de la costa, Cathedral Couples Group, Amigas de las Am., Cultura Hispanica. Avocations: oil painting; jogging; knitting; gourmet cooking; gardening. Office: Del Mar Coll Baldwin and Ayers Corpus Christi TX 78404

PEREZ, FRANCISCO IGNACIO, clinical psychologist; b. Havana, Cuba, May 21, 1947; came to U.S., 1960; s. Francisca J. and Maria F. (Villa) P.; m. Georgina Montero, Aug. 27, 1971; children—Francisco A., Teresa M. B.A., U. Fla., 1969, M.A., 1971, Ph.D., 1972. Lic. psychologist, Tex. Asst. prof. edn. U. Houston, 1972-74; asst. prof. neurology & psychiatry Baylor U. Coll. Medicine, Dallas, 1974-80; pvt. practice clin. psychology, Houston, 1980—; clin. asst. prof. neurology and phys. medicine Baylor Coll. Medicine, Houston, 1980—. Bd. dirs. Houston Community Youth Ctr., Stroke Club, Houston. NIMH research grantee, 1976-77. Mem. Am. Psychol. Assn., Internat. Neuropsychology Soc., Assn. Advancement Behavior Analysis, Biofeedback Soc. Am. Roman Catholic. Contbr. articles to profl. jours. Home: 3407 Fawn Creek Dr Kingwood TX 77339 Office: 6560 Fannin Suite 1224 Houston TX 77030

PEREZ, GENARO JESSE, Spanish language educator; b. Barranquilla, Colombia, Jan. 26, 1943; came to U.S., 1958, naturalized, 1964; s. Nestor Alfonso Perez and Ligia Zunilda (Llinas) Lehn; m. Janet Isabel Coon, July 18, 1981; children—Julie, Nicole, Paul. B.A., La. State U., 1967; M.A., Tulane U., 1973, Ph.D., 1976. Teaching asst. Tulane U., 1971-76; instr. U. New Orleans, 1975-78; asst. prof. U. Tex.-Permian Basin, Odessa, 1978-83, assoc. prof. Spanish, 1983—. Author: Formalist Elements in the Novels of Juan Goytisolo, 1979; La Novelistica de J. Leyva, 1985; (poetry) Prosapoemas, 1980; also articles. Editor Jour. New South Quarterly, 1967-69; Monographic Rev. Revista Monografica, 1984—. Mem. Am. Assn. Tchrs. Spanish and Portuguese, MLA, (exec. com. 1985—), Assn. Internat. de Hispanistas, South Central MLA, Sigma Delta Mu. Roman Catholic. Avocations: jogging; photography. Office: Dept Literature & Spanish U Tex-Permian Basin Odessa TX 79762

PEREZ, JEFFREY JOSEPH, optometrist; b. Aberdeen, Md., July 26, 1952; s. Jack Joseph and June C. (Champlin) P.; B.A. (scholar), U. Miss., 1974; B.S., So. Coll. Optometry, 1977, O.D., 1979; m. Sharon S. Cooper, June 10, 1979; 1 son, Justin Joseph. Asso. with Dr. W.H. Starr, Gulfport, Miss., 1979-80; pvt. practice optometry, Gulfport, 1980—. Mem. Am. Optometric Assn., Miss. Optometric Assn. (dir.), South Miss. Optometric Soc., Jaycees, Omega Delta. Roman Catholic. Club: Elks. Home: 520 Popps Ferry Rd Biloxi MS 39532 Office: 3113 11th St PO Box 805 Gulfport MS 39501

PÉREZ, MARIÁ LUISA, librarian; b. Santa Clara, Cuba, Oct. 22, 1932; came to U.S., 1979; d. Gustavo and Elena (Ruíz) Pérez. M.Library Sci., U. Ariz., 1980; Ph.D., Universidad de la Habana (Cuba), 1955. Lic. social worker, Fla. Social worker State of Fla. Refugee Assistance Program, Miami, 1980-81; librarian, research div. Dade County Planning Dept., 1981-82; reference librarian Miami-Dade Pub. Library System, Miami, 1982—. Glisa fellow, 1979. Mem. ALA, Seminar on Acquisition of Latin Am. Library Materials. Roman Catholic. Home: 10215 SW 26th Terr Miami FL 33165 Office: Miami Dade Pub Library System Coral Gables Br Segovia 3443 Miami FL 33134

PEREZ, ROBERTO, educator; b. San Antonio, Aug. 17, 1933; s. Felipe and Amalia Perez; B.A. in Social Sci., Fla. State U., 1971; M.Ed., U. Tex., Austin, 1974, Ph.D. in Ednl. Adminstrn., 1979; m. Grace Campos, Jan. 27, 1957; children— Maria Elena, Roberto, Patricia Ann, Rey. Aerospace edn. instr. Holy Cross High Sch., San Antonio, 1972; asso. dir. Tchr. Corps, U. Tex.,

Austin, 1974-76, clin. prof., 1976-78; asst. prof., program devel. specialist St. Edwards U., Austin, 1979-81; participant symposia. Chmn., Coalition for Ednl. Betterment of Chicanos, 1978. Served with USAF, 1951-71; Korea. Decorated AF Commendation medal; cert. elem. tchr., Tex. Mem. Nat. Council States on Inservice Edn., Assn. Supervision and Curriculum Devel., Assn. Tchr. Educators, Nat. Assn. Bilingual Edn., World Future Soc., Research Inst. Am. Democrat. Roman Catholic. Contbr. chpts. to books. Conceived sch.-based model for inservice edn. Home: 2409 Robin Rd Manchaca TX 78652

PEREZ-COMAS, ADOLFO, physician; b. Mayaguez, P.R., Nov. 27, 1941; s. Adolfo and Alma Luz (Comas-Lugo) Perez-Sosa; B.S., U. P.R., 1961; M.D., U. Barcelona (Spain), 1967, Ph.D., 1975; m. Maria del Rosario Fraticelli, Mar. 30, 1985; children—Adolfo, Alberto. Intern, San Juan City Hosp., 1968, fellow in endocrinology, 1970-72; resident in pediatrics San Juan City Hosp., P.R. Med. Center, Rio Piedras, 1969-70; practice medicine specializing in endocrinology and med. genetics, Mayaguez, P.R., 1972—; asst. prof. physiology and biochemistry Sch. Medicine, U. Barcelona, 1963-67; dir. pediatric endocrinology and med. genetics sect. Mayaguez Med. Center, 1972—, sec. of faculty, 1972-73, chief of staff, 1975-79; vis. prof. U. Salamanca (Spain), 1981-84; lectr. physiology U. P.R., Mayaguez, 1973—, assoc. prof. pediatrics, 1974—. Counselor, Growth Hormone Fund, Inc., 1974; advisor to Senate of P.R., 1980—. Named Citizen of Year, Mayaguez, 1974, Most Disting. Young Man in Fields of Sci. and Medicine, Rio Piedras Jaycees, 1974. Fellow Superior Council Sci. Investigations (hon.) (Spain); mem. Am. Acad. Pediatrics (ann. award 1968), Am. Soc. Human Genetics, Am. Soc. Andrology, Internat. Diabetes Fedn., Fedn. Latinoam. de Assns. de Lucha Contra la Diabetes (exec. council) (Venezuela), Am. Diabetes Assn., Latinam. Assn. Diabetes (dir., v.p. 1980—) (Argentina), AAAS, N.Y. Acad. Sci., Am. Med. Writers Assn., Soc. Nuclear Medicine P.R., Western Dist. Med. Soc. (dir. med. edn.), Govtl. Physicians Assn. P.R. (pres. 1979—), Iberoam. Med. Assn. (Madrid) (v.p. 1980—), Craniofacial Genetics Assn. N.Am., P.R. Med. Assn., Endocrine Soc., Dominican Republic Acad. Sci. (hon.), Peru Diabetic Assn. (hon.), Ecuador Diabetic Assn. (hon.), Nu Sigma Beta. Mormon. Contbr. articles on research in endocrinology, diabetes and med. genetics to med. jours. Home: 90 Alhambra Mayaguez PR 00708 Office: 22 N Dr Basora Mayaguez PR 00708 also Condominio Ada Ligia 1452 Ashford Ave Suite 310 Condada-Santurce PR also PO Box 20 Mayaguez PR 00709-0020

PEREZ-CRUET, JORGE, psychiatrist, psychopharmacologist; b. Santurce, P.R., Oct. 15, 1931; s. Jose Maria Perez-Vicente and Emilia Cruet-Burgos; m. Anyes Heimendinger, Oct. 4, 1958; children—Antonio, Mikie, Graciela, Isabela. B.S. magna cum laude, U. P.R., 1953, M.D., 1957; diploma psychiatry McGill U., Montreal, Que., Can., 1976. Diplomate Am. Bd. Psychiatry and Neurology, Nat. Bd. Med. Examiners; lic. Can. Council Med Examiners. Rotating intern Michael Reese Hosp., Chgo., 1957-58; fellow in psychiatry Johns Hopkins U. Med. Sch., 1958-60, instr., then asst. prof. psychiatry, 1962-73; lab. neurophysiologist Walter Reed Army Inst. Research, Washington, 1960-62, cons., 1963-68; research asso. lab. chem. pharmacology, also research asso. adult psychiatry br. and lab. clin. sci. NIMH, Bethesda, Md., 1969-73; psychiatry resident diploma course in psychiatry McGill U. Sch. Medicine, Montreal Gen. Hosp., 1973-76, Montreal Children's Hosp., 1975; prof. psychiatry U. Mo.-Mo. Inst. Psychiatry, St. Louis, 1976-78; chief psychiatry service San Juan (P.R.) VA Hosp., also prof. psychiatry U. P.R. Med. Sch., 1978—; spl. adviser on mental health P.R. Senate, P.R. sec. health; spl. cons. NASA, 1965-69. Served to capt. M.C., USAR, 1960-62. Recipient Coronas award, 1957, Ruiz-Arnau award, 1957, Diaz-Garcia award, 1957, Geigy award, 1975, 76, AMA Recognition award, 1971, 76, 81, Horner's award, 1975, 76, Pavlovian award, 1978. Fellow Interam. Coll. Physicians and Surgeons, Royal Coll. Physicians and Surgeons (Can.); mem. AMA, Am. Psychiat. Assn., Am. Physiol. Soc., N.Y. Acad. Scis., Pavlovian Soc., Am. Fedn. Clin. Research, Can. Psychiat. Assn., Am. Soc. Clin. Pharmacology and Therapeutics, Soc. Neurosci., Internat. Soc. Research Aggression, Nat. Assn. VA Chiefs Psychiatry, P.R. Med. Assn. Republican. Roman Catholic. Home: PO Box 1797 Guaynabo PR 00657-7002 Office: Chief Psychiatry Service 116 A PO Box 4867 VA Med Ctr San Juan PR 00936

PERFETTI, THOMAS ALBERT, research chemist; b. Jeannette, Pa., Mar. 22, 1952; s. Bruno M. and Ruth M. (Peters) P.; m. Patricia Ann Finley, Aug. 16, 1975; 1 child, Michael Thomas. B.S. in Chemistry, Indiana U. of Pa., 1974; Ph.D., Va. Poly. Inst. and State U., 1977. Chemist, R.J. Reynolds Tobacco Co., Winston-Salem, 1977, sr. research chemist, 1979, sr. research and devel. chemist, 1981-84, sr. staff scientist, 1984-86, master scientist, 1986—; cons. in field. Mem. Winston-Salem Fire Brigade; active emergency med. tng. ARC. Recipient Outstanding Teaching award Va. Poly. Inst. and State U., 1977. Fellow Am. Inst. Chemists; mem. Am. Chem. Soc., AAAS, N.Y. Acad. Sci., Sigma Xi, Phi Lambda Upsilon, Chi Beta Phi. Democrat. Roman Catholic. Contbr. articles to profl. jours. Home: 2116 Newcastle Dr Winston-Salem NC 27103 Office: Bowman Gray Tech Ctr Reynolds Blvd Winston-Salem NC 27102

PERINI, PATRICIA PAUL, television executive; b. N.Y.C., July 7, 1944; d. Bernard James and Ann (Hudlin) Paul; 1 dau., Elizabeth M. B.A., U. Tex., 1966; M.A., Johns Hopkins U., 1967. Asst. to editor Delos Mag., Nat. Transl. Ctr., Austin, Tex., 1967-69; graphics designer Rep. Nat. Bank, Dallas, 1969; pub. info. dir. Sta. KERA-TV, Dallas, 1969-77, dir. creative services and programming, 1977, v.p. broadcasting services, 1977-81, v.p. program devel. and prodn., 1981-83, v.p. programming, 1983—. Contbr. editorial to Dallas Morning News, 1983. Adv. council bd. trustees Ft. Worth Art Mus., 1983-84; trustee Greenhill Sch., 1983-85; mem. leadership devel. subcom. Women and Minority Econ. Issues Joint com. Dallas Citizens Council and C. of C., 1983-84; mem. task force adult edn. program goals com. Dallas Mus. Art, 1982-83; mem. Goals for Dallas, 1977-79; chmn. media adv. panel Tex. Commn. on Arts, 1983-84; mem. Gt. Performances Program Mgmt. Consortium, 1982-84; panelist Children's Media Panel, Nat. Endowment Humanities, 1983; mem. Leadership Dallas, 1980-81; adv. com. arts Magnet Sch. for Dallas Ind. Sch. Dist., 1978-83; mem. Charter 100. Mem. Exec. Women of Dallas (v.p. 1980-81). Episcopalian. Office: KERA 3000 Harry Hines Blvd Dallas TX 75201

PERINO, GREGORY HERMAN, archeologist, researcher, consultant; b. St. Helena, N.C., Feb. 25, 1914; s. Henry and Virginia (Bonincontri) P.; m. Dorothy Elmore, Apr. 3, 1937; children—Charles, Robert, Sandra, Sue Ann. Curator, researcher Thomas Gilcrease Found., Tulsa, 1955-65, Thomas Gilcrease Inst., Tulsa, 1965-73; sr. archeologist Northwestern U., Evanston, Ill., 1973-75; archeologist, dir. Mus. of Red River, Idabel, Okla., 1975-85. Leader, participant numerous excavations Ill., Mo., Ark., Okla., 1955-85; cons. authentication and identification of artifacts for museums, univs., pvt. individuals. Author: Selected Preforms, Points, Knives of North American Indians, Vol. I, 1985, Guide to Identification of American Indian Projectile Points; numerous other publs. Contbr. Central States Archaeol. Jour., Artifacts (Soc. of Ohio), Am. Antiquity, Redskin, others. Author surveys in field. Mem. Southeast Archeol. Conf., Midwest Archeol. Conf., Soc. Profl. Archeologists (cert.), Soc. for Am. Archeology, Central States Archeol. Soc. (mem. editorial staff), Club: McCurtain Gems & Mineral (Idabel, Okla.). Avocations: gardening; carving. Home and office: 1509 Cleveland St Idabel OK 74745

PERKEL, ROBERT SIMON, photojournalist; b. Jersey City, Apr. 23, 1925; s. Louis Leo and Flora Sonia (Levin) P.; B.S., NYU, 1948; M.S., Barry U., 1964; postgrad. Columbia U. Owner, operator Gulfstream Color Labs., Miami Beach, Fla., 1955-61; graphic instr. Dade County Pub. Schs., 1962-66; freelance photojournalist, 1967—; rep. News Events Photo Service, Ft. Lauderdale, Fla.; instr. photography Broward Community Coll., 1982-85; rep. Patch Pub. Co., Titusville, Fla., 1985—; contbr. photo stories, and photographs to numerous mags. and indsl. trade publs. including Women's World, Merck, Sharp & Dohme's Frontline Mag., Gt. Am. Combank News, Nat. Utility Contractor, Mainstream, Nat. Jewish Monthly, Delta Digest, Textile Rental, Sprint Communicator, Rag, the All-Music Mag., DAV Mag., Hallandale Digest, record jacket C.P. Records, Inc.; exhibited at Met. Mus. and Art Center, Coral Gables, Fla. Served with AUS, 1943-46; ETO. Recipient Community Spirit award Zonta Club Greater Miami, 1980. Mem. NYU Alumni Fedn. (Leadership award for 1982-83 fund campaign), Barry U. Alumni Assn., Nat. Press Photographers Assn., Profl. Photographers Am., DAV (nat. citation for disting. service 1969, trustee Jack Schwartz chpt., past comdr. Miami Beach-Surfside chpt.), Alpha Mu Gamma. Clubs: L'Alliance Française de Dade County, B'nai B'rith. Home: 20500 W Country Club Dr North Miami Beach FL 33180

PERKINS, CARL C., congressman; b. Washington, Aug. 6, 1954; s. Carl D. and Verna (Johnson) P.; m. Cathy Whitaker, 1975. B.A., Davidson Coll., 1976; J.D., U. Louisville, 1978. Lawyer, farmer, mem. Ky. Ho. of Reps., 1981-84; mem. 99th Congress from 7th Dist. Ky. Active Appalachian Regional Hosps., 1981-84. Office: US House of Reps Washington DC 20515*

PERKINS, DAVID LAYNE, SR., architect; b. Picayune, Miss., Mar. 3, 1925; s. Robert E. and Henrietta (Browne) P.; m. Edna Blanche Rice, Jan. 10, 1954; children—David Layne Jr., Richard Scott. B.Arch., Tulane U., 1954. Registered architect, La., Ga., Ala., Tex. Designer, draftsman Curtis & Davis, New Orleans, 1948-53; designer M. Wayne Stoffle, New Orleans, 1954; assoc. prof. U. Southwest La., Lafayette, 1954-57; architect David L. Perkins, Architect, Lafayette, La., 1955-75; pres., sr. ptnr. Perkins, Guidry & Young, Lafayette, 1975-85, Perkins, Guidry, Beazley & Ostteen, Architects, Lafayette, 1985—. Prin. works include office bldg. design Riverstone, office bldg. College Oaks, Lafayette Pub. Library, neuropsychiat. clinic. Served to capt. USAF, 1943-45, 51-52. Fellow AIA (regional bd. dirs. 1975-78); mem. So. La. Chpt. of AIA (pres. 1963-64), La. Architects Assn. (pres. 1965-66, Honor awards 1970, 74, 82, 83), Nat. Archl. Accrediting Bd. (pres. 1981-82). Republican. Presbyterian. Avocation: boating. Home: 503 Marjorie Blvd Lafayette LA 70503 Office: Perkins Guidry Beazley Ostteen 300 Heymann Blvd Lafayette LA 70503

PERKINS, DOSITE HUGH, JR., lawyer; b. Shreveport, La., Jan. 8, 1930; s. Dosite Hugh and Cora Lee (Henry) P.; m. Dolores Bates, Apr. 27, 1956; children—Dosite John, Dolores Ann, Desmond Lee. J.D., Tulane U., 1953. Bar: La. 1953, U.S. Ct. Appeals (5th cir.) 1981, U.S. Dist. Ct. (we. dist.) La. 1953. Asst. city atty. City of Shreveport, 1953-57; asst. U.S. Atty. Dept. Justice, Shreveport, 1957—. Republican. Episcopalian. Club: Shreveport Country. Home: 551 McCormick St Shreveport LA 71104 Office: Room 3B12 US Fed Bldg 500 Fannin St Shreveport LA 71101

PERKINS, JAMES ALLEN, lawyer; b. Oakland, Calif., May 15, 1952; s. Robert Cone Perkins and Doris Jean (Steinberg) Perkins Goltz; m. Barbara Carol Bellinghausen, Dec. 19, 1983. B.A. with honors, U. Tex., 1975; J.D., St. Mary's U., 1980. Bar: Tex. 1981, U.S. Dist. Ct. (we. dist.) Tex. 1981, (so. dist.) Tex. 1981, U.S. Ct. Appeals (5th cir.) 1982, U.S. Supreme Ct., 1985. Briefing atty. Fourth Ct. Appeals, San Antonio, 1980-81; assoc. Pat Maloney, San Antonio, 1982-84; sole practice, San Antonio, 1984—; v.p. Bexar County Health Facilities Corp., San Antonio, 1984—; dir. Bexar County Housing Fin. Authority, 1984—. County commr. Precinct 2 Bexar County Commrs. Ct., San Antonio, 1984—; campaign dir. Com. to Elect Rudy Esquivel Assoc. Justice, San Antonio, 1980, Com. to Elect Paul Elizondo County Judge, San Antonio, 1984. Mem. Tex. Bar Assn., Am. Trial Lawyers Assn., ABA, San Antonio Trial Lawyers Assn., Tex. Trial Lawyers Assn. Democrat. Presbyterian. Office: 314 E Commerce San Antonio TX 78205

PERKINS, JAMES FRANCIS, physicist; b. Hillsdale, Tenn., Jan. 3, 1924; s. Jim D. and Laura Pervis (Goad) P.; A.B., Vanderbilt U., 1948, M.A., 1949; Ph.D., 1953; m. Ida Virginia Phillips, Nov. 23, 1949; 1 son, James F. Sr. engr. Convair, Fort Worth, Tex., 1953-54; scientist Lockheed Aircraft, Marietta, Ga., 1954-61; physicist Army Missile Command Redstone Arsenal, Huntsville, Ala., 1961-77; cons. physicist, 1977—. Served with USAAF, 1943-46. AEC fellow, 1951-52. Mem. Am. Phys. Soc., Sigma Xi. Contbr. articles to profl. jours. Home and office: 102 Mountainwood Dr Huntsville AL 35801

PERKINS, MARTHA BAUGH, nursing educator; b. Valdosta, Ga., Nov. 10, 1943; d. John Thomas and Martha Eberhart (Thompson) Baugh; m. James Summers Perkins III, Dec. 29, 1967. Diploma Valdosta Vocat.-Tech. Sch., 1966; A.D.N., Albany Jr. Coll., 1970; B.S.N., Albany State Coll., 1974; M.S.N., Med. Coll. Ga., 1976. R.N., Ga. Staff and charge nurse Palmyra Park Hosp., Albany, Ga., 1971-74; instr. nursing Albany State Coll., 1974-77; asst. prof. nursing Albany Jr. Coll., 1977—. Mem. Am. Nurses Assn., Ga. Nurses Assn. (sec. 2d dist. 1983-85). Democrat. Baptist. Office: Albany Jr Coll 2400 Gillionville Rd Albany GA 31707

PERKINS, MICHAEL JAMES, clinical psychologist; b. Columbia, S.C., Aug. 9, 1945; s. Joseph Augustus and Loretta (Giller) P.; m. Cynthia Arline Carreiro, Oct. 14, 1967; children—Sarah Anne, Carrie Lorine. B.A., Boston U., 1974; M.A., Va. Commonwealth U., 1976, Ph.D., 1979. Lic. psychologist, Va. Staff psychologist Community Mental Health Ctr., Norfolk, Va., 1979-80, dir. child unit, 1980-81; med. staff Charter Colonial Psychiat. Inst., Newport News, Va., 1981—, exec. com., 1983-84, sec., treas., 1984-85, v.p., 1986—; psychologist Clin. Assocs., Tidewater, Norfolk, 1981—. Contbr. articles to profl. jours. Mem. Am. Psychol. Assn., Va. Acad. Clin. Psychologists, Tidewater Acad. Clin. Psychologists (bd. dirs. 1984-85, v.p. 1985-86). Office: Clin Assocs Tidewater Bldg 20 Koger Exec Ctr Norfolk VA 23502

PERKINS, RANDALL CURTIS, physician; b. Alexandria, La., Feb. 24, 1947; s. Dee M. Jr. and Elaine (Posey) P.; m. Pamela Allison Perkins, Feb. 19, 1972; 1 child, Allison Lee. B.A., North Tex. State U., 1970; D.O., Kansas City Sch. Osteo. Medicine, 1974. Pvt. practice Granbury Med. Clinic, Tex., 1976—; health officer City of Granbury; head obstetrics Hood Gen. Hosp., Granbury. Bd. dirs. Pecan Valley Health-Mental Retardation, Granbury. Mem. Tex. Osteo. Med. Assn. Methodist. Avocation: sports fan. Office: Granbury Med Clinic 1312 Paluxy Hwy Granbury TX 76048

PERKINS, RONALD DEE, geology educator, consultant; b. Covington, Ky., May 1, 1935; s. Stanley E. and Pauline L. (Green) P.; m. Beverly Lou Hughes, June 9, 1957; children—Lisa Lou, Debra Dee. B.S. U. Cin., 1957, M.S., U. N.Mex., 1959; Ph.D., Ind. U., 1962. Research geologist Shell Devel. Co., Houston, also Coral Gables, Fla., 1962-68; assoc. prof. geology Duke U., Durham N.C., 1968-75, prof., 1975—, chmn. dept., 1978—; pres. Perkins Exploration and Cons., Inc., 1979; ptnr. Flamingo Assocs. seminars-modern carbonate field trips to Caicos Islands; cons. numerous oil cos. Mem. Am. Assn. Petroleum Geologists, Geol. Soc. Am., Internat. Assn. Sedimentologists, Soc. Econ. Paleontologists, Mineralogists (nat. sec. 1980-82, chmn. fin. com.). Author: Quaternary Sedimentation in South Florida: Geol. Soc. Am. Memoir 147, 1977; contbr. articles to profl. jours. chpts. to books. Home: 2719 Montgomery St Durham NC 27705 Office: Dept Geology Duke U Room 206 Old Chemistry Bldg Durham NC 27706

PERKINS, STANLEY LVAN, petroleum exploration company executive, petroleum geologist; b. Kingsville, Tex., Nov. 29, 1930; s. Voyd Homer and Lillie Belle (Pilgrim) P.; m. Sandra J. Gaskin, Jan. 18, 1975; children—Stanley L., Lynn, Jondyle Leslie, Michelle, Kimberley, Janece, David C., Douglas. B.S., Tex. A & M Coll., 1952. Exploration geologist Continental Oil Co., 1954-65; ind. petroleum geologist, South Tex. and Texas Gulf Coast, 1965-68; founder, pres. Arrow Petroleum Co., San Antonio, 1969-79; ind. petroleum geologist, 1979—; pres., owner Pexco, Inc., San Antonio, 1979—. Pres. So. Hills Civic Club, Shreveport, La.; mem. steering com. Tex. A&M Scholarship Fund, Class of 1952. Served to maj. USAF, 1952-72. Named Boss of Yr., Desk & Derrick Assns., 1982. Mem. Tex. Mid-Continent Oil and Gas Assn., Ind. Petroleum Assn. Am., Am. Assn. Petroleum Geologists, Soc. Ind. Profl. Earth Scientists, South Tex. Geol. Soc., East Tex. Geol. Soc. Clubs: Petroleum (pres. bd. govs.) (San Antonio); University. Home: 11403 Raindrop San Antonio TX 78216 Office: 8620 N New Braunfels Suite 308 San Antonio TX 78217

PERKINS, WALTER RAY, university coach, educator; b. Mount Olive, Miss., Dec. 6, 1941.; m. Carolyn Martin; children—Tony, Mike. B.S., U. Ala., 1967. Football player Balt. Colts, 1967-71; asst. coach Miss. State U., 1973, New Eng. Patriots, 1974-77, San Diego Chargers, 1978; head coach N.Y. Giants, 1979-82; football coach U. Ala., University, 1983—. Address: Univ of Ala Rose Adminstrn Bldg University Blvd University AL 35486*

PERKINS, WILLIAM MAX, business executive; b. Evansville, Ind., Feb. 3, 1947; s. John F. and Glenna (Eble) P.; B.S. in Mktg., Ind. State U., 1974; 1 son, Christopher Michael. Mem. mgmt. ops. tng. program Danville (Ill.) Terminal of Ryder Truck Lines, 1974, ops., mgr. Rock Island (Ill.) Terminal, 1974-76, internal auditor, 1976-79, mktg. adminstr., Jacksonville, Fla., 1979-83; mgr. sales adminstrn. Ryder/P.I.E. Nationwide Inc., Jacksonville, 1983-85; facility mgr. Frito-Lay, Inc., Jacksonville, Fla., 1985—; mem. supervisory com. Ryder Truck Lines Credit Union, 1978. Coach, Jacksonville Youth Baseball, 1976-79; active Jr. Achievement. Served with USAF, 1966-70. Mem. Am. Mktg. Assn. Roman Catholic. Club: Masons. Home: 2413 Maple Leaf Dr Jacksonville FL 32211 Office: Frito-Lay Inc 2908 W Beaver St Jacksonville FL 32205

PERLIS, HOWARD WILLIAM, educator; b. Paterson, N.J., June 20, 1941; s. Leo and Betty Francis (Gantz) P.; B.A., Adelphi U., 1969; Ph.D., U. Ala., 1978; m. Loretta J. Stodel, Dec. 26, 1965; children—Jonathan Andrew, Melissa Amy. Research asst. Albert Einstein Coll. Medicine, N.Y.C., 1965-67; project engr. MIRU, U. Ala. Med. Center, Birmingham, 1967-70, mgr. obstetrics computer center, 1970-79, asst. prof. biophysics dept. ob-gyn, 1979—; instr. Sch. Bus., U. Ala., Birmingham, 1979—; pres. Compu-Train, Inc., office automation, tng. and custom software development, 1985—. Recipient cert. of Merit, Central Assn. Obstetricians and Gynecologists. Mem. AAAS, Sigma Xi. Home: 2621 Chandalar Ln Pelham AL 35124 Office: U Ala University Station Birmingham AL 35294

PERLMUTTER, ARNOLD, physics educator, researcher; b. Bklyn., Nov. 4, 1928; s. Bernard and Luba (Rapoport) P.; m. Ruth Pines, July 9, 1949 (div. 1975); children—Bernard Pines, Joseph Philip; m. Lynn Meyer, Nov. 28, 1980. B.S., U. Calif., 1949; M.S., NYU, 1951, Ph.D., 1955; Instr. physics Cooper Union Coll., N.Y.C., 1954-55, Bklyn. Coll., 1955-56; asst. prof. U. Miami, Coral Gables, Fla., 1956-63, assoc. prof., 1963-68, prof., 1968—, sec. Ctr. for Studies, 1965—; vis. prof. Imperial Coll. Sci. and Tech., London, 1973-74, U. Mich., Ann Arbor, 1978-81, U. Torino, Italy, 1983-84. Contbr. articles to profl. jours.; contbg. editor sci. books. Bd. dirs. ACLU South Fla., 1982—. Fulbright Travel grantee, Italy, 1961-62; vis. fellow Inst. Nazionale Fisica Nucleare, U. Trieste, Italy, 1961-62; vis. fellow Israel AEC, Weizmann Inst., 1962-63; guest fellow Ukrainian Acad. Scis., Kiev, USSR, 1970. Mem. Am. Phys. Soc. Democrat. Jewish. Avocations: tennis; sailing; chamber music. Office: Ctr Theoretical Studies U Miami PO Box 249055 Coral Gables FL 33124

PERLMUTTER, BARRY F., developmental psychologist; b. Detroit, June 28, 1951; s. Isadore and Marian (Lewis) P.; m. Maryanne Elizabeth Smith, Mar. 30, 1974; children—Jennifer Lynn, Kristen Michelle. B.S., Mich. State U., 1973; M.S., Northwestern U., 1980, Ph.D., 1981. Licensed psychologist, Tex. Cons. Inst. for Learning Disabilities, 1977-80; postdoctoral fellow devel. psychology, Wayne State U., Detroit, 1981-83, instr., 1981-83; asst. prof. Tex. Tech U. Med. Sch., Amarillo, 1983—; ednl. cons. to various pub. schs., Ill., Mich., Tex., 1980—. Mem. editorial bd. Jour. Youth and Adolescence, 1985—, Techniques: Jour. Remedial Edn. and Counseling, 1985—. Contbr. articles to profl. publs., chpt. to book. Bd. dirs. Parenting Services, Inc., Amarillo, 1984—. Recipient Seed Research award Tex. Tech Med. Sch., 1984-85; Northwestern U. fellow, 1980. Mem. Am. Psychol. Assn., Council for Learning Disabilities, Council for Exceptional Children, Rodin Remediation Found., Jean Piaget Soc., Soc. Research in Child Devel., Evans Scholars Alumni Assn. Avocations: racquetball; bicycling; soccer, wrestling referee. Home: 1538 Stubbs Amarillo TX 79106 Office: Dept Pediatrics Sch Medicine Tex Tech U Health Scis Ctr 1400 Wallace Blvd Amarillo TX 79106

PERLMUTTER, MARTIN ALLEN, research geologist; b. N.Y.C., July 13, 1951; s. Robert and Helen (Peller) P.; m. Judith Ann Ficcadenti, Mar. 20, 1982. B.S., SUNY-Stony Brook, 1972, M.S., 1973; Ph.D., U. Miami, 1982. Geology curator marine geology dept. U. Miami, Fla., 1976-81; sr. geologist Texaco Houston Research Ctr., 1981—. Author: (with others) A Source Book Oceanographic Properties Affecting Biofouling and Corrosion of OTEC Plants and Selected Sites, 1978. Contbr. articles to profl. jours. Recipient Ann. award Miami Geol. Soc., 1979. Mem. Am. Assn. Petroleum Geologists, Soc. Econ. Paleontologists and Mineralogists. Avocations: scuba diving; fishing; canoeing; hiking; camping.

PERMENTER, SHIRLEY LEE, nurse; b. Cold Springs, Ky., July 9, 1931; d. John R. Wooten and Meredith (Alderman) Goodley; R.N., Warren A. Candler Hosp. Sch. Nursing, 1952; student Armstrong State Coll., 1950; children—Cynthia Faye, David, Wayne. Asst. dir. nurses Warren A. Candler Hosp., Savannah, Ga., 1963-65; asst. dir. nurses Chatham Nursing Home, Savannah, 1965-73, dir. inservice edn., 1967-73; founder, registrar Nursing Services Registry of Savannah, Inc., 1978—. Address: PO Box 14482 Savannah GA 31406

PERMENTER, VIVIAN KAY, college dean, educator; b. Evarts, Ky., Sept. 6, 1940; d. William Marion and Ollie Jane (Howard) Baker; children—Debra Kay, David Nelson, Donna Gayle. B.S., East Central State U., Okla., 1969; M.S., Okla. State U., 1970. Cert. profl. sec. Acct. Blackman & McBee, C.P.A.s, McAlester, Okla., 1970; instr. South Fla. Jr. Coll., Avon Park, 1970-74; assoc. prof. dept. bus. adminstrn., dean of admissions and student affairs Pan Am. U., Brownsville, Tex., 1974—; condr. seminars and communications, 1973—. Mem. Tex. Bus. Edn. Assn., South Tex. Assn. Registrars and Admissions Officers (pres.), So. Tex. Assn. Admission Officers and Registrars (mem.-at-large), Delta Pi Epsilon, Alpha Kappa Psi. Lodge: Order Eastern Star. Avocations: music; dancing. Office: Pan Am U Brownsville 1614 Ridgely Rd Brownsville TX 78520

PEROT, H. ROSS, data processing company executive; b. 1930; married. Ed. U.S. Naval Acad., 1953. With IBM, 1957-62; with Electronic Data Systems Corp., Dallas, 1962—, now chmn. bd., chief exec. officer, also dir. Served with USN, 1953-57. Office: Electronic Data Systems Corp 7171 Forest Ln Dallas TX 75230*

PERRA, BARBARA ANNE, nurse; b. Utica, N.Y., Jan 31, 1949; d. Lewis Richard and Katherine Anne (Lyons) P. Diploma St. Elizabeth Hosp., Utica, N.Y., 1970; B.S.N., Fla. Internat. U., 1977, M.S., 1980. R.N., Fla. Staff nurse St. Elizabeth Hosp., Utica, 1970-73; head nurse ICU/CCU, Fla. Med. Ctr., Lauderdale Lakes, 1973-78; regional inservice coordinator S.E. U.S. consultative capacity Am. Optical Med. Div., Pompano, Fla., 1978-80; dir. edn. Humana Hosp. Bennett, Plantation, Fla., 1980—. Recipient spl. recognition award Am. Heart Assn., 1978, 81, 82, 83. Mem. Am. Assn. Critical Care Nurses (pres. 1978-79, dir. 1979-81), South Fla. Nurse Educators. Democrat. Roman Catholic. Office: Humana Hosp Bennett 8201 W Broward Blvd Plantation FL 33324

PERREIAH, ALAN, philosophy educator; b. Los Angeles, Apr. 11, 1937; s. Charles S. and Helen M. (Rossiter) P.; m. Eleanor Grace Sievert, June 14, 1958; children—Carmen Covert, Paul, Peter, Martin, Scott. B.A., Loyola U., Los Angeles, 1959; M.A., Marquette U., 1961; Ph.D., Ind. U., 1967. Asst. prof. U. Wis.-Whitewater, 1966-67; asst. prof. U. Ky., Lexington, 1967-69, assoc. prof., 1969-82, prof. philosophy, dept. chmn., 1982—. Translator: Paul of Venice: Logica Magna Suppositions, 1971; Paul of Venice: Logica Parva, 1984; Paul of Venice: Bibliographical Guide, 1986. Villa i Tatti fellow Harvard U., 1980-81, Fulbright Found. fellow, 1965-66. Mem. Am. Philos. Assn., Ky. Philos. Assn., Inst. Advanced Study. Home: 2339 Maplewood Dr Lexington KY 40503 Office: Dept Philosophy U Ky Lexington KY 40506

PERRICONE, CATHERINE ROSE, foreign language educator; b. Bogalusa, La., Sept. 12, 1935; d. Joseph J. and Rosa Mae (Powe) P.; m. David L. Martin, June 6, 1975. B.A. in Spanish, Notre Dame Coll., 1959; M.A. in Spanish, U. Okla., 1965; Ph.D. in Spanish, Tulane U., 1973. Tchr. Redemptorist High Sch., New Orleans, 1957-64; mem. faculty U. Dallas, 1965-68; prof. fgn. langs., 1982-84, Auburn U. (Ala.), 1972—, mentor, translator, fgn. lang. dept., mem., sec. univ. senate. La. State U. NDEA fellow, 1960; Fulbright scholar, 1966; Vanderbilt U. Mellon Found. Inst. fellow, 1983. Mem. MLA, Assn., South Atlantic MLA, Am. Council Teaching Fgn. Langs., So. Conf. Teaching Fgn. Langs., Am. Assn. Tchrs. Spanish and Portuguese, AAUW, AAUP, Ala. Assn. Fgn. Lang. Tchrs. (sec.-treas., editor Alahispania). Author: Alma y corazón: antología de las poetisas hispanoamericanas, 1977; contbr. articles to fgn. lang. publs. (sec.-treas., v.p., pres., editor Alahispania). Author: Alma Office: Auburn U Dept Foreign Languages Auburn AL 36849

PERRIN, SARAH ANN, lawyer; b. Neoga, Ill., Dec. 13, 1904; d. James Lee and Bertha Frances (Baker) Figenbaum; LL.B., George Washington U., 1941, J.D., 1964; m. James Frank Perrin, Dec. 24, 1926. Bar: D.C. 1942. Assoc. atty. Mabel Walker Willebrandt, law office, Washington, 1941-42; atty. various fed. housing agys., 1942-69, asst. gen. counsel FHA, Washington, 1959-60, asst. gen. counsel HUD, Washington, 1960-69; sec. Nat. Housing Conf., Washington, 1970-80; research cons. housing and urban devel., Palmyra, Va., 1970—; acting sec. Nat. Housing Research Council, Washington, 1973-80; bd. dirs. Nat. Housing Conf., 1972—. Trustee Found. for Coop. Housing, 1975—; mem. Blue Ridge Presbytery Div. Mission, Presbyterian Ch., 1979-80. Mem. Am. Bar Assn., Fed. Bar Assn., Women's Bar Assn. D.C. (pres. 1959-60), Nat. Assn. Women Lawyers, George Washington Law Assn., Charlottesville Women's Bar Assn., Phi Alpha Delta (internat. pres. 1955-57), Fluvanna County Hist.

Soc. (pres. 1973-75). Lodge: Order Eastern Star. Home: Solitude Plantation Palmyra VA 22963

PERRIN, SHEPARD FRANCIS, JR., consulting engineer, real estate marketer; b. New Orleans, June 3, 1922; s. Shepard Francis and Leila Winans (Joffrion) P.; B.S. in Chem. Engring., Tulane U., 1942; m. Elizabeth Rice, June 20, 1947; children—Leila Joffrion, Cidette St. Martin, Shepard Francis. Supr. petroleum refining Esso Standard Oil, Baton Rouge, 1946-57; head splty. products sales Esso & Humble Oil Co., N.Y.C., 1957-66; sr. adviser Esso Inter Am., Coral Gables, Fla., 1966-70; head lube oil sales Exxon Internat., N.Y.C., 1970-72; sr. adviser Esso Asia, Singapore, 1972-74; exec. dir. La. Superport Authority, Baton Rouge, 1975-81; exec. dir. Gov.'s Task Force on Deepening Mississippi River, 1982; dir. bus. devel. Pyburn & Odom, Odom Offshore Surveys, Inc., 1981-83. Chmn. com. United Way, Baton Rouge, 1977, 78; adv. council Gulf South Research Inst.; adv. bd. La. State U. Sea Grant Program; mem., past pres. Tulane Engring. Bd. Advs. Served to lt. USNR, 1942-46. Registered profl. engr., La. Mem. SAR, Tulane U. Alumni Assn. (past pres.), Am. Inst. Chem. Engrs., La. Engring. Soc. Presbyterian. Clubs: N.Y. Yacht, Storm Trysail, Baton Rouge City, Baton Rouge Country, New Orleans, Plimsoll; Singapore Island Country, Tanglin (Singapore). Address: 7465 Boyce Dr Baton Rouge LA 70809

PERRITT, R. T., clergyman; b. Winnsboro, Tex., May 20, 1926; s. James Hogg and Clara (White) P.; A.A., Jacksonville (Tex.) Coll., 1948; B.D., Bible Bapt. Sem., Arlington, Tex., 1958; Th.M., Okla. Missionary Bapt. Inst. and Sem., 1960, Th.D., 1961; m. Betty Ruth Powell, Nov. 23, 1944; children—Robert Lynn, John Mark, Ruth Ann, James Lance. Ordained to ministry Baptist Ch., 1945; pastor Calvary Missionary Bapt. Ch., Sherman, Tex., 1949-51, Liberty Missionary Bapt. Ch., Ft. Worth, 1951-56, Cavanaugh Missionary Bapt. Ch., Fort Smith, Ark., 1956-59, 5th St. Missionary Bapt. Ch., Marlow, Okla., 1959-80, Broadway Heights Baptist Ch., Clinton, Okla., 1983—; dean Okla. Missionary Bapt. Coll., Inst. and Sem., 1961-63, pres., 1963—; asst. moderator Bapt. Gen. Assembly Okla., 1970-72, moderator, 1973-75. Pres., Unique Christian Ministries, Inc., 1974-79, 83—; chmn. bd. Leisure Village, Norman, Okla., 1976-79; pres. Myrtle Springs Perpetual Care Cemetary Assn., Quitman, Tex., 1977-84. Pres., Cavanaugh Baseball Club, 1957-59. Served with U.S. Maritime Service and Mcht. Marine, 1944-45. Named Community Leader Am., 1969. Mem. Am. Bapt. Assn. (v.p. 1970-80, asst. parliamentarian 1980—, chmn. missionary com. 1966-75). Democrat. Lion. Author: The Natural and the Spiritual, 1960; Kindling Fires for Church Growth, 1965; Mastery in Sorrow, 1969; Studies in Daniel, 1973; also numerous religious tng. course quars. Home: 418 S 16th St Clinton OK 73601 Office: 807 S 9th St Marlow OK 73055 also 431 S 16th St Clinton OK 73601

PERROT, PAUL NORMAN, museum director; b. Paris, July 28, 1926; came to U.S., 1946, naturalized 1954; s. Paul and Kate Norman (Derr) P.; m. Joanne Stovall, Oct. 23, 1954; children—Paul Latham, Chantal Marie Claire, Jeannine, Robert. Student Ecole du Louvre, 1945-46, N.Y.U. Inst. Fine Arts, 1946-52. Asst. The Cloisters, Met. Mus. Art, 1948-52; asst. to dir. Corning Mus. Glass, N.Y., 1952-54, asst. dir. mus., 1954-60, dir., 1960-72; editor Jour. Glass Studies, 1959-72; asst. sec. for mus. programs Smithsonian Instn., Washington, 1972-84; dir. Va. Mus. Fine Art, 1984—; lectr. glass history, aesthetics, museology; v.p. Internat. Council Mus. Found.; past pres. Northeast Conf. Mus.; v.p. Internat. Centre for Study of Preservation and Restoration of Cultural Property, Rome, mem. council, 1974—. Author: Three Great Centuries of Venetian Glass, 1958, also numerous articles on various hist. and archael. subjects. Recipient Chevalier des Arts et Lettres French Ministry of Culture, 1981. Mem. Am. Assn. Museums (v.p., council 1967-78), N.Y. State Assn. Museums (past pres.), Internat. Assn. History Glass (v.p.), Corning Friends of Library (past pres.), So. Tier Library System (past pres.). Office: Va Mus of Fine Arts Blvd and Grove Ave Richmond VA 23221

PERRY, ANTHONY JOHN, cons. engr.; b. Boston, Sept. 7, 1905; s. Anthony A. and Ellen M. (Connors) P.; A.B., Boston Coll., 1926; B.S., M.I.T., 1929; m. Ruth Jane Saunders, June 2, 1979. Civil and elec. engr. Bur. Reclamation, Dept. Interior, 1930-65; spl. assignment State Dept. in Iran, Iraq, Lebanon, Italy, 1952, Cambodia, 1958, Brazil, 1964; pvt. cons., 1965—. Registered profl. engr., Colo., D.C. Fellow ASCE (life); mem. Nat. Soc. Profl. Engrs., Am. Defense Preparedness Assn. (life.). Democrat. Roman Catholic. Club: K.C. Home and Office: Route 3 Box 519 Moneta VA 24121

PERRY, EDWARD OWEN, III, forest products company executive; b. Augusta, Ga., Oct. 29, 1948; s. E. Owen Jr. and Joy (O'Brien) P.; m. Betty Laura Brand, Aug. 21, 1971; children—Laura Claire, Elizabeth O'Brien. B.S., Washington and Lee U., 1970; M.B.A., U. Ga., 1972. Mgmt. trainee, supr. Deering Milliken Inc., LaGrange, Ga., 1972-73; adminstrv. mgr. Canal Wood Corp. Augusta d/b/a Southland Timber Co., 1973-77, v.p., ops. mgr., 1977-81, pres., 1981—. Served to capt. U.S. Army, 1970-72. Mem. Ga. Forestry Assn. (v.p., pres. elect 1985—, dir. 1981—, Pres. award 1984), Am. Pulpwood Assn. (supplier com.). Republican. Episcopalian. Clubs: Augusta Country, Ducks Unlimited (dir. 1980-84). Lodge: Kiwanis. Home: 774 Camellia Rd Augusta GA 30909 Office: Southland Timber Co PO Box 250 Augusta GA 30903

PERRY, GERALD KEITH, state educational official; b. Jeffrey, W.Va., Apr. 13, 1934; s. Charles Freeman and Nina Jane (Cook) P.; m. Ruth Ann Pennington Perry, Dec. 21, 1957; children—Geoffrey, Gregory. B.A., Marshall U., 1955, M.A., 1960, cert. advanced study, 1977. Jr. high sch. tchr. Logan County Schs., W.Va., 1955-57; elem. tchr. Kanawha County Schs., Charleston, W.Va., 1957-61, prin., 1962-69, coordinator tutorial services, 1969-73; asst. dir. elem. schs. W.Va. Dept. Edn., Charleston, 1973-76, coordinator textbook adoptions, 1976—; instr. W.Va. U., Morgantown, 1970-75; state chmn.-elem. North Central Assn. Colls. and Schs., Charleston, 1975-79; nat. chmn. Adv. Commn. on Textbook Specifications, Stamford, Conn., 1981-82. Author: Generic Guidelines for Textbook Adoptions, 1975; editor State Multiple Lists Approved Textbooks, 1974—. Mgr., Glendale Swim Club, South Charleston, W.Va., 1964-67, Highlawn Swim Club, St. Albans, W.Va., 1968; exec. sec. Charleston Schs. Shoe Fund, 1970-73; bd. dirs. Vol. Service Bur., Charleston, 1970-73. Served to staff sgt. Army N.G., 1956-62. W.Va. Dept. Edn. scholar Marshall U., 1951. Mem. W.Va. Assn. Social Services and Attendance (pres. 1971-73, Recognition award 1973), Internat. Assn. Pupil Personnel Workers (state dir. 1981), Nat. Assn. State Textbook Adminstrs. (nat. pres. 1980). Democrat. Presbyterian. Lodges: Kiwanis, Shriners, Masons. Avocations: mechanics; fishing; hunting. Home: 2323 S Walnut Dr Saint Albans WV 25177 Office: W Va Dept Edn Capitol Complex Bldg 6 Room 330 Charleston WV 25305

PERRY, HARRY A., II, wholesale food distributing corporation executive; b. 1922; married. Student, U. Colo.; B.S., U. Kans., 1947. Pres. Perry Packing Co., 1947-50; commodity salesman Seymour Packing Co., 1950-52; pres. Seymour Foods Inc., 1952-66, Morris Foods Co., 1966-70; v.p. affiliated ops. Fleming Cos. Inc., Oklahoma City, 1970-72, exec. v.p., dir., 1972—; also pres. Fleming Industries. Office: Fleming Companies Inc 6601 N Broadway Box 26647 Oklahoma City OK 73126*

PERRY, JACK BIRL, bailiff; b. Granbury, Tex., Jan. 31, 1923; s. William Walter and Mary Ellen (Smith) P.; m. Oma Lee Boase, Dec. 5, 1953; 1 dau., Mary Lee Perry Gilliland. Cert. peace officer, Tex. With Posten Feed Store, Stephenville, Tex., 1949-65; dep. sheriff Erath County, Tex., 1965-77, sheriff, 1977-85, bailiff, 1985—; bd. dirs. continuing edn. Tarleton State U., Stephenville, 1983-85. Democrat. Baptist. Avocations: fishing; camping. Office: Erath County Seat County Courthouse Stephenville TX 76401

PERRY, JAMES LAWRENCE, JR., government social services administrator; b. Elizabeth City, N.C., Sept. 27, 1946; s. James Lawrence and Maggie Ethel (Lane) P.; B.A., N.C. Wesleyan Coll., 1968; postgrad. Birmingham Sch. Law, 1973-74; M.P.A., U. Ala., Birmingham, 1983; cert. credit union mgmt. U. Ala., 1977; also various courses CSC; m. Sandra Jo Norman, Dec. 27, 1968; children—Rebecca, Gwendolyn, James Lawrence III. Social ins. claims rep. Social Security Adminstrn. Field Ops., Miami, Fla., 1968-69; social ins. claims examiner Southeastern Program Service Center, Social Security Adminstrn. Central Ops., Birmingham, 1969-74, social ins. claims specialist, 1974-76, asst. process module mgr., 1976-79, chief auditor, 1979-80, process mgr., 1980—; dir. Nat. Task Force to Rewrite Social Security Adminstrn. Audit Procedures, 1980, mem. nat. task force to formulate new performance Standards. Vol., Big Bros., Birmingham, 1974—; adminstrv. advisor to Jr. Achievement, Birmingham, 1974-75; dir. employees activities assn. Southeastern Program Service Center, Birmingham, 1974-76, vice chmn. combined fed. campaign, 1975; legis. del. Social Security Employees Credit Union, 1978—, chmn. credit com., 1978-81, 82—; vice chmn. Council on Ministries, First United Methodist Ch., Hueytown, Ala., 1980—, lay speaker, 1980—; advocacy chmn. Ala. Friends of Adoption, 1980-83, bd. dirs., 1981-84; mem. state adv. council Ala. Dept. Pensions and Security, 1981-84; advisor Dixie Youth Softball, Hueytown, 1980-81; participant White House Conf. Voluntarism, 1982; mem. adv. bd. U. Ala.-Birmingham, 1984—. Recipient award for outstanding contbn. to religious life Wesleyan Campus, 1968; Spl. Achievement award Social Security Adminstrn., 1973, 80, Commr.'s citation, 1975; cert. merit Fed. Service Campaign for Nat. Health Agys., 1978, letter of commendation Social Security Adminstrn., 1981. Mem. Social Security Adminstrn. Mgmt. Assn., Am. Mgmt. Assn., Inst. Internal Auditors, Am. Soc. for Public Adminstrn., U.Ala. Birmingham Alumni Assn. (exec. com.). Club: Hueytown Swim. Home: 232 Highland Dr Hueytown AL 35023 Office: 2001 12th Ave N Birmingham AL 35285

PERRY, JESSE JAMES, business educator; b. Norfolk, Va., Mar. 5, 1933; s. Jesse James Perry and Stella (Maie) Ferbee. A.A. in Bus., Old Dominion U., 1954, B.S. in Bus., 1956; M.S. in Bus., Va. Poly. Inst. and State U., 1958, M.Ed., 1962. Distributive edn. coordinator Galax City Schs., Va., 1959-67; assoc. prof. bus. Richard Bland Coll., Petersburg, Va., 1967—. Named Outstanding Tchr. of Yr., Richard Bland Coll., 1969. Fellow AAUP (local chpt. pres.). Lodge: Kiwanis (lt. gov. staff 1980—; Legion of Honor 1985). Avocations: numismatist; reading; traveling. Home: 1940 Westover Ave Petersburg VA 23805 Office: Richard Bland Coll Johnson Rd Ext Petersburg VA 23805

PERRY, KENNETH DWIGHT, museum director; b. Lubbock, Tex., Sept. 1, 1946; s. Robert Ross and Billie Louise (Zimmerman) P.; m. Judy Andersen, Sept. 7, 1968. B.A., Tex. Tech. U., 1969, M.A., 1975. Teaching asst. Tex. Tech. U., Lubbock, 1973-74, mus. intern, 1974-75; dir. mus. and archives Sul Ross State U., Alpine, Tex., 1975—. Editor: Museum Forms Book, 1980. Contbr. articles to profl. jours., booklets. Charter mem., pres. Davis Mountains Art League, Alpine, 1983; charter mem. Alpine Humane Soc., 1983-85. Recipient Founders cert. Centennial Com., Alpine, 1982. Mem. Tex. Assn. Mus. Bd., Permian Basin Mus. Inst. Bd., Am. Assn. Mus., Am. Assn. State and Local History, Soc. Am. Archivists. Club: Alpine Country (bd. dirs.). Lodge: Rotary. Avocations: watercolor painting; golf; reading.

PERRY, MATTHEW J., JR., U.S. district judge; b. 1921. B.S., S.C. State U., 1948, LL.B., 1951. Atty., Spartanburg, S.C., 1951-61, Columbia, S.C., 1961-76; instr. law U. S.C., 1973-75; judge U.S. Ct. Mil. Appeals, Washington, 1976-79; judge U.S. Dist. Ct. for S.C., Columbia, 1979—. Address: 1845 Assembly St PO Box 7307 Columbia SC 29202*

PERRY, MOZELLE (MRS. ORVAL PERRY), museum executive; b. Denton, Tex., Aug. 8, 1913; d. Richard Oscar and Clemmie Cleo (Dunaway) Martin; m. Orval R. Perry, Apr. 6, 1935; 1 child, Penny Lee. Student North Tex. State U., Sul Ross State U.; Winedale seminar grad. Tex. Hist. Commn., 1973. Tire clerk War Price and Rationing Bd., Seagraves, Tex., 1942-45; tchr. elem. sch., Seagraves, 1936; dir. Gaines County Mus. and Art Ctr., Seagraves-Loop Div., 1973—. Art editor: Gaines County Story, 1974 (state award 1974). Edn., church sec. First Bapt. Ch., Seagraves, 1952-57; mem. Gaines County Hist. Commn.; mem. Seagraves Sesquicentennial Commn. Named Best Artist Seagraves C. of C. Arts and Crafts Show, 1970. Mem. Tex. Fedn. of Women's Club (homelife chmn. Caprock dist. 1968-69, art chmn. 1967, Outstanding Clubwoman Caprock dist. 1972, life mem. 1975). Republican. Baptist. Club: Cultus (pres. Seagraves 1941-42, 64-65, 80-81). Avocation: painting. Home: 606 12th St Seagraves TX 79359 Office: Gaines County Mus and Art Ctr Seagraves-Loop Div Main & Hill Sts Seagraves TX

PERRY, NANCY JO, investment company executive; b. Olean, N.Y., Dec. 12, 1931; d. Thomas Bronson and Doris Marjory (Bacon) White; student Gustavus Adolphus Coll.; grad. Bethesda Hosp. Sch. Nursing, St. Paul, 1952; m. Charles Robert Perry, Apr. 9, 1955; children—Elizabeth Perry Sewell, Charles Thomas, Nancy Marie. Asst. head nurse U. Colo. Gen. Hosp., 1953-55; co-owner, dir. Perry Gas Co., Perry Energy Co., Odessa, Tex., 1967-82; v.p. Perry Investments, Perry Found., 1982—; past sec.-treas. Perry Energy Co., Perry Gas Processors, Perry Gas Transmissions, Inc., PGP Gas Products, Inc., Rockies Oil and Gas Corp. Past bd. dirs. Odessa Council on Alcoholism; past mem. Task Force on Women; past sec., bd. dirs. Our New Beginnings recovery house for women alcoholics; past pres., bd. dirs. West Tex. Pastoral Counseling Center; mem. Tex. Commn. on Alcohol and Drug Abuse, 1986—. Mem. Jr. League (sustaining). Presbyterian (elder). Home: 9 San Miquel Sq Odessa TX 79762 Office: 621 State National Plaza Odessa TX 79762

PERRY, PRISCILLA ROSENFELD, community, political and media relations consultant; b. Brockton, Mass., July 2, 1932; d. Michael Louis and Lena Sylvia (Altman) Rosenfeld; m. Morton L. Perry, Apr. 6, 1958 (div. June 1974); children—Pamela, Aaron; m. 2d, Eugene H. Man, Sept. 15, 1976. B.Ed., U. Miami, 1955, M.A., 1971. Assoc. dir. Anti-Defamation League, B'nai B'rith Fla. Regional Office, Miami, 1954-58; coordinator urban affairs project U. Miami, Coral Gables, Fla., 1968-71, instr. dept. human relations, 1968-70, assoc. dir. Ctr. for Urban and Regional Studies, 1971-73, dir. ctr., 1973-75, founder and dir. Inst. for Study Aging, 1975-80; cons. community, polit. and media relations, South Miami, Fla., 1980—. Editor, Miami Interaction, 1968-75; contbr. articles to prof. jours. Founder, League of Working Mothers, Miami-Dade County, Fla., 1972; chmn. health planning council Environ. Health Planning Com., Miami, 1978; dir. Sta.-WLRN-TV, Miami-Dade County, 1979—. Bd. dirs. Greater Miami C. of C. New World Com., 1983; charter bd. dirs. Area Agy. on Aging/United Way Dade County, 1980—; mem. Miami Mayor's Com. on Budget; mem. Ade County Commn. on Status of Women. Recipient Women in Bus. and Industry award YWCA, 1983; Adminstrn. on Aging grantee U. Miami, 1976-79, 77. Mem. Fla. Council on Aging (trustee 1979), So. Gerontol. Soc. (v.p. 1979-80; founding mem.), Council Univ. Insts. for Urban Affairs, Am. Soc. Pub. Adminstrn., Am. Inst. Planners, Gerontol. Soc. Democrat. Jewish. Home and Office: Priscilla R Perry and Assocs Inc 5740 SW 64th Pl South Miami FL 33143

PERRY, ROBERT THOMAS, oral and maxillofacial surgeon; b. Houston, Aug. 28, 1947; s. John Harold and Betsy (Taylor) P.; m. Sue Ellen Claybaugh, Dec. 23, 1972; children—Laura Sue, Katherine Rene, Beth Ann. B.S. in Zoology, Tex. A&M U., 1970; D.D.S., Baylor Dental Coll., 1974; cert. Oral and Maxillofacial Surgery, Ohio State U., 1983. Resident gen. dentistry Dallas VA Hosp., 1975-76; gen. practice dentistry, College Station, Tex., 1976-80, practice dentistry specializing in oral and maxillofacial surgery, 1983—. Fellow Am. Assn. Oral and Maxillofacial Surgeons, Am. Dental Soc. Anesthesiology mem. ADA, Tex. Dental Assn., Brazos Valley Dist. Dental Soc. (sec., treas. 1984-85), Southwest Soc. Oral and Maxillofacial Surgeons, College Station C. of C. (chmn. health services com.), Psi Omega (v.p. 1973-74). Republican. Methodist. Lodge: Rotary Internat. (College Station) (bd. dirs. 1984-85). Avocations: gardening; picture framing; photography; tennis; swimming. Home: 2806 Apple Creek Bryan TX 77802 Office: 303 Arguello Dr College Station TX 77840

PERRY, RUSSELL H., insurance executive; b. Cornell, Ill., Nov. 8, 1908; s. Walter O. and Mabel (Hilton) P.; student N.Y. U., 1937; J.D. cum laude, Bklyn. Law Sch., 1940; D.C.L., Atlanta Law Sch.; m. Phoebe Sherwood, June 2, 1956. Clk., Chgo. Fire & Marine Ins. Co., 1925-32; underwriter Republic Ins. Co., N.Y.C., 1934-38, charge eastern dept. underwriting, 1939-42, asst. to v.p., 1942-43, spl. agt. for L.I. and Westchester, 1943, mgr. eastern dept., 1945-47, resident sec., 1947-49, v.p., 1949-59, exec. v.p., 1959-61; pres., chief exec. officer Republic Fin. Services, Inc., holding co. for Republic Ins. and Allied Fin. Groups, Dallas, 1961-71, chmn. bd., pres., chief exec. officer, 1971-72, chmn. bd., chief exec. officer, 1972—; dir. USA Cafes, Inc., Met. Savs. & Loan Assn., Dallas, TACA, Inc.; adv. dir. Union Bank & Trust, Dallas. Bd. dirs. Ins. Info. Inst., N.Y.C.; bd. dirs., chmn. emeritus Dallas Council on World Affairs; pres. Trinity Improvement Assn.; bd. dirs. Dallas Citizens Council; mem. devel. bd. Dallas Bapt. Coll.; adv. chmn. Salvation Army, Dallas, nat. bd. dirs.; chmn. bd. trustees, mem. exec. com. Communities Found. Tex.; nat. bd. dirs. Am. Cancer Soc.; bd. dirs. Big Bros./Big Sisters Am., Citizen's Choice, Dallas UN Assn., Texas Research League, Dallas County Community Coll. Found., Inc.; bd. dirs., past pres. Tex. Bur. Econ. Understanding, Inc.; adv. council Airline Passengers Assn.; bd. dirs. Tex. Soc. Prevention of Blindness, Dallas Summer Musicals, Greater Dallas Planning Council, Better Bus. Bur. Met. Dallas, Hwy. Users Fedn.; chmn. polit. action com. Nat. Ctr. Policy Analysis. Recipient G. Mabry Seay award Dallas Assn. Ins. Agts., 1970, Headliner of Yr. award Press Club Dallas, 1975, Orchid for Uncommon Support Free Enterprise, Students in Free Enterprise, So. Meth. U., 1977, Person of Vision award Tex. Soc. for Prevention of Blindness, 1977, Linz award for public service Linz Bros. Jewelers-Dallas Times Herald, 1978, Torch of Liberty award Anti-Defamation League, 1979, Horatio Alger award, 1981; named Boss of Yr., Ins. Women Dallas, 1976, Disting. Salesman of Dallas, 1976, Sales and Mktg. Execs. Dallas, 1977. Mem. Philonomic Soc., Am., N.Y., Dallas bar assns., State Bar Tex. (dir.), Tex. Good Roads Assn. (dir., exec. com.), Am. Ins. Assn. (past pres., mem. nominating com.), Nat. Assn. Casualty and Surety Execs. (dir.), Tex. Assn. Taxpayers, Newcomen Soc. N.Am., E. Tex. C. of C. (dir.), Delta Theta Phi. Clubs: Knife and Fork, Dallas Petroleum, Dallas Country, Rotary, Lancers, 2001 (Dallas); Austin; Tower; University (N.Y.C.). Home: 2817 Park Bridge Ct Dallas TX 75219 Office: 2727 Turtle Creek Blvd Dallas TX 75219

PERRY, STYLES SAMUEL, insurance loss control representative; b. Greenville, S.C., Dec. 30, 1938; s. William Edwin and Evangeline (Barker) P.; m. Iris Gantt, June 6, 1964; children—Robin, Scott, Jennifer. B.S., Clemson U., 1964. Cert. safety profl. Tchr. Montaview Jr. High Sch., Greenville, 1964-65; engring. trainee Burlington Industries, Mooresville, N.C., 1966; loss control rep. CIGNA Loss Control Services, Inc., Charlotte, N.C., 1967—. Served with USAR, 1956-62. Mem. Am. Soc. Safety Engrs. Republican. Baptist. Home: Route 1 Box 212 Twin Oaks Rd Indian Trail NC 28079 Office: CIGNA Loss Control Services Inc PO Box 220647 6000 Monroe Rd Charlotte NC 28222

PERRY, THOMAS BERNARD, engineering and construction company executive, accountant; b. Roanoke, Ala., June 26, 1948; s. Thomas Bernard Perry and Mary (Benefield) Woody; m. Vernell Stewart, Dec. 23, 1967; children—Thomas Bernard, Heather Michele. B.S., U. Ala.-Tuscaloosa, 1970. C.P.A. Sr. auditor Arthur Andersen & Co., Birmingham, Ala., 1972-77; v.p. fin. Rust Internat. Corp., Birmingham, 1977—. Cub master Birmingham area Council Boy Scouts Am., Birmingham, 1977-80, asst. scout master, 1983, dist. commr., 1979. Served to 1st lt. U.S. Army, 1970-72, to Capt. USAR, 1972-77. Mem. Am. Inst. C.P.A.s, Ala. Soc. C.P.A.s, Nat. Assn. Accts., (dir. 1979-81, 84-85, v.p. 1985—), Constrn. Fin. Mgmt., Fin. Execs. Inst., Beta Alpha Psi. Presbyterian (elder). Clubs: Birmingham Canoe, Les Amis du Vin, Rust Mgmt. (dir. 1983-84), Optimist. Office: Rust Internat Corp PO Box 101 Birmingham AL 35201

PERRY, WILLIAM DALE, control systems company executive, electrical engineer; b. Hazard, Ky., Nov. 19, 1952; s. Bill Chad and Kila (Hensley) P.; m. Norma Hodge, Dec. 23, 1972; 1 son, Russell. B.S.E.E., U. Ky., 1979. Electronic technician U. Ky., Lexington, 1972-74; jr. engr. Corning Glass Co., Danville, Ky., 1974-78; elec. controls engr. Richard Equipment Co., Cin., 1978-81; pres. Intelligent Control Systems, Inc., Lexington, 1981—. Served with USN, 1970-72; Vietnam. Decorated Purple Heart; recipient Leadership award DAR, 1980. Mem. Soc. Mfg. Engrs. Republican. Baptist. Club: Wildcat (Lexington). Home: 1481 Mt Rainier Dr Lexington KY 40502 Office: Intelligent Control Systems Inc PO Box 22194 Lexington KY 40522

PERRY, WILLIE JOE, newspaper official; b. Montgomery, Ala., May 30, 1944; s. Clinton and Juanita (White) P.; m. Ethrl M. Andrews, Aug. 18, 1970; children—LaTonya and LaCole (twins), Sanciare. B.S., Ala. State U., 1971; M.A., U. Houston, 1978. Store mgr. Western Auto Supply, Montgomery, Ala. and Houston, 1968-75; dept. buyer Foleys Dept. Store, Houston, 1975-77; dist. mgr. Houston Post Co., 1977-79, field renewals mgr., 1981—; dist. rep. Nat. Convience, Houston, 1979-81; coordinator Sch. Vocat. Edn. Program, Houston, 1981—. Recipient Arm award Western Auto Supply, 1971, Sales Club, 1972, Mgr. of Month award, 1973; U. Houston grantee, 1978. Mem. Nat. Small Bus. Assn., Nat. Geog. Assn., Internat. Karate Assn., Uechi-Ryu Karate Assn., Ala. State U. Alumni Assn. Democrat. Clubs: Hill Wood Civic (Houston); Veterans (agt. at arms 1972) (Montgomery, Ala.). Home: 12818 Segrest Dr Houston TX 77047

PERRYMAN, MARLIN RAY, economist, educator; b. Tyler, Tex., Dec. 25, 1952; s. Merrill A. and Oneta (Davis) P.; B.S. in Math., Baylor U., 1974; Ph.D. in Econs., Rice U., 1978; m. Nancy Beth Satterwhite, July 14, 1973. Founder, dir. Center for the Advancement of Econ. Analysis, Baylor U., Waco, Tex., 1979—, dir. honors program, 1980—, mem. grad. faculty, 1978—, Herman Brown prof. econs., 1980—, mem. publ. com. Baylor Bus. Studies, 1977—, dir. econs. div. Inter-U. Consortium for Polit. and Social Research, 1978—; sr. asso. Center for Communication Research, 1981—, Resource Econs. and Mgmt. Assos.; dir. State of Tex. Econometric Model Project, 1979—; founder, dir. Baylor U. Forecasting Service; econ. cons. to Comptroller Public Accounts, State Tex., 1979—; reviewer numerous acad. jours. and research grant orgns., 1978—; guest lectr. econs. various radio and TV programs, 1977—. Mem. urban and regional policy planning bd. Heart of Tex. Council of Govts., 1978, 79, 80. Named Outstanding Alumni in Econs. Research, Rice U., 1979, Most Popular Prof., Hankamer Sch. of Bus., 1979, Outstanding Young Economist and Social Scientist in U.S., NSF, 1979, 80; recipient Disting. Prof. award Hankamer Sch. Bus., 1979, Teaching Excellence citation Baylor U., 1978, 79, 80, 81; Nat. Merit scholar, 1971-74. Mem. Am. Econ. Assn., Am. Statis. Assn., Midwest Econ. Assn., Mo. Valley Econ. Assn., Post-Keynesian Econ. Assn., Atlantic Econ. Soc., Am. Fin. Assn., Econometric Soc., Nat. Tax Assn., Southern Econ. Assn., Western Econ. Assn., Southwestern Soc. for Economists, Inst. of Math. Statistics, Internat. Assn. of Math. Modeling, Internat. Time Series Assn. (exec. sec. interaction com.), Math. Assn. of Am., Inst. for Socioecon. Studies, Assn. for Evolutionary Econs., AAAS, Am. Acad. Arts and Scis., Royal Econ. Soc. of Eng., Southwestern Fedn. Acad. Disciplines, La. Acad. Scis., History of Econs. Soc., Southwestern Econ. Assn., Southwestern Social Sci. Assn., Sherlock Holmes Soc. London, Alpha Chi, Omicron Delta Epsilon, Omicron Delta Kappa, Phi Eta Sigma, Beta Gamma Sigma. Baptist. Author: Trends in the Texas Economy, 1982—; Fluctuations in Economic Activity: Analysis and Forecasting, 1983; (with Nancy B. Perryman) Problems in Economic Forecasting, 1983. Editor: Time Series Analysis, 1981; Applied Time Series Analysis, 1981; Economic Modelling, 1981—. Contbr. numerous articles on econ. analysis and theory to scholarly jours. Home: 309 Brookwood St Waco TX 76710 Office: Center for the Advancement of Econ Analysis Baylor Univ Waco TX 76798

PERSKY, DAVID WILLIAM, college official; b. Boston, Feb. 2, 1950; s. Lester and Mary Elizabeth (Connor) P.; m. Mary Easler, Nov. 28, 1980. B.A., So. Methodist U., 1972; M.S., Miami U., 1973; Ph.D., Fla. State U., 1979. Asst. dir. housing U. South Fla., Tampa, 1973-77; coordinator alcohol awareness Fla. State U., Tallahassee, 1977-79; asst. to v.p. acad. affairs U. South Fla., Tampa, 1979-80, asst. to v.p. student affairs, 1980-84, assoc. dean students, 1985—. Bd. dirs. Alcohol Community Treatment Services, Tampa, 1984—, Tampa Bay Council on Alcoholism, 1984-86, DWI Counterattack, Inc., 1984-85. Mem. Nat. Assn. Student Personnel Administrs., Am. Coll. Personnel Assn., Am. Assn. Counseling and Devel., So. Assn. Coll. Student Affairs, Blue Key, Kappa Sigma, Omicron Delta Kappa. Jewish. Club: Civitan (pres. 1983-84). Avocations: tennis; running; rugby. Home: 14737 Morning Dr Lutz FL 33549 Office: U South Florida ADM 151 Tampa FL 33620

PERSON, BILL S., industrial relations manager; b. Hobbs, N.Mex., Feb. 11, 1948; s. Wilton and Mary Nell (Denton) P.; m. Beverly Rasco. B.B.A. in Mgmt., Tex. Tech U., 1974. With Rowan Cos., Inc., Houston, 1967—, field ops., 1967-74, safety dir., 1974-78, mgr. safety and tng., 1978-82, mgr. indsl. relations, 1982—; speaker at profl. confs. Campaign vol. various elections, Houston. Mem. Am. Soc. Safety Engrs., Internat. Assn. Drilling Contractors (chmn. human resources Houston 1985—, bd. dirs. 1982—), Am. Petroleum Inst. (prodn. safety regulation 1978—), Am. Mgmt. Assn., Sigma Iota Epsilon. Republican. Mem. Ch. of Christ. Office: Rowan Cos Inc 5051 Westheimer S-1900 Houston TX 77056

PERSON, CURTIS S., JR., lawyer, state senator; b. Shelby County, Tenn., Nov. 27, 1934; B.S., Memphis State U.; LL.B., U. Miss.; married. Practice law, Memphis; former mem. Tenn. Ho. of Reps.; now mem. Tenn. Senate, Republican whip, 1973-74, minority caucus chmn., 1977-82. Pres., Memphis-Shelby County Mental Health Assn., 1969-73, Handicapped, Inc.; chmn. Memphis Commn. on Drug Abuse, 1970; charter pres. Memphis State Tiger Rebounders; past trustee Memphis State U. Found.; exec. committeeman Danny Thomas Memphis Open Golf Classic; co-chmn. Shelby County Legis. Del., 1973-74, sec., 1969, vice chmn., 1970; chmn. Shelby Rep. Del., 1977. Named Memphis and Tenn. Outstanding Young Man of Yr., Jaycees, 1969; recipient Liberty Bell Freedom award Memphis/Shelby County Bar Assn., 1969, Tenn. Adv. of Year for Handicapped children, 1978. Mem. Tenn. Bar Assn., Miss. Bar Assn., Memphis/Shelby County Bar Assn., Memphis State U. Nat. Alumni Assn. (pres. 1970), So. Golf Assn. (past dir.), Nat. Rifle Assn.

(life), Phi Alpha Delta, Phi Alpha Theta, Kappa Sigma. Presbyterian. Clubs: Masons, Shriners. Office: Room 308 War Meml Bldg Nashville TN

PESCE, VINCENT JOSEPH, JR., electronics company executive; b. N.Y.C., Aug. 27, 1935; s. Vincent J. and Irene (Corbani) P.; m. Camille DeMaso, June 10, 1961; children—Marie Angela, Vincent III. B.S.E.E., Pratt Inst., N.Y.C., 1961. Sr. sales engr. Westinghouse Electric, N.Y.C., 1961-68; regional mgr. Amerace-Esna, Hackettstown, N.J., 1969-71; regional mgr. Allis Chelmers, Union, N.J., 1971-79; mgr. training and personnel devel., Siemens-Allis, Atlanta, 1979-84; v.p. sales and mktg. Electronic Systems Internat., Atlanta, 1985—. Author: We Are in the People Business; A Complete Manual of Professional Selling, 1985. Served with USAF, 1953-57. Recipient Pres.' award Westinghouse Electric, 1963-66; named Outstanding Sales Mgr. Allis-Chalmers, 1974. Mem. Ga. Speakers Assn. (pres. 1983-84, Leadership award 1984), Atlanta Sales and Mktg. Execs. (bd. dirs. 1982-83 Participation award), Nat. Speakers Assn., Toastmasters. Avocations: writing; teaching profl. salesmanship and mgmt. Home: 1149 Pedfield Ridge Atlanta GA 30338 Office: Electronic Systems Internat 2797 Peterson Pl Norcross GA 30071

PESKOE, IRVING, lawyer, mayor; b. Long Branch, N.J., Feb. 16, 1918; s. Herman and Natalie (Marshall) P.; m. Beatrice Peskoe, Mar. 16, 1941; children—Riva, Dan, Anne. B.S., MIT, 1939; J.D., U. Miami, 1950. Bar: Fla., U.S. Supreme Ct. Sole practice law, Homestead, Fla., 1950—; mayor City of Homestead, 1981—. Pres. Homestead Jewish Ctr., 1964-65. Served to col. USAFR. Mem. Ret. Officers Assn. (past pres. Homestead), Homestead C. of C. (v.p. 1966-68), Homestead Bar Assn. (pres. 1968-70), ABA, Fla. Bar. Democrat. Jewish. Lodge: Rotary. Bus. mgr., contbg. editor U. Miami Law Quar. Office: 1000 N Krome Ave Homestead FL 33030

PESTINGER, JAMES MORITZ, JR., chiropractor, dentist; b. Beloit, Kans., Jan. 13, 1943; s. James Moritz and Margaret (Young) P.; m. Kathleen A. Overlander, Dec. 20, 1974. B.S., U. Kans., 1964; D.D.S., U. Mo., 1968; D.C., Los Angeles Coll. Chiropractic, 1983. Pvt. practice dentistry, Kansas City, Mo., 1968-79; real estate salesman Lelah T. Pierson Realty, Brentwood, Calif., 1979-83; mem. faculty U. Mo., 1972; cons. dentist, Los Angeles, 1979-83; orthopedic resident in chiropractic, Los Angeles Coll. Chiropractic, Whittier, 1983; practice chiropractic medicine, Clearwater, Fla., 1984—. Contbr. articles to publs. Active Nat. Republican Com., 1979-84. Mem. ADA (life), Am. Chiropractic Assn., Fla. Chiropractic Assn., Am. Dental Acad. Gen. Practice (life), Flying Dentists, Psi Omega, Phi Delta Theta (pres. 1983), Sigma Chi Alpha. Roman Catholic. Clubs: Optimist (life mem.; Outstanding Pres. award 1980), Univ. Study. Home: 160 Foxfire Ln Oldsmar FL 33557 Office: 3135 US 19 N Clearwater FL 33575

PETEET, FRANK Y., II, architect, consultant; b. Gadsden, Ala., Jan. 1, 1943; s. Frank Y. and E.L. (Little) P.; m. Jennie Graham (dec. 1981); children—Frank, Chanel, Ginger. Student Miss. So. U., 1961-62, Auburn U., 1963-65, UCLA, 1970-71. Regis. architect, Calif., S.C. Owner, architect Peteet Co., Georgetown, S.C., 1973—. Dir. Sertoma, Pawley Island, S.C., 1982—; advisor Presbyterian Coll., Climon, S.C., 1985. Served with USMC, 1968-69. Mem. AIA, Soc. Am. Registered Architects, Nat. Council Architects and Registration Bds. Presbyterian. Club: DeBordieu Beach. Avocations: sailing; stamps; landscaping.

PETER, LILY, plantation operator, writer; b. Marvell, Ark.; d. William Oliver and Florence (Mowbrey) P. B.S., Memphis State U., 1927; M.A., Vanderbilt U., 1938; postgrad. U. Chgo., 1930, Columbia U., 1935-36; L.H.D., Moravian Coll., Bethlehem, Pa., 1965, Hendrix Coll., Conway, Ark., 1983; LL.D., U. Ark., 1975. Owner, operator plantations, Marvell and Ratio, Ark.; writer poetry, feature articles pub. in S.W. Quar., Delta Rev., Cyclo Flame, Etude, Am. Weave, others; mem. staff S.W. Writers Conf., Corpus Christi, Tex., 1954—, sponsor Ark. Writers' Conf. Chmn., Poetry Day in Ark., 1953—; chmn., sponsor music Ark. Territorial Sesquicentennial, 1969. Author: The Green Linen of Summer, 1964; The Great Riding, 1966; The Sea Dream of the Mississippi, 1973; In the Beginning, 1983. Bd. dirs. Ark. Arts Festival, Little Rock, Grand Prairie Festival Arts; chmn. bd. Phillips County Community Center, 1969-73; hon. trustee Moravian Music Found. Recipient Moramus award Friends of Moravian Music, 1964, Disting. Alumni award Vanderbilt U., 1964, Gov.'s award as Ark. Conservationist of Year, Ark. Wildlife Fedn., 1975, Whooping Crane award Nat. Wildlife Fedn., 1976; named Poet Laureate Ark., 1971, Democrat Woman of Year, 1971, 1st Citizen of Phillips County, Phillips County C. of C., 1985, Most Disting. Woman of Ark., Ark. C. of C., 1985. Mem. DAR, (hon. state regent), Nat. League Am. Pen Women, Ark. Authors and Composers Soc., Poets' Roundtable Ark., poetry socs. of Tenn., Tex., Ga., Met. Opera Assn., So. Cotton Ginners Assn. (dir. 1971—), Big Creek Protective Assn. (chmn. 1974—), Sigma Alpha Iota (hon.). Democrat. Episcopalian. Clubs: Pacaha (Helena, Ark.); Woman's City (Little Rock). Home: Route 2 Box 69 Marvell AR 72366

PETER, MARY ANN, nursing administrator; b. Plainfield, N.J.; d. William and Minna Louise (Zepp) Rohrhurst; m. Robert H. Peter, Aug. 24, 1961; children—Jon Miles, William Alexander, Jennifer Lauren. B.S.N., Duke U., 1962, M.S.N., 1965. Pub. health nurse Durham County Health Dept., Durham, N.C., 1962-63; instr. Maryview Hosp. Sch. Nursing, Portsmouth, Va., 1965-66; clin. specialist Duke U. Hosp., Durham, 1967-69, profl. adminstrv. asst., 1969-73, dir. quality assurance, 1973-78, dir. nursing, 1978—; dir. Security Fed. Savs. and Loan, Durham, 1984—. Editor: Quality Assurance Process and Outcome, 1980. Patentee in field. Mem. Am. Orgn. Nurse Execs., Am. Nurses Assn., N.C. Nurses Assn. Mem. United Ch. Christ. Office: Box 3714 Duke U Hosp Durham NC 27705

PETERS, C. WILBUR, retail fabric chain executive; b. Hospers, Iowa, Dec. 16, 1922; s. Cornelius and Tena (Mulder) P.; m. Bessie Van Essen, Dec. 20, 1943; children—Judith Ann Peters Becklund, Roger. B.B.A., U. Minn., 1947; D. Humanities (hon.), Pillsbury Baptist Bible Coll., 1979. Chief indsl. engr. McQuay, Inc., Mpls., 1947-60; pres., chmn., chief exec. officer Minnesota Fabrics Inc., Charlotte, N.C., 1960—; dir. Nat. City Bank, Mpls.; bus. cons. Pillsbury Bapt. Bible Coll. Baptist. Office: PO Box 32606 Charlotte NC 28232*

PETERS, DANIEL JOSEPH, educator; b. Pensacola, Fla., Feb. 12, 1948; s. Harlan Harris and Margaret Mary (Malcrone) P. B.S., Christopher Newport Coll., 1971; M.S. Zoology, Va. Poly. Inst. and State U., 1974. Researcher invertebrate zoology Smithsonian Instn., Washington, 1969—; tchr. sci. York High Sch., Yorktown, Va., 1972—, team leader, chmn. sci., math. dept., 1976—; adj. instr. biology Christopher Newport Coll., Newport-News, Va., part-time, 1977—, St. Leo Coll., Ft. Eustis, Va., part-time, 1979—. Treas. York Polit. Action Com., 1977-85; area rep. Youth for Understanding, 1981—. Mem. York Edn. Assn. (v.p., mem. exec. bd.), Assn. Southeastern Biologists, Biol. Soc. Washington, Sigma Xi. Democrat. Roman Catholic. Contbr. articles to various publs. Home: Box 510 Hayes VA 23072 Office: 2890 George Washington Hwy Yorktown VA 23692

PETERS, GEORGE NICHOLAS, surgical oncologist; b. Clarksdale, Miss., Apr. 8, 1947; s. Nicholas Emanuel and Lillie (Lemonis) P.; m. Janet Lee Straub, July 28, 1973; children—Nicholas George, Barton Frederick. B.A., U. Miss.-Oxford, 1970; M.D., U. Miss.-Jackson, 1974. Diplomate Am. Bd. Surgery. Surg. resident Baylor U. Med. Ctr., Dallas, 1974-79; vis. fellow in surgery Columbia Presbyn. Hosp., N.Y.C., 1979-80; surg., oncology fellow Roswell Park Meml. Inst., Buffalo, 1980-80; assoc. attending in surgery Baylor U. Med. Ctr., 1980—; attending staff Gaston Episcopal Hosp., Dallas, 1980—. Contbr. articles to profl. jours. Mem. parish bd. Holy Trinity Greek Orthodox Ch., 1984-85, bd. v.p., 1985. Recipient award for achievement in pub. edn. Am. Cancer Soc., Tex. div., 1984. Fellow ASC; mem. Am. Soc. Clin. Oncology, Tex. Med. Assn., AMA, Dallas Soc. Gen. Surgeons, Dallas County Med. Soc., Am. Cancer Soc. (bd. dirs., med. v.p. 1985), Titanic Hist. Soc. Republican. Greek Orthodox. Lodge: Am. Hellenic Edn. Progressive Assn. Avocations: chess; painting; bicycling. Office: Baylor U Med Ctr 3600 Gaston Suite 510 Dallas TX 75246

PETERS, GERALD ROBERT, real estate executive; accountant; b. New Orleans, Mar. 30, 1944; s. George Harold and Althea Barbara (Burns) P.; m. Margaret Ann Duncan, Aug. 13, 1966; children—Douglas Robert, Kyle David. B.S. in Acctg., U. Southwestern La., 1966. C.P.A., La. Audit supr. Peat, Marwick, Mitchell & Co., New Orleans, 1966-71; controller, treas. Morris Kirschman & Co., Inc., New Orleans, 1971-73; exec. v.p. Sizeler Realty Co., Inc., New Orleans, 1973-80; exec. v.p. Sunbelt, Inc., New Orleans, 1980-82; pres. Coldwell Banker/Sunbelt, Inc., New Orleans, 1982-85; pres. Re/Max Real Estate Ptnrs., Inc., New Orleans, 1985—. Mem. Nat. Assn. Realtors, La. Realtors Assn., Am. Inst. C.P.A.s, La. Soc. C.P.A.s. Democrat. Roman Catholic. Home: 5 Pearl Ct Kenner LA 70065 Office: 5600 Veterans Blvd Suite C Metairie LA 70003

PETERS, LINDA ANN, nurse; b. New Orleans, Mar. 2, 1949; d. Junius Herbert and Wilhelmina (Jones) P.; m. Henry Lee Francis, Aug. 30, 1972 (div. Aug. 1982); 1 son, Tevis Mark. Cert. in practical nursing L.E. Rabovin Hosp., New Orleans, 1970-71; B.S.N. magna cum laude, Dillard U., New Orleans, 1985. Staff nurse Ochsner Found., New Orleans, 1976-81, Tulane Med. Ctr., New Orleans, 1981—. Fin. sec. Zamani Sasa, New Orleans, 1981.

PETERS, MICHAEL W., insurance company executive; real estate broker; b. Martinsville, Va., Apr. 8, 1947; s. Clovis Woodrow and Virginia (Watkins) P.; m. Patricia Ann Eddins, July 4, 1971; children—Michael Clovis, James David. Degree of Retail Mgmt., NYU, 1972. Lic. real estate broker, N.C. Mgr., buyer Williams & Co., Inc., Eden, N.C., 1972-74; home improvement mgr. Sears Roebuck & Co., Reidsville, N.C., 1974-76; broker Lee Dillard Richardson Co., Reidsville, 1976—; ins. agt. Life & Casualty of Tenn., Reidsville, 1978-83; agy. mgr. Am. Gen. Life Ins., Danville, Va., 1983—; moderator personal ins. Danville Assn. Life Underwriters, 1984-85, moderator bus. ins., 1985-86. Chmn. profl. div. Heart Fund, Reidsville, 1983. Recipient Grant for Nat. Sales Achievement, Nat. Assn. Life Underwriters, 1983-84. Mem. Nat. Assn. Life Underwriters. Democrat. Methodist. Clubs: Millionaire, Top of Tower. Avocations: golf; rabbit hunting. Home: 217 Sheraton Rd Reidsville NC 27320 Office: Am Gen Life and Accident PO Box 9610 Danville VA 24541

PETERS, NANCY GOULD, loss control consultant; b. Whitinsville, Mass., Aug. 14, 1957; d. Clyde Stuart and Margaret (Cawley) Gould; m. Donald Gregory Peters, Aug. 21, 1982; children—Jessica Laine, Kristen Nicole. B.S. in Adminstrv. Mgmt., Clemson U., 1979. Loss control rep. I Kemper Group Inc., Long Grove, Ill., 1979, rep. II, 1980-83, rep. III, 1983-85, cons., 1985—. Mem. Am. Soc. Safety Engrs., Bd. Cert. Safety Profls. (assoc.). Roman Catholic. Avocations: skiing; swimming; arts and crafts; camping; hiking. Office: Kemper Group 1800 East Gate Garland TX 75041

PETERS, PHILIP LEE, insurance company administrator; b. Roanoke, Va., Jan. 10, 1954; s. Cloyd Muncie and Jean Frances (Naff) P.; m. Patricia Rankin Myers, June 23, 1979; children—Sarah Blackburn, Brian Anderson. B.A. with distinction, U. Va., 1976; M.Adminstrn., Lynchburg Coll., 1982. Profl. in human resources. Client coordinator Mgmt. Data Communications Corp., Rosemont, Ill., 1978, account mgr., 1978-79; supr. CHAMPUS Blue Cross Blue Shield Southwestern Va., Roanoke, 1979-81, supr. major med., 1981-83, tng. and devel. coordinator, 1983-84, mgr. human resources, 1984-85, dir. human resources, 1985—. Vice chmn. March of Dimes Birth Defects Found., Roanoke, 1984-85; vol. Am. Cancer Soc., Roanoke, 1983—. Mem. Am. Soc. Tng. and Devel. (v.p. membership Valleys of Va. chpt. 1984-85), Personnel Assn. Roanoke, Am. Soc. Personnel Adminstrn., Am. Mgmt. Assn. Avocations: reading; traveling. Office: Blue Cross and Blue Shield of Southwestern Va 602 S Jefferson St Roanoke VA 24011

PETERS, RALPH MARTIN, university dean; b. Knoxville, Tenn., May 9, 1926; s. Tim C. and Alma (Shannon) P.; m. Lorraine Daniel, Apr. 12, 1928; children—Teresa (Mrs. Joe A. Eaton, Jr.), Marta (Mrs. R.R. Roberts). B.S., Lincoln Meml. U., Harrogate, Tenn., 1949; M.S., U. Tenn.-Knoxville, 1953, Ed.D., 1960. Tchr. history and govt. Clinton High Sch., Tenn., 1949-56; dir. adminstrn. and alumni Lincoln Meml. U., 1956-59, chmn. dept. edn., 1961-62, exec. v.p., 1963; dean of students Tenn. Tech. U., Cookeville, 1963-68, dean grad. sch., 1968—. Served with USN, 1944-46, World War II. Mem. NEA, Phi Kappa Phi (chpt. pres. 1976-78), Phi Delta Kappa, Omicron Delta Kappa. Lodge: Rotary. Avocations: tennis, other amateur sports. Home: 927 Mt Vernon Rd Cookeville TN 38501 Office: Grad Sch Tenn Tech U Cookeville TN 38505

PETERS, RONALD GREGORY, oil company official; b. Tulsa, Sept. 28, 1944; s. Stanley Ray and Margie (Smith) P.; B.S. in Bus. Adminstrn., Tulsa U., 1966, cert. in mgmt., 1974; m. Bonnie LaVerne Swenke, June 12, 1965; children—Gregory James, Ronda JoAnn. Market analyst Sunray DX Oil Co., Terre Haute, Ind., 1966, mgr. planning and analysis LP Gas div., Tulsa, 1967, mktg. research and econs. analyst, Tulsa, 1968, mgr. sales promotion, 1969; sr. staff asso. Sun Oil Co., Phila., 1970; mktg. research coordinator Cities Service Co., Tulsa, 1971-74, mgr. internal communications, 1974-81, mgr. policy devel., 1981—, dir. govt. and industry affairs, 1981-83, dir. state relations, 1983—. Drive coordinator Tulsa Area United Way, 1977; former chmn. Christian edn. Ascension Lutheran Ch. Recipient Editor of Year award Am. Petroleum Inst., 1979. Mem. Am. Mktg. Assn. (past pres. Tulsa chpt., citation for outstanding service), Tinker Soc. Profl. Engrs. and Scientists (cert. of appreciation). Editor Public Affairs News, 1977-83. Home: 10836 E 26th Pl Tulsa OK 74129 Office: PO Box 300 Tulsa OK 74101

PETERS, SID RALPH, association executive; b. Cambridge, Md., Jan. 31, 1927; s. Ralph Hicks and Ruth Steele (Lowe) P.; m. Patricia Reider, Dec. 14, 1957; children—Scott, Drew, John. B.S., Temple U., 1954, M.B.A., 1963. Founder, Brandywine Coll., Wilmington, Del., 1965, pres., 1965-75; pres. Martingham Real Estate Devel., St. Michaels, Md., 1969-76; exec. Nat. Assn. Indsl. and Office Parks, Arlington, Va., 1976—; dir. Americas Competitive Free Enterprise System, Wilmington, 1965-75. Author: (with Walter Brower) Supplies, Equipment & Facilities for Business Education, 1964; (with Jay W. Miller) Meetings, Change in Technical Preparation for business, 1965. Vice pres. ARC, Del. chpt., Wilmington, 1969-74; treas. Older Youth-Young Adult Research project Nat. Bd. Edn. United Meth. Ch., Wilmington, 1960-61. Served with USAAF, 1944-45. Decorated Air medal with oak leaf cluster. Mem. Adminstrv. Mgmt. Soc., United Bus. Sch. Assn., Eastern Bus. Tchrs. Assn. (bd. dirs. 1960-65). Republican. Club: University & Whist (pres. 1966-67). Office: Nat Assn Indsl and Office Parks 1215 Jefferson Davis Hwy Arlington VA 22202

PETERS, TED HOPKINS, insurance company executive; b. Greenville, Tex., Dec. 30, 1943; s. Joe Becton and Teddy Rose (Hopkins) P.; B.B.A., E. Tex. State U., 1965; postgrad. U. Tex., 1965-66; m. Fonda Lynn Carter, June 3, 1966; children—Amy Teigh, Andrew Lathen. Fire rate actuary State Bd. Ins., Austin, Tex., 1966; agency dir. Union Security Life Ins. Co., Greenville, Tex., 1967-72, exec. v.p., dir., 1972—; sec. Greenville Hosp. Dist., 1975-78. Bd. dirs. East Tex. State U. Found., 1977-78; mem. exec. bd. N. Central Tex. Council Govts., 1978-80; foreman Hunt County Grand Jury, 1974; dir. Salvation Army adv. bd., sec. Greenville Indsl. Devel. Fund, 1966-70, pres., 1970—; mem. Nat. Eagle Scout Assn., Nat. Genealogy Soc.; tchr. Bible study class Aldersgate Ch., 1985—; mem. bd. regents East Tex. State U., 1983; mem. Hunt County Juvenile Bd. Recipient Spl. Service award Greenville United Fund, 1971. Mem. Tex. Assn. Life Ins. Ofcls. (pres. 1970-71), Life Ins. Advertisers Assn., Lambda Chi Alpha. Democrat. Author: Peters Family History, 1977. Home: 5401 Vale St Greenville TX 75401 Office: Union Security Life Bldg Box 1299 Greenville TX 75401

PETERSEN, DAVID LEE, air force officer; b. Louisville, Dec. 17, 1943; s. Clifford Warren and Martha Lee (Schmidt) P.; m. Edwina Marie Stiles, June 22, 1968; children—Christopher Lee, Jennifer Wood, Joshua Kulk. B.S. in Bus. Adminstrn., Marquette U., 1966; M.B.A., U. Utah., 1971. Commd. 2d lt. U.S. Air Force, 1967; advanced through grades to maj., 1979; chief maintenance 601st Tactical Control Maintenance Squadron, Sembach AFB, Germany; navigator 437 Mil. Airlift Wing, Charleston AFB, S.C., 1972-73; instr. navigator 374 Tactical Airlift Wing, Clark AB, Philippines, 1973-74; navigator flight examiner 314 Tactical Airlift Wing, Little Rock AFB, Ark., 1974-76; chief ops. programs 61 Mil. Airlift Support Wing, Hickam AFB, Hawaii, 1976-79; asst. chief inspections 317 Tactical Airlift Wing, Pope AFB, N.C., 1979-83; chief plans and policy HQ Tactical Air Command Info. Systems, Langley AFB, Va., 1983—. Vice pres. Wendwood Assn., Newport News, Va., 1984-85, pres., 1985-86. Decorated 2 Air Force Meritorious Service medals, 3 Air medals, 2 Humanitarian Service medals. Mem. Air Force Assn., Armed Forces Communications-Electronics Assn. Republican. Roman Catholic. Club: Langley Officers (Va.). Avocations: woodworking; antique and art collecting; consumer advocate. Home: 335 Wendwood Dr Newport News VA 23602 Office: HQ TAC/SI Langley AFB VA 23665

PETERSON, ALVIN OTIS, architect, specification writer; b. Coleman, Fla., July 31, 1925; s. Henry Turner and Trudy (Zipperer) P.; student Butler U., 1942-43; grad. Chgo. Tech. Coll., 1956; m. Alice Joyce McKay, Dec. 9, 1945; 1 son, David Eric. Design estimator Williams Devel. Co., Orlando, Fla., 1960-63; with Rogers, Lovelock & Fritz, Winter Park, Fla., 1963—, head specifications dept., 1971—. Bd. dirs. College Park Towers, 1976—; mem. Orlando Fire Prevention Code Bd. Appeals and Adjustments, 1980—. Served with USNR, 1942-45, 50-52. Mem. Nat. Fire Protection Assn. (bldg. constrn. com. 1973—, life safety code/detention and correctional occupancies subcom. 1976—), ASTM (fire hazards and fire tests com. 1974—), So. Bldg. Code Congress, Internat. Congress of Bldg. Ofcls., Constrn. Specifications Inst., Internat. Platform Assn. Baptist (deacon 1959—, chmn. deacons 1977-78, ch. clk. 1959-60, Sunday sch. tchr. 1965—, ch. tng. dir. 1971-72, asso. Sunday sch. dir. 1961-62). Home: 1643 Crestwood Dr Orlando FL 32804 Office: 145 Lincoln Ave Winter Park FL 32789

PETERSON, CURTIS, state senator, landscape architect; b. Lakeland, Fla., Aug. 23, 1922; m. Ethel Schultz, Apr. 8, 1944; children—Curtis III, Peter. Student George Washington U.; LL.D., Fla. So. Coll., 1984. Landscape architect Peterson Nursery, Lakeland, 1945—. Apptd. to Fla. Agrl. Adv. Council and Plant Industry Tech. Council, 1961-72; mem. Fla. Senate, 1972—, pres. pro tem, 1980-82, pres. 1982-84, chmn. edn. com., mem. agrl. com.; mem. Gov.'s Commn. on Secondary Schs. Del. Democratic Charter Conf., 1974; mem. Edn. Commn. of States. Bd. dirs. Polk County Assn. for Retarded Citizens; past scoutmaster and cubmaster Gulf Ridge Council Boy Scouts Am.; mem. Southside Bapt. Ch., Lakeland; past pres. Lakeland Little League Baseball. Served with USCG, World War II. Recipient Allen Morris award-Most Effective Senator, 1981; Gavel of Authority award Fla. Assn. Sch. Adminstrs., 1985; Legis. Leadership award Fla. Vocat. Assn., 1983; Disting. Leadership award Fla. Community Devel. Assn., 1982; recipient numerous other awards and honors. Mem. Fla. Nurseryman and Growers Assn. (past pres., nurseryman of yr. 1962), Agribus. Inst. Fla. (past pres.), Lakeland C. of C., Lodge: Optimist (charter Lakeland). Office: Office of the State Senate Tallahassee FL 32301

PETERSON, D. WAYNE, telecommunications company executive; b. 1936. Formerly with Southwestern State Telephone Co., Southwestern Bell Telephone Co.; v.p. mktg. United Telecommunications, Inc., 1968-80; pres., chief exec. officer, dir. Carolina Telephone & Telegraph Co., Tarboro, N.C., 1980—; pres., dir. N.C. Ind. Telephone Assn.; dir. Planters Nat. Bank & Trust Co. Address: Carolina Telephone & Telegraph Co 122 E Saint James St Tarboro NC 27886*

PETERSON, DAVID WINFIELD, artist; b. Chgo., Feb. 6, 1913; s. David Richard Peterson and Marie (Diehl) Peterson Penniman; m. Beulah Lillian Johnson, Dec. 27, 1945; children—James K., Timothy David. B.S., U. Wis., 1935. Sales supr. Kellogg Co., Battle Creek, Mich., 1946-56; pres. Peterson-King Co., Battle Creek, 1956-61; pres. The Peterson Co., Battle Creek, 1961-74, chmn. bd., 1963—, cons., 1974—, also dir.; profl. artist Studio 101 Naples, Fla., 1974—. Editor: Animal Feeding, 1951. Exhibited in group shows at Grand Central Galleries, N.Y.C., Mus. Arts and Scis., Daytona Beach, Fla., Salmagundi Club, N.Y.C., Brevard Mus., Fla. Illustrator: Hunting is for the Birds, 1981. Chmn. Battle Creek chpt. ARC, 1959. Served with U.S. Army, 1940-41. Recipient Niven Landscape award Ft. Myers Beach Art Assn., 1978, Gold Room award Waterfowl Festival, Easton, Md., 1980, 81, 82. Mem. Am. Soc. Marine Artists, Internat. Soc. Marine Painters (award 1980), Am. Artists Profl. League, Naples Art Assn. (bd. dirs. 1979-82, chmn. scholarship com. 1977-83), Salmagundi Club. Republican. Christian Scientist. Club: Quail Creek Country (Naples, Fla.). Lodges: Masons, Rotary. Avocations: golf; fly fishing. Home and Studio: Studio 101 Miramar 2750 Gulf Shore Blvd N Naples FL 33940

PETERSON, ELIZABETH BOWMAN, speech pathologist; b. Dallas, Dec. 22, 1937; d. Leonard Clifford and Aleene (Perry) Bowman; B.A. magna cum laude, So. Meth. U., 1961; M.A., U. So. Calif., 1964; m. Harold W. Peterson, June 14, 1969; 2 adopted children. With Houston Speech and Hearing Inst., 1963-68, Houston Assos. in Psychiatry and Neurology, 1968-70; speech pathologist, resource tchr. Houston Ind. Sch. Dist., 1970-82; mem. adv. bd. Spaulding S.W. Treas., Houston Council on Adoptable Children, 1979, pres., 1980; vol. tchr. English as second lang. Citizens for Animal Protection, 1976—. Named 1978 Tchr. of Yr., Houston Assn. Children with Learning Disabilities. Mem. Am. Speech and Hearing Assn., Tex. Speech and Hearing Assn., Houston Assn. Communication Disorders, Houston Assn. Children with Learning Disabilities, Delta Kappa Gamma. Episcopalian. Clubs: Angelo State U. Women's (v.p.), Civic Action Group. Home: 2641 Oxford San Angelo TX 76904

PETERSON, HENRY ALBERT THOMAS, JR., banker; b. Fredricksburg, Va., Oct. 26, 1957; s. Henry Albert Thomas and Shirley (Cable) P. B.A. in Philosophy, George Mason U., 1983. Tchr., Gar-Field Sr. High Sch., Woodbridge, Va., 1975-77; teller, customer service rep. Va. Nat. Bank, Dumfries, Va., 1978, customer service rep. Sovran Fin. Corp., Dumfries, 1978-84; asst. br. mgr. Central Fidelity Bank, Springfield, Va., 1984—. Republican. Episcopalian. Mem. Magna Charter Barons, Mayflower Soc. Club: Montclair Country (Dumfries). Avocations: swimming; tennis; biking; geneology. Home: 307 W Duke St Dumfries VA 22026 Office: 6200 Backlick Rd Springfield VA 22150

PETERSON, JAMES ROBERT, engring. psychologist; b. St. Paul, Apr. 16, 1932; s. Palmer Elliot and Helen Evelyn (Carlson) P.; B.A. in Psychology cum laude, U. Minn., 1954; M.A. in Exptl. Psychology, 1958; Ph.D. in Engring. Psychology, U. Mich., 1965; m. Marianna J. Stockvig, June 26, 1954; 1 dau., Anne Christine. Devel. engr. Honeywell Inc., 1961-65, sr. devel. engr., 1965-67, staff engr., 1967—. Served with USMC, 1954-57. Assoc. fellow AIAA; mem. Am. Psychol. Assn., Human Factors Soc., Soc. Engring. Psychologists. Club: Mason. Contbr. articles to profl. jours. Home: 3303 San Gabriel St Clearwater FL 33519 Office: Honeywell Inc Clearwater FL 33546

PETERSON, JOHN EDGAR, JR., agricultural executive, retired textile company executive; b. Radford, Va., Mar. 26, 1916; s. John Edgar and Mary Elizabeth (Dolan) P.; B.S. in Bus. Adminstrn., Va. Polytech. Inst., 1936; m. Mary Jane Crowell, May 8, 1943; children—John Edgar III, Mary Stuart Peterson Henegar, William Early. Jr. auditor Arthur Andersen & Co., N.Y.C. and Atlanta, 1937-39, sr. auditor, 1939-44; sec.-treas. Magnet Cove Barium Corp., Jamestown, Tenn. and Houston, 1944-46; asst. to controller Burlington Industries, Inc., Greensboro, N.C., 1946-47, sec.-treas., dir. Burlington Mills Internat. Corp., 1947-48, co-div. mgr., 1948-49, div. controller, 1949-56, area controller, 1956-58, asst. corp. controller, 1958-70, asst. corp. v.p., from 1970, now ret.; chmn. bd. dirs., pres. Lane Processing, Inc.; dir. Custom Industries, Inc., Everetts' Lake Corp.; examiner U.S. Bankruptcy Ct.; chmn. bd. The Evergreens, Inc.; commr. Greensboro Housing Authority. Mem. adv. com. Coll. Bus. Va. Polytech. Inst., 1969—. C.P.A., N.Y., Ga., Tenn., N.C.; certified internal auditor. Mem. Am. Inst. C.P.A.s, N.C. Soc. C.P.A.s, Inst. Internal Auditors. Presbyterian. Clubs: Starmount Forest Country, Off Island Gun, Three Lakes (dir.), Brush Creek Hunting (dir.), Masons. Home: 1001 Kemp Rd W Greensboro NC 27410

PETERSON, KENT GRAHAM, mental health counselor, consultant, clinician; b. N.Y.C., Nov. 17, 1951; s. O. Victor and Edith Jane (McEntee) P.; m. Linda J. Chapman, Nov. 11, 1979; 1 son, Colin Chapman. B.A. in Psychology, Stetson U., 1974; M.S. in Applied Psychology, Nova U., 1981. Lic. mental health counselor, Fla. Youth supr. Mills Sch., Ft. Lauderdale, Fla., 1974-78; 1st mate corp. sailboat Paper Doll, Paper Sales Corp., Darien, Conn., 1978-80; pvt. practice Couples Counseling, Ft. Lauderdale, 1981—; biofeedback clinician Ctr. for Neurol. Services, Ft. Lauderdale, 1982—; cons. mental health counselor Broward Ctr. for Male Sexual Dysfunction, 1985—; lectr., cons. Health Info. Assocs., Ft. Lauderdale. Mem. Am. Assn. Counseling and Devel., Fla. Personnel and Guidance Assn., Soc. for Sci. Study Sex, Biofeedback Soc. Am., Biofeedback Soc. Fla. Republican. Episcopalian. Home: 1836 SW 3d Ave Fort Lauderdale FL 33315 Office: 2701 E Sunrise Blvd Suite 101 Fort Lauderdale FL 33304

PETERSON, LEROY LEONARD, chemical engineer, paper company executive; b. Taconite, Minn., May 23, 1922; s. Leonard Axel and Lila Marie (Lundeen) P.; m. Mary Elizabeth Linker, June 28, 1947; children—David Leonard, John Linker, Steven LeRoy. B.S. in Chem. Engring., Mich. State U., 1947, M.S., 1949. Cert. engr. Tenn., Wis. Researcher in chem. engring. Mich. Hwy. Dept., Lansing, 1947-49; process engr. Kimberly Clark, Memphis, 1949-53, engring. mgr., 1953-58, Neenah, Wis., 1958-73, v.p. mfg., Coosa Pines, Ala., 1973-80, sr. v.p. mfg., research and engring., Neenah, Wis., 1980-84, sr.

exec., Coosa Pines, 1984—. Patentee cellulose product and method, cellulose product and package, method of compression, paper making fabric. Served to sgt. U.S. Army, 1942-45, ETO. Decorated Purple Heart, Bronze Star. Mem. Am. Inst. Chem. Engrs. Club: Relay House (Birmingham, Ala.). Lodges: Masons, Shriners. Home: 1106 Pine Ridge Circle Sylacauga AL 35150 Office: Kimberly Clark Corp Coosa Pines AL 35044

PETERSON, PAMELA PARRISH, business educator, researcher; b. Harvey, Ill., Nov. 18, 1954; d. Robert Roy and Virginia Elaine (Towne) Parrish; m. David Robert Peterson, Sept. 4, 1976; 1 child, Kenneth. B.S., Miami U., Oxford, Ohio, 1975; Ph.D. in Bus., U. of N.C., 1981. Tax acct. Arthur Andersen & Co., Chgo., 1976-77; asst. prof. Fla. State U., Tallahassee, 1981—. Contbr. articles to profl. jours. McKnight faculty devel. fellow, 1985-86. Mem. Am. Econ. Assn., Am. Fin. Assn., Eastern Fin. Assn., Western Fin. Assn., So. Fin. Assn., Fin. Mgmt. Assn. Office: Fla State U Coll Bus Tallahassee FL 32306

PETERSON, PAUL CARSON, political science educator; b. Washington, Mar. 19, 1946; s. Murray Rundell Peterson and Billie Louise (Payne) Capes. B.A., Brigham Young U., 1968; M.A., U. Calif.-Riverside, 1969; Ph.D., Claremont Grad. Sch., 1980. Instr. Memphis State U., 1973-77; asst. prof. Ill. State U., Normal, 1977-79, No. Ill. U., DeKalb, 1979-82; assoc. prof. polit. sci. U. S.C., Conway, 1982—; bd. advisors Ctr. Study Constitution, Carlisle, Pa., 1982—. Author, editor: (with others) Readings in American Democracy, 1979. Author (with others) : Taking The Constitution Seriously, 1981; The American Founding: Politics, Statesmanship, and the Constitution, 1981. Fellow NSF, 1969-70; NEH grantee 1984. Mem. Am. Polit. Sci. Assn. Republican. Mormon. Home: 104 Caropine Dr Myrtle Beach SC 29577 Office: Dept Govt and Internat Studies U SC Coastal Carolina Coll Conway SC 29526

PETERSON, RICHARD AUSTIN, sociologist, educator, consultant; b. Moussorie, India, Sept. 28, 1932 (parents Am. citizens); s. Harold Hill and Edna Elisa (Wildman) P.; m. Helen, McHenry, Apr. 24, 1955 (div. 1960); m. Claire Lenore Clark, June 2, 1962; children—Michael Gaga, David Chandler, Ruth Hill. A.B., Oberlin Coll., 1955; M.A., U. Ill., 1958, Ph.D., 1961. Instr. Washington U., St. Louis, 1959-60; from instr. to asst. prof. U. Wis.-Madison, 1960-64; from asst. prof. to prof. sociology Vanderbilt U., Nashville, 1965—, chmn. dept., 1982—; vis. prof. Stanford U., Calif., 1975, Harvard U., Cambridge, Mass., 1978; research specialist Nat. Endowment for Arts, Washington, 1979-80; vis. lectr. Leeds U., Eng., 1985-86; bd. visitors So. Culture Ctr. U. Miss.; contract study dir. Pres.'s Adv. Commn. on Civil Disorders, 1967-68; cons. in field. Editor, author: (anthology) Patterns of Cultural Choice, 1983; Production of Culture, 1976. Assoc. editor Sociol. Inquiry Jour., 1981, Am. Jour. Sociology, 1978-80, Jour. Jazz Studies, 1972-81, Am. Sociologist Jour., 1968-71. Grantee NSF, 1975, Treuhoff Found., 1984, Nat. Parks Service, 1984. Mem. Am. Sociol. Assn., So. Sociol. Assn., Nashville Music Assn., Country Music Assn. Mem. Soc. of Friends. Avocations: sailboat racing; model boat building; photography. Home: 3301 Orleans Dr Nashville TN 37212 Office: Dept Sociology Anthropology Box 1635B Vanderbilt U Nashville TN 37235

PETERSON, ROSS ERIK, automotive company executive; b. Orange, N.J., July 10, 1954; s. Ross Spencer and Doris Lorraine (Cox) P.; m. Denyse Gisele, Oct. 20, 1984. B.S., Syracuse U., 1976; M.Mgmt., Northwestern U., 1977. Analyst, Lincoln Mercury Div., Teterboro, N.J., 1979, zone mgr., Buffalo and Phila., 1980-83, ops. mgr., Falls Church, Va., 1983-84, merchandising mgr., 1984, market representation mgr., 1984-85, retail mgmt. mgr., 1985—. Mem. exec. com. Alumni Adv. Bd. Syracuse U., 1985. Served to 2d lt. U.S. Army, 1978-79; served to capt. USAR, 1985—. Avocations: Skiing; basketball; running; horseback riding. Home: 5927 Waters Edge Landing Ln Burke VA 22015 Office: Lincoln Mercury Div 8051 Gatehouse Rd Falls Church VA 22046

PETERSON, WILLIAM CANOVA, architect; b. Cleve., Nov. 3, 1945; s. William Canova Peterson and Phyllis Imogene (Hill) Smith; m. Anne Lee Deitz, June 3, 1967 (div. Nov. 1981); children—Lisa Ann, Amanda Rebecca. B.Arch., Va. Poly. Inst., 1968; postgrad. Va. Commonwealth U., 1975-77. Registered architect, Va. Specification writer R.P. Fox, Architect, Newark, Del., 1970-72; project mgr. Highfill Assoc., Richmond, Va., 1972-73; project architect Wrigh, Jones & Wilk, 1973-79; prin. W. Canova Peterson, Architects, Mechanicsville, Va., 1979—. Prin. works include Tuckaway Ctr., 1984, Yen Ching West, 1985. Mem. exec. com. United Va. Bank-Sr. PGA, Richmond, 1984. Served to 1st lt. U.S. Army, 1968-70; Vietnam Mem. AIA, Constrn. Specifications Inst. (bd. dirs.). Republican. Episcopalian. Lodges: Rotary (pres. 1982-83), Masons, Shriners. Office: 1125 Hanover Green Dr Mechanicsville VA 23111

PETRAGNANI, RALPH FRANCIS, helicopter marketing company official; b. Phila., Sept. 27, 1946; s. Ralph Frank and Antoinette (Raneri) P.; m. Elisa Novelli, Oct. 5, 1968; 1 dau., Janine. Student mgmt. Dallas Community Coll., 1974-76, Dallas Baptist Coll., 1977-79. Lic. airframe and power plant technician. With Aerospatiale Helicopter, Grand Prairie, Tex., 1973—, tech. instr., 1973-74, supr. tng., 1974-77, prodn. supr., 1977-79, mktg. tech. specialist, 1979-82, mgr. mktg. services, 1982-85, dir. mktg. services, 1986—. Bd. mgrs. Ft. Worth Aviation Com., 1983. Mem. Westchester Aviation Maintenance Assn., Profl. Aviator Maintenance Assn., Helicopter Assn. Internat., Nat. Bus. Aircraft Assn. (transp. chmn. Dallas 1983), Dallas C. of C. (heliport chmn. aviation com. 1983). Republican. Roman Catholic. Club: K.C. (lector Duncanville, Tex. 1982-83). Office: Aerospatiale Helicopter Corp 2701 Forum Dr Grand Prairie TX 75051

PETRIK, EUGENE VINCENT, college president; b. N.J., May 25, 1932; s. Ferdinand V. and Anna (Komarek) P.; m. Helen Veliky, June 26, 1955; children—John, Mark, Thomas, James. B.S. in Physics, Fairleigh Dickinson U., 1955, H.H.D. (hon.), 1982; M.A. in Sci. Edn., Columbia U., 1957, Ed.D., 1959. Instr., Fairleigh Dickinson U., 1957-59; asst. prof. gen. sci. NYU, N.Y.C., 1959-60; assoc. prof. physics Seton Hall U., South Orange, N.J., 1960-65, prof., 1965-68, chmn. dept., 1962-68; v.p. Mt. St. Mary's Coll., Los Angeles, 1968-73; pres. Bellarmine Coll., Louisville, 1973—; bd. dirs. Kentuckiana Metroversity, 1973—, pres., 1980-82; mem. adv. council Nat. Ctr. Higher Edn. Mgmt. Systems, 1969, Danforth Found. Inst. Coll. Devel., 1969-73, also colls.; dir. The Cumberland, Commonwealth Life Ins. Co. subs. Capital Holding Corp. Author: Inductive Calculus, 1967; Manual for Academic Planning, 1969. Co-author: Modern High School Physics: A Recommended Course of Study, 2d edit., 1959. Founding bd. dirs. Leadership Louisville Found., 1979—, vice-chmn. bd., 1983-84, chmn. bd., 1984-85; bd. dirs. Louisville Central Area, Inc., 1976-84; founding bd. dirs. Spirit of Louisville Found., 1979—, vice-chmn., 1979, chmn., 1981; bd. dirs. Old Ky. Home council Boy Scouts Am., 1979-81; chmn. Louisville div. Am. Heart Assn., 1981-82; chmn. pub. service div. Louisville Met. United Way, 1978, 79, 80, 82, pres. bd. dirs., 1983-85; bd. dirs. Louisville Community Found., Inc., 1984, Methodist Evang. Hosp., 1984—, Louisville Collegiate Sch., 1985—. Columbia U. Sci. Manpower fellow, 1957, 59; recipient Ottenheimer award Louisville Jewish Community Ctr., 1984, Trinity High Sch. peace medal, 1985; Man of Yr. award Louisville Ad Club and Better Bus. Bur., 1984. Mem. Assn. Ind. Calif. Colls. and Univs. (dir. 1968-73), Assn. Cath. Colls. and Univs. (dir. 1977-79), Council Ind. Ky. Colls. and Univs. (pres. 1975-77), Louisville C. of C. (dir. 1978-81), English-Speaking Union (br. dir. 1973—, br. pres. 1982-83). Lodge: Rotary (dir. 1979-81, 1st v.p. 1983-84, pres. 1984-85) (Louisville). Office: Bellarmine College Louisville KY 40205

PETRINI DE MONTFORT, COUNT RINALDO ARISTIDE ANTONIO, architect, interior designer; b. Pistoja, Tuscany, Italy, Mar. 18, 1931; came to U.S., 1978; s. Count Alfredo A.A. and Katrina Vida (von Benaz) P de M.; m. Princess Rodika Gabriela Mirea, 1971. 1 child, Tania Vida Josephine. Diploma architecture LDV Polytechnic, Alessandria, United Arab Republics, 1954; M.S., U. Tenn., 1968; Docteur es Lettres, LaSorbonne, Paris, 1974; postgrad. restoration Ecole des Hautes Etudes, Paris, 1973-74. Registered architect Tex. Pres., Petrini Architects and Designers, Rome, Florence, Paris, Houston, 1960—; v.p. Pierluigi Nervi & Assocs., Rome, Florence, Houston, N.Y.C., Houston, 1983—; Prof. architecture Beaux Arts, Paris, 1973-79; dir. research U. Nairobi, 1970-73; dir. internat. studies U. Houston, 1978—; disting. lectr. U. Tex., San Antonio, 1985. Chmn. internat. edn. commn. ICSID/UNESCO, 1961-71; dir., founder Internat. Restoration Brigade, France and Italy, 1973; dir. Lunar Habitat Design and Research Team, Washington, 1979 . Author: Framework for Design Education, 1968; Space, 1978. Decorated knight Royal Order Cyprus, Royal Order Norman Crown, Order Malta, Order St. George, Order Sword of Silence; grand bailiff Sovereign Mil. Hospitaller Order St. George; academician Internationale Burkhardt Academie, 1982, Accademia Clementina, Bologna, Italy, 1984; recipient Bene Merenti Gold medal Pope Paul VI, 1973, Golden Legion, L'Accademia Tiberina, 1977. Mem. AIA, Indsl. Design Inst. Am. (v.p. Tx. chpt. 1980-81), Nat. Trust Historic Preservation, Soc. Archlt. Historians, U.S. Inst. Theatre Technology, Constrn. Specification Inst., Alpha Rho Chi. Republican. Clubs: Florence, Circolo della Nobilta di Firenze. Avocations: Dressage, cross countryhunt; polo; fencing; pistol. Office: Pierluigi Nervi and Assocs 2001 Kirby TX 77019

PETRONE, WILLIAM FRANCIS, physician, microbiologist; b. Bklyn., Sept. 12, 1949; s. Arthur Carmen and Helen (Kenny) P.; B.A., U. Conn., 1972; M.S., U. Mass., 1974; Ph.D., U. R.I., 1978; M.D., U. South Ala., 1984; m. Kathleen Anne Baron, Aug. 25, 1979; children—William Gaetano, Katherine Bridget. Research asso. Coll. Medicine, U. South Ala., Mobile, 1978-80; resident in pediatrics Orlando (Fla.) Regional Med. Ctr., 1984-85, W.Va. U. Med. Ctr., 1985—. Mem. AAAS, AMA, Am. Med. Student Assn., N.Y. Acad. Scis., Sigma Xi. Roman Catholic. Contbr. articles on inflamation and white blood cell function to sci. jours. Office: WVa U Med Ctr Morgantown WV 26506

PETROSKO, JOSEPH MICHAEL, JR., education educator; b. Joliet, Ill., Mar. 19, 1947; s. Joseph Michael and Mary (Orenic) P. B.A., Lewis Coll., 1969; Ph.D., N.Mex. State U., 1972. Asst. research educator Grad. Sch. Edn., UCLA, 1972-75; from asst. to assoc. prof. edn. U. Louisville, 1975—. Contbr. articles on ednl. research to profl. jours. Lewis Coll. scholar, 1965; fellow U.S. Office Edn., 1969. Mem. Am. Psychol. Assn., Am. Ednl. Research Assn., Nat. Council on Measurement in Edn., AAUP, Phi Delta Kappa. Office: Sch Edn U Louisville Louisville KY 40292

PETTEE, ROGER CHARLES, financial planner; b. St. Paul, Dec. 9, 1942; s. Robert A. and Beatrice (Lahah) P.; m. Macye L. Crowder, Apr. 22, 1965; children—Roger M., Nicole M. B.S. in Bus. Adminstrn., U. Fla., 1961-65. Cert. fin. planner. Stockbroker Dean Witter, Orlando and Miami, Fla., 1969-71; pres. The Pettee Group, Inc., Atlanta, 1971—. Mem. Internat. Assn. Fin. Planners. Republican. Presbyterian. Home: 1400 N Riverside Circle Atlanta GA 30328 Office: The Pettee Group Inc 101 Village Pkwy Suite 200 Marietta GA 30067

PETTEY, MARY RUTH, training specialist; b. Jackson, Miss., Jan. 26, 1954; s. James Reeder and Martha Ann (Bradford) P. B.S. in English, Miss. U. for Women, 1976. Tchr., Bessemer Bd. Edn., Ala., 1976-77; tchr. New Hope Sch., Columbus, Miss., 1977-79; methods analyst So. Farm Bur., Jackson, Miss., 1979-81; tng. coordinator McRae's, Inc., Jackson, 1981-82; tng. specialist Deposit Guaranty Nat. Bank, Jackson, 1982—. Vol. worker Miss. Bapt. Med. Ctr., Jackson, 1984. Mem. Am. Soc. Tng. and Devel., Career Forum (co-founder 1982), Miss. U. for Women Alumnae. Episcopalian. Avocations: writing children's stories; sailing; reading.

PETTID, GLADYS MARIE, school principal, counselor; b. Olewein, Iowa, May 7, 1932; d. Harry Lewis and Mabel (Beckner) Gray; m. Michael John Pettid, Jr., July 14, 1956; children—Carole Marie, Catherine Diane, Michael John. B.A., No. Iowa U., 1954; M.A. in Edn., Ariz. State U., 1973, M.Counseling, 1975. Cert. classroom tchr., spl. edn. tchr., counselor, supr., prin., Tex. Tchr. Peoria Elem. Sch., Glendale, Ariz., 1954-55, Roosevelt Elem. Sch., Phoenix, 1955-57, Washington Elem. Sch. Dist. 6, Phoenix, 1969-79; counselor, coordinator Ft. Worth Ind. Sch. Dist., 1979-83, prin., 1983—; mem. task force Site Based Mgmt., Ft. Worth, 1982—; presenter workshops, Ft. Worth, 1983—. Mem. Tarrant County Council Adminstrv. Women in Edn. (treas. 1984-85), Ft. Worth Pub. Sch. Adminstrs. Assn., Assn. for Supervision and Curriculum Devel., Tex. Personnel and Guidance Assn. Inc., LWV, Phi Lamba Theta. Democrat. Lutheran. Avocations: painting; swimming; jogging; boating; reading. Home: 2327 L Don Dodson 164 Bedford TX 76021 Office: Metro Opportunity Sch 2100 Cooper St Fort Worth TX 76104

PETTIETTE, ALISON YVONNE, lawyer; b. Brockton, Mass., Aug. 16, 1952; d. David and Loretta (LeClair) Waters; m. Tom Lee Pettiette, Dec. 23, 1976 (div. Aug. 1982). B.A., Newcomb Coll. of Tulane U., 1972; student Sorbonne U., Paris, 1971-72; M.A., Rice U., 1974; J.D., U. Houston, 1978. Bar: Tex. 1979, U.S. Dist. Ct. (so. dist.) Tex. 1979, U.S. Ct. Appeals (5th cir.) 1981. Ptnr., Harvill & Hardy, Houston, 1979-83; sole practice, Houston, 1983-84; mem. O'Quinn & Hagans, Houston, 1984—; mem. Agt. Orange Plaintiffs' Mgmt. Com., Bklyn., 1984—. Editor U. Houston Law Rev., 1977-78. NDEA fellow, 1972-74; recipient Am. Jurisprudence award, 1978; Woodrow Wilson scholar, 1972. Mem. Tex. Trial Lawyers Assn., Assn. Trial Lawyers Am., Houston Trial Lawyers Assn., Phi Beta Kappa, Phi Delta Phi. Club: Warwick Breakfast (Houston). Home: 2336 North Blvd Houston TX 77006 Office: O'Quinn & Hagans 3200 Texas Commerce Tower Houston TX 77002

PETTINGER, WILLIAM A., physician, educator; b. Cumberland, Iowa, May 26, 1932; B.S. in Math., Creighton U., Omaha, 1954, M.S. in Physiology, 1957, M.D., 1959. Intern in medicine N.J. Coll. Medicine, 1959-60, asst. resident in medicine, 1960-61; clin. investigator clin. pharmacology and exptl. therapeutics Nat. Heart Inst., 1961-63; sr. asst. resident in medicine Yale U./Grace New Haven Hosp., 1963-64; postdoctoral fellow, instr. clin. pharmacology Vanderbilt U. Med. Sch., 1964-66, asst. prof., 1966-67; with dept. clin. pharmacology and pharmcology Hoffman-LaRoche, Inc., Nutley, N.J., 1967-71, dir. div. cardiovascular-renal research, 1969-71; asst. prof., then asso. prof. medicine N.J. Coll. Medicine, 1967-71; asso. prof. pharmacology and internal medicine U. Tex. Southwestern Med. Sch., Dallas, 1971-74, dir. div. clin. pharmacology, 1971—; sr. attending physician Parkland Meml. Hosp., Dallas, 1971—; prof. pharmacology and internal medicine U. Tex. Health Sci. Center, Dallas, 1974—; William N. Creasy vis. prof. La. State U., 1977, U. Miami, 1981, Tex. A&M U., 1984; mem. pharmacology test com. Nat. Bd. Med. Examiners, 1970-80; med. adv. bd. council high blood pressure research Am. Heart Assn., 1972—. Burroughs-Wellcome scholar, 1974-79; recipient Rawl's Palmer award Am. Soc. Clin. Pharmacology and Therapeutics, 1982; diplomate Am. Bd. Internal Medicine. Fellow Am. Coll. Cardiology, ACP; mem. Am. Soc. Clin. Investigation, Soc. Exptl. Biology and Medicine, Am. Soc. Clin. Pharmacology and Therapeutics (dir.), AMA, Am. Fedn. Clin. Research, AAAS, Fedn. Am. Soc. Exptl. Biology and Medicine, So. Soc. Clin. Investigation, Dallas County Med. Soc. Author over 100 articles in field of hypertension, cardiovascular and renal research. Editor-in-chief Jour. Cardiovascular Pharmacology, 1978-80; mem. editorial bds. profl. jours. Office: 5323 Harry Hines Blvd Dallas TX 75235

PETTIT, JOSEPH MAYO, college president; b. Rochester, Minn., July 15, 1916; s. Joseph Asahel and Florence (Anderson) P.; m. Florence Rowell West, June 8, 1940; children—Marjorie Pettit Wilbur, Joseph Roy, Marilyn Pettit Backlund. B.S., U. Calif. at Berkeley, 1938; E.E., Stanford, 1940, Ph.D., 1942. Registered profl. engr., Calif. Instr. U. Calif. at Berkeley, 1940-42; spl. research assoc., asst. exec. engr. Radio Research Lab. Harvard U., 1942-45; tech. observer USAF, India-China, 1944; assoc. tech. dir. Am. Brit. Lab., ETO, 1945; supervising engr. Airborne Instruments Lab., Inc., N.Y.C., 1945-46; faculty Stanford U., 1947-72, prof. elec. engring., 1954-72, assoc. dean engring., 1955-58, dean, 1958-72; pres. Ga. Inst. Tech., Atlanta, 1972—; Dir. Varian Assocs., Sci. Atlanta, Inc., Ga. Motor Club, Inc.; Mem. Army Sci. Adv. Panel, 1957-63; mem. Nat. Sci. Bd., 1977-82. Author: Electronic Switching, Timing and Pulse Circuits, 1959, 2d edit, (with M.M. McWhorter) Electronic Switching, Timing and Pulse Circuits, 1970, (with others) Very-High-Frequency Techniques, 1947, (with F.E. Terman) Electronic Measurements, 1952, (with McWhorter) Electronic Amplifiers, 1961. Recipient Presdl. Certificate of Merit; Electronics Achievement award IRE. Fellow IEEE (Founders medal 1983), AAAS; mem. Nat. Acad. Engring., Am. Soc. Engring. Edn. (pres. 1972-73), Ga. Acad. Scis. Congregationalist. Clubs: Rotary; University (N.Y.C.); Cosmos. Home: 292 10th St NW Atlanta GA 30318*

PETTIT, LAWRENCE KAY, university system adminstrator; b. Lewistown, Mont., May 2, 1937; s. George Edwin and Dorothy Bertha (Brown) P.; m. Sharon Lee Anderson, June 21, 1961 (div. Oct. 1976); children—Jennifer Anna, Matthew Anderson, Allison Carol, Edward McLean; m. Elizabeth DuBois Medley, July 11, 1980; stepchildren—Mark Adron Medley, Lee Emmett Medley, Bryce Matthew Medley. B.A., U. Mont., 1959; A.M., Washington U., St. Louis, 1962; Ph.D. (Univ. fellow, Vilas fellow), U. Wis., 1965. Legis. asst. U.S. Senate, 1959-60, 62; mem. faculty dept. polit. sci. Pa. State U., 1964-67; mem. adminstrv. staff Am. Council Edn., Washington, 1967-69; chmn. dept. polit. sci. Mont. State U., 1969-72; adminstrv. asst. to Gov. of Mont., 1973; chancellor Mont. Univ. System, 1973-79; dep. commr. for acad. and health affairs Tex. Coordinating Bd. for Higher Edn., 1981-83; chancellor Univ. Systems of South Tex., 1983—; mem. various nat. and regional bds. and coms. on higher edn. Author: (with H. Albinski) European Political Processes, 2d edit. 1974; (with E. Keynes) Legislative Process in the U.S. Senate, 1969; (with S. Kirkpatrick) Social Psychology of Political Life, 1972. Mem. Mont. Democratic Reform Commn., 1971. Served with USAR, 1955-63. Mem. Am. Polit. Sci. Assn., AAUP, State Higher Edn. Exec. Officers (exec. com.), Am. Assn. Higher Edn., Sigma Chi. Episcopalian. Clubs: Rotary, Kingsville Country, Nueces, Masons, Shriners. Office: Univ System of South Tex PO Box 1238 Kingsville TX 78363

PETTY, OLIVE SCOTT, geophysical engineer; b. Olive, Tex., Apr. 15, 1895; s. Van Alvin and Mary Cordelia (Dabney) P.; student Ga. Inst. Tech., 1913-14; B.S. in Civil Engring., U. Tex., 1917, C.E., 1920; m. Mary Edwina Harris, July 19, 1921; 1 child, Scott. Adj. prof. civil engring. U. Tex., 1920-23; structural engr. R.O. Jameson, Dallas, 1923-25; pres. Petty Geophys. Engring. Co., Petty Labs., Inc., San Antonio, 1925-52, chmn. bd., 1952-73; chmn. bd. Petty Geophys. Engring. Co. de Mex. S.A. de C.V., 1950-73; partner Petty Ranch Co., 1968—; ranching, minerals, timber and investment interests, 1937—. Benefactor, San Antonio Symphony Soc., McKay Art Mus.; mem. exec. com., founding mem. chancellor's council U. Tex. System Austin, also adv. council, founding mem., hon. life mem. Geology Found. Adv. council. Served as lt., inf. U.S. Army, 1917-18; AEF in France. Named hon. adm. Tex. Navy; recipient Disting. Grad. award U. Tex. Coll. Engring., Austin, 1962; registered profl. engr., Tex. Fellow N.Y. Acad. Sci., Wisdom Soc., Am. Geol. Inst. (Centurian Club), Tex. Acad. Sci. (hon. life); mem. ASCE (hon. life; life Tex. sect.), AIME (Legion of Honor), Am. Assn. Petroleum Geologists (life mem. trustees assn.), AAAS, Am. Petroleum Inst., Nat. Soc. Profl. Engrs. (life), Am. Geophys. Union, Internat. Platform Assn., Houston Geophys. Soc., South Tex. Geol. Soc., Soc. Petroleum Engrs. (Legion of Honor), Friends of Alec Club of U. Tex. Coll. Engring., (founding mem.), Am. Assn. Petroleum Geologists Trustee Assn., Soc. Am. Mil. Engrs., Soc. Exptl. Geophysicists (hon. life), Newcomen Soc. N.Am., Soc. 1st Inf. Div. (founding), Tex. Ind. Producers and Royalty Owners Assn., La. Ind. Producers and Royalty Owners Assn., Tex. Soc. Profl. Engrs., Ind. Petroleum Assn. Am., Tex. and Southwestern Cattle Raisers Assn., Nature Conservancy (life), Explorers Club (life), Chi Epsilon (hon. life), Theta Xi, Tau Beta Pi. Baptist. Clubs: San Antonio Country, Argyle, St. Anthony (San Antonio), Girard. Author: Seismic Reflections, Recollections of the Formative Years of the Petroleum Exploration Industry, 1976; A Journey to Pleasant Hill; The Civil War Letters of Captain E.P. Petty, C.S.A.; patentee geophys. methods, instruments, equipment. Home: 101 E Kings Hwy San Antonio TX 78212 Office: 711 Navarro St San Antonio TX 78205

PETTY, ROY WILLIAM, orthopedic surgeon, educator; b. Little Rock, Oct. 18, 1942; s. Roy H. and Mary Lee (Harrell) P.; m. Betty Blackmon, Dec. 27, 1963; children—David William, Mark Aaron, Julie Allison. B.S., U. Ark., 1962, M.D., 1966, M.S., 1968. Diplomate Am. Bd. Orthopaedic Surgery. Intern, Tampa Gen. Hosp. (Fla.), 1966-67; fellow in orthopedics Mayo Clinic, Rochester, Minn., 1970-74; orthopedic surgeon, Naples, Fla., 1974-75; asst. prof. U. Fla., Gainesville, 1975-79, assoc. prof., 1979-81, prof. and chmn. dept. orthopedics, 1981—; chief orthopaedic surgeon VA Hosp., Gainesville, 1979-84. Served to capt. USAF, 1967-69. Mem. Am. Acad. Orthopedic Surgeons, Orthopedic Research Soc., Fla. Orthopedic Soc., Fla. Med. Assn., Alachua County Med. Soc., Community Med. Services Assn., Inc., AMA, N.Y. Acad. Sci., Sigma Xi., Alpha Omega Alpha. Methodist. Contbr. articles to profl. jours. Office: Dept Orthopedics PO Box J-246 U Fla Coll Medicine Gainesville FL 23610

PETTY, RUTH ROBERTS, financial analyst and consultant; b. Greensboro, N.C., Aug. 12, 1947; d. David Herbert and Mary Viginia (Ketner) P.; divorced; children—R. David Petty-Lindholtz. B.A., Wheaton Coll., 1969; M.A., Calif. State U.-Sacramento, 1977. C.L.U.; chartered fin. cons. Real estate agt. Coldwell-Banker Fair Oaks, Calif., 1977-81; fin. cons. Equitable Fin. Services, Richmond, Va., 1982—; pres. Crosswoods Homeowners Assn., Citrus Heights, Calif., 1976-77; prin., cons., fin. planner Petty & Assocs., Richmond, 1985—. Author: (with Roberts, Kloss and Dorn) Sociology with a Human Face, 1975. Mem. com. Citrus Heighs Inc., Calif., 1976. Mem. Nat. Assn. Life Underwriters, Am. Sociol. Assn., Women's Life Underwriter Council, Richmond Assn. Life Underwriters. Avocations: bicycling; photography; tennis. Home: PO Box 29495 Richmond VA 23229 Office: Equitable Financial Services 1801 Libbie Ave Richmond VA 23229

PETTY, TRAVIS HUBERT, business executive; b. Clarksville, Tex., July 31, 1928; s. Joseph H. and Kathleen (Mauldin) P.; student U. Tex., 1945-46; m. Berenice Wieland, Feb. 10, 1948; children—Brian, Paul, David, Kevin, Sean, Karen, Michael. With El Paso Natural Gas Co., 1946—, asst. controller, 1961-65, controller, 1965-69, v.p., 1969-73, dir., 1971—, exec. v.p., 1973-76, pres., 1976-78, chmn., 1978-85; dir. The El Paso Co., 1974—, exec. v.p., 1974-78, vice-chmn., 1978, chmn., 1979—, pres., 1980—; vice chmn. bd. Burlington No., Inc., 1983—, also dir.; dir. El Paso Nat. Bank, El Paso Nat. Corp., Tex. Commerce Bancshares, El Paso Products Co. Mem. Am. Gas Assn., Pacific Coast Gas Assn. (past chmn.), Interstate Natural Gas Assn. (dir.), So. Gas Assn. (past chmn. adv. council). Office: Burlington Northern Inc PO Box 1492 El Paso TX 79978

PEW, JUDY GARLAND, nurse; b. Saco, Maine, Aug. 19, 1942; d. Bernard Cyril and Bertha Edna (Johnstone) G.; m. John Paul Pew, Feb. 5, 1965; children—John Paul, Wallace Garland. Diploma Maine Med. Ctr., Portland, 1963; nursing student, 1985—. Charge nurse Burton Hollis Hosp., Bar Mills, Maine, 1963-64; staff nurse Greenville Gen. Hosp., S.C., 1964-70, head nurse, 1970-71; head nurse St. Francis Hosp., Greenville, 1971, supr., 1971-72, infection control nurse, 1972—; Tb program planner Am. Lung Assn., Columbia, S.C., 1983; cons. to nursing homes, Greenville, 1984—; instr. Greenville Tech. Coll., 1984. Active McCarter Presbyn. Ch., Greenville; Mem. Nat. Assn. Practitioners in Infection Control, S.C. Assn. Practitioners in Infection Control, S.C. Hosp. Assn., Am. Heart Assn. (instr.). Republican. Club: Community (sec. 1975-76). Avocations: crafts; reading; rose growing. Office: St Francis Hosp 1 Saint Francis Dr Greenville SC 29601

PEWITT, EDITH MARIE, educational administrator; b. Greenville, Tex., Feb. 27, 1926; d. Charles Ambrose, Jr. and Beulah Edna (King) Hendrix; B.S., Tex. Women's U., 1961; M.Ed., North Tex. State U., 1964, Ed.D., 1967; m. Edgar Lee Pewitt, Feb. 23, 1945; children—Edith Pamela Pewitt Chatagnier, Robert Lewis, II, Edgar Lee. Supr. sch. lunches, then tchr. Grapevine (Tex.) Ind. Sch. Dist., 1958-66; research asst., lab. instr., then asst. prof. edn. North Tex. State U., 1966-68; coordinator curriculum Edn. Service Center, Region XI, Ft. Worth, 1968-70; cons. Novato (Calif.) Unified Sch. Dist., 1970-71, adminstrv. asst., 1971-72; staff devel. coordinator Partners in Career Edn., Arlington, Tex., 1972-74; tchr. high sch. sci., instructional leader, coordinator, prin. Career Planning Acad., Ft. Worth Ind. Sch. Dist., 1974—; cons. in field. Mem. NEA, Adminstrv. Women in Edn. (membership chmn. 1980-81), Assn. Supervision and Curriculum Devel., Soc. Study Edn., Nat. Sci. Tchrs. Assn., Tex. Tchrs. Assn., Tex. Assn. Supervision and Curriculum Devel., Ft. Worth Classroom Tchrs. Assn., Ft. Worth Public Schs. Adminstrs. Assn., Kappa Delta Pi (past chpt. pres.), Delta Kappa Gamma (v.p. 1980-82), Phi Delta Kappa. Methodist. Home: 303 Ridge Rd Grapevine TX 76051 Office: 3813 Valentine St Fort Worth TX 76051

PEYROUSE, JOHN CLAUDE, JR., theatre educator; b. Ovid, Colo., June 29, 1928; s. John Claude and Ruth (Young) P.; m. Jane Harton, May 6, 1956; children—Jane VanVoorhees, Marcia Melanie, John Claude. B.A., U. Denver, 1949, M.A., 1953; postgrad. U. Ark., 1956, U. Mo., 1957-58, Northwestern U., 1960-62; Ph.D., U. Nebr., 1978. Tchr., Logan County High Sch., Sterling, Colo., 1950-51, Centennial High Sch., Pueblo, Colo., 1955-56; various teaching positions Drury Coll., Springfield, Mo., 1957-60, Kendall Coll., Evanston, Ill., 1960-61, Doane Coll., Crete, Nebr., 1961-70, U. Central Ark., Conway, 1971-72, Ark. Coll., Batesville, 1972-73, E. Tenn. State U., Johnson City, 1973-76; dir. theatre Methodist Coll., Fayetteville, N.C., 1977—; theatre critic Sta. WFNC; arts tour guide; youth theatre dir.; artistic dir. Shakespearean Summer Festival. Bd. dirs. Fayetteville Arts Council, mem. July 4th celebration com. Served with USAF, 1951-55. Recipient grants for theatre prodns.; Cumberland Found. grantee, 1981. Mem. Am. Theatre Assn., Speech Communication Assn., Southeast Theatre Conf., Nat. Collegiate Players (hon.), Alpha Psi Omega (hon.). Democrat. Episcopalian. Lodge: Elks. Contbr. articles to profl. jours. Home: 746 Buena Vista Dr Fayetteville NC 28301 Office: Methodist Coll Raleigh Rd Fayetteville NC 28301

PFAFFENBERGER, CARL DALE, bioanalytical chemist, consultant; b. Houston, Oct. 18, 1938; s. Carl Fredrick and Katie Elizabeth P.; m. Marta Elena Ariel, Jan. 7, 1983. B.S. with honors, U. Tex.-Austin, 1962; Ph.D. with distinction, Purdue U., 1967. Research chemist Union Carbide, South Charleston, W.Va., 1967-69; vis. assoc. prof. organic chemistry Nat. Taiwan U., 1969-70; assoc. prof. bioanalytical chemistry Baylor Coll. Medicine, Houston, 1970-76; prof. bioanalytical chemistry, dir. chem. epidemiology U. Miami Sch. Medicine, 1976-85; chief environ. planning Dade County Dept. Environ. Resources Mgmt., 1985—, EPA grantee, 1977—. Mem. Am. Chem. Soc., Am. Soc. Mass Spectrometry. Home: 3301 NE 5th Ave #1107 Miami FL 33137 Office: 111 NW First St Miami FL 33128

PFEFFER, PHILIP MAURICE, book company executive; b. St. Louis, Jan. 20, 1945; s. Philip McRae and Jeanne (Kaufman) P.; m. Pamela Jean Korte, Aug. 28, 1965; children—John-Lindell Philip, James Howard, David Maurice. B.A. in Math., So. Ill. U., 1966, M.A. in Econs., 1966; postgrad., Vanderbilt U., 1966-68. Dir. fin. planning Ingram Book Co., Nashville, 1976-77, v.p. fin. and administrn., 1977-78, exec. v.p., 1978, pres. and chief exec. officer, 1978-81, chmn. bd. and chief exec. officer, 1981—, dir., 1978—; exec. v.p. Ingram Industries, Inc., Nashville, 1981—; dir. Gulfco Industries, Inc., Oklahoma City, 1981—, Telco Research Co., Nashville, 1977—, Tenn Book Co., 1977—. Mem. exec. bd. dir. Boy Scouts Am., Nashville, 1978, mem. nat. exploring com., Dallas, 1982; mem. campaign com. Nashville Area United Way, 1981; bd. assocs. Owen Grad. Sch. Mgmt. Vanderbilt U., Nashville, 1981; bd. dirs. So. Ill. U. Alumni Assn., 1982. Recipient Long Rifle Boy Scouts Am., Nashville, 1981. Mem. Fin. Execs. Inst. (pres. 1978-79). Club: Percy Priest Yacht (Nashville). Lodge: Rotary-Nashville. Office: Ingram Book Co 347 Reedwood Dr Nashville TN 37220*

PFEIFFER, ASTRID ELIZABETH, utility executive; b. N.Y.C., Nov. 15, 1934; d. Ernest and Alice (Strobel) P.; B.A., Cornell U., 1955; J.D. cum laude, Wayne State U., 1967; grad. exec. program in bus. adminstrn. Columbia U. Grad. Sch. Bus., 1976; m. Edmund Lee Gettier, III, May 28, 1956 (div. 1966); children—Evan Ernest, Elizabeth Lee, Edmund Lee, Sheila Anne, David Brian. Mng. editor Detroit Inst. Arts, 1962-67; admitted to Mich. bar, 1968, N.Y. bar, 1969, Fla. bar, 1975; atty. J.P. Mattimoe, Detroit, 1967-68, Chubb & Son, Inc., N.Y.C., 1969-70, firm Cadwalader, Wickersham & Taft, N.Y.C., 1971-73; corp. sec. Fla. Power & Light Co., Miami, 1973—. Mem. Am. Bar Assn., Fla. Bar Assn., Dade County Bar Assn., Am. Soc. Corp. Secs. (past pres. S.E. region, nat. bd. dirs. 1982—). Club: Coral Gables Country. Office: Fla Power & Light Co 9250 W Flagler St PO Box 029100 Miami FL 33102

PFEIFFER, CARL E., manufacturing company executive; b. 1930; B.S. in M.E., Mich. State U. With Quanex Corp., 1953—, plant mgr. Gulf States Tube Corp. subs., v.p., 1958-68, exec. v.p., 1968-71, pres., 1971-72, chmn. exec. com., pres., chief exec. officer, dir., 1972—. Office: Quanex Corp 1900 West Loop S West Houston TX 77027*

PFISTER, ROSWELL ROBERT, ophthalmologist, administrator; b. Buffalo, Jan. 19, 1938; s. Milton Albert and Florence P. (Nachreiner) P.; m. Darlene, Nov. 13, 1976; children—Daryl, Yvonne, Damien, Erin, Kyle. M.D., U. Mich., 1962, M.S., 1969. Diplomate Am. Bd. Ophthalmology. Intern, Los Angeles County Hosp., 1962-63; resident in ophthalmology U. Mich. Med. Sch., Ann Arbor, 1966-69; clin. fellow Cornea Service, Mass. Eye and Ear Infirmary, 1969-71; research fellow dept. cornea research, Retina Found., Boston, 1969-71; asst. prof. ophthalmology U. Colo., Denver, 1971-75, assoc. prof., 1975-76; med. dir. Colo. Eye Bank, 1974-76; prof. ophthalmology U. Ala., 1976—, chmn. dept., 1976-81; dir. Brookwood Eye Research Labs., 1982—; pvt. practice corneal and external diseases, Birmingham; trustee Eye Found. Inc., 1976-81. Served with USAF, 1963-65. Mem. Med. Assn. State Ala., Jefferson County Med. Soc., Assn. Research in Vision and Ophthalmology, Research Prevent Blindness, Inc., Am. Acad. Ophthalmology Ala. Acad. Ophthalmology, AMA, Colo. Ophthal. Soc., Mich. State Med. Soc., Corneal Soc., Colo. Soc. Prevention of Blindness (med. adv. bd. 1974-76), David J. Kelman Research Found., Kerato-Refractive Soc., Contact Lens Assn. Am., Am. Intraocular Implant Soc., Internat. Corneal Soc., N.Y. Acad. Scis. Home: 4622 Battery Ln Birmingham AL 35213 Office: 2022 Brookwood Med Ctr Dr Birmingham AL 35209

PFOST, WILLIAM LOUIS, JR., fiber co. exec.; b. Orange, N.J., Oct. 13, 1936; s. William Louis and Dorothy May (Kustler) P.; student Fairleigh Dickinson U., 1958-65; B.S. in B.A., Widener Coll., 1970; grad. exec. program U. Va., 1979; m. Jane Ellen Berger, Apr. 6, 1957; children—William Louis, Penni, Patti, Ricky. With Thiokol Corp., Denville, N.J., summer 1955, draftsman, 1955-59, procedures analyst, 1959-62, employment rep., 1962-65, employee relations supr., Elkton, Md., 1965-66, personnel mgr., 1966-74, dir. indsl. relations, Waynesboro, Va., 1974-79; v.p. adminstrn., corp. sec. Wayn-Tex Inc., Waynesboro, 1979-80, v.p. ops., 1980-83, pres., chief operating officer, 1983—; mem. faculty Cecil Community Coll., 1973-74, Goldey Beacom Coll., 1973-74. Pres., United Way, Cecil County, 1970-71; chmn. adv. bd. Cecil County Bd. Edn., 1971-73; pres. Economic Devel. Council for Staunton, Waynesboro, Augusta County, Va., 1976-77. Mem. Elkton C. of C. (dir. 1972-73), Waynesboro-E. Augusta C. of C. (pres. 1977-78), Va. C. of C. (dir. 1979-80, pres. 1984—), Am. Soc. Personnel Adminstrn. Presbyn. Clubs: Masons, Kiwanis, Ruritan. Home: Route 1 PO Box 338 Waynesboro VA 22980 Office: 901 S Delphine Ave Waynesboro VA 22908

PFOUTS, RALPH WILLIAM, economics educator; b. Atchison, Kans., Sept. 9, 1920; s. Ralph Ulysses and Alice (Oldham) P.; B.A., U. Kans., 1942, M.A., 1947; Ph.D., U. N.C., 1952; m. Jane Hoyer, Jan. 31, 1945 (dec. Nov. 1982); children—James William, Susan Jane Pfouts Portman, Thomas Robert, Elizabeth Ann Pfouts Klenowski; m. Lois Bateson, Dec. 21, 1984. Research asst., instr. econs. U. Kans., 1946-47, U. N.C., Chapel Hill, 1947-50, lectr., 1950-52, asso. prof., 1952-58, prof., 1958—, chmn. grad. studies dept. econs. Sch. Bus. Adminstrn., 1957-62, chmn. dept. econs., 1962-68. Social Sci. Research Council fellow U. Cambridge, 1953-54; Ford Found. faculty research fellow, 1962-63; vis. prof. U. Leeds (Eng.), 1983; vis. scholar Internat. Inst. for Applied Systems Analysis, Laxenburg, Austria, 1983. Served as deck officer USNR antisubmarine duty, 1943-46. Mem. Am., N.C. (pres. 1951-52) statis. assns., Am., So. (pres. (1965-66) econ. assns., Population Assn. Am., Econometric Soc., AAAS, Atlantic Econ. Soc. (v.p. 1974-76, pres. 1977-78), Royal Econ. Soc., Phi Beta Kappa, Pi Sigma Alpha, Alpha Kappa Psi, Omicron Delta Epsilon. Author: Elementary Economics: A Mathematical Approach, 1972. Editor So. Econ. Jour., 1955-75; editor, contbr.: Techniques of Urban Economic Analysis, 1960; Essays in Economics and Econometrics, 1960; editorial bd. Metroeconomica, 1961-80, Atlantic Econ. Jour., 1973—, Quar. Jour. Ideology, 1976—. Contbr. articles to profl. jours. Home: 307 Cameron Ave Chapel Hill NC 27514

PHAM, QUANG HUU, state official, engineer; b. Thanh Hoa, Viet Nam, Dec. 24, 1942; s. Ba Van and Oanh Thi (Le) P.; came to U.S., 1975; B.S. in C.E., U. Saigon, 1966; M.S. in C.E., U. Okla., 1971; m. Thanh Thi, Apr. 15, 1969; children—Tuyet, Tuan. Asst. chief bur. City of Saigon (Viet Nam), 1966-67, chief bur., 1969-70, asst. chief dept., 1972-75; instr. Engring. Sch. Corps. of Engrs., Viet Nam, 1967-68; dist. engr. Okla. State Health Dept., Oklahoma City, 1975-80, dir. public water supply engring., 1980-82, chief engr., permits and compliance, 1982—; lectr. U. Saigon, 1974-75; chmn. Okla. com. to revise and update constrn. standards for public water supply facilities, 1981. Vice pres. Vietnamese Buddhist Assn. Okla. Recipient awards City of Saigon, 1972-75; AID scholar, 1971-72. Registered profl. engr., Okla. Mem. Am. Water Works Assn., Sao Viet Athletic Assn. (pres.). Buddhist. Author: Proposal for Improving the Solid Waste System Management of Saigon City, 1971. Home: 6913 Greenway Dr Oklahoma City OK 73132 Office: NE 10th and Stonewall Sts Oklahoma City OK 73152

PHAN, PETER CHO, theology educator, reseacher; b. Nha Trang, Viet Nam, Jan. 5, 1943; came to U.S., 1975, naturalized, 1982; s. Hien Van Phan and So Thi Le. B.A., U. London, 1968; B.D., Salesian Pontifical U., Italy, 1971, S.T.L., 1972, S.T.D., 1978. Asst. prof. theology U. Dallas, Irving, 1975-80, assoc. prof., 1980—, chmn. dept. theology, 1980—, dir. Ph.D. program theology, 1980-85. Author: Social Thought, The Message of the Fathers of the Church, 1984, Culture and Eschatology, 1985. Arthur Vining Davis faculty devel. grantee U. Dallas, 1979, NEH faculty devel. grantee, 1985. Mem. Cath. Theol. Soc. Am., Coll. Theology Soc., Am. Acad. Religion, Council S.W. Theol. Schs. (v.p. 1984—), Sch. Theology Laity (bd. dirs. 1984—).

PHARIES, DAVID ARNOLD, linguistics educator; b. Levelland, Tex., Nov. 7, 1951; s. Roy Edward and Emma Mauryce (Giles) P.; m. Elizabeth Jean Harrington, June 16, 1973; children—Stefan, Alice, Hilary. A.B., Austin Coll., 1973; Ph.D., U. Calif.-Berkeley, 1979. Vis. asst. prof. Ariz. State U., Tempe, 1979-80; asst. prof. Spanish and linguistics U. Fla., Gainesville, 1980-86, assoc. prof., 1986—. Author: C.S. Peirce and the Linguistic Sign, 1985; Structure and Analogy in the Playful Lexicon of Spanish, 1986. Contbr. articles to profl. jours. Fellow NEH, 1982, 85, U. Fla., 1982. Mem. MLA (mem. exec. com. div.), South Atlantic MLA. Democrat. Mem. Society of Friends. Office: Dept Romance Languages U Fla Gainesville FL 32611

PHARO, GWEN MCRAE, management consultant, government affairs specialist; b. Lafayette, Ala., Aug. 5, 1927; d. Wesley Talmadge and Mary Louise (Tyson) McRae; m. Milam Bernard Pharo, June 23, 1951 (div. Sept. 1979); children—Milam Randolph, Mark Langston. Student Cottey Jr. Coll. for Women, 1945-46, U. Houston, 1946-48, Exec. Sch. of Protocol, 1981. Adminstrv. asst. to dep. adminstr. Gen. Services Adminstrn., Dallas, 1950-51; advt. copy writer Bonwit Teller, Phila., 1951; civic worker, Dallas, 1952-74; mng. ptnr. Maley, Pharo & Holloman, Inc., Dallas, 1974; corp. v.p. for nat. and internat. pub. relations Intercontinental Translations, Austin, Tex., 1975-81; Washington rep. O.I.L. Energy, Inc. subs. Kidde, Inc., Dallas; cons. to pub. Tex. Tribune, Austin, 1979-82; pub. relations cons. Tex. Free Enterprise Found., also dir. Press liaison and advance worker for state and nat. candidates, 1960s and 1970s; co-chmn. Reagan for Pres. Com., Dallas, 1968; mem. del. selection com. 3d Congl. Dist., mem. del.-at-large selection com. state conv., 1968-76; del. to dist. and state conv., Dallas, 1980; pres. Park Cities Republican Women's Club, 1966, 67; served on Presdl. Rank awards for Sr. Exec. Service, Dallas, 1983; pres. Pub. Affairs Luncheon Club, Dallas, 1965-66; pres. Dallas Health and Sci. Mus. Guild, mem. adv. com. Mus. Bd. Govs.; charter mem. Dallas chpt. Freedoms Found. at Valley Force; charter mem. Fair Campaign Practices Com.; bd. dirs. Rosalind Kress Haley Library, Northwood Inst. Mem. League of Rep. Women, Fgn. Policy Assn., Internat. Assn. Drilling Contractors, Am. League Lobbyists, Tex. Ind. Producers and Royalty Owners, Tex. State Soc., Coolidge Soc., English Speaking Union. Episcopalian. Clubs: Tex. Breakfast, Capitol Hill, Monday (Washington); Chaparral, Public Affairs Luncheon, Sci. Place (Dallas). Home: 6310A Bandera Dallas TX 75225

PHARO, MARK LANGSTON, jewelry company executive, jewelry designer; b. Dallas, May 12, 1955; s. Milam Bernard and Edith Gwendolyn (McRae) P.; m. Sandra Gail Thurlo, Aug. 18, 1979; 1 dau., Rachelle. Student Tex. Tech U., 1973-75; East Tex. State U., 1976. Vice pres. Internat. Diamonds, 1974-77; owner Internat. Gems, 1977-80; owner, pres. Pharo Fine Jewelry, Dallas, 1980—, Diamond Services Co. Inc., Dallas, 1982—. Bd. dirs. Dallas Civic Opera; del. Republican State Conv., 1976-83. All Univ. Weight Lifting and Wrestling champion Tex. Tech U., 1975. Mem. Dallas C. of C., Dallas Better Bus. Bur., Jewelry Security Alliance, Sigma. Episcopalian. Clubs: Pub. Affairs Luncheon, 24kt. (Dallas). Office: 17130 N Dallas Pkwy Suite 230 Dallas TX 75248

PHARR, DWIGHT DOUGLAS, SR., pharmacy administrator, pharmacy consultant, minister; b. Wurtzberg, Germany, July 16, 1952; (parents Am. citizens); s. George Thomas and Nellie (Scott) P.; m. Cindy Carol Jones, Dec. 31, 1973; children—Dwight Douglas, Jr., Cindy Michelle, Jonathan, Daniel. A.A. in Sci., N.E. Miss. Jr. Coll.; B.S. in Pharmacy, U. Miss. Registered pharmacist, Miss. Staff pharmacist Roy's prescriptions, Tupelo, Miss., 1976, Kilmichael Drugs, Kilmichael, Miss., 1976-77; dir. pharmacy Tishomingo City Hosp., Iuka, Miss., 1977—; substitute preacher Carters Chapel Ch., Booneville, Miss., 1984—. Deacon, Iuka Ch. of Christ, 1982—. Mem. Miss. Pharm. Assn., Miss. State Hosp. Pharm. Assn., Am. Soc. Hosp. Pharm., Rho Chi. Club: Tri State Bassmasters (asst. tour dir. 1985, treas. 1985) (Iuka). Avocations: fishing; hunting; aquariums. Home: Route 4 Box 890 Iuka MS 38852 Office: Tishomingo County Hosp 1410 W Quitman Iuka MS 38852

PHELAN, JOHNNY EUGENE, data processing executive; b. Borger, Tex., Nov. 6, 1942; s. John William and Lela Ordel (Selvidge) P.; B.B.A., W. Tex. State U., 1969; m. Tommye Kaye Simmons, Sept. 24, 1977; children—Deborah Lynn, Rebecca Jean, Michael Joe, Christopher Glen, Terry Duane. With Am. Nat. Bank, Amarillo, Tex., 1963-69, data processing officer, 1967-69; with Western Data Centers, Inc., Amarillo, 1969—, v.p. charge prodn., 1973-76, sr. v.p. prodn. and communication, 1976-83, exec. v.p., 1983—; adv. com. EDP, Tex. State Tech. Inst., Waco. Mem. Nat. Assn. Bank Servicers, Data Processing Mgmt. Assn. Mem. Ch. of God. Home: PO Box 548 Amarillo TX 79105 Office: PO Box 1308 Amarillo TX 79105

PHELAN, MARY ALICE BARRETT, medical center administrator; b. Cin., Jan. 19, 1943; d. William Joseph and Harriet Alice (Hogan) Barrett; m. William Joseph Phelan, Oct. 4, 1967 (dec. 1984); children—Pauline, William, Patricia Higgins, Michael, John, Thomas, Mary, Louise Smith, Michele Ross, Colleen Outlaw, Kevin, Kathleen Ward. A.B. in Polit. Sci., Trinity Coll., 1964; M.A. in Govt., Fla. State U., 1966. Dir. community relations St. Vincent's Med. Ctr., Jacksonville, Fla., 1984—. Author: Districting in Florida During the 1980's, 1981. Officer LWV, Fla., 1979-84; participant Leadership Jacksonville, 1983-84; bd. dirs. Downtown Devel. Authority, Jacksonville, 1979—. Mem. Fla. Hosp. Assn., Jacksonville Women's Network, Fla. Downtown Devel. Assn., Jacksonville C. of C. Democrat. Roman Catholic. Clubs: River (Jacksonville), Timuquana Country (Jacksonville), Ponte Verda (Fla.). Avocations: Swimming; tennis; reading. Home: 1025 Brierfield Dr Jacksonville FL 32205 Office: St Vincents Med Ctr 2565 Park St. PO Box 40341 Jacksonville FL 32203

PHELAN, WESLEY THOMAS, geologist; b. Fort Worth, Dec. 3, 1950; s. Arthur Thomas and Dorothy Jean Phelan; m. Deborah Kennemer, Nov. 25, 1978; children—Cameron Allen, Julia Louise. B.S., Tex. Christian U., 1982, B.A., 1973. Asst. advt. mgr. Mid Cities Daily News, Hurst, Tex., 1973-75; advt. mgr. News Tribune, Fort Worth, 1975-76; salesman Cockrell Printing, Fort Worth, 1976-78; geologist Command Energy Corp., Fort Worth, 1980-83; geologist Tex. Oil & Gas Corp., Fort Worth, 1983—; pres. Ju-Roo Petroleum Co., Fort Worth, 1972-73. Vice pres. Fort Worth Young Democrats, 1967-69. Recipient Miller Lite award Advt. Club Fort Worth, 1977. Mem. Am. Assn. Petroleum Geologists, Soc. Exploration Geophysicists, Fort Worth Geol. Soc., Dallas Geol. So., Soc. Profl. Well Log Analysts, Phi Delta Sigma. Republican. Methodist. Avocations: racquetball; golf. Home: 2220 Ashland St Fort Worth TX 76107 Office: Tex Oil and Gas Corp 200 W 7th St Suite 1200 Fort Worth TX 76102

PHELPS, ASHTON, JR., newspaper publisher; b. New Orleans, Nov. 4, 1945; s. Ashton and Jane Cary (George) P.; m. Mary Ella Sanders, Apr. 10, 1976; children—Cary Clifton, Mary Louise. B.A., Yale U., 1967; J.D., Tulane U., 1970. Trainee, Times-Picayune, New Orleans, 1970-71, asst. to pub., 1971-79, pres. and pub., 1979—. Bd. dirs. Bur. Govt. Research, New Orleans, 1973—; com; mem. Bus. Task Force on Edn., New Orleans, 1981—; bd. dirs. Council for a Better La., 1982—, Met. Area Com., New Orleans, 1983—; bd. trustees Ochsner Found. Hosp., New Orleans, 1982—; bd. dirs. So. Newspaper Pubs. Found., 1982, Pub. Affairs Research Council, 1982—, La. Children's Mus., 1983—, Metairie Park Country Day Sch., 1982—, Xavier U. La., 1979-82; deacon St. Charles Ave. Presbyn. Ch., 1981-82, now trustee. Mem. So. Newspaper Pubs. Assn. (dir. 1982-85), La. Press Assn. (dir.), Young Pres.'s Orgn., Order of the Coif. Presbyterian. Clubs: Boston, New Orleans Country, New Orleans Lawn Tennis, City. Avocations: tennis. Office The Times Picayune Pub Corp 3800 Howard Ave New Orleans LA 70140

PHELPS, C. PAUL, state agency secretary; b. Baton Rouge, Nov. 8, 1932; s. C. Paul and Auril (Williams) P.; m. Betty Halbert, Aug. 27, 1955; children—Andrea, Cynthia. B.A. in Econs., La. State U., 1957, M. Social Work, 1963. Cert. social worker, La. Various positions East Baton Rouge Parish Family Ct., 1957-67; various positions La. Dept. Corrections, 1967-81; program dir. Alliance House, Baton Rouge Mental Health Assn., 1981-84; sec. La. Dept. Pub. Safety & Corrections, Baton Rouge, 1984—; ct. expert witness U.S. Dist. Ct., Baton Rouge, 1981-84; cons. various archtl. firms, Baton Rouge, 1981-84. Mem. Gov.'s Prison Overcrowding Policy Task Force; mem. La. Commn. Law Enforcement and Adminstrn. of Criminal Justice; mem. adv. com. Edn. Handicapped Children. Named La. Social Worker of Yr., 1978. Mem. Nat. Council Crime and Delinquency, Am. Correctional Assn., Nat. Assn. Social Workers, Acad. Cert. Social Workers, La. Bd. Cert. Social Workers, State Bd. Cert. Social Work Examiners, Nat. Assn. Juvenile Court Judges, Assn. State Correctional Adminstrs., Kappa Sigma, Omega Chpt. Democrat. Episcopalian. Lodge: Masons. Avocations: flying; boating; duck hunting. Office: Dept Pub Safety and Corrections PO Box 94304 Capitol Sta Baton Rouge LA 70804-9304

PHELPS, HOLLY ALPINE, bibliographer; b. Trenton, Oct. 13, 1952; d. Girard William and Eugenia (Filbert) P.; m. Joel R. Gardner, July 7, 1980. B.A., Johns Hopkins U., 1974, M.L.A., 1977; M.L.S., UCLA, 1979. Library asst. Johns Hopkins U., Balt., 1974-75, circulation supr., 1975-76; asst. reference librarian UCLA, 1977-79, research asst., 1978-79; bibliographer 18th Century Short-Title Catalogue N.Am., Baton Rouge, 1980—. Copy editor (syllabus) Introduction to Bibliography, 1978. Mem. ALA, Assn. Coll. and Research Libraries, La. Assn. Coll. and Research Libraries, La. On-Line Assn., Friends Hist. Assn. Soc. Friends. Home: 1011 Forge Ave Baton Rouge LA 70808 Office: ESTC/NA Coll Arts and Scis La State Univ Baton Rouge LA 70803

PHILIPS, ALFRED MCKENZIE, college president; b. Normal, Ill., July 19, 1923; s. Alfred W. and Ruth (Cleland) P. B.S., Emporia State U., 1945, M.S., 1948; Ed.D., Wash. State U., 1958. Chmn. dept. physics, registrar Gray's Harbor Coll., Aberdeen, Wash., 1948-59, dean instrn., 1957-59; pres. Sheridan (Wyo.) Coll., 1959-62, Big Bend Coll., Moses Lake, Wash., 1962-66; vice chancellor Dallas County Jr. Coll. Dist., Dallas, 1966-69; pres. Tulsa Jr. Coll., 1969—; pres. Council North Central Community and Jr. Colls., 1979-80; chmn. Okla. Coll. and Univ. Pres. Council, 1975-83; bd. dirs. Am. Assn. Community and Jr. Colls., 1964-66, 77-80; mem. Okla. State Adv. Council Vo-Tech. Edn., 1971-76. Bd. dirs. Downtown Tulsa Unltd.; mem. Gov.'s Com. Sci. and Tech., 1983. Mem. Econ. Devel. Commn., 1977. Recipient Disting. Alumnus award Emporia State U., 1982. Office: Tulsa Jr Coll 6111 E Skelly Dr Suite #200 Tulsa OK 74135

PHILLABAUM, LESLIE ERVIN, editor; b. Cortland, N.Y., June 1, 1936; s. Vern Arthur and Beatrice Elizabeth (Butterfield) P.; m. Roberta Kimbrough Swarr, Mar. 17, 1962; children—Diane Melissa, Scott Christopher. B.S., Pa. State U., 1958, M.A., 1963. Editor Pa. State U. Press, 1961-63; editor-in-chief U. N.C. Press, 1963-70; asso. dir., editor La. State U. Press, Baton Rouge, 1970-75, dir., 1975—. Served to 1st lt. AUS, 1959-61. Mem. Assn. Am. Univ. Presses (dir. 1978-80, pres.-elect 1983-86, pres. 1984-86), Am. Hist. Assn., So. Hist. Assn., Orgn. Am. Historians, Acacia, Omicron Delta Kappa, Alpha Kappa Psi. Democrat. Home: 670 Burgin Ave Baton Rouge LA 70808 Office: La State U Press Baton Rouge LA 70893

PHILLIPS, CHARLES A. SPEAS, retired surgeon; b. Bonlee, N.C., Sept. 15, 1922; m. Olivia Womble Long, Mar. 27, 1971; m. Carol Huebner, Oct. 12, 1946 (div. 1968); children—Janet, Charles, Nancy, Elizabeth, Mary, Joan. B.S. in Physics, U. N.C., 1942; M.D., Northwestern U., 1947. Diplomate Am. Bd. Surgery. Instr. math. U. N.C., 1942-43, lectr. anatomy, 1957-58, clin. asst. prof. anatomy, 1959-62, instr. surgery, 1968, clin. asst. prof. surgery, 1969-72; intern Cook County Hosp., Chgo., 1946-47; resident in gen. surgery VA Hosp., Hines, Ill., 1950-52, resident in urology, 1953-54; chmn. dept. health edn., Sandhills Community Coll., Carthage, N.C., 1975-77; attending surgeon Moore Meml. Hosp., Pinehurst, N.C., 1954-80, chief surg. services, 1968-73, vice-chmn. staff, 1959, chief of staff, 1962, chief gen. surgery sect., 1979-80, courtesy staff, 1981—; attending physician St. Joseph of Pines Hosp., Southern Pines, N.C., 1954-60, cons., 1961—; med. examiner FAA; field rep. Joint Commn. on Accreditation of Hosps., 1980-83. Pres. Pinehurst Forum, 1972, mem. program com., 1963-64, chmn., 1965-66, 66-67; vice chmn. ARC, 1958-61; pres. Sandhills Music Assn., 1962-63; bd. dirs. Sandhills Art Council, 1980—; candidate Moore County Bd. Edn., 1964; commr. Moore County, 1980-84, chmn. bd., 1980-82. Served to lt. (j.g.) USN, 1947-50. Fellow ACS (state adv. com., 1974—, com. on applicants 1970—), N.C. Surg. Assn. (sec.-treas. 1965-70, pres. 1980), Hines Surg. Assn., Charles B. Puestow Surg. Soc., Karl A. Meyer Surg. Soc., Moore County Med. Soc. (v.p. 1957, pres. 1958), 5th Dist. Med. Soc. (sec. 1958-64, pres. 1966, vice counselor 1964-67), N.C. Med. Soc., AMA, Moore County Mental Health Assn. (pres. 1958-61, dir.-at-large 1962-64, N.C. Mental Health Assn. (state dir. 1959-64, regional v.p. 1961), Phi Beta Kappa, Alpha Epsilon Delta. Republican. Presbyterian. Clubs: Country of N.C., Pinehurst Country. Lodge: Kiwanis. Contbr. articles to profl. jours. Office: PO Box 430 Pinehurst NC 28374

PHILLIPS, CHARLTON RAY, geophysical contractor; b. McAdams, Miss., Apr. 22, 1940; s. Charlton Festus and Edna Hildred (Armstrong) P.; B.S. in Production Mgmt. and Math., U. Southwestern La., 1963; m. Cindy Ellen Segraves, July 25, 1964; children—Charlton Allen, Christopher Matthew. With Seiscom Delta, Inc., Jackson, Miss., 1964-72; co-founder, pres., chief exec. officer Gephys. Field Surveys, Inc., Jackson, 1972—, prin. organizer Jackson Seismic Processing and Southeastern Seismic Data subs. Geophys. Field Surveys, Inc. Mem. Jackson Geophys. Soc. (past pres.), Internat. Soc. Exploration Geophysicists, Miss. Geol. Soc., N. Am. Hunting Club, Nat. Rifle Assn. Methodist. Home: 250 Sundial Rd Madison MS 39110 Office: PO Box 12304 Jackson MS 39211

PHILLIPS, CLINTON A., university administrator, consultant; b. Easton, Mass., Apr. 10, 1925; s. Edward Clinton and Mathilde Phillips; m. Julia Elizabeth Herbert, Nov. 12, 1953; children—Lauralee, Edward Clinton. A.B., Baldwin-Wallace Coll., 1949; Ph.D., Vanderbilt U., 1956. Asst. prof. U. Tenn., Knoxville, 1954-58, prof., assoc. dean, 1958-67; prof. Tex. A&M U., Coll. Sta., 1967-85, dept. head fin., 1969-77, interim dean, assoc. dean coll. bus., 1978-80, dean faculties, assoc. provost, 1980—. Co-author: Economics: Principles, Practices and Perspectives, 1957; also articles and revs. Active City Adv. Com. Mem. Am. Assn. Colls. Home: 1704 Glade College Station TX 77840 Office: Tex A&M U Dean Faculties College Station TX 77843

PHILLIPS, DONALD HERMAN, physicist; b. Knoxville, Tenn., Mar. 10, 1941; s. Sanford Murphy and Ruth R. (Reagan) P.; m. Andrea Lane Wallace, June 14, 1959 (div. Feb. 1972); children—Donna L., Deborah G.; Jan D. McQurk, July 14, 1973; children—Jenifer C., Claiborn L. B.S. in Physics, Tenn. Poly. Inst., 1963; M.S. in Physics, Va. Poly. Inst., 1968, Ph.D. in Physics, 1971. Research scientist NASA, Hampton, Va., 1963—; vis. scholar Harvard U., Cambridge, Mass., 1980-81. Contbr. articles to profl. jours. Cons. CARE, Norfolk, Va., 1978-80. Thompson fellow Langley Research Ctr., Hampton, Va., 1980. Mem. Am. Phys. Soc., Am. Chem. Soc. (bd. dirs. 1985—), Sigma Pi Sigma. Office: NASA Langley Research Ctr mail stop 234 Hampton VA 23665

PHILLIPS, DONALD RAY, landscape architect; b. Wilmington, N.C., July 19, 1950; s. Bennie Battle and Norma (Lawler) P.; m. Vicky Young, Feb. 6, 1971; 1 child, Benjamin Young. B.Landscape Architecture, U. Ga., 1975. Registered landscape architect, Ala. Owner, Tinga Landscape Co., Muscle Shoals, Ala., 1970—. Recipient Nat. Landscape award Am. Nurserymen Assn., 1972, 1st place Urban Improvement award Fed. Transit Systems, 1974. Mem. Am. Soc. Landscape Architects (St. Gerrad award 1980, Honor award 1984), AIA (assoc.). Republican. Avocations: golf; fencing. Office: Tinga Landscape Co PO Box 2365 Muscle Shoals AL 35660

PHILLIPS, EARL NORFLEET, JR., financial company executive; b. High Point, N.C.; May 5, 1940; s. Earl Norfleet Phillips and Lillian Jordan; m. Sarah Boyle, Oct. 19, 1971; children—Courtney Dorsett, Jordan Norfleet. B.S. in Bus. Adminstrn., U. N.C., 1962; M.B.A., Harvard U., 1965. Security analyst Wertheim & Co., N.Y.C., 1965-67; exec. v.p. Factors Inc., High Point, N.C., 1967-71, exec. v.p. First Factors Corp., High Point, 1972-83, pres., 1983—; dir. Process Systems Inc., Styrex, Inc. Trustee U. N.C., Chapel Hill, 1983-87, bd. dirs. N.C. Bus. Found.; mem. N.C. Econ. Devel. Bd., Raleigh, N.C., 1984-87. Named Young Man of Yr., High Point Jaycees, 1971; named One of Five Outstanding Young Men, N.C. Jaycees, 1971. Mem. Nat. Comml. Fin. Assn. (bd. dirs.). Clubs: The Brook (N.Y.C.); Country of N.C. (Pinehurst); Willow Creek, String and Splinter (High Point). Lodge: Gorgons Head. Office: First Factors Corp 101 S Main St High Point NC 27261

PHILLIPS, JAMES ALLEN, clergyman; b. Monahans, Tex., Aug. 21, 1952; s. James Allen and Margeret (Webb) P.; m. Marcella Darlene Zachry, Nov. 24, 1972; 1 child, Amber Mashea. Assoc. in Bibl. Studies, Nazarene Bible Coll., Colorado Springs, Colo., 1980; student U. Colo., 1981. Ordained to ministry Ind. Holiness Ch., 1985. Registered evangelist Ch. of Nazarene, Colorado Springs, 1979-81; assoc. pastor Trinity Ch. of Nazarene, Abilene, Tex., 1982-83, Moore Ch. of Nazarene, Okla., 1984; founder. dir. S.O.L.O. Sch. Ministry, Moore, 1985—. Served with USN, 1971-77. Mem. Am. Assn. Counseling and Devel., Wesleyan Theol. Soc. Avocations: technical rock climbing; ice climbing; mountaineering. Home and Office: 616 S W 8th St Moore OK 73160

PHILLIPS, JAMES DICKSON, JR., federal judge; b. Scotland County, N.C., Sept. 23, 1922; s. James Dickson and Helen (Shepherd) P.; B.S. cum laude, Davidson Coll., 1943; J.D., U. N.C., 1948; m. Jean Duff Nunalee, July 16, 1960; children—Evelyn Phillips, James Dickson, III, Elizabeth Duff, Ida Wills. Admitted to N.C. bar; asst dir. Inst. Govt., Chapel Hill, N.C., 1948-49; partner firm Phillips & McCoy, Laurinburg, N.C., 1949-55, Sanford, Phillips, McCoy & Weaver, Fayetteville, N.C., 1955-60; from asst. prof. to prof. law U. N.C., 1960-78, dean Sch. Law, 1964-74; circuit judge U.S. Ct. Appeals, 4th Circuit, 1978—. Mem. N.C. Wildlife Resources Commn., 1961-63; mem. N.C. Cts. Commn., 1963-75, also vice chmn.; chmn. N.C. Bd. Ethics, 1977-78. Served with parachute inf. U.S. Army, 1943-46. Decorated Bronze Arrowhead, Bronze Star, Purple Heart; recipient John J. Parker Meml. award; Thomas Jefferson award. Mem. Am. Law Inst., N.C. Bar Assn. Democrat. Presbyterian. Home: 529 Caswell Rd Chapel Hill NC 27514 Office: PO Box 3617 Durham NC 27702*

PHILLIPS, JAMES WILLIAM, data processing educator, consultant; b. Logansport, Ind., Nov. 6, 1947; s. William B. and Rosalie (Kruzick) P.; m. Karen Casteel, July 8, 1938. B.S.I.M., Purdue U., 1972; M.S., U. Ky., 1985. Programmer, systems analyst Purdue U., West Lafayette, Ind., 1965-77; assoc. prof. data processing U Ky. Community Coll., Lexington, 1978—; cons. in field. U.K. Summer Teaching Improvement fellow, 1979. Mem. Assn. for Computing Machinery. Contbr. articles to profl. jours. Address: Univ KY Lexington Community Coll Lexington KY 40506

PHILLIPS, JAQUITA DEANN, marketing executive; b. Berryville, Ark., May 2, 1954; d. Thomas Martin and Norma Jeannine (Hale) P. B.A., U. Ark., 1976. Account exec. Ark. Democrat, Little Rock, 1976; news artist, reporter Sta. KARK-TV, Little Rock, 1976-78, asst. promotion mgr., 1978-79; dir. pub. relations United Way, Little Rock, 1979-85; mktg. exec. St. Vincent Infirmary, Little Rock, 1985—; cons. pub. relations, non-profit agys. Nat. press sec. Young Democrats Am., 1981-83, state press sec. Young Democrats Ark., 1983-85; past sec. Pulaski County Young Democrats. Recipient Radio Commls. spl. award United Way Am., 1979. Mem. Pub. Relations Soc. Am., Internat. Assn. Bus. Communicators, Am. Soc. Tng. and Devel., Nat. Ctr. Citizen Involvement (assoc.), Pi Beta Phi. Methodist. Home: 6412 Kenwood St Little Rock AR 72207 Office: 2 St Vincent Circle Little Rock AR 72205

PHILLIPS, JAYNE LYNNE, retail executive; b. Louisville, July 17, 1946; d. Robert Earl and Loraine Elizabeth (Zoeller) Riddle; m. Richard Kenneth Phillips, June 7, 1970; children—Carter Russell, Clayton Johnson. B.A., Randolph-Macon Woman's Coll., 1968. Trainee Rich's Dept. Store, Atlanta, 1970-71, asst. buyer, 1971-73, buyer, 1974-79, divisional mdse. mgr., 1980-83, divisional v.p. merchandising, 1984, divisional v.p. stores, store mgr. Lenox Sq., 1985—, symphony coordinator Young People's Concerts, Rich's Atlanta, 1984—. Mem. Randolph-Macon Woman's Coll. Alumni Assn., Buckhead aBus. Assn., Women's C. of C. Republican. Presbyterian. Avocations: swimming; tennis; gardening. Office: Richs Lenox Sq 3393 Peachtree St NE Atlanta GA 30326

PHILLIPS, JOHN GURLEY, oil company executive; b. Camden, Ark., Sept. 8, 1922; s. John Gurley and Thalia (DuBose) P.; B.S., U. Ark., 1948; m. Evelyn Richards, Dec. 16, 1950; children—Fran Evelyn (Mrs. Roger Alan Grayson), Cherry Thalia (Mrs. John G. Scott). Staff accountant Peat, Marwick, Mitchell & Co., 1948-51; with La. Land & Exploration Co., 1951—, exec. v.p., 1962-67, dir., 1962—, pres., 1967-74, chief exec. officer, 1972-83, chmn. bd., 1974-84; dir. Bank of N.Y., Allis-Chalmers Corp., Delta Air Lines, Inc., Whitney Nat. Bank, Travelers Corp.; mem. nat. adv. bd. First Comml. Bank, Little Rock; former mem. Nat. Petroleum Council; former trustee Com. Econ. Devel.; hon. mem. bd. dirs. Am. Petroleum Inst. Vice pres. mktg., nat. exec. bd. Boy Scouts Am.; mem. Tulane Bd. Adminstrs.; former trustee Tax Found., Inc. Served to 1st lt. USAAF, 1942-45. Mem. Am. Inst. C.P.A.s Clubs: Country, Boston, Pickwick (New Orleans); Racquet and Tennis (N.Y.C.); Wildcat Cliffs Country (Highlands, N.C.). Home: 2524 St Charles Ave New Orleans LA 70130 Office: PO Box 60350 New Orleans LA 70160

PHILLIPS, JOSEPH HOYTE, optometrist; b. Odessa, Tex., Nov. 6, 1956; s. Hoyte Eugene and Mary Nell (Foshee) P. B.S., Okla. Bapt. U., 1979; student Oklahoma City U., 1977; O.D., Northeastern State U., 1983. Optometrist specializing in contact lenses Omni Park Eye Ctr., Oklahoma City, 1983—; clin. investigator FDA, 1983—. Contbg. author: Rx For Success, 1983. Bd. dirs. Okla. Soc. to Prevent Blindness, 1984—. Mem. Am. Optometric Assn. (polit. action com. 1979—, mem. contact lenses sect.), Oklahoma City C. of C., Canterbury Choral Soc., Okla. Optometric Assn., Central Okla. Optometric Assn. (pres. 1985—), Soc. Contact Lens Specialists (research award 1984), Heart of Am Contact Lens Soc. (grantee 1981, 82), Beta Sigma Kappa. Republican. Episcopalian. Club: Young Men's Dinner. Home: 6500 NW Grand Blvd Condo 185 Oklahoma City OK 73116 Office: Omni Park Eye Ctr 5000 NW Expressway Oklahoma City OK 73132

PHILLIPS, KAY ELLEN, interior designer; b. Elkhart, Ind., Oct. 9, 1945; d. Charles Raymon and Bernetha (Threlkeld) Cook; m. Ronald Lee Phillips, Aug. 25, 1967; children—Eric Wayne, Dana Lynne. B.A., Ariz. State U., 1967, M.A., 1970; color analysis cert., Beauty for All Seasons, Orlando, Fla., 1983; postgrad. in interior design Seminole Community Coll., 1984—. Color analyst, ind. rep. Beauty for All Seasons, 1983—; interior designer Anne Spalla Interiors, Inc., Longwood, Fla., 1985—. Mem. assoc. bd. Fla. Symphony, Orlando, 1980—, sec., 1984; vol. Additions program Orange County Sch. System, Orlando, 1980—. Recipient Service award Orange County Sch. System, 1980-85. Mem. Pi Lambda Theta, Phi Theta Kappa. Republican. Presbyterian. Club: Semoran Jr. Woman's (treas. 1977-79). Avocations: travel; gourmet cooking; aerobics; reading. Home: 8755 Larwin Ln Orlando FL 32817

PHILLIPS, MICHAEL DON, optometrist; b. Wichita Falls, Tex., June 15, 1954; s. Lemuel Harrison and Opal Oleta (Robertson) P.; m. Cirrie Ann Lomax, Aug. 18, 1974; children—Nichole, Jennifer, Alisha, Shelly. Assoc. Sci., Lubbock Christian Coll., 1974; B.S., U. Houston, 1977; O.D., 1977. Optometrist pvt. practice, Pittsburg, Tex., 1977-84; pres. Optometric Relief Service, Carrollton, Tex., 1984—; co-owner Primary Eye Care, Dalals, 1984—. Chmn. Camp County Tourism Com., Pittsburg, 1982-84. Pittsburg Rotary fellow, 1983. Mem. Camp County C. of C. (dir. 1978-84, pres. 1983-84). Republican. Mem. Ch. of Christ. Lodge: Rotary. Avocations: travel; skiing. Office: Primary Eye Care 13131 Preston Rd Dallas TX 75240

PHILLIPS, MICHAEL LYNN, business official; b. Erwin, Tenn., June 18, 1952; s. M. L. and Margaret Virginia (Jones) P.; B.S.M.E., Tenn. Tech. U., 1976, M.A. in Bus. Adminstrn. (Citizens Bank scholar), 1978. Night clk. Clinchfield YMCA, Erwin, 1970; machine operator Crystal Ice Coal and Laundry, Erwin, 1970; with engring. dept. Union Carbide Corp., Oak Ridge, 1971-72, 73-74; salesman Southwestern Co., Nashville, 1975; report and instrns. manual writer Citizens Bank, Cookville, Tenn., 1977-78; team mgr. Buckeye Cellulose Corp., Memphis, 1978-80, team mgr., Huntsville, Ala., 1980, contract mfg. mgr., 1980-83; sales rep. Procter & Gamble, Dallas, 1983—. Youth chmn. Snodgrass for Gov. Tenn., 1970; coordinator ptnrs. for Christ class 1st United Meth. Ch., Lewisville, Tex., 1984—. Mem. ASME, Nat. Soc. Profl. Engrs., Order of Engrs., Tenn. Tech. Alumni Assn. (nat. dir., pres. North Ala. chpt. 1981-82), Huntsville C. of C. (free enterprise day instr. and luncheon com. 1981-83), Theta Tau, Tau Beta Pi, Pi Tau Sigma, Kappa Mu Epsilon, Phi Kappa Phi, Omicron Delta Kappa. Republican. Home and office: PO Box 1910 Dallas TX 75221

PHILLIPS, RAYMOND FOY, real estate company executive; b. Vernon, Tex., July 26, 1935;; s. Robert Raymond and Margie Fay (Fowler) P.; B.S. in Chem. Engring., Tex. Tech. U., 1957; m. Maidie Bassett Baldwin, Aug. 28, 1960; children—Maidie Bland, Robert Foy, Fowler Scott. Engaged in new product and new venture mktg. research Humble Oil and Refining Co., Baytown, Tex., Houston and N.Y.C., 1957-63; petroleum product mktg., advt. research Internat. Petroleum, Coral Gables, Fla. and Bogotá, Colombia, 1963-65; chem. and environ. resource adviser Houston Research Inst., 1965-67; with Pennzoil Co., Houston, 1967-74, dir. land and water resources div., 1970, 71, with new products and new ventures, 1972-74; pres. Mondo Chem. & Supply Co., Houston, 1974-76, R. Foy Phillips & Assocs., real estate, Houston, 1977—, Phillips Energy Resources, Inc., Ranch Country Products, Inc., Phoenix Rockport. Mem. Chem. Mktg. Research Assn., S.W. Chem. Assn., Soc. Petroleum Engrs. Contbr. articles to profl. jours. Home: 5603 Tatteridge Houston TX 77069 Office: 14405 Walters Rd Houston TX 77014

PHILLIPS, RICHARD WILLIAM, optometrist; b. Pittsfield, Ill., Oct. 4, 1952; s. George Richard and Rebecca Rose (Brumett) P.; m. Janie Rhea Wexler, Aug. 30, 1975; children—Melissa Rhea, Richard Jerome. Student U. South, 1971, East Tenn. State U., 1972; B.S. in Biology, Milligan Coll., 1974; O.D., So. Coll. Optometry, 1978. Licensed to practice optometry, 1978. Assoc. Gaby & Parris PC, Johnson City, Tenn., 1978-80; gen. practice optometry, Gray, Tenn., 1980-84; ptnr. Wilson Eye Clinic, Johnson City, 1985—. Pres. Johnson City Community Theatre, 1981-83, 85—, treas. 1984-85. Served to capt. USAFR, 1980-83. Mem. N.E. Tenn. Optometric Soc. (pres. 1980-81, 85—), Tenn. Optometric Assn., Am. Optometric Assn. Avocations: acting, directing. Home: 1032 Grace Dr Johnson City TN 37601 Office: Wilson Eye Clinic 118 E Watauga Ave Johnson City TN 37601

PHILLIPS, THELMA, library administrator; b. York County, S.C., Mar. 27, 1924; d. Adam I. and Maggie (Falls) McDaniel; m. Paul Phillips, Aug. 10, 1947; children—Paula Lorraine, Elaine Freddye, Paul, Janet Yvonne. A.B. in Social Scis. N.C. Coll., Durham, 1945; B.L.S., U. Chgo., 1946; postgrad., Tuskegee (Ala.) Inst., 1947-48, Reference librarian Tuskegee Inst., 1946-50; librarian hosp. VA Hosp., Tuskegee, 1950-52; librarian St. Mary's High Sch., Fredericksburg, Tex., 1964-66; librarian County Gillespie, Fredericksburg, 1966-73; extension coordinator Arlington (Tex.) Pub. Library, 1973-76, assoc. dir., 1977—; workshop presenter Central Tex. Library System, 1984; steering com. Tex. Gov.'s Conf., Austin, 1973; project dir. Library Vol. Program, 1980-81; del. White House Conf. Libraries Info. Services, Washington, 1979; adv. bd. Tex. Library Systems Act., 1969-74. Project dir. City of Arlington City-Wide Vol. Program, 1983-84. Named The Arlington Woman, Biog. Feature, 1974. Mem. Southwest Library Assn. (developed Southwest cultures bibliographies 1975-76), ALA, Tex. Library Assn. (Librarian Yr. 1971, pub. library div. pres. 1973-74, dist. 7 chmn. 1979-80, planning. com. 1980-81), Arlington C. of C., Nat. Assn. Vol. Adminstrn., Nat. Conf. Citizen Involvement. Clubs: Soroptimist (Arlington); Democratic Women (Fredericksburg). Home: 1700 Meadowlane Terr Fort Worth TX 76112 Office: Arlington Pub Library 101 E Abram St Arlington TX 76010

PHILLIPS, WADE TERRY, personnel official; b. Lebanon, Tenn., Oct. 31, 1950; s. James Edward and Joy Evelyn (Trapp) P.; m. Julie Nellene Belcher, Dec. 29, 1972. B.S. in Psychology, Middle Tenn. State U., 1973. M.A. in Psychology, 1976. Employee relations mgr. Carrier Air Conditioning Co., McMinnville, Tenn., 1977-78; employee relations coordinator Heil Co., Ft. Payne, Ala., 1978-79, indsl. relations mgr., 1980-81; dir. personnel Coyne Cylinder Co., Huntsville, Ala., 1981-84; personnel mgr. Chromalox-Emerson Electric Co., Murfreesboro, Tenn., 1984—. Served to 2d lt. U.S. Army, 1974-75. Decorated Nat. Def. ribbon, Armed Forces Res. medal; recipient cert. recognition Ala. Rehab. Assn., cert. appreciation Huntsville ARC. Mem. Am. Soc. Personnel Adminstrn., Indsl. Mgrs. Assn., Personnel Mgrs. Assn.

PHILLIPS, WILLIAM AULT, pediatric dentist; b. Louisville, June 28, 1946; s. Clyde Custer, II, and Geraldine (Ault) P.; m. Karen Walters, June 28, 1969; children—Taylor Brett, Hayden Reign. D.M.D., U. Ky., 1971; M.S.D., Boston U., 1973. Diplomate Am. Acad. Pedodontics; mem. Am. Bd. Pedodontics. Pvt. practice pediatric dentistry, Louisville, 1973—; clin. instr. U. Louisville, 1973-78. Trustee Council Retarded Citizens, 1978-81; dir. Community Coordinated Child Care, 1980—. Fellow Am. Acad. Pedodontics, Am. Soc. Dentistry for Children, Pierre Fauchard Acad. Republican. Presbyterian. Clubs: Louisville Boat, Hobie Cat Fleet. Home: 2406 Henley Ct Louisville KY 40222 Office: 1001 Dupont Sq N Louisville KY 40207 also 5512 Bardstown Rd Fern Creek KY 40291

PHILLIPS, WILLIAM SPURGEON, police official; b. Durham, N.C., Aug. 19, 1931; s. Ewart Spurgeon and Edna Gwendolyn (Farmer) P.; m. Sigrid Elsa Hagen, Dec. 3, 1970. Student Va. State Police Tng. Sch., 1953, FBI Nat. Acad., 1975; A.A.S. summa cum laude, Southwest Va. Community Coll., 1977. State police trooper Va. State Police, Richmond, 1952-69; pub. safety adviser U.S. Dept. State/AID, South Vietnam, 1969-73; chief of police Abingdon, Va., 1973—. Pres., Tri State Crime Clinic, Abingdon, 1977-78. Served with USCG, 1949-52, USMCR, 1957-61. Named Policeman of Yr., Exchange Club of Williamsburg, Va., 1964; recipient Nat. Police Honor medal, 1970, J. Edgar Hoover Meml. award, 1974, Patriotic Activities award Congl. Medal of Honor Soc., 1985. Mem. Va. Assn. Chiefs of Police, Internat. Assn. Chiefs Police, FBI Nat. Acad. Assocs. (state pres. 1980-81), Va. State Police Alumni Assn. (div. rep. 1975—), Hargrave Mil. Acd. Almuni Assn. (pres. 1977-78), Am Legion, Nat. Rifle Assn. Anglican. Lodge: Masons. Avocations: U.S. military history; Appalachian folk music. Home: 445 Circle Dr Abingdon VA 24210 Office: Police Dept Abingdon VA 24210

PHILPOT, EDWARD JERRY, personnel administrator; b. Heidrick, Ky., Oct. 2, 1947; s. Edward B. and Dorothy (Main) P.; m. Brenda Bond, Apr. 19, 1973; 1 child, Jonathan Edward. A.B. in Polit. Sci., Eastern Ky. U., 1970; M.A. in Edn., Counseling and Psychology, Union Coll., 1972; M. Pub. Adminstrn. and Personnel, Ky. State U., 1975. Asst. pub. hearing officer Ky. Dept. Econ. Security, Frankfort, 1972-73; rep. claims Fed. Social Security Adminstrn., Frankfort, 1973-74; personnel officer Ky. Dept. Human Resources, Frankfort, 1974-78; mgr. indsl. relations Environdyne Coal, Harlan, Ky., 1978-79; mgr. br. Ky. Dept. Human Resources, Frankfort, 1979-81; personnel adminstr. Govt. Services Ctr., Frankfort, 1981—. Mem. Mil. Fraternity, Associated Industries of Ky. (bd. dirs.) Lodge: Lions. Home: 193 Blueridge Dr Frankfort KY 40601 Office: Govt Services Ky State U 4 W Acad Service Bldg Frankfort KY 40601

PHIPPS, WILLIAM EUGENE, educator religion and philosophy; b. Waynesboro, Va., Jan. 28, 1930; s. Charles Henry and Ruth LaVell (Patterson) P.; m. Martha Ann Swezey, Dec. 21, 1954; children—Charles, Anna, Ruth. B.S., Davidson Coll., 1949; M.Div., Union Theol. Sem., 1952; M.A., U. Hawaii, 1963; Ph.D., U. St. Andrews (Scotland), 1954; hon. M.H.L., Davis and Elkins Coll., 1972. Ordained to ministry Presbyterian Ch., 1952. Prof. Bible Peace Coll., Raleigh, N.C., 1954-56; prof. religion and philosophy Davis and Elkins Coll., Elkins, W.Va., 1956—, pres. faculty assn., 1973-75. Author: Recovering Biblical Sensuousness, 1975; Influential Theologians on Wo/Man, 1980; Encounter through Questioning Paul, 1983; Paul against Supernaturalism, 1986. Recipient Scholarly and Creative Accomplishments award Davis and Elkins Coll., 1980. Mem. Am. Acad. Religion. Democrat. Home: Lincoln Ave Elkins WV 26241 Office: Davis and Elkins Coll Elkins WV 26241

PHUNG, DOAN LIEN, nuclear engineer; b. Battrang, Vietnam, Jan. 1, 1940; came to U.S., 1958, naturalized, 1975; s. Thanh Van and Phong Thi (Le) P.; m. Thu Le Doan, June 28, 1970; children—LiLi, GiGi. B.S. in Physics, Fla. State U., 1961, B.S. in Math., 1961; M.S. in Physics, MIT, 1963, M.S. in Nuclear Engring., 1963, Sc.D. in Nuclear Engring., 1972. Registered profl. engr., Pa. Scientist, Dalat (Vietnam) Research Inst., 1964-67; engr., project mgr. United Engrs. and Constructors, Inc., Phila., 1967-72, sr. cons., 1972-75; chief scientist Oak Ridge Associated Univs., 1975-78, sr. scientist, 1978-83; pres. Profl. Analysis, Inc., Oak Ridge, 1983—. Vice pres. Aid to the Children of Vietnam, San Jose, Calif., 1972-75. Mem. Am. Nuclear Soc., AAAS, N.Y. Acad. Sci., Sigma Xi, Phi Beta Kappa, Phi Kappa Phi, Pi Mu Epsilon, Sigma Pi Sigma. Contbr. over 70 sci. articles to profl. publs. Office: 11 Brewster Ln Oak Ridge TN 37830

PICARD, THOMAS JOSEPH, JR., manufacturers representative; b. Boston, Dec. 7, 1933; s. Thomas Joseph and Bertha Mildred (Brightman) P.; B.S. in Mech. Engring., U. Mass., 1959; M.B.A., Rollins Coll., 1985; m. Renee E. Coulmas, Aug. 20, 1977; children by previous marriage—T. Gerald, Pamela P. Mfg. engr. Gen. Electric Co., 1959-60; application and sales engr. Masoneilan Div., McGraw Edison Co., 1960-65; v.p. M.D. Duncan & Assocs., Inc., Orlando, Fla., 1965-74, pres., 1974—. Pres., Brookshire Sch. PTA, Winter Park, Fla., 1969-71, Glenridge Jr. High Sch. PTA, Winter Park, 1972-73; v.p. Winter Park Little League, 1968; mem. Orange County Republican Exec. Com., 1973. Served with AUS, 1953-55. Named Exec. of Month, Orlando Area, Sta. WDBO, June 1977; profl. tennis umpire. Mem. Instrument Soc. Am. (sr.; chmn. 1980, dist. v.p. 1981-83, nominating com., chmn. dist. honors and awards com., mem. nat. edn. com., profl. cert. com., parliamentarian 1984-86, dir. edn. dept. 1985-87), U.S. Tennis Assn. Conglist. Clubs: Rotary Orange County East (pres. 1972-73), Masons.

PICKARD, DORIS ANN, property management executive; b. Atlanta, Aug. 20, 1937; d. Theodore Roosevelt and Ola Braye (Happerfield) Ahern; children—Cheryl, Charles, Thomas, Glenn. Student Barry Coll., 1958-60. Instr., So Bell Co., 1969-71; office mgr. Seidman & Seidman, 1971-78; pres. Adminstrv. Design, 1978-80; mgr. Racal Milgo, 1980-83; chief adminstr. Sengra Corp., 1983— (all Miami, Fla.). Author: (seminar) How To Start Your Own Small Business, 1979. Task force chmn. Dade County Commn. on Status of Women, 1982; founder pres. Human Resource Devel., 1982—. Mem. Am. Bus. Women Assn. (bull. chmn. 1976), Nat. Assn. Women Bus. Owners (legis. chmn. 1979-80). Democrat. Baptist. Home: 10463 SW 124th Pl Miami FL 33186 Office: Sengra Corp 6843 Main St Miami FL 33014

PICKARD, MYRNA RAE, college dean; b. Sulphur Springs, Tex., Oct. 10, 1935; d. George Wallace and Ellie (Williams) Swindell; m. Bobby Ray Pickard, 1957; 1 child, Bobby Dale. B.S., Tex. Wesleyan Coll., 1957, M. Ed., 1964; M.S., Tex. Women's U., 1974; Ed. D., Nova U., 1976. Instr. John Peter Smith Hosp., Ft. Worth, 1956-58; Pub. Health Nurse Forest County Health Dept., Hattiesburg, Miss., 1958-60; asst. nurse adminstr. John Peter Smith Hosp. Sch. of Nursing, Ft. Worth, 1960-70, nurse adminstr., 1970-73; dean Arlington Sch. of Nursing, Tex., 1971—; cons. Kuwait U., 1983, Southwestern Coll., Keene, Tex., 1984. Midwestern U., Wichita Falls, Tex., 1984, Cath. U., Ponce, P.R., 1984. Contbr. articles to profl. jours. Bd. dirs., mem. exec. com. Multiple Sclerosis Soc., Tarrant County, Tex., 1978—; mem. adv. com. for health program Southwest Adventist Coll., Keene, 1982—; chmn. by-laws com. So. Regional Edn. Council on Nursing, 1983—; pres.-elect Tex. League for Nursing, 1985. Mem. Am. Nurse's Assn., Nat. League for Nursing, Am. Rural Health Assn. (editorial bd., 1985), Nat. Identification Program for Women in Higher Edn., Sigma Theta Tau. Methodist. Avocations: jogging; gardening. Home: 8301 Anglin Dr Fort Worth TX 76119 Office: Univ Tex at Arlington Sch of Nursing Box 19407 Arlington TX 76019

PICKARD, TERESA JEAN, nurse; b. Oklahoma City, Aug. 29, 1952; d. James Henry and Naomi Bess (Tharp) P. B.S.N., Central State U., Edmond, Okla., 1976. R.N., Okla. Nursing asst. Edmond Meml. Hosp., 1972-74; medication technician Baptist Med. Ctr., Oklahoma City, 1974-76; staff/charge nurse St. Anthony Hosp., Oklahoma City, 1976—, preceptor, 1981—; instr. CPR, ARC, Oklahoma City, 1983—. Scholar Wagner High Sch. and RN Club, Clark AFB, Philippines, 1970. Mem. Okla. Students Nurses Assn. (treas. 1972-73), Central State U. Nursing Club, Mothers Against Drunk Drivers, Central State U. Nursing Alumni Assn.

PICKARD, WILLIAM CHARLES, oil company executive; b. Miles City, Mont., Feb. 26, 1939; s. Claud Dennis and Violet (Stepher) P.; m. Margot R. Ames; children—Steven, Alison, Dean. B.S. in Petroleum Engring., Mont. Sch. Mines, 1962; Hon. Degree in Petroleum Engring., Mont. Tech. Inst., 1978. Registered profl. engr., Colo. Field engr. Johnston Testers, Casper, Wyo., 1962-63; drilling engr. Signal Drilling Co., Denver, 1963-68; area mgr. Brinkerhoff Drilling Co., Denver, 1968-73; pres. Eastman Whipstock, Houston, 1973-83; pres., chief exec. officer Prodn. Operators, Houston, 1983—. Mem. Soc. Petroleum Engrs., Petroleum Equipment Suppliers Assn. Presbyterian.

PICK DE WEISS, SUSAN EMILY, social psychologist, educator, researcher; b. Mexico City, July 31, 1952; d. Richard Ludwig and Lore (Steiner) Pick; m. Jaime Weiss, Aug. 19, 1972; children—Daniel, Arturo, Sonia. B.S. in Social Psychology with honors, London Sch. Econs., U. London, 1975, Ph.D. in Social Psychology with honors, 1978. Prof. social psychology U. Mexico, Mexico City, 1978—, head dept., 1981-84; dir. Transnat. Family Research Inst. Mex., 1985—; cons. Secretaria de Hacienda y Crédito Pblico, 1980-81, Secretaria de Programación y Presupuesto, 1980-81, Instituto Mexicano de Psiquiatría, 1982-85. Editor: Revista de la Asociación Latinoamericana de Psicología Social, 1980-85. Author: Estudio Social Psicológico de la Planificación Familiar, 1979; Como Investigar en Ciencias Sociales, 1980. Author articles in field. Research grantee Ford Found., 1976-78, Conacyt, Mex., 1979, Interam. Bank for Devel., 1981, Panam. Health Orgn., 1986—. Mem. Am Psychol. Assn., Interam. Soc. Psychology, London Sch. Econs. Soc. in Mex. (founder), Asociación Mexicana de Psicología Social (founder), Population Assn. Am., Asociación Mexicana de Psicología, Am. Pub. Health Assn. Jewish. Home: Bosque de Avellanos 156 Mexico DF 11700 Mexico Office: Facultad de Psicología Universidad Nacional Autónoma de México Mexico DF Mexico

PICKELL, CHARLES NORMAN, clergyman, educator; b. Haddonfield, N.J., Dec. 18, 1927; s. William Norman and Ada Marie (Kelley) P.; m. Sarah Louella Mitchell, Nov. 20, 1982; children by previous marriage—Rachel Grace, Stuart Charles, Arthur John, Luke Andrew, Heather Lee; step-children—Ellen Landon Harlow, Ethan John Harlow. B.A., Juniata Coll., 1949; M.Div., Pitts. Theol. Sem., 1952, Th.M., 1957; D.D., Sterling Coll., 1964; postgrad. Harvard U., 1959-60, Andover-Newton Theol. Sem., 1960-61, No. Va. Community Coll., 1973, George Mason U., 1982. Ordained to ministry Presbyterian Ch. U.S.A., 1952. Pastor Chelsea Presbyn. Ch., Atlantic City, 1952-55, 1st Presbyn. Ch., Monongaleha, Pa., 1955-57, United Presbyn. Ch., Newton, Mass., 1957-63, Wallace Meml. United Presbyn. Ch., Hyattsville, Md., 1963-70, Vienna Presbyn. Ch., Va., 1970-80, Ashburn Presbyn. Ch., Va., part-time 1980-85, full-time, 1985—; mem. adminstrv. faculty George Mason U., Fairfax, Va., 1980-83; mgr. adminstrv. and support services Creative Mgmt. Systems, McLean, Va., 1983-84; adj. prof. Gordon Div. Sch., Wenham, Mass., 1958-63; moderator Presbytery Boston, United Presbyn. Ch. U.S.A., 1959, chmn. ministerial relations, 1961-63; moderator Synod New Eng., 1960; asst. stated clk. Presbytery Washington City, 1969; chmn. nominating com. Nat. Capital Union Presbytery of United Presbyn. Ch. U.S.A. and Presbyn. Ch. U.S., 1974-77, moderator, 1978; mem. council Synod of Vas., Presbyn. Ch. U.S., 1976-82, chmn. council, 1980-82; mem. adv. bd. Salvation Army, Fairfax, 1981-83; mem. governing bd. United Coll. Ministries in No. Va., 1982—; mem. hunger com. Nat. Capital Presbytery, 1984—; trustee Westminster Coll., New Wilmington, Pa., 1957-61, Gordon Div. Sch., Wenham, Mass., 1959-70; trustee Gordon Coll., Wenham, 1959-82, chmn. acad. affairs, 1965-82; mem. governing bd., incorporator Gordon-Conwell Theol. Sem., Hamilton, Mass., 1969-71. Author: Preaching to Meet Men's Needs, 1957, Colossians, A Study Manual, 1965, Works Count Too!, 1966, also ch. sch. curricula, poetry and numerous articles in religious periodicals; author, editor: Presbyterianism in New England, 1960. Mem. Vienna Vol. Fire Dept., 1973-83, pres., 1978-80; chief chaplain Fairfax County Fire and Rescue Dept., 1974-81; mem., chaplain Burke Vol. Fire Dept., Va., 1983—. Mem. Hymn Soc. Am., Presbyn. Hist. Soc., Am. Soc. Ch. History. Republican. Club: Kiwanis (chmn. spiritual aims) (Fairfax). Avocations: writing, history, hymnody, spectator sports, theatre. Home: 5756 Lakeside Oak Ln Burke Centre VA 22015 Office: Ashburn Presbyn Ch PO Box 57 Ashburn VA 22011

PICKENS, DAVID RICHARD, JR., surgeon; b. Nashville, Apr. 16, 1920; s. David Richard and Corinne (Waddey) P.; m. Harriet Palmer, May 12, 1945; children—David Richard III, Mary, John, Robert. B.S., Vanderbilt U., 1941, M.D., 1944. Diplomate Am. Bd. Surgery. Intern Western Res. U. Hosp., Cleve., 1944-45; resident in urol. surgery Roosevelt Hosp., N.Y.C., 1945-46; resident in gen. surgery St. Thomas Hosp., Nashville, 1946-47; resident in surgery Bellevue Hosp., N.Y.C., 1947-51; Nat. Tb Assn. fellow in chest surgery Triboro Hosp., N.Y.C., 1951-52, resident in thoracic surgery, 1951-52; practice medicine specializing in surgery, Nashville, 1952-53, 55—; mem. staffs St. Thomas Hosp., Bapt. Hosp.; asst. clin. prof. surgery Vanderbilt U. Hosp., 1968—. Served to capt., M.C., U.S. Army, 1953-55. Mem. AMA, ACS, Am. Soc. Colon and Rectal Surgeons, Southeastern Surg. Congress, Tenn. Med. Assn., Davidson County Med. Soc., Nashville Acad. Medicine, Piedmont Soc. Colon and Rectal Surgeons, So. Surg. Assn., So. Med. Assn., Soc. for Surgery Alimentary Tract, Delta Kappa Epsilon. Clubs: Belle Meade Country, University. Contbr. articles to profl. jours. Home: 224 Lynwood Blvd Nashville TN 37205 Office: 1919 Hayes St Nashville TN 37203

PICKENS, WILLIAM GARFIELD, realtor, educator; b. Atlanta, Dec. 27, 1927; s. William Garfield and Eula (Reese) P.; m. Theresa Smith, Aug. 20, 1950 (div. 1977); children—Leslie Rochelle, Kelsey Reese, Peter Todd; m. Ernestine McCoy, Sept. 30, 1977; 1 child, Marcos. B.A. in English magna cum laude, Morehouse Coll., 1948; M.A. in English, Atlanta U., 1950; Ph.D. in English and Linguistics, U. Conn., 1969. Tchr., Hartford Pub. Schs., Conn., 1954-68; head dept. English, 1968-70; chmn. dept. English, Morehouse Coll., Atlanta, 1970-84; owner, broker Pickens Realty, Hartford, 1956-71; assoc. broker B.J. Alexander Realty, Atlanta, 1984—; pres., founder Realty Bd. Greater Hartford, 1960-62. Editor: Trends in Southern Sociolinguistics, 1975. Served with U.S. Army, 1950-52, Korea. Mem. Phi Beta Kappa. Democrat. Baptist. Home: 2617 Peyton Woods Trail Atlanta GA 30311 Office: Morehouse Coll 830 Westview Dr Atlanta GA 30314

PICKENS, WILLIAM STEWART, cardiologist; b. Bentonville, Ark., Dec. 16, 1940; s. William Craig and Mary Elizabeth (McFarland) P.; B.S., U. Ark., Fayetteville, 1962; M.D., U. Ark., Little Rock, 1966; m. Patricia Dee Hughes, Nov. 8, 1975; children—Holly, Heather, Brian. Rotating intern Tampa (Fla.) Gen. Hosp., 1966-67; resident in radiology U. Fla. Med. Ctr., Gainesville, 1970-72; resident in internal medicine, then fellow in cardiology U. South Fla. Med. Center, Tampa, 1972-75; fellow in cardiovascular radiology U. Fla. Med. Center, 1974; staff physician VA Hosp., Tampa, 1974-75; practice medicine specializing in cardiology, Pensacola, Fla., 1976—; mem. staff Baptist Hosp., Sacred Heart Hosp.; asst. prof. radiology and internal medicine U. Ark., Little Rock, 1975-76 clin. assoc. prof. medicine Tulane U., 1983—; v.p. ECG Systems Inc. Served as officer M.C., USAF, 1967-72; maj. Res. Rockefeller scholar, 1958-59; U. Ark. Alumni scholar, 1958-60; Edn. Found. scholar, 1958-62; Barton Found. scholar, 1965; C.V. Mosby scholar, 1966; diplomate Am. Bd. Internal Medicine. Mem. Sigma Xi (assoc.), Alpha Omega Alpha, Phi Eta Sigma, Alpha Epsilon Delta. Republican. Episcopalian. Office: 1717 North E St Suite 503 Pensacola FL 32501

PICKERING, CLARA LEE, geologist; b. Austin, Tex., Apr. 27, 1959; d. George Franklin and Lyla Lee (Woodruff) Vance; m. William Michael Pickering, May 26, 1984. B.S. in Geology, U. Minn., 1981. Petroleum geologist Gulf Oil Exploration and Prodn., Odessa, Tex., 1982—. Mem. Am. Assn. Petroleum Geologists, West Tex. Geol. Soc., Houston Geol. Soc. Avocations: golf; swimming; travelling. Home: 1415 Burgoyne Houston TX 77077

PICKERING, JAMES H., university dean, English language educator; b. N.Y.C., July 11, 1937; s. James Henry and Anita (Felber) P.; m. Patricia Noel Paterson; children—David Scott, Susan Elizabeth. B.A., Williams Coll., 1959; M.A., Northwestern U., 1960, Ph.D., 1964. English instr. Northwestern U., Evanston, Ill., 1963-65; asst. prof., prof. Mich. State U., East Lansing, 1965-81, assoc. chmn., grad. chmn. English dept., 1969-75, dir. The Honors Coll., 1975-81; dean, Coll. of Humanities and the Fine Arts, U. Houston, 1981—. Editor: Fiction 100, 4th edit., 1985, (with others) Literature, 1982, 2d edit., 1986; contbr. articles to profl. jours. Mem. Coll. English Assn. (pres. 1980-81), Nat. Collegiate Hon. Council, Conf. of Urban Colls. of Arts and Letters. Presbyterian. Home: 13602 Queensbury Ln Houston TX 77079 Office: Office of Dean U Houston Coll of Humanities and Fine Arts Cullen Blvd Houston TX 77004

PICKETT, GEORGE BIBB, JR., retired military officer; b. Montgomery, Ala., Mar. 20, 1918; s. George B. and Marie (Dow) P.; B.S., U.S. Mil. Acad., 1941; student Nat. War Coll., 1959-60; m. Beryl Arlene Robinson, Dec. 27, 1941 (dec. 1980); children—Barbara Pickett Harrell, James, Kathleen, Thomas; m. 2d, Rachel Copeland Peeples, July 1981. Commd. 2d lt. U.S. Army, 1941, advanced through grades to maj. gen., 1966; instr. Inf. Sch., Fort Benning, Ga., 1947-50, instr. Armed Forces Staff Coll., Norfolk, Va., 1956-59; comdg. officer 2d Armored Cav. Regt., 1961-63; chief of staff Combat Devel. Command, 1963-66; comdg. gen. 2d inf. div., Korea, 1966-67; ret., 1973; field rep. Nat. Rifle Assn., 1973-85. Decorated Purple Heart with oak leaf cluster, D.S.M. with two oak leaf clusters, Bronze Star with two oak leaf clusters and V device, Silver Star, Legion of Merit with two oak leaf clusters, Commendation medal with two oak leaf clusters. Mem. SAR, Old South Hist. Assn., Ala. Assn. Engrs. and Land Surveyors, Am. Legion, VFW. Episcopalian. Club: Kiwanis (chmn. 1974—). Author: (with others) Joint and Combined Staff Officers Manual, 1959; contbr. articles on mil. affairs to profl. jours. Home: 3525 Flowers Dr Montgomery AL 36109 Office: PO Box 4 Montgomery AL 36101

PICKETT, MARK RAYMOND, electrical engineer; b. Waycross, Ga., Jan. 17, 1957; s. Lester Raymond and Linda Margret (Lee) P. Student Ware Vo-Tech., 1973-74, North Ga. Coll., 1975-77, Ga. Inst. Tech., 1978—. Elec. apprentice Ware Electric, Inc., Waycross, 1973-78; computer printer ribbon reprocessor Wespac, S.E., Atlanta, 1979; electronic maint. technician Maxell Am., Inc., Conyers, Ga., 1980—; v.p. Ware Electric, Inc., Waycross, 1981—. Mem. IEEE. Baptist. Home: 335 Peachtree Ave NE Atlanta GA 30305 Office: Ware Electric Inc 912 Albany Ave Waycross GA 31501

PICKETT, NANCY ELIZABETH, government council executive, consultant, trainer; b. Barksdale AFB, La., Nov. 7, 1948; d. Richard Dewey and Evelyn (Weis) P.; m. Wendell Alfred Smith III, May 31, 1968 (div. 1976); children—Melinira Lynne, Wendell Alfred, IV. B.A., Nicholls State U., 1970, Ed.M., 1972. Tchr. St. Charles Sch. Bd., Luling, La., 1970-71; counselor, coordinator River Parishes Council Govt., Convent, La., 1973-74, exec. dir., Boutte, La., 1974—, pres. pvt. industry council, LaPlace, La., 1981-83; pvt. practice trainer, cons., Boutte, La., 1979—; mem. adv. bd. La. Family Planning Program, New Orleans, 1976—. Editor: Directory Community Resources, 1977. Del. White House Conf. Families, Mpls., 1978, La. Gov.'s Conf. Libraries, Baton Rouge, 1978; founding bd. dirs. St. Charles Community Theatre, Luling, La., 1979-84; bd. dirs., v.p. S.E. La. Girl Scout Council, New Orleans, 1978-83. Nat. Merit scholar, 1966. Mem. Am. Soc. for Tng. and Devel. (bd. dirs., treas. 1984, chmn. position referral 1983), Nat. Assn. Female Execs. (charter), Service Delivery Area Dirs. Assn. Office: River Parishes Council Govt PO Box 440 Boutte LA 70039

PICKETT, NELL ANN, English language educator, author; b. Utica, Miss., Oct. 22, 1935; d. Fred Newman and Yancy Eva (Reed) Pickett; m. Harry Johnson Partin, Aug. 14, 1976. A.A., Hinds Jr. Coll., 1955; B.A., Miss. U. for Women, 1957; M.A., Peabody Coll., 1958; Ph.D., Univ. Miss., 1977. Chmn. English dept. Rolling Fork High Sch., Miss., 1958-61; instr. English, Delta State U., Cleveland, Miss., 1962-65; cons. dept. sociology Miss. State U., Starkville, 1965-66; prof. English, Hinds Jr. Coll. Dist., Raymond, Miss., 1966—. Author: Technical English, 1970, 4th rev. edit., 1984, Occupational English, 1974, 4th rev. edit., 1985. Contbr. articles on writing to profl. jours. Originator, donor Best Article of Yr. award for teaching of English in two-yr. coll., 1981—. Recipient Cowan Excellence in Teaching award S.E. Conf. on English in the Two-Yr. Coll., 1985. Nat. Teaching fellow U.S. Office Edn., 1969-70. Fellow Assn. Tchrs. of Tech. Writing (exec. sec., treas. 1974—); mem. Nat. Council Tchrs. of English (chmn. com. on tech. and sci. communication 1984—), MLA, AAUP. Avocations: European travel; fishing; farming; reading. Office: Hinds Jr Coll Dist Raymond MS 39154

PICKLE, JAMES C., hospital administrator; b. Memphis, June 8, 1943; s. John Lott and Sarah Elizabeth (Adams) P.; m. Peggy Jean Massey, Dec. 18, 1965; children—Jeff, Matt. B.S. in Liberal Arts, Memphis State U., 1967, M.P.A., 1977. Asst. to pres. Store Devel. Corp., Memphis, 1967-69; investment analyst First Tenn. Adv. Corp., Memphis, 1972-73; v.p., dir. Care Inns Inc., Memphis, 1973-76; dir. shared services Meth. Hosps., Memphis, 1978, v.p. adminstrn., 1978-83, sr. v.p., 1983-84, exec. v.p., 1985. Mem. health and welfare ministry bd. Memphis Conf., United Meth. Ch., 1983—; mem. health adv. bd. Memphis State U., 1984—; chmn. bd. dirs. Dogwood Village of Memphis and Shelby County Inc., 1984-85. Served to lt. (J.G.), USN, 1969-72. Mem. Am. Coll. Hosp. Adminstrs., Am. Health Planning Assn., Am. Coll. Health Care Adminstrs., Tenn. Hosp. Assn. (numerous coms.), Memphis Hosp. Council (sec.-treas. 1985). Republican. Methodist. Avocations: snow skiing; sailing. Home: 3054 Carrick Dr Germantown TN 38138 Office: Methodist Hosps of Memphis 1265 Union Ave Memphis TN 38104

PICKLE, JAMES JARRELL (JAKE), congressman; b. Roscoe, Tex., Oct. 11, 1913; s. J. B. and Mary P.; B.A., U. Tex.; m. Beryl Bolton McCarroll; children—Peggy Pickle Norris, Richard McCarroll and Graham McCarroll. Area dir. Nat. Youth Adminstrn., 1938-41; co-organizer Sta. KVET, Austin, Tex.; pub. relations and advt. bus.; dir. Tex. Democratic Exec. Com., 1957-60; mem. Tex. Employment Commn., 1961-63; mem. 88th-99th congresses 10th Dist. Tex. Served with USNR, World War II. Office: 242 Cannon House Office Bldg Washington DC 20515

PICOU, EDWARD BEAUREGARD, JR., paleontologist; b. Baton Rouge, Mar. 26, 1932; s. Edward Beauregard and Eugenia Violet (Babin) P.; B.S., La. State U., 1955. Paleontologist, Shell Oil Co., Baton Rouge, New Orleans, 1957-65, div. paleontologist, Lafayette, La., New Orleans, Houston, 1966-70, New Orleans, 1971-81, paleontol. adv. and div. paleontologist, New Orleans, 1981—. Served with U.S. Army, 1955-57. Cushman Found. Foraminiferal Research fellow. Fellow AAAS; mem. Soc. Econ. Paleontologists and Mineralogists (v.p.), Am. Assn. Petroleum Geologists, Paleontol. Soc., Paleontol. Research Inst., New Orleans Geol. Soc., Houston Geol. Soc. Republican. Roman Catholic. Contbr. articles to profl. jours. Home: 6901 Canal Blvd New Orleans LA 70124 Office: Shell Offshore Inc PO Box 61933 New Orleans LA 70161

PIEPER, PATRICIA R., artist, photographer; b. Paterson, N.J., Jan. 28, 1923; d. Francis William and Barbara Margareth (Ludwig) Farabaugh; student Baron von Palm, 1937-39, Deal (N.J.) Conservatory, summers 1939, 40, Utah State U., 1950-52; m. George F. Pieper, July 1, 1941 (dec. May 1981); 1 child, Patricia Lynn. One-woman shows Charles Russell Mus., Great Falls, Mont., 1955, Fisher Gallery, Washington, 1966, Tampa City Library, 1977, 78, 79, 80, 81, Ctr. Pl. Art Ctr., Brandon, Fla., 1985; 2-man show: St. Joseph's Hosp. Gallery, Tampa, Tampa City Library, 1983; exhibited in group shows Davidson Art Gallery, Middletown, Conn., 1968, Helena (Mont.) Hist. Mus., 1955, Dept. Commerce Alaska Statehood Show, 1959, Joslyn Mus., Omaha, 1961, Denver Mus. Natural History, 1955; represented in pvt. collections. Pres., Bell Lake Assn., 1976-80, 83-84, 85-86; mem. Pasco County (Fla.) Water Adv. Council, 1978—, chmn., 1979-80, 82, 83-84, 85-86; mem. Hillsborough River Basin Bd., 1981—, vice chmn., 1983-86; mem. ad hoc com. Fla. Save Our Rivers program. Recipient 2d and 6th pl. prizes Gen. Tel. All-Fla. Photo Competition, 1979, 82, Best of Show award Dist. 8 Show, Fla. Fedn. Women's Clubs, Save Our Roivers Ad Hock, 1986. Mem. Nat. League Am. Pen Women (v.p. Tampa 1976-78, Woman of Year award 1977-78), Land O' Lakes C. of C. (dir. 1979-82; award), Fla. Geneal. Soc., Cambria County (Pa.) Geneal. Soc., Fla. West Coast Archeol. Soc., Ret. Officers Assn. Clubs: Lutz, Land O' Lakes Women's. Home and Studio: PO Box 15 Land O' Lakes FL 33539

PIEPER, WYLIE BERNARD, diversified company executive; b. Beeville, Tex., 1932; married. B.A., Rice U., 1953, B.S.C.E., 1954. Engring. supr. Brown & Root Inc., a company of Halliburton Co., Houston, 1957-72, v.p., 1972-74, sr. v.p., 1974-77, group v.p., from 1977, now sr. exec. v.p., also dir. Office: Brown & Root Co 4100 Clinton Houston TX 77001*

PIERCE, ANITA MAE, business executive; b. Johnson City, Tenn., June 21, 1946; d. Robert Bruce and Kathryn Ina (Heaton) Pierce; m. Arthur Steve Fair, Feb. 20, 1965 (div. Apr. 1969); m. 2d, John Randolph Maher, Nov. 26, 1974 (div. 1984). Student East Tenn. State U., 1964-67. Sec. Tenn. Eastman Co. div. Kodak, Kingsport, 1964-65, 66-67; purchasing adminstrv. asst. solar aircraft div. Internat. Harvester Co., Inc., San Diego, 1965-66; with IBM Corp., Raleigh, N.C., Kingsport, Tenn., Cin., Armonk, N.Y., White Plains, N.Y., Atlanta, 1967—, mgr. central employment office, south-west mkgt. div. Atlanta, 1978—. Baptist. Home: 58 Middleton Ct Smyrna GA 30080 Office: IBM Central Employment Suite 440 400 Colony Sq Atlanta GA 30361

PIERCE, DARRELL LEE, exploration geologist; b. Corpus Christi, Tex., May 15, 1951; s. Lowell Rheudell and Arliss Bernadine (Gundy) P.; m. Leslie Ann Barry, Aug. 4, 1979. Student, Navarro Coll., 1969-70; A.A., Del Mar Coll., 1971; B.S. in Geology, U. Houston, 1980. Tennis profl. H.E. Butt Tennis Ctr., Corpus Christi, Tex., 1971-72, Corpus Christi Country Club, 1972-73, Pharaoh's Country Club, Corpus Christi, 1973-76; geol. technician Superior Oil, Houston, 1976-78, Amoco Internat., Houston, 1978-80; exploration geologist Tex. Eastern, Houston, 1980—. U.S. Savs. Bond coordinator, 1985—; tennis tchr. Head Start Program, Corpus Christi, 1968, 69, 70, Dad's Club YMCA, Houston, 1984. Mem. Am. Assn. of Petroleum Geologists, Soc. Profl. Well Log Analysts, Houston Geol. Soc., Corpus Christi Geol. Soc. Republican. Mem. Church of Christ. Avocations: tennis, fishing; gardening; arts. Home: 10039 Briarwild Ln Houston TX 77080 Office: Tex Eastern Corp PO Box 2521 Houston TX 77252

PIERCE, GEORGE FOSTER, JR., architect; b. Dallas, June 22, 1919; s. George Foster and Hallie Louise (Crutchfield) P.; student So. Methodist U., 1937-39; B.A., Rice U., 1942, B.S. in Architecture, 1943; diplome de architecture Ecole Des Beaux Arts, Fountainbleau, France, 1958; m. Betty Jean Reistle, Oct. 17, 1942; children—Ann Louis Pierce Arnett, George Foster III, Nancy Reistle Pierce Dietrich. Founding partner Pierce, Goodwin, Alexander, Architects, Houston,Dallas, Austin, Tex., 1947-85. Trustee, Tex. Archtl. Found., 1960-84, pres. 1974-75; trustee Mus. Nat. Sci., Houston; pres. Houston Contemporary Arts Mus., 1956-57, chmn. bd., 1957-58 mem. exec. bd., area council Boy Scouts Am.; Served as ensign USNR, World War II. Named One of 5 Outstanding Young Texans, 1954. Fellow AIA (nat. chmn. com. on aesthetics 1963-64, nat. chmn. com. on chpt. affairs 1958-60), Sociedad de Architectos Mexicanos (hon.); mem. Tex. Soc. Architects (pres. 1964, L.W. Pitts award for most outstanding service to community and archtl. profession), Houston C. of C. (chmn. future studies com. 1977-78). Methodist. Clubs: Houston Country, Petroleum of Houston, Rotary (Houston); Crown Colony Country (Lufkin, Tex.). Architect: 4 prin. terminals and airport master planning Houston Intercontinental Airport, Petroleum Club of Houston, Two Houston Center, Houston Mus. Natural Sci., 7 bldgs. Rice U., 2 bldgs. U. Houston. Office: PO Box 13319 Houston TX 77019

PIERCE, GERALD SWETNAM, financial planner; b. Sapulpa, Okla., Aug. 17, 1933; s. Harold Ellis and Mary Katherine (Snell) P.; student U. Tex., Austin, 1953-54; A.B., Harvard U., 1955; M.A. (Univ. fellow), U. Miss., Oxford, 1956, Ph.D. (NDEA fellow), 1963; postgrad. U. N.Mex., 1956-57; m. Janis Fay Vaughn, May 27, 1956; children—Ann Elizabeth Swetnam, John Willard. Fgn. service officer U.S. Dept. State, Washington and Rio de Janeiro, Brazil, 1957-60; asst. prof. history U. Miss., Oxford, 1963-64; asst. prof. history Memphis State U., 1964-67, assoc. prof., 1967-70, prof., 1970-83, dir. internat. studies, 1974-75; pres. Consultants System Inc., 1975—; mem. firm Burleigh-/Pierce, 1980-81; v.p., head fin. planning dept. Morgan, Keegan & Co., Inc., 1981—; adj. faculty Coll. Fin. Planning, Denver, 1982—. Chmn., Tenn. Council on Internat. Edn., 1974-75; mem. Memphis Hist. Heritage Com., 1974-80, Forum for a Better Memphis. Recipient Author's award for Tex., Theta Sigma Phi, 1969; Am. Philos. Soc. grantee, 1966-67; C.L.U.; cert. fin. planner. Mem. Mo., Okla. hist. assns., Inst. Cert. Fin. Planners, Internat. Assn. Fin. Planners (chpt. dir., v.p. 1982-83, pres. 1983-84), Phi Kappa Phi. Club: Harvard (pres. 1980-81). Author: Texas Under Arms, 1969, Travels in the Republic of Texas, 1842, 1971. Gen. editor: Narratives of the American West, a series, 1971-77; assoc. editor Mil. History of Texas and the Southwest, a jour., 1969-77. Contbr. articles to profl. jours. Home: 4743 Park Ave Memphis TN 38117 Office: Morgan Keegan & Co Inc One Commerce Sq Memphis TN 38103

PIERCE, JANIS VAUGHN, ins. exec.; b. Memphis, Dec. 23, 1934; d. Jesse Wynne and Dorothy Arnette (Lloyd) Vaughn; B.A. (univ. scholar), U. Miss., 1956, M.A., 1964; m. Gerald Swetnam Pierce, May 27, 1956; children—Ann Elizabeth Swetnam, John Willard. High sch. tchr., 1957-58; mem. faculty Memphis Univ. Sch., 1964-66, Memphis State U., 1968-75; agt. Aetna Life Ins. Co., Memphis, 1977-80, career supr., 1980—, mgr., 1981—, supt. of prime, 1983; v.p., dir. Consultants System, Inc., bus. cons., 1975—; mem. Aetna Women's Task Force, chmn., 1982, 83, 84. Pres., Women's Resources Center, Memphis, 1974-77; sec. Tenn. chpt. Women's Polit. Caucus, 1975-76; bd. dirs., treas., sec., mem. exec. com. Memphis YWCA, 1979—; mem. steering com. Women in Bus. Conf., 1981; mem. Tenn. action com. U.S. Civil Rights Commn., 1980; bd. dirs. Memphis Area Transit Authority, 1981—. Mem. Million Dollar Roundtable, 1978, 79, Women Leaders Roundtable, 1978—. C.L.U. Mem. Nat. Assn. Life Underwriters, Tenn. Life Underwriters Assn., Memphis Life Underwriters Assn. (bd. dirs. 1982—, chmn. pub. service), Women's Life Underwriters Conf. (pres.-elect), Am. Pub. Transp. Assn. (chmn. fin. com., nominating com. governing bd.), Memphis PTA (council 1971-72), LWV, AAUW, Mortar Bd. (regional coordinator 1972-78), Leadership Memphis, Republican Career Women (dir., sec. 1983), Memphis C. of C., Memphis State U. Women's (pres. 1978), Alpha Lambda Delta, Sigma Delta Pi. Republican. Episcopalian. Club: Le Bonheur (dir.). Home: 4743 Park Ave Memphis TN 38117 Office: 1355B Lynnfield Rd Suite 109 Memphis TN 38119

PIERCE, NORMA FAYE, psychology educator; b. Mobile, Ala., Sept. 3, 1934; d. Murl and Eva Mae (Coggin) Scribner; m. Donald Fay Pierce, June 5, 1954; children—Kathryn, Donald, John Charles, Jeffrey. B.S., Blue Mountain Coll., 1953; M.A., U. Ala., 1956; M.S., U. So. Ala., 1980; Ph.D., U. So. Miss., 1983. Cert. tchr., Ala.; lic. psychologist. Tchr., J.T. Wright Sch. for Girls, Mobile, 1956-62; instr. U. South Ala., Mobile, 1967-68, instr. psychology, 1979-80; instr. U. So. Miss., 1982-83; psychologist, ptnr. Clin. Psychology Services, Mobile, 1980—; mediator Divorce Mediation Ctr.; psychometrist, psychotherapist Vietnam Outpatient VA Ctr., Mobile. Founder, pres. UMS Prep Sch. Mothers' Club, 1978-80; pres. Jr. and Sr. Bd. FCH, 1970-75; pres. Woman's Missionary Union of Dauphin Way and Springhill Baptist Ch.; mem. Home Mission Bd., So. Bapt. Conv. NSF scholar, 1956, 57. Mem. Am. Psychol. Assn., Southeastern Psychol. Assn., Am. Assn. Marriage and Family Therapists (clin.) Acad. Family Mediators (assoc.), Registry for Psychometrists, Psi Chi, Alpha Mu Delta, Alpha Theta Chi, Sigma Xi. Republican. Clubs: Mobile Country, Athelstan, Bienville. Contbr. articles on psychology to profl. jours. Office: 266 S McGregor Mobile AL 36608

PIERCE, NORMA JANE HAND, computer scientist, management consultant; b. Memphis, May 11, 1956; d. Albert Moore and Wanda Jean (Momon) Hand; m. Edward Augustus Pierce, June 20, 1981. B.S. in Computer Sci. magna cum laude, So. Meth. U., 1977; M.B.A., Harvard U., 1982. Programmer-/analyst Lawrence Livermore Lab. (Calif.), 1977; systems analyst Tex. Instruments Inc., Dallas, 1978-82; mgmt. cons. Booz, Allen & Hamilton, 1982-85, Pierce Jackson Kennedy, 1986—. Vol., H.E. Egleston Hosp. for Children, Atlanta, 1982-85; charter mem. High Mus. Art, Atlanta, 1983—; block capt. Collier Hills Civic Assn., Atlanta, 1983-85. Mem. Assn. for Computing, Young Women of Arts, So. Ctr. for Internat. Studies, Harvard Bus. Sch. Alumni Assn. (sect. sec. 1982—). Baptist. Clubs: Junior League, Harvard Business Sch.; Demoiselle (Shreveport, La.). Home: 3783 Elmora at Auden Houston TX 77005

PIERCE, REBECCA LYNN, mathematics educator, consultant; b. Traverse City, Mich., Dec. 14, 1950; d. W. Keith and Mildred Anita (Wendel) Potter; m. Martin James Pierce, Nov. 17, 1973. B.S. in Math., Olivet Coll., 1973; M.A. in Edn., Eastern Mich. U., 1978; postgrad. in Math., U. Tex.-Arlington, 1980—. Chmn. math. dept. Hartland Consolidated Schs., Mich., 1974-79; instr. Ga. State U., Atlanta, 1979-80; instr. math U. Tex., Arlington, 1980—; research assoc. Pierce Johnson Mgmt. Cons., Dallas, 1983—. Editor: Curriculum Objectives K-8 Mathematics Program, 1978. Sponsor Am. Cancer Soc. Arlington, 1983, United Way, Arlington, 1984; treas. Nat. Edn. Assn., Hartland, 1978. Mem. Nat. Council Tchrs. Math., Math. Assn. Am., Am. Math. Soc. Am. Statis. Assn. Pi Mu Epsilon. Republican. Methodist. Avocations: writing; ornithology; gardening. Home: 2206 Sexton Dr Arlington TX 76015 Office: U Tex Dept Math Arlington TX 76019

PIERCE, RICHARD ANDREW, banker; b. Key West, Fla., Nov. 13, 1945; s. Joseph Austin and Ruth Amelia (Page) P.; student St. Leo (Fla.) Coll.; m. Jean Marie Alvarez, Dec. 21, 1964; children—Terri Lynn, Troy Coburn. Asst. cashier, asst. v.p., Fla. First Nat. Bank, Key West, 1969-76; v.p., then pres., chmn. bd. Fla. Nat. Bank, Gainesville, 1976-80; pres., chmn. bd. Fla. First Nat. Bank Fla. Keys, Key West, 1980-81; pres., chief exec. officer Fla. Keys First State Bank, 1981—. Bd. dirs. Mental Health Assn., Gainesville, Friends of Five Ednl. TV; adv. bd. Salvation Army, Key West; mem. Fla. Com. 100; Monroe County (Fla.) campaign chmn., 1980 1980. Recipient Spl. Service award Gainesville chpt. Beta Sigma Phi, 1979; named Banker of Yr., 1981, 83. Mem. Southernmost C. of C., Key West C. of C. (dir.), U.S. Navy League (pres.) Assn. Naval Aviation (dir., treas.). Office: 1201 Simonton St Key West FL 33040

PIERCE, RORY WAYNE, chiropractic physician; b. Kansas City, Mo., Feb. 10, 1948; s. C.M. and Hazel (Fletcher) P.; m. Marilyn Sue Florence, Mar. 7, 1970. B.A., Park Coll., 1974; D.Chiropractic, Cleve. Chiropractic Coll., 1978. Practice chiropractic medicine, Lansing, Kans., 1978-79; assoc. dir. Fernandez Clinic, St. Petersburg, Fla., 1979-82, dir., pres., 1982—. Mem. Am. Chiropractic Assn., Fla. Chiropractic Assn., Pinellas County Chiropractic Soc., Parker Chiropractic Research Found., Gonstead Clin. Studies Soc., Cleve. Chiropractic Coll. Ambassador Soc., Circus Saints and Sinners of Am. (pres. 1983). Republican. Mem. Christian Ch. Lodge: Masons. Home: 7500 21st N St Saint Petersburg FL 33702 Office: Fernandez Chiropractic Clinic 4800 4th St N Saint Petersburg FL 33703

PIERCE, VERLON LANE, pharmacist, store proprietor; b. Greensburg, Ky., July 13, 1949; s. Ogle Lee and Aleene (Hall) P.; m. Brenda Mildred Russell, May 20, 1973; children—Amanda Lee, Daniel Russell. B.S. in Math. and Chemistry, Western Ky. U., 1972; B.S. in Pharmacy, U. Ky., 1975. Relief pharmacist Shugart & Willis Drug Store, Franklin, Ky., 1975-78; staff pharmacist Franklin Simpson Meml. Hosp., Franklin, 1976-79; owner, pres. pharmacist Medicine Shoppe, Bowling Green, Ky., 1978—; pres. Westland Drug Inc., Bowling Green, 1984—; sec. 21st Investment Group, Bowling Green, 1984—. Recipient Franny award Internat. Franchise Assn., 1980; Hall of Fame bust Medicine Shoppe, St. Louis, 1983. Mem. 4th Dist. Pharmacy Group (pres. 1983-84), Ky. Pharmacy Assn. Democrat. Baptist. Avocations: golf; swimming. Home: Route 6 Box 507 Franklin KY 42134 Office: Medicine Shoppe 816 US 31 W Bowling Green KY 42101

PIERSON, DONALD, research sociologist, social anthropologist; b. Indpls., Sept. 8, 1900; s. William Gilbert and Ada May (Brown) P.; m. Helen Joy Batchelor, June 12, 1929; A.B., Coll. Emporia, 1927; A.M., U. Chgo., 1933, Ph.D., 1939. Fellow sociology U. Chgo., 1933-35, research asst. Social Sci. Research Com., 1935-37; research assoc. Fisk U., 1937-39; prof. sociology, social anthropology Escola de Sociologia e Politica of São Paulo, Brazil, 1939-59, chmn. dept. sociology and anthropology, 1941-43, dean grad. div. 1943-57, Inter-Am. exchange prof. U.S. State Dept., 1943-45; anthropologist Inst. Social Anthropology, Smithsonian Instn. in charge Brazilian program of research and research tng. in cooperation with Escola de Sociologia e Politica of São Paulo, 1945-52; vis. prof. Inter Am. Program Advanced Tng. Applied Social Scis., Orgn. Am. States, Escuela Nacional de Antropologia, Mex., 1960-61; Guggenheim fellow, Portugal, Spain, 1963-64; Fulbright lectr., Portugal, 1966. Recipient medal of merit União Cultural Brasil-Estados Unidos, São Paulo, 1980. Fellow Am. Anthrop. Assn., Am. Sociol. Assn. Conglist. Author: Negroes in Brazil: A Study of Race Contact at Bahia, 1942 (Anisfield award 1942, Portuguese edits. 1945, 71, 2d U.S. edit. 1967; Teoria e pesquisa em Sociologia, 1945, 18th edit., 1981; Survey of Literature on Brazil of Sociological Significance, 1945; Cruz das Almas; A Brazilian Village, 1951, Portuguese edit., 1966, O Homen no Vale do Sao Francisco, 3 vols., 1972. Contbr. articles, rev. to U.S., Latin Am. learned jours. Editor: Biblioteca de Ciencias Sociais (book series), 1942-55; co-editor Sociologia, Sao Paulo, 1950-57. Home: 65 Great Oak Dr Fruitland Park FL 32731

PIETERS, MARIA MATILDE, bilingual educator; b. Guatemala City, Guatemala, May 5, 1957; d. Frans George and Jane (Cutts) Pieters. B.S., Peabody Coll., 1979; M.S., Wheelock Coll., 1982. Tchr. Colegio Americano de Guatemala, Guatemala City, 1979-80; tchr. bilingual Felix Tijerina Elem. Sch., Houston Ind. Sch. Dist., 1982—; pvt. tutor, Guatemala City, 1980-81; tchr. Spanish, Amigos de Las Americas, Boston, 1981-82; translator DePauw U. Constrn. Team, Guatemala City, 1977, DePauw U. Med. and Constrn. Team, Guatemala, 1978. Mem. Internat. Reading Assn., Tex. Reading Assn., Council for Exceptional Children, Kappa Delta Epsilon.

PIETY, KENNETH RALPH, psychologist, consultant; b. South Bend, Ind., Feb. 19, 1924; s. Zadoc John and Ora Frances (Watson) P.; m. Jachie Patton, Aug. 17, 1960 (dec. Nov. 1971) 1 child, Maria Annette; m. Virginia Quiñones, Sept. 30, 1972; 1 child, Michael José. B.A., David Lipscomb Coll., 1950; M.A., George Peabody Coll., 1951; Ph.D., Vanderbilt U., 1958. Lic. psychologist, Fla. Instr., David Lipscomb Coll., Nashville, 1950-54; psychologist VA Hosp., Murfreesboro, Tenn., 1957-67; chief psychologist Orange Meml. Hosp., Orlando, Fla., 1958-74; practice psychology, Orlando, 1974—. Contbr. articles to profl. jours. Served with U.S. Army, 1942-46, PTO. Mem. Am. Psychol. Assn., Fla. Psychol. Assn., Am. Assn. Disability Examiners. Republican. Mem. Ch. of christ. Home: 451 Woodbury Rd Orlando FL 32826 Office: 988 Woodcock Rd Suite 100 Orlando FL 32803

PIGOTT, RALPH ELLIS, pharmacist, consultant; b. Tylertown, Miss., Nov. 21, 1926; s. John Ellis and Lessie Cleo (Bailey) P.; m. Clara LaRita Varnado, July 26, 1953; children—Randall Ellis, Lisa Michele. B.S. in Bus. Adminstrn., U. So. Miss., 1949; M.S. in Pharmacy, U. Miss., 1961; D.Pharmacy, State Bd. Pharmacy, Tenn., 1982. Registered pharmacist, Miss., Tenn. Ptnr., mgr. Pigott's Dry Goods, Tylertown, 1949-58; pharmacist Med. Arts Pharmacy, Nashville, 1961-62, Frasier's Pharmacy, Waynesboro, Miss., 1962-65, Woolridge Drug Store, Columbia, Tenn., 1965-68; mgr., buyer Gibson's Pharmacies, Inc., Hattiesburg, Miss., 1968—; cons. pharmacist S.E. Miss. Community Action Agy., Hattiesburg, 1981—. Served with USNR, 1944-46, 51-53. Recipient award of merit ARC, 1957. Mem. Hattiesburg C. of C., Hattiesburg Jr. C. of C., VFW, Nat. Assn. Retail Druggists. Baptist (treas.). Lodge: Moose. Home: 905 Monterrey Ln Hattiesburg MS 39401 Office: 1602 W Pine St Hattiesburg MS 39401

PILCHER, JAMES BROWNIE, lawyer; b. Shreveport, La., May 19, 1929; s. James Reese and Mattie (Brown) P.; m. Frances M. Pettit, Jan. 28, 1951; children—Lydia, Martha, Bradley. B.A., La. State U., 1952; J.D. summa cum laude, John Marshall Law Sch., 1955; postgrad. Emory U. Bar: Ga., 1955. Sole practice law, Atlanta, 1955—; legal aide to speaker Ga. Ho. of Reps., 1961-64; assoc. city atty. City of Atlanta, 1965-70; prof. law John Marshall Law Sch., 1955-59, 65—; pres. Trans-Atlanta Properties, Inc., 1959—. Mem. Ga.

Democratic Exec. Com., 1962-66; pres. Atlanta Jaycees, 1961-62, Active Voters, 1966-69; pres. Young Dem. Club Fulton County, 1964-65, Ga., 1965-66; chmn. Fulton County Dem. Party, 1969-71, mem. exec. com., 1972—; bd. dirs. Whitehead Boys Club, 1961—. Served with USNR, 1946-48. Mem. ABA, Ga. Bar Assn., Atlanta Bar Assn., Am. Trial Lawyers Assn., Nat. Assn. Criminal Def. Lawyers (dir. 1980-84, sec. 1984-85), Ga. Assn. Criminal Def. Lawyers (pres. 1980-82), Ga. Trial Lawyers Assn. (exec. com. 1980—), Ga. Assn. Claimants Attys. (pres. 1983-84). Baptist. Lodge: Kiwanis (pres. Atlanta 1983-84). Office: 63 14th St NE Atlanta GA 30309

PILCHER, WALTER HAROLD, apparel company executive; b. Washington, Oct. 21, 1941; s. Milton Alfred and Elizabeth (Haywood) P.; m. Carol Ann Beebe, July 17, 1965; children—Walter Todd, Jennifer Beebe, Carolyn Elizabeth. B.A., Wesleyan U., 1963; M.B.A., Stanford U., 1966. Product mgr. L'Eggs Products, Winston-Salem, N.C., 1969-73, v.p. mktg., 1979-83, pres., 1983—; v.p. mktg. Hanes Knitwear, Winston-Salem, 1973-75; mktg. mgr. Wix Corp., Gastonia, N.C., 1975-77; v.p. mktg. L'Erin Cosmetics, Winston-Salem, 1977-79. Mem. allocations com. Forsyth United Way, Winston-Salem, 1978. Served to 1st lt. USAR, 1963-70. Republican. Presbyterian. Avocations: creative writing; photography. Office: L'Eggs Products Inc PO Box 2495 Winston-Salem NC 27102

PILKO, GEORGE, industrial real estate/environmental consultant; b. N.Y.C., Feb. 21, 1949; s. Peter J. and Martha (Tonti) P.; B.S.E. in Chem. Engring., U. Mich., 1971, M.B.A., 1973; m. Susan M. Wasvary, Apr. 28, 1973; children—Brian George, David Alan. Energy planner, project mgr., coal project Olin Chems., Stamford, Conn., 1973-75, sales rep., indsl. chems., Houston, 1975-77, coll. recruiter, 1974; chem. mktg. cons. Pace Cons. & Engrs., Houston, 1977-78, mgr. environ. mgmt. services, 1978-80; pres. Pilko & Assos., Inc., Houston, 1980—; speaker on econ. devel. issues at local, state and nat. confs. Vice pres. Trailwood Village Community Assn., 1978-79; co-founder Houston Personal Devel. Forum, 1983. Recipient Branston prize U. Mich., 1968; Eiseman scholar, 1967-71. Mem. Houston Mgmt. Council, U. Mich. Alumni Club (dir. Houston chpt.). Club: Houston Forum. Contbr. articles to profl. jour. Home: 2606 Woodland Ridge Kingwood TX 77345 Office: 2707 North Loop W Suite 960 Houston TX 77008

PILLER, HERBERT, physics educator, researcher; b. Hartmanitz, Bohemia, May 18, 1926; came to U.S., 1960; s. Johann and Rosa (Piller) Landauer Rankl; m. Hertha Hlavacek, Jan. 20, 1955; children—Ingrid A., Herbert J., Helga C., Suzanne H. Ph.D., U. Vienna, Austria, 1955. Research physicist Siemens Labor, Munich, W.Ger., 1955-60; supervisory research physicist Michelson Labor, China Lake, Calif., 1960-69; assoc. prof. dept. physics La. State U., Baton Rouge, 1969—; cons. Naval Air Systems Command, Washington, 1971-75. Contbr. articles to profl. jours., chpts. to books. Patentee in field. Judge State Sci. Fair, Baton Rouge, 1984. Ford Found. fellow, Vienna, Austria, 1955; research grantee Office Naval Research, Washington, 1981. Mem. Am. Phys. Soc. Democrat. Roman Catholic. Home: 12467 Sherbrook Dr Baton Rouge LA 70815 Office: Dept Physics and Astronomy La State U Baton Rouge LA 70803

PILLOW, GEORGE DURDEN, JR., manufacturing company executive; b. Greenwood, Miss., Apr. 22, 1947; s. George Durden and Frances Elaine (Dale) P.; m. Martha Ruth Robbins, Apr. 29, 1972; children—Martha Rachel, Frances Rebecca, Celeste Robbins. B.S. in Bus. Adminstrn., Miss. State U., 1969. With sales mgmt. tng. program Mut. of N.Y., Jackson, Miss., 1969-71, asst. mgr. for Miss., 1971-73; spl. assignments worker Nat. Floor Products Co., Florence, Ala., 1973-75, plant mgr., 1975-76, v.p. ops., 1976-80, exec. v.p., 1980—; bd. dirs. Resilient Floor Covering Inst., pres., 1985-86, past chmn. tech. affairs com. Chmn. bd. dirs. Trinity Episcopal Ch., Florence, 1979-82, 85, also chmn. fin. com.; founding mem. Riverhill Sch., St. Florian, Ala., chmn. bd. trustees, 1980—; bd. dirs. Met. YMCA, Lauderdale County United Way, Jr. Achievement. Served with USAR, 1969-75. Mem. ASTM, Florence C. of C. (bd. dirs.). Club: Turtle Yacht and Country (Killen, Ala.). Lodge: Rotary. Home: Route 2 Box 173-A Killen AL 35645 Office: PO Box 354 Florence AL 35631

PILLOW, ROBERT EDWARD, ice manufacturing corporation executive; b. Childress, Tex., Nov. 14, 1943; s. John Houston and Flossie (Majors) P.; m. Jeannie Knisley, Sept. 4, 1965; children—Robert Edward, Jeannie Renea. Bus. degree, Lubbock Christian Coll., 1965; B.B.A., in Mktg., Tex. Tech U., 1967. Sales mgr. Pillow Ice Co., Inc., Seagraves, Tex., 1967-75, pres., 1975—; pres. S. Plains Oil, Inc., Seagraves, 1975—, Real Estate Investments, Seagraves, 1975—; dir. First State Bank, Seagraves. Pres. Sch. Bd., Seagraves, 1982—. Mem. Seagraves C. of C. (dir. 1976, pres. 1977). Democrat. Mem. Ch. of Christ. Club: Industrial Found. (pres. 1975—). Lodge: Lions (dir. 1975). Avocations: private pilot; skiing; hunting; fishing; reading. Home: Box 245 Seagraves TX 79359 Office: Pillow Ice Co Inc 708 11th Seagraves TX 79359

PILLSBURY, EDMUND PENNINGTON, museum director; b. San Francisco, Apr. 28, 1943; s. Edmund Pennington and Priscilla Keator (Giesen) P.; m. Mireille Marie-Christine Bernard, Aug. 30, 1969; children—Christine Bullitt, Edmund Pennington III. B.A., Yale U., 1965; M.A., U. London, 1967, Ph.D., 1973. Curator European art Yale U. Art Gallery, New Haven, 1972-78; asst. dir. Yale U. Gallery, New Haven, 1975-76; dir. Yale Ctr. Brit. Art, New Haven, 1976-80; chief exec. officer Paul Mellon Ctr. Studies in Brit. Art, London, 1976-80; dir. Kimbell Art Mus., Ft. Worth, 1980—; chmn. Villa I Tatti Exec. Council, N.Y.C., 1979-84; adj. prof. Yale U., 1976-80, lectr., 1972-75; adj. prof. Tex. Christian U., Ft. Worth, 1985—. Author: Florence and the Arts, 1971, David Hockney: Travels with Pen, Pencil and Ink, 1977, The Graphic Art of Federico Barocci, 1978. Trustee Ft. Worth Country Day Sch., 1982—, St. Paul's Sch., David E. Finley fellow Nat. Gallery Art, Washington, 1967-69; Ford Found. fellow Cleve. Mus. Art, 1970-71; Morse fellow Yale U., 1974; Nat. Endowment Arts research fellow, 1975. Mem. Assn. Am. Mus. Dirs., Coll. Art Assn., Indemnity Adv. Panel, Am. Fedn. Arts (trustee). Episcopalian. Clubs: Ft. Worth, City Club (Ft. Worth), Rivercrest (Ft. Worth). Home: 4511 Ridgehaven Rd Fort Worth TX 76116 Office: Kimbell Art Museum 3333 Camp Bowie Blvd Forth Worth TX 76107

PILTZ, BARRY SIEVERS, retail store executive; b. Greenville, Miss., Nov. 30, 1954; s. Julius and Vivian (Sievers) P.; m. Rebecca Sue Zatopek, May 11, 1980. B.S. in Fin., La. State U., 1976; M.B.A., Delta State U., Cleveland, Miss., 1978. Sec./treas., gen. mgr. J's Hub, Inc., Greenville, 1976—. Sec. Jewish Community Ctr., Greenville, 1980-83, v.p., 1984; mem. Greenville Jewish Welfare Fund Com.; bd. dirs. Jr. Achievement; bd. dirs. Hebrew Union Congregation, Greenville, 1983-87; chmn. retail div. Washington County (Miss.) Heart Fund, 1980; co-chmn. Mainstream Festival, Greenville, 1980; rep. to Miss. Gov.'s Conf. on Tourism, 1982. Mem. Assn. M.B.A. Execs., Greenville Area C. of C. (v.p. mktg. div. 1982, chmn. retail com. 1983, chmn. tourism com. 1984-85, Outstanding Vol. award 1984), Greenville Downtown Mchts. Assn. (bd. dirs. and v.p. 1980-85), Delta Mu Delta. Club: Met. Dinner (bd. dirs. 1981-84). Lodges: Lions (v.p. and bd. dirs. 1982-86), B'nai B'rith (Greenville). Home: 1129 Oxford Pl Greenville MS 38701 Office: 737 Washington Ave Greenville MS 38701

PINCUS, JEFFREY HOWARD, dentist, educator, educational administrator; b. Bklyn., Oct. 22, 1950; s. Bernard and Sally (Azan) P.; m. Janie Weiss, Aug. 20, 1972; children—Loren Weiss, Benjamin Leonard. B.S., U. Fla., 1972; D.D.S., U. Md., 1977. Pvt. practice dentistry, Seminole, Fla., 1979-81; prof., chmn. dental sci. Indian River Community Coll., Ft. Pierce, Fla., 1981-82, dir. allied health edn., 1982—; dental cons. Pinellas Assn. Retarded Citizens, St. Petersburg, Fla., 1979-81; dir., agt. Indian River Community Coll. Dental Research Clinic, Ft. Pierce, 1981—; cons. testmaking Dental Assisting Nat. Bd., Chgo., 1982—. Co-author multi-media: Rationale for Initial Mouth Preparation, 1977. Co-inventor enveloped food product and process for making thereof, 1983. Served to lt. USN, 1977-79. Video grantee Fla. Dept. Vocat. Edn., Tallahassee, 1983. Mem. Fla. Assn. Community Colls., Tri County Dental Soc., JAFCO, Inc. (sec.), Gorgas, Gamma Pi Delta. Democrat. Jewish. Avocations: athletics; automobiles. Office: Indian River Community Coll 3209 Virginia Ave Fort Pierce FL 33450

PINEDA, URIEL, building designer; b. Matagalpa, Nicaragua, Sept. 9, 1955; came to U.S., 1974; s. Uriel and Delia (Cuadra) P. B.S., U. So. Miss., 1981. Bldg. designer Simmons & Walker, Hattiesburg, Miss., 1978-81, F-S Prestress, Hattiesburg, 1982-85, Breland & Farmer, Jackson, Miss., 1985—; design instr. U. So. Miss., Hattiesburg, 1984-85. Recipient 3d prize Miss. Dept. Energy, Jackson, 1983. Mem. Am. Inst. Bldg. Design (2d v.p., sec.). Republican. Roman Catholic. Home: 1045 Flynt Dr Apt K-6 Jackson MS 39208 Office: Breland & Farmer 631 Lakeside E Dr Jackson MS 39208

PINGREE, DAVID HARRISON, human services agency administrator; b. Boston, Dec. 11, 1938; s. Ralph Harrison and Adeline (Templeman) P.; children—Kristin, Karin, Benjamin. Student Harvard U., 1957-60; B.A., Drew U., 1963; postgrad. Boston U., 1962, Emory U., 1963-64, Fla. State U., 1967-70. Project coordinator for Citizens Com. on Ga. Gen. Assembly, instr. polit. sci. U. Ga., Athens, 1969-70; dir. research and info. services Pub. Research and Mgmt., Inc., Atlanta, 1970-71; asst. dir. so. office Council of State Govts., Atlanta, 1971; pres. David H. Pingree, Inc., Govtl. Cons., Atlanta, 1971-73; staff dir. Com. on Health and Rehab. Services Fla. Ho. of Reps., Tallahassee, 1972-74; dir. Cntr. for State Legis. Research and Services, Eagleton Inst. Politics, Rutgers State U.-Wood Lawn, New Brunswick, N.J., 1974-75; legis. planning and analysis dir. Fla. Dept. Health and Rehab. Services, Tallahassee, 1975-76, asst. sec. for ops., 1976-77, asst. sec. for adminstrv. services, 1977-79, sec., 1979-80, 81—; dep. chief of staff Office of Gov. State of Fla., Tallahassee, 1980-81. Contbr. articles to legis. jours. Mem. Winchester Ann. Town Meeting, (Mass.), 1960-61; del. White House Conf. on Children and Youth, 1960. Mem. Am. Polit. Sci. Assn., Am. Soc. for Pub. Adminstrn., So. Polit. Sci. Assn., Presidents' Assn., Fla. Adv. Council for Intergovtl. Affairs, So. Inst. for Human Resources (pres. Atlanta). Democrat. Episcopalian. Office: Dept Health and Rehab Services 1317 Winewood Blvd Tallahassee FL 32301

PING-ROBBINS, NANCY REGAN, musicologist, educator; b. Nashville, Dec. 19, 1939; d. Charles Augustus and Ruby Phyllis (Perdue) Regan; m. Robert Leroy Ping, June 19, 1959 (div. 1980); children—Robert Alan, Michael Regan, Bryan Edward; m. 2d, William Edwards Robbins, Jr., Mar. 14, 1981. B.Music, Ind. U., 1964; M.A., U. No. Colo., 1972; Ph.D., U. Colo., 1979. Organist, Armed Forces Chapels, Frankfurt and Kaiserslautern, Germany, 1962-66; staff pianist U.S. Armed Forces Spl. Services Theater, Frankfurt, 1963-65; music tchr. Fayetteville (Ind.) pub. schs., 1966-67, Stratton (Colo.) pub. schs., 1967-70; instr. piano, staff piano accompanist U. No. Colo., Greeley, 1970-72; instr. music history U. Colo., Boulder, 1974; instr., asst. prof. music U. N.C.-Wilmington, 1974-79; assoc. prof. music, coordinator music Shaw U., Raleigh, N.C., 1979—; pvt. instr. piano and flute, 1960-79; profl. harpsichord accompanist Internat. Inst. in Early Music, summer 1983. Bd. dirs. Piedmont Council Traditional Music, Community Theater Project, St. Augustine Coll. Raleigh Chamber Music Guild; sec. Bach Festival Com., Raleigh, 1984. John H. Edwards fellow Ind. U., 1961; U. Colo. grad. fellow, 1972-74; Mellon Found. grantee, 1982; N.C. Arts Council grantee, 1985; NEH summer seminar fellow, 1984. Mem. Am. Musicological Soc. (sec.-treas. chpt. 1981-83), Soc. for Ethnomusicology (chmn. regional chpt. 1983-84), Coll. Music Soc., (com. on status minorities 1985), Sonneck Soc., Alpha Lambda Delta, Pi Kappa Lambda, Sigma Alpha Iota. Democrat. Unitarian. Recs. include: Early Popular Music on Piano/Harpsichord, 1984; author: The Piano Trio in the Twentieth Century, 1984; editor, compiler: The Music of Gustave Blessner, 1985; music reviewer News & Observer, Raleigh, 1981—; contbr. articles to profl. jours. Office: PO Box 58265 Raleigh NC 27658

PINKARD, RAYMOND FLOYD, firefighter; b. Madison, Fla., Jan. 3, 1929; s. James Burton and Viola (Dempsey) P.; m. Evelyn Mary Albritton, Jan. 16, 1960; children—Jerome Edward, Kenneth Patrich. Grad., Madison High, Fla. Firefighter Madison Fire Dept., 1957-59, 1961-74, fire chief, 1974—; Gen. Merchant, Madison, 1959-61. Served to sgt. U.S. Army, 1947-54. Home: 415 S Horry St Madison FL 32340 Office: Fire Dept 116 W Dade St Madison FL 32340

PINKENBURG, RONALD JOSEPH, ophthalmologist; b. Houston, Nov. 25, 1940; s. William Joseph and Winnie Vale (Downs) P.; B.A. cum laude, U. St. Thomas, 1963; M.D., Baylor U., 1967; m. Patricia Anne Regan, Oct. 21, 1967; children—Lisa, Anne Marie, Steven, Renée. Intern, U. Iowa, 1967-68; resident U. Okla., 1971-74, asst. clin. prof. ophthalmology, 1974—; gen. practitioner So. Calif. Permanente Med. Group-Kaiser Found. Hosp., Fontana, 1970-71; pvt. practice medicine specializing in ophthalmology, Tyler, Tex., 1974—; mem. staff Med. Center Hosp., Tyler, Mother Francis Hosp., Tyler. Served with USAF, 1968-70. Fellow ACS, Royal Soc. Medicine; mem. Smith County Med. Soc., Tex. Med. Assn., AMA, Tex. Ophthalmology Assn., Am. Acad. Ophthalmology, Am. Intraocular Implant Soc. Roman Catholic. Home: 311 Cumberland Rd Tyler TX 75703 Office: 820 S Baxter St Tyler TX 75701

PINKERTON, MIQUE FERRELL, photographer, artist; b. Norfolk, Va., May 20, 1920; d. William Edmond and L'Ona Mae (Holton) Ferrell; m. Robert S. Pinkerton, Mar. 7, 1939 (div. 1946); 1 child, Dyanna Ferrell Pinkerton Byers; m. C.E. Pinkerton, May 17, 1958. Student U. Hawaii, 1961-65. Photographer Pinkerton Studio, Wink, Tex., 1936-39, Mathews, Va., 1939-42, Luray, Va., 1942-58, Port Isabel, Tex., 1958-60; photographer, artist George's Studio, Honolulu, 1961—; seashell dealer Mique's Molluscs, Warrenton, Va., 1975—; free lance photographer, Tex., Va., 1961-78; docent dept. malacology Smithsonian Instn., Washington, 1976-77; lectr. in field, 1975—. Contbr. articles to profl. jours. Vol., Mustard Seed, Gainesville, Va., 1973-81, FISH, Warrenton, 1984-85, FORE, Warrenton, 1984-85. Mem. Hawaiian Malacological Soc. (sec. 1967, 68, 69), Nat. Capital Shell Club, Conchologist Am., Am. Malacological Union, Smithsonian Assocs. Avocations: malacology; paleontology. Home: 1324 Westmoreland Dr Warrenton VA 22186

PINKSTON, JOHN WILLIAM, JR., hospital administrator; b. Valdosta, Ga., Aug. 11, 1924; s. John William and Fannie L. (Smith) P.; B.B.A., Emory U., 1946; m. Jane G. Grant, Nov. 12, 1959; children—Carol Grant, John William III. Trainee, Western Electric Co., 1947-48; with Grady Meml. Hosp., Atlanta, 1948—, exec. dir., 1964—. Sec. health and social service adv. council Atlanta Regional Commn., 1975; bd. dirs. North Central Ga. Health Systems Agy., 1976—; trustee Atlanta Music Festival Assn., 1984—; bd. dirs. Blue Cross/Blue Shield, 1986. Served with C.E., AUS, 1944-46. Mem. Am. (chmn. pub. hosp. sect. 1976, 83, mem. council on legis. 1975—, Ho. of Dels. 1978-87, Council on Patient Services 1985-88), Ga. (treas. 1975, pres. 1977), hosp. assns., Assn. Am. Med. Colls. (mem. adminstrv. bd. council of teaching hosps. 1974-75). Home: 3176 Verdun Dr NW Atlanta GA 30305 Office: 80 Butler St SE Atlanta GA 30335

PINNELL, GARY RAY, lawyer; b. San Antonio, Oct. 2, 1951; s. Raymond A., Jr., and Mary Ruth (Waller) P. B.B.A., U. Tex.-Austin, 1973, postgrad., 1976-77; J.D., St. Mary's U., San Antonio, 1976. Bar: Tex. 1976, U.S. Supreme Ct. 1982, U.S. Ct. Appeals (all cirs.), U.S. Tax Ct. 1976, U.S. Ct. Claims 1977, U.S. Tax Ct. 1976, U.S. Ct. Claims 1977, U.S. Ct. Customs and Patent Appeals 1978. Sole practice, Austin, Tex., 1976-77. San Antonio, 1977—; legis. asst. to Rep. Danny E. Hill, 1977; instr. U. Tex.-Austin, 1976-77. Bd. govs. Soc. Colonial Wars, Tex., 1978—; mem. Tex. Soc. Sons Revolution, 1979—. Decorated comdr. Order St. John, Queen Elizabeth II, 1985; officer Order Polonia Restituta (Poland), 1982, knight Teutonic Order (Vatican), 1979. Mem. Internat. Bar Assn., State Bar Tex., Mexican Acad. Internat. Law, Omicron Delta Kappa, Delta Sigma Pi, Phi Alpha Delta. Republican. Roman Catholic. Club: St. John's (London). Contbr. articles legal jours. Home: 2611 Eisenhauer Rd 603 San Antonio TX 78209 Office: 432 Dwyer St San Antonio TX 78204

PINNELL, HOWARD EUGENE, hospital administrator, real estate broker, independent oil producer; b. Scotia, Mo., Feb. 26, 1931; s. Howard Everet and Zella Christine (Lewis) P.; m. Virginia Faye Miller, Dec. 17, 1950; children—David, Penny, Patty. B.B.A., St. Mary's U., 1958. Adminstr. Meml. Hosp., Uvalde, Tex., 1959-62, Polly Ryon Meml. Hosp., Richmond, Tex., 1962-83, El Campo Meml. Hosp., Tex., 1983-85. Deacon, First Bapt. Ch., El Campo, 1984. Served to cpl. U.S. Army, 1952-54. Mem. Am. Coll. Hosp. Adminstrs., Am. Hosp. Assn., Tex. Hosp. Assn., El Campo C. of C. Republican. Lodge: Rotary.

PINNEY, EDWARD LOWELL, JR., physician, educator; b. Gauley Bridge, W.Va., Nov. 11, 1925; s. Edward Lowell and May (Vencill) P.; A.B., Princeton U., 1949; B.S., W.Va. Med. Sch., 1947; M.D., Washington U., St. Louis, 1949; m. Arline Claire Caldwell, Aug. 2, 1957 (div. May 1980); children—David Edward, Diane Arline, Michael Leslie. Intern, St. Louis City Hosp., 1949-50; resident Bklyn. State Hosp., 1952-54, sr. psychiatrist, 1954-55; practice medicine specializing in psychiatry, Bklyn., 1955-68; mem. staff St. John's Episcopal Hosp., 1956-68, Meth. Hosp., 1956-67, Bklyn. Cumberland, Gracie Square hosps., Beekman Downtown Hosp., N.Y.C., 1968-78; partner, med. dir. Bklyn. Med. Assos. Psychiatry and Neurology, 1958-64; psychiat. cons., dir. Mental Hygiene Clin. Cumberland Hosp. div., Bklyn.-Cumberland Med. Center, 1964-68, attending psychiatrist, 1968-76, psychiat. cons., 1976-82; psychiat. cons. Bklyn. Eye and Ear Hosp., 1967-76; attending psychiatrist Manhattan Eye, Ear and Throat Hosp., 1976-82; clin. instr. SUNY, Down State Med. Center, 1958-68; clin. asst. prof. psychiatry Cornell U. Med. Coll., 1968-71, clin. asso. prof., 1971-78; clin. asso. prof. N.Y. U., 1978-82; physician health service L.I. U., 1962-82; psychiat. cons. Bd. Edn. N.Y.C.; dir. psychiatry N.Y.C. Dept. Correction, 1979-80; co-dir. tng. program in group psychotherapy N.Y. U. Postgrad. Med. Sch., 1979-82; psychiat. cons. VA Hosp. Bklyn., 1972-82; med. dir. Austin-Travis County (Tex.) Mental Health/Mental Retardation Center, 1982-83; mem. faculty dept. psychiatry U. Tex. Med. Br., Galveston, 1983-84; dir. residency tng. program Austin State Hosp., 1984—. Bd. mgrs. Bklyn. Central YMCA, 1964-68; chmn. profl. adv. com. Archeus Found., N.Y.C., 1968—, pres., 1975-76; mem. profl. adv. com. Epilepsy Soc. for Social Service, 1970-82. Served as lt., M.C., USNR, 1950-52. Fellow Am. Psychiat. Assn., Am. Soc. Psychoanalytic Physicians (pres. 1973-74), Am. Group Psychotherapy Assn.; mem. Schilder Soc., AMA, Kings County, N.Y. County med. socs., N.Y. Soc. Clin. Psychiatry, Assoc. Physicians L.I., Pan Am. Med. Assn., Assn. Mil. Surgeons U.S., Med. Soc. N.Y. State (chmn. sect. psychiatry 1976-77, alt. del. 1978), Eastern Psychiat. Research Assn. (sec.-treas.), Assn. Research Nervous and Mental Diseases, AAAS, N.Y. State Hosps. Med. Alumni Assn. (pres. 1968-72), Phi Beta Pi. Club: N.Y. Athletic. Author: A First Group Psychotherapy Book, 1970; A Glossary for Group and Family Therapy, 1982; contbr. articles to profl. jours.; assoc. editor The Bull. Area II dist. brs. Am. Psychiat. Assn. Home: 8403A Cima Oak Ln PO Box 49680 Austin TX 78765 Office: Austin State Hosp 4110 Guadalupe Austin TX 78751

PINZONE, JOHN ANTHONY, computer company executive; b. Springfield, Mass., July 16, 1943; s. Victor E. and Jennie (Colletti) P.; m. Mary Jane Cruz, June 8, 1963; 1 dau., Sheryl Lynne. B.A., Am. Internat. Coll., 1965; M.B.A., Pepperdine U., 1982. Div. mgr. Dataserv, Burlingame, Calif., 1973-75; div. mgr. Hybrid Electronics, Burlingame, Calif., 1975-77; pres., chmn. bd. dirs. U.S. Brokers, Dallas, 1977-79; pres., chmn. bd. dirs. Pinzone Internat., Inc., Duncanville, Tex., 1979—; dir. Internat. Computer. Mem. Republican Nat. Com., 1979. Mem. Nat. Fedn. Small Businesses, Computer Dealers Syndicate, Republican Inner Circle. Roman Catholic. Club: Oak Cliff Country. Home: 1218 Coventry Ln Duncanville TX 75137 Office: 1103 S Cedar Ridge Duncanville TX 75137

PIOTROWSKI, GEORGE, engineering educator, consultant; b. Konigsberg, Germany, Jan. 4, 1942; came to U.S., 1953, naturalized, 1960; s. John and Alice (Nausner) P.; m. Linda Joyce Lewis, Aug. 7, 1966; children—Mark Andrew, Eric Steven. B.S. in Mech. Engring., MIT, 1964, M.S. in Mech. Engring., 1965; Ph.D. in Biomed. Engring., Case Western Res. U., 1975. Registered profl. engr., Fla. Asst. prof. dept. mech. engring. U. Fla., Gainesville, 1969-76, assoc. prof., 1976—; ptnr. Design Analysis Services Co., Gainesville, 1983—; cons. USFDA, Silver Spring, Md., 1975-83. Contbr. numerous articles to profl. jours. Mem. ASTM (chmn. sect. F4.2.5 1974—), ASME, Am. Soc. Engring. Edn., Vet. Orthopaedic Soc. Avocation: model railroading. Home: 2011 NW 57th Terr Gainesville FL 32605 Office: U Fla Dept Mech Engring Gainesville FL 32611

PIPER, GARY NELSON, banker; b. Albion, Mich., Jan. 1, 1946; s. Ezra Burton and Madonna (Hughes) P.; m. Kathryn Joyce Shook, Aug. 23, 1969; children—Mary Kathryn, Matthew Burton. B.S. in Mktg., Ind. State U., 1969. Asst. v.p. So. Nat. Bank, Houston, 1973-79; v.p. Central Bank, Houston, 1979; asst. v.p. First City Nat. Bank of Houston, 1979-85, v.p., 1985—. Bd. mgmt. YMCA, Pearland, Tex., 1984—; treas. Sagemont Area Soccer Club, Houston, 1983-84, St. Andrew's Episcopal Ch., Pearland, 1982-84, mem. vestry, 1983—; v.p. Sagemont Area Jaycees, 1976. Served with U.S. Army, 1969-72. Avocation: youth sports. Office: First City Nat Bank of Houston 1001 Fannin Houston TX 77002

PIPER, LLOYD LLEWELLYN, II, engineering and construction executive; b. Wareham, Mass., Apr. 28, 1944; s. Lloyd Llewellyn and Mary Elizabeth (Brown) P.; B.S.E.E., Tex. A&M U., 1966; M.S. in Indsl. Engring., U. Houston, 1973; m. Jane Melonie Scruggs, Apr. 30, 1965; 1 son, Michael Wayne. With Houston Lighting & Power Co., 1965-74; project engring. mgr. Dow Chem. Engring. & Constrn. Services, Houston, 1974-78; project mgr. Ortloff Corp., Houston, 1978-83, mgr. engring., 1979-80, v.p., 1980-83; pres., dir. Plantech Engrs. and Constructors, Inc. subs Dillingham Corp., Houston, 1983—; pres. Delta Plantech Co., Houston, 1985—. Bd. dirs. Harris County Water Control and Improvement Dist., 1973-83, pres., 1973-83; trustee Ponderosa Joint Powers Agy. Harris County, 1977-83, pres., 1977-83. Recipient Disting. Service award Engrs. Council Houston, 1970; Outstanding Service award Houston sect. IEEE, 1974, Tex. Young Engr. of Yr., 1976, Nat. Young Engr. of Yr., 1976; registered profl. engr., Tex. Mem. Nat. Soc. Profl. Engrs. (chpt. pres. 1978, nat. chmn. engrs. in industry div. 1977, nat. v.p. 1977, chmn. nat. polit. action com. 1980-83), IEEE, Project Mgmt. Inst., Phi Kappa Phi. Roman Catholic. Contbr. articles to profl. jours. Home: 4310 Oxhill Rd Spring TX 77388 Office: PO Box 60587 Houston TX 77205

PIPER, WILLIAM FRED, JR., acctg. co. exec.; b. Nashville, May 26, 1944; s. Willima Fred and Burnease (Towns) P.; B.S., U. Tenn., 1966; Asso. in Data Processing, Nashville State Tech., 1967; m. Juanita E. Hicks, Mar. 28, 1978; children—Deborah C., William F., Tiffany E., Keith B. Jr. acct. M.B. Cottle P.A., 1963-66; from jr. acct. to dir. prodn. control Phillips & Buttorff Corp., Nashville, 1966-76; mgr. prodn. control Tappan Appliance, Springfield, Tenn., 1976-77; owner, mgr., dir. Diversified Services of Nashville, 1977—; dir. ABC Bldg. & Maintenance Co., El Taco of Tenn., William F. Piper Acctg. and Tax Service; acct. Office of Criminal Ct. Clk., City of Nashville, 1980. Mem. Republican Nat. Com. Mem. Nat. Soc. Public Accts., Tenn. Soc. Public Accts., Nat. Assn. Tax Consultors, Mcht. Brokers Exchange, Am. Prodn. and Inventory Control Soc. Jehovah Witness. Author acctg. and taxation articles for small bus. man; also prodn. control manuals. Office: 4114 Gallatin Rd Box 4669 Nashville TN 37216

PIPES, STANLEY HOWARD, sugar company executive; b. Shreveport, La., Dec. 13, 1934; s. Luther Frank and Mary Sue (Stanley) P.; m. Virginia Ann Ponder, July 9, 1953; children—Stanley Howard, Cynthia Ann. B.S. in Acctg., La. State U., 1966. C.P.A., La. Sr. auditor Touche Ross & Co., New Orleans, 1966-71; v.p., treas. Sterling Sugars, Inc., Franklin, La., 1971—. Served with USN, 1962-63. Mem. Am. Inst. C.P.A.s, Soc. La. C.P.A.s. Republican. Baptist. Club: Belleview Golf and Country (pres. 1981-83). Lodge: Rotary (pres. local club 1983-84). Home: Route 1 Box 159 Franklin LA 70538 Office: PO Box 572 Franklin LA 70538

PIPKIN, RICKY REED, therapist; b. Memphis, Oct. 23, 1952; s. J.C. and Susie (Reed) P.; m. Janet Reasons, Dec. 29, 1972; 1 child, Rachel. A.A., Freed-Hardeman Coll., Henderson, Tenn., 1976; B.A., Western Ill. U., 1985; postgrad. U. Tex.-Arlington, 1985, E. Tex. State U., 1985. Lic. social worker, Tex. Counselor, minister Broad St. Ch. of Christ, Lexington, Tenn., 1974-77; v.p. Metro Mktg., Inc., Memphis, 1978-81; therapist, counselor Boles Home, Inc., Quinlan, Tex., 1982—; football coach Boles High Sch., 1982-85. Mem. sch. bd. trustees Boles Ind. Sch. Dist., Quinlan, 1985. Named Ambassador of Goodwill, State of La., 1979; Hon. lt. col., Ala. State Militia, 1981; hon. citizen City of New Orleans, 1983, City of Dallas, 1983. Mem. Nat. Assn. Social Workers, Am. Assn. Counseling and Devel., Am. Mental Health Counselors Assn., Assn. Trainers in Clin. Hypnosis (cert. clin. hypnotherapist). Republican. Mem. Ch. of Christ. Home: Route 3 Box 40 Quinlan TX 75474 Office: Boles Home Inc Route 3 Box 40 Quinlan TX 75474

PIRKLE, DAVID EUGENE, mech. engr.; b. Atlanta, Aug. 8, 1927; s. David Ambrose and Eugenia (Bragg) P.; B.S., Ga. Inst. Tech., 1952; m. Mildred Ransie Edgens, Jan. 31, 1959. Mech. engr. Lockheed Aircraft Co., Marietta, Ga., 1952-59; individual engring. practice, Atlanta, 1959-63, 70—; mech. engr. Atlanta Army Depot, Forest Park, Ga., 1963-70. Recipient award Lockheed Mgmt. Club, 1954; award for outstanding performance in engring. Dept. Army, 1966, 69. Registered profl. engr., Ga. Address: 2203 Polar Rock Pl SW Atlanta GA 30315

PIRKLE, GEORGE EMORY, television writer, producer, director, consultant; b. Atlanta, Sept. 3, 1947; s. George Washington and Glanna Adeline (Palmer) P.; m. Karen Leigh Horn, Oct. 20, 1973; 1 child, Charity Caroline. Student North Ga. Coll., 1965-66; B.A. in Journalism, U. Ga., 1969, M.A., 1971. Radio announcer, sportscaster for various radio stas., North Ga. area, 1968-70; TV producer, dir. Instructional Resources Ctr., Athens, Ga., 1969-70;

pub. info. officer Ga. Dept. Revenue, Atlanta, 1973-78; coordinator TV prodn. services So. Co. Services, Inc., Birmingham, Ala., 1978—; exec. v.p. Mgmt. and Human Devel. Assocs., Inc., Birmingham, 1984—; producer Prodn. Works, Birmingham, 1984—; actor for various radio and TV commercials, radio dramas, stage plays, 1975—. Editor monthly newsletter Ga. Revenews, 1973-78; writer, producer, exec. producer numerous TV and film programs. Mem. communications com. Birmingham Area Council Boy Scouts Am., 1983-85; Master of ceremonies gov.'s vet. awards presentation World Peace Luncheon, Birmingham, 1981, 82, 84; exec. producer videotape for Birmingham Film Council, 1985. Served to 1st lt. U.S. Army, 1971-73. Recipient various awards. Mem. Internat. TV Assn. (charter pres. Birmingham chpt. 1984-85, pres. pro tem 1984), So. Electric System Media Resources Rev. Group (founding). Republican. Baptist. Avocations: photography; genealogy; computers; archaeology; reading. Home: 3801 Buckingham Pl Birmingham AL 35223 Office: So Co Services In PO Box 2625 Birmingham AL 35202

PIRKLE, WILLIAM ARTHUR, geology educator, researcher; b. Atlanta, May 11, 1945; s. Earl C. and Valda Nell (Armistead) P.; m. Rachel Isabel Batts, Aug. 25, 1968; children—Owen William, Elizabeth Anne. B.S. in Geology, Emory U., 1967; M.S., U. N.C., 1970, Ph.D., 1972. Cert. profl. geologist, Ga. Asst. prof. geology U. S.C.-Aiken, 1972-75, assoc. prof. geology, 1975-82, prof. geology, 1982—, chmn. div. natural scis., 1984—; geologist Rosario Resources, Inc., 1969; project geologist, S.C. Geol. Survey, 1973—. Mem. Geol. Soc. Am., Am. Inst. Mining, Metall. and Petroleum Engrs., Carolina Geol. Soc., Sigma Xi. Methodist. Contbr. articles to profl. jours. Home: 318 Lakeside Dr Aiken SC 29801 Office: Div Natural Scis U SC Aiken SC 29801

PIRTLE, GEORGE WILLIAM, geologist, petroleum consultant; b. Cecilia, Ky., Nov. 1, 1902; s. Thomas Louis and Laura (Shipley) P.; B.S., U. Ky., 1924, M.S., 1925; m. El Freda Taylor, July 16, 1928; 1 son, George William. Geologist, Ky. Geol. Survey, 1924-25; cons. geologist, partner Hudnall & Pirtle, Tyler, Tex., 1925-69; ind. petroleum cons., 1969—; dir. Peoples Nat. Bank. Past trustee Tyler Jr. Coll.; dir. South Central region Boy Scouts Am., mem. nat. exec. bd. Recipient Silver Beaver, Silver Antelope, Silver Buffalo awards Boy Scouts Am.; named Tyler's Outstanding Citizen, 1962. Mem. Tex. Acad. Sci., East Tex. C. of C. (past v.p.), Geol. Soc. Am., Am. Assn. Petroleum Geologists, Mich. Acad. Sci., AIME, Sigma Xi, Omicron Delta Kappa. Methodist. Endowed George W. Pirtle Tech. Center, Tyler Jr. Coll., 1979-83. Home: 115 E 2d St Tyler TX 75701 Office: 610 Interfirst Plaza Bldg Tyler TX 75702

PIRTLE, IVYL LEORA FLEMING (MRS. J. MAX PIRTLE), librarian; b. nr. Ottumwa, Iowa, Jan. 11, 1906; d. Barton Earl and Lillie (Roberts) Fleming; student Iowa State Coll., 1931; B.A., U. Fla., 1944; M.A., Fla. State U., 1951; m. J. Max Pirtle, Sept. 17, 1938. Tchr. elementary schs., Iowa, 1924-39; tchr. Grace Stern Pvt. Sch., Miami Beach, Fla., 1939-40; tchr. elementary schs., Indiantown, 1940-43; tchr. primary grades, Stuart, 1943-50; demonstration tchr. Fla. State U., Tallahassee, summer 1949; tchr. Palmetto Sch., West Palm Beach, 1950-55; supr. elementary edn. Palm Beach County, 1955-65, dir. library services, 1965-70; mem. Fla. steering com. NDEA, 1958-68. Trustee Jr. Mus. Palm Beach County, 1960-63. Recipient certificate of appreciation Fla. Dept. Edn., 1969. Mem. Assn. Childhood Edn. Internat. (br. pres. 1953-55, primary edn. com. 1954-56), Fla. Assn. Sch. Librarians (area chmn. 1959-62), NEA, Fla. Edn. Assn. (state chmn. dept. suprs. 1959-60, dept. suprs. citation for meritorious service 1968), Assn. Supervision and Curriculum Devel., Delta Kappa Gamma (chpt. pres. 1955-59), Kappa Delta Pi, Phi Kappa Phi. Club: Zonta. Contbr. articles to profl. jours. Home: 340 Nottingham Blvd West Palm Beach FL 33405

PISACANO, NICHOLAS JOSEPH, physician, educator; b. Phila., June 6, 1924; s. Joseph Harry and Rafaella (Saquella) P.; B.A., Western Md. Coll., 1943, D.Sc. (hon.), 1980; M.D., Hahnemann Med. Sch., 1951; m. Virginia Leigh Burleson, May 9, 1978; children—Toni Ann, Nicki Rae, Dean Alan, Don Arlie, Lori Sue. Intern, Stamford, (Conn.) Hosp., 1951-52, resident, 1952-53; gen. practice medicine, South Royalton, Vt., 1953-55, Phila., 1955-62; med. dir. Am. Cancer Soc., 1958-62; dir. continuing med. edn. U. Ky., Lexington, 1962-69, asst. dean Coll. Arts and Scis., 1966-72, asst. to v.p. Med. Center, 1966-72, prof., chmn. dept. allied health edn. and research, 1975—, asso. dean Coll. Allied Health Professions, 1974—; prof. biology-medicine U. Ky. Med. Center; exec. dir., and sec. Am. Bd. Family Practice, 1969—. Pres., Bluegrass Mental Health Assn. Served with U.S. Army, 1943-46. Recipient Disting. Teaching award U. Ky., 1967; Most Outstanding Alumnus of Yr. award Hahnemann Med. Coll., 1979. Mem. Am. Acad. Family Physicians (Thomas Johnson award 1977, Max Cheplove, M.D., award Erie County (N.Y.) chpt. 1977), Canadian Coll. Family Physicians (hon.), AMA, AAAS, Pan Am. Med. Assn. (v.p.), Assn. Am. Med. Colls., Soc. for Health and Human Values, Royal Soc. Medicine (Eng.), Soc. Tchrs. of Family Medicine, So. Med. Assn., N.Y. Acad. Scis., Ky. Med. Assn., Internat. Ctr. Family Medicine. Office: 2228 Young Dr Lexington KY 40505

PISCHNER, JOHN CHARLES, labor relations management consultant; b. Green Bay, Wis., May 24, 1944; s. Charles R. and Alice M. (Gallagher) P.; m. Teresa Wright, Feb. 26, 1981; children—Kristen, Kathleen, Stephanie. B.S. magna cum laude, U. Wis.-Green Bay, 1972; postgrad. Neuro-Linguistic Programming Inst., Washington, 1985, Inst. for Ethical and Clin. Hypnosis, Washington, 1986. Health planner Northeastern Wis. Health Planning Council, Inc., Green Bay, 1972-74; dir. planning St. Vincent Hosp., Green Bay, 1974-79; psychotherapist Am. Found. Religion and Psychiatry, Green Bay, 1974-79; mgr. tng. and orgn. devel. Modern Mgmt., Inc., Chgo., 1979-81; pres. John C. Pischner & Assocs., Knoxville, Tenn., 1981—. Served with USAF, 1962-66. Mem. Am. Soc. Tng. and Devel. Lodge: Masons.

PISCIOTTA, JOHN LEE, economics educator; b. Pueblo, Colo., July 10, 1944; s. Fred and Rose Lee (Corsentino) P.; m. Sharleen Jo Parlapiano, June 12, 1965; children—Sunny, John, Fred, Nicole. B.A., U. Colo., 1966; Ph.D., U. Tex., 1971. Teaching asst., lectr. U. Tex., Austin, 1968-71; asst. to assoc. prof. U. So. Colo., Pueblo, 1971-77, chmn. econs. dept., 1977-80; Stevens prof. pvt. enterprise Baylor U., Waco, Tex., 1980—. Editor: Macroeconomics 85/86, 1985. Contbr. articles to profl. jours. Recipient George Washington Medal of Honor, Freedoms Found. at Valley Forge, 1984; Leavey Found. award Freedoms Found. at Valley Forge 1982; Top Prof. award Baylor U., 1981. Mem. Southwestern Econs. Assn. Joint Council Econ. Edn. (Internat. Paper Co. Found. award 1982), Tex. Council Social Studies. Roman Catholic. Home: 8224 Teakwood Waco TX 76710 Office: Ctr Pvt Enterprise Hankamer Sch Bus Waco TX 76798

PISKE, RICHARD A., JR., consulting mechanical engineer; b. New Orleans, May 23, 1924; s. Richard A. and Myrtle L. (Mackenroth) P.; m. Louise Oldert, July 6, 1946; children—Richard, Gregory. B.M.E., Tulane U., 1944. Registered profl. engr., Tenn. Regional engring. mgr. Carrier Corp., Atlanta, 1955-62, programs mgr. Mil. Equipment dept., Syracuse, N.Y., 1962-65; prin. in charge I.C. Thomasson Assoc., Cons. Engrs., Knoxville, Tenn., 1966-81; mgr. bldg. systems dept. Allen & Hoshall, Inc., Cons. Engrs., Knoxville, 1981—. Mem. Nat. Soc. Profl. Engrs., Am. Cons. Engrs. Council (past nat. dir.), Cons. Engrs. Tenn. (past pres.), Tenn. Soc. Profl. Engrs., ASHRAE, Knoxville Tech. Soc. Lutheran. Home: 5516 River Pt Cove Knoxville TN 37919 Office: Box 90345 Knoxville TN 37990

PISTOR, CHARLES HERMAN, JR., banker; b. St. Louis, Aug. 26, 1930; s. Charles Herman and Virginia (Brown) P.; B.B.A., U. Tex., 1952; M.B.A., Harvard U., 1956, So. Meth. U., 1961; grad. Stonier Sch. Banking, Rutgers U., 1964; m. Regina Prikryl, Sept. 20, 1952; children—Lori Ellen, Charles Herman III, Jeffrey Glenn. Pres., dir. RepublicBank Dallas (formerly Republic Nat. Bank), to 1980, chmn., chief exec. officer, 1980—; dir. Republic Financial Services, Inc., Dallas, RepublicBank Corp., Am. Airlines, Inc., Am. Brands, Inc. Chmn. SMU Bus. Sch. Found.; mem. Dallas Citizens Council. Served to lt. USNR, 1952-54. Mem. Am. Bankers Assn. (dir.), Assn. Res. City Bankers (dir.). Presbyterian (elder). Club: Dallas Country. Office: PO Box 225961 Dallas TX 75265

PITCHFORD, HENRY GRADY, sociology educator; b. Dadeville, Ala., June 5, 1929; s. Henry Grady and Bernice Lillian (Casaday) P. B.A., Auburn U., 1948; M.S., Syracuse U., 1950; M.A., U. Denver, 1958; Ph.D., Emory U., 1960. Librarian San Jose State U., Calif., 1954-57, prof. sociology, 1963-69; librarian U. Denver, 1957-58; prof. sociology U. Southwestern La., Lafayette, 1969—, dept. head, 1972-75. Contbr. articles in profl. jours. Pres. Catholic Interracial Council, San Jose, 1965-66. Recipient Disting. Prof. award U. Southwestern La., 1972, Amoco award for Excellence in Teaching, 1982; spl. honor fellow Emory U., 1958-60. Mem. Am. Sociol. Assn., AAUP, Kappa Sigma (faculty adv. 1979-84). Roman Catholic. Home: 185 Whittington Dr Lafayette LA 70503 Office: U Southwestern La Box 40198 Lafayette LA 70504

PITISCI, JAMES HARRELL, psychologist, educator; b. Miami, Fla., Feb. 14, 1947; s. Joseph Spoto and Marguerite (Harrell) P.; m. Mary Louise Moxness, June 8, 1974; 1 child, Gina Marie. B.S. in Psychology, Wofford Coll., 1969; M.Ed. in Counseling, Fla. Atlantic U., 1971; Ed.D. in Behavioral Sci., Nova U., 1979. Cert. sex therapist, sex educator, sex counselor, marriage and family therapist, sch. psychologist, mental health counselor. Research analyst Miami-Dade Community Coll., Fla., 1969-72, instr. to assoc. prof. 1972-80, prof., 1981—; clin. intern in human sexuality, Sch. Medicine U. Calif., San Francisco, 1980, assoc. staff, 1980-81; psychotherapist Miami Lakes Med. Ctr., Fla., 1981—; dir. counseling SHE Ctr., North Miami, Fla., 1980-82; lectr. U. Miami Med. Sch., 1980—; cons. Random House Publs., N.Y.C., 1982—, stas. WIOD, WNWS, WCIX-TV, Miami, 1981—. Author: Study Guide to Sexuality, 1985; cons. editor: Random House Publs., 1984, West Publishing, 1981; author jour. articles. Coach Miami Springs Optimist Club, 1969-72; lectr. civic, polit., ch. groups. Recipient Disting. Service award, Miami-Dade Community Coll., 1979, Spl. Merit award, 1985; named Best News Source, Falcon Times Newspaper, Miami, 1982. Mem. Am. Psychol. Assn., Am. Assn. Marriage and Family Therapy (clin.), Acad. Psychologists in Sex/Marital Therapy (clin.), Am. Assn. Sex Educators, Counselors and Therapists, Soc. for Sci. Study of Sex, Sex Info. and Edn. Council of U.S. Republican. Baptist. Clubs: Optimist, Dawn Patrol, Miami Lakes Athletic. Avocations: flying; marathon running; fishing; golf. Home: 14580 English Rd Miami Lakes FL 33014 Office: Miami Lakes Med Ctr 15175 Eagle Nest Ln Miami Lakes FL 33014

PITMAN, SHARON GAIL, school counselor; b. Dayton, Ohio, June 13, 1946; d. Finley Andrew and Lena Kay (Wells) Jennings; m. Benjamin Pitman III, Jan. 19, 1980; stepchildren—Scott, Todd. B.S. in Edn., Miami U., Oxford, Ohio, 1968, M.Ed. in Edn., 1970; sch. counseling cert. Ga. State U., 1979, M.Ed. in Counseling, 1981. Tchr. pub. schs., Hamilton, Ohio, 1968-73, Gwinnett County, Ga., 1973-80; interim counselor Lilburn Elem. Sch., Gwinnett County, 1981, Five Forks Middle Sch., Gwinnett County, 1981; sch. counselor Buford Middle Sch., Ga., 1981—; conductor workshops in field. Fellow Am. Assn. Counseling and Devel., Am. Sch. Counseling Assn., Ga. Sch. Counselors Assn., NEA, Ga. Assn. Educators, Gwinett County Assn. Counselors, Ga. League Middle Grade Educators. Avocations: writing poetry; photography; gardening. Office: Buford Middle Sch 601 Hill St Buford GA 30518

PITSENBERGER, THOMAS MORRIS, dentist; b. Philippi, W.Va., Dec. 21, 1939; s. Isaac Irvin and Ada (Morris) P.; children—James, Ashley. B.A., W.Va. U., 1960, D.D.S., 1964. Dentist Davis Meml. Assocs. Inc., Elkins, W.Va., 1970-80, Dental Assocs. Inc., Elkins, 1980—; dir. Kane and Keyser Hardware, Inc., Belington, W.Va., Belington Bank; founder, pres. Primacare Services Inc., Elkins, 1981—. Pres. Randolph County United Way, 1975; mem. Regional Health Adv. Council, Buckhannon, W.Va., 1979—. Served as capt. U.S. Army, 1964-67. Mem. ADA; Monongahola Valley Dental Assn. (pres. 1981). Lodge: Lions. Avocations: skiing; flying. Home: 206 Westview Dr Elkins WV 26241 Office: Dental Assocs Inc 108 3rd St Elkins WV 25241

PITTILLO, JACK DANIEL, biology educator, researcher, consultant; b. Hendersonville, N.C., Oct. 25, 1938; s. Louia and Mattie Ruth (Hill) P.; m. Jean Henri Farr, Aug. 23, 1966; children—Heather Ann, Shane Keven. A.B., Berea Coll. (Ky.), 1961; M.S., U. Ky.-Lexington, 1963; Ph.D., U. Ga.-Athens, 1966. Grad. and research asst. U. Ky., 1961-63, U. Ga., 1963-66; asst. prof. biology Western Carolina U., 1966-71, assoc. prof., 1971-77, prof., 1977—; researcher Nat. Park Service, Atlanta, 1975-77. Pres. N.C. Bartram Trail Soc., Inc., 1980—; active Cullowhee United Meth. Ch., 1968—, mem. adminstrv. bd., 1968—. NSF grantee, 1982-85. Mem. Assn. Southeastern Biologists (research award 1985), Bot. Soc. Am., Ecol. Soc. Am., N.C. Acad. Sci., So. Appalachian Bot. Club (pres. 1977-78, editor 1983—), N.C. Bartram Trail Soc. (pres. 1979-85), Sigma Xi. Democrat. Office: Dept Biology Western Carolina Univ Cullowhee NC 28723

PITTMAN, CARLA BRYANT, social worker, administrator; b. Waco, Tex., Aug. 25, 1949. B.S. in Psychology, Austin Peay State U., 1971; M.S.S.W., U. Tex.-Arlington, 1973; postgrad. George Washington U., 1974-75, Georgetown U., 1976-77. Lic. clin. social worker, Va. Dir. recreation dept. Downtown br. YWCA, Dallas, 1971; field placement counselor Arlington pub. schs., 1971-72, Dist. VI, Mental Health, Mental Retardation Ctr., Dallas, 1972-73; social worker John Peter Smith Hosp., Ft. Worth, 1973; social worker Fairfax County Dept. Social Services, Fairfax, Va., 1973-75, social work supr., 1976-82; dir. Fairfax County Area Agy. on Aging, 1982—; instr. social casework Va. Commonwealth U., Richmond, 1980—; presenter numerous workshops tng. sessions. Active Mt. Vernon Alliance for Housing, Mt. Vernon Ctr. for Community Mental Health, Route 1 Coalition, Fairfax County Commn. for Women Task Force on Battered Women, Crossroads Adv. Bd. Mem. Nat. Assn. Social Workers, Am. Pub. Welfare Assn., Va. Council Social Welfare (dir.). Office: Area Agency on Aging 4100 Chain Bridge Rd Fairfax VA 22030

PITTMAN, DONALD LYNN, SR., building contractor; b. Greenwood, Miss., May 28, 1947; s. John Emmett and Eula Christine (Chapman) P.; m. Sandra Darlene Sanders, July 22, 1969; children—Donald Lynn, Joshua Adam. B.B.A. in Acctg., Delta State U., 1975. Vice pres., controller First Fed. Savs., Greenwood, 1975-78; sec., treas., 1978-80; sr. auditor Lamar Savs., Austin, Tex., 1980-81, sr. v.p. acctg., 1981, exec. v.p., 1981-84, pres., 1984-85, mng. officer, 1982-85, dir., 1982-85. Mem. Inst. Fin. Edn., Fin. Mgrs. Soc., Greenwood Jr. C. of C., Austin Jr. C. of C. Republican. Baptist. Lodge: Lions. Home: 415 Warwick Rd Clinton MS 39056 Office: EPC Inc PO Box 378 Clinton MS 39056

PITTMAN, EDWIN LLOYD, state official; b. Hattiesburg, Miss., Jan. 2, 1935; s. Lloyd H. and Pauline P.; m. Barbara Peel, Aug. 24, 1957; children—Malanie, Win, Jennifer. B.S., U. So. Miss.; J.D., U. Miss., 1960. Bar: Miss. Practiced law until, 1964; mem. Miss. Senate, 1964-72; treas. State of Miss., Jackson, 1976-80, sec. of state, 1970—. Served to 2d lt., Inf. U.S. Army. Mem. U. Miss. Alumni Assn., U. So. Miss. Alumni Assn., Miss. Jaycees (past state dir.), ABA, South Central Miss. Bar Assn. Democrat. Baptist. Clubs: Lions, Masons. Office: PO Box 136 Jackson MS 39205*

PITTMAN, GEORGE HENRY, JR., airport executive, former air force officer; b. Falkland, N.C., Mar. 16, 1920; s. George Henry and Daisy Pauline (Carman) P.; m. Anne Lamoreaux Crawford, June 12, 1941 (div. 1960); children—Theresa Anne, George Henry; m. 2d, Christine Halbhuber, Nov. 1, 1960; 1 dau., Gabriele Antonia. B.S., U.S. Mil. Acad., 1941; grad. Air U., 1950; postgrad. various schs. Commd. 2d lt. U.S. Army, 1941, advanced through grades to col., 1961; pilot Air Navigation Sch., Kelly Field, Tex., 1942; test pilot Air Depot, Duncan Field, Tex., 1942-43; chief insp. maintenance div. San Antonio Air Service Command, Kelly Field, 1943-44; comdr. 5th Floating Air Depot, Tex. and Ala., 1944; base ops. officer, Tinker Field, Okla., 1944; maintenance chief Air Service Ctr., Tinian Island, 1944-45; chief maintenance 20th Air Force, Guam, 1946-47; chief plans Mil. Air Transp. Service, Calif. wing and Mass. div., 1948-50, air transport wing ops., Mass., 1951; comdr. and ops. officer for resupply and communications, Idaho and Philippines, 1951-54; div. chief, exec. U.S. Air Force Directorate for Flight Safety Research, Calif., 1954-58; comdr., tactical missile squadron and dep. comdr. materiel 38th Tactical Missile Wing, W.Ger., 1958-63; dep. comdr. 1st Fighter Wing, Mich., 1963-66; electronics maintenance chief Aerospace Def. Command, 1966-68, ret., 1968; dep. and asst. dir. aviation Melbourne (Fla.) Regional Airport, 1968—; active pilot; guest lectr. Fla. Inst. Tech., also various aviation groups; participant in seminars; tobacco, peanut, corn, soybean farmer, Falkland. Mem. tech. adv. com. Met. Planning Orgn.; former program chmn. Port Malabar Civic Assn.; mem. Melbourne Com. of 100; past mem. Palm Bay Mayor's Adv. Com. Mem. Am. Assn. Airport Execs., Southeastern Airport Mgrs. Assn., Fla. Airport Mgrs. Assn., Palm Bay Area C. of C. (dir. 1974-76), Air Force Assn., Space Coast West Point Soc., Nat. Pilots Assn. (disting. pilot), Aircraft Owners and Pilots Assn., Melbourne Comets (past pres.), Bahia Comets (pres. 1976-77), Quiet Birdman. Democrat. Lutheran. Lodges: Masons, Shriners (past pres. Greater Melbourne), Fla. Shrine Flying Fezzes Assn. (comdr. 1984-85, vice comdr. 1985-86), Azan Aviators (founder, comdr. 1981-82), Royal Order Jesters (past dir. Melbourne). Home: 1490 Country Club Dr NE Palm Bay FL 32905 Office: 1050 S Joe Walker Rd Suite 220 Melbourne FL 32901

PITTMAN, JAMES ALLEN, JR., university dean, physician; b. Orlando, Fla., Apr. 12, 1927; s. James Allen and Jean C. (Garretson) P.; B.S., Davidson Coll., 1948; M.D., Harvard U., 1952, D.Sc. (hon.), 1980; m. Constance Ming-Chung Shen, Feb. 19, 1955; children—James Clinton, John Merrill. Intern, asst. resident medicine Mass. Gen. Hosp., Boston, 1952-54; teaching fellow medicine Harvard U., 1953-54; clin. asso. NIH, Bethesda, Md., 1954-56; instr. medicine George Washington U., 1955-56; chief resident medicine U. Ala. Med. Center, Birmingham, 1956-58, instr. medicine, 1956-59, asst. prof., 1959-62, asso. prof., 1962-64, prof. medicine, 1964-71, dir. endocrinology and metabolism div., 1962-71, co-chmn. dept. medicine, 1969-71, asso. prof. physiology and biophysics, 1966-71; asst. chief med. dir. research and edn. in medicine U.S. VA, 1971-73; prof. medicine Georgetown U. Med. Sch., Washington, 1971-73; dean U. Ala. Sch. Medicine, 1973—; mem. pharmacology, endcrinology fellowships rev. commn. NIH, 1967-68, mem. endocrinology study sect., 1964-68; mem. drug research bd. Nat. Acad. Scis., 1972-75. Fellow ACP (life); Inst. Medicine-Nat. Acad. Scis., mem. Assn. Am. Physicians, Endocrine Soc. (council 1971-74), Am. Thyroid Assn. (v.p. 1972-73, dir. 1974-76), N.Y. Acad. Scis. (life), Soc. Nuclear Medicine, Am. Diabetes Assn., Harvard Med. Alumni Assn. (pres. 1986-87), Am. Chem. Soc., Wilson Ornithol. Club, Am. Ornithologists Union, Am. Fedn. Clin. Research (pres. So. sect., mem. nat. council 1962-66), So. Soc. Clin. Investigation, Inst. of Medicine, Phi Beta Kappa, Alpha Omega Alpha, Omicron Delta Kappa. Author: Diagnosis and Treatment of Thyroid Diseases, 1963; contbr. articles to profl. jours. Home: 5 Ridge Dr Birmingham AL 35213

PITTMAN, JOHN ISHAM, safety engineer; b. Atlanta, Jan. 12, 1948; s. Isham Watson and Katherine (Mathis) P.; m. Leta Loraine Hall, May 19, 1979; 1 child, John Christopher. B.S. in Indsl. Mgmt., Ga. Inst. Tech., 1970. Cert. safety profl., N.C. Mgmt. trainee S.S. Kresge Co., Atlanta, 1971-72; loss prevention cons. Liberty Mut. Ins. Co., Roanoke, Va., 1972-77; safety engr. Burlington Industries, Greensboro, N.C., 1977—. Mem. Am. Soc. Safety Engrs. (profl.; pres. N.C. chpt. 1985-86). Republican. Baptist. Home: 5303 Bayberry Ln Greensboro NC 27405 Office: Burlington Industries 3330 W Friendly Ave Greensboro NC 27410

PITTMAN, JOYCE JANITA, builder; b. Dallas, Aug. 31, 1940; d. O. B. and Thelma Louise Howard; student So. Methodist U., 1961-64, M.A. in Civic Affairs, U. Dallas, 1980; postgrad. U. Tex.-Arlington, 1980-82; m. Clyde H. Pittman, Nov. 7, 1958; children—Craig Howard, Clarissa Dawn. Exec. sec., 1960-67; owner, operator Curiosity Corner, Irving, 1969-71; v.p., co-owner Epic Cos., Dallas, 1975—; pres. Indigo Builders, Inc.; owner AAA Storage; cons. North Tex. Commn.; adv. dir. Am. Bank & Trust. Mem. Irving City Council, 1974-77; pres. Irving chpt. Am. Heart Assn., 1978; dist. dir. Tex. Republican Women's Orgn., 1974-77; mem. Irving Symphony Assn. Named Outstanding Council Woman, Irving, 1976, Outstanding Republican Woman Tex., 1977. Mem. Irving C. of C. Methodist. Clubs: Irving Rep. Women's (sec.-treas. 1968-70, pres. 1971-72), Irving Noon Toastmasters. Home: 1401 Colony Irving TX 75061 Office: 8585 N Stemmons Freeway Dallas TX 75247

PITTMAN, RICHARD FRANK, JR., newspaper publisher; b. Tampa, Fla., Mar. 12, 1923; s. Richard Frank and Jette (Robinson) P.; B.S. in Bus. Adminstrn., U. Fla., 1944; m. Dada Andrews, Apr. 15, 1952; children—Richard Andrews, Dada Katherine. With IRS, 1946; with Tribune Co., Tampa, 1946—, bus. mgr., 1965-69, v.p., gen. mgr., 1970-77, pub. Tampa Tribune and Tampa Times, 1978—, also v.p., dir. Elder, 1st Presbyn. Ch., 1976-79; past pres. Tampa chpt. ARC; campaign chmn., pres., dir., treas. United Way of Greater Tampa; past v.p., bd. dirs. United Cerebral Palsy; vice chmn. S.W. Fla. Blood Bank; bd. dirs. Community Coordinating Council, Fla. Gulf Coast Symphony Assn., Family Service Assn., Sta. WEDU, Fla. Council of 100; trustee St. Joseph's Hosp. Served to 1st lt., Tank Corps, AUS, 1942-46; PTO. Recipient Vol. Activist award, 1977. Mem. Am. Newspaper Pubs. Assn., So. Newspaper Pubs. Assn., Fla. Press Assn., Inst. Newspaper Controllers and Finance Officers, Tampa C. of C. (dir., mem. exec. com.), Pi Kappa Alpha. Clubs: Rotary (past pres.), Tampa Yacht and Country (commodore), Univ. (past dir.), Merrymakers (past pres.), Tower (dir.) (Tampa); Ye Mystic Krewe of Gasparilla (past king and capt.). Office: Tribune Co 202 S Parker St PO Box 191 Tampa FL 33601

PITTMAN, TERRY LEE OBERT, business statistics educator, consultant; b. Camden, N.J., June 2, 1954; s. Charles Leonard and Lee (Blackwell) Obert; m. Walter Earl Pittman, July 27, 1973. B.S., Miss. U. for Women, 1974; M.S. Miss. State U., 1976; postgrad. U. Ala. Instr. dept. math Miss. State U., Mississippi State, 1976-83, instr. stats., dept. bus. info. systems and quantitative analysis, 1983—. Contbr. articles to profl. jours. Sigma Xi grantee, 1985. Mem. Am. Statis. Assn. (mem. com. on quality and productivity 1984—), Am. Soc. for Quality Control (sponsor student chpt. 1984—, treas. local chpt. 1985-86). Avocations: jogging; aerobics; racquetball. Home: 3626 Azalea Dr Columbus MS 39701 Office: Mississippi State U Dept Business Info Systems and Quantitative Analysis Drawer DB Mississippi State MS 39762

PITTS, BEN ELLIS, media specialist, educator; b. Pennington Gap, Va., Sept. 20, 1931; s. Ellis R. and Mary Kelly P.; B.S., Lincoln Meml. U., 1954; M.Ed., U. Ga., 1970, Ed.S., 1971, Ed.D., 1973; M.Div., Emory U., 1974. Tchr., prin. Lee County (Va.) Public Schs., 1950-54; ordained to ministry, United Meth. Ch., 1959; minister chs., 1955-67; media specialist Gwinnett County (Ga.) Public Schs., 1968-73; media specialist Rockdale County (Ga.) Public Schs., 1973-74; coordinator learning resource center Tenn. Tech. U., Cookeville, 1974-79; asso. prof. library/media Delta State U., Cleveland, Miss., 1979-81; media specialist South Ga. Coll., Douglas, 1981—, head librarian, 1983—; cons. Upper Cumberland Regional Library System, Tenn. Mem. Phi Kappa Phi, Kappa Delta Pi, Pi Delta Kappa. Club: Masons. Contbr. articles to profl. jours. Home: Box 1604 Douglas GA 31533 Office: South Ga Coll Douglas GA 31533

PITTS, CHARLOTTE ANN, nursing educator; b. Fort Knox, Ky., Feb. 9, 1952; d. Terrell Lee and Stefanie (Berger) Skelton; m. Harvey Curtis Pitts, Feb. 11, 1981; 1 child, Curtis Fitzpatrick. B.S. in Nursing, U. Ala., 1974; M.S. in Nursing, Med. Coll. of Ga., 1976; Ed.D., Auburn U., 1982. Clin. instr. Columbus Coll., Ga., 1974-75, emergency room charge Med. Ctr., 1974-76, in-service instr. Med. Ctr., 1977-78; in-service dir. Cobb Hosp., Phenix City, Ala., 1977-78; dir. of nursing Chattahoochee Valley Community Coll., Phenix City, 1978—; chmn. council Ala. Assoc. Degree in Nursing Programs; cons. in field. Bd. dirs. Auto Repair Centers, Inc., Columbus, 1983—; mem. adv. bd. Columbus Vocat. Tech. Inst., 1983—. Mem. Ala. Assn. Women Deans, Nat. League for Nursing (accreditation visitor), Am. Nursing Assn., Sigma Theta Tau, Alpha Epsilon Delta. Republican. Roman Catholic. Home: 3900 Lakeview Ct Phenix City AL 36867

PITTS, DONALD GRAVES, optometrist, researcher, educator, consultant; b. Hagarville, Ark., Apr. 11, 1926; s. William Lawrence and Edith (Graves) P.; m. Laura Belle McFarland, Sept. 22, 1946; children—Donna Jeanette Pitts Smith, Gayle Faith Pitts Garner, Susan Michele Pitts Webb. D.Optometry, So. Coll. Optometry, Memphis, 1950; M.S., Ind. U., 1959, Ph.D., 1964. Lic. optometrist, Okla., Nev. Practice optometry, Tulsa, 1950-51; base optometrist U.S. Air Force Hosps., 1951-57; commd. 2d lt. U.S. Air Force, 1957; advanced through grades to lt. col., 1965; research optometrist Wright-Patterson AFB, Ohio, 1959-62, Brooks AFB, Tex., 1962-69; ret., 1969; prof. Coll. of Optometry, U. Houston, 1969—. Co-author: UV-A Biologic Effects, 1979; Effects of Aging on Selected Visual Functions, 1982. U. Houston grantee, 1978-79; George H. Giles Meml. lectr. Brit. Optical Assn., London, 1981; named Disting. Practitioner in Optometry Nat. Acads. of Practice, San Francisco, 1984. Fellow Am. Acad. Optometry (Glenn A. Fry award lecture 1977), AAAS; mem. Am. Optometric Assn., Optical Soc. Am., Sigma Xi. Avocations: photography; golf; travel. Home: 4368 Graduate Circle Houston TX 77004 Office: College of Optometry U of Houston University Park Houston TX 77004

PITTS, E(ARL) HAMPTON, educator; b. Lexington, N.C., Sept. 11, 1936; s. Romaine William and Winnie Lee (Lookabill) P.; m. E. Lawana Carver, Mar. 21, 1970; 1 dau., Katherine Sarah. B.A., Oglethorpe U., 1971; M.A., West Ga. Coll., Carrolltown, 1973; Ph.D., U. Miss.-Oxford, 1975; cert. coll. bus. mgmt. U. Ky.-Lexington, 1982. Evening mgr. Coronodo Motor Hotel, Ft. Walton Beach, Fla., 1961-65; sr. buyer Lockheed Aircraft Corp., Marietta, Ga., 1965-71; dean students Palm Beach Atlantic Coll., West Palm Beach, Fla., 1975-79; asst. dir. bus. and fin. Wingate (N.C.) Coll., 1979-81; dir. bus. and fin. Chesterfield-Marboro Tech. Coll., Cheraw, S.C., 1981-84; asst. prof. bus. Wingate Coll., N.C., 1984—. Served with USMC, 1954-57; PTO. Recipient

Cost Savs. award Lockheed Aircraft Corp., 1966, 70; Outstanding Adminstr. of Yr. Palm Beach Atlantic Coll., 1977, 79. Mem. Nat. Assn. Colls. and Univs. Bus. Officers, So. Assn. Colls. and Univs. Bus. Officers, Acad. Mgmt., Phi Alpha Theta, Phi Delta Kappa, Theta Chi. Democrat. Baptist. Lodge: Kiwanis (Cheraw). Contbr. articles to profl. jours. Office: Wingate Coll Wingate NC 28174

PITTS, GERALD NELSON, computer science educator; b. Brownwood, Tex., June 14, 1943; m. Paula K. Pitts, Aug. 27, 1964; 4 children. B.A., Tex. A&M U., 1966, M.S., 1967, Ph.D., 1971; M.S. in Mgmt. Sci., Am. Tech. U., 1974. Asst. prof. computer sci. U. Southwestern La., Lafayette, 1971-72; assoc. prof., head dept. computer sci. Central Tex. Coll., Killeen, 1972-74; assoc. prof. computer sci. Miss. State U., 1975-81; assoc. prof. computing and informational scis. Trinity U., San Antonio, 1981—; v.p. Sigma Systems, Inc., Brownwood, 1973-81. Contbr. articles to profl. jours. Mem. La. Acad. Sci., Tex. Acad. Sci., Am. Ordnance Soc., Assn. Computing Machinery (past pres.), Sigma Xi, Epsilon Delta Pi, Upsilon Pi Epsilon. Office: Dept Computing and Info Scis Trinity Univ San Antonio TX 78284

PITTS, RUTH ELEANOR, music educator; b. Ft. Worth, Sept. 11, 1939; d. James Henry and Irene Ingalls (Pearson) Landes; m. William Lee Pitts, Sept. 15, 1961; children—William Robert, James Lee. B.Mus.Ed., Baylor U., 1960; M.A., George Peabody Coll., 1960, Ph.D., 1968. Lectr., Free Will Bapt. Bible Coll., 1962-66, Houston Bapt. U., 1969-70, Dallas Bapt. U., 1970-71, 74-75, Baylor U., Waco, Tex., 1977, McLennan Community Coll., Waco, 1977—; tchr. Arapano Elem. Sch., Richardson, Tex., 1972-74; pvt. tchr. piano, voice, 1961—. Reviewer, Choice mag., 1976—. Music dir. First Bapt. Ch., Centerville, Ga., 1966-69; dir. youth choir First Bapt. Ch., Waco, 1977-82; organist, choir dir. VA Hosp., Waco, 1976—. NDEA scholar, 1960. Mem. Am. Coll. Musicians, Music Tchrs. Nat. Assn., Tex. Music Tchrs. Assn. (theory com. 1984—, world music com. 1983—), Waco Music Tchrs. Assn. (pres. 1976-78, chmn. theory 1976-82). Democrat. Avocation: giving musical programs and inspirational talks. Home: 717 Ivyann St Waco TX 76710 Office: McLennan Community Coll 1400 College Dr Waco TX 76710

PIXLEY, JOHN SHERMAN, SR., research company executive; b. Detroit, Aug. 24, 1929; s. Rex Arthur and Louise (Sherman) P.; B.A., U. Va., 1951; postgrad. Pa. State U., 1958-59; m. Peggy Marie Payne, Oct. 16, 1949; children—John Sherman, Steven, Lou Ann. Asst. cashier Old Dominion Bank, Arlington, Va., 1953-56; tech. dir. John I. Thompson & Co., research and engring. firm, Bellefonte, Pa., 1956-65; co-founder, exec. v.p. Potomac Research Inc., Alexandria, Va., 1965-80; v.p. Gov. Sevs. Div. Electronic Data Systems, 1980-81; co-founder, pres. PRI, Inc., Alexandria, Va., 1981—. Owner Edgeworth Farm, Orlean, Va. Mem. Fairfax County Republican Com., Annandale, Va., 1964-72; mem. fin. com. for U.S. Rep. Joel T. Broyhill, Republican, Va., 1970-72. Served to 1st lt. AUS, 1952-53; maj. Res. ret. Decorated Army Commendation medal. Mem. IEEE, Sleepy Hollow Woods Civic Assn. (v.p., pres. 1969-71). Presbyterian. Club: Quantico (Va.) Flying (charter mem.). Home: 3711 Sleepy Hollow Rd Falls Church VA 22041 Office: PRI Inc 6121 Lincolnia Rd Alexandria VA 22312

PIZARRO, ANTONIO, mathematics educator; b. Coquimbo, Chile, Nov. 21, 1942; came to U.S., 1975; s. Luis and Berta (Geraldo) P.; m. Celina Ramirez, Jan. 14, 1967; children—Fernando, Antonio, Pedro. B.S., U. Chile, 1963; M.S. in Math., Tech. U. Chile, 1972; M.S. in Math., U. Iowa, 1978, Ph.D. in Math., 1979. Teaching asst. U. Chile, 1963-67; mem. math. and physics faculties various fgn. colls., 1967-75; teaching and research asst. U. Iowa, 1976-79; vis. prof. Oberlin (Ohio) Coll., 1980-81; asst. prof. math. dept. Centenary Coll. of La., Shreveport, 1982—. Tech. U. scholar, 1972-73. Mem. Am. Math. Soc., AAAS, La. Acad. Sci., Sigma Xi. Office: 2911 Centenary Blvd Shreveport LA 71134

PLAISTED, JAMES REGINALD, psychologist; b. Kearney, Nebr., Jan. 18, 1949; s. James Dale and Loretta Marie (Pruett) P.; m. Donna Kaye Droneburg, Aug. 30, 1975; children—Elizabeth Anne, James Reginald Jr., Ronald Michael, Laura Marie. B.A. in Psychology and Philosophy summa cum laude, Fla. Tech. U., 1975; M.S. in Psychology, Auburn U., 1977, Ph.D., 1981. Lic. psychologist, Tex. Practicing clin. psychology, clin. neuropsychology, Corpus Christi, 1982—; asst. prof. U. Tex.-Galveston, 1983—, Driscoll Children's Hosp., Corpus Christi, 1984—. Assoc. editor Tex. Psychologist, 1984—; Jour. Clin. Child Psychology, 1984—. Contbr. articles to profl. jours. Served to capt. U.S. Army, 1969-73. Mem. Am. Psychol. Assn., Tex. Psychol. Assn., Nueces County Psychol. Assn. (pres. 1986—), Nat. Acad. Neuropsychologists, Am. Coll. Psychology. Baptist. Home: 4409 Bluefield Dr Corpus Christi TX 78413 Office: 5315 Everhart Suite 5 Corpus Christi TX 78411

PLAIT, ALAN OSCAR, electronic engineer; b. Chgo., Aug. 14, 1926; s. Hyman and Katie (Greenfield) P.; m. Evelyn Faye Schain, Jan. 18, 1953; children—Sidney Ross, Merril Eliot, Marcia Beth, Philip Cary. B.S. in Math., Ill. Inst. Tech., 1951; B.S. in Elec. Engring., 1957; M.S. in Systems Engring., Va. Poly. Inst., 1975. Registered profl. engr., Calif. With Magnavox Co., Ft. Wayne, Ind., 1959-62; dept. mgr. Melpar Co., Falls Church, Va., 1962-67, Computer Scis. Co., Falls Church, 1967-75. Litton Amecom, College Park, Md., 1975-77; tech. dir. ManTech Support Technology, Inc., Alexandria, Va., 1977—; instr. Ill. Inst. Tech., 1954-57; tchr. U.S. Dept. Agr. Grad. Sch., Washington, 1963—. Contbr. articles on reliability engring. and quality control to profl. and indsl. jours. Fellow Am. Soc. for Quality Control (sect. chmn. 1970); mem. IEEE (sr. mem., pres. Reliability Soc. 1985—), Nat. Soc. Profl. Engrs. Home: 5402 Yorkshire St Springfield VA 22151 Office: ManTech Support Technology Inc 2320 Mill Rd Alexandria VA 22314

PLAMONDON, WILLIAM NELSON, JR., oil company executive; b. Chgo., Sept. 5, 1924; s. William Nelson and Elisabeth Cecile (Hauck) P.; B.Engring., M.E., Yale U., 1945; M.S. in Mgmt. Engring., N.J. Inst. Tech., 1954; m. Mary Elizabeth Heller, Aug. 17, 1946; children—William Nelson, Jeffrey, Donna Plamondon Scully, Mark. With Caltex Petroleum Corp., N.Y.C., 1951-55; with Continental-Emsco Co., N.Y.C. and Houston, 1956-73, mgr. sales-internat. div., 1967-73; mgr. mktg. Dixilyn Corp., Houston, 1973-76; v.p. sales and contracts Zapata Off-Shore Co., Houston, 1976-77; v.p. mktg. Dixilyn-Field Drilling Co., Houston, 1977-80; v.p. market devel. Global Marine Drilling Co., Houston, 1981-82; v.p. mktg. and sales Houston Offshore Internat., Inc., 1982—; lectr. marine offshore seminars Tex. A. and M. U., 1975, 76, 80. Served to lt. (j.g.) USN, 1943-46; PTO. Mem. Soc. Petroleum Engrs., Internat. Assn. Drilling Contractors (dir., past chmn. Houston chpt.), Am. Petroleum Inst., Nomads (past pres. N.Y. chpt.). Republican. Roman Catholic. Clubs: Petroleum of Houston, Petroleum of Lafayette, Warwick. Contbr. articles to trade jours. Home: 629 Chadbourne Ct Houston TX 77079 Office: One West Loop S Suite 804 Houston TX 77027

PLANAS, WILLIAM, manufacturing company executive; b. Ponce, P.R., Oct. 16, 1936; s. Miguel A. and Leocadia (Delgado) P.; m. Rosa M. Montes, Nov. 29, 1958; children—Rosa, William, Nilda. Student Ponce pub. schs. Engring. technician Union Carbide Caribe, Penuelas, P.R., 1965-71; prodn. mgr. Digital Equipment Corp., San German, P.R., 1971-79; mfg. mgr. Storage Tech. Corp., Ponce, 1979-81; dir. P.R. Adminstrn. Atari Caribe, Fajardo, 1981—; electronics tchr. Framingham Tech. Sch. Served with USAF, 1954-64. Mem. P.R. Mfrs. Assn., Electronic Industries Assn., Fajardo C. of C. Roman Catholic. Home: Reparto Sagrado Corazón Calle 3 E 23 Ponce PR 00731 Office: Mfg Dept and Plant Facilities Dept MDS QANTEI Inc Juncos PR

PLANCK, ROBERT DEMPSEY, food company executive; b. Texas City, Tex., July 1, 1948; s. Henry Ver and Elizabeth (Dempsey) Planck; m. Sharon Brieger, Dec. 27, 1969; 1 son, Jeffrey. B.S. in Hotel and Restaurant Mgmt., U. Houston, 1971. Dir. corp. food service Humana Hosp. Corp., Louisville, 1975-77; dir. edn. and quality assurance SYSCO Corp., Houston, 1977-81; v.p. mktg. Compton Foods Div. Sysco, Houston, 1981-84, chmn. product standards com., 1983—, chmn. product devel. council, 1982—; v.p. mktg. Sysco Food Services, Houston, 1984-86; v.p. Compton Foods, Houston, 1986—. Chmn. bd. trustees Tau Kappa Epsilon, U. Houston, 1980-83. Recipient Outstanding Alumni award Tau Kappa Epsilon, 1981, 85; Hon. Alumni of Yr., Hilton Coll., U. Houston, 1982. Mem. Soc. Advancement of Foodservice Research, Am. Dietetic Assn., Am. Soc. Food Technologists, Dietitians in Bus. and Industry (nat. dir. 1981), Nat. Restaurant Assn., Ky. Cols. Republican. Home: 11831 Westmere St Houston TX 77077

PLANK, CHARLES ANDREWS, chemical engineering educator; b. Charlotte, N.C., Oct. 12, 1928; s. Charles Andrews and Janett (Fayssoux) P.; m. Joyce Cecilia Clayton, Aug. 12, 1950; children—Steven Eric and Karl Andrews (twins), Mark Clayton. B.S.Chem.E., N.C. State U., 1949, M.S., 1951, Ph.D., 1957. Assoc. prof. chem. engring. U. Louisville, 1957-67, prof., 1967—, dir. interdisciplinary programs in engring., 1971-73, chmn. dept. chem. engring., 1973-79; spl. projects engr. Olin Mathieson Corp., Brandenburg, Ky., 1963, 67; cons. to various chem. and design cos. Host radio program Time Out for Jazz, 1979—. Mem. Am. Inst. Chem. Engrs., Am. Soc. Engring. Edn. Contbr. articles to profl. jours., chpts. to books. Home: 1852 Woodfill Way Louisville KY 40205 Office: Dept Chem Engring U Louisville Louisville KY 40292

PLANT, RICHARD, retired dentist; b. Madison, Fla., July 12, 1924; s. Clarence Mosely and Marie (Garbutt) P.; m. M. Mae Pickins, Aug. 26, 1954; children—Rachel Hubbs, Rebecca Dees. B.S., U. Fla., 1949; D.M.D., U. Louisville, 1953. Intern, Fla. State Hosp., Chattahoochee, 1953-54, asst. dir., 1959-62; gen. practice dentistry, Tallahassee, Fla., 1962-79; univ. dentist Fla. State U., Tallahassee, 1979-85. Contbr. articles to profl. jours. Dental missionary United Meth. Ch., Mex., Honduras, Haiti. Mem. Fla. Dental Assn., ADA. Club: Gideons. Avocation: artist. Home: 808 Piedmont Dr Tallahassee FL 32312

PLASTERR, NORMA LIVELY, English educator; b. St. Louis, Nov. 8, 1928; d. Charles Elmer and Beulah Almedia (Strawhun) Lively; m. Charles Henderson Plasterr, Nov. 27, 1948; children—Adele, Stephen, Michael. Student U. Mo., 1946-48, Washington U., summer 1948; A.B., U. Charleston, 1961; M.A., Marshall U., 1965, postgrad., 1968-78. Tchr., Chapmanville Pub. Schs. (W.Va.), 1958-67; instr. English, Marshall U., Logan, W.Va., 1967-71; prof. English, So. W.Va. Community Coll., Logan, 1971—. Recipient Nick Savas Outstanding Faculty award, 1983. Methodist. Lodge: Eastern Star.

PLATT, ALLAN, state official, consulting engineer; b. Bayonne, N.J., Aug. 24, 1925; s. David and Jane (Shilkoff) P.; m. Ann Heryla, Aug. 2, 1958; children—C. Jay, D. Glenn. B.M.E., Clarkson Coll. Tech., 1950. Registered profl. engr., Ala., Va. Inspection engr. Picatinny Arsenal, Dover, N.J., 1950-56, chief quality assurance spl. munitions, 1956-59; mgr. ballistic missile warhead sects. Army Munitions Command, 1959-64; dep. project mgr. guided missile system Army Missile Command, Redstone Arsenal, Ala., 1964-70, chief engring. services, 1970-71; gen. plant mgr. Fed. Copper and Aluminum Co., Pulaski, Tenn., 1971-74; fgn. tech. analyst Army Intelligence Agy., Huntsville, Ala., 1974-75; chief armaments and munitions U.S. Logistic Ctr., Ft. Lee, Va., 1975-81; dir. Bur. Bldgs. and Grounds, Commonwealth of Va., Richmond, 1982—. Served with USAAF, 1943-45, AUS, 1951-52. Recipient Meritorious Civilian Service award Dept. Army, 1966; Sr. Exec. award Army Missle Command, 1970. Home: 7701 Ardendale Rd Richmond VA 23225-1959 Office: Bur Buildings and Grounds 203 Governor St Richmond VA 23219

PLATTEN, MARVIN ROGER, educator; b. St. Paul, Dec. 29, 1926; s. Roger W. and Olga (Terland) P.; m. Marion Caroline Middlestaedt, Sept. 8, 1951; children—Andrea Kay, Steven Charles, Kathryn Marie, Charles Webster. B.S., U. Minn., 1952, M.Ed., 1956; Ph.D., Tex. Tech U., 1976. Art tchr., Detroit Lakes, Minn., 1952-54, Mpls., 1954-66, HEW, Ramey AFB, P.R., 1966-68; instr. art history Met. Jr. Coll., Mpls., 1965-66, Inter-Am. U., P.R., 1967-68; elem. tchr. art Dept. of Def. Schs., Japan, 1968-69, art cons., 1969-71; lectr. Coll. Edn., Tex. Tech U., Lubbock, 1971-76, asst. prof., 1976-80, assoc. prof., 1980—, dir. South Plains aesthetic and creativity edn. program. Pres., Luth. Council for Community Action, 1981-83. Served with USN, 1944-46. Recipient Amoco Disting. Teaching award, 1983; ednl. research grantee Tex. State research funds 1975-81; cert. of merit Japanese Soc. Calligraphers, 1971; 1st prize for watercolors and acrylics Soc. Fine Arts, Ramey, P.R., 1968. Mem. Nat. Art Edn. Assn., Tex. Art Edn. Assn. (pres. 1975-77), Seminar for Research in Art Edn., Phi Delta Kappa. Democrat. Lutheran. Contbr. articles to profl. jours. Home: 4512 W 15th St Lubbock TX 79416 Office: Coll of Edn PO Box 4560 Tex Tech Univ Lubbock TX 79409

PLATZER, MARTIN MEYER, clinical chaplain; b. Highland Park, Ill., Mar. 28, 1946; s. Hans K. and Edith E. (Meyer) P. B.A., Concordia Coll., 1968; M.Div., Concordia Sem., 1972; Th.M., Columbia Sem., 1982. Parish pastor, Lariat, Tex., 1972-74; chaplain intern Tex. Med. Ctr., 1974; chaplain resident Ga. Mental Health Inst., 1975; clin. chaplain North DeKalb Family and Children's Clinic, Atlanta, 1976—; chaplain families and children Lutheran Ch./Mo. Synod, 1978—. Program planning com. Lutheran Ministries Ga. Mem. Am. Assn. Marriage and Family Therapy, Step-Family Assn. Am., Inc., Am. Assn. Pastoral Counselors, Am. Acad. Psychotherapy. Contbr. articles to profl. jours. Office: 3921 New Peachtree Rd Doraville GA 30340

PLAXCO, JAMES HENRY, JR., chiropractor; b. Kansas City, Mo., Oct. 11, 1954; s. James Henry and Melba Louise (Bryant) F.; m. Pamela Lee Nix, Jan. 13, 1981; 1 dau., Jamie Lee. D.Chiropractic, Cleve. Chiropractic Coll., 1975. Owner, Plaxco Chiropractic Clinic, Moulton, Ala., 1976-80, 83—, ptnr., Russellville, Ala., 1980-83; team physician Hatton High Sch., 1977-80, Mount Hope High Schs., 1980-83. Mem. Internat. Coll. Applied Nutrition, Parker Chiropractic Research Found., Ala. State Chiropractic Assn., Moulton Jaycees. Baptist. Clubs: Ala. Cattleman's Assn., Franklin County Conservation, Tenn. Bowhunters. Lodge: Gideons Internat. Home: Route 8 Box 395 1902 Mulberry St Russellville AL 35653 Office: 207 N Main St Moulton AL 35650

PLAYER, JANE DIXON, pharmacist, manager; b. Lake City, S.C., Oct. 26, 1954; d. Julian Spencer and Mary Ellen (Richardson) Dixon; m. Spencer McGill Player, June, 1977; 1 child, Mary Ellen Richardson. B.S. in Pharmacy, Med. U. S.C., 1978. Hosp. pharmacist Bylery Hosp., Hartsville, S.C., 1978; pharmacist Revco Co., Hartsville, S.C., 1978-79, pharmacist, asst. mgr., Florence, S.C., 1979-81, asst. to supr. 14 area stores, 1981—; pharmacist Price Wise Pharmacy, Kingstree-Florence, S.C., 1983. Founder, Pharmacists Against Drug Abuse, Lake City, S.C., 1985. Dean's List awardee, recipient Dean's award Med. U. S.C., 1978; named Outstanding Young Adult, Lake City Presbyn. Ch., 1982. Mem. S.C. Pharm. Orgn., Pee Dee Pharm. Orgn. Presbyterian. Clubs: Gentry Dance, Country (Lake City, S.C.). Avocations: reading; traveling; teaching. Home: 212 Academy Ave Lake City SC 29560

PLAZA, SERGIO FERNANDO, civil engineer, geodesist, public surveyor, retailer, construction and real estate management consultant; b. El Paso, Tex., Dec. 9, 1931; s. Sergio Fernando and Ana Balbina (Nevarez) P.; m. Irma Antonieta Alvarez, Feb. 27, 1960; children—Sergio III, Irma, Claudia, Marizza. B.S. in Civil Engring., U. Tex.-El Paso, 1955, M.S. in Geotech. and Structural Engring., 1969. Registered profl. engr., Tex.; registered pub. surveyor, Tex. Instrument man Tex. Hwy. Dept., El Paso, 1955-56; geodesist White Sands Missile Range (N.Mex.), 1957-59, civil engr., 1960-65, civil engr. design and constrn., 1966-73; civil engr. design, constrn. and ops. mgmt. U.S. Army Directorate of Engring. and Housing, Ft. Bliss, Tex., 1974—; mem. com. devel. pavement design standards engring. dept. City of El Paso. Recipient Outstanding Services award Dept. Def., 1970. Mem. Nat. Soc. Profl. Engrs., ASCE, Soc. Am. Mil. Engrs. (pres. El Paso 1983), Tex. Soc. Profl. Engrs. Republican. Roman Catholic. Home: 9229 Turrentine St El Paso TX 79925 Office: DEH Bldg Suite 1165 Fort Bliss TX 79916

PLIKAYTIS, BRIAN DAVID, mathematical statistician; b. Seattle, Sept. 9, 1951; s. Edward Joseph and Josephine (Nyland) P.; m. Bonnie Jean Brake, Dec. 30, 1983. B.S. in Molecular and Cellular Biology, U. Wash., 1973, M.S. in Biomath., 1977. Chief spl. pathogens activity Statis. Services Br., Bacterial Diseases Div., Bur. of Epidemiology, Ctr. for Disease Control, Atlanta, 1977-80, chief Statis. services activity Chronic Diseases Div., 1980-82, math. statistician, statis. services aativity Div. Bacterial Diseases, Ctr. for Infectious Diseases, 1982—; teaching asst. dept. biostatistics Sch. Pub. Health and Community Medicine, U. Wash., 1975-76, statis. cons. dept. biostatistics, 1977. Contbr. articles to profl. jours. Mem. Am. Statis. Assn., Biometric Soc., Southeastern Photog. Soc. (v.p. 1980-82). Avocation: photography. Home: 2739 Livsey Trail Tucker GA 30084 Office: Statis Services Activity Div Bacterial Diseases Ctr for Infectious Diseases Ctrs for Disease Control Atlanta GA 30333

PLUMMER, JACK MOORE, psychologist; b. Galveston, Tex., Apr. 19, 1940; s. Jack Moore and Sarah Carroll (Cochran) P.; B.A., St. Mary's U., 1962; M.S., Trinity U., 1968; Ph.D., Tex. Tech. U., 1969; A.A.S., Garland County Community Coll., 1978; m. Rose Marie Taylor, July 22, 1960; children—Cynthia Marie, Edward Moore, Elizabeth Anne, Sarah Lorraine, Jack Moore. Psychologist Okla. rehab. div. Okla. State Reformatory, Granite, 1968-69; dir. tng. Ark. Rehab. Research and Tng. Center, Hot Springs, 1970-71; pvt. practice psychology, Hot Springs, 1971—; exec. dir. Plummer Assocs. for Consultation and Tng., 1982—; dir. Ark. Behavioral Services Clinic, 1983—; exec. officer Tng. Inst. for Edn. in Security, 1983—; psychol. cons. to Rehab. Services, Dept. Correction, Probation and Parole Div., also to physicians, attys., cts., law enforcement agys.; instr. Garland County Community Coll., Hot Springs, 1973—; continuing edn. instr. nursing degree program Coll. St. Francis, Joliet, Ill., 1979—; cons. Parents Without Partners. Mem. bd. L.P.N. nurse program Ouachita Vocat.-Tech. Sch., Hot Springs, 1979—. Fellow Ark. Psychol. Assn.; mem. Nat. Rehab. Assn., Nat. Rehab. Counseling Assn., Am. Psychol. Assn., Ark. Psychol. Assn. (chmn. fellow status rev. com. 1980, 81, chmn. profl. standards rev. com. 1982, 83), Hot Springs Psychol. Assn. (pres. 1979, 80), Internat. Soc. for Study Symbols. Democrat. Roman Catholic. Elk, Lion. Contbr. articles to profl. jours., chpt. in Handbook of Measurement and Evaluation in Rehabilitation. Home: 614 Ridgeview Dr Hot Springs AR 71901 Office: 207 Hagen St Hot Springs AR 71913

PLUMMER, WILLIAM MORRIS, relocation co. exec.; b. Oklahoma City, Mar. 13, 1943; s. Loren Morris and Alice Mae (Simmering) P.; A.C., No. Okla. Coll., 1963; B.S., Okla. State U., 1966; children—Nedra Leigh, Christopher Edwards. Trust officer Republic Nat. Bank, Dallas, 1969-74; pres. Relocation Services Inc., Dallas, 1974-77; v.p. mktg. Employee Transfer Corp., Dallas, 1977-81; regional dir. mktg. The Equitable Relocation Mgmt. Corp., Dallas, 1981—. Mem. Am. Soc. Personnel Adminstrs., Employee Relocation Council. Republican. Baptist. Home: 1313 N Trail St Carrollton TX 75006 Office: 1166 Park Central VII 12750 Merit Dr Dallas TX 75251

PLUSQUELLEC, PAUL LLOYD, oil company executive; b. Steubenville, Ohio, Apr. 4, 1941; s. Peter and Martha Ann (Evans) P.; m. Betty Joan Borgeson, Aug. 21, 1965; children—Paul Lloyd Jr., Alan Robert, John Cristopher. B.A., Coll. Wooster, 1963; M.S., U. Ill., 1966, Ph.D., 1968. Cert. petroleum geologist. Postdoctoral fellow U. Ill., Urbana, 1968-69; geologist to dist. geologist Texaco, New Orleans, 1969-79; div. geologist, exploration mgr. Natomas N.Am., New Orleans, Houston, Tulsa, 1979-83; v.p. exploration and devel. CNG Producing Co., New Orleans, 1984—; dir. CNG Producing Co., New Orleans, 1984—. Contbr. articles to profl. jours. Mem. Am. Assn. Petroleum Geologists, New Orleans Geol. Soc., Rocky Mountain Assn. Geologists, Sigma Xi. Republican. Presbyterian. Clubs: Stonebridge Country (Gretna, La.); Rivercenter Tennis, City (New Orleans). Avocations: tennis; wood working; gardening. Home: 3708 Lake Aspen West Dr Gretna LA 70056 Office: CNG Producing Co One Canal Pl Suite 3100 New Orleans LA 70130

POAGE, WALLER STAPLES, III, architect; b. Wythe County, Va., Apr. 25, 1936; s. Waller Staples and Mary Simmerman (Crockett) P.; B.Arch., Va. Poly. Inst. and State U., 1960; m. Elizabeth B., June 21, 1975; children—Mary Elizabeth, Mary Margaret. Asso., Dales Y. Foster, Inc., Architects, Dallas, 1974-76; pvt. practice Waller S. Poage & Asso., Architects, Planners, Houston, 1965-67, Wytheville, Va., 1967-69, Arlington, Tex., 1973-76; owner, prin. Community Planners Inc. of Laredo, Tex., 1976-82; ptnr. Gondeck-Poage Partnership, architects, San Antonio, 1983-84; prin. Waller S. Poage AIA Inc., San Antonio, 1984—; instr. architecture U. Tex., San Antonio, 1980-83. Commr., Airport Zoning Bd., City of Laredo, 1979-83; adv. to city council, Constrn. Industry Council, Houston, 1969-71. Recipient Award of Merit for residential design, House and Home Mag., 1968; Award of Merit, Constrn. Specifications Inst., 1971; registered architect, Tex., La., Va. Okla., Colo., Ark., Kans., Mo., Tenn., Miss., N.Mex. Mem. AIA, Tex. Soc. Architects, Constrn. Specifications Inst. (ofcl. rep. and exec. v.p. 1970-72, 1st. v.p. 1972, dir. 1970-73), Laredo C. of C., Am. Inst. Planners. Republican. Episcopalian. Clubs: Rotary (dir. 1978-83), Exchange (bd. dirs. 1967-68, pres. 1969). Archtl. works include Jim Hogg County Jail, Hebbronville, Tex., 1978, Webb County Facilities Master Plan, Laredo, 1978, Westgate Pl., 1977, Country Club Estates, 1978, The Quadrangle, 1978, The Century Bldg., Laredo, 1976, Wytheville (Va.) Community Hosp., 1969-70, Wythe County Vocational Sch., 1969-70, various County jails and law enforcement ctrs. in Tex. Home and Office: 323 Fantasia St San Antonio TX 78216

POARCH, NADINE CLARKE, occupational health nurse; b. Lenoir, N.C., Feb. 4, 1936; d. Charlie Clifton and Frances (Clark) C.; m. Ned Lester Poarch, Nov. 23, 1954 (div. Nov. 1973); 1 child, Nancy Pamela Poarch Walker. Student secretarial sch. Caldwell Coll., 1955-57; L.P.N., Caldwell Community Coll., 1971, cert. audiometric tech., 1973; cert. loss control mgmt. Western Carolina U., 1985. Emergency room nurse Dula Hosp., Lenoir, 1959-70; audiometric technician Singer Furniture, Lenoir, 1973—, occupational health nurse, 1971—. Mem. N.C. Occupational Nurses, Western Piedmont Safety Council, Soc. Safety Engrs. of S.C., Foot Hill Occupational Health Nurses, Am. Soc. Engrs. Democrat. Methodist. Clubs: Parents Without Partners, Zodiac (Hickory, N.C.). Avocations: dancing; flower arrangement, research. Home: Rt 7 Box 485 Lenoir NC 28645 Office: Singer Furniture Div PO Box 1588 Lenoir NC 28645

PODEIN, GEORGE CLEMENT, JR., psychologist, marriage and family therapist; b. Valdosta, Ga., Oct. 6, 1945; s. George Clement and Jeannette Claire (Lawry) P.; m. Barbara Anne Masters, Apr. 28, 1973. B.S. in Psychology, Valdosta State Coll., 1968; M.Ed. in Counseling, Auburn U., 1971; grad. Walden U., 1981—. Lic. marriage and family counselor, Ga. Tchr. high sch., Madison, Fla., 1968-69; counselor Vocat. Rehab. dist. Jacksonville (Fla.), 1971-73; psychologist Valdosta-Lowndes Comprehensive Community Mental Health Ctr., 1973-75, coordinator community mental health services, 1975-76; asst. coordinator mental health services Tri-County Mental Health Ctr., Nashville, Ga., 1975; satellite ctr. dir., psychologist Coosa Valley Community Mental Health Ctr., Rome, Ga., 1976-79, coordinator satellite services, supr. Haralson County Sattelite Office, 1979—. Bd. dirs. Haralson County Library, Bremen, Ga. Recipient Outstanding Service award Haralson County Nursing Home, 1981-82; fund raising award Ga. Health Care Assn., 1981; fund raising award Am. Heart Assn., 1982. Mem. Am. Psychol. Assn., Ga. Psychol. Assn., Nat. Rehab. Assn., Ga. Rehab. Assn., Nat. Assn. Rural Mental Health, SAR, Auburn Alumni Assn., Tau Kappa Epsilon. Clubs: Rotary, Bremen. Democrat. Mem. Ch. of Christ. Home: 609 Valley Run St Bremen GA 30110 Office: 100 Poplar St Bremen GA 30110

PODGORNY, GEORGE, emergency physician; b. Tehran, Iran, Mar. 17, 1934; s. Emanuel and Helen (Parsian) P.; came to U.S., 1954, naturalized, 1973; B.S., Maryville Coll., 1958; postgrad. Bowman Gray Sch. Medicine, 1958; M.D., Wake Forest U., 1962; m. Ernestine Koury, Oct. 20, 1962; children—Adele, Emanuel II, George, Gregory. Intern in surgery N.C. Bapt. Hosp., Winston-Salem, 1962-63, chief resident in gen. surgery, 1966-67, in cardiothoracic surgery, 1967-69; sr. med. examiner Forsyth County, N.C., 1972—; dir. dept. emergency medicine Forsyth Meml. Hosp., Winston-Salem, 1974-80; sec.-treas. Forsyth Emergency Services, Winston-Salem, 1970-80; clin. prof. emergency medicine East Carolina U. Sch. Medicine, Greenville, 1984—. Dir., Emergency Med. Services Project Region II of N.C., 1975—; chmn. bd. trustees Emergency Medicine Found.; chmn. residency rev. com. emergency medicine Accreditation Council Grad. Med. Edn.; founder Western Piedmont Emergency Med. Services Council, 1973; mem. N.C. Emergency Med. Services Adv. Council, 1976-81; assoc. prof. clin. surgery Bowman Gray Sch. Medicine, Wake Forest U., Winston-Salem, 1979—. Bd. dirs. Piedmont Health Systems Agy., 1975-84; trustee Forsyth County Hosp., Authority, 1974-75; bd. dirs. N.C. Health Coordinating Council, 1975-82, Medic Alert Found. Internat. Fellow Internat. Coll. Surgeons, Internat. Coll. Angiology, Royal Soc. Health (Gt. Britain), Southeastern Surg. Congress; mem. Am. Coll. Emergency Physicians (charter; pres. 1978-79), AMA, (chmn. council of sect. emergency medicine 1982—), Am. Bd. Emergency Medicine (pres. 1976-81). Contbr. articles to profl. publs. on trauma, snake bite and history of medicine; editorial bd. Annals of Emergency Medicine, Med. Meetings. Office: 2115 Georgia Ave Winston-Salem NC 27104

POE, PENNY, counselor; b. San Diego, June 9. M.A., Central State U., Edmond, Okla., 1977. Cert. tchr., counselor, Okla. Tchr., dept. chmn. Putnam City Schs., Oklahoma City, 1972-80; owner, counselor Central Intermediate Sch., Oklahoma City, 1980—; cons. active parenting seminars, Oklahoma City, 1984—. Columnist Counselor's Corner, Oklahoma City Tribune Rev., 1983—. Named Outstanding Contbr. to Student Body, Oklahoma City PTA, 1983; recipient Golden Apple of Excellence, Putnam City Excellence Com., 1985. Mem. Okla. Sch. Psychol. Assn., Okla. Assn. Counseling and Devel., Am. Assn. Counseling and Devel., Nat. Bd. Cert. Counselors. Avocations: tennis, travel. Office: Central Intermediate Sch 5430 NW 40th St Oklahoma City OK 73122

POE, PHYLLIS ANN, former religious gift shop owner; b. Altus, Okla., Jan. 16, 1942; d. Noah Lee and Nellie Faye (Pendergrass) Futrell; m. Rev. Jack O'Brian Poe, Aug. 18, 1961; children—David O'Brian, Robin Denise. Grad. pub. high sch. Del City, Okla. Sec. Baptist Gen. Conv., Oklahoma City, 1961-65; ch. sec. Truett Chapel, Dallas, 1966-69; sec. Thomas A. Massey, Atty., Oklahoma City, 1976-80; owner, mgr. Gifts of Praise, Oklahoma City, 1982-86; dir. Associational Acteens Women's Missionary Union, Ada, Okla., 1970-71, Kingfisher, Okla., 1972-74; Author local newspaper column, Reflections, 1984—. Mem. Rockwell Plaza Mchts. Assn. (sec. 1982-83). Democrat. So. Baptist. Avocation: gospel singing. Home: 6920 Stony Creek St Oklahoma City OK 73132 Office: Gifts of Praise #2 8527 N Rockwell Oklahoma City OK 73132

POELMAN, KAREN CHRISTINE, psychologist, nurse; b. Highland Park, Ill., Jan. 13, 1944; d. Dirk Adrian and Diane V. (Liukkonen) P. R.N., Ill. Masonic Hosp. Sch. Nursing, 1964; B.S., Ga. State U., 1973, M.A., 1977, Ph.D., 1980. Lic. clin. psychologist; R.N., Ill., Ga. Nurse, Ill. State Psychiat. Inst., Chgo., 1964-66; U.S. Peace Corps vol., Kabul, Afghanistan, 1966; nurse Highland Park Hosp. Found., Ill., 1967-68, St. Joseph's Hosp., Atlanta, 1969-78; clin. psychologist Fulton County Health Dept., Atlanta, 1979—; clin. psychologist in pvt. practice, Atlanta, 1981—; cons. U.S. Postal Service, Atlanta, 1983; mem. panel psychologists Ga. Dept. Human Resources, Div. Vocat. Rehab., Atlanta, 1984—. Mem. Am. Psychol. Assn., Southeastern Psychol. Assn., Ga. Psychol. Assn., Nat. Register Health Service Providers in Psychology, Mental Health Assn. Met. Atlanta, Alpha Lambda Delta, Phi Kappa Phi, Psi Chi. Office: SW Atlanta Psychology Clinic 2001 MLK Jr Dr SW Suite 421 Atlanta GA 30310 also Acworth-Woodstock Psychology Clinic 1147 Alabama Rd Suite D Acworth GA 30101

POFF, RICHARD HARDING, justice; b. Radford, Va., Oct. 19, 1923; s. Beecher David and Irene Louise (Nunley) P.; m. Jo Ann R. Topper, June 24, 1945 (dec. Jan. 1978); children—Rebecca, Thomas, Richard Harding; m. Jean Murphy, Oct. 26, 1980. Student, Roanoke Coll., 1941-43; LL.B., U. Va., 1948, LL.D., 1969. Bar: Va. 1947. Partner law firm Dalton, Poff, Turk & Stone, Radford, 1949-70; mem. 83d-92d congresses, 6th Dist. Va.; justice Supreme Ct. Va., 1972—; Vice chmn. Nat. Commn. on Reform Fed. Crime Laws; chmn. Republican Task Force on Crime; sec. Rep. Conf., House Rep. Leadership. Named Va.'s Outstanding Young Man of Year Jr. C. of C., 1954; recipient Nat. Collegiate Athletic Assn. award, 1966, Roanoke Coll. medal, 1967, Distinguished Virginian award Va. Dist. Exchange Clubs, 1970, Presdl. certificate of appreciation for legislative contbn., 1971, legislative citation Assn. Fed. Investigators, 1969, Thomas Jefferson Pub. Sesquicentennial award U. Va., 1969, Japanese Am. Citizens League award, 1972. Mem. Am., Va. bar assns., Am. Judicature Soc., V.F.W., Am. Legion, Pi Kappa Phi, Sigma Nu Phi. Clubs: Mason, Moose, Lion. Office: Supreme Ct Bdlg Richmond VA 23210

POGUE, FORREST CARLISLE, historian; b. Eddyville, Ky., Sept. 17, 1912; s. Forrest Carlisle and Frances (Carter) P.; m. Christine Brown, Sept. 4, 1954. A.B., Murray State Coll., 1931, LL.D., 1970; M.A., U. Ky., 1932, Litt.D., 1983; Ph.D., Clark U., 1939, L.H.D., 1975; Am. Exchange fellow Inst. des Hautes Etudes Internationales, U. Paris, 1937-38; Litt.D., Washington and Lee U., 1970. Instr., Western Ky. State Coll., 1933; from instr. to assoc. prof. Murray (Ky.) State Coll., 1933-42, prof. history, 1954-56; mem. hist. sect. U.S. Forces, ETO, 1944-46; with Office Chief Mil. History, Dept. Army, 1946-52; ops. research analyst Ops. Research Office, Johns Hopkins, U.S. Army Theater Hdqrs., Heidelberg, Germany, 1952-54; dir. George C. Marshall Research Center, 1956-64, George C. Marshall Research Library, 1964-74, Dwight D. Eisenhower Inst. Hist. Research, Smithsonian Instn., Washington, 1974-84; exec. dir. George C. Marshall Research Found., 1964-74, life mem. adv. com., 1974—; Mary Moody Northen vis. prof. history Va. Mil. Inst., 1972; former mem. adv. bd. Air Force Army and Navy Hist. Offices, Dept. Navy; chmn. adv. com. Senate Hist. Office; mem. Am. Com. History World War II (former chmn.); mem. adv. com. publ. Eisenhower papers Johns Hopkins U.; mem. adv. com. Nat. Hist. Soc.; chmn. adv. com. coll. campus program Former Mems. of Congress Assn.; nat. adviser Ky. Oral History Commn.; former regent Omar N. Bradley Found.; trustee U.S. Capitol Hist. Soc.; bd. dirs. Harry S. Truman Library Inst. Author: The Supreme Command, 1954; George C. Marshall: Education of a General, vol. 1, 1963; George C. Marshall: Ordeal and Hope, 1939-42, vol. 2, 1966; George C. Marshall: Organizer of Victory, 1943-45, vol. 3, 1973. Co-author: The Meaning of Yalta, 1956. Contbr. to Command Decisions, 1960, Total War and Cold War, 1962, D-Day: The Normandy Invasion in Retrospect, 1971, Soldiers and Statesmen, 1973, The Continuing Revolution, 1975, Bicentennial History of the U.S., 1976; The War Lords, 1976. Contbg. editor: Guide to American Foreign Relations, 1983. Served with AUS, 1942-45; ETO. Decorated Bronze Star; Croix de Guerre (France); recipient Disting. Alumnus award Murray State Coll., 1964, Disting. Alumnus Centennial award U. Ky., 1965. Fellow Am. Mil. Inst. (past pres.), Soc. Am. Historians; mem. Am., So. hist. assns., Orgn. Am. Historians, NEA, Oral History Assn. (past pres.), Am. Legion. Democrat. Presbyterian. Club: Cosmos. Address: 1111 Army-Navy Dr Arlington VA 22202

POHL, GAIL PIERCE, author, assn. exec.; b. Stigler, Okla., Nov. 18, 1938; d. William James and Kathleen Louise (McConnell) Pierce; B.A., U. Okla., 1960; m. Lee W. Pohl, July 7, 1962; 1 dau., Leslie Kathleen. Reporter, Okla. Bus. News, Oklahoma City, 1960-65, news editor, 1966-72; pub. relations asso. Am. Mut. Ins. Alliance, Chgo., 1972; editor Jour. Am. Ins., 1973-76; dir. publs. Alliance Am. Insurers, Chgo., 1976-78, dir. policy communications, 1978-79; exec. dir. Nat. Self-Service Storage Assn., Eureka Springs, Ark., 1981—. Pres., trustee 1st Montessori Sch. Atlanta Parents Assn., 1980-81. Mem. Women in Communications, Mut. Ins. Communicators (1st place award for editorial excellence 1977, 78), Chgo. Assn. Bus. Communicators (awards for bus. news writing 1978, mag. editing 1978, feature writing 1978; competition judge mag. editing 1979), Ins. Distaff Execs. Assn. Chgo. (legis. com. 1977-78, pub. relations com. 1976-78, exec. bd. 1978-79), Nat. Assn. Ins. Women (ethics com. 1977-79), Soc. Consumer Affairs Profls. in Bus., Am. Soc. Assn. Execs., Bus. and Profl. Women (v.p. chpt.). Home: 270 Spring St Eureka Springs AR 72632

POHLMANN, GARY LEE, risk management representative; b. Davenport, Iowa, Sept. 13, 1956; s. Henry Paul and Marilyn June (Ragan) P.; m. Katie R. Van Balen, May 3, 1980. B.S. in Indsl. Tech., U. No. Iowa, 1978. Loss control rep. St. Paul Cos., Atlanta, 1978-80, state loss control rep., Columbia, S.C., 1980-85, risk mgmt. rep., Atlanta, 1985—; cons. Internat. Human Factors Loss Control Inst., Mpls., St. Paul, 1984—, Internat. Loss Control Inst., Atlanta, 1983—. Mem. Am. Soc. Safety Engrs. Avocations: skydiving; photography; sports. Home: 1315 Blankenship Lane Lilburn GA 30247 Office: St Paul Cos 2220 Parklane Dr Atlanta GA 30345

POINSETTE, LEO JEROME, real estate executive; b. Indpls., Nov. 7, 1945; s. Donald Eugene and Anne Katherine (Farrell) P.; m. Mary Catherine Shouvlin, Nov. 8, 1969; children—Jason J., Amanda M. B.A. in Econs., Xavier U., 1968. Sales rep. Uniroyal Inc., Cin., 1968-71; dist. sales rep. Castle-Sybron, Cin., 1972-76; pres. Champion Restaurants, Cin., 1976-79; Zone sales mgr. Memorex Corp., Cin., 1979-81; pres., pub. America's Home Guide, Winter Park, Fla., 1981-83; pres. Spectrum Real Estate Brokers, Winter Park, 1983—; chmn. Autolease, Inc., Orlando, Fla.; v.p., dir. Trico Investments Inc., Cin. Mem. Orlando/Winter Park Bd. Realtors, Xavier U. Alumni Assn., Orlando C. of C. Republican. Roman Catholic. Clubs: Xavier U. All for One (Cin.); Lodge: Kiwanis. Office: 2265 Lee Rd Suite 123 Winter Park FL 32789

POINTER, SAM CLYDE, JR., federal judge; b. Birmingham, Ala., Nov. 15, 1934; s. Sam Clyde and Elizabeth Inzer (Brown) P.; m. Paula Purse, Oct. 18, 1958; children—Minge, Sam Clyde. A.B., Vanderbilt U., 1955; J.D., U. Ala., 1957; LL.M., NYU, 1958. Bar: Ala. 1957. Ptnr., Brown, Pointer & Pointer, 1958-70; judge U.S. Dist. Ct. (no. dist.) Ala., Birmingham, 1970—; judge Temporary Emergency Ct. of Appeals, 1980—; mem. Jud. Panel on Multi-dist. Litigation, 1980—. Bd. editors Manual for Complex Litigation, 1979—. Vice chmn., gen. counsel Ala. Republican Party, 1965-69; bd. dirs. Ala. Found. Hearing and Speech, 1965-70, Vol. Bur. Greater Birmingham, 1966-72; trustee Crippled Children's Clinic, 1967-72. Mem. ABA, Ala. Bar Assn., Birmingham Bar Assn., Am. Law Inst. Farrah Order of Jurisprudence, Phi Beta Kappa. Episcopalian. Office: US Dist Ct 138 Fed Courthouse Birmingham AL 35203

POIRIER, ROBERT HAROLD, ophthalmologist; b. Springfield, Ohio, July 3, 1939; s. Bernard Harold and Mary Ann (Kerkering) P.; B.A., St. Mary's Coll., 1961; M.D., Marquette U., 1965. Diplomate Am. Bd. Ophthalmology. Intern, St. Mary's Hosp., Mpls., 1965-66; resident trainee Med. Coll. Wis., Milw., 1968-70, 1971-72; research fellow Moorfields Eye Hosp., London, 1970-71; research fellow U. London, 1970-71; ophthalmologist Audie Murphy VA Hosp., San Antonio, 1973-78, Brooke Army Med. Ctr., San Antonio, 1974—, Bapt. Meml. Med. Ctr., San Antonio, 1972—; Jacaltenango Hosp. Guatemala, 1973—; Humana Hosp., 1980—; practice medicine specializing in ophthalmology (cataracts and refractive surgery), San Antonio, 1972—. Contbr. articles to profl. jours. Served in USAF, 1966-68. Carl and Elizabeth Eberbach Found. fellow, 1970-71; recipient numerous grants in med. field. Mem. AMA (recipient Recognition award in continuing med. edn., 1973-76), Am. Acad. Ophthalmology, ACS, Am. Ophthal. Assn., Oxford Congress (Eng.), Assn. for Research in Vision and Ophthalmology, Tex. Med. Assn., Delta Epsilon Sigma, Alpha Omega Alpha, Beta Beta Beta. Office: 7810 Louis Pasteur Dr San Antonio TX 78229

POLAN, NANCY MOORE, artist; b. Newark, Ohio; d. William Tracy and Francis (Flesher) Moore; A.B., Marshall U., 1936; m. Lincoln Milton Polan, Mar. 28, 1934; children—Charles Edwin, William Joseph Marion. One-man shows Charleston Art Gallery, 1961, 67, 73, Greenbrier, 1963, Huntington Galleries, 1963, 66, 71, N.Y. World's Fair, 1965, W.Va. U., 1966, Carroll Reese Mus., 1967, Mountaineer Dinner Theatre, Winfield, W.Va., 1972; exhibited in group shows: Am. Watercolor Soc., Allied Artists of Am., Nat. Arts Club, 1968, 69, 70, 71, 72, 73, 74, 76, 81, Pa. Acad. Fine Arts, Opening of Creative Arts Center W.Va. U., 1969, Internat. Platform Assn. Art Exhibit, 1968-69, 72, 73-80, Allied Artists W.Va., 1968-69, Joan Miro Graphic Exhbn., Barcelona, Spain, 1970, XXI Exhibit Contemporary Art, La Scala, Florence, Italy, 1971, Ressegna Internazionale d'Arte Grafica, Siena, Italy, 1973, Opening of Parkersburg (W.Va.) Art Center, 1975, traveling exhbn. Am. Watercolor Soc., 1972-73, Accademia Leonardo da Vinci, Rome, 1979, Nuevo Acropoli, Rome, 1979, numerous others. Mem. internat. com. Centro Studi e Scambi Internazionale, Rome, Italy, 1968, spl. rep., 1970, hon. v.p., 1979. Recipient Norton Meml. award 3d Nat. Jury Show Am. Art, Chautauqua, N.Y., 1960; purchase prize, Jurors award for Watercolor Huntington Galleries, 1960, 61; Gold medal Masters of Modern Art exhbn., La Scala Gallery, Florence, 1975; Grumbacher award Pen and Brush, 1978, many others. Mem. Composers, Authors & Artists Am., D.A.R., Allied Artists W.Va., Huntington Galleries, Internat. Platform Assn. (3d award 1977), Allied Artists Am. (asso.), Tri-State Arts Assn., Sunrise Found., Pen and Brush, Am. Watercolor Soc. (asso.), Am. Fedn. Arts, Nat. Arts Club (watercolor award 1969), Leonardo da Vinci Acad., Accademia Italia (Gold medal 1979, 84; painting award 1985), Sigma Kappa. Episcopalian. Address: 2 Prospect Dr Huntington WV 25701 also 2106 Club Dr Vero Beach FL 32960

POLANIS, MARK FLORIAN, banker; b. Milw., Jan. 11, 1944; s. Henry Anthony and Adele Rose (Czarnecki) P.; m. Gloria Jean Grebe, Feb. 16, 1963; children—Laura J., James A., Henry C., Julie D., Rex A. B.S. in Acctg., Marquette U., 1965, M.A. in Econs., 1973. C.P.A., Wis., Ill.; chartered bank auditor. Audit mgr. First Wis. Bankshares, Milw., 1965-69; sr. corp. auditor Montgomery Ward, Inc., Chgo., 1969-72; gen. auditor Lake View Trust & Savs. Bank, Chgo., 1972-76; v.p., dir. Bank Adminstrn. Inst., Rolling Meadows, Ill., 1976-81; sr. v.p. audit Pan Am. Banks, Inc., Miami, Fla., 1981—; mem. cons. bd. bank publs. Am. Acctg. Assn., 1981-83. Mem. Am. Inst. C.P.A.s (task force on EDP fraud 1979-81), Bank Adminstrn. Inst. (task force on audit standards 1976-77), Inst. Internal Auditors, Beta Alpha Psi, Beta Gamma Sigma. Republican. Roman Catholic. Author: Audit Organization and Practice in Banks Over $50 Million, 1977; co-author: Statement of Principles and Standards for Internal Auditing in the Banking Industry; contbg. author: Internal Auditing in the Banking Industry, 3 vols., 1977; editor books in field. Office: Pan Am Banks Inc 150 SE 3d Ave Miami FL 33101

POLATTY, ROSE JACKSON, civic worker; b. Atlanta, Sept. 17, 1922; d. James Wilmot and Esther Ann (Sweeny) Jackson; A.B. in Journalism, U. Ga., 1943; postgrad. Oglethorpe U., 1962-63, Ga. State U., 1963; m. George Junius Polatty, Nov. 27, 1942; children—George Junius, Robert Wilmot, Rose Crystal, Richard James. Active U. Ga. Alumni Soc., pres. Class of 1943 Alumni, 1948-58, bd. mgrs., 1966-69, v.p., 1971-73, chmn. seminar, 1971; exec. sec. Atlanta Boy Choir, 1968-69; bd. dirs. Atlanta Arts Council, 1968-69; adv. com. Kennesaw Coll. on Wheels, 1974-78; bicentennial chmn., City of Roswell, Ga., 1975-76, sec. hist. preservation commn., 1978-82, chmn., 1983-84; active Ga. Trust for Hist. Preservation, Ga. Conservancy, Roswell Hist. Soc., Atlanta Symphony Assocs.; adminstrv. bd., chmn. altar guild, Roswell United Meth. Ch. Recipient recognition award Nat. 4-H Alumni, 1959, service award City of Roswell, 1976, community service award Roswell Optimist Club, 1977, Roswell Jaycee Leadership award, 1977, community service award Zion Bapt. Ch., 1977. Mem. Women in Communications, Colonial Dames XVII Century (v.p. chpt. 1980-81, pres. 1982-83) UDC, Atlanta Audubon Soc., High Mus. Art, Delta Omicron, Phi Beta Kappa, Phi Kappa Phi, Kappa Delta Pi. Clubs: Kappa Delta, P.E.O. (chpt. AA, Ga., charter 1977), DAR (Joseph Habersham chpt.), Roswell Women's (charter 1948, pres. 1966-68), Roswell Garden (charter 1951, pres. 1975-77), N. Fulton Council Garden Clubs (charter 1975, pres. 1975-77). Home: 889 Mimosa Blvd Roswell GA 30075

POLHEMUS, MARY ANN, educator; b. Adrian, Mich., May 3, 1947; d. Charles Robert and Melva Jane Bartholemew; B.S., La. State U., 1969; M.Ed., U. Houston, 1972; m. John Philip Polhemus, Mar. 25, 1972. Tchr., Houston Ind. Sch. Dist., 1969-75, reading cons., 1975-80, reading and lang. arts cons., 1980-81, secondary reading supr., 1981—. Mem. Assn. for Supervision and Curriculum Devel., Internat. Reading Assn., Nat. Council Tchrs. English, Delta Kappa Gamma. Republican. Cons., Spelling for Writing series Charles E. Merrill Pub. Co., 1979-80. Home: 2419 Robinhood St Houston TX 77005

POLIAKOFF, GARY A., lawyer, educator; b. Greenville, S.C., Nov. 25, 1944; s. Herman and Dorothy (Ravitz) P.; m. Sherri D. Dublin, June 24, 1967; children—Ryan, Keith. B.S., U. S.C., 1966; J.D., U. Miami, 1969. Bar: Fla. 1969, D.C. 1971. Sr. ptnr. Becker, Poliakoff & Streitfeld, P.A., Ft. Lauderdale, Miami, Sarasota, North Palm Beach, Clearwater, Fla., 1973—; adj. prof. law Nova U.; panelist Nat. Confs. Community Assns.; lectr. ann. condominium seminars Fla. Bar; participant Fla. Law Revision Council; cons. to White House in drafting Condominium and Coop. Abuse Relief Act, 1980. Mem. exec. com. Anti-Defamation League So. Region. Mem. Fla. Bar (co-chmn. condominium and coop. law sect., chmn. legis. subcom. condominium and coop. law). Author: (with others) Florida Condominium Law and Practice, 1982; contbr. articles to profl. jours.

POLICHINO, JOSEPH ANTHONY, JR., wholesale company executive; b. Houston, Oct. 17, 1948; s. Joseph Anthony and Josephine Adeline P.; student Spring Hill Coll., 1966-67; A.A. cum laude, S. Tex. Jr. Coll., 1969; student U. Houston, 1969-71; m. Jean Elliott McDowell, Oct. 7, 1978; children—Joseph Anthony III, Sara Gale. Sales posting clk. Jax Beer Co., Houston, 1971-72, route salesman asst., 1972; sales supr. Nat. Beverage Co., Houston, 1972-74, pres., 1974-76; owner, pres. Coors Northeast Distbg. Co., Houston, 1976-84; founder, v.p. Alessandra Import Co., Houston, 1980—; exec. v.p. Internat. Brands, 1984—. Bd. dirs. Houston Livestock Show and Rodeo, 1978—, Houston Muscular Dystrophy Assn., 1977—, Bill Williams Capon Charity Dinner, 1977—, Strake Jesuit Coll. Prep. Sch., 1986—; commr. City of West University Place (Tex.), 1981-83, councilman, 1983-85. Mem. Sons of Bosses Internat. (regional v.p. 1974-75), Jesuit Coll. Prep. Alumni Assn. (pres. 1977-79), Houston Citizens C. of C. (dir. 1977—), Nat. Beer Wholesalers Assn., Wholesale Beer Distbrs. Tex., Harris County Wholesale Beer Distbrs. Assn. Roman Catholic. Club: Toastmaster.

POLING, WAYNE ALLEN, minister; b. Amarillo, Tex., July 29, 1950; s. Clifford Harold and Ruby Lorena (McClellan) P. B.A., Hardin Simmons U., 1972; M.Religious Edn., S.W. Baptist Theol. Sem., 1976. Ordained to ministry So. Baptist Ch., 1982. Minister youth Colonial Bapt. Ch., Dallas, 1973-76; minister edn. Lamar Bapt. Ch., Wichita Falls, Tex., 1976-81; leader, tng. cons. Bapt. Sunday Sch. Bd., Nashville, 1981—. Mem. Am. Soc. Tng. and Devel., So. Baptist Religious Edn. Assn., S.W. Bapt. Religious Edn. Assn. Republican. Office: Baptist Sunday Sch Bd 127 9th Ave N Nashville TN 37234

POLITE, BERNARD, pulp and paper products company training manager; b. Savannah, Ga., May 8, 1943; s. Richard and Gertrude (Jenkins) P.; m. Frances Roberta Mackey, Sept. 16, 1964; 1 child, Vincent Bernard. B.S., Knoxville Coll., 1966. Lab. technician So. Research Inst., Birmingham, Ala., 1966-69; program exec. Robert Treat council Boy Scouts Am., Newark, 1969-73, dir. exploring div. Greater N.Y. council, N.Y.C., 1973-80; tng. mgr. Union Camp Corp., Savannah, 1980—. Co-chmn. Savannah State Coll. fundraising campaign, 1983; trustee Savannah Tech. Sch. Found., 1983—; mem. Southeastern Consortium for Minorities in Engring., Savannah, 1983-84; mem. Leadership Savannah, 1984—; vice chmn. allocations Com., Savannah United Way, 1984—, mem. children of change com., 1984—, bd. dirs., 1985—, trustee, 1985—. Mem. Am. Soc. Tng. and Devel., Savannah C. of C. (mem. edn. com. 1984—, bus. edn. partnership, 1984—, mem. fundraising campaign 1984—, host exec. for a day program 1984—, mem. speaker's bur. 1984—). Methodist. Home: 10613 Dorchester Rd Savannah GA 31419 Office: Union Camp Corp PO Box 570 Savannah GA 31402

POLITZ, HENRY ANTHONY, federal judge; b. Napoleonville, La., May 9, 1932; s. Anthony and Virginia (Russo) P.; B.A., La. State U., 1958, J.D. (mem. bd. Law Rev. 1958-59), 1959; m. Jane Marie Simoneaux, Apr. 29, 1952; children—Nyle, Bennett, Mark, Angela, Scott, Jane, Michael, Henry, Alisa, John, Nina. Admitted to La. bar, 1959; asso., then partner firm Booth, Lockard, Jack, Pleasant & LeSage, Shreveport, 1959-79; judge U.S. 5th Circuit Ct. Appeals, Shreveport, 1979—; vis. prof. La. State U. Law Center; bd. dirs. Am. Prepaid Legal Services Inst., 1975—; mem. La Judiciary Commn., 1978-79. Mem. Shreveport Airport Authority, 1973-79, chmn., 1977; bd. dirs. Rutherford House, Shreveport, 1975—, pres., 1978; pres. Caddo Parish Bd. Election Suprs., 1975-76; mem. Electoral Coll., 1976. Served with USAF, 1951-55. Named Outstanding Young Lawyer in La., 1971. Mem. Am. Bar Assn., Am. Judicature Soc., Internat. Soc. Barristers, La. Bar Assn., La. Trial Lawyers Assn., Shreveport Bar Assn., Justinian Soc., Omicron Delta Kappa. Democrat. Roman Catholic. Club: K.C. Home: 938 Linden St Shreveport LA 71104 Office: 2B04 500 Fannin St Shreveport LA 71101

POLK, EVELYN PHILYAW, nursing practice consultant; b. Tuskegee, Ala., Aug. 23; d. Harrison and Carrie Bell (Walton) Philyaw; children—Brenda Polk Maxey, Theodore C. B.S., Tuskegee Inst., 1975. R.N., Ohio, Ga. Asst. head nurse, head nurse, supr. Hanna Pavilion U. Hosps., Cleve., 1957-66; head nurse Ga. Mental Health Inst., Atlanta, 1967; alcohol, drug abuse program specialist U.S. Army Hosp., Frankfurt, W. Ger., 1977-79; tng. program coordinator Ga. Regional Hosp., Atlanta, 1979-80; developer, coordinator day treatment program West Mental Health Ctr., Atlanta, 1980-81; nursing practice cons. Ga. Bd. Nursing, Atlanta, 1981—, liaison impaired nurse com., 1981—; chmn. nominating com. Nat. Council State Bds. Nursing, Chgo., 1983-84; guest lectr. Emory Sch. Nursing, Atlanta, 1981—. Vol. Just Us Theatre, Atlanta, 1983-84. Recipient merit award Ga. Regional Hosp., Atlanta, 1981; outstanding service award dept. nursing Malcolm Grow Med. Ctr., Andrews AFB, Washington, 1983. Mem. Am. Nurses Assn., Ga. Nurses Assn. (liaison impaired nurse com. 1981—). Democrat. Office: Ga Bd Nursing 166 Pryor St SW Atlanta GA 30303

POLK, HIRAM CAREY, JR., surgeon; b. Jackson, Miss., Mar. 23, 1936; s. Hiram Carey and Dorris (Hemby) P.; m. Wanda Waddell, Sept. 1, 1956; children—Susan Elizabeth, Hiram Cary. B.S., Millsaps Coll., 1956; M.D., Harvard U., 1960. Intern, Barnes Hosp., St. Louis, 1960-61, resident, 1961-65; instr. surgery Washington U., St. Louis, 1964-65; asst. prof. surgery U. Miami, Fla., 1965-69, assoc. prof., 1969-71; prof., chmn. dept. surgery U. Louisville, 1971—; pres., chmn. bd. Univ. Surg. Assocs., P.S.C., 1971—; chmn. bd. Clin. Services Assn., Inc. Bd. govs. Trover Clinic Found., Madisonville, Ky. Mem. Allen O. Whipple Soc. (exec. council 1968-72), Am. Assn. Surgery of Trauma, Am. Burn Assn., Am. Cancer Soc., ACS (gov. 1972-78, commn. on cancer 1975-80), AMA, Am. Surg. Assn. (sec. 1984—), Acad. Surgery (pres. 1975-76), Central Surg. Assn., Assn. Am. Med. Colls. (chmn. ad hoc com. on Medicare and Medicaid 1978—), Collegium Internationale Chirurgiae Digestivae (sec.-treas. 1981—), Council on Pub. Higher Edn. (task group on health scis.), Halsted Soc., Internat. Soc. Burn Injuries, Jefferson County Med. Soc., Ky. Med. Assn., Ky. Surg. Soc., (pres. 1982-83), Louisville Surg. Soc., Societe Internationale de Chirurgie, Soc. Surgery Alimentary Tract (treas. 1975-78, pres. 1985-86), Soc. Clin. Surgery, Soc. Surg. Chairmen, Soc. Surg. Oncology (pres. 1984-85), Soc. Univ. Surgeons (pres. 1979-80), Southeastern Surg. Congress, So. Med. Assn. (chmn. sect. on surgery 1972-73, sec. 1970-72), So. Surg. Assn. (treas. 1982—), Alpha Omega Alpha. Author: (with H.H. Stone) Contemporary Burn Management, 1971; Hospital-Acquired Infections in Surgery, 1977; (with N.J. Ehrenkranz) Therapeutic Advanced and New Clinical Implications: Medical and Surgical with Betadine Microbicides; (with others) Basic Surgery: A Sympton Oriented Approach, 1978. Contbr. articles to med. jours. Mem. editorial bd. So. Med. Jour., 1970-72, Jour. Surg. Research, 1970-72, 75—, Current Problems in Surgery, 1973—, Surgery, 1975-85, Current Surgery, 1977—, Current Surg. Techniques, 1977—, Emergency Surgery: A Weekly Update, 1977—, Collected Letters in Surgery, 1978—, Brit. Jour. Surgery, 1981—. Chief editor Am. Jour. Surgery, 1985—. Home: 18 River Hill Rd Louisville KY 40207 Office: Dept Surgery U Louisville Louisville KY 40292

POLK, JAMES EDWARD, grain company executive; b. Port Tampa, Fla., Nov. 28, 1947; s. James Charles and Mary Fae (Laws) P.; m. Diane Elizabeth Lowery, Nov. 26, 1968; children—Paul, Jennifer. B.S. in Acctg., Miss. Coll., 1971. Acct., Skill-Craft Builders, Jackson, Miss., 1970-72; controller Char-Mac, Jackson, 1972-74, Instnl. Foods, Jackson, 1974-79; sec.-treas. Johnston Enterprises, Enid, Okla., 1979—, also dir.; sec.-treas., dir. W. B. Johnston Grain, 1979—, Johnston Seed Co., 1979—, Johnston's Port 33, 1983—. Bd. dirs., treas. Heritage Hills Homeowners, Enid, 1981, dir. and sec.-treas., 1982; chmn. bd. dirs. Enid Opportunity Sch., 1985; bd. dirs. Enid United Way, 1985. Served with Miss. N.G., 1966-76. Mem. C. of C. (chmn. com. 1985, bd. dirs. 1985—). Democrat. Baptist. Club: Enid Civitan (dir. 1982, dir., sec. 1983, pres.-elect, 1985). Lodge: Elks. Home: 2726 Heritage Trail Enid OK 73701 Office: Johnston Enterprises PO Box 1307 Enid OK 73702

POLK, OTIS CHARLES, JR., educational administrator; b. Electra, Tex., Mar. 15, 1928; s. Otis Polk and Annie Mae (Jackson) Reed; m. Evelyn Vivian Dawkins, Dec. 21, 1951 (dec. 1972); children—Lyn R., Alicia W., Otis Charles, III. B.S. in Chemistry, Mary Allen Coll., 1950; M.S. in Adminstrn. and Supervision, Prairie View A&M U., 1959. Chemistry tchr. B.T. Washington High Sch., Wichita Falls, Tex., 1954-56, vice prin., 1954-67, project dir., 1969-70; vice prin., coach East Side Jr. High Sch., Wichita Falls, 1967-69; prin. G.H. Kirby Middle Sch., Wichita Falls, 1970—; Chmn., East br. YMCA, Wichita Falls, 1966-68, acting exec. dir., 1967-68; chmn. East Tex. Dist. Southwest Area YMCA, Wichita Falls, 1967-69, Rosewood Neighborhood Group #1, Wichita Falls, 1974—; mem. bd. reps. Community Action, Wichita Falls, 1974-80. Recipient Service to Youth award YMCA, 1969, Brotherhood award NCCJ, 1973, Adminstr. of Yr. award Wichita Falls Classroom Tchrs., 1975; Outstanding Prin. award Tex. Congress PTA, 1982, Outstanding Community Service award Community Action, 1981-82. Mem. Tex. Middle Sch. Assn., Nat. Middle Sch. Assn., Tex. Assn. Secondary Sch. Prins., Phi Delta Kappa. Democrat. Avocations: fishing; hunting. Home: 1400 Normandy Dr Wichita Falls TX 76303 Office: GH Kirby Middle Sch 1715 N Loop 11 Wichita Falls TX 76305

POLK, THOMAS DUNCAN, manufacturing executive, air force officer; b. Johnson City, Tenn., May 22, 1946; s. Harold Grady and Dorothy Lee (Duncan) P.; m. Carolyn Jean Gentry, June 22, 1968; children—Amy Christen, Carrie Susan. B.S., Georgetown (Ky.) Coll., 1968. Air pollution control insp. City of Dayton (Ohio), 1968-69; commd. 2d lt. U.S. Air Force, 1969, advanced through grades to maj.; squadron avionics officer 84th Fighter Interceptor Squadron, 1971-73; squadron relocation officer, 1973, squadron quality control officer, 1974; discharged from active duty, 1974, assumed res. commn.; unit maintenance staff officer 4950th Test Wing, Air Force Systems Command, Avionics Maintenance Squadron, Wright-Patterson AFB, Ohio, 1975-80; dep. chief maintenance scheduling and inventory control Air Force Logistics Command, Hill AFB, Utah, 1980-82, dep. chief maintenance tng., 1983-85; div. quality control engr. O-Ring div. Parker Hannifin Corp., Lexington, 1978-80, mgr. applications engring., 1980-85, div. quality assurance mgr. O-Ring div., 1985—. Decorated Air Force Commendation Medal with 2 oak leaf clusters. Mem. Rubber Mfrs. Assn. (chmn. O-ring tech. com. Sealing Products div. 1984—), Soc. Automotive Engrs., ASTM, Res. Officers Assn., Am. Soc. Quality Control, Beta Beta Beta. Baptist. Office: 2360 Palumbo Dr Lexington KY 40509

POLLARD, JOSEPH AUGUSTINE, retail marketing executive; b. N.Y.C., June 22, 1924; s. Joseph Michael and Mary Theresa (Sheerin) P.; m. Helen Frances O'Neill, Jan. 18, 1947 (dec.); children—Christopher (dec.), Kenneth, Eugene, Daniel, Theresa, Michael; m. 2d, Lee Sharon Rivkins, Jan. 1, 1981. Student Pratt Inst., 1946-50. Advt. mgr. Boston Store, Utica, N.Y., 1951-53; sales promotion dir. Interstate Stores, N.Y., 1954-60, 67-70; v.p. sales Community Discount Stores, Chgo., 1960-63; dir. sales S. Klein, N.Y., 1964-66; v.p. advt. and pub. relations Peoples Drug Stores, Alexandria, Va., 1970—. Pres., trustee D.C. div. Am. Cancer Soc., 1985-86; pres. Modern Retailers Ill.,

1962. Served with USAF, 1943-46, 50-51. Recipient Am. Advt. Fedn. Silver medal award, 1982, St. George's medal Am. Cancer Soc., 1984. Mem. Advt. Club Met. Washington (pres. 1975-76). Club: Country of Fairfax (Va.). Home: 5848 Kara Pl Burke VA 22015 Office: Peoples Drug Stores 6315 Bren Mar Dr Alexandria VA 22312

POLLARD, KATHARINE MILLER, state government organization executive; b. Norfolk, Va., Dec. 8, 1943; d. William Roland and Katharine (Byrd) Miller; children—John Garland Pollard IV, K.C. Pollard. A.A., St. Mary's Coll., Raleigh, N.C., 1963; B.A., Old Dominion U., 1972. Asst. dir. Inst. Scottish Studies Old Dominion U., Norfolk, 1982-85; program dir. Va. World Trade Ctr., Norfolk, 1985—; dir. Virginia Beach Tommorrow, mem. econ. devel. com.; cons. Tidewater Scottish Festival, Inc. Editor Internat. Network Directory of Greater Hampton Roads, 1985. Vice pres. Lynn Haven Clean Waters Assn., Virginia Beach, Virginia Beach chpt. Soc. Prevention Cruelty to Animals; past pres. St. Mary's Coll. Alumnae Assn.; chmn. Internat. Scottish Festival of Art, Music and Drama, Norfolk, 1981 (filmed by BBC-TV, BBC radio). Grantee Univ. Edinburgh summer study, 1979. Fellow Soc. Antiquaries of Scotland; mem. The Hist. Assn., Scottish History Soc., Econ. History Soc., Hampton Roads Fgn. Commerce Club, No. Va. Trade Assn., Colonial Dames Am. (life). Avocations: sailing, gardening, travel. Office: Virginia World Trade Ctr 600 World Trade Center Norfolk VA 23510

POLLARD, OVERTON PRICE, lawyer, commission administrator; b. Ashland, Va., Mar. 26, 1933; s. James Madison and Anne Elizabeth (Hutchinson) P.; m. Anne Aloysia Meyer, Oct. 1, 1960; children—Mary O., Price, John, Anne, Charles, Andrew, David. B.A., Washington & Lee U., 1954, J.D., 1957. Bar: Va. 1962. Claims supr. Travelers Ins. Co., Richmond, Va., 1959-64; spl. asst. Va. Sup. Ct., Richmond, 1968-70; asst. atty. gen. City of Richmond, 1967, 70-72; exec. dir. Pub. Defender Commn., Richmond, 1972—; ptnr. Moore, Pollard, Boice & Seymour, Richmond, 1972—. Pres. Metro Legal Aid, Richmond, 1978. Mem. ABA, Va. Bar Assn., Richmond Bar Assn. Democrat. Baptist. Club: Bull & Bear (Richmond). Lodge: Lions. Home: 7726 Sweetbriar Rd Richmond VA 23229 Office: Moore Pollard Boice & Seymour 8550 Mayland Dr Richmond VA 23229

POLLARD, THOMAS NICHOLAS, JR., university dean; b. Richmond, Va., Sept. 20, 1931; s. Thomas Nicholas and Katherine (Bell) P.; m. Carter Smith, May 10, 1958; children—Thomas N. III, Katherine Carter, Garnett Tinsley. B.A., U. Richmond, 1953; M.A., George Washington U., 1957. Probation officer Juvenile and Domestic Ct., Arlington, Va., 1955-56; personnel officer Richmond Pub. Schs., Va., 1957-59, asst. dir. research, 1959-60; dean admissions U. Richmond, 1960—. Episcopalian. Home: 7103 Club Vista Ln Richmond VA 23229 Office: U Richmond Richmond VA 23173

POLLARD, WILLIAM LAWRENCE, social worker, educator; b. Raleigh, N.C., Nov. 27, 1944; s. Linwood and Betty (Burrell) P.; m. Merriette Maude Chance, Dec. 21, 1968; children—William Lawrence, Frederick Touissaint. A.B., Shaw U.; M.S.W., U. N.C., 1969; Ph.D., U. Chgo., 1976. Instr. Livingstone Coll., Salisbury, N.C., 1969-71; asst. prof., dir. social welfare program, 1973-76; asst. prof. Sch. Social Work, U. Pitts., 1976-80, assoc. prof., chmn. Community Orgn. Skillset, 1980-82; dir. social work program Grambling State U. (La.), 1982-84, dean Sch. Social Work, 1984—; sec. Allegheny County Bd. Pub. Assistance, Pitts.; mem. Pa. Bd. Pub. Welfare, 1981-82. Fellow Met. Applied Research Corp.; mem. Council Social Work Edn. (bd. dirs.), Assn. Black Social Workers (editorial bd. Black Caucus Jour.), Kappa Alpha Psi. Baptist. Author: A Study of Black Self-Help, 1978; also book revs., articles, papers. Home: PO Box 907 Grambling LA 71245 Office: Grambling U Social Work Program Grambling LA 71245

POLLEY, RICHARD DONALD, microbiologist; b. Bklyn., Feb. 23, 1937; s. George Weston and Evelyn (Tuttle) P.; student Trinity Coll., 1954-57; B.S., B.A., Hofstra U., 1960; m. Ruth Margaret Sullivan, May 2, 1958; children—Gordon MacHeath, Jennifer Elizabeth, Tabitha Isabelle, Sean Sullivan. Asst. advt. mgr. tech. Permatex Chem. Corp., Huntington, N.Y., 1960-61, Sun Chem. Corp., 1961-63; advt. mgr. Celanese Plastics Co., Newark, 1963-67; account dir. McCann Indsl. Tech. Sci. Mktg., N.Y.C., 1967-68, v.p., gen. mgr., Miami, 1968-70; pres. Intercapital Belgium S. Am., Brussels, 1970-72; pres., tech. dir. Iodinamics Corp., Lancaster, Pa., El Paso, Tex., 1972-76; pres., tech. dir. Hydrodine Corp., Miami, 1976-80, Omnidine Corp., Miami, 1980—; dir. Hydrodine Corp., Miami; pres. Skin Care Labs., Inc., Miami, 1979—; chmn. bd. Polymorphic Polymers Corp., Miami, 1978—; overseas dir. Field Iodine Goiter Med. Demonstration Projects, Beth Israel Hosp.-Harvard Med. Sch., 1977—; cons. water microbiology and disinfection control Pan Am. Health Orgn., others. Mem. Water Quality Assn., Internat. Iodine Disinfection Inst. (chmn. bd.). Republican. Patentee in field. Office: 74 NE 74th St Miami FL 33138

POLLOCK, DAN HERRICK, clinical psychologist; b. Newbern, N.C., Apr. 2, 1943; s. Swindell and Anne (Herrick) P. B.S. in Psychology, Old Dominion U., 1965; M.S., Va. Commonwealth U., 1973, Ph.D., 1977. Cert. biofeedback clinician. Coordinator dept. psychology Averett (Va.) Coll., 1977-80; dir. biofeedback Pain Control Ctr., Danville, Va., 1979-82; cons. Forsyth Meml. Hosp., Whitaker Rehab. Ctr., Winston-Salem, N.C., 1981-82; pvt. practice, co-owner Ctr. for Counseling and Therapy, Winston-Salem, 1981—; psychologist, staff adj. Mandula Ctr., Forsyth Meml. Hosp. Mem. Mental Health Services Bd. Served as capt. U.S. Army, 1966-70; Vietnam. VA grantee, 1982. Mem. AAAS, Am. Psychol. Assn., Biofeedback Soc. Am., N.C. Psychol. Assn. Author: The Measurement of Assertiveness, 1976. Home: 220 Heatherton Way Winston-Salem NC 27104 Office: 1409 E Plaza West Rd Winston-Salem NC 27103

POLLOCK, JACK PADEN, biology and dental educator, consultant, retired army officer; b. Columbus, Miss., May 12, 1920; s. Samuel Lafayette and Pauline Elizabeth (Pollock) O'Neal; m. Anne Olamae Silbernagel, Aug. 25, 1945; children—Poli A., Elizabeth D. Student, Tulane U., 1938-41; B.S., Southeastern La. U., 1942; D.D.S. cum laude, Loyola U., New Orleans, 1945; diploma, Army War Coll., 1965, Indsl. Coll. Armed Forces, 1966. Asst. prof., Loyola U., New Orleans, 1945-46, prof., 1977—; commd. 1st lt. U.S. Army, 1946, advanced through the grades to brigadier gen., 1972; career officer U.S. Army, 1946-77; dental advisor to Sec. of Defense, 1970-73; cons. Surgeon Gen. U.S. Army, Washington, 1981-84; U. rank and tenure com. Loyola U., New Orleans, 1982—. Author: International Communism: Its Future Prospects, 1965. Contbr. articles to profl. jours. Active in Nat. Council Boy Scouts Am., 1973—, nat. exploring com., 1973—. Decorated D.S.M., Legion of Merit with oak leaf cluster, Bronze Star with one oak leaf cluster, Master Paracutist badges; numerous others. Fellow Am. Coll. Dentistry, Internat. Coll. Dentistry; mem. Am. Dental Assn., La. Dental Assn., New Orleans Dental Assn., Am. Coll. Dentists, Internat. Coll. Dentists, Fedn. Dentaire Internationale, Assn. Mil. Surgeons of U.S. (life), Pierre Fauchard Acad., C. Victor Vignes Odontological Soc., Am. Assn. Dental Schs., Delta Sigma Delta, Kappa Sigma, Phi Kappa. Clubs: Army and Navy (Washington), Univ. (San Antonio). Avocations: gardening; writing; travel; conservation. Home: 118 Bayberry Dr Covington LA 70433 Office: Loyola U 6363 St Charles Ave New Orleans LA 70118

POLLOCK, JOHN T., corporation executive; b. Jackson, Miss., 1925; (married). B.A., Colgate U., 1949. With Thatcher Glass Mfg. Co., 1949-68; chief exec. officer Thatcher Glass div. Dart Industries, 1968-75; exec. v.p. Dorsey Corp., 1975-77, 1977, pres., 1979—, chmn. bd., chief exec. officer, 1979—. Address: 400 W 45th St Box 2189 Chattanooga TN 37410*

POLLOCK, STEVEN RICHARD, management educator, executive; b. Louisville, Dec. 26, 1957; s. Richard Horace and Sue Anne Pollock; m. Denise Michelle Hager, June 23, 1978; children—Emily Michelle, Erica Suzanne. B.B.A. with high distinction, Eastern Ky. U., 1980, M.P.A., 1981; postgrad. in higher edn. adminstrn. U. Louisville, 1984—. Adminstrv. intern dept. natural resources State of Ky., 1979; grad. teaching asst. dept. polit. sci. Eastern Ky. U., Richmond, 1980-81; prodn. mgr. Poly-Cycle, Inc., Louisville, 1981-83; instr. mgmt. Jefferson Community Coll., Louisville, 1983—. Mem. Eastern Ky. U. Alumni Assn., Sigma Chi, Phi Kappa Phi. Democrat. Presbyterian. Home: 201 Urton Ln Middletown KY 40223

POLLOW, CHARLES ERNEST, banker; b. Bethesda, Md., Dec. 17, 1948; s. Charles Howard and Eleanor (Collins) P.; B.A. in Sociology, Coll. William and Mary, 1970; postgrad. Stonier Grad. Sch. Banking, Rutgers U., 1975-77; m. Linda Jean Reese, Sept. 12, 1970. Mgmt. trainee Clarendon Bank and Trust, Arlington, Va., 1970-72, asst. treas., credit dept. mgr., 1972-73, comml. loan officer, 1973-78; v.p., corp. banking officer 1st Am. Bank Va., McLean, 1978-81, v.p., head fin. instns. dept., 1981-84; v.p., mgr. Va. Loan Prodn. Office, Equitable Bank, N.A., Balt., 1984—. Mem. Robert Morris Assocs., Va. Bankers Assn., Bank Adminstrn. Inst. Club: Shannon Green Golf (Fredericksburg, Va.). Home: 4520 Airlie Way Annandale VA 22003

POLOZOLA, FRANK JOSEPH, federal judge; b. Baton Rouge, Jan. 15, 1942; s. Steve A., Sr., and Caroline C. (Lucito) P.; student Bus. Adminstrn., La. State U., 1955-59. LL.B., J.D., 1965; m. Linda Kay White, June 9, 1962; children—Gregory Dean, Sheri Elizabeth, Gordon Damian. Admitted to La. bar, 1965; law clk. to U.S. Dist. Judge E. Gordon West, 1965-66; asso. firm Seale, Smith & Phelps, Baton Rouge, 1966-68, partner, 1968-73; part-time U.S. magistrate, Middle Dist. La., Baton Rouge, 1972-73, U.S. magistrate, 1973-80, U.S. dist. judge Middle Dist. La., 1980—; spl. lectr. Law Center La. State U., 1977—. Mem. La. State Bar Assn., Baton Rouge Bar Assn., Fifth Circuit Dist. Judges Assn., Omicron Delta Kappa. Roman Catholic. Clubs: KC, La. State U. Alumni Fedn., La. State U. L Club. Home: 9589 El Cajon Dr Baton Rouge LA 70815 Office: 307 US Courthouse 707 Florida Ave Baton Rouge LA 70801*

POLTROCK, STEVEN EDWARD, scientist; b. Seattle, Sept. 6, 1946; s. Robert William and Jeanne (Coulson) P.; m. Kathleen Louise Brown, Oct. 9, 1970 (div. 1973). B.S. in Engring., Calif. Inst. Tech., 1968; M.A. in Math., UCLA, 1970; Ph.D. in Psychology, U. Wash., 1977. Tech. staff TRW Systems Group, Redondo Beach, Calif., 1967-70; engr., programmer Honeywell Marine Systems Ctr., West Covina, Calif., 1970-72; research, teaching asst. U. Wash., Seattle, 1972-77; asst. prof. U. Denver, 1977-82; postdoctoral fellow AT&T Bell Labs., Murray Hill, N.J., 1982-84; mem. tech. staff Microelectronics and Computer Tech. Corp., Austin, Tex., 1984—. Contbr. articles to profl. jours. Grantee Biomed. Research Support, 1978, NIMH, 1978, Air Force Office Sci. Research, 1980, Nat. Inst. Child Health and Human Devel., 1979. Mem. Am. Psychol. Assn., Psychonomic Soc., AAAS, N.Y. Acad. Scis. Home: 8200 Neely Dr 149 Austin TX 78759 Office: Microelectronics and Computer Tech Corp 9430 Research Blvd Austin TX 78759

POLVAY, MARINA SCHERBATOFF, public relations executive, food consultant; b. Krasnojars, USSR, July 24, 1928; came to U.S., 1952, naturalized, 1955; d. Konstantine Scherbatoff and Eugenia Szenutovits-Berezsni; B.S., Innsbruck (Austria) U., 1949; m. Murray Polvay, Feb. 26, 1960. Exec. v.p. Slenderella Internat., 1952-60; owner Marina Polvay Assos. Inc., food cons. and public relations, Miami Shores, Fla., 1968—; author for mags., cookbooks, 1962—; host radio and TV talk shows. Past pres. Miami Ballet Soc., Theatre Arts League, Pearl S. Buck Found. Mem. Sommelier Guild, Confrerie de la Chaine des Rotisseurs. Writers Guild and League, Writers Club, Am. Soc. Journalists, Food and Wine Soc. Republican. Mem. Russian Orthodox Ch. Author: Marina Polvay's Best International Recipies, 1972; Florida Heritage Cookbook, 1976; The Dracula Cookbook, 1978; All Along the Danube, 1979; The Energy Saver's Cookbook, 1980; Slimming and Healthy Cooking of Italy, 1981. Home: 9250 NE 10th Ct Miami Shores FL 33138 Office: 9315 Park Dr Suite A1 Miami Shores FL 33138

POLYSON, JAMES ATHAN, clinical psychologist, educator; b. Hinton, W.Va., Apr. 26, 1953; s. Van and Katherine (Mathews) P.; m. Susan Perry, 1980; 1 child, John Athan. B.S., Old Dominion U., 1975; Ph.D., U. Ala., 1980. Lic. clin. psychologist, Va. Clin. psychology intern Va. Treatment Ctr. Children, Richmond, 1978-79; asst. prof. psychology Ind. State U., Terre Haute, 1979-83, U. Richmond, 1983—; staff psychologist Ctr. Psychol. Services U. Richmond, 1983—; pvt. practice clin. psychology, Richmond, 1984—. Author articles, book reviews, short stories, poetry. Grantee Ind. State U., 1980, U. Richmond, 1984. Mem. Am. Psychol. Assn., So. Soc. for Philosophy Psychology, Psychologists for Social Responsibility, Richmond Peace Edn. Ctr., APA Dev. 9 Task Force Peace. Democrat. Avocations: sci. fiction; astronomy; swimming; record collecting; basketball. Office: Dept Psychology 118 Richmond Hall U Richmond Richmond VA 23173

POMANTE, AUGUST ERIC, drug store executive; b. Harrisville, R.I., Aug. 1, 1925; s. Attilio and Gaetana (Trinchini) P.; m. Laura June Mercuro, Sept. 10, 1950; children—Donna, Richard, Dolce, Gina. B.Sc. in Pharmacy, Rutgers U., 1950. Registered pharmacist, N.J., Fla. Treas., chief pharmacist Discount Drugs, Inc., West Palm Beach, Fla., 1969-75, v.p. ops., chief pharmacist, 1975—; owner Shake & Roll Tablet, West Palm Beach, 1985—; dir. Riverton Investment Corp., Va., Capitol Cement Corp., Martinsburg, W.Va., Riverton Corp. Patentee in field. Democrat. Mem. Nat. Assn. Retail Druggists, Fla. Pharm. Assn., Palm Beach County Pharm. Assn. Democrat. Roman Catholic. Avocations: coins; stock market; investor. Office: Discount Drugs Inc PO Box 3686 West Palm Beach FL 33402

POMERANTZ, MARTIN, chemistry educator, researcher; b. N.Y.C., May 3, 1939; s. Harry and Pauline (Sietz) P.; m. Maxine Miller, June 4, 1961; children—Lee Allan, Wendy Jane, Heidi Lauren. B.S., CCNY, 1959; M.S., Yale U., 1961, Ph.D., 1964. NSF postdoctoral fellow U. Wis.-Madison, 1963-64; asst. prof. Case Western Res. U., 1964-69; assoc. prof. Belfer Grad. Sch. Sci., Yeshiva U., 1969-74, prof., 1974-76, acting chmn., 1971-72, chmn. chemistry dept., 1973-76; vis. assoc. prof. U. Wis.-Madison, 1972; vis. prof. Columbia U., part-time 1970-75; Alfred P. Sloan Found. fellow, 1971-76; vis. prof. Ben-Gurion U., Negev, Beer Sheva, Israel, summer, 1981, 85; prof. chemistry U. Tex., Arlington, 1976—; cons. various cos. Woodrow Wilson fellow, 1959-60; NSF, hon. Sterling fellow, 1962-63; Leeds and Northrup grad. fellow, 1960-62; grantee NSF, Petroleum Research Fund, Alfred P. Sloan Found., Robert A. Welch Found. Mem. Am. Chem. Soc., Royal Soc. Chemistry, Phi Beta Kappa, Sigma Xi. Contbr. numerous articles to profl. jours. Home: 5521 Williamstown Dallas TX 75230 Office: Dept Chemistry U Tex PO Box 19065 Arlington TX 76019

POMPIAN, RICHARD OWEN, consulting company executive, communications educator; b. Chgo., July 17, 1935; s. Bertram Edwin and Molly Mavis (Pumpian) P.; m. Rita Lillian Beyers, Dec. 20, 1970 (div. 1984). A.B. in Journalism, U. Mich., 1958, Cert. in Journalism, 1958, Internship Cert. in Advt., 1961; M.B.A. in Mktg. with distinction, NYU, 1965, Cert. in Publishing and Graphics, 1966, Cert. in TV, Radio and Film, 1967, Cert. in Data Processing and Systems, 1970; postgrad. in psychology New Sch. for Social Research, 1968-70; postgrad. in bus. communication U. Tex.-Austin, 1982—. Copywriter Dancer-Fitzgerald-Sample, Inc., N.Y.C., 1960-68; advt. cons., N.Y.C., 1968-69; advt. agt., prin. ProSell Communications, N.Y.C., 1970-74; pres. Pompian Advt., Inc., N.Y.C., 1974-82; ptnr. Pompians/Tng. Cons., N.Y.C. and Austin, Tex., 1977—; guest lectr. Pace U., N.Y.C., 1974-75; adj. lectr. Fordham U., N.Y.C., 1979-80; adj. lectr. communication arts Marymount Manhattan Coll., N.Y.C., 1979-80; adj. asst. prof. communication arts St. John's U., N.Y.C., 1979-80, asst. prof., 1980-84. Author: Advertising: a First Book, 1970; Writing for Professionals, 1981. Editor: The Rhythm Book, 1971; Northeast Gazette, 1976-80. Served to 1st lt. art. U.S. Army, 1958-60. NEA grantee. Mem. Soc. Profl. Journalists, Nat. Acad. TV Arts and Scis., AAAS, AAUP, Assn. for Bus. Communication formerly Am. Bus. Communication Assn. (presentation at nat. conv. 1984), N.Y. Acad. Scis., Soc. for Gen. Systems Research, U. Mich. Alumni Assn., NYU Alumni Assn., Delta Sigma Phi, Phi Kappa Phi. Club: Deadline (N.Y.C.). Home: 4313 Charlemagne Court Austin TX 78727 Office: Dept Gen Bus Grad Sch Bus U Tex-Austin CBA 5.202 Austin TX 78712

POND, HARRY SEARING, urologist, educator; b. New Orleans, Jan. 22, 1939; s. Harry Searing and Elizabeth (Lewis) P.; student Tulane U., 1960; M.D., U. Tenn., 1963. Intern, Phila. Gen. Hosp., 1963-64; resident in urology Johns Hopkins Hosp., Balt., 1967-71; staff physician Ochsner Clinic, New Orleans, 1971-73; practice medicine, specializing in urology, Mobile (Ala.) Urology Group, 1973—; assoc. prof. U.S. Ala., Mobile, 1973—; pres. med. staff Providence Hosp., 1982-83. Trustee, St. Paul's Sch., Mobile, 1976-83; warden of vestry St. Paul's Episcopal Ch., 1978-79. Served with USPHS, 1964-66. Recipient First prize for research, Am. Urologic Assn., 1970; Med. Assn. of Ala. award for services to humanity, 1977. Mem. Am., So. med. assns., Am. Urologic Assn., Am. Bd. Urology, Ala. Med. Assn., Am. Assn. Clin. Urologists, ACS, Mobile County Med. Soc. (pres. 1983-84). Club: Country, Fairhope Yacht. Contbr. articles in field to med. jours. Home: 4 Kingsway St Mobile AL 36608 Office: 1720 Center St Mobile AL 36608

PONDER, ELYMAS YATES, sheriff; b. Madison County, N.C., Nov. 11, 1909; s. Zadie and Emma (Ramsey) P.; m. Orla O'Neil, Dec. 29, 1929; 1 son, Warren. Student pub. schs., Madison County, Marshall, N.C. Sheriff Madison County, N.C., 1950—; mem. N.C. Crime Commn., 1977-84; mem. N.C. Sheriff Tng. Standard Com. Mem. Madison County Bd. Health, 1930-40; mem. Marshall Bd. Edn., 1941-51. Office: Madison County Sheriff's Office County Courthouse Marshall NC 28753

PONDER, FRED THOMAS, psychologist, adminstr.; b. Coosa County, Ala., Mar. 6, 1940; s. Ruben Thomas and Gladys Elfreda (Guy) P.; A.B., U. Ala., 1967, M.A., 1968, Ed.S., 1971; postgrad. Miss. State U., 1974; 1 son, Thomas Eric. Outpatient therapist Spoon River Community Health Center, Galesburg, Ill., 1970-81; program dir. St. Mary's Sq. Living Center, Galesburg, 1970-81; psychologist Galesburg Mental Health Center, 1981-82; dir. Clarendon (Tex.) Family Services Center, 1981—. Served with USAF, 1961-63. Mem. Am. Psychol. Assn., Ala. Psychol. Assn., Ill. Psychol. Assn. Southeastern Psychol. Assn. Democrat. Unitarian-Universalist. Club: Lions. Office: Med Center PO Box 1007 Clarendon TX 79226 Home: PO Box 180 Lelia Ike TX 79240

PONDER, JAMES ALTON, clergyman, evangelist; b. Ft. Worth, Jan. 20, 1933; s. Leo A. and Mae Adele (Blair) P.; B.A., Baylor U., 1954; M.A. in Edn., Southwestern Bapt. Theol. Sem., 1965; m. Joyce Marie Hutchison, Sept. 1, 1953; children—Keli, Ken. Ordained to ministry Baptist Ch., 1953; pastor Calvary Bapt. Ch., Corsicana, Tex., 1953-57, First Bapt. Ch., Highlands, Tex., 1957-62, Ridglea West Bapt. Ch., Ft. Worth, 1963-66, First Bapt. Ch., Carmi, Ill., 1966-67; dir. evangelism Ill. Bapt. State Conv., 1967-70, Fla. Bapt. Conv., 1970-81; pres. Jim Ponder Ministries, Inc., 1981—; fgn. mission bd. evangelist in various countries of Asia, Central Am., Middle East, 1960—; project dir. Korea Major Cities Evangelization Project, 1978-80; evangelist ch. revivals, area crusades and evangelism confs., 1951—; mem. faculty Billy Graham Schs. Evangelism, 1970—; co-founder Ch. Growth Inst. Fla., 1976; co-dir. Ch. Growth Crusades, 1978-79; sports announcer Sta. KIYS, Waco, Tex., 1950-54. Bd. dirs. N. Fla. chpt. Leukemia Soc. Am. Mem. Internat. Platform Assn., Fellowship Christian Athletes, Smithsonian Inst. Democrat. Club: Kiwanis. Author: The Devotional Life, 1970; Evangelism Men...Motivating Laymen to Witness, 1975; Evangelism Men...Proclaiming the Doctrines of Salvation, 1976; Evangelism Men...Preaching for Decision, 1979; contbr. articles to religious publs. Home: Arlington By the River Jacksonville FL 32211 Office: PO Box 8881 Jacksonville FL 32239

PONS, JOSEF MANUEL, public relations cons.; b. Washington, Feb. 28, 1947; s. Juan Antonio and Gladys Violeta (Janer) P.; m. Sara Maria Castro, Apr. 6, 1972; children—Josef Antoine, Ricardo Juan, Sariela, Julio, Irene. B.Sc., U. P.R., 1970. Dir. public affairs P.R. Maritime Shipping Authority, San Juan, 1974-76; v.p. Welbeck/Carl Byoir & Assocs., Hato Rey, P.R., 1976-80; pres. Viewpoint, Pub. Relations, Hato Rey, P.R., 1980-83; pub. relations and advt. cons. Internat. Charter Mortgage Corp., Hato Rey, 1983—; instr. U. Sacred Heart, San Juan, 1976—. Served with Air NG, 1965-72. Recipient Top Mgmt. award Sales and Mktg. Exec. Assn. San Juan, 1978, Class of 99 award Transport 2000 Mag., 1976. Mem. Pub. Relations Soc. Am. (accredited; Silver Anvil award 1976), Overseas Press Club P.R., Pub. Relations Assn. P.R., Phi Sigma Alpha. Democrat. Roman Catholic.

PONTIUS, PAUL ELMER, mathematics educator; b. Algonac, Mich., Feb. 14, 1934; s. Elmer Wallace and Aileen Grace (Endelman) P.; m. Louise Rutherford, Dec. 15, 1973; 1 dau., Carole Louise. B.B.A., U. Tex.-Austin, 1956; M.A. in Math., U. Ill., 1965; postgrad. Pan Am. U., 1956-61, Tex. A&I U., 1960-61, Kingsville and Eastern Mich. U., 1962. Cert. tchr., Tex. Tchr. math. La Joya High Sch. (Tex.), 1956-61, McAllen High Sch. (Tex.), 1961-64, Pensacola Jr. Coll. (Fla.), 1965-66; instr. math. Pan Am. U., Edinburg, Tex., 1966-77, asst. prof., 1977—; cons. to pubs. including Academic Press, Scott Foresman, Wadeworth, Brooks/Cole, Prindle, Weber & Schmidt, others. Active Valley Astron. Assn., Rio Grande Valley Assn. for Gifted/Talented Children. Recipient John H. Shary award John H. Shary Found., 1952; NSF grantee, 1963; recipient Merit award Pan Am. U., 1982, 83. Mem. Am. Math. Assn. Two Year Colls., Phi Eta Sigma, Alpha Kappa Psi. Republican. Methodist. Author student guides. Home: 1514 Highland McAllen TX 78501 Office: Dept Math Pan Am Univ Edinburg TX 78539

POOLE, CALVIN, III, lawyer; b. Greenville, Ala., July 6, 1955; s. Elisha Calvin and Juanita (Cumbie) P.; m. Mary Rogers Weiss, Aug. 21, 1982; 1 child, Calvin Crenshaw. B.S., U. Ala., 1977, J.D., 1980. Bar: Ala. 1980, U.S. Dist. Ct. (mid. dist.) Ala. 1980, U.S. Ct. Appeals (11th cir.) 1982. Ptnr. Poole & McFerrin, Greenville, 1980—; spl. asst. atty. gen. State of Ala., Greenville, 1982-83; asst. dist. atty. State of Ala., 2d Jud. Circuit, Greenville, 1983—; dir. First Nat. Bank, Greenville. Pres. Am. Heart Assn. Butler County, 1981, 82, United Fund Butler County, Inc., 1982, 83, 84. Mem. Ala. Trial Lawyers Assn., Nat. Dist. Attys. Assn., Assn. Trial Lawyers Am., Ala. Dist. Attys. Assn. Republican. Presbyterian. Club: Rotary (pres. 1985—). Club: Ridge Expeditions Ltd. (chmn. 1980—). Home: 200 College St Greenville AL 36037 Office: Poole & McFerrin 600 E Commerce St Greenville AL 36037

POOLE, DAVID RAWLINGS, psychologist; b. D.C., Sept. 23, 1945; s. Rawlings Stine and Frances Anne (Childers) P.; m. Donna Faye McDaniel, Mar. 6, 1976; children—John Rawlings, Katherine Louise. B.A. in Philosophy, St. Marys Sem., 1967; M.Ed. in Counseling, Johns Hopkins U., 1969; Ph.D. in Counseling Psychology, U. Tex., 1972. Lic. psychologist, Tex. Psychologist, Austin, Tex., 1972—; cons. Meridell Achievement Ctr., Austin, 1975—, Dept. Human Resources, Austin, 1975—, Darden Hill Ranch Sch., Dripping Springs, Tex., 1980—. Mem. Am. Psychol. Assn. Democrat. Avocations: reading; civil war history; running; family; real estate. Home: 4111 Edwards Mountain Dr Austin TX 78731 Office: 4404 Burnet Rd Austin TX 78756

POOLE, EDGAR MORGAN, JR., optometrist; b. Gaffney, S.C., Dec. 9, 1946; s. Edgar Morgan and Malinda (Black) P.; m. Marilyn Babb, June 6, 1969; children—Jennifer Michelle, Craig Michael, Brian James, Chad Edgar. B.S., Brigham Young U., 1969; O.D., So. Coll. Optometry, 1973. Prin. Family Vision Care, Spartanburg, S.C., 1974—, Chesnee, S.C., 1983—. Mem. Am. Optometric Assn., S.C. Optometric Assn., Appalachian Optometric Soc. (pres. 1981-83). Mormon. Lodge: Lions (eye care chmn. 1976—). Home: 4347 Conrad Dr Spartanburg SC 29301

POOLE, ELIZABETH GRACE, communications company executive; b. Chapel Hill, N.C., Aug. 10, 1954; d. James Ralph and Mary (Haley) P., Jr. B.S. in Phys. Edn., U. N.C.-Greensboro, 1976. Tchr., coach Allendale Fairfax High Sch., Allendale, S.C., 1977-79; communication technician AT&T Long Lines, Memphis, 1980-82; Quality of worklife trainer/FAC, 1983-84, AT&T Divestiture Task Force, Atlanta, 1982-83; mgmt. devel. trainer AT&T Communications Co., Atlanta, 1983-84, ops. supr., 1985—, fast track mgmt. devel. program 1984—; co-coordinator quality of worklife symposium, 1984. Developer curriculum materials. Recipient Tchr. of Yr. award Allendale County Schs., 1979. Mem. Am. Soc. Tng. and Devel., Internat. Assn. Quality Circles. Democrat. Roman Catholic. Avocations: running; softball; photography; landscaping. Home: 615 Hillpine Dr NE Atlanta GA 30306 Office: AT&T Communications 51 Ivy St Atlanta GA 30303

POOLE, RICHARD WILLIAM, educator; b. Oklahoma City, Dec. 4, 1927; s. William Robert and Lois (Spicer) P.; B.S., U. Okla., 1951, M.B.A., 1952; Ph.D., Okla. State U., 1960; m. Bertha Lynn Mehr, July 28, 1950; children—Richard William, Laura Lynne, Mark Stephen. Research analyst Okla. Gas & Electric Co., Oklahoma City, 1952-54; mgr. Sci. and Mfg. Devel. dept. Oklahoma City C. of C., 1954-57; asst. to pres. Frontiers of Sci. Found., 1956; mgr. Office of James E. Webb, Washington, 1957-58; instr. econs., asst. prof., asso. prof., prof., Okla. State U., 1960-65, dean Coll. of Bus., 1965-72, v.p. univ. relations and devel., 1972-74, v.p. Univ. relations and extension, 1974—; cons. NASA, Midwest Research Inst.; mem. Gov's. gen. adv. com., tech. com. Statis. Standards, 1964-66; mem. adv. exec. com. Nat. Govs. Conf., 1965. Bd. dirs. Stillwater Indsl. Found., 1967-78, Stillwater YMCA, 1966, Mid-Continent Research and Devel. Council, 1965-78, chmn., 1969; bd. dirs. Okla. Council on Econ. Edn., 1965—, mem. exec. council, 1965—. Served from pvt. to 2d lt., AUS, 1946-48. Mem. Am., So. econ. assns., Okla. (dir. 1965—), Stillwater (dir. 1965-78, pres. 1968) chambers commerce, Am. Assembly Collegiate Schs. Bus. (dir. 1971-72), Southwestern Econ. Assn. (pres. 1968), Res. Officers Assn., Southwestern Bus. Adminstrn. Assn. (pres. 1973), Phi Eta Sigma, Beta Gamma Sigma (dir. 1979-82), Pi Gamma Mu, Phi Kappa Phi, Omicron Delta Kappa. Contbr. articles to profl. jours. Home: 124 Georgia Ave Stillwater OK 74075

POPADIC, JOSEPH STEPHEN, architect, educator; b. Bridgeport, Conn., Nov. 6, 1945; s. Joseph Peter and Pauline Katherine (Vrabel) P.; B.Landscape

Arch., SUNY, 1967, M.Landscape Arch., 1974; m. Mary K. Rountree, Dec. 16, 1978. Landscape architect New Haven Redevel. Agy., 1967-68; with Reimann & Buechner, Landscape Architects, Syracuse, N.Y., 1970-71, Moriece and Gary, Landscape Architects, Cambridge, Mass., 1974; prin. Haynes, Popadic, Abbey Asso., Landscape Architects, Baton Rouge, 1978-80, Haynes-Popadic, Landscape Architects, Baton Rouge, 1980—; prof. Landscape Architecture, La. State U., Baton Rouge, 1972—, mem. faculty senate, 1977-80, dir. grad. studies in landscape architecture Sch. Landscape Architecture, 1980—; with Canoeing Adventures, instrn. and guide service, Baton Rouge. Served to 1st lt., U.S. Army, 1968-70, now maj. USAR. Mem. Am. Soc. Landscape Architects, La. Soc. Landscape Architects. Home: 565 Castle Kirk Dr Baton Rouge LA 70808 Office: Sch Landscape Arch La State Univ Baton Rouge LA 70803

POPE, DAVID E., geologist, micropaleontologist; b. Forrest City, Ark., Dec. 20, 1920; s. Jesse Ellis and Mary Ruth (Remley) P.; m. Dorothy Angeline Salario, June 8, 1947 (dec. Jan. 1982); children—David Brian, Mark Alan. B.S., La. State U., 1947, M.S., 1948; grad. U.S. Army Command and Gen. Staff Coll., 1967. Cert. petroleum geologist. Paleontologist, Union Producing Co., Houston, 1948-49, New Orleans, 1949-55, dist. paleontologist, New Orleans, 1955-63, Lafayette, La., 1963-67; cons., Lafayette, La., 1967-75; sr. research geologist La. Geol. Survey, Baton Rouge, 1975—; lectr. La. State U., 1979, 80, N.E. La. U., 1983. Mem. nat. adv. bd. Am. Security Council, 1983—; bd. dirs. La. State U. Mus. Geosci. Assocs., 1980—, pres. 1981-82. Served to capt. U.S. Army, 1942-46, to lt. col. USAR, 1945-70. Decorated Silver Star medal with oak leaf cluster, Purple Heart, Combat Inf. badge. Mem. Am. Assn. Petroleum Geologists (Ho. of Dels. 1980—), Soc. Econ. Paleontologists and Mineralogists (pres. Gulf Coast sect. 1959-60), New Orleans Geol. Soc. (v.p. 1962-63), Lafayette Geol. Soc., Baton Rouge Geol. Soc. (pres. 1980-81), Gulf Coast Assn. Geol. Socs. (exec. com. 1979—, historian 1984—), Res. Officers Assn. (life), Mil. Order World Wars, La. State U. Sch. Geology Alumni Assn. (pres. 1958-59, 84-85), La. Petroleum Council. Contbr. articles to profl. jours. Home: 299 Roselawn Blvd Lafayette LA 70503 Office: La Geol Survey PO Box G Univ Sta Baton Rouge LA 70893

POPE, DOROTHEA NEALMA, retail store manager, hair stylist; b. Youngstown, Ohio, Sept. 2, 1931; d. Gustav Paul and Elizabeth M. (Heidenrich) Scholz; m. Rebo Pope, May 4, 1963. Diploma, Canton Acad. Beauty Sch., 1948; student Dale Carnegie Mgrs. Course, 1979. Cert. cosmetologist, Ohio; notary, Fla. Hair stylist Taylor Bros. Dept. Store, Cleve., 1949; cosmetology tchr., stylist, Gary, Ind., 1951; mgr. Beauteria Salons, Sarasota, Fla., 1952; owner, operator beauty salons, Miami and Hollywood, Fla., 1957-63; dept. mgr., buyer Grant's Co., Las Vegas, 1964-67; salesman, dept. mgr. Ford Window Shades, North Miami Beach, Fla., 1968; with Super X Drugs, Ft. Lauderdale, Fla., 1969—, store mgr., Opalocka, Fla., 1975-80, Lorida, Fla., 1980—. Dir. Lorida Vol. Fire Dept. Aux., 1981-82, v.p., 1982-83; lector Roman Catholic Ch.; tchr. Confraternity of Christian Doctrine; active Community Ctr. of Lorida, Cath. Youth Orgn. Recipient Silver Razor award, 1950. Mem. Nat. Notary Assn., Nat. Cometologists Assn., Nat. Assn. Female Execs. Democrat. Clubs: Columbette's (v.p.) (Lake Placid, Fla.); Toastmasters (Sebring, Fla.). Lodges: Elks, Lions. Home: Lorida FL Office: Super X Drugs 1040 SE Lakeview Dr Sebring FL 33870

POPE, JACK, retired chief justice Supreme Court of Texas; b. Abilene, Tex., Apr. 18, 1913; m. Allene Nichols. B.A., Abilene Christian U., 1934, LL.D. (hon.), 1980; LL.B., U. Tex., 1937; LL.D. (hon.), Pepperdine U., 1981, St. Mary's U., San Antonio, 1982., Okla. Christian Coll., 1984. Practice law, Corpus Christi, Tex., 1937-46; judge 94th Dist. Ct. Tex., 1946-50; justice Tex. Ct. Civil Appeals, 1950-65, chmn. jud. sect., 1961-62; justice Supreme Ct. Tex., Austin, 1965-82, chief justice, 1982-85, chmn. appellate judges sect., 1972, chmn. ethics com. of jud. sect., 1972-73; rules mem. Supreme Ct. Adv. Com.; chmn. Tex. Law Library Bd. Author numerous published opinions; contbr. numerous articles to law jours.; editorial bd. Tex. Law Rev., 1936-37; chmn. bd. editors Appellate Procedure in Tex.; pres. Council for Christian Chronicle, 1986; editorial bd. The Tex. Lawyer, 1985—. Elder Jefferson Congregation, San Antonio, 1957-64; trustee Abilene Christian U. (Tex.), 1954—. Served with USN. Recipient Law Rev. award Tex. Bar Found., 1979, 80, 81, Rosewood Gavel award St. Mary's U. Sch. Law, 1962, St. Thomas More award St. Mary's U., 1982, Joe Greenhill Jud. award, 1982, Silver Beaver award Alamo council Boy Scouts Am. Mem. Nueces County Bar (pres. 1946), San Antonio Bar, Travis County Bar, Hill Country, Bar, Am. Judicature soc., ABA, Law-Sci. Inst., Am. Soc. Legal History, Order of Coif, Phi Delta Phi. Mem. Ch. of Christ. Club: Austin Knife & Fork (pres. 1980). Address: 2803 Stratford Dr Austin TX 78746

POPE, JAMES GLEN, ophthalmologist; b. Cawood, Ky., Mar. 12, 1929; s. Henry Harrison and Kila (Ball) P.; m. Janelle Hogg, Aug. 19, 1954 (div. 1967); m. Helen P. Hackney, Nov. 17, 1984; children—Mary Beth, Cynthia Leigh, James G. B.A., Vanderbilt U., 1950; M.D., U. Louisville, 1955. Diplomate Am. Bd. Ophthalmology. Intern Phila. Gen. Hosp., 1955-56; resident ophthalmology Henry Ford Hosp., Detroit, 1959-62; practice medicine specializing in ophthalmology, Lexington, Ky., 1962—; chmn. dept. ophthalmology Good Samaritan Hosp., Lexington, 1983—. Served to capt USAF, 1956-58. Democrat. Presbyterian. Lodge: Rotary. Avocations: golf; roses; travel. Home: 2013 Bixby Way E Lexington KY 40502 Office: 2368 Nicholasville Rd Lexington KY 40503

POPE, JANET CORAL CAMPBELL, architect; b. Albuquerque, Nov. 24, 1953; d. Ovid Sylvester and Evelyn Grace (Kistler) Campbell; student DeKalb Jr. Coll., 1970-71; B.S., Ga. Inst. Tech., 1975, M.Arch., 1977; m. Rodney Lee Pope, June 12, 1977. Registered architect, Ga. Asso. urban designer Met. Atlanta Rapid Transit Authority, Atlanta, 1977-78; architect intern Toombs Amisano & Wells, Atlanta, 1978-80; architect Thompson, Ventulett, Stainback & Assocs., Atlanta, 1980-84, Dimery, Corbet, West & Assocs., 1984, Dan Harmon & Assocs., 1984-85; pres. Campbell Pope & Assocs., 1985—. Mem. AIA (award for excellence of studies Atlanta chpt. 1977), Constrn. Specifications Inst., Mem. Plymouth Brethren. Home: 1500 Chantilly Dr NE Atlanta GA 30324 Office: 1500 Chantilly Dr NE Atlanta GA 30324

POPE, MARY ANN IRWIN, graphic design artist; b. Louisville, Mar. 8, 1932; d. James Cecil Irwin and Margaret E. Taylor; m. Richard Coraine Pope, Nov. 25, 1954; children—Margaret Neil, Zachary Taylor, Richard Trent. Draftsman U.S. Army, Louisville, 1953-54; fashion artist Byck's, Louisville, 1956-59; freelance fashion artist, Louisville, 1960-66; design asst. Planning, Huntsville, Ala., 1979—; tchr. Huntsville Art League, 1966-78; dir. Huntsville Art League & Mus. Assn., 1966-75. One woman shows include Birmingham So. U., Ala., 1974, Montevallo Coll., Ala., 1977, U. Ala., Huntsville Gallery, 1979; exhibited numerous group shows in Ky., La., Ala.; represented in permanent collections Fine Arts Mus. of South, Mobile, Ala., Mint Mus. Art, Charlotte, N.C., Huntsville Mus. Art, Ala., and numerous other pub. and pvt. collections. Recipient Purchase award Aqueous 84 Ky. Watercolor Soc., 1984, Museum award Watercolor USA Springfield Art Mus., Mo., 1982, Purchase prize Ala. Craftsmen Council Annual, 1975, Purchase prize Piedmont Painting Exhibition Mint Mus. Art, Charlotte, 1972, and numerous other awards. Mem. Ky. Watercolor Soc. (bd. mem. 1977), Birmingham Art Assn., Ala. Art League (v.p. 1975), Watercolor Soc. Ala. (bd. mem. 1976-78), Ga. Watercolor Soc. Home and Office: 1705 Greenwyche Rd SE Huntsville AL 35801

POPE, MARY FAYE LORMAND, food service administrator; b. Kaplan, La., Aug. 8, 1941; s. Percy and Velma (Broussard) Lormand; m. Marlin G. Kerkman, Dec. 27, 1964 (div. July 1976); children—Marlin G., Karla Mary; m. Jesse Lee Pope, Feb. 18, 1977; children—David Lee, Lisa Renee. B.S. in Instl. Mgmt., U. Southwestern La., 1963. Registered dietitian. Asst. dir. O. K. Allen Dining Hall, U. Southwestern La., Lafayette, 1963-64, dir., instr., 1964-65, O.K. mgr., instr. Northeastern La. State U., Monroe, 1965-67; Allen Dining Hall, 1967-70; dir. dietary Am. Legion Hosp., Crowley, La., 1970-77; assoc. dir. U. Tex. M. D. Anderson Hosp., Houston, 1977—. Named Outstanding Dietitian, Southeastern Hosp. Conf., Atlanta, 1974, Outstanding Alumna, Coll. Agrl. U. Southwestern La., 1976. Mem. Am. Dietetic Assn., Am. Soc. Hosp. Food Service Adminstrs. (Tex. Gulf Coast chpt.), La. Dietetic Assn. (pres. 1974-75), Tex. Dietetic Assn., South Tex. Dietetic Assn., Phi Kappa Phi. Avocations: cooking; writing; reading; bike-riding. Home: 4729 Brian Haven Houston TX 77018 Office: U Tex M D Anderson Hosp 6723 Bertner St Box 58 Houston TX 77030

POPE, RENEÉ GRAVITT, college administrator; b. Columbia, S.C., Dec. 8, 1956; d. Rinnard and Christine (Hendrix) Gravitt; m. Don Addison Pope, Nov. 17, 1984. A.A. in Bus., Midlands Tech. Coll., 1978; B.A., U. S.C., 1979, M.Ed., 1982, Ednl. Specialist, 1986. Asst. U. S.C. Alumni Assn., Columbia, 1976, asst. to Visitors Ctr. and Student Activities Office, 1977-78; dir. residence life Columbia Coll., 1979—. Contbr. articles to profl. jours. Vol. ARC. Recipient Achievements Dir. Residence Life award, 1983. Mem. S.C. Housing Officers Assn. (founder 1981, v.p. 1982), Southeastern Assn. Housing Officers (state chairperson 1982, state editor 1980, 81), Assn. Coll. and Univ. Housing Officers Internat., Delta Zeta, Phi Kappa Sigma. Office: Columbia Coll Box 1001 Columbia SC 29203

POPE, ROBERT R., bank executive; b. Oxford, Ala., June 16, 1934; s. Robert R. and Annie (Allen) P.; m. Virginia Voss, Dec. 21, 1957; children—Pamela Pope Fowler, Patrice Voss, Robert R. III. LL.B., U. Ala., 1955; postgrad. in banking U. Wis., 1962; postgrad. in pub. relations and mktg. Northwestern U., 1964; postgrad. in banking Harvard U., 1966, Columbia U., 1968. Chmn., pres. Bank of Heflin, Ala., 1956-74; pres. Exchange Nat. Bank, Montgomery, Ala., 1974; chmn., pres. Comml. Bank, Douglasville, Ga., 1975—; chmn. First Fulton Bank and Trust Co., Palmetto, Ga., 1976-83; chmn., pres. West Ga. Bank, Tallahoosa, 1965; dir. Ga. Credit Life Ins. Co., Butler, 1982—; pres. Metro BanCorp Inc., Douglasville, 1984. Exec. council Boy Scouts Am., Atlanta, 1980—; active Indsl. Devel. Authority Douglas County, 1980—; dir. Douglas County Civilian Club, 1983—; pres. Douglas County C. of C., 1984. Recipient Outstanding Young Banker of Ala. award, 1966; Leadership award Cleburne County, 1973; Pres.'s award Douglas County C. of C., 1982; Outstanding Service award United Meth. Women, 1982. Mem. Ind. Bankers Assn. (pres. elect 1984, mem. regulation rev. com. 1984), Leadership Atlanta, Scabbard and Blade, Phi Mu Alpha, Delta Sigma Kappa, Sigma Phi Epsilon (pres. 1953-54, pledge award 1952). Republican. Methodist. Clubs: Atlanta City, Ga., Chattahoochee Country, Montgomery Country. Home: 6896 Heritage Pkwy Lithia Springs GA 30057 Office: Comml Bank PO Box 1178 Douglasville GA 30133

POPE, SELMA DARLENE, educational counselor; b. Abilene, Tex., Dec. 12, 1934; d. John Clabourn and Selma Lee (Russell) Warlick; m. William Franklin Pope, Dec. 20, 1952; children—Becky Lee, Gregory Franklin, Russell Marion. B.S., Hardin Simmons U., 1970, M.Ed., 1976. Lic. profl. guidance counselor, Tex. Tchr. Eula Ind. Sch. Dist., Clyde, Tex., 1970-75; cons. Region 14 Edn. Service Ctr., Abilene, 1976-83; counselor Abilene Ind. Sch. Dist., 1983—; cons. in field, Abilene, 1983—. Mem. adopt-a-sch. task force Abilene C. of C., 1983. Named Hon. State Farmer, Tex. Future Farmers of Am., 1976; Hardin-Simmons U. grantee, 1976. Mem. Tex. State Tchrs. Assn., NEA, Tex. Assn. Counseling and Devel. (senator 1983-85, Service award 1985), Am. Assn. Counseling and Devel., Delta Kappa Gamma. Democrat. Baptist. Avocations: music (piano); travel; agriculture. Home: Route 2 PO Box 547 Abilene TX 79601 Office: Jane Long Sch Abilene TX 79603

POPE, SUZETTE STANLEY, accountant; b. Florala, Ala., Sept. 15, 1925; d. Raymond T. and Vashti Viola (Williams) Stanley; b. W. Norelle Pope, June 22, 1947; children—Stephanie Suzanne, Brently Preston. Assoc. Sci., Miami-Dade Community Coll., 1967; B.B.A., U. Miami, Coral Gables, Fla., 1969, M.B.A., 1971; Edn. Specialist, U. Fla.-Gainesville, 1976. Grad. asst. acctg. U. Miami, Coral Gables, 1967-69; staff acct. Stuzin C.P.A.s, Hialeah, Fla., 1968; supr. gen. acctg. Dade County Pub. Sch., Miami, Fla., 1969-71, supr. fiscal control, 1972-75, spl. adminstr. fed. funds program, 1976, chief acct. acctg., 1976-83, chief acct. accounts payable, 1983—. Club rep. Women's Com. 100, Miami, 1982-85; activist, mem. UN Am./U.S.A., Miami, 1983—; bd. dirs. Panel B, Agy. Ops. Div., Miami United Way, 1983-85; founder, com. mem. Sharing Human Resources and Skills, Inc., Miami, 1980-83; dir. United Manpower Service, Inc., Miami, 1976-80; mem., activist Coral Gables People to People, Coral Gables, Miami, 1981-85; trustee Bay Oaks Home. Recipient Ednl. and Profl. Scholarship, U.S. Office Edn., Washington, 1975; named Most Outstanding Adminstr., Dade County Pub. Schs., Miami, 1982, Outstanding Bus. Woman, Am. Bus. Woman's Assn., Miami, 1984, Most Outstanding Woman Vol. of Dade County, North Miami Woman's Club, 1985, Woman of Distinction, Internat. Goodwill-Soroptimist Internat., Miami, 1985. Mem. Assn. Sch. Bus. Ofcls. (chmn. fed. programs com. 1983-85, Fred Hill grad. scholar 1977), Nat. Council on Govt. Accts. (HUD users com. 1979-81), Am. Soc. Women Accts. (v.p. 1982-83), Southeastern Assn. Sch. Bus. Ofcls. (bd. dirs. 1984), Fla. Support Adminstr. Assn. (dir., treas. 1981-86), Fla. Sch. Fin. Council (bd. dirs. 1982-86), AAUW, Coral Gables Bus. and Profl. Women's Club (v.p. 1984-85). Clubs: Soroptimists (Miami) (pres. 1981-83, chmn. tng. awards so. region 1982-84), United Home Care (bd. dirs. 1979-86). Office: Dade County Pub Schs 1450 NE 2d Ave Room 602 Miami FL 33132

POPE, WILLIAM RAY, educational administrator; b. Gadsden, Ala., July 8, 1952; s. Jesse Ray and Jimmie Lou (Waldrop) P. B.S., Middle Tenn. State U., 1975, M.A., 1977; Ph.D., Va. Commonwealth U., 1981. Personnel research analyst State of Tenn., Nashville, 1977-78; asst. prof. Mary Washington Coll., Fredericksburg, Va., 1981-83, assoc. dir. acad. computing, 1984—; research cons. Va. Commonwealth U., Richmond, 1978-81; presenter to numerous convs. Contbr. articles to profl. publs. State Council of Higher Edn. grantee, 1984. Mem. Am. Psychol. Assn. Home: PO Box 1183 Fredericksburg VA 44202

POPE, WILLIAM ROBERT, lawyer, former state rep.; b. Mt. Mourne, N.C., Feb. 24, 1918; s. James Robert and Mary (Kelly) P.; grad. Brevard Jr. Coll., 1938; B.S., Davidson Coll., 1940; LL.B., U. N.C., 1948; m. Esther Maria Johnson, July 31, 1976; children—William Robert, James Shuford, Charles Vance, Elizabeth Barber, Deborah, Caroline Amelia. Admitted to N.C. bar, 1948; pvt. practice, Mooresville, 1948—; judge Mooresville Recorder's Ct., 1952-63; gen. counsel Crescent Electric Membership Corp.; dir. Cornelius Devel. Co., Inc.; atty. Town of Mooresville; pres. Braco, Inc., Rocky River Investment Co.; bd. mgrs. Northwestern Bank. Mem. N.C. Ho. of Reps., 1951-52, 63-64; chmn. adv. com. Iredell County Govtl. Complex; mem. Lowrance Hosp., Inc.; past pres. bd. regents Barium Springs Home for Children. Served to lt. USNR, 1940-46. Decorated D.F.C. Mem. Am., N.C., Iredell County bar assns., Phi Delta Phi. Democrat. Presbyterian. Clubs: Masons, Rotary. Home: US 21 Mooresville NC 28115 Office: PO Box 27 Mooresville NC 28115

POPENOE, JOHN, botanical garden administrator; b. Los Angeles, Jan. 24, 1929; s. Paul and Betty (Stankowitch) P.; B.S., UCLA, 1950; M.S., U. Md., 1952, Ph.D., 1955; m. Geraldine V. Mann, June 29, 1952; children—Deborah Irene, Natalie, Juanita, Jennifer. Asst. horticulturist U.S. Dept. Agr., Miami, 1955-58; asso. prof. horticulture Ala. Poly. Inst., 1958-59; asso. horticulturist U. Fla. Subtropical Experiment Sta., 1960-63; dir. Fairchild Tropical Garden, Miami, 1963—. Served with U.S. Army, 1952-54. Mem. Am. Assn. Bot. Gardens and Arboreta, Am. Soc. Hort. Sci. Home: 11925 Old Cutler Rd Miami FL 33156 Office: 10901 Old Cutler Rd Miami FL 33156

POPOVICH, EDWARD ANTHONY, statistician, educator, consultant; b. Detroit, Mar. 2, 1957; s. Edward John and Colette Helene (Szymanowski) P. B.S., U. Fla., 1977, M.Stats., 1979, Ph.D., 1983. Instr. depts. math. and stats., U. Fla. Gainesville, 1977-83; adj. prof. U. Central Fla., Orlando, 1984—; cons. Harris Corp., Melbourne, Fla., 1984—. Mem. Am. Statis Assn., Am. Soc. Quality Control, Phi Kappa Phi. Democrat. Roman Catholic. Avocations: tennis; swimming. Home: 1125 Hwy AIA 706 Satellite Beach FL 32937 Office: Harris Corp-Corp Hdqrs 1025 W Nasa Blvd Melbourne FL 32919

POPPINO, ALLEN GERALD, structural engineering company executive; b. Wichita, Kans., Oct. 30, 1925; s. Allen G. and Margaret V. (Eye) P.; children—Robert Allen, Susan L. Smith. B.S.C.E., Okla. State U., 1950. Registered profl. engr., 22 states. Structural engr. Sverdrup & Parcel & Hudgins Thompson Ball, 1950-51; chief structural engr. Benham-Blair & Affiliates Inc., 1951-65; ptnr. Benham-Blair-Poppino-Stealy, 1965-72; exec. v.p., dir. The Benham Group, Oklahoma City, 1972-74, pres., dir., 1974-81, vice chmn. bd., 1981—. Fellow Am. Cons. Engrs. Council; mem. ASCE, Nat. Soc. Profl. Engrs., Soc. Am. Mil. Engrs., Internat. Soc. Shell and Spatial Structures, Internat. Soc. Bridge and Structural Engrs., Met. Assn. Urban Designers and Environ. Planners, Transp. Research Bd., Air Force Assn., Internat. Bridge, Tunnel and Turnpike Assn., Oklahoma City C. of C. Democrat. Presbyterian. Clubs: Oklahoma City Golf and Country, Quail Creek Golf and Country. Lodges: Masons, K.T., Shriners. Contbr. articles to profl. publs. Home: 3008 Thorn Ridge Rd Oklahoma City OK 73120 Office: 1200 NW 63 PO Box 10400 Oklahoma City OK 73156

PORIES, WALTER JULIUS, surgery educator, researcher; b. Munich, Germany, Jan. 18, 1930; s. Theodore Francis and Frances (Lowin) P.; came to U.S., 1940; m. Mary Ann Rose, June 4, 1977; children—Susan, Mary Jane, Carolyn, Kathy, Mary Lisa, Michael. B.A., Wesleyan U., 1951; M.D. with honors, U. Rochester, 1955. Diplomate Am. Bd. Surgery, Am. Bd. Thoracic Surgery. Intern, Strong Meml. Hosp., Rochester, 1955-56, resident in gen. and thoracic surgery, 1958-62, fellow head and neck cancer U. Nancy (France), 1956-58; fellow research AEC, 1959-60; asst. prof. surgery and oncology U. Rochester (N.Y.), 1967-69; prof., vice-chmn. dept. surgery Case Western Res. U., Cleve., 1969-77; prof., chmn. dept. surgery East Carolina U., Greenville, N.C., 1977—; founder U. Rochester Cancer Ctr., Cancer Ctr. Cleve., Hospices Cleve., Greenville. Dir., Am. Cancer Soc., Ohio chpt., 1973-77, N.C. chpt., 1978—; dir. Boy Scouts Am., Cleve., 1975-77; dir. Greenville Mus. Art, 1981-83, 85; founder, chmn. bd. Pitt County Day Care Ctr. for Adults. Served with USAF, 1955-67. Decorated Legion of Merit; recipient McLester award U.S. Air Force, 1967. Mem. ACS (pres. N.C. chpt. 1985—), Am. Surg. Assn., AMA, Soc. Univ. Surgeons, Soc. Vascular Surgery, N.C. Watercolor Soc., Sigma Xi, Alpha Omega Alpha. Republican. Roman Catholic. Club: Country (Greenville, N.C.). Co-author: Clinical Applications of Zinc Metabolism, 1974; co-editor: Operative Surgery, 4 vols., 1983; contbr. articles on surgery and trace element chemistry to profl. jours. Home: 203 Chowan Dr Greenville NC 27834 Office: East Carolina U Sch Medicine Greenville NC 27834

PORTEE, CORA COLEMAN, educator; b. Stuart, Fla., Nov. 18, 1946; d. Preston and Catherine Lucretia (Christopher) Coleman; m. Alree Portee, Feb. 12, 1970 (div. May 1980); children—Cecil Levan, Catherine Laverne, Colby Levar. Tchr. pub. schs., Dade County, Fla., 1976-82; chmn. dept. math. Lake Stevens Jr. High Sch., Miami, Fla., 1984—; cons. on cotillions and weddings. Elder Presbyn. Ch. Named Tchr. of Yr., Lake Stevens Jr. High Sch., 1981. Mem. Nat. Council Tchrs. Math., Dade County Tchrs. Math., Assn for Supervision and Curriculum Devel., AAUW, Nat. Council Negro Women, Fla. A&M U. Alumni Assn., Zeta Phi Beta (Educator of Yr. award 1981, Zeta of Yr. award 1984). Democrat. Home: 11140 NW 25th Ave Miami FL 33167

PORTER, ALAN LESLIE, industrial and systems engineering educator; b. Jersey City, June 22, 1945; s. Leslie Frank and Alice Mae (Kaufman) P.; m. Claudia Loy Ferrey, June 14, 1968; children—Brett, Doug, Lynn. B.S. in Chem. Engring., Calif. Inst. Tech., 1967; M.S., UCLA, 1968, Ph.D. in Psychology, 1972. Research assoc. program social mgmt. tech. U. Wash., Seattle, 1972-73, research asst. prof., 1973-74; asst. prof. indsl. and systems engring. Ga. Inst. Tech., Atlanta, 1975-78, assoc. prof., 1979—; cons. Dept. Commerce, State of Md. NIH fellow, 1968; NSF grantee, 1974-75, 78-85; Dept. Transp. grantee, 1977-79; Fund for Improvement Post Secondary Edn. grantee, 1977-79; Dept. Labor grantee, 1973-74; Hazen Found. grantee, 1983-84. Mem. Internat. Assn. Impact Assessment (sec.), IEEE Systems Man and Cybernetics Soc. (chmn. tech. forecasting com.), Am. Soc. Engr. Edn. (chmn. engrs. and pub. policy div. 1982-83), AAAS, Am. Psychol. Assn., Sigma Xi. Author: (with others) A Guidebook for Technology Assessment and Impact Analysis, 1980; editor: (with T.J. Kuehn) Science Technology and National Policy, 1981; (with F.A. Rossini) Integrated Impact Assessment; Impact Assessment Bull., 1981-84. Home: 110 Lake Top Ct Rosewell GA 30076 Office: Indsl and Systems Engring Dept Sch Indsl and Systems Engring Georgia Tech Atlanta GA 30332

PORTER, AUBREY L., lawyer; b. Mt. Pleasant, Tex., July 6, 1898; s. R. J. and Lavenia (Hall) P.; student E. Tex. Tchr's Coll., 1917-21; LL.B., Kent Coll. Law, Chgo., 1925; m. Hazel Harvey, Jan. 2, 1927 (dec. Dec. 1969); 1 son, Robert M. Admitted to Fla. bar, 1926; pros. atty. Wakulla County (Fla.), 1926-32; county judge, 1932-57; gen. law practice, 1957—; cert. tree farmer. Mem. Wakulla County Welfare Assn.; trustee Tallahassee Community Coll., 1965-68, pres., 1968. Mem. Am. Legion, 40 and 8, Fla. Bar, 2d Jud. Circuit Bar Assn. (past pres.), Wakulla County C. of C. (past pres.). Democrat. Methodist (ofcl. bd. mem., past chmn.). Club: Masons. Address: Crawfordville FL 32327

PORTER, BETTY MELISSA GRIFFITH, nursing education administrator; b. Greenup, Ky., Aug. 28, 1940; d. Ruben David and Virgie J. (Rose) Griffith; m. Arvis Porter, Dec. 29, 1962; children—Anthony Wayne (dec.), Roger Dewane. Diploma in nursing Kings' Daus. Hosp. Sch. Nursing, Ashland, Ky., 1961; B.S., Morehead State U., 1971, M.H.Ed., 1973, M.S., 1977, Ed.S., 1977; B.S.N., U. Ky., 1979, M.S.N., 1981, Ed.D., 1984. Staff nurse Kings' Daus. Hosp., 1961; team leader U. Ky. Med. Ctr., Lexington, 1962; nurse in physician's office, Morehead, Ky., 1964-68; asst. prof. nursing Morehead State U., 1972-79, acting coordinator A.D.N. program, 1979-80, head dept. nursing and allied health sci., 1983—; workshop presenter; mem. exec. bd. Area Health Edn. System, 1976-79. Recipient Disting. Faculty award Morehead State U. Sch. Applied Scis. and Tech., 1979. Mem. Ky. Nurses Assn. (pres. dist. 19 1972-75), Am. Nurses Assn., Nat. League Nursing, Ky. League Nursing (chmn. membership 1979—), AMA Aux., Ky. Med. Assn. Aux., Ky. Council Higher Edn. (sub-com. on nursing edn. 1979), Sigma Theta Tau (research com. delta Psi chpt. 1982). Republican. Baptist. Avocations: needlepoint; water sports.

PORTER, CATHERINE TIFT, Realtor; b. Atlanta, July 15, 1922; d. Thomas Willingham and Catherine Hill (Terrell) Tift; m. James Tinsley Porter, Dec. 7, 1944; children—Catherine Porter Fuller, Pattie Porter Firestone, James Tinsley, Thomas T., Russell T. A.B., Sweet Briar Coll., 1944. Realtor, Harry Norman Realtors, Atlanta, 1973—; dir. Atlanta Air Ctr., Tiftona Industries, Porter Carpet Mills. Chmn. bd. Cerebral Palsy Ctr., 1970-72; bd. dirs. Atlanta Jr. League, 1946-50, Women of Ch., Presbyn. Ch., 1956-58. Mem. Nat. Soc. Colonial Dames Am. (chmn. Atlanta town Com., 1983-85), Atlanta Bd. Realtors, Ga. Assn. Realtors, Nat. Assn. Realtors.

PORTER, E. MELVIN, state senator; b. Okmulgee, Okla., May 22, 1930; s. Victor E. and Mary (Cole) P.; m. Jewel Ewing, 1955; children—E. Melvin, Joel Anthony. B.S., Tenn. State U., 1956; LL.B., Vanderbilt U., 1959. Mem. Okla. Senate, 1965—. Mem. NAACP, YMCA. Recipient Kappa of Month award. Served with C.E., U.S. Army, 1948-52. Mem. ABA, Am. Judicature Soc., Oklahoma City C. of C., Sigma Rho Sigma, Kappa Alpha Psi. Democrat. Baptist. Office: Okla Senate Room 412A Oklahoma City OK 73105*

PORTER, ERNEST LEE, finance company executive; b. Jacksonville, Fla., Jan. 8, 1939; s. Cliff and Annie Ruth (Rogers) P.; m. Bunny Chambers, June 26, 1970; 1 son: Charles C. A.B., Stetson U., 1961. Cert. review appraiser; registered mortgage underwriter. Mortgage dept. mgr. Peninsular Life Ins., Jacksonville, Fla., 1969-71; chief loan analyst 1st Mortgage Investors, Miami Beach, Fla., 1971-72, MGIC Fin., Miami, 1972-73; v.p. South Atlantic Trust Co., Miami, 1973-78, Atico Mortgage Corp., Miami, 1978-79, DMG, Inc., West Palm Beach, Fla., 1979—. Sec. Jaycees, Jacksonville Beach, Fla., 1968. Served to capt. U.S. Army, 1962-70. Mem. Mortgage Bankers Assn., Fla. Assn. Realtors, Nat. Assn. Realtors, Nat. Assn. Rev. Appraisers and Mortgage Underwriters. Democrat. Episcopalian. Clubs: Ponte Vedra (Fla.), Ocean Reef (Key Largo, Fla.). Home: 213 Bracken Wood Terrace Palm Beach Gardens FL 33410 Office: Diversified Mortgage Investors Inc 1645 Palm Beach Lakes Blvd West Palm Beach FL 33401

PORTER, H. LEONARD, III, hospital administrator, genealogist; b. Denver, July 12, 1945; s. Howard Leonard and Margaret (Johnson) P.; B.A., Monmouth (Ill.) Coll., 1967; M.S., U. Ill., Champaign, 1968; m. Mary Ellen Biciste, June 22, 1968; 1 son, Andrew James. Dir. public relations Monmouth Coll., 1968-69, asst. dir. devel., 1972-73; dir. public relations Detroit Osteo. Hosp. Corp., 1973-78, Greenville (S.C.) Hosp. System, 1978-81; pres. The Porter Co., 1981—; dir. devel. and community relations Anderson (S.C.) Meml. Hosp., 1981-84; v.p. strategic planning and mktg. Winter Haven Hosp., Fla., 1984—. Served with Med. Service Corps, USAF, 1969-72. Republican. Presbyterian. Author: Beginning Your Search...Your Family History, 1981; Secrets of Genealogical Research in Abbeville County, 1983; Destiny of the Scotch-Irish from Ballybay, Ireland to the Central Illinois Prairie—1720 to 1853, 1984; contbr. articles to profl. publs. Home: 2068 Katie Ct Winter Haven FL 33883 Office: 200 Ave NE Winter Haven FL 33880

PORTER, HOWARD JULIAN, JR., real estate developer; b. Birmingham, Ala., Dec. 30, 1950; s. Howard J. and Dorothy (Murfee) P.; m. Gayle Murrah, Apr. 7, 1973; children—Emily Catherine, Sarah Murfee. B.S. in Bus. Adminstrn., Auburn U., 1974. Staff appraiser Hearn Co., Birmingham, 1974-76; pres. H.J. Porter & Assocs., Inc., Birmingham, 1976-83, Crossland Properties, Inc., Auburn, Ala., 1983—; tchr. coll. level appraisal course; speaker seminars and tng. sessions. Mem. Am. Inst. Real Estate Appraisers (M.A.I. designee), Soc. Real Estate Appraisers (cert.; past state chmn. Market Data Ctr., past chpt. pres.), Real Estate Securities and Syndication Inst., Urban Land Inst., Nat. Assn. Realtors. Republican Presbyterian. Clubs: The Club; Sugalutchee Country. Lodge: Kiwanis. Home: 400 Kimberly Ave Auburn AL 36830 Office: 753 E Glenn Ave Auburn AL 36830

PORTER, JAMES EDUARDO, lawyer; b. Laredo, Tex., May 10, 1948; s. Leo Victor and Beatrice Elia (Leal) P.; m. Bessie Ximenez (div. 1981); children—Sandra Marie, James Eduardo. A.A., San Antonio Community Coll., 1972; B.A. cum laude, St. Mary's U. 1974, J.D., 1976. Bar: Tex. 1976. Pvt. practice law, San Antonio, 1976-79; v.p. Botello, Porter & Serna, Inc., San Antonio, 1979-80; pres. James E. Porter, Inc., Atty.-at-Law, San Antonio, 1980—. Served with USMC, 1966-70. Mem. San Antonio Bar Assn., Tex. Bar Assn., ABA, San Antonio Trial Lawyers Assn., Assn. Trial Lawyers Am. Roman Catholic. Club: Plaza. Office: 515 S Main Ave San Antonio TX 78204

PORTER, JANE CARROLL, management consultant; b. Brattleboro, Vt., May 9, 1955; d. William Carroll and Mary (Bolton) P.; m. Robert Mark Kolodner, May 26, 1985. B.A., Beloit Coll.; M.P.P.M., Yale U.; student U. Rennes, France. Analyst, project officer EPA, Washington, 1979-82; cons. Tarkenton & Co., Atlanta, 1982-84, prin., 1984-85, v.p., 1985—; cons. Baha'i Internat. Community at UN, 1983—. Treas. Local Spiritual Assembly of Baha'is, Washington, 1981-82; charter mem. Nat. Mus. of Women in Arts, Washington, 1985. Khashoggi Found. grantee, 1978. Mem. Nat. Assn. Exec. Women, Am. Soc. for Tng. and Devel., Organizational Devel. Network, World Future Soc., Mortar Bd., Phi Beta Kappa, Omicron Delta Kappa, Phi Sigma Iota. Club: Atlanta Ski. Office: Tarkenton & Co 3340 Peachtree Rd NE Suite 444 Atlanta GA 30326

PORTER, KENT ARLO, media broker, hotel marketing consultant; b. Keokuk, Iowa, May 29, 1929; s. Arlo Kenneth Porter and Olive (Nagel) Burroughs; m. Jan Hooker Porter, Apr. 14, 1957; children—Wallace Kent, Patrick Paul. Student Matherly Coll., Keokuk, 1945-46, Quincy Coll. (Ill.), 1946-49; M.A., UCLA, 1955. Exec. v.p. Am. Physicians Investment Corp., New Orleans, 1962-64; pres., owner Wallace Agy., New Orleans, 1961-70, London Ct. Ltd., New Orleans, 1970—; cons. Hilton Hotels, Olaf C. Lambert Assocs., New Orleans, Hotels Mgmt. Ltd., Kenner, La. Home: 4808 Folse Dr Metairie LA 70002 Office: London Company Ltd PO Box 7634 Metairie LA 70010

PORTER, LEON JAMES, educational administrator; b. Belen, N. Mex., Mar. 6, 1958; s. Luther Lee and Barbara (Hunton) P. B.S., N. Mex. State U., 1980, M.S., 1982. Research asst., Las Cruces, N. Mex., 1980-81; farm and ranch mgmt. program chmn. Murray State Coll., Tishomingo, Okla., 1981-83, agr. economist, chmn. div. agrl., 1983—; research asst., Las Cruces, N. Mex., 1980-81. Contbr. articles to profl. jours. Player ROTC Basketball Benefit, Milburn, Okla., 1984. Mem. Johnston County Livestock Assn., Jr. Livestock Assn., Am. Agrl. Econs. Assn., Western Agrl. Econs. Assn., Nat. Vocat. Agr. Tchrs. Assn., Alpah Zeta. Lodge: Lions. Office: Murray State Coll Tishomingo OK 73460

PORTER, PEGGY RANSOM, English language educator, writing consultant; b. Beaumont, Tex., Oct. 13, 1946; d. Grover Cleveland and Ruth (Calip) Ransom; m. Willie Robert Porter, Aug. 17, 1968; children—Sherri Denise, Michelle Renee, Michael Robert. B.A., Lamar U., 1968; M.A., Tex. So. U., 1975; postgrad. U. Houston, 1977-83, Purdue U., 1983. Tchr. Houston Ind. Sch. Dist., 1970-73; instr. Tex. So. U., Houston, 1975—, freshman coordinator dept. English, 1983—; recorder Coll. Conf. on Communication and Composition, San Francisco, 1982. Workshop presenter Cities in Schs., Houston, 1983-84; vol. Houston Area Women's Ctr., 1984. Mem. Nat. Council Tchrs. English, Assn. Profl. Writing Cons., Am. Assn. Bus. Communication, Coll. Lang. Assn., South Central MLA. Democrat. Baptist. Clubs: Armstrong Acres (Houston); Civic. Avocations: oil painting; scrabble; gardening. Office: English Dept Tex So U 3100 Cleburne St Houston TX 77004

PORTER, PHIL, geologist, petroleum consultant; b. Norman, Okla., Nov. 8, 1915; s. Earle Sellers and Mary Pearl (Goodrich) P.; m. Doris Joan Smith, Sept. 14, 1940; children—Earle Stephen, Robert David, Mollie Suzanna. A.B. in Chemistry, Princeton U., 1937; B.S. in Geology, U. Okla., 1938; postgrad. U. Tex., 1940. Registered profl. engr., Calif., Tex. Geologist, Atlatl Royalty Corp., Houston, 1938-40; v.p. DeGolyer & MacNaughton, Dallas, 1940-58; pres. DeGolyer & MacNaughton, Inc., Dallas, 1958-70; pres., chmn. TerraMar Cons., div. SEDCO, Dallas, 1970-78; pres. Methane Gas Co., Dallas, 1981-84; ind. petroleum cons., Dallas, 1978—. Chmn. Council Sci. and Engring. Socs., Dallas-Fort Worth, 1978-79; mem. exec. com. regional sci. fair, Dallas, 1970—; chmn. sci. adv. com. Skyline High Sch., Dallas, 1978—; chmn. bd. trustees Dallas Acad., 1983—. Served to lt. (sr. grade), USNR, 1942-46. Named Father of Yr., Altrusa Club of Oak Cliff, Dallas, 1971. Mem. Soc. Petroleum Engrs. of AIME, Soc. Ind. Profl. Earth Scientists, Dallas Assn. Petroleum Geologists, Dallas Geol. Soc. (pres. 1967-68), Houston Geol. Soc., Dallas Petroleum Club. Republican. Presbyterian. Clubs: Tanglewood (Pottsboro, Tex.); Garden of Gods (Colorado Springs, Colo.). Avocations: travel; photography; education of young people. Home: 4322 Lively Ln Dallas TX 75220 Office: 4625 Greenville Ave Suite 201 Dallas TX 75206

PORTER, RAYMOND EARL, international marketing executive, consultant; b. Ft. Worth, Aug. 25, 1926; s. Edward Kinney and Eula Mable (Barton) P.; m. Mae Gwendolyn Westbrook, June 17, 1944 (dec. 1967); children—Rama Jean Porter Jordan, Gwendolyn Ann Porter Reed; m. 2d, Florinda Grace Humphrey, Nov. 17, 1977. B.S. in Mech. Engring., U. Tex.-Austin, 1947; B.A. in Bus., Tex. Christian U., 1953. Chief engr. heat transfer div. Cobell Industries, Inc., Ft. Worth, 1953, gen. mgr., 1954; pres. Mathes-Porter Engring. Co., Ft. Worth, 1955-61; Southwest mfrs. rep. York div. Borg-Warner Corp., Ft. Worth, 1961-69; v.p. mktg. and sales Pitts Industries Inc., Electro-Lock and Surfaces Inc. Divs., Dallas, 1970-77; mktg. mgr. Condensers Inc., Jacksonville, Tex., 1977-78; chief exec. officer Profl. Mktg. Co. Am. (PROMARK), Ft. Worth, 1979—. Mem. Petroleum Engrs., ASHRAE, AAAS, Internat. Mobile Air Conditioning Assn. Republican. Methodist. Lodges: Masons, Shriners. Contbr. articles, designs in field; patentee clutch pulley measuring device. Office: PO Box 18768 North Richland Hills TX 76118

PORTER, ROBERT LAW, acoustic engineer, computer systems analyst; b. Camden, S.C., Apr. 8, 1939; s. William Salter and Mary English (Law) P.; m. Sara Allen Behrens, June 10, 1962; children—David, John, Elizabeth. B.S., Ga. Inst. Tech., 1961; M.S., U.S. Naval Postgrad. Sch., 1969; postgrad. Cath. U. Am., 1977—. Commd. ensign USN, 1961, advanced through grades to lt. comdr.; weapons officer USS Epperson, 1965-67; nav. USS Inchon, 1970-72; test and eval. resources Coordinator Office Chief Naval Ops., 1975-81; sr. engr. Gen. Physics Corp., Arlington, Va., 1981-84; project cons. Aquidneck Data Corp., Manassas, Va., 1984—; continuing edn. lectr. acoustics Cath. U. Am., 1983—. Pres., commr. Prince William Soccer, Inc., 1981-82; cubmaster Cub Scout Pack 1378, 1977-78, 80-81; mem. commrs. staff Prince William dist. Boy Scouts Am., 1978-79. Mem. Acoustical Soc. Am., Audio Engring. Soc., Sigma Xi. Presbyterian. Office: 9380A Forestwood Ln Manassas VA 22110

PORTER, ROBERT WILLIAM, district court judge; b. Monmouth, Ill., Aug. 13, 1926; s. William Benson and Vieva Laurel (Drew) P.; A.B. cum laude, Monmouth Coll., 1949; J.D., U. Mich., 1952; m. Lois Virginia Freeman, July 4, 1956; children—Robert William, William Benson, John David. Admitted to Tex. bar, 1953; home office counsel Res. Life Ins. Co., Dallas, 1952-54; asso. and partner Thompson, Coe, Cousins, & Irons, Dallas, 1954-74; judge U.S. Dist. Ct., No. Dist. Tex., 1974—; spl. counsel County of Dallas, 1972-74; lectr. Robert A. Taft Inst. of Govt., U. Tex., Arlington, 1972-73. Vice chmn. bd. trustees Lamplighter Sch. Inc., 1967-74, trustee, 1979—; councilman, Richardson, Tex., 1965-66, mayor pro tem., 1966, mayor, 1967; pres. Tex. Assn. Mayors, Councilmen and Commrs., 1965-66; pres. Greater County League of Municipalities, 1966-67; mem. exec. com. N. Central Tex. Council of Govts., 1966-67, 70-72, regional citizen rep., 1967-72; mem. Dallas County Election Bd., 1972-74; original conferee Goals for Dallas, chmn. neighboring communities com., mem. task force com., vice chmn. task force on transp. and communications, chmn. achievement com. for transp. and communications, 1965-74; mem. State Rep. Exec. Com., 1966-68, chmn. Task Force on Modernization of State and Local Govts., 1967; dep. state chmn. Rep. Party of Tex., 1969-71; Dallas County Rep. chmn., 1972-74; mem. adv. council S.W. Center Advanced Study, 1966-69. Served in USN, 1944-46; PTO. Mem. Richardson, Dallas bar assns., State Bar Tex., Barristers Soc., Delta Theta Phi, Alpha Tau Omega. Presbyterian. Office: 1100 Commerce St Room 15E26 Dallas TX 75242

PORTER, RONALD WEBSTER, physical therapist; b. Knoxville, Tenn., May 4, 1952; s. James Bert and Alice G. (Webster) P. B.S. in Zoology, U. Tenn., 1974; Cert. in Phys. Therapy, Emory U., 1979. Registered phys. therapist, Ga. Staff phys. therapist DeKalb Gen. Hosp., Decatur, Ga., 1979-80, Atlanta Falcons Profl. Football Team, Atlanta, 1979-80; instr. Back Sch. of Atlanta, 1980-81, dir., 1981—. Cons. to Pub. Broadcasting System TV series: Back Pain-Cause, Treatment and Prevention, 1983-85. Mem. Am. Phys. Therapy Assn., Am. Assn. Safety Engrs. Avocations: sports; gardening. Home: 965 Crane Rd Atlanta GA 30324 Office: Back Sch of Atlanta 1401 W Paces Ferry Rd A210 Atlanta GA 30327

PORTER, WAYNE RANDOLPH, dermatologist; b. Washington, Jan. 10, 1948; s. James Randolph and Betty (Burgess) P. B.Sc., M.I.T., 1970; M.D., Duke U., 1973. Diplomate Am. Bd. Internal Medicine, Am. Bd. Dermatology. Intern, U. Miami Fla., 1971-74, resident, 1974-76, resident in dermatology, 1976-78; practice medicine, specializing in dermatology, N. Miami Beach, Fla., 1979—; asst. prof. clin. medicine, dermatology U. Miami Sch. Medicine, 1982-85, assoc. prof., 1985—; cons. Lupus Found. Am.; cons. in dermatology Miami Vice TV series. Fellow Am. Acad. Dermatology, Am. Soc. Dermatologic Surgery; mem. ACP, AMA, Fla. Med. Assn., Dade County Med. Assn., Miami Dermatol. Soc. (pres. 1984-85), So. Med. Assn., Internat. Soc. Pediatric Dermatology. Democrat. Presbyterian. Office: Wayne R Porter 909 N Miami Beach Blvd North Miami Beach FL 33162

PORTER, WILLIAM RANDOLPH, computer co. exec.; b. Phila., Oct. 13, 1942; s. Harry and Edith Clair (Wiggins) P.; m. Mary Ann E. Porter, May 1, 1965; children—Michael Scott, Anthony Scot. Student Monmouth Coll., 1961-63, U. Md., 1964-65, Framingham State Coll., 1967-69. With CIA, Washington, 1962-65; programmer Air Force Cambridge Research Lab., Bedford, Mass., 1965-69; data processing mgr. Secret Service, Washington, 1969-73; with Def. Intelligence Agy., Washington, 1973-78; mgr. facility and services System Devel. Corp., Fredericksburg, Va., 1978—; cons. Dir. Worcester (Mass.) CD, 1976-78; mem. Mendon (Mass.) Sr. Citizens Adv. Com., 1977-79. Democrat. Roman Catholic. Office: System Devel Corp 601 Caroline St Fredericksburg VA 22401

PORTERA, FREIDA, infection control nurse; b. New Albany, Miss., Feb. 19, 1952; d. Dewey and Verba Haynes; div. 1977; 1 child, Laneisa. R.N., Bapt. Hosp., Memphis, 1973; student Memphis State U., 1970-85; B.S. in Health Adminstrn., So. Ill. U., 1985. Cert. in hosp. epidemiology Ctrs. for Disease Control, Atlanta. Infection control nurse Bapt. Hosp., Memphis, 1973-82, mem. faculty Nursing Sch., 1982; head dept. infection control St. Joseph Hosp., Memphis, 1982—; cons. in epidemiology Memphis and Shelby County Health Dept., 1984—. Recipient Merit award for investigative work in Legionnaires epidemic Bapt. Meml. Hosp., 1978. Mem. Assn. Practitioners in Infection Control (bd. dirs. 1983, pres. 1982). Avocation: camp nursing for children. Office: St Joseph Hosp 220 Overton Ave Memphis TN 38101

PORTMAN, GLENN ARTHUR, lawyer; b. Cleve., Dec. 26, 1949; s. Alvin B. and Lenore M. (Marsh) P.; m. Katherine Seaborn, Aug. 3, 1974 (div. Oct. 1984). B.A., Case Western Res. U., 1972; J.D., So. Meth. U., 1975. Bar: Tex. 1975. Assoc. Johnson, Bromberg & Leeds, Dallas, 1975, ptnr., 1980—. Bd. dirs. So. Meth. U. Council Law Alumni, 1980—. Mem. ABA, State Bar Tex., Dallas Bar Assn., Order of Coif. Republican. Methodist. Clubs: 500, Assemblage, Dallas Knife and Fork (Dallas). Asst. editor-in chief Southwestern Law Jour., 1974-75; contbr. articles to profl. jours. Home: 9503 Winding Ridge Dr Dallas TX 75238 Office: 2600 Lincoln Plaza 500 N Akard Dallas TX 75201

PORTNER, DAVID MICHAEL, clinical psychologist; b. Bklyn., May 9, 1952; s. Frank and Ruth (Leibowitz) P.; m. Elayne Desimone, July 23, 1975 (div. 1978); m. Kay Ellen Schroeder, Sept. 25, 1982. B.A., Hofstra U., 1974; Ed.M., Columbia U., 1977; Ph.D., St. Louis U., 1982. Lic. clin. psychologist, Va. Staff psychologist Pilgrim Psychiatric Ctr., Brentwood, N.Y., 1977-78; clin. dir. Community Mental Health Ctr., Dinwiddie, Va., 1982-84; assoc. Joe W. King and Assocs., Richmond, Va., 1984—; clin. cons. dist. 18 Mental Health, Petersburg, Va., 1983—. Chmn. Parents Adv. Council for Exceptional Children, Dinwiddie, 1983-84. Mem. Am. Psychol. Assn., Va. Psychol. Assn. Avocations: fishing; tennis. Office: Psychiatric Inst Richmond 3001 5th Ave Richmond VA 23222

PORTNOY, WILLIAM MANOS, electrical engineering educator; b. Chgo., Oct. 28, 1930; s. Joseph and Bella (Salzman) P.; m. Alice Catherine Walker, Sept. 9, 1956; children—Catherine Anne, Michael Benjamin. B.S., U. Ill., 1952, M.S., 1952, Ph.D., 1959. Registered profl. engr., Tex. Mem. tech. staff Hughes Aircraft Co., Newport Beach, Calif., 1959-61, Tex. Instruments Inc., Dallas, 1961-67; assoc. prof. elec. engring. Tex. Tech U., Lubbock, 1967-72, prof. biomed. engring. sch. of medicine, 1973-75, prof. physics, 1985, prof. elec. engring., 1972—; cons. in field. Editor: Emergency Medical Care, 1977; contbr. articles to profl. jours. Patentee in field. Bd. dirs. Am. Heart Assn., 1972-75. Named Fulbright Prof., Eng. 1976 recipient Abell Faculty award, 1984. Fellow IEEE; mem. Am. Soc. Engring. Edn. (Western Electric Fund award 1980), Am. Phys. Soc., Internat. Soc. Hybrid Microelectronics, Sigma Xi. Office: Tec Tech Univ Elec Engring Dept Lubbock TX 79409

PORTWOOD, WARREN THOMAS, JR., dentist, lawyer; b. Washington, Ga., Jan. 2, 1943; s. Warren Thomas and Anna (Saine) P.; m. Katharyn Aderholdt, July 29, 1967; children—Anna Katharyn, Jettie Caroline. B.A., N.C. State U., 1965; D.D.S., U. N.C., 1970; J.D., Campbell U., 1984. Bar: N.C., 1985. Practice dentistry, Hickory, N.C., 1970—; sole practice law, Hickory, 1985—. Articles editor Campbell Law Observer, 1983-84. Co-chmn. Heart Fund, 1974, fundraiser, 1973, 76, 85. Mem. Acad. Trial Lawyers, N.C. Dental Soc., N.C. Bar Assn. Republican. Mem. United Ch. of Christ. Lodge: Rotary (dir.). Avocations: Sailing; fishing. Home: 535 2d Ave Hickory NC 28601 Office: 260 1st Ave NW Hickory NC 28601

POSEY, ELIZABETH FITZGERALD, university dean, educator; b. Pecos, Tex., Apr. 26, 1940; d. Johnnie S. and Margaret Elizabeth (Duncan) Fitzgerald; m. John Mahoney, Sept. 19, 1959 (div. 1983); children—Teri, Tana; m. Bob Posey, Nov. 19, 1983. B.A., U. Ariz., 1965; M.Ed., Sul Ross State U., 1969; Ed.D., No. Ariz. U., 1979. Tchr. Balmorhea (Tex.) Elem. Sch., 1965-66, Alpine (Tex.) Elem. Sch., 1967-70; vocat. coordinator, cons. West Tex. Edn. Service Ctr., Region XVIII, 1970-71; counselor Ft. Stockton High Sch., 1971-72; career edn. coordinator Demonstration in Career Edn. Project, 1972-74; v.p. Career Edn. Media, Inc., 1974-78; career and affective edn. cons. Edn. Achievement Corp., 1974-75; v.p., mgmt. cons., program developer Synergistic Ednl. Systems, Inc., 1975-79; mem. part-time faculty Rio Salado Coll., Phoenix, 1979; asst. dean student life Sul Ross State U., Alpine, Tex., 1979-82, dean student life, 1982—, asst. prof. edn., 1979—; cons. and lectr. in field; counselor Neighborhood Youth Corps, 1969. Mem. adv. bd. Tri County Drug Edn. Program, 1980-81, Alpine Centennial Com., 1980-82. Recipient Sponsor-of-Yr. awards Sul Ross State U. Student Pres.'s Assn., 1981, 82, 83, 84; U.S. Dept. Edn. spl. services grantee, 1982-83, 83—; 4-H Club Parents Award, 1980; cert. of recognition Boy Scouts Am., 1981. Mem. Am. Assn. for Counseling and Devel., Assn. Humanistic Edn. and Devel., Nat. Vocat. Guidance Assn. (del. 1979), Am. Coll. Personnel Assn., Assn. for Counselor Edn. and Supervision, Am. Vocat. Assn., Assn. for Curriculum Supervision and Devel., Tex. Assn. Coll. and Univ. Personnel Adminstrs., Tex. Soc. Coll. Tchrs. Edn., Tex. Personnel and Guidance Assn., Tex. Assn. Humanistic Edn. and Devel., Tex. Counselor Educators and Suprs., Tex. Sch. Counselor Assn., Tex. Career Guidance Assn., Phi Delta Kappa, Kappa Delta Pi. Democrat. Contbr. articles to profl. jours. Home: PO Box 951 Alpine TX 79831 Office: Sul Ross Box C115 Alpine TX 79832

POSEY, GEORGE GARDNER, hospital administrator; b. Philadelphia, Miss., Mar. 6, 1934; s. Herman Gardner and Cora Bernice (Parker) P.; m. Martha Sue Cox, July 30, 1953; 1 child, Suzanne. A.D., Jones Jr. Coll., Ellisville, Miss., 1979; D. in Personnel Mgmt., U. So. Miss., 1980; D. in Health Services Adminstrn., U. Ala.-Birmingham, 1982. Enlisted U.S. Air Force, 1952, served to master sgt., ret., 1972; med. adminstrv. supr. USAF, 1952-72; adminstr. Thaggards Hosp., Madden, Miss., 1972-74; adminstr. Perry County Gen. Hosp., Richton, Miss., 1974—. Decorated Air Force Commendation medal. Mem. Hosp. Fin. Mgmt. Assn. Republican. Roman Catholic. Lodge: Scottish Rite (Richton). Office: Perry County Gen Hosp 208 Bay St Drawer Y Richton MS 39476

POSEY, GLENNIS BAILEY, educator; b. Arab, Ala., July 19, 1936; d. Loyd Marion and Iva Irene (Maze) Bailey; m. Donald S. Posey, May 27, 1957; 1 child, Donald Loyd. B.S., Florence State U., 1957, M.A., 1962. Tchr. Lauderdale Bd. Edn., Florence, Ala., 1957-58, Winston County Bd. Edn., Double Springs, Ala., 1959—, chmn. bus. dept., 1973—; adviser Future Bus. Leaders Am., Ala., 1957—. Mem. Double Springs Library Bd., 1960-68, Double Springs Recreation Bd., 1978-84. Mem. Ala. Vocat. Assn. (v.p. 1985-86; named Outstanding Bus. Edn. Tchr. 1983, Outstanding Vocat. Tchr. Ala. 1983), Tenn. Valley Bus. Tchrs. Assn., NEA, Data Processing Mgmt. Assn., Delta Pi Epsilon, Alpha Delta Kappa. Republican. Mem. Ch. of Christ. Club: Double Springs Study. Avocations: tole painting; crocheting. Home: PO Box 244 Double Springs AL 35553 Office: Winston County Vocat Ctr PO Box 146 Double Springs AL 35553

POSEY, JOHN MICHAEL, insurance company executive; b. Waco, Tex., Feb. 19, 1955; s. J.P. and Elvira Anne (Homburg) P.; m. Rebecca JoDel Dean, June 23, 1977; 1 son, Seth Michael. Student McLennan Community Coll., 1973-75; B.B.A. magna cum laude, Baylor U., 1977. Staff cons. Arthur Andersen & Co., Houston, 1977-79; ins. exec. Tex. Life Ins. Co., Waco, 1979—, asst. sec., 1981-82, asst. v.p., dept. mgr., 1982—; city councilman City of Riesel, 77, 84—, mayor, 1980-83; sect. chmn. United Way Loaned Exec. Program, 1981—. Chmn. deacons First Bapt. Ch., Riesel, Tex., 1981—, also music dir.; active Riesel Hist. Soc. Fellow Life Mgmt. Inst.; mem. Am. Soc. Pension Actuaries (assoc.), Phi Theta Kappa, Sigma Iota Epsilon, Beta Gamma Sigma, Gamma Beta Phi. Office: Tex Life Ins Co Texas Ctr 9th and Washington Waco TX 76703

POSEY, KENNETH CLAYTON, SR., carpet company executive; b. Dalton, Ga., Feb. 5, 1931; s. William Henry and Jessie Frances (Sissom) P.; B.B.A., U. Ga., Atlanta, 1956; m. Hellen Deloris Kinsey, Mar. 6, 1955; children—Kenneth Clayton, William Stephen Griggs, Penelope Helen. Asst. personnel mgr. H.W. Lay & Co., Atlanta, 1957-61; personnel and advt. mgr. Paramount Dairies, Inc., Dalton, 1961-64; personnel mgr. Thomas Pride Mills Co., Calhoun, Ga., 1964-65, Star Finishing Co., Dalton, 1965-67; personnel mgr. carpet div. Collins & Aikman Co., Dalton, from 1967, now dir. human resources, floor coverings div. Bd. dirs. Whitfield County (Ga.) United Appeal, 1963-72, sec., 1965-72, co-chmn. employees div., 1963—, publicity dir., 1964; advisor Atlanta Jr. Achievement, 1959-60, sec., 1965-69, pres., dir. Dalton Jr. Achievement, 1969-70, dir., 1970-78; active Boy Scouts Am., Dalton, 1972—; deacon 1st Presbyterian Ch., Dalton, 1967-69, 75-77, elder, 1982—; bd. dirs. Dalton chpt. ARC, 1978—, Big Bros./Big Sisters Whitfield County, 1986—. Served with USAF, 1950-52. Mem. Am. Soc. for Personnel Adminstrn., Tufted Textile Mfg. Assn. (sec. indsl. relations club 1962-63, v.p., 1963-64, chmn., 1964-65), Carpet and Rug Inst. (chmn. indsl. relations club 1968-69), N.W. Ga. Personnel Assn. (v.p. 1972, pres. 1973, dir. 1974), N.W. Ga. Pvt. Industry Council, Delta Sigma Pi. Clubs: The Nine O'Clocks, Tut Skiers & Kite Flyers, Inc. (dir.), Elks. Home: 1401 Braiden Rd Dalton GA 30720 Office: Smith Indsl Blvd Dalton GA 30720

POSEY, LAWRENCE OWEN, dentist; b. Austin, Tex., July 24, 1928; s. Meredith Neill and Lillian Frances (Ott) P.; m. Margaret Carolyn Cashion, May 30, 1952 (div. 1970); children—Frances Kathleen, Lawrence Owen, Malinda Claire; m. Linda Marie DeLellis, June 12, 1970; children—Laura Lynn, Lee Owen. B.S., East Carolina Coll., 1949, M.A. in Edn. Adminstrn., 1952; D.D.S., U. N.C., 1964. Tchr., North High Sch., Mecklenberg County, N.C., 1952-53; supr. E.I. Dupont Co., Kinston, N.C., 1953-60; tchr. Broward Community Coll., Fort Lauderdale, Fla., 1974-76; gen. practice dentistry, Pompano Beach, Fla., 1964—. Editor: Handbook for High School Principals, 1951. Served with U.S. Mcht. Marine, 1945-47. Mem. Atlantic Coast Dist. Dental Soc., Fla. Dental Assn., Broward County Dental Assn. (pres. 1972-73). Republican. Roman Catholic. Club: Mensa. Home: 6511 NE 21 Way Fort Lauderdale FL 33308 Office: 572 E McNab Rd Pompano Beach FL 33060

POSNER, CALVIN STUART, banker, human resource development consultant; b. Balt., Sept. 2, 1942; s. Albert Sylvan and Beatrice (Cohen) P.; m. Barbara Ellen Vantilburg, Aug. 9, 1972. B.A., Columbia (Mo.) Coll., 1976; M.S., U.S. Internat. U., 1978; Ed.S., Ball State U., 1981, Ed.D. (fellow), 1982. Asst. prof. Def. Info. Sch., Indpls., 1977-81; mgr. staff devel. U. Ala., 1982-83; mgr. corp. tng. Amsouth Bank, N.A., Birmingham, Ala., 1983—; cons. State of Ala., 1982—. Mem. Jefferson County Vocat. Adv. Com., 1984—. Served to capt., USAR, 1967—; Vietnam, Korea. Recipient cert. of achievement Adv. Council Mgmt. Devel. Programs, U. Ala., 1983. Mem. Am. Soc. for Tng. and Devel. (v.p. 1982-83), Nat. Soc. Performance and Instrn., Assn. Supervision and Curriculum Devel., Orgnl. Behavior Teaching Soc., Res. Officers Assn., 101st Airborne Div. Assn. (life), VFW, Phi Delta Kappa. Democrat. Jewish. Office: PO Box 11007 Birmingham AL 35228

POSNER, KENNETH JAMES, administrator; b. Stamford, Conn., Apr. 30, 1958; s. Marshall Norman Posner and Rosalie (Falk) Langrock. B.A., Mich. State U., 1980, M.A., 1982. Grad. asst. Mich. State U., East Lansing, 1980, resident dir., 1981-82; residence coordinator U. Miami, Coral Gables, Fla., 1982-85, dir. conf. services, 1983-85; dist. mgr. Carico, 1985—. Mem. Assn. Coll. and Univ. Housing Officers, Am. Coll. Personnel Assn., S.E. Assn. Housing Officers, Sigma Alpha Epsilon (v.p. 1979-80). Republican. Avocations: reading; computers; horseback riding; swimming; creative writing. Home: 8700 SW 133 Ave Rd Miami FL 33183

POSPISIL, EVA SUE, programmer analyst; b. Hobby, N. Mex., May 6, 1953; d. Earl Lee and Ruby Pearl (Bryan) Holdridge; m. Charles Henry Beecroft, Oct. 2, 1971 (div.); m. Francis Joseph Pospisil, Oct. 10, 1980. A.S., Baylor U., 1977; B.S., NYU, 1983; M.S. in Sci. Counseling Psychology, Am. Technol. U., 1985, postgrad., 1985—. Med. technologist, instr. Acad. Health Sci., Fort Sam Houston, Tex., 1971-81; med. technologist Darnall Army Community Hosp., Fort Hood, Tex., 1982-84; programmer analyst DOIM, Fort Hood, 1984—; research project coordinator Central Tex. Coll., Killeen, 1984—. Served with U.S. Army, 1971-81. Fellow Am. Med. Technicians, Tex. Assn. Counseling and Devel., Nat. Assn. Underwater Diving Instrs., Nat. Assn. Parachute Clubs, Copperas Cove C. of C. Democrat. Roman Catholic. Club: Fort Hood Parachute. Home: 918 Deorsam Dr Copperas Cove TX 76522

POST, HAZEL GERALDINE GREEN, pharmacist; b. Morrisville, N.C., Mar. 31, 1936; d. William Augustus and Ruby Lucille (Moore) Green; m. William Earl Post, Jr., Aug. 30, 1957; children—William Thomas, Amy Elizabeth Post Bivins. B.S. in Pharmacy, U. N.C., 1961. Registered pharmacist, N.C., Ga. Staff pharmacist Grady Meml. Hosp., Atlanta, 1961-62, DeKalb Gen. Hosp., Decatur, Ga., 1962-63; asst. mgr., pharmacist Reed Drug Co., Atlanta, 1963-65; pharmacist Embry Hills Pharmacy, Atlanta, 1965-67; staff pharmacist Ga. Mental Health Inst., Atlanta, 1967-68; indsl. pharmacist Am. Tobacco Co., Reidsville, N.C., 1971-74; pharmacist Eckerd Drugs, Reidsville, Greensboro, N.C., 1969-79; asst. mgr., pharmacist Revco Drugs, Reidsville, 1979-84; co-owner, pharmacist Rockingham Ctr. Pharmacy, Reidsville, 1984—, v.p., 1984—. Co-chmn. rural div. Reidsville United Way, 1985; membership chmn. Saura dist. Cherokee council Boy Scouts Am., 1982, asst. dist. commr., 1979-81, dist. commr., 1983-84, asst. council commr. Cherokee council, 1985, dist. award of merit, 1982, Silver Beaver award, 1985. Mem. N.C. Pharm. Assn., Rockingham County Soc. Pharmacists (pres. 1985; Woodbadge award 1985), Kappa Epsilon. Episcopalian. Home: 910 Courtland Ave Reidsville NC 27320 Office: Rockingham Ctr Pharmacy Route 8 Box 126 1/4 Reidsville NC 27320

POST, WILLIAM JON, interior designer; b. Grand Rapids, Mich., Mar. 27, 1944; s. Louis George and Katherine (Mohler) P. Diploma, Kendall Sch. Design, 1966. Designer, Post Fixture Co., Grand Rapids, Mich., 1966-68; sr. designer Steelcase Inc., Grand Rapids, 1968-73; mgr. interior dept. Barrett and Assoc. AIA, Atlanta, 1973-76; dir. design The Classics, Jeddah, Saudi Arabia, 1976-77; sr. v.p. Design Continuum Inc., Atlanta, 1977—. Served with USMC, 1962-68. Mem. Am. Soc. Interior Designers, Inst. Bus. Designers. Republican. Avocations: tennis; fishing; camping; boating. Office: Design Continuum Inc 1819 Peachtree Rd Suite 410 Atlanta GA 30309

POSTAL, STEVE JON, motion picture director, writer; b. Bklyn., Mar. 9, 1941; s. Julius and Naomi (Schwartzman) P.; m. Gail Agatha Dino, May 31, 1974; children—Elena Paulette, Maurice Simeon. B.S., CUNY-Bklyn., 1963; postgrad. New Sch. for Social Research, 1964. Motion picture dir. Cinevue Prodns., Miami, Toronto, N.Y.C., 1966—, Tele-Sci. Prodns., N.Y.C., 1957-66; TV engr. Fla. Atlantic U., Boca Raton, 1970-72; library book selection clk. Scarboro Pub. Library, Ont., Can., 1965-70; motion picture/TV producer-writer Steve Postal Prodns., Miami, Fla., 1976—. Author/dir.: Growing Away, 1985, Holiday Beach, Everglades, 1983 (films). Mem. Soc. Motion Picture and TV Engrs., Profl. Film and Video Assn., Dirs. Guild of Can. Democrat. Jewish. Avocations: photography; nature study; painting; studying Oriental languages. Home: PO Box 428 Bostwick FL 32007 Office: Cinevue PO Box 398475 1921 Bay Rd #15 Miami Beach FL 33139

POSTMA, HERMAN, nuclear physicist; b. Wilmington, N.C., Mar. 29, 1933; s. Gilbert and Sophie (Verzaal) P.; m. Patricia Ann Dunigan, Nov. 25, 1960; children—Peter, Pamela. B.S. summa cum laude, Duke U., 1955; M.S., Harvard U., 1957, Ph.D., 1959; postgrad. bus. adminstrn. U. Tenn., 1970-73. Registered profl. engr., Calif. With Oak Ridge Nat. Lab., 1959—, asst. dir., then assoc. dir. thermonuclear div., 1966-67, dir. thermonuclear div., 1967-73, lab. dir., 1974—; v.p. Martin Marietta Energy Systems, Inc., 1984—; cons. Lab. Laser Energetics, U. Rochester, Gas Research Inst., 1986—; mem. adv. council Coll. Bus. Adminstrn. U. Tenn., Knoxville, 1976—; mem. bd. sci. adv. N.C. Energy Inst., 1978-82; mem. tech. council Union Carbide Corp., 1977—; co-chmn. Indsl. Research Inst./Nat. Lab. Task Force, 1982; chmn. WATTec Pub. Awareness Symposium, Knoxville, 1980; mem. govt. coms. Nat. Acad. Scis., AEC, ERDA, EPA, Dept. Energy; mem. Tenn. Gov.'s Task Force to Study Tech. Corridor; bd. dirs., mem. exec. com. Tenn. Tech. Found. Pres. bd. trustees Oak Ridge Hosp. of United Meth. Ch., 1978-80; commr. Tenn. Higher Edn. Commn., 1984—. Fellow AAAS, Am. Nuclear Soc., Am. Phys. Soc.; mem. Internat. Sci. Forum on Changes in Energy, Assn. Am. Univs., Am. Phys. Soc. (exec. com. div. plasma physics 1969-70), Am. Nuclear Soc. (exec. com. tech. group for controlled nuclear fusion; dir. 1976-79), Am. Mgmt. Assn. (research and devel. council 1981-82), Oak Ridge C. of C. (v.p.). Mem. editorial bd. Nuclear Fusion, 1968-74; contbr. articles to profl. jours. Lodge: Oak Ridge Breakfast Rotary. Office: PO Box X Oak Ridge TN 37830

POSTON, JAMES STUART, hospital administrator; b. Ripley, Tenn., July 15, 1936; s. Lester William and Catherine (Lohman) P.; m. Irene Boque, June 9, 1957; children—Mary Lynn, James Stuart Jr. Cert. in Med. Tech., Hawkins Sch. Med. Tech., 1956; B.B.A., Memphis State U., 1968; M.S., Trinity U., 1970. Med. technician Fulton Hosp., Ky., 1957-64; admitting supr. Meth. Hosp., Memphis, 1965-68, adminstrv. resident, 1969; asst. adminstr. Blount Meml. Hosp., Maryville, Tenn., 1970-72; adminstr. Murray Calloway County Hosp., Murray, Ky., 1972—; dir. Ky. Hosp. Assn., Louisville, Nursing Home Adminstrn. State Ky. adv. council Murray State U. Nursing Program. Chmn. Murray Leadership, 1984-85, Murray chpt. Am. Red Cross, 1982-85; bd. dirs. Murray United Fund, 1985. Recipient Disting. Service award Jaycees, Fulton, Ky., 1964, award of Excellence, Ky. Hosp. Assn., 1985. Mem. Am. Coll. Hosp. Adminstrs., Twin Lakes Hosp. Dist. (pres. 1975-76). Republican. Methodist. Lodges: Rotary (pres. 1979-80, dir. 1975-81), Masons. Avocations: golf; quail hunting; fishing.

POSTON, JOHN WARE, health physicist educator, consultant; b. Sparta, Tenn., July 8, 1937; b. John Gordon and Martha Estella (Ware) P.; m. Lillian Yvonne Plunkett, June 20, 1958; children—Martha Ruth, Vera Frances, John Ware, Jr., B.S., Lynchburg Coll., 1958; M.S., Ga. Inst. Tech., 1969, Ph.D., 1971. Experimental physicist Babcock & Wilcox, Lynchburg, Va., 1957-64; health physicist Oak Ridge Nat. Lab., Tenn., 1964-77; assoc. prof. Ga. Inst. Tech., Atlanta, 1977-84; prof. Tex. A&M U., Coll. Sta., Tex., 1985—; cons. Ga. Power, Baxley, 1983—, Nuclear Data, Smyrna, Ga., 1977—, Babcock & Wilcox, Lynchburg, 1984—. Co-author (with others) Principles of Nuclear Radiation Detection, 1979, 2d rev., 1980. Mem. AAAS, Am. Nuclear Soc., Soc. Nuclear Medicine, Health Physics Soc. (pres.-elect 1985-86). Home: 2304 Longmire Dr Apt D College Station TX 77840

POTASH, LAWRENCE MARTIN, applied psychologist; b. Binghamton, N.Y., June 20, 1940; s. Leonard Saul and Mildred Rose (Pencig) P.; divorced; 1 child, Tamara Lyn. B.S., U. Md., 1961, M.A., 1963; Ph.D., Cornell U., 1969. Lic. psychologist, Washington. Asst. prof. U. Alberta, Edmonton, Can., 1969-74; research psychologist U.S. Army Research Inst., Alexandria, Va., 1975-79; research scientist EG&G Idaho, Inc., Idaho Falls, Idaho, 1979-80; project mgr. Inst. Nuclear Power Ops., Atlanta, 1980-85; psychologist Colin Anderson Ctr., St. Marys, W.Va., 1985—. Author numerous poems. Contbr. articles to profl. jours. NIH fellow, 1967, 68. Mem. Human Factors Soc., Am. Psychol. Assn., Acad. Am. Poets. Democrat. Jewish. Avocations: poetry; verse satire.

POTEAT, JOHN ALEXANDER, aerospace company manager, retired army officer, civil engineer; b. Charlotte, N.C., Oct. 24, 1931; s. John Alexander and Margaret (Blythe) P.; m. Madelyn Schreffler, June 12, 1954; 1 dau., Alexandra Blythe. B.S. in Engring., U.S. Mil. Acad., 1954; M.S. in Civil Engring., MIT, 1959. Registered profl. engr. D.C., Wash. Commd. lt. U.S. Army C.E., 1954, advanced through grades to col., 1974; asst. dir. civil works Office Chief of Engrs., Washington, 1975-76, comdr., dist. engr. Seattle Dist., 1976-79, exec. asst. to asst. sec. Army Civil Works, Washington, 1979-80; comdr., div. engr. Huntsville Div. (Ala.), 1980-84; ret., 1984; aerospace program mgr. Boeing Co., 1984—. Mem. adv. bd. U. Ala.-Huntsville Sch. Engrs. Decorated Legion of Merit (2), Meritorious Service medal (3), Bronze Star. Fellow Soc. Am. Mil. Engrs.; mem. ASCE, Assn. U.S. Army, Phi Kappa Phi. Presbyterian. Club: Huntsville Rotary. Home: 2203 DeRussey Rd SE Huntsville AL 35801 Office: 220 Wynn Dr Research Park Huntsville AL 35807

POTEET, MICHAEL ALLEN, computer company sales executive; b. Houston, Dec. 26, 1953; s. Lee Allen and Madelyn Ann (Ingram) P.; m. Sandi Kay Scherler, Nov. 21, 1981; 1 child, Ryan Michael. B.B.A. in Mktg., U. Houston, 1980. Mktg. rep. IBM Corp., Houston, 1972-74; owner, mgr. FMI Inc., Houston, 1974-77; operations controller Texaco Inc., Houston, 1977-80; account exec. Xerox Corp., Houston, 1980-82; nat. acct. mgr. Tandy Corp., Houston, 1982-84; regional mgr. Protocol Computers, Houston, 1984—; profl. singer, 1974-82; cons. MA Interest, Houston, 1974—; real estate agt. Bofysil Assocs., Houston, 1976—. Named to Gov.'s staff State of Miss., 1975. Mem. Houston Bd. Realtors. Republican. Avocations: Sailing; tennis; golf; cinematography; reading. Home: 260 Wilcrest Houston TX 77042 Office: Protocol Computers Inc 2925 Briar Park Suite 420 Houston TX 77042

POTNIS, KRISHNARAO SHRINIVAS, obstetrician and gynecologist; b. Vengurla, India, Apr. 16, 1934; s. Shrinivas Shantaram and Laxmi Vishnu (Chitnis) P.; came to U.S., 1963; B.A., U. Bombay (India), 1957, M.D., 1962. Intern, Bridgeport (Conn.) Hosp., 1964; resident in obstetrics and gynecology State U. N.Y. Hosp., Buffalo, 1965-69; instr. obstetrics and gynecology U. Miss. Sch. Medicine, Jackson, 1969-71, asst. prof., 1971-83, asst. prof. family medicine, 1979—; chief dept. obstetrics and gynecology Kuhn Meml. State Hosp., Vicksburg, Miss., 1974—, med. dir., 1978—; cons. Jackson-Hinds Comprehensive Health Center, 1973-78; med. dir. Vicksburg div. Issaguena-Warren-Sharkey County Health Improvement Project, 1971-72; cons. Ob-Gyn programs dist. VII-B, Miss. Bd. Health, 1978—. Diplomate Am. Bd. Obstetrics and Gynecology. Fellow Am. Coll. Ob-Gyn., A.C.S.; mem. AMA, Miss. Med. Assn., West Miss. Med. Soc., So. Med. Assn., AAAS, Miss. Obstet. and Gynecol. Assn., Am. Inst. Ultrasound in Medicine, Assn. Practitioners in Infection Control, Bombay Ob-Gyn Soc., Fedn. Ob-Gyn Socs. India, Miss. Ultrasound Soc., Soc. Obstetricians and gynecologists in Ultrasound. Hindu. Home: 1201 South St Vicksburg MS 39180 Office: Vicksburg Ob-Gyn Clinic 1011 Mission 66 Vicksburg MS 39180

POTOCKO, RICHARD JOHN, psychologist, educator; b. Poughkeepsie, N.Y., Dec. 4, 1927; s. John and Mary Magdalen (Krivda) P.; m. Monika Liesbeth Cordes, July 5, 1961; children—Katherine Sue, Peter Richard, Stephanie Ann. Student Hobart and William Smith Coll., 1945-46; B.S., Union Coll., 1949; Ph.D., Freie U. Berlin and Walden U., 1979. Cons., U.S. Govt., Dept. Def., Washington, 1952-63, adj. prof., 1982—; asst. prof. stats. Sch. Govt., George Washington U., Washington, 1963; sr. info. systems specialist Documentation Inc., Bethesda, Md., 1963-65; project mgr. Tech./Ops. Inc., Hampton, Va., 1965-67; math. analyst Communications Satellite Corp., Washington, 1967-69; research psychologist Systems Resources Corp., Plainview, N.Y., 1969-70; pres. Indexed Info. Inc., 1967—; tchr. Hampton City Schs., 1970—; adj. prof. psychology Hampton Inst., 1971—, Thomas Nelson Community Coll., Hampton, 1971-72, Golden Gate U. Sch. Bus. Adminstrn. and Sch. Pub. Adminstrn., San Francisco, 1972—, St. Leo Coll., Naples, Fla., 1980—, Christopher Newport Coll., 1982; cons., lectr. in field. Served with USN, 1945-47, USAF, 1950, U.S. Army, 1951-55, USAR, 1956-63; lectr. Army Intelligence, 1956-62. Mem. AAAS, AAUP, Am. Psychol. Assn., Hampton Edn. Assn., Hampton Taxpayers Assn., IEEE, Internat. Platform Assn., NEA, Nat. Microfilm Assn., Ops. Research Soc. Am., Va. Edn. Assn., Delta Phi. Republican. Roman Catholic. Contbr. articles to profl. jours. Home: 311 Alcove Dr Hampton VA 23669 Office: 339 Woodland Rd Hampton VA 23669

POTTER, ANNE LOUISE, political scientist; b. Eugene, Oreg., Sept. 1, 1949; d. Daniel Oliver and Betty Louise (Harder) P.; B.A., Reed Coll., 1971; M.A., Stanford U., 1973, Ph.D., 1979. Vis. scholar Inst. Torcuato di Tella, Buenos Aires, Argentina, 1974-76; asst. prof. govt. Oberlin (Ohio) Coll., 1978-79; project mgr. Tech. Applications, Inc., Falls Church, Va., 1980-81; project mgr. Daedalean Assos., Inc., Woodbine, Md., 1981-82, Technology Applications, Inc., Falls Church, Va., 1982—. OAS research fellow, 1976. AAUW dissertation fellow, 1975-76; Woodrow Wilson fellow, 1971-72; NSF grad. fellow, 1972-75. Mem. Am. Polit. Sci. Assn. (Gabriel A. Almond award), Women's Caucus for Polit. Sci., Latin Am. Studies Assn., Acad. Polit. Sci., Soc. Internat. Devel., AAAS, NOW, Phi Beta Kappa. Home: 4901 Seminary Rd Alexandria VA 22311 Office: 5201 Leesburg Pike Suite 800 Falls Church VA 22041

POTTER, ANTHONY NICHOLAS, JR., security company executive, security consultant; b. N.Y.C., Jan. 6, 1942; s. Anthony Nicholas Sr. and Alta Lorene (Downing) P.; m. Patricia Anne Tlumac, Apr. 4, 1964 (div. Oct. 1981); children—Merika Elizabeth, Victoria Hope Nora; m. Cheryl Kay Dittman, Oct. 15, 1983. A.A., Westchester Community Coll., 1970; B.S. in Criminal Justice, U. Cin., 1975. Cert. protection profl. Chief police Tampa Internat. Airport, Fla., 1970-73; prin. cons. Booz, Allen & Hamilton, Cin., 1973-75; chief police City of Danville, Ill., 1976-78; police commr. City of York, Pa., 1978-80; v.p. Omni Internat. Security, Atlanta, 1980-83; exec. dir. Internat. Assn. Shopping Ctr. Security, Atlanta, 1981—; cons. shopping ctr. developers, operators, retailers; faculty mem. Internat. Council Shopping Ctr. Mgmt. Insts., 1970—. Author: Shopping Center Security, 1976. Contbr. articles to profl. jours. Various positions local, council, regional, nat. Boy Scouts Am., 1950—. Served to sgt. USMC, 1959-65. Recipient Disting. Service award Internat. Security Conf. 1970; Merit award Security World Mag., 1972. Mem. Met. Atlanta Crime Commn., Internat. Assn. Chiefs Police (pvt. security com. 1978—), Am. Soc. Indsl. Security (chmn. St. Petersburg chapt. 1970-71, chmn. nat. transp. security com. 1971-74, regional v.p. region VI 1975-76, com. standards and codes 1977-80), ABA (assoc.). Republican. Lutheran. Avocations: model railroading; gun collecting; scuba diving. Home: 2493 Willow Wood Ct NE Atlanta GA 30345 Office: Internat Assn Shopping Ctr Security Suite 300 2830 Clearview Pl NE Atlanta GA 30340-2117

POTTER, DAVID CHARLES, telecommunications executive, consultant, remarketing expert; b. Santa Monica, Calif., Feb. 23, 1949; s. Ronald Eric and Doris May (Halsey) P.; m. Carol Jean Craig, July 9, 1983. B.B.A. in Acctg., So. Meth. U., 1972. Co-founder, pres. Source, Inc., Dallas, 1971—; v.p. Telemation Inc., Dallas, 1982—; bd. dirs. Ken Sutherland Prodns., Inc., Dallas, 1980—; cons. Gen. Electric Credit Corp., U.S. Telephone, Inc. Mem. N.Am. Telephone Assn., U.S. Ind. Telephone Assn., Am. Assn. Equipment Leasors. Episcopalian. Contbr. articles to jours. in field. Office: 1201 Peters St Dallas TX 75215

POTTER, JAMES DOUGLAS, pharmacology educator; b. Waterbury, Conn., Sept. 26, 1944; s. Herbert Eugene and Jean Gladys (Troske) P.; m. Priscilla F. Strang, Aug. 9, 1985; children—Liesse, Andrew. B.S., George Washington U., 1965; Ph.D., U. Conn., 1970; postgrad. (fellow) Boston Biomed. Research Inst., 1970-74. Staff scientist Boston Biomed. Research Inst., 1974-75; assoc. in neurology Harvard U. Med. Sch., 1974-75; asst. prof. cell biophysics Baylor Coll. Medicine, 1975-77; assoc. prof. pharmacology U. Cin., 1977-81, prof., 1981-83; chmn., prof. pharmacology U. Miami, 1983—; grant reviewer in field. Grantee NIH, 1978-81, 83—, Nat. Heart Lung and Blood Inst., 1978—, Muscular Dystrophy Assn., 1983. Fellow Muscular Dystrophy Assn.; mem. Am. Heart Assn. (established investigator 1974-79), Am. Soc. Biol. Chemists, Cardiac Muscle Soc., Biophysical Soc., Sigma Xi. Contbr. articles to profl. jours. Office: Univ of Miami Dept Pharmacology PO Box 016189 Miami FL 33101

POTTER, JAMES H(ENRY), software company executive; b. Bridgeport, Conn., May 1, 1941; s. Henry V. and Marion G. (Booth) P.; m. Marie L. Donovan, July 11, 1964; children—Lynn Marie, David Booth, James Michael, Mark William, William Joseph. B.S., Fairfield U., 1963, postgrad., 1964; postgrad. Yale U., 1965. Sr. assoc. Booz, Allen & Hamilton, N.Y.C., 1968-71; pres. Effective Mgmt. Assocs., Hartford, Conn., 1971-77; v.p. Info. Systems Am., Atlanta, 1977-79, sr. v.p., 1979-80, exec. v.p., 1980-82, pres., chief exec. officer, 1982—, also dir.; chmn., dir. Constrn. Data Control, Atlanta, 1982—. Mem. Pres.'s Assn. Republican. Roman Catholic. Club: Dunwoody Country, Georgian (Atlanta).

POTTER, JOHN LEITH, consulting engineer, aerospace and mechanical engineering educator; b. Metz, Mo., Feb. 5, 1923; s. Jay Francis Lee and Pearl Delores (Leeth) P.; m. Dorothy Jean Williams, Dec. 15, 1957; children—Stephen, Anne, Carol. B.S. in Aero. Engring., U. Ala., 1944, M.S. in Engring., 1949; M.S. in Engring. Mgmt., Vanderbilt U., 1976, Ph.D. in Mech. Engring., 1974. Regis. profl. engr., Tenn. Aerodynamicist Curtiss Propeller div., Curtiss-Wright Corp., 1944-47; instr. aero. engring. U. Ala., Tuscaloosa, 1947-48; aerodynamicist N.Am. Aviation, Inc., 1949; asst. prof. aero. engring. U. Ala., 1949-51; research engr. Naval Ordnance Lab., summer 1950, 51-52; research engr. to chief Flight and Aerodynamics Lab., Ordnance Missle Labs., Redstone Arsenal, 1952-56; from mgr. research br. to dep. dir. von Karman Facility, ARO, Inc., Tullahoma, Tenn., 1956-77; dep. tech. dir., dep. for technology, sr. staff scientist Sverdrup Tech., Inc., Tullahoma, 1977-83; cons. engr. and research prof. mech. engring. Vanderbilt U., Nashville, 1983—; adj. prof. U. Tenn., 1956-84; cons. NASA, U.S. Army, U.S. Air Force, aerospace cos., NATO; invited lectr. USSR, various U.S. univs., Organizing Com. Internat. Symposia on Rarefied Gas Dynamics; mem. Engring. Accreditation Commn., 1985—. Pres. Sheffield Homeowners Assn., 1983-84. Fellow AIAA (Gen. H.H. Arnold award for outstanding contbns. 1964), Sigma Xi, Tau Beta Pi, Theta Tau, Sigma Gamma Tau. Clubs: University, Cheekwood (Nashville). Editor: Rarefied Gas Dynamics, parts 1 and 2, 1977; assoc. editor AIAA Jour., AIAA Progress Series books; contbr. chpts. to books, numerous articles to profl. jours. Office: Dept Mech and Materials Engring Box 1673 Sta B Vanderbilt U Nashville TN 37235

POTTER, ROBERT D., U.S. district judge; b. 1923; m. Catherine Neilson; children—Robert D., Jr., Mary Louise, Catherine Ann. A.B., Duke U., 1947, LL.B., 1950. Atty., Charlotte, N.C., 1951-53; practiced with B. Irvine Boyle, 1952-57; sole practice, Charlotte, 1957-81; commr. Mecklenburg County, 1966-68; judge U.S. Dist. Ct. for Western N.C., Charlotte, 1981—, chief judge, 1984. Office: 195 Charles R Jonas Fed Bldg 401 W Trade St Charlotte NC 28202*

POTTER, ROBERT ELLIS, librarian; b. Knoxville, Tenn., Mar. 16, 1937; s. Pollye Jack and Violet Belle (Walker) P.; B.S.J., U. Tenn., 1961; M.S. in L.S., U. Tenn., 1978; postgrad. U. South Fla.; postgrad. U. So. Calif., Miami U., Oxford, Ohio, 1983; m. Rosemary Byrd Lee, Dec. 28, 1963; children—Robert Ellis and Kenyon David (twins). Student asst. U. Tenn. Libraries, 1959-61; copyreader The Knoxville News-Sentinel, 1961-62; library asst. U. Tenn. Libraries, 1962-63; library aide Los Angeles County Library System, El Monte, Calif., 1963-65; reference librarian, bus. and sci. collection City of Hialeah Library div. Hialeah John F. Kennedy Library (Fla.), 1966-73, head librarian bus., sci. and tech. dept., 1973-80; head tech. services Dunedin (Fla.) Public Library, 1980-83, dir. tech. services, 1983—. Counselor, Trail Blazer's Camps, Inc., N.Y.C., 1958; chaplain's asst. U.S. Army Res., 1959-64; cubmaster Boy Scouts Am., 1976-77, 83-84, asst. cubmaster, 1984—, asst. Webeloes leader, 1977-78, committeeman, 1978-80, advancement chmn., 1980—, mem. publicity com. West Central Fla. council, 1983—, chmn. post 468 com., 1986—, publicity chmn. fall encampment Central Fla. Council, 1986—; 1st v.p. Clearwater High Sch. Parent Tchr. Student Assn., 1984-85, treas., 1985—; scouting coordinator United Meth. Ch., 1984—; mem. stewardship com. St. Paul United Meth. Ch. Served with AUS, 1959. Mem. Am., Southeastern (mem. nominating com. resources and tech. services sect. 1984), Fla. (vice-chmn., chmn. elect tech. services Caucus 1985—), Dade County (pres. 1970-71, historian 1976-77, archivist 1975), library assns., Pinellas County Librarian's Assn. (sec. 1982-83, mem.-at-large 1983-84, v.p., pres. elect 1984-85, pres. 1985—, editor newsletter 1985—), Hialeah Library Div. Staff Assn. (pres. 1974-75, sec. 1976, 80), U. Tenn. Century Club, U. Tenn. Nat. Alumni Assn. (bd. govs. Greater Miami chpt., v.p. 1973-74, pres. 1975-77), Maryville Coll. Alumni Assn. (sec.-treas. Fla. chpt. 1982-85), Toastmasters Internat. (adminstrv. v.p. Dunedin 1983, ednl. v.p. 1983-84, sargeant-at-arms 1984-85, pres. 1985—, editor weekly bull. 1983-84), Sigma Delta Chi. Mem. United Ch. of Christ (treas. 1974-77, pres., 1977, chmn. ch. council 1977, mem. mission council Dade-Monroe counties). Author various library publs. Editor newsletter Dade County Library Assn., 1970-75, bull. SORT, ALA, 1971-74, The Wind Word newsletters, 1982-83; contbr. articles to profl. jours. Office: 223 Douglas Ave Dunedin FL 33528

POTTER, ROBERTO HUGH, human resource development specialist, researcher; b. Avon Park, Fla., Dec. 21, 1953; s. Robert Hugh and Margaret Elva (Ellerbee) P.; m. Susan Elizabeth Doyle, May 10, 1980 (div. 1980); m. Susan Pamela Boyles, Jan. 1, 1984. B.A., U. South Fla., 1975; M.A., U. Fla., 1977, Ph.D., 1982. Instr. dept. sociology U. Fla., Gainesville, 1976-78, research assoc., 1979-81; assoc. planner Bur. Criminal Justice, Tallahassee, 1981-82; dir. Fla. Juvenile Justice Inst., Tallahassee, 1982-84; tng. dir. Fla. Network of Youth and Family Services, Inc., Tallahassee, 1984-85. Co-author jour. articles. Mem. Am. Soc. Criminologists, Am. Sociol. Assn., Am. Soc. Tng. and Devel., Fla. Soc. Assn. Execs. Democrat. Avocations: bicycling; gardening; hiking; reading. Home: 1037-C Jamestown Rd Decatur GA 30033

POTTER, TED, JR., art center executive, artist, consultant; b. Springhill, Kans., Dec. 6, 1936; s. Ted and Blanche Ruth (Harris) P.; m. Laura Kienan Carpenter, June 20, 1983; 1 child, Kelly Palmer. B.A., Baker U., 1955; M.F.A., Calif. Coll. Arts, 1961. Cert. arts adminstr., Kans., Calif. Art dir. Glide Found., San Francisco, 1966-67; dir. Southeastern Ctr. for Contemporary Art, Winston-Salem, N.C., 1968—; cons., panelist N.C. State Arts Council, Raleigh, N.C., 1970—, Nat. Endowments Arts, Washington, 1970—; cons. numerous corps., museums. One man shows include Vanderbilt U., V.P.I. Gallery, Blacksburg, Va., Salem Coll., Barbara Fiedler Gallery, Washington, Morehead Galleries, Greensboro, N.C., New Orleans Acad. Fine Arts; exhibited in group shows at Wake Forest U., U. N.C., Chapel Hill. Founder, dir. Awards in Visual Arts. Served with U.S. Army, 1956-57. Avocations: tennis; squash. Office: Southeastern Ctr for Contemporary Art 750 Marguerite Dr Winston-Salem NC 27106

POTTS, AVERY CLARK, geologist, oil exploration; b. Mar. 8, 1956; s. Forrest Clark and Audrey Belle (Kitchens) P.; m. Cathy Lee Flatt, Jan. 22, 1977; 1 child, Bryan Clark. Student indsl. arts Abilene Christian U., 1974-77. Draftsman, Crown Exploration Co., Abilene, Tex., 1976-78; geologist Westwood Energy Inc., Abilene, 1978—; well site work Delta Hydrocarbon Co., Abilene, 1984—. Jr. mem. Am. Assn. Petroleum Geologists. Republican. Mem. Ch. of Christ. Avocations: fishing; hunting; geology; golf. Home: 1466 Minter Ln Abilene TX 79603 Office: Westwood Energy Inc 1166 N 3d St Abilene TX 79604

POTTS, DONALD RALPH, religion educator, clergyman; b. St. Louis, June 10, 1930; s. Benjamin Sedwick and Ethel Dorothy (Deitz) P.; m. Jeanne Daugherty, June 10, 1951; children—Cynthia Diane Chamberlin, Donald Mark. A.A., S.W. Bapt. Coll., 1950; B.A. in Psychology, Okla. Bapt. U., 1952; B.D., Southwestern Bapt. Theol. Sem., 1955, Th.D. in Homiletics, 1959, M.Div., 1973. Instr. Southwestern Bapt. Theol. Sem., Fort Worth, 1959-60; pastor Central Bapt. Ch., Lawton, Okla., 1960-64; prof. religion Cameron Coll., Lawton, 1960-64; pastor First Bapt. Ch., Groves, Tex., 1964-76; prof., chmn. dept. religion East Tex. Bapt. U., Marshall, 1976—. Contbr. articles to ch. publs. Pres. Lawton-Fort Sill Ministerial Alliance, 1963, Groves Ministerial Alliance, 1968. Oxford U. grantee, 1980. Mem. Am. Acad. Religion, Assn. Bapt. Tchrs. Religion, Bibl. Archeol. Soc., Nat. Geog. Soc., Smithsonian Inst. Lodge: Rotary (dir. 1984-85, pres. 1986—). Avocations: reading; travel; hunting; numismatics; fishing. Home: 702 Ambassador Marshall TX 75670 Office: East Tex Baptist U Dept Religion 1209 N Grove Marshall TX 75670

POTTS, JUDITH CLAIRE, hospital administrator, nurse; b. Columbia, S.C., Nov. 18, 1947; d. William John and Ruth (Yancey) Rybka; m. John Sanderson Pace, June 21, 1969 (div. Feb. 1976); children—Christopher, Carrie; m. 2d, Joseph LeRay Potts, Dec. 17, 1983; stepchildren—Laura, Brian. B.S. in Nursing, U. N.C., 1969; M.Edn., N.C. State U., 1981. Registered nurse. Staff nurse psychiatric dept. Jackson Meml. Hosp., Miami, Fla., 1969-71, instr. diploma nursing program, 1971-74; instr. Operation Awareness, Fayetteville Tech. Inst., Ft. Bragg, N.C., 1974-76; instr. program Fayetteville Tech. Inst., 1976-80; adult program dir. Cumberland Hosp., Fayetteville, 1980-82, clin. coordinator, 1982-83, asst. adminstr. clin. services Health Services Adminstrn., 1983—; cons. Central Carolina Community Coll., 1983. Mem. Mental Health Assn., N.C. Nurses' Assn. (Dist. 14). Democrat. Episcopalian. Office: HSA Cumberland Hosp 3425 Melrose Rd Fayetteville NC 28304

POTTS, NANCY DEE, psychologist, business consultant; b. Houston, Dec. 21, 1947; d. Sidney Boyd and Katie Sue (McDonald) N.; m. Lloyd L. Potts, Mar. 21, 1970. B.A., Baylor U., 1970; M.Ed., Sam Houston U., 1974; Ed.D., U. Houston, 1979. Tchr. Spring Branch (Tex.) Ind. Sch. Dist., 1971-73; therapist, program cons. Ctr. for Counseling, Houston, 1973-75; psychologist, ptnr. Marriage, Family & Divorce Cons., Houston, 1975—; bus. cons., ptnr. Choice Unltd., Houston, 1981—. Mem. Am. Psychol. Assn., Am. Orthopsychiat. Assn., Am. Personnel and Guidance Assn., Am. Assn. Marriage and Family Therapists, AAUW. Author: Beginning Again: Challenge of Formerly Married, 1976; Counseling Single Adults, 1978; Loneliness: Living Between the Times, 1978. Home: 1605-C Nantucket Houston TX 79057

POTTS, TERRI HEARN, lawyer; b. Cedartown, Ga., June 18, 1950; d. Thomas H. and Joyce (Camp) Hearn; m. Frank Stanley Potts, Feb. 10, 1973; 1 child, Carter Reston. A.B., Agnes Scott Coll., 1972; J.D., U. S.C., 1975. Bar: S.C. 1975, Ga. 1981. Atty., Family Cts., S.C., 1975-77; gen. counsel S.C. Dept. Labor, 1977-80; assoc. Constangy, Brooks & Smith, Columbia, S.C. and Atlanta, 1981—. Editor newsletter Labor and Employment Law Newsletter, 1980-82. Contbr. articles to profl. jours. Mem. exec. com. Richland County Republican Party, 1982—. Mem. S.C. Bar Assn. (chmn. employment and labor law sect. 1984—), S.C. C. of C. (vice chmn. safety and health com. 1985), Am. Soc. Safety Engrs., Richland County Profl. Women, Ga. Bar Assn. Episcopalian. Office: Constangy Brooks & Smith 920 Bankers Trust Columbia SC 29201

POTTS, WILLIAM EDWARD, retired army officer, government-military consultant; b. Oklahoma City, Nov. 9, 1921; s. Joel C. and Floyce E. (Wise) P.; m. Elaine Marie Whitaker, Sept. 6, 1942; children—William E. A.A., Okla. Mil. Acad., 1942; postgrad. Command and Gen. Staff Coll., 1946; B.S. in Polit. Sci., U. Md., 1951; M.S., George Washington U., 1955, M.A., 1962; postgrad. Armed Forces Staff Coll., 1958, Nat. War Coll., 1961, Oxford U., 1963, Advanced Mgmt. Program Harvard U., 1965, Am. U., 1983. Commd. 2d lt. U.S. Army, 1942, advanced through grades to lt. gen., 1973; participated in 15 campaigns during three wars with U.S. Armed Forces; comdr. armor bn. in combat during both World War II and Korean War, then armored cav. Squadron on East-West German border and armored cav. regt. responsible for Fulda Gap and Frankfort-Berlin Autobahn, 1958-59; asst. chief of staff G3 VII Corps, 1959-60, G3 U.S. Army Vietnam during accelerated buildup of allied forces, 1965-66; served numerous tours in key positions on Army Gen. Staff, in Office Joint Chiefs of Staff, in Office Sec. of Def. and in joint, combined and allied staff assignments; U.S. rep. on Intelligence and Security coms. of NATO Standing Group and NATO Mil. Com. in Permanent Sessions, 1963-65; chief of staff Army Security Agy., 1966-67; dir. intelligence U.S. Army Pacific, 1967-68, U.S. Armed Forces in Vietnam, 1968-72; asst. chief of staff for intelligence U.S. Army, 1972-73; dep. dir. Def. Intelligence Agy., 1973-74, ret., 1974; sr. ops. analyst Gen. research Corp., McLean, Va., 1975-76, project mgr. Indochina Refugee authored monograph program, 1976-81; sr. ops. analyst Electrospace Systems, Inc., McLean, 1981—. Decorated Disting. Service medal with one oak leaf cluster, Silver Star, Legion of Merit with two oak leaf clusters, Bronze Star with four oak leaf clusters and V clasp, Air medal with four oak leaf clusters, Joint Service Commendation medal with one oak leaf cluster, Army Commendation medal with one oak leaf cluster, Purple Heart; Nat. Order of Legion of Honor, Croix-de-Guerre with Silver Star (France); spl. cravat Order of Cloud and Banner (Republic of China); knight grand cross Order of White Elephant (Thailand); Outstanding Achievement medal (Philippines); Nat. Order of Vietnam 4th Class, Armed Forces Honor medal 1st Class, Nat. Police Honor medal 1st Class, Civil Actions medal 1st Class, Mil. Social Service Honor medal 1st Class, Navy Service medal Honor Class, Gallantry Cross Unit Citation with Palm (Vietnam); Presdl. citation, Order of Mil. Merit-Chungmu, Chungmu Disting. Service medal with Gold Star (Korea); others. Mem. Am. Soc. French Legion of Honor, Harvard U. Alumni Assn., Nat. War Coll. Alumni Assn., U.S. Armor Assn., U.S. Army Assn., Am. Def. Preparedness Assn., Nat. Assn. Uniformed Services, Assn. Former Intelligence Officers, Mil. Order World Wars, Ret. Officers Assn., 2d Cav. Assn., 2d Inf. Div. Assn., George Washington U. Alumni Assn., U. Md. Alumni Assn., Am.

Mgmt. Assn. Methodist. Home: 1872 N Patrick Henry Dr Arlington VA 22205 Office: 7921 Jones Branch Dr McLean VA 22102

POULIOT, STUART HARLAND, tobacco company executive, industrial hygienist; b. Worcester, Mass., July 25, 1950; s. L. Paul and Mildred Elizabeth (Wilson) P.; m. Jeannette Hodges, June 30, 1973. B.S. in Biology, Wake Forest U., 1972; M.S.P.H. in Indsl. Hygiene, U. N.C., 1973. Cert. indsl. hygienist, Am. Bd. Indsl. Hygiene; cert. hazard control mgr. Planning engr. indsl. hygiene Western Electric Inc., Richmond, Va., 1974-79, sr. engr. environ. health and safety, 1979-80; mgr. indsl. hygiene Philip Morris USA, Richmond, 1980-82, mgr. indsl. hygiene and safety, 1982-84, mgr. loss prevention and environ. protection, 1984—; mem. adj. faculty J. Sargeant Reynolds Community Coll., 1979-80; mem. safety com. Va. Mfrs. Assn., 1982—. Mgr. Christian Tape Ministry, Richmond, 1984—; vice chmn. Central Va. Health Systems Agy. Task Force on Prevention of Disease and Disability, Richmond, 1979-81. Named Outstanding Tech./Profl. Western Electric Inc., 1979. Mem. Am. Indsl. Hygiene Assn. (founder Central Va. Sect., pres. 1980-82, exec. com. 1982-83), Am. Soc. Safety Engrs., Am. Acad. Indsl. Hygiene, ASTM (E-34 com.). Avocations: Mustang restoration; bicycling. Home: 4030 Litchfield Dr Chesterfield VA 23832 Office: Philip Morris USA PO Box 26603 Richmond VA 23261

POULOS, CHRISTINE ELIZABETH, business executive; b. Jacksonville, Fla., Mar. 15, 1950; d. Theodore C. and Angela (Savvas) P. B.S., U. Fla., 1972, M.S., 1973. Asst. biologist Dames & Moore, Atlanta, 1973-75; staff biologist, 1975-78, project biologist, 1978-84; systems sales specialist Flow Labs., Inc., Tampa, Fla., 1984—; dist. rep. Nalco Chem. Co., Tampa, 1984—. Mem. Nat. Assn. Profl. Saleswomen, Sierra Club, Sigma Xi. Mem. Unity Ch. Club: Toastmasters (Tampa).

POULOS, MICHAEL JAMES, life insurance company executive; b. Glens Falls, N.Y., Feb. 13, 1931; s. James A. and Mary P.; B.A., Colgate U., 1953; M.B.A., N.Y. U., 1963; m. Mary Kay Hutcheson; children—Denise, Peter. With sales and mgmt. depts. U.S. Life Ins. Co., N.Y.C., 1958-65, asst. v.p., 1965-67, 2d v.p., chief adminstrv. officer for sales, 1967-68, sec., treas., dir., 1968, v.p. adminstrn., 1969, mem. exec. com., 1970; v.p. adminstrn. Cal.-Western States Life Ins. Co., Sacramento, 1970, dir., 1971, sr. v.p., 1972, exec. v.p., chmn. investment com., 1974, pres., chief exec. officer, dir., 1975—; sr. v.p., div. head life ins. Am. Gen. Corp., 1979-81, pres., chief operating officer, mem. exec. com., dir., 1981—; dir., chmn. bd. AG Life Ins. Co., AG Life Ins. Co. Del., AG Life Ins. Co. N.Y., Am. Amicable Life Ins. Co., Equitable Life Ins. Co., Am. Gen. Fire and Casualty Co., Nat. Standard Ins. Co., Cal-Western States Life Ins. Co., Gulf Life Ins. Co., Hawaiian Life Ins. Co., Variable Annuity Life Ins. Co.; dir., sr. chmn. Life and Casualty Ins. Co. of Tenn. Mem. Am. Soc. C.L.U.s, Nat. Assn. Life Underwriters, Life Office Mgmt. Assn., Am. Mgmt. Assn., Beta Gamma Sigma, Delta Sigma Pi. Greek Orthodox. Clubs: Heritage, Univ. Office: 2929 Allen Pkwy Houston TX 77019

POULTON, BRUCE ROBERT, university chancellor; b. Yonkers, N.Y., Mar. 7, 1927; s. Alfred Vincent and Ella Marie (Scanlon) P.; B.S. with honors, Rutgers U., 1950, M.S., 1952, Ph.D., 1956; LL.D. (hon.), U. N.H.; m. Elizabeth Charlotte Jerothe, Aug. 26, 1950; children—Randall Lee, Jeffrey Jon, Cynthia Sue, Peter Gregory. Asst. prof. Rutgers U., 1952-56; asso. prof., then prof. animal and vet. scis. U. Maine, 1958-66, chmn. dept., 1958-66, dir. Bangor campus, 1967-68, dean, dir. Coll. Life Scis. and Agr., 1968-71, v.p. research and public service, U. Maine, Orono, 1971-75; chancellor Univ. System N.H., 1975-82, N.C. State U., Raleigh, 1982—; vis. prof. Mich. State U., 1966-67. Trustee Unity Coll.; bd. dirs. Research Triangle Inst., Microelectronics Center, Triangle Univs. Center for Advanced Studies, Aubrey Brooks Found. Served with AUS, 1944-46. Mem. Nat. Assn. Land Grant Univs. and Colls., Am. Council Edn. Author articles in field. Home: 1903 Hillsborough St Raleigh NC 27607 Office: Box 7001 NC State U Raleigh NC 27695

POUNCEY, ALICE GERTRUDE MOORE, psychology and home economics educator; b. Lauderdale County, Miss., July 9, 1939; d. Robert Erby and Julia (Bullard) Moore; m. Kenneth Warren Pouncey, Dec. 20, 1959; children—Alicia Ann, Amy Dawn, Nick Alan. A.A., Jones Jr. Coll., 1959; B.S., U. So. Miss., 1961; M.Ed., Livingston U., 1968; postgrad. Miss. State U., 1970, 82, U. So. Miss., 1969-70, 83. Tchr., Enterprise Jr. High Sch., Miss., 1961-63, Beatrice High Sch., Ala., 1963-65; prof. psychology and home econs. East Central Jr. Coll., Decatur, Miss., 1969—. Mem. ch. adminstrv. bd., chancel choir Meth. Ch.; mem 4-H Adv. Council. Recipient State 4-H Alumni award. Mem. NEA, Miss. Jr. Coll. Faculty Assn., Miss. Profl. Educators, Miss. Assn. Educators, Delta Kappa Gamma. Republican. Methodist. Club: 4-H Vols. (pres. 1963-65), Garden, Woman's, 4-H Honor Club. Avocations: sewing; traveling. Home: PO Box 121 Decatur MS 39327 Office: Dept Social Studies E Central Jr Coll Decatur MS 39327

POUNDS, CAROL JEANNE, pharmacist; b. Gadsden, Ala., July 4, 1955; d. Carl Raymond and Allene Jeanne (Roden) P.; A.S., Gadsden State Jr. Coll., 1975; B.S. in Pharmacy, Samford U., 1977. Pharmacist, asst. mgr. Eckerd Drug, Birmingham, Ala., 1979-80, pharmacist, mgr., 1980-82; staff pharmacist, chmn. continuing edn. St. Vincent Hosp., Birmingham, 1982-83; pharmacist Big B Inc., Birmingham, 1983-84, pharmacist, mgr., Gadsden, 1984—. Contbr. poetry and photographs to mags. Recipient award of merit World of Poetry, 1985. Avocations: photography; creative writing.

POURIAN, HEYDAR, financial analyst, economist, educator; b. Tehran, Iran, Apr. 23, 1948; came to U.S., 1972, naturalized, 1984; s. Pasha and Moneer (Hamidi-Khaleghi) P. Student Nat. U. Iran, 1966-70, B.A., 1972; English lang. cert. U. Mich., 1972; M.A. (Internat. Scholar) U. Wis.-Oshkosh, 1974; Ph.D., U. Wis.-Milw., 1980; pub. econs. cert. MIT, summer, 1979. Research asst. dept. econs. and C. of C., U. Wis.-Milw., 1974, teaching asst. dept. econs., 1975-78, lectr. econs., dept. econs. and Sch. Bus. Adminstrn., 1978-79; asst. prof. econs. U. Mo.-St. Louis, 1979-84; asst. prof. fin. Western Carolina U., Cullowhee, N.C., 1984—; research asst. U. N.C., summer, 1981, Grad. Sch. Bus., U. Chgo., summer 1982, Fletcher Sch. Law and Diplomacy, Tufts and Harvard Univs., summer 1983, 84, 85; coordinator IRS Tax Assistance Program. Author: The Essence of Money and Banking, 1983; contbr. articles to profl. jours. Served as 2d lt. Iranian Army, 1970-72. Recipient Grad. Sch. award U. Wis.-Milw., 1975. Mem. Am. Econ. Assn., Econometrics Soc., Am. Fin. Assn., Fin. Mgmt. Assn., Soc. Fin. Assn., Internat. Inst. Forecasters, N.Am. Econs. and Fin. Assn., UN Assn. U.S.A., Omicron Delta Epsilon, Phi Kappa Phi. Home: Box 1960 Cullowhee NC 28723 Office: Sch Business Western Carolina U Cullowhee NC 28723

POWE, KAREN WATKINS, educator, former association executive; b. St. Joseph, Mo., Aug. 15, 1941; d. Hugh Ransom and Viola Violet (Clark) Watkins; m. Marc Bracken Powe, Dec. 9, 1961; children—D. Michelle, Laura Elizabeth. B. Liberal Scis., U. Okla., 1975. Personnel mgr. Tiaffay Assocs., Inc., Monterey, Calif., 1962-63, Barrett Assocs., Inc., Alexandria, Va., 1975-77; gen. mgr. Am. Embassy Community Assn., Am. embassy, Moscow, 1977-79; exec. asst. Nat. Assn. State Bds. Edn., Alexandria, Va., 1979-83, project dir. Alcohol Edn. Guidelines Project, 1983-85; tchr. ESL, Baghdad, Iraq, 1985—. Coach Girls' Soccer, Springfield Youth Club (Va.). Mem. AAUW, Alliance Traffic Safety, Nat. Sch. Health Edn. Coalition, NOW, Nat. Abortion Rights Action League, Va. Orgn. Keep Abortion Legal. Office: USDAO Am Embassy Baghdad US State Dept Washington DC 20520

POWE, RALPH ELWARD, university administrator; b. Tylertown, Miss., July 27, 1944; s. Roy Elward and Virginia Alyne (Bradley) P.; m. Sharon Eve Sandifer, May 20, 1962; children—Deborah, Ryan, Melanie. B.S. in Mech. Engring., Miss. State U., 1967, M.S. in Mech. Engring., 1968; Ph.D. in Mech. Engring., Mont. State U., 1970. Student trainee NASA, 1962-65; research asst., lab. instr. Miss. State U., 1968, instr. dept. mech. engring., 1968; research asst., teaching asst. Mont. State U., Bozeman, 1968-70, asst. prof. dept. mech. engring., 1970-74; assoc. prof. Miss. State U., 1974-78, prof., 1979-80, assoc. dean engring., dir. engring. and indsl. research sta., 1979-80; assoc. v.p. research, 1980—; cons. energy conservation programs, coal fired power plants, torsional vibrations, accident analysis. Mem. Internat. Center Heat and Mass Transfer, ASME (service award Miss. sect.), Soc. Automotive Engrs., Am. Soc. Engring. Edn., AAAS, Wind Energy Soc. Am., Miss. Acad. Scis., Miss. Engring. Soc., Blue Key, Sigma Xi (Miss. State U. research award), Tau Beta Pi, Kappa Mu Epsilon, Pi Tau Sigma, Phi Kappa Phi, Omicron Delta Kappa. Baptist. Lodge: Rotary. Home: 110 Pinewood Dr Starkville MS 39759 Office: Miss State U PO Drawer G Mississippi State MS 39762

POWELL, ANICE CARPENTER, librarian; b. Moorhead, Miss., Dec. 2, 1928; d. Horace Aubrey and Celeste (Brian) Carpenter; student Sunflower Jr. Coll., 1945-47, Miss. State Coll. Women, 1947-48; B.S., Delta State U., 1961, M.L.S., 1973; m. Robert Wainwright Powell, July 19, 1948; children—Penelope Elizabeth, Deborah Alma. Librarian, Sunflower (Miss.) Pub. Library, 1958-61; instr. English, Isola (Miss.) High Sch., 1961-62; dir. Sunflower County Library, 1962—; mem. adv. council State Instl. Library Services, 1967-71; mem. adv. com. Miss. Gov.'s Conf. Libraries, 1978-79; mem. Library Services and Constrn. Act adv. com. Miss. Library Commn., 1978-80. Chmn. Miss. Heart Assn., Sunflower, 1963-73; chmn. library category Sunflower County Merit Program, 1973. Mem. Miss. Library Assn. (cert. of appreciation 1975, Peggy May award 1981; sect. chmn. 1965, treas. 1970, fed. relations coordinator 1973-74, chmn. intellectual freedom com. 1975, exec. dir. Nat. Library Week 1975, chmn. right to read com. 1976, mem. legis. com. 1973-77, 79, 81, mem. constn. bylaws com. 1978, chmn. legis. com. 1979, mem. nominating com. 1981, chmn. membership com. 1982-83, v.p. 1983, pres. 1984, chmn. nominating com., budget com., edn. com., legis. com., all 1986), Sunflower County Hist. Soc. (pres. 1983-86). Methodist. Home: Box 310 Sunflower MS 38778 Office: 201 Cypress Dr Indianola MS 38751

POWELL, ANNABELLE COUNCIL, geology educator, geoscience resources company executive; b. Burlington, N.C., Nov. 23, 1953; d. Thomas Edward and Annabelle (Council) P. B.A., Wellesley Coll., 1975; Ph.D., Oxford U., Eng., 1980. Asst. to curator Mus. of Basel, Switzerland, 1980; asst. prof. geology Rutgers U., New Brunswick, N.J., 1981-82; founder, pres. Geosci. Resources, Inc., 1982—. Mem. Geol. Soc. Am., Am. Assn. Petroleum Geologists, Soc. Econ. Palentol. Mineralogists. Republican. Avocations: piano; organ; flying. Home: 120 N Gurney St PO Box 1992 Burlington NC 27215

POWELL, CLIFFORD KEITH, insurance company administrator, consulting actuary; b. Corbin, Ky., Aug. 19, 1948; s. Clifford Everett Powell and Nannie (Messer) Baker; m. Colleen Ann Gibbons, Dec. 22, 1970; 1 child, Richard Keith. B.A. magna cum laude, Union Coll., 1968; M.B.A., U. Ky., 1975. Mgr. pensions, pension actuary Textron Corp., Providence, 1980-82; dir. div. medicare cost estimates Health Care Financing Adminstrn., Balt., 1982-84; actuary Group Hospitalization, Washington, 1984; dir. actuarial div. Blue Cross Ins. Ky., Louisville, 1984—. Mem. Soc. Actuaries (assoc.), Am. Acad. Actuaries (mem. subcom. fed. impact on role of health actuary 1982-84). Avocation: reading. Home: 504 Rothbury Ln Louisville KY 40243 Office: Blue Cross Ky Linn Statron Rd Louisville KY 40243

POWELL, EVERETT G., college dean, educator; b. Corpus Christi, Apr. 25, 1934; s. Everett L. and Imogene B. (Peck) P.; m. Gloria Hood, June 5, 1953; 1 child, Katherine. B.A., U. Corpus Christi, 1955; M.A., Tex. A&I U., 1961; Ph.D., U. Tex., 1970. Cert. tchr., Tex. Tchr., West Oso Sch. Dist., Corpus Christi, 1957-61; prof. Tex. A&I U., Kingsville, 1961-66; prof. Del Mar Coll., Corpus Christi, 1966-82, asst. dean arts and sci., 1980-82, dean arts and scis., 1982—. Founding co-editor Tex. A&I U. Studies jour., 1965; contbr. articles to publs. Served with U.S. Army, 1955-57. Mem. Acad. Dean of So. States, Tex. Assn. Jr. and Community Coll. Instructional Adminstr., Tex. Joint Council Tchrs. of English (hon. life). Democrat. Episcopalian. Home: 1400 Ocean Dr 1001C Corpus Christi TX 78404 Office: Del Mar College Baldwin at Ayers Corpus Christi TX 78404

POWELL, IRIS CUNDIFF, nurse; b. Pittsylvania County, Va., Nov. 22, 1935; d. Beverly Davis and Helen Josephine (Southall) Cundiff; m. James Frederick Powell, June 27, 1959; 1 son, James Frederick. Diploma, Roanoke Meml. Hosp. Sch. Nursing, 1957; B.S., U. Va., 1959; postgrad. Catholic U. Am., 1968-69; M.S., Radford Coll./Univ., 1971. Supr., U. Va. Hosp., Charlottesville, 1959-61; instr. nursing Va. Baptist. Hosp., Lynchburg, 1962-67; asst. prof. nursing Radford Coll. (Va.), 1970-72; pub. health nurse Montgomery County Health Dept., 1972-74; assoc. prof. nursing. Va. Western Community Coll., 1975-83, dir. nursing program, 1982-83. Active Mothers March of Dimes, Cancer Crusade, Red Cross Bloodmobile, United Way. Mem. Va. Council Assoc. Degree Nursing Edn., Va. Dist. II Nurses Assn., Am. Nurses Assn., Va. Nurses Assn. Baptist. Lodge: Order Eastern Star. Home: Rt 4 Box 366-A Burlington NC 27215

POWELL, JAMES LEE, psychologist, educator; b. Reidsville, N.C., Nov. 4, 1944; s. John James and Martha Lee (Martin) P.; m. Mary Julia Parker, Mar. 2, 1974; 1 child, Julia Ellen. A.B., Duke U., 1967, M.Div., 1970; Ph.D., N.C. State U., 1984. Lic. psychologist, Ga.; ordained to ministry Methodist Ch., 1968. Minister, Hornes United Meth. Ch., Wilson, N.C., 1970-74; psychology intern Smoky Mountain Area Mental Health, Hazelwood, N.C., 1974-75, ctr. dir., Hayesville, N.C., 1975-82; psychologist Affiliated Counseling and Psychol. Services, Jonesboro, Ga., 1982—; acting pres. Psychol. Studies Inst., Atlanta, 1984-85, pres., 1985—; mem. adj. staff Hinton Rural Life Ctr., Hayesville, 1979—; part time instr. Tri-County Community Coll., Murphy, N.C., 1979-82; adj. faculty Mars Hill Coll., N.C., 1980-82; Ga. State U., Atlanta, 1984—. Contbr. articles to profl. publs. Pres. bd. dirs. Clay County Hist. and Arts Council, Hayesville, 1980, Appalachian Hospice, Hayesville, 1981; chmn. Clay County Crime Prevention Assn., Hayesville, 1981-82; mem. Leadership Clayton, Morrow, Ga., 1983-84. Recipient Disting. Service award N.C. Mental Health Ctrs. Assn., 1979, Dist. award of Merit Daniel Boone Council, Boy Scouts Am., 1980, Disting. Vol. Leadership award Pisgah chpt. March of Dimes, 1979. Mem. Am. Psychol. Assn., Southeastern Psychol. Assn., Ga. Psychol. Assn., Christian Assn. for Psychol. Studies, Am. Assn. for Counseling and Devel., Clay County Jaycees (v.p. 1977-78). Democrat. Club: Burns (Atlanta). Lodge: Masons. Avocations: reading; sailing; computers. Home: 9165 Woodhill Ln Jonesboro GA 30236 Office: Affiliated Counseling and Psychol Services 7099 Tara Blvd Jonesboro GA 30236

POWELL, JOHN KEY, life insurance executive; b. Dallas, Dec. 14, 1925; s. Floyd Berkeley and Eloise (Sadler) P.; m. Ann Penniman, July 14, 1950; children—Nena Ann, Scott Key, Elliott Edward. Student U. Ala., 1946-50; grad. Inst. Ins. Mktg., So. Meth. U., 1955. C.L.U. Agt. various firms, Tuscaloosa, Ala., 1950-54; asst. gen. agt. John Hancock Life Ins. Co., Lubbock, Tex., 1954-57, asst. supt., Boston, 1957-59, gen. agt. for S.C., Columbia, 1959-85; prin. J. Key Powell CLU & Assocs, Columbia; mem. adv. bd. Bankers Trust S.C., Columbia, 1977—. Bd. dirs. Salvation Army, Columbia, 1983—, Citizens Advocating Decency and Revival of Ethics, Columbia, 1984—. Served with USAAF, 1943-45. Mem. Gen. Agts. and Mgrs. Assn. (pres. 1967-68), John Hancock Gen. Agts. Assn. (pres. 1969-71), Million Dollar Round Table (life, qualifying mem.), Am. Soc. C.L.U.s, Greater Columbia C. of C. (bd. dirs. 1979-81), Sigma Alpha Epsilon. Presbyterian. Clubs: Forest Lake, Wildewood Country, Litchfield Country. Lodges: Rotary (past pres.), Kiwanis (past pres.). Avocations: golf; fishing; hunting. Home: 212 Holliday Rd Columbia SC 29223 Office: J Key Powell CLU & Assocs 1332 Main St Columbia SC 29201

POWELL, JOSEPH ROBERT, microbiologist, educator; b. Jacksonville, Fla., Sept. 6, 1947; s. Julius Stenson and Mary Elizabeth (Feher) P.; m. Elizabeth Morris, Aug. 28, 1971; 1 dau., Meredith Ann. B.S., St. Bernard Coll., 1969; M.C.S., U. Miss., 1975; postgrad. Hahnemann Med. Coll., 1983; Ph.D., Columbia Pacific U., 1985. Instr. anatomy, physiology, and chemistry Bishop Kenny High Sch., Jacksonville, 1969-71; instr. biology, chmn. dept. sci. Robert E. Lee High Sch., Jacksonville, 1971-76; prof. microbiology, anatomy, and physiology Fla. Jr. Coll., Jacksonville, 1976—, pres. faculty senate, 1981-82. Mem. AAUP, Am. Soc. Microbiology, Fla. Assn. Community Colls. Home: 7904 Jolliet Dr Jacksonville FL 32217 Office: Fla Jr Coll North Campus 4501 Capper Rd Jacksonville FL 32218

POWELL, JOUETT LYNN, college dean, philosophy and religious studies educator; b. Dallas, Dec. 2, 1941; s. Hiram Wheeler and Evelyn Ruth (Foster) P.; m. Mary Ellen Beall, Aug. 15, 1964; 1 child, Kristen Lynn. B.A., Baylor U., 1964; B.D., So. Bapt. Theol. Sem., 1967; M.Phil., Yale U., 1970, Ph.D., 1972. Instr. religion U. N.C., Chapel Hill, 1971-72, asst. prof. religion, 1972-78; asst. prof. philosophy and religious studies Christopher Newport Coll., Newport News, Va., 1978-80, assoc. prof., 1980—, dean Sch. Letters and Natural Sci., 1983—; vis. assoc. prof. religion Coll. William and Mary, 1984-85. Contbr. articles to profl. jours. Recipient summer seminar stipend NEH, 1981, summer research stipend NEH, 1982; Rockefeller doctoral fellow Yale U., New Haven, 1969-70; Smith-Reynolds Found. grantee, 1974. Mem. Am. Acad. Religion, Am. Philos. Assn., Am. Assn. Higher Edn., AAUP, So. Humanities Conf. Democrat. Episcopalian. Avocation: listening to classical music; carpentry. Home: 65 Rivermont Dr Newport News VA 23601 Office: Christopher Newport Coll 50 Shoe Ln Newport News VA 23606

POWELL, LOUISA ROSE, psychologist; b. Highland Park, Mich., Oct. 10, 1942; d. Albert and Mildred Loraine (Bos) Feldman; B.S. Roosevelt U., 1966; M.S., U. Chgo., 1969, Ph.D., 1973; m. Philip Melancthon Powell, Jr., Dec. 29, 1962; children—David, Aaron, Robert. Intern in psychology VA Hosp., Newington, Conn., 1973-75; instr. So. Conn. State Coll., New Haven, 1975-76; psychologist Austin (Tex.) Evaluation Ctr., 1979-80, 81-82; dep. dir. gen. clin. services Austin Child Guidance and Evaluation Ctr., 1982-84, interim clin. dir., 1984-86; adj. prof. dept. psychology U. Tex., Austin, 1984—; sch. psychologist San Rafael (Calif.) Schs., 1980-81; instr. SW Tex. State U., San Marcos, 1978-79; pvt. practice psychology. Chmn. Cub Scouts Pack #54, 1977-78; violincellist Austin Civic Orch. psychologist, health services provider, Tex.; listed Nat. Health Service Providers in Psychology. Mem. Am. Psychol. Assn., Am. Orthopsychiat. Assn., Southwestern Psychol. Assn., Tex. Psychol. Assn., Capital Area Psychol. Assn. (sec. 1985-86), Soc. for Research in Child Devel., Nat. Assn. Gifted Children Central Tex. Assn. Gifted Children (co-v.p. 1984-85). Democrat. Home: 3910 Edgerock Dr Austin TX 78731 Office: 612 W 6th St Austin TX 78701

POWELL, ROBERT MORGAN, trucking company executive; b. Cleve., Sept. 28, 1934; s. David Kelso and Rachel Kirk (Alford) P.; m. Janice Hobbs, Sept. 2, 1973. B.S., U. N.C., 1956. With Ark.-Best Freight System, Inc., 1960; ops. mgr., St. Louis, 1960-62, asst. dir. terminals, Fort Smith, Ark., 1962-63, br. mgr., St. Louis, 1963-67, dir. research and planning, Fort Smith, 1967-68, v.p. spl. commodities, 1968-69, v.p. ops., 1969-73, exec. v.p., 1973-86; sr. v.p. Ark. Best Corp. Mem. Fort Smith Airport Commn.; active fund-raising drives United Way. Served with USN, 1956-60, 61-62. Mem. Am. Trucking Assn. (dir. ops. council), Ark Trucking Assn. (past pres.). Club: Fort Smith Town (dir., past pres.). Office: Ark-Best Freight System Inc PO Box 48 Fort Smith AR 72901*

POWELL, STEVEN KARL, builder, developer; b. Phila., July 27, 1947; s. Lee and Jean (Saslow) P.; m. Terri Buckhantz, July 13, 1969; children—Kimberly, Michael, Stacey, Brian. B.S. in Biology, Baldwin-Wallace Coll., 1969. Chmn. bd. PAR Constrn. Corp., Vienna, Va., 1974-82; pres. United Devel. Corp., Vienna, 1982—, United Carpentry Corp., Vienna, 1984—, E.S. Service Corp., 1985—. Bd. dirs. Langley Sch., McLean, Va., 1983-84. Served with U.S. N.G., 1970-76. Mem. No. Va. Builders Assn., Home Owners Warranty Corp. of No. Va. (bd. dirs.). Avocations: scuba diving; flying; racquetball. Office: United Devel Corp PO Box 1120 Vienna VA 22180

POWELL, THOMAS EDWARD, III, physician, bus. exec.; b. Alamance County, N.C., Aug. 1, 1936; s. Thomas Edward, Jr. and Sophia Maude (Sharpe) P.; A.B. in Biology, Va. Mil. Inst., 1957; M.D., Duke U., 1961; M.A., Harvard U., 1965; m. Betty Durham Yeager, June 19, 1965; children—Frances Elizabeth, Thomas Edward, IV, Caroline Yeager. Surgeon, USPHS, 1966-68; exec. v.p., then chmn. bd. Carolina Biol. Supply Co., Burlington, N.C., 1969-80, pres., 1980—; co-founder Biomed. Reference Labs., Inc., 1969, chmn. exec. com., 1979—; pres. Granite Diagnostics, Inc., Waubun Labs., Inc., Wolfe Sales Corp., Bobbitt Labs., Inc.; dir. Wachovia Bank, Burlington; mem. N.C. Bd. Sci. and Tech., 1979-84. Author articles in field. Trustee Elon Coll., 1968—; chmn. bd. Burlington Day Sch.; bd. dirs. N.C. Citizens Bus. and Industry, United Way Alamance County. Served in arty. U.S. Army, 1957; to capt. Res. Recipient Citizens Service award Elon Coll. Alumni Assn., 1980. Mem. N.C. Acad. Family Physicians, Assn. Microbiol. Media Mfrs. (dir.), AMA, Am. Cancer Soc., N.C. Med. Soc., Alamance-Caswell Med. Soc., Newcomen Soc., Alamance Investors Club. Mem. United Ch. Christ. Clubs: Burlington Rotary, Alamance Country (Burlington); Hope Valley Country (Durham, N.C.); Greensboro (N.C.) City; Capital City (Raleigh, N.C.); Congl. Country (Washington). Home: 950 E Lake Dr Burlington NC 27215 Office: 2700 York Rd Burlington NC 27215

POWELL, TIMOTHY FRANKLIN, geologist, geophysicist; b. Tulsa, June 3, 1956; s. Frank Wilkins and Ethel Mae (O'Brien) P.; m. Vivian Marie Fredericks, Aug. 18, 1979; children—Natalie Marie, Gary Alan. B.S. in Geology, Tex. A&M U., 1979. Core analyst Core Labs., Houston, 1980; geologist Pennzoil Exploration and Prodn., Houston, 1980-84, geophys. specialist, 1984—. Mem. Houston Geol. Soc., Am. Assn. Petroleum Geologists. Avocations: rebuilding British sports cars; softball; camping. Home: 13306 Oak Ledge Dr Houston TX 77065 Office: Pennzoil Exploration and Prodn 700 Milam Houston TX 77001

POWELL, VANCE EDWARD, III, real estate appraiser, consultant; b. Dallas, Nov. 3, 1955; s. Vance E. and W. Patricia (Waters) P.; m. Nancy E. Hur, June 10, 1978. Student S.W. Tex. State U., 1974-76; B.B.A., U. Tex.-Austin, 1980. Appraiser trainee Osenbaugh & Assocs., Houston, 1973-74; staff appraiser to mgr. Bolton/Graef & Co., Austin, Tex., 1975-81; assoc. to sr. faculty Am. Coll. Real Estate, Austin, 1978-84; owner Vance Powell & Assocs., Austin, 1981-83; chmn. bd. Powell, Osenbaugh & Assocs. Inc., Austin, 1983—. Outstanding Working Student scholar, U. Tex., 1980. Mem. Soc. Real Estate Appraisers (dir. 1981-83, chmn. edn. com. 1981-84, admissions com. 1983-84, treas. 1984—, Young Adv. Council 1983—), Am. Inst. Real Estate Appraisers, Nat. Assn. Rev. Appraisers, Austin Bd. Realtors. Republican. Methodist. Office: Powell Osenbaugh and Assocs Inc 1016 MoPac Circle Suite 202 Austin TX 78746

POWELL, WILLIAM ALLAN, chemistry educator, consultant; b. Wallace, N.C., May 28, 1921; s. Purvey Oglesby and Anna Bailey (Maynard) P.; m. Edna Rae Bradshaw, Mar. 29, 1941; children—William Allan, Richard Bradshaw, Elizabeth Maynard. B.S., Wake Forest U., 1942; postgrad. U. Pitts., 1947-48; Ph.D., Duke U., 1953. Asst. chief chemist Carolina Aluminum Co., Badin, N.C., 1942-46; indsl. hygiene chemist, New Kensington, Pa., 1946-48; instr. Wake Forest U., 1948-49; parttime instr. Duke U., Durham, N.C., 1949-51; DuPont fellow, 1951-52; asst. prof. U. Richmond (Va.), 1952-56, assoc. prof., 1956-66, prof. chemistry, 1966—, chmn. dept. chemistry, 1959-82; cons. Philip Morris Research Labs. Pres., Westham Civic Assn., 1975. Mem. Am. Chem. Soc. (chmn. Va. sect. 1964, councilor 1970—; disting. service award 1977), Va. Acad. Sci. (pres. 1976-77), AAAS, Phi Beta Kappa, Sigma Xi, Omicron Delta Kappa, Gamma Sigma Epsilon. Democrat. Baptist. Lodge: Mason. Developed instrumental methods in study of toxins of jellyfish. Home: 48 E Lock Ln #4 Richmond VA 23226 Office: Gottwald Sci Ctr W-111 U Richmond Richmond VA 23173

POWELL, WILLIAM ARNOLD, JR., banker; b. Verbena, Ala., July 7, 1929; s. William Arnold and Frances (Baxter) P.; B.S. in Bus. Adminstrn., U. Ala., 1953; grad. Sch. Banking, La. State U., 1966; m. Barbara Ann O'Donnell, June 16, 1956; children—William Arnold, Barbara Ann Powell McCaleb, Susan Frances, Patricia Baxter. With First Nat. Bank (now Am. South Bank, N.A.), Birmingham, Ala., 1953—, v.p., br. supr., 1968-71, sr. v.p., 1971-73, exec. v.p., 1973-79, pres., 1979-83, vice chmn., 1983, also dir.; pres. AmSouth Bancorp., Birmingham, 1979—, also dir.; dir. AmSouth Mortgage Co. Inc.; instr. Banking Sch., La. State U., 1977-79, 81—, pres.-elect, dir., 1985-86. Bd. dirs. Brookwood Med. Center, Inc., Am. Cancer Soc., Birmingham Children's Theatre, Warrior-Tombigbee Waterway Assn., Ala. Sports Festival; bd. visitors U. Ala.; pres. Birmingham Festival Arts, 1986; trustee Ala. Assn. Ind. Colls. and Univs. Served to 1st lt. U.S. Army, 1954-56. Mem. Birmingham Area C. of C. (dir., v.p.), Birmingham Hist. Soc. (dir.). Methodist. Clubs: Downtown, The Club, Green Valley Country, Mountain Brook, Riverchase Country, Birmingham Country, Kiwanis (pres. 1970). Home: 3309 Thornton Dr Birmingham AL 35226 Office: PO Box 11007 Birmingham AL 35288

POWELL, WILLIAM COUNCIL, manufacturing company executive; b. Burlington, N.C., Nov. 5, 1948; s. Thomas Edward and Annabelle (Council) P.; B.S., Va. Mil. Inst., 1971; M.B.A., Wake Forest U., 1974; student Elon Coll., 1971, U.S.C., 1968-70; m. Jacqueline Garrison, July 3, 1976; children—Ashley C., William Council. Vice pres. Bobbitt Labs., Burlington, N.C., 1974-77, pres., 1977-82; chmn. bd. Home Entertainment & Decor Systems, Inc., Burlington, 1978—; v.p. Warren Land Co., 1978—; pres. Granite Diagnostics, Inc., 1978-84; chmn. bd. dirs. Excalibur Lock Co. Inc., 1982—; dir. Carolina Biol. Supply Co. Inc., 1980—. Served to capt. USAR, 1971-79. Real estate broker, N.C. Mem. Soc. Plastics Engrs., NAM, Safari Club Internat. (pres. N.C. chpt. 1985), Ducks Unltd. (chmn.). Democrat. Methodist. Home: 1109 W Front St Burlington NC 27215-3610 Office: HEADS Inc Rt 3 Box 115A Elon College NC 27244

POWELL, WILLIAM GENE, insurance company executive; b. Robersonville, N.C., Oct. 31, 1940; s. William Olive and Ruth (White) P.; m. Nancy Coltrain, Jan. 27, 1963; children—William Gene, Jr., Cynthia Leigh. B.S. in

Edn., N.C. State U., 1963. C.P.C.U., A.L.C.M. Adjuster, Nationwide Ins. Co., Elizabeth City, N.C., 1966-72, master adjuster, Spartanburg, S.C., 1972-74, regional hail mgr., Raleigh, N.C., 1974-78, loss control cons., Robersonville, 1978—; defensive driving instr. Nat. Safety Council, Chgo., 1983. Mem. N.C. State U., Alumni Assn. (county chmn. 1980, area chmn. 1983), Am. Soc. Safety Engrs. Club: Gold Point Ruritan (Robersonville). Democrat. Baptist. Home: PO Box 1240 Robersonville NC 27871 Office: Nationwide Mutual Ins Co PO Box 30000 Raleigh NC 27612

POWER, BETTY JOAN, nurse; b. Altoona, Pa., Nov. 15, 1949; d. Robert Elsworth and Verna Bernice (Holmes) Fulton; m. Hugh Irvin Power, Sept. 15, 1973. R.N., Marion County Gen. Hosp., 1970. R.N., Ind., Tex. Staff nurse Marion County Hosp., Indpls., 1970-71; staff nurse U. Tex. Med. Br., Galveston, 1971-79, charge nurse Child Health Ctr., 1981-84, asst. head nurse, 1984—; staff nurse St. Mary's Hosp., Galveston, 1979-81; CPR instr. Galveston chpt. ARC. Recipient Galveston ARC Vol. Recognition award, 1981; named John Sealy Hosp. Employee of Month, Nov. 1984. Home: 4400 Ave N Apt 156 Galveston TX 77550 Office: Child Health Center U Tex Med Br Unit 6 N Galveston TX 77550

POWER, JACK, JR., clergyman; b. Littlefield, Tex., Apr. 26, 1945; s. Larkin Jackson and Eva L. (Cole) P.; m. Jo Beth Pettus, Aug. 14, 1965; children—Jack, III, Jacquelyn. Student, Howard County Jr. Coll., 1963-64, Arlington Bapt. Coll. and Sem., 1965-66. Ordained to ministry Bapt. Ch., 1966; dept. mgr. J.C. Penney Co., Big Springs, Tex., 1961-64, Fort Worth, 1965-66; assoc. pastor Rolling Hills Bapt. Ch., Fort Worth, 1966-67, First Bapt. Ch., Englewood, Colo., 1967-69; pastor Houston Bapt. Temple, Houston, 1969—. Rotarian (sec.). Home: 2603 Wood River Dr Spring TX 77373 Office: 15620 Sellers Rd Houston TX 77060 also PO Box 60967 Houston TX 77205

POWERS, CARSON HARDIE, financial services executive, consultant; b. N.Y.C., Nov. 24, 1934; s. Harry Grell and Gladys Lillian (Mars) P.; m. Jon Grenville Dodson, May 4, 1957 (div. May 1978); children—Torii Heath, Elliott Grell; m. Kathleen Ann Osage, July 1, 1978. A.B. in Econs., Princeton U., 1956; postgrad. Harvard U., 1971. Media buyer Cunningham & Walsh, Inc., N.Y.C., 1960-62; account exec. Dancer-Fitzgerald-Sample, Inc., N.Y.C., 1963-68; v.p., dir. mktg. Chem. Bank, N.Y.C., 1968-79; nat. dir. service mktg. Price Waterhouse, N.Y.C., 1979-83, dir. smaller bus. practice devel., Washington, 1983-85; pres. Hardie Powers & Co., Alexandria, Va., 1985—; cons. India Internat., Inc., Washington; dir. R.S. Carmichael & Co., Inc., White Plains, N.Y., Harrison Powers Assocs., New Caanan, Conn. Rep., Town Meeting, Greenwich, Conn., 1974-77; trustee Greenwich Library, 1975-77; class fund agt. Harvard Bus. Sch., Boston, 1982-84. Served to lt. USNR, 1956-60. Mem. Am. Mktg. Assn. Presbyterian. Clubs: Princeton of N.Y., University, St. Andrews Soc. N.Y. State. Home: 315 S Union St Alexandria VA 22314

POWERS, ELLIOTT HOLCOMB, oil company executive; b. Overton, Tex., Oct. 20, 1907; s. James Shelton and Lynn Alberta (Bagwell) P.; m. Alice Jane Leighton, Aug. 11, 1935; 1 child, Patricia Powers Freel. B.A., Tex. Tech U., 1930; M.S., U. Iowa, 1933, Ph.D., 1935. Exploration geologist Gulf Oil Corp., Midland and Fort Worth, Tex., 1935-49, asst. v.p., Houston, 1949-52; v.p., dir. So. Prodn. Co., Fort Worth, 1952-56; v.p. exploration Union Tex. Petroleum, Houston, 1956-70; Ind. oil operator, Houston, 1970—; chmn. bd. Bayou Bend Petroleum Corp., Houston, 1983—. Fellow Geol. Soc. Am.; mem. Am. Assn. Petroleum Geologists (sec., treas. 1953-55). Clubs: Houston, Petroleum (Houston). Avocation: travel. Home: 101 Westcott St Apt 302 Houston TX 77007 Office: Bayou Bend Petroleum Corp 7715 San Felipe St Ste 200 Houston TX 77063

POWERS, GEORGIA M., state senator; b. Springfield, Ky., Oct. 29; d. Ben and Frances (Walker) Montgomery; ed. Louisville Municipal Coll., 1940-42; m. James L. Powers; 1 son from previous marriage, William F. Davis. Supr. IBM Data Processing div. U.S. Census Bur., 1959-62; asst. hosp. adminstr., Louisville, 1966; mem. Ky. Senate, 1968—. Mem. Gov.'s Adv. Council on Mental Retardation, 1967-68. Dist. chmn. Jefferson County Democratic Exec. Com., 1964-66; chmn. Blume for Congress campaign, 1966; del. Dem. Nat. Conv., 1968. Bd. dirs. Louisville area chpt. ARC, 1970-72. Recipient Kennedy-King Meritorious award Ky. Young Dems., 1968; Achievement award Zion Bapt. Ch., 1968; certificate of appreciation Ky. Sch. Bds. Assn., 1968; Woman of Yr. award YWCA, 1978, Watson Meml. award, 1979; award Ky. State U., 1981; Pres.'s award Simmons Bible Coll., Martini Luther King, Jr.-Drum Maj. for Justice award, 1983, Disting. Citizen award Kappa Alpha Psi, 1983, many others. Mem. NAACP (Ky. Conf. award 1979, Isaac Murphy award 1981, Clarence Mitchell award 1983), Urban League.

POWERS, HUBERT PAUL, accountant, former ednl. adminstr.; b. Anson, Tex., Apr. 7, 1906; s. Si Thomas and Dibbon Mary (Barker) P.; B.A., Tex. Tech U., 1934, M.A., 1938; m. Lula Mae Carter, June 1, 1980; children by previous marriage—Patsy Vee Powers Nichols, Paula Deniece Powers Jones. Prin. rural schs., Mitchell County, Tex., 1927-34, McCaulley, Tex., 1934-38; supt. schs. McCaulley, Tex., 1938-42, Avoca, Tex., 1942-46, Throckmorton, Tex., 1946-54; prin. elem. schs., Childress, Tex., 1954-71; acct. Income Tax Service, Public Bookkeeping Service, Childress, 1971—. Pres., ARC, Childress, 1972-75; sec. Am. Cancer Soc., Childress County, 1972-77. Recipient citation plaque for war effort, Pres. Roosevelt, 1942. Mem. C. of C., Tex. State Tchrs. Assn., NEA, Nat. PTA, Tex. PTA. Baptist. Clubs: Rotary (pres. 1979-80), Masons. Home: 803 H-NW Avenue H Childress TX 79201 Office: 208 Commerce St Childress TX 79201

POWERS, JACK W., college executive; b. Fort Wayne, Ind., Oct. 28, 1929; s. Dorsey Byrl and Winnifred Cecelia (Kundred) P.; m. Ruth Margaret Ollhoff, Aug. 24, 1952; children—Tod W., David E., Alicia A., Laura J. B.S., Purdue U., 1952, M.S., 1956, Ph.D., 1957. Regional dir. Research Corp., Atlanta, 1969-75, v.p. resource devel., N.Y.C., 1975-79; v.p. external affairs Rensselaer Poly. Inst., Troy, N.Y., 1979-81; v.p. devel. Davidson Coll., N.C., 1981-85, St. Andrews Presbyterian Coll., Laurinburg, N.C., 1985—. Mem. Am. Chem. Soc., Nat. Soc. Fund Raising Execs., Council for Advancement and Support of Edn., Sigma Xi. Republican. Presbyterian. Lodge: Masons (grand master Ripon, Wis. 1967-68). Avocations: golf; sailing; fishing. Office: St Andrews Presbyn Coll Laurinburg NC 28352

POWERS, LINDA JEANNE, librarian, writer, storyteller; b. Richlands, Va., Mar. 5, 1958; d. Kline Reed and Negetha Lee (Gourley) P. B.A. in English, Clinch Valley Coll., 1980; M.S. in L.S., U. Tenn.-Knoxville, 1981. Children's librarian Bristol Pub. Library (Va.), 1981—, mem. Jefferson Cup Com., 1982. Contbr. short stories, poems, and book revs. to publs. (Cohen award 1979). Recipient William Elbert Fraley award, Clinch Valley Coll., 1980. Mem. ALA, Va. Library Assn., Beta Phi Mu. Republican. Presbyterian. Office: Bristol Pub Library 701 Goode St Bristol VA 24201

POWLEY, DAVID EDWARD, geologist; b. Sask., Can., Dec. 13, 1927; came to U.S. 1964; m. Doris Evelyn Johnson, July 16, 1951; children—Kenneth, Beverly, Brian, Sheryl. B.Engring., U. Sask., 1950, M.S. in Geology, 1951. Registered profl. engr., Alberta, Can. Geologist Amoco Prod. Co., Can., U.S.A., 1951-64, worldwide and research mgr., 1964—; advisor in geology of geothermal energy Am. Petroleum Inst. and Dept. Energy, Washington, 1979-82. Patentee in field. Mem. Am. Assn. Petroleum Geologists (lectr., chmn. research com.), Soc. Exploration Geophysicists, AIME. Home: 5735 E 62nd Pl Tulsa OK 74136 Office: Amoco Prod Co PO Box 591 Tulsa OK 74102

POYNOR, KENNETH J., Realtor; b. Chelsea, Okla., July 3, 1916; s. James Madison and Nova K. (Aldridge) P.; B.S., Okla. State U., 1937; m. Dorothy O. Smith, May 24, 1937. With U.S. Dept. Agr., Stillwater, Okla., 1938-43; tchr. vocat. agr., Noble, Okla., 1943-44, Altus, Okla., 1944-45; owner, operator Ken Poynor Agy. real estate and ins., Norman, Okla., 1951—; owner, operator farms and ranches. Mem. Okla. Ho. of Reps., 1958-62. Named Norman Realtor of Year, 1969. Mem. Okla. Realtors (state chmn. legis. com. 1965-73, agrl. research and edn. com. 1965-73), Norman Bd. Realtors (pres. 1960-71), C. of C., Okla. State U. Alumni Assn. (life). Clubs: Masons, Shriners, Kiwanis. Home: 1306 Melrose Dr Norman OK 73069 Office: 708 W Main St Norman OK 73069

POYNOR, ROBERT WILSON, JR., heating and air conditioning executive; b. Malvern, Ark., June 14, 1930; s. Robert Wilson and Maedelle (Daniel) P.; m. Patsy Fern Gregg, Mar. 29, 1951 (div. 1966); children—Daena Sue, Terry Lynn, Randall David; m. Charlene Burk, July 14, 1966; stepchildren—Bobby Glenn, Danny Joe, Roy Lynn, Clifford Wayne; 1 child, Robert Wilson, III. B.S., Tex. Tech U., 1961. Evangelist, Ch. of Christ, Lubbock, Tex., 1951-59; owner, operator White Auto Store, Slaton, Tex., 1959-66; research and devel. engr. Lubbock Mfg. Co., 1966-72; v.p., gen. mgr. State Heating and Air Conditioning Co., Lubbock, 1972—. Pres. Roosevelt Sch. Bd. Trustees, Lubbock County, 1972—, South Plains Sch. Bd. Assn.; trustee Tex. Assn. Sch. Bds. Dist. 10, 1985—. Mem. Tex. Air Conditioning Contractors. Republican. Avocations: woodworking; yard work. Home: 35 Highland Dr Ransom Canyon TX 79366 Office: State Heating Air Conditioning Co 614 E Slaton Hwy Lubbock TX 79404

PRABHAKAR, VISHVAJIT DILBAGH, geological engineer; b. Nairobi, Kenya, Nov. 25, 1954; came to U.S., 1973; s. Dilgagh Rai and Nirmala (Dikshit) P. B.S. in Biology, Utah State U., 1977; B.S. in Geol. Engring., U. Utah, 1980. Geol. engr. Shell Oil Co., New Orleans, 1981—, unitization engr., 1982—. Mem. Am. Assn. Petroleum Geologists, Soc. Petroleum Engrs. Republican. Office: Shell Western E & P Inc 2212 One Shell Square New Orleans LA 70161

PRADIA, REYNALDO JAMES, project manager, planning consultant; b. Mar. 16, 1947, Houston; s. Robert James and Ruby Mary (Wells) P.; m. Wanda Ruth Cole, Aug. 12, 1978 (div. 1982); 1 child, Reynaldo James, II. B.S. in Archtl. Design, Prairie View A&M U., 1969; M.A. in Urban Planning, Tex. So. U., 1973; cert. in Mgmt., U. Pa., 1982. Cert. secondary tchr., Tex. Tchr., coach Houston I.S.D., 1969-70; account mgr. Lever Bros., Detroit, 1970-71; adminstr., planner City of Houston, 1971-73; dir. planning and design Tex. So. U., Houston, 1973-77; project mgr. Spaw-Glass Inc., Houston, 1978—; planning cons. Democratic Party, Houston, 1972—, City of Houston, 1983—; guest lectr Prairie View A&M U., Tex., 1984—. Vita mem. Vols. in Tech. Asst., Houston, 1972—; mem. Our Mother of Mercy Parish Council, Houston, 1981-84, City of Houston Planning Commn., 1983—. Mem. Constrn. specification Inst., Am. Planning Assn., Urban Designers Inc., Nat. Rifle Assn. (life). Democrat. Roman Catholic. Club: Hidden Valley Civic (Houston). Lodges: Knights of Peter, Claver Council "72". Avocations: hunting; fishing; swimming; designing and building furniture; collecting jazz albums. Home: 815 Helms Rd Houston TX 77088 Office: Project Mgmt Systems 2900 Wesleyan Houston TX 77027

PRADO, EDWARD CHARLES, judge; b. San Antonio, June 7, 1947; s. Edward L. and Bertha (Cadena) P.; m. Maria Anita Jung, Nov. 10, 1973; 1 son, Edward C. A.A., San Antonio Coll., 1967; B.A., U. Tex.-Austin, 1969, J.D., 1972. Bar: Tex. 1972. Asst. dist. atty. Bexar County Dist. Atty.'s Office, San Antonio, 1972-76; asst. pub. defender U.S. Pub. Defender's Office, San Antonio, 1976-80; state dist. judge Tex., San Antonio, 1980; U.S. atty. Dept. Justice, San Antonio, 1980-84; U.S. Dist. judge, Western Tex., 1984—. Served to capt. U.S. Army. Named Outstanding Young Lawyer Bexar County (Tex.), 1980. Mem. ABA, Tex. Bar Assn., San Antonio Bar Assn., San Antonio Young Lawyers, Assn., Fed. Bar Assn. Republican. Roman Catholic. Office: U S Courthouse 655 E Durango Blvd San Antonio TX 78206*

PRADO, WILLIAM MANUEL, psychologist, educator; b. N.Y.C., Oct. 20, 1927; s. Manuel Fernando and Amor Maria (Bango) P.; m. Elizabeth Ann Avery, Aug. 16, 1953; children—Cheryl, Stuart, Mark. B.A., Johns Hopkins U., 1950; M.A., U. Ala., 1953; Ph.D., U. Okla., 1958. Staff psychologist VA Hosp., Little Rock, 1958-85, asst. chief psychology services, 1961-82; asst., assoc. and adj. prof. psychology Philander Smith Coll., Little Rock, 1967—; instr. Little Rock U., 1959-69; clin. psychologist in pvt. practice, Little Rock, 1961—; cons. in field. Contbr. articles to profl. jours. Served with U.S. Army, 1946-47. Recipient Math and Sci. Gold medal Rensselaer Poly. Inst., 1944. Mem. Am. Psychol. Assn., Ark. Assn. Profl. Psychologists. Democrat. Roman Catholic. Avocations: music; art; movies.

PRAGER, GERALD DAVID, geologist, petroleum researcher; b. Norfolk, Va., Oct. 25, 1940; s. Omar Raymond and Evelyn Juanita (Melville) P.; m. Brenda Gayle Stamm, Apr. 15, 1973. B.S., U. Kans., 1962; Ph.D., U. Cin., 1971; C.A.G.S., Northeastern U., 1978. Geologist, Valley Geoservices, Cin., 1971-73; asst. prof. Northeastern U., Boston, 1973-78; assoc. prof. Ohio U., Athens, 1978-80; chief geologist Howard Donley Assocs., Redwood City, Calif., 1980-81; exploration stratigrapher Texaco Inc., New Orleans, 1981-85; offshore mgr. Energy Devel. Corp., Houston, 1985—; cons. Boston Edison Co., 1976-77, N.Y. State Electric and Gas Co., 1977-78, Pitts. Plate Glass Co., 1980. Contbr. articles to profl. jours. NSF fellow 1966. Mem. Am. Assn. Petroleum Geologists, Geol. Soc. Am., History Earth Scis. Soc., New Orleans Geol. Soc., Sigma Xi. Avocations: tennis; skiing; archery; astronomy; military history. Home: 2027 St Nick Dr New Orleans LA 70114 Office: Energy Devel Corp Suite 3040 1200 Smith Houston TX 77002

PRAHAN, AVINASH CHINTAMANI, physician; b. Thana, India, June 13, 1948; s. Chintamani Gopal and Suhasini C. Pradhan; m. Medha A. Pradhan, Oct. 27, 1973; children—Pradnya, Vidya. Student, R. Ruia Coll., Bombay, India; M.B.B.S., G.S. Med. Coll., Bombay. Diplomate Am. Bd. Internal Medicine, Am. Bd. Nephrology. Intern, Highland Park Gen. Hosp. (Mich.), 1972-73, resident VA Med. Ctr., Bklyn., 1973-76; fellow in nephrology Albany Med. Ctr. (N.Y.), 1976-78; chief med. service Fort Lyon VA Med. Ctr. (Colo.), 1978-82, Dublin VA Med. Ctr. (Ga.), 1983—; cons. in medicine. Mem. AMA, Assn. VA Chiefs Med. Service. Home: 1201 Shamrock Dr Dublin GA 31021 Office: Dublin VA Med Center Dublin GA 31021

PRAHL, HELMUT FERDINAND, research foundation executive, scientist; b. Ludwigshafen, Germany, Oct. 16, 1933; came to U.S., 1947; s. Walter Hugo and Gertrude (Unkelbach) P.; m. Marian Alice White, July 15, 1953; (div. 1969); children—Juliana, Walter, Ralph. B.S., U. Rochester, 1954; M.S., U. Wis., 1959, Ph.D., 1958. Head polypropylene fiber Chemstrand Corp., Decatur, Ala., 1958-60; head polymer applications Standard Oil Co. (Ohio), Cleve., 1960-62; dir. organic and polymer Bjorksten Research Labs., Madison, Wis., 1962-66; pres. Dynatron Research Corp., Madison, 1966—, exec. dir. Dynatron Research Found., Madison, 1967—. Mem. Fiber Soc., Plant Growth Regulator Soc. Avocations: sailing; amateur astronomy; photography.

PRASSEL, FREDERICK FRANZ, construction company executive; b. San Antonio, Nov. 14, 1934; s. Victor, Sr. and Eda Marie (Groos) P.; student U. Tübingen (Ger.), Trinity U.; B.A., U. Tex., Austin, 1959; postgrad. Calif. Western U.; m. Barbara Fry, July 2, 1959; children—Charlotte, Victor B., Edie C. Owner, pres. Prassel Constrn. Co., San Antonio, 1959—; v.p., sec.-treas. Pras-Mel Corp.; public speaker. Bd. dirs. YMCA; deacon First Presbyterian Ch., chmn. property com., 1982-83; pres. Arthur Gray Jones Choir, 1978, 79; mem. Leadership San Antonio Program, 1979-80; mem. allocations com. United Way, 1981; bd. dirs. Palmer Drug Abuse Program, 1981-82. Served with AUS, 1957-59. Mem. Am. Mgmt. Assn., Builders Exchange Tex., Constrn. Specifications Inst., Internat. Platform Assn., YMCA, Jaycees (dir. 1961-62). Clubs: Toastmasters (pres. 1976, gov. 1978), Oak Hills Country, Beethoven Maennerchor (chmn. bldg. com. 1982), Rotary (sec. 1978-79, service chmn. 1979-80, sgt. at arms 1980-81, program chmn. 1981-82, pres. 1984-85). Home: 116 Cardinal Ave San Antonio TX 78209 Office: 1000 S Comal St PO Box 526 San Antonio TX 78292

PRATER, ROBERT WAYNE, industrial hygienist, safety engineer; b. Meta, Mo., Feb. 24, 1937; s. Leonard F. and Ida P. (Champlain) P.; m. Darla J. Gibson, Feb. 18, 1961 (div. 1978); children—Robert M., Laura J.; m. Montague Lupo Herlong, Mar. 2, 1979; stepchildren—Deanne Herlong, Heidi Herlong Malone. B.S. in Biology, Central Mo. State U., 1977, M.S. in Indsl. Hygiene, 1978, M.S. in Indsl. Safety Engring., 1985. Cert. indsl. hygienist comprehensive practice. Enlisted U.S. Navy, 1955, advanced through grades to sr. chief petty officer, 1975; ret., 1975; indsl. hygienist Bendix Corp., Kansas City, Mo., 1978-81, The Williams Cos., Tulsa, 1981-85; cons. indsl. safety and indsl. hygiene, Tulsa, 1985—. Guest speaker Tulsa Area Safety Council, 1982. Mem. Am. Indsl. Hygiene Assn. (personal protective devices com. 1983—), Am. Acad. Indsl. Hygiene, Am. Soc. Safety Engrs. Avocations: photography, canoeing, hiking. Home: 6825 S 29 West Ave Tulsa OK 74132

PRATHER, HENRY LEON, SR., history educator, trombonist; b. Nashville, Jan. 6, 1921; s. Toby Lee and Essie Beatrice (Speight) P.; m. Audrey Minga, June 5, 1953; children—Henry Leon, Lawsanne Geraldine. A.B., S.C. State Coll.-Orangeburg, 1948; postgrad. NYU, 1952, Ph.D., 1961. Profl. trombonist, arranger, 1945-47; bandmaster, mem. social sci. faculty Elizabeth City (N.C.) State Tchrs. Coll., 1948-58; assoc. prof. history Del. State Coll., Dover, 1961-63; prof. history Tenn. State U., Nashville, 1963—. Served with USAAF, 1941-45. Recipient Martin Luther King, Jr. Black Author's award, 1981; Interdenominational Ministers fellow, 1982. Mem. Orgn. Am. Historians, So. Hist. Assn., Assn. for Study of Negro Life and History, Assn. Social and Behavioral Scis., Ted Rhodes Nat. Golfing Found., Alpha Lambda Delta, Omega Psi Phi. Author: Resurgent Politics and Educational Progressivism in the New South, North Carolina, 1890-1913, 1979; We Have Taken A City: Wilmington Racial Massacre and Coup of 1898, 1984. Home: 2495 Walker Ln Nashville TN 37207 Office: 3500 John Merritt Blvd Nashville TN 37203

PRATHER, LENORE LOVING, state supreme court justice; b. West Point, Miss., Sept. 17, 1931; d. Byron Herald and Hattie Hearn (Morris) Loving; m. Robert Brooks Prather, May 30, 1957; children—Pamela, Valerie Jo, Malinda Wayne. B.S., Miss. State Coll. Women, 1953; LL.B., U. Miss., 1955. Bar: Miss. 1955. Practice with B. H. Loving, West Point, 1955-60, sole practice, 1960-71; mcpl. judge City of West Point, 1965-71; chancery ct. judge 14th dist. State of Miss., Columbus, 1971-82, supreme ct. justice, Jackson, 1982—; v.p. Conf. Local Bar Assn., 1956-58; sec. Clay County Bar Assn., 1956-71. Mem. Miss. State Bar Assn., Miss. Conf. Judges, DAR. Episcopalian. Clubs: Pilot, Jr. Aux. Columbus. First woman in Miss. to become chancery judge (1971) and supremecourt justice (1982). Office: Supreme Court State of Mississippi Gartin Bldg Jackson MS 39205

PRATT, JESSE (JACK) PALMER, retired state corrections official, educator; b. Barnwell, S.C., Sept. 19, 1932; s. S. J. and M. Earidene (Price) P.; m. Margaret Bryant, Feb. 4, 1956; children—Tony, John. A.A. with high honors, Palmer Coll., 1972; B.A., U. S.C., 1973, M.P.A., 1975. Probation and parole agt., Greenville, S.C., 1955-65, agt. in charge S.C. Dept. Parole and Community Corrections, Pickens County, 1955-58, tng. officer, Columbia, S.C., 1965-68, dep. dir., Columbia, 1968-81, exec. dir., 1981-83; instr. (part-time) U.S.C. and Midlands Tech. Coll., Columbia. Pres. Quail Hollow Community Assn., 1976-79; mem. Citizens Adv. and Action Council, Campbell Work-Release Center, Columbia. Named Disting. Alumnus Coll. Applied Profl. Scis., U.S.C., 1982. Mem. Am. Correctional Assn., Am. Probation and Parole Assn., S.C. Law Enforcement Officers Assn., S.C. State Employees Assn., S.C. Corrections Assn., Alston Wilkes Soc., U.S.C. Alumni Assn. Democrat. Baptist.

PRATT, STEPHEN MICHAEL, lawyer; b. Los Angeles, Sept. 28, 1945; s. George Lyon and Margaret Louise (Duff) P.; children—Jennifer Victoria, Stephanie Lyon. B.A. cum laude, Hobart Coll., 1967; J.D., U. Va., Charlottesville, 1970. Bar: Va. 1970, U.S. Supreme Ct. 1976, Md. 1984. Title officer Titlesearch, Inc., Charlottesville, 1970-71; assoc. John H. Rust, Fairfax, Va., 1971-74; ptnr. Rust, Rust & Pratt, Fairfax, 1974-80, Pratt, Buonassissi & Henning, P.C., Fairfax, 1980-84, of counsel, 1984-85; of counsel Buonassissi, Henning, Campbell & Moffet, P.C., 1985—; v.p. RCH Land Sales Inc., 1984—, Copper Land Co., 1984—, T & K, Inc., 1984—, Raymond C. Hawkins Constrn. Co., Inc., 1984—; bd. govs. estates and property sect. Va. State Bar, 1974-78. Pres. Century I Condominium Assn., Ocean City, Md., 1978; treas. Hampton Woods Homes Assn., Inc., 1978-79. Mem. ABA, Va. State Bar Assn., Md. Bar Assn., Fairfax County Bar Assn., Phi Beta Kappa. Episcopalian. Club: Fairfax Swim. Home: 10601 Railroad Ct Fairfax VA 22030 Office: Route 2 Box 985 Catlett VA 22019

PRATT, SUZANNE GARRETT, physician; b. Ga., Mar. 9, 1948; d. Roswell and Susie (Keller) Garrett; m. Frank Graham Pratt, III, Sept. 18, 1971; children—Frank Graham, Edward Garrett. B.S. summa cum laude, U. Ga., 1970; M.D., Med. Coll. Ga., 1973. Diplomate Am. Bd. Ob-Gyn. Resident Med. Coll. Ga., Augusta, 1973-77; physician D.D. Eisenhower Army Med. Ctr., Ft. Gordon, Ga., 1977-79; practice medicine specializing in ob-gyn, Rome, Ga., 1980—; coordinator ob-gyn family practice residency program Floyd Med. Ctr., Rome, 1983-84. Nat. Merit scholar U. Ga. Found., 1966-70. Fellow Am. Coll. Obstetricians and Gynecologists; mem. Floyd-Polk-Chattooga Med. Soc. (sec. 1982-84), AMA, Ga. Soc. Obstetricians and Gynecologists, Med. Assn. Ga., Zodiac, Phi Beta Kappa, Phi Kappa Phi. Office: Three Rivers Ob-Gyn 909 N 5th Ave Rome GA 30161

PRAY, RICHARD WADSWORTH, pharmacist; b. Syracuse, N.Y., Feb. 4, 1956; s. R. Ford and Joan Leslie (Wadsworth) P.; m. Dayna Elizabeth Brown, Oct. 19, 1985. A.A., Wesley Jr. Coll., 1976; student U. Del., 1976-77; B.S., Auburn U., 1980. Pharmacist Moulton's Drugs, Pensacola, Fla., 1980-82; pharmacist, asst. mgr. Revco Drugs, Pensacola, 1982-84, pharmacist, mgr., 1984-85. mem. Am. Pharmacy Assn., Escambia County Pharmacy Assn. (sec. 1983, treas. 1984-85). Republican. Presbyterian. Clubs: Auburn of West Fla., Soc. Am. Baseball Research. Avocations: sports; sailing; gardening. Home: 7800 Lanain Dr Pensacola FL 32514 Office: Revco Drug Stores Inc 8187-D W Fairfield Dr Pensacola FL 32506

PREBLUDA, HARRY JACOB, consulting chemist; b. Fall River, Mass., May 19, 1911; s. Barney and Esther (Chernock) P.; B.S. magna cum laude, U. R.I., 1932, M.S., 1933; Ph.D. in Biochemistry (Eli Lilly fellow), Johns Hopkins U., 1937; m. Renetta Berkman, June 16, 1946; children—Jeffrey Lee, Ellen Sue Prebluda Chilton. Instr. organic chemistry U. R.I., Kingston, 1933-35; cons. chemist U.S. Indsl. Alcohol Co., Balt., 1937-38; devel. biochemist U.S. Indsl. Chems. Co., Balt., 1938-44; mgr. spl. products div. Nat. Distillers & Chem. Corp., N.Y.C., 1944-52, mgr. spl. products sales, 1952-61; cons. chemist, Miami Beach, Fla., 1961—; asso. Roger Williams Tech. and Econ. Services, Inc., Princeton, N.J., 1973-75, project leader, 1975-85, dir., 1979-85; dir. R.I. Found., pres. Option Fund, 1964-75. Mem. Forward Trenton Com., 1972-73. Research Corp. fellow, 1937-38. Fellow Inst. Chemists AAAS, N.Y. Acad. Scis.; mem. Nat. Farm Chemurgic Council (dir., sec.), Am. Chem. Soc., World Poultry Sci. Assn., Inst. Food Technologists, Animal Nutrition Research Council, Assn. Cons. Chemists and Chem. Engrs., Fla. Inst. Chemists (pres.), Controlled Release Soc., Research and Devel. Assocs. for Mil. Food and Packaging Systems, Soc. Indsl. Microbiology, Sigma Xi. Club: Johns Hopkins Faculty Chemists. Lodge: Mason. Editor Chemurgic Digest, 1963—; author: Introduction to Organic Chemistry, 1936; The Newer Knowledge of Animal Nutrition, 1978; adv. panel Chemtech, 1978—, chmn., 1980; contbr. articles to profl. jours. Patentee in field. Home and Office: 4101 Pine Tree Dr #803 Miami Beach FL 33140

PREDDY, RAYMOND RANDALL, newspaper pub.; b. Texarkana, Ark., Feb. 1, 1940; s. Raymond Watson and Dorothy Belle (Long) P.; B.S., Northwestern U., 1961, M.S. in Journalism, 1962; m. Sarah Elizabeth Mitchell, Nov. 20, 1965; children—Lewis, Tiffany. Copy editor Louisville Courier-Jour., 1965-69; with Dayton (Ohio) Daily News, 1969-74, asst. city editor, 1971, met. editor, 1971-74; systems mgr. Dayton Newspapers, Inc., 1974-76; with Waco (Tex.) Tribune-Herald, 1976—, asst. pub., 1977-78, pub., 1978—. Served with U.S. Navy, 1962-65. Presbyterian. Club: Rotary. Office: 900 Franklin Ave Waco TX 76701

PRENG, DAVID EDWARD, executive search consultant; b. Chgo., Sept. 30, 1946; s. Edward Marion and Frances (Maras) P.; m. JoAnne Ferzoco, Dec. 6, 1969; children—Mark, Laura, Stephen, Michael. B.S. in Fin., Marquette U., Milw., 1969; M.B.A., DePaul U., Chgo., 1973. Acct., supr. Shell Oil Co., Chgo., Houston, 1969-73; div. controller Litton Industries, Houston, 1973-74; v.p. Addington & Assocs., Houston, 1974-76; v.p. S.W. Industries, Houston, 1976-77; sr. assoc. Korn/Ferry Internat., Houston, 1977-78; v.p. Kors Marlar & Assocs., Houston, 1978-80; pres. Preng & Assocs., Houston, 1980-85, Preng Zant & Assocs., Houston, 1985—; dir. Citizens Nat. Bank of Bellaire (Tex.), Bear Creek Nat. Bank, Houston, Plaza del Oro Nat. Bank, Houston. Roman Catholic. Home: 3010 Bucknell Ct Sugar Land TX 77478

PRENTICE, NANCY HUTCHISON, public relations and commerical art executive; b. Slab Fork, W.Va., Sept. 28, 1940; d. Wayman Joseph and Grace Figgett (Dudley) H.; children—Helen Grace Hall, Adrianne Christine; m. Jay H. Prentice, July 10, 1982. Student Atlanta Sch. Art, 1958-60. Comml. artist, 1960-67; v.p., creative dir. The Art Factory, 1975-77; pres., creative dir. So. Belle/Nancy Prentice, Atlanta, 1978—; v.p. Prentice & Langford Pub. Relations, Atlanta, 1982—; pres., creative dir. So. Belle Print Prodns. Ltd., 1983—. Democrat. Presbyterian. Home: 305 Peachtree Ave NE Atlanta GA 30305 Office: 375 Pharr Rd Suite 116 Atlanta GA 30305

PRESBURY, JOHN (JACK) HARDING, JR., psychology educator; b. Kansas City, Kans., Jan. 10, 1938; s. John Harding and May Anita (Ostertag) P.; m. Katharine Lindley Perkins, July 4, 1969. B.S. in Edn., Central Mo. State U., 1965; M.Ed., U. Pitts., 1968, Ph.D., 1972. Lic. profl. counselor, Va.; cert. social sci. tchr., Mo. Instr. SUNY-Brockport, 1969-70; assoc. prof., head dept.

psychology Lyndon State Coll. (Vt.), 1971-74; psychologist Columbia Area Mental Health Center (Tenn.), 1974-80; assoc. prof. psychology James Madison U., Harrisonburg, Va., 1980—, also coordinator counseling psychology programs; cons., counselor. Mem. Va. Counselors Assn., Central Valley Counselors Assn. (pres.). Democrat. Co-author: Save Tomorrow for the Children; Ways of Knowing. Contbr. articles to profl. publs.; composer songs; Save Tomorrow for the Children, Creation, 1983. Home: 501 E Beverley St Staunton VA 24401 Office: Johnston Hall 123 James Madison Univ Harrisonburg VA 22807

PRESSER, STEPHEN LEE, insurance and investment counselor; b. Blytheville, Ark., Feb. 19, 1944; s. Broadus Lee and Mary Iola (Pyland) P.; divorced; children—Stephanie Diane, Todd Stephen. A.A., Sch. of Ozarks, 1964; B.S., U. Ark., 1967. C.L.U. Ins. and investment counselor Equitable Fin. Services Inc., Atlanta, 1971—. Bd. dirs. Peachtree-Atlanta Kiwanis Club, 1985-87. Served with U.S. Army, 1967-70. Decorated Bronze Star (2), Purple Heart; recipient Outstanding Kiwanian award, 1985, Rookie of Yr. award, 1985. Mem. Nat. Assn. Life Underwriters, Atlanta Assn. Life Underwriters, Am. Soc. C.L.U.s, Million Dollar Roundtable, U. Ark. Alumni Assn. Met. Atlanta (bd. dirs. 1985—). Republican. Avocations: jogging; nautilus; racquetball. Home: 1431 B Willow Lake Dr Atlanta GA 30329 Office: 2635 Century Pkwy Atlanta GA 30345

PRESSLY, CLAUDE LOWRY, surgeon; b. Statesville, N.C., July 13, 1916; s. James Hearst and Julia Mabel (Lowry) P.; m. Margaret Amelie Mechlin, Feb. 5, 1949; children—Amelie, Sara, Margaret. A.B., Erskine Coll., Due West, S.C., 1938; M.D., U. Pa., 1943. Diplomate Am. Bd. Surgery, Am. Bd. Thoracic Surgery. Intern, Pa. Hosp., Phila., 1943, resident in surgery, 1944-45, 47-48; resident in surgery Meml. Hosp., N.Y.C., 1948-49; practice medicine specializing in gen. and thoracic surgery, Charlotte, N.C., 1950—; past pres. staff Presbyn. Hosp., Mercy Hosp., Charlotte Meml. Hosp. Served to capt., M.C., U.S. Army, 1945-47. Mem. ACS, Soc. Surg. Oncology, Am. Coll. Chest Physicians. Democrat. Presbyterian. Contbr. articles to med. jours. Home: 1863 Cassamia Pl Charlotte NC 28211 Office: 2300 Randolph Rd Charlotte NC 28207

PRESSLY, WILLIAM LAURENS, headmaster; b. Louisville, Ga., July 24, 1908; s. Paul and Lois (Moffatt) P.; m. Alice Fletcher McCallie, Aug. 28, 1940; children—Paul Moffatt, William Laurens. A.B., Princeton U., 1931; M.A., Harvard U., 1947; D.Litt., Washington and Lee U., Lexington, Va., 1949; LL.D., Hanyang U., 1978; D.H.L., Erskine Coll., 1982. Co-headmaster, McCallie Sch., Chattanooga, 1936-51; founding pres., headmaster Westminster Schs., Atlanta, 1951-73; adminstr. Atlanta Hist. Soc., 1973-79; past pres. Nat. Council Ind. Schs., So. Assn. Schs. and Colls., Headmasters Assn.; past trustee Coll. Entrance Exam. Bd., Ednl. Testing Service, Nat. Assn. Ind. Schs., Erskine Coll., Rabun-Gap Nacooche Sch., Atlanta Hist. Soc.; past chmn. President's Commn. Presdl. Scholars. Chmn. trustees Atlanta Coll. Art; life trustee Atlanta Arts Alliance; elder, trustee First Presbyn. Ch., Atlanta. Recipient Edward S. Noyes award Coll. Entrance Exam. Bd., 1976. Mem. Am. Assn. Museums, Nat. Trust Hist. Preservation.

PRESSON, CHARLES ARNOLD, ins. co. exec.; b. Jackson, Miss., Oct. 30, 1942; s. Ewart Knox and Mary Elizabeth (Mobley) P.; A.A., Itawamba Jr. Coll., 1960; B.S. in Bus., Miss. Coll., 1964; m. Norma Kay Storm, Nov. 11, 1967; children—Charles Anthony, Dawn Elizabeth. Cashier trainee Jefferson Standard Life Ins. Co., Jackson, 1965-66, officer mgr., Tulsa, 1966-67, San Antonio, 1967-77, sales service supr., Houston, 1977—. Served with USAF, 1964-65. Baptist. Club: Masons (sr. warden 1976-77). Office: 8323 SW Freeway Suite 700 Houston TX 77074

PRESTON, JACK, chemist, consultant; b. Birmingham, Ala., Aug. 7, 1931; s. Earl Walter and Ada Idella (Aldridge) P.; children—John Brock, Joan Catherine; m. Sue Waterman, Aug. 4, 1974 (div. 1984). B.S., Howard Coll., 1952; M.S., U. Ala., 1954, Ph.D., 1957. Research chemist Chemstrand Corp., Decatur, Ala., 1957-60, Chemstrand Research Ctr., Durham, N.C., 1960-65, fellow, 1965-74, sr. fellow, 1974-81; sr. fellow Monsanto Fibers Co., Pensacola, Fla., 1981-85, cons., 1985—; sr. research assoc. dept. chemistry Duke U., Durham, 1977—. Co-editor 5 books. Contbr. articles to profl. jours. Patentee in field. Mem. Am. Chem. Soc., Fiber Soc. Democrat. Home and office: 11409 High Springs Rd Pensacola FL 32514

PRESTON, LOYCE ELAINE, educator; b. Texarkana, Ark., Feb. 25, 1929; d. Harvey Martin and Florence (Whitlock) P.; student Texarkana Jr. Coll., 1946-47; B.S., Henderson State Tchrs. Coll., 1950; certificate in social work La. State U., 1952; M.S.W., Columbia U., 1956. Tchr. pub. schs., Dierks, Ark., 1950-51; child welfare worker Ark. Dept. Public Welfare, Clark and Hot Spring counties, 1951-56, child welfare cons., 1956-58; casework dir. Ruth Sch. Girls, Burien, Wash., 1958-60; asst. prof. spl. edn. La. Poly. Inst., Ruston, 1960-63; asst. prof. Northwestern State Coll., Shreveport, La., 1963-73; asst. prof. La. State U., Shreveport, 1973-79; ret., 1979. Chpt. sec. La. Assn. Mental Health, 1965-67, Gov's. adv. council, 1967-70; mem. Mayor's Com. for Community Improvement, 1972-76. Mem. AAUW (dir. Shreveport br. 1963-69), Acad. Cert. Social Workers, Nat. Assn. Social Workers (del. 1964-65, pres. North La. chpt., state-wide com. 1968-69), La Conf. Social Welfare, La. Fedn. Council Exceptional Children (pres. 1970-71), La. Tchrs. Assn. Home: 9609 Hillsboro Dr Shreveport LA 71112

PRESTON, THOMAS RONALD, English educator; b. Wyandotte, Mich., Oct. 31, 1936; s. Thomas and Marie Katherine (Nettlow) P.; m. Mary Ruth Atkinson, June 4, 1960; children—Lorel, Mary, Thomas. B.A., U. Detroit, 1958; M.A., Rice U., 1960, Ph.D., 1962. Asst. prof. English, U. Fla., Gainesville, 1963-67; assoc. prof., chmn. Loyola U., New Orleans, 1967-69; prof., chmn. U. Tenn., Chattanooga, 1969-73, U. Wyo., Laramie, 1973-82; prof., dean arts and scis. North Tex. State U., Denton, 1982—; chmn. Wyo. Council for Humanities, Laramie, 1976-77. Author: Not in Timon's Manner, 1975. Editor Jour. 18th Century: A Current Bibliography, 1985. Contbr. articles to profl. jours. Recipient NEH research stipend, 1979; George Duke Humphrey award U. Wyo., 1982; Am. Council Learned Soc. grantee, 1980. Mem. South Central MLA, Am. Soc. 18th Century Studies (editor jour. 1985), Coll. English Assn., South Central Soc. for 18th Century Studies (v.p. 1985—). Democrat. Anglican. Home: 2608 Jamestown St Denton TX 76201 Office: Coll Arts and Scis Denton TX 76203

PRESTWOOD, ALVIN TENNYSON, lawyer; b. Roeton, Ala., June 18, 1929; s. Garret Felix and Jimmie Mae (Payne) P.; m. Sue Burleson Lee, Nov. 27, 1974; children—Ann Celeste, Alison Bennett, Cynthia Joyce Lee, William Alvin Lee, Garret Courtney. B.S., U. Ala., 1951, J.D., 1956. Bar: Ala. 1956, U.S. Supreme Ct. 1972, U.S. Ct. Appeals (6th and 11th cirs.) 1981. Law clk. Supreme Ct. Ala., 1956-57; asst. atty. gen. of Ala., 1957-59; commr. Ala. Dept. Pensions and Security, 1959-63; sole practice, Montgomery, Ala., 1963-65, 77-81, 85— ptnr. Volz, Capouano, Wampold, Prestwood & Sansone, Montgomery, 1965-77, Prestwood, & Rosser, Montgomery, 1982-84. Chmn. legal com. Am. Nursing Home Assn., 1972; bd. dirs. Montgomery Bapt. Hosp., 1958-65; chmn. bd. mgmt. East Montgomery YMCA, 1969; pres. Morningview Sch. PTA, 1970. Served to 1st lt. U.S. Army, 1951-53. Recipient Sigma Delta Kappa Scholastic Achievement award U. Ala., 1956; Law Day Moot Ct. award U. Ala., 1956. Mem. Ala. State Bar (chmn. adminstrv. law sect. 1972, 78, 83), ABA, Fed. Bar Assn., Am. Trial Lawyers Assn., Montgomery County Bar Assn. (chmn. exec. com. 1971), Farrah Order of Jurisprudence, Phi Alpha Delta. Democrat. Baptist. Clubs: Montgomery Country, Capital City. Contbr. articles to legal jours. Home: 1431 Magnolia Curve Montgomery AL 36106 Office: One Court Sq Suite 209 Montgomery AL 36101

PRETLOW, CAROL JOCELYN, fashion consultant; b. Salisbury, Md., Nov. 9, 1946; d. Kenneth H. and Vivian Virginia (Hughes) P. B.A., Fish U., 1976; M.A., Norfolk State U., 1982. Fashion columnist The Smithfield Times (Va.), 1977-80; talk show hostess Sta. WAVY-TV, 1978-81; fashion editor Tidewater Life Mag., 1979; reporter, asst. news dir. Sta. WSNB News, Norfolk, Va., 1980-81; press sec. Com. to Elect Fred D. Thompson Jr. Treas. Isle of Wight County, 1981; ind. fashion cons., Smithfield, Va., 1982—. Coordinator Sesquitricentennial Celebration, Isle of Wight County, 1984. Home: RR3 Box 697 Smithfield VA 23430

PRETO-RODAS, RICHARD ANTHONY, modern language educator; b. N.Y.C., May 30, 1936; s. Manuel and Beatrice A. (Carvalho) P-R. B.A., Fairfield U., 1958; M.A. in Philosophy, Boston Coll., 1960; M.A. in Spanish, U. Mich., 1963, Ph.D. in Romance Langs., 1966. Asst. prof. modern langs. U. Fla., Gainesville, 1966-70; assoc. prof. U. Ill., Urbana, 1970-74; prof., dept. chmn., 1974-81; dir. div. langs. U. South Fla., Tampa, 1981—; reviewer Library of Congress Latin Am. Handbook, Washington, 1984. Author: Negritude in Poetry in Portuguese, 1972; Courtly Lore in Renaissance, 1972. Editor: (with others) Cronicas Brasileiras, 1973; 40 Historinhas, 1985; Empire in Transition, 1985. Mem. MLA, Assn. Depts. Fgn. Lang., Assn. Tchrs. of Spanish and Portugese, Phi Beta Kappa. Democrat. Avocations: swimming; gardening; running; biking. Home: 4483 Vieux Carre Circle Tampa FL 33613 Office: Div of Lang U South Fla Tampa FL 33620

PREUS, WILLIAM ALAN, marketing and insurance executive, mortgage broker; b. Montclair, N.J., June 14, 1950; s. S. William and Jean Ella (Pierson) P.; m. Ann Shirley Paulhus, July 20, 1974; children—Jeffery William, Sarah Anne. Student St. Petersburg Jr. Coll., 1968-70, U. South Fla., Tampa, 1970-71. Lic. mortgage broker, Fla. Sec., treas. Corp. Fin. Planning, Inc., St. Petersburg, 1971-73; v.p. Corp. Fin. Planning of Fla., Inc., St. Petersburg, 1973—; v.p. Mktg. Services of Am., Inc., St. Petersburg, 1980—; instr. in field. Ambassador-at-large City of St. Petersburg, 1970. Recipient numerous ins. awards. Mem. Internat. Platform Assn. Republican. Club: St. Petersburg Yacht. Lodges: Elks, Moose. Home: 758 61st Ave S Saint Petersburg FL 33705 Office: 1641 1st Ave N Saint Petersburg FL 33713

PREVATT, ROBERT WALDEMAR, citrus culture educator, consultant; b. Seville, Fla., May 15, 1925; s. Wallie A. and Elizabeth Mable (Frierson) P.; m. Edna Harmon, Sept. 12, 1953; children—Suzanne Kay, Carol Anne. B.S.A., U. Fla., 1948, M.S., 1951, Ph.D., 1959. Asst. to prodn. mgr. Dr. Phillips Co., Orlando, Fla., 1951-54; teaching asst. Agronomy Dept. Cornell U., Ithaca, N.Y., 1954-56; research agronomist Internat. Mineral & Chem. Corp., Mulberry, Fla., 1959-70; prof. Citrus Inst., Fla. So. Coll., Lakeland, 1970—, dir., 1980—, John and Ruth Tydall citrus chair, 1981. Mem. Am. Soc. Hort. Sci., Fla. State Hort. Soc. (v.p. 1983), Am. Rose Soc. (dir. 1971-76, 83—). Democrat. Methodist. Lodge: Kiwanis. Avocations: growing and lecturing on rose culture. Home: 2705 Collins Ave Lakeland FL 33803 Office: Fla So Coll Lakeland FL 33802

PREWITT, LENA VONCILLE BURRELL, educator; b. Feb. 17, 1932; m. Moses Kennedy Prewitt, Sept. 5, 1959; 1 child. B.S., Stillman Coll., 1954; M.S., Ind. U., 1955, Ph.D., 1961. Asst. prof. Stillman Coll., Tuscaloosa, Ala., 1955-57, assoc. prof., 1958, prof., 1960-67; assoc. prof., dept. chmn. Tex. So. U., Houston, 1967-69; assoc. prof. Florence (Ala.) State U., 1969-70; assoc. prof. human resource mgmt. U. Ala.-Tuscaloosa, 1970-74, prof., 1974—. Mem. Tuscaloosa Zoning Bd. Mem. Nat. Bus. Edn. Assn., AAUW, Acad. Mgmt., So. Mgmt. Assn., European Found. for Mgmt. Devel., Alpha Kappa Mu, Delta Pi Epsilon. Office: Dept Human Resource Mgmt U Ala 10 Woodridge Tuscaloosa AL 35401

PREYSZ, LOUIS ROBERT FONSS, III, management consultant, educator; b. Quantico, Va., Aug. 1, 1944; s. Louis Robert Fonss, Jr., and Lucille (Parks) P.; B.A., U. Wis., Madison, 1966; M.B.A., U. Utah, 1973; grad. Stonier Grad. Sch. Banking, Rutgers U., 1983; m. Claudia Ann Karpowitz, Sept. 9, 1967; children—Louis Robert Fonss IV, Christine Elizabeth, Michael Anthony, Laura Ann. Teaching and research asst. U. Utah, 1972-73; mktg. and personnel officer Security 1st Nat. Bank of Sheboygan (Wis.), 1973-76; mktg. dir. 1st Nat. Bank Rock Island (Ill.), 1976-77; asst. v.p., mktg. sales mgr. 1st Nat. Bank Birmingham (Ala.), 1977-78; v.p., mktg. mgr. Sun 1st Nat. Bank Orlando (Fla.), 1978-80; pres. Preysz Assos. (Fla.), 1980—; asst. prof. mgmt. and banking Flagler Coll., St. Augustine, Fla., 1982—; mem. part-time faculty U. Wis., 1973-76, Fla. Inst. Tech., 1976-77, St. Ambrose Coll., Davenport, Iowa, 1976-77, U. Central Fla., 1979-81, Columbia Coll., Mo., 1982; mem. Tng. and Profl. Devel. Council, Bank Mktg. Assn., 1976-78, chmn., 1978; mem. mktg. and public relations com. Wis. Bankers Assn., 1975; v.p. Ala. Automated Clearing House Assn., 1978; mem. Wis. Automated Clearing House Assn., 1975-76; mem. Rep. Presdl. Task Force, Rep. Nat. Com. Served to capt. U.S. Army, 1968-72; officer Fla. Army N.G. Mem. U. Wis. Alumni Assn., U. Utah Alumni Assn., Soc. Advancement Mgmt. (v.p., dir.), Nat. Geog. Soc., Phi Gamma Delta. Republican. Roman Catholic. Club: St. Augustine Officers. Lodge: Rotary. Author: How to Introduce a New Service, 1976; Energy Efficiency Programs and Lending Practices for Florida's Financial Institutions, 1980; Credit Union Marketing, 1981; An Effective Management Structure for Multi-Bank Holding Companies, 1983; contbg. editor: Target Market, an Instructional Approach to Bank Cross Selling of Services, New Accounts Training Manual, 1977; Tested Techniques in Bank Marketing, 1977; contbr. articles to mags. Home: 42 Southwind Circle Saint Augustine FL 32084 Office: PO Box 1027 Saint Augustine FL 32085

PREZIOSI, ROBERT CHARLES, management consultant; b. Washington, Feb. 6, 1946; s. Emil C. and Charlotte (Rohder) P.; B.A., Fla. Atlantic U., 1968, M.Ed., 1972; M.P.A., Nova U., 1976, D.P.A., 1977; m. Barbara Sue Brant, July 1, 1972; children—Lauren Marie, Carly Elizabeth. Tng. supr. Burger Castle, Miami, Fla., 1969; exec. dir. Youth Activities, Miami, 1970-74; program adminstr. Cath. Service Bur., Miami, 1974-78, personnel dir., 1978-80; v.p. staff devel. Am. Savs., Miami, 1980-83; v.p. Mgmt. Assocs., 1983-84, pres., 1984—; mem. faculty U. Miami, 1980, Biscayne Coll., 1980—, Nova U., 1979-84; cons. in field. Vice chmn. citizens adv. com. Dade County Schs., 1975-76; bd. dirs. Greater Miami Athletic Conf. Ofcls. Assn., 1973-78, Jr. Achievement, 1982-83. Recipient Man of Yr. award K.C., 1973; Contbn. to Edn. award Dade County Public Schs., 1975. Mem. Miami C. of C., Am. Soc. Tng. and Devel. (treas. Miami chpt. 1981, pres. 1983), Am. Mgmt. Assn. Democrat. Roman Catholic. Author articles in field. Home and Office: 18493 SW 83d Pl Miami FL 33157

PRICE, CHARLES EUGENE, lawyer, educator, consultant; b. Apalachicola, Fla., Mar. 13, 1926; s. Charles P. and Lela Frances (Joseph) P.; m. Lennie Florence Bryant, Nov. 30, 1946; 1 son, Charles Eugene (dec.). B.A., Johnson C. Smith U., 1946; A.M., Howard U., 1949; LL.B., Am. Sch. of Law, 1951; J.D., John Marshall Law Sch., 1968, also postgrad.; postgrad. Johns Hopkins U., Boston U., LaSalle Extension U., Carnegie-Mellon U., Emory U., Harvard U. Law Sch. Bar: Ga. 1968. Tchr. Ballard High Sch., Macon, Ga., also Rosenwald High Sch., Panama City, Fla., 1948-49; prof., dean Butler Coll., 1950-53, Fla. Meml. Coll., 1953-55; prof. Livingstone Coll., 1957-59; mem. nat. staff NAACP, 1955-57; sole practice law, Atlanta, 1968—; assoc. prof. Morris Brown Coll., Atlanta, 1960—, asst. dean, 1970-72; adj. prof. law John Marshall Law Sch., 1973-76; freelance writer; cons. Thomas & Russell Cons. Firm. Dir. Dekalb EOA, 1966-70; presdl. elector, 1972; adv. bd. SBA, 1974-82. Recipient award for outstanding service Ga. NAACP, 1966, Dekalb NAACP, 1967; named Tchr. of Yr., 1973, 82, Centennial Tchr. of Yr., Morris Brown Coll., 1981. Mem. State Bar Ga., ABA, Nat. Bar Assn., Gate City Bar Assn., Am. Polit. Sci. Assn., Alpha Kappa Mu, Alpha Phi Alpha. Presbyterian (ruling elder). Author: The Garvey Movement; columnist Atlanta Daily World, 1965-82, Pitts. Courier, 1955-57.

PRICE, GAIL ELIZABETH, public relations director, author, educator; b. Camden, N.J., Apr. 19, 1945; d. Joseph Washington and Elizabeth (Ahern) P.; m. Robert Alan Price, Apr. 5, 1969 (div. 1974); 1 child, Benjamin Joshua; m. Donald Ferrill Liscomb, Nov. 2, 1985; stepchildren—Dawn, Chance, Samuel, Lindy, Amy, Liberty, Mary Liscomb. A.B. in Polit. Sci. History, Douglass Coll., 1967; M.A. in Social Scis., Antioch U., 1969; M.A. in Lit. and Writing, Rutgers U., 1979; postgrad. Temple U., 1976-77, Glassboro State U., 1976. Cert. tchr., Calif. Tchr. English and social studies Unified Sch. Dist., San Francisco, 1969-74; asst. prof. English and sociology Camden County Coll., Blackwood, N.J., 1974-77; instr. English, Phila. Coll. Art, 1976-79, Rutgers U., Camden, N.J., 1977-79; regional tng. coordinator Legal Services Corp., Phila., 1980-84; dir. pub. relations Rocco Enterprises, Harrisonburg, Va., 1984—; adj. prof. communication arts James Madison U., 1985—; cons., writing instr. various univs., cos. and assns. Author-editor: (monthly column) Clearinghouse Review, 1983—. Author: Training Skills Development Manual, 1982; The Community as Textbook, 1970. Contbr. articles to profl. jours. Women's platform writer for George McGovern's Presdl. Campaign, 1972. Organizer, pres. Melville St. Neighbors, Phila., 1982-84; coordinator Rocco United Way Drive, Harrisonburg, 1984-85. Recipient Recognition of Service award Legal Services Corp., 1984. Mem. Am. Soc. Tng. and Devel. (v.p. 1983-84; Nat. recognition 1984), Internat. Assn. Bus. Communicators, Pub. Relations Soc. Am., Harrisonburg-Rockingham C. of C. (bd. dirs. 1985—). Democrat. Roman Catholic. Home: Price-Liscomb Farm Luray VA 22835 Office: Rocco Enterprises Inc 1 Kratzer Rd Harrisonburg VA 22801-0549

PRICE, JACK ERNEST, building materials company executive; b. Balt., Mar. 26, 1946; s. Roy Melvin and Claire Elizabeth (Baxter) P.; m. Linda Mary Rose, Nov. 20, 1971; children—Kenneth Edward, Daniel Allen. A.S.B., Ctr. for Degree Studies, Scranton, Pa., 1979; B.S.B.A., Thomas Edison Coll., Trenton, 1985. Key account mgr. Z-Brick, subs. VMC Corp., Woodinville, Wash., 1972-78; Eastern regional sales mgr. U.S. Gypsum Co., Chgo., 1978-82; nat. sales mgr. Hoyne Industries, McDonough, Ga., 1982-85; sales mgr. Perma-Bilt Industries, Atlanta, 1985—. Coach, Stone Mountain Soccer, Ga., 1985—. Served with USAF, 1966-69. Republican. Baptist. Lodges: Lions, Masons. Avocations: hunting; fishing; camping. Office: Perma-Bilt Industries 5350 Bucknell Dr Atlanta GA 30336

PRICE, JAMES, ophthalmologist, medical educator; b. Phila., July 13, 1935; s. Thomas H. and Kathryn E. (Redmond) P.; m. Ann L. Cottone; children—Victoria A., Pamella, Kathryn. M.D., Jefferson Med. Coll., 1963; M.Sc., Georgetown U., 1967; Ph.D., U. Calif.-Berkeley, 1972. Diplomate Am. Bd. Ophthalmology. Intern, Geisinger Med. Ctr., Danville, Pa., 1964; resident Georgetown U. Med. Sch., 1965-67; cons. Lawrence Radiation Lab., Berkeley, 1968-72; asst. prof. Tufts Med. Sch., Boston, 1971-74; prof., founding chmn. ophthalmology dept. Tex. Tech Med. Sch., Lubbock, 1974—; chief of service Boston VA Hosp., 1971-74, Lubbock Gen. Hosp., 1974—. Editor various ophthalmic lit., 1969-72. Bd. dirs. dist. 2-T2 Eye Bank, Lubbock, 1974—, Light House for Blind, Lubbock, 1971. Served with USMR, 1956-59. Research to Prevent Blindness grantee, 1974—. Fellow ACS; mem. Am. Acad. Ophthalmology, Assn. Research in Vision and Ophthalmology, AAAS. Home: 3303 58th St Lubbock TX 79413 Office: Tex Tech U Health Sci Ctr Lubbock TX 79430

PRICE, JOYCE ELLEN, real estate development company executive; b. Huntington, W.Va., Sept. 2, 1945; d. James Wallace and Estelle Elizabeth (Pemberton) P.; B.A., Ohio State U., 1968, B.F.A., 1968; Pres., Price, Ltd., Inc., Huntington, 1970—, Wallace Constrn. Co., Huntington, 1976-82, The P.C.T. Co. of Huntington, 1977-83; v.p., sec. James W. Price, Inc., Huntington, 1976—; partner The Ellenco Corp., Huntington, 1980-82; pres. Ellenco Corp., Huntington, 1983—. Bd. dirs., trustee The Herschel C. Price Ednl. Found., 1976—; mem. Republican exec. com. 9th Dist. Cabell County. Recipient Key to City of Huntington, 1979; trustee W.Va. Found. for Ind. Colls.; mem. adv. bd. Salvation Army. Mem. AAUW, Ohio State U. Alumni Assn., DAR, Huntington Area Businesswomen's Network, Ky.-Ohio-W.Va. Geneal. Soc., Altrusa Internat., Bus. and Profl. Women's Club (treas.), Huntington Area C. of C., Huntington-Cabell Rep. Women's Club, Nat. Fedn. Rep. Women (regent), Order Ky. Cols. Republican. Methodist. Club: Huntington Cotillion. Home: 2785 3d Ave Huntington WV 25702 Office: 3035 Merrill Ave Huntington WV 25702

PRICE, LIONEL FRANKLIN, lawyer; b. New Orleans, Mar. 14, 1940; s. Samuel and Elmay (Lightell) P.; m. Cory Jean Smith, Nov. 15, 1974; children—Daniel Saxon, Cassia Amber. B.A., La. State U., 1963; J.D., Tulane U., 1971; Bar: La. 1971, U.S. Dist. Ct. (ea. dist.) La. 1971, U.S. Ct. Appeals (5th cir.) 1971. Assoc. Flanders & Flanders, New Orleans, 1971-74; sole practice, Slidell, La. and New Orleans, 1974—; dir. Gulf Caribe Transport, Inc., New Orleans. Bd. dirs. Jefferson Mil. Coll. Found., 1983-84. Contbr. articles to profl. publs. Served to comdr. USNR, 1963—. Mem. ABA, La. Bar Assn., Naval Res. Assn. (chpt. v.p. 1978-80), Slidell Bar Assn., Delta Theta Phi (Outstanding Student award 1971). Home: 1509 Lakewood Dr Slidell LA 70458 Office: PO Box 1236 500 Pontchartrain Dr Slidell LA 70459

PRICE, MADELINE HOWELL, printing company executive; b. Bay Minette, Ala., Sept. 11, 1938; d. Julius Elvin and Annie Mae (Walker) Howell; 1 child, Cynthia Denise Jones Weathermon; m. Roy Franklin Price, June 2, 1973. Grad. Huffstetler Bus. Coll., Mobile, Ala., 1956. Sec., U.S. Air Force, Mobile, Ala., 1961-64, writer, editor, 1964-67; writer, editor U.S. Navy, Pensacola, Fla., 1967-70; personnel mgr. Den-Tal-Ez Mfg. Co., Bay Minette, Ala., 1973-80; personnel mgr. Poser Bus. Forms, Fairhope, Ala., 1980—. Mem. Am. Soc. Safety Engrs., South Baldwin Personnel Mgrs. Avocations: painting; reading; crafts. Home: 200 Jeff Davis St Fairhope AL 36532 Office: Poser Business Forms Fairhope Ave PO Box 409 Fairhope AL 36532

PRICE, ROSALIE PETTUS, artist; b. Birmingham, Ala.; d. Erle and Ellelee (Chapman) Pettus; m. William Archer Price, Oct. 3, 1936. A.B., Birmingham-So. Coll., 1935; M.A., U. Ala., 1967. One woman shows include Samford U., Birmingham, 1964, Birmingham Mus. Art, 1966, 73, 82, Town Hall Gallery, 1968, 75, South Central Bell, 1977; exhibited in group shows at Am. Watercolor Soc., N.Y.C., 1947, 74, Nat. Watercolor Soc., Los Angeles, 1945-48, 70, Watercolor U.S.A., Springfield, Mo., 1968, 71, 72, Rocky Mountain Nat., Golden, Colo., 1974, 80, Butler Mus., Youngstown, Ohio, 1970, Audubon Artists, N.Y.C., 1981, Ball State U., Muncie, Ind., 1972, 74, 78-82, Del Mar Mus., Corpus Christi, Tex., 1971, 73, 78, 83; represented in permanent collections at Birmingham Mus. Art, Springfield Mus. Art, South Central Bell, Birmingham, Samford U. Gallery, Southtrust Bank, Birmingham, First Ala. Bank, Birmingham; instr. Birmingham Mus. Art, 1967-70, Samford U., 1969-70. Bd. dirs. Birmingham Mus. Art, 1950-54, vice chmn., 1950-51. Recipient purchase award Watercolor, U.S.A., 1972; Silver Bowl award Birmingham Festival Arts, 1960. Mem. Birmingham Art Assn. (pres. 1947-49), Watercolor Soc. Ala. (sec. 1948-49), Nat. Watercolor Soc., Nat. Soc. Painters in Casein and Acrylic (W. Alden Brown Meml. award 1970, Joseph A. Cain Meml. award 1983), La. Watercolor Soc., So. Watercolor Soc., Watercolor Honor Soc. of Springfield (Mo.), Jr. League of Birmingham (chmn. art com. 1947-50), Pi Beta Phi. Episcopalian. Clubs: Window Box Garden, Birmingham Music (trustee 1956-66). Home: 300 Windsor Dr Birmingham AL 35209 Office: 2132 S 20th Ave Birmingham AL 35223

PRICE, SANDRA FREDERICK, business education educator; b. Hutchinson, Kans., Nov. 15, 1935; d. Homer William and Sarah Fern F.; m. Clifford Eugene Price, Sept. 9, 1956; children—Penny L., Tammy S. B.S., Athens Coll., 1969; M.S., Ala. A&M U., 1973; Ed.D., U. Tenn., Knoxville, 1982. Exec. sec. Thiokol Chem. Corp., Huntsville, 1960-63; instr. bus. edn. Oakwood Coll., Huntsville, 1967-78, head bus. edn. dept., 1978—; vis. prof. Ala. A&M U. Sch. Bus., NASA. Bd. dirs. North Huntsville Health Services, Inc., 1980-81, Big Cove Seventh Day Adventist Jr. Acad., 1980—. Named Tchr. of Yr., Oakwood Coll., 1983; Union Coll. scholar, 1954 Mem. Nat. Bus. Edn. Assn., So. Bus. Edn. Assn., Ala. Bus. Edn. Assn., Am. Vocat. Assn., Office Systems Research Assn., Adminstrv. Mgmt. Soc., Delta Pi Epsilon, Phi Delta Kappa, Pi Lambda Theta, Omicron Tau Theta. Seventh Day Adventist. Club: Big Cove Homemakers. Home: 188 Haden Rd Brownsboro AL 35741 Office: Dept Bus Oakwood Coll Huntsville AL 35896

PRICE, WILLIAM SOLOMON, JR., archives administrator; b. Asheboro, N.C., Jan. 19, 1941; s. William Solomon and Elizabeth (Rodwell) P.; m. Pia Tavernise, Dec. 19, 1964; children—Marie Elizabeth, Katherine Reynolds. A.B., Duke U., 1963; M.A., U. N.C., 1969, Ph.D., 1973. Head colonial records unit N.C. Div. Archives and History, Raleigh, 1971-75, asst. dir., 1975-81, dir., 1981—. Author: Not a Conquered People, 1975; editor: The Way We Lived in North Carolina (James Harvey Robinson prize 1984), 1983. Served to lt. USNR, 1963-66. Mem. Nat. Assn. Govt. Archives and Records Adminstrs. (v.p. 1984-86), So. Hist. Assn., Soc. Am. Archivists, Am. Assn. State and Local History, N.C. Lit. and Hist. Assn. (sec./treas. 1981-85). Methodist. Club: Raleigh Hist. (sec. 1983—). Avocation: jogging. Home: 3008 Mayview Rd Raleigh NC 27607 Office: NC Div Archives and History 109 E Jones St Raleigh NC 27611

PRICHARD, JOHN FRANKLIN, periodontist; b. Lancaster, Tex., Apr. 16, 1907; s. John Allen and Lillie (Hood) P.; m. Edna Crabtree, Nov. 6, 1928; 1 dau., Catherine Prichard Kaplan. D.D.S., Baylor U., 1928. Pvt. practice dentistry, Lamesa, Tex., 1928-30, Ft. Worth, 1930—; sr. cons. periodontal dept. U. Wash., Seattle, 1950—; vis. lectr. periodontal dept. U. Pa., Phila., 1946—; cons. in field to various jours. and publishers; periodontal cons. 27th edit. Dorland's Medical Dictionary; bd. dirs. Dental Services Corp., 1967-74. Trustee Baylor U. Coll. Dentistry, 1985—. Recipient Outstanding Alumnus award Baylor U. Coll. Dentistry, 1978; named to Baylor U. Hall of Fame, 1984; diplomate Am. Bd. Periodontology (vice chmn. bd. dirs. 1970-76). Fellow Tex. Dental Assn., Am. Acad. Periodontology, Am. Coll. Dentists, Am. Med. Writers Assn., S.W. Soc. Periodontology (ann. research prize named in his honor 1985), mem. Am. Soc. Periodontists (pres. 1964-65), Am. Acad. Oral Roentgenology, Internat. Assn. Dental Research, Southwestern Soc. Dental Medicine (pres. 1940-41), Ft. Worth Dist. Dental Soc. (pres. 1942), Delta Sigma Delta, Omicron Kappa Upsilon. Baptist (deacon 1936-70). Author: Advanced Periodontal Disease, 1965, 2d edit., 1972; Diagnosis and Treatment of Periodontal Disease, 1979, others; editorial cons. Internat. Jour. Periodontics and Restorative Dentistry; contbr. articles to profl. jours. Home: 5662 Westover Court Fort Worth TX 76107 Office: 3833 Camp Bowie Blvd Fort Worth TX 76107

PRICHARD, SANDRA SAVAGE, insurance agency executive; b. Springfield, Tenn., July 23, 1936; d. Thomas Mac and Mary Frances (Crocker) Savage; m. Grady Smith Prichard, Jan. 6, 1956; children—William, Robert, Teresa. B.S., Tenn. Tech. U., Cookeville, 1956; cert. of gen. ins. Ins. Inst. Am., Malvern, Pa., 1976. CPCU. Co-owner Prichard Ins. Agy., Inc., Clarksville, Tenn., 1967-70, Norman, Okla., 1970—; mem. ins. adv. bd. Moore-Norman Vo-Tch., Norman, Okla., 1978—. Mem. Soc. CPCUs, Nat. Assn. Ins. Women, Ins. Women Cleveland County (v.p. 1973, pres. 1974, 76), Bus. & Profl. Women. Baptist. Office: Prichard Ins Agy Inc 115 S Peters St Suite 5 PO Box 1372 Norman OK 73070

PRICKETT, GARY JAMES, paper products company executive; b. Paul's Valley, Okla., Oct. 21, 1950; s. Loy E. and Roberta (Wynn) P.; student Southwestern State U., 1968-69; B.A., So. Oreg. State Coll., 1973; m. Janet L. Haney, Sept. 21, 1971; 1 dau., Pamela Jean. Sales rep. Splevin's Music Corp., Los Angeles, 1973-74; asst. mgr. Thrifty Drug Stores, Inc., Los Angeles, 1974-75; store mgr., student store buyer UCLA, 1975-77; with Recycled Paper Products, Inc., Houston, 1977—, S.W. regional sales mgr., 1978-81, v.p. Western sales div., 1981—, dir., 1980—. Office: 4420 FM 1960 West Suite 227 Houston TX 77068

PRIDE, HERMAN ELFONNO, accounting educator; b. Delray Beach, Fla., Aug. 30, 1932; s. Herman A. and Gertrude Pride (Carter) P.; B.S., Savannah (Ga.) State Coll., 1965; M.B.A., Atlanta U., 1966; M.S.D., Am. Bible Inst., 1977; m. Joan Brown, June 12, 1964; children—Jamel, Laurie, Lasharn. Instr. acctg. and fin. Ala. State U., Montgomery, 1966-69; asst. dir. Am. Savs. & Loan League, Washington, 1969-70; exec. v.p. State Mut. Fed. Savs. & Loan Assn., Jackson, Miss., 1970-74; prof. bus. Tougloo Coll., Jackson, 1972-78; exec. v.p. TAG Ins. Agy., Dublin, Ga., 1978-82; instr. acctg. Palm Beach Jr. Coll., Lake Worth, Fla., 1982—. Served with USMCR, 1953-57. Mem. Internat. Assn. Fin. Planners, Profl. Inst. Agts. Assn., Life Underwriters Council, Full Gospel Businessmen's Fellowship (v.p.). Presbyterian. Club: Optimist. Author articles in field. Home: 1100 Stoneway Ln W Palm Beach FL 33409 Office: 4200 Congress Ave Lake Worth FL 33461

PRIEST, HARTWELL WYSE, artist; b. Brantford, Ont., Can., Jan. 1, 1901; d. John Frank Henry and Rachel Thayer (Gavet) Wyse; m. A.J. Gustin Priest, Aug. 4, 1927; children—Paul Lambert, Marianna Thayer. B.A., Smith Coll. Former tchr. graphic art Va. Art Inst., Charlottesville; former lectr. on prints and lithography. Exhibited one-woman shows Arjent Gallery, N.Y.C., 1955, 58, 60, 73, 77, 81, Va., 1969, 71, Pen & Brush, N.Y.C., 1973, invitational retrospective exhbn. McGultey Art Ctr., Charlottesville, Va., 1984; work represented in permanent collections Library of Congress, Washington, Norton Gallery, Palm Beach, Fla., Soc. Am. Graphic Artists, Hunterdon County Art Ctr., Longwood Coll., Smith Coll., Va. Mus., Richmond, Hunt Bot. Library, Pitts. Recipient awards for lithograph Field Flowers, Longwood Coll., 1965, Nat. Assn. Woman Artists, 1965, lithograph West Wind, A Buell award, 1961, print Streets of Silence, T. Giorgi Meml. award, 1973, lithograph Blue Lichen, Pen & Brush, 1984, award for collage, 1985; 1st award for graphics Blue Ridge Art Show, 1985. Mem. Nat. Assn. Women Artists, Pen & Brush, Soc. Am. Graphic Artists, Washington Print Club, 2d St. Gallery, Charlottesville, McGuffey Art Ctr. Avocations: playing recorder and piano, walking, singing. Home: 41 Old Farm Rd Bellair Charlottesville VA 22901 also Georgian Bay ON Canada

PRIGMORE, CHARLES SAMUEL, retired educator; b. Lodge, Tenn., Mar. 21, 1919; s. Charles H. and Mary Lou (Raulston) P.; A.B., U. Chattanooga, 1939; M.S., U. Wis., 1947, Ph.D., 1961; m. Shirley Melaine Buuck, June 7, 1947; 1 child, Philip Brand. Social caseworker Children's Service Soc., Milw., 1947-48; social worker Wis. Sch. for Boys, Waukesha, 1948-51; supr. tng. Wis. Bur. Probation and Parole, Madison, 1951-56; supt. Tenn. Vocational Tng. Sch. for Boys, Nashville, 1956-59; asso. prof. La. State U., 1959-64; ednl. cons. Council Social Work Edn., N.Y., 1962-64; exec. dir. Joint Commn. Correctional Manpower & Tng., Washington, 1964-67; prof. Sch. Social Work, U. Ala., 1967-84, cons., 1984—; chmn. com. on Korean relationships; Fulbright lectr., Iran, 1972-73; cons. Iranian Ministry Health and Welfare, 1976-78; Fulbright research scholar U. Trondheim (Norway), 1979-80; part-time cons. with four research projects, 1959-76; part-time tchr. U. Md., 1965-67; frequent lectr. and workshop leader. Chmn. Ala. Citizens Environ. Action, 1971-72, Tuscaloosa Council Environ. Quality, 1970-72; former mem. adv. com. Former Prisoners of War, VA; chmn. Ala. Prisoner of War Bd., 1984—; comdr. Ala. dept. Am. Ex-POWS, Inc., 1985-86; gov.'s liaison to U.S. Holocaust Meml. Council, 1983—. Served to 2d lt. USAAF, 1940-45; lt. col. Res. (ret.). Decorated Air medal with oak leaf cluster. Recipient Conservation award Woodmen of the World, 1971. Mem. Acad. Certified Social Workers, Am. Correctional Assn., AAUP, Am. Soc. Criminology, Am. Sociol. Assn., Council Social Work Edn., Nat. Assn. Social Workers, Nat. Council Crime and Delinquency, Royal Soc. Health, Tuscaloosa C. of C., Tuscaloosa Civitan Club, Alpha Kappa Delta, Beta Beta Beta. Club: Tuscaloosa County. Author: Textbook on Social Problems, 1971; Social Work in Iran Since the White Revolution, 1976; sr. author: Social Welfare Policy Analysis and Formulation, 1979; editor 2 books; contbr. articles to profl. jours. Office: Box 1935 University AL 35486

PRIGMORE, DONALD GENE, utility company executive; b. Leon, Kans., Sept. 26, 1932; s. Harry Edward and Mary Julia (Doyle) P.; m. June Mary O'Connell, May 15, 1970; children—Marc, Elizabeth Ann, Mary Kathryn, Christine. B.S.C.E., Kans. State Coll., 1955; M.B.A., U. Mich., 1958. Registered profl. engr., Mich., Ind., Tex. Spl. studies engr. Gen. Telephone Co. of Mich., Muskegon, 1958-62, div. mgr., Three Rivers, 1962-69, pres., Muskegon, 1979-81; plant dir., service dir. GTE Service Corp., N.Y.C., 1969-72, regional v.p. mktg. and customer services, Irving, Tex., 1978-79; v.p. ops. Gen. Telephone Co. of Ind., Ft. Wayne, 1972-76, Gen. Telephone Co. S.W., San Angelo, Tex., 1976-77; v.p. mktg. and customer services Gen. Telephone Co. S.W., 1977-78; pres. Gen. Telephone Co. S.E./Ky., Durham, N.C., 1981—; dir. Hackley Bank & Trust, 1979-81, Detroit Bank Corp., 1981. Mem. adv. bd. Ft. Wayne United Way, 1972-75; gen. chmn. Tom Green County (Tex.) United Way, 1978; bd. dirs. Mfrs. and Employers, Muskegon, Mich., 1980, West Shore Symphony, 1980, Muskegon County United Way; exec. com. ARC, 1980; trustee Greater Muskegon Indsl. Fund, 1980; bd. dirs. United Way of Durham and Durham County; mem. N.C. Citizens for Bus. and Industry; trustee Durham Acad., Historic Preservation Soc. Durham; bd. visitors Duke U. Engrng. Sch. Mem. Am. Mktg. Assn. (dir. Dallas chpt. 1978), Nat. Soc. Profl. Engrs., Durham C. of C. (bd. dirs.), Phi Delta Theta. Clubs: Hope Valley Country, Capital City. Home: 5 Littlewoods Ln Durham NC 27707 Office: 4100 N Roxboro Rd Durham NC 27704

PRIGOGINE, ILYA, physics educator; b. Moscow, Jan. 25, 1917; s. Roman and Julie (Wichmann) P.; m. Marina Prokopowicz, Feb. 25, 1961; children—Yves, Pascal. Ph.D., Free U. Brussels, 1942; hon. degrees, U. Newcastle (Eng.), U. Poitiers (France), U. Chgo., U. Bordeaux (France), numerous others. Prof., U. Brussels, 1947—; dir. Internat. Insts. Physics and Chemistry, Solvay, Belgium, 1962—; dir. Ilya Prigogine center statis. mechanics and thermodynamics U. Tex., Austin, 1967—. Author: (with R. Defay) Traite de Thermodynamique, conformement aux methodes de, Gibbs et de De Donder, 1944, 50, Etude Thermodynamique des Phenomenes Irreversibles, 1947, Introduction to Thermodynamics of Irreversible Processes, 1962, (with A. Bellemans, V. Mathot) The Molecular Theory of Solutions, 1957, Statistical Mechanics of Irreversible Processes, 1962, (with others) Non Equilibrium Thermodynamics, Variational Techniques and Stability, 1966, (with R. Herman) Kinetic Theory of Vehicular Traffic, 1971, (with R. Glansdorff) Thermodynamic Theory of Structure, Stability and Fluctuations, 1971, (with G. Nicolis) Self-Organization in Nonequilibrium Systems, 1977, From Being to Becoming-Time and Complexity in Physical Sciences, 1979, Order Out of Chaos, 1979, La Nouvelle Alliance, Les Métamorphoses de la Science, 1979. Recipient Prix Francqui, 1955; Prix Solvay, 1965; Nobel prize in chemistry, 1977; Honda prize, 1983; medal Assn. Advancement of Sci., France, 1975; Rumford gold medal Royal Soc. London, 1976; Descartes medal U. Paris, 1979. Mem. Royal Acad. Belgium, Am. Acad. Sci., Royal Soc. Scis. Uppsala (Sweden), Fgn. Assn. Nat. Acad. Scis. U.S.A., Soc. Royale des Scis. Liege Belgium (corr.), Acad. Gottingen Ger., Deutscher Akademie der Naturforscher Leopoldine (medaille Cothenius 1975), Osterreichische Akademie der Wissenschaften (corr.), Chem. Soc. Poland (hon.), others. Address: 67 ave Fond'Roy 1180 Brussels Belgium also Ilya Prigogine Ctr Statis Mechanics U Tex Austin TX 78712*

PRINCE, BILLY D., law enforcement official. Chief of police, Dallas. Office: City Hall Dallas TX 75201*

PRINCE, G. L. (JACK), JR., retail grocery executive; b. Carroll County, Ga., Feb. 4, 1922; s. Golie L. and Maude (Maxwell) P.; m. Catherine Pennington, Apr. 30, 1947; children—Mark M., Mitzi Prince Henley. Student W. Ga. Jr. Coll., 1940-41. Store mgr. to store trainer Kroger Co., Atlanta, 1945-55; gen. mgr. retail ops. Hudson & Thompson Co., Montgomery, Ala., 1955-59; owner, mgr. Piggly Wiggly Supermarket, Ft. Walton Beach, Fla., 1959—, Niceville, Fla., 1979—; dir. 1st City Bank, Prince, Inc., Wright Grocery Co., Penn-Max, Inc., Northgate, Inc., Wright Shopping Ctr., Inc., Prince Enterprizes. Former chmn. Okaloosa County Planning and Zoning Commn.; bd. dirs., past pres. local Humane Soc.; bd. dirs. Fla. Arthritis Found., 1969—, past pres. Northwest Fla. Region chpt. Served with U.S. Army, World War II; ETO. Mem. Food Mktg. Inst., Retail Grocers Assn. Fla., Nat. Grocers Assn., Ft. Walton C. of C. (past dir., com. chmn.), Com. 100 Okaloosa County. Lodges: Civitan, Elks.

PRINCE, M. DAVID, electronics and technical manager, computer graphics educator; b. Greensboro, N.C., Mar. 27, 1926; m. Fay Wright, June 8, 1947; children—Stephen, Nicholas, Timothy, Rebecca. B.E.E., Ga. Inst. Tech., 1946, M.S. in E.E., 1949. Project mgr. Ga. Tech. Engrng. Expt. Sta., Atlanta, 1952-57; sr. mem. tech. staff ITT Labs., Atlanta, 1957-59; sr. staff specialist Lockheed-Ga. Co., Marietta, 1959—; prof., lectr. Ga. Inst. Tech., 1980—; cons. Systems Cons. Assocs., Atlanta, 1970—; chmn. Electronics Automation Program, Computer-Aided Mfg. Internat., 1982-83. Author: Interactive Graphics for Computer-Aided Design, 1971; author articles; patentee computers and electronics. Served to ensign USNR, 1944-47. Named Engr.-Scientist of Yr., Lockheed-Ga. Co., 1981. Fellow IEEE. Avocations: Astronomy; bicycling; book collecting. Home: 3132 Frontenac Ct Atlanta GA 30319 Office: Lockheed-Ga Co D/72-96 Zone 410 Marietta GA 30063

PRIOR, DANIEL WALTER, human relations educator; b. Buffalo, Nov. 25, 1947; s. Walter A. and Mary F. (Green) P.; m. E. Dianne Hubbard, Aug. 14, 1971 (div. Dec. 1983); children—Shana R., Shawn R.; m. Mary Grimes, Dec. 25, 1983. A.A.S., Erie Community Coll., 1968; B.S., Evangel Coll., 1975; M.S., Pittsburg State U., 1977, Ed.S., 1978; Ph.D., Kans. State U., 1980. Nat. cert. counselor. Grad. asst. Pittsburg State U., Kans., 1976-78; instr. Kans. State U., Manhattan, 1978-80; asst. prof. Evangel Coll., Springfield, Mo., 1980-81; asst. prof. behavioral scis. La. Tech. U., Ruston, 1981—. Group facilitator Parents Anonymous, Ruston, 1984-85. Served with USN, 1968-73. La. Dept. Edn. grantee, 1983. Mem. Am. Soc. for Tng. and Devel., Am. Assn. for Counseling and Devel. Avocations: racquetball; fishing; cooking. Home: 2008 W California Ruston LA 71270 Office: La Tech U PO Box 10048 TS Ruston LA 71272

PRITCHETT, ALLEN HENRY, educational administrator; b. Mobile, Ala., Sept. 1, 1948; s. Ivan Murry and Elaine Rose (Struck) P.; m. Marion Patricia Valentine, Sept. 4, 1969 (div. July 1983); children—Allen Glenn, Michael Todd; m. Margaret Ann Cazalas, May 3, 1984. B.S., U. South Ala., 1970. Auditor Office Insp. Gen. USDA, Atlanta, 1970-73; internal auditor Babcock and Wilcox Co., Augusta, Ga., 1974-76; budget mgr. U. South Ala., Mobile, 1976-81, bus. mgr. coll. medicine, 1981—; treas. South Ala. Med. Sci., Mobile, 1982—; pres. bd. South Ala. Fed. Credit Union, Mobile, 1985, v.p., 1984. Asst. treas. South Ala. Polit. Action Com. Higher Edn., Mobile, 1981-82, treas., 1983, chmn., 1984, adv. com. 1985. Mem. Assn. Am. Med. Colls., Med. Group Mgmt. Assn. Methodist. Club: USA Coaches. Avocations: golf; fishing; travel. Home: 1009 Shady Brook Dr Mobile AL 36606 Office: U South Ala Coll Medicine CC/CB 290 Mobile AL 36688

PRITCHETT, ANNA MARIE WHITE, fashion consultant, pianist; b. Vienna, Ga., Feb. 10, 1941; d. James Edward White and Vivia Trippe (Waters) White-McDuffie; m. Carl Blair Pritchett, Jr., May 2, 1959 (div. 1965); children—Carl Blair III, Laura White. Student Perry Bus. Sch., Albany, Ga., 1966-68, U. Ga., Athens, 1974; student Alliance Theatre Sch., Atlanta, 1984—; grad. Columbia Sch. Broadcasting, 1985. Asst. to curator Swan House, Atlanta Hist. Soc., 1981-84; fashion cons. The Clothes Bin, Atlanta, 1984—, Play it Again, Atlanta, 1984—; pianist, network television performances include: Bob Crosby Show, 1955, Art Linkletter Show, 1955; classical pianist Bids for Broadway, WMAZ-TV, Macon, Ga., 1955-57; participant USA Honors Tour on television stas. in major cities, 1955. Contbr. articles to mags. Newsletter editor St. Patrick's Ch., Albany, Ga., 1968-70; asst. publicity chmn. Atlanta Met. Opera, 1979-81. Mem. Jr. League Atlanta (chmn. juvenile justice com. 1975, rep. to Council for Children, 1974-76), Nat. Council on Crime and Delinquency, Republican Senatorial Inner Circle, Successful Singles Internat., Nat. Trust for Hist. Preservation, Ga. Trust for Hist. Preservation. Episcopalian. Avocations: gourmet cooking, sewing, race walking, body building, water skiing. Address: 20 Springlake Pl NW Atlanta GA 30318

PRITCHETT, HOWARD CLEO, JR., pharmacist; b. Enterprise, Ala., Dec. 10, 1951; s. Howard C. and Winifred (Blair) P.; m. Suzanne Cox, June 12, 1971; children—Shay, Chad. A.S., Enterprise Jr. Coll., 1971; B.S. in Pharmacy, Auburn U., 1973. Registered pharmacist, Ala., Fla. Pharmacy intern Clark's Pharmacy, Opelika, Ala., 1974-75; pharmacist Smith's Pharmacy, Winter Haven, Fla., 1975-76, Liggett Rexall Drugs, Haines City, Fla., 1976-78; pharmacist, mgr. Lakeside Pharmacy, Avon Park, Fla., 1978—. Mem. Am. Pharm. Assn., Fla. Pharm. Assn. Baptist. Home: 1490 Silver Oak Dr Avon Park FL 33825 Office: Lakeside Pharmacy 2390 Beach Dr Avon Park FL 33825

PRITCHETT, LOIS JANE, counselor, educator; b. Phoenix; d. Harold Bruce Brown and Cora Jane (Burgin) Goodrich; m. David Lowrey Pritchett, Nov. 26, 1976; m. Lloyd Graper, Mar. 29, 1964 (dec. Dec. 1975); 1 child, Samuel Blair. A.B. in Edn., U. Ky., 1963; M.A. in Guidance and Counseling, Georgetown Coll., 1975; Ed.S. in Counseling, U. So. Miss., 1981. Cert. school psychologist, adminstr., supr., counselor, tchr. Tchr., Monticello Sch. System, N.Y., 1963-65, Fayette County Sch. System, Lexington, Ky., 1965-72, 76-77, 84—; tchr. Ocean Springs Sch. System, Miss., 1977-78, counselor/sch. psychologist, 1978-84. Den mother Pine Burr council Boy Scouts Am., 1980; Sunday Sch. tchr. 1st Bapt. Ch., Ocean Springs, 1982-84; cons. for teenage workshop Biloxi-Ocean Springs Jr. Aux., 1984. Recipient Outstanding Personnel and Guidance Program award Miss. Personnel and Guidance Assn., 1981. Mem. Nat. Bd. Cert. Counselors, Am. Assn. for Counseling and Devel., Am. Sch. Counselors Assn., Ky. Edn. Assn., Miss. Assn. for Psychology in the Schs., Alpha Delta Kappa. Democrat. Avocations: piano; raising plants; drawing; painting; bridge. Home: 2218 Bahama Rd Lexington KY 40509

PROCTOR, MELVIN P(ORCH), constrn. co. exec.; b. Cisco, Tex., Aug. 8, 1928; s. Jess and Ima (Leveridge) P.; student Cisco Jr. Coll., 1945, 47, U. Houston, 1949-51; m. Rita B. Henderson, Apr. 28, 1950; children—Stephen Jeffrey, Donna Rae, Linda Diane, Gwen Ann. Salesman, Able Supply Co., Houston, 1950-56; v.p. Thorpe Insulation Co., 1956-60; v.p. J.T. Thorpe Co., constrn., 1960-75, exec. v.p., 1975—, chief operating officer, dir., 1980—; dir., sec. Thorpe Realty Co., Houston, 1963-69; dir., sec.-treas. Thorpe Insulation Co., Corpus Christi, Tex., 1966—; dir., pres. Thorpe Equipment Sales Co., 1980—; exec. v.p. Thorpe Corp., 1984—; chmn., pres., chief exec. officer Sunbelt Constructors, Inc., 1985—; chmn., pres., chief exec. officer Thorpe Products Co., 1985—. Active, Boy Scouts Am. Served with AUS, 1946-47. Mem. Thermal Insulation Soc. (dir. 1959-61). Republican. Clubs: Glenbrook Valley Civic (dir. 1970-72), Golfcrest Country (Houston). Home: 7515 Rockhill St Houston TX 77061 Office: 6833 Kirbyville St Houston TX 77033

PROCTOR, RUTH NESBITT, marketing consultant; b. Cordele, Ga., Mar. 4, 1927; d. Thomas and Claire (Fletcher) Nesbitt; children—Claire Proctor Scheer, Sara Proctor Wakley, Rebecca Grier. A.B., Wesleyan Coll., 1948. With Fairhaven: Life-Care Retirement Home, Balt., 1977-80; dir. Evergreen House Found., Balt., 1981-82; with Bon Secours Heart Lands, Howard County, Md., 1982-83, Len Brook Sq. Found., Atlanta, 1983—. Sec., 2d Presbyn. Home of Md., Towson, 1974-77. Republican. Clubs: Woodland Garden (pres. 1962, 63, 64,; nat. award touch and smell garden), Federated Garden of Md. (publicity chmn.), Jr. League, Huguenot Soc. S.C. Home: 88 Sheridan Dr Atlanta GA 30305 Office: Lenbrook Sq Found 3747 Peachtree Rd Atlanta GA 30319

PROCTOR, TERRELL WILLIAM, lawyer, art gallery owner; b. Austin, Tex., Aug. 4, 1934; s. William Owen and Arlene G. (Holdeman) P.; m. Joan Farrar, Dec. 20, 1958 (div.); children—Douglas, David, Donna Proctor Kester, Diana. B.S. in Bus. Adminstrn., Tulsa U., 1957, postgrad., 1958; J.D., South Tex. Coll. Law, Houston, 1964. Bar: Tex. 1963, U.S. Dist. Ct. (so. dist.) Tex., U.S. Ct. Appeals (5th cir.) 1965. Pres., owner San Jacinto Gallery, also Proctor Supply, Houston, 1967—; mcpl. judge, Jacinto City, Tex., 1967-71, 73-74, city sec., 1967; city atty., Lomax, Tex., 1968-70; master 246th Dist. Ct., Houston, 1984; dean Proctor's Acad. Fine Arts, 1977—; prin. T.W. Proctor & Assocs., attys., Houston. Magician, 1958—; exhibited art, 1966—; represented in permanent collections Tex. Supreme Ct., Tex. Ct. Criminal Appeals, also other jud. offices; theatre and TV actor. Mem. Democratic Exec. Com., Houston, 1968-70; pres. Greater N.E. C. of C., 1970-72, Northshore Area Art League, 1980-81; bd. dirs. Baytown Art League, 1981-82, 82-83; del. Tex. Republican Conv., 1982. Served with USAF, 1952-60. Recipient awards for writing, 1963, 77, also awards for art. Mem. Tex. Bar Assn., Houston Bar Assn., North Channel Bar Assn. (treas.), Greater Northshore Area Bar Assn. (sec.-treas. 1967-81), Watercolor Art Soc., North Harris County Bar Assn. (pres. 1982), Assn. Trial Lawyers Am., Am. Judicature Soc., Harris County Criminal Lawyers Assn. (charter). Methodist (past trustee). Address: 630 Uvalde St Houston TX 77015

PROEFROCK, DAVID WAYNE, psychologist; b. Geneseo, Ill., June 26, 1950; s. Loren Wayne and Clara Darlene (Reiss) P.; m. Vicki Ialeen Gaither, June 20, 1970; children—Amy Elizabeth, Benjamin Wayne. B.S., U. Ill., 1972; M.S., Memphis State U., 1977, Ph.D., 1980. Lic. psychologist, Ga. Asst. prof. Augusta Coll., Ga., 1980-84; pvt. practice clin. psychology, Augusta, 1984—; cons. Richmond County Juvenile Ct., Augusta, 1981—, Project Head Start, Augusta, 1984—, Neuro Devel. Tng., Inc., Augusta, 1984—. Contbr. articles to profl. jours. Author weekly newspaper column Families, 1985—. Bd. dirs. Unitarian Ch. Augusta, 1985—, Girls Ctr., Augusta, 1985—, Augusta Area Mental Health Assn., 1985—. Served with U.S. Army, 1972-75. Mem. Am. Psychol. Assn., Assn. for Humanistic Psychology, Southeastern Psychol. Assn., Ga. Psychol. Assn., Augusta Area Psychol. Assn. (pres. 1983-84), Sigma Xi. Club: Augusta Track (v.p. 1983-84). Avocation: running. Home: 4684 Oakley Pirkle Rd Martinez GA 30907 Office: 551 Greene St Augusta GA 30901

PROEHL, ROBERT FRANCIS, marketing consultant; b. LaSalle, Ill., May 19, 1945; s. Arthur Francis and Ethel Hannah (Manahan) P.; student U. Md., 1964-67, Tarrant County Jr. Coll., 1969-70; m. Kathy Nell Kinser, Sept. 28, 1964; children—Sammye, Robert Francis. Writer, Allied Research Assos., Balt., 1968-71; tech. writer LTV Aerospace Corp., Dallas, 1968-71; tech. writer Electronic Data Systems, Dallas, 1971-73; pres. Omnigraphix Advt. Co. subs. Electronic Data Systems, Dallas, 1973-76; mktg. support mgr. Equimatics div. Informatics Inc., Dallas, 1976-78, dir. mktg., 1978-82, dir. microcomputer ops., 1982-83; pres. Robert F. Proehl & Assocs., 1983—. Area chmn. College Hills Fort Worth Republican Com., 1968. Served with USAF, 1963-67. Fellow Life Mgmt. Inst. (dir. North Tex. FLMI Soc.); mem. CUEFS Fin. Systems User Group (sec.-treas.), LIFE-COMM User Group (sec.-treas.). Home and Office: PO Box 12199 Saint Thomas VI 00801

PROFIT, LORETHA SPURS, educator; b. Monroe, La., Aug. 15, 1947; d. James and Willie Mae (Kiper) Spurs; B.A., N.E. La. U., 1976; m. Simon Profit, Jr., June 6, 1966; children—Anthony Simeon, Adriane Sirena, Simon, III. Asst. mgr. Nelsons Drive In and Motel, Monroe, 1966-68, mgr., 1970-73, co-owner, 1980-84; substitute tchr., vol. tutor Ouachita Prish Sch. Bd., Monroe, 1968-69, paraprofl. Swayze Elem. Sch., Monroe, 1973-76; tchr. 2d grade Woodlawn Elem. Sch., West Monroe, La., 1976—. Mem. NEA, La. Assn. Educators (polit. action com.), Ouachita Assn. Educators (faculty rep.), Classroom Tchrs. Assn., Northeast La. Reading Assn., Assn. Supervision and Curriculum Devel., Internat. Platform Assn. Lodge: Order Eastern Star. Home: 4005 Gaston St Monroe LA 71203 Office: Route 3 Box 126-C West Monroe LA 71291

PROPST, ROBERT B., U.S. district judge; b. 1931; m. Jo Griffin; children—Stephen, David, Joanne. B.S., U. Ala., 1953, J.D., 1957. Mem. Wilson, Propst, Isom, Jackson, Bailey & Bolt, 1957-80; judge U.S. Dist. Ct. for No. Ala., Birmingham, 1980—. Office: 341 Federal Courthouse Birmingham AL 35203*

PROSCHAN, FRANK, statistics educator; b. N.Y.C., Apr. 17, 1921; s. Israel and Rose (Gelman) Proschansky; m. Edna Mae Green, Mar. 21, 1952; children—Virginia, Michael. B.S., CCNY, 1941; M.A., George Washington U., 1948; Ph.D., Stanford U., 1960. Research statistician Sylvania Elec. Products Inc., Waltham, Mass., 1952-60; Boeing Co., Seattle, 1960-70; disting. prof. stats. Fla. State U., Tallahassee, 1970—. Author: Statistical Theory of Reliability, 1975; Mathematical Theory of Reliability, 1965. Named Disting. Alumnus, CCNY, 1980, Disting. Alumnus, George Washington U., 1978. Fellow Am. Statis. Assn. (Wilks award 1982), Inst. Math. Stats.; mem. Internat. Statis. Inst. Avocations: walking; swimming. Office: Fla State U Dept Stats Tallahassee FL 32306

PROVANCHER, ROBERT LEE, safety operations administrator; b. Portland, Oreg., Sept. 28, 1935; s. Arthur Irving and Louise Marie (Durrie) P.; m. Ruby Kate Johnson, Nov. 11, 1958 (div. 1966); m. Carol Ann Weber, Oct. 26, 1967; children—Anthony Lee, Michael Ray, Karen Marie. A.A. in Gen. Studies, Daytona Beach Community Coll., 1977; B.A. magna cum laude in Pub. Adminstrn., U. Central Fla., 1979, M.Pub. Policy, 1981. Cert. safety prof. Personnel technician U.S. Air Force, Korea, Caribou, Maine, 1956-59; nuclear weapons technician U.S. Army, U.S. Air Force, Washington, 1959-74; indsl. safety rep. Fla. Dept. Labor, Tallahassee, 1974-77; coordinator risk mgmt. Daytona Beach Community Coll., Fla., 1977-81; sr. safety engr. Martin Marietta Corp., Orlando, Fla., 1982-84, chief safety ops., 1984—. Pres. Daytona Beach Community Coll. Fed. Credit Union, 1981. Mem. Am. Soc. Safety Engrs., Central Fla. Chpt. of Am. Soc. Safety Engrs., Nat. Safety Council, Civitan Club (sec.-treas. 1976-77). Republican. Avocations: golf; model building. Home: 565 N Yonge St Ormond Beach FL 32074 Office: Martin Marietta Orlando Aerospace Sand Lake Rd PO Box 5837 Orlando FL 32855

PRUDEN, PETER DEWITT, III, packing company executive; b. Suffolk, Va., Mar. 8, 1945; s. Peter DeWitt and Judith Kline (Brothers) P.; m. Margaret Elizabeth Boucher, Mar. 23, 1968 (div. 1975); children—Peter DeWitt IV, Jonathan; m. 2d, Pamela Cutherell Taylor, June 11, 1977; children—Emily Brooke, Taylor Randolph. Student Coll. William and Mary, 1963-64; B.S., U. Richmond, 1968. Sales rep. R.J. Reynolds Tobacco Co., Norfolk, Va., 1968; treas. Pruden Packing Co., Inc., Suffolk, Va., 1969-72, pres., chmn. bd., 1980—; asst. trust officer Am. Nat. Bank, Portsmouth, Va., 1972-74; trust officer, v.p., sr. v.p. Citizens Trust Bank, Portsmouth, 1974-80; pres. Pruden Foods, Inc., Suffolk, 1981—; dir. Bunker Hill Foods, Inc., Bedford, Va.; dir., v.p. DeWitt Stuart, Inc., Suffolk; chmn. bd. Smithfield (Va.) Ham & Products Co., Inc.; dir. Old Dominion Investors Trust, Inc. Bd. dirs. Tidewater Estate Planning Counsel, 1979-80; sec., treas. Pruden Found., 1972—. Served with Army N.G., 1968-74. Republican. Episcopalian. Club: Norfolk Yacht and Country.

PRUETT, LILIAN PIBERNIK-BENYOVSZKY, music educator; b. Zagreb, Croatia, Yugoslavia, Oct. 15, 1930; came to U.S. 1950; naturalized 1955; d. Ivan I. and Mathilde (von Benyovszky) Pibernik; m. James Worrell Pruett, July 20, 1957; children—Mark Worrell, Ellen Sharon. Student Mozarteum, Salzburg, Austria, 1946-50; A.B., Vassar Coll., 1952; M.A., U. N.C., 1957, Ph.D., 1960. Instr. Miss Hall's Sch., Pittsfield, Mass., 1952-54, U. N.C., Chapel Hill, 1960-63; asst. prof. N.C. Central U., Durham, 1965-68, assoc. prof., 1968-73, prof. of mus., 1973—. Author and editor: (with others) Directory of Music Research Libraries: Czechoslovakia, Hungary, Poland, Yugoslavia. Mem. Am. Musicological Soc. (southeast chpt. pres. 1957-60, sec., treas. 1973-75), Am. Assn. for the Advancement of Slavic Studies, Southeastern Hist. Keyboard Soc. Home: 343 Wesley Dr Chapel Hill NC 27514 Office: NC Central U Durham NC 27707

PRUETT, THOMAS WILLIAM, optometrist; b. Pecos, Tex., Oct. 18, 1931; s. Thomas Benton and Bessie Mae (Sewell) P.; m. Carolyn Pessarra, Dec. 18, 1960; children—Tamara Tomlyn, Thomas Lloyd. A.A., Schreiner Inst., 1950; student Tex. Tech U., 1950-52; B.S., U. Houston, 1954, O.D., 1955. Mem. faculty Coll. Optometry U. Houston, 1954-55, 85; gen. practice optometry, Lake Jackson, Tex., 1956—; vol. dir. Methodist Eyecare Program in Mexico, 1982—; Tex. state dir. Vol. Optometric Service to Humanity, 1985—; optometric coordinator Christian Hands in Action, El Paso, Tex., 1984—. Mem. Brazosport C. of C. Methodist. Lodge: Rotary. Avocations: stamp collecting; public speaking. Home: 104 Post Oak St Lake Jackson TX 77566 Office: 109 Circle Way Lake Jackson TX 77566

PRUITT, CHARLES PINCKNEY, music educator, bandmaster; b. Williamston, S.C., Feb. 26, 1924; s. Jack Spear and Caroline Elizabeth (Koon) P. A.B., Newberry Coll., 1950; M.A., Columbia U., 1961. Tchr. music (band) York High Sch. (S.C.), 1950-56; assoc. prof. music Newberry Coll. (S.C.), 1956—; bandmaster 246th Army Band, S.C. N.G. Band, 1950—. Served with USAAF, 1943-46. Recipient Outstanding Prof. award Newberry Coll. Alumni Assn., 1969. Mem. Nat. Jazz Educator's Assn. (past pres. S.C. unit, outstanding music educator award 1973, Charles P. Pruitt music scholar 1983), Coll. Band Dirs. Nat. Assn., Nat. Guard Assn. U.S., N.G. Assn. S.C., Pi Mu Alpha. Home: 1241 Clarkson Ave Newberry SC 29108 Office: Newberry Coll Newberry SC 29108

PRUITT, PATRICIA NORDAN, safety specialist, occupational nurse consultant; b. Raleigh, N.C., Nov. 15, 1945; s. James Wilson and Annie Mitchell (Hogwood) Nordan; m. L. Frank Floyd, Jan. 26, 1962 (div. 1972); children—L. Frank, Jr., Amy Michell; m. Larry Wayne Pruitt, Apr. 14, 1984. B.S. in Nursing, N.C. Wesleyan Coll., 1980; A.A.S. in Nursing, Beaufort Community Coll., 1974. Registered nurse, N.C., Va. Nurse intensive care unit Rex Hosp., Raleigh, 1975-76; safety, med. adminstr. Rockwell Internat., Raleigh, 1976-81; fire, security inspector Miller Brewing Co., Eden, N.C., 1981-84; nurse, house mgr. Danville-Pittsylvania County Mental Health Service Bd., Va., 1984—. Mem. Am. Soc. Safety Engrs. Office: Danville-Pittsylvania County Mental Health Service Bd 506 Middle St Danville VA 24540

PRUZZO, NEIL ALAN, physician; b. Marion, Ohio, Sept. 25, 1941; s. Samuel Francis and Dorothy Fay (Burnoskey) P.; m. Judith Josephine Engel; children—Maria, Eric, Brian, Lisa. Cert. med. tech., radiol. tech. Midwest Med. Tech. Inst., 1964; B.S., Southwest State Coll., Weatherford, Okla., 1968; D.O., Kansas City Coll. Osteo. Medicine, Mo., 1973. Diplomate Nat. Bd. Physicians and Surgeons. Intern East Town Osteo. Hosp., Dallas, 1973-74; clin. asst. prof. dept. osteo. philosophy, principles and practice Tex. Coll. Osteo. Medicine, Ft. Worth, 1974—; practice medicine specializing in cranial osteopathy, Richardson, Tex., 1974—. Co-author: An Evaluation and Treatment Manual of Osteopathic Medicine, 1973, An Evaluation and Treatment Manual of Osteopathic Muscle Energy Procedures, 1979. Contbr. articles to profl. jours. Mem. Am. Osteo. Assn., Am. Coll. Sports Medicine (founding), Tex. Acad. Osteopathy, Cranial Acad., Am. Acad. Osteopathy. Jehovah's Witness. Avocation: reading. Home: 19 Willow Creek Pl Richardson TX 75080 Office: 1109 Hampshire Ln Richardson TX 75080

PRYOR, BOBBY JOE, insurance executive; b. Gallatin, Tenn., Aug. 7, 1948; s. Henry T. and Lillie Mae (Walker) P.; m. Paula J. Tyler, May 3, 1968. B.A., Fla. State U., 1970. Intelligence analyst Fla. Dept. Law Enforcement, 1970-73; spl. agt. Northwestern Mut. Life Ins. Co., 1973-74; sub-contractor, Tallahassee, 1974-76; loss control specialist Mobile Home Industries, Inc., Tallahassee, 1976—, asst. v.p., 1976—. Instr., ARC, Tallahassee, 1976-82; United Fund worker. Haydon Burns scholar, 1966. Mem. Fla. Assn. Ins. Agts., Profl. Ins. Agts. Assn. Fla. (dir.). Republican. Baptist. Club: Foremost Ins. Co. Hall of Fame. Office: 1309 Thomasville Rd Tallahassee FL 32303

PRYOR, DAVID HAMPTON, U.S. senator; b. Camden, Ark., Aug. 29, 1934; s. Edgar and Susan (Newton) P.; m. Barbara Lunsford, Nov. 27, 1957; children—David, Mark, Scott. B.A. in Polit. Sci, U. Ark., 1957, LL.B., 1961. Bar: Ark. bar 1964. Practiced in, Camden; mem. firm Pryor and Barnes; founder, pub. Ouachita Citizen newspaper, Camden, 1957-60; mem. Ark. Ho. of Reps., 1961-67, 89th-92d Congresses from 4th Dist., Ark.; gov., Ark., 1974-79, senator from, 1979—. Address: Russell State Office Bldg Washington DC 20510*

PRYOR, SANDRA JEANNE, clinical social worker; b. Miami, Fla., June 24, 1950; d. Leroy and Rosemary (Dailey) Stringer; m. Joe T. Pryor, Nov. 4, 1978 (div.); children—Archibald Claudius, Zenobia Joëlle. B.A., Barry Coll., 1972, M.S.W., 1976. Clk. Dade County Pub. Health Dept., Miami, 1972-74, clin. social worker, 1976-80; counsellor P.R.I.D.E., Inc., Homestead, Fla., summers 1974, 75; adminstrv. asst. Div. Aging Adult Services, Miami, 1975-76; clin. social worker United Family & Children Services, Miami, 1980-81; clin. social worker Jackson Meml. Hosp., Miami, 1981—, courtesy postor person for med. social workers, 1983. co-rep. Nat. Natural Hist. Study Sickle Cell Diseases, 1982-83; dir. psycho-social summer camp Dade County Sickle Cell Found., Miami, 1983; Chmn. citizen rating com. Dante Fascell's Office, Miami, 1973-74; area campaign coordinator for Pres. J. Carter, Miami, 1975. Elected to Hall of Fame Sta. WQAM, Miami, 1968; spl. minority scholar Barry U., 1974-76. Mem. Nat. Black Assn. Social Workers, Quintessence. Office: 794 NW 18th St Miami FL 33125

PRYOR, SHEPHERD GREEN, III, aeronautical engineer, lawyer; b. Fitzgerald, Ga., June 27, 1919; s. Shepherd Green, Jr. and Jeffie (Persons) P.; B.S. in Aero. Engring., Ga. Inst. Tech., 1947; J.D., Woodrow Wilson Coll. Law, Atlanta, 1974; m. Lenora Standifer, May 17, 1941; children—Sandra Anita Pryor Clarkson, Shepherd Green IV, Robert Stephen, Patty Jeanne, Alan Persons, Susan Lenora; m. Ellen Wilder, July 13, 1984. Engr., Hartford Accident and Indemnity Co., 1947-56; with Lockheed Ga. Co., 1956—, nuclear engr., 1958-64, research and devel. rep., 1964—; real estate salesman Cole Realty Co., Nelson Realty Co. Ga., also Valiant Properties, Marietta, Ga., 1955—; admitted to Ga. bar, 1974, U.S. Supreme Ct. bar; practiced in Atlanta, 1974—. Past pres. Loring Heights Civic Assn., Atlanta; mem. Sandy Springs Civic Assn., Devonwood br., Atlanta; trustee Masonic Children's Home, Atlanta. Served to capt. USAAF, 1942-45. Registered profl. engr., Ga.; lic. pilot. Mem. Am. Bar Assn., State Bar Ga., Mensa, Intertel, Sigma Delta Kappa, Pi Kappa Phi, Kappa Kappa Psi. Methodist. Club: Masons, Shriners. Home: 135 Spalding Dr NE Atlanta GA 30328

PRYOR, WILLIAM LEE, humanities educator; b. Lakeland, Fla., Oct. 29, 1926; s. Dahl and Lottie Mae (Merchant) P.; A.B., Fla. So. Coll., 1949; M.A., Fla. State U., 1950, Ph.D., 1959; postgrad. U. N.C., 1952-53; pvt. art study with Florence Wilde; pvt. voice study with Colin O'More and Anna Kaskas. Asst. prof. English, dir. drama Bridgewater Coll., 1950-52; vis. instr. English Fla. So. Coll., MacDill Army Air Base, summer 1951; grad. teaching fellow humanities Fla. State U., 1953-55, 57-58; instr. English, U. Houston-University Park, 1955-59, asst. prof., 1959-62, assoc. prof., 1962-71, prof., 1971—, assoc. editor Forum, 1967, editor, 1967-82; vis. instr. English, Tex. So. U., 1961-63; vis. instr. humanities, govt. U. Tex. Dental Br., 1962-63; lectr. The Women's Inst., Houston, 1967-72; lectr. humanities series Jewish Community Center, 1972-73; originator, moderator weekly television and radio program The Arts in Houston on KUHT-TV and KUHF-FM, 1956-57, 58-63. Bd. dirs. Houston Shakespeare Soc., 1964-67; bd. dirs., program annotator Houston Chamber Orch. Soc., 1964-76; narrator Houston Symphony Orch., Houston Summer Symphony Orch., Houston Chamber Orch., U. Houston Symphony Orch., St. Stephen's Music Festival Symphony Orch., Ind.; narrator world premier of The Bells (Jerry McCathern), U. Houston Symphony Orch., Am. premier Symphony No. Seven, Antartica (Vaughn-Williams), Houston Symphony Orch., Am. premier Babar the Elephant (Poulec-Francaix), Houston Chamber Orch., Le Roi David (Honegger), Voice of God in Opera Noye's Fludde (Britten), St. Stephen's Music Festival, 1981; bd. dirs., program annotator Music Guild, Houston, 1960-67, v.p., 1963-67, adv. bd. 1967-70; bd. dirs. Contemporary Music Soc., Houston, 1958-63; mem.-at-large bd. dirs. Houston Grand Opera Guild, 1966-67; mem. repertory com. Houston Grand Opera Assn. 1967-70; bd. dirs. Houston Grand Opera, 1970-75, adv. bd., 1978-79; mem. cultural adv. com. Jewish Community Center, 1960-66; bd. dirs. Houston Friends Pub. Library, 1962-67, 73-75, 1st v.p., 1963-67; adv. mem. cultural affairs com. Houston C. of C., 1972-75. Recipient Master Teaching award Coll. Humanities and Fine Arts U. Houston, 1980. Mem. Coll. English Assn., Modern Langs. Assn. L'Alliance Francaise, English-Speaking Union, Alumni Assn. Fla. State U., AAUP, South Central Modern Lang. Assn., Coll. Conf. Tchrs. English, Am. Studies Assn., Conf. of Editors of Learned Jours., Phi Beta (patron), Phi Mu Alpha Sinfonia, Alpha Psi Omega, Pi Kappa Alpha, Sigma Tau Delta, Tau Kappa Alpha, Phi Kappa Phi. Episcopalian. Contbg. author: National Poetry Anthology, 1952; Panorama das Literaturas das Americas, 4 vols., 1958-60; contbr. articles to scholarly jours. Home: 2625 Arbuckle St Houston TX 77005 Office: Dept English U Houston-University Park 3801 Cullen Blvd Houston TX 77004

PRYSBY, CHARLES LEE, political science educator; b. Olympia, Wash., May 11, 1945; s. Charles C. and Rose G. (Hakemian) P.; m. Anita D. Ebert, June 17, 1967; children—Nicole D., Michelle D. B.S. in Polit. Sci., Ill. Inst. Tech., 1966; Ph.D. in Polit. Sci., Mich. State U., 1973. NDEA fellow Mich. State U., East Lansing, 1966-69, instr. 1969-71; instr. U. N.C. at Greensboro, 1971-73, asst. prof., 1973-78, assoc. prof., 1978—; N.C. state mgr. News Election Service, N.Y.C., 1980—. Co-author: Voting Behavior: 1972 Election, 1975; Voting Behavior 1976 Election, 1978; Voting Behavior: 1980 Election, 1981; Political Choices, 1980. Contbr. articles to profl. jours. NEH summer seminar fellow, 1978, 83. Mem. N. C. Polit. Sci. Assn. (past-pres. 1984-85), Am. Soc. Pub. Adminstrn. (council mem. Piedmont Triad chpt. 1984-85), Am. Polit. Sci. Assn., Southern Polit. Sci. Assn., Midwest Polit. Sci. Assn. Democrat. Home: 3505 Redington Dr Greensboro NC 27410 Office: Univ North Carolina at Greensboro Dept Polit Sci Greensboro NC

PRZIREMBEL, CHRISTIAN ERNST-GEORG, mechanical engineering educator, consultant; b. Brunn, Germany, Mar. 30, 1942; s. Walter Louis and Irene Gertrude (von Wallenberg) P.; m. Donna Lee Faust, June 15, 1963; children—Christian Faust, Dawn Alee. B.S., Rutgers U., 1963, M.S., 1964, Ph.D., 1967. Asst. prof. mech. engring. Rutgers U., New Brunswick, N.J., 1967-71, assoc. prof. mech. engring., 1971-79, prof. mech. engring., 1979-81, assoc. dean acad. affairs, 1977-81; prof. and head mech. engring. Clemson U., S.C., 1981—; project engr. Exxon Research and Engring. Co., Linden, N.J., summer 1963, Florham Park, N.J., summer 1964; faculty fellow USAF/ASEE Research Program, Wright-Patterson AFB, summer 1976; cons. several indsl./law firms, N.J., 1971-81. Resources person bd. edn., Chester, N.J., 1978-81. Fellow ASME (Mid-Jersey sect. award 1963), AIAA (assoc.); mem. Am. Soc. Engring. Edn. (v.p., bd. dirs.), Sigma Xi, Pi Tau Sigma (gold medal 1973), Tau Beta Pi. Contbr. articles to profl. jours. Office: Dept Mech Engring Clemson U Clemson SC 29631

PSILLAS, GEORGE NICHOLAS, retail executive; b. Greenville, S.C., Jan. 26, 1946; s. Nicholas G. and Helen (Kurlas) P.; m. Della Trainor, Mar. 2, 1964 (div. 1982); children—Nicholas George; m. 2d, Frankie Sandra Wolfe, June 10, 1983. Student Furman U., 1964-65, Greenville Tech. Coll., 1965-68. Cert. pedorthist, S.C. With McMahan Shoes, Inc., 1965—, store mgr., Spartanburg, S.C., 1968, pres. Spartanburg office, 1980—; tax preparer H. & R. Block, 1984—; seminar chmn. fall seminar Prescription Footwear Assn., Spartanburg, 1978. Mem. Prescription Footwear Assn., Nat. Shoe Retailers Assn., C. of C., Southeastern Prescription Footwear Assn. (chmn. 1977-78). Home: PO Box 915 Spartanburg SC 29304 Office: 247 E Main St PO Box 955 Spartanburg SC 29304

PUCKETT, JAMES MANUEL, JR., genealogist; b. Oakman, Ga., Dec. 8, 1916; s. James Manuel and Alma (Willkie) P.; student West Ga. Coll., Emory U.; m. Robbie Horton, Sept. 13, 1944; 1 son, James William (dec.). Retail mcht., 1937-42; with Treasury Dept., 1944-53; public acct., 1955-60; feature writer Ga. Geneal. Soc. quar., 1965-75; genealogist, lectr., 1965—. Mayor of Oakman, 1940-42. Served with USNR, 1942-44. Mem. SAR, Sons Confederate Vets., Order Stars and Bars (Ga. comdr. 1966-70), Am. Hist. Soc., So. Hist. Soc., Ga. Hist. Soc., Internat. Platform Assn., Nat. Geneal. Soc., Nat. Hereditary Soc. Home: 1563 Runnymeade NE Atlanta GA 30319 Office: 240 Peachtree St NE Suite 10-J-10 Atlanta GA 30303

PUCKETT, LEON STEVENS, medical products company executive; b. Gladewater, Tex., June 3, 1934; s. Everett and Ruby (Stevens) P.; m. Dixie Joyce Mason, June 20, 1959; children—Tamela Dawn, Steven Ray, Robert Brian. B.B.A., Tex. Tech U., 1955. Test engr. Continental Oil Co., Ozana, Tex., 1959-64; mfg. mgr. Ethicon Inc., San Angelo, Tex., 1964—. Pres. Grape Creek Pulliam Ind. Sch. Dist., San Angelo, 1982-85, trustee, 1975-85; trustee Grape Creek Baptist Ch., San Angelo, 1982-85. Served with USN, 1955-61. Office: Ethicon Inc PO Box 511 San Angelo TX 76902

PUGA, SISTER MARY OF THE ANGELS, registered nurse; b. Mexico City, Sept. 12, 1925; came to U.S., 1956, naturalized, 1961; d. Franeisco de Puga and Guadalupe (Fuentes) deP. B.S., Chapman Coll., 1980. Joined Carmelite Sisters of the Sacred Heart, 1956; obstet. supr. St. Tevesita Hosp., Los Angeles, 1958-61, nursing service dir., Duaerte, Calif., 1961-64, ICU/CCU dept. supr., Los Angeles, 1964-79, ins. education dir., 1979-81, paramedic liaison instr., 1981-83; nursing service dir. Dimmit County Meml. Hosp., Carrizo Springs, Tex., 1983—; cons. Am. Heart Assn., Los Angeles, 1964, Paramedic Office, Los Angeles, 1973. Recipient award of merit Am. Heart Assn. Greater Los Angeles, Los Angeles County Heart Assn., 1973, Los Angeles County Paramedic Office, 1983. Mem. Am. Assn. Critical Care Nurses. Avocations: prayer life; classical music; reading; opera; tennis; trips to beach. Home: 1113 N 9th St Carrizo Springs TX 78834 Office: Dimmit County Meml Hosp 704 Hospital Dr Carrizo Springs TX 78834

PUGH, DONALD WAGNER, music educator, academic administrator; b. Houston, June 25, 1931; s. Tom H. and Nora Laverne (Wagner) P.; m. Dolores Earlene Taylor, Jan. 28, 1956; children—Mark Taylor, Keith Wayne, Andria Dawn. Mus.B., North Tex. State U., 1955, M. Music Edn., 1957; D. Music Arts, U. Tex., 1970; Dir. chorus Killeen Pub. Sch., Tex., 1956-67; teaching asst. U. Tex., Austin, 1967-69; chmn. music dept. Panola Coll., Carthage, Tex., 1970-72, Brazosport Coll., Lake Jackson, Tex., 1972-75, dean acad. edn., 1975—. Contbr. articles to profl. jours. Served with USN, 1951-53. Mem. Tex. Assn. Jr. and Community Coll. Instructional Adminstrs. (pres. 1982-83), Tex. Jr. Coll. Tchrs. Assn., Phi Delta Kappa, Pi Kappa Lambda, Phi Mu Alpha Sinfonia. Baptist. Lodge: Masons. Avocations: camping; music. Home: 113 Meadowbrook St Lake Jackson TX 77566 Office: Brazosport Coll 500 College Dr Lake Jackson TX 77566

PUGH, IRBY GENE, lawyer; b. Montgomery, Ala., Jan. 22, 1943; s. Bert O'Neal and Eliza Jordan (Owen) P.; m. Betsy Ann Kerner, June 18, 1961 (div. July 1967); children—Glenn Edward, Eric Norman, Lisa Michelle. B.S., Calif., Poly. Inst., 1966; postgrad. in engring. U. Fla., 1967-69, J.D., 1972. Bar: Fla. 1972, U.S. Ct. Appeals (5th and 11th cirs.) 1973, U.S. Supreme Ct. 1979. Sr. engr. Martin-Marietta Co., Orlando, Fla., 1966-69; mem. staff U. Fla., Gainesville, 1970-72; assoc. Groshorn, Nabors, Miller & McClelland, Titusville, Fla., 1972-73, Fernandez & Scarito, Orlando, 1973-75; ptnr. Barco & Pugh, Orlando, 1975-78; sole practice, Orlando, 1978—; numerous media appearances. Coach Little League baseball and football, Orlando, 1973-76; del. Fla. Democratic Conv., 1982; mem. Dem. Exec. Com., Orange County 1984, chmn., 1986—; Dem. candidate Fla. Ho. of Reps., 1984; appt. com. to preserve parks and open spaces Orange County Commns., 1986—. Recipient several awards Rotary, Kiwanis. Mem. Assn. Trial Lawyers Am., ABA, Nat. Assn. Criminal Def. Lawyers, Fla. Bar Assn, Sierra Club (various awards), League Conservation Voters (bd. dirs. 1982—, awards 1982-83). Office: 218 Annie St Orlando FL 32806

PUGH, NELDA JORDAN, business administrator educator; b. Birmingham, Ala., Aug. 5, 1935; d. Gordon Brookins and Nell (Jones) Jordan; m. Tillman William Pugh Jr., Dec. 18, 1954; children—Gordon Irwin, Tillman W., III (dec.). B.S., Samford U., 1955; M.A., U. Ala., 1961; postgrad., Cumberland Sch. Law, 1970-1972; Ed.D., Nova U., 1981. Instr. Jefferson County, Birmingham, 1965-69; educator Jefferson State Coll., Birmingham, 1969—; speaker Civic orgns., Birmingham, 1980—; sponsor Women on the Way, Birmingham, 1979-83; coordinator Ala. Bus. Communication Assn., 1983. Editor newsletter Jordans Journeys, 1980—; textbook editor. Seminar coordinator Winners Circle, Jamaica, 1981, YMCA, Birmingham, 1980. Mem. Nat. Bus. Law Assn., Am. Bus. Communication Assn. (proceedings reviewer 1984), Nat. Bus. Edn. Assn., Depta Pi Epsilon. Republican. Presbyterian. Club: Internat. Toastmistress (treas., pres., v.p., sec., del., 1976—). Avocations: genealogy; needlework. Home: 3723 Brookwood Rd Birmingham AL 35223 Office: Jefferson State Coll 2601 Carson Rd Birmingham AL

PUGLIESE, DONATO JOSEPH, political science educator, consultant, researcher; b. West Trenton, N.J., Mar. 25, 1930; s. Nicola and Candida (Rossi) P.; m. Margaret Snyder, Sept. 10, 1955; children—Donna Jeannette Pugliese Price, Philip Nicholas. A.B., U. Pa., 1951, M.Govt. Adminstrn., 1953; D.Pub. Adminstrn., Syracuse U., 1960. Research asst. Phila. Bur. Municipal Research, 1958-59; instr. Temple U., Phila., 1956-58; from asst. prof. to assoc. prof. U. Detroit, 1959-69; assoc. prof. U. Tenn., Knoxville, 1969-73; prof. polit. sci. Ga. State U., Atlanta, 1973—; asst. dir. pub. affairs program U. Detroit, 1962-65; cons. Citizens Research Council, Detroit, 1965-67, Gov.'s Office, Lansing, Mich., 1967-68, U.S. Office Personnel Mgmt., Atlanta, 1978-79. Author: Voluntary Associations: An Annotated Bibliography, 1985. Editor: (with others) Symposium on State Local Govt. Adminstrn. Jour., 1984. Contbr. articles to profl. jours., chpt. to book. Pres. Worthington Valley Neighbors, Decatur, Ga., 1979; pres. Family Sch. Assn. Friends Sch., Detroit, 1967; legis. reporter Phila. Com. City Policy, 1957, 59. Served with U.S. Army, 1953-55. Recipient Meritorious Service award S.E. Conf. for Pub. Adminstrn., 1982; Fed. Exec. Inst. fellow, 1971. Mem. Am. Soc. for Pub. Adminstrn. (mem. council 1972-75), Am. Polit. Sci. Assn., Am. Acad. Polit. Social Scis., S.E. Conf. Pub. Adminstrn., So. Polit. Sci. Assn., Omicron Delta Kappa. Avocation: woodworking. Home: 1565 Stoneleigh Way Stone Mountain GA 30088 Office: Ga State U University Plaza Atlanta GA 30303

PUGLIESE, TINA L(ORRAINE), public relations consultant; b. Summit, N.J., Nov. 6, 1943; d. Sante J. and Laura M. (Ghizzoni) Scarcia; m. Frank P. Pugliese, Jr., Aug. 25, 1968. B.A., Trinity Coll., 1965. Fashion coordinator Atlas Buying Corp., N.Y.C., 1965-67; asst. advt. dir. Vanity Fair Mills, Inc., N.Y.C., 1967-69; advt. pub. relations mgr. Roots Inc., N.J., 1969-70; treas. Inverness Capital Corp., Alexandria, Va., 1973-77; pvt. practice pub. relations cons. to businesses and assns. and polit. candidates, Washington met. area, 1977—. Mem. Pub. Relations Soc. Am. (accredited), Nat. Press Club, Publicity Club N.Y., Alexandria (Va) C. of C. (v.p., dir.), Nat. Assn. Female Execs. Republican. Roman Catholic. Office: 610 Madison St Alexandria VA 22314

PUJOL, HENRY LOUIS, semiconductor company executive; b. Havana, Cuba, Feb. 5, 1944; came to U.S., 1960; s. Henry Louis and Olga Teresa (Radelat) P.; m. Aida Maria Mata, July 4, 1964; children—Henry Louis, Mary Jean. B.E.E., CCNY, 1968; M.S. in Elec. Engring., Rutgers U., 1974. Technician, Consol. Edison Co., N.Y.C., 1963-68; asst. engr., 1968-69; mem. tech. staff RCA Corp., Somerville, N.J., 1969-74, mgr. applications engring., 1974-78; mgr. ops. solid state div., Palm Beach Garden, Fla., 1978—; instr. electronics Somerset County Vocat. Inst., Somerville, N.J., 1976-77. Pres., Band Parents Assn., Palm Beach Gardens High Sch., Fla., 1982—. Served with USNR, 1961-64. Recipient Outstanding Achievement award RCA Corp., 1983. Mem. Electronics Industries Assn., Am. Soc. Quality Control, IEEE. Republican. Roman Catholic. Club: National Exchange. Home: 10146 Daisy Ave Palm Beach Gardens FL 33410 Office: RCA Solid State Div 3900 RCA Blvd Palm Beach Gardens FL 33410

PULIDO, MIGUEL LAZARO, industrial and agricultural chemical marketing company executive; b. Cuba; s. José F. and María D. (Pérez) P.; m. María M. G. Tellechea, Oct. 4, 1957; children—Maria, Miguel; m. 2d, Janie Ham, Nov. 28, 1980; 1 son, Miguel James. Agrl.Engr., Havana U. (Cuba), 1956, Sugar Technologist, 1956; M.S., La. State U., 1961, Ph.D., 1965. Div. mgr. Agrl. and Indsl. Devel. Bank of Cuba, 1956-59; agrl. engr., Havana, 1959-60; asst. mgr. tech. services Velsicol Chem. Co., Chgo., 1965-67; with Bockman Labs, Inc., Memphis, 1967—, v.p. agrl. mktg., 1975-79, v.p. mktg. Western Hemisphere, 1979-80; v.p. internat. mktg. south Buckman Lars Inc., Memphis, 1980—; grad. asst. La. State U., 1962-65. Contbr. articles to profl. jours.; editor Fitopatología Mag., 1969-74; patentee. Pan Am. Union fellow, 1960-62. Mem. AAAS, Am. Phytopath. Soc., Weed Sci. Soc., Plant Growth Regulator Soc., Assn. Am. Inst. Biol. Scis., Internat. Sugarcane Technologists Soc., Am. Mgmt. Assn. Club: Holly Hills Country (Cobdoba, Tenn.). Lodge: Moose (Memphis). Home: 3083 Rising Sun Memphis TN 38134 Office: 1256 N McLean Blvd Memphis TN 38108

PULLEY, HUBERT CONLEY, English literature educator; b. Nashville, July 5, 1948; s. Leo and Mae Sue (Conley) P.; m. Semetta Mae Coure, June 10, 1972; children—Kristin, Tristan. B.S., Tenn. State U., 1974, M.A., 1977; postgrad. Vanderbilt U. Div. Sch., 1983—. Lic. to ministry Methodist Ch., 1972. Pastor, Key United Meth. Ch., Cookeville, Tenn., 1971-74; tchr. Nashville pub. schs., 1974-76; asst. pastor John Wesley United Meth. Ch., Nashville, 1975-84; assoc. pastor Gordon Meml. United Meth. Ch., Nashville, 1984-85; pastor Elder's Lillard's United Meth. Ch., Murfreesboro, Tenn., 1985—; instr. English, Tenn. State U., Nashville, 1976-85; instr. Middle Tenn. State U., Murfreesboro, 1985—. Recipient Crusade scholar award United Meth. Ch., 1975; Ethnic Minority scholar award Vanderbilt U., 1983. Mem. NAACP, Nat. Council Tchrs. English, United Methodist Ministers Alliance, Tenn. Edn. Assn., Nashville Council Tchrs. English, Southeastern Conf. on English in the Two-Yr. Coll., Tenn. State U. Alumni Assn. Democrat. Methodist. Author: Through a Glass Darkly, 1979; Turning Over A College Poetry Anthology, 1982; Reflections, Emotions, Experiences, Feelings, 1981. Office: Dept English Middle Tenn State U Murfreesboro TN 37132

PULLIAM, WALTER TILLMAN, newspaper publisher; b. Knoxville, Nov. 5, 1913; s. James Richardson and Jennie Blanche (Badgett) P.; m. Julia Hill Brownlow, Apr. 18, 1970; 1 child, Mrs. (Mary) Everette L. Doffermyre. B.A., U. Tenn., 1936. Copy editor Knoxville Jour., 1936; reporter Knoxville News-Sentinel, 1936-42, polit. writer, 1946; nat. affairs reporter, asst. city editor Washington Post, 1947-49; editor, pub. Harriman Record, Tenn., also pres., gen. mgr. Record Printing Co., Inc., 1949-77; pres. La Follette Press, Inc., 1968—; pub. La Follette Press, Tenn., Jellico Advance-Sentinel, Tenn., Town Crier, Lake City, Tenn. Author: Harriman: The Town that Temperance Built, 1977; also articles. Chmn. Indsl. Devel. Commn. Harriman; active Harriman Pub. Library Bd., Tenn. Hist. Commn., 1981—; founder, chmn. Tenn. Newspaper Hall of Fame, 1965—; v.p. Knoxville Opera Co.; pres. Tenn. Newspaper Found., 1980-84, Monteagle Assembly (Tenn.), 1979-83. Served with Mediterranean edit. Stars and Stripes, U.S. Army, 1942-46. Mem. Tenn. Press. Assn. (past pres.), East Tenn. Hist. Soc. (pres.), Tenn. Hist. Soc. (v.p.), Sigma Delta Chi. Presbyterian. Clubs: Nat. Press (Washington); Cherokee Country, LeConte (Knoxville). Rotary (past dist. gov.). Home: 1400 Kenesaw Ave Knoxville TN 37919

PULS, RICHARD JOHN, physician; b. Ft. Worth, July 14, 1925; s. George and Ada (Reinhardt) P.; m. Mary Janina Rentschler, June 11, 1950; children—Alan R., Gloria R., Larry E. B.A., U. Tex., 1947; M.D., Washington U., St. Louis, 1950; postgrad. So. Meth. U., 1962-68, U. Tex.-Dallas, 1970-75. Diplomate Am. Bd. Internal Medicine. Intern, Wesley Meml. Hosp., Chgo., 1950-51; resident Univ. Hosp., Columbus, Ohio, 1951-53, Parkland Hosp., Dallas, 1953-54; practice medicine specializing in internal medicine, Dallas, 1954—; med. dir. Procter & Gamble Mfg. Co., 1958—, Northhaven Nursing Home, Dallas, 1976-82; clin. asst. prof. medicine U. Tex. Health Sci. Ctr., Dallas, 1977—. Served with USNR, 1942-44, 46-50. Mem. ACP, Am. Soc. Internal Medicine, AMA, Tex. Med. Assn. (alt. del. 1982—), Dallas County Med. Soc., Dallas Internist Club. Republican. Presbyterian. Contbr. articles to profl. jours. Home: 6849 Greenwich Ln Dallas TX 75230 Office: 8215 Westchester St Suite 327 Dallas TX 75225

PULSIFER, ROY, transportation and financial consultant; b. Schenectady, Oct. 20, 1931; s. Joseph R. and Marie (Phillips) P.; B.A., Columbia U., 1953, M. Internat. Affairs, 1958, J.D., 1958; m. Maryann Foreman, Dec. 18, 1963. Bar: N.Y. 1958, U.S. Supreme Ct. Enforcement officer Internat. Air Transport Assn., N.Y.C., 1959-60; atty. adviser FAA, Washington, 1960-63; with CAB, Washington, 1963-82, asst. chief, routes div., office gen. counsel, 1968-70, asst. dir. Bur. Operating/Rights, 1970-78, assoc. dir. for licensing programs and policy devel. Bur. Domestic Aviation, 1978-82; transp. and fin. cons. Served with AUS, 1954-56. Recipient Meritorious Service award CAB, 1975. Mem. Am. Bar Assn., Am. Econ. Assn. Co-author govt. studies; contbr. articles to profl. jours. Home: 210 Lawton St Falls Church VA 22046

PULSIPHER, ALLAN GILBERT, economist; b. Denver, Sept. 24, 1938; s. Gilbert E. and Lois (Blanchard) P.; m. Lydia M. Mihelic, June 1, 1964; children—Anthony, Alexander. B.A. magna cum laude, U. Colo., 1961; Ph.D., Tulane U., 1971. Asst. prof. Tex. A&M U., Coll. Sta., 1964-68; assoc. prof. Southern Ill. U., Carbondale, 1968-77; sr. staff economist Pres.'s Council Econ. Advs., Washington, 1973-75; program officer Ford Found., N.Y.C., 1977-80; chief economist TVA, Knoxville, Tenn., 1980—. Mem. Phi Beta Kappa. Home: 4013 Alta Vista Way Knoxville TN 37919 Office: TVA 400 W Summitt Hill Dr Knoxville TN 37902

PULTE, WILLIAM JOHN, linguist, educator; b. Gainesville, Tex., Jan. 13, 1941; s. William John and Harriet Elizabeth (Thompson) P.; m. Kathleen Helene Burrow, Jan. 13, 1968; 1 child, Gregory Brian. B.A., North Tex. State U., 1964, M.A., 1966; Ph.D., U. Tex.-Austin, 1971. Staff linguist, dir. Cherokee Bilingual Program, Tahlequah, Okla., 1971-73; asst. prof. linguistics So. Meth. U., Dallas, 1973-78, assoc. prof., 1978—, dir. Bilingual Edn. Programs, 1975—; cons. Ctr. for Applied Linguistics, Arlington, Va., 1972-74, Cherokee Nation of Okla., Tahlequah, 1975—. Editor: Cherokee-English Dictionary, 1975. Contbr. articles on linguistics to profl. jours. Grantee U.S. Dept. Edn., 1979, 82, NSF, 1981. Fellow Am. Anthrop. Assn.; mem. Linguistic Soc. Am., Nat.

Assn. for Bilingual Edn. Democrat. Roman Catholic. Home: 9607 Kilarney Dr Dallas TX 75218 Office: Southern Meth Univ Dallas TX 75275

PURCELL, ED MILTON, banker; b. Las Vegas, N. Mex., Feb. 13, 1940; s. J.M. and Knight E. (Kornegay) P.; m. Susan Walker, Feb. 4, 1966; children—Paul, Patrick. Grad. U. Colo., 1973; So. Meth. U. Sch. Banking, 1979, Tex. Tech. U. Banking Sch., 1975. Mgr. Kroger Food Stores, Dallas, 1959-62, Patton Hood & Food Store, Duncanville, Tex., 1965-70; exec. officer Tex. Am. Bank, Duncanville, 1970—, dir., 1983—. Bd. dirs. Meth. Hosp., Dallas, 1980—; pres. Duncanville Ind. Sch. Dist., 1979-80, Am. Cancer Soc., Duncanville, 1979. Named one of Outstanding Young Men Am. 1970, Duncanville Jaycees Man of Yr., 1971. Mem. Duncanville C. of C. (dir. 1982—, pres. 1971), Am. Legion (comdr. 1970). Roman Catholic. Lodge: Lions (pres. 1983-84, dir. 1980—). Office: care Lions Internat PO Box 70 Duncanville TX 75116

PURCELL, GWENDOLYN, chemist; b. Maysville, Ga., July 5, 1933; d. Thornton and Lou Etta (Rumsey) P.; B.S. in Biology, Ga. State U., 1964. Dept. and shift supr. Linden Labs. Inc. (Upjohn Co.), Atlanta, 1959-74; chemistry supr. Cobb Gen. Hosp., Austell, Ga., 1976-77; chemist, med. technologist Kennestone Hosp., Marietta, Ga., from 1977; safety officer, mem. hosp. safety edn. com., nat. lab. week com., career counselor for hosp. in ref. to allied health, now clin. chemistry analyst; supr. Perimeter Med. Lab., Atlanta, 1984—. Active YWCA. Named Lab. Employee of Yr., 1982. Mem. Nat. Registry Clin. Chemistry, Am. Assn. for Clin. Chemistry, Am. Bus. Women's Assn., Am. Soc. Clin. Pathologists, Alpha Xi Delta. Baptist. Club: Order Eastern Star. Home: 1135 Corner Rd SW Powder Springs GA 30073 Office: St Joseph's Doctors Bldg II Suite 255 5665 Peachtree Rd NE Atlanta GA 30342

PURCELL, MICHAEL RAYMOND, architect; b. Niles, Mich., Dec. 30, 1948; s. Ray and Golda Mae (Lambert) P.; m. Nancy Elizabeth Cooper, Sept. 4, 1982; children—Colby Cooper, Wesley Amanda. B.S. in Architecture, U. Mich., 1971. Registered architect, Tex. Designer Skidmore Owings Merrill, Chgo., 1972-75; mgr. project, designer Interiors Inc., Chgo., 1976-79; project mgr. ASD Inc., Atlanta, 1979-80, Cooper Carry Interiors, Atlanta, 1980-82; mgr. interior architecture Gresham Smith & Ptnrs., Dallas, 1982-83; dir. interior architecture Pierce Goodwin Alexander, Dallas, 1983—. Mem. Speakers Bur. Dallas Sch. Dist., 1985; 1st v.p. Robert E Lee PTA, Dallas, 1985-86, recording sec., 1984-85. Recipient award Inst. Bus. Design, 1985. Avocations: tennis; martial arts; real estate investment. Office: Pierce Goodwin Alexander 2121 San Jacinto 1900 Dallas TX 75201

PURDIE, ALEXANDER M. (SANDY), JR., fin. corp. exec.; b. Atlanta, Aug. 12, 1945; s. Alexander M. and Nancy E. P.; B.B.A. in Mgmt., Ga. State U., 1969; m. Edie Crocker, Aug. 24, 1968; children—Heather, Scott, Craig. Mgr. instl. trading Fin. Service Corp., Atlanta, 1969-72; mgr. instl. trading, block trader, first v.p., mgr., dept. head Robinson Humphrey/Am. Express, Atlanta, 1972—, now sr. v.p., dir. block trading. Elder Clairmont Presbyterian Ch.; bd. dirs. Young Life Urban Atlanta. Served with USNR, 1965-68. Mem. Nat. Securities Traders Assn., Ga. Securities Traders Assn., Midwest Stock Exchange. Home: 1297 Heards Ferry Rd NW Atlanta GA 30328 Office: 3333 Peachtree St NE Atlanta GA 30326

PURDOM, HAROLD, diversified company executive; b. 1924; married. B.S., Abilene Christian Coll., 1947. Drilling engr., Shell Oil Co., 1947-57; gen. mgr. Buck Fishing Tool Co., 1957-61; div. mgr. Nitrogen Oil Well Service Co., a company of Big Three Industries Inc., 1961-63, br. mgr., 1963-70, mktg. mgr., 1970-72; v.p.-so div. Big Three Industries Inc., from 1972, now exec. v.p., also dir. Served to maj. USAR, 1944-66. Office: Big Three Industries Inc 3535 W 12th St Houston TX 77253*

PURDY, DEBORAH MITCHELL, information manager; b. Radford, Va., Mar. 15, 1954; d. Kenneth Willard and Lena Rachel (Quesenberry) M.; m. Jeffrey Ellison Purdy, Oct. 11, 1980; 1 child, Laura Kendra. B.A., Hollins Coll., 1975, M.A., 1976. Research scientist B, Va. Hwy. Transp. Research Council, Charlottesville, Va., 1975-80; sr. research scientist Kinton, Inc., Alexandria, Va., 1980-82; sr. systems analyst Advanced Tech., Inc., Reston, Va., 1982-83; mgr. fed. proposal group Data Gen. Corp., McLean, Va., 1983—. Contbr. articles to profl. jours. NSF fellow, 1972-74. Mem. Am. Psychol. Assn., Human Factors Soc., Fed. Ednl. Tech. Assn. Avocation: quilting. Office: Data Gen Corp 7927 Jones Branch Dr Suite 200 McLean VA 22102

PURDY, HELEN CARMICHAEL, librarian; b. Miami, Jan. 17, 1920; d. James B. and Alice Cornelia (Brown) C.; m. Joseph Lynn Purdy, Feb. 12, 1946 (div. Aug. 1971). A.B., U. Miami-Coral Gables, 1943; M.S., Fla. State U.-Tallahassee, 1957. Asst. dept. head U.S. Censorship, Miami, 1944-45; library asst. catalog dept. U. Miami, Coral Gables, 1946-56, cataloger, 1957-60, Fla. cataloger, 1961-77/78, head archive and spl. collections dept., 1978, 79—, senator Faculty Senate, 1967-71, mem. council, 1969-71; mem. Women's Adv. Com. on Acad. Affairs, Coral Gables, 1972-81. Mem. Citizens Crime Watch, Miami, 1980—; mem. Republican Nat. Com., Washington, 1981—; mem. Republican Party of Fla., Tallahassee, 1983—. Mem. ALA, Southeastern Library Assn., Fla. Library Assn. (div. vice chmn. 1958-59, chmn. 1959-60), Beta Phi Mu. Episcopalian. Home: 5824 SW 50th St Miami FL 33155 Office: Univ Miami Library Coral Gables FL 33146

PURI, RAJENDRA KUMAR, business and tax consultant; b. Hoshiarpur, Punjab, India, Dec. 22, 1932; came to U.S., 1965, naturalized, 1969; s. Harbans Lal and Satya Vati (Jerath) P.; children—Neena, Veana, Ram. B.S., Agra U., 1952; diploma in Russian Lang. and Lit., U. Delhi, 1958; postgrad. U. Wash., 1965-66, B.A., 1968, M.B.A., 1969: M.S. in Taxation, Golden Gate U., 1982. Customs officer Govt. of India, New Delhi, 1955-60; asst. treas. Merc. Bank Ltd., New Delhi, 1960-65; mem. staff Peat, Marwick, Mitchell & Co., C.P.A.s, Seattle, 1969-70; state exminer State of Wash., 1970-72, asst. supervising state examiner, 1972-74, supervising state examiner, 1974-77; internal auditor Lockheed Missiles and Space Co., Sunnyvale, Calif., 1977-79, sci. programming analyst, 1979-80, data processing specialist, 1980-84, sci. programming specialist, 1984—. Del., Wash. State Republican Conv., 1976, Snohomish County Rep. Conv., 1976; spl. advisor U.S. Congl. Adv. Bd., 1982-83. Mem. Am. Inst. C.P.A.s, Wash. Soc. C.P.A.s. Home: 2608 Hunlac Cove Round Rock TX 78681 Office: Lockheed Austin Div PO Box 17100 Austin TX 78760

PURKEY, WILLIAM WATSON, counseling and guidance educator; b. Shenandoah, Va., Aug. 22, 1929; s. Watson Shenk and Elizabeth (Reynolds) Purkey; children—William Watson, Jr., Cynthia Ann. Registered counselor, N.C. Tchr. Chatham Pub. Schs., N.J., 1958-61; prof. counseling, guidance U. Fla., Gainesville, 1964-76, U. N.C., Greensboro, 1976—. Author: Self Concept and School Achievement, 1970; (with others) Helping Relationships, 1978; (with others) Helping Relationship Sourcebook, 1978; (with others) Inviting School Success, 1984. Served with USAF, 1951-55, Recipient Disting. Alumnus award U. Va., 1983, Disting. Contbn. to Edn. award Lehigh U., 1983. Mem. Am. Psychol. Assn., Am. Assn. Counseling and Devel., Am. Ednl. Research Assn., Assn. for Supervision Curriculum Devel., Alliance for Invitational Edn. Home: 4407 Williamsburg Rd Greensboro NC 27410 Office: Sch Edn U NC Greensboro NC 27412

PURNELL, CHARLES GILES, lawyer; b. Dallas, Aug. 16, 1921; s. Charles Stewart and Ginevra (Locke) P.; m. Sarah Ellen Hupp, Feb. 21, 1945 (dec. Mar. 1981); children—Neva Marie, Sara Elizabeth Purnell Smith, Charles Hupp, John William. Student Rice Inst., 1938-39; B.A., U. Tex., 1941; postgrad. Harvard U. Bus. Sch., 1942; LL.B., Yale U., 1947. Bar: Tex. 1948. Ptnr., Locke, Purnell, Boren, Laney & Neely, Dallas, 1947—; exec. asst. to gov. of Tex., Austin, 1973-75; lectr. Taft Inst., U. Tex.-Arlington, 1972-74. Gov.'s Liaison Constl. Conv., 1973; chmn. Youth Care and Rehab. Task Force, Tex. Exec. Dept., 1973-74; vice chmn. Tex. Energy Adv. Council, 1974; mem. Med. Profl. Liability Study Commn., 1975—; bd. dirs. Dallas Council on World Affairs, 1965—, Tex. Soc. to Prevent Blindness, 1975—, Trinity River Authority of Tex., 1975-81, Tex. Good Roads/Transp. Assn., 1982—. Served to lt. USNR, 1942-45. Mem. ABA, Tex. Bar Assn., Tex. Bar Found., Beta Theta Pi, Phi Delta Phi. Episcopalian. Clubs: Yale, Dallas, Dallas Country; Headliners, Town and Gown (Austin); La Jolla (Calif.) Beach and Tennis. Home: 4502 Watauga Rd Dallas TX 75209 Office: Locke Purnell Boren Laney & Neely 3600 Republic Nat Bank Tower Dallas TX 75201

PURRINGTON, EDWARD C., opera administrator; b. Dec. 6, 1929; B.A., U. Mass., Amherst, 1951; M.F.A., Columbia U., 1958. Asst. to Gian Carlo Menotti in revival The Consul, N.Y.C. Opera, City Center, 1960; asso. prof. theatre and speech Notre Dame Coll. of S.I., N.Y., 1958-67; dir. devel. and public relations Opera Assn. of N.Mex., Santa Fe, 1969-71, bus. mgr., 1967-69, prodn. coordinator, stage dir., stage mgr., instr. apprentice artist program, co. mgr. 1961 tour to West Berlin and Belgrade, summers, 1959-67; chmn. dep. performing arts Coll. of Santa Fe, 1972-74, devel. officer for spl. acad. programs; gen. dir. Tulsa Opera, Inc., 1975—; grants panelist Nat. Endowment for Arts, opera, mus. theater, 1980-83, on-site evaluator Nat. Opera Inst., 1980—, grant rev. panelist, 1980, 81; mem. com., judge Met. Opera Auditions, Tulsa Dist.; chmn. San Francisco Opera Auditions, Tulsa, 1977-79; founding dir. Okla. Summer Arts Inst., pres. bd., 1978-79; dir., v.p. Opera Am., Inc., 1981-82; dir. numerous seminars and classes. Mem. Sigma Alpha Iota. Office: Tulsa Opera 1610 S Boulder St Tulsa OK 74119

PURTLE, JOHN INGRAM, justice Ark. Supreme Ct.; b. Enola, Ark., Sept. 7, 1923; s. John Wesley and Edna Gertrude (Ingram) P.; m. Marian Ruth White, Dec. 31, 1951; children—Jeffrey, Lisa K. Student, U. Central Ark., 1946-47; LL.B., then J.D., U. Ark., Fayetteville, 1950. Bar: Ark. bar 1950, Fed. bar 1950. Individual practice law, Conway, Ark., 1950-53, Little Rock, 1953-78; mem. Ark. State Legislature, 1951-52, 69-70; asso. justice Ark. Supreme Ct., 1979—. Tchr., deacon Baptist Ch. Served with U.S. Army, 1940-45. Mem. Ark. Bar Assn., Am. Judicature Soc., Am. Bar Assn., Ark. Jud. Council. Democrat. Office: Justice Bldg Little Rock AR 72201*

PURVIS, JOHN TAYLOR, neurological surgeon; b. Morristown, Tenn., Feb. 4, 1929; s. Robert Averette and Katherine (Taylor) P.; student Carson-Newman Coll., 1948-49; M.D., U. Tenn., 1953; m. Patricia Ann Lane, Sept. 24, 1971; 1 son, Robert Henson; children (by previous marriage)—Katherine Purvis Sharp, Elizabeth Harrison Purvis Grace, John Taylor, Allyn Hunter, David Chilton. Intern, McGill U. Royal Victoria Hosp., Montreal, Que., Can., 1953-54; resident in gen. surgery and neurol. surgery U. Va. Hosp., Charlottesville, 1956-60; commd. 1st lt. M.C., U.S. Air Force, 1953, advanced through grades to maj., 1963; chief dept. neurol. surgery USAF Hosp., Wright-Patterson AFB, Ohio, 1961-65; chief dept. neurol. surgery USAF Hosp., Clark Air Base, Philippines, 1965-66; ret., 1966; pvt. practice medicine specializing in neurol. surgery, Birmingham, Ala., 1966-67, Richmond, Va., 1967-68, Knoxville, Tenn., 1968—; asst. prof. neurol. surgery U. Ala. Med. Center, 1966—; attending neurosurgeon Ft. Sanders Presbyn. Hosp., chief surgery, 1976; attending neurosurgeon St. Mary's Meml., East Tenn. Baptist, East Tenn. Children's hosps.; clin. asso. prof. neurol. surgery U. Tenn., Knoxville; cons. Oak Ridge Asso. Univs. Bd. dirs. Park West Hosp., 1975-76; mem. exec. bd. Kidney Found. East Tenn. Diplomate Am. Bd. Neurol. Surgery. Fellow ACS; mem. Am., Tenn. (del. 1975-77) med. assns., Knoxville Acad. Medicine (chmn. legis. com. 1973-75), Congress Neurol. Surgeons, So. Neurosurg. Soc., Am. Assn. Neurol. Surgeons, Assn. Air Force Mil. Surgeons, Phi Gamma Delta, Phi Ki. Methodist. Club: Elks. Contbr. chpt. to book; papers to profl. jours. Home: Route 2 Smith Rd Concord TN 37720 Office: Ft Sanders Profl Bldg Knoxville TN 37916

PURVIS, WILLIAM ALEXANDER, educator; b. Kingstree, S.C., May 16, 1927; s. Dottie A. and Annie (Bradley) P.; m. Annie L. Green, Aug. 25, 1951; children—Bily, Barbara, Carl. B.A., Claflin Coll., 1975; M.Ed., S.C. State Coll., 1978. Joined U.S. Air Force, 1949; served in France, Japan, Vietnam; ret., 1969; supr. U.S. Post Office, Wilmington, Del., 1970-73; tchr./adminstr. Norway Jr. High Sch., S.C., 1975—; chmn. project com. PTA, Norway, 1974-82. Organizer Brookdale Civic Assn., 1974. Mem. S.C. Adminstrs. Assn., NAACP, Pi Gamma Mu, Omega Psi Phi. Democrat. Methodist. Lodge: Masons. Avocations: reading; gardening; travel. Office: PO Box 128 Norway SC 29113

PUSTAY, MICHAEL WALTER, management educator; b. N.Y.C., June 20, 1947; s. Walter and Catherine Bernice (Fay) P.; m. Zandra Leannette Zak, May 27, 1973; children—Scott Buckley, Katherine Duffy. B.A. summa cum laude, Washington and Lee U., 1969; M.Phil., Yale U., 1971, Ph.D., 1973. Asst. prof. econs. Purdue U., West Lafayette, Ind., 1973-78; assoc. prof. Bowling Green State U., Ohio, 1978-80; assoc. prof. mgmt. Tex. A&M U., College Station, 1980—, coordinator research Coll. Bus. Adminstrn., 1981—. Mem. Assn. Univ. Bus. and Econs. Research, Am. Econs. Assn., Phi Beta Kappa. Home: 201 Hensel Bryan TX 77801 Office: Dept Mgmt Tex A&M U College Station TX 77843

PUTNAM, JEB STUART, geophysicist; b. Corning, N.Y., Aug. 20, 1958; s. Harold Leonard and Betty Mae (Canfield) P.; m. Louise Bannister McCormick, July 10, 1982. B.S. in Botany, Kent State U., 1981, B.A. in Geology, 1981. Geophysicist, Profl. Geophys., Inc., Midland, Tex., 1981-84; group leader Geo-Mid Seismic Services, Midland, 1984—. Mem. Soc. Exploration Geophysicists, Am. Assn. Petroleum Geologists, Permian Basin Geophys. Soc. Republican. Avocations: gardening; racketball; fossil and mineral collecting. Home: 708 W Cuthbert St Midland TX 79701 Office: Geo-Mid Seismic Services 1515 Idlewilde Midland TX 79701

PUTNAM, RICHARD JOHNSON, SR., U.S. judge; b. Abbeville, La., Sept. 27, 1913; s. Robert Emmett and Mathilde (Young) P.; m. Dorethea Gooch, Jan. 27, 1940; children—Richard Johnson, Claude Robert, Mary Stacy, Cynthia Anne. B.S. cum laude, Springhill Coll., Mobile, 1934; LL.B., Loyola U., New Orleans, 1937. Bar: La. 1937. Pvt. practice, Abbeville, 1937-54; dist. atty. 15th Jud. Dist., La., 1948-54; judge 15th Jud. Dist. Ct., La., 1954-61; U.S. dist. judge West Dist., La., 1961—; sr. U.S. dist. judge, 1975—; temporary judge U.S. Ct. Appeals for 5th circuit; rep. of fed. cts. council La. Law Inst., 1976—; liaison judge for Western dist. 5th Circuit Archives-Hist. Com., 1980. Served from ensign to lt. (s.g.) USNR, 1942-45. Recipient Student Council Key Loyola U., 1937. Mem. Dist. Judges Assn., Am., La. bar assns., Fifth Circuit Dist. Judges Assn., Am. Legion, V.F.W., C. of C., St. Thomas Moore Soc. (Service award 1937), Delta Theta Phi. Club: K.C. (4 deg.). Office: US District Court Lafayette LA 70501

PUTNAM, RICHARD WORCESTER, dentist; b. Gainesville, Fla., Dec. 20, 1945; s. Charles Worcester and Jean Madden (Hampson) P.; m. Joanne White, Dec. 23, 1967; children—Joseph Worcester, Charles Jason. B.S. in Biology, Emory U., 1967, D.D.S., 1971. Instr. Camp Cherokee for boys, Clarksville, Ga., 1966-67; bus driver Atlanta Transit System, Atlanta, 1968-69; gen. practice dentistry, Blairsville, Ga., 1973—; staff mem. Blairsville Gen. Hosp., 1973-76, Union Gen. Hosp., Blairsville, 1974—; lctrs. Am. Cancer Soc., Union County Sch. System. Chmn. awards, publicity Union County Bicentennial Com., 1976. Served as capt. U.S. Army Dental Corps, 1971-73. Featured Country Dentist, Dental Mgmt. Mag., 1979; Fla. Bd. Regents scholar, 1967-71. Mem. Mountain Area Dental Study Group (founder), ADA, Ga. Dental Assn., Eastern Dental Assn., No. Dist. Dental Soc., N. Am. Norwegian Red Cattle Assn. (bd. dirs. 1983—, first registered breeder Norwegian Red cattle in Ga., 1974), Jaycees, Phi Gamma Delta (charter, treas. 1964-65, historian 1965-66), Delta Sigma Delta (social chmn. 1969-70). Lodge: Kiwanas (bd. dirs. 1974—, chmn. various coms. 1979-82). Avocations: kayaking; physical fitness. Home and Office: PO Box 827 Blairsville GA 30512

PYE, MARILYN ANN SHANHART, nursing home administrator, nurse; b. Rochester, N.Y., Nov. 11, 1943; d. Delos and Mildred Marie (Stabel) Shanhart; m. John Joseph Pye, Jan. 22, 1972 (div. Dec. 1982). Diploma Rochester State Hosp. Sch. Nursing, 1964. Registered nurse, N.Y., N.C.; lic. nursing home adminstr., N.C. Staff nurse Rochester (N.Y.) State Hosp., 1965-66, ARC, Rochester, 1966-72; staff nurse to dir. nursing to to adminstr. Lamb's Nursing Home, High Point, N.C., 1973-78; dir. nursing Unifour Med. Mgmt., Hickory, N.C., 1978-79, adminstr., various locations, 1979-85, Lexington and Winston Salem, N.C., 1979-85; adminstr. Michael Gerard, Inc., speech, phys., occupational therapies. Named Runner-Up Adminstr. of Yr., Unifour Med. Mgmt., 1983. Mem. N.C. Health Care Facilities Assn. Club: Southeastern Loners on Wheels Camping. Home: Route 6 Box 130B Winston Salem NC 27107 Office: Koger Exec Ctr Suite 25 Kinston Bldg 2303 W Meadowview Rd Greensboro NC 27407

PYFER, JEAN LOUISE, physical education educator, administrator; b. Downers Grove, Ill., June 6, 1936; d. Louis Aaron Pyfer and Florence (Swier) Luchene. B.S., Bradley U., 1963; M.S., Ind. U., 1967, D.Phys. Edn., 1970. Teaching asst. Bradley U., Peoria, Ill., 1961-63; tchr. Toulon Grad. and High Schs., Ill., 1963-65, Limestone High Sch., Bartonville, Ill., 1965-67; teaching assoc. Ind. U., Bloomington, 1967-70; prof. U. Kans., Lawrence, 1970-81; chmn. dept. phys. edn. Tex. Woman's U., Denton, 1981—; project dir. tng. personnel in edn. handicapped, Denton, 1982—. Author: (with others) Principles and Methods of Adapted Physical Education and Recreation, 1985. Contbr. phys. edn. manual, chpt. to book, articles to profl. jours. Mem. com. Am. Heart Assn. Tex. Affiliate, 1983—; bd. dirs. Assn. for Retarded Citizens, Douglas County, Kans., 1972-77. Mem. Am. Alliance for Health, Phys. Edn., Recreation and Dance (chmn. therapeutics council 1977-78, chmn. adapted phys edn. acad. 1982-83), Tex. Assn. Health, Phys. Edn., Recreation and Dance, Council Exceptional Children. Roman Catholic. Home: 1815 Creek St Denton TX 76201 Office: Tex Woman's U PO Box 23717 Denton TX 76204

PYLANT, KENNETH DEAN, II, association executive; b. Tampa, Fla., Dec. 10, 1950; s. Kenneth Dean and Faye (Ables) P.; m. Bethany Sharman, Dec. 19, 1981; 1 son, Kenneth Dean, III. B.B.A., Auburn U., 1973, M.B.A., 1975. Grad. tchr. mgmt. dept. Auburn U., 1973-75, sr. programmer, research data analyst, 1975-77, project leader adminstrv. data processing, 1977-79; coordinator alumni and devel. Auburn Alumni Assn., Auburn, Ala., 1979—; owner Pylant Enterprises; pres. Video Terminal Inc.; data processing instr.; cons. data processing various savs. and loan assns. Mem. Am. Assn. Info. Mgrs., Nat. Pilots Assn., Nat. Fedn. Ind. Bus., Asso. Info. Mgrs., Delta Nu Alpha. Republican. Mem. Ch. of Christ. Clubs: Saugahatchee Country, Elks. Home: 552 Sundilla Ct Auburn AL 36830 Office: 116 Foy Union Auburn University AL 36849

PYLE, FRANK LEFOREST, SR., lawyer; b. Lewiston, Maine, Aug. 9, 1919; s. Guy LeForest and Marguerite Marie (Chauvin) P.; m. Beatrice DeBacker, Nov. 29, 1968; children—Michael A., Susan B., Patricia M., Frank LeForest, Jr. A.B., U. Fla., 1946, J.D. with honors, 1949. Bar: Fla. 1949, U.S. Dist. Ct. (so. dist.) Fla. 1949. Sr. ptnr. Kinsey, Vincent & Pyle, P.A., Daytona Beach, Fla., 1949—. Chmn. Peabody Auditorium Adv. Bd., Daytona Beach, 1960-70; chmn. County Law Library Trustees, Daytona Beach, 1977-85, Jud. Nominating Commn., Fla., 1977-79; treas. Daytona Beach Art League, 1980—. Served to capt. U.S. Army, 1941-46, ETO; col. Res. Decorated Bronze Star (2), Purple Heart. Mem. ABA, Fla. Bar Assn., Volusia County Bar Assn. (pres. 1975-76), Judge Advocate's Assn., Fla. Bar (real property, probate and trust sects.), Am. Judicature Soc., U. Fla. Law Rev. Alumni, Res. Officers Assn., Mil. Order World Wars, Phi Delta Phi, Kappa Sigma (v.p. 1941). Democrat. Clubs: Halifax Yacht (commodore 1961), Daytona Playhouse (pres.). Lodge: Halifax Kiwanis (pres. 1962). Home: 416 Pelican Bay Dr Daytona Beach FL 32019 Office: City Center E 150 S Palmetto Ave Daytona Beach FL 32014

PYLE, RAYMOND JAMES, JR., outdoor advertising executive; b. Oak Park, Ill., Jan. 15, 1932; s. Raymond James and Bessie Inez (Osborn) P.; student U. Wis., 1951-56, U. Notre Dame, 1968; student mgmt. U. South Fla., 1972; m. Mabel Lee Freeman, June 28, 1952; children—Dale, David, Steven, Carol Lynn. Sales rep. Leader Dept. Store, 1955-57, London Wholesale Hardware, 1957-58; sales rep. Martin Outdoor Advt., 1958-65, gen. mgr., 1965-66, v.p., 1966-69, pres., 1969-76; Fla. regional mgr., v.p. Foster & Kleiser div. Metromedia, Tampa, Fla., 1976-82, sr. v.p., mgr. Eastern U.S.; bd. fellows, counselor U. Tampa, 1970-77. Former treas. Easter Seal Soc. Tampa, now bd. dirs.; bd. dirs. ARC Tampa; active Heart Fund, United Fund, Boy Scouts Am. Mem. Outdoor Advt. Assn. Fla. (pres.; Disting. Service award 1981), Inst. Outdoor Advt. S.E. U.S.A. (treas.), Tampa Advt. Fedn. (past pres.; Advt. Man of Year 1969, Silver Medal award 1979-80), Sales and Mktg. Execs. Tampa (past pres.; Sales and Mktg. Exec. of Yr. 1970, Top Mgr. of Yr. 1983), Mchts. Assn. Tampa (past dir.), Pi Sigma Epsilon. Democrat. Baptist. Clubs: University, Rotary (Tampa); Palma Ceia Golf and Tennis; Feather Sound Golf and Tennis; Masons. Home: 1206 S Suffolk Dr Tampa FL 33609 Office: 5555 Ulmerton Rd Clearwater FL 33520

PYLE, RONALD EDWARD, manufacturing company executive, scientist; b. Kerrville, Tex., Mar. 24, 1947; s. Gilbert Edward and Mary Ann (Treiber) P.; m. Katharine Reid Macpherson, Aug. 1, 1973 (div.); children—Keely Campbell, Trevor Reid. B.S. in Chemistry with honors, U. Tex.-Arlington, 1969; M.A. in Chem. Physics, Johns Hopkins U., 1970, Ph.D., 1974. Post-doctoral research assoc. dept. chemistry Johns Hopkins U., Balt., 1974-75; staff scientist chemistry div. Radian Corp., Austin, Tex., 1975-76, sr. scientist, group leader, 1976-77, sr. scientist Advanced Systems div., 1977-78; sr. scientist Analysis and Applied Research div. Tracor, Inc., Austin, Tex., 1978-81; prin. staff scientist, mgr. Analytical Labs, R. & Q.A. div. Motorola, Inc., Austin, 1981—. NSF fellow, 1971; Comml. Credit Corp. scholar. Mem. Am. Phys. Soc., Am. Chem. Soc., Instrument Soc. Am., Alpha Chi, Epsilon Phi, Sigma Xi, Phi Lambda Upsilon. Contbr. articles to profl. jours. Home: 13400 Wisterwood Austin TX 78729 Office: 3501 Ed Bluestein Austin TX 78721

QASIM, MOHAMMAD MUSTAFA, chemistry educator, researcher; b. Jerusalem, Aug. 2, 1936; came to U.S., 1958, naturalized, 1976; s. Mustafa Taha and Na'Ama Qasim; m. Marcia Mary Morgan, Feb. 18, 1960; children—Amal Mary, Laila Jihad. B.S., Findlay Coll., 1962; M.A. in Chemistry, Bowling Green State U., 1964; Ph.D., U. Cin., 1969. Postdoctoral research assoc. U. N.C., Chapel Hill, 1968-73, researcher dept. neurology, 1976-80; med. technologist, supr. N.C. Meml. Hosp., Chapel Hill, 1973-76; asst. prof. chemistry Shaw U., Raleigh, N.C., 1980-82, assoc. prof., 1982—; cons. chemistry dept. neurology U. N.C., Chapel Hill; del. Nat. Bur. Standards seminars, 1982, 83. Fulbright scholar Williams Coll., 1958-59; grantee Williams Coll., 1958-59, Bowling Green State U., 1962-64, U. Cin., 1965-68. Mem. N.Y. Acad. Sci., AAAS, Arab Am. Univ. Grads., Sigma Xi. Moslem. Club: Civitan (bd. dirs.) (Chapel Hill). Developer gen. technique for extraction polypeptides and inhibition of their enzymatic degradation; refined arginine vasopressin assay; developed radioimmunoassays for oxytocin, methionine, leucine enkephalins.

QUACKENBUSH, JOHN FREDERICK, clinical psychologist; b. Port Monmouth, N.J., Jan. 20, 1933; s. Charles Garner and Emily (Gross) Q.; B.S., Tulane U., 1954; M.A., Pa. State U., 1959, Ph.D., 1965; m. Mary Jane Campbell, Mar. 8, 1957; children—Stuart, Johanna, Diana, John. Dir. psychology Laurelton (Pa.) State Sch., 1960-68; dir. psychol. services Devereux Found., Victoria, Tex., 1968-82; lectr. U. Houston, 1972—; pvt. practice clin. psychology, 1968—; behavior scientist Victoria Family Practice Residency Program, 1982-84; mem. jurisprudence com. Tex. Bd. Examiners. Served with U.S. Army, 1954-56. Mem. Am. Psychol. Assn., Sigma Xi, Phi Kappa Phi. Club: Exchange. Office: 2701 Azelea St Victoria TX 77901

QUAKENBUSH, JOHN STEPHEN, linguist, Bible translator; b. Asheville, N.C., Sept. 29, 1956; s. John William and Louise (Hipps) Q.; m. Janice Ruth Noren, Jan. 9, 1983; 1 child, Amanda Noren. B.A., U. N.C., 1978; M.S., Georgetown U., 1981, Ph.D., 1986. Linguistic researcher Summer Inst. Linguistics, Huntington Beach, Calif., 1979-84, Quezon City, Philippines, 1984—. Nat. Merit Scholar U. N.C., 1974-78; Georgetown U. Grad. Sch. fellow, 1979-82. Mem. Wycliffe Bible Translators, Linguistic Soc. Am., Linguistic Soc. Philippines. Home: 108 Adams Hill Rd Asheville NC 28806 Office: Summer Inst Linguistics 12 Big Horseshoe Dr Quezon City Philippines

QUALLS, CORINNE, nurse, nursing adminstr.; b. DeQueen, Ark., July 17, 1932; d. Roy L. and Clarice M. (Brizendine) Johnson; diploma St. Joseph's Sch. Nursing, 1953; cert. in nursing home adminstrn. Grayson County Coll., 1974; lic. nursing home preceptor; children—Steven Qualls, Stacy Gaston, Shelta Quins, Sherri Brawner. Operating room, emergency room nurse Leflore County Hosp., Poteau, Okla., 1953-54; pvt. duty nurse, Okla. and Calif., 1954-63; night supr. Van Buren (Ark.) Hosp., 1963-65, Broken Bow (Okla.) Nursing Home, 1967-68; dir. of nurses, asst. adminstr. Morgan Nursing Home, Broken Bow, 1968-70; pres., owner Yes-Ter-Year, Inc., Saint Jo, Tex., 1970—, Muenster Manor, Inc., Saint Jo, 1977—. R.N., Tex., Ark., Okla., Calif.; lic. nursing home adminstr., Tex. Mem. Nat. Fire Protection Assn. (health care sect.), LWV. Republican. Baptist. Clubs: 20th Century (pres. 1973-74), St. Jo Band Booster (pres. 1972-73), St. Jo Riding. Home: 2 Capps Corner Rd Saint Jo TX 76265 Office: 405 W Boggess St Saint Jo TX 76265

QUALLS, PAUL DAVID, economics educator; b. Wichita, Kans., Nov. 6, 1938; s. Paul Matthew and Mae Elizabeth (McKinney) Q.; B.A., U. Fla., 1960, M.A., 1961; Ph.D., U. Calif., Berkeley, 1968; m. Wanda Fay Smith, June 3, 1961; children—Kimara Jean, Caroline Elizabeth. Asst. prof. econs. U. Md., College Park, 1968-74; vis. asst. prof. econs. U. Calif., Berkeley, 1969-72; cons. U.S. Dept. Transp., 1972-74; sr. staff economist Bur. of Econs., FTC, Washington, 1974-75, dep. asst. dir., 1976, asst. dir., 1977-78, dep. dir., 1978-79; prof., U. Tenn., Knoxville, 1979—, head dept. econs., 1979-83; cons. Assn. of Am. R.R.'s, 1979. Recipient Award for Excellence in Supervision, FTC, 1977; U. Fla. fellow, 1960-61; Nat. Resources fellow, Resources for the Future, Inc., 1966-67. Mem. Indsl. Orgn. Soc. (dir. 1977—, pres. 1979—), Am.

Econs. Assn., So. Econs. Assn., Phi Beta Kappa, Beta Gamma Sigma, Phi Kappa Phi. Editorial bd. Indsl. Orgn. Rev., 1977-82; co-editor Rev. Indsl. Orgn., 1983—; author: (with others) The U.S. Steel Industry and Its Internat. Rivals, 1977; editor: (with R.T. Masson) Essays on Industrial Organization in Honor of Joe S. Bain, 1976. Home: 9600 Perth Circle Knoxville TN 37922 Office: 512 Stokely Mgmt Center U Tenn Knoxville TN 37996

QUALLS, RODDY LEE, exploration company executive, geology consultant; b. Dublin, Tex., June 19, 1958; s. Robert Lee and Sonja Gail (Evans) Q.; m. Leann Rye, Aug. 21, 1982. Student Tarleton State U., 1978-79; B.S., Hardin-Simmons U., 1984. Petroleum geologist Chalmers Operating Co., Abilene, Tex., 1980-84; co-owner, mgr. Ron-Lan Exploration Co., Abilene, 1984—. Vol. Am. Heart Assn., Abilene, 1985—. Mem. Am. Assn. Petroleum Geologists, Abilene Assn. Petroleum Geologists, Abilene Gem Mineral Soc., Sigma Delta Sigma. Republican. Mem. Ch. of Christ. Avocations: water skiing, hunting, fishing, weight lifting. Home: 3742 Duke Ln Abilene TX 79605 Office: Rod-Lan Exploration Co 1502 N Second St Abilene TX 79601

QUAN, ALICE BROWNE, civic worker, clubwoman, philanthropist; b. Ft. Worth, Apr. 4, 1908; d. Virgil and Maimee Lee (Robinson) Browne; A.B., U. Okla., 1930, M.A. in History, 1939; m. Frank James Quan, Feb. 22, 1966; 1 son by previous marriage, Floyd Davis Raupe. Substitute tchr. history jr. and sr. high schs., Oklahoma City, 1941-45; Okla. state pres. Children Am. Revolution, 1941-45, hon. pres., 1945, nat. v.p., 1945-47, nat. librarian, curator 1947-51, editor 1st and 2d state yearbook, 1941-47; organizing regent, hon. regent DAR, Paul's Valley, Okla., 1947, Okla. state chmn. bldg. fund, 1950-52, Okla. state membership chmn., 1946-50, rec. sec. Okla. state officers club, 1960; Okla. state women's com. chmn. savings bond div. U.S. Treasury Dept., 1950-64; docent Bklyn. Children's Mus., 1940-41; mem. pres.'s council Sch. of the Ozarks, Mo., 1973—; mem. pres.'s council Oklahoma City, U., 1974-79; mem. women's com. Okla. Symphony Soc., chmn. 1950-52; v.p. Okla. Art Center, 1945-46, bd. dirs., 1972—; decoration chmn. Beaux Arts Ball, 1958; hospitality chmn. Town Hall, Oklahoma City, 1967-70; v.p. Civic Music Assn., 1974-75, bd. dirs., 1976-83; adv. com. Oklahoma City Sch. Music, 1975-81; program chmn. First Presbyn. Ch., 1978-81; bd. dirs. Oklahoma City Opera, Southwestern Hospitality; chmn. Phoebe Circle, 1976-77, Priscilla Circle, 1977-78; chmn. Oklahoma City chpt. UN Assn., 1981—; patron, mem. nat. council Met. Opera, 1977—; mem. Bishop's Council, 1980—. Recipient Outstanding Service award U.S. Treasury Dept. 1962; Spl. Service cert. ARC, 1942-46; Alice B. Quan wing dedicated Sch. Ozarks, 1981. Mem. Okla. Soc. Mayflower Descs., Soc. Old Plymouth Colony Descs., Soc. Descs. Knights Order of Garter (life), Jr. League Oklahoma City (sustaining), Okla. Sci. and Arts Found. (life), Sovereign Colonial Soc. Ams. Royal Descent (life), Order of Washington (life), English Speaking Union (travel chmn. 1974-76, chmn. membership com. 1976-78, program chmn. 1979-81), Colonial Order of Crown, Plantagenet Soc. (life), Okla. Assn. Women Hwy. Leaders (dir. 1966—), Magna Carta Dames (life; state regent 1982-84), Okla. Art League (pres. 1968-69), Okla. Heritage Assn. (dir. 1982-84), Gamma Phi Beta. Clubs: Ladies Music (v.p. 1957-64), Redbud Women's (pres. 1968-69), Oklahoma City Golf and Country, The Beacon, The '75, Lotus, Mayfair, Embassy (charter), Aristophanian, Colonial Bridge (trophy 1935). Address: 1304 Huntington Ave Oklahoma City OK 73116

QUATAERT, DONALD GEORGE, history educator; b. Rochester, N.Y., Sept. 10, 1941; s. William Leonard and Norine Louise (Katzenberger) Q.; m. 1963 (div. 1965); 1 dau., Laurie Ann; m. 2d, Jean Helen Grebler, Jan. 24, 1970; 1 son, Eliot James. Student, John Carroll U., 1959-60; A.B., Boston U., 1966; A.M., Harvard U., 1968; Ph.D., UCLA, 1973. Research, Turkey, W. Germany, Eng., 1970-71, Turkey, W. Germany, E. Germany, 1975; asst. prof. dept. history U. Houston, 1974-78, assoc. prof., 1978—, research Turkey, East Germany, West Germany, France, Austria, 1980-81. Fgn. Area Fellowship, 1970-72, Social Sci. Research Council fellow, 1975; U. Houston Research Initiation grantee, 1976, Faculty Devel. Leave and Research Enabling grantee, 1981; research grantee, Eng., 1985; Inst. Turkish Studies grantee, 1985; NEH Sr. fellow, 1986-87. Mem. Am. Hist. Assn., Middle East Studies Assn., Turkish Studies Assn.; assoc. mem. Inst. Turkish Studies. Author: Social Disintegration and Popular Resistance in the Ottoman Empire, 1881-1908: Reactions to European Economic Penetration, 1983. Book rev. editor Internat. Jour. Turkish Studies. Contbr. articles to profl. jours., bulletins. Office: Dept History U Houston Houston TX 77004

QUATTLEBAUM, LUCILLE SCONYERS, hospital administrator; b. Cottondale, Fla., Apr. 9, 1930; d. John Grady and Ida Mae (Roberts) Sconyers; m. Houston J. Quattlebaum, Aug. 2, 1947; children—Wayne, Fred, Tom, Michael. Grad. Campbell's Bus. Coll., 1950; grad. Sch. Allied Health Services Adminstrn. U. Ala. Sec. to adminstrn. S.E. Ala. Med. Center, Dothan, 1956-60, exec. sec., 1960-70, adminstrv. asst. to adminstrn., 1970-80, adminstrv. asst., 1980-84, asst. adminstr., 1984—. Mem. Community Services Com., Dothan, Ala. Recipient awards for outstanding service S.E. Ala. Med. Center, 1981, 82. Mem. Nat. Assn. Profl. Women, Ala. Hosp. Assn., Henry County Hist. Soc., Dothan C. of C. Baptist.

QUESENBERRY, KENNETH HAYS, agronomy educator; b. Springfield, Tenn., Feb. 28, 1947; s. James William and Cora Geneva (Moore) Q.; m. Joyce Ann Kaze, July 28, 1947; children—James Kenneth, Kendra Joyce. B.S., Western Ky. U., 1969; Ph.D. U. Ky., 1975. D. F. Jones predoctoral fellow U. Ky., Lexington, 1972-75; asst. prof. U. Fla., Gainesville, 1975-80, assoc. prof. agronomy, 1980—; pres. So. Forage Br., Gainesville, 1979-80. Contbr. articles to profl. jours. Deacon First Baptist Ch., Gainesville, 1979-82. Served with U.S. Army, 1969-71, Vietnam. Named Prof. of Yr., Coll. Agr., U. Fla., 1976. Mem. Am. Soc. Agronomy, Crop Sci. Soc. Am., Can. Genetics Soc., Gamma Sigma Delta. (pres. 1984-85). Democrat. Avocations: sports; antique furniture refinishing. Office: Univ Fla 2183 McCarty Hall Gainesville FL 32611

QUESTER, ALINE OLSON, economist, researcher; b. Rockford, Ill., Feb. 9, 1943; s. Rudolph Harold and Ethel Mildred (Hagge) Olson; m. George Herman Quester, June 20, 1964; children—Theodore, Amanda. B.A., Wellesley Coll., 1965; M.A., Tufts U., 1968, Ph.D., 1976. Instr. econs. Boston U., 1966-68; asst. prof. SUNY, Cortland, 1970-74, assoc. prof., 1974-81; mem. profl. staff Ctr. Naval Analyses, Alexandria, Va., 1981—; reviewer NSF, 1980—. Contbr. articles to profl. jours. Mem. editorial bd. Social Sci. Quarterly, 1978—. Woodrow Wilson fellow, 1966, 68; NSF grantee, 1982-83. Mem. Am. Econ. Assn., Mil. Ops. Research Soc. Home: 5124 N 37th St Arlington VA 22207 Office: Ctr Naval Analyses 4401 Ford Ave Alexandria VA 22302

QUIANTHY, RICHARD LEE, association executive; b. Memphis, Feb. 16, 1944; s. Louis Paul and Anne Loraine (Dunning) Q.; m. Pamela Catherine Rodriguez, Apr. 23, 1966; children—Patricia, Robert. B.A.E., U. Fla., 1966, M.A.E., 1967; Ed.D., Nova U., 1980. Faculty, Fla. Jr. Coll., Jacksonville, 1967-69; instr. Broward Community Coll., Pompano Beach, Fla., 1969-79, div. chmn. communications, 1979-80, div. dir. communication and humanities, 1981-85; exec. dir. Internat. Listening Assn. cons. in field. Mem. Fla. Speech Communication Assn., So. Speech Communication Assn., Speech Communication Assn., Assn. Communication Adminstrs., Fla. Assn. Communication Adminstrs., Fla. Devel. Edn. Assn., Fla. Assn. Community Colls. Democrat. Roman Catholic. Author: A Resource Manual to Aid in the Teaching of Nonverbal Communication, 1978; contbr. articles to profl. jours. Office: 1000 Coconut Creek Blvd Pompano Beach FL 33066

QUICK, ROBERT CARL, III, petroleum exploration company executive, geologist, geophysicist; b. Rochester, Ind., Mar. 26, 1945; s. Robert Carl II and Bette Jean (Hayden) Q.; m. Susan Marie Manley, Dec. 20, 1969; children—Rebecca Sue, Robert Carl IV, Joseph Brian, Bradley Thomas. B.A., Purdue U., 1964-71; M.S., Bowling Green State U., 1976. Geologist Ohio Civil Service, Bowling Green State U., Ohio, 1971-77; sr. geophysicist Gulf Oil, Houston, 1977-80; sr. geologist Natomas N.Am., Tulsa, 1980-82; pvt. practice cons. geologist, geophysicist, Tulsa, 1982-83; pres. Anchor Resources, Inc., Tulsa, 1983—, also dir.; cons. U.S. Geol. Survey, Kansas City, Mo., 1982. Tech. resource person Pub. Schs., Boy Scouts Am., Broken Arrow, Okla., 1980—; coach Youth Athletics, Broken Arrow, 1980—. Mem. Tulsa Geol. Soc., Oklahoma City Geol. Soc., Am. Assn. Petroleum Geologists; Soc. Exploration Geophysicists. Club: Young Men's (Tulsa). Avocations: photography; camping; hiking; tennis. Home: 6410 S 221 E Ave Broken Arrow OK 74014 Office: Anchor Resources Inc 1851 E 71st St Tulsa OK 74136

QUICK, T.C., dentist; b. Jasper, Tex., Sept. 13, 1935; s. Roy C. and Versie N. (Hyden) Q.; m. Mary E. Byerly, June 8, 1957; children—Paul Tyson, Thomas Randall. Student, Sam Houston State U., 1957; D.D.S., U. Tex., 1961. Gen. practice dentistry, Jasper, Tex., 1961—. Mem. Sabine Dist Dental Soc., Tex. Dental Assn., ADA. Democrat. Baptist. Lodge: Kiwanis (pres. Jasper chpt. 1965). Avocations: hunting; bass fishing. Office: 364 N Zavalla St Jasper TX 75951

QUICK, VAN DYKE, college administrator; b. Hazlehurst, Miss., Mar. 26, 1933; s. H.T. and Mary V. (Gillis) Hurst; m. Shelly Marie Smyly, June 12, 1955; children—Karon Lynn Quick McMillan, Sharon Lee. M.Div., No. Bapt. Sem., New Orleans, 1958; M.Ed., Miss. Coll., 1965; Ed.D., Miss. State U., 1974. Minister of youth Bellevue Bapt. Ch., Memphis, 1958-60; adminstr. Miss. Coll., Clinton, 1960-84, v.p., 1975—. Served to col. U.S. Army, 1957-84. Mem. Reserve Officers Assn., Soc. Mil. Engrs., Assn. Mil. Chaplains, Nat. Assn. Student Personnel Adminstrs., Miss. Ofcls. Assn., Phi Delta Kappa. Home: Box 211 Clinton MS 39056 Office: Miss Coll Box 4066 Clinton MS 39058

QUIETT, KENNETH RAY, sociology educator; b. Levelland, Tex., Nov. 8, 1934; s. Norris Harbin and Ida Veomia (Lobstein) Q.; m. Connie Claude Gerlach, Mar. 4, 1956; children—Karry Brent, Karis Lachelle. B.A., Baylor U., 1956; M.Div., Southwestern Theol. Sem., 1959; M.A., Okla. U., 1967; Ph.D., Okla. State U., 1977. Dir. Baptist Student Union, Ada., Okla., 1959-64; asst. prof. East Central U., Ada., 1964-77, assoc. prof., 1977-81, prof. sociology, 1981—, chmn. dept. sociology, 1972-84, chmn. div. social sci., 1984—; cons. State Dept. Edn., Oklahoma City, 1974-79. Author: Modern Memory Course, 1974; Building Self Esteem, 1980; Dealing with Personal Criticism, 1980. Editor Free Inquiry, 1972-74. Bd. dirs. Arts and Humanities Council, Ada, 1979-81, Area Services for Battered Women, Ada, 1982-84, Ada Airport Commn., 1979—. NSF faculty fellow, 1971-72. Mem. Am. Sociol. Assn., Okla. Sociol. Assn. (pres. 1979-80), USA Transactional Analysis Assn., Internat. Transactional Analysis Assn. (cert.), Assn. for Counseling and Devel. Republican. Baptist. Lodge: Bd. dirs. 1973-74). Avocations: woodworking; flying private airplane. Home: 515 Hillcrest Ada OK 74820 Office: East Central U Social Scis Div Ada OK 74820

QUIGLEY, JOHN CALVIN, JR., lawyer; b. Montgomery County, Va., July 15, 1945; s. John Calvin Quigley and Nellie Marie (Helms) Quigley Waggoner; m. Patricia Ann Burnett, Sept. 14, 1965; 1 child, Cristin Monca. A.A.S., New River Community Coll., 1972; B.S., Radford Coll., 1974; J.D., U. Richmond, 1979. Bar: Va. 1979, U.S. Bankruptcy Ct. 1980, U.S. Dist. Ct. (we. dist.) Va. 1980, U.S. Ct. Appeals (4th cir.) 1980. State tax rep. Va. Dept. Taxation, 1974-76; ptnr. Jenkins, Quigley & Craig, Radford, Va., 1979—; registered agt. Christiansburg Jaycees, Inc., Va., 1980—, Demon Booster Club, Christiansburg, 1982—; legal counsel Holiday Datsun, Inc., Christiansburg, 1984—, Montgomery County Democratic Party, 1983. Mem. Assn. Trial Lawyers Am., Jaycees (pres. 1975-76, dist. dir. 1980-81). Democrat. Methodist. Home: PO Box 144 Christiansburg VA 24073 Office: PO Box 886 513 Norwood St Radford VA 24141

QUIGLEY, RICHARD JAMES, sociology educator; b. St. Louis, Aug. 15, 1946; s. Edward A. and Virginia Jane (McCormick) Q.; m. Lidia Victoria Aravena, Dec. 31, 1970; children—Brenna Aileen, Bridget Colleen. B.A. in History, St. Louis U., 1968; M.A. in Edn., U. Ill., 1973, postgrad. in sociology. Vol. Peace Corps, Chile, 1968-70; extension agt. Servicio Agricola y Ganadero, Cañete, Chile, 1968-70; prof. social studies Coll. San Mateo, Osorno, Chile, 1970-72; prof. English, Osorno Coll., 1970-72; prof. sociology Cath. U. P.R., Ponce, 1977-84, chmn. polit. sci. and sociology depts., 1984—; dir., counselor PTA, Colegio Sagrado Corazón, Ponce, 1982-84; dir. Ctr. of Orientation Services, Ponce, 1977—, treas., 1980-81. Author: (with others) Introductory Sociology Text, 1983, 85; (with others) Investgative Study of Government Agencies, 1978. Contbr. articles to profl. jours. Mem. Am. Sociol. Assn., AAUP, Acad. Art Hist. and Archeology P.R., Phi Alpha Theta, Pi Gamma Mu (sec., treas. 1982-85). Roman Catholic. Avocations: swimming; camping; reading. Office: Catholic U PR Avenida Las Americas Ponce PR 00731

QUILLEN, JAMES H(ENRY), congressman; b. Wayland, Va., Jan. 11, 1916; s. John A. and Hannah (Chapman) Q.; ed. high sch.; LL.D. (hon.), Milligan Coll., Tenn., 1978; m. Cecile Cox, Aug. 9, 1952. With Kingsport Press, 1934-35, Kingsport Times, 1935-36; founder, pub. Kingsport Mirror, 1936-39; founder, pub. Johnson City Times, 1939-44, converted to daily, 1940; mem. Tenn. Ho. of Reps., 1954-62, legis. council, 1957-59, 61; mem. 88th-98th Congresses from 1st Tenn. Dist., ranking minority mem. house rules com., mem. Republican leadership of House. Served to lt. USNR, 1942-46. Mem. Am. Legion, VFW, C. of C. Methodist. Clubs: Lions; Ridgefield Country (Kingsport); Capitol Hill (Washington). Office: 102 Cannon House Office Bldg Washington DC 20515

QUIMBY, MYRON JAY, author, lecturer, writer; b. San Antonio, June 17, 1922; s. Myron Jay and Martha Eller (Dane) Q.; divorced; children—Myron J., Martha J. Quimby Aumond, Pamela J. Quimby Jordan. Student U. Md., 1952. Joined U.S. Army, 1941, advanced through grades to 1st lt., 1959; served in Scotland, Eng., France, Luxembourg, Belgium, Germany, Austria, Czechoslovakia; with 4th armored div. 3d Army; tng. officer Radio Intelligence Ethiopia, 1952-53; with Army Security Agy.; French interpreter NATO, Fontainbleau, France, 1957-59; ret. 1959; with Pinkerton's, Burns Internat. Security Service, St. Petersburg, Fla., 1972-78; lectr. pub. libraries Pinellas County, Fla., 1970-78; monthly columnist Evening Ind., St. Petersburg. Contbr. articles to profl. jours. Author: Scratch Ankle, U.S.A., 1969; The Devil's Emissaries, 1969, 4th edit., 1974; Twilight of the Gods, 1976; Cherokee Gold, 1977. Decorated Croix de Guerre with palm (France). Mem. St. Petersburg Writers Club (pres. 1972-73), DAV. Home and office: 1461 52d Ave N Saint Petersburg FL 33703

QUINIF, ALICE MCELHANNON, radiologist; b. Athens, Ga., Jan. 17, 1955; d. Fayette Monroe and Daisy Grace (Howell) McElhannon; m. Nicholas James Quinif, May 20, 1978; 1 son, Brian Patrick. B.S., Emory U., 1975; M.D., Med. Coll. Ga., 1979. Diplomate Am. Bd. Radiology. Resident radiology Akron Gen. Med. Ctr., Northeastern Ohio U. Coll. Medicine, 1979-83; radiologist Delta Med. Ctr., Greenville, Miss., 1983—. Mem. Am. Coll. Radiology, Radiol. Soc. N.Am., AMA, Miss. Med. Assn., Delta Med. Soc. Republican. Methodist. Office: Delta Med Center 1400 E Union St Greenville MS 38701

QUINN, JOSEPH ALLAN, music company executive; b. Owensboro, Ky., Oct. 23, 1942; s. Joseph Allan and Bessie Lee (Crabtree) Q.; m. Carol Ann Quinn, May 29, 1971; children—Celecia Allana. Student Ky. Wesleyan U., 1960-64. Registered electronic engr. in organ design. Mgr., Smith Music Co., Owensboro, 1958-64; design cons. Kimball Organ Co., Jasper, Ind., 1962-66; pres., chmn. bd. Allan Quinn Music, Owensboro, 1964—, Allan Quinn Real Estate, 1968—; organist Walnut Street Bapt. Ch., 1962-71, Nat. Assn. Music Mchts., Chgo., 1963-68, World Trade Fair, Frankfurt, W.Ger., 1964. Organist LP record album Say it With Music, 1964, also others; author: The Church Organist, 1979. Bd. chmn. Paraochial Bd. Music Edn., Owensboro, 1968-74; bd. dirs. Owensboro Symphony Orch., 1971-77, Settle Meml. United Meth. Ch., 1979-82, Bicentennial Com. of United Meth. Ch., 1984. Mem. Am. Guild Organists, Phi Mu Alpha. Home: 1449 Kentucky Hwy 144 Owensboro KY 42301 Office: Allan Quinn Music Inc PO 218 Owensboro KY 42301

QUINN, JULIA PROVINCE, civic worker; b. Franklin, Ind., Feb. 23; d. Oran Arnold and Lillian (Ditmars) Province; B.A., Franklin Coll., 1937; M.S., Smith Coll. Sch. Social Work, 1939; m. Robert William Quinn, Jan. 21, 1942; children—Robert Sean, Judith Ditmars. Caseworker, student supr. Community Service Soc., N.Y.C., 1939-44; caseworker community research Family Service Soc., New Haven, 1946; social worker in research, dept. preventive medicine Yale U. Sch. Medicine, New Haven, 1946-49; research asst. dept. preventive medicine Vanderbilt U. Sch. Medicine, Nashville, 1969-70. Bd. dirs. Tenn. Bot. Gardens and Fine Arts Center, 1976-81, Friends of J. F. Kennedy Center, 1976-81, Family and Children's Service, Nashville, 1977-83, Friends of Cheekwood, 1966-81, Nashville Symphony Assn., 1978-85, Tenn. Performing Arts Found., 1979-85; chmn. public relations Friends of Cheekwood, 1966-68, 72-74, 76-78, Tenn. Performing Arts Found., 1978—, Family and Children's Service, 1978-83; mem. adv. bd. C-Farr program Vanderbilt U. Med. Center, 1981-85; bd. dirs. Nashville Opera Assn., 1984—, also chmn. pub. relations. Recipient Nashville Vol. Activist award Cain-Sloan and Germaine Monteil, 1979. Mem. Nat. Assn. Social Workers, Acad. Cert. Social Workers, Ladies Hermitage Assn., Vanderbilt Med. Center Aux., Nashville Area C. of C. (cultural affairs com. 1979-85). Democrat. Presbyterian. Clubs: Smith Coll., Centennial (bd. dirs. 1982-85), (Nashville); Vanderbilt Garden, Vanderbilt Woman's. Contbr. articles to social work and med. jours. Home: 508 Park Center Dr Nashville TN 37205

QUINN, PHILIP FRANCIS, psychologist, educator; b. Chgo., Feb. 8, 1932; s. William Martin and Helen Gertrude (Coffey) Q.; m. Jo Ann Farina, June 10, 1974; children—Allain, Megan, Colleen. Student Loyola U., Chgo., 1949-51, M.A. in Sociology, 1960, Ph.D. in Counseling, 1972; B.A., Xavier U., 1955; S.T.B., West Baden Coll., 1965; diploma div. Religion and Psychiatry, Menninger Sch. Psychiatry, 1966. Ordained priest Roman Catholic Ch., 1964; laicized, 1973. Instr. sociology Xavier U., Cin., 1967-69; teaching asst. dept. counseling and guidance Grad. Sch. Edn., Loyola U., Chgo., 1970-71; dir. pastoral counseling ctr. St. Joseph's Hosp. Mental Health Ctr., Tampa, Fla., 1971-73; clin. asst. prof. psychiatry U. South Fla. Coll. Medicine, Tampa, 1972-73; assoc. prof. dept. social sci. U. Tampa, 1973—; pvt. practice psychology, Tampa, 1973—; cons. Tampa Community Correctional Ctr., 1975, Dixie Hollins High High Sch., 1979. Bd. dirs. DWI Counter Attack, 1977-80, 84—, Cath. Social Services, Tampa, 1981-83; vol. psychol. services Tampa Police Dept., 1981-84. Mem. Am. Psychol. Assn., Am. Soc. Criminology, Am. Assn. Marriage and Family Therapy, Fla. Assn. Marriage and Family Therapists, Am. Personnel and Guidance Assn., Acad. Criminal Justice Scis., Fla. Assn. Practicing Psychologists, Contbr. articles to profl. jours. Office: University Profl Ctr Suite 212B 3500 E Fletcher Ave Tampa FL 33613

QUINN, SANDRA LAVERN, political science educator, consultant; b. Grand Rapids, Mich., Oct. 30, 1935; d. Rex Earl and Lavern Emaline (Conner) Nowland; m. James Fenton Arbing, July 16, 1954 (div. 1966); m. C. John Quinn, Nov. 16, 1966; children—Joan B., John J., Jane M., Julie T., Sandra M. B.A., U. Las Vegas Nev., 1975, M.A., 1976; Ph.D., Claremont Grad. Sch., 1978. Interior decorator Montgomery Ward, Grand Rapids, 1964-66, mdse. specialist, N.Y.C., 1966-72; asst. community affairs dir. Sta. KORK-TV, Las Vegas, Nev., 1975-76; exec. officer Norman Kaye R.E. Inc., Las Vegas, 1976-78; dir. edn., writer Polit. Research, Dallas, 1978-80; prof., dept. chmn., San Jacinto Coll., Houston, 1980—; mem. speaker's bur., 1980—; dir. Friendswood Indsl. Devel. Corp., Texas; ptnr. QUIMUS, Tri-County Analysts, Friendswood, 1984—. Co-author: America's Royalty: All the Presidents Children, 1983; How to Pass An Essay Exam, 1983; (newspaper column) On Education, 1984—. Contbr. articles to profl. jours. Program dir. Am. Bus. Women's Assn., Pearland, Tex., 1982-83; founder Friendswood Literary Forum, 1980; del. Rep. Nat. Conv., 1981. Recipient Outstanding Member award Multiple Sclerosis Assn., Las Vegas, 1977. Mem. Women in Polit. Sci., Southwest Humanities Assn., Southwest Polit. Sci. Assn., Tex. Jr. Coll. Tchr.'s Assn. Roman Catholic. Avocations: painting; reading; gardening; tennis; swimming. Home: 516 Avondale Friendswood TX 77546 Office: San Jacinto Coll South 13735 Beamer Rd Houston TX 77089

QUINN, THOMAS CLAUDE, sales and marketing executive; b. Lexington, Ky., Aug. 18, 1930; s. Faye Osborne and Irene Olive (Gibson) Q.; m. Carol Anne Clark, Aug. 20, 1960; s. Thomas Edward, Karen Anne, Colleen Anne. B.A. in Bus., U. Cin., 1954. Salesman, sales trainer Savage Lab., Belleaire, Tex., 1962-64; div. sales mgr. hosp. sales Warner-Chillott Lab., Morris Plains, N.J., 1964-80; salesman Fisher Sci., Cin., 1982-85; v.p. Thoroughbred Moulding, Louisville, 1985—. Bd. dirs. Kidney Found., Columbus, Ohio, 1968-70; adv. com. Westerville Bd. Edn. (Ohio), 1971; asst. campaign mgr. Congressman Gene Synder, Oldham County, Ky., 1980; asst. campaign mgr. Jim Bunning for Congress, 1985. Recipient Sports awards, 1952-70; Civatan Club Speech award, 1966; Elmer H. Bobst award Warner Chillott Lab., 1971; Ky. col. Republican. Club: Am. Legion (asst. commr. 1968-69). Avocations: sports; reading; photography; travel. Home: 3101 Pin Oak Dr LaGrange KY 40031

QUINON, JOSE MANUEL, lawyer; b. Camaguey, Cuba, Jan. 15, 1950; came to U.S., 1962, naturalized, 1973; s. Jose Manuel and Gladys Orlinda (Sarduy) Q.; m. Louise Teza, July 9, 1977; 1 child, Samantha. B.S. in Bus. Adminstrn., Seton Hall U., 1972; J.D., Rutgers U., 1975. Bar: Fla. 1975, U.S. Dist. Ct. (so. dist.) Fla. 1975, U.S. Ct. Appeals (5th and 11th cirs.) 1982. Assoc., A.M. Schwitalla, Miami, Fla., 1975-77; ptnr. Schwitalla & Quinon, 1977-79; asst. state atty. Major Crimes Div., Dade County, 1979-83; sole practice, Miami, 1983—. Mem. ABA, Fla. Criminal Def. Lawyers Assn. (bd. dirs.), Nat. Assn. Criminal Def. Lawyers, Fla. Bar Assn., Dade County Bar Assn. Office: Jose M Quinon PA 2600 Douglas Rd Penthouse One Coral Gables FL 33134

QUIRK, JOHN JAMES, training administrator; b. Bayonne, N.J., Apr. 1, 1947; s. John James and Elizabeth Ann (Decker) Q.; m. Anny Katherine Lukas, June 6, 1972 (div. 1982); m. Paula Madonna Mooney, Dec. 4, 1982; B.A. in English, Ricker Coll., 1976. Dir. continuing edn. Ricker Coll., Houlton, Maine, 1976-78, Husson Coll., Bangor, Maine, 1978-80; tng. assoc. New Eng. Inst., Bangor, 1980-83; dir. tng. ProSync, Melbourne, Fla., 1983—. Author: Introduction to Soldering, 1984. Co-author: Socialization to Work, 1981; Adaptation to Work, 1982; Maintenance of Work, 1982. Mem. Mullet Creek Preservation Soc., Melbourne, Fla., 1984—. Served to sgt. USAF, 1967-71, Fed. Republic of Germany. Mem. Am. Soc. Tng. and Devel. (council on continuing edn. 1983—, chpt. program chmn. 1984—, chpt. pres. 1985, conf. on productivity 1984—), Internat. High-Tech. Tng. Assn. (conf. coordinator 1985), Melbourne C. of C., Audubon Soc. Democrat. Roman Catholic. Avocations: environmental issues; counseling youth on drug and alcohol problems. Home: 2368 Eden Park Dr Melbourne FL 32935 Office: ProSync Inc 2006 Vernon Pl Melbourne FL 32901

RA, JONG OH, political science educator; b. Seoul, Republic Korea, Aug. 23, 1945, came to U.S. 1959; s. Iong Gwyn and Gye Nye (Park) R.; m. Carol Fae Hawn, June 30, 1962 (div. 1981); m. Young Sun Yang, Sept. 30, 1984; children—Stephanie Susan, Alison Emily. A.B., Ind. State Coll., 1961, M.S., 1962; M.S.L.S., U. Ill., 1965, Ph.D., 1972. Asst. prof. Hollins Coll., Va., 1969-75, assoc. prof., 1977-83, prof., 1984—; vis. assoc. prof. U. Ill., Urbana, 1976-77, 80; vis. prof. Va. Poly. Inst. & State U., Blacksburg, 1981—. Author: Labor at the Polls: Union Voting in Presidential Elections, 1952-76, 1978. Contbr. articles to profl. jours. Mem. editorial bd. Polit. Studies Rev., 1984—. Mem. Am. Polit. Sci. Assn., Southern Polit. Sci. Assn., Midwest Polit. Sci. Assn. Office: Hollins Coll Dept Polit Sci Hollins College VA 24020

RAAD, VIRGINIA, pianist, lecturer; b. Salem, W.Va., Aug. 13, 1925; d. Joseph M. and Martha (Joseph) Raad. B.A., Wellesley Coll., 1947; spl. student New Eng. Conservatory Music, 1947-48; diplome Ecole Normale de Musique, Paris, 1950; Doctorate (French Govt. grantee 1950-52, 54-55), U. Paris, 1955. Artist-in-residence Salem Coll., 1959-70; musician-in-residence N.C. Arts council, 1971-72; concerts, lectures, master classes at Carleton Coll., Viterbo Coll., Portland State U., Notre Dame U., Mt. Mary Coll., Mundelein Coll., Trinity Coll., Washington, Phillips Gallery, Washington, Norton Gallery, Rollins Coll., Marietta Coll., Huntington (W.Va) Galleries, W.Va. U., Coll. William and Mary, Channel 13 (WQED), Pitts., Channel 24 (WNPB), Morgantown, W.Va., Lincoln (Pa.) U., U. Pitts., U. Mich., Dearborn, Fordham U., N.Y. Piano Tchrs. Congress, So. Conn. State Coll., Wellesley (Mass.) Coll., Middlebury (Vt.) Coll., Manhattanville (N.Y.) Coll., Elmira (N.Y.) Coll., Ladycliff Coll., numerous others; Am. rep. Debussy Colloque, Paris, 1962; adjudicator W. Va. Music Tchrs. Assn., W.Va. Fedn. Music clubs, Nat. Guild Piano Tchrs. Mem. com. Nat. Endowment Arts, 1979; panelist, grants reviewer NEH, 1978—; active Urgent Action Network, Amnesty Internat. Contbg. author Debussy et l'evolution de la musique au XXe siècle, 1965; also articles in profl. jours. Named Outstanding W.Va. Woman Educator, Delta Kappa Gamma, 1965; Am. Council Learned Socs. grantee, 1962. Mem. Soc. Française de Musicologie, Am. Musicol. Soc. (regional officer 1960-65), Am. Soc. for Aesthetics, Internat. Musicol. Soc., Coll. Music Soc., Music Tchrs. Nat. Assn. (musicology program chmn. 1983-87). Republican. Roman Catholic. Avocations: gardening, birding. Home: 60 Terrace Ave Salem WV 26426

RABAUT, CHARLES PAUL, JR., human services program specialist; b. Detroit, May 13, 1933; s. Charles Paul and Myra Jane (Mills) R.; m. Freida Grace Martin, Dec. 9, 1962; children—Lila Marie, Patricia Antionette, Charles Paul, James Keith, Catherine Lue. A.A., Orlando Jr. Coll., 1966; B.S., Rollins Coll., 1971, M.S., 1973. Cert. Assoc. Alcoholism Counselor, Fla. Personnel mgr. Plymouth Citrus Products Corp., Fla., 1973; occupational program cons. Fla. Dept. Health and Rehab. Services, Tallahassee, 1973-77, dir. employee assistance program, 1977-80, dir. productivity enhancement program, 1980-81, research assoc., 1981-82, mental health program analyst, 1982-84, sr human services program specialist, 1984—; bd. dirs., cons. Fla. Occupational Program Com., Tallahassee, 1973—, Fla. Alcoholism Counselors Cert. Bd., 1979—; regular guest lectr. Fla. Hwy. Patrol Acad., Tallahassee, 1975—; bd.

dirs., sec. Fla. Sch. Substance Abuse Studies, 1981—. Author tng. manual: Supervisory Training Guide, 1978. Author booklet: Supervisor's Handbook, 1979. Tech. cons. The EAP and Me, 1980. Pub. speaking group leader Sr. Citizens Ctr., Tallahassee, 1981, Jake Gaither Community Ctr., Tallahassee, 1983; youth leadership coordinator 4-H Leon County, Tallahassee, 1982; career planning instr. Lincoln High Sch., Tallahassee, 1984. Served with U.S. Air Force, 1951-60. U.S. Civil Service Commn. grantee 1978, 79; recipient Meritorious Service medal Gov. Fla., 1983; Army Commendation medal Sec. of Army, 1985. Mem. Am. Soc. 1 Tng. and Devel. (conf. presenter 1974-82), Assn. Labor-Mgmt. Adminstrs. and Cons. on Alcoholism (Conf. Workshop Leader 1975, 83), Nat. Assn. Alcohol and Drug Abuse Counselors (conf. presentor 1984), Southeastern Sch. Alcohol and Drug Abuse Studies (group leader 1976, 80), Fla. Personnel Assn. (workshop leader 1975-84). Democrat. Roman Catholic. Clubs: Toastmasters Internat. (div. lt. gov. 1984—), Tallahassee Bowhunters. Lodges: Masons, Scottish Rite. Office: Alcohol Drug Abuse and Mental Health Program Dept Health and Rehabilitative Services 1317 Winewood Blvd Tallahassee FL 32301

RABIN, ALAN ABRAHAM, economics educator; b. N.Y.C., June 16, 1947; s. Sidney and Claire R. B.A., Hamilton Coll., 1969; Ph.D., U. Va., 1977. NSF trainee U. Va., 1970-71, 71-72; asst. prof. Calif. State U.-Northridge, 1973-74, Georgetown U., Washington, summer 1975; asst. prof. econs. Sch. Bus. Adminstrn., U. Tenn.-Chattanooga, 1977-81, assoc. prof., 1981—. Contbr. articles to profl. jours. NDEA fellow, 1969-70; U. Tenn.-Chattanooga faculty research grantee, 1982. Mem. Am. Econ. Assn., So. Econ. Assn., Atlantic Econ. Soc., U. Tenn. Chattanooga Council Scholars, Omicron Delta Epsilon. Jewish. Avocations: sports; stamp collecting; bridge. Home: 3501 Dayton Blvd Apt B26 Chattanooga TN 37415 Office: U Tenn-Chattanooga Chattanooga TN 37403

RABIN, STANLEY ARTHUR, metals company executive; b. N.Y.C. B.A.B.S., Columbia U.; M.B.A., U. Santa Clara. With Comml. Metals Co., Dallas, 1970—, pres., 1978—, now also chief exec. officer, dir. Office: Comml Metals Co 3000 Diamond Park Dr Dallas TX 75221*

RABINOWITZ, GEORGE E., obstetrician and gynecologist, educator; b. San Antonio, Feb. 16, 1918; s. Abraham and Sadie (Ladabaum) R.; B.S., St. Mary's U., 1937; M.D., U. Tex., 1942; m. Johanna Bass, June 17, 1947; children—A. Charles, Michael Leigh, Joan Elise. Intern, Mt. Sinai Gen. Hosp., Cleve., 1946-47; resident St. Ann's Hosp., Cleve., 1947-48, Wesley Hosp., Wichita, 1948-49; practice medicine specializing in obstetrics and gynecology, McAllen, Tex., 1949—; assoc. prof. U. Tex., Med. Br., Galveston, 1965; clin. prof. U. Tex. Health Sci. Center, San Antonio, 1949—; staff McAllen Med. Ctr., Mission Mcpl. Hosp., Edinburgh Gen. Hosp., Rio Grande Regional Hosp., McAllen. Chmn. Sub-standard Housing Com., City of McAllen, 1976-77, emergency ambulance vice chmn., 1978-79. Served with USAAF, 1943-46. Diplomate Am. Bd. Obstetrics and Gynecology. Fellow Am. Coll. Obstetricians and Gynecologists (founding fellow), A.C.S.; mem. Phi Delta Epsilon. Jewish. Office: 222 E Ridge Rd Suite 214 McAllen TX 78503

RABORN, MONA JANE, nursing administrator; b. Walnut Grove, Miss., June 12, 1934; d. J.T. and Myrice Rozelle (Tyner) Phillips; m. James Clifford Duncan, Jr., Aug. 3, 1956 (div. Oct. 1976); children—James Clifford III, David Philip, Thomas William, Paul Truitt; m. James Purser Raborn, July 30, 1983. Diploma in Nursing, Gilfoy Sch. Nursing, Miss. Bapt. Hosp., 1955. Dir. nursing Leake County Meml. Hosp., Carthage, Miss., 1961-70, Jefferson Davis Meml. Hosp., Natchez, Miss., 1978—; dir. nursing Drs. Hosp., Jackson, Miss., 1971-72, nursing supr., 1970-71; staff nurse Thaggard Hosp., Madden, Miss., 1973-74, hosp. adminstr., 1974-78. Contbr. articles to profl. jours. Mem. Am. Nurses Assn., Dist. Nurses Assn. (bd. dirs. 1980-82), Miss. Hosp. Assn. Soc. Nursing Services Adminstrs. (bd. dirs. 1981—, pres. 1984, com. mem. 1981—), Miss. Nurses Assn., Am. Orgn. Nurse Execs. Am. Hosp. Assn. Republican. Baptist. Avocations: reading; fishing; gardening. Home: HC 66 Box 219 Ferriday LA 71334 Office: Jefferson Davis Meml Hosp PO Box 1488 Natchez MS 71334

RABURN, JOSEPHINE, librarian, educator; b. Norman, Okla., Dec. 6, 1929; d. Albert E. and Josephine D. (Hudson) Riling; m. James Winston Raburn, Sept. 29, 1950; children—Catherine Anne Heller, Dora Lynn Greenleaf. B.S., U. Okla., 1950, M.L.S., 1964, Ph.D., 1981. Library asst. Spl. Services, Ft. Sill, Okla., 1962-63, reference, adminstrv. librarian, 1964-66; reference and circulation librarian Morris Sweatt Tech. Library, 1966-67; spl. instr. U. Okla. Sch. Library Sci., 1966-67; reference librarian Cameron A&M Jr. Coll., 1967-68; instr. Cameron U., Lawton, Okla., 1968-72, asst. prof., 1972-81, assoc. prof., 1981, dept. chmn., 1982-83, head lang. arts div., 1983—, prof., 1985—; trustee Lawton Pub. Library, pres. bd., 1973-76, also systems analyst; library tech. asst. adv. com. Rose State Coll.; cons. in field. Mem. mammography bd. Meml. Hosp., 1979-81, sec., 1979-80. Recipient Disting. Faculty award Cameron U., 1976; Helen Olander scholar, 1979. Mem. ALA, Okla. Library Assn. (Sequoyah Children's Book award com. chmn. elect 1986), Okla. Orgn. Ednl. Tech., Assn. Ednl. Communications and Tech., Adolescent Lit. Assn., Am. Inst. Tng. and Devel., AAUW, Friends of Library, Beta Phi Mu (pres. Lambda chpt. 1973), Phi Kappa Phi, Delta Kappa Gamma (pres. chpt. 1985-87), Alpha Delta Kappa. Democrat. Methodist. Contbr. articles to profl. jours., chpts. to books, presentations in library sci. Home: 511 NW 40th St Lawton OK 73505 Office: Cameron U Lawton OK 73505

RABY, KENNETH ALAN, lawyer, army officer; b. Edgemont, S.D., Dec. 29, 1935; s. Carl George and Helen Josette (Milne) R.; m. Shirley Rae Nelson, June 2, 1957; children—Randolph Carlton, Shelly Ann. B.A., U. S.D., 1957, J.D., 1960; grad. with honors Command And Gen. Staff Coll., 1975, U.S. Army War Coll., 1981. Bar: S.D. 1960, D.C. 1983. Commd. 2d lt. U.S. Army, 1957, advanced through grades to col. JAGC, 1979; dep. staff judge adv. Am. Div., Chu Lai, Vietnam, 1968-69; chief legal team U.S. Army Inf. Sch., Ft. Benning, Ga., 1969-71; team chief, acting div. chief, adminstrv. law div. Office JAG, Dept. Army, 1971-74; staff judge adv. Hdqrs., 24th Inf. Div., Ft. Stewart, Ga., 1974-79; staff judge adv. U.S. Army Armor Ctr., Ft. Knox, Ky., 1979; chief criminal law div. Office of JAG, Washington, 1981-84; sr. judge Army Ct. Mil. Rev., Falls Church, Va., 1984—; former chmn., mem. Joint Service Com. on Mil. Justice, 1981-84; mem. Mil. Justice Act of 1983 Adv. Commn., 1984—; army liaison to criminal law sect. ABA, 1981-84. Decorated Bronze Star with oak leaf cluster, Meritorious Service medal with 2 oak leaf cluster, Joint Service Commendation medal, Air medal, Army Commendation medal with oak leaf cluster. Mem. S.D. Bar Assn., D.C. Bar Assn., Assn. U.S. Army, Delta Theta Phi, Theta Xi. Lodges: Masons, Shriners. Home: 8102 Backlash Ct Springfield VA 22153 Office: Army Ct Mil Rev Panel 6 Room 212 NASSIF Bldg 5611 Columbia Pike Falls Church VA 22041

RACE, GEORGE JUSTICE, physician, educator; b. Everman, Tex., Mar. 2, 1926; s. Claude Ernest and Lila Eunice (Bunch) R.; m. Annette Isabelle Rinker, Dec. 21, 1946; children—George William Daryl, Jonathan Clark, Mark Christopher, Jennifer Anne (dec.), Elizabeth Margaret Rinker. M.D., U. Tex., Southwestern Med. Sch., 1947; M.S. in Pub. Health, U. N.C., 1953; Ph.D. in Ultrastructural Anatomy and Microbiology, Baylor U., 1969. Intern, Duke Hosp., 1947-48, asst. resident pathology, 1951-53; intern Boston City Hosp., 1948-49; asst. pathologist Peter Bent Brigham Hosp., Boston, 1953-54; pathologist St. Anthony's Hosp., St. Petersburg, Fla., 1954-55; staff pathologist Tex. Children's Hosp., Dallas, 1955-59; dir. labs. Baylor U. Med. Ctr., Dallas, 1959—, chief dept. pathology, 1959—, vice-chmn. exec. com. med. bd., 1970-71; cons. pathologist VA Hosp., Dallas, 1955-75; adj. prof. anthropology and biology So. Meth. U., Dallas, 1969; instr. pathology Duke U., 1951-53, Harvard Med. Sch., 1953-54; asst. prof. pathology U. Tex. Southwestern Med. Sch., 1955-58, clin. assoc. prof., 1958-64, clin. prof., 1964-73, prof., 1973—, dir. Cancer Ctr., 1973-76, assoc. dean continuing edn., 1973—; pathologist-in-chief Baylor U. Med. Ctr., 1959—, prof. microbiology, 1962-68, prof. pathology, 1964-68, prof., chmn. dept. pathology, 1969-73; dean A. Webb Roberts Continuing Edn. Ctr., 1973—; spl. adv. on human and animal diseases Gov. Tex., 1979-83; chmn. Gov.'s Task Force on Higher Edn., 1981-83. Pres., Tex. div. Am. Cancer Soc., 1970. Served with AUS, 1944-46; from 1st lt. to maj. USAF, 1948-51. Decorated Air medal. Fellow Coll. Am. Pathologists, Am. Soc. Clin. Pathologists, AAAS, Am. Coll. Legal Medicine; mem. AMA (chmn. multiple discipline research forum 1969), Am. Assn. Pathologists, Internat. Acad. Pathology, Soc. Parasitologists, Am. Assn. Med. Colls., Am. Assn. Cancer Research, Am. Assn. Phys. Anthropologists, Soc. Med. Coll. Dirs. Continuing Med. Edn. (pres.), Sigma Xi. Editor: Laboratory Medicine (4 vols.), 1973, 6th edit., 1979; contbr. articles in field to profl. jours., chpts. to textbooks. Home: 3429 Beverly Dr Dallas TX 75205

RACKLEY, AUDIE NEAL, journal editor; b. Oney, Okla., Oct. 11, 1934; s. Emmet Irvin and Jesse Lela (Morrison) R.; m. Willie Mae Holsted, Aug. 26, 1956; children—Leicia Leann, Renee, Audette Marshelle. B.S. in Animal Sci., Okla. State U., 1957. Mgr. Hissom A&M Farm, Okla. State U., Sand Springs, 1957, swine herdsman, 1959-61; field rep., advt. salesman Cattleman Mag., Ft. Worth, 1961-67; pub. relations and field rep. Am. Angus Assn., St. Joseph, Mo., 1967-70; dir. advt. Quarter Horse Jour., Amarillo, 1970-72, editor, 1972—. Served with U.S. Army, 1957-59. Mem. Am. Horse Publs. (dir. 1972, pres. 1976), Soc. Nat. Assn. Publs. (dir. 1978, 2d v.p. 1981), Livestock Publs. Council (bd. dirs.). Republican. Baptist. Home: Route 4 Box 58 Amarillo TX 79119 Office: PO Box 32470 Amarillo TX 79120

RACKLEY, CLIFFORD WALKER, oil company executive; b. Tifton, Ga., Sept. 19, 1923; s. Thomas B. and Datie (Ross) R.; m. Julia Susan Old, Feb. 6, 1945; children—Jennifer Rackley Sullivan, Clara Anne Rackley Eller, Sherrie Gail Rackley Webb. B.Ch.E., Ga. Inst. Tech., 1949. Supervisory process engr. Mobil Oil, Beaumont, Tex., 1949-56; sr. process engr. Tenneco Oil Co., New Orleans, 1956-60, sr. v.p. marketing, Houston, 1960-72, exec. v.p., refining and mktg., 1972-74, pres., 1974—, chmn. bd., 1978—; sr. v.p., group exec. Tenneco Inc., 1982—. Served to 1st lt. USAAF, 1943-45. Decorated D.F.C., Air Medal. Mem. Am. Inst. Chem. Engrs., Am. Petroleum Inst., Profl. Engrs. La., Alumni Assn. Ga. Inst. Tech. Presbyterian. Office: PO Box 2511 1010 Milam St Houston TX 77001

RACZ, GABOR BELA, anesthesiologist, educator; b. Budapest, Hungary, July 6, 1937; came to U.S., 1963; s. Lukacs and Ethel R.; m. Enid Gugi, June 25, 1961; children—Gabor, Yvonne, Tibor, Sandor. M.B.Ch.B., U. Liverpool, 1962. Intern, United Liverpool Hosps. and Royal So. Hosp., 1962-63; resident SUNY Upstate Med. Ctr., Syracuse, 1963-66, asst. prof., 1966-69, assoc. prof. anesthesiology, 1969-77; prof., chmn. dept. anesthesiology Tex. Tech. U. Health Sci. Ctr., Lubbock, 1977—, med. dir. Pain Ctr., 1978—, med. dir. respiratory therapy, 1978—. Contbr. articles to profl. jours. Fellow Am. Coll Anesthesiologists; mem. AMA, Am. Soc. Anesthesiology, Internat. Anesthesia Research Soc., Tex. Soc. Anesthesiology, Tex. Med. Assn. Club: Rotary. Home: 4504 17th St Lubbock TX 79416 Office: 3601 4th St Lubbock TX 79430

RAD, RITA MARIA, counties administrator, consultant; b. Havana, Cuba, Nov. 27, 1949; d. Severo Jose and Hilda Margarita (Hernandez) Chica; m. Jesus Salomon Rad, Sept. 14, 1974; children—Stephanie Anne, Andrea Victoria. Cert. achievement Fla. Computer Coll., 1970; A.A., Miami Dade Community Coll., 1972; B.A. in Psychology, Fla. Internat. U., 1974, M.P.A., 1982. Screening specialist Dade County Pub. Schs., Miami, Fla., 1974-76; tchr. Francisco Baldor Sch., Miami, 1976-77; social service worker State of Fla., Miami, 1977-79, counselor, 1979-80, mental health cons., 1980-82; fiscal dir. Dade-Monroe Mental Health Bd., Miami, 1982-83; rehab. cons. Constn. Rehab. Co., Miami, Fla., 1984—. Mem. Am. Soc. Pub. Adminstrn., Fla. Internat. U. Student Psychol. Assn. (charter), Zool. Soc. Fla. Republican. Roman Catholic. Office: Constitution Rehab Co 150 S Pine Island Rd Plantation FL 33324

RADDE, PAUL O(LIVER), change agent, psychologist, consultant, author; b. Wahpeton, N.D., Nov. 11, 1940; s. Oliver James and Marcella M. (Morris) R. B.A., U. Notre Dame, 1962; M.A., U. Tex., 1969, Ph.D., 1974. Lic. psychologist, Tex., D.C. Project asst. USAID, Washington, 1962-63; instr. English, St. George Coll., Santiago, Chile, 1964; clin. psychologist Austin Mental Health, Tex., 1972-75; edn. dir. Tex. State Dept. Human Resources, Austin, 1975-76; pres. Thrival Systems (R), Arlington, Va., 1976—. Author: Supervising: A Guide for All Levels, 1981, The Supervision Decision. Mem. Tex. Partners of the Alliance, Austin, 1968-74. Mem. Nat. Speakers Assn., Am. Group Psychotherapy Assn., Am. Psychol. Assn., Assn. Humanistic Psychology. Mem. Dignity Party. Avocations: racquetball; sailing; skiing; music. Home: 4824 S 29th St Arlington VA 22206 Office: Thrival Systems/21st Century Mgmt PO Box 6633 Arlington VA 22206

RADECKI, CATHERINE, psychologist; b. Franklin, N.J., Jan. 23, 1953; s. Alexander Edward and Mary Catherine (Poncharik) R. B.S. in Psychology, U. Md., 1975; M.A. in Psychology, U. Del., Ph.D. in Clin. Psychology, 1982. Lic. psychologist, N.C., N.J., Va. Psychol. examiner West Memphis Mental Health Ctr., West Memphis, Ark., 1978-80; coordinator emergency services N. Ocean Counseling Services, Lakewood, N.J., 1980-83; coordinator adult services Pitt County Mental Health Ctr., Greenville, N.C., 1983-84; dir. Psychol. Services Ctr., Va. Commonwealth U., Richmond, 1984—. Contbr. articles to profl. jours. Mem. com. Task Force Domestic Violence, Richmond, Va., 1985—; mem. United Way of Pitt County, 1984-85. Mem. Am. Psychol. Assn., Psi Chi, Phi Beta Kappa. Home: 2420 Maplewood Ave Richmond VA 23220 Office: Center for Psychol Services Va Commonwealth Univ 806 W Franklin St Richmond VA 23284-0001

RADER, NORVIN ELWOOD, consulting company executive, retired air force officer; b. Elnora, Ind., June 22, 1922; s. John Louis and Flossie May (Poindexter) R.; m. Evelyn Joyce Edwards, July 29, 1944; children—John Randolph, Toni Christine, Roger Timothy. B.A. in Psychology, U. Okla., 1949, M.A. in Pub. Adminstrn., 1949; grad. Indsl. Coll. of Armed Forces, 1970. Commd. 2d lt. U.S. Air Force, 1950, advanced through grades to col., 1975; dir. manpower Hdqrs. U.S. Air Forces Europe, W.Ger., 1969, Air Force Systems Command, Andrews AFB, Md., 1970-72; chief programs div. Hdgrs. Air Force, Pentagon, 1972-73; dep. dir. Manpower Air Force, 1973-75; ret., 1975; dir. personnel Internat. Tech. Products Corp., Washington, 1975-77; cons., TRW Teheran, Iran, 1977-79; dir. human resource systems Gen. Research Corp., McLean, Va., 1979-83; exec. v.p. Syllogistics, Inc., Springfield, Va., 1983—. Decorated Legion of Merit, D.F.C., Air medals (5). Mem. Ret. Officers Assn., Air Force Assn., Indsl. Coll. Armed Forces, Order Daedalians. Club: Bolling Officers. Avocations: golf; flying. Home: 4031 38th Pl N Arlington VA 22207 Office: Syllogistics Inc 5514 Alma Ln Suite 400 Springfield VA 22151

RADEZ, DAVID CHARLES, financial planning and investment company executive; b. Cobleskill, N.Y. Apr. 23, 1946; s. John Edward and Cora (Drumm) R. B.S., Union Coll., Schenectady, 1968; M.P.A., Cornell U., 1970; cert. real estate studies NYU, 1978. Asst. dir. Kings County Hosp. Ctr., Bklyn., 1970-73; adminstrv. coordinator Meml. Hosp., N.Y.C., 1973-74; dir. clin. ops. Exec. Health Examiners, N.Y.C., 1974-76; real estate salesman Heights-Cranford, Bklyn., 1976-80; real estate broker Whitebread-Nolan, N.Y.C., 1980-81, Montague St. Realty, Bklyn., 1981-82, First Investors Corp., Lexington, Ky., 1984-85, FSC Securities Corp., Lexington, 1985—, Assoc. Fin. Cons., Inc., 1985—; real estate cons., Lexington, 1982—. Assoc. agt. Union Coll. Ann. Fund, 1975—. Mem. Nat. Assn. Securities Dealers (registered rep.), Ashland Park Assn. Home: 225 S Ashland Ave Lexington KY 40502

RADFORD, CAROL ANN, oilfield lease service company executive; b. Kingsville, Tex., Sept. 5, 1938; d. Harlan Waite and Gladness Mae (Knight) Laws; m. William Fred Radford, June 28, 1957; children—William Dean, Darrin Lee. Student Tex. A&I U., 1971-73. Office clk. May-Nix Chevrolet, Kingsville, Tex., 1957-59; sec. Gen. Maintenance, Inc., Kingsville, 1978-80, v.p., 1980—. Pres. jr. dept. Kingsville Woman's Club, 1971-72, v.p., 1976-77; bd. dirs. Ricardo Ind. Sch. Dist., Tex., 1976—, pres., 1983-85; asst. supt. Kleberg-Kenedy County Queen Contest, Kingsville, 1978—. Methodist. Home and Office: Route 1 Box 418 Kingsville TX 78363

RADIN, ALLEN STEWART, pension consultant, accountant; b. N.Y.C., Dec. 31, 1942; s. Joseph and Gertrude (Sherman) R.; m. Isabel R. Radin, June 6, 1974 (div.); children—Vania, Elisa. B.S., Fla. State U., 1965; M.B.A., U. Ga., 1966. C.P.A., Fla., Ga.; cert. employee benefits specialist. Instr. acctg. U. Miami, 1977-81; instr. acctg. and taxes Barr U., Miami, part time, 1981-83; agt. IRS, Miami, 1971-76; pension auditor U.S. Dept. Labor, Miami, 1976-81; pension cons. ESZM Ltd., Ft. Lauderdale, Fla., 1981-83; pension plan cons. Allen Radin Assocs., Inc., Hollywood, Fla., 1983—. Mem. Cert. Employee Benefits Assn., Am. Inst. C.P.A.s, Fla. Inst. C.P.A.s, Internat. Found. Employee Benefit Plans, South Fla. Employee Benefits Assn. Republican. Jewish. Home: 9701 SW 131st St Miami FL 33176 Office: 2535 N 40th Ave Hollywood FL 33021

RADO, STUART ALAN, consumer advocate, consultant; b. Atlanta, Nov. 17, 1945; s. Jerome and Jeanne Antoinette (Gusman) R.; B.B.A., U. Ga., 1971. Exec. dir. Nat. Network Youth Adv. Bds., Inc., Miami Beach, Fla., 1975—; coordinator ENOUGH campaign against waste in govt., 1978—. Mem. Pres. Reagan's pvt. sector survey on cost control, 1982; adv. com. Miami Beach Citizens Adv. Com. for Community Improvement, 1982; mem. Miami Beach Energy Bd., 1982—; bd. dirs. Dade County Young Democrats, 1972-75, alt. del. Dem. Nat. Conv., 1972; mem. Orange Bowl Staging Com., 1973—. Recipient Nat. Vol. Activist award Nat. Ctr. Voluntary Action, 1977; Silver Key award Greater Miami Jaycees, 1972-73; Disting. Service award 1981-82, Dir. of Yr. award 1982, Presdl. award of Honor 1983 (all Miami Beach Jaycees; also numerous awards Fla. Jaycees and U.S. Jaycees. Jewish. Mem. U. Ga. Alumni Soc. (v.p. Miami chpt. 1973-74, pres. 1974-75). Author: Youth Advisory Boards: Organize, Advise, Implement, 1974; Organizing an Effective Youth Involvement Unit, 1977; Towards Better Communication Through Resource Identification, 1977; The Waste Watchers Guide to Government for Everything You Never Wanted to Know About the Bureaucracy, But Paid for Anyhow, 1982. Home: 1500 W 23d St Sunset Island 3 Miami Beach FL 33140 Office: PO Box 402036 Ocean View Branch Miami Beach FL 33140

RADVIC, STEPHAN, management consultant, linguist; b. Mar. 5, 1940; s. Melko and Theresa (Cini) R. B.Econs. and Commerce, U. Melbourne (Australia), 1963; M.A. in Internat. Mgmt., U. Tex.-Dallas, 1976. C.P.A., Australia, 1965-69; profl. soccer player, 1963-65; exec. asst. to Lamar Hunt, Hunt Oil Co., Dallas, 1969-73; controller, chief fin. officer electronics group Rockwell Internat., London and Paris, 1973-79; v.p. fin. Europe, United Technologies, Barcelona and Geneva, 1979-81; pres. Atlantic Group, Inc., Madeira Beach, Fla., 1981—; lectr. internat. corp. fin. U. Tex.-Dallas, 1976-77. Mem. Am. Inst. C.P.A.s. Catholic. Office: PO Box 8856 Madeira Beach FL 33738

RADZEWICZ, PAUL ANTHONY, oil company executive; b. nr. Hudson County, N.J., Apr. 7, 1925; s. Anthony Radzewicz and Helen (Lewicki) R.; grad. Fort Trumble Maritime Acad., 1944; student Millsaps Coll., 1950-51; LL.B., Jackson Sch. Law, 1951; m. Ethel Odel Cole, Sept. 15, 1949; children—Gene Anthony, Maureen Ethel. Instr. nav. machinery USN, Pearl Harbor, Honolulu, 1941-43; organizing sec., chief engr. internat. S.S. Line, Long Beach, Calif. and Buenos Aires, Argentina, 1947-49; pres. Starboard Oil Co., Jackson, Miss., 1949—; prin. Radzewicz Oil Ctr., Jackson, Natchez and New Orleans; pres. Anthony's Yachts Co., Jackson, 1968—; chmn. bd. Radzewicz Operating Corp., Radzewicz Exploration and Drilling Corp.; pres. Ashwood Oil & Gas Corp. Chmn. bd. Magellan Victoria Found. Served with U.S. Maritime Service, 1943-46; PTO. Mem. Am. Petroleum Inst. (pres. Miss. chpt. 1968), Jackson Power Squadrons, Ind. Petroleum Assn. Am., Internat. Oil Scouts Assn., Marine Engrs. Benefit Assn., Miss. Acad. Scis., Natural Gas Men New Orleans, Internat. Assn. Petroleum Landmen, Miss. Landmen's Assn. Clubs: Gulfport (Miss.) Yacht; Patio Jackson Yacht, Jackson Country, University, Capital City-Petroleum (Jackson). Home: 1802 Eastover Dr Jackson MS 39211 Office: Radzewicz Oil Center 1647 Lakeland Dr Jackson MS 39216

RAE, GLEN ALLAN, hazardous waste services company marketing executive, health physicist; b. Fresno, Calif., Oct. 25, 1946; s. Harold Wilson and Erma Mae (Lawrence) R.; m. Judith Vassar, Sept. 22, 1968; children—Carolyn Jean, Allison Lynn. Student, Fresno City Coll. (Calif.), 1964-65, Fresno State U., 1965-66. Health physics supt. Fla. Power & Light Co., Miami, 1972-78; dir. mktg. Chem-Nuclear Systems, Inc., Columbia, S.C., 1978-82, exec. dir. mktg. and sales, 1983—. Served with USN, 1966-72. Mem. Am. Nuclear Soc., Internat. Brotherhood of Magicians (sec. 1976-78), Columbia C. of C. Lutheran. Lodge: Sertoma (Lexington). Home: 213 Wood Dale Dr Lexington SC 29072 Office: Chem Nuclear Systems Inc 240 Stoneridge Dr Columbia SC 29210

RAESSLER, DANIEL M., college educator music; b. Los Angeles, Sept. 16, 1948; s. Christian and Marjorie (Jacobson) R.; m. Deborah Clement, June 25, 1977; children—Jonathan, Sarah. B.A., Fresno State Coll., 1970; M.A., U. Calif.-Santa Barbara, 1972, Ph.D., 1976. Assoc. prof. music Randolph-Macon Woman's Coll., Lynchburg, Va., 1974—. Contbr. articles to profl. jours. Presbyterian. Avocations: woodworking; tennis. Office: Randolph-Macon Woman's Coll Rivermont Ave Lynchburg VA 24503

RAFF, SUANN RAYLENE, pharmacist; b. Joplin, Mo., Aug. 17, 1957; d. Danny Ray and Nancy Darlene (Stogsdill) Beck; m. Charles L. Raff, June 20, 1981. A.A., Northea. Okla. A&M U., 1977; B.S. in Pharmacy, Southwestern Okla. State U., 1980. Registered pharmacist, Okla., Mo. Intern pharmacist V & V Pharmacy, Vinita, Okla., 1980; pharmacy mgr., pharmacist Vista Pharmacy, Miami, Okla., 1980—. Mem. Okla. Pharm. Assn., Beta Sigma Phi (corr. sec. chpt. 1984-85). Democrat. Methodist. Lodge: Order Rainbows (various offices). Avocations: collecting antique glassware; needlework; reading. Office: Vista Pharmacy 1500 N Main Miami OK 74354

RAFFLE, ROBERT LESLIE ROGER, architect, engineer; b. Rochester, Pa., Oct. 20, 1951; s. Walter Robert and Bertha Dolores (Halon) R.; children—Lenore, Christopher; m. Charline Jean Harper, Mar. 20, 1982; children—Barbara, Darian. B. Arch. Engring., Pa. State U., 1975. Registered engr., Tex., W.Va., N.C., Col.; registered architect, Tex. Jr. design engr. ZMM, Inc., Charleston, W.Va., 1975-77; architect-engr., designer Bernard Lively, Architects, Charleston, 1977-78; architect-engring. dept. mgr. TAG Architects, Inc., Charleston, 1978-82, Sinclair-Wright, Architects, Tyler, Tex., 1982-83; pres. RR, Inc., Tyler, 1983-85; architect, project mgr. R.E. Shafer, AIA, Tyler, Tex., 1985—; instr. indsl. engring. Pa. State U., University Park, 1974; instr. steel design, passive solar energy design W.Va. State Coll., Institute, 1980-82. Lighting designer: Charleston Nat. Bank (award 1982), 1979, Heart-O-Town Hotel (award 1982), 1980, Charleston Area Med. Ctr. (award of merit 1982), 1981. Mgr. Sr. Little League Baseball, North Charleston, 1976-78; active W.Va. Energy Com., Charleston, 1976; W.Va. Energy Conservation Commn., Charleston, 1976-77, 79-82. Recipient Outstanding Achievement award Pa. State U. Dept. Archtl. Engring., 1975; U. Ill. Dept. Archtl. Engring. fellow, 1975. Mem. Nat. Fire Protection Assn., ASCE, ASHRAE, Tex. Soc. Architects, AIA (mem. energy conservation and codes and standards com. 1976-78). Republican. Roman Catholic. Avocations: soccer; chess; racquetball; baseball. Home: 3100 Colgate Tyler TX 75701

RAFTIS, MICHAEL JOSEPH, advertising agency executive; b. Waterloo, Iowa, Apr. 12, 1941; s. Harold J. and Coletta M. Raftis; grad. Leadership Terre Haute (Ind.), 1980; children—Wendy, Connie, Jill, Robin, Lacy, Jennifer. With Sears, Roebuck & Co., Mpls., 1962-64; profl. musician, 1962-68; sales and sta. mgr. Sta. WSMJ, Greenfield, Ind., 1968-70; account exec. Sta. WIFE, Indpls., 1970-72; owner, gen. mgr. Sta. WVTS, Terra Haute, 1972-77; partner Eisenhardt & Assocs., Terre Haute, 1977-78; air personality Sta. WBOW, Terre Haute, 1978-81, WDBO Radio, 1982-84; pres. Raftis: The Agy., Terre Haute, 1980-81, Cedar Key Marina, Inc., 1984—; owner, pub. TV Facts of Terre Haute, 1980-81; partner Pink Flamingo Bar & Restaurant, Terre Haute, 1980-81; owner, operator RIA Advt. Agy., 1981-84. Bd. dirs. Terre Haute Girls Club, Heart Assn. Served with USN, 1958-62. Mem. Advt. Rev. Council (dir.), Better Bus. Bur. (dir.), Terre Haute Ad Club (past pres.), Cedar Key C. of C. (v.p.), Am. Legion, VFW Cedar Key C. of C. (v.p.). Democrat. Roman Catholic. Clubs: Lions, Elks. Home: Whiddon Ave Cedar Key FL 32625 Office: PO Box 292 Cedar Key FL 32625

RAGAN, ELIZABETH HOFFMAN, wholesale company executive; b. Albemarle, N.C., Nov. 11, 1916; d. Joseph Filson and Lilly Bassett (Carter) Hoffman; certificate bus. adminstrn. High Point Coll., 1937; m. Herbert Tomlinson Ragan, Oct. 14, 1939 (div. Sept. 9, 1984); 1 son, Herbert Tomlinson. Head bond dept. Sunflower Ordnance Works, Hercules Powder Co., DeSota, Kan., 1942-45; sec.-treas. Ragan-Carmichael, Inc., High Point, N.C., 1956-74, Staple Products, Inc., High Point, 1956-74, R & C Holding Co., Inc., High Point, 1956-74; sec. Ragan Hardware Co., Inc. (merger), High Point, 1974-81; trustee Ragan Hardware, Inc. Profit Sharing Trust and Pension Trust. Cellist N.C. Symphony, 1932-35; mem. adv. bd. Maryfield Nursing Home, 1975-79; bd. visitors High Point Coll., 1979-82; bd. dirs. Guilford Coll. Friends of Library, 1980-82. Mem. High Point Hist. Soc. (dir. 1977-81, pres. 1979-80). Democrat. Mem. Soc. of Friends (organist, choir dir.). Author, compiler: The Lineage of the Amos Ragan Family, 1976. Home: 201 Lake Dr E Thomasville NC 27360

RAGIN, NOEL WALKER, architect, real estate developer; b. Columbia, S.C., Aug. 28, 1951; s. Donald Walker and Elizabeth Pope (Noel) R.; m. Evelyn Diane Davis, Apr. 15, 1978 (div. Feb. 1980); m. Robin Lea Smith, June 5, 1982. B.Arch., U. Tex., 1974. Registered architect, Tex. Architect, Hellmuth, Obata, Kassabaum, Dallas, 1979-83; Craycroft Architects, Dallas, 1983-84; v.p. Kenneth H. Hughes Interests, Dallas, 1984—. Bd. dirs. Oak Lawn Forum,

Dallas, 1985, The Vineyard Assn., Dallas, 1984-85. Mem. AIA, Tex. Soc. Architects, Urban Land Inst. Mem. Ch. of Christ. Avocations: racquetball; sailing; gardening; carpentry. Office: Kenneth H Hughes Interests 2020 Americas Tower LB 110 Dallas TX 75201

RAGLAND, ALWINE MULHEARN, judge; b. Monroe, La., July 28, 1913; m. LeRoy Smith, 1947 (dec.); children—LeRoy, Caroline Smith Christman; m. 2d, L. Percy Ragland, Mar. 8, 1978. A.A., Principia Coll., St. Louis; J.D., Tulane U., 1935. Bar: La. 1935. Sole practice, Tallulah, La., 1935-74; mem. firm Mulhearn & Smith, 1972-74; judge 6th Jud. Dist. Ct., Lake Prvidence, La., 1974—; atty. for inheritance tax collector Madison Parish, La., 1968-74; former city atty., Delta, La.; temporary judge La. Ct. Appeals (2d cir.), 1976. Charter bd. dirs. Silver Waters council Girl Scouts U.S.A.; past pres. Band Boosters Assn. Tallulah High Sch., Tallulah High Sch. PTA; past dist. dir., past bd. dirs, lay reader 1st Ch. Christ Scientist, Vicksburg, Miss.; past bd. dirs. Delta Christian Sch. Mem. ABA, La. Bar Assn., 6th Jud. Bar Assn., Am. Judges Assn., La. Judges Assn., Am. Judicature Soc., La. Council Juvenile and Family Ct. Ct. Judges (pres.), Nat. Council Juvenile Ct. Judges, So. Juvenile Ct. Judges, Assn. Trial Lawyers Am., La. Trial Lawyers Assn., Family Conciliation Cts. and Services, Nat. Juvenile Ct. Service Assn., La. Conf. Social Welfare, Practicing Law Inst., Nat. Assn. Women Judges, La. Assn. Def. Counsel. Club: Ladies Golf and Tennis Assn. Home and Office: PO Box 392 Lake Providence LA 71254

RAGLAND, JAMES BLACK, wholesale food distribution co. exec.; b. Murfreesboro, Tenn., Jan. 28, 1917; s. Charles Burton and Bess (Black) R.; m. Evelyn Claire Kingins, Nov. 14, 1940; children—Evelyn Claire Ragland McKnight, James Black. B.A., Vanderbilt U., 1938. With C.B. Ragland Co., Nashville, 1938—, pres., 1961—; dir. 3d Nat. Bank Nashville. Served with USNR, 1942-45. Mem. Nat.-Am. Wholesale Grocers' Assn., Tenn. Wholesale Grocers Assn., Nashville C. of C. Methodist. Clubs: Rotary, Belle Meade Country. Home: 415 Jackson Blvd Nashville TN 37205 Office: 2720 Eugenia Ave Nashville TN 37204

RAGLAND, WILLIAM LAUMAN, III, educator, pathologist; b. Richmond, Va., Aug. 24, 1934; s. William Lauman Jr. and Alma Josephine (Tatum) R.; m. Lois Camilla Witcher, July 16, 1961; children—Karen Renee, Alexander Shelton, Amy Elizabeth. B.S. in Biology, Coll. William and Mary, 1956; postgrad. Va. Poly Inst., summer 1956; D.V.M., U. Ga., 1960; postgrad. in med. pathology, Tulane U., 1961-62; Ph.D. in Pathology and Biochemistry, Wash. State U., 1966. Instr. Tulane U. dept. pathology, New Orleans, 1961-62; NIH postdoctoral fellow dept. vet. pathology Wash. State U., Pullman, 1962-66; NIH spl. research fellow depts. oncology and pathology U. Wis., Madison, 1966-68, asst. prof. dept. pathology, 1968-70; assoc. prof. depts. avian medicine, med. microbiology, and vet. pathology U. Ga., Athens, 1970-76, prof., 1976—; pathologist Wis. Regional Primate Research Ctr., Madison, 1968-70; pres., chmn. Ragland Research, Inc., Athens, 1980—; adj. prof. dept. pathology and lab. medicine Emory U., Atlanta, 1984—; dir. Custom Adjuvants, Inc., Atlanta, 1983—, Vetrepharm Research, Inc., Detroit, 1985—. Patentee Flourescence gel scanner, 1974. Traveling fellow Brit. Horserace Betting Levy Bd., 1968. Mem. AAAS, Internat. Acad. Pathology, Biochem. Soc., Soc. Toxicology, Am. Assn. Cancer Research, Am. Assn. Avian Pathologists, Am. Assn. Pathologists, Southeastern Immunology Conf. (dir.). Avocation: swimming. Office: Poultry Disease Research Ctr U Ga 953 College Station Rd Athens GA 30605

RAGSDALE, CHARLENE SEELY, educator, consultant; b. O'Donnell, Tex., Feb. 15, 1934; d. William Ernest Seely and Eva Edna (Mayfield) Seely Boyd; m. Bob J. Ragsdale, Nov. 7, 1953 (div. 1977); children—Cheryl Ragsdale Nieto, Cathy Ragsdale Chitwood, Jim; m. Ronald F. Chess, Apr. 2, 1983. B.A. with high honors, Tex. A&M U., 1970, M.E.D., 1975; cert. Sam Houston State U., 1983. Cert. secondary and elem. tchr., Tex. Tchr. Bryan Ind. Sch. Dist., Tex., 1970-76; dept. chmn., tchr. Spring Ind. Sch. Dist., Houston, 1976-83; acad. dean Episcopal High Sch., Bellaire, Tex., 1984—; editor curriculum Ohio U., 1982; seminar presentor Regional Edn. Ctr., Richardson, Tex., 1983; in-service presentor Tex. and N. Mex. schs., 1973-84. Author: (with others) Brazos Valley Historical, 1976; Spring: Lofts & Lore, 1978. Author, editor: World History Curriculum, 1978. Recipient Tchr. of Yr. award Spring Ind. Sch. Dist., 1978, Outstanding Tchr. Performance award, 1983. Mem. Assn. Secondary Curriculum Devel., Am. Soc. Training and Devel., Nat. Speakers' Assn. Presbyterian. Avocations: travel; pub. speaking. Office: Episcopal High Sch 4621 Fournace Pl Bellaire TX 77401

RAGSDALE, MARK STEPHEN, optometrist; b. Sherman, Tex., Jan. 13, 1954; s. Richard Warren and Patricia (Baker) R.; m. Jennifer Merrimon Worthington, July 20, 1977; children—Jason Warren, Shane Michael. B.S. in Optometry, O.D., U. Houston. Ptnr., Ragsdale Vision Ctr., Denton, Tex., 1981-84, owner, pres., 1984—. Unit commr. Denton Council Boy Scouts Am., 1983—. Mem. Am. Optometric Assn., Tex. Optometric Assn., North Tex. Optometric Soc., Better Vision Inst., Beta Sigma Kappa. Republican. Mem. Ch. of Jesus Christ of Latter-day Saints. Lodge: Rotary Internat. Avocations: hunting; skiing; sports; outdoor activities. Home: 12 Highview Ct Denton TX 76205 Office: Ragsdale Vision Ctr 526 N Locust St Denton TX 76201

RAHAIM, GEORGE LOUIS, JR., psychologist; b. Quincy, Mass., June 2, 1948; s. George Louis, Sr. and Ethel (Allsbury) R. A.B. in Psychology cum laude, Boston Coll., 1972; M.Ed. in Counseling, Boston U., 1976; Ph.D. in Clin. Psychology, U. Ala.-Tuscaloosa, 1983. Lic. psychologist, Fla. Mem. Mayor's Coordinating Council on Drug Abuse, Boston, 1969-70; teaching asst. dept. psychology Boston Coll., 1971-72; psychiat. counselor Melrose Wakefield Hosp., Mass., 1975-76; dir. classification South Middlesex Pre-Release Ctr., Mass. Dept. Corrections, 1976-79, tchr., 1978; co-leader Indian Rivers Mental Health Ctr. Jail Group, Tuscaloosa, Ala., 1980; instr. dept. psychology U. Ala., spring 1980, 82; psychotherapist Psychol. Clinic, U. Ala., 1980-81; cons. psychometrist N.W. Ala. Rehab. Ctr., Muscle Shoals, 1980-82; co-dir. crisis line Indian Rivers Mental Health Ctr., Tuscaloosa, 1981-82; intern McLean Hosp., Belmont, Mass., 1982-83; clin. fellow Harvard Med. Sch., 1982-83; clin. psychologist Fla. State Hosp., Chattahoochee, 1983-84; adj. faculty mem. dept. psychology Fla. State U., Tallahassee, fall 1984; instr. dept. psychology Fla. State U., Tallahassee, fall 1984, Dept. Profl. and Human Services Fla. Atlantic U., Boca Raton, spring 1985; practice clin. and forensic psychology, West Palm Beach, Fla., 1985—; adj. faculty mem. dept. profl. and human services Fla. Atlantic U., Boca Raton, 1985—; project dir. Forensic Mental Health Services, West Palm Beach, 1985—; cons. in field. dir. Roxbury Multi-Service Ctr., Mass. Contbr. articles to profl. publs. Expert witness U.S. House of Reps. Select Com. on Crime, Boston, 1971; mem. U.S. Coast Guard Power Squadron, Palm Beach, Fla., 1985. Served to seaman apprentice USN, 1965-66, South Vietnam. NIMH grad. traineeship, 1979-81. Mem. Am. Assn. Correctional Psychologists, Am. Psychol. Assn. (divs. 1, 12, 41), Southeastern Psychol. Assn., Psi Chi. Avocations: micro-computers; scuba diving; travel; skiing; photography. Home: 500 N Congress Ave 31 W Palm Beach FL 33401 Office: Forensic Mental Health Services 224 Datura St 8th Floor West Palm Beach FL 33401

RAHALL, NICK JOE, II, congressman; b. Beckley, W.Va., May 20, 1949; s. Nick Joe and Alice R.; A.B., Duke U., 1971; postgrad. George Washington U.; m. Helen McDaniel, Aug. 19, 1972; children—Rebecca Ashley, Nick Joe, Suzanne Nichole. Staff asst. U.S. Sen. Robert C. Byrd (D-W.Va.), 1971-74; sales rep. WWNR Radio, Beckley, 1974; pres. Mountaineer Travel, Inc., Beckley, 1975-77; mem. 95th-98th Congresses from 4th W.Va. Dist.; mem. Interior and Insular Affairs and Pub. Works and Transp. Coms. Ho. of Reps., mem. ethics com.; pres. W.Va. Broadcasting. Del., Democratic Nat. Conv., 1972, 74, 76, 78. Named Outstanding Young Man in W.Va., 1977. Mem. Beckley Jr. C. of C. (Young Man of Year 1972). Presbyterian. Clubs: Masons, Shriners, Rotary, Elks, Moose. Office: 440 Cannon House Office Bldg Washington DC 20515

RAHI, GURCHARAN S., soil physicist; b. Pathankot, India, Oct. 14, 1941; came to U.S., 1968; s. Amar Singh Subbarwal and Rajinder Kaur; B.S. with honors, U. P.A. Univ., Pantnagar, India, 1963, M.S., 1965; Ph.D., Miss. State U., 1971; m. Gurdeep K. Malhotra, June 4, 1970; children—Navneet A., Gagandeep S. Postdoctoral fellow Miss. State U., State College, 1971-72; research asso. Tuskegee (Ala.) Inst., 1972-75; prof. math. and sci. Saints Coll., Lexington, Miss., 1975-76; asso. prof. Edward Waters Coll., Jacksonville, Fla., 1976-78; asso. in agrl. engring. Research and Edn. Center, U. Fla., Belle Glade, 1978-83; asst. dir. agr., probationer Indian Standards Instn., New Delhi, 1966-68. Vice pres. exec. com. of parents Justina Elementary Sch., Jacksonville, 1978. Mem. Am. Soc. Agronomy, Soil Sci. Soc. Am., Internat. Soc. Soil Sci., Am. Water Resources Assn. Sikh. Condr. research, contbr. articles to publs. Office: Agr Research and Education Center PO Drawer A Belle Glade FL 33430

RAHMES, MARY RUTH, geologist; b. Dover, Del., Mar. 10, 1960; d. Frank and Ruth (Weathers) Giampietro. B.S., Emory U., Atlanta, 1982. Geologist, Eason Oil, Oklahoma City, 1982-85, Sonat Exploration, Oklahoma City, 1985—. Mem. Young Republicans, Oklahoma City, 1984—. Geol. summer field camp scholar, Amax, 1981. Mem. Oklahoma City Geol. Soc., Am. Assn. Petroleum Geologists, Delta Delta Delta (reference and panhellenic advisor, artist chmn. for Holiday Bouquet of Art). Episcopalian. Avocations: skiing; camping; aerobics; running; piano. Home: 5757 W Hefner Rd 905 Oklahoma City OK 73132 Office: So Natural Exploration 2601 NW Expressway Oklahoma City OK 73112

RAHMLOW, K(ATHERINE) LAVINA, retired federal employee, author; b. Viroqua, Wis., Feb. 1, 1912; d. Berent Ole and Tena Julia (Christianson) Dahl; m. Herbert Rahmlow, Sept. 25, 1936 (dec. 1980); children—Bruce Arlan, Bonnie Lynn Rahmlow Dennison. Grad. with honors, La Crosse Tchrs. Coll., 1933; postgrad. U. Wis. Sch. Journalism, 1935-36. Civilian personnel specialist in adminstrn. U.S. Air Force Def. Intelligence Agy., Washington, 1958-68; freelance artist, author and toy designer, Springfield, Va., 1968—. Author: (juvenile) Granny Glee and Whoppity Sock, 1979, Granny Glee and Sockabye Land, 1984. Creator Granny Glee doll, 1983. Recipient Spl. Service award U.S. Air Force, 1961-62; First Place award for toy bear design U.S. Bear Force, 1982. Mem. Am. Assn. Ret. Persons. Republican. Episcopalian. Avocations: art; needlecraft; toy making; writing; playing organ and accordion. Home: 5987 Queenston St Springfield VA 22152

RAI, CHARANJIT, educator; b. Barabanki, U.P., India, July 19, 1929; came to U.S., 1954, naturalized, 1964; s. Hans Raj and Phool Chambi (Bedi) Ghai; B.S., Agra U., 1948; M.S., U. Ill., 1956; Ph.D., Indian Inst. Sci., 1959; Ph.D., Ill. Inst. Tech., 1960; m. Mary Jane Haug, Dec. 30, 1967. Sr. research scientist The Pure Oil Co. div. Union Oil, Crystal Lake, Ill., 1959-66; dept. mgr. Cities Service Oil Co., Cranbury, N.J., 1966-72; dept. head NL Industries, Hightstown, N.J., 1972-73; asso. prof. U. Wyo., 1973-77; chief synthetic fuels research and devel. br. U.S. Dept. Energy, Morgantown, W.Va., 1977-79; prof. chem. and natural gas engring. Tex. A. and I. U., Kingsville, 1979—; cons. in field. Grantee in field. Registered profl. engr., Tex. Mem. AAUP, Am. Chem. Soc., Am. Inst. Chem. Engrs., Soc. Petroleum Engrs., Am. Petroleum Inst., Catalysis Club. Club: Kiwanis. Contbr. articles in field; patentee in field. Home: Route 1 Box 322-A Kingsville TX 78363 Office: PO Box 193 Tex A and I University Kingsville TX 78363

RAIA, PATSY ANGELLE, pharmacist; b. Cecilia, La., Dec. 28, 1954; d. Willie and LouAnna (Guidry) Angelle; m. Albert Dennis Raia, May 7, 1977; 1 child, Katherine Angelle. Student U. Southwestern La., 1972-73; B.S. in Pharmacy, Northeast La. U., 1976. Assoc. dir. pharm. services Franklin Found. Hosp., La., 1976-77; relief pharmacist various inds., Baton Rouge, 1977—; pharmacist, owner The Medicine Stop, Baton Rouge, 1983—. Mem. Profl. Compounding Ctrs. Am., Houston, 1984—; instr. nursing Franklin Found. Hosp., 1976-77. Mem. Homeowners Assn., Baton Rouge, 1982—; campaign worker Sec. State La., 1976, Gov. La., 1980. Mem. Am. Pharm. Assn., Baton Rouge Pharm. Soc. Republican. Roman Catholic. Avocations: stained glass; needlework; quilting; dance; aerobics. Office: Medicine Stop 9944 Florida Blvd Baton Rouge LA 70815

RAINES, JEFF, biomed. scientist, med. research dir.; b. N.Y.C., Sept. 5, 1943; s. Otis J. and Mildred C. (Wetzler) R.; B.S. in Mech. Engring., Clemson U., 1965; M. in Mech. Engring., U. Fla., 1967; Ph.D. in Biomed. Engring. (NIH fellow), M.I.T., 1972; m. Arnita Marlene Halyburton, July 1, 1978; children—Gretchen Christena, Victoria Jean. Mem. staff M.I.T., Cambridge, 1968-70; biophysicist dept. surgery Mass. Gen. Hosp., Boston, 1972-77, dir. Vascular Lab., 1972-77; instr. surgery Harvard Med. Sch., Boston, 1973-77; preceptor Harvard/M.I.T. Sch. Health Scis., 1976-77; research dir., dir. Vascular Lab., Miami (Fla.) Heart Inst., Miami Beach, 1977—; adj. asso. prof. bioengring. U. Miami, Coral Gables, 1977—; adj. prof. surgery U. Miami (Fla.) Sch. Medicine, 1977—; prin. investigator series NIH programs and pharm. firms, 1977—; Harvard Travelling fellow lectr. in Europe, 1975. Recipient Apollo Achievement award NASA, 1969. Fellow Am. Coll. Cardiology, Am. Assn. of Physicists in Medicine; mem. Biomed. Engring. Soc., Instrument Soc. Am., Am. Heart Assn., Internat. Cardiovascular Soc., Cardiovascular System Dynamics Soc. (founding mem.; editor 1976—, pres. 1980-82), New Eng. Cardiovascular Soc., AAAS, ASME, Sigma Xi, Tau Beta Pi. Republican. Presbyterian. Clubs: Kiwanis; La Gorce Country; Marco Island Country; Harvard, M.I.T. Contbr. numerous articles on biomechanics, cardiovascular diagnosis, dynamics and instrumentation to sri. jours.; patentee med. devices; developer math. models of arterial hemodynamics and clin. use of autotransfusion. Home: 5025 N Bay Rd Miami Beach FL 33140 Office: 4701 N Meridian Ave Miami Beach FL 33140

RAINEY, BOBBY STANLEY, educational administrator; b. Kinston, Ala., Jan. 4, 1934; m. Margaret Mozley, June 2, 1957. B.S., Troy State Coll., 1957; M.A., George Peabody Coll., 1960; postgrad. Rollins Coll., 1970. Tchr. Baldwin High Sch., Fla., 1958; tchr. Covington County High Sch., Florala, Ala., 1958-60, head football coach, 1958-60, head basketball coach, 1958-60; tchr. Antioch High Sch., Nashville, 1961; tchr. Abbeville High Sch., Ala., 1961-62, head football coach, 1960-61; tchr. Apopka High Sch., Fla., 1962-63, asst. basketball and football coach, 1961-62; tchr. Oak Ridge High Sch., Orlando, Fla., 1963-68, asst. basketball coach, asst. football coach, golf coach, 1962-63, head basketball coach, golf coach, 1963-68; tchr. Fla. Keys Jr. Coll., Key West, 1968-69, head basketball coach, 1968-69, athletic dir., phys. edn. chmn., 1968-69; tchr. Sanford Middle Sch., Fla., 1969-77, dean students, 1973-75, asst. prin., 1975-77; prin. Jackson Heights Middle Sch., Oviedo, Fla., 1977—. Instr. ARC, Central Fla., Served with U.S. Army, 1954-56. Recipient Recognition award Seminole County County-wide Adv. Com., 1981-82. Mem. Seminole Assn. Sch. Adminstrs. (bd. dirs. 1975, pres. 1984-85), Nat. Assn. Secondary Sch. Prins., Fla. Assn. Sch. Adminstrs., Am. Assn. Sch. Adminstrs. Democrat. Methodist. Avocations: reading history; fern and orchid growing. Home: 3620 Shamrock Ct Orlando FL 32806 Office: Jackson Heights Middle Sch 141 Academy Ave Oviedo FL 32765

RAINEY, DUDLEY LIPSCOMB, geologist; b. Denver, Oct. 5, 1918; s. John W. Rainey and Nell (Lipscomb) Gleaves; m. Blythe Bailey, July 12, 1947; children—Lynn Rainey Shanks, Ann. Mining Engr., Colo. Sch. Mines, 1942; M.S., Columbia U., 1951. Registered profl. engr., Tex. Engr., shift boss N.J. Zinc Co., Franklin, 1946-49; engr., pit foreman Foote Mineral, Kings Mountain, N.C., 1951-53; foreman, geologist Ringwood Iron Mines, N.J., 1953-54; geologist Texasgulf, Inc., Newgulf, Tex., 1954-82; ret., 1982. Served to 1st lt. C.E., U.S. Army, 1942-46; ETO. Krumb scholar, 1951. Mem. AIME, Am. Assn. Petroleum Geologists., Houston Gem and Mineral Soc. Episcopalian. Avocation: mineral collecting. Home: 418 Neal Rd Wharton TX 77488

RAINEY, GENE EDWARD, political science educator; b. Angleton, Tex., Nov. 28, 1934; s. Paul J. and Alice (Mullins) R.; m. Dorma Lee Rogers, Oct. 24, 1958; children—Cheryl Lee, Eric Edward. B.A., George Washington U., 1957; B.S., Harding U., 1959; M.A., Fletcher Sch. Law and Diplomacy, 1960; Ph.D., Am. U., 1966. Assoc. dean Grad. Sch., Am. U., Washington, 1964-66; asst. prof. polit. sci. Ohio State U., Columbus, 1966-69; prof. polit. sci., U. N.C., Asheville, 1969—, chmn. dept., 1969—. Mem. Asheville City Council, 1975-79. Woodrow Wilson fellow, 1959-60. Mem. Polit. Sci. Assns., N.C. Polit. Sci. Assn. (pres.). Democrat. Mem. Ch. of Christ (lay minister). Author: American Foreign Policy: The Official Voice, 1969; Patterns of American Foreign Policy, 1975; editor Policy and Politics, 1984—. Home: 19 Reynolds Pl Asheville NC 28804 Office: Dept Political Science U NC One University Heights Asheville NC 28804

RAINEY, JAMES LEE, JR., chemical manufacturing company executive; b. Nashville, Dec. 4, 1929; s. James Lee and Elsie Mallory R.; B.S., Purdue U., 1952; m. Edith Esther Normington, Feb. 17, 1952; children—James, Patrick J., Robert L., Sarah Lee, Jason N. Gen. mgr. eastern agri-chem. ops. Kerr-McGee Chem. Corp., Balt., 1968-72, v.p., gen. mgr. agri-chem. ops., Oklahoma City, 1968-72, v.p. chem. mktg. div., 1972-75, pres. Kerr-McGee Chem. Corp., 1975-85, sr. v.p., 1985—. Mem. Deer Creek Sch. Bd., 1975-79; dir. Oklahoma County ARC, 1971-73; mem. Deer Creek Sch. Planning Com.; mem. Episcopal Diocesan Bishop's Planning Commn. Served with U.S. Army, 1952-54. Mem. Chem. Mfr.'s Assn. Republican. Episcopalian. Home: 4009 Birdneck Route 1 Edmond OK 73034 Office: PO Box 25861 Oklahoma City OK 73125

RAINEY, MILDRED JEAN, risk and insurance official; b. Mt. Pleasant, Tex., Aug. 26, 1950; d. Renford Sidney and Mildred Aline (Campbell) Justiss; m. Danny Floyd Rainey, Aug. 8, 1969 (div.); children—Shawnna, Daniel, Kevin. Student pub. schs., Mt. Pleasant. Cert. profl. ins. woman. Sr. rater Travelers Ins., Dallas, 1971-76; account exec. asst. Alexander & Alexander, Dallas, 1976-82; risk mgr. Sammons Corp. Services, Inc., Dallas, 1982—; instr. ins. El Centro Coll., Richland Coll., Ins. Women of Dallas, 1977-82. Mem. Ins. Women of Dallas. Democrat. Baptist. Home: 6910 Abilene Sachse TX 75040

RAINEY, ROBERT EDWARD, human resource management consultant; b. Erie, Pa., Apr. 6, 1943; s. Thomas James and Ellen Elizabeth (Stockman) R.; B.A. in Psychology, Gannon Coll., Erie, 1969; M.A. in Indsl.-Orgnl. Psychology, U. New Haven, 1976; m. Marie Fava, Sept. 2, 1967; children—R. Gregory, Allison E. Supr. recruiting Welch Foods, Inc., Westfield, N.Y., 1969-72; mgr. mgmt. devel. and recruiting Pepsico Internat., Purchase, N.Y., 1972-76; mgr. mgmt. and orgn. devel. Am. Can Internat. Co., Greenwich, Conn., 1976-78; dir. human resources Mitsubishi Aircraft Internat., Inc., Dallas, 1978-82; v.p. Drake Beam Morin, Inc., Dallas, 1983-85, sr. v.p., San Antonio, 1985—; mem. adj. faculty Western Conn. State Coll.; cons. in field. Served with USNR, 1962-65. Mem. Am. Compensation Assn., Nat. Orgn. Devel. Network, Dallas Personnel Assn., Psi Chi. Republican. Roman Catholic. Home: 5502 Summit Ridge Trail Arlington TX 76017 Office: 12500 San Pedro San Antonio TX 78216

RAINS, DALE OSBORN, educator; b. Natchitoches, La., Oct. 22, 1936; s. John Franklin and Vera Mae (Osborn) R.; m. JoAnne Bradley; 3 children. B.A., Baylor U., 1958, M.A., 1963; Ph.D., La. State U., 1976. Tchr., Bay City (Tex.) High Sch., 1960-63, LaPorte (Tex.) High Sch., 1963-67; mem. faculty dept. speech and drama Presbyn. Coll., Clinton, S.C., 1967—, assoc. prof., 1979—. Bd. dirs. Laurens County Theater, 1982—, v.p., 1982-83, pres. 1983-84. Recipient Disting. Service citation Bay Area Fine Arts Assn., La Porte, 1967. Mem. Am. Theatre Assn., Southeastern Theatre Conf., S.C. Theatre Assn. (dir., v.p. 1978-79, pres. 1979-80), Laurens County Arts Council, Mensa. Democrat. Episcopalian. Home: PO Box 57 Clinton SC 29325 Office: Presbyterian Coll Clinton SC 29325

RAINS, JOHN HARRISON, JR., environ. cons.; b. Champaign, Ill., Feb. 16, 1925; s. John Harrison and Nora Alle Belle (Guffey) R.; B.A., U. Ill., 1949; postgrad. various mil. service schs., Furman U., 1968; m. Gloria Wentworth Cann, Jan. 15, 1946; children—Michael W., Gordon C., Deborah C., John Harrison. Served as enlisted man U.S. Marine Corps, 1943-46; commd. 2d lt. U.S. Air Force, 1950, advanced through grades to maj., 1967; comdr. 2044-1 Airways and Air Communications Squadron, Washington, 1953-55, maintenance adv. Chinese Combat Air Command, Taipei, Taiwan, 1955-57, communications-electronics staff officer 63d Troop Wing, Donaldson AFB, S.C., 1957-60, comdr. Thorsup Air Force Sta., Iceland, 1961-62, telecommunications staff officer Mil. Airlift Command, Scott AFB, Ill., 1963-67, ret., 1967; advanced math. instr. Traveler Rest High Sch., Greenville County, S.C., 1967; dir. Neighborhood Youth Corps OEO, Greenville County, 1968-69; environ. cons., 1975—; cons. Manasota-88, Inc., Palmetto, Fla., 1978—. Mem. 208 water quality com. Tampa Bay Regional Planning Council, St. Petersburg, Fla., 1975-80, mem. coastal zone mgmt. com., 1976-78, local citizens and tech. adv. com., 1978; chmn. transp. com. Fla. Gov.'s Local Govt. Study Commn., Manatee County, 1976-77; precinct committeeman Republican Exec. Com. Manatee County, 1975-80; pres. Bay Colony Property Owners Assn., 1977; mem. Environ. Info. Center, Fla. Conservation Found. Waste Alert Task Force, 1980; mem. adv. com. Fla. Defenders of Environment's Environ. Service Center, 1980-81; mem. Manatee Save Our Bays Assn., 1978-82. Decorated Purple Heart with Gold Star. Mem. Fla. Wildlife Fedn. (Outstanding Conservationist award 1980), Environ. Confedn. S.W. Fla. (dir. 1974-82), Izaak Walton League Am. (pres. Manatee chpt. 1976-80, Fla. div. 1978-80, exec. dir. Fla. div. 1980-82, Judge Tobin award 1978, Nat. Conservation award 1981), Fla. Indigenous Plan Soc., Air Force Assn., Manasota Geneal. Soc. (pres. 1972-73). Home: 5314 Bay State Rd Palmetto FL 33561

RAINS, MARY JO, banker; b. Konawa, Okla., Oct. 27, 1935; d. Albert Wood and Mary Leona (Winfield) Starns; student Okla. Sch. Banking, 1969, Seminole Jr. Coll., 1970-72, E. Central State U., 1978-79; diploma Am. Inst. Banking, 1981, 83; m. Billy Z. Rains, June 17, 1956; 1 son, Nicky Z. Accounting div. Universal C.I.T., Oklahoma City, 1953-56; cashier Okla. State Bank, Konawa, 1957—, now sr. v.p. Sec., 1st Baptist Ch., Konawa, 1969-79, mem. budgeting com., 1982—. Mem. Okla. Bankers Assn. (dir. women's div. 1974-76), Konawa C. of C., Am. Legion. Club: Order Eastern Star. Home: Route 2 Box 26 Konawa OK 74849 Office: PO Box 156 Konawa OK 74849

RAINWATER, CRAWFORD, JR., carbonated beverage company executive; b. Fairfield, Ala., Feb. 4, 1945; s. Crawford and Betty (Gregg) R.; m. Freddie Barrett, Jan. 24, 1970; children—Crawford III, Blanche. Ed. U. of South, 1963-67; B.A. in Fin. and Acctg., U. West Fla., 1968; M.B.A., U. S.C., 1972. Market mgr., asst. mgr. Beaumont (Tex.) Coca-Cola Bottling Co., 1974-78; regional mgr., Hygeia Coca-Cola Bottling Co. and Associated Cos., Pensacola, Fla., 1978-79, v.p. ops., 1979-81, chmn., chief exec. officer 1981—, dir., 1976—; dir. Ala. Coca-Cola Bottling Co., Oxford, Beaumont Coca-Cola Bottling Co., Columbia Coca-Cola Bottling Co. (S.C.), Paris Coca-Cola Bottling Co. (Tex.), Tex. Bank Beaumont, 1983-85, Tallahassee Coca-Cola Bottling Co. Bd. dirs. Escambia County United Way, 1979-82; mem. Escambia County Appeals Rev. Bd., 1979—; pres. Gulf Coast council Boy Scouts Am., Pensacola, 1982-84. Mem. Soc. Soft Drink Technologists. Republican. Episcopalian. Lodge: Rotary. Office: Hygeia Coca-Cola Bottling Co 7330 N Davis St Pensacola FL 32504

RAINWATER, WANDA KAYE, nurse; b. Asheville, N.C., July 26, 1947; d. Woodson Walter and Edith Irene (Owens) R. Emergency med. technician cert. Asheville-Buncombe Tech. Coll., 1976, A.S. in Nursing, 1981. R.N., N.C.; cert. emergency med. technologist. Clerical coordinator dept. radiology Meml. Mission Hosp., Asheville, 1969-76, med. sec., 1969-76; health care technician State of N.C., Black Mountain, 1976-80, ambulance driver, 1977-80; urology and oncology staff nurse St. Joseph Hosp., Asheville, 1981—. Mem. Am. Assn. Emergency Med. Technicians, Buncombe County Assn. Emergency Med. Technicians, Am. Assn. R.N.s, N.C. Assn. R.N.s. Democrat. Baptist. Home: 153 Edwards Ave Swannanoa NC 28778 Office: St Joseph Hosp Biltmore Ave Asheville NC 28801

RAIZADA, MOHAN KISHORE, physiologist, educator, reseacher; b. Fatehpur, India, Oct. 21, 1948; s. Maharaj Bahadur and Bittan Kuvar; m. Laura Carlson, Nov. 20, 1979; children—Kristen, Keely. Student U. Kanpur (India), 1968-72, Ph.D., 1972. Postdoctoral fellow Med. Coll. Wis., Milw., 1973-74; postdoctoral assoc. Jewish Gen. Hosp., Montreal, Que., Can., 1974-76; assoc. U. Iowa, Iowa City, 1976-79, asst. prof., 1979-80; assoc. prof. J. Hillis Miller Health Ctr., U. Fla., Gainesville, 1980—. Recipient Young Scientist medal Indian Nat. Sci. Acad., 1974. Mem. Am. Physiol. Soc., Endocrine Soc., Am. Soc. Cell Biology, Tissue Culture Assn., AAAS, Contbr. articles to profl. publs. Home: 6509 NW 33d Terr Gainesville FL 32606 Office: Box J274 JHMHC Univ Fla Gainesville FL 32610

RAKESTRAW, REBECCA JONES, family therapist; b. Greenville, S.C., Sept. 18, 1943; d. Joseph Clyde and Mildred Idel (Smith) Jones; m. James Wilburn Rakestraw, June 4, 1965; children—Bryan Robert, Paige Allison, Brooke Lauren. B.A., Mercer U., 1979; M.S.W., U. Ga., 1981. Flight attendant Eastern Airlines, Boston, Atlanta, 1963-65, cons., 1982-83; counselor Ga. Regional Hosp., Atlanta, 1979-80; social worker South DeKalb Mental Health Ctr., Atlanta, 1980-81; therapist Peachtree Parkwood Hosp., Atlanta, 1981-82, aftercare coordinator, 1982-83; family program coordinator Substance Abuse Free Existence, Atlanta, 1983-84, program dir., 1984—; cons. City of Atlanta, Republic Airlines, 1983. Mem. Nat. Assn. Social Workers, Nat. Assn. Clin. Social Workers, Acad. Cert. Social Workers, Ga. Clin. Social Workers. Republican. Baptist. Home: 2659 Smoke Tree Way NE Atlanta GA 30345 Office: SAFE 6255 Barfield Rd Atlanta GA 30328

RAKOCY, WILLIAM J., curator, artist, painter; b. Youngstown, Ohio, Apr. 14, 1924; s. Joseph Rakocy and Anna Mae (Kollar) R.; children—Wendy, Diane, Bill, Lisa, Dan; m. Gloria Ann Canterbury, June 17, 1950; 1 child, Wendy Sue. B.F.A., Kans. City Art Inst., 1950; M.F.A., U. Kansas City, 1951.

Dir. Community Art Studio, Youngstown, 1952-53; adv. mgr. Isaly Dairy Co., Youngstown, 1954-62, Nat. Tea Co., Youngstown, 1962-66; prof. Coll. Artesia, N.Mex., 1966-71; curator El Paso Mus. Art, 1971—; art instr. Choffin Voc. Ctr., Youngstown, 1952-60, Community Art Sch., Youngstown, 1952-60, Mohn Sch. Art, Youngstown, 1952-66. Editor, founder artist newspaper, 1960. One-man shows include Kansas City, Cleve., Butler Inst., El Paso, El Paso Mus. Art; exhibited in several nat. shows receiving many awards. Author: For Art, Anything; Images/Paso del Norte; Artists and Writers; Saya of the Kid. Mem. Rio Bralo Watercolorists Assn. (founder, pres. 1974), Mogollon Hist. Soc. Avocation: auto restoration. Office: El Paso Mus Art 1211 Montana El Paso TX 79902

RAKOWSKI, PAUL ALAN, environmental engineer, consultant; b. Bayonne, N.J., July 7, 1951; s. Joseph Stanley and Stella (Jakubowski) R.; m. Julie Ann Catherine Wagner, June 15, 1974; children—Susan Marie, Jeffrey Joseph. B.S. in Civil Engring., Newark Coll., 1974; M. Engring. in Civil Engring., Old Dominion U., 1979. Registered profl. engr., Va.; cert. hazardous materials mgr. With Atlantic div. Naval Facilities Engring. Command, Norfolk, Va., 1974—, supervisory environ. engr., 1980—; rep. to Hampton Rds. Water Quality Agy. Named Employee of Yr. Atlantic div. Naval Facilities Engring. Command, 1978. Mem. Water Pollution Control Fedn., ASCE, Nat. Soc. Profl. Engrs., Am. Electroplaters Soc., Tau Beta Pi, Chi Epsilon. Roman Catholic. Office: Atlantic Div Code 114 Naval Facilities Engring Command Norfolk VA 23511

RALSTON, CARL CONRAD, construction executive; b. Owensboro, Ky., Nov. 1, 1927; s. Carl C. and Elizabeth (Little) R.; Asso. B.B.A., Ky. Bus. Coll., 1949; B.A., Ky. Wesleyan Coll., 1956; m. Patricia Warren, Nov. 12, 1971; children—Pamela Kay, Kelly Michelle. Pub. acct., 1956; chief acct., estimator Mills & Jones Inc., 1957-60, project mgr., 1960-65; v.p. Mills & Jones Constrn. Co., St. Petersburg, Fla., 1965-82; exec. v.p. Fed. Constrn. Co., 1982—, also dir., dir. Mills & Jones Constrn. Co. Pres., Cross Bayou Little League, Seminole, Fla., 1959-61; treas. Seminole Lake Civic Assn., Seminole, 1959-62; trustee Southeastern Ironworkers' Health and Welfare Fund; bd. dirs. St. Petersburg Gen. Hosp., chmn. bd., 1983. Served with USAAF, 1945-47. Mem. Am. Mgmt. Assn., Assn. Gen. Contractors (chpt. dir. 1969-70), Am. Inst. Constructors, Am. Soc. Profl. Estimators. Clubs: Seminole Lake Country (gov. 1964-67, chmn. bd. 1967-68); Bardmoor Country; Feather Sound Country, Polywogs. Lodges: Masons, Elks. Home: 6328 Augusta Blvd Seminole FL 33543 Office: 800 2d Ave S Saint Petersburg FL 33701

RALSTON, FREDERICK LANGILL, educator for deaf; b. Brockton, Mass., Jan. 17, 1939; s. Raymond Henry and Doris Helen R.; m. Karen Marie Chewey, Apr. 17, 1982. Diploma Mass. Trades Shops Sch., 1961; B.A., Gallaudet Coll., 1969; M.Ed. (fellow), U. Wash., 1974. Journeyman machinist Mathewson Machine Works, Quincy, Mass., 1961-65; coordinator field testing Project Lang. Instrn. to Facilitate Edn., Washington, 1969-71; supervising tchr. Amego, Inc., Quincy, 1972-74; tchr. Middle Sch., R.I. Sch. for Deaf, Providence, 1974-75, Multi-Handicapped Deaf Program, Protestant Guild Program, Watertown, Mass., 1975-76; head, tchr. multi-handicapped classroom Sch. Bd. Lee County, Fort Myers, Fla., 1977—; S.W. chmn. Fla. Registry Interpreters for the Deaf, 1978—; cons. local Instructional Methods for Parents and Children Together Program, 1979—. Scoutmaster Troop 112, Palm dist. Southwest Fla. council Boy Scouts Am., 1981—; pres. bd. dirs. Speech and Hearing Service Ctr. of Southwest Fla., 1981—. Mem. Lee County Handicap Adv. Com., 1979-84. Mem. Assn. for Supervision and Curriculum Devel., Nat. Assn. of Deaf, Conv. Am. Instrs. of the Deaf. Democrat. Home: 23380 Olean Blvd Port Charlotte FL 33952 Office: Sch Bd Lee County Allen Park Sch 3345 Canelo Dr Fort Myers FL 33901

RALSTON, STEPHEN KENT, architect, designer; b. Ft. Walton Beach, Fla., Mar. 27, 1958; s. William Kent and Clarice (McDuffie) R. B.Arch., Tex. Tech. U., 1981. Draftsman, S.H.W.C., Inc., Dallas, 1981-83; draftsman, asst. project mgr. Woo, James, Harwick, Peck Architects & Planners, Inc., Dallas, 1983-84; project mgr. WJHP/Murray Interiors, Inc., Dallas, 1984—; mem. Young Architects Task Force, Dallas, 1981—; bus. rep. Dallas Area Rapid Transit Bd., 1983. Mem. Dallas Mus. Art, 1982—, Nat. Geog. Soc., Washington, 1983—, 500, Inc., Dallas, 1985—. Photographer photograph: Three Faces (hon. mention Dallas AIA 1984). Assoc. mem. AIA (Dallas chpt.), Tex. Soc. Architects, Kappa Sigma Internat. (Lubbock, Tex.). Republican. United Methodist. Avocations: photography; running; art; skiing; travel. Home: 9747 Whitehurst No 175 Dallas TX 75243 Office: WJHP/Murray Interiors Inc 7557 Rambler Rd Suite 300 Dallas TX 75231

RAMAKUMAR, RAMACHANDRA GUPTA, electrical engineering educator; b. Coimbatore, Tamil Nadu, India, Oct. 17, 1936; came to U.S., 1967; s. Gopalakrishna Ramachandra and Saraswathi (Bai) Gupta; m. Tallam Gokuladevi, June 13, 1963; children—Sanjay, Malini, B.E. U. Madras, 1956; M.Tech., Indian Inst. Tech., 1957; Ph.D., Cornell U., 1962. Registered profl. engr., Okla. Asst. lectr., lectr elec. engring. Coimbatore Inst. Tech., 1957-62, asst. prof., 1962-67; vis. and assoc. prof. Okla. State U., Stillwater, 1967-76, prof. elec. engring., 1976—; cons. JPL, Pasadena, Calif., 1978-79; cons. UN, UNU, NSF, Kuwait U., others. TCM scholar, 1959-62; NSF grantee, 1978. Mem. IEEE (sr.), Power Engring. Soc. (energy devel. subcom., power generation com.), Internat. Solar Energy Soc., Okla. Soc. Profl. Engrs. (outstanding achievement award 1972). Contbr. articles to profl. jours.; patentee in field. Home: 2623 N Husband St Stillwater OK 74075 Office: 202 Engring South Okla State U Stillwater OK 74078

RAMAN, ARAVAMUDHAN, metallurgy educator, consultant; b. Landhakkottai, India, Oct. 13, 1937; s. Aravamudhan and Pankajavalli Iyengar; m. Edelgard Sieglinde Zimpel, Jan. 15, 1965; children—Vasudevan, Padhmavathi, Lakshmi-Kalavani. M.A. in Physics, Madras U., 1958; B.E. in Metallurgy, Indian Inst. Sci., Bangalore, 1960; Ph.D., Tech. U. Stuttgart, W.Ger., 1964. Assoc. lectr. in metallurgy Indian Inst. Tech., Bombay, 1960-61; research assoc. in metallurgy U. Ill., Urbana, 1964-65; postdoctoral fellow in materials sci. U. Tex., Austin, 1965-66; asst. prof., assoc. prof. prof. materials group, mech. engring. dept. La. State U., Baton Rouge, 1966—; vis. chemist dept. chemistry UCLA, summer 1969; cons. various chem. and petroleum cos., dept. transp. State of La.; instr. spl. extension course on electronic materials Western Electric Co., 1971. Author: Experiments and Problems in Metallurgy for Engineers, 1978; contbr. articles to sci. jours. Mem. Am. Soc. Metals, Nat. Assn. Corrosion Engrs., Sigma Xi. Brahmin Hindu. Avocations: tennis; swimming; listening to classical music; meditating. Home: 6919 N Rothmer Dr Baton Rouge LA 70808 Office: Dept Mech Engring La State Univ Baton Rouge LA 70803

RAMBERG, STEVEN HAROLD, petroleum engineer; b. Portland, Oreg., June 30, 1956; s. Harold Chris and Avon Jean (Simmons) R.; m. Helen Marie Keefer, June 22, 1983; children—Michael, Matthew. B.S. cum laude in Engring. Geology, Brigham Young U., 1980. Field engr. Gulf Oil Co., New Orleans, 1980, secondary/EOR engr., 1980-81, reservoir engr. exploration and prodn.-Delta area, 1981-85; reservoir engr. Eastern region Chevron U.S.A., New Orleans, 1985—. Named Outstanding Geology Student, Brigham Young U., 1980. Mem. Soc. Petroleum Engrs., Am. Assn. Petroleum Geologists. Republican. Mormon. Avocations: running; sports; music. Home: 916-B Trianon Sq W Gretna LA 70056 Office: Chevron USA PO Box 6056 New Orleans LA 70174

RAMBO, GEORGE DAN, lawyer; b. Marietta, Okla., Apr. 23, 1928; s. Joseph Daniel and Maebelle (Raum) R.; m. Carroll Ann Imle, Feb. 19, 1969 (div. 1976); m. Cindy Ann Davenport, June 7, 1980; children—Blake Ryan, Grier Daniel. B.B.A., U. Okla., 1951, M.S. in Geology, 1955, J.D., 1965. Bar: Okla. 1965. Sole practice, Norman, Okla., 1965-68, 75-78, Oklahoma City, 1984—; campaign coordinator Humphrey-Muskie Campaign, States of Wash. and Oreg., Seattle and Portland, 1968, David Hall for Gov. Campaign, State of Okla., 1969-70, George Nigh for Gov. Campaign, State of Okla., Oklahoma City, 1978, John Glen Campaign, State of Fla., Orlando, 1983-84, Mondale-Ferraro Campaign, State of Ky., Frankfort, 1984; legal counselor to gov. State of Okla., Oklahoma City, 1971-74; rep. of sec. U.S. Dept. Energy, Region VI, Dallas, 1978-80; v.p. Monjeb Minerals, Inc., Oklahoma City, 1981-83; judge Okla. Workers Compensation Ct., State of Okla., Oklahoma City, 1982-83; appointee of gov. Okla., Interstate Oil Compact Commn., Oklahoma City, 1981—. Served with USMC, 1946-47. Democrat. Presbyterian. Home: 2503 Walnut Rd Norman OK 73069 Office: 511 Couch Dr Oklahoma City OK 73102

RAMEY, GEORGE GROVER, theology educator, university administrator; b. Dixon, Mo., Aug. 17, 1938; s. Donald Edward and J. Ruth (Crum) R.; m. Patricia Ann Perkins, June 7, 1959; children—Jonathan Edward, Steven Wesley. A.A., S.W. Baptist Coll., 1958; B.A., William Jewell Coll., 1960; B.Div., Midwestern Baptist Sem., 1963; M. Theology, So. Bapt. Sem., 1965, Ph.D., 1968. Pastor Hopewell Bapt. Ch., Barnett, Mo., 1958, New Hope Bapt. Ch., Bethany, Mo., 1961-63; asst. prof. Cumberland Coll., Williamsburg, Ky., 1968-72, assoc. prof., 1972-82, prof. religion, 1982—, dir. bus. affairs, treas., 1976—; field supr. Joint Archaeol. Expdn. to Ai, Jordon, 1966, lab. technician, 1971. Cubmaster Williamsburg Pack 15, Boy Scouts Am., 1973-80. Mem. Soc. Bibl. Lit., Am. Sch. Oriental Research, Nat. Assn. Profs. Hebrew (mem. nat. exec. com. 1974—), Council Ind. Ky. Coll. and Univ. Bus. Officers, Nat. Assn. Coll. and Univ. Bus. Officers. Home: Route 4 Box 728 Williamsburg KY 40769 Office: Cumberland Coll Bus Office Williamsburg KY 40769

RAMIREZ, ALEXANDER, police detective; b. N.Y.C., July 29, 1953; s. Baltasar and Maria (Rodriguez) R.; m. Catherine Stepinski, Aug. 3, 1975 (div. July 1979). B.A., John Jay Coll., N.Y.C., 1975, postgrad., 1979-80; postgrad. Biscayne Coll., 1982-83. postgrad. Cert. on state standards for police, Fla. Police officer Port Authority Police, N.Y.C., 1975-80, Dade County Police, Miami, Fla., 1980—; adviser Hispanic Officer's Assn., Miami, 1981—. Contbr. articles to various publs. Recipient numerous citations N.Y.C. Police Dept., 1975, Port Authority Police Dept., 1980, appreciation award Post Authority Hispanic Soc., N.Y.C., 1980; Mem. Internat. Blue Knights (internat. gov. 1982—, pres./founder Miami chpt. IV 1981—, founder, chmn. So. Conf. 1981—), Dade County Patrolman's Benevolent Assn. (dir. 1982—, interviewer polit. screening 1983). Democrat. Roman Catholic. Home: 1185 NE 134th St North Miami FL 33161 Office: Blue Knights Fla IV PO Box 610052 Miami FL 33161

RAMIREZ, SALVADOR MANUEL, orthopedic surgeon; b. N.Y.C., Mar. 17, 1936; s. Salvador H. and Providencia (Torres) R.; m. Janis Tarpo, Nov. 26, 1960; children—Sally Ann, Robert, Elena, Elizabeth. B.S., St. John's U., 1956; M.D., Chgo. Med. Sch., 1960. Intern Kings County Hosp., Bklyn., 1960-61; resident Jewish Hosp. and Med. Ctr., Bklyn., 1963-67; chief orthopedics Mercy Hosp., Miami, Fla., 1980-83, pres. med. staff, 1983—. Served with USN, 1961-63. Mem. AMA, ACS, Internat. Coll. Surgeons, Am. Acad. Orthopedic Surgeons. Republican. Roman Catholic. Address: 1797 Coral Way Miami FL 33145

RAMIREZ PEREZ, MIGUEL ANGEL, economics researcher, economic consultant; b. Cabo Rojo, P.R., Nov. 3, 1929; s. Angelino and Manuela (Perez) R.; m. Norma I. Rivera, July 24, 1960 (div. June 1973); children—Angeles I., Miguel A.; m. Wanda C. Rodriguez, Dec. 22, 1973; 1 child, Yuri Waldemar. B.A. in Econs., U. P.R., Rio Piedras, 1957; M.A. in Econs. and Pub. Adminstrn., Syracuse U., 1958; Ph.D. in Econs., Rutgers U., 1970. Instr. econs. U. P.R., Mayaguez, 1958-59; chief sect. statistician P.R. Dept. Labor, San Juan, 1959-60; instr. to prof. econs. U. P.R., Rio Piedras, 1960-84, researcher in econs., 1985—; project dir. P.R. Dept. Health, San Juan, 1965-66; cons., researcher Gov.'s Labor Council, San Juan, 1978-84, CETA Council, San Juan, 1980-82. Contbr. articles to profl. jours. Served with U.S. Army, 1951-53. P.R. Govt. Personnel Office fellow, San Juan, 1957-58. Mem. Am. Econ. Assn., P.R. Econ. Assn. Avocations: classical music and opera; gardening; internal tourism. Office: PO Box 23010 U PR Sta Rio Piedras PR 00931

RAMIS, GUILLERMO JUAN, advertising agency executive, vehicle company executive; b. Habana, Cuba, Mar. 29, 1945 (parents U.S. citizens); s. Guillermo and Carmen (Galdo) R.; m. María Celeste Arrarás, Oct. 12, 1984. B.B.A., U. Notre Dame, 1966; M.B.A., Boston U., 1968; Ph.D., U. Pitts., 1975. Researcher Fed. Deposit Insurance, Washington, 1967; v.p. Tropicair Mfg. Corp., San Juan, P.R., 1968-74; dir. Aluminum Extrusion Corp., Canovanas, P.R., 1968-74; prof. U. P.R., Rio Piedras, 1973-76; pres. The Atlantic Orgn., San Juan, 1975—. Dir., producer Un Dia en la vida de.. documentary, 1976. Mem. Am. Econ. Assn., Am. Film Inst., P.R. Hotel and Tourism Assn., P.R. C. of C. (pres. tourism com. 1984—), P.R. Nat. Swimming Team. Avocations: tennis; swimming; photography. Office: Caleta de las Monjas #17 Old San Juan PR 00901

RAMOS, MANUEL, JR., hospital administrator; b. Wichita Falls, Tex., July 25, 1941; s. Manuel Arredondo and Erlinda (Gonzalez) R.; m. Patricia Arlene Ramos, Sept. 4, 1962 (dec. 1979); children—James Howard, Michael Arlie, Timothy Daniel; m. 2d, Emma Ochoa, Aug. 5, 1980. B.S. in Edn., Midwestern State U., 1972, M.S. in Edn., 1973. Tchr., athletic coach various schs., Tex. and Calif., 1962-75; personnel dir. Tex. Dept. Mental Health Retardation, San Antonio, 1975-79, hosp. adminstr., Laredo, 1979-83; hosp. adminstr. Charter Med. Corp., Laredo, 1983—; chmn. bd. San Antonio Fed. Credit Union, 1977-79; advisor Kingsville Health Systems Agy. (Tex.), 1979-82. Treas. March of Dimes, Laredo, 1979; chmn. Tex. United Way Campaign, 1982. Served with USMC, 1962-65. Named to Football Hall of Fame, Latin Am. Internat., 1982. Mem. Am. Soc. for Personnel, Nat. Assn. Supts. Pub. Residential Facilities for Mentally Retarded, Am. Assn. Mental Deficiencies. Republican. Roman Catholic. Home: 701 Laurel St Laredo TX 78041 Office: Charter Rio Grande Hosp PO Box 2769 Laredo TX 78041

RAMOS LÓPEZ, CARMEN ROSA, counselor; b. Caguas, P.R., Aug. 31, 1939; d. Agustin Ramos and Rafaela Lopez. B.A., U. P.R., 1961, postgrad., 1979; M.Ed., Catholic U. of P.R., 1971; student NYU, 1981. Cert. counselor; nat. cert. career counselor. Mem. employment interview staff Dept. Labor, Humacao, P.R., 1961-65, occupational counselor, 1965-73; college counselor, U. P.R., Cayey, 1973—; camp dir. Child Commn., Humacao, 1965; tchr. Cayey U. Coll., U. P.R., 1974—. Mem. Am. Assn. Counseling and Devel., Am. Coll. Personnel Assn., Am. Rehab. Counseling Assn., P.R. Athenaeum. Roman Catholic. Avocation: travel. Home: Munoz Rivera St PO Box 6414 Caguas PR 00626 Office: Cayey Univ Coll Antonio R Barcelo Ave Cayey PR 00633

RAMPACEK, CARL, metallurgy educator, consultant; b. Omaha, Aug. 7, 1913; s. Max and Marie (Skala) R.; m. Mary Caroline Kull, Nov. 15, 1939; children—George Bruce, Charles Max. B.S., Creighton U., 1935, M.S., 1937; postgrad. in metallurgy U. Mo.-Rolla, 1937-39. Chemist Phillips Petroleum Co., 1939-41; metallurgist U.S. Bur. Mines, Tuscaloosa, Ala., 1941-45; supervisory metallurgist S.W. Expt. Sta., Tucson, 1945-60; research dir. Tuscaloosa Metallurgy Research Ctr., U.S. Bur. Mines, 1960-63, asst. dir. adminstrn., Washington, 1963-67, research dir., College Park, Md., 1967-69, acting asst. dir., Washington, 1969-70, asst. dir. metallurgy, Washington, 1970-75; dir. Mineral Resources Inst., U. Ala., University, 1976-83, assoc. dir., 1983—, also prof. metallurgy; cons. in field. Recipient Alumni Achievement award Rolla U., 1974, Disting Service medal U.S. Dept. Interior, 1967. Mem. Am. Chem. Soc., AIME (Henry Krumb Lectr., Robert Earll McConnell award 1977-78), AAAS, Sigma Xi, Alpha Chi Sigma. Lodge: Rotary. Contbr. numerous articles to profl. jours; patentee in field.

RAMSEY, FEBBIE L., school counselor; b. Alligator, Miss., June 21, 1952. B.A., Tougaloo Coll., 1974; M.Ed., Auburn U., 1983. Cert. tchr. English tchr. Bay County Sch. Bd., Panama City, Fla., 1978-84, sch. counselor, 1984—. Nat. merit scholar, 1970; Internat. Paper Co. Found. fellow, 1979-83; Nat. Ednl. finalist NEH, 1984. Fellow Nat. Council Tchrs. of English, Lang. Arts Council, Am. Assn. Counseling and Devel., Fla. Assn. Counseling and Devel.; mem. Black Educators Caucus (treas. 1981-85). Avocations: sewing; reading; writing; shell collecting. Home: 1023 Kurze Ave Panama City FL 32401

RAMSEY, INEZ LINN, librarian, educator; b. Martins Ferry, Ohio, Apr. 25, 1938; d. George and Leona (Smith) Linn; m. Jackson Euguene Ramsey, Apr. 22, 1961; children—John Earl, James Leonard. B.A. in Hist. SUNY-Buffalo, 1971; M.L.S., 1972; Ed.D. in Audiovisual Edn., U. Va., 1980. Librarian Iroquois Central High Sch., Elma, N.Y., 1971-73, Lucy Simms Elem. Sch., Harrisonburg, Va., 1973-75; instr. James Madison U., Harrisonburg, 1975-80, asst. prof., 1980—; mem. Va. State Library Bd., Richmond, 1975-80; cons.; librarian, book reviewer Harrisonburg-Rockingham County Assn. for Retired Citizens. Contr. to Enclopedia, articles to profl. jours.; project dir. Oral (tape) History Black Community in Harrisonburg, 1977-78; storyteller, puppeteer. Mem. Harrisonburg Republican City Com., 1981-83. Recipient spl. citation for service Va. Readathon Program, Harrisonburg, 1977; research grantee James Madison U., Harrisonburg, 1981. Mem. ALA, Am. Assn. Sch. Librarians, Assn. Edn. Communications, Tech., Children's Lit. Assn., Puppeteers Am., Nat. Assn. Preservation and Perpetuation of Storytelling, Va. Ednl. Media Assn. (sec. 1981-83, citation 1983 pres. 1985-86, Educator of Yr. award 1984-85), Phi Beta Kappa (pres. Shenandoah chpt. 1980-81), Children and Young Adults Round Table (exec. bd. 1977-80), Va. Library Assn., Beta Phi Mu. Home: 282 Franklin St Harrisonburg VA 22801 Office: Dept Ednl Resources James Madison U Harrisonburg VA 22807

RAMSEY, JACKSON EUGENE, educator; b. Cin., Dec. 20, 1938; s. Leonard Pershing and Edna Willa (Blakeman) R.; B.S. in Metall. Engring., U. Cin., 1961; M.B.A., SUNY, Buffalo, 1969, Ph.D., 1975; m. Inez Mae Linn, Apr. 22, 1961; children—John Earl, James Leonard. Welding engr. Gen. Electric Co., Cin., 1961-62, Westinghouse-Bettis Lab., Pitts., 1962-66; prodn. control mgr. Columbus-McKinnon Corp., Buffalo, 1966-71; asst. prof. mgmt. SUNY, Buffalo, 1971-73; prof. mgmt. James Madison U., Harrisonburg, Va., 1973—; cons. in field. Chmn. Harrisonburg Republican Party, 1978-84, vice chmn., 1974-78; vice chmn. Sixth Dist. Rep. Party, 1984—. Served with USMCR, 1956-62. Named Outstanding Young Scholar, Xerox Corp., 1976; registered profl. engr., Va., Ohio. Mem. Acad. of Mgmt., Am. Inst. for Decision Scis., Inst. of Mgmt. Sci., Am. Soc. for Metals, Nat. Soc. Profl. Engrs. Republican. Baptist. Author: R * D Strategic Decision Criteria, 1986; editor: Handbook for Professional Managers, 1985; Budgeting Basics, 1985; Library Planning and Budgeting, 1986; contbr. articles to profl. jours. Home: 282 Franklin St Harrisonburg VA 22801 Office: Dept Mgmt and Mktg James Madison U Harrisonburg VA 22807

RAMSEY, JETTIE CECIL, county official; b. Daytona Beach, Fla., Aug. 31, 1925; s. Joseph James and Nonnie (Mann) R.; B.B.A., Massey Coll., 1955; postgrad. Fla. Jr. Coll., 1968, 73, Ga. U., 1972, Fla. Technol. U., 1972, U. Colo., 1983; m. Pauline Cordelia Thaden, May 9, 1942; children—Wilson Lujack, Joseph Cecil (dec.), Pauline Diana (dec.). Engr., Duval Engring. & Constrn. Co., Jacksonville, Fla., 1946-66; with Office of Sheriff, Duval County, Fla., 1966—, warden Duval County Prison, 1969-71, rehab. officer, 1971-73, supt. jails, 1973—. Mem. Duval County Exec. Com., 1958—; capt. Jacksonville Police Res., 1968-75; troop scoutmaster Boy Scouts Am., 1962-64. Served with USNR, 1943-46. Mem. So. Genealogists Soc., VFW (vice comdr. 1975), Correctional Officers Assn., Fla. Peace Officers Assn., Fraternal Order Police, Assn. Preservation Tenn. Antiquities, Soc. Confederate Vets. Democrat. Clubs: Masons (32 deg., worshipful master) (Shriners), Order Eastern Star (worthy patron 1960, 81). Author: Road Back to the Mainline. Home: 1039 Hood Ave Jacksonville FL 32205 Office: 400 E Bay St Jacksonville FL 32201

RAMSEY, LINDA HORNER, nurse; b. Denver, Oct. 16, 1942; d. Robert Frederick and Thelma Delores (Winn) Horner; m. Terry LeRoy Ramsey, Mar. 1, 1964; children—Ann Marie, Felicia Lynn. R.N., St. Luke's Hop., 1961; postgrad. Colo. Womans Coll., 1963-64, Tulsa U., 1964. Recovery room nurse St. Luke's Hosp., Denver, 1961-63, Bartlesville Meml. Hosp. (Okla.), 1964-65; lectr. weight reduction, Dallas, 1982—. Trustee, Dallas Ballet, 1975-77, lectr., 1975, v.p. women's com., 1979-80, pres. women's com., 1980-82; mem. women's bd. Friends of Ctr., Swiss Ave. Counseling Ctr., 1985-86; commentator Heirloom Fashion Shows, Goodwill Industries, 1985-86; core leader Community Bible study, 1984, 85, 86. Mem. Beta Sigma Phi. Republican. Presbyterian.

RAMSEY, MARY ELIZABETH, nurse, nursing director; b. Walnut, Ark., May 27, 1937; d. Cecil and Mary Rose (Meadows) R.; m. Cletis James Fellabaum, Nov. 1967 (div. 1980). R.N., Bapt. Hosp. Sch. Nursing, 1957; B.A. in Bus. Adminstrn. and Psychology, Stephens Coll., 1983. Staff nurse Crossett Health Ctr., Ark., 1957-58; asst. night supr. Springdale Meml. Hosp., Ark., 1958-60; stewardess nurse No. Pacific Railway, Seattle, Chgo., 1960-61; staff and asst. head nurse USPHS Hosp., Seattle, 1961-66; float staff nurse, asst. head nurse Ob unit, Alaska Native Health Ctr., Anchorage, 1969-71; asst. night supr. Springdale Meml. Hosp., Ark., 1971-72; mgr. GBS Record Keeping Systems, Rogers, Ark., 1972-74; asst. dir. Shared Inservice Northwest Ark., 1972-74; dir. nursing service Springdale Meml. Hosp., 1976—; chmn. LPN Adv. Com., Springdale, 1983—. Served to capt. USAF, 1967-70. Mem. Nat. League Nurses, Ark. Hosp. Assn., Am. Nurses Assn. Republican. Presbyterian. Avocations: racquetball; golf; fishing. Home: 613 N Mill Springdale AR 72764 Office: Springdale Meml Hosp PO Box 47 Springdale AR 72765

RAMSEY, ROBERT RUSSELL, JR., higher education consultant; b. Stewart County, Tenn., Apr. 22, 1929; s. Robert Russell and Bonnie Kate (Goforth) R.; B.A., Yale U., 1950; Ed.M., Harvard U., 1954, Ed.D., 1959; LL.D. (hon.), Alderson-Broaddus Coll., 1981; m. Susan Charlotte Randolph, June 30, 1962. Asst. to dir. admissions Harvard U. Law Sch., 1954-57; asst. in financial aid office, head proctor, mem. bd. freshman advisers Harvard Coll., 1957-59; asst. dean freshman year, asst. dir. Office Ednl. Research, Yale U., 1959-61, asst. master Branford Coll., 1960-63, univ. dir. admissions and freshman scholarships, 1961-66; asst. dir. program devel. Va. Council Higher Edn., 1966-68, asso. dir., 1968-69; dir. evaluation Commn. Instns. Higher Edn., New Eng. Assn. Schs. and Colls., 1969-76; sec. edn. Gov.'s Cabinet, Commonwealth of Va., 1976-78; Va. commr. Edn. Commn. States, 1976-78; ednl. cons., 1978-80; chancellor W.Va. Bd. Regents, 1980-83; W.Va. mem. So. Regional Edn. Bd., 1981-83; W.Va. mem. Edn. Commn. States, 1982-83; dep. commr. coordinating bd. Tex. Coll. and Univ. System, Austin, 1983-85; higher edn. cons., 1985—. Served with AUS, 1950-53. Mem. Am. Psychol. Assn., Am. Sociol. Assn. (assoc.). Home and Office: 102 S Highland St Paris TX 38242

RAMSEY, VIRGINIA CAROL MARSHALL, educator; b. Alcoa, Tenn., Aug. 7, 1935; d. Arthur Glenn and Dorothy Alexander (Huff) Marshall; m. David Lawrence Ramsey, July 5, 1957; children—Stephanie Lea, Jennifer Lynne, Thomas Marshall. B.A., Maryville Coll., 1957; Ed.M., W. Ga. Coll., 1981; Ed.S., U. Ga., 1984. Cert. tchr., counselor, art supr., data collector. Instr. art Maryville Coll., Tenn., 1957-58; supr. art Alcoa City Sch. System, Tenn., 1958-59; art instr. Cobb County Pub. Schs., Marietta, Ga., 1972—, Cobb Community Sch., Marietta, 1980-83; bd. dirs. Student Art Symposium, Athens, Ga.; presenter art shows, confs., 1972—. Author: Student Teacher Handbook, 1982. Mem. Kennestone Hosp. Guild, Marietta, 1967—; mem. Cobb PTA, 1967—, treas., 1974-76, pres., 1970-71, 76-77; mem. Sprayberry High Sch. Booster Club, 1972—; panelist Gov.'s Conf. on Career Devel., Macon, 1972; leader Girl Scouts U.S.A., 1971-72; v.p. Sprayberry Adv. Council, Marietta, 1981-82, pres., 1982-85; active Robert Woodruff Mus. Art, 1969—, Cobb Arts Council, 1975—, Marietta/Cobb Fine Arts Orgn., 1970—. Mem. Nat. Art Edn. Assn., Ga. Art Edn. Assn. (middle sch. chmn. 1984—, high sch. chmn. 1977-79), Atlanta Area Art Tchrs. Assn., Huguenot Soc. (v.p. Tenn. 1974-75), Bells Ferry Homeowners Assn. Republican. Presbyterian. Avocations: photography; hiking; bridge; golf; history. Office: Mabry Sch Cobb County Sch System 2700 Jims Rd Marietta GA 30066

RAMSKI, RUSSELL, systems engineer, financial advisor; b. Miami, July 18, 1953; s. Joseph Anthony and Mary (Halasz) R.; m. Jennifer Lynn Evans, Oct. 13, 1984. A.S., Fla. Inst. Tech., 1974, B.S., 1975; M.B.A., Rollins Coll. Systems engr. Geophys. Services, Inc., Dallas, 1975-79, navigation supr., 1979-83; systems engr./analyst Sci. Applications, Inc., Orlando, Fla., 1983-84. Mem. Mensa. Home: 3225 N Helen Ave Orlando FL 32804

RANA, JAIME M., physician; b. Bolivia, S.Am., Apr. 26, 1936; came to U.S., 1971; s. Manuel and Candelaria (Gaite) R.; m. Haydee Vega, June 13, 1964; children—Fernando, Silvina. M.D., U. de La Plata, 1964. Intern, Cook County Hosp., Chgo., 1971-72, resident, 1972-74; fellow in cardiology Med. coll. Wis., Milw., 1974-76; practice medicine specializing in cardiology; mem. staff Meml. City Hosp., Spring Br. Hosp., Katy Community Hosp. Fellow Am. Coll. Cardiology; mem. AMA, Am. Hosp. Assn., Am. Coll. Cardiology. Office: 902 Frostwood St Suite 290 Houston TX 77024

RAND, ANTHONY EDEN, state senator, lawyer; b. Garner, N.C., Sept. 1, 1939; s. Walter and Geneva (Yeargan) R., Jr.; m. Karen Skarda; children—Ripley E., Craven M. A.B., U.N.C., 1961, LL.B., 1964. Ptnr. Mitchiner, Andrews, Rand, Raleigh, N.C., 1965-68, Rose, Thorp, Rand & Ray, Fayetteville, N.C., 1968-81, Rose, Rand, Winfrey & Gregory, Fayetteville, 1982—; mem. N.C. Senate, 1981—. Mem. N.C. State Democratic Exec. Com., 1975-77; chmn. exec. com. Cumberland County Dem. party (N.C.), 1977-81; bd. visitors U. N.C.-Chapel Hill; bd. dirs., mem. exec. com. Pub. Sch. Forum. Mem. ABA, N.C. Bar Assn., Assn. Trial Lawyers Am. (state committeeman 1968-72), Am. Judicature Assn., Alpha Tau Omega, Delta Theta Phi. Episcopalian. Office: NC Senate State Capitol Raleigh NC 27611*

RAND, MARGARET MARY, counselor; b. Richmond, Va., June 14, 1959; d. Patrick Charles and Margaret Barbara (Regenhold) R. B.A., Va. Poly. Inst. and State U., 1981; M.S., Va. Commonwealth U., 1984. Counselor Parmadale Family Treatment Program, Parma, Ohio, 1982-83; alcoholism cons. Beyond

Inc., Richmond, Va., 1983-85, treatment services supr., 1985—; com. mem. Alcohol Awareness, Richmond, 1984-85. Active in Child Devel. Council, Parmadale, St. Anthony's, 1981-83; speaker Teenage Inst. Drug Prevention Workshops, Cleve., 1982; chmn. Mid Eastern Alateen Conf., Va., 1981-82; bd. dirs. Eastern Seaboard Alateen Conf., Va., 1980; foster parent, Montgomery County, Va., 1981. Mem. Va. Assn. Alcohol and Drug Abuse Counselors, (bd. dirs. 1985—), Nat. Assn. Alcohol and Drug Abuse Counselors, Am. Assn. Counseling and Devel. Baptist. Clubs: Rebos (sec. 1984-85). Home: 1500 Stony Force Dr Richmond VA 23228 Office: Beyond Inc 6952 Forest Hill Ave Richmond VA 23228

RANDALL, CAROLYN DINEEN, federal judge; b. Syracuse, N.Y., Jan. 30, 1938; d. Robert E. and Carolyn E. (Bareham) Dineen; A.B. summa cum laude, Smith Coll., 1959; LL.B., Yale U., 1962; children—James, Philip, Stephen. Admitted to D.C. bar, 1962, Tex. bar, 1963; pvt. practice, Houston, 1962-79; circuit judge U.S. Ct. Appeals 5th Circuit, Houston, 1979—. Trustee, exec. com., treas. Houston Ballet Found., 1967-70; mem. Houston dist. adv. council SBA, 1972-76; mem. Dallas regional panel President's Commn. White House Fellowships, 1972-76, mem. commn., 1977; bd. dirs. Houston chpt. Am. Heart Assn., 1978-79; nat. trustee Palmer Drug Abuse Program, 1978-79; trustee, chmn. audit com. United Way Tex. Gulf Coast, 1979-85. Mem. Am. Bar Assn., Fed. Bar Assn., State Bar Tex., Houston Bar Assn., Phi Beta Kappa. Roman Catholic. Home: 3830 Wickersham Ln Houston TX 77027 Office: 11020 US Courthouse 515 Rusk St Houston TX 77002

RANDALL, CLIFFORD WENDELL, civil engineering educator, water pollution control researcher and consultant; b. Somerset, Ky., May 1, 1936; s. William Lesbert and Geneva (James) R.; m. Phyllis Amis, Aug. 15, 1959; children—Andrew Amis, William Otis. B.S. in Civil Engring., U. Ky., 1959, M.S. in Civil Engring., 1963; Ph.D., U. Tex., 1966. Asst. prof. civil engring. U. Tex.-Arlington, 1965-68; asst. prof. civil engring. Va. Poly. Inst. and State U., Blacksburg, 1968-69, assoc. prof., 1969-72, prof., 1972-81, Charles P. Lunsford prof. civil engring., 1981—; cons. to indsl. plants; mem. Va.-N.C. Chowan River Tech. Liaison Com.; mem. Va. Bd. Cert. for Water and Wastewater Works Operators, 1980—; vis. prof. civil engring. U. Cape Town (South Africa), 1983; water supply project analyst So. Bapt. Fgn. Mission Bd., Kenya, 1983; WHO Cons. for lectures to Nat. Environ. Engring. Research Inst. India, Nagpur, 1983; mem. sci. and tech. adv. com. Chesapeake Bay Project, EPA; mem. James River water quality monitoring com. State of Va. Co-author: Biological Process Design for Wastewater Treatment, 1980; Stormwater Runoff Management in Urbanizing Areas, 1983. Contbr. numerous articles on civil engring. and water pollution control to profl. jours. Served to lt. U.S. Coast and Geodetic Survey (now ocean survey of NOAA), 1959-62. Moderator Highlands Baptist Assn., Va., 1982-83; pres. Montgomery Gideon Camp, Va., 1986-78, 82; chmn. troop 44 com. Boy Scouts Am., 1980-82; deacon Blacksburg Bapt. Ch., 1972-76, 79-82, chmn., 1976. Mem. Water Pollution Control Fedn. (dir. 1981-84, Morgan cert. of merit 1982, Bedell award 1983), ASCE (rep. on U.S.A. nat. com. of Internat. Assn. Water Pollution Research and Control 1980—, meritorious tech. paper award 1969, service award, 1978, 80), Am. Water Works Assn. (cert. of recognition 1980), Internat. Assn. on Water Polution Research and Control, Assn. Environ. Engring. Profs. (sec.-treas. 1978-80, dir. 1977-80, service award 1981, officers award 1982), Va. Water Pollution Control Assn. (past pres. award 1977, dir. 1975-76, 81-84, pres. 1976). Democrat. Baptist.

RANDALL, JOHN DEL, nuclear engineer, consultant; b. Whittier, Calif., Nov. 19, 1932; s. Francis Marion and Mary LaVerne (Gardner) R.; m. Marilyn Verle Shirk, Feb. 5, 1953; children—Cathleen Gail, Deborah Jean, John Robert, Carolyn Lisa. B.S., U. Calif.-Berkeley, 1955, M.S., 1956; Ph.D., Tex. A&M U., 1965. Assoc. head nuclear sci. ctr. Tex. A&M U., College Station, 1963-65, assoc. prof., 1968-72, dir. sci. ctr., 1965-82, prof., 1972-83; sr. exec. cons. NUS Corp., College Station, 1983-85; mgr. S.W. region Gen. Physics Corp., 1985—; cons. Internat. Atomic Energy Agy., Vienna, Austria, Inst. for Atomic Energy, São Paulo, Brazil, 1976-79, USNRC, R.O. lic. examiner, 1981-82. Pres., Oak Hills Owners Assn., College Station, 1978—. Fellow Am. Nuclear Soc. (chmn. reactor operations 1982, Silver Anniversary Exceptional Service award 1980); mem. Nat. Orgn. Test, Research, and Tng. Reactors (chmn. 1982), Health Physics Soc., Sigma Xi, Phi Kappa Phi. Republican. Mormon. Avocations: golf; fishing. Home: Route 5 Box 1273 College Station TX 77840 Office: Gen Physics Corp Route 5 Box 1273 College Station TX 77840

RANDALL, QUEEN FRANKLIN, college president; b. Pine Bluff, Ark., Jan. 28, 1935; d. Samuel and Ollie (Boykins) Franklin; 1 dau., Barbara Joyce. B.S. in Edn., Lincoln U., 1956; A.M., Ind. U., 1961; Ed.D., Nova U., 1975. Instr. math. Lincoln U., 1956-58; instr. math. Am. River Coll., Sacramento, 1962-70, chmn. math. and engring. div., 1972-76, assoc. dean instrn., 1972-76, dean instrnl. systems and student devel., 1976-78; pres. Pioneer Community Coll., Kansas City, Mo., 1978-80; asst. to chancellor Met. Community Coll. Dist., Kansas City, 1980-81; pres. El Centro Coll., Dallas, 1981—; dir. Indsl. Devel. Corp. Dallas. Mem. Contact Dallas Advt. Bd., Treescape Dallas Adv. Bd. Fellow John Hay Whitney Found., 1961, Delta Kappa Gamma, 1974. Mem. Am. Assn. Women in Community and Jr. Colls., Tex. Jr. Coll. Tchrs. Assn. Club: Soroptimists. Home: 7123 Murdock Way Carmichael CA 95608 Office: Main and Lamar Sts Dallas TX 75202

RANDALL, ROBERT ALDEN, anthropology educator; b. Montclaire, N.J., Apr. 14, 1942; s. Alden Lawson and Wanda Mary Allen (Danne) R.; m. Nancy Evelyn Edwards, Aug. 23, 1968; 1 child, Colin Ross. B.S., Bucknell U., 1964; postgrad., Columbia Tchrs. Coll., 1964; M.A., SUNY-Binghamton, 1968; Ph.D., U. Calif.-Berkeley, 1977. Head math. Birnin Kudu SS, Nigeria, 1964-66; vis. lectr. U. Victoria, B.C., Can., 1975-76, U. Calif., Riverside, 1976-79; asst. prof. anthropology U. Houston, Tex., 1979—; anthrop. researcher U. Calif., Berkeley, 1971-72. TV commentator on Vietnam War Series PBS, Houston, 1984. Contbr. articles to profl. jours. Coach Little League, Houston, 1983—; active Westwood Civic Assn., Houston, 1979—; bd. dirs. Streetfarmer's Coop., Houston, 1982-83. U. Calif.-Berkeley fellow 1975; U. Houston grantee 1980, 84. Recipient Excellence in Teaching award U. Houston 1985. Mem. Am. Anthrop. Assn., Am. Ethnol. Soc., Linguistic Soc. Am. Democrat. Avocation: rare fruit tree growing. Office: U Houston Dept Anthropology University Park Houston TX 77004

RANDEL, JO STEWART, museum executive; b. Clarendon, Tex., Dec. 14, 1915; d. William Cole and Mae (Clarke) Stewart; m. Ralph E. Randel, Sept. 23, 1937; 1 dau., Margaret Stewart-Randel Koons. Student Clarendon Coll., 1932-34. Reporter, editor Tex. newspapers, 1935-37; founder Carson County Sq. House Mus., Panhandle, Tex., 1965, dir., 1965-83, chmn. bd., 1983—; mem. exec. com. Tex. Panhandle Heritage Found., 1960—; bd. dirs. Amarillo Symphony, Tex., 1970—; trustee Amarillo Art Ctr., 1975-81; active West Tex. State U. Fine Arts Found., 1977—. Author history coloring book for children—Land of Coronado, 1973. Editor, contbg. author: A Time To Purpose, 4 vols., 1967 (state award 1967). Contbr. feature articles to various nat. publs. Active Girl Scouts U.S., 1937—; mem. Tex. Gov.'s Com. on Aging, Austin, 1961-65; mem. Tex. Com. on Higher Edn., Austin, 1968-70; chmn. West. Tex. State U. Found., Canyon, 1980-83. Recipient Hist. Preservation award Tex. Hist. Commn., 1971; Outstanding Citizen award Amarillo C. of C., 1976; Outstanding Contbn. to Arts award Tex. Commn. on Arts, 1979; Summit awards Golden Nail, 1984; named Disting. Woman, West Tex. State U., 1977; named to West Tex. State U. Hall of Fame, 1985. Mem. Tex. Hist. Found. (bd. dirs. 1969-83), Tex. Assn. Mus. (council; Outstanding Service to Council award 1981), Nat. trust Hist. Preservation, Am. Assn. State and Local History, Am. Assn. Mus. (council Mountain Plains region 1970-73), Fine Arts Club (pres. 1960-62), Philos. Soc. Tex., DAR. Methodist. Avocations: golf; swimming; fly fishing. Home: 400 Charles PO Box 186 Panhandle TX 79068 Office: Carson County Sq House Mus 5th and Elsie PO Box 276 Panhandle TX 79068

RANDLE, JUDY MARY, small business counselor, realtor, accountant; b. Teaneck, N.J., Apr. 1, 1943; d. Andrew Benjamin and Susan Catherine (Gibney) Mroczek; m. William Malcolm, Dec. 31, 1963; children—William Malcolm, Andrew Francis. Student Colgate U., 1958-59; B.A., U. North Fla., 1976, M.B.A., 1978. Sales rep. Jacksonville (Fla.) C. of C., 1975; instr. St. Johns River Jr. Coll., 1977; grad. research asst. U. North Fla., 1977-78; programmer Ind. Life Ins. Co. Inc., Jacksonville, 1979-81; market research analyst Blue Cross Blue Shield Fla., 1981; small bus. counselor Randle and Randle Cons., Orange Park, Fla., 1977 83; realtor assoc. Watson Realty Corp., 1983-84; broker-salesman Coldwell Banker, 1984—. Mem. reelection com. Congressman Chappell; mem. Town Gov. Charter Rev. Com.; 1st v.p. Democratic Women's Club Clay County, 1982; com. woman Dem. Exec. Com. Clay County; del. Dem. State Conv., 1983; candidate Town Council, 1985. Mem. Nat. Assn. Accts. (sec. 1981, treas. 1982), Data Processing Mgmt. Assn. (outstanding service award 1982, profl. newspaper staff, trade show vendor chmn. 1982), Clay County C. of C. (chmn. edn. com., chmn. econ. devel. com.), Clay County Bd. Realtors (polt. action com., legis. day com.), Am. Mgmt. Assn. Episcopalian. Clubs: Sawgrass Country (Ponte Vedra, Fla.); Continental Country (Orange Park, Fla.); Fla Striders Track.

RANDLE, RODGER A., state senator; b. Oct. 26, 1943; B.A., U. Okla., 1967; LL.B., U. Tulsa, 1978. Mem. Okla. Ho. of Reps., 1971-72; mem. Okla. Senate, 1973—, now chmn. Senate Appropriations Com., Joint Legis. Com. on Fed. Funds, pres. pro tem 40th Legis. Session, past chmn. Senate Edn. Com.; admitted to Okla. Bar, 1978. Office: PO Box 514 Tulsa OK 74101

RANDLE, THOMAS EARL, educational administrator; b. Brenham, Tex., Jan. 25, 1953; s. Mary D. (Graves) Randle Burton; m. Rubye Whiting, Dec. 8, 1973; children—Gayland, Brian, Clayton. B.S., Tex. A&M U, 1975, Ed.M., 1979; Ed.D., Okla. State U., 1981. Tchr. vocat. agr. Sweeny Ind. Sch. Dist., Tex., 1975-79; research asst. Okla. Dept. Vocat. Tech., Stillwater, 1979-80; asst. dir. student teaching Okla. State U., Stillwater, 1980-81; asst. prin. McCullough High Sch., The Woodlands, Tex., 1981-84; prin. Knox Jr. High Sch., The Woodlands, 1984—. Contbr., co-contbr. articles to profl. publs. Active Kiwanis Spl. Olympics, Woodlands, Tex., 1984. Okla. Regents Scholar, 1980; named Hon. State Farmer, Tex. Future Farmers Am., 1978; named to Outstanding Young Men Am., U.S. Jaycees, 1981. Mem. Nat. Assn. Secondary Sch. Prins., Vocat. Agrl. Tchrs. Assn. (dist. v.p. 1977-78). Democrat. Baptist. Lodge: Kiwanis (Woodlands, Tex.). Home: 12 Spurwood Court The Woodlands TX 77381 Office: Knox Jr High Sch 12104 Sawmill Rd The Woodlands TX 77380

RANDLES, HARRY EDWARD, educational administration educator; b. Rutland, N.Y., Nov. 12, 1919; s. George Wilson and Fannie (Babcock) R.; m. Christine Lorraine Farrow, Jan. 31, 1944; children—Karen Spiekerman, Bruce. B.F.A., Syracuse U., 1950; M. Edn. Adminstrn., Miami U., Oxford, Ohio, 1958; Ph.D. in Ednl. Adminstrn., Ohio State U., Miami U.-Oxford, 1964. Cert. pub. sch. adminstr. Tchr. Argyle Central Sch., N.Y., 1953-54, Univ. Jr. High Sch., Austin, Tex., 1954-56, Wilson Jr. High Sch., Hamilton, Ohio, 1956-59; prin. Vandalia Jr. High Sch., Ohio, 1959-61; grad. fellow Miami and Ohio State Univs., Oxford, Columbus, 1961-63; personnel adminstr. Akron City Schs., Ohio, 1963-64; prof. ednl. adminstrn. Sch. Edn. Syracuse U., N.Y., 1964-78, Peabody/Vanderbilt U., Nashville, 1978—; cons. pub. sector labor relations. Author: Handbook for Negotiators in the Public Sector, 1982; also articles. Served to capt. USAF, 1942-46. NDEA fellow, 1961-63. Mem. Am. Assn. Sch. Adminstrs., Tenn. Council Sch. Adminstrs., Tenn. Profl. Edn. Adminstrs., Phi Delta Kappa (pres.-elect 1984—). Democrat. Methodist. Avocation: creative writing. Home: 1504 Dresden Circle Nashville TN 37215 Office: Peabody Coll Vanderbilt Univ Box 514 Peabody St Nashville TN 37203

RANDOLPH, JAMES HARRISON, SR., realty co. exec.; b. Springfield, Tenn., Feb. 17, 1917; s. Bayless Jones and Effie Lee (Cummings) R.; B.S. in Bus. Adminstrn., U. Tenn., 1940; m. Millicent Roma Lincoln, Aug. 14, 1943; 1 son, James Harrison. Spl. agt., adminstrv. asst. to dir. FBI, Washington, 1942-52, also Bur. speaker, insp.; personnel dir. Dallas Housing Authority, 1952-54; real estate broker Bolanz & Bolanz, Dallas, 1954-58; real estate broker, investor Jim Randolph & Co., Realtors, Dallas, 1958—. Bd. govs. U. Tenn. Mem. Soc. Former Spl. Agts. of FBI (chmn. chpt. 1960), Soc. Indsl. Realtors, Dallas C. of C. (hon. life), Scarabbean, Phi Sigma Kappa. Baptist. Club: Brookhaven Country (Dallas). Subject of articles in Nat. Real Estate Investor, July, 1961. Home: 11433 Lamplighter St Dallas TX 75229 Office: 211 N Ervay Bldg Dallas TX 75201

RANDOLPH, LINDA DARLENE LASHMET, marketing executive; b. Highland Park, Mich., Sept. 14, 1950; d. Franklin A. and Dolores B. (Maciejewski) Lashmet; m. Ronald Glenn Randolph, Aug. 18, 1984. B.A., No. Mich. U. With Travelodge, Orlando, Fla., 1972-73; sales rep. Seaworld, Orlando, 1973-74, sales mgr., 1974-75; field mgr. Am. Motor Inns, Roanoke, Va., 1975-79, v.p., 1980—; owner Shuckers Seafood Restuarants, Roanoke, 1982—, Luxury Limousine Service, 1983—. Mem. Am. Soc. Tng. and Devel. (chpt. dir. 1982-84), Meeting Planners Internat. (com. chair 1980), Profl. Bus. Women Roanoke, Sales and Mktg. Execs., Soc. Advancement of Travel for Handicapped. Democrat. Roman Catholic. Avocations: skiing; gardening; swimming. Home: Rt 4 Box 411 Salem VA 24153 Office: PO Box 14100 Roanoke VA 24022

RANDUK, RAY PAUL, food and design consultant; b. Chgo., Mar. 7, 1933; s. Sam Joseph and Mary (Brnich) R.; m. Audrey Mae Agnis, July 5, 1956; 1 child, Susan. B.A., Mich. State U., 1956, M.B.A., 1960. Hotel and restaurant cons. U.S. Dept. State, Tel Aviv, Israel, 1960-61; resident mgr. Cabana Hotel, Dallas, 1961-62; asst. to pres. C.H. Alberding-44 Hotels, Chgo., 1962-72; pres. H.R.I. Cons. Internat., Inc., Dallas, 1972—. Editor: Bar Management, 1981. Contbr. articles to profl. jours. Served with U.S. Army, 1956-58. Recipient Design award Blue Cross/Blue Shield, 1980, 81. Mem. Dallas Hotel Assn. (pres. 1969-71), Food Service Cons. Soc. Internat., Cert. Hotel Adminstrs., Food Facilities Cons. Soc., Tex. Restaurant Assn., Food Research Soc. Internat., Mich. State U. Alumni Assn. Republican. Presbyterian. Club: Engineers. Lodge: Lions. Avocations: reading; golfing. Home: 9240 Shoreview Rd Dallas TX 75238 Office: H R I Cons Internat Inc 3505 Turtle Creek #502 Dallas TX 75219

RANFT, ARTHUR NEAL, pharmaceutical company executive; b. N.Y.C., Dec. 13, 1945; s. Arthur R. Ranft and Lilyan M. Ranft Hennessy; m. Susan Felts, Dec. 12, 1970 (div. Dec. 1984). Student pub. schs., N.Y.C. Div. mgr. Sears Roebuck and Co., Bossier City, La., 1969-71; mfg. supr. Rucker Pharm. Co., Shreveport, La., 1971-78; purchasing mgr. Boots Pharms., Inc., Shreveport, 1978—. Served with USMC, 1965-68, Vietnam. Mem. Nat. Assn. Purchasing Mgrs. Democrat. Roman Catholic. Lodge: Lions. Avocations: sailing; scuba; photography; art. Office: Boots Pharmaceuticals Inc 6540 Line Ave Shreveport LA 71106

RANGANAYAKI, RAMBABU POTHIREDDY, geophysicist; b. Secunderabad, India, Jan. 15, 1942; came to U.S. 1970; d. Gajapathirao L. Pasupulate and Dwarakabai V. Cola; m. Rambabu Pothireddy, Mar. 24, 1968; children—Anita R. Pothireddy, Anuja R. Pothireddy. B.S., Osmania (India) U., 1962, M.Sc. in Physics, 1964; M.S. in Geophysics, U. Hawaii, 1972; Ph.D. in Geophysics, MIT, 1978. Sr. scientific asst., Nat. Geophys. Research Inst., Hyderabad, India, 1964-69, scientist A., 1969-70; research assoc. Carnegie Instn. of Washington, 1978-80; sr. staff geophysicist Mobil Research and Devel. Corp., Dallas, 1980-84, research geophysicist, 1984-85, sr. research geophysicist, 1985—. East-West Ctr. grantee, 1970-72. Home: 3212 Executive Circle Dallas TX 75234 Office: Mobil Research Devel Corp Dallas TX

RANGE, ROBERT L., utility executive; b. Cuero, Tex., 1933; married. Grad. Southwest Tex. State U., 1957; M.B.A., Pepperdine U., 1976. With Central Power & Light Co. a company of Central & Southwest Corp., Corpus Christi, Tex., 1957-67, 79—, supr. tax acctg., 1963-66, mgr. gen. acctg., 1966-67, exec. v.p., 1979—, also dir.; v.p., controller parent co., 1967-79. Office: Central Power & Light Co 120 N Chapparal Corpus Christi TX 78401*

RANK, MARK ROBERT, sociologist; b. Milw., May 18, 1955; s. Robert Arthur Hallie Jean (Hughes) R.; m. Anne Elizabeth Deutch, Sept. 15, 1984. B.A. with honors, U. Wis., 1978, M.S., 1980, Ph.D., 1984. Demography trainee U. Wis., Madison, 1978-79, project asst., 1979-81, lectr., 1982, research asst., 1981-84; profl. fellow U. N.C., Chapel Hill, 1984—. Contbr. articles to profl. jours. Bush Inst. for Child Family Policy fellow, 1984; Nat. Inst. Child Health Human Devel. demography traineeship, 1978. Mem. Am. Sociol. Assn., Nat. Council Family Relations, Midwest sociol. Assn. Avocations: Tennis; music; skiing, basketball; cooking. Office: Frank Porter Graham Child Devel Ctr U NC Hwy 54 Bypass West 071A Chapel Hill NC 27514

RANKIN, HENRY HOLLIS, JR., lawyer; b. Mission, Tex., Jan. 11, 1915; s. Henry Hollis and Iva (Adams) R.; A.A., Edinburg Jr. Coll., 1933; LL.B., U. Tex. at Austin, 1936; m. Ann Lucille Chesnutt, July 24, 1939; children—Henry Hollis III, Robert Carlton, Deborah Ann (Mrs. Gary Paul Wagner). Admitted to Tex. bar, 1936; gen. practice law, Edinburg, Tex., 1936-58; former ptnr. Rankin & Kern, Inc., McAllen, Tex.; now legal cons./advisor judge Hidalgo County Ct. at Law, 1951-53; dir. Tex. Hist. Commn., 1969-76. Trustee, Mission Ind. Sch. Dist., 1963-69. Bd. dirs. Tex. Hist. Found., 1969-71, 80—, mem. exec. com., 1980-82; bd. dirs. Tex. Law Enforcement Found., 1969, Project Child Abuse; former col. Confederate Air Force. Named Ky. col. Cert. in civil trial law Tex. Bd. Legal Specialization. Fellow Tex. Bar Found. (life); mem. Am. Bar Assn., Hidalgo County Bar Assn. (dir. 1973-75, pres. 1976-77), Tex. Bar Assn., 1936— (legal publs. com. 1972-77, com. on assistance to local bar assns. 1977—), Tex. Assn. Def. Counsel, SAR, Ky. Col., Phi Theta Kappa, Theta Xi. Republican. Baptist. Clubs: McAllen Country. Home and office: 400 St Augustine St Center TX 75935

RANKIS, OLAF EGILS, educator, marketing and statistical research consultant; b. Kiel, Fed. Republic Germany, Apr. 23, 1948; came to U.S., 1951, naturalized, 1960; s. Reinhold Visvaldis and Susan Kaethe-Marie (Herrmann) R.; m. Brenda Kay Morman, Dec. 17, 1977; children—William Konrad, Susanne-Marie. B.S., Heidelberg Coll., 1970; M.S., Xavier U., 1975; Ph.D., Ohio U., 1981. Sr. case analyst Ohio Adult Parole Authority, Columbus, 1970-74; instr. Hocking Tech. Coll., Nelsonville, Ohio, 1974-77, Ohio U., Athens, 1979-81; asst. prof. SUNY-Canton, 1977-79, U. Miami, Coral Gables, Fla., 1981—; research assoc. Police Found., Washington, 1982—, Dade County Grand Jury, Miami, 1984—; sr. research assoc. Behavioral Sci. Research Corp., Coral Gables, 1983—; staff cons. Nigerian Polit. Digest, Lagos, 1984—. Contbr. articles to profl. jours. Chmn. UN Assn. Miami, 1985; presdl. advisor UN Assn. Mem. Am. Psychol. Assn., Internat. Communication Assn., World Communication Assn., Speech Communication Assn. P.R., Fla. Speech Communication Assn. Democrat. Avocations: marksmanship, art collecting, microcomputers, gardening. Home: 9490 SW 64th St Miami FL 33173 Office: Sch Communication Univ Miami 105 Merrick Bldg Coral Gables FL 33124

RANNEY, RICHARD RAYMOND, dental educator, researcher; b. Atlanta, July 11, 1939; s. Russell Ballou and Maureen Joan (Bannon) R.; m. Beverly Anne Toton, June 10, 1961 (div.); children—Christine Marie, Kathleen Anne; m. 2d, Patricia Marie DeNoto, Feb. 22, 1969; children—Maureen Frances, Russell Christopher. D.D.S., U. Iowa, 1963; M.S., U. Rochester, 1969. Asst. prof. periodontology U. Oreg., 1969-72; assoc. prof. periodontics Va. Commonwealth U., Richmond, 1972-78, prof., 1978—, dir. grad. periodontics, 1972-76, chmn. dept. periodontics, 1974-77, asst. dean research and grad. affairs, 1977-84, asst. dean research, 1984—; dir. Clin. Research Ctr. for Periodontal Diseases, 1978—. Served with USPHS, 1963-66. Nat. Inst. Dental Research grantee, 1970—. Fellow Internat. Coll. Dentists; mem. ADA, Am. Acad. Periodontology, Internat. Assn. Dental Research (basic research in periodontology award 1985), Am. Assn. Dental Schs., AAAS, Am. Soc. Microbiology, Sigma Xi, Omicron Kappa Upsilon. Contbr. chpts. to books, articles to profl. jours. Office: PO Box 566 MCV Sta Va Commonwealth U Richmond VA 23298

RANSOM, NANCY ALDERMAN, university official; b. New Haven, Feb. 25, 1929; d. Samuel Bennett and Florence (Opper) Alderman; m. Harry Howe Ransom, July 6, 1951; children—Jenny Alderman, Katherine Marie, William Henry Howe. B.A., Vassar Coll., 1950; postgrad. Columbia U., 1951, U. Leeds (Eng.), 1977-78; M.A., Vanderbilt U., 1971. Instr. sociology U. Tenn.-Nashville, 1971-76; grant writer Vanderbilt U., Nashville, 1976-77, dir. Women's Ctr., 1978—, instr. sociology, 1972, 74, lectr. women's studies, 1983—; speaker profl. meetings. Vol. counselor family planning Planned Parenthood Assn. of Nashville, 1973-77, bd. dirs., 1978—, v.p., 1981—. Columbia U. residential fellow, 1951; Vanderbilt U. fellow, 1971, Mem. Am. Sociol. Assn., So. Sociol. Assn., Nat. Women's Studies Assn., Southeastern Women's Studies Assn., AAUW, Women's Ctrs. Network, Women in Higher Edn. Tenn., NOW, Nat. Women's Polit. Caucus, LWV, Phi Beta Kappa. Club: Cable. Office: PO Box 1513 Sta B Vanderbilt U Nashville TN 37235

RANWEZ, JEAN-LOUIS FERNAND, engring. co. exec.; b. Montigny-sur Sambre, Belgium, Feb. 5, 1918; s. Fernand Edouard and Helene Urbina (Scheins) R.; came to U.S., 1945, naturalized, 1960; B.A., Sacred Heart Coll., Argentina, 1936; E.E., Institut Gramme, Liège, 1940; m. Jane Thatcher Moses, June 25, 1946; children—Helene Taylor, Francis, Corinne Clark. Student engr., Combustion Engring. Inc., 1945, field supr. France, 1946-56, supr. research and devel., N.Y.C., 1956-60, European rep., Paris, 1960-63, Madrid, 1963-65, Australian mgr., Sydney, New South Wales, 1965-69, project mgr. Windsor, Conn., 1969-85; v.p. Logical Systems, Inc. Served with Signal Corp, Belgian Army, attached to Brit. Army, 1940-45. Mem. ASME. Republican. Roman Catholic. Home: Whitehall 908 Whitehall Rd Apt 12-J Chattanooga TN 37405 Office: PO Box 246 Senoia GA 30276 also 911 W Main St Chattanooga TN 37405

RAPAPORT, BENJAMIN, scientific corporation executive; b. Boston, Aug. 21, 1936; s. Israel and Rose (Cohen) R.; m. Elizabeth Ann Rice, June 23, 1971; 1 child, Darren Alexis. B.A., Northeastern U., 1959; M.B.A., U. Ala., 1968. Commd. 2d lt. U.S. Army, 1959, advanced through grades to lt. col., 1975; with U.S. Army Signal Corps, U.S. Army, 1959-79; ret., 1979; program mgt. IIT Research Inst., Annapolis, Md., 1980-81; sr. analyst Sci. Applications Internat. Corp., McLean, Va., 1981—; lectr. Tinder Box Internat. Ltd., Santa Monica, Calif., Tobacco Assn. Am. Author: A Complete Guide to Collecting Antique Pipes, 1979; A Tobacco Source Book, 1973. Assoc. editor Pipe Smoker Mag., 1983-84; columnist Smokeshop mag. Contbr. articles to profl. jours. Named to Pipe Smokers Hall Fame 1974. Mem. l'Académie Internationale de la Pipe, Am. Soc. Appraisers, New Eng. Appraisers Assn., Phi Alpha Theta, Beta Gamma Sigma. Republican. Avocations: pipe collecting; bibliophile on tobacco and smoking; writer and researcher on tobacco lore; racquetball; handball. Home: 5101 Willowmeade Dr Fairfax VA 22030

RAPER, BOBBY JOE, airlines company executive, mayor; b. McKinney, Tex., Feb. 9, 1933; s. Roy S. and Grace Lorene (McIrvin) R.; student public schs., McKinney; m. Vennie Ann Thompson, Feb. 17, 1956; children—Risa Jo, Gayla Deann, Wade. With Braniff Airlines, from 1956, now maintenance quality control insp. Mem. Irving (Tex.) City Council, 1972—, mayor, 1981—. Served with USN, 1951-55. Baptist. Office: Office of Mayor PO Box 2288 Irving TX 75015*

RAPHAEL, COLEMAN, engineer, manufacturing company executive; b. N.Y.C., Sept. 16, 1925; s. Morris and Adella (Leav) R.; B.Civil Engring., CCNY, 1945; M.C.E., Poly. Inst. Bklyn., 1951, Ph.D. in Applied Mechanics, 1965; m. Sylvia Moskowitz, Feb. 28, 1948; children—Hollis, Gordon. Structural research engr., test research engr. Republic Aviation Corp., 1945-47; instr. mech. engring. Pratt Inst., Bklyn., 1947-51; from sr. research engr. to mgr. space systems div. Republic Aviation Corp., 1951-65; gen. mgr. space and electronics systems div., then v.p. Fairchild Hiller Corp., Germantown, Md., 1965-70; with Atlantic Research Corp., Alexandria, Va., 1970—, chmn. bd., chief exec. officer, 1980—; chmn. bd. SJI Industries, 1968-70, Night Owl Security, 1983—. Mem. engring. adv. com. Montgomery Coll., Md., 1968-69, George Washington U., 1977-80; mem. Gov. Va. Task Force Nuclear Power Plants, 1969; chmn. energy com. Gov. Md. Sci. Adv. Council, 1974-76; bd. visitors U. Pitts., 1980—; chmn. U.S. Bond drive, Alexandria, 1975-76, Montgomery County Task Force on Compensation, 1983-85; bd. dirs. Ctr. for Innovative Tech.; chmn. adv. com. Montgomery County Bldg. Codes, 1976-77. Recipient Citizenship award Montgomery County Press Assn., 1967, Disting. Service award Montgomery County C. of C., 1969, Disting. Citizenship award State of Md., 1970; registered profl. engr., N.Y., Fla. Assoc. fellow AIAA (chmn. mgmt. com. 1976). Author textbook, papers, reports in field. Home: 508 Hermleigh St Silver Spring MD 20902 Office: 5390 Cherokee Ave Alexandria VA 22324

RAPP, JAMES ALAN, marketing executive; b. St. Louis, Dec. 30, 1946; s. William Albert and Catherine Celeste (Book) R.; B.A., St. Benedicts Coll., 1969; student St. Johns U., 1965-66; m. Esther Nelson, May 25, 1979. Mng. editor Apt. Living Mag., St. Louis, 1972-73; mng. editor Daily Record, New Orleans, 1973; dir. devel. and mktg. WYES-TV, New Orleans, 1974-78; dir. mktg. services Stewart Enterprises, Inc., New Orleans, 1978-85; v.p. mktg. Perez Ltd., New Orleans, 1985—. Devel. advisor New Orleans Opera Assn., 1981-83. Mem. Advt. Club New Orleans (Addy award 1984), Pub. Relations Soc. Am. (Anvil award for excellence 1983), U.S. Fencing Assn., La. Hist. Soc. Editor: Metairie Cemetery: An Historical Memoir, 1981. Home: 509 Mandeville St New Orleans LA 70117 Office: 110 Veterans Blvd New Orleans LA 70005

RAPP, SANDU Z., architect; b. Targoviste, Romania, Mar. 23, 1917; came to U.S., 1959, naturalized, 1965; s. Zissu Benjamin and Berthe (Loebel) R.;

diploma in architecture Poly. Inst., Bucharest, Romania, 1941; grad. Conservatory of Music, Bucharest, 1940; m. Katherine Gruenberg, Jan. 12, 1958. Pvt. practice architecture, Bucharest, Romania, 1940-50, Tel Aviv, 1950-59; assoc. P. Birnbaum, Architect, N.Y.C., 1959-65, Evans & Delehanty, Architects, N.Y.C., 1965-73; pvt. practice architecture, Miami Beach, Fla., 1973—. Served as 2nd lt. Romanian Army, 1940-41. Registered architect, Israel, N.Y., Fla.; cert. Nat. Council Archtl. Registration Bds. Mem. AIA. Democrat. Archtl. works include Palace of the Swedish Legation, Bucharest, 1941-43, project for Swedish Legation, Jerusalem, 1951; (with Evans and Delehanty) expansion of Bklyn. Coll., Marymount Manhattan Coll. high rise, 1965-73. Composer various works for piano, orch., chamber music, songs. Home: 1865 79th St Causeway Apt 15-I North Bay Village FL 33141 Office: 1666 79th St Causeway Suite 402 North Bay Village FL 33141

RAPPAPORT, MARTIN PAUL, physician; b. Bronx, N.Y., Apr. 25, 1935; s. Joseph and Anne (Kramer) R.; B.S., Tulane U., 1957, M.D., 1960; m. Bethany Ann Fitzgerald; children—Karen, Steven, Sheila. Intern, Charity Hosp. of La., New Orleans, 1960-61, resident in internal medicine, 1961-64; practice medicine specializing in internal medicine, Seabrook, Tex., 1968-72, Webster, Tex., 1972—; mem. courtesy staff Mainland Ctr. Hosp. (formerly Galveston County (Tex.) Meml. Hosp.), 1968—, Bapt. Meml. System, 1969-72; mem. staff Humana Hosp Clear Lake Clear Lake Hosp.), 1972—; cons. staff St. Mary's Hosp., 1973-79; cons. nephrology St. John's Hosp., Nassau Bay, Tex.; fellow in nephrology Northwestern U. Med. Sch., Chgo., 1968; clin. instr. in medicine and nephrology U. Tex., Galveston, 1969—; lectr. emergency med. technician course, 1974-76; adviser on respiratory therapy program Alvin (Tex.) Jr. Coll., 1976-82; cons. nephrology USPHS, 1979-80. Served to capt. M.C., U.S. Army, 1961-67. Diplomate Am. Bd. Internal Medicine, Nat. Bd. Med. Examiners. Fellow Am. Coll. Chest Physicians, A.C.P.; mem. Internat., Am. socs. nephrology, So. Med. Assn., Tex. Med. Assn., Am. Soc. Artificial Internal Organs, Am. Diabetes Assn., Tex. Acad. Internal Medicine, Galveston County Med. Soc., Am. Diabetes Assn., Am. Geriatrics Soc., Bay Area Heart Assn. (bd. govs. 1969-75), Clear Lake C. of C., Phi Delta Epsilon, Alpha Epsilon Pi, Tulane Alumni Assn. Jewish. Lodge: Rotary. Home: 16515 Laurelfield Dr Houston TX 77059 Office: 450 Blossom St Webster TX 77598

RAPPAPORT, YVONNE KINDINGER, educator, lecturer; b. Crestline, Ohio, Feb. 15, 1928; d. Paul Theodore and Florence Iona (Cover) Kindinger; m. Norman Lewis Rappaport; children—Michael. Laura, Hilray, Stephen, Jocelyn. B.S. summa cum laude, Northwestern U., 1949; M.A., Va. Poly. Inst. and State U., 1973; C.A.G.S., 1979; Ph.D., 1980. Personnel officer, then cons. and mgmt. analyst USAF, 1953-63; cons. mgmt. analysis, personnel and pub. relations, 1963-67; cons. program devel., instr. U. Va., 1967-70, dir. continuing edn. for women, 1970-76, dir. continuing edn. for adults, 1976—; dir., performer theatre, children's theatre, radio and TV, 1953—; mem. editorial adv. bd. New Viewpoints div. Franklin Watts, Inc., pubs., 1979—; cons. in field. Author handbooks and work books, also radio, TV scripts. Mem. Va. Adv. Legis. Com. Continuing Edn., 1970-71, No. Va. Adv. Com. Ednl. Telecommunications, 1971—; bd. dirs. Home and Sch. Inst., Washington, 1971-79; mem. adv. bd. Service League Va., 1976-78; U.S. del. gen. assembly Internat. Council Adult Edn., Paris, 1982, UNESCO, Paris, 1985, ICAE World Assembly, Buenos Aires, 1985. Recipient Meritorious Service award USAF, 1959; Leadership award Am. Assn. Adult and Continuing Edn., 1982, 84, Human Resource Devel. award ASTD/TOC, 1982. Mem. Nat. Assn. Women Deans, Adminstrs. and Counselors (S.E. regional coordinator 1973-83), Adult Edn. Assns. U.S. (Nat. Leadership award 1973, 74, 76, 77, 78, 79; chmn. commn. status women in edn. 1972-84, dir. 1973—, chmn. council affiliate orgns. 1974-75, chmn. pub. affairs, 1975-78, v.p. 1978-79), Va. (pres. 1971-73; Recognition of Merit award 1971-73), LWV (state dir. 1968-73, nat. pub. relations com. 1970—), AAUW, PTA, Washington Soc. Assn. Execs., Internat. Assos. Adult Edn. (treas. 1981—), Am. Personnel and Guidance Assn., Nat. Univ. Extension Assn., Assn. Continuing Higher Edn., Coalition Adult Edn. Orgns. U.S. (sec.-treas. 1981-83, pres. 1985-86), Am. Bus. Women Assn. (award 1960), Phi Delta Kappa. Club: Order Eastern Star. Home: 3225 Atlanta St Fairfax VA 22030 Office: Sch Continuing Edn Univ Va Charlottesville VA 22903

RASBERRY, CHARLES L., broadcasting educator; b. Brookland, Ark., Sept. 14, 1934; s. Roy H. and Nellie I. (Shockney) R.; m. Rebecca Kay Gardner, Oct. 10, 1975; 1 child, Catherine Nell. B.S., Ark. State U., 1956; M.Television, U. Ill., 1961. Reporter, The Daily Big Picture, Paragould, Ark., 1953, reporter, announcer KDRS Radio, Paragould, 1953-56; reporter WILL-AM-FM-TV, Urbana, Ill., 1960, KDRS Radio, Paragould, 1961; chmn. dept., dir. broadcasting Ark. State U., Jonesboro, 1961—, dir. Indian Sports Network, Jonesboro, 1961—, mgr., gen. mgr., KASU Radio, Jonesboro, 1961—; cons. in field. Contbr. articles to profl. jours.; producer numerous broadcasts. Mem., Cable TV Franchising Com., Jonesboro, 1984-85. Served to lt. USNR, 1956-60. U. Ill. grad. fellow, 1960; recipient Plaque, City Council, Jonesboro, 1983. Mem. Broadcast Edn. Assn., Soc. Profl. Journalists, Sigma Delta Chi. Methodist. Office: Ark State U Dept Radio-TV PO Box 2160 State University AR 72467

RASCH, ELLEN MYRBERG, biophysics educator; b. Chicago Heights, Ill., Jan. 31, 1927; d. Arthur August and Helen Catherine (Stelle) Myrberg; m. Robert W. E. Rasch, June 17, 1950; 1 son, Martin Karl. Ph.B. with honors, U. Chgo., 1945, B.S. in Biol. Sci., 1947, M.S. in Botany, 1948, Ph.D., 1950. Asst. histologist Am. Meat Inst. Found., Chgo., 1950-51; USPHS postdoctoral fellow U. Chgo., 1951-53, research assoc. dept. zoology, 1954-59; research assoc. Marquette U., Milw., 1962-65, assoc. prof. biology, 1965-68, prof. biology, 1968-75, Wehr Disting. prof. biophysics, 1975-78; research prof. East Tenn. State U., Quillen-Dishner Coll. Medicine, Johnston City, 1978—. Mem. Wis. Bd. Basic Sci. Examiners, 1971-75, sec. bd., 1973-75. Recipient Pre-doctoral fellowship USPHS, 1951-53, Research Career Devel. award, 1967-72; Teaching Excellence award Marquette U., 1975; Kreeger-Wolf disting. vis. prof. in biol. sci. Northwestern U., 1979. Fellow AAAS, Royal Microscopic Soc.; mem. Am. Microscopical Soc., Am. Soc. Cell Biology, Am. Soc. Zoologists, Am. Soc. Ichthyologists and Herpetologists, The Histochem. Soc., Phi Beta Kappa, Sigma Xi. Contbr. articles to various publs. Home: 1504 Chickels St Johnson City TN 37601 Office: PO Box 15130a East Tenn State Univ Quillen Dishner Coll Medicine Johnson City TN 37614

RASE, BEVERLY WILLS BONELLI, school administrator, civic worker; b. Ft. Worth, Mar. 14, 1928; d. Louis Benedict and Venne Armstrong (Wills) Bonelli; m. Howard Frederick Rase, June 12, 1954; children—Carolyn Victoria, Howard Frederick. B.A., Wellesley Coll., 1950. Vol., Ft. Worth Art Assn., 1949; editor West Side Post, Ft. Worth, 1951-53; vol. Ft. Worth Children's Mus., 1952-54; organizer Ft. Worth Wellesley Club, 1954; founding co-chmn. Wellesley Children's Art Show, Austin, Tex., 1955; v.p. U. Tex. Univ. Ladies Club Newcomers, Austin, 1955-56; charter mem. Laguna Gloria Art Guild, Austin, 1955-60; v.p. Laguna Gloria Art Mus., Austin, 1960; pres. Austin Wellesley Club, 1961; founder Eastern Coll. Parents Com., Austin, 1961; pres. Tex. Fine Arts Assn., Austin, 1963-64; dir. Wellesley Fund, Tex. and La., 1964-67; leader Camp Fire Girls of Good Shepherd, 1968-71; area program chmn. Balcones council Camp Fire Girls, Austin, 1969-72; founder, pres. Elisabet Ney Mus. Guild, 1969; pres. Casis Elem. Sch. PTA, Austin, 1970-71; mem. Altar Guild Episcopal Ch. of Good Shepherd, 1971-73; founder, dir., chmn. bd. trustees Kirby Hall Sch., Austin, 1976—; mem. Symphony League of Austin. Recipient appreciation award Tex. Fine Arts Assn., 1969, Camp Fire Leader award, 1971, Order of the Unicorn appreciation award Kirby Hall Sch., 1979. Mem. Delta Delta Delta. Republican. Author: Tales of a Texas Grandfather, 1957, student and faculty handbooks. Home and Office: 3700 River Rd Austin TX 78703

RASHKIND, PAUL MICHAEL, lawyer; b. May 21, 1950; s. Harvey Rashkind and Norma (Dorfman) Nash Weinstein; m. Robin Shane, Dec. 20, 1975; children—Adam Charles, Noah Hamilton, Jennifer Elizabeth. A.A., Miami-Dade Jr. Coll., 1970; B.B.A., U. Miami, 1972, J.D., 1975. Bar: Fla. 1975, U.S. Dist. Ct. (so. dist. Fla.) 75, U.S. Ct. Appeals (5th cir.) 1976, U.S. Supreme Ct. 1978, U.S. Dist. Ct. (middle dist. Fla.) 1979, U.S. Ct. Appeals (2d cir.) 1981, U.S. Ct. Appeals (11th cir.) 1981, N.Y. 1981, D.C. 1981; cert. criminal trial atty. Nat. Bd. Trial Advocacy. Debate coach U. Miami, Coral Gables, Fla., 1972-73; asst. state atty. Dade County State Attys. Office, Miami, 1975-78, chief asst. state atty. in charge of appeals, 1977-78; assoc. firm Sams, Gerstein & Ward, P.A., Miami, 1978-83; mem. firm Bailey, Gerstein, Rashkind & Dresnick, Miami, 1983—; spl. master 11th Jud. Circuit Ct., Miami, 1982—; arbitrator Dade County Jail Inmates Grievance Program, Miami, 1981—; mem. Fla. Bar Unauthorized Practice of Law Com. 11th Jud. Cir., Miami, 1980-84. Contbr. articles on ethics and criminal law to profl. jours. Pres., bd. dirs. Lindgren Homeowners Assn., Miami, 1981—. Fellow Am. Bd. Criminal Lawyers (gov. 1980—); mem. ABA, Dade County Bar Assn., Acad. Fla. Trial Lawyers (chmn. criminal law sect. 1985-86), Hon. Order Ky. Cols., Soc. Bar and Gavel, Iron Arrow, Delta Theta Phi, Omicron Delta Kappa, Delta Sigma Rho-Tau Kappa Alpha, Pi Sigma Alpha. Democrat. Jewish. Office: Bailey Gerstein Rashkind & Dresnick 4770 Biscayne Blvd Miami FL 33137

RASMUS, JO GOSS, sales manager, management training specialist; b. Oklahoma City, Okla., Nov. 27, 1952; d. Eddie Kendall and Johnnie Mae (Renfro) G.; m. James Lee Rasmus, Jan. 28, 1984. B.S. in Bus., Okla. State U., 1975. Market support specialist Xerox Office Products Div., Tulsa, 1976-78, sales tng. specialist Internat. Tng. Ctr., Leesburg, Va., 1978-80, market support mgr. OPD, Dallas, 1980-81, mgmt. tng. devel. mgr. OPD, Dallas, 1981-83, mgr. human resources Systems Mktg. Div., Dallas, 1983-84, sales mgr. Infomart, Dallas, 1984—. Recipient Outstanding Market Support Mgr. award Xerox OPD, 1981, Special Merit award Xerox at Infomart, 1985. Mem. Am. Soc. Tng. and Devel., Women in Computing. Democrat. Baptist. Avocations: jogging, dance. Home: 7628 Village Trail Dr Dallas TX 75240 Office: Xerox at Infomart 1950 Stemmons St Suite 3001 Dallas TX 75207

RASMUSSEN, BRIAN ROBERT, insurance company executive; b. LaPorte, Ind., June 5, 1953; s. Robert Frederick and Rose Elizabeth (Conner) R. B.A., Ind. U., 1975; Ph.D., U. Tex., 1981. Health analyst AFSCME, Washington, 1977-78, 80-83; legis. analyst Blue Cross and Blue Shield Assn., Washington, 1983—; cons. Rasmussen and Assocs., Arlington, Va., 1983—; vice chmn. Forum on Long-Term Care, Washington, 1983—. Contbr. articles to profl. jours. Mem. Am. Psychol. Assn. Democrat. Home: 2019 N 20th Rd Arlington VA 22201

RASMUSSEN, DAVID WILLIAM, economist, educator, consultant; b. Chgo., Dec. 20, 1942; s. William Reinholt and Mabel Elizabeth (Houser) R.; m. Jeanne M. McFarland, Aug. 20, 1979 (dec. Sept. 1980); m. Joanne Thersa Oliveri, Dec. 26, 1982; 1 child, Sarah Elizabeth. B.A., Earlham Coll., 1964; M.S., Washington U., St. Louis, 1967, Ph.D., 1969. Asst. prof. Fla. State U., Tallahassee, 1968-72, assoc. prof., 1972-79, prof., 1979—; spl. asst. for research U.S. Dept. HUD, 1978-79; cons. Urban Inst., 1979-83. Author: Elements of Economics, 1984; Economics: Principles and Applications, 1979; Urban Economics, 1973; also articles. Mem. Regional Sci. Assn., Am. Econ. Assn., So. Regional Sci. Assn., So. Econ. Assn., Am. Real Estate and Urban Econ. Assn. Home: 3127 Ferns Glen Dr Tallahassee FL 32308 Office: Dept of Econs Florida State U Tallahassee FL 32306

RASMUSSEN, JULIE SHIMMON, educator, cellist; b. Aberdeen, S.D., June 3, 1940; d. George Bar and Clara (Lange) Shimmon; m. Frederick Robert Rasmussen, Apr. 1, 1961 (div. May 1971). B.Music, Ind. U., 1963; M.Ed., U. Fla., 1967. Cert. tchr., Fla. Coordinator music Bradford County Sch. Bd., Starke, Fla., 1965-68; tchr. Duval County Sch. Bd., Jacksonville, Fla., 1968-69, community edn., 1972-79, program devel., 1979—; master tchr. Clay County Sch. Bd., Orange Park, Fla., 1969-72; facilitator, mem. planning com. Duval County Sch. Bd., Jacksonville, 1985-86. Grant writer in ednl. areas, 1979—. Com. mem. Jacksonville Community Council, Inc., 1973; cellist Jacksonville Symphony, 1963-65; tech. asst. Arts Assembly of Jacksonville, Inc., 1979-82; mem. Cummer Art Gallery, Jacksonville, 1983. Recipient Little Red Schoolhouse award Fla. Dept. Edn., 1977-78, Sense of Community award Duval County Community Edn., 1979; Internat. String Congress grantee Musician's Union, 1961. Mem. Fla. Ednl. Research Assn., Pi Kappa Lambda, Phi Delta Kappa, Kappa Delta Pi (parliamentarian 1985-86). Democrat. Lutheran. Club: Pilot. Avocations: physical fitness; jogging; swimming; cycling; psychology. Home: 3946 St John's Ave Jacksonville FL 32205 Office: Duval County Sch Bd Adminstrn Bldg 1701 Prudential Dr Jacksonville FL 32207

RASNAKE, MONROE, agricultural extension specialist; b. Bee, Va., Feb. 8, 1942; s. Ira and Sarah Ercil (Sykes) R.; m. Florence Marie Long, June 6, 1965; children—Sara Elizabeth, Matthew Monroe. B.S. in Agr., Berea Coll., 1965; M.S. in Agronomy, Va. Poly. Inst., State U., 1967; Ph.D. in Soil Chemistry, U. Ky., 1973. Conservationist trainee USDA, Ky., 1963-65; tchr. Buchanan County Sch., Va., 1967-70; asst. prof. Va. Poly. Inst. State U., Blacksone, 1973-77; land mgmt. specialist Dept. Defense U.S. Army, Blacksone, Va., 1977-78; extension specialist U. Ky., Princeton, 1978—. Contbr. articles to profl. jours., mags. Recipient Outstanding Young Man Am., 1975. Mem. Am. Soc. Agronomy, Am. Forage Grassland Council (chmn. affiliate adv. commn.), Ky. Forage Grassland Council (sec.), Pub. Service to Forages award 1985), Assn. Ky. Extension Specialists (Outstanding New Specialist award 1983). Baptist. Avocations: gardening; hunting; fishing. Home: Route 6 Box 23G Princeton KY 42445 Office: U Ky PO Box 469 Princeton KY 42445

RATARD, RAOULT CLAUDE-BERNARD, physician; b. Santo, New Hebrides, Dec. 13, 1944; came to U.S., 1977; s. Aubert and Suzanne Marie-Louise (Lafforgue) R.; B.S., U. Paris, 1967, M.D., 1968; D.M.&I, Institut Pasteur, Paris, 1970; M.S., La. State U., 1976; M.P.H., Tulane U., 1976; m. Margaret S. Francez, Dec. 14, 1970; children—Laennec, Marceau, Paulin. Intern, Hosp. Vaugirard, Paris, 1968-69; chief med. officer Rural Health Services, Vila, New Hebrides, 1972-77; dep. dir. region 9, Tex. Dept. Health, Uvalde, 1977-79, leprosy cons., 1977-79; dir. Jefferson Parish Health Dept., Metairie, La., 1980-81; chief Tb, venereal disease and toxic disease control sect. La. Dept. Health, 1980-85; chief Schistosomiasis Research Project, Yaounde, Cameroon, 1985—; leprosy cons. WHO, Suva, Fiji, 1979. WHO fellow, 1973, 75-76. Mem. Am. Public Health Assn., La. Public Health Assn., La. Med. Assn., Am. Soc. Tropical Medicine and Hygiene, Royal Soc. Tropical Medicine and Hygiene, Internat. Health Soc., Am. Coll. Preventive Medicine. Contbr. articles to profl. jours. Home: 4109 Cleveland Pl Metairie LA 70003 Office: BP817 Yaounde Cameroon

RATCLIFFE, CARL JAMES, college counselor; b. Bluefield, W.Va., Dec. 9, 1946; s. Charles James and Mary Lee (Brooks) R.; m. Janice Kathleen Milligan, June 7, 1969. B.S., U. S.C., 1972; M.A., Ball State U., 1975; Ed.D., Nova U., 1983. Teaching cert., Ala., S.C. Tchr. pub. schs., Huntsville, Ala., 1975-78; counselor youth program NASA, Huntsville, 1977; counselor-dir. youth program U.S. Army, Redstone Arsenal, Ala., 1978; counselor J.C. Calhoun Coll., Decatur, Ala., 1979—; counselor summer camp Assembly of God, Clanton, Ala., 1985. Tchr. Christian Missionary Alliance, Udorn, Thailand, 1970; elder First Christian Ch., Huntsville, 1977; tchr. young adults Weaterly Christian, Huntsville, 1984—. Served with USAF, 1968-75. Mem. Am. Assn. Counseling and Devel., Ala. Assn. Counseling and Devel., Ala. Jr. and Community Coll. Assn., J.C. Calhoun Community Coll. Edn. Assn., Nat. Evang. Assn., World Evang. Assn. Democrat. Mem. Assemblies of God. Avocations: speaking to church groups; providing marriage and pre-marriage seminars; slide programs on countries visited; fishing. Home: 11003 Jean Rd SE Huntsville AL 35803 Office: JC Calhoun Community Coll PO Box 2216 Decatur AL 35602

RATHGEBER, JUERGEN OSCAR, plastics company executive; b. Wuppertal, Northrhine-Westfalia, Germany, Dec. 29, 1938; s. Fritz and Irene Beate (Otto) R.; m. Jo Lovella Foster, Sept. 4, 1965. B.S. in Engring., U. Wuppertal (Germany), 1961; B.S. in Econs., U. South Calif., 1965, M.B.A., 1968. Project engr. Akzona, Asheville, N.C., 1961-63; project engr. Mattel, Inc., Hawthorne, Calif., 1968-74; v.p. engring. Milton Bradley, Nuernberg, Germany, 1974-77; dir. engring. Kenner Toys, Cin., 1978-80; v.p. engring. Southern Case, Raleigh, 1980-84, v.p. ops., 1984—. Dean's scholar U. So. Calif., 1964-65. Mem. Am. Mktg. Assn., Soc. Plastics Engrs., N.C. World Trade Orgn. Republican. Lutheran.

RATICK-STROUD, SHERI, theatre arts administrator; b. Bklyn., Nov. 3, 1947; d. Martin and Dorothy (Berlin) Ratick; m. Kenneth E. Stroud, Aug. 5, 1972; 1 child, Dori Evette. B.A., U. Md., 1970. Office adminstr., editor Socio-Systems, Inc., Falls Church, Va., 1978-79; office mgr., bookkeeper Musifex, Inc., Arlington, Va., 1979-80; asst. supr. Opinion Ctrs., Inc., Springfield, Va., 1980-81; dir. group sales and vol. services Paper Mill Playhouse, Millburn, N.J., 1982-84; holiday festival coordinator John F. Kennedy Ctr. for Performing Arts, Washington, 1985. Dir. play Dear Me, The Sky is Falling. Vol. co-host weekly show Electronic Info. Edn. Service; vol. office helper Paper Mill Playhouse. Recipient 1st Place award VFW, 1964. Mem. Am. Film Inst., Am. Council for Arts, Cultural Alliance Greater Washington, Friends of Kennedy Ctr. (sustaining), Women's Am. Orgn. for Rehab. through Tng. (pres. Fairfax chpt. 1977-79, v.p. No. Va. area council 1985—). Jewish. Avocation: collecting fans, music boxes, frog figurines. Home: 7812 Mulberry Bottom Ln Springfield VA 22153

RATLEDGE, WILBERT HAROLD, JR., educational administrator; b. Atlanta, May 2, 1940; s. Wilbert Harold and Nora Mae (Coleman) R.; m. Helen Marie Siemens, Aug. 28, 1965; children—Philip Wilbert, Rebekah Ruth. B.A., Tenn. Temple Coll., 1962; Th.M., Dallas Theol. Sem., 1966; M.A., N.Tex. State U., 1970, Ph.D., 1982. Instr. Dallas Bible Coll., 1966-67, athletic dir., 1968-70, asst. registrar, dir. admissions, registrar, 1970-79, dean acad. affairs, 1978-85; instr. Bamboo River Acad., West Borneo, Indonesia, 1967-68; v.p. acad. affairs Woodcrest Coll., Lindale, Tex., 1985—; pastor First Bapt. Ch., Cunningham, Tex., 1964-67. Editor: Satan, 1973; author articles. Mem. Evang. Theol. Soc., Soc. Christian Philosophers, Phi Alpha Theta. Baptist. Avocations: chess; reading; table tennis; basketball. Office: Woodcrest Coll Route 1 Box 106 Lindale TX 75771

RATLIFF, RICHARD WAYNE, oil company executive, sporting goods store executive; b. Rotan, Tex., June 28, 1945; s. A.D. and Bertha Jewel (Chism) R.; m. Janice Kay Albert, May 4, 1974; children—Ryan, Courtney, Ashlee. B.S. in Bus. Adminstrn., St. Edwards U., 1975. Office mgr. State Farm Ins., Dallas, 1964-66; div. dir. Dept. Community Affairs State of Tex., Austin, 1970-81; controller Three B Oil Co., Monahans, Tex., 1981—. Bd. dirs. Ward Meml. Hosp., Monahans, 1985. Served with U.S. Army, 1966-68. Mem. Nat. Assn. Accts., Permian Basin Petroleum Assn., Monahans C. of C. (Ambassadors). Republican. Mem. Ch. of Christ. Lodge: Rotary (pres.-elect 1985).

RATNER, MAX, building products company executive, land developer; b. Bialystok, Poland, 1907. J.D., Cleve. Marshall Law Sch. With Forest City Enterprises, Inc., Cleve., 1928—, chmn. bd., 1974—, dir.; pres. Am. Electrochem. Industries, inc., Israel. Office: Forest City Enterprises Inc 10800 Brookpark Rd Cleveland OH 44130*

RATTI, GINO ARTURO, III, general contractor; b. Balt., Sept. 8, 1944; s. Gino Arturo and Mary Margaret (King) R.; m. Barbara Ann Bertelsman, Aug. 23, 1969; children—Michael Gerard, Kristen Amanda. B.S., Rutgers U., 1967; M.Agr., U. Fla., 1970. Cert. gen. contractor, resdl. contractor. County supr. FMHA, U.S. Dept. Agr., Orlando, Fla., 1971-74; sales/constrn. supr. Mark V Ltd., Inc., Apopka, Fla., 1974-78; self employed builder, Altamonte Springs, Fla., 1978—; pres. Glenstone Corp., Altamonte Springs, 1984—. Mem. Altamonte Springs Transp. Study, 1983. Mem. Nat. Assn. Home Builders, Home Builders Assn. Mid Fla. Republican. Roman Catholic. Club: Downtown Athletic (Orlando). Lodge: Rotary. Address: 1140 Virginia Ave Altamonte Springs FL 32701

RATTRAY, JAMES BAILEY, lawyer; b. Watertown, N.Y., July 26, 1950; s. Clifford M. and Dora M. (Bailey) R.; m. Brenda C. Tyree, Sept. 1, 1978. A.B. cum laude, Syracuse U., 1972; J.D., Coll. William and Mary, 1975, M.L.T., 1982. Bar: Va. 1975, D.C. 1976. Assoc. firm Ernest C. Consolvo, Norfolk, Va., 1975; dep. city atty. City of Hampton (Va.), 1976—; instr. St. Leo Coll., Tidewater Center, Langley AFB, Va., 1982—, Golden Gate U., Resident Ctr., Langley AFB, 1978—, Hampton U., Va., 1985—. Mem. ABA, D.C. Bar Assn., Va. Bar Assn., Nat. Inst. Mcpl. Law Officers, Local Govt. Attys. of Va. Episcopalian. Contbr. articles to profl. jours. Home: PO Box 146 Hampton VA 23669 Office: 22 Lincoln St Hampton VA 23669

RAU, WILLIAM HENRY, educator, pharmacist; b. Hanceville, Ala., Sept. 6, 1922; s. Adolph Johann and Alma Bernardine (Schuster) R. Assoc. Sci., St. Bernard Coll., 1943; B.S. in Pharmacy, Samford U., 1948, B.S. in Sci., 1951. Instr. pharmacy Samford U., Birmingham, Ala., 1948-58; lab. asst. U. Ala.-Birmingham Med. Sch., 1952-58; pharmacist Pharmacy and Nursing Home, Hanceville, 1958-80; tchr. high sch. sci. Cullman County Commn. on Edn., Hanceville, 1958—; cons. pharmacy Hanceville Nursing Home, 1973-78. Author: Pharmaceutical Math, 1950, Pharmacology Laboratory, 1952. Served to cpl. U.S. Army, 1942-46, PTO. Mem. NEA (life), Ala. Edn. Assn. (life), Cullman County Edn. Assn. (pres. 1967-68), Phi Kappa Phi. Lutheran. Lodge: Lions (pres. 1984-85, Melvin Jones fellow 1985). Avocations: sports; photography. Home: 301 Alabama Ave NE Route 6 Box 203 Hanceville AL 35077 Office: Hanceville High Sch 801 Commercial St SE Hanceville AL 35077

RAUH, RICHARD PAUL, architect; b. Covington, Ky., Mar. 27, 1948; s. Robert Paul and Pauline (Farmer) R.; m. Mary Darlene Bailey, Oct. 6, 1975. A.B., Columbia U., 1970; B.Arch., M.Arch., Harvard U., 1974; D.M.D., U. Ky., 1980. Registered architect, 25 states; lic. dentist, Ky., Va. Assist. prof. U. Ky. Coll. Arch., Lexington, 1976-80, adj. asst. prof., 1980-81; prin. Carpenter/-Rauh, Lexington, 1978-80; prin. Rabun Hatch Portman McWhorter Hatch & Rauh Architects, Atlanta, 1981-85; prin. Richard Rauh & Assocs., Architects, Atlanta, 1984—. Works include: Norfolk Hilton Hotel, Va., 1985, Netherland Plaza Hotel restoration, Cin., 1982-83, Bridgeport Plaza Hotel, Conn., 1985, Carew Tower Block restoration, Cin., 1983, master plan Ctr. for Humanities U. Ky. Lexington, 1984; author (with David G. Wright) Design Courses at Schools of Architecture in Western Europe: A Documentary Study, 1975. Pres., Historic South Hill Assn., Lexington, 1978-80. Sheldon fellow, Harvard U., 1974-75, Appleton fellow, 1974-75; recipient LUMEN excellence award Illuminating Engring. Soc. N.Am., 1985; Harvard Book award Harvard Club Cin., 1965; U.S. Dept. Interior grantee Ky. Heritage Commn., 1978; recipient honor awards Nat. Trust Historic Preservation U.S., 1985, AIA South Atlantic Regional council, 1984, Ga. Assn. AIA, 1984; Greater Cin. Beautiful award City of Cin., 1984. Democrat. Presbyterian. Home: 3605 Stratford Rd NE Atlanta GA 30342 Office: Richard Rauh & Assocs 3300 Piedmont Rd NE Atlanta GA 30305

RAUSCHER, JANE KATHLEEN, beverage company project manager; b. Hackensack, N.J., Aug. 8, 1957; d. David Albert and Mary-Gray (Maison) R. B.S. in Interdisciplinary Studies, U. S.C., 1980. Mng. dir. Sales & Mktg. Execs., Internat., N.Y.C., 1981-82; territorial sales mgr. Coca-Cola, USA, Atlanta, 1982-84, project mgr., 1984—. Sponsor, Eagles Nest Boys Ranch, Gainesville, Ga., 1984, sponsor, co-chmn. auction benefit Ga. Alliance for Children, Atlanta, 1984. Mem. Am. Soc. Tng. and Devel., Pi Sigma Epsilon (pres. 1980-81, mng. dir. 1981-82, Outstanding New Mem. 1979). Club: Atlanta Lawn and Tennis Assn. Home: 308 Wedgewood Way Dunwoody GA 30338 Office: Coca-Cola USA 1197 Peachtree St 100 Colony Sq Suite 1801 Atlanta GA 30361

RAVENSCRAFT, HOWARD LEE, physician, lawyer; b. Williamstown, Ky., Oct. 25, 1930; s. James Lee and Ethel Mae (Sargent) R.; m. Joyce Anne Prall, Dec. 10, 1954; children—Krista, Valorie, Natalie, David, Janelle, Bruce. B.S. magna cum laude, Georgetown (Ky.) Coll., 1951; M.D., U. Louisville, 1955; J.D., Chase Coll., 1983. Diplomate Am. Bd. Family Practice; bar: Ky. 1983. Intern, resident St. Elizabeth Hosp. Med. Center, Covington, Ky., 1955-58; practice family and legal medicine Covington and Hebron, Ky., 1955—; pres. Ravenscraft & Yates, P.S.C., 1970—; asst. clin. prof. U. Ky. Sch. of Medicine, Lexington, 1978—; mem. staff William Booth Mem. Hosp., St. Elizabeth Hosp. Served to maj. U.S. Army, 1960-68. Fellow Am. Coll. of Legal Medicine; mem. AMA, Am. Acad. of Family Practice, Ky. Med. Assn., Boone County Med. Soc. (past pres.). Lutheran. Clubs: Mason, Shriner. Home: Box 2635 Riverview Dr Hebron KY 41048 Office: Box 1789 Petersburg Rd Hebron KY 41048

RAVOIRA, JAMES, artist; b. Weirton, W.Va., Sept. 4, 1933; s. James and Josephine; B.A., W. Liberty State Coll., 1962; M.A., Kent State U., 1966, M.F.A., 1977; m. LaWanda Faye Pugh, Nov. 19, 1977. Asst. prof. Indian River Community Coll., Ft. Pierce, Fla., 1967-69; faculty Thornton Community Coll., Harvey, Ill., 1969-70; asst. prof. The Citadel, Charleston, S.C., 1971-74; prof. art U. S.C., Myrtle Beach, 1974-77; art dir. State Fla. grant U. North Fla., Jacksonville, 1983; one-man show Myrtle Beach Conv. Center, 1977, Lynn Kottler Galleries, N.Y.C., 1977, 78; group shows include Fed. Bldg., Ft. Lauderdale, Fla., 1986; pub. in Artist/USA, 1977, The Experiment, 1978; actor Guys and Dolls, 1984. Recipient Eleanor D. Caldwell award Bethany (W.Va.) Coll., 1961, Carnegie Library award, 1961. Mem. Coll. Art Assn., Accademia Italia delle Arti e del Lavoro (Gold medal). Included in Internat. Dictionary of Contemporary Artists. Home: 2633 Middle River Dr Fort Lauderdale FL 33306

RAWLINGS, ANNETTE, painter; b. Birmingham, Ala., Feb. 23, 1943; d. Henry Buchanan and Doris Naomi (Williams) Rawlings; m. Richard Tucker Sinclair, Mar. 30, 1976; 1 dau., Vanessa. Certificate of Completion, U. Heidleburg, 1961, Escuolade Estraneira, Perugia, Italy, 1967; B.A., U. Miami, 1969. Faculty, Met. Mus. and Art Center, Miami, Fla., 1980-83; cons., lectr. Dade County Pub. and Pvt. Schs., Miami, 1980-83, Coconut Grove Art Assn., 1982-83; one man shows Yellowplush Gallery, London, 1976, Rogue Gallery Art, Medford, Oreg., 1981, Union St. Gallery, San Francisco, 1981, Virginia

Miller Gallery, Miami, 1981; group shows include Met. Mus. of Miami, 1983, Birmingham Mus., 1983, Fla. Internat. U., 1983, Internat. Center Contemporary Art, Paris, 1984, Metropolis Internationale Galerie d'Art, Geneva, 1985, Mandragore Internationale Galerie d'Art, Paris, 1986; represented in permanent collections Raimondos, Corp., Plaza Bank, Miami, Michael Butter, Miami, Brunswick Corp., N.Y.C., Internat. Sch. Art and Design, Miami; also pvt. collections. Mem. Met. Mus. and Art Center, Birmingham Mus. Art, Women in Art, Community Art Alliance. Democrat. Episcopalian. Home: 4286 Douglas Rd Miami FL 33133

RAWLINS, HARRY ERLE, JR., realtor; b. Lancaster, Tex., Oct. 13, 1907; s. H. Erle and Maude Trigg (White) R.; m. Virginia Louise Marvin, Dec. 5, 1944 (dec. 1967); children—H. Erle, Susan Rawlins Weaver. B.A., Rice U., 1931, postgrad. Lic. realtor, Tex. With Remington Rand, Houston, 1931-35; officer mgr. Diamond Alkali, Dallas, 1936-39; co-owner Erle Rawlins Jr. Realtors, Dallas, 1945—; restorer town square, Lancaster, Tex. Bd. dirs. Dallas Ballet, Hist. Preservation League, Oak Lawn Preservation Soc., Dallas Mus. Fine Art. Served to lt. comdr. USNR, 1941-45. Mem. Dallas Bd. Realtors. Episcopalian. Clubs: Dallas Country, Lancers. Office: 6725 Snider Plaza Dallas TX 75205

RAWLINS, SALLY EASTHAM, educator; b. Midland, Tex., Oct. 26, 1943; d. Harris Grant and Clara Williams (Murchison) Eastham; m. Leonard Norman Rawlins, Nov. 28, 1982. B.A. in Lit., Queens Coll., 1965; M.Ed., Ga. State U., 1970, postgrad., 1970-72. Instr. Ga. State U., Atlanta, 1970-72; psychologist adolescent unit Ga. Mental Health Inst., Atlanta, 1972-76; behavior specialist Atlanta Pub. Schs., Atlanta, 1976—; cons. in field. Developer programs in edn. middle schs. Dept. Edn. fellow, 1969-70. Mem. Council Exceptional Children. Democrat. Avocations: rug design; photography. Home: 8 Freeman St Maysville GA 30558 Office: PO Box 184 Maysville GA 30558

RAWLS, FRANK MACKLIN, lawyer; b. Suffolk, Va., Aug. 24, 1952; s. John Lewis and Mary Helen (Macklin) R.; m. Sally Hallum Blanchard, June 26, 1976; children—Matthew Christopher, John Stephen. B.A. cum laude in History, Hampden Sydney Coll., 1974; J.D., U. Va., 1977. Bar: Va. 1977, U.S. Dist. Ct. (ea. dist.) Va. 1977, U.S. Ct. Appeals (4th cir.) 1977. Assoc. Rawls, Habel & Rawls, Suffolk, 1977-78, ptnr., 1978—. Elder, clk. of session Westminster Presbyn. Ch., Suffolk, 1984—; chmn. bd. dirs. Suffolk Crime Line, 1982—, Suffolk Cheer Fund, 1982—, Covenant Christian Schs., Suffolk, 1982-84; bd. dirs. Greater Hampton Roads Crime Lines, 1984—; mem. adv. bd. dirs. Salvation Army, Suffolk, 1977—. Mem. Suffolk Bar Assn., Va. Bar Assn., Christian Legal Soc., Va. State Bar, Va. Trial Lawyers Assn., ABA, Assn. Trial Lawyers Am., Suffolk Bar Assn. Lodge: Suffolk Ruritan. Home: 613 N Broad St Suffolk VA 23434

RAWLS, MARTHA GROGAN (MOLLY), librarian; b. Winston-Salem, N.C., Feb. 18, 1949; d. Joseph Cherry and Angelia (Mackie) Grogan; B.A., U. N.C., 1971, M.S.L.S., 1972; m. Jeffrey D. Rawls, June 4, 1978; children—Curtis Grogan, Allen Worthington. Mktg. research librarian R.J. Reynolds Tobacco Co., Winston-Salem, 1973-75, mgmt. info. librarian R.J. Reynolds Industries, Winston-Salem, 1976-79, mgr. mgmt. info. services, 1979-84; former cons. Mandala Center, Inc., Winston-Salem. Mem. Spl. Libraries Assn., Nat. Micrographics Assn., Assn. Records Mgrs. and Adminstrs. Democrat. Baptist. Home: 1839 Barnstable Rd Clemmons NC 27012

RAY, ALBERT BARTOW, psychologist, psychotherapist; b. Washington, July 2, 1946; s. Albert B. and Virginia Lee (Young) R.; m. Barbara Susan Hopkins, Dec. 17, 1972; 1 son, Albert Bartow. B.S. in Psychology, U. Ga., 1969, M.S., 1971, Ph.D., 1976. Lic. psychologist, Fla., Ga.; cert. addiction counselor, Ga. Addiction Counselors Assn. Research asst. Animal Behavior Lab., dept. psychology U. Ga., Athens, 1968-69, equipment coordinator, 1969-70, teaching asst., 1970-71; research asst. to the dir. Athens Unit, Ga. Retardation Ctr., 1970-75; neuroanatomy, neurophysiology and neurology instr. Emergency Med. Tech. Courses and guest instr. practical nursing Athens Area Vocat. Tech. Sch., 1973-75; instr. dept. psychology U. Ga., Athens, 1974; asst. prof. biol. psychology SUNY-Brockport, 1975-77; asst. and assoc. prof. psychology Ga. Southwestern Coll., Americus, 1977-81; staff Sumter Regional Hosp. dir., pres. Alcoholism Recovery Services, Americus, 1979—; instr. Sumter County Driver Improvement Clinic, 1980-82; substance abuse/addiction and mental health counselor, cons. Peach County Hosp., Ft. Valley, Ga., 1981-82; program co-dir. Ithica Place, Treatment Ctr. for Chem. Dependence, Goldenrod, Fla., 1981-82; adj. counselor Pastoral Inst. of Americus, 1981-82; dir. Horizons Unltd. Counseling and Enrichment Ctr., Americus, Ga., 1982—; lectr. in field; conductor workshops. Meritorious scholar, Dept. Psychology, SUNY-Brockport, 1975-76, 76-77; Cert. of Appreciation, Sumter County Mental Health Assn., 1980, Ga. Citizens Council on Alcoholism, Atlanta, 1981. Mem. So. Soc. for Philosophy and Psychology, Sumter County Mental Health Assn. (dir. 1979-80), Ga. Citizens Council on Alcoholism, Ga. Addiction Counselors Assn. (bd. dirs.), Ga. Psychol. Assn., Fla. Psychol. Assn., Aircraft Owners and Pilots Assn., Nat. Assn. Alcoholism Counselors, Ga. Addiction Counselors Assn., Fla. Assn. Practicing Psychologists, Psi Chi. Contbr. articles to profl. jours. Office: 808 Elmo St Americus GA 31709

RAY, ALICE TAYLOR, dietitian; b. Clay County, Tenn., Jan. 19, 1933; d. George Clemons and Clora (Cole) T.; B.S., Tenn. Technol. U., 1952; postgrad. U. Tenn., 1962-63; m. Bascom Ray, May 28, 1952 (dec.); children—Barbara, Kenneth, Sylvia. Supr. food service Vanderbilt U. Hosp., Nashville, 1953-54; supr. spl. diet kitchen St. Thomas Hosp., Nashville, 1954-56; dietitian's asst. Sumner County Meml. Hosp., Nashville, 1962-63; chief dietitian Jesse H. Jones Hosp., Nashville, 1963-69; dir. dietetic services Middle Tenn. Mental Health Inst., Nashville, 1969—; dietetics cons. Med. Quality Assurance div. Tenn. Dept. Health and Environment, 1969-84; cons. in field. Adv. com. Nashville Area Vocat.-Tech. Sch., 1975-76, Vol. State Community Coll., 1977—; organizer, dir. Jolly Sixties sr. citizens group. Mem. Am. Dietetic Assn. (registered dietitian), Tenn. Dietetic Assn., Nashville Dist. Dietetic Assn., Am. Soc. Hosp. Food Service Adminstrs. (area rep. Tenn. chpt. 1974-75, chpt. pres. 1975-76), Hosp., Instn. and Ednl. Food Service Soc. (state adv. 1976—). Baptist. Home: Route 3 Box 315 Springfield TN 37172 Office: Middle Tenn Mental Health Inst 1501 Murfreesboro Rd Nashville TN 37217

RAY, ARLISS DEAN, environmental consultant; b. Hot Springs, Ark., Apr. 3, 1929; s. Clyde E. and Gladys Lorraine (Wofford) R.; B.Engring., Yale U., 1951; M.S., Oreg. State U., 1957; Ph.D., U. Calif., Berkeley, 1962; m. Ardyth Lee Sharman, Aug. 23, 1952; children—Sandra Lee, Nancy Lynn, Laurie Jean, James Clyde. Asst. prof. environ. engring. Vanderbilt U., 1961-63; assoc. prof., then prof. U. Mo., Columbia, 1963-71; v.p. Woodward-Envicon, also Woodward Clyde Cons., Clifton, N.J. and Houston, 1972-75; pvt. cons., 1975-77; co-founder, 1978, since exec. officer EMANCO Inc., environ. mgmt. and cons., Houston, 1978—; adv. EPA, NSF. Served with USNR, 1951-55. Recipient award merit Mo. Water Pollution Control Assn., 1967. Mem. ASCE, Am. Water Works Assn., Air Pollution Control Assn., Water Pollution Control Fedn., Sigma Xi, Tau Beta Pi, Chi Epsilon, Pi Mu Epsilon. Author papers in field. Home: 1319 W Brooklake St Houston TX 77077

RAY, CECIL ARMSTRONG, clergyman; b. Fort Worth, Dec. 9, 1922; s. William Paul and Annie (Armstrong) R.; m. Charlene Andrews, June 15, 1942; children—Barbara Susan, Robert Lanny. B.A., Howard Payne U., 1943, D.D., 1968; Th.M., Southwestern Bapt. Theol. Sem., 1946. Ordained to ministry Baptist Ch., 1939; pastor Arnett-Benson Bapt. Ch., Lubbock, Tex., 1946-56; associational dir. missions San Antonio Bapt. Assn., 1956-61; sec. coop. program dept. Bapt. Gen. Conv. Tex., Dallas, 1961-67, dir. stewardship devel., 1967-75; gen. sec.-treas. Bapt. State Conv. N.C., Raleigh, 1976-83; nat. dir. So. Bapt. Conv. Planned Growth in Giving, Nashville, 1984—. Named Tex. Bapt. Father of Yr., Bapt. Gen. Conv. Tex., 1961. Office: Southern Bapt Conv 460 Jones Robertson Pkwy Nashville TN 37219

RAY, CECIL ARTHUR, JR., lawyer; b. Ft. Smith, Ark., June 2, 1936; s. Cecil Arthur and Sunbeam Ross (Carmichael) R.; m. Gail Elizabeth Collier, Sept. 3, 1964 (dec. Nov. 1977); 1 dau., Harper Elizabeth; m Cynthia Waltermire, Aug. 31, 1979; 1 dau., Carlyn Ashley; stepchildren—Tracy Lee Edelman, Wendy Marie Edelman. B.B.A., So. Meth. U., 1957, J.D., 1960; LL.M., Harvard U., 1961. Bar: Tex. 1960. Assoc. Coke & Coke, Dallas, 1961-67, ptnr., 1967-77; ptnr. Hughes & Hill, Dallas, 1977—; lectr. So. Meth. U. Law Sch., 1966, 73-74, 75; lectr. in field. Mem. adv. council Dallas County Community Chest Trust Fund; bd. mgmt. Camp Grady Spruce br. of Dallas YMCA, chmn., 1977; v.p. Pastoral Counseling and Edn. Center, 1980. Fellow Tex. Bar Found., Am. Coll. Probate Counsel; mem. Dallas Bar Assn. (sec.-treas. probate and trusts sect. 1984-85), State Bar Tex. (chmn. sect. taxation 1976-77). ABA (com. on employee benefits 1968-73, 75—, mem. subcom. on ERISA litigation, chmn., 1982—, mem. subcom. on fiduciary responsibility 1975-78, subcom. on employee death benefits, chmn. 1980— sect. real property, probate and trust law, mem. tax lawyers-IRS liaison com. for SW region, chmn. 1978-79), Southwestern Legal Found., Dallas Estate Planning Council, Phi Alpha Delta, The Barristers. Democrat. Episcopalian. Clubs: Insurance, T Bar M Raquet, Chaparral (Dallas). Contbr. articles to legal jours.; editor Southwestern Law Jour., 1959-60. Home: 12436 Hillcrest Rd Dallas TX 75230 Office: 1000 Mercantile Dallas Bldg Dallas TX 75201

RAY, CREAD L., JR., judge; b. Waskom, Tex., Mar. 10, 1931; s. Cread L. and Antonia (Hardesty) R.; B.B.A., Tex. A. and M. U., 1952; J.D., U. Tex., 1957; m. Janet Watson Keller, Aug. 12, 1977; children—Sue Ann, Robert E., Glenn L., David B. Keller, Marcie Lynn, Anne Marie. Admitted to Tex. bar, 1957; asso. law firm Smith & Hall, Marshall, Tex., 1957-59; partner law firm Taylor & Ray, Marshall, 1960-66; judge Harrison County Ct., Marshall, 1959-61; sr. partner law firm Ray, Kirkpatrick, Grant, Dennis & Baxter, Marshall, 1966-70; justice Tex. Supreme Ct., Austin, 1980—. Mem. nat. council Boy Scouts Am.; rep. Tex. Ho. Reps., 1967-70; asso. justice 6th Dist., Ct. Civil Appeals, Texarkana, Tex., 1971-80. Served with USAF, 1952-54, lt. col. Res. Recipient Boy Scouts Am. Silver Beaver award, 1976, Silver Antelope award, 1980, Disting. Eagle Scout award, 1982. Mem. State Bar of Tex., Northeast Tex. Bar, Harrison County Bar, Bowie County Bar, Am. Legion, VFW, Delta Theta Phi. Democrat. Methodist. Clubs: Rotary, Elks, Tex. Aggie. Home: 4800 Wild Briar Pass Austin TX 78746 Office: PO Box 12248 Austin TX 78711

RAY, DONALD HENSLEY, aquatic biologist; b. Hamilton AFB, Calif., Sept. 23, 1952; s. Cecil C. and Harriet Ellen (Graham) R.; m. Joni Lynn Rogers, June 26, 1976. A.A., Okaloosa Walton Jr. Coll., 1972; B.S. in Biology, U. West Fla., 1974. Range technician Vitro Services, Eglin AFB, Fla., 1972; survey asst. Lowe Engrs., Fort Walton Beach, Fla., 1972; research asst. Hennison, Durham, Richardson Engrs., Pensacola, Fla., 1973-74; research asst. U. West Fla., Pensacola, 1974; v.p. Theta Analysis, Inc., Pensacola, 1974-75, pres., 1975; aquatic biologist Fla. Dept. Environ. Regulation, State of Fla., Pensacola, 1976—; charter affiliate Jour. Freshwater Invertebrate Biology, 1982; mem. staff Gov.'s Fla. Rivers Study Com., 1985. Mem. North Am. Benthol. Soc., Southeastern Water Pollution Biologist Assn., Sigma Xi. Contbr. articles to profl. jours. Discovered Hydroperla phormidia (Plecoptera) species, 1981. Office: 160 Governmental Center Dept Environmental Regulation Pensacola FL 32501

RAY, DONALD WILLIS, communications company executive; b. Nashville, Ga., Aug. 24, 1942; s. Joe S. and Effie C. (Buckholtz) R.; m. Susan E. Bryant, Oct. 26, 1965; children—Tanya Nicole, Jamie Allison. B.A. in Indsl. and Tech. Edn., U. So. Fla., 1985. Cert. indsl. electronics instr., Fla. Telecom technician Continental Telephone Co., Freeport, Bahamas, 1964-69; ops. mgr. ITT, Ft. Lauderdale, Fla., 1969-75; telcom engr. Telcom Plus, Orlando, Fla., 1975-78; tech. tng. supr. Stromberg-Carlson, Sanford, Fla., 1978-82; tech. tng. mgr. Com Dev, Sarasota, Fla., 1982—; pres. Systems Test Services, Sarasota, 1978—. Served with USAF, 1960-63. Mem. Am. Soc. Tng. and Devel., Nat. Soc. Performance and Instrn. Republican. Avocation: stained glass. Home: 1477 Georgetowne Dr Sarasota FL 33580

RAY, GERALD LYNN PETE, stock broker; b. Oklahoma City, Aug. 12, 1946; s. August Erwin and Bessie Mary (Bunyard) R.; m. Margy Lynn Weisman; 1 child, Gregory Lynn. Student North Tex. U., 1964-66, East Tex. State U., 1966-68, Texarkana Coll., 1968-69. Vice-pres. Fin. Strategies, Shreveport, La., 1971-79; sr. stock broker Merrill Lynch, Shreveport, 1979-83; v.p., resident mgr. Prudential Bache Securities, Shreveport, 1983-85; v.p. A.G. Edwards & Sons, Shreveport, 1985—. Contbr. articles to profl. jours. Bd. dirs. Jr. Achievement, Shreveport, 1983—, Shreveport Council on Alcoholism, 1985-88; v.p. Greater Shreveport Econ. Devel. Found., 1983-86, Shreveport C. of C., 1984, Econ. Devel. Shreveport, 1985-86. Recipient Fund Raiser of Yr. award Shreveport Found., 1982; Best Performing Chmn. award United Way North La., 1983; Fund Raiser of Yr. award Lion's Club Eye Bank, 1983; Shreveport Vol. of Yr. award Shreveport C. of C., 1983, Young Bus. Leader of Yr. award, 1985; Fund Raiser award Shreveport Jr. Achievement, 1984. Mem. Nat. Assn. Security Dealers (prin. 1982—), Internat. Assn. Fin. Planners Jewish. Lodge: Lions. Avocations: civic affairs; politics; charities; fishing; golf. Home: 6137 Horton Shreveport LA 71163

RAY, HAROLD TREYNOR, JR., rental housing company executive; b. Chgo., June 12, 1918; s. Harold Treynor and Verena Adele (Kloess) R.; m. Dorothy Glenn Adams, July 25, 1942; children—Harold T., III, Herbert Glen, Beth Adrienne. B.S. in Edn., Tex. A&M U., 1970. Certified Housing Mgmt. Dir. Joined USAC, 1940, advanced through grades to lt. col. USAAF, 1967; command pilot, served with SAC; exec. dir. Brenham Housing Authority, 1968—; instr. Tex. Housing Assn. Seminars, 1976-79; pres., mem. bd. dirs. Northeast Washington County Water Supply Corp., 1983-84. Chmn. Services for Handicapped and Aged Persons, Home Health-Home Care Adv. Council; mem. Brenham State Sch. Adv. Com. Decorated Air medals with two oak leaves, Commendation medal with one oak leaf, Bronze Stars (2), Silver Star. Recipient award Assn. Retarded Citizens, 1983. Mem. Tex. Housing Assn. (v.p.), Nat. Assn. Housing and Redevel. Orgn. Methodist. Lodge: K.T. Home: Route 5 Box 331 Brenham TX 77833 Office: PO Box 623 Brenham TX 77833

RAY, JOSEPH COCHRAN, educational administrator, political science educator; b. Oklahoma City, Dec. 22, 1936; s. Joseph Franklin and Mary Ellen (Cochran); m. Glenda Ann Pullin, Feb. 17, 1964; children—Stephanie Marie, Cynthia Joann, Christopher Joseph. B.A. with highest honors, U. Okla., 1959, Ph.D., 1985; A. M. in Polit. Sci., Stanford U., 1961; M. City Planning, Harvard U., 1963, study Inst. Edn. Mgmt., 1974. Research asst. Stanford U., 1960; legis. analyst U.S. Bur. Budget, Exec. Office of President, Washington, 1963-68; with U. Okla., 1968—, asst. dir. Research Inst., 1968, asst. to v.p. acad. affairs, 1968-70, asst. to provost, 1970-72, assoc. provost adminstrn., 1972, acting provost, 1973, exec. asst. to pres., 1973-79, adj. asst. polit. sci., 1969, asst. prof., 1970, assoc. prof., 1979—, assoc. provost, Norman campus, 1979—; mem. Norman Comprehensive Planning Task Force, 1978-80. Vol. YWCA Richardson Project for underpriviledged Washington children, 1965-66, chmn. Washington U. Okla. Alumni Devel. Fund Campaign, 1967; Norman United Fund budget com., 1972; adminstrv. bd. chmn. St. Stephens United Methodist Ch., 1976, Urban Issues Citizens com., Norman, 1977-78; bd. govs. Okla. Ctr. Sci., Arts (Kirkpatrick Ctr.), Oklahoma City, 1979—; bd. dirs. Wesley Found., 1981-85; chmn. Radio Sta. KGOU-FM Community Adv. Bd., 1983-85; vice chair adminstrv. bd. McFarlin United Meth. Ch., 1985-86. Robert Dean Bass Meml. scholar, U. Okla., 1958, 59; Woodrow Wilson Nat. fellow, Stanford U, Woodrow Wilson Found., 1959-60, Loula D. Lasker fellow, Harvard U., 1962-63. Mem. Am. Polit. Sci. Assn. Norman C. of C., Phi Beta Kappa (chpt. pres. 1982-83), Omicron Delta Kappa. Democrat. Methodist. Lodge: Lions (Norman) (v.p. 1982-84, pres. 1984-85, dir. 1981—). Home: 1412 Cherry Laurel Dr Norman OK 73072 Office: 660 Parrington Oval Norman OK 73019

RAY, LINDA M., retail business executive; b. N.Y.C., Feb. 17, 1947; d. Salvatore C. and Yolanda (Del Guidice) Caruso; m. Wendell E. Ray, Oct. 18, 1964; children—Y. Michele, Wende Elizabeth. B.A., U. Miami, 1968. Sec. Discountland Furniture, Miami, Fla., 1968-70; v.p. Ray's Furniture, Miami, 1970-73, Ray Enterprises, 1973-75; pres. Linda Ray Enterprises, Miami, 1975—; ops. mgr. Miami Internat. Merchandise Mart, 1979—; Bd. dirs. Pub. Broadcasting System, Miami, 1980-83. Mem. AAUW, Bldg. Owners and Mgrs. Assn., Nat. Found. for the Arts, Blowing Rock C. of C., Miami Baller Soc. (treas. 1977-78), Opera Guild. Club: Women's Variety. Office: Miami Internat Merchandise Mart 777 NW 72d Ave Miami FL 33134

RAY, PATRICIA COOPER, manufacturing executive, office automation consultant; b. Prattsville, Ark., Mar. 19, 1932; s. Joseph Elwood and Agnes Mildred (Keesee) Cooper; m. Gene Thomas Ray, Feb. 6, 1959; children—Reynaldo, Kimberley (Mrs. Andrew Landon). B.A. in Music, Tex. Woman's U., 1953, M.A., 1954. Tchr., Dallas Ind. Sch. Dist., 1954-59; landman S.W. Prodn. Co., Dallas, 1959-65; adminstrv. asst. Johnson Investment Corp., Austin, Tex., 1965-72; mgr. adminstrv. services Victor Equipment Co., Denton, Tex., 1972—; owner, operator Office Systems Cons. Mem. LWV, AAUW. Mem. Am. Mgmt. Assn., Assn. Records Mgrs. and Adminstrs., Assn. Info. System Profls., Assn. Info. and Image Mgmt., Office Tech. Mgmt. Assn. Office: PO Drawer 1007 Denton TX 76202

RAY, RICHARD BELMONT, congressman; b. Crawford County, Ga., Feb. 2, 1927; m. Barbara Elizabeth Giles, 1947; children—Susan, Charles, Alan. Grad., U. Ga., 1956. Farmer, 1946-50; founder, operator Ray Services Inc., 1950-62; mgr. Southeastern region Getz Inc., 1962-72; adminstrv. asst. to Senator Sam Nunn of Ga., 1972-82; mem. 98th Congress, 1982—; mayor Perry, Ga., 1964-70. Mem. Perry City Council, 1962-64; pres. Ga. Mcpl. Assn., 1969-70; bd. stewards Perry 1st United Meth. Ch. Democrat. Office: Room 514 Cannon House Office Bldg Washington DC 20515*

RAY, WALTER JOSEPH, engineering company executive; b. Yonkers, N.Y., Jan. 21, 1938; s. Sylvester Thomas and Eleanor Francis (Cunningham) R.; m. Patricia Anne Brady, Oct. 26, 1957 (div. Oct., 1981); children—Dennis Walter, Pamela Anne; m. 2d. Donna Eva Hudson, Nov. 7, 1981. B.S. in Bus., Ind. U., 1964; A.S. in Indsl. Mgmt., East Carolina U., 1969. Enlisted U.S. Marine Corps, 1955, commd. 2d lt., advanced through grades to capt., ret., 1976; sr. systems analyst Unified Industries, Alexandria, Va., 1976-78; program mgr. Wheeler Industries, 1978-80, dir. corp. devel., 1980-82; dir. integrated logistics support div., 1982-83; fin. dir. Resources Cons., Inc., McLean, Va., 1983—. Pres. Little League, 1970-71; mgr. Babe Ruth team, 1972-75; coach, mgr., Pop Warner Football League, 1972-75. Decorated Vietnam Service medal, Combat Action ribbon; Cross of Gallantry (Vietnam). Mem. Am. Mgmt. Assn., Am. Soc. Naval Engrs., Soc. of Logistics Engrs., Soc. Mil. Comptrollers. Republican. Roman Catholic. Lodges: Moose, Elks. Home: 201 S Reynolds St Apt L502 Alexandria VA 22304 Office: Resources Cons Inc 8200 Greensboro Dr Suite 600 McLean VA 22102

RAYBORN, WILLIAM LEE, state senator; b. McComb, Miss., May 15, 1936; student Am. Sch., Chgo.; m. Doris Nettles; 5 children. Mem. Miss. Senate; dental technician, denturist. Mem. Am. Acad. Denturists, Nat. Denturists Assn. Democrat. Baptist. Lodges: Civitan, Moose, Masons, Shriners, Order Eastern Star. Home: Rt 1 Box 532 Brookhaven MS 39601 Office: Miss Senate Jackson MS 39205

RAYBURN, B.B., farmer, cattleman, state senator; b. Aug. 11, 1916; student Sullivan Trade Sch., Bogalusa, La.; hon. doctorate Loyola U., New Orleans, 1959; m. Hazel Eugene Blanchard. Pipefitter, Crown-Zellerback Corp., 30 yrs.; mem. La. Ho. of Reps., 1948-51; mem. La. Senate, 1951—, currently chmn. Senate Fin. Com., Joint Legis. Com. on Budget, former mem. numerous coms. including conservation, edn., transp., pub. works, indsl. relations, labor, others; del. 1973 Constl. Conv., chmn. com. on revenue, fin. and taxation. Mem. Washington County Police Jury, 1944-48. Rayburn Sch. Vet. Sci., La. State U., named in his honor, 1978. Mem. La. Vet. Med. Assn. (hon.). Democrat. Baptist. Clubs: Masons, Shriners, Lions. Office: Route 1 Box 234 Bogalusa LA 70427

RAYFORD, ORREN LEWIS, college counselor; b. Charleston, W.Va., Feb. 1, 1939; s. Dandridge Thomas and Delilah (Burks) R.; m. Nell Miller, Apr. 13, 1968. B.A. in Edn., W.Va. State Coll., 1963; M.Ed., Ohio U., 1969, Ph.D., 1972. Nat. cert. counselor. Elem. sch. tchr. Cleve. pub. schs., 1963-68; instr., asst. prof. counseling Ohio U., Athens, 1969-72; research asst. Norfolk pub. schs., Va., 1973-74; assoc. prof., counselor Norfolk State U., 1974—, computer literacy instr., 1984—; cons. human relations tng., 1972-73; practicum supr. Ohio U., 1968-71. Author pamphlets. NDEA fellow, 1967, 68. Mem. Am. Assn. Counseling and Devel., Nat. Vocat. Guidance Assn., NAACP, Urban League Hampton Roads. Home: 5500 State St Virginia Beach VA 23455

RAYL, RACHEL LETHEA, nurse, hospital nursing administrator; b. Gulfport, Miss., May 15, 1955; d. David McMurtrie Rayl and Doris (Burnett) Rayl-Anthony. B.S. in Nursing, Northwestern State U., Natchitoches, La., 1978; postgrad. in nursing U. Ark. for Med. Scis. R.N., Tex.; cert advanced cardiac life support instr. Staff nurse Houston N.W. Med. ctr., 1979, nursing supr., 1979-81, 83, head nurse emergency room, 1981, profl. recruiter, 1983-84; nursing supr. Diagnostic Hosp., Houston, 1982; dir. nursing service Dardanelle Hosp., Ark., 1984—; coordinator Dardanelle Health Fair, 1985, Dardanelle Hosp. Aux., 1985—; county coordinator Red Cross Blood drive, Yell County, Ark., 1985—. Coach City Tee-Ball Team, Dardanelle, 1985—. Mem. Ark. Soc. Hosp. Nursing Service Dirs., Beta Sigma Phi (treas. chpt. 1985—). Republican. Baptist. Avocations: golf; skiing; camping; fishing; tennis. Home: PO Box 267 Dardanelle AR 72834 Office: Dardanelle Hosp 200 N Third St Dardanelle AR 72834

RAYMOND, CHARLES MICHAEL, lawyer; b. Chester, Pa., May 22, 1953; s. Charles Anthony and Theresa (Curney) R.; m. Sandra H. Brabham, May 22, 1984. B.A., La. State U., 1975; J.D., Loyola U., New Orleans, 1978. Bar: La. 1979, U.S. Supreme Ct. 1984, U.S. Ct. Appeals (5th cir.) 1979, U.S. Dist. Ct. (mid. dist.) La. 1981, (so. dist.) Tex. 1984, (we. dist.) Mo. 1984, (ea. dist.) La. 1983, U.S. Ct. Appeals (11th cir.) 1985. Asst. city-parish atty. City of Baton Rouge and Parish East Baton Rouge, 1979-84; atty. Gill & Bankston, Baton Rouge, 1982-84, Camp, Carmouche, Barsh, Hunter, Gray Hoffman & Gill, Baton Rouge, 1984-86, Camp, Carmouche, Barsh, Gray, Hoffman & Gill, Baton Rouge, 1986—. Exec. v.p. La. Young Democrats, 1977-78; mem.-at-large East Baton Rouge Parish Dem. Exec. Com., 1979-83; coordinator City-Parish Atty.'s Office United Way Campaign, Baton Rouge, 1983. Moot Ct. judge, So. U. Sch. Law, 1983. Mem. Assn. Trial Lawyers Am., ABA, La. Bar Assn., Fed. Bar Assn., Pi Sigma Alpha. Democrat. Roman Catholic. Home: 16215 Morel Ave Baton Rouge LA 70817 Office: Camp Carmouche Barsh et al 3071 Teddy Dr Baton Rouge LA 70809

RAYNER, STEVE, cultural anthropologist, technology policy researcher; b. Bristol, Eng., May 22, 1953; came to U.S., 1980; s. Harold Frank and Esmé (Britton) R. B.A. in Philosophy, Theology, U. Kent, Canterbury, Eng., 1974; Ph.D. in Social Anthropology, U. Coll. London, 1979. Lectr. U. London, 1977-78; research assoc. Ctr. Occupational Community Research, London, 1978-80, Russell Sage Found., N.Y.C., 1980-81; sr. research assoc. Ctr. Occupational Community Research, 1981—; research staff. Oak Ridge Nat. Lab., Tenn., 1983—. Author: (with J.L. Gross) Measuring Culture, 1985. Contbr. articles to profl. jours. Vis. scholar Boston U. Sch. Pub. Health, 1982, Columbia U. dept computer sci., 1981, 82. Fellow Royal Anthropol. Inst.; mem. Am. Anthropol. Assn., Am. Sociol. Assn., Assn. Social Anthropologists of Commonwealth, Soc. for Risk Analysis, So. Sociol. Soc., East Tenn. Wine Soc., Sigma Xi. Avocations: cooking; wine tasting; canoeing; folk music. Home: 111 Grandcove Ln Oak Ridge TN 37830 Office: Oak Ridge Nat Lab PO Box X Oak Ridge TN 37831

RAZDAN, MAHARAJ KRISHAN, physician; b. Kashmire, India, June 10, 1940; came to U.S., 1971; s. Jagan Nath and Rupawati (Gadoo) Razdan (Hashia); M.B., B.S., Gandhi Med. Coll., Bhopal, 1962; M.D., All-India Inst. Med. Sci., New Delhi, 1967; m. Vijay Sadhu, Oct. 12, 1962; children—Ashutosh, Aurobindo. Instr. clin. pharmacology Med. Coll., Kashmir, 1963-66; sr. research fellow Council Sci. and Indsl. Research, India, 1967-70; teaching fellow in medicine and nephrology Case Western Res. U., Cleve., 1973-76; sr. instr. internal medicine, 1977-78; practice medicine specializing in internal medicine and nephrology, McAllen, Tex., 1978—; clin. assoc. prof. U. Tex., McAllen, 1978—; cons. McAllen Gen. Hosp., Edinberg Gen. Hosp., Mission Mcpl. Hosp., Valley Community Hosp., Brownsville, Tex. Served to maj. USAR. Mem. ACP, AMA, Tex. Med. Assn., Am. Soc. Internal Medicine, Kidney Found. N.E. Ohio, Tex. Med. Soc., Hidelgo-Starr County Med. Soc. Contbr. articles to profl. jours. Office: McAllen Med Plaza Suite 116 222 E Ridge Rd McAllen TX 78503

REA, PHILLIP ALTON, pharmacist; b. Mishawaka, Ind., Jan. 13, 1942; s. Kenneth Alton and Phyllis (Hixson) R.; m. Naomi Joan Cumberland, June 18, 1967; children—Jeffrey, Julie, Joel. B.S., Butler U., 1967. Pharmacist, mgr. Tribe-O-Rea Drug, Mishawaka, 1967-77; pharmacist, owner Tribe-O-Rea Drug Inc., 1977-82; pharmacist Eckerd Drugs, Charlotte, N.C., 1982—. Pres., Mishawaka Campfire Girls, 1975, Preservation of Reservation Ind., 1976. Named Man of Yr., Mishawaka Enterprise, 1976. Mem. Mishawaka Jaycees (Disting. Service award 1976), Am. Heart Assn. (Disting. Service award 1981), N.C. Pharmacists Assn., Mecklenberg Pharmacists Assn. (sec. 1984—), Ind. Pharmacists Assn. Republican. Methodist. Lodges: Kiwanis (pres. Mishawaka chpt. 1976), Masons. Home: 4101 Foxmoor Dr Charlotte NC 28226 Office: Eckerd Drugs Pineville-Matthews Rd Charlotte NC 28226

READ, DAVID WISE, national guard non-commissioned officer, model railroad retailer and manufacturer; b. Atlantic, Va., Oct. 18, 1938; s. Norbourne D. and Lois Mason (Cale) R.; m. Carole Ann Shields, Oct. 23, 1959 (div. Sept. 1975); children—Franklin Ervin, Charles Alan; m. Patricia Paulus Bennett,

Nov. 22, 1976 (div. Sept. 1981); m. Barbara Lou Rainey, Feb. 26, 1982. Student Miss. State U., 1959-61, Carson-Newman Coll., 1969, Augusta Coll., 1971-75. Store mgr. The Krystal Co., Augusta, Ga., 1970-71; dist. credit mgr. SCM Glidden-Durkee, Augusta, 1971-74; unit adminstr. Ga. Army N.G., Augusta, 1974-77, ops. tng. and readiness specialist, 1978-82, state retention non-commd. officer, 1982—; owner North Marietta Depot, 1983-85; chmn., pres. Depot Products Ltd., Marietta, Ga., 1985—; v.p., dir. So. Rails Ltd., Belmont, N.C., 1985—; instr. N.G. Profl. Edn. Center, North Little Rock, Ark., 1979—. Served with USMCR, 1956; with USAF, 1956-69; mem. USAF Res., 1969-73, Ga. Army N.G., 1973—. Mem. Air Force Assn. (life), Enlisted Assn. N.G. Ga. (by-law com. chmn. 1983), Nat. Model R.R. Assn. (life), Assn. U.S. Army, Non-Commd. Officers Assn. (life; sec.-treas., trustee Ga. Minuteman chpt.), Mideastern Region Nat. Model R.R. Assn. (life), 8th Air Force Hist. Soc. (life), Chattanooga Area Model R.R. Club, Nat. Ry. Hist. Soc., Pa. R.R. Tech. and Hist. Soc., Soc. Am. Baseball Research, Southeastern Region Nat. Model R.R. Assn. (life). Democrat. Baptist. Office: 935 E Confederate Ave PO Box 17965 Atlanta GA 30316

READ, WILLIAM SQUIERS, thoroughbred farm manager; b. Boston, Sept. 26, 1941; s. Robert Scudder and Virginia Estabrook (Squiers) R.; m. Nita Ann Pillow, Jan. 18, 1963; 1 dau., Tifany Rene. Student Adams State Coll., 1959-60, Colo. State U., 1960-65. Material handling engr. Chrysler Corp., Belvidere, Ill., 1965-69; farm mgr. Flamingo Farm, Ocala, Fla., 1970-75, Happy Valley Farm, Ocala, 1975—. Bd. dirs. Fla. Horsemen's Children's Home. Mem. Fla. Thoroughbred Farm Mgrs. Club (pres. 1984). Republican. Presbyterian. Club: Elks. Home: 4074 NW 95th Ave Rd Ocala FL 32675 Office: Happy Valley Farm 4076 NW 95th Ave Rd Ocala FL 32675

REAGAN, ABBIE JAMES, JR., county official; b. Emory, Ga., Oct. 7, 1929; s. Abbie James and Ruth (McConnell) R.; m. Margaret Stivarius, Jan. 3, 1953; children—James Walter, Julie Anne, Jeffrey Dale. Student, U. Miami, 1953. Mng. dep. Clk. of Criminal Ct. of Record, Dade County, 1954-69; exec. dir. Office State Atty., Dade County, 1969—; cons. on prosecutors mgmt. and fiscal matters. Served with U.S. Army, 1948-53. Mem. Fla. Pros. Attys. Assn., Nat. Dist. Attys. Assn., Cousteau Soc., Sierra Club, Nat. Audubon Soc., Defenders of Wildlife, Aircraft Owners and Pilots Assn., Am. Bonanza Soc., Nat. Rifle Assn., Good Sam Club. Democrat. Roman Catholic. Home: 5438 SW 91st Ave Miami FL 33165 Office: Suite 653 Metro Justice Bldg 1351 NW 12th St Miami FL 33125

REAGAN, BARBARA BENTON, economics educator; b. San Antonio; d. Loren William and Cora Atalee (Martin) Benton; m. Sydney Chandler Reagan; children—Patricia, Chad. B.S. with honors, U. Tex., 1941; M.A. in Stats., Am. U., 1947; M.A. in Econs., Harvard U., 1949, Ph.D. in Econs., 1952. Economist, Dept. of Agr., Washington, 1942-47, sr. project leader Agrl. Research Service, 1949-55; prof., Tex. Woman's U., 1959-67; prof. econs. So. Meth. U., Dallas, 1967—, dir. undergrad. studies in econs., 1972-75, assoc. dean Univ. Coll., 1975, asst. to pres., 1975-76, chairperson econs. dept., 1984—, rep. Assn. Am. Colls., 1983—; disting. vis. prof. econs. Kenyon Coll., 1979; dir. Fed. Home Loan Bank Region IX, 1981-85; adv. bd. Tex. Bank and Trust, 1986—; faculty rep., bd. govs., bd. trustees So. Meth. U., 1981-83; cons. Ford Found., 1980; cons. econs. curriculum Office of Edn., 1980; adv. com. White House Conf. Balanced Nat. Growth and Econ. Devel., 1977-78; econ. research adv. com. Dept. of Agr., 1965-70; Internat. Econs. Assn. observer World Conf. Internat. Women's Yr., Mexico City, 1975. Tex. adv. bd. Tex. Coastal Mgmt. Program, 1977-78; univ. adv. council Am. Council Life Ins., 1977-81; adv. com. Nat. Research Inst. on Family, 1973-76; mem. Nat. Adv. Food and Drug Council, 1968-71; agrl. adv. com. to bd. dirs. and pres. Tex. A&M U., 1967-68; adv. com. on Agrl. Policy Inst., N.C. State U. and Kellogg Found., 1965-70; co-chair com. on skills bank Dallas Urban League, 1977-79, dir., 1975-79; manpower council Nat. Tex. Council Govts., 1972-74; trustee Pub. Communication Found. North Tex., 1973-76; dir. League Ednl. Advancement, Dallas, 1972-75; com. urban affairs Dallas C. of C., 1975; adv. bd. Women's Ctr. Dallas, 1975-79, pres., 1981; founder, dir. Women for Change, Dallas, 1971. Recipient Willis M. Tate award So. Meth. U., 1982, M. award for service, 1972, named Outstanding Tchr., 1972; recipient Women Helping Women award, 1980, Laurel award AAUW, 1983. Mem. Am. Econs. Assn., Southwestern Social Sci. Assn. (pres. 1978-79, exec. com. 1977-80), Dallas Economists Club, Phi Beta Kappa. Club: So. Meth. U. Women's (pres. 1981). Contbr. articles to profl. jours. Home: 10 Duncannon Ct Dallas TX 75275 Office: Dept of Economics Southern Methodist University Dallas TX 75275

REAGAN, BILLY R., educational administrator. Supt. of schs. Houston. Office: 3830 Richmond Houston TX 77027*

REAGAN, JOY PARTNEY, family services executive; b. St. Louis; d. Donald Richard and Ruth Barber P.; m. L. David Reagan, Aug. 26, 1948; children—Cyndy Reagan Klinger, Bonnie Ruth, Eric David. B.S., Lamar U., 1967; M.A., Sam Houston State U., 1971; postgrad. Baylor U., 1946-48, U. Houston, Lamar at London, 1980. Adminstr., Buckner Children's Village and Family Care Ctr., Beaumont, Houston and Conroe, Tex. Mem. adv. bd. Tex. Dept. Human Resources; bd. dirs. Am. Heart Found.; mem. adv. bd. Beaumont State Ctr. Human Devel. Named Social Worker of Yr., S.E. Tex. Social Welfare Assn., 1973. Mem. Nat. Assn. Homes for Children, Am. Assn. Psychiat. Services for Children, Tex. Assn. Execs. Homes for Children, Southwestern Assn. Child Care Execs., Tex. Assn. Licensed Children's Homes. Baptist. Club: Etudier Literary (Houston). Contbg. editor Residential Group Care. Office: 9055 Manion Dr Box 12420 Beaumont TX 77706

REAGAN, RONALD DEAN, architect; b. New Castle, Ind., Aug. 29, 1949; s. James Junior and Marie Jane (Whitsell) R.; m. Connie Jean Phillips, Aug. 8, 1969; children—Jeffrey David, Michael Scott, Melanie Marie-Michelle. Assoc. Applied Sci., Indian River Jr. Coll., 1969, A.A., 1974; B.A., Clemson U., 1978. Registered architect S.C., Ga., N.C. Project architect J.E. Sirrine Co., Greenville, S.C., 1978-81, Neal Prince & Browning, Greenville, 1981-83; prin., owner Ron Reagan, Architect, Easley, S.C., 1983—. City council candidate City of Easley, 1983; active in Planning and Zoning Commn., Easley, 1984, Mayors Adv. Council Downtown Revitalization, Easley, 1984. Served to sgt. USAF, 1970-73, Vietnam. Mem. AIA, Greenville Council Architects (sec. 1982), Easley C. of C.. Republican. Baptist. Avocations: photography; art; sports. Home: 310 Lavonne Ave Easley SC 29640 Office: 106 Bradley Ave Easley SC 29640

REAGIN, WALLIS EDWIN, optometrist; b. Atlanta, May 6, 1927; s. Thomas Edwin and Era Bernice (Pace) R.; m. Joan O. Gaby, June 26, 1952; children—Thomas Gaby, Elizabeth Marie, Richard Stephen, Kimberlee Joan. Student Vanderbilt U., 1944-45; O.D., So. Coll. Optometry, 1950. Assoc. in practice optometry with Dr. W.R. Gilbert, Griffin, Ga., 1950-51; practice optometry, Decatur, Ga., 1951—; lectr. in field. Served with U.S. Army, 1945-46. Fellow Coll. Optometrists in Visual Devel., Am. Pub. Health Assn., Am. Sch. Health Assn.; mem. Am. Optometric Assn. (Optometric Recognition award 1980-85), 5th Dist. Optometric Assn. (past pres.), Ga. Optometric Assn. (past pres., Optometrist of Yr. award 1965), Am. Optometric Found., Optometric Extension Program (clin. assoc.), Mensa. Christian Scientist. Lodges: Lions, Masons. Home: 2740 Briarlake Woods Way NE Atlanta GA 30345 Office: 104 Church St Decatur GA 30030

REAK, OSCAR J., diversified company executive; b. Randolph, Wis., 1922. Student, Tex. A. and M. U., Wayne State U. Pres. Cutter-Hammer, Inc., 1941-79, Blount, Inc., Montgomery, Ala., 1979—, also chief operating officer, dir. Address: Blount Inc 4520 Executive Park Dr Montgomery AL 36192*

REAL, LINDA MCBROOM, educator; b. Haleyville, Ala., May 20, 1950; d. Clifford Wallace and Rachel (Wilkinson) McBroom; m. Michael Douglas Real, June 1, 1969; children—Rhonda Renee, Rachel Lanice. Student Freed Hardeman Coll., 1968-69; B.S., Livingston U., 1972, M.A.T., 1981. Tchr. phys. edn., coach Marion County High Sch., Guin, Ala., 1972-73; tchr. phys. edn. N.W. Ala. State Jr. Coll., 1981-83; coach, tchr. phys. edn. Phillips High Sch., Bear Creek, Ala., 1973—. Named Volleyball Coach of Yr., Marion County Coaches and Prins. Assn., 1982, 83, N.E. Ala. Athletic Conf., 1982, 83, Track Coach of Yr., N.W. Ala. Athletic Conf., 1983, Marion County Coaches and Prins. Assn., 1983. Mem. Marion County Coaches and Prins. Assn. (sec.), N.W. Ala. Conf. Home: Route 1 Detroit AL 35552 Office: Phillips High Sch Route 1 Box 3 Bear Creek AL 35543

REAMER, RICHARD ERVEL, air force officer; b. Detroit, Dec. 26, 1941; s. Richard Harding and Louise (Benedict) R.; m. Karen Isabel Kukey, Sept. 5, 1964; children—Jeannine L., Lisa M., Richard Harding. B.S., Ohio State U., Columbus, 1964; M.S., U. So. Calif., Kadena Air Base, Japan, 1972; postgrad. Squadron Officers Sch., Air Command and Staff Coll. Commd. U.S. Air Force, advanced through grades to maj., 1984; flight safety officer 16th Squadron, Tan Son Nhut AFB, Vietnam, 1968-69; standarization/evaluation officer 18th Tactical Fighter Wing, Kadena AFB, Japan, 1969-72; system program mgr. Aero. Systems Div., Wright-Patterson AFB, Ohio, 1972-75; chief spl. reconaissance ops. 26th Tactical Reconnaissance Wing, Zwetbrucken AB, W.Ger., 1975-78; chief flight safety 67th Tactical Reconnaissance Wing, Bergstrom AFB, Tex., 1978-81; chief reconnaissance ops. div. HQ Tactical Air Command, Langley AFB, Va., 1981—. Co-chmn. Bellbrook Planning Bd. (Ohio), 1975; parish council pres. Zwetbrucken Cath. Chapel, 1978; group leader Spl. Olympics, Hampton, Va., 1982. Decorated D.F.C., Meritorious Service medal, Air medal (10), Air Force Commendation medal (2). Mem. Air Force Assn., Daedalians, Arnold Air Soc., Delta Upsilon. Home: 7 Stirrup Ct Hampton VA 23664 Office: HQ TAC/DOFR Langley AFB VA 23665

REAMY-STEPHENSON, MICHAELIN, marriage and family therapist, educator, consultant; b. N.Y.C., Feb. 20, 1938; d. Judson Reamy and Eleanor Stevens (McMichael) R.; m. James Donald Cowie, Aug. 29, 1959; children—Jennifer D., James J., David K., Laura S.; m. Richard Ward Stephenson, Aug. 31, 1979. B.S. with Distinction in Human Ecology, Cornell U., 1960; M.S.W., U. Ga., 1979. Tchr. swimming, Conn., E. Africa, Lebanon, 1968-75; social work intern, grad. asst., Atlanta, 1978-79; dir. social services, assoc. dir. and coordinator family therapy adult treatment program Brawner Psychiat. Inst., Atlanta, 1980-82; dir. extramural tng., marriage and family therapist Atlanta Inst. Family Studies, 1982—. Mem. Atlanta Com. Children, 1983—; instr. Water Safety ARC, 1957—. Recipient DAR Citizen award, 1956; YMCA award for Disting. Service, White Plains, N.Y., 1958. Mem. Nat. Assn. Social Workers, Am. Assn. Marriage and Family Therapists, Ga. Assn. Marriage and Family Therapists, Cornell U. Human Ecology Alumni Assn., Internat. Platform Assn., Mortar Bd., Omicron Nu, Phi Kappa Phi. Contbr. articles to profl. jours. Home: 1733 Kellogg Springs Dr Dunwoody GA 30338 Office: Atlanta Inst Family Studies 61 8th St Atlanta GA 30309

REAVLEY, THOMAS MORROW, judge; b. Quitman, Tex., June 21, 1921; s. Thomas Mark and Mattie (Morrow) R.; B.A., U. Tex., 1942; J.D., Harvard, 1948; LL.D., Austin Coll., 1974, Southwestern U., 1977, Tex. Wesleyan, 1983; LL.M., U. Va., 1984; m. Florence Montgomery Wilson, July 24, 1943; children—Thomas Wilson, Marian, Paul Stuart, Margaret. Admitted to Tex. bar, 1948; asst. dist. atty., Dallas, 1948-49; mem. firm Bell & Reavley, Nacogdoches, Tex., 1949-51; county atty., Nacogdoches, 1951; mem. firm Fisher, Tonahill & Reavley, Jasper, Tex., 1952-55; sec. state Tex., 1955-57; mem. firm Powell, Rauhut, McGinnis & Reavley, Austin, Tex., 1957-64; dist. judge, Austin, 1964-68; justice Supreme Ct. Tex., 1968-77; judge U.S. Ct. Appeals, 5th Circuit, Austin, 1979—; pres. Tex. Jud. Council, 1971-76; lectr. Baylor U. Law Sch., 1976—; adj. prof. U. Tex. Law Sch., 1958-59, 78-79. Chancellor S.W. Tex. conf. United Methodist Ch., 1972—. Bd. dirs. Southwestern U., Georgetown, Tex.; pres. Meth. Home, Waco, Tex. Served to lt. USNR, 1943-45. Mason (33 deg.). Home: 1312 Meriden Ln Austin TX 78703 Office: Am Bank Tower Austin TX 78701

REBER, SIDNEY CRAFT, JR., religious organization executive; b. Jackson, Miss., June 12, 1918; s. Sidney Craft and Robbie Edna (Merrill) R.; m. Alwilda Montgomery, Dec. 4, 1943; children—Rebecca Alwilda Reber Washington. B.S., Trinity U., San Antonio, 1950; postgrad. Trinity U., 1950-52, Miss. Coll., Clinton, 1952-53, Southwestern Bapt. Theol. Sem., 1967-68. With War Dept., Washington and Atlanta, 1940-43; classification analyst U.S. Civil Service Commn., Dallas, 1945-46; personnel officer VA, Dallas, San Antonio, Jackson, Miss., 1946-53; regional tng. officer, taxpayer assistance officer IRS, Dallas, 1953-63; bus. mgr., treas. Malaysia-Singapore Bapt. Mission, So. Bapt. Conv., Fgn. Mission Bd., Singapore, 1963-69; dir. mgmt. services div. So. Bapt. Fgn. Mission Bd., Richmond, Va., 1969-80, v.p. mgmt. services, 1980—. Served to 2d lt. USAAF, 1943-45. Mem. Am. Mgmt. Assn., Soc. Advancement Mgmt. Baptist. Lodge: Rotary. Home: 7800 Ardendale Rd Richmond VA 23225 Office: Fgn Mission Bd So Bapt Conv 3806 Monument Ave Richmond VA 23230

RECTOR, ANNE BEST, real estate marketing executive; b. Columbia, S.C., Apr. 10, 1942; d. Fred Benjamin and Harriette (Burckhalter) Best; m. Edwin Rector, Mar. 13, 1971. B.A., Salem Coll., 1964. Vice pres. Manarin, Odle and Rector, Inc., Alexandria, Va., 1976-81; pres. Rector Assocs., Inc., Alexandria, 1981—. Bd. dirs. Am. Cancer Soc., Alexandria, 1979-85. Mem. Nat. Assn. Relators, Va. Assn. Realtors (bd. dirs. 1983—), Alexandria C. of C. (bd. dirs. 1981-84).

REDDEN, ROBERT HARDING, energy/construction company executive; b. Oklahoma City, Apr. 29, 1943; s. Gene Robert and Jamsie R.; B.A., Northeastern State U., 1965; postgrad. U. Okla. Sch. Law, 1965-66; m. Mary Claire Detjen, June 3, 1965; 1 dau., Michelle Ann. Asst. ins. mgr. Pan Am. Petroleum Corp., 1965-70; asst. ins. mgr. Williams Cos., Tulsa, 1970-77; dir. treasury and ins. Willbros Energy Services Co., Tulsa, 1977-82, dir. ins. and pub. relations, 1982—; v.p., dir. Langside Ltd., Hamilton, Bermuda, 1971-77; cons. corp ins. programs, internat. ins. Trustee, v.p. exec. bd. Broken Arrow Community Playhouse (Okla.). Mem. Risk and Ins. Mgmt. Soc. (sec.-treas. Okla. chpt. 1972-73, sec. 1983-84). Home: 6630 S 218 Ave Broken Arrow OK 74014 Office: 2530 E 71st St Tulsa OK 74136

REDDICK, ROBERT JOHN, english educator; b. Mpls., July 8, 1939; s. James Lee Sr. and Evelyn (Thorne) R.; m. Roseann Patricia Jennrich, Sept. 9, 1967; children—Andrea Leigh, Carissa Ann. B.S., U. Minn., 1966, M.A., 1969, Ph.D., 1975. Asst. prof. Ball State U., Muncie, Ind., 1973-75; assoc. prof. English U., Tex., Arlington, 1975—. Asst. editor Allegorica Scholarly Jour. 1978—, Harold Frederic Edition 1978-85. Contbr. articles to profl. jours. Served to cpl. USMC 1957-61. Mem. Linguistic Soc. Am., Modern Language Assn., Internat. Soc. Anglo-Saxonists, Dallas Area Medieval Assn. (dir. 1981-83). Office: U Tex English Dept Box 19035 Arlington TX 76019

REDDICK, W(ALKER) HOMER, social worker; b. River Junction, Fla., Mar. 26, 1922; s. Walker H. and Lillian (Anderson) R.; B.S., Fla. State U., 1951, M.S.W., 1957; m. Anne Elizabeth Hardwick, Sept. 7, 1947; children—Walker Homer, Andy Hardwick (dec.). Chief juvenile probation officer Muscogee County Juvenile Ct., Columbus, Ga., 1952-53; sr. child welfare worker Floyd County Dept. Pub. Welfare, Rome, Ga., 1955-56; chief social worker Montgomery County Dept. Pub. Health, Montgomery, Ala., 1957-59; dir. social services Ala. Bapt. Children's Home, Troy, 1959-64; casework supr. Youth Devel. Center, Milledgeville, Ga., 1964-71; dir. Family Counseling Center, Macon, Ga., 1972-81. Cons. Appleton Ch. Home for Girls Group Homes, Macon, 1974-81; community columnist Macon (Ga.) Telegraph, 1980-81. Pres. Council Service Agys., Macon, 1975. Mem. Ala. State Adv. Com. on Children and Youth, 1961-64. Bd. dirs. Middle Ga. Drug Council. Served with AUS, 1940-43. Licensed marriage and family counselor, Ga. Fellow Royal Soc. Health; mem. Nat. Assn. Social Workers (charter; bd. mem.-at-large Ga. chpt.), Acad. Cert. Social Workers, Am. Assn. Marriage and Family Therapists, Transactional Analysis Study Group of Macon (dir. 1974), DAV, 121st Inf. Assn. (historian 1981-86). Episcopalian. Club: Masons. Contbr. articles to profl. jours. Address: 2485 Kingsley Dr Macon GA 31204

REDDING, BARBARA ANN, nurse educator; b. Gettysburg, Pa., Aug. 30, 1939; d. Leonard Francis and Helen Margaret (Yohe) R. B.S., St. Joseph Coll., 1961; M.S.N., U. Pa., 1964; Ed.D., U. Fla., 1983. Faculty, St. Joseph Coll., Emmitsburg, Md., 1964-69; asst. prof. U. Mass., Amherst, 1969-73; assoc. prof. Holyoke (Mass.) Community Coll., 1973-75; asst. prof. nursing U. South Fla., Tampa, 1975-78, assoc. prof., 1978—. Mem. Fla. Nurses Assn., Fla. League Nursing, Assn. Care of Children's Health, Sigma Theta Tau, Phi Delta Kappa, Kappa Delta Pi. Roman Catholic. Home: 8621 Cattail Dr Tampa FL 33617 Office: U South Fla 12901 N 30th St Box 22 Medical Ctr Tampa FL 33612

REDDING, MORRIS G., law enforcement official. Chief of police, Atlanta. Office: City Hall 68 Mitchell St SW Atlanta GA 30335*

REDFERN, JOHN JOSEPH, III, financial analyst; b. Oklahoma City, Jan. 9, 1939; s. John Joseph and Rosalind (Kapps) R.; m. Doris Purcell, Jan. 25, 1963; children—Mary Randall, John Joseph, IV. B.A., U. Tex., 1961, M.B.A., 1964. Chartered fin. analyst. Security analyst, trust dept. Ft. Worth Nat. Bank, 1964-66; treas., sec., fin. analyst, dir. Flag-Redfern Oil Co., Midland, Tex., 1966—. Mem. Houston Soc. Fin. Analysts. Home: 4 Greenwich Midland TX 79705 Office: Flag-Redfern Oil Co 1200 Wall Towers W Midland TX 79701

REDMAN, WILLIAM WALTER, JR., realtor, state senator; b. Statesville, N.C., Oct. 15, 1933; s. William Walter and Mildred Huie R.; B.S., Embry-Riddle Aeronaut. U., 1972; student U. So. Calif., 1966; m. Elizabeth Ann Wilhelm, Dec. 28, 1956; children—Lisa Dawn, Kathryn Marlene, Adrienne Ann. Enlisted U.S. Army, 1954, advanced through grades to lt. col., 1974, ret., 1974; dir. public relations Northwestern Bank, Statesville, N.C., 1974-76; pres. Redman Realty, Statesville, N.C., 1976—; mem. N.C. State Senate, 26th dist., 1978—. Bd. advisors Gardner-Webb Coll. Named to Inf. Officers' Sch. Hall of Fame, Ft. Benning, Ga., 1981. decorated DFC with oak leaf cluster, Bronze Star medal with two oak leaf clusters, Air medal with sixteen oak leaf clusters, Meritorious Service medal. Mem. Ret. Officers Assn., VFW, Am. Legion. Republican. Baptist. Clubs: Civitan, Elks. Address: Route 2 Box 43 Chipley Ford Rd Statesville NC 28677

REDMANN, DAVID EDMUND, lighting supply company executive; b. New Orleans, Nov. 13, 1938; s. Morris Benjamin and Esther Alice (Joyce) R.; m. Rose Marie Rapier, June 30, 1968; children—David Jr., Michael, Thomas, Kevin, Jonathan. B.B.A., Tulane U., 1964. Research asst. City Council, New Orleans, 1967-69; account exec. E. F. Hutton and Co., New Orleans, 1969-75; owner, pres. Gen. Lighting Supply, New Orleans, 1975—. Mem. New Orleans C. of C., Delta Sigma Pi. Republican. Roman Catholic. Clubs: Pickwick, Stratford (New Orleans). Avocations: piano; electronics. Office: Gen Lighting Supply 1601 Lafitte St New Orleans LA 70112

REDMON, AGILE HUGH, JR., allergist; b. Galveston, Tex., Dec. 17, 1924; s. Agile H. and Natalie Mary (Collins) R.; m. Dora Mary Bastiani, May 18, 1957; children—James Joseph, John Gerard. Student Tex. A&M U., 1942-43, U. Southwestern La., 1943-44; M.D., Baylor U., 1948. Diplomate Am. Bd. Allergy and Immunology. Intern U.S. Naval Hosp., San Diego, 1948-49; resident in allergy, 1955-56; resident in internal medicine VA Hosp., Houston, 1950-53; assoc. prof. medicine Baylor U., Houston, 1957—; sr. ptnr. Redmon-Barrick Allergy Assocs., Houston, 1970—. Served with M.C., USN, 1943-48, 53-57. Fellow Am. Acad. Allergy and Immunology; mem. AMA, Tex. Med. Assn., Harris County Med. Soc. (v.p. 1984), Tex. Allergy Soc. (pres. 1984-85), Houston Allergy Soc. (past pres.). Republican. Roman Catholic. Home: 5223 Contour Pl Houston TX 77096 Office: 7505 Fannin St Suite 515 Houston TX 77054

REDMOND, GAIL ELIZABETH, petroleum company executive; b. Milw., July 28, 1946; d. George Foote and Doris Ruth (Roethke) R.; m. John Thomas Happ; stepchildren: Amy, Julie, Tammi. Student Coll. St. Catherine, 1964-66; B.S. magna cum laude, Utah State U., 1968. Tchr. public schs., Milw., 1968-70; staff coordinator Med. Personnel Pool, Milw., 1973-76; corp. manpower devel. mgr. Clark Oil & Refining Corp., Milw., 1976-80; sr. advisor communications, employee benefits Conoco, Inc., Ponca City, Okla., 1980-81, coordinator profl. recruiting, 1981-82, coordinator benefit communications, 1982-84, asst. mgr. phase II evaluation, 1985—. Active USNR. Mem. AAUW, Phi Kappa Phi. Office: Conoco Inc PO Box 1267 Ponca City OK 74603

REECE, BENNY RAMON, educator; b. Asheville, N.C., Dec. 7, 1930; s. Judson Jones and Ina Marie (Blalock) R.; B.A., Duke, 1953; M.A., U. N.C., 1954, Ph.D., 1957; postgrad. U. Munich, 1957-58; m. Ethel Patricia Van Dyke, June 4, 1960; 1 son, Judson Benjamin. Instr., U. N.C., 1954-57; asst. prof. Mercer U., 1957-60; asso. prof. classical langs. Furman U., Greenville, S.C., 1960-80, prof., 1980—, chmn. dept. classical langs., 1960-72; vis. prof. U. N.C., 1968. Fulbright fellow, 1957-58; So. fellow, 1959; Am. Philos. Soc. fellow, 1967, 71. Mem. Am. Philol. Assn., Classical Assn. Middle West and South, Eta Sigma Phi, Alpha Phi Omega. Presbyn. Author: Documents Illustrating Cicero's Consular Campaign, 1967; Sermones Ratherii Episcopi Veronensis, 1969; Learning in the Tenth Century, 1972; A Bibliography of First Appearances of the Writings by A. Conan Doyle, 1975; The Role of the Centurion in Ancient Society, 1976; translator Plautus: Epidicus, 1967. Home: Route 7 Roe Ford Rd Greenville SC 29609

REECE, MAX GARDNER, JR., pharmacist, pharmacy manager; b. High Point, N.C., Feb. 19, 1953; s. Max Gardner and Virginia Alice (Weaver) R.; m. Susan Jane Boling, June 26, 1976; 1 child, Max Gardner, III. Assoc. in Sci., Louisburg Coll., 1973; B.S. in Pharmacy, U. N.C., 1977. Pharmacist-mgr. Revco Drug Co., Inc., Siler City, N.C., 1977—. Adv. bd. mem. Chatham Middle Sch., Siler City; mem. Ednl. Found., Chapel Hill, N.C., 1977—; bd. dirs. United Way Chatham County. Mem. N.C. Pharm. Assn., Siler City C. of C. (bd. dirs. 1985-86), U. N.C. Sch. Pharmacy Alumni Assn., Phi Theta Kappa. Republican. Baptist. Club: Siler City Country. Lodges: Optimist Club, Rotary Club (Paul Harris fellow, 1985). Avocations: golf; tennis. Home: Rt 1 Box 193 Siler City NC 27344

REED, ALFRED, composer, conductor; b. N.Y.C., Jan. 25, 1921; s. Carl Mark and Elizabeth (Strasser) Friedman; student Juilliard Sch. of Music, 1946-48; B.M., Baylor U., 1955, M.M., 1956; Mus. D., Internat. Conservatory of Music, Lima, Peru, 1968; m. Marjorie Beth Deley, June 20, 1941; children—Michael Carlson, Richard Judson. Composer, arranger, N.Y.C., 1941—; exec. editor Hansen Publs., N.Y.C., 1955-66; prof. music U. Miami (Fla.) Sch. of Music, 1966—; condr. Tri-State Music Festival, Okla., 1956-57, 60-66, 70, 73, Midwest Nat. Band Clinic, 1960-75, Bemidji (Minn.) Summer Music Camp, 1970-71, 75, Mid-East Instrumental Music Conf., Pitts., 1957-60, Canadian Music Educators Assn., Edmonton, Alta., 1975. Served with AUS, 1942-46. Mem. ASCAP, Am. Bandmasters Assn., Am. Fedn. Musicians, Nat. Band Assn., Music Educators Nat. Conv. Composer: Russian Christmas Music, 1944, Symphony for Brass and Percussion, 1952; Rhapsody for Viola and Orch., 1956, Choric Song, 1966, Titania's Nocturne, 1967, A Festival Prelude, 1962, Passacaglia, 1968, Music for Hamlet, 1973, Armenian Dances, 1974-75, Punchinello, Overture to a Romantic Comedy, 1974, Testament of an American, 1974, First Suite for Band, 1975, Othello, A Symphonic Portrait in Five Scenes, 1976, Prelude and Capriccio, 1977, Second Symphony, 1978, Siciliana Notturno, 1978, Second Suite for Band, 1978, The Enchanted Island, 1979, others. Home: 1405 Ancona Ave Coral Gables FL 33146 Office: Sch of Music Univ of Miami Coral Gables FL 33124

REED, BETTY JO, microbiologist; b. Houston; d. James Henry and Annie M. (Waite) Reed; B.S., Tulane U., 1966, M.S., 1968, postgrad., 1968-71. Instr. infectious diseases Tulane U. Sch. Medicine, New Orleans, 1968-74; chmn. immunology dept. Universidad Del Valle, Cali, Colombia, 1968-74; microbiologist W. Jefferson Hosp., New Orleans, 1974-80, Montelepre Meml. Hosp., New Orleans, 1980—; cons. WHO; infection control instr.; lectr. alcohol and drug abuse program LWV, 1978—. USPHS fellow, 1966-71; HEW cert. in environ. control. Mem. Am. Soc. Med. Technologists, Am. Soc. Microbiologists, Am. Soc. Clin. Pathologists. Republican. Methodist. Author: Manual of Infection Control, 1975. Home: 206 E Maplridge Metairie LA 70001 Office: 3125 Canal St New Orleans LA 70119

REED, GLEN ALFRED, lawyer; b. Memphis, Sept. 24, 1951; s. Thomas Henry and Evelyn Merle (Roddy) R.; m. Edith Jean Renick, June 17, 1972; children—Adam Christopher, Alec Benjamin. B.A., U. Tenn.-Knoxville, 1972; J.D., Yale U., 1976. Bar: Ga. 1976. Project dir. Tenn. Research Coordinating Unit, Knoxville, 1972-73; assoc. firm Alston Miller & Gaines, Atlanta, 1976-77; assoc. firm Bondurant, Miller, Hishon & Stephenson, Atlanta, 1978-81, partner, 1981-85; ptnr. King & Spalding, 1985—. Contbr. articles to profl. jours.; author: (seminar book) Practical Hospital Law, 1979-81. Gen. counsel Assn. for Retarded Citizens, Atlanta, 1979—. Mem. Am. Acad. Hosp. Attys., Ga. Acad. Hosp. Attys., ABA, Phi Beta Kappa. Home: 4379 Tree Haven Dr Atlanta GA 30342 Office: King & Spalding 2500 Trust Co Tower Atlanta GA 30342

REED, HELEN TARASOV, translator, interpreter, economist; b. Toronto, Ont., Can., Nov. 23, 1915; came to U.S., 1916, naturalized, 1927; d. Peter P. and Claudia M. (Yurevich) Tarasov; m. Haldee Lee Reed, Feb. 18, 1946 (dec. 1978); children—Claudette Reed Upton, Ronald Peter, Andrew Douglas. B.A., Western Res. U., 1936; full credit Ecole libre Sci. Po., Paris, 1934-35; M.A., Fletcher Sch. Law and Diplomacy, 1937; postgrad. New Sch. Social Research, 1939. Economist, U.S. Govt., Washington, 1939, Berlin, 1945-46; instr. U. N.C., Asheville, 1945-46; coordinator fgn. lang. Asheville Country Day Sch., 1959-73; contract cert. interpreter Russian-English, U.S. State Dept., throughout U.S., 1973-84; pvt. practice as sci. translator, Asheville, 1952—; instr., adv. in English South China Inst. Tech., Guangzhou, Peoples Republic of China,

1984—, Nanjng Inst. Posts and Telecommunications, 1985-86, Gansu Province Inst. Membrane Sci. and Tech., 1986; held workshops in fgn. lang. teaching Independent Schs. Assn., evening course U. N.C. in Russian, spl. courses YWCA in parliamentary law, procedure; parliamentarian for N.C. convs. LWV, other orgns. Del. N.C. State Dem. Conv., Raleigh, 1968, 76, 80; mem. County Bd. Edn., Asheville, 1953-57, N.C. State Pub. Water Adv. Commn., Raleigh, 1980-82, Buncombe County Energy Commn., Asheville, 1981-84; mem., sec. Western Carolina Devel. Assn. Forestry commn., 1980-84; mem. energy task force AAUW, Washington, 1977-79. Recipient All-State Environ. Service award N.C. Sierra Club, 1983, French Broad River award Land of Sky, 1982, and others. Mem. AAUW (past pres., treas.), Am. Econ. Assn., Am. Forestry Assn., Am. Translators' Assn., Am. Soc. Interpreters, Sierra Club, League of Women Voters, Carolina Mountain Club. Unitarian-Universalist. Club: Am. Enka. Avocations: hiking; swimming; tennis; travel; reading. Home: 26 Dogwood Rd Asheville NC 28806

REED, JACKIE TOLBERT WILLIAM, educator; b. Big Lake, Tex., Oct. 9, 1951; s. Earl James and Fannie Irene (Payne) R.; m. Shethelia Ilene Lewis, Dec. 19, 1981; 1 child, Michael Scott. B.S. in Edn., Angelo State U., San Angelo, Tex., 1974; M.A. in Counseling, U. Tex.-Permian Basin, Odessa, 1986. Tchr. Kermit Ind. Sch. Dist., Tex., 1975—. Author: (children's play) Who Really Shot J.R.?, 1983. Mem. Kermit PTA, 1984—; historian Future Tchrs. Assn., Rankin, Tex., 1970. Mem. Assn. Tex. Profl. Educators, Kermit Classroom Tchrs. Assn., Tex. State Tchrs. Assn. Avocations: photography; music; writing; sports. Home: PO Box 554 Kermit TX 79745

REED, JIMMY BURL, SR., auto supply co. exec.; b. Williamson, W.Va., June 30, 1924; s. William Sidney and Mary (Purdy) R.; B.S. in Bus. Adminstrn., U. Palm Beach, 1949; m. Lorene Helen Alderman, Aug. 11, 1947; children—Jimmy Burl, William Michael, Helen Lynn. Retail salesman Goodyear Tire & Rubber Co., Inc., West Palm Beach, Fla., 1949-51, retail store mgr., Miami, Fla., 1951-53, retail store mgr., Tampa, Fla., 1953-59, dist. truck tires sales mgr., Jacksonville, Fla., 1959-62, dist. petroleum sales mgr. State of Ala., 1962-65, regional petroleum sales mgr. So. region, 1965-67; propr., pres. Dublin Auto Supply Co. (Va.), 1967—, Leisure Living Homes, Inc., Dublin, 1973—. Pres. Dublin United Way, 1973-74; chmn. Pulaski County (Va.) United Way, 1975; mem. New River Community Coll. Adv. Bd., 1975—; bd. dirs. Pulaski County Lifesaving, 1974-75. Served with USN, 1943-46; PTO. Mem. Nat. Assn. of Ind. Bus., Pulaski County C. of C. (dir. 1976-77), Dublin Mchts. and Profl. Assn. (dir. 1980-81). Club: Lions (dir. 1974-76). Methodist. Home: 7th and Jordan Sts Radford VA 24141 Office: Dublin Auto Supply PO Box 1107 Dublin VA 24084

REED, JOHN JACK RODMAN, chemist; b. Eunice, La., Oct. 2, 1932; s. Wesley and Lucy (Guillory) R.; B.S., U. S.W. La., 1957; Ph.D., Tulane U., 1963; m. Vernell Caldwell, Apr. 9, 1965; 1 child, Angela. Research chemist Exxon Research & Engring. Co., Baytown, Tex., 1961-82, sr. staff chemist, 1980-82; with Exxon Chem. Co., 1983-84; pvt. cons., 1984—. Precinct chmn. Republican Party, 1976-80. Served with USAF, 1953-55. Roman Catholic. Club: Elks. Author: NMR Data Sulfur Compounds, 1971. Research on analytical applications of Fourier transform infrared spectrometry. Home: 707 Inwood St Baytown TX 77521

REED, JOSEPH HOWARD, banker, investor, independent oil operator, farmer; b. Medford, Okla., June 15, 1930; s. Harold Dehorty and Verna Lee (Elder) R.; m. Paula Sue Nyswonger, Dec. 20, 1952; children—Jason Howard, Renee Suzanne. B.S., Okla. State U.-Stillwater, 1952; postgrad. Mexico City Coll., 1953; J.D., Georgetown U., Washington, 1957; M.A., Calif. Western U., Santa Ana, 1976. Bar: D.C. 1957, Okla. 1957. Vice pres. Grant County Bank, Medford, Okla., 1957-68, pres., 1968—; pres. Reed Enterprise, Inc., Medford, 1977—, Reed Properties, Inc., Medford, 1977—; farmer, rancher, Medford, 1954—; dir. Adams Hard-Facing Co., Inc., Guymon, Okla., 1975—. Contbr. articles in field. Commr., Gov. Commn. on Reform of State Govt., Okla., 1984—; state chmn. Com. of Employer Support for the Guard and Res., Okla., 1984—; mem. Gov.'s Com. Jobs for Veterans, 1984—, Democratic Nat. Fin. Council, Washington, 1984—, Sen. Nickels Veterans Adv. Com., Okla., 1985, Okla. State U. Centennial Adv. Commn., 1985; dir. Grant County Indsl. Devel. Authority (Okla.), 1984—; trustee, bd. dirs. Donna Nigh Found. for Mentally Retarded, 1984—. Served to 1st lt. U.S. Army, 1953-55; served to brig. gen. USNG, 1985—. Decorated Legion of Merit, Meritorius Service medal, others. Mem. Okla. Bankers Assn., Res. Officers Assn., Nat. Mil. Intelligence Assn., Former Intelligence Officers Assn., Nat. Guard Assn. U.S., Medford C. of C. (pres. 1975), Phi Kappa Phi. Lodges: VFW, Am. Legion. Office: Grant County Bank 1122 S Main St Medford OK 73759

REED, LEON BRANNON, II, dentist; b. Clarksburg, W.Va., Oct. 1, 1947; s. Leon Brannon and Laura Belle (Pritt) R.; m. Jeanne Lynn Law, Aug. 10, 1968 (div.); children—Joshua Law, Joel Ashley. Student Tex. A&M U., 1965-66; D.D.S., W. Va. U., 1972. Gen. practice dentistry, Williamsburg, Va., 1976—. Coach basketball teams Jamestown Acad., Williamsburg, 1982—; bd. dirs. Big Brothers, Big Sisters, Williamsburg, 1978-81. Served as capt. U.S. Army, 1972-75, Germany. Mem. ADA, Va. Dental Assn., Acad. Gen. Dentistry, Peninsula Dental Soc., Psi Omega. Democrat. Avocations: scuba diving, running, basketball, windsurfing, horseback riding. Home: 2133 #53 S Henry St Williamsburg VA 23185 Office: 1115 B Profl Dr Williamsburg VA 23185

REED, MARGARET CAROL, nurse; b. Frankfort, Ky., Nov. 29, 1935; d. Regis Francis and Margaret Frances (Moore) Whitehead; m. Clyde E. Reed, May 9, 1964 (div.); children—Suzanne, Rebecca Lynn. Diploma, Nazareth Sch. Nursing, 1958. Registered nurse, Ky.; lic. ins. rep., Ky. Head nurse critical care unit, intensive care unit King's Daus. Hosp., Frankfort, Ky., 1970-77; sr. regional adminstr. Ky. Peer Rev. Orgn., Louisville, 1977-81, assoc. care service dir., 1982—; dir. Assoc. Care Service, 1983—. Pres. Franklin County (Ky.) Republican Women, 1966, 78; 4th v.p. Ky. Fedn. Rep. Women, 1979; activities dir. Good Shepherd Parish Council, 1976, 77, 78. Mem. Ky. Nurses Assn. (bd. dirs. polit. action com., 1979). Roman Catholic.

REED, RICHARD KENT, geologist; b. Portsmouth, Va., June 5, 1942; s. Karl Edwin and Helen Elizabeth (McIlwain) R.; m. Sharon Sammis, 1978; children—Erin, Allison, Susannah, Christopher Owen (dec.). A.B. in Geology, Cornell U., 1964; M.S. in Geology, U. Ariz., 1967; Ph.D. in Geology, U. N.Mex., 1971. Geologist Texaco-Eastern Hemisphere, Bellaire, Tex., 1971-77, Union Tex. Petroleum, Houston, 1977-80; sr. geologist Monsanto Oil, Houston, 1980-84; advanced sr. geologist Marathon Internat., Houston, 1984—. Councilman Bellaire City Council, 1980-82; sr. warden St. Thomas Anglican Ch., Houston, 1985-86. Served with U.S. Army, 1967-69. Mem. Am. Assn. Petroleum Geologists, Houston Geol. Soc., Sigma Xi. Republican. Anglican. Clubs: Eire (Houston); Friends of Bellaire Parks. Home: 502 Mulberry Ln Bellaire TX 77401 Office: Marathon Internat Oil Co PO Box 3128 5555 San Felipe Houston TX 77253

REED, ROBERT GEORGE, III, petroleum company executive; b. Cambridge, Mass., Aug. 9, 1927; s. Robert George and Marjorie B. Reed; m. Maggie L. Fisher, Mar. 22, 1974; children—Sandra McNickle, Valerie Sloan, Jonathan J., John-Paul. B.A. in Econs., Dartmouth Coll., 1949; A.M.P., Harvard U., 1970. Mktg. mgr. Tidewater Oil subs. Getty Oil Co., Los Angeles, 1957-64; v.p. mktg. CitiesService Co., Tulsa, 1964-72; exec. v.p. Tesoro Petroleum Corp., San Antonio, 1972-79; chmn. bd., chief exec. officer Clark Oil & Refining Corp., Milw., 1979-81, pres., chief exec. officer div. Apex Oil Co., St. Louis, 1981—; chmn. bd., chief exec. officer Energy Sources Exchange, Inc., Houston, 1981—; gen. mgr. Sanchez-O'Brien Mgmt. Corp., 1983—; dir. Marine Nat. Bank, Marine Corp. Chmn. Com. for Equitable Access to Crude Oil, 1980-82. Served with USN, 1945-46. Mem. Am. Petroleum Inst., Nat. Petroleum Refiners Assn. (bd. dirs.). Clubs: University; Houston City. Office: 17 S Briar Hollow Ln Suite 200 Houston TX 77027

REED, ROBERT LEONARD, JR., boot manufacturing company executive; b. Nashville, Nov. 28, 1932; s. Robert L. and Lillian Theresa (Morris) R.; m. Janet Lee Davis, June 26, 1954; children—Robert Matthew, Elizabeth Leigh. B.B.A., U. Ga., 1954. With GENESCO, Nashville, 1957-79, plant mgr., 1962-65, div. mgr., 1965-72, gen. mgr., 1972-74, group pres., 1974-79; exec. v.p. Tex. Boot Co., Lebanon, Tenn., 1979—. Served to 1st lt. USAF, 1954-56. Recipient Superior Achievement Recognition awards GENESCO, 1967, 75. Republican. Presbyterian. Club: Wildwood Swim (Brentwood, Tenn.). Contbr. articles to profl. jours. Office: Texas Boot Co E Forest Ave Lebanon TN 37087

REED, SCOTT, judge; b. Lexington, Ky., July 3, 1921; s. Wilbur S. and Florence (Young) R.; m. Sue Charles, Oct. 12, 1946; 1 son, Geoffrey. J.D., U. Ky., 1945; LL.D., No. Ky. U., 1977. Bar: Ky., 1944. Pvt. practice, Lexington, 1944-64; county atty. Fayette County, Ky., 1952; judge Fayette Circuit Ct., Lexington, 1964-69; justice Ky. Ct. Appeals, Lexington, 1969-75; justice, chief justice Supreme Ct. Ky., 1976-79; judge U.S. Dist. Ct., 1979—; acting assoc. prof. U. Ky., 1946-53. Recipient Sullivan medal U. Ky., 1945; Nat. Coll. Judiciary fellow, 1965. Mem. ABA, Ky. Bar Assn. (award 1977), Fayette County Bar Assn. (Henry T. Duncan award 1977, citation for outstanding service, 1979, 84), Am. Law Inst., Order of Coif, Phi Delta Phi. Clubs: Lexington Civil War Roundtable. Editor-in-chief Ky. Law Jour., 1944.

REED, TERRY ALLEN, accountant; b. Ft. Payne, Ala., Oct. 13, 1948; s. Carl and Burma (Benefield) R.; B.S. in Acctg., Jacksonville State U., 1971; m. Sharon Elizabeth Phillips, Sept. 11, 1971; children—Allison Elizabeth, Phillip Allen. Staff acct. Goolsby and Walkley, C.P.A.s, Birmingham, Ala., 1971-72; controller law firm Bradley, Arant, Rose & White, Birmingham, 1972-82; office mgr. firm Haskell Slaughter Young & Lewis, Birmingham, 1982—. Treas. Grace United Methodist Ch., Birmingham, 1981-83. Assn. Legal Adminstrs. (Birmingham chpt.). Home: 5724 Overton Rd Birmingham AL 35210 Office: 800 1st Nat So Natural Bldg Birmingham AL 35203

REEDER, WILLIAM GLASE, museum administrator, zoologist; b. Los Angeles, Feb. 4, 1929; s. William Hedges and Gladys Ella (Glase) R.; B.A., UCLA, 1950; M.A., U. Mich., 1953, Ph.D., 1957; m. Lynn Roseberry Rohrer, Jan. 27, 1951; children—Elisabeth H., Jeffrey W., Heather L., Kathleen A. Asst. curator ornithology and mammalogy Los Angeles County Mus., 1949-51; vis. asst. prof. zoology UCLA, 1955-56; curatorial asst. Mus. Zoology, U. Mich., 1956-58; asst. prof. zoology U. Wis., Madison, 1958-62, asso. prof., 1962-66, prof., 1966-78, dir. Zool. Mus., 1967-78; prof. zoology, dir. Tex. Meml. Mus., U. Tex., Austin, 1978—. Chmn. Tex. Antiquities Commn., 1983—. Mem. Am. Soc. Mammalogy, Am. Soc. Zoologists, Soc. Study Evolution, Soc. Systematic Zoology, Am. Arachnological Soc., Am. Assn. Mus., Soc. Vertebrate Paleontology. Research, publs. in systematic biology and ecology. Office: 2400 Trinity St Austin TX 78705

REEFE, NORA LEA, management consultant; b. Danville, Va., Sept. 22, 1946; d. Bryan Jones and Marian Natalie (Stevens) Rogers; m. Edward Michael Reefe, May 10, 1969; children—Donna Christine, Kathryn Lea. B.A. in History, Duke U., 1967; postgrad. U. N.C.-Greensboro, 1967-68; M.B.A., U. South Fla., 1980. Instr. history Radford (Va.) Coll., 1968-69; tchr. history Antilles High Sch., San Juan, P.R., 1969-70; exec. sec., adminstrv. asst. Ctr. for Textual and Editorial Studies, U. Va., 1972-74; tchr. social studies, Charlotte, N.C., 1975-77; tech. asst., cons. Mgmt. Inst., U. South Fla., Tampa, 1979-80; dir. organizational devel., asst. to chief exec. officer Greiner Engring., Tampa, 1980-83; pres. Cons. Mgmt. Services, Inc., Tampa, 1983—; adj. prof. bus. U. South Fla. speaker various civic and profl. orgns. Bd. dirs. U. Tampa, Human Devel. Ctr.; solicitor Arthritis Found.; industry chmn. United Way; mem. parish council, ch. lector, tchr. St. Mary's Cath. Ch., Tampa. Mem. Profl. Services Mgmt. Assn., Am. Soc. Tng. and Devel., Planning Execs. Inst., Internat. Assn. Bus. Communicators, Soc. for Mktg. Profl. Services. Republican. Club: Davis Island Yacht (Tampa). Author: The Economic Impact of Land Use Planning: Land Developers and the Horizon 2000 Plan, 1979; Marketing and Promoting Professional Design Services, 1980; Identification and Selection of an Export Market for a Small Firm, 1980; Competitive Bidding: A Cost/Benefit Analysis, 1981; Professional Development Programs: Key to The Future, 1984; Creating a Competitive Edge: The Case for Professional Human Resource Management in A/E Firms, 1985. Office: 5445 Mariner St Suite 210 Tampa FL 33609

REEL, JERRY ROYCE, researcher, educator; b. Washington, Ind., May 4, 1938; s. Royce Howard and Anna Belle (Valin) R.; m. Joan Kay Wedberg, Aug. 14, 1965; 1 dau., Justine Jeanette. B.A., Ind. State U., 1960; M.S., U. Ill., 1963, Ph.D., 1966 Diplomate Am. Bd. Toxicology. Am. Cancer Soc. postdoctoral fellow Oak Ridge Nat. Lab. (Tenn.), 1966-68; dir. endocrinology sect. Park-Davis/Warner-Lambert Pharm. Research Labs., Ann Arbor, Mich., 1968-78; sr. endocrinologist Research Triangle Inst., Research Triangle Park, N.C., 1978-80, research dir. Life Scis. and Toxicology div., 1980-85; dir. dept. endocrinology Sterling-Winthrop Research Inst., Rensselaer, N.Y., 1985—; research rev. panelist U.S. Govt., WHO, Geneva; adj. prof. endocrinology Wayne State U. Sch. Medicine, 1974—. Mem. Soc. Toxicology, Endocrine Soc., Am. Chem. Soc., Soc. for the Study Reproduction, AAAS, Am. Physiol. Soc. Contbr. numerous articles to profl. jours.; editor 2 books; developer novel progestational agt. Home: 156 Darroch Rd Delmar NY Office: Endocrinology Dept Sterling-Winthrop Research Inst Rensselaer NY 12144

REESE, CLARA COOK, educator; b. Burke County, N.C., Nov. 11, 1931; m. Ned Ervin Reese, Aug. 25, 1950; children—Jerry Alan, Susan Clarice. A.B., Lenoir Rhyne Coll., 1969; M.A., N.C. State U., 1972, Ed.D., 1980. With finishing dept., supr. irregular dept. Ellis Hosiery Co., Inc., Hickory, N.C., 1952-62, payroll clk., receptionist, 1962-64; sales staff J.C. Penney Co., Hickory, N.C., 1968-69; tchr. Catawba Valley Tech. Inst., 1972-77, Newton-Conover City Schs., Newton, N.C., 1969-77; asst. prof. dept. occupational, adult and safety edn. Marshall U., Huntington, W.Va., 1980—. Chmn. bd. dirs. Career Exploration Clubs N.C., 1974-76; state advisor Career Exploration Clubs W.Va. Mem. Am. Vocat. Assn., W.Va. Vocat. Assn., Phi Delta Kappa, Epsilon Pi Tau. Democrat. Methodist. Office: Marshall U Dept OAS Huntington WV 25701

REESE, DALE OWEN, petroleum geologist; b. Newman, Ill., Aug. 15, 1934; s. Paul Everett and Mabel Bertha (Dever) R.; m. Carolyn Norwood. B.S., U. Ill., 1956; M.S., U. Kans., 1959. Geologist, Arabian Am. Oil Co., Dhahran, Saudi Arabia, 1959-61, Pan Am. Petroleum Co., Jackson, Miss., 1962-65; cons., Jackson, 1965-70; geologist Fla. Gas Exploration Co., Jackson, 1970-74, Bridger Petroleum Co., Dallas, 1974-77; exploration mgr. Lear Petroleum Co., Dallas, 1977-79, Vaughn Petroleum Co., Dallas, 1979-83; cons. petroleum geologist, Dallas, 1983—. Served with U.S. Army, 1957-58. Richland County scholar, 1952. Mem. Am. Assn. Petroleum Geologists, Am. Inst. Profl. Geologists, Soc. Exploration Geophysicists, Sigma Xi. Republican. Baptist. Club: Brookhaven Country (Dallas). Home and Office: 6816 Roundrock St Dallas TX 75248

REESE, DAVID JOHN, physician, educator; b. Danville, Pa., May 16, 1940; s. Robert E. and Helen (Deppen) R.; A.B., Princeton U., 1962; M.D., U. N.C., 1968; m. Eleanor Jane Sullivan, Aug. 7, 1965. Intern, U. Va. Hosp., 1968-69, resident in pediatrics, 1968-71; practice medicine specializing in pediatrics, Arlington, Va., 1973—; dir. pediatric edn. Arlington Hosp., 1973—, chmn. dept. pediatrics, 1974—; asso. prof. pediatrics Georgetown U. Sch. Medicine, 1979—, also assoc. prof. family and community medicine; mem. com. for hypothyroid screening program for infants, State of Va., 1977-79; mem. tech. adv. panel on neonatal intensive care Health Systems Agy. of No. Va., 1977-80. Mem. Juvenile Services Study Task Force, No. Va. Planning Dist. Commn., 1976-80; pres. Arcturus Park Assn., 1975-79; mem. community adv. bd. No. Va. Community Service League, 1976-78. Served to maj. M.C., U.S. Army, 1971-73. Recipient Tchr. of Yr. award Georgetown U. Dept. Pediatrics, 1976, Cert. of Recognition, Gov. Va., 1978. Diplomate Am. Bd. Pediatrics. Mem. No. Va. Pediatric Soc., Arlington County Med. Soc. Home: 824 Arcturus on the Potomac Alexandria VA 22308 Office: 1701 N George Mason Dr Arlington VA 22205

REESE, JACK EDWARD, university chancellor; b. Hendersonville, N.C., Apr. 12, 1929; s. William James and Alyce Genevieve (Pace) R.; A.B. in English, Berea (Ky.) Coll., 1951; M.A., U. Ky., 1953, Ph.D., 1961; m. Nancy Anne Larsen, Aug. 31, 1957; children—Matthew Bradley, Kristin Alyce. Teaching asst. U. Ky., 1957-58, vis. prof., summer 1968; mem. faculty U. Tenn., Knoxville, 1961—, assoc. prof. English, dean grad. studies, asso. vice chancellor acad. affairs, 1972-73, chancellor, 1973—; acad. adminstrv. intern. Am. Council Edn., U. Ariz., 1969-70. Chmn. Tenn. Arts Commn., 1967-68; mem. Gov. Tenn. Adv. Com. Minority Econ. Devel., 1974—. Served with USNR, 1953-57. Mem. Southeastern Renaissance Conf., Phi Kappa Phi. Episcopalian. Contbr. articles to profl. jours. Office: 506 Andy Holt Tower U Tenn Knoxville TN 37916*

REESE, KENNETH WENDELL, diversified company executive; b. Orange, Tex., Aug. 1, 1930; s. Richard W. and Florence (Mulhollan) R.; m. Mary A. Broom, Aug. 22, 1955; children—Jimmy, Michael, Gary. B.B.A., U. Houston, 1954. Asst. treas. Firestone Tire & Rubber Co., Akron, Ohio, 1968-70, treas., 1970—, v.p., 1973-75, exec. v.p. finance, 1975; sr. v.p. fin. Tenneco Inc., Houston, 1975-78, exec. v.p., 1978—; dir. Tex. Commerce Bancshares, Inc., Fleming Cos., Inc., Tenneco Inc. Bd. dirs. Better Bus. Bur., Met. Houston, Tex. Council on Econ. Edn.; trustee U. Houston Found.; mem. adv. com. Coll. Bus. Adminstrn., U. Houston. Served to 1st lt. AUS, 1954-56. Mem. U. Houston Athletic Lettermans Assn. Baptist. Clubs: Petroleum, Heritage (Houston). Office: Tenneco Bldg PO Box 2511 Houston TX 77001

REESE, LOWELL D., association executive; b. Pikeville, Ky., Mar. 12, 1940; s. Palmer R. and Ollie (Rose) R.; m. Carol Jean Rowe, Dec. 26, 1970; 1 stepson, Tracy Lee Huffman. B.A. in History, Berea Coll., 1963. Chief Bur. Child Devel., Commonwealth of Ky., Frankfort, 1969-71; exec. dir. Our Common Heritage, Lexington, Ky., 1971-72; v.p. Ky. C. of C., Frankfort, 1972-79; exec. v.p. S.C. C. of C., Columbia, 1979—. Bd. dirs. Greater Columbia Jr. Achievement; exec. dir. for Ky. Pres. Ford Election Campaigns, 1976. Served to 1st lt. U.S. Army, 1963-67; Vietnam. Decorated Purple Heart, Bronze Star, Air medal, Commendation medal with V; Vietnamese Cross of Gallantry. Republican. Home: 1335 Elm Abode Columbia SC 29210 Office: SC C of C PO Box 11278 Columbia SC 29211

REESE, SUE BRYSON, nurse, educator; b. Moundsville, W.Va., Oct. 6, 1931; d. Harry A. and Virginia Elizabeth (Moore) Bryson; B.S.N., Hartwick Coll., Oneonta, N.Y., 1955; postgrad. Syracuse U., 1967; M.S.N., Cath. U. Am., 1974; m. Charles David Reese, Dec. 7, 1957; children—Becki, Cyndi, Suzi. Clin. coordinator Wheeling (W.Va.) Hosp., 1955-57; instr. Monongalia Gen. Hosp., Morgantown, W.Va., 1958-61, staff nurse, 1962; staff nurse Indiana (Pa.) Hosp., 1963, instr., 1963-66; instr. Syracuse (N.Y.) U., 1966-67; coll. health nurse, instr. West Liberty (W.Va.) State Coll., 1968-71; inservice edn. and asst. dir. nursing service Greater S.E. Community Hosp., Washington, 1971-73; assoc. prof. nursing, dir. nursing edn. Shepherd Coll., Shepherdstown W.Va., 1974-81; nursing quality assurance coordinator VA Med. Ctr., Martinsburg, W.Va., 1981—. Mem. Am. Nurses Assn., W.Va. Nurses Assn., W.Va. Heart Assn., W.Va. Lung Assn., AAUW, DAR (nat. defense chmn. Pack Horse Ford chpt.), Sigma Theta Tau, Zeta Tau Alpha. Republican. Methodist. Clubs: Order Eastern Star (Shepherdstown, W.Va.). Home: PO Box 220 Shepherdstown WV 25443 Office: VAMC Martinsburg WV 25401

REESE, WILBUR ROY, retired clinical psychologist; b. Wilson, N.Y., Sept. 20, 1918; s. Walter Everett and Edna (Smith) R.; m. Hope Elizabeth King, Apr. 24, 1942; children—William Jerome, Sandra F. Hoyer, Linda Reese Tortorici. B.S. in Edn., SUNY-Buffalo, 1938; postgrad. SUNY-Albany, 1938-40, Ohio State U., 1946-48. Cert. sch. psychologist, Ohio. Sch. psychologist Akron Bd. Edn. (Ohio), 1948; research psychologist Psychol. Corp., N.Y.C., 1947; teaching asst. Ohio State U., Columbus, 1947-48; evening coll. prof. Coll. William and Mary, Williamsburg, Va., 1952-74; clin. psychologist, acting dir. Tidewater Mental Health Clinic, Williamsburg, 1949-78; pvt. practice clin. psychology, Williamsburg, 1962-64, ret., 1978. Mental health chmn., bd. dirs. Va. Congress PTAs, 1963-65; bd. dirs. Community Action Agy., Williamsburg, 1970-79. Served to lt. comdr., USNR, 1941-45; PTO. Mem. Am. Psychol. Assn. Home: 410 Griffin Ave Williamsburg VA 23185

REEVES, ALEXIS SCOTT, journalist; b. Atlanta, Feb. 4, 1949; d. William Alexander and Marian (Willis) Scott; m. Marc Anthony Lewis, Sept. 14, 1968 (div. 1973); m. David Leslie Reeves, Mar. 16, 1974; 1 child, Cinque Scott. Student Barnard Coll., 1966-68. Reporter, asst. city editor, cable TV editor, mgr. video edit. Atlanta Jour. & Constn., Atlanta, 1974—; vis. instr. summer program for minority journalists, Berkeley, Calif., 1980, 81, 84, 85, Grady High Sch., Atlanta, 1982-83; journalist-in-residence Clark Coll., Atlanta, 1983. Researcher, writer: The History of Atlanta NAACP, 1983 (NAACP award, 1984). Recipient Disting. Urban Journalism award Nat. Urban Coalition, 1980. Michele Clark fellow Columbia Univ. Sch. Journalism, 1974. Mem. Nat. Assn. Media Women (Media Woman of Yr. award, 1983, Media Woman of Yr. nat. award 1983, pres. Atlanta chpt. 1985-86), Atlanta Assn. Black Journalists (Commentary Print award 1983), Nat. Assn. Black Journalists, Sigma Delta Chi (bd. dirs. 1980-84, treas. 1985). Moderator, First Congl. Ch.. Office: Atlanta Jour-Constn 72 Marietta St Atlanta GA

REEVES, CARROLL DON, history and political science educator, clergyman; b. Gainesville, Tex., Jan. 9, 1935; s. Troy Virgil and Roxie Ann (Waggoner) R.; m. Clydanne Montgomery, Aug. 31, 1961 (div. 1980); children—Michael Alan, David Kevin. Student Harding Coll., 1954; B.S. in Edn., North Tex. State U., 1956, M.S. in History, 1961; postgrad. Abilene Christian U., 1957, 59, U. Tex., Austin, 1962, 65-68, Baylor U., 1975, Westbrook Coll., 1979. Cert. tchr., Tex.; ordained to ministry Ch. of Christ, 1954. Minister, Ch. of Christ, Valley View, Tex., 1954-57, Ethel, Tex., 1957-59, Bolivar, Tex., 1959-61; tchr. English, Denton Sr. High Sch. (Tex.), 1958-59; grad. teaching asst. North Tex. State U., Denton, 1960; instr. history and polit. sci. Laredo Jr. Coll. (Tex.), 1961-65; prof. history and polit. sci. McLennan Community Coll., Waco, Tex., 1967—, history area coordinator, 1977-78, chmn. dept. social scis., 1978-82, 84—. Reporter Cedar Ridge Elem. Sch. PTA, Waco, 1975, treas., 1976; deacon, elder Ch. of Christ, 1963-78; precinct sec. Republican Party, 1972; bd. dirs. Waco Christian Sch., 1975-79. Am. Studies fellow Abilene Christian U., 1957; mem. Master Tchrs. Seminar, 1979. Mem. Tex. Jr. Coll. Tchrs. Assn. (sec. history sect. 1963, vice chmn. 1966, chmn. 1974), Phi Alpha Theta. Sponsor chess clubs Laredo Jr. Coll. and McLennan Community Coll. and Phi Theta Kappa, Waco, also Coll. Republicans. Home: 3616 Pine Ave Waco TX 76708 Office: 1400 College Dr Suite 202 Waco TX 76708

REEVES, GENE, lawyer; b. Meridian, Miss., Feb. 27, 1930; s. Clarence Eugene and May (Philyaw) R.; m. Brenda Wages, Sept. 26, 1980. LL.B., John Marshall U., 1964. Bar: Ga. 1964, U.S. Ct. Appeals (11th cir.) 1965, U.S. Supreme Ct. 1969. Ptnr., Craig & Reeves, Lawrenceville, Ga., 1964-71; sole practice, Lawrenceville, 1971—; judge City Ct., Lawrenceville, 1969-70. Served to sgt. USAF, 1951-54. Mem. Am. Jud. Soc., ABA, Gwinnett County Bar Assn. (pres. 1970-72). Baptist. Home: 221 Pineview Dr Lawrenceville GA 30245 Office: 125 Perry St Lawrenceville GA 32045

REEVES, GEORGE PAUL, bishop; b. Roanoke, Va., Oct. 14, 1918; s. George Floyd and Harriett Faye (Foster) R.; m. Adele Beer, Dec. 18, 1943; children—Cynthia Reeves Pond, George Floyd II. B.A., Randolph-Macon Coll., 1940; B.D., Yale U., 1943; D.D., U. of South, 1970, Nashotah House, 1970. Ordained priest Episcopal Ch., 1948, consecrated bishop, 1969; chaplain U.S. Naval Res., 1943-47, Fla. State U., 1947-50; rector All Saints Ch., Winter Park, Fla., 1950-59, Ch. of Redeemer, Sarasota, Fla., 1959-65, St. Stephens Ch., Miami, Fla., 1965-69; bishop of Ga., Savannah, 1969—. Mem. Phi Beta Kappa. Office: 611 E Bay St Savannah GA 31401*

REEVES, JIMMY HARPER, banker; b. Montezuma, Ga., Apr. 7, 1938; s. Charlie George and Luna Mae (Kirkland) R.; m. Evelyn Cross, May 9, 1959; children—Deborah Denese, Michael Mark. B.B.A. in Mgmt., Ga. State U., 1963, M.B.A. in Fin., 1966; postgrad. La. State U. Sch. of Banking, 1981-83. Adminstrv. asst. trust dept. Trust Co. Bank, 1963-67; tech. dir. finishing plant Riegel Textile Corp., Ware Shoals, S.C., 1967-70; asst. to v.p. fin. Southwire Co., Carrollton, Ga., 1970-77; v.p. West Ga. Nat. Bank, Carrollton, 1977—. Chmn. dist. camping com. Boy Scouts Am., 1976; pres. Central High and Middle Schs. PTA, Carrollton, 1977-78, Central High Sch. Athletic Booster Club, 1985-86; treas. Carroll County Early Childhood Ctr.; sec. Carroll County unit Am. Heart Assn.; fund raiser Am. Cancer Soc., ARC, Am. Heart Assn., Boy Scouts Am. Recipient Order of Arrow, Boy Scouts Am., 1975, Silver Beaver award, 1977, Carroll Dist. award of merit, 1977. Mem. Bank Adminstrn. Inst. (dir. West Ga. chpt.), Carroll County C. of C., Blue Key, Beta Gamma Sigma. Republican. Baptist. Clubs: Kiwanis (past pres., past lt. gov.), Carroll County Cattlemen's Assn. Home: 685 Thomas-Wilson Rd Roopville GA 30170 Office: PO Box 280 Carrollton GA 30117

REFICE, LINDA JOSEPHINE, school counselor; b. Flint, Mich., Apr. 14, 1948; d. Louie and Mary Gloria (Conti) R. B.A., Central Mich. U., 1970, M.A., 1977. Cert. tchr., Mich., Tex.; lic. counselor, Tex., Mich. Tchr. schs. Flint, Mich., 1970-76; middle sch. counselor Merrill Community Schs., Mich., 1977-81; tchr. Humble High Sch., Tex., 1981-82; middle sch. counselor Klein Ind. Sch. Dist., Spring, Tex., 1982—; tchr. supr. Central Mich. U., Flint, 1973; asst. arts and crafts dir. Central Mich. U., Summer Speech and Hearing Clinic, Mt. Pleasant, 1976-77; counselor ct. referrals, Stanton, Mich., 1977-81. Mem. Tex. State Tchrs. Assn., Tex. Assn. Counseling and Devel., Tex. Sch. Counselors Assn., NEA, Am. Assn. Counseling and Devel., Am. Sch. Counselors Assn.

Roman Catholic. Avocations: music; sports; cooking. Office: Hildebrandt Intermediate Klein Ind Sch Dist 22800 Hildebrandt Rd Spring TX 77389

REGALADO, ELISA, university administrator; b. Remedios, Cuba, Dec. 2, 1940; d. Rene Mederos and Rafaela (Rodriguez) Mederos Sales; children—Elisa, Jose. B.A., U. Villanueva (Cuba), 1960; M.B.A., U. Miami (Fla.), 1983. Dir. med. budgeting and fin. reporting U. Miami Med. Sch. (Fla.), 1966—. Mem Nat. Assn. Accts., Am. Mgmt. Assn., Nat. Assn. Female Execs., Assn. Am. Med. Colls. (group bus. affairs). Republican. Roman Catholic. Club: U. Miami Bowling (sec. 1979, treas. 1980). Office: U Miami Sch Medicine PO Box 016960 D2-3 Miami FL 33101

REGALADO, MARK EDWARD, art history educator; b. El Paso, Tex., Feb. 3, 1942; s. Edward and Lupe (Paredes) R.; m. Rosemary Louise Carlon, June 16, 1967; 1 child, Joseph Edward. Student U. Guam, 1963; B.A., U. Tex.-El Paso, 1968. Cert. tchr., Tex. Tchr. art Ysleta Ind. Schs., El Paso, 1968-75, Dept. Def. Overseas Dependent Schs., Goose Bay, Can., 1975-77; instr. art history and comml. art El Paso Community Coll., 1978—; cons. in field. Legis. asst. to Rep. Paul Moreno, Tex. Served with USNR, 1961-66. Fulbright Hayes grantee, 1982. Mem. NEA, Tex. Tchrs. Assn., Profl. Assn. Coll. Educators. Illustrator (head start manual record albums) Mis Primeros Pasos; set designer for amateur theatre U.S., Can. Home: 1564 Dale Douglas El Paso TX 79936 Office: El Paso Community Coll Valle Verde Campus S132 El Paso TX 79998

REGELBRUGGE, ROGER RAFAEL, steel company executive; b. Eeklo, Belgium, May 22, 1930; came to U.S., 1953, naturalized, 1961; s. Victor and Rachel (Roesbeke) R.; B.S. in Mech. Engring., State Tech. Coll., Ghent, Belgium, 1951; B.Sc. in Indsl. Engring., Gen. Motors Inst., Flint, Mich., 1955; M.S. in Mech. Engring., Mich. State U., 1964; m. Dorcas Merchant, June 7, 1980; children—Anita, Marc, Laurie, Jon, Craig, Kurt, Christine. Supr. product engring. dept. Gen. Motors Corp., Antwerp, Belgium, 1955-58; chief devel. engr. Hayes Industries Inc., Jackson, Mich., 1958-62, gen. mgr. Airmaster div., 1962-66; tech. dir. Koehring Co., Milw., 1966-67, group v.p. internat. ops., 1969-74, pres. Menck & Hambrock GmbH subs., Hamburg, W. Ger., 1967-69; exec. v.p. Georgetown Industries, Inc. (formerly Korf Industries, Inc.), Charlotte, N.C., 1974-77, pres., chief exec. officer, 1977—; chmn. bd. Georgetown Steel Corp., Georgetown Internat. Corp. Bd. visitors Davidson Coll., N.C., Johnson C. Smith U., Charlotte. Mem. ASME, Am. Soc. Automotive Engrs., Am. Iron and Steel Inst. (dir.). Roman Catholic. Clubs: Carmel Country, Charlotte Athletic; George Town (Washington). Home: 4000 Foxcroft Rd Charlotte NC 28211 Office: Georgetown Industries Inc 1901 Roxborough Rd Suite 200 Charlotte NC 28211

REGER, MICHAEL FRANK, public relations executive; b. Akron, Ohio, Sept. 20, 1957; s. P.G. and Charlotte J. (Rockhold) R. B.A., Taylor U., Upland, Ind., 1979. Coordinator community events Maj. Hosp., Shelbyville, Ind., 1979-81; dir. community relations Huntington Meml. Hosp. (Ind.), 1981-82; dir. pub. relations and mktg. Am. Med. Internat., Oklahoma City, 1982-83; dir. pub. relations Bapt. Med. Ctr., Oklahoma City, 1982—, asst. v.p. pub. relations, 1986—; dir. pub. relations ProGraphics, Inc., 1982-86, asst. v.p. pub. relations, 1986. cons. to rural hosps. Exec. adv. bd. Computers in Healthcare mag. Bike-a-thon dir. Am. Diabetes Assn., Shelbyville, Ind., 1981, Huntington, Ind., 1982, nat. bd. dirs.; vol. March of Dimes of Okla., Oklahoma City, 1983; bd. dirs. Am. Diabetes Assn. Mem. Am. Soc. Hosp. Pub. Relations, Oklahoma City Hosp. Pub. Relations Council (v.p. 1983-84) Pub. Relations Soc. Am. (dir. 1983—), Am. Mktg. Assn., Am. Acad. Hosp. Pub. Relations. Exec. adv. bd. Computers in Healthcare Mag. Republican. Baptist. Contbr. articles in field. Home: 4120 NW 62d Terr Oklahoma City OK 73112 Office: Baptist Medical Ctr of Okla Inc 3300 Northwest Expressway Oklahoma City OK 73112

REGISTER, BILLY DEAN, accountant; b. Tallahassee, July 6, 1934; s. Abbott Drafus and Ivy Grace (Benton) R.; m. Judith Elaine Wilkinson, Nov. 1, 1957; children—Marcus, Matthew, Martha. B.S., Fla. State U., 1961. C.P.A., Fla. Agt., IRS, 1961-74; pvt. practice acctg., Havana, Fla., 1974—. Served with USN, 1952-55. Mem. Am. Inst. C.P.A.s, Fla. Inst. C.P.A.s, Naval Res. Assn., Tallahassee Regional Estate Planning Council, Havana Businessmen's Assn. Republican. Club: Country (Havana, Fla.). Home and Office: Route 2 Box 130 Havana FL 32333

REGNIER, CLAIRE NEOMIE, business and communications consultant; b. Fort Riley, Kans., May 2, 1939; d. Eugene Arthur and Claire Janet (Macfarlane) Regnier; m. James Lewis Pipkin, Jr. B.S. cum laude in Journalism, Trinity U., San Antonio, 1961. Advt. cons., San Antonio, 1961-68; editor Paseo del Rio Showboat newspaper, San Antonio, 1968-81; exec. dir. San Antonio River Assn., San Antonio, 1968-81; pres. Metro Cons., San Antonio, 1981—. Mem. Centro 21 Downtown Revitalization Task Force, San Antonio, chmn., 1979-81; rep. San Antonio River Corridor Com., 1970-80; bd. dirs. San Antonio Area council Girl Scouts U.S.A., 1973-83; mem. adv. bd. San Antonio Parks and Recreation Dept. Recipient awards of excellence for Showboat, Alamo Bus. Communicators, 1970, 71, 73, 74. Mem. Internat. Assn. Bus. Communicators (Merit award San Antonio chpt. 1984), Women in Communications (Headliner for Public Endeavor, San Antonio chpt. 1980, Southwest Region award 1981, Merit award San Antonio chpt. 1984), Univ. Roundtable of San Antonio, Tex. Public Relations Assn., Internat. Assn. Bus. Communicators (Communicator of Yr. 1977), San Antonio Council Internat. Relations, Tex. Recreation and Parks Assn., San Antonio Mus. Assn., San Antonio Conservation Soc. Club: Altrusa of San Antonio. Home: 7772 Woodridge St San Antonio TX 78209 Office: 8958 1H 10 West Suite 201 San Antonio TX 78230

REGNIER, REX WALTER, entertainer, band leader, surveyor; b. Denver, Dec. 6, 1938; s. E. Carney and Peggy M. (Laude) R. Student Miami Dade Community Coll., 1975-76. Engring. technician Colo. Hwy. Dept., Burlington, 1963-71; entertainer USO prodns. in South Pacific, 1971-73; band leader Alabama Jacks, Homestead, Fla., 1973—. Entertainer for various non-profit groups and schs., 1973—. Served with U.S. Army, 1961-63. Recipient Cert. of Appreciation, Dept. Def., 1972, Am. Legion, 1982; recipient Cert. Achievement, U.S. Army Support, 1972; Cert. Participation, Am. Legion, 1983. Mem. Internat. Musicians Union. Baptist. Avocations: welding; machine work; fishing; hunting; boats. Home and Office: 30030 SW 168th Ct Homestead FL 33030

REHG, JEROLD ELMER, veterinary pathologist; b. St. Louis, Oct. 14, 1942; s. George H. and Maxine M. (Mullen) R.; m. Betsy Griffith Warwick, Dec. 27, 1969; 1 dau., Jamie Christine. B.S., U. Mo-Columbia, 1964, D.V.M., 1966. Diplomate Am. Coll. Vet. Pathologists, Am. Coll. Lab. Animal Medicine. USPHS-NIH postdoctoral fellow exptl. pathology Washington U. Sch. Medicine, St. Louis, 1968-72; resident in comparative pathology and comparative medicine Johns Hopkins U. Sch. Medicine, Balt., 1972-75, dir. animal pathology autopsy service, instr. pathology and comparative medicine, 1975-76, asst. prof. pathology and comparative medicine, 1976; asst. prof. comparative medicine and pathology U. Tex. Health Sci. Ctr.-Dallas, 1976-82; dir. div. comparative medicine, assoc. mem. pathology St. Jude Children's Research Hosp., Memphis, 1982—; cons. Dallas Zoo. Served as capt. U.S. Army, 1966-68. Mem. Am. Coll. Vet. Pathologists, Internat. Acad. of Pathology, Am. Coll. Lab. Animal Medicine, AVMA, Am. Assn. Lab. Animal Sci. (research award 1982), Mo. Vet. Med. Assn., Mid-Atlantic Comparative Pathology Colloquy, N. Tex. Soc. Pathologists, Comparative Gastroenterology Soc., Sigma Xi, Alpha Zeta. Lodge: K.C. Contbr. articles on vet. pathology to profl. jours.; mem. editorial bd. Vet. Pathology and Lab. Animal Sci. Office: 332 N Lauderdale Memphis TN 38101

REHM, GERALD S., real estate and business management consultant, former state senator; b. West Palm Beach, Fla., Mar. 10, 1927; children—Gregory, Pamela, Scott. B.S., U.S. Mcht. Marine Acad., 1948; postgrad. Hofstra Coll. Commr., Dunedin, Fla., 1963-65, mayor, 1965-72; mem. Fla. Senate, 1980-84; owner, pres. Krueger Candy Factory Inc.; owner pres. Gerald S. Rehm & Assocs. Mem. exec. com. Pinellas County Republican Party, Fla.; exec. dir. Eckerd Found., 1968-80; trustee Eckerd Coll.; active Boy Scout Am. Served with USNR, 1948-55. Recipient citation of service VFW; Sertoma Service to Mankind award, 1969; Mr. Delightful Dunedin award, 1970; numerous legis. awards. Mem. Southeastern County Found., So. Assn. Colls. and Schs., Aluminum Assn. Am. (pres. 1975), jaycees (Citizen of Yr. award 1969). Roman Catholic. Republican. Lodge: Kiwanis (Dunedin pres. 1962).

REHM, KENNETH BRUCE, podiatrist; b. Cleve., June 26, 1946; s. Arnold and Cecile (Appel) R.; m. Donna Lee Klein, June 20, 1971; children—Jamie, Lindsey, B.S., Ohio State U., 1969; D.P.M., Calif. Coll. Podiatric Medicine, 1976; M.S., Cleve. State U., 1977. Diplomate Am. Bd. Podiatric Surgery. Grad. asst., instr. dept. biology, Cleve. State U., 1970-72; tchr. biology Woodbury Jr. High Sch., Shaker Heights, Ohio, 1967-71; x-ray technician asst. Calif. Coll. Podiatric Medicine, San Francisco, 1972-76, instr. physiology, 1975-76; podiatry and surgery resident, Jacksonville Gen. Hosp. (Fla.), 1976-77; pvt. practice podiatry, Coral Springs, Fla., 1977—; instr. Fla. Jr. Coll., Miami Dade Jr. Coll.; dir. Upjohn Corp.; med. dir. Foot Function and Sports Improvement Lab.; cons. Tampa Bay Buccaneers, Cleve. Browns, Tampa Bay Rowdies, Los Angeles Raiders, Phoenix Wranglers, Tampa Bay Bandits; adj. clin. instr. W.M. Scholl Coll. Podiatric Medicine, U. Tampa; health service occupation tchr. Coral Springs High Sch. Assoc. bd. dirs. Health Planning Council of Broward County. Fellow Acad. Ambulatory Foot Surgery; Mem. Fla. Podiatry Assn., Broward County Podiatry Assn., Am. Podiatry Assn., Arthritis Found. (v.p. bd. dirs., Disting. Service award 1980), Am. Acad. Podiatric Acupuncture, C. of C., Coral Springs Profl. and Bus. Assn., Roadrunners Club Am.; assoc. Am. Coll. Foot Surgeons, Am. Acad. Podiatric Sports Medicine. Clubs: Executive, Toastmasters (Coral Springs). Author: Restless Leg Syndrome, A Common Podiatric Complaint in Current Podiatry, 1977. Home: 997 NW 82d Ave Coral Springs FL 33065 Office: 3000 N University Dr Coral Springs FL 33065

REICH, KATHLEEN JOHANNA, educator; b. Mannheim, Germany, May 1, 1927; came to U.S., 1955, naturalized, 1958; d. Robert and Luise Charlotte Helene (Kurowsky) Weichel; M.A.T. in English, Rollins Coll., 1976, Ed.S., 1978; 1 son, Robert Weichel. With Orlando (Fla.) Pub. Library, 1955-57; cataloguer, instr. U. Detroit, 1957-60, Trinity U., San Antonio, 1960-61; adminstr. Fla. Book Processing Center, Orlando, 1961-68; bur. chief, div. library services Fla. State Dept., Winter Park, 1968-71; assoc. prof. library sci. Rollins Coll., Winter Park, 1971—, asst. dean faculty, 1981-83, dir. overseas studies, 1983-84; co-owner, acad. dean Prew Prep. Sch., Sarasota, Fla. Mem. AAUP, African Literature Assn., Nat. Assn. Fgn. Student Affairs, Am. Water Ski Assn. Home: 211 Fawsett Rd Winter Park FL 32789 Office: Rollins College Winter Park FL 32789

REICHARD, SHERWOOD MARSHALL, radiobiologist, educator; b. Easton, Pa., June 24, 1928; B.A., Lafayette Coll., 1948; M.A. in Physiology, N.Y. U., 1950, Ph.D. in Endocrine Physiology (AEC fellow), 1955; postgrad. (fellow) McCollum Pratt Inst., Johns Hopkins U., 1957-60, Army Chem. Sch., summer 1964, Inst. Biophysics, U. Freiburg (Ger.), summer 1970; m. Janet Williamson, June 24, 1954; children—Jon Lanier, Deborah L., Stuart B. Vis. investigator Armed Forces Inst. Pathology, Washington, 1958-60; asst. prof. physiology dept. biol. scis. Fla. State U., Tallahassee, 1960-63, dir. Radiation Biology Inst., 1961-63; asso. prof. radiology and physiology Med. Coll. Ga., Augusta, 1964-69, prof. radiology and physiology, 1969—, regents' prof. radiology, 1979—, prof. physiology Sch. Grad. Studies, 1969—, dir. div. radiobiology, 1969—; radiobiologist Talmadge Meml. Hosp., Augusta, 1966—; disting. lectr. Bryn Mawr Coll., 1965; sci. adv. EPA, 1979; research adv. E.I. Du Pont de Nemours & Co., 1973, Warner-Lambert/Parke-Davis, 1978; vis. lectr. various univs. in U.S., Japan, Europe and Israel, 1958-80; participant various internat. symposia on radiology and shock, 1958-82; cons. NASA, 1963-67, Graniteville Co., 1978-80; pres. Chem. Cons., Augusta, 1978—. Bd. dirs. Health Center Credit Union, 1976—, chmn., 1976-81, pres., 1976-81. Served with M.S.C., U.S. Army, 1955-57. Recipient Zoology medal Internat. Congress Zoology, 1963; Outstanding Tchr. award U.S. Army Chem. Sch., 1964; Outstanding Faculty award Med. Coll. Ga., 1978, Chair's Disting. Service award, 1982; NIH grantee, 1966-80; Upjohn grantee, 1981. Fellow AAAS, N.Y. Acad. Sci.; mem. Am. Physiol. Soc., Am. Soc. Zoologists, Radiation Research Soc., Radiol. Soc. N. Am., Reticuloendothelial Soc. (pres. 1973-74, council 1965—, Silver Medallion award 1976, parliamentarian 1977-82, exec. dir. 1982—), Endocrine Soc. (Fred Conrad Koch travel award 1970), Soc. Nuclear Medicine, Shock Soc. (sec. 1978-80, pres. 1981-82, exec. dir. 1982—), Internat. Union Reticuloendothelial Socs. (pres. 1978-82), Internat. Inflammation Club, Am. Assn. Anatomists, Soc. Exptl. Biology and Medicine, AAUP (pres. 1970-72), Mgmt. Assn. Profl. Socs. (pres.), Sigma Xi (pres. 1982), Beta Beta Beta, Sigma Pi Sigma. Author: RES Functions, 1974; Tax Sheltered Annuities: A Comparative Analysis, 1980; contbr. numerous articles on radiobiology and reticuloendothelial systems to sci. publs.; editor Jour. Reticuloendothelial Soc., 1970-73; editor: Advances in Biology and Medicine, 1976; The Reticuloendothelial System: A Comprehensive Treatise, 1980; Advances in Shock Research, 1982; Progress in Leukocyte Biology; reviewer books in biology; contbr. numerous articles on physiology and radiation research to jours. in sci. Home: 1122 Johns Rd Augusta GA 30904 Office: Med Coll Ga Div Radiobiology Augusta GA 30912

REICHENBACH, DAVID LESTER, plasma chemist, consultant; b. Waterbury, Conn., Dec. 16, 1942; s. Lester A. and Margaret M. (Guffie) R.; m. Nancy Lee Benner, May 30, 1980; children—Jennifer, Derik. B.S. in Biology, Antioch Coll., 1965; Ph.D. in Microbiology, U. Miami, 1970. Research scientist Dade div. Am. Hosp. Supply Corp., Miami, Fla., 1970-71, process improvement head, 1971-73; pvt. clin. chemistry cons., Hollywood, Fla., 1973-75; prodn. mgr. Lab. Serums, Davie, Fla., 1975-80, plant mgr., 1980—; pres. Bioresource Tech., Pembroke Pines, Fla., 1983—; cons. mfg. diagnostic controls. Mem. Woodbridge Homeowners Assn. Fellow NIH, 1967-70. Mem. N.Y. Acad. Sci., AAAS, Sigma Xi. Contbr. articles to profl. jours.; developer 1st comml. prodn. normalized control serum from recovered plasma. Home: 10220 Sheridan St Pembroke Pines FL 33026 Office: 4210 So University Dr Davie FL 33028

REID, BRUCE WALLACE, JR., investment executive; b. Charlotte, N.C., Sept. 29, 1941; s. Bruce Wallace and Virginia W. (Harrison) R.; student U. Tenn., 1961-62; m. Sereda Ann Pasquariello, Aug. 4, 1961; children—Lisa Ann, Bruce Philip, Angela, Andrew Vincent. With UMIC, Inc., Memphis, 1966-76; with Donald Sheldon & Co., Inc., 1976—, br. mgr., Houston, 1980—. Served with USMCR, 1959-60. Republican. Roman Catholic. Club: KC. Home: 5917 Burgoyne Houston TX 77057 Office: 2401 Fountainview Suite 102 Houston TX 77057

REID, CHERYLON BENTON, training specialist, consultant; b. Ashdown, Ark., Mar. 17, 1951; d. Phillip and Johnnie Lou (Bailey) Benton; m. Ulys Ray Reid, July 30, 1972; 1 child, Sarah Layne. B.S.E., U. Ark., 1972; postgrad., U. Houston, 1975; M.S.M., Houston Bapt. U., 1986. Cert. tchr., Tex., Ark. Tchr. Little Rock Pub. Sch., 1972-75, Houston Ind. Sch., 1975-79; tng. specialist ENTEX, Houston, 1980-81; tng. mgr. Eastman Whipstock, Houston, 1981—; cons. Management Tree, Dallas, 1981—. Author (with others) (supervisory workbook) Supervising for Greater Productivity, 1983. Referral agt. United Way, Houston, 1981-84; mem. adv. com. Houston Community Coll. Recipient President's award Eastman Whipstock, 1983; Shell grantee, 1978. Mem. Am. Soc. Tng. and Devel., Houston Personnel Assn., Health Care Coalition. Republican. Methodist. Club: Braeburn Glen Civic. Home: 9011 Altamont St Houston TX 77074 Office: 2525 Holly Hall Houston TX 77021-14609

REID, ISHMAEL SAMUEL, JR., physician; b. Pine Bluff, Ark., Jan. 12, 1949; s. Ishmael Samuel and Bernice Vivian (Sheppard) R.; m. Vernetta A. Sanders, Aug. 31, 1969; children—Tanya, Catherine. B.A., So. Ill. U., 1970; M.D., U. Ark., 1974. Diplomate Am. Bd. Internal Medicine. Intern, U. Ark., Little Rock, 1974-75, resident medicine, hematology fellow, 1980-81, instr. medicine, 1981-83; fellow Nat. Cancer Inst., 1981-83; staff physician Little Rock VA Hosp., 1983-84; dir. practice medicine specializing in internal medicine, hematology and oncology, Pine Bluff, 1984— Served with M.C., USAF, 1976-78. Mem. AMA, Am. Soc. Hematology, Alpha Omega Alpha. Office: 817 Cherry St Pine Bluff AR 71601

REID, RALPH WALDO EMERSON, management consultant; b. Phila., July 5, 1915; s. Ralph Waldo Emerson and Alice Myrtle (Stuart) R.; m. Ruth Bull, Dec. 7, 1946; 1 child, Robert. Student, Temple U., 1932-34; B.S., Northwestern U., 1936; M.A., U. Hawaii, 1938; Ph.D., Harvard U., 1948. Cert. mgmt. cons. Asst. to v.p. Northwestern U., Evanston, Ill., 1938-40; chief mcpl. govt. br., spl. asst. govt. sect. Supreme Comdr. Allied Powers, 1946-47; spl. asst. Under Sec. of Army, 1948-49; chief Far Eastern affairs div. Office Occupied Areas, chief econs. div. Office Civil Affairs and Mil. Govt., Dept. of Army, 1950-53; asst. to dir. U.S. Bur. of Budget, Washington, 1953-55, asst. dir., 1955-61; resident mgr. A.T. Kearney Inc., Washington, 1961-72, mng. dir., Tokyo, 1972-81, cons., Alexandria, Va., 1981—; former dir. Nihon Regulator Co., Tokyo, Yuasa-Ionics Ltd., Tokyo, Japan DME, Tokyo. Served to comdr. USNR, 1941-46, PTO. Decorated Commendation Ribbon, Order of Rising Sun (3d class) (Japan); recipient Exceptional Civilian Service award U.S. Army, 1954. Mem. Inst. Mgmt. Consultants, Am. Polit. Sci. Assn., Am. Soc. Pub. Adminstrn. Republican. Am. Baptist. Clubs: Cosmos, Capitol Hill (Washington); Union League (Chgo.). Home: 412 Monticello Blvd Alexandria VA 22305 Office: A T Kearney Inc PO Box 1405 Alexandria VA 22313

REID, ROBERT JOHN, architect; b. La Jolla, Calif., Oct. 24, 1947; s. Robert Osborne and Marjorie Ada (Ferry) R.; m. Pamela Ann Theberge, July 31, 1971; children—Kimberlee Erin, Wesley George. B.Arch., U. Tex., 1975. Registered architect, Tex. Designer, Fluor Engring., Houston, 1975-77; sr. project mgr. MRW Architects, Houston, 1977-81; project architect Sikes Jennings Kelly, Houston, 1981-84; assoc. PBR Architects, Houston, 1984; sr. project architect CRS Sirrine, Houston, 1985—. Author pamphlet. Speaker Office of Mayor-Econ. Redevel., Houston, 1982. Served with USN, 1966-71. Mem. AIA, Tex. Soc. Architects, Constrn. Specifications Inst., Nat. Trust for Hist. Preservation, Tex. Ex Students Assn. Episcopalian. Home: 10207 Overview Sugar Land TX 77478 Office: 1111 W Loop S PO Box 22427 Houston TX 77277

REID, WILLIAM TYRELL, JR., dentist; b. Corpus Christi, Tex., Aug. 23, 1943; s. William Tyrell and Suzanne (Jackson) R.; m. Jackie Lee Cornelius, June 4, 1966; children—Stacie Lea, Jessica Lyn. B.S. in Pharmacy with high honors, U. Fla., 1966; D.D.S. with highest honors, Emory U., 1971. Corp. pres. W. T. Reid, D.D.S., P.C., 1974-85; co-dir. Hairston-Redan Profl. Ctr., 1984—; clin. prof. Emory U. Sch. Dentistry, Atlanta, 1977-78. Supr. Jour. Pharm. Scis., 1964. Contbr. articles to profl. jours. Bd. dirs. Am. Cancer Soc., Dekalb, Ga., 1978-81; co-pres. PTA, Stone Mountain, Ga., 1984-85. Served to capt. USAF, 1971-73. Recipient Appreciation award Atlanta Dental Soc., 1977, cert. Merit Am. Cancer Soc., 1978, 79, 80. Mem. ADA (treas. 1967—), Ga. Dental Assn., No. Dist. Dental Soc. (seminarian 1977), Dekalb Dental Study Group (pres. 1974-75). Republican. Roman Catholic. Clubs: Stoneleigh (capt. 1976, 1978, 80, 82); Atlanta Lawn Tennis Assn. Avocations: tennis; skiing; scuba diving; triathlons; marathoner. Age group finisher Cape Cod Ironman Triathlon, 1985. Home: 5810 Stonehaven Dr Stone Mountain GA 30083 Office: Hairston-Redan Profl Ctr 1183-D S Hairston Rd Stone Mountain GA 30083

REIFF, JACK W., jewelry manufacturing company executive, mail order promotion company executive; b. N.Y.C., May 17, 1927; s. Lawrence and Mollie (Schneider) Wisotsky; m. Judith Morris, June 27, 1948; children—Amy, Claudia. Salesman, William Schneider, Inc., Miami, 1946-50, sales mgr., 1950-64, v.p., 1964-74, pres., 1974—; pres., mktg. dir. Impac Ltd., Chgo., 1980—. Asst. sec. Nat. Parkinson Found., 1979—; pres. Sunshine State Indsl. Park, 1972—; mem. Am. Red Mogen David, Foster Parents Plan, Children's Asthmatic Research Inst. Hosp., Miami. Served with USN, 1944-46. Recipient First Prize nat. sales contest Union Carbide, 1963; plaque United Jewish Appeal, 1970. Mem. Sales Execs. Club N.Y. Democrat. Jewish. Lodge: B'nai B'rith. Home: 251 174th St Apt 1204 Miami Beach FL 33160 Office: 16400 NW 15th Ave Miami FL 33169

REIFSNIDER, KENNETH LEONARD, metallurgist, educator; b. Balt., Feb. 19, 1940; s. David Leonard and Daisy Pearl (Hess) R.; m. Loretta Lieb, June 15, 1963; children—Eric Scott, Jason Miles. B.A., Western Md. Coll., 1963; B.S. in Engring., Johns Hopkins U., 1963, M.S. in Engring., 1965, Ph.D., 1968. Jr. instr. John Hopkins U., Balt., 1966-67; asst. prof. Va. Poly. Inst. and State U., Blacksburg, 1968-72, assoc. prof., 1972-75, prof., 1975-83, Reynolds Metals prof. engring. sci. and mechanics, 1983—, , also chmn. materials engring. sci. Ph.D. program, chmn. adminstrn. bd. Ctr. Composite Materials and Structures, 1984; engr. Lawrence Livermore Nat. Lab., 1981; cons. in materials sci. NATO, 1969, 75. Mem. troop 44 com. Boy Scouts Am., Blacksburg, Va. Recipient Va. Acad. Sci. J. Shelton Horsley award, 1978, Va. Poly. Inst. Alumni award, 1982. Fellow ASTM (founder Jour. of Composites standing com. on publs., award of merit 1982); mem. ASME, Council on Engring. Editor, co-editor, author books, book chpts., articles for profl. publs.

REILING, CECILIA POWERS, hospital chaplain; b. Boston, Mar. 23, 1926; d. Edward Thomas and Delia (Hehir) Powers; m. Thomas Leonard Reiling, Nov. 11, 1960; stepchildren—Elizabeth, Kathleen, Mary, Eileen. B.A., Northeastern U., 1964, M.A., 1973; M.Ed., Boston U., 1979. Instr., advisor Chamberlayne Jr. Coll., Boston, 1964-73; instr. Bryant Coll., North Smithfield, R.I., 1973-79; chaplaincy vol. Sherrill House, Boston, 1972-79, researcher, 1977-79; program dir., v.p. College Club, Boston, 1970-72; chaplaincy vol. Martin Meml. Hosp., Stuart, Fla., 1980—. Mem. Am. Sociol. Assn., Mass. Sociol. Soc., Christian Sociol. Soc., Assn. for Clin. Pastoral Edn. Republican. Roman Catholic. Clubs: Stuart Yacht and Country (Fla.); Kittansett (Marion, Mass.). Avocations: golf, music. Home: 4264 SE Fairway E Stuart FL 33494

REILY, MICHAEL GORDON banker, real estate and insurance broker; b. Groveton, Tex., Dec. 15, 1929; s. Gordon Clinton and Julia Belle (Holly) R.; m. Jean Dudley, Mar. 22, 1951; children—Michael Jr., Sharon, Taylor. B.B.A. So. Meth. U., 1951. Pres., Citizen's State Bank, Corrigan, Tex., 1951-76, also dir.; mayor City of Corrigan, 1960—; chmn. Corrigan Hosp. Dist., 1981—; pres. Corrigan Housing Corp., 1971—; chmn. Citizens State Fin. Corp., 1982—; bd. dirs. 1st Bank, Groveton, Tex. Democrat. Methodist. Lodge: Mason. Home and Office: PO Box 20C Corrigan TX 75939

REIMANN, JOACHIM OSKAR FERDINAND, vocational employment counselor; b. Berlin, Fed. Republic Germany, Jan. 24, 1951; came to U.S., 1960, naturalized, 1967; s. Bernhard Erwin Ferdinand and Beate Eleonore (Hedwig) R. B.A. in Psychology, U. Tex.-El Paso, 1973, M.Ed., 1985. Musician Fox Harbour, Neoga, Ill., 1973-75, Highway, El Paso, 1975-77; caseworker youth Dept. Human Devel., El Paso, 1978-79, counselor, 1979-82; counselor Pvt. Industry Council, Inc., El Paso, 1982—. Contbr. articles to profl. jours. Instr. guitar N.E. YMCA, 1978-84. Mem. Am. Assn. Counseling, Nat. Employment Counselors Assn. Democrat. Avocations: martial arts; writing. Office: Upper Rio Grande PIC Skill Ctr 909 Hawkins St El Paso TX 79915

REIMERS, DONALD RAY, architectural firm executive, consultant; b. Douglas, Ariz., June 4, 1934; s. Raymond Henry and Faye Ellen (Bratton) R.; m. Barbara Ann Bonvillain, Nov. 27, 1955 (div. July 20, 1972); children—Terri, Kirste, Stacey, Erin; m. Clara Cecilia Morrison, Apr. 17, 1974; stepchildren—Cecilia, Cristina, John. B.Arch., U. Tex., 1958. Registered architect, Tex. Draftsman, various firms, 1957-65; project asst. for gen. services Humble Oil Co., 1965-66; prodn. mgr. Herman Kelling, 1966-67; assoc. architect W. Jackson Wisdom, 1967-69; prodn. mgr. Lucian T. Hood, 1969-71; project architect Pitts, Phelps & White, 1971-73; pvt. practice, 1973-76; project architect Arenco, Inc., Houston, 1976-79; asst. v.p. H.C. Hwang & Ptnrs., Inc., Houston, 1977—; constrn. mgr. Grupo Cydsa S.A. Monterrey, Mex., 1979-81. Designer ambient light tower furniture, 1981, pottery plant light, 1981, residential storage system, 1983. Sustaining mem. Rep. Nat. Com.; charter mem. Rep. Presdl. Task Force. Recipient Disting. Bldg. award Fed. Com. for Architecture, Monterrey, Mex., 1981; 1st award Landscape Houston C. of C., 1983. Assoc. Nat. Trust for Historic Preservation, mem. Tex. Hist. Found, Tau Kappa Epsilon (pres., nat. bd. dirs. 1953-55). Avocations: landscaping-horticulture; rehab. of historic properties. Office: H C Hwang & Ptnrs Inc 1900 W Loop South #200 Houston TX 77027

REIN, MARTIN, college administrator; b. Bklyn., Aug. 31, 1933; s. Samuel and Jennie (Simon) R. B.A., L.I.U., 1957. Editorial asst. N.Y. Herald Tribune, 1952-57; program editor TV Guide Mag., San Francisco, 1959-60; reporter Miami Beach (Fla.) Sun, 1961-62; copyreader The Miami News, 1962-63; copywriter Leo Jay Rosen Advt., Miami, 1963-64; mng. editor Swimming Pool Weekly, Swimming Pool Age, Swimming Pool Reference & Data Manual, 1964-69; mng. editor Gift & Tableware Reporter, 1969-75; info. specialist Miami-Dade Community Coll., 1975-83, dir. publs./media relations, 1983—. Bd. dirs. Dade County Hispanic Heritage Festival, 1981—, Coconut Grove Family Ctr., Inc., 1983—. Served with U.S. Army, 1957-59. Mem. Pub. Relations Soc. Am., Advt. Fedn. Greater Miami, Fla. Assn. Community Colls. Democrat. Home: 3251 McDonald St Miami FL 33133 Office: Miami-Dade Community Coll 11011 SW 104th St Miami FL 33133

REINA, DOROTHY LEE FORRESTER, ceramic company executive; b. Crockett, Tex., Feb. 10, 1932; d. Emmett Ray and Grace Lee (Hallmark) Forrester; divorced; children by previous marriage—Teri Nanette, James Dennis, Catherine Lee. Student Rice U., 1954-55, U. Houston, 1958. Sec. Engrs. & Fabricators, Inc., Houston, 1958-63; sec., office mgr. Interkiln Corp. Am., Houston, 1963-66, part-owner, 1966—, v.p. fin., 1970—; prin. Reina & Co., fin. cons. firm, 1983—; dir. various fgn. cos. Mem. Gulf Coast Council Fgn. Affairs, Asia Soc., Nat. Assn. Accts., UN Assn. U.S.A., Am. Ceramic Soc. Episcopalian. Clubs: University, Warwick (Houston); Directors (London).

REINHEIMER, SUSAN RUTH, emergency room physician; b. Riverside, Calif., Nov. 15, 1948; d. Herbert Stanley and Dorothy (McLleland) R. B.S.N., Med. Coll. Va., 1970; M.P.H., Yale U., 1975; M.D., Med. U. S.C., 1979. Diplomate Am. Bd. Family Practice. Nurse, U.S. Army, Ft. Gordon, Ga. and Danang, Vietnam, 1970-72, nursing instr., Ft. Belvoir, Va., 1972-73; resident U. Tenn.-Chattanooga, 1979-82, Vanderbilt U., Nashville, 1982-83; emergency room physician Bapt. Med. Ctr., Columbia, S.C., 1983—; vol. faculty Richland Family Practice, Columbia, 1983—. Served to maj. USAR, 1973—. Mem. Tenn. Acad. Family Practice (pres. residents assn. 1979-83, dir. 1981), Am. Acad. Family Practice, Am. Coll. Emergency Physicians, AMA, Alpha Sigma Chi, Sigma Zeta. Republican. Presbyterian. Club: Toastmasters. Home: 400 Mallet Hill Rd Apt C-1 Columbia SC 29206 Office: Bapt Emergency Room Taylor St Columbia SC 29220

REKAU, RICHARD ROBERT, architect; b. Chicago Heights, Ill., June 6, 1936; s. Robert Richard and Charlotte (Ryan) Rekau Altier; m. Carolyn Pritchett, Dec. 20, 1962; 1 son, Ryan Richard. B.Arch., B.S., Ga. Tech Inst., 1965. Registered architect Ga., N.C., Ala.; cert. Nat. Council Archtl. Registration Bds. Project mgr. John Portman & Assocs., Atlanta, 1970-76; assoc. Herndon & Harris, Atlanta, 1976-77; v.p. Devel. Contractors, Inc., Atlanta, 1979-81; prin. Richard R. Rekau, Architect, Atlanta, 1977—; pres. Rekau Properties, 1984—. Prin. works include Lanier Plaza, Gainesville, Ga. Corp. Plaza Northwest, Atlanta, Pkwy. Village, Macon, Ga. Mem. Ga. Canoeing Assn., Gainesboro 500. Mem. AIA, Hist. Preservation Found. N.C., Nat. Trust Hist. Preservation. Home: 1771 Beverly Wood Ct Chamblee GA 30341 Office: 2900 Chamblee Tucker Rd Bldg 12 Atlanta GA 30341

REKERDRES, CHARLES A. H., insurance agency executive; b. Rochester, N.Y., Oct. 5, 1920; s. Henry and Emma (Braun) R.; m. Susan Elizabeth Strouss, June 3, 1947 (div. 1975); children—Charles Theodore, Ralph Craig, Douglas Randall; m. 2d, Renate Bontrempts, Nov. 28, 1976. B.S.B.A. in Fin., Columbia U., 1949. Lic. ins. agt., Tex. Broker, Orvis Bros. & Ira Haupt, 1950-54; prin. Rekerdres & Sons Ins. Agy., Inc., Dallas, 1955—, chief exec. officer, 1961—; chief exec. officer Salamander, Inc., Dallas, 1964—. Served in Danish Mcht. Marines, 1934; to lt. USN, 1937-41, 42-45. Mem. Am. Cotton Shippers Assn., Lubbock Cotton Exchange, Tex. Cotton Assn., Lloyds of London (corr.), Western Cotton Shippers, Internat. Trade Assn. Dallas, Dallas Council World Affairs, Nat. Arbitration Assn., Dallas C. of C. Republican. Episcopalian. Clubs: Tower, Cipango, Mariners (all Dallas). Home: 5601 Dittmar Pl Dallas TX 75229 Office: 1000 Cotton Exchange Bldg Dallas TX 75201

RELPH, MARTHA HELEN, librarian; b. Madison, Kans., Mar. 8, 1930; d. Glen and Hattie (Harlan) Cannon; m. Kenneth Relph, Apr. 10, 1950 (dec. May 1982); children—Geneva Bauman, Daniel. B.S., U. Kans., 1950; M.L.S., Emporia State U., 1971. Tchr. pub. schs., Kans., Md., Utah, Idaho, 1958-69; asst. librarian tech. library Reactor Testing Sta., Idaho Falls, Idaho, 1971-73; librarian Altoona (Kans.) Jr. High Sch., 1973-74, Morris Swett Library, U.S. Army Arty. Sch., Ft. Sill, Okla., 1975—. Editor: Subject Headings Used at the Morris Swett Library, 1980. Clk. Lawrence (Kans.) Election Bd., 1952-60. Mem. ALA, Spl. Library Assn., Co. Mil. Historians. Club: Arty. Toastmistress (Ft. Sill) (past pres.). Home: Lawton OK 73505 Office: Morris Swett Library Snow Hall Ft Sill OK 73503

REMENCHIK, ALEXANDER PAVLOVICH, physician; b. Chgo., Sept. 13, 1922; s. Paul Samuelovich and Irina Alexandra (Babich) R.; m. Mary Margaret Mays, Apr. 19, 1947; children—Alex Kevin, Ellen Jean, Karen Ann, Margaret Lynn. B.S. in Physics, U. Chgo., 1943, M.D., 1951. Intern, Cook County Hosp., Chgo., 1951-52; resident U. Ill. Research and Ednl. Hosps., 1952-53, fellow, 1953-54; clin. investigator VA Hosp., Hines, Ill., 1960-62; practice medicine specializing in internal medicine, Chgo., 1953-72, Montclair, N.J., 1972-74, Houston, 1974—; asst. med. supt. Mcpl. Contagious Disease Hosp., Chgo., 1953-59; instr. medicine U. Ill., Chgo., 1954-59; asst. prof. medicine Stritch Sch. Medicine, Loyola U., Maywood, Ill., 1960-63, assoc. prof., 1964-67, prof., 1967-72, pres. Faculty Collegium, 1970-71, asst. chmn. dept. medicine, 1964-70; dir. dept. nuclear medicine Loyola U. Hosp., 1969-71; attending physician Cook County Hosp., 1959-72; Mountainside Hosp., Montclair, 1972-74, dir. med. edn., 1972-74; attending mem. active staff Parkway Hosp., 1974-79, courtesy staff, 1986—; mem. active staff Citizens Gen. Hosp., 1974—, chief med. service, 1977, chief of staff, 1979, 81-82, mem. governing bd., 1977-86; mem. staff Eastway Gen. Hosp., 1974—, chmn. dept. medicine, 1976-80; pres. East Loop Emergency Med. Clinic, Houston, 1979-81, East Loop Cardio Pulmonary Center, Inc., 1979-85; courtesy staff Meth. Hosp.; cons. staff Doctor's Hosp. Editor: (with P.J. Talso) Mechanisms of Disease, 1968. Contbr. over 50 articles on internal medicine to profl. jours. Mem. Zoning Commn. Oak Park (Ill.), 1969-72; trustee Unitarian-Universalist Ch. of Oak Park, 1969-70. Served to lt. (j.g.) USN, 1943-46. Diplomate Am. Bd. Internal Medicine. Fellow A.C.P.; mem. Tex. Soc. Internal Medicine, Soc. Critical Care Medicine, Houston Soc. Internal Medicine, Houston Cardiol. Soc., Soc. Exptl. Biology and Medicine, Am. Fedn. Clin. Research, Harris County Med. Soc., AMA, Tex. Med. Assn., Am. Soc. Internal Medicine, Am. Heart Assn., Am. Diabetes Assn. Sigma Xi. Home: 9330 Oakford Ct Houston TX 77024 Office: 8799 N Loop East Houston TX 77029

REMINGTON, PATRICIA JANE, educational administrator, nun; b. Detroit, Jan. 25, 1920; d. William H. and Josephine E. (Marvin) R.; B.A., Marygrove Coll., 1955; M.A., U. Detroit, 1966; Ph.D., Wayne State U., 1981. Joined Order of Immaculate Heart of Mary, Roman Catholic Ch., 1941; tchr. elem. schs., Detroit, 1943-66, secondary schs., 1966-71; supr. student teaching Marygrove Coll., Detroit, 1971-72, dir. spl. services, 1981-83; reading cons. pub. schs., 1972-81; asst. dir. reading and study skills Wayne State U., 1972-81; assoc. prof. edn. St. Leo Coll. (Fla.), 1983—. U. San Francisco grantee, 1968. Mem. Mich. Coll. Reading Council (pres.), North Central Reading Assn., Nat. Reading Conf., Internat. Reading Assn., Assn. Supervision and Curriculum Devel., Phi Delta Kappa, Pi Lambda Theta.

REMPEL, PETER LOYD, architect, educator; b. Hamilton, Ont., Can., Mar. 25, 1939; s. George Hilburn and Reine (Loyd) R.; m. Nancy Henrietta Schmidt, Aug. 1962; children—Hillary, Reine. B.Arch., U. Fla., 1961. Registered architect, Fla., Architect Clements, Rumpel Assocs., Jacksonville, Fla., 1976-84, Clements, Rumpel, Goodwin, Jacksonville, 1984-85; adj. prof. architecture U. Fla., Gainesville, 1982-84, assoc. prof., 1984—; v.p. Jacksonville Community Design Ctr. Contbr. articles to profl. publs. Mem. AIA (numerous awards Fla. Assn. and Jacksonville chpt.; state honor award 1981, John Dyal award Jacksonville chpt. 1985). Office: Clements Rumpel Goodwin Inc 45 W Bay St Jacksonville FL 32202

REMSEN, JOHN LOCKWOOD, lawyer; b. New Brunswick, N.J., Apr. 5, 1928; s. Frank W. and Helen (Lockwood) R.; m. Dorothy Lee Vasser, Sept. 9, 1951; children—John Lockwood, Helen Michelle Remsen Fisher, Stephanie E. Grad. Palm Beach Jr. Coll., 1950; LL.B. cum laude, U. Miami, 1953. Bar: Fla. 1953, U.S. Dist. Ct. Fla. 1953. Ptnr. Cromwell & Remsen, Riviera Beach, Fla., 1955—; founding dir. Citizens Bank Palm Beach County. Vice chmn. Palm Beach County (Fla.) Area Planning Bd., 1970-72; gen. chmn. PGA Team Championships, 1965, 66, PGA Championship, 1971; chmn. Palm Beach County Bd. Pub. Instrn., 1961-64. Served with USMC, 1946-47. Recipient Community Appreciation award, 1984. Mem. Palm Beach County Bar Assn., Fla. Bar Assn. (mem. grievance com. 1967-70, 75-78, 82—, chmn. unauthorized practice com. 1972-75; mem. profl. ethics com. 1978-82, mem. and chmn. 15th Circuit Fla. Jud. Nominating Commn., 1978-82, 83—), ABA. Democrat. Presbyterian. Clubs: Kiwanis, Jaycees, Elks (North Palm Beach), Governors of Palm Beaches. Home: 11960 Lake Shore Pl North Palm Beach FL 33408 Office: 6th Floor Barnett Bank Bldg 2001 Broadway Riviera Beach FL 33404

REMY, WILLIAM QUENTIN, architect; b. Norman, Okla., Sept. 10, 1946; s. William Edward and Dorella (Constant) R.; m. Jane Elizabeth Meyer, Mar. 29, 1969; children—Katherine, Amanda, Anne, David. Student Okla. State U., 1965; B.Arch., U. Okla., 1970. Lic. architect Tex., Okla.; cert. Nat. Council Archtl. Registration Bds. Architect, Turnbull & Mills, Oklahoma City, 1971, Hudgins, Thompson, Ball, Oklahoma City, 1972; architect Quentin Remy Assocs., Norman, Okla., 1974—, chief exec. officer, 1983—. Served with USAF, 1970-76. Recipient design awards Boston Soc. Architects, 1981, design awards E. Fay Jones, 1983. Mem. AIA (awardee Okla. chpt.), Nat. Trust Hist. Preservation, Am. Inst. Graphic Arts, Inst. Urban Design, Beta Theta Pi (v.p., bd. dirs. corp.). Home: 25 Walnut Hill Norman OK 73069 Office: 3200 Marshall Norman OK 73069

RENFROE, JACKIE LOUISE, interior consultant; b. Dalton, Ga., Jan. 23, 1944; d. James Turner and Helen Beatrice (Jergian) Phillips; m. Donnie Renfroe, July 23, 1961; children—Donna, Tracy, Karen. Student pub. schs., Dalton, Interior cons. Aero Drapery, Dalton, 1972-78, Decorating Den, Dalton, 1978-80, Fashion, Inc., Dalton, 1980—. Vice pres. PTA, Dawnville Elem. Sch., 1972, pres., 1973-75; bd. dirs. Cherokee Estate, Dalton, 1978-82; mem. adv. bd. Dawnville Elem. Sch., 1978-82, Dalton Retail Trade Commn., 1984—; mem. Small Bus. Council Bd., 1984—. Mem. Dalton C. of C., LWV (dir. 1980-85). Democrat. Mormon. Home: 2056 Dawnville Beaverdale Rd Dalton GA 30720 Office: Fashion Inc 201 W Morris St Dalton GA 30720

RENFROW, EDWARD, state auditor; b. Johnston County, N.C., Sept. 17, 1940; s. Donnie T. and Ilamae (Lewis) R.; m. Rebecca Stephenson, Dec. 4, 1960; children—Candace, Paige. Grad. Hardbarger Bus. Coll., 1960; postgrad. Duke U., 1961-62, East Carolina U., 1977-78, Atlantic Christian Coll., 1962-63, Johnston Tech. Inst., 1977-78. Acct., Daniel G. Matthews & Assocs., Inc., Smithfield, N.C., 1960-63; practice acctg., 1963-80; mem. N.C. Senate, 1974-80; state auditor State of N.C., Raleigh, 1980—. Mem. exec. com. Baptist State Conv., 1972-74; treas. Johnston Bapt. Assn., 1972-79, mem. fin. com., 1972-79; treas. N.C. Democratic Exec. Com., 1973-74; chmn. Commn. Pub. Sch. Laws N.C.; chmn. Gov.'s Commn. Pub. Sch. Fin.; mem. N.C. Council State; chmn. bd. dirs. N.C. Firemen's and Rescue Squad Workers' Pension Fund; mem. Capitol Planning Commn.; bd. dirs. N.C. Wildlife Fedn. Served with N.G., 1962-66. Recipient awards including Disting. Service award Smithfield Jaycees, 1974; Gov.'s awards as Conservation Legislator of Yr., N.C. Wildlife Fedn., 1977, 79. Mem. N.C. State Employees Assn., N.C. Assn. Ednl. Office Personnel (advisor), Nat. State Auditors Assn. (pres.), Nat. Assn. State Auditors, Comptrollers and Treas., Nat. Intergovtl. Audit Forum and Southeastern Intergovtl. Audit Forum, Govt. Fin. Officers Assn., Am. Legion. Home: PO Box 2175 Smithfield NC 27577 Office: 300 N Salisbury St Raleigh NC 27611

RENICK, RALPH APPERSON, journalist; b N.Y.C., Aug. 9, 1928; s. Ralph Apperson and Rosalie (Dwyer) R.; A.B., U. Miami (Fla.), 1949; m. Elizabeth Jane Henry, June 5, 1949 (dec. July, 1964); children—Patricia Garrard, Kathryn Chaille, Ralph A., Susan Joseph, Pamela, Michele. News dir. TV Sta. WTVJ, Miami, 1950-58, v.p. for news, 1958-85, v.p. Wometco Enterprises, Miami, 1959-77, v.p. in charge Wometco Broadcast News Ops., 1977-84; dir. Fed. Home Loan Bank of Atlanta, 1979-83; instr. TV news reporting U. Miami, 1952-58. Mem. Fla. State Library Adv. Council. Recipient Radio-TV Mirror award, 1967. Mem. Radio Television News Dirs. Assn. (nat. pres. 1958-59), AP Broadcasters Assn. (pres. 1979-81), Nat. Press Club, Radio-TV Corrs. Assn., Miami-Dade C. of C., Iron Arrow, Soc. Profl. Journalists/Sigma Delta Chi (chpt. pres. 1958-59). Club: Kiwanis. Home: 1579 NE 104 St Miami Shores FL 33138

RENNER, HELEN LOUISE, art gallery executive, counselor; b. Independence, Mo., Jan. 12, 1943; d. Walter Red Breckenridge and June Jeannetta (Combs) Gambrill; m. Robert Louise Renner, June 4, 1961; children—Lori Ann, Scott Robert. Student U. Md., 1972-73, Park Coll., 1977; cert. of completion Inchbald Sch. Design, London, 1975; B.A., La. Tech. U., 1983, M.A. in Guidance and Counseling, 1985. Program dir. Recreation Ctr., Rickenbacker AFB, Ohio, 1977-79, Skyclub Recreation Ctr., Barksdale AFB, La., 1980; sec. La. Tech. U., Barksdale AFB, 1980-81; mgr. So. Gallery, Shreveport, La., 1981—. Counselor Ctr. for Displaced Homemakers, Shreveport, 1984—, Hospice of La., Shreveport, 1984—, Open Ear Crisis Line, Shreveport, 1984-85. Named Outstanding Young Women Am., 1968; recipient Cert. of Achievement Upper Heyford Anglo-Am. Com., Eng., 1968. Mem. Am. Assn. for Counseling and Devel. Republican. Clubs: Officers Wives (Barksdale AFB); Questers. Home: 406 Kenshire Ct Shreveport LA 71115

RENOLL, ELMO SMITH, agricultural engineering educator; b. Glen Rock, Pa., Jan. 25, 1922; s. Paul K. and Mazie C. (Smith) R.; m. Margaret W. Waid, Sept. 15, 1945; children—Lynn A. and Jean Renoll Cockrell. B.S., Auburn U., 1947; M.S., Iowa State U., 1949. Engr. U.S. Dept. Agr., Auburn, Ala., and Ames, Iowa, 1945-49; asst. prof. Auburn U., Auburn, Ala., 1949-52, assoc. prof., 1952-72, prof., 1972-83. Served with U.S. Army, 1942-45. Decorated Purple Heart. Recipient Hon. State Farm Degree Ala. Future Farmers Am., 1973; named Outstanding Educator of Am., 1975. Mem. Am. Soc. Agrl. Engrs., Am. Soc. Engring. Educators, AAAS. Methodist. Contbr. numerous articles to various profl. jours.; presenter before various national and internat. meetings. Home: 939 South Gay St Auburn AL 36830 Office: Agric Engring Dept Auburn Univ Auburn AL 36849

RENTENBACH, THOMAS JOSEPH, civil engineer; b. Hancock, Mich., Mar. 30, 1911; s. Thomas Michael and Margaret Helen (O'Neill) R.; m. LaReine Brelsford, Oct. 10, 1936; children—Thomas Michael, LaReine, William Brelsford, Robert Patrick. B.S. in Civil Engring. with honors, Mich. Tech. U., Houghton, 1932, C.E. with honors, 1933. Registered profl. engr., Tenn., 15 other states. Civil engr. Corps Engrs., 1933-40; engr. spl. engring. div. Panama Canal, 1941-42; founder Rentenbach Engring. Co., Knoxville, Tenn., 1946, pres., 1956-71, chmn. bd., chief exec. officer, 1971-82, chmn. bd., 1982—; dir. United Am. Bank (N.A.), Knoxville, 1972-75, exec. bd., 1975—; dir. Home Fed. Savs. & Loan Assn., Knoxville, 1971-82, Hamilton Nat. Bank, 1972-75; exec. bd. United Am. Bank (N.A.), 1971-82; mem. Tenn. adv. bd. Liberty Mut. Ins. Cos., 1976-82. Mem. lay adv. bd. St. Mary's Med. Center, Knoxville, 1967-79, chmn., 1975-76; trustee devel. fund Mich. Tech. U., 1970-80, mem. president's club, 1971—; bd. dirs. United Way Greater Knoxville, 1965-76, chmn. fund appeal, 1969, pres. bd. dirs., 1972; bd. dirs. Child and Family Services Knoxville, 1965-71; chmn. Knoxville Center City Task Force, 1973-77; bd. dirs. Dulin Gallery Art, Knoxville, 1970-79, v.p., 1973-78, chmn., 1979-80; adv. council Jr. Achievement Greater Knoxville, 1973—. Served to maj. C.E. AUS, 1942-46. Fellow ASCE; mem. Nat. Soc. Profl. Engrs. (pres. Knoxville chpt. 1959), Knoxville Tech. Soc., Asso. Gen. Contractors Am. (pres. Tenn. br. 1970), Tau Beta Pi (nat. exec. council 1970-74), Chi Epsilon. Roman Catholic. Clubs: Elks, Cherokee Country, LeConte. Office: 2400 Sutherland Ave Knoxville TN 37919

RENTZ, MICHAEL JAMES, air traffic control specialist; b. Bartow, Fla., Sept. 14, 1950; s. George W. and Ann (Moroney) R.; 1 son, Michael J.; m. 2d Iris Arline McLaughlin, Apr. 23, 1982; 1 son, Mark Christianson. Student pub. schs., Fort Meade, Fla. Registered paramedic, Fla.; cert. pvt. pilot; cert. air traffic control specialist. Air traffic control specialist FAA, 1977—. Advanced first aid and CPR instr. Ft. Myers (Fla.) chpt. ARC. Served with USNR, 1969-70. Recipient Commendation Letter, FAA, 1981. Mem. Aircraft Owners and Pilots Assn., Nat. Assn. Air Traffic Specialists, Facility Tech. Adv. Com. Republican. Baptist.

REPPERT, NANCY LUE, city official; b. Kansas City, Mo., June 17, 1933; d. James Everett and Iris R. (Moomey) Moore; student Central Mo. State U., 1951-52, U. Mo., Kansas City, 1971-75; cert. legal asst., Rockhurst Coll., Kansas City, Mo., 1980; cert. risk mgr., 1979; m. James E. Cassidy, 1952 (div.); children—James E., II, Tracy C. With Kansas City (Mo.) chpt. ARC, 1952-54, N. Central region Boy Scouts Am., 1963-66, Clay County Health Dept., Liberty, Mo., 1966-71, City of Liberty, 1971-80; risk mgr. City of Ames (Iowa), 1980-82; risk mgr. City of Dallas, 1982-84; dir. risk mgmt. Pinellas County, Fla., 1984—; mem. faculty William Jewell Coll., Liberty, 1975-80; vis. prof. U. Kans., 1981; seminar leader, cons in field. Lay minister United Meth. Ch., 1965—; dir. youth devel. Hillside United Meth. Ch., Liberty; co-chmn. youth dir. Collegiate United Meth. Ch., mem. Council of Ministries; advancement chmn. Mid-Iowa Council Boy Scouts Am., membership chmn. White Rock Dist. council, chmn. council health and safety com. West Central Fla. council. Recipient Order of Merit, Boy Scouts Am., 1979, Living Sculpture award, 1978,79; Service award Rotary Internat., 1979. Mem. Am. Mgmt. Assns., Internat Platform Assn., Risk and Ins. Mgrs. Soc., Public Risk and Ins. Mgmt. Assn., Am. Soc. Profl. and Exec. Women, Am. Film Inst., U.S. Naval Inst., Nat. Assn. Female Execs., Nat. Inst. Municipal Law Officers. Author: Kids Are People, Too, 1975. Pearls of Potentiality, 1980; also articles. Home: Blind Pass Marina 9555 Blind Pass Rd St Petersburg Beach FL 33706 Office: 520 Oak Ave Clearwater FL 33516

RESER, DON CLAYTON, lawyer; b. San Antonio, Dec. 14, 1950; s. Richard Stair and Mary Luella (Clayton) R.; m. Rebecca Jo Reser, Mar. 30, 1974. A.B. in Econs., Stanford U., 1973; M.B.A., U. Tex., 1976; J.D., U. Houston, 1978. Bar: Tex. 1977, U.S. Dist. Ct. (we. and so. dists.), U.S. Ct. Appeals (5th and 11th circs.) 1981, U.S. Supreme Ct. 1981, U.S. Tax Ct. 1980. Jr. law clk. to judge U.S. Dist. Ct. Western Dist. Tex., 1977-78, sr. law clk., 1978-79; assoc. Mathis & Bevil, San Antonio, 1979-80, Plunkett, Gibson & Allen, San Antonio, 1980-83; sole practice, 1983—. Bd. dirs. U. Houston Law Alumni Assn. Mem. ABA, Fed. Bar Assn., Tex. Bar Assn., San Antonio Bar Assn., Nat. Assn. Securities Dealers. Republican. Presbyterian. Contbr. article to law jour. Securities. Office: 311 E Ramsey Rd San Antonio TX 78216

RESNIK, ROBERT (BUDDY), furniture manufacturing company executive; b. Louisville, Apr. 26, 1939; s. Jacob and Hazel Hennesey (Duckworth) R.; m. Sharen McClelland, July 5, 1984; children by previous marriage—Geoffrey, Garth, Jessica Beth. B.A., U. Wash., 1967. Vice pres. Long Bank Note Co., Salt Lake City, 1961-65; pres. Nat. Talent Cons., Beverly Hills, Calif., 1965-67; v.p., pres. Hollywood Furniture, Seattle, 1967-69; pres. Western Resources, San Francisco, 1969-81; v.p. Royal Creations, Villa Rica, Ga., 1981-86; v.p. L. Powell Co., Culver City, Calif., 1986—; dir. Rancho Cucamonga, Calif. Recipient Recognition award Furniture Rental Assn. of Am., 1983. Republican. Jewish. Avocation: university athletic recruiter. Home: 31 Ivy Chase NE Atlanta GA 30342

RESO, ANTHONY, geologist; b. London, Eng., Aug. 10, 1934; s. Harry and Marion (Gerth) R.; came to U.S., 1940, naturalized, 1952. A.B., Columbia Coll., N.Y.C., 1954; M.A., Columbia U., 1955; postgrad. U. Cin., 1956-57; Ph.D. (fellow) Rice U., 1960; postgrad. Grad. Sch. Bus. U. Houston, 1964-68. Instr. geology Queens Coll., Flushing, N.Y., 1954; geologist Atlantic Richfield Corp., Midland, Tex., 1955-56; asst. prof. geology and curator invertebrate paleontology Pratt Mus., Amherst (Mass.) Coll., 1959-62; staff research geologist Tenneco Oil Co., Houston, 1962—. Cons. in geol. research Tenn. Gas and Oil Co., 1960-61; lectr. U. Houston, 1962-65; vis. prof. Rice U., 1980; mem. bd. advisers Gulf Univs. Research Corp., Galveston, Tex., 1967-75, chmn., 1968-69; dir. Stewardship Properties, Houston, 1968—. Recipient research grants Am. Assn. Petroleum Geologists, 1958, 59, Geol. Soc. Am., 1958, Eastman Fund, 1962; NSF fellow, 1959. Fellow Geol. Soc. Am. (mem. com. investments 1984—, chmn. 1985—), AAAS; mem. Am. Assn. Petroleum Geologists (life, mem. com. on convs. 1977-83, chmn. 1980-83, gen. chmn. nat. conv. 1979, com. on investments 1982—; Disting. service award 1985), Paleontol. Soc., Soc. Econ. Paleontologists and Mineralogists, Paleontol. Research Instn., Marine Tech. Soc., Tex. Acad. Sci., Houston Geol. Soc. (v.p. 1973-75, pres. 1975-76, chmn. constn. revision com. 1981; Disting. service award 1985), English-Speaking Union U.S. (dir. Houston chpt. 1978-81, v.p. 1982—), Sigma Xi, Sigma Gamma Epsilon, Beta Theta Pi. Episcopalian. Club: Shadyside Tennis. Contbr. profl. jours. Home: 1801 Huldy Houston TX 77019 Office: Tenneco Oil Co PO Box 2511 Houston TX 77001

RESO, SIDNEY JOSEPH, oil company executive; b. New Orleans, Feb. 12, 1935; s. James Anthony and Josephine Agnes (Shindler) R.; m. Patricia Marie Armond, Aug. 20, 1955; children—Robin, Cyd, Gregory, Christopher, Renee. B.S. in Petroleum Engring., La. State U., 1957. Registered profl. engr., Tex. Engr. Humble Oil & Refining Co. (name changed to Exxon U.S.A.), 1957-65; ops. mgr. East Tex. div., Houston, 1970-71, asst. mgr. Southeastern div., New Orleans, 1971-72, div. mgr. East Tex. div., 1973-74, ops. mgr. prodn. Hdqrs., Houston, 1974-75, v.p. Gas Exxon Corp., N.Y.C., 1978-80, v.p. prodn., Houston, 1980-81, sr. v.p., 1981-85, exec. v.p., 1985—; chief engr. prodn. Esso Standard Oil (Australia) Ltd., Sydney, 1965-67, mgr. nat. gas dept., 1967-69, dir., 1972-73, v.p. Esso Europe, 1975-78, Mem. Soc. Petroleum Engrs., Am. Petroleum Inst., Tex. Mid-Contenent Oil and Gas Assn., Pi Epsilon Tau, Tau Beta Pi. Roman Catholic. Clubs: Country of Darien (Conn.); River Oaks Country, Petroleum (Houston); Galveston Country (Tex.). Office: Exxon USA PO Box 2180 Houston TX 77001

RESSLER, PARKE E(DWARD), lawyer, accountant; b. Lancaster, Pa., Aug. 21, 1916; s. Parke H. and Sadie (Weiser) R.; B.S., U. Pa., 1947; B.B.A., Baylor U., 1947, LL.B., 1952, J.D., 1969; M.B.A., U. Houston, 1949; m. Margaret B. Tucker, June 3, 1944; children—Nancy Parke, Margaret Anne. Agt. Internal Revenue Service, 1947-50; part time instr. Baylor U., 1950-65; admitted to Tex. bar, 1952, since practiced in Waco; asso. firm Edwin P. Horner. Mem. Am. Inst. C.P.A.'s, Tex. Soc. C.P.A.'s, Am., Tex., McLennan County bar assns., Am. Assn. Atty.-C.P.A.'s, Phi Alpha Delta, Delta Sigma Pi. Mem. Christian Ch. Rotarian. Clubs: Ridgewood Country, Hedonia, Ridgewood Yacht, Baylor Bear. Home: 2209 Arroyo Rd Waco TX 76710 Office: 4800 Lakewood Dr Waco TX 76710

RETIF, THOMAS NEWTON, music educator; b. Baton Rouge, La., May 16, 1942; s. Alfred Sr. and Tommie Alene (Hutchinson) R. Mus.B., La. State U., 1964; Mus. M., U. Tex., 1968; Mus.D., Southwestern Bapt. Theol. Sem., 1980. With Tarrant County Jr. Coll., Fort Worth, 1968-75, U. Tex., Arlington, 1975-76, Southwestern Bapt. Theol. Sem., Fort Worth, 1976-80, Hardin Simmons U., Abilene, Tex., 1980-81; assoc. prof. Brewton-Parker Coll., Mount Vernon, Ga., 1981—; profl. singer Santa Fe Opera Co., N. Mex., 1964-65; dir. Ohoopee Council Arts, Vidalia, Ga., 1982—. Chmn. bd. dirs. Schola Cantorium of Tex., Fort Worth, 1976-77. Mem. Nat. Assn. Tchrs. Singing, Am. Musicological Soc., Am. Guild English Handbell Ringers, Coll. Music Soc. Republican. Presbyterian. Office: Brewton Parker Coll Mount Vernon GA 30445

RETTIG, TERRY, veterinarian, wildlife consultant; b. Houston, Jan. 30, 1947; s. William E. and Rose (Munves) R.; m. Anne Calhoun Martin, Aug. 29, 1970; children—Michael Thomas, Jennifer Suzanne. B.S. in Zoology, Duke U., 1969, M.A.T. in Sci., 1970; D.V.M., U. Ga., 1975. Resident veterinarian, mgr. animal health The Wildlife Preserve, Largo, Md., 1975-76; wildlife veterinarian Dept. Environ. Conservation, State of N.Y., Delmar, 1976-77; owner Atlanta Animal Hosp., 1976—; pres., chmn. Atlanta Animal Services, P.A., 1983—; sec., dir. Atlanta Pet Supply, Inc., 1983—; cons. Six Flags Over Ga., Yellow River Game Ranch, Stone Mountain Park Animal Forest, Atlanta Zoo; Author: (with Murray Fowler) Zoo and Wild Animal Medicine (Aardvark award 1978), 1978, 2d edit., 1986; contbr. articles to profl. jours. Del., Dekalb County Republican Conv., 1983. Spl. scholar Cambridge U. Coll. Vet. Medicine, 1973-74. Mem. AVMA, Ga. Vet. Med. Assn., Greater Atlanta Vet. Med. Assn., Dekalb Vet. Soc., Acad. Vet. Medicine, Am. Assn. Zoo Veterinarians, Am. Assn. Zool. Parks and Aquaria, Nat. Wildlife Health Found., Nat. Wildlife Assn., Atlanta Zool. Soc., Am. Fedn. Aviculturists, Cousteau Soc., Am. Assn. Avian Veterinarians, Am. Animal Hosp. Assn., Internat. Wildlife Assn., Soc. Aquatic Veterinary Medicine, Am. Buffalo Assn. Presbyterian. Home: 5082 Wickford Way Dunwoody GA 30338 Office: Atlanta Animal Hosp 2482 C Mt Vernon Rd Dunwoody GA 30338

REUTHER, ROSANN WHITE, advertising executive; b. Nashville, Nov. 24, 1943; d. Wiley Butler and Mildred Elizabeth (Little) White; m. Peter Martin Reuther, Oct. 3, 1964. Student George Peabody Coll. for Tchrs., Vanderbilt U., 1961-64. Copywriter, Sta. WHMA Radio, Anniston, Ala., 1964-65; advt. copywriter Broadman Press, Nashville, 1965-72; copywriter Thomas Nelson Pubs., Nashville, 1972-73; account exec. Holder-Kennedy Pub. Relations, Nashville, 1973-74; pub. relations dir. Thomas Nelson Pubs., Nashville, 1974-75; pension adminstr. Wood, Bateman, Nord and Assocs., Nashville, 1975-76; owner In-Vision Advt. and Pub. Relations, Nashville, 1976—; guest lectr. Tenn. State U.; part-time instr. Continuing Edn. program Nashville State Tech. Inst. Recipient Paul M. Hinkhouse award Religious Pub. Relations Council, 1974. Mem. Am. Women in Radio and TV (former S.E. dist. dir.), Nashville Advt. Fedn., Brentwood C. of C. Republican. Baptist. Club: Country (Brentwood, Tenn.). Home: 1315 Haber Dr Brentwood TN 37027 Office: 20 Academy Pl Nashville TN 37210

REVELEY, LOUIS RAMON, pathologist; b. San Antonio, Nov. 13, 1951; s. Marciano Contreras Gonzalez and Marietta Augusta Reveley; m. Suzanne Morrissey, Jan. 14, 1978; 1 child, Todd Raymond. B.A. with honors, U. Tex., Austin, 1973; M.D., U. Tex.-Dallas, 1978. Diplomate Am. Bd. pathology, Nat. Bd. Med. Examiners. Resident in pathology Parkland Meml. Hosp., Dallas, 1978-82; assoc. pathologist Brown & Assocs. Med. Labs., Houston, 1982—, tech. dir. clin. pathology reference lab., 1982—; staff pathologist Park Plaza Hosp., Houston, 1982-83; dir. labs. Polly Ryan Hosp., Richmond, Tex., 1983—, sec. med. staff, 1985—; med. dir. med. lab. technologist tng. program San Jacinto Coll. Central, Pasadena, Tex., 1984—. Am. Cancer Soc. clin. fellow in radiation oncology St. Paul Hosp., Dallas, 1974; Southwestern Med. Found. scholar, 1974. Fellow Am. Soc. Clin. Pathologists, Coll. Am. Pathologists (insp. lab. accreditation program); mem. N.Y. Acad. Scis., Internat. Acad. Pathology, AMA, Am. Assn. Blood Banks, Am. Soc. Cytology, So. Med. Assn., Tex. Med. Assn., Tex. Soc. Pathologists, Harris County Med. Soc., Houston Soc. Clin Pathologists, Am. Soc. Microbiology, Tex. Hist. Assn., San Jacinto Mus. History Assn. Republican. Methodist. Club: The Briar (Houston). Home: 2130 Swift St Houston TX 77030 Office: Brown & Assocs Med Labs Suite 220 1213 Hermann Dr Houston TX 77004

REYER, RANDALL WILLIAM, anatomist, educator; b. Chgo., Jan. 23, 1917; s. William Cleveland and Elsie Mary (Hardy) R.; A.B., Cornell U., 1939; M.A., 1942; Ph.D., Yale U., 1947; m. Carolyn Elizabeth Murray, June 12, 1943; children—Elizabeth Ann, Mary Louise. Instr. in Biology, Conn. Wesleyan U., 1946-47; instr. in Zoology, Yale U., 1947-50; asst. prof. Anatomy, U. Pitts., 1950-57; assoc. prof. anatomy, W.Va., U., 1957-67, prof., 1967—, acting chmn. dept., 1977-78. Recipient research grants NIH, 1951-81. Mem. Am. Assn. Anatomists, Am. Soc. Zoologists, Internat. Soc. Differentiation, Internat. Soc. Devel. Biologists, AAAS, Soc. for Devel. Biology, Assn. for Research in Vision and Ophthalmology, So. Soc. Anatomists, Am. Inst. Biol. Sci., Assn. Am. Med. Colls., Sigma Xi, Phi Beta Kappa, Phi Kappa Phi, Pi Kappa Alpha, Phi Rho Sigma. Presbyterian. Research on devel. and regeneration of lens in amphibian eye, 1948—. Office: Dept Anatomy Med Center W Va U Morgantown WV 26506

REYES, MAXIMILIAN ORTEGON, tax auditor; b. San Antonio, June 12, 1940; s. Abraham and Teodora (Ortegon) R.; m. Rose Marie Lagunas, Nov. 23, 1961; children—Cheryl Yvette, Karen Renee, Max Eric. A.A., San Antonio Coll., 1972; B.B.A., S.W. Tex. State U., 1974. Credit mgr. Globe Fin. Co., San Antonio, 1962-64; mgr. Termplan Fin. Co., 1964-68, Gt. Western Investment Co., Harlingen, Tex., 1968-70; credit mgr. Richard Gill Investment Co., San Antonio, 1975; tax auditor Tex. Employment Commn., San Antonio, 1975—. Served with USNR, 1958-64. Mem. Tex. Employees Union. Democrat. Lutheran. Home: 3330 Rosetti San Antonio TX 78247 Office: 1248 Austin Hwy Suite 100 San Antonio TX 78209

REYNA, LEO J., psychologist, educator; b. N.Y.C., Oct. 26, 1918; s. Samuel J. and Alegria (Azuz) R.; B.A., U. Mo., 1943, M.A., U. Iowa, 1944, Ph.D., 1946; lic. psychologist, Fla., Mass.; m. Priscilla Deane Trick (dec.); children—Stephen, Christopher, Susan, Patrick, Alix. Lectr., sr. lectr. U. Witwatersrand, Johannesburg, South Africa, 1946-50; asst. prof. to prof., Boston U., 1950-78; prof. psychology Nova U., Ft. Lauderdale, Fla., 1978—; mem. faculty extension div. Harvard U., 1959-76; cons. VA hosps., Boston and Bedford, Mass., Northport VA Hosp. (N.Y.), Tufts U. Med. Sch., Worcester Youth Guidance Ctr. (Mass.), U. Va. Med. Sch., Temple U. Med. Sch., Epilepsy Found. Mass., R.I. Div. Vocat. Rehab., Cambridge Psychiat. Day Ctr., others; founding mem., adv. bd. Cambridge Ctr. Behavioral Studies. Research grantee USPHS, 1957-61, 64-67. Mem. Am. Psychol. Assn., Eastern Psychol. Assn., Mass. Psychol. Assn., Behavior Therapy and Research Soc. (dir.), Assn. for Advancement of Behavior Therapy, Nat. Inst. for Psychotherapies, Fla. Assn. Behavior Analysis, AAUP, Sigma Xi. Co-author: Conditioning Therapies, 1964; co-founder, asso. editor Jour. Behavior Therapy and Exptl. Psychiatry, 1970—; contbr. articles in field to profl. publs. Home: 2431 SW 82d Ave Fort Lauderdale FL 33324 Office: Nova U College Ave Fort Lauderdale FL 33314

REYNOLDS, ARDEN FAINE, JR., neurosurgeon; b. Woodbury, N.J., Mar. 20, 1944; s. Arden Faine and Charlotte Elizabeth (Janeka) R.; m. Mary Judith Hicks, June 8, 1965; children—Joshua Daniel, Seth Elijah, Micah Jonathan and Paul Nathaniel (twins). B.A., Loma Linda U., 1965. M.D., 1969. Intern in surgery U. Minn.-Mpls., 1969-70; resident in neurosurgery U. Wash.-Seattle, 1972-76, instr. neurosurgery, 1976; asst. prof. neurosurgery U. N.Mex.-Albuquerque, 1977-78; assoc. prof. neurosurgery U. Ariz.-Tucson, 1978-82; assoc. prof. neurosurgery U. Okla.-Oklahoma City, 1983—; practice medicine specializing in neurosurgery, Albuquerque, 1977-78, Tucson, 1978-82, Oklahoma City, 1983—; mem. staff Okla. Meml. Hosp., Oklahoma City VA Hosp., Okla. Meml. Childrens Hosp. Served with USPHS, 1970-72. Mem. Am. Acad. Neurol. Surgeons (Research award 1973, 76), Western Soc. Neurol. Surgeons, Am. Assn. Neurol. Surgeons, Rocky Mountain Neurosurg. Soc., Congress Neurol. Surgeons, Neurosci. Soc., Alpha Omega Alpha. Office: PO Box 26307 Everett Bldg Room 6E210 Oklahoma City OK 73126

REYNOLDS, ARLEN BARTON, hospital executive; b. Watseka, Ill., Aug. 10, 1941; s. Barton Elmer and J. Arlene (Young) R.; m. Arlene Alice Auterman, Aug. 1, 1965; children—Michelle, Nicole. B.S. in Pharmacy, Purdue U., 1964; M.P.A., Roosevelt U., 1976. Registered pharmacist, Ill. Owner, operator, pharmacist Arlen's Drug, Champaign, Ill., 1967-79; asst. exec. dir. Cermak Meml. Hosp., Chgo., 1973-76; mgr. HCA-King Faisal Hosp., Riyadh, Saudi Arabia, 1976-80; project dir. HCA-King Saud Univ. Hosp., Riyadh, 1980-82; chief exec. officer North Monroe Hosp., Monroe, La., 1982—; pres. Nat. Drug Abuse Council, Washington, 1969-71; lectr. Chgo. Jr., Coll., 1974-76; King Saud U., Riyadh, 1976-82; mem. White House Task Force on Drug Abuse, Washington, 1982. Del. UN Protocol on Dangerous Drugs, Geneva, 1970-71; mem. Rep. Nat. Task Force, Washington, 1980—. Nominee Am. Coll. Hosp. Adminstrs.; mem. Am. Hosp. Assn., Fedn. Am. Hosps., Purdue U. Alumni Assn. (life). Lutheran. Lodge: Lions. Avocations: boating; backpacking; cubist art. Home: 2409 Marie Pl Monroe LA 71201 Office: HCA-North Monroe Hosp 3421 Medical Park Dr PO Box 7050 Monroe LA 71211

REYNOLDS, DAVID PARHAM, metals company executive; b. Bristol, Tenn., June 16, 1915; s. Richard S. and Julia L. (Parham) R.; m. Margaret Harrison, Mar. 25, 1944; children—Margaret A., Julia P., Dorothy H. Student, Princeton U. With Reynolds Metals Co., Louisville, 1937—, salesman, 1937-41, asst. mgr. aircraft parts div., 1941-44, asst. v.p., 1944-46, v.p., 1946-58, exec. v.p., 1958-69, exec. v.p., gen. mgr., 1969-75, vice chmn., chmn. exec. com., 1975-76, chmn. bd., chief exec. officer, 1976—, also dir.; chmn. Eskimo Pie Corp.; Chmn. bd., dir. Robertshaw Controls Co.; dir. Reynolds Internat., Inc., United Va. Bankshares. Trustee Lawrenceville Sch. (N.J.), U. Richmond; bd. dirs. United Negro Coll. Fund. Mem. Aluminum Assn. Office: 6601 Broad Street Rd Richmond VA 23261

REYNOLDS, DONALD WORTHINGTON, publisher; b. Fort Worth, Sept. 23, 1906; s. Gaines Worlie and Anna Louise (Elfers) R. BJ., U. Mo., 1927. Pub. Southwest-Times Record, Ft. Smith, Ark., Okmulgee (Okla.) Times, 1940—, Moberly (Mo.) Monitor-Index, Las Vegas (Nev.) Rev. Jour., 1949—, Ely (Nev.) Times and Carson City (Nev.) Appeal, 1950—, Blackwell (Okla.) Jour. Tribune, 1955—, Chickasha (Okla.) Express, 1956—, Guthrie (Okla.) Leader, 1958—, Hawaii Tribune-Herald of Hilo, 1961—, Pawhuska (Okla.) Daily Jour.-Capital, 1964—, Guymon (Okla.) Daily Herald, 1966—, Aberdeen (Wash.) Daily World, 1968, The Daily Report, Ontario, Calif., Northwest Arkansas Morning News, Pomona (Calif.) Progress-Bull., Frederick (Okla.) Daily Leader, Borger (Tex.) News Herald, 1977, Pauls Valley (Okla.) Daily Democrat, Wewoka (Okla.) Daily Times, 1967—, Jacksonville (Tex.) Progress, 1978, Cleburne (Tex.) Times Rev., 1976, Red Bluff (Calif.) Daily News, 1968—, Booneville (Ark.) Democrat, 1968—, Macon (Mo.) Chronicle-Herald, Holdenville (Okla.) News, 1969—, Weatherford (Tex.) Democrat, 1967, Washington (Ind.) Times Herald, 1972—, Sherman (Tex.) Democrat, 1977, Springdale (Ark.) News, Kailua-Kona (Hawaii) West Hawaii Today, 1968—, Henryetta (Okla.) Freelance, Lompoc (Calif.) Record, Picayune (Miss.) Item, Bartlesville (Okla.) Examiner-Enterprise, Kilgore (Tex.) News Herald, Gainesville (Tex.) Daily Register, Chico (Calif.) Enterprise-Record, Auburn (Wash.) Daily Globe News, Kent (Wash.) Daily News Journal, Renton (Wash.) Daily Record Chronicle, Sweetwater (Tex.) Reporter, 1973—, Glasgow (Ky.) Daily Times, Oskaloosa (Iowa) Herald, Redlands (Calif.) Daily Facts, Vallejo (Calif.) Times-Herald, Poplarville (Miss.) Democrat, Durant (Okla.) Daily Democrat, Donrey Cablevision, Guymon, Bartlesville, and Blackwell, Okla., Vellejo, Calif., Rogers, Ark.; pres. Donrey Outdoor, Inc., Las Vegas, Reno, Albuquerque, Spokane, Tulsa, Oklahoma City and Ft. Smith, Donrey Outdoor Advertising, Little Rock, Columbus, Ohio, Amarillo, Tex.; owner, operator radio stas. KEXO, Grand Junction, Colo., radio stas. KBRS, Springdale, Ark., 1949—, radio stas. KORK-AM/FM, Las Vegas, radio stas. KOCM-FM, Newport Beach, Calif., KOLO, Reno, 1955—, KOLO-TV, 1954—, Wichita (Kans.) Donrey Outdoor Co., 1973—. Hon. disch., maj. M.I., 1945. Awarded Legion of Merit, Bronze Star, Purple Heart, 5 combat stars; Broadcaster of Year award Nev. Broadcasting Assn., 1978. Mem. Nat. Assn. Radio-TV Broadcasters, Am. Soc. Newspaper Editors, So. Newspaper Pubs. Assn., Am. Legion, Sigma Delta Chi, Pi Kappa Alpha. Clubs: Overseas Press (San Francisco); Hillcrest Country (Bartlesville); Tulsa, Dallas Athletic; Hardscrabble Country (Ft. Smith); Prospector's (Reno); Pacific (Honolulu). Home: PO Box 70 1111 N Bonanza Las Vegas NV 89101 Office: Donrey House 920 Rogers Ave PO Box 1359 Fort Smith AR 72902*

REYNOLDS, GREGG M., public relations executive; b. Seattle, Nov. 10, 1935; s. M.E. and Maxine Ruth (Finlay) R.; m. Anne Whiting, 1958 (div.); children—Diana, Candace, Valerie; m. 2d, Joyce Borovac, Feb. 7, 1976. Student bus. adminstrn. U. Wash., 1953-55, 57-58; B.A. in Pub. Relations, San Jose State U., 1959. Pub. relations account exec. Ricks & Assocs., Seattle, 1959-60; with Boeing Co., 1960-69, pub. relations mgr., Seattle, 1962-64, 68-69, Cape Canaveral, 1964-66, pub. relations dir., Washington, 1966-68; dir. pub. relations western region Heublein, Inc., San Francisco, 1969-80; v.p. pub. affairs Ky. Fried Chicken, Louisville, 1980—; dir. Internat. Franchise Assn., Washington, also chmn. mktg.-pub. relations com. Bd. dirs. Ky. Derby Festival, Jr. Achievement Ky; active United Way, Louisville. Served with USNR, 1955-57. Mem. Pub. Relations Soc. Am. Club; Nat. Press. Home: 9004 Denington Dr Louisville KY 40222 Office: Ky Fried Chicken Corp 1441 Gardiner Ln Louisville KY 40232

REYNOLDS, HERBERT HAL, university president; b. Frankston, Tex., Mar. 20, 1930; s. Herbert Joseph and Ava Nell (Taylor) R.; B.S., Trinity U., San Antonio, 1952; M.S., Baylor U., Waco, Tex., 1958, Ph.D., 1961; m. Joy Myria Copeland, June 17, 1950; children—Kevin Hal, Kent Andrew, Rhonda Sheryl. Entered USAF, 1948, advanced through grades to col., 1966; service in Japan, Europe; dir. research Aeromed. Lab., Alamogordo, N. Mex., 1961-67; comdr. Air Force Human Resources Lab., San Antonio, Tex., 1968; ret., 1968; exec. v.p. Baylor U., 1969-81, pres., 1981—. Mem. Am., Tex. psychol. assns., Sigma Xi. Contbr. articles profl. jours. Address: Baylor Univ Waco TX 76703*

REYNOLDS, JOSEPH JAY, lawyer; b. New Haven, May 23, 1941; s. Joseph Patrick and Elizabeth Kathryn (Sherin) R.; m. Maxine V. E. Evans, June 23, 1962; children—Bradley, Jay Pat, Janelle. B.A., Stetson U., 1963, J.D., 1966. Bar: Fla. 1966. State's atty. Fla., 1966-69; div. chief, 1968-69; sr. ptnr. Reynolds & Reynolds, 1969—; mcpl. judge City of Boca Raton (Fla.), 1970-72; pub. defender City of Boynton Beach (Fla.), 1970-72; city atty. Boca Raton, 1974-75; mem. Fla. Legislature, 1972-74; tchr. jr. coll. adult edn. course. Bd. dirs. YMCA, Boca Raton, Fla. Mem. ABA, Fla. Bar Assn., Palm Beach County Bar Assn. (sec., treas.), South Palm Beach County Bar Assn. Republican. Lutheran. Clubs: Boca Pointe Country, Boca Raton Hotel and Club; King Mount (Scaly, N.C.), Kiwanis. Office: Reynolds & Reynolds 301 Crawford Blvd Suite 201 Boca Raton FL 33432

REYNOLDS, LESLIE B(OUSH), JR., physician; b. Lakeland, Fla., Aug. 16, 1923; s. Leslie Boush and Verna (Powell) R.; B.S., Randolph-Macon Coll., 1949 M.S., Ga. Inst. Tech., 1951; Ph.D., Med. Coll. S.C., 1941; M.D., Northwestern U., 1966; m. Alma Carter, Oct. 24, 1947; children—Alma Mary, Margaret Mary. Engr., E.I. du Pont de Nemours & Co., Inc., Kinston, N.C., 1951-53, group leader, 1954-55, lab. supr., 1956-57; asst. prof. physiology Northwestern U. Med. Sch., Chgo., 1961-64, research asso. medicine, 1964-66; intern St. Joseph Hosp., Chgo., 1966-67; practice medicine specializing in pulmonary disease, Memphis, 1968-76, now Kingsport, Tenn.; mem. staff Holston Valley Hosp., Kingsport; asst. prof. medicine U. Tenn., 1971-76, assoc. prof. physiology and biophysics, 1967-76, acting chmn. dept. physiology and biophysics, 1968-69; assoc. prof. family practice East Tenn. State U. Coll. Medicine, Kingsport, 1977-79, prof., 1979—, prof. physiology, 1977—, asst. dean, dir. med. edn., 1979—; dir. AL-Med Corp., Dresden, Tenn., 1976-77. Served with USNR, 1942-46. Mem. Am. Physiol. Soc., AMA, Am. Thoracic Soc., Am. Coll. Chest Physicians, Aerospace Med. Assn., Am. Acad. Family Practice, Am. Chem. Soc., Sigma Xi, Phi Lambda Upsilon. Research in respiratory reflexes, treatment of respiratory diseases. Home: Box 924 Kingsport TN 37662 Office: 202 Ravine Kingsport TN 37660

REYNOLDS, LINDA CAROLINE, writer, consultant; b. Fort Worth, Jan. 20, 1940; d. James Daniel and Martha Caroline (Valigura) Little; m. Robert Morgan Reynolds, May 5, 1961 (div. 1973). B.A. in Bus. Adminstrn., Tex. Christian U., 1965, M.B.A., 1970. Cert. secondary tchr., Tex. Instr., Fort Worth Pub. Sch., 1965-74, Tarrant County Coll., Fort Worth, 1975-76, Tex. Christian U., Fort Worth, 1976-85; writer, cons., Fort Worth, 1974—; lectr., seminar participant various colls. and profl. mtgs., 1974—. Author: Air Country Typewriting Practice Set, 1974, Dimensions in Personal Development, 1977, Snow Country Typewriting Practice Set, 1981, Dimensions in Professional Development, 1983. Editor: Inside the M.J. Neeley School of Business, 1981-83. Mem. bd. dirs. Tarrant County Mus. of Western Transp., Fort Worth, 1977. Recipient Gold Book award South-Western Pub. Co., 1983. Mem. Am. Vocat. Assn., Am. Bus. Communication Assn., Nat. Bus. Edn. Assn.

REYNOLDS, MARK FLOYD, II, lawyer, management and labor consultant; b. Phila., Apr. 14, 1943; s. Marcus Reuben and Ella Mae (Van Why) R.; m. Pauline D. Reynolds, Sept. 17, 1965; children—Meredith Lynn, Douglass Scott. B.A., Lincoln U., Pa., 1970; J.D., U. Balt., 1975. Bar: Pa. 1975, U.S. Dist. Ct. (ea. dist.) Pa. 1975, U.S. Supreme Ct., 1980, N.C. 1985, U.S. Dist. Ct. (mid. dist.) N.C. 1985, U.S. Ct. Mil. Appeals 1985. Atty., Bethelehem Steel Corp., Pa., 1976-84; ptnr. Robert Sheahan & Assocs., High Point, N.C., 1985—; dir. Ready Supply Corp., Johnstown, Pa., 1982—. Vice pres. Penns Woods council Boy Scouts Am., 1981-84; chmn. United Way Greater Johnstown, 1981-84; trustee Slatington Presbyterian Ch., Pa., 1976-81. Served with AUS, 1962-65. Mem. Pa. Bar Assn. (council labor law 1984), ABA (labor law sect. com. on OSHA), N.C. Bar Assn., Lehigh County Bar Assn., Guilford County Bar Assn., Alpha Phi Omega. Republican. Lodge: Masons. Home: 151 Wolfetrail Rd Greensboro NC 27406 Office: Robert Sheahan & Assocs PO Box 29 High Point NC 27261

REYNOLDS, PAUL JOSEPH, osteopathic physician; b. McCloud, Okla., Mar. 18, 1921; s. Fred A. and Bridgette Lendre (McMorrow) R.; m. Jeanne Maxine Posey, June 11, 1944; children—Michael, Paul David, Jeffrey, Brian. Student Okla. Bapt. U., 1949-50, Okla. U., 1950-51; D.O., Kansas City Coll. Osteopathy, 1956. Dir. Brookwood Weight Clinic, Oklahoma City, 1982—. Author: Sex and the Bathroom Scales, 1969; author weight control program: Personalized Weight Control, 1967-82. Served with USMC, 1942-46. Mem. Soc. Bariatric Physicans, Okla. Osteo. Assn. Democrat. Roman Catholic. Club: Oak Tree Golf. Avocations: golf; sporting events; reading; movies; crossword puzzles. Home: 10101 Kingsgate Rd Oklahoma City OK 73159 Office: Brookwood Weight Clinic 1684 SW 86th Suite C/D Oklahoma City OK 73159

REYNOLDS, RANDOLPH NICKLAS, aluminum company executive; b. Louisville, Nov. 22, 1941; s. William Gray and Mary (Nicklas) R.; m. Susan Van Reypen, Aug. 6, 1964; children—Randolph Nicklas, Ralph Seymour, Robert Gray. B.A., Bellarmine Coll., 1966; postgrad., U. Louisville, 1967-68. Market dir. chems. Reynolds Metals Co., Richmond, Va., 1975-77, gen. mgr. chem., 1977-78; pres. Reynolds Internat. Inc., Richmond, 1978—; pres., chief exec. officer Reynolds Aluminum Internat. Services Inc., Richmond, 1981—; dir. 30 susidiaries Reynolds Metals Co.; dir. Dominion Nat. Bank, Richmond. Bd. dirs. Bellarmine Coll., Louisville, 1981, YMCA, Richmond, 1983—. Democrat. Episcopalian. Home: 8605 River Rd Richmond VA 23229 Office: 6603 W Broad St Richmond VA 23261*

REYNOLDS, ROBERT GREGORY, toxicologist; b. Chgo., July 29, 1952; s. Robert G. and Loys Delle (Kever) R.; m. Phyllis Thurrell, May 1983. B.S. in Nutrition and Food Sci., M.I.T., 1973, postgrad. in toxicology, 1973-78, postgrad. Sloan Sch. Mgmt., 1977-78. Mng. editor The Graduate mag., M.I.T., 1975-78; v.p. Internat. Contact Bur., Ft. Lauderdale, Fla., 1977—; staff toxicologist, asst. to v.p. mktg. Enviro Control, Inc., Rockville, Md., 1978-79; dir. tech. resources Borriston Research Labs., Inc., Temple Hills, Md., 1979-80; dir. mktg. Northrop Services Inc., Research Triangle Park, N.C., 1980-85; mgr. bus. devel., 1985—; toxicol. cons. Energy Resources Co., Inc, Cambridge, 1976-77. NSF fellow, 1973. Mem. Air Pollution Control Assn., Am. Acad. Clin. Toxicology, AAAS. Episcopalian. Contbr. chpts. to textbook, lab. manual, sci. jours. and govt. publs. Office: PO Box 12313 Research Triangle Park NC 27709

REYNOLDS, THOMAS ANTHONY, oil company executive; b. Worcester, Mass., Jan. 29, 1950; s. Robert William and Violet Ann (Lorusso) R.; B.S., Worcester Poly. Inst., 1972; M.S., U. Houston, 1984. Prodn. supr. Uniroyal Co., Midlebury, Conn., 1972-74; prin. Sci. Placement, Inc., Houston, 1974-77; exec. recruiter Internat. Systems & Controls, Houston, 1977-78; dir. physician relations Lifemark Corp., Houston, 1978-80; mgr. corp. internal audit Occidental Petroleum Corp., Houston, 1980—; cons. precious metals extraction; mgr. Reynolds Investments, Houston, 1981—. Bd. dirs. Houston Mcpl. Utility Dist. #1. Mem. Am. Inst. Chem. Engrs., Am. Petroleum Inst., Inst. Mining Engrs., Aircraft Owners and Pilots Assn., U.S. Chess Fedn., Phi Theta Kappa, Phi Kappa Theta. Republican. Roman Catholic. Lodge: Elks. Author: Extractive Metallurgy of Gold and Silver—A Study of the Finer Points of Heap Leaching, 1981; Corporate Aircraft—Control, Cost and Utilization, 1982. Home: 6912 S 78th East Ave Tulsa OK 74133 Office: PO Box 46 Tulsa OK 74102

RHEA, GENE STEVE, geophysicist, seismic data processing educator; b. Beaumont, Tex., Aug. 26, 1948; s. Eugene and Edna (Bell) R.; m. Sandra Ann Hoops, Dec. 6, 1980. B.S., Lamar U., 1970. Geologist, Tech. & Field Surveys, Sydney, Australia, 1970-75, Pressure Control Systems, Houston, 75-77; data processing analyst Western Geophys., Houston, 1977-78, Digicon, Inc., Houston, 1980—. Mem. Mus. Area Mcpl. Assn., Houston, 1984—. Mem. Soc. Exploration Geophysicists, Geophys. Soc. Houston, Lamar U. Geol. Soc. (life; sec. 1969-70). Democrat. Methodist. Avocations: travel; collecting edged weapons; wargaming. Home: 302 Portland Pl 2 Houston TX 77006 Office: Digicon Inc 3701 Kirby Dr Houston TX 77098

RHETT, WILLIAM PATERSON, JR., teacher educator, psychologist, clergyman; b. Charleston, S.C., Aug. 4, 1931; s. William Paterson and Margaret Fishburn (Hughes) R.; m. Dorothy Irene Carson, Feb. 28, 1968. B.S., Coll. of Charleston, 1953; M.Div., Va. Theol. Sem., 1960; M.Ed., Temple U., 1968; Ed.D., Auburn U., 1971. Ordained priest Episcopalian Ch., 1961. Rector Christ-St. Paul's Parish, Adams Run, S.C., 1960-62; asst. rector St. Michael's Parish, Charleston, 1962-63; prof. The Citadel, Charleston, 1968—, also coordinator grad. studies in counselor edn.; pvt. practice psychology, Charleston, 1973—. Served with USAFR. Mem. Am. Psychol. Assn., Am. Assn. Marriage and Family Therapists, Res. Officers Assn., Soc. of Cincinnati, Soc. Colonial Wars, St. Cecelia Soc., First Families S.C. Club: Carolina Yacht. Address: 2 St Michaels Alley Charleston SC 29401

RHOADES, CHARLES VANCE, psychology educator, counselor; b. Vicksburg, Miss., Apr. 18, 1956; s. Charles William and Donnie Harris (Rogillio) R.; m. Paula Marie Landrum, May 27, 1978. A.A. with spl. honors, Copiah-Lincoln Jr. Coll., 1976; B.S. with honors, U. So. Miss., 1978, M.Sc., 1979, postgrad., 1983. Recreational counselor Natchez Recreation Dept., 1974; census enumerator R.L. Polk & Co., Natchez, 1975; asst. prof. psychology, counselor Brewton-Parker Coll., Mount Vernon, Ga., 1979—, golf coach, 1983—; adj. prof. psychology Tift Coll., Forsyth, Ga., 1980—. Recipient Psychology award Copiah-Lincoln Jr. Coll., 1976; named Tchr. of Yr., Brewton-Parker Coll. 1981. Mem. Am. Personnel and Guidance Assn., Assn. Student Devel. in So. Bapt. Colls. and Univs., Nat. Assn. Student Personnel Adminstrs., Am. Coll. Personnel Assn., Psi Chi, Phi Theta Kappa. Republican. Baptist. Home: Route 1 Box 45D Mount Vernon GA 30445 Office: PO Box 205 Brewton-Parker Coll Mount Vernon GA 30445

RHOADS, STEVEN ERIC, political science educator; b. Abingdon, Pa., May 12, 1939; s. John Reginald and Barbara Ann (Dugan) R.; m. Diana Cabanis Akers, May 17, 1944; children—Christopher, Nicholas, John. B.A., Princeton U., 1961; M.P.A., Cornell U., 1965, Ph.D., 1972. Mem. staff Office Mgmt. and Budget, Washington, 1965-66; asst. prof. dept. govt. and fgn. affairs U. Va., Charlottesville, 1970-76, assoc. prof., 1977-86, prof. 1986—. Served to lt. (j.g.) USN, 1961-63. NEH, Inst. Ednl. Affairs, Earhart Found. fellow. Mem. Am. Polit. Sci. Assn., So. Polit. Sci. Assn., Assn. Pub. Policy and Mgmt., Am. Soc. Pub. Adminstrn. Author: Policy Analysis in the Federal Aviation Administration, 1974; Valuing Life: Public Policy Dilemmas, 1980; The Economist's View of the World: Government, Markets and Public Policy, 1985; contbr. articles to profl. publs. Home: 3190 Dundee Rd Earlysville VA 22936 Office: Dept Government 232 Cabell Hall U Virginia Charlottesville VA 22901

RHODES, ANN L(OUISE), construction company executive; b. Ft. Worth, Oct. 17, 1941; d. Jon Knox and Carol Jane (Greene) R.; student Tex. Christian U., 1960-63. Vice pres. Rhodes Enterprises Inc., Ft. Worth, 1963-77; owner-mgr. Lucky R Ranch, Ft. Worth, 1969—, Ann L. Rhodes Investments, Ft. Worth, 1976—; pres., chmn. bd. ALR Enterprises, Inc., Ft. Worth, 1977—, pres. Sunergos Prodns. div., 1983—. Bd. dirs. Tarrant Council Alcoholism, 1973-78, hon. bd. dirs., 1978—; bd. dirs. N.W. Tex. council Arthritis Found., 1977—, Ft. Worth Farm and Ranch Club; exec. com. Tarrant County Republican Party, 1964-69; adv. bd. mem. Circle Theatre, Ft. Worth. Recipient various service awards. Mem. Am. Mgmt. Assns., Nat. Fedn. Ind. Bus., Am. Horse Council, Kappa Kappa Gamma. Episcopalian. Office: Suite 908 Ridglea Bank Bldg Fort Worth TX 76116

RHODES, CLOPELL, bookstore manager; b. Narion, S.C., Jan. 1, 1954; s. John Tillman and Clotell (Miller) R.; B.S., Morris Coll. Shipping clk. L'egg Co., Marion, S.C., 1972-73, Ratex Inc., Marion, 1974-75; officers mass Sun Oil Co., Chester, Pa., 1973-74; bookstore mgr. Morris Coll., Sumter, S.C., 1979—. Reserve officer Sumter County Law Enforcement Recipient Outstanding Young Men of Am. award. Mem. NAACP, Phi Beta Lambda, Phi Beta Sigma. Democrat. Baptist. Lodges: Masons, C.C. Johnson Consistency. Avocations: tennis; bowling; golfing. Home: 154 Briarcliff MHP Dalzell SC 29040 Office: Morris Coll Bookstore Box 19 Sumter SC 29150

RHODES, DONALD EVERETT, JR., investment company executive; b. Bethlehem, Pa., Aug. 26, 1945; s. Donald E. and Anne Jeanette (Deetz) R.; m. Cheryl Ainbender, May 15, 1977; 1 dau., Rachel Anne. B.S., Yale U., 1967, B.A., 1968; postgrad. MIT, 1971-73. Registered profl. engr. Mass. Faculty Commonwealth Sch., Boston, 1968-72; project mgr. Stone & Webster, Boston, 1973-79; v.p. Roe, Martin & Neiman, Atlanta, 1979-83, First Equities Corp., 1983—. Clubs: Kiawah Island (S.C.); East Lake Country (Atlanta). Office: First Equities Corp 6201 Powers Ferry Rd Atlanta GA 30339

RHODES, JOHN CECIL, oil producer; b. Kansas City, Mo., Oct. 9, 1929; s. W. Gordon and Carrie Lee (Bond) R.; m. Joan White, Sept. 12, 1953; children—Celia Rhodes Wilson, Lisa, William Jay (dec.). Student Tex. Christian U., 1947-49, U. Tex., 1949-50; B.S., Evansville Coll., 1951; postgrad. U. Tex., 1952. Cert. petroleum geologist. Exploration geologist Ashland Oil & Refining Co., 1952-55; exploration geologist Tex. Pacific Oil Co., Midland, 1955-63; cons. geologist, Midland, 1963-68; ind. oil producer, Midland, 1968—. Mem. Am. Assn. Petroleum Geologists, Soc. Ind. Earth Scientists. Republican. Presbyterian. Clubs: Midland Country, Midland, Racquet; Jockey (Ruidosa, N.Mex); Horsehoe Bay (Granite Shoals, Tex.). Home: 1905 Crescent Pl Midland TX 79701 Office: 399 One Marienfeld Pl Midland TX 79701

RHODES, JOHN WILEY, college official, consultant; b. Montgomery, Ala., May 17, 1944; s. John Albert and Erma (Bush) R.; m. Mary Alice Potts, Aug. 31, 1968; children—Kristin, Kimberly. B.S., Troy State U., 1965; M.Music, Fla. State U., 1968; Ph.D., Ga. State U., 1979. Cert. elem. and secondary music. Music cons. Ga. Dept. Edn., Atlanta, 1973-77, asst. dir. grants mgmt., 1977-80, coordinator tchr. edn., 1980-83; v.p. acad. affairs Shenandoah Coll. and Conservatory, Winchester, Va., 1983—; cons. edn., Atlanta, 1978-83. Editor Ga. Jour. Tchr. Edn., 1983; contbr. articles to profl. jours. Bd. dirs. Salvation Army Adv. Bd., Winchester, Va., 1984—; conf. del. Market St. United Meth. Ch., Winchester, 1985; lay leader Harmony Grove United Meth. Ch., Lilburn, Ga., 1982-83. Mem. Phi Delta Kappa. Avocations: photography, astronomy. Office: Shenandoah Coll and Conservatory 660 Millwood Ave Winchester VA 22601

RHODES, LORD CECIL, dentist; b. Norfolk, Va., May 26, 1920; s. Edward C. and Ella H. (Spence) R.; m. Anna Louise Allen, Feb. 1, 1952 (div. 1961); 1 child, Lord Cecil; m. Muriel Holmes, May 25, 1969. B.S. Shaw U., 1941; D.D.S., Howard U., 1951; postgrad. U. Iowa, 1941-42, Middlesex Med. Coll., 1943-44. Gen. practice dentistry, City Dental Clinic, Portsmouth, Va., 1952-56, Norfolk, 1956—; asst. in research pharmacology Sch. Medicine Howard U., 1947-50; founder, dental dir., adminstr. Rhodes Dental Hosp., Norfolk, 1962—; staff Norfolk Community Hosp.; dir. Berkley Citizens Bldg. and Loan Assn.; co-owner Profl. Assocs. Inc. Med. Bldg. Author: History Black Dentists in Virginia, 1985; contbr. articles in field. Served pvt. to staff sgt. M.C. AUS, 1944-46, ETO. Mem. Nat. Dental Assn., Old Dominion Dental Soc., John L. McGriff Dental Soc. (past pres.), Am. Acad. Implant Dentures, AAAS, Am. Assn. Dental Hosp. Chiefs, Internat. Platform Assn., Norfolk C. of C., Frontiers of Am. (dir.), Chi Delta Mu. Home: 748 Stanwix Sq Norfolk VA 23502 Office: 501 E Brambleton Ave Norfolk VA 23501

RHODES, PATRICK L., social services administrator, counselor; b. Santa Barbara, Calif., Mar. 17, 1946; s. George and Edwina (Burruss) R.; B.A., Guilford Coll., 1972; M.S., James Madison U., 1974; Ed.D., U. N.C., Greensboro, 1981. Dir. behavior modification Youth Rehab. Center, Roanoke, Va., 1972-73; asst. prof. Tidewater Community Coll., Portsmouth, Va., 1974-77; mgr. Youth Care Inc., Greensboro, N.C., 1982-83; dir. Office of

Youth Services, Waynesboro, Va., 1983—; project adminstr., Va. Dept. Corrections, 1983—; youth counselor City of Waynesboro, 1983—; VISTA site supr., 1985-86. Served with AUS, 1968-70. Mem. Am. Soc. Pub. Adminstrn., Phi Delta Kappa, Psi Chi. Club: Rotary Internat. Office: PO Box 894 120 N Wayne St Waynesboro VA 22980

RHODES, THOMAS CLELLMONT, fire chief, educator; b. Indpls., Dec. 5, 1948; s. Robert Clellmont and Esther Ruth (Watts) R.; m. Loretta Ann Williams, July 16, 1976; children—Kathy, Robert, Noel, Jeannie, Michael. Student Fire Sci. Inst., Ocala Fire Coll., 1980-84. Cert. in fire sci., cert. mcpl. insp., instr., co. officer, Fla. Firefighter Greenacres City Fire/Rescue Dept., Fla., 1974-75, driver, 1975-77, lt., 1977-80, capt., 1980-81, fire chief, 1981—; instr. fire sci. South Tech. Inst., Boynton Beach, Fla., 1984—, also instr. Emergency Med. Technician, 1984—. Served with USN, 1967-70, Vietnam. Recipient commendation Greenacres City, 1982, Fla. State Firemen's Assn., 1984. Mem. Internat. Assn. Fire Chiefs, Nat. Fire Protection Assn., Fla. Fire Chiefs Assn., Palm Beach County Fire Chiefs Assn., Internat. Assn. City Mgrs. Republican. Presbyterian. Avocations: softball; golf; electronics. Office: Greenacres City Fire/Rescue Dept 301 Swain Blvd Greenacres City FL 33463

RHOTON, ALBERT LOREN, JR., neurological surgery educator; b. Parvin, Ky., Nov. 18, 1932; s. Albert Loren and Hazel Arnette (Van Cleve) R.; m. Joyce L. Moldenhauer, June 23, 1957; children—Eric L., Albert J., Alice S., Laural A. B.S., Ohio State U., 1954; M.D. cum laude, Washington U., St. Louis, 1959. Diplomate Am. Bd. Neurol. Surgery (mem. 1985—). Intern, Columbia Presbyn. Med. Center, N.Y.C., 1959; resident in neurological surgery Barnes Hosp., St. Louis, 1961-65; cons. neurol. surgery Mayo Clinic, Rochester, Minn., 1965-72; chief div. neurol. surgery U. Fla., Gainesville, 1972-80, R.D. Keene prof. and chmn. dept. neurol. surgery, 1980—; developer microsurg tng. center; guest lectr. Neurol. Socs. Switzerland, Japan, Venezuela, France, Columbia, Middle East; invited faculty and guest lectr. Harvard U., Washington U., Emory, U., UCLA, U. Calif.-San Francisco, U. Miami, U. Okla., U. So. Calif., Northwestern U., U. Chgo., U. Pa., Johns Hopkins U., Ohio State U., Temple U., Duke U. Recipient Disting. faculty award U. Fla., 1981; Alumni Achievement award Washington U. Sch. Medicine, 1985; Jones award for outstanding spl. med. exhibit of yr. Am. Assn. Med. Illustrators, 1969; grantee NIH, VA, Am. Heart Assn. Mem. Congress Neurol. Surgeons (pres. 1978), Fla. Neurosurgical Soc. (pres. 1978), ACS (bd. govs. 1978-84), Am. Assn. Neurol. Surgeons (chmn. vascular sect., treas. 1983-86), Soc. Neurol. Surgeons (treas. 1975-81), So. Neurol. Soc. (v.p. 1976), Alachua County Med. Soc. (exec. com. 1978), AMA (Billings Bronze medal for sci. exhibit 1969), Fla. Med. Assn., Am. Surgical Assn., Soc. Univ. Neurosurgeons, Am. Heart Assn. (stroke council, outstanding achievement award 1971), Am. Acad. Neurol. Surgery, Neurol. Soc. Am. Designed over 100 microsurgery instruments; editorial bd. Neurosurgery, Jour. Microsurgery, Surgical Neurology, Jour. Fla. Med. Assn., Am. Jour. Otology; contbr. numerous articles to profl. jours. Home: 2505 NW 22d Ave Gainesville FL 32605 Office: Dept Neurosurgery PO Box J-265 U Fla Gainesville FL 32610

RHYMES, JOHN LONGSTREET, business executive; b. Macon, Miss., Dec. 30, 1927; s. Ray Lewis and Annie Ella (Ames) R.; 1 son, Michael Longstreet. B.A., U. Miss., 1951; B.D., Kenyon Coll., 1954; M.Ed., Tulane U., 1963. Ordained priest Episcopal Ch., 1954. Priest of Episcopal Ch., 1954-70; vicar, St. John's Ch., Leland, Miss., 1954-57; headmaster St. Michael's Farm for Boys, Picayune, Miss., 1957-58, St. Andrew's Sch., New Orleans, 1958-64; prin. St. Martin's Sch., Metairie, La., 1964-74; owner Longstreet & Co., New Orleans, 1972—; ednl. adminstr., ednl. psychologist. Served with M.C., U.S. Army, 1946-47, USNR, 1947-51. St. Luke's Sem. scholar, 1951, Tulane U. scholar, 1961. Mem. Mensa, Sigma Chi. Republican. Buddhist. Lodge: Masons. Home: 508 Madison Pl Apt 2 New Orleans LA 70116 Office: First Nat Bank Bldg Suite 305F 7809 Airline Hwy Metairie LA 70003

RICE, CHARLES EDWARD, banker; b. Tenn., Aug. 4, 1935; s. Charles Edward and Louise (Goodson) R.; m. Dianne Tauscher; children—Danny, Celeste, Michelle. B.B.A., U. Miami, 1958; M.B.A., Rollins Coll., Winter Park, Fla., 1964; grad., Advanced Mgmt. Program, Harvard U., 1975. Vice pres., then pres. Barnett Bank, Winter Park, 1965-71; exec. v.p. Barnett Banks Fla., Inc., Jacksonville, 1971-73, pres., 1973—, chief exec. officer, 1979—, also dir. Bd. dirs. St. Vincent Med. Center, Jacksonville; trustee Rollins Coll. Club: Jacksonville Country. Office: Barnett Banks Fla Inc 100 Laura St Jacksonville FL 32203*

RICE, DONADRIAN LAWRENCE, psychology educator; b. Spartanburg, S.C., Nov. 21, 1948; s. Marion Jefferson and Louise Rice; m. Cheryl Ann Sink. B.A., Wofford Coll., 1971; M.A., Western Carolina U., 1972; Ph.D. in Clin. Psychology, Saybrook Inst., 1977. Asst. prof. psychology Auburn (Ala.) U., 1973-78; clin. psychologist East Ala. Mental Health Clinic, Opelika, 1973-78; asst. prof. psychology West Ga. Coll., Carrollton, 1978—; cons. Sara Murphy Home for Children, Haralson County Tng. Ctr., 1980—. Gardner Murphy fellow. Mem. Am. Psychol. Assn. Mem. Ch. of God. Home: 127 Peachtree St Carrollton GA 30117 Office: 328 Social Sci Bldg West Ga Coll Carrollton GA 30118

RICE, GEORGE LAWRENCE (LARRY), III, lawyer; b. Jackson, Tenn., Sept. 24, 1951; s. George Lawrence and Judith W. (Pierce) R.; m. Joy Gaia, Sept. 14, 1974; children—George Lawrence, Amy Colleen. B.A. with honors, Southwestern Coll., 1974; student Oxford U., 1972-73; J.D., Memphis State U., 1976; student Nat. Coll. Advocacy, 1978. Bar: Tenn. 1977, U.S. Supreme Ct. 1980. Assoc. Pierce, Rice, Nichols, Rice & Stone, Memphis, 1976-81, ptnr., 1981—; lectr. Memphis Cablevision, 1983-84, Sta. WHBQ, Memphis, 1983-85, U. Chgo., 1982. Mem. Memphis Bar Assn. (chmn. divorce and family law sect.), Shelby County Bar Assn., Tenn. Bar Assn. (litigation sect. council, family law com.), ABA, Memphis Trial Lawyers Assn., Tenn. Trial Lawyers Assn., Assn. Trial Lawyers Am. Unitarian. Office: Pierce Rice Nichols Rice & Stone 147 Jefferson St Suite 600 Memphis TN 38103

RICE, IVAN GLENN, gas turbine engineer; b. Phoenix, July 24, 1924; s. Harvey Clifford and Charlotte Abegail (Burre) R.; student Phoenix Coll., 1946-47; B.S.M.E. with high distinction, U. Ariz., 1950; Carolyn Ruth Keyes, June 16, 1950; children—Thomas Glenn, Kathleen Elizabeth, James Nelson. With Gen. Electric Co., 1950-69, gas turbine application engr., for S.W. U.S.A., Houston, 1957-64, regional turbine engr. for U.S., Can. and Mexico, Houston, 1964-69; mgr. nat. and worldwide mktg. DeLaval Turbine Inc., Houston, 1969-74; cons. engr., Spring, Tex., 1974—. Mem. adv. com. Turbo-Machinery Symposium, Tex. A&M U., 1972—; mem. planning com. First Offshore Tech. Conf., Houston, 1969. Pres. Spring High Sch. PTA, 1972-73; mem.-at-large Sam Houston Area council Boy Scouts Am.; chmn. Harris County Republican Precinct 110, 1976-78. Served with Transp. Corps, AUS, 1943-46; ETO. Recipient Mgmt. awards Gen. Electric Co., 1955, 61, 66, Breakthrough 60 award Gen. Electric Co., 1960, Scouters award Boy Scouts Am., 1966. Fellow ASME (Meritorious Service award 1968, gas turbine div. commendation 1971, chmn. South Tex. sect. 1975-76, chmn. div. gas turbine 1976-77, Council award 1977, 79, Centennial medallion 1980, Region X award 1984); mem. Nat., Tex. socs. profl. engrs., Soc. Petroleum Engrs., Houston Engring. and Sci. Soc., Pi Mu Epsilon, Phi Kappa Phi, Tau Beta Pi, Pi Tau Sigma. Republican. Methodist (adminstrv. bd. 1975-76). Contbr. articles on gas turbines to profl. jours. Patentee gas turbine heat rate control reheat-gas turbine combined cycle, steam-blade cooling of reheat-gas turbine. Home: 1007 Lynwood St Spring TX 77373 Office: PO Box 233 Spring TX 77383

RICE, JAMES ROY DAVID, podiatrist; b. Altoona, Pa., Feb. 10, 1928; s. William John and Anna Matilda Rice; D.S.C., Temple U.; D.P.M., Pa. Coll. Podiatric Medicine; m. M. Louise, June 26, 1951; children—Carol Ann Rice Rentz, David. Gen. practice podiatry, Greenville, S.C.; mem. S.C. Bd. Podiatry Examiners; chief podiatry clinic Greenville Gen. Hosp.; clin. instr. family practice medicine Med. U. S.C., Greenville. Served to capt. U.S. Army, 1950-53; mem. Res. (ret.). Mem. Am. Podiatry Assn., S.C. Podiatry Assn., Am. Assn. Hosp. Podiatrists, Acad. of Ambulatory Foot Surgeons, Greenville Podiatry Assocs. (pres.). Lutheran. Lodges: Rotary (Greenville), Masons. Office: #1 Pelham Pointe Greenville SC 29615

RICE, JOANN MCDONALD, pharmacist; b. Pineville, Ky., Apr. 2, 1958; d. Alvin Kenneth and Beulah (Fortney) McDonald; m. Timothy Eugene Rice, May 28, 1983. Student, Eastern Ky. U., 1976-79; B.S. in Pharmacy, U. Ky., 1983, Pharm. D., 1983. Registered pharmacist, Ky. Pharmacy intern St. Joseph Hosp., Lexington, Ky., 1979-83, pharmacist, 1983; dir. pharmacy Berea Hosp., Ky., 1983—; speaker. Mem. Ky. Hosp. Pharmacists Assn., Am. Soc. Hosp. Pharmacists. Office: Berea Hosp Inc Estill St Berea KY 40403

RICE, JOHN THOMAS, educational administrator; b. Wilmington, Del., Apr. 9, 1939; s. William Thomas and Jacquelyn Palm (Johnston) R.; m. Grace Carrington Arendall, Sept. 4, 1960; children—W. Thomas II, Sarah Cunningham, Anne Carrington, Robert Coleman. B.S., Va. Poly. Inst., 1961; M.A., U. Tenn., 1963; L.H.D. (hon.), Va. Episcopal Sem., 1985. Dean men James Madison U., Harrisonburg, Va., 1965-69; v.p. Fla. Jr. Colls., Jacksonville, 1969-70; headmaster St. Anne's Sch., Charlottesville, Va., 1970-72; dean student affairs Sweet Briar Coll., Va., 1972-76; pres. St. Mary's Coll., Raleigh, N.C., 1976—; chmn. bd. Amherst Acad., Va., 1974-76; dir. Cooperating Raleigh Colls., 1976—. Bd. dirs. United Way Wake County, Raleigh, 1981-84, Mus. History Assocs., Raleigh, 1977-83; vestry mem. Christ Episcopal Ch., Raleigh, 1982—. Served to capt. U.S. Army, 1962-66. Mem. Cooperating Raleigh Colls. (pres. 1981-82), Ind. Coll. Fund N.C. (v.p. 1984—), N.C. Assn. Ind. Colls., Southern Assn. Colls. and Schs. (commn. colls. 1985—), Assn. Am. Colls. Republican. Clubs: Carolina Country (Raleigh), Coral Bay (Atlantic Beach, N.C.). Lodge: Rotary. Avocations: sports; jogging; weight lifting; travel; music. Home: Pres House 900 Hillsborough St Raleigh NC 27603 Office: St Mary's Coll 900 Hillsborough St Raleigh NC 27603

RICE, MARION, university chancellor. B.A., Wayne State U., 1964, M. Ed., 1966; Ph.D., Mich. State U., 1973. Provost Auburn Hills Campus, Oakland Community Coll., Auburn Heights, Mich., 1974-84; chancellor Fla. Inst. Tech.-Jensen Beach Campus, Fla., 1984—. Bd. dirs. Martin County chpt. ARC. Mem. Robotics Internat. Soc. Mfg. Engrs., East Central Fla. Consortium for Higher Edn. and Industry, Fla.-Colombia Ptnr., Hist. Soc. Martin County, Jensen Beach C. of C., Stuart/Martin County C. of C., Delta Kappa Gamma. Club: Martin County Econ. Office: Fla Inst Tech 1707 NE Indian River Dr Jensen Beach FL 33457*

RICE, MAX MCGEE, business executive, lay religious administrator; b. Belton, S.C., Aug. 19, 1928; s. Max and Janie (Grier) R.; m. Vivian Barker Rice, Feb. 18, 1956; children—Vivian Ann, Carolyn, Eunice. B.A., Furman U., 1949. Vice pres. Rice Mills., Belton, S.C., 1953-61; pres. Rice Corp., Travelers Rest, S.C., 1961—; exec. dir. Lay Christian Assocs.; founder, exec. dir. Look-Up Lodge, Christian Retreat Ctr. Author: Commonsense Christianity, 1974, When Can I Say "I Love You"?, 1977; Your Rewards in Heaven, 1981. Served to 1st lt. USAF, 1950-53. Baptist. Home: Route 1 Box 322-B Travelers Rest SC 29690 Office: Lay Christian Assocs Hwy 11 Box 322-B Travelers Rest SC 29690

RICE, PAUL RANDALL, accountant; b. Beaumont, Tex., Sept. 5, 1951; s. Jack M. and Frances A. (Scarborough) R. B.B.A., Lamar U., 1973. C.P.A., Tex. Asst. to v.p. trust div. First Security Nat. Bank, Beaumont, Tex., 1974; auditor Melton & Melton, C.P.A.s, Houston, 1974-75; auditor/consolidations acct. Service Corp. Internat., Houston, 1975-76; asst. controller Telxon Corp., Houston, 1976-77; sr. auditor/acctg. mgr. Riviana Foods, Houston, 1977-79; mgr. acctg. systems and practices Occidental Chem. Corp., Houston, 1979—. Treas., Inwood N. Civic Club, 1976-78; mem. Republican. Presdl. Task Force, 1980—. Mem. Am. Inst. C.P.A.s, Internat. Investment Council. Republican. Baptist. Club: River Safari (Houston). Office: 2000 Post Oak Blvd Apt 704G Houston TX 77056

RICE, ROGER BURNHAM PIERCE, oil company executive; b. Martins Ferry, Ohio, Apr. 29, 1944; s. Roger Fred and Shirley (Pierce) R.; m. Lynda Patterson, Aug. 13, 1966; children—Roger Pierce, Lynda Katherine. B.A., Tex. Tech. U., 1966, M.B.A., 1968. With Shell Oil Co., 1968-80, div. employee relations mgr., Midland, Tex., 1972-74, mgr. employee relations, Houston, 1974-75, mgr. fed. affairs, 1975-77, supt., Wood River, Ill., 1977-79, sr. staff economist, Houston, 1980; dir. employee relations Superior Oil Co., Houston, 1980-82, v.p., mem. mgmt. com., chmn. investment com., 1981-85; ptnr. Chancellor Properties, Houston, 1985—. Bd. dirs. ARC, Alton, Ill., 1979—; v.p. Ginger Creek Civic Assn., Edwardsville, Ill., 1977-79; life col. La. Gov.'s staff Gov., 1982. Mem. Tex. Assn. Bus. (life), Houston Livestock and Rodeo Assn. (life), Forum Club. Republican. Methodist. Clubs: Houston, Pine Forest Country. Home: 13831 Pinerock Ln Houston TX 77079 Office: Chancellor Properties 1616 Voss Suite 250 Houston TX 77057

RICE, THOMAS JAMES, III, health care executive, hospital administrator; b. Richmond, Va., Mar. 1, 1952; s. Thomas James, Jr. and Betty Larus (Morrissette) R.; m. Linda Kay Beaver, May 29, 1976; children—Kathryn Anne, Thomas Johnathan, Michael Benjamin. B.A. in English, Coll. William and Mary, 1974, M.B.A., 1976; M.H.A., Med. Coll. Va., 1978. Sales interpreter Colonial Williamsburg Found., Va., 1972-76; evening supr. Petersburg Gen. Hosp., Va., 1977-78; v.p. Health East, Inc., Roanoke, Va., 1978—; asst. adminstr. Wythe County Community Hosp., Wytheville, Va., 1978—; asst. adminstr. Wythe County Community Hosp., Wytheville, Va., 1978-79; adminstr. Lonesome Pine Hosp., Big Stone Gap, Va., 1979-85, Southside Community Hosp., Farmville, Va., 1985—; mem sub-area council Planning Dist. II, S.W. Va. Health Services Agy., also dir.; treas. Chpt. 10 Mental Health and Mental Retardation Bd.; bd. dirs., mem. personnel com. Holston Mental Health Agy.; advisor Heritage Hall Health Care Agy.; v.p., dir. S.W. Va. Emergency Med. Services Council, Inc. Treas., mem. vestry Christ Episcopal Ch., Big Stone Gap; mem. exec. com. S.W. Va. Episcopal Diocese; trainer Powell Valley High Sch. Football; bd. dirs. Norton Community Bloodbank, Va. Mem. Va. Hosp. Assn., S.W. Va. Hosp. Council (v.p.), Va. Hosp. Assn., Am. Coll. Hosp. Adminstrs., Appalachia Downtown Bus. Assn. Lodge: Kiwanis. Avocations: Sailing; tennis; golf; photography; skiing. Office: Southside Community Hosp 800 Oak St Farmville VA 23901

RICE, WILLIAM VAUGHN, JR., air force officer, educator; b. Hiawassee, Ga., Dec. 5, 1926; s. William Vaughn and Anne Julia (O'Quinn) R.; B.S., U.S. Mil. Acad., 1949; M.B.A., USAF Inst. Tech., 1958; Ph.D., La. State U., 1974; m. Claire L. Mikulin, Aug. 24, 1950; children—Michael D., William Vaughn III, Tamara Anne. Commd. 2d lt. USAF, 1949, advanced through grades to col., 1967; air crew mem. SAC, 1950-57; ednl. adviser Republic of Korea Air Acad., Seoul, 1958-59; asst. prof. aerospace studies La. State U., 1960-66; sr. instr. Acad. Instr. Sch., Air U., Montgomery, Ala., 1967-68, chief, labor-mgmt. relations div., 1969-75; instr. econs. Troy State U. Adult Edn. Program, 1966-75; asst. prof. econs. and mgmt. U. Houston at Clear Lake City, Tex., 1975-78, asso. prof., 1978-82, prof., 1982—, also dir. Center for Econ. Edn. Mem. Am., So. econ. assns., Air Force Assn., Omicron Delta Epsilon. Mason. Author: Introduction to Air Force Labor Relations, Vol. I, 1971; Supersimulation, 1983. Contbr. articles to profl. jours. Address: 2700 Bay Area Blvd Houston TX 77058

RICE, WINSTON EDWARD, lawyer; b. Shreveport, La., Feb. 22, 1946; s. Winston Churchill and Margaret (Coughlin) R.; student Centenary Coll. La., 1967; J.D., La. State U., 1971; m. Barbara Reily Gay, Apr. 16, 1977; 1 son, Andrew Hynes; children by previous marriage—Winston Hobson, Christian MacTaggart. Bar: La. Cons. geologist Crosby Mineral Co., Gulfport, Miss., 1968-70; ptnr. Phelps, Dunbar, Marks, Claverie & Sims, New Orleans, 1971—; instr. law La. State U., Baton Rouge, 1970-71. Mem. ABA (vice-chmn. com. on admiralty and maritime law 1979—), La. Bar Assn., New Orleans Bar Assn., New Orleans Assn. Def. Counsel, Maritime Law Assn. U.S. (chmn. subcom. on offshore exploration and devel.), Assn. Average Adjusters U.S., Assn. Average Adjusters (U.K.), Southeastern Admiralty Law Inst., Order of Coif, Phi Delta Phi, Phi Kappa Phi, Kappa Alpha. Republican. Episcopalian. Clubs: Mariners of Port of New Orleans (treas. 1974-75, 78-79, sec. 1975-76, v.p. 1976-77, pres. 1977-78), Boston, Stratford, Bayou Racquet, Mariners (Houston and New Orleans), Petroleum (New Orleans); Coral Beach and Tennis (Bermuda). Asso. editor La. Law Rev., 1970-71. Home: 204 Robinhood St Covington LA 70433 Office: 30th Floor Texaco Ctr 400 Poydras St New Orleans LA 70130

RICH, CLAYTON, university administrator; b. N.Y.C., May 21, 1924; s. Clayton Eugene and Leonore (Elliot) R.; m. Mary Bell Hodgkinson, Dec. 19, 1953 (div. May 2, 1974); 1 son, Clayton Greig.; m. Carolyn Sue Miller, Apr. 8, 1982. Grad., Putney Sch., 1942; student, Swarthmore Coll., 1942-44; M.D., Cornell U., 1948. Diplomate Am. Bd. Internal Medicine. Intern Albany (N.Y.) Hosp., 1948-49, asst. resident, 1950-51; research asst. Cornell U. Med. Coll., 1949-50; asst. Rockefeller U., 1953-58, asst. prof., 1958-60; asst. prof. medicine U. Wash. Sch. Medicine, 1960-62, assoc. prof., 1962-67, prof. 1967-71, assoc. dean, 1968-71; chief radioisotope service VA Hosp., Seattle, 1960-70, assoc. chief staff, 1962-71, chief staff, 1968-70; v.p. med. affairs, dean Sch. Medicine; prof. medicine Stanford U., 1971-79, Carl and Elizabeth Naumann prof., 1977-79; chief staff Stanford U. Hosp., 1971-77, chief exec. officer, 1977-79; sr. scholar Inst. Medicine, Nat. Acad. Sci., Washington, 1979-80; Mem. gen. medicine B study sect. NIH, 1969-73, chmn., 1972-73; mem. spl. med. adv. group VA, 1977-81; provost U. Okla., Oklahoma City, 1980—, v.p. for health scis., 1983—, also exec. dean, prof., 1980-83. Editorial bd.: Calcified Tissue Research, 1966-72, Clin. Orthopedics, 1967-72, Jour. Clin. Endocrinology and Metabolism, 1971-72; Contbr. numerous articles to med. jours. Bd. dirs. Children's Hosp. at Stanford, Stanford U. Hosp., 1974-79; chmn. Gordon Research Conf. Chemistry, Physiology and Structure of Bones and Teeth, 1967; bd. dirs., exec. Com. Okla. Med. Research Inst. Served to lt. USNR, 1951-53. Fellow ACP; mem. Assn. Am. Physicians, Western Assn. Physicians, Am. Soc. Mineral and Bone Research (adv. bd. 1977-80), Am. Soc. Clin. Investigation, Assn. Am. Med. Colls. (exec. council 1975-79), Inst. of Medicine, Western Soc. Clin. Research (v.p. 1967-68), Endocrine Soc., Sigma Xi, Alpha Omega Alpha. Home: 115 Lake Aluma Dr Oklahoma City OK 73121 Office: Provost Office U Okla Oklahoma City OK 73190

RICH, GARY CLAYTON, business executive; b. Jacksonville, Fla., Apr. 2, 1950; s. Charles Franklin and Alma Janelle (Coggin) R.; m. Deborah Ann Nunes, Apr. 13, 1985. A.A., N. Fla. Jr. Coll., 1970; B.A., U. W. Fla., 1972. Ops. mgr. Ryder Systems, Jacksonville, Fla., 1972-76; regional distbn. mgr. Duracell, U.S.A., Jacksonville, 1976—. Mem. Am. Mgmt. Assn., Nat. Council Profl. Distbn. Mgrs., Southside Businessmen's Club, Jacksonville C. of C. (com. of 100), Pi Kappa Alpha. Club: Sertoma. Home: 10908 Great Southern Dr Jacksonville FL 32223 Office: Durcell USA 6805 Southpoint Pkwy Jacksonville FL 32216

RICH, HELEN WALL (MRS. ARTHUR L. RICH), educator; b. Chester, S.C., May 4, 1912; d. George Addison and Georgia (Hardin) Wall; student Queen's Coll., 1930-32; B.S. summa cum laude, Catawba Coll., 1934 diploma in piano Juilliard Sch. Music, 1938; diplomas Christiansen Choral Sch., 1950, 51; m. Arthur Lowndes Rich, July 26, 1934; children—Arthur Lowndes, Ruth Anne. Instr. music Catawba Coll.; Salisbury, N.C., 1934-43; organist Mercer U., Macon, Ga., 1944-50, asst. prof. music, 1950-74, emeritus prof., 1974—; organ recitalist throughout Southeast; v.p. Tudor Apts., Atlanta, 1960-68; sec.-treas. Richelieu Apts., Macon, 1955-68. Mem. Federated Music Clubs (chmn. scholarship contest), Ga. Piano Tchrs. Guild, Nat. Assn. Schs. Music (asso.), Am. Coll. and U. Concert Mgrs. Assn. (asso.), Cardinal Key Soc. Mercer U. (hon.), Delta Omicron. Club: Morning Music (dir.) (Macon). Home: 369 Candler Dr Macon GA 31204

RICH, WAYNE ADRIAN, retired lawyer; b. Piner, Ky., Aug. 8, 1912; s. Shirley S. and Edna Jane (Mann) R.; m. Ellen Peters, Sept. 4, 1937 (dec. Dec., 1966); children—Wayne A., Ellen Randolph Williams; m. Frances Runyan, Oct. 4, 1968; 1 stepchild, Charles Hamilton West. A.B., U. Cin., 1935; J.D., Harvard U., 1938. Bar: W.Va., U.S. Supreme Ct., U.S. Tax Ct. Sole practice law, Charleston, W.Va., 1938-77, ret., 1977—; dir. City Nat. Bank, Charleston, 1956-77, pres., 1967-68, chmn. bd., trust officer, 1968-77. Mem. Kanawha Juvenile Council, Charleston, 1955-62; bd. dirs. Kanawha Welfare Council, 1957-63; trustee Greater Kanawha Valley Found., 1968-77; mem. City Council, Charleston, 1955-59, Municipal Planning Commn., Charleston, 1962-77. Served to comdr. USN, 1943-46. Mem. W.Va. State Bar Assn., Kanawha County Bar Assn. (v.p. 1953, 59), Tau Kappa Alpha, Omicron Delta Kappa, Sigma Chi. Republican. Presbyterian. Club: Kingsmill Golf (Williamsburg). Avocation: golf. Home: 12 Ensigne Spence Williamsburg VA 23185

RICHARD, ADRINA, university administrator; b. New Rochelle, N.Y., Mar. 25, 1947; d. Aram and Hermine (Hovanessian) Grayson; m. Lee Donald Richard, Apr. 5, 1969; children—Melanie Helene, Aram David. A.B., Ga. State U., 1965-69, postgrad. 1970, 73. Mgr., Books Can., Ottawa, Ont., 1970-73; asst. mgr. B. Dalton Bookseller, Atlanta, 1973-74; mgr. bookstore Oglethorpe U., Atlanta, 1974-85, dir. purchasing, 1983-85, dir. auxiliary services, 1985—. Bd. dirs. Armenian Ind. Cultural Orgn. of Atlanta, 1981, 82, 85-86. Mem. Ga. Assn. Coll. Stores (program chmn. 1976-77, sec., treas. 1977-78, pres. 1978-79, edn. com. 1984, 85), Nat. Assn. Coll. Stores (diploma mgmt. seminar), Nat. Assn. Ednl. Buyers, Nat. Assn. Purchasing Mgmt., Nat. Assn. Coll. Aux. Services. Avocations: piano; reading; real estate investing. Office: Oglethorpe Univ 4484 Peachtree Rd Atlanta GA 30319

RICHARD, DARLENE DOLORAS, advertising manager, marketing firm executive; b. Mansfield, Ohio, Jan. 4, 1946; d. Charles Alvertis and Marjorie Elaine (Foster) Swander; m. David Allen Richard, Aug. 14, 1965 (div.). A.A., Famous Artist Sch., 1964; B.A. in Edn., Ohio State U., 1969. Asst. to controller Johnstown Properties, Atlanta, 1978-79, adminstrv. mgr. TCG Communications, Atlanta, 1979; promotional dir. Am. Health Cons., Atlanta, 1979-82; pres. Direct Mktg./R&D, Ltd., Atlanta, 1982—, Georgia Fed. Bank, Atlanta, 1985—. Mem. Newsletter Assn. Am., Atlanta Ad Club, Nat. Assn. Female Execs., AAUW, Am. Mgmt. Assn., Internat. Oceanographic Found. Republican. Address: Direct Marketing/R&D Peachtree Park Dr NE Suite 0-1 Atlanta GA 30309 and Georgia Fed Bank 20 Marietta St Atlanta GA 30303

RICHARD, ROBERT ALAN, architect; b. Miami, Fla., Oct. 11, 1946; s. Robert Sowers and Pauline Juel (Flaten) R.; B.Arch., U. Fla., 1970; m. Shirley F. Hendry, Aug. 19, 1967; children—Robert Alan, Lisa Michelle. Staff architect First Planning Internat. Co., Miami, 1975; staff architect SKBB Architects, Coral Gables, Fla., 1975-76; propr. Robert A. Richard Assos., Miami, 1976-78; chief architect Gen. Devel. Corp., Miami, 1978-83, also chmn. innovative design com.; ptnr. Greenberg & Richard Architects & Planners, Coral Gables, 1983—; prin. works include Oakwood Villas Townhouses, Port Malabar, Fla., 1981, Faith United Meth. Ch., Miami, 1980, Villas of Village Green Townhouses, Port St. Lucie, Fla., 1981, Country Club Vistas Townhouses, Port Malabar, 1980, Fifth Rib Restaurant, Miami, 1981, Camelot Housing Project Bonvaventure, Sunrise, Fla., 1983, also pvt. residences. Mem. AIA, Builders Assn. S. Fla., Urban Land Inst., Constrn. Specifications Inst., Am. Planning Assn. Lutheran. Home: 13111 SW 83d St Miami FL 33183 Office: 4111 Laguna St Coral Gables FL 33146

RICHARD, ROGER PAUL, international freight forwarder, customhouse broker; b. New Orleans, Sept. 28, 1941; s. William and Una Marie (Gremillion) R.; m. Jeanette Randon, Nov. 9, 1963; children—Roger Paul, Mark Michael. Student Loyola U., New Orleans, 1959-60, 61, U. New Orleans, 1971, 72, U. Colo., 1974. Br. mgr. Schenkers Internat. Forwarders, New Orleans, 1964-69; v.p. First Nat. Bank of Commerce, New Orleans, 1969-74; exec. v.p., dir. Quast & Co., Inc., New Orleans, 1974—; pres. Intership of La., Inc., New Orleans, 1977—; v.p., dir. S.T.O.W., Inc., Chgo., 1981—. Served with USAF, 1960-66. Mem. New Orleans Traffic and Transp. Bur. (2d v.p., dir. 1974—), World Trade Club Greater New Orleans (pres. 1973, Outstanding Mem. award 1979), Miss. Valley World Trade Conf. (past gen. chmn.), Miss. Valley World Trade Council (past pres.), Internat. House (dir. 1973), Internat. Trade Mart (dir. 1973), New Orleans and River Region C. of C., Latin-Am. C. of C. (dir. 1980), Sugar Equipment and Service Exporters Assn. U.S. (treas. 1975), Pont chartrain Shores Civic Assn. Republican. Roman Catholic. Office: Quast & Co Inc 2445 Aberdeen St Kenner LA 70062

RICHARDS, ALYS PRICE, personnel assistant; b. Fort Worth, Nov. 12, 1937; d. Duel Robert and Wilene (Wilson) Price; m. George Arthur Richards, Aug. 13, 1960; children—Lyn Ann, George Arthur II. B.A., So. Meth. U., 1960. Cert. tchr., Tex. Elem. tchr. Dallas Ind. Sch. Dist., 1960-62, 65-66; mgr., owner Green & Price Co., Italy, Tex., 1972-80; bus. mgr. Dr. George Richards, Richardson, Tex., 1980—; owner, mgr. farm, Italy, Tex., 1975—; personnel asst. So. Meth. U., Dallas, 1982—, worker's compensation coordinator, 1983-84, coordinator spl. events, 1984—. Bd. dirs. Dallas County Dental Aux.; pres. Richardson Symphony Orch. (Tex.), 1979-80, Richardson Symphony Orch. Guild, 1971-73, Tex. Women's Assn. for Symphony Orch., 1976-77; mem. adminstrv. bd., chmn. council on ministries 1st United Methodist Ch., Richardson. Recipient Five-Yr. award, 1976, Ten-Yr. award, 1981, both Richardson Symphony Orch.; Cert. of Appreciation, Exchange Club, 1982. Mem. Alpha Delta Pi (pres. 1968-69), Zeta Phi Eta. Clubs: Prairie Greek Garden (pres. 1976-77), Criterion Book (pres. 1977-78), Mustang, So. Meth. U. Faculty, Richardson Woman's. Home: 4 Forest Park Dr Richardson TX 75080 Office: So Meth U Dallas TX 75275

RICHARDS, ANN WILLIS, state treasurer; b. Waco, Tex., Sept. 1, 1933; d. R. Cecil and Ona Willis; m. David R. Richards; children—Cecile, Dan, Clark, Ellen. B.A., Baylor U., 1954; teaching cert. U. Tex., 1955. Tchr. govt. and history Austin Ind. Sch. Dist. (Tex.), 1955-57; adminstrv. asst. to Tex. State Rep. Sarah Weddington, 1973-75; co-commr. Travis County, Tex., 1977-82;

state treas. Tex., 1983—; mem. Pres.'s Adv. Com. on Women, 1978-80, Tex. Criminal Justice Adv. Bd., 1981-82, Spl. Com. on Delivery of Human Services in Tex., 1979-80; chmn. Tex. State Depository Bd., 1983—; mem. Tex. State Banking Bd., 1983—. Mem. Travis County Dem. Party; mem. Austin Transp. Study, 1977-82. Recipient Woman of Yr. award Women in Communications, 1978; One of Austin's Ten Most Influential Citizens award Austin Am.-Statesman, 1978; Outstanding Woman of Central Tex. award AAUW, 1979; Woman of Yr. award Tex. Women's Polit. Caucus, 1981. Mem. Nat. Assn. State Treas.', Nat. Assn. Unclaimed Property Adminstrs., nat. Women's Polit. Caucus. Club: Sierra. Democrat. Office: State Treasurer PO Box 12404 Captiol Sta Austin TX 78711

RICHARDS, CURTIS VANCE, fire chief; b. Quail, Tex., Nov. 30, 1932; s. Elbert and Connie M. R.; m. Wanda Ann Richards, June 5, 1955; children—Rodney, Randy, Sheree. A.A., Amarillo Coll. Firefighter Amarillo Fire Dept., Tex., 1954-57, driver, 1957-63, lt., 1963-65, capt., 1965-73, fire chief, 1973—. Served with USAF, 1951-52. Democrat. Lodge: Kiwanis. Home: 2212 S Harrison St Amarillo TX 79109 Office: Amarillo Fire Dept 400 S Van Buren St Amarillo TX 79101

RICHARDS, GEORGE ARTHUR, dentist; b. Payette, Idaho, Oct. 9, 1938; s. Fred F. and Dorothy L. (Taylor) R.; m. Alys Janice Price, Nov. 12, 1937; children—Lyn Ann, George A. B.S., So. Meth. U., 1959; D.D.S., Baylor U., 1963. Assoc. prof. dept. removable prosthodontics Baylor U. Coll. Dentistry, Dallas, 1965-77; gen. practice dentistry, Richardson, Tex., 1965—, Dallas, 1982—. Pres. Richardson Symphony Orch., 1977-78. Served to capt. Dental Corps, U.S. Army, 1963-65. Fellow Internat. Coll. Dentists; mem. Dallas County Dental Soc. (pres. 1983-84), Greater Dallas Dental Research Group (past pres.), Tex. Dental Assn. (del.), ADA (del.), Pierre Fauchard Dental Soc. (hon.), Xi Psi Phi, Omicron Kappa Upsilon. Methodist. Club: Mustang (Dallas). Lodges: Masons, Shriners. Home: 4 Forest Park Dr Richardson TX 75080 Office: 8600 NW Plaza Dr Suite 3A Dallas TX 75225

RICHARDS, GEORGE LEROY, exploration geologist; b. El Paso, Tex., July 18, 1926; s. George Eaton and Mamie (Oden) R.; m. Ann Carlin, Sept. 3, 1948; children—Julie McNeil, Jack C. B.S., U. Tex.-El Paso, 1948. Cert. petroleum geologist, Tex. Dist. geologist Standard Oil Co. Tex., Houston, 1948-64; sr. v.p. Coastal Corp. Houston, 1964-78; exploration mgr. Bright & Co., Dallas, 1978—. Served with USNR, 1944-46. Mem. Am. Assn. Petroleum Geologists, Am. Inst. Profl. Geologists (mem. rep. dist. II). Republican. Presbyterian. Clubs: San Antonio, San Antonio Petroleum; Houston Petroleum. Avocations: boating; water skiing. Home: Route 5 Box 637 New Braunfels TX 78130 Office: Bright & Co 8918 Tesuro Dr 575 San Antonio TX 78217

RICHARDS, JANET LEACH, lawyer, educator; b. Somerville, Tenn., Jan. 19, 1948; d. Wilmer Homer and Loraine Lottie (Robertson) Leach; m. William Michael Richards, Mar. 6, 1976; children—Jamie, Robert. B.S., Memphis State U., 1969, J.D., 1976. Bar: Tenn. 1976, U.S. Dist. Ct. (we. dist.) Tenn. 1976. Stewardess, methods analyst Delta Airlines, Atlanta, 1969-74; assoc. J.B. Cobb & Assocs., Memphis, 1976-78; asst. prof., asst. dean students affairs Memphis State Law Sch., 1978-1980, assoc. prof., 1981—, assoc. dean, 1986—. Recipient Sam A. Myar, Jr. Meml. award for Outstanding Young Lawyer in Memphis. Mem. Memphis and Shelby County Bar Assn. (pres. Young Lawyers' 1981, bd. dirs. 1980-81, 83-84), Memphis State Law Alumni Assn. Home: 1605 Vinton Memphis TN 38104 Office: Memphis State U Sch Law Memphis TN 38152

RICHARDS, JOE EDWARD, health care consultant; b. S. Charleston, W.Va., July 31, 1947; s. Guy Edward and Margaret Jane (Gray) R.; m. Barbara Jean Evans, Aug. 11, 1971 (div.); m. Janet Louise Knudson, Feb. 4, 1982. B.A., W.Va. State Coll., 1976; postgrad. Marshall U., 1976, 82, 83, W.Va. Coll., 1981. Chief research and devel. Office Emergency Med. Services, W.Va. Dept. Health, 1977-81, dir. regulatory services div., 1981-82, dir. cert. of need, 1983-84; mgr. health care cons. Ernst & Whinney, Charleston, 1984—; adminstrv. law cons.; adj. instr. health law and legis. W.Va. Inst. Tech. Dist. chmn., bd. dirs. Buckskin council Boy Scouts Am.; bd. dirs. W.Va. Easter Seal Soc. Served with USAF, 1966-69. Decorated Nat. Def. medal. Mem. Sigma Xi. Democrat. Presbyterian. Developed and implemented statewide emergency med. services mgmt. info. system, 1981. Home: 1134 Oakmont Rd Charleston WV 25314 Office: 716 Charleston National Plaza Charleston WV 25330

RICHARDS, LEONARD MARTIN, investment executive, consultant; b. Phila., June 4, 1935; s. Leonard Martin and Marion Clara (Lang) R.; m. Phyllis Janelle Mowrey, Aug. 26, 1961 (div. Aug. 1978); children—Lisa, David Reed. B.S., Pa. State U., 1957; M.B.A., Wharton Sch., U. Pa., 1963. Asst. to sr. ptnr. Van Cleef, Jordan & Wood, N.Y.C., 1963-68; v.p., portfolio mgr. Bernstein-Macaulay, Inc., N.Y.C., 1968-72; ptnr. G. H. Walker, Laird Co., N.Y.C., 1972-74; v.p., trust officer Republic Bank N.A., Dallas, 1974-77; v.p. investments Variable Annuity Life Ins. Co., Houston, 1977—; dir., pres. L.M. Richards & Co., Houston. Bd. dirs. Sand Dollar Youth Ctr., Houston, 1985—. Served as capt. U.S. Army, 1958-64. Fellow Fin. Analysts Fedn.; mem. Houston Soc. Fin. Analysts. Republican. Avocations: tennis, travel, scuba. Home: 9023 Briar Forest Dr Houston TX 77024 Office: Variable Annuity Life Ins Co 2929 Allen Pkwy Houston TX 77019

RICHARDS, MERLON FOSS, retired diversified technical services company executive; b. Farmington, Utah, May 18, 1920; s. Ezra Foss and Mertie Malinda (Hunt) R.; B.S., U. Utah, 1942; M.B.A., Harvard U., 1947; m. Caryle Jane Vandenberg, July 18, 1945; children—Craig M., Cathy Jean, Cynthia Jane, Julie Ann. Public acct. Arthur Andersen & Co., Chgo., 1947-52, asst. treas. to exec. v.p., 1952-59; from v.p. vice chmn. and chief exec. officer Dynalectron Corp., Washington, 1959-85, dir., mem. exec. and audit com., 1961—. Served to maj. F.A., AUS, 1942-46; ETO. Decorated Bronze Star, Silver Star. C.P.A., Ill. Mem. Pi Kappa Alpha. Republican. Mem. Ch. Jesus Christ of Latter-day Saints. Club: Kenwood Country (Bethesda, Md.). Home: 5502 Newington Rd Bethesda MD 20816 Office: 1313 Dolley Madison Blvd McLean VA 22101

RICHARDS, PAMELA MOTTER, lawyer; b. Columbus, Ohio, Feb. 24, 1950; d. L. Clair and Mildred Jo (Williams) Motter; m. John W. Richards, II, Mar. 1, 1975 (div. 1984); children—Christine Elizabeth, Teresa Jo. B.A., DePauw U., 1972; J.D., Ohio No. U., 1975. Bar: Ga. 1975. Assoc., Cowart, Varner & Harrington, Warner Robins, Ga., 1977-82; ptnr. Cowart, Varner, Harrington & Richards, Warner Robins, 1982-83, Cowart, Varner & Richards, 1983-84; sole practice, 1984—. Bd. dirs., sec. Kids Stuff Learning Ctrs. of Am., Warner Robins, 1983—, Warner Robins Day Care Ctr., 1976-80, Am. Cancer Soc., 1981—; v.p. Warner Robins C. of C., 1981-82, dir., 1980-82; bd. dirs., chmn. Hospice of Houston County, Inc., 1985; bd. dirs. Houston County Assn. Exceptional Children, 1985—. Mem. State Bar of Ga., Houston County Bar Assn., ABA. Club: Civitan. Office: PO Box 3044 Warner Robins GA 31099

RICHARDS, PATRICIA POOLE, automobile dealership manager; b. Greenville, S.C., June 29, 1953; d. Lushion Norwood and Cecillia Florence (Stowe) Poole; m. Christopher Jay Richards, May 16, 1976 (div.). B.A., Greenville Inst. Tech., 1973. Bus. mgr. Marion Burnside Chrysler-Plymouth, Columbia, S.C., 1973-79, Columbia Chrysler-Plymouth, 1979-80, Moore-Hudson Olds, 1980-83, Minyard Datsun-Volvo, Greenville, 1983—; cons. Timmerman Datsun, Aiken, S.C., 1981-83. Mem. Volvo Bus. Mgrs., Datsun Bus. Mgmt., Gen. Motors Bus. Mgrs., Chrysler Bus. Mgrs. Republican. Episcopalian. Home: 91 Jamestowne Commons Taylors SC 29687

RICHARDSON, C(ARL) LEIGH, employee benefit plan design and implementation company executive; b. Norfolk, Va., July 16, 1945; s. Carl Blueford and Edith Lewis (Lacy) R.; m. Shanna Griggs, Aug. 16, 1969; children—Shanna Leigh, Jennifer Stacy, John Paul Carr, Heather Lacy, Todd Neal Lewis, Kelly Lee. B.S. in Psychology, Va. Poly. Inst., 1968; cert. in bus. ins. La. State U. Inst. Ins. Mktg., 1973; grad. Life Underwriting Tng. Council, Washington, 1973. Agt. Fidelity Union Life Ins. Co., Norfolk, 1969-71, gen. agt., mgr., 1971-74, personal producing gen. agt., Virginia Beach, Va., 1974-75; life ins. agt. New Eng. Mut. Life, Norfolk, 1975-77; dist. agt. Union Mut. Life Ins. Co., Norfolk, 1977-81; pres. Leigh Co., Norfolk, 1981—. Exhibited paintings in art shows, Va., 1968—. Mem. Republican Nat. Com., Washington; football ofcl. Va. High Sch. League, Norfolk, Eastern Va. Ofcls. Assn., Virginia Beach. Recipient Nat. Quality award Life Ins. Mktg. and Research Assn., 1974, 75, 83. Mem. Nat. Assn. Life Underwriters (nat. sales achievement award 1972-76); qualifying mem. Million Dollar Round Table 1973, 74, 75, 76, 83-84), Va. Assn. Life Underwriters, Norfolk Life Underwriters Assn. (moderator Life Underwriter Tng. Council 1977, 78, 84), Union Mut. Life Ins. Co. Pres. Club. Baptist. Home: 769 Brinson Arch Virginia Beach VA 23455 Office: Leigh Co 2 Koger Exec Ctr Suite 16 PO Box 12597 Norfolk VA 23502

RICHARDSON, DOROTHY VIRGINIA, controller; b. Bennington, Okla., Sept. 26, 1937; d. William Lycurgus and Mittie Mae (Richardson) Ray; m. Charles Howard Richardson, Dec. 28, 1958; children—Charles Timothy, Michael Todd. Student Eastern Okla. A&M, 1955-56; B.B.A., U. Alaska, 1974. Asst. acct. Peat, Marwick, Mitchell & Co., Omaha, 1975-76; gen. acct. U. Alaska Statewide System, Fairbanks, 1976; asst. bus. mgr. Geophys. Inst., Fairbanks, 1976-77; dir. grant and contract services U. Alaska, Fairbanks, 1977-80; controller Alaska Legal Services Corp., Anchorage, 1980-81; bus. mgr. div. community colls., rural edn. and extension U. Alaska, 1981-84; assoc. controller U. Fla., Gainesville, 1984—. Active Cub Scouts, Mothers March of Dimes, PTA. Served with USAF, 1957-59. Mem. Am. Soc. Women Accts., Am. Woman's Soc. C.P.A.s, Alaska State Soc. C.P.A.s, Am. Inst. C.O.A.s (bd. dirs.), Soc. Research Adminstrs. Lodge: Soroptimists.

RICHARDSON, EMILIE WHITE, manufacturing company executive, investment company executive, lecturer; b. Chattanooga, July 8; d. Emmett and Mildred Evelyn (Harbin) White; B.A., Wheaton Coll., 1951; 1 child, Julie Richardson Morphis. With Christy Mfg. Co., Inc., Fayetteville, N.C., 1952—, sec. 1956-66, v.p., 1967-74, exec. v.p., 1975-79, pres., chief exec. officer, 1980—; v.p. E. White Investment Co., 1968-83, pres., 1983—; cons. Aerostatic Industries, 1979—; v.p. Gannon Corp., 1981—; cons. govt. contacts and offshore mfg., 1981—. Vice pres. public relations Ft. Lauderdale Symphony Soc., 1974-76, v.p. membership, 1976-77, adv. bd., 1978—; active Atlantic Found., Ft. Lauderdale Mus. Art, Beaux Arts, Freedoms Found.; mem. E. Broward Women's Republican Club, 1968—, Americanism chmn., 1971-72. Mem. Internat. Platform Assn., Nat. Speakers Assn., Fla. Speakers Assn. Presbyterian. Clubs: Toastmasters, Green Valley Country. Home: 151 NE 51st St Fort Lauderdale FL 33334 Office: PO Box 35375 Fayetteville NC 28303

RICHARDSON, ERNESTINE GORDON, educator, coach; b. Whigham, Ga., Dec. 13, 1930; d. Johnny and Eunice (Strange) Gordon; m. Robert Earl Richardson, June 25, 1955; children—Fert R., Rebecca Richardson Sanders, LaVerne Richardson Murphy. B.S., Savannah State Coll., 1951; M.Ed., Fla. A&M U., 1960. Cert. tchr. phys. edn. and social studies, Ga. Tchr., coach Attapulgus High Sch., Ga., 1951-54; tchr., basketball coach Attapulgus-Mt. Moriah High Sch., 1954-65; girls' basketball coach Havanah Northside High Sch., Fla., 1975—. Named Coach of Yr., Gulf Coast Athletic Conf., 1979-80, 81, 82, 84, 85, Tchr. of Yr., Havana Northside High Sch., 1983-84. Mem. Fla. Teaching Profession, Classroom Tchrs.' Assn. (sec.-treas. 1970-73), Fla. Coaches' Assn., Am. Assn. Health, Recreation and Dance, Am. Legion Aux. Democrat. Methodist. Club: Fam U Boosters (Tallahassee, Fla.). Home: 214 First St SE Havana FL 32333 Office: Havana Northside High Sch PO Box 618 Havana FL 32333

RICHARDSON, GORDON BANNING, insurance company executive, investment consultant; b. N.Y.C., May 19, 1937; s. Ogden Barker and May Thistle (Shirres) R.; m. Judy Carolyn Williams, May 7, 1966; children—Gordon Banning II, Randall S. Student Ashbury Coll., Ottawa, Ont., Can., 1956; B.S. in Bus. Adminstrn., Boston U., 1962; C.L.U., Am. Coll., 1974. Owner, pres. Ins. Assocs., Caldwell, Tex., 1968—. County chmn. Republican party; mem. Tex. Commn. on Blind Made Products, 1982—, Tex. Film Commn., 1983—. Recipient Hon. State Farmer award Future Farmers Am., 1975. Mem. Tex. Assn. Life Underwriters (v.p. legis.), Confederate Air Force. Baptist. Lodge: Lions (dist. gov. 1981-82).

RICHARDSON, MOZELLE GRONER, author; b. Hereford, Tex., Jan. 26, 1914; d. Grover Cleveland and Jessie Leah (Head) Groner; student E. Tex. Bapt. Coll., 1930-33, Central State U., Edmond, Okla., 1967-69, Okla. U., 1969-71; m. William T. Richardson, Aug. 25, 1939; children—William T., Judy Richardson Markley, Susan Ann Richardson Gumerson, Rock Grover. Novels include: The Curse of Kalispoint, 1971, Portrait of Fear, 1971, Masks of Thespis, 1973, Candle in the Wind, 1973, The Song of India, 1975, Daughter of the Sacred Mountain, 1977; speaker to writer-related groups, high schs. Recipient Writer's award Okla. U., 1973. Mem. Mystery Writers Am., Authors Guild, PEN. Democrat. Home: 1611 Guilford Ln Oklahoma City OK 73120

RICHARDSON, ROBERT RICHMOND, lawyer; b. Atlanta, July 29, 1927; s. Leaver and Virginia (McLane) R.; m. Mary Anne Wagstaff, June 9, 1948; children—Robert Richmond, Mark W., Vaughan Richardson Cooper. Student, Ga. Inst. Tech., 1944-45; B.A., Emory U., 1948, LL.B., 1950. Bar: Ga. 1950, U.S. Dist. Ct. (all dists.) Ga. 1951, U.S. Ct. Appeals (5th cir.) 1962, U.S. Supreme Ct. 1966, U.S. Ct. Appeals (11th cir.) 1982. Assoc., Gambrell, Harlan & Russell, 1949-54; ptnr. Gambrell, Harlan, Russell, Moye & Richardson, Atlanta, 1954-64, Hurt, Hill & Richardson, Atlanta, 1964-74; sr. ptnr. Hurt, Richardson, Garner, Todd & Cadenhead, Atlanta, 1974—; instr. Ga. State U., 1951-55; dir. So. Turf Nurseries, Inc., Techsteel, Inc. Mem. platform com. Democratic Nat. Conv., 1964; chief staff Gov. of Ga., 1962-66; bd. dirs. Central Atlanta Progress, 1984—. Served to 1st lt. U.S. Army, 1946-47. Fellow Am. Coll. Trial Lawyers, Internat. Assn. Ins. Counsel, ABA, Am. Judicature Soc., Lawyers Club Atlanta, Atlanta C. of C. (dir. 1966-70). Democrat. Episcopalian. Clubs: Piedmont Driving, Atlanta Country, Commerce, World Trade. Office: Suite 1100 233 Peachtree St NE Atlanta GA 30303

RICHARDSON, RUPERT NORVAL, history educator, author; b. nr. Caddo, Tex., Apr. 28, 1891; s. Willie Baker and Nannie (Coon) R.; A.B., Hardin-Simmons U., Abilene, Tex., 1912; Ph.B., U. Chgo., 1914; A.M., U. Tex., 1922, Ph.D., 1928; LL.D., Baylor U., 1982; m. Pauline Mayes, Dec. 28, 1915; 1 son, Rupert Norval. Prin. high sch., Cisco, Tex., 1915-16, Sweetwater, 1916-17; prof. history Hardin-Simmons U., 1917—, dean students, 1926-28, v.p., 1928-38, exec. v.p., 1938-40, acting pres., 1943-45, pres., 1945-53, pres. emeritus, prof., 1953-67, Piper prof., 1963, Distinguished prof., 1967—; assoc. prof., prof. history U. Tex. 8 summers, also 1940-41. Mem. So. Bapt. Edn. Commn., 1952-55; mem. Tex. Hist. Survey Com., 1953-67, pres., 1961-63. Served 2d lt. U.S. Army, 1918. Recipient Cultural Achievement in Lit. award West Tex. C. of C., 1967; Ruth Lester award Tex. Hist. Commn., 1972; award of merit Nat. Assn. State and Local History, 1953, 76; Leadership award Tex. State Hist. Assn., 1976; Citizen of Year award Abilene C. of C., 1975; citation of honor Tex. Soc. Architects, 1978. Fellow Tex. State Hist. Assn. (pres. 1969-70); mem. Tex. Philos. Soc. (pres. 1962-63). Baptist. Mason. Lion (past pres., dist. gov.). Author: The Comanche Barrier to the South Plains Settlement, 1933; (with C. C. Rister) The Greater Southwest, 1934; Texas: the Lone Star State, 1943; Adventuring with a Purpose, 1952; The Frontier of Northwest Texas, 1963; Colonel Edward M. House: The Texas Years, 1964; Famous Are The Halls: Hardwin-Simmons University as I Have Seen It, 1975; Caddo, Texas: The Biography of a Community, 1966; Along Texas Old Forts Trail, Abilene, 1972; This I Remember, 1983. Editor: West Tex. Hist. Assn. Yearbook, 1929—. Contbr. to hist., ednl. publs. Home: 1102 N 19th St Apt 45 Abilene TX 79601

RICHARDSON, THOMAS LYNN, chemical engineer; b. Sheffield, Ala., Apr. 2, 1955; s. Thomas Luther and Opal Agnes (Jackson) R.; m. Marilyn Ward, June 21, 1980; 1 child, Jonathan. B.S. in Chem. Engring., Auburn U., 1979. Engr.-in-tng., Ala. Project and process engr. Monsanto Co., Anniston, Ala., 1979-81; product devel. engr. Fiber Industries Inc., Salisbury, N.C., 1981-82; process engr. Kendall Co., Bethune, S.C., 1982-83; plant engr. Lyndal Chem. Co., Dalton, Ga., 1983—. Recipient Pres.' award, Ala. Soc. Profl. Engrs., 1981. Mem. Am. Soc. Safety Engrs., Nat. Soc. Profl. Engrs. (assoc.), Ga. Soc. Profl. Engrs. (assoc.), Am. Inst. Chem. Engrs. (profl. mem.; profl. devel. cert.). Republican. Mem. Ch. of Christ. Club: Optimist (Dalton). Avocations: amateur radio; tennis; racquetball; bowling. Home: 1809 Shadow Ln Apt 6 Dalton GA 30720 Office: Lyndal Chem Co PO Box 1740 Dalton GA 30722-1740

RICHARDSON, W. DANIEL, real estate consultant and investor; b. Columbia, S.C., Nov. 30, 1953; s. Winfrie Daniel and Louise (Lowman) R.; m. Donna Muhlheizler, Dec. 19, 1981. B.S., U. S.C., 1975. Pres. Winrich Corp., Hope Mills, N.C. and Charleston, S.C., 1981—. Office: W Daniel Richardson PO Box 433 Hope Mills NC 28348

RICHARDSON, WILLIAM ALLEN, JR., state senator; b. Maury County, Tenn., Mar. 20, 1932; married; 8 children. B.S. in Civil Engring., Tenn. Technol. U., 1954; M.A., Harding Grad. Coll., 1961. Registered surveyor. Mem. 89th, 90th, 91st, 92d Tenn. Gen. Assemblies; mem. Tenn. Senate, 1982—. Bd. dirs. Korean Christian Edn. Fund. Recipient commendations from Korean Govt. for service to Korean Orphans, 1970; commendations from Korean Army for promotion of Better Korean-Am. Relationships, 1958. Mem. Tenn. Assn. Surveyors, Jr. Order, Farm Bur. Mem. Churches of Christ. Democrat. Office: Tenn Senate War Meml Bldg Nashville TN 37219*

RICHEY, JAMES POTTER, furniture manufacturing company executive; b. Poughkeepsie, N.Y., Feb. 27, 1929; s. Alban and Lucy Christiana (Rafter) R.; m. Dorothy Lee Davis, Oct. 10, 1953 (div. Oct. 1975); children—Meghan Thorpe, Matthew Potter, Andrew Seabury. Student Bates Coll., Lewiston, Maine, 1946, Bard Coll., 1948-50, George Washington U., 1950-51. Apprentice cabinet maker Albert Wood & Five Sons, Port Washington, N.Y., 1942-44; with retail buying and sales div. J.C. Penney and Hecht Co., 1951-57; with woodworking/furniture prodn., engring. and mgmt. div. Brunswick Corp., 1957-61, Howard Miller Clock, 1961-64, Freedman Artcraft Corp., 1964-69; founder, pres., chief exec. officer Butler Furniture Industries, Inc., Carrollton, Ky., 1970—. Served with USN, 1946-48. Mem. Aircraft Owners and Pilots Assn., Carroll County Mental Retardation Assn. (pres. 1970-74). Democrat. Episcopalian. Club: Jefferson (Louisville). Lodges: Kiwanis, Moose. Home: 502 4th St Carrollton KY 41008 Office: 600 4th St Carrollton KY 41008

RICHEY, RONALD KAY, diversified financial company executive; b. Erie, Kans., June 16, 1926; s. Earle Jacob and Mary Wintress (Oakleaf) R.; m. Florence E. Kane, Nov. 24, 1949; children—Linda, Robert, Christopher. B.A., Washburn U., 1949, LL.B., 1951. Bar: Ill. 1959, Okla. 1965. Vice pres. Central Plains Ins. Group, Hutchinson, Kans., 1955-57; legis. mgr. Am. Mut. Ins. Alliance, Chgo., 1957-64; exec. v.p. Globe Life & Accident Ins. Co., Oklahoma City, 1964-78, chmn. bd., chief exec. officer, 1978-82, chmn. bd., 1978—; pres., dir. Torchmark Corp., Birmingham, Ala., 1982—; chmn. bd. United Am. Ins. Co., Liberty Nat. Life Ins. Co. Served with U.S. Army, 1944-46. Mem. Am. Council Life Ins. Assns., ABA, Okla. Bar Assn., Oklahoma City C. of C. Republican. Methodist. Clubs: Quail Creek Golf and Country (Oklahoma City); Oaktree Golf and Country (Edmond, Okla.); Shoal Creek Golf and Country, Relay House (Birmingham). Office: 2001 3d Ave S Birmingham AL 35233

RICHIE, JACK LEROY, insurance agency official; b. Flint, Mich., Sept. 16, 1934; s. John and Vera (Walt) R.; m. R. Maurine Genshaw, Sept. 13, 1958; children—Jacqueline, Sharon, Robert, Nancy. Student Gen. Motors Inst., 1956-58. C.L.U. Skilled trades trainee Gen. Motors Corp., Flint, 1956-58; sales engr. Hydraulic Supply Co., Flint and Miami, Fla., 1959-66; sales agt. First Fin. Advisors, Miami, 1966-73; gen. agt., owner Richie & Assocs., Miami, 1974—. Ambassador, Life Underwriters Polit. Action Com., 1982-83; active United Way of Dade County, 1983. Served with USAF, 1952-56. Recipient awards including Found. Builder award Midland Mut. Life, Columbus, Ohio, 1981, Winner's Circle Gen. Agts., 1981, Six-Plus award/Full Circle of Success, 1980-82; named Man of Yr., Mich. Life Ins. Co., Southfield, 1969, 73; recruiting and retention award Am. United Life, Indpls., 1976-79, mem. Pres. Club, 1975-80. Mem. Gen. Agts. and Mgrs. Assn. Miami (pres. 1982, dir. 1983), Fla. Gen. Agts. and Mgrs. Assn. (sec.-treas. 1983, recognition agy. mgmt. award Tallahassee, 1982). Republican. Lutheran. Home: 9895 SW 141st St Miami FL 33176 Office: Richie & Assocs 3900 NW 79th Ave Suite 815 Miami FL 33166

RICHMOND, JOHN MELVYN, jewelry company executive; b. Chgo., Feb. 13, 1939; s. Harry and Clarice (Costulas) R.; student pub. schs., Chgo., Los Angeles; m. Dotty Anne Finberg Nov. 28, 1959; children—Kelly, Robyn, Shannan. Salesman Sarong Inc., div. Playtex, Dover, Del., 1964-66; key account coordinator Exquisite Form, Pelham Manor, N.Y., 1964-66; regional mgr., nat. trainer Benrus Corp., Ridgefield, Conn., 1966-70, regional mgr. Wells Inc., div. Benrus Corp., Attleboro, Mass., 1970-74, nat. sales mgr., 1974-75; v.p., nat. sales mgr. Imperial Pearl Syndicate, Chgo., 1975-76; nat. sales mgr., v.p. Gall Fashion Jewelry Co., Dallas, 1977—; pres. JMR Fine Jewelry, 1977—, Classique D'Or Inc., Dallas, Shoe Biz Inc., Auric, Inc.; dir. Town North Nat. Bank, Dallas. Served with U.S. Army, 1958-61. Mem. Retail Jewelers of Am., Jewelers Mfg. Guild. Home and Office: PO Box 172 Carrollton TX 75006

RICHMOND, SAMUEL BERNARD, university dean; b. Boston, Oct. 14, 1919; s. David E. and Freda (Braman) R.; A.B. cum laude, Harvard U., 1940; M.B.A., Columbia U., 1948, Ph.D., 1951; m. Evelyn Ruth Kravitz, Nov. 26, 1944; children—Phyllis Gail, Douglas Emerson, Clifford Owen. Mem. faculty Columbia U., N.Y.C., 1946-76, asso. prof., 1957-60, prof. econs. and stats., 1960-76, asso. dean Grad. Sch. Bus., 1971-72, acting dean, 1972-73; dean Owen Grad. Sch. Mgmt., Vanderbilt U., Nashville, 1976—, Ralph Owen prof. mgmt., 1984—; vis. prof. U. Sherbrooke (Que.), 1967, U. Buenos Aires (Argentina), 1964, 65, Case Inst. Tech., Cleve., 1958-59, Fordham U., N.Y.C., 1952-53; dir. IMS Internat. Inc., N.Y.C., Corbin Ltd., N.Y.C., First Am. Corp., Nashville, Ingram Industries Inc., Nashville, Winners Corp., Nashville; cons. to maj. comml., ednl., profl. and govtl. orgns. Trustee, Ramapo Coll. N.J., 1975-76; bd. govs. Haifa U. Served to 1st lt. USAAF, 1943-45. Recipient Honor award CAB, 1971. Mem. Am. Statis. Assn. (chmn. adv. com. research to CAB 1966-74, dir. 1965-67), Am. Econ. Assn., Inst. Mgmt. Sci., Ops. Research Soc. Am., Beta Gamma Sigma. Author: Operations Research for Management Decisions, 1968; Statistical Analysis, 1957, 2d. edit., 1964; Regulation and Competition in Air Transportation, 1961. Home: 5404 Camelot Rd Brentwood TN 37027 Office: Owen Grad Sch Mgmt Vanderbilt U Nashville TN 37203

RICHTER, JACKIE WILSON, business executive; b. Hornbeck, La., Oct. 30, 1933; d. Jack Caraway Wilson; m. Clyde Joseph Richter; children—Lisa Anne, Clyde Joseph, Sarah Elizabeth; student Nacogdoches Bus. Coll., 1951, Victoria Coll., 1972, Del Mar Coll., 1979-80; cert. in mgmt. Corpus Christi State U., 1980. With R.W. Hill Co., Victoria, Tex., 1952, So. Pacific R.R., 1952-57; co-owner Richter's Precision Air Co., Victoria, 1962—, Intra Coastal Enterprises, Corpus Christi, 1975—. Patron, Harbor Playhouse, Corpus Christi Symphony Guild, Art Mus. S. Tex., Art Community Ctr.; alt. del. Republican State Conv., 1980, del., 1982; v.p. Corpus Christi Rep. Women's Club, 1983, pres., 1984; del. Tex. Fedn. Rep. Women's State Conv., 1983. Recipient Internat. Silver medal Photog. Soc. Am., 1981, Internat. Salon Silver medal, 1983, Endres Silver Medal award, 1981. Mem. C. of C. (women's group; trade with Mex. com. 1982), Refrigeration Service Engrs. Aux. (pres. 1967), Tex. Restaurant Assn., Tex. Retail Grocers Assn., Internat. Platform Assn., DAR (Corpus Christi 2d vice regent 1986), Daus. Am. Colonists (Martha Heron Douglas chpt. sec. 1983-85), Daus. Republic of Tex., Corpus Christi Camera Club (dir. 1981-82). Republican. Lutheran. Photographs pub. in newspapers and mags. Home: 3546 Denver Corpus Christi TX 78411 Office: PO Box 226 909 N Staples St Corpus Christi TX 78403

RICHTER, RANDA SAMUELS, architect; b. St. Louis, June 4, 1954; d. I. David and Sue Rose Samuels; B.A. in Architecture, Washington U., St. Louis, 1976; M.Arch., U. Houston, 1979. Interior architect, space planner Kinetic Systems Co., also R. Fitzgerald Architect, Houston, 1976-80, Ferendino-Grafton-Spillis-Candela, Miami, Fla., 1980; architect Wolfberg-Álvarez-Taracido, lvarez-Taracido, Miami, 1980-81; project architect Baldwin-Sackman & Assocs., Coconut Grove, Fla., 1981-83; owner, prin. Randa L. Samuels, Architects, Miami, 1983—, prin. Samuels Richter Architects. Home: 4474 Nautilus Dr Miami Beach FL 33140

RICHWINE, DAVID ALAN, marine corps officer; b. Oakland, Calif., Oct. 4, 1943; s. David William and Violet Elaine (Cohoon) R.; m. Gayle Lydia Kreutzer, June 30, 1968; children—Heather Louise, Carrie Anne. B.A., U. Kans., 1965; student Basic Sch., 1965, Flight Tng. Sch., 1969-70, Amphibious Warfare Sch., 1973, Air Command and Staff Coll., 1978-79, Nat. War Coll., 1984-85. Commd. 2d lt. U.S. Marine Corps, 1965, advanced through grades to col., 1985; platoon comdr., co. comdr. 3d Bn. 4th Marine regiment, 1966-67, officer selection officer 9th Marine Corps Dist., 1967-69, basic tng. officer fighter/attack tng. Squadron 201, 1970-71, asst. maintenance officer Tng. Squadron 4, 1971-72, Fighter/Attack Squadron 232, 1973-74; standardization officer Fighter/Attack Squadron 212, 1974-76, aide-de-camp to comdg. gen. and plans officer Fleet Marine Force Pacific Hdqrs., 1976-78, comdg. officer Fighter/Attack Squadron 251, Beaufort, S.C., 1980-81, exec. officer Marine Aircraft Group 15, Japan, 1981-82, spl. ops. officer Hdqrs., Arlington, Va., 1982, spl. analyst Office Undersec. Def., Washington, 1983-84, comdg. officer Air Sta., Beaufort, 1985—. Mem. Partnerships in Edn., Beaufort, 1985; mem. Japan-Am. Community Council, Japan, 1981-82; mem. PTA, Burke, Va., 1982-85. Decorated Silver Star, Purple Heart, Defense Meritorious Service medal; recipient Chgo. Tribune award, 1965, DAR award, 1965. Mem. U.S. Marine Corps Assn., U.S. Naval Aviation Mus. Soc., Marine Corps Aviation Assn., Phi Delta Theta. Lodge: Rotary. Avocations: Woodworking; scuba diving; sports; running. Home: 3 Bay Circle Laurel Bay SC 29902 Office: Comdg Officer Marine Corps Air Sta Beaufort SC 29904-5001

RICKENBACHER, TED, publishing executive, printing company owner; b. Fredonia, Kans., Sept. 1, 1936; s. Ted and Lucienne (Hudson) R.; children—Jeff, David, Ann. Student Tex. Christian U., 1955-59. Vice pres., gen. mgr. Fredonia Daily Herald (Kans.), 1960-62, Trinity Publs., Ft. Worth, 1962-69; pres., owner Times-Chronicle Newspapers, Dallas, 1969-80, Rickenbacher Publs., Dallas, 1980—; bd. dirs. Suburban Newspapers Am., Chgo., 1973-79. Trustee Greenhill Sch., Dallas, 1977—. Mem. Am. Mgmt. Assns. (trustee N.Y.C. 1980-83, mgmt. council 1980—), Metrocrest C. of C. (bd. dirs. Dallas County 1974-80). Republican. Episcopalian. Clubs: Rotary (pres. Grapevine 1969, also mem. Carrollton). Office: Rickenbacher Publs PO Box 810195 13950 Distribution Way Dallas TX 75234

RICKERT, DOUGLAS EDWARD, toxicologist, pharmacologist; b. Sioux City, Iowa, Jan. 27, 1946; s. Waldo Henry Herman and Genevieve Lucille (Hahn) R.; m. Sharlene Joyce Nordblom, Sept. 2, 1967 (div. 1979); m. Terrie Sue Baker, June 27, 1981. B.S. in Chemistry, U. Iowa, 1968, M.S. in Pharmacology, 1972, Ph.D. in Pharmacology, 1974. Diplomate Am. Bd. Toxicology. Asst. prof. pharmacology Mich. State U., East Lansing, 1974-77; scientist Chem. Industry Inst. Toxicology, Research Triangle Park, N.C., 1977—. Editor: Toxicity of Nitroaromatic Compounds, 1984; contbr. articles to profl. jours. Served with U.S. Army, 1969-71. NIH grantee, 1978. Mem. Soc. Toxicology, Am. Soc. Pharmacology and Exptl. Therapeutics, Am. Soc. Mass Spectrometry, Am. Chem. Soc., AAAS. Democrat. Office: Chem Indsl Inst Toxicology PO Box 12137 Research Triangle Park NC 27709

RICKETSON, J(AKE) E(DWIN), clinical psychologist; b. Ft. Monmouth, N.J., Oct. 19, 1952; s. Marion S. and Louise Ricketson; m. Janice S. Martin, Sept. 3, 1980. B.S. in Psychology, U. S.C., 1974, M.Ed., 1975; Psy.D., Fla. Inst. Tech., 1983. Lic. psychologist, N.C. Vocat. evaluator S.C. Dept. Vocat. Rehab., Columbia, 1976-77; student counselor Midland Community Coll., Columbia, 1977-80; clin. psychology intern VA Med. Ctr., Tuskegee, Ala., 1982-83; clin. psychologist Forsyth Meml. Hosp., Winston-Salem, N.C., 1984—. Fed. Trainship grantee, 1974-75. Mem. Am. Psychol. Assn., S.E. Psychol. Assn. (editor 1982). Avocations: skiing, golf, camping. Office: Forsyth Meml Hosp 3333 Silas Creek Pkwy Winston-Salem NC 27103

RICKETTS, DIANE WILLS, business exec.; b. Chgo., Dec. 19, 1955; d. Lowell E. and Violet (Heery) Wills; B.Chemistry, Wheaton Coll., Mass., 1975; postgrad. Bus. Sch. Tulane U., 1977; m. Philip Malone Ricketts, June 26, 1976; 1 son, Jason Malone. With Procter & Gamble, 1975-80, tech. brand asst., Cin., 1975, supr. manufacture synthetic granules package soap and detergent, Kansas City, Kans., 1976, supr. packing synthetic granules, 1977, prodn. planning mgr. Folger Coffee, New Orleans, 1978, warehouse and maintenance mgr. Folger Coffee, 1979-80; pres. DARCON, Broussard, La., 1980-83, Chip's Ice Cream, 1983—; sponsor summer engr. program, 1977. Bus. cons. Jr. Achievement project, 1976, 77; chmn. Wheaton Coll. recruiting, 1976—; pres. Wheaton Coll. New Orleans Alumnae Chpt., 1978-79; Bible sch. tchr. Autumn Woods Alliance, 1980-82. Mem. Am. Chem. Soc., AAAS, AAUW. Republican. Baptist. Club: UDC. Home: 212 Country Club Dr Lafayette LA 70501

RICKS, DAVID ARTEL, business educator, editor; b. Washington, July 21, 1942; s. Artel and Focha (Black) R.; m. Lesley A. Williams, July 3, 1976. B.S., Brigham Young U., 1966; M.B.A., Ind. U., 1968, Ph.D., 1970. Asst. prof. Ohio State U., 1970-75, assoc. prof., 1975-81; prof. internat. bus. U. S.C., Columbia, 1981—; editor Kent Pub. Co., Boston, 1978—. Author books, articles in field, including Directory of Foreign Manufactures in the U.S. (Best Reference Book 1974 ALA, 1975). Editor-in-chief Jour. of Internat. Business Studies, 1984—. Mem. Acad. Internat. Bus. (treas. 1981-82). Home: 828 Kilbourne Rd Columbia SC 29205 Office: USC Coll of Bus Columbia SC 29208

RICKS, JOYCIA CAMILLA, equal opportunity specialist, lawyer; b. Atlanta, Feb. 17, 1949; d. George Palmer and Johnnie Mae (Ricks) Redd. B.B.A., Albany State Coll., 1971; M.S., Ga. State U., 1977; J.D., Woodrow Wilson Coll. Law, Atlanta, 1979. Bar: Ga. 1979, U.S. Dist. Ct. (no. dist.) Ga. 1979, U.S. Ct. Appeals (5th cir.) 1979, Acctg. clk. Gulf Oil Corp., Atlanta, 1971; clk. EEOC, Atlanta, 1971-73, paralegal specialist, 1971-79, equal opportunity specialist, 1979—. Mem. NAACP, Atlanta, 1983—. Recipient Presdl. citation award Equal Opportunity in Higher Edn., Washington, 1981; Spl. Achievement award EEOC, Atlanta, 1982-84. Mem. ABA, Atlanta Bar Assn., Ga. Assn. Black Women Attys., Albany State Coll. Alumni Assn. (pres. Atlanta chpt. 1983-85), Assn. Trial Lawyers Am., Ga. State U. Alumni Assn., Woodrow Wilson Coll. Law Alumni Assn., Am. Bus. Women's Assn. (Woman of Yr., Tara chpt. 1985). Democrat. Presbyterian. Club: Spreading Oak Community. Office: EEOC 75 Piedmont Ave NE Suite 1100 Atlanta GA 30335

RIDDLE, ALVIN I., conservationist; b. Waxahachie, Tex., Jan. 7, 1947; s. Raymond Ozelle Riddle and Annie Lou (Hamby) Plumhoff; m. Fay Elaine Laughlin, Aug. 21, 1969; children—Jennifer Denise, Kelly Don. B.S., Tarleton State U., 1969. Dist. conservationist U.S. Dept. Agrl. Soil Conservation Service, Stanton, Tex. Pres. Martin County Hist. Mus., Stanton, 1979— mem. Martin County Hist. Commn., 1983—. Recipient Cert. Merit, USDA Soil Conservation Service, Temple, Tex., 1983, cert. of Congratulations Texas Senate, Austin, 1985. Mem. Nat. Assn. Conservation Dists. Soil Conservation Soc. Am. (Pres. Permian Basin chpt. 1982-83), Tex. State Tchrs. Assn., Martin County C. of C. (pres. 1984-85) Democrat. Mem. Church of Christ. Lodge: Stanton Noon Lions (pres. 1984—). Avocation: carpentry. Home: Box 657 Stanton TX 79782 Office: USDA Soil Conservation Service Box 1070 Stanton TX 79782

RIDDLE, DENNIS RAYMOND, banker; b. Oglethorpe, Ga., 1934. Grad., Ga. Inst. Tech., 1955. Now pres., dir. First Nat. Bank Atlanta; exec. v.p., chief operating officer, dir. First Atlanta Corp.; dir. Atlantic Am. Corp., Munich Am. Reassurances Co., Atlanta Gas Light Co. Mem. Ga. Bankers Assn., Am. Bankers Assn. (credit com.). Address: First National Bank Atlanta 2 Peachtree St NW Atlanta GA 30383*

RIDDLE, JAMES TONY, sales and marketing company executive; b. Muncie, Ind., Nov. 24, 1946; s. James Welby and Vivian Pearl (Shiply) R.; m. Sandra Gwen Andrews, Aug. 26, 1977. Student U. Miss., 1964-65, U. So. Miss., 1965, Memphis State U., 1970-72. Field mktg. rep. F. Schumacher & Co., N.Y.C., 1975-80; nat. account sales mgr. Blumenthal Mills, New Orleans, 1981-82; pres. T. Riddle & Co., New Orleans, 1982—; guest speaker Interior Bus. Designers Assn., New Orleans, 1983, No. La. chpt. AIA. Bd. dirs. Chardonnary Village Homeowners Assn., 1983. Mem. La. Restaurant Assn., La. Hotel and Motel Assn., Am. Soc. Interior Designers, Friends of Audubon Zoo. Republican. Methodist. Home: 17 E Rue Chardonnay Kenner LA 70062 Office: T Riddle & Co PO Drawer 50200 New Orleans LA 70150

RIDDLE, MICHAEL LEE, lawyer; b. Abilene, Tex., Oct. 7, 1946; s. Joy Lee and Francis Irene (Brandas) R.; m. Suzan Ellen Shaw, May 25, 1969 (div.); m. 2d, Carol Jackson, Aug. 13, 1977; 1 son, Robert Andrew. B.A., Tex. Tech U., 1969, J.D. with honors, 1972. Bar: Tex. 1972. Assoc. Geary Brice Barron & Stahl, Dallas, 1972-75; ptnr. Baker Glast Riddle Tuttle & Elliot, Dallas, 1975-80; ptnr. Riddle & Brown, Dallas, 1980—, sr. ptnr., 1980—; chmn. bd. Provident Bancorp., Tex. Bd. dirs. USA Film Festival, pres., 1984-86; bd. dirs. Am. Legal Found. Mem. ABA, Tex. Bar Assn., Dallas Bar Assn. Democrat. Lutheran. Clubs: University, Lincoln City, Lakewood Country (Dallas). Office: 4004 Belt Line Rd Suite 200 Dallas TX 75244

RIDDLES, JERRY LYNN, safety and environmental engineer; b. Paris, Tex., Feb. 27, 1947; s. Amis Edward and Margaret (Pinson) R.; m. Vera Jean Browning, Oct. 10, 1970; children—Jerry Lynn, Jr., Timothy Edward. B.S. in Indsl. Tech., Tarleton State U., 1969. Personnel and safety dir. Mosher Steel Co., Dallas, 1974-76; asst. corp. safety and environ. dir. Trinity Industries, Inc., Dallas, 1976—. Served to capt. U.S. Army, 1970-73. Mem. Am. Soc. Safety Engrs., N. Tex. Hazardous Material Assn. (mem. exec. com. 1985), Am. Indsl. Hygiene Assn., RR. Carbuilder's Safety Group. Home: 1710 Lexington Ct Ennis TX 75119 Office: Trinity Industries Inc 2525 Stemmons Freeway Dallas TX 75207

RIDDLESPERGER, JAMES WARREN, JR., political science educator; b. Denton, Tex., Oct. 28, 1953; s. James Warren and Carol Ruth (Jertson) R.; m. Kristina Reinhardt Lindenblad, July 17, 1982; 1 child, James Warren, III. B.A., North Tex. State U., 1975, M.A., 1980; Ph.D., U. Mo., 1983. Instr., U. Mo., Columbia, 1981-82; asst. prof. polit. sci. Tex. Christian U., Ft. Worth, 1982—; dir. Vet. Clin. Lab., St. Louis, 1983—. Contbr. articles to profl. jours. Mem. Am. Polit. Sci. Assn., Ctr. for Study of Presidency, Midwest Assn. Polit. Sci. Democrat. Methodist. Home: 4433 Donnelly Ave Fort Worth TX 76107 Office: Dept Polit Sci Tex Christian U Fort Worth TX 76129

RIDENOUR, JAMES FRANKLIN, college administrator; b. Peoria, Ill., Aug. 2, 1932; s. Arthur S. and Ruth O. (Ohlzen) R.; m. Doris K. Maxeiner, June 21, 1958; children—James, David Arthur, Eric Carl, Anne Catherine. B.S., Ill. Wesleyan U., 1954; M.S., Ill. State U., 1970. Mktg. rep. Armstrong Cork Co., 1955-67; assoc. dir. devel. Ill. Wesleyan U., 1967-73; v.p. devel. Western Md. Coll., Westminster, 1973-84; v.p. devel. Berry Coll., Mount Berry, Ga., 1984—. Chmn. Carroll County Tourism Council, 1976-79; active Boy Scouts Am.; bd. dirs. YMCA; chmn. Families of Evenglow. Mem. Council Advancement and Support Edn. (com. gift standards 1977—, nat. awards com.), Council for Fin. Aid to Edn. (adv. com.), Pi Gamma Mu, Gamma Upsilon. Republican. Episcopalian. Club: Center (Balt.). Office: Berry Coll Mount Berry GA 30149

RIDER, KATHERINE LOVETA THOMPSON, clinical social worker; b. Roswell, N.M., Apr. 18, 1945; d. Donald and Setta Loveta (Jones) Thompson; B.A., U. Tex., 1967, M.S.S.W., 1969; m. Kent Morrison Rider, June 8, 1968; children—Tracy Lyn, Courtney Elizabeth, Kelley Michelle. Social worker adult mental health staff, Austin-Travis County Mental Health-Mental Retardation Center, 1969-77; cons. Model Cities Project, Austin, Tex., 1971-72, community orgn. specialist alcohol-related services, 1974-76; clin. field faculty Sch. Social Work, U. Tex., Austin, 1977-81; pvt. practice social work, 1977—; clin. staff mental health dept. Austin Regional Clinic, 1982-84; mem. homemaker services bd. Child and Family Service Austin, 1970-75. Mem. First Baptist Day Sch. Bd., Austin, 1980-82; pres. L.L. Campbell Elem. Sch. PTA, 1984-86; mem. Austin Family Mediation Assn. Bd., 1985-87. Lic. Social Psychotherapist, Tex. Mem. Nat. Assn. Social Workers (dir. Tex. chpt. 1980-84), Tau Beta Sigma. Baptist. Home: 3221 Clearview Dr Austin TX 78703 Office: 812 San Antonio St Suite 304 Austin TX 78701

RIDER, TOMMYE LOU, insurance underwriter; b. Okla., Aug. 20, 1929; d. John Thomas and Minnie J. (Putt) Holley; m. James Hubert Rider, Aug. 13, 1946; 1 dau., Cherie Danette Rider Louthan. Student No. Okla. Coll., Tonkawa, 1954; Sr. Ins. Underwriter, Ins. Inst. Am., Malvern, Pa., 1980. CPIW (cert. profl. ins. woman). Loss clk. Roberts Ins. Agy., Tonkawa, 1961-74; sr. underwriter Burton Ins. Agy., Tonkawa, 1974-82, office mgr., 1982—. Mem. Ins. Women of Kay County (pres. 1973-75, 81-83, dir. 1973—). Democrat. Mem. Ch. of Christ. Home: 1102 N 5th St Tonkawa OK 74653 Office: Burton Ins Agy Inc 108 W Grand St Tonkawa OK 74653

RIDGE, CLAIRE LILLIAN, general contractor; b. Bklyn., Jan. 2, 1936; d. William Carl and Elizabeth Claire (Braun) Edwards; student Palm Beach Jr. Coll., 1981—; m. William J. Ridge, Nov. 6, 1968; children by previous marriage—Glenn A. Simonin, Diane C. Graziano. Lic. real estate broker; notary pub. Real estate saleswoman Provident Properties, Inc., 1965-67; owner, real estate broker Piper Realty, Inc., 1967-73; owner, builder St. Mark's Estates, Inc., Fieldcrest Homes, Inc., 1971—; owner, builder Sunshine Custom Builders, Inc. and Sunshine Builders of Palm Beach, Inc., 1977—; owner C. Ridge Realty, Inc. Mem. Singer Island Civic Assn.; mem. minority bus. enterprise staff com. Palm Beach County Commrs. Mem. North Palm Beach County Bd. Realtors, Home Builders Assn. Palm Beach County, Nat. Assn. Notaries, Nat. Assn. Women in Constrn., Palm Beach Gardens C. of C. Republican. Lutheran. Home: 1037 Morse Blvd Singer Island Riviera Beach FL 33404 Office: 1960 W 9th St Port Commerce Ctr Riviera Beach FL 33404

RIDGILL, JAMES LEE, JR., patent examiner, civil engineer; b. High Point, N.C., Sept. 17, 1926; s. James Lee and Ruth E. (Ward) R.; m. Janie Marline Weaver; children—Stephen, James, Jerrold. B.C.E., Clemson U., 1948; M.B.A., Tex. Christian U., 1956; LL.B., So. Meth. U., 1960; postgrad. George Washington U., 1960-63, Newberry Coll., 1949-50, St. Mary's U., San Antonio, 1953, Indsl. Coll. Armed Forces, 1961, Naval War Coll., 1973, 78. Bar: D.C. 1968, U.S. Supreme Ct. 1971. Field engr. Vannort Engrs., Charlotte, N.C., 1948-49, Patterson & Dewar, Decatur, Ga., 1950; planning engr. E.I. Dupont deNemours & Co., Jackson, S.C., 1952-53; design engr. Convair, Ft. Worth, 1954-59; sr. reliability engr. Ling-Temco-Vought, Garland, Tex., 1959-60; patent examiner/civil engr. U.S. Patent Office, Arlington, Va., 1960—, primary examiner, 1977—. Served to 1st lt. USMC, 1950-52, to col. Res., 1971—. Registered profl. engr., Tex. Mem. Marine Corps Res. Officers Assn., Patent Office Soc., Patent Office Profl. Assn. (sec. 1978-81), PTO-Fed. Credit Union (chmn. supervisory com. 1983). Baptist. Lodge: Rotary. Club: Toastmasters (pres. 1986) (Arlington). Home: 2516 Appaloosa Ct Reston VA 22091 Office: PO Box 2745 Arlington VA 22202

RIDINGS, DOROTHY SATTES, organization executive, communications consultant; b. Charleston, W.Va., Sept. 26, 1939; d. Frederick Lyle and Katharine (Backus) Sattes; m. Donald J. Ridings, Sept. 8, 1962; children—Donald J., Matthew Lyle. Student Randolph-Macon Woman's Coll., 1957-59; B.S. in Journalism, Northwestern U., 1961; M.A., U. N.C., 1968; D.Pub. Service (hon.), U. Louisville, 1985. Feature writer, polit. reporter Charlotte Observer, N.C. 1961-66; copy editor Washington Post, summer 1967; instr. U. N.C. Sch. Journalism, Chapel Hill, 1966-68; freelance writer, 1969-77; tech. asst. Resident Mgmt. Corp., Iroquois Homes pub. housing project, Louisville, 1977-79; news editor Ky. Bus. Ledger, 1977-80, editor, 1980-83; producer/host Ky. Entrepreneur, weekly ednl. TV series, 1982-83, Ky. Reports, 1983; adj. prof. U. Louisville, evenings 1982-83; communications cons., 1983—; human resources coordinator LWV U.S., 1976-80, 1st v.p., 1980-82, pres., 1982—, trustee LWV Edn. Fund, 1976-80, 1st vice chmn., 1980-82, chmn., 1982—; mem. adv. commn. spl. com. on election law and voter participation ABA; mem. Gov.'s Commn. for Full Equality, 1982-83, Com. on Higher Edn. in Ky.'s Future, 1980-83; mem. state adv. council U.S. Commn. Civil Rights, 1975-79; mem. exec. com., Ky. Coordinating Com. for Internat. Women's Yr., 1977-78. Bd. govs. dept. Christian edn. Presbytery of Louisville-Union and chmn. communications task force, 1973-77; bd. dirs. Leadership Louisville, 1983—, Louisville YWCA, 1978-80, Jr. League Louisville, 1972-74; mem. session 2d Presbyn. Ch., 1972-75, 78-81, sec.-treas. ch. sch., 1972-76, mem. weekday sch. bd., 1972-75; mem. Jefferson County Sunshine Commn., 1973; mem. steering com. Task Force for Peaceful Desegregation, 1974-75; pres. LWV Louisville and Jefferson County, 1974-76, bd. dirs., 1969-76; mem. adv. council on financing higher edn. Nat. Inst. Ind. Colls. and Univs.; mem. task force Project '87. Am. Polit. Sci. Assn. and Am. Hist. Assn.; mem. exec. com. Bretton Woods Com., Leadership Conf. on Civil Rights; mem. leadership com. Campaign for Free Speech, Commn. on Constl. System, Nat. Com. on U.S.-China Relations; bd. dirs. Com. for Study Am. Electorate, Ind. Sector, Com. on Constl. System, Nat. Com. against Discrimination in Housing, Leadership Ky., 1984—; mem. adv. bd. Nat. Com. for Citizen Participation in Adminstrn. of Justice; trustee Overseas Edn. Fund, Citizens Research Found., 1982-84; mem. adv. council on ch. and society United Presbyn. Ch. in U.S.A., 1978-84; mem. governing council Nat. Mcpl. League, 1980-83, v.p., 1985—; jurist All-Am. City awards, 1976, 78, 81, jury foreman, 1983; mem. Ky. Gov.'s Council on Ednl. Reform, 1984; chmn. Prichard Com. for Acad. Excellence; chmn. communications and info. systems com. Ky. Tomorrow, 1984—. Mem. Women in Communications (pub. affairs adv. bd.). Home: 11 Eastover Ct Louisville KY 40206 Office: 1730 M St NW Washington DC 20036 also 1009 S 4th St Louisville KY 40203

RIDINGS, JENNIFER LYNN, pharmacist; b. Greenville, S.C., Jan. 1, 1956; d. Charles Luther and Norma Jean (Shelton) R. B.S. in Pharmacy, U. Tex., 1978. Registered pharmacist, Tex. Mgr., pharmacist Eckerd Drug, Austin, Tex., 1979—, Western Trails Pharmacy, Austin, 1984—. Mem. Am. Pharm. Assn., Capitol Area Pharm. Assn. (bd. dirs. 1983-84), pres. 1985—), Tex. Pharm. Assn. (membership chmn. local sect. 1984-85, vice chmn. 1985—), Jaycees (bd. dirs. 1984), LWV. Baptist. Avocation: travel. Home: 3831 Cologne Ln Austin TX 78759

RIDLEY, BETTY ANN, educator, church worker; b. St. Louis, Oct. 19, 1926; d. Rupert Alexis and Virginia Regina (Weikel) Steber; B.A., Scripps Coll., Claremont, Calif., 1948; m. Fred A. Ridley, Jr., Sept. 8, 1948; children—Linda Drue Ridley Archer, Clay Kent. Christian Sci. practitioner, Oklahoma City, 1973—; Christian Sci. tchr., 1982—; mem. Christian Sci. Bd. Lectureship, 1980-85, Found. Bibl. Research and Preservation Primitive Christianity. Mem. Jr. League Am. Home: 7908 Lakehurst Dr Oklahoma City OK 73120 Office: 3000 United Founders Blvd Suite 100-G Oklahoma City OK 73112

RIDLON, MARGARET AGNES, social worker; b. Pittsburg, Kans., Feb. 27, 1923; d. Evan Anthony and Agnes Jessie (Staib) Naylor; B.A., B.S., Pittsburg State U., 1943; M.S. in Social Work (fellowship 1969-71, univ. grantee 1971), U. Tenn., 1971; divorced; children—Evan Anthony, William Frank, II. Lic. social worker, Ark. Med. supr. Ark. Social Services, 1967-71, utilization rev. supr., 1971-73; social work supr. Ark. State Hosp., Little Rock, 1973-76; counselor supr. Ark. Mental Retardation Dept., 1976-81; client and family support dir. S.E. Ark. Devel. Center, Warren, 1981—; field instr. U. Ark. Grad. Sch. Social Work, 1983—; mem. Ark. Comprehensive Health Planning Commn., 1972-76, Environ. Barriers Council, 1977-83; bd. dirs. North Central Ark. Mental Health, 1974-76. Mem. Am. Assn. Mental Deficiency (chmn. social work Ark. 1979-85), Nat. Assn. Social Workers, Acad. Cert. Social Workers, Sigma Delta Chi, Alpha Sigma Alpha. Democrat. Methodist. Home: 602 Halligan Warren AR 71671 Office: SE Ark Human Devel Center Route 3 1 Center Circle Warren AR 71671

RIEDER, GREGORY FRANK, police psychologist; b. St. Louis, Jan. 13, 1948; s. Oscar Edgar and Anna (Feduniszyn) R.; m. Karen Anne Black, May 31, 1969; children—Meredith Rene, Allison Michelle. B.A. in Psychology, U. Mo.-Rolla, 1970; M.S. in Clin. Psychology, Central Mo. State U., 1972; Ph.D. in Counseling Psychology, U. Mo., 1975. Lic. psychologist, Tex.; cert. psychologist Nat. Register Health Services Providers. Intern, Fulton State Hosp., Mo., 1971-72; prof. psychology Central Mo. State Hosp., Warrensburg, 1972-74; prof. criminal justice Tex. Criminal Justice Ctr., Huntsville, 1974-79; dir. psychol. services div. Houston Police Dept., 1979—; instr. FBI Acad., 1984—; instr., speaker Internat. Assn. Chiefs of Police, 1984—; cons. to industry on extortion, terrorism and kidnapping Multi-Nat. Corp., 1983—; speaker, advisor Harris County Mental Health Assn., 1983—. Contbr. articles to Badge and Gun, Police Mag., others. Dir. research coms. on child abuse, hostage negotiation and selection of police officers Tex. Ho. of Reps., Austin, 1972-79. Mem. Am. Psychol. Assn., Nat. Orgn. Black Law Enforcement Execs. (mem. mgmt. team 1985—), Psi Chi, Phi Delta Kappa, Kappa Delta Pi. Episcopalian. Avocations: radio control models. Office: Houston Police Dept #61 Riesner Houston TX 77002

RIEGER, SAM LEE, insurance company executive; b. Durango, Colo., May 14, 1946; s. Lee Roy and Ruth (Harris) R.; student U. Tex., 1964-68; m. Pamela J. Robinson, Apr. 7, 1973. Sales agt. Prudential Ins. Co., Dallas, 1970-72; sales supr. Great Am. Res. Inc. Co., San Antonio, 1972-74, dir. manpower devel., 1974-76, agy. mgr., Austin, Tex., 1974-76, S.W. Agy., San Antonio, 1976-82, v.p. sales, Dallas, 1982—. Served with U.S. Army, 1969. Recipient Nat. Mgmt. award Gen. Agts. and Mgrs. Conf., 1979, 80, 81, 82. C.L.U. Mem. Nat. Assn. Life Underwriters, Dallas Assn. Life Underwriters, Gen. Agts. and Mgrs. Assn. Republican. Methodist. Club: Prestonwood Country. Home: 6139 Copperhill Dallas TX 75248 Office: 2020 Live Oak Dallas TX 75201

RIEMENSCHNEIDER, JOHN BOLESLAW, lawyer; b. Fond du Lac, Wis., Sept. 23, 1948; s. John Albert and Ann (Woicek) R. B.S., U. Wis.-Oshkosh, 1971; J.D., U. Miss., 1974. Bar: Miss. 1974, Wis. 1985, U.S. Dist. Ct. (no. dist.) Miss. 1974, (so. dist.) Miss. 1985, U.S. Supreme Ct. 1979, U.S. Ct. Appeals (5th cir.) 1981, U.S. Dist. Ct. (ea. dist.) Wis. 1984, U.S. Ct. Appeals (D.C. cir.) 1984. Mem. editorial staff West Pub. Co., St. Paul, 1974-75; assoc. Farese Farese & Farese P.A., Ashland, Miss., 1976—; county pros. atty. Benton County, Miss., 1980—. Pres. Ashland Civic Club, 1980-81, 84-85, sec., 1983-84. Named winner legal essay competition Assn. Trial Lawyers Am., 1974. Mem. Miss. State Bar, State Bar Wis., ABA, Miss. Prosecutors Assn., Nat. Dist. Attys. Assn. Roman Catholic. Office: Farese Farese and Farese PA PO Box 98 Ashland MS 38603

RIERSON, RICHARD TROY, magazine editor; b. Charlotte, N.C., Nov. 6, 1955; s. Robert L. and Bobbie Jean (McLeod) R. Student Leicester Coll., Mass. Exec. asst. Rierson Broadcast Cons., N.Y.C., 1974; asst. film editor Ralph Koch, Inc., N.Y.C., 1974; printing asst. Radiator Splty. Co., Charlotte, N.C., 1975; assoc. editor Am. Jewish Times Outlook, Charlotte, 1976-80, editor, 1980—; mem. stock company Charlotte Summer Theatre, 1963-66. Author short stories and editorials. Tchr., Adult Basic Literacy Edn. Ctr., Charlotte, N.C., 1984. Episcopalian. Avocations: films; music; theatre; books. Office: American Jewish Times-Outlook 1400 W Independence Blvd Charlotte NC 28208

RIES, EDWARD RICHARD, independent petroleum geologist, consultant; b. Freeman, S.D., Sept. 18, 1918; s. August and Mary F. (Graber) R.; student Freeman Jr. Coll., 1937-39; A.B. magna cum laude, U. S.D., 1941; M.S., U. Okla., 1943, Ph.D. (Warden-Humble fellow), 1951; postgrad. Harvard, 1946-47; m. Amelia D. Capshaw, Jan. 24, 1948 (div. Oct. 1956); children—Rosemary Melinda, Victoria Elise; m. Maria Wipfler, June 12, 1964. Asst. geologist Geol. Survey S.D., Vermillion, 1941; geophys. interpreter Robert Ray Inc., Oklahoma City, 1942; jr. geologist Carter Oil Co., Mont., Wyo., 1943-44, geologist Cutbank, Mont., 1944-49; sr. geologist Standard Vacuum Oil Co., India, 1951-53, sr. regional geologist, Indonesia, 1953-59, geol. advisor for Far East, Africa and Australia, White Plains, N.Y., 1959-62; geol. advisor Far East, Africa, Oceania, Mobil Petroleum Co., N.Y.C., 1962-65; staff geol. advisor for Europe, Far East, Mobil Oil Corp., N.Y.C., 1965-71, sr. regional explorationist Far East, Dallas, 1971-73, Asia-Pacific, Dallas, 1973-76, sr. geol. advisor, 1976-79, annuitant petroleum cons., 1983-85; ret., 1983; assoc. geol. advisor (regional geology-geophysics) Mobil Exploration and Producing Services, Inc., Dallas, 1979-82, geol. cons. regional geology-geophysics, 1982-83; ind. petroleum geologist and cons., 1985—; Grad. asst., teaching fellow U. Okla., 1941-43, Harvard, 1946-47. Served with AUS, 1944-46. Mem. N.Y. Acad. Scis., Am. Assn. Petroleum Geologists (assoc. editor 1976-83), Geol. Soc. Am., Am. Hort. Soc., Internat. Platform Assn., Am. Geol. Inst., A.A.A.S., Nat. Audubon Soc., Nat. Wildlife Fedn., Soc. Exploration Geophysicists, Wilderness Soc., Am. Legion, Phi Beta Kappa, Sigma Xi, Phi Sigma, Sigma Gamma Epsilon. Republican. Mennonite. Club: Harvard (Dallas). Contbr. articles to profl. jours. Home: 6009 Royal Crest Dr Dallas TX 75230 Office: 7200 N Stemmons Dallas TX 75247

RIESCO, ARMANDO, II, management consultant, educator; b. Cuba, May 21, 1943; s. Armando Riesco Puyol and Bertha Cartaya Gutierrez; m. Blanca Rosa Farinas Torres, Dec. 16, 1972; children—Natascha Beatrice, Armando, Alejandro Jose. Student U. Bridgeport, 1960-61; B.S. in Indsl. Engring. magna cum laude, U. Fla., 1965, M.S. in Indsl. Engring., 1967, Ph.D. in Indsl. and Systems Engring. and Ops. Research, 1970. Prof. indsl. engring. U. P.R., Mayaguez, 1970-79; pres. Sistema Inc., Guaynabo, P.R., 1979—; vis. prof. indsl. and systems engring., U. Fla., Gainesville, 1976-77; sr. cons., co-founder Mgmt. Systems Design and Analysis, 1974-79; pvt. practice cons., 1967-74, corps. including Citibank, Electronic Data Systems, govt. agys. including NASA, govts. P.R., Costa Rica, Dominican Republic; chmn., dir. organizational meetings profl. orgns.; lectr. in field. OAS fellow, 1968-70. Mem. Inst. Indsl. Engrs., Ops. Research Soc. Am., The Inst. Mgmt. Scis., Phi Kappa Phi, Alpha Pi Mu (past regional v.p.), Sigma Xi, Tau Beta Pi. Roman Catholic. Contbr. sci. papers to profl. confs. and publs. Office: SISTEMA Inc Call Box BSJ Suite 515 Banco de San Juan Center Guaynabo PR 00657

RIGAU, JORGE IVAN, architect; b. Arecibo, P.R., Aug. 7, 1953; s. Gabriel Juan and Carmen Cecilia (Perez) R.; m. Sonia Yumet, June 1, 1979; children—Alberto José, Susana. B.A. in Architecture, Cornell U., 1975. Registered profl. architect, P.R. Architect, Hist. Dist., Inst. Puerto Rican Culture, San Juan, 1976; dir. cultural affairs U. P.R., Río Piedras, 1976-80, instr. Sch. Architecture, 1976-80, asst. dean of students, 1979-80; exec. dir. Architects Assn., San Juan, 1981—. Treas., Colación, 1979—; bd. dirs. Art Students League, 1980—. NEA grantee, 1980-81. Mem. Colegio de Arquitectos de Puerto Rico, AIA. Roman Catholic. Home: 221 Tous Soto St Hato Rey PR 00918

RIGBY, KENNETH, lawyer; b. Shreveport, La., Oct. 20, 1925; s. Samuel and Mary Elizabeth (Fearnhead) R.; m. Jacqueline Carol Brandon, June 10, 1951; children—Brenda, Wayne, Glen. B.S. magna cum laude, La. State U., 1950, J.D., 1951. Bar: La. 1951, U.S. Ct. Appeals (5th cir.) 1966, U.S. Supreme Ct. 1971, U.S. Tax Ct. 1981, U.S. Ct. Appeals (11th cir.) 1982. Ptnr. Love, Rigby, Dehan, Love & McDaniel, 1951—; mem. Marriage-Persons Com. La. Law Inst., 1981—. Served with USAAF, 1943-46. Fellow Am. Acad. Matrimonial Lawyers; mem. ABA, Assn. Trial Lawyers Am., La. Trial Lawyers Assn., Shreveport Bar Assn. (pres. 1973-74), La. Bar Assn. (chmn. com. on continuing legal edn. 1974-75, chmn. family law sect. 1981-82, bd. govs. 1986—). Methodist. Contbr. articles to profl. jours. Office: 6th Floor Johnson Bldg 412 Milam Street Shreveport LA 71101

RIGBY, PERRY GARDNER, university dean, medical educator, physician; b. East Liverpool, Ohio, July 1, 1932; s. Perry Lawrence and Lucille Ellen (Orin) R.; m. Joan E. Worthington, June 16, 1957; children—Martha, Peter, Thomas, Matthew. B.S. summa cum laude, Mt. Union Coll., 1953, D.Sc. hon., 1976; M.D., Western Res. U., 1957. Diplomate: Am. Bd. Internal Medicine. Intern in medicine U. Va. Hosp., Charlottesville, 1957-58, asst. resident in medicine, 1958-60; research fellow in hematology Mass. Meml. Hosp., Boston, 1960-62; clin. asst. in medicine Boston City Hosp., 1961-62; research assoc. in medicine Mass. Meml. Hosp., Boston U. Med. Ctr., 1961-62; asst. prof. internal medicine and anatomy U. Nebr., Omaha, 1964-66; assoc. prof. internal medicine and anatomy, 1966-69, prof. internal medicine, 1969-78, prof. anatomy, 1969-74, prof. med. edn., 1973-74, head sect. hematology Eugene C. Eppley Inst. for Research in Cancer and Allied Diseases, 1964-68, dir. hematology div., 1968-74, asst. dean for curriculum Coll. Medicine, 1971-72, assoc. dean for acad. affairs, 1972-74, dir. office ednl. services, 1972-74, acting assoc. dean for allied health professions, 1973-74, vice chmn. dept. med. and ednl. adminstrn., 1974, dean, 1974-78, chmn. dept. med. and ednl. adminstrn., 1974; prof. internal medicine La. State U., Shreveport, 1978—, assoc. dean acad. affairs Sch. Medicine, 1978-81, acting dean, 1981-82, dean, 1982-85, chancellor, 1985—, mem. clin. bd. Univ. Hosp., 1978—, chmn. clin. bd., 1978—, program dir. biomed. research support grant program, 1980-81; chmn. dean's com. VA Hosp., Shreveport, 1978—; mem. courtesy staff Immanuel Med. Ctr.; bd. dirs. Health Planning Council of Midlands, Omaha, 1976-78; cons. WHO, Kabul, Afghanistan, 1976. Bd. dirs. Fontenelle Forest, Omaha, 1976-78, River Cities High Tech. Group, Shreveport, 1982—. Served as capt. M.C. U.S. Army, 1962-64. Markle scholar, 1965. Fellow ACP; mem. Am. Fedn. Clin. Research (councillor 1971), AMA (del.), Am. Soc. Hematology, N.Y. Acad. Scis., Am. Assn. Med. Colls. (council of deans of Midwest-Gt. Plains 1974-78, chmn. Midwest-Gt. Plains 1976), Am. Assn. Cancer Research, AAAS, Am. Heart Assn., Central Soc., Clin. Research, Internat. Soc. Hematology, Health Edn. Media Assn., Am. Assn. Physicians' Assts., So. Soc. Clin. Investigation, Shreveport C. of C. (dir. 1982—), Sigma Xi, Alpha Omega Alpha, Phi Rho Sigma. Office: La State U Med Ctr 1501 Kings Hwy Shreveport LA 71130

RIGGS, ARTHUR J(ORDY), lawyer; b. Nyack, N.Y., Apr. 3, 1916; s. Oscar H. and Adele (Jordy) R.; A.B., Princeton U., 1937; LL.B., Harvard U., 1940; m. Virginia Holloway, Oct. 15, 1942; children—Arthur James (dec.), Emily Adele, Keith Holloway, George Bennett. Admitted to Mass. bar, 1940, Tex. bar, 1943; asso. Warner, Stackpole, Stetson & Bradlee, Boston, 1940-41, Solicitor's Office U.S. Dept. Labor, 1941-42; mem. firm Johnson, Bromberg, Leeds & Riggs, Dallas, until 1981; of counsel Geary, Stahl & Spencer, Dallas, 1981—. Cert. specialist in labor law. Mem. State Bar Tex., Am., Dallas bar assns., Southwestern Legal Found., Phi Beta Kappa. Home: 4116 Amherst St Dallas TX 75225 Office: 2800 One Main Pl Dallas TX 75250

RIGGS, CARL DANIEL, higher education administrator, biologist; b. Indpls., Dec. 7, 1920; s. Josiah Miller and Margaret Helen (Schleicher) R.; m. Patricia Bynum, June 1, 1952; children—Margaret Clare Riggs Johnson, Carl D., Jeffrey B., Catherine. B.S. in Zoology, U. Mich., 1944, M.S. in Zoology, 1946, Ph.D. in Zoology, 1953. Teaching fellow dept. zoology U. Mich., Ann Arbor, 1946-47; instr. to prof. dept. zoology U. Okla., Norman, 1948-65, dean Grad. Coll., 1965-71, v.p. grad. studies, 1966-71, acting provost, 1970-71; v.p. for acad. affairs U. South Fla., Tampa, 1971-80, acting pres., 1977-78, dean Grad. Sch. and coordinator univ. research, 1980—, interim dean Coll. Pub. Health, 1983-84; pres. Conf. So. Grad. Schs., 1986-87; cons. NSF, NIH, CGS. Mayor pro tem, Norman, 1963-64; bd. dirs. and long range planning com. United Way of Greater Tampa; bd. dirs. Tampa Mus. Fedn., 1979-84, pres., 1980-81; bd. dirs. Children's Home, Inc., 1974—, pres., 1984-86, also mem. exec. com.; chmn. Scouting for the Handicapped, Gulf Ridge council Boy Scouts Am., 1974-86. Served with USAF. Recipient Conservation Edn. award Sears Roebuck Found., 1966; grantee NSF, 1957-66, NASA, 1966-70, John S. Zink Found., 1976, 70; fellow NDEA, 1966-70. Fellow Okla. Acad. Sci. (pres. 1966-67); mem. AAAS, Am. Inst. Biol. Scis., Am. Fisheries Soc., Am. Soc. Ichthyologist and Herpetologists, Fla. Acad. Sci., Phi Beta Kappa, Sigma Xi, Phi Kappa Phi, Beta Gamma Sigma, Omicron Delta Kappa. Democrat. Presbyterian. Contbr. articles on biology to profl. jours. Office: Grad Sch U South Fla Tampa FL 33620

RIGGS, KARL ALTON, JR., geologic consultant; b. Thomasville, Ga., Aug. 12, 1929; s. Karl A. and Marjorie Elizabeth (Urquhart) R.; m. Patricia Ann Hartrick, June 28, 1952; children—George Hartrick, Kathryn Ann Riggs Keen, Linda Kay. B.S. with honors, Mich. State U., 1951, M.S., 1952; Ph.D., Iowa State U., 1956. Sr. research technologist Mobil Research and Devel. Lab., Dallas, 1956-59; research assoc. Iowa State U., Ames, 1953-56, instr., 1952-56; asst. prof. Western Mich. U., Kalamazoo, 1966-68; assoc. prof. geology Miss. State U., Mississippi State, 1968—; geologic cons., 1952—; v.p., dir. Con Oil Drilling Programs, Inc., N.Y.C., 1982. Dist. chmn. Dallas County Republicans, 1960-62; vol. messenger CD Service, World War II. Fellow Geol. Soc. Am.; mem. Am. Inst. Profl. Geologists (cert.), Am. Assn. Petroleum Geologists, Assn. Engring. Geologists, Mineral. Soc. Am., Soc. Econ. Paleontologists and Mineralogists, Am. Mgmt. Assn., Miss. Acad. Sci., Nat. Mil. Intelligence Assn., Gideons Internat. Methodist. Author: Principles of Rock Classification, 1975; abstractor Mineral. Abstracts, 1968—, organizer for Am., 1978—. Home: 109 Grand Ridge Dr Starkville MS 39759 Office: Box KR Mississippi State MS 39762

RIGGS, LEONARD MORRISON, landscape architect; b. Deridder, La., Nov. 27, 1905; s. Samuel Leonidas and Adah Alice (Matthews) R.; m. Fleeta Walker, Apr. 1, 1934; 1 child, Leonard Morrison. B.A., Centenary Coll., 1928. Landscape architect Walnut Hill Co., Shreveport, La., 1927-36, R. Lacy Co., Longview, Tex., 1936-49, Riggs Landscape Co., Longview, 1949-76, Riggs Enterprises, Longview, 1976—. Recipient Gold Medal award Nat. Flower Show, 1939, Beautification award City of Longview, 1982. Mem. Tex. Assn. Nurserymen (pres. 1942-43), Tex. Landscape Assn. (pres. 1954-55), Club: Civitan (gov. 1946-47). Lodge: Rotary (Paul Harris award 1982). Avocation: fishing.

RIGGS, OLEN LONNIE, JR., electrochemical and corrosion engineer; b. Bethany, Okla., Aug. 25, 1925; s. Olen Lonnie and Lena Louvene (Sparkman) R.; m. Ann Rose France, June 3, 1947; children—Debra Ann Riggs Bundy, Michael Olen. B.S. in Chemistry and Math., Eastern Nazarene Coll., Boston, 1949. Registered profl. engr., Calif.; cert. profl. chemist; accredited corrosion specialist. Research supr. Continental Oil Co., Ponca City, Okla., 1952-56, group supr., 1956-68; research dir. Wichita, Kans., 1968-69; sr. research assoc. Getty Oil Co., Houston, 1969-71; sr. staff chemist Kerr-McGee Corp., Oklahoma City, 1971—. Author: Anodic Protection, 1981; Electrochemistry: Introduction for Technologists, 1985; also tech. articles. Patentee inhibitors, instrumentation and metals. Served with USAF, 1943-45. Recipient Outstanding Alumni award Eastern Nazarene Coll., 1985. Fellow Am. Inst. Chemists; mem. Electrochem. Soc., Nat. Assn. Corrosion Engrs. Avocations: golf, painting. Office: Kerr-McGee Corp Tech Ctr 3301 NW 150th St Oklahoma City OK 73125

RIGGS, ROBERT OWEN, university president; b. Gallatin, Tenn., Oct. 15, 1942; s. Clyde O. and Sue L. (Cullbreath) R.; B.A., Vanderbilt U., 1964; M.Ed., Memphis State U., 1968, Ed.D., 1970; m. Judith Mathis, July 1968; children—Robert Owen, Susan Lea. Asst. to chancellor U. Tenn., Martin, 1970-71; dir. budget and planning Memphis State U., 1971-72; asst. to pres. James Madison U., Harrisonburg, Va., 1972-73, asso. dean, 1973-74, dean, 1974-76; pres. Austin Peay State U., Clarksville, Tenn., 1976—; dir. 1st Trust & Savs. Bank. Served with USMC, 1964-67. Named Outstanding Young Man Clarksville Jaycees, 1976. Mem. Am. Assn. for Higher Edn., Am. Ednl. Research Assn., Assn. for Instl. Research, Am. Assn. of State Colls. and Univs., Alpha Phi Omega, Phi Kappa Pi, Phi Delta Kappa, Phi Kappa Sigma. Methodist. Clubs: Rotary, Clarksville Country. Contbr. articles to profl. jours. Office: Austin Peay State U College St Clarksville TN 37040

RIGGS, ROSA KATHLEEN, psychiatrist; b. Evansville, Ind., Feb. 20, 1937; d. Charles W. and Helen (Robbins) R.; 1 adopted dau., Barbara Jean Watson. B.S., U. Ky., 1958, M.S., 1962, Ph.D., 1966, M.D., 1974. Diplomate Am. Bd. Psychiatry and Neurology. Tchr. biology and physics Versailles (Ky.) High Sch., 1959-64, head dept., 1960-64; asst. prof. biology Transylvania U., Lexington, Ky., 1966-70; intern in psychiatry Ind. U., Indpls., 1974-75; resident in psychiatry U. Ky., Lexington, 1975-77; staff psychiatrist for Cornelia B. Wilbur, M.D., Lexington, 1977-79; practice medicine specializing in psychiatry, Lexington, 1980—; mem. staff Good Samaritan Hosp., Central Bapt. Hosp., Woodford County Hosp.; cons. to hosps.; tchr. seminars. Mem. Fayette County Med. Assn., Ky. Med. Assn., AMA, Ky. Psychiat. Assn., Am. Psychiat. Assn. Mem. Christian Ch. (Disciples of Christ). Home: 1616 Versailles Rd Lexington KY 40504 Office: 660 N Broadway Lexington KY 40508

RIGO DE RIGHI, FABRIZIO ARISTIDE, geologist, oil company executive; b. Urbino, Italy, Feb. 27, 1925; came to U.S., 1983; s. Alessandro E. and Maria (Bernardini) Rigo de R.; m. Neli Da Silva, Apr. 25, 1974; children—Yara, Alan; m. Maria G. Nicastro, Apr. 18, 1955 (div. 1972); children—María Teresa, Giuseppe, Claudia. D. Geol. Scis., State U. Milan, 1951. Jr. asst., lectr. Faculty of Geology, U. Milan, 1951-53; party chief Edison S.P.A., Milan, 1953-64; pres. Seagull Exploration, Rome, 1965-77; pres. Euromin Internat. S.A., Vaduz-Liechtenstein, 1978—; pres. Euromin Oil Inc., Houston, 1983—, Italmin Petroli SA, Rome, 1971—; v.p. Seaxe Energy Corp., Jackson, Miss., 1982—; pres. Euromin Can. Ltd., Calgary, Alta., 1984—; owner, mgr. Rigo & Assocs., Rome, 1964—. Contbr. articles to profl. jours. Served with Italian Army, 1950-51. Fellow Sci. Acad. Yugoslavia, 1969. Mem. A. Assn. Petroleum Geologists, Italian Geol. Soc., Italian Assn. Profl. Geologists. Roman Catholic. Home: 10907 Pama Circle Houston TX 77024 Office: Euromin Oil Inc Suite 156 8552 Katy Fwy Houston TX 77024

RIGOS, PLATON NICOLAS, urban affairs/public administration educator; b. Alexandria, Egypt, Nov. 17, 1942; came to U.S., 1961, naturalized, 1970; s. Nicolas Platon and Stella Rigos; m. Barbara A. Hodges, Dec. 26, 1962 (div. 1968); m. Margaret Jane Orr, Dec. 17, 1977. B.A., U. Colo., 1965; M.A., UCLA, 1968; Ph.D., Mich. State U., 1974. Asst. prof. U. Miami, Fla., 1972-76, U. South Fla., Tampa, 1976-83; assoc. prof. polit. sci., 1983—; cons. NSF, Brandon C. of C. Contbr. articles to profl. jours. Asst. to campaign Mary Figg, 1982-83. Mem. Am. Soc. Pub. Adminstrn. (pres. Suncoast chpt. 1984-85), LWV. Greek Orthodox. Home: 13818 Capitol Dr Tampa FL 33613 Office: U S Fla Dept Polit Tampa FL 33620

RILEY, JOSEPH P., JR., mayor. Mayor City of Charleston, S.C. Office: PO Box 652 Charleston SC 29402*

RILEY, RICHARD WILSON, governor S.C.; b. Greenville, S.C., Jan. 2, 1933; s. Edward Patterson and Martha Elizabeth (Dixon) R.; m. Ann Osteen Yarborough, Aug. 23, 1957; children—Richard Wilson, Anne Y., Hubert D., Theodore D. B.A., Furman U., 1954; J.D., U. S.C., 1960. Bar: S.C. bar 1959. Partner firm Riley & Riley, Greenville, 1959-78; gov., S.C., 1978—; spl. asst. to subcom. U.S. Senate Jud. Com., 1960; mem. S.C. Ho. of Reps., 1963-66, S.C. Senate senate from Greenville-Laurens Dist., 1966-76. Vice pres. S.C. Young Democrats, 1968. Served to lt. (j.g.) USNR, 1954-56. Named Outstanding Young Man of Greenville and S.C. Jr. C. of C., 1965. Mem. S.C., Greenville bar assns., Furman U. Alumni Assn. (pres. 1968-69). Rotarian. Office: Office of Gov State House Columbia SC 29211*

RILEY, WILLIAM O., steel company executive; b. 1921; student Ga. Inst. Tech.; LL.B., Atlanta Law Sch. With Atlantic Steel Co., Atlanta, 1940—, sr. v.p., then exec. v.p., 1971-78, pres., 1978—, also dir.; dir. Atlantic Bldg. Systems Inc. Office: Atlantic Steel Co PO Box 1714 Atlanta GA 30301*

RILING, EUGENE HAROLD, engineer; b. Spiro, Okla., Aug. 23, 1936; s. Lester and Eva Rowena (Clark) R.; B.S., Calif. State U., 1968; m. Irla Kay Hughey, May 6, 1960; children—Barton, Quentin. Engring. asst. E.B. Hall, 1960-62; br. mgr. Grant Oil Tool, Compton, Calif., 1962-65; prodn. engr. Thums Long Beach Co., Long Beach, Calif., 1965-71; sr. application engr. Byron Jackson Pump Co.-Centrilift, Midland, Tex., 1971-76; mgr. field service TRW Reda Pump, Bartlesville, Okla., 1976—. Mgr., Little League, 1969-70, 71-74; active YMCA. Section leader Republican party, 1968-69. Served with AUS, 1956-59. Mem. Am. Inst. Mining, Metall. and Petroleum Engrs., Am. Petroleum Inst., Am. Soc. Plant Engrs. Baptist. Club: Sunset Country. Author, illustrator: Handbook for Oilfield Subsurface Electrically Driven Pumps, 1975; Tee Up in the Oilpatch, 1976. Patentee in field. Cartoonist. Home: 934 Briarwood Dr Bartlesville OK 74003 Office: 4th and Dewey Bartlesville OK 74003

RILLING, JOHN ROBERT, history educator; b. Wausau, Wis., Apr. 28, 1932; s. John Peter and Esther Laura (Wittig) R.; m. Joanne Marilyn McCrory, Dec. 21, 1953; children—Geoffrey Alan, Andrew Peter. B.A. summa cum laude, U. Minn., 1953; A.M., Harvard U., 1957, Ph.D., 1959. Asst. prof. history U. Richmond, Va., 1959-62, assoc. prof. history, 1962-68, prof. history, 1968—, chmn. dept. history, 1977-83; chmn. Westhampton Coll. dept. history, 1965-71. Served with U.S. Army, 1953-55. Woodrow Wilson fellow, 1955-59; Harvard U. Travelling fellow, 1958; Coolidge fellow, 1955-56; Folger Library fellow, 1960; recipient U. Richmond Disting. Educator award, 1975, 76, 77, 80. Mem. Am. Hist. Assn., Econ. History Soc., Conf. Brit. Studies, AAUP, Phi Beta Kappa, Omicron Delta Kappa. Presbyterian. Contbr. articles to profl. jours. Home: 1507 Wilmington Ave Richmond VA 23227 Office: U Richmond Richmond VA 23173

RINDFUSS, JOAN HAYNES, school administrator; b. Mpls., Oct. 11, 1928; d. James Arthur and Lyla (Waterbury) Haynes; m. Loren Perry Henkel, May 19, 1952 (div. 1977); children—Richard James Henkel, Julie Anne Henkel McKinney; m. 2d, A. Donald Rindfuss, Mar. 31, 1978. A.B., Hillsdale Coll. (Mich.), 1950; M.Adminstrn. and Supervision, Western Carolina U., 1969. Cert. tchr., adminstr., Fla. Advt. copywriter Montgomery Ward, Marshall Field & Co. and Henry C. Lytton's, Chgo., 1950-53; tchr. Dade County Pub. Schs., Miami, Fla., 1962—; asst. prin. West Homestead Elem. Sch., 1973-78, Pine Villa Elem. Sch., 1978-81, Coral Reef Elem. Sch., 1980—; producer ednl. slide presentations. Steering com. South Area Region I Adv. Com., 1981—. Alpha Delta Kappa Internat. Enrichment grantee, 1977. Mem. Am. Bus. Women's Assn. (finalist as Woman of Yr.), South Area Asst. Prins. (chmn. 1981-82), Dade County Sch. Adminstrs. Assn., Fla. Assn. Sch. Adminstrs., Theater Arts League, Miniplayers, Alpha Psi Omega, Alpha Delta Kappa. Congregationalist. Home: 15115 SW 89th Ct Miami FL 33176 Office: Coral Reef Elem Sch 7955 SW 152d St Miami FL 33157

RINGOLD, JAMES ROBERT, manufacturing company executive; b. Arkansas City, Kans., May 5, 1940; s. James Robert and Anna Marie (McKeever) R.; B.A. in Mktg., Pan Am. U., Edinburg, Tex., 1969; m. Sidney Marie Neidhart, Aug. 10, 1962; children—Shelley Ann, Lorinda Lea. With Humble Oil and Refining Co., Dallas, 1969-72, Pitney Bowes Co., Dallas, 1972-73, Diebold, Inc., Dallas, 1973-76; with Nat. Safe Corp., Clearwater, Fla., 1976-83, internat. mktg. mgr., 1980-83; pres. Protection Group Inc., Palm Harbor, Fla., 1983—. Vice pres. Dallas Jaycees, 1975. Served with USAF, 1962-66. Mem. Nat. Ind. Bank Equipment and Systems Assn., ASTM (security com.). Office: 3440 E Lake Rd Suite 110 Palm Harbor FL 33563

RINK, WESLEY WINFRED, banker; b. Hickory, N.C., June 14, 1922; s. Dewey L. and Mable E. (Yount) R.; m. Doreen M. Warman, Sept. 7, 1946; children—Rebecca S., Christopher L.; B.S. in Acctg., U. Ill., 1947, M.S., 1948. Div. controller The Glidden Co., Chgo., 1948-58; adminstrv. mgr. Central Soya Co., Chgo., 1958-65; v.p., controller State Nat. Bank, Evanston, Ill., 1965-71; exec. v.p., dir. Pioneer Bank & Trust Co., Chgo., 1971-76; corp. v.p. Exchange Bancorp., Inc., Tampa, Fla., 1977-82; sr. v.p. NCNB Nat. Bank Fla., Tampa, 1982—. Served with USAAF, 1942-46. Republican. Lutheran. Clubs: Westmoreland Country (Wilmette, Ill.); Temple Terrace Golf and Country. Lodges: Kiwanis, Rotary. Home: 523 Garrard Dr Temple Terrace FL 33617 Office: NCNB National Bank of Florida PO Box 25900 Tampa FL 33630

RINKER, MARSHALL EDISON, cement company executive; b. Cowan, Ind., Dec. 8, 1904; s. Jacob E. and Alberta May (Neff) R.; m. Vera Lea Keesling, Nov. 26, 1925; children—Marshall Edison, David B., John J. Student, Ball State Tchrs. Coll., Muncie, Ind., 1921-23; With Rinker Materials Corp. (and predecessor), chief exec. officer, chmn. bd., West Palm Beach, Fla., Rinker Portland Cement Corp., Rinker Southeastern Materials Inc. Chmn. West Palm Beach Community Chest, 1954; bd. dirs. W. Palm Beach chpt. ARC, 1930-50; trustee Stetson U., DeLand, Fla.; chmn. bd. deacons First Baptist Ch., West Palm Beach, 1960-62. Mem. Nat. Concrete Masonary Assn. (pres. 1954), Nat. Ready Mixed Concrete Assn. (pres. 1973, bd. dirs.), Fla. Concrete and Products Assn. (pres. 1967), West Palm Beach C. of C. (pres. 1954-55). Clubs: Rotary, Everglades, Old Guard Soc. (Palm Beach); Garden of Gods (Colorado Springs, Colo.); Ocean Reef (Key Largo, Fla.); Govs. (Palm Beach) (lifetime); River (Jacksonville, Fla.). Home: 561 Island Dr Palm Beach FL 33480 Office: 1501 Belvedere Rd West Palm Beach FL 33402 Office: PO Drawer K West Palm Beach FL 33402

RIONDA, CARLOS SILVESTRE, engring., metal stamping company executive; b. Havana, Cuba, June 26, 1947; s. Carlos A. and Olga (Duany) R.; m. María I. González, Aug. 24, 1968; children—Carlos S., Ileana O., Luis A. B.S.M.E., U. Miami, 1968, M.B.A., 1977; grad. advanced mgmt. program Harvard U., 1983. Registered profl. engr., Fla. Factory service engr. Gen. Tire, Akron, Ohio, 1968; from design engr. to sr. v.p. and gen. mgr. Gang Nail Systems Inc., Miami, Fla., 1969-82, pres., 1983—, chief exec. officer, 1984—, also dir.; dir. gang Nail Can., Toronto, Ont., 1981—, Gang Nail Europe, Brussels, 1981—. Editorial bd., contbr. tech. articles Mfg. Today Mag., 1978-79; patentee in field. Mem. Fla. Engring. Soc. Republican. Roman Catholic. Club: Kings Bay Yacht (Miami). Office: Gang Nail Systems Inc 7525 NW 37 Ave Miami FL 33147

RIOS, REBECCA ARMANDINA, nurse; b. Los Angeles, Oct. 27, 1954; d. Natividad V. and Georgina (Alvarado) R. B.S.N., Incarnate Word Coll., 1976. R.N., Tex.; cert. in advanced cardiac life support Am. Heart Assn. Obstetrics supr. Maverick County Hosp., Eagle Pass, Tex., 1977, operating room supr., 1977-78, nursing supr., 1978, hemodialysis dir., 1979-80, LVN sch. dir., 1980-82, emergency room head nurse, 1982—; nurse cons. Stonebrook Care Ctr., Eagle Pass, 1983—. Sec., March of Dimes, 1978. Mem. Am. Assn. Nephrology Nurses and Technicians, Tex. Nurses Assn., Nurses Book Soc. Roman Catholic. Address: PO Box 3299 Eagle Pass TX 78853

RIPPE, PETER MARQUART, museum administrator; b. Mpls., Dec. 16, 1937; s. Henry Albert and Zelda (Marquart) R.; m. Maria Boswell Wornom, Aug. 10, 1968. B.A., U. Puget Sound, 1960; M.A., U. Del., 1962. Dir., Confederate Mus., Richmond, Va., 1962-68; exec. dir. Harris County Heritage Soc., Houston, 1968-79, Roanoke Mus. Fine Arts (Va.), 1979—. Mem. Roanoke Arts Commn., 1983—. Fellow Old Deerfield Found., 1958, H.F. duPont Winterthur Mus., 1960-62. Mem. Am. Assn. Mus. (chmn. small mus. com. 1981-83, sr. examiner, 1983—, councillor-at-large 1985—), Tex. Assn. Mus. (pres. 1975-77, Tex. award 1979), Va. Assn. Mus. (pres. 1983-84), Southeast Mus. Conf. Democrat. Episcopalian. Home: 2318 Avenham Ave SW Roanoke VA 24014 Office: Roanoke Mus Fine Arts Ctr in the Square One Market Sq Roanoke VA 24011

RIST, HOYET ANDREW, III, broker; b. Richmond, Va., Dec. 11, 1946; s. Hoyet Andrew and Geraldine Koontz R.; m. Janet Hardee, Nov. 24, 1966; children—Stacy Gale, Todd Andrew. Student Va. Commonwealth U., 1974-77, Northwestern U., 1975. Traffic safety specialist Richmond (Va.) Bur. Police, 1971-76, safety and tng. officer, 1976-77; regional transp. safety coordinator Va. Dept. Transp. Safety, Richmond, 1977-78, state mgr. ops. and fin. Va. Alcohol Safety Action Program, 1978-82, state dir., 1982-83; account exec. Dean Witter Reynolds, 1983—; mem. Central Va. Safety Council, 1979—, v.p., bd. dirs., 1979-81; instr. trainer Nat. Safety Council, 1978—. Mem. Forest View Vol. Rescue Squad, 1969-79, ops. lt., 1974-76; mem. Fraternal Order of Police, 1971-75; safety clinic staff instr. trainer ARC, 1969—; deacon, assoc. Sunday Sch. Dir. Oak Grove Bapt. Ch., 1980—. Served with USMC, 1963-64. Recipient Meritorious Service award VA, 1962; Excellent Police Duty medal Richmond Bur. Police, 1974; Outstanding Vol. Service award ARC, 1976, medal for humanity, 1977, Outstanding Vol. Service award, 1977; Invaluable Vol. Service award Commonwealth Va., 1979; Disting. and Meritorious Service award Va. Shorthand Reports Assn., 1980; Jefferson Cup, Va. Bar Assn., 1983. Mem. Am. Mgmt. Assn., Am. Acad. Judicial Edn. (nat. com. devel. curriculum 1980), Va. Crime Prevention Assn., Va. Assn. Chiefs Police, Va. Alcohol Safety Action Program Dirs. Assn. Baptist. Home: 6319 Claudehart Rd Richmond VA 23234 Office: 700 Bldg 7th and Main St Richmond VA 23219

RITCHIE, ERIS ALTON, JR., business executive, mayor; b. Athens, Ala., Apr. 18, 1935; s. Eris Alton and Mary Ethel (Tackett) R.; B.S. cum laude, Abilene Christian U., 1957, M.Ed., 1961; m. Annita Hartsell, July 29, 1960; children—Matthew Eris, Robin Annette, Holly Hart, Michael Christopher. Band dir. Trent (Tex.) Public Schs., 1957-59, Cisco (Tex.) Public Schs., 1959-68; public relations dir., band dir. Cisco Jr. Coll., 1968-73, coordinator Band-Belles, 1973-77, promoter 5 appearances in Macy's Thanksgiving Day Parade, N.Y.C., 1971, 73, 77, 81, 84, also nat. TV appearances; dir. Cisco Jr. Music Festival, 1960-77; owner women's and children's retail store, 1969-79, 82—, embroidered emblems mfg. and mktg. firm, 1975—; mayor City of Cisco, 1981—; dir. summer camp clinics for baton twirlers, cheerleaders, drill teams, 1960—. Bd. dirs. Cisco Community Chest, West Tex. Fair, 1975-78; mem. adv. bd. Abilene Christian U., 1982—; chmn. com. for restoration and rehab. 1st hotel owned by Conrad Hilton, 1982—. Mem. Cisco C. of C. (pres. 1970-71, Outstanding Young Citizen award 1964, Outstanding Citizen 1968, Community Service award 1985). Mem. Ch. of Christ. Club: Rotary. Home: PO Box 350 Cisco TX 76437

RITCHIE, JOHN, lawyer, educator; b. Norfolk, Va., Mar. 19, 1904; s. John and Edith (Kensett) R.; B.S., U. Va., 1925, LL.B., 1927; J.S.D. (Sterling fellow 1930-31), Yale U., 1931; LL.D. (hon.), Coll. William and Mary, Williamsburg, Va., 1979; m. Sarah Dunlap Wallace, Apr. 20, 1929; children—John, Albert. Bar: Nebr. 1927, Va. 1942, Mo. 1952, Wis. 1953, Ill. 1957. Practice in Omaha, 1927-28; mem. faculty Furman U. Law Sch., 1929-30, U. Wash. Law Sch., Seattle, 1931-36, U. Md. Law Sch., 1936-37, U. Va. Law Sch., 1937-52; Kirby prof., dean Law Sch., Washington U. Law Sch., St. Louis, 1952-53; prof., dean Law Sch., U. Wis., Madison, 1953-57; Wigmore prof., dean Law Sch., Northwestern U., 1957-72, emeritus, 1972—; prof. law U. Va. Law Sch., 1972-74, scholar-in-residence, 1974—; pres. Judge Advs. Assn., 1952-53, Assn. Am. Law Schs., 1964; Tucker lectr. Washington and Lee U., 1964; De Tocqueville lectr. Marquette U., 1967; Tazewell prof. Coll. William and Mary, 1976; vis. prof. U. Tenn., 1974, U. Okla., 1975; mem. Ill. Jud. Adv. Council, 1964-68. Bd. dirs. Am. Council Edn., 1964-68, United Charities Chgo., 1966-72. Served to col. AUS, 1942-45. Decorated Bronze Star, Commendation medal. Life fellow Am. Bar Found.; mem. ABA (ho. of dels. 1952-72), Va. Bar Assn., Ill. Bar Assn., Chgo. Bar Assn., Raven Soc., Phi Beta Kappa, Order of Coif (nat. pres. 1952-55), Omicron Delta Kappa, Phi Kappa Psi, Phi Delta Phi. Episcopalian. Clubs: Wayfarers, Colonnade, Greencroft, Law of Chgo. Author: The First Hundred Years-A History of the University of Virginia Law Sch., 1978; co-author: Decedents' Estates and Trusts, 6th edit., 1982; contbr. articles to legal publs. Editorial bd. Found. Press, 1963—. Home: 1848 Westview Rd Charlottesville VA 22903 Office: Sch of Law U Va Charlottesville VA 22901

RITCHIE, JOSEPH C., mayor. Mayor City of Newport News, Va. Office: 2400 Washington Ave Newport News VA 23607*

RITTER, PHILIP WAYNE, library administrator; b. Ft. Myers, Fla., May 29, 1945; s. Ozzie Clarence and Connie (Copeland) R.; m. Barbara Ann Barnes, June 3, 1967; children—Andrew Philip, Cynthia Leigh. B.A., Atlantic Christian Coll., Wilson, N.C., 1967; M.Div., Vanderbilt U., 1970; M.S. in L.S., U. N.C., Chapel Hill, 1971. Cert. librarian, N.C., Va. Librarian, Southside Va. Community Coll., Alberta, Va., 1971-72; extension librarian Wake County Dept. Library, Raleigh, N.C., 1972-75; dir. Central N.C. Regional Library, Burlington, 1976-80; dir. Gaston-Lincoln Regional Library, Gastonia, N.C., 1980—, Gaston County Pub. Library, 1980—. Mem. United Arts and Sci. Council, 1981—; bd. dirs. Gaston Skills, Inc., Gastonia, N.C., 1982—; pres. Sherwood Elem. Sch. Parent Tchr. Orgn., 1984-85. Mem. United Way Community Resources Div. Bd., Gastonia, 1983—. Mem. ALA, Southeastern Library Assn., N.C. Library Assn. (past v.p.), N.C. Pub. Library Dirs. Assn., Metrolina Library Assn. (past pres.), Alpha Chi, Sigma Pi Alpha, Beta Phi Mu. Lodge: Rotary (bd. dirs. 1985—). Contbr. in field. Office: 1555 E Garrison Blvd Gastonia NC 28054

RITTERMAN, STUART I., speech pathologist, educator; b. Bklyn., May 21, 1937; s. Nathan and Ettie (Fried) R.; B.A., N.Y. U., 1959; postgrad Coll. City N.Y., 1962-64; Ph.D., Case Western Reserve U., 1968; m. Sharen Bruneau; 1 son, Joshua Nathaniel; 1 dau. by previous marriage, Moriah. Speech clinician Bklyn. Coll. Clinic, City Univ. N.Y., Bklyn., 1963, Bergan Pines County Hosp., Paramus, N.J., 1963-64; Vocational Rehab. Adminstrn. trainee Cleve. Hearing and Speech Center, 1964-66; speech clinician Benjamin Rose Hosp., Cleve., 1965-66; NIH career investigator trainee Case Western Res. U., Cleve., 1966-68, research asso. in dental edn., 1967-68; asst. prof. dept. communication disorders U. Okla. Med. Center, Oklahoma City, 1968-69, dir. diagnostic services in speech pathology, 1968-69; asst. prof. speech pathology and audiology inst. U. S. Fla., Tampa, 1969-71, asso. prof., 1972-76, prof., 1976—, dir. diagnostic services, 1969-71, dir. research in communicology, 1976—, acting dir. program in speech pathology and audiology Coll. Social and Behavioral Sci., 1971; vis. prof. phonetics U. Lille (France), 1984; cons. U. Okla. Med. Ctr., Oklahoma City, 1968-69; exec. dir. Cypher Research Consortium, Wesley Chapel, Fla., 1986—. Dept. Dept. Health Edn. and Welfare grantee, USPHS, 1971, Office Edn., 1971, Fla. Dept. Edn., 1971. Fellow Royal Soc. Health; mem. Am., Fla. speech and hearing assns., Am. (research com. 1972—), S.E. Am. (chmn. speech pathology and audiology sec. 1969-74) assns. on mental deficiency, Southeastern Conf. on Linguistics, Fla. Acad. Sci. (program chmn. behavioral sci. 1975-76), Linguistic Soc. Am., IEEE Computer Soc., Sigma Xi. Contbr. articles to profl. jours. Home: 181 Ellerbee Rd Wesley Chapel FL 34249 Office: U S Fla CBA 241 Tampa FL 33620

RIVAS, ERNESTO, newspaper columnist; b. N.Y.C., Dec. 19, 1924; s. Gabry and Sara (Solis) R.; m. Maria Coco, Dec. 8, 1969; children—Martin Javier, Maria Gabriela. B.A. and Sci., Colegio Centroamerica, Granada, Nicaragua. Press div. clk. UN, N.Y.C., 1947-48; reporter La Nueva Prensa, Managua, Nicaragua, 1949-52; dir. Radio Panamericana, Managua, 1952-60; with pub. relations dept. Nicaragua Mission, N.Y.C., 1960-62; news dir. Radio 590, Managua, 1963-79; columnist Diario Las Americas, Miami, Fla., 1979—; UPI corr., Managua, 1978-79; pub. relations cons. Nat. Power & Light Co., Managua, 1967-77, Union Democratica Nicaraguense, Miami, 1981—. Republican. Roman Catholic. Clubs: Nejapa Country, Terraza (Managua).

RIZAN, JANET KAY WASHINGTON, nurse, administrator; b. Griffin, Ga., Nov. 13, 1953; d. Stanley Allmon and Emma Sue (Potts) Washington; m. Philip John Rizan, Dec. 22, 1984. Diploma, Ga. Bapt. Hosp. Sch. Nursing, 1975. Registered nurse, Ga.; cert. trauma nurse specialist. Staff nurse, Ga. Bapt. Med. Ctr., Atlanta, 1975-76, charge nurse, 1976-77, asst. head nurse, 1977-81, chief flight nurse, 1981-83, dir. emergency nursing, 1983—. Co-coordinator: (course) Trauma Nurse Specialist, 1983. Mem. Nat. Flight Nurses' Assn., Emergency Nurses Assn., Am. Soc. Hosp.-Based Emergency Air Med. Services. Baptist. Avocations: aerobics; jogging; gardening; reading; sports. Office: Ga Baptist Med Ctr 300 Blvd NE Atlanta GA 30312

RIZZO, ANTHONY TONII, real estate executive; b. Buffalo, N.Y., Apr. 30, 1947; s. Samuel Anthony and Sara (Deconeck) R.; m. Aug. 11, 1973 (div. Oct. 1983); children—Scott Anthony, Shannon Ann; remarried, 1985. B.S., Western Ky. U.-Bowling Green, 1969, M.P.S., 1973; grad. Army Command and Gen. Staff Coll., 1978; M.B.A., Bellarmine Coll., Louisville, 1976. Mgmt. trainee Sears Roebuck & Co., Chgo., 1969; mktg. rep. Proctor & Gamble, Louisville, 1973-76; region cons. Xerox Corp., Louisville, 1976-80; sr. v.p. NTS Devel., Louisville, 1980-85; exec. v.p. Nat. Fin. Investment Corp., Louisville, 1985—. Served to maj. U.S. Army. Mem. Internat. Council Shopping Ctrs., Ky. Indsl. Devel. Council, Am. Mgmt. Assn., Sales Mktg. Assn., Bldg. Office Mgmt. Assn., Nat. Assn. Security Dealers (registered rep.). Roman Catholic. Home: 14501 Ashmont Pl Louisville KY 40223 Office: National Financial Investments Corp 2100 Citizens Plaza Louisville KY 40223

ROACH, SISTER JEANNE, nun, hospital administrator; b. Denver, Aug. 25, 1934. R.N., Regina Sch. Nursing, 1956; B.S., Coll. Mt. St. Joseph, 1964; M.S., Trinity U., 1973. Joined Sisters of Charity, Roman Catholic Ch., 1951; med. supr. St. Mary-Corwin Hosp., Pueblo, Colo., 1956-58; operating room supr. San Antonio Hosp., Kenton, Ohio, 1958-61; dir. nursing service Mt. San Rafael Hosp., Trinidad, Colo., 1961-67; speciality supr. Penrose Hosp., Colorado Springs, Colo., 1967-69, dir. nursing service, 1969-70, asst. adminstr., 1970-71, asst. adminstr. profl. services, 1973-75; assoc. adminstr. and coordinator St. Joseph Hosp., Mt. Clemens, Mich., 1975-78; v.p. Good Samaritan Hosp., Cin., 1978-82; adminstr. Our Lady of the Way Hosp., Martin, Ky., 1982-85; chief exec. officer St. Joseph Hosp., Huntingburg, Ind., 1985—. Trustee, treas. Ohio Valley Renal Disease Network, Inc., Louisville, 1981-83; bd. dirs. Mud Creek Clinic, Grethel, Ky., 1982-85. Fellow Am. Coll. Hosp. Adminstrs.; mem. Am. Mgmt. Assn., Am. Hosp. Assn., Cath. Health Assn., Ky. Hosp. Assn., Nat. League for Nursing. Office: St Joseph Hosp Leland Heights Huntingburg IN 47542

ROACH, JERRY VAN, dentist, Bible researcher; b. Cordell, Okla., Feb. 17, 1945; s. Weldon Van and Winnie B. (Nix) R.; m. Linda Kay Potosky, June 4, 1966; children—Kyle C., Kasey S. B.S. in Zoology, Eastern N.Mex. U., 1967, B.A. in Chemistry, 1967; D.D.S., Baylor U., 1971. Gen. practice dentistry, San Angelo, Tex., 1973—. Bd. dirs. West Tex. Rehab. Ctr., San Angelo, 1976—. Named Dentist of Yr., Tex. Dental Soc. 1977. Fellow Acad. Gen. Dentistry; mem. San Angelo Dist. Dental Soc. (pres. 1981-82). Republican. Lodge: Kiwanis (pres. San Angelo 1981-82). Avocations: running; snow skiing. Home: 2805 Palo Dura San Angelo TX 76904 Office: 4333 College Hills Blvd San Angelo TX 76904

ROACH, JOHN VINSON, II, manufacturing/retail company executive; b. Stamford, Tex., Nov. 22, 1938; s. John V. and Agnes (Moudy) R.; m. Jean Wiggin, Mar. 31, 1962; children—Amy, Lori. B.A., Tex. Christian U., 1961; M.B.A., 1965; D.Bus. Enterprise (hon.), Central New Eng. Coll., 1982. Mgr. data processing Consumer Fin. Co., Ft. Worth, 1965-67; gen. mgr. Tandy Computer Services, Ft. Worth, 1967-73; v.p. gen. distbn. Radio Shack, Ft. Worth, 1973-75, v.p. mfg., 1975-78, exec. v.p., 1978-80; pres., chief ops. officer Tandy Corp. & Radio Shack, Ft. Worth, 1980-81; pres., chief exec. officer Tandy Corp., Ft. Worth, 1981—, chmn. bd., 1982—; dir. Tex. Am. Bankshares, Justin Industries. Mem. Pres. Regan's Adv. Council on Pvt. Sector Initiatives, 1983; mem. Tex. Gov.'s Task Force on Unemployment and Jobs, 1983; pres. Arts Council Ft. Worth, 1982-83; bd. dirs. Tex. Christian U., Ft. Worth Country Day Sch., North Tex. Commn., Assn. Higher Edn. North Tex., Van Cliburn Found., Univ. Christian Ch.; mem. Tex. Gov.'s Blue Ribbon Commn. on Criminal Justice Corrections. Named Chief Exec. Officer of Yr., Fin. World, 1981, Salesman of Yr., Sales and Mktg. Execs. Ft. Worth, 1981, Top 100 in Tech., Tech. Mag., 1981, Best Chief Exec. Audio/Video Home Products, 1983; recipient Man of Yr. award Anti-Defamation League, 1983. Mem. Delta Pi Epsilon (disting. lectr. 1983), Sigma Chi. Lodge: Rotary. Office: 1900 One Tandy Center Fort Worth TX 76102

ROACH, WILLIAM LESTER, JR., guidance counselor, psychologist; b. Brookhaven, Miss., Sept. 4, 1948; s. W. Lester and Ethie Doris (Young) R.; m. Debra Cheryl Clements, May 29, 1971; children—William Lester III, Brian Lamar. B.A. in Edn., U. Miss., 1970, M.Ed., 1971; Ph.D., 1976. Cert. counselor Nat. Bd. Counselor Cert.; lic. psychologist, Miss.; cert. sch. psychologist. Tchr. math. W.P. Daniel High Sch., New Albany, Miss., 1970, Oxford Jr. High Sch., Miss., 1970-71; grad. asst. U. Miss., University, 1971-72; dir. guidance Lafayette County Schs., Oxford, 1972—; mem. adj. faculty counseling and edn. psychology dept. U. Miss., 1977—; mem. adj. faculty dept. psychology N.W. Jr. Coll., Senatobia, Miss., 1982—; psychologist North Central Regional Screeing Team, Oxford, 1980—. Author: Registration Guide for Students and Parents, 1980—. Named Outstanding Counselor, U. So. Miss., 1980. Mem. Am. Psychol. Assn., Nat. Assn. Sch. Psychologists, Miss. Counseling Assn., Miss. Sch. Counselor Assn. (pres.-elect 1981-82, pres. 1982-83). Avocations: hunting; fishing; golf; working with summer baseball program. Home: 15 La Rhonda Dr Route 5 Oxford MS 38655 Office: Lafayette High Sch Route 5 Oxford MS 38655

ROADEN, ARLISS LLOYD, higher education administrator; b. Corbin, Ky., Sept. 27, 1930; s. Johnie Samuel and Nora Ethel (Killian) R.; student (Am. Legion scholar) Cumberland Jr. Coll., 1949; A.B., Carson Newman Coll., 1951; M.S., U. Tenn., 1958, Ed.D., 1961; m. Mary Etta Mitchell, Sept. 1, 1951; children—Janice Arletta Roaden Skelton, Sharon Kay Roaden Hagen. Tchr. elem. sch., 1949-50; staff asst. Univ. Relations div. Oak Ridge Inst. Nuclear Studies, 1957-59; asst. prof. Auburn U., 1961-62; asst. prof., dir. grad. studies Ohio State U., 1962-64, asso. prof., 1964-65, asst. dir. Sch. Edn., 1965, asso. dir., 1966, prof., 1967, assoc. dean Coll. Edn., 1968, acting dean, 1969, vice provost for research, dean grad. sch., 1970-74; pres. Tenn. Technol. U., 1974-85; exec. dir. Tenn. Higher Edn. Commn., 1985—; vis. prof. Marshall U., summer 1961, Nat. Inst. for Study of Ednl. Change, Ind. U., summer 1967; mem. council, v.p. Div. I-A, NCAA, 1983-86; dir. Am. Bank and Trust, Cookeville, Tenn.; cons. sch. systems, univs., ednl. instns., profl. groups. Former chmn. bd. govs. Phi Delta Kappa Found.; exofficio mem. several bds.; mem. So. Regional Edn. Bd.; bd. dirs. Japan Ctr. of Tenn.; nat. bd. dirs. Project 714. Served with AUS, 1951-53. Recipient Centennial medallion for Disting. Faculty and Alumni, Coll. Edn., Ohio State U., 1970, Disting. Alumnus award Cumberland Coll.; Silver Beaver award Boy Scouts, 1983; Jaycees Boss of Year, 1985. Mem. Tenn. Coll. Assn. (pres. 1978), Nat. Assn. State Colls. and Land Grant Univs., Am. Assn. Higher Edn., Nat. Soc. for Study of Edn., AAAS, Am. Ednl. Research Assn., Nat. Acad. Polit. and Social Sci., Phi Delta Kappa (Distinguished Service award), Phi Kappa Phi, Kappa Phi Kappa, Kappa Delta Pi. Lodges: Lions (v.p.), Rotary (dir., Rotarian of Yr. award 1984). Author: Problems of Schoolmen in Depressed Urban Centers, 1968; (with Blaine R. Worthen) The Research Assistantship, 1975; contbr. editor Nat. Forum. Contbr. numerous articles to profl. jours. Home: 1242 Jefferson Davis Dr Brentwood TN 37027 Office: 501 Union Bldg Suite 300 Nashville TN 37219

ROAN, FORREST CALVIN, lawyer; b. Waco, Tex., Dec. 18, 1944; s. Forrest Calvin and Lucille Elizabeth (McKinney) R.; children—Amy Katherine, Jennifer Louise. B.B.A., U. Tex., Austin, 1973, J.D., 1976. Bar: Tex. 1976, U.S. Dist. Ct. (we. dist.) Tex. 1977, U.S. Ct. Appeals (5th cir.) 1977, U.S. Ct. Appeals (11th cir.) 1981, U.S. Supreme Ct. 1979. Prin. Roan & Assos., Austin, 1969-73; assoc. Heath, Davis & McCalla, Austin, 1976-78; sr. prin. Roan & Gullahorn, P.C., Austin, 1978—; dir. Pioneer Title Co., Alro Corp., Natesco Underwriters, Hull & Co. of Tex., G & R Communications, Waterloo Fin. Services, Capital Nat. Life Ins. Co. Mem. Tex. State Democratic Exec. Com., 1967-69; counsel Tex. Ho. of Reps., 1973-76; v.p. bd. dirs. Tex. Lyceum Assn. Served with Army NG, 1966-74. Mem. State Bar Tex., Travis County Bar Assn., ABA, Heritage Soc. Austin, Knights of the Symphony Sq. Com., Austin C. of C., E. Tex. C. of C., Delta Theta Phi, Delta Upsilon. Methodist. Clubs: Ins. of Dallas; Citadel, Austin, Headliners, Capital, Masons, Shriners; Rotary (Austin). Office: Roan and Gullahorn Box 896 Austin TX 78767

ROARK, JACQUELYN DEVORE, college official; b. Newberry, S.C., Sept. 12, 1950; d. William N. and Julia E. (Coleman) DeVore; m. Walter Lynch Roark, III, Apr. 21, 1979; children—Walter Lynch, Julia Elizabeth. B.S. in Home Econs. Edn., Lander Coll., 1972; M.Ed., Clemson U., 1975. Admissions counselor Lander Coll., Greenwood, S.C., 1971-75, dir. admissions, 1976—. Bd. dirs. S.C. Lung Assn., 1974; program mem. S.C. League Nursing, 1980; mem., officer Greenwood Woman's Forum. Mem. Am. Personnel and Guidance Assn., Am. Council Higher Edn., Am. Assn. Collegiate Registrars and Admissions Officers, S.C. Assn. Coll. Registrars and Admissions Officers, So. Assn. Collegiate Registrars and Admissions Officers. Democrat. Home: 100 Gracemont Dr Greenwood SC 29646

ROARK, JAMES E., mayor of Charleston, lawyer; b. Charleston, W.Va., Aug. 31, 1945; s. James M. and Geneva (Ash) R.; children—Taylor, Campbell. B.A., U. Va., 1967; J.D., W.Va. U., 1973. With U.S. Dept. Justice, Washington, 1973-75; asst. U.S. atty. Western Dist. Pa., 1975-77; assoc. Steptoe & Johnson, Clarksburg, W.Va., 1977-78; pros. atty. Kanawha County, Charleston, 1978-83; mayor City of Charleston, 1983—. Vice pres. Charleston Renaissance Corp. Served to lt. USMC, 1968-71. Recipient W.Va. Lawyers award, 1981. Mem. U.S. Conf Mayors, Nat. League Cities, W.Va. Mcpl. League, Stageworks, Kanawha Players, Fund for Arts, Ducks Unltd. Republican. Episcopalian. Lodge: Lions. Office: City of Charleston City Hall Court and Virginia Sts Charleston WV 25301

ROBB, CHARLES SPITTAL, lawyer, former governor Virginia; b. Phoenix, June 26, 1939; s. James Spittal and Francis Howard (Woolley) R.; m. Lynda Bird Johnson, Dec. 9, 1967; children—Lucinda Desha, Catherine Lewis, Jennifer Wickliffe. Student, Cornell U., 1957-58; B.B.A., U. Wis., 1961; J.D., U. Va., 1973. Bar: Va. 1973, U.S. Supreme Ct. 1976. Law clk. to John D. Butzner, Jr., U.S. Ct. Appeals, 1973-74; atty. Williams Connolly & Califano, 1974-77; lt. gov. Va., 1978-82, gov., 1982-86; v.p., dir. LBJ Co., 1971-81, No. Va. Radio Co., 1978-81; ptnr. Hanton & Williams, 1986—; chmn. Va. Forum on Edn., 1978-81, Concerned Citizens of the Commonwealth, 1978-81; vice-chmn. Local Govt. Adv. Commn., 1978-81; mem. exec. com., chmn. So. Region, chmn. intergovtl. affairs com., vice chmn. econ. devel. com. Nat. Conf. Lt. Govs., 1979-80; chmn. Am. Council Young Polit. Leaders del. to Peoples Republic of China, 1979; chmn. Edn. Comm. of the States, 1985, Jobs for Am.'s Graduates, 1986; mem. exec. com. So. Growth Policies Bd.; mem. So. Regional Edn. Bd.; dir. United Va. Bank, The Enterprise Found. Mem. various bds. U. Va., 1974—, U. Richmond, 1974—, Hampton Inst. Tech., 1977-81; mem. Nat. Capital Area exec. bd. Boy Scouts Am., 1976—; chmn. No. Va. Scout Expo, 1976, 77; mem. Fairfax County bd. Am. Cancer Soc., 1976—; profl. gifts chmn. United Way of Fairfax County, 1976; dep. gen. counsel, asst. parliamentarian Democratic Nat. Com. Platform Com., 1976; mem. Fairfax County Dem. Com., 1975—, Dem. State Central Com., 1976—. Served with USMC, 1961-70; co. comdr., aide to comdg. gen. 2d Marine Div.; social aide to White House; Washington; inf. co. comdr.; Vietnam. Decorated Bronze Star, Vietnam Service medal with 4 Stars; Vietnamese Cross of Gallantry with Silver Star; recipient Raven award, 1973, Seven Socs. Orgn. award U. Va. Mem. Am., Va. bar assns., Va. Trial Lawyers Assn., Nat. Govs. Assn. (chmn. standing com. criminal justice and pub. protection, mem. transp., commerce and tech. com., mem. energy and environ. com.), So. Govs. Assn. (chmn.), Dem. Govs. Assn. (chmn.), Res. Officers Assn., USMC Res. Officers Assn., Am. Legion, Raven Soc., Omicron Delta Kappa. Episcopalian. Office: Office of Gov State Capitol Richmond VA 23219

ROBBIE, JOSEPH, lawyer, professional football team executive; b. S.D., July 7, 1916; s. Joseph Robbie and Jennie (Ready) R.; A.B., U. S.D., 1943, LL.B., 1946, LL.D. (hon.), 1979; LL.D. (hon.), Biscayne Coll., 1970; Ph.D. (hon.), Mt. Marty Coll., Yankton, S.D., 1979; H.H.D., St. Leo Coll., 1982; D.B.A. (hon.), Dakota Wesleyan U., 1984; m. Elizabeth Ann Lyle, Dec. 28, 1942. Admitted to S.D. bar, 1946, Minn. bar, 1951; practiced in Mitchell, S.D., 1946-53, Mpls., 1953—; founder, 1965, since pres., mng. gen. partner Miami Dolphins, Ltd.; dep. state's atty. Davison County, S.D., 1947-49; regional counsel, acting regional enforcement dir. Office Price Stblzn., Mpls., 1951-52, regional dir., 1952-53; author Minn. Mcpl. Commn. Act., 1959-60, 1st chmn. commn., 1959-65; charter mem., sec.-treas. Twin Cities Met. Planning Commn., 1957-67; spl. counsel com. for hearings to create Dept. Urban Affairs, U.S. Senate, 1961; exec. sec., legal counsel Commn. Mcpl. Annexation and Consol. Minn. Legislature, 1957-59, Commn. Mcpl. Laws Minn. Legislature, 1959-61; exec. dir. Minn. Candy and Tobacco Distbrs. Assn., 1959—; asst. prof. econs. Dakota Wesleyan U., 1946-48; spl. instr., debate coach Coll. St. Catherine, St. Paul, 1953-54. Vice pres., presiding officer Am. Lebanese Syrian Asso. Charities, 1966-68; co-chmn. Notre Dame Summa Fund Raising Campaign, 1967; chmn. Biscayne Coll. Challenge Fund Raising Campaign, 1968-69; hon. chmn. challenge for Century III campaign De La Salle High Sch., Mpls., 1982; chmn. Miami Easter Seal Campaign, 1969; gen. chmn. Heart Fund Greater Miami; mem. steering com. Friends of Religion, U. Miami, 1979—. Chmn. Am. Football League Player Relations Com., 1969; exec. com. Nat. Football League Mgmt. Council, 1972-77, 83—; mem. S.D. Legislature, 1949-51, joint caucus leader; chmn. S.D. Democratic Com., 1948-50; candidate gov. S.D., 1948, U.S. Congress from Minn., 1956, 58; chmn. Minn. adv. com. Nat. Dem. Com., 1954-58; chmn. Dade County (Fla.) Dem. Exec. Com., 1972; campaign chmn. Humphrey for Pres., Charleston, W.Va., 1960; bd. govs. St. Jude Children's Research Hosp., Memphis, 1959-80; bd. dirs. Crippled Children's Soc., Miami, 1967-73, Boys Town Fla., Variety Children's Hosp.; mem. adv. bd. Fla. Meml. Coll., Miami, 1967—, Fla. Internat. U., 1972—; mem. nat. adv. council St. Jude Children's Research Hosp., 1981—; bd. advisors Miami Lighthouse for the Blind, 1983; past bd. dirs. Operation South Help; bd. dirs., mem. exec. com. United Fund of Dade County; trustee Dade Found., Dade County Community Relations Bd., Public Health Trust, Jackson Meml. Hosp., 1973-79, 81—, St. Leo Coll., 1984—; trustee emeritus Biscayne Coll.; mem. citizens bd. U. Miami; hon. chmn. Century of Service Fund Campaign, Yankton, 1978; bd. dirs. Jesuit Program for Living and Learning, 1978—; past bd. dirs. Cath. Service Bur., Archdiocese of Miami, chmn. bd. dirs., from 1977. Served with USNR, 1941-45. Decorated Bronze Star, Knights of Malta, Order of Knights of St. Gregory; recipient Nathan Burkan Meml. award for essay copyright law, 1946; J. Ernest O'Brien Commendation award Nat. Assn. Tobacco Distbrs., 1966; Horatio Alger award, 1979; CHIEF award Ind. Colls. and Univs. of Fla., 1981; Humanitarian award Big Bros./Big Sisters Greater Miami, 1982; named Nat. Football League Owner of Yr., Minutemen of Mpls. and St. Paul, 1971; Profl. Football Exec. of Year, L.I. Athletic Club, 1972. Outstanding Ambassador for S.D., S.D. Press Assn., 1984; named to Hall of Fame, U. S.D., 1982. Mem. Greater Miami C. of C. (gov. 1971-74). Office: 4770 Biscayne Blvd Miami FL 33137 also 1123 Plymouth Bldg Minneapolis MN 55402

ROBBINS, ANN CAROTHERS, nursing administrator; b. Detroit, May 21, 1936; d. George Gregory and Pauline Elise (Tucker) Carothers; m. Theodore C. Robbins, Nov. 14, 1959; children—Susan Catherine, Karen Elizabeth, Thomas Charles. R.N., Norfolk Gen. Hosp., 1959; B.S.N., Tex. Woman's U., 1973, M.S.N., 1976. Supr. Woodlawn Hosp., Dallas, 1973-75; instr. Tex. Woman's U., Denton, 1975-79; cons. U. Tex. Health Scis. Ctr., Dallas, 1980-81; cons. Buckner Baptist Nursing Home, Dallas, 1982-83; asst. prof. Dallas Baptist Coll., 1981-83; dir. nurses Parkland Hosp., Dallas, 1983—; cons., Dallas, 1980—; mem. disaster nursing team ARC, Dallas, 1981-82; mem. Tex. Nurses' Coalition for Action in Politics, Dallas, 1975—. Mem. Am. Nurses Assn., Tex. Nurses Assn. (treas. dist. 4, 1981-82, pres. 1983-84), Sigma Theta Tau. Republican. Methodist. Contbr. articles to profl. jours., chpts. to books. Office: Outpatient Services Parkland Hosp Harry Hines Blvd Dallas TX 75235

ROBBINS, BRUCE RANDELL, human resources administrator; b. San Diego, Sept. 2, 1953; s. William Franklin and Ione Carol (Mapes) R.; m. Barbara Rose Schrieber, Aug. 12, 1978 (div. 1985). A.A., N.Mex. Mil. Inst., 1973; B.S., SUNY-Albany, 1977; M.A., Webster Coll., 1981. Tech. recruiter Potomac Electric Power Co., Washington, 1982-83; mgr. adminstrv. recruiting MCI Telecommunications, Washington, 1983-84; mgr. human resources No. Telecom, Inc., Vienna, Va., 1985—. Campaign vol. Reagan for Pres., 1976, Frank Wolf for Congress, 1983-84; commn. mem. Law Enforcement Adv. Commn., Falls Church, Va., 1983-85. Served to capt. U.S. Army, 1978-81; terrorism specialist Res. Mem. Am. Soc. Personnel Adminstrn. (editorial reviewer 1981—). Republican. Avocations: tennis; racquetball; camping. Home: 8139 Prescott Dr Apt 204 Vienna VA 22180 Office: No Telecom Inc 8401 Old Courthouse Rd Vienna VA 22180

ROBBINS, CAREY ANGELYN MAY, nurse; b. Fayette, Ala., Feb. 24, 1952; d. Carey Milton and Billie Angelyn (Wilson) May; m. Berlin Jackson Robbins, Jr., June 5, 1980; children—Berlin Jackson, John Michael; 1 son by previous marriage, William Alan Potter. Student Athens Coll., 1970-72, B.S.N., U. Ala.-Birmingham, 1974. B.S. supr. Bryce Hosp., Tuscaloosa, Ala., 1974-75, 76-78, nurse recruiter, 1975-76; psychiat. charge nurse Huntsville Hosp. (Ala.), 1978-80, staff nurse emergency dept., 1980—. Mem. Huntsville Civic Ballet Assn., Huntsville Historic Soc. Served with Army Res. Mem. Am. Nurse Recruiters Assn., Internat. Platform Assn. Republican. Baptist. Home: 6100 University Dr Huntsville AL 35806 Office: 2124 S Memorial Pkwy Huntsville AL 35801

ROBBINS, EARL L., oil operator; b. Detroit, Mar. 9, 1921; s. Louis and Ida Robbins; m. Dorothy D. Robbins, Nov. 12, 1949 (div. Mar. 1974); children—T. Paul, Louis J., Loralee. B.A., Wayne State U., 1949; M.B.A., U. Chgo., 1951. Owner, Enurtone of Tex., Houston, 1951-55; v.p. Continental Securities Co., Houston, 1955-57; owner, mgr. Robbins & Co., Houston, 1957-59; div. mgr. Great Books, Houston, 1960-74; owner, mgr. Robbins Oil Co., Houston. Bd. dirs. Cancer Assistance League, Houston, 1983-84, Children's Resource and Info. Soc. chmn. Alley Theater Gala, Houston, 1983; com. mem. Houston Live Stock Show, 1978-81. Served to maj. USAAF, 1941-46. Recipient Disting. Service award Am. Diabetes Assn., Houston, 1982. Office: Robbins Oil Co PO Box 35322 Houston TX 77035

ROBBINS, GERALD DUANE, JR., petroleum geologist; b. Clinton, Ind., June 6, 1952; s. Gerald Duane and Arleen Velma (Marshall) R.; m. Elaine Alice Rarey, Dec., 1976; children—Bryan William, Jeanette Arleen. B.S. in Geology, Ind. U., 1976; M.S. in Geology, Okla. State U., 1979. Petroleum geologist Union Oil of Calif., Oklahoma City, 1979-81; cons. geologist CEC Drilling, RCTX Corp, Eason Oil, Oklahoma City, 1982-84; sr. geologist Wagner & Brown Oil Producers, Oklahoma City, 1985—. Mem. Am. Assn. Petroleum Geologist, Oklahoma City Geol. Soc. Republican. Presbyterian. Club: Music Assocs. (Oklahoma City). Avocation: classical piano. Office: Wagner & Brown Oil Producers 2500 Liberty Tower Oklahoma City OK 73102

ROBBINS, LARRY JACK, college administrator; b. Chesapeake, Ohio, Aug. 8, 1935; s. Lawrence Loring and Blanche Margaret (Earls) R.; m. Wanda Lee True, Aug. 20, 1961; 1 child, Katherine Loring Robbins Herald. B.A., Lexington Bapt. Coll., 1964, B.Th., 1969, B.Religious Edn., 1973; B.S., Cumberland Coll., 1976; M.Religious Edn., Lexington Bapt. Coll., 1977; M.Higher Edn., Morehead State U., 1978; D.Div., Lexington Bapt. Coll., 1981. Ordained minister, Baptist Ch., 1964. Pastor Stewartsville Bapt. Ch., Williamstown, Ky., 1964-68, Lusby's Mill Bapt. Ch., Owenton, Ky., 1968-72; asst. pastor Devondale Bapt. Ch., Lexington, Ky., 1972-79; registrar to exec. v.p. Lexington Bapt. Coll., 1968—. Served with U.S. Army, 1958-60. Democrat. Avocations: fishing; hunting; reading; golf. Home: 188 N Ashland Ave Lexington KY 40502 Office: Lexington Bapt Coll 163 N Ashland Ave Lexington KY 40502

ROBBINS, LILLIAN ANDREWS, educational administrator; b. High Point, N.C., Sept. 10, 1930; d. Charles Ray and Ruby (Harris) Andrews; m. Hal G. Robbins, Jr., Mar. 27, 1949; children—Jewell Yvonne, Joel Edward, Jeffrey Ray. Student Central Wesleyan Coll., 1946-47, Woman's Coll., Greensboro, N.C., 1954, Summer Inst.-N.C. State U., 1974, Tri-County Tech. Coll., 1971-72, Greenville Tech. Coll., 1976. Supr. office force for fund-raising Hampden Sydney (Va.) Coll., 1958-60; acct. Clanton's Drug Store/Booker's Garage, Alta Vista, Va., 1961-69; with Bruton Developer, Builder, Realtor, Charlottesville, Va., 1969-70; staff bus. office Central Wesleyan Coll., Central, S.C., 1970-71, alumni and admissions dir., 1977—; coordinator profl. devel. program Clemson U., 1971-77; seminar leader for women's, children's programs Central Wesleyan Coll. Recipient Service award Central Wesleyan Coll. Alumni Assn., 1978-80; Disting. Service award Central Wesleyan Coll. Bd. Trustees, 1981. Mem. Carolina Assn. Collegiate Registrars and Admissions Officers, Women in Higher Edn. Networks. Club: Sailing. Home: 105 Hillendale Rd Liberty SC 29657 Office: PO Box 518 Central SC 29630

ROBBINS, RIMA, journalist, public relations specialist; b. N.Y.C., Apr. 3, 1934; d. Maurice and Ruth (Ackerman) R.; m. Michael John Greenberg, June 10, 1954; children—Peter A., John K., Karl P. Student Cornell U., 1951-54; B.A., Fla. State U., 1955; M.S. in Journalism, Boston U., 1957; M.A. in East Asian Studies, Fla. State U., 1970. Tech. editor office engring. publs. U. Ill., Urbana, 1962-64; free-lance journalist, Fla., 1971-73; info. specialist Fla. Dept. State, Tallahassee, 1977-80; dep. dir. pub. info. Fla. Hosp. Cost Containment Bd., Tallahassee, 1980-81; pres. The Shadow Communication Service, 1983—; nat. coordinator documentary radio series category Clarion awards competition Womem in Communications; adj. prof. Flagler Coll., St. Augustine, Fla., 1986; free-lance writer, book reviewer, pub. relations cons. NDEA fellow, 1968; recipient So. Pub. Relations Fedn. award, 1979. Mem. Nat. Assn. Am. Pen Women, Soc. Tech. Communication, Women In Communications, Fla. Pub. Relations Assn., Pub. Relations Soc. Am., Am. Med. Writers Assn. Home: Route 1 Box 112 B Saint Augustine FL 32086 Office: PO Box 4287 Saint Augustine FL 32085

ROBERSON, DALE EDWARD, pharmacist, songwriter, musician; b. Pikeville, Tenn., July 5, 1952; s. Rhubert Blake and Mary Gene (Roberson) R.; m. Liza Ault Burns, Aug. 18, 1974; children—Phillip Edward, Anna Elizabeth. Student U. Tenn.-Chattanooga, 1970-71; B.S. in Pharmacy, Samford U., 1975; B.S. in Chemistry, Tenn. Tech. U., 1975; D. Pharmacy, Tenn. Bd. Pharmacy, 1981. Musician The Playboys, Chattanooga, 1966-72; pharmacist Big B Inc., Midfield, Ala., 1975-78, chief pharmacist, asst. mgr., Huntsville, Ala., 1978-82; pharmacy mgr. Kroger, Huntsville, 1982—; songwriter. Exec. mem. mass communications Calhoun Community Coll., 1984. Mem. Ala. Pharm. Assn., Madison County Pharm. Assn., Muscle Shoals Songwriters Assn., North Ala. Songwriters Assn. Democrat. Methodist. Club: Huntsville Athletic. Avocations: handball; racquetball; tennis; basketball; softball. Home: 2509 Galahad Dr SE Huntsville AL 35803

ROBERSON, GARY DON, oil company executive; b. Hereford, Tex., Jan. 3, 1947; s. Deward Bernard and Tiny Lee (Springer) R.; m. Dana Shumard, May 23, 1970; children—Leslie Renee, Jonathan Kristopher. B.S., Baylor U., 1969, M.S., 1972. Geologist, Union Oil of Calif., Lafayette, La., 1971-74; exploration geologist Atlantic Richfield, Bogota Colombia, S.Am., 1974-76, Tex. Pacific Oil Co., Lafayette, 1976-80; v.p. exploration Tarandus Exploration, 1980-84; v.p., ptnr. Isla Exploration, Lafayette, 1984-85; ind. geologist, 1985—. Youth choir dir. Asbury United Methodist Ch., Lafayette, 1972-74, bd. dirs., 1980—; student adv. U. Southwestern La., 1980; bd. dirs. Lafayette Log Assn., 1983-84, Jr. Achievers of Lafayette, 1974-75; soccer coach Lafayette Parish Youth Soccer Assn., 1984—. Mem. Soc. Econ. Petrologists and Minerologists (sec. 1977-78), Lafayette Geol. Soc., Gulf Coast Assn. Geol. Soc. (publicity chmn. 1980), Am. Assn. Petroleum Geologists, Southwest Geophys. Soc. Republican. Methodist. Avocations: golfing; camping; soccer; skiing.

ROBERSON, HOUSTON FRANKLIN, JR., pharmacist; b. Cedartown, Ga., Nov. 11, 1951; s. O.E. and Syble (Wilson) Brannan R.; m. Teresa Kay Davis, Aug. 27, 1977; children—Benjamin Jacob, Claire Elizabeth, Houston Franklin III. B.S., U. Ga., 1976; M.Div., Southwestern Sem., Fort Worth, 1985. Registered pharmacist. I.V. pharmacist Floyd Med. Ctr., Rome, Ga., 1976-80; staff pharmacist Mercy Hosp., Watertown, N.Y., 1980-81; chief pharmacist E.J. Noble Hosp., Alexander Bay, N.Y., 1981; relief pharmacist Riverside Drug, Fort Worth, 1982-84, Shields Pharmacy, Euless, Tex., 1984—. Mem. Tex. Pharm. Assn. Baptist. Avocations: hunting; jogging; reading; sports; fishing.

ROBERSON, JAMES O., association executive. Pres., Louisville C. of C. Office: Louisville C of C 1 Riverfront Plaza Louisville KY 40202*

ROBERSON, JANIS LANELL, library adminstrator; b. Sherman, Tex., Nov. 22, 1947; d. Eddie Loyd and Thelma Ilene (Kerr) Helton; m. Richard David Roberson, May 22, 1971; children—Brian Devin, David Curtis. B.S., Tex. Woman's U., 1970, M.L.S., 1976. Cert. county librarian, Tex. Cataloger, head tech. processing Grand Prairie (Tex.) Meml. Library, 1970-77; dir. Grapevine (Tex.) Pub. Library, 1978—. Mem. Tarrant Regional Librarians Assn. (pres. 1982-83), Pub. Librarians Assn. North Tex. (pres. 1983), Grapevine Women's C. of C., Grapevine Hist. Soc. (oral history com. chmn.), Grapevine C. of C., ALA, Tex. Library Assn., Tex. Mcpl. Library Dirs. Assn. Republican. Baptist. Home: 2929 Harvest Hill Grapevine TX 76051 Office: Grapevine Public Library 307 W Dallas Rd Grapevine TX 76051

ROBERSON, THOMAS GLENN, b. Walterboro, S.C., Sept. 26, 1955; s. Thomas Guy and Juanita E. (Sullins) R.; m. Susan Elaine Andrews, Oct. 24, 1957. Grad. in acctg. U. South Fla., 1978. Field rep. GMAC, Nashville, 1978-81; bus. mgr. Brentwood (Tenn.) Acad., 1981-82; fiscal officer Fla. Coll., Temple Terrace, 1982—. Mem. U.S. Congl. Adv. Bd., 1983-84, Republican Presdl. Task Force, 1983-84. Mem. Am. Assn. Accts., Nat. Assn. Student Fin. Aid Adminstrs., Nat. Assn. Coll. and Univ. Bus. Officers, So. Assn. Student Fin. Aid Adminstrs., Assn. Sch. Bus. Officers, Western Assn. Coll. and Univ. Bus. Officers, So. Assn. Coll. and Univ. Bus. Officers, Fla. Assn. Student Fin. Aid Adminstrs., Nat. Jr. Coll. Athletic Assn., Nat. Council Community Coll. Bus. Ofcls., C. of C. Mem. Ch. of Christ. Club: U.S. Senatorial. Office: 119 Glen Arven Ave Temple Terrace FL 33617

ROBERT, JOSEPH CLARKE, historian, consultant; b. State College Miss., June 2, 1906; s. Joseph Clarke and Hallie Christian (Cavett) R.; A.B. magna cum laude, Furman U., 1927, LL.D., 1959; A.M., Duke U., 1929, Ph.D., 1933; Litt.D., Washington and Lee U., 1958; L.H.D., Med. Coll. Va., 1962; m. Evelyn Mercer Bristow, June 15, 1931 (dec.); children—Frank Chambers, Carol Mercer Robert Armstrong; m. Sara Cross Squires, May 12, 1985. Ranger-historian Nat. Park Service, Yorktown, Va., 1934; instr. history Ohio State U., Columbus, 1934-38; asst. prof. Duke U., 1938-44, asso. prof., 1944-49, asso. dean Grad. Sch., 1949-52, prof., 1949-52; pres. Coker Coll., Hartsville, S.C., 1952-55; pres. Hampden-Sydney (Va.) Coll., 1955-60; prof. history U. Richmond (Va.), 1961-71, prof. history emeritus, 1972—; cons. Psychol. Cons., Inc., Richmond, 1966, Newport News Shipbldg. & Dry Dock Co. (Va.), 1961-64, others. Pres., So. Carolina Assn. Colls., 1952-53. Watauga fellow Harvard U., 1929-30, Duke U. fellow, 1930-31, Fund for Advancement of Edn. travel and study grantee, 1960-61, Humanities fellow U. N.C., Duke U., 1966-67. Mem. So. Hist. Assn. (life), Va. Hist. Soc. (pres. emeritus), Phi Beta Kappa, Omicron Delta Kappa, Sigma Chi. Presbyterian. Club: Commonwealth (Richmond). Author: THe Tobacco Kingdom, 1938; The Road From Monticello, 1941; The Story of Tobacco in America, 1949; Ethyl: A History of the Corporation and the People Who Made It, 1983; People Who Made It, 1983; Gottwald Family History, 1984; contbr. articles to profl. jours. Home: 103 Tuckahoe Blvd Richmond VA 23226

ROBERTO, LAURA GIAT, clinical psychologist, educator; b. N.Y.C., Dec. 22, 1952; d. Ouriel and Ann Giat; m. Frank Andre Roberto, June 21, 1981; 1 son, Aaron Jesse. B.A., U. Conn., 1974; Psy.D., U. Ill., 1979; postdoctoral fellow U. Wis. Sch. Medicine, 1979-80. Lic. clin. psychologist, Va. Research assoc. Wis. Psychiat. Inst., U. Wis. Sch. Medicine, Madison, 1980-81; pvt. practice psychology, Madison, Wis. and Norfolk, Va., 1980-83; asst. prof. Eastern Va. Med. Sch., Norfolk, 1982—. NIMH trainee, 1974. Mem. Am. Assn. Marriage and Family Therapists (approved supr.), Am. Psychol. Assn., Nat. Register Health Care Providers, Tidewater Acad. Clin. Psychologists, Am. Family Therapy Assn., Sigma Xi Research Found., Phi Beta Kappa, Phi Kappa Phi. Office: Eastern Va Family Therapy Inst 205 Business Park Dr Virginia Beach VA 23462

ROBERTON, DONALD K., telecommunications executive; b. Las Vegas, Nev., Oct. 29, 1941; s. Donald Nesbit and Mary Helen (Paterson) R.; m. Jennifer J. Roberton, Apr. 9, 1968; children—Shannon Eillen, Dawn Christy. Cert., Colgate Darden, U. Va., 1981; cert. Mich. State U., 1977; Gen. plant supr. Centel Corp., Chgo., 1973-75; plant mgr. Central Telephone of N.C., Hickory, N.C., 1975-77, engring. mgr., 1977-78, gen. mgr., 1978-80; gen. mgr. Central Telephone of Va., Charlottesville, 1980-84; v.p. Fisk div. Centel Bus. Systems, Houston, 1984—. Bd. dirs. Jr. Achievement, Charlottesville, 1982-83; group chmn. United Fund, Hickory, N.C., 1978; bd. dirs. Adminstrv. Mgmt. Soc. Hickory, 1979-80. Served with U.S. Army, 1959-62. Recipient award for most improved operating performance Centel Corp., 1981. Republican. Lutheran. Club: Rotary. Home: 7918 Northbridge Spring TX 77373 Office: Fisk Div Centel Bus Systems 2100 Travis Suite 900 Houston TX 77002

ROBERTS, BILL GLEN, fire chief, investor, consultant; b. Deport, Tex., June 2, 1938; s. Samuel Westbrook and Ann Lee (Rhodes) R.; m. Ramona Downs, June 1, 1963; 1 dau., Renee Ann. A.A.S., El Centro Jr. Coll., Dallas, 1980. Lt., Dallas Fire Dept., 1964-67, capt., 1967-71, div. fire chief, 1971-79, asst. fire chief, 1979-83; fire chief Austin Fire Dept. (Tex.), 1983—; tech. bd. dirs. Found. Fire Safety, Washington, 1982—. Author: EMS Dallas, 1978; (with others) Anesthesia for Surgery Trauma, 1976, EMS Measures to Improve Care, 1980; contbr. articles to periodicals. Com. chmn. Dallas Jaycees, 1962-65; task force Am. Heart Assn., Austin, 1973-83. Served to tech. sgt. USAF, 1960-66. Recipient John Stemmons Service award Dallas Fire Dept., 1978; Internat. Assn. Fire Chiefs scholar, 1968. Mem. Internat. Assn. Fire Chiefs, Nat. Fire Protection Assn., Am. Trauma Soc. (founding mem.), Am. Assn. Trauma Specialists. Methodist. Home: 4009 Cordova St Austin TX 78759 Office: Austin Fire Dept 1622 Festival Beach Rd Austin TX 78702

ROBERTS, BOBBY GENE, protective service official; b. Bristol, Va., Sept. 5, 1941; s. Robert Dale and Rowena Mae (Shull) R.; m. Patsy Barger, Oct. 22, 1965; 1 child, David Allen. Student E. Tenn. State U., 1963, Va. State Police Acad. Asst. mgr. Inter-Mountain Telephone Co., Abingdon, Va., 1961-63; fireman Bristol Fire Dept., 1963; police lt. Bristol Police Dept., 1963—; v.p. Southeastern Security Inc., Bristol, 1984—; active Bur. Narcotics and Dangerous Drugs, Dept. Justics, Community Devel. Alternatives to Drug Abuse; hostage situation negotiator Commonwealth of Va. Active Radiol. Emergency Preparedness, Bristol Va. Life Saving Crew, Bristol Central Little League Baseball. Recipient Police Officer of Yr. award Bristol Jaycees, 1972, 76, Officer Appreciation award Bristol Police Aux., 1979. Mem. Tri State Crime Clinic, Va. Security Assn. (state v.p. 1985-86), Va. Assn. Drug Enforcement Officers. Democrat. Presbyterian. Avocations: firearms; carpentry; yard work. Home: 415 Randolph St Bristol VA 24201 Office: Police Dept 415 Cumberland St Bristol VA 24201

ROBERTS, BRENDA FAYE, psychotherapist, educator; b. Lake Charles, La., Aug. 13, 1949; d. Adam and Mabel Louanna (Primeaux) Thibodeaux; m. Michael Thomas Roberts, June 19, 1971; children—Bree Michelle, Rhiannon Lea, Vanessa. B.A., Jamestown State U., 1970, M.Ed., 1974, Ed.D., 1981. Lic. profl. counselor; nat. cert. counselor; nat. cert. mental health counselor, cert. reality therapist. Elem. tchr. Brazosport Ind. Sch. Dist., Freeport, Tex., 1970-73; therapeutic counselor Edn. and Treatment Council, Lake Charles, 1975-80; family counselor Family and Youth Agy., Lake Charles, La., 1980-81; grad. asst. in psychology McNeese State U., Lake Charles, 1980-81, vis. lectr. dept. psychology, 1981—; practice psychotherapy, Lake Charles, 1981—. Appointee La. Statewide Health Coordinating Council, Baton Rouge, 1983—; bd. dirs. Chem. Dependency Treatment Ctr. of St. Patrick's Hosp., Lake Charles, 1984—. Mem. Am. Assn. for Counseling and Devel., La. Assn. for Counseling and Devel., Inst. for Reality Therapy, Am. Mental Health Assn. Republican. Roman Catholic. Avocation: golf. Home: 344 Venessa St Lake Charles LA 70605 Office: 184 Williamsburg St Lake Charles LA 70605

ROBERTS, (BUFORD) DEWAYNE, pharmacologist; b. Bartlesville, Okla., Sept. 7, 1927; s. Otley Leon and Nina Ruth (Coleman) R.; m. Nira Jean Rosebrough, Dec. 7, 1951; children—Leslie Susan Roberts Graves, Valerie Ann Roberts Wiseman, Kevin DeWayne. B.S. in Chemistry Okla. State U., 1950; Ph.D. in Pharmacology, Washington U., St. Louis, 1957. Assoc. chemist Phillips Chem. Co., Dumas, Tex., 1951-53; research asst. Washington U., St. Louis, 1953-57; cancer research scientist Roswell Park Meml. Inst., Buffalo, 1957-62; research assoc. Harvard U. Med. Sch., Boston, 1962-68; pharmacologist St. Jude Children's Research Hosp., Memphis, 1968—; mem. adj. faculty Brandeis U., Waltham, Mass., 1962-65, Northeastern U., Boston, 1966-67, U. Tenn. Sch. Med., Memphis, 1968—. Served with U.S. Army, 1946-48. Grantee Nat. Cancer Inst., NIH. Mem. Am. Assn. Cancer Research, Am. Soc. Pharmacology and Exptl. Therapy, Am. Fedn. Clin. Research, Sigma Xi. Contbr. to profl. jours. and books.

ROBERTS, DAN HAYNES, psychologist; b. Beaumont, Tex., Dec. 3, 1951; s. Sam Swinford and Billie Joyce (Haynes) R.; m. Kimberly Ann Warrick, Nov. 2, 1984. B.S., Lamar U., 1973; M.S., North Tex. U., 1975, Ph.D., 1982. Lic. psychologist, Tex. Psychol. assoc. Central Tex. Mental Health/Mental Retardation Ctr., Brownwood, 1976-79; psychologist S.E. Tex. Mental Health/Mental Retardation Ctr., Beaumont, 1982-83, Beaumont Neuropsychiat Clinic, 1983—; advisor Head Start programs, Brownwood, 1976-79. Mem. Am. Psychol. Assn., S.E. Tex. Psychol. Assn. (treas. 1984—), Tex. Psychol. Assn., Am. Acad. Neuropsychologists, Brownwood Jaycees (bd. dirs. 1976-77, Outstanding Dir. award, 1977). Avocations: guitar; reading. Office: Beaumont Neuropsychiatric Clinic 3240 Fannin St Beaumont TX 77701

ROBERTS, DARRYL J(AY), cemetery executive; b. Columbus, Ohio, Nov. 12, 1944; s. Chester Grant and Clara Marzetta (Hite) R.; m. Hazel Ann King, May 25, 1968; 1 son, Adam Grant. B.S., U. Tenn.-Knoxville, 1967. Salesman, Blue Ridge Meml., Beckley, W.Va., summers 1962-68; mgr. Greenhills Memory, Richlands, Va., 1968-69; bus. mgr. Associated Cemetery Estates, Beckley, 1969-80, pres., 1980—; v.p. Cemetery Consumer Service Council, Washington, 1983-84. Mem. Ohio Assn. Cemeteries (dir. 1977-78), Prearrangement Interment Assn. Am. (pres. 1976-77), W.Va. Cemetery Assn. (pres. 1975-76), Beckley, C. of C. (dir. 1975-78). Democrat. Home: 117 Phil Ave Beckley WV 25801 Office: Associated Cemetery Estates Box 1586 Beckley WV 25801

ROBERTS, GARY ANTHONY, clinical pharmacist; b. Jacksonville, Fla., Apr. 14, 1956; s. Tillman Garrett and Mildred Ann (Rogero) R.; m. Karen Jo Maida, Dec. 9, 1978 (div. Mar. 1982); m. Terry Ann Russell, June 22, 1985. Student U. Fla., 1976; A.A., Fla. Jr. Coll., 1977; B.Pharm., Mercer U., 1980, D.Pharm., 1981. Registered pharmacist, Fla., Ga. Clin. pharmacist Riverside Hosp., Jacksonville, 1981-84; clin. pharmacist Home Health Systems, Jacksonville, 1983—, pres., 1983—; pharmacist Hyde Park Pharmacy, Jacksonville, 1984—, v.p., 1984—; tchr., lectr. in field, 1981—; cons. pharmacist Cathedral Convalescent Ctr., Jacksonville, 1984—. Author monthly newsletter: Metabolic Support Rounds, 1982. Mem. Northeast Fla. Soc. Hosp. Pharmacists (sec. 1984), Am. Soc. Hosp. Pharmacists, Nat. Intravenous Therapy Assn., Am. Geriatrics Soc. Democrat. Club: Univ. (Jacksonville). Lodges: Lawtonwood Hunting, Sertoma. Avocations: racquetball; tennis; contact sports; woodworking; music listening. Home: 5338 Colonial Ave Jacksonville FL 32210 Office: Home Health Systems Inc 1959 Lane Ave S Jacksonville FL 32210

ROBERTS, GEARY DEAN, fire chief; b. Holdenville, Okla., May 8, 1942; s. Orlan O. and Birdie Juanita (White) R.; m. Deanna Joan Crook, Sept. 9, 1966; 1 son, Geary Dean II. B.B.A., Washburn U., 1964; M.Poly. Sci., Ariz. State U., 1968; Assoc. in Fire Sci., Phoenix Coll., 1969. Firefighter, Rural/Met. Fire Dept., Scottsdale, Ariz., 1965-66, fire insp., 1966-68, fire marshall, 1968-70; bn. chief Rural/Met. Fire Dept., Mesa, Ariz., 1970-77; fire chief Rural/Met. Fire Dept., Sun City, Ariz., 1977-81; fire chief Rural/Met. Fire Dept., Knoxville, Tenn., 1981—. Mem. Fire Protection Engrs., Internat. Fire Chiefs Assn., Nat. Fire Protection Assn., Fire Marshalls Assn., Internat. Soc. Fire Instrs. Republican. Presbyterian. Lodge: Masons. Home: 616 Banbury Rd Knoxville TN 37922 Office: Rural/Metro Fire Dept 318 Erin Dr Knoxville TN 37919

ROBERTS, GENE, mayor. Mayor City of Chattanooga. Office: Municipal Bldg Chattanooga TN 37402*

ROBERTS, GEOFFREY ARTHUR SEBRY, international business consultant, electronic manufacturing company executive; b. London, Sept. 25, 1913; came to U.S., 1945, naturalized, 1952; s. Arthur Bell and Elizabeth Kate (Sebry) R.; B.Sc. in Elec. Engring., London U., 1937; m. Clara Diana Meruelo, Jan. 22, 1954; children—Diane Elizabeth, Ian Geoffrey. With Marconi's Wireless Telegraph Co., London, 1937-40; spl. overseas rep. for Latin Am., RCA, 1945-59; founder OKI Electronics Am., Inc. (now subs. OKI Am., Inc.), Ft. Lauderdale, Fla., 1959, chmn. bd., 1959-78, chmn. emeritus, 1978—; founder, past chief exec. officer PEC Industries subs. Reliance Electric of Ohio (now subs. Exxon Corp.). Former mem. Broward Indsl. Bd., Ft. Lauderdale; chmn., bd. dirs. Fla. Oaks Sch., Ft. Lauderdale. Served with RAF, 1940-45. Recipient Key to Port Everglades, Fla., 1969. Mem. Aircraft Owners and Pilots Assn., Nat. Pilots Assn. (Safe Pilot award 1970, Flight Proficiency award 1974), Nat. Aero. Assn., Nat. Bus. Aircraft Assn., N.Am. Telephone Assn. (past dir.), Opera Guild (dir. Ft. Lauderdale), Silver Wings Frat., RAF Ferry Command Assn. (Can.), Royal Air Force Assn. (Gt. Britain), Fla. C. of C., Ft. Lauderdale C. of C. Republican. Roman Catholic. Clubs: Le Club Internat., Lauderdale Yacht, Tower (Ft. Lauderdale). Address: PO Box 290128 Davie FL 33329

ROBERTS, GEORGE PRESTON, JR., lawyer; b. St. Louis, June 23, 1947; s. George P. and Eleanor Roberts; m. Barbara A. Smith, June 30, 1973; children—Christopher Dent, Craig Dane, Carrie Diana. B.A., U. Tulsa, 1969; J.D. with honors, 1975. Legal intern Harris Gladd & Dyer, Tulsa, 1974-75; assoc. Fleming, O'Bryan & Fleming, Ft. Lauderdale, Fla., 1976-81, mng. ptnr., West Palm Beach, Fla., 1981—. Served with USAF, 1969-73. Mem. ABA, Palm Beach County Bar Assn., Broward County Bar Assn. Presbyterian. Office: 319 Clematis St Suite 308 West Palm Beach FL 33401

ROBERTS, (GRANVILLE) ORAL, clergyman; b. nr. Ada, Okla., Jan. 24, 1918; s. Ellis Melvin and Claudius Priscilla (Irwin) R.; student Okla. Bapt. U., 1942-44, Phillips U., 1947; m. Evelyn Lutman, Dec. 25, 1938; children—Rebecca Ann (dec.), Ronald David (dec.), Richard Lee, Roberta Jean. Ordained to ministry Pentecostal Holiness Ch., 1936, trans. ordination to United Meth. Ch., 1968; evangelist, 1936-41; pastor, Fuquay Springs, N.C., 1941, Shawnee, Okla., 1942-45, Toccoa, Ga., 1946. Enid, Okla., 1947; began worldwide evengelistic ministry thru crusades, radio, TV, printed page, 1947; founder Oral Roberts Evangelistic Assn., Inc.; founder Univ. Village Retirement Center, City of Faith Health Care Ctr.; Ptnr.'s Healing Outreach Ctr.; founder, pub. Abundant Life mag., Daily Blessing, quar. mag.; founder pres. Oral Roberts U., Tulsa, 1963—; appears on weekly half-hour TV program, prime-time TV spls.; dir. Bank Okla. Club: Rotary. Author over 50 books including If You Need Healing, Do These Things, 1947; God is a Good God, 1960; If I Were You, 1967; Miracle of Seed-Faith, 1970; (autobiography) The Call, 1971; The Miracle Book, 1972; A Daily Guide to Miracles, 1975; Better Health and Miracle Living, 1976; How to Get Through Your Struggles, 1977; Receiving Your Miracle, 1978; Don't Give Up, 1980; Your Road to Recovery, 1986; Attack Your Lack, 1986; producer 52-cassette-tape series reading and oral commentary of N.T., 1982; also numerous tracts and brochures. Office: Oral Roberts University 7777 S Lewis Ave Tulsa OK 74171

ROBERTS, HYMAN JACOB, physician; b. Boston, May 29, 1924; s. Benjamin and Eva (Sherman) R.; M.D. cum laude, Tufts U., 1947; m. Carol Antonia Klein, Aug. 9, 1953; children—David Barry, Jonathan Stuart, Mark Elliott, Stephen, Scott F., Pamela Beth. Intern Boston City Hosp., 1947-48, resident, 1948-49; resident Municipal Hosp., Washington, 1949-50; fellow in medicine Lahey Clinic, Boston, 1950-51; instr. in medicine, research fellow Tufts U. Med. Sch., Boston, 1948-49, Georgetown Med. Sch., Washington, 1949-50; pvt. practice medicine, West Palm Beach, Fla., 1955—; sr. attending staff St. Mary's Hosp., Good Samaritan Hosp.; 1st Eugene Dibble ann. lecture Tuskegee Inst., 1967; dir. Palm Beach Inst. for Med. Research, 1964—. Mem. Palm Beach Philanthropic Council; trustee Am. Physicians Fellowship for Israel Med. Assn.; pres. Jewish Community Day Sch. Palm Beaches, 1975-76; mem. SHARE (Spl. Help for Agrl. Research and Edn.) council; dising. mem. president's council U. Fla. Served from lt. (j.g.) to lt. USNR, 1943-45, 51-54. Recipient Fla.'s Outstanding Young Men award Jr. C. of C., 1959; named hon. Ky. col. Paul Harris fellow Rotary Found. Diplomate Am. Bd. Internal Medicine. Fellow Am. Coll. Angiology (Fla. gov.), Royal Soc. Health, Am. Coll. Chest Physicians, Am. Coll. Nutrition; mem. Am. Fedn. Clin. Research, Endocrine Soc., Am. Assn. Study Headache, Am. Soc. Internal Medicine, N.Y. Acad. Scis., A.C.P., Am. (stroke council), Fla. heart assns., Am. Diabetes Assn., AAAS, Internat. Assn. for Accident and Traffic Medicine, Am., So., Fla. med. assns., Internat. Acad. Metabology, Fla. Thoracic Soc., Physicians for Automotive Safety, Am. Assn. for Automotive Medicine, Alpha Omega Alpha. Mem. B'nai B'rith (v.p. 1958-59). Rotarian (charter mem., dir. 1956-58) (West Palm Beach, Fla.). Clubs: Millennium Tufts U. Sch. Medicine, Confrérie de la Chaine des Rôtisseurs. Author: Difficult Diagnosis; A Guide To The Interpretation of Obscure Illness, 1958; The Causes, Ecology and Prevention of Traffic Accidents, 1971; Is Vasectomy Safe? Medical, Public Health and Legal Implications, 1979; also numerous sci. papers; contbg. editor Tufts Med. Alumni Bull.; donor Hyman and Carol Roberts Med. Library to Tufts U. Coll. Medicine, Hyman and Carol Roberts Room of Jewish Community Day Sch. of Palm Beach County. Home: 6708 Pamela Ln West Palm Beach FL 33405 Office: 300 27th St West Palm Beach FL 33407

ROBERTS, JAMES LEONARD, lawyer, bank executive; b. Livingston, Tenn., Aug. 31, 1924; s. Hubert Claud and Maggie Thomas (Davis) R.; student Washington U., St. Louis, 1943, David Lipscomb Coll., 1946-47, George Peabody Coll., 1948; J.D., Vanderbilt U., 1950; m. Nevagene Almonrode, Sept. 13, 1946; children—Janice Roberts Wingfield, Kenneth W., Donald J., Douglas C. Admitted to Tenn. bar, 1950; U.S. dist. ct., 1950; U.S. Ct. Appeals (6th cir.), 1953; U.S. Supreme Ct., 1971; asst. U.S. atty. Middle Dist. Tenn., 1952-55; individual practice law, Nashville, 1955-60; asso. firm Farris, Evans & Evans, Nashville, 1960, partner, 1969; partner firm Parker, Nichol & Roberts, Nashville, 1969-73; sr. v.p., staff counsel Third Nat. Bank, Nashville, 1973—. Served with USAAF, 1943-46. Mem. Nashville Bar Assn., Tenn. Bar Assn., Am. Bar Assn. Republican. Home: 1604 Peerman Dr Nashville TN 37206 Office: 201 4th Ave North Nashville TN 37219

ROBERTS, JOHN ELGIN, magazine editor; b. Shelby, N.C., Sept. 14, 1926; s. John Ellis and Annie (Spake) R.; diploma Gardner-Webb Jr. Coll., 1947-49; B.A., Furman U., 1951, LL.D., 1972; M.A., George Peabody Coll. Tchrs., 1952; D.Litt., Bapt. Coll. at Charleston, S.C., 1971; m. Helen E. Goodwin, Sept. 8, 1950; children—Wayne, Mark, Glenn, Jonna, Jill, Julie. Tchr. Gastonia (N.C.) City Schs., 1951-54; dir. pub. relations Gardner-Webb Coll., 1954-60; dir. pub. relations, editor Charity and Children Bapt. Children's Homes of N.C., Thomasville, 1960-65; editor, bus. mgr. The Bapt. Courier, Greenville, S.C., 1966—. Mem. So. Bapt. Editors Conf. (pres. 1979), So. Bapt. Inter-Agy. Council; bd. advisers New Orleans Bapt. Theol. Sem.; mem. Thomasville (N.C.) Bd. Edn., 1963-65; trustee So. Bapt. Radio and TV Commn., 1978—, chmn. bd. trustees, 1984-85 pres. S.C. Bapt. Conv., 1980. Served with AUS, 1945-46. Mem. So. Bapt. Pub. Relations Assn. (pres. 1962-63), Bapt. World Alliance Commn. on Communication. Baptist (deacon). Lodge: Rotary. Home: 106 Trinity Way Greenville SC 29609 Office: 100 Manly St Greenville SC 29602

ROBERTS, JOHN HAROLD, metallurgical engineer; b. Peoria, Ill., Feb. 24, 1943; s. John Gerald and Helen Ruth (Gauger) R.; m. Catherin Ann Duncan, Nov. 15, 1985. B.S. in Engring., U. Ill., 1965; M.B.A., U. Tex., Dallas, 1982. Engr., Sundstrand Aviation, Rockford, Ill., 1965-69; engr. Tex. Instruments Co., Dallas, 1969-71; mgr. process engring. Consol. Casting Corp., Dallas, 1971-78, chief engr., 1978-80, plant mgr., 1980-84; chief engr. Castex div. GSC Foundries, 1984—; v.p. Rochester Gauges Credit Union, 1983-84; pres. JHR Enterprises, 1983—. Registered profl. engr. Mem. ASME, Am. Soc. Metals, Investment Casting Inst., Mensa. Club: Mason (32d deg.). Home: 13677 Purple Sage Rd Dallas TX 75240 Office: 1004 Dalworth Mesquite TX 75149

ROBERTS, JOYCE ANN, sales coordinator; b. Brookhaven, Miss., Dec. 19, 1947; d. Jim Ben and Alice Naomi (Mayo) Hughes; m. Carl C. Sealey, Apr. 28, 1964 (div. Apr. 1972); children—Carl C., Joseph D., Amber Dawn, Byron J.; m. 2d, Allen Paul Roberts, Oct. 6, 1976 (div. July 1983). Internat. sales coordinator Oil Ctr. Research, Inc., Lafayette, La., 1975-82, 83—; mgr. Jedwin Internat. Mktg., Lafayette, 1982-83. Mem. La. Dist. Export Council, 1979-81. Mem. Am. Bus. Womens Assn. Democrat. Baptist.

ROBERTS, LORI GAYE, soft drink marketing executive; b. Manitowoc, Wis., Nov. 9, 1955; d. Albert William and Betty Lou (Brunner) B.; m. Ronald Winfred Roberts, Dec. 1985. Student U. Wis.-Madison, 1973-75; B.B.A., U. Wis.-Milw., 1977. Ter. sales mgr. Coca-Cola USA, Chgo., 1977-79, sales devel. mgr., Madison, 1979-80, asst. mgr. market planning, Atlanta, 1980-84, mgr. telemarketing, 1981—; speaker bus. seminars, 1981—. Counselor, Rape Crisis Center, Madison, 1974; harpist U. Wis. Symphonic Orch., Milw., 1976; youth edn. advisor Jr. Achievement, 1981—; profl. women's fund raiser Atlanta Symphony Orch., 1984. Mem. Sales and Mktg. Execs. (dir. Chgo. 1979-80, dir. Atlanta 1984—), Am. Harp Soc., Pi Sigma Epsilon (nat. alumni dir. 1980—, founder Chgo. Alumni chpt., pres. 1978-80, profl. advisor Atlanta 1981—), Atlanta City Women's Exec. Club (founder, mktg. dir. 1983-84). Republican. Lutheran. Home: 331 Wood Ridge Dr Atlanta GA 30339 Office: Coca-Cola USA PO Drawer 1734 Atlanta GA 30301

ROBERTS, MARION STAMPER, optometrist, researcher; b. Hyden, Ky., Aug. 10, 1912; s. William B. and Arminta (Stamper) R.; m. Mattie Kathryn Tolbert, July 23, 1939; 1 child, Barbara Lynn. A.B., Eastern Ky. Tchrs. Coll., 1935; M.S., La. State U., 1938; O.D., So. Coll. Optometry, 1949. Tchr. pub. schs., Ky., La., Ala., Va., 1935-42; pvt. practice optometry, London, Ky. and Richmond, Ky., 1950—. Served to capt. U.S. Army, 1942-46. Mem. Am. Optometric Assn., Ky. Optometric Assn., Eastern Ky. Optometric Soc. (pres. 1950-51). Democrat. Baptist. Lodges: Rotary (pres. 1954), Masons. Home: 112 Westwood Dr Richmond KY 40475

ROBERTS, NANCY LEE, geophysicist; b. Tyler, Tex., Apr. 11, 1957; d. C.B. and Leola (Deitrich) Roberts. A.A., Tyler Jr. Coll., 1977; B.S., Tex. A&M U., 1980. Geophysicist Cities Service Oil, Houston, 1980-81, Placid Oil Co., Dallas, 1981—. Vol. tutor Buckner Children's Home, Dallas, 1984—; vol. Scottish Rite Hosp. for Crippled Children, Dallas, 1984—. Mem. Am. Assn. Petroleum Geologists, Dallas Geophys. Soc., Phi Theta Kappa. Republican. Lutheran. Office: Placid Oil Co 3900 Thanksgiving Tower Dallas TX 75201

ROBERTS, NOBLE LEE, nurse; b. Port Arthur, Tex., June 9, 1949; s. Noble Lee and Dorothy Jean (Armstrong) Hawkes; m. Mary Frances Roberts, June 24, 1984. Student Tex. Tech. U., 1976-78; R.N., Cooke County Coll., 1980; postgrad. in cardiovascular clinician, Tex. Women's U., 1981-83. Air-sea rescue nurse U.S. Air Force, Clark AFB, Philippines, 1973-76; ambulance and rescue squad nurse Cooke County Emergency Med. Service, Gainesville, Tex., 1978-80; intensive care nurse Garland Meml. Hosp. (Tex.), 1981-83; paramedic examiner medi-test div. Kimberly Nurses Inc., Dallas, 1983—; emergency room nurse Presbyn. Hosp., Dallas, 1983—; paramedic instr. Tex. Dept. Health, Dallas, 1982-83; dir. tng. rescue and scuba teams Dallas Fire Dept., 1985. Author poem: Remember Me Please, 1970. Para-rescue instr. Cooke County Coll., 1979. Served to 1st lt. U.S. Army, 1969-71; Vietnam. Decorated Purple Heart with cluster, Bronze Star; Vietnamese Cross of Gallantry; recipient Order of Blue Knights award U.S. Air Force Drill Team, 1974; Bob Bachworth Meml. award U.S. Parachute Assn., 1975, U.S. parachute Team award, 1982, 83. Mem. Nat. Assn. Underwater Instrs., VFW. Democrat. Baptist. Clubs: Metroplex Skydiving (instr. 1978—), Tex. Motorcycle Riders. Office: PO Box 740332 556 Bondstone Dallas TX 75374

ROBERTS, PETER JAMES, dentist; b. Poughkeepsie, N.Y., June 14, 1942; s. Oran Merl and Mary Aline (Petrosky) R.; m. Betha Lee Stubbe, Aug. 15, 1970 (div. 1983); children—Peter Jonathan, Martin William. B.A. with honors, West Tex. State U., 1965; D.D.S., U. Tex.-Houston, 1968. Rotating intern Fla. State Hosp., Chattahoochie, 1968-69. Sole practice gen. dentistry Perryton, Tex., 1969-71, Pampa, Tex., 1971-75, Amarillo, Tex., 1976—. Served with USPHS, 1966-68. Fellow Acad. Gen. Dentistry; mem. ADA, Panhandle Dist. Dental Soc., Tex. Dental Assn., Acad. Gen. Dentistry, Am. Assn. Functional Orthodontia. Republican. Avocations: fishing, photography, choral music. Home: 3400 Royal Rd Amarillo TX 79109 Office: 2300 W 7th St Suite 102 Amarillo TX 79106

ROBERTS, RAYMOND URL, exploration geologist, explorer; b. Camp Kilmer, N.J., Oct. 4, 1949; s. William Martin and Francis (Prozibek) R.; m. Pamela Ruth Mercer, June 15, 1980. B.S. in Geology, Oreg. State U., 1977. Cert. profl. geologist, Okla. Command Ctr. officer Salem Police Dept., Oreg., 1977; geologist Core Labs., Oklahoma City, 1978-80, Gulf Oil Co., Oklahoma

City, 1980-81; exploration geologist Sabine Corp., Oklahoma City, 1981—. Sec., Trinity Lutheran Ch., Norman, Okla., 1985—; tribal mem. citizens bd. Pottawatomi Indians. Served with U.S. Army, 1967-71, Vietnam. Mem. Am. Inst. Profl. Geologists, Am. Assn. Petroleum Geologists, Oklahoma City Geol. Soc. Democrat. Lutheran. Avocations: writing; exploration. Home: 9925 Aztec Dr Norman OK 73071 Office: Sabine Corp 6401 NW Grand Blvd Oklahoma City OK 73116

ROBERTS, RAYMOND WILLIAM, pharmacist, health care consultant; b. Coral Gables, Fla., Sept. 16, 1951; s. William Leonard and Rita Joan (Szanik) R.; m. Diane Elizabeth Willyoung, June 9, 1973; children—Daniel Joseph, John William, Emily Katherine. B.S., U. Fla., 1973, D. Pharmacy, 1977. Asst. prof. St. Louis Coll. Pharmacy, 1977-80; clin. pharmacist Washington U. Med. Ctr., St. Louis, 1977-80; dir. pharmacy Riverside Hosp., Jacksonville, Fla., 1980—; v.p. Rivercorp, Inc., Jacksonville, 1984—; cons. Mandarin Manor, Jacksonville, 1981—; educator, cons. U. Fla., Gainesville, 1980—. Contbr. articles to profl. jours. Speaker Sta. WJCT-TV, Jacksonville, 1980—; moderator PBS Broadcasting, Jacksonville, 1981; campaign coordinator United Way, Jacksonville, 1981. Recipient Eagle Scout award Boy Scouts Am., 1965; Pres.'s Scholar award Jacksonville U., 1970-71; Narco award St. Louis Coll. Pharmacy, 1980. Mem. Am. Pharm. Assn. (trustee 1985-86, speaker of house 1985-86), Nat. High Blood Pressure Edn. Coordinating Com. (exec. com. 1985—), Am. Soc. Hosp. Pharmacists, Am. Pharm. Assn. Found. Republican. Roman Catholic. Avocations: philately; reading. Office: Riverside Hosp 2033 Riverside Ave Jacksonville FL 32073

ROBERTS, ROBERT FRANKLIN, oil company executive; b. Austin, Tex., Nov. 29, 1924; s. Allen Pickney and Lillian (Lane) R.; m. Leila Crain, Dec. 23, 1951; 1 son, Mark Allen. LL.B., J.D., U. Tex., 1945. Bar: Tex. bar 1945. Mem. firm Hamilton, Hamilton, Turner & Hutchison, Dallas, 1945-47; ind. oil producer, La., 1947-63; pres., chmn. bd., chief exec. officer Crystal Oil Co., Shreveport, 1963—, also dir.; dir. La. Bank and Trust Co., Shreveport. Episcopalian. Clubs: University (gov.), Shreveport Petroleum, Shreveport Country. (Shreveport). Address: Crystal Oil Bldg PO Box 21101 Shreveport LA 71120*

ROBERTS, ROBERT RAYMOND, engineering educator; b. Willacoochee, Ga., Jan. 17, 1933; s. Owen Russell and Gladys Merle (Gaskins) R.; m. Gail Elizabeth Woodard, June 17, 1959; children—Lisa Gail, Jennifer Lee. B.C.E., Ga. Tech. Inst., 1956, M.S.C.E., 1963; Ph.D., W.Va. U., 1975. Sr. designer Ga. Hwy. Dept., Tifton, 1956-60; assoc. engr. Wilbur Smith & Assocs., Columbia, S.C., 1962-65; asst. prof. U.S.C., Columbia, 1965-70, assoc. prof., 1973—. Served with U.S. Army, 1958-59. NSF grantee, 1967; UMTA fellow, 1970; Nat. Hwy Inst. grantee, 1980. Mem. Inst. Transp. Engrs., Transp. Research Bd., Soc. Automotive Engrs., Nat. Soc. Profl. Engrs., Nat. Acad. Forensic Engrs., Sigma Xi, Chi Epsilon. Contbr. articles to profl. jours. Home: 6016 Poplar Ridge Rd Columbia SC 29206 Office: Coll Engring U S C Columbia SC 29208

ROBERTS, ROBIN WATSON, public health educator; b. Birmingham, Ala., July 18, 1947; s. David and Cecil (Johnson) R. B.A., Rollins Coll., 1969; M.S., Ga. State U., 1973; Ph.D., Emory U., 1980. Postdoctoral fellow U. Ala., Birmingham, 1980-83, asst. prof. Sch. Pub. Health, 1983—. Vol. March of Dimes, Birmingham, 1984; co-chmn. Red Mountain Mus., Birmingham, 1984; bd. dirs. Teenage Suicide Prevention Task Force, Birmingham, 1983-85. Mem. Am. Sociol. Assn., Am. Burn Assn., Am. Assn. Suicidology, Mid-South Sociol. Assn., So. Sociol. Soc. Democrat. Episcopalian. Avocations: skeet shooting; fishing; boating. Office: Sch Pub Health 3150 Tidwell University Sta Birmingham AL 35294

ROBERTS, SUSAN WADSWORTH, judge; b. Daytona Beach, Fla., June 16, 1944; d. William Littledale and Frances (Faulkner) Wadsworth; A.A., Daytona Beach Jr. Coll., 1964; B.A., Fla. State U., 1966, J.D., 1969; m. Dan P. Brawley, June 9, 1979; 1 child, Carson James. Admitted to Fla. bar, 1970; research aide 2d Dist. Ct. Appeal, Lakeland, Fla., 1969-70; pvt. practice law, Lakeland, 1971-76; public defender, Lakeland, 1972-73; prosecutor City of Lakeland, 1973-75; staff atty. Polk County Legal Aid, 1972-76; mcpl. judge City of Lakeland, 1975-76; judge County Ct., Polk County, Fla., 1977-84; judge 10th Jud. Circuit, 1984—; mem. adv. bd. Rape Crisis Center. Mem. Tri-County Mental Health Bd. Dist. VIII-A, Inc.; mem. Driver Improvement Adv. Com.; mem. adv. bd. Police Acad. Polk Community Coll., Displaced Homemakers; mem. traffic ct. rev. com. Fla. Supreme Ct. mem. Pride of Lakeland Mem. ABA, Fla., Lakeland bar assns., Am. Judicature Soc., Fla. Assn. Women Lawyers, Polk County Trial Lawyers Assn. Baptist. Clubs: Pionette Bus. and Profl. Women's. Home: PO Box 5686 Lakeland FL 33803 Office: PO Box 928 Bartow FL 33830

ROBERTS, THERESE MARGARET, educational guidance counselor, educator; b. Ft. Lauderdale, Fla., Nov. 16, 1926; d. Carey Reid Roberts and Frances (Smith) McAllister. B.S., Siena Heights Coll., 1951; M.S., Barry U., 1960. Joined Adrian Dominican Order, Roman Catholic Ch., 1945; guidance counselor Pub. Sch. Bd., Ft. Lauderdale, 1975—; chmn. Dist. X Health and Rehab. Services, 1979-82; adj. prof. Nova U., 1980—. Chmn. selection com. Port Everglades Authority, Ft. Lauderdale, 1981; chmn. non-pub. sch. United Way, Ft. Lauderdale, 1972. Mem. Am. Sch. Counselors Assn., Fla. Sch. Counselors Assn. (pres. 1976-78), Assn. for Values in Edn. (pres. 1977-78), Phi Delta Kappa. Home: 308 NE 14th Ave Fort Lauderdale FL 33301 Office: Piper High School 8000 NW 44th St Sunrise FL 33121

ROBERTS, WALKER EDWARD, journalist, magazine editor; b. Whitefish, Mont., May 19, 1941; s. John David and Mary Ellen (Westrom) R.; B.A. in Econs., Wash. State U., 1964, cert. in journalism, 1964; M.A. in Journalism, Mich. State U., 1971; m. Deanne Dewey, Nov. 27, 1976. With various newspapers, Pacific N.W., 1966-70; state editor Lewiston (Idaho) Morning Tribune, 1968-70; bus. writer Miami (Fla.) Herald, 1972-73; editor Fla. Trend mag., St. Petersburg, 1973-81, Fla. Bus./Tampa Bay, 1985—; prin., pub. Fla. Constructor mag.; cons. on mag. matters. Pres. Tampa Bay Maritime Soc. Served to lt. U.S. Army, 1964-66, Vietnam. Decorated Purple Heart. Mem. Fla. Mag. Assn., Kappa Alpha Theta. Home: 836 S Delaware St Tampa FL 33606 Office: 5005 W Laurel Tampa FL 33607

ROBERTS, WILLIAM LAWRENCE, appraiser, broker, realtor; b. Boston, Jan. 20, 1924; s. James Joseph and Mary Margaret (Galvin) R.; student Northeastern U., 1949-51, Rutgers U., 1952-54; LL.B., Blackstone Sch. Law, 1959; grad. Realtors Inst., 1975; m. Josephine Mary DeLeo, July 22, 1945; children—James Joseph, Linda Marie (Mrs. John Hamilton Glover), William Lawrence. With RCA, Camden, N.J., 1951-58, Midwest regional rep., 1955, N.E. regional rep., 1956; sr. mem. tech. staff Thompson Ramo Wooldridge Co., Redondo Beach, Calif., 1958-60, N.E. regional mgr., 1960-61; mgr. marketing Sperry Rand Research Center, Sudbury, Mass., 1961-62; research and devel. marketing mgr. Litton Industries, Beverly Hills, Calif., 1962-65, dir. data systems, div. aero Service Corp., 1965-66; with Collins Radio Co., Dallas, 1966-74, venture analyst, mgr. sales service div., 1973-74; with Paula Stringer Realtors Inc., Plano, Tex., 1974-81, v.p., 1977-81; partner Burchett & Roberts Appraisers, Plano, 1975—. Chmn. cub scouts Fort Stanwix council Boy Scouts Am., 1956-57, asst. dist. commr., 1965-66; pres. Meadowbrook P.T.A., Pennsauken, N.J., 1953-54; capt. fund drive Plano YMCA, 1975. Campaign mgr. Kennedy/Johnson, Rome, N.Y., 1960. Served with USNR, 1942-45: PTO. Recipient Citizens award City Utica (N.Y.), 1963; cert. residential specialist, residential broker. Mem. IEEE (sr. mem., nat. exec. com. 1960-64), Am. Rocket Soc., Am. Inst. Aero. and Astronautics, Armed Forces Communications and Electronics Assn. (nat. dir. 1959-67), Am. Angus Assn., Nat. Mktg. Inst., Nat. Assn. Review Appraisers (sr. mem.), Soc. Real Estate Appraisers (dir., sr. residential appraiser), Tex. Assn. Realtors (edn. com.), Collin County Bd. Realtors (pres.). Home: 3021 Princeton Dr Plano TX 75074 Office: 1007 20th St Plano TX 75074

ROBERTSON, C. R., insurance company executive; b. 1930; married. B.B.A, U. Tex., 1952. Mgr. audit staff Ernst & Ernst, 1955-65; staff asst. Am. Nat. Ins. Co., Galveston, Tex., 1965-67, asst. sec., 1967-69, controller, asst. sec., 1969-70, v.p., controller, 1970-74, sr. v.p., controller, 1974-77, exec. v.p. adminstrn., then exec. v.p. home office adminstrn., 1977—. Office: Am Nat Ins Co One Moody Pl Galveston TX 77550*

ROBERTSON, CHARLES SEDWICK, economics, business law and government educator, retired marine corps officer, farmer; b. Anniston, Ala., Dec. 11, 1919; s. Elias Richard and Hattie Leola (McCall) R.; m. Mary Betty Hughes, May 11, 1943; children—Marsha Lynne, Ellen Gayle, Carlos Jay. M.L.S., U. Okla., 1975; M.A. in Teaching, Rollins Coll., 1978. Served to 1st sgt. U.S. Marine Corps, 1938-42, commd. 2d lt., 1942, advanced through grades to brig. gen., 1969; combat comdr. W.W. II, Korea, Vietnam; joint strategic planner, Washington, 1964-69; CINCPAC Staff, Hawaii; instr. Brazilian Naval War Coll., 1957-60; dep. fiscal dir., fiscal dir. USMC, 1970-74; instr. econs., bus. law, govt. Morris Jr. Coll. bus., Melbourne, Fla., 1978—. Vice pres. Nat. Soc. Mil. Comptrollers, Washington, 1972-74; pres. Honor Am., Melbourne, 1975-76. Decorated Legion of Merit with 4 gold stars (U.S.); Cloud and Banner (Nationalist Republic China); Order Naval Merit (Brazil); Hwarang medal (Republic of Korea). Republican. Avocation: tennis. Home: 7025 S Tropical Trail Merritt Island FL 32952 Office: Morris Jr Coll Bus 4635 N Harbor City Blvd Melbourne FL 32935

ROBERTSON, DAVID, clinical pharmacologist, physician, educator; b. Sylvia, Tenn., May 23, 1947; s. David Herlie and Lucille Luther (Bowen) R.; m. Rose Marie Stevens, Oct. 30, 1976; 1 child, Rose. B.A., Vanderbilt U., 1969, M.D., 1973. Diplomate Am. Bd. Internal Medicine. Intern, Johns Hopkins U., Balt., 1973-74, asst. resident, 1974-75, asst. chief service in medicine, 1977-78; fellow in clin. pharmacology Vanderbilt U., Nashville, 1975-77, asst. prof. medicine and pharmacology, 1978-82, assoc. prof., 1982—; practice medicine specializing in disorders of blood pressure regulation, Nashville, 1978—; mem. staff Vanderbilt Hosp., Burroughs Welcome scholar in clin. pharmacology, 1985—. Recipient Research Career Devel. award NIH, 1981; Adolph-Morsbach grantee Bonn, W.Ger., 1968; Logan Clendening fellow Reykjavik, Iceland, 1969. Fellow Am. Heart Assn. Council Hypertension; mem. ACP (teaching and research scholar 1978-81), U.S. Pharmacopeial Conv., Nat. Bd. Med. Examiners, Aerospace Med. Assn. MLA, Am. Fedn. for Clin. Research, Brit. Pharmacological Soc., So. Soc. for Clin. Investigation, Am. Soc. for Clin. Pharmacology and Therapeutics, Phi Beta Kappa. Baptist. Author: (with B.M. Greene and G.J. Taylor) Problems in Internal Medicine, 1980, (with C.R. Smith) Manual of Clinical Pharmacology, 1981. Home: 4003 Newman Pl Nashville TN 37204 Office: Pharmacology Dept Vanderbilt Hosp Nashville TN 37232

ROBERTSON, DAVID WINFIELD, transportation engineer, civil engineering consultant; b. Winston-Salem, N.C., Sept. 27, 1952; s. Henry Winfield and Ruby (Leftwich) R. B.S. with honors in Civil Engring., N.C. State U., 1974, M.S. in Civil Engring., 1975. Registered profl. engr., N.C. Transp. engr. intern City of Greensboro (N.C.), summers 1972-74; traffic signals engr. City of Raleigh (N.C.), 1974, assoc. traffic engr., 1974-80, traffic engr., 1980-84; hwy. engr. N.C. Dept. Transp., 1984—. traffic engring. cons. Research Engrs., Inc., Research Triangle Park, N.C. Mem. exec. bd. March of Dimes, 1981; West Raleigh coordinator Heart Fund, 1981; bus. coordinator United Fund Raleigh, 1981. Recipient Friendship Force Ambassador to Eng., 1980; Fed. Hwy. Adminstrn. grad. fellow, 1974; Vocat. Rehab. grantee, 1970. Mem. Nat. Soc. Profl. Engrs., ASCE, Inst. Transp. Engrs., Soil Conservation Soc. Am., N.C. Land Use Congress, Inc., Jaycees (dir. 1980-81, 83). Republican. Methodist. Author reports in field. Home: 2504 Vanderbilt Ave Raleigh NC 27607 Office: NC Dept Transp PO Box 25201 Raleigh NC 27602

ROBERTSON, DOROTHEA RUTH-LOUISE, rehabilitation counselor; b. Richmond, Va., July 31, 1952; d. Elmer Shackleford and Margaret Hannah (Armstrong) R. B.A., Stratford Coll., 1974; M.Ed., U. S.C., 1975. Counselor pvt. office of physician, Richmond, 1976-80; validity team mem. Commonwealth of Va., Richmond, 1980; rehab. counselor Intracorp, Richmond, 1980—; co-sponsor Parents Anonymous, Richmond, 1984—. Mem. Jr. League. Republican. Presbyterian. Home: 4010 Grove Ave Richmond VA 23221 Office: Intracorp 4198 Cox Rd Richmond VA 23294

ROBERTSON, EVELYN CRAWFORD, JR., mental institution administrator, county official; b. Winchester, Tenn., Nov. 19, 1941; s. Evelyn Crawford and Pearl (Brewer) R.; m. Hugholene Ellison, Oct. 13, 1963; children—Jeffrey Bernard, Sheila Yvette. B.S., Tenn. State U., 1962, M.A., 1969; postgrad. Memphis State U., 1976-77. Cert. tchr., ednl. supt. Tchr., Allen-White Elem. Sch., Whiteville, Tenn., 1962-68, prin., 1968-69; asst. prin. Central High Sch., Bolivar, Tenn., 1970-74; asst. supt. Western Mental Health Inst., Bolivar, 1974-79, supt., 1983—; supt. Nat T. Winston Devel. Ctr., Bolivar, 1979-83; cons. in field. Pres., Whiteville Civic League, Tenn., 1969-74, mem. Hardeman County Comm., Bolivar, 1981—; chmn. bd. dirs. Hardeman County Devel. Services Ctr., Bolivar, 1976-77. Named Outstanding Young Tchr. Hardeman County Jaycees, 1972; honored Evelyn C. Robertson Day, Whiteville, Tenn., 1983; Outstanding Citizens award Sigma Gamma Rho, Bolivar, 1983. Mem. Am. Assn. on Mental Deficiency, Southeastern Assn. on Mental Deficiency (chmn. adminstrv. div. 1982-83), Inst. on Hosp. and Community Psychiatry, Tenn. State U. Alumni (pres. Bolivar chpt. 1978-80). Baptist. Club: Civitan (pres. 1981-82) (Bolivar). Lodges: Silver Star (pres. 1968-73), Shriners (past pres.). Avocations: spectator sports; reading; gardening; fishing; photography. Home: Route 1 Box 178 Whiteville TN 38075 Office: Western Mental Health Inst Hwy 64 W Western Institute TN 38074

ROBERTSON, GAYLE PRICE, mortician; b. Levelland, Tex., Dec. 22, 1947; d. George Copeland and Ophelia (Eudaly) Price; student Tex. Tech. U., 1967-68, Dallas Inst. Mortuary Sci., 1970-71; A.S., South Plains Coll., 1967; m. Jerry D. Robertson, Aug. 23, 1975; children—Lindsay Riann, Mika Leigh. With Geo. C. Price Funeral Dirs., Levelland, 1962—, funeral dir., embalmer, 1972—. Mem. Ranching Heritage Assn. (charter), Nat. Assn. Female Execs., Panhandle Funeral Dirs. Assn., Tex. Funeral Dirs. Assn., Nat. Funeral Dirs. Assn., Nat. Tole and Decorative Painters Soc., Democrat. Methodist. Clubs: South Plains Horsemen Assn., Order Eastern Star, Jr. Womens. Home: PO Box 657 Levelland TX 79336 Office: PO Box 517 Levelland TX 79336

ROBERTSON, HARRIET COCHRAN, real estate broker; b. Shreveport, La., June 2, 1943; d. Allen Douglas and Elizabeth Freeman (Parsons) Murray; m. John Paul Robertson; children—John Stuart, Rachelle Renee. B.A., N.E. La. State U., 1966. Lic. real estate broker, Tex. Art tchr., New Orleans and Dallas, 1966-74; real estate broker Chandlers Landing, Rockwall, Tex., 1976-82; pres. Harriet Robertson, Inc., Rockwall, 1982—. Pres. Rockwall County Friends of Library, 1982, parliamentarian, 1983; pres. Lone Star chpt. Nat. Charity League, 1983-84; chmn. square beautification Rockwall Beautiful, 1982-83; mem. 500, Inc.; mem. bd. Salvation Army, Rockwall. Mem. Home and Apt. Builders Assn. Met. Dallas (assoc.), Greater Dallas Bd. Realtors, Rockwall Bd. Realtors, Rockwall C. of C. (dir.), Dallas Mus. Fine Arts, Delta Delta Delta. Methodist. Clubs: Chandlers Landing Yacht (Rockwall); Shores Country, 2001. Office: 2313 Ridge Rd Suite 104B Rockwall TX 75087

ROBERTSON, HORACE CARROLL, marketing consultant; b. Littleton, N.C., Nov. 29, 1943; s. Ben N. and Lila (Chichester) R.; m. Eunice Blalock, Aug. 29, 1965; children—Christina Carroll, Johnathan Lee. B.S. in Bus. Edn., East Carolina Coll., 1966, M.A. in Edn., 1968. Cert. secondary tchr., N.C. Mem. erection crew Howell Steel Service, Weldon, N.C., 1961-65; salesman J.C. Penney, Co., Greenville, N.C., 1962-66; tchr. introduction to vocations J.H. Rose High Sch., Greenville, 1966-67, distributive edn. coordinator, 1967-71; cons. distributive edn. N.C. Dept. Pub. Inst., Raleigh, N.C., 1971-75, chief cons. mktg., 1975—; edn. policy fellow Inst. Ednl. Leadership, Washington, 1984—; bd. dirs. Interstate Distributive Edn. Curriculum Consortium, Columbus, Ohio, 1985—. Co-author: Simulation Training Package, 1974. Editor numerous curriculum guides for mktg., 1971-84. Contbr. articles to profl. jours. Sec., Gideons Internat., Raleigh, 1978-79; chmn. bd. deacons 1st Baptist Ch., Cary, N.C., 1982-84, chmn. fin. com., 1984—; treas. Raleigh Boychoir Inc., Raleigh, 1983-84. Named Outstanding Young Educator, Greenville Jaycees, 1971; recipient Dirs. award N.C. Div. Vocat. Edn., 1985. Mem. Am. Vocat. Assn., N.C. Vocat. Assn., Nat. Mktg. Educators Assn. (v.p. so. region 1981), Distributive Edn. Clubs Am., Sales and Mktg. Execs. (bd. dirs. Raleigh 1984—). Democrat. Clubs: Scottish Hills Recreation (Cary). Avocations: fishing; swimming; water skiing; yard work and general repair. Home: 1120 Balmoral Dr Cary NC 27511

ROBERTSON, JAMES ARTHUR, JR., art educator, artist; b. Houston, May 3, 1949; s. James Arthur and Jean Ramsey (Kuykendall) R.; m. Dorothy Lisa Williams, May 27, 1978. B.F.A., U. Houston, 1974; M.F.A., U. Tex., 1979. Mem. faculty North Harris City Coll., Houston, 1980—, prof. art, gallery dir., 1980—; artist, Toni Jones Gallery, Houston, 1980-81; Hansen Galleries, N.Y.C., 1979-80; 40 Walls Gallery, Houston, 1981—; represented in permanent collections: Pensacola Jr. Coll., City of Baytown, Nat. Bank of Shreveport and numerous pvt. collections. Served with U.S. Army, 1967-70. Recipient 1st place award Assistance League of Houston, 1977; 1st place N.Mex. Internat. Art Exhibit, 1976; numerous art competiton awards. Mem. Coll. Art Assn. Home: 23938 Creekridge Spring TX 77373 Office: N Harris City Coll 22700 W Thorne Dr Houston TX 77073

ROBERTSON, JAMES MONROE, III, psychologist, probation services administrator, consultant, researcher; b. Birmingham, Ala., July 21, 1942; s. James Monroe, Jr. and Laura Yvonne (Dixon) R.; m. Linda Jo Schilleci, Aug. 27, 1967; children—James M. IV, Linda Michelle. B.S. in Polit. Sci., U. Ala., 1967, M.A. in Counseling, 1972, Ed.D. in Behavioral Studies, 1983. Organizational analyst U.S. Steel Corp., Pitts., 1967-70; chief psychol. services Birmingham City Cts., Ala., 1971-72; U.S. probation officer U.S. Dist. Ct., Birmingham, 1972-85, supr. probation services, 1985—, researcher on deviant behavior, 1983—; cons. U. Ala., 1980—, Office Spl. Investigations, U.S. Air Force, 1984—. Author: Required Counseling, 1983; Fraud Surveys: An Outline, 1983; Base Expectancy Scales, 1984. Mem. Atty. Gens. staff State of Ala., Montgomery, 1978. Mem. Nat. Rehab. Counselors Assn., Fed. Probation officers Assn., Am. Criminal Justice Assn., Am. Psychol. Assn., Res. Officers Assn., West Ala. Bus. Profl. Assn., Officers Club. Clubs: U. Faculty (Tuscaloosa, Ala.). Avocation: boating. Office: US Probation Office 1800 5th Ave N Birmingham AL 35401

ROBERTSON, JEFFREY WAYNE, optometrist; b. Pitts., Mar. 16, 1952; s. Edward Romell and Margaret Catherine R.; m. Linda Ferguson, June 16, 1979 (div. 1984). B.S. in Biology, Albright Coll., 1974; B.S. in Optometry, Pa. Coll. Optometry, 1975, Dr. Optometry, 1978. Pvt. practice optometry, Suffolk, Va., 1978—. Vice chmn. Suffolk Indsl. Devel. Authority, 1985; pres. Suffolk United way, 1985—. Mem. Am. Pub. Heart Assn., Better Vision Inst. Baptist. Lodges: Kiwanis (pres. 1982), Ruritan. Avocation: golf. Home: 300 Westgate Ave Suffolk VA 23434 Office: 418 N Main St Suffolk VA 23434

ROBERTSON, MARTIN WESLEY, JR., clergyman; b. Hawesville, Ky., July 13, 1962; s. Martin Wesley and Thelma Lee (Bruner) R.; m. Stephanie Wayne Touchton, Aug. 10, 1985. B.A., Campbellsville Coll., 1985. Lic. So. Baptist Conv., 1980; Ordained to ministry So. Baptist Conv., 1983. Assoc. pastor, minister youth Cloverport Bapt. Ch., Ky., 1982; pastor Tell St. Bapt. Ch., Tell City, Ind., 1983-85, Flint Missionary Bapt. Ch., Murray, Ky., 1985—. Page, Ky. State Senate; Ky. col. Fellow Blood River Bapt. Assn., Am. Psychol. Assn., Am. Assn. Counseling and Devel., Assn. Religious Values in Counseling. Republican. Avocations: fishing; golf. Home: Rt 2 Box 83-A Murray KY 42071

ROBERTSON, STEVEN KENT, mechanical engineer; b. Long Beach, Calif., June 7, 1956; s. Isaac Frank and Mary (Butera) R.; m. Joan Shearer, Mar. 12, 1966; children—Tiffany Hope, Jason Everett. B.Eng., Vanderbilt U., 1968. Registered profl. engr., Tenn., Va. Planning engr. Newport News Shipbldg. (Va.), 1968-71; mgr. program planning Newport News Reactor Services, Burnt Hills, N.Y., 1971-75; mgr. planning Newport News Indsl. Corp., 1975-78; spl. projects coordinator Va. Electric Power Co., Surry, Va., 1978-79; asst. engring. mgr. Rust Engring. Co., Oak Ridge, Tenn., 1979—. Indian guide leader YMCA, 1975-78; leader Boy Scouts Am., 1981-82. Mem. Aircraft Owners and Pilots Assn., ASME (assoc.), E. Tenn. Pilots Assn. Baptist. Home: 9701 Cortez Dr Knoxville TN 37923 Office: PO Box 587 Oak Ridge TN 37830

ROBERTSON, TED ZANDERSON, judge; b. San Antonio, Sept. 28, 1921; s. Irion Randolf and Aurelia (Zanderson) R.; m. Avis Cole, Dec. 29, 1955. Student, Tex. A&I, 1940-42; LL.B., St. Mary's U., San Antonio, 1949. Bar: Tex. 1949. Chief civil dept. Dist. Atty.'s Office, Dallas County, Tex., 1960-65; judge Probate Ct. 2, Dallas County, 1965-69, Juvenile Ct. 2, 1969-75, 95th Dist. Ct., 1975-76, Ct. Civil Appeals, 5th Supreme Jud. Dist., 1976-82, Supreme Ct. Tex., Austin, 1982—; guest lectr. So. Meth. U., Dallas, Dallas County Juvenile Bd., Tex. Coll. of the Judiciary, 1970-82. Active Dallas Assn. for Retarded Children, Dallas County Commn. on Alcoholism, Dallas County Mental Health Assn. Served to yeoman USCG, 1942-46. Recipient Golden Gavel St. Mary's U., San Antonio, 1979; named Outstanding Alumnus St. Mary's U., 1981. Mem. Am. Judicature Soc., Tex. Bar Assn., Dallas Bar Assn., Dallas County Juvenile Bd. Democrat. Methodist. Lodges: Masons; Lions. Home: 6233 Highgate Ln Dallas TX 75214 Office: Supreme Ct Tex Capitol Sta PO Box 12248 Austin TX 78711*

ROBERTSON, WILLIAM HOWARD, physician, educator; b. Nashville, July 1, 1921; s. William Perry and Mary (Henderson) R.; student Birmingham So. Coll., 1939-41: B.S., U. Ala., 1947; M.D., Med. Coll. Ala., 1951; m. Jennie May Webb, Oct. 29, 1940; children—Melissa Turpin, Jennifer Webb, William Webb. Intern, Univ. Hosp., Birmingham, Ala., 1951-52, resident in ob-gyn, 1953-56; practice medicine specializing in ob-gyn, Birmingham, 1956—; asso. clin. prof. Med. Coll. Ala., 1975—; med. writer Miles Pharms., West Haven, Conn. Chmn. United Way, Birmingham, 1977—; chmn. bd. dirs. Birmingham Civic Ballet; chmn. Arts Hall of Fame, Birmingham. Served to 1st lt. U.S. Army, 1942-46. Recipient medal Bayer AG Grer; diplomate Am. Bd. Ob-Gyn. Fellow ACS, Internat. Soc. Study of Vaginal Diseases; mem. AMA, So. Med. Assn., Royal Soc. Medicine, Pan Am. Med. Assn., Am. Fertility Soc., Birmingham Ob-Gyn Soc., Ala. Ob-Gyn Soc., Birmingham Surg. Soc., AAAS, Nat. Arts Club, N.Y. Acad. Sci., Alpha Omega Alpha. Contbr. articles to profl. jours. Office: 2660 10th Ave S Birmingham AL 35205

ROBERTSON, WILLIAM SHORE, judge; b. Richmond, Va., June 20, 1939; s. Alexander Cralle and Eugenia Bailey R.; m. Barbara Brewster Williams, June 26, 1966; children—Stuart Alexander. A.B., Coll. William and Mary, 1961; J.D., U. Va., 1964. Bar: Va. 1964. Assoc. Martin & Alexander, Warrenton, Va., 1966-67, ptnr. Martin, Alexander & Robertson, 1967-78; mem. Martin, Walker & Lawrence P.C., Warrenton, 1978-80; asst. Commonwealth atty. of Fauquier County (Va.), 1968-74; judge 20th Jud. Cir. Va., 1980—; bd. govs. Criminal Law, 1982—; mem. Va. Jud. Inquiry and Rev. Commn., 1985—. Vice Mayor, Town Council, Warrentown, 1973-80; lay leader Warrenton-United Methodist Ch., 1973-75, 82-83, chmn. bd., 1970-72; pres. Fauquier chpt. Va. Mus., 1968-69; adv. bd. Fauquier Family Guidance Ctr., 1974-76; chmn. Fauquier County Schs. Study Adv. Com., 1970; bd. dirs. Fauquier County Mental Health Assn., 1970-74; bd. dirs. maternity clinic Fauquier Hosp., 1971-74; mem. Welfare Bd. Fauquier County, 1975-80, Library Bd., 1974-77; mem. Highland Sch. Bd., 1972-83. Served to capt. U.S. Army, 1964-66. Mem. ABA, Va. State Bar (council 1969-73), Va. Bar Assn., Fauquier County Bar Assn. (pres. 1976-77), Jud. Conf. Va., Warrenton-Fauquier C. of C. (v.p. 1978-80, external v.p. jaycees 1968-69, outstanding man of yr. 1969), Lambda Chi Alpha, Omicron Delta Kappa, Phi Alpha Delta. Clubs: Rotary (hon. Warrenton Fauquier) Fauquier, Chestnut Forks Tennis, Vint Hill Officer's (hon.). Home: 28 Smith St Warrenton VA 22186 Office: PO Box 985 Warrenton VA 22186

ROBICHAUD, CAROL ANNE, investment banker; b. Uchitomari, Okinawa, Sept. 4, 1957; d. Oliver Valmore and Margaret Frances (Biles) R.; m. John Patrick Haley, Aug. 20, 1977; 1 dau., Elise Robichaud. B.B.A., Loyola U., New Orleans, 1977; M.B.A., U. North Fla., 1981. Mgmt. trainee Hibernia Nat. Bank, New Orleans, 1977-78; credit analyst Barnett Bank of Jacksonville, Fla., 1979-80; cash mgmt. officer Barnett Banks Fla., Jacksonville, 1980-81; investment officer Gulfco Capital Mgmt., Jacksonville, 1981-83; 1st v.p. investment banking Blackstock & Co. Inc., Jacksonville, 1983-85; pvt. fin. cons., 1985—. Mem. Jacksonville Fin. Analysts Soc. (bd. dirs. 1984-85). Republican. Roman Catholic.

ROBICHAUD, PHYLLIS IVY ISABEL, artist, educator; b. Jamaica, West Indies, May 16, 1915; came to U.S., 1969, naturalized, 1977; d. Peter C. and Rose Matilda (Rickman) Burnett; grad. Tutorial Coll., 1933, Kingston, Jamaica, Munro Coll., St. Elizabeth, Jamaica, 1946; student Central Tech. Sch., Toronto, Ont., Can., 1960-63, Anderson Coll., Can., 1968-69; m. Roger Robichaud, July 22, 1961; children by previous marriage—George Wilmot Graham, William Henry Heron Graham, Mary Elizabeth Graham Watson, Peter Robert Burnett Graham. Sec. to supr. of Agr., St. Elizabeth, 1940-50; loans officer and cashier Confederation Life Assn., Kingston, 1950-53; tchr. art Jamaica Welfare Ltd., 1963; tchr. art recreation dept. New Port Richey, Fla., 1969-77; tchr. art Pasco Hernando Community Coll., New Port Richey, 1977—; judge art shows, propr., mgr. Band Box Dress Shop, Kingston, Jamaica, 1954-57; numerous one-woman shows of paintings including various banks, libraries, Kingston, 1963-64, 67, Toronto, 1968, New Port Richey, 1969, 70, 73, 76, Tampa, Fla., 1974, 75, 76; numerous group shows, latest being: Sweden House, Tampa, 1977-78, Chasco Fiesta, New Port Richey, 1977, Magnolia Valley Golf and Country Club, New Port Richey, 1978, West Pasco Art Guild, New Port Richey, 1978, 79, Indian Rocks Beach exhbn., Clearwater, Fla., 1985; other cities in Fla.; executed murals, New Port Richey and

Kingston; represented in permanent collections: New Port Richey C. of C., Magnolia Valley Golf and Country Club, also pvt. collections. Patron, St. Alban's 4H Club, 1942; sec. Sunday sch. Ch. of Eng., Kingston, 1937-39. Recipient award T. Eaton Co. of Can., 1961, cert. of merit, Mayor of New Port Richey, 1976, appreciation award New Port Richey Recreation Dept., 1977, award Fla. Heart Fund, 1982. Mem. Nat. League Am. Pen Women (v.p. Tampa br. 1978-80, dir. 1969—), W. Pasco Art Guild (Blue ribbons 1978, 79), Fla. Fine Arts Guild. Republican. Roman Catholic. Lodge: Holiday Lioness (v.p. 1983; Gov.'s Achievement award 1982, Golden Chain award 1982). Address: 1053 Lenox Circle New Port Richey FL 33552

ROBIE, WILLIAM RANDOLPH, lawyer, government official; b. Balt., Sept. 15, 1944; s. Fred Smith and Mary Louise (Kent) R. B.A., Northwestern U., 1966, J.D., 1969. Bar: Ill. 1969, D.C. 1975, U.S. Ct. Mil. Appeals 1971, U.S. Supreme Ct. 1973. Assoc. Hubachek, Kelly, Rauch & Kirby, Chgo., 1969-70; asst. gen. counsel, Office Consumer Affairs, HEW, 1974-75; assoc. dir. legal edn. inst. Civil Service Commn., 1975-78; counsel to assoc. atty. gen. for atty. personnel, 1978-79, dep. assoc. atty. gen., 1979-81, assoc. dep. atty. gen. U.S. Dept. Justice, 1981; dir. Office Atty. Personnel Mgmt., Office Dep. Atty. Gen., U.S. Dept. Justice, Washington, 1981-83; chief immigration judge Exec. Office for Immigration Rev., Falls Church, Va., 1983—; instr., chmn. adv. bd. Paralegal Studies Project, U. Md., 1976—. Richard Weaver fellow, 1966-67. Served to capt. JAGC, U.S. Army, 1970-74. Mem. ABA (chmn. spl. com. delivery of legal services 1979-82), Fed. Bar Assn. (chmn. council on the fed. lawyer 1978-82, nat. sec. 1985-86), Judge Advocates Assn. (dir. 1975-82, chmn. field organization com. 1983—), Ill. Bar Assn., Chgo. Bar Assn., D.C. Bar. Republican. Presbyterian. Club: Nat. Lawyers Contbr. articles to profl. jours. Home: 111 Roberts Ct Alexandria VA 22314 Office: Suite 1501 5201 Leesburg Pike Falls Church VA 22041

ROBIN, JON ALAN, geologist; b. Conroe, Tex., Feb. 3, 1956; s. Alonzo Herbert and Dorothea Nell (Griffith) R.; m. Barbara Joan Atteridg, Sept. 2, 1978. B.S. in Geology, U. Tex., 1979. Research asst. Bur. Econ. Geology, Austin, Tex., 1976-79; geologist Northwestern Resources, Huntsville, Tex., 1979-81; prod. geologist Superior Oil, The Woodlands, Tex., 1981-84; exploration geologist Maggert Energy, Houston, 1984—. Mem. Am. Assn. Petroleum Geologists. Republican. Baptist. Avocations: watersports, snow skiing. Home: 26 Southfork Pines Pl The Woodlands TX 77381

ROBIN, THEODORE TYDINGS, JR., engineer; b. New Orleans, Aug. 29, 1939; s. Theodore Tydings and Hazel (Corbin) R.; B.M.E., Ga. Inst. Tech., 1961, M.S.N.E., 1963, Ph.D., 1967; LL.B., Blackstone Sch. Law, 1979; m. Helen Jones, June 8, 1963; children—Corbin, Curry, Ted, Phil. Bar: Calif 1980, U.S. Patent and Trademark Office 1982. Registered profl. engr., Ala., Calif. Research engr. Oak Ridge Nat. Lab., 1967; asst. prof. radiology and physics Emory U., 1968-69; project engr. Atomic Internat. div. N.Am. Rockwell, Canoga Park, Calif., 1970-72; program mgr. pooled inventory mgmt. program So. Co. Services, Birmingham, Ala., 1973—. Mem. Am. Bar Assn. Presbyterian. Club: Mountain Brook Swim and Tennis. Lodge: Rotary. Research on power plant performance and reliability, space radiation effects on human cells, boiling heat transfer. Home: 4524 Pine Mountain Rd Birmingham AL 35213 Office: PO Box 2625 Birmingham AL 35202

ROBINETT-WEISS, NANCY GAY, nutritionist, state agency administrator; b. Bluefield, W.Va., Mar. 16, 1948; d. Adam and L. Anne (Terry) R.; m. D. Bruce McCutcheon, May 16, 1970 (div. 1978); m. 2d, Dayne Mitchell Weiss, Aug. 2, 1980. B.S. in Foods and Nutrition, W.Va. U., 1970; M.S. in Nutrition Edn., Drexel U., 1975; postgrad. U. Utah, 1979-81. Dietitian, Logan Gen. Hosp. (W.Va.), 1968; staff therapeutic dietitian Our Lady of Loudres Hosp., Camden, N.J., 1970-71; therapeutic dietitian Temple U. Hosp., Phila., 1971-74; nutritionist, instr. Temple U. Dental Sch., Phila., 1974-75; instr. nutrition Camden County Vocat. and Tech. Schs. (N.J.), 1975-76; chief nutrition services Woodhaven Ctr., Phila., 1975-77; nutrition cons. family and health services, maternal and child health, handicapped children's services Utah Dept. Health, Salt Lake City, 1977-80, nutrition coordinator Utah Family Health Services, 1980-82; dir. nutrition services Tex. Dept. Health, Austin, 1982—; cons. ednl. program Sta. WHYY-TV, Phila., 1975; intern nutrition and pregnancy Montreal Diet Dispensary (Que., Can.), Feb. 1980; mem. program com., participant Tex. Conf. on Disease Prevention and Health Promotion, 1983. Mem. Utah Gov.'s Conf. Nutrition, co-chmn. pregnancy and early childhood sect., 1978; mem. Tex. Gov.'s Com. on Nutrition and Wellness, 1984; participant nat. and regional coms. on nutrition, child health, and crippled children's services, 1977—. Mem. Am. Dietetic Assn. (pub. health nutritionists practice group), Utah Dietetic Assn. (co-chmn. statewide meeting 1979, 80), Utah Nutrition Council, Tex. Dietetic Assn. (legis. workshop presenter 1983, legis. info. and pub. policy rep. 1984-85; chmn. elect food and nutrition sect.), Am. Pub. Health Assn. (chmn. program planning food nutrition sect. ann. meeting 1983), Utah Pub. Health Assn. (planning com. ann. meeting 1981), Tex. Nutrition Council, Assn. State and Territorial Pub. Health Nutrition Dirs. (exec. bd. 1983-86). Office: 1100 W 49th St Austin TX 78756

ROBINOWITZ, RALPH, psychologist; b. Houston, Sept. 21, 1929; s. Isadore and Esther (Levinson) R.; m. Chana Freedman, Nov. 6, 1960; children—Howard, Don E., Jill, Kevin. B.A., U. Tex., 1950, M.A., 1952, Ph.D., 1954. Staff psychologist VA Med. Ctr., Waco, Tex., 1958-61; staff psychologist VA Med. Ctr., Dallas, 1961-72, chief drug dependence treatment program, 1972—; adj. prof. psychology East Tex. State U., Commerce; clin. assoc. prof. psychology U. Tex. Health Scis. Ctr., Dallas; mem. Tex. State Drug Abuse Adv. Council, 1979-83; mem. mental health task force Tex. Area 5 Health Systems Agy., 1977-83. Served to 1st lt. U.S. Army, 1955-58. VA grantee, 1980—. Fellow Am. Psychol. Assn., Soc. for Personality Assessment. Cons. editor Jour. Personality Assessment, 1978-85. Home: 7149 Blairview Dr Dallas TX 75230 Office: VA Med Center Dallas TX 75216

ROBINS, HUGH PERK, university official; b. Louisville, May 5, 1930; s. Hugh and Lillian (Driskell) R.; m. Mary Lou Rutz, June 20, 1953; children—Richard, Rebecca Robins Galvin, Patricia Robins Dailey. B.S. in Edn., Wittenberg U., Springfield, Ohio, 1952. First baseman Cin. Reds, 1955-56; alumni dir. Wittenberg U., 1956-67; dir. devel. Ball State U., Muncie, Ind., 1967-73; v.p. U. Ga., Athens, 1973—; cons. U. N.C., Luth. Sch. Theology, Chgo., S.E. La. U., Newberry Coll. Served with U.S. Army, 1953-55. Recipient U.S. Steel award Council for Advancement and Support of Edn., 1958, 80, 81. Home: 155 Dunwoody St Athens GA 30605 Office: U Ga Athens GA 30605

ROBINS, RICHARD LEE, college official, consultant; b. Louisville, Dec. 8, 1954; s. Hugh Perk and Mary Lou (Rutz) R.; m. Janice Annette Henderson, Apr. 2, 1977; children—Jason, Jeremy. B.B.A., U. Ga., 1977. Asst. dir. ann. support Purdue U., West Lafayette, Ind., 1978; dir. devel. and alumni services West Ga. Coll., Carrollton, 1978-79; dir. annual support East Carolina U., Greenville, N.C., 1979-81; dir. devel. Valdosta State Coll., Ga., 1981-85; asst. v.p. for devel. Oglethorpe U., Atlanta, 1985—; mem. faculty Case Summer Inst., Lexington, Ky., 1985; cons. Southeastern La. U., Hammond, 1984-85, Fla. Jr. Coll., Jacksonville, 1983, Brunswick Jr. Coll., Ga., 1983. Fin. chmn. Circle 7 dist. Boy Scouts Am., 1985; stewardship chmn. Park Avenue United Meth. Ch., Valdosta, 1984-85; hon. Dir. Spectrum II TV Marathon VSC-TV 1983. Recipient Case/U.S. Steel Alumni Giving Incentive award, 1980, 81. Mem. Valdosta-Lowndes County C. of C., Council Advancement and Support Edn., Ga. Ednl. Advancement Com., Nat. Assn. Athletic Mktg. and Devel. Dirs. Republican. Club: Valdosta Country. Avocations: athletics; model trains. Home: 4023 Timberbrook Trail Valdosta GA 31602 Office: Valdosta State Coll 205 Powell Hall West Valdosta GA 31698

ROBINSON, ADELBERT CARL, lawyer; b. Shawnee, Okla., Dec. 13, 1926; s. William H. and Mayme (Forston) R.; student Okla. Baptist U., 1944-47; LL.B., Okla. U., 1950, J.D., 1970; m. Marilyn Ruth Stubbs, Dec. 28, 1963 (div.); children—William, James, Schuyler, Donald, David, Nancy, Lauri. Admitted to Okla. bar, 1950; practiced in Muskogee, 1956—; with legal dept. Phillips Petroleum Co., 1950-51; adjuster U.S. Fidelity & Guaranty Co., 1951-54, atty., adjuster-in-charge, 1954-56; partner Fite & Robinson, 1956-62; partner Fite, Robinson & Summers, 1963-70, Robinson & Summers, 1970-72, Robinson, Summers & Locke, 1972-76, Robinson, Locke & Gage, 1976-80, Robinson, Locke, Gage & Fite, 1980—; police judge, 1963-64; mcpl. judge, 1964-70; prin. justice Temp. Div. 36 Ct. Appeals of State of Okla., 1981—. Pres., dir. Wall St. Bldg. Corp., 1969-78, Three Forks Devel. Corp., 1968-77, Rolo Leasing, Inc., 1971—, Suroya II, Inc., 1977—; sec., dir. P & H Supply, Inc., Weddles Food Stores, Muskogee Tom's, Inc., Helmer Printing Co., Inc., Blue Ridge Corp., Harborcliff Corp.; dir. First Bancshares of Muskogee, Inc., First of Muskogee Corp.; adv. dir. First Nat. Bank & Trust Co. of Muskogee; mng. ptnr. RLG Ritz, 1980—; ptnr. First City Real Estate Parnership, 1985—. Chmn. Inter-Organizational Relations Com., 1960-63; chmn. Muskogee County Law Day, 1963; chmn. Muskogee Area Redevel. Authority, 1963; chmn. Muskogee County chpt. Am. Cancer Soc., 1956; chmn. Profl. Cooperation Com., 1965-69. Pres., bd. dirs. Muskogee Community Council; bd. dirs. United Way of Muskogee, Inc., Muskogee Community Concert Assn., Muskogee Tourist Info. Bur., 1964-68; bd. dirs., gen. counsel United Cerebral Palsy Eastern Okla., 1964-68; trustee Connors Devel. Found., Connors Coll., 1981—; v.p. United Way of Muskogee, 1982, pres., 1983, exec. com., 1983—. Served with inf. AUS, 1945-46. Mem. Am. Bar Assn., Okla. Bar Assn. (chmn. uniform laws com. 1970-72, past regional chmn. grievance com.), Muskogee County Bar Assn. (pres. 1971, mem. exec. council), Okla. Assn. Def. Counsel (dir.), Okla. Assn. Mcpl. Judges (dir.), Muskogee C. of C., Delta Theta Phi. Methodist. Rotarian (pres. 1971-72). Home: 2800 Robin Ln Muskogee OK 74401 Office: 530 Court St PO Box 87 Muskogee OK 74401

ROBINSON, BERNETTA DENISE, librarian, biologist; b. Phila., May 1, 1953; d. Rudolph and Evelyn (McCarter) Robinson. B.A., Cheyney State Coll., 1974; M.L.S., Atlanta U., 1981. Sci. tchr. Phila. Sch. Dist., 1974-75; manpower planner City of Phila., 1975-78; grad. research asst. Atlanta U., 1979-80; forestry technician U.S. Dept. Agr. Forest Service, Delaware, Ohio, 1979; tech. info. specialist Lawrence Livermore Lab. (Calif.), 1981; reference librarian Atlanta U. Ctr., 1981—. Mem. Urban League, Phila., 1976-78, NAACP, Phila., 1977-78. Recipient Women in Non-Traditional Occupations award U.S. Dept. Labor, 1978, Co-op award U.S. Dept. Agr. Forest Service, 1979-80. Mem. ALA, Atlanta Online Users Assn., Met. Atlanta Library Assn., Ga. Library Assn., Delta Sigma Theta. Baptist. Office: Robert W Woodruff Library Atlanta U Ctr 111 Chestnut St Atlanta GA 30314

ROBINSON, BRENDA COOMBS, city official; b. Goldsboro, N.C., Dec. 16, 1947; d. Rhem Horace and Mary Kathleen (Davis) Coombs; student Meredith Coll., 1965-67; B.S. in Bus. Adminstrn., U. Central Fla. 1977, M.A. in Econs., 1979; married; children—Lisa Reed Donnan, Christopher Scott Donnan, Allison Ann Robinson. Grad. asst. U. Central Fla., 1978-79; sr. planner manpower div. County of Seminole, Fla., 1979, sr. budget and mgmt. analyst, 1979-81; dir. fin. City of Altamone Springs, Fla., 1981-83; mgmt. and budget ofcl. City of Orlando (Fla.), 1983—. Recipient Orlando C. of C. Gold Telephone award 1976. Mem. Govtl. Fin. Officers Assn., Beta Gamma Sigma, Omicron Delta Kappa. Republican. Presbyterian. Home: 186 Monterey Isle South Longwood FL 32779 Office: 400 S Orange Ave Orlando FL 32801

ROBINSON, BRENDA PERRY, business executive; b. Richlands, Va., June 21, 1946; d. Joseph Franklin and Irene (Jessee) Perry; student public schs., Va. and Md., also various seminars; m. Walter Warren Robinson, Aug. 24, 1977; 1 dau. by previous marriage, Lori Kay White. File clk. Tabb Brockenborough & Ragland, Richmond, Va., 1963-64; acctg. clk. So. states R.H. Donnelley Co., Richmond, 1965; with Reynolds Metals Co., Richmond, 1966—, mgr. employee med. benefits, 1975-78, mgr. adminstrv. services, 1978-81, mgr. office systems implementation and automation edn., 1981-83, mgr. automation cons. and edn., 1981-86; pres. Innovative Resources, 1985—; v.p. sales Riddick Communication/MG1, 1986—. Editor: Innovation. Chmn. adv. council Va. Dept. Bus. Edn.; sec. Miss Softball Am., Richmond; co. rep. United Way, Richmond; substitute rep. Va. Nutrition Com.; cons. project bus. Jr. Achievement, 1985; mem. adv. com. Incubator Task Force, to Congressman Gliley. Named Boss of Yr., Am. Businesswomen's Assn., 1976. Mem. Adminstrv. Mgmt. Soc. and Speakers Bur. (chmn. edn. com.), Richmond Office Automation Roundtable (sec.), Va. Advanced Tech. Assn. (bd. dirs.), Office Automation Roundtable, Women's Network, Nat. Assn. Female Execs. Baptist. Home: 702 Sleepy Hollow Rd Richmond VA 23229 Office: 6601 W Broad St Richmond VA 23261

ROBINSON, FLOYD WALTER, JR., hospital director; b. Chambersburg, Pa., Dec. 22, 1947; s. Floyd Walter, Sr. and Nellie Jeanettie (Payton) R. B.S. in English and Speech, Shippensburg U., 1969. English master Mercersburg Acad., Pa., 1969-76; asst. to v.p. human resources Gulf Oil Chems., Houston, 1976-79; mgr. Am. Express Co., St. Thomas, Virgin Islands, 1979-82; assoc. dir. patient supply, processing and distbn. U. Tex. System Cancer Ctr.-M.D. Anderson Hosp. & Tumor Inst., Houston, 1982—; career counselor Career Mgmt., 1978-79. Author short stories. Advisor, Mayor's Youth Council, Houston, 1976-79; bd. dirs. Mental Health/Mental Retardation Central Pa., 1970-77, Community Concert Assn., Chambersburg, Pa., 1974-76; dir. youth employment program Houston Metropolitan Ministries, 1978-79. Mem. Am. Soc. Hosp. Central Service Personnel, Tex. Hosp. Assn., Houston Soc. for Central Service Personnel, Am. Mgmt. Assn. Democrat. Episcopalian. Avocations: traveling; reading; public speaking; acting and singing. Home: 4119 Graustark 10 Houston TX 77098 Office: MD Anderson Hosp 6723 Bertner Ave Houston TX 77030

ROBINSON, FRED L. JACK, former mil. newspaper publisher; b. Pickens, S.C., Oct. 13, 1909; s. Mark Frank and Hattie (White) R.; student naval tng. schs.; m. Lillian E. Surman, July 4, 1953; children—Linda Lee, Casey F. Staff mem. mil. papers, 1927—; author syndicated column Horseshoe Robinson; 74 Served war corr. 1926-30. Served with USN, 1926-30. Mem. Va. Boating Assn. (founder, sr. commodore). Home: 2101 Cocoa Circle Virginia Beach VA 23454

ROBINSON, GARY CHARLES, geophysicist; b. Phila., May 11, 1956; s. Charles Huston and Carmela (Villari) R.; m. Carol Ann Wallace, June 7, 1980; 1 child, Corey Charles. B.S. in Geology, Stanford U., 1978; postgrad. U. Houston, 1985—. Summer field geologist Mobil Oil Corp., Denver, 1978; geophysicist Denver Processing Ctr., 1978-79; geophysicist Compagne Generale de Geophysique, Denver, 1979-83, mgr. interpretation, Denver, 1983-84; sr. geophysicist Elf Aquitaine Petroleum, Houston, 1984—. Contbr. articles to profl. jours. Mem. Soc. Exploration Geophysicists, Am. Assn. Petroleum Geologists, Rocky Mountain Assn. Geologists, Geophys. Soc. Houston, European Assn. Exploration Geophysicists, Alpha Sigma Phi. Roman Catholic. Avocation: photography. Home: 22935 Benbury Dr Katy TX 77450 Office: Elf Aquitaine Petroleum 1000 Louisiana Suite 3800 Houston TX 77002

ROBINSON, HAROLD FRANK, university administrator, educator; b. Bandana, N.C., Oct. 28, 1918; s. Fred Herbert and Geneva (Jarrett) R.; m. Katherine Palmer Robinson, Feb. 9, 1944; children—Karen Elizabeth Dail, Mary JoAnne Bewsey. Student Mars Hill Coll., 1935-37; B.S. with high honors in Plant Breeding, N.C. State Coll., 1939, M.S. in Plant Breeding, 1940; Ph.D. in Genetics and Plant Breeding, U. Nebr., 1948, D.Sc. (hon.), 1966. Seed specialist N.C. Crop Improvement Assn., 1940-41; asst. prof. dept. exptl. stats. N.C. State Coll., Raleigh, 1945-48, assoc. prof., 1948-51, prof., 1951-58, prof. genetics and exptl. stats., 1958-62, head dept. genetics, 1958-62, dir. Inst. Biol. Scis., 1962-65, asst. dir. Agrl. Expt. Sta., 1962-65, adminstrv. dean for research N.C. State U., 1965-68; exec. dir. Pres.'s Sci. Adv. Com. Panel on World Food Supply, 1966-67; vice chancellor Univ. System of Ga., 1968-71; prof. biology Ga. Inst. Tech., Atlanta, 1968-71; prof. stats. Ga. State U., 1968-71; prof. genetics U. Ga., Athens, 1968-71; prof. microbiology Med. Coll. Ga., 1968-71; prof. biol. scis. and stats. Purdue U., West Lafayette, Ind., 1971-74, provost, 1971-74; prof. biology and math. Western Carolina U., Cullowhee, N.C., 1974—, chancellor, 1974-84; cons. and lectr. to numerous state, local and nat. profl. orgns.; mem. found. com. Sultan Qubuos Univ. Project, Muscat, Oman. Contbr. articles to profl. jours. Mem. numerous civic orgns., profl. coms. and univ. orgns. Served to lt. USN, 1941-45. Recipient award for contbns. in genetics and plant breeding Nat. Council Comml. Plant Breeders, 1964. Fellow Am. Soc. Agronomy, AAAS; mem. Am. Assn. Higher Edn., Am. Soc. Naturalist, Am. Inst. Biol. Scis., Assn. Allied Health Professions, Biometric Soc., Genetics Soc. Am., Beta Beta Beta, Gamma Sigma Delta, Phi Kappa Phi, Sigma Xi, Phi Sigma, Omicron Delta Kappa, Alpha Kappa Psi (hon.). Methodist. Research on quantitative genetics, heterosis and related phenomena in maize genetics, population and food supply. Office: Office of Univ Studies Western Carolina U Cullowhee NC 28723

ROBINSON, JAMES ARTHUR, college president; b. Blackwell, Okla., June 9, 1932; s. William L. and Ethel Bell (Hicks) R.; A.B., George Washington U., 1954, D.P.S. (hon.), 1977; M.A., U. Okla., 1955; Ph.D., Northwestern U., 1957; LL.D. (hon.), Kyungpook (Korea) Nat. U., 1979; m. Lucia Adelaide Walton, Dec. 11, 1965 (div. 1984); children—Adelaide Ethel, William Luke Walton. Instr. polit. sci. Northwestern U., 1958-59, asst. prof., 1959-62, asso. prof., 1962-64; prof. polit. sci. Ohio State U., Columbus, 1964-71, dir. Mershon Center, 1967-70, v.p. acad. affairs, provost, 1969-71; pres., prof. polit. sci. Macalester Coll., St. Paul, 1971-74; pres., prof. polit. sci. U. West Fla., Pensacola, 1974—; dir. Baptist Care Inc. Trustee, chmn. Episcopal Day Sch.; bd. dirs. Nat. Center Higher Edn. Mgmt. Systems. Congl. fellow Am. Polit. Sci. Assn., 1957-58. Mem. Nat. Commn. Coop. Edn., Fla. Assn. Colls. and Univs. (past chmn.). Democrat. Episcopalian. Club: Cosmos (Washington); Univ. (N.Y.C.). Author: (with R.C. Snyder) National and International Decision Making, 1961; Congress and Foreign Policy Making, rev. edit., 1967; House Rules Committee, 1964. Address: U West Fla Pensacola FL 32514

ROBINSON, JAMES VAYDEN, psychology educator; b. Summerland, Miss., Mar. 28, 1930; s. James Vayden and Lessye Maxine (McDaniel) R. B.S., U. So. Miss., 1954; M.A., U. Miss., 1959, Ph.D., 1961. Instr. psychology Miss. U. for Women, Columbus, 1961-63; asst. prof. William Woods Coll., 1963-65; assoc. prof. Ga. So. Coll., Statesboro, 1965-70; assoc. prof. psychology Coll. of Charleston, S.C., 1970—. Served with USAF, 1953-57, Korea. Mem. AAUP, Am. Psychol. Assn. Home: PO Box 12143 Charleston SC 29412 Office: Dept Psychology Coll of Charleston Charleston SC 29424

ROBINSON, JAY, educational administrator. Supt of schs. Mecklenburg County, N.C. Office: PO Box 30035 Charlotte NC 28230*

ROBINSON, JOE ADAMS, writer, retired foreign service officer; b. Union, S.C., Apr. 2, 1912; s. Hurvy H. and Mary Brannon (Adams) R.; m. Lenore Thomas, Aug. 15, 1942; children—Joseph Adams, Walter Thomas, James McGill Hervey, Olivita Mary Robinson Koach. B.S., U. Okla., 1935; M.A., George Washington U., 1937, Ph.D., 1945; grad. Nat. Def. U., Ft. McNair, Washington, 1952. With Fed. Home Loan Bank Bd., 1935-41; economist U.S. Tarriff Commn., 1941-42; commd. fgn. service officer Dept. State, 1946; U.S. del. numerous internat. negotiations; U.S. del. European office UN, Geneva, 1955-58; 1st sec., econ. officer Am. embassy, Paris, 1962-64; counselor, chief trade div. OECD, Paris, 1964-66, ret., 1970; freelance fiction writer, 1972—; short stories pub. in various mags. Active in local, state and nat. polit. affairs. Served as comdr. USN, 1942-45. Mem. Washington Ind. Writers, Diplomatic and Consular Corps, Fgn. Service Assn., Alumni Assn. U. Okla., Alumni Assn. George Washington U., Alumni Assn. Nat. Def. U., Order of Artus, Beta Gamma Sigma, Pi Gamma Mu. Clubs: Fgn. Service, Ft. Myer Officers, Ft. Lesley J. McNair Officers (Washington). Home: 3019 Cedarwood Ln Falls Church VA 22042

ROBINSON, JOHN CLIFTON, oilman, petroleum landman, geologist; b. Shreveport, La., Dec. 8, 1951; s. Clifton Hight, Jr. and Helen Cora (Baker) R.; m. Audrey Marie Martin, May 31, 1974 (div. 1978); 1 child, Christine Anne; m. Sharon Sue Wesson, Sept. 27, 1980; 1 child, John Clifton, Jr. B.S. in Geology, Centenary Coll., 1985. Carpenter, Shreveport, 1978-79; petroleum land mgr. C.H. Robinson, Jr. & Assocs., Shreveport, 1979-82; ind. oilman, Shreveport, 1982—. Served with U.S. Army, 1974-78; 2d lt. Res. Mem. Am. Assn. Petroleum Geologists, Am. Assn. Petroleum Landmen, Shreveport Geol. Soc. Ark-La-Tex Landmans Assn. Republican. Mem. Assembly of God Ch. Avocations: photography; canoeing; camping; hunting; fishing. Home and office: 320 Merrick Shreveport LA 71104

ROBINSON, JOHN HAROLD, mechanical engineer; b. Jackson, Tenn., Oct. 14, 1921; s. Charles Albert and Katie May (Reeder) R.; student State Tenn. Tchrs. Coll., 1941; B.S.M.E., Internat. Corr. Schs., 1964; postgrad. State Tech. Inst. Memphis; m. Virginia Elizabeth Marbury, Sept. 21, 1942; children—Sandra Elizabeth, Sharon Lane, Wanda Jane, John Harold. Chief engr. Claridge Hotel, Memphis, 1939-42, 45-47, Tenn. Tb Control, State of Tenn. Tb Hosps., 1948-57, Humko Products Co., Champaign, Ill., 1957-58; cons. engr. to Tb Bd. Fla., Fla. Tb Control, W.T. Edwards-Fla. State Hosp., 1958-61; engring. mgr., Cudahy Refining Co., Memphis, 1961-63; engring. mgr. Humko Chem. div. Witco Corp., Memphis, 1963—; pres. AME Assocs. Inc.; past mem. Memphis Elec. Code Adv. Bd. Active Chickasaw council Boy Scouts Am., 1970-78. Served to staff sgt. USAAF, 1942-45; ETO. Decorated Air medal with 3 oak leaf clusters, D.F.C.; recipient Scouters award Boy Scouts Am., 1974, 75, named Leader of Distinction, 1975; registered profl. engr., Tenn. Mem. Am. Inst. Plant Engrs. (cert. plant engr.; Engr. of Yr. award 1972-73, pres. local chpt. 1975-76), Engring. Joint Council, Am. Hosp. Assn. Hosp. Engrs., Refrigeration Engrs. and Technicians Assn. (pres. chpt. 1955-57). Presbyterian (elder 1983). Home: 3336 Chancellor St Memphis TN 38118 Office: 1231 Pope St Memphis TN 38108

ROBINSON, LEWIS WILLIAM, architect; b. Guatemala City, Guatemala, Sept. 1, 1944; s. Lewis J. and Elisa A. (Cruz) R.; B.Arch., U. Nebr., 1962-68; m. Deborah A. Taylor, Aug. 20, 1966; children—Lewis A., John C., Anne E. Architect Nebr. Dept. Roads, 1966-68; architect Black & Veatch, Cons. Engrs., 1971-73; architect, project mgr., v.p. Henningson Durham & Richardson, Omaha, mgr. archtl. dept., Alexandria, Va., 1973—. Troop com. chmn. Boy Scouts Am., 1980-82. Served to capt., C.E., U.S. Army, 1968-71. Registered profl. architect, Nebr., Minn., Va., WIs., Fla., N.C. Mem. AIA. Republican. Roman Catholic.

ROBINSON, LILA WISTRAND, linguistics, folklore and anthropology educator; b. Chgo., May 12, 1931; d. Elmer George m. Albert Robinson, Jr., July 31, 1971. B.A., U. Tex., 1966, M.A., 1968, Ph.D., 1969. Field worker, educator Summer Inst. Linguistics Peru, 1954-65; asst. prof. linguistics, speech Kans. State U., Manhattan, 1969-72; dir. grant project Christian Children's Fund, Park Hill, Okla., 1975-76, Kans. State U., 1976-77; prof. linguistics and anthropology Liberty U., Lynchburg, Va., 1978—; dir. folklore workshop Summer Inst. Linguistics, Mitla, Oaxaca, Mex., 1975. Author: Otoe and Iowa Indian Language, 1977, vol. 2, 1978; (with Rose Garcia) Italian Immigrant Coal-Miner's Daughter, 1977; Cashibo Biota, 1984; editor: A Transformational Approach to Mandarin Grammar, 1981. Mem. Am. Anthrop. Assn., Linguistic Soc. Am., Va. Folklore Soc., Soc. Linguistic Anthropology, Am. Folklore Soc. Avocations: hiking; oil painting. Office: Div Social Scis Liberty Univ PO Box 20000 Lynchburg VA 24506

ROBINSON, LOUIS WADE, geologist, consultant; b. Ipswich, Eng., Oct. 26, 1956; came to U.S., 1958; s. H.C. and Gloria (Akins) R.; m. Nora Lou Thompson, Aug. 3, 1979. B.S., La. Tech. U., 1979. Geologist, River Rouge Minerals, Mansfield, La., 1979-81, Griffin So., Denver, 1981-82, M.G.F. Oil Co., Midland, Tex., 1982; cons. geologist, Mansfield, 1982—. Mem. Am. Assn. Petroleum Geologists, Soc. Econ. Paleontologists and Mineralogists, Shreveport Geol. Soc. Democrat. Baptist. Avocations: tennis; golf. Home and office: 710 Debra Dr Mansfield LA 71052

ROBINSON, LYNN BROWN, marketing educator; b. Mobile, Ala., July 29, 1938; d. Samuel and Carolyn D. (Greenfield) B.; m. John Kenneth Robinson, Feb. 27, 1963; children—Jennifer Kay, John Kenneth Jr. B.B.A., Emory U., 1960; M.B.A., U. Ala., 1965, Ph.D., 1972. Asst. prof. to prof. U. South Ala., Mobile, 1968—, dir. grad. studies Coll. Bus., 1977-80, chmn. dept. mktg. and transp., 1983—; v.p. Engineered Textile Products, Inc. Bd. dirs. St. Mary's Home for Children, Ala. Easter Seal Soc. Mem. Am. Mktg. Assn., So. Mktg. Assn., Sales and Mktg. Execs. Internat., Beta Gamma Sigma. Office: Coll of Bus and Mgmt Studies U of So Ala Mobile AL 36688

ROBINSON, MARIE RACHELLE, artist; b. De Ridder, La., Oct. 14, 1919; d. Thomas Benjamin and Bertha (Allemoure) Genna; student Warner Sch. Art, 1927, Sophie Newcomb U., 1936-37, pvt. study Hans Hofman, Maine, 1960-62, U. Paris, 1964; m. King H. Robinson, May 29, 1935. Pres., Design Fashions, Inc., 1967; owner Interior Planning by Marie, Houston, 1969-70, Bayou Art Sch., Dickinson, Tex., 1970, Marie Robinson Art Studio and Gallery, Houston, 1970—; partner Mar-King Co., Houston, 1970—; one-man shows Davis Gallery, Houston, Alley Gallery, Houston, Broken Arrow-Strandart Gallery, Galveston, Tex., Biloxi (Miss.) Art Gallery, River Oaks Gallery, Houston, Rice Hotel, Houston. Mem. Appraisers Assn. Am., New Eng. Appraisers Assn., La. Art Advisory Comm., Am. Assn. Master Artists, Internat. Soc. Appraisers, Internat. Soc. Fine Arts Appraisers. Republican. Roman Catholic. Author: Painting Scapes—Land and Sea, 1968; A Walk with the Old Masters, 1967; The Importance of Perspective, 1968. Office: PO Box 64 Rusk TX 78785

ROBINSON, MARTHA A., psychologist, educator; b. Reidsville, N.C., Sept. 7, 1940; d. John William and Louise Thacker (Pettigrew) Allen; m. Linville Carleton Robinson, Aug. 28, 1971. B.A., U.S.C., 1962; M.Ed., Duke U., 1968; doctoral candidate U. S.C. Tchr., Charleston (S.C.) Schs., 1962-67, tchr. emotionally handicapped, 1968-70; cons. Office Programs for Handicapped, S.C. State Dept. Edn., 1970-72; spl. edn. cons. Greenville (S.C.) County Schs., 1972-74; spl. edn. dir. Pickens County Schs., 1974-75; dir. Programs for

Handicapped, Spartanburg (S.C.) Sch. Dist. 7, 1976-81, sch. psychologist, 1981—; guest instr. Converse Coll., Clemson U., U. S.C.; dir. Learning Disabilities Project, Greenville County, 1973. Bd. advisors Assn. Retarded Citizens; bd. dirs. Ballet Guild Spartanburg. Mem. Council Exceptional Children, Assn. Children with Learning Disabilities, S.C. Sch. Psychologists Assn., Assn. Retarded Citizens, Assn. Supervision and Curriculum Devel., S.C. Assn. Children Under Six, Spartanburg County Internat. Reading Assn. Republican. Presbyterian. Co-editor: Good Mental Health in the Classroom, 1974. Home: 265 Lake Forest Dr Spartanburg SC 29302 Office: 640 Cummings St DSOC Spartanburg SC 29303

ROBINSON, MARY LOU, judge; b. Dodge City, Kans., Aug. 25, 1926; d. Gerald J. and Frances Strueber; B.A., U. Tex., 1948, LL.B., 1950; m. A.J. Robinson, Aug. 28, 1949; children—Rebecca Aynn Gruhlkey, Diana Ceil, Matthew Douglas. Admitted to Tex. bar, 1949; practice law, Amarillo, 1950-55; judge County Ct., Potter County, Tex., 1955-59; judge 108th Dist. Ct., Amarillo, 1961-73; asso. justice Ct. of Civil Appeals for 7th Supreme Jud. Dist. of Tex., Amarillo, 1973-77, chief justice, 1977-79; U.S. dist. judge No. Dist. Tex., Amarillo, 1979—. Named Woman of Year Tex. Fedn. Bus. and Profl. Women, 1973. Mem. Nat. Assn. Women Lawyers, Am. Bar Assn., Tex. Bar Assn., Amarillo Bar Assn., Delta Kappa Gamma. Presbyterian. Office: US Dist Ct PO Box 13248 Amarillo TX 79189

ROBINSON, MICHAEL FRED, anesthesiologist; b. Oklahoma City, May 17, 1951; s. Charles George and Elaine Meryl (Goldberg) R.; m. Diana Asnes, Jan. 14, 1984. Student Tulane U., 1969-70; A.B., Washington U., St. Louis, 1973; M.D., U. Okla., 1978; postgrad. Oklahoma City U. Sch. Law, 1982-83. Med. research technician, summers 1969-73; resident physician in anesthesiology U. Okla., 1978-81; mem. Affiliated Anesthesiologists, Oklahoma City, 1981—. Mem. Jewish Community Council. Mem. Oklahoma Couty Med. Soc., Okl. State Med. Assn., AMA, Am. Soc. Anesthesiologists, Okla. Soc. Anesthesiologists, Internat. Anesthesia Research Soc. Democrat. Club: Oklahoma City Ski. Lodge: B'nai B'rith. Home: 1212 Westchester Dr Oklahoma City OK 73114 Office: 10301 N May Oklahoma City OK 73120

ROBINSON, MICHAEL WARREN, SR., solid waste manager; b. Little Rock, Ark., June 29, 1947; s. Murriel Warren and Grace Lee (Martin) R.; m. Queen Ester Prowell, June 14, 1970; children—Michael Warren, Katrina Latice. B.S., Ark. Baptist Coll., 1980. Asst. dir. Safety and Civil Def., Little Rock, Ark., 1973-75; sanitation operator, officer City of Little Rock, 1975-77, chief sanitation operator, 1977—. Active Boys Club Am. Served in U.S. Army, 1967-69. Decorated Bronze Star. Mem. Am. Pub. Works Assn., Govtl. Refuse Collection Disposal Assn. Democrat. Methodist. Lodge: Masons. Home: 1 Shelby Circle Little Rock AR 72206 Office: 3312 J E Davis Dr Little Rock AR 72209

ROBINSON, ORMSBEE W., educational consultant; b. Bklyn., June 17, 1910; s. Harry Alexander and Claire (Wright) R.; m. Janet MacNaughton Miller, June 22, 1935; children—Heather (Mrs. Phillips Thorp), John Alexander. A.B. cum laude, Princeton U., 1932; M.S.S., New Sch. for Social Research, 1937; M.A., Columbia U. Tchrs. Coll., 1942, Ed.D., 1949. Exec. sec. Plainfield (N.J.) Inst., 1934-35; high sch. tchr., 1935; dir. adult edn. Soc. for Ethical Culture, N.Y.C., 1935-41; tchr. ethics Fieldston Sch., N.Y.C., 1935-42; assoc. Region II, OPA, 1942-46; dir. admissions and pub. relations Bard Coll., 1946-50, v.p., 1950-54; ednl. cons. for higher edn. Conn. Dept. Edn., 1954-55, chief Bur. Higher and Adult Edn., 1955-57; exec. sec. Conn. Council Higher Edn., 1954-57; cons. in exec. devel. IBM, 1957-61, dir. ednl. affairs, 1962-70, dir. univ. relations planning, 1970-75; program dir. IBM Exec. Sch., 1962; dir. internat. program Nat. Council on Philanthropy, 1975-79, acting pres., 1977-78; cons. Eugenio Mendoza Found. and Venezuelan Fedn. Pvt. Founds., Caracas, 1979-83, Technoserve, Inc., 1980-83; assoc. seminar on tech. and social change Columbia U., 1962-75; chmn. bus. edn. adv. bd. Com. Econ. Devel., 1963-68; mem. council devel. edn. and tng. Nat. Indsl. Conf. Bd., 1960-68; mem. faculty Salzburg Seminar in Am. Studies, 1968; mem. U.S. Nat. Commn. for UNESCO, 1971-74, mem. exec. com., 1972-74, chmn. adv. com. on bus. and internat. edn., 1971-72, chmn. membership com., 1974; mem. standards com. Am. Assembly Coll. Schs. Bus., 1971-72, chmn. internat. affairs com., 1973-75, bd. dirs., 1974-75; mem. task force on bus. and internat. edn. Am. Council on Edn., 1975-76. Co-author: Education in Business and Industry, 1966; mem. editorial adv. bd. Indian Adminstrv. and Mgmt. Rev., New Delhi, 1966-75; 75; contbr. articles to profl. jours. Bd. dirs. World Affairs Ctr., Hartford, Conn., 1981-83; mem. adv. council Am. Ditchley Found., 1969—; mem. Granby (Conn.) Bd. Edn., 1979-83. bd. founders U. Hartford; chmn. adv. council Orinoco Found., Palo Alto, Calif., 1980-83; bd. dirs. United Way of Chatham County, 1985—. Mem. Assn. for Internat. Practical Tng. (sr. adviser 1984—), Acad. Ind. Scholars, Soc. Internat. Devel. S.R., Soc. Colonial Wars. Club: Princeton (N.Y.C.). Home: Fearrington Post Box 241 Pittsboro NC 27312

ROBINSON, RALPH CARLAN, dentist; b. Pulaski, Va., Feb. 7, 1925; s. Glenn R. and Ruth (Brian) R.; m. Jean Shirley Romm, Aug. 16, 1952; children—Carlan Marie, Robin B., Ralph Carlan, Roland C., Candace R. B.S., U. Miami, 1951; D.D.S., Med. Coll. Va., 1955. Gen. practice dentistry, Miami, Fla., 1955—. Mem. ADA, Fla. Dental Assn., Miami Dental Soc. Methodist. Clubs: Spares and Pairs (pres. 1961-62) (Coral Gables, Fla.); Sertoma (pres. 1963-64), Toastmasters (pres. 1964-65), Exchange (bd. dirs. 1985) (Miami). Avocations: boating; tennis. Home: 160 Sunrise Ave Coral Gables FL 33133 Office: 316 Ingraham Bldg Miami FL 33133

ROBINSON, RICHARD IRVINE, oil company executive; b. Corsicana, Tex., Dec. 26, 1930; s. Luther Irvine and May Alice Robinson; m. Mary Marie Bier, Dec. 27, 1951; children—John Randal, Richard Mark, Mary Kay. B.S. in Chem. Engring., Tex. Tech. U., 1952. Registered profl. engr. Tex., Okla. With Phillips Petroleum Co., 1952—, plant supt., Sweeny, Tex., 1973-79, gen. mgr., Tesside, Eng., 1979-80, v.p. refining, Bartlesville, Okla., 1980—. Named Disting. Engr. Tex. Tech. U., 1981. Mem. Nat. Soc. Profl. Engrs., Am. Petroleum Inst., Nat. Petroleum Refinery Assn., Okla. Soc. Profl. Engrs. Lodge: Bartlesville Rotary. Office: 1170 Adams Bldg Bartlesville OK 74004

ROBINSON, ROBERT MCCOLLUM, psychologist; b. Great Bend, Kans., Mar. 3, 1952; s. Robert McCollum and Billie Virgene (Brookshear) R.; m. Pamela Jo Pennington, Mar. 19, 1977; 1 child, Morgan Elizabeth. B.A. with honors in psychology U. Tex., Austin, 1974; M.A. in Psychology, Ohio State U., 1977, Ph.D., 1979. Lic. psychologist, Tex. Cons. LWFW, Inc., Houston, 1978-81; tng. research specialist Pennzoil Co., Houston, 1981-84; mgr. tng. Sohio Petroleum Co., Houston, 1984-85; mgr. mgmt. devel. Frito-Lay, 1985—. Deacon Meml. Ch. of Christ, Houston, 1984-85. Mem. Am. Psychol. Assn., Houston Area Indsl. Orgnl. Psychologists, Psi Chi. Avocations: music; reading.

ROBINSON, ROBERT OBIE, ophthalmolgist; b. Beaumont, Tex., Aug. 1, 1943; m. Linda Parent; children—Craig, Blake, Alan. B.S., Lamar U., 1964; M.D., U. Tex.-Galveston, 1968. Diplomate Am. Bd. Ophthalmology. Intern Hermann Hosp., Houston, 1968-69; resident in ophthalmology U. Tex. Med. Br., Galveston, 1971-74, tchr., 1971-74; practice medicine specializing in ophthalmology, Beaumont, 1974—; mem. staff Bapt. Hosp. S.E. Tex., St. Elizabeth Hosp., Beaumont Med.-Surg. Hosp., Surg. Ctr. S.E. Tex.; apptd. to Tex. State Bd. Health, 1985. Jefferson County Democratic campaign coodinator Bob Krueger for U.S. Senate; served on numerous state fund raising coms. and campaigns; del. to precinct, county, state convs. 1979—. Mem. AMA, Am. Acad. Ophthalmology, Tex. Med. Assn. (del. ho. of dels.), Jefferson County Med. Soc., Tex. Soc. Ophthalmology and Otolaryngology, Tex. Soc. for Prevention Blindness, Tex. Ophthal. Assn. (v.p. 1985-86). Avocations: politics; scuba diving; traveling; chinese art. Office: Beaumont Eye Assocs 3129 College Beaumont TX 77701

ROBINSON, RONALD ALAN, oilfield manufacturing company executive; b. Louisville, Mar. 23, 1952; s. J. Kenneth and Juanita M. (Crosier) R. B.S., Ga. Inst. Tech., 1974; M.B.A. with honors, Harvard U., 1978. Staff engr., asst. to exec. v.p. ops. Dual Drilling Co., Wichita Falls, Tex., 1978-80; v.p. Dreco, Inc., Houston, 1980-84, pres., dir. Triflo Industries Internat. Inc., 1984—, Ramteck Systems, Inc., 1984—. Recipient Optimist Internat. Citizenship award, 1970; Gardiner Symonds fellow, 1977. Mem. Am. Welding Soc., Internat. Assn. Drilling Contractors, Am. Petroleum Inst., Harvard Alumni Assn. Baptist. Club: University (Houston). Home: 12123 Attlee St Houston TX 77077 Office: PO Box 227 Houston TX 77001

ROBINSON, RONALD DERRICK, rehabilitation agency counselor; b. Columbia, S.C., Oct. 4, 1954; s. Kirkman George and Dorothy Mae (Boozer) R. A.A., Midlands Tech. Coll., West Columbia, S.C., 1980; B.A., U. S.C., 1981; Ed.M., 1984; postgrad. Columbia Pacific U., San Francisco, 1985—. Adminstrv. clk. TransAm. Title Ins. Co., Anchorage, 1976-77; bldg. custodian Oxford Bldg. Co., West Columbia, 1978-81; adminstrv. specialist 120th ARCOM, U.S. Army Res., Columbia, 1981-83; rehab. counselor Rehab. Services, Columbia, 1985—. Author: Autobiography of Ronald Robinson, 1984. Youth counselor Bros. and Sisters, Columbia, 1979, Boys Club, Cayce, S.C., 1979-80, Valley Park Community Ctr., Columbia, 1979-80; rehab. counselor VA Hosp., Columbia, 1983-84. Served with USAF, 1972-76. Mem. Am. Assn. for Counseling and Devel., Am. Mental Health Counselors, Am. Rehab. Counseling Assn., Assn. for Humanistic Edn., VFW. Democrat. Avocations: auto repair; photography; reading; biking; traveling. Home: 1401 Poplar St Cayce SC 29033

ROBINSON, RONALD EDWARD, foundation executive; b. Buffalo, Dec. 13, 1950; s. Charles Alfred and Kathleen (Mohan) R.; m. Michelle Easton, Sept. 14, 1974; 2 sons, Ronald Easton, Daniel Easton. B.A., Canisius Coll., 1972; J.D., Cath. U., 1983. Bar: Va. 1983. State and chpt. dir. Young Ams. for Freedom, Reston, Va., 1973-77, exec. dir., 1977-79, sr. dir., 1979—; pres. Young America's Found., 1979—. Vice pres. U.S. Youth Council, 1979-84, pres., 1984—; chmn. Fund for a Conservative Majority, 1975-79. Recipient Disting. Leadership award Am. Security Council, 1980. Mem. Di Gamma. Republican. Roman Catholic. Assoc. editor New Guard, 1975-77, pub., 1977-79; pub. Dialogue, 1977-79, Libertas, 1978—. Office: Suite 812 11800 Sunrise Valley Dr Reston VA 22091

ROBINSON, RUBEN PAUL, dentist; b. Knoxville, Tenn. B.A., U. Tenn.-Knoxville, 1949; D.D.S., U. Tenn.-Memphis, 1953; postgrad. U. Pa., U. Tenn., Boston U., UCLA, U. Ala., Emory U. Pub. health extern U. Tenn.-Memphis, 1953, instr. Dental Coll., 1954; practice gen. dentistry, Knoxville, 1957—; mem. staff, instr. dept. nursing edn. East Tenn. Baptist Hosp., Knoxville, 1965-82, chief dental dept., 1983—, lectr., 1979—; chief of staff Knox County Dental Health Dept., Knoxville, 1965-75; co-founder, instr. Dental Assts. Sch., Knoxville, 1975-83; dir. Registered Dental Assts. Evening Sch., Knoxville, 1978—; lectr. U. Tenn.-Nashville Study Club, Ft. Sanders Hosp. Nurses Sch. Pres., Heska Amuna Synagogue, 1983—, trustee, 1971-75; charter bd. dirs. Cooper House; patron Dulin Art Gallery; mem. roundtable NCCJ; charter mem. Delta Dental Plan; developer MEDIC blood donor program Knoxville, 1962; mem. Knoxville Tourist Bur.; bd. dirs. Knoxville Symphony Soc.; bd. dirs. Knox Area Mental Health Assn., pres., 1965-66; nat. bd. dirs. Joint Distbn. Com. for Displaced Jews Throughout World; mem. Zionist Orgn. Am., Tenn. Conservation Soc., Fed. Task Force for Health Services, East Tenn. Devel. Dist. Served with USN, 1954-56. Named Young Man of Yr., City of Knoxville, 1961; recipient Tenn. disting. service award, 1962; Mayor's award for contbn. to Knoxville's World's Fair, 1982; named hon. Ky. Col. Fellow Acad. Craniomandibular Orthopedics, Acad. Gen. Dentistry; mem. Tenn. Dental Assn. (state peer review com.), 2d Dist. Dental Soc. (pres. 1970-71, Dentist of Yr. award 1978-79), Nat. Soc. Lit. and Arts, Knoxville C. of C. (past dir.), Tenn. Mental Health Assn. (bd. 1964), Knoxville C. of C., Jr. C. of C. (pres. Knoxville 1961-62), ADA, Dental Health Edn. (Tenn. council), Pierre Fouchard Acad., Fedn. Dentaire Internationale, Collegium Internationale Oris Implantorum, Odontological Soc., Alpha Epsilon Pi (charter pres.), Alpha Omega. Clubs: Deane Hill Country; LeConte; Kiwanis (Knoxville); Pres.'s (U. Tenn.). Author: (video tapes) On the Diagnosis and Treatment of Temporomandibular Joint Dysfunction; featured on TV and radio programs; producer Little Theatre shows. Office: 604 Blount Profl Bldg Knoxville TN 37920

ROBINSON, RUSSELL AUSTIN, utility company strategic planner; consultant; b. Miami, Fla., Nov. 1, 1947; s. Austin Wirt and Mayre (Zoric) R.; m. Barbara Ann Helms, Aug. 8, 1970; children—Meredith Graham, Whitney Elizabeth. B.S., U. N.C., 1969; M.B.A. in Fin., Ga. State U., 1975. Chartered fin. analyst. Corp., trust officer Citizens and So. Nat. Bank, Atlanta, 1970-76; sr. staff strategic planner So. Co. Services, Atlanta, 1976—; program chmn. Southeastern Stock Transfer Assn., Atlanta, 1974-75; pvt. investment cons., Atlanta, 1980—. Fellow Fin. Analysts Fedn.; mem. Inst. Chartered Fin. Analysts, Atlanta Soc. Fin. Analysts, U. of N.C. Alumni Assn. (treas. Atlanta chpt. 1980-84). Episcopalian. Clubs: Ansley Golf, U. N.C., Atlanta Bus. Sch. Avocations: tennis; history; investment counseling. Home: 3258 Argonne Dr NW Atlanta GA 30305 Office: So Co 64 Perimeter Ctr East Strategic Planning Dept Atlanta GA 30346

ROBINSON, SANDRA LAWSON, state health official, physician; b. New Orleans; d. Alvin James Lawson and Elvera Stewart Lawson Martin; children—Michael, Carla. B.S., Howard U., 1965, M.D., 1969; M.P.H. in Health Care Adminstrn., Tulane U., 1977. Intern, Children's Hosp. Nat. Med. Ctr., D.C., 1969-70, resident in pediatrics, 1970-71; resident in pediatrics, fellow in ambulatory care U. Calif.-San Francisco, 1971-72; med. dir. Neighborhood Health Clinics, New Orleans, 1973-77; dir. ambulatory care-/outpatient services Charity Hosp., New Orleans, 1977-81; dir. ambulatory care service Children's Hosp., New Orleans, 1981-84; sec. Dept. Health and Human Resources, Baton Rouge, 1984—; clin. asst. prof. pediatrics La. State U., Tulane U. Schs. Medicine; adj. asst. prof. Tulane U. Sch. Pub. Health and Tropical Medicine; med. cons. learning disabilities team Mission Area Sch. Unified Sch. Dist., San Francisco, 1971-72; med. cons. sch. and behavior unit Mt. Zion Hosp., San Francisco. Active Med. Adv. and Sickle Cell Anemia Research Found., San Francisco; Coordination Prevention Medicine Program, Nat. Med. Assn. Conv., 1974; Ross Roundtable, Upper Respiratory Disease, 1974; bd. dirs. Kingsley House, 1976-79, Family Service Soc., 1976-79; cons. Westinghouse Corp. Headstart Program, 1976-80; bd. dirs. New Orleans Area Bayou River Health Systems Agy., 1977-82, Urban League Greater New Orleans, 1967-82, Isidore Newman Sch., 1978—; active Plan Devel. Com. Health Systems Agy., 1978-82, Com. to Use Human Subjects Tulane U., 1974-84; chmn. steering com. Orleans Parich Coordination Council High Blood Pressure Control, 1978; adv. com. Sch. Anesthesia for Nurses, Charity Hosp., New Orleans, 1979-84; cons. Raintree House, Meth. Home, Vols. Am., 1981-84; nat. adv. com. Hosp. Sponsored Ambulatory Dental Services, Robert Wood Johnson Found., 1978—; bd. dirs. Women Execs. in State Govt., 1984—; La. rep. So. Regional Task Force on Infant Mortality, 1984—; gov. designate Commn. Health and Human Services, 1984—. Recipient Outstanding Community Service award Black Orgn. Leadership Devel. Mem. Assn. State and Territorial Health Ofcls., La. Women's Network, Inc., Nat. Med. Assn., Ambulatory Pediatric Soc., New Orleans Grad. Med. Assembly, Orleans Parish Women's Med. Assn., Tulane Women's Assn., Pediatric Soc. New Orleans, New Orleans Med. Soc., Delta Sigma Theta. Office: Dept Health and Human Resources 755 Riverside 2d Floor Baton Rouge LA 70821

ROBINSON, THOMAS HART, lawyer, educator; b. Richmond, Va., Feb. 3, 1948; s. Carey Hart and Rose (Strauss) R. B.S. in Econs., Va. Commonwealth U., 1970, postgrad., 1978; J.D., Coll. William and Mary, 1973. Bar: Va. 1973, U.S. Dist. Ct. 1974. Clk., Richmond Legal Aid, 1972-73; asst. prof. Va. Commonwealth U., 1973-78; ptnr. Deal Felts & Robinson, Richmond, 1976-86, Felts & Robinson, Richmond, 1986—; guest lectr. various univs., 1973—; dir. Va. Ski Inc., Richmond; gen. counsel Lowrey Organ Ctr., Inc., Fairmont, W. Va., 1977-83. Author: Handbook for Name Changes, 1972; contbr. articles to profl. jours. Del., Democratic Com., Henrico County, Va., 1980; chmn. Credit Consumers Counsil, Richmond, 1981; spl. commr. Henrico County Ctr. Ct., 1982. Recipient B.E. Major award R.P.I. of Richmond; Man of Yr. award Va. Ski Inc. Mem. Va. State Bar (mem. pres.'s council), Henrico Bar Assn. (pres. 1982-83), Richmond Criminal Bar Assn., Am. Trial Lawyers Assn., Phi Delta Phi (v.p.). Office: 4799 S Laburnum Ave Richmond VA 23231

ROBINSON, TOMMY F., congressman; b. Little Rock, Mar. 7, 1942; m. Carolyn Barber; children—Bill, Fran, Deborah, Leslie, Gregory, Jeff. B.A., U. Little Rock, 1959. Officer North Little Rock Police Dept., 1963-66, 68-71, Ark. State Police Dept., 1966-68, U.S. Marshall Service, 1971-74; dir. pub. safety U. Ark. Med. Scis., 1974-75; police chief, Jacksonville, Ark., 1975-79; dir. pub. safety State of Ark., 1979-80; sheriff Pulaski County, 1980-84; mem. 99th Congress from 2d Dist. Ark., freshman whip, mem. armed services and house affairs on vets. coms. Served with USN, 1959-63. Address: US Ho of Reps Washington DC 20515*

ROBINSON, WILLIAM CARY, electronic engineer, educator; b. Norwalk, Ohio, Dec. 24, 1910; s. Junius Cary and Marion Lois (Lucas) R.; m. Thelma Marguerite Pheanis, Aug. 1, 1940; children—Penn Robinson Ansorg, Quinn Cary. B.A., Miami U., Oxford, Ohio, 1932, postgrad., 1937; B.S.Ed., Bowling Green State U., 1937; postgrad. U. Chgo., 1941. Cert. tchr., Ohio. Tchr. pub. schs., Ohio, 1937-42; radar instr. USAF Tech. Sch., Boca Raton, Fla., 1942-44, chief instr., chief tng. research and devel., 1944-47; tng. supr. Air Force Radar Tech. Sch., 1947-49; staff supervisory aircraft electronics research and devel. engr. USAF Hdqrs, Washington, 1949-57, U.S. Army Signal Corps Hdqrs., 1957-62, U.S. Army Material Command, 1962-71; tech. rep. Dept. Def., various mil. and civilian orgns., Washington, 1949-71. Del. Americans for Democratic Action, Washington, 1972—; founder Friends World Coll., L.I., N.Y., 1964; candidate Bd. Suprs., Buckingham County, Va., 1979; pres. Community Health Ctr., Buckingham County, 1979-80; pres. Buckingham County Indsl. Devel. Corp., 1979-81, v.p., 1981—; bd. dirs. Va. Action, Richmond, 1982-85. Recipient Meritorious Civilien Service award, Dept. Army, 1962. Mem. AAAS, Fedn. Am. Scientists, Inst. Navigation, Sigma Tau Delta. Club: Ruritan (v.p. 1974, pres. 1975, dir. 1976-80, Burckingham County Citizenship award 1978). Address: RD 3 Box 79 Dillwyn VA 23936

ROBINSON, WILSON SCOUT, safety engineer; b. Jacksonville, Fla., Sept. 29, 1943; s. Perke S. and Annie S. (Scout) R.; m. Jane Rachael Wallace, Sept. 18, 1966; children—Julie, Lauren. Scout, Brett. B.S. in Indsl. Engring., Tenn. Tech. U., 1968. Registered profl. engr., Calif.; cert. safety profl. Safety engr. Atlas Machine & Iron Works, Gainesville, Va., 1970-72; safety supt. Washington, Intercounty Assocs., Inc., 1972-75; safety engr. Atlantic div. U.S. Naval Facilities Engring. Command, Norfolk, Va., 1975-78; safety engr. Power and Engring., TVA, Chattanooga, 1978—; chmn. Field Fed. Safety and Health Council, Norfolk, 1978. Served as 1st lt. USAR, 1968-70. Mem. Am. Soc. Safety Engrs. (profl. mem., regional v.p. 1985—, pres. Chattanooga area chpt. 1983-84, v.p. greater Tidewater chpt. 1978-79, President's award 1976, 78), TVA Engrs. Assn. Club: Chattanooga Engrs. Methodist. Avocations: fishing; tennis; coaching Little League ball. Home: 17 Whispering Pines Dr Signal Mountain TN 37377 Office: 1150 Chestnut St 4N 91B Missionary Ridge Pl Chattanooga TN 37402

ROBISON, BARTON F., jewelry company executive; b. Paris, Tenn., Sept. 6, 1940; s. G. Dan and Nelle (McSwain) R.; m. Regina Smith, Dec. 18, 1964; children—Becky, Cathy, David, Merritt. B.A., Vanderbilt U., 1962; M.S., U. Tenn., 1974; J.D., YMCA Night Law Sch., 1985. Tchr., dept. chmn. Henry County Bd. Edn., Paris, Tenn., 1962-81; pres., chmn. bd. Murray-McKenzie Jewelry Co., Inc., Paris, 1983—, also dir.; pres. Par Ten Investment Club, Paris, 1966-74; Bd. dirs. Henry County Edn. Assn., 1968-78, pres., 1970-76; adviser Young Democratic Club, Paris, 1966-70; historian Poplar Street Beautification Assn., 1980—. NDEA grantee Peabody U., 1967. Mem. NEA, Paris Henry County C. of C. (mem. com.), Tenn. Edn. Assn. (cons. 1972), Phi Kappa Sigma, Sigma Delta Kappa. Episcopalian. Club: Paris Country. Home: 702 N Poplar St Paris TN 38242 Office: Murray-McKenzie Jewelry Co Inc 119 N Poplar St Paris TN 38242

ROBISON, CORWIN MILTON, II, insurance company executive; b. Logan, W.Va., Sept. 3, 1950; s. Gerald Dean and Betty Lou (Clay) R.; m. Amanda Davis, July 5, 1981. B.A., U. S.C., 1972. With Richway div. Rich's Inc., Atlanta, 1972; ins. agt. State Farm Ins., Marietta, Ga., 1973-75; ind. contractor agt. State Farm Ins. Cos., Marietta, 1975-83, agy. mgr., Lexington, Ky., 1983—. Mem. Marietta Jr. C. of C. (dir. 1973-74, pres. 1978-79), Am. Soc. Risk and Ins., Am. Platform Assn. Club: Civitan. Author: Vietnam: China's China, 1972. Home: 2172 Island Dr Lexington KY 40502

ROBISON, JOHN THOMAS, architect; b. Evanston, Ill., Jan. 7, 1943; s. Clinton Starin and Helen (Gram) R.; m. Rebecca Sue Waul, Sept. 2, 1967; children—Laurel Ann, Birch Mariner. B.Arch., U. Okla., 1967. Intern architect J Gale Brown, Wilmette, Ill., 1967-68; project architect JHBR Inc., Oklahoma City, 1968-75; prin. John Robison Architects, Oklahoma City, 1975—; co-founder Sunspace, Inc., Ada, Okla., 1976-78; founder Soft Path Ctr., Oklahoma City, 1979-85; vis. prof. U. Okla., Okla. State Tech. Inst.; lectr. Oklahoma City Community Coll., Central State U., Edmond, Okla., Oklahoma City Pub. Schs. Prin. works include pvt. residences, F.P.S. Clinic, numerous historic preservations, comml. and urban design projects. Pres., bd. dirs. Neighborhood Devel. and Conservation Ctr., 1976—; bd. dirs. Met. Alliance for Safer Cities, 1980—, Central Okla. Preservation Alliance, 1978; v.p. bd. dirs., sec. 3 Oklahoma City neighborhood assns., 1976—. Grantee, US. Dept. Energy, 1976, 79, 81. Mem. AIA (bd. dirs. Oklahoma City 1978-79), Internat. Solar Energy Soc., Okla. Solar Energy Soc. (bd. dirs. 1978-79), Action Linkage, Sierra Club (bd. dirs. 1977-78). Avocations: music; art; nature; sailing. Office: John Robison Architects 2927 The Paseo Oklahoma City OK 73103

ROBISON, RONALD DEE, pharmacist; b. Carthage, Tex., Aug. 3, 1953; s. Horace Glen and Sue Clara (Lawhorn) R. B.S. in Pharmacy, N.E. La. U., 1976. Registered pharmacist, Tex., La. Pharmacist, Gibson Pharmacy, Marksville, La., 1976-77, Louis Morgan Drug, Longview, Tex., 1977-80; staff pharmacist Longview Regional Hosp., 1981-82; pharmacist Kilgore Pharmacy, Tex., 1982-84, K and B Drug, Longview, 1984—; cons. pharmacist Roy H. Laird Meml. Hosp., Kilgore, 1982-85. Baptist. Lodge: Kiwanis (v.p. Kilgore 1984-85). Avocations: guitar; numismatics; antiques; poetry; classic cars. Home: 4 Serendipity St Longview TX 75601 Office: K and B Drug 803 Gilmer Rd Longview TX 75601

ROBISON, RONALD WAYNE, architect; b. Birmingham, Ala., Dec. 3, 1935; s. Ira Leonard and Willie Louise (Mankin) R.; m. Merle Delores Williams, Jan. 21, 1984. B.Arch., U. Fla. Registered architect, Fla. Draftsman, architect Steward-Skinner Assocs., Miami, Fla., 1959-63; architect cons. Nat. Gypsum Co., Miami, 1963-64; motor lodge architect Howard Johnson Co., Miami, 1964-67; dept. head Richard Plumer Design, Miami, 1967-70; pres. Robison & Assocs., Inc., Coral Gables, Fla., 1970—; dir. Bank of Coral Gables; adj. prof. U. Fla., Gainesville, 1983—; mem. vis. architecture com. U. Miami, Coral Gables, 1984—; mem. adv. bd. Fla. Internat. U., Miami, 1980—. City commr. City of Coral Gables, 1982-85; mem. Miami Citizens Against Crime, 1981-84. Served with Army N.G., 1959-65. Mem. AIA (bd. dirs. Fla. South chpt. 1979-83, chmn. nat. com. on interiors 1981-82), Greater Miami C. of C. (bd. govs. 1983-84), Coral Gables C. of C. (pres. 1978-79). Republican. Methodist. Lodge: Rotary (pres. Coral Gables 1975-76). Home: 822 Jeronimo Dr Coral Gables FL 33134 Office: Robison & Assocs Inc Interior Architecture 4217 Ponce de Leon Coral Gables FL 33146

ROBSON, ANN MARIE, nurse; b. Marion, Ohio, Aug. 21, 1957; d. John D. and Patricia Ann (Oelebracht) R. B.Nursing Scis., Kent State U., 1979. R.N., N.C., Ohio. Nurse gynecology service Univ. Hosps. of Cleve., 1979-80; med./surg. nurse Wake County Med. Ctr., Raleigh, N.C., 1980-81, 83, med./surg. unit preceptor, 1982, operating room nurse, 1983—. Mem. U.S. Equestrian Team, 1982—. Mem. Am. Nurses Assn., N.C. Cancer Assn. Club: J & S Flying (Raleigh). Home: 5604 Lane Ave Raleigh NC 27610 Office: 3000 New Bern Ave Raleigh NC 27610

ROBSON, JOHN THEODORE, surgeon; b. Kirksville, Mo., May 18, 1912; s. Theodore T. and Edith M. (Kelly) R.; B.A., U. Wash., 1938, B.S., 1937; M.D., U. Oreg., 1942; M.S. in Neurology, U. Minn., 1946; J.D., U. Wash., 1956; m. Gail Mottishaw, Aug. 18, 1973; children—John Theodore, Farrand Cory, Leila, Burr, Hannah, Matthew Hill. Intern, St. Vincent Hosp., Portland, Oreg., 1942-43; fellow Mayo Found., Minn., 1943-47; practice medicine specializing in neurol. surgery, Tacoma, 1947-60, Minot, N.D., 1973-80, Nacogdoches, Tex., 1980—; chief neurosurgery Miners Meml. Hosp. Assn., 1960-63; mem. staff St. Joseph and Trinity hosps., Meml. Hosp. Med. Center; chief med. officer Dept. Justice, 1979-80; sr. ptnr. Robson, Khatari, Nacogdoches, 1981—; asst. prof. neurosurgery N.D. Med. Sch., 1973—; fellow Karolinsat Inst., Stockholm, 1955; instr., London, 1956, Copenhagen, 1957; pres. Puget Sound Corp., Nacogdoches. Diplomate Am. Bd. Neurology, Am. Bd. Neurosurgery. Fellow A.C.S.; mem. Harvey Soc., AMA, Mayo Alumni Assn., Am. Acad. Neurology, Am. Soc. Neurologic Surgeons, Am. Trauma Soc., Pan Am. Surg. Soc., Congress Neurologic Surgeons, Alpha Omega Alpha. Club: Rotary. Contbr. articles on neurosurgery to profl. jours.; contbr. chpts. to med. texts. Home: 624 Crooked Creek Dr Nacogdoches TX 75961 Office: Nacogdoches Diagnostic Center Nacogdoches TX 75961

ROCHELLE, ROBERT THOMAS, lawyer, state senator; b. Nashville, Nov. 25, 1945; s. James Marcell and Katherine (Purnell) R.; m. Janice Johnson, Aug. 18, 1973; 1 son, Aaron Marcellus. B.S., Cumberland Coll. Bar; Tenn. Sole practice law, Lebanon, Tenn.; county atty. Wilson County (Tenn.), 1974—, mem. Tenn. Senate, 1982—. Democratic del. Nat. Conv. from Wilson County, Tenn., 1974; coordinator 4th Congl. Dist. for Carter for Pres., 1976, 80; state vice chmn. Mondale for Pres., 1984; bd. dirs. YMCA, 1971-76; chmn. Children's Hosp. Fund Drive, 1977-78; legacies chmn. Cancer Crusade, 1977-83; bd. dirs. Wilson County Promotions, Inc. Served with U.S. Army, 1969-71. Decorated Army Commendation medal with oak leaf cluster, Bronze Star, Vietnam Service medal; recipient Service to Youth award YMCA, 1974; named Outstanding Young Man of Yr., Lebanon Jr. C. of C., 1978. Mem. ABA, Wilson County Bar Assn., Tenn. Bar Assn., U. Tenn. Alumni Assn. (pres. 1974), Lebaon/Wilson County C. of C., West Wilson C. of C. Methodist. Office: 325 W Main St Lebanon TN 37087

ROCHESTER, BRADFORD ALLEN, college official; b. Summit, N.J., Apr. 15, 1945; s. Alfred Andrew and Elizabeth Bradford (Winkler) R.; m. Mary S. Pyle, Apr. 5, 1984 (dec. Nov. 1984). B.A., Washington and Lee U., 1967. Staff reporter Winston-Salem Jour., N.C., 1967-75; assoc. editor The Courier, Clemmons, N.C., 1976-78; editor The Sun, Madison-Mayodan, N.C., 1978-79; pub. info. officer Rockingham Community Coll., Wentworth, N.C., 1979—. Contbr. articles to newspapers. Sec. Rockingham County Democratic Com., 1984—; pres. Rockingham County Young Dems., 1979-80; del. N.C. State Dem. Conv., Raleigh, 1976, 78, 80, 82, 84; pres., v.p. Clemmons Community Devel. Council, 1978. Recipient Pulitzer prize, 1969. Mem. Assn. Community Colls. Pub. Info. Officers (bd. dirs. 1982-84, Ben Fountain award 1982, 85). Democrat. Unitarian. Avocations: gardening; sailing; swimming; traveling; volunteer work. Home: 1394 Tellowee Rd Route 3 Sauratown Estates Eden NC 27288 Office: Rockingham Community Coll PO Box 38 Wentworth NC 27375

ROCHESTER, EUGENE WALLACE, JR., agricultural engineering educator; b. Greenville, S.C., July 15, 1943; s. Eugene Wallace and Mary Usona (Hughey) R.; m. Phyllis Rowena Parker, June 2, 1968; children—Paul Wallace, Alan Parker. B.S., Clemson U., 1965; M.S., N.C. State U., 1968, Ph.D., 1970. Registered profl. engr., Ala. NSF trainee N.C. State U., Raleigh, 1965-68, research asst., 1968-70; assoc. prof. agrl. engring. Auburn (Ala.) U., 1970—. Named Young Engr. of Yr., Auburn chpt. Ala. Soc. Profl. Engrs., 1976; W.H. Smith Faculty fellow Auburn U., 1976. Mem. Am. Soc. Agrl. Engrs., Irrigation Assn. Baptist. Contbr. articles to tech. publs. Home: 625 Jennifer Dr Auburn AL 36830 Office: Dept Agrl Engring Auburn U Auburn AL 36849

ROCHON, SANDRA PALMA, banker; b. Laredo, Tex., Sept. 16, 1947; d. Edward Anthony and Ofelia (Dickinson) Palma; A.A., San Antonio Jr. Coll., 1967. Credit dept. mgr. Del Rio Bank & Trust Co. (Tex.), 1964-71; mgmt. trainee Household Fin. Corp., Silver Spring, Md., 1975; asst. v.p., comml. loan officer Dominion Nat. Bank, Vienna, Va., 1975-79; v.p., compliance officer, collections supr., br. adminstr. Enterprise Bank Corp., Falls Church, Va., 1979—. Sec. Reflection Homeowners Assn., 1980-81, pres. 1981—. Mem. Nat. Assn. Bank Women (vice chmn. No. Va. chpt.). Office: 7787 Leesburg Pike Falls Church VA 22043

ROCKEFELLER, JOHN DAVISON, IV, United States senator; b. N.Y.C., June 18, 1937; s. John Davison III and Blanchette Ferry (Hooker) R.; A.B., Harvard U., 1961; student Japanese lang. Internat. Christian U., Tokyo, 1957; postgrad. in Chinese, Yale U. Inst. Far Eastern Langs.; m. Sharon Percy, Apr. 1, 1967; children—Jamie, Valerie, Charles, Justin. Mem. nat. adv. council Peace Corps, 1961, spl. asst. to dir. corps, 1962, ops. officer in charge work in Philippines, until 1963; desk officer for Indonesian affairs Bur. Far Eastern Affairs, Dept. State, 1963, later asst. to asst. sec. for Far Eastern affairs; cons. Pres.'s Commn. on Juvenile Delinquency and Youth Crime, 1964; field worker Action for Appalachian Youth program, from 1964; mem. W.Va. Ho. of Dels., 1966-68; sec. state W.Va., 1968-72; pres. W.Va. Wesleyan Coll., Buckhannon, 1973-77; gov. W.Va., 1977-85; senator from W.Va., 1984—. Trustee U. Chgo., 1967—, U. Notre Dame, 1974—. Contbr. articles to mags. including Life, N.Y. Times Sunday mag. Home: 1515 Barberry Ln South Hills Charleston WV 25314 Office: 241 Dirksen Office Bldg Washington DC 20510 also 812 Quarrier St Suite 800 Charleston WV 25301

ROCKETT, KAY, civic worker; b. Jackson, Miss., Nov. 2, 1941; d. Louis Newbern and Rita (Hall) R.; 1 child, Barbara. B.A., U. Miss., 1963; M.A., Miss. Coll., 1975. Past treas. Rockett Enterprises; social columnist Northside Sun, Jackson. Chmn.'s advisor U.S. Congrl. Adv. Bd.; bd. dirs. Hinds County Heart Assn. (Outstanding Service award 1975), Miss. Opera Assn. (chmn. statewide opera gala 1980), Miss. Ballet Theatre, Juvenile Diabetes Found of Jackson, Miss. Mus. Art; membership chmn. Jackson Music Assn., 1979; active mem. Jackson Symphony Encore Club, Hinds County Heart Assn. Century Club, Miss. Opera Curtain Raisers. Mem. D.A.R., United Daus. Confederacy, First Families of Va., Colonial Dames XVII Century, Chi Omega. Republican. Baptist. Clubs: Country of Jackson, Capitol City Petroleum of Jackson, Cotillion of Jackson (advisor), University, Miss. Debutantes Mothers of Miss. (2d v.p.). Home: 354 St Andrews Dr Jackson MS 39211

ROCKWELL, ROBIN MARKLE, aviation co. exec.; b. Hazleton, Pa., Nov. 14, 1939; s. Charles Embree and Mary Orme (Markle) R.; student U. Hawaii, Wilkes Coll., Pa., N.Y. Inst. Fin., 1969-70; m. Barbara Jo Russell, Apr. 23, 1971; children—Stephanie Orme R. Account exec. Walston & Co., Honolulu; pres. Hawaii Trade Enterprises, Honolulu; v.p. Airport Tractors, Inc., Montpelier, Vt., 1971-74, Tilfords Aviation Center, Palm Beach, Fla., 1974-77; founder, pres. Rockwell Gen. Aviation Center, Inc., West Palm Beach, Fla., 1980-85, Gardens Aviation, Inc., 1980-85; founder, pres. Rockwell, Inc., 1985—. Served with Air NG. Mem. Nat. Air Transport Assn., Nat. Bus. Aircraft Assn., Greater West Palm Beach C. of C., Palm Beach C. of C., Air Force Assn., Aircraft Owners and Pilots Assn. Republican. Clubs: Outrigger Canoe (Honolulu); Elks, Rotary. Home: 3140 Washington Rd West Palm Beach FL 33405 Office: 3140 Washington Rd West Palm Beach FL 33405

ROCKWELL, STANLEY BALDWIN, JR., hospital official; b. Farmville, Va., May 18, 1954; s. Stanley Baldwin and Marion Ann (Martin) R.; m. Shelley Rae Rubenking, June 17, 1978. B.A., Coll. of William and Mary, 1976, M.Ed., 1977, cert. advanced grad. study, 1981. Research asst. Social Skills Tng. Grant, Williamsburg, Va., 1978; psychology asst. research dept. Eastern State Hosp., Williamsburg, 1978-80, counselor substance abuse unit, 1979-84, adminstrv. asst. safety office, 1983—. Vol. Sexual Assault Victims Assistance, Williamsburg, 1982-83, Parents Anonymous, Williamsburg, 1982; vol. tutor Adult Skills Program, Williamsburg, 1978. Recipient vol. services award Eastern State Hosp., 1979. Mem. Am. Psychol. Assn., Am. Assn. Counseling and Devel., Am. Mental Health Counselors Assn. Methodist. Home: PO Box 2022 Williamsburg VA 23187 Office: Safety Office Eastern State Hosp Drawer A Williamsburg VA 23187

RODE, ELMER GILBERT, JR., university dean and official; b. Port Authur, Tex., Oct. 28, 1937; s. Elmer Gilbert and Evelyn Rode. B.B.A., Lamar U., Beaumont, Tex., 1960; M.Ed., Sam Houston U., Huntsville, Tex., 1966. Asst. registrar Lamar U., 1961-70, assoc. dean admissions and records, 1970-79, dean of admissions and registrar, 1979—. Bd. dirs. Land Manor, Beaumont, 1979-80, Young Men's Bus. League, Beaumont, 1980—. Served with U.S. Army, 1960-65. Avocations: jogging. Home: 730 Adams Beaumont TX 77705 Office: Lamar Univ PO Box 10010 Beaumont TX 77710

RODEN, MARVIN DICK, educational administrator; b. Clarksville, Tex., Jan. 19, 1943; s. Robert Alvin and Edith Eleanor (Brooks) R.; m. Linda Joyce Presley, Mar. 27, 1967; children—Robert David, Richard Ray. A.A., Paris Jr. Coll., 1963; B.S., East Tex. State U., 1965, M.Ed., 1967, postgrad., 1983—. Cert. profl. counselor, Tex. Counselor, dir. adult basic edn. Ennis Ind. Sch. Dist. (Tex.), 1965-70; mgr. interface service Edn. Service Center, Richardson, Tex., 1970-74; dir. pupil personnel services Garland Ind. Sch. Dist. (Tex.), 1974-78, asst. supt. for adminstrn., 1979—; mem. Tex. State steering com. for computer procurement, 1974-76. Chmn. Sch. Night for Scouting, 1982—; bd. dirs. Dallas Council on Alcoholism, 1982—. Recipient Leadership award City of Garland Leadership Class, 1982-83. Mem. Dallas County Assn. Sch. Adminstrs. (pres. 1983-84), Nat. Assn. Sch. Adminstrs., Council of Facility Planners Internat., Am. Personnel and Guidance Assn., Am. Assn. Sch. Bus. Ofcls., Garland C. of C., Phi Delta Kappa. Baptist. Lodge: Mason. Author: State User Guide for Computer Services, 1969. Office: 720 Stadium Dr Garland TX 75040

RODEN, MARY LEE, superintendent schools; b. Rush Springs, Okla., May 25, 1929; d. Cecil C. and Velan V. (Harris) Jinks; m. Bob C. Roden, Mar. 11, 1950; 1 child, Rodne R. B.S., Okla. Coll. for Women, 1954-55; M.S., U. Okla., 1964. Elem. tchr., Marlow, Okla., 1958-62, 64-66, Duncan, Okla., 1962-64, Claremore, Okla., 1966-77; supt. schs. Rogers County Office Edn., Claremore, 1977—; co-owner Men's Shop Claremore, 1984—. Active local campaigns Am. Heart Assn., Am. Cancer Assn., United Way; mem. exec. bd. N.E. Counties of Okla. Econ. Devel. Assn., 1984—; mem. foster rev. bd. Jud. System of Okla., 1985. Mem. N.E. Counties Officers County Supt. Group (pres. 1983-85), Okla. Assn. Sch. Adminstrs., Okla. Heritage Assn., Delta Kappa Gamma (state memership chmn. 1979-81, state profl. affairs chmn. 1983, Outstanding Woman of Achievement for Okla. 1982), past pres. Alpha Alpha and Beta Theta chpts., Club: Federated Women's (past pres.). Lodge: Order Eastern Star (past worthy matron). Office: Rogers County Supt of Schs 219 S Missouri Room 1-103 Claremore OK 74017

RODENBERGER, CHARLES ALVARD, engineering consultant; b. Muskogee, Okla., Sept. 11, 1926; s. Darcy Owen and Kathryn Martha (Percival) R.; student U. Ark., 1944-45; B.S. in Gen. Engring., Okla. State U., 1948; M.S.M.E., So. Meth. U., 1959; Ph.D. in Aero. Engring., U. Tex., Austin, 1968; m. Molcie Lou Halsell, Sept. 3, 1949; children—Kathryn Sue Rodenberger Wilcox, Charles Mark. Jr. petroleum engr. Amoco, Levelland, Tex., 1948-51; chief engr. McGregor Bros., Odessa, Tex., 1953; petroleum engr. Gen. Crude Oil Co., Hamlin, Tex., 1954; sr. design engr. Gen. Dynamics, Ft. Worth, 1954-60; aerospace engr. NASA, Houston, summer 1962; prof. aerospace engring. Tex. A&M U., College Station, 1960-82, prof. emeritus, 1982—; chmn. bd. Meiller Research, Inc., College Station, 1967-82; pres. JETS, Inc., N.Y.C., 1977-79; cons. S.W. Research Inst., Gen. Motors Corp., Gen. Dynamics. Served with USAAF, 1945, USAF, 1951-53. NSF fellow, 1964-65; recipient Disting. Teaching award Tex. A&M U., 1962. Mem. Nat. Soc. Profl. Engrs. (v.p. 1980-81), Tex. Soc. Profl. Engrs., ASME, Am. Soc. Engring. Edn., Tau Beta Pi, Sigma Gamma Tau; assoc. fellow AIAA. Methodist. Patentee hypervelocity gun and orthotic device. Home: Star Route 1 Box 60 Baird TX 79504 Office: Star Route 1 Box 60 Baird TX 79504

RODER, DENNIS LEE, geologist; b. Port Clinton, Ohio, Feb. 13, 1948; s. Ralph Frederick and Irene Elizabeth (Hansen) R. B.S., Bowling Green State U., 1970; M.S., U. Wis., 1973. Geologist, Bear Creek Mining Co., Ladysmith, Wis., 1974; area staff geologist Enserch Exploration Inc., Dallas, 1975—. Served to capt. USAR, 1972-73. Fellow U. Wis., 1970. Mem. Am. Assn. Petroleum Geologists (jr.), Soc. Exploration Geologists, Dallas Geol. Soc. Lutheran. Avocation: jogging. Home: 3340 Hedgerow Apt 3228 Dallas TX 75235 Office: Enserch Exploration Inc 4849 Greenville Ave Dallas TX 75206

RODGERS, CHRISTINE ANN, aerospace manufacturing company official; b. Huntsville, Ala., Apr. 22, 1953; d. Emmett Horton and Virginia Ruth (Wilson) R. B.A., Southwestern at Memphis, 1974; M.B.A., Fla. Inst. Tech., 1982. Research cons. Top of Ala. Regional Council Govt., 1976-77; tech. editor United Space Boosters, Inc., Huntsville, Ala., 1977, data mgmt. analyst, 1977-80, supr. publs. services, 1980-82, mgr. mgmt. services office, 1982—. Recipient awards Dale Carnegie Course, 1983. Presbyterian. Home: 2020 Princeton Blvd Huntsville AL 35801 Office: PO Box 1626 Huntsville AL 35807

RODGERS, EMANUEL, college financial administrator, consultant; b. Winston-Salem, N.C., Oct. 31, 1951; s. Willie S. and Sallie (Hughes) R.; Shirley Baskerville, Dec. 22, 1974; children—Michaela Leatrice, Janella Lisette, Camillia Zanette. Student Winston-Salem State U., 1970-72; B.S. in Bus. Adminstrn., Oakwood Coll., Huntsville, Ala., 1974; postgrad. Ohio State U. Research asst. Budget and Research Dept. Forsyth County, Winston-Salem, 1971; advt. and sales rep. Home Health Inst., Phila., 1972; procurement asst. U.S. Dept. Commerce, Rockville, Md., 1973; asst. to dean men Oakwood Coll., 1972-74, dir. industries, 1981—; bus. mgr., treas. Pine Forge Acad (Pa.), 1974-77; fin. exec. trainee Weyerhaeuser Co., Mt. Vernon, 1978-81; pvt. practice fin. consulting, 1981; cons. O.M. Martin & Sons, Inc., Columbus, Ohio, 1981, Snak Skins, Inc., Huntsville and Atlanta, 1983. Mem. exec. com. Huntsville Council on Human Relations. Mem. Huntsville C. of C. Adventist. Lodge: Kiwanis. Home: 4020 Summerhill Dr NW Huntsville AL 35810

RODGERS, ILLA SWING, accountant; b. Westel, Tenn., Dec. 9, 1932; d. William Hammet and Edna (Phillips) Swing; m. Wheeler Eugene Rodgers, Sept. 21, 1956; 1 child, Eric. Pub. acct., Tenn. Acct. Smith & Coppinger, Rockwood, Tenn., 1950-57, 1958-59; bookkeeper Charles E. Smith Co., Washington, 1962-67; acctg. clk. U.S. Govt., Edgewood, Md., 1957-58, Washington, 1959-62; acct. Braddock Supply Corp., Chantilly, Va., 1971—. Meml. chmn. Fairfax unit Am. Cancer Soc., 1975—. Mem. Nat. Soc. Pub. Accts., Accts. Soc. Va. Republican. Mem. Ch. of Christ. Club: Fairfax Country. Home: 11205 Sedgefield Rd Fairfax VA 22030

RODGERS, KATHERINE VIRGINIA, chemist; b. Moorehead, Miss., June 16, 1937; s. Robert D. and Annie Laurie R.; B.S. in Chemistry, Ouachita Bapt. Coll., Arkadelphia, Ark., 1959; postgrad. numerous specialized courses. Clin. chemistry technologist Meml. Bapt. Hosp., Houston, 1959; nuclear medicine technologist U. Tex. Med. Sch., Galveston, 1960-61; research chemist U. Tex. Dental Sch., Houston, 1961; research asst. Rice U., Houston, 1961-62, 64-65; med. technologist Tex. Children's Hosp., Houston, 1963; tchr. secondary sch. sci. Houston Ind. Sch. Dist., 1962-65, edn. cons., 1968-69; sr. engr. Lockheed Electronics Co., Houston, 1966-72, sr. scientist, 1972-79; sci. supr. Lockheed Engring. and Mgmt. Services Co., Houston, 1979—. Recipient Apollo Achievement award NASA, 1969; Acad. Year Inst. grantee, 1965. Mem. Am. Chem. Soc., Tex. Tchrs. Assn., Alpha Chi, Gamma Sigma Epsilon. Author numerous papers in field. Home: 18034 Bal Harbour Dr Houston TX 77058

RODGERS, MARC MICHAEL DAVID, accounting company executive; b. Valdosta, Ga., Dec. 3, 1948; s. Arnie Jackson and Marie (Hooker) R.; B.S. in Acctg., John Quincy Adams U., Las Vegas, Nev., 1975, M.S., 1975; D.Sc. in Acctg., Am. U., 1977. Sales rep. Holiday Inns, Inc., 1969-71; with Brundick Co. Inc., Jacksonville, Fla., 1971—, treas., controller, 1973—, exec. v.p., 1982—; exec. v.p. St. Johns Ins. Mgmt., Inc., 1982—; pres., chmn. bd. Advanced Acctg. Concepts, 1982—; v.p. St. Johns Aviation, Inc., 1976—. Pres., Citizens for Mandarin Devel., 1980—. Mem. Nat. Assn. Accts., Ins. Acctg. and Statis. Assn., Aircraft Owners and Pilots Assn. Club: University. Home: 5400 Julington Creek Rd Jacksonville FL 32223 Office: 3030 Hartley Rd Suite 6 Jacksonville FL 32217

RODGERS, RAY VERN, JR., oil company executive; b. Pampa, Tex., Feb. 18, 1942; s. Ray V. and Frankie E. (Wilson) R.; m. Charlotte F. Allen, Aug. 12, 1961; children—Mary Ellen Rodgers Jacks, Demaris Lee. Newscaster, KPDN Radio, Pampa, 1960-61; reporter-newscaster KFDA-TV, Amarillo, Tex., 1961-62; editor Pampa Daily News, 1962-64; ops. mgr. nat. hdqrs. U.S. Jaycees, Tulsa, 1964-66; personnel and adminstrv. mgr. Cabot Corp., 1966-76; pres. Rodgers Hydrocarbon Corp., Wichita Falls, Tex., 1976—. Mem. Nat. Petroleum Inst., Oil and Gas Assn. Tex., Assn. Oilwell Service Contractors, Am. Quarter Horse Assn. Republican. Baptist. Developer system for removing liquid hydrocarbons and liquified natural gas from high pressure lines without vaporizing liquids.

RODICH, NANCY ANN, librarian; b. Fresno, Calif., Aug. 15, 1931; d. Clyde Bergner and Marjorie Elizabeth (Fairgrieve) Gentle; m. Grover William Rodich, June 13, 1951 (div. Dec. 1976); children—Susan, Lorraine, Donald, Bruce, Scott. B.A. in Math., U. Oreg., 1953, M.L.S., 1968. Tchr. math. Hughson, Calif. pub. schs., 1955-57; library asst. San Joaquin County Library, Tracy, Calif., 1959-64, Oreg. System Higher Edn., Corvallis and Portland, 1963-67; catalog librarian U. Oreg. Med. Ctr., Portland, 1968-73; tech. services librarian Georgetown Med. Ctr., Washington, 1974-76; tech. services librarian Mid-Miss. Regional Library, Kosciusko, 1976—; instr. caltaloging U. Md.-College Park, 1974-76. U. Oreg. Med. Ctr. Nat. Library Medicine grantee, 1971-73. Mem. ALA, Am. Soc. Info. Sci., Miss. Library Assn., Kosciusko Bus. and Profl. Women (pres.), NOW. Democrat. Presbyterian. Home: Route 4 Box 415 Green Acres Kosciusko MS 39090

RODMAN, KENNETH LLEWELLYN, JR., lawyer; b. East Hartford, Conn., May 3, 1951; s. Kenneth L. and Verna M. (Robinson) R.; m. Charlotte Patricia Booth, Mar. 25, 1972 (div. 1978); m. 2, Donna Jean Dorman, June 2, 1979; 1 dau., Sandra Michelle. A.A. with honors, Hillsborough Jr. Coll., 1970; B.A., U. South Fla., 1971; J.D., Stetson U., 1976. Bar: Fla. 1976, U.S. Dist. Ct. (mid. dist.) Fla. 1976, U.S. Ct. Appeals (5th cir.) 1979. Research asst., clk. Ira Weinstein, Esq., Tampa, Fla., 1974-76; spl. asst. to pub. defender Pinellas County, St. Petersburg, Fla., 1975-76; ptnr. Lawrence, Rodman & Gold, P.A., Tampa, 1976-80; pres., ptnr. Kenneth L. Rodman, Jr., P.A., Tampa, 1980—; atty. Fla. Assn. Sch. Resource Officers; producer Reach TV series; lectr., TV appearances on real estate investment counselling. Atty., bd. dirs. Kiwanis Children's Clinic, Inc., Tampa, 1982—, Hospice of Hillsborough, Inc., Tampa, 1982—; bd. dirs. Condominium Assocs., local chpt. Boys Club. Mem. Fla. Bar Assn. (bd. dirs.), Hillsborough County Bar Assn., Hillsborough County Criminal Def. Lawyers, Hillsborough County Real Estate Attys., Suncoast Investors Soc. (past pres.). Republican. Lodges: Kiwanis (past pres.), Masons. Contbr. articles to profl. publs. and real estate investment jours. Home: 8221 La Serena Dr Tampa FL 33604 Office: 501 E Jackson St Suite 208 Tampa FL 33602

RODMAN, NATHANIEL FULFORD, III, statistician, computer programmer; b. Phila., Dec. 16, 1953; s. Nathaniel F., Jr. Rodman and Martha (Shmidheiser) DuBarry. B.A. in Physics, U. N.C., 1978, M.S. in Biostats., 1984. Computer programmer Frank Porter Graham Researcher Ctr., Chapel Hill, 1978-83; statistician Research Triangle Inst., Research Triangle Park, N.C., 1984—. Mem. Am. Statis. Assn. Avocations: kaleidoscope making; stained glass design; tennis. Office: Research Triangle Inst PO Box 12194 Research Triangle Park NC 27709

RODRIGUEZ, ALEJANDRO JAVIER, diversified industry executive; b. Monterrey, N.L., Mex., Apr. 19, 1939; s. Servando and Enriqueta (Miechielsen) R.; B.S. in Chem. Engring., Universidad de Nuevo Leon, Monterrey, 1960; postgrad. Notre Dame U., 1962; M.B.A., U. Pa., 1964; m. Carmen Bonetti de Rodriguez, Aug. 31, 1961; children—Alejandro, Carmen Teresa, Ivonne, Karla. High sch. prof. chemistry and math., 1957-58; plant operator Fierro Esponja, 1959, research and devel., 1960; procurement mgr. Empresas Industriales, 1960-62; asst. to metall. supt. Hojalata y Lamina, 1964-65, prodn. planning and control mgr., 1965-66, mktg. mgr., 1966-69; corp. planning dir. Valores Industriales, Monterrey, 1969-73; v.p. planning Alfa, 1973-75; pres. Nylon de Mexico, S.A., 1975—; pres. Fibras Quimicas, S.A., 1977—; exec. v.p. Alfa Industrias, 1979—, pres. consumer goods sector; pres. Industries Synkro, S.A. de C.V., 1981—. tchr. engring. econs. State U., Nuevo Leon, 1964; tchr. adminstrn. grad. level U. N.L., 1965-69, mktg. mgmt., 1966-67; prof. tech. planning and fin. U. Anahuac. Mem. Am. Soc. Metals (v.p.), Am. Mktg. Assn., Instituto Mexicano de Ingenieros Quimicos. Clubs: Futbol Monterrey (pres.), Casino (Monterrey); Campestre; Chapultepec Golf. Home: Bosque de Frambo-yanes 420 Mexico City 11700 Mexico Office: PO Box 10-969 Mexico City Mexico

RODRIGUEZ, CALIXTO MANUEL, economist, consultant; b. Havana, Cuba, Aug. 13, 1938; came to U.S., 1960, naturalized, 1970; s. Calixto Ramon and Lelia (Gonzalez) R. M.A. in Econs. summa cum laude, Interam. U., San Juan, P.R., 1971-72; licenciate in Econs. cum laude, U. Villanova, Havana, 1959. Economist P.R. Planning Bd., San Juan, 1961-63; cons. Urban Renewal & Housing Adminstrn., San Juan, 1963-66, research dir., 1966-72; prin. cons. C. Rodriguez & Assocs., San Juan, 1973-75; prin. R-E & Assocs., San Juan, 1976—; cons. Agy. for Internat. Devel. U.S. Dept. State, Managua, Nicaragua, 1973, OAS, Santo Domingo, Dominican Republic, 1976. Contbr. books, articles to profl. jours. Pres. Aranjuez Condominium Inc., Hato Rey, P.R., 1969-73, bd. dirs., 1978-80. Recipient Lion of Yr. award Lions Club San Juan, 1972. Mem. Am. Econ. Assn., P.R. Econ. Assn., P.R. Planning Soc. (dir. 1966-72), Am. Mensa Ltd. Roman Catholic. Lodge: Lions. Avocations: semi-classical music; reading; numismatics; photography; art films. Office: R-E Assocs Box 1785 Hato Rey Puerto Rico 00919

RODRIGUEZ, FRANCISCO BERNARDO, III, pharmacist; b. Laredo, Tex., May 15, 1938; s. Francisco B. and Lilia (Dickinson) R.; m. Leticia Garza, Dec. 26, 1960; children—Diana Leticia, Cynthia Teresa, Francisco B. IV. B.S. in Chemistry, St. Mary's U., 1959; B.S. in Pharmacy, U. Tex., 1962. Pharmacist Sommers Drug Stores, San Antonio, 1962; asst. mgr. pharmacy Walgreen Drug Stores, San Antonio, 1964-67; head pharmacist City Drug Co., Laredo, 1967-69; owner, pharmacist Rodriguez Pharmacy, Laredo, 1969—; mem. adv. bd. Upjohn Health Care, Laredo, 1980-83, APC Home Health Care, Laredo, 1983—; dir. Laredo Savs. & Loan, 1974—. Served to capt. U.S. Army, 1962-64. Recipient Citation for Achievement, Army Med. Service Corps., 1964. Mem. Am. Pharm. Assn., Tex. Pharm. Assn., Webb County Pharm. Assn., Nat. Assn. Retail Druggists, Laredo Jr. C. of C. (bd. dirs. 1968-69). Roman Catholic. Club: Cosmopolitan (Laredo). Lodge: Elks. Avocation: hunting. Office: Rodriguez Pharmacy Ltd 819 Corpus Christi Laredo TX 78040

RODRIGUEZ, FRED HENRY, JR., pathologist, educator b. New Orleans, Oct. 5, 1950; s. Fred Henry and Lorraine Esther (Fitzpatrick) R.; B.S. in Biology, U. New Orleans, 1972; M.D., La. State U., 1975; m. Susan Marilyn Miller, Dec. 22, 1973; children—Alison Patricia, Fred Henry, Kathryn Lorraine, David Miller. Diplomate Am. Bd. Pathology. Pathology intern Charity Hosp., New Orleans, 1975-76, pathology resident, 1976-79, vis. pathologist, 1979—; instr. dept. pathology La. State U. Med. Center, New Orleans, 1978-80, asst. prof., 1980-83, assoc. prof., 1983—, asst. prof. dept. med. tech., 1980-83, assoc. prof., 1983—, assoc. dir. diagnostic electron microscopy lab., 1978—; staff pathologist VA Med. Center, New Orleans, 1979—, dir. Sch. Med. Tech., coordinator pathology residency tng., dir. serology and immunology lab. sects., assoc. dir. diagnostic electron microscopy sect., 1979—, chief lab. service, 1984—. Bd. dirs. Ronald McDonald House, New Orleans. Recipient biol. scis. faculty award U. New Orleans, 1972; Am. Cancer Soc. grantee, 1978. Fellow Coll. Am. Pathologists; mem. AMA (physician's recognition award, 1981, 84), So. Med. Assn., Am. Soc. Clin. Pathologists, Internat. Acad. Pathology, Phi Eta Sigma, Beta Beta Beta, Phi Kappa Phi. Author, co-author sci. articles; author course manual for slides series, course manual for clin. pathology. Office: 1901 Perdido St New Orleans LA 70112

RODRIGUEZ, JOHN BAPTIST, JR., geophysicist; b. New Orleans, July 8, 1951; s. John Baptist and Alix (Vath) R.; m. Louise Campbell, Oct. 6, 1973; children—Karen, Craig. B.S. in Geology, U. So. Miss., 1973; postgrad. in geophysics and math. U. Houston, 1975-78; M.B.A., Houston Bapt. U., 1985. Geophys. engr. Geophys. Service Inc., Houston, 1973-75; processing geophysicist Digicon Geophys. Corp., 1975-77; dist. geophysicist for So. La. dist. Pennzoil Exploration & Prodn. Co., Houston, 1977—. Sustaining mem. Republican Nat. Com., 1980—. Named Most Valuable Player, Houston Padres Amateur Baseball, 1974, 76, Outstanding Young Man Am., U.S. Jaycees, 1984. Mem. Soc. Exploration Geophysicists, Am. Assn. Petroleum Geologists (jr. mem.), So. Geol. Soc., U. So. Miss. Alumni Assn. (bd. dirs. 1984—). Republican. Roman Catholic. Clubs: Bro. Martin High Sch. Century, U. So. Miss. M. Avocations: softball; golfing; reading. Home: 1931 Michele Dr Sugar Land TX 77478 Office: Pennzoil Exploration & Prodn Co 700 Milam St Houston TX 77001

RODRIGUEZ, JUAN CARLOS, college administrator; b. Marti, Cuba, Dec. 27, 1951; came to U.S., 1960; s. Pedro Oscar and Amelia R.; m. Magda Farina, Dec. 29, 1973; children—Cassandra, Alejandro. Student U. Miami (Fla.), 1971-73, S.E. Fla. Inst. Criminal Justice, Miami, 1973; M.D., U. Central Del Este, San Pedro de Macoris, Dominican Republic, 1983. Police officer Dade County Pub. Safety, Miami, 1973-74; organized crime investigator Broward Sheriff's Dept., Ft. Lauderdale, Fla., 1974-79; youth counselor Youth Coop., Miami, 1983; asst. dir. Jobs Program InterAm. C. of C., Miami, 1984; br. dir. Lincoln-Marti br. Martin Tech. Coll., Hialeah, Fla., 1984—. Mem. Miami Folk Festival Com., 1984; spl. asst. to commr. City Miami Commn., 1984. Recipient Achievement award Organized Crime Bur. Broward County, 1979; named Outstanding Program Coordinator City of Miami, 1983. Democrat. Episcopalian. Home: 3647 SW 16th Terr Miami FL 33145 Office: 180 Jose Marti Blvd Hialeah FL 33012

RODRIGUEZ, JUAN GUADALUPE, entomologist, acarologist, educator; b. Espanola, N.Mex., Dec. 23, 1920; s. Manuel D. and Lugardita (Salazar) R.; B.S., N.Mex. State U., 1943; M.S., Ohio State U., 1946, Ph.D., 1949; m. Lorraine Ditzler, Apr. 17, 1948; children—Carmen, Teresa, Carla, Rosa. From asst. prof. to assoc. prof. entomology U. Ky., Lexington, 1949—; prof. entomology, 1961—; adviser entomology Universidad de San Carlos, Guatemala, 1961; vis. scientist Warsaw U., Poland, 1971; del. Internat. Congress Entomology, Vienna, Austria, 1960, Moscow, 1968, Kyoto, Japan, 1980, Hamburg, W.Ger., 1984, 1st Internat. Conf. Insects and Diseases of Coffee, San Jose, Costa Rica, 1965; del. 1st Internat. Congress Acarology, Ft. Collins, Colo., 1963, 2d Internat. Congress, Nottingham, Eng., 1967, 3d Internat. Congress, Prague, Czechoslovakia, 1971, 4th Internat. Congress, Saalfelden, Austria, 1974, sec. V Internat. Congress, Edinburgh, Scotland, 1982; dir. pest mgmt. curriculum Coll. Agr. Bd. dirs. Lexington chpt. NCCJ; chmn. agr. com. Ky.-Ecuador Ptnrs. of Ams. Served with inf. AUS, World War II. Recipient U. Ky. Alumni Assn. award for disting. research, 1963; Thomas Poe Cooper award for disting. achievement in research U. Ky. Coll. Agr., 1972; Disting. Scientist award Ky. Acad. Sci., 1985. Mem. Am. Inst. Biol. Scis., Acarological

Soc. Am. (gov. bd.), Ky. Acad. Sci. (pres. 1982-83, disting. scientist award 1985), Ky. Acad. Sci. Found. (pres. 1982—), AAAS, entomol. socs. Can., Ont., Am. (br. sec.-treas. 1963-65; br. com. man-at-large 1968—, pres. 1981-82), Hon. Order Ky. Cols., Sigma Xi, Gamma Alpha, Gamma Sigma Delta. Roman Catholic. Editor: Insect and Mite Nutrition, 1972; Recent Advances in Acarology, Vols. I and II, 1979; co-editor: Current Topics in Insect Endocrinology and Nutrition, 1981, Leafhoppers and Planthoppers, 1985; mem. editorial bd. Internat. Jour. Acarology, 1981—, Transactions of Ky. Acad. Sci., 1982—; contbr. numerous sci. and tech. publs. Researcher nutritional ecology and physiology of insects and mites, axenic arthropoda. Home: 1550 Beacon Hill Rd Lexington KY 40504

RODRIGUEZ, JULIO RAMON, manufacturing executive; b. Havana, Cuba, Sept. 2, 1939; s. Julio Pastor and Obdulia (Abella) R.; came to U.S., 1961, naturalized, 1971; A.A., Miami-Dade Jr. Coll., 1970; B.B.A., U. Miami (Fla.), 1972; postgrad. Fla. Internat. U.; m. Osmilda Silva, Aug. 6, 1966; children—Linda Maria, Julio Ramon. Head accountant Canadian Gulf Line of Fla., Miami, 1968-72; pvt. practice pub. accounting and cons., Coral Gables, Fla., 1973-80; exec. v.p. Gali Mfg. Corp. Mem. Interam. Assn. of Businessmen, Hialeah Latin C. of C. Clubs: Country (Coral Gables); Kiwanis (Miami); Latin Am. (sec. 1976-77, v.p. 1977-78, pres. 1978-79). Home: 1415 Lisbon St Coral Gables FL 33134 Office: Gali Mfg Corp 215 W 21st St Hialeah FL 33010

RODRIGUEZ, LAVINIA, clinical psychologist; b. Aguadilla, P.R., Nov. 21, 1952; d. Jose Luis and Lillian (Yulfo) R. B.A. in Psychology and B.A. in Italian with honors, U. South Fla., 1974; M.A. in Psychology, 1977, Ph.D. in Clin. Psychology, 1981. Lic. psychologist, Fla. Clin. psychologist U. South Fla. Counseling Ctr., Tampa, 1981—; pvt. practice psychology, Tampa, 1981—; outreach dir. U. South Fla. Counseling Ctr., 1981—; cons. eating disorders, 1981—. Mem. Am. Psychol. Assn., Phi Kappa Phi, Sierra Club, World Wildlife Fund. Democrat. Roman Catholic. Avocations: running; bodybuilding (2d place award Ms. Superior 1984); drawing; reading; traveling. Office: 3403 Jamis Woodway Tampa FL 33618

RODRIGUEZ, LOUIS JOSEPH, university president; b. Newark, N.J., Mar. 13, 1933; m. Ramona Dougherty, May 31, 1969; children—Susan, Michael, Scott. B.A., Rutgers U., 1955; M.A., La. State U., 1957, Ph.D., 1963. Dean, Coll. Bus. Adminstrn., Alcee Fortier Disting. prof. Nichols State U., Thibodaux, La., 1958-71; dean Coll. Bus. U. Tex.-San Antonio, 1971-72, v.p. acad. affairs, dean faculty, 1972-73; dean Sch. Profl. Studies U. Houston-Clear Lake City, 1973-75, vice-chancellor, provost, 1975-80; pres. Midwestern State U., Wichita Falls, Tex., 1981—; cons. Cane Mech. & Engring. Co., Thibodaux, 1976-77. Contbr. articles to profl. jours. Chmn. bd. Tex. Council on Econ. Edn., Houston, 1981-83; bd. dirs. Joint Council on Econ. Edn., N.Y.C., 1981-83, Goodwill Industries Am., Washington, 1976-82, United Way Tex., Austin, 1982—; pres. Clear Lake City Devel. Found., Houston, 1976-77, Goals for Wichita Falls, Inc., 1983. Ford Found. grantee, 1964; Fulbright fellow, 1976. Mem. Am. Econs. Assn., Council of Presidents (Tex. coll. exec. com. 1982). Mem. Ch. of Christ. Home: 2405 Midwestern Pkwy Wichita Falls TX 76308 Office: Midwestern State U 3400 Taft Blvd Wichita Falls TX 76308

RODRIGUEZ, LUIS FRANCISCO, financial analyst, investment consultant; b. Havana, Cuba, Oct. 10, 1952; came to U.S., 1959; s. Francisco and Antonia (Rivero) R. A.A., Miami Dade Community Coll., 1973; B.B.A, Fla. Internat. U., 1977; M.B.A. U. Miami, 1979. C.P.A., Fla. Fin. analyst Rodriguez and Assocs., Miami, Fla., 1973—; acct. Miami Caribe Investments, Miami, 1972-75. Mem. Internat. Assn. Fin. Planners, Am. Inst. C.P.A.s, Inst. Cert. Fin. Planners. Home: 1929 SW 21st St Miami FL 33145 Office: Rodriguez and Assocs 100 Biscayne Blvd Miami FL 33101

RODRIGUEZ, MARIA AMELIA, educational administrator; b. Guaynabo, P.R., Mar. 21, 1932; d. Ramon and Amelia (Rivera) R.; Normal Diploma (fellow P.R. Govt.), U. P.R., 1950, B.A. in Elem. Edn., 1957, B.A. in Secondary Edn., 1966, Profl. Diploma (Dept. Edn. fellow), 1967, M.A. in Edn., 1968; postgrad. (Dept. Edn. fellow), NYU, 1977-79; m. Jose E. Torres, Sept. 24, 1965; children—Ruth, Arlyn, Arnaldo. Tchr. elem. schs., P.R., 1962-65, secondary schs., 1950-56, elem. sch. prin., 1966-68, secondary sch. prin., 1968-69, regional gen. supr., 1969-74, social studies gen. supr., Hato Rey, 1974—; cons. police acad., gerontology dept.; coll. prof. Counsellor Esposas Miembros de la Policia, 1977-80. Office Edn. grantee, 1980, 83. Mem. NEA, P.R. Tchrs. Assn., P.R. Math. Tchrs. Assn., Assn. Supervision and Curriculum Devel., Nat. Council Social Studies, Am. Psychol. Assn. (affiliate). Roman Catholic. Home: B-5 Santa Elvira Caguas PR 00625 Office: Hato Rey PR 00919

RODRIGUEZ, PEDRO A(SENCIO), psychiatrist, educator; b. Santiago, Cuba, June 18, 1948; came to U.S., 1960; s. Pedro Jose and Elva (Elias) R.; m. Magdalena Hilda Averhoff, July 19, 1969; children—Pedro Alejandro, Magda Christina. M.D., Universidad de Salamanca (Spain), 1974. Diplomate Am. Bd. Psychiatry and Neurology. Intern Jackson Meml. Hosp., Miami, Fla., 1975-76; resident in psychiatry U. Miami, 1975-79, asst. clin. instr., 1979, clin. instr., 1980, asst. clin. prof., 1983—, clin. psychiatry cons., 1981-82; practice medicine specializing in psychiatry, Miami, 1980—; mem. staff Cedars Med. Ctr., Victoria Hosp., Coral Gables Hosp. (Fla.), Mercy Hosp., Am. Hosp.; cons. psychiatry. Recipient cert. appreciation City of Miami, 1982. Mem. AMA, Dade County Med. Assn., Fla. Med. Assn., South Fla. Psychiat. Soc., Am. Psychiat. Soc. Club: Cuidamar Yacht (Miami). Office: 333 Palermo Ave Coral Gables FL 33134

RODRIGUEZ, RENE ANTONIO, banker; b. Havana, Cuba, Jan. 17, 1944; came to U.S., 1963; s. Rene A. and Raquel (Beltran) R. B.S. in Bus. U. Miami, 1972; M.B.A. in Fin., Fla. Internat. U., 1973. Chief acct. Royal Castle Systems, Miami, Fla., 1969-72; div. comptroller Gondas Corp., Miami, 1972-73; v.p., chief fin. officer Totalbank Corp. of Fla., Miami, 1974—, also alt. dir.; dir., v.p., treas. Total Properties Inc.; sr. v.p., comptroller Totalbank; dir., pres. Nerod Investments Corp., Reba Corp., Duto Corp.; dir., v.p., comptroller Eduardo Furniture Sales, Inc.; dir., v.p. Lime Groves Inc.; dir., sec. Woodview Corp., Peche Corp., Cato Corp. CDR Corp. Served with U.S. Army, 1967-69; Vietnam. Republican. Roman Catholic. Home: 13199 SW 9th Terr Miami FL 33184 Office: Totalbank Corp Fla 2720 Coral Way Miami FL 33145

RODRIGUEZ, ROQUE CARLOS, JR., army officer; b. Laredo, Tex., Mar. 22, 1941; s. Roque and Beatriz (Novoa) R.; m. Beverly Jean Bauer, Oct. 15, 1967. B.A. in Math., Tex. A.&M. U., 1963; M.S., U. Tex.-El Paso, 1974. Commd. lt. U.S. Army, 1963, advanced through grades to lt. col., 1980; battery comdr., Vietnam, 1967, mfg. supr. Tex. Instruments, 1969, comdt. of cadets U. Tex., 1974, comdr. S.W. Dist. Recruiting, San Antonio, 1980, chief studies and analysis div., Ft. Bliss, Tex., 1981, chief plans and analysis div. Combat Devel. Experimentation Ctr., El Paso, 1982—; cons. airline ops.; real estate planner Benchmark Investments. Decorated Bronze Star, Air medal, Army Commendation medal. Mem. Am. Legion. Roman Catholic. Club: Vista Hills Country. Lodge: Elks. Home: 1654 Common Dr El Paso TX 79936

RODRIGUEZ, WILLIAM, law enforcement official. Chief of police, El Paso, Tex. Office: City Hall 2 Civic Ctr Plaza El Paso TX 79999*

RODRÍGUEZ-CAMILLONI, HUMBERTO LEONARDO, architect, architectural historian, educator; b. Lima, Peru, May 30, 1945; came to U.S., 1963; s. Alfonso and Elda (Camilloni) R.; B.A. magna cum laude, Yale U., 1967, M.Arch., 1971, M.Phil., 1973, Ph.D., 1981; m. Mary Ann Alexanderson, July 1, 1972; children—Elizabeth Marie, William Howard. Asst. research Yale U. Sch. Architecture, 1964-70, teaching fellow dept. history art, 1971-72, 74-75; chmn. research dept. Centro de Investigación y Restauración de Bienes Monumentales, Instituto Nacional de Cultura, Lima, 1973; restoration architect OAS, Washington, 1976—; asst. prof. Sch. Architecture, Tulane U., New Orleans, 1975-82; vis. prof. U. Ill.-Chgo., 1982-83; assoc. prof. architecture and urban studies Va. Poly Inst. and State U., 1983—, dir. Ctr. for Theory and History of Architecture, 1985—; reviewer-cons. Choice, 1975—; mem. interim bd. dirs. Center Planning Handbook Latin Am. Art, 1978—; cons., adv. Internat. Exhbn. and Symposium Latin Am. Baroque Art and Architecture, 1980; co-organizer Mountain Lake Symposium VI, Post-Modern Art and Architecture, 1985. Ellen Battell Eldridge fellow, 1970-71; Robert C. Bates jr. fellow, Jonathan Edwards Coll., Yale U., 1970-71; Social Sci. Research Council fellow, 1972-73, 73-74; Yale Concilium Internat. Studies fellow, 1972-73; Giles Whiting fellow, 1974-75; Nat. Endowment Humanities fellow Columbia U., 1983. Mem. Soc. Archtl. Historians (dir. 1977-80, past pres., past sec. South Gulf chpt.), Coll. Art Assn. Am., Southeastern Coll. Art Conf., Latin Am. Studies Assn., Assn. Latin Am. Art, Assn. Preservation Va. Antiquities, Nat. Trust Historic Preservation, Save our Cemeteries (past dir.), Preservation Resource Center (past dir.). Roman Catholic. Author: (with Walter D. Harris) The Growth of Latin American Cities, 1971; (with Charles Seymour, Jr.) Italian Primitives, The Case History of a Collection and Its Conservation, 1972. Office: Coll Architecture and Urban Studies Va Poly Inst and State U Blacksburg VA 24061

RODRIGUEZ-CHOMAT, LEONORA MARIE, travel agent, educator; b. N.Y.C., May 21, 1950; d. George and Irene (Bernabei) Ramagnoli; m. Jorge Rodriguez-Chomat, Mar. 6, 1976; children—Rodolfo Jorge, Irene Maria. B.Edn., U. Miami, 1973. Tchr. spl. edn. Dade County Pub. Schs., Miami, Fla., 1973-75, 1982-83; travel cons. Ambassadors Travel, Miami, 1975-82, Transcontinental Travel, 1983—; tchr. St. Joseph Sch., Miami, 1983—. Mem. P.T.A., 1982-83. Mem. United Tchrs. Dade. Democrat. Roman Catholic. Club: Big Five (Miami, Fla.). Home: 5400 Alton Rd Miami Beach FL 33141

RODRIGUEZ-DIAZ, JUAN E., lawyer; b. Ponce, P.R., Dec. 27, 1941; s. Juan and Auristela (Diaz-Alvarado) Rodriguez de Jesus; m. Sonia de Hostos-Anca, Aug. 10, 1966; children—Juan Eugenio, Jorge Eduardo, Ingrid Marie Rodriguez. B.A., Yale U., 1963; LL.B., Harvard U., 1966; LL.M. in Taxation, N.Y.U., 1969. Bar: N.Y. 1968, P.R. 1970. Assoc. Baker & McKenzie, N.Y.C., 1966-68; assoc. McConnell, Valdes, Kelley, Griggs, Sifre & Ruiz-Suria, San Juan, P.R.; undersec. Dept. Treasury P.R., 1971-73; mem. Sweeting, Pons, Gonzalez & Rodriguez, 1973-81; sole practice, Hato Rey, P.R., 1981—; dir. Ochoa Indsl. Sales Corp., Camaleglo Corp., Ochoa Telecom, Inc., Las Americas Trust Co. Bd. govs. Acqueduct and Sewer Authority P.R., 1979-84; mem. adv. com. collective bargaining negotiation of P.R. Elec. Power Authority to Gov. P.R., 1977-78; bd. govs. P.R. council Boy Scouts Am., mem. transition com., 1984-85. Mem. ABA, N.Y. State Bar Assn., P.R. Bar Assn. Roman Catholic. Club: AFDA. Home: Calle Fresno #1 Urb San Patricio Caparra Heights PR 00921 Office: Suite 920 Housing Investment Corp Bldg 416 Ponce de Leon Ave Hato Rey PR 00918

RODRIGUEZ ESQUERDO, PEDRO JUAN, statistics educator, researcher, consultant; b. Mayaguez, P.R., Sept. 4, 1956; s. Juan Rodriguez Cruz and Aida L. Esquerdo Andujar; m. Mildred I. Rivera Vazquez, Oct. 2, 1976; children—Mariana L., Pedro J. B.S. in Math., U. P.R., 1976; M.S. in Statistics, U. Calif.-Santa Barbara, 1980, M.A. in Econs., 1981, Ph.D. in Math., 1983. Mathematician, Def. Mapping Agy., Washington, 1977-78; teaching asst., lectr. U. Calif.-Santa Barbara, 1978-83; research assoc. Minicars, Goleta, Calif., 1981; research assoc. U.S. Bur. Census, Washington, 1983-84; asst. prof. dept. math. U. P.R., Rio Piedras, 1984—. Author writings in field. Campus fellow U. Calif.-Santa Barbara, 1978-82; ABD fellow, 1982-83; Pres.' scholar U. P.R., San Juan, 1979-82. Mem. Am. Statis. Assn. (research assoc. 1983-84), Econometric Soc., Inst. Math. Stats. Avocations: microcomputing; jogging; softball. Office: Dept Math Univ PR Rio Piedras PR 00931

RODY, WALTER WILLIAM, shipbuilding company executive; b. St. Petersburg, Fla., Aug. 16, 1926; s. Walter and Mary (Fleitas) R.; B.E. in Civil Engring., Tulane U., 1948; M.B.A., La. State U., 1969; m. Joyce Dolores Van Sandt, July 27, 1949; children—Walter Wayne, Wendelyn Wren, Wendell Wesley. Office engr. Mene Grande Oil Co., San Tome, Venezuela, 1948-50; constrn. engr. A.N. Goldberg, New Orleans, 1950-52; prodn. engr. Avondale Shipyards, New Orleans, 1952-53, chief cost engr., 1953-54, chief engr., 1954-58, asst. to pres., 1958-59, prodn. mgr., 1959-65, v.p., 1966-69; dir. prodn. planning and control Ingalls/Litton Shipbldg., Inc., Pascagoula, Miss., 1969-71, dir. shipbldg., 1971-72; marine and indsl. cons., 1972-78; pres. Port Allen Marine Services, Inc., Baton Rouge, 1978—. SME chmn. Boy Scouts Am., Baton Rouge, 1984-85; v.p. United Way, Baton Rouge, 1984-85; chmn. adv. bd. Salvation Army, New Orleans, 1965, Baton Rouge, 1983; pres. Met. Crime Commn. New Orleans, 1965-66. Recipient Disting. Service award New Orleans Jaycees, 1962; Citizen of Yr. award Jefferson Parish Sheriffs Assn., 1966. Mem. Am. Waterway Operators (bd. dirs. 1985-87), Am. Waterway Shipbuilders Conf. (chmn. ship repair com.), ASTM (chmn. Gulf Region 1969), Traffic Club Baton Rouge, Tulane Engrs. Club. Methodist. Clubs: Skyline Country; Sherwood Forest Country, City (Baton Rouge); Rotary; Masons (past master), Shriners, Grand Consistory of La. (knights comdr. ct. of honor) (New Orleans). Contbr. articles to profl. jours. Home: 10 Oak Alley Baton Rouge LA 70806 Office: PO Box 108 Port Allen LA 70767

ROE, NEWTON CHARLES, geologist; b. Guthrie, Okla., July 20, 1931; s. James Coleman and Ruth (Hill) R.; m. Jean Clark, Mar. 26, 1955; children—Susan Cherlace, Sally Ruth. Student Tex. A&M U., 1949-50; B.S., U. Okla., 1954, M.S., 1955. Prodn. geologist Exxon Co., USA, Kingsville, Tex., 1972-75, sr. prodn. geologist, Corpus Christi, Tex., 1975-77, geol. assoc., 1977-80, geol. advisor, 1980-81, div. adminstrv. geologist, 1981-82, div. ops. geologist, 1982—. Chmn. City Park Bd., Portland, Tex., 1971-72. Served to 1st lt. USAF, 1955-57. Mem. Am. Assn. Petroleum Geologists, Corpus Christi Geol. Soc., Am. Inst. Profl. Geologists. Republican. Methodist. Lodge: Lions. Avocations: golf; fishing; shelling. Office: Exxon Co USA PO Box 2528 Corpus Christi TX 78403

ROE, SHELDON FORD, JR., chemical engineer; b. Elmira, N.Y., May 16, 1932; s. Sheldon and Florence Gertrude (Knapp) R.; m. Shirley Ann Shaffer, Nov. 1, 1959. B.S. in Chem. Engring., Bucknell U., 1954; postgrad. U. Miami, 1956. Registered profl. engr., Fla.; cert. hazardous waste mgr. Research dir., asst. prof. Thatcher Glass, Elmira, N.Y., 1953-62; mgr. material research Owens Ill. Inc., Toledo, 1962-69; dir. field services Applied Research Labs., Miami, Fla., 1970-75; cons. Munters Corp., Ft. Myers, Fla., 1975—. Author numerous tech. articles and book chpts.; patentee in field. Served with AUS, 1956-58. Mem. Am. Chem. Soc., Am. Inst. Chem. Engrs., Am. Soc. Metals, ASTM, Am. Water Works Assn., Assn. Energy Engrs., Fla. Engring. Soc., Fla. Pollution Control Assn., Soc. Plastics Engrs., Water Pollution Control Fedn., World Future Soc. Republican. Presbyterian. Clubs: Sailing, Engineers (Cape Coral, Fla.). Home: 5375 Coral Ave Cape Coral FL 33904 Office: Munters Corp 5375 Coral Ave Cape Coral FL 33904

ROE, THOMAS ANDERSON, building company executive; b. Greenville County, S.C., May 29, 1927; s. Thomas Anderson and Leila Maydell (Cunningham) R.; m. Shirley Marie Waddell, Aug. 2, 1980; children by previous marriage—Elizabeth Overton Roe Mason, Thomas Anderson III, Philip Stradley, John Verner. Vice pres. Am. Holdings, Inc., 1964-70; chmn. bd. 1st Piedmont Corp. and subs. 1st Piedmont Bank & Trust Co., Greenville, S.C., 1967-74; chmn. bd. Builder Marts of Am., Inc., Greenville, 1974—. Chmn. adv. council Furman U.; bd. dirs. Heritage Found., Washington, 1985—; bd. govs. Council Nat. Policy; trustee Greenville Sumphony, Coker Coll., S.C. Found. Ind. Colls., S.C. Coll. Council, Found. Francisco Marroquin, Intercollegiate Studies Inst., Internat. Policy Forum, Inst. Research on Econs. of Taxation; chmn. Roe Found., 1968—; former bd. dirs. Greenville United Cerebral Palsy, ARC; trustee Christ Ch. Episcopal Sch., 1970-72; mem. Greenville County Redevel. Authority, 1971-75; trustee Greenville Chamber Found., 1971-85; bd. dirs. Nat. Found. Ilietis and Colitis, 1975-76. Recipient Disting. Service award Sertoma Club, 1960, Outstanding Leadership award, 1961. Mem. Carolina Lumber and Bldg. Material Dealers Assn. (pres. 1964), Greenville Home Builders Assn. (past v.p., Builder of Yr. 1962), Nat. Assn. Home Builders (pres. Greater Greenville 1970), Greater Greenville C. of C. (pres. 1970), Com. Monetary Research and Edn., Mt. Pelerin Soc. Episcopalian. Clubs: Greenville Country, Poinsett, World Trade Ctr. (N.Y.C.), Peidmont Econs. Address: 712 Crescent Ave Greensville SC 29601

ROECKLE, CHARLES ALBERT, university official, lecturer; b. St. Louis, Nov. 6, 1942; s. Albert Edgar and Audrey Jovita (Camacho) R.; m. Katherine Anne Elsey, May 24, 1980. B.Music, St. Louis Inst. Music, 1964; M.Music, U. Tex., Austin, 1966, Ph.D., 1978. Asst. band dir. Harlingen Ind. Sch. Dist., Tex., 1966-67; instr. St. Martin's Coll., Olympia, Wash., 1967-69; exec. asst. Tex. State Solo-Ensemble Contest, Austin, 1969-72; asst. to dean Coll. Fine Arts, U. Tex., Austin, 1974-81, asst. dean., 1981—; clarinetist, bass clarinetist Am. Wind Symphony, Pitts., 1964, 65, Tacoma Symphony, 1967-69, Austin Symphony Orch., 1964-66, 69-70, 76-82, 84. Mem. Am. Musicol. Soc., Am. Soc. 18th Century Studies, South Central Soc. 18th-Century Studies, Am. Fedn. Musicians. Home: 10208 Willfield Dr Austin TX 78753 Office: Coll Fine Arts Office of Dean U Tex Austin TX 78712

ROEDDER, WILLIAM CHAPMAN, JR., lawyer; b. St. Louis, June 21, 1946; s. William Chapman and Dorothy (Reifeiss) R.; m. Gwendolyn Arnold, Sept. 13, 1968; children—William Chapman, Barcley Shane. B.S., U. Ala., 1968; J.D., Cumberland U., 1972. Bar: Ala. Law clk. to chief justice Ala. Supreme Ct., Montgomery, 1972; ptnr. Hand, Arendall, Bedsole, Greaves & Johnston, Mobile, Ala., 1973—. Comments editor Cumberland-Samford Law Rev. Contbr. articles to legal publs. Mem. ABA, Ala. State Bar, Mobile County Bar Assn., Fed. Ins. and Corp. Counsel, Ala. Def. Lawyers Assn., Curia Honoris, Order of Barristers, Def. Research Inst., Phi Alpha Delta (pres. 1971-72). Home: 211 Levert Ave Mobile AL 36607 Office: Hand Arendall Bedsole Greaves & Johnston PO Box 123 Mobile AL 36601

ROEMER, CHARLES ELSON, III, congressman; b. Shreveport, La., Oct. 4, 1943; s. Charles E. and Adeline (McDade) R.; m. Patti Crocker; children—Caroline Elizabeth, CarlesxCharles Elson, Dakota Frost. B.A., Harvard U., 1964, M.B.A., 1967. Vice pres. sales Innovative Data Systems Inc.; partner Scopena Plantation; mem. 97th-98th Congresses from 4th Dist. La. Chmn. Bossier Heart Fund Drive, 1973; past v.p. La. Alliance for Good Govt.; mem. Bossier and La. Farm burs.; trustee Physicians and Surgeons Hosp., Shreveport Bossier Urban League, Alliance for a Better Community; chmn. Minuteman Orgn.; bd. dirs. Diabetic Bd. N. La.; del. La. Constl. Conv., 1972. Named Outstanding Young Man Bossier Parish, 1970. Democrat. Methodist. Office: 125 Cannon House Office Bldg Washington DC 20515*

ROESCHEISE, ROSANNA INEZ, psychotherapist, staff development consultant; b. Monterrey, Mex., July 25, 1956 (parents Am. citizens); d. Donald Ray Roescheise and Irene Benita (Jacuzzi) Davidson. B.S. in Health Sci. and Safety, San Diego State U., 1978; M.A. in Marriage and Family Therapy, U.S. Internat. U., 1980, Ph.D. in Psychology, 1983. Counselor Polomar Jr. Coll., San Diego, 1981-82; eating disorders specialist San Diego State U., 1981-82; psychol. intern U. Houston, 1982-83; psychotherapist 45th Street Mental Health Ctr., West Palm Beach, Fla., 1984—. Mem. Am. Psychol. Assn., Mental Health Assn. West Palm Beach, Calif. Assn. Marriage and Family Therapists. Roman Catholic. Avocations: dancing; fishing; swimming; diving.

ROESLER, ROBERT HARRY, newspaper sports editor; b. Hammond, La., Oct. 5, 1927; s. Albert and Hilda (Schwartz) R.; m. Cloe Huth, May 6, 1955; children—Kim, Robert, Toby. Student Tulane U. Sports editor The Times Picayune, New Orleans, 1964; exec. sports editor, Times Picayune States Item, 1980—. Served with USN, World War II and Korea. Recipient writing awards La. Sportswriters Assn., AP. Mem. Profl. Football Writers Assn. (pres. 1976-76). Club: New Orleans Press (pres. 1967-68, Writing awards). Office: 3800 Howard Ave New Orleans LA 70140

ROESS, MARTIN JOHN, lawyer, banker, corporate executive; b. Ocala, Fla., Dec. 18, 1907; s. Martin John and Mary R. (Anderson) R.; m. Alice Guion, Nov. 21, 1981; children—Diane Celeste, Robert Thornton, Martin John, Mary Susan, Morgen Leslie, Sherry Allison. A.B., Cornell U., 1930, LL.D., 1931. Bar: Fla. 1932, D.C. 1938, U.S. Supreme Ct. 1935. Assoc. firm Rogers and Towers, Jacksonville, Fla., 1931-34, Holland & Runyon, St. Petersburg, Fla., 1948-51; chief counsel Large Scale Housing div. FHA, Washington, 1934-37, dist. dir., Jacksonville, 1947-48; assoc. gen. counsel Internat. Paper & Power Co., N.Y.C., 1937-38; sole practice, St. Petersburg, 1938—; gen. counsel A. Lloyd Goode Contracting Co., Washington, 1938-43; pres., gen. counsel Builders Mortgage Corp., St. Petersburg, 1948-51; acting dir. Shelter div. FCDA, Washington, 1951-52; owner, operator Martin Roess Co., Jacksonville, 1952-55; organizer, chmn. N.Am. Mortgage Corp., St. Petersburg, 1955-74, Am. Bank Tyrone, St. Petersburg, 1972-74; owner, chmn., pres. N.Am. Ins. Agy., Inc., St. Petersburg, 1955—; owner, dir. Lawyers Land Title Corp., St. Petersburg, 1958—; founder, chmn., pres. Guaranty Savs. and Loan Assn., St. Petersburg, 1960-83; organizer, owner, chmn. Am. Nat. Bank South Pasadena, St. Petersburg, 1963-74; purchaser, chmn. Am. Nat. Bank, Clearwater, Fla., 1967-74; judge 6th Jud. Cir., St. Petersburg, 1967-68; founder, pres. Internat. Travel Assocs., Inc., St. Petersburg, 1976—, Tour Hosts of Fla., Inc., St. Petersburg, 1977—; of counsel Jacobs, Robbins & Gaynor P.A., St. Petersburg, 1981—; past dir. Ind. Bankers Fla.; past chmn. Oceanography Com. Fla. Served to lt. USNR, World War II. Boldt scholar, 1928. Mem. ABA, St. Petersburg Bar Assn., Fla. Bar Assn., Fla. Bankers Assn., Am. Bankers Assn., Mortgage Bankers Assn., St. Petersburg Bd. Realtors, Fla. Savs. and Loan League, U.S. League Savs. Assns., U.S. C. of C., Fla. C. of C., St. Petersburg C. of C., Fla. council of 100 (past dir.), Cornell Law Assn., Phi Beta Kappa, Phi Delta Pi, Sigma Alpha Epsilon. Clubs: Univ. (Washington; Tampa (Fla.), Jacksonville; Cornell (N.Y.C.); River (Jacksonville), St. Petersburg Yacht. contbr. articles to profl. jours. Home: 424 Park St N Saint Petersburg FL 33710 Office: Goldome Savs Bank 2100 66th St N Saint Petersburg FL 33710

ROESSNER, GILBERT GEORGE, financial company executive; b. Irvington, N.J., Arp. 27, 1918; s. John K. and Emma Dora (Kurz) R.; m. Dorothy Anne Hector, Oct. 24, 1942; children—D. Anne Roessner Atherton, Martha, Gilbert George, Jane Roessner Ritchie, Barbara Roessner Baggott, Katherine Roessner Thorndike. With City Fed. Savs. & Loan, Elizabeth, N.J., 1958—, chmn., pres., chief exec. officer, 1978-79, chmn., chief exec. officer, 1979-85, chmn., 1985—; chmn., pres., chief exec. officer City Fed. Fin. Corp., Palm Beach, Fla., 1984—. Pres., Overlook Hosp. Assn., Summit, N.J., 1963; chmn. N.J. Bd. Higher Edn., 1973-75; mem. Reagan Housing Policy Task Force, 1980; chmn. N.J. Gov.'s Pension Study Commn., 1983. Served with armed forces, 1942-45, PTO. Recipient Cert. of Distinction as chief exec. officer of yr. Fin. World, 1982. Republican. Roman Catholic. Clubs: Baltusrol Golf (Springfield, N.J.); N.Y. Yacht (N.Y.C.); Lost Tree (North Palm Beach). Office: City Fed Financial Corp 293 S County Rd Palm Beach FL 33480

ROETTGER, NORMAN CHARLES, JR., U.S. judge; b. Lucasville, Ohio, Nov. 3, 1930; s. Norman Charles and Emma Eleanora Roettger; B.A., Ohio State U., 1952; LL.B. magna cum laude, Washington and Lee U., 1958; children—Virginia, Peggy. Bar: Ohio 1958, Fla. 1958. Assoc. firm Frost & Jacobs, Cin., 1958-59; assoc. firm Fleming, O'Bryan & Fleming, Ft. Lauderdale, Fla., 1959-63, partner, 1963-69, 71-72; dep. gen. counsel HUD, Washington, 1969-71; judge U.S. Dist. Ct., So. Dist. Fla., Ft. Lauderdale, 1972—. Served to lt. (j.g.) USN, 1952-55, to capt. Res., 1972. Mem. ABA, Fed., Fla., Broward County bar assns., Order of Coif, Omicron Delta Kappa, Kappa Delta Rho. Presbyterian. Clubs: Masons; Coral Ridge Yacht (Ft. Lauderdale). Office: US Courthouse 299 E Broward Blvd Fort Lauderdale FL 33301

ROFF, JOHN HUGH, JR., natural gas company executive; b. Wewoka, Okla., Oct. 27, 1931; s. Hugh and Louise Roff; m. Ann Green, Dec. 23, 1956; children—John, Charles, Andrew, Elizabeth, Jennifer. A.B., U. Okla., 1954, LL.B., 1955. Bar: Okla., Mo., N.Y. Law clk. Hon. A.P. Murrah U.S. Ct. Appeals 10th Cir., 1958; atty. Southwestern Bell Telephone Co., St. Louis, 1959-63, AT&T Co., N.Y.C., 1964-68, v.p., gen. atty. Long Lines, N.Y.C., 1969-73, gen. atty., 1973-74; chmn., pres., chief exec. officer United Energy Resources, Houston, 1974—. Chmn. Central Houston, Inc.; mem. adv. bd. Ctr. for Strategic and Internat. Studies, Georgetown U.; mem. council of overseers Rice U. Sch. Adminstrn.; bd. dirs. Houston Symphony; treas. Houston Ballet Found. Served to 1st lt. JAGC, U.S. Army, 1955-58. Mem. Interstate Natural Gas Assn. Am., Inst. Gas Tech., Am. Gas Assn. (dir. 1980-83, exec. com. 1981-82), Order of Coif, Phi Beta Kappa. Clubs: Houston Country, Houston, Coronado, Houstonian. Office: PO Box 1478 Houston TX 77001

ROGEL, TODD STEPHEN, lawyer; b. Newark, Nov. 11, 1952; s. Max and Theresa Rich (Grosman) R.; m. Mary Bryant Hurst, June 17, 1978. B.A. with honors, U. N.C., 1975; J.D. cum laude, Georgetown U., 1978. Bar: Va. 1978, Fla. 1979, U.S. Dist. Ct. (so. dist.) Fla. 1982, N.C. 1982, U.S. Ct. Appeals (5th cir.) 1981, U.S. Ct. Appeals (11th cir.) 1982. Law clerk to presiding justice U.S. Ct. Appeals (5th cir.), 1978-79; assoc. Greenberg, Traurig et al, Miami, Fla., 1979-80; assoc. Fromberg, Fromberg, Gross, Shore, Lewis, Rogel & Kern, P.A., Miami, 1980-82, ptnr., 1982—; ptnr. Clark & Rogel, Sylva, N.C., 1982. Contbr. articles to profl. jours. Mem. Dade County Bar Assn. (mem. gen. jurisdiction com. 1981—, med. profession liaison com. 1982—), N.C. Bar Assn. (mem. litigation sect. 1982-83), ABA (mem. litigation sect., tort and ins. practice sect., civil practice rules com. 1983, automobile law com. 1985), Fla. Bar (mem. civil procedure rules com. 1983—, health law com. 1983—, trial lawyers sect. 1983—), Va. Bar Assn., N.C. State Bar Assn., N.C. Acad. Trial Lawyers Assn. (mem. litigation sect.), Assn. Trial Lawyers Am., Acad. Fla. Trial Lawyers, Am. Judicature Soc., Internat. Assn. Jewish Lawyers and Jurists. Democrat. Jewish. Lodges: Rotary (South Miami); Optimists (Sylva, N.C.); Lions (Ackerman, Miss.). Home: 13611 SW 110th Terr Miami FL 33186 Office: Fromberg Fromberg Gross & Shore PA 420 S Dixie Hwy 3rd Floor Coral Gables FL 33143

ROGERS, BENNIE CLYDE, JR., oil company executive; b. Morton, Miss., Oct. 10, 1947; s. Bennie Clyde and Martha Janelle (Patrick) R.; m. Mary

Randle Melton, June 25, 1971; children—Mary Alison, Bennie Clyde III. B.S. in Econs., Miss. Coll., 1969. Vice pres. B.C. Rogers and Sons, Morton, 1969-81, pres., 1981—; v.p. Rogers Farms, Inc., 1969-81, pres., 1981—; v.p. B.C. Rogers Oil Co., Morton, 1969-81, pres., 1981—; chmn. bd. Bank of Morton, 1984—. Bd. dirs. Miss. Econ. Council, 1982-83, Scott County Hosp., Morton, 1972-82; mem. exec. bd. Jackson council Boy Scouts Am., 1974; deacon 1st Bapt. Ch., Morton, 1978; mem. adv. council Patriotic Am. Youth, 1979. Recipient Wall St. Jour. award Miss. Coll., 1969; Dist. award of merit Boy Scouts Am., 1976. Mem. Miss. Poultry Assn. (chmn. bd. 1976-77), Young Pres. Orgn. Home: 231 E 4th Ave Morton MS 39117 Office: BC Rogers Oil Co Inc 151 S 5th St Morton MS 39117

ROGERS, BRENDA GAYLE, educational administrator; b. Atlanta, July 27, 1949; d. Claude Thomas and Louise (Williams) Todd; m. Emanuel Julius Jones, Jr., Dec. 17, 1978; children—Lavelle, Brandon. B.A., Spelman Coll., 1970; M.A., Atlanta U., 1971, Ed.S., 1972; Ph.D., Ohio State U., 1975; postgrad. Howard U., 1980, Emory U., 1986. Program devel. specialist HEW, Atlanta, 1972; research assoc. Ohio State U., Columbus, 1973-75; asst. prof. spl. edn. Atlanta U., 1975-78, program adminstr., 1978—, CIT project dir., 1977—; tech. cons. Dept. Edn., Washington, 1978, 80, 82, 85; due process regional hearing officer Ga. State Dept Edn., Atlanta, 1978-84, adv. bd., 1980-84. Mem. Hidden Lake Civic Assn., Decatur, Ga., 1978—; bd. dirs. Southwest Montessori Sch., Atlanta, 1980, Malibu Civic Assn., College Park, Ga., 1977-78; mem. Grady Meml. Hosp. Community Action Network, Atlanta, 1982-83. Recipient disting. service award Atlanta Bur. Pub. Safety, 1982, award Atlanta Pub. Sch. System, 1980, 82, 83; fellow Ohio State U., 1972-74, Howard U., 1980. Mem. Assn. for Retarded Citizens, Council for Exceptional Children: Phi Delta Kappa, Phi Lambda Theta. Democrat. Roman Catholic. Avocation: gourmet cooking. Office: Atlanta U 233 James P Brawley Atlanta GA 30314

ROGERS, BRUCE N., dentist; b. Warren, Ohio, Sept. 8, 1949; s. Richard Watson and Mary Elizabeth (Glinn) R.; m. Jane Christine Hunter, Sept. 11, 1971; children—Michael, Ryan. B.S., Davidson Coll., 1971; D.D.S., Ohio State U., 1974; postgrad. Babcock Sch. Bus., Wake Forest U., 1985—. Gen. practice dentistry Winston-Salem Dental Care Plan, N.C., 1979-85, dir., 1985—. Decorated D.S.M. with two oak leaf clusters. Fellow Acad. Gen. Dentistry, Am. Dental Soc. Anesthesiology; mem. ADA, Am. Assn. Dental Group Practice, Winston-Salem Dental Care Plan Study Club, 310th Study Club, Omicron Kappa Upsilon. Republican. Presbyterian. Avocations: TV repair; cabinetry; home remodeling. Office: Winston-Salem Dental Care Plan Inc 201 Charlois Blvd Winston-Salem NC 27103

ROGERS, CAL JOSEPH, advertising agency executive, consultant, lecturer; b. Wilkes-Barre, Pa., July 4, 1947; s. Carroll Smith and Margaret Mary (Garbett) R.; m. Marydell Smith, June 12, 1971; 1 son, Michael Randolph. B.A., West Ga. Coll., 1972. Salesman/mgr. Chesebrough-Ponds, Inc., Atlanta, 1972-75; regional mgr. Gillette Inc., Atlanta and Cleve., 1975-78; owner, pres. Cal J. Rogers & Assocs., Dunwoody, Ga., 1978—; lectr. on mktg. ideas for specialty advt. to coll. mktg. classes, 1980—. Rutgers U. Alumni Fund grantee, 1965. Mem. Specialty Advt. Mfrs. Resp. Assn. (v.p., bd. dirs., founding mem. 1983—), Ala. Advt. Specialty Assn. (program dir. and bd. dirs. 1982—), Specialty Advt. Assn. Inst., Specialty Advt. Assn. Internat. (Golden Pyramid award 1982), Democrat. Roman Catholic. Home and Office: 220 River Pass Tr Dunwoody GA 30338

ROGERS, CHARLES GLORE, physician; b. Atlanta, Aug. 4, 1932; s. Henry Relly and Annie (Glore) R.; m. Laura Pritchett, Aug. 24, 1954; children—Charles Griffin, Stephen Richard. B.A., Emory U., 1953, M.D., 1957. Diplomate Am. Bd. Ob-Gyn. Intern, U. Okla. Hosp., Oklahoma City, 1957-58; resident Ga. Bapt. Hosp., Atlanta, 1962-65; practice medicine specializing in ob-gyn; vice chief of staff Northside Hosp.; mem. staff St. Joseph, Ga. Bapt., Shallowford hosps. Fellow Am. Coll. Obstetricians and Gynecologists; mem. AMA, Ga. Med. Assn., South Atlantic Assn. Obstetricians and Gynecologists, Atlanta Ob-Gyn. Soc. (sec., treas. 1982-85, pres. elect), Med. Assn. Atlanta, Alpha Omega Alpha. Republican. Baptist. Office: 993 D Johnson Ferry Rd NE Atlanta GA 30342

ROGERS, COLONEL HOYT, agricultural consultant; b. Mullins, S.C., Jan. 6, 1906; s. Colonel Cross and Mary (Page) R.; B.S., Clemson Coll., 1926; M.S. (Research fellow), U. Ky., 1927; Ph.D. in Plant Physiology (Teaching research fellow), Rutgers U., 1930; m. Justine Frances Harris, Sept. 27, 1927; children—James H., Richard L. Instr. biology Ark. State Coll., Jonesboro, 1927-28; instr. botany Rutgers U., New Brunswick, N.J., 1928-29, asst. research plant physiology, 1929-31; plant pathologist Tex. A&M U., Temple, 1931-42; plant pathologist tobacco and cotton research Coker's Pedigreed Seed Co., Hartsville, S.C., 1942-60, v.p., 1960-72, cons. U.S. and fgn. agr., 1972—; mem. bd. rev. tobacco N.C. State U. Mem. faculty adv. com. plant pathology and physiology and bd. visitors Clemson U., 1972-74. Named Man of Year, Progressive Farmer, 1969, Man of Year, Farmer Coops., 1972, Man of Year, Mullins (S.C.) C. of C., 1977, Man of Year in Agr., N.C. State U., 1976; recipient Disting. Service award S.C. Tobacco Warehouse Assn., 1969, N.C. State U., 1976; Disting. Alumnus award Clemson U., 1982. Mem. Am. Soc. Agronomy, Crop Sci. Soc. Am., Bot. Soc. Am., Am. Phytopathol. Soc., Am. Farm Bur., S.C. Farm Bur., Sigma Xi. Contbr. sci. and popular articles to profl. jours. Developer 21 varieties tobacco; leader tobacco breeding program in Italy. Address: Route 4 Box 532 Mullins SC 29574

ROGERS, DONALD ONIS, educator; b. Springfield, Mo., Oct. 9, 1938; s. Onis Lee and Wilma (Gideon) R.; B.S., S.W. Mo. State U., 1961; M.A., La. State U., 1968; Ph.D., U. Southwestern La., 1979; m. Mora Jeannine, Aug. 19, 1961; children—Donald Scott, Anne Margaret. Lang. coordinator Ralls County Pub. Schs., Ralls County, Mo., 1961-66; grad. teaching asst. La. State U., Baton Rouge, 1966-68; asst. prof. La. State U., Eunice, 1968-74, asso. prof., 1974-79, head div. liberal arts, dir. acad. Affairs, 1973-78, prof. English, dean acad. affairs and services, 1979—. Bd. dirs. Bayouland Library System, 1974-78. Served with USNR, 1957-59. Mem. Ralls County Tchrs. Assn. (pres. 1965-66), Coll. English Assn., La. Council Tchrs. English, S.W. Regional Conf. English in 2-Yr. Colls., Mod. Lang. Assn., South Central Mod. Lang. Assn. Democrat. Mem. Ch. of Christ. Contbr. articles to profl. jours. Home: PO Box 301 Cheneyville LA 71325 Office: PO Box 1129 Eunice LA 70535

ROGERS, DOROTHY NELL, speech communication and theatre arts educator; b. Waco, Tex., Aug. 17, 1920; d. Albin Hoyt and Mildred Notley (Roberts) Short; m. Quinton Rogers; children—Mildred Elaine Rogers Michero, William Quinton. B.A., Baylor U., 1941, M.A., 1949; Litt.D. (hon.), East Tex. Baptist Coll., 1984. Tchr. speech and English, Gatesville Sr. High Sch., Tex., 1941-43, Harlingen Sr. High Sch., Tex., 1943-44; assoc. prof. speech communication and theatre arts East Tex. Bapt. U., Marshall, 1944—, chmn. dept. speech communication and theatre arts, 1944—, assoc. dean profl. studies, 1986; Piper prof. Minnie Stevens Piper Found., 1981. Mem. exec. bd. Community Concert Assn., Marshall, 1982-85, Marshall Regional Arts Council, 1981-85; charter mem. Symphony League, Marshall. Recipient Woman of Achievement award Bus. Profl. Women's Club, 1982. Mem. Speech Communication Assn. Am., Delta Kappa Gamma (Woman of Achievement award 1983). Mem. Christian Ch. Clubs: Univ. Women's, Harrison County Rep. Women (v.p. 1985-86). Home: 1005 Pine Crest West Marshall TX 75670 Office: E Tex Bapt U Marshall TX 75670

ROGERS, ERNEST MABRY, lawyer; b. Demopolis, Ala., Sept. 22, 1947; s. James B. and Ernestine B. (Brewer) R.; m. Jeanne Edwards, Dec. 15, 1979; children—Gilbert B., Katherine B., Mary C. B.A., Yale U., 1969; J.D., Harvard U., 1974. Bar: Ala. 1974, U.S. Dist. Ct. (no. dist.) Ala. 1975, U.S. Ct. Appeals (5th cir.) 1975, U.S. Ct. Appeals (11th cir.) 1981, U.S. Supreme Ct. 1981, U.S. Ct. Claims 1983. Ptnr. Bradley, Arant, Rose & White, Birmingham, Ala., 1980—. Contbr. articles to profl. jours. Episcopalian. Lodge: Kiwanis. Office: Bradley Arant Rose & White 1400 Park Pl Tower Birmingham AL 35203

ROGERS, GARY LIN, petroleum geologist, consultant; b. Silsbee, Tex., Sept. 14, 1946; s. Robert Thomas and Jenny Fay (Moore) R.; m. Judy Lynn Stillwell, Aug. 7, 1976; children—Dana Michelle, Kyla Jewell, Sara Lin. B.S. in Geology, East Tex. State U., 1979, B.S. in Biology, 1979. Dist. supr., profl. well cons., Oklahoma City, 1979-81; cons. in drilling and completion, Tyler, Tex., 1981-84; field supr. Clayhill Prodns., Inc., Dallas, 1984—. Served with U.S. Army, 1969-70. Mem. Am. Assn. Petroleum Geologists, East Tex. Geol. Soc., Beta Beta Beta. Avocations: sailing; hunting; archery; golf. Home: 1304 Highland Rockdale TX 76567 Office: Clayhill Prodns Inc PO Box 1554 Rockdale TX 76567

ROGERS, GUY NORTHCROSS, lawyer; b. New Albany, Miss., Mar. 20, 1924; s. Herbert Graham and Opal (Pannell) R.; m. Frieda Vallatos, June 8, 1947; children—Guy Northcross, Steven Graham, Nancy Elizabeth. Student Miss. State U., 1942-43; B.A., U. Miss., 1948, J.D., 1950. Bar: Miss. 1950, U.S. Dist. Ct. (no. dist.) Miss. 1950, U.S. Dist. Ct. (so. dist.) Miss. 1962, U.S. Ct. Appeals (5th cir.) 1962, U.S. Supreme Ct. 1969. Assoc. Hugh N. Clayton, New Albany, Miss., 1950, 52-54; 1st asst. U.S. atty. no. dist. Miss., Dept. Justice, Oxford, 1954-61; assoc. Sam Lumpkin, Tupelo, Miss., 1961-62; asst. atty. gen., Jackson, Miss., 1966-75; assoc. Watkins, Pyle, Edwards & Ludlam, Jackson, 1964-65, Williams, Rogers & Gunter, Jackson 1975-76; asst. adj. gen. State of Miss., Jackson, 1976-80 asst. atty. gen., 1980-84, exec. dir. Consumer Protection Div., 1980-84; lectr. workshops for law enforcement agys.; tchr. civil and criminal law U. Miss., 1950, Miss. Coll. Sch. Law, 1975-76. Served as Msgt. U.S. Army, 1943-46, ETO; served to 1st lt. U.S. Army, 1950-52, Korea; served to maj. gen. Miss. N.G., 1980 (ret.). Decorated Bronze star. Fellow Am. Bd. Criminal Lawyers; mem. Miss. Bar Assn., VFW, Am. Legion, Miss. N.G. Assn., N.G. Assn. U.S., Kappa Sigma, Phi Alpha Delta. Episcopalian. Lodges: Masons, Shriners, Lions. Home: 607 Hampton Circle Jackson MS 39211 Office: Scales and Scales PA 414 S State St PO Box 1176 Jackson MS 39205

ROGERS, HAROLD DALLAS, congressman; b. Barrier, Ky., Dec. 31, 1937; student Western Ky. U., 1956-57; A.B., U. Ky., 1962, LL.B., 1964; m. Shirley McDowell, 1957; children—Anthony, Allison, John Marshall. Admitted to Ky. bar, 1964; partner firm Smith & Blackburn, Somerset, Ky., 1964-67; individual practice, 1967-69; Commonwealth atty. Pulaski and Rockcastle counties (Ky.), 1969-80; del. Republican Nat. Conv., 1972; mem. 97th-98th Congresses from 5th Dist. Ky. Bd. dirs. Pulaski County Indsl. Found. Served with N.C. and Ky. N.G., 1957-64. Mem. Somerset Pulaski County C. of C. Republican. Office: 1028 Longworth House Office Bldg Washington DC 20515

ROGERS, JAN D., public relations executive, journalist, photographer; b. Oklahoma City, Mar. 17, 1953; s. William E. and Jo E. Rogers; B.A. in Journalism/Pub. Relations, U. Okla., 1975, postgrad. in bus. adminstrn. Pub. relations intern Oklahoma City Dept. Airports, 1975; pub. relations asst. Okla. Med. Research Found., Oklahoma City, 1975-78, assoc. dir. pub. info., 1979; pub. info. dir. State Arts Council Okla., Oklahoma City, 1979—; vis. instr. journalism U. Okla., Norman, spring 1981, 85. Sec. Oklahoma City Rugby Football Club, 1982-84, Ozark Rugby Union, 1981-84; sec./treas. Ozark Referees Soc. Mem. Pub. Relations Soc. Am. (accredited), Internat. Assn. Bus. Communicators (Communicator of Yr. award Central Okla. chpt. 1978), Sigma Delta Chi. Office: State Arts Council Okla Jim Thorpe Bldg Room 640 Oklahoma City OK 73105

ROGERS, JENNIFER ENGLES, TV production executive; b. Batesville, Ark., July 28, 1943; d. Jake Raymond and Bess Ermine (Goodin) Engles; B.A., Ark. Coll., 1965; M.A., Memphis State U., 1973; m. Francis Xavier Rogers, Jr., Jan. 26, 1974; 1 son, Joshua Francis. Debate, drama tchr. Malden (Mo.) High Sch., 1965-66; sec. Dan River Mills, N.Y.C., 1966; drama tchr. Bald Knob (Ark.) High Sch., 1966-68; entertainer Silver Dollar City, Branson, Mo., 1967-69; actress Bloody Mama, Mt. Home, Ark., 1969; asst. mgr. Melba Theatre, Batesville, Ark., 1969-70; actress H & H Productions, So. states, 1970; remedial reading tchr. Newark (Ark.) Elem. Sch., 1970-71; producer, dir. Sta. WREG-TV, Memphis, Tenn., 1973-81; asst. prof. broadcasting Okla. State U., Stillwater, 1981-83; producer, dir. Cox Cable OKC, Oklahoma City, 1983-84. Named Miss Ark. Coll., 1965. Mem. Batesville Community Theatre (pres.), Alpha Psi Omega. Republican. Mem. Ch. of Christ. Author: The Autobiography of Miss Punkin Jones, 1977. Office: Channel 2 CSU 100 N University Edmond OK 73034

ROGERS, JOANN VEDDER, library and information science educator; b. Pitts., July 28, 1940; d. Sanford Elihu and Helen (Gottbraith) Vedder; m. John C. Rogers, 1970 (div. 1974). B.A., Conn. Coll., 1962; M.L.S., Columbia U., 1967; Ph.D., U. Pitts., 1977. Cert. library media specialist, N.Y., secondary tchr., N.Y., Va. Assoc. prof. Coll. Library Info. Sci., U. Ky., Lexington, 1974—. Author, editor: Libraries and Young Adults, 1979; author: Nonprint Cataloguing for Multimedia Collections, 1982. Contbr. articles to profl. jours. Ctr. for Devel. Change fellow, Lexington, 1978. Mem. ALA (council 1984—), Assn. Library Info. Sci. Edn., AAUP, Beta Phi Mu. Home: 620 Seattle Dr Lexington KY 40503 Office: Coll Library Info Sci U Ky Lexington KY 40506

ROGERS, JOHN D., state senator; b. Somerset, Ky., July 18, 1940; s. John M. and Beulah (Redman) R.; m. Debra Godby, 1975. B.A., Eastern Ky. U., 1964, M.A., 1967; J.D., U. Louisville, 1972. Mem. Ky. Senate, 1975—. Mem. ABA, Ky. Bar Assn., Pulaski County Bar Assn., Delta Theta Phi. Baptist. Office: Ky Senate State Capitol Frankfurt KY 40601*

ROGERS, JOHN RICHARD, lawyer; b. Ashburn, Ga., June 30, 1924; s. Edwin A. and Ella Mae (Evans) R.; LL.D., U. Ga., 1949; m. Reginald Ann Cox, Aug. 6, 1953; children—Sylvia, Starr. Admitted to Ga. bar, 1949, since practiced in Ashburn; pres. Monroe Mall Corp., 1965—, First Fed. Savs. & Loan Assn. of Turner County. Served to 1st lt. AUS, 1944-46. Mem. Turner County C. of C. (pres., past dir.), Am., Tifton Circuit bar assns., Ga. Trial Lawyers Assn. (pres. 1982-83), Am. Trial Lawyers Assn., Am. Judicature Soc., Phi Eta Sigma, Sigma Chi, Phi Alpha Delta. Home: Madison Ave Ashburn GA 31714 Office: Rogers Plaza Ashburn GA 31714

ROGERS, JOHN THOMAS, JR., state police administrator; b. Cleburne, Johnson County, Tex., Oct. 20, 1927; s. John Thomas and Lonnie (Wilbanks) R.; m. Juanita Elizabeth Shelley, Dec. 24, 1945; 1 dau., Linda Susan Rogers Barber. Grad. Gulf Coast Bus. Sch., 1948; student U. Tex.-Austin, 1962, 68-69, Northwestern U., 1970; B.S. in Law Enforcement and Police Adminstrn., Sam Houston State U., 1974; M.P.A., Nova U., 1978, D.P.A., 1979. With Tex. Dept. Pub. Safety, Austin, 1951—, hwy. patrolman, Houston, 1951-57, sgt. hwy. patrol, Brenham, 1957-61, Houston, 1961-72, spl. services sgt. regional hdqrs., Houston, 1972-78, adminstrv. asst. dir.'s office, Austin, 1978—; instr. Southwestern Bell Telephone Accident Investigators Sch., 1964; guest lectr. U. Houston, Downtown Coll., 1974-75. Mem. exec. com. Brenham PTA, 1960-61; mem. Washington County Traffic Safety Com., 1959-61; advisor Civil Def., Washington County, 1959-61; counselor Boy Scouts Am., 1960-61; mem. Tex. Gov.'s Task force on Mgmt. by Objectives, 1979-84; chmn. United Way campaign, 1979; adv. council for mgmt. tng. div. Tex. Engring. Ext. Service, Tex. A&M U. System, 1982—; mem. Gov.'s MBO Task Force Subcom. on personnel, 1982-84, subcom. on implementation of Tex. 2000 Commn. Recommendations, 1982-84; state coordinator for implementation of results mgmt. Dept. Pub. Safety, 1979—; mem. Tex. State Agy. Coordinating Com., 1984—; mem. Gov.'s Council on Exec. Devel., 1982—; cluster developer and pub. relations liaison Nova U., D.P.A. program, 1983-84; sustaining mem. Republican Nat. Com. Served with U.S. Army, 1946-47. Mem. Tex. Police Assn., Tex. Pub. Employees Assn. (dir.), Tex. Law Enforcement Educators Assn., Am. Acad. Polit. and Social Sci., Am. Soc. Pub. Adminstrn., Internat. Assn. Chiefs of Police, Austin Soc. Pub. Adminstrs., East Tex. Peace Officers Assn., Sam Houston State U. Alumni Assn., Nova U. Alumni Assn., Internat. MBO Inst., Tex. Capital Area Law Enforcement Assn., Pi Gamma Mu, Alpha Kappa Delta, Lambda Alpha Epsilon. Club: Rotary (sec., dir. 1960-62). Lodge: Masons (dist. dep. grand master 1968-69). Address: 1502 Desert Quail Ln Austin TX 78758

ROGERS, JONATHAN W., mayor of El Paso, investment counselor; b. New Haven, June 5, 1928; s. Maurice and Harriet B. (Woodruff) R.; m. Patricia Beach Murchison, Sept. 11, 1954; children—Jonathan W., Louise, Patricia, Samuel. B.S., Yale U., 1950. Sales engr. Alcoa, Los Angeles, 1953-56; broker Quinn & Co., El Paso, Tex., 1960-63; pres. Mortgage Investment Co., El Paso, 1963-84; mayor City of El Paso, 1981—. Served to 1st lt. arty. U.S. Army, 1950-53. Named Outstanding Border Mayor, Pres. of Mexico, 1982, Outstanding Citizen, El Paso Homebuilders, 1981, El Paso Realtors, 1982. Mem. Mortgage Bankers Assn. (gov.), Tex. Mortgage Bankers (pres. 1974-75, bd. dirs.; Disting. Service award 1980). Avocation: golf. Office: Office of Mayor City of El Paso 2 Civic Ctr Plaza El Paso TX 79999

ROGERS, JOSEPH CONNOLLY, geologist; b. Detroit, June 10, 1953; s. Joseph Voorheis and Mary Anna (Connolly) R. B.S. in Geology, Eastern Mich. U., 1975. Reporter, dist. mgr. Petroleum Info. Corp., Houston, 1976-79, methods analyst, Denver, 1979-80, dist. mgr., Houston, 1980-85, data adminstrn. analyst so. region, 1985—. Mem. Am. Assn. Petroleum Geologists, Rocky Mountain Assn. Geologists, Houston Geol. Soc. Republican. Lutheran. Avocation: sailing. Home: 6385 Dryad Dr Houston TX 77035 Office: Petroleum Info Corp 4150 Westheimer Rd Houston TX 77027

ROGERS, LON B(ROWN), retired lawyer; b. Pikeville, Ky., Sept. 5, 1905; s. Fon and Ida (Brown) R.; B.S., U. Ky., 1928, LL.B., 1932; L.H.D. (hon.), 1979; m. Mary Evelyn Walton, Dec. 17, 1938; children—Marylon Walton, Martha Brown, Fon II. Admitted to Ky. bar, 1932; practiced law in Lexington, 1932-38, Pikeville, 1939-80. Dir. East Ky. Beverage Co., Pikeville, Pikeville Nat. Bank & Trust Co. Mem. Pikeville City Council, 1951; mem. local bd. SSS, 1958-69; mem. Breaks Interstate Park Commn., Ky.-Va., 1960-68, chmn., 1960-62, 64-66, vice chmn., 1966-68; chmn. Community Services Commn., Pikeville Model Cities, 1969-71; mem. Ky. Arts Commn., 1965-72, Ky. Travel Council, 1967-70, 73-75; pres. Ky. Mountain Laurel Festival Assn., 1971-72. Chmn. bd. trustees Presbytery Ebenezer, U.S.A., 1950-71; trustee Pikeville Coll., 1951-72, 73-79, trustee emeritus, 1979—; trustee Presbytery of Transylvania, 1971-83; mem. bd. nat. missions United Presbyn. Ch. Am., 1954-66; trustee Appalachian Regional Hosps., Inc., 1963-67, Ky. Ind. Coll. Found., 1973-82; bd. dirs. Meth. Hosp. of Ky., 1966-82. Mem. Ky. C. of C. (regional v.p. 1962-64, 69-74), Ky. Hist. Soc., S.A.R., Civil War Round Table, Sigma Alpha Epsilon, Phi Delta Phi. Republican. Presbyn. (elder). Clubs: Kiwanis (past lt. gov.); Filson, Green Meadow Country, LaFayette, Blue Grass Automobile (pres. 1971-74, dir.). Home: 505 E Main St Lexington KY 40507 Office: 181 N Mill St Suite 5 Lexington KY 40507

ROGERS, MARGARET GAY, executive assistant; b. Ketona, Ala., Mar. 25, 1937; d. James Elbert and Margaret Louis (Nolde) Haigler, Jr.; student Massey Bus. Coll., 1957; m. Douglas Earl Rogers, June 30, 1975. Tng., inventory clk. Goodwill Industries, Ft. Wayne, Ind., 1959; with Ala. Title Co., Inc., Birmingham, 1963, file clk., asst. bookkeeper, 1965, policy clk., asst. bookkeeper, 1966, asst. bookkeeper, exec. asst. to pres., 1975—. Vol. hosps. for vets.; active Boys and Girls Ranches. Mem. Nat. Assn. Female Execs., Nat. Fraternal Soc. of the Deaf, Caption Club, Ala. Sheriffs' Assn., North Shore Animal League. Republican. Lutheran. Home: 3024 Forest Dr Fultondale AL 35068 Office: 615 N 21st St Birmingham AL 35203

ROGERS, MARGARET NITA BRABHAM, social worker; b. Clinton, S.C., Aug. 13, 1950; d. Thomas Jefferson and Margaret Emily (Workman) Brabham; B.S., U. S.C., 1971, M.S.W., 1976; m. Francis Drew Rogers, Jan. 23, 1971. Caseworker I, Aid to Families with Dependent Children Services, Dept. Social Services, Beaufort, S.C., 1972-74, asst. to dir., 1975, case mgr. II, Children and Family Services, 1976-78; social worker III, maternal and child care Low Country Dept. Health and Environ. Control, Beaufort, 1978-82; genetic assoc. U. S.C. Sch. Medicine, 1982-83; nephrology social worker Low Country Dialysis Facility, 1983-86, home health social worker, 1985—, social work cons., 1981-82; mem. Head Start Policy Adv. Council, 1977-80; Child Abuse and Neglect Treatment Team, 1979-82; mem. adv. com. S.C. Perinatal Assn., 1978-83; social work cons. Beaufort Meml. Hosp., 1979-81. Registered social worker, S.C. Mem. Nat. Assn. Social Workers, Acad. Cert. Social Workers, Council Nephrology Social Workers (sec. 1984-86), AAUW, Am. Bus. Women's Assn. (treas. 1985-86), NOW. Democrat. Methodist. Home: 705 Sunset Circle River Reach Burton SC 29902 Office: PO Box 459 Beaufort SC 29902

ROGERS, MICHAEL BRUCE, orthodontist; b. Augusta, Ga., Oct. 25, 1945; s. Bruce Latimer and Dorothy (Baird) R.; m. Elizabeth Bennett, Dec. 21, 1968; children—Bruce, Kay, Alison, Lisa. Student Emory U., 1963-65, D.D.S., 1969; cert. in Orthodontics, Med. Coll. Ga., 1973. Diplomate Am. Bd. Orthodontists. Pvt. practice orthodontia, Augusta, Ga., 1973—; part time asst. clin. prof. Sch. Dentistry, Med. Coll. Ga., Augusta, 1973—. Dir. August chpt. Am. Cancer Soc., 1980—. Served to capt. Dental Corps U.S. Army, 1971-73. Fellow Internat. Acad. Dental Studies; mem. ADA, Am. Assn. Orthodontists, Eastern Dist. Dental Soc. (pres. 1982-83), Ga. Soc. Orthodontists (v.p. 1983-84), Med. Coll. Ga. Orthodontic Alumni Assn. (pres. 1985-86), Psi Omega, Omicron Kappa Upsilon. Roman Catholic. Club: Rotary. Avocations: golf; boating. Home: 3214 Candace Dr Augusta GA 30909 Office: 1717 1/2 Central Ave Augusta GA 30904

ROGERS, NATHANIEL SIMS, banker; b. New Albany, Miss., Nov. 17, 1919; s. Arthur L. and Elizabeth (Bouton) R.; m. Helen Elizabeth Ricks, July 3, 1942; children—Alice, John, Lewis. A.B., Millsaps Coll., 1941; M.B.A., Harvard, 1947. With Deposit Guaranty Bank and Trust Co., Jackson, Miss., 1947-69, 1st v.p., 1957-58, pres., dir., 1958-69; chmn. dir. 1st City Nat. Bank Houston, 1969-84; pres. First City Bancorp. of Tex., 1970-84, chmn., 1984-86; dir. Standard Life Ins. Co., Lomas & Nettleton Fin. Corp., Gulf States Utilities Co., Beaumont, Tex., Sonato, Inc., Eastover Corp. Chmn. Jackson United Givers Fund, 1957, pres., 1959, bd. dirs., 1958-61; pres. Andrew Jackson area council Boy Scouts Am., 1962; trustee Miss. Found. Ind. Colls., 1959-69; past pres., trustee Millsaps Coll.; trustee Methodist Hosp., Houston. Served to lt. (s.g.) USNR, 1942-46. Named Outstanding Young Man of Year Jackson Jr. C. of C., 1955. Mem. Am. Bankers Assn. (pres. 1969-70), Miss. Bankers Assn. (pres. jr. banker sect. 1952-53, pres. 1964-65), Robert Morris Assos. (pres. S.E. chpt. 1954-55, nat. dir. 1959-62), Assn. Res. City Bankers, Jackson C. of C. (pres. 1962), Houston C. of C. (chmn. 1979-80), Young Pres.'s Orgn., Millsaps Coll. Alumni Assn. (pres. 1955-56), Newcomen Soc., Omicron Delta Kappa, Kappa Alpha. Methodist (chmn. ofcl. bd.). Office: PO Box 2557 Houston TX 77001

ROGERS, OSCAR ALLAN, JR., college president; b. Natchez, Miss., Sept. 10, 1928; s. Oscar Allan and Maria Pinkie (Jackson) R.; m. Ethel Lee Lewis, Dec. 20, 1950; children—Christopher, Christian, Christoff. A.B., Tougaloo Coll., 1950; S.T.B., Harvard U., 1953, M.A.T., 1954; Ed.D., U. Ark., 1960; postgrad. U. Wash., 1968-69. Ordained to ministry Congl. Ch., 1953, Baptist Ch., 1955, Methodist Ch., 1962. Asst. pastor St. Mark Congl. Ch., Roxbury, Mass., 1951-54; dean-registrar Natchez Jr. Coll., Miss., 1954-56; pres. Ark. Bapt. Coll., Little Rock, 1956-59; dean students prof. social sci. and edn. Jackson State U., Miss., 1960-68, dean Grad. Sch., 1969-84; pres. Claflin Coll., 1984—; postdoctoral fellow U. Wash., Seattle, 1968-69; pastor Asbury-Kingsley Charge, Bolton and Edwards (Miss.) United Meth. Ch., 1962-84. Served with USN, 1946-47. Mem. Conf. Deans of Black Grad. Schs. (pres. 1975-76, treas. 1979-84), AAUP, NAACP, Phi Delta Kappa, Kappa Delta Pi, Alpha Phi Alpha. Democrat. Author: My Mother Cooked My Way Through Harvard with These Creole Recipes, 1973; Mississippi: The View from Tougaloo, 1979. Home: Claflin College 700 College Ave Orangeburg SC 29115 Office: Claflin College Orangeburg SC 29115

ROGERS, REINE ROCHELLE ROBINSON, contractor, company executive; b. Painesville, Ohio, Oct. 17, 1943; d. Herbert L. and Ilah Irene (Bowersox) Robinson; m. Kenneth George Handley, July 29, 1961 (div.); children—Susan Ann, Dawn Christine, Gerald Lee, Wendy Lynn; m. 2d, Jarold James Rogers, June 29, 1973 (div.); 1 dau., Anne Marie. Degree in gen. contracting Allstate Constrn. Coll., 1977. Sec. to asst. adminstr. City of Rock Island (Ill.), 1963-65; sec./bookkeeper Manhard Realty Co., Rock Island, 1970-71; fin./exec. sec. Mercy Hosp., Davenport, Iowa, 1971-73; ptnr. Rogers Constrn. Co., Pinellas Park, Fla., 1976-79; pres./treas. Rogers Constrn. Contractors Co., Pinellas Park, 1979-83; pres./treas./sec. Reine R. Rogers Constrn., Inc., Pinellas Park, 1982—. Mem. Contractors and Builders Assn. Pinellas County. Republican. Lutheran. Office: Reine R Rogers Constrn Inc 6695 69th Ave N Pinellas Park FL 33565

ROGERS, ROBIN KENT, social worker, educator; b. Evansville, Ind., Jan. 2, 1947; s. William Kenton and Virginia Rosalee (Phares) R.; m. Ruth Lynn Massey, July 21, 1973. B.A., Baylor U., 1969; M.A. in Christian Edn., So. Bapt. Theol. Sem., 1973; M.S.S.W., U. Louisville, 1974; postgrad. Sch. Social Work, U. Pitts., 1985—. Cert. Acad. Cert. Social Workers. U.S.-2 missionary, Christian social ministries cons. Home Mission Bd., So. Bapt. Conv., L.I., N.Y., 1969-71; mgr. info. services br. Dept. for Human Resources, Frankfort, Ky., 1974-77; assoc. prof. social work Carver Sch. Ch. Social Work, So. Bapt. Theol. Sem., Louisville, 1977-85, dir. social work program, 1982-84; gerontology cons. Assn. Theol. Schs. in U.S. and Can., 1979; research cons. Sch. Social Work, U. Pitts., 1986—; mem. bd. advisors and rev. Inst. Cultural Affairs, Ky.-Ind. region, 1982-85. Author, producer videotapes on gerontology. Vol. Ky. Ctr. for Performing Arts, Louisville, 1984; mem. steering com. Ky. Action for Human Needs, Frankfort, 1980-84. Recipient Instructional Devel. award Kentuckiana Metroversity, Louisville, 1979. Mem. Assn. Gerontology in Higher Edn. (institutional rep. 1983), Nat. Assn. Social Workers (treas. Ky. chpt. 1980-82, treas. polit. action com. 1983-85, Ky. chmn. project block grant 1981-83, Social Worker of Yr. Ky. chpt. 1983), So. Baptist Assn. of Ministries with Aging (v.p. 1981-82), Nat. Interfaith Coalition on Aging. Democrat. Avocations: running; woodworking; reading biographies and historical novels. Office: 2203 Cathedral of Learning U Pitts Pittsburgh PA 15260

ROGERS, SHANNON UZ, consulting company executive; b. Dickson, Tenn., Oct. 6, 1948; s. Charlie Robert and Viola Elizabeth (Powell) R.; m. Wanda Gayle Durham, June 10, 1968 (div. 1978); 1 child, Jennifer Annette; m. Marie Antoinette Moss, Dec. 29, 1978; children—Sharon Danielle, Birdie Michelle, Shannon Nicole. Student Chgo. Tech. Coll., 1966-69; State Vocat. Sch., 1970, Alexander Hamilton Inst., 1971-74. Designer Rogers Industries, Gallatin, Tenn., 1966-69; div. mgr. Hunt Constrn. Co., Lebanon, Tenn., 1969-72; project mgr. B. Tucker & Assoc. Architects, Nashville, 1972-76; owner, gen. mgr. S. Rogers & Assoc., Nashville, 1976-81; pres. Associated Bldg. Services, Gallatin, 1981—. Mem. Assembly of God Ch. Avocations: reading; writing; bicycling; music. Home: 207 Ross St Gallatin TN 37066 Office: Associated Bldg Services 366 E Eastland Ave Gallatin TN 37066

ROGERS, TERESA SBUTTONI, public accounting auditor; b. Nashville, July 1, 1961; d. Bartholomew Natale and Dorothy (Scott) Sbuttoni; m. Asa Scobey Rogers III, June 8, 1984. B.A. in Econs., Vanderbilt U., 1983, M.B.A., 1984. Mem. acctng. staff Hosp. Corp. Am., Nashville, 1983-84; staff auditor Touche Ross and Co., Nashville, 1984—. Mem. Friends of Cheekwood, 1984—. Scholastic scholar, 1979-83. Mem. DAR, Vanderbilt U. Alumni Assn., Assn. M.B.A. Execs., Nat. Assn. Accts., Nat. Assn. Female Execs., Gamma Phi Beta, Mu Alpha Theta. Office: Touche Ross and Co 401 Church St Nashville TN 37219

ROGERS, TERRELL RANDOLPH, clergyman; b. Seminole, Okla., May 28, 1952; s. Terrell Chester and Joyce Welcome (Cheatwood) R.; m. Ida Marie Ables, June 3, 1978; children—Jeremy, Shekinah. B.A., Baylor U., 1976; M.R.E., Southwestern Bapt. Theol. Sem., 1981. Ordained to ministry So. Baptist Ch., 1977. Youth minister Harris Creek Ch., Waco, Tex., 1976, Whispering Pines Ch., Conroe, Tex., 1977-78, Henderson Hills Ch., Edmond, Okla., 1978-80, Killarney Bapt. Ch., Winter Park, Fla., 1981-82, Calvary Bapt. Ch., Tulsa, 1983-85, First Bapt. Ch., Enid, Okla., 1985; pastor First Bapt. Ch., Porter, Okla., 1986—; founder, pres. Powerlife Ministries, 1981-85. Home: PO Box 198 Porter OK 74454 Office: PO Box 18 Porter OK 74454

ROGERS, VERNIS DALE, school superintendent; b. Nacogdoches, Tex., Sept. 2, 1947; s. Vernis V. and Bennie Dale (Pearce) R.; m. Mary Jo Hendrick, Apr. 20, 1967; children—Teresa Ann, Sherry Lynn. B.S., Stephen F. Austin U., 1969, M.E., 1972. Tchr. pub. schs., Tex., 1969-73; elem. prin. Garrison Sch. Dist., Tex., 1974-82, supt., 1982—; dir. Nacog-County Spl. Edn. Cooperative, Tex., 1983—, Deep East Tex. Council of Govts., 1983—. Chmn. Nacodocha Community Action Com., 1984—; chmn. bd. trustees Meth. Ch., Garrison, 1980-82; bd. dirs. East Tex. area council Boy Scouts Am., 1984—. Mem. Tex. Assn. Community Schs., Tex. Assn. Secondary Adminstrn., Nacogdoches County Tex. State Tchrs. Assn. (pres. 1979-80), Phi Delta Kappa. Democrat. Lodges: Lions (sec. 1980—), Masons (sr. warden). Avocations: hunting; cattle raising. Home: PO Box 202 Garrison TX 75946

ROGERS, WALTER IRVIN, hotel and casino executive; b. Eureka, Calif., Nov. 30, 1932; S. Dwight O. and Norma Leigh (Lane) R.; B.A. in Biology, Fresno State Coll., 1956; m. Bonnell Kepple, Apr. 12, 1962; children—Cynthia Lynn, David Walter, Tami Lynn. Casino mgr. Aladdin Hotel Casino, Parvin-Dohrmann, Las Vegas, 1970-71; Castaways Hotel Casino, Hughes Tool Co., Las Vegas, 1971, Desert Inn Hotel Casino, 1971-72, gen. mgr. Silver Slipper, 1972-73; gen. mgr. Paradise I. Casino, Resorts Internat., Nassau, Bahamas, 1973-77, v.p. casino ops., Atlantic City, 1977-79, v.p. casino devel., North Miami, Fla., 1979—, also officer parent corp. Resorts Internat., Inc. Served with U.S. Army, 1956-58. Mem. Miami C. of C. Roman Catholic. Office: 915 NE 125th St North Miami FL 33161

ROGERS, WILLIAM FENNA, JR., supermarket executive; b. Higginsville, Mo., Dec. 25, 1912; s. William Fenna and Emily S. (Moose) R.; m. Thelma Ann Hooper, June 15, 1940 (dec. Mar. 1982); m. Ethel Allene Burgess, Aug. 6, 1983; stepchildren—Dorothy H. Nance, Linda H. Connors. B.A., Ark. Coll., 1933; postgrad. U. Ark., 1933, Tulane U., 1935, U. Fla., 1938-39. Vocat. adv. Nat. Youth Adminstrn., Little Rock, 1936-38; chief field ops. U.S. Employment Service, Little Rock, 1938-43, chief supr. tng., Washington, 1946-47; asst. dir. Civilian Personnel Div., U.S. Dept. Navy, Washington, 1947-55; v.p. indsl. relations Giant Food, Inc., Washington, 1955-75; mgmt. cons., Falls Church, Va., 1975—; trustee Teamster Warehouse Fund, 1956—, Carpet Layers Funds, 1968—; lectr. Am. U., 1949-69; pres. Chateau Devel. Corp., Fairfax, Va., 1978-83. Mem. selection bd. U.S. Postal Service, 1969-77; elder New York Ave. Presbyterian Ch., Washington, 1948-72, Falls Church Presbyn. Ch., 1980-83; mem. Falls Church Village Preservation and Improvement Soc., 1967—; cons. Lincoln commn. New York Ave. Presbyn. Ch., 1984—; chmn. bur. edn. and employment Greater Washington Bd. Trade, 1974-76. Served to lt. comdr. USNR, 1943-64. Mem. Am. Soc. Tng. and Devel. (life), Alpha Psi Omega, Kappa Gamma, Pi Kappa Delta, Iota Lambda Sigma. Club: International Town and Country (dir. 1959-61) (Fairfax, Va.). Avocations: golf; fishing. Home: 214 Van Buren St Falls Church VA 22046

ROGOW, BRUCE SYLVAN, law educator, consultant; b. Hartford, Conn., Nov. 28, 1939; s. Jack and Jeanne (Sherr) R.; m. Norma Watkins, June 6, 1967 (div. 1976); m. 2d, Jacquelyn Steinberg, June 26, 1978; children—Bryce Linden, Brooks Trystan, Alyna Jace. B.B.A., U. Miami, Fla., 1961; J.D., U. Fla., 1963. Bar: Fla. 1964. Staff counsel Lawyer's Constl. def. Com., Jackson, Miss., 1965-66; asst. dir. Legal Services Greater Miami, 1967-72; of counsel Pearson & Josefsberg, Miami, 1972-76; asst. prof. U. Miami Law Sch., 1969-74; prof. law Nova U. Law Ctr., Ft. Lauderdale, Fla., 1974—, co-dean, 1978, acting dean, 1984-85; spl. counsel ACLU, Fla., 1972, gen. counsel, 1979-86. Served with U.S. Army, 1964. Recipient Reginald Heber Smith award Nat. Legal Aid & Defender Assn., 1972. Author: (with others) Lawyers Clients and Ethics, 1974; also legal articles. Home: 2097 S W 27th Terr Fort Lauderdale FL 33312 Office: Nova U Law Ctr 3100 S W 9th Ave Fort Lauderdale FL 33315

ROHE, JAMIE M., architect; b. Pasadena, Tex., Jan. 3, 1945; s. James M and Billie Jean (Fields) R.; m. Vickie Nesom, Nov. 26, 1966 (dec. 1980); m. Cherry Whitener, June 5, 1981. B.Arch., Tex. A&M U., 1968, M.Arch., 1971. Registered architect, Tex. Draftsman for Mies Van Der Rohe, Chgo., 1966, Oglesby Group, Dallas, 1971-72; head interiors Greener & Sumner, Dallas, 1972-73; prin. Concept Cons., Inc., Dallas, 1973-80, Inspace, Inc., Dallas, 1980—. Prin. works include office design Swearingen Co., offices for State Music Hall in Majestic Theater, retail space Christopher Lawrence, numerous office spaces. Mem. admissions com. Step Up Ministry, 1st Presbyn. Ch., Dallas, 1984-85; mem. Historic Preservation League, Dallas, 1978—. Served to lt. USN, 1968-70. Recipient Reynolds Aluminum Design award, 1967. Mem. AIA (interiors bd.). Democrat. Avocations: designing and building own home. Home: 4411 Gilbert Apt 5 Dallas TX 75219 Office: Inspace Inc 1201 Griffin St W Dallas TX 75215-0033

ROHLFS, HENRY D., educator; b. Yonkers, N.Y., May 7, 1938; s. Henry Herman and Teresa (Helminger) R.; m. Filomena Teresa DeGrego, May 16, 1964; children—Maria, John. B.A., Biscayne Coll., 1983; M.A., Norwich U., 1984. Tchr. Dade County Schs., Miami, Fla., 1979-84, Annuncian Sch., Hollywood, Fla., 1984-85, Pace High Sch., Opa Locka, Fla., 1985—. Author: Environmental Biology, 1983; Taxonomic Key of Local Flora, 1983. Mem. Am. Inst. Biol. Sci., Nat. Assn. Biology Tchrs., Am. Hort. Soc., Fla. Acad. Sci. Avocations: horticulture; show Horses. Home: 920 NE 130th St North Miami FL 33161

ROHMILLER, REED ALLEN, personnel administrator; b. Miami, Okla., May 8, 1955; s. Nicholas J. and Lavenia (Griffith) R. B.S., Okla. State U., 1977; M.S., East Tex. State U., 1979. Cert. compensation profl. Personnel cons. Personnel Service, Inc., Dallas, 1979-80; asst. personnel officer Preston State Bank, Dallas, 1980-81, cons., 1982; sr. compensation analyst So. Union Co., Dallas, 1981—; cons. T.H.E. Travel Agy., 1984, Gas Co. N.Mex., 1985. Instr. water safety ARC, 1975-81. Mem. Am. Psychol. Assn. (assoc.), Am. Compensation Assn., Dallas Personnel Assn. Republican. Club: Dallas Chess. Avocations: chess; swimming. Office: So Union Co 1800 Interfirst Two Dallas TX 74270

ROHRER, MARY ANNE SCHOBER, human resource consulting company executive; b. Milw., Apr. 10, 1946; d. Herman Frederick and Bernice Louise Schober; m. Arthur Thomas Harrison, June 15, 1974 (div. July 1981); children—Zachary Watkins, Jesse Josef; m. 2d, Dallas L. Rohrer, May 31, 1984. B.S.W., U. Calif.-Berkeley, 1970. Customer service rep. Blue Cross-Blue Shield, Oakland, Calif., 1967-68; pub. relations dir. Phipps Land Co., Atlanta, 1972-74; sec.-treas. Village Planter, Inc., Atlanta, 1974-76; exec. v.p. I.D., Inc., Atlanta, 1979-81; pres., cons. F.S.C. Cons. Services, Inc., Atlanta, 1982—. Counselor underprivileged teens, YWCA, emotionally disturbed-mentally retarded Goodwill Industries, Milw., 1966-67; counselor Berkeley Suicide Prevention Ctr., 1970-71; counselor, facilitator Pacific Psychotherapy, San Francisco, 1970-71; vol. tchr. Fulton County Schs., Atlanta 1974-75. Mem. Am.Soc. Personnel Adminstrs., Sales and Mktg. Execs., Alpha Chi Omega. Home: 1145 Edgewater Dr NW Atlanta GA 30328 Office: SCR Inc PO Box 550263 Atlanta GA 30355

ROLAND, BILLY RAY, retired electronics company executive; b. Grandview, Tex., June 12, 1926; s. Marvin Wesley and Minnie Mae (Martin) R.; B.S., Tex. Christian U., 1954; m. Ruth Ranell, Mar. 9, 1950 (div. May 1982); children—Carl R. and Darla K. (twins); m. Linda Sue Leslie, Feb. 21, 1986. With So. Greyhound Bus Co., Ft. Worth, 1943-44, 46-51; supr. acctg. dept. Tandy Leather Co., Ft. Worth, 1954-60; controller, asst. sec., treas. Tandy Corp., Ft. Worth, 1960-75; asst. sec.-treas. controller Tandy Crafts, Inc., Ft. Worth, 1975-78; v.p. Tandy Corp., Ft. Worth, 1978—. Vice pres., treas. David L. Tandy Found.; mng. trustee James L. and Eunice West Chritable Trust. Served with inf., AUS, 1944-46; CBI. C.P.A., Tex. Mem. Ft. Worth C. of C., Am. Inst. C.P.A.s, Tex. Soc. C.P.A.s, Ft. Worth C.P.A.s. Methodist. Clubs: Colonial Country, Petroleum.

ROLAND, JOHN LARRY, financial executive; b. Batesburg, S.C., July 23, 1947; s. John Blanton and Viola (Senterfeit) R.; m. Dorothy Gale Smith, Aug. 17, 1968. B.S. in Bus. Adminstrn., The Citadel, 1976, M.B.A., 1981. Lic. acctg. practitioner, S.C. Asst. mgr. Termplans, Inc., Charleston, S.C., 1968-69; staff acct. Sherman Yarborough P.A., Charleston, 1972-77; sr. staff acct. Schleeter, Monsen, & Debacker C.P.A.s, Charleston, 1977-78; v.p., treas., chief fin. officer Atlantic Services Charleston, Inc., 1978—; sec.-treas. Palmetto Shipping & Stevedoring Co., Inc., Charleston, 1980—; officer, dir. Comml. Bonded Warehouse, Inc., Charleston, 1980—, Palmetto Travel Service, Inc., Charleston, 1980—, Maybank Fertilizer Corp., Charleston, 1980—, Hopkins Transfer & Storage, Inc., Charleston, 1980—. Mem. Nat. Assn. Accts., Trident C. of C., S.C. Assn. Pub. Accts. Methodist. Club: Sertoma (sec./treas. 1974-75) (Goose Creek, S.C.). Home: 103 Ashfield Pl Goose Creek SC 29445 Office: Atlantic Services Charleston Inc PO Box 591 Charleston SC 29402

ROLF, HOWARD LEROY, mathematics educator; b. Laverne, Okla., Nov. 25, 1928; s. James Walter and Edith May (Yoho) R.; m. Anita Jane Ward, June 24, 1961; children—James, Jennifer, Stephanie, Rhonda. B.S., Okla. Baptist U., 1951; M.A., Vanderbilt U., 1953, Ph.D., 1956. Instr. math. Vanderbilt U., Nashville, 1954-56, dir. computer ctr., 1959-64; asst. prof. math. Baylor U., Waco, Tex., 1956-57, prof., 1964—, dept. chmn., 1971—; assoc. prof. math. Georgetown Coll., Ky., 1957-59. Author: Mathematics, 1982. Editor conf. proc. Author articles. Mem. Math. Assn. Am. (chmn. Tex. sect. 1978), Am. Math. Soc., Sigma Xi. Baptist. Home: Route 12 Box 565 Waco TX 76710 Office: Math Dept Baylor Univ Waco TX 76798

ROLLANS, MARY ANN, university official, consultant; b. Fort Smith, Ark., Sept. 23, 1946; d. Ronald R. and Mary Josephine (Korkames) Hobaica; m. David Carter Rollans, Aug. 10, 1968; children—Mary Alicia, Carrie Ann, Russell David. B.A., Ark. Tech. U., 1968; M.A., U. Central Ark., 1974; Ed.D., U. Ark., 1986. Cert. tchr., Ark. Tchr. Russellville High Sch., Ark., 1968-70; instr. Capital City Bus. Coll., Russellville, 1971-76; pub. relations rep. Ark. Employment Security Div., Russellville, 1976-79; affirmative action officer, grant coordinator Ark. Tech. U., Russellville, 1980—; profl. devel. cons., 1980—. Mem. Russellville Planning Commn., 1979-85; mem. bd. edn. Cath. Diocese of Little Rock, 1978-82; bd. dirs. Ark. River Valley Arts Ctr., Russellville, 1980-83. Recipient Ark. Merit award, 1978. Mem. Bus. and Profl. Women (pres. 1981-82, Young Career Woman award 1968, 70), Ark. Council Women in Higher Edn., Russellville C. of C. (bd. dirs. 1984-85), Ark. Tech. U. Alumni Assn. (bd. dirs. 1980-83), Delta Kappa Gamma (sec. 1978-79; doctoral fellow 1983-84). Avocations: water skiing, camping, running, boating, fishing. Home: 2017 Skyline Dr Russellville AR 72801 Office: Ark Tech U N Arkansas Ave Russellville AR 72801

ROLLINS, ALAN CHARLES, human resources developer; b. Pittsfield, Mass., May 2, 1945; s. Charles and Mildred E. (Hayden) Warren; student Rockland Community Coll., 1964-65, McConnell Airline Sch., 1965, Daytona Beach Community Coll., 1969-71, Fla. Technol. U., 1971-72, U. Miami (Fla.), 1973, U. Ga., 1976, Fla. State U., 1979, Eckerd Coll., 1979; m. Sue Kathryn Curry, Dec. 28, 1968 (dec. Apr. 1981); 1 child, Mariah. Community organizer Vista Vol., Ga., 1966-68; counselor Reality House, Daytona Beach, Fla., 1972-73, asst. dir., 1973-74; substance abuse counselor Human Resources Center, Daytona Beach, 1974-75; program planner and coordinator Mental Health Bd. Daytona Beach, 1975-76; exec. dir. Community Out-Reach Services, Inc., DeLand, Fla., 1977-81; asso. dir. Mental Health Bd. HRS Dist. IV, 1981-82; dir. staff devel. Human Resources Ctr., Daytona Beach, Fla., 1982—; bd. dirs. mental health tech. program and social services program Daytona Beach Community Coll., 1983—. Chmn. City of Holly Hill (Fla.) Charter Rev. Commn., 1978-79; mem. Planning Bd. City of Holly Hill, 1977-78; pres. Young Democrats of Volusia County, 1978-79; mem. Volusia County Dem. Exec. Com. bd. dirs. Wiser Women's Center, Daytona Beach, 1977-78, Miss Daytona Beach Pageant, 1979-80, Jr. Athletic Championship, 1978-79, WMFE Pub. Broadcasting; mem. adv. bd. Highlands Elem. Sch., 1985-86, chmn. spl. needs com. Served with USN, 1962-63. Recipient Nat. Collegiate Sports Festival Good Sport award, 1986; Volusia County Sch. System award, 1985. Mem. Fla. Assn. for Health and Social Services (exec. bd. 1977-78), State Assn. Alcoholism Coordinators (sec.-treas. 1976-77), Fla. Assn. of Halfway Houses (dir. 1978), Fla. Alcohol and Drug Abuse Assn. (founder), Am. Soc. Tng. and Devel., Am. Mgmt. Assn., Nat. Mgmt. Assn. Daytona Beach Jaycees (Man of the Year award nominee 1979, 80, 81), Mus. Arts and Scis. Daytona Beach, DAV. Mem. Unity Ch. Home: 828 N Ridgewood Ave Ormond Beach FL 32074 Office: 1220 Willis Ave Daytona Beach FL 32014

ROLLINS, ALBERT WILLIAMSON, cons. engr.; b. Dallas, July 31, 1930; s. Andrew Peach and Mary (Williamson) R.; B.S. in Civil Engring., Tex. A. and M. U., 1951, M.S. in Civil Engring., 1956; m. Martha Ann James, Dec. 28, 1954; children—Elizabeth Ann, Mark Martin. Engring. asst. Tex. Hwy. Dept., Dallas, 1953-55; dir. pub. works City of Arlington (Tex.), 1956-63, city mgr., 1963-67; partner Schrickel, Rollins & Assos., land planners-engrs., Arlington, 1967—. Mem. Gov.'s Energy Adv. Council; chmn. Tex. Mass Transp. Commn.; bd. dirs. Tex. Turnpike Authority. Served as 1st lt. AUS, 1951-53. Registered profl. engr., Tex., La., Okla. Mem. Internat. City Mgmt. Assn., Nat. Soc. Profl. Engrs., ASCE, Am. Water Works Assn., Water Pollution Control Fedn., Sigma Xi, Phi Eta Sigma, Tau Beta Pi, Phi Kappa Phi, Chi Epsilon. Contbr. articles to profl. jours. Home: 3004 Yellowstone Dr Arlington TX 76013 Office: 604 Ave H East Arlington TX 76011

ROLLINS, RONALD ROY, metallurgist, educator; b. Tooele, Utah, Oct. 2, 1930; s. Warren Leroy and Marcella (Miller) R.; m. Monique Thaon, Sept. 6, 1957; children—Michael, Aline, Bruce, Scott, Daniel. B.S. in Fuels Engring., U. Utah, 1959, Ph.D. in Metallurgy, 1962. Metallurgist, ceramist Vallecitos Atomic Lab., Pleasanton, Calif., 1962-64; assoc. prof. Rock Mechanics and Explosives Research Ctr., U. Mo.-Rolla, 1964-79; prof. mining engring. W.Va. U., Morgantown, 1979—, chmn. mineral processing engring., 1981—; research assoc. Argonne Nat. Lab., 1965, Sandia Corp., 1966, 69, Picatinny Arsenal, 1968, Naval Weapons Ctr., 1983; cons. in field. Served with USNR, 1948-52; with AUS, 1953-54. Sandia Corp. fellow 1959-62. Mem. AIME, Am. Soc. for Engring. Edn., AAAS, Internat. Soc. Rock Mechanics, Sigma Xi. Republican. Mormon. Contbr. articles to profl. publs. Home: 1433 Dogwood Ave Morgantown WV 26505 Office: White Hall West Virginia U Morgantown WV 26506

ROLLINSON, MARK, lawyer; b. Chattanooga, Dec. 8, 1935; s. Turner Earl and Josephine (Orput) R.; m. Barbara Crain, Sept. 7, 1957; children—Barbara Louis, Alice Orput, Marjorie Ann, Amy Claire; m. 2d, Carole Seliger, Oct. 30, 1971. A.B. in Econs., Duke U., 1958; LL.B., George Washington U., 1962. Bar: D.C. 1964, Md. 1975, Va. 1982, U.S. Dist. Ct. Md. 1976, U.S. Dist. Ct. (ea. dist.) Va. 1982, U.S. Ct. Appeals (D.C. cir.) 1963, U.S. Ct. Appeals (4th cir.) 1984. Asst. trust officer Nation Savs. and Trust Co., 1958; staff economist Foster Assoc., 1959; treas., exec. com. Human Scis. Research, Inc., 1960-62; v.p. Greater Washington Investors, Inc., 1963-71; ptnr. Rollinson & Schaumberg, Washington, 1972-77; resident ptnr. Dykema, Gossett, Spencer, Goodnow & Trigg, Washington, 1978-81; ptnr. Rollinson & Zusman, Alexandria, Va., 1982—; mem. task force on inflation White House Conf. on Small Bus., 1979-80, exptl. research and devel. incentives program NSF, 1974-75. Mem. ABA (taxation sect., corp., banking and bus. law sect., internat. law sect., standing com. on law and tech., 1980-81, governing com. of forum com. on franchising, 1976-81, planning coms. confs.), D.C. Bar Assn. (chmn. com. on computer-assisted legal research), Internat. Bar Assn. (sect. bus. law), U.S. C. of C. (small bus. council 1985—), Va. Trial Lawyers Assn. Republican. Episcopalian. Clubs: Belle Haven Country, Lawyers, Alexandria Businessmen's. Contbr. writings to legal publs.; speaker in field seminars and sch. Office: 603 King St Alexandria VA 22314

ROLLISON, DAVID JAKE, II, accountant; b. Savannah, Ga., Jan. 1, 1947; s. James Calhoun, III and Martha Thomas (Duffield) R.; 1 dau., Aimee Christine. B.B.A., U. Ga., 1966; M.B.A., Harvard U., 1974. C.P.A., Va., D.C., Ga. Audit staff Ernst & Ernst, Miami, Fla., 1969-70; v.p. fin. Comed, Inc., Ft. Lauderdale, Fla., 1970-72; dir. bus. mgmt. Nat. Assn. Home Builders, Washington, 1975-79; v.p. fin. Yeonas Co., Fairfax, Va., 1980-81; mgr. mgmt. adv. services Suries & Assocs., Ltd., Warrenton, Va., 1981-82; pres., cons. strategic planning C.P.A. Mgmt. Services, Warrenton, 1982-83; v.p., controller Ross Industries Inc., Midland, Va., 1983—. Served to capt. U.S. Army, 1969. Decorated Purple Heart, Silver Star. Mem. Am. Inst. C.P.A.s, Va. Soc. C.P.A.s. Episcopalian. Clubs: City Tavern (Washington); Farmington Country (Charlottesville, Va.); Potomac Polo. Contbr. articles to profl. jours. Office: PO Box 458 Warrenton VA 22186

ROLSTON, LEONARD EDWARD, tourism/convention executive; b. Detroit, July 31, 1932; s. Reginald S. and Mildred I. (Sovereen) R.; B.S. in Bus. Adminstrn., Wayne State U., 1954; m. Janet Marie Randall, Sept. 4, 1953; children—Susan, Pamela and Patricia (twins), Kathleen. Methods and systems analyst Ford Motor Co., 1954-56; conv. sales mgr. Met. Detroit Conv. & Visitors Bur., 1956-64, pres., chief exec. officer, 1964-77; pres., chief exec. officer Greater Houston Conv. & Visitors Council, 1977—. Mem. Internat. Assn. Conv. and Visitors Burs. (past-pres.), Tex. Assn. Conv. and Visitors Burs. (past pres.), Mich. Assn. Conv. and Visitors Bus. (past pres.), Travel Industry Assn. (past dir.), Conv. Liaison Council (past chmn.), Wayne State U. Alumni Assn. (past dir., past dir. fund), Houston C. of C. Office: 3300 Main St Houston TX 77002

ROM, FRANK ERNEST, mechanical engineer, consultant; b. Queens, N.Y., Aug. 16, 1926; s. Frank and Josefa (Kobetitsch) R.; m. Marilyn A. McNamara, Oct. 21, 1950; children—Mary Anne, Paul, Frank Ernest, Barbara, Kathleen, Laura, Mark. B.S.M.E., Cornell U., 1946, M.S.E., 1948. Registered profl. engr., Ohio. Jr. aerodynamicist Cornell Aero. Lab., 1947; research scientist NASA-Lewis Research Ctr., Cleve., 1948-73, 1948-52, sect. head, 1952-56, br. chief, 1956-73; pres. Rom-Aire Solar Corp., Lorain, Ohio, 1973-80; energy and solar cons. Mem. Epiphany Cathedral Council. Served with USN, 1944-46. Mem. Internat. Solar Energy Soc., AIAA, Phi Kappa Phi, Tau Beta Pi. Roman Catholic. Club: Marriage Encounter (Venice, Fla.) Contbr. articles to profl. jours.; patentee in field. Home and office: 1306 Pinebrook Way Venice FL 33595

ROMAGUERA, MARIANO ANTONIO, consulting engineer; b. Mayaguez, P.R., May 4, 1928; s. Jose Mariano and Aminta (Martinez) R.; B.S., M.I.T., 1950; M.S., U. P.R., 1975; m. Virginia Casablance, July 3, 1952; children—Jose Mariano, Jorge Enrique, Alberto, Ana Maria. Asst. engr. Arturo Romaguera, Cons. Engr., Colombia, 1950-51; asst. engr. Ingenio Providencia, Palmira, Colombia, 1951; shift engr. Central Igualdad and Western Sugar Refinery, Mayaguez, 1953-54; erection engr., asst. project mgr., Pradera Valle, Colombia, 1954-55, plant supt., chief engr., 1955-57; project engr. Ingenior Providencia, Palmira, Colombia, 1957, chief engr. ops. and maintenance, 1958-64; exec. v.p. Romaguera & Vendrell Devel. Corp., Mayaguez, P.R., 1964-68; pres. RomaVel, Inc., Mayaguez, 1965-68, Yagueka Equipment, Inc., 1968-78, Mariano A. Romaguera and Assocs., Engrs., Appraisers and Cons., Mayaguez, 1974—; sr. ptnr. Camino, Romaguera & Assocs., 1976—; sr. ptnr. M/E Appraisers, 1976—; cons. engr. Sugar Corp. P.R., Commonwealth of P.R. Pres., Yagueka dist. P.R. council Boy Scouts Am., 1965-69, mem. exec. bd. P.R. council; chmn. ARC, 1966; bd. dirs. Mayaguez YMCA; mem. MIT Ednl. Council. Recipient Silver Beaver award P.R. council Boy Scouts Am., 1969. Mem. Colegio de Evaluadores de P.R., Colegio Ingenieros y Agrimensores de P.R. (past pres. Mayaguez dist.), ASME (pres. S.W. P.R. group), Instituto de Ingenieros Mecanicos de P.R., P.R. Soc. Profl. Engrs., Assn. Engring. Socs., Nat. Soc. Profl. Engrs., Am. Soc. Appraisers, Am. Right of Way Assn., Internat. Soc. Sugar Cane Technologists, P.R. Assn. Real Estate Bds., Mayaguez Bd. Realtors, M.I.T. Alumni Assn., Nu Sigma Beta, Alpha Phi Omega. Roman Catholic. Lodge: Rotary. Home: Peral 16 N Penthouse Mayaguez PR 00708 Office: PO Box 1340 Mayaguez PR 00709

ROMAINE, LEON MARTIN, JR., optometrist, educator; b. Huntingdon, Pa., June 26, 1954; s. Leon Martin and Katherine Cecelia (Houseknecht) R.; m. Lana Cheryl Cornwell, Oct. 30, 1981; 1 child, Cortni Beth. B.S. in Visual Sci., Ill. Coll. Optometry, 1976, O.D., 1978. Ophthalmic asst. John D. Janney, O.D., Oak Hill, W.Va., 1976; optometric asst. Michael Lipsich, M.D., Chgo., 1976-78; ophthalmic technician Sol Rocke, O.D., P.C., Homewood, Ill., 1977-78; pvt. practice optometry, Summersville, W.Va., 1978-84; asst. prof. optometry Northeastern Okla. State U., Tahlequah, 1984—, dir. ocular pathology clinic, 1984-85; optometric cons. Nicholas County Bd. Edn., W.Va., 1978-84; mem. So. Council Optometry, Atlanta, 1978-84; area chmn. W.Va. Optometric Assn., 1982-84. Mem. area adv. council W.Va. Spl. Olympics, Summersville, W.Va., 1983-84. Mem. Am. Optometric Assn. (chmn. W.Va. area 1982-84). Democrat. Methodist. Lodge: Kiwanis. Avocations: music; oil painting. Office: Northeastern Okla State U 206 Wyly Hall Tahlequah OK 74465

ROMAN-ENRIQUEZ, MANUEL FRANCISCO, planning educator, consultant, researcher, actuary; b. Mexico City, Nov. 6, 1951; s. Manuel Roman-Diaz de Leon and Beatriz Enriquez-Escallon; m. Blanca E. Mireles, July 9, 1983. B.S. in Actuarial Sci., Nat. U. Mex., 1975, B.S. in Math., 1981, M.Sc., 1976; M.A., Universidad Ibero Americana, 1982. Enrolled actuary, Mich.; registered survey statistician, Mich. Head ops. research group Facultad de Ciencias, Nat. U. Mex., 1978-80, head planning group, 1980-84, lectr., 1975—, head planning and systems group, 1984—; sr. researcher dept. math. Centro de Investigacion y Docencia Economicas, Mex., 1983-84; chief cons. Direccion General de Programacion, Sec. Pub. Edn., Mex., 1981-83; councillor and advisor. Author: La Planeacion Educativa, 1975; Planeacion y Planeacion Prospectiva, 1983; Political Implications of Planning, 1985. Assoc. editor Revista de Estadistica, Mex., 1984—. Scholar Consejo Nacional de Ciencia y Tech., Mex., British Council. Fellow Colegio Nacional de Actuarios (under sec. 1982-85), Instituto Mexicano de Sistemas (under sec. 1982-85), mem. Sociedad Interamericana de Planificacion, Internat. Orgn. Human Ecology. Roman Catholic. Avocations: cinema; archaeology; tennis; history of ancient and modern warfare. Home: Castana 189 Mexico City DF 02800 Mexico Office: Dept Math Facultad de Ciencias Mexico City DF 04510 Mexico

ROMANO, PAUL EDWARD, pediatric ophthalmologist, educator; b. N.Y.C., Oct. 30, 1934; s. Paul Salvatore and Mary Elizabeth (Simms) R.; m. Judith Ann Robinson, Oct. 18, 1969. A.B., Cornell U., 1955, M.D., 1959; M.S. with distinction in Ophthalmology, Georgetown U., 1967. Diplomate Am. Bd. Ophthalmology. Intern in surgery Albany Med. Ctr. Hosp., N.Y., 1959-60, residency in gen. surgery, 1960-61; residency in ophthalmology Georgetown U. Hosp., Washington, 1964-67; fellow in ophthalmology Armed Forces Inst. Pathology, Washington, 1967, Wilmer Ophthal. Inst., Johns Hopkins Hosp., Balt., 1967-69; dir. ophthalmology Children's Meml. Hosp., Chgo., 1970-80; asst. prof. Northwestern U. Med. Sch., Chgo., 1969-73, assoc. prof., 1973-80; prof. ophthalmology U. Fla. Coll. Medicine, Gainesville, 1980—; cons. VA Med. Ctr., Gainesville, 1980—, Naval Regional Med. Ctr., Jacksonville, Fla., 1981—. Founding editor Binocular Vision Jour., 1985—. Contbr. over 100 articles to sci. jours. Served to capt. U.S. Army, 1961-64. Fellow Heed Found., 1968, NIH, 1968-69. Fellow Am. Acad. Ophthalmology, Am. Acad. Pediatrics; mem. Internat. Assn. Ocular Surgeons (charter), Internat. Strabismus Assn., Am. Assn. for Pediatric Ophthalmology (charter), Assn. for Research in Vision and Ophthalmology, AAUP, Fla Med. Assn., Fla. Soc. Ophthalmology, Alachua County Med. Soc., Soc. Heed Fellows, Wilmer Residents' Assn. Avocation: auto racing (owner and driver). Home: 2500 NW 23d Terr Gainesville FL 32605 Office: Dept Ophthalmology U Fla Coll Medicine Box J-284 Gainesville FL 32610

ROMANS, RALPH HAYS, educational administrator; b. McHenry, Ky., Sept. 25, 1937; s. Gerome Orville and Eva Margurite Romans; m. Judith Ann Moore, June 27, 1961; children—Lisa Renee, Jared Brown. B.A., Campbellsville Coll., 1961; M.A., Western Ky. U., 1964; Ed.D., Ind. U., 1974. Tchr. Hardin County Pub. Schs., Elizabethtown, Ky., 1960-61, Butler County Pub. Schs., Morgantown, Ky., 1961-62; prin. Daviess County Pub. Schs., Owensboro, Ky., 1962-73, 75—; research asst. Ind. U., Bloomington, 1973-74. Author: Ind. School Boards Jour., 1974; Financing American Education, 1974. Patentee blow injection plastic, 1973, insect trap, 1972. Pres. Audubon Soc., Owensboro, 1972; precinct capt., Owensboro, 1984; bd. dirs. Family Y, Owensboro, 1973, Welfare League, Owensboro, 1976. Tex. Gas Corp. grantee, 1984; Dept. Vocat. Edn. grantee, 1983. Mem. NEA, Ky. Ednl. Assn., Daviess County Edn. Assn., Ky. Assn. Sch. Adminstrs. Democrat. Baptist. Club: Toastmasters (treas. 1973-74). Lodge: Masons. Avocations: art; angling; writing. Home: 1621 Roosevelt Rd Owensboro KY 43201 Office: Owensboro Treatment Ctr 3001 Leitchfield Rd Owensboro KY 42301

ROMBERG, LESLIE HOLMES, international marketing management company executive; b. Bklyn., Aug. 11, 1941; d. Alton Butler and Margaret Nichol (Arnett) H.; m. Jon Word Blaschke, Aug. 20, 1966 (div. June 1968); m. Conrad Louis Romberg, Jan. 6, 1985. Student, Baylor Coll. Dentistry, 1959-60, U. Tulsa, 1962-64; B.S. in Chemistry and Biology, Central State U., Edmond, Okla., 1966; Ph.D. in Chemistry, U. Okla., 1968. Head internat. ops. New Eng. Nuclear Corp., Boston, 1969-77; sales engr. Tracor Analytic, Des Plaines, Ill., 1977-79; internat. mktg. and product mgr. Zoecon Industries, Dallas, 1979-80; owner, operator Tex-Am. Internat., Dallas, 1980—. Named Most Outstanding Former Student Central State U., 1975. Republican. Unitarian.

ROMERO, FRANK, school administrator, musician; b. Williams, Ariz., Nov. 18, 1933; s. Francisco A. and Andrea (Acosta) R.; m. Armida Juarez, Jan. 25, 1956; children—Yvonne Romero Garza, Armida, Frances Deane. B.A., Tex. Western Coll., 1962; M.Ed., U. Tex.-El Paso, 1967; postgrad. East Tex. State U., 1975-76, U. Tex.-Austin, 1975-82. Freight carman South Pacific RR, El Paso, 1956-58; tchr. sci. El Paso Ind. Sch. Dist., 1962-68, dir. personnel, 1968-75; title I cons. Tex. Edn. Agy., Austin, 1975-76; ednl. adminstr. Dallas Ind. Sch. Dist., 1976—; cons. Noble and Noble Pub., N.Y.C., 1974-75, Coronado Pub. Co., San Diego, 1981-85. Author: Concepts in Science, 1980; patentee removeable golf cleats, 1973. Treas. McCall Day Nursery, El Paso, 1974; fellow Boy Scouts Am., Dallas, 1982; dir. St. Luke Computer Edn. Program, Dallas, 1983. Recipient Tchr. of Yr. award Ben Milam Sch., El Paso, 1967; Prin. of Yr. award Dallas Subdist. II, 1983, 84. Fellow Dallas Assn. Sch. Adminstrs., Dallas Assn. Bilingual Educators, Spl. Edn. PTA (treas. 1983-85, prin. of yr. award 1984). Republican. Roman Catholic. Home: 823 Brook Valley Ln Dallas TX 75232 Office: LV Stockard Middle Sch 2300 S Ravinia Dr Dallas TX 75211

ROMERO, KATHERINE NORRIS, nursing adminstrator; b. Orlando, Fla., Apr. 15, 1948; d. Floyd Hubert and Evelyn (Thompson) N.; m. Joseph J. Lee, June 7, 1969 (div. 1974); m. Cristobal J. Romero, Dec. 22, 1978; children—Paul, Anthony. Grad. Charity Hosp. Sch. Nursing, New Orleans, 1969; B.S., Loyola U., New Orleans, 1976; postgrad. Xavier U., 1985. Cert. nurse adminstr. Staff nurse Charity Hosp., 1969-71, instr., Sch. Nursing, 1971-73, supr., 1973-76, asst. dir. nursing Charity Hosp., 1977-83, clin. dir., 1983—, dir. operating room nursing, 1983—. Vol. YMCA Crisis Line, New Orleans, 1979; leader Girl Scouts U.S.A., St. Rose, La., 1983; vol. ARC, New Orleans, 1969—; mem. Mothers Against Drunk Driving, New Orleans, 1984. Mem. Assn. Operating Room Nurses, La. Assn. Post Anesthesia Nurses. Democrat. Baptist. Avocations: camping; shooting; fishing; festivals. Office: Charity Hosp 1532 Tulane Ave New Orleans LA 70087

ROMERO, RICHARD MICHAEL, coal company executive; b. Pensacola, Fla., Jan. 17, 1948; s. Richard and Anna Elizabeth (McLaughlin) R.; student Catholic U., Washington, U. Mo.; m. JoAnn Day, Apr. 22, 1983; children—Paige, Erin. Bookkeeper, ACR Electronics Co., Westbury, N.Y., 1969-70; corp. staff Peabody Coal Co., St. Louis, 1970-75, mem. underground ops. services staff, Evansville, Ind., 1975-77, adminstrv. supr. underground ops. East div., Greenville, Ky., 1977-79; dir. adminstrn. and fin. Pyro Mining Co., 1979-81, acctg. mgr., comptroller, 1980—; controller Pyramid Mining Co., 1982—. Republican. Roman Catholic. Mem. Lancer Yacht Assn., U.S. Yacht Racing Union. Home: Route 1 Box 464 Ditto Rd Philpot KY Office: PO Box 686 Owensboro KY 42302

ROMEY, CAROL MERCED, educator, clinical psychologist; b. San Francisco, Jan. 25, 1947; d. Roy Lee and Frances Elizabeth (Lillyblad) R.; m. Carlos G. Ramos-Bellido, June 13, 1970; children—Alexandra, Magdalena, Cristina. B.A. in Sociology, U. Calif.-Berkeley, 1968, M.A. in Criminology, 1971; Ph.D. in Clin. Psychology, Caribbean Ctr. for Advanced Studies, 1981. Prof. sociology U. P.R., Mayaguez, 1970-72, Rio Piedras Campus, 1972—; cons. Legal Services P.R., 1975—; pro-bono P.R. Bar Assn., 1982—. Contbr. articles to profl. jours. Patentee in field. Mem. Am. Psychol. Assn., P.R. Psychol. Assn. Office: Box 22425 University Sta Rio Piedras PR 00931

ROMIG, WILLIAM JAMES, railroad holding company executive; b. Manhattan, Kans., Apr. 16, 1944; s. James Edward and Ruth Elizabeth (Walker) R.; m. Elizabeth Paige Gannon, Aug. 31, 1968; children—Curtis James, Nicholas Ward. B.S., Kans. State U., 1966; M.B.A., U. Md., 1971, D.B.A., 1975. Sr. ops. research analyst Assn. Am. R.R.s, Washington, 1973-74, dep. dir. research, 1975-77; dir. operating systems Norfolk & Western Ry., Roanoke, Va., 1977-80, asst. v.p. mgmt. info., 1980-82; asst. v.p. costs and ins. Norfolk So. Corp. (Va.), 1982-83, asst. v.p. fin., 1983—; com. chmn. Transp. Research Bd., Nat. Acad. Scis., 1983—. Contbr. articles to publs. Trustee United Way, Roanoke, 1982. Served as 1st lt. U.S. Army, 1967-69. Decorated Bronze Star. Mem. Ops. Research Soc. Am., Phi Kappa Phi, Delta Upsilon. Republican. Episcopalian. Clubs: Roanoke Country, Norfolk Yacht and Country. Lodge: Kiwanis. Home: 1418 Brunswick Ave Norfolk VA 23508 Office: Norfolk So Corp 1 Commercial Pl Norfolk VA 23510

ROMINE, KENNY FLOYD, federal government administrator; b. Memphis, Feb. 1, 1927; s. William Armory and Ollie Nora (King) R.; m. Dorothy Schmus, Oct. 20, 1952 (div. 1956); m. Toni Toyoko Murata, Dec. 20, 1957; 1 child, Kenneth Wayne. Enlisted as pvt. U.S. Marine Corps, 1945, advanced through grades to gunnery sgt., 1958, retired, 1965; salesman Sears Roebuck Co., Jacksonville, N.C., 1965-67; ins. agt. Life and Casualty Ins. Co., Jacksonville, 1967-69; fire prevention insp. U.S. Govt. Employment, Camp Lejeune, N.C., 1971-75, occupational safety and health specialist 1975—. Mem. Am. Soc. Safety Engrs. (pres. eastern Carolina chpt. 1984-85, sec. region IX 1984-85). Democrat. Baptist. Office: Naval Air Rework Facility Code 015 Marine Corps Air Sta Cherry Point NC 28533

ROMINE, THOMAS BEESON, JR., cons. engring. firm exec.; b. Billings, Mont., Nov. 16, 1925; s. Thomas Beeson and Elizabeth Marjorie (Tschudy) R.; student Rice Inst., 1943-44; B.S. in Mech. Engring., U. Tex. at Austin, 1948; m. Rosemary Pearl Melancon, Aug. 14, 1948; children—Thomas Beeson III, Richard Alexander, Robert Harold. Jr. engr. Gen. Engring. Co., Ft. Worth, 1948-50; design engr. Wyatt C. Hedrick, architect/engr., Ft. Worth, 1950-54, chief mech. engr., 1954-56; pres., chief mech. engr. Thomas B. Romine, Jr., cons. engr. (now Romine, Romine & Burgess, Inc., cons. engrs.), Ft. Worth, 1956—. Mem. Plan Commn., City of Ft. Worth, 1958-62; mem. Supervisory Bd. Plumbers, City of Ft. Worth, 1963-71, chmn., 1970-71, chmn. Plumbing Code Review Com., 1968-69; mem. Mech. Bd., City of Ft. Worth, 1974-80, chmn., 1976-80; chmn. plumbing code bd. North Central Tex. Council Govts., Ft. Worth, 1971-75. Bd. mgrs. Tex. Christian U.-South Side YMCA, Ft. Worth, 1969-74; trustee Ft. Worth Symphony Orch., 1968—; v.p. Orch. Hall, 1975—. Served with USNR, 1943-45. Registered profl. engr., Tex., Okla., La., Ga. Fellow Am. Soc. Heating, Refrigeration and Air Conditioning Engrs. (pres. Ft. Worth chpt. 1958, nat. committeeman 1974—), Automated Procedures Engring. Cons. (trustee 1970-71, 75, 1st v.p. 1972-73, internat. pres. 1974), Am. Cons. Engrs. Council; mem. Nat., Tex. (dir. 1956, treas. 1967) socs. profl. engrs., Cons. Engrs. Council of Tex. (pres. North Tex. chpt., also v.p. state orgn. 1965, dir. state orgn. 1967), Starfish Class Assn. (nat. pres. 1970-73, nat. champion 1976), Delta Tau Delta (v.p. Western div. 1980—), Pi Tau Sigma. Episcopalian. Rotarian. Club: Colonial Country. Author numerous computer programs in energy analysis and heating and air conditioning field. Contbr. articles to profl. jours. Home: 3232 Preston Hollow St Fort Worth TX 76109 Office: 300 S Greenleaf St Fort Worth TX 76107

RONDEAU, CLEMENT ROBERT, petroleum geologist; b. Ironwood, Mich., July 6, 1928; s. Clement Matthew and Beatrice Ida (Johnson) R.; B.S., Tulane U., 1955; m. Irmtraut Juliana Gretler, Aug. 7, 1949; children—Robert M., Stephen R., Paul H. (dec.), Charles R. Geol. supr. Texaco Inc., New Orleans, 1955-63; area mgr. Pubco Petroleum Corp., New Orleans, 1963-69; cons. petroleum geologist, Harahan, La., 1969—; owner Natural Gas Exploration Co., 1977—. Served with AUS, 1946-49, 50-51. Mem. Am. Assn. Petroleum Geologists, Soc. Exploration Geophysicists, New Orleans Geol. Soc., AAAS, Explorers Club, Ind. Petroleum Assn., N.Y. Acad. Sci., Internat. Platform Assn., Internat. Oil Scouts Assn., Phi Beta Kappa, Sigma Gamma Epsilon. Democrat. Roman Catholic. Clubs: New Orleans Athletic; Bay/Waveland Yacht (Miss.). Home: 632 Stratford Dr Harahan LA 70123 Office: 958 Hickory Suite A Harahan LA 70123

RONEY, PAUL H., federal judge; b. Olney, Ill., Sept. 5, 1921; married; 3 children. Student, St. Petersburg Jr. Coll., 1938-40; B.S. in Econs., U. Pa., 1942; LL.B., Harvard U., 1948; LL.D., Stetson U., 1977; LL.M., U. Va., 1984. Bar: N.Y. 1949, Fla. 1950. Asso. firm Root, Ballantine, Harlan, Bushby & Palmer, N.Y.C., 1948-50; with firm Mann, Harrison, Roney, Mann & Masterson (and predecessors), St. Petersburg, Fla., 1950-57; individual practice law, 1957-63; partner firm Roney & Beach, St. Petersburg, 1963-69; firm Roney, Ulmer, Woodworth & Jacobs, St. Petersburg, 1969-70; judge U.S. Circuit Ct. 5th Circuit, St. Petersburg, 1970-81, U.S. Circuit Ct. 11th Circuit, 1981—; mem. adv. com. on adminstrv. law judges U.S. CSC, 1976-77. Served in U.S. Army, 1943-46. Fellow Am. Bar Found.; mem. Am. Bar Assn. (chmn. legal adv. com. Fair Trial-Free Press 1973-76, mem. task force on cts. and public 1973-76, jud. adminstrn. div., chmn. appellate judges conf. 1978-79, mem. Gavel Awards com. 1980-83), Am. Judicature Soc. (dir. 1972-76), Am. Law Inst., Fla. Bar, St. Petersburg Bar Assn. (pres. 1964-65), Nat. Jud. Coll. (faculty 1974, 75), Jud. Conf. U.S. (subcom. on jud. improvements 1978-84). Office: 601 Federal Office Bldg Saint Petersburg FL 33701

RONY, PETER R., chemical engineering educator; b. Paris, June 29, 1939; came to U.S., 1940; s. George Jury and Rosette R.; m. Myriam Eliette Paiz, Dec. 23, 1961; children—Karen, Karl, Paul, Glenn, Marianne. B.S., Calif. Inst. Tech., 1960; Ph.D., U. Calif.-Berkeley, 1965. Assoc. prof. chem. engring. Va. Poly. Inst., Blacksburg, 1971-75, prof., 1975—; trustee CACHE, Inc., Austin, Tex. Author: 8080A Microcomputer Programming and Interfacing, 1975, also 8 other books. recipient Faculty Service award Nat. Univ. Extension Assn., 1978; Delos/Tektronix award for Excellence in Lab. Instrn., Am. Soc. Engring. Educators, 1984; Dreyfus Found. tchr.-scholar, 1973. Mem. IEEE (sr.; editor-in-chief IEEE Micro 1983-85), Am. Chem. Soc., Am. Inst. Chem. Engrs. Avocations: swimming; microcomputers. Home: 1501 Highland Circle Blacksburg VA 24060 Office: Dept Chem Engring Va Inst Blacksburg VA 24061

ROOF, BETTY SAMS, physician; b. Columbia, S.C., Apr. 13, 1926; s. Grover Melton Saunders and Lucinda Wood (Sams) R.; m. Herman Hugh Fudenberg (div.); children—Drew Douglas, Brooks Roberts, David Melton, Hugh Haskell. B.S., U. S.C.-Columbia, 1944; M.D., Duke U., 1949. Diplomate Am. Bd. Internal Medicine, Am. Bd. Endocrinology and Metabolism. Vol. vis. investigator Rockefeller Inst., N.Y.C., 1949-50; intern Presbyn. Hosp., N.Y.C., 1950-51, asst. resident, 1951-53, asst. physician, 1953-55; attending physician Francis Delafield Hosp., N.Y.C., 1954-55; clin. and research fellow dept. medicine Mass. Gen. Hosp., Boston, 1955-56, research fellow dept. pathology, 1957-58; research fellow Harvard U., 1955-56; research assoc. dept. microbiology and pathology Rockefeller Inst., 1958-59; asst. research physician Cancer Research Inst. U. Calif., San Francisco, 1962-63, assoc. research physician, 1967-71, lectr. medicine, 1971-74, assoc. clin. prof., 1974; assoc. prof. medicine Med. U. S.C., 1974-80, prof., 1980—. Mem. Library Bd., Mill Valley, Calif., 1965-68; mem. Tamalpais Nursery Sch. Bd., Mill Valley, Calif., 1968. Am. Cancer Soc. trainee, 1953-55; grantee Am. Cancer Soc., USPHS, Koebig Trust Fund; USPHS fellow, 1949-50. Mem. Am. Assn. Cancer Research, Western Soc. Clin. Research, Endocrine Soc., Internat. Endocrine Soc., Am. Soc. for Bone and Mineral Research, Charleston Med. Soc., ACP, Am. Fedn. Clin. Research, So. Soc. Clin. Investigation, Waring Library Soc., Soc. for Destitute Widows and Children of Dec. Physicians, Phi Beta Kappa, Alpha Omega Alpha. Contbr. articles to profl. jours. Home: 675 Fort Sumter Dr Charleston SC 29412 Office: 171 Ashley Ave Charleston SC 29425

ROOKS, FLOYD JEFFERSON, public relations executive, non-profit-corporation executive; b. Umatilla, Fla., June 26, 1923; s. Floyd J. and Bessie (Golden) R.; m. Marjorie Ann Fowler, Oct. 9, 1954; children—Virginia Ann, Sharon Elaine, Deborah Ann, Christina Carol. A.B., U. Fla., 1948, M.A. in Polit. Sci., 1949; M.S., Medill Sch. Journalism, Northwestern U., 1950. Account exec. Internat. Nickel Co., Inc., N.Y.C., 1952-56; regional pub. relations Celanese Corp. Am., Charlotte, N.C., 1956-58; prin. Jeff Rooks Assos., Inc., Pub. Relations, Charlotte, 1958-63, Miami, Fla., 1966-76; pres. Christians Afloat, Inc., Melbourne, Fla., 1976—. Served with AUS, 1943-46. Mem. Pub. Relations Soc. Am. Democrat. Clubs: Eau Gallie Yacht, Indian Harbour Beach (Fla.). Office: Box 1442 Melbourne FL 32901

ROOP, JERRY PAUL, oil company executive; b. Poteau, Okla., Aug. 14, 1950; s. James Ralph and Imogene (Cooper) R.; m. Nancy Ann Parham, June 2, 1973; children—Jay Paul, Melinda Ann. B.B.A., Central State U., Edmond, Okla., 1976, M.B.A., 1977. Systems Analyst Halliburton Services Co., Duncan, Okla., 1977-79; adminstrv. mgr. Perkins Prodn. Co., Duncan, 1980; v.p. adminstrn. Perkins Energy Co., Duncan, 1980—, also dir. Advisor Jr. Achievment, Duncan, 1977-79; campaign worker United Way, 1983. Served with USAF, 1968-72, Vietnam. Mem. So. Okla. Assn. Petroleum Landmen, Duncan C. of C. (Leadership Duncan participant 1983), Alpha Chi. Democrat. Baptist. Lodge: Elks. Office: Perkins Energy Co 15 N 9th St PO Box 878 Duncan OK 73534

ROOS, PHILIP, consulting and training company executive, psychotherapist; b. Brussels, Belgium, Jan. 24, 1930, came to U.S., 1939; s. Maurice and Berthe (Matheissens) R.; m. Susan Gail Morgan, June 9, 1958; 1 dau., Valerie Gail. B.A., B.S., Stanford U., 1949; Ph.D., U. Tex., 1955. Cert. lic. clin. psychologist, Tex.; cert. Nat. Register Health Service Providers; cert. Gestalt psychotherapist. Dir. psychology dept. Timberlawn Sanitarium, Dallas, 1959-60; chief psychol. services Tex. Dept. Mental Health/Mental Retardation, Austin, 1960-64; supt. Austin State Sch., 1964-67; assoc. commr. N.Y. State Dept. Mental Hygiene, Albany, 1967-69; nat. exec. dir. Assn. Retarded Citizens, Arlington, Tex., 1969-83; pres. P.S. Roos & Assocs., Inc., Hurst, Tex., 1980—; nat. exec. dir. Mothers Against Drunk Drivers, Hurst, 1983-84; pvt. practice psychology, Ft. Worth, Austin and Hurst, 1955-68, 80—; cons.; lectr. U. Tex., Austin, 1965-67; adj. prof. U. Tex.-Arlington, 1975—. Served to capt. USPHS, 1955-57. Lic. clin. psychologist, Tex. Fellow Am. Orthopsychiat. Assn., Am. Assn. Mental Deficiency (chmn. planning bd. 1973-77); mem. Pres.' Commn. Employment of Handicapped, Am. Psychol. Assn., Mental Health Law Project (dir.). Club: CAP (group comdr. Ft. Worth-Dallas 1957-60). Designer Time Reference Inventory, 1963. Contbr. numerous articles to profl. jours., chpts. to books. Home: 6100 Tiffany Park Ct Arlington TX 76016 Office: P S Roos & Associates Inc 235 NE Loop 820 Suite 508 Hurst TX 76053

ROOT, MICHAEL RAY, oil and gas exploration company executive, geologist; b. Middletown, Ohio, Oct. 30, 1953; s. Arthur Ray and Joyce Marlene (Auerbach) R.; m. Elaine Debra Moody, Aug. 25, 1979; children—Branden Ryan, Christina Leialoha. A.A. in Geology, Shasta Coll., 1974; B.S. in Geology, U. Ala., 1976, M.S. in Geology, 1978. Cert. profl. geol. scientist, Ala., Colo., Okla. Jr. geologist ARCO, Anchorage, 1977-78, sr. geologist AMOCO, Denver, 1978-80; exploration mgr. Basic Earth Sci. Systems, Inc., Denver, 1980-81; sr. geologist Lear Petroleum Exploration, Inc., Oklahoma City, 1981-85; pres. Terraquest Corp., Oklahoma City, 1985—; cons. Maven Land Mgmt., Oklahoma City, 1985—. Contbr. articles to profl. jours. Mem. Am. Assn. Petroleum Geologists, Am. Inst. Profl. Geologists (Oklahoma City rep. 1984), Internat. Assn. Math. Geology, Okla. Computer User Group. Republican. Avocation: rare stamp and coin collecting. Home: 1913 Glen Eagle Edmond OK 73034 Office: Terraquest Corp 2 E 11th Suite 23 Edmond OK 73034

ROOZEN, KENNETH JAMES, microbiologist, educator, university dean; b. Milw., Jan. 17, 1943; s. Roger and Bernice R.; m. Sandra Giles, Feb. 26, 1981; children—Karla, Kevin, Kristin. B.S., Lakeland Coll., 1965; M.A., U. S.D., 1968; Ph.D., U. Tenn., 1971. NSF summer trainee U. S.D., 1966; postdoctoral fellow Washington U., St. Louis, 1971-73, instr., 1973-74; asst. prof. microbiology U. Ala.-Birmingham, 1974-80, assoc. prof., 1980—, vice chmn. microbiology dept., 1977-81, assoc. dean Grad. Sch., 1979-81, acting chmn. microbiology, 1983, chmn., 1984—, dean Grad. Sch., 1981—; cons. Oak Ridge Nat. Lab., 1977—, Technicon Corp., Tarrytown, N.Y., 1972-74, Monsanto Co., St. Louis, 1978-80. Contbr. articles to sci. jours. NDEA fellow U. S.D., 1966-67; NIH postdoctoral fellow, 1971-73; Robert Wood Johnson Health Policy fellow, 1983-84. Mem. Am. Soc. Cell Biology, Am. Soc. for Microbiology, AAAS, Ala. Acad. Scis., Sigma Xi (chpt. pres. 1980-81). Methodist. Avocations: tennis; skiing; antique foreign cars. Home: 361 Laredo Dr Birmingham AL 35294 Office: U of Ala at Birmingham University Blvd Birmingham AL 35294

ROPER, BILLY JOE, water utility executive; b. Wilmot, Ark., June 20, 1939; s. Mode F. and Veda B. (Hughes) R.; student La. State U., 1965; m. Edith L. Westmoreland, Oct. 12, 1968; children—Ricky, Dennis, Trey, Billy. Mgr., Central La. Electric Co., Monroe, 1958-67; automobile dealership, Wilmot, Ark., 1967-70; gen. mgr. Conway County Regional Water Distbn. Dist., Morrilton, Ark., 1970—. Treas., Boiling Springs Cemetery Assn. Named Mgr. of Yr., Central Dist. Water, 1978-79. Mem. Am. Waterworks Assn., Ark. Waterworks and Pollution Control Fedn. (pres.; Disting. Service award 1979), Ark. Water and Waste Mgrs. Assn. (past chmn.), Baptist. Club: Kiwanis (dir. 1973—, Kiwanian of Yr. 1978). Home: Route 4 Box 447 Russellville AR 72801 Office: 108 E Railroad Ave Morrilton AR 72110

ROPER, JOHN LONSDALE, III, shipyard executive; b. Norfolk, Va., Jan. 19, 1927; s. John Lonsdale, II and Sarah (Dryfoos) R.; m. Jane Harman Preston, Sept. 29, 1951; children—Susan, John Lonsdale IV, Sarah Preston Tekamp, Jane Harman Van Sciver, Katherine Hayward Stout. B.S. in Mech. Engring., U. Va., 1949; B.S. in Naval Architecture and Marine Engring., MIT, 1951. With Norfolk Shipbldg. & Drydock Corp., 1946—, chmn. bd., chief exec. officer, dir.; pres., dir. Lonsdale bldg. Corp., Marepcon Corp.-Internat.; v.p., sec. Schooner Point, Inc.; dir. John L. Roper Corp., Cruise Internat., Inc., Dominion Nat. Bank Tidewater, The Flagship Group, Ltd. Active Norfolk Community Hosp. Commn.; bd. dirs. United Communities Fund, Med. Ctr. Hosps. Served with USCG, 1945-46. Mem. Am. Bur. Shipping (dir.), Shipbuilders Council Am. (dir.), Nat. Propeller Club U.S., Soc. Naval Architects and Marine Engrs., Am. Soc. Naval Engrs., Chiselers Club N.Y., Am. Legion. Episcopalian. Clubs: Virginia, Princess Anne Country, Norfolk Assembly, Norfolk Yacht and Country, Harbor of Norfolk, Cedar Point Country, Norfolk German. Home: 8005 Blanford Rd Norfolk VA 23505 Office: PO Box 2100 Norfolk VA 23501

ROPER, PAUL HOLMES, hospital administrator; b. San Antonio, Aug. 9, 1932; s. Gwilt Roper and Mable (Holmes) Roper McCartney; m. Dana Janelle Furr, Feb. 26, 1955; children—M. Brian, M. Boyce. B.B.A., Tex. A&M Coll., 1954; M.S., U. Iowa, 1958. Adminstr., Bapt. Med. Ctr., San Antonio, 1978—. Served to 1st lt. U.S. Army, 1954-56. Fellow Am. Coll. Hosp. Adminstrs. Baptist. Home: 1127 Haltown St San Antonio TX 78213 Office: Bapt Med Ctr 111 Dallas St San Antonio TX 78286

RORISON, MARGARET LIPPITT, reading consultant; b. Wilmington, N.C., Feb. 6, 1925; d. Harmon Chadbourn and Margaret Devereux (Lippitt) R.; A.B., Hollins Coll., 1946; M.A., Columbia U., 1956; Diplôme de langue, L'Alliance Française, Paris, 1966; postgrad. U. S.C., 1967-70, 81—. Market and editorial researcher Time, Inc., N.Y.C., 1949-55; classroom and corrective reading tchr. N.Y.C. public schs., 1956-65; TV instr. ETV-WNDT, Channel 13, N.Y.C., 1962-63; grad. asst., TV instr. U. S.C., Columbia, 1967-70; instrnl. specialist in reading S.C. Office Instrnl. TV and Radio, S.C. Dept. Edn., Columbia, 1971-81; reading cons. S.C. Office Instructional Tech., 1982—. Active Common Cause. Mem. Internat. Reading Assn., Am. Ednl. Research Assn., Assn. Supervision and Curriculum Devel., Nat. Soc. Study of Edn., AAUW. Phi Delta Kappa, Delta Kappa Gamma. Episcopalian. Author instrnl. TV series: Getting the Word (So. Ednl. Communications Assn. award 1972, Ohio State award 1973, S.C. Scholastic Broadcasters award 1973), Getting the Message, 1981. Home: 1724 Enoree Ave Columbia SC 29205

ROS, ILEANA, state legislator, educational administrator; b. Havana, Cuba, July 15, 1952; came to U.S., 1960; m. Dexter W. Lehtinen. A.A., Miami-Dade Community Coll., 72; B.A., Fla. Internat. U., 1975. Prin., owner Eastern Acad., Miami, Fla.; mem. Fla. Ho. of Reps., 1982—; writer weekly articles for Spanish newspaper. Mem. adv. bd. Parenting Inst., Miami-Dade Community Coll.; mem. edn. bd. U.S. Senate; bd. dirs. Miami Mental Health Assn.; mem. adv. bd. City of Miami, 1981. Mem. Bilingual Pvt. Sch. Assn. (pres. 1980-84), Council Bilingual Schs. (v.p. 1979—), Fla. Reading Council, AAUW, Assn. Curriculum Devel., Miami C. of C., Kappa Delta Pi, Phi Theta Kappa, Sigma Delta Chi. Republican. Roman Catholic. Home: 724 SW 99th Court Circle Miami FL 33174 Office: 8421 NW 56th St Miami FL 33166 also 411 House Office Bldg Tallahassee FL 32301

ROSE, ALVIN CARNEY, educational administrator; b. Dyersburg, Tenn., Feb. 27, 1945; s. Alvin C. and Hattie Frances (Hendren) R.; m. Jeanne Roberts, June 8, 1969; children—James, Benjamin. B.A., David Lipscomb Coll., 1968; M.A. in Tchg., Vanderbilt U., 1969; M.Ed., Austin Peay State U., 1977, Edn. Specialist, 1977; postgrad. Vanderbilt U., 1984—. Cert. elem. tchr., prin., cert. secondary prin., elem. and secondary supr., supt. schs. Tchr. social studies Cheatham County Central High Sch., Ashland City, Tenn., 1969-75, asst. prin., 1975-76, prin., 1976—. Chmn. Cheatham County Curriculum Council, Ashland City, Tenn., 1974—, Tenn. Secondary Schs. Athletic Assn. Basketball Dist. 10-AAA, Ashland City, 1980—; mem. adj. faculty Austin Peay State U., Clarksville, Tenn., 1982—. Weekly columnist Dyer County Tennessean, 1966—, Ashland City Times, 1968—. Contbr. articles to profl. jours. Minister music Ashland City Ch. of Christ, 1977—. Recipient Participant award The Master Teacher, 1984; Vanderbilt U. fellow, 1968-69; R.J. Reynolds Tobacco Co. fellow, 1970. Mem. Assn. Supervision and Curriculum Devel., Nat. Assn. Secondary Prins., Tenn. Assn. Secondary Prins., NEA, Tenn. Edn. Assn., Cheatham county Edn. Assn. (pres. 1971-72, exec. bd. 1970-80). Democrat. Mem. Ch. of Christ. Lodge: Masons. Avocations: jogging; gardening; reading; baseball; educational travel. Home: Route 1 Box 87-H Ashland City TN 37015 Office: Cheatham County Central High Sch Route 6 Box 93 Ashland City TN 37015

ROSE, CAROLYN BRUCE, interior designer, educator; b. Gunnison, Miss., Oct. 10, 1930; d. John Douglas and Emmye Elizabeth (Bowe) Simmons; m. James Frederic Rose, Sept. 7, 1953; children—James Frederic, Phillip Douglas, Elizabeth Bowe. B.S., Miss. Women's U., 1952; M.S., Delta State U., 1952. Tchr. Inverness (Miss.) High Sch., 1952; elem. sch. tchr. John D. Overstreet Elem. Sch., Starkeville, Miss., 1952-53, Misawa (Japan) AFB Dependent Sch., 1954-55; nursery sch. tchr., Long Island, N.Y., 1954-55; owner Rose Designs, Dallas, 1975—. Sec. women's com. Dallas Theatre Ctr., 1965-74; bd. dirs. women's com. Dallas Civic Opera, 1978-83; mem. Opera Action, 1965-70; research com. head Noted Cookery Cookbook, Dallas Symphony Orch., 1968; chmn. charity events Investment Bankers Wives' Com., 1978; local chmn., judge Dallas County 4-H; bd. dirs. Chorus of Santa Fe, 1985; contbr. Santa Fe Opera. Home chosen for Dallas Designer's Homes Tour, 1981. Mem. Miss. Edn. Assn. Republican. Episcopalian.

ROSE, CHARLES ALEXANDER, lawyer; b. Louisville, Ky., June 14, 1932; s. Hector Edward and Mary (Shepard) R.; m. Katherine Claire Adams, Aug. 2, 1973; children—Marc, Craig, Lorna, Gordon, Alex, Sara. B.A., U. Louisville, 1954, J.D., 1960. Bar: Ky. 1960. U.S. Ct. Appeals (6th cir.) 1970, Ind. 1978, U.S. Supreme Ct. 1978. Sole practice, Louisville, Ky., 1960-63; assoc. Jones, Ewen & McKenzie, Louisville, 1963-65; ptnr. Curtis & Rose, Louisville, 1965-81, Handmaker, Weber & Rose, Louisville, 1981—. Served to lt. USAF, 1954-56. Mem. ABA, Ky. Bar Assn., Ind. Bar Assn., Louisville Bar Assn., Am. Soc. Hosp. Attys., Brandeis Soc., Fedn. Ins. Counsel. Republican. Episcopalian. Clubs: River Road Country, Pendennis (Louisville), Jefferson. Office: 2300 Citizens Plaza Louisville KY 40202

ROSE, CHARLES GRANDISON, III, congressman; b. Fayetteville, N.C., Aug. 10, 1939; s. Charles Grandison, Jr. and Anna Frances (Duckworth) R.; m. Joan Ray Teague, Sept. 25, 1982; children—Charles Gradison IV, Sara Louise. A.B., Davidson Coll., 1961; LL.B., U. N.C., 1964. Bar: N.C. bar 1964. Chief prosecutor Dist. Ct., 12th Judicial Dist., 1967-70; mem. 93d-99th congresses from 7th Dist. N.C., mem. agrl. and adminstrn. coms. Pres. N.C. Young Democrats, 1968. Presbyterian. Office: 2230 Rayburn House Office Bldg Washington DC 20515*

ROSE, CHERYL ROMPREY, counselor; b. Laconia, N.H., Nov. 15, 1949; d. Thomas Adrian Romprey and Vera Irene (Swift) Curry; m. Clinton Richard Rose, Nov. 26, 1981; children—Cydney Ryanne Rose. B.S., Plymouth State Coll., 1971; M.Ed., Wayne State U., 1976; Ph.D., Brigham Young U., 1981. Lic. profl. counselor, Ala. Treatment adminstr. Odyssey House, Salt Lake City, 1975-76; dir. counseling and guidance Jordan Sch. Dist., Copperton, Utah,

1976-81; counselor Family Counseling Ctr., Mobile, Ala., 1982—; counselor Lyons Park Evaluation and Counseling Ctr., Mobile, Ala., 1983-84; supr. practice and grad. students U. South Ala., Auburn, 1983—, instr. edn. service, 1985—. Contbr. articles to profl. jours. Trainer, instr. Contact Mobile, 1985—; presentor Barton Acad.-Mobile Sch. Dist., 1984; pres. Community Health Fairs, Mobile, 1982—; group leader Community Activities Workshop, Mobile, 1982—. Served to capt. U.S. Army, 1970-75. Decorated Army Commendation medal; Lakes Region scholar, 1967. Mem. Am. Psychol. Assn., Mobile Assn. Psychologists. Republican. Roman Catholic. Clubs: New Mobilians, St. Andrews County. Avocations: golf; creative writing; sports. Home: 105 E Claridge Rd Mobile AL 36608

ROSE, DONALD MACLEAN, marketing executive; b. New Haven, Oct. 30, 1934; s. Robert Nelson and Louise (Herman) R.; m. Gail Whitaker, July 19, 1971 (div. Jan. 1981); children—Helen, Denis, Susan Louise. Student St. Lukes Coll., 1953, Hobart Coll., 1957. Salesman, Reynolds Metal Co., N.Y.C., 1959; sales and mktg. mgr. Reynolds Extrusion, Toronto, Ont., Can., 1968-71, Iranian Aluminum, Tehran, 1971-77, Alcasa, Caracas, Venzuela, 1977-79, Reynolds Aluminum Internat., Richmond, Va., 1979—. Served with U.S. Army, 1954-56. Mem. Soc. Automotive Engrs., Archtl. Aluminum Assn. Republican. Episcopalian. Clubs: Deep Run Hunt, Snooty Fox Soc. (sec-treas. 1984—). Avocations: horses; tennis; sailing; golfing; art; hunting. Office: Reynolds Aluminum Internat 6603 W Broad St Richmond VA 23223

ROSE, ERMA L., music educator; b. LaCygne, Kans., Dec. 20, 1941; d. William Phillip and Dorothy L. (Holman) R. B.Mus. Edn., Pittsburg (Kans.) State U., 1963, M.S. in Piano, 1964; postgrad. U. So. Calif., 1965-66; Ph.D. in Mus. Edn., N. Tex. State U., 1981. Temp. instr. Pittsburg State U., 1964-65; tchr., Marion, Va., 1966-67; asst. prof. music Ferrum (Va.) Coll., 1969-71, assoc. prof., 1971-82, prof. music, 1982—; piano accompanist. Mus. dir. Showtimers, Roanoke, Va., 1982, 83. Mem. Coll. Music Soc., Golden Crest, Sigma Alpha Iota, Pi Kappa Lambda, Kappa Delta Pi. Republican. Home: PO Box 2657 Ferrum Coll Ferrum VA 24088 Office: Music Dept Ferrum Coll Ferrum VA 24088

ROSE, ERNEST WRIGHT, architect; b. Richmond, Va., Mar. 12, 1939; s. Ernest Wright and Josie (Peebles) R.; m. Diane Hickman, Sept. 7, 1959 (div. 1964); m. Connie Coffman, Apr. 17, 1971; children—David Christopher, Andrew Frederick, Jonathan Wright. B.Arch., Va. Poly Inst., 1963. Registered architect, Va., Ala., Conn., Fla., Ga., Md., Pa., N.C., S.C., Tenn., W.Va., N.Y. Designer, project mgr. Alan McCullough, Richmond, 1963-70; prin. Ernie Rose Architect, Richmond, 1970-75, pres., 1975—; dir. Dragon Chem., Roanoke, Va. Pres. Rock Creek Park Civic Assn., Richmond, 1975-78. Mem. AIA, Constrn. Specifications Inst. (pres. 1981-83). Club: Engineers (pres. 1983-84) (Richmond). Avocations: sailing; antique auto restoration; woodworking. Office: Ernie Rose Inc 4190 Innslake Dr Glen Allen VA 23060

ROSE, MICHAEL DAVID, hotel corporation executive; b. Akron, Ohio, Mar. 2, 1942; s. William H. and Annabel L. (Kennedy) R.; B.B.A., U. Cin., 1963; LL.B., Harvard U., 1966; children—Matthew Derek Franco, Gabrielle Elaine Franco, Morgan Douglas. Bar: Ohio 1966. Lectr. U. Cin., 1966-67; atty. firm Strauss, Troy & Ruehlmann, Cin., 1966-72; exec. v.p. Winegardner Internat., Cin., 1972-74; v.p. hotel group Holiday Inns, Inc., Memphis, 1974-76, pres. hotel group, 1976-78, corp. exec. v.p., 1978-79, pres., 1979-84, chief exec. officer, 1981—, chmn., 1984—; dir. First Tenn. Nat. Corp., Po Folks Inc., Gen. Mills, Inc. Bd. dirs. Memphis Arts Council, 1979—, Lausanne Sch., 1978—; mem. Future Memphis, 1979—; mem. nat. adv. com. U. Cin., 1979—. Mem. Ohio Bar Assn., Young Pres.'s Orgn., Conf. Bd. Club: Econ. of Memphis. Office: Holiday Corp 1023 Cherry Rd Memphis TN 38117

ROSE, NORMAN, lawyer; b. N.Y.C., July 7, 1923; s. Edward J. and Frances (Ludwig) R.; div.; children—Ellen Rose Scharf, Michael. B.B.A., CCNY, 1947; J.D., N.Y. Law Sch. 1953. Bar: Fla. 1979, N.Y. 1954, U.S. Dist. Ct. (ea. dist.) N.Y. 1956, U.S. Dist. Ct. (so. dist.) N.Y. 1960, U.S. Dist. Ct. (so. dist.) Fla. 1981, U.S. Ct. Appeals (2d cir.) 1967, U.S. Tax Ct. 1956, U.S. Supreme Ct. 1961. Sole practice, N.Y.C., 1954-69, Garden City, N.Y., 1969-79, Ft. Lauderdale, Fla., 1979—; assoc. Dean, Falanga & Rose, Carle Place, N.Y., 1979—; referee Small Claims Ct., N.Y.C., 1959-69; arbitrator Accident Claims Tribunal, Am. Arbitration Assn., 1960-65; C.P.A., N.Y.C., 1951-57; lectr. in field. Author law note Liability of Golfer to Person Struck by Ball, 1959 (Hon. mention 1960). Pres. Nassau S. Shore Little League, Lawrence, N.Y., 1966-68; treas. 5 Towns Democratic Club, Woodmere, N.Y., 1966-67; chmn. United Fund, Village of Lawrence, 1967. Served to cpt. USAF, 1943-45, ETO. Decorated Disting. Flying Cross (ETO), Air medal, Silver star, Purple Heart. Mem. Assn. Trial Lawyers Am. (sustaining), Acad. Fla. Trial Lawyers (sustaining), Assn. N.Y. State Trial Lawyers, N.Y. State Bar Assn., Fla. Bar Assn., Nassau County Bar Assn., Lawyer/Pilots Bar Assn. Democrat. Jewish. Club: Lawrence Country (bd. govs. 1966-68); Old Westbury Country (bd. govs. 1975). Lodges: Masons, Shriners. Home: 3200 Port Royale Dr N Fort Lauderdale FL 33308 Office: 1995 E Oakland Blvd Fort Lauderdale FL 33306

ROSE, SCOTT, educational administrator. Supt. of schs., Clearwater, Fla. Office: PO Box 4688 Clearwater FL 33518*

ROSE, STEPHEN ELLIS, developmwnt administrator; b. Bklyn, Dec. 27, 1939; s. Benjamin and Edna H. R.; m. Ellen Schwartz, Dec. 24, 1977; children—Brian, David, Mark, Patti. B.S. in Bus. Adminstrn., Fin., Boston U., 1957-61; M.B.A. in fin. investments, CCNY, 1968. Br. mgr. Bache & Co., N.Y.C., Dallas, 1961-72; regional dir. B'nai B'rith Found., Southwest, Dallas, 1973-74; dir. Found. Jewish Philanthropies, Miami, Fla., 1975-81; dir. devel. Miami Jewish Home and Hosp. for Aged, Miami, 1982—. Bd. dirs. Temple Solel. Served to sgt. USAR, 1961-68. Mem. Jewish Communal Workers South Fla., Nat. Soc. Fund Raising Execs., Nat. Assn. Hosp. Devel. Jewish. Lodge: B'nai B'rith. Home: 4866 Sheridan St Hollywood FL 33021 Office: 151 N E 52 St Miami FL 33137

ROSE, VERNON EUGENE, public health educator, researcher; b. Chgo., Mar. 24, 1940; s. John Vernon and Marjorie Pearl (Kennedy) R.; m. Nancy Ann Abig, Dec. 8, 1971. B.S. in Civil Engring., Ill. Inst. Tech., 1961; M.S. in Civil Engring., Ga. Inst. Tech., 1962; D.P.H., U. Tex.-Houston, 1977. Registered profl. engr., Calif. Indsl. hygienist USPHS, Rockville, Md., 1967-78; prof. pub. health U. Ala., Birmingham, 1978—; cons. Profl. Examination Service, N.Y.C., 1979-84; dir. Am. Bd. Indsl. Hygiene, Lansing, Mich., 1983-89. Contbr. articles to profl. jours. Served to capt. USAF, 1962-67. Recipient Outstanding Achievement award USPHS, 1977. Mem. Am. Indsl. Hygiene Assn., Am. Soc. Safety Engrs. Home: 3317 Castle Crest Dr Birmingham AL 35216 Office: U Ala Sch Pub Health Birmingham AL 35294

ROSEBERRY, MARGARET BRELAND, nursing adminstrator; b. Marianna, Fla., Feb. 28, 1955; d. Jabe Armistead and Betty (Baker) Breland; m. Robert Clarence Roseberry, July 16, 1977; children—Robert Breland, Margaret Amanda. B.S. in Nursing, U. Ala.-Birmingham, 1977. Staff nurse CCU, U. Ala., Birmingham, 1977-79, research coordinator, 1979-81, staff nurse CCU, 1981; dir. nursing Hale County Hosp., Greensboro, Ala., 1982—. Pres. Hale County unit Am. Heart Assn., Greensboro, 1982—. Mem. Ala. Soc. Nursing Service Adminstrs., West Ala. Council Nursing Service Adminstrs., DAR. Home: 701 1st St Greensboro AL 36744 Office: Hale County Hosp 1st and Greene Sts Greensboro AL 36744

ROSELLO, NARCISO VINCENT, business executive; b. Havana, Cuba, July 1, 1913; s. Vincent N. and Angela Rosello; m. Minerva Martha, Dec. 29, 1944; children—George, Vivian; came to U.S. Dec. 30, 1959. C.P.A., Havana Sch. Commerce, 1934; D. Econs., Havana U., 1944. Pres., Rosello Trading Co., Havana, 1944-59; chmn. New Telephone Co., Havana, 1950-59; chmn. Newtel Inc., Miami, Fla., 1960—; pres. Intercontinental Airways Cuba, 1948-59; comml. pilot. Life mem. Republican party; sr. adviser U.S. Congl. Adv. Bd. Recipient honor awards Cuban Red Cross, 1949, Spanish Red Cross, 1950, Silver Cross, Mexican Red Cross, 1951. Episcopalian. Club: Lions (Cuba). Address: 10381 SW 64th St Miami FL 33173

ROSEN, BENSON, business administration educator; b. Detroit, Oct. 9, 1942; s. David and Laura R.; m. Brenda M. Liebroder, Dec. 17, 1966; children—Gregory Scott, David Loren. B.S., Wayne State U., 1964, M.A., 1968, Ph.D., 1969. Asst. prof. U. N.C., 1969-74, assoc. prof., 1974-80, prof. bus. adminstrn., 1980—; vis. prof. U. Minn., 1981; cons. to bus., industry, govt. Recipient Young Scholars award Spencer Found., 1976, 78; NSF grantee, 1973-75; Adminstrn. on Aging grantee, 1978-80. Mem. Am. Psychol. Assn., Acad. Mgmt. Author: Becoming Aware, 1976; Older Employees: New Roles for Valued Resources, 1984; contbr. numerous articles to profl. jours.; mem. editorial rev. bd. Acad. Mgmt. Jour., 1978-85. Office: Grad Sch Bus Adminstrn U NC Chapel Hill NC 27514

ROSEN, CATHERINE ELKIN, psychologist; b. Chgo., Oct. 31, 1927; d. Francis William and Catherine Thresa (Lavin) Elkin; m. Sidney Rosen, Apr. 29, 1951; children—Mark Eben, Daniel Kurt, Steven Craig, Amy Susan. B.Ed., Chgo. State Coll., 1949; M.A., U. Mich., 1953; Ph.D., U. Ga., 1971. Lic. applied psychologist, Ga., Wis. Child clin. psychologist Easter Seal Child Devel. Ctr., Milw., 1966-68, U. Ga., 1968-72; dir. research and evaluation Northeast Ga. Community Mental Health Ctr., Athens, 1972-79; sr. clin. psychologist Central State Hosp., Milledgeville, Ga., 1980—; adj. prof. U. Ga.; expert witness; mem. Ga. Task Force on Privacy and Confidentiality in Mental Health. Adminstrn. on Aging grantee, 1977-79. Mem. Gerontol. Soc., Am. Psychol. Assn., So. Regional Conf. Mental Health Stats. Contbr. articles to sci. jours., chpts. in books. Home: 198 Sunnybrook Dr Athens GA 30605 Office: Central State Hosp Box 325 Milledgeville GA 31061

ROSEN, DANIEL BERNARD, social services executive; b. Worcester, Mass., May 7, 1950; s. Harry Joseph and Estelle Rose (Goldin) R.; B.S., Cornell U., 1972; postgrad. Columbia U., 1972-73; M.S., Fordham U., 1976, Ph.D., 1985; m. Susan Carol Poetter, June 4, 1972; children—Michael, Jonathan. Dir. spl. services programs Ednl. Alliance, Inc., N.Y.C., 1973-75; adj. faculty Coll. S.I., CUNY, 1978; exec. dir. Working Orgn. for Retarded Children, Inc., Flushing, N.Y., 1975-80, Bost Human Devel. Services, Inc., Ft. Smith, Ark., 1980—; cons. in field; mem. children's services com. N.Y.C. Mental Health, Retardation and Alcoholism Services, 1974; mem. Queens Mental Retardation and Devel. Disabilities Council, 1975-80, vice-chmn., 1979-80; mem. Queens Boro Devel. Services Office, 1978-80, chmn. children's services com., 1978-80; mem. Bklyn. Mental Retardation and Devel. Disabilities Council, 1976-80, Bronx Mental Retardation and Devel. Disabilities Council, 1976-80. Recipient individual achievement award Nat. Soc. for Children and Adults with Autism, 1983. NIMH grantee, 1972-73. Mem. Autism Soc. Ark. (bd. dirs. 1981—), Human Service Providers Assn. Ark., Am. Assn. Mental Deficiency (vice chmn. adminstrn. region V 1982-83, mem. nat. research adv. com. 1983—, pres. Ark. chpt. 1985, spl. award for significant contbn. to devel. disabled Ark. chpt. 1983), Community Providers Assn. for Devel. Disabled (regional coordinator 1983-84). Contbr. articles to profl. jours. Home Address: 4015 Free Ferry Rd Fort Smith AR 72903 Office: Bost Human Devel Services 1801 S 74th St Fort Smith AR 72903

ROSEN, EDWARD, retired commodity house executive; b. New Orleans, July 10, 1928; s. Louis Leucht and Nita Mildred (Silverstein) R.; m. Carol Elizabeth Heinberg, Sept. 30, 1950; children—Catherine Elizabeth Rosen Hinnant, Geri Anne Rosen Rubin. B.S., Tulane U., 1950. Salesman Leon Israel Bros., New Orleans, 1950-61, v.p., N.Y.C., 1961-70; exec. v.p. Coffee div. ACLI Internat., N.Y.C., 1970-79, pres., 1979-84, ret.; bd. mgrs. N.Y. Coffee, Cocoa, Sugar Exchange, 1982-84; former advisor for coffee to U.S. Trade Rep., Washington. Bd. govs. Tulane U. Hosp. and Clinic, New Orleans, 1985—. Served to lt. U.S. Army, 1951-52, Korea. Mem. Republican. Jewish. Club: Lakewood Country. Avocations: golf; swimming; fishing. Home: 837 Nashville Ave New Orleans LA 70115

ROSEN, ROBERT JAMES, ophthalmologist; b. Newark, Aug. 13, 1942; s. Emanuel P Peter and Pearl Pauline (Pollack) R.; m. Jane Ruth Jacobs Sept. 17, 1967; children—Andrew Todd, Brooke Danielle. B.A., Brown U., 1964; M.D., Chgo. Med. Health Scis. Coll., 1968. Intern Bellevue Med. Ctr., N.Y.C., 1968-69; resident Albert Einstein Coll. Medicine, N.Y.C., 1969-72; staff U. N.Mex. Med. Ctr., Albuquerque, 1972-74, Tex. Tech U. Med. Ctr., Lubbock, 1974—; chief ophthalmologist Thomason Gen. Hosp., El Paso, Tex., 1977—, Sierra Med. Ctr., El Paso, 1980-82. Bd. dirs. El Paso Aqua Posse, 1980-82, United Way, 1982—, Sunturians, 1983—; mem. El Paso Mus. Collectors Council; sec., bd. dirs. Mt. Sinai Temple; pres. Hospice of El Paso, 1984-85. Served to maj. U.S. Army, 1972-74. Fellow Am. Acad. Ophthalmologists; mem. AMA, Tex. Med. Assn., West Tex. Ophthalmologists Soc. (pres. 1978-80). Democrat. Jewish. Home: 921 Cherry Hill Ln El Paso TX 79912 Office: 10400 Vista Del Sol El Paso TX 79925

ROSEN, ROBERT STEWART, neuropsychologist, school psychologist; b. Phila., Jan. 20, 1953; s. Albert and Mollie (Kramer) R.; m. Deborah Ann Goldstein, Dec. 27, 1975. Student Penn. State U., 1970-73; B.A., Temple U., 1974, Ed.M., 1976; Ph.D., U. Ga., 1982. Lic. sch. psychologist, Fla. Sch. psychologist Maurice River Schs., Port Elizabeth, N.J., 1976-78, Upper Township Schs., Tuckahoe, N.J., 1978-79, Hillsborough County Schs., Tampa, Fla., 1982-84; neuropsychologist Tampa Gen. Rehab. Ctr., Tampa, 1984—. Mem. Am. Psychol. Assn., Nat. Assn. Sch. Psychologist, Fla. Assn. Sch. Psychologist, Nat. Acad. Neuropsychologist, Internat. Neuropsychological Soc., Phi Kappa Phi. Home: 5502 Carrollwood Meadows Dr Tampa FL 33625 Office: Tampa Gen Rehab Ctr Davis Island Tampa FL 33606

ROSENBAUM, MICHAEL S., clinical psychologist; b. N.Y.C., Apr. 15, 1951; s. Sidney and Estelle (Krantman) R.; m. Susan Lehrer, June 23, 1973; children—Lisa Beth, Jeffrey David. B.A. in Psychology U. Rochester, 1973; M.A., Inst. Behavior Research, 1974; Ph.D. in Clin. Psychology, Ga. State U., 1979. Lic. psychologist, Ala. Psychology resident U. Miss. Med. Ctr., Jackson, 1977-78, research assoc., 1978-79; asst. prof. pediatrics U. So. Ala., Mobile, 1979-83; psychologist West Mobile Psychology Ctr., 1983—; dir. TERRAP, Mobile, 1983—; state coordinator Phobia Soc. Am., Mobile, 1985—. Contbr. articles to profl. jours. Mem. com. Assn. for Adults and Children with Learning Disabilities. Recipient Intramural Research award U. So. Ala., 1980. Mem. Am. Psychol. Assn., Assn. Advancement Behavior Therapy, Phobia Soc. Am., Ala. Psychol. Assn. Avocations: jogging, weight lifting, softball, tennis. Home: 5756 Vendome Dr N Mobile AL 36609 Office: West Mobile Psychology Ctr 4325 Midmost Dr Suite B Mobile AL 36609

ROSENBAUM, ROY ISRAEL, association executive; b. Chgo., Jan. 30, 1947; s. Irving J. and Ruth (Groner) R.; m. Judith M. Mann, July 7, 1968; children—Rebecca, David, Morton. B.A., U. Chgo., 1968, M.A., 1972; Rabbi, Hebrew Theol. Coll., 1971. Community relations assoc. Jewish Community Fedn. Cleve., 1973-76, asst. dir. community relations, 1976-77, dir. community relations, 1977-80, dir. spl. projects, 1980-81; exec. dir. Jewish Community Fedn. Richmond (Va.), 1982—. U. Chgo. rep. Conf. U.S. Affairs, U.S. Mil. Acad., 1967. Ford Found. fellow, 1969-72. Mem. Assn. Jewish Community Orgn. Personnel. Author, producer, dir. multi-media presentations Jews in Arab Lands, We Are All Zionists, 1975; Prisoners of Conscience, 1976; contbr. to newspapers and mags. Home: 118 Seneca Rd Richmond VA 23226 Office: 5403 Monument Ave Richmond VA 23226

ROSENBAUM, WALTER ANTHONY, political science educator, consultant, researcher; b. Pitts., Oct. 20, 1937; s. Walter and Julia Margarite (Luther) R.; m. Jean Annette Camfield, July 9, 1960; children—Brian Anthony, Douglas Michael. B.A. magna cum laude, U. Redlands, 1959; M.A., Princeton U., 1962, Ph.D., 1964. Asst. prof. polit. sci. U. Fla., Gainesville, 1962-68, assoc. prof., 1969-74, prof., 1975—; policy analyst U.S. EPA, Washington, 1974-75. Author: Energy Policy, 1979; Environmental Politics and Policy, 1985, others. Contbr. articles to profl. jours. Nat. Assn. Schs. Pub. Adminstrn. fellow, 1974; Woodrow Wilson fellow, 1978. Democrat. Presbyterian. Avocation: cert. ofcl. swimming. Home: 2629 NW 10th Ave Gainesville FL 32611 Office: Dept Polit Sci U Fla Gainesville FL 32611

ROSENBERG, JAN GREGG, safety consultant, safety engineer; b. Bethpage, N.Y., Jan. 28, 1958; s. Nathan and Dorothy Beatrice (Arie) R. B.S. in Bus. Adminstrn., U. Ariz., 1979, M.S. in Safety Mgmt., 1980. Assoc. safety profl; assoc. in Risk Mgmt. Circulation mgr. Newsday, Inc., Melville, N.Y., 1977-78; risk mgmt. services rep. St. Paul Ins. Cos., Lubbock, Tex., 1980-85; sr. loss control rep. CIGNA Ins. Co., Irving, Tex., 1985—. Scholar John R. Stilb, C.L.U. & Assocs., 1978, So. Ariz. Assn. Life Underwriters, 1978, Ariz. Ctr. for Occupational Safety and Health, 1979. Mem. Am. Soc. Safety Engrs., Nat. Safety Mgmt. Soc. Republican. Jewish. Avocations: competitive sports; music; science fiction; travel. Home: 4047 N Beltline Rd Irving TX 75062 Office: 600 Las Colinas Blvd Irving TX 75039

ROSENBERG, JEROME, psychology educator; b. Bklyn., May 28, 1940; s. Barney and Ruth R.; divorced; children—Stephen G., Robert E., Tony M. A.B., U. Miami, 1962; M.S., Fla. State U., 1965, Ph.D., 1968. In-service tng. coordinator, asst. supt. programs-services Sunland Hosp., Tallahassee, 1967; instr. dept. psychology Counseling Ctr., Fla. State U., 1968-69; asst. prof. dept. psychology U. Ala., 1969-70, assoc. prof. dept. psychology, also The New Coll., 1971—; cons., lectr. Bd. dirs. Tuscaloosa Assn. Retarded Citizens Crisis Ctr. Mem. Southeastern Psychol. Assn. Jewish. Co-author (with W. H. Rivenbark): Human Behavior II: Man in Society, 1973, 2d edit., 1974, Issues in Human Behavior, 1974; co-author: Issues in Human Adjustment, 1980; contbr. chpts. to books; contbr. articles to profl. jours. Home: 1602 Briarcliff Northport AL 35476 Office: Box CD also Box 2968 U Ala University AL 35486

ROSENBERG, MARSHAL E., financial consultant, banker; b. Miami, Dec. 11, 1936; s. Morris and Myra R.; m. Patricia Eileen Rosenberg, May 14, 1982; children by previous marriage—Lynne, Daniel H. B.B.A., U. Miami, 1959, M.B.A., 1982; Ph.D., Calif. Western U., 1982. Pres., Marshal E. Rosenberg Orgn., Inc.; hon. pres. Mfrs. Life Ins. Co. Prodn. Club, Toronto; mem. faculty U. Miami Sch. Bus.; dir. Pan Am. Bank N.A., also chmn. trust com. Life trustee, founder Mt. Sinai Med. Ctr., also sec. bd.; trustee Miami Heart Inst.; bd. dirs. Am. Cancer Soc., Dade County Unit; chmn. coaches com. U. Miami Baseball Program. Mem. Assn. Advanced Life Underwriters, Top of the Table Million Dollar Round Table, Am. Club: Ocean Reef (Key Largo, Fla.). Home: 10205 SW 68th Ct Miami FL 33156 Office: 1500 Monza Ave Suite 202 Coral Gables FL 33146

ROSENBERG, PETER DAVID, lawyer, patent examiner, educator; b. N.Y.C., Aug. 2, 1942; s. Frederick and Martha (Grossman) R. B.A., NYU, 1962, B. Chem. Engring., 1963; J.D., N.Y. Law Sch., 1968; LL.M., George Washington U., 1971. Bar: N.Y. 1970, U.S. Ct. Appeals (2d cir.) 1970, U.S. Dist. Ct. (so. and ea. dists.) N.Y. 1971, U.S. Supreme Ct. 1973, U.S. Dist. Ct. (no. and we. dists.) N.Y. 1979, U.S. Ct. Appeals D.C. 1982, U.S. Ct. Internat. Trade 1982, U.S. Ct. Mil. Appeals 1982. Examiner U.S. Patent and Trademark Office, Washington, 1968—; assoc. professorial lectr. George Washington U.; Recipient Silver Medal award U.S. Dept. Commerce, 1981. Mem. Am. Intellectual Property Law Assn., ABA (antitrust sect.). Republican. Author: Patent Law Fundamentals, 1975, 2d edit. 1980; assoc. editor Jour. Patent and Trademark Office Soc.; contbr. articles to profl. jours. Home: 1400 S Joyce St Arlington VA 22202

ROSENBERGER, FRANCIS COLEMAN, lawyer, writer, editor; b. Manassas, Va., Mar. 22, 1915; s. George L. and Olive D. (Robertson) R.; m. Astra Lazdins, Dec. 12, 1966. Student U. Va., 1932-36, 37-40; J.D., George Washington U., 1942. Bar: Va. 1939, U.S. Supreme Ct. 1949. Counsel U.S. Senate and Ho. of Reps. com. staffs, 1942-54; counsel U.S. Senate Com. on Judiciary, 1955-75; chief counsel and staff dir. U.S. Senate Com. on Judiciary, 1976-78; guest scholar Brookings Instn., Washington, 1979-80; Washington rep. Nat. Conf. of Bankruptcy Judges, 1981-85. Author: (poetry) One Season Here, 1976; An Alphabet, 1978; The Visit, 1984; Pattern and Variation, 1986. Editor: Virginia Reader, 1948; Jefferson Reader, 1953; Washington and the Poet, 1977, Records of Columbia Hist. Soc. Washington, D.C., 8 vols.; mem. editorial bd. Fed. Bar Jour., 1957-63. Contbr. poetry to anthologies, articles to mags. and newspapers. Mem. Fed. Bar Assn. (pres. Capitol Hill chpt. 1965-66). Democrat. Presbyterian. Clubs: Cosmos (Washington); Writers (Richmond, Va.). Home: 6809 Melrose Dr McLean VA 22101

ROSENBERG-FOWLER, DEBRA, high technology/communications company sales executive; b. Tallahassee, Fla., Jan. 16, 1950; d. Charles Herbert and Charlotte Rosenberg; m. Walter Guy Fowler, Sept. 20, 1983. A.S., Endicott Coll., Beverly, Mass., 1971; B.B.A. in Mktg., Ga. State U., 1974. Asst. buyer, jr. exec. Davison's, Atlanta, 1974-75, dept. mgr., 1975, divisional mdse. mgr., 1975-76; area sales rep. Xerox Corp., Atlanta, 1977-78, geog. sales rep., 1978-80, maj. account rep., 1980-82, nat. account mgr., 1982-84, account mgr., 1984—. Supporter Egleston Children's Hosp., Atlanta, 1981-83; sponsor Atlanta Ballet, 1983; patron sponsor High Mus. Art. Named Number One Mktg. Rep., Xerox Atlanta, 1981. Democrat. Jewish. Club: Southeastern Chinese Sharpei (treas. 1981—) (Atlanta). Home: 4075 Northside Dr Atlanta GA 30342

ROSENBLATT, CY HART, health care management consultant, state senator; b. Jackson, Miss., Apr. 5, 1954; s. William Harold and Margaret (Dreyfus) R.; m. Judy Clinton, Dec. 1, 1979; 1 child, Sara Hart. B.A. in Polit. Sci., So. Methodist U., 1976; M.A. in Pub. Adminstrn., U. Va., 1981. Health planner Jackson Dept. Health, Miss., 1977-78, dir. planning, 1979; adminstrv. asst. to gov. of Miss., Jackson, 1979-80; mgmt. cons., Jackson, 1981—; mem. Miss. Senate, since 1984—. Mem. Jackson Diabetes Coordinating Council, 1984-85; bd. govs. Jackson Symphony Orch., 1985-87; bd. dirs. Jackson chpt. Miss. Kidney Found., 1985—. Democrat. Methodist. Lodge: Rotary. Office: Office of State Senate Jackson MS 39205

ROSENBLUM, MARTIN JEROME, eye surgeon; b. N.Y.C., Apr. 7, 1948; s. Phillip and Rita (Steppel) R.; m. Zina Zarin, May 31, 1975; children—Steven David, Richard James. B.S., Bklyn. Coll., 1968; M.D., U. Ariz., 1973. Diplomate Am. Bd. Ophthalmology. Intern Cornell U., N.Y.C., 1974-75; resident N.Y. Med. Coll., 1975-78, instr., 1978-79; resident Columbia U., 1977; practice medicine specializing in eye surgery, St. Petersburg, Fla., 1979—. Fellow Am. Acad. Ophthalmology, ACS, Am. Intraocular Implant Soc.; mem. AMA, Fla. Med. Assn. Republican. Jewish. Club: Seminole Lake Country. Avocation: tennis. Home: 9035 Baywood Park Dr Seminole FL 33543 Office: 3637 4th St N Fla Fed Bldg 290 Saint Petersburg FL 33704

ROSENBLUTH, MORTON, periodontist, educator; b. N.Y.C., Sept. 28, 1924; s. Jacob and Eva (Bigeleissen) R.; B.A., N.Y.U., 1943, grad. program in periodontia, oral medicine, D.D.S., 1946; m. Sylvia Fradin, July 2, 1946; children—Cheryl Bonnie, Hal Glen. Intern, Bellevue Hosp. N.Y.C., 1946-47, resident, 1947; individual practice dentistry, N.Y.C., 1947-59; individual practice periodontia, North Miami Beach, Fla., 1960—; periodontist Mt. Sinai Hosp., N.Y., Polyclinic Hosp. and Med. Sch. N.Y., Mt. Sinai Hosp., Miami Beach, Fla., Parkway Gen. Hosp.; chief dental dept. North Miami Gen. Hosp.; chmn. periodontia sect. Dade County Research Ctr.; clin. assoc. prof. div. oral and maxillofacial surgery U. Miami Sch. Medicine; assoc. clin. prof. Southeastern Osteo. Coll. Medicine; lectr. throughout U.S.A., Israel, Mexico, Rome, Teheran, Bangkok, Hong Kong, Tokyo, Honolulu, Jamaica, Paris, London, Sicily, Budapest, Berlin, Luxembourg, South Africa, and others; vis. lectr. U. Tenn. Dental Coll., N.Y.U. Dental Coll.; cons. VA Hosp., Miami. Mem. adv. bd. U. Fla. Coll. Dentistry; mem. profl. adv. bd. North Dade Children's Center, Hope Sch. Mentally Retarded Children; mem. sci. adv. com. United Health Found. Chmn. Dental div. United Fund of Dade County, Combined Jewish Appeal; nat. chmn. Hebrew U. Sch. Dental Medicine; bd. dirs. Health Planning Council S. Fla. Served with AUS, 1943-44, as capt. USAF, 1951-52. Recipient Maimonides award State of Israel, 1979; diplomate Am. Bd. Periodontology. Fellow Am. Coll. Dentists, Internat. Coll. Dentists; mem. Am. Acad. Periodontology, Am., Fla. socs. periodontists, Am. Assn. Hosp. Dental Chiefs, Am. Acad. Dental Medicine, Am. Soc. Advancement Gen. Anesthesia in Dentistry, ADA, Northeastern Soc. Periodontists, Fla. (chmn. council on legislation), Miami, Miami Beach, East Coast (sec.-treas. 1968, pres. 1971-72), North Dade (pres. 1963-64) dental socs., Fedn. Dentaire Internationale, Fla. Acad. Dental Practice Adminstrn., Alpha Omega (pres. 1967-68, internat. regent 1973-75, internat. editor 1975-77, internat. pres.-elect 1977-78, internat. pres. 1979, vice chmn. Alpha Omega Found.) Am. Dental Interfrat. Council (pres. 1981-82). Jewish (trustee congregation 1961-64). Clubs: Nocoma (pres. 1958-60), N.Y.U. Century (local chmn.), KP, Masons, Kiwanis (dir. 1965). Contbr. articles to profl. jours. Home: 11111 Biscayne Blvd Apt 857 North Miami FL 33161 Office: Profl Center 1100 NE 163d St North Miami Beach FL 33162

ROSENE, LINDA ROBERTS, organizational consultant, researcher; b. Miami, Fla., Nov. 1, 1938; d. Wilbur David and Dorothy Claire (Baker) Roberts; m. Ralph W. Rosene, Aug. 3, 1957; children—Leigh, Russ, Tim. M.A., Fielding Coll., 1981, Ph.D. in Clin. Psychology, 1983. Counselor Rapid City Regional Hosp., S.D., 1978-81, Lutheran Social Services, Rapid City, 1978-83; v.p. Target Systems Inc., Dallas, 1983-85, cons., 1985—; cons. S.W. Home Furnishing Assn., Dallas, 1984, Northwestern Bell, Omaha, 1985; presenter, developer seminars. Bd. mem. Assn. Children with Learning Disabilities, S.D., 1983-84, West River Alcoholism Services, S.D., 1983-84, Health Adv. of Head Start, S.D., 1980-84, St. Martins Acad., S.D., 1971-75; mem. Rapid City Mayor's Commn. on Racial Conciliation, 1971-73. Research grantee Nat. Lutheran Ch., 1981. Mem. Am. Psychol. Assn., Am. Soc. Tng. and Devel., S.W. Home Furnishing Assn. Unitarian. Avocations: bicycling; racquetball; music; birdwatching. Home: 300 Shinoak Valley Irving TX 75063

ROSENFELD, GARY MARTIN, psychotherapist; b. N.Y.C., Nov. 30, 1938; s. David L. and Sadie (Schwebel) R.; m. Marcia R. Elkin, Dec. 17, 1960 (div. 1978); children—Robyn J., Alan J.; m. Marcia L. Girolomoni, May 24, 1980. B.S., Columbia U., 1961; M.S. in Psychology, Nova U., 1978. Lic. mental health counselor; lic. marriage and family therapist. Sales rep. Eli Lilly & Co., Indpls., 1970-76; dir. Hollywood Counseling Ctr., Pembroke Pines, Fla., 1976—; adj. prof. behavioral scis. Nova U., 1984—. Bd. dirs. Coalition of Psychol. Services Profls., Orlando, Fla., 1984—. Mem. Nat. Mental Health Counselors Assn., Nat. Acad. Cert. Clin. Mental Health Counselors, Fla. Mental Health Profls. Assn. (pres. 1985-86), Fla. Mental Health Counselors Assn. Avocations: raising orchids; photography; woodworking. Office: Hollywood Counseling Ctr 2225 N University Dr Pembroke Pines FL 33024

ROSENFELD, IRENE KANTOR, editorial linguist; b. Boston, Aug. 8, 1919; d. Samuel and Alice (Katz) Kantor; m. Leonard S. Rosenfeld, June 7, 1942; 1 dau., Lynn. B.A., NYU, 1940, postgrad., 1940-42; M. Ed., Harvard U., 1956. Lic. tchr. Mass., Mich., N.Y. Performing pianist, singer, classical guitarist, 1940-55; elem., high sch., grad. sch. tchr., 1955-66; registrar, dir. admissions and student fins. Beth Israel Med. Ctr. Sch. Nursing, N.Y.C., 1966-70; asst. dir. dept. community medicine Hosp. for Joint Diseases and Med. Ctr., N.Y.C., 1971-73; asst. to gen. dir. N.C. Meml. Hosp., Chapel Hill, 1973, cons. ambulatory services, 1974-76; editor Internat. Fertility Research Program, Research Triangle, N.C., 1976-81; freelance multilingual editor, Chapel Hill, 1981—. Founding mem., mem. 1st bd. dirs. Am. Hosp. Assn. Soc. Patient Reps., 1st chmn. conf. and edn. com. Mem. Pi Lambda Theta, Mu Sigma. Author manuals, monographs and articles for profl. publs. Address: 1309 Arboretum Dr Chapel Hill NC 27514

ROSENFELD, RACHEL ANN, sociologist, educator; b. Balt., Nov. 15, 1948; d. Jerome and Ethel Marie (Hanners) R. B.A., Carleton Coll., 1970; M.S., U. Wis.-Madison, 1974, Ph.D., 1976. Planning aide Iowa State Hwy. Commn., Ames, 1970-72; asst. prof. McGill U., Montreal, Que., Can., 1976-80; sr. study dir. Nat. Opinion Research Ctr., U. Chgo., 1978-81; asst. prof., then assoc. prof. sociology U. N.C., Chapel Hill, 1981—. Author: Farm Women: Work, Farm and Family in U.S., 1985. Contbr. articles to profl. jours. Fellow Carolina Population Ctr.; mem. Am. Sociol. Assn. (mem. com. nat. stats.), So. Sociol. Soc. (publs. com.), Population Assn. Am., Internat. Soc. Assn. Mem. Soc. Friends. Home: 123 Robin Rd Chapel Hill NC 27514 Office: Dept Sociology U NC Chapel Hill NC 27514

ROSEN-GRANDON, JANE RAY, marriage and family therapist; b. Miami Beach, Fla., Aug. 8, 1953; d. Jerald I. and Vivian J. (Rosenthal) Rosen; m. Gary M. Grandon, June 2, 1974; children—Jessica, Benjamin. B.A., U. Fla., 1973; M.A., U. Conn., 1977. Lic. therapist, Fla. Dir. human services Town of Tolland, Conn., 1977-80; therapist Rosen Grandon Assocs., Tolland, 1980-81, Discovery Inst., Tampa, Fla., 1981-85; marriage and family therapist Rosen Grandon Assocs., Greensboro, N.C., 1985—. Fellow Internat. Council Sex Edn. and Parenthood of Am. U.; mem. Am. Assn. Marriage and Family Therapy, Tampa Bay Area Assn. Marriage and Family Therapy (treas. 1985), Nat. Council Family Relations, Am. Assn. Counseling and Devel. Home: 3106 Edgewater Dr Greensboro NC 27403

ROSENKOETTER, MARLENE M., nursing education administrator, consultant; b. St. Louis, Feb. 26, 1943; d. Ernest Ralph and Katherine Elizabeth (Ahrens) Merifield; m. John Louis Rosenkoetter, June 4, 1967. Diploma in Nursing, Barnes Hosp., St. Louis, 1964; B.A., U. Mo.-St. Louis, 1970, M.Ed., 1972; Ph.D., St. Louis U., 1979; M.S. in Nursing, East Carolina U., 1983. R.N. Asst. prof. Maryville Coll., St. Louis, 1970-74; cons. Gordan Friesen, Inc., Washington, 1974-75; chmn. div. health sci., chmn. dept. nursing West Piedmont Community Coll., Morganton, N.C., 1975-81; dean sch. nursing U. N.C., Wilmington, 1984—; pvt. practice cons., 1975—. Contbr. articles to profl. publs. Mem. Nat. League for Nursing (vice chmn. So. Regional Assembly 1985—), N.C. League for Nursing (pres. 1982-84; citation 1984), Am. Nurses Assn., N.C. Nurses Assn., Delta Soc., Sigma Theta Tau, Phi Delta Kappa, Pi Lambda Theta. Avocations: Music; photography. Office: U NC at Wilmington 601 S College Rd Wilmington NC 28403-3297

ROSENN, KEITH SAMUEL, legal educator, consultant, lawyer; b. Wilkes-Barre, Pa., Dec. 9, 1938; s. Max and Tillie Rose (Hershkowitz) R.; m. Nan Raker, June 19, 1960 (div. 1965); 1 dau., Eva; m. 2d, Silvia Cordeiro Rudge, Mar. 21, 1968; children—Jonathan, Marcia. B.A., Amherst Coll., 1960; LL.B., Yale U., 1963. Bar: Pa. 1964, Fla. 1981. Law clk. to Judge Smith, U.S. Ct. Appeals 2d circuit, 1963-64; assoc. firm Rosenn, Jenkins & Greenwald, Wilkes-Barre, 1964-65; asst. prof. Law Sch., Ohio State U., Columbus, 1965-66, assoc. prof., 1968-70, prof., 1970-79; prof. law U. Miami (Fla.) Sch. Law, 1979—, assoc. dean, 1982-83; cons. Ford Found., Rio de Janeiro, 1966-67, Dept. State, 1981-82, Hudson Inst., 1979, Escritorio Augusto Nobre, Rio de Janeiro, 1980-81; vis. lectr. Nat. Law Sch. of Paraguay, 1970; vis. prof. program in Guadalajara, U. San Diego, 1983; vis. prof. in Mexico City, U. San Diego, 1985; vis. prof. Stanford Chilean Law Program, 1968, U. Francisco Marroquin, Guatemala, 1983. Social Sci. Research Council grantee, 1970; Dana Found. grantee, 1982. Mem. ABA, Inter-Am. Bar Assn., Fla. Bar Assn., Am. Soc. for Comparative Study of Law, Am. Law Inst., Brazilian-Am. C. of C. (sec. 1982-83). Jewish. Author: Law and Inflation, 1982; (with K. Karst) Law and Development in Latin America, 1975; mem. bd. editors Am. Jour. Comparative Law; contbr. articles to scholarly jours. Home: 7700 SW 146th Terr Miami FL 33158 Office: Univ Miami Law Sch PO Box 248087 Coral Gables FL 33124

ROSENQUIST, DAVID ALEX, hospital administrator; b. Princeton, Ill., Aug. 17, 1946; s. Holton Albee and Cherry Ann (Landis) R.; m. Patricia Lynn Nordstrom, Sept. 1, 1968; children—Jared Andrew, Colin Matthew. B.S., Bradley U., 1968, M.A., 1970; M.H.A., U. Minn., 1980. Psychologist Oaklawn Ctr., Elkhart, Ind., 1973-78; adminstrv. resident No. Va. Mental Health Inst., Falls Church, 1979-80; dir. Southwestern State Hosp., Marion, Va., 1980—. Served with USAF, 1970-73. Mem. Assn. Mental Health Adminstrs. Methodist. Lodge: Rotary. Avocations: antiques; gardening; photography. Office: Southwestern State Hosp 502 E Main St Marion VA 24354

ROSENSWEIG, LAWRENCE FREDERICK, museum curator; b. Kingston, Pa., Nov. 4, 1950; s. William and Lois Barbara (Levy) R.; m. Nora Katherine Nobles, Nov. 11, 1979; 1 child, Clark Jeffrey. B.A., Harvard U., 1973; M.A., U. Mich., 1975. Curator The Morikami Mus. Japanese Culture, Delray Beach, Fla., 1976—. Pres. Japan-Am. Soc. South Fla., Miami, 1979-81. Mem. Am. Assn. Mus., Southeastern Mus. Conf., Palm Beach County Cultural Execs. Com. (chmn. 1984—). Office: The Morikami Mus Japanese Culture 4000 Morikami Park Rd Delray Beach FL 33446

ROSENTHAL, GARY MARK, educational administrator; b. Washington, Mar. 9, 1954; s. Jacob Aaron and Elaine Beverly (Wasserman) R. B.A., Va. Poly. Inst. and State U., 1975, M.A., 1977. Cert. secondary tech., Va.; cert. secondary administr., Va. Tchr., cons. Fairfax County Pub. Schs. Area IV, Springfield, Va., 1973-74, 75-82, adult edn. tchr. Annandale Adult Ctr., 1978-80, asst. prin. summer sch., Reston and McLean Va., 1983-84; adminstrv. aide George C. Marshall High Sch., Falls Church, Va., 1982-85, dir. student activities, 1985—; participant Va. Secondary Prins. Inst., Richmond, 1983-84; presenter Fairfax Schs. Mgmt. Conf., 1983; participant, presenter Fairfax County Sch. Based Mgmt. Program, 1984-85; presenter legal and policy issues conf. Va. Tech. U., 1986; participant Inst. Sch. Climate and Goverance, Harvard U., 1986. Asst. dir. ticket ops. Com. for 50th Am. Presdl. Inauguration, 1985; mem. Va. Tech. Student Aid Assn., Blacksburg, 1976—; mem. com. on youth edn. for citizenship ABA, Recipient cert. of achievement Harvard U. Prins. Ctr., 1984. Fellow Acad. Polit. Sci.; mem. Va. Council for Social Studies (no. dir. 1981-82), No. Va. Secondary Sch. Adminstrs. Assn. (bd. dirs. region III, 1985 v.p. 1986—), Phi Delta Kappa (condr. 1982-83). Republican. Jewish. Club: Century (appreciation award 1984) (Va. Tech. U.). Lodge: B'nai B'rith. Home: 3701 George Mason Dr Apt 2503N Falls Church VA 22041 Office: George C Marshall High Sch 7731 Leesburg Pike Falls Church VA 22043

ROSENTHAL, J. WILLIAM, ophthalmologist; b. New Orleans, Oct. 30, 1922; s. Jonas William and Marjorie Florence (Oppenheimer) R.; m. Harriet Beth Stern, Mar. 27, 1945; children—Paul William, Susan Ann Rosenthal Farrell. B.S., Tulane U., 1942, M.D., 1945; M.Sc., U. Pa., 1952, D.Sc., 1956. Diplomate Am. Bd. Ophthalmology. Intern, Charity Hosp., New Orleans, 1945-46, resident, 1948-51; practice medicine specializing in ophthalmology, New Orleans, 1951—; pres. New Orleans Eye Specialists, 1981—; clin. prof. ophthalmology Tulane U. Med. Sch., New Orleans, 1970-85; chief curator Am. Acad. Ophthalmology Found. Mus. Editor: New Orleans Acad. Ophthalmology Series, 1962-65. Contbr. articles to profl. publs. Served to lt. (j.g.) USNR, 1945-48. Fellow ACS, Internat. Coll. Surgeons (regent 1981—), Am. Acad. Ophthalmologists (1st Service award 1985), Royal Soc. Medicine, French Ophthal. Soc., Orleans Parish Med. Soc., La. Med. Soc., Beta Mu. Lodge: Lions (pres. 1984, sec. 1984—). Avocations: collecting edged weapons; fishing. Home: 2720 Jefferson Ave New Orleans LA 70115 Office: New Orleans Eye Specialists 3715 Prytania St New Orleans LA 70115

ROSENTHAL, MARK ELLIOTT, hospital administrator; b. Columbus, Ohio, May 30, 1952; s. Bert L. and Betty L. (Robbins) R.; m. Phyllis Bidnick, Aug. 3, 1975; children—Heather, Emily. B.A. in Pre-med. Sci., U. Mo., 1974, M.S. in Pub. Health-Health Services Mgmt., 1977. Adminstrv. staff asst. Meml. Med. Ctr., Springfield, Ill., 1977-79, adminstrv. dir. phys. medicine and rehab., 1979-81; adminstr. Rehab. Inst. Okla., Oklahoma City, 1981-83; assoc. adminstr. Dallas Rehab. Inst., 1983—; mem. consumer cons. com. Tex. Rehab. Commn., 1983—; mem. nat. adv. com. Commn. Accreditation of Rehab. Facilities; mem. Ill. Gov's. steering com. Internat. Yr. Disabled Persons, 1981, chmn. Springfield Mayor's Exec. Com., 1981. Mem. Plano Cable TV Adv. Bd., Tex., 1984—. Mem. Am. Coll. Hosp. Adminstrs., Assn. Med. Rehab. Dirs. and Coordinators (Tex. Lone Star region rep. 1984—), Am. Hosp. Assn., U. Mo. Grad. Studies Health Services Mgmt. Alumni Assn. Jewish. Avocations: golf; water sports; photography; computers. Office: Dallas Rehab Inst 9713 Harry Hines Blvd Dallas TX 75220

ROSENTHAL, RICHARD RAPHAEL, physician, medical researcher; b. N.Y.C., Apr. 5, 1939; s. Louis and Augusta (Dubovah) R.; m. Eileen Pressman, Jan. 1, 1968. B.A., Rutgers U., 1961, M.S., 1962; M.D., SUNY-Bklyn., 1966. Diplomate Am. Bd. Allergy and Immunology. Intern Kings County Hosp., Bklyn., 1966-67, resident in internal medicine, 1967-68; resident in internal medicine L.I. Jewish Med. Ctr., New Hyde Park, N.Y., 1970-71; fellow in medicine Johns Hopkins U. Sch. Medicine, Balt., 1971-73, asst. in medicine, 1973-74, instr. medicine, 1974-75, asst. prof. medicine clin. immunology div., 1975—; practice medicine specializing in allergy and clin. immunology, Fairfax, Va., 1973—; chief allergy sect. Fairfax (Va.) Hosp., 1973—; cons. Nat. Inst. Allergy and Infectious Diseases, NIH. Served with USPHS, 1968-70. NIH grantee, 1973—. Fellow Am. Acad. Allergy, ACP; mem. AMA (continuing edn. award 1969, 72), Am. Thoracic Soc., Am. Soc. Internal Medicine, Va. Acad. Medicine, Johns Hopkins Med. Soc., Lung Assn. No. Va., Greater Washington Allergy Soc. (sec-treas. 1978), Md. Allergy Soc., Md. Thoracic Soc., Va. Thoracic Soc., Am. Lung Assn., Fairfax County Med. Soc. Club: West River (Md.) Sailing. Mem. editorial bd. Jour. Allergy and Clin. Immunology; contbr. numerous articles to med. jours.; patentee nebulization dosimeter. Home: 4303 Ann Fitz Hugh Dr Annandale VA 22003

ROSENTHAL, SUSAN BARBARA, librarian; b. Elberon Park, N.J., Apr. 7, 1946; d. Joseph and Anna (Warar) Rosenthal. B.A., Montclair State Coll., 1967; M.Ed. in L.S., U. Miami, 1973. Cert. media specialist, tchr., Fla., N.J. Tchr., Manasquan Bd. Edn. (N.J.), 1967-71; tech. services librarian Oakland Park Library (Fla.), 1978—. Author: (mag.) Galumph, 1965-67. Mem. Humane Soc., Broward County, Fla., 1981. Recipient St. Cloud Teaching award Société d'Enseignement, St. Cloud, France, 1966. Mem. ALA, Fla. Library Assn. (continuing edn. com. 1980), Broward County Library Assn. (treas. 1981-83), Apple Computer Enjoyment Soc. (chpt. sec. 1984—, corp. sec. 1985—), Mensa, Pi Delta Phi. Club: Procrastinators Am. (Phila.). Office: Oakland Park Library 1298 NE 37th St Oakland Park FL 33334

ROSENTHAL, WARREN W., restaurant chain executive; b. Paducah, Ky., 1923; married. Grad., U. Ky., 1947. With Long John Silver's Inc., Lexington, Ky., chmn. bd. and pres., from 1957, now chmn. bd., dir.; chmn. Jerrico, Inc. Office: Long John Silver's Inc 101 Jerrico Dr Box 11988 Lexington KY 40579*

ROSIN, LINDSAY ZWEIG, clinical psychologist; b. San Antonio, Oct. 28, 1954; s. Morris and Ethel (Rosenberg) R.; m. Susana Aceituno, Sept. 3, 1981. B.A., U. Tex., 1975; M.A., Xavier U., 1979; Ph.D., Fla. Inst. Tech., 1985. Psychology assoc. Dayton Mental Health Ctr., Ohio, 1980-82, Cin. Neurol. Assocs., Cin., 1981-82; intern VA Med. Ctr., Houston, 1982-83; coordinator outpatient service Houston Child Guidance Ctr., 1983-84; fellow Med. Ctr. Del Oro, Houston, 1984-85; staff psychologist Mid City MHMR, 1985—; pvt. practice clin. psychology, 1985—. Recipient Outstanding Contbn. to Psychology in Ohio, Ohio Assn. Psychologists, 1982. Mem. Am. Psychol. Assn., Tex. Psychol. Assn., Houston Psychol. Assn., Soc. Clin. and Exptl. Hypnosis, Soc. Behavioral Medicine. Home: PO Box 20671 Houston TX 77225 Office: 7515 S Main 510 Houston TX 77030

ROSIN, MORRIS, real estate, land development company executive; b. San Antonio, Feb. 21, 1924; s. Berco and Leia (Dupchansky) R.; student Tex. A&M U., 1942, St. Mary's U., 1941, 45-47; m. Ethel Rosenberg; children—Susan, Charles, Lindsay. Sec.-treas. Bimbi Mfg. Co., 1949-67; pres. Bimbi Shoe Co. div. Athlone Industries, San Antonio, 1970-72; v.p. Athlone Industries, Parsippany, N.J., 1967-72; pres. Ardo Pro, San Antonio, 1966-74, Yoakum Bend Corp., San Antonio, 1968—, Broadway Devel. Corp., 1984—; sec.-treas. R & R Corp., San Antonio, 1970-72. Served with USAAF, 1942-45. Clubs: Masons (32 deg.), Shriners. Home: 4 Parliament Pl Dallas TX 75225 Office: 4813 Broadway Dallas TX 75248

ROSINEK, JEFFREY, judge, lawyer, educator, consultant; b. N.Y.C., Sept. 13, 1941; s. Isidore and Etta (Kramer) R.; m. Sandra Gwen Rosen, Aug. 7, 1977; 1 son, Ian David. B.A. in History, U. Miami, 1963; J.D., 1974, postgrad. in history, polit. sci. and edn. Bar: Fla. 1974. Tchr., Dade County (Fla.) Pub. Schs., 1963-78; instr. Boston U., 1975; sole practice, Miami, Fla., 1975-77; assoc. firm Tendrich & Todd, Miami, 1977-78; ptnr. Rosinek & Blake, Miami, 1978-86; judge, Dade County, 1986—; ednl. dir. Temple Judea, Coral Gables, Fla.; cons. Dade County Sch. System. Chmn. City of Miami Environ. Adv. com., 1970-73; mem. Dade County Youth Relations Bd., 1974; chmn. Civilian Rev. Bd. Selection of Nominees to U.S. Service Acads., 1978; chmn. Dade County Walk for Mankind-Project Concern, 1983; pres. Dade County Young Democrats, 1969-70; campaign mgr. Congressman Dante B. Fascell, 1974—; chmn. Dade County Adv. Council Close-Up; asst. adminstr. Fla. Dist. Key Club Internat., 1977-82, counselor, 1982-83; chmn. Fla. Walk for Mankind-Project Concern Internat., 1984-85. Recipient Outstanding Achievement award Jewish Theol. Sem. Am., 1978; Key of Honor Fla. Dist. Key Club, 1976, conv. honoree, 1984; Outstanding Educator of Yr. Dade County, 1968-69. Fellow Kiwanis Internat. Found. (life); mem. ABA, Fla. Bar Assn., South Miami Kendal Bar Assn. (pres.), Coral Gables Bar Assn., U. Miami Law Sch. Alumni (treas. 1984-85, sec. 1985-86), Democrat. Jewish. Club: Miami. Lodge: Kiwanis (lt. gov. Fla. dist. 1982-83; maj. emphasis chmn. 1985-86). Home: 535 Bird Rd Coral Gables FL 33146 Office: Miami Beach Ct 100 Meridian Ave Miami Beach FL 33139

ROSKOPF, JAMES JOSEPH, independent insurance agent; b. St. Louis, May 20, 1954; s. William J. and Louise D. (Stevens) R.; m. Sherilyn Joy Laukhuf, Oct. 20, 1979; 1 child, Lindsey Nicole. B.S. in Geology, U. Tex., Austin, 1975, M.S. in Fin., U. Tex.-Dallas, 1984. Geologist, Texaco Inc., Corpus Christi, Tex., 1977-78, Phillips Coal Co., Richardson, Tex., 1978-84; sales rep. Bright Ins. Services, Dallas, 1984—. Counselor Methodist Youth Found., Plano, Tex., 1983-85; mem. Meth. Men's Club, Plano, 1983-85. Mem. Life Underwriters Tng. Council, Plano C. of C. Republican. Lodges: Rotary, Toastmasters. Avocations: reading; running; fishing. Home: 1620 Throwbridge Ln Plano TX 75023 Office: Bright Ins Services 2129 W Parker Rd Suite E Plano TX 75023

ROSLOW, SYDNEY, marketing educator; b. N.Y.C., July 29, 1910; s. Joseph and Anna (Lipman) R.; B.S., N.Y. U., 1931, M.A., 1932, Ph.D., 1935; m. Irma Sternberg, Oct. 21, 1932; children—Richard Jay, Susan Jane, Peter Dirk. Research asst. in market, indsl., personnel research Psychol. Corp., 1931-41; sch. psychologist, mem. bd. edn., Hastings on Hudson, N.Y., 1937-48; pub. opinion research program surveys div. Dept. Agr., 1939-43; founder Pulse, Inc., market and audience research in radio, television, advt. industries, N.Y.C., 1941-78; adj. assoc. prof. Baruch Coll. CUNY, 1967-75; assoc. prof. dept. mktg. Fla. Internat. U., 1976-83, prof. mktg., assoc. dean Coll. Bus. Adminstrn., 1983—. Fellow Am. Psychol. Assn.; mem. Am. Mktg. Assn. (pres. Miami chpt. 1980-82), Market Research Council, Radio-Television Research Council (past pres.) Radio and Television Execs. Soc., Phi Beta Kappa. Contbr. articles to profl. jours. Home: 1035 NE 202d Terr N Miami Beach FL 33179

ROSNER, EDMOND, surgeon; b. Bucharest, Romania, Nov. 14, 1925; s. Isaak and Jenny (Ekstein) R.; came to U.S., 1960, naturalized, 1965; M.D. magna cum laude, U. Bucharest, 1949; m. Lucia C. Cergau, Oct. 3, 1951. Intern, 1st Surg. Clinic, U. Bucharest, 1949-50; 1st surgeon U. Bucharest Surg. Clin., 1950-59; vis. surgeon U. Vienna (Austria) Med. Sch., 1959-60; chief of surgery Central State Hosp., Petersburg, Va., 1961-64; practice medicine specializing in surgery, Colonial Beach, Va., 1964—; mem. staff Tidewater Meml. Hosp. Founder, pres., bd. dirs. Historyland Playground Inc., 1965—. Fellow Am. Soc. Abdominal Surgeons; mem. Am. Med. Soc. of Vienna (life), World Med. Assn., Colonial Beach C. of C. (pres. 1966-68, dir.), Republican. Roman Catholic. Clubs: Lions, Moose. Contbr. articles to med. jours. Home: 2525 Riverview Dr Colonial Beach VA 22443 Office: 35 Colonial Ave Colonial Beach VA 22443

ROSOVSKY, JAY M., computer company executive; b. N.Y.C., Oct. 28, 1945; s. Kermit and Ruth R.; m. Barbara Jane Wolder Rosovsky; children—Lisa, Adam. B.S., SUNY-Albany, 1967. Systems engr., mktg. rep. IBM, Albany, N.Y., 1967-71; ops. mgr. Ocean Data Systems, Albany, 1971-74; pres. C.R. Ernst Assocs., Albany, 1974-75; pres. Jay M. Rosovsky Assoc., Albany, 1975-77, MCT/The Computer Room, Albany, 1977-83; pres., dir. Computone Systems, Inc., Atlanta, 1983—; dir. Nervene, Inc., Saratoga Springs, N.Y., 1977—. Contbr. articles to profl. jours. Fundraiser Congregation Beth Shalom, Clifton Park, N.Y., 1980; membership com. Schenectady Jewish Community Ctr., 1973; advisor Albany St. Acad., 1972, Jr. Achievement, Albany, 1970. Recipient 100% Club award IBM, 1971. Mem. Kappa Mu Epsilon, Alpha Pi Omega. Republican. Jewish. Home: 880 Waddington Ct Dunwoody GA 30338 Office: Computone Systems Inc 1 Dunwoody Park Atlanta GA 30338

ROSS, CLARK GRANT, economics educator; b. Gloucester, Mass., June 24, 1950; s. Norman C. and Helen (Blecher) R. B.A., U. Pa., 1971; Ph.D., Boston Coll., 1975. Asst. prof. dept. econs. College of William and Mary, 1975-76; research scientist U. Mich., 1976-79; asst. prof. econs. Davidson Coll., N.C., 1979-83, assoc. prof., 1983—, chmn. dept., 1983—; cons. in field. Contbr. articles to profl. jours. Mem. Am. Econs. Assn., So. Econs. Assn. Roman Catholic. Home: Route 2 Box 283CC Davidson NC 28036 Office: Dept Economics Davidson Coll Davidson NC 28036

ROSS, CLAY CAMPBELL, JR., mathematics and computer science educator, consultant; b. Lexington, Ky., June 17, 1936; s. Clay Campbell and Vera Florence (Kite) R.; m. Andrea Valborg Lundeberg, Sept. 1, 1964; 1 child, Helen. B.S., U. Ky., 1959; M.A., U. N.C., 1961, Ph.D., 1964. Assoc. prof. math. Emory U., Atlanta, 1967-73; prof. math. and computer sci. U. of South, Sewanee, Tenn., 1973—; vis. prof. U. Mo.-Rolla., 1979-80. Served to capt. U.S. Army, 1965-66. Mem. Math. Assn. Am., Assn. Computing Machinery, AAAS, Sigma Xi. Republican. Presbyterian. Avocations: playing piano and organ; nature and portrait painting. Home: SPO 1220 Sewanee TN 37375 Office: Computer Sci Dept U of South SPO 1220 Sewanee TN 37375

ROSS, DANIEL BLEASE, business educator; b. Bowman, S.C., May 27, 1946; s. Blease and Myrtle (Bruce) R. B.S., S.C. State Coll., 1972; M.B.A., NYU, 1974; Ed.D., Columbia U., 1982. Tchr. Elizabeth Schs., N.J., 1974-75; prof. bus. Voorhees Coll., Denmark, S.C., 1975—. Assoc. del. Orangeburg Democrats, S.C., 1970. Served with U.S. Army, 1964-68, Vietnam. Mem. Nat. Bus. Edn. Assn., Assn. Supervision and Curriculum Devel., S.C. Bus. Edn. Assn. Avocations: computer operations; photography; hiking. Home: Route 1 Box 137 Branchville SC 29042 Office: Voorhees Coll Voorhees Rd Denmark SC

ROSS, DENISE GUINN, pathologist; b. San Antonio, Feb. 21, 1946; d. John Alonzo and Bessie Alice (Mitchell) Guinn; m. William Bruce Ross, Aug. 2, 1969; children—Rebecca, Christina, Michael Guinn. B.A., B.S., Tex. Woman's U., 1967; M.D., U. Tex.-Dallas, 1971. Diplomate Am. Bd. Pathology in Anatomic and Clin. Pathology, Blood Banking. Rotating intern, resident in pathology Naval Regional Med. Ctr., Portsmouth, Va., 1971-76, staff pathologist, 1976-79; instr. pathology Eastern Va. Med. Sch., Norfolk, 1972-78, asst. prof. pathology, 1978-85, assoc. prof. pathology, 1985—; staff pathologist DePaul Hosp., Norfolk, 1978-81; asst. med. dir. ARC, Norfolk, 1981, med. dir., 1982—. Contbr. sci. articles to med. jours. Served from ensign to comdr., M.C., USNR, 1970-79. Recipient scholastic achievement award Kiwanis Internat., Denton, Tex., 1967, Physician's Recognition award AMA, 1977, 80, 83. Fellow Am. Soc. Clin. Pathologists (pathology continuing med. edn. award 1977, 80, 83); mem. Am. Assn. Blood Banks, Am. Soc. Cytology, Am. Soc. Apheresis, Mid-Atlantic Assn. Blood Banks, Va. Soc. Pathology, Va. Soc. Cytology, Va. Soc. Hematology, Tidewater Pathology Soc. Presbyterian. Office: Am Red Cross Blood Services PO Box 1836 Norfolk VA 23501

ROSS, GERALD NICHOLAS, mental health clinic executive, psychologist; b. Lorain, Ohio, Aug. 7, 1940; s. Gerald Nicholas Ross and Harriette (Grondin) Ross Tartaglia; m. Patricia Josephine Jones, May 1, 1965; children—Jennifer Louise, Julie Marie. B.A.E., U. Fla., 1967, M.Ed., 1967; Ed.D., U. Ga., 1973; postgrad. in bus. adminstrn. U. of South Fla., 1985—. Lic. psychologist, Fla. Dir. counseling and testing South Ga. Coll., Douglas, 1967-70; psychologist West Palm Beach Community Mental Health, Fla., 1972-74; psychologist Charlotte County Mental Health Clinic, Fla., 1974—, exec. dir., 1985—; bd. dirs. Rape Crisis Ctr., Punta Gorda, Fla., 1982—; psychol. cons. police depts., Punta Gorda, Port Charlotte and Northport, Fla., 1983—. Served with USN, 1958-64. Mem. Am. Psychol. Assn., Fla. Assn. for Practicing Psychologists (cert.). Roman Catholic. Avocation: avid runner and bicyclist. Home: 1243 Rommel St Port Charlotte FL 33952 Office: Charlotte County Mental Health Clinic PO Box 366 PO Box 366 Punta Gorda FL 33950

ROSS, HOWARD PHILIP, lawyer; b. Chgo., May 10, 1939; s. Bernard and Estelle (Maremont) R.; children—Glen Joseph, Cynthia Ann; m. Jennifer Kay Shirley, 1984. B.S., U. Ill., 1961; J.D., Stetson Coll. Law, 1964. Bar: Fla. 1964, U.S. Ct. Appeals (5th cir.) 1965, U.S. Ct. Appeals (11th cir.) 1981, U.S. Supreme Ct. 1969. Bd. cert. civil trial lawyer Fla. Bar. Assoc., Parker & Battaglia and predecessor firm, St. Petersburg, Fla., 1964-67; ptnr. Battaglia, Ross, Hastings, Dicus & Andrews and predecessor firms, St. Petersburg, 1967—; lectr. Stetson Coll. Law, St. Petersburg, 1971-72. Recipient Woman's Service League Best Groomed award, 1979; Fla. Bar merit citation, 1974. Mem ABA, Fla. Bar Assn., St Petersburg Bar Assn., Am. Soc. Writers on Legal Subjects, Assn. Trial Lawyers Am., Assn. Fla. Trial Lawyers, Smithsonian Assocs. Republican. Jewish. Club: Treasure Island Tennis and Yacht (bd. govs.). Contbr. articles to profl. jours. Address: PO Box 41100 Saint Petersburg FL 33743

ROSS, JAMES KENNETH, architect, consultant; b. Johnson City, Tenn., June 15, 1941; s. Charles Thomas and Sarah Alice (Brockwell) R.; m. Carole Yvonne Arnett, Dec. 26, 1964; children—Jami Allyson, Yvonne Caroline, Jeremy Brett. A.S. in Engring., So. Tech. Inst., Marietta, Ga., 1964. Registered architect Nat. Council Archtl. Registration Bds. Draftsman, Beeson & Beeson Architects, Johnson City, 1957-64, 65-74, assoc., 1974-76; instr. architecture Steed Coll., 1964-65; pres. Ken Ross Architects, Inc., Johnson City, 1976—. Mem. plumbing bd. City of Johnson City; chmn. bd. Hosp. Guest House, 1983. Named Bus. Assoc. of the Yr. Franklin chpt. Am. Bus. Women's Assn., 1983. Mem. Johnson City C. of C. (treas. 1983), Nat. Fire Protection Assn., Nat. Home Bldrs. Assn. Jehovah's Witness. Club: North Johnson City Bus. Home: Route 11 Box 18 Jonesboro TN 37659 Office: 2700 S Roan St Suite 400 Johnson City TN 37601

ROSS, JANICE KOENIG, artist, art educator; b. Harrisburg, Pa., May 2, 1926; d. Paul Lindenmuth and Edna Rachel (Lowe) Koenig; m. Conrad H. Ross, Apr. 19, 1954; children—Katherine Ann, Joseph Aaron, Lucie Rachel. B.A., Pa. State u., 1947; M.F.A., U. Ill., 1954. Prof. art Tuskegee U., Ala., 1968—; artist in residence art studies abroad Program U. Ga., Cortona, Italy, 1984; lectr. in field. NEH fellow 1981; grantee Com. for Humanities in Ala., 1982. Mem. Coll. Art Assn., Southeastern Womens Caucus for Art (sec.-treas. 1978-80), Womens Caucus for Art, Studio 218 (founder; pres. 1980-82, 84-86, sec.-treas. 1982-84). Democrat. Unitarian. Home: 447 Wrights Mill Rd Auburn AL 36830 Office: Art Dept Tuskegee U Tuskegee Institute Ala 36088

ROSS, LEO HAROLD, manufacturing company pharmacist; b. Malvern, Ark., July 11, 1946; s. Will and Mary (Whitmore) R.; m. Beverly Elaine Dove, Aug. 25, 1973; 1 child, Joy Nicole. B.S. in Math., Wilberforce U., 1968; B.S. in Pharmacy, Phila. Coll. Pharmacy, 1973; M.B.A., Va. Commonwealth U., 1985. Registered pharmacist, Va., Ind. Programmer, IBM Co., Rochester, Minn., 1968-69; pharmacist Dow Chem. Co., Indpls., 1973-77, A.H. Robins,

Richmond, Va., 1977-81, research pharmacist, 1981-85, pharmacy mgr., 1985—. Recipient Wheel award Indpls. Jaycees, 1976. Mem. Am. Pharm. Assn., Va. Pharm. Assn., Richmond Pharm. Assn., Acad. Pharm. Scis., NAACP, Richmond Urban League, Richmond Council Boy Scouts Am., Alpha Phi Alpha (pres. 1982-85), Wilberforce U. Alumni Assn. (Outstanding Alumnus award 1977), Chi Delta Mu. Avocations: photography; music; sports; tennis. Home: 5210 Bonington Rd Richmond VA 23234 Office: AH Robins Co 1407 Cummings Dr Richmond VA 23220

ROSS, MARY DERBIGNY, librarian; b. Newport News, Va., Sept. 3, 1938; d. Irving Anthony and Maurice Ethelred (Newsome) Derbigny; children—Lisa Gail, Valerie Antoinette. B.S., Tuskegee Inst., 1954; M.S. in Library Sci., SUNY-Albany, 1956; postgrad., Columbia U., Tulane U., U. New Orleans, Loyola U.-New Orleans, London Poly. Inst. Children's librarian N.Y. Pub. Library, N.Y.C., 1956-59; librarian Mid./Sr. High Sch., Westchester County, N.Y., 1960-66, Elem. Library Processing Ctr., New Orleans, 1966-67; ednl. cons. Tulane U., New Orleans, 1970-73; librarian Orleans Parish Schs., New Orleans, 1975—(on leave); media specialist U.S. Dept. Def. Dependent Schs., Mannheim APO New York NY 09084 Contbr. articles to profl. jours. Mem. ALA, LWV, Council for Devel. of French in La., Kappa Delta Pi. Home: 7005 Lawrence Rd Apt 337 New Orleans LA 70126 Office: US Dept Def Dependent Schools Mannheim APO New York NY 09084

ROSS, MIRIAM DEWEY, book store executive; b. Cleve., Oct. 3, 1927; d. Kirk Martin and Grace Gray (Thomas) Dewey; m. James F. Ross, May 30, 1949; children—Deborah Jane, Steven Kirk, Rebekah Ruth. B.A., Doane Coll., 1949; M.A.T., George Washington U., 1972; M.S.L.S., Catholic U., 1976. Tchr. Riverside Ch. Nursery, N.Y.C., 1949-52, Short Hills Country Day, N.J., 1967-68; librarian Adv. & Learning Exchange, Washington, 1972-76; communications specialist D.C. Pub. Schs., Washington, 1978-81; owner Ross Book Service, Alexandria, Va., 1981—. Author numerous book revs. Active North Shore Hist. Soc., Pugwash, N.S., Can., 1975—; registrar joint archeol. expdn. Tell el-Hesi, Israel, 1979; bd. dirs. Am. Schs. Oriental Research, Phila., 1980-82, Albright Inst. Archeol. Research, Jerusalem, 1982-85. Mem. D.C. Library Assn., Am. Bookseller Assn., Soc. for Scholarly Pub., D.C. Writers Ctr. Democrat. Mem. United Ch. of Christ. Avocations: travel; archaeology; textile arts. Home: Seminary PO Alexandria VA 22304-0993 Office: Ross Book Service 3718 Seminary Rd Alexandria VA 22304

ROSS, PATTI JAYNE, physician; b. Brookfield, Ohio, Nov. 17, 1946; d. James J. and Mary (Nicastro) R.; B.A. with honors in Zoology, DePauw U., 1968; M.D., Tulane U., 1972; m. Allan R. Katz, May 23, 1976. Intern in ob-gyn Johns Hopkins Hosp., Balt., 1972-73; resident in ob-gyn Jackson Meml. Hosp., Miami, Fla., 1973-75, chief resident, 1975-76; assoc. prof. dept. ob-gyn U. Tex. Med. Sch., Houston, 1977—, dir. adolescent unit, 1977—. Active, Houston Orgn. for Parent Edn. Diplomate Am. Coll. Ob-Gyn. Mem. AMA, Am. Women's Med. Assn., Tex. Med. Assn., Harris County Med. Soc., Am. Fertility Soc., Tex. Assn. Obstetricians and Gynecologists, Houston Obstet. and Gynecol. Soc., So. Perinatal Assn., Sigma Xi, Beta Beta Beta. Roman Catholic. Contbr. articles to profl. jours. Home: 12214 Drakemill Dr Houston TX 77077 Office: 6431 Fannin Houston TX 77030

ROSS, PAUL, radiologist; b. Germany, Nov. 29, 1927; m. Penelope Braham, July 3, 1958; children—Andrea, Shelley, Lisa. M.D., U. Melbourne, 1951. Diplomate Am. Bd. Radiology. Rotating intern Hamilton Hosp., 1952-53; pediatrics intern Children's Hosp., Perth, Australia, 1953; resident in radiology Strong Meml. Hosp., U. Rochester (N.Y.), 1953-56; asst. radiologist St. Vincent's Hosp., Univ. Teaching Hosp., Melbourne, 1956-58, Royal Children's Hosp., 1958-65; ptnr. Melbourne Diagnostic Group, 1958-65; asst. prof. radiology, assoc. radiologist U. Rochester Med. Ctr., 1967-70, assoc. prof. radiology, assoc. radiologist, 1967-70, prof. diagnostic radiology, radiologist, neuroradiologist, 1970-75; prof., chmn. dept. radiology Med. U. S.C., Charleston, 1975—; vis. prof. Nat. Hosp. for Nervous Diseases, London, 1972-73; Mem. Am. Coll. Radiology, Assn. Univ. Radiologists, Radiol. Soc. N.Am. (chmn. audiovisual com.), Am. Soc. Neuroradiology (sr.), Soc. Chairmen Acad. Radiology Depts., Southeastern Neuroradiol. Soc. (com.), Am. Coll. Med. Imaging. Contbr. articles to profl. publs. Home: 490 Old Dock Rd Kiawah Island SC 29455 Office: 171 Ashley Ave Med Univ SC Charleston SC 29425

ROSS, ROBERT DWAIN, lawyer; b. Hope, Ark., Dec. 3, 1932; s. George Raymond and Alma Lillian (Putman) R.; m. Frances Roots Mitchell, June 15, 1963; children—Robert Mitchell, Virginia Frances, Mary Starr. Student So. State Coll., 1951-53; B.S.L., U. Ark., 1962, J.D., 1962. Bar: Ark. 1961, U.S. Dist. Ct. (ea. dist.) Ark. 1962, U.S. Supreme Ct. 1966. Law clk. Ark. Supreme Ct., 1961-62, 63; assoc. Pope, Shamburger, Buffalo & Ross, Little Rock, 1963-65, ptnr., 1965—; sec., exec. dir. Ark. Constl. Conv., 1980. Bd. dirs. Elizabeth Mitchell Children's Ctr., 1972-78, 83—, treas., 1974, pres., 1978, 84-85, v.p. and treas., 1983; bd. dirs. Quapaw Quarter Assn., 1977-80, pres., 1979. Served with U.S. Army, 1956-58. Fellow Ark. Bar Found.; mem. ABA, Ark. Bar Assn. (sec.-treas. 1969-72, ho. of dels. 1973-76, 78-81, mem. exec. council 1973, 75-78, chmn. 1981-82, bd. dirs. 1982-85, Pulaski County Bar Assn. (bd. dirs. 1978-79), Assn. Trial Lawyers Am. Democrat. Episcopalian. Office: 300 Spring Bldg Suite 400 Little Rock AR 72201

ROSS, WESLEY FREDERICK, clinical psychologist; b. Erie, Pa., Feb. 23, 1941; s. Wesley K. and Lucille (Schurz) R.; m. Shirley Ann Cody, Apr. 7, 1962; 1 child, Wesley Charles. A.B., U. Ky., 1962, M.A., 1964, Ph.D., 1969. Psychologist VA Hosp., Lexington, Ky., 1964-66; instr. U. Ky., Lexington, 1964—; psychologist, unit chief NIMH Clinic Research Ctr., Lexington, 1966-74; unit mgr. Fed. Correction Inst., Lexington, 1974—. Contbr. articles to profl. publs., chpt. to book. Mem. allocations panel United Way, Lexington, 1982—, mem. campaign panel, 1983, mem. Speakers Bur., 1982-84; instr. wellness program YMCA, Lexington, 1983—, bd. dirs., 1981—. Served to col. USPHS, 1966—. Recipient Superior Performance award USPHS Hosp., 1962, Vocat. Rehab. award Vocat. Rehab. Adminstrn., 1964. Mem. Psyhcologists in Pub. Service, Am. Psychol. Assn., Central Ky. Psychol. Assn. (sec. 1965-66, v.p. 1966-67), Kappa Delta Pi (pres. 1963). Lutheran. Clubs: Antique Automobile (bd. dirs. 1971-73); Bluegrass R.R. (pres. 1975, 82) (Lexington); Nat. Ry. Hist. Soc. (Louisville). Avocations: collecting antique automobiles, collecting railroadainia, photography. Home: 1749 Bahama Rd Lexington KY 40509 Office: Fed Correctional Instn Leestown Pike Lexington KY 40512

ROSSER, JOHN BARKLEY, JR., economics educator; b. Ithaca, N.Y., Apr. 12, 1948; s. John Barkley and Annetta Louise (Hamilton) R.; m. Sue A. Vilhauer, Aug. 31, 1968 (div. 1979); children—Meagan Rebecca, Caitlin Elizabeth. B.A., U. Wis., 1969, M.A., 1972, Ph.D., 1976. Project specialist Inst. Environ. Studies, Madison, Wis., 1972-75; planning analyst Dept. Natural Resources, Madison, 1975-76; assoc. prof. econs. James Madison U., Harrisonburg, Va., 1976—. Contbr. articles to profl. jours. Mem. Am. Econs. Assn., So. Econs. Assn., Va. Social Sci. Assn. Unitarian. Home: 107 Clinton St Harrisonburg VA 22801 Office: Dept Econs James Madison U Harrisonburg VA 22807

ROSSIE, CARLOS ENRIQUE, educational administrator, consultant; b. Havana, Cuba, Oct. 7, 1948; s. Dionisio M. and Edelmira (Blanco) R.; came to U.S., 1966; m. Claudia V. Velilla, Mar. 24, 1972; children—Cynthia Patricia, Claudette Marie, Carlos Fernando. Assoc. in Sci., Miami Dade Jr. Coll., 1970; postgrad. Fla. Internat. U., 1978—. Dir., owner Programar Computer Sch., Colombia, 1972-78; computer system and procedures analyst, dir. programmers and analysts tng. Burger King Corp., Miami, Fla., 1978-79; asst. v.p. computer dept. Flagler Fed. Savs. and Loans, Miami, 1979-81; dir., owner Fla. Programming Computer Sch., Miami, 1981—; computer cons. for Cuban-Am. Orgn. program, Dade County (Fla.), 1981—; computer presentations Dade County High Schs. Author: Cobol Computer Language, 1974 (Best Cobol Book award Columbia, S.Am.); 3 other computer books and intro. to data processing computer book. Cons. econ. com. Colombian Conservative Party; cons. candidate Manny Iglesias in U.S. Republican. Roman Catholic. Office: Fla Programming and Ednl Ctr 8578 SW 8 St Miami FL 33144

ROSSIE, WILLIAM LOUIS, JR., sanitary engineer, county official; b. Norton, Va., Oct. 17, 1932; s. William Louis and Sethelle (Barclift) R.; B.S. in Civil Engring., Va. Mil. Inst., 1956; postgrad. U. N.C., 1959; m. Elizabeth S. Rossie, Nov. 9, 1957; children—William Louis III, Steven Britt. Sanitary engr. Va. Health Dept., Lexington and Richmond, 1956-62; regional engr., Lexington, 1962-74; exec. dir., sec., treas. Roanoke County (Va.) Pub. Service Authority, 1974-80, county utility dir., Salem, Va., 1974-80, assoc. county adminstr., 1980-81; chief engr. Albemarle County Service Authority, 1982—. Served with U.S. Army, 1957, col. Res. Mem. Am. Water Works Assn., ASCE, Am. Public Works Assn., Water Pollution Control Assn., Res. Officers Assn. Methodist. Club: Elks. Office: PO Box 1009 Charlottesville VA 22902

ROSSINI, FREDERICK ANTHONY, social scientist, educator; b. Washington, Sept. 20, 1939; s. Frederick Dominic and Anne Kathryn (Landgraff) R.; m. Maria P. Miranda, June 5, 1964; children—Anthony J., Laura M., Jon D. B.S. in Physics, Spring Hill Coll., 1962; Ph.D. in Physics, U. Calif.-Berkeley, 1968. Acting asst. prof. physics U. Calif.-Berkeley, 1968, NIMH postdoctoral fellow, 1969-71; research assoc. Nat. Acad. Sci.-NRC, Nasa Ames Research Ctr., 1971-72; asst. prof. social scis. Ga. Inst. Tech., Atlanta, 1972-76, assoc. prof. social scis., 1976-80, prof. social scis., 1980—, dir. tech. and sci. policy program, 1980-82, dir. Tech. and Policy Assessment Ctr., 1981—, assoc. dir. Office Interdisciplinary Programs, 1983-85, dir., 1985—. NSF predoctoral fellow, 1962-64. Mem. AAAS, Internat. Assn. Impact Assessment (founder, treas.), Policy Studies Orgn., Soc. Philosophy and Tech., Internat. Assn. for Study Interdisciplinary Research, Sigma Xi. Founding editor-in-chief Impact Assessment Bull.; assoc. editor Technol. Forecasting and Social Change; editor, contbr. to sci. books; contbr. numerous articles to profl. publs. Office: Office Interdisciplinary Programs Georgia Institute Technology Atlanta GA 30332

ROSSLER, WILLIS KENNETH, JR., petroleum company executive; b. Houston, Nov. 17, 1946; s. Willis Kenneth and Fay Lee (Olle) R.; B.S. in Indsl. Engring., Tex. Tech. U., 1969; m. Melva Sue Booker; children—Nancy Kay, Kristen Sue, Deborah Anne, Ryan Konrad, Eric George. Dist. mgr. Tex.-La. ops. Continental Pipe Line Co., Lake Charles, La., 1974-75, mgr. engring., Houston, 1976-77; asst. mgr. corp. planning and devel. Conoco, Inc., Houston, 1977-78; v.p. project devel. PetroUnited, Inc., Houston, 1978-80, pres., 1981—, also dir. Pres., Village Pl. Community Assn., Houston, 1978. Mem. Am. Inst. Indsl. Engrs., Am. Petroleum Inst., Houston Mgmt. Council, Ind. Liquid Terminals Assn. (vice chmn.), Am. Mgmt. Assn., Planning Forum (pres. chpt.). Republican. Episcopalian. Club: Petroleum of Houston. Office: 600 Travis St Houston TX 77001

ROSSMAN, JOSEPH HARRY, distillery company executive; b. Atlanta, Nov. 19, 1945; s. Philip G. and Helen (Wheldon) R.; m. Pamela J. Wilson, Oct. 1, 1982. B.S., Middle Tenn. State U., 1968, M.S., 1970. Aquatic biologist Tenn. Water Quality Control Div., Nashville, 1970-77, regional office mgr., 1977-79; environ. cons. Hickerson & Assocs., Murfreesboro, Tenn., 1980-81; asst. environ. coordinator Jack Daniel Distillery, Lynchburg, Tenn., 1981-83, dir. safety, security, 1982—, human resources mgr., 1983—. Author tech. reports. Mem. Nat. Assn. Underwater Instrs., Am. Soc. Safety Engrs., Nat. Safety Council, Am. Soc. Personnel Adminstrn., Highland Rim Personnel Assn. (v.p., program chmn. 1984-85). Club: Highland Yacht. Avocations: sailing; scuba diving; reading. Home: Route 4 Box 123 Winchester TN 27298 Office: Jack Daniel Distillery PO Box 199 Lynchburg TN 37352

ROSSON, WILLIAM M., corporate executive; b. Springfield, Tenn., 1922; B.S., Tenn. Poly. Inst., 1944; married. With Conwood Corp., 1955—, asst. mgr. Clarksville leaf dept., 1965-67, mgr. dept., 1967-69; asst. v.p., 1969-71, v.p. leaf dept., 1971, exec. v.p. ops., 1972-74, pres., chief exec. officer, 1974—, also dir. Address: 813 Ridge Lake Blvd Memphis TN 38117

ROTGIN, CHARLES, JR., real estate devel., constrn. and mgmt. co. exec.; b. Charleston, W.Va., July 31, 1942; s. Charles and Helaine M. (Kaufman) R.; B.A. in Econs., U. Va., 1966; m. Whitley Vogler, Oct. 12, 1968; children—Sarah Mosby, Forrest Vogler. Life underwriter Equitable Life Assurance Soc. U.S., Charlottesville, Va., 1967-69; v.p. Amvest Corp., Charlottesville, 1969-72; pres. Great Eastern Mgmt. Co., Inc., Charlottesville, 1972-78, prin., 1978—, also dir.; chmn. Wasteco, Inc., Charlottesville, 1973-82; dir. Albemerle Bank & Trust Co., Culpepper Country Hams, Inc. Pres., Blue Ridge Homebuilders Assn., 1980-81, also dir.; trustee St. Annes Belfield Sch. Served with USCG, 1966. Clubs: Boar's Head Sports, Farmington Country. Home: 2409 Angus Rd Charlottesville VA 22901 Office: PO Box 5526 Charlottesville VA 22905

ROTH, BRYAN LEO, research scientist, physician; b. Missoula, Mont., Dec. 15, 1954; s. Urban Leo and Phyllis (Blank) R.; m. Jane Howard, June 23, 1977 (div. 1983); m. Judith Paris, Sept. 1, 1985. B.A., magna cum laude, Carroll Coll., Mont., 1977; Ph.D., St. Louis U., 1983, M.D., 1983. Intern in psychiatry Nat. Naval Med. Ctr., Bethesda, Md., 1983-84; guest scientist NIMH, Washington, 1983; scientist Naval Med. Research Inst., Bethesda, 1984—. Contbr. chpts. to books, articles to profl. jours. Served to lt. USN, 1977—. Health Professions scholar U.S. Navy, 1977-83; March of Dimes Research fellow St. Louis U., 1978, St. Louis U. fellow, 1979-83. Mem. Soc. Neurosics., Shock Soc., Phi Beta Kappa, Delta Epsilon Sigma. Democrat. Avocations: Creative writing; chess; skiing. Home: 2157 Evans Ct #304 Falls Church VA 22043 Office: Naval Med Research Inst Surg Research Br Bethesda MD 20814

ROTH, STEPHANIE CAMILLE (STEPHANIE STEPHENS), radio personality, promotions manager; b. Asheville, N.C., Oct. 18, 1952; d. John Frances and Mary Louise (Phillips) R. B.A. cum laude, Wake Forest U.-U. London, 1974; M.A., NYU, 1980. Prodn. asst. CBS-TV, N.Y.C., 1977; with corp. communications dept. United Airlines, N.Y.C. and Chgo., 1977-80; mgr. media relations Tex. Internat. Airlines, 1980-81; sr. mgr. media relations Continental Airlines, Houston, 1981-83, mgr. promotions, 1984-85; morning drive, evening and weekend on-air personality disc jockey, promotions coordinator, copywriter sta. KT-FM, San Antonio, 1985—. freelance writer, voiceover. talent Recipient United Airlines Corp. award of merit, 1980, Toys for Tots recognition U.S. Marine Corps, 1981, KUHT-TV award, 1983. Mem. Pub. Relations Soc. Am. (Silver Anvil award 1984), Soc. Am. Travel Writers, Am. Women in Radio and TV, Tex. Press Women Aviation/Space Writers Assn. Office: KTFM Radio 4050 Eisenhauer Rd San Antonio TX 78218

ROTH, STEVEN ALAN, psychologist, consultant; b. Phila., Jan. 15, 1940; s. Nathan Harry and Esther (Carlin) R.; m. Anne Glass, Aug. 21, 1966; 1 child, David. B.S., Temple U., 1966; M.A., Columbia U., 1967; Ph.D., U. Wyo., 1975. Lic. psychologist, Fla., Wyo. Assoc. dir., psychologist S.E. Wyo. Mental Health Ctr., Inc., Cheyenne, 1973-84; assoc. Kaslow Assocs., P.A., West Palm Beach, Fla., 1984—; assoc. dir. Fla. Couples and Family Inst., West Palm Beach, 1984—. Bd. dirs. Substance Abuse Cert. of State of Wyo., Cheyenne, 1982-84, Safe House, Cheyenne, 1983-84. Served with USAR, 1962-68. NIMH fellow, 1971-72. Mem. Fla. Psychol. Assn. (sec.-treas. 1984-86), Internat. Acad. Profl. Counseling Psychotherapy (diplomate), Am. Psychol. Assn., Nat. Register Health Service Providers in Psychology (council). Jewish. Avocations: boating; swimming; photography. Home: 4185 Larch Ave Palm Beach Gardens FL 33418 Office: Fla Couples and Family Inst 2617 N Flagler Dr Suite 204 West Palm Beach FL 33407

ROTH, SUSAN, psychologist, educator; b. N.Y.C., Apr. 16, 1948; d. Milton Irving and Beatrice (Teichman) R.; m. Philip R. Costanzo, Mar. 10, 1979; 1 child, Anthony Roth. B.A., Barnard Coll., 1970; M.A., Northwestern U., 1972, Ph.D., 1973. Lic. psychologist, N.C. Dir. psychology clinic Duke U., Durham, N.C., 1979-81, dir. clin. tng. program, 1982—, asst. prof. psychology, 1973-79, assoc. prof., 1979—. Mem. adv. bd. Durham Rape Crisis Ctr., Durham, 1984—; bd. dirs. YWCA, 1985—. Mem. Am. Psychol. Assn., N.C. Psychol. Assn., Council Univs. Dirs. Clin. Psychology, Phi Beta Kappa. Office: Dept Psychology Duke Univ Durham NC 27706

ROTH, THOMAS JEROME, financial executive; b. Hagerstown, Ind., May 14, 1930; s. Raymond Frank and Elizabeth Marie (Brown) R.; B.G.E., U. Omaha, 1965; postgrad. U.S. Army Command and Gen. Staff Coll., 1968; m. Louise Morton Cole, Dec. 21, 1961; children—Margaret Morton, Elizabeth Cole. Enlisted U.S. Army, 1951, commd. officer and advanced through grades to lt. col., 1970; served in Korea and Vietnam; assigned to Army Gen. Staff and Joint Chiefs of Staff; ret., 1976; financial mgr. Sperry Corp., Vienna, Va., 1976—. Decorated Bronze Star medal. Mem. Am. Legion, Mil. Order World Wars, SAR, Soc. Ind. Pioneers, Magna Charta Barons. Presbyterian. Club: Belle Haven Country (Alexandria). Home: 7618 Leith Pl Alexandria VA 22307 Office: Sperry Corp Info Systems Group 8500 Leesburg Pike Vienna VA 22180

ROTH, WILLIAM STANLEY, hospital foundation executive; b. N.Y.C., Jan. 12, 1929; s. Sam Irving and Louise Caroline (Martin) R.; A.A., Asheville-Biltmore Jr. Coll., 1948; B.S., U. N.C., 1950; m. Hazel Adcock, May 6, 1963; children—R. Charles, W. Stanley. Dep. regional exec. Nat. council Boy Scouts Am., 1953-65; exec. v.p. Am. Humanics Found., 1965-67; dir. devel. Bethany Med. Center, Kansas City, Kans., 1967-74; exec. v.p. Geisinger Med. Center Found., Danville, Pa., 1974-78; pres. v.p. Found., Baptist Med. Centers, Birmingham, Ala., 1978—. Mem.-at-large Nat. council Boy Scouts Am., 1972-86; ruling elder John Knox Kirk Presbyn. Ch., Kansas City, Mo., Grove Presbyn. Ch., Danville, Pa. Recipient Silver award United Methodist Ch., 1970, Mid-West Health Congress, 1971; Outstanding Fund Raising Exec., Ala. Soc. Fund Raising Execs., 1983; Seymour award Outstanding Hosp. Devel. officer, 1983. Fellow Nat. Assn. Hosp. Devel. (nat. pres. 1975-76, chmn. ednl. fund 1980-82); mem. Nat. Soc. Fund Raising Execs. (pres. Ala. chpt. 1980-82, nat. dir. 1980-85), Am. Hosp. Assn., Am. Soc. Hosp. Mktg., Ala. Soc. Sleep Disorders, Ala. Heart Inst., Mid-Am.Hosp. Devel. Assn. (pres. 1973-74), Mid-West Health Congress (devel. chmn. 1972-74), Alpha Phi Omega (nat. pres. 1958-62, dir. 1950—, Nat. Disting. Service award 1962), Delta Upsilon (pres. N.C. Alumni 1963-65). Clubs: Rotary (pres. club 1976-77), Relay House, Green Valley, Elks, Order Holy Grail, Order Golden Fleece, Order of The Arrow (Nat. Disting. Service award 1958). Editor Torch and Trefoil, 1960-61. Home: 341 Laredo Dr Birmingham AL 35226 Office: 2700 Hwy 280 S Birmingham AL 35223

ROTHE, ERNST, paper manufacturing company executive; b. N.Y.C., Feb. 19, 1941; s. Tyge Ernst and Delight Dawson (Hall) R.; A.B. in Econs., Brown U., 1963; m. Nancy Louise Eberhart, Feb. 28, 1976; children—Ernst, Alden Augustus, Whitney Knowlton. Salesman, S.D. Warren Products Co., Geneva, Switzerland, 1967-69; asst. v.p. for Latin Am., Moller & Rothe Inc., N.Y.C., 1969-76; sales mgr. Caribbean Forest Products Co., Arecibo, P.R., 1977-78; project mgr. McLean Securities Inc., N.Y.C., 1979-84; internat. sales mgr. Manville Forest Products Co., Monroe, La., 1984—; pres. Bunzl Export Corp., N.Y.C., 1980-81, cons. 1982; computer cons. Fish and Neave. Served to lt. USN, 1963-67. Mem. Gen. Soc. Mayflower Descendants, Soc. Colonial Wars State of New York, SR (asst. sec.). Club: Badminton of N.Y.

ROTHENBERG, IRWIN Z., lab. mgr.; b. Bklyn., Feb. 17, 1944; s. Alex and Tillie (Rothstein) R.; B.S., Bklyn. Coll., City U. N.Y., 1965; M.S., Colo. State U., 1969; M.T., Good Samaritan Sch. Med. Tech., 1973. Staff technologist in microbiology Carl Hayden Community Hosp., Tucson, 1974; adminstrv. technologist McKee Med. Center, Loveland, Colo., 1974-79; lab. mgr. Crittenden Meml. Hosp., West Memphis, Ark., 1979—; lab. mgmt. cons. Performance Improvement Cons., Inc., 1979; state med. technologist rep. to Colo. PSRO, 1977-78. NSF exchange scientist, Antarctica, 1967-68. Mem. Am. Soc. Clin. Pathology, Am. Soc. Med. Tech., Clin. Lab. Mgmt. Assn., Black and White Men Together (nat. bd. dirs., co-founder Memphis chpt.), Sigma Xi, Phi Kappa Phi. Jewish. Home: 1471 North Pkwy Memphis TN 38112 Office: 200 Tyler St West Memphis AR 72301

ROTTON, JAMES, psychology educator, researcher; b. Black Oak, Ark., Feb. 14, 1944; s. Matt L. and Viola (Forbes) R.; m. Cheryl R. Allen, Mar. 11, 1968; children—Allen, Mischele. B.S., Purdue U., 1965, M.S., 1971, Ph.D., 1973. Vis. instr. Miami U., Oxford, Ohio, 1972-73; asst. prof. U. Dayton, Ohio, 1973-77; assoc. prof. psychology Fla. Internat. U., North Miami, Fla., 1977—. Contbr. articles to profl. jours. Mem. Am. Psychol. Assn., Psychonomic Soc., Environ. Design Research Assn., Com. for Sci. Investigation of Claims of Paranormal, Sigma Xi. Democrat. Avocations: biking; canoeing. Office: Fla Internat U North Miami FL 33181

ROTTY, RALPH MCGEE, research analyst, engineer, meteorologist; b. St. Louis, Aug. 1, 1923; s. Oscar John and Louise (McGee) R.; m. Maxene W. Young, Nov. 14, 1944; children—Jocelyn S., Cynthia G., John W., Daniel R. B.S.E.E., State U. Iowa, 1947; M.S. in Meteorology, Calif. Inst. Tech., 1948, M.S. in Mech. Engring., 1949; Ph.D. in Mech. Engring., Mich. State U., 1953. Registered profl. engr., La. Instr., Mich. State U., 1949-53, asst. prof., 1953-55, assoc. prof. mech. engring. dept. 1955-58; prof., head mech. engring. dept. Tulane U., New Orleans, 1958-66; prof., dean Sch. Engring., Old Dominion U., Norfolk, Va., 1966-72; sr. research assoc. Air Resources Labs., NOAA, Silver Spring, Md., 1972-74; sr. scientist Inst. for Energy Analysis, Oak Ridge Assoc., Univs., Oak Ridge, 1974—. Served to 1st lt. USAAF, 1943-46. Sr. Research assoc. NRC, 1972-73. Mem. AAAS, ASME, Am. Meteorology Soc., Tau Beta Pi, Sigma Xi, Pi Tau Sigma, Eta Kappa Nu. Contbr. articles to various publs. Home: PO Box 136 Oak Ridge TN 37831 Office: Inst for Energy Analysis Oak Ridge Assoc Univs PO Box 117 Oak Ridge TN 37831

ROUBEY, LESTER WALTER, clergyman, educator; b. Balt., Feb. 11, 1915; s. Abraham and Sara (Cordish) R.; A.M., Johns Hopkins, 1936, Ph.D., 1938; M.H.L. and Rabbi, Hebrew Union Coll., 1947, D.D. (hon.), 1972; m. Charlotte Helen Stern, June 1, 1947; 1 son, Robert Arthur. Rabbi, 1947; rabbi, Lancaster, Pa., 1947-53, Reading, Pa., 1954-64, East Orange, N.J., 1964-66, Baton Rouge, 1966-80, rabbi emeritus, 1980—; adj. prof. religion Franklin and Marshall Coll., Lancaster, 1951-53; asso. prof. Romance langs. Kutztown (Pa.) State Coll., 1961-64; lectr. Romance langs. La. State U., Baton Rouge, 1966-70, assoc. prof., 1970-82, assoc. prof. religious studies and bibl. Hebrew, 1982—. Mem. civic com., Lancaster, 1950-53; mem. adv. bd. Baton Rouge Gen. Hosp., 1967—, trustee, 1972—; mem. religious com. Reading round table NCCJ; chmn. Reading com. Am. Jewish Tercentenary, 1954-55; bd. dirs. ARC, 1968-71, Mental Health Assn. Baton Rouge, 1980-83. Mem. Central Conf. Am. Rabbis, Hebrew Union Coll.-Jewish Inst. Religion Alumni Assn. (trustee 1953-56), Am. Assn. Tchrs. French, Am. Assn. Tchrs. Italian, AAUP, MLA, South Central Modern Lang. Assn. (chmn. Italian sect. 1969), Phi Sigma Iota. Mason (32 deg., Shriner), Rotarian. Club: Baton Rouge Country. Producer, conductor series of TV worship programs, Lancaster, 1951-53. Office: Dept Philosophy La State U Baton Rouge LA 70803

ROUECHE, JOHN EDWARD, II, educator; b. Statesville, N.C., Sept. 3, 1938; s. John Edward and Mary (Harris) R.; B.A., Lenoir Rhyne Coll., Hickory, N.C., 1960; M.A., Appalachian Coll., Boone, N.C., 1961; Ph.D., Fla. State U., 1964; m. Suanne Davis; children by previous marriage—Michelle Renee, John Edward, III. Dean coll. Gaston Coll., Gastonia, N.C., 1964-67; asso. research educator U. Calif., Los Angeles, 1967-69; dir. jr. coll. div. Nat. Lab. Higher Edn., 1968-71, also asso. prof. edn. Duke U.; prof. edn., dir. community coll. leadership program U. Tex., Austin, 1971—; community coll. editor Jossey-Bass Publishers, 1971-82. Pres. Doss Sch. PTA, 1974-75; chmn. bd. Northwest Hills United Methodist Ch., 1973-76. Recipient Distinguished Service award A.M.E. Ch., 1971, awards Council of Univs. and Colls., 1978, 84, 85; Outstanding Alumnus award Appalachian State U., 1979; Disting. Grad. award Fla. State U., 1981; Teaching Excellence award U. Tex., 1982, Outstanding Researcher award, 1985 Excellence award for Outstanding Learned Article, U.S. Edn. Press Assn., 1983; Disting. Research award Nat. Assn. Devel. Edn., 1984, 86, other disting. research awards, 1985—; lifetime Research Contbn. award, 1986; Disting. Service award Council Univs. and Colls., 1984, Nat. Research Publ. award, 1985; Disting. Nat. Leadership award Am. Assn. Community and J. Colls., 1986; Disting. Research award Nat. Council Staff, Program, and Organizational Devel.; named lifetime ambassador for N.C., 1978; Kellogg fellow, 1962-64. Mem. Am. Assn. Community and Jr. Colls., Am. Assn. Higher Edn., Council Univs. and Colls. (dir.), Phi Beta Kappa, Phi Delta Kappa. Author books, articles, monographs; mem. editorial bds. profl. jours.; editor Creative Teaching Series, Media Systems Corp., 1980—. Home: 6804 Edgefield Dr Austin TX 78731 Office: EDB 348 Univ Tex Austin TX 78712

ROUNTREE, BETTY NEUMANN, pharmacist; b. Galveston, Tex., Jan. 16, 1946; d. Edgar Ernest and Madalena (Vaglienti) Neumann; m. Allen DeWitt Rountree, June 20, 1970 (div. Oct. 1978); 1 child, Allen DeWitt II. B.S. in Pharmacy, U. Houston, 1969. Registered pharmacist, Tex. Staff pharmacist St. Mary's Hosp., Galveston, 1969-70, St. Anthony's Ctr., Houston, 1970-77, Meml. Hosp. Galveston County, Texas City, Tex., 1977-81; staff pharmacist Danforth Meml. Hosp., Texas City, 1981—, cardiac rehab. cons., 1982—, pharm. antibiotic rev. coordinator to pharmacy and therapeutics com., 1983—, mem. speakers bur., 1983—. Mem. Galveston Hist. Found., 1983—; mem. Diocesan Council of Catholic Women, Houston, 1970-77, Galveston, 1977—. Mem. Am. Soc. Hosp. Pharmacists, Tex. Soc. Hosp. Pharmacists, Houston, Galveston Area Soc. Hosp. Pharmacists, Am. Pharm. Assn., Tex. Pharm. Assn., Galveston County Pharm. Assn., Nat. Assn. Female Execs., Phi Mu (life; Galveston county key alumnae 1979—, circle contact 1980—), Kappa Epsilon. Roman Catholic. Lodge: Lioness Club (Texas City). Avocations: breeding Cairn terriers; designing women's apparel; silk flower arranging. Home: #7 Back Bay Circle East Galveston TX 77551 Office: Danforth Hosp Pharmacy Pharmacy Mgmt Services 519-9th Ave North Texas City TX 77590

ROUNTREE, GEORGE DENTON, health services management consultant; b. Houston, Mar. 14, 1937; s. George Washington and Verda Mae (Wagnon) R. B.S., Lamar U., 1960; M.H.A., Washington U., St. Louis, 1963; postgrad. Grad. Sch. Bus. and Public Health, Harvard U., 1976. Vice pres. Methodist Hosp., Houston, 1963-75; pres. Quadrus Internat. Inc. Tex., Houston, 1977—. Adj. asst. prof. Washington U. Med. Sch., St. Louis, 1978-85; guest lectr. U. Tex. Health Sci. Ct., Houston, 1983. Contbr. articles to profl. jours. Mem. profl. adv. com. Mental Health Assn. Houston and Harris County; adv. and instl. rep. Boy Scouts Am. Served with USNR, 1956-63. Fellow Am. Coll. Hosp. Adminstrs.; mem. Houston C. of C. (chmn. art com. Ronald McDonald House), Am. Assn. Hosp. Planning, Greater Houston Hosp. Council, Nat. Council Internat. Health, Assn. Univ. Programs in Health Adminstrn. Club: Rotary. Home: 4323 Ivanhoe St Houston TX 77027 Office: 3401 Louisiana St 230 Houston TX 77002

ROUNTREE, JOHN GRIFFIN RICHARDSON, business and association executive; b. Ocala, Fla., Oct. 31, 1936; s. Otis J. and Harriet (Griffin) R.; 1 child: Robert Ivan Shreve-Rountree. Student graphic arts and advt. Ringling Sch. Art, Sarasota, Fla., 1957. Hon. accademico corrispondento L'Accademia Tiberina, Rome, 1970. Pres., Rountree Printing & Advt. Co., Miami, Fla., 1959-63; asst. exec. v.p., statistician Inst. Shortening & Edible Oils, Washington, 1963-65; asst. exec. v.p. Automotive Trade Assn., Washington, 1965-67; exec. dir. DP&S Inc., Washington, 1968-73; pres., pub. The Hereditry Register of the U.S.A., Washington, 1971-75; pres. St. Johns Printing & Office Supply, Inc., St. Augustine, 1976—. Served with F.A., U.S. Army, 1958-60. Decorated Grand Cross Magistral Grace, Sovereign Greek Order St. Dennis of Zante; Gran Cruz, Soberana e Imperial Orden de la Corona Azteca; grand officer Sovereign Mil. Order Temple of Jerusalem; lt. col., aide de camp Gov. Jimmy Carter Staff, Ga., 1971; Gov. George Wallace Staff, Ala. 1972; col. Gov. Edwin Edwards Staff, La., 1972; hon. col., aide de camp Gov. Robert Ray, Iowa, 1972; hon. citizen State Tex., 1973; hon. sec. state State Ind., 1972; hon. Silver State plenipotentiary, Gov. O'Callaghan, Nev., 1973; Disting. Hooser, Gov. Ind., 1973; Hon. citizen W. Va., 1973; recipient 1st place award hard bound volumes Printing Industries Virginias, 1971. Mem. Welsh Soc., St. Andrews Soc., Royal Soc. St. George, London, Gen. Soc. War 1812, St. David's Soc., Gen. Soc. SAR (bd. dirs. Washington 1970), Nat. Soc. SAR (librarian gen. nat. soc. 1969-71), Gen. Soc. Colonial Wars (gentleman of council D.C. 1976), Mil. Order Fgn. Wars U.S., Sons. Confederate Vets., Nat. Soc. Sons and Daus. of the Pilgrims, Soc. Descendants of the Colonial Clergy, Order Stars and Bars (1st vice comdr. D.C. 1970), Nat. Huguenot Soc., Order of Lafayette, Hereditary Order Descendants of the Loyalists and Patriots of the Am. Revolution (librarian general 1972), Colonial Order of the Crown, Soc. Descendants of the Knights of the Most Noble Order of the Garter, Clan MacArthur Soc. Republican. Episcopalian. Clubs: Ponte Vedra (Fla.); St. Augustine Yacht (chmn. bd. 1982), St. Augustine Beach and Tennis; St. George's (London). Lodges: Masons, K.T., Shriners, Nat. Sojourners. Avocations: Boating; tennis. Office: St Johns Printing & Office Supply Inc 107 King St Saint Augustine FL 32084

ROUP, WALTER GLENN, dentist; b. Houston, May 6, 1925; s. Marion G. and Betty (Torres) R.; m. Jeanne Martin, Mar. 25, 1944; children—Walter Glenn, Robert W., Cynthia, Nancy. B.S., U. Houston, 1949; D.D.S., St. Louis U., 1953. Pvt. practice gen. dentistry, Houston, 1953—. Lit. reviewer Acad. Gen. Dentistry Jour., Chgo., 1984-85, examination cons., 1984-85. Patentee in field dental articulators. Served with U.S. Army, 1942-45. Fellow Acad. of Dentistry; mem. ADA, Tex. Dental Assn., Houston Dental Assn., Acad. Dentistry (master). Republican. Roman Catholic. Clubs: Brae Burn Country, Doctors. Avocations: reading dental research; hunting; fishing; golf; swimming.

ROUS, STEPHEN NORMAN, physician, educator; b. N.Y.C., Nov. 1, 1931; s. David H. and Luba (Margulies) R.; A.B., Amherst Coll., 1952; M.D., N.Y. Med. Coll., 1956; M.S., U. Minn., 1963; m. Margot Woolfolk, Nov. 12, 1966; children—Benjamin, David. Intern, Phila. Gen. Hosp., 1956-57, resident, 1959-60; resident Flower-Fifth Ave. and Met. Hosp., N.Y.C., 1957-59, Mayo Clinic, Rochester, Minn., 1960-63; practice medicine specializing in urology, San Francisco, 1963-68; asso. prof. urology N.Y. Med. Coll., N.Y.C., 1968-72, asso. dean, 1970-72; prof. surgery, chief div. urology Mich. State U., East Lansing, 1972-75; prof., chmn. dept. urology Med. U. S.C., Charleston, 1975—; urologist-in-chief Med. U. S.C. and County hosps., Charleston, 1975—; cons. urologist Saginaw VA Hosp., 1972-75, Charleston VA Hosp., 1975—; hon. cons. in urology St. Peter's Hosps., London, 1981-82; sr. vis. fellow Inst. Urology, London, 1981-82; mil. cons. in urology to surgeon gen. U.S. Air Force, 1982-85. Mem. East Lansing Planning Commn., 1974-75; Vestryman, jr. warden Episcopal Ch., 1974-75, layreader, 1975—, chmn. layreaders, 1983—, mem. diocesan com. continuing edn., 1975—; vestryman St. Michael's Episc. Ch., 1979-82, chmn. every mem. canvass, 1979, 80; del. Diocesan Conv., 1978. Col., M.C., USAR 1981-85. Served to col. M.C. USAR, 1985—. Diplomate Am. Bd. Urology. Fellow ACS, Am. Acad. Pediatrics mem. Soc. Univ. Urologists, Internat. Soc. Urology, Am. Urol. Assn., AMA, Nat. Urol. Forum. Soc. Pediatric Urology, Mayo Alumni Assn. (v.p. 1979-81, chmn. devel. com. 1979-83, pres. 1983-85). Republican. Clubs: Lotos (N.Y.C.); Seabrook Island; Army and Navy (Washington); Lotos (N.Y.C.). Author: Understanding Urology, 1973; Urology in Primary Care, 1976; Urology: A Core Textbook, 1985. Contbr. articles to profl. jours. Office: Dept Urology Med U South Carolina 171 Ashley Ave Charleston SC 29425

ROUSAKIS, JOHN PAUL, mayor of Savannah, insurance broker; b. Savannah, Ga., Jan. 14, 1929; s. Paul V. and Antigone (Alexopoulos) R.; m. Irene Fotopoulos, Sept. 5, 1953; children—Rhonda, Paul, Thea, Tina. B.B.A., U. Ga., 1952. Ins. broker, Savannah, 1956—; mayor City of Savannah, 1970—; past pres., dir. Nat. League Cities; mem. adv. bd. U.S. Conf. Mayors; dir. Pub. Tech., Inc. Served with U.S. Army, 1953-56. Named Outstanding Young Man of Savannah, also Outstanding Young Man of Ga., 1962. Mem. Ga. Mcpl. Assn. (dir., past pres.), Am. Legion. Club: Sertoma. Lodges: Masons, Shriners, Elks, Ahepa. Office: City Hall Savannah GA 31401

ROUSE, BRENDA BEVERLY, respiratory therapist, nurse; b. Chgo., Sept. 10, 1952; d. Raymond John and Ila Jean (Neeley) R.; m. Rick Alan Bair, May 11, 1974 (div.). A.D. in Nursing, Purdue U.-Ft. Wayne, 1974; diploma in Advanced Respiratory Therapy U. Chgo., 1976; B.S. in Allied Health Adminstrn., Ind. U.-Indpls., 1978. Respiratory therapy technician Luth. Hosp., Ft. Wayne, Ind., 1972-74, profl. therapist, 1974-76, respiratory care nurse, 1976-78, respiratory therapy supr., 1978-79, asst. dir. respiratory therapy, 1979-81; program dir. respiratory therapy sch. St. Vincent Hosp. and Marian Coll., Indpls., 1981-82; dir. respiratory therapy dept. Lubbock Gen. Hosp. (Tex.), 1982-85; dir. pulmonary services dept. Seton Med. Ctr., Austin, 1985—; adv. bd. Ind. Vocat. Tech. Coll., Ft. Wayne, 1976-81, South Plains Coll., Lubbock, 1982-85, S.W. Tex. State U., San Marcos, 1985—; CPR instr. Am. Heart Assn.; active N.E. Ind. Interagy. Council Smoking and Health, 1979. Mem. Am. Assn. Respiratory Therapy, Am. Assn. Critical Care Nurses, Tex. Soc. Respiratory Therapy, Tex. Thoracic Soc. Methodist. Home: 12130-B Thompkins Dr Austin TX 78753 Office: Seton Med Ctr 1201 W 38th St Austin TX 78705

ROUSE, DORIS JANE, physiologist, research administrator; b. Greensboro, N.C., Oct. 3, 1948; d. Welby Corbett and Nadia Elizabeth (Grainger) R.; B.A. in Chemistry, Duke U., 1970, Ph.D. in Physiology and Pharmacology, 1980; m. Blake Shaw Wilson, Jan. 6, 1974; 1 dau., Nadia Jacqueline. Sci. instr. Peace Corps, Liberia, 1970-71; research scientist Burroughs Wellcome Co., Research Triangle Park, N.C., 1971-76; dir. biomed. applications team NASA, Research Triangle Inst., Research Triangle Park, 1976-83, dir. Ctr. Tech. Applications, 1983—; adj. asst. prof. U. N.C. Sch. Medicine, 1983—; adminstr. com. for wheelchair standards Am. Nat. Standards Inst., 1982—; mem. spl. rev. com. small bus. applications NIH, 1983—; cons. VA. Mem. adv. bd. Assn. Retarded Citizens. Recipient group achievement award NASA, 1979. Mem. Assn. Advancement Med. Instrumentation, Rehab. Engring. Soc. N.Am. (chmn. wheelchair com. 1981—), Am. Soc. on Aging (tech. and aging info. adv. bd.), Club: Triangle Drive. Contbr. articles prof. jours. Home: 2410 Wrightwood Ave Durham NC 27705 Office: PO Box 12194 Research Triangle Park NC 27709

ROUSE, ELOISE MEADOWS, foundation executive; b. Shreveport, La., July 22, 1931; d. Curtis Washington and Lucille Eloise (Loyd) Meadows; m. Dudley Lee Rouse, Aug. 26, 1952; children—Deborah L., Lee, Elizabeth M. B.Mus. Ed., Baylor U., 1952. 1st grade tchr. Brentwood Elementary Sch., Austin, Tex., 1953-55; v.p., dir., mem. grants rev. com. The Meadows Found., Dallas, 1979—. Mem. honor bd. New Horizons Ranch & Center Home for Troubled Youth, Goldthwaite, Tex.; mem. trustee's com. Meadows Sch. of the Arts, So. Meth. U.; mem. exec. com., bd. dirs. Dallas Summer Musicals; mem. adv. com. Baylor U. Sch. Music; mem. Baylor U. Devel. Council; active First Bapt. Ch. Dallas. Clubs: Village Gardeners Garden (1st v.p.); Wadley Guild; Dallas Woman's; Marianne Scruggs Garden Crystal Charity Ball com.; Park Cities Hist. Soc.; Dallas Summer Musicals Guild; DAR, Internat. Platform Assn. Clubs: Dallas Country (Women's Tennis Assn.), Ponte Vedra (Fla.). Home: 4540 Lorraine Ave Dallas TX 75205 Office: The Meadows Found 2922 Swiss Ave Dallas TX 75204

ROUSE, JANE, hospital administrator; b. Port Arthur, Tex., July 4, 1922; d. Robert Emmett and Lou Victor (Tunis) McKay Lynch; m. Philip Milton Rouse, Feb. 19, 1943 (dec. 1984); children—Robert Wilson (dec.), John Philip, Phyllis Anne Chudleigh, Linda Jane Pickering. Diploma, Port Arthur Bus. Coll., 1942. Sec., Gulf Oil Corp., Port Arthur, 1942-47; mgr. Swanson Mech. Contractor, Bellaire, Tex., 1959-63; adminstr. Colo.-Fayette Med. Ctr., Weimar, Tex., 1967—. Mem., Tex. Sesquecentennial Com., Colorado County, 1984—. Mem. Am. Hosp. Assn. (del. 1984—, governing council 1983—), Tex. Hosp. Assn. (com. chmn. 1983-85, trustee 1985—), Tex. Assn. Hosp. Fin. Adminstrn. (bd. dirs. 1982-84), Weimar C. of C. (pres. 1978). Republican. Methodist. Avocations: Sewing; painting; traveling. Home: PO Box 621 Weimar TX 78962 Office: Colo-Fayette Med Ctr 104 N East St Weimar TX 78962

ROUSE, WILLIAM BRADFORD, systems engineering researcher, educator; b. Fall River, Mass., Jan. 20, 1947; s. Gaylor Louis Rouse and Barbara (Peirce) Rouse Sherman; m. Sandra Howard Kane, Sept. 8, 1968; 1 child, Rebecca Kane. B.S.M.E., U. R.I., 1969; S.M., MIT, 1970, Ph.D., 1972. Postdoctoral research assoc. MIT, Cambridge, 1972; asst. prof. Tufts U., Medford, Mass., 1973; prof. U. Ill., Urbana, 1974-81; prof. indsl. and systems engring. Ga. Inst. Tech., Atlanta, 1981—; prin. scientist, chief exec. officer Search Tech., Inc., Norcross, Ga., 1980—; chief exec. officer Search Aeronautics, Inc., Norcross, 1984—. Author books including: Systems Engineering Models of Human-Machine Interaction, 1980; also numerous chpts., articles. Recipient O. Hugo Schuck award Am. Automatic Control Council, 1979. Fellow IEEE (Centennial medal 1984); mem. Systems, Man and Cybernetics Soc. of IEEE (pres. 1982-83), Am. Inst. Indsl. Engrs. (sr.), Human Factors Soc. Methodist. Home: 1886 Vanderlyn Dr Dunwoody GA 30338 Office: Search Tech Inc 25-B Tech Park Norcross GA 30092

ROUSSEAU, JAMES ARTHUR, technical institute administrator; b. Adah, Pa., July 16, 1940; s. James Arthur Rousseau and Nettie (Robinson) Rousseau Smith; m. Jean E. Edwards, July 18, 1970; children—James Arthur, Inge' Dawn. B.S., Knoxville Coll., 1962; M.S., A&T State U., Greensboro, N.C., 1972; Ed.S., Appalachian State U., 1983. Asst. prin., athletic dir. Carver High Sch., Winston-Salem, N.C., 1973-76; asst. prin. East Forsyth Sr. High Sch., Winston-Salem, 1976; prin. Philo Jr. High Sch., Winston-Salem, 1977-80, Paisley High Sch., Winston-Salem, 1980-82; v.p. planning and devel. Forsyth Tech. Inst., Winston-Salem, 1982—; moderator, toastmaster ednl. orgns., Winston-Salem, 1963—; condr. staff devel. activities, Winston-Salem, 1976-82. Author numerous grant proposals. Chmn. Pub.-Pvt. Sector-Arts Council Fund Drive, Winston-Salem, 1981; mem. Citizens for Jobs and Edn. Com., Winston-Salem, 1983; com. chmn. Project Self-Sufficiency, City of Winston-Salem, 1984; bd. dirs. Forsyth County Ct. Vols., N.C., 1984. Named Most Outstanding Prin., Winston-Salem/Forsyth County PTA Council, 1978; R.J. Reynolds scholar Loretta Heights Coll., Denver, 1981; IDEA fellow, 1981-82. Mem. N.C. Council Resource Devel. (exec. com. 1982-84), N.C. Assn. Instl. Research (exec. com. 1983-84), N.C. State Employees Assn., Council for Advancement Secondary Edn., Learning Resource Assn., Flonnie Anderson Theatrical Assn., Forsyth Prins. Assn. (treas. 1980-81, pres.-elect 1981-82), Omega Psi Phi (basileus 1984-86, Omega Man of Yr. 1981). Democrat. Presbyterian. Avocations: fishing; reading; sports. Home: 5017 Timbrook Ln Winston-Salem NC 27103 Office: Forsyth Tech Inst 2100 Silas Creek Pkwy Winston-Salem NC 27103

ROUSSOS, CONSTANTINE, computer science educator, software systems design consultant; b. Kingston, N.Y., Sept. 22, 1947; s. Christos Constantine and Sylvia Martha (Amrod) R.; m. Gail Darlene Phillips, Nov. 27, 1969; children—Miriam, Damon. B.A. in Math, Old Dominion U., 1969; M.S. in Math., Coll. William and Mary, 1974; Ph.D. in Computer Sci., U. Va., 1979. Grad. asst. U. Va., Charlottesville, 1975-79; instr. computer sci. and math. Washington and Lee U., Lexington, Va., 1977-78; v.p. software systems Three Ridges Corp., Lovingston, Va., 1979-81; dir. computer services Lynchburg Coll., Va., 1981-85, chmn. computer sci. dept., 1985—. Chmn., Nelson County Recreation Bd., Lovingston, 1985. Served with USN, 1970-73. Named Outstanding Young Man of Am., U.S. Jaycees, 1983. Mem. Digital Equipment Users Soc., Assn. for Computing Machinery, Va. Ednl. VAX Users (founder, pres. 1983-85), Nelson Jaycees (sec. 1982-84). Avocations: rugby; gardening; hiking; ice skating; softball. Home: Route 1 Box 186 Arrington VA 22922 Office: Lynchburg Coll Computer Ctr Lynchburg VA 24501

ROVE, KARL CHRISTIAN, direct marketing company executive; b. Denver, Dec. 25, 1950; s. Louis C. and Reba Louise R.; m. Darby Hickson, Jan. 25, 1986. Student U. Utah, 1969-71, George Mason U., 1973-75, U. Tex., 1977, 79. Exec. dir. Coll. Republican Nat. Com., Washington, 1971-73; legis. asst. Rep. Richard Mallary, Washington, 1973; spl. asst. to George Bush, Republican Nat. Chmn., 1973-74, exec. asst. to Richard Obenshain, Rep. Nat. Co-Chmn., 1974-75; fin. dir. Republican. Com. Va., 1976; asst. to George Bush, Houston, 1977-78; dep. dir. Gov. Clements Com., Austin, Tex., 1979-80; dep. exec. asst. to Gov. William P. Clements Jr., 1980-81; pres. Karl Rove & Co., Austin, Tex., 1981—; spl. asst. for adminstrn. Gov. Clements, Jr., 1981. Chmn., Coll. Rep. Nat. Com., 1973-77; mem. Rep. Nat. Exec. Com., 1973-77; chmn. U.S. Youth Council, 1977-78; treas. Tex. Women's Employment and Edn., 1981-84; regent Tex. Womans U., 1981-83. Episcopalian. Home: 616 Crystal Creek Austin TX 78746 Office: PO Box 1902 Austin TX 78767

ROVENGER, SCOTT ELLIOT, lawyer; b. Miami Beach, Fla., July 14, 1953; s. Ben and Sylvia (Schoenberg) R.; m. Holli L. Harwin, Dec. 26, 1983; 1 child, Dani Samantha. B.A., U. Miami, 1974, J.D., 1977. Bar: Fla. 1978, U.S. Dist. Ct. (so. dist) Fla. 1978. Assoc. Vogler & Postman, Miami, 1978-80; ptnr. Linet, Rovenger, Perkins & Krakower, North Miami Beach, Fla., 1980—. Mem. ABA, Am. Trial Lawyers Assn. Democrat. Jewish. Lodge: B'nai B'rith. Office: Linet Rovenger Perkins & Krakower 1899 NE 164th St North Miami Beach FL 33162

ROW, THOMAS HENRY, nuclear engineer; b. Blacksburg, Va., Feb. 9, 1935; s. Stuart Blake and Ruth (Turner) R.; m. Marian Joyce Bonham, Dec. 1958 (div. 1973); m. 2d, Carole Jane Robbins, Mar. 27, 1975; children—Deborah Lynne, Stuart Bonham, Thomas Christopher, Robert Blake. B.S., Roanoke Coll., 1957; M.S., Va. Poly. Inst. and State U., 1959. With nuclear safety program Oak Ridge Nat. Lab., 1959-66, PWR spray program, 1966-71, environ. impact program, 1971-74, environ. impact section head, 1974-81, dir. nuclear waste programs, 1981—. Mem. Am. Nuclear Soc., Sigma Xi. Lodge: Elks. Home: 231 Louisiana Ave Oak Ridge TN 37830 Office: Oak Ridge National Lab PO Box X Oak Ridge TN 37831

ROWAN, JO, ballerina, educator; d. Joseph T. and Nona (Meyer) R.; m. John Richard Bedford. Student ballet Cin. Sch. Am. Ballet, Ballet Theatre Sch.; B.F.A., M.A.D., U. Cin.; student ballet Bolshoi Sch. Moscow. Ballet mistress Dallas Ballet; soloist Met. Opera, Phila. Opera, Dallas Civic Opera, Cin. Summer Opera, Tulsa Civic Opera; ballet soloist and guest artist Kans. City Philharm., Balt. Symphony Orch., Cin. Symphony Orch.; lectr. history Am. Dance; founder, dir. Am. Spirit Dancers, Oklahoma City U.; founder Oklahoma City U. Liturgical Dancers; guest tchr. Okla. Dance Masters Assn., St. Louis Dancing Tchrs. Assn., Dance Troup, Dance Makers, Tex. Assn. Tchrs. Dance, Am. Dance Assn., Miami Valley Assn. Dance Tchrs.; actress, singer, commedienne, choreographer; artist-in-residence U. Wyo., Laramie; guest artist U. Nebr., Lincoln; guest artist and artist-in-residence Cin. Sch. Creative and Performing Arts; toured nationally Dance Caravan Red, Dance Olympus; faculty mem. Nilo Toledo's Summer Fine Arts Camp, Tampa, Fla., also Dance Camp Am.; guest lectr. on dance injuries Am. Acad. Orthopaedic Surgeons sport injury clinics and convs. Producer 10 nationally distributed dance instrn. records on Statler, Hoctor, Stepping Tones labels. Home: 745 Jenkins Ave Norman OK 73069 Office: Dance Dept Oklahoma City U 2501 NW Blackwelder Ave Oklahoma City OK 73106

ROWAN, JOHN ROBERT, medical center director; b. Joliet, Ill., Aug. 19, 1919; s. Hugh Hamilton and Elizabeth Margaret (Maloney) R.; m. Ruth Elaine Boyle, June 17, 1944; 1 son, Robert J. Student, Butler U., 1952-53, Ind. U., 1953-54. Personnel specialist VA Br. Office 7, Chgo., 1946; personnel officer VA Hosp., Ft. Benjamin Harrison, Ind., 1946-51, Indpls., 1951-56, asst. dir., 1960-67, asst. mgr., Iron Mountain, Mich., 1956-60; hosp. adminstrn. specialist VA Central Office, Washington, 1967-69; dir. VA Hosp., Manchester, N.H., 1969-71, Buffalo, 1971-72, VA Med. Center, Lexington, Ky., 1972—, VA Med. Dist. 11, 1975—. Bd. dirs. Marion County (Ind.) unit Am. Cancer Soc., 1960-67, pres., 1964-66, bd. dirs. Ind. div., 1966-67; bd. dirs. Western N.Y. Regional Med. Program, 1971-72, Eastern Ky. Health Systems Agy., 1976—, United Way of Bluegrass, 1976—; mem. regional advisory council Ohio Valley Regional Med. Program, 1972-76; mem. State Health Planning Council, 1982—; bd. dirs. Hosp. Hospitality House of Lexington, 1981, United Way of the Bluegrass, 1983. Served in USAAF, 1942-46. Decorated Bronze Star; recipient Meritorious Service citations Ind. dept. DAV, 1964, Ky. dept. Am. Legion, 1975, Ky. dept. VFW, 1976, Eastern Ky. U., 1974, Ky. dept. DAV, 1978, Spl. Recognition award VFW, 1982, cert. of Merit DAV, 1982. Fellow Am. Coll. Hosp. Adminstrs.; mem. Am. Hosp. Assn., Ky. Hosp. Assn. (trustee), Bluegrass Dist. of Ky. Hosp. Assn., Lexington Hosp. Council, Assn. Mil. Surgeons U.S., Fed. Hosp. Inst. Alumni Assn., Fed. Exec. Interagy. Alumni Assn., Lexington Fed. Exec. Assn. (pres. 1975-76). Roman Catholic. Home: Quarters 8 VA Med Center Leestown Rd Lexington KY 40511 Office: VA Med Center Leestown Rd Lexington KY 40511*

ROWE, A(RIEL) PRESCOTT, chemical company executive; b. Fredericksburg, Va., Jan. 6, 1938; s. William J. and Otelia R. (Cline) R.; m. Jane F. Fenlon, Sept. 2, 1961; children—John Prescott, Virginia Peyton. B.A., Washington and Lee U., 1960. Dir. info. services Washington and Lee U., Lexington, Va., 1960-63; mgr. consumer and packaging pub. relations Reynolds Metals Co., Richmond, Va., 1963-65; dir. info. services Central Va. Ednl. TV Corp., Richmond, 1965-68; dir. devel. Queens Coll., Charlotte, N.C., 1968-70; dir. corp. communications Ethyl Corp., Richmond, 1970-85, v.p. corp. communications, 1985—. Bd. dirs. Richmond Goodwill Industries, Inc.; chmn. Central Va. Ednl. TV. Served to sgt. U.S. Army, 1961-66. Mem. Pub. Relations Soc. Am. (accredited), Met. Richmond C. of C. (former dir.), Omicron Delta Kappa, Sigma Delta Chi. Episcopalian. Clubs: Commonwealth, Bull & Bear, Country Club Va. (Richmond). Lodge: Rotary (pres. 1984-85). Home: 102 Tuckahoe Blvd Richmond VA 23226 Office: Ethyl Corp 330 S 4th St Richmond VA 23219

ROWE, BONNIE GORDON, music co. exec.; b. Buford, Ga., May 3, 1922; s. Bonnie Gordon and Alma (Poole) R.; student Ga. Evening Coll., 1939-41, U. Wichita, 1948-49, Ga. State Coll., 1949-52; m. Mary Wilburta Shidler; 1 dau., Sharon Lynn; m. 2d, Gloria Lucille Fairfax, Feb. 17, 1962 (div.); 1 dau., Susan Rebecca. Traffic mgr. Bonanza Air Lines, Las Vega, 1946-48; music tchr. 1948-52; owner Rowe Accordion Distbg. Co., Rowe Accordion Center, Atlanta, 1952-56, Atlanta Music Pub. Co., 1956—, B. Rowe Music Co., Atlanta, 1957—; pres.-treas. B.C.R. Corp. Bd. dirs. Sandtown Found. Served to lt. col. USAAF, World War II; ETO. Decorated Air medal with three oak leaf clusters. Mem. Southeastern Accordion Assn. (past pres.), Nat. Assn. Music Mchts., Atlanta Fedn. Musicians, Travelers Protective Assn., Atlanta C. of C. Res. Officers Assn., Internat. Platform Assn., Am. Legion, Gamma Delta Phi. Clubs: Sandtown Civitan (past pres., lt. gov., past pres. Met. Atlanta Council), Elks, Ft. McPherson Officers. Composer: Accordionique, 1953, Vivolet, 1956, More and More and More, 1964, Dedication, 1964, All I Really See Is You, 1965, I Love Only You, 1965, Predudio Reminisci, 1969. Home: 5085 Erin Rd SW Atlanta GA 30331 Office: 6102 Gordon Rd Mableton GA 30059

ROWE, GENEVA LASSITER, psychotherapist, counseling center administrator; b. Atlanta, Aug. 11, 1927; d. Hoyt Cleveland and Tinie (Gresham) Lassiter; m. Fred Earnest Rowe, May 3, 1958; children—Carol, Vickie, Randall. B.A., Oglethorpe U., 1968; M.S.W., U. Ga., 1970; Ph.D., Fla. State U., 1978. Accredited Acad. Cert. Social Workers; lic. marriage and family therapist, Ga. Alcohol and drug counselor Georgian Clinic, Atlanta, 1968; outpatient counselor DeKalb Guidance Clinic, Atlanta, 1969; protective services supr. DeKalb Family and Children Services, Decatur, Ga., 1970-72; outpatient therapist DeKalb Mental Health Ctr., 1972-75; marriage and family therapist Fla. State U., 1977; lectr. sociology Oglethorpe U., 1978-81; psychotherapist, dir. Northeast Counseling Ctr., P.C., Atlanta, Marietta and Lawrenceville, Ga., 1978—; clin. supr. master's students in practicum Ga. State U., 1980—. Fellow Am. Orthopsychiat. Assn., Internat. Council Sex Edn. and Parenthood; mem. Am. Assn. Marriage and Family Therapy (clin. mem.), AAUW, Ga. Assn. Marriage and Family Therapy (pub. relations chmn. 1984-86), Gwinnett County C. of C., Cobb County C. of C., Young Women of Arts. Methodist. Home: 2005 Woodsdale Rd NE Atlanta GA 30324 Office: Northeast Counseling Ctr PC 2995 Lawrenceville Hwy Lawrenceville GA 30245 also 3823 Roswetl Rd NE Marietta GA 30062

ROWE, JAMES WILLIAM, SR., engineer; b. Richmond, Va., Mar. 10, 1944; s. William Walter and Margaret Lucille (Brauer) R.; m. Janet O'Neal Parker, Mar. 30, 1968; children—James William, Rhett Nelson. B.S., Va. Commonwealth U., 1968. Cert. wastewater plant operator. Chief operator City of Richmond, 1974-76; supr. Park 500 div. Phillip Morris, Richmond, 1976-79; quality control chemist Gen. Metals Tech., Richmond, 1979-81; process engr. Synertech, Richmond, 1981-83, FN Mfg., Inc., Columbia, S.C., 1983—. Coach NE Columbia Soccer Assn., 1983—, Dale Youth Soccer Assn., Richmond, 1982-83. Mem. Am. Soc. for Metals, Am. Electroplaters Soc. Republican. Baptist. Club: Va. Motor Sports (Richmond). Home: 304 N Chateau Dr Columbia SC 29223 Office: FN Mfg Inc 797 Clemson Rd Columbia SC 29223

ROWE, MARY ETHEL, nurse; b. Shelby, N.C., Oct. 21, 1939; d. James Marvin and Lincey Mae (Morgan) Hall; m. Talmadge Rowe, Sept. 30, 1960; children—Mary Beth, Donna Hope. Diploma, Gaston Meml. Sch. Nursing, 1961. Staff nurse Newberry County Hosp., S.C., 1961-62; staff nurse S.C. State Hosp., Columbia, 1962-63, head nurse, 1963-64; staff nurse Baptist Med. Ctr., Columbia, 1964-66, head nurse, 1966—; mem. nurse mktg. com. Bapt. Med. Ctr., Columbia, 1983—. Mem. ARC, Columbia, 1980—; mem. Mid-Carolina Jr. High PTO, Prosperity, S.C., 1984—; pres. bd. dirs. S.C. Bapt. Hosp. Credit Union, Columbia, 1984—. Recipient 20 Yr. Service award Congaree council Girl Scouts U.S., 1982, Bapt. Med. Ctr., 1984. Lutheran. Home: Route 3 Box 141 A Prosperity SC 29127 Office: Bapt Med Ctr 1519 Marion St Columbia SC 29220

ROWE, ROBERT CLARK, electronic manufacturing executive; b. Champaign, Ill., Mar. 17, 1930; s. Johny Clifford and Margaret Ann (Moore) R.; m. Patricia Ann Mason, May 29, 1952; children—Randy C., Robin A. Student Joplin (Mo.) Jr. Coll., 1950, U. Wichita, 1959, Tulsa Jr. Coll., 1980-81; U. Tulsa, 1971, Oral Roberts U., 1983. Indsl. engr. Boeing Co., Wichita, 1955-59; prodn. supr. Dayton Rubber Co., Springfield, Mo., 1959-63; systems analyst Rockwell Internat., Tulsa, 1963-76; adminstrv. mgr. telephone and telemetry products Seiscor div. Seismograph Service Corp., Tulsa, 1976-83, mgr. corp. info. systems, 1983-84; mgr. material control Lowrance Electronic, Inc., Tulsa, 1984—. Past drive chmn. United Fund; sponsor Jr. Achievement. Served with Army NG, 1948-85. Mem. Am. Prodn. and Inventory Control Soc. Republican. Club: Internat. Fitness (Tulsa). Lodge: Masons, Elks. Home: 305 W 4th St Owasso OK 74055 Office: 12000 E Skelly Dr Tulsa OK 74128

ROWE, THOMAS DUDLEY, JR., lawyer, educator; b. Richmond, Va., Feb. 26, 1942; s. Thomas Dudley and Georgia Rosamond (Stripp) R. B.A. summa cum laude, Yale U., 1964; M.Phil. (Rhodes scholar), Oxford (Eng.) U., 1967; J.D. magna cum laude, Harvard U., 1970. Bar: D.C. 1971, N.C. 1976. Law clk. to Assoc. Justice Potter Stewart, U.S. Supreme Ct., Washington, 1970-71; asst. counsel U.S. Senate Adminstrv. Practice Subcom., Washington, 1971-73; pvt. practice, Washington, 1973-75; assoc. prof. law Duke U., Durham, N.C., 1975-79, prof., 1979—, assoc. dean for research, 1981-84; vis. prof. law Georgetown U., 1979-80, U. Mich., 1985; bd. dirs. Pvt. Adjudication Ctr. U.S. Dept. Justice fellow, 1980-81; recipient Disting. Teaching award Duke Bar Assn., 1985. Mem. Am. Law Inst., ABA. Democrat. Contbr. articles to profl. jours. Home: 712D Constitution Dr Durham NC 27705 Office: Sch of Law Duke U Durham NC 27706

ROWLAND, BRET, geologist; b. Calif., July 3, 1950; s. David and Jane (Willis) R.; m. Trinia Lynn Howell, Sept. 25, 1976; 1 child, Forrest Dustin. B.S. in Geology, Va. Poly. Inst., 1972; M.S. in Geology, Memphis State U., 1974. Wellsite geologist Mobil Oil Corp., Dallas, 1974-76, staff geologist, New Orleans, 1977-79, supr. South Alaska exploration, Dallas, 1984—; prodn. geologist Arabian Am. Oil Co., Saudi Arabia, 1980-84, 85; geol. advisor Mobil producing Tex., N.Mex., Midland, Tex., 1985—. Mem. Am. Assn. Petroleum Geologists, Geol. Soc. Am. Mormon. Avocations: family, farming. Home: 2613 Fannin Dr Midland TX 79705 Office: MPTM PO Box 633 Midland TX 79701

ROWLAND, JAMES ROY, congressman; b. Wrightsville, Ga., Feb. 3, 1926; s. J. Roy and Jerradine R.; m. Luella Price, July 28, 1924; children—Lou Rowland Neal, Jane Rowland Wood, Jim. Ed. Emory U., 1943, South Ga. Coll., 1946, U. Ga., 1946-48; M.D., Med. Coll. Ga., 1952. Intern Macon Hosp., Ga., 1952-53, resident in family practice, 1953-54; practice medicine specializing in family practice, Dublin, Ga., 1954-82; state rep. Ga. Ho. of Reps., Atlanta, 1976-82; mem. 98th Congress from 8th Ga. Dist., 1983—. Served with U.S. Army, 1942-46; ETO. Decorated Bronze Star. Democrat. Methodist. Office: US House of Representatives 423 Cannon House Office Bldg Washington DC 20515

ROWLEY, CHARLES KERSHAW, economics educator; b. Southampton, Eng., June 21, 1939; came to U.S., 1984; s. Frank and Ellen (Beal) R.; m. Betty Silverwood, June 19, 1961 (div. 1971); m. Marjorie Isobel Spillets, July 17, 1972; children—Amanda, Sarah. Lectr. U. Nottingham, Eng., 1962-65; lectr., then sr. lectr. U. Kent, Canterbury, Eng., 1965-70; reader U. York, Eng., 1970-72; prof. econs. U. Newcastle, Eng., 1972-83, George Mason U., Fairfax, Va., 1984—; cons. Office Fair Trading, London, 1980-83; research assoc. Wolfson Coll., Oxford, 1984—. Author numerous books in field. Contbr. articles to profl. jours. Grantee Bank of Eng., 1965, Social Sci. Research Council, London, 1970-72, Dept. Environ., London, 1974-80. Mem. Mont Pelerin Soc., Am. Econ. Assn., Royal Econ. Soc., Pub. Choice Soc., European Pub. Choice Soc. (pres. 1980-82) Home: 4973 Swinton Dr Fairfax VA 22032 Office: Ctr Study Public Choice George Mason U Fairfax VA 22030

ROWLEY, HORACE PEREZ, III, lawyer; b. Houston, Dec. 7, 1940; s. Horace Perez Jr. and Monita (Hohenstein) R.; m. Wendy B. Kornegay, Oct. 20, 1979; 1 child, Hardin Parisher. B.B.A., Tulane U., 1962, LL.B., 1967. Bar: La. 1967, U.S. Ct. Appeals (5th cir.) 1967, U.S. Dist. Ct. (ea. dist.) La. 1967, D.C. 1970, U.S. Supreme Ct. 1970, N.Y. 1971, U.S. Tax Ct. 1971, U.S. Ct. Mil. Appeals 1971, U.S. Ct. Claims 1971, U.S. Ct. Custom and Patent Appeals 1971, U.S. Dist. Ct. (mid. dist.) La. 1973, U.S. Dist. Ct. (we. dist.) La. 1983. Asst. U.S. atty. Dept. Justice, New Orleans, 1967-70; sole practice law, N.Y.C., 1971-75, New Orleans, 1976—. Founder Suburban Rural Rights Coalition, N.Y., N.J. and Conn., 1972, editor, pub. newsletter, 1972-75. Served to lt. (j.g.) USN, 1962-64. Mem. La. State Bar Assn., Assn. Trial Lawyers Am., N.Y. State Trial Lawyers Assn., New Orleans Bd. Trade. Roman Catholic. Home and Office: 116 Fairway Dr Covington LA 70433

ROWSON, RICHARD CAVANAGH, publisher; b. Hollywood, Calif., Apr. 7, 1926; s. Louis Cavanagh and Mable Louise (Montney) R.; m. Elena Louisa Costabile, Nov. 22, 1952; children—Peter Cavanagh, John Cummings. A.B., U. Calif., Berkeley, 1946; certificate, Sorbonne, 1949; M.I.A., Columbia U., 1950. Trainee Fgn. Policy Assn., 1950; dir. World Affairs Council R.I., 1951-52; with Fgn. Policy Assn., 1951-62, dir. finance and devel., 1960-62; with Radio Free Europe, 1962-69, dir. policy and planning, 1964-69; dir. spl. studies Praeger Pubs., Inc., N.Y.C., 1969-77, pres., 1975-77, Pergamon Press, 1977-80. R.R. Bowker, 1980; info. and pub. cons., 1981; dir. Duke U. Press, 1981—; lectr., condr. workshops, roundtables. Contbr. articles to profl. jours. Served to lt. (j.g.) USNR, 1944-47. Mem. Am. Polit. Sci. Assn., Am. Econ. Assn., N.Y. Acad. Scis., Am. Assn. Advancement Slavic Studies, U. Calif., Columbia U. alumni assns., Soc. Internat. Devel. Democrat. Club: Overseas Press (N.Y.C.). Home: 5 Sylvan Rd Durham NC 27701 Office: Duke U Press 6697 College Station Durham NC 27708

ROY, CHARLES EDWARD, religion educator; b. Birmingham, Ala., July 15, 1917; s. Moses Eugene and Bessie (Bennett) R.; m. Brona Nifong, Dec. 20, 1947; children—Rebecca Roy Benfield, A.A., Young Harris Coll., 1938; A.B. cum laude, Piedmont Coll., 1940; M.Div., Candler Sch. Theology, 1944; M.A., George Peabody Coll., 1949; D.D. (hon.), Greensboro Coll., 1980. Ordained elder United Methodist Ch. Chaplain, prof. religion, chmn. div. humanities Brevard Coll., N.C., 1944-84, emeritus, 1984—, acting pres., 1968-69. Pres. Translyvania County Youth Assn., 1965-68; bd. dirs. Transylvania-Henderson Counties Justice Alternatives, 1981—; bd. mem. Community Relations Council, Schenck Job Corps, Brevard, 1980—; chmn. Transylvania County Human Relations Council, Brevard, 1965—; chmn. Transylvania County United Way, Brevard, 1971-72. Mem. Soc. Bibl. Lit., Am. Schs. Oriental Research, Transylvania County Ministerial Assn. Democrat. Lodge: Lions (pres. Brevard 1973-74). Avocations: travel; archeology; gardening; woodworking.

ROY, CLARENCE LESLIE, landscape architect; b. Ironwood, Mich., Mar. 6, 1927; s. Theodore Gideon and Myrtle May (Mathews) R.; m. Ruth Serou, Nov. 11, 1959. B.S. in Landscape Architecture, U. Mich., 1951. Landscape architect Lambert Assoc. Cos., Dallas, 1951-59; assoc. Eichstedt-Johnson Assoc., Grosse Pointe, Mich., 1960; prin. Johnson Johnson & Roy/inc., Ann Arbor, Mich., 1961-81, Dallas, 1982—; dir. The Smith Group, Detroit, 1979-82. Founder Old West Assn., Ann Arbor, 1966, pres., 1968-73; pres. Ann Arbor Tomorrow, 1978-79. Served with USN, 1945-46. Fellow Am. Soc. Landscape Architects; mem. Am. Planners Assn., U. Mich. Alumni Assn. (bd. dirs. 1976-79), Tau Sigma Delta. Office: Johnson Johnson & Roy/inc 3000 Carlisle Suite 200 Dallas TX 75204

ROY, ELSIJANE TRIMBLE, U.S. dist. judge; b. Lonoke, Ark., Apr. 2, 1916; d. Thomas Clark and Elsie Jane (Walls) Trimble; m. James M. Roy, Nov. 23, 1943; 1 son, James Morrison. J.D., U. Ark., Fayetteville, 1939, LL.D. (hon.), 1978. Bar: Ark. 1939. Atty. Ark. Revenue Dept., Little Rock, 1939-64; mem. firm Reid, Evrard & Roy, Blytheville, Ark., 1947-54, Roy & Roy, Blytheville, 1954-63; law clk. Ark. Supreme Ct., Little Rock, 1963-65, assoc. justice, 1975-77; U.S. dist. judge for Eastern and Western Dists. Ark., Little Rock, 1977—; judge Pulaski County (Ark.) Circuit Ct., Little Rock, 1966; asst. atty. gen., Ark., Little Rock, 1967; sr. law clk. U.S. Dist. Ct., Little Rock and Ft. Smith, 1968-73; Mem. med. adv. com. U. Ark. Med. Center, 1952-54; Committeewoman Democratic Party 16th Jud. Dist., 1940-42; vice chmn. Ark. Dem. State Com., 1946-48; mem. chmn. com. Ark. Constnl. Commn., 1967-68. Recipient Disting. Alumna citation U. Ark., 1978; named Ark. Woman of Yr., 1976. Mem. Nat. Assn. Women Lawyers, Am. Bar Assn., Ark. Bar Assn., AAUW, Little Rock Women Lawyers (pres. 1939, 42), Ark. Women Lawyers (pres. 1940-41), Mortar Bd., P.E.O., Delta Theta Phi., Chi Omega. Club: Altrusa. Home: Riviera Apts Apt 1101 Little Rock AR 72202 Office: US Post Office and Courthouse PO Box 3255 Little Rock AR 72203*

ROY, JOHNNY BERNARD, urologist; b. Baghdad, Iraq, Jan. 21, 1938; s. Bernard Benedict and Regina V. (Saka) R.; came to U.S., 1965, naturalized, 1976; M.D., U. Baghdad, 1962; m. Sandy L. Gaede, Sept. 23, 1978; children—Jennifer Anne, John II, Geoffrey Benedict. Diplomate Am. Bd. Urology. Chief resident in urology U. Ky. Hosp., 1969-70; NIH research fellow U. Okla. Med. Center, 1970-71; chief urology Kaiser Found. Hosps. Hawaii, 1972-75; chief urology VA Med. Center, Oklahoma City, also assoc. prof. urology U. Okla. Med. Center, 1981—. Contbr. articles to med. jours. Mem. AMA (Physicians Recognition award 1970—), Am. Urol. Assn., A.C.S., Internat. Coll. Surgeons, Am. Fertility Soc., Soc. Univ. Urologists, So. Med. Assn., Okla. Med. Assn., Okla. County Med. Assn., Okla. Kidney Found. (pres. 1979-80), Okla. Urol. Assn. (exec. sec., pres. 1980-81), Sigma Xi. Republican. Roman Catholic. Home: 808 Glenridge Dr Edmond OK 73034 Office: U Okla Health Scis Center PO Box 26901 Oklahoma City OK 73190

ROY, MARIA GAUDALUPE LUPE, nursing services administrator; b. Del Rio, Tex., Oct. 22, 1936; d. Frank Moreno and Julia (Felan) Valdez; m. Lawrence Friedrich Roy, May 30, 1959; children—Carol Lynn Roy Smith, Douglas Edward, Leslie Sue Roy Litteral. B.S., Incarnate Word Coll., 1958, postgrad., 1973. R.N., Tex. Charge nurse Robert B. Green Hosp., San Antonio, 1958-59, Blessing Hosp., Quincy, Ill., 1964-65; staff nurse ob-gyn Santa Rosa Med. Ctr., San Antonio, 1965-67; mem. labor delivery staff Nix Meml. Hosp., San Antonio, 1968-73, supr. ob-gyn, 1974-75; dir. nursing services Meml. Med. Ctr., San Antonio, 1973-74; asst. dir. nursing services Humana Hosp., San Antonio, 1975-86; staff nurse substance abuse program Hays Meml. Hosp., San Marcos, Tex., 1986, dir. eating disorders program, 1986—; cons. for area nursing homes. Served to 1st lt. Army Nursing Corps, 1958-61. Mem. Nurses Assn. Am. Coll. Ob-Gyn (del. 1979-81, chairperson 1979-80), Confraternity of Christian Doctrine Recorder (bd. dirs.), Alumni Assn. Incarnate Word Coll., Nat. Council Cath. Women. Democrat. Avocations: bowling; crafts; sewing; church volunteer work. Home: Route 10 PO Box 24W New Braunfels TX 78130

ROY, NAOMI JEAN, nursing educator; b. Charleston, W.Va., Mar. 12, 1929; d. John Henry and Lena Estis (Hill) Hoy; m. Henry Thomas Roy, Sept. 5, 1952; 1 child, John Thomas. B.S. in Nursing, Alderson-Broaddus Coll., 1951; M.A. in Sociology, W.Va. U., 1960, Ed.D., 1980. Nursing supr. Myers Clinic Hosp., Philippi, W.Va., 1951-54, Broaddus Hosp., Philippi, 1954-57; from instr. to assoc. prof. Alderson-Broaddus Coll., 1957-69, chmn. dept. nursing, 1969-79; vice chmn. dept. nursing W.Va. Wesleyan Coll., Buckhannon, 1979-80, prof., 1980—, chmn. dept., 1980—; pres. W.Va. Bd. Examiners for Registered Nurses, 1963-73. Reviewer (textbook) New Clinical Nursing Procedures, 1979. Contbr. articles to profl. jours. Bd. dirs. Meml. Found. for Nurses in W.Va., 1982—; mem. Gov's Adv. Council Comprehensive Health Planning, 1969-74. Mem. W.V. League for Nursing (bd. dirs.), Nat. League for Nursing, Am. Nurses Assn., W.Va. Nurses Assn., (editorial bd. 1978—). Democrat. Baptist. Lodge: Order of Eastern Star. Avocation: swimming. Home: Route 1 Box 61 Philippi WV 26416 Office: W Va Wesleyan Coll Middleton Hall Buckhannon WV 26201

ROY, RAYMOND ALBERT, JR., pharmacist; b. Matewan, W.Va., Mar. 3, 1954; s. Raymond Albert and Mary (Howerton) R. B.S. in Pharmacy, W.Va. U., 1977. Registered pharmacist, Va., W.Va., N.C., S.C. Pharmacist, buyer Strosnider Drug Co., Williamson, W.Va., 1977-78; pharmacy mgr. Rite Aid Pharmacy, Morgantown, W.Va., 1978-80; pharmacist in charge, pharmacy mgr. K Mart Pharmacy 4084, Lynchburg, Va., 1980—; elder care and child care pharmacist Park-Davis Pharms., Morris Plains, N.J., 1985—. Recipient Pharmacy Edn. Program award Burroughs Wellcome Co., 1982. Mem. Am. Pharm. Assn., Va. Pharmacist Assn. Roman Catholic. Home: 3501 Fort Ave Rutherford 28 Lynchburg VA 24501 Office: K Mart Pharmacy 4084 2315 Wards Rd Lynchburg VA 24502

ROY, ROBERT EDWARD, psychologist; b. Matewan, W.Va., Oct. 5, 1946; s. Raymond Albert and Mary Louise (Howerton) R.; m. Vivian Anna Loret de Mola, Jan. 21, 1984. Staff psychologist Pioneer Community Mental Health Ctr., Seward, Nebr., 1974-76; staff psychologist, program dir. VA Med. Ctr., Lincoln, Nebr., 1976-78; clin. psychologist VA Med. Ctr., Bay Pines, Fla., 1978-80, chief alcohol dependence treatment program, 1980—; clin. assoc. prof. psychology U. Nebr.-Lincoln, 1976-78; clin. asst. prof. psychiatry U. South Fla. Coll. Medicine, Tampa, 1984—. Contbr. articles to profl. jours. Mem. Am. Psychol. Assn., Soc. Psychologists in Addictive Behavior, Nebr. Psychol. Assn., Nebr. Soc. Clin. Hypnosis. Office: Alcohol Dependence Treatment Program 116A2 Psychiatry Service VA Med Ctr Bay Pines FL 33504

ROYAL, SELVIN WAYNE, library science educator; b. Clanton, Ala., Nov. 2, 1941; s. Glen Herman and Aline (Bowen) R.; m. Shirley Ann Cooper, Oct. 10, 1964; B.A., Coll. of Ozarks, 1964; M.A., Central Mo. State U., 1969, Ednl. Specialist, 1976; Advanced Masters, Fla. State U., 1979, Ph.D., 1981. Cert. library media specialist, instructional technologist. Tchr. Sedalia Pub. Schs., Mo., 1964-73, head librarian, 1973-76; asst. prof. Central Mo. State U., Warrensburg, 1976-78; asst. prof. U. Central Ark., Conway, 1979-80, assoc. prof., chmn. dept. library scis., 1980—; cons. in field. Co-author: Manual of Library Skills, 1979. Contbr. articles to profl. jours. Mem. ALA, Assn. Edn. and Communication Tech., Ark. Library Assn., Ark. Audiovisual Assn. (editor News and Views 1982-84), Phi Delta Kappa. Lodge: Lions. Avocations: photography; reading; carpentry. Home: 900 W 28th St Sedalia MO 65301 Office: Univ of Central Arkansas Bruce St Conway AR 72032

ROYALL, ROBERT VENNING, JR., banker; b. Montgomery, Ala., Dec. 11, 1934; s. Robert Venning and Eleanor (Williams) R.; m. Edith G. Frampton, July 30, 1955; children—Eleanor, Margaret, Edith. A.B., U. S.C., 1956; postgrad. Stonier Sch. Banking, Rutgers U., 1969, Advanced Mgmt. Program, Harvard U., 1975. With Citizens & So. Nat. Bank, Columbia, S.C., 1961—, exec. v.p., 1968-70, exec. v.p. retail div., 1970-74, pres., 1974—, chief exec. officer, 1986—, dir., vice chmn. The C&S Corp., 1974—. Chmn. S.C. State Ports Authority, treas., 1983-84; bd. visitors Med. U. S.C., chmn., 1983-84; mem. Pres.'s Nat. Adv. Council, U. S.C.; chmn. Midlands Bd. Econ. Devel.; chmn. S.C. Pvt. Industry Council. chmn. State Job Tng. Coordinating Council. Served to capt. USMC, 1956-59. Named Outstanding Young Man of Yr., Florence Jaycees, 1968; One of 3 Outstanding Young Men in S.C., S.C. Jaycees, 1968. Mem. S.C. Bankers Assn. (Outstanding Young Banker award 1971, dir., 1st v.p., pres.-elect 1983, pres. 1985-86), Am. Mgmt. Assn., Robert Morris Assn., Pres. Assn. Episcopalian. Home: 6 Old Mill Ct Columbia SC 29206 Office: Citizens & So Bank 1801 Main St Columbia SC 29201

ROYCE, RAYMOND WATSON, lawyer, rancher, citrus grower; b. West Palm Beach, Fla., Mar. 5, 1936; s. Wilbur E. and Veda (Watson) R.; m. Catherine L. Setzer, Apr. 21, 1979; children—Raymond, Steven, Nancy, Kathryn. B.C.E., U. Fla., 1958, J.D., 1961. Bar: Fla. 1961, U.S. Dist. Ct. (so. dist.) Fla. 1961, U.S. Ct. Appeals (5th cir.) 1961, U.S. Ct. Appeals (11th cir.) 1981. Assoc. William W. Blakeslee, Palm Beach, Fla., 1961-62; ptnr. Scott, Royce, Harris & Bryan P.A., Palm Beach, 1962—, pres., 1982—; lectr. continuing legal edn. program Fla. Bar. Active Am. Cancer Soc., 1965-75; mem. Econ. Council Palm Beach County; chmn., bd. dirs. Palm Beach County Zoning Task Force. Mem. Fla. Bar (gov. 1974-78), Palm Beach County Bar Assn. (pres. 1973-74, chmn. long range planning com.), Am. Judicature Soc., Fla. Trial Lawyers Assn., Phi Delta Phi, Blue Key. Democrat. Presbyterian. Home: 5550 Whirlaway Rd Palm Beach Gardens FL 33410 Office: 450 Royal Palm Way Palm Beach FL 33480

ROYER, ROBERT L., utility co. exec.; b. 1928; B.S. in Elec. Engring., Rose Hulman Inst. Tech., 1949; married. With Louisville Gas and Electric Co., Inc., 1949—, v.p., gen. supt., 1964-69, v.p. ops., 1969-78, exec. v.p., from 1978, now pres., chief exec. officer, dir. Served in Armed Forces, 1953-55. Office: Louisville Gas and Electric Co PO Box 32010 Louisville KY 40232

ROYSTER, MARGARET ANNE, insurance company administrator; b. Dallas, Oct. 20, 1937; d. Woodrow Wilson and Johnnie (Jones) Buckmeyer; student Baylor U., 1956-57; children—Cynthia Annice Smith, Richard Gregory Smith. Stenographer, Blue Cross/Blue Shield Tex., Dallas, 1957-60, legal sec., part-time 1962-67, exec. sec., 1971-77, sr. supr. employment, 1977—; cons. coll. career fairs, 1978-81. Recipient Campaign award United Way Met. Dallas, 1981. Mem. Dallas Personnel Assn. Home: 521 San Clemente Dr Garland TX 75043 Office: 8150 Brookriver Dr Dallas TX 75247

ROYSTER, WIMBERLY CALVIN, university official, mathematics educator; b. Robards, Ky., Jan. 12, 1925; s. Fred and Ruth Furman (Denton) R.; m. Betty Jo Barnett, July 1, 1950; children—David Calvin, Paul Barnett. B.S., Murray State U., 1946; M.A., U. Ky., 1948, Ph.D., 1952. Asst. prof. Auburn U., Ala., 1952-56; from asst. prof. to prof. math. U. Ky., Lexington, 1956-63, chmn. dept. math., 1963-69, dean Coll. Arts and Scis., 1969-72, vice chancellor for research, dean Grad. Sch., 1972—; chmn. bd. dirs. Council Grad. Schs., Washington, 1983; chmn. Grad. Record Exam. Bd., Princeton, N.J., 1983-84. Contbr. articles to profl. jours. Bd. dirs Oak Ridge Assoc. Univs., 1978-84. Mem. Am. Math. Soc., Math. Assn. Am. (bd. govs. 1959-62), AAAS, Council So. Grad. Schs. (pres. 1981-82), S.E. Consortium for Internat. Devel. (chmn. bd. dirs. 1982-83), Sigma Xi. Methodist. Lodge: Rotary. Home: 773 Malabu Dr Lexington KY 40502 Office: Grad Sch U Ky Lexington KY 40506

ROYSTON, LLOYD LEONARD, college administrator; m. Marion Grant, Nov. 12, 1983; children by previous marriage—Sharon, Le'Nard, Jayston. A.B., Talladega Coll., 1958; M.Ed., Tuskegee Inst., 1971; Ed.D., U. Ala., 1980. Cert. tchr., counselor. Tchr. Ala. State Bd. Edn., Dadeville, 1959-63; social caseworker N.Y.C. Social Services, 1963-65; continuing edn. Tuskegee Inst., Ala., 1965-77, dir. human resources, 1980; faculty devel. coordinator U. Ala., University, 1977-80; dean continuing edn. Pensacola Jr. Coll., Fla., 1982—; cons. AID, 1976-78, Multi-Racial Corp., New Orleans, 1970-72. Author: Methods of Teaching Adults, 1968; Planning Practices At Predominantly Black Institutions, 1980. Bd. dirs. PUSH, Pensacola, 1983, Wedgewood Homeowners Assn., Pensacola, 1982, Fla. Inst. Govt., U. West Fla., 1982—, Pvt. Industry Council, Pensacola, 1984—; mem. Ganett Found. Scholarship Com., 1984. Recipient Service award Dept. Social Service N.Y.C., 1964; Outstanding service award Ala. Migrant Council, 1974; Youth Services award Tuskegee Inst., 1977; Service award Equal Opportunity Commn., Pensacola, 1985. Mem. Fla. Adult Edn. Assn., Lifelong Learning Commn., Continuing Edn. Standing Com., Pensacola C. of C., Talladega Alumni Assn. (v.p. 1984—), Kappa Delta Pi. Baptist. Avocations: Fishing; camping; swimming. Office: Pensacola Jr Coll 1000 College Blvd Pensacola FL 32504

ROZAS, CARLOS JOAQUIN, physician, medical educator; b. Havana, Cuba, Apr. 16, 1952; s. Jose R. and Amalia (Delgado) R.; m. Marisela Castellon, Dec. 21, 1951; children—Daniel, Marissa, Alexandra. B.S. cum laude, U. Miami, 1973, M.D., 1976. Diplomate Am. Bd. Internal Medicine, subsplty. Bd. Pulmonary Disease. Intern, Maricopa County Gen. Hosp., Phoenix, 1976-78, resident in medicine, 1978-80; pulmonary fellow U. South Fla. Affiliated Hosp., Tampa, 1980-82, clin. instr., 1980-82, asst. prof. internal medicine, 1982—. Contbr. articles, papers, abstracts in field to profl. lit. Assoc. fellow Am. Coll. Chest Physicians; mem. ACP, Am. Thoracic Soc., Dade County Med. Soc. Office: Suite 402 4700 N Habana St Tampa FL 33514

ROZENDAL, ROGER ANTHONY, oil company executive; b. Volga, S.D., Jan. 30, 1934; s. Bernard and Josephine (Wobbema) R.; m. Patricia Ann Thebedeaux Scott, Jan. 14, 1961; children—Robert Bertrand, Paul Bernard, Keith Anthony. B.S. in Geol. Engring., S.D. Sch. Mines and Tech., 1956; M.S. in Geology, U. Minn., 1957. Geologist, Shell Oil Co., Midland, Tex., Houston and New Orleans, 1957-70, mgr. new ventures Alaska div., Houston, 1974-79, mgr. exploration econs. head office, Houston, 1979-85; sr. staff geologist Shell Can., Calgary, Alta., 1970-73; chief exploration ops. Pecten Internat. Co., Houston, 1985—. Contbr. articles to profl. publs. Mem. Am. Assn. Petroleum Geologists, Houston Geol. Soc. Republican. Episcopalian. Avocations: Boy Scouts. Home: 5910 Pinewilde Houston TX 77066 Office: Pecten Internat Co PO Box 205 Houston TX 77001

ROZON, ALAN EDWARD, zoo administrator; b. Ft. Pierce, Fla., June 16, 1933; s. Victor Pickering and Dorothy Edna (Railsback) R.; m. Mary Lou McMillan, Feb. 27, 1955; children—Alan Edward Jr., Cynthia Louise. Student, Clemson A&M Coll., 1952-53. Commd. officer U.S. Army, 1953, advanced through grades to lt. col., 1973; ret., 1973; exec. dir., chief operating officer Central Fla. Zool. Soc. Inc., Lake Monroe, 1973—. Co-author study: Urban Insurgency in U.S., 1973. Mem. Seminole County Tourism Devel. Adv. com. Recipient 19 mil. decorations, Central Fla. Zool. Soc. Achievement citation, 1974, Sanford, Fla. C. of C. Outstanding Community Service award, 1975. Fellow Am. Assn. Zoll. Parks and Aquariums. Baptist. Home: 120 Partridge Circle Winter Springs FL 32708 Office: Central Florida Zool Soc PO Box 309 Lake Monroe FL 32747

RUA, MILTON FRANCISCO, lawyer; b. San German, P.R., Dec. 8, 1919; s. Urbano F. and Josefa A. (Gonzalez-Ferrer) R.; B.A. cum laude, U. P.R., 1941, LL.B., 1943; m. Barbara Ann Becher; children by previous marriage—Milton J., Jaime L. Admitted to P.R. bar, 1943; legal counsel Dept. Finance of P.R., 1943-46; sr. partner Rivera-Zayas, Rivera-Cestero & Rua, San Juan, P.R., 1950-73; founder, sr. partner Ra & Mercado, San Juan, P.R., 1973—; founder, counsellor Banco Mercantil de P.R., Rio Piedras, 1966—, chmn. bd. dirs., 1975—; founder Asso. Ins. Agencies, Inc., San Juan, 1972, Fajardo Fed. Savs. & Loan Assn. (P.R.), 1972—; pres., dir. Lincoln Fin. Mortgagees, Inc., San Juan. Mem. bar exam. com. Supreme Ct. P.R., 1955-56; spl. counsel com. natural resources and beautification P.R. Ho. of Reps., 1967-68; mem. citizens com. nuclear plants Environ. Quality Bd. of P.R., 1972; chmn. Electoral Reform Commn., 1973—; mem. organizing com. First Latin Am. Biennal Graphic Arts, P.R., 1970; bd. dirs. Casa el Libro, chmn., 1960-70; bd. dirs. Inst. of Culture of P.R., 1968-79, Students Art League of San Juan, Mus. P.R., P.R. Found. for Humanities, 1981-84. Mem. Found. Bar Assn. P.R. (hon. pres. 1976-78), Bar Assn. P.R., Am., Inter-Am. bar assns., Iberoamerican Inst. Aero. Law. Clubs: Bankers, Union League (N.Y.C.), Elks. Office: 261 Tanca St Old San Juan PR 00902

RUANE, EDWARD MICHAEL, construction company executive; b. Miami, Fla., Jan. 21, 1950. B.A., Loyola U., New Orleans, 1971. With J.A. Jones Constrn. Co., Charlotte, N.C., 1974—, mgr. procurement and logistics, 1978—. Mem. Purchasing Mgmt. Assn. Carolinas-Va., Nat. Assn. Purchasing Mgmt. (cert. purchasing mgr.). Office: JA Jones Constrn Co One South Executive Park Charlotte NC 28287

RUBACK, RICHARD BARRY, psychology educator, lawyer; b. Omaha, Mar. 29, 1950; s. Norman and Mary (Piha) R. B.A., Yale U., 1972; J.D., U. Tex., 1975; M.S., U. Pitts., 1977, Ph.D., 1979. Bar: Tex. 1975, Ga. 1981, U.S. Dist. Ct. (no. dist.) Ga. 1981, U.S. Ct. Appeals (11th cir.) 1981. Asst. prof. psychology Ga. State U., 1979-84, assoc. prof., 1984—; Fulbright lectr. Andhra U., India, 1985-86. Co-author: Social Psychology of the Criminal Justice System, 1982. Contbr. articles to profl. jours., chpts. to books. Andrew Mellon fellow U. Pitts., 1978-79. Mem. Am. Psychol. Assn., Am. Psychology-Law Soc., Soc. Southeastern Social Psychologists (pres. 1984-85), Soc. for Psychol. Study Social Issues. Democrat. Jewish.

RUBENSTEIN, HARVEY MERRILL, landscape architect; b. Pitts., Feb. 14, 1941; s. Jack and Anne (Reznick) R.; m. Toby Weisberg, Aug. 26, 1965; children—Lynne Rose, Steven Alan. B.S. in Landscape Architecture, Pa. State U., 1963; M.Landscape Architecture, Harvard U., 1965. Registered landscape architect. Landscape architect The Architects Collaborative, Cambridge, Mass., 1964-66; assoc. prof. U. Kans., Lawrence, 1966-71; assoc. ptnr. Bellante, Clauss, Miller & Ptnrs., Scranton, Pa., 1971-80; pvt. practice landscape architecture, Clarks Summit, Pa., 1980-83; sr. landscape architect Carter & Burgess, Inc., Fort Worth, 1983-84; assoc. Hellmuth, Obata & Kassabaum, Inc., Dallas, 1984—. Author: A Guide to Site and Environmental Planning, 1969, 2d edit., 1980, Japanese edit., 1974, Central City Malls, 1978, Spanish edit., 1984. Mem. Am. Soc. Landscape Architects (v.p. Pa.-Del. chpt. 1981-82, nat. award of merit 1970, 80, state honor award 1978, state merit awards 1978, 81, 83). Club: Harvard (Dallas). Avocations: photography; boating; fishing; skiing. Office: Hellmuth Obata & Kassabaum Inc 2501 Cedar Springs Dallas TX 75201

RUBENSTEIN, RICHARD LOWELL, educator, theologian, public policy consultant; b. N.Y.C., Jan. 8, 1924; s. Jesse George and Sara (Fine) R.; m. Ellen van der Veen, Apr. 1948 (div.); children—Aaron, Hannah Rachel, Jeremy; m. 2d, Betty Rogers Alschuler, Aug. 21, 1966. A.B., U. Cin., 1946; M.H.L., Jewish Theol. Sem., 1952; S.T.M., Harvard U., 1952, Ph.D., 1960. Ordained rabbi, 1952. Interim chaplain to Jewish students Harvard U., 1956-58; chaplain to Jewish students U. Pitts., 1958-70, adj. prof. humanities, 1969-70; prof. religion Fla. State U., Tallahassee, 1970-77, Lawton disting. prof. religion, 1977—; Nat. Humanities Inst. fellow Yale U., 1976-77; pres. Washington Inst. Values in Pub. Policy, 1982—; sr. cons. Internat. Cultural Edn. Recipient Portico d'Ottavia Literary prize, Rome, 1977; Disting. Prof. of Yr. award Fla. State U., 1977-78; NEH grantee, 1978-79. Fellow Soc. Values Higher Edn., Rabbinical Assembly Am.; mem. Am. Acad. Religion, Soc. Bibl. Lit., Western Soc. German Studies. Clubs: Governor's (Tallahassee); Cosmos (Washington); Internat. House of Japan (Tokyo). Author: After Auschwitz: Radical Theology and Contemporary Judaism, 1966; The Religious Imagination, 1968; Morality and Eros, 1970; My Brother Paul, 1972; Power Struggle: An Autobiographical Confession, 1974; The Cunning of History, 1975; Modernization: The Humanist Response to Its Promise and Problems, 1982; The Age of Triage, 1982; mem. editorial adv. bd. Washington Times; works translated into Dutch, German, Polish, Russian, Swedish, Japanese, French, Hungarian, and Italian; contbr. numerous articles and revs. to profl. jours. Home: 751 Lake Shore Dr Tallahassee FL 32312 Office: Dept Religion Fla State U Tallahassee FL 32306 also Washington Inst Values in Pub Policy 1333 New Hampshire Ave NW Suite 910 Washington DC 20036

RUBI, JOSE MANUEL, food company executive; b. Barcelona, Spain, Dec. 10, 1939, came to U.S., 1961; s. Jose and Antonia (Martinez) R.; children—Alicia, Joseph, John. B.A., U. Barcelona, 1960; postgrad. U. Geneva, 1962; B.S. in Chemistry, U. Dallas, 1966, M.B.A., 1968; A.B.D., U. Tex.-Dallas, 1979. Fgn. service officer Embassy of Spain, Washington, 1962-66; v.p. Campbell Taggart, Inc., Dallas, 1973-80, sr. v.p., 1980-82, exec. v.p., 1982-84, also dir.; chmn. bd., pres. Suoro, Inc., 1984—; Bartush-Schnitzius Foods Co. Mem. AAAS, Am. Chem. Soc., M.B.A. Assn., Chem. Mktg. and Econ. Soc. Roman Catholic. Club: Brook Hollow Golf (Dallas). Office: Suoro Inc 11242 Indian Trail Dallas TX 75229

RUBIN, ALVIN BENJAMIN, judge; b. Alexandria, La., Mar. 13, 1920; s. Simon and Frances (Prussack) R.; m. Janice Ginsberg, Feb. 19, 1946; children—Michael H., David S. B.S. in Bus. Adminstrn., La. State U., 1941, LL.B., 1942. Bar: La. 1942. Practice in, Baton Rouge, 1946-66; ptnr. Sanders, Miller, Downing, Rubin & Kean, 1946-66; U.S. dist. judge Eastern Dist. La.,

1966-77; U.S. circuit judge 5th Circuit Ct. Appeals, 1977—; adj. prof. law La. State U. Law Sch., 1946—; lectr. taxation Am. Law Inst., Tulane U. Tax Inst., Ga. Tax Inst., La. State U. Mineral Law Inst.; arbitrator Fed. Mediation and Conciliation Service, 1964-66. Author: (with McMahon) Louisiana Pleadings and Judicial Forms Annotated, (with Janice G. Rubin) Louisiana Trust Handbook, (with Gerald LeVan) Louisiana Wills and Trusts, (with Anthony D. Leo) Law Clerk's Handbook; bd. editors: Manual for Complex Litigation, 1983—. Chmn. Baton Rouge Zoning Study Com.; mem. La. Legislative Adminstrv. Procedure Com. Sec. Baton Rouge United Givers Fund, 1954-66; bd. dirs. C.L.E.P.R., 1970-80, Cornell U., 1980—, New Orleans Jewish Welfare Fedn., 1972-76; mem. vis. com. Law Sch., U. Chgo., 1972-75, U. Miami, 1974-80, Harvard U., 1975-82, Cornell Law Sch., 1981—; disting. jud. visitor U. Notre Dame, 1980, U. Iowa, 1983, U. Conn., 1984; past bd. dirs. Baton Rouge chpt. Girl Scouts Am., Mental Health Guidance Center, Community Chest, Community Services Council, Nat. Assn. Crippled Children and Adults; past adv. bd. local Salvation Army, YWCA, Blundon Orphanage; trustee Temple B'nai Israel, 1966-74, Temple Sinai, 1973-76. Served to capt. AUS, 1942-46; ETO. Recipient Golden Deeds award for civic service, 1964; Brotherhood award NCCJ, 1968; named Disting. Alumnus La. State U., 1982. Mem. ABA (bd. editors jour. 1976-82, mem. task force competency in legal edn. 1978—, chmn. estate and gift tax com. 1964, chmn. sect. bar activities 1963, chmn. lawyer referral com. 1969-72), La. Bar Assn. (chmn. sect. trust estates, probate and immovable property law 1961, chmn. labor law sect. 1957, jr. bar sect. 1955, com. on ct. adminstrn. Jud. Conf.), Nat. Acad. Arbitrators, Am. Arbitration Assn., La. Law Inst., Order of Coif, Phi Beta Kappa, Phi Delta Phi, Omicron Delta Kappa, Blue Key (hon.). Lodge: Mason (32 deg.). Office: 2440 One American Place Baton Rouge LA 70825*

RUBIN, EVELYN ANN GOLDBERG, small business owner; b. Chgo., Aug. 23, 1919; d. Manuel and Leah (Cohen) Goldberg; student Art Inst. Chgo., 1937; A.A., Miami Dade Jr. Coll., 1973; B.A., Shaw U., 1974; m. Herman P. Rubin, Nov. 22, 1939; children—Michael Allen, Jeffrey Charles, Sherry Ellen. Contract rep. Field Enterprises Ednl. Corp., Miami, Fla., 1952, area mgr., 1952-56, dist. mgr., 1954-56, div. mgr., 1956-57, co-regional mgr., 1957-58, div. mgr., 1959-60, br. mgr., 1960-68, asst. v.p. and gen. mgr., 1968-81 (name changed to World Book-Childcraft, Internat.); owner antique clothing boutique. Mem. women's com. Variety Children's Hosp., 1962—, life trustee, 1962—; program chmn. Kinlock Park Elementary Sch. P.T.A., 1953-54; mem. U. Miami Lowe Art Gallery, Miami Opera Guild; founder pres. Orlando chpt. B'nai B'rith, 1944; interfaith chmn. Coral Gables Jewish Center, 1946-52, Dade and Broward Counties Conf. Jewish Women's Orgns., 1947-52, Greater Miami Council Ch. Women, 1947-52; mem. Nat. Council Jewish Women, 1963. Recipient various awards Fields Enterprises Ednl. Corp., Meritorious Service award for promoting interfaith in Dade County, Coral Gables Jewish Center, 1959. Mem. Assn. Humanistic Psychology. Jewish. Home: 1111 Crandon Blvd #901A Key Biscayne FL 33149 Office: 3434A Main Hwy Coconut Grove FL 33133

RUBIN, MARVIN ALEXANDER, motel exec.; b. San Antonio, Oct. 17, 1921; s. Frank and Gussie (Finesilver) R.; B.S. in Civil Engring., Ind. Inst. Tech., 1956; postgrad. So. Meth. U., 1957; m. Edith Solomon, Sept. 27, 1947; children—Glenda Rubin Kane, Jan Rubin Newland. Asst. to v.p. engring. Mo., Kans. & Tex. R.R., 1952-57; dynamics engr. Chance Vought Aircraft Co., Dallas, 1957-58; partner Frank Rubin & Son, San Antonio, 1958-69; v.p., prin. Travis-Braun & Assos., Cons. Engrs., San Antonio, 1973—; v.p. project devel. LaQuinta Motor Inns, Inc., San Antonio; pres. Marci Inc., 1980—, Marvin & A. Rubin & Co., Syn-Cor Constrn.; mng. ptnr. Oro Partnership; cons. energy conservation, modular bldg. Served with USMC, 1942-45, 50-51; Decorated Purple Heart. Mem. Am. Assn. Cost Engrs., Tex. Soc. Solar Engrs., Internat. Soc. Solar Engrs., Precast Concrete Inst., Constrn. Specifications Inst. Jewish. Designer, developer solar energy project for motor inns. Home: 1321 Grey Oak St San Antonio TX 78213 Office: 6808 West Ave San Antonio TX 78213

RUBIN, MELVIN LYNNE, physician, educator; b. San Francisco, May 10, 1932; s. Morris and May (Gelman) R.; m. Lorna Isen, June 21, 1953; children—Jan, Daniel, Michael. A.A., U. Calif.-Berkeley, 1951, B.S., 1953; M.D., 1957; M.S., State U. Iowa, 1961. Diplomate Am. Bd. Ophthalmology (dir. 1977, chmn. exams. 1977-83, pres. 1984). Intern U. Calif. Hosp., San Francisco, 1957-58; resident in ophthalmology State U. Iowa, 1958-61; attending surgeon Georgetown U., Washington, 1961-63; asst. prof. surgery U. Fla. Med. Sch., Gainesville, 1963-66, assoc. prof. ophthalmology, 1966-67, prof., 1967—, chmn. dept., 1978—; research cons. Dawson Corp.; ophthalmology cons. VA Med. Ctr., Gainesville. Co-founder Gainesville Assn. Creative Arts, Citizens for Public Schs., Inc., Pro Arte Musica Gainesville, Inc., 1969; pres. Pro Arte Musica Gainesville, Inc., 1971-73; mem. Thomas Center Adv. Bd. for Arts, 1978-83; bd. dirs. Hippodrome, 1981—, v.p., 1983—. Served with USPHS, 1961-63. Recipient Best Med. Book for 1978 award Am. Med. Writers Assn., 1979. Fellow Am. Acad. Ophthalmology (sec. 1978-85), ACS; mem. Assn. for Research in Vision and Ophthalmology (trustee 1973-78, pres. 1979), Retina Soc., Macula Soc., Club Jules Gonin, N.Y. Acad. Scis., Fla. Ophthal. Soc., Am Ophthal. Soc., Pan Am. Soc. Ophthalmology, Ophthalmic Photographers Soc., Alachua County Med. Soc., Fla. Med. Assn., AMA, N.Fla. Eye Bank (dir.), Sigma Xi, Alpha Omega Alpha, Phi Kappa Phi. Author: Studies in Physiological Optics, 1965; Fundamentals of Visual Science, 1969; Optics for Clinicians, 1971, 2d edit., 1974; The Fine Art of Prescribing Glasses, 1978; Dictionary Eye Terminology, 1984; mem. editorial bd. Survey Ophthalmology, AMA Archives Ophthalmology; contbr. numerous articles to med. jours. Home: 1122 NW 20th Dr Gainesville FL 32605 Office: Box J-284 Univ Florida Med Center Gainesville FL 32610

RUBIO, HERMAN FRANK, lawyer, educator; b. Miami, Aug. 11, 1952; s. Herman Frank and Carmen (Sanchez) R. B.A., U. Miami-Coral Gables, 1973, J.D., 1976. Bar: Fla. 1976, D.C. 1981, N.Y. 1982. Cert. legal intern P.A. Hubbart, Miami, 1975-76; asst. pub. defender City of Miami, 1975-77; ptnr. Flynn & Rubio, Miami, 1977; ptnr. Flynn, Rubio & Tarkoff, Miami, 1977-83; sole practice, Miami, 1983—. Recipient Am. Jurisprudence award The Lawyers Coop., 1975. Mem. ABA, Fed. Bar Assn., Dade County Bar Assn., N.Y. State Bar Assn., Fla. Bar, D.C. Bar, Assn. Trial Lawyers Am., Nat. Assn. Criminal Def., Acad. Fla. Trial Lawyers. Democrat. Office: Law Office H Frank Rubio PA 1481 NW N River Dr Miami FL 33125

RUBIO, PEDRO ANTONIO, cardiovascular surgeon; b. Mexico City, Dec. 17, 1944; came to U.S., 1970; s. Isaac and Esther; children—Sandra, Eduardo. M.D., U. Nacional Autónoma de Méx., 1968; M.S. in Surg. Tech., Pacific Western U., 1981, Ph.D. in Biomed. Tech., 1982. Diplomate Am. Bd. Surgery; profl. cert. law enforcement sci., Nat. Com. Profl. Law Enforcement Standards, 1972. Prof. sect. neurology Escuela Normal de Especialización, Secretaria De Educación Pblica, Mexico City, 1968-69; asst. instr. dept. surgery Baylor Coll. Medicine, Houston, 1971-76; clin. instr. dept. surgery U. Tex. Med. Sch., Houston, 1978—; clin. supr. psychiatry residency tng. program Tex. Research Inst. Mental Scis., Houston, 1979-85; surgeon, dir. Cardiovascular Surg. Ctr., Houston, 1976—; chmn. surgery dept. Med. Ctr. Del Oro Hosp., Houston, 1978—; researcher projects with FDA, NCI, HEW, VA, 1977; chmn. bd. Ibex Internat., Associated Film Co., Concorde Limousines, Automotive Research, Inc., Gerhard Wurzer Galleries, Pedro A. Rubio Interests, Saturn Security Services. Chmn. bd. dirs., pres. exec. com. Houston Chamber Singers, 1982-83. Decorated Palms Honor Cross (hon.), Mex. Army; recipient Recognition diploma bachelor's class Universidad Nacional Autonoma de Mex., 1961, Facultad de Medicina, 1966; named Outstanding Surg. Intern, Baylor Coll. Medicine, 1970-71. Fellow Academia Mexicana de Cirugia, ACS (Best Paper award South Tex. chpt. 1976), Am. Coll. Angiology, Am. Coll. Chest Physicians, Am. Soc. Contemporary Medicine and Surgery, Houston Acad. Medicine, Interam. Coll. Physicians and Surgeons, Internat. Coll. Angiology, Internat. Coll. Surgeons (pres. Tex. div. 1983-85, historian 1985—, chmn. membership Com. U.S. sect. 1984—. 3d pl. sci. motion picture 1980), Israel Med. Assn. USA, Royal Soc. Medicine, Am. Heart Assn. (stroke council), S.W. Surg. Congress; mem. Am. Coll. Cardiology, Am. Geriatrics Soc., AMA (Recognition award 1971, 73-82), Am. Trauma Soc., Corr. Soc. Surgeons, Denton A. Cooley Cardiovascular Soc., Harris County (Tex.) Med. Soc., Houston Cardiology Soc., Houston Surg. Soc. (1st pl. essay 1973, 75), Internat. Assn. Study Lung Cancer, Internat. Cardiovascular Soc., Pan-Pacific Surg. Assn., Sociedad Mexicana de Angiologia (1st pl. nat. contest 1974), Soc. Internat. Chirurgie, Tex. Med. Assn., World Med. Assn. Lodge: Rosicrucian. Author: (with E.M. Farrell) Atlas of Angioaccess Surgery, 1983; Staple Techniques in Surgery, 1986; contbr. 150 sci. articles to publs.; patentee med. instrumentation. Office: 7400 Fannin Suite 1200 Houston TX 77054

RUBLE, ROBERT LEE, police chief; b. St. Louis, Mar. 16, 1933; s. Robert E. Lee and Dolores (Fields) R.; m. Patricia Evelyn Scott (div. 1973); children—Rebecca, Lisa; m. 2d, Sheila Margaret Cooper, Oct. 12, 1974. A.A. in Criminal Justice, Kennesaw Coll., 1983; B.S., Brenau Coll., 1983. Enlisted man U.S. Marine Corps, 1950-61, 65-77; ret., 1977; patrolman Tampa (Fla.) Police Dept., 1961-65; spl. agt. frauds VA, Atlanta, 1977-80; chief of police City of Kennesaw (Ga.), 1980—. Chmn. St. Judes and Nat. Kidney Found., 1980-83. Decorated Navy Commendation medal with combat V. Mem. Nat. Assn. Chiefs of Police (exec. bd. 1980—, state pres. 1980-83), Ga. Assn. Chiefs of Police. Democrat. Episcopalian. Lodges: Shriners. Office: Kennesaw Police Dept 2844 S Main St Kennesaw GA 30144

RUCH, WILLIAM HARVEY, business official; b. Sunbury, Pa., July 7, 1928; s. Joseph Isaac and Helen Dorothy (Derr) R.; m. Lois Eilene Wildsmith, Sept. 28, 1951; children—Dennis Allen, Michael William. Grad. pub. schs., Sunbury. Precision machinist Am. Safety Razor Co., Staunton, Va., 1962-66, machine shop planner, 1966-67, supr. apprentices, 1967-72, maintenance engr. asst., 1972-77; maintenance planner Merck & Co., Inc. Elkton, Va., 1977-79, mech. tng. supr., 1979—; chmn. apprenticeship adv. com. Massanutten Tech. Ctr., Harrisonburg, Va., 1983—, curriculum cons., 1981—, part-time tchr., 1981—. Served with USAF, 1946-49. Mem. Am. Soc. for Tng. and Devel., Nat. Marfan Found. (chmn. Shenandoah Valley chpt. 1985), Nat. Rifle Assn., Nat. Assn. Primitive Riflemen. Republican. Lutheran. Avocations: leather carving; black powder gunsmithing; target shooting. Home: Route 4 Box 164 Staunton VA 24401

RUCKEL, JOHN MARVIN, insurance agent; b. Galveston, Tex., July 27, 1948; s. Pete E. and Sybil V. R.; B.B.A. in Mgmt., Stephen F. Austin U., 1970; m. Deborah Laros, Aug. 31, 1968; children—John Damon, Kendall Grant. Life agt. Mass. Mut. Life Ins. Co., Nacogdoches, Tex., from 1969, agy. mgr., 1975-78; now asso. Price, Ruckel & Assos., Nacogdoches. County chmn. Phil Gram U.S. senatorial campaign, 1976; county co-chmn. John Tower U.S. senatorial campaign, 1978; Republican candidate Tex. Ho. of Reps., 1978; county chmn., mem. state steering com. John Connally presdl. campaign, 1979-80; pres. Nacogdoches County Rep. Men; bd. dirs. Community Theater; found. assoc. Stephen F. Austin U. Found.; active fund drives various local charitable orgns. Mem. Tex. Assn. Life Underwriters (dir., v.p.), Pineywood Assn. Life Underwriters (past pres., past dir.), Million Dollar Round Table, Nacogdoches C. of C., East Tex. C. of C., East Tex. Estate Planning Council, Tex. Leaders Round Table. Mem. Ch. of Christ. Club: Piney Woods Country (dir.). Lodge: Rotary. Home: 524 Inwood Ln Nacogdoches TX 75961 Office: 521 E Main St Nacogdoches TX 75961 also Price Ruckel & Assos PO Drawer 1762 Nacogdoches TX 75961

RUCKER, HAROLD JAMES, lawyer; b. Paducah, Ky., Dec. 8, 1921; s. Morton Val Dean and Birdie (Flora) R.; A.B., U. Ky., 1947, J.D., 1949; children—Carol Jane, Morton Val Dean, Douglas McCauley, Helen Lynne Louise. Bar: Ky. 1949, Tex. 1950, U.S. Dist. Ct. (no. dist.) Tex. 1954, U.S. Supreme Ct. 1957, U.S. Dist. Ct. (we. dist.) Tex. 1959, U.S. Ct. Appeals (5th cir.) 1981. Mem. staff land dept. Shell Oil Co., Midland, Tex., 1949-50; practiced in Midland, 1950—; mem. firm Perkins, German, Mims & Bell, 1951-54, Perkins & Bezoni, 1955-56, Rucker & Rassman, 1958-60; dir. Chancellor Chair Co., Optic Boutique, Inc. Past pres., bd. dirs. Am. Cancer Soc., Midland, 1960-61; mem. Midland YMCA, 1961-68, pres., bd. dirs., 1962-68, chmn. endowment com., 1964-65, chmn. Century Club, 1965-66, pres., bd. dirs. S.W. Area Council, 1962-66, mem. program com., chmn. workshop area council meeting, Dallas, 1963; past bd. dirs. Midland County Child Welfare Unit, 1957-58; pres., bd. dirs. Midland Diagnostic Cancer Clinic, 1961-62; pres. bd. trustees Trinity Sch., Midland; trustee St. Andrew's (Tenn.) Sch., Sch. Bd. Diocese N.W. Tex. (Episcopal). Served to 1st lt. AUS, 1942-46. Named Boss of Year, Legal Secs. Assn., Midland, 1963; named Ky. col., 1974. Mem. ABA, Midland County, Ky. bar assns., State Bar Tex., Am. Judicature Soc., Phi Alpha Delta, Sigma Chi. Episcopalian (vestryman). Kiwanian (pres., dir. 1955-57). Clubs: Petroleum, Racquet (dir. 1962) (Midland). Office: Rucker & Rucker 4305 N Garfield Suite 221 Midland TX 79705

RUDACILLE, SHARON VICTORIA, medical technologist; b. Ranson, W. Va., Sept. 11, 1950; d. Albert William and Roberta Mae (Anderson) R.; B.S. cum laude, Shepherd Coll., 1972. Med. technologist VA Center, Martinsburg, W. Va., 1972—, instr. Sch. Med. Tech., 1972-76, asso. coordinator edn., 1976-77, edn. coordinator, 1977-78, quality assurance officer clin. chemistry, 1978-80, lab. service quality assurance and edn. officer, 1980-84, clin. chemistry sect. leader, 1984—; adj. faculty mem. Shippensburg (Pa.) State Coll., 1977-78. Mem. Am. Soc. Med. Tech., Am. Soc. Clin. Pathologists, W.Va. Soc. Med. Technologists, Shepherd Coll. Alumni Assn., Sigma Pi Epsilon. Baptist. Home: PO Box 14 Ranson WV 25438 Office: Route 9 Martinsburg WV 25401

RUDDLE, ELEANOR STEELE, retired business educator; b. Roanoke, Va., July 19, 1924; d. Olin Harrison and June (Wright) R.; B.S., Madison U., Harrisonburg, Va., 1944, M.S., 1966. Tchr. bus. edn., Hawaii, 1944-48, Ohio, 1948-50, Va., 1951-82, ret., 1982; speaker at profl. meetings. Contbr. articles to profl. publs. Mem. Nat. Bus. Edn. Assn. Democrat. Presbyterian. Avocations: tennis; bridge; golf; travel. Home: 203 Yoakum Pkwy 619 Alexandria VA 22304

RUDERT, CYNTHIA SUE, gastroenterologist; b. Cin., Mar. 17, 1955; d. John Wayne and Hilda Wanda (Loftus) R. B.S. with honors, U. Ky., 1975; M.D., U. Louisville, 1979. Diplomate Am. Bd. Internal Medicine. Intern internal medicine Emory U., Atlanta, 1979-80, resident, 1980-82, fellow gastroenterology, 1982-84. Member's guild, patron mem. High Mus. Art, Atlanta, 1983; mem. Southeastern Hist. Keyboard Assn. Recipient Morris Hewburg award U. Louisville, 1979. Mem. AMA, Am. Med. Women's Assn., Nat. Assn. Residents and Interns, ACP, Am. Gastroent. Assn. (assoc.), Am. Assn. for Study Liver Diseases, So. Med. Assn. Club: Young Careers (Atlanta).

RUDLOFF, WILLIAM J., lawyer; b. Bonne Terre, Mo., Feb. 19, 1941; s. Leslie W. and Alta M. (Hogenmiller) R.; m. Rita Howton, Aug. 5, 1965; children—Daniel, Andrea, Leslie, Susan. A.B., Western Ky. U., 1961; J.D., Vanderbilt U., 1965. Bar: Ky. 1965, Tenn. 1965, U.S. Supreme Ct. 1975; cert. civil trial specialist Nat. Bd. Trial Advocacy. Mem. Harlin, Parker & Rudloff and predecessors, Bowling Green, Ky., 1965—; U.S. magistrate Western Dist. Ky., 1971-75. NDEA fellow U. Nebr. 1961-62. Mem. Assn. Ins. Attys., Trial Attys. Am., Am. Bd. Trial Advocates, Am. Counsel Assn., Def. Research Inst., Ky. Def. Counsel, Assn. Trial Lawyers Am., ABA, Ky. Bar Assn., Bowling Green Bar Assn., Am. Coll. Forensic Psychiatry, Internat. Assn. Ins. Counsel. Home: 517 Ashmoor Dr Bowling Green KY 42101 Office: 519 E 10th St Bowling Green KY 42101

RUDOLPH, ARNOLD J(ACK), medical educator; M.B. B.Ch., U. Witwatersrand, 1940. Resident in neurology and dermatology Transvaal Meml. Hosp. for Children, Johannesburg, South Africa, 1941; resident in pediatrics U. Witwatersrand, Johannesburg, 1942-46; tng. in neonatology Harvard Med. Sch., 1956-59; asst. prof. pediatrics, Coll. Medicine Baylor U., Houston, 1961-66, assoc. prof. pediatrics, 1966-70, prof. pediatrics, 1970—, prof. pediatrics, dept. ob gyn, 1973—. Recipient Sr. Class award for Teaching, 1981, award for Outstanding Tchr., Pediatric Housestaff, 1981, Twenty Year Service award, 1982, Outstanding Faculty Hall of Fame award for Teaching, 1982. Mem. AMA, Am. Pediatric Soc., Brit. Med. Assn., Ambulatory Pediatric Assn., Soc. Soc. for Pediatric Research, So. Perinatal Assn., Tex. Med. Assn., Tex. Perinatal Assn., Tex. Med. Assn., Tex. Perinatal Assn., Harris County Med. Soc., Houston Pediatric Soc., Philippines Pediatric Soc. (hon. fellow), Alpha Omega Alpha. Jewish. Contbr. writings to profl. publs. in field. 5239 Birdwood Houston TX 77096 Office: Dept Pediatrics Baylor Coll Medicine One Baylor Plaza Tex Med Ctr Houston TX 77030

RUDOLPH, MALCOLM ROME, investment banker; b. Balt., Sept. 22, 1924; s. Louis and Sara E. (Rome) R.; A.B., Harvard U., 1947; postgrad. U. Grenoble, U. Paris (France), 1948, Hayden Stone Mgmt. Sch., 1965; m. Zita Herzmark, July 1, 1956 (div. 1979); children—Madelon R. II, Margot R.; m. 2d, Barbara J. Girson, 1979. With div. internat. confs. State Dept., Paris, 1949; registered rep. trainee Orvis Bros. & Co., N.Y.C., 1949, registered rep., asst. mgr., acting mgr., 1950-64; mgr. Hayden Stone, Inc., Washington, 1964-68, partner, 1968-69; chmn. bd. Donatelli, Rudolph & Schoen, Inc., Washington, 1970-74; chmn. Multi-Nat. Fin. Corp., Inc., Washington, 1974-79, pres., 1979—; chmn. bd. Multi-Nat. Precious Metals Corp., Washington, 1974-75; chmn. bd. Multi-Nat. Money Mgmt. Co., Inc., Washington, 1974-79, pres., 1979—; chmn. bd. Rudolph & Schoen Inc., Washington, 1975—; sr. v.p., dir. Laidlaw Adams & Peck, Inc., 1975-79; pres. Laidlaw Resources, Inc., 1976—, Sutton Energy, Inc., 1976—; pres., chief exec. officer DeRand Resources Corp., 1979—; sr. v.p., dir. DeRand Corp. Am., 1979—; dir. Jack Hoag & Assos., Inc.; chmn. bd. Arlington Energy Corp., 1980—; mem. Phila.-Balt.-Washington Stock Exchange, 1972-75; pres. Rome Resources Corp., Investment Bankers and Cons.; asso. mem. Pitts., Boston, Montreal stock exchanges, 1972-75; allied mem. N.Y. Stock Exchange, 1975-79. Mem. presdl. Inaugural Com., 1960, 64. Served with USNR, 1943-46. Mem. Assn. Investment Brokers Met. Washington (v.p. 1965-66, pres. 1967), Bond Club Washington Ind. Oil and Gas Assn. W.Va., Ohio Oil and Gas Assn., Ind. Petroleum Assn. Am., Southeastern Ohio Oil & Gas Assn., Washington Met. Bd. Trade, Internat. Assn. Fin. Planners. Clubs: Internat., Harvard (asst. treas. 1957-60, treas. 1960-64, chmn. investment com. 1958-59, exec. com. 1957-67), Nat. Aviation (Washington). Home: Willow Oak Farm Bozman MD 21612 Office: 2201 Wilson Blvd Arlington VA 22201

RUENHECK, JEROME B., fast food chain executive; b. Aug. 25, 1938; B.S. in Bus. Adminstrn., U. Denver; m. Karen; 3 children. With Burger King Corp., 1969—, div. mgr., 1970-73, exec. v.p., dir. ops., Miami, Fla., 1973-80, pres., chief operating officer, 1980—. Mem. exec. bd. S. Fla. council Boy Scouts Am. Served with USMC, 1961-64. Mem. Nat. Restaurant Assn. Office: Burger King Corp 7360 N Kendall Dr Miami FL 33156

RUFFIN, CRAIGE, lumber and millwork executive; b. Richmond, Va., May 11, 1902; s. Thomas Chmpion and Grace Helen (Spear) R.; m. Marjorie Belvin, Oct. 20, 1934; 1 dau., Marjorie Belvin Ruffin Cain. B.S., U. Va., 1923. With Ruffin and Payne, Inc., Richmond, 1923—, exec. v.p., 1971-78, pres., 1978-83, pres., chmn. bd., chief exec. officer, 1983—. Past pres. Salvation Army Hosp.; past Sunday sch. supt., past Vestryman St. Stephen's Episcopal Ch. Mem. Nat. Bldg. Materials Dealers Assn. (dir., exec. com.), Va. Bldg. Materials Assn. (pres.), Archtl. Woodwork Inst. (dir. 1956-59), Richmond Retail Mchts. Assn. (dir. 1956-72), Met. Richmond C. of C. (dir. 1970-73). Republican. Clubs: Country of Va. (dir. 1961-64), Commonwealth (Richmond, Va.). Lodge: Masons (past master).

RUFFIN, PATTI YVONNE, learning disabilities specialist; b. Columbus, Ohio, Aug. 16, 1958; d. Richard David and Yvonne (White) R. B.A., Emory U., 1980, M.Med. Sci., 1981, student L'Alliance Français, Paris, summer 1977. Teaching specialist, Ga. Learning disabilities specialist Atlanta Speech Sch., 1981—, staff rep. Parent Tchr. Study Group, 1982-83; pvt. practice remediation, learning disabilities specialist, Atlanta. Presenter paper profl. assn. confs. Mem. Assn. Children with Learning Disabilities, Ga. Assn. Children with Learning Disabilities. Office: Atlanta Speech Sch 3160 Northside Pkwy Atlanta GA 30327

RUFFNER, CHARLES LOUIS, lawyer, accountant; b. Cin., Nov. 7, 1936; s. Joseph H. and Edith Louise (Solomon) F.; B.S. in Bus. Adminstrn., U. Fla., 1958; LL.B. cum laude, U. Miami (Fla.), 1964; m. Mary Ann Kaufman, Jan. 30, 1966; children—Robin Sue, David Robert. Bar: Fla. 1964, U.S. Supreme Ct. 1966; cert. in taxation Fla. Bar Bd. Cert. IRS agt., Miami, 1959-64; trial atty. tax div. U.S. Dept. Justice, Washington, 1964-67; pres. Ruffner, Hagen & Rifkin, P.A., Miami, 1975-79; pres. Charles L. Ruffner, P.A., Miami, 1980-82; tax ptnr. Myers, Kenin, Levinson, Ruffner, Frank & Richards, 1982-84; pres. Charles L. Ruffner, P.A., 1984—; lectr. tax law Fla. Internat. U., 1977—; guest speaker on taxation and profl. service corps. to various profl. groups throughout U.S., Mex., Europe, Caribbean, 1969—; tax columnist Miami Rev., newspaper. Mem. Am., Fed., Dade County bar assns., Fla. Bar (exec. council tax sect. 1967—), Greater Miami Tax Inst., Greater Miami Estate Planning Council, Phi Kappa Phi, Phi Alpha Delta, Pi Lambda Phi. Jewish. Clubs: Bankers, Standard. Lodges: Masons, Shriners, B'nai B'rith (pres. Scopus lodge 1977). Contbr. articles to legal jours.; editorial bd. U. Miami Law Rev., 1963-64. Home: 6250 SW 135th St Miami FL 33156 Office: 3001 SW 3d Ave Suite 100 Miami FL 33129-2799

RUFUS, ANITA LEE, human resources executive; b. Newark, May 17, 1941; d. Herbert S. Goldstein and Evelyn (Goodman) G.; children—Michael David and Susan Adella (twins); m. James K. Devlin, Apr. 24, 1983. Asst. to pres. Diversified Industries Internat., Los Angeles, 1966-71, Aist Market Research, Los Angeles, 1971-73; owner Arriba Typesetting and Sec. Service, Los Angeles, 1973-75; asst. to pres., corp. sec. Carterfone Communications Corp., Dallas, 1975-78; asst. to chmn. bd., dir. advt., v.p. human resources U.S. Telephone, Inc., Dallas, 1979—. Mem. NOW, Am. Soc. Personnel Adminstrs., Am. Soc. Tng. and Devel., Internat. Orgn. Women in Telecommunications, Nat. Assn. Female Execs., Human Potential Inst. N. Tex. Home: 3504 Crescent Dr Dallas TX 75205 Office: US Telephone Inc 108 S Akard Dallas TX 75202

RUIZ, ALDELMO, consultant; b. Yauco, P.R., June 12, 1923; s. Hipolito and Mercedes (Santiago) R.; B.S. in Civil Engring., Va. Poly. Inst. and State U., 1949, M.S. in San. Engring., 1950; postgrad. U. Va., 1954, George Washington U., 1971-72, Fgn. Service Inst., 1969, Indsl. Coll. Armed Forces, 1972; m. Mary Tosca Lonardelli, July 29, 1949; children—Stella Ann, Michael Linvil. Design engr. Washington Suburban San. Commn., Hyattsville, Md., 1950-51; san. and project engr. Research and Devel. Labs., Fort Belvoir, Va., 1952-55; chief civil, san. and mech. engring. depts. Far East div. Thomas B. Bourne & Assos., Washington, 1955-58, also tech. coordinator, 1957-58; propr., pres. Caribbean Engring. Services, Cons. Engrs., Santurce, P.R., 1958-62; chief engr. AID, Taiz, Yemen, 1962-64, dir. water supply and environ. sanitation dept. Yemen, 1964-66, devel. officer, Sana, Yemen, 1966-67, chief engring. adv. to Kabul, Afghanistan, 1967-68, gen. engring. officer, Kabul, 1968-71, interregional engring. coordinator AID, Washington, 1971-72, affairs officer, Yemen, 1973, AID rep. in Yemen, 1974-75, mission dir., Yemen, 1975-77, El Salvador, 1978-79, Panama, 1979-81, cons., 1981—; mem. U.S. com. irrigation, drainage and flood control Internat. Commn. Irrigation and Drainage. Bd. dirs. Sana Internat. Sch., Yemen, 1973-77, Mill Creek Park Citizens Assn., Annandale, Va., 1952—. Served with U.S. Army, 1942-45. Recipient Disting. Honor award AID, 1966, Outstanding Career Achievement award, 1981; Disting. Cert., Pres. Yemen, 1977; Order Vasco Nuñez de Balboa (Panama); registered profl. engr., Del., Md., D.C., Mass., P.R. Fellow ASCE; mem. Nat. Soc. Profl. Engrs., Am. Water Works Assn. (life), Colegio de Ingenieros, Agrimensores de P.R., Washington Soc. Engrs., Am. Fgn. Service Assn. Club: Lions. Contbr. numerous articles on san. and civil engring. to profl. jours. Home: 3816 Lake Blvd Annandale VA 22003 Office: PO Box 126 Annandale VA 22003

RULE, GERALDINE LEVINGSTON, nurse; b. Houston, Nov. 23, 1924; d. Charles Graham and Clara Theresa (Hebert) Levingston; m. Carl Allen Rule, Mar. 17, 1947 (div. 1968); children—Charles Ernest, Judy Kaye, Peggy Jean. Lic. vocat. nurse St. Francis Sch. Practical Nursing, Carlsbad, N.Mex., 1962; A.S., San Jacinto Jr. Coll., Pasadena, Tex., 1980. R.N., Tex. Staff vocat. nurse Carlsbad Meml. Hosp., 1963-67, Northshore Med. Plaza, Houston, 1967-76, Eastway Gen. Hosp., Houston, 1976-78; staff nurse Jefferson Davis Hosp., Houston, 1980—. Democrat. Baptist. Home: 11900 Barryknoll Ln 1405 Houston TX 77024

RUMAGGI, LOUIS JACOB, ret. army officer, cons.; b. Memphis, Dec. 3, 1900; s. Louis and Garnet (Huntsbarger) R.; student Miami U., Oxford, Ohio, 1917-18; B.S., U.S. Mil. Acad., 1922; B.S. in Civil Engring., U. Calif. at Berkeley, 1927; m. Miriam Louise Tuggle, Mar. 30, 1950; 1 dau., Louise Herron (Mrs. Alan Lyndal Reed). Commd. 2d lt. C.E., U.S. Army 1922, advanced through grades to maj. gen., 1953; acting chief engr. Army Forces, S.W. Pacific, 1945-46; engr. 8th U.S. Army, Korea, 1952-53; dep. chief engrs. U.S. Army, 1954-55; chief staff 6th U.S. Army, 1955-57; div. engr. North Central div., Corps Engrs., 1957-59; asso. Tex. Instruments, Inc., 1959-62. Decorated Legion of Merit with oak leaf cluster, D.S.M.; Ulchi medal (Korea). Fellow ASCE; mem. Mil. Order World Wars, SAR (v.p. gen. south central dist.), Soc. Am. Mil. Engrs., Am. Legion. Clubs: Rotary; Army and Navy (Washington). Home: 10556 Barrywood Dr Dallas TX 75230

RUMMERFIELD, BENJAMIN FRANKLIN, geophysicist; b. Denver, May 25, 1917; s. Lawrence L. and Helen A. (Roper) R.; Engr. Geology, Colo. Sch. Mines, 1940; grad. Harvard U. Advanced Mgmt. Program, 1947, Aspen Inst. Humanistic Studies, 1958, Indsl. Coll. Armed Forces, 1963; m. Mary Merchant, Feb. 16, 1979; children—Ann S., Michael J., Benjamin F., Mary Susan, Lila, Sonya, Karim. Asst. mgr. Seismograph Service Corp., Mexico City, 1947-50, Venezuela and Colombia, 1945-47; exec. v.p. Century Geophys. Corp., Tulsa, 1950-60, also dir.; pres. GeoData Corp., Tulsa, 1960—, Gulf Coast GeoData, Houston, 1962—; dir. GeoData Index Internat., East Grinstead, West Sussex, U.K., Permian Exploration, Custom Data Services;

cons. Petróleos Mexicanos. Bd. dirs. YMCA, Tulsa, 1955—, pres., 1956-59. Recipient Outstanding Service award YMCA, Tulsa, 1958, 63, Disting. Achievement medal Colo. Sch. Mines, 1978, hon. mention for painting Philbrook Art Mus., 1961. Mem. Tulsa Geol. Soc., Colo. Sch. Mines Alumni Assn. (pres. 1953), Asociación Mexicana de Geólogos Petróleos, Am. Assn. Petroleum Geologists, Soc. Exploration Geophysicists (nat. v.p. 1958), Sigma Gamma Epsilon. Clubs: Tulsa, Harvard (Tulsa). Contbr. numerous articles to profl. jours. Home: 6787 Timberlane Dr Tulsa OK 74105 Office: GeoData Bldg Box 3476 Tulsa OK 74101

RUMPFF, CORNELIS JAN, marketing executive; b. Groningen, Netherlands, Feb. 20, 1946; came to U.S., 1976; D. in Econs., Erasmus U., Rotterdam, Netherlands, 1972; m. Barbara Bryant, May 15, 1976; 1 son, Ronald. Corp. planner, Schuitema, Netherlands, 1972-74; mktg. mgr. Spar Orgn., Gieten, Netherlands, 1974-76; v.p. fin. Grolsch Importers, N.Y.C., 1976-78, Atlanta, 1978, pres., 1978-85; pres. European Am. Mktg. Corp., 1985—. Recipient Vivo award, 1973. Mem. Nat. Assn. Beverage Importers, Assn. Distbn. Economists Netherlands, Netherlands C. of C. (exec. mem., dir.). Clubs: Sleepy Hollow Country (Briarcliff Manor, N.Y.); Horseshoe Bend (Roswell, Ga.); World Trade (Atlanta). Author: (in Dutch) The Development of the Systems Approach in the Retailing Industry, 1973. Office: 669 Gunby Rd Marietta GA 30067

RUMSEY, DAVID LAKE, JR., lawyer; b. Dallas, Aug. 24, 1944; s. David Lake and Eva Linn (Carter) R.; B.A., U. Tex., Austin, 1970; J.D., U. Tex. and City Coll. London, 1972; m. Penelope Williams, Aug. 18, 1973. Admitted to Ga. bar, 1973; partner firm Kutah, Rock & Huie, Atlanta, 1972-81; partner firm Bird, Scherffius & Rumsey, Atlanta, 1981—; adj. prof. trial advocacy Emory U. Served to 1st lt. U.S. Army, 1967-69. Decorated Bronze Star with V device and oak leaf cluster. Mem. Atlanta C. of C. (hon., life; mem. Downtown Council), Am., Ga., Atlanta bar assns., Lawyers Club Atlanta, Sigma Alpha Epsilon. Office: 604 Grant Blvd 44 Broad St NW Atlanta GA 30303

RUNION, ROBERTA LYNN, editor, communications professional; b. Alexandria, Va., May 24, 1957; d. Wayne Godolphin and Gladys Roberta (Whetzel) R. B.A., George Mason U., Fairfax, Va., 1979. Editorial asst. Am. Hist. Assn., Washington, 1981-82; editorial asst. Washingtonian Mag., Washington, 1982-83, also contbr. articles; editor Soc. Neuroscience, Washington, 1985-86; freelance editor/writer, 1983-85. Editorial asst. Writings on Am. History, 1980-81, Recently Pub. Articles, 1981-82; asst. editor Guide to Departments of History, 1981-82; editor Neurosci. Tng. Programs in N.Am., 1986, Ann. Meeting Promotional Materials, 1986. Mem. Women in Communications, Washington Edn. Press Assn. Home: Route 1 Box 548 Chantilly VA 22021

RUPE, ROBERT WILLIAM, electrical engineer; b. Ontario, Oreg., Sept. 30, 1948; s. Raymond Edward and Mary Theresa (Bodewig) R. B.S. in Physics, Wash. State U., 1977, M.S. in Elec. Engring., 1984. IC electrician U.S. Navy, 1967-73; ops. engr. Westinghouse Co., Richland, Wash., 1977-79; field engr. Schlumberger Co., Enid, Okla., 1980; assoc. engr. IBM, Boca Raton, Fla., 1984—. Served with USN, 1967-73. Mem. IEEE, Quantum Electronics and Applications Soc., Aerospace and Electronic Systems Soc., Antennas and Propagation Soc., Computer Soc., Phi Beta Kappa. Home: 2945 SW 22d Ave #202 Delray Beach FL 33445 Office: IBM Bldg 203 Dept 33V Boca Raton FL 33432

RUPEL, LAWRENCE MICHAEL, clergyman, psychotherapist; b. South Bend, Ind., Sept. 5, 1948; s. Maurice Eugene and Mary Elizabeth (Tamplen) R.; B.A., U. Tex., Austin, 1971; M.Div., Josephinum Sch. Theology, 1975. Ordained priest Roman Catholic Ch., 1975; mem. staff Marriage Tribunal Diocese Corpus Christi, 1975—; chaplain Incarnate Word Sisters, 1975-76; asso. pastor Our Lady of Guadalupe Ch., Corpus Christi, 1976-77; asso. pastor St. Paul Cath. Ch., Corpus Christi, 1977-79; asso. pastor St. Elizabeth Cath. Ch., Alice, Tex., 1979—; chmn. dept. measurement and evaluation Office Cath. Schs., 1976-78; alcoholism and drug abuse counseling, 1979; cons., primary therapist Coastal Bend Rehab. for Alcoholics; cons. Coastal Bend Council Alcoholism. Lic. profl. counselor. Mem. Am. Personnel and Guidance Assn., Canon Law Soc. Am., Nat. Cath. Guidance Assn., Am. Measurement and Evaluation in Guidance, Tex. Psychotherapy Assn. Democrat. Office: 3350 S Alameda Corpus Christi TX 78411

RUPNIK, JOHN JOSEPH, geophysicist, geologist, consultant; b. Denver, Dec. 9, 1910; s. John and Barbara (Mahr) R.; m. Dorothy Baugher, July 28, 1935; children—Daille, J. Kenyon. B.S. in Geol. Engring., Colo. Sch. Mines, 1933; M.S. in Geology, Calif. Inst. Tech., 1941, postgrad., 1941-42. Registered profl. engr., Okla.; registered geologist, geophysicist, Calif. Party chief The Tex. Co., La., Calif., Tex., 1933-39; research and party chief United Geophys. Co., Calif., 1942-46; review and interpretation Sun Oil Co., Beaumont, Tex., 1946; spl. services, interpretation Sinclair Oil & Gas Co., La., Miss., Okla., Tex., Colo., Wyo., Can., 1947-51; cons. geophysicist, worldwide, 1951—. Contbr. articles to profl. jours. Mem. Am. Inst. Profl. Geologists (past 2d v.p. Okla. sect.), Am. Assn. Petroleum Geologists, Soc. Exploration Geophysicists, Tulsa Geol. Soc., Geophys. Soc. Tulsa, Oklahoma City Geol. Soc., Kans. Geol. Soc., Colo. Sch. Mines Alumni Assn., Calif. Inst. Tech. Alumni Assn., Sigma Xi, Sigma Gamma Epsilon. Club: Tulsa Petroleum. Home: 1507 E 34th St Tulsa OK 74105 Office: 324 Main Mall Ste 708 Tulsa OK 74103

RUSH, GRACE CAMERON, counselor, family life education coordinator; b. Lumberton, Miss., Apr. 6, 1936; d. Lee L. and Lucile (Dickens) C.; m. Robert Frank Rush, Mar. 13, 1959; children—George Franklin, Greg L. B.A., U. So. Ala., 1979, M.S., 1983. Family life edn. coordinator Family Counseling Ctr., Mobile, Ala., 1979-83, counselor, 1983—; mgr., dir. Vols. Community Program, Mobile, 1979—; supr., dir. grad. students, Mobile, 1983—; facilitator Community Health Fairs, Mobile, 1983—. Producer psychodramas Plays for Living, 1979. Mem. program planning and devel. com. Mobile Domestic Violence Com., Mobile, 1980; mem. adv. com. Disaster Counseling Project Council Against Violence, Mobile, 1979-80. Recipient Cert. of Merit, S.W. Ala. Council, 1980. Mem. Ala. Lic. Profl. Counselors, Am. Psychol. Assn. (assoc.), Mobile Lic. Profl. Counselors. Republican. Baptist. Clubs: Internat. Preview Soc. (Indpls.); Monday (Mobile). Avocations: music, tennis. Home: 6609 Devondale Ct Mobile AL 36609 Office: Family Counseling Ctr 6 S Florida St Mobile AL

RUSH, PAMELA JEANNE TURBOW, financial institution executive; b. Jacksonville, Fla., Sept. 28, 1958; d. Morton B. and Cleta (Spencer) Turbow; m. John Alfred Rush, III, Apr. 26, 1980. B.A., Jacksonville U., 1977, M.B.A., 1984. Chartered fin. analyst. Adminstrv. dir. Barnett-PAC, Jacksonville, 1978-79; staff auditor Barnett Banks of Fla., Jacksonville, 1979-81; investment officer Barnett Banks Trust Co., Jacksonville, 1981-82; sr. investment analyst Charter Security Life, Jacksonville, 1982-84; v.p. First Charter Savs. Bank, Jacksonville, 1984—, also dir.; treas. Charter Savs. Corp., Jacksonville, 1984—. Pres. scholar Jacksonville U., 1975. Mem. Jacksonville Fin. Analyst Soc. (bd. dirs. 1984—), Alpha Kappa Psi. Republican. Baptist. Home: 726 Granada Blvd S Jacksonville FL 32207 Office: First Charter Savs Bank 1 Charter Plaza Jacksonville FL 32202

RUSHING, JOE B., college chancellor; b. Zephyr, Tex., May 23, 1921; s. Cordie M. and Vallie (Parson) R.; B.A., Howard Payne Coll., 1946; M.A., East Tex. State Coll., 1949; Ph.D., U. Tex., 1952; postdoctoral study U. Mich., 1959; m. Elaine Whitis, Dec. 21, 1946; children—Anita Sherron, Cynthia Ann, Robert Scott. Tchr. sci., adminstr. Levelland (Tex.) High Sch., then Mt. Pleasant (Tex.) High Sch., 1946-50; teaching fellow U. Tex., 1950-52; dir. adult edn. Wharton Jr. Coll., 1952-54; dean grad. div. Howard Payne Coll., 1954-58, adminstrv. v.p., 1956-60; pres. Jr. Coll. of Broward County, Ft. Lauderdale, Fla., 1960-65; pres. Tarrant County Jr. Coll. Dist., Ft. Worth, 1965-69, chancellor, 1969—. Chmn. council of Presidents of Assn. of Higher Edn., N.Tex., 1980-81. Mem. Nat. Endowment for Humanities Com., 1976—, State Adv. Panel Am. Council on Edn. Nat. Identification Program for Women in Higher Edn., 1980. Served with U.S. Army, 1942-46. Recipient Carl Bredt award U. Tex., 1977; Paul Harris fellow, 1972; named Educator of Year, Press Club Ft. Worth, 1974; Disting. Alumnus Howard Payne U., 1976, E. Tex. State U., 1979; Boss of Year Nat. Secs., 1971. Mem. Nat. Council on Humanities, Am. Assn. Community and Jr. Colls. (chmn. 1981-82), Pi Sigma Alpha, Phi Delta Kappa, Kappa Delta Pi. Baptist. Address: Tarrant County Junior College 1500 Houston St Fort Worth TX 76102

RUSHLOW, PHILIP LEO, marketing systems company executive; b. Covington, Ky., Feb. 2, 1929; s. Leo Bernard and Elinor Victoria (Slater) R.; m. Bonnie Miller, June 25, 1945; children—Philip Lee, David Robert. B.A., Wayne U., 1949; M.A., Mich. State U., 1956. Regional mgr. B.F. Goodrich Co., Detroit, 1945-56; pres. Lansing Gen. Co., East Lansing, Mich., 1956-59, Azure Internat. Corp., Lansing Mich., 1959-61, Fashion Industries, Inc., Miami, Fla., 1961-71; pres., chmn. Group Three Corp., Ft. Lauderdale, Fla., 1971—; mktg. cons., dir. The First Bankers Corp., Pompano Beach, Fla., 1973—; ptnr. Leo Bernard & Co., Pompano Beach, Fla., 1978—; dir. Richelieu Assocs., Inc., Ft. Lauderdale, Rushlow, Philips & David Corp., Ft. Lauderdale. Contbr. to mktg., advt. and research publs. Fellow Aspen Inst. Humanities. Clubs: Lighthouse Point (Fla.); Beech Mountain Country (N.C.). Home: Hillsboro Shores FL Office: Group Three Corp 3200 NE 14th Causeway Pompano Beach FL 33062

RUSKELL, VIRGINIA ANN, librarian, educator; b. Nashville, June 4, 1948; d. George Channing Ruskell and Douglass (McFerrin) Rudkoff; A.A., Reinhardt Coll., 1967; B.A. in history, Emory U., 1969; M.L.S., George Peabody Coll., 1970; M.A. in English, West Ga. U., 1975. Library asst. George Peabody Coll. Library Sch., 1969-70; interlibrary loan librarian West Ga. Coll., Carrollton, 1970-76, bibliog. instrn. librarian, 1977-80, reference coordinator, 1980—, assoc. prof., 1980—. Treas., LWV, Carrollton, 1975-77; chmn. social concerns St. Andrew United Meth. Ch., Carrollton, 1981-82, fin. sec., 1980-81, chmn. fin. com., 1982. Council Library Resources Library Services Enhancement grantee, 1976-77. Mem. Southeastern Library Assn., AAUP (sec. 1974-75, v.p. 1975-76), AAUW (v.p. programs 1982—), Beta Phi Mu, Phi Kappa Phi. Democrat. Home: PO Box 844 Carrollton GA 30117 Office: W Ga Coll Library Carrollton GA 30118

RUSSELL, ANN NICHOLS, college administrator; b. Birmingham, Ala., May 10, 1940; d. Olas Clarence and Emma (Spurgeon) Nichols; m. Jim W. Russell, May 14, 1961 (div. 1979); children—Mark Acton, Craig Nichols. Student, Auburn U., 1958-61; B.A., Am. U., 1965; M.Ln., Emory U. 1981; postg. Ednl. asst. First United Meth. Ch., Cedartown, Ga., 1970-73; pub. relations rep. Ethel Harpst Home, Cedartown, 1973-78; TV producer Tri-County Regional Library, Rome, Ga., 1978, pub. relations/grants coordinator, 1978-81; grants coordinator Berry Coll., Mt. Berry, Ga., 1981-82, dir. corp. and found. programs, 1982—; mem. state planning com. Am. Council on Edn. Nat. Identification Program, 1983—; info. cons. Infosearch, Rome, 1981—; project cons. Ga. Com. for Humanities and NEH, 1980. Contbr. articles to profl. jours.; producer video series Folk Art: Bridge Between The Mountains and the Plains, 1978. Pres., Jr. Service League, Cedartown, Ga., 1975-76; mem. adv. com. Congressman Newt Gingrich, 1982; chmn. bd. dirs. Polk Tng. Ctr. Mentally Retarded, 1972-75, First United Meth. Presch., 1977-78. Recipient Cokesbury Grad. award Emory U., 1980; John Whouley fellow, 1980. Mem. Council for Advancement and Support of Edn., ALA, AAUW (editor/br. pres. 1976-77). Club: Cherokee Golf and Country. Home: 318 W Girard Ave Cedartown GA 30125 Office: Berry Coll Mount Berry GA 30149

RUSSELL, CAROLYN TURNER, lawyer, governmental analyst; b. Dallas, Mar. 27, 1949; d. John Thomas and Zeta B. (Turner) R. B.S., Howard U., 1968; M.A., George Washington U., 1972; J.D., Harvard U., 1977. Bar: Mass. 1977, D.C. 1980. Policy planner Dept. Def., Washington, 1968-72; dir. urban environ. programs EPA, Washington, 1972-74, dir. civil rights, Atlanta, 1978-80; dir. civil rights HHS, Atlanta, 1980-82, intergovtl. and congl. liaison, 1982-83; policy analyst/atty. Council State Govts., Atlanta, 1983—; vis. prof. Spelman Coll., Atlanta, 1984. Bd. dirs. Coalition Internat. Programs, Atlanta, 1982-84; mem. allocations bd. United Way, Atlanta, 1983-84; mem. Leadership Atlanta, 1983-84. Named Outstanding Young Woman of Washington, U.S. Jaycees, 1972; recipient Outstanding Service award Fed. Exec. Bd., Atlanta, 1979, Combined Fed. Campaign, Atlanta, 1980, Bronze medal EPA, Atlanta, 1980. Mem. ABA, Nat. Bar Assn., Ga. Assn. Black Women Attys., Delta Sigma Theta. Republican. Mem. African Methodist Episcopal Ch. Home: 1038 Oglethorpe Ave SW Atlanta GA 30310 Office: Council State Govts 3384 Peachtree Rd NE Atlanta GA 30310

RUSSELL, CHARLES RAYFIELD, state official; b. West Palm Beach, Fla., Mar. 22, 1931; s. Charles Edward and Alma Ernestine (Johnson) R.; B.S., Fla. A&M U., 1952; M.S., Ind. U., 1962; Ph.D., Fla. State U., 1972; m. Nancy Ellen Mosley, Dec. 8, 1953; children—Tamara Verline Russell White, Leslie Ann, Gail Trinise, Carla Raye, Charles Rayfield. Tchr. jr. high sch., Palm Beach County, Fla., 1956-68; specialist labor relations Fla. Edn. Assn., Tallahassee, 1968-69; grad. asst. mgmt. systems Fla. State U., Tallahassee, 1970; adminstrv. asst. Fed. Higher Edn. Programs, Fla. Dept. Edn., Tallahassee, 1971-72; registrar Fla. A&M U., Tallahassee, 1972-76, asst. prof. mgmt. sci., 1976-80, acting dir. div. mgmt. sci., 1978-79; dir. Fla. Div. Employment and Tng., Tallahassee, 1980-83; asst. dir. Fla. Div. Unemployment Compensation, Tallahassee, 1983—; cons. mgmt. systems, planning and budgets. Chmn. bd. dirs. Palm Beach County (Fla.) Community Action Council, 1964-65. Served to 1st lt. U.S. Army, 1952-55; Korea; maj. Res. ret. Mem. Internat. Assn. Personnel in Employment Security, Interstate Conf. Employment Security Agys., Res. Officers Assn., NAACP, Tallahassee Urban League, Capital City Voters League, Fla. A&M U. Alumni Assn., Phi Delta Kappa, Alpha Phi Alpha. Democrat. Baptist. Clubs: Charmers; Jack and Jill Am. Home: 433 Mercury Dr Tallahassee FL 32301 Office: 210 Caldwell Bldg Tallahassee FL 32301

RUSSELL, CHARLES STEVENS, judge, educator; b. Richmond, Va., Feb. 23, 1926; s. Charles Herbert and Nita M. (Stevens) R.; m. Carolyn Elizabeth Abrams, Mar. 18, 1951; children—Charles Stevens, David Tyler. B.A., U. Va., 1946, LL.B., 1948. Bar: Va. 1949, U.S. Dist. Ct. (ea. dist.) Va. 1952, U.S. Ct. Appeals (4th cir.) 1955, U.S. Supreme Ct. 1958. Assoc. firm Jesse, Phillips, Klinge & Kendrick, Arlington, Va., 1951-57, ptnr., 1957-60, Phillips, Kendrick, Gearheart and Aylor, Arlington, 1960-67; judge 17th Jud. Ct. Va., Arlington, 1967-82, Supreme Ct. Va., Richmond, 1982—; mem. jud. council Va., 1977-82; adj. prof. law George Mason U., Arlington, 1977—; mem. exec. com. Va. State Bar, Richmond, 1964-67; mem. faculty Nat. Jud. Coll., Reno, 1980—. Mem. Adv. Com. on Youth, Arlington. Served to lt. comdr. USNR, 1944-51. Mem. ABA, Arlington County Bar Assn., Va. Bar Assn., Va. Trial Lawyers Assn., Am. Judicature Soc. Episcopalian. Clubs: Annapolis (Md.) Yacht; Downtown (Richmond). Home: 4618 N Dittmar Rd Arlington VA 22207*

RUSSELL, DAVID EMERSON, consulting mechanical engineer; b. Jacksonville, Fla., Dec. 20, 1922; s. David Herbert and Wilhelmina (Ash) R.; B.Mech. Engring., U. Fla., 1948; postgrad. Oxford (Eng.) U. Mech. engr. United Fruit Co., N.Y.C., 1948-50, U.S. Army C.E., Jacksonville, 1950-54, Aramco, Saudi Arabia, 1954-55; v.p. Beiswenger Hoch and Assocs., Inc., Jacksonville, 1955-57; owner, operator David E. Russell and Assos., cons. engrs., Jacksonville, 1957—. Chmn. Jacksonville Water Quality Control Bd., 1969-73; bd. dirs. Jacksonville Hist. Soc., 1981-82; mem. Jacksonville Bicentennial Commn., 1973-79. Served to 2d lt. AUS, 1943-46. Recipient Outstanding Service award City of Jacksonville, 1974. Registered profl. engr., Fla., Ga. Mem. ASME (chmn. N.E. Fla. 1967-68), Nat. Soc. Profl. Engrs., ASHRAE, Assn. Energy Engrs., Am. Soc. Inventors, Fla. Engring. Soc. Episcopalian. Club: University (Jacksonville). Contbr. articles to profl. jours. Patentee in field. Office: 110 Riverside Ave Jacksonville FL 32202

RUSSELL, DAVID LYNN, federal judge; b. Sapulpa, Okla., July 7, 1942; s. Lynn and F. Elizabeth (Brown) R.; m. Dana J. Russell, Apr. 16, 1971; 1 dau., Sarah E. B.S., Okla. Bapt. U., 1963; J.D., Okla. U., 1965. Bar: Okla. Asst. atty. gen State of Okla., Oklahoma City, 1968-69; legal advisor to gov. of Okla., Oklahoma City, 1969-70; legal advisor to sen. Dewey F. Bartlett, Washington, 1973-75; U.S. atty. Western Dist. Okla., Oklahoma City, 1975-77, 81-82; judge U.S. Dist. Ct., Oklahoma City, 1982—. Chmn. bd. Crown Heights Meth. Ch., Oklahoma City, 1980. Served to lt. comdr. JAGC, USNR, 1965-72. Mem. ABA, Okla. Bar Assn., Fed. Bar Assn. (pres. 1981). Republican. Methodist. Club: Men's Dinner (Oklahoma City). Lodge: Rotary. Home: 2309 NW 119 Terr Oklahoma City OK 73120 Office: US Dist Ct 3321 US Courthouse Oklahoma City OK 73102

RUSSELL, DEMPSEY RANDOLPH, financial manager; b. Hartford, Ky., July 17, 1919; s. Orville William and Ina Gray R.; m. Jane Catherine Jones, Nov. 5, 1949, children—Randolph Lee, Marsha Ann, Nancy Jean, Raymond Wayne, Robert Edward, Richard Alan. B.S., U. Md., 1961. Commd. officer U.S. Army, 1961, advanced through grades to lt. col., 1964; service in Vietnam, 1963; adj. gen. 25th Inf. Div., Hawaii, 1956-58; dir. adminstrn. office Chief of Staff, U.S. Army, 1965-67; resigned, 1967; fin. mgr. computer systems div. Sperry Corp., Charlotte, N.C., 1967—. Mem. Pres. Nat. Campaign Com. Decorated Bronze Star; recipient Presdl. Excellence award Sperry Corp., 1976. Mem. Am. Mgmt. Assn. Republican. Baptist. Clubs: Toastmasters; Sharon View Country (Charlotte). Lodges: Masons, Shriners (Charlotte). Home: 7416 Folger Dr Charlotte NC 28226 Office: 301 S McDowell St Charlotte NC 28204

RUSSELL, DONALD STUART, judge; b. Lafayette Springs, Miss., Feb. 22, 1906; s. Jesse and Lula (Russell) R.; m. Virginia Utsey, June 15, 1929; children—Donald, Mildred, Scott, John. A.B., U. S.C., 1925, LL.B., 1928; student, U. Mich., 1929. Bar: S.C. 1928. Practiced law, Spartanburg, 1930-42; with Nicholls, Wyche & Byrnes, Nicholls, Wyche & Russell, and Nicholls & Russell, 1930-38; pvt. practice, 1938-42; mem. Price Adjustment Bd., War Dept., Washington, 1942; asst. to dir. econ. stablzn., 1942, asst. to dir. war moblzn., 1943; dep. dir. Office War Moblzn. Reconversion, 1945; asst. sec. state, 1945-47; pres. U. S.C., 1951-57; pvt. law practice, 1957-63, gov. S.C., 1963-65, mem. U.S. Senate from S.C., 1965-66, U.S. Dist. Ct. judge, 1967-71, U.S. Ct. Appeals judge, 1971—. Mem. Wriston Com. on Reorgn. Fgn. Service, 1954; trustee emeritus Emory U., Atlanta; trustee Converse Coll., Spartanburg, S.C., Benedict Coll., Columbia, S.C. Served as maj. AUS, 1944, SHAEF, France. Mem. Phi Beta Kappa. Methodist. Home: 716 Otis Blvd Spartanburg SC 29302 Office: Fed Bldg Spartanburg SC 29304*

RUSSELL, DOROTHY SCHOEBERLEIN, educator; b. Oradell, N.J., Feb. 19, 1935; d. John and Dorothy Hanna (Erwin) Schoeberlein; m. Ronald W. Zuersher, Dec. 17, 1955; children—William Eugene, Lori Ann; m. Donald W. Russell, May 22, 1976. B.A., Fairleigh Dickinson U., 1956; M.A.T., William Paterson Coll., 1969; Ed.D., U. N.C.-Greensboro, 1974. Tchr., Westwood (N.J.) Sch. Dist., 1970, Greensboro (N.C.) Pub. Schs., 1971; asst. prof. Cleve. State U., 1974-78; dir. tchr. edn., assoc. prof. Salem Coll., Winston-Salem, 1978—, assoc. dean, 1982—. Mem. NOW, Nat. Council Tchrs. of Math., N.C. Assn. Colls. Tchr. Edn. (pres.). Contbr. articles to profl. jours. Home: 900 Brintonial Way Winston-Salem NC 27104 Office: Salem Station Winston-Salem NC 27108

RUSSELL, H(ARRY) AL(MON), banker, creative consultant; b. Houma, La., Aug. 30, 1947; s. Harry Almon Russell and Claudia Howard (Wallis) Russell Tharp; m. Linda Theresa Walker, June 6, 1970; 1 child, Benjamin Matthew. B.S. in Premedicine, La. State U., 1970; M.H.A. Acad. Health Scis., 1979; M.B.A., Kennedy Western U., 1986. Clin. adminstr. Mannheim (W.Ger.) Health Clinic, 1974-77; med. team chief U.S. Army Readiness Region IX, San Francisco, 1977-78; exec. officer, aide-de-camp to comdg. Gen., Readiness Region IX, San Francisco, 1978-80; v.p. ops. Am. Bank & Trust, Houma, La., 1981, chief ops. officer, sr. v.p., 1981-85, sr. v.p. personal banking 1985-86, chmn. mgmt. com., 1983-84, chmn. ops. com., 1981-85, chmn. mktg. com., 1984-86. Mem. Sch. Bd., St. Matthew's Episcopal Sch., Houma, pres. PTA, 1984; participant Pub. Affairs Research Council, Baton Rouge, 1982-86; sponsor Nat. Republican Congl. Com. Victory Fund, Nat. Rep. Senatorial Com.; cons. Downtown Revitalization Project, 1984. Served to capt. U.S. Army, 1970-80. Decorated Army Commendation medal, others. Mem. Assn. Mil. Surgeons, Am. Legion. La. Bankers Assn., Nat. Assn. Security Dealers (registered rep.). Episcopalian. Home: Hwy 24 Route 1 Box 515-C Bourg LA 70343 Office: Am Bank and Trust Co 801 Barrow St Houma LA 70361

RUSSELL, HARRY FRANK, contract security executive; b. Calhoun, Ga., May 14, 1938; s. Harry Frank and Halloween (Stephens) R.; m. Reba Wynette Rickett, Dec. 14, 1958 (div. Mar. 1962); children—Alesia Lynne, Harry Wade; m. Judith Hall, Apr. 22, 1972; 1 son, Scott Harrison. B.S., Ga. State U., 1974, postgrad. Dir. alcohol and tobacco tax unit Ga. Dept. Revenue, Atlanta, 1972-74; dir. investigation Ga. Sec. of State, Atlanta, 1974-76; pres. Russell Marine & Field, Atlanta, 1976-77; gen. mgr. So. Security Services, Atlanta, 1977-79; dir. corp. security Charter Co., Jacksonville, Fla., 1979-82; area mgr. Wackenhut Corp., Atlanta, 1982—; cons. Charter Oil Co., Jacksonville, 1977-79. Asst. coordinator Jimmy Carter for Gov., Atlanta, 1970. Served to capt. U.S. Army, 1965-70; Vietnam. Decorated Bronze Stars (3), Purple Heart, 18 others. Mem. Riverside/Avondale Preservation Socl. (chmn. 1980-81, exec. com. 1981-82), Am. Soc. for Indsl. Security (cert. protection profl.). Baptist. Clubs: Sawgrass (Ponte Vedra Beach, Fla.); Atlanta Sporting. Home: 209 Brighton Rd Atlanta GA 30309 Office: Wackenhut Corp 1945 Cliff Valley Way Atlanta GA 30329

RUSSELL, JAMES MADISON, III, scientist; b. Newport News, Va., June 12, 1940; s. James Madison, Jr., and Sue Estelle (Thomas) R.; m. Virginia Bell Rollings, June 18, 1960; children—Amy E., David M., Jennifer A. Student Va. Mil. Inst., 1958-60; B.S.E.E., Va. Poly. Inst. and State U., 1962; M.E.E., U. Va., 1966; Ph.D. in Atmospheric Sci., U. Mich., 1970. Aerospace engr. NASA Langley Research Center, Hampton, Va., 1962-68, research scientist, 1970-75, head chemistry and dynamics br. Atmospheric Sci. div., 1976-84, head theoretical studies br. Atmospheric Sci. div., 1984—; research asst. meterology U. Mich., 1968-70; vis. scientist Nat. Center Atmospheric Research, 1974; lectr. physics Christopher Newport Coll., 1971-73, 84; lectr. remote sensing George Washington U., 1973. Bishop, stake pres. Ch. of Jesus Christ of Latter-day Saints. Recipient Disting. Achievement award U. Mich. Coll. Engring., 1970; medal for exceptional sci. achievement NASA, 1982. Mem. Am. Meteorol. Soc., Sigma Xi, Tau Beta Pi, Eta Kappa Nu. Patentee in field. Home: 124 Breezy Point Dr Grafton VA 23692 Office: MS401B NASA Langley Research Center Hampton VA 23665

RUSSELL, JAMES MICHAEL, exploration geologist; b. Falfurrias, Tex., Dec. 6, 1952; s. James Charles and Willie Anita (Zimmerman) R.; m. Catherine May Leslie, Jan. 8, 1979; children—Caroline Anne, Angela Michelle. B.S. in Geology, Tex. A&I U., 1977. Exploration geologist Uranium Resources, Inc., Corpus Christi, Tex., 1977-82, sr. geologist, 1982—. Contbr. articles to profl. jours. Mem. Am. Assn. Petroleum Geologists (energy minerals div.), AIME, Corpus Christi Geol. Soc. Republican. Mem. Christian Ch. Avocations: fishing; tennis; archaelogical hunting. Office: Uranium Resources Inc 5333 Everhart St Suite 126 Corpus Christi TX 78411

RUSSELL, JERRY LEWIS, public relations counselor, political consultant; b. Little Rock, July 21, 1933; s. Jerry Lewis and Frances (Lieb) R.; m. Alice Anne Cason, Feb. 14, 1969; children—Leigh Anne, Andrew J. III, Christopher R.; children by previous marriage—Jerry Lewis III, Susan Frances. B.A. in Journalism, U. Ark., 1958; postgrad. in history U. Central Ark., 1978-82. Pub. relations dir. Little Rock C. of C., 1958; editor, pub. The Visitor, Little Rock, 1959-60; sec.-mgr. Ark. Press Assn., Little Rock, 1960-61; account exec. Brandon Agy., Little Rock, 1961-65; founder, pres. Guide Advt. (now part of River City Enterprises, Inc.), also River City Pubs., Little Rock 1965-70, 72—; pres. River City Enterprises, Inc., 1974—; dir. public relations service S.M. Brooks Agy., Little Rock, 1970-72; founder, pres. Campaign Cons., Inc., 1974—; pub., editor Grass Roots Campaigning newsletter, 1979—, Hog Call Fanletter, 1979—. Served with AUS, 1953-56. Mem. Ark. Advt. Fedn. (pres. 1967-68), Public Relations Soc. Am. (pres. Ark. chpt. 1974), Am. Assn. Polit. Cons., Orgn. Am. Historians, Co. Mil. Historians, Western Hist. Assn., Council on Am.'s Mil. Past (state dir. 1979—), So. Hist. Soc., Victorian Mil. Soc., Little Big Horn Assos., Ark., Pulaski County hist. socs., Civil War Round Table Ark. (charter pres. 1964-65), Civil War Round Table Assos. (founder 1968, nat. chmn.), Order Indian Wars (founder 1979, nat. chmn.), Circus Fans Assn. Am. (pres. Little Rock chpt. 1981-83), Westerners Internat. (charter pres. Little Rock Corral 1974—), Confederate Hist. Inst. (founder, nat. chmn.), Victorian Mil. History Inst. (founder, colonial chmn.). Home: 9 Lefever Ln Little Rock AR 72207

RUSSELL, JOHN EDWIN, physician, physical therapist; b. Teaneck, N.J., July 13, 1941; s. John E. and Betty (Habersaat) R. Student Gettysburg Coll., 1959-61; B.S., McMurry Coll., Abilene, Tex., 1963; B.S., U. Houston, 1964; R.P.T., Kansas City Coll. Osteo. Medicine, 1970. Lic. phys. therapist. Fellow phys. medicine and rehab. Kansas City Clinic, 1968-70; intern Suncoast Hosp., Largo, Fla., 1970-71; therapist, cons. Meml. Hosp., Midway Hosp., Los Angeles, Beverly Glen Hosp., Beverly Hills, Calif.; med. chmn. Fla. State Gov.'s Council Phys. Fitness and Sports, 1976-81; chmn. sports medicine Men's Olympic Devel., Track, Field Com., 1980-84; physician U.S. Olympic Gymnastic Team Trials, Jacksonville, Fla., 1980, Tampa (Fla.) Amateur Boxing Assn., 1980-83, Nat. Collegiate Track and Field Championships, Baton Rouge, 1981, 82, 83, 85, Internat. Swimming Championships, Gainesville, Fla., 1981, 82, World Mixed Pair Gymnastics Championships, Gainesville, 1982, Pan Am. Games, Caracus, Venezuela, 1983, NCAA Track and Field

Championships, 1981-84, U.S. vs. China Master's Team Asian Games, Hong Kong, 1982, U.S. Nat. Jr. Track Team tour, Sherbrooke, Can., Italy, 1983, U.S. Nat. Jr. Basketball Team tour, Russia, 1983, Olympic Games, Los Angeles, 1984, Caribbean Championships, Las Tunas, Cuba, 1984; chmn. Fla. AAU com. Submaster's, Master's Track, Field. Recipient Sports Illustrated Merit Achievement award, 1977. Mem. Fla. Osteo. Med. Assn. (chmn. sports medicine, phys. fitness 1976-82), Am. Osteo. Coll. Sports Medicine (founder mem. 1976, pres. 10 dist. Fla. 1979-80), Hillsborough (Fla) Council Hosps. Clubs: Tampa Bay Track (pres. 1976-78), Phila. Track (internat. team). Author: How to Look and Feel Ten Years Younger, 1982; The —I Don't Have Time To Exercise— Weight Loss Program, 1982; co-author: DMSO, Arthritis Cure, Miracle Drug or Fraud, 1982. Office: Beacon Sq Physical Therapy 1034 W Hillsborough Ave Tampa FL

RUSSELL, JOHN FRANCIS, librarian; b. Mt. Carmel, Ind., Apr. 30, 1929; s. David Freeman and Bertha (Major) R.; B.A., DePauw U., 1951; postgrad. Ind. U., 1951-52; M.A., Johns Hopkins U., 1954; student Cath. U. Am., summer 1955; M.S., Grad. Sch. Library Sci. Drexel U., 1977; m. Edith Raymond Hyde, June 27, 1953; 1 dau., Anne Marie. Tchr. English, Park Sch. Balt., 1954-75, chmn. dept., 1957-75; tchr. speech, dir. Ira Aldridge Players Morgan State Coll., fall 1965-66; tchr. drama Loyola Coll., 1964, 66. Pres. Tchrs.' Assn. Ind. Sch. Balt. Area, 1960-62, advisory bd., 1966-67, chmn. com. on English, 1966-68; exec. com. Assn. Ind. Md. Sch., 1967-68. Dir., costumer Johns Hopkins U. Playshop, 1963-64; lectr. Lecture Group, Woman's Club Roland Park, others, 1964—. Bd. dirs. Balt. area council World Federalists U.S.A., 1961-67, vice chmn., 1964-67, nat. exec. council, 1963-65; bd. dirs. Center Stage, 1964-77; dir. Pasadena Little Theatre, v.p., 1979-83, pres., 1983-85; mem. adminstrv. bd. First United Meth. Ch., 1980—; sec. Houston Shakespeare Festival Angels, 1982—. Recipient Nat. Citation of Merit Am. Shakespeare Festival, 1961; Critics Choice award Houston Post, 1984. Mem. Harris County Heritage Soc., Am. Film Inst., Nat. Film Soc., Am. Theatre Assn. (v.p. Mid-Atlantic dist. 1967-68, pres. 1968-69, nat. dir. 1970-73, Mid-Atlantic chpt. award for achievement and contbn. to theatre 1973), Secondary Sch. Theatre Assn. (v.p. devel. 1974-75), Tex. Non-Profit Theatre, Nat. (bd. dirs. 1969), Md. (pres. 1969-70) councils tchrs. English, Capital Area Media Educators Orgn. (exec. com. 1970-73, screening chmn. 1971-73), ALA, Tex. Library Assn. (audiovisual chmn. conv. planning com. 1981), Assn. for Ednl. Communication and Tech., Council Info. and Referral Services (newsletter editor 1984-86), Tex. Alliance Info. and Referral Services (conv. speaker 1981, 83, 84, 85), Alliance of Info. and Referral Services, Houston Public Library Staff Assn. (pres. 1981-82), Literacy Vols. Am. (sec. Houston 1984—), Reading, Edn. and Devel. Council (recruitment chmn., exec. com. 1984-86), Phi Beta Kappa, Phi Eta Sigma, Beta Phi Mu. Editor: The Secondary School Theatre, 1972-74. Home: 7817 Grove Ridge Houston TX 77061 Office: Park Pl Br Library 8145 Park Pl Blvd Houston TX 77017

RUSSELL, LAO, philosopher, author, educator; b. Ivinghoe, Buckinghamshire, Eng.; d. Alfred William and Florence (Hills) Cook; naturalized, 1947; ed. pvt. tutors; m. Walter Russell, July 29, 1948. Founder, Walter Russell Found. (now known as U. Sci. and Philosophy), Waynesboro, Va., 1948, mng. dir., 1948—, pres., 1949—; founded Shrine of Beauty known as Swannanoa Palace and Sculpture Gardens, 1948. Founder Man-Woman Equalization League, 1955, Internat. Age of Character Clubs, 1966. Author: God Will Work With You But Not For You (named 1 of 6 best books of year N.Y. Herald Tribune 1955), 1955; An Eternal Message of Light and Love, 1964; My Love I Extend To You, 1966; Love-A Scientific and Living Philosophy of Love and Sex, 1966; Why You Cannot Die! The Continuity of Life-Reincarnation Explained, 1972; (with Walter Russell) Home Study Course in Universal Law, Natural Science and Living Philosophy, 1950, Scientific Answer to Human Relations, 1951, Atomic Suicide?, 1957, The World Crisis-Its Explanation and Solution, 1958, The One-World Purpose-A Plan to Dissolve War by a Power More Mighty Than War, 1960. Executed 5-foot statue (with husband) The Christ of the Blue Ridge, 1948, also colossal model, 1950; presented colossal bronze bust of George Washington (sculpted by Walter Russell) to Fredericksburg Bicentennial Commn., 1976. Address: Univ Science and Philosophy Swannanoa Waynesboro VA 22980

RUSSELL, LYNN DARNELL, mechanical engineer, educator; b. Pontotoc, Miss., Nov. 1, 1937; s. Clyde Austin and Clytee Lora (Faulkner) R.; m. Elaine Lowery, June 16, 1966; children—Kathy, Brent, Mark, Jeffrey. B.S., Miss. State U., 1960, M.S., 1961; Ph.D., Rice U., 1966. Profl. engr. Ala., Miss., Tenn. Engr. NASA Marshall Space Flight Ctr., Johnson Spacecraft Ctr., 1961-64; research scientist Lockheed, Huntsville, Ala., 1966-67; mem. tech. staff TRW, Huntsville, 1967-69; dean engring. U. Tenn.-Chattanooga, 1969-79; prof. mech. engring. Miss. State U., 1979—; energy cons. Recipient numerous fellowships and grants. Mem. Chattanooga Engrs. Club (pres. 1975); pres. Tenn. Soc. Profl. Engrs., 1978-79. Mem. ASME, AAAS, Miss. Engring. Soc., Nat. Soc. Profl. Engrs., Am. Soc. Engring. Edn., Miss. Acad. Sci., Internat. Solar Energy Soc., Sigma Xi, Pi Tau Sigma (past pres. Miss. chpt.). Contbr. articles to profl. jours. Home: 20 Greenbriar Rd Starkville MS 39759 Office: PO Drawer ME Mississippi State MS 39762

RUSSELL, MICHAEL ANDRÉ, marketing executive; b. Tyler, Tex., Aug. 19, 1956; s. Jeraldine (Lane) R. A.S., Tyler Jr. Coll., 1977, A.A., 1977; B.A., Fisk U., 1979; M.B.A., Atlanta U., 1981. Mktg. rep IBM, Atlanta, 1980-82; asst. brand mgr. USA Nat. Coca-Cola Hdqrs., Atlanta, 1983—; cons. The Phoenix Group, Atlanta, 1984. Vice chmn. bd. trustees Simpson St. Ch. of Christ, Atlanta, 1982; bd. dirs. Butler St. YMCA, Atlanta, 1983; active High Mus. Art/Young Careers, Atlanta, 1984, NAACP, Atlanta, 1983. Mem. Nat. Black M.B.A. Assn. (mktg. chmn. 1979), Am. Mktg. Assn. (pres. chpt. 1979-80), Fisk U. Alumni Assn. (exec. com. 1980, chpt. pres. 1984), Kappa Alpha Psi. Democrat. Mem. Ch. of Christ. Club: Atlanta City.

RUSSELL, OSCAR CECIL (BUD), JR., banker; b. Huntsville, Ala., Nov. 10, 1945; s. Oscar Cecil and Lovena (Moss) R.; B.S., U. Ala., 1968; postgrad. Ga. State U., 1974-77. With Citizens & So. Nat. Bank, Atlanta, 1973-77; sr. v.p., cashier, ops. group exec. Hibernia Nat. Bank, New Orleans, 1977—; bd. dirs. New Orleans Clearing House Assn., 1977—, bd. dirs., mem. exec. com. La.-Ala.-Miss. Automated Clearing House Assn., 1977—. Bd. dirs., treas. New Orleans Ballet, 1981-83; trustee New Orleans City Ballet, bd. dirs., v.p., 1983; trustee Artistic Resource Corp. Cin. Served to capt. U.S. Army, 1968-73. Mem. Am. Inst. Banking, Bank Adminstrn. Inst., Phi Kappa Psi. Republican. Roman Catholic. Home: 2733 Hudson Pl New Orleans LA 70114 Office: PO Box 61540 New Orleans LA 70161

RUSSELL, PAUL JAMES, JR., broadcast equipment company executive, broadcasting company engineering executive; b. East Orange, N.J., Apr. 7, 1948; s. Paul James and Loretta (Connolly) R.; m. Sandra Lynn Reynolds, Apr. 18, 1969; children—Paula Lynn, Brian Eugene. Student, U. Miami, 1972-76; cert. transmitter repair U.S. Army Signal Sch., Sony Service Schs. Engring. supr. U. Miami (Fla.), 1969-76, Sta.-WTVJ-TV, Miami, 1976—; pres. E.N.G. Communications Service, Inc., Miami, 1982—. Served with U.S. Army, 1966-68; Vietnam. Mem. Soc. Broadcast Engrs. Democrat. Baptist. Lodge: Am. Legion. Home and Office: 7700 SW 146 Rd Miami FL 33183

RUSSELL, PEGGY TAYLOR, soprano, educator; b. Newton, N.C., Apr. 5, 1927; d. William G. and Sue B. (Cordell) Taylor; Mus.B. in Voice, Salem Coll., 1948; Mus.M., Columbia U., 1950; postgrad. U. N.C., Greensboro, 1977; student Am. Inst. Mus. Studies, Austria, 1972, 78; student of Clifford Bair, Nell Starr, Salem Coll., Winston-Salem, N.C., Edgar Schofield, Chloe Owen, N.Y.C.; student opera-dramatics Boris Goldovsky, Southwestern Opera Inst., Ande Andersen, Max Lehner, Graz, Austria; m. John B. Russell, Feb. 23, 1952; children—John Spotswood, Susan Bryce. Mem. faculty dept. voice Guilford Coll., Greensboro, 1952-53, Greensboro Coll., 1971-72; pvt. tchr. voice, Greensboro, 1963—; vis. instr. in voice U. N.C., Chapel Hill, 1973-77; founding dir. Young Artists Opera Theatre, Greensboro, 1983; lectr. on music history and opera, High Point, N.C., Center for Creative Leadership, Greensboro, 1979-80, First Presbyn. Ch., 1982; debut in light opera as Gretchen in The Red Mill, Winston-Salem Opera Assn., 1947; debuts include: Rosalinda in Die Fledermaus, Piedmont Festival Opera Assn., 1949, Lola in Cavalleria Rusticana, Greensboro Opera Assn., 1951, Violetta in La Traviata, Greensboro Opera Assn., 1953, Fiordiligi in Cosi fan tutte, Piedmont Opera Co., 1956; appeared as Marguerite in Faust, Brevard Music Center Resident Opera Co., 1967, First Lady in The Magic Flute, Am. Inst. Mus. Studies, Graz, Austria, 1972; mem. Greensboro Oratorio Soc., 1955-59, soprano soloist in The Messiah, 1952, 58, The Creation, 1955, Solomon, 1958; soprano soloist Presbyterian Ch. of the Covenant, Greensboro, 1958-71; guest appearances Sta. WFMY-TV, Greensboro, 1958-62; soprano soloist with Greensboro Symphony Orch., 1964, 80, Eastern Music Festival Orch. 1965, Greensboro Civic Orch., 1980; soloist in numerous recitals including: Wesleyan Coll., 1964, Roanoke Symphony Guild, 1967, Am. Inst. Mus. Studies, Austria, 1972, 78, U. N.C., Chapel Hill, 1974, 75, 76, 77, N.C. Mus. of Art, 1978; recital, masterclass Mars Hill Coll., 1981. Bd. dirs. Music Theater Assocs., Greensboro Friends of Music, N.C. Lyric Opera. Mem. Nat. Opera Assn. (chmn. regional opera cos. com. 1985—), Central Opera Service, Nat. Assn. Tchrs. of Singing (state gov. 1976-82, coordinator Regional Artist Contest 1982—), N.C. Fedn. Music Clubs (dir. 1956-58), Music Educators Nat. Conf., Greensboro Music Tchrs. Assn. (pres. 1966-67), Symphony Guild (dir. 1977-78), Broadway Theater League (chmn. 1961-63), Atlanta Opera Guild, Civic Music Assn. (chmn. 1963-64). Presbyterian. Clubs: Sherwood Swim and Racquet, Altrusa. Home: 3012 W Cornwallis Dr Greensboro NC 27408

RUSSELL, ROBERT LEONARD, association executive; b. Mt. Vernon, Ill., July 18, 1916; s. Charles Arthur and Edna Mabel (Yearwood) R.; student St. Petersburg Jr. Coll., 1971-72; B.Sc., U. Mid-Fla., 1973, M.S., 1974; m. Jeanne Lucille Tackenberg, May 21, 1942. Reporter, Peoria (Ill.) Jour., 1939-42, 46-47, Chgo. Daily News, 1947-57; asst. exec. dir. Profl. Golfers Assn., Dunedin, Fla., 1957-65; exec. dir. United Vol. Services, San Mateo, Calif., 1965-66; reporter St. Petersburg (Fla.) Evening Ind., 1967-70; exec. v.p. Fla. Health Care Assn. (formerly Fla. Nursing Home Assn.), Orlando, 1970-77; exec. v.p. Mortgage Bankers Assn. Fla., Orlando, 1977—, Mortgage Bankers Assn. Central Fla., Orlando, 1978—; exec. dir. Mortgage Bankers Ednl. Found. Fla., Orlando, 1983—; adminstr. Fla. Health Care Self Insurers Fund, 1972-78; sec.-treas. Mortgage Bankers Fla. Polit. Action Com., 1977-85; pres. Profl. Assn. Services, Inc., 1977-81. Pres., Aldrich & Assos., 1967-70. Elder, Park Lake Presbyn. Ch., Orlando, 1979-83, St. Paul's Presbyn. Ch., Orlando, 1983—. Served with USAAF, 1942-46. Mem. Am. (certified), Fla., Central Fla. socs. assn. execs., Am. Coll. Health Care Adminstrs. (hon.), Fla. Sheriffs Assn. (hon.), U.S. Basketball Writers Assn. (pres. 1956-57), Football Writers Assn. Am. (dir. 1955-57), Nat. Rifle Assn. (life). Republican. Presbyterian. Editor: Profl. Golfer mag., 1957-65; Nat. Golfer mag., 1965-66; Communicator, 1977-80, Bull., 1980-81, The Messenger, 1985—; exec. editor Rx Sports and Travel mag., 1966-67. Home: 6586 Kreidt Dr Orlando FL 32818 Office: PO Box 3586 Orlando FL 32802

RUSSELL, STEVE ALLEN, broadcasting announcer, radio and television commercial producer; b. Bamberg, S.C., Nov. 7, 1954; s. Leroy Russell and Eva Lee (Whetstone) Greenwood; m. Rene Lannette Jervey, Oct. 9, 1982. Grad. high sch. Announcer Sta. WWBD AM-FM, Bamberg, 1970-73, Sta. WTMA-WPXI, Charleston, S.C., 1973-75; announcer, program dir. Sta. WNCG-WKTM, North Charleston, 1975-81; announcer, prodn. dir. Sta. WCSC-WXTC, Charleston, 1981-85; program announcer Sta. WCSC-TV, Charleston, 1981—; owner, prin. Steve Russell Audio, Charleston; cons. in field. Recipient Silver, Bronze awards 3d Dist. chpt. Advt. Fedn., 1984, 85, 1st place Spot Prodn. award S.C. Broadcasters Assn., 1982. Mem. Advt. Fedn. of Charleston (recipient numerous awards 1979—). Avocations: tennis; fishing; traveling. Home: 1789 Banbury Rd Charleston SC 29407 Office: Steve Russell Audio 4 Carriage Ln Suite 305 Charleston SC 29407

RUSSELL, STEVEN ARTHUR, dentist; b. Shreveport, La., Dec. 24, 1956; s. Jimmy Ray and Elizabeth (Mills) R. B.S. in Biology, Centenary, Coll., 1978; D.D.S., La. State U., 1982. Gen. practice dentistry, Shreveport, 1982—. Mem. ADA, NW La. Dental Assn., La. Dental Assn. Democrat. Episcopalian. Home: 5710 Marina Bay Dr Shreveport LA 71119 Office: 9308 Mansfield Rd Suite 500 Shreveport LA 71118

RUSSELL-WORTHAM, JEANETTE STRATTON PORTER, mathematics educator; b. Liberty, Ky., Apr. 3, 1931; d. Welby Herbert and Doretta Ethel (Thomas) Russell; A.A., Lindsey Wilson Coll., 1950; B.S., Eastern Ky. U., 1952, M.A., 1953; postgrad. Central Wash. U., 1964, U. Puget Sound, 1965, summers U. Idaho, 1958, 59, U. Louisville, 1980; m. L. Glenn Collins (dec.); children—Patrick Glenn, Susan Jean; m. 2d, Francis L. Wortham, July 9, 1971. Tchr. math. Versailles (Ky.) High Sch., 1952-56; Marston Jr. High Sch., San Diego, 1956-57, Moscow (Idaho) High Sch., 1957-60, Clover Park High Sch., Tacoma, 1960-65, Waggener High Sch., Louisville, 1966-69; cons. elem. math Jefferson County Schs., Louisville, 1969-79, elem. math. program devel. specialist, 1979-80, elem. math and curriculum specialist, 1980—; mem. summer faculty U. Louisville, 1974-80, 85. NSF grantee, summers 1958, 59. Mem. Nat. Council Suprs. Math., Nat. Council Tchrs. Math., Ky. Assn. Sch. Adminstrs., Jefferson County Assn. Sch. Adminstrs., Ky. Assn. Ednl. Suprs. (exec. bd.), NEA, Ky. Council Tchrs. Math. (exec. bd.), Greater Louisville Council Tchrs. Math. (past pres.), Assn. Supervision and Curriculum Devel., Idaho Acad. Sci. (charter), Women in Sch. Adminstrn., Metric Assn., Computer Users in Edn., Filson Club Hist. Soc., DAR, Eastern Ky. Alumni Club (past pres. Greater Louisville chpt.), Delta Kappa Gamma (past pres. Xi chpt.). Republican. Clubs: Friendship Class Bridge. Home: 1902 Warrington Way Louisville KY 40222 Office: Van Hoose Edn Center 3332 Newburg Rd Louisville KY 40218

RUST, ROLAND THOMAS, marketing educator; b. Indpls., Apr. 27, 1952; s. R.B. and Mary Ellen (Shutt) R. B.A., DePauw U., 1974; M.B.A., U. N.C., 1977, Ph.D., 1979. Asst. prof. mktg. U. Tex., Austin, 1979-85, assoc. prof., 1985—. Editorial rev. bd. Jour. Mktg. Research, 1982—; contbr. articles to profl. jours. Avocations: running; music; chess. Office: Dept Mktg U Tex Austin TX 78712

RUTA, THEODORE RALPH, retail automotive company executive; b. Norwalk, Conn., Nov. 19, 1940; s. Ralph Robert and Josephine Ann (Angerio) R.; B.S. in Math., Fla. State U., 1962, B.S. in Stats., 1962; postgrad. in acctg. Stetson U., 1970; m. Charlotte Mae Sims, Aug. 13, 1960; children—Ralph Steven, Debra Jovonne, Michelle Christine, Theodore Scott. Fin. analyst TRW, Inc., Kennedy Space Center, 1966-71; comptroller McCotter Motors, Inc., Titusville, Fla., 1971-75, v.p., 1976—; pres. Contractor Operated Parts System, Inc., 1981—. Chmn. North Brevard (county, Fla.) Park and Recreation Commn., 1979, 80, 81; mem. Titusville Planning and Zoning Commn., 1982-84; vice chmn. bd. North Brevard Hosp., 1984—; officiated Sun Bowl, 1984, Freedom Bowl, 1985. Served with USAF, 1962-65. Mem. Arnold Air Soc., Mid-Coast Ofcls. Assn. (pres. 1973-74), So. Coaches and Ofcls. Assn., So. Ind. Collegiate Ofcls. Assn. (bd. dirs.), Sunshine State Conf., The Athletic Congress, Amateur Softball Assn., Fla. Recreation Softball Assn. (umpire in chief 1977-78), Fla. High Sch. Activities Assn., Sigma Phi Epsilon. Club: Rotary. Office: PO Box 6295 Titusville FL 32782

RUTFORD, ROBERT HOXIE, university administrator; b. Duluth, Minn., Jan. 26, 1933; s. Skuli and Ruth (Hoxie) R.; m. Marjorie Ann, June 19, 1954; children—Gregory, Kristian, Barbara. B.A., U. Minn., 1954, M.A., 1963, Ph.D., 1969. Football and track coach Hamline U., 1958-62; research fellow U. Minn., 1963-66; asst. prof. geology U. S.D., 1967-70, asso. prof., 1970-72, chmn. dept. geology, 1968-72, chmn. dept. physics, 1971-72; dir. Ross Ice Shelf Project U. Nebr., Lincoln, 1972-75, vice chancellor for research and grad. studies, prof. geology, 1977-82, interim chancellor, 1980-81; pres. U. Tex., Dallas, 1982; dir. div. Polar Programs, NSF, Washington, 1975-77. Served to 1st lt. U.S. Army, 1954-56. Recipient Antarctic Service medal, 1964, Distinguished Service award NSF, 1977, Ernie Gunderson award for service to amateur athletics S.D. AAU, 1972. Fellow Geol. Soc. Am.; mem. Antarctican Soc., Arctic Inst. N.Am., Explorers Club, Am. Polar Soc., Nat. Council Univ. Research Adminstrs., Sigma Xi. Lutheran. Club: Cosmos. Home: 6809 Briar Cove Dr Dallas TX 75240 Office: Univ of Texas at Dallas PO Box 830688 Richardson TX 75083-0688

RUTH, BYRON EDWARD, civil engineering educator; b. Chgo., Mar. 25, 1931; s. Edward Luther and Evelyn Pearl (Wells) R.; m. Margarete Rohweder, Sept. 10, 1960; children—Boyd Owen, Toni Karen. B.S., Mont. State U., 1955; M.S., Purdue U., 1959; Ph.D., W.Va. U., 1967. Registered profl. Engr., Ind., W.Va., Fla. Field engr. Walter H. Knapp, Drummond Island, Mich., 1959; asst. dir. research and devel. Symons Mfg. Co., Des Plaines, Ill., 1960-61; instr. civil engring. W. Va. U., Morgantown, 1961-67, asst. prof., 1967-70; assoc. prof. civil engring. U. Fla., Gainesville, 1970-77, prof., 1977—; cons. transp., materials and design. Served with AUS 1956-58. Mem. ASCE, ASTM, Assn. Asphalt Paving Technologists, Can. Tech. Asphalt Assn., Transp. Research Bd., Am. Soc. Photogrammetry, Sigma Xi, Tau Beta Pi. Contbr. numerous articles to profl. jours. Patentee concrete forming equipment. Office: 346 Weil Hall U Fla Gainesville FL 32611

RUTH, WILLIAM AUGUSTUS, III, illustrator; b. Albany, N.Y., Oct. 16, 1925; s. William Augustus and Loretta Mary (Kilmade) R.; student George Peabody Tchrs. Coll., 1943, U. Pa., 1946-48. Illustrator U.S. Army Engr. Sch., Ft. Belvoir, Va., 1956-80; painter in oils and acrylics. Served in USAAF, 1943-46, U.S. Army, 1950-53. Mem. Internat. Graphics Inc. Roman Catholic. Home: 10317 Burke Lake Rd Fairfax Station VA 22039

RUTLAND, ADELE DUCHARME, educational administrator; b. Alexandria, La., Mar. 2, 1943; d. Robert James and Mary Elizabeth (Holly) Ducharme; children—Shannon M. Rutland, Shawn H. Rutland. B.S. in Elem. Edn., La. State U.-Baton Rouge, 1964, M.Ed., 1981, Ed.D., 1984. Tchr., Parkview Elem. Sch., Baton Rouge, 1977, Trinity Episcopal Sch., Baton Rouge, 1977-82; grad. teaching asst. La. State U., Baton Rouge, 1982-84; asst. prof. elem. edn. Troy State U., Montgomery, Ala., 1984—; cons. Trafton Acad., Baton Rouge, 1984; dir., cons. Learning Unltd., Baton Rouge, 1983-84. Contbr. articles to profl. jours. Mem. Internat. Reading Assn., Nat. Reading Conf., Nat. Council Tchrs. English, Am. Ednl. Research Assn., Assn. for Supervision and Curriculum Devel., Kappa Kappa Iota. Avocations: painting; gardening. Home: 105 Holly Ln Prattville AL 36067 Office: TSUM Bldg 625 Maxwell AFB AL 36112

RUTLEDGE, GARY RAY, state official, lawyer; b. Asheville, N.C., Nov. 13, 1950; s. Robert Earl and Mary Elizabeth (Rogers) R.; m. Danna Louise Depew, Aug. 7, 1976. Student Fla. Jr. Coll., 1969-70; B.A., U. Fla., 1972, J.D., 1976. Bar: Fla. 1976. Assoc., Bolton-Margulies Law Firm, Miami, Fla., 1976-79; ptnr. Margulies-Rutledge, P.A., Miami, 1979; dir. div. pari-mutuel wagering Miami Dept. Bus. Regulation, State of Fla., 1979-81, sec., 1981-84; sec. dept., 1984—; assoc. Sparber, Shevin, Shapo & Heilbronner. Mem. Fla. Bar Assn., Dade County Bar Assn., ABA, Nat. Assn. State Racing Commrs. (former mem. exec. com.). Democrat. Congregationalist. Club: U. Fla. Blue Key Alumni. Home: 6449 Count Turf Trail Tallahassee FL 32301 Office: Sparber Shevin Shapo & Heilbronner PA 315 S Calhoun St Suite 348 Barnett Bank Bldg Tallahassee FL 32301

RUTLEDGE, KEVIN JOSEPH, music educator, singer; b. Miami, Fla., Nov. 26, 1960; s. Henry Joseph and Rutledge Vera Leona (McIntosh) Forbes; m. Shirley Ann Woodard, Apr. 6, 1985. B. Music Edn., Howard U., 1983. Asst. conductor Howard U., Washington, 1982-83; minister music St. John Baptist Ch., Miami, 1983-84; tchr. music N. Glade Elem. Sch., OpaLocka, Fla., 1983—; music dir. Artistic Prodns., Miami, 1985; instr. music Madie Ives Community Sch., North Miami, Fla., 1985—. Recipient Outstanding Musical Leadership award St. John Bapt. Ch., 1980-82; fine arts scholar Howard U., 1981-83. Fellow United Tchrs. Dade, Howard U. Alumni Assn., Music Educators Nat. Conf. Democrat. Baptist. Avocations: singing; music arranging; playing piano. Home: 494 NW 165th St Rd C 303 Miami FL 33169 Office: 5000 NW 177 St Opalocka FL 33055

RUTLEDGE, PAMELA LEE, nurse; b. Hamilton, Ohio, Apr. 29, 1951; d. Raymond Jarvis and Adah (Lynch) Feltner; m. Justin Clark Rutledge, July 23, 1976. Assoc. in Nursing, Miami U., Oxford, Ohio, 1974; B.S. in Nursing, Austin Peay State U., 1983. Nurse Vanderbilt Hosp., Nashville, 1974-79, St. Thomas Hosp., Nashville, 1979—; instr. CPR, ARC, Nashville, 1983—. Mem. Am. Nurses Assn., Am. Assn. Critical Care Nurses (cert. in critical care). Home: 865 Bellevue Rd Apt J22 Nashville TN 37221

RYALS, SHIRLEY ANNE, banker; b. Tampa, Fla., Jan. 15, 1933; d. Gilbert J. and Elizabeth M. Miller; m. Lester J. Ryals, Dec. 19, 1953; children—Karen, Lester J. Student U Tampa, 1949-51, U. Colo., 1978-80. With Sun Banks, Tampa, 1976—, sr. v.p. mktg., 1978—. Vice pres. ARC; mem. exec. com. United Way; chmn. Tampa Sports Authority. Mem. Sales and Mktg. Execs., Pub. Relations Soc. Am., Tampa C. of C. Democrat. Methodist. Club: Tower. Home: 4514 Beachway Dr Tampa FL 33609 Office: 315 Madison St Tampa FL 33602

RYAN, GAIL BATTY, music educator; b. Miami, Mar. 7, 1929; d. Raymond H. and Mary E. Batty; m. Byron Dean Ryan, Sept. 15, 1929 (div. June 1960); 1 son, Randolph Raymond. B.Mus., U. Miami, 1950; postgrad. U. Mich., 1950-57, U. Perugia (Italy), 1957. Tchr. music, Dade County, Fla., 1950—; tchr. music edn. and humanities Nova U., Ft. Lauderdale, Fla., 1979—; tchr. music edn. U. Miami, 1966-67, tchr. black music/art/lit., 1968; music edn. intern Barry Coll., 1970-71. Profl. bassoonist U. Miami Symphony, Miami Beach Symphony, N.H. Symphony, Fort Lauderdale Symphony, U. Mich. Symphony, 1946-58; coordinator, narrator Symphonies for Children, Miami Beach Symphony, U. Miami, N.H. Symphony, 1955-58; producer, dir. Opera Amahl and the Night Visitors, 1963, 64, 70; founder The Fla. Renaissance Guild, Inc., 1979-83; choir dir., ch. sch. dir. Miami Shores Community Ch. U. Miami scholar, 1946-50; scholar Nat. Music Camp Interlocken, Mich., 1946-52; recipient award Better Homes and Gardens, 1961; award Valley Forge Freedom Found., 1968; Service award City of North Miami, 1970, 83; award VFW, 1970. Mem. Miami Shores Bus. and Profl. Women's Club, Sigma Alpha Iota, Delta Kappa Gamma. Republican. Presbyterian. Home: 860 NE 78th St Apt 504 Miami FL 33138 Office: 10351 NE 5th Ave Miami Shores FL 33138

RYAN, JOHN BERNARD, educator; b. Mt. Vernon, Ohio, Mar. 16, 1944; s. Edgil and Ruth Anastatia (Shaw) R.; m. Janic Carolyn Cooper, Dec. 1971; 1 child, Reuben. B.A.A.S., S.W. Tex. State U., 1977. Enlisted U.S. Air Force, 1962, advanced through grades to master sgt., 1978; TAC aircrew scheduling, Randolph AFB, Tex., 1976-78; Congl. Inquiries staff, 1978-80, chief retention reports, 1980-82; ret., 1982; ops. mgr. Pritchard Services, Dallas, 1982-83; EET instr. ITT Tech. Inst., Arlington, Tex., 1983-84, chief EET instr., 1984—. Active Harwood Baptist Ch., Bedford, Tex., 1985. Republican. Club: Toastmasters (pres. 1981-82, area gov. 1981-82). Avocations: model railroads; reading; chess; baseball; latch hook rugs. Office: ITT Tech Inst 2202 Rd to Six Flags Arlington TX 76011

RYAN, JOHN RANDOLPH, coast guard officer; b. Gadsden, Ala., Jan. 26, 1951; s. Roland Monroe and Goldie Vee (Moore) R.; m. Bonnie Gail Oliver, Jan. 26, 1974; children—Jennifer, Sean. Student Gadsden State Jr. Coll., 1969-71, Auburn U., 1975-76; B.S., SUNY-Albany, 1978. Served with USN, 1971-78; enlisted man U.S. Coast Guard, 1978, advanced through grades to lt., 1984; non-appropriated funds activities officer, St. Petersburg, Fla., 1980—. Pres. Autumn Run Homeowners Assn., 1983. Decorated Coast Guard Commendation medal. Mem. Am. Soc. Mil. Comptrollers, Retail Mchts. Assn. Baptist. Office: 600 8th Ave SE St Petersburg FL 39701

RYAN, JON MILLER, educational administrator, real estate teacher, investor; b. Falfurrias, Tex., May 4, 1934; s. Thomas Franklin and Agnes Clara (Miller) R.; m. Sylvia Ann Wentworth, Dec. 24, 1958; children—Tim, Steve, Kathy, Julie. B.A., Baylor U., 1955, M.A., 1960; M.Div., Southwest Bapt. Theol. Sem., 1959; cert. work Sam Houston State U., 1962-72. Lic. profl. counselor, real estate salesman, sch. supt., Tex.; ordained to ministry Bapt. Ch., 1959. Tchr. Aldine Ind. Sch. Dist., Houston, 1959-62, counselor, 1962-63, prin., 1963-68, dir. secondary schs., 1968-74; supt. schs. Kingsville Ind. Sch. Dist., Tex., 1974-76, Ft. Stockton Ind. Sch. Dist., Tex., 1976—; dir. Marketplace Ministeries, Dallas; mem. state elem. com. So. Assn. Colls. and Schs., Austin, 1980—, commn. mem., 1982—. Boss ambassador Ft. Stockton Ambassadors, 1983; chmn. personnel com. First Bapt. Ch., Ft. Stockton, 1979-84; pres. Panther Booster Club, Ft. Stockton, 1980-81. Named Educator of Month, Tex. Sch. Bus. Assn., 1985; recipient Booster of Yr. award Panther Booster Club, 1976-77, life membership award Tex. PTA, 1976. Mem. Am. Assn. Sch. Adminstrs., Tex. Assn. Sch. Adminstrs. (state chmn. membership com. 1985—), Tex. Assn. for Counseling and Devel., Nat. Assn. Ednl. Office Personnel (bd. dirs. 1985—), Fort Stockton C. of C. (pres. 1980), Phi Delta Kappa. Lodges: Rotary (pres. 1981-82), Masons. Avocations: game hunting, refinishing antique furniture. Home: 1804 W 7th St Fort Stockton TX 79735 Office: Fort Stockton Ind Sch Dist 101 W Division Fort Stockton TX 79735

RYAN, MARGUERETTE GERALDENE, registered nurse; b. Hillsdale, Okla., Aug. 23, 1933; d. Edward Joseph and Lottie Isabelle (Shorter) R. Diploma in Nursing, St. Anthony Sch. Nursing, 1954. Cert. nurse adminstr.

Staff nurse Okla. Children's Meml. Hosp., Oklahoma City, 1954-55, head nurse, 1955-60, asst. supr., 1960-62, 63-64, supr., 1962-63, 64-70, asst. dir., 1971-80, dir. nurses, 1980-82, infection control practitioner, 1982—. Mem. Assn. for Practitioners in Infection Control, Central Okla. Practitioners in Infection Control. Democrat. Roman Catholic. Avocations: piano, fishing. Home: 3317 N Utah Oklahoma City OK 73112 Office: Oklahoma Children's Meml Hosp Box 26307 Oklahoma City OK 73126

RYAN, NOLAN, professional baseball player; b. Refugio, Tex., Jan. 31, 1947; s. Lynn Nolan and Martha (Hancock) R.; m. Ruth Elsie Holdruff, June 26, 1967. Student, Alvin (Tex.) Jr. Coll., 1966-69. Pitcher N.Y. Mets, N.Y.C., 1966-71, Calif. Angels, 1972-79, Houston Astros, 1979—; mem. Am. League All-Star Team, 1972, 73, 75, 79. Author: (with Steve Jacobson) Nolan Ryan: Strike-Out King, 1975, (with Bill Libby) Nolan Ryan: The Other Game, 1977, (with Joe Torre) Pitching and Hitting, 1977. Served with AUS, 1967. Holder maj. league record for most strikeouts in one season since 1900. *

RYAN, PATRICK J., utility company executive; b. Chgo., July 31, 1938; s. Phillip W. and Estelle F. Ryan; m. Grace M. Marko, Sept. 5, 1959; children—Rachel, Nicole. B.S.E.E., U. Okla., 1961; grad. mgmt. (hon.), Edison Electric Inst., 1976. Cert. profl. engr., Okla. Service mgr. western div. Okla. Gas Electric Co., Oklahoma City, 1971-73, chief environ. affairs, 1973-76, asst. treas., 1976-78, treas., 1978-80, v.p., treas., 1980-81, sr. v.p., treas., 1981-84, exec. v.p. fin. and adminstrn., 1984—. Bd. dirs. Okla. Bus. Develop., Oklahoma City, 1980—, United Way Fund Dr., Oklahoma City, 1982—, ARC, Oklahoma City, 1981—, Last Frontier Council Boy Scouts Am., Oklahoma City, 1985, Community Council Central Okla. Served with U.S. Army, 1962. Mem. Okla. Soc. Fin. Analysts, Okla. Econ. Club, U. Okla. Assocs. Republican. Episcopalian. Clubs: Whitehall, The Greens. Avocation: sailing. Office: Okla Gas Electric Co 321 N Harvey PO Box 321 Oklahoma City OK 73101

RYAN, WILLIAM GRADY, psychologist; b. Bklyn., July 27, 1942; s. Leo R. and Peggy (Grady) R.; m. Nancy Jo Lutman; children—Anjali Rani, Brie Erin. B.A., St. Paul's Coll., Washington, 1964; Ph.D. in Clin. Psychology, Adelphi U., 1969. Lic. psychologist, Fla. Lectr. Adelphi U., 1964-69; staff psychologist Henderson Clinic of Broward County, Fla., 1969-70; adj. assoc. prof. Behavioral Scis. Ctr., Nova U., Fort Lauderdale, Fla., 1971-73, 81-82; co-founder Bio-Feedback Labs., Inc., Fort Lauderdale, 1973; clin. cons. juvenile div. Circuit Ct. Broward County, 1973; practice psychology, Broward County, 1972-80; dist. mental health program specialist Health and Rehabilitative Services, 1978; founder, clin. dir. Family Inst. of Broward and Palm Beach, 1980-84, exec. dir., sr. ptnr., 1984—; clin. cons. Broward County Div. Alcohol and Drug Abuse, 1978-80; mem. Fla. Health and Rehabilitative Services Forensic Task Force, 1978, Fla. Gov.'s Task Force on Substance Abuse, 1985, Broward County Community Mental Health Bd., 1980-82; mem. adv. bd. Postdoctoral Psychoanalytic Inst., Nova U., 1984—; pres. Psychol. Care South Fla., 1985; mem. peer counseling adv. bd. Broward County Sch. Systems. cons. Olympic Com. Tng. Ctr., Colorado Springs, Colo., 1979, Voices, 1984—; condr. workshops. Author: (autobiography) Irish Mist; Innovations in Clinical Practice: A Source Book. Editorial advisor Voices, 1984—. Contbr. articles to profl. jours. Elder, 2d Presbyn. Ch., Fort Lauderdale, 1976-78; pres. Epilepsy Found. Broward County, 1974; bd. dirs. Spl. Gerontology Project, 1977-79. NIMH fellow, 1964-65. Mem. Am. Psychol. Assn., Fla. Psychol. Assn., Nat. Register Health Care Providers in Psychology, Fla. Assn. Advancement of Psychology (bd. dirs. 1979), Broward County Psychol. Assn. (past mem. ethics com., past treas., past v.p.). Avocations: boating; jogging; racquetball. Office: Family Inst Broward and Palm Beach 1144 SE 3d Ave Fort Lauderdale FL 33316 also 1 W Camino Real Boca Raton FL 33432

RYANT, CARL GEORGE, historian, educator; b. Cleve., June 28, 1942; s. George Charles and Lolita Margaret (Burwell) R.; B.A., Case-Western Res. U., 1964; M.A. (Wis. Alumni Research Found. fellow), U. Wis., 1965, Ph.D. (Univ. fellow, Knapp fellow), 1968; m. Mary Louise Neville, Aug. 5, 1970; 1 son, Neville George. Asst. prof. history U. Louisville, 1968-72, asso. prof., 1972-85, prof., 1985—, co-dir. Oral History Center, 1971—. Mem. exec. bd. Ky. Civil Liberties Union, 1978-84. Mem. Am., So. hist. assns., Orgn. Am. Historians, Oral History Assn., Oral History Soc., Soc. Historians Am. Fgn. Relations. Filson Club. Democrat. Contbr. articles to profl. jours. Home: 1839 Roanoke Ave Louisville KY 40205 Office: Dept History U Louisville Louisville KY 40292

RYBACK, DAVID, psychologist, consultant; b. Montreal, Que., Can., Mar. 8, 1941; came to U.S., 1974; s. Isaac and Celia (Becker) R. A.A., Los Angeles City Coll., 1962; B.Sc., McGill U. (Que.), 1963; M.A., San Diego State U., 1964; Ph.D., U. Hawaii, 1969. Lic. psychologist, Ga. Lectr. overseas div. U. Md., 1969-74; asst. prof. West Ga. Coll., Carrollton, 1974-80; pvt. practice psychology, Atlanta, 1980—. Contbr. articles to profl. jours. Mem. Am. Psychol. Assn., Assn. Humanistic Psychology. Home: 1534 N Decatur Rd Atlanta GA 30307

RYBURN, BETTY CORNETT, sociology educator; b. Northfolk, W.Va., Jan. 12, 1935; d. Clyde Jefferson and Berthelda Alice (Northen) Cornett; 1 dau., Pam. A.S., Marshall U., 1955, B.A., 1957; M.A., Ohio U., 1958; Ph.D., Laurence U., 1975. Mem. faculty Towson State Coll. (Md.), 1959-61, 67-68, U. Md.-Balt., 1967, George Mason U., 1970-75, Am. Tech. U., 1979-82; pvt. practice Family Counseling Service, Harker Heights, Tex., 1979-82; assoc. prof. sociology Mobile Coll. (Ala.), 1982—; cons., lectr. on human relations, leadership skills and mil. families. Author: The Relationship Between Certain Sociological Factors and Grade Achievement, 1958; Alienation: Generative Social Structural Conditions, Role Conflict/Strain, and Resulting Social Consequences, 1975; contbr. articles to profl. jours., papers to profl. confs. Chmn. Am. Heart Assn. Drive, Am. Cancer Soc. Drive; bd. advisers U. West Fla. Ctr. on Aging. Mem. Am. Sociol. Assn., Mid-South Sociol. Assn., So. Sociol. Soc., Ala.-Miss. Sociol. Assn., AAUP, AAUW, Alpha Lambda Delta, Alpha Kappa Delta. Baptist. Home: 25 Cobblestone Way W Mobile AL 36608 Office: Mobile Coll Dept Sociology Coll Pkwy Mobile AL 36613

RYDMAN, JAY, television production company executive, TV producer; b. Bklyn., Mar. 1, 1943; s. Edward and Jean (Storey) R.; m. Debra Lane, Feb. 28, 1970 (div. Oct. 1978); m. Karen A. Cummings, Apr. 5, 1980; children—Emily Brooke, Jessica. B.A. in Sociology, U. Tex., 1968. Reporter, cameraman WBNS-TV, Columbus, Ohio, 1970-72; radio TV supr. Gov. of Ohio, Columbus, 1972-73; producer, camerman KDFW TV, Dallas, 1973-77; producer, pres. Rydman Prodns., Inc., Dallas, 1977—. Producer TV series Caring, 1981, TV Recruitment program Its Your Move, 1982. Recipient awards including Silver award for cinematography Internat. Film and TV Festival, 1978, Bronze Award for cinematography, 1980-81, Silver award for producing, 1981, Bronze award, 1982. Mem. Internat. TV Assn. (Golden Reel of Excellence 1981, Golden Reel of Merit 1983), Tex. Assn. Film/Tape Profls., Informational Film Producers Assn. (Cindy awards 1981, 83), Dallas Communications Council, Sigma Delta Chi. Unitarian. Home: 8910 Capri Dr Dallas TX 75238 Office: Rydman Prodns Inc 2211 N Lamar Dallas TX 75202

RYLAND, WALTER MONCURE, III, writer, air force officer; b. Pine Bluff, Ark., May 11, 1938; s. Walter Moncure and Audra Virginia (Hammond) R.; B.A., La. Poly. Inst., 1959; M.S., Boston U., 1969; m. Pearl Chachi Pagano, Aug. 27, 1961; children—William Norman, Robert Walter, Ada Virginia. Commd. 2d lt. U.S. Air Force, 1959, advanced through grades to maj. 1971; press officer, Cape Canaveral, Fla., 1959-62; comdr. Am. Forces Network, Verdun, France, 1962-65; info. officer Tactical Air Command, Langley AFB, Va., 1965-71; chief public info. UN Command, Seoul, Korea, 1971-72; chief of info., Nellis AFB, Nev., 1972-75, Beale AFB, Calif., 1975-79; ret., 1979; freelance writer and investor, 1979—; author: Cape Canaveral, 1961; Downrange, 1962; Space Exploration USA, 1965, rev. edit., 1975; Space Flight Communications, 1966, rev. edit., 1967; contbr. to N.Y. Times mag., Films in Rev., Stamp World, Mil. Media Rev., Saga, Stars and Stripes, Air Force, Airman, others; editor The Tech Talk, 1957-59, TAC Facts, 1966-68. Bd. dirs. Better Bus. Bur. So. Nev., 1972-75; public affairs officer Joint Task Force, Kinshasa, Congo, 1967; escort for returning POWs, 1973; chmn. North Las Vegas (Nev.) Bicentennial Commn., 1974-76; sec. Las Vegas Base-Community Council, 1972-75; bd. dirs. Yuba-Sutter (Calif.) United Way, 1978-79. Decorated Meritorious Service medal (2), numerous others; recipient USAF Jr. Officer Achievement award, 1961; cert. of commendation Greater Las Vegas C. of C., 1972, 73, 75; cert. of appreciation Calif. Hwy. Patrol, 1976, U.S. Air Force Band, 1968, Smithsonian Instn., 1983, Am. Revolution Bicentennial Adminstrn., 1976; Mil. Pubs. award, 1977, 78. Mem. Ret. Officers Assn., Nat. Bd. Rev. Motion Pictures, Am. Film Inst., Am. Philatelic Soc., Armed Forces Broadcasters Assn., Phi Kappa Phi, Omicron Delta Kappa, Kappa Alpha Order. Home and Office: 4024 Fechin Circle Plano TX 75023

RYMER, S. BRADFORD, JR., appliance manufacturer; b. Cleveland, Tenn., May 30, 1915; s. S. Bradford and Clara Ladosky (Gee) R.; grad. Fishburne Mil. Sch., 1933; B.S. in Indsl. Mgmt., Ga. Inst. Tech., 1937; m. Anne Roddye Caudle, Nov. 7, 1942; children—Anita Elise, S. Bradford III. Indsl. engr. Dixie Foundry Co., Inc., Cleveland, Tenn., 1937-40, sec.-treas., dir. prodn., 1940-50, pres., 1950—, now Magic Chef, Inc., Cleveland, Tenn., chmn., 1976—; chmn. Dixie-Narco, Inc., Ranson, W. Va.; dir. Navarne Corp. Chattanooga, Coca-Cola Bottling Co., Miami, Munford Co., Provident Life & Accident Ins. Co., Citizens & So. Nat. Bank, Atlanta. Past pres. Cleveland Asso. Industries. Past trustee Tenn. Wesleyan Coll.; past bd. dirs. Bradley County Meml. Hosp. Civilian flight instr., World War II. Mem. Am. Gas Assn. (past exec. com., dir.), NAM (past dir.), Chief Execs. Forum (pres. 1971, dir.), Gas Appliance Mfrs. Assn. (pres. 1965), Young Pres. Orgn. (past dir., area v.p., chmn. Rebel chpt.), Ga. Tech. Nat. Alumni Assn. (past trustee), Phi Gamma Delta. Methodist (trustee). Home: 1790 Ocoee St NE Cleveland TN 37311

RYON, THOMAS S(HIPLEY), tobacco co. exec.; b. Washington, May 29, 1917; s. Norman Eugene and Mary (Shipley) R.; A.B., Duke U., 1938; postgrad. Law Sch., George Washington U., 1938-40; m. Ruth Elizabeth Green, Apr. 12, 1940; children—Thomas Shipley, David Osmond. Real estate and income tax specialist, Washington, 1938-39; mgr. A.C. Monk Enterprises, Farmville, N.C., 1940-43; comptroller A.C. Monk & Co., Inc., Farmville, 1943-45, asst. sec., 1945-54, sec., 1954—, v.p., 1971—; pres. Security Savs. & Loan, Farmville, 1960-72, dir., 1959-71; sec., dir. Eastern Tobacco Co.; sr. v.p., dir. First Fed. Savs. & Loan Pitt County, 1972—; v.p. Dixon-Hamilton Tobacco Suppliers Co., 1968—; sec., dir. Mohenco Corp., Wendell, N.C., 1976—; pres. T.S. Ryon & Co., 1967—, Ryon & Assos., 1975—, Farmville Tobacco Bd. Trade, 1966-68. Chmn. Farmville com. Boy Scouts Am., 1957-63; bd. dirs. Farmville Little League, Farmville Community Chest, Farmville United Fund; vice chmn. Farmville Sch. Bd., 1957, chmn., 1958-63; chmn. Farmville Houseing Authority, 1974-79; treas. Jones for Congress Com., 1967—. Mem. N.C. World Trade Assn. (dir.), Farmville C. of C. (dir.). Democrat. Episcopalian. Clubs: Wilson Coin; Farmville Coin, Farmville Country (past sec.-treas.). Home: 1007 Fountain Hwy Farmville NC 27828 Office: West Marlboro Rd Farmville NC 27828

SAAB, ANN POTTINGER, history educator, educational administrator; b. Boston, Dec. 18, 1934; m. Elias Saab; children—Georges, David. B.A. with honors, Wellesley Coll., 1955; M.A., Radcliffe Coll., 1957, Ph.D. (AAUW fellow), 1962. Teaching fellow Harvard U., 1958-59, 1961-62; instr. Wellesley Coll., 1959-60, 1962; instr. Middlebury Coll., 1962-64; postdoctoral grantee, researcher Social Sci. Research Council, Turkey, France and Eng., 1964-65; lectr. U. N.C.-Greensboro, 1965-66, asst. prof., 1966-70, assoc. prof., 1970-75, prof., 1975—; head history dept., 1978-84, head western civilization program, 1979-84, acting head classical civilization dept., 1980-83, asst. to chancellor, 1981-82, various com. mems.; cons. in field. Grantee NEH, 1981. Mem. Am. Hist. Assn., AAUP, Middle East Studies Assn., So. Assn. Women Historians, Carolinas Symposium on Brit. Studies, Alliance Française, Archeol. Inst. Am., Phi Beta Kappa (past v.p., exec. com. local chpt.) Author: The Origins of the Crimean Alliance, 1977; Napoleon III and The German Crisis, 1865-66, 1966; translator: The Peace of Paris 1856 (Winfried Baumgart), 1981; contbr. numerous articles and revs. to profl. jours.

SABATO, LARRY JOSEPH, government educator; b. Norfolk, Va., Aug. 7, 1952; s. N.J. and Margaret F. (Simmons) S. B.A., U. Va., 1974; postgrad. Princeton U., 1974-75; D. Phil., Oxford U., 1977. Lectr. politics New Coll., Oxford U., 1977-78; assoc. prof. dept. govt., U. Va., Charlottesville, 1978—; guest scholar Brookings Instn., 1980; Thomas Jefferson vis. prof. Downing Coll., Cambridge U., 1982; sr. fellow Ctr. Study Governorship, Duke U., Durham, N.C., 1982—. Danforth fellow, 1975; Kellogg fellow, 1983; Rhodes scholar. Mem. Am. Polit. Sci. Assn., Am. Assn. Polit. Cons., Phi Beta Kappa. Author: The Rise of Political Consultants: New Ways of Winning Elections, 1981; Goodbye to Goodtime Charlie: The American Governorship Transformed, 1983; PAC Power: Inside the World of Political Action Committees, 1984. Home: 2020 Minor Rd Charlottesville VA 22903 Office: Dept Govt U Va 232 Cabell Charlottesville VA 22901

SABBAGHA, GEORGE ZACKARY, international trade executive; b. Columbia, S.C., Sept. 3, 1944; s. Zackary and Agnes (Davis) S.; m. Janice Scott, July 17, 1971. Student in econs. and prelaw, U. S.C., 1968-71. Founder, operator Cobb and Sabbagha Estate and Constrn. Co., West Columbia, S.C., 1971—; internat. sales and mktg. exec. Trans World Investment, Ltd., 1974—; chmn. Sun World Corp., West Columbia, 1980—; cons., lectr. U.S. Commerce Dept. and other agys. on internat. trade; vice chmn. U.S. Argl. Corp., Washington; chmn. U.S.-Caribbean JACC, vice chmn. U.S.-Nigerian JACC. Mem. S.C. Dist. Export Council. Served with USN, 1962-67; Vietnam. Decorated various mil. commendations; recipient Presdl. E award for excellence in exporting. Mem. Bd. Realtors, Home Builders Assn., other export and trade councils. Office: 1730 Augusta Rd West Columbia SC 29169

SABINES, LUIS, retail company executive; b. Havana, Cuba, Nov. 18, 1917; s. Ramon and Cecilia (Ortiz) S.; m. Mary Ortiz; 1 son, Luis, Jr. Student pub. schs. Propr., Sabines Distbrs., Inc., Miami, Fla., 1970—; with Latin C. of C., Miami, 1965—, exec. v.p., 1983—; pres. Saber Inc. Chmn. Small Bus. Opportunity Ctr. Inc., Miami, 1976—; vice chmn. bd. dirs. Little Havana Devel. Authority, 1982-83; founder Home for Blind, Miami, 1978-81; v.p. Little Havanna Devel. Authority; active Boy Scouts Am. Mem. Vet. Med. Assn., Flor De Liz, Cuban Dental Assn. in Exile. Lodge: Lions. Home: 1417 W Flagler St Miami FL 33135 Office: Latin C of C 1417 W Flagler St Miami FL 33135

SABLIK, MARTIN JOHN, research physicist; b. Bklyn., Oct. 21, 1939; s. Martin C. and Elsie M. (Fuzia) S.; m. Beverly Ann Shively, Nov. 26, 1965; children—Jeanne, Karen, Marjorie, Larry. B.A. in Physics, Cornell U., 1960; M.S. in Physics, U. Ky., 1965; Ph.D., Fordham U., 1972. Jr. engr. The Martin Co., Orlando, Fla., 1962-63; half-time instr. U. Ky., Lexington, 1963-65; research assoc. Fairleigh Dickinson U., Teaneck, N.J., 1965-67, instr. physics, 1967-1972, asst. prof., 1972-76, assoc. prof., 1976-80; sr. research scientist Southwest Research Inst., San Antonio, 1980—. Contbr. articles to profl. jours. Mem. Am. Phys. Soc., Acoustical Soc. Am., Am. Soc. Nondestructive Testing (chmn. So. Tex. sect. 1983-84), IEEE, Am. Assn. Physics Tchrs. Roman Catholic. Office: Southwest Research Inst PO Drawer 28510 San Antonio TX 78284

SACASAS, RENE, lawyer; b. N.Y.C., July 10, 1947; s. Anselmo and Orlanda (Soto) S.; m. Cathy Lee Van Natta, Jan. 24, 1970. B.A., Am. U., 1969; J.D., Emory U., 1975. Bar: Fla. 1976, U.S. Dist. Ct. (so. dist.) Fla. 1976, U.S. Ct. Appeals (5th cir.) 1976, U.S. Ct. Appeals (11th cir.) 1983, U.S. Supreme Ct. 1980. Law clk. McLarty and Aiken, Atlanta, 1974-76; assoc. Welbaum, Zook, Jones, Williams, Miami, Fla., 1976-79; ptnr. Darrach, Merkin and Sacasas, Miami, 1979-83, Merkin & Sacasas, Miami, 1984-86; of counsel Welbaum, Zook, Jones & Williams, Miami, 1986—; asst. prof. bus. law U. Miami, Coral Gables, 1985—. Mem. Fla. Bar Assn. (vice chmn. grievance com. 1981-84), ABA, Dade County Bar Assn., Latin Am. C. of C., U.S. Jaycees, Cuban Am. Bar Assn., Phi Sigma Kappa (pres. 1968). Democrat. Home: 12715 SW 102d Terr Miami FL 33186 Office: 2701 S Bayshore Dr Penthouse Suite Miami FL 33132

SACHS, WILLIAM LEWIS, clergyman; b. Richmond, Va., Aug. 22, 1947; s. Lewis S. and Dorothy M. (Creasy) S.; m. Elizabeth Austin Tucker, May 17, 1986. B.A., Baylor U., 1969; M.Div., Vanderbilt U., 1972; S.T.M., Yale U., 1973; Ph.D., U. Chgo., 1981. Ordained to ministry Episcopal Ch., 1973; curate Emmanuel Episc. Ch., Richmond, 1973-75; asst. rector St. Chrysostom's Ch., Chgo., 1975-80, St. Stephen's Ch., Richmond, 1980—; mem. bd. Richmond Clericus, 1981—; exam. chaplain Diocese of Va., 1981—; dir. Episc. Book Store, Richmond, In-Home Health Care, Inc.; program chmn. Richmond Episc. Clergy; chaplain Boston State Hosp., 1972; adj. faculty U. Richmond. Bd. dirs. Va. Planned Parenthood, 1981—. Stevenson fellow, 1971-72; Episc. Ch. Found. fellow, 1976-80. Mem. Arts Club Chgo. Club: Chgo.-Vanderbilt (pres. 1978-80). Author: One Body; Improving the Times. Contbr. articles to theol. jours.; researcher Huntington Library; producer cable TV documentaries. Home: 6003 York Rd Richmond VA 23226 Office: 6004 Three Chopt Rd Richmond VA 23226

SACINO, SHERRY WHEATLEY, international relations specialist, public relations consultant; b. Wilmington, Del., July 14, 1959; d. Lawrence McClusky and Carolyn (Alexander) W.; m. Ronald Anthony Sacino, Dec. 29, 1984. B.A. in Journalism, Ariz. State U., 1980. News dir. KAAA-KZZZ Radio, Kingman, Ariz., 1977; pub. relations rep. McDonald's, Los Angeles region, 1974-79; pub. relations dir. KUPD-KUKQ Radio, Phoenix, 1978-79, Phoenix Pro Soccer, 1979-80; owner, pres. Sherry Wheatley Sacino Ltd., St. Petersburg, Fla., 1980—; chief exec. officer, founder Tampa Bay Council for Internat. Visitors, Fla., 1983—; tchr. Internat. Acad. Mdse. and Design, Tampa, 1984—. Com. chmn. Clean Community System, Phoenix, 1983, Super Task Force, Tampa Bay, 1984; bd. dirs. March of Dimes, Pinellas County, Fla., 1985; com. mem. Latin Am. Scholarship Found., Tampa Bay, 1985; mem. Gov.'s Council on Health and Fitness, Phoenix, 1983. Named Nat. Rep. McDonald's, 1979. Mem. Phoenix Ad Club 2 (v.p. 1982-83), Aircraft Owners and Pilots Assn. Republican. Roman Catholic. Avocations: traveling abroad; foreign languages; flying airplanes. Office: Tampa Bay Council for Internat Visitors 2507 Pass a Grille Way Pass a Grille FL 33741

SACKMAN, DON, architect; b. N.Y.C., Jan. 7, 1944; s. Herman E. and Phyllis (Bowles) S.; student public schs.; m. Arlene Samuels, July 7, 1968. With firm Robert M. Shrum, 1962-68, Gail Baldwin, Coconut Grove, Fla., 1968-72; partner Baldwin Sackman & Assocs., Coconut Grove, 1972—. Served with USNG, 1970-76. Mem. AIA (nat. com. on design 1981—, v.p. state assn. 1986-87, recipient 16 state, local awards for design excellence). Democrat. Jewish. Office: Baldwin Sackman and Assocs 2869 SW 27th Ave Miami FL 33133

SACONAS, EDWARD SHERMAN, real estate developer, banker; b. Elkhart, Ind., May 7, 1939; s. George and Louise (Tamburine) S.; B.A. summa cum laude, St. Mary's U., San Antonio, 1960; LL.D. cum laude, U. Houston, 1965. Pres., Bayou Vista Land Corp., Hitchcock, Tex., 1963—; dir. Mainland Bank, Texas City, Tex., 1966—, vice chmn., 1969-73; dir. Citizens Nat. Bank, Beaumont, Tex., Vidor State Bank; chmn. East Tex. State Bank, Buna; pres. Vistacorp, Hitchcock, Tex., 1983—. Bd. dirs. Galveston County Homebuilders Assn., 1980—; pres. Tex. Assn. Ind. Water Cos., 1980-81; bd. dirs. Coll. of Mainland Founds., 1981-83. Served to capt. AUS. Named Galveston County Builder of Yr., 1982. Mem. Hitchcock C. of C. Lodge: Rotary (West Galveston County) (charter pres. 1985—, Paul Harris Fellow award). Home: 1318 Blue Heron Dr Hitchcock TX 77563 Office: PO Box 8 Hitchcock TX 77563

SADDLER, CHARLES CLARK, III, city official; b. Abilene, Tex., Sept. 21, 1956; s. Charles Clark and Virginia Anne (Berg) S.; m. Peggy L. Chandler, Apr. 29, 1978. B.S., Union Coll., Barbourville, Ky., 1976; M.P.S., Western Ky. U., 1977. City coordinator/adminstr. City of Cumberland (Ky.), 1978-79; community devel. adminstr. Bluegrass Area Devel. Dist., Lexington, Ky., 1979-80; exec. town mgr. Mcpl. Corp. of Cape Charles (Va.), 1980—. Mem. Cape Charles Vol. Fire Co., 1982, sec., 1983—; bd. dirs. Union Coll. Alumni. Mem. Internat. City Mgmt. Assn., Va. Mcpl. League (legis. policy com.), Va. City Mgmt. Assn., Alpha Kappa Delta, Gamma Beta Phi, Iota Sigma Nu. Lodge: Lions. Home: 506 Monroe Ave Cape Charles VA 23310 Office: PO Box 391 Cape Charles VA 23310

SADLER, ROBERT EDWARD, electronics company executive; b. Eagle Grove, Iowa, Sept. 3, 1925; s. Edward Anthony and Elsie June (Sherman) S.; m. Kathleen Irene English, Nov. 17, 1951 (dec.); children—Kathe Sadler Wright, Janet T. McKee, Robert E.A., John C., Michael S., Kathleen T. B.S.E.E., U. Colo., 1961; postgrad. Air War Coll., 1967, Armed Forces Staff Coll., 1967. Enlisted U.S. Army, 1943, commd. 2d lt., 1945, advanced through grade to maj. gen., 1975, ret. 1979; comdr. 1964th Communicators Group, dir. Communications Electronics 7th Air Force, Vietnam, 1970-71; comdr. No. Communications Area, Griffis AFB, N.Y., 1971-72, dir. communications electronics U.S. Rediness Command, MacDill AFB, Fla., 1972-74; vice comdr. Air Force Communications Service, Richards Gebaur AFB, Mo., 1974; dep. dir. Command Control and Communication, Hdqrs. U.S. Air Force, Washington, 1974-75; dir. J-6, Communications and Electronics, Office of Joint Chiefs of Staff, Washington, 1975-76; dep. dir. Def. Communications Agy., Plans and Programs, Washington, 1976-77; comdr. Air Force Communications Service, Scott AFB, Ill., 1977-79; dir. def. systems Telecommunications and Electronic Warfare, Magnavox Govt. Indsl. Electronics Co., Ft. Wayne, Ind., 1979-81; v.p., gen. mgr. No. Va. ops. Magnavox, Inc., Falls Church, 1981—. Editor Navigator Mag., 1953-56. Editor: Air Navigation, 1948. Author: Air Navigation for Pilots, 1952; In-Flight Maintenance of The APQ-24, 1953. Decorated DSM, Def. Superior Service medal with oak leaf cluster, Legion of Merit with 2 oak leaf clusters, Meritorious Service medal; Cross of Gallantry with palm (Republic of Vietnam). Mem. Armed Forces Communications Electronics Assn. (internat. v.p., dir. 1982-84, recipient Medal of Merit, 1976, Gold medal, 1978, Disting. Service medal, 1979). Republican. Roman Catholic. Avocations: hunting; fishing; hiking. Home: 247 Springvale Rd Great Falls VA 22066 Office: Magnavox No Va Systems Div 2990 Telestar Ct Falls Church VA 22042

SADOWSKY, PERCIVAL LIONEL, orthodontist, educator; b. Johannesburg, South Africa, Apr. 30, 1940; came to U.S., 1976, naturalized, 1982; s. Hyman Joseph and Sadie Leah (Tooch) S.; m. Carole Sue Zeitler, Jan. 1, 1978. B.D.S., U. Witwatersrand, Johannesburg, 1963, diploma in orthodontics, 1973, M.Dentistry, 1974; D.M.D., U. Ala., 1978, diploma in orthodontics, 1979. Diplomate Am. Bd. Orthodontics. Gen. practice dentistry, London, 1964, Johannesburg, 1964-69; practice orthodontics, 1972-76; last sr. lectr. U. Witwatersrand, 1969-76; asst. prof. U. Ala. Sch. Dentistry, Birmingham, 1976-80, assoc. prof., 1980-85, prof., 1985—; sci. lectr., South Africa, U.K., Australia, U.S., Can., 1969—. Contbr. articles to profl. jours. Recipient Colgate prize, 1973; Elida Gibbs award Dental Assn. S. Africa, 1974. Mem. ADA, Am. Assn. Dental Research, Am. Assn. Dental Sch., Am. Assn. Orthodontists, Coll. of Diplomates of Am. Bd. Orthodontics, Sigma Xi, Omicron Kappa Upsilon. Avocations: computers; sports; reading. Home: 3424 Oakdale Dr Birmingham AL 35223 Office: U Ala Sch Dentistry 1919 7th Ave South Birmingham AL 35294

SAENZ, MICHAEL, college president; b. Laredo, Tex., Oct. 25, 1925; s. C. A. and Pola R. Saenz; B.S. with honors in Accounting, Tex. Christian U., 1949, M.Ed., 1952; Ph.D. in Econs., U. Pa., 1961; m. Nancy Elizabeth King; children—Michael King, Cynthia Elizabeth. Dep. collector IRS, Ft. Worth, Dallas, 1949-52; adminstr. United Christian Missionary Soc., Bayamon, P.R., 1954-57, 59-65, exec. sec., Indpls., 1965-71; acad. dean Laredo Jr. Coll., 1971-74; pres. N.W. campus Tarrant County Jr. Coll., 1975—; trustee Tex. Christian U., Brite Div. Sch. Bd. dirs. Civic Ballet of Laredo (Tex.), Ft. Worth chpt. NCCJ, Juliette Fowler Homes, Dallas; chmn. Aztec Dist., dir. Gulf Coast council Boy Scouts Am., 1971-75; gov. Career Devel. Center, Arlington, Tex.; chmn. Laredo's Bicentennial Com., 1973-76; trustee, bd. dirs. United Way Ft. Worth, 1979—; mem. gen. bd. Christian Ch. (Disciples of Christ), 1981—. Mem. Tex. Jr. Coll. Tchrs. Assn., Tex. Assn. Jr. Coll. Instructional Adminstrs., Am. Acad. Polit. and Social Scis., Urban Ministries in Higher Edn, Civic Music Assn. Laredo, N. Ft. Worth C. of C. (dir. 1978—). Lodge: Rotary (North Ft. Worth). Home: 4201 Westmont Ct Fort Worth TX 76109

SAENZ, NANCY ELIZABETH KING (MRS. MICHAEL SAENZ), civic worker; b. Greenville, Tex., Jan. 28, 1930; d. Henry M. and Vallie (Wheatley) King; A.B. with honors, Tex. Christian U., 1950, B.S. magna cum laude, 1952; postgrad. Hartford Sem. Found., 1952-53, Escuela de Idiomas, 1953; Lexington Theol. Sem., 1953; m. Michael Saenz, July 28, 1950; children—Michael King, Cynthia Elizabeth. Missionary, United Christian Missionary Soc., Indpls., serving in P.R., 1954-65; bd. dirs. Adminstrv. Bd. Christians Chs., P.R., 1950-65; counselor and tchr. State Christian Youth Fellowship Conf., P.R., 1954-57; chmn. dept. Christian edn. Christian Chs., P.R., 1962-64, sec., 1959-61, state dir., 1963; dept. Christian edn. P.R. Council Chs., 1959-64, sec., 1959-60; sec. and counsellor State Christian Women Fellowship of Christian Chs., P.R., 1955-57, 59-63, dist. chmn., Indpls., 1968-71; pres.-elect Christian Ch. in Southwest, 1974-76, pres., 1976—; mem. gen. bd. Christian Ch. in U.S. and Can., 1974—. Sec., Disciples of Christ Acad. PTA, Bayamon, P.R., 1962-63; mem. state com. Home for Aged, United Ch. Women, P.R., 1963; women's com. Ind. State Symphony Soc., 1967-71; women's com. Internat.

Christian U. Japan, 1962-64, 65-75, pres. Indpls. chpt. 1967-68; mem. exec. bd. Indpls. council PTA, 1967-70; mem. vocat.-tech. adv. council Laredo Ind. Sch. Dist., 1971—; vol. coordinator Am. Bible Soc., 1974—; mem. Laredo Mercy Hosp. Aux., 1973-75, pres.-elect, 1974-75; dist. cons., mem. adminstrv. com. Christian Women's Fellowship in Tex., 1972-75; mem. nominating com. Internat. Christian Women's Fellowship, 1974-78; mem. Tarrant County Vol. Center Com., 1975-81, vice chmn., 1978-79, chmn., 1980-81; bd. dirs. Hostesses to Overseas Guests, 1982—. Bd. dirs. Greater Indpls. Fedn. Chs., 1970-71; pres.-elect Tarrant Area Community of Chs., 1980, pres., 1981-82; bd. sponsors Laredo Civic Ballet Soc., 1971-75; bd. dirs. Laredo Planned Parenthood Assn., 1972-75, v.p., 1973-74, pres.-elect, 1974-75; bd. dirs. Ruthe B. Cowle Rehab. Center, 1974-75; bd. dirs. Ft. Worth Area Council Chs., exec. interim dir., 1979; mem. adv. council Vols. in Public Schs., Ft. Worth, 1977-78, chmn., 1981-82; bd. dirs., mem. ch. fin. council Christian Ch., Disciples of Christ, 1978—, mem. exec. com., 1981-82; chmn. emergency assistance com. United Way of Met. Tarrant County, also mem. allocations com. Mem. Irvington Union of Clubs (exec. bd. 1966—, 2d v.p. 1968-70), Young Mothers Club Irvington (v.p. 1965, pres. 1967), Marion County Guardian Home Guild (pres. 1968-70), Art Assn. Indpls., Thistle Hill Docent Guild, Tex. Heritage, Inc. (originator, editor Heritage Highlights newsletter 1980—), Art League, Irvington, AAUW, Laredo and Ft. Worth Table II, Ch. Women United (pres. 1980-81), Pan Am. Roundtable, Alpha Chi, Phi Sigma Iota. Clubs: Rotary Anns, Women's College (P.R.); Tex. Christian U. Women Execs. (Ft. Worth); Irvington Women's; Laredo Tuesday Music and Lit. (pres. 1973); Women's City. Author: Winds of Change, 1968; Step by Step to a Successful Volunteer Program, 1984. Home: 4201 Westmont Ct Fort Worth TX 76109

SAFA, HELEN ICKEN, anthropology educator, educational administrator; b. N.Y.C., Dec. 4, 1930; d. Gustav and Erna (Keune) Icken; m. Manouchehr Safa-Isfahani, Dec. 23, 1962; 1 dau., Mitra; stepchildren—Kaveh, Arya. B.A., Cornell U., 1952; M.A., Columbia U., 1956, Ph.D., 1962. Sr. research assoc. Youth Devel. Ctr., Syracuse U. (N.Y.), 1962-67; asst. prof. anthropology Maxwell Grad. Sch., Syracuse U., 1962-67; assoc. prof. anthropology, urban planning, Livingston Coll., 1967-72, prof., 1972-80, assoc. dir. Latin Am. Inst., 1969-72, dir., 1973-74, New Brunswick chmn. dept. anthropology, 1974-80; dir. Ctr. for Latin Am. Studies, U. Fla., Gainesville, 1980-85, prof. anthropology, 1985—, pres. Latin Am. Studies Assn., 1983-85. Tinker Found. grantee, 1981; Ford Found. grantee, 1982; NIMH grantee, 1980; Soc. Sci. Research Council grantee, 1976. Mem. Am. Anthrop. Assn., Council on Internat. Exchange of Scholars (bd. dirs. 1983-86). Democrat. Author: The Urban Poor of Puerto Rico, 1974; editor: Sex and Class in Latin America, 1976; Migration and Development, 1976; Towards a Political Economy of Urbanization in Third World Countries, 1982; Women and Change in Latin America, 1985. Home: 2021 NW 15 Ave Gainesville FL 32605 Office: Ctr for Latin Am Studies Univ Fla Gainesville FL 32611

SAFFIR, HERBERT SEYMOUR, consultant civil and structural engineer; b. N.Y.C., Mar. 29, 1917; s. A.L. and Gertrude (Samuels) S.; B.S. in Civil Engring. cum laude, Ga. Inst. Tech., 1940; m. Sarah Young, May 9, 1941; children—Richard Young, Barbara Joan. Civil engr. TVA, Chattanooga, 1940, NACA, Langley Field, Va., 1940-41; structural engr. Ebasco Services, N.Y.C., 1941-43, York & Sawyer & Fred Severud, N.Y.C., 1945; engr. Waddell & Hardesty, Cons. Engrs., N.Y.C., 1945-47; asst. county engr. Dade County, Miami, Fla., 1947-59; cons. engr. Herbert S. Saffir, Coral Gables, Fla., 1959—. Adj. lectr. civil engring. Coll. Engring., U. Miami, 1964—; adviser on civil engring. Fla. Internat. U., 1975-80; cons. Govt. Bahamas on bldg. codes; cons. on engring. in housing to UN, govt. and industry; chmn. Met. Dade County Unsafe Structures Bd.; mem. Nat. Adv. Group on Glass Design. Served with AUS, 1943-44. Recipient Outstanding Service award Fla. Profl. Engrs., 1954, NOAA Pub. Service award, 1975; named Miami Engr. of Yr., 1978. Registered profl. engr., Fla., N.Y., Tex., P.R., Miss. Fellow ASCE (sect. past pres.), Fla. Engring. Soc. (award for outstanding tech. achievement 1973, community service award 1980); mem. Soc. Am. Mil. Engrs., Am. Concrete Inst., ASTM (com. on performance bldg. constrn.), Prestressed Concrete Inst., Colegio de Ingenieros P.R., Wind Engring. Research Council (dir.), Am. Meteorol. Soc., Am. Nat. Standards Inst. (com. bldg. design loads), Internat. Assn. for Bridge and Structural Engring., Nat. Panel Arbitrators, Am. Arbitration Assn., Coral Gables C. of C. (bd. dirs., past pres.), Tau Beta Pi. Club: Country of Coral Gables. Author: Housing Construction in Hurricane Prone Areas, 1971; Nature and Extent of Damage by Hurricane Camille, 1972; contbg. author: Wind Effects on Structures, 1976; also papers presented at seminars, articles in profl. jours., chpts. to books. Designer Saffir/Simpson hurricane scale. Home: 4818 Alhambra Circle Coral Gables FL 33146 Office: 255 University Dr Coral Gables FL 33134

SAFFY, EDNA LOUISE, rhetoric educator; b. Jacksonville, Fla., Mar. 8, 1935; d. Habib Solomon and Sadie (Daumit) S.; B.A., U. Fla., 1966, M.A., 1968, Ph.D., 1976; m. Grady Earl Johnson, Jr., Aug. 9, 1969. Asst., then instr. English, U. Fla., 1967, speech, 1972-75; prof. rhetoric Fla. Jr. Coll., Jacksonville, 1968—; speaker, writer, lectr., cons. polit. activist. Mem. Democratic Exec. Com. Duval County; del. Dem. Nat. Conv., N.Y.C.; mem. affirmative action com. Fla. Dem. party; mem. Fla. coordinating com. Internat. Women's Year; mem. Jacksonville Area Planning Commn.; founder Jacksonville Women's Network; bd. dirs. Fla. Women's Network; mem. devel. council Univ. Hosp., also chmn. community relations com. Recipient various recognition awards. Mem. South Atlantic MLA, Speech Communication Assn., So. Speech Communication Assn., Fla. Speech Communication Assn., Fla. Coll. English Assn., U. Fla. Grad. Speech Assn. (pres. 1975), NOW (dir., co-convenor Jacksonville chpt. 1970, dir. Gainesville chpt. 1973), Jacksonville Women's Network (founder), Fla. Women's Network (exec. bd.), Alachua County Women's Polit. Caucus (charter), Duval County Women's Polit. Caucus (v.p. 1976, 82, exec. bd. 1976-84), Fla. Women's Polit. Caucus (pres.), Jacksonville Citizens for Nuclear Freeze (steering com. 1982), Gen. Fedn. Women's Clubs, Alpha Chi Omega. Democrat. Club: Jacksonville Women's (Jacksonville). Author publs. in field. Home: 4273 Point La Vista Rd Jacksonville FL 32207 Office: Fla Jr Coll South Campus Beach Blvd Jacksonville FL 32216

SAFRA, IVAN ISAAC, accountant; b. Phila., Dec. 30, 1950; s. Morris and Reba (Haltzman) S.; m. Deborah J. Maisel, June 25, 1978; children—Michael Eric, Steven Russell. Student Rutgers U., 1968-70; B.B.A., U. Miami, 1972. C.P.A., Fla. Acct. August, Weintraub & Safra, 1970-72; revenue agt. IRS, 1972-77; acct. Rachlin & Cohen, 1977-79; staff supr. Rapaport, Krissel & Co., Miami, Fla., 1979-81; ptnr. Krissel & Safra, P.A., Miami, 1981—. Treas. Dade County Young Democrats, 1981-82, Caravel Shores Calusa Homeowners Assn., 1980-85, pres., 1984-85; fin. sec. Temple Samu-El Synagogue. Rooney acctg. scholar U. Miami, 1970. Mem. Fla. Inst. C.P.A.s, Am. Inst. C.P.A.s, South Miami-Kendall Area C. of C. Lodge: B'nai B'rith. Office: 10691 N Kendall Dr Suite 207 Miami FL 33176

SAFRIET, MARIAN LAMBETH, hospital administrator; b. Fayetteville, N.C., Dec. 14, 1923; d. Alva Sherwood and Nell (Wilson) Lambeth; B.S. in Acctg. and Fin., Fla. State U., Tallahassee, 1945; postgrad. Columbia U., U. N.C., Chapel Hill; m. Hubert Wilson Safriet, July 26, 1951; children—Nancy Lambeth, Philip Wilson; 1 stepdau., Barbara S. Carpenter. Instr. acctg. Fla. State U., 1946-47, Queens Coll., Charlotte, N.C., 1948-50, Kings Coll., Charlotte, 1950-51, Crofts Bus. Coll., Concord, N.C., 1955-61, Crofts Bus. Coll., Greensboro, N.C., 1963-69; dir. fin. services Annie Penn Meml. Hosp., Reidsville, N.C., 1971-82, dir. auditing, 1982—. Mem. Hosp. Fin. Mgmt. Assn. (chmn. ednl. council N.C. chpt. 1977-78, pres. chpt. 1981), DAR (regent 1973). Democrat. Episcopalian. Club: Woman's (pres. 1954, 85-86). Home: 1017 Shadyview Dr PO Box 1222 Reidsville NC 27320 Office: Annie Penn Meml Hosp S Main St Reidsville NC 27320

SAGAN, HANS, mathematics educator, author; b. Vienna, Austria, Feb. 15, 1928; came to U.S., 1954, naturalized, 1960; s. Hans and Josefa (Seif) S.; m. Ingeborg Ulbrich, Mar. 20, 1954; 1 child, Ingrid. Ph.D. in Math., U. Vienna, 1950. Asst. prof. U. Tech., Vienna, 1950-54; asst. prof. Mont. State U., Bozeman, 1954-57; assoc. prof. U. Idaho, Moscow, 1957-61, prof., head dept., 1961-63; prof. N.C. State U., Raleigh, 1963—; vis. prof. U. Tech., Munich, 1964, U. Vienna, 1972; vis. lectr. Math. Assn. Am., 1963-73, 77—. Co-author: Die Laplace Transformation and Ihre Anwendung, 1953; author: Boundary and Eigenvalue Problems in Mathematical Physics, 1961, Integral and Differential Calculus-an Intuitive Approach, 1962, Introduction to the Calculus of Variations, 1969, Advanced Calculus, 1974, Beat the Odds, 1980, Calculus-Accompanied on the Apple, 1984; co-author: Ten Easy Pieces, 1980; also articles. Recipient Outstanding Faculty award U. Idaho, 1959-60; Poteat award N.C. Acad. Sci., 1966. Mem. Math. Assn. Am., AAUP, Oesterreichische Mathematische Gesellschaft, Sigma Xi. Avocations: swimming; sailing. Office: NC State U Dept Math Raleigh NC 27695

SAGE, ANDREW PATRICK, systems and computer engineering educator; b. Charleston, S.C., Aug. 27, 1933; s. Andrew P. and Pearl (Britt) S.; m. Laverne Galhouse, Mar. 3, 1962; children—Theresa, Karen, Philip. B.S. in Elec. Engring., Citadel, 1955; S.M. in Elec. Engring., MIT, 1956; Ph.D., Purdue U., 1960. Registered profl. engr., Tex. Instr. elec. engring. Purdue U., West Lafayette, Ind., 1956-60; assoc. prof. elec. engring. U. Ariz., Tucson, 1960-64; prof. elec. engring., U. Fla., Gainesville, 1964-67; prof. info. and control sci. So. Meth. U., Dallas, 1967-74; Quarles prof. systems engring. U. Va., Charlottesville, 1974-84; prof. info. tech. George Mason U., 1984—, assoc. v.p. acad. affairs, 1984-85, dean Sch. Info. Tech. and Engring., 1985—; cons. in field. Fellow IEEE, (Carlton award 1970, Wiener award 1980), AAAS; mem. Am. Inst. Decision Scis., Ops. Research Soc. Am., Inst. Mgmt. Sci., Am. Inst. Engring. Sci., Am. Soc. for Engring. Edn. (Terman award 1970). Author: Optimum Systems Control, 1968, 2d edit., 1977; Estimation Theory, 1971; System Identification, 1971; An Introduction to Probability and Stochastic Processes, 1973; Systems Engineering: Methodology and Applications, 1977; Methodology for Large Scale Systems, 1977; Linear Systems Control, 1978; Economic Systems Analysis, 1983; editor: Transactions on Systems, Man and Cybernetics, IEEE, 1970—; co-editor-in-chief Large Scale Systems, 1979—; editor Automatica; contbr. numerous articles on engring. to profl. jours. Office: Sch Info Tech and Engring George Mason University VA 22030

SAGE, EARL RICHARD, educator; b. Cardington, Ohio, Feb. 19, 1926; s. Walter J. and Lulu Inez (Caris) S.; B.Sc., Ohio State U., 1949; M.B.A., Harvard U., 1960; Ph.D., Ohio State U., 1973; m. Dorotha Ann Dufford, Apr. 12, 1958; children—Anne Leslie, Bradley James, Audrey Lynn. Buyer, Hydraulic Press Mfg. Co., Mt. Gilead, Ohio, 1949-53; traffic rep. No. Consol. Airlines, Fairbanks, Alaska, 1953-54; buyer, mng. buyer Radio Corp. Am., Findlay, Ohio, 1954-58, budget mgr., adminstr. standards and cost estimating, Mountaintop, Pa., 1960-63; research asso., course dir. chmn. Dept. Mgmt. and Quantitative Techniques Ohio State U., Columbus, 1963-73; asst. prof. U. N.C., Charlotte, 1973, dir. mgmt. devel. programs, 1973-76, asso. prof., 1976—. Served with USN, 1943-46. Sarnoff fellow, 1958-60. Mem. Acad. Mgmt., Beta Gamma Sigma. Republican. Methodist. Home: 4414 Barwick Rd Charlotte NC 28211 Office: Coll of Bus Univ of NC Charlotte NC 28223

SAHLI, BRENDA PAYNE, consultant, educator, toxicologist; b. Richmond, Va., Sept. 28, 1942; d. Thomas Frederick and Nancy (Rhoades) Payne; m. Muhammad Saleh Sahli, Oct. 14, 1967; children—Andrea, Kevin, Heather. B.S. in Applied Sci. with honors, Richmond Profl. Inst. (Va.), 1964; M.S. in Pharm. Chemistry, Med. Coll. Va., Richmond, 1967; Ph.D., Va. Commonwealth U., 1974. Research asst. Am. Tobacco Co., Richmond, 1964-65; chemist Firestone Synthetic Fibers and Textiles Co., Hopewell, Va., 1967-69; research chemist E.I. duPont de Nemours & Co., Richmond, 1974-77; toxicologist Toxic Substances Info., Va. Dept. Health, Richmond, 1977-82, dir., 1983-84, voluntary compliance dir. Bur. Occupational Health, 1982-83; adj. prof. Va. Commonwealth U., 1975-77, U. Va.-Falls Church Regional Ctr., 1984—; occupational health/environ. toxicology cons., 1984—; lectr. and speaker in field of occupational health, toxicology and related topics. Contbr. articles to profl. jours. Mem. Springhill-Gatewood Civic Assn., Richmond; corr. sec. Reams Road Elem. Sch. PTA; sec./treas. Cub Scout Pack; asst. leader Brownie troop; discussion leader Jr. Great Books. Mem. Am. Conf. Govt. Indsl. Hygienists, Am. Coll. Toxicology, ASTM (former chmn. task force), Sigma Xi, Rho Chi, Iota Sigma Pi. Methodist. Home and office: 1950 Camborne Rd Richmond VA 23236

SAIDI, AHMAD, export company executive; b. Khoy, Iran, Jan. 28, 1904; came to U.S., 1931, naturalized, 1950; s. Abol Hassan and Khanombozorg (Abolghassemi) S.; B.A., U. Okla., 1935; M.A., George Washington U., 1937; m. Elizabeth Gettner, Feb. 12, 1954; 1 child, Ali Emerson. Asst. to pres. M. Dilmaghani & Co., Scarsdale, N.Y., 1938-41; instr. Persian Inst., 1942; chief Persian Desk, OWI, N.Y.C., 1942-43; chief Persian sect. Dept. Def., N.Y.C., 1943-45; exec. sec. Iran Am. C. of C., N.Y.C., 1945-75; pres. Gen. Fgn. Sales Corp., Scarsdale, N.Y., 1946-68, chmn. bd. 1968-75; pres. Iran Trading Corp., Scarsdale, 1949-68; chmn. bd. Export Promotion Center, Tehran, Iran, 1967-68. Inaugurated, dir. Voice of Am. broadcasts to Iran, 1943. Mem. high coordinating econ. com., Tehran, Iran, 1967-68. Mem. nat. gift com. NCCJ, 1964. Decorated Order of Homayoon, Shah of Iran, 1962. Mem. Nat. Geog. Soc., Pi Sigma Alpha. Contbg. author: Sufi Studies: East and West. Editor: Iran Am. Monthly Newsletter, 1950-75, Iran Am. Rev., 1945-75. Numerous articles in Persian and English. Home: 1416 Gray Bluff Trail Chapel Hill NC 27514

ST. CLAIR, HAL KAY, electrical engineer; b. Los Angeles, Oct. 11, 1925; s. Millard T. and Ruth (McGrew) St. C.; student U. So. Calif., 1943-44; B.S., U. Calif., Berkeley, 1946, M.S., 1948; m. Jane Creely, June 24, 1949; children—Gregory, Russell, Elizabeth. Research engr. Marchant Calculators, Emeryville, Calif., 1948-52; project engr. RCA, Camden, N.J., 1953-54; program mgr. IBM, San Jose, Calif., 1954-69, tech. staff, Boca Raton, Fla., 1969-72, mgr. input/output devel., 1972-75, mgr. gen. lab. devel., 1975-81, mgr. small comml. systems engring., 1981-83, mgr. ergonomics project office, div. hdqrs., 1983-85, devel. edn. mgr., 1986—; instr. U. Calif. Extension Div., 1951-52. Tech. adv. U.S. Nat. Com. Internat. Electrotechnical Commn., 1967-69. Mem. Republican Central Com. of Calif., 1962-66. Served to lt. (j.g.) USNR, 1943-46. Mem. IEEE, SAR, Mensa, Phi Beta Kappa, Sigma Xi, Tau Beta Pi, Eta Kappa Nu. Home: 875 Oleander St Boca Raton FL 33432 Office: 1000 NW 51st St Boca Raton FL 33432

ST. CLAIR, HELEN ALLISON, assn. exec.; b. Stevenson, Ala., July 23, 1932; d. George Milton and Frances Carolyn (Grider) Allison; student U. Ala., 1949-51, U. Va., 1961; m. Fred Weems St. Clair, Aug. 4, 1950 (div. 1983); children—Loyce Anne, Fred Weem, Thomas Reid. Cert. assn. exec. Supr., Camp Lejeune Officers' Wives Club Sitting Service, 1956-60; tchr. Prince William County Schs., 1960-64, substitute tchr., 1967-69, 73; staff spl. events Miss. Optometric Assn., 1974-76, exec. dir., 1976—; cons. Am. Optometric Assn., So. Council Optometrists. Trustee, So. Coll. Optometry, Memphis, 1979-82; bd. dirs. Miss. Inst. Aging, 1976-81; mem. Miss. Council Aging, 1976-83; mem.-at-large Central Miss. sub-area council Miss. Health System Agy., 1978—, com. chmn. plan and devel. com., vice chmn. council, then chmn., 1980-83; mem. exec. com., sec. to bd. dirs., chmn. vols. Central Miss. chpt. ARC. Recipient cert. ARC. Mem. PTA (life), Am. Soc. Assn. Execs. (bd. dirs., membership devel. com.), Am. Public Health Assn., Internat. Assn. Optometric Execs. (past pres.), Miss. Soc. Assn. Execs. (v.p., program chmn., pres. 1984-85, past pres. 1985-86). Democrat. Methodist. Club: Ofcl. Miss. Women's. Contbg. editor: So. Jour. Optometry, 1976—; editor MOA News, 1976—. Home: 102 Meadowlane Jackson MS 39213 Office: 5420 I-55 North Suite D Jackson MS 39211

ST. JEAN, JOSEPH, micropaleontologist, educator; b. Tacoma, July 24, 1923; s. Joseph Leger and Ruby Pearl (Burg) St. J.; m. Josephine Elizabeth Boulton, Aug. 28, 1948 (div.); m. 2d, Elena Mikhailovna Melnikova, Sept. 21, 1971. B.S., Coll. Puget Sound, 1949; A.M., Ind. U., 1953, Ph.D., 1956. Field asst., party chief Ind. Geol. Survey, summers 1950-53; instr. Kans. State U., Manhattan, 1951-52; instr., asst. prof. Trinity Coll., Hartford, Conn., 1955-57; mem. faculty U. N.C., Chapel Hill, 1957—, prof. geology, 1966—, gen. coll. advisor, 1979-85. Second violinist Durham (N.C.) Symphony, Village Orch. Chapel Hill, and others. Served with USNR, 1942-45. Geol. Soc. Am. grantee, 1956-58; AEC grantee, 1958-60; NSF grantee, 1960-62; U. N.C. Faculty Research Council grantee, 1960-62; U.S. Acad. Sci. grantee, Soviet Acad. Sci. grantee, 1965. Mem. Paleontol. Soc., Soc. Econ. Paleontologists and Mineralogists, AAAS, N.Y. Acad. Scis., N.C. Acad. Scis., Paleontol. Assn. Gt. Britain, Internat. Paleontol. Union, Sigma Xi. Contbr. articles to profl. jours. Home: 7 Riffel Wood Chapel Hill NC 27514 Office: Dept Geology U NC Chapel Hill NC 27514

ST. JOHN, ADAM, artist, interior designer; b. Tampa, Fla., Feb. 24, 1952; 1 child, Aprile Danyse. Prin., ASJ Assoc., Houston and Dallas, 1980—; lectr. seminar The Simplified Art of Faux Finishing, 1985—. Contbr. to Designers West, Texas Homes, Houston Home & Garden, Dallas Fort Worth Home & Garden, D Mag., Houston City, Austin Home & Garden, So. Living Classics, San Antonio Home and Garden. Represented in permanent collection Houston Mus. Fine Arts. Mem. Mensa. Office: ASJ Assoc 2615 Waugh Dr Suite 216 Houston TX 77006

ST JOHN, ARDITH POTTER, career and personal counselor; b. Drew, Maine, Apr. 10, 1931; d. Ardron Clark and Florence Mae (McKay) Potter; m. Joseph Winfield St. John, Aug. 15, 1959; children—Andrew, Evan. B.S., U. Maine-Farmington, 1952; M.S., NYU., 1955; M. Human Devel. and Learning, U. N.C.-Charlotte, 1985. Cert. secondary tchr., N.Y. Home econs. extension agent Agrl. Coop. Extension Service, Wallingford, Conn., 1957-59; instr. home econs. Hunter Coll., N.Y.C., 1960-61; instr. adult vocat. edn. Rowan Tech. Coll., Kannapolis, N.C., 1981-82; instr. vocat. edn. Ulster Occupation Ctr., Port Ewen, N.Y., 1977-78, Dutchess County Occupational Ctr., Poughkeepsie, N.Y., 1978-79; pvt. practice Cabarrus Counseling & Psychotherapy Assocs., Concord, N.C., 1985—. Chmn. Cabarrus Council Women, 1982—; adv. com. Cabarrus County Extension Service, Concord, 1982—. Mem. Am. Assn. Counseling and Devel., N.C. Assn. Counseling and Devel., Metrolina Assn. Counseling and Devel. Democrat. Avocations: American historic preservation; music; theatre; handcrafts; gardening. Office: Cabarrus Counseling and Psychotherapy Assocs 238 Church St N Concord NC 28025

ST. JOHN, HENRY SEWELL, JR., utility company executive; b. Birmingham, Ala., Aug. 18, 1938; s. H. Sewell and Carrie M. (Bond) St. J.; student David Lipscomb Coll., 1956-58, U. Tenn., 1958-59, U. Ala., 1962-64; m. J. Ann Morris, Mar. 7, 1959; children—Sherri Ann, Brian Lee, Teresa Lynn, Cynthia Faye. Engring. aide Ala. Power Co., Enterprise, 1960-62, Birmingham, 1962-66; asst. chief engr. Riviera Utilities, Foley, 1966-71, sec.-treas., gen. mgr., 1971—; vice-chmn. bd. dirs. Ala. Mcpl. Electric Authority, 1981—; vice chmn., 1981-82, chmn., 1983—. Deacon, Foley Ch. of Christ, 1975-82, elder, 1983—; active Am. Cancer Soc., chmn. bd. Baldwin County unit, 1977; bd. dirs. AGAPE of Mobile, 1977-80; bd. dirs., treas. Christian Care Center, Inc., 1981—; bd. dirs. South Baldwin Civic Chorus, pres., 1979—. Mem. IEEE, South Ala. Power Distbrs. Assn. (chmn. 1973-74), Ala. Consumer-Owned Power Distbrs. Assn. (chmn. 1974-75, 82-83, sec.-treas. 1980, vice-chmn. 1981), Municipal Electric Utility Assn. Ala. (exec. com., dir. 1971—), Southeastern Electric Reliability Council (assoc.), United Mcpl. Distbrs. Group (bd. dirs. 1972—), Am. Public Power Assn. (cable communications com.), South Baldwin C. of C. (pres. 1974, dir. 1981—). Clubs: Gulf Shores Golf (dir. 1974-75), Foley Quarterback (sec.-treas. 1984-85). Lodge: Rotary. Home: PO Box 818 Foley AL 36536 Office: PO Box 550 Foley AL 36536

ST. JOHN, MARCO, actor; b. New Orleans, May 7, 1939; s. Marco John Figuerga and Iris (Davidson) Springer; m. Barbara Lincoln Bonnell (dec. 1971); 1 child, Marco II. B.S., Fordham U., 1960. Appeared in Broadway plays Forty Carats, Weekend, The Unknown Soldier and His Wife, Things That Go Bump in the Night, Poor Bitos, You Can't Take it with You, War and Peace, others; films include Tightrope, Contract on Cherry Street, Night of the Juggler, The Next Man, The Mind Snatchers; TV programs include Remington Steele, The Insiders, The Mississippi, Beulah Land, Hot Pursuit, Hardcase, Kojak, Gunsmoke, Bonanza, Naked City, As the World Turns, others. Served to 1st lt. U.S. Army, 1960-61. Democrat. Roman Catholic. Lodge: K.C. Avocation: Jogging. Home: PO Box 521 Ocean Springs MS 39564

SAKS, BONNIE RAE, psychiatrist, sex therapist; b. Chgo., Mar. 13, 1950; d. Seymour and Charlotte Ann (Shapiro) S.; m. Mark Charles Maltzer, Sept. 18, 1977. B.A., Brown U., 1972, M.D., 1975. Diplomate Am. Bd. Psychiatry and Neurology. Intern Montefiore Hosp., Bronx, N.Y., 1975-76; resident in ob-gyn Yale-New Haven Hosp., 1976-78; resident in psychiatry Yale-West Haven (Conn.) VA Hosp., 1978-80; chief resident in psychiatry Yale U. Mental Health Ctr., 1980-81, clin. instr. psychiatry and ob-gyn Yale U. Sch. Medicine, New Haven, 1981-82; asst. prof. psychiatry U. South Fla., Tampa, 1982—, dir. Sexual Cons. Clinic, 1982-83; practice medicine specializing in psychiatry, Tampa, 1982—. Mem. Health Council, Tampa. Contbr. to Handbook for Prescribing Medications During Pregnancy, 1980; contbr. articles to profl. jour. Mem. Cultural Affairs Council, Tampa. Mem. Am. Psychiatric Assn., Am. Assn. Sex. Educators, Counselors and Therapists (cert.), Am. Soc. Psychosomatic Ob-Gyn., Marce Soc., Hillsborough County Med. Assn., C. of C. Tampa. Jewish. Club: Tampa. Office: 201 E Kennedy Suite 906 Tampa FL 33602

SAKS, JUDITH-ANN, artist; b. Anniston, Ala., Dec. 20, 1943; d. Julien David and Lucy-Jane (Watson) S.; student Tex. Acad. Art, 1957-58, Mus. Fine Arts, Houston, 1962, Rice U., 1962; B.F.A., Tulane U., 1966; postgrad. U. Houston, 1967; m. Haskell Irvin Rosenthal, Dec. 22, 1974; 1 son, Brian Julien. One-man shows include: Alley Gallery, Houston, 1969, 2131 Gallery, Houston, 1969; group shows include: Birmingham (Ala.) Mus., 1967, Meinhard Galleries, Houston, 1977; Galerie Barbizon, Houston, 1980, Park Crest Gallery, Austin, 1981; represented in permanent collections including: L.B. Johnson Manned Space Mus., Clear Lake City, Tex., Harris County Heritage Mus., Windsor Castle, London, Smithsonian Instn., Washington: commns. include: Pin Oak Charity Horse Show Assn., Roberts S.S. Agy., New Orleans; curator student art collection U. Houston, 1968-72; artist Am. Revolution Bicentennial project Port of Houston Authority, 1975-76. Recipient art awards including: 1st prize for water color Art League Houston, 1969, 1st prize for graphics, 1969, 1st prize for sculpture, 1968. Mem. Art League Houston, Houston Mus. Fine Art, DAR (curator 1983-85). Home: PO Box 1793 Bellaire TX 77401

SALACUSE, JESWALD WILLIAM, law educator, dean; b. Niagara Falls, N.Y., Jan. 28, 1938; s. William Leonard and Bessie (Buzzelli) S.; m. Donna Claire Booth, Oct. 1, 1966; children—William, Maria. Diploma, U. Paris, France, 1959; A.B., Hamilton Coll., 1960; J.D., Harvard U., 1963. Bar: N.Y. 1965, Tex. 1980. Lectr. law Ahmadu Bello U., Zaire, Nigeria, 1963-65; assoc. Conboy, Hewitt, O'Brien & Boardman, N.Y.C., 1965-67; assoc. dir. African Law Ctr., Columbia U., N.Y.C., 1967-68; prof. law, dir. research Nat. Sch. Adminstrn., Kinshasa, Zaire, 1968-71; adviser Middle East regional law and devel. Ford Found., Beirut, Lebanon, 1971-74, rep. in the Sudan, Khartoum, 1974-77; vis. prof. U. Khartoum, 1974-77; vis. scholar Harvard Law Sch., Cambridge, Mass., 1977-78; prof. law So. Meth. U., Dallas, 1978—, dean Sch. of Law, 1980—; cons. Ford Found., N.Y.C., 1978-82, U.S. Dept. State, Washington, 1978-84, UN Centre on Transnat. Corps., N.Y.C., 1984-85; lectr. Internat. Law Inst., Washington, 1978—. Author: An Introduction to Law in French Speaking Africa, 2 vols., 1969-75; (with Streng) International Business Planning: Law and Taxation, 6 vols., 1982-85; (with Kasunmu) Nigerian Family Law, 1966. Mem. ABA, Am. Bar Found., Am. Soc. Internat. Law, Tex. Bar Found., Dallas Bar Assn. Roman Catholic. Avocations: tennis; music. Home: 3312 Purdue St Dallas TX 75225 Office: Sch of Law So Meth U Dallas TX 75275

SALAMON, STEVEN JAY, advertising and public relations agency executive, writer, producer; b. Balt., Apr. 3, 1945; s. Alexander Salamon and Vera (Emden) Schuman-Cohen; m. Bonnie House, June 22, 1968; 1 son, Scott Jarod. B.S. in Broadcasting, U. Fla., 1967; postgrad. in mktg. Ga. State U., 1974-75. Dir. sta. WTVM-TV, Columbus, Ga., 1968-69; producer, dir., sta. WQXI-TV, Atlanta, 1969-71; account exec. Mgmt. Search, Atlanta, 1972-73; writer/producer Charal Assocs., Atlanta, 1974; pres. Salamon & Assocs., Inc., Atlanta, 1974—; dir. Rand Agy., Inc., Atlanta, 1980—. Treas. Am. Assn. for Mentally Retarded Offenders, Decatur, Ga., 1977. Mem. Sales and Mktg. Execs. (chmn. coms. 1982-84). Club: Atlanta City Sales (pub. relations dir. 1983—). Lodge: B'nai B'rith (dir. 1980—, treas. 1982-83). Home: 62 Lancaster Ct Lilburn GA 30247 Office: Salamon & Assocs Inc 2900 Chamblee Tucker Rd Bldg 15 Atlanta GA 30341

SALATICH, JOHN SMYTH, physician; b. New Orleans, Nov. 28, 1926; s. Peter B. and Gladys (Malter) S.; B.S. cum laude, Loyola U., New Orleans, 1946; M.D., La. State U., 1950; m. Patricia L. Mattison, Sept. 26, 1959; children—John Smyth, Elizabeth, Allison, Stephanie. Intern Charity Hosp., New Orleans, 1950-51, resident, 1951-54, also asso. dir. emergency rooms; practice medicine, specializing in cardiology and internal medicine, New Orleans, 1954—; dir. EKG dept. Southeastern La. Hosp., Mandeville, La.; prof. clin. medicine La. State U.; mem. staff Touro Infirmary, St. Charles Gen. Hosp.; chmn. dept. medicine Hotel Dieu, 1974-86 pres., New Orleans Emergency Room Corp., Physician Supplemental Services; adv. bd. Bank La. Bd. dirs. La. Regional Med. Program, 1972. Served to capt. M.C., AUS, 1954-56; Korea. Decorated Medallion of Greek Army. Diplomate Am. Bd. Internal Medicine. Fellow Am. Coll. Chest Physicians, ACP; mem. Am. Heart Assn., La. Heart Assn., New Orleans Acad. Internal Medicine, La. Thoracic Soc., La. Soc. Internal Medicine, AMA, La. Med. Soc., Orleans Parish Med. Soc., Theta Beta, Alpha

Sigma Nu, Delta Epsilon Sigma. Club: New Orleans Country. Contbr. articles to profl. and bus. jours. Home: 433 Country Club Dr New Orleans LA 70124 Office: 2025 Gravier St New Orleans LA 70112

SALATINO, ANTHONY BERNARD, ballet director; b. Utica, N.Y., Apr. 17, 1947; s. Vincent James and Mary Jane (Sacco) S.; m. Sirpa Hannele Jorasmaa, Feb. 21, 1970; 1 son, Teo Aatos. B.F.A., Juilliard Sch., 1969. Dancer, Tanz Form, N.Y.C., Opera Germany, N.Y.C., 1969-72; dir. Kirkland Coll., Clinton, N.Y., 1972-74; dir. Syracuse Ballet, 1974-79; assoc. dir. Hartford (Conn.) Ballet, 1979-82; artistic dir. Fort Worth Ballet, 1982—. Choreographer numerous ballets, 1972—. Fellow Council Arts. Lodge: Rotary. Home: 3424 Wedgworth Rd South Fort Worth TX 76133 Office: Fort Worth Ballet Assn 1301 5th Ave Fort Worth TX 76104

SALATKA, CHARLES ALEXANDER, archbishop; b. Grand Rapids, Mich., Feb. 26, 1918; s. Charles and Mary (Balun) S.; student St. Joseph's Sem., Grand Rapids, 1932-38; M.A., Cath. U. Am., 1941; J.C.L., Inst. Civil and Canon Law, Rome, 1948. Instr. St. Joseph's Sem., Grand Rapids, Mich., 1945; ordained priest Roman Catholic Ch., 1945; assigned chancery office Diocese of Grand Rapids, 1948-54, vice chancellor, 1954-61; aux. bishop, 1961, vicar gen., 1961; consecrated bishop, 1962; pastor St. James Parish, Grand Rapids, 1962-68; bishop of Marquette, 1968-77; archbishop of Oklahoma City, 1977—. Mem. Canon Law Soc. Am. Office: PO Box 23205 Oklahoma City OK 73123

SALAZAR, RAMIRO, librarian; b. Del Rio, Tex., Mar. 3, 1954; s. Jesus and Juanita (Suarez) S.; m. Cynthia Castillo, Dec. 19, 1976; children—Ramiro Orlando, Selinda Yvette. B.A., Tex. A&I U., 1978; M.L.S., Tex. Woman's U., 1979. Asst. library dir. Val Verde County Library, Del Rio, Tex., 1975-76; librarian Robert J. Kleberg Library, Kingsville, Tex., 1977-78; library dir. Eagle Pass Pub. Library (Tex.), 1980—. Mem. AMA, Tex. Library Assn. Democrat. Roman Catholic. Lodge: Lions. Home: 1298 Grand Park Ln Eagle Pass TX 78852 Office: Eagle Pass Pub Library 589 Main St Eagle Pass TX 78852

SALAZAR-CARRILLO, JORGE, economics educator; b. Havana, Cuba, Jan. 17, 1938; came to U.S., 1960; s. Jose Salazar and Ana Maria Carrillo; m. Maria Eugenia Winthrop, Aug. 30, 1959; children—Jorge, Manning, Mario, Maria Eugenia. B.B.A., U. Miami, 1958; M.A. in Econs., U. Calif.-Berkeley, 1964, cert. in econ. planning, 1964, Ph.D. in Econs., 1967. Sr. fellow, non-resident staff mem. Brookings Instn., Washington, 1965—; dir., mission chief UN, Rio de Janeiro, Brazil, 1974-80; prof. econs. Fla. Internat. U., Miami, 1980—, chmn. dept. econs., 1980—; adviser, contbg. editor Library of Congress, Washington, 1972—; econs. cons. InterAm. Devel. Bank, Washington, 1979—; council mem. Internat. Assn. Housing, Vienna, 1981—; co-chmn. discussion group Internat. Ctr. of Fla., Miami, 1981—; bd. dirs. Cuban Nat. Planning Council, Miami, 1982—, Insts. of Econ. and Social Research of Caribbean Basin, Dominican Republic, 1983—, U.S.-Chile Council, Miami, 1984—. Co-author: Trade, Debt and Growth in Latin America, 1984; Prices for Estimation in Cuba, 1985; The Foreign Debt and Latin America, 1983; External Debt and Strategy of Development in Latin America, 1985. Author: Wage Structure in Latin America, 1982. Fellow Brit. Council, London, 1960, Georgetown U., Washington, 1961-62, OAS, Washington, 1962-64, Brookings Instn., Washington, 1964-65. Mem. Am. Econ. Assn., Internat. Assn. Research in Income and Wealth, Econometric Soc. Latin Am., N.Am. Econs. and Fin. Assn., Latin Am. Studies Assn. Roman Catholic. Home: 1105 Almeria Ave Coral Gables FL 33134 Office: Fla Internat U Tamiami Campus DM 347 Miami FL 33199

SALE, MICHAEL MCCLENDON, oil company executive, petroleum geologist; b. Shreveport, La., Mar. 22, 1957; s. William Milton and Nancy (McClendon) S. B.B.A., So. Meth. U., 1979; B.A., Centenary Coll., 1983. Dist. landman Marathon Oil Co., Shreveport, 1980-81; petroleum geologist Braddock Exploration, Shreveport, 1982-84; founder, pres. Sale Prodn. Co., Inc., Shreveport, 1985—. Mem. Am. Assn. Petroleum Geologists, La. Assn. Ind. Producers and Royalty Owners, Shreveport Geol. Soc., So. Meth. U. Alumni Assn. (bd. dirs. Shreveport chpt.). Republican. Clubs: Shreveport Country, Cambridge (Shreveport). Avocations: tennis; swimming. Office: Sale Prodn Co PO Box 212 Shreveport LA 71101

SALET, EUGENE ALBERT, retired army officer, college official; b. Standish, Calif., May 25, 1911; s. August and Marie (Irigary) S.; B.A., U. Nev., 1934, LL.D. (hon.), 1968; LL.D. (hon.), Dickinson Law Sch., 1966; D.D. (hon.), Am. Theol. Sem., 1985; m. Irene Taylor, June 13, 1936; children—Suzette Taylor Salet Cook, Eugene Michael. Commd. 2d lt. U.S. Army, 1934, advanced through grades to maj. gen., 1963, ret., 1970; trust devel. officer 1st Nat. Bank & Trust Co., Augusta, Ga., 1970-73; pres. Ga. Mil. Coll., Milledgeville, 1973-85. Decorated D.S.M., Silver Star, Legion of Merit with 2 oak leaf clusters, Bronze Star with 2 oak leaf clusters, Army Commendation medal with oak leaf cluster, Combat Inf. badge; Mil. Valor Cross (Italy), Croix de Guerre (France), Fourragere (France); recipient Decoration for Disting. Civilian Service, U.S. Army, 1983; named Disting. Nevadan, 1967. Mem. Assn. Mil. Colls. and Schs. of U.S. (pres.), Assn. Pvt. Colls. and Univs. Ga. (v.p. 1983-84, pres. 1984-85), Internat. Platform Assn., So. Assn. Colls. and Schs., 3d Inf. Div. Assn., VFW, Ret. Officers Assn., Ryukyuan Bar Assn. (hon.). Republican. Roman Catholic. Clubs: Kiwanis; Harvard (Atlanta). Home: 108 Spruce Point SE Eatonton GA 31024

SALINAS, MANUEL, JR., science educator; b. Robstown, Tex., Aug. 25, 1931; s. Manuel and Ofelia (Shutter) S.; m. Clara Vasquez, Feb. 12, 1956; children—Nilda Irene, Manuel, III, Linda Anna. B.A., Tex. A&I U., 1957, M.S., 1959; Ph.D., U. Nebr., 1977. Asst. to chancellor Tex. A&I U., Kingsville, 1972-75, vice chancellor, 1975-76, v.p., 1978-83, assoc. prof., 1983—; dir. acads. Univ. System South Tex., Kingsville, 1977-78; cons. in edn. Brooks County, Tex., 1983—, Tex. Edn. Agy., Austin, 1985; referee profl. books. Chmn. United Way Campaign, 1978; mem. Kleberg Hosp. Found., 1983—. Served with USAF, 1950-55, Korea. U. Tex. scholar, 1960; council for Advancement Edn. scholar, 1980; U. Idaho fellow, 1965-66; NSF grantee, 1960-64. Mem. Sci. Tchrs. Assn. Tex. (life; pres. 1963-64), Nat. Assn. Adult Educators, Tex. Assn. Coll. Tchrs., Nat. Assn. Biology Tchrs. (bd. dirs. chpt. 1962-64), Phi Delta Kappa (pres.). Democrat. Roman Catholic. Lodge: K.C. (treas. 1978-83). Avocations: hunting; travel; reading; target shooting. Office: Tex A&I U Santa Gertrudis Kingsville TX 78363

SALISBURY, JAMES DAVID, regional government official; b. Salyersville, Ky., Nov. 6, 1934; s. James William and Marie (Stephens) S.; m. Betty Hall, Mar. 20, 1954; children—Rebecca Ann, Rhonda Gayle, Jami Lynn, James David III. A.B., Morehead State U., 1960, M.A., 1968. Prin. Boyd County Pub. Schs., Catlettsburg, Ky., 1960-67; exec. dir. FIVCO Area Devel. Dist., Catlettsburg, 1968—. Chmn. Big Sandy Water Dist., 1976-83; pres. Boyd County 4-H Council, 1976-80, Boyd County Extension Council, 1977-81. Mem. Ky. Assn. of Area Devel. Dist. Assn. Methodist. Lodge: Masons. Office: FIVCO Area Devel Dist PO Box 636 Catlettsburg KY 41129

SALITURI, JEFF ROBERT, safety management and environmental consultant; b. N.Y.C., Aug. 29, 1950; s. Francis Joseph and Aurora Louise (Ferro) S.; m. Jeanne Marie Jatz, Sept. 7, 1974; children—Sarah Marie, Melissa Anne. Student U.S. Coast Guard Acad., 1968-70; B.S. in Phys. Oceanography, Fla. Inst. Tech., 1973, M.S. in Bio-environ. Oceanography, 1975. Cert. safety profl., hazard control mgr., product safety mgr., healthcare safety profl., hazardous materials mgr. Cons. loss prevention Liberty Mut. Ins. Co., Miami and Orlando, Fla., 1976-81, M&M Protection Cons., Winter Park, Fla., 1981—. Block capt. Community Crime Watch program, Winter Park, 1983—. Served with USCG, 1968-70. Mem. Am. Soc. Safety Engrs. (profl. mem.; chpt. pres. 1983-84, assembly del. 1983-84, exec. com. 1984—), Soc. Fire Protection Engrs. (affiliate), Nat. Fire Protection Assn. Avocations: sailing; bicycling; softball; gardening; reading. Office: M&M Protection Cons 1091 S Semoran Blvd Winter Park FL 32792

SALLER, M(AX) DAVID, oil and gas landman; b. Memphis, Mar. 28, 1946; s. Max Charles and Julia Rae (Greer) S.; m. Sharon Doreen Boyd, June 11, 1966; children—Stephanie Rene, Robyn Anne, Lauren Elizabeth, David Boyd. B.S. in Journalism and Mktg., Memphis State U., 1971. Cert. profl. landman, oil and gas. Sales mgr. Gen. Motors Corp., Memphis, 1971-72, dist. mgr., Little Rock, Ark., 1972-74; ind. petroleum landman, Tyler, Tex., 1974—. Served with USMC, 1964-70. Mem. Am. Assn. Petroleum Landmen, East Tex. Assn. Petroleum Landmen, Am. Security Council, Confederate Air Force. Republican. Roman Catholic. Clubs: Petroleum, Timber Creek Racquet (Tyler), Athletic, Serra of East Texas, Rotary. Home: 6212 Bedford Dr Tyler TX 75703 Office: M David Saller Mineral Properties 100 Independence Pl Suite 415 Tyler TX 75703

SALLEY, VIRGINIA SUTTON, business executive; b. Miami, Fla.; d. Durward Belmont and Sarabelle (Burns) Sutton; student Sullins Coll., Rollins Coll.; m. George H. Salley, Aug. 28, 1961. Asso., jr. partner D.B. Sutton Jewelry Co., Miami, 1948-50; singer (Gloria Manning, profl. name) with Vincent Lopez Orch., Ben Ribble Orch., 1951-60; owner, operator Wiscasset Antiques, 1960-62; owner, mgr., pres. Sutton Manning Corp., 1962—. Mem. Met. Dade County Zoning Apls. Bd., 1966-70, vice-chairperson, 1970-71; bd. dirs. Big Bros., 1971-72; founder, pres. Theatre Arts League, 1959, Jr. Theatre Guild of Miami, 1961; bd. dirs., Gilded Lilies, Crippled Children's Soc. of Dade County (Fla.), 1982-83; mem. pres.' adv. council Barry Coll., 1978-79. Mem. Nat. League Am. Pen Women, Miami Young Patroness of Opera (life), DAR, English Speaking Union, Am. Guild Variety Artists, Screen Actors Guild. Mem. Christian Ch. Clubs: Miami Yacht, Ocean Reef, Indian Creek, Boothbay Harbour Yacht. Co-author: Royal Bayreuth China, 1970. Contbr. articles in field to profl. jours. Office: Sutton Manning Corp 100 N Biscayne Blvd Suite 700 Miami FL 33132

SALLOT, LYNNE MARIE, marketing communications corporation executive, writer; b. Cleve., Jan. 26, 1948; d. Kenneth Charles Funk and Rose Marie (Shoup/Clark) Pyle; m. Jeffry George Sallot, Oct. 5, 1968 (div. Dec. 1974); 1 child, Kenneth Edward. B.A., Kent State U., 1970. Editorial asst. Cleve. Press, 1967-68; bur. reporter Beacon-Jour., Akron, Ohio, 1969-71; asst. editor Maclean-Hunter, Toronto, Ont., Can., 1973-75; editor Southam Publs., Toronto, 1975-76; N.Am. mgr. Internat. Mktg. Ptnrs./Cayman Islands News Bur., Miami, Fla., 1977-80; v.p., dir. Creative Resources, Inc., Miami, 1980—; freelance writer contbg. to Redbook, Chatelaine, Quest, Miami Herald, others, U.S., Can., 1972—. Author: Bearwalk, 1977. Promotion, publicity activities for various charity orgns. including Am. Cancer Soc., City of Hope, Cystic Fibrosis Found., 1973—. William Randolph Hearst Found. scholar, 1969, award for feature writing, 1970; Scripps-Howard Found. scholar, 1968; Can. Arts Council grantee, 1977; Nat. Gaspar award Am. Cancer Soc., 1984; spl. award Ronald McDonald House, 1985. Mem. Women in Communications. Democrat. Home: 7550 S W 60th St Miami FL 33143 Office: Creative Resources Inc 2000 S Dixie Hwy Miami FL 33133

SALLOUM, ANTOINE ABDULLAH, pharmacist; b. Amyoun, Lebanon, Feb. 20, 1913; came to U.S., 1937, naturalized, 1943; s. Albert and Fontaine (Easa) S.; m. Violet Khouri, Dec. 31, 1943; children—Lulie (dec.), Leah. B.A., Am. U. Beirut, 1936; B.S., U. Pitts., 1940; Ph.D. in Pharmacy (hon.), Mass. Coll. Pharmacy and Assoc. Health Services, 1982. Owner, mgr. Sullivan's Pharmacy, Roslindale, Mass., 1945—. Recipient citations Am. Legion, 1956, White House, 1965, Pres. Nixon, 1971, Mass. Ho. of Reps., 1974, Pa. Ho. of Reps., 1982. Clubs: Home and Sch. (Roslindale pres. 1965—); Kiwanis, Am. Legion. Lodges: Masons (trustee), Shriners, Lebanese Internat., Sultural Union Breater Boston. Home: 2772 NE 3rd St Pompano Beach FL 33062

SALMONS, JOANNA, nursing adminstr.; b. Smiths Grove, Ky., Nov. 7, 1933; d. Walter Scott and Birdie Wilma (Jackson) Parker; R.N., Fla. Hosp. Sch. Nursing, 1954; student So. Missionary Coll., 1979; cert. in health systems mgmt. Harvard U., 1980; B.S.N. SUNY, 1982; postgrad. Trinity Coll.; cert. in healthcare mgmt. Yale U., 1985; m. William L. Salmons, June 6, 1970; children by previous marriage—Robert B. Morrow, Scott Alan Morrow. Dir. nursing Larkin Gen. Hosp., Miami, Fla.; adminstr., Ft. Walton Beach (Fla.) Hosp., 1974-75; dir. surg. nursing Fla. Hosp., Orlando, 1976-78; dir. profl. standards Adventist Health Systems/Sunbelt Corp., Orlando, 1978-79; sr. v.p. patient care services Fla Hosp. Orlando, 1979—; cons. in field. Mem. A Thousand Plus com. Am. Cancer Soc. Recipient Outstanding Achievement award, Larkin Gen. Hosp., Miami, 1969 Mem. Fla. Nurses Assn. (bd. dirs. 1980-81, 83-84), Am. Heart Assn., Retarded Children's Assn. Orange County, Fla. Hosp. Assn., Am. Nurses Assn. (cert. nurse adminstr.), Fla. Soc. Nursing Adminstrs., Am. Soc. Nursing Adminstrs., Assn. Seventh-Day Adventist Nursing Club: Buena Ventura Lakes Golf and Tennis. Home: Lake Pickett Woods 2621 S Hwy 419 Chuluota FL 32766 Office: 601 Rollins St Orlando FL 32803

SALOKAS, G. MICHAEL, bank executive; b. Waterbury, Conn., May 11, 1950; s. George and Helen (Bakaitis) S.; m. Linda Joan Martino, Sept. 17, 1977; 1 child, Kenneth Martin Michael. B.A., Western Conn. State U., 1973; M.S., Southern Conn. State U., 1976. Personnel adminstr. Hinton Mortgage Co., Dallas, 1979-80; asst. personnel dir. Tex. Credit Union League, Dallas, 1980-82; asst v.p. human resources Richardson Savings & Loan, Dallas, 1982—; program devel., instr. Richland Coll., Dallas, 1980-83. Mem. Dallas Personnel Assn., Am. Soc. of Personnel Adminstrs., Am. Soc. of Tng. and Devel. Republican. Roman Catholic. Avocations: travel; sports; reading. Office: Richardson Savings and Loan Assn 12700 Park Central Dr Suite 1500 Dallas TX 75251

SALOMONE, WILLIAM GERALD, consultant; b. Flushing, N.Y., Apr. 14, 1948; s. Harry and Mary (Tartaro) S.; m. Mary Jo Piano, July 22, 1978. B.Civil Engring., Manhattan Coll., 1970; M.S. in Civil Engring. UCLA, 1971; Ph.D. in Civil Engring., Purdue U., 1978; J.D., U. Fla., 1985. Registered profl. engr., N.Y., N.J., Ill., Fla., Md., Ga., Ala. Research fellow UCLA, 1970-71; project engr. Dames & Moore, Cranford, N.J., 1971-75; research asst. Purdue U., West Lafayette, Ind., 1975-78; project mgr. Woodward-Clyde Cons., Chgo., 1978-80; prin. geotech. engr. Fluor Power Services, Chgo., 1980-81; v.p., dir. geotech. engring. Bromwell Engring., Inc., Lakeland, Fla., 1981-82; cons. William G. Salomone, Lakeland, 1982—; adj. prof. bus. law U. Fla., 1985—; adj. prof. U. South Fla., 1985; judge Lakeland Regional High Sch. Sci. Fair, 1983. NDEA Title IV fellow UCLA, 1970-71; recipient Letters of Commendation, ASCE, Mayor of Lakeland, Sheriff of Bartow, Fla., Dept. Army-C.E. Mem. ASCE (Young Civil Engr. of Yr. 1982), Earthquake Engring. Research Inst., Seismol. Soc. Am., Internat. Soc. Soil Mechanics and Found. Engring., Nat. Soc. Profl. Engrs. (coll. scholarship com. 1983), ASTM, Fla. Engring. Soc. (Young Engr. of Yr. 1983), Chi Epsilon, Tau Beta Pi. Office: 3520 Cleveland Heights Blvd Suite 111 Lakeland FL 33803

SALOOM, KALISTE JOSEPH, JR., judge; b. Lafayette, La., May 15, 1918; s. Kaliste and Asma (Boustany) S.; B.A. with high distinction, Southwestern La. U., 1939; J.D., Tulane U., 1942; m. Yvonne Adelle Nassar, Oct. 19, 1958; children—Kaliste Joseph III, Douglas, Leanne, Gregory John. Admitted La. bar, 1942; pvt. practice, 1942—; city atty. Lafayette, 1948-52, city judge Div. A, 1953—; mem. judicial council La. Supreme Ct.; bd. dirs. La. Jud. Coll., 1976-79. Chmn. La. Parish Draft Bd., 1950-71; mem. La. Youth Commn., 1958-72, chmn., 1970-72; mem. com. cts., codes and laws La. Hwy. Safety Commn.; mem. Nat. Com. on Uniform Traffic Laws, Washington, 1975—; mem. La. Pub. Affairs Research Council; chief U.S. del. World Congress Christian Bros. Sch. Alumni, Spain, 1964, Can., 1967; del. White House Conf. on Children and Youth, 1960; invitee 1st Nat. Conf. on Bail and Criminal Justice, Dept. Justice, Washington, 1963; chmn. com. on traffic law revision Jud. Council of La. Supreme Ct.; mem. U.S. Dept. Transp. Nat. Hwy. Safety Adv. Com., 1977-80; Am. Bar Assn. rep. to adv. com. model non-resident violators compact Council State Govts., 1977. Dir. La. Gulf Coast Oil Expn.; exec. bd. Evangeline area council Boy Scouts Am.; bd. dirs. United Givers Fund, Southwest La. Mardi Gras Assn., United Democrats La., 1957-59; trustee Am. Lebanon-Syrian Asso. Charities, 1957-65; founder Acadiana Safety Council, 1961; mem. bd. Lafayette Mental Health Assn.; bd. dirs. Nat. Center for State Cts., Williamsburg, Va., 1977-84, Lafayette Diocese Cath. Youth Orgn. Served as spl. agt. CIC, U.S. Army, 1942-45. Recipient Alumni award U. Southwestern La., 1939, grant-in-aid Esso Safety Found., Traffic Safety Conf., 1958, award traffic safety program Am. Bar Assn., 1958, 59, 61, 63, 64, Lafayette Civic Cup award, 1965; award for public service U.S. Dept. Transp., 1980; Appreciation award Acadiana Safety Council, 1983; named Man of Year, Salvation Army, 1966. Fellow Law-Science Acad. Am.; mem. ABA (lectr. traffic ct. advance seminars, mem. traffic ct. program, standards of criminal justice, automobile law coms. 1975—, mem. assoc. and adv. com., recipient Outstanding Traffic Ct. judge award 1969, Flaschner Found. award 1981), Lafayette Bar Assn. (pres. 1955-56), Am. Judicature Soc., Nat., La. (pres. 1963-64) councils juvenile court judges, N.Am. (bd. govs. 1969-73), Am. (bd. govs. 1973-77, William H. Burnett award 1982), La. City judges assns. (past pres.), La. Law Inst. (adv. com.), Am. Legion (judge adv. La. 1953-56), La. Conf. Social Welfare (dir. 1961), Nat. Inst. Municipal Law Officers, World Assn. Judges, S.W. La. Univ. Alumni Assn. (pres. 1959-60), Nat. Council on Crime and Delinquency, Nat. Council Spl. Ct. Judges (chmn. traffic ct. com. 1975-83), Nat. Council Municipal Judges, La. Hist. Soc., Council for Devel. of French in La. (pres. Lafayette Parish chpt. 1975), Blue Key, Order Coif, Kappa Sigma, Pi Gamma Mu, Pi Kappa Delta, Alpha Phi Omega, Phi Alpha Theta, Phi Kappa Phi. Clubs: Knife and Fork (dir.), Lafayette Town House (dir.), Rotary. Author: Traffic Court Judge's Check List, 1965, rev. edit., 1984, also articles. Home: 502 Marguerite Blvd Lafayette LA 70503 Office: 211 W Main St Lafayette LA 70501

SALTZMAN, BENJAMIN NATHAN, physician; b. Ansonia, Conn., Apr. 24, 1914; s. Joseph N. and Frances (Levine) S.; A.B., U. Oreg., 1935, M.A., 1936, M.D., 1940; m. Ruth Elizabeth Bohan, Dec. 19, 1941; children—Sue Ann, John Joseph, Mark Stephen. Intern Gorgas Hosp., Ancon, C.Z., 1941, resident, 1942; pvt. practice, Mountain Home, Ark., 1946-74; past mem. staffs Mountain Home, Ark., Boone County Hosp., Harrison, Ark., Marion County Hosp., Yellville, Ark.; past chief of staff Baxter Gen. Hosp.; pres. Saltzman-Guenthner Clinic Ltd.; preceptor Sch. Medicine, U. Ark., Little Rock, also asso. clin. prof., 1972-74, prof., chmn. dept. family and community medicine U. Ark. for Med. Scis., 1974-76, dir. rural med. devel. programs, 1976-81, coordinating dir. family practice programs Coll. Medicine, 1977-78, dir. flexible internship program, 1980-81, prof. emeritus, 1981—; dir. Ark. Dept. Health, 1981—; mem. staff Univ. Hosp., St. Vincent Hosp., Ark. Bapt. Med. Center, Ark. Children's Hosp., Little Rock VA Hosp. (all Little Rock). Mem. Ark. Bd. Health, 1972-80, pres., 1976-77; mem. Gov.'s Health Council Ark.; mem. rev. com. Community Health Services, Washington, 1965-67; mem. Nat. Adv. Health Services Council, 1970-72; mem. Gov.'s Com. on Mental Retardation, Ark., 1962-66, Ark. Comprehensive Health Planning Council, 1967-70, Gov.'s Adv. Council Developmental Disabilities, 1970—, Gov.'s Adv. Council on Community Mental Health Centers; Baxter County health officer, Mountain Home, 1948-74. Pres. Ark. Tb Assn., 1958-63, nat. rep. dir., pres. So. Tb Conf., 1969-70; past pres., dir. Tri-States Assn. for Cripples, 1959-60; pres. bd. Ozark Regional Mental Health Center, 1970-74; mem. bd. Baxter County Day Service Center; bd. dirs. Ark. Health Systems Found., 1974-76, Ark. Regional Med. Program, 1969-76; alderman Mountain Home City Council, 1947-52; bd. dirs. First Ark. Devel. Finance Corp, Hosp. Crippled Adults, Memphis; bd. dirs., regional v.p. Nat. Assn. Retarded Citizens; pres. Ark. div. Am. Cancer Soc., 1970-71, Ark. Assn. Retarded Children, 1971-73; pres. Ark. Endowment for Humanities, 1979-80. Served from lt. to capt. AUS, 1942-46; lt. col. USAF Res. ret. Named Man of Year, Ark. Conf. Tb Workers, 1960, Ark. Democrat, 1975; recipient outstanding award Nat. Tb Assn., 1961, Will Ross medal Am. Lung Assn., 1979, mem. Hall of Fame, 1980; Human Relations award Ark. council NCCJ, 1980; Glenn W. Rollins award North Ark. Human Services System, 1984; Disting. Leadership award Am. Rural Health Assn., 1985; diplomate Am. Bd. Family Practice. Fellow Am. Acad. Family Physicians; mem. Ark. Acad. Gen. Practice (pres. 1954-55, Family Dr. of Yr. award 1984), Ark. Med. Soc. (pres. 1974-75), World, Am. (chmn. council rural health), So. Ark. (treas.), Baxter County (past pres., sec.), Pulaski County med. assns., Am., Ark. thoracic socs., Am., Ark. (Tom T. Ross award 1975; outstanding achievement award 1970) pub. health assns., Am. Sch. Health Assn. (com. mem.), Aeromed. Assn., Assn. Mil. Surgeons, Ark. Heart Assn. (dir. 1972-76, 79—), Ark. Soc. for Clin. Hypnosis (pres. 1978-80), Ark. Gerontol. Soc. (dir. 1971-75, 81—), Res. Officers Assn., Am. Legion (former comdr.), Flying Physicians Assn. (nat. v.p.), Mountain Home C. of C. (pres. 1954-56, 65-67), V.F.W., Sigma Xi. Democrat. Unitarian. Lodges: Masons (33 deg.), Shriners, Elks (pres. Ark.), Rotarian (dist. gov. 1952-54, pres. Mountain Home, 1949, internat. dir. 1961-63, trustee Internat. Found. 1965-67; Paul Harris award 1973, internat. chmn. health, hunger and humanity com. 1978-80, meritorious Service award Rotary Found. 1984). Home: PO Box 823 Mountain Home AR 72653 Office: 4815 W Markham St Little Rock AR 72201

SALYER, LAVERNA HARRISON, educator; b. Gracemont, Okla., June 16, 1924; d. Leonard Cornelius and Ocie Ruth (Carr) H.; m. Delbert E. Salyer, Aug. 3, 1941 (dec. 1968), D'Lynn, Mary Beth Goodridge. B.A., Trinity U., San Antonio, 1959; M.Ed., Okla. U., 1969, Ph.D., 1975. Tchr. Latin and English, San Antonio pub. schs., 1959-64, Oklahoma City pub. schs., 1966-70; instr. Rose State Coll., Midwest City, Okla., 1970-80, div. chmn., 1980—. Bd. dirs. Ret. Citizens Vols., Oklahoma City, 1983—. Mem. Internat. Reading Assn. (pres. S.W. region jr. coll. 1977), Okla. Jr. Coll. Assn., Phi Theta Kappa, Delta Psi Omega, Sigma Tau Sigma, Alpha Delta Kappa. Republican. Avocations: art collector; seamstress. Home: 10016 S Rose St Oklahoma City OK 73159 Office: Rose State Coll 6420 SE 15th St Midwest City OK 73110

SAMELSON, WILLIAM, foreign language and literature educator, author; b. Sosnowiec, Poland, Sept. 21, 1928; s. Harry and Bela (Stibel) S.; m. Rosa Salinas, Aug. 22, 1954; children—James, Regina Faye, Henry, Morris. B.A., Western Res. U., 1950; M.A., Kent State U., 1954; Ph.D., U. Tex., 1960. Instr., U. Tex., Austin, 1955-56; prof. fgn. langs. and lit. San Antonio Coll., 1956—; cons. in langs. Bd. dirs. Epilepsy Found., Leukemia Found., Tex. Commn. on Arts and Humanities. Served with U.S. Army, 1951-53. Decorated War medal. Recipient Fed. Republic Germany scholarship award, 1970; Americanism medal DAR, 1977; named Piper Professorship Outstanding Tex. Coll. Tchr. of Yr., 1982. Mem. Internat. Speakers Forum, Authors League Am., Authors Guild, Inc., Tex. Jr. Coll. Tchrs. Assn., TESOL. Author: Gerhart Herrmann Mostar: A Critical Profile, 1965; Der Sinn Des Lesens, 1968; All Lie in Wait, 1969; Romances and Songs of the Sephardim, The Sephardi Heritage, 1972; English as a Second Language, Phase One: Let's Converse, 1974, Phase Two: Let's Read, 1975, Phase Three: Let's Write, 1976, Phase Four: Let's Continue, 1979, Phase Zero Plus: Let's Begin, 1980. Home: 4119 Sylvan Oaks San Antonio TX 78229 Office: 1300 San Pedro Ave San Antonio TX 78284

SAMENOW, STANTON ETHAN, psychologist, consultant, author; b. Washington, Oct. 16, 1941; s. Charles U. and Sylvia L. Samenow; m. Dorothy Kellman, Apr. 4, 1971; children—Charles P., Jason P. B.A. cum laude, Yale U., 1963, M.A., U. Mich., 1964, Ph.D., 1968. Lic. psychologist, Va., Washington. Psychologist Northville State Hosp., Mich., 1968-70; clin. research psychologist Saint Elizabeths Hosp., Washington, 1970-78; clin. psychologist Stanton E. Samenow, Ph.D., P.C., Alexandria, Va., 1978—; cons. in field. Author: Inside the Crimmal Mind, 1984, (with Dr. Samuel Yochelson) The Criminal Personality, vol. 1, 1976, vol. 2, 1977. TV appearances: 60 Minutes, Donahue, Merv Griffin, CBS Morning News, David Susskind Show. Nat. radio: The Larry King Show. Appointed by Pres. Reagan to: Law Enforcement Task Force, 1980, Talk Force on Victims of Crime, 1982. Mem. Am. Psychol. Assn., Va. Psychol. Assn., D.C. Psychol. Assn. Home: 6359 Crosswoods Dr Falls Church VA 22044 Office: Stanton E Samenow PhD P C 4921 Seminary Rd 104 Alexandria VA 22311

SAMFIELD, MAX MARCUS, chemical engineer; b. Memphis, Apr. 20, 1918; s. Marcus and Henrietta (Hirsch) S.; m. Isabel Miriam Leon, Nov. 16, 1944; children—Frieda Werden, Max Milton, Dina, Emily. B.S., Rice U., 1940; M.S., U. Tex., 1941, Ph.D., 1945. Chem. engr., Bur. Indsl. Chemistry, Austin, Tex., 1945-47; unit engr. Servel, Inc., Evansville, Ind., 1947-52; supr. engring. research and devel. Liggett & Myers, Durham, N.C., 1952-64, asst. dir. research, 1964-73; project officer EPA, Research Triangle Park, N.C., 1973-80; cons. in tobacco and environ. protection, Durham, 1980—. Author: Research and Manufacturing in U.S. Cigarette Industry, 1980; contbr. articles to profl. jours. Pres., Judea Reform Congregation, Durham, 1960-62. Recipient Bronze medal EPA, 1980. Mem. Durham Engrs. Club (v.p. 1964-66), N.C. Soc. Engrs., Durham C. of C. Clubs: Toastmasters (pres. 1952-54, dist. gov. 1964-66), Kiwanis, Rotary. Avocations: bridge; chess; gardening; travel. Home: 915 W Knox St Durham NC 27701 Office: PO Box 610 Durham NC 27702

SAMFORD, FRANK PARK, JR., life insurance company executive; b. Montgomery, Ala., Jan. 29, 1921; s. Frank Park and Hattie (Noland) S.; student Auburn U., 1937-38; B.A., Yale, 1942; LL.B., U. Ala., 1947; m. Virginia Carolyn Suydam, May 27, 1942; children—Frank Park III, Laura Alice, John Singleton Pitts, Mae Virginia. With Liberty Nat. Life Ins. Co., Birmingham, Ala., 1947—, v.p., 1955-60, pres., 1960-73, chmn. bd., 1973—, pres., 1980—, also dir.; chmn. bd. Torchmark Corp. Pres. Ala. Safety Council, 1968-70. Past exec. com. Am. Life Conv.; past chmn. Life Insurers. Conf., 1970; chmn. Jefferson County United Appeal, 1963. Bd. dirs. Jefferson County Community Chest pres., 1965-66. Served to lt. (s.g.) USNR, 1942-45. Mem. Assn. C.L.U.s, Alpha Tau Omega, Phi Delta Phi, Berzelius. Presbyterian. Clubs: Rotary, Birmingham Country, Mountain Brook Country (Birmingham). Office: 2001 Third Ave S Birmingham AL 35202

SAMMONS, CHARLES A., corporate executive; b. 1901; married. With Postal Mut. Indemnity Co., 1929-48, past pres., chmn. bd., dir. Res. Life Ins. Co.; now chmn. bd., dir. Sammons Enterprises Inc., Dallas. Office: Sammons Enterprises Inc 403 S Akard Dallas TX 75265*

SAMOLE, MYRON MICHAEL, lawyer; b. Chgo., Nov. 29, 1943; s. Harry Lionel and Bess Miriam (Siegel) S.; m. Sandra Rita Port, Feb. 2, 1967; children—Stacey Ann, Karen Lynn, Rena Mara, David Aaron. Student U. Ill. (Jewish Vocat. Service scholar), 1962-65; J.D., DePaul U., 1967; postgrad. John Marshall Lawyer's Inst., 1967-69. Bar: Ill. 1967, U.S. Ct. Appeals 1968, U.S. Dist. Ct. (no. dist. Ill.) 1968, Fla. 1981. Sole practice law, Chgo., 1967-79, Miami, Fla., 1981—; chmn. bd. Fidelity Electronics Ltd. and subs., Miami, 1969-83; pres. Fidelity Hearing Instruments, Inc., Miami, 1983—; dir. Fidelity Computer Products, Inc., Miami; adv. bd. dirs. Enterprise Bank Fla. Bd. dirs. Brandeis Acad., Congregation Beth David. Recipient award Soc. Univ. Founder, U. Miami, 1981. Mem. ABA, Chgo. Bar Assn., Ill. Bar Assn., Fla. Bar Assn., Dade County Bar Assn., Ill. Trial Lawyers Assn., Miami C. of C., Phi Alpha Delta. Democrat. Jewish. Club: Masons, Shriners. Address: 6000 NW 153 St PO Box 9318 Miami FL 33178 33014-9318

SAMPLE, DOROTHY EATON, lawyer; m. Richard L. Sample. B.A. in Econs., Duke U., 1933, J.D. Bar: N.C. 1933. Asst. atty. HOLC, Salisbury, N.C.; sec., dept. mgr. automobile fin. co. Mem. Fla. Children's Commn., Pinellas Presch. Lic. Bd., State Welfare Bd., Save Our Bays; v.p., regional dir. Fla. Wildlife Fedn.; pres. PTA, Pasadena Property Owners Assn.; active Band Boosters; legis. chmn. LWV; active Jr. Coll. Service Club; bd. dirs. Gulf Coast and Fla. Tb Assn.; v.p. West St. Petersburg Property Owners' Assn.; mem. Community Welfare Council, St. Petersburg Hist. Soc., Multiple Scleroris and United Fund Drive Suncoast Active Vols. for Ecology, C. of C. Steering Council on Econs. and Environ., Citizens Council on Crime, St. Petersburg Bicentennial com., Pinellas Pkwy. Adv. Bd., Coastal Coordinating Council, Pinellas County Edn. Study Commn., Mental Health Assn. Pinellas County, Pinellas C. of C. Govt. Action com.; mem. Ho. of Reps. State of Fla.; bd. dirs. Council of Neighborhood Assns., March of Dimes; adminstrv. Pasadena Community Ch.; dir. Gulf Beach-Seminola Republican Club. Recipient St. Petersburg Homeowners Assn. Outstanding Pub. Official award, 1982; Tampa Women for Responsible Legis. Freedom award, 1982; Good Govt. award, 1981; Fla. Wildlife Fedn. Spl. Service award, 1977; Sertoma Club Outstanding Service to Mankind award, 1974. Mem. Chi Phi, Delta Phi Rho. Alpha. Clubs: St. Petersburg Yacht, Jr. Coll. Service. Home: 200 Sunset Dr S Saint Petersburg FL 33707 Office: 3110 1st Ave N Saint Petersburg FL 33713

SAMUELS, GEORGE, agricultural consultant; b. Phila., July 7, 1922; s. Philip and Dora (Spitalnick) S.; m. Mollie Freed, May 27, 1945; children—Lynn Barbara Samuels Mandon, Sharon Ann Samuels Johnsen. B.Sc. in Agronomy, U. Del., 1946; Ph.D. in Soils, Rutgers U., 1949. Research asst. Rutgers U., New Brunswick, N.J., 1946-49; plant physiologist Agrl. Expt. Sta., U. P.R., Rio Piedras, 1949-55, sr. agronomist, 1955-77, biomass energy cons. Ctr. for Energy and Environment, 1979-85; research cons. Agrl. Research Assocs., Rio Piedras, 1955-77, tech. dir., Winter Park, Fla., 1978—. Author: Foliar Diagnosis for Sugar Cane, 1969; also numerous sci. papers. Served as 2d lt. U.S. Army, 1943-46, ETO. Mem. Caribbean Food Crop Soc. (sec.-treas. 1969-77), Am. Soc. Agrl. Scis. (pres. 1970-72), Am. Soc. Sugar Cane Technologists, Phi Kappa Phi, Sigma Xi, Gamma Sigma Delta. Avocations: woodworking, painting. Home: 825 Carvell Dr Winter Park FL 32792 Office: Agrl Research Assocs 825 Carvell Dr Winter Park FL 32792

SAMUELS, LAWRENCE WILLIAM, dietitian, food management consultant; b. San Angelo, Tex., Oct. 19, 1951; s. Lawrence Samuels Jr. and Wanda Jane (Adams) Samuels Martin; m. Carolyn Michele Martin, Apr. 20, 1973; children—Adam Martin, Aaron Charles. A.A., Tarrant County Jr. Coll., 1971; B.S. in Foods and Nutrition, N. Tex. State U., 1974. Registered and lic. dietitian. Assoc. dir. dietary dept. Harris Hosp. Methodist, Fort Worth, 1975-80, Med. Plaza Hosp., Fort Worth, 1980; dietitian, med. rep. Edward Don & Co., Dallas, 1980-81; dietitian, sales rep. BIH-Food Service, St. Louis, 1981-84; dir. nutrition and food service Walls Regional Hosp., Cleburne, Tex., 1984—. Bd. dirs. Johnson County United Way, Cleburne, 1984-86, allocation chmn., 1985, campaign sub chmn., 1985; bd. dirs. Johnson County Heart Assn., 1985. Mem. Am. Dietetic Assn., Am. Soc. Hosp. Food Service Adminstrs., Tex. Soc. Hosp. Food Service Dirs., Ft. Worth Dietetic Assn. (pres. 1978-79, area rep. 1984—), Tex. Dietetic Assn. Republican. Methodist. Lodge: Kiwanis (pres. Cleburne 1985-86). Avocations: cooking; camping; golf; swimming. Home: 314 Meadow View Dr Cleburne TX 76031 Office: Memorial Hosp PO Box 118 Cleburne TX 76031

SAMUELS, MARION AUGUSTUSGOTIER, educator; b. Augusta, Ga., Mar. 6, 1951; s. Percy L. and Constance B. Quinn; m. Almeta Lee Colbert, July 1, 1983; 1 son, Eric. B.S., Paine Coll., 1976. Asst. registrar Paine Coll., Augusta, Ga., 1972-76; tchr. Houghton Elem. Sch., Augusta, 1976, Terrace Manor Elem. Sch., Augusta, 1976-77; tchr., coach Wrens High Sch. (Ga.), 1977—, head track coach, 1977—, head basketball coach, 1977—, head cross country coach, 1978—. Scoutmaster Boys Club Am., Augusta, 1976—. Served with U.S. Army. Decorated Purple Heart, Bronze Star with cluster; recipient Positive Living award K.C., 1977; named Tchr. of Yr., Wrens High Sch., 1981, Coach of Yr., Ga. Athletic Coaches Assn., 1982-83. Democrat. Roman Catholic. Club: Optimist (Wrens, Ga.). Home: 3722 Beacon Hill Dr Hephzibah GA 30815 Office: Wrens High Sch Griffin St Wrens GA 30833

SAMUELS, SEYMOUR, JR., lawyer; b. Nashville, Oct. 23, 1912; s. Seymour and Maude Stella (Rosenfeld) S.; B.A., Vanderbilt U., 1933, LL.B., J.D., 1935; m. Essie Schoen Wenar, July 7, 1937; children—Seymour III, Charles Wenar. Admitted to Tenn. bar, 1935, admitted to practice before U.S. Supreme Ct., Supreme Ct. Tenn., U.S. Ct. Appeals 6th Circuit, U.S. Dist. Ct. and Trial Cts. Tenn.; practicing atty., 1935-40; partner Samuels & Allen, 1940-42; area rent atty., dep. rent dir. OPA, 1942-43; partner Nashville Bag & Burlap Co., 1946-62; dep. dir. law Met. Govt. of Nashville, 1963-67; with Hooker & Willis, 1967; partner Hooker, Hooker, Willis & Samuels, 1968, Farris, Evans & Evans, 1969-71, Farris, Warfield & Samuels, Nashville, 1972-74; affiliate Schulman, LeRoy & Bennett and predecessor firms, Nashville, 1975—; lectr., met. govt. Malone Coll. Mem. Met. Traffic and Parking Commn., 1967-70; chmn. Davidson County Dem. Campaign Com., 1968; mem. Met. Govt. Charter Revision Com.; mem. Met. Transit Authority, 1972-73; mem. Tenn. Bot. Gardens and Fine Arts Center, Nashville Symphony Assn., The Temple. Served with USNR, 1943-46. Mem. Am., Tenn., Nashville bar assns., Am. Judicature Soc., Order of Coif, Artus Club, Phi Beta Kappa. Club: Nashville City. Home: 4487 Post P 68 Nashville TN 37205 Office: 501 Union St Nashville TN 37219

SAMUELS, WILLIAM BENJAMIN, scientist, biology educator; b. Bklyn, Jan. 20, 1952; s. Nathan Lester and Beverly Anne (Yemin) S.; m. Bernice Ellen Marcus, Aug. 15, 1976. B.S. in Biology and Geology, U. Rochester, 1974; M.S. in Marine Sci., L.I. U., 1976; Ph.D. in Biology, Fordham U., 1979. Research fellow N.Y. Ocean Sci. Lab., Montauk, 1975-76, Louis Calder Conservation and Ecology Ctr., Fordham U., Armonk, N.Y., 1976-79; cons. Aquatic Research Systems, Ltd., Ossining, N.Y., 1977-79; oceanographer U.S. Geol. Survey, Reston, Va., 1979-82, U.S. Minerals Mgmt. Service, Reston, 1983-84; sr. scientist Sci. Applications Internat. Corp., McLean, Va.; adj. prof. biology No. Va. Community Coll., Annandale, 1980—. Active, Foster Parents Plan. Jessie Smith Noyes fellow, 1975-76; Fordham U. research fellow, 1976-79; recipient U.S. Geol. Survey Superior Performance award, 1979, 82. Mem. AAAS, Am. Soc. Limnology and Oceanography, N.Y. Acad. Sci., Am. Geophys. Union, Sigma Xi., Contbr. articles to profl. jours. Office: Sci Applications Internat Corp Spl Studies Div 1710 Goodridge Dr McLean VA 22071

SAMUELSON, CHARLES HARRY, energy and commuter company executive; b. Mpls., Oct. 22, 1929; s. Edward E. and Dorothy H. Samuelson; B.A., U. Minn. 1951; M.B.A., U. Pitts., 1961; grad. Naval War Coll., 1966; m. Mary C. Mullen, June 19, 1951; children—Leslee J., Michael E., Mary S. Commd. ensign U.S. Navy, 1951, advanced through grades to comdr., 1966; service in Vietnam, 1966-67; various assignments, U.S., 1967-70, 72; stationed in Philippines, 1970-72; ret., 1972; asst. v.p. Fed. Compress and Warehouse Co., 1973, v.p. and treas., 1974-75; treas. Southwide, Inc., Memphis, 1976-79, v.p., 1978-81; pres. Delinting Systems, Inc., Memphis, 1979-81; exec. v.p. Ring Around Products, Montgomery, Ala., 1981, pres., 1981-82; chmn. bd. G.H. Avery Co., Inc., Memphis, 1982—; chmn. bd. Samuelson-Avery Co., Inc., 1982—, Energy Tech. Fin. Services Co., Inc. Pres., bd. dirs. Jr. Achievement, Memphis, 1975-84; vice chmn., bd. dirs. United Way, Memphis, 1977-80; bd. dirs., trustee Porter Leath Children's Home, Memphis, 1977-84; bd. dirs. Memphis Orchestral Soc.; mem. pres.'s council Southwestern U., Memphis; elder Presbyn. Ch. United States. Decorated Meritorious Service medal, Joint Service medal, Navy Commendation medal; cert. fin. analyst (asso.). Mem. Fin. Analysts Soc., Nat. Cotton Found., Alumni Assn. U. Minn., Alumni Assn. U. Pitts., Memphis Symphony Assn., Landmarks Found., Delta Tau Delta. Republican. Clubs: Chickasaw Country, Summit (Memphis). Lodges: Kiwanis (Memphis); Masons (Mpls.). Home: 4033 Baronne Way Memphis TN 38117 Office: 946 Rayner Memphis TN 38114

SANBORN, RICHARD DYER, lawyer, railroad executive; b. Sanbornville, N.H., June 3, 1936; s. Richard Dyer and Bernice (McCrillis) S.; m. Hilda Joan Penner, July 1, 1977; 1 dau., Cynthia Marie. B.A., U. N.H., 1957; LL.B., Harvard U., 1960. Bar: Fla. Atty., Atlantic Coast Line R.R., Jacksonville, Fla., 1961-73; spl. asst. to pres. Seaboard Coastline R.R., Jacksonville, 1973-80, vice pres., asst. to chmn., 1980-82; sr. v.p. admstrn. Family Lines Rail System, 1982; pres., chief exec. officer Seaboard System R.R. 1982-86; pres., chief exec. officer CSX Distbn. Services, 1986—; dir. 1st Ky. Nat. Corp., RF&P RR. Pres. Central Jacksonville Improvement, Inc., 1984; bd. govs. Jacksonville C. of C., 1982—. Mem. ABA, Mass. Bar Assn., Fla. Bar Assn., Assn. Am. RRs, Am. RR Found. Clubs: River, Timuquana, San Jose, Fla. Yacht (Jacksonville); Commonwealth (Richmond, Va.). Office: Seaboard System RR 500 Water St Jacksonville FL 32202

SANCHEZ, ALBERTO J., SR., consulting engineer; b. Havana, Cuba, Feb. 5, 1939, came to U.S., 1963; s. Manuel and Manuela (Sanchez) S.; m. Nancy M. Montes, Jan. 13, 1962; children—Alberto J., Jr., Beatriz, Diana. B.E. in Mech. Engring., Villanova U., 1965; M.S. in Environ. Engring., Drexel U., 1971. Registered profl. engr., 9 states; cert. energy mgr. Project engr. M. Michael Garber, Phila., 1968-70; project mgr. Kling-Lindquist, Phila., 1970-74; dept. head Watson & Co., Tampa, Fla., 1974-75; div. mgr. DSA Engrs., Tampa, 1975-78; assoc. Best & Hickman, St. Petersburg, Fla., 1978-79; v.p. Carastro, Aguirre & Assocs., Inc., Tampa, 1979—. Author: (with others) Respectful Rehabilitation: A Guide to Housing Rehabilitation in Tampa, 1979. Adv. com. Tampa Bay Vocat. Tech. Sch., 1979—. Mem. ASHRAE (chpt. pres. 1981-82, regional vice chmn. edn. Region XII, 1st place award in energy conservation 1982); Fla. Engring. Soc., Nat. Soc. Profl. Engrs., Assn. Energy Engrs. Republican. Roman Catholic. Clubs: Cuban Civic (dir.), Commerce (Tampa). Lodge: Tampa Rotary. Home: 6836 Mitchell Circle Tampa FL 33614 Office: Carastro Aguirre & Assocs Inc 3636 S Westshore Blvd Tampa FL 33629

SANCHEZ, E. RAMON, banker, engineer, real estate developer; b. Havana, Cuba, Oct. 31, 1944; came to U.S., 1961; s. Jose R. and Bertha (Verdes) S.; m. Idania Dominguez, Dec. 18, 1965; children—Lilly Ann, Lisette, Loury. B.S. in Mech. and Indsl. Engring., U. Nebr., 1966; M.S. in Bus., Bradley U., 1968. Mfg. trainee Internat. Harvester Co., Peoria, Ill., 1966-68; chief engr. Precision Industries, Miami, Fla., 1968-70; plant mgr. Brunor, Miami, 1970-72; pres. Panther Equipment Co., Miami, 1972-83; chmn. bd. under orgn. The Trust Bank, Miami, 1983—; builder Ray San Constrn. Co., Miami, 1974-77. Mem. Inner Circle of U.S. Senate. Roman Catholic. Lodge: Kiwanis (pres., sec., treas.) (Hialeah, Fla.). Home: 7521 Los Pinos Blvd Coral Gables FL 33143 Office: 4445 W 16th Ave Hialeah FL

SANDDAL, ROSS BENNETT, photographer; b. St. Paul, Mar. 21, 1927; s. Ross Carl and Gertrude Annebelle (Bennetts) S.; m. Yvonne Bergman, May 25, 1948; children—Sherry Ann, Jan Marie. B.S., U. Houston, 1949, M.S. in Photography, 1957; M.A. in Photography (hon.), Brooks Inst., Santa Barbara, Calif., 1985. Mgr. photo services group Hughes Tool Div., Houston, 1954—. Monthly columnist The Profl. Photographer, 1979—; contbr. articles to photography mags. Served with USAF, 1945-46, P.R. Mem. Profl. Photographers Am. (hon. life; pres. 1985), Tex. Profl. Photographers Assn. (hon. life; pres. elect 1985, Nat. award 1982), Soc. Photographers in Industry (hon. life; charter mem., 1st pres. 1954-55), Brit. Inst. Profl. Photographers. Republican. Baptist. Lodges: Masons, Shriners. Avocations: writing, auto mechanics, motorcycles. Home: 5827 Cerritos St Houston TX 77035 Office: Hughes Tool Div Photog Services PO Box 2539 Houston TX 77001

SANDERCOX, ROBERT ALLEN, college administrator, clergyman; b. Akron, Ohio, May 20, 1932; s. Monroe John and Elverda Mae (Arnold) S.; m. Nancy Lee Wertz, Sept. 13, 1958; children—Alison Grace, Megan Louise, Robert Philip. B.A., Bethany Coll., 1954; M.Div., Yale U., 1957; postgrad. W.Va. U., U. Buffalo. Ordained to ministry Christian Ch. (Disciples of Christ), 1954. Dir. admissions Bethany Coll., W.Va., 1957-63, v.p., dean students, 1963-75, v.p., provost, 1975—; trustee Christian Ch. (Disciples of Christ), W.Va., 1984—; nat. dir Alpha Sigma Phi, 1980—, v.p., 1985—. Democrat. Clubs: Symposiarchs (Wheeling, W.Va.), Duquesne (Pitts.); Lodge: Rotary. Home: 117 Roosevelt Ave Bethany WV 26032 Office: Bethany Coll Bethany WV 26032

SANDERS, CARL MILLARD, JR., optometrist; b. Sumter, S.C., Nov. 30, 1926; s. Carl M. and Metha (Schnaidt) S.; m. Joan Fite, Sept. 26, 1949 (div. June 1977); m. Patricia Ann Gibson, Nov. 19, 1977; children—Gary, Sharon. Student, Clemson Coll., 1943-44; O.D., So. Coll. Optometry, Memphis, 1949. Lic. optometrist, S.C. Gen. practice optometry, Dillon, S.C., 1950—. Served with USN, 1944-46. Mem. S.C. Optometric Assn., Am. Optometric Assn., Pee Dee Optometric Soc., So. Council Optometry, Sigma Alpha Sigma, Beta Sigma Kappa. Methodist. Lodges: Rotary (past sec., v.p., pres.), Am. Legion, Masons. Avocations: fishing; golfing. Home: 123 Dr Hardy Circle Dillon SC 29536 Office: 106 W Harrison St Dillon SC 29536

SANDERS, HAROLD BAREFOOT, JR., judge; b. Dallas, Feb. 5, 1925; s. Harold Barefoot and May Elizabeth (Forrester) S.; m. Jan Scurlock, June 12, 1931; children—Janet, Martha, Mary, Harold Barefoot III. A.B., U. Tex., 1949, J.D., 1950. State rep. Tex. Ho. of Reps., Austin, 1952-58; U.S. atty. U.S. Dept. Justice, Dallas, 1961-65, asst. dep. atty. gen., Washington, 1965-66, asst. atty. gen. civil div., Washington, 1966-67; legis. counsel to Pres. Lyndon B. Johnson, Washington, 1967-69; U.S. Dist. judge No. Dist. Tex., Dallas, 1979—; trustee Dallas Bar Found., 1981-84. Served to lt. (j.g.) USNR, 1943-46; PTO. Mem. State Bar Assn. Tex., Dallas Bar Assn. (chmn. bd. dirs. 1975-79), ABA. Democrat. Methodist. Office: 1100 Commerce St Dallas TX 75242

SANDERS, JIMMY ROE, safety specialist; b. Nashville, Ark., Oct. 2, 1954; s. Roe Washington and Mabel Elizabeth (Richardson) S.; m. Linda Elaine Hoelscher, June 3, 1973; 1 child, Jason Roe. B.S.M.E. with high honors, U. Ark., 1977. Registered profl. engr., Okla. Facilities engr. Cities Service Co., Tulsa, 1976-78, terminal mgr., Meridian, Miss., 1978-80, engr. III, Tulsa, 1980-81, staff engr., Tulsa, 1981-83; safety mgr. Citgo Petroleum Corp., Tulsa, 1983—; cons. Southeast Tulsa Homeowners Assn., 1985—. Author (reports) Motorcycle Turbo-charging, 1976, Pipeline Tariff Penalties, 1983. Rep. Cities Service Govtl. Action Program, Meridian, 1979-80; youth leader Thornton YMCA, Tulsa, 1984—; mem. Tulsa Area Safety Council, 1984—. Mem. ASME, Nat. Soc. Profl. Engrs., Okla. Soc. Profl. Engrs., Am. Soc. Safety Engrs., Phi Eta Sigma, Tau Beta Pi. Republican. Methodist. Club: Pipeliners (Tulsa). Avocations: coaching; woodworking; automobiles; fishing; boating. Home: 6936 E 76th St Tulsa OK 74133 Office: Citgo Petroleum Corp 6100 S Yale Ave Tulsa OK 74136

SANDERS, LAVINIA GRIFFITH, rancher, conservationist; b. Terrell, Tex., June 25; d. Thomas Bond and Ada Lee (Girand) G.; m. Jan. 15, 1930. Student, St. Mary's Coll., Dallas, Ariz. Sch. Music, So. Meth. U. Legis. chmn. LWV, 1948-52; bd. dirs. Tex. Welfare Assn., Austin, 1950-54; v.p. Daus. Republic of Tex., pres. Charles S. Taylor chpt., 1968; owner, mgr. Griffith League Ranch, Paige, Tex., 1950—. Mem. adv. bd. Atty. Gen. J.B. Shepperd. Democrat. Episcopalian. Clubs: San Antonio Country, Argyle, Dallas Woman's, Dallas City, Browning. Donor Meml. Park to Signers of Declaration of Independence, 1985.

SANDERS, LAWRENCE DOW, IV, system cons., ins. co. exec.; b. San Antonio, Mar. 29, 1939; s. Lawrence Dow and Margaret Helen (Lincecum) S.; B.A. in Math., U. Tex., Austin, 1963; m. Judith Elizabeth Carrabba, Aug. 8, 1971; children—Holly Vincele, Robin Elizabeth. Actuarial asst. Gt. So. Life Ins. Co., Houston, 1965-69; sr. programmer analyst Blue Cross-Blue Shield Tex., Dallas, 1969-71; mgr. actuarial systems TCC, Inc., Austin, 1971-73; project mgr. Am. Nat. Ins. Co., Galveston, Tex., 1973-75, sr. staff analyst, 1976-79, system cons. and mgr. systems planning and coordination, 1979—; data processing cons.; developer generalized computer software; v.p. G&M Investment Group. Served with U.S. Army, 1963-65. Mem. Ins. Accounting and Statis. Assn., Life Office Mgmt. Assn., Data Processing Mgmt. Assn. Home: 1018 Montour St Houston TX 77062 Office: 1 Moody Plaza Galveston TX 77550

SANDERS, LOUIS LEE, JR., internist, educator; b. Little Rock, May 18, 1929; s. Louis Lee and Helen Lucile (Mann) S.; m. Catherine Lenore Schanche, Nov. 9, 1958; children—Leslie, Meredith, Kimberly, Shari. B.S., U. Ark., 1951, M.D., 1955, M.S., 1961. Diplomate Am. Bd. Internal Medicine. Intern, Phila. Gen. Hosp., 1955-56, resident in internal medicine, 1956-57, 59-61; asst prof. internal medicine U. Ark. for Med. Scis., Little Rock, 1962-69, assoc. prof., 1969-80, prof., 1980—; chief endocrinology Little Rock VA Hosp., 1969-75, asst. chief med. service, 1975—. Vice-pres. Ark. chpt. Arthritis Found.; pres. Friends of KLRE-FM, 1983. Served to lt. USNR, 1957-59. Recipient Golden Apple award U. Ark. for Med. Scis., 1964, 78; Outstanding Vol. Service award Arthritis Found., 1981. Fellow ACP; mem. Sigma Xi, Alpha Omega Alpha. Democrat. Methodist. Contbr. articles to med. jours. Home: 6 Pamela Ct Little Rock AR 72207 Office: 4300 W 7th Little Rock AR 72205

SANDERS, LOYD ASTOR, drug abuse consultant; b. Oklahoma City, July 7, 1948; s. Sidney Loyd and Ruth Ester (Hildreth) S.; m. Phyllis A. Sanders, June 25, 1972; children—Kia Ashaun, Sakari Allayne. B.A. in Psychology, Ga. State U., 1977. News trainee WQXI, Atlanta, 1969-70; intake counselor Alcohol & Drug Services, Atlanta, 1972-74, drug counselor, 1974-76, manpower specialist, 1976-77, dir. Southside Drug Ctr., Atlanta, 1977-78; ADC II intake coordinator, 1978—; lectr. Ga. State U., 1979-83, Atlanta U., 1981-83; co-chmn. resource Statewide Minority Advocacy, Atlanta, 1983—. Author/editor: People Feelings I Have Known (poetry book), 1977; screenplay: The Great Hurt-Why People Use Drugs, 1983. Mem. Alpha Phi Alpha. Office: Midtown Intake and Treatment Center 228th St NE Atlanta GA 30309

SANDERS, MARGUERITE DEES, retired educational administrator; b. Many, La., Sept. 1, 1914; d. W.E. and Mary J. (White) Dees; B.A. in Edn., Mathematics and Physics, La. State Normal Coll., Natchitoches, La., 1934; M.Ed. in Secondary Edn., Stephen F. Austin U., Nacogdoches, Tex., 1955; postgrad. U. Colo., Stephen F. Austin U., Baylor U., Northwestern U., 1959-69; m. Horace I. Sanders (dec.); 1 dau., Dorothy Sanders Tidwell. Mathematics coordinator, N. La. Supplemental Edn. Center, Natchitoches, La., 1967-69; curriculum coordinator Title 1, Sabine Parish Sch. Bd., Many, La., 1970-73, dir. Title I, 1973-74, dir. federal programs, 1974-76, asst. supt. Sabine Parish Schs., 1976-80, ret., 1980. Mem. NEA, La. Tchrs. Assn., La. Assn. Sch. Adminstrs. (federally assisted programs), La. Unit Assn. Sch. Curriculum Developers, La. Suprs. Assn., La. Sci. Tchrs. Assn. (pres., sec.), La. Mathematics Assn. Nat. Ret. Tchrs. Assn., So. Ret. Tchrs. Assn., La. Ret. Tchrs. Assn., Delta Kappa Gamma (Psi chpt.), Kappa Delta Pi. Recipient La. Sci. Tchrs. Honor Award, 1963. Author revision of sch. bd. policy manual Sabine Parish Sch. Bd. Home: Route 1 Box 55 Many LA 71449 Office: PO Box 1153 Sabine Parish Sch Bd Many LA 71449

SANDERS, MARIAN AUGUSTA, parent education trainer; b. Detroit, Oct. 11, 1949; d. Louis Raymond and Hula M. (Anderson) Parker; m. Rubin Wardell Sanders, Aug. 7, 1971; children—James Douglas, Marcus William. B.A. in Social Work, U. Detroit, 1971, M.A. in Counseling and Guidance, 1972. Fin. aid counselor, freshman studies counselor Detroit Inst. Tech., 1973-74; asst. fin. aid officer Wayne State U., Detroit, 1974-75; project trainer Pride in Parenting Program Planning Council Virginia Beach (Va.), 1983—; cons. Comprehensive Mental Health Virginia Beach, 1983—. Bd. dirs. Crisis Ctr., Tidewater Child Care Assn., Norfolk Com. for Prevention of Child Abuse. Mem. AAUW, Am. Personnel Guidance Assn. Home: 3797 Lake Tahoe Trail Virginia Beach VA 23456 Office: 1100 First Virginia Bank Tower Norfolk VA 23410

SANDERS, PAUL HERSHEL, JR., architect; b. Houston, Sept. 13, 1945; s. Paul Hershel and Claudia Mae (Ricks) S.; m. Janet Ross Sanders, Oct. 7, 1972; children—Jonathan Ross, Mae Margaret, Leigh Stacey, Laura Elizabeth. B.Arch., Tex. A&M U., 1969, M.Arch., 1970. Registered architect, Tex. Project designer 3/D Internat., Houston, 1969-70; project architect Golemon & Rolfe Assocs., Houston, 1970-72; project mgr. Morris Aubry Assocs., Houston, 1972-74; pres., mng. prin. Sanders & Sanders Assocs., Inc., Houston, 1974—; v.p., sec. Cucine Inc., Houston, 1984—. Prin. archtl. works include Houston Telephone Fed. Credit Union, 1977, Tex. Commerce Bank, Corpus Christi, 1984. Pres. Municipal Utility Dist. 21, Ft. Bend County, Tex., 1980-82; mem. South Main Assn., Houston, 1979—; mem. bd. deacons First Baptist Ch., Houston, 1975—, mem. deacon adminstrv. com., 1980-82, 84-87. Mem. AIA (practice mgmt. com. Houston chpt. 1983-85), Tex. Soc. Architects (com. on interior architecture 1977-79), Houston C. of C. Republican. Clubs: Houston City, Houstonian (Houston). Avocations: jogging; hunting; fishing; reading. Home: 2348 Bolsover St Houston TX 77005 Office: Sanders & Sanders Assocs Inc 2412 South Blvd Houston TX 77098

SANDERS, RICHARD, clinical psychologist; b. N.Y.C., Sept. 15, 1920; s. Charles Sambursky and Ethel Swedelson; m. Gertrude Gallant, June 21, 1942; children—Lee Alan, Kenneth Robert. B.S., CCNY, 1941; M.A., U. Mich., 1948, Ph.D., 1951. Cert. clin. psychologist, Pa., Fla. Clin. psychologist VA Clinic, Madison, Wis., 1950-51, chief clin. psychologist, Milw., 1951-52; asst. chief clin. psychologist VA Hosp., Perry Point, Md., 1952-56; clin. medicine research dir. Phila. State Hosp., 1956-68; dir. research and eval. Thomas Jefferson U., Phila., 1968-71; assoc. regional health adminstr. for mental health HEW, Phila., 1971-80; dir. Sch. Profl. Psychology, Nova U., Ft. Lauderdale, Fla., 1981-84, prof. psychology, 1981-84; pvt. practice psychology, 1984—; assoc. prof. psychiatry Thomas Jefferson Med. Coll., Phila.; mem. small grants com., hosp. improvement grants com. NIMH, mental health projects grants NIMH. Gerontology com. Broward County Bd. Commrs. Served with Signal Intelligence, U.S. Army, 1942-46. NIMH grantee, 1958-64, 64-68, 64-67, 65-68. Fellow Am. Psychol. Assn., Pa. Psychol. Assn., Eastern Psychol. Assn., Phila. Soc. Clin. Psychology. Author: (with Robert S. Smith and Bernard Weinman) Chronic Psychosis and Recovery-An Experimental Approach, 1967; contbr. articles to profl. jours. Home and Office: 4800 NW 73d Ave Lauderhill FL 33319

SANDERS, ROBERT RAYMOND, corporation safety and security administrator; b. Arthur, Ill., Apr. 27, 1944; s. John William and Norma Jean (Schuetz) S.; children—Julie, Rebecca, Patricia. B.S., Maryville Coll., 1976; M.S., Webster Coll., 1978. Cert. safety profl.; cert. protection profl. Police officer, detective Kirkwood Police Dept., Mo., 1969-77; dir. safety, security St. Joseph Hosp., Kirkwood, 1977-80; regional dir. loss prevention Marriott Corp., Washington, 1980-84; corp. dir. safety, security La Quinta Motor Inns, Inc., San Antonio, 1984—; instr. St. Louis Community Coll., Mo., 1977-80, Tarkio Coll., St. Louis, 1977-80, U. Mo., St. Louis, 1977-80. Cardiopulmonary resuscitation instr. Am. Heart Assn., St. Louis, Washington, San Antonio, 1977—. Served with USMC, 1962-66. Named Police Officer of Yr., Optimist Club Am., 1976. Mem. Am. Soc. Safety Engrs. (cert.), Am. Soc. for Indsl. Security (cert., com. chmn. 1982-84), Internat. Assn. Chiefs Police (assoc.), Am. Heart Assn. (affiliate faculty 1982—), Nat. Fire Protection Assn. Office: La Quinta Motor Inns Inc PO Box 32064 San Antonio TX 78216

SANDERS, SHIRLEY, clinical psychologist; b. Phila., Nov. 8, 1935; d. Samuel and Nellie (Shor) S. A.B., U. Miami, 1963; M.A., U. Ky., 1965, Ph.D., 1967. Lic. psychologist, N.C. Asst. prof. U. N.C., Chapel Hill, 1968-77, assoc., 1977-81, clin. assoc. prof., 1981-84, clin. prof., 1984—; practice psychology, Chapel Hill, 1981—; cons. Randolph County Mental Health, Asheboro, N.C., 1968-70; dir. Project Redirect, Siler City, N.C., 1975-78. Contbr. articles to profl. jours. Recipient N.C. State Dept. Catthel award, 1976. Fellow Am. Psychol. Assn., Am. Soc. Clin. Hypnosis (pres. 1982; recognition award 1982), Soc. Clin. and Exptl. Hypnosis (recipient Morton Prince award 1981). Avocations: photography; dance; music. Home: Route 5 Box 228 B Chapel Hill NC 27514 Office: 1829 E Franklin St Suite 101 Chapel Hill 27514

SANDERS, WALTER MACDONALD, III, sanitary engineer; b. Bluefield, W.Va., Dec. 5, 1930; s. Walter M. and Mary E. Sanders, II; m. Emily Joyce, Aug. 4, 1956; children—Emily Graham, Walter McDonald, IV, Albert Brian, Steven Craig. B.S. in Civil Engring., Va. Mil. Inst., 1953; M.S. in Sanitary Engring., John Hopkins U., 1956, Ph.D. in Environ. Engring., 1964. San. engr. officer USPHS, 1956-64; chief freshwater ecosystems br. Environ. Research Lab., EPA, Athens, Ga., 1964-76, assoc. dir. water quality research, 1976-85; environ. cons., 1985—; chmn. tech. adv. com. Chesapeake Bay Program; mem. N.E. Ga. Water Resources Adv. Com., Mem. toxicology program guidance com. U. Ga., research assoc., mem. grad. faculty in ecology, 1967—. Contbr. articles to profl. jours., chpts. to books. Elder, Friendship Presbyn. Ch., 1966—; v.p. Timothy Estates Assn., 1967-68; mem. synods com. on campus Christian Life Presbyn. Ch., 1969-72, chmn., 1972-74, mem. com. on minister and his works; pres. Alps Rd. PTA, 1970-71. Served to 1st lt. USAF, 1953-55.

Recipient citation EPA, 1984, Gold medal, Disting. Career award EPA, 1985; Paul Harris fellow Athens West Rotary, 1985. Mem. Am. Soc. Civil Engrs., AAAS, Am. Orchid Soc., Am. Iris Soc., Sigma Xi. Democrat. Clubs: University of Ga., Athens Torch. Lodge: Rotary (bd. dirs. 1975-79, 80-81, 83—, pres. 1977-78, dist. gov. 1984—). Avocations: photography; raising orchids and other flowering plants. Home: 195 Xavier Dr Athens GA 30606 Office: 195 Xavier Dr Athens GA 30606

SANDERS, WILLIAM EVAN, bishop; b. Natchez, Miss., Dec. 25, 1919; s. Walter Richard and Agnes Mortimer (Jones) S.; B.A., Vanderbilt U., 1942; B.D., U. of South, 1945, D.D., 1959; S.T.M., Union Theol. Sem., 1946; m. Kathryn Cowan Schaffer, June 25, 1951; 4 children. Curate St. Paul's Episcopal Ch., Chattanooga, 1945-46; asst. St. Mary's Cathedral, Memphis, 1946-48, dean, 1948-62; bishop coadjutor Tenn., Knoxville, after 1962, now bishop. Address: PO Box 3807 Knoxville TN 37917*

SANDFORD, CHARLES WILLIAM, JR., chemical engineer; b. Ft. Worth, May 13, 1939; s. Charles William and Maudallen (Young) S.; B.S. in Mech. Engring., Tex. A&M U., 1961; m. Karen Johnson, June 4, 1971; children—James Allen, Elizabeth Anne, Susan Michelle, Marcie Kay. With Union Carbide Co., Seadrift, Tex., 1961-69, sr. process engr., 1965-68, dept. head, 1968-69; mgr. co. projects S.W. Chem. Co., Seabrook, Tex., 1969-71; mgr. ops. and tech. Allied Chem. Co., Baton Rouge, 1971-75; sr. project mgr. Crawford & Russell Co., Houston, 1975; cons. Pace Engrs., Houston, 1975-76; mgr. projects Mobil Chem. Co., Houston, 1976-78, mgr. distbn. engring., 1980—, mgr. chem. planning and coordinator Mobil Sekiyu K.K., Tokyo, 1978-80. Deacon, 1st Presbyn. Ch., Victoria, Tex., 1965-69. Registered profl. engr., Tex. Mem. Soc. Plastics Engrs., Am. Mgmt. Assn. Republican. Co-developer gas phase polymer process; winner Kirkpatrick award for Union Carbide, 1971. Home: 1702 Mossy Stone Dr Houston TX 77077 Office: 15600 Drummet Blvd Houston TX 77032

SANDIFER, BEVERLY ANN, psychologist, educator, consultant; b. Houston, Miss., Sept. 23, 1948; s. George Arnold and Wilma Joyce (McGreger) Hannaford; m. Eddie N. Sandifer, July 9, 1966 (div. Aug. 1982); children—Gregory Neal, Amy LeWynn. B.S., U. So. Miss., 1969, M.Ed., 1976, Ph.D., 1981. Lic. psychologist, Miss. Clin. services supr. Regional Mental Health Complex, Starkville, Miss., 1979-80; asst. prof. counseling psychology U. So. Miss., Hattiesburg, 1980-81, 83—; clin. dir., psychologist Pine Belt Mental Health Services, Hattiesburg, 1981-84; psychologist, exec. dir. Psychol. Services, P.A., 1984—; exec. dir., cons. Potential, Inc., Hattiesburg, 1984—. Contbr. articles to profl. jours. Editor The Miss. Psychologist, 1982-84. Vol. worker United Way, Hattiesburg, 1984-85. Mem. Am. Psychol. Assn., Assn. for Advancement of Behavior Therapy, Miss. Psychol. Assn. Methodist. Avocations: playing organ and piano; scuba diving. Home: 207 Chesterfield Rd Hattiesburg MS 39401 Office: Psychol Services PA 105 Asbury Circle Hattiesburg MS 39401

SANDIFORD, CAROL ANN, mental health administrator; b. Decatur, Ga., Aug. 30, 1941; d. Harold McCall and Catherine Melba (DuVal) Sandiford. Diploma in Nursing, Barrett Sch. Nursing, 1962; B.S.N., U. Cin., 1967; M.Nursing, Emory U., 1972. Team leader, sr. nurse Ga. Mental Health Inst., Atlanta, 1967-68, NIMH project instr., 1968-70, asst. dir. nursing edn., 1972-73; coordinator adult services Gwinnett County Community Mental Health/Mental Retardation, Lawrenceville, Ga., 1973-77; dir. quality assurance Ga. Div. Mental Health/Mental Retardation, Atlanta, 1977-80; dep. supt. Ga. Mental Health Inst., 1980-85; asst. dir. DeKalb County Div. Mental Health/Mental Retardation, 1985—; instr. Floyd County Hosp. Sch. Nursing, Rome, Ga., 1969-70; educator/cons. Continuing Edn., Nursing Unltd., Atlanta, 1977; cons. Annewakee Found., Douglasville, Ga., 1975—; assoc. prof. Emory U. Sch. Nursing, 1983—. Contbr. articles to profl. jours. Mem. Mental Health Assn. Atlanta, 1970—. NIMH scholar, 1966. Mem. Am. Nurses Assn., Ga. Nurses Assn., Sigma Theta Tau. Democrat. Unitarian. Office: DeKalb County Health Dept 440 Winn Way Decatur GA 30030

SANDITEN, EDGAR RICHARD, retail company executive; b. Okmulgee, Okla., Feb. 1, 1920; s. Herman and Anna (Sanditen) S.; student Western Mil. Acad., 1934-37; m. Isabel Raffkind, Jan. 26, 1945; children—Linda Caryl, Judith Marie, Ellen Jane, Michael Jay. B.S. in Bus., Okla. U., 1941. With Otasco, Inc., Tulsa, 1941—, pres., 1974-77, chmn., chief exec. officer, 1977-83, chmn., 1983—; dir. BancOkla. Corp., dir. Bank of Okla., Tulsa. Chmn. United Jewish Appeal, Tulsa, 1960; mem. adv. bd. Tulsa YMCA, 1966—, March of Dimes, 1983—; mem. adv. com. Jr. League, 1977—; chmn. Tulsa Charity Horse Show, 1969-71, 83—; bd. dirs. Tulsa Opera, 1967—, Civic Ballet, 1960-68, Tulsa Econ. Devel. Commn., 1970-84, Tulsa chpt. NCCJ, 1983—; bd. dirs. St. John Med. Center, 1973-83, chmn., 1979-80; trustee Children's Med. Center, 1983—; pres. Temple Israel, 1968-70. Served with USAAF, 1943-46. Recipient Honor award Tulsa Jaycees, 1943. Mem. Tulsa C. of C. (dir. 1977-83, v.p. 1978-79), Okla. C. of C. (dir. 1978—), Quarter Century Club Automotive Industry. Clubs: Summit (dir. 1971-77), So. Hills Country, Meadowbrook Country (Tulsa). Home: 2140 E 30th St Tulsa OK 74114 Office: PO Box 885 Tulsa OK 74102

SANDLE, FLOYD LESLIE, speech educator; b. Magnolia, Miss., July 4, 1913; s. Leslie and Essie Samantha (Hampton) S.; m. Marie Johnson, June 11, 1941; children—Gail, Ava, Wanda, Floyd Jr., Anthony. A.B., Dillard U., 1937; M.A., U. Chgo., 1947; Ph.D., Wash. State U., 1959. Head dept. speech and drama Grambling State U., La., 1952-63, dean div. gen. studies, 1963-78; prof. speech La. State U., Baton Rouge, 1972-73; chmn. humanities div. Dillard U., New Orleans, 1978—; pres. Conf. La. Colls. and Univs., 1976-77. Author: (textbook) Orientation: An Image of the College, 1967; (textbook) The Negro in the American Educational Theatre, 1964. Served with USN, 1944-45. Mem. Nat. Assn. Dramatics and Speech Arts (pres. 1955-57). Office: Dillard Univ Div Humanities 2610 Gentilly Blvd New Orleans LA 70122

SANDLIN, GEORGE WALTER RAOUL, real estate investment broker, realtor; b. Austin, Tex., Nov. 27, 1943; s. George Wilson and Ruth Ina (Zollinger) S.; m. Susan Scarborough, June 11, 1983. Realtor assoc. Sandlin & Co., Austin, 1970-72, mgr. residential dept., 1972-75, mgr. comml. and investment dept., 1975-77, dir. property mgmt. and investment div., 1977—; v.p. Realty Investment Corp.; dir. Internat. Creations; v.p. Sandlin Mortgage Corp. Served with USNR, 1966-70; Vietnam. Recipient citation for spl. combat ops. Vice Adm. M.F. Weisner, 1970. Mem. Nat. Assn. Realtors, Tex. Assn. Realtors, Austin Bd. Realtors (bd. dirs. 1984—, sec.-treas. 1984, pres. bd. govs. comml. investment div. 1976-79, bd. govs. 1984—. Republican. Episcopalian. Home: 8330 Summerwood Dr Austin TX 78759 Office: 308 W 15th St Austin TX 78701

SANDLIN, GEORGE WILSON, real estate broker, mortgage banker; b. Glen Rose, Tex., May 13, 1912; s. Walter Algie and Margaret (Parks) S.; student pub. schs., also Schreiner Inst.; m. Ruth Ina Zollinger, Sept. 21, 1941 (dec. Feb. 27, 1975); children—George Walter Raoul, Carole Ruth, Sarah Louise, Margaret Ina. Field rep. HOLC, San Antonio, 1934-36; pres. Sandlin Mortgage Corp., Austin, Tex.; owner Sandlin & Co., 1936—; chmn. bd., pres. Internat. Creations, Inc.; pres., dir. Trans-Pacific Resorts, Inc.; pres. Profl. Arts, Inc.; ind. fee appraiser. Chmn., Tex. Real Estate Commn., 1949-55. Mem. Austin City Planning Commn., 1947-52, chmn., 1951-52. Chmn. Tex. Dem. Exec. Com., 1954-56. Pres. chmn. bd. Tex. Found., 1955—. Served as lt. comdr. USNR, World War II; PTO. Recipient silver citizenship medal Vets. Fgn. Wars, 1957. Mem. Tex. Assn. Realtors (pres. 1979), Austin Real Estate Bd. (past pres.), Inst. Real Estate Mgmt., Mortgage Bankers Assn., Nat. Assn. Realtors (dir.), Am. Legion, V.F.W. Episcopalian. Clubs: Austin Country, Headliners. Home: 1801 Lavaca St Apt 7L Austin TX 78701 Office: 6010 Balcones Dr Austin TX 78731

SANDLIN, MICHAEL ARTHUR, home builder; b. Ft. Worth, July 5, 1954; s. Johnny Bartow and Mary Louise (DeGrauwe) S.; m. Eva Julia Zeller, June 28, 1980; 1 son, Jonathan Behn. B.S. in Home Building, Trinity U., 1976. Registered real estate broker, Tex. Pres. Mike Sandlin Homes, Ft. Worth, 1976—; dir. Bank of Hurst, Active Rotary Internat., C. of C. Mem. Homebuilders Assn. Ft. Worth and Tarrant County (dir.), Nat. Assn. Homebuilders (life spike 1981). Republican. Roman Catholic. Home: 604 Live Oak Dr Euless TX 76040 Office: 5137 Davis Blvd Ft Worth TX 76118

SANDOZ, THOMAS REYNOLDS, JR, newspaper executive; b. San Antonio, June 4, 1947; s. Thomas Reynolds and Mary (Frandolig) S.; m. Brenda Bayless, June 16, 1979; 1 child, Thomas Reynolds III. B.B.A., Tex. Tech U., 1969. Maj. account rep. Dallas Morning News, 1971-73, exec. trainee, 1974-77, asst. to dir., 1977-78, classified advt. mgr., 1978-81, retail advt. mgr., 1982—. Mem. Leadership Dallas, 1983, Leadership Dallas Alumni Assn., 1984—. Mem. Dallas Advt. League (pres. 1985-86, Outstanding Mem. award 1979), Tex. Tech Mass Communications Alumni Assn. (pres. 1981-83), Internat. Newspaper Advt./Mktg. Execs. Republican. Presbyterian. Clubs: Lakewood Golf, Calyx Mens (Dallas). Avocations: golf, skeet shooting. Home: 3436 Stanford St Dallas TX 75225 Office: Dallas Morning News Communications Ctr Dallas TX 75222

SANDRIDGE, ROBERT LEE, chemist; b. Junior, W.Va., June 12, 1932; s. Howard C. Sandridge and Ariel (Putnam) Morris; m. Frances Ilene Mahon, May 22, 1953; children—Michael, Jennifer, Becky, Brian, Susan. B.S., West Liberty State Coll., 1954; M.S., W.Va. U., 1958, Ph.D., 1969. Sr. chemist Mobay Chem. Corp., New Martinsville, W.Va., 1958-67, group leader, 1967-73, sr. group leader, 1973-78, analytical mgr., 1978-82, mgr. analytical and environ. research, 1982—. Contbr. articles to encys. Bd. dirs., treas. Mobay Employees Fed. Credit Union, New Martinsville, 1970—. Served to lt. (j.g.) USNR, 1954-56. Mem. Am. Chem. Soc., Internat. Isocyanate Inst. (chmn. analytical com. 1978—), Chem. Mfrs. Assn. (mem. phosgene safety com.). Republican. Methodist. Club: Spieler's (Proctor, W.Va.) (bd. dirs.). Avocation: sailboat cruising and racing. Office: Mobay Chem Corp New Martinsville WV 26155

SANDS, DON WILLIAM, agricultural products company executive; b. Durant, Okla., Aug. 30, 1926; s. William Henry and Mary (Crutchfield) S.; m. Joan Cantrell, Mar. 28, 1947; children—Susan Sands Stone, Stan W., Steve J. B.S., Southeastern Okla. State U., 1949. Office mgr. Durant Cotton Oil & Peanut Corp., Okla., 1949-53; asst. mgr. Greenwood Products Co., Graceville, Fla., 1953-57; with Cotton Producers Assn., (changed name to Gold Kist Inc., 1970); exec. v.p. GoldKist Inc., Atlanta, 1978-84, pres., 1984—; dir. C & S Agribusiness Adv. Bd., Atlanta, C & S Comml. Bank, Ill. Coop. Futures Co., Chgo., Roper Corp., Kankakee, Ill., In Trade, Inc., Curacao, Netherlands Antilles. Adv. bd. mem. Inst. Internat. Edn., Atlanta, 1980, Japan-U.S. Southeast Assn., Atlanta, 1975; bd. dirs. Ga. Bd. Industry and Trade, Atlanta, 1979. Served with USN, 1944-46. Mem. Ga. C. of C. (dir.). Democrat. Presbyterian (elder). Club: Atlanta Athletic (pres.). Office: Gold Kist Inc 244 Perimeter Ctr Parkway Atlanta GA 30346

SANDS, DORIS MARIE, worldwide directional drilling company administrator; b. Louisville, Sept. 4, 1934; d. Bruce W. and Edith F. (Young) Franklin; m. George G. King Jr., July 31, 1953 (div.); children—Cynthia L. and Kimberly E. Bryce; m. 2d Milton Howard Sands, Jr., Aug. 21, 1976. Bus. degree, Atherton Bus. Coll., 1954. Cert. exec. sec. Sec. Ky. Village State Correction Home, Lexington, 1954-56; with Registrar's Office, San Jacinto Coll., Houston, 1966-74; sec. to 10 coaches Houston Oilers Profl. Football Team, Houston, 1974-76; sec. to dir. broadcasting Houston Astros Baseball Team, 1976-78; exec. sec. to v.p. Eastern Hemisphere Eastman Whipstock, Inc., Houston, 1978-79, adminstrv. services supr., 1979—; mem. exec. bd. U.S. Postal Forum. Sec. Arlington Hts. Civic Club, Houston, 1966-68; pres. Arlington Hghts. Garden Club, Houston, 1965-68; vol. Harris County Mentally Retarded Assn., Houston, 1968-74; ednl. dir. Eta Omicron Internat. Ednl. Orgn., 1968-69, pres., 1969-70; v.p. Pasadena Jr. Forum, (Tex.), 1970-71, sec., 1971-72; pres. Shell Oil Co. Wives Club, 1971-73; mem. Rep. Nat. Com; Rep. Party Precinct Judge, Harris County, Houston, 1970-75; vol. Crisis Hotline, Houston, Heart Found., PARA Orgn., Rep. Party, Galveston County, Tex. Recipient Presdients' award Eastman Whipstock, Inc., 1981-82. Mem. LWV. Lutheran. Author many in-house administrative manuals for Eastman Whipstock, Inc., 1979-82. League City TX Office: 2525 Holly Hall Houston TX 77054

SANDS, KITI, financier, designer, realtor, health, nutrition, beauty and fashion consultant; b. N.J.; d. Frank and Muriel (Kulla) Reiner; m. Ira Sands, 1975; children—Nelson Anthony, Tiffany Ivy, Summer Paige. Student NYU, 1974 Cosmetology and Estheticians Sch. Cert. cosmetologist and esthetician. Asst. to Monsieur Jacques as dir. of Antoines de Paris; ptnr. Claredon Capital Group, N.Y., Fla.; pres., dir. Tiffany Ivy Yacht Interiors Inc., Tiffany Sands, Inc., Tiffany Ivy Interiors Inc.; founder, pres. Bio Cellular Systems, Inc., Fla.; Dr.'s Diet Day Spas, Fla., v.p. dir. New Capital Mgmt. Inc., Fla., Bio-Med Acne Ctr., Fla.; sec. L.K. Inc., Fla.; propr., mgr., dir. Park Ave. Salon for Hair Color Cons., N.Y.; researcher and developer of skin care and hair-coloring processes and formulae; columnist and feature writer on diet control, nutrition, hair coloring; lectr. on image creation and nutrition mgmt. for working persons to women's orgns., med. personnel, tchrs., bank officials; former Aquacade swimmer. Recipient Disting. Service citation Indsl. Home for Blind, 1976, Disting. Mem. award City of Hope, 1977, Diploma of Jingles Internat., Certs. of Achievement for Acad. and Inst., Clairol, Clairol Certs. of award for outstanding hair coloring expertise, Certs. of Achievement for higher edn. in art of profl. hair coloring. Mem. Congress of Colorists (qualified), Ind. Cosmetic Mfrs. and Distbrs. Assn. Miami FL

SANDS, LU ALICE, librarian; b. Montgomery County, Tenn., Dec. 30, 1926; d. Bailey Gay and Betty Marable (Minor) Lyle; B.A., George Peabody Coll., 1947; M.A., Fla. State U., 1961; postgrad. Emory U., 1967, Christ Church Coll., Oxford, Eng., 1983; m. John Earl Sands, Nov. 25, 1947; 1 son, Alan Minor. Head children's services S. Ga. Regional Library, Valdosta, 1956-59; dir. library and learning resources N. Fla. Jr. Coll., Madison, 1960—; cons. in field. Trustee Suwannee River Regional Library, Live Oak, Fla., 1972-74. Mem. Fla., Southeastern library assns. Democrat. Methodist. Author: Basic Materials for Junior College Libraries: Books: Philosophy, Religion, Art, and Music, 1963. Editor: Fla. Libraries, 1971-72. Home: 115 Hancock St SE Madison FL 32340 Office: North Florida Jr Coll Madison FL 32340

SANDT, HARTLEY, fiberglass company executive; b. N.Y.C., Apr. 4, 1924; s. Robert and Alberta (Hartley) S.; B.S. in Mech. Engring., CCNY, 1948; M.B.A., U. Dayton, 1978; m. Muriel Turnbell, Apr. 6, 1945; children—Mary Lou Kesting, Peter Hartley, Richard John. Sales rep., product mgr. Johns-Manville Sales Corp., N.Y.C., 1948-67, v.p., gen. mktg. mgr. Johns-Manville Internat. Corp., N.Y.C., 1967-70; v.p. Price Brothers Co., Dayton, 1970—; pres. McClean-Anderson Inc., Milw., 1977-83; pres. H-C Composites, Inc., Green Cove Springs, Fla., 1978—; adj. prof. Grad. Sch. Bus. Adminstrn., U. Dayton, 1979-80; instr. mgmt. Fla. Jr. Coll., Jacksonville, 1982—. Served with AUS, 1943-46. Mem. Am. Water Works Assn. Clubs: Timuquana Country, University, Elks, Rotary. Author: The Public Relations Manual, 1st edit. 1965. Home: 2425 Dogwood Ln Orange Park FL 32073 Office: PO Box B Green Cove Springs FL 32043

SANFORD, LESLIE MCHENRY, JR., naval officer; b. Penola, Va., Apr. 20, 1946; s. Leslie McHenry and Aleeyne Genivieve (Peatross) S.; B.S., Va. Poly. Inst., 1968, also B.A.; postgrad. U. West Fla., 1974-77; m. Brenda Ann Hayes, Aug. 14, 1971; children—Shelley Wray, Kristin Ann, Brian Wade, Albert Earl, Sara Beth. Commd. ensign U.S. Navy, 1968, advanced through grades to lt. comdr., 1979; bombardier, navigator Attack Squadron 75, 1972-74; instr. Naval Air Tng. Command, Pensacola, Fla., 1974-77; aircraft schedules coordinator Aircraft Ferry Squadron 31, Norfolk, Va., 1977-80; A-6 project officer Naval Air Rework Facility, Norfolk, 1980—. Decorated Air medal (16); Vietnamese Cross of Gallantry; numerous other decorations and awards. Mem. U.S. Naval Inst. (life), Am. Def. Preparedness Assn. (life), Tailhook Assn. (life), AAUP, Rotating Beacon Assn., Va. Poly. Inst. and State U. Alumni Assn. Republican. Methodist. Home: 4599 Steeplechase Dr Virginia Beach VA 23464 Office: Naval Air Rework Facility Naval Air Station Norfolk VA 23511

SANFORD, MARION, JR., lawyer, lobbyist; b. Lubbock, Tex., Jan. 2, 1941; s. Marion and Mary McGrath (Drane) S.; m. Judith Kendall Forsythe, Jan. 29, 1966; children—Alexis Walcott, Marion Kendall. B.A., U. Tex.-Austin, 1963, LL.B., 1966. Bar: Tex. 1966. Assoc., Liddell, Sapp, Zivley, Brown & LaBoon, Houston, 1966-74; assoc. Vinson & Elkins, Houston, 1974-76, ptnr., 1977—; adj. prof. So. Tex. Coll. Law, Houston, 1980—. Chmn. small firms United Fund, Houston, 1968; active local polit. campaigns. Named Outstanding Lobbyist in Tex., Tex. Monthly, 1976; recipient Presdl. award Houston Apt. Assn., 1982; Outstanding Service award Assn. Exec. Council Nat. Apt. Assn., 1984. Mem. ABA, Tex. Bar Assn., Houston Bar Assn. (chmn. legislation com. 1978-80), Houston C. of C. (chmn. various coms.). Democrat. Roman Catholic. Clubs: Tejas Breakfast, Headliners, Houston (Houston). Office: Vinson & Elkins 2809 First City Tower Houston TX 77002

SANFORD, TERRY, university president emeritus, lawyer; b. Laurinburg, N.C., Aug. 20, 1917; s. Cecil and Elizabeth (Martin) S.; A.B., U. N.C., 1939, J.D., 1946; m. Margaret Rose Knight, July 4, 1942; children—Elizabeth Knight, Terry. Asst. dir. Inst. of Govt., U. N.C., 1940-41, 46-48; spl. agt. FBI, 1941-42; admitted to N.C. bar, 1946; practiced in Fayetteville, 1948-60; partner firm Sanford, Adams, McCullough & Beard, Raleigh, N.C., 1965—; gov. N.C., 1961-65; pres. Duke U., Durham, N.C., 1969-85, pres. emeritus, 1985—; public gov. Am. Stock Exchange. Dir. Study of Am. States. Duke, 1965-68; mem. Carnegie Commn. Ednl. TV, 1964-67; pres. Urban Am., Inc., 1968-69; chmn. ITT Internat. Fellowship Com.; chmn. Am. Council Young Polit. Leaders; adv. council Pacific Am. Inst., Inc. Sec.-treas. N. C. Port Authority, 1950-53, mem. N.C. Senate, 1953-54; pres. N.C. Young Dem. Clubs, 1949-50; del. Nat. Dem. Conv., 1956, 60, 64, 68, 72, 84; chmn. Nat. Dem. Charter Commn., 1972-74; mem. governing bd. Nat. Com. for Citizens in Edn., Am. Art Alliance; trustee Cordell Hull Found. Internat. Edn., Am. Council Learned Socs., 1970-73, Nat. Humanities Center, Meth. Coll., Howard U.; bd. dirs. Children's TV Workshop, 1967-71. Council on Founds., 1971-76, N.C. Outward Bound, 1981—, Nat. Acad. Public Adminstrs.; chmn. So. Regional Edn. Bd., 1961-63. Appalachian Community Service Network, 1980—, Assn. Am. Univs., 1980-81, com. for Dem. Studies, 1981—. Served to 1st lt. AUS, 1942-46. Mem. Am. Bar Assn., Am. Acad. Polit. and Social Sci., Am. Judicature Soc., Am. Arbitration Assn. (dir.), Nat. Municipal League (v.p.). Methodist. Author: But What About the People?, 1966; Storm Over the States, 1967; A Danger of Democracy, 1981. Office: Duke U Durham NC 27706

SANG, HERB, educational administrator. Supt. of schs. Duval County, Fla. Office: 1701 Prudential Dr Jacksonville FL 32207*

SANGSTER, ESTHER VIRGINIA, hospital official, nurse; b. Clermont, Fla., Feb. 2, 1950. B.S. in Nursing, U. North Fla., 1981; M.S. in Nursing, U. South Fla., 1986. Cert. advanced nurse practitioner. Dir. profl. services Upjohn Co., Jacksonville, Fla., 1980-82; dir. organizational devel. Tampa Gen. Hosp., Fla., 1983—. Mem. Am. Nurses Assn., Fla. Nurses Assn. (chmn. com. continuing edn. 1983—, dir. 1979-82, chmn. legis. com. 1981-83), LWV. Democrat. Avocations: jogging, tennis; scuba diving; skiing. Home: 909 S Fremont Tampa FL 33606 Office: Tampa Gen Hosp Davis Island Tampa FL 33606

SANII, EZAT TOLLAH, engineering educator; b. Bojnord, Iran, Apr. 21, 1951; came to U.S., 1974; s. Amanollah and Fatemeh Sanii; B.Sc. in Indsl. Engring., Arya-Mehr U. Tech., Iran, 1973; M.Sc. in Indsl. Engring., Purdue U., 1975, Ph.D., 1982. Registered profl. engr. N.C. Mfg. engr. Brown & Sharp Mfg. Co., North Kingstown, R.I., 1975-76; instr. Purdue U., West Lafayette, Ind., 1976-80; asst. prof. U. Miami, Coral Gables, Fla., 1980-83; asst. prof. engring. N.C. State U., Raleigh, 1983—; cons. various orgns. Miami, 1980-83, Raleigh, 1983—; mem. professionalism com. N.C. State U., 1985, mem. artificial intelligence com., 1984-85. Recipient Research Project awards Integrated Mfg. Systems, Engring., 1984-85. Mem. Inst. Indsl. Engrs. (sr.), Soc. Mfg. skiing. (sr.), Computer Automated Systems Assn., Robotics Internat. Avocations: tennis; skiing. Home: 1299 A Schaub Dr Raleigh NC 27606 Office: N C State U Dept Indsl Engring Box 7906 Raleigh NC 27695

SANSBURY, OLIN BENNETT, JR., university administrator; b. Florence, S.C., Dec. 10, 1937; s. Olin Bennett and Gladys Ruth (Snipes) S.; m. Helen Cecile Hyman, Aug. 24, 1963; 1 son, Olin Bennett, III. B.A. in History, Wofford Coll., 1959; Ph.D. in Internat. Studies, U. S.C., 1972. Reporter, editorial writer WBTW-TV, Florence, 1963-64, 1966-67; asst. dir. student affairs U. S.C., Florence, 1969-70; dean students Francis Marion Coll., Florence, 1970-71; asst. vice provost, asst. prof. govt. and internat. studies U. S.C., Columbia, 1971-73; chancellor, assoc. prof. govt. and internat. studies, U. S.C., Spartanburg, S.C., 1973—. Bd. dirs. S.C. Council Econ. Edn., 1977—; founding com. Leadership Spartanburg, 1980—. Served with U.S. Army, 1960-63. H.B. Earhart fellow, 1965-66, 69. Mem. Am. Assn. State Colls. and Univs., Internat. Studies Assn., So. Polit. Sci. Assn., S.C. Polit. Sci. Assn. Episcopalian. Office: U South Carolina Spartanburg SC 29303

SANSONE, FREDRICK RAWLS, television producer; b. Miami, May 11, 1952; s. Alfred G. and Rose Anne (Malyk) S. B.G.S., U. Miami, 1974. Producer, The Larry King Show, Sta. WIOD, Miami, 1975-78; ops. mgr. Sta. WNWS, Miami, 1978-79; producer To the Point, Sta. WCIX, Miami, 1979-81; exec. producer Frankly Speaking with Dr. Kathy Peres, Sta. WCIX, Miami, 1981-84, exec. producer Frankly Speaking with Chuck Zink, 1984-85, sta. editorial coordinator, 1983-85; v.p. Sadler Galleries, Inc., 1983—; producer/-dir. Miami-Dade Community Coll., 1985—. Recipient Outstanding Media award Dade County Psychol. Assn., 1982. Mem. Assn. Media Psychology, Nat. Acad. TV Arts and Scis. (Emmy award 1979, 82), Mensa. Office: 3000 N Ocean Blvd Suite 103 Fort Lauderdale FL 33308

SANTANDER, JULIO ALEJANDRO, mechanical engineer, educator; b. Caracas, Venzezuela, Sept. 24, 1943; s. Julio Emigdio and Solita Margarita (Palmero) S.; came to U.S. Aug. 1963; m. Mary Melissa Middleton, 1966; children—Andrew Michael, Jessica Elizabeth, Allison Mary. B.S.M.E., U. Mich., 1968; M.S.M.E., Ga. Inst. Tech., 1975. Plant supt. Internat. Milling Co., Valencia, Venezuela, 1968-69; resident engr. Ford Motor Co., Valencia, 1969-70; assoc. prof. U. Carabobo, Valencia, 1970-82, head physics dept., 1970-72, head mech. engring. research ctr., 1977-78; design engr. Williams-Russell-Johnson, Atlanta, 1981-82; research assoc. Ga. Inst. Tech., Atlanta, 1982-83; asst. prof. So. Tech. Inst., Marietta, Ga., 1983—. Author: Experimental Physics, 1973; Applied Thermodynamics, 1977; also monographs, articles. Treas. Troop 651, Boy Scouts Am., Atlanta, 1983. Gulf Oil Co. scholar, 1964. Mem. ASME, ASHRAE. Home: 3422 Ashwood Ln Chamblee GA 30341 Office: Southern Technical Institute 1112 Clay St Marietta GA 30060

SANTANGELO, NICOLO ANTHONY, economist; b. Bklyn., Feb. 22, 1930; s. Philip and Maria (Costa) S.; m. Alma Joyce Hopkins, May 11, 1953; children—Susan L., Judith E., M. John, Philip N., William J., Nicolo A., Jr. B.B.A., U. Tex.-El Paso, 1972. Field economist U.S. Dept. Labor, Dallas, 1973-78; chief econ. analysis and info. Bur. Labor Stats., U.S. Dept. Labor, Dallas, 1979—. Served to lt. col. U.S. Army, 1948-70; Korea, Viet Nam. Decorated Bronze Star, Air medal, Joint Services Commendation medal, Commendation medal with four oak leaf clusters. Home: 4021 Greenway Garland TX 75041 Office: US Dept of Labor Bur of Labor Statistics 525 Griffin St Room 221 Dallas TX 75202

SANTIAGO, EUGENIO MARDONIO, civil engineer; b. Placetas, Cuba, Aug. 7, 1944; came to U.S., 1961; s. Mardonio Rodrigo and Aleida Estela (Retana) S.; B.S., U. Miami, 1972; m. Pury López; children—Patricia Cristina, Amalia Eugenia, Daniel Eugenio. Draftsman, chief draftsman, structural engr. Crain & Crouse Engrs., Miami, Fla., 1968-69; structural engr. Planas, Franyie & Santiago, Inc., Miami, 1969-70, head structural dept., 1970-76, v.p., 1976; v.p., br. mgr. Mich. Testing Engrs. of Fla., Inc., Miami, 1976-79; v.p., head structural dept. Profl. Assoc. Cons. Engrs., Coral Gables, Fla., 1979-80; pres. Santiago & Assos./Engrs., Inc., Miami, 1980—. Registered profl. engr., Fla. Mem. Am. Concrete Inst. (past v.p. South Fla. chpt., mem. joint Am. Concrete Inst.-ASCE 421 com.), Portland Cement Assn., Prestressed Concrete Inst., Am. Welding Soc., Am. Soc. Nondestructive Testing, Film Soc. Miami (founder, pres., program dir. Cine-Club film series). Home: 9460 SW 31st Terr Miami FL 33165 Office: 3383 NW 7th St Suite 210 Miami FL 33125

SANTIAGO, GLADYS, govt. librarian; b. Guaynabo, P.R., Jan. 12, 1929; d. Pedro and Julia (Rodríguez) S.; B.A., U. P.R., 1955, M.L.S., 1971; m. Ángel Meléndez, July 20, 1974. Asst. librarian P.R. Dept. Health, Bayamón Dist. Hosp., 1949-60, P.R. Bur. of Budget, Office of Gov., 1960-72; chief librarian reference dept. Inter-Am. U., Met. Br., P.R., 1972-75; dir. library P.R. Office of Mgmt. and Budget, San Juan, 1975—; del. White House Conf. Libraries and Info. Services, 1981. Recipient merit certs. for disting. public service Govt. of P.R., 1968, 71, 79, 81; P.R. Govt. grantee, 1970-71. Mem. NEA, P.R. Tchrs. Assn., Sociedad de Bibliotecarios de P.R., Alumni Assn. of Sch. Library Sci. of U. P.R., Found. Christian Living. Club: Loyalty. Home: 4th St H-25 Urb Monte Verde Toa Alta PR 00758 Office: 254 Cruz y Tetuan San Juan PR 00904

SANTIAGO, RAUL JORGE, accounting executive; b. Havana, Cuba, Nov. 2, 1936; s. Raul and Margarita (Andino) S.; m. Carmen Garcia, May 3, 1958; children—Ana Maria, Raul Jose, Carmen; came to U.S., 1967. B.B.A. in Acctg., Fla. Internat. U. C.P.A., Fla. Br. mgr. Godoy Sayan Bank, Havana, 1955-63, chief acct. Havana constrn. co., 1963-64; owner, mgr. R.J. Santiago C.P.A., Hialeah, Fla., 1968—. Mem. Cuban Am. C.P.A.s (treas. 1981-82); Fla.

Inst. C.P.A.s, Am. Inst. C.P.A.s. Republican. Roman Catholic. Club: Big Five. Address: Raul J Santiago CPA 221 E 49th St Hialeah FL 33013

SANTIAGO, ROSA EMILIA, sales and marketing executive; b. Havana, Cuba, Nov. 17, 1935; came to U.S., 1960; d. Emilio and Rosa (Fernandez) S.; m. Pedro P. Llaguno, July 19, 1963 (div. 1976); children—Rosa E., Peter E., Paul E. B.A. with honors, Fla. Internat. U., 1977. With sales and mktg. dept. Holiday Inn, Coral Gables, Fla., 1975-78, mktg. dir., 1983—; sales mgr. Holiday Rent-a-Car, Miami, Fla., 1978-79, v.p., 1981; mktg. dir. Ramada Inn/Airport, Miami, 1981; S.E. dist. mktg. dir. Holiday Rent-a-Car System, Miami, 1981-82; pres. U.S. Aviation Showcase, Inc., 1986—; instr. div. tourism St. Thomas U., Miami, 1979-84, also mem. student adv. com.; mktg. dir. Holiday Inn/Coral Gables (Fla.); assoc. editor tourism mag., 1976—; free-lance rep. Vice chmn. Tequesta dist. Boy Scouts Am.;past mem., media dir. Coalition Hispanic Am. Women; co-chmn. pub. relations Council for Internat. Visitors; mem. Congl. Citizens Council on Hispanic and Minority Affairs; trustee Hispanic United Families Assn. Recipient Wood badge Boy Scouts Am., 1978, Dist. award of merit, 1984, Silver Beaver award, 1985. Mem. Coral Gables C. of C., Alexander von Humboldt Soc. Ams. (v.p.), Internat. Platform Assn., Venezuelan C. of C. (dir. pub. relations), Phi Lambda Pi. Democrat. Roman Catholic. Home: 9412 SW 4th Ln Miami FL 33174 Office: Holiday Inn 2051 LeJeune Rd Coral Gables FL 33134

SANTIESTEBAN, H. TATI, lawyer, state senator; b. El Paso, Tex., Nov. 3, 1934; s. Ricardo and Carmen S.; m. Sue McMillen, Dec. 26, 1956; children—Volorie Lynn Santiesteban Whittenton, Stephanie Diane Santiesteban Salinas, Ricardo Tati. B.A., N.Mex. Mil. Inst.; J.D., U. Tex. Austin. Bar: Tex. Practice law, El Paso, ptnr. Santiesteban and Assocs., El Paso; mem. Tex. Senate. Com. chmn. presdl. campaign Johnson-Humphrey, 1964; keynote speaker State Democratic Conv., 1976. Roman Catholic. Office: Santiesteban and Assocs 747 E San Antonio St El Paso TX 79901

SAPOSNIK, RUBIN, economics educator; b. Chgo., July 11, 1929; m. Marlene Taber, June 6, 1960; children—Alicia Anne, Andrea Lynn. Ph.B., U. Chgo., 1949, B.S., 1950, M.A., 1951; Ph.D., U. Minn., 1959. Instr., then asst. prof. Purdue U., Lafayette, Ind., 1956-63; assoc. prof. SUNY-Buffalo, 1963-66; prof. econs. U. Kans.-Lawrence, 1966-70, Ga. State U., Atlanta, 1970-77, 81—, U. Ky.-Lexington, 1977-81; article reviewer Am. Math. Soc., Ann Arbor, Mich., 1976—. Co-author: General Equilibruim and Welfare, 1968. Contbr. articles to profl. publs. Mem. Am. Econ. Assn., Econometric Soc., So. Econ. Assn. (editorial bd. 1973-76), Pub. Chioce Soc. Home: 2595 Woodwardia Rd Atlanta GA 30345 Office: Ga State U Dept Econs Atlanta GA 30303

SARGENT, LEALON LEE, oil company executive; b. Clinton, Okla., July 16, 1930; s. Luther Guy and Inez (Cooke) S.; m. S. Elizabeth Gumm, Dec. 28, 1955; children—Steven, Patti, Mike. B.S. in Geology, U. Okla., 1958; Advanced Mgmt. Program in Bus., Harvard U., 1976. Sr. v.p. Tenneco Oil, Houston, 1958-81; pres. Hamilton N.Am., Denver, 1981-82, ENI Exploration, Houston, 1982-83; chmn. chief exec. officer, pres. Petro Corp., Inc., Houston, 1983—; dir. Allied Bank, North Belt, Houston, Sch. Geology, U. Okla., Monument Energy, Houston. Chmn. friends of scouting Polaris council Boy Scouts Am., 1978-80. Served to sgt. USAF, 1948-52, Korea. Mem. Am. Assn. Petroleum Geologists, Am. Gas Assn., Ind. Petroleum Assn. Am., Houston N.W. C. of C. (dir. 1976-80). Republican. Baptist. Clubs: Raveneaux Country, Greenspoint (dir. 1985—). Avocations: fishing, bird hunting. Home: 16023 Mickleham Dr Houston TX 77379 Office: Petro Corp Inc 16800 Greenspoint Park Dr Suite 300 N Atrium Houston TX 77060

SARGENT, WILLIAM EARL, educator; b. Balt., Aug. 2, 1919; s. Edward Brown and Lucy Edna (Simms) S.; B.A. in History, Am. U., 1953, M.Ed. in Adminstrn. and Supervision, 1963; postgrad. Va. Poly. Inst. and State U. Cert. elem. tchr., sch. counselor, Va. Dir., Burgundy Farm Country Day Sch., Alexandria, Va., 1960-63; elem. classroom tchr., Arlington County, Va., 1954-60, 67-70, 77-78, tchr. seminar for gifted elem. students, 1963-67, sch. social worker, 1970-72, child devel. cons., 1972-76, elem. sci. tchr., 1976-77, tchr. English as 2d lang., 1978-79; team leader, asst. to dir. Arlington-Trinity Tchr. Corps Project in Bilingual and Multicultural Edn., 1979—, tchr. English as 2d Lang., 1980—; free lance writer 1981—; vol. Spanish Speaking Com. Va. Mem. Fairfax County Dem. Com., 1970; mem. Greenbelt Consumer Services Inc., 1979—. Served with USN, 1942-46; PTO. Mem. Am. Orthopsychiat. Assn., Am. Assn. Counseling and Devel., Am. Sch. Counselors Assn., United Teaching Profession, Assn. Tchr. Edn., Irish Am. Cultural Inst., Clan Fraser Soc. N.Am., Clan Stewart Soc. in Am., Sims-Simms Family Geneal. and Meml. Soc. (founder, chmn.), Internat. Platform Assn., Alpha Psi Omega. Unitarian. Clubs: Leabhar, Comunn na Canain Albannaich (Isle of Lewis, Scotland); Conradh na Gaeilge (Washington); An Comunn Gaidhealach, Am. and Scotland. Home and office: 902 Myers Circle SW Vienna VA 22180

SARKIS, FREDERICK DERR, lawyer, educator; b. Jan. 25, 1912; s. E.D. and Anna Sarkis; m. Margaret Travis, Mar. 12, 1938; children—Edwin, Sally. B.S.C., Temple U., 1936, J.D., 1942. Bar: Pa. 1948, U.S. Dist. Ct. (ea. dist.) Pa. 1958, U.S. Supreme Ct. 1959, U.S. Ct. Appeals (fed. cir.) 1982. Chief contract claims U.S. Army, Phila., 1940-46; asst. treas. B-L-H Corp., Phila., 1946-52; counsel Vertol-Boeing, Phila., 1952-57; sr. ptnr. Stassen, Kephart, Sarkis & Kostos, Phila., 1959-70; now ptnr. Murphy and Sarkis, Melbourne, Fla.; lectr. industry groups, Fla. and Pa., 1960—, U. Central Fla., Orlando, 1979-83, Rollins Coll., Winter Park, Fla., 1983—. Trustee Wyoming Sem., Kingston, Pa., 1970-84; gen. counsel Pa. Sports Hall of Fame, Phila., 1960-70; pres. Fla. Sports Hall of Fame, Inc., Maitland, 1978—; active community civic assns. Mem. Fed. Bar Assn. (pres. Orlando chpt. 1978-80, del. nat. council 1978—, bd. dirs. Phila. chpt. 1960-78), ABA. Methodist. Club: Union League. Lodges: Masons, Shriners. Home: 2569 Newfound Harbor Dr Merritt Island FL 32952 Office: Murphy and Sarkis 1811 S Riverview Dr Melbourne FL 32901

SARMIENTO, GUILLERMO, commodities trader; b. Bogota, Colombia, July 26, 1951; came to U.S., 1968, naturalized, 1981; s. Dario and Flor (Acosta) S.; m. Mary-Dolly Escobar, Feb. 20, 1980; children—Flor Alejandra, Guillermo. B.A., Brown U., 1973, M.A., 1974. Vice pres. E.F. Hutton, N.Y.C., 1975-81, Refco Inc., Chgo., 1981-82, AceAmerican, Miami, Fla., 1982—; pres. Commodity Futures Internat., Miami, 1985—; coffee cons. Berkshire Enterprises, Charlotte, 1983—; editor Cafe Coffee Newsletter, Miami, 1983—. Mem. Commodity Futures Trading Commn., Nat. Coffee Assn., Interam. Businessmen's Assn. Colombian Am. C. of C., Greater Miami C. of C. Republican. Roman Catholic. Contbr. articles to profl. jours. Home: 742 Sevilla Ave Coral Gables FL 33134 Office: 2050 Coral Way Suite 405 Miami FL 33145

SARMIENTO, ROBERT FOCION, psychologist; b. Oakland, Calif., Sept. 14, 1945; s. Roberto and Hazel Sarmiento; m. Sue E. Sodke; children—Robert, Eric, Adam, Laura. B.A., Harvard U., 1967; Ph.D., U. Rochester, 1973. Lic. psychologist, Tex. Asst. prof. psychology SUNY-Brockport, 1972-76; psychologist, prin. Sarmiento Assocs., Houston, 1976—. Contbr. articles to sci. and popular publs.; advice columnist Career Doctor, Nationwide Careers, 1985—. Mem. Am. Psychol. Assn., Houston Assn. Organizational/Indsl. Psychologists, Sigma Xi. Office: Sarmiento Assocs 2200 Post Oak Blvd Suite 533 Houston TX 77056

SARMIENTOS-DE LEON, JORGE ALVARO, composer, conductor, educator; b. San Antonio, Guatemala, Feb. 19, 1931; s. Julio Vicente and Maria Brtha (DeLeon) Alvarado Sarmientos Morales; m. Amparo Barillas-Carranza, Oct. 12, 1954 (div. 1957); 1 child, Jorge Alvaro; m. Matilde Roldan-Salguero, Nov. 13, 1960; children—Dphnis Igor, Chloe Monica. Student Nat. Conservatory, Guatemala City, 1947-54, Nat. U., Guatemala City, 1972-79; Emeritissimun, 1982. With Nat. Symphony Orch. Guatemala, 1955—, musical and artistic dir., 1972—; prof. composition Nat. Conservatory, Guatemala, 1957—, prof. orch. directing, 1969—; prof. musical aesthetics U. R. Landivar, Guatemala, 1969-80; prof. harmony U. F. Marroquin, Guatemala, 1982-85. Composer: numerous works for symphonies, concerts, sonatas, chorales, numerous others. Recipient composition awards C.A. Bellas Artes, Guatemala, 1953, 56, 57, Juegos Florales, Guatemala, 1965; acad. awards include Gobierno de Francia, 1976, UNESCO/Colombia, 1979. Mem. Guatemalan Philharm. Assn. (pres. 1979-80), Guatemalan Union Musicians, Assn. Am. and Latino-Am. Composers, UNESCO. Avocations: sports; music. Home: 3a Ave 2-25 Guatemala City Guatemala Zone 2 Office: Nat Symphony Orchestra 3a Ave 4-61 Guatemala City Guatemala Zone 1

SARNER, ALLAN DAVID, textile executive; b. N.Y.C., July 30, 1924; s. Jack and Jeanne S.; m. Kay Rachel Sebiry, Sept. 1, 1956; children—Jon, Laurence. B.A., Colby Coll., 1948; postgrad. Sorbonne, Paris, 1946; U. Berne (Switzerland), 1946. Pres. Arrowhead Assocs., Dallas, 1967—. Served to col. USAR. Mem. PsyWar Soc., Res. Officers Assn., Mensa.

SARNOFF, ARTHUR SARON, artist; b. Pitts., Dec. 30, 1912; s. Samuel and Lena (Wagner) S.; m. Lillian, Dec. 14, 1935 (div.); children—Susan, Linda; m. Muriel Zapolean, June 21, 1966. Student Indsl. Sch. Art, N.Y.C., 1930-32, Grand Central Sch. Art, N.Y.C., 1932-36, Art League, N.Y.C., 1930's. Art dir. Mitchel Studios, N.Y.C., 1933-37; represented by Deligny Gallery, Ft. Lauderdale, Fla., Shorr Goodwin Gallery, Phoenix, Zantman Gallery, Carmel, Calif. and Palm Desert, Calif.; illustrator books, mags., advt. Represented in numerous pvt. collections. Recipient ann. advt. award Art Dirs. Club, 1957, ann. exhbn. 1st prize Profession Art League, 1965. Mem. Allied Aritsts Am. (7th ann. exhbn. award for realism 1985), Profl. Art League, Boca Raton Mus. Art, Grand Central Galleries, Soc. Illustrators. Club: Boca Raton Country. Avocations: squash, tennis, sailing, golf. Home and Studio: 6462 Woodbury Rd Boca Raton FL 33433

SARPALIUS, BILL, state senator; b. Los Angeles, Jan. 10, 1948; A.S., Clarendon Coll.; B.S., Tex. Tech. Coll.; M.S., West Tex. State U.; m. Donna Sue Ritchie, Nov. 19, 1969; 1 son, David William. Vocat. agrl. tchr. Cal Farleys Boys Ranch; dist. office mgr. to speaker Tex. Ho. of Reps.; with Center Plains Industries, Inc., now dir. bus. devel.; now mem. Tex. Senate. Democrat. Methodist. Clubs: Masons, Lions. Office: PO Box 7926 Amarillo TX 79114

SARRELL, WARREN GLEA, cardiologist; b. Rockwood, Tenn., Oct. 16, 1924; s. James Edgar and Doris (Kindred) S.; m. Martha Jean Pope, Nov. 28, 1950 (dec. Mar. 1967); m. Lela Jane Blocker Sarrell, Mar. 5, 1970; children—Warren Glea, Debra Jean, Doris Marie, Martha Beth, Catherine Ann, April Jane. B.S., U. W.Va., 1946; M.D., Cornell U., 1948. Diplomate Am. Bd. Internal Medicine. Intern. N.C. Bapt. Hosp., Bowman Gray Sch. Medicine, Winston-Salem, 1948-49, Grady Meml. Hosp., Atlanta, 1949-51; resident Emory U. Hosp., Atlanta, 1952-54; pres. Anniston Med. Clinic, Ala., 1979—. Served to capt. U.S. Army, 1950-52, Korea. Decorated Combat Medical award, 1950; Bronze Star; named Kiwanian of Yr., Anniston Kiwanis Club, 1973, Man of Yr., Anniston Star, 1975. Fellow ACP, Am. Coll. Cardiology, Am. Coll. Nuclear Medicine (pres. Southeastern chpt. 1970); mem. Ala. Heart Assn. (pres. 1976), Anniston C. of C. (bd. dirs. 1972-74). Avocations: fishing; gardening. Home: 300 Fairway Dr Anniston AL 36201 Office: Box 2127 1010 Christian Ave Anniston AL 36201

SARTIN, JAMES LEWIS, JR., physiologist; b. Jacksonville, N.C., Feb. 15, 1952; s. James Lewis and Exa (Halford) S.; m. Eva Ann Martin, Dec. 29, 1976; 1 child, Matthew McCullough. B.A., Auburn U., 1973, M.S., 1976; Ph.D., Okla. State U., 1978. Teaching assoc. Okla. State U., Stillwater, 1978-79; postdoctoral fellow Temple U., Phila., 1979-81, staff biologist, 1981-82; asst. prof. physiology Auburn (Ala.) U., 1982—. Mem. Am. Physiol. Soc., Am. Soc. Animal Sci., Ala. Acad. Sci., Endocrine Soc., So. Study of Reprodn., N.Y. Acad. Scis., Sigma Xi. Democrat. Baptist. Editor: Domestic Animal Endocrinology. Office: Auburn Univ Dept Physiology Auburn AL 36849

SASEK, GLORIA BURNS, English language educator; b. Springfield, Mass., Jan. 20, 1926; d. Frederick Charles and Minnie Delia (White) Burns; B.A., Mary Washington Coll. of U. Va., 1947; Ed.M., Springfield Coll., 1955; postgrad. Sorbonne, summer 1953; M.A., Radcliffe Coll., 1954; postgrad. Universita per Stranieri, Perugia, Italy, summer 1955; m. Lawrence Anton Sasek, Sept. 5, 1960. Tchr., head dept. jr. and sr. high sch. English, Somers, Conn., 1947-51, 52-59; tchr. English, Winchester (Mass.) pub. schs., 1959-60; faculty La. State U., Baton Rouge, 1961—, asst. prof. English, 1971—, chmn. freshman English, 1969-70. Recipient George H. Deer Disting. Tchr. award La. State U., 1977. Mem. MLA, South Central Modern Lang. Assn., South Central Renaissance Soc., AAUP (chpt. v.p. 1981-84). Address: 1458 Kenilworth Pkwy Baton Rouge LA 70808

SASMOR, JAMES CECIL, publishing representive; b. N.Y.C., July 29, 1920; s. Louis and Cecilia (Mockler) S.; m. Jeannette L. Fuchs, May 30, 1965; 1 dau., Elizabeth Lynn. B.S., Columbia U., 1942; M.B.A., Calif. Western U., 1977, Ph.D., 1979. Advt. exec. N.Y. World Telegram, 1946-48, Chain Store Age, 1948-50, Am. Girl mag., 1950-59; registered rep. Nat. Assn. Security Dealers, 1956-57; founder, owner J.C. Sasmor Assocs. Publishing Reps., N.Y.C., 1959—; co-founder, pres., dir. adminstrn. Continuing Edn. Cons., Inc., Tampa, 1976—; pub. cons., 1959—; lectr. U. S. Fla. Coll. Nursing. Team tchr. childbirth edn. Am. Soc. Childbirth Educators; bd. dirs. Tampa chpt. ARC, also chmn. instructional com. on nursing and health; county nursing ednl. cons. ARC; edn. counselor U. So. Fla. Comprehensive Breast Cancer Ctr. Served with USN, 1942-46. Recipient cert. appreciation ARC, 1979; Dept. Health and Rehab. Services award for Fla. Mental Health Inst. service, 1980; cert. sex educator Am. Assn. Sex Educators, Counselors and Therapists. Internat. Council of Sex Edn. and Parenthood Am. U. fellow, 1981—. Mem. Assn. Pubs. Reps. (pres. 1965-66), Am. Soc. Psychoprophylaxis in Obstetrics (dir. 1970-71), Am. Assn. Childbirth Educators (co-founder, dir. 1972—), Nurses Assn. of Am. Coll. Obstetricians and Gynecologist (dir. Tampa chpt.), Health Edn. Media Assn., Nursing Educators Assn. Tampa. Contbr. chpts. Childbirth Education: A Nursing Perspective, 1979. Contbr. articles to profl. jours. Office: PO Box 16159 Tampa FL 33687

SASSER, HAROLD JEARL, chemical engineer; b. Bogue Chitto, Miss., Oct. 17, 1945; s. Harold Eben Sasser and Marguerite (Scott) Boyd; m. Betty Gail Goodman, Dec. 20, 1970; children—Autumn Leigh, Heather Michelle, Amber Dawn. A.A., Copiah Lincoln Jr. Coll., 1966; B.S. in Chem. Engring., Miss. State U., 1969; postgrad. U. Louisville, 1970, Marshall U., 1979. Project engr. B.F. Goodrich, Louisville, 1969-73; mgr. plasticizer prodns. Haywood Co., Brownsville, Tenn., 1973-77; supt. polymerization USS Chems., Kenova, W.Va., 1977-79, prodn. mgr., 1980—. Vice pres. Beverly Hills Youth Football League, Huntington, W.Va., 1984-85, bd. dirs., 1986—. Mem. Am. Inst. Chem. Engrs. Democrat. Mem. Ch. of Christ. Lodge: Lions (3d v.p. 1985). Avocation: sports. Home: 5 Garwood Dr Huntington WV 25705 Office: USS Chems PO Box 189 Kenova WV 25530

SASSER, JAMES RALPH, U.S. Senator; b. Memphis, Sept. 30, 1936; s. Joseph Ralph and Mary Nell (Gray) S.; m. Mary Gorman, Aug. 18, 1962; children—Gray, Elizabeth. B.A., Vanderbilt U., 1958, LL.B., 1961. Bar: Tenn. 1961. Partner firm Goodpasture, Carpenter, Woods & Sasser, Nashville, 1961-76; mem. U.S. Senate from Tenn., 1976—. Chmn. Tenn. State Dem. Exec. Com., 1973-76; so. vice chmn. Assn. Dem. State Chmn., 1975-76. Served with USMCR, 1958-65. Mem. Am. Bar Assn., NCCJ (dir. Nashville chpt.), UN Assn., Nashville Com. Fgn. Relations, Am. Judicature Soc. Office: SR298 Russell Senate Office Bldg Washington DC 20510*

SASSER, JOSEPH NEAL, plant nematologist, educator; b. Goldsboro, N.C., May 19, 1921; s. John A. and Minnie Gertrude (Neal) S.; m. Laura Elizabeth Long, Nov. 4, 1945; children—Anita Gail Chappell, Joseph Neal, Betty Louise Bitting, Luara Ann Young. B.S. in Agrl. Edn., N.C. State U., 1943, M.S. in Plant Pathology, 1950; Ph.D. in Plant Pathology, U. Md., 1953. Asst. nematologist U.S. Dept. Agr., Beltsville, Md., 1950-53; asst. prof. plant pathology N.C. State U., Raleigh, 1953-55, assoc. prof. plant pathology, 1955-64, prof. plant pathology, 1964—; prin. investigator Internat. Meloidogyne Project. Served to lt. (j.g.) USNR, 1943-46. Recipient IX Internat. Congress Plant Protection Adventurers in Agrl. Sci. Award of Distinction, 1979, U.N.C. Bd. Govs. Oliver Max Gardner award, 1982. Mem. Soc. Nematologists (v.p. 1961-63, pres. 1963-64, Cert. Merit 1979, Ciba-Geigy Recognition award 1981), Orgn. Tropical Am. Nematologists, Council Agrl. Sci. and Tech., Sigma Xi, Kappa Phi Kappa. Democrat. Baptist. Author, co-author approximately 150 sci. publs. Home: 628 Grove Ave Raleigh NC 27606 Office: NC State U Dept Plant Pathology PO Box 7616 Raleigh NC 27695

SASSER, WILLIAM GRAY, music educator; b. Wilson, N.C., July 25, 1927; s. Oscar William and Nell Gray (Wilkerson) S.; m. Thelma Margarita Paiewonsky; Dec. 1, 1955; children—C. David, Paul W. B.A., U. N.C., 1947, M.A., 1949, Ph.D., 1960; L.H.D. (hon.), N.C. Wesleyan Coll., 1985. Choral dir. Landon High Sch., Jacksonville, Fla., 1955-57, Ch. Good Shepherd, Rocky Mount, N.C., 1966-85; instr. Jacksonville Coll. Music, 1955-57; grad. instr. U. N.C., Chapel Hill, 1957-60; chmn. music dept. N.C. Wesleyan Coll., Rocky Mount, 1960-85, prof. emeritus, 1985—. Profl. pianist with various orchestras. Contbr. articles to mus. jours. Bd. dirs. Rocky Mount Arts Ctr., 1970-74. Served with U.S. Army, 1953-55. Mem. N.C. Music Tchrs. Assn. (pres. 1967-69, Pres.'s citation 1984, piano clinician 1963-85), N.C. Music Educators Assn. (choral clinician 1968-73), Music Tchrs. Nat. Assn., Music Educators Nat. Assn. Episcopalian.

SATCHER, DAVID, physician, administrator; b. Anniston, Ala., Mar. 2, 1941; s. Wilmer and Anna Mattie (Curry) S.; m. Nola R. Smith, Oct. 12, 1979; children by previous marriage—Gretchen, David Lorone, Daraka, Daryl. B.S., Morehouse Coll., 1963; M.D., Case Western Res. U., 19—, Ph.D., 19—. Resident, U. Rochester, 1970-72; Macy faculty fellow King-Drew Med. Ctr., Los Angeles, 1972-74, chmn. dept. family medicine, acting dean, 1976-79; Robert W. Johnson clin. scholar UCLA, 1975-76; chmn. community medicine Morehouse Sch. Medicine, Atlanta, 1979-82; pres. Meharry Med. Coll., 1982—; mem. adv. com. Nat. Heart Lung and Blood Inst. Mem. Am. Acad. Family Physicians, Soc. Tchrs. Family Medicine, NAACP, Phi Beta Kappa, Alpha Omega Alpha. Home: 6305 E Valley Rd Nashville TN 37205

SATTERFIELD, GEORGE HARRIS, real estate broker; b. Houston County, Ga., May 10, 1934; s. John Moses and Eris (Guinn) S.; m. Betty Jean Yates, Apr. 11, 1959; 1 dau., Lisa Karen (Mrs. Mark L. Hunt). Student Middle Ga. Coll., 1952-54. Field rep. Gen. Motors Acceptance Corp., Newman, Ga., 1961-66, credit rep., Atlanta, 1966-71, credit supr., LaGrange, Ga., 1971-81, purchase office mgr., LaGrange, 1981; v.p., part owner Spinks-Brown Realty Assocs., LaGrange, 1982—. Deacon 1st Baptist Ch., LaGrange, 1973—, chmn. deacons, 1985; past pres. Troop County chpt., dir. Ga. div. Am. Cancer Soc. Served with U.S. Army, 1955-58. Mem. Ga. Assn. Realtors, Realtors Nat. Mktg. Inst., Troup County Bd. Realtors (pres. 1986). Club: Lions (pres. LaGrange chpt. 1978—, gov. Ga. Dist.). Home: 615 Piney Woods Dr La Grange GA 30240 Office: 207 N Lewis St LaGrange GA 30240

SATTLER, RAYMOND LOUIS, neurosurgeon; b. Concord, Calif., July 16, 1944; s. Ernest Louis and Dorothy Alberta (Bright) S.; m. Deborah L. Kiehl, Apr. 2, 1982. A.B., U. Calif.-Berkeley, 1967; Pharm. D., U. Calif.-San Francisco, 1971; M.D., Case Western Res. U., Cleve., 1977. Spl. asst. to adminstr. Health Services and Mental Health Adminstrn., Dept. HEW, Rockville, Md., 1971-72; spl. asst. to dir. Bur. Health Manpower Edn., NIH, Dept. HEW, Bethesda, Md., 1972-73; planning assoc. Devel. Planning Group, Office of Dean, Sch. Medicine, Case Western Res. U., Cleve., 1973-74, research assoc. dept. medicine, 1973-75, fellow in gen. surgery, 1977-78, fellow in neurol. surgery, 1978-82; intern, resident in neurol. surgery Univ. Hosp., Cleve., 1976-82; neurosurgeon Southeastern Gen. Hosp., Lumberton, N.C., 1982—. Served to lt. USPHS, 1971-73. Mem. Student Am. Pharm. Assn. (pres. 1970-71), Internat. Fedn. Med. Students Assn. (treas., mem. exec. com. bd. trustees 1974-75), Nat. Coalition of Student Profl. Orgns. (chmn., co-founder 1969-71), AMA, N.C. Med. Soc., Robeson County Med. Soc., Am. Pharm. Assn., ACS (participant candidate's group), Congress Neurol. Surgeons, Alpha Omega Alpha. Republican. Home: 411 Duart Rd Lumberton NC 28358 Office: Lumberton Neurosurgical Assocs PA 202 W 27th St Lumberton NC 28358

SAUCIER, ROGER THOMAS, research geographer, consulting earth scientist; b. New Orleans, Aug. 30, 1935; s. Richard August Thomas and Marjorie (Saucier) Thatcher; m. Anita Ruth Wood, Apr. 18, 1957; children—Connie Jean, Brian Gene. B.A., La. State U., 1957, M.A., 1958, Ph.D., 1967; postgrad., UCLA, 1958-59. Research fellow La. State U., Baton Rouge, 1958-61; geographer Waterways Experiment Sta., Vicksburg, Miss., 1961-72, spl. asst., 1972-82, phys. scientist, 1982—; cons. earth scientist, Vicksburg, 1970—. Contbr. articles to profl. jours. Recipient Meritorious Civilian Service decoration Dept. Army 1973; Research Achievement award Waterways Experiment Sta. 1979. Fellow Geol. Soc. Am.; mem. Soc. Am. Archeology (Roald Fryxell medal 1985), Am. Quaternary Assn., Assn. Engring. Geologists (sec. Lower Miss. Valley chapt. 1985), Soc. Profl. Archeologists. Republican. Methodist. Avocations: woodworking; cabinet making. Home: 4325 Winchester Rd Vicksburg MS 39180-8969 Office: USAE Waterways Experiment Sta PO Box 631 Vicksburg MS 39180-0631

SAUL, IRA STEPHEN, lawyer; b. West Reading, Pa., Apr. 2, 1949; s. Charles Ryweck and Florence Rebecca (Sussman) S.; m. Elizabeth Claire Barclay, Nov. 30, 1974; children—Barclay Charles, Amanda Emerson. B.A., Dickinson Coll., 1971; J.D., Am. U., 1975. Bar: Va. 1975, U.S. Dist. Ct. (ea. dist.) Va. 1976, U.S. Ct. Appeals (4th cir.) 1977, D.C. 1978, U.S. Dist. Ct. D.C. 1978, U.S. Ct. Appeals (D.C. Cir.) 1985. Assoc. Miller, Gattsek, Tavenner, Rosenfeld & Schultz, Bailey's Crossroads, Va., 1975-77; prin. Saul & Barclay, P.C., Fairfax, Va., 1978—. Recipient cert. of Appreciation Inst. Real Estate Mgmt., 1982, 83. Mem. ABA, Am. Trial Lawyers Assn., Fairfax Bar Assn., Va. Trial Lawyers Assn. Republican. Jewish. Office: Saul & Barclay PC 4055 Chain Bridge Rd Fairfax VA 22030

SAULNER, HENRY SIDDALL, geologist, exploration company executive; b. Phila., Aug. 11, 1923; s. Theophile and Alice (Siddall) S.; m. Janice Raus, Dec. 18, 1948; children—Suzanne, Scott, Steven. B.S., Ohio U., 1948; M.S., U. Mass., 1950. Geologist to dist. geologist Amerada Petroleum Corp., Tulsa, 1950-71; geologist Kewanee Oil Co., Tulsa, 1971-73; exploration mgr. Tex. Pacific Oil Co., Oklahoma City, 1974-81; v.p. exploration South Ranch Oil Co., Oklahoma City, 1981-82; exploration mgr. Bracken Exploration, Oklahoma City, 1982-83; v.p. exploration Devon Energy Corp., Oklahoma City, 1983-85; cons. petroleum geologist, 1985—. Bd. dirs. YMCA, Edmond, Okla., 1972; sr. warden St. Mary's Episc. Ch., Edmond, 1974. Served to sgt. USMC, 1942-45. Mem. Am. Assn. Petroleum Geologists, Oklahoma City Geol. Soc., Geophys. Soc. Oklahoma City, Oklahoma City Assn. Petroleum Landmen, Am. Assn. Petroleum Landmen. Republican. Club: Oklahoma City Petroleum. Avocations: jogging, mineral and fossil collecting. Home: 2802 Randolph Rd Edmond OK 73034 Office: 2802 Randolph Rd Edmond OK 73013

SAUNDERS, EDWARD DEXTER, small business owner; b. Coral Gables, Fla., Dec. 3, 1936; s. Dexter and Irene Mildred (Morden) S.; m. Patricia Bennett, June 22, 1957; children—Debra Jeanne, William Edward, Richard Graham, Michael James. B.S.B.A., U. Fla., 1959. Owner, Saunders Hardware, Miami, Fla., 1969—; treas. Brickell Bank Savs. & Loan, 1981—. Active South Miami Hosp. Found. Mem. Ga.-Fla. Hardware Assn. (past pres.), So. Hardware and Implement Assn. (past pres.), Nat. Retail Hardware Assn. (dir.), Better Bus. Bur., Bus. Inc. Democrat. Lutheran. Clubs: Kiwanis (pres. 1976), Country Club (Coral Gables) (pres. 1977, fleet commodore 1978), Executive (pres. 1976), Riviera Country. Home: 7300 SW 72d Ave Miami FL 33143 Office: 10550 Kendall Dr Miami FL 33176

SAUNDERS, HOMER LEE, business educator, consultant; b. Batavia, Ark., May 30, 1927; s. Tinzley Porter and Verlia Mae (Branson) S.; m. June Louise Pinkley, July 31, 1949; 1 child, Kenneth Alan. B.S. in Edn., U. Ark., 1952, B.A., 1952, M.B.A., 1965, Ph.D. in Bus. Adminstrn., 1976. Salesman, Saunders Agy., Bentonville and Springdale, Ark., 1954-61; asst. placement dir. U. Ark., Fayetteville, 1964-67; prof. U. Central Ark., Conway, 1967—, dir. Small Bus. Inst., 1980—; pres. Manco, Inc., Conway, 1974—, Cen-Ark Enterprises, Conway, 1975-78; cons. mgr. Merchant Security Service, Conway, 1978-81. Contbr. articles to profl. jours. Served to 2d lt. U.S. Army, 1945-46, 53. Recipient Outstanding Performance award SBA, 1976, Best Case award Small Bus. Inst. Little Rock Dist. SBA, 1981; Disting. S.W. Fedn. Adminstrv. Disciplines Paper award Bus. Publs., Inc. and Richard D. Irwin, Inc., 1984. Mem. M.B.A. Dirs. Assn., Southwestern Fedn. Acad. Disciplines, Southwestern Small Bus. Inst. Assn. (v.p. 1985—), Beta Gamma Sigma, Phi Delta Kappa. Democrat. Lodges: Masons, Shriners, Order Eastern Star. Home: #9 Deerwood Dr Conway AR 72032 Office: U Central Ark Bruce and Donaghey Conway AR 72032

SAUNDERS, JOHN VAN DYKE, sociology educator; b. Porto Alegre, Brazil, Feb. 25, 1930; parents Am. citizens; s. John Rouzie and Sara Van Dyke (Stout) S.; m. Julia Vissotto, Dec. 20, 1952; children—Thomas Lee, Edward Paul, Andrew William. B.A., Vanderbilt U., 1951, M.A., 1955; Ph.D., U. Fla., 1955; postgrad. U. Chgo., 1956. Instr. to asst. Miss. State U., Mississippi State, 1955-59, prof. sociology, 1973—, head dept. sociology, 1973-81; asst. to assoc. prof. La. State U., Baton Rouge, 1959-62; assoc. to prof. U. Fla., Gainesville, 1962-73; dir. Latin Am. Ctr. U. Fla., Gainesville, 1962-66; population adv. Ford Found., Lima, Peru, 1967-68. Author and editor: Population Growth in Latin America and U.S. National Security, 1986; Modern Brazil: New Patterns and Development, 1971. Sr. author: Rural Electrification and Development, 1978. Author: The Population of Ecuador: A Demographic Analysis, 1960. Fulbright fellow, 1966; Tinker Found. grantee 1985; recipient Fulbright award 1958-59, 81-82. Mem. Rural Sociol. Soc. (exec. council 1972-75), Latin Am. Studies Assn. (exec. council 1971-73), So. Sociol. Soc. (chmn. program com.

1980-81), Southeastern Council Latin Am. Studies (council 1960-62), Internat. Union Sci. Study of Population, Populations Assn. Am. Home: PO Box 84 Mississippi State MS 39762 Office: Dept Sociology Miss State Univ PO Drawer C Mississippi State MS 39762

SAUNDERS, KAREN, nursing educator; b. Stamford, Eng., Sept. 4, 1951; d. Coleman Robert and Doreen (Beasley) S. R.N., Petersburg Gen. Hosp. Sch. Nursing, 1972; B.S. Nursing, Med. Coll. Va., 1976; M.S. Nursing, U. Va., 1982, L.P.N.P., 1982. Staff nurse pediatrics Petersburg (Va.) Gen. Hosp., 1972-75, instr. Sch. Nursing, 1975-80; staff nurse Martha Jefferson Hosp., Charlottesville, Va., 1980-81; teaching asst. U. Va., Charlottesville, 1981-82; asst. prof. pediatric nursing Petersburg Gen. Hosp. Sch. Nursing, 1982—; basic cardiac life support instr. Am. Heart Assn., 1978—. Chmn., Crater Child Protection Team, Petersburg, 1983-85. Mem. Nat. League Nursing. Democrat. Episcopalian. Home: 2144 Armistead Ave Petersburg VA 23803 Office: Dept Pediatrics Petersburg Gen Hosp Sch Nursing 801 S Adams St Petersburg VA 23803

SAUNDERS, KIM DAVID, physical oceanographer; b. Chgo., Jan. 21, 1945; s. David and Jane (Keough) S.; m. Barbara Gail Briedenbach, June 12, 1968 (div. Sept. 1984); children—Evan David Bjorn, Jennie May. B.Sc., Rose Poly. Inst., 1966; Ph.D., MIT and Woods Hole Oceanographic Inst., 1971. Research assoc. MIT, Cambridge, 1971-72; postdoctoral fellow U. Bergen (Norway), 1972-74; environ. scientist Argonne Nat. Lab., 1974-78; oceanographer GM-13 Naval Ocean Research and Devel. Activity, NSTL Station, Miss., 1978—; adj. prof. U. New Orleans; cons. in field. MIT fellow, 1966-67; NSF fellow, 1967-71; NATO fellow, 1972-73; recipient publ. award Naval Ocean Research and Devel. Activity, 1981. Mem. Am. Geophys. Union, AAAS, Miss. Acad. Sci., Sigma Xi. Lodge: Masons. Contbr. articles to profl. jours. Home: 302 Country Club Dr Picayune MS 39466 Office: Code 331 Naval Ocean Research and Development Activity NSTL Station MS 39529

SAUNDERS, MARYBETH KENNER, management consultant; b. Norfolk, Va., June 16, 1954; d. Robert H. and Edith (Itzkowitz) K.; m. Kenneth Allen Saunders, Aug. 13, 1977. B.S., Old Dominion U., 1975; M.Ed., U. Ga., 1976; Cert. Advanced Study in Edn., Coll. William and Mary, 1980; Ph.D., Ga. State U., 1982. Tchr. Virginia Beach Pub. Schs., Va., 1976-78; instr. Old Dominion U., Norfolk, Va., 1978-80; research assoc. Ga. Secondary Com., Atlanta, 1980-82; mgmt. cons. Tng. & Devel. Concepts, Norfolk, 1982—; adj. prof. Va. Wesleyan Coll. and Golden Gate U., Norfolk, 1982—. Author: The Teaching Game, 1985; also profl. articles. Mem. Am. Soc. for Tng. and Devel., Norfolk Women's Forum. Avocations: travel, walking. Office: Tng & Devel Concepts One Koger Exec Ctr Suite 200 Norfolk VA 23502

SAUNDERS, RICHARD AMES, ophthalmologist, educator; b. N.Y.C., Nov. 9, 1946; s. Dero Ames and Beatrice (Nair) S.; m. Anne Elizabeth Leslie, Oct. 20, 1973; children—Jean, Carter. A.B., Dartmouth Coll., 1969; M.D., Columbia U., 1973. Intern, St. Luke's Hosp. Ctr., N.Y.C., 1973-74; resident in ophthalmology Presbyn. Hosp., N.Y.C., 1974-77; fellow Ind. U. Sch. Medicine, Indpls., 1977-78; asst. prof. ophthalmology Med. U. S.C., Charleston, 1978-81, assoc. prof., 1981—. Mem. Internat. Strabismological Assn., Am. Acad. Ophthalmology, Am. Assn. Pediatric Ophthalmology and Strabismus, AMA, S.C. Med. Assn. Republican. Avocations: athletics; flying. Home: 89 Rutledge Ave Charleston SC 29401 Office: Dept Ophthalmology Med U SC 171 Ashley Ave Charleston SC 29425

SAUNDERS, WILLIAM JAMES, educational administrator; b. Pasquotank, County, N.C.; Nov. 27, 1942; s. Julian Parker and Dorothy (Carter) S.; m. Ida Paulette Pace, Dec. 26, 1965 (separated); children—Nicolle Marie, William Parker. B.S., East Carolina Coll., 1965, M.A.Ed., 1972. Cert. in indsl. and tech. edn., pub. sch. adminstrn. Tchr., Portsmouth Pub. Schs., Va., 1965-70, asst. prin., 1970-73, tchr., 1976-77; prin. P.D. Pruden Vocat. Tech. Ctr., Suffolk, Va., 1973-76, Churchland Jr. High Sch., Portsmouth, 1977-80, Alf J. Mapp Middle Sch., Portsmouth, 1980—. Pres., bd. dirs. Lions Charity Found. Norfolk, Va., 1984-85. Named Outstanding Young Educator, Portsmouth Jaycees, 1973; life mem. PTA, 1981; Ky. Col., 1983. Methodist. Lodges: Lions (pres. Cradock 1975-76, dist. gov. Southeast Va. 1982-83), Moose. Office: Alf J Mapp Jr High Sch 21 Alden Ave Portsmouth VA 23702

SAVAGE, ROBERT L., political science educator; b. Fort Worth, Feb. 26, 1939; s. Henry Carroll and Helen Marie (Donahue) Goldman; m. Naomi Lee Stedman, Nov. 8, 1963 (div. June 1976); 1 child, Naomi Lynne; m. Barbara Grace Brown, Jan. 4, 1980. A.S. in Math., Tarleton State Coll., 1961, B.A. in Govt., 1963; M.A. in Polit. Sci., U. Houston, 1966; Ph.D. in Polit. Sci., U. Mo., 1971. Asst. prof. Auburn U., Montgomery, Ala., 1971-74; U. Ark., Fayetteville, 1974-77, assoc. prof., 1977-82, prof., 1982—; mem. adv. bd. dirs. Ark. Household Research Panel, Coll. Bus. Adminstrn. U. Ark., Fayetteville, 1980—; mem. exec. council Nat. Network State Polls, Tuscaloosa, Ala., 1984—. Author: (with others) Candidates and Their Images, 1976. Author and co-author of monographs and contbr. articles to profl. jours. Staff cons. Ala. Energy Mgmt. Office, Montgomery, 1974; chmn. Community Devel. Com., Fayetteville, 1977-78; regional Humanist Ark. Endowment Humanities, 1978—. Served with USAF, 1956-59. Grantee U.S. Dept. Housing & Urban Devel. 1975, First Ark. Bank Co. 1979, Ark. Endowment Humanities, 1980, J. William Fulbright Coll Arts & Sci. U. Ark. 1981, Mem. Internat. Communication Assn., Midwest Polit. Sci. Assn. (mem. editorial bd. Am. Jour. Polit. Sci. 1983-85), Southern Polit. Sci. Assn., Southwestern Polit. Sci. Assn. (exec. council 1981-83), Ark. Polit. Sci. Assn. (pres. 1978-79), Am. Polit. Sci. Assn., Speech Communication Assn., Southern Speech Communication Assn., Ga. Polit. Sci. Assn., Conf. Fed. Studies, Policy Studies Orgn., Classification Soc., Assn. Politics and Life Scis., Consortium Math. and Its Applications, Pi Sigma Alpha. Democrat. Avocations: record collecting; reading. Home: 109 N School #3 Fayettville AR 72701 Office: U Ark Dept Polit Sci Kimpel 619 Fayettville AR 72701

SAVARESE, DONALD LOUIS, mayor; b. N.Y.C., Jan. 7, 1936; s. Louis F. and Dorothy E. (Krafft) S.; m. Arline Marie Cloutier; children—Donald L., Rory Marie. Student U. N.C., NYU, Pace Coll. Mem. council City of Coconut Creek (Fla.), 1975-84, vice mayor, 1975-77, mayor, 1979-83. Mem. Gov.'s Council on Crime, 1982-83; chmn. adv. bd. Broward Vocat. Tech. Edn., 1983; mem. adv. bd. vocat. tech. edn. State of Fla., 1983-84. Mem. Fla. League Cities (bd. dirs. 1978-79), Internat. Chiefs of Police, Am. Planning Assn. Roman Catholic. Home: 300 Lake Dr Coconut Creek FL 33066 Office: City of Coconut Creek 1071 NW 45th Ave Coconut Creek FL 33066

SAVIA, STEVEN ALFRED, management consultant; b. Arlington, Va., July 15, 1951; s. Alfred Angelo and Jean (Leitch) S.; m. Janet Marie Sykes, June 14, 1975. B.A., George Mason U., 1973; M.A., Fla. Atlantic U., 1978. Adminstrv. intern Dept. Justice, Washington, 1973-74; asst. dir. govt. devel. programs Fla. Atlantic U., Boca Raton, 1974-76; cons. Steven A. Savia Assocs., Boca Raton, 1977-79; project mgr. Mgmt. Improvement Corp. of Am., Durham, N.C., 1979-81; mgr. mgmt. adv. services Deloitte, Haskins & Sells, Charlotte, N.C., 1981-85, San Francisco, 1986—; lectr. in field. Mem. Community Relations Bd., City of Boca Raton, 1976, candidate for city council, 1977. Mem. Am. Soc. Pub. Adminstrn., Nat. Corp. Cash Mgmt. Assn., Am. Bankers Assn., Am. Polit. Sci. Assn., Policy Scis. Orgn., Phi Kappa Phi. Baptist. Contbr. articles to profl. jours. Office: 2100 Southern National Center Charlotte NC 28202

SAVILLE, ROYCE BLAIR, lawyer; b. Cumberland, Md., Aug. 5, 1948; s. Earl Blair and Audrey(Cosner) S.; m. Sharon Ann Brinkman, Apr. 3, 1981; children—Melissa Ann, Lauren Ashley, Meagan Elizabeth. B.A., W.Va. U., 1970, J.D., 1974. Bar: W.Va. 1974; assoc. William J. Oates Jr., Romney, W.Va., 1974-75; ptnr. Oates & Saville, 1975-77; sole practice, 1978—; pres. Potomac Land Co., Romney, 1975—; mcpl. judge City of Romney, 1980—. Served with USAR, 1970-76. Mem. ABA, W.Va. Bar Assn., Assn. Trial Lawyers Am., W.Va. Trial Lawyers Assn., W.Va. U. Alumni Assn. (life), W.Va. Law Sch. Assn. (life), Phi Alpha Delta. Democrat. Episcopalian. Lodge: Masons. Home: Liberty Hall 276 E Main St Romney WV 26757 also Mill Island Moorefield WV 26836 Office: 95 W Main St Romney WV 26757

SAVING, THOMAS ROBERT, economics educator, consultant; b. Chgo., Dec. 27, 1933; s. Harold John and Frances Josephine (Fillipino) S.; m. Barbara Jean Sorby, Aug. 22, 1959; children—Jason Lee, Nicole Aline. B.A. in Econs., Mich. State U., 1957; M.A. in Econs., U. Chgo., 1958, Ph.D. in Econs., 1960. Asst. prof. U. Wash., Seattle, 1960-61; asst. prof. Mich. State U., East Lansing, 1961-63, assoc. prof., 1965-66, prof., 1966-68; head dept. econs. Tex. A&M U., College Station, 1985—, prof. econs., 1968—; pres. RRC, Inc., College Station, 1980-85. Author: Money, Wealth, Economic Theory, 1966. Mem. Western Econ. Assn. (pres. 1971-72), So. Econ. Assn. (pres. 1981-82), Am. Econs. Assn. Home: 1402 Post Oak Circle College Station TX 77840 Office: Tex A&M U Dept Econs College Station TX 77843

SAVINO, EVELYN GOLDSTEIN BUHLER, retired lawyer, insurance broker; b. N.Y.C., Aug. 11, 1916; d. Max and Rachel Leah (Goldstein) Goldstein; m. David George Buhler, Oct. 6, 1940 (dec. 1970); children—Alan S., Barry R., Robert L., Gwen B. Dreilinger; m. Peter John Savino, Dec. 18, 1971. B.A., Hunter Coll., 1936; LL.B., Bklyn. Law Sch., St. Lawrence U., 1940. Bar: N.Y., 1943. Practicing atty. Buhler & Buhler, Esqs., N.Y.C., 1943-70. Del., Dem. Nat. Conv., Atlantic City, 1964; 1st v.p. Boca Greens Assn. Homeowners; bd. dirs. Delray Sr. Citizens' Ctr. Mem. Women's Am. ORT (legacy and endowment chmn. 1983—, pres. Boca Glades chpt. 1982-84), Bklyn. Law Sch. Alumni Assn. Avocations: golf, music, public charity. Home: 19760 Boca Greens Dr Boca Raton FL 33434

SAVITZ, ALAN DAVID, wholesale import-export company executive; b. Wilkes-Barre, Pa., Dec. 19, 1937; s. Abe and Sylvia (Strauss) S.; B.B.A., U. Miami (Fla.), 1960; m. Lucille Mona Kahn, Feb. 25, 1961; children—Lisa Ann, David Alan, Michael Charles. Vice pres., dir. Am. Star Co., Miami, 1961-65; chmn. bd., pres., dir. Universal Home Products, Inc., Miami, 1965—. Served as 2d lt. USAR. Mem. Nat. Assn. Textile Apparel Wholesalers, Res. Officers Assn., U. Miami Alumni Assn. Inter-Am. Businessmen's Assn. Internat. Clubs: U.S. Power Squadron, Masons, Shriners. Home: 11094 Paradela St Coral Gables FL 33156 Office: 1920 N Miami Ave Miami FL 33136

SAWYER, GLADYS KNIGHT, civic worker, ret. sch. adminstr.; b. El Paso, Tex., Mar. 31, 1921; d. Oscar Kenneth and Lula Kate (Beaty) Knight; student Catawba Coll., 1937-38; B.A., Lenoir Rhyne Coll., 1957; M.A., Appalachian State U., 1968; m. Clyde Wesley Sawyer, July 21, 1938 (dec. Jan. 1979); children—Kathryn Anne, Gay Virginia, Kay Margaret, Clyde Wesley. Farmer, 1941-64; machine operator clothing factory, 1945-53; classroom tchr., 1955-68; high sch. supr., 1968-81; dir. ESEA Middle Sch. Project, Title IV-C, Caldwell County Schs., Lenoir, N.C., 1977-79, middle sch. supr., 1977-81, ret., 1981; former chmn. dept. fgn. lang. and English, Oak Hill High Sch., Hibriten High Sch.; workshop tchr.; dir. CETA remediation. Sec. adv. com. Caldwell County Social Services, 1974; youth chmn. ARC, 1970-72; chmn. youth task force Community Based Alternatives, Caldwell County, 1980-81; RSVP vol. library and schs.; vol. Hospice of Caldwell County, Caldwell County Home Health Adv. Bd.; elder, sec. consistory United Ch. Christ, vol. Retirement Ctr., peace task force; bd. dirs. Am. Lung Assn., N.C., also Western dist. assn.; mem. Caldwell County Council to Prevent Teenage Pregnancy; coordinator vol. service Caldwell County Schs. Mem. N.C. League Middle and Jr. High Schs. (founder), Am. Assn. Ret. Persons (chpt. publicity chmn.). Democrat. Club: Altrusa (dir. 1979-80, v.p. 1980-82). Contbr. articles to edn. jour. Home: 921 Millers Creek Rd SE Lenoir NC 28645

SAWYER, HUGH LUCAS, accountant, financial planning consultant; b. Norfolk, Va., Apr. 30, 1952; s. John Wilkins, II, and Vallie (Lucas) S.; m. Melanie Ann Basham, Dec. 21, 1972; children—Chadwick, Christina. B.B.A. summa cum laude, Roanoke Coll., 1974. C.P.A., Va. Supr. Brown Edward & Co., C.P.A.s, Roanoke, 1974-78; tax mgr. Ernst & Whinney, C.P.A.s, Roanoke, 1978-84; pres. Fin. Planning of Va., Roanoke, 1984—; owner Hugh L. Sawyer, C.P.A., Roanoke and Radford, Va., 1984—. Author publs. in field. Bd. advisors Roanoke Coll., 1983—, Radford U., 1983—; sect. chmn. United Way, Roanoke, 1980-81. Recipient Wall St. Jour. award, 1974; jr. scholar Roanoke Coll., 1973. Fellow Va. Soc. C.P.A.s (tax com. 1983); mem. Am. Inst. C.P.A.s (tax sect.), Nat. Assn. Accts. (pres. Roanoke chpt. 1982-83), Internat. Assn. Fin. Planning (bd. dirs. Roanoke chpt. 1984-85), Roanoke C. of C., Phi Beta Kappa. Republican. Baptist. Clubs: The Boardroom (pres. Roanoke 1981-82), Rotary. Avocations: tennis; racquetball. Home: 2704 Summit Ridge Rd NE Roanoke VA 24012 Office: Dominion Bank Bldg Suite 1413 Roanoke VA 24011

SAWYER, JAMES EDWARD, real estate executive; b. San Antonio, May 4, 1943; s. James Eldren and Freida Loyce (Pannill) S.; B.B.A., Tex. Christian U., 1967; m. R. Eileen Massey, Dec. 27, 1967; children—Bryan Lynn, Yolonda Lynn. Sr. acct. Arthur Young & Co., Ft. Worth, 1967-70, Bogotá, Colombia, 1970-71; bus. mgr. Johnson Chevrolet, Dallas, 1971-73: sr. tax acct. First Nat. Bank, Dallas, 1973; controller Malouf Co., Dallas, 1973-75; partner Ellis, Martin & Sawyer, C.P.A.s, Lawton, Okla., 1976-79; owner, prin. James E. Sawyer, C.P.A., Lawton, 1979-80; pres. Sawyer, Liester & Stabler, Inc., C.P.A.s, Lawton, 1980-83, D.B. Harrell Co., Comml. Realtors, San Antonio, 1983—. Co-chmn. drive Arts for All Lawton, 1978, bd. dirs., 1978— pres., 1978-79; bd. dirs. Lawton Philharm. Orch., 1978—, v.p., 1979; chmn. Redcoat-Ambassadors of Lawton C. of C., 1978-79; mem. high council Lawton Stake Ch. Jesus Christ of Latter-day Saints, 1976-79. C.P.A., Tex., Okla. Mem. Am. Inst. C.P.A.s, Am., Okla. (pres. SW chpt., 1977-79, 80-81, state dir. 1977-79, 80-83), Tex. socs. C.P.A.s, Beta Alpha Psi, Beta Gamma Sigma. Republican. Mormon. Club: Kiwanis (dir. 1979-83). Home: 9318 Northbend Dr San Antonio TX 78239 Office: 801 N St Mary's San Antonio TX 78205

SAWYER, LINDA G., veterinarian; b. Ft. Huachuca, Ariz., Nov. 3, 1954; d. James W. and Mae Dean (Woodburn) S. A.A. magna cum laude, Vol. State Community Coll., 1974; D.V.M. with honors, Auburn U., 1979. With Memphis Animal Hosp., Inc., 1979, Americus Vet. Hosp. (Ga.), 1979-82; owner, veterinarian Whispering Pines Animal Hosp., Americus, 1982—. Mem. AVMA, South Ga. Vet. Med. Assn., Phi Kappa Phi, Phi Zeta. Baptist. Office: Whispering Pines Animal Hosp RR5 Box 200 Vienna Rd Americus GA 31709

SAWYER, MARGERY ANN MERCER, hospital administrator; b. Tacoma, Sept. 13, 1940; d. Marshal Carlton and Elsie Irene (Harm) Mercer; m. John Bowen Sawyer, Sept. 2, 1961; 1 dau., Mylinda Ann. Diploma, Tacoma Gen. Hosp. Sch. Nursing, 1961. Cert. operating room nurse. Asst. operating room supr. DeKalb Gen. Hosp., Decatur, Ga., 1967-69; operating room supr. Doctor's Meml. Hosp., Atlanta, 1973-79; dir. surg. services Humana Hosp. Gwinnett, Snellville, Ga., 1979—. Mem. Assn. Operating Rm. Nurses (chpt. Nurse of Yr. 1976-77, recommended practices com. 1981-83, nursing practices com. 1984-86, chmn. planning com. Atlanta congress 1984). Baptist. Avocations: gardening; travel; fishing. Home: 2536 Britt Rd PO Box 141 Snellville GA 30278 Office: Humana Hosp Gwinnett 2160 Fountain Dr Snellville GA 30278

SAWYER, MARIANNE SUTTON, motion picture-television producer; b. Houston, Oct. 14, 1958; d. Jimmy and Sue Sutton; m. Joseph Brion Sawyer, Apr. 16, 1983. B.A. in communications, Trinity U., San Antonio, 1981. TV reporter-anchor woman, hosted 30 minute weekly pub. affairs show KTPX-TV, Midland, Tex., 1981-83; producer TV-film commls. and documentaries Hayes Prodns., San Antonio, 1983—. Recipient UPI Regional award, 1982, two news stories picked up by ABC network, one by Good Morning Am. Mem. Tex. Assn. Film/Tape Profls. (bus. mgr.), Sigma Delta Chi Delta, Gamma Chi Delta. Produced docu-drama: Anyman, 1981. Home: 3435 River N San Antonio TX 78205

SAXON, NEAL HARRIS, pharmacist; b. Iron Mountain, Mich., May 20, 1957; s. Warren Harris and Clarice Inez (Waites) S. B.S. in Pharmacy, Auburn U., 1980. Pharmacy intern Harco Drug, Tuscaloosa, Ala., 1980-81, asst. store mgr., Greenville, Ala., 1981-84; dir. pharmacy LV Stabler Meml. Hosp., Greenville, 1985—. Vice-pres. chancel choir 1st United Meth. Ch., Greenville, 1985—. Mem. Greenville Jaycees (v.p. 1985—), Ala. Pharm. Assn., Ala. Soc. Hosp. Pharmacists, Am. Pharm. Assn., Am. Soc. Hosp. Pharmacists. Methodist. Avocations: tennis; jogging; biking. Home: 700 Ft Dale Rd Greenville AL 36037 Office: LV Stabler Meml Hosp PO Box 1000 Greenville AL 36037

SAYE, ALBERT B., emeritus political scientist, educator, author; b. Rutledge, Ga., Nov. 29, 1912; s. William Bibb and Suvinnie (Whitten) S.; m. Ruth Kendrick, Dec. 20, 1939. A.B., U. Ga., 1934, M.A., 1935, LL.B., 1957; diplôme de français degré supèrieur U. Dijon, France, 1938; Ph.D., Harvard U., 1941. Assoc. prof. history U. Ga., Athens, 1938-41, assoc. prof. polit. sci., 1941-47, prof., 1947-54, prof. law, 1957-75, R.B. Russell prof. polit. sci., 1975-79, prof. emeritus, 1979—. Author 20 books including: New Viewpoints in Georgia History, 1943; American Constitutional Law, 2d edit., 1979; Georgia History and Government, 3d edit., 1982; Principles of American Government, 10th edit., 1986. Named Disting. Prof., Ga. Alumni Found. Mem. Internat. Polit. Sci. Assn., Ga. Polit. Sci. Assn., Ga. Hist. Soc., Phi Beta Kappa. Baptist. Home: 190 W Lake Pl Athens GA 30606 Office: U Ga Dept Polit Sci Athens GA 30602

SAYER, WILLIAM H., chiropractic physician; b. Wilmington, Del., Jan. 5, 1948; m. Lorraine Sayer, Jan. 16, 1972; children—Jessica Alexandra, Gabriel Ian, Maxwell Ely. B.A., Oglethorpe U., 1970; D.C. summa cum laude, Palmer Coll. Chiropractic, Davenport, Iowa, 1976. Diplomate Nat. Bd. Chiropractic Examiners. Practice chiropractic, Winter Haven, Fla., 1976—; personal injury and family practice, Atlanta, 1977—; instr. Life Chiropractic Coll., Atlanta, 1976. Mem. Am. Chiropractic Assn., Ga. Chiropractic Assn., Fla. Chiropractic Assn., Am. Chiropractic Assn. (councils on roentgenology, sports injuries, chiropractic orthopedics, physiotherapy, nutrition), Pi Tau Delta. Office: 5075 Roswell Rd NE Suite 124 Atlanta GA 30342

SAYFIE, EUGENE JOSEPH, cardiologist internist; b. Charleston, W.Va., Sept. 13, 1934; s. Snow and Selma (Zakaib) S.; B.S. magna cum laude, W.Va. U., 1956; M.D., Washington U., St. Louis, 1960; m. Suzanne Morin, Feb. 22, 1969; children—Stephanie, Nicole, Lisa, Amy Jo. Practice medicine specializing in internal medicine and cardiology, Miami, Fla.; mem. staff Miami Heart Inst., chief med. staff, 1978-80, chief of medicine, 1981—; cons. staff physician Jackson Meml. Hosp., Miami; clin. asso. prof. Sch. Medicine, U. Miami. Bd. dirs. Miami Heart Inst., Heart Assn. Greater Miami; trustee Antiochian Orthodox Christian Archdiocese N.Am. Recipient Silver Meritorious award Miami Heart Inst., 1977. Fellow ACP, Am. Coll. Cardiology, Am. Coll. Angiology, Am. Coll. Chest Physicians; mem. AMA, Am., Fla., Greater Miami (pres. 1981-82, dir.) heart assns., Fla., Dade County med. assns., Alpha Omega Alpha. Mem. Eastern Orthodox Ch. Clubs: LaGorce Country, Palm Bay, Bath, Jockey. Office: 550 Brickell Ave Miami FL 33131

SAYLES, DAVID CYR, engineer, consultant; b. Scollard, Alta., Can., Mar. 23, 1917; came to U.S., 1939; s. Maxine and Gertrude S.; m. Marion Katherine Zelter, July 29, 1952 (dec. 1969); children—Lance Howard, Lynn Robert. B.S. with honors in Chemistry, U. Alta., 1939; M.S. in Chemistry, U. Chgo., 1941; Ph.D. in Chemistry, Purdue U., 1946, B.S. in Chem. Engring., 1946. Profl. engr., Ala. Chief, Gun and Rocket Br., Wright Air Devel. Ctr., 1954-56; tech. advisor Air Munitions Lab., Eglin AFB, Fla., 1956-57; group leader Army Missile Command, Redstone Arsenal, Ala., 1958-63, scientist, 1963-70; engr. Ballistic Missile Def. Advanced Tech. Ctr., Huntsville, Ala., 1970—; cons. Lockheelly Distillery, Calgary, Alta., 1946-75, Harrow Enterprises, Montreal, 1946-75, Hopestone, Montreal, 1946-75, R & D Corp., Chgo., 1940-73. Author publs. in field; inventor. Councilman, Ft. Walton Beach, Fla., 1957; bd. dirs. Redstone Fed. Credit Union, Huntsville, 1982. Served as capt. Royal Canadian Engrs., 1944-46. Eli Lilly fellow, 1940-41; Internat. House fellow, 1940-43; du Pont fellow, 1942-43; Alrose chem. fellow, 1943-46; research fellow Purdue U., 1945-46; Recipient James T. Grady award, 1977, So. Chemists award, 1978, Am. Inst. Chemists honor scroll, 1979. Mem. Am. Chem. Soc., Am. Inst. Chemists, Ala., Soc. Profl. Engrs., JANNAF Propulsion. Avocations: sailing; bridge; square dancing. Home: PO Box 4741 Huntsville AL 35815-4741 Office: Ballistic Missile Defense Advanced Tech Ctr 106 Wynn Dr NW Huntsville AL 35807-3801

SBARATTA, RICHARD MARK, lawyer; b. Jersey City, July 1, 1948; s. Philip and Carmela (Dono) S.; m. Corinne MacMahon, June 11, 1977; children—Brianne, Ryan, Kyle. B.A., Montclair State Coll., 1970; M.A. in Econs., Pa. State U., 1974; J.D., N.Y. Law Sch., 1978. Bar: N.Y. 1979. Econ. analyst Nat. Econ. Research Assocs., N.Y.C., 1974-78; regulatory atty. AT&T, N.Y.C., 1978-83; v.p., gen. counsel Nat. Exchange Carrier Assn., Whippany, N.J., 1983-85; solicitor Bell South, Atlanta, 1985—. Served with U.S. Army, 1971-72. Mem. ABA, N.Y. State Bar Assn., Am. Econ. Assn., Omicron Delta Epsilon. Home 1382 Wyntercreek Ln Dunwoody GA 30338 Office: So Bell Ctr 675 W Peachtree St NE Atlanta GA 30375

SBREGA, JOHN JOSEPH, history educator; b. Holyoke, Mass., July 8, 1941; s. John Bruno and Rita Alice (Counter) S.; m. Jo-Anne Manijak, Dec. 14, 1974; children—Daniel Joseph, Christianne. A.B., Union Coll., 1963; M.A., Georgetown U., 1972, Ph.D., 1974. Dept. chmn. social scis. J.S. Reynolds Comml. Coll., Richmond, Va., 1974-79; div. chmn. social scis. Tidewater Comml. Coll., Virginia Beach, Va., 1979—. Author: Anglo-American Relations and Colonialism in East Asia, 1941-45, 1983. Contbr. articles to profl. jours. Baseball coach Little League, Virginia Beach, 1983—. Served to capt. USAF, 1963-68. Recipient Moncado prize Am. Mil. Inst., 1983; Beveridge grantee Am. Hist. Assn., 1983; research grantee Va. Social Scis. Assn., 1983; Fulbright scholar Council for Internat. Exchange of Scholars, 1972-73. Mem. Am. Hist. Assn., Am. Com. Historians of the Second World War, Soc. Historians of Am. Fgn. Relations. Greater Hampton Roads World Affairs Council (trustee 1983) Democrat. Roman Catholic. Avocations: reading, sports. Home: 404 Loyalist Ct Virginia Beach VA 23452 Office: Tidewater Community Coll 1700 College Crescent Virginia Beach VA 23456

SCALES, ARCHIBALD HENDERSON, II, lawyer; b. Greensboro, N.C., Oct. 26, 1916; s. Alfred Moore and Mary Leigh (Pell) S.; m. Carolyn Evans, June 23, 1940; children—Archibald Henderson III, Richard Erskine. A.B., U. N.C., 1936. Bar: N.C. 1937. Sole practice, Currituck, N.C., 1938-42; adjudication officer VA, Charlotte, N.C., 1946-48, Winston-Salem, N.C., 1948-73; assoc. Hall, Scales & Cleland, Winston-Salem, 1974-77; ptnr. Scales & Scales, Winston-Salem, 1977-78; sole practice, Winston-Salem, 1978—. Br. dir. CD, Forsyth County, N.C., 1963—; chmn. bd. dirs. Crisis Control Ministry, Inc., Winston-Salem, 1974-75, bd. dirs., 1975-83; bd. dirs. Sr. Services, Inc., Winston-Salem, 1984—. Served to comdr. USN, 1942-46; PTO, MTO. Recipient commendation VA, 1973, citation for disting. service DAV, 1973, resolution of appreciation Crisis Control Ministry, Inc., 1983. Mem. N.C. Bar Assn., Forsyth County Bar Assn. Democrat. Presbyterian. Lodge: Kiwanis (various local offices 1971—). Avocations: horticulture; reading; genealogy. Home and Office: 2912 Robin Hood Rd Winston-Salem NC 27106

SCALES, HAZEL HELEN, educational administrator; b. Shawmut, Ala., Sept. 6, 1926; d. Johnie Hamilton and Afton Hazelton (Nichols) Daniel; m. Charles Drew Scales, June 1, 1951; 1 son, Charles Donald. B.S., State Tchrs. Coll., Jacksonville, Ala., 1950, B.S., 1950; M.A., U. South Ala., 1972. Cert. tchr., supr-adminstr., Fla., Ala., Ga. Tchr. pub. schs., Ala., 1946-52, Ga., 1952-55, Fla., 1956-75; dept. chairperson Escambia High Sch., Pensacola, Fla., 1965-75; asst. prin. Pine Forest High Sch., Pensacola, 1975-80, prin., 1980—. Vol. United Way, Pensacola, 1980-85, ARC, Pensacola, 1980s; mem. adv. council West Fla. Hosp., Pensacola, 1980—; speaker to civic clubs, chs., Pensacola, 1980—. Named Tchr. of Yr., Exchange Clubs, Pensacola, 1964; recipient Woman of Yr. award Gateway Ch. of Christ, Pensacola, 1985. Mem. Nat. Assn. Secondary Prins., Fla. Assn. Sch. Adminstrs., Escambia Assn. Adminstrs. in Edn. (bd. dirs. 1984-85), Fla. Council on Ednl. Mgmt., Delta Kappa Gamma (pres. local chpt. 1966-68), Phi Delta Kappa (bd. dirs. local chpt. 1984-85). Democrat. Baptist. Avocations: reading; gardening; cooking. Home: 6556 Lake Charlene Dr Pensacola FL 32506 Office: Pine Forest High Sch 2500 Longleaf Dr Pensacola FL 32506

SCALES, JAMES RALPH, university president emeritus; b. Jay, Okla., May 27, 1919; s. John Grover and Katie (Whitley) S.; B.A., Okla. Baptist U., 1939; M.A., U. Okla., 1941, Ph.D., 1949; postgrad. U. Chgo., 1945-47, U. London, 1958; LL.D., Alderson Broaddus Coll., 1971. Duke U., 1976; Litt.D., No. Mich. U., 1972; L.H.D., Belmont Abbey Coll., 1981, Winston-Salem State U., 1984; m. Elizabeth Ann Randel, August 4, 1944; children—Laura (dec.), Ann Catherine. Reporter, Miami (Okla.) News Record, 1934-35, Shawnee (Okla.) News-Star, 1935-36; instr. Okla. Baptist U., Shawnee, 1940-42, asst. prof., 1946-47, asso. prof., 1947-51, prof. history, govt., 1951-61, v.p., 1950-53, exec. v.p., 1953-61, pres., 1961-65; dean arts and scis. Okla. State U., Stillwater, 1965-67; pres. Wake Forest U., Winston-Salem, N.C., 1967-83, pres. emeritus, 1983—; founder Cimmaron Rev., 1967—. Mem. Pres.'s Com. Edn. Beyond High Sch., 1957; mem. adv. com. U.S. Army Command and Gen. Staff Coll., Ft. Leavenworth, Kans., 1969-72, chmn., 1971-72; mem. U.S. del. UNESCO, 1978-81. Mem. Okla. del. Democratic Nat. Conv., 1956; trustee Belmont Abbey Coll., 1977-80. Served as officer USNR, 1942-45. Named to Okla. Hall of Fame, 1983. Mem. Am. Hist. Assn., Am. Polit. Sci. Assn., Am. Assn. U. Profs., So. Assn. Bapt. Colls. (pres. 1969-70), Am. Guild Organists, N.C. Assn. Ind. Colls. (pres. 1969-71), Winston-Salem C. of C. (dir.), Phi Beta Kappa, Omicron Delta Kappa, Phi Eta Sigma. Baptist (deacon). Rotarian. Clubs: University (N.Y.C.); Reform (London); Bay Hill Golf and Country (Orlando, Fla.); Cape Fear (Wilmington, N.C.); Miles Grant Country (Port Salerno, Fla.). Address: PO Drawer 7228 Winston-Salem NC 27109

SCALES, JIMMY VERDELL, school administrator; b. Idabel, Okla., Sept. 25, 1943; s. Walter Scales and Lodiska (Young) Scales Spagner; m. Cynthia Sherrilyn Gray, Feb. 7, 1980; 1 child, Jimmy V. Jr. B.S., East Central U., 1966,

M.Ed., 1969. Tchr., coach Okmulgee Pub. Sch., Okla., 1966-71; athletic dir. N.E. High Sch., Oklahoma City, 1971-74; asst. prin. John Marshall High Sch., Oklahoma City, 1974-77; prin. Millwood Jr./Sr. High Sch., Oklahoma City, 1977-85; prin. McLain High Sch., Tulsa, 1985—. Active NAACP, Oklahoma City, 1977—, YMCA, Oklahoma City, 1979—; treas. Okla. Curriculum Improvement Commn., Oklahoma City, 1979-84; bd. dirs. Mgmt. Acad., Stillwater, Okla., 1981-84; vice-chmn., sec. Okla. Commn. Children and Youth, Oklahoma City, 1982-84; bd. dirs. Okla. State Sch. Bd., Oklahoma City, 1984—. Recipient Outstanding Young Man Am. award U.S. Jaycees, 1971; Outstanding Young Man Okla. award Jaycees, 1977; Civic Leader award Set Club, 1983. Mem. Nat. Assn. Secondary Sch. Prins., Assn. Curriculum Devel., Okla. Assn. Secondary Prins. (Outstanding Adminstr. award 1984-85), Nat. Assn. State Bds. Edn. (nat. program com. 1984—). Democrat. Methodist. Avocations: fishing; jogging. Home: 1702 N 24th West Ave Tulsa OK 74127 Office: McLain High Sch 4929 N Peoria Tulsa OK 74126

SCANDALIOS, JOHN GEORGE, geneticist; b. Nisyros Isle, Greece, Nov. 1, 1934; s. George John and Calliope (Broujos) S.; came to U.S., 1946; B.A., U. Va., 1957; M.S., Adelphi U., 1962; Ph.D., U. Hawaii, 1965; m. Penelope Anne Lawrence, Jan. 18, 1961; children—Artemis Christina, Melissa Joan, Nikki Eleni. Asso. in bacterial genetics Cold Spring Harbor Labs., 1960-62; NIH postdoctoral fellow U. Hawaii Med. Sch., 1965; asst. prof. Mich. State U., East Lansing, 1965-60, asso. prof., 1970-72; prof., head dept. biology U. S.C., Columbia, 1973-75; prof., head dept. genetics N.C. State U., Raleigh, 1975—, Disting. Univ. prof. of genetics, 1985—; vis. prof. genetics U. Calif., Davis, 1969; vis. prof. OAS, Argentina, Chile and Brazil, 1972; mem. NIH-Recombinant DNA Adv. Com., 1980—. Served with USAF, 1957. Alexander von Humboldt travel fellow, 1976; mem. exchange program NAS, US/USSR. Mem. Genetics Soc. Am., Am. Soc. Human Genetics, Am. Genetic Assn. (pres. 1981), AAAS, Soc. Devel. Biology, Sigma Xi. Greek Orthodox. Author: Physiological Genetics, 1979; editor: Developmental Genetics Jour.; Advances in Genetics; co-editor: Isozymes: Current Topics in Biological and Medical Research, 1975; Monographs in Developmental Biology, 1968—. Office: PO Box 7614 Raleigh NC 27695

SCANLON, PAT H., lawyer; b. Houma, La., Aug. 4, 1936; s. Leo Joseph and Mary (Ezell) S.; m. Carlene Myers, June 10, 1961; children—Margaret, Pat, Jr., Cissy, John. B.S. in Geology, La. State U., 1957; LL.B. with distinction, U. Miss., 1960. Assoc. Satterfield, Shell, Williams & Bo, Jackson, Miss., 1960-62; ptnr. Young, Scanlon & Sessums, Jackson, 1962—; chmn., commnr. Miss. Jud. Performance Commn., Jackson, 1980-83; instr. Jackson Sch. Law, 1963-66; chmn. Miss. Law Inst., Jackson, 1970. Mem. editorial bd. Miss. Law Jour., 1959-60. Mem. vestry St. James Episcopal Ch., Jackson, 1972-75, 79—). Served to capt. USAR. Fellow Am. Coll. Trial Lawyers, Internat. Soc. Barristers, Am. Bar Found., Miss. Bar Found. (trustee 1980-83); mem. Miss. Bankruptcy Conf. (pres. 1984—), Miss. Young Lawyers Assn. (pres. 1969-70), Miss. State Bar Assn. (2d v.p. 1970-71), Hinds County Bar Assn. (pres. 1974-75), Fed. Bar Assn. (pres. Miss. chpt. 1972-73). Lodge: Kiwanis (sec. 1966-70). Office: 1440 Deposit Guaranty Plaza Jackson MS 39201

SCANLON, WILLIAM NEIL, professional tennis player; b. Dallas, Nov. 13, 1956; s. Philip James and Hannah Neil (Daniel) S. Student Trinity U., 1974-76. Singles champion NCAA, 1976; semi-finalist U.S. Open Tennis, 1983; rank 9, Tennis World, 1983; pres. Scanlon Corp., Dallas, 1980—. Founder, pres. Dallas Youth Found., 1983—. Mem. Assn. Tennis Profls. Republican. Roman Catholic. Clubs: Northwood, T Bar M Tennis. Home: 13418 Hughes Ln Dallas TX 75240 Office: Scanlon Corp 6335 NW Hwy 516 Dallas TX 75225

SCARBOROUGH, CLARENCE VIRGIL, college administrator, minister; b. Bossier City, La., Sept. 11, 1945; s. Clarence V. Scarborough and Norma Maxine (Strayhan) Scarborough Smith. B.A., Rhodes Coll., 1967; M.Div., Princeton Theol. Sem., 1971. Ordained minister Presbyterian Ch. Asst. minister First Presbyn. Ch., Bklyn., 1971-72; minister to community First Presbyn. and Grace Episcopal chs., Bklyn., 1971-73; asst. dean students Rhodes Coll., Memphis, 1975-76, assoc. dean students, 1976-80, dean students, 1980—. Candidates chmn. Presbetery W. Tenn., 1980-84; candidates com. Presbytery Memphis, 1984—. Recipient Algeron Sydney Sullivan award Rhodes Coll., 1967, 84. Rockefeller Theol. fellow, 1967. Democrat. Home: 1792 Forrest Ave Memphis TN 38112

SCARBOROUGH, CLAUDE MOOD, JR., lawyer; b. Columbia, S.C., Dec. 7, 1929; s. Claude M. and Gelene (Stallworth) S.; student U. of South, 1947-49; A.B., U.S.C., 1951, LL.B., 1952; m. Sarah Carpenter, June 30, 1955; children—Sarah Catherine, Elizabeth Ann, Claude M. III, Gelene Bivins. Admitted to S.C. bar, 1952, U.S. Dist. Ct., 1956; U.S. Ct. Appeals, 1957; assoc. firm Nelson, Mullins & Grier, Columbia, S.C., 1955-61, ptnr. Nelson, Mullins, Grier & Scarborough, 1961—, mng. ptnr., 1964—; mem. Columbia adv. bd. Nat. Bank S.C., 1979—, chmn., 1982—, also dir.; dir. NBSC Corp. Spl. hearing officer U.S. Dept. Justice, 1962-68. Trustee Legal Aid Soc. Richland Co., 1960-67, pres., 1960-64; mem. Gov.'s Com. to Study Prison and Community Relations, 1975-76; mem. indsl. adv. bd. S.C. Dept. Corrections, 1974-76; bd. dirs. Com. of 100, 1980-85, chmn., 1983-84; bd. trustees Episc. Diocese of Upper S.C., 1981—, pres., 1985—; chmn. bd. dirs. S.C. Research Authority, 1983—, S.C. Council Econ. Devel., 1984—. Served to 1st lt. AUS, 1952-55. Mem. Internat. Assn. Ins. Counsel, Am., S.C. (treas. 1968-72, exec. com. 1972-74, chmn. exec. com. 1973-74, pres. 1975-76), Richland County bar assns., S.C. Bar Found. (dir. 1976-81, chmn. bd. 1977-80), U.S. 4th Circuit Jud. Conf. (permanent mem.), S.C. Def. Attys. Assn., Def. Research Inst., Am. Judicature Soc. (Herbert Harley award 1976), Greater Columbia C. of C. (pres. 1986-87, dir. 1985—), Phi Delta Phi. Episcopalian (lay reader, vestryman, warden). Clubs: Palmetto, Summit, Wildewood, Forest Lake Country, Kiwanis. Home: 1514 Tanglewood Rd Columbia SC 29205 Office: 3d Floor Keenan Bldg Columbia SC 29201

SCARBOROUGH, ESMOND GREGORY, petroleum geologist; b. Ft. Worth, July 2, 1949; s. Esmond Luther and Lena Mae (Fenner) S.; m. Rita Claire McCudden, Nov., 1974 (div. 1984). A.A., Tarrant County Jr. Coll., 1977; B.S. in Geology, U. Tex., Arlington, 1981. Geologist, field supr. KCA Baron Inc., Weatherford, Tex., 1980-81; geologist, field supt. Geohawk Exploration, Ft. Worth, 1981-82; cons. geologist Coastline Oil and Gas Co., Ft. Worth, 1982-84; staff geologist InterAm. Minerals Inc., Mineral Wells, Tex., 1984—. Dep. Tarrant County Sheriff's Dept., Ft. Worth; vol. Dist XI Spl. Olympics, Ft. Worth. Served with USN, 1969-70, Vietnam. Mem. Am. Assn. Petroleum Geologists. Avocations: hunting; fishing; outdoor activities.

SCARBOROUGH, STUART MARSHALL, oil company executive; b. N.Y.C., Dec. 8, 1952; s. Moliere and Eleanor Margaret (Scarborough) S.; m. Sandra Lynn Smith, June 28, 1980; 1 child, Courtney Munson. B.B.A., Tex. A&M U., 1975. Landman, Placid Oil Co., Shreveport, La., 1975-78, sr. field landman, San Antonio, 1978-80, mgr. office, area rep., Houston, 1980-81; landman Southland Royalty Co., Houston, 1981—. Canvasser Houston Symphony League, 1983. Mem. Am. Assn. Petroleum Landmen (cert.), Houston Assn. Petroleum Landmen, Ark. La. Tex. Landmens Assn., S. Tex. Geol. Soc., Producers Forum, Assn. Former Students Tex. A&M U., S.A.R. Republican. Episcopalian. Club: Houston Highlanders Pipe Band. Lodge: Masons. Avocations: hunting; fishing; travel; jogging; painting. Home: 4236 Byron St Houston TX 77005 Office: Southland Royalty Co 5251 Westheimer St Suite 400 Houston TX 77056

SCARBOROUGH, TRUMAN GUY, JR., lawyer, mayor; b. St. Augustine, Fla., Jan. 16, 1944; s. Truman and Mary Catherine (Nuzum) S.; m. Barbara Jean Lowry, June 21, 1969; children—Truman Guy III, Mary Catherine. B.S., U. Fla., 1966, J.D., 1968; postgrad. George Washington U., 1970-71. Bar: Fla. 1971, U.S. Dist. Ct. D.C. 1971, U.S. Supreme Ct. 1974, U.S. Dist. Ct. (mid. dist.) Fla. 1974, U.S. Ct. Appeals D.C. 1971, U.S. Ct. Appeals (5th and 11th cirs.) 1981. Loan officer Ex-Im Bank, Washington, 1969-72; sole practice, Titusville, Fla., 1972—; prosecutor City of Cocoa and Titusville, 1972-75; mayor City of Titusville, 1980—. Chmn. Ch. Bd. Deacons, Titusville, 1978; vice chmn. Brevard Symphony Orch., Melbourne, Fla.; co-chmn. Fla. Theatre, Titusville. Recipient Good Govt. award Jaycees, 1982; Key to City of Cocoa, 1984; honored by Spl. Program Brevard Community Coll., 1984. Mem. D.C. Bar Assn., Fla. Bar Assn., Brevard County Bar Assn. Republican. Presbyterian. Club: Rotary. Office: Harrison St Titusville FL 32780

SCARBOROUGH, CLEVE KNOX, JR., museum director; b. Florence, Ala., July 17, 1939; s. Cleve Knox and Emma Lee (Matheny) S.; m. Sharon K. Smith, Sept. 9, 1972. B.S., U. No. Ala., 1962; M.A., U. Iowa, 1967. Asst. prof. art history U. Tenn., 1967-69; dir. Mint Mus. Art, Charlotte, N.C., 1969-76, Hunter Mus. Art, Chattanooga, 1976—; pres. N.C. Museum Council, 1976; bd. mem., adv. com. Tenn. Arts Commn., 1976-77, chmn. visual arts com., 1978—; mem. art selection com. TVA, 1983—, Provident Life Ins. Co., 1983—. Compiler, editor: North Carolinians Collect, 1970, Pre Columbian Art of the Americas, 1971, Graphics by Four Modern Swiss Sculptors, 1972, British Paintings from the North Carolina Museum, 1973, Montain Landscapes by Swiss Artists, 1976. Mem. Chattanooga Landmark Com., City Planning Bd.; Bd. dirs. Chattanooga Conv. and Visitors Bur., 1977-79; advisor Chattanooga Central City Council, 1981—, Tenn. State Mus., 1981. Served with USN, 1962-64. Mem. Am. Assn. Museums (councilman 1986—), Southeastern Muss. Assn. (councilman 1986—), Southeastern Mus. Conf. (council 1976-80, chmn. publs. com. 1979). Club: Rotary. Office: Hunter Museum of Art 10 Bluff View Chattanooga TN 37403

SCARBROUGH, DAPHNE, designer, fabricator; b. Long Beach, Calif., June 24, 1954; d. DeLayne Myers and Marjory Alice (Nunnery) S. B.A., U. Tex., 1978. Sales rep. Sakowitz, Houston, 1979-80; designer, gen. mgr. George Allens Brass Works, Houston, 1980-82; pres., designer, fabricator The Brass Maiden, Houston, 1982—. Docent Children's Mus. Houston, 1985; mem. Mus. Fine Arts, Houston, 1985, San Antonio Mus. Fine Arts, 1985, Mus. Art Am. West, Houston, 1985, Tex. Hist. Soc. Mem. Houston C. of C., Nat. Fedn. Ind. Bus., Cultural Arts Council Houston, Houston Ctr. for Photography, Zool. Soc. Houston, Nat. Trust for Hist. Preservation, Art League Houston. Methodist. Club: Houston Livestock Show. Avocations: horse training; antiques. Office: The Brass Maiden 2035 Portsmouth St Houston TX 77098

SCARBROUGH, PAULA RENEE, clinical geneticist; b. Mobile, Ala., July 13, 1954; d. Albert Owen and Margaret (Leigh) Scarbrough. B.S. in Biology, Spring Hill Coll., 1974; M.D., U. Ala., 1978. Intern in pediatrics U. So. Ala., Mobile, 1978-79, resident in pediatrics, 1979-80; fellow in med. genetics U. Ala., Birmingham, 1980-82, clin. instr., fellow med. genetics, 1982-83; staff clin. geneticist Lab. Med. Genetics, 1983—; mem. staff U. Ala. Hosps. and Clinics, Birmingham; cons. St. Vincent's Hosp., Brookwood Med. Ctr., Bapt. Med. Ctr.-Montclair, all Birmingham. Recipient Toolen award Spring Hill Coll., 1974; President's scholar in biology Spring Hill Coll., 1974. Mem. Am. Woman's Med. Assn. Republican. Baptist. Contbr. articles to profl. jours. Home: 306 Poinciana Dr Birmingham AL 35209 Office: Lab Med Genetics Univ Sta Birmingham AL 35294

SCARBROUGH, WILLIAM LEON, geohydrologist; b. Thomasville, Ala., Apr. 19, 1929; s. William Young and Louise (Hill) S.; B.S. in Geology, U. Ala., 1959; m. Kathryn Tew, Dec. 24, 1950; children—William Blakely, Katheryn Lynne. With Ala. Geol. Survey, 1963-74, chief water resource div., 1971-74; chief Fla. ops. P.E. Lamoreaux & Assos., 1974-77; pres., owner Hydrosci. Research Group Inc., Lakeland, Fla., 1977-81, Scarbrough & Assos., Lakeland, 1981—; pres. Ala. Geol. Soc., 1972-74. Served with AUS, 1950-52. Mem. Nat. Water Well Assn., Am. Inst. Profl. Geologists, Am. Inst. Mining Engrs. Author, patentee in field. Home and Office: 3880 Cleveland Heights Blvd Lakeland FL 33802

SCARPELLO, VIDA, social scientist; b. Kaunas, Lithuania, Dec. 17, 1940; came to U.S., 1949; m. Thomas P. Scarpello, June, 14 1962 (div. 1978); children—Thomas, Paul. B.S., U. Minn., 1974, M.A., 1975, Ph.D., 1980. Bus. agt. Minn. Nurses Assn., St. Paul, 1974-75; sr. compensation analyst Honeywell Inc., Mpls., 1975-76; instr. U. Minn., Mpls., 1975-79; assoc. prof. dept. mgmt. Coll. Bus. Adminstrn., U. Ga., Athens, 1979—; vis. assoc. prof. N.Y. State Sch. Indsl. and Labor Relations, Cornell U., Ithaca, N.Y., 1984-85; cons. Minn. Nurses Assn., St. Paul, 1977, Manville Bldg. Materials Corp., Denver, 1980—. Author: Personnel/Human Resource Management, 1987. Contbr. articles to profl. jours. Mem. Am. Psychol. Assn., Acad. Mgmt., Am. Inst. Decision Sci., Indsl. Relations Research Assn. Avocations: art; swimming; travel. Home: 155 Whippoorwill Circle Athens GA 30605 Office: Dept Mgmt Coll Bus Adminstrn U Ga Athens GA 30602

SCERBO, FRANCES CAROLYN GARROTT, architectural technician; b. Bowling Green, Ky., Mar. 10, 1932; d. Irby Reid and Carrie Mae (Stahl) Cameron; m. Leslie Othello Garrott, Oct. 12, 1951 (dec. Feb. 1978); children—Dennis Leslie, Alan Reid; adopted children—Carolyn Maria, Karen Roxana; m. 2d, Raymond William Scerbo, May 31, 1978. Student Fla. State U., 1951, St. Petersburg Jr. Coll., 1962-74; grad. Pinellas Vocat. Tech. Inst., 1975. With Sears, Roebuck and Co., Rapid City, S.D., 1951-52, St. Petersburg, Fla., 1961-62; bookkeeper Ohio Nat. Bank, Columbus, 1953-54, Sunbeam Bakery, Lakeland, Fla., 1955-56; with Christies Toy Sales, Pennsauken, N.J., 1958-60; exec. sec. Gulf Coast Automotive Warehouse, Inc., Tampa, Fla., 1970-73, office mgr., 1975-78; sec.-treas., chief pilot, co-owner Tech. Devel. Corp., St. Petersburg, Fla., 1970-78; freelance archtl. draftsman and designer, archtl. cons., constrn. materials estimator, 1975—. Nat. Assn. Women in Constrn. scholar, 1974. Mem. Nat. Assn. Women in Constrn., Alpha Chi Omega. Democrat. Home and Office: 11298 53d Ave N Saint Petersburg FL 33708

SCHACHTEL, BARBARA HARRIET, behavioral scientist, epidemiologist, educator; b. Rochester, N.Y., May 27, 1921; d. Lester and Ethel (Neiman) Levin; m. Hyman Judah Schachtel, Oct. 15, 1941; children—Bernard, Ann. Student Wellesley Coll., 1939-41; B.S., U. Houston, 1951, M.A. in Psychology, 1967; Ph.D., U. Tex.-Houston, 1979. Psychol. examiner Meyer Ctr. for Devel. Pediatrics, Tex. Children's Hosp., Houston, 1967-81; instr. dept. pediatrics Baylor Coll. Medicine, Houston, 1967-81, asst. prof. dept. medicine, 1982—; asst. dir. biometry and epidemiology Sid W. Richardson Inst. for Preventive Medicine, Houston, 1981—; mem. instl. rev. bd. for human research Baylor Coll. Medicine, Houston, 1981—. Contbr. articles to profl. jours. Vice pres., bd. dirs. Houston-Harris County Mental Health Assn., 1966-67; vice-chmn. bd. mgrs. Harris County Hosp. Dist., Houston, 1974—, bd. dirs., 1970—. Named Great Texan of Yr., Nat. Found. for Ilietis and Colitis, Houston, 1982, Outstanding Citizen, Houston-Harris County Mental Health Assn., 1985; recipient Good Heart award B'Nai B'rith Women, 1984. Mem. Am. Psychol. Assn., Am. Pub. Health Assn., Southwest Psychol. Assn., Tex. Psychol. Assn., Houston Psychol. Assn. (psychol. assoc. rep. 1974). Avocations: golf; tennis; books. Home: 2527 Glenhaven St Houston TX 77030 Office: Sid W Richardson Inst for Preventive Medicine Meth Hosp MS 400 6560 Fannin St Houston TX 77030

SCHAD, THEODORE GEORGE, JR., food company executive; b. N.Y.C., Mar. 4, 1927; s. Theodore George and Helen (Tennyson) S.; B.S. in Bus. and Econs., Ill. Inst. Tech., 1950, M.S., 1951; m. Karma Rose Cundell, Mar. 21, 1957 (dec. June 1978); children—Roberta, Theodore George III, Olive (Mrs. Richard L. Smith), Peter; m. Mary Nell Jennings, June 20, 1981. Vice pres. mktg. Gt. Western Savs., Los Angeles, 1961-63; prin., nat. dir. mktg., and econs. Peat, Marwick, Mitchell & Co., C.P.A.'s, Los Angeles and N.Y.C., 1964-71; chmn. bd., pres., chief exec. officer Lou Ana Industries, Inc., 1971—, Lou Ana Foods, Inc., Opelousas, 1971—, Lou Ana Industries Internat., Inc., Opelousas, 1971-84, Schad Industries Internat., 1985—. Pres. Mamaroneck (N.Y.) Parents of Retarded Children. 1970-71; bd. dirs., mem. exec. com. dir. U.S. Indsl. Council, 1978—; bd. dirs. La. Assn. Bus. and Industry, 1981-85; trustee Va. Mil. Inst. Found., 1979—; v.p., mem. exec. com., bd. dirs. Evangeline council Boy Scouts Am., 1984-86. Served as 2d lt. C.E., AUS, World War II; ETO, PTO. Mem. Am. Mktg. Assn. (pres. So. Calif. chpt. 1961-62, dir. 1962-63), Greater Opelousas C. of C. (pres. 1972-73). Republican. Methodist. Clubs: Indian Hills Country (Opelousas); World Trade Ctr. (New Orleans). Brentwood (Calif.) Sertoma (founding pres. 1963). Contbr. articles on mktg. and econs. to profl. jours. Home: 1155 Prudhomme Ln Opelousas LA 70570 Office: 731 N Railroad Ave Opelousas LA 70570

SCHADLER, DANIEL LEO, biology educator; b. Dayton, Ky., Apr. 5, 1948; s. Alvin Peter and Irma Catherine (Schack) S. A.B., Thomas More Coll., 1970; M.S., Cornell U., 1972, Ph.D., 1974. Research assoc. U. Wis., Madison, 1974-75; prof. biology Oglethorpe U., Atlanta, 1975—, also chmn. sci. div. Recipient Outstanding 4-H Alumnus award Ky. 4-H Clubs, 1985, Best Novice Exhibit award Ga. Chrysanthemum Soc., 1983. Mem. Am. Chem. Soc., Am. Phytopath. Soc., Sigma Xi, Phi Kappa Phi, Sigma Zeta, Catholic Alumni Club. Ga. Chrysanthemum Soc. Democrat. Avocations: growing chrysanthemums; music of original Carter family; gardening. Home: 4218 Admiral Dr Chamblee GA 30341 Office: Oglethorpe U 4484 Peachtree Rd NE Atlanta GA 30319

SCHAEFER, EARL SIMON, health educator; b. Adeville, Ind., May 13, 1926; s. Bernard John and Emma Anna (Jasper) S.; m. Patricia Anne Coyle, Dec. 29, 1956; children—Stephen, Thomas, Anne, Cecilia. B.S., Purdue U., 1948; M.A., Cath. U. Am., 1952, Ph.D., 1954. Research psychologist NIMH, Bethesda, Md., 1953-71, research reviewer, 1976-79, 82—; prof. maternal and child health U. N.C., Chapel Hill, 1971—. Served with U.S. Army, 1944-46. Recipient Commendation medal USPHS, 1967; Nat. Inst. Child Health and Human Devel. grantee, 1975-78; March of Dimes grantee, 1983-85. Fellow Am. Psychol. Assn.; mem. Soc. for Research in Child Devel., Am. Ednl. Research Assn., Am. Pub. Health Assn. Democrat. Roman Catholic. Home: 2325 Honeysuckle Rd Chapel Hill NC 27514 Office: U NC SPH Rosenau Hall 201H Chapel Hill NC 27514

SCHAEFFER, STEPHEN GLEIM, concert organist, music educator; b. York, Pa., Jan. 23, 1947; s. Marlin Thomas and Barbara Krell (Gleim) S. B.A., Davidson Coll., 1968; Mus.M., U. Cin., 1970, D.M.A., 1977. Mem. faculty Presbyn. Coll., Clinton, S.C., 1971—; organist, chorimaster Grace Episcopal Ch., Cin., 1968-71; organist Broad St. United Meth. Ch., Clinton, S.C., 1971-78, dir. music, 1978-80; organist All Saints Episc. Ch., 1982—; organ cons. throughout state, 1976—. Bd. dirs. Laurens County Community Concerts, 1972-80, pres., 1977-79; bd. dirs. Laurens County Arts Commn., 1977—, treas., 1983—. Mem. Am. Guild Organists (pres. Greenwood chpt. 1978-80), S.C. Music Tchrs. Assn. (state organ chmn. 1985-86). Organ Hist. Soc. Democrat. Episcopalian. Avocations: swimming; walking; gourmet cooking; traveling. Home: 601 S Adair St Clinton SC 29325 Office: Presbyn Coll Dept Fine Arts S Broad St Clinton SC 29325

SCHAETTI, HENRY JOACHIM, oil company executive; b. Kodaikanal, India, Aug. 10, 1921; came to U.S., 1952, naturalized, 1955; s. Henry Martin and Clara (Brunnschweiler) S.; m. Rachel Miller, Aug. 23, 1950 (dec. 1984); children—Margery C., Barbara F., Susan E. Ph.D., U. Bern, Switzerland, 1949. Research geologist Carter Research, Tulsa, 1952-60; chief geologist Esso Sahara Inc., Algiers, Algeria, 1960-66; exploration mgr. Esso Exploration, London, 1966-68, venture mgr., Senegal, Morocco, Malaysia, 1968-72, v.p., Singapore, London, Houston, 1972—, also dir. Served to 1st lt. Swiss Army, 1940-50. Mem. Am. Assn. Petroleum Geologists, Am. Geophys. Union, AAAS, N.Y. Acad. of Scis., Geol. Soc. of London, Swiss Geol. Soc. Home: 13722 Alchester Houston TX 77079 Office: Esso Exploration Inc PO Box 146 Houston TX 77001

SCHAFFER, ALAN, history educator; b. N.Y.C., Oct. 29, 1930; s. Louis and Elsa (Hecht) S.; m. Carole A. Abrams (div. 1974); children—Cullen, Dylan, Wendy, Guthrie; m. Jane Walker Herndon, June 16, 1979. B.A., NYU, 1958; M.A., U. Va., 1959, Ph.D., 1962. Asst. prof. history Mich. State U., East Lansing, 1962-69; assoc. prof. CUNY, 1969-74; prof. Clemson U., S.C., 1974, head dept. history, 1974-84; mem. S.C. Commn. on Archives and History, 1974-84, vice chmn., 1981-83, chmn. 1983-84. Served with U.S. Army, 1951-53. Office: Clemson U Dept History Clemson SC 29631

SCHAFFER, DENNIS RICHARD, management consultant; b. Allentown, Pa., Apr. 28, 1944; s. Claude Granville and Edna Aquilla (Wimmer) S.; m. Marlene Margaret Pachuta, Sept. 5, 1970; 1 child, Kathleen Denise. B.A., Pa. State U., 1969, M.Ed., 1971, Ed.D., 1972. Counselor Pa. State U., University Park, 1968-70; trainer Ill. Dept. Mental Health, Decatur, 1972-73; instructional designer U. Del., Newark, 1973-77; prof. Health Sci. Ctr., U. Tex.-Houston, 1977-80; cons. Geosource, Inc., Houston, 1980-83; pres. Career Circles, Inc., Houston, 1983—; mem. adj. faculty Goldey Beacom Coll., Wilmington, Del. 1975-77, U. Del., Newark, 1974-77, Houston Bapt. U., 1984-85. Served with USN, 1965-68; Vietnam. Mem. Internat. Assn. Quality Circles (v.p. Houston chpt. 1985), Am. Soc. for Tng. and Devel. Presbyterian. Avocations: travel; model railroading; pen and ink drawing; video productions.

SCHAFFER, WARREN DEUPERT, personnel executive; b. Balt., Oct. 18, 1939; s. William Martin and Laura Ruth (Worley) S.; m. Zelma Gwendolyn Allen, Dec. 27, 1960; children—Alice Catherine, Laura Suzanne. B.S., U. Md., 1961; M.B.A., Stetson U., 1972. Internal auditor Nat. Dairy Products, N.Y.C., 1961-63; personnel/safety dir. Sealtest Foods, Jacksonville, 1963-65; employment rep. Bendix Field Engring., Columbia, Md., 1965-67, bus. adminstr., 1967-77, supr. employee relations, 1977-80; dir. human resources ICSD Corp., Kissimmee, Fla., 1980—. Mem. Employers Assn. of Fla. (dir.), Central Fla. Personnel Assn., Am. Soc. Personnel Adminstrn., Am. Def. Preparedness Assn. Republican. Baptist. Home: 751 Will Barber Rd Kissimmee FL 32743 Office: ICSD Corp 2931 N Poinciana Blvd Kissimmee FL 32758

SCHALLY, ANDREW VICTOR, medical research scientist; b. Europe, Nov. 30, 1926; came to U.S., 1957; s. Casimir Peter and Maria (Lacka) S.; m. Ana Maria Comaru, Aug. 12, 1976. B.Sc., McGill U. (Can.), 1955, Ph.D. in Biochemistry, 1957. Research asst. biochemistry Nat. Inst. Med. Research, London, 1949-52, dept. psychiatry. McGill U., Montreal, Que., 1952-57; research asso., asst. prof. physiology and biochemistry Coll. Medicine. Baylor U., Houston, 1957-62; chief endocrine and polypeptide labs. VA Hosp., New Orleans, 1962—; asso. prof. Sch. Medicine, Tulane U., New Orleans, 1962-67, prof., 1967—. Contbr. articles to profl. jours. Recipient Dir.'s award for outstanding med. research VA Hosp., New Orleans, 1968, Van Meter prize Am. Thyroid Assn., 1969, Ayerst-Squibb award Endocrine Soc., 1970, William S. Middleton award VA, 1970, Ch. Mickle award U. Toronto, 1974, Gairdner Internat. award, 1974, Albert Lasker Basic Med. Research award, 1975, Nobel Prize in Physiology and Medicine, 1977; USPHS sr. research fellow, 1961-62; sr. med. investigator VA, 1973. Mem. Endocrine Soc., Am. Physiol. Soc., Soc. Biol. Chemists, Nat. Acad. Scis., AAAS, Am. Acad. Arts and Scis., Soc. Exptl. Biol. Medicine, Internat. Soc. Research Biology Reprodn., Soc. Study Reprodn., Soc. Internat. Brain Research Orgn., Mexican Acad. Medicine, Am. Soc. Animal Sci., Nat. Acad. Medicine (Brazil), Sigma Xi, others. Home: 5025 Kawanee St Metairie LA 70002 Office: 1601 Perdido St New Orleans LA 70146

SCHANIE, CHARLES FREDERICK, industrial psychologist, employee relations consultant; b. Louisville, July 27, 1947; s. Raymond L. and Anna L. (Linton) S.; m. Connie Redmon, Nov. 23, 1966; children—Christian, Craig, Cameron. B.A. in Psychology, U. Louisville, 1969, M.A. in Psychology, 1972, Ph.D. in Psychology, 1974. Dir. evaluation River Region, Louisville, 1974-77; cons. Riddick & Flynn, Louisville, 1977-78, Schanie Assocs., Louisville, 1978-82; prin. Mercer-Meidinger, Inc., Louisville, 1982—. Editor manuals: The Compensation Institute, 1984; author jour. articles. NSF fellow, 1969-73; named Outstanding Male Student, Univ. Coll., U. Louisville, 1969. Mem. Am. Psychol. Assn., Am. Compensation Assn., Woodcock Soc., Phi Kappa Phi. Avocation: Recreational soccer coach. Home: 10408 Grazing Ct Louisville KY 40223 Office: Wm M Mercer-Meidinger Inc 2600 Meidinger Tower Louisville KY 40202

SCHANZMEYER, LAWRENCE P., bank holding company executive; b. 1946; married. B.S.B.A., U. Mo., 1969. Analyst Barnett Winston Mortgage Co., 1973-74; v.p. Citicorp Real Estate Inc., 1974-80; exec. v.p. MBank Houston Subs. MCorp, Houston, 1980—. Office: MBank Houston NA 910 Travis St Houston TX 77002

SCHAPER, DARWIN EARL, quality control executive; b. State Center, Iowa, June 26, 1935; s. Arnold Frederick and Ruie Francis (Kolbe) S.; m. Beverly Ann Blish, Jan. 17, 1962; children—John Arnold, Steven Earl. B.A., U.S. Naval Post Grad. Sch., 1974; M.S. in Safety, U. So. Calif., 1984. Commd. U.S. Navy, 1956, advanced through grades to lt. comdr., 1978; supr. safety Hayes Internat. Corp., Dothan, Ala., 1979-85, dir. quality control, 1985—. Chief, treas. Vol. Fire Dept., Wicksburg, Ala., 1981—. Mem. Am. Soc. Safety Engrs. (vice pres. chpt. 1981-83). Lutheran. Avocations: reading, bee keeping, hunting, golf. Home: Rt 1 Box 381 Newton AL 36352 Office: Hayes Internat Corp PO Box 929 Dothan AL 36302

SCHAPIRO, BETH S., public affairs and political consultant; b. Rockville Centre, N.Y., Sept. 23, 1949; d. Irwin A. and Jeanne (Goldman) S. B.S., U. Md., 1971; M.A., Emory U., 1977, Ph.D., 1979. Sr. planner, Ga. Office of Planning & Budget, Atlanta, 1979-81; exec. dir. Research Atlanta, 1981-84; pres. Beth Schapiro & Assocs., Atlanta, 1984—. Mem. exec. com. Leadership Atlanta, 1982-84; bd. visitors Grady Meml. Hosp., Atlanta, 1983—; chair adv. council Council on Battered Women, Atlanta, 1984—; bd. dirs. Ga. Women's Polit. Caucus, Atlanta, 1981—. Mem. Am. Polit. Sci. Assn. Office: Beth Schapiro & Assocs 134 Peachtree St Suite 1130 Atlanta GA 30303

SCHAPPE, GERALD LEE, fire/safety program consultant; b. St. Charles, Mo., Nov. 2, 1941; s. Nicholas Isadore and Margaret Marie (Schuttenberg) S.;

m. Doris Fay Keilers, Nov. 26, 1966; children—Nicholas Allen, Jennifer Lee. B.A.A.S., Southwest Tex. State U., 1981. Cert. safety profl. EOD technician U.S. Air Force, 1964-68; lt. investigator Fire Dept., Austin, Tex., 1969-72; fire insp. Office of State Fire Marshal, Austin, 1972-80; program dir. safety Tex. Dept. Mental Health/Mental Retardation, Austin, 1981—. Commr. Girls South Austin Youth Soccer Assn., 1984-85. Served with USAF, 1964-65. Mem. Am. Soc. Safety Engrs., Tex. Safety Assn., Mensa. Lutheran. Avocation: coaching youth soccer. Home: 7229 S Brook St Austin TX 78736 Office: Tex Dept Mental Health and Mental Retardation PO Box 12668 Austin TX 78711

SCHARBO, RONALD WILLIAM, advertising agency executive; b. Northfield, N.J., Aug. 14, 1938; s. William Warren and Lillian May (Rice) S.; m. Marianne Martin Lowry, Oct. 20, 1962; children—Mark, Grant, Dana. B.A., Duquesne U., 1960. Account supr. Young & Rubicam, N.Y.C., 1962-66, Carl Ally, N.Y.C., 1966-68, BBDO, N.Y.C., 1968-69; mng. dir. Cargill, Wilson, Acree, Atlanta, 1969-73; exec. v.p. McDonald & Little, Atlanta, 1973-74; chmn., pres. Burton-Campbell, Inc., Atlanta, 1974—. Trustee The Paideia Sch., Atlanta, 1980—; mem. adv. bd. U. Ga. Sch. Journalism, Athens, 1984—. Mem. Am. Assn. Advt. Agys. (sec.-treas. Atlanta council 1984-85), Affiliated Advt. Agys. Internat. (trustee 1983-85), Atlanta Advt. Club (pres. 1973-74). Clubs: Duquesne (Pitts.); Ansley (Atlanta). Home: 61 Barksdale Rd Atlanta GA 30309 Office: Burton-Campbell Inc 100 Colony Sq Suite 2400 Atlanta GA 30361

SCHARFF, ERIC MATISON, industrial supply company executive; b. N.Y.C., July 4, 1942; s. Morris Adrian ; Peggy Myrtle (Hertzberg) S.; m. Helene Goldberg, Aug. 25, 1963; children—Michael, Kevin. B.S. in Bus., Oglethorpe U., 1963. Founder, pres. Mr. E. Ltd., Loganville, Ga., 1964-79; exec. v.p. Walton Clothes, Loganville, 1963-79; pres. Petrofax Internat., 1981-84; exec. v.p., dir. Industries, Atlanta, 1984—; dir. Gaines Industries (Pte) Ltd.; Singapore, Gaines Industries Ltd., Hong Kong. Mem. bd. visitors Oglethorpe U., Atlanta, 1978-84; coordinator Nat. Collegiate Athletic Assn. Nat. Basketball Tournament, 1977; bd. dirs. Sandy Springs Youth Sports, Atlanta, 1972-79; sec. Pace Acad. Parents Club, 1983-84. Mem. Am. Philatelic Soc., Cobb County C. of C. Clubs: Kiawah Island, Standard. Office: Gaines Industries Inc 1300 Gresham Rd Marietta GA 30062

SCHARLATT, HAROLD, management consultant; b. N.Y.C., Dec. 9, 1947; s. Bertram and Miriam Louise (Stone) S.; B.A. in Edn., SUNY, 1969, M.Liberal Studies, 1973; advanced cert. adminstrn. and supervision, Oxford U., 1975; m. Mary Moore, June 10, 1978. Tchr., in-service instr. N.Y.C., 1970-77; mgmt. devel. specialist Union Carbide Corp., N.Y.C., 1977, mgmt. devel. cons., 1978-80; regional dir. Vector Mgmt. Systems, Inc., Lexington, Ky., 1980-83; pres. Tng. and Devel. Assocs., Inc., Lexington, 1983—. Mem. Am. Soc. Tng. and Devel., Am. Mgmt. Assn. Office: 3314 Pimlico Pkwy Lexington KY 40502

SCHATTEN, WILLIAM EUGENE, surgeon; b. Nashville, Oct. 3, 1928; s. Sam and Eva (Hurwitz) S. B.S., Emory U., 1946, M.D., 1950. Diplomate Am. Bd. Surgery, Am. Bd. Plastic Surgery. Intern, Univ. Hosps. Cleve., 1950-51, asst. resident surgery, 1952-53, research fellow surgery, 1952-53, resident surgery, 1953-54, 54-55; sr. asst. surgeon USPHS, NIH, Nat. Cancer Inst., 1955-57; acting chief surgery Nat. Cancer Inst., 1956; fellow plastic surgery Barnes Hosp., St. Louis, 1957-58, resident plastic surgery, 1958-59; practice medicine, specializing in plastic surgery, Atlanta; staff West Paces Ferry, Piedmont, St. Joseph's and Northside hosps.; clin. asst. prof. plastic surgery Emory U.; guest examiner Am. Bd. Plastic Surgery, 1970, 76, 79, 81. Campaign chmn. Atlanta Jewish Fedn., 1983, 84, Atlanta Israel Bonds, 1971-77, mem. Nat. Israel Bond Cabinet, 1978—; pres. Ahavath Achim Synagogue, 1976-78; bd. dirs. Am. Jewish Com. Named Man of Yr., B'nai B'rith, 1981; recipient award for original research Ednl. Found. Am. Soc. Plastic and Reconstructive Surgery, 1957. Fellow ACS; mem. Am. Soc. Plastic and Reconstructive Surgery, Am. Assn. Plastic Surgeons, Am. Soc. Aesthetic Plastic Surgeons, Plastic Surgery Research Council, Soc. Head and Neck Surgeons, Southeastern Soc. Plastic and Reconstructive Surgeons, Internat. Soc. Aesthetic Plastic Surgeons, Ga. Soc. Plastic Surgery, AMA, So. Med. Assn., Ga. Med. Assn., Atlanta Med. Assn. Contbr. articles to profl. jours. Address: 3280 Howell Mill Rd NW Atlanta GA 30327

SCHATZ, MARTIN, college dean, business educator; b. N.Y.C., Aug. 1, 1936; s. Murray and Florence (Hollander) S.; m. Harriet M. Cohen, June 26, 1970; children—Karen, Lauren. B.S., U. Ala.-Tuscaloosa, 1959; M.B.A., U. Fla., 1965; Ph.D., NYU, 1972. Asst. to dean N.Y.U., N.Y.C., 1966-69; asst. prof. Worcester Poly. Inst., Mass., 1972-74; assoc. dean Adelphi U., Garden City, N.Y., 1974-76; dean sch. bus. SUNY-Utica, 1976-78; dean grad. sch. bus. Rollins Coll., Winter Park, Fla., 1979—. Contbr. articles to profl. jours. Mem. Acad. Mgmt., Am. Inst. for Decision Scis., Inst. Mgmt. Scis., Fin. Mgmt. Assn. Home: 102 Coveridge Ln Longwood FL 32779 Office: Roy E Crummer Grad Sch Bus Rollins Coll Winter Park FL 32789

SCHATZMAN, ROBERT A., lawyer; b. Miami, Fla., Jan. 14, 1945; s. Moe and Sylvia (Rayvis) S.; m. Lorraine Berger, Nov. 30, 1969; children—Staci Leigh, Kevin Todd. B.B.A., U. Miami, 1967; law student Loyola U., 1968-69; J.D., U. Miami, 1971. Bar: Fla. 1971, U.S. Dist. Ct. (so. dist.) Fla. 1972, U.S. Ct. Appeals (5th cir.) 1972, U.S. Ct. Appeals (11th cir.) 1982. Assoc., Whitman & Wolfe, Miami, Fla., 1971-72, Friedman & Britton, Miami, 1972-78; ptnr. Schatzman & Schatzman, P.A., Miami and Coral Gables, Fla., 1978-85; ptnr. Britton, Cassel, Schantz & Schatzman, P.A., 1985—. Mem. profls. com. United Fund, 1977. Mem. Bankruptcy Bar Assn. South Fla. (pres. 1983-84), Comml. Law League Am., ABA, Dade County Bar Assn., Econ. Soc. South Fla., U. Miami Athletic Fedn., Phi Delta Phi, Zeta Beta Tau. Democrat. Jewish. Club: Progress of Miami (pres. 1982-83, dir. 1978). Office: 1500 S Dixie Hwy Suite 350 Coral Gables FL 33146

SCHAUDIES, JESSE P., lawyer; b. Knoxville, Tenn., Aug. 27, 1954; s. Jesse P. and Adele (Thompson) S.; m. Elizabeth D. Schaudies, Sept. 15, 1979; children—Jesse P. III, Frederick T. B.A. magna cum laude, Duke U., 1976; J.D., Georgetown U., 1979. Assoc. Troutman, Sanders, Lockerman & Ashmore, Atlanta, 1979—. Mng. editor Am. Criminal Law Rev., 1978-79. Charter mem. High Mus. Art, Atlanta. Mem. ABA, Ga. State Bar Assn. (labor sect., litigation sect.), Atlanta Bar Assn. (labor sect., litigation sect.), Author's Court Ga. (charter). Republican. Presbyterian. Office: Troutman Sanders Lockerman & Ashmore 127 Peachtree St Atlanta GA 30043

SCHAUER, PAMELA JO, management consultant, financial planner; b. Cleve., Oct. 21, 1947; m. William Edward Schauer, Sept. 14, 1968 (div. June 1975); 1 child, William Edward. B.S., U. Chgo., 1969, M.B.A., 1971. Orders and movement clk. Shell Chem. Co., Chgo., 1966-69; sr. internal auditor IBM, Chgo., 1969-71; asst. dir. fin. Key West, Fla., 1975-79; bus. mgr. Pediatric Assocs., Gainesville, Fla., 1979-83; mgmt. cons. Profl.'s Cons., Gainesville, 1983—; cons. in field. Treas. Namvets, Gainesville, 1983—, Terwilliger PTA, Gainesville, 1981—. Democrat. Home: 3434 NW 53d Terr Gainesville FL 32606

SCHAUER, WILLIAM RICHARD, architect; b. Birmingham, Ala., Dec. 4, 1933; s. John and Mary Alicia (Swygert) S.; children—Thomas William, James Robert. B. Arch., Auburn, U., 1958. Registered architect, Ala.; cert. Nat. Council Archtl. Registration Bds. Architect intern Northington, Smith, Kranert, Architects, Florence, Ala., 1958-64, Lawrence S. Whitten & Sons, Architects, Birmingham, 1965-67; architect Carlton Lawrence Jr., Architect, Birmingham, 1967-69; prin. architect, owner William R. Schauer-Architect, Birmingham, 1970—; architect Directorate of Facilities Engring., Fort Gordon, Ga., 1978—. Served with U.S. Army, 1954-56. Recipient Commendation award Directorate Facilities Engring., Dept. Army, 1980. Mem. Constrn. Specifications Inst. Avocation: golf. Home: 15th Terrace Circle NE Apt 20D Birmingham AL 35215 Office: 3814 5th Ct North Birmingham AL 35222

SCHECHTER, ARTHUR LOUIS, lawyer; b. Rosenberg, Tex., Dec. 6, 1939; s. Morris S. and Helen Ruth (Brilling) S.; m. Joyce Proler, Aug. 28, 1965; children—Leslie Rose, Jennifer Paige. B.A., U. Tex., 1962, J.D., 1964; postgrad. U. Houston. Cert. trial lawyer Tex. Bd. Legal Specialization; bar: Tex. Pres., Dowman, Jones & Schechter, Houston, 1964-77, Schechter, Eisenman & Solar, Houston, 1977—; lectr. Marine Ins. Seminar; dir. Bank of Harris County, Bank of Haris County N.W. Mem. U. Tex. Law Sch. Dean's Council. Author: Rights of Foreign Nationals in the Courts of the U.S. Bd. dirs. Theatre Under the Stars, 1965-70, Congregation Beth Israel, 1971-78, 82—, Am. Jewish Com., 1982—; mem. dean's council U. Tex. Law Sch.; mem. Nat. Democratic Fin. Council, 1978; co-chmn. lawyers div. Jewish Fedn. Houston. Recipient Jewish Fedn. Houston Young Leadership award. Fellow Jewish Chautauqua Soc.; mem. Roscoe Pond Assn., Assn. Trial Lawyers Am. (sustaining). Clubs: Westwood Country, Houston Racquet.

SCHECHTERMAN, LAWRENCE, lawyer; b. Elizabeth, N.J., June 23, 1943; s. Josef and Sylvia (Berger) S.; m. Suzanne Lois Hilzenradt, May 31, 1981; children—Jill Laura, Danielle Sara, Danielle Beth, Nicole Corin, Gregory Jared. B.A., U. Miami, Fla., 1966; J.D., Suffolk U., 1969; LL.M., NYU, 1973. Bar: N.J. 1969, U.S. Dist. Ct. N.J. 1969, U.S. Ct. Appeals (D.C. cir.) 1970, U.S. Tax Ct. 1970, U.S. Supreme Ct. 1972, N.Y. 1980, U.S. Ct. Appeals (11th cir.) 1982, Fla. 1983, U.S. Dist. Ct. (so. dist.) Fla. 1983, U.S. Dist. Ct. (mid. dist.) Fla. 1984. Tax assoc. Coopers & Lybrand, N.Y.C., 1969-70; assoc. Bendit, Weinstock & Sharbaugh, Newark, 1970-72; sole practice, Plainfield, N.J., 1972-75, East Brunswick, N.J., 1975-81; gen. counsel Equinox Solar, Inc., Miami, Fla., 1981-83; mem. Lawrence Schechterman, P.A., Boca Raton, Fla., 1983—. Author: (poetry) New Dimensions: An Anthology of American Poetry, 1967. Contbr. articles to legal jours. Councilman, Twp. of East Brunswick, 1976-80. Mem. ABA, N.J. State Bar Assn., Fla. Bar, Middlesex County Bar Assn. (trustee 1977-80, sec. 1980-81), Palm Beach County Bar Assn., South Palm Beach County Bar Assn. Democrat. Jewish. Home: 11937 Sandlake Dr Boca Raton FL 33428 Office: One Lincoln Pl 1900 Glades Rd Suite 301 Boca Raton FL 33431

SCHEFFER, CHERI ROSE, artist; b. Kansas City, Mo., Nov. 12, 1950; d. Jules Emile and Francis Willamena (Doman) S.; 1 child, Tangi Katzer. Student, Kans. State Tchrs. Coll., 1969-71. Treas. Island Art Shoppe, Dunedin, Fla., 1974—; assoc. Surfcoast Realty, Dunedin, 1984—; v.p. Sheffer Studio Inc., Dunedin, 1980—; cons. Nat. Edn. Ctr., Tampa, 1983—. Prin. sculpture includes The Protected Child, 1981. Bd. dirs. Pinellas County Arts Council, Fla., 1984—. Recipient Cert. of Achievement, Minolta, 1985. Mem. Contractors and Builders Assn., Nat. Assn. Female Execs. Republican. Club: Ducks Unlimited. Avocations: photography; yachting; media research. Home: 1897 Stancel Dr Clearwater FL 33546 Office: Scheffer Studio 240 Causeway Blvd Dunedin FL 33528

SCHEFFER, JULES EMILE, architectural delineator, artist; b. Tjimahi, Java, Indonesia, Jan. 29, 1924; came to U.S. 1947, naturalized 1950; s. August Jules Willem and Petronella Emile (Velds) S.; m. Francis Wilhelmina Doman, Apr. 21, 1945; children—Terrance J., Cheryl R., Daryl J., Karyl S., Merrie R. Student Westlawn Sch. Yacht Design, 1982-85. Fighter pilot Dutch Air Force, East Indies, 1941-47; editorial artist Kansas City Star, Mo., 1948-49; retoucher Macy's Adv. Dept., Kansas City, 1949-50; owner, architectural delineator Scheffer Studio, Kansas City, 1950-83, Clearwater, Fla., 1974—; chmn. art com. Ducks Unlimited, Clearwater, 1982—; judge tech. drawing Tampa Tech. Inst., Fla., 1982, adv. bd., 1983. Artist of several limited edition prints, 1972; contbr. to book, Design Graphics, 1968. Mem. Island Estates Civic Assn.; dress circle mem. Performing Arts Centre/Theatre, Clearwater, 1983-84. Served to lt. Air East Indies, 1941-47. Recipient 3rd place award for stamp design Nat. Soc. Art Dirs., 1956. Mem. Nat. Assn. Home Builders, Contractors and Builders Assn., Nat. Fed. Independent Bus. Republican. Roman Catholic. Club: Clearwater Yacht (Commodore 1978-81). Office: Scheffer Studio 240 Causeway Blvd Dunedin FL 33528

SCHEFFLER, IRENE CLARE, safety engineer; b. Dallas, Sept. 20, 1955; d. Vincent H. and Virginia A. (Mattox) Schoeneberger; m. Laurel Lee Scheffler, Sept. 2, 1978; children—Elaine Laurene, Steven Vincent. B.S. in Indsl. Engring., Tex. A&M U., 1977. Safety engr. Alcoa Corp., Point Comfort, Tex., 1978-81, sr. safety engr., 1982-84, safety supr., Bauxite, Ark., 1984—. Mem. Am. Soc. Safety Engrs. (chpt. sec. 1982-84). Republican. Roman Catholic. Avocations: crafts; gardening; hiking. Home: Rt 5 2887 Woodridge Benton AR 72015 Office: Alcoa PO Box 300 Bauxite AR 72011

SCHEID-COOK, TERESA LINNEA, sociologist; b. Syracuse, N.Y., Sept. 22, 1957; d. Charles and Patricia Ann (Babcock) Scheid; m. Stephen Phillip Cook, Dec. 29, 1979. A.A., Onondaga Coll., Syracuse, 1977; B.A., Heidelberg Coll., 1979; M.S., Tex. A&M U., 1982. Teaching asst. Tex. A&M U., 1980-82, U. N.C., Chapel Hill, 1982; teaching asst. N.C. State U., Raleigh, 1983-84, research asst., 1984—; speaker in field. Mem. Am. Sociol. Assn., Alpha Kappa Delta. Club: Grad. Students Assn. N.C. State U. Office: Dept Sociology NC State Univ Raleigh NC 27650

SCHEIE, PAUL OLAF, physics educator; b. Marietta, Minn., June 24, 1933; s. Olaf Johan and Selma Pricilla (Varhus) S.; m. Mary Anna Harrison, May 18, 1963; children—Eric, Maren. B.A., St. Olaf Coll., Northfield, Minn., 1955; M.S., U. N.Mex., 1957; Ph.D., Pa. State U., 1965. Asst. prof. physics Oklahoma City U., 1958-63; asst. prof. biophysics Pa. State U., State Coll., 1965-73; prof. physics Tex. Lutheran Coll., Seguin, 1973—, interim acad. dean, 1976. Contbr. articles to profl. publs. Recipient Faculty Alumni award, Tex. Luth. Coll., 1985. Mem. Biophys. Soc., AAAS, Am. Assn., Physics Tchrs., Sigma Xi. Lutheran. Lodge: Lions. Avocations: woodworking; gardening. Home: 207 Leonard Seguin TX 78155 Office: Tex Luth Coll 1000 W Court St Seguin TX 78155

SCHEIN, EUGENIE, dance teacher; s. Adolph and Freda (Bergknopf) S. Student Hunter Coll., Columbia U., U. Mex., Martha Graham Sch. of Dance, N.Y.C. Instr., Hunter Coll., N.Y.C., U. Miami, Coral Gables, Fla., Coral Gables Youth Ctr. Docent Bass Mus., Miami Beach; mem. Ctr. for Fine Arts. Represented by Cooley Square Art Gallery, South Miami, Fla. Mem. Artists Equity Assn. Inc. (treas. Fla. chpt., v.p., pres.) Avocations: crafts; batik; stained glass.

SCHELL, DIANNE W(ILSON), psychologist, consultant; b. Clinton, S.C., Oct. 17, 1947; d. James Cleveland and Edith Ora (Wright) Wilson. B.S., U. S.C., 1971; M.Ed., Winthrop Coll., 1972. Lic. psychologist, tchr. Tchr., York (S.C.) City Schs., 1970-72; psychologist Rock Hill (S.C.) Schs., 1972-76, Charleston (S.C.) County Schs., Charleston, 1976-81; cons. Custom Creations, Ltd., Charleston, 1981—; fin. cons. Custom Car Stereo Inc., Charleston, 1982—; cons. Faith Ventures, Ltd., Charleston, 1983—; Charleston County Bd. Edn., 1983. Fellow Trident C. of C.; mem. Assn. Psychologists (v.p. Charleston 1980-81), S.C. Sch. Psychol. Assn., Nat. Assn. Retail Advertisers, Nat. Fedn. Ind. Bus., Phi Kappa Phi. Republican. Methodist. Club: Bus. and Profl. Women. Office: Custom Creations Ltd PO Box 32138 Charleston SC 29417

SCHELLHAMMER, PAUL FREDERICK, urologist, educator; b. N.Y.C., June 1, 1940; m. Barbara Ann Barnett; children—Christopher, Scott. B.S. magna cum laude, U. Notre Dame, 1962; M.D., Cornell Med. Coll., 1966; Intern, Univ. Hosps. Cleve., 1966-67, resident in surgery, 1967-68; resident in urology Med. Coll. Va. Hosps., 1970-73; hon. clin. asst. urology R.T. Turner-Warwick, Middlesex, Hosp., 1973; fellow Am. Cancer Soc., Meml. Hosp., N.Y.C., 1973-74; assoc. Devine-Poutasse-Fiveash Assocs., Ltd., Norfolk, Va., 1974—; prof. urology Eastern Va. Med. Sch., dir. urology tng. program; mem. staff Med. Ctr. Hosps., Inc., Children's Hosp., King's Daughters, Norfolk, De Paul Hosp., Norfolk; cons. Gen. Hosp. Virginia Beach, Bayside Hosp., Virginia Beach; lectr. urology Dept. Navy, Naval Regional Med. Ctr., Portsmouth, Va. Served to capt. USAF, 1968-70. Am. Cancer Soc. Fellow, 1974; hon. clin. fellow, Middlesex, Eng., 1973. Fellow ACS, Am. Acad. Pediatrics; mem. Am. Urol. Assn., Soc. Surg. Oncology, Am. Assn. Clin. Urology, Alpha Omega Alpha. Roman Catholic. Researcher numerous areas of carcinoma and radiation; contbr. articles and tech. papers to profl. jours. Office: Devine-Poutasse-Fiveash Assocs Ltd, 400 W Brambleton Ave Suite 100 Norfolk VA 23510

SCHELLY, ZOLTAN ANDREW, physical chemistry educator; b. Budapest, Hungary, Feb. 15, 1938; came to U.S., 1968, naturalized, 1974. B.S., Tech. U., Vienna, Austria, 1962, D.Sc., 1967. Postdoctoral fellow U. Wis.-Milw., 1968, U. Utah, Salt Lake City, 1969-70; asst. prof. U. Ga., Athens, 1970-76; A. von Humboldt fellow Max-Planck Inst. for Biophys. Chemistry, Gottingen, Fed. Republic Germany, 1974; prof. phys. chemistry U. Tex. at Arlington, 1977—; cons. indsl. orgns. and univs., 1977—. Contbr. research articles to profl. jours. Editorial bd. Jour. Molecular Liquids, Amsterdam, The Netherlands, 1980—. Recipient M.G. Michael award U. Ga., 1975; Disting. Research award U. Tex.-Arlington, 1982. Mem. Am. Chem. Soc., Am. Phys. Soc., Austrian Chem. Soc., Sigma Chi. Office: U Tex at Arlington Chemistry Dept Arlington TX 76019

SCHENCK, ALEXANDER FAIRCHILD, forest industry executive; b. Greensboro, N.C., Sept. 7, 1912; m. Laurinda Carlson, June 22, 1946; children—Michael Weldon, Alexander Lewis. B.S., Davidson Coll., 1934; M.B.A., Harvard U., 1936. Div. mgr. Vick Chem. Co., N.Y.C., 1936-41; ptnr., pres. Indsl. Equipment Co., Charlotte, N.C., 1946-61; exec. v.p., dir. Richardson Found., Greensboro, N.C., 1961-66; owner-mgr. tree farms, forest lands, nurseries, N.C., S.C., 1955—. Chmn. Charlotte Planning Bd., 1951-54; trustee Mint Mus. Art, Charlotte, 1952-60; co-founder N.C. Fellows Program U. N.C., Davidson Coll., N.C. State U., A&T U., 1967—; bd. dirs., organizer Hist. Flat Rock, N.C., 1968—, pres., 1968-74; bd. visitors Davidson Coll., 1969—; bd. dirs. N.C. Nature Conservancy, 1981—. Served to lt. col. AUS, 1942-46. Decorated Silver Star, Legion of Merit. Mem. Hist. Preservation Soc. N.C. (Merit award 1980). Episcopalian. Clubs: Charleston, Yeamans Hall; Biltmore Forest (Asheville, N.C.). Home: Yeamans Hall Club Charleston SC also Flat Rock NC

SCHENCK, ARTHUR CARL, consulting engineer; b. Phila., July 31, 1910; s. Rev. Dr. A. Clarence and Hattie Olive (Ritter) S.; B.S., U. Ala., 1934; m. Eloise Elena Williams, July 6, 1934; children—Nancy Elizabeth Schenck Smith, Jean Gray Schenck Rice. Field, resident engr. Stone & Webster Engring. Corp., 1934, 1936-42; insp. U.S. C.E., Phila., 1935-36; v.p. Carpenter Constrn. Co., Inc., Norfolk, Va., 1942-63; prin. A. Carl Schenck and Assos., constrn. mgmt. and engring. cons., Norfolk, 1963—. Mem. Bd. Rev. Real Estate Assessments; past chmn. lay adv. bd. DePaul Hosp.; adv. council Norfolk Area Med. Center Authority; mem. public relations and grad. sch. med. coms. Eastern Va. Med. Authority, 1975-84; mem. Citizens Adv. Com., Norfolk, 1964-65; mem. Va. Airports Authority, 1958-80; bd. dirs. Norfolk-Portsmouth Builders, Contractors Exchange, 1960-63; mem. adv. bd. Tidewater council Boy Scouts Am.; mem. engring. com. Devel. Council, U. Ala., 1958-62; mem. Fire Prevention Adv. Com., Norfolk. Mem. Nat., Va. (past pres.) socs. profl. engrs., Asso. Gen. Contractors Am. (hon. mem., pres. Va. br. 1962), Am. Arbitration Assn. (nat. panel mem.), Tau Beta Pi, Theta Tau, Chi Beta Phi. Lutheran (mem. council 1950—). Clubs: Engineers of Hampton Roads (pres. 1953-54); Kiwanis (pres. 1966); Harbor, Virginia (Norfolk). Home: 5601 Huntington Pl Norfolk VA 23509 Office: PO Box 7097 Norfolk VA 23509

SCHENCK, BETSY BROWN, osteopathic physician; b. Auburn, Ind., June 27, 1950; d. Max Stanley and Betty (Betts) Brown; m. W. Larry Schenck, Jr., Dec. 18, 1969; 1 child, Charles. B.A., North Tex. State U., 1973; D.O., Tex. Coll. Osteo. Medicine, 1978. Diplomate Am. Coll. Family Practice. Osteo. physician, emergency medicine Westgate Hosp., Denton, Tex., 1979-80; family practice medicine, Denton, 1980-84; osteo. physician emergency medicine Flow Meml. Hosp., Denton, 1984—; med. dir. Good Samaritan Nursing Ctr., Denton, 1980—; safety chmn. Westgate Hosp., Denton, 1982-84, employee health physician, 1979-84; chief of staff Denton Osteo. Hosp., Denton, 1981. Mem. Am. Osteo. Assn., Tex. Osteo. Med. Assn., Delta Zeta. Methodist.

SCHENCK, KENNETH L., JR., oral and maxillofacial surgeon; b. Dayton, Ohio, May 28, 1939; m. Patricia Kathleen Bowen, Mar. 10, 1961; children—Jason Charles, Brian Kenneth. D.D.S., U. Tenn., 1967. Diplomate Am. Bd. Oral and Maxillofacial Surgery. Pvt. practice oral surgery, Memphis, 1970-82; instr. oral surgery, U. Tenn., Memphis, 1970-82; pvt. practice oral surgery, Hixson, Tenn., 1982—; instr. pharmacology Chattanooga State Community Coll., 1983—. Trustee North Park Hosp., Hixson, 1984—. Served with USAF, 1958-62. Mem. Am. Assn. Oral and Maxillofacial Surgeons, Tenn. Dental Assn., ADA, Southeastern Soc. Oral and Maxillofacial Surgeons, Tenn. Soc. Oral and Maxillofacial Surgeons (sec./treas. 1983-84), 3d Dist. Dental Soc., Memphis Soc. Oral and Maxillofacial Surgeons (pres. 1972-73), Memphis Dental Legion (Pres. 1979), Omicron Kappa Upsilon. Republican. Presbyterian. Home: 46 Rockcrest Dr Signal Mountain TN 37377 Office: 4845-C Hixson Pike Hixson TN 37343

SCHENEMAN, CARL STEPHEN, continuing education educator, consultant; b. Monette, Mo., Mar. 7, 1948; s. Carl Norman and Phyllis Dean (Miller) S.; m. Mary Ann Sadich, Aug. 31, 1973; children—Carl Andrews, Melissa Ann. B.S. in Pub. Adminstrn., U. Mo., 1970, M.S. in Community Devel., 1971; Ph.D. in Extension Edn., Ohio State U., 1980. Extension agt. Va. Tech. U., Appomattox, 1972-73, Charlottesville, 1973-74, dist. dir., Blacksburg, 1974-77, extension specialist, staff devel., 1980-83, extension leader, staff devel., 1983—; cons. So. States Cooparative, Richmond, Va., 1981-82; mem. conf. planning com. So. Region Extension Staff Devel., Asheville, N.C., 1984-85; mem. adv. bd. So. Region Extension Summer Grad. Sch., Raleigh, N.C., 1984—. Editor profl. devel. sect. Adult and Continuing Edn. Today, 1985—, tools of trade sect. Jour. of Extension, 1986—. Author articles, lectr. to prof. groups. Bd. dirs. Blacksburg in the 80's-Citizens Planning for Tomorrow, 1981-82, Blacksburg United Way, 1983—; chmn. leadership devel. com. Moneton dist. Boy Scouts of Am., Va., 1981-82; head baseball coach Montgomery County Parks and Recreation Dept., Christiansburg, Va., 1983. Mem. Am. Assn. for Adult and Continuing Edn. (chmn. profl. devel. unit 1985—), Am. Soc. for Tng. and Devel. (mem. ethics com. 1984), Am. Soc. Tng. and Devel. (bd. dirs. Valleys of Va. chpt. 1984—), Am. Mgmt. Assn., Va. Tech. Extension Faculty Assn. (sec.-treas. 1986), Phi Kappa Phi, Epsilon Sigma Phi (chmn. extension profl. com. 1983—). Lodge: Rotary (Christiansburg-Blacksburg) (chmn. ethics com. 1980-82, chmn. youth com. 1982-83, chmn. rural-urban relations com. 1984-85). Home: 2513 Plymouth St Blacksburg VA 24060 Office: Va Tech U 107 Hutcheson Hall Blacksburg VA 24061

SCHERER, DONALD ROY, geologist; b. New Orleans, May 5, 1927; s. Ludwig Theodore and Louise (Kieffer) S.; m. Frances Bernice Huber, Nov. 23, 1949; children—Donald Alvin, Linda Frances. B.S., Tulane U., 1949. Draftsman, Gulf Oil Corp., New Orleans, 1949-51; draftsman, lab. technician Gulf Research and Devel. Co., New Orleans, 1951-52; dist. geologist So. Natural Gas Co., New Orleans and Houston, 1952-76, Tex. Crude, Inc., Houston, 1976-79; div. geol. mgr. Weaver Oil and Gas Co., Houston, 1979-82, McCormick Oil and Gas, Houston, 1982-83; sr. staff geologist Williams Exploration Co., Houston, 1983-85; ind. geologist, 1986—. Contbr. articles to profl. publs. Served with USN, 1945-46, PTO. Mem. Houston Geol. Soc. (treas. 1982-83), Am. Gas Assn. (chmn. subcom. 1955—), Am. Assn. Petroleum Geologists, Am. Inst. Profl. Geologists (cert.), Miss. Geol. Soc., Geophys. Soc. Houston. Methodist. Avocations: philately; tennis. Home: 5806 Rutherglenn Houston TX 77096

SCHERER, ROBERT W., utility executive; b. 1925; married. B.S., Yale, 1946; LL.B., Emory U., 1950. With Ga. Power Co., Atlanta, 1946—, v.p., div. mgr. Rome div., 1965-69, exec. v.p., 1969-75, pres., 1975-82, chmn. bd., chief exec. officer, 1982—, chief exec. officer, 1978—, also dir.; dir. So. Co., So. Electric Internat., Inc., Atlanta & West Point R.R. Co., So. Co. Services, Inc., Trust Co. of Ga., First Trust Co. Bank, So. Electric Generating Co., Equifax, Inc. Office: 333 Piedmont Ave NE Atlanta GA 30308

SCHERMERHORN, KENNETH DEWITT, symphony conductor; b. Schenectady, N.Y., Nov. 20, 1929; s. Willis B. and Charlotte (Raes) S.; m. Lupe Serrano, Dec. 30, 1957 (div. 1974); children—Erica Louise, Veronica Lynn; m. Carol Neblett, Dec. 31, 1974 (div. 1979); 1 child, Stefan Gerrit. Diploma, New Eng. Conservatory of Music, Boston, 1950; D.Music (hon.), Ripon Coll., 1975. Music dir. Am. Ballet Theatre, N.Y.C., 1956-68; asst. condr. N.Y. Philharm., 1959-60; music. dir. N.J. Symphony, Newark, 1963-68; Milw. Symphony, 1968-80, Nashville Symphony, 1983—, Hong Kong Philharm., 1984—. Served with U.S. Army, 1951-55. Recipient Elisabeth Sprague Coolidge medal, 1954; Beebe Found. grantee, 1956; Sibelius medal Finnish Govt., 1978; MacDowell Colony resident, 1979. Office: Nashville Symphony 208 23rd Ave Nashville TN 37203

SCHERMERHORN, WILLIAM LYNN, soft drink company executive; b. Salinas, Calif., June 28, 1942; s. Lynn George and Irma Genevive (Farnsworth) S.; B.S., U. S.D., 1966; m. Lynda Rae Cowley, Jan. 21, 1967; 1 son, Jonathan Tyler. Asso. product mgr. A.E. Staley Mfg. Co., Decatur, Ill., 1968-72; product mgr. Gen. Foods Corp., White Plains, N.Y., 1972-74; sr. product mgr. tobacco products Brown and Williamson Tobacco Corp., Louisville, 1974-77; v.p. mktg. Dr. Pepper Co., Dallas, 1977—. Served with U.S. Army, 1966-68. Mem. Am. Mktg. Assn., Assn. Nat. Advertisers, Delta Tau Delta. Republican. Roman Catholic. Clubs: Dallas Athletic Country, Hunting Creek Country. Office: 5523 E Mockingbird Ln Dallas TX 75222

SCHETZ, JOSEPH ALFRED, aerospace and ocean engineering educator; b. Orange, N.J., Oct. 19, 1936; m. Katherine Frances, Jan. 31, 1959; 4 children. B.S., Webb Inst. Naval Architecture, 1958; M.S.E., Princeton U., 1960, M.A.,

1961, Ph.D., 1962. Sr. scientist, then supr. Combustion Research Gen. Applied Sci. Lab., Westbury, N.Y., 1961-64; assoc. prof. aerospace engring. U. Md., 1964-69; prof., chmn. dept. aerospace and ocean engring. Va. Poly. Inst. and State U., 1969—; cons. Applied Physics Lab. Johns Hopkins U., 1964—; guest prof. Inst. Theoretical Gas Dynamics, Aachen, Ger., 1970; lectr. in field. Author: Injection and Mixing in Turbulent Flow, 1980; Foundations of Boundary Layer Theory, 1984. Assoc. tech. editor: Jour. Applied Thermal Process, 1964-65. Fellow ASME, AIAA (assoc. tech. editor jour. 1975-77); mem. Soc. Naval Architects and Marine Engrs. Sigma Xi, Sigma Gamma Tau. Home: 607 Rainbow Ridge Dr Blacksburg VA 24060 Office: Va Poly Inst Aerospace & Ocean Engring Dept Blacksburg VA 24061

SCHEUERLE, WILLIAM HOWARD, university dean, English language educator; b. Irwin, Pa., Mar. 12, 1930; s. Lewis Jacob and Alice Elizabeth (Ramsey) S.; m. Jane Francis Walker, June 21, 1958; children—Angela Elizabeth, Ramsey William. B.A., Muskingum Coll., New Concord, Ohio, 1952; M.A., U. Pa.-Phila., 1954; Ph.D., Syracuse U., 1964. Instr. Westminster Coll., New Wilmington, Pa., 1956-58; asst. prof. to prof. English, U. South Fla., Tampa, 1964—, asst. v.p., 1972-78, assoc. v.p., 1978-81, dean undergrad. studies, 1981—; coordinator humanities and fine arts State Univ. System Fla., Tallahassee, 1969-71; cons. Nat. Inst. Social Scis., N.Y.C., 1973-77. Author: The Neglected Brother, 1971. Editor: Ravenshoe, 1967. Contbr. chpts. to books. Bd. dirs., sec. Serve, Tampa, Fla., 1981—; v.p. Fla. Bibliophile Soc., Tampa, 1984; pres. Friends of Hillsborough County Pub. Library, 1984—; presiding chmn. State Univ. Presses Fla., Gainesville, 1984. Grantee, Am. Philos. Soc., 1966, NEH, 1967. Mem. South Atlantic MLA, Research Soc. for Victorian Periodicals (v.p. 1973-75, pres. 1975-77, bd. dirs.), Southeastern 19th Century Soc. (bd. dirs. 1982—). Avocations: needlepointing, reading. Home: 18412 Timberlan Dr Lutz FL 33549 Office: U South Fla SVC 251 Tampa FL 33620

SCHEWEL, ELLIOT SIDNEY, state senator, furniture company executive; b. Lynchburg, Va., June 20, 1924; m. Rosel H. Hoffberger. B.S. in Econs., Washington and Lee U. Vice pres. Schewel Furniture Co.; mem. Va. Senate, 1976—. Served with U.S. Army, World War II. Democrat. Office: Va Senate Gen Assembly Bldg 9th and Broad Sts Richmond VA 23219*

SCHIELD, HARVEY WILLIAM, dentist, educator; b. Detroit, Jan. 22, 1925; s. Harvey William and Madora Matilda (Bourget) S.; m. Violet Wassel, July 5, 1952 (div. 1974); children—Brian Calvin, Andrea Lynn; m. Penny Nagi, Mar. 11, 1976. B.A., Albion Coll., 1949; D.D.S., U. Mich., 1952, M.S., 1956. Sole practice dentistry, Ann Arbor, Mich., 1952-69; asst. prof. dentistry U. Mich., Ann Arbor, 1955-60, assoc. prof., 1961-65, prof. dentistry, 1965-81, dir. pre-clin., 1969-81, prof. emeritus, 1981—; pvt. practice dentistry, North Myrtle Beach, S.C., 1981—; cons. Horry County Sports Medicine Com., Myrtle Beach, 1982—, KAVO-Am. Dental Mfg. Co., Chgo., 1985. Author: (with L.M. Carter and P. Yaman) Dental Instruments, 1981; contbg. author: Introduction to Functional Occlusion, 1982. Contbr. articles to profl. jours. Bd. dirs. Am. Jr. Bowling Congress, Colonial Lanes, 1961-81; pres. Resident Owners Assn., Ann Arbor, 1970; bd. dirs. Am. Heart Assn., 1982—. Served with U.S. Army, 1943-45; ETO. Decorated Bronze Star; recipient Citation for Service award, Wyo. State Dental Assn., 1960; Tchr. of Year award, Sophomore Dental Class, Ann Arbor, 1973, 74, 77, 78; Plaque of Recognition as pres. Washtenaw Dist. Dental Soc., Block Drug Co., 1964-65; Citation for Service, Mich. Dental Assn., 1975; Plaque of Appreciation, Colonial Bowling Lanes, 1981; Cert. of Service award S.C. Heart Assn., 1982-84. Fellow Internat. Acad. Dentistry, Internat. Coll. Dentistry, Fedn. Dentaire Internat.; mem. Mich. Assn. Professions, Francis B. Vedder Prosthodontic Soc., Grand Strand Dental Assn., Pee Dee Dist. Dental Assn., S.C. Dental Assn., Am. Dental Assn., Ann Arbor Occlusion Study Club, C. of C., Omicron Kappa Upsilon. Republican. Lutheran. Lodge: Masons. Avocations: Astronomy; golfing; running; forestry; bowling. Home: PO Box 3216 North Myrtle Beach SC 29582 Office: 803 2nd Ave N North Myrtle Beach SC 29582

SCHIFF, JON EDWARD, dentist; b. Evansville, Ind., Dec. 23, 1940; s. Edward George and Anna Marie (Barthel) S.; m. Judy Ruth Cole, Mar. 12, 1963 (div. 1967); children—Michelle Rene, Jon Scott, Melissa Marie; m. Linda Frances Black, Mar. 10, 1985. D.D.S., Ind. U., 1964. Practice dentistry, Ormond Beach, Fla., 1972—. Pres. Ormond Beach Hist. Trust; v.p. Greater Daytona Beach Republican Club, City of Ormond Beach Adv. Bd.; active Volusia County Rep. Exec. Com., VFW. Served with USN, 1964-72, served to maj. USAFR, 1983—. Decorated Bronze Star medal, Vietnamese Cross of Gallantry. Mem. Acad. Gen. Dentistry, ADA, Central Dist. Dental Assn., Volusia County Dental Assn., Res. Officers Assn. Am. Roman Catholic. Home: 349 Ocean Shore Blvd Ormond Beach FL 32074 Office: Halifax Dental Assocs 1089 W Granada Blvd Ormond Beach FL 32074

SCHIFF, LEON, physician, educator; b. Riga, Latvia, May 1, 1901; s. Mordecai and Esther (Liebschutz) S.; came to U.S., 1906, naturalized, 1913; B.S., U. Cin., 1922, M.D., 1924, M.S., 1927, Ph.D., 1929; m. Augusta Miller, June 9, 1925; children—Herbert Nolan (dec.), Gilbert Martin, Eugene Roger. Intern, then resident Cin. Gen. Hosp., 1924-27, 28-30; fellow medicine U. Munich and U. Leipzig (Germany), 1927-28; mem. faculty U. Cin. Med. Sch., 1930-70; prof., clin. prof. medicine U. Miami Med. Sch., Miami, Fla., 1970—; cons. gastroenterology and liver diseases. Recipient award Nat. Commn. Digestive Diseases, 1977; Doris Faircloth Auerbach award, 1985; Leon Schiff ann. lectureship at U. Cin. Med. Center established in his honor, 1981. Master A.C.P.; mem. Am. Soc. Clin. Investigation, Am. Fedn. Clin. Research, Central Soc. Clin. Research, Am. Gastroenterol. Assn. (Friedenwald medal 1973), Am. Soc. Gastroent. Endoscopy, Am. Assn. Study Liver Disease (past pres.; Disting. Service award 1981), Internat. Assn. Study Liver, European Assn. for Study of Liver, French Assn. for Study of Liver Disease, Am. Med. Writers Assn., Sigma Xi, Alpha Omega Alpha. Author: Differential Diagnosis of Jaundice, 1946; Clinical Approach to Jaundice, 1954; sr. editor: Diseases of the Liver, 5th edit., 1982; co-editor: Bile Salt Metabolism, 1969.

SCHIFFMAN, NANCY ELIZABETH, corporate executive; b. Everett, Mass., May 6, 1937; d. Joseph Coelho and Helen (Buchanan) Perry; B.A. cum laude, Boston U., 1973, M.S. in Urban Affairs, 1976; m. Yale M. Schiffman, June 23, 1974; children—David, Steven. Community relations specialist YWCA, Natick, Mass., 1975-76; regional transp. planner Central Mass. Regional Planning Commn., Worcester, 1977-79; Congressional research staff Rockwell Internat., Arlington, Va., 1980-82; v.p. SES, Inc., Springfield, Va., 1982-84, chief exec. officer, 1984—. Mem. women's and minority com. Area Manpower Planning Bd., Marlboro, Mass., 1976; mem. subcom. Sudbury Housing Authority, 1977; chairperson bd. dirs. Offender Aid and Restoration of Arlington, Va., 1980; mem. Republican County Com., Fairfax, Va., 1982, chmn. Springfield dist.; mem. exec. com. Fairfax Rep. Com.; candidate for Va. Senate, 1983. Mem. Am. Pub. Transit Assn. (council on preserving urban motility), Nat. Fedn. Rep. Women (patron). Contbr. articles to profl. jours. Home: 7406 Forest Hunt Ct Springfield VA 22153

SCHIFFMAN, YALE MARVIN, environmental scientist, corporate executive; b. Boston, July 31, 1938; s. Benjamin and Sara (Reznick) S.; m. Nancy Elizabeth Perry, June 23, 1974. B.L.S., Boston U., 1972, M.S., 1974. Tech. project specialist Gen. Electric Co., Weisbaden, Germany, 1962-66; program mgr. Raytheon Co., Bedford, Mass., 1966-75; prin. investigator Stone & Webster Engring. Corp., Boston, 1975-78; tech. dir. Camp Dresser McKee, Boston, 1978; group leader community applications Metrek div. Mitre Corp., McLean, Va., 1978-82; pres. SES Inc., Springfield, Va., 1982—; teaching fellow Harvard U. Grad. Sch. Design, 1978—; exec. dir. Ctr. Earth Resource Mgmt. Mem. nat. adv. bd. Am. Security Council, 1982—; Va. state sec. B'nai B'rith, 1984; mem. Fairfax County Wetlands Bd., 1984. Served with USAF, 1957-61. Recipient Raytheon Authors award, 1975; Meritorious award Internat. Congress Applied Systems Engring. and Cybernetics, 1980. Mem. Council of Environ. Design Orgns. (co-chmn. bd. dirs.), Am. Planning Assn. (past pres. energy div.), Nat. Council Energy Mgmt. Profls., Boston U. Alumni Assn. (past dir.). Home: 7406 Forest Hunt Ct Springfield VA 22153 Office: PO Box 2697 Springfield VA 22152

SCHIFFRIN, MILTON JULIUS, physiologist; b. Rochester, N.Y., Mar. 23, 1914; s. William and Lillian (Harris) S.; A.B., U. Rochester, 1937, M.S., 1939; Ph.D. cum laude, McGill U., 1941; m. Dorothy Euphemia Wharry, Oct. 10, 1942; children—David Wharry, Hilary Ann. Instr. physiology Northwestern U. Med. Sch., 1941-45; lectr. pharmacology U. Ill. Med. Sch., 1947-57, clin. asst. prof. anesthesiology, 1957-61; with Hoffmann-La Roche, Inc., Nutley, N.J., 1946-79, dir. drug regulatory affairs, 1964-71, asst. v.p., 1971-79; pres. Wharry Research Assn., Port St. Lucie, Fla., 1979—. Served from 2d lt. to capt. USAAF, 1942-46. Mem. Am. Med. Writers Assn. (dir. 1967—; pres. N.Y. chpt. 1967-68; pres. 1972-73), Am. Physiol. Soc., Internat. Coll. Surgeons, Am. Therapeutic Soc., Coll. Clin. Pharmacology and Therapeutics, Am. Chem. Soc. Author: (with E.G. Gross) Clinical Analgetics, 1955. Editor: Management of Pain in Cancer, 1957. Office: 1430 Sans Souci Ln Port Saint Lucie FL 33452

SCHIFLETT, MARY FLETCHER CAVENDER, researcher/educator; b. El Paso, Tex., Sept. 23, 1925; d. John F. and Mary M. (Humphries) Cavender; 1 son, Joseph Raymond. B.A. in Econs. with honors, So. Meth. U., 1946, B.S. in Journalism with honors, 1947; M.A. in English, U. Houston, 1971. Writer, historian Office Price Adminstrn., Dallas, 1946-47; asst. editor C. of C. Publs., Dallas, 1947-48; bus. writer Houston Oil, 1948-49; market analyst Cravens-Dargan, Ins., Houston, 1949-52; bus. writer Bus. Week and McGraw-Hill Pub. Co., Houston, 1952-56; freelance writer in bus. econs., banking and ins., 1956-68; faculty U. Houston, 1969-85, spl. projects coordinator Center for Human Resources, Houston, 1969-73, dir. publs. Energy Inst., 1974-78, sr. research assoc. Inst. Labor and Indsl. Relations, 1973-80, adj. faculty Coll. Architecture, 1976-85, dir. Ctr. for Health Mgmt., Coll. Bus. Adminstrn., 1980-83; assoc. dir. research and planning Tex. Med. Ctr., Inc., Houston, 1984, dir. pub. affairs, 1985—. Pres., Houston Ct. Humanities, 1978-80; project dir. Houston Meets Its Authors I-IV, 1980-84; pub. program dir. Houston: Internat. City, 1980-83. Mem. Internat. Council Indsl. Editors, World Future Soc., Tex. Folklore Soc., Friends of the Library, Houston C. of C. (future studies com. 1975-84, small bus. council 1981-83), Nat. Assn. Bus. Economists, AIA (profl. affiliate; profl. devel. com., health com.), Cultural Arts Council Houston, Mortar Bd., Theta Sigma Phi, Alpha Theta Phi, Delta Delta Delta. Methodist. Author: (with others) Dynamics of Growth, 1977, Applied Systems and Cybernetics, 1981. Office: Tex Med Ctr 406 Jesse H Jones Library Bldg Houston TX 77030

SCHILLER, MARCIA JANE, sales executive; b. Charlotte, N.C., June 20, 1954; d. Martin Frederick, Sr., and Margaret (Moore) S.; B.S. in Bus. Adminstrn. (Vets.' scholar), East Carolina U., 1976. With John Deere Co., Atlanta Sales Br., Conyers, Ga., 1976—, mktg. rep., 1976, fin. services rep., 1977-79, sales promotion supr., 1979-82, agrl. ter. mgr. 1983-85, consumer products ter. mgr., 1985—. Mem. Conyers-Rockdale C. of C. (pres.'s club 1980), Alpha Omicron Pi. Republican. Presbyterian. Home: 5420 Forest East Ln Stone Mountain GA 30088 Office: 2001 Deere Dr Conyers GA 30208

SCHILLING, JO ANNE, radio and television producer, public relations executive; b. Los Angeles, May 13, 1940; d. Bruce and Dorothy Elizabeth (Loynes) Cooper; m. Karl Henry von Krog, IV, July 29, 1961 (div. 1964); m. Paul Wesley Schilling, June 18, 1965; children—Marcellaine Dawn, Matthew Damon. B.A. in Social Sci., Los Angeles Pacific Coll., 1961. Tchr., Los Angeles City Sch. System, 1961-64, U.S. Dept. Def., London, 1964-66; dir./producer The Little Theatre, Rio de Janeiro, Brazil, 1974-77; dialog specialist Internat. Film Enterprises, Rio de Janeiro, 1977; dir. Minacapelli's Dinner Theatre, Slidell, La., 1977; pres./owner Burgundy Circle, Inc., Slidell, 1978-85; coordinator social galas Office Surgeon Gen., Washington, 1969; exec. dir. La Fete Summer Celebration, New Orleans, 1982; bd. dirs. New Orleans Food Festival, 1982—. Author, editor, dir. musical Ring Freedom!, 1976; producer radio show: Good News, New Orleans!, Sta. WWL, 1983-84, cable TV show: Goodtime News, 1983, TV show Lady!, 1984, 85. Founder, Peanut-Butter Bridge, Washington, 1969; rep. White House Conf. on Small Bus., New Orleans, 1978; founder Olde Towne Tree-Lighting Ceremony, Slidell, 1978; founder Slidell Trade Fair, 1978—; pub. relations coordinator, parish pres. St. Tammany, La., 1979. Mem. Nat. Fedn. Press Women, Nat. Assn. Parliamentarians, La. Talent Bank of Women (co-chmn.), Bus. and Profl. Women (pres.-elect, NIKE award 1979, Woman of Year 1984), Am. Council for Career Women (co-chmn. pub. relations), Slidell C. of C. (top salesperson award 1979). Republican.

SCHILLING, LOUIS ROBERT, JR., aerospace company executive; b. Hackensack, N.J., Nov. 24, 1931; s. Louis Robert and Frances Elizabeth (Loehwing) S.; B.S., Villanova U., 1954; m. Joan Patricia Coughlin, Apr. 21, 1956 (div. 1978); children—Louis Robert III, Lynn Patricia; m. 2d, Patricia Ann Howard, June 27, 1981. Staff accountant Shell Chem. Corp., N.Y.C., 1958-61; cost mgr. I.T. & T., Paramus, N.J., 1962-65; accounting mgr. Gen. Foods Corp., White Plains, N.Y., 1965-67; fin. mgr. R.J.R. Foods, Inc., N.Y.C., 1967-69; controller, sec. Henkel Inc. (formerly Standard Chem. Products), Teaneck, N.J., 1969-73; fin. dir. Polyester div. W.R. Grace Co., 1973-74; pres. L.R. Schilling & Assocs., Montvale, N.J., 1974-76; budget mgr., bus. mgr. govt. products div. Pratt and Whitney Group United Technologies Corp., 1976—. Served to lt. USNR, 1954-58, 61-62. Mem. Financial Execs. Inst., Assn. Systems Mgmt., N.Am. Yacht Racing Union. Club: Englewood (N.J.) Yacht. Home: 745 Dogwood Rd North Palm Beach FL 33408 Office: PO Box 2691 West Palm Beach FL 33402

SCHILLMOLLER, CHARLES MARIE, chemical engineer, consulting materials engineer; b. Indonesia, May 24, 1923; s. Bernhard Frits Anton and Anna Johanna Maria (Quant) S.; m. Freda Walker Jones, June 13, 1946 (div. Oct. 1975); children—Anthony Frederick, Paul Charles, Peter Jan, Anne Louise; m. 2d, Verena Lydia Braunschweiler, Dec. 31, 1975. B.S. in Chem. Engring., U. Sydney (Australia), 1952. Registered profl. engr., Calif. Process engr. Atlantic Richfield Corp., Los Angeles, 1952-56; with market devel. dept. Internat. Nickel Co. Inc., Los Angeles, 1956-66, N.Y.C., 1966-70, mgr. minerals investigation Internat. Nickel Australia Ltd., Sydney, 1970-72; mng. dir. Nickel Alloys Internat. S.A., Brussels, 1972-74; pres. Schillmoller Assocs., Mgmt. Cons., Brussels and The Hague, 1974-78; tech. mktg. mgr. VDM Technologies Corp., Houston, 1978-83, pres. Schillmoller Assocs., mgmt. Consultants, Houston, 1983—. Served to 1st lt. Royal Netherlands Air Force, 1941-47. Recipient award of Merit Nat. Swimming Pool Inst., 1964. Mem. Am. Petroleum Inst., Nat. Assn. Corrosion Engrs., Am. Inst. Chem. Engrs., Am. Water Works Assn., Materials Tech. Inst. Republican. Clubs: Royal Sydney Yacht. Contbr. numerous articles on chem. engring. and control of corrosion to profl. jours.

SCHIMEK, ROBERT ALFRED, ophthalmologist, educator; b. Beaver Falls, Pa., May 1, 1926; s. Hugo and Wilma (Alberty) S.; m. Sara Ellen Ray, 1951 (div. 1971); children—Robert Alfred, Ray Alan; m. Denise Villere, Dec. 1, 1979. Student Geneva Coll., 1943-44; B.S., Franklin and Marshall Coll., 1945; M.D., Johns Hopkins U. Med. Sch., 1950. Diplomate Am. Bd. Ophthalmology, 1954. House officer, resident Johns Hopkins Hosp., Balt., 1950-53; staff ophthalmologist Henry Ford Hosp., Detroit, 1953-57; head dept. ophthalmology Ochsner Clinic and Found. Hosp., New Orleans, 1957-78, staff ophthalmologist, 1978-84, EENT Hosp., 1957—, Touro Infirmary, 1957—, E. Jefferson Hosp., 1972—, Lakeside Hosp., 1984—, St. Jude Hosp., 1985—, Mercy Hosp., 1985—; assoc. prof. ophthalmology Tulane U. Med. Sch., New Orleans, 1957-76, clin. prof., 1977—; clin. prof. ophthalmology La. State U., 1979—. Served with USNR, 1944-46. Mem. New Orleans Acad. Ophthalmology (pres. 1982-84), Am. Acad. Ophthalmology (honor award 1961, sr. honor award 1984), So. Med. Assn. (chmn. ophthalmology 1984), ACS (coordinator ophthalmic movie), Eye Study Club, Am. Soc. Ophthalmic Plastic and Reconstructive Surgery, Pan-Am. Assn. Ophthalmology, AMA, La. Med. Assn., Phi Beta Kappa. Episcopalian. Clubs: New Orleans Country, So. Yacht. Lodge: Masons. Contbr. numerous articles to sci. jours. Home: 6565 Oakland Dr New Orleans LA 70118 Office: 4720 I-10 Service Rd Suite 2 Metairie LA 70001 also St Jude Med Office Bldg 200 W Esplanade Kenner LA 70065

SCHINDLER, GAIL LEWIS, psychologist; b. Houston, Sept. 3, 1930; d. Abraham Boris Lewis and Mary Frances (Dorenfield) Lowry; m. William Joseph Schindler, Dec. 17, 1972; children—Steven Sean Callahan, Cynthia Gail Orman, Marc Benjamin Schindler. Student, So. Meth. U., 1947-48, Rice U., 1949-51; B.A., U. Houston, 1952, M.Ed., 1969, Ed.D., 1979. Tchr. Houston Ind. Sch. Dist., 1955-63, Spring Branch Ind. Sch. Dist., Houston, 1963-65, Houston Community Coll., 1972; tchr., staff devel. counselor, coordinator Deer Park Ind. Sch. Dist., Tex., 1967-77, cons., 1980—; research asst., teaching fellow U. Houston, 1975; sole practice psychology, Houston, 1980—; cons. Tex. Edn. Assn., Houston, 1973, Pre-Menstrual Syndrome Clinic, Houston, 1983. Mem. Southwest Civic Club, Houston; contbr. Democrats of Tex. Paige Besch grantee Baylor Coll. Medicine, 1978-79. Mem. Houston Psychol. Assn., Tex. Psychol. Assn., Am. Psychol. Assn., Soc. for Clin. and Exptl. Hypnosis, NOW. Democrat. Jewish. Avocations: reading; aerobics; bridge; theater; grandchildren. Home and Office: 4027 Tartan Ln Houston TX 77025

SCHINDLER, NEWELL HILARY, freelance journalist, musician, retired oil company executive; b. New Orleans, May 29, 1928; s. Charles Frederick and Jeanne Cecile (Solzano) S.; m. Jacqueline Ruth Jahn, Sept. 4, 1955; children—Johanna, Newell Hilary, Christina. B.Music Edn., Loyola U., New Orleans, 1952. Newsman The Times-Picayune, New Orleans, 1949-54, 60-62, UPI, Dallas and Cheyenne, Wyo., 1954-57; tchr. Rawlins (Wyo.) Pub. Schs., 1957-59; tchr. Holy Cross Sch., New Orleans, 1959-60; chief feature writer, reporter Clarion Herald, New Orleans, 1962-66; employee relations specialist eastern region Chevron U.S.A. Inc., New Orleans, 1966-77, pub. affairs counsel, 1977-83, environ. affairs rep., 1983-85. Chmn. Alumni Fund Campaign for Loyola, 1979; mem. exec. bd. Holy Cross Sch. Alumni, 1980-84, chmn. Decade of 40s Fund campaign, 1982-85; mem. Jefferson Performing Arts Soc. Community Chorus. Served with USN, 1946-48. Recipient Order of St. Louis award Archidocese of New Orleans, 1975. Mem. Am. Fedn. Musicians, Press Club New Orleans, Loyola U. Alumni Assn. (dir. 1978-82, pres. 1980-81). Democrat. Roman Catholic. Club: Brechtel Golf (dir. 1978-81, pres. 1980-81) (New Orleans). Home: 8001 Danube Rd New Orleans LA 70126

SCHINDLER, STEPHEN NEIL, ophthalmologist; b. Bklyn., Feb. 17, 1949; s. Alfred Lawrence and Edith (Astrachan) S.; m. Diane Perry Morse, July 14, 1974; children—Margaret, Douglas. A.B., Colgate U., 1971; postgrad. Syracuse U., 1971-72; M.D., Case Western Res. U., 1977. Diplomate Am. Bd. Ophthalmology. Intern Cleve. Clinic, 1977-78; resident Baylor Coll. Medicine, Houston, 1978-81; ptnr. Clearwater Eye Assn., Fla., 1982-83; gen. practice ophthalmology, Clearwater, 1983—; med. advisor retinitis Pigmentosa Found., Tampa, Fla., 1983—, Med. Explorers, Morton Plant Hosp., Clearwater, 1983—, Lions Eye Bank, Clearwater, 1983-84; cons. Vision Works, Clearwater, 1984—; med. dir. AMI Single Day Surgery Ctr. Contbr. articles to profl. jours., chpts. to med. texts. Fellow Internat. Coll. Surgeons. Mem. Am. Acad. Ophthalmology, AMA, Baylor Coll. Medicine Ophthalmology Alumni Assn., Pinellas County Med. Soc., Fla. Med. Assn., Fla. Soc. Ophthalmology, Outpatient Ophthalmic Surgery Soc., Contact Lens Assn. Am., Kerato-refractive Soc., Internat. Soc. Ocular Surgeons, Am. Intra-ocular Implant Soc., Internat. Soc. Refractive Keratoplasty, Am. Soc. Contemporary Ophthalmology, Internat. Glaucoma Congress, Pan Am. Assn. Ophthalmology, Alpha Omega Alpha. Avocations: tennis; violin. Home: 1470 Maple Forest Dr Clearwater FL 33546 Office: 417 Corbett St Clearwater FL 33516

SCHIPPER, RANDALL J., retail exec.; b. Holland, Mich., Oct. 24, 1956; student Western Mich. U., 1974-75; B.S., Hope Coll., 1978; postgrad. U. Pa., 1978; m. Lynne Gaeb Jennings, May 25, 1978; children—Bradford Vincent, Matthew Alexander. Law intern Pepper, Hamilton & Scheetz, Phila., 1978; advt. dir., founder LMI Advt. Agy., Holland, Mich., 1979; v.p., mgr. ops. Jennings Corp., Macatawa, Mich., 1980—; exec. v.p. Bradford's, Naples, Fla., Jennings Mercantile Corp., Naples, Fla. Dist. mgr. Arlen Specter's campaign for gov. Pa., 1977-78. Bd. dirs. Am. Cancer Soc., 1985—. Republican. Clubs: Macatawa Bay Yacht. Office: 2244 N Tamiami Trail Naples FL 33940 also 2150 S Shore Dr Macatawa MI 49434

SCHISLER, GILBERT CHARLES, accounting executive; b. Phila., Dec. 10, 1953; s. Charles Herbert and Dorothy Marie (Piening) S.; m. Lisa D. Nearhouse, Nov. 19, 1977; 1 dau., Jennifer N. Student U. South Fla., 1978-80; B.S. in Acctg., SUNY, 1983. Lic. ins. and real estate salesman, Fla. State medicaid specialist Budget Prescription Ctrs., Tampa, Fla., 1977-82; mng. ptnr. L & L Acctg. & Tax Service, Tampa, 1979-82; pres. Li-cole Inc., Tampa, 1982—, also dir.; dir. C.P.S. Inc.; mem. B-O-D Tahitian Co-op Inc. Mem. Univ. Square Civic Assn. Mem. Fla. Accts. Assn., Nat. Bd. Realtors, Fla. Bd. Realtors, Tampa Bd. Realtors. Republican. Club: Univ. Lions (Tampa). Home: 8506 Caledesi Island Dr Tampa FL 33617

SCHLAGETER, ROBERT WILLIAM, museum administrator; b. Streator, Ill., May 10, 1925; B.A., U. Ill., 1950, M.F.A., 1955; postgrad. U. Heidelberg (Ger.), 1949-50, U. Chgo., 1956, Harvard U., 1957. Asst. prof. art history U. Tenn., 1952-58; dir. Mint Mus. Art, Charlotte, N.C., 1958-66; asso. dir. Downtown Gallery, N.Y.C., 1967, Ackland Art Center at U. N.C., Chapel Hill, 1967-76; dir. Cummer Gallery Art, Jacksonville, Fla., 1976—. Mem. Fla. Art Mus. Assn. (treas. 1981-84). Office: 829 Riverside Ave Jacksonville FL 32204

SCHLAKE, DENISE LYNETTE, educational administrator; b. Beatrice, Nebr., July 30, 1957; d. Wilmer Harlan and Eleanor Tina (Folkerts) S. B.S. in Home Econs., U. Nebr., 1979, M.S. in Ednl. Psychology, 1981. Activities advisor Tex. Tech U., Lubbock, Tex., 1981-84, activities advisor student orgn., 1984-85; coordinator orientation and orgns. U. Mo.-Columbia, 1986—; asst. ednl. services coordinator Nat. Assn. Campus Activities, South Central Regional Conf., 1984. Contbr. articles to profl. jours. Mem. leadership devel. com. Nat. Assn. Campus Activities, 1981, evaluation coordinator, 1982, mem. host com., Lincoln, Nebr., 1980; mem. health of life com., Tex. Tech. U., 1983—, mem. student affairs staff devel. com., 1981-82. Mem. Am. Coll. Personnel Assn. (conf. coordinator 1981), Am. Assn. Counseling and Devel. Lutheran. Avocation: creative activities.

SCHLECTE, MARVIN CHARLES, JR., ophthalmologist; b. Houston, May 26, 1947; s. Marvin Charles and Ruth Evelyn (Gardner) S.; m. P. Diane Shaughnessy, May 9, 1970; 1 child, Charlie. B.S. in Elec. Engring., Tex. Tech U., 1970; M.D., U. Tex. Health Sci. Ctr., 1974. Diplomate Am. Bd. Ophthalmology, 1979. Clin. assoc. prof. Family Practice Program, Baylor U., Waco, Tex., 1979—. Mem. Am. Acad. Ophthalmologists, Tex. Med. Assn. (del. 1980—), Tex. Ophthal. Soc. Home: 2900 Deerwood Waco TX 76710 Office: Waco Eye Assocs 3500 Hillcrest Waco TX 76708

SCHLENKER, BARRY RICHARD, psychologist, researcher, educator; b. Passaic, N.J., Feb. 21, 1947; s. Henry Walter Schlenker and Ruth Stephanie (Gammelin) Allis; m. Patricia Anne O'Rorke, July 22, 1972; children—David Richard, Kristine Anne. B.A. summa cum laude, U. Miami, Fla., 1969; M.A., U.S. Internat. U., 1970; Ph.D., SUNY-Albany, 1972. Asst. prof. U. Fla., Gainesville, 1972-76, assoc. prof., 1976-80, prof. psychology, 1980—, dir. social-personality program, 1984—, prof. mktg., prof. clin. psychology, 1976—. Cons. editor 4 psychology jours.; author 4 books including: A Contemporary Introduction to Social Psychology, 1976; Impression Management, 1980; editor: Self and Social Life, 1985. NSF research grantee, 1977-80, predoctoral fellow, 1970-72; recipient Research Scientist Devel. award NIMH, 1979-83. Fellow Am. Psychol. Assn., Soc. for Psychol. Study of Social Issues; mem. Southeastern Psychol. Assn., Phi Kappa Phi, Phi Eta Sigma. Avocation: Baseball. Home: 3218 NW 46th Pl Gainesville FL 32605 Office: Dept Psychology Univ Fla Gainesville FL 32611

SCHLESINGER, LOUIS MICHAEL, air force officer, optometrist; b. Brookhaven, Miss., Oct. 31, 1955; s. Milton Abrams and Cecile Ruth (Ginsberg) S. B.S., La. State U., 1977; O.D., So. Coll. of Optometry, Memphis, 1982. Commd. 2d lt. USAF, 1979, advanced through grades to capt., 1982; staff doctor USAF Hosp., Abilene, Tex., 1982-85; chief eye services USAF Hosp. Warner Robins, Ga., 1985—. Fellow Am. Coll. Optometric Physicians; mem. Armed Forces Optometric Soc., Tex. Optometric Assn., Am. Optometric Assn. Republican. Jewish. Lodge: Lions (bd. dirs. 1983—). Avocations: private pilot; bicycling; computer programming. Office: USAF Hosp Robins Optometry Clinic/SGHGO Robins AFB GA 31098

SCHLICK, JOHN TERRANCE, safety engineer; b. Madison, Ind., May 23, 1950; s. John Edward and Roseann Patricia (Behr) S.; m. Catherine Patricia Holloran, 1973. B.S. in Safety Mgmt., Ind. State U., 1973. Safety engr. Stone and Webster Engring. Corp., Boston, 1973-76, Western State Hosp., Staunton, Va., 1976-79; mgr. loss prevention services Henderson and Phillips, Inc., Norfolk, Va., 1979—. Developer safety program, 1978. Vol. Big Bros./Big Sisters Tidewater, Virginia Beach, 1983—. Mem. Am. Soc. Safety Engrs., Nat. Safety Mgmt. Soc. Roman Catholic. Avocations: music; sports. Home: 8965 Saint George Ave Norfolk VA 23503 Office: Henderson and Phillips Inc 235 E Plume St M Norfolk VA 23501

SCHLOSSER, MARSHA LINKWALD, commercial/industrial lighting company executive, management development trainer; b. Balt., Jan. 9, 1949; d. William and Lena (Ronin) Linkwald; m. Robert Lee Schlosser, July 2, 1972 (div. 1980); children—Melanie, David. B.S. cum laude in Edn., Kent State U., 1970, M.A. summa cum laude in Sociology, 1971. Cert. secondary edn., Ohio. Spl. project dir. Tng. and Research Ctr., Planned Parenthood, Chgo.; with mgmt. edn. ctr. Gould, Inc., Chgo., 1979, program adminstr., 1979-80; systems trainer Lithonia Lighting div. Nat. Service Industries, Atlanta, 1981, mgr. tng. and edn., 1981—. Author: (booklet) Putting Your Best Foot Forward (award Am Soc. Tng. and Devel.), 1982. Facilitator single parenting interaction group, Atlanta, 1984-85. U.S. Office Edn. grantee, 1971. Mem. Lithonia Lighting Mgmt. Club (v.p. 1982-83), Am. Soc. of Tng. and Devel. (bd. dirs. 1982, spl. projects. dir. Atlanta chpt. 1982, Vol. of Yr.) Jewish. Avocation: reading. Office: Lithonia Lighting Div of Nat Service Industries 1400 Lester Rd Conyers GA 30207

SCHLUTERMAN, BENNO, educational administrator; b. Chgo., Sept. 11, 1935; s. August and Gertrude (Leding) S. B.A., Subiaco Coll., 1957; M.Ed., Loyola U., Chgo., 1962. Ordained priest Roman Catholic Ch., 1960. Instr. Subiaco Acad., Ark., 1960-61, dean, 1962-64, headmaster, 1964—; chmn. religious dept. Subiaco Acad. Mem. Nat. Cath. Edn. Assn. Avocations: nurseryman; stained glass; art. Home and Office: Subiaco Acad Subiaco AR 72865

SCHMELZER, RONALD VINCENT, JR., psychology educator; b. Mpls., Feb. 26, 1944; s. Ronald Vincent and Doris Ann (Wellman) S.; m. Claire Dobson, Nov. 24, 1972; children—Erika Elizabeth, Stephen Paul. B.S., St. Cloud State U., 1968; M.A., Wash. State U., 1970; Ph.D., U. Minn., 1975. Elem. tchr. Orono pub. schs., Maple Plain, Minn., 1968-69; dir. reading ctr. Anoka Ramsey Community Coll., Coon Rapids, Minn., 1970-77; assoc. dean Steed Coll., Johnson City, Tenn., 1977-78; asst. dir. counseling U. S.C., Columbia, 1978-83; chmn. learning skills Eastern Ky. U., Richmond, 1983—; indsl. psychologist Lindbom and Assocs., St. Paul, 1975-77; faculty Met. State U., St. Paul, 1974-77; cons. in field. Author: Word Attack and Spelling, 1981; Setting the Pace, 1984, others. Contbr. articles to profl. jours. Co-chmn. Madison County Republican Com., Ky., 1984; mem. oversight com. Diocese of Covington, Ky., 1984-85. Served with USN, 1962-64. Mem. Am. Psychol. Assn., Internat. Reading Assn., Coll. Reading Assn., Nat. Reading Conf. Avocations: flying; camping; fishing; metal and woodworking. Office: Eastern KY U 225 Keith Hall Richmond KY 40475

SCHMIDLEY, AUDREY DIANNE, telecommunications executive, demographer; b. Nacogdoches, Tex., May 11, 1942; d. Francis Xavier and June Delores (Hage) S.; m. Darrell G. Johnson, June 17, 1959 (div. July 1975); children—Constance Adele, Richard Darrell, John Eric; m. David Anderson Foster II, July 31, 1982. B.A., Mary Washington Coll., 1975; M.A., Georgetown U., 1977; postgrad., U. Md., 1983—. Staff demographer U.S. Ho. of Reps., Washington, 1977-79, C & P Telephone Co., Washington, 1979-83; corp. demographer Bell Atlantic Corp., MSI, Arlington, Va., 1983—; mem. bus. demographer PAA Com., Washington, 1982—, chmn., 1982-84, chmn. COPS subcom. on 1990 Census, 1985—. Georgetown U. scholar, 1975. Mem. Am. Sociol. Assn., Population Assn. Am., Am. Statis. Assn., Assn. Pub. Data Users, So. Regional Demographic Group. Avocations: gardening, travel. Office: Bell Atlantic MSI 1310 N Court House Arlington VA 22201

SCHMIDT, ARTHUR LOUIS, state senator, banker; b. Cold Spring, Ky., May 1, 1927; s. Joseph E. and Elizabeth (Bertsch) S.; m. Marian Seibert, Apr. 28, 1951; children—Karen, Marianne. Mgr. mktg. Cin. Bell, 1946-83; dir. No. Ky. Bank and Trust, 1964-85. Mem. City Council, Cold Spring, Ky., 1962-63; mem. Ky. Ho. of Reps., 1963-83; mem. Ky. Senate, 1983—. Office: Office of the State Senate Frankfort KY 40601

SCHMIDT, DALTON MORRIS, electrical engineer; b. Mt. Vernon, Ind., Feb. 22, 1924; s. Charles W. and Edna (Bockstahler) S.; m. Susan Mildred Harbin, June 19, 1965; children—Charles H., William A. B.S.E.E., Purdue U., 1949; M.S., U. Fla., 1950; student Ind. U., 1942-43, Rutgers U., 1943, U. Ala.-Huntsville, 1968-69. Registered profl. engr., Ala. With Harza Engring. Co., Chgo., 1951-53, Van Dyck-Johnson Constrn. Co., Blue Island, Ill., 1953-57; U.S. Army Ballistic Missile Agy., Huntsville, Ala., 1957-60; with NASA, Huntsville, 1960—, supervising test condr. assembled rocket boosters, 1958-62, project engr. lab. dept., 1962-64, sr. launchsite staff engr., 1964-65, lab. staff engr., 1966-69, payload components test supr., 1969—. Mem. Ala. Conservancy, 1968—; active Boy Scouts Am.; mem. Secretariat for Electronic Test Equipment, U.S. Navy, 1967-68. Served with USAAF, 1943-46. Mem. IEEE, Tau Beta Pi, Eta Kappa Nu, Theta Chi. Baptist. Contbg. author books on automatic test equipment. Home: 411 Cole Dr SE Huntsville AL 35802 Office: ET45 Marshall Space Flight Ctr Huntsville AL 35812

SCHMIDT, DOROTHY (DOREY) SHERMAN, educator, editor; b. Comfort, Tex., Dec. 19, 1931; d. Valentine L. and Gladys Fern (Hedges) Sherman; B.A., Pan Am. U., 1963; M.S., Tex. A & I U., 1973; Ph.D., Bowling Green U. (Ohio), 1979; m. Robert J. Schmidt, May 27, 1950; children—Richard W., Virginia K., Janice L., Karyl Lea. Elem. tchr., Edinburg and La Villa, Tex., 1958-63; secondary English and reading tchr. Edcouch-Elsa High Sch., Edinburg High Sch., 1963-73; assoc. prof. English, Pan Am. U., Edinburg, 1973—, editor Living Author Series, 1977-83, dir. Pan Am. Univ. Press, 1983—; editor-pub. RiverSedge Press, Edinburg, 1977—; editor Margaret Drabble: Golden Realms, 1982, Am. Mag., Wilmington, Del., Del. Art Mus., 1979, Larry McMurtry: Unredeemed Dreams, 1978. Mem. Am. Culture Assn., MLA, Am. Studies Assn., Western Lit. Assn., Popular Culture Assn., Tex. Pubs. Assn., Coll. English Assn., Council Small Mag. Editors and Pubs., Tex. Assn. Coll. Tchrs. Home: PO Box 1450 Wimberley TX 78676 Office: Dept English Pan Am Univ Edinburg TX 78539

SCHMIDT, EVERETT PAUL, college administrator; b. Yorktown, Tex., Aug. 15, 1930; s. Paul A. and Ida B. (Brieger) S. B. in Music Edn., Southwest Tex. State U., 1951; M. in Music, U. Tex., 1952; D. Edn., U. Houston, 1973. Cert. secondary tchr., Tex. Asst. band dir. El Campo Ind. Sch. Dist., Tex., 1952-53; high sch. prin., band dir. Giddings Ind. Sch. Dist., Tex., 1953-61; instr. music dept. San Jacinto Coll., Pasadeno, Tex., 1961-64, chmn. music dept., 1964-74, acad. dean north campus, Houston, 1974—. Mem. Tex. Jr. and Community Coll. Tchrs. Assn., Tex. Assn. of Collegiate Registrars and Admissions Officers, Tex. Assn. of Community Coll. Instl. Adminstrs., Assn. of Acad. Deans and Vice Pres., N. Channel Area C. of C. (mem. com. 1977—). Lodge: Rotary (Galena Park). Home: 5830 S Lake Houston Pkwy Apt T-30 Houston TX 77049 Office: San Jacinto Coll North 5800 Uvalde Houston TX 77049

SCHMIDT, HAROLD EUGENE, land company executive; b. Cedar Rapids, Iowa, Oct. 12, 1925; s. Alfons W. and Lillie (Schlegel) S.; B.S. in Civil Engring., U. Iowa, 1949; M.S. in San. Engring., Mass. Inst. Tech., 1953; m. Lucy Hermann, Apr. 13, 1957; children—Harold, Sandra. Research and devel. engr. Chgo. Pump Co., 1949-51; engr. A.B. Kononoff, Miami, Fla., 1956-58; with Gen. Devel. Corp., 1958—, v.p. utilities, asst. v.p. ops., 1967-72, v.p., 1972-73, v.p. communities, 1973-82; pres. Gen. Devel. Utilities, Inc.; pres. Kingsway Properties, Inc., 1982—; dir. Port Charlotte Bank. Served to capt. USAF, 1951-56. Registered profl. engr., Fla. Mem. Am. Water Works Assn., Water Pollution Control Fedn., Sigma Xi, Chi Epsilon. Home: Westchester Woods 25 Port Charlotte FL 33952 Office: 908 Kings Hwy Lake Suzy FL

SCHMIDT, PAUL JOSEPH, physician, educator; b. N.Y.C., Oct. 22, 1925; s. Joseph and Anna (Schwanzl) S.; B.S. Fordham U., 1948; M.S., St. Louis U., 1952; M.D., NYU, 1953; m. Louise Kern Fredericks, June 18, 1953; children—Damien, Matthew, Thomas, Maria. Intern, St. Elizabeth's Hosp., Boston, 1953-54; staff asso. Nat. Microbiol. Inst., Bethesda, Md., 1954-55; chief blood bank dept. NIH, Bethesda, Md., 1955-74, asst. chief clin. pathology dept., 1963-65; sr. asst. surgeon, USPHS, 1954, advanced through grades to med. dir., 1964-74; assoc. clin. prof. pathology, then clin. prof. Georgetown U., Washington, 1965-75; dir. S.W. Fla. Blood Bank, Inc., Tampa, 1975—; prof. pathology U. So. Fla., Tampa, 1975—; cons. to surgeon gen. U.S. Navy, 1976—. Mem. service and rehab. com. Fla. div. Am. Cancer Soc., 1976-84; bd. dirs. Am. Assn. Blood Banks, 1981—, v.p., 1986. Served with U.S. Army, 1944-46. Recipient Silver medal Spanish Red Cross, 1960; Emily Cooley award Am. Assn. Blood Banks, 1974. Mem. Am. Soc. Clin. Pathologists, Coll. Am. Pathologists, Am. Assn. Blood Banks, Internat. Soc. Blood Transfusion, Fla. Assn. Blood Banks (pres. 1980-81). Roman Catholic. Club: Rotary. Contbr. articles to profl. jours.; described etiology of renal failure after hemolytic blood transfusion reactions, 1967, Rh null disease, 1967. Office: PO Box 2125 Tampa FL 33601

SCHMIDT, RAYMOND HARRY, industrial hygienist; b. Phila., Nov. 7, 1950; s. Louis and Katherine (Wild) S. A.A. in Biology, Atlantic Community Coll., 1971; B.A. in Chemistry, Trenton State Coll., 1973, B.A. in Biology, 1973; M.S. in Occupational Health, Temple U., 1985. Cert. indsl. hygienist. Chemist, Bio/Dynamics, Inc., East Millstone, N.J., 1974-75; operating engr. Wilputte Corp., Murray Hill, N.J., 1975-77; chemist Union Camp Corp., Princeton, N.J., 1978-81; lab. dir. Reliance Ins. Co., Phila., 1981-83; mgr. field studies EnviroScis., Inc., Raleigh, N.C., 1984—. Recreational counselor Children's Seashore House, Margate, N.J., 1971-72. Nat. Inst. Occupational Safety and Health Grad. fellow, 1984-85. Mem. Am. Chem. Soc., Am. Indsl. Hygiene Assn., Assn. Ofcl. Analytical Chemists. Club: Capital City. Avocations: backpacking; bycycling; photography; tennis; sailing; horseback riding. Office: EnviroScis Inc 3509 Haworth Dr Suite 310 Raleigh NC 27609

SCHMIDT, WALLACE VERE, speech communication educator; b. Aberdeen, S.D., July 31, 1946; s. Clarence W. and Sylvia (Tarnasky) S.; m. Susan Ruth Osborn, Dec. 21, 1969; 1 child, Matthew Wallace. B.A. cum laude, Midland Coll., Nebr., 1968; M.A., U. Nebr., 1972; Ph.D., NYU, 1979. Tchr., Glenwood High Sch., Iowa, 1968-73; asst. prof. Hofstra U., Hempstead, N.Y., 1973-80, Tex. Tech. U., Lubbock, 1980-83; assoc. prof. speech communication U. Tex.-Tyler, 1983—. Author: (with Jo-Ann Graham) The Public Forum: A Transactional Approach to Public Communication, 1979; Organizational Communication: Principles and Practices, 1988; (with Keith Erickson) Relating, Communicating Interpersonally; also articles. Democratic precinct chair, Tyler, 1984—; bd. dirs. Tyler chpt. Am. Diabetes Assn., 1984—. Mem. Internat. Soc. History of Rhetoric (program planning com. U.S. br. 1983-84), Tex. State Speech Communication Assn. (pres. rhetoric group 1983-84, v.p. group 1982-83), Internat. Communication Assn., Am. Bus. Communication Assn., Rhetoric Soc. Am., others. Lutheran. Avocations: golf; fishing; chess. Office: U Tex Tyler TX 75701

SCHMIDT, WILLIAM JAY, geophysicist, researcher; b. Houston, Nov. 18, 1952; s. Donald Walter and Joyce L. (Johnson) S. B.S., U. Minn.-Duluth, 1977; M.A., Rice U., 1980, Ph.D., 1985. Geophysicist assoc. Conoco, Houston, 1981-82, geophysicist, Ponca City, Okla., 1982-84, geophysicist research, 1984—. Contbr. articles to profl. jours. Rice U. fellow, 1977-80. Mem. Am. Assn. Petroleum Geologists. Republican. Methodist. Avocations: sailing; squash; tennis. Home: 2129 N Osage St Ponca City OK 74601 Office: Conoco 6423 R&D W 1000 S Pine St Ponca City OK 74603

SCHMIED, ELSIE ANN, health care administrator; b. Milwaukee, July 12, 1926; d. Oscar August and Anna Theresa (Kilbert) Friedrich; m. Walter Ralph Schmied, Aug. 23, 1947; children—Paul Steven, Linda Lee Zagroba, John Fredric, Donald Walter. B., Roosevelt U., Chgo., 1972; M. in Mgmt. (Wharton nurse fellow), Northwestern U., 1977. Registerd profl. nurse, Wis., Ill., La. Head nurse Passavant Hosp., Chgo., 1962-66, med. supr., 1966-72, staff devel. coordinator, 1972-74, dir. methods improvement, 1974-77; project mgr. Olson Pavilion Constrn., Chgo., 1977-80; asst. to v.p. Northwestern Meml. Hosp., Chgo., 1980-83; v.p. patient services So. Baptist Hosp., New Orleans, 1983—; cons. in field; pres. 4-P Fed. Credit Union, Chgo., 1974-77. Pres. Women Health Execs. Network, Chgo., 1981-82. Fellow Inst. Medicine of Chgo.; mem. Am. Coll. Hosp. Adminstrs., Nat. League for Nursing, Am. Orgn. Nurse Execs., Hosp. Mgmt. Systems Soc., Chgo. Health Execs. Forum, La. Hosp. Assn., New Orleans Area Nursing Adminstrs., Sigma Theta Tau. Lutheran. Editor: Maintaining Cost Effectiveness, 1979, Organizing For Care, 1982; contbr. articles to profl. jours. Office: Southern Baptist Hospital 2700 Napoleon Ave New Orleans LA 70115

SCHMITT, CARLOS RAY, college administrator, educator, consultant; b. Keyesport, Ill., Jan. 26, 1941; s. John Henry and Leauvon (Elliott) S.; m. Janice Barnes, June 7, 1964; 1 child, Carla Janice. B.S., Murray State U., 1963, M.A., 1964; Ph.D., Mich. State U., 1971. Nat. teaching fellow Lansing Community Coll., Mich., 1968-69; instr. Mich. State U., East Lansing, 1970-71; assoc. prof. Fla. Internat. U., Miami, 1971-75; dir. S. Tech. Edn. Ctr., Boynton Beach, Fla., 1975-80; prof., dept. chmn. Clayton Jr. Coll., Morrow, Ga., 1980—. Recipient Cert. of Meritorious Service, Murray State U., 1973. Mem. Am. Tech. Edn. Assn., Am. Vocat. Assn., Ga. Vocat. Edn. Assn., Kappa Delta Pi. Republican. Methodist. Avocations: custom furniture building; farming. Home: 405 Dix-Lee'On Dr Fairburn GA 30213

SCHMITT, FREDERICK ADRIAN, gerontologist, neuropsychologist; b. Cin., July 22, 1953; s. Werner and L. Gerlinde (Adrian) S.; m. Melinda Greenlese, Oct. 16, 1984. B.S., Rensselaer Poly., 1975; Ph.D., U. Akron, 1981. Lic. psychologist, N.C. Postdoctoral fellow Duke Aging Ctr., Durham, N.C., 1981-83, fellow in geriatrics, 1983-84; vis. asst. prof. psychology, U. N.C., Chapel Hill, 1984-85; research assoc. Duke Med. Ctr., Durham, 1984-85; dir. neuropsychology service U. Ky., Lexington, 1985—; cons. Shaw U., Raleigh, N.C., 1983-84. Contbr. chpts. to books, articles to profl. jours. Mem. Am. Psychol. Assn., Gerontol. Soc. Am., Internat. Neuropsychol. Soc., Soc. for Research Child Devel., AAAS. Mem. of Baha'i Faith. Office: Dept Neurology U Ky Med Ctr Lexington KY 40536

SCHMITT, GEORGE THEODORE, exploration manager, geologist; b. Hamilton, Ohio, Nov. 29, 1920; s. George Fredrick and Katherine (Vahl) S.; m. Harriet Louise Sneed, Feb. 16, 1945; children—Theodore Rankin, William Andrew. B.S. in Meterology, NYU, 1943; B.A. in Geology, Miami U., 1947; M.S. in Geology, Mich. State U., 1949; Ph.D. in Geology, Northwestern U., 1952. Staff geologist Sohio Petroleum Co., Midland, Tex., 1952-56, asst. mgr. fgn. ops., Oklahoma City, 1957-62, mgr. staff studies, 1963-70, area geologist, 1971-76; exploration mgr. The Appalachian Co., Houston, 1981—. Mem. vestry All Souls Ch., Oklahoma City, 1965-68. Served to maj. USAF, 1942-46. Fellow Geol. Soc. Am.; mem. Am. Assn. Petroleum Geologists, Houston Geol. Soc. Republican. Episcopalian. Avocation: collector and dealer antiques. Home: 5849 Sugar Hill St Houston TX 77057 Office: The Appalachian Co PO Box 56646 Houston TX 77256

SCHMITT, GREGORY CHARLES, English and communication educator; b. Albuquerque, Aug. 22, 1945; s. Charles Christian and Mary Ellen (Reeve) S.; m. Linda Lu Buddecke, June 2, 1972; children—Sarah Elizabeth, Geoffrey Charles. B.A., Central Washington State Coll., 1968; M.A., U. Mo., 1974. Reporter Ellensburg Daily Record, Wash., 1967-68; contracting officer U.S. Air Force, Offutt AFB, Nebr., 1975-81, photographer, writer, Warner Robins, Ga., 1981-84; asst. prof. English, communications Coll. Charleston, S.C., 1984—, communications program coordinator, 1984—; chief photojournalist Air Force Reserve, Warner Robins, Ga., 1981-84. Served to sgt. USAF, 1968-72; Vietnam. U. S.C. Inst. So. Studies fellow, 1985. Mem. Nat. Press Photographers Assn., S.C. Press Assn., Assn. for Edn. in Journalism and Mass Communication, SAR, Soc. Profl. Journalists, Guild S.C. Artists. Democrat. Lutheran. Avocation: photography. Home: 412 Red Fox Run Summerville SC 29483 Office: College of Charleston English Dept Charleston SC 29424

SCHMITT, PATRICIA ANN, health and physical education educator; b. Crystal City, Tex., July 19, 1938; d. Joseph Frances and Clara Constance (Conring) S. B.S., Tex. A&I U., 1960; M.A., Tex. Woman's U., 1965, Ph.D., 1974. Tchr. Driscoll Jr. High Sch., Corpus Christi Ind. Sch. Dist., Tex., 1960-62, Mary Carroll High Sch., Corpus Christi, 1962-65; prof. Del Mar Coll., Corpus Christi, 1965—; waterfront dir. Heart o' the Hills Camp, Kerrville, Tex., 1960-63, 66-71. Water safety instr. trainer ARC, Nueces County, 1970—; chmn. pastor parish relations com. Wesley United Methodist Ch., Corpus Christi, 1981-83. Named Woman of Yr. in Edn., YWCA, 1984; recipient Disting. Service award Tex. Assn. Intercollegiate Athletics for Women, 1981. Mem. Tex. Assn. for Health, Phys. Edn., Recreation and Dance (chmn. coll. adminstrs. sect. 1981), Tex. Volleyball Ofcls. Assn. (dist. dir. 1977-83, ofcl.). Avocations: jogging; gardening; travel. Home: 5005 Marylands Corpus Christi TX 78413 Office: Del Mar Coll 101 Baldwin Corpus Christi TX 78404

SCHMITT, ROBERT CHRISTIAN, architect, interior designer; b. Las Vegas, N.Mex., Aug. 21, 1946; s. Robert Mikelsen and Alice Gertrude (Hastings) S.; m. Marilyn Clewley Merchant, Sept. 6, 1969; children—Sabrina Hastings, Cullen Carrier. B.Arch., U. Ariz., 1970; M.Arch., Harvard U., 1972. Registered architect, Mass., S.C., Fla., N.C. Designer S.B.A. & A. Architects, Boston, 1969-70, E. Flansburgh & Assocs., Cambridge, Mass., 1970-73; design mgr. Sea Pines Co., Hilton Head, S.C., 1973-75, Kiawah Island Co., Charleston, 1977-79; project architect DRA Architects, Wellesley, Mass., 1975-77; prin., owner Glick, Schmitt & Assocs., Charleston, S.C., 1979—. Recipient Aurora Design award Southeastern Builders Conf., 1983, 84. Mem. AIA (pres. 1985—), Constrn. Specifications Inst., Am. Soc. Interior Designers. Republican. Club: James Island Yacht. Avocations: sailing; tennis; photography. Home: 678 Deepwood Dr Charleston SC 29412 Office: Glick Schmitt & Assocs 247 Meeting St Suite 100 Charleston SC 29401

SCHMITT, THOMAS LEE, clinical social worker, deputy constable, educator; b. Louisville, Oct. 30, 1931; s. Albert A. and Elsie M. S.; m. Betty Marie Childers, Sept. 4, 1954; children—Maria, Thomas Lee, Angela, Michael, Christopher, Theresa, Albert, Vincent. B.S. in Biology, U. Louisville, 1968, M.S. in Social Work, Kent Sch. Social Work, 1973. Lic. clin. social worker, Ky. Social service worker, adminstr. Central State Psychiat. Hosp., Louisville, 1954-71; dir. social services Hazelwood Facility, Louisville, 1973—; pvt. practice clin. social worker, Louisville, 1976—; part-time tchr. adult edn. Jefferson County Bd. Edn.; field instr. social work U. Louisville; dep. constable Jefferson County; cons. Jefferson County Ct., 1973-75; cons./evaluator grant programs Fed. Devel. Disability Service Adminstrn., 1976. Dir. ops., maj. Ky. Wing of CAP. Served with USAF and USAFR, 1950-54. Recipient various CAP awards; commd. Ky. col., 1978. Mem. Nat. Assn. Social Workers, Jefferson County Med. Social Workers Assn., Louisville Med. Social Workers Assn., Ky. Clin. Social Workers Assn. Contbr. stories and photographs to newspaper. Home: 5800 Emmalee Dr Louisville KY 40219 Office: 1800 Bluegrass Ave PO Box 14506 Louisville KY 40214

SCHMITZ, CHARLES EDISON, clergyman; b. Mendota, Ill., July 18, 1919; s. Charles Francis and Lucetta M. (Foulk) Schmitz Kaufmann; student Wheaton Coll., 1936-37, summer 1937, 38, 39; A.B., Wartburg Coll., Waverly, Iowa, 1940; B.D., Wartburg Theol. Sem., Dubuque, Iowa, 1942, M.Div., 1977; m. Eunice M. Ewy, June 1, 1942; children—Charles Elwood, Jon Lee. Home mission developer and parish pastor Am. Luth. Ch., 1942-65, 73—, serving as founding pastor 12 parishes including Ascension (Los Angeles), Am. Evang. Luth. Phoenix, others in Prescott, Glendale, Ariz., Scottsdale, Ariz., Portales, N.Mex., Sebastian and West Palm Bay, Fla.; founder and prin. parochial schs. in Los Angeles, Phoenix, Palm Bay; synodical Bible evangelist Am. Luth. Ch., 1965-73; dir. Intermountain Missions, 1948-60; dir. parish mission builder program; pastor Peace Luth. Ch., Palm Bay, Fla., 1973—. Former chmn., bd. mem. Ariz. Christian Conf., Christian Instnl. Ministry, Camelback Girls Residence, Ariz. Alcohol and Narcotics Edn. Assn., Phoenix Council Chs., Evang. Ministers Assn.; pres. Intermountain Conf., 1954-65; vice chmn. Nat. Worship and Ch. Music Commn., 1961-65; chmn. Billy Graham Ariz. Crusade, 1964, Nat. Luth. Social Welfare Conf., 1944-70; chmn. Space Coast Conf., Am. Luth. Ch., 1980—, mem. southeastern dist. council, 1980-84; chief chaplain Maricopa County CD, 1961-65; chaplain Palm Bay C. of C., Melbourne Area C. of C., 1973—; chmn., organizer Palm Bay Pastors Assn., 1979—. Mem. Ariz. Conf. Crime and Delinquency Control, 1957-65; referee Maricopa County Juvenile Ct., 1959-61; mem. Gov.'s Com. Marriage and Divorce Problems, 1962-64; mem. Palm Bay Planning Commn., 1975-82. Recipient Dist. Alumni award Wartburg Coll., 1959; City of Palm Bay Citizen of Yr. award, 1979. Mem. South Brevard Ministerial Assn. (chmn.). Lion (founding sec. and bd. mem. North Phoenix 1952-65, founding officer Palm Bay 1975—). Co-editor: The ABC's of Life; editor: Body of Christ-Evangelism for the Seventies; contbg. editor Good News mag., 1965-71. Home: 1801 Port Malabar Blvd NE Palm Bay FL 32905

SCHMITZ, MARY ALICE, educational administrator; b. Harlingen, Tex., Aug. 23, 1938; d. Sidney Vernon and Ernestine (Ramsey) Neely; m. Robert R. Allgood, Aug. 27, 1960 (div. Apr. 1973); children—Angela E., Andrea C., Robert Stephen; m. Calvin O. Schmitz. Mus.B., Southwestern U., Georgetown, Tex., 1960; Mus.M., So. Meth. U., 1962; adminstrv. cert. Stephen F. Austin U., 1983. Cert. educator, adminstr., Tex. Tchr. music Hudson Prep. Sch., Longview Ind. Sch. Dist., Tex., 1974-80, elem. prin. McClure Elem. Sch., 1980-82, prin. Forest Park Middle Sch., 1982—. Composer: Sing For Joy, 1976; Long Ago, 1977; A Song Is Such A Joyful Thing, 1977. Bd. dirs. Longview Community Theatre, 1964-73, Longview Symphony League, 1972-74, 82-83, YMCA, Longview, 1983, Commn. on Arts and Culture, 1985—. Named to Outstanding Young Women Am., U.S. Jaycees, 1969; named premier prin. Tex. State PTA, 1983. Mem. Tex. Middle Sch. Assn., Tex. Assn. Secondary Sch. Prins., Nat. Assn. Secondary Sch. Prins., Jr. League. Methodist. Lodge: Zonta. Home: 1821 Miles Dr Longview TX 75601 Office: Forest Park Middle Sch 1515 Lake Dr Longview TX 75601

SCHMITZ, THOMAS PAUL, pharmacist; b. Monroe, Mich., July 4, 1951; s. Paul Albert and Ruth Elizabeth (Foshag) S.; m. Stephanie Michelle Werner, Shrum, Dec. 27, 1981; children—James, Jonathan, Andrew Jacob. B.S. in Chemistry, U. Mich., 1973. B.S. in Pharmacy, Idaho State U., 1977, M.S., 1983, M.B.A., 1985. Registered pharmacist, Fla., Mich., Idaho. Asst. mgr. Perry Drug Stores, Inc., Pontiac, Mich., 1977-78; hosp. pharmacist Bannock Regional Med. Ctr., Pocatello, Idaho, 1978-80, VA, Bay Pines, Fla., 1984; teaching asst. Idaho State U., 1981-83, instr. pharmacy, 1983; dir. pharmacy Mariners Hosp./Owen Healthcare, Inc., Tavernier, Fla., 1984—. Scholar Mich. Higher Edn. Assn., 1969, Monroe City Fine Arts Council, 1968. Mem. Am. Soc. Hosp. Pharmacists, Am. Pharm. Assn., Fla. Soc. Hosp. Pharmacists, Phi Kappa Phi, Rho Chi. Avocations: cross-country skiing; bicycling; snorkeling; jogging. Home: PO Box 215 Tavernier FL 33070 Office: Mariners Hosp/Owen Healthcare Inc 50 High Point Rd Tavernier FL 33070

SCHMORR, JOHN ARTHUR, dentist; b. Bronx, N.Y., Dec. 23, 1942; s. Arthur and Florence (Ehrlinger) S.; m. Mary Dilene Reneer, Aug. 17, 1963 (div. 1985); 1 child, Rebecca Ann. D. Dental Surgery, U. Tenn., 1973. Dentist, New Bern, N.C., 1975—; adv. bd. Area Health Edn. Com. Eastern Sec. of N.C., Greenville, N.C., 1981—. Served to lt. USN, 1973-75. Fellow Acad. Gen. Dentistry; mem. ADA, Am. Acad. Implant Dentistry (supporting mem), Internat. Coll. Craniomandibular Orthopedists, Craven County Dental Soc. (pres. 1976-77). Republican. Lutheran. Clubs: New Bern Golf and Country, Capital City (Raleigh). Avocations: boating; golf. Office: 1917 Trent Blvd New Bern NC 28560

SCHNAPER, HAROLD WARREN, medical educator; b. Boston, Nov. 11, 1923; s. Julius Hasse and Minnie Ruth (Galler) S.; m. Edna Ruth Stern, Jan. 21, 1951; children—Jonathan Hasse (dec.), Ann Rebecca, Brett Eliot, Michelle Helene, Deborah Lynn. A.B., Harvard U., 1945; M.D., Duke U., 1949. Diplomate Am. Bd. Internal Medicine. Intern, Boston City Hosp., 1949-50; resident Mt. Sinai Hosp., N.Y.C., 1953-54; cardiovascular research fellow Georgetown U. Sch. Medicine, Washington, 1951-52, instr. 1954-56, asst. prof., 1956-67; chief med. research VA Central Office, Washington, 1960-62, assoc. dir., nat. acting dir. research service, 1962-67; assoc. prof. U. Ala., Birmingham, 1967-69, prof., 1969—, co-dir. cardiovascular research and tng. ctr., 1967-73, exec. vice chmn. dept. medicine, 1967-73, dir. hypertension programs, 1973—, dir. Ctr. for Aging, 1976—; dir. div. gerontology and geriatric medicine. Served to 1st lt. AUS, 1943-46, 51-53; ETO. Mem. ACP, Council on Epidemiology-Am. Heart Assn., Am. Coll. Cardiology, Am. Pub. Health Assn., AAAS, Gerontol. Soc., Am. Geriatric Soc., So. Gerontol. Soc., Ala. Gerontol. Soc., N.Y. Acad. Scis. Clubs: Harvard, Duke Med. Alumni (Birmingham). Contbr. numerous articles to med. jours. Office: U Ala Birmingham Birmingham AL 35294

SCHNAPER, LARRY BRUCE, construction management engineer, consultant; b. Balt., Jan. 28, 1954; s. Sheldon Bernard and Elaine Sylvia (Godel) S.; m. Michelle Lee Coady, June 27, 1981. Student Catonsville Community Coll., 1972-74; B.S. in Civil Engring., U. Ariz., 1976. Registered profl. engr., Fla.; cert. gen. contractor, Fla.; lic. real estate agt., mortgage broker. Tunneling engr. Fruin-Colon Constrn., Balt., 1977-78; field engr. Hensel Phelps Constrn., Balt., 1978-79; project mgr. Tishman Constrn. Corp., Lake Buena Vista, Fla., 1980-83; owner MLS Constrn. Cons., Orlando, 1983—. Mem. Nat. Soc. Profl. Engrs. Republican. Jewish. Home: 3700 Curry Ford Rd Apt B-2 Orlando FL 32806

SCHNECK, HERMINIA MALARET, guidance counselor; b. Preston, Cuba, July 6, 1925; d. Pedro Salvador and Herminia (Ponce de Leon) Malaret; B.A., Bryn Mawr Coll., 1946, M.A., 1948; m. George W. Schneck, Sept. 17, 1949 (div. June 1978); children—Karen Elizabeth, Laura Isabel; m. Vladimir Trenka, Oct. 2, 1982. Psychometrician, Johnson O'Connor's Human Engring. Lab., Phila., 1947-48; research worker U. Pa. Press, Phila., 1948-50; translator Sharp & Dohme, Inc., Phila., 1950-52; tchr. St. John Sch., San Juan, P.R., 1958-62; prof. English Catholic U., Bayamon, P.R., 1966-68; English tchr. Academia del Perpetuo Socorro, Miramar, P.R., 1968-69, guidance coordinator, 1969-80; prin. St. John's Sch., 1980-81; prin. Baldwin Sch., 1981-83, guidance counselor, 1983—; mem. Middle States regional council Coll. Bd., 1980-81. Mem. adv. com. Title IV Dept. Edn., chmn. coordinating com. Cath. Schs. Guidance Services, 1976-77. Mem. Am. Personnel and Guidance Assn., Caribbean Counselors Assn. (pres. 1976-79, v.p. 1979—). Mem. Partido Nuevo Progresista (Statehood Party). Home: Box 3957 Bayamon Gardens Sta PR 00620 Office: Baldwin Sch PR Box 1827 Bayamon PR 00619

SCHNEEFLOCK, ROBERT DONALD, JR., petroleum geologist; b. Beatrice, Nebr., May 25, 1945; s. Robert Donald and Norma Margaret (Kilmer) S.; m. Janice Diane Jefcoat, Mar. 3, 1968 (div. 1981); 1 child, Stacie Michelle; m. Susan Parker Enis, Feb. 14, 1983; 1 stepson, Richard Brian Enis. B.S. in Geology, U. So. Miss., 1969; M.S. in Geology, U. Ala., 1972; B.A. in Econs., Calif. State U., 1977. Geologist, Chevron Oil Co., Harvey, La., 1969-71, Tenneco Oil Co., Lafayette, La., 1972-75, Bakersfield, Calif., 1975-78; dist. geologist Hunt Energy Corp., Jackson, Miss., 1978-80; exploration mgr. Clayton W. Williams, Jr., Jackson, 1980-81; petroleum geologist Schneeflock Corp., Jackson, 1981—, pres., chmn. bd. dirs., 1981—; pres., chmn. bd. dirs. Dallas Energy Corp., Jackson, 1981—; chmn. bd. dirs. Carribean Exploration, Charlotte Amalia, V.I., 1982—. Contbr. articles to profl. jours. Named Outstanding Young Man of Am., Jaycees, 1972. Mem. Am. Assn. Petroleum Geologists, Miss. Geol. Soc., Toastmasters Internat. (Mem. of Yr. 1977). Republican. Methodist. Home: 50 Fenceway Dr Brandon MS 39042 Office: Schneeflock Corp 208 Landmark Ctr 175 E Capitol St Jackson MS 39201

SCHNEIDER, CHARLES FREDERICK, college administrator; b. Victoria, Tex., Dec. 27, 1937; children—Kimberly, Colin. B.F.A., U. Houston, 1960, M.A., 1964; Ph.D., U. Tex.-Austin, 1976. Teaching fellow U. Houston, 1962-63; tchr. Victoria Ind. Sch. Dist., 1963-64; radio news dir. Sta. KVIC, Victoria, 1963-67; faculty Victoria Coll., 1964—, dir. pub. relations, 1968—; info. officer U. Houston-Victoria, 1974-82. Active Victoria County Hist. Commn., 1978—, bd. advisors Victoria Bronte Pub. Library, 1980—; bd. dirs. Victoria Symphony Soc., 1975—, pres., 1982-83. Served with U.S. Army, 1960-62. Decorated Army Commendation medal, 1962. Mem. Nat. Council Tchrs. of English, So. Speech Communication Assn., Tex. Jr. Coll. Tchrs. Assn., Victoria Interagy. Council (chmn. 1981-82), Conf. Coll. Tchrs. English, Tex. Joint English Com. Schs. and Colls. (hon. emeritus). Presbyterian. Avocations: musicology; ranching. Office: Victoria Coll 2200 E Red River Victoria TX 77901

SCHNEIDERMAN, RICHARD S., museum director, curator; b. N.J., June 27, 1948; s. Rubin and Dorothy (Fleer) S.; B.A., Hartwick Coll., 1970; M.A., U. Cin. (scholar), 1973; Ph.D., SUNY, Binghamton, 1976; m. Kathleen Matteson, Sept. 1, 1969; children—Matthew, Adam, Justin, Jessica. Lectr. dept. art SUNY-Binghamton, 1974, 76; adj. prof. art history Tompkins Cortland Community Coll., 1976; curator prints and drawings Ga. Mus. Art, 1976—, acting dir., 1980-81, dir., 1981—. Samuel H. Kress Found. research grantee, 1975-76; SUNY, Binghamton Grad. Provost's grantee, 1974-75. Mem. Print Council Am., Coll. Art Assn. Am., Am. Assn. Mus., Assn. Art Mus. Dirs., Am. Soc. Aesthetics. Author: A Catalogue Raisonne of the Prints of Sir Francis Seymour Haden. Home: 1395 Belmont Rd Athens GA 30605 Office: Ga Mus Art U Ga Athens GA 30602

SCHNELL, RONALD OTTO, art educator, art collections director; b. Stuttgart, W.Ger., July 1, 1929; came to U.S., 1958; s. Otto Franz and Frieda Maria (Woehrle) S.; m. Ruthanne Delong, June 19, 1958; children—David, Inge. B.A., Schickhardt-Realgymnasium, Stuttgart, 1949; M.A., State Acad. Fine Arts, Stuttgart, 1952, M.F.A., 1953; M.A., Tuebingen U., 1957, postgrad., 1958; cert. Los Angeles County Art Inst., 1959. State diploma for art edn. and German, Baden-Wuerttemberg. Asst. prof. Tougaloo Coal., Miss., 1959-64, assoc. prof., 1964-70, prof. art, 1970—, curator art collections, 1965-82, dir. art collections, 1982—; adj. prof. Jackson State U., Miss., 1970, 73, 74. Painter; author catalogues Tougaloo Coll. art collections, 1978. Participant City Spirit, Jackson Arts Alliance, 1979, 80; co-dir. Tougaloo Coll.-Miss. Mus. Art Coop, Jackson, 1978-85. Howard fellow in painting, Brown U., Providence, 1968; recipient Merril F. Ingram award in painting, 1964, Griot award, SE Conf. Afro-Am. Studies, 1984, award for Dissemination Afro-Am. Art, Miss. Cultural Arts Coalition, Jackson, 1984; NEH fellow, 1984. Mem. Coll. Art Assn., Miss. Mus. Art. Home: Tougaloo Coll Tougaloo MS 39174 Office: Art Dept Tougaloo Coll Tougaloo MS 39174

SCHNELLENBERGER, HOWARD LESLIE, football coach; b. St. Meinrad, Ind., Mar. 16, 1934; s. Leslie B. and Rosena S. (Hoffman) S.; m. Beverlee Donnelly, May 2, 1959; children—Stephen, Stuart, Timothy. B.S., U. Ky., 1956. Asst. football coach U. Ky., Lexington, 1959-60, U. Ala., Tuscaloosa, 1961-65, Los Angeles Rams, 1966-69, Miami Dolphins, 1970-72, 75-78; head football coach Balt. Colts, 1973-74, U. Miami, Coral Gables, Fla., 1979-84, U. Louisville, 1985—; coach Blue-Gray All-Star Game, 1981, East-West Shrine Game, 1982, 83. Chmn. findraising drive Archdiocese of Miami, 1984; bd. dirs. Dade County Easter Seal Soc., 1981; mem. spl. com. on edn. State of Fla., 1983; co-chmn. Dade County Ptnrs. for Youth Program, 1980-84; chmn. Am. Cancer Soc., Ky., 1986. Named So. Independent Coach of Yr., Assoc. Press., 1980, Coach of Week, United Press Internat., 1981, Coach of Yr., Football News, 1981; coached Miami Hurricanes to nat. championship, 1983. Mem. AFTRA. Roman Catholic. Clubs: Bankers, Jockey, Miami (Miami); Audubon Country, Wildwood Country, Hurstbourne (Louisville). Home: 9825 Willowbrook Circle Louisville KY 40223 Office: U Louisville Football Complex Louisville KY 40292

SCHNORRENBERG, JOHN MARTIN, art educator; b. N.Y.C., Dec. 1, 1931; s. Rudolph Hubert and Laura (Schaeffer) S.; m. Barbara Brandon, July 7, 1962; children—David Martin, Katherine Laura. A.B., U. N.C., 1952, M.A., 1953; M.F.A., Princeton U., 1957, Ph.D., 1964. Tchr. Patterson Sch., Lenoir, N.C., 1953-54; instr. Columbia U., N.Y., 1958-59; from asst. prof. to prof. U. N.C., Chapel Hill, 1959-76; prof. art, chmn. dept. art U. Ala., Birmingham, 1976—. Editor: (with J. Folda) (catalogue) Medieval Treasures SE Collection, 1971, (with H. Risatti) Comedy in Western Art, 1979; contbr. Edith Harker Frohock, 1984. Bd. dirs. Community Kitchens of Birmingham, 1983—. Mem. Coll. Art Assn. Am., Soc. Archtl. Historians, Medieval Acad. Am., Southeastern Coll. Art Conf. (pres. 1975, 80), Southeastern Nineteenth Century Studies Assn. (dir. 1984-86). Democrat. Episcopalian. Avocation: choral singing. Home: 3824 11th Ave S Birmingham AL 35222 Office: U Ala Dept Art Birmingham AL 35294

SCHNUR, JAMES OLIVER, university dean; b. Dunkirk, N.Y., Aug. 25, 1936; s. Walter H. and Frances H. (Kalfas) S.; m. Mary Ann Goulding, May 25, 1957; children—Kathleen Ann, Jeffrey Michael. B.S., State U. Coll., Fredonia, N.Y., 1959, M.S., 1962; D.Ed., SUNY-Buffalo, 1970; cert. Inst. Ednl. Mgmt., Harvard U., 1980. Cert. tchr., N.Y. Asst. prof., then assoc. prof. State U. Coll., Geneseo, N.Y., 1966-71, asst. dean div. edn. studies, 1971-72; head dept. curriculum and instrn. U. No. Iowa, Cedar Falls, 1972-78, assoc. dean Coll. Edn., 1978-80; dean Coll. Edn. Lamar U., Beaumont, Tex., 1980-84; dean Coll. Edn. and Psychology U. So. Miss., Hattiesburg, 1984—; project dir. N.Y. State Ctr. for Migrant Studies, Geneseo, 1970-71; project dir. Title IV, Found. Desegregation Tng. Inst., Cedar Falls, 1973-74; cons. Office Spl. Edn., U.S. Dept. Edn., 1981—; team chmn. Nat. Council for Accreditation Tchr. Edn., 1982—. Author: A Synthesis of Research in Migrant Education, 1970; Calculators—A Case for Minicalculators, 1979. Author ednl. materials. Del., Blackhawk County Republican Conv., 1980, Iowa State Rep. Party Conv., Cedar Rapids, 1980; bd. dirs. Fairway Houses, Inc., Beaumont, 1981-84. Mem. Miss. Assn. Colls. Tchr. Edn. (bd. dirs. 1984—), Am. Assn. Colls. Tchr. Edn. (as force profl. devel. com. 1984—), Assn. Tchr. Educators (com. fiscal affair 1985), Tex. Assn. Colls. Tchr. Edn. (pres. 1984). Republican. Roman Catholic. Avocations: photography, travel, swimming, fishing, hunting. Office: U So Miss So Sta Box 5023 Hattiesburg MS 39406

SCHNUR, JOEL MARTIN, chemical biophysicist; b. Washington; s. Leon Herman and Lillian Florence (Feldman) S.; m. Anita Koosman, Sept. 5, 1964 (div. Dec. 11, 1969); m. 2d, Sara Lee McKinney, Nov. 22, 1971; 1 dau., Tatiana. B.S., Rutgers U., 1966; Ph.D., Georgetown U., 1971. Cons. Display Scis., Upper Saddle River, N.J., 1965-68; postdoctoral fellow Naval Research Lab., Washington, 1971, Parma, Italy, 1972, research physicist, Washington, 1973, dep. head optical probes br., 1979-84, head biomolecular engring. br., 1984—; head energetic materials programs, 1980-84; v.p. Concepts Unltd., Burke, Va., 1971—; adjoint prof. U. Paris, 1982—. Mem. Am. Chem. Soc., N.Y. Acad. Scis., Sigma Xi. Contbr. numerous articles to profl. jours.; patentee in field.

SCHNUR, SIDNEY, physician; b. Bklyn., June 23, 1910; s. Joseph and Sadie (Broadman) S.; B.S., Coll. City of N.Y., 1930, M.S., 1931; M.D., N.Y. U., 1935; m. Wilma Adalene Boyce, Mar. 23, 1944; 1 stepson, Joseph Parnell. Intern, Morrisania City Hosp., N.Y.C., 1935-37; resident internal medicine Kings County Hosp., Bklyn., 1937-39; practice medicine, specializing in cardiology, Houston, 1939—; chief of staff St. Joseph Hosp., Houston, 1962-65, chmn. dept. medicine, 1960-70, acad. chief, 1962-70 med. dir. electrocardiography, 1954-82; emeritus clin. prof. medicine Baylor Coll. Med., Houston, 1977—, U. Tex. Med. Sch., Houston, 1977—; mem. hosp. licensing advisory council State of Tex., 1975-81. Bd. trustees, exec. com. Houston Mus. Natural Sci., 1970-80. Served to lt. col., M.C., USAAF, 1940-45. Decorated Bronze Star medal; recipient awards, Houston Heart Assn., 1975, Tex. Heart Assn., 1975; diplomate Am. Bd. Internal Medicine, subsplty bd. cardiovascular disease. Fellow ACP (emeritus), Am. Coll. Chest Physicians, Am. Coll. Cardiology, Am. Heart Assn. (v.p. 1976); hon. mem. Harris County Med. Soc. (pres. 1972), Houston Heart Assn. (pres. 1964), Tex. Heart Assn. (pres. 1972), Houston Soc. Internal Medicine (pres. 1965). Contbr. articles in field to med. jours. Home: 2139 Sunset Blvd Houston TX 77005 Office: Tenneco Inc PO Box 2511 Houston TX 77001

SCHOBER, CHARLES COLEMAN, III, psychiatrist, psychoanalyst; b. Shreveport, La., Nov. 30, 1924; s. Charles Coleman and Mabel Lee (Welsh) S.; B.S., La. State U., 1946, M.D., 1949; m. Martha Elizabeth Welsh, Dec. 27, 1947 (dec.); children—Irene Lee, Ann Welsh; m. 2d, Argeree Maburl Stiles, Feb. 4, 1972; 1 son, Charles Coleman. Intern, Phila. Gen. Hosp., 1949-51; resident in psychiatry Norristown (Pa.) State Hosp., 1953-57; practice medicine specializing in psychiatry and psychoanalysis, Phila., 1957-71; asso. clin. dir. Inst. Pa. Hosp., Phila., 1957-60, clin. dir., 1960-64, attending psychiatrist, 1960-68, sr. attending psychiatrist, 1968-71; mem. faculty Phila. Psychoanalytic Inst., 1966-71; clin. instr. U. Pa. Sch. Medicine, 1957-62, clin. asso., 1962-68, clin. asst. prof., 1968-71; prof., chmn. dept. psychiatry La. State U. Med. Center, Shreveport, 1971-73, chief psychiatry service, 1971-73; chief psychiatry service VA Hosp., Shreveport, 1971-73; faculty New Orleans Psychoanalytic Inst., 1972-73; mem. faculty St. Louis Psychoanalytic Inst., 1973-78; clin. prof. psychiatry St. Louis U. Med. Sch., 1973-78; clin. prof. psychiatry St. Louis U. Med. Sch., 1973-78; active med. staff psychiatry St. Louis U. Hosp., 1973-78; cons. psychiatry Jefferson Barracks VA Hosp., St. Louis, 1973-78; pvt. practice medicine, specializing in psychiatry and psychoanalysis, Shreveport, 1978—; clin. prof. psychiatry, mem. med. staff psychiatry La. State U. Med. Center Hosp., Shreveport, 1978—; chief psychiatry service Schumpert Med. Center, 1982—; active staff psychiatry Humana Brentwood Psychiat. Hosp., Shreveport. Trustee Humana Brentwood Psychiat. Hosp. Served to capt. M.C., USAF, 1951-53. Diplomate Am. Bd. Psychiatry and Neurology (examiner). Fellow Am. Coll. Psychiatrists, Am. Psychiat. Assn.; mem. Am. Psychoanalytic Assn., AMA, La. Psychiat. Soc., La. Med. Soc., New Orleans Psychoanalytic Soc., Phila. Psychoanalytic Soc. Club: Rotary. Contbr. articles to profl. and med. jours. Home: 626 Wilder Pl Shreveport LA 71104 Office: 1513 Line Ave Suite 305 Shreveport LA 71101

SCHOEFFLER, RONALD WILLIAM, municipal official; b. Gloversville, N.Y., July 4, 1949; s. William Charles and Helena Bertha (Bruse) S.; m. Vada Susan Cheshire, Aug. 25, 1974; children—Bryan Hall, John Howard, Rachel Helena. A.A., Fulton-Montgomery Community Coll., 1969; B.S., High Point Coll., 1971; M.Ed., U. N.C. at Greensboro, 1973; Ed.D., U. Ga., 1979. Resident hall mgr. High Point (N.C.) Coll., 1969-71; grad. residence hall counselor U. N.C., Greensboro, 1971-73; dist. scout exec. Boy Scouts Am., Tifton, Ga., 1973-75; family housing resident mgr. U. Ga., Athens, 1976-79; asst. dir. Athens Community Council on Aging, Inc., 1980-81, exec. dir., 1981—. Treas. Morton Theatre Corp., 1982-84, pres., 1985—; mem. Ga. Social Services Adv. Council, Ga. Dept. Human Resources, 1980—, 2d vice chmn., 1985-86, 1st vice chmn., 1986—; mem. dist. X social services adv. council, 1980—, 2d vice chmn., 1984—; chmn. citizens adv. bd. So. Bell-Ga., 1983-85, mem., 1985—; program dir. Boy Scouts Am., Camp Osborn, Albany, Ga., 1974, camp dir., 1975, dist. commr. Cherokee dist., N.E. Ga. council, 1980-82, award of merit, 1981, exec. bd. N.E. Ga. council, 1982—, chmn. council scout show, 1985—; leadership devel. cons. U. Ga. Student Devel. Lab., 1976-78; exec. officer U. Ga. Family Housing Council, 1976-79; cons. and sml. group facilitator Program of Edn. and Career Exploration, Div. Vocational Edn., Ga. Dept. Edn., 1977-78; facilitator or co-facilitator various workshops on student devel., leadership devel, 1975-79; mem. ch. council St. Anne's Episcopal Ch., Tifton, Ga., 1975; mem. Tift County Bicentennial Com., 1974-75; mem. outreach com. and pastoral care team Emmanuel Episcopal Ch., Athens, 1980—, mem. vestry, 1986—; del. Ga. State Democratic Conv., 1982; membership chmn. Clarke County (Ga.) Dem. Com., 1980-82, sec., 1983—; pres. Northeast Ga. Community Resource Council, 1981. Bd. dirs. Northeast Ga. Community Resource Council, 1981-83; loaned exec. United Way N.E. Ga., 1982; mem. legal claims adjudication bd. 15, State of Ga., SSS, 1981—; mem. steering com. Hospice of Athens, 1981—; treas. Athens Area Human Relations Com., 1982—; a founder, v.p. Hospice of Athens, Inc., 1984-85, pres., 1985—; mem. Leadership Athens, Class of 1985; peer reviewer Nat. Home Caring Council, 1985—. Recipient Scouter's Tng. award, Boy Scouts Am., 1970, Pro Deo Et Patria Religious award, 1964, named to Vigil, Order of Arrow, 1974—. Mem. Gerontol. Soc. Am., Gerontol. Soc. Ga., Nat. Eagle Scout Assn., Athens Area C. of C. (conv. and visitors bur. com. 1986—), Ga. Gerontol. Soc. (chmn. awards com. 1986), Nat. Service Fraternity Alpha Phi Omega. Democrat. Lodge: Athens Rotary (bd. dirs. 1985-86). Assoc. editor The Viewpoint, 1976-77; contbr. articles to profl. jours. Home: 240 Winterberry Dr Athens GA 30606 Office: Athens Community Council on Aging Inc 230 S Hull St Athens GA 30605

SCHOEN, GERARD, insurance broker; b. New Orleans, Nov. 1, 1930; s. Gerard L. and Stella (Ravain) S.; m. Aline J. Crovetto, Sept. 10, 1952; children—Mary, Gerard, Anne, Aline, Patrick, Joan, James. B.B.A., Tulane U., 1952. With Jacob Schoen & Son, New Orleans, 1954—, also sec.-treas., dir. 1953—; chmn. bd. Schoen Funeral Home, Inc., Covington, La., 1957—; pres. Schoen Energy Mgmt. Corp., New Orleans, 1977—; pres. La. Insurers Conf., 1974. Author: (with Ronald Smith) The Funeral Service Industry, 1975. Served to 1st lt. USN, 1952-54, Korea. Recipient Medallion Circle award Nat. Assn. Holy Name Socs., 1971; decorated Order St. Gregory the Great, Pope Paul VI, 1977; elected to Hall of Fame, St. Stanislaus Coll., Bay St. Louis, Miss. Mem. Sales and Mktg. Execs. Assn. Republican. Roman Catholic. Clubs: Lions, Vista Shores Country (pres. 1970-72), New Orleans Athletic. Home: 6043 Chamberlain Dr New Orleans LA 70122 Office: Schoen Services Inc 3827 Canal St New Orleans LA 70119

SCHOENFELD, LAWRENCE STEVEN, medical educator; b. N.Y.C., Dec. 22, 1941; s. Irving and Muriel (Levy) S.; m. Heide Ellen Buchbinder, Aug. 19, 1967; children—Jennifer Dawn, Jessica Leah. B.A., Ohio Wesleyan U., 1963; M.A., U. Fla., 1965, Ph.D., 1967. Diplomate Am. Bd. Profl. Psychology. Dir. resident tng. U. Tex. Health Sci. Ctr., San Antonio, 1976-81, chmn.-IRB, 1977-78, prof. anesthesiology, 1980—, prof. psychiatry, 1979—; adj. prof. Trinity U., San Antonio, 1979—; cons. psychology Audie Murphy VA Hosp., San Antonio, 1975—; ethics chmn. Tex. Psychol. Assn., Austin, 1980—; cons. City of San Antonio, 1973—, S.W. Research Inst., San Antonio, 1978—. Contbr. articles to profl. jours. Trustee Planned Parenthood, San Antonio, 1979-85, Julie Jordan Free Clinic, San Antonio, 1978-80; bd dirs. Alamo chpt. Big Bros./Big Sisters, 1983—; exec. dir., founder Crisis Ctr. for San Antonio, 1972-79; bd. dirs. Hidden Forest, 1984—. Mem. Am. Psychol. Assn., Tex. Psychol. Assn., Southwestern Psychol. Assn., Rocky Mountain Psychol. Assn. Home: 16002 Wolf Creek San Antonio TX 78232 Office: U Tex Health Sci Center at San Antonio Dept Psychiatry 7703 Floyd Curl Dr San Antonio TX 78284

SCHOFIELD, CALVIN ONDERDONK, JR., bishop; b. Delhi, N.Y., Jan. 6, 1933; s. Calvin O. and Mabel (Lenton) S.; B.A., Hobart Coll., 1959, S.T.D. (Hon.), 1980; M.Div., Berkeley Div. Sch., 1959, D.D. (hon.), 1979; m. Elaine Marie Fullerton, Aug. 3, 1963; children—Susan Elaine, Robert Lenton. Ordained priest Episcopal Ch., 1962; curate St. Peter's Episcopal Ch., St. Petersburg, Fla., 1962-64; vicar St. Andrew's Episcopal Ch., Miami, Fla., 1964-70; rector, 1970-78; bishop coadjutor Diocese SE Fla., Miami, 1978-79, diocesan bishop, 1980—; exec. bd. Presiding Bishops Fund for World Relief. Served with U.S. Army, 1955-56; served to comdr. chaplain corps USNR, 1960—. Mem. Naval Res. Assn., Naval Inst. Republican. Office: 525 NE 15th St Miami FL 33132

SCHOLIN, ALLAN RICHARD, journalist; b. Chgo., July 16, 1915; s. Lars Eric and Olga Richardina (Moberg) S.; A.B. in Communications, Am. U., Washington, 1959; postgrad. Air War Coll., Maxwell AFB, Ala., 1972; m. Mary Virginia Burke, Mar. 29, 1941; children—Allan Richard, Blain Taylor, Michael Bruce. Reporter, Bloomington (Ill.) Pantagraph, 1937; jr. writer U.S. Office Edn., Washington, 1940-42; commd. 2d lt. USAF, 1942, advanced through grades to col., 1968; ret., 1973; sr. info. specialist Hdqrs. USAF, 1946-58; asst. chief, pub. affairs N.G. Bur., Washington, 1958-62; assoc. editor Air Force mag., Washington, 1962-68; spl. asst. to pub. affairs officer Hdqrs. U.S. Readiness Command, MacDill AFB, Fla., 1968-75; free lance writer non-fiction, Tampa, Fla., 1975—; staff officer U.S. Air N.G., Pa., 1946-48, D.C., 1948-53, 55-68, Mo., 1953-55; mil. editor Air Progress mag., 1963-75; mil./aerospace editor Aviation Yearbook, 1976-80; contbg. editor arration publs. of Communication Channels, Inc., Atlanta, 1982—; res. dir. info. Hdqrs. Air U., Maxwell AFB, Ala., 1968-73. Decorated Meritorious Service medal; recipient Meritorious Civilian Service medal U.S. Govt., 1975, Lewis H. Brereton award Fla. Air Force Assn., 1980. Mem. Nat. Press Club, Aviation/Space Writers Assn. (award for best article on aviation subject 1969, 75), Soc. Profl. Journalists-Sigma Delta Chi (pres. student chpt. Am. U. 1962), Air Force Assn. (pres. Tampa 1970-71, 77-78). Clubs: Army-Navy Country (Arlington, Va.); Tampa Yacht and Country. Home and office: 8703 Bay Crest Ln Tampa FL 33615

SCHOMP, JOY JANETT, investor, lobbyist; b. Weatherford, Okla., Sept. 20, 1932; d. Ranza Bennett and Nettie Alice (Pollock) Boggess; m. Dale Loyd Schomp, Mar. 23, 1951; children—Bonnie, DaLynne, Jacqueline. B.S., Okla. State U., 1957, M.S., 1962. Cert. tchr., Okla. Extension home economist Okla. State U., Payne and Custer counties, 1957-69; mgr.-owner Mini Storage Co., Weatherford, 1974—; with Add-vance Co., Weatherford, 1981-82; pvt. investor, Weatherford, 1983—; bd. dirs. Okla. Mineral Owners Assn., Weatherford, 1984—, pres., 1984, sec., 1985—, lobbyist, 1985—. Pres. Weatherford Sch. Bd., 1982, Okla. Vet. Assn. Aux., 1971. Recipient Outstanding Service citation Nat. Assn. Royalty Owners, 1985. Mem. Okla. State Sch. Bds. Assn. Democrat. Mem. Disciples of Christ. Avocations: reading, sewing, travel. Home: 722 Maple Dr Weatherford OK 73096 Office: Okla Mineral Owners Assn PO Box 96503 Weatherford OK 73096

SCHON, HERBERT LAWRENCE, communications cons.; b. Lynn, Mass., May 31, 1915; s. Edward and Evelyn L. (Baker) S.; student Boston U., 1934-35; m. Marion Bergson, Oct. 23, 1946. Reporter, Lynn Item, 1935-42; info. specialist Army War Coll., Washington, 1942-46; info. officer Army Quatermaster Gen., Washington, 1946-48; public affairs exec. Office Sec. of Def., Washington, 1949-63; asst. for public affairs Def. Supply Agy., Alexandria, Va., 1963-73; communications cons., Alexandria. Served with U.S. Army, 1942-46. Decorated Army Commendation medal. Mem. Public Relations Soc. Am., Thoreau Soc., Am. Jewish Hist. Soc. Club: Nat. Press. Contbr. articles to profl. jours. Address: 7807 Elba Rd Alexandria VA 22306

SCHONFELD, LAWRENCE, mental health institute administrator, educator; b. Yonkers, N.Y., Oct. 23, 1951; s. Abraham M. and Lucille G. (Freeman) S.; m. Krista Kutash, June 7, 1980. B.A., Fla. Atlantic U., 1973, M.A., 1975; Ph.D., U. South Fla., 1981. Instr. psychology U. South Fla., Tampa, 1978-81; research psychologist Fla. Mental Health Inst., Tampa, 1980-84, dir., asst. prof. Community Aging Program, 1985-86, dir., asst. prof. Elderly Substance Abuse Program, 1986—; cons. in field. Contbr. articles to profl. jours. Mem. Am. Psychol. Assn., So. Gerontol. Soc., Southeastern Psychol. Assn., Phi Kappa Phi, Psi Chi. Democrat. Home: 2506 Chateau Dr Lutz FL 33549 Office: Fla Mental Health Inst Dept Aging & Mental Health 13301 N 30th St Tampa FL 33612

SCHONHOFF, ROBERT LEE, marketing/advertising executive; b. Detroit, May 24, 1919; s. John Clement and Olympia Regina Diebold S.; student Wayne State U., 1940-41; m. 2d, Kathleen O'Hara, Dec. 24, 1971; children—Rita, Elise, Robert. Artist, J.L. Hudson, 1939-42; v.p. advt./mktg. Dillard Dept. Stores, Little Rock and San Antonio, 1963-77; owner R.L. Schonhoff Advt./Mktg., San Antonio, 1977—; mem. faculty Bus. Sch., St. Marys U., 1975-81. Permanent deacon Roman Catholic Ch., San Antonio Diocese. Served to 1st lt. USAF, World War II. Mem. Am. Mktg. Assn. (founding dir. San Antonio). Clubs: Tapatio Springs Country; University (San Antonio). Home: 501 Hillside Dr San Antonio TX 78212 Office: 1520 Contour St Suite 5 San Antonio TX 78212

SCHOOLS, CHARLES HUGHLETTE, banker, business executive, lawyer; b. Lansing, Mich., May 24, 1929; s. Robert Thomas and Lillian Pearl (Lawson) S.; B.S., Am. U., 1952, M.A., 1958; J.D., Washington Coll. of Law, 1963; LL.D., Bethune-Cookman U., 1973; m. Rosemarie Sanchez, Nov. 22, 1952; children—Charles, Michael. Dir. phys. plant Am. U., 1952-66; pres., chmn. bd. Consol. Ventures, Ltd., Instl. and Environ. Services, Inc.; owner Gen. Security Co., Washington, 1969—; pres., chmn. bd. McLean Bank (Va.) 1974—, Community Assn. Services Va.; dir. Computer Data Systems Inc., DAC Devel. Ltd., Am. Indsl. Devel. Corp., Intercoastal of Iran; mem. Met. Bd. Trades. Pres. McLean Boys' Club; bd. dirs. D.C. Spl. Olympics, Nat. Kidney Found., Washington; trustee Bethune Cookman Coll., Randolph Macon Coll., Western Md. Coll. Served with USAAF, 1946-47, USAF, 1947-48. Mem. Va. C. of C., Profl. Businessman's Orgn., Alpha Tau Omega. Democrat. Clubs: Georgetown, Touchdown of Washington, Univ. of Washington, Washington Golf and Country, Pisces (Washington); Halifax (Daytona Beach, Fla.); Masons. Home: 1320 Darnall Dr McLean VA 22101 Office: The McLean Bank PO Box 309 McLean VA 22101

SCHOONOVER, JACK RONALD, appellate judge; b. Winona, Minn., July 23, 1934; s. Richard M. and Elizabeth A. (Hargeisheimer) S.; student Winona State Coll., 1956-58; LL.B., U. Fla., 1962; m. Ann Marie Kroez, June 18, 1965; children—Jack Ronald, Wayne J. Admitted to Fla. bar, 1962; since practiced in Charlotte County; atty. Charlotte County Sch. Bd., 1969-75; asst. state's atty., 1970-72; city judge, Punta Gorda, Fla., 1973-74; judge Fla. Circuit Ct., 1975-81; appellate judge, 1981—. Served with USAF, 1952-56. Mem. Am. Legion. Home: 1224 Stratton Dr Lakeland FL 33803 Office: PO Box 327 Lakeland FL 33802

SCHOPPET, RICHARD ALLEN, architect; b. Washington, June 13, 1941; s. Charles Horace and Dorothy Ann (Senior) S.; m. Nancy Ann Smith, Dec. 20, 1978; children—Angela Dale, Laurel Ann, Pamela Marie Tribino, Richard Manuel Tribino, Thomas Richard. Grad. Columbia Tech. Inst., U. Va. Designer, Walton & Assocs., Arlington, Va., 1958-61; chief designer Alexandria Prestressed, Va., 1961-63; project dir. R.W. Jenkins, McLean, Va., 1963-69; asst. coordinator architect Marriott Corp., Bethesda, Md., 1969-72; asst. v.p., chief designer Reid Contracting Corp., McLean, Va., 1972-73; assoc. A.G. Van Laarhoven, McLean, 1973-75; office dir. Bushey-Burrey, McLean, 1975-78; sr. assoc. Lynwood E. Brown, AIA, Alexandria, 1978—. Contbr. articles to profl. jours. Served with U.S. Army. Recipient 1st Place award Better Homes & Garden's Mag., 1984. Mem. AIA, Va. Solar Energy Assn., Internat. Solar Soc., Constrn. Specifications Inst., Am. Inst. Design and Drafting, Assn. Bldg. and Apt. Owners, Internat. Platform Assn., Nat. Soc. Lit. and Arts, Nat. Fire Protection Assn. Avocations: photography; art; architectural collections. Home: Route 1 Box 141 Blue Knoll Castleton VA 22716 Office: Lynwood E Brown AIA 1220 Prince St Alexandria VA 22314 also Moonglo Architecture Route 1 Box 141 Castleton VA 22716

SCHOPPMEYER, MARTIN WILLIAM, educator; b. Weehawken, N.J., Sept. 15, 1929; s. William G. and Madeline (Haas) S.; B.S., Fordham U., 1950; Ed.M., U. Fla., 1955, Ed.D., 1962; m. Marilyn M. Myers, Aug. 8, 1958; children—Susan Ann, Martin William. Tchr., Fla. public schs., 1955-59; instr. U. Fla., Gainsville, 1960-62, asst. prof., 1962-63; asso. prof. Fla. Atlantic U., Boca Raton, 1963-65, prof., 1965-68, dir. continuing edn., 1965-67; asso. prof. U. Ark., Fayetteville, 1968-71, prof., 1971—, program coordinator ednl. adminstrn., 1983—; mem. nat. adv. council on Edn. Professions Devel., 1973-76; exec. sec. Ark. Sch. Study Council, 1976—; evaluator instr. tng. program, Nat. Tng. Fund, 1978. Bd. dirs. Womans Ednl. and Devel. Inst., Little Rock, 1977—, Nat. Sch. Devel. Council, 1979—. Served with U.S. Army, 1951-53; Korea. Mem. NEA, Ark. Edn. Assn., Ark. Assn. of Ednl. Adminstrs., Phi Delta Kappa. Roman Catholic. Club: Fayetteville Country. Lodges: Rotary, K.C. Author: (with VanPatten, Belok and Roucek) Conflict, Permanency, Change and Education, 1976; asso. editor Jour. of Thought, 1974-80, La. Ednl. Research Jour., 1976-80; mem. editorial bd. Jour. Ednl. Equity and Leadership, 1982—; mem. editorial adv. bd. Jour. Edn. Fin., 1982—; also articles, chpts. in books. Home: 2950 Sheryl Ave Fayetteville AR 72701 Office: 244 Graduate Education Bldg University of Arkansas Fayetteville AR 72701

SCHORR, JAMES LEE, hotel company executive; b. Columbus, Ohio, May 14, 1942; s. Harold S. and Rita (Odea) S.; children—James Lee, John Ross, Michael Odea, Christopher Owen. B.S., Ohio State U., 1964. Mktg. mgr. Procter & Gamble Co., Cin., 1966-71; dir. mktg. U.S. Postal Service, Washington, 1971-73; cons. to Pres. of U.S. White House, 1974; exec. v.p. Holiday Inns Inc., Memphis, 1975-80, pres., 1980—. Office: Holiday Inns Inc 3742 Lamar Ave Memphis TN 38195*

SCHORRE, L(OUIS) CHARLES, JR., artist; b. Cuero, Tex., Mar. 9, 1925; s. Louis Charles and Anna (Barthlome) S.; m. Margaret Storm, July 17, 1948; children—Alice Ann Stultz, Martha Jackson, Robin Glover. B.F.A., U. Tex., 1948. Instr. Mus. Sch., Mus. Fine Arts, Houston, 1949-55; asst. prof. Rice U., Houston, 1960-72; artist-in-residence Ossabaw Island, Ga., 1972, Mobil Oil Corp., Saudi Arabia, 1979. Grantee Nat. Endowment for Arts, 1979. One man shows include: CEPA Gallery, Buffalo, Contemporary Arts Mus., Houston, 1981; group shows include: Contemporary Arts Mus., Houston, 1982, New Orleans Mus., 1980, Mus. Fine Arts, Houston, 1985; represented in permanent collections Mus. Fine Arts, Houston. Episcopalian. Home: 2406 Tangley Rd Houston TX 77005

SCHOTT, JAMES, educational administrator. Supt. of schs. Orange County, Fla. Office: PO Box 271 Orlando FL 32802*

SCHOTT, RICHARD LOCKWOOD, public affairs educator; b. Kansas City, Mo., Dec. 29, 1939; s. Edward Lockwood and Mary Jane (Chalkley) S.; m. Pamela Jean Butler, May 25, 1964 (div. June 1978); children—Colin Lockwood, Whitney Butler. B.A. magna cum laude, Stanford U., 1961; M.A., Johns Hopkins U., 1964; Ph.D., Syracuse U., 1972. Asst. dir. tng. The Experiment, Putney, Vt., 1964-65; fgn. service officer USIA, Bonn, London and Washington, 1965-69; asst. prof. U. Tex., Austin, 1972-78, assoc. prof., 1978-82, prof., 1982—; cons. U.S. Dept. Transp., Washington, 1972, Gov. Tex., Austin, 1974, HEW, Washington, 1976-79. Author: Professionals in Public Service, 1973; (with L. Dodd) Congress and the Administrative State, 1979; (with D. Hamilton People, Positions and Power, 1983. Editor: The Presidency and Congress, 1979. Woodrow Wilson fellow, 1962-64; Pub. Service Edn. grantee HEW, 1976-82. Mem. Am. Soc. Pub. Adminstrn., Acad. Polit. Sci., Am. Polit. Sci. Assn., Internat. Soc. Polit. Psychology, Phi Beta Kappa. Avocations: sailing; jazz music; amateur radio. Home: 3513 Lakeland Dr Austin TX 78731 Office: LB Johnson Sch Pub Affairs U Tex Austin TX 78713

SCHOTTLAND, EDWARD MORROW, hospital administrator; b. N.Y.C., Aug. 5, 1946; s. Leo Edward and Harriet (Morrow) S.; m. Nancy Resnick, July 25, 1977; 1 son, David. B.A., Queens Coll., CCNY, 1968; M.P.S., Cornell U., 1973. Asst. adminstr. Mercy Hosp., Rockville Centre, N.Y., 1973-75, asst. adminstr. and dir. planning, 1975-79; pres. Kosair Crippled Children's Hosp., Louisville, 1979-81, sr. v.p., chief adminstrv. officer, 1986—; v.p. NKC Inc., Louisville, 1981-83, sr. v.p., 1983-85. Chmn. Jefferson County Child Abuse Authority, Louisville, 1981-83, dir., 1979—; bd. dirs. Suicide Prevention and Edn. Ctr., Louisville, 1982—. Fellow Am. Coll. Health Execs. Home: 8114 Barbour Manor Dr Louisville KY 40222 Office: Kosair-Children's Hosp 200 Chestnut St Louisville KY 40232

SCHOUEST, PAUL DARYL, security consultant; b. Houma, La., Nov. 9, 1951; s. Paul O. and Gladys B.; m. Debra Ann Guidry, June 9, 1973; 1 son, Paul Justin. B.S.B.A., U. Southwestern La., 1975, M.B.A., 1979. Police officer U. Southwestern La., 1973-75; dir. U. Southwestern La. Transit System, 1975-79; dir. Acadiana Law Enforcement Tng. Acad., Lafayette, La., 1976-79; pres. Exec. Protection Systems, Lafayette, 1978—; adj. prof. criminal justice U. Southwestern La., 1981; mem. La. Peace Officer Standards and Tng. Council, 1976-79, chmn. cert. and curriculum com., 1976-79. Mem. Acadiana Safety Assn. (v.p. home and sch. div. 1980), Acadiana Security Officers Assn. (exec. dir. 1980), Am. Soc. Indsl. Security, Nat. Fedn. Ind. Bus., Lafayette C. of C. (chmn. health and safety com. 1983). Club: Rotary (1st v.p. 1983-84) (Lafayette). Office: 4702-I Johnston St Lafayette LA 70503

SCHRAMM, TEXAS E., football club official; b. Los Angeles, June 20, 1920. Publicity dir., then gen. mgr. Los Angeles Rams, 1947-57; asst. dir. sports CBS, 1957-60; gen. mgr. Dallas Cowboys, 1960—, pres., 1966—. Office: Dallas Cowboys 6116 N Central Expressway Dallas TX 75206*

SCHRANK, WILBURN REINHOLD, educational administrator; b. Aleman, Tex., Jan. 28, 1930; s. Herbert Bruno and Hattie Amanda (Moerbe) S.; m. Lynda Beth Graves, June 5, 1953; children—Lisa Ann, James Gene, Lori Beth. B.S. in Indsl. Engring., Tex. A&M U., 1952, Ph.D. in Edn., 1967; M.S. in Meteorology, NYU, 1953. Commd. 2d lt. U.S. Air Force, 1953, advanced through grades to lt. col., 1969, ret., 1976; chief electronics br. Chanute Tech. Sch., Rantoul, Ill., 1957-62; assoc. prof. math U.S. Air Force Acad., Colorado Springs, Colo., 1964-69; chief instr. and resources div. Air U., Maxwell AFB, Ala., 1969-73; chief spl. tng. div. Air Tng. Command, Randolph AFB, Tex., 1973-76; dir. sci. div. Andelina Coll., Lufkin, Tex., 1976—. Contbr. articles to profl. publs. Mem. Nat. Soc. Profl. Engrs., Tex. Soc. Profl. Engrs. (bd. dirs. chpt. 1985—). Lutheran. Lodge: Rotary. Avocations: numismatics; music. Office: Sci Div Angelina Coll Lufkin TX 75901

SCHRECK, MICHAEL H., painter, sculptor; b. Austria (father Am. citizen). One-man shows include Dominion Gallery, Montreal, 1950, 52, Selected Artists Gallery, N.Y.C., 1961, Collectors Gallery, L.I., N.Y., 1968, Roslyn Gallery, L.I., 1968, Gloria Luria Gallery, Miami, Fla., 1973, 76, Palm Beach Galleries, Fla., 1974, 77; exhibited in group shows, Vienna, 1932-38, London, 1938-48, Mus. Fine Arts, Montreal, 1953-56, Salon Internat., Montecarlo, 1963, 64, Musee D'Art Moderne, Paris, 1964, Galerie des Arts, Lyon, France, 1965, Galerie Lacloche, Paris, 1965, Sculptors of Fla., 1975; represented in permanent collections Mus. Fine Arts, Lausanne, Switzerland, Mus. Art, Ft. Lauderdale, Mus. Modern Art, Haifa, Israel, Heckscher Mus., Huntington, N.Y., Norton Gallery and Mus. Palm Beaches, NYU Art Dept., Tel Aviv Mus., Israel, Jacksonville Art Mus. (Fla.), Currier Gallery of Art, Manchester, N.H. Recipient numerous awards and prizes including Grand Prix Internat., Deauville, France; Prix Internat., Vichy, France; award City of Hollywood, 1975; elected Academician with Gold medal Academia Italia, 1980. Life fellow Royal Soc. Arts (Eng.); mem. Artists Equity Assn., Am. Fedn. Arts, Sculptors of Fla., Smithsonian Instn. Subject of books: Michael Schreck Sculpture, 1975; Michael Schreck Life and Work 1931-81, 1982. Address: 3111 N Ocean Dr Hollywood FL 33019

SCHREINER, LAURIE ANNE, psychology educator, consultant; b. Louisville, Apr. 29, 1958; d. Joseph Edward and Sue Rose (Zimmerman) Sutherland; m. Dale Edward Schreiner, Aug. 16, 1980. B.A., Milligan Coll., 1978; Ph.D., U. Tenn., 1982. Cons. Urban Studies Ctr., Louisville, 1982-83; instr. Watterson Coll., Louisville, 1982-83; prof. psychology, head social scis. dept. Ky. Christian Coll., Grayson, 1983—; bd. advs. Milligan Coll., Tenn., 1978—. Recipient Outstanding Young Woman Am. award, 1985. Mem. Am. Psychol. Assn., S.E. Psychol. Assn. Democrat. Mem. Christian Ch. Avocation: skiing. Home: Route 4 Box 458 Grayson KY 41143 Office: Ky Christian Coll 617 Carol Malone Blvd Grayson KY 41143

SCHREMSER, DONNA BARRETT, library executive; b. Kittery, Maine, July 29, 1949; d. Russell Joseph and Helen (Dunlap) Thompson; m. Robert F. Schremser; children—Caroline, Hannah. B.A., Miss. U. for Women, 1971; M.L.S., 1976. Library asst. Birmingham Pub. Library, Ala., 1971-72, reference librarian, 1972-76; children's librarian Wheeler Basin Regional Library, Decatur, Ala., 1976-77; head reference dept. Huntsville Pub. Library, 1977-78, asst. dir., 1978-81, exec. dir., 1981—. Bd. dirs. Pub. Relations Council Ala., 1981—, Am. Inst. for Psychotherapy, Huntsville, 1985—; mem. Venture grant com. United Way of Huntsville and Madison County, 1985—; mem. adv. panel on state and fed. funding Urban Libraries Council; v.p. Library Mgmt. Network, Inc., 1984—. Mem. Pub. Library Assn. (goals, guidelines and standards com. 1982—), Ala. Library Assn. (pres. pub. library div. 1981-82), Library Adminstrn. and Mgmt. Assn., Democrat. Presbyterian. Home: 1410 E Olive Dr Huntsville AL 35801 Office: Huntsville-Madison County Public Library 108 Fountain Circle PO Box 443 Huntsville AL 35804

SCHROCK, SIMON, book company executive; b. Oakland, Md., Dec. 28, 1936; s. Noah and Cora (Burkholder) S.; m. Eva Lena Yoder, June 7, 1959 (dec. Apr. 1962); m. Pauline Yoder, Sept. 29, 1963; children—Janice Yvonne, Eldon Laverne, Ivan Dale. With Eastern States Farm Supply Co., Oakland, Md., 1957-59, Children's Hosp., Washington, 1959-61, Copp Properties, 1961-75; pres. Choice Books of No. Va., Fairfax, 1975—; chmn. Choice Books Caribbean, 1976—; chmn. adv. council Blue Ridge Christian Home, Stuarts Draft, Va., 1980—. Author: Get on With Living, 1976, Price of Missing Life, 1981. Contbr. articles to ch. jours. Chmn. Faith Christian Sch. Bd., 1977—; bishop Faith Christian Fellowship, Catlett, Va., 1981—. Avocations: traveling; camping; biking. Office: 11923 Lee Hwy Fairfax VA 22030

SCHRODER, GEORGE TORRINGTON, ophthalmologist, physician; b. Pickneyville, Ill., Nov. 5, 1942; s. George William and Lorraine Antoinette (Wilson) S.; m. Mary Olivia Gann, Dec. 18, 1964; children—George F., Mary Lorraine, John Orman, Daniel Walter. Student Vanderbilt U., 1963; M.D., U. Tenn., 1966. Diplomate Am. Bd. Ophthalmology. Resident U. Ark Med. Ctr., Little Rock, 1970-73; practice ophthalmology, Little Rock, 1973—. Bd. dirs. Family, Life, Am. God., Little Rock, 1977—; state del. nat. conf. White House Conf. Families, 1980. Served with USPHS, 1968-69. Fellow Am. Acad. Ophthalmology; mem. Ark. Med. Soc., Pulaski County Med. Soc., Christian Ophthalmological Soc. Republican. Baptist. Avocations: hunting; bicycling. Home: 149 Pleasant Valley Little Rock AR 72212 Office: 260 Doctors Park 9600 Lile Dr Little Rock AR 72205

SCHROEDER, WALTER ALLEN, lawyer; b. San Francisco, July 29, 1954; s. Carl Walter and Mary (Lee) S.; B.S. in Bus. Adminstrn., Georgetown U., 1976; J.D., U. Houston, 1979. Asst. treas. G.U. Fed. Credit Union, Washington, 1976-77; asst. to pres. U.S.E. Credit Union, Houston, 1977-79; analyst Banc Systems, Inc., Houston, 1979; bar: Tex. 1979, D.C. 1984, U.S. Dist. Ct. (we., no. and so. dists.) Tex., U.S. Ct. Appeals (5th and 11th cirs.), U.S. Supreme Ct. 1984; briefing atty. Tex. Ct. Civil Appeals, Ft. Worth, 1979-80; asst. counsel Am. Ins. Assn., Houston, 1980-81, Rolston & Hausler, Houston, 1981-85, Chamberlain, Hrdlicka, White, Johnson & Williams, Houston, 1985—. Trustee Found. Amateur Radio, Inc., Washington, 1972-76, chmn. audit com., 1975-76; treas. Houston Echo Soc., Inc., 1979. Recipient Indsl. Peace award Georgetown U., 1976. Mem. ABA, Houston Bar Assn., D.C. Bar Assn., State Bar Tex. Republican. Lutheran. Author articles in field. Home: 2333 Bering Dr #104 Houston TX 77057 Office: 1400 Citicorp Ctr 1200 Smith St Houston TX 77002

SCHROYER, RONALD EUGENE, police chief; b. Chattanooga, Oct. 6, 1946; s. Harry E. and Espa Lois (Holder) S.; m. Cynthia C. Delashmitt, Aug. 21, 1953; 1 child, William. Student Middle Tenn. State U., Murfreesboro, 1965-66, U. Chattanooga, 1966-67. Fireman, asst. tillerman Chattanooga Fire Dept., 1966-69; police officer City of Red Bank, Tenn., 1969-78, chief of police, 1978—. Named Officer of Yr., Red Bank Optimist Club, 1979-80. Mem. Tenn. Assn. Chiefs of Police, Nat. Assn. Chiefs of Police, Internat. Assn. Chiefs of Police, Tenn. Law Enforcement Officers Assn., Internat. Assn. Criminology, Nat. Area Safety Council. Democrat. Baptist. Lodges: Kiwanis, Masons, Scottish Rite. Avocations: golf; fishing; hunting. Home: 512 Heidi Circle Chattanooga TN 37415 Office: City of Red Bank Police Dept 3117 Dayton Blvd Red Bank TN 37415

SCHRUM, JAKE BENNETT, university administrator; b. Greenville, Tex., Feb. 9, 1946; s. Jake M. and Julia (Bennett) S.; m. Alice Woodman, Dec. 28, 1968; children—Julia Elizabeth, Emily Katharine. B.A., Southwestern U., 1968; M.Div., Yale U., 1973; postgrad. Harvard U., 1983. Ordained to ministry Methodist Ch., 1969. Devel. officer Yale U., New Haven, 1973-77; dir. devel. Muhlenberg Coll., Allentown, Pa., 1977-78; v.p. Tex. Wesleyan Coll., Fort Worth, 1978-82; v.p. univ. relations Southwestern U., Georgetown, Tex., 1982-85; v.p. Emory U., Atlanta, 1985—; dir. Landmark Savs. Assn. Chmn. bd. Learning Tree, Georgetown, 1983-85. Mem. Council Advancement and Support Edn. Lodge: Rotary. Avocations: squash; golf; racquetball; tennis. Office: Emory U 403 Adminstrn Bldg Atlanta GA 30322

SCHUCK, MARJORIE MASSEY, publisher, editor, lectr.; b. Winchester, Va., Oct. 9, 1921; d. Carl Frederick and Margaret Harriet (Parmele) Massey; student U. Minn., 1941-43, Sch., N.Y.C., 1948, N.Y. U., 1952, 54-55; m. Ernest George Metcalfe, Dec. 2, 1943 (div. Oct. 1949); m. Franz Schuck, Nov. 11, 1953 (dec. Jan. 1958). Mem. editorial bd. St. Petersburg (Fla.) Poetry Assn., 1967-68; co-editor, pub. Poetry Venture Mag., St. Petersburg, Fla., 1968-69, editor, pub., 1968-74; founder, owner, pres. Valkyrie Press, Inc. (reorganized as Valkyrie Pub. House, Inc. 1981), St. Petersburg, 1972—, MS Records, Inc., 1974-79, Marjorie Schuck Pub., Inc., 1974-79; founder, co-dir., lectr., chmn. poetry Fla. Suncoast Writers' Confs., U. South Fla., 1973-83, mem. adv. bd., 1983—; lectr. in field. Founder Valkyrie Press Round Table Writers' Workshop and Forum, 1975-79, Valkyrie Press Reference Library for Writers and Poets, 1976-81. Corr.-rec. sec. Women's Aux. Hosp. for Spl. Surgery, N.Y.C., 1947-59; active St. Petersburg Mus. Fine Arts (charter), St. Petersburg Sister City Com., St. Petersburg Arts Center Assn.; chmn. Pinellas County Arts Council, 1977-78, mem., 1977-79; lectr., mem. Friends of Library St. Petersburg; mem. adminstrv. bd. Suncoast Mgmt. Inst., 1977-78, chmn. women in mgmt. confs., 1977-78; bd. dirs., pub. relations chmn. Soc. for Prevention Cruelty to Animals 1968-71. Named One of 76 Fla. Patriots, Fla. Bicentennial Commn., 1976. Recipient 1st Ann. People of Dedication award Salvation Army, Tampa, 1984. Mem. Nat. Fedn. Am. Press Women, Acad. Am. Poets, Fla. Poets Assn., Pi Beta Phi. Democrat. Episcopalian. Author: Speeches and Writings for Cause of Freedom, 1973; contbr. poetry to profl. jours. Home: 8245 26th Ave N Saint Petersburg FL 33710 Office: 8245 26th Ave N Saint Petersburg FL 33710

SCHUDER, RAYMOND FRANCIS, lawyer; b. Wickford, R.I., Dec. 27, 1926; s. Rollie Milton and Selma (Ball) S.; A.B., Emory U., 1949, J.D., 1951; m. Betty Jo Williams, Mar. 14, 1948; children—Gregg Williams, Glen Arva. Admitted to Ga. bar, 1951; with Trust Co., Ga., Atlanta, 1951-54; asso. firm Wheeler, Robinson & Thurmond, Gainesville, Ga., 1954-59; pvt. law practice, Gainesville, 1959-70, 76—; partner firm Schuder & Brown, Gainesville, 1971-76; dir. Lanier Securities, Inc. Municipal ct. judge, Gainesville, 1956-60, 73-75; supr. Upper Chattahoochee Soil and Water Conservation Dist., 1971-74. Bd. dirs. Charles Thompson Estes Found., Inc., Gainesville. Served to cpl. USMCR, 1944-50; 1st lt. USA Res. (ret.). Mem. Gainesville-Northeastern (pres. 1969-70) Bar Assn., State Bar Ga. (gov. 1966-70), Am. Legion, V.F.W., Phi Alpha Delta. Methodist. Clubs: Chattahoochee Country, Elks. Home: 2224 Riverside Dr NE Gainesville GA 30501 Office: Lanier Bldg 500 Spring St Gainesville GA 30501

SCHULER, THEODORE ANTHONY, city ofcl., civil engr.; b. Louisville, July 1, 1934; s. Henry R. and Virginia (Meisner) S.; B.C.E., U. Louisville, 1957, M.Engring., 1973; m. Jane A. Bandy, July 29, 1979; children—Marc, Elizabeth, Eric, Ellen. Design, constrn. engr. Brighton Engring. Co., Frankfort, Ky., 1960-65; design engr. Hensley-Schmidt Inc., Chattanooga, 1965-68, asso. mem., 1969-73, sr. asso. mem., 1973-75, prin., asst. v.p., head Knoxville office, 1975-81; asst. dir. engring. dept. City of Knoxville, 1981—. Served to lt. (j.g.) USNR, 1957-60. Registered profl. engr., Ky., Tenn.; registered land surveyor, Ky. Fellow ASCE. Home: 5907 Adelia Dr Knoxville TN 37920 Office: Dept Engring Room 483 City-County Bldg Knoxville TN 37901

SCHULERT, ARTHUR ROBERT, engineering company executive, chemist; b. Gladwin, Mich., Feb. 26, 1922; s. Oscar Edward and Ruth Olive (Sanford) S.; m. Ruth Barbara Darling, June 17, 1949; children—Barbara, Mark, Jean, Philip, Andrew, Peter, Timothy. B.S., Wheaton Coll., 1943; M.A., Princeton U., 1947; Ph.D., U. Mich., 1951. Research asst. Manhattan Project, Princeton, N.J., 1943-46; fellow medicine NYU, 1951-53; research assoc. Columbia U., N.Y.C., 1953-61; dir. biochemistry dept. U.S. Naval Med. Research Unit, Cairo, 1961-66; from asst. prof. to assoc. prof. Vanderbilt U., Nashville, 1961-73; pres. Environ. Sci. and Engring. Corp., Mount Juliet, Tenn., 1970—; cons. Isotopes, Inc., Westwood, N.J., 1957-61, NIH, Bethesda, Md., 1958-64. Co-author: Strontium-90 in Man, 1961, 62. Bd. dirs. Mount Juliet Christian Acad., Mount Juliet, 1981—. Fellow Am. Assn. Clin. Chemists, Am. Inst. Chemists; mem. Am. Chem. Soc., AAAS, Am. Inst. Nutrition, Nat. Speakers Assn., Sigma Xi, Phi Lambda Upsilon. Baptist. Avocations: tennis; camping. Home: 83 E Hill Dr Mount Juliet TN 37122 Office: Environ Sci and Engring Corp 1776 Mays Chapel Rd Mount Juliet TN 37122

SCHULMAN, CLIFFORD A., lawyer; b. Dec. 6, 1947; s. George and Henrietta Schulman; m. Michele Weissman, June 28, 1969; 1 child, David Michael. B.S. in Journalism and Communications cum laude, U. Fla., 1969, J.D., 1972. Bar: Fla. 1972, U.S. Supreme Ct. 1981, U.S. Ct. Appeals (5th cir.) 1975. Law clk. to Eugene P. Spellman, Miami, Fla., 1970-71; research aide to Judge Norman Hendry, Miami, 1972-73; asst. county atty. Met. Dade County, Miami, 1973-79; ptnr. Greenberg, Traurig, Askew, Hoffman, Lipoff, Rosen & Quentel, Miami, 1979—. Editor-in-chief continuing legal edn. manual Environ. Regulation and Litigation in Fla., 1981 edit. Mem. Gov.'s Task Force on Biscayne Bay Rules, 1978; del. 57th biennial conv. Am. Hebrew Congregations, 1983. Served to capt. USAR, 1969-73. Mem. Fla. Bar (co-editor environ. law sect. newsletter 1977-80; exec. council environ. and land use law sect. 1979-83, sec.-treas. 1981-83, chmn. 1984-85). Home: 21311 NE 23d Ave North Miami Beach FL 33180 Office: Greenberg Traurig Askew Hoffman Lipoff Rosen & Quentel 1401 Brickell Ave PH-1 Miami FL 33131

SCHULMAN, NORMA JANEAU, psychologist, marriage and family counselor; b. N.Y.C., Mar. 4; d. Samuel N. and Ruth (Berman) Janeau; children—Sharan L. Levine, David H. Schulman. B.A. in English and Humanities, U. Chgo.; M.S.W., Wayne State U.; Ph.D. in Ednl. and Clin. Psychology. Lic. psychologist, Fla.; lic. marriage and family therapist, Fla., Mich. Clin. social worker Northville State Hosp., Northville, 1964-66; social work supr., continuing edn. for pregnant girls Detroit Bd. Edn., 1966-67; grad. fellow, instr. Wayne State U., Detroit, 1968-70; clin. dir. Children's Orthogenic Ctr., Detroit, 1970-72; field work instr. Wayne State U., 1970-72; ind. practice clin. psychology, marriage and family counseling, West Palm Beach, Fla., 1975—; cons. Chosen Children, adoption service, 1983—; cons. to pvt. law firms; mem. staff Humana Hosp. of Palm Beaches, Fla., 1975—; mem. adj. faculty Fla. Family Inst., West Palm Beach, 1983—. Instr. vol. tng. classes Crisis Line Info. and Referral Service Palm Beach County, 1977—, profl. adviser, 1980—, mem. exec. bd. 1982—, v.p. exec. bd. 1984-85, chmn. edn. com. 1984-85, Spl. Recognition award, 1979; former mem. Council on Child Abuse and Neglect; mem. exec. bd. Children's Home Soc., 1983-86; guest lectr., instr. numerous humanist, spl. interest and personal growth groups. Mem. Fla. Psychol. Assn. (chpt. sec.-treas. 1981-82, pres. 1984, rep. exec. council 1985—, mem. ethics com. 1981—), Fla. Soc. for Clin. Hypnosis (mem. tng. workshop faculty 1981, liaison to exec. council Fla. Psychol. Assn. 1984—), Am. Soc. for Clin. Hypnosis, Am. Psychol. Assn. (clin. mem.), Am. Assn. Marriage and Family Therapists (clin. mem.), Mich. Psychol. Assn., Am. Orthopsychiat. Assn. Avocation: skiing. Office: 2151 45th St Suite 109 West Palm Beach FL 33407

SCHULTZ, ARTHUR HENRY, geologist; b. Cumberland, Md., July 15, 1925; s. Henry Michael and Helen Marie (Schaidt) S.; m. Alicia Mercedes Bolivar, Sept. 10, 1954; children—Tadeo Henry, Arturo Ernest, Lloyd Frederick, Carmen Helen. B.S., Case Western Res. U., 1951; M.S., U. Mich., 1953. Petroleum geologist Creole Petroleum Corp., Maracaibo, Venezuela, 1953-58; regional geologist Mobil Oil de Venezuela, Caracas, 1958-67, div. geologist, Anaco, Venezuela, 1967-71, adv. to mgmt., Caracas, 1971-75; sr. geol. adviser Mobil Oil Internat., Dallas, 1975—; unitization coordinator Agua-Lac Unit, Caracas, 1971-75, Budare Unit, Caracas, 1971-75; researcher in field. Mem. Am. Assn. Petroleum Geologists, Assn. Profl. Geol. Scientists, Dallas Geol. Soc., Asociacion Venezolano de Geologos, Instituto Para la Conservaccion del Lago de Valencia (lifetime), Delta Upsilon. Roman Catholic. Avocations: minerals; gems. Home: 7008 Town Bluff Dr Dallas TX 75248 Office: 300 Diamond Park Dr Dallas TX 75247

SCHULTZ, JOEL SIDNEY, architect; b. Buffalo, Feb. 3, 1945; s. Raymond Abraham and Emilia Mimi (Citron) S.; B.Arch., Kans. State U., 1970; m. Betty Krul, Aug. 18, 1968; children—Andrea, Jennifer. Designer, draftsman John Highland Asso., Buffalo, 1970-71, Cannon Partnership, Buffalo, 1971-72, Connell Asso., Miami, Fla., 1972-73, Charles McAlpine, Architect, Ft. Lauderdale, 1973-75; pres. Summit Tech. Archtl. Group (doing bus. as J.S. Schultz Architect and Assocs.), Coral Springs, Fla., 1975—; faculty arch. Broward Community Coll., Ft. Lauderdale, 1972-73. Moeller Archtl. scholar, Kans. State U., 1965-70. Mem. AIA, Nat. Assn. Home Builders, Coral Springs C. of C. Office: 1750 N University Dr Suite 206 Coral Springs FL 33065

SCHULTZ, JOHN CARL, JR., real estate consultant appraising firm executive; b. Savannah, Ga., Oct. 27, 1939; s. John Carl and Adele (Helmly) S.; B.B.A. in Real Estate, U. Ga., Athens, 1963; m. Margaret Bellinger Johnson, Sept. 1, 1962; children—John Carl III, Angela Porcher, Druella Helmly. Appraiser, Stewart Wight Co., Atlanta, 1963-68; partner Wight, Couch & Schultz, Atlanta, 1968-72; v.p. Landauer Assocs. of N.Y. subs. Marsh & McLennan, Atlanta, 1972-83; pres. Albritton, Schultz, Martin, Carr & Assocs., Atlanta, 1976—. Mng. partner Campbellton Plaza Joint Venture, Atlanta, 1972-76; tchr. appraisal courses Am. Inst. Real Estate Appraisers, Soc. Real Estate Appraisers, Atlanta Area Tech. Sch., Atlanta Multiple Listing Service, Atlanta Bd. Realtors. Chmn., Property Comm., Cath. Archdiocese of Atlanta, 1974-76. Named Distinguished lectr., practitioner, Coll. Bus. Adminstrn., U. Ga. at Athens, 1975. Mem. Am. Soc. Real Estate Counselors (sec.-treas. Ga. chpt. 1984), Am. Inst. Real Estate Appraisers (pres. Ga. chpt. 1980, profl. recognition award 1976-81, nat. governing council 1982-84), Soc. Real Estate Appraisers (sr. real estate analyst; pres. Atlanta chpt. 8 1973-74, young men's council 1976-77, v.p. 1977), Atlanta Bd. Realtors (pres. 1984, dir. 1980—, Realtor of Yr. award 1978), Nat., Ga. (dir. 1974—, regional v.p. 1984) assns. realtors, Nat. Inst. Farm and Land Brokers, Rho Epsilon (nat. pres. 1974-76). Roman Catholic. Lodges: Elks, K.C., Jaycees (conv. com. nat. conv. 1971). Home: 383 Springdale Dr NE Atlanta GA 30305 Office: 121 Alexander St NW Atlanta GA 30313

SCHULTZ, LESLIE KRENN, petroleum geologist, consultant; b. Visalia, Calif., Jan. 6, 1928; s. Rudolph August Schultz and Berniece Emily (Kalb) Putnam; m. Darlene Betty Jean, Oct. 2, 1950; children—Stephen, Karen, Eric. A.B., U. Calif.-Berkeley, 1952. Geologist Mobil, Houston, 1971-75, mgr. exploration, Denver, 1975-76, Dallas, 1976-81, coordinator new plays fgn., 1981-85; pres. SFC Petroleum Inc., Lake Dallas, Tex., 1985—. Served with USAF, 1946-48, PTO. Mem. Am. Assn. Petroleum Geologists, Houston Geol. Soc. Avocations: travel; photography; fishing. Home: 3624 Candelaria Dr Plano TX 75023 Office: SFC Petroleum Inc 1010 Stemmons St PO Box 1261 Lake Dallas TX 75065

SCHULTZ, NANCY REILLY, retail tennis shop exec.; b. N.Y.C., July 20, 1930; d. John Francis and Eunice Genevieve (Crowley) Reilly; B.A., Smith Coll. for Women, 1951; m. Frederick Henry Schultz, Aug. 11, 1951; children—Catherine, Frederick, Clifford, John Reilly. Pres., The Smash Tennis Shop, Inc., Jacksonville, Fla., 1976—. Chmn., Duval County Mothers March, March of Dimes, 1958-59; head docent Cummer Gallery of Art, 1963-70; caseworker Family Counciling Center, Jacksonville, 1961-62; vol. worker Community Public TV, Am. Cancer Soc.; supporter WTA Tennis Championships, Amelia Island, Fla., 1981. Mem. Jr. League of Jacksonville. Democrat. Roman Catholic. Home: 4314 Ortega Forest Dr Jacksonville FL 32210 Office: 3657 Saint Johns Ave Jacksonville FL 32205

SCHULTZ, STEVEN EUGENE, steel company executive; b. Dayton, Ky., Apr. 11, 1948; s. George Bowling and Elizabeth Mary (Schottler) S.; m. Linda Mary Boswell, Dec. 27, 1969; 1 child, Jeffrey Steven. B.B.A., Eastern Ky. U., 1971. Mgr. restaurant Roy Rogers Restaurants, Cin., 1971-72; claims examiner Ky. Dept. Human Resources, Covington, 1972-81; safety supr. Newport Steel Corp., Ky., 1981—. Mem. Am. Soc. Safety Engrs. Avocations: manager knothole team; bowling; softball; basketball. Office: Newport Steel Corp 9th and Lowell St Newport KY 41072

SCHULTZ, THOMAS WILLIAM, health services administrator; b. Elmhurst, Ill., Oct. 29, 1949; s. William Albert and Marion Frances (Fanning) S.; B.A., Coll. of St. Thomas, St. Paul, 1971; M.H.A., Duke U., 1973. Adminstrv. fellow Mass. Gen. Hosp., Boston, 1973-75, asst. dir. adminstrv. services, 1975-78; cons. Booz, Allen & Hamilton, Inc., N.Y.C., 1978-80; dir. planning Brookwood Health Services, Birmingham, Ala., 1980-81; mgr. Arthur Young & Co., Birmingham, 1981-83, prin., 1983—. Mem. Am. Coll. Hosp. Adminstrs., Duke U. Alumni Assn. Home: 35 Pine Crest Rd Birmingham AL 35223 Office: 2110 First Nat-So Natural Bldg Birmingham AL 35203

SCHULZ, LAWRENCE EUGENE, political science educator; b. Santa Ana, Calif., Apr. 21, 1943; s. Kenneth M. and Lucille Theresa (Lohse) S.; m. Dixie Lee Grant, June 11, 1966 (dec. 1976); 1 child, Brian; m. Sue Ervin Hedrick, June 10, 1978; 1 stepchild, Michael. B.A., U. Redlands, 1965; M.A., Claremont Grad. Sch. and U. Ctr., 1967, Ph.D., 1972. Instr. So. Calif. Coll., Costa Mesa, 1969-71; asst. prof. St. Andrews Presbyn. Coll., Laurinburg, N.C., 1971-79, assoc. prof. polit. sci., 1979—. Contbr. articles to profl. jours. Elder Laurinburg Presbyn. Ch., 1983—; 2d vice chmn. 3d precinct Scotland County Democratic Party, Laurinburg, 1985. NEH fellow, 1977; grantee St. Andrews Presbyn. Coll., 1982, 84, Lilly, 1980. Mem. Assn. Asian Studies, Internat. Studies Assn., Am. Polit. Sci. Assn., Arms Control Assn., N.C. Polit. Sci. Assn. Avocations: gardening; tennis; swimming; fishing. Home: 705 Highland Dr Laurinburg NC 28352 Office: St Andrews Presbyn Coll Laurinburg NC 28352

SCHULZ, RALPH JEAN, insurance executive; b. Alton, Ill., Mar. 9, 1926; s. Edmund F. and Helen C. (Merkle) S.; m. Teresa E. Lusher, Oct. 27, 1951; children—Ralph J., Frederick, Richard, Paul, Nora, Therese, Mary, Anne. Student St. Joseph's Coll., Mo., 1944-45; B.A., U. Louisville, 1949, M.A., 1950. C.L.U. Tchr., Louisville, 1949-51; fin. planner Home Life Ins. Co., Bankers Life Ins. Co., 1951-57; sales mgr. Prudential Ins. Co., Occidental Life Ins. Co.,

Bankers Life Ins. Co., 1957-63; regional supt. Provident Life and Accident Ins. Co., Chattanooga, 1963-65, divisional mgr., 1965-68, asst. v.p., 1968-82; pres., gen. agt., cons. Arjay Enterprises, Chattanooga, 1982—. Served with JAGC, U.S. Army, 1945-47; ETO. Recipient various local and regional awards in sales and mgmt. Mem. Am. Soc. C.L.U.s, Nat. Assn. Life Underwriters, Am. Soc. Tng. and Devel., Internat. Assn. Fin. Planners, C. of C. Roman Catholic. Club: Serra (past local pres., past dist. gov.) (Louisville and Chattanooga). Home: 616 Sweetbriar Ave Chattanooga TN 37412 Office: Provident Bldg Fountain Sq Chattanooga TN 37402

SCHULZ, REX, SR., criminal justice educator, consultant; b. Kansas City, Mo., Mar. 2, 1934; s. August W. and Billie A. (Bathurst) S.; m. Valerie Ann Blackman, Feb. 1, 1953 (div. Mar. 1983); children—Rex, Jr., Sandy, Erik, Rey, Regina; m. Paula Joan Rowe, Apr. 27, 1983 (div. Mar. 1984); m. Carol Carey, Aug. 18, 1985. B.S. in Law Enforcement and Corrections, U. Nebr., 1970; M.S. in Counseling and Guidance, Nova U., 1976, Ed.D., 1979. Enlisted in U.S. Army, 1952; service in Ger., 1956-59, 66-69, Korea, 1963-64, Vietnam, 1969-71; mem. faculty Broward Community Coll., Ft. Lauderdale, Fla., 1972—, prof. police sci., 1972—, dept. chmn. police sci., 1981—; cons. police depts., pvt. investigation agys., attys., 1972—. Recipient Honor Grad. award Assn. U.S. Army, 1958-62. Mem. AAUP, NEA, Soc. Pen and Sword, Lambda Alpha Epsilon. Democrat. Home: 7081 NW 16th St Apt 309B Plantation FL 33313 Office: 3501 SW Davie Rd Fort Lauderdale FL 33314

SCHULZE, LOUANN THOMPSON, college administrator; b. Oklahoma City, June 27, 1957; d. Louis Hamilton and Patricia Ann (Murrell) Thompson; m. Frederick Allen Schulze, Jan. 6, 1979. B.A., S.W. Tex. State U., 1979; M.S., Tex. A&M U., 1980. Off campus adviser Tex. A&M U., College Station, 1980-81, coordinator off-campus ctr., 1981-84; career counselor U. Tex., Arlington, 1984-85, coordinator orientation, 1985—. Mem. Am. Coll. Personnel Assn. (bd. dirs. Com. XVII exec. com. 1983-85), Tex. Assn. Coll. and Univ. Student Personnel Adminstrs. (exec. com. 1983-85), Nat. Orientation Dirs. Assn. (com. 1985-86), Am. Assn. Counseling and Devel. Avocations: photography; aerobics; water sports; racquetball. Office: Counseling Testing and Career Placement U Tex Arlington PO Box 19156 Arlington TX 76019

SCHUMACHER, ROBERT ALAN, forest products company executive; b. Marshall, Tex., Jan. 13, 1923; m. Dorothy Wemyss, July 23, 1945. B.A., U. Va., 1944. Vice pres. Groveton Paper Co., 1946-56; pres. Vanity Fair Paper Co., 1956-63; v.p. Northeast div. Georgia-Pacific Corp., 1963-74, sr. v.p. Northeast div., 1974-82, exec. v.p. pulp and paper, 1982-85, pres. and chief operating officer, Atlanta, 1985—, also dir. Bd. dirs. New Canaan Red Cross, Conn.; chmn. Heart Fund, Stamford, Darien, New Canaan, Conn., 1967; chmn. Cancer Fund, 1964; dir.-at-large U. Maine Pulp and Paper Found. Office: Georgia-Pacific Corp 133 Peachtree St NE Atlanta GA 30303

SCHUMACHER, SALLY ANN, teacher educator; b. Washington, July 23, 1935; d. Francis and Muriel (McBride) S. B.A., Duke U., 1957; M.A., Northwestern U., 1961; M.Ed., U. N.C., 1963; Ph.D., Washington U., St. Louis, 1975. Tchr. high sch. Caroline County Schs., Denton, Md., 1957-59; tchr. high sch., counselor Kern County Pub. Schs., Bakersfield, Calif., 1963-69; evaluation asst., assoc. CEMREL, Inc., St. Louis, 1972-73; vis. asst. prof. research and adminstrn. U. Ill.-Urbana, 1973-74; asst. prof. research and adminstrn. Va. Commonwealth U., Richmond, 1974-80, assoc. prof. ednl. studies, 1980—; cons. Va. Dept. Edn., sch. dists. Delta Gamma scholar, 1957; Nat. Experience Tchr. fellow, 1969-70; Va. Dept. Edn. grantee, 1979-81, 84-88. Mem. Am. Ednl. Research Assn. (treas., sec.-treas. politics of edn. spl. interest group 1975-79), Va. Ednl. Research Assn. (pres. 1979-80, Service award 1983), Am. Ednl. Studies Assn., Am. Assn. Colls. for Tchr. Edn., Nat. Soc. Study of Edn., Nat. Council Measurement in Edn. Phi Delta Kappa, Phi Kappa Delta. Democrat. Methodist. Co-author: Research in Education, 1984. Contbr. articles to profl. jours.; co-author textbook, 1984. Office: Sch Edn Va Commonwealth Univ Richmond VA 23284

SCHUMANN, AL, architectural engineer, interior designer; b. Southampton, Eng., June 5, 1925; s. Irving and Ray (Friend) S.; came to U.S., 1926, naturalized, 1934; B.S. in Archtl. Engring., U. Tex., Austin, 1949; m. Shirley Breger, June 13, 1946; children—Alan, Paul, Marla Schumann Shivers. Archtl., structural designer Jack Corgan, Architect, Dallas, 1954-57; constrn. mgmt. engr. Gen. Services Adminstrn., Dallas, 1957-63; archtl. engr., also design coordinator of various computerized service centers IRS, Washington, 1963-65, interior designer, archtl. engr., Dallas, 1970-84; archtl. and interior designer Army and Air Force Exchange Service, Dallas, 1966-70; pres. Bus. Euthenics, Richardson, Tex., 1984—; lectr. Office Landscape Users Group, 1977—; speaker in field. Bd. dirs. Temple Emanu-el Brotherhood, Dallas, 1974-82. Served as flight officer Air Corps, AUS, 1944-46. Recipient Office Design award Adminstrv. Mgmt. Mag., 1976, Office of the Year award, 1975. Registered profl. engr., Tex. Mem. Inst. Bus. Designers (profl. mem., v.p. edn. North Tex. chpt. 1981-83, pres. North Tex. chpt. 1983-84, trustee 1985-87), Nat. (profl. mem.), Tex. (profl. mem.) socs. profl. engrs., Tex. Soc. Architects (profl. affiliate), AIA (Dallas chpt. profl. affiliate), Ops. Mgmt. Edn. and Research Found. (bd. dirs., sec.-treas. 1980-83, chmn. 1983—). Developer, tchr. tng. course for govt. employees on office space planning and design. Office: Business Euthenics PO Box 835991 Richardson TX 75083

SCHUNCKE, GEORGE MONMONIER, educator, researcher; b. Balt., Apr. 21, 1943; s. John Joseph and Marie Anne (Stadter) S.; m. Barbara Lee Brandon, Mar. 19, 1976 (div. 1983); 1 child, Mark Elliott Stadter. B.A., LaSalle Coll., 1965; M.A., San Francisco State Coll., 1970; Ph.D., Stanford U., 1974. Prof. U. Fla., Gainesville, 1974-84; prof., head dept. Elem. edn. Western Carolina U., Cullowhee, N.C., 1984—. Author: Helping Children Choose, 1983; also articles; editor: Jour. Humanistic Edn., 1981—. Mem. Assn. Humanistic Edn. (exec. bd. 1981—), Nat. Council Social Studies. Democrat. Episcopalian. Home: 31 Jackson St Sylva NC 28779 Office: Western Carolina U Dept Elem Edn and Reading Cullowhee NC 28723

SCHUNK, DALE HANSEN, psychology educator; b. Chgo., Aug. 14, 1946; s. Elmer Charles and Mildred Augusta (Hansen) S.; m. Caryl Sue Cook, June 29, 1984. B.S., U. Ill., 1968; M.Ed., Boston U., 1974; Ph.D., Stanford U., 1979. With dept. psychology and edn. Stanford U., 1974-79; assoc. prof. ednl. psychology U. Houston, 1979—. Served to capt. USAF, 1968-74. NSF grantee, 1980, 85; NIMH grantee, 1980, 84; Spencer Found. grantee, 1983, 84. Mem. Am. Psychol. Assn., Am. Ednl. Research Assn., Soc. Research in Child Devel., Southwestern Psychol. Assn., S.W. Ednl. Research Assn., N.Y. Acad. Scis., AAAS, Council for Exceptional Children, Phi Beta Kappa, Phi Kappa Phi. Contbr. articles in field to profl. jours. Home: 8711 Ariel St Houston TX 77074 Office: Coll Edn U Houston Houston TX 77004

SCHUSTER, GEORGE SHEA, microbiologist, dentist; b. Geneva, Ill., Sept. 22, 1940; s. Marvin Sander and Sarah (Kuntz) S.; m. Betty Jean Eisenmayer, Aug. 19, 1963; 1 child, Jennifer. A.B., Washington U., St. Louis, 1962; D.D.S., Northwestern U., Chgo., 1966, M.S., 1966; Ph.D., U. Rochester, 1970. Prof. microbiology Sch. Dentistry, Med. Coll. Ga., Augusta, 1977—. Author: Oral Microbiology and Infectious Diseases, 1983. Contbr. articles to profl. jours. Served to capt. U.S. Army, 1967-73. Mem. ADA, Internat. Assn. Dental Research, Am. Assn. Dental Schs. Office: Med Coll Ga Sch Dentistry Augusta GA 30912

SCHUSTER-CRAIG, JOHN, music educator, critic; b. St. Louis, Jan. 13, 1949; s. John William and Ramey Cleo (Vaughn) Craig; m. Sharon Schuster, Sept. 6, 1980; children—Johanna, Sean. Mus.B., U. Louisville, 1971; M.A., U. N.C., 1976. Lectr. U. Louisville, 1975—, Bellarmine Coll., Louisville, 1978-84; music critic Louisville Times, 1976-84. Editor musical compositions. Mem. Am. Musicological Soc. Democrat. Episcopalian. Home: 2220 Walterdale Terr Louisville KY 40205 Office: U Louisville Sch Music Louisville KY 40292

SCHUTTS, PHILIP LOWDON, printing co. exec.; b. Ft. Worth, Oct. 6, 1947; s. Robert and Kathryn (Lowdon) S.; B.B.A., Tex. A&M U., 1970; m. Carolyn Elizabeth Reeves, July 12, 1969 (div.); children—William Lowdon, Emily Elizabeth. With Stafford-Lowdon, Inc., Ft. Worth, 1970—, pres. Stafford-Lowdon Bank Stationery Co., 1979—; sr. v.p. Am. Bank Stationery Co., 1980—; pres., chief exec. officer Schutts & Royer, Inc., 1984—. Chmn. bd. Cutting Horse Heritage Found.; bd. dirs. Sister Cities Orgn. Served with USMCR, 1970-76. Mem. Nat. Cutting Horse Assn., Am. Quarter House Assn., Ft. Worth C. of C. (bd. dirs.). Republican. Presbyterian. Clubs: Rotary, Rivercrest Country, Fort Worth, Forth Worth Boat, Century II, Steeplechase, Petroleum, Julian Field Lodge. Home: Rt 7 Box 23 Weatherford TX 76086 Office: Am Bank Stationery Co Suite 200 108 W 8th St Fort Worth TX 76102

SCHUTZ, ROBERT, physical scientist; b. Meadville, Pa., Mar. 9, 1926; s. Harold and Edith (Frost) S.; m. Gloria Mae Howard, Oct. 3, 1959; children—Patricia Ellen, Elizabeth Ann. B.S., Allegheny Coll., 1949. Chemist U.S. Bur. Mines, Pitts., 1949-64, supr. chemist, 1964-72; chief, testing and cert. br. NIOSH, Morgantown, W.Va., 1972-79, spl. asst. to dir., 1979—; chmn. respirator com. Am. Nat. Standards Inst., 1968-72. Contbr. articles to profl. jours. Served with USNR, 1944-46, PTO. Mem. Am. Conf. Govtl. Indsl. Hygienists, Am. Soc. Safety Engrs., Am. Printers Assn. Club: Baker Street Irregulars. Lodge: Masons. Avocations: amateur letter press printing. Office: NIOSH 944 Chestnut Ridge Rd Morgantown WV 26505

SCHUTZMAN, RALPH AUGUST, bookkeeping systems manufacturing company executive; b. Milw., Sept. 13, 1914; s. Alfred Lee and Angeline Therese (Kurtz) S.; m. Mary Elizabeth Coupé, Sept. 13, 1941; children—James, Christine, William, John, Mary Beth, Joseph. Student Marquette U., 1933-35. Gen. mgr. A.L. Schutzman Co., Milw., 1938-51; sales mgr. North Tex. area Grolier Soc., Dallas, 1951-53; salesman, asst. br. mgr. Burroughs Corp., Dallas, 1953-60; pres. Ralph Schutzman & Assocs., Dallas, 1960—; dir. NBS Systems, Inc., Whittier Calif., Narco Products, Inc., Dallas. Mem. Dallas C. of C., Delta Sigma Pi. Roman Catholic. Club: Lakewood Country. Lodge: Rotary. Office: Ralph Schutzman & Assocs 1717 Baylor St Dallas TX 75226

SCHUYLER, LAMBERT, JR., management consultant; b. Seattle, Aug. 4, 1938; s. Lambert and Nora Patricia (Briggs) S.; m. Barbara Poole Rick, June 16, 1962; children—Stephen Dodds, Bradley Rick. B.S. in Bus. Adminstrn., Babson Coll., 1964. Mgmt. trainee Reading Trust Co. (Pa.), 1964-66; sr. cons. Arthur Andersen & Co., Phila., 1966-69; controller Trojan Yachts Co. subs. Whitaker Corp., Lancaster, Pa., 1969-70; sr. cons. Gilbert Assocs., Inc., Reading, 1970-73; v.p. Billington, Fox-Ellis, Inc., Atlanta, 1973-79, Lamalie Assocs., Inc., Atlanta, 1979-82; pres. Schuyler Assocs., Ltd., Atlanta, 1982—. Pres., Winding Vista Assn., 1979-80; treas., co-chmn. task force Goals for DeKalb (Ga.), 1980-83. Mem. Bus. Council Ga. Clubs: Georgian (founding mem.), Atlanta City. Office: Century Springs Suite 430 6100 Lake Forrest Dr NW Atlanta GA 30328

SCHWALM, FRITZ EKKEHARDT, biology educator; b. Arolsen, Hesse, Germany, Feb. 17, 1936; came to U.S., 1968; s. Fritz Heinrich and Elisabet (Wirth) S.; m. Renate Gertrud, Feb. 10, 1962; children—Anneliese, Fritz-Uwe, Karen. Ph.D., Philipps U., Marburg, Germany, 1964, Staatsexamen, 1965. Anglo Am. Corp. advanced postdoctoral research fellow U. Witwatersrand, Johannesburg, Republic South Africa, 1966-67; postdoctoral trainee U. Va., Charlottesville, 1968; research assoc. U. Notre Dame, South Bend, Ind., 1968-70; asst. prof. biology Ill. State U., Normal, 1970-74, assoc. prof., 1974-82; chmn. dept. biology Tex. Woman's U., Denton, 1982—. Contbr. research articles on insect embryology to profl. jours., 1965—. Vice pres. Glenn Sch. PTA, Normal, Ill., 1976; treas. Singing Y'ers. NATO advanced research fellow, Freiburg, 1977. Mem. AAAS, Deutsche Zoologische Gesellschaft, Am. Soc. Zoologists, Soc. Devel. Biology, S.W. Regional Conf. Devel. Biology (chmn. 1985), Club: University (pres. 1983-85) (Denton). Lodge: Kiwanis. Home: 116 Linden Dr Denton TX 76201 Office: Tex Woman's U Dept Biology Denton TX 76204

SCHWARTZ, BARRY DAVID, psychologist; b. Boston, May 8, 1947; s. Isadore and Helen (Lipofsky) S.; m. Roselyn Barbara Koretzky, June 17, 1984. B.S., U. Mass., 1971; M.A., U. Nebr., 1974; Ph.D., Tulane U., 1978. Head recreational therapist Mass. Mental Health Ctr., Boston, 1971-72; co-prin. investigator-psychiat. research VA Med. Ctr., New Orleans, 1979—; assoc. prof. psychiatry/neurology Tulane Med. Sch., New Orleans, 1981—; cons. Wellness Inst., Gretna, La., 1983—. Contbr. articles to profl. jours. Grantee VA, Washington, 1980-83, 84-87, NIMH, 1982-83; recipient Outstanding Performance award VA, New Orleans, 1982, 83, 84. Mem. Soc. Biol. Psychiatry, Am. Psychol. Assn., AAAS, N.Y. Acad. Scis., Sigma Xi, Psi Chi. Lodge: B'nai B'rith. Avocations: handball; running; bicycling; theatre. Office: VA Med Ctr Perdido St New Orleans LA 70146

SCHWARTZ, CHARLES, JR., federal judge; b. New Orleans, Aug. 20, 1922; s. Charles and Sophie (Hess) S.; B.A., Tulane U., 1943, J.D., 1947; m. Patricia May, Aug. 31, 1950; children—Priscilla May, John Putney. Admitted to La. bar, 1947; practiced in New Orleans, until 1976; ptnr. firm Little, Schwartz & Dussom, 1970-76, dist. counsel Gulf Coast dist. U.S. Maritime Adminstrn., 1953-62, U.S. dist. judge Eastern Dist. La., New Orleans, 1976—; asso. prof. Tulane U. Law Sch.; lectr. continuing law insts. Pres. New Orleans unit Am. Cancer Soc., 1956-57; v.p., chmn. budget com. United Fund Greater New Orleans Area, 1959-61, trustee, 1963-65; bd. dirs. Cancer Assn. Greater New Orleans, 1958—, pres., 1958-59, 72-73; bd. dirs. United Cancer Council, 1962-80, pres., 1971-73; mem. com. on grants to agencies Community Chest, 1965—; men's adv. com. League Women Voters, 1966-68; chmn. com. admissions of program devel. and coordination com. United Way Greater New Orleans, 1974-76; mem. comml. panel Am. Arbitration Assn., 1974-76; bd. dirs. Willow Wood Home, 1979—; trustee Metairie Park Country Day Sch., 1977—; mem. La. Republican Central Com., 1961-76; mem. Orleans Parish Rep. Exec. Com., 1960-74, chmn., 1965-75; mem. Jefferson Parish Rep. Exec. Com., 1975-76; del. Rep. Nat. Conv., 1960, 64, 68. Served to 2d lt. AUS, 1943-46; maj. U.S. Army Res. ret. Mem. Am., La., New Orleans bar assns., Am. Judicature Soc., Fgn. Relations Assn. New Orleans (past dir.), Phi Beta Kappa. Club: Lakewood Country (dir. 1967-68, pres. 1975-77). Address: US Dist Ct US Courthouse Chambers C-255 500 Camp St New Orleans LA 70130*

SCHWARTZ, DARRELL MICHAEL, banker, economist; b. Chgo., July 17, 1958; s. Fred and Irene (Kahn) S.; m. Mary Irene Strok, June 28, 1982. A.A. in Econs., Miami Dade Community Coll., 1980; B.A. in Econs., Fla. Atlantic U., 1982. Mgr. trainee Eckerd Drugs, Miami, 1974-77; sales mgr. Jefferson/Ward, Miami, 1981-82; br. mgr., asst. v.p. Coral Gables Fed. Savings and Loan, Fla., 1982—; dir. Inst. Fin. Edn., 1984—. Recipient Outstanding Young Men of Am. award U.S. Jaycees, Montgomery, Ala., 1981. Mem. Am. Econ. Assn., Econ. Soc. South Fla., Fla. Acad. Scis., Fla. Atlantic U. Alumni Assn. (life, bd. dirs. 1984—), Mirimar-Pembroke Pines C. of C. Democrat. Jewish. Clubs: DECA (North Miami Beach) (pres. 1975-77), Fla. Atlantic U. Sailing (pres. 1981-82). Home: 16806 Royal Poinciana Dr Fort Lauderdale FL 33326 Office: Coral Gables Fed Savings and Loan 8900 Hollywood Blvd Hollywood FL 33024

SCHWARTZ, HAROLD ALAN, obstetrician/gynecologist; b. Atlanta, July 29, 1911; s. Julius J. and Rebecca Ann (Borisky) S.; m. Eleanor Sylvia Miller, Apr. 2, 1914; children—Harold Alan, Patti Ann, Ellen Schwartz Yellin. B.A. magna cum laude, Vanderbilt U., 1932; M.D., Johns Hopkins U., 1936. Diplomate Am. Bd. Ob-Gyn. Intern, Union Meml. Hosp., Balt., 1936-37, Rotunda Hosp., Dublin, 1937-38; asst. resident to chief resident ob-gyn Bellevue Hosp., N.Y.C., 1938-42; instr. ob-gyn NYU, 1939-42; practice medicine specializing in ob-gyn, Chattanooga, 1946—; pres., mem. Gynecologists Assocs., Inc., 1971—; asso. clin. prof. U. Tenn., Chattanooga, 1974-84; mem. staff Baroness Erlanger Meml. Hosp., 1950—, chief ob-gyn, 1966-70, 72-74. Pres., Chattanooga Jewish Welfare Fedn., 1957, Mizpah Congregation, 1966; bd. dirs. Am. Cancer Soc., 1958-65. Served to maj. M.C., U.S. Army, 1942-46. Decorated Legion of Merit. Fellow Am. Coll. Obstetricians and Gynecologists (founding fellow), ACS, Tenn. Ob-Gyn Soc. (founding fellow; 3d pres.), mem. Central Assn. Ob-Gyn, So. Med. Assn., AMA, Am. Fertility Soc., Am. Legion (vice comdr. 1958), Phi Beta Kappa. Democrat. Club: Chattanooga Golf and Country. Lodge: Elks. Contbr. articles to profl. jours. Home: 1414 Continental Dr Apt 1201 Chattanooga TN 37405 Office: 1000 E 3d St 202 Medical Towers Bldg Chattanooga TN 37403

SCHWARTZ, J. BRAD, economics educator; b. Belleville, Ill., Aug. 25, 1949; s. Cletus Edward and Colores Ann (Faltus) S.; m. Priscilla Anne Bratcher, Oct. 25, 1975; 1 child, Rosalind. B.A., U. South Fla., 1972; M.A., U. Iowa, 1978; Ph.D., U. N.C.-Chapel Hill, 1982. Asst. prof. econs. U. South Fla., Tampa, 1982-84, U. N.C.-Chapel Hill, 1984—; research assoc. Carolina Population Ctr., Chapel Hill, 1984—. Fellow Bush Ctr. for Child and Family Policy, 1980. Mem. Am. Econ. Assn., So. Econ. Assn. Office: U NC Dept Econs Chapel Hill NC 27514

SCHWARTZ, LEONARD JAY, lawyer; b. San Antonio, Sept. 23, 1943; s. Oscar S. and Ethel (Eastman) S.; m. Sandra E. Eichelbaum, July 4, 1965; 1 dau., Michele Fay. B.B.A., U. Tex. 1965, J.D., 1968. Bar: Tex. 1968, Ohio 1971, U.S. Dist. Ct. (no., ea., we., so. dists.) Tex., U.S. Dist. Ct. (no., so. dists.) Ohio, U.S. Dist. Ct. Nebr., U.S. Ct. Appeals (5th, 6th, 7th, 11th cirs.), U.S. Supreme Ct. 1971. Assoc. Roberts & Holland, N.Y.C., 1968-70; ptnr. Rigely, Schwartz & Fagan, San Antonio 1970-71; staff counsel ACLU of Ohio, Columbus, 1971-73; ptnr. Schwartz, Fisher, Spater, McNamara & Marshall, Columbus, 1973-77, Schwartz & Fishman, Columbus, 1977-79; elections counsel to sec. of state of Ohio, Columbus 1979-80; ptnr. Waterman & Schwartz, Austin, Tex., 1981-83; sr. mem., dir. Schwartz, Waterman, Fickman & Van Os, P.C., Austin, 1984-85; sole practice, 1985—; lectr. Recipient Outstanding Teaching Quizmaster award U. Tex. Sch. Law, 1968. Mem. ABA, Tex. Bar Assn., Travis County Bar Assn., Am. Trial Lawyers Assn., Tex. Trial Lawyers Assn., Internat. Platform Assn., Tex. Assn. Union Lawyers, Nat. Assn. Tchr. Attys., Phi Delta Phi. Jewish. Home: 5800 Back Ct Austin TX 78731 Office: 1300 Guadalupe PO Box 26946 Austin TX 78755

SCHWARTZ, NATALA BELLE, small business owner, clinic manager; b. Dayton, Ohio, Sept. 23, 1946; d. Beacher McKay Tillman and Virginia Ruth (Blair) T.; m. Michael Jacob Schwartz, June 3, 1968; children—Tatia Lynn, Michael Colby. R.N., Mercy Sch. Nursing, 1968. R.N., Children's Hosp., Oklahoma City, 1968-69, 71-73; ob-gyn supr., Moscow, Idaho, 1969-71; built and opened Yukon Car Wash, Yukon, Okla., 1981—, now pres.; clinic mgr. Town Plaza Med. Ctr. Active Yukon C. of C., Yukon PTA, Girl Scouts U.S.A. Mem. Aircraft Owners and Pilots Assn., U.S. Parachute Assn. Contbr. articles to jours. in field. Office: Yukon Car Wash 401 S Ranchwood Blvd Yukon OK 73099

SCHWARTZ, SEYMOUR (SY), education consultant; b. N.Y.C., Mar. 15, 1919; s. Irving and Ida Schwartz; M.B.A., U. Mich., 1940; m. Elizabeth Hall Bennett; 1 son, Karl B. Joined U.S. Army Air Force, 1942; commd. 2d lt., 1943, advanced through grades to col., 1964-68; ret., 1968; asst. to dean Coll. Bus. Adminstrn., U. Tex., Austin, 1968-71, asst. dean Grad. Sch. Bus., 1971-83; pvt. cons. to colls., univs., pvt. founds. Med. evacuation specialist NATO, Paris, 1960-61. Decorated Bronze Star medal. Mobil Oil Found. Small Bus. grantee, 1972-83; SBA grantee, 1972-83. Mem. Internat. Council Small Bus., Small Bus. Inst. Dirs. Assn., Southwest Fedn. Adminstrn. Disciplines, Ret. Officers Assn. Home and Office: 1717 Bay Shores Dr Rockport TX 78382

SCHWARTZ, THOMAS, educator, philosopher, social scientist; b. Elizabeth, N.J., Jan. 17, 1943; m. Ellana Susan Shriber, June 10, 1964; children—Mary Ann, Robert Thomas. A.B., Brandeis U., 1965; Ph.D., U. Pitts., 1969. Asst. prof. philosophy Stanford U., Calif., 1969-73; assoc. prof. philosophy, urban pub. affairs Carnegie-Mellon U., Pitts., 1973-76; assoc. prof. U. Tex., Austin, 1976-80, prof. govt., 1980—. Author: Freedom and Authority, 1973; The Art of Logical Reasoning, 1981; The Logic of Collective Choice, 1985. Contbr. articles to profl. jours. Recipient Grad. Teaching award U. Tex., 1983; grantee Carnegie Found., 1975-76, Sid Richardson Found., 1977-78, Hogg Found., 1984, Univ. Research Inst., 1976-84. Mem. Am. Polit. Sci. Assn. (mem. com. profl. ethics), Am. Philos. Assn., Pub. Choice Soc. Republican. Home: 6715 Shoal Creek Blvd Austin TX 78731 Office: Dept Govt U Tex Austin TX 78712

SCHWARTZ, WILLIAM (ALLEN), broadcasting executive; b. Detroit, Nov. 29, 1938; B.A. in Mktg. and Broadcasting, Wayne State U., 1961; postgrad. Bernard Baruch Grad. Sch. Bus.; m. Marlene J. Cohen; children—Jonathan, Cynthia, Michael. Mgr. research projects NBC, 1963-66; asst. dir. research Columbia Pictures, 1966; v.p., gen. mgr. Sta. WUAB-TV, Cleve., 1968-73; v.p. ops. Telerep, Inc., N.Y.C., 1973-74; v.p., gen. mgr. Sta. KTVU-TV, Oakland, Calif., 1974-79; pres. Broadcast div. Cox Broadcasting Corp. (now Cox Communications, Inc.), Atlanta, 1979-81, pres., chief operating officer corp., Atlanta, 1981-83, pres., chief exec. officer corp., 1983—. Home: 265 Cameron Ridge Dr Atlanta GA 30328 Office: 1601 W Peachtree St NE Atlanta GA 30309

SCHWARZ, MARTIN, foreign language educator; b. Halle, Germany, June 17, 1931; came to U.S., 1951, naturalized, 1956; s. Edgar and Hilda (Spielberg) S. B.A., U. Louisville, 1955; M.A., Washington U., 1957; PH.D., U. Mich., 1963. Asst. prof. French, U. Mich., Ann Arbor, 1963-69; assoc. prof. French, Rice U., Houston, 1969-71; prof. fgn. langs. U. Tulsa, 1971-81, head fgn. lang. dept., 1971-76; prof. fgn. lang. East Carolina U., Greenville, 1981—, chmn. fgn. lang. dept., 1981—. Am. Assn. Tchrs. of French, South Atlantic Modern Lang. Assn., MLA. Author: O Mirbeau, Vie et Oeuvre, 1966, Variété de Contes, 1969. Contbr. articles to profl. publs. Home: PO Box 8393 Greenville NC 27834 Office: East Carolina U Greenville NC 27834

SCHWEIKART, GERALD THEODORE, development company executive, real estate broker; b. Jacksonville, Fla., Jan. 22, 1934; s. Elmer T. and Dorothy (Fulcher) S.; m. Grace Miller, Sept. 18, 1952; children—Allen R., Charlotte L. Exec. adminstr., dir. planning and mktg. Bert Rodgers Sch. Real Estate, Inc., Orlando, Fla., 1969-73; exec. adminstr. Henry Hoche, Inc., Realtor, Orlando, Fla., 1973-74; assoc. Fletcher Properties, Inc., Altamonte Springs, Fla., 1974-75; self-employed sales/mgmt/mktg. cons., Orlando, 1975-77; dir. mktg. Sunreco, Inc., New Smyrna Beach, Fla., 1977-78, pres., 1978—. Chmn., Citizens Code Enforcement Bd., New Smyrna Beach, Fla., 1981—. Mem. Am. Mgmt. Assn. Home: 21 Fore Dr New Smyrna Beach FL 32069 Office: Sunreco Inc Box 565 1 Fairgreen Ave New Smyrna Beach FL 32070

SCHWEIKHART, KENNETH A., advertising executive; b. Cin., Mar. 29, 1938. B.S. in Indsl. Design, U. Cin., 1961; postgrad. in Bus. Mgmt., Xavier U., 1965-66; diploma in bus. mgmt. LaSalle U., 1963. Sales designer Display Sales, Inc., Cin., 1958-62; gen. mgr. Evans/Baucom, Inc., Canton, Ohio, 1962-64; mgr. advt. and pub. relations Avco Corp., Cin., 1964-70; mgr. mktg. services Briggs div. Jim Walter Corp., Detroit, 1970-74; mgr. sales promotion Celotex Corp., Tampa, Fla., 1974-76, mgr. communications, 1976-78, mgr. advt., 1978-82, dir. advt., 1982—, dir. mktg. communications. Served with U.S. Army, 1967-68. Mem. U. Fla. Advt. Council (chmn.). Home: 2203 Venus St Tampa FL 33629 Office: Celotex Corp 1500 N Dale Mabry Tampa FL 33607

SCHWEITZER, JEROME WILLIAM, educator; b. Tuscaloosa, Ala., Dec. 28, 1908; s. Abraham and Mary (Spiro) S.; A.B., U. Ala., 1930, M.A., 1932; Ph.D., Johns Hopkins, 1940; postgrad. U. Mexico, 1946; m. Anne Rachael Stoler, Oct. 1, 1931. Reporter, Tuscaloosa News, 1928-30; dir. News Bur., U. Ala., Tuscaloosa, 1930-37; instr. romance langs. U. Ala., University, 1930-40, asst. prof., 1940-47, asso. prof., 1947-51, prof., 1951-76, prof. emeritus, 1976—, mem. univ. com. for selection Rhodes, Fulbright, Truman scholars, 1980—; fgn. corr. Cahiers Tristan l'Hermite, 1979—. Served with AUS, 1942-45; lt. col. Res. (ret.). U. Ala. research grantee, 1961-65. Mem. MLA, South Atlantic Modern Lang. Assn., Am. Assn. Tchrs. Spanish and Portuguese, The Comediantes, Ala. Edn. Assn., Nat. Ret. Tchrs. Assn., Ala. Ret. Tchrs. Assn., Société des Amis de Tristan L'Hermite, Société des études du dix-septième siècle, Am. Assn. Ret. Persons, Phi Beta Kappa. Jewish. Author: (with C.B. Wicks) The Parisian Stage, 1961; Almahide, 1939, 73. Editorial bd. Revista De Estudios Hispánicos, 1967-75; co-editor: Théâtre Complet de Tristan l'Hermite, 1975. Home: 14 Arcadia Dr Tuscaloosa AL 35404-0571 Office: Drawer B Eastside Sta Tuscaloosa AL 35404-0571

SCHWEIZER, RUDOLPH JAMES, oil company executive; b. L.I., N.Y., Sept. 21, 1948; s. Rudolph J. and Dorothy Ruth (Rankin) S.; m. Charlotte Langston Williams, July 10, 1970 (div. Sept. 1979); m. 2d, Marilyn Mileham, Apr. 5, 1980; children—Ryan James, Jamie Erin. B.S.C.E., The Citadel, 1970; M.S.C.E., U. Tex., 1975. Registered profl. engr., Okla. Sr. engr. Williams Bros. Engring. Co., Tulsa, 1975-77, Santa Fe Pipeline Co., Tulsa, 1977-78; pres. RJS Constrn., Inc., Tulsa, 1978-80; profl. engr. Aminoil USA, Inc., Houston, 1980-82, plant mgr., 1982—. Author: Stability of Earth Slopes, 1975. Chmn. Wagoner County Rural Water Dist., Broken Arrow, Okla., 1978-80. Serving to maj. USAFR. Recipient George Walker White award in engring. The Citadel, 1970. Mem. Am. Gas Assn., ASCE, Res. Officers Assn. (life), Air Force Assn., Nat. Rifle Assn. (life), YMCA. Republican. Presbyterian. Club: Pipeliners (Tulsa). Lodge: Elks. Home: 4009 Harpers Ferry Enid OK 73701 Office: Aminoil USA Box 94193 Houston TX 77292

SCHWENDLER, WILLIAM THEODORE, JR., manufacturing company executive; b. Mineola, N.Y., May 23, 1940; s. William Theodore and Mabel Rebecca (Jorden) S.; m. Barbara Ann Deiss, Feb. 20, 1971; children—Rebecca Helena, William Theodore III. A.B., Princeton U., 1964; M.B.A., Harvard U., 1966. Fin. analyst Grumman Aerospace Corp., 1966-70; exec. v.p., treas., dir. Grumman Ecosystems Corp., 1971-73, pres., treas., dir., 1974-76; asst. to chmn. Grumman Corp., 1976-78, mgr. S.E. region, 1978-84, dir. S.E. region, 1984—; dir. Paumanock Devel. Corp., 1978-85; pres., dir. Solar Energy

Industries Assn. Ga., Inc., Atlanta, 1979-85; dir. Ga. Solar Coalition, 1982-85. Clubs: Wynterhall Swim and Tennis (pres., dir. 1982); Rotary, Harvard Bus. Sch. (Atlanta); Princeton of Ga. Office: 301 Perimeter Center N Suite 220 Atlanta GA 30346

SCHWING, CHARLES EDWARD, architect; b. Plaquemine, La., Nov. 21, 1929; s. Calvin Kendrick and Mary Howard (Slack) S.; m. Cynthia Benjamin (div. 1967); children—Calvin Kendrick III (dec.), Therra Cynthia; m. Geraldine Fleniken Hofmann, Dec. 27, 1969; 1 stepchild, Steven Blake. Student La. State U., 1947-51; B.S., Ga. Inst. Tech., 1953, B.Arch., 1954; postgrad. Assesite de Arch., Ecole Des Beaux-Arts. Field insp. Bodman, Murrell and Smith Baton Rouge, 1954-55; assoc. architect Post and Harelson, Baton Rouge, 1955-59; ptnr. Hughes and Schwing, Baton Rouge, 1959-61; prin. Charles E. Schwing, Baton Rouge, 1961-69, Charles E. Schwing and Assocs., Baton Rouge, 1969—; v.p. Schwing Inc. Fellow AIA (treas., exec. com., dir., planning com., chmn. fin. com. 1976-77, pres. 1980), Royal Archtl. Inst. Can. (hon.); mem. La. Solar Design Assn. (bd. dirs.), La. Archtl. Assn. (pres. 1973), Venezuelan Soc. Architects (hon.), Bolivian Inst. Architects (hon.), La Soc. de Architects of Mexico (hon.), Baton Rouge C. of C., La. State U. Alumni Fedn., Ga. Tech. Alumni Club, Sigma Alpha Epsilon. Episcopalian. Clubs: Baton Rouge Country, City. Office: Schwing and Assocs 721 Government St Baton Rouge LA 70802

SCIACCA, WILLIAM WAYNE, hospital administrator; b. New Orleans, June 20, 1945; s. Thomas John and Pauline Louise Sciacca; B.A., La. State U., 1967; m. Margaret A. D'Abadie, June 11, 1983; children—William, Deborah, Mark, Scott. Asst. mgr. Brennan's Restaurant, New Orleans, 1971-73; dir. dietary Hotel Dieu Hosp., New Orleans, 1973-76; dir. food service and housekeeping Tulane Med. Center Hosp. and Clinic, New Orleans, 1976—; cons. in field. CPR instr. Am. Heart Assn., New Orleans. Served to capt. U.S. Army, 1967-71. Decorated Bronze Star. Mem. Am. Soc. Hosp. Food Service Adminstrs. (pres. La. Bayou chpt. 1980-81), La. Restaurant Assn., Internat. Food Service Execs. Assn., Nat. Exec. Housekeepers Assn., Les Chefs de Cuisine de la Louisianne (trustee), Res. Officers Assn., Theta Xi. Democrat. Roman Catholic. Clubs: Lions, Confederation Mondiale des Activites Subquatiques. Home: 316 28th St New Orleans LA 70124 Office: 1415 Tulane Ave New Orleans LA 70112

SCIMECCA, JOSEPH ANDREW, sociologist, educator; b. N.Y.C., Aug. 26, 1940; s. Francis and Frances (Mula) S.; m. Elsie M. Lundberg, Nov. 23, 1968; children—Kirsten, Faith. B.A., Hunter Coll.-CUNY, 1962; M.A., NYU, 1965; Ph.D., 1972. Instr. Upsala Coll., East Orange, N.J., 1966-68; lectr. Herbert H. Lehman Coll., Bronx, N.Y., 1968-69; asst. prof. U. Maine, Orono, 1969-70, disting. prof., 1970; assoc. prof., SUNY-Albany, 1970-77; prof., chmn. dept. sociology George Mason U., Fairfax, Va., 1977—; fellow Ctr. for Conflict Resolution, George Mason U., 1982—. Author: Society and Freedom, 1981; Education and Society, 1980; The Sociological Theory of C. Wright Mills, 1977; (with Roland Damiano) Crisis at St. John's, 1968. Mem. Am. Sociol. Assn., Am. Soc. Criminology, Eastern Sociol. Soc., Soc. Study Social Issues, Assn. for Humanist Sociology (v.p. 1982-83). Democrat. Roman Catholic. Home: 11391 Bantry Terr Fairfax VA 22030 Office: George Mason U 4400 University Dr Fairfax VA 22030

SCOLARO, REGINALD JOSEPH, geologist; b. Tampa, Fla., Oct. 19, 1939; s. Joseph Domenic and Louise Rita (Guiffria) S.; m. JoAnn Olinski, June 6, 1966 (div. 1976); children—Larra, Ryan; m. Susan Lea Fink, Apr. 29, 1982. B.A., U. Fla., 1960, B.S., 1962, M.S., 1964; Ph.D., Tulane U., 1968. Prof., chmn. dept. geology Radford U., Va., 1969-79; project geologist Gulf Oil Corp., New Orleans, 1979-82, Houston, 1982; area geologist Sohio Petroleum Co., Houston, 1982-85, sr. geologist II, 1985—. Served to sgt. U.S. Army, 1961. Mem. Geol. Soc. Am., Am. Assn. Petroleum Geologists, Paleontol. Soc., Paleontol. Research Inst. Roman Catholic. Avocation: Racquetball. Office: Sohio Petroleum Co 9401 Southwest Freeway Houston TX 77074

SCOLASTICO, JOHN SYLVIN, JR., marketing company executive, real estate investor; b. Reading, Pa., Oct. 1, 1954; s. John Sylvin and Shirley Jane (Hertz) S.; m. Chris Brace Coe, May 7, 1983. B.S., Drexel U., 1977. Mgr. aftermarket mktg. White Motor Corp., Cleve., 1977-80; dist. sales mgr. Volvo White Trucks Co. Dallas, 1980-82; dist. mgr. Steelcase Inc., Dallas, 1982-86; pres. Mara Co. div. CDG, Inc., Dallas, 1984—, also dir.; pres. L.C.H.A., Inc., Dallas, 1981-83, dir., 1983—; dir. CDG, Inc., Dallas; bd. dirs. C.V.H. Assn., Carrollton, Tex., 1984—. Active Dallas County Young Men's Republican Club, 1981—. Mem. Nat. Trust Hist. Preservation, Hist. Preservation League, Nat. Geog. Soc., Tex. Hist. Soc., Dallas Bd. Realtors, Presbyterian. Clubs: Towne, President's (Dallas). Lodge: Order Demolay (master councilor 1969-70). Office: Mara Co div CDG Inc 3403 Wylie Dr Dallas TX 75235

SCOLNICK, JOSEPH MENDELSOHN, JR., political science educator; b. Jamaica, N.Y., Mar. 4, 1940; s. Joseph Mendelsohn and Louise Bland (Roane) S. B.A., U. Va., Charlottesville, 1961, M.A., 1965; Ph.D., U. Ky., 1980. Asst. prof. Longwood Coll., Farmville, Va., 1965-69; grad. instr. U. Ky., Lexington, 1971; asst. prof. Clinch Valley Coll., Wise, Va., 1973-80, assoc. prof., 1980—. Teaching editor Comparative Fgn. Policy Notes, comparative fgn. policy sect. Internat. Studies Assn., 1985—. Contbr. articles and book revs. to profl. jours. Treas. Library Gallery, Lonesome Pine Regional Library, Wise, 1984—. Served to lt. (j.g.) USNR, 1961-63. Mem. Internat. Studies Assn. (award 1971), Am. Polit. Sci. Assn., So. Polit. Sci. Assn., S.W. Va. Council for Social Studies (sec.-treas. 1985—). Office: Clinch Valley Coll of U Va PO Box 16 Wise VA 24293

SCOPA, PATRICIA MORRIS, chemistry educator; b. Cumberland, Ky., Aug. 24, 1945; d. Luther Edward and Maxine Mae (Smith) Morris; m. Joseph Anthony Scopa, Jr., Aug. 16, 1980; children—Elana, Christa, Clarissa. B.S., U. Ky., 1967; M.A., Eastern Ky. U., 1974. Cert. standard secondary tchr. Tchr. gen. sci. Clark County High Sch., Winchester, Ky., 1967-71; tchr. chemistry-biology Lynch High Sch., Ky., 1971-75; assoc. prof. U. Ky. Southeast Community Coll., Cumberland, 1975—, chmn. phys. sci. div., 1980—. Council on Higher Edn. Ky. grantee, 1980. Mem. Am. Chem. Soc., Ky. Assn. Community Coll. Profs., Com. For Chemistry in Two-Yr. Colls. Republican. Avocation: reading. Office: U Ky Southeast Community College Cumberland KY 40823

SCORCELLETTI, PIER GIORGIO, geologist; b. Pistoia, Tuscany, Italy, May 6, 1930; came to U.S., 1977; s. Ferruccio and Clementina (Chini) S.; m. Dunia Polizio, Sept. 28, 1955; children—Sabrina Scorcelletti Jones, Marco. D.Geol.Sci., U. Pisa, Italy, 1954. Geologist Gulf Italia Co., Ragusa, Sicily, Italy, 1954-58; regional geologist Gulf Oil Co. Libya, Tripoli, 1958-62, acting mgr., 1969-70; geol. supr. Mozambique Gulf Oil Co., Lourenco Marques, 1962-68; acting mgr. Gulf Oil Co. Ethiopia, Asmara, 1968-69; geol. supr. Cabinda Gulf Oil Co., Luanua, Angola, 1970-73; chief geologist Gulf Oil Co. Gabon, Libreville, 1973-77; regional ops. geologist Gulf Oil Exploration and Prodn. Co. Internat., Houston, 1977-85; staff geologist Amoco Prodn. Co., Houston, 1985—. Pres. PTA, Luanda, 1974-75; chmn. Africa Scout Group of Houston. Mem. Ordine Nazionale Dei Geologi, Am. Assn. Petroleum Geologists. Avocations: swimming; gardening; filmmaking. Home: 1707 Westmere Ct Houston TX 77077 Office: Amoco Prodn Co 501 Westlake Park Blvd Houston TX 77253

SCOTT, ANN MARTIN, English educator; b. Knoxville, Tenn., Mar. 24, 1943; s. William Martin and Clara Oleeta (Sallee) Breeding. B.A., Peabody Coll., 1964; M.A., Fla. State U., 1969, M.L.S., 1972, Ph.D., 1975. Cert. tchr., Tenn., Fla., La. Tchr., Kissimmee Jr. High Sch., Fla., 1967-68; instr. S. Fla. Jr. Coll., Avon Park, 1969-70; chmn. English dept. Lake Placid Jr. High Sch., Fla., 1970-71; asst. prof. Ind. State U., Evansville, 1975-76; prof. English U. Southwestern La., Lafayette, 1976—; cons. Fla. State Dept. Edn., Tallahassee, 1974-75; writer Am. Coll. Testing Program, 1976—. Contbr. articles to profl. jours. Active Save Our Oaks, The Hunger Project, Save the Children. Recipient Experienced Tchr. award HEW, 1968. Mem. Nat. Council Tchrs. English, La. Language Arts Assn., Linguistic Soc. Am. Avocations: swimming; flute; stained glass; stone masonry; camping. Home: Box 186 Cecilia LA 70521 Office: U Southwestern La Dept English Griffin Hall Lafayette LA 70504

SCOTT, BLAKELY NELSON, clergyman; b. Columbia, S.C., Feb. 11, 1948; s. Blakely, Jr. and Lillie Mae (Neal) S.; m. Mary Cornell Brooks, Aug. 31, 1969. Student S.C. State Coll., 1965-68; A. in Acctg., Palmer Coll., 1974; B.A., U. S.C., 1975; B.D., Morris Coll., 1980; postgrad., Lutheran Theol. Sem., 1982—. Teller, So. Bell Co., Columbia, 1976-78; pastor Mill Creek Bapt. Ch., Columbia, 1977-79, Mt. Moriah Bapt. Ch., Hopkins, S.C., 1978—, 1st Nazareth Bapt. Ch., Columbia, 1979—; asst. dir. of aux. services Benedict Coll., Columbia, 1978—; moderator Wateree Bapt. Assn.-U.D., Columbia, 1982—, dean Young People's Christian Assembly, Benedict Coll., 1985—. Mem. Hospice Bd. Bapt. Med. Ctr., Columbia, 1983. Served with USAF, 1969-73. Recipient Living the Legacy award Nat. Council of Negro Women, 1982. Mem. Chamber of Bapt. Ministers, S.C. Bapt. Edn. and Missionary Conv., Nat. Bapt. Conv. of Am., Gethsemene Bapt. Assn. (exec. com. mem. 1983—, asst. sec.), Omega Psi Phi (chaplain 1983-84), Alpha Phi Omega (adv. 1981—). Lodge: Masons. Avocations: reading; fishing; carpentry. Home: 408 Portchester Dr Columbia SC 29203 Office: Benedict Coll Harden and Blanding Sts Columbia SC 29204

SCOTT, CECYLE DARLYNE, nurse; b. Bokchita, Okla., Jan. 11, 1941; d. Thomas Richard and Annie Mae (Herrington) Harper; m. Gary Clinton Scott, Dec. 7, 1962; 1 dau., G. Victoria. Student South Oklahoma City Jr. Coll., 1975, U. Okla., 1965; nursing diploma, Mercy Hosp. Sch. Nursing, 1962. R.N., Okla. Staff nurse Mercy Hosp., Oklahoma City, 1962-68, asst. dir. inservice, 1968-69, supr., 1969-74; head nurse urology Bapt. Med. Ctr., Oklahoma City, 1974-79, mgr. surgery supply, 1979-82, head nurse post coronary care unit, 1982—; mem. adv. bd. Okla. State U. Tech. Inst. Sch. Nursing, Oklahoma City, 1973-81. Bd. dirs. Bapt. Med. Ctr. Credit Union, 1983—. Horton Ins. Co. scholar, 1960-62. Mem. ARC, Am. Heart Assn. Republican. Mem. Church of Christ. Avocation: thimble collecting. Office: Bapt Med Ctr 3300 NW Expressway Oklahoma City OK 73112

SCOTT, CHARLES DAVID, chemical engineer; b. Chaffee, Mo., Oct. 24, 1929; s. Charles Perry and Alma Gertrude (Kendall) S.; m. Alice Reba Bardill, Feb. 11, 1956; children—Timothy Charles, Mary Alice, Lisa Ann. B.S. in Chem. Engring., U. Mo., 1951; M.S. in Chem. Engring., U. Tenn., 1961, Ph.D., 1966. Registered profl. engr., Tenn. Devel. engr. Union Carbide Corp., Oak Ridge, 1953-57; research engr. Oak Ridge Nat. Lab., 1957-73, sect. chief, 1973-76, assoc. div. dir., 1976-83, research fellow, 1983—; lectr. chem. engring. U. Tenn., Knoxville. Served to 1st lt. AUS, 1951-53. Recipient U.S. Dept. Energy E.O. Lawrence award, 1980; Union Carbide Corp. fellow, 1983. Mem. AAAS, Am. Chem. Soc., Am. Assn. Clin. Chemistry (chmn. com. advanced analytical concepts, nat. award 1980), Am. Inst. Chem. Engrs., Nat. Acad. Engring., Sigma Xi, Alpha Chi Sigma. Lutheran. Contbr. articles to profl. jours.; patentee in field. Office: Oak Ridge National Laboratory PO Box X Oak Ridge TN 37830

SCOTT, CHARLES ERNEST, publishing company executive; b. Memphis, July 25, 1938; s. Charles E. and Lois Margaret (Brock) S.; m. Betty Jean Strickland, Oct. 8, 1955; children—Michael Steven, Patrick Ernest. Student U. Tex., 1966-69. Salesman, Nabisco, Inc., Austin, Tex., 1960-70; mem. mgmt. staff Kroger, Inc., Austin, 1970-74; salesman Prentice-Hall, Inc., Austin, 1974-76; pres. Scotsman Law Books, Inc., Austin, 1976—, also library cons. and computer cons.; owner SCS Systems, Austin, 1984—. Served with USMC, 1956-58. Republican. Avocations: woodworking; photography; traveling; reading; fishing. Office: Scotsman Law Books Inc 5537 Loyola Ln Austin TX 78724

SCOTT, CHARLOTTE HANLEY, business administration educator, researcher; b. Yonkers, N.Y., Mar. 18, 1925; d. Edgar Bernard and Charlotte Agnes (Palmer) Hanley; m. Nathan Alexander Scott, Dec. 21, 1946; children—Nathan Alexander, Leslie Kristin Scott Ashamu. A.B., Barnard Coll., 1947; postgrad. Am. U., 1949-52; M.B.A., U. Chgo., 1964; LL.D. (hon.) Allegheny Coll., 1981. Research assoc. Nat. Bur. Econ. Research, N.Y.C., 1947-48; research assoc. R.W. Goldsmith Assocs., Washington, 1948-55; economist U. Chgo., 1955-56; economist Fed. Res. Bank of Chgo., 1956-71, asst. v.p., 1971-76; prof. bus. adminstrn. and commerce U. Va., Charlottesville, 1976—; sr. fellow Tayloe Murphy Inst.; mem. consumer adv. council, bd. govs. FRS, 1980, vice chmn. 1981, chmn., 1982; nat. adv. council U.S. SBA, 1979-81; mem. Charlottesville bd. Sovran Bank. Mem. Gov.'s Commn. on Va. Future; mem. Va. Commn. on Status of Women; bd. dirs., treas. Va. Women's Cultural History Project. Mem. Am. Fin. Assn., Va. Assn. Economists, Acad. Mgmt., Internat. Assn. Personnel Women, Am. Soc. Personnel Adminstrn. Episcopalian. Contbr. articles to profl. jours.

SCOTT, DEBORAH ANNE, geologist; b. San Antonio, Nov. 20, 1954; d. Louis George and Jerry Anne (Beard) Wehman; m. Richard Wayne Bennett, Aug. 26, 1978 (div. Dec. 1983); m. David Ellsworth Scott, Feb. 14, 1985. B.A., Bryn Mawr Coll., 1976; postgrad. Princeton U., 1976-77. Research technician U. Tex. Med. Br., Galveston, 1977-78; info. coordinator Smithsonian Inst., Washington, 1978-81; geologist Cities Service Co., Houston, 1981-82; sr. analyst Gulf Oil Corp., Houston, 1983-85; applications analyst Chevron Geoscis. Co., Houston, 1985—. Supt. Sunday Sch., Luth. Ch., Houston, 1985—, mem. choir, 1978—. Mem. Am. Assn. Petroleum Geologists (assoc.), Houston Geol. Soc., Assn. Records Mgrs. and Adminstrs. Avocations: scuba diving; playing piano; archaeology. Home: 9510 Sandstone Rd Houston TX 77036 Office: Chevron Geoscis Co PO Box 42832 Houston TX 77242

SCOTT, FLOYD LEE, management information executive; b. Norfolk, Va., Oct. 6, 1949; s. Floyd Albin and Kathleen (Garrett) S. B.S. in Math. and Edn., Va. Poly. Inst. and State U., 1973. Cert. data processor. Gen. mgr. Eastern Water Works Supply, Virginia Beach, Va., 1977; spl. projects mgr. Davis Water & Waste, Thomasville, Ga., 1978-79; systems analyst McNichols Co., Tampa, Fla., 1980-83; mgmt. info. systems mgr. ABA Industries, Largo, Fla., 1983-85; sr. systems analyst Abbott Labs., Rocky Mount, N.C., 1985—. Served with U.S. Army, 1973-76. Mem. Assn. of Inst. Cert. Computer Profls., Data Processing Mgmt. Assn. Home: 225 Old Colony Way Rocky Mount NC 27804 Office: Abbott Labs Rocky Mount NC 27801

SCOTT, GAYLE CASH, social worker; b. Richmond, Va., Dec. 5; d. Benjamin F. and Ruth (Taylor) Cash; m. Herbert C. Scott, Feb. 19, 1977; 1 child, Ryan Carnell; m. Leonidas B. Morton, Jr., Sept. 3, 1968 (div. 1975). B.S., Central State U., Wilberforce, Ohio, 1970; B.S.W., 1970; Postgrad Golden State U. Social worker City of Richmond, Va., 1970-75; job developer Operation Service, Dallas, 1975-77; social worker U. Dallas, 1978-82, Denton State Sch., Tex., 1982—. Mem. Tex. Public Employers Assn. (treas. 1984—), Nat. Black Assn. Social Workers, Nat. Assn. Social Workers, Am. Bus. Womens Assn. Home: 14 Chisholm Trail McKinney TX 75069 Office: Denton Sch Mental Retardation PO Box 368 Denton TX 76202

SCOTT, GAYNELLE ELY, real estate company executive, beauty institute executive, investor; b. Harlan, Ky., Nov. 3, 1958; d. Byril Winfield and Edna Earle (Hill) S. Student internat. politics No. Va. Community Coll., 1975-77, 85—; student bus. and econs. Am. U., 1978-81. Spl. asst. to Julian R. Adame (Mex.), Washington, 1978-81; realtor, investor Town & Country, Alexandria, Va., 1981-82, Paul Garmirian Realty, McLean, Va., 1984; realtor, owner Chain Bridge Realty, McLean, 1982-84; pres., owner Ganelle, Inc., McLean, 1983—; real estate advisor Embassy of Jordan, Washington, 1982-83; pres. Empire Properties Internat. Council mem. Nat. Conservative Polit. Action Com., Alexandria, 1983-84; active Citizens for Am., Washington, 1985—. Recipient Merit and Salon of Yr. award Modern Salon, 1984. Mem. Charter-100. Republican Methodist. Clubs: Greater McLean Rep. Women's, Pisces. Avocations: travel; art; music; reading; politics; sports. Home: 7570 Potomac Fall Rd McLean VA 22102 Office: Ganelle Inc 6744 Old McLean Village Dr McLean VA 22101

SCOTT, GEORGE COLE, III, stockbroker; b. N.Y.C., July 9, 1937; s. George Cole Scott and Anne Martindell (Blair) Clark; m. Leslie Jane Daniels, Apr. 12, 1969; children—Jane Leslie, Anne Blair, John Cole. B.A., U. Wash., 1969. Advt. reporter Am. Weekly, London, 1966-68; stockbroker Anderson & Strudwick, Richmond, Va., 1969-73, Scott & Stringfellow, Richmond, 1973-78, Piper, Jaffray & Hopwood, Seattle, 1978-82; v.p., investment officer Wheat, First Securities, Inc., Richmond, 1982—; dir. Claremont Capital Corp., Seattle, 1976—. Chmn. emeritus, founder Seattle-Christchurch, New Zealand Sister City Com. Served with USCG, 1960-64. Recipient Disting. Citizen award State of Wash., 1981. Mem. Richmond Soc. Fin. Analysts (assoc.), Seattle Soc. Fin. Analysts (assoc.). Democrat. Episcopalian. Clubs: Soc. Cin.; Wash. Athletic (Seattle); Va. Country (Richmond). Lodge: Kiwanis. Avocation: free-lance writing in history. Office: Wheat First Securities 707 E Main St Richmond VA 23219

SCOTT, GEORGE GALLMANN, accountant; b. Hattiesburg, Miss., July 8, 1928; s. John Havers and Rebecca Evelyn (Gallmann) S.; B.S., Millsaps Coll., 1949; m. Patsy T. Womack, June 27, 1953; 1 child, George Gallmann. Clk., Spanish Trail Transport, Mobile, Ala., 1949-50, asst. auditor, 1953-55; bookkeeper Met. Engraving & Electrotype Co., Richmond, Va., 1952-53; chief clk. Central Truck Lines of Tampa, Fla., Mobile, 1955-56; gen. auditor M.R.&R. Trucking Co., Crestview, Fla., 1956-66, sec.-treas., 1967-77; public acct. enrolled to represent taxpayers before IRS, 1979—. Mem. data processing adv. com. Okaloosa-Walton Jr. Coll., Niceville, Fla., 1965-66, 72-73; mem. Okaloosa County Gen. Advisory Com. for Devel. Vocat. Edn., 1973, 79; bd. dirs. Okaloosa Community Concert Assn., 1982—. Served with U.S. Army, 1950-52. Accredited in acctg. and taxation Nat. Accreditation Council for Accountancy. Mem. Am. Trucking Assn. (nat. acctg. and fin. council 1956-77), Southeastern Acctg. and Fin. Council (dir. 1974-77), Crestview Downtown Mchts. Assn. (dir. 1980—, treas. 1980—), Greater Crestview C. of C. (chmn. bus. ethics com. 1973-74, dir. 1981-83, treas. 1982-83), Fla. Accts. Assn. (bd. govs. 1979-80, pres. N.W. Fla. chpt. 1979-80), Pi Kappa Alpha. Methodist (choir dir. 1966-83, chmn. ofcl. bd. 1971-73, chmn. fin. com. 1974-75, 79-81 chmn. audit com. 1977—, mem. com. on lay personnel 1979—, chmn. 1983—, mem. com. on pastor-parish relations 1980—, council ministries 1985—). Lodge: Kiwanis (trustee 1985—). Home: 244 Seminole Trail NW Crestview FL 32536

SCOTT, HAROLD HOPHIEUS, JR., army officer, educator; b. Ora, Ind., Aug. 1, 1947; s. Harold Hophieus and Maxine Louise (Strevy) S.; m. Trudy Lynn Hall, Aug. 27, 1966; children—Deonne, Tiffany. B.S. in Computer Sci., U. So. Miss., 1975; M.A. in Mgmt. and Supervision, Central Mich. U., 1983; grad. U.S. Army Command, 1978. Commd. 2d lt. U.S. Army, 1967, advanced through grades to maj., 1978; platoon leader to sr. staff officer C.E., 1966—; stationed in Viet Nam, 1968-69, W.Ger., 1978-81; asst. prof. mil. sci. Ga. So. Coll., Statesboro, 1981—. Decorated Bronze Star. Mem. Assn. U.S. Army, Soc. Am. Mil. Engrs., Am. Legion, Sigma Iota Epsilon. Methodist. Home: 104 Simmons Rd Statesboro GA 30458 Office: Dept Mil Sci Ga So Coll Statesboro GA 30460

SCOTT, JAMES FRANCIS, real estate appraiser; b. Geneva, N.Y., June 30, 1921; s. Frank Edward and Agatha Ethel (James) S.; student SUNY, Extension Geneva and Rochester, 1939-41, U. Wis., 1969, U. Conn., 1971; m. Arleen Marie Masucci, Apr. 1, 1944 (div. 1982); children—Gary F., Cheryl M., Margaret Mary Scott James. m. 2d, Barbara J. Edwards, 1983. Photo paper prodn. Eastman Kodak Co., Rochester, N.Y., 1948-50; sr. appraiser Gokey & Galion, Ft. Lauderdale, Fla., 1950-53; owner, operator James F. Scott & Assos., realtors, appraisers, Rochester, 1955-63; pres. Scott Appraisal Service, Rochester, 1963-72, Atlanta, 1972—; cons., lectr. in field. Served to maj. USAAF, 1942-47; PTO. Decorated Silver Star with oak leaf cluster, Air medal with 5 oak leaf clusters. Mem. Soc. Real Estate Appraisers (internat. v.p. 1974), Am. Right of Way Assn. (sr.), Nat. Assn. Corp. Real Estate Execs. (chmn. appraising and taxation com.). Republican. Roman Catholic. Home: 3844 Longview Dr Atlanta GA 30341 Office: 5775 Peachtree-Dunwoody Rd Suite 510-C Atlanta GA 30342

SCOTT, JANET ELAINE, counselor, consultant; b. Aug. 21, 1948; d. James Samuel and Gladys May Scott. B.S. Calif. State Coll., 1969; M.A., Ohio State U., 1973, Ph.D., 1976. Nat. cert. counselor, Secondary tchr. Spanish, Painesville Bd. Edn., Ohio, 1969-72; resident dir. Ohio State U., Columbus, 1973-77; asst. prof. counseling Memphis State U., 1977-84; prin. Janet Scott, Ph.D. and Assocs., Memphis, 1983—; cons. Memphis Fed. Correctional Inst., 1981—, Dogwood Village, Eads, Tenn., 1984—. Contbr. articles to profl. jours. Bd. dirs. Vollintine Boys' Club, Memphis, bd. dirs. Transitional Ctrs. Inc., Memphis, pres. 1982-83. Mem. Nat. Council Negro Women (v.p. 1983—), Am. Assn. Counseling and Devel., Assn. for Splists. in Group Work (editorial bd. 1984—), Nat. Assn. Urban Edn. (mem. exec. bd. 1977-78), West Tenn. Correction Assn. (v.p. 1982-83), Bus. and Profl. Federated Club. Methodist. Home: 939 Mt Vernon St Memphis TN 38111 Office: 27 North Cleveland St Suite 208 Memphis TN 38104

SCOTT, JIMMIE DOW, health facility administrator; b. Milo, Okla., Jan. 1, 1930; s. Preston William and Elnora Mae (Hancock) S.; B. Liberal Studies, U. Okla., 1974, M.P.A., 1976, M.H.R., 1982; m. Wanda Mae Tippit, Oct. 5, 1952; children—Jimmie Dow, Dwain Dawson. Seaman recruit U.S. Navy, 1948, advanced through grades to lt. comdr., 1968; asst. adminstr. patient affairs, security and edn. U.S. Naval Hosp., Pensacola, Fla., 1959-63; asst. adminstr. Yokosuka (Japan) Naval Hosp., 1963-67; chief patient relations br. Bur. Medicine and Surgery, Washington, 1967-71; ret., 1971; exec. asst. for adminstrn. Univ. Hosp. and Clinics, Oklahoma City, 1980-83; adminstrv. asst. for adminstrn., assoc. adminstr. Okla. Meml. Hosp. and Clinics, Oklahoma City, 1983—. Mem. Am. Acad. Med. Adminstrs., Am. Soc. Public Adminstrs., Am. Coll. Hosp. Adminstrs., Acad. Polit. Sci., Am. Acad. Polit. and Social Sci. Republican. Baptist. Home: 2107 Fox Ave Moore OK 73160 Office: PO Box 26307 Oklahoma City OK 73126

SCOTT, JOHN ATWOOD, JR., hypnoanalyst; b. Darby, Pa., July 14, 1949; s. John Atwood and Mary Joyce (Forrester) S.; B.S., Empire State Coll., 1976; M.A.R., Harding Grad. Sch. Religion, 1979; postgrad. Memphis State U., 1979—; m. Edna Vera Newhouse, June 12, 1971; children—Abigail Rae, John Benjamin. Ordained to ministry Ch. of Christ, 1969; minister, youth worker Shiloh, Inc., N.Y.C., 1969-71; youth worker, adminstrn. Central Coleman Youth Devel. Project, Rochester, N.Y., 1971-75; counselor, hypnoanalyst John A. Scott, Ph.D. & Assos., P.C., Memphis, 1975—. Bd. dirs. Drug and Alcohol Council, Rochester, 1973-75; mem. 16th Ward Coalition for Neighborhood Devel., Rochester, 1973-75, chmn., 1974; mem. adv. bd. Genesee Valley Mental Health Center, 1974-75, chmn., 1975; neighborhood rep. to bd. dirs. Action for Better Community, 1974-75; founder, dir. Rochester City-Wide Basketball League, 1974-75; minister outreach to city program White Station Ch. of Christ, Memphis, 1976—. Mem. Soc. Med. Hypnoanalysts, Am. Inst. Hypnosis, Hypnosis Research Found., Am. Assn. Sex Educators, Counselors and Therapists, Nat. Alliance for Family Life. Assoc. editor Med. Hypnoanalysis, 1980-81; contbr. articles and book revs. to profl. publs. Office: 5100 Poplar Ave Suite 2404 Memphis TN 38137

SCOTT, KAREN JANE, osteopathic physician; b. Sweetwater, Tex., July 30, 1955; d. Thomas Eugene and Wanda Ruth (Pence) S. B.S. in Chemistry, Tex. Tech U., 1977; D.O., Tex. Coll. Osteo. Medicine, Ft. Worth, 1981. Intern Okla. Osteo. Hosp., Tulsa, 1981-82; gen. practice medicine, Denver City, Tex., 1982—. Mem. Tex. Osteo. Polit. Activation Com., 1983—. Nat. Health Service Corps scholar, 1977-81. Mem. Am. Osteo. Assn., Tex. Osteo. Med. Assn., Am. Coll. Osteo Gen. Practitioners, Alpha Epsilon Delta (sec. 1976-77), Epsilon Sigma Alpha, Iota Sigma Pi, Alpha Lambda Delta. Republican. Episcopalian. Club: Atlas. Home: Drawer 1390 522 E Elm St Denver City TX 79323 Office: Drawer 1390 412 N Ave F Denver City TX 79323

SCOTT, KENNETH DAVIS, development specialist; b. Richmond, Va., Aug. 8, 1944; s. Lester Dew and Helen Earlyne (Davis) S.; m. Susan Lang Blanton, Mar. 17, 1968 (div. 1985); children—Steven Lester, Melissa Blanton, Kimberly Dawn. B.S. in Mgmt., Va. Commonwealth U., 1974. Lab. tech. Reynolds Metals Co., Richmond, Va., 1964-68, research asst., 1968-70, engring. tech., 1970-74, devel. engr., 1974-84, sr. devel. specialist, 1984—. Pres. Henrico Vol. Rescue Squad, Richmond, 1977-78, sec., 1978—. Mem. Soc. Automotive Engrs., Am. Soc. Safety Engrs. Methodist. Office: Reynolds Metals Co PO Box 27003 Richmond VA 23261

SCOTT, KERRIGAN DAVIS, investor; b. Magdalene, Fla., Sept. 26, 1941; s. Thurman Thomas and Jacqueline (Glenister) S.; children—Katherine, Stephanie, Jennifer. Student U. Va., 1964 Investor Mcht. Marine and Plantation Properties, Hilton Head Island, S.C., 1965—. Author: Aristocracy and Royalty of the World, 1983. Capt. U.S. Mcht. Marine. Mem. Million Dollar Round Table, RMS Queen Mary Hist. Soc. (founder). Episcopalian. Club: Shipyard Plantation Racquet (Hilton Head Island). Avocations: maritime subjects, Southern history, art. Home: 10 Windflower Ct Hilton Head Plantation Hilton Head Island SC 29928

SCOTT, LEE HANSEN, utility company executive; b. Atlanta, Sept. 25, 1926; s. Elbert Lee and Auguste Lillian (Hansen) S.; m. Margaret Lee Smith, July 20, 1951; children—Bradley Hansen, Randall Lee. Student Davidson Coll., 1944, North Ga. Coll., 1945, Fla. State U., 1947; B.E.E., U. Fla., 1949. Registered profl. engr., Fla. Engr. Fla. Power Corp., St. Petersburg, 1949-60, supr. distbn. engring., 1960-62, asst. div. mgr., 1962-65, supt. transmission and distbn., 1965-68, dir. constrn., maintenance and operating, 1968-71, v.p. customer ops., 1971-77, sr. v.p. ops., 1977-83, pres., 1983—; dir. Sun

Bank/Tampa Bay. Pres. Pinellas Com. of 100, 1980, Pinellas chpt. ARC, 1980, St. Petersburg Progress, 1983, pres. Pinellas Bus. and Industry Devel. Council, 1983; pres. Community Service Council; v.p. United Way, 1985. Served with USAF, 1944-46. Mem. Am. Mgmt. Assn., IEEE, Elec. Council of Fla. (pres. 1981), Fla. C. of C. (v.p. 1985). Presbyterian. Club: Suncoasters. Office: Fla Power Corp 3201 34th St S Saint Petersburg FL 33733

SCOTT, LEIGH SHARINE, school psychologist; b. Bonham, Tex., Jan. 26, 1949; d. Jimmie Dude and Sandra Lee (Lowe) Mills; m. Clyde Edward Scott, Feb. 2, 1968; children—Bryan Clyde, Bradley Christopher. B.S., East Tex. State U., 1974, M.S., 1975. Lic. assoc. sch. psychologist, Tex. Instr. for disavantaged Paris Jr. Coll., Tex., 1974-75; adaptive behavior researcher Corpus Christi Ind. Sch. Dist., 1976-79, assoc. sch. psychologist, 1979-80, cons. for appraisal services, 1980—; sec. Allen's Convenience Stores, Kingsville, Tex., 1980-85. Editor: Adaptive Behavior Newsletter, 1977-79; assoc. editor: Texas Psychologist, 1984-85. Contbr. articles to profl. jours. Mem. Am. Psychol. Assn., Tex. Psychol. Assn. (dir. div. psychol. assocs. 1984), Nueces County Psychol. Assn. (pres. 1985), Alpha Chi. Democrat. Avocations: swimming, oil painting. Office: Corpus Christi Ind Sch Dist 820 Buffalo Office of Appraisal Services Corpus Christi TX 78401

SCOTT, MAE RANKIN, mortgage company executive; b. Birmingham, Ala., Jan. 1, 1940; d. William Roscoe and Annie Mae (Dobbs) Rankin; student extention U. Ala., 1959-61; children—Leslie Ann Scott Garris, William Eugene, Jr. Sr. cert. rev. appraiser and registered underwriter; sr. cert. valuer Internat. Inst. Valuers. With Heritage Corp. of N.Y., 1962-67; asst. v.p. King's Way Mortgage Co., Miami, Fla., 1967-73, sr. v.p., 1973-78, exec. v.p., 1978—; corp. sec. Veritas Ins. Co., Alpha, Inc.; sr. v.p. Pan Am. Mortgage Corp.; approved underwriter Fed. Home Loan Bank, Fed. Nat. Mortgage Assn.; approved HUD direct endorsement underwriter. Active Prevention of Blindness, South Fla. Mem. Mortgage Bankers Assn. South Fla., Mortgage Bankers Assn. Am., Mortgage Bankers Fla., Manufactured Housing Cert. Appraisers (sr.), South Fla. Home Builders Assn., Nat. Assn. Rev. Appraisers (cert. rev. appraiser), various South Fla. real estate bds. Democrat. Baptist. Contbr. articles to pubis. Office: 150 SE 3d Ave Room 325 Miami FL 33131

SCOTT, NATHAN ALEXANDER, JR., religion educator; b. Cleve., Apr. 24, 1925; s. Nathan Alexander and Maggie (Martin) S.; m. Charlotte Hanley, Dec. 21, 1946; children—Nathan Alexander III, Leslie K. A.B., U. Mich., 1944; B.D., Union Theol. Sem., 1946; Ph.D., Columbia U., 1949; Litt.D., Ripon Coll., 1965; L.H.D., Wittenberg U., 1965, Fed. City Coll., 1976; D.D., Phila. Div. Sch., 1967, Va. Theol. Sem., 1985; S.T.D., Gen. Theol. Sem., 1968; Litt.D., St. Mary's Coll., Notre Dame, 1969, Denison U., 1976, Brown U., 1981, Northwestern U., 1982. Ordained priest Episcopal Ch., 1960; canon theologian Cathedral St. James, Chgo., 1967-76; William R. Kenan prof. religious studies, U. Va., Charlottesville, 1976—; Shailer Mathews prof. theology and lit. U. Chgo., 1955-76. Author: The Broken Center, 1966; Negative Capability, 1969; The Wild Prayer of Longing, 1971; Three American Moralists, 1973; The Poetry of Civic Virtue, 1976; The Poetics of Belief, 1985. Co-editor Jour. Religion, 1963-77. Adv. editor Va. Quar. Rev. Religion and Lit. Mem. Soc. Arts, Religion and Contemporary Culture, Soc. for Values in Higher Edn. (Kent fellow), Am. Philos. Assn., MLA., Am. Acad. Religion (pres. 1986). Office: Dept Religious Studies U Va Charlottesville VA 22903

SCOTT, NAUMAN S., fed. judge; b. New Roads, La., June 15, 1916; s. Nauman Steele and Sidonie (Provosty) S.; B.A., Amherst Coll., 1938; LL.B., Tulane U., 1941; m. Blanche Hammond, Jan. 8, 1942; children—Ashley Scott Smith, Nauman S., III, John W., Arthur Hammond. Admitted to La. bar, 1942; practiced law, Alexandria, 1942-70; chief judge U.S. Dist. Ct. for La. Western Dist., 1970—; mem. Jud. Council La. Supreme Ct., 1961-70. Chmn. United Fund, Alexandria, ARC, Alexandria; bd. dirs. La. Assn. Mental Health, Vocat. and Rehab. Center, YMCA, YWCA. Mem. Alexandria (pres. 1965-66), La. State, Am. bar assns., Alexandria C. of C., Young Men's Bus. Assn. Roman Catholic. Club: Kiwanis. Office: US Dist Ct PO Box 312 Alexandria LA 71301*

SCOTT, RALPH LEE, librarian; b. N.Y.C., July 23, 1942; s. Roy Lee and Martha Artelia (Derrick) S.; B.A., Columbia U., 1968, M.S., 1970; M.A., East Carolina U., 1979. Bibliog. asst. Burgess-Carpenter Library, Columbia U., N.Y.C., 1960-62, Spl. Collections Library, 1962-69; asst. prof. library services East Carolina U., Greenville, N.C., 1970-79, assoc. prof., 1979—, unit head documents N.C. Collection, 1985—. Vice pres. Pitt County Hist. Soc., 1977-80; mem. Pitt County Bicentennial Commn., 1975-76, exec. com. Democratic Party, 1981-86; mem. history com. Immanuel Baptist Ch., 1981-82, chmn. usher com., 1978-81. Mem. Outreach com. Meml. Bapt. Ch., 1983—, chmn. usher com., 1985; spl. elections commr. Pitt County, 1983-84. Recipient Annual award N.Y. Library Club, 1969; Tech. Services award Tauber-Bergman, 1971. Mem. ALA, N.C. Library Assn., N.C. On-Line Users Group, Sierra Club. Democrat. Mem. editorial bd. N.C. Libraries, 1979-83; contbr. articles to profl. publs. Home: 2702 Jackson Dr Greenville NC 27834 Office: 104 Joyner Library East Carolina U Greenville NC 27834

SCOTT, RANDOLPH JOHN, mining engineer, consultant; b. Lynch, Ky., Mar. 26, 1955; s. John D. and Shirley Yvonne (Mullins) S.; m. Katrina Sue Turner, May 27, 1978. B.S. in Civil Engring., U. Ky.-Lexington, 1977. Registered profl. engr., Ky. Mining engr. Benham Coal Inc., Ky., 1977-80, project engr. 1984—; staff engr. Paul Weir Co., Chgo., 1980-84; tchr. Community Coll., Cumberland, Ky., 1978. Mem. Soc. Mining Engr., ASCE, Nat. Soc. Profl. Engrs., U. Ky. Alumni Club (Cumberland Valley chpt.), Chi Epsilon. Republican. Methodist. Lodge: Lions. Office: Benham Coal Inc 158 Central Ave Benham KY 40807

SCOTT, ROBERT EMMERSON, JR., computer company executive; b. Pitts., Mar. 18, 1942; s. Robert Emmerson and Sarah Ann (Waller) S.; m. Anita Louise Bingel, Aug. 30, 1969. M.B.A., Ga. State U., 1985. Engr., Control Data Co., Atlanta, 1967-76, salesman, Charlotte, N.C., 1976-79; dist. sales mgr. Intergraph Corp., Charlotte, N.C., 1979-81, region sales dir., Atlanta, 1981-84; nat. sales mgr. Automation Intelligence, Orlando, Fla., 1984—. Served with USAF, 1962-66. Avocations: fishing; boating; home construction projects. Home: 220 Autumn Wood Ln Roswell GA 30075 Office: Automation Intelligence Inc 1200 W Colonial Dr Orlando FL 32804

SCOTT, ROBERT WILLIAM, geologist; b. Davenport, Iowa, June 7, 1936; s. Robert Simon and Catherine (Volz) S.; m. Carole Ann Riedmiller, June 2, 1962; children—Paul, Theresa, Michael. B.A. in Philosophy, Maryknoll Coll., 1958; B.A. in Geology, U. Wyo., 1960, M.A., 1961; Ph.D. in Geology, U. Kans., 1967. Asst. prof. Waynesburg Coll., Pa., 1966-70, U. Tex.-Arlington, 1970-74; research assoc. Amoco Prodn. Co., Tulsa, 1974-82, spl. research assoc., 1982—. Mem. Am. Assn. Petroleum Geologists, Soc. Econ. Paleontologists and Mineralogists, Paleont. Soc., Sigma Xi. Home: 3734 S Darlington Tulsa OK 74135 Office: Amoco Prodn Co PO Box 3385 Tulsa OK 74102

SCOTT, ROY VERNON, history educator; b. Wrights, Ill., Dec. 26, 1927; s. Roy J. and Edna (Dodson) S.; m. Jane Angeline Brayford, July 9, 1959; children—John, Elizabeth, Sarah. B.S., Iowa State U., 1952; M.A., U. Ill., Urbana, 1953, Ph.D., 1957. Asst. prof. U. Southwest La., 1957-58; research assoc. Bus. History Found., 1958-59; asst. prof. U. Mo., 1959-60; asst. prof. Miss. State U., Mississippi State, 1960-62, assoc. prof., 1962-64, prof., 1964-78, disting. prof. history, 1978—. Active Republican Party. Served with USAF, 1946-48. Baptist. Author: Agrarian Movement in Illinois, 1962; The Reluctant Farmer: The Rise of Agricultural Extension to 1914, 1970; The Public Career of Cully A. Cobb: A Study in Agricultural Leadership, 1973; co-editor: Southern Agriculture since the Civil War, 1979; Railroad Development Programs in the Twentieth Century, 1985. Home: 207 Seville Pl Starkville MS 39759 Office: PO Box 1018 Miss State U Mississippi State MS 39762

SCOTT, SHIELDS LAMAR, safety and training executive; b. Meridian, Miss., June 28, 1939; s. Shields Lamar and Mary Evelyn (Parker) S.; m. Mary Louise Davis, June 28, 1962; children—Shields Lamar III., Melissa Davis, Rebecca Dawn. B.S. La. Coll., 1962. Coach and athletic dir. Leakesville High Sch., Miss., 1962-67, Kaplan High Sch., La., 1967-74; mgr. safety audit Brown & Root, Inc., Houston, 1974-79; fgn. safety Diamond M Co., Houston, 1980-81, mgr. safety, 1981—, mgr. safety and tng., 1983—. Mem. Am. Soc. Safety Engrs., Am. Soc. Tng. and Devel. Democrat. Baptist. Home: 213 E Temperance Ln Deer Park TX 77536 Office: Diamond M Co 14141 Southwest Freeway Houston TX 77210

SCOTT, STANLEY TINNIS, appliance distbr.; b. Portsmouth, Ohio, May 2, 1927; s. Edward Dewey and Effie (Edmonson) S.; B.S., Wilmington (Ohio) Coll., 1960; m. Hope Scott; children—Michele Dian, Kevin Alan. With Frigidaire div. Gen. Motors Corp., 1950-71, sales mgr. Frigidaire Sales Corp., Detroit, 1965-68, zone mgr., Houston, 1968-71, Phila., 1971; v.p., gen. mgr. Straus-Frank Co., San Antonio, 1971—. Chmn. Film Industry Com., 1974-80. Served with USNR, 1945-46. Mem. Greater San Antonio C. of C., Gen. Motors Exec. Club (past pres. Houston), San Antonio Advt. Fedn., San Antonio Appliance Assn., La sociedad de los buenos compañeros. Office: 1970 S Alamo St San Antonio TX 78292

SCOTT, T. GORDON, chemistry educator, consultant; b. Laconia, N.H., Nov. 27, 1941; s. W. Stafford and Jeanne Frances (Richardson) S.; A.B., U. Pa., 1963; B.A. with honors, Cambridge U. (Eng.), 1965, M.A., 1969; Ph.D., U. Ill., 1969. Thouron scholar Cambridge U., 1963-65; teaching and research asst. U. Ill.-Urbana, 1965-69; asst. prof. chemistry Oberlin Coll. (Ohio), 1969-70; lectr. biochemistry U. Calif.-Santa Barbara, 1971; ednl. cons., Uniontown, Pa., 1972-74, 79-81; supr. secondary studies Westminster Acad., Carmichaels, Pa., 1975-79; asst. prof. chemistry Alderson-Broaddus Coll., Philippi, W.Va., 1981-84; assoc. prof., chmn. dept. chemistry Bryan Coll., Dayton, Tenn., 1984—; cons. organic chemistry. Mem. Am. Chem. Soc., Sigma Xi, Phi Lambda Upsilon. Presbyterian. Contbr. chpt. to book, articles to profl. jours. Office: Bryan College Box 7585 Dayton TN 37321

SCOTT, WALTER COKE, sugar company executive, lawyer; b. Norfolk, Va., July 20, 1919; s. Walter Coke and Rosemary (White) S.; B.S., Hampden-Sydney Coll., 1939; J.D., U. Va., 1948; m. Virginia Kemper Millard, May 14, 1949; children—Mary Lyman Scott Jackson, Roberta Coke Scott Gatewood, Alexander McRae, Buford Coke. Bar: Va. 1947, Ga. 1954. Atty., U.S. Dept. Justice, Jacksonville, Fla., 1948; commerce atty. S.A.L. Ry., Norfolk, 1948-54; commerce counsel, gen. solicitor Central of Ga. Ry., Savannah, 1954-60, v.p., 1960-62, dir., 1960—; ptnr. firm Hitch, Miller & Beckmann, Savannah, 1956-60; sr. v.p., sec. Savannah Foods & Industries, Inc. (formerly Savannah Sugar Refining Corp.), 1962-72, exec. v.p., mem. exec. com., 1972—, also dir.; exec. v.p., sec., mem. exec. com. dir. Everglades Sugar Refinery, Inc., Clewiston, Fla.; sec., mem. exec. com., dir. The Jim Dandy Co., Birmingham, Ala., 1968-81; dir. Savannah Bank & Trust Co., Transales Corp., Dixie Terminal Co., Biomass Corp., Chatham Corp., Savannah, Wells Pet Food Corp., Monmouth, Ill. Pres., chmn. exec. com. Historic Savannah Found., 1963-64; bd. dirs. United Community Services, 1965-68, pres., 1967; gen. chmn. United Community Appeal, 1966; mem. Chatham-Savannah Met. Planning Commn., 1963-68; trustee, chmn. fin. com. Telfair Acad. Arts and Scis., 1964-67; trustee, vice chmn. Savannah Country Day Sch., 1967-69, chmn., 1970-72. Bd. dirs., chmn. fin. com. Savannah Speech and Hearing Center, 1967-70; bd. dirs. Savannah chpt. ARC, Savannah Symphony Soc. Mem. U.S. C. of C., Va. State Bar, ICC Practitioners Assn., Ga. State Bar, St. Andrews Soc., Savannah Benevolent Assn., Kappa Sigma, Omicron Delta Kappa, Phi Alpha Delta, Chi Beta Phi, Pi Delta Epsilon. Episcopalian (past vestryman, sr. warden). Clubs: Chatham, Oglethorpe, Savannah Golf. Home: 56 E 54th St Savannah GA 31405 Office: Savannah Bank Bldg Savannah GA 31401

SCOTT, WILLIAM ARNOLD, social worker; b. Bay Shore, N.Y., Jan. 18, 1949. B.A. in Sociology, Mercy Coll., 1970; M.Social Work, SUNY-Albany, 1977. With Harris County Ctr. for Retarded, Houston, 1977-78; asst. dir. to vocat. counseling workshop U. Houston, 1978-80; founder, adminstrv. dir. Montrose Counseling Ctr., Houston, 1978-80, psychotherapist, clin. supr., 1978-84, clin. dir., 1984—; field instr. Grad. Sch. Social Work, U. Houston, 1979—; pres., psychotherapist William A. Scott and Assocs., Houston, 1983—; lectr. in field. Mem. Nat. Assn. Social Workers, Am. Assn. Sex Educators, Counselors, and Therapists, Tex. Psychotherapist Assn., Houston Group Psychotherapist Assn., Houston C. of C. Office: 900 Lovett Suite 209 Houston TX 77006

SCOTT-QUEENIN, DEBORAH RUTH, marketing analyst, researcher; b. Balt., Feb. 14, 1954; d. John Tivis, Jr. and Viola Dorothy (Atkinson) Scott; m. Lawrence George Queenin, May 9, 1981. B.A., U. Md., 1978, M.A., 1980; M.B.A., Nova U., 1986. Mktg. analyst Port Everglades Authority, Fort Lauderdale, Fla., 1981—. Mem. Am. Sociol. Assn., World Trade Council, Women in Transp. Democrat. Avocation: swimming. Home: 7751 NW 44 Ct Lauderhill FL 33321 Office: Port Everglades Authority PO Box 13136 Fort Lauderdale FL 33321

SCRANTON, MARGARET EAHOLTZ, political science educator, consultant in foreign policy and inter-American relations; b. Jacksonville, Fla., Mar. 25, 1949; d. Galen Martin and Margaret (George) Eaholtz; m. Robert Forest Scranton, Dec. 22, 1973. B.A., Randolph-Macon Woman's Coll., 1972; M.A., U. Pitts., 1975, Ph.D., 1980. Asst. prof. U. Ark., Little Rock, 1978-82, assoc. prof., 1982—; guest lectr. Fgn. Service Inst., Washington, 1984. Co-author: Managing Interstate Conflict, 1976; Dynamics of U.S. Foreign Policy Making: The President, Congress and the Panama Canal, 1984. Bd. dirs. Ark. Endowment for Humanities, 1980-81, 83-85; active Ark.-East Bolivia Ptnrs. of Ams., 1978-81, Little Rock Com. Fgn. Relations, 1979—. Recipient Am. Polit. Sci. Rev. fellow, 1976-77; Fgn. Policy Research fellow Brookings Instn., 1977-78; Japan fellow So. Ctr. Internat. Studies, 1982; Ark. Internat. Ctr. grantee USIA, 1983. Mem. Internat. Studies Assn., Ark. Polit. Sci. Assn. (editorial bd. 1982-85), Am. Polit. Sci. Assn. (Helen Dwight Reid award 1981). Avocation: fencing. Home: 1400 Old Forge Dr 101 Little Rock AR 72207 Office: U Ark Dept Polit Sci 33d and University Little Rock AR 72204

SCREEN, PAT, city official. Mayor, City of Baton Rouge. Office: 222 Saint Louis St Baton Rouge LA 70821*

SCRIBNER, BEVERLY KINNEAR, lawyer; b. Chandler, Okla., Mar. 8, 1941; d. Howard James and Helen Vista (Smith) Kinnear; m. Edward Leon Scribner, Aug. 26, 1961 (div. Aug. 1970); 1 son, John Edward; m. 2d, Don Martin Claunch, July 9, 1983; 1 stepdau., Diane Melissa. B.S. with distinction, U. Okla., 1963, J.D., 1977. Bar: Okla. 1977. Office mgr. McAfee & Taft, attys. at law, Oklahoma City, 1970-72; adminstr. asst. GHK Cos., Oklahoma City, 1972; legal asst. Hines & Smith, Oklahoma City, 1972-74; dir. legal asst. program U. Okla. Sch. Law, Norman, 1974-77; atty. Kerr Davis et al, Oklahoma City, 1977-79; ptnr. Bryant & Scribner, Oklahoma City, 1979-83, Claunch, Bryant & Scribner, Oklahoma City, 1983—; mem. adv. bd. legal asst. program Okla. U. Coll. Law, Norman, 1977—. Mem. ABA, Okla. Bar Assn., Oklahoma County Bar Assn., Oklahoma City Title Attys. Assn. (mem. exec. bd. 1983-84, treas. 1984, v.p. 1985), Oklahoma City Mineral Lawyers Soc. (sec.-treas. 1984-85, v.p. 1985-86), Oklahoma City Mgmt. and Profl. Women (pres. 1982). Republican. Presbyterian. Office: 710 Energy Plaza 3030 Northwest Expressway Oklahoma City OK 73112

SCRIVNER, BARBARA E., piano teacher; b. Oreg., May 25, 1931; student (piano student of Lawrence Morton), Bob Jones U., 1962-66; corr. student Inst. Children's Lit., Redding Ridge, Conn., 1974-76; children—R. Dick. Lawrence C., Barbara Ann, Betty Jo. Part time sec., Oreg., 1948-50, 60-62, 74-76, 80-82, Census Bur., S.C., 1980; piano tchr., Greenville, S.C., 1963—. Active Republican Nat. Com., Nat. Rep. Senatorial Com., Nat. Rep. Congressional Com., S.C. Rep. Party. Mem. S.C. Music Assn., Music Tchrs. Nat. Assn., Liberty Found. Contbr. articles, letters to newspapers and columns; editor, pub. Golden Nuggets of Truth, 1982—.

SCRUGGS, JOHN MARK, architect; b. Dallas, Aug. 11, 1951; s. C.G. and Miriam June (Wigley) S.; m. Drew F. Larvin, June 2, 1971; children—Evan Grey, Travis Larvin. B.Arch., U. Tex., 1974. Registered architect, Tex. Project mgr. ANPH Inc., Architects, Dallas, 1974-76; project architect Hatfield-Holcomb, Inc., Dallas, 1976-78; ptnr. ArchiTexas, Dallas, 1978—; adj. prof. U. Tex.-Arlington, 1984-85. Pres. BL Lacerta cultural corp., Dallas, 1982—. Mem. AIA. Office: ArchiTexas 1907 Marilla St Dallas TX 75201

SCRUGGS, RICHARD TURNER, aluminum co. exec.; b. Birmingham, Ala., Apr. 4, 1915; s. Josiah Hubert and Willye (Turner) S.; student Birmingham So. Coll., 1933-34, U. Ala., 1934-36; m. Marilyn Perkins Bade, Sept. 7, 1938; children—Marilyn Craig (Mrs. Charles L. Tucker), Margaret Sarah (Mrs. Jarrel Estes), Richard Turner, John Hubert. Salesman, So. Culvert Co., Birmingham, Ala., 1936-38, v.p., 1938-42; asst. chief aircraft insp. Bechtel-McCone Corp., Birmingham, 1942-46; co-founder Vulcan Metal Products, Inc., Birmingham, 1946, pres., 1956—; pres. Scruggs Investment Co., Inc. Mem. adv. council Salvation Army; chmn. gen. council Lee Assos. Washington and Lee U., Lexington, Va., 1976-77. Recipient Silver Circle award Alpha Tau Omega, 1959, hon. award Washington and Lee U. chpt. Omicron Delta Kappa, 1973. Mem. Screen Mfrs. Assn. (dir.), C. of C., S.A.R., Birmingham-Jefferson Hist. Soc., Sales Exec. Club, Newcomen Soc., Delta Sigma Pi. Methodist (steward). Clubs: Rotary, Shoal Creek Country, Birmingham Country, Downtown, The Club. Home: 3524 Victoria Rd Birmingham AL 35223 Office: PO Box 6788 Birmingham AL 35210

SCUDDER, JOHN RALPH, JR., philosophy and education educator; b. Taylorsville, N.C., Mar. 9, 1926; s. John Ralph and Fodell Love (Adams) S.; m. Mary Ethel Clayton, Dec. 16, 1951; children—Cynthia A. Scudder Lester, John Ralph III, Catherine J. Scudder Burke. B.A., Vanderbilt U., 1950; M.A., U. Ala., 1952; M. Div., Lexington Theol. Sem., 1955; Ed.D., Duke U., 1961. Asst. prof. history Atlantic Christian Coll., Wilson, N.C., 1956-57, assoc. prof. religion and philosophy, 1957-61, prof. edn., 1961-67; prof. philosophy and edn. Lynchburg Coll. (Va.), 1967—, chmn. dept. philosophy, 1971-83; vis. scholar Vanderbilt U., 1974. Author: (with Algis Mickunas) Meaning, Dialogue, and Enculturation: Phenomenological Philosophy of Education, 1985. Editor: (with Anne Bishop) Coping, Curing, and Caring: Relationships of Physician, Nurse, and Patient, 1985. Contbr. articles to profl. jours. Served with U.S. Army, 1944-46. Mem. Am. Philos. Assn., Soc. Existential and Phenomenological Philosophy, Philosophy Edn. Soc., South Atlantic Philosophy Edn. Soc. (pres. 1973-75). Democrat. Home: 3229 Landon St Lynchburg VA 24503 Office: Dept Philosophy Lynchburg Coll Lynchburg VA 24501

SCUDDER, MARY CLAYTON, library administrator; b. Tuscaloosa County, Ala., Nov. 29, 1928; d. Fred Lee Clayton and Helen Josephine (Hunt) C.; m. John Ralph Scudder, Jr., Dec. 16, 1951; children—; Cynthia A. Scudder Lester, John R. III, Catherine J. Scudder Burke. B.S., U. Ala., 1951; M.L.S., Peabody Coll. of Vanderbilt U., 1974. Periodicals librarian U. Ala., 1952-53; cataloguer U. Ky., 1953-54; asst. librarian Atlantic Christian Coll., Wilson, N.C., 1955-58, 61-67; asst. librarian pub. services Lynchburg (Va.) Coll., 1969-75, dir. Knight-Capron Library, 1975—. Mem. ALA, Southeastern Library Assn., Va. Library Assn. Democrat. Mem. Disciples of Christ Ch. Home: 3229 Landon St Lynchburg VA 24503 Office: Knight-Capron Library Lynchburg Coll Lynchburg VA 24501

SCUDDER, RICHARD B., publishing executive; b. Newark, May 13, 1913; s. Edward W. and Katherine (Hollifield), S.; m. Elizabeth A. Shibley, June 24, 1944; children—Elizabeth H. (Mrs. Philip Difani), Charles A., Carolyn (Mrs. Peter M. Miller), Jean. A.B., Princeton, 1935. Reporter Newark News, 1935-37, v.p., 1941-51, pub., 1951-72; reporter Boston Herald, 1937-38; pres. Hollifield, Inc.; chmn. bd. Garden State Paper Co.; now pres. Garden State Newspapers, Inc., Gloucester County Times, Inc., Media News Group, pubs. Hayward Daily Rev., Calif., North Jersey Herald News N.J., 13 others; dir. Midlantic Bank; mem. Nat. Adv. Com. on Indsl. Innovation, 1978—. Trustee Riverview Hosp., Frost Valley YMCA, N.J. Conservation Found.; v.p., bd. dirs. Paper Mill Playhouse, Millburn, N.J.; pres. Duryea Found. Served from pvt. to maj. AUS, 1941-45. Decorated Bronze Star; recipient TAPPI award, 1971; Nat. Recycling award Nat. Assn. Secondary Materials Industries, 1972; Nat Resource Recovery Man of Year award, 1978; Papermaker of Year award Paper Trade Jour., 1978. Clubs: Rumson Country, Seabright Beach, Seabright Lawn Tennis and Cricket, Essex Adirondack League. Home: Brown's Dock Rd Navesink NJ 07752 Office: Park 80 Plaza East Saddle Brook NJ 07662

SCULLY, JOHN ROBERT, oral and maxillofacial surgeon; b. N.Y.C., Mar. 2, 1949; s. Frank Edward and Helen Veronica (Sawyer) S.; m. Bonnie Diane Baron, Aug. 28, 1971; 1 child, Amanda Rose. B.S. Chemistry, Spring Hill Coll., 1970; D.D.S., Med. Coll. Va., 1974; M.S., U. Iowa, 1980. Diplomate Am. bd. Oral and Maxillofacial Surgery. Resident in oral and maxillofacial surgery U. Iowa, 1980; pvt. practice dentistry, Asheville, 1980—; chief oral and maxillofacial surgery St. Josephs Hosp., Asheville, 1984—, Meml. Mission Hosp., 1984—; cons. Pardee Hosp., Hendersonville, N.C., 1983—. Served to capt. USAF, 1974-77. USAF Merit scholar, 1972-74. Fellow Am. Assn. Oral and Maxillofacial Surgery; mem. ADA, N.C. Dental Soc., Buncombe County Dental Soc., Asheville C. of C., Zebulon Vance Debating Soc., Delta Sigma Delta. Club: Asheville Country. Avocations: music; rock and folk guitar; dance; tennis; autoracing. Home: 17 Bluebriar St Asheville NC 28804 Office: 5 Doctors Park Asheville NC 28801

SCURA, DOROTHY MCINNIS, English educator; b. Elizabeth, La., Mar. 18, 1933; s. James Edgar and Elizabeth (Cherry) McInnis; m. Alban E. Woolley, Jr., June 6, 1951 (div. May 1962)); m. George W. Scura, Dec. 5, 1964 (dec. Oct. 1981); children—Wynne Elizabeth, Michael Edward, Jill Caroline. B.S., La. State U., 1956; M.A., Columbia U. Tchrs. Coll., 1968; Ph.D., U. N.C., 1973. Asst. prof. English, U. Richmond, 1975-78; asst. prof. Va. Commonwealth U., Richmond, 1974-75, 78-81, assoc. prof., 1981—, chmn. dept., 1983—. Bd. dirs. Va. Women's Cultural History Project, 1982—; bd. dirs. Ellen Glasgow Soc., Ashland, Va., 1972—. Editor: Henry James, 1960-1974: A Reference Guide, 1979. Mem. MLA (del. Assembly 1980-82), Womens Caucus MLA (pres. 1981-83), Soc. Study So. Lit., Assn. Depts. English. Home: 1511 West Ave Richmond VA 23220 Office: Dept English Va Commonwealth U 900 Park Ave Richmond VA 23284

SCURO, JOSEPH E., JR., lawyer; b. Jersey City, Mar. 28, 1948; s. Joseph E. and Phyllis (Amato) S.; m. Charalyn M. Bishop. B.A., Manhattan Coll., 1970; J.D., Ohio State U., 1972. Bar: Tex., Ohio, U.S. Dist. Cts., U.S. Tax Ct., U.S. Mil. Appeals, U.S. Supreme Ct., U.S. Ct. Appeals (5th, 6th and 10th cirs.). Asst. atty. gen. Ohio, 1973-81; chief legal counsel Ohio State Hwy Patrol, 1975-81; practice law, 1973—; counsel Nicholas & Barrera, San Antonio, 1982—; atty.-counsel San Antonio Police Officers Assn.; counsel Combined Law Enforcement Assn. Tex., Alamo Heights Police Officers Assn., Tex. Mcpl. League, Bexar County Sheriffs Assn., cities of Devine, Laredo, Dilley, Kyle, Universal City, Austin, Irion County, Hondo, Greenville, Del Rio, Leon Valley and Hondo Police Officers Assns., Bexar County Constables Assn.; police legal adv. to cities of San Marcos, New Braunfels, Balcones Heights, La Vernia and Poteet (Tex.); spl. counsel on tng. San Antonio Police Dept.; condr. seminars Bd. dirs. Nat. Hispanic Arts Endowment. Served to capt. USAF, 1970-75. Fellow Southwestern Legal Found.; mem. Tex. Bar Assn., Ohio Bar Assn., ABA, San Antonio Bar Assn., Columbus (Ohio) Bar Assn., Am. Trial Lawyers Assn., Police Exec. Research Forum, Internat. Assn. Chiefs of Police (ins. bd. advs., program), Ams. for Effective Law Enforcement (bd. advs.), Southwestern Law Enforcement Inst. (bd. advs.), Internat. Soc. Law Enforcement and Criminal Justice Instrs., Combined Law Enforcement Assn. Tex., Fed. Criminal Investigators Assn., Ohio Assn. Polygraph Examiners. Democrat. Presbyterian. Contbr. articles on police and law enforcement to profl. jours. Office: 424 E Nueva St San Antonio TX 78205

SEABORN, JAMES BYRD, physics educator; b. Panama City, Fla., Dec. 15, 1932; s. James Baker and Mary Emma (Byrd) S.; m. Gwendolyn Consuelo Penton, Jan. 2, 1953; children—Jill, Carol, Richard, Thomas, Katrina. B.S., Fla. State U., 1960, M.S., 1962; Ph.D., U. Va., 1965. Asst. prof. U. Richmond, Va., 1965-66, prof., chmn. dept. physics, 1970—; research assoc. U. Frankfurt, W.Ger., 1966; asst. prof. N. Tex. State U., Denton, 1967-69; vis. lectr. Iowa State U., Ames, 1969-70; summer research appointee Cath. U. Am., 1973, 81, Inst. for Atomic Research, Ames, 1969, 70, 71, U. Mainz, W.Ger., 1980, 85; cons. Lawrence Livermore Lab., Calif., 1978-82. Contbr. articles to profl. jours. including Phys. Rev., Physics Letters, Nuclear Physics, Can. Jour. Physics, Zeitschrift für Physik. Served with USAF, 1953-57, Greece. Home: 970 Manakin Rd Midlothian VA 23113 Office: Dept Physics U Richmond Richmond VA 23173

SEABRIGHT, HUNTER STANLEY, accountant; b. Morganton, N.C., Jan. 29, 1925; s. Hunter Stanley and Carolyn (McConnell) S.; B.S. in Bus. Adminstrn., U. N.C., 1953; m. Ethel D. Myers, May 27, 1967. Accountant various firms, 1962-66, 67-72; agt. IRS, 1966-67; social worker, 1960-61; pvt. practice public acctg., North Wilkesboro, N.C., 1972—. Served with USNR, 1943-46, with AUS, 1954-57. C.P.A. Mem. Nat. Assn. Public Accts. Contbr. articles on taxation to profl. jours. Office: Hayes Brothers Bldg PO Box 1068 9th St North Wilkesboro NC 28659

SEABROOK, BONNIE MERCIER, risk and insurance executive; b. Atlanta, Oct. 13, 1947; d. D.B. and Louise (McCurry) Mercier; divorced; 1 son, Robert Hunter Seabrook. B.A., Clemson U., 1969; M.Ed., Clemson U., 1971. Tchr., Pickens County (S.C.) Sch. System, 1969-73; adult instr. Tri-County Tech, 1973-74; adminstrv. officer, personnel dir. W.B. Johnson Properties, Atlanta, 1976-77; ins. mgr. McBurney Corp., Atlanta, 1978-85; owner, risk mgr. Indsl. Risk Mgmt. Services, Atlanta, 1985—, AIG Ins. Co., 1985—; ins. cons.

Panhellenic House Corp. Assn., Emory U., Chi Omega. Named Miss Summerville (S.C.), 1967, 68; participant Miss S.C. Pageant, 1967, 68. Mem. Risk and Ins. Mgmt. Soc., Jaycees (hon.), Assoc. Builders and Contractors of Ga. (chmn. safety com., 1984-85, bd. dirs. 1985; Nat. award of excellence 1985), Angel Flight, Jr. League, Chi Omega (personnel advisor Emory U. chpt., nat. chmn. ins. 1982—, del. nat. conv. 1982, 84, leader Firesides House Corp. 1983), Kappa Delta Pi. Republican. Presbyterian. Home: 6830 Sunny Brook Ln Atlanta GA 30328

SEAGO, DALTON GILBERT, JR., energy company executive; b. Calhoun County, Miss., Aug. 10, 1929; s. Dalton Gilbert and Lena Rosella (Taylor) S.; grad. high sch.; m. Etta Vera Freeman, June 30, 1948; children—Larry Wayne, Robert Glenn, Sharon Allyse. Founder, Seago Enterprises, Inc., McComb, Miss., 1948 (merged with Mid Continent, Inc. 1974; name changed to Mid Continent Systems, Inc. 1976), now chmn. bd., chief exec. officer, chmn. exec. com., chmn. fin. com., West Memphis, Ark.; dir. Tallahatchie County Bank, Charleston, Miss. Bd. dirs. Life Action Ministries, 1976—, Kim's Ministries, 1978-79, Moody Adams Evangelistic Assn., 1977—, Mid-Am. Bapt. Theol. Sem., 1978—; past pres., bd. dirs. East McComb Activities Community Service; charter mem. Men of Miss., 1978. Mem. Nat. Assn. Truck Stop Operators, Nat. Petroleum Refiners Assn., Am. Trucking Assn., Nat. Automobile Transporters Assn., Am. Mgmt. Assn. Baptist. Office: 310 Mid Continent Plaza West Memphis AR 72301*

SEAGO, JOHN DURST, psychology educator; b. Greenwood, S.C., June 13, 1937; s. Pierce Turner and Helen Reid (Keith) S.; m. Frances Milburn Ratteree, June 27, 1964; 1 child, John Durst, III. A.A., Manatee Jr. Coll., 1960; B.S., Fla. State U., 1962, M.S., 1964; Ph.D., Tex. Christian U., 1970; Instr. biol. scis. Abraham Baldwin Coll., Tifton, Ga., 1964-66; prof. psychology Concord Coll., Athens, W.Va., 1971—, chmn. div. social scis., 1974—. Contbr. articles to profl. jours. Bd. dirs. Athens Med. Clinic, 1975-78, So. West Va. Area Agy. on Aging, Athens, 1976-78; mem. adminstrv. bd. Athens United Methodist Ch., 1976-78; town councilman Town of Athens, 1977-79. Grantee NASA, 1967, NSF, 1970. Mem. So. Soc. for Philosophy and Psychology (treas. 1985—), Animal Behavior Soc., Internat. Neuropsychology Soc., Sigma Xi. Democrat. Lodge: Lions (pres. 1976-77). Avocations: racquetball; golf. Home: PO Box 744 Athens WV 24712

SEAL, ENOCH, JR., college administrator; b. Poplarville, Miss., June 14, 1925; s. Enoch and Leo (Kirkland) S.; m. E. Layne Trickey, Dec. 27, 1951; children—Melva Layne, James Enoch, Ellis Clark, Mary Lee. B.S., Miss. State U., 1950, M.S., 1951. Instr., Pearl River Coll., Poplarville, 1951-64, registrar, 1964-71, dean acad. affairs, 1971—. Contbr. articles to profl. jours. Pres. Booster Club, Poplarville, 1971, Rotary Club, Poplarville, 1972. Recipient Alumnus of Yr. award Pearl River Jr. Coll., 1969. Mem. Miss. Jr. Coll. Deans' Assn. (pres. 1983-84), Phi Theta Kappa. Republican. Baptist. Home: 232 Highway 26 E Poplarville MS 39470 Office: Dean Acad Affairs Pearl River Coll Station A Poplarville MS 39470

SEAL, WILLIAM ASA, JR., exploration company executive, geophysicist; b. Wellington, Kans., July 29, 1925; s. William Asa and Mary Elizabeth (Mathew) S.; m. Leila E. Baucum, Nov. 24, 1950; children—Bradford, Jeffrey, Craig, Sally. B.S. in Geol. Engring., U. Okla., 1949. Jr. geophysicist Stanolind Oil & Gas Co., Vernal, Utah, 1949-50; party chief So. Geophys. Co., Tex. and N.Mex., 1950-53; supr., div. mgr. Continental Geophys. Co., Midland, Tex., 1953-67; div. mgr., v.p. Teledyne Exploration Co., Midland, 1967—; v.p. West Tex. Drilling Co., Midland, 1954-57. Served to lt. (j.g.) USNR, 1943-47; PTO. Mem. Am. Assn. Petroleum Geologists, Soc. Exploration Geophysicists (chmn. trustees 1973), West Tex. Geol. Soc., Permian Basin Geophys. Soc. (v.p. 1955-56). Republican. Episcopalian. Avocations: traveling; golf; hunting; fishing. Home: 1602 Winfield Rd Midland TX 79705 Office: Teledyne Exploration Co 2014 N Big Spring St Midland TX 79701

SEALE, MARGARET RUTH, music educator, bus. exec.; b. Knoxville, Ala., Apr. 20, 1915; d. James Andrew and Edna Lee (Phillips) Lamb; student Tulane U., 1958-59; B.Ch.Music, New Orleans Bapt. Theol. Sem., 1960, M.Ch. Music, 1962; m. Clifton Carter Seale, Nov. 9, 1941 (dec. May 20, 1977); children—Clifton Carter, Joy Ruth, Robert Hamilton. Soloist, chorister New Orleans Opera Co., 1943-53; ch. soloist, concerts in New Orleans, Mobile, Ala., Meridian, Miss., others, 1944-70; contract tchr., voice and piano New Orleans Bapt. Theol. Sem., 1945-62; music therapist Willowwood Home for Ret., 1972-74; owner, operator Marsile Music Co., New Orleans, 1974—; pres. Big Parade Corp., 1975—; pres. Marsile Music Pub. Co. Mem. adv. bd. Delta Festival Ballet Co. Music Therapy Fund, 1950—; active LWV, 1972—. Recipient New Orleans Mayor's awards, 1971, 75. Mem. La. Council for Music and Performing Arts, Nat., La., New Orleans (exec. bd.) music tchrs. assns., Nat. Fedn. Music Clubs (chmn. folk music 1975-79, chmn. sacred music 1979-87), Nat. Music Council (bicentennial coordinator), Nat. (bicentennial coordinator), La. (New Orleans dist. coordinator 1964-74, v.p. 1972-74, pres. 1974-76) fedns. music clubs, Gottschalk Soc., Greater New Orleans Music Club, Jr. Philharm. Soc., New Orleans C. of C. Aux., Gamma Xi, Mu Phi Epsilon. Author: (musical) Lil' Ol' Looziana; (songs) Welcome to New Orleans, Get-A-Goin', Lil' Ol' Looziana, Welcome to Louisiana, The Big Parade, Lovesong; (record) In The Now, 1975; (anthems) He Is Risen, Allelujah, Return To Me, It's So Wonderful; (solos) Oh that Men Would Praise the Lord, Unworthy As I Am; author, composer piano teaching series Fun for (Student's Name) and Friend. Home and office: 4674 Franklin Ave New Orleans LA 70122

SEALER, DAVID ARTHUR, electronics engineer; b. Ashland, Ohio, June 2, 1939; s. Elmer David and Florence Ellen (Britenbucher) S.; m. Constance Kay Marvin, Dec. 16, 1961; children—Tracey Sue, Kay Elizabeth. B.Sc., Ohio State U., 1962, Ph.D., 1965. Mem. tech. staff Bell Telephone Labs., Murray Hill, N.J., 1966-78; product dept. mgr. United Technologies Mostek, Carrollton, Tex., 1978-82; mng. dir. Advanced Micro Devices, Austin, Tex., 1982—. Mem. IEEE, Am. Phys. Soc., Sigma Xi, Phi Eta Sigma, Sigma Pi Sigma, Pi Mu Epsilon, Tau Beta Pi. Home: 7620 Kevin Dr Dallas TX 75248 Office: Advanced Micro Devices Ben White Blvd Austin TX 78744

SEALS, RYAN BROWN, electronics engineer; b. Coleman, Tex., July 23, 1920; s. William Harrison and Ocia Mae (Brown) S.; m. Mary Jo Taylor, Aug. 31, 1941 (div. Feb. 1942); m. Doris Jo Brown, Mar. 29, 1942 (div. Nov. 1961); 1 child, Sandra Jean Seals Harmes; m. Jeanette Ceil Meadows, July 28, 1967. B.A., North Tex. Agrl. Coll./Tex. A&M, 1941; B.S. in Physics and Math., Daniel Baker Coll., 1952; postgrad. So. Meth. U., Tex. Christian U., U. So. Miss., 1953-78. Cert. flight instr. Asst. chief engr. KNET Radio, 1941-42; asst. head electronics tng. Kelly Field, San Antonio, 1942-44; chief engr. KSTA Radio, Coleman, 1947-52; design engr. through project dir. Collins Radio Co., Dallas, 1952-71; cons. electronics, Dallas, Austin (Tex.), Los Angeles, 1972; systems engr., program mgr. Litton Data Systems div., Pascagoula, Miss., 1972-81, sr. staff engr., 1981-86; instr. Jackson County Jr. Coll., Gautier, Miss., 1972-80. Adviser, Elec. Ectronics Sch., Jackson County Jr. Coll., 1972-84; chief check pilot CAP Squadron Group 3 Miss., 1973-79. Served with USN, 1944-46. Mem. IEEE (sr.), Aircraft Owners and Pilots Assn., Exptl. Aircraft Assn. (chpt. founder, pres. 1980-83), Internat. Aerobatics Club (chpt. founder, pres. 1979-85, profl. ari show pilot). Presbyterian. Home: 3415 Princess Ann Dr Ocean Springs MS 39564 Office: PO Box 1618 Pascagoula MS 39567

SEALY, TOM, lawyer; b. Santa Anna, Tex., Feb. 18, 1909; s. Thomas Richard and Bessie Elizabeth (Harper) S.; m. Mary Velma McCord, Jan. 16, 1936; 1 dau., Nancy Sealy Thompson. LL.B., U. Tex., 1931. Bar: Tex. 1931. Atty., State Hwy Dept., State of Tex., 1933-35; mem., mng. ptnr. Stubbemann McRae, Sealy, Laughlin & Browder, Inc., Midland, Tex., 1935-81, sr. ptnr., 1981—; hon. dir. First City Nat. Bank of Midland. Chmn. bd. regents U. Tex., 1952-56, devel., 1963-65; trustee U. Tex. Law Sch. Found., pres., 1969-80; chmn. coordinating bd. Tex. Coll. and Univ. Systems, 1965-70; dir. Tex. Research League, chmn., 1965; bd. govs. Midland Meml. Found., 1984—. Recipient Disting. Alumnus award Ex-Students Assn., U. Tex., 1966; Outstanding Alumnus award U. Tex. Law Sch. Found., 1970; 50-Yr. award Tex. Bar Fellows, 1985; establishment by Atlantic Richfield Co. U. Tex. Law Sch. of Tom Sealy Research Professorship in Energy Law. Fellow Am. Bar Found., Tex. Bar Found.; mem. State Bar Tex., ABA, Internat. Assn. Ins. Counsel, Tex. Def. Counsel (pres. 1966), Southwestern Legal Found. (hon. trustee). Presbyterian. Clubs: Midland Country, Petroleum, Plaza, Racquet (Midland); Headliners (Austin); Chaparral (Dallas); Century II (Fort Worth); St. Anthony (San Antonio). Lodges: Mason, Shriners.

SEAMAN, JOHN GATES, lawyer; b. Galveston, Tex., Mar. 9, 1919; s. Harry Milton and Bera (Gates) S.; student U. Houston, summers 1938, 39; B.A., U. Tex., 1940, LL.B., 1942; m. Henri Etta Rester, Mar. 7, 1946; children—John G., Stephen H., Sandra Jane. Admitted to Tex. bar, 1942; practiced in Houston, 1946-51, Corpus Christi, Tex., 1951—; mem. firm Neel & Seaman, 1951-65, Keys, Russel, Watson & Seaman, 1965-75, Keys. Russell & Seaman, 1975—. Trustee, Art Mus. South Tex. Served to lt. USNR, 1942-46. Named adm. Tex. Navy. Mem. State Bar Tex., Am., Nueces County bar assns., Am. Judicature Soc., Am., Corpus Christi assns. petroleum landmen, Navy League, Phi Beta Kappa, Phi Delta Phi, Alpha Tau Omega. Democrat. Episcopalian. Kiwanian. Clubs: Century, Houston, Corpus Christi Town. Home: 618 Santa Monica St Corpus Christi TX 78411 Office: 1st City Bank Tower Corpus Christi TX 78477

SEAMANS, FRANCIS AUGUSTUS, oil company executive; b. Salem, Mass., Sept. 11, 1927; s. Richard D. and Nathelie P. (Gifford) S.; m. Mary Page, June 21, 1950; children—Stephen, David, Wendy, Timothy. B.S. in Physics, Harvard U., 1949. Geophysicist Texaco Inc., 1949-60, div. geophysicist, Colo., 1960-65, staff geophysicist, N.Y.C., 1965-70, mgr. div., Los Angeles, 1970-71, gen. mgr., N.Y.C., 1971-73, v.p., Bellaire, Tex., 1973—. Home: 222 Sugarberry Circle Houston TX 77024 Office: 1111 Rusk St Houston TX 77002

SEAR, ALAN MARTIN, public health educator; b. Chattanooga, Jan. 25, 1944; s. Louis and Rose E. (Rosenthal) S.; divorced; children—Celeste Elaine, Jacqueline Elise. B.S., U. Tenn., 1965, M.A., 1967; Ph.D. Purdue U., 1971. Research assoc., asst. prof. Tulane U., New Orleans, 1970-74; population studies researcher Inst. Health Services Research, New Orleans, 1973-74; chief research design and analysis unit Internat. Inst. Study of Human Reprodn., Columbia U., N.Y.C., 1974-76, research assoc., asst. prof. Regional Perinatal Network, 1976-78; assoc. prof. U. S.C., Columbia, 1978—; cons. numerous nat. and internat. agys. Campaign coordinator Eugene McCarthy presdl. campaign, Clinton County, Ind., 1968. Fellow Purdue Research Found., 1967-69. Mem. Am. Pub. Health Assn., AAAS, Population Assn. Am., Am. Sociol. Assn., S.C. Pub. Health Assn., Alpha Kappa Delta. Contbr. articles to profl. jours. Home: 2828 Larkhall Rd Columbia SC 29206 Office: Sch Public Health U SC Columbia SC 29208

SEAR, MOREY LEONARD, judge; b. New Orleans, Feb. 26, 1929; s. William and Yetty (Streiffer) S.; J.D., Tulane U., 1950; m. Lee Edrehi, May 26, 1951; children—William Sear II, Jane Lee. Admitted to La. bar, 1950; asst. dist. atty. Parish Orleans, 1952-55; individual practice law, New Orleans, 1955-71; spl. counsel New Orleans Aviation Bd., 1956-60; U.S. magistrate Eastern Dist. La., 1971-76; judge U.S. Dist. Ct. Eastern Dist. La., 1976—; judge Temporary Emergency Ct. Appeals, 1982—; mem. faculty Fed. Jud. Center, Washington, 1971—; adj. prof. Tulane U. Coll. Law; chmn. adv. com. on bankruptcy rules Jud. Conf. U.S., also ad hoc com. on bankruptcy legislation; mem. Jud. Conf. Com. on Adminstrn. Fed. Magistrates System Founding dir. River Oaks Pvt. Psychiat. Hosp., 1968; pres. Congregation Temple Sinai, 1977-79; bd. govs. Tulane Med. Center, 1976—; pres. Tulane Med. Center Hosp. and Clinic, 1976—. Mem. Am., New Orleans, La. bar assns. Office: 500 Camp St New Orleans LA 70130

SEARCY, KENNETH PAUL, petroleum geologist; b. Fort Bragg, N.C., Oct. 23, 1954; s. Paul Robert and Helen Ruth (Snyder) S. B.S. in Geology and Geophysics, U. Mo.-Rolla, 1977. Geologist, Mo. Dept. Natural Resources, Rolla, 1977-81, 82-83, Jefferson City, Mo., 1981-82; geologist Gulf Oil Corp., Oklahoma City, 1982-85; petroleum geologist Chevron U.S.A., 1985—. Mem. Oklahoma City Geol. Soc., Am. Assn. Petroleum Geologists (jr. mem.), Soc. Profl. Well Logging Engrs. Avocations: photography; mineral collecting; camping; travel. Home: 4307 NW 12 Oklahoma City OK 73107 Office: PO Box 12116 3625 NW 56th Oklahoma City OK 73157

SEARCY, WILLIAM NELSON, lawyer; b. Moultrie, Ga., June 26, 1942; s. Floyd Hartsfield and Anna (Pidcock) S.; m. Camille Heery, June 17,1967; 1 dau., Amelia Ashburn. A.B., U. Ga., 1964, J.D., 1967; LL.M. in Taxation, Washington U., St. Louis, 1968. Bar: Ga. 1967, U.S. Dist. Ct. (so. dist.) Ga. 1970, U.S. Ct. Appeals (5th cir.) 1976, U.S. Ct. Appeals (11th cir.) 1984. Assoc. Bouhan, Williams & Levy, Savannah, Ga., 1970-73; ptnr. Brannen, Wessels & Searcy, Savannah, 1973—; dir. Citizens Bank, Cairo, Ga.; asst. sec. Managed Industries, Inc.; sec. Am. Fed. Savs. and Loan Assn., 1978-81; adv. dir. Liberty Fed. Savs. & Loan Assn. Pres. Chatham-Savannah Voluntary Action Ctr., Inc., 1978-80. Served to lt. col. Air N.G., 1967—. Mem. ABA (sec. liaison tax com. S.E. region, chmn. 1984-85, sec. 1983-84), State Bar Ga. (chmn. taxation sect. 1983-84, mem.-at-large exec. council Young Lawyers Sect. 1975-78, chmn. conf. with Ga. Soc. C.P.A.s. 1979-81), Savannah Bar Assn. (pres. Younger Lawyers Sect. 1975-76), Am. Judicature Soc., Savannah Estate Planning Council. Clubs: Oglethorpe, Savannah Golf, Plimsoll (Savannah); Georgian (Atlanta). Office: PO Box 8002 Savannah GA 31412

SEARLE, PHILIP FORD, banker; b. Kansas City, Mo., July 23, 1924; s. Albert Addison and Edith (Thompson) S.; A.B., Cornell U., 1949; grad. Stonier Grad. Sch. Banking, Rutgers U., 1957, 64; m. Jean Adair Hanneman, Nov. 22, 1950; 1 son, Charles Randolph. With Geneva Savs. and Trust Co. (Ohio), 1949-60, pres., 1959-60; pres., sr. trust officer Northeastern Ohio Nat. Bank, Ashtabula, 1960-69, also dir.; pres., chief exec. officer BancOhio Corp., Columbus, 1969-75, also dir.; chmn., chief exec. officer Flagship Banks, Inc., Miami, Fla., 1975-84, also dir.; chmn. bd., dir. Sun Banks, Inc., Orlando, Fla., 1984—; dir. ALLTEL Corp.; former mem. faculty Ohio Sch. Banking. Ohio U., 1959-70, Nat. Trust Sch., Northwestern U., 1965-68. Past chmn. bd. regents Stonier Grad. Sch. Banking, Rutgers U., 1974-76, past mem. faculty; mem. corp. adv. com. Nat. Assn. Securities Dealers, 1981-83; v.p., mem. fed. adv. council to bd. govs. Fed. Res. System. Served to capt. AUS, 1943-46, 51-52. Decorated Bronze Star; named Outstanding Citizen in Ashtabula County, 1967. Mem. Am. Bankers Assn. (dir. 1972-74, governing council), Fla. Bankers Assn. (dir. 1979-81, council 1981), Ohio Bankers Assn. (pres. 1970-71), Assn. Bank Holding Cos. (dir. 1979-81, exec. com. 1981), Fla. Assn. Registered Bank Holding Cos. (pres. 1979-81), Fla. Council 100, Fla. C. of C. (dir. 1978-82), Phi Kappa Tau. Clubs: Bay Hill, Citrus (Orlando, Fla.). Co-author: The Management of a Trust Department, 1967. Mem. editorial adv. bd. Issues in Bank Regulation, 1978—. Address: 200 S Orange Ave Orlando FL 32801 also PO Box 2848 Orlando FL 32802

SEARLES, ANNA MAE HOWARD, educator, civic worker; b. Osage Nation Indian Terr., Okla., Nov. 22, 1906; d. Frank David and Clara (Bowman) Howard; A.A., Odessa (Tex.) Coll., 1961; B.A., U. Ark., 1964; M.Ed., 1970; postgrad. (Herman L. Donovan fellow), U. Ky., 1972—; m. Isaac Adams Searles, May 26, 1933; 1 dau., Mary Ann Rogers (Mrs. Herman Lloyd Hoppe). Compiler news, broadcaster sta. KJBC, 1950-60; corr. Tulsa Daily World, 1961-64; tchr. Rogers (Ark.) High Sch., 1964-72; tchr. adult class rapid reading, 1965-76; tchr. Rogers extension North Ark. Community Coll., 1972—; tchr. adult edn. Learning Center Benton County (Ark.), Bentonville, 1973-77, supr., 1977-79. Sec. Tulsa Safety Council, 1935-37; leader, bd. dirs. Kilgore council Girl Scouts U.S.A., 1941-44, leader, Midland, Tex., 1944-52, counselor, 1950-61; exec. sec. Midland Community Chest, 1955-60; gray lady Midland A.R.C., 1958-59; organizer Midland YMCA, Salvation Army; dir. women's div. Savings Bond Program, Midland; mem. citizens com. Rogers (Ark.) Hough Meml. Library, women's aux. Rogers Meml. Hosp.; sec. Beaver Lake Literacy Council, Rogers, 1973-85; bd. dirs. Globe Theatre, Odessa, Tex., Midland Community Theatre, Tri-County Foster Home, Guadalupe, Midland youth centers, DeZavala Day Nursery, P.T.A., Adult Devel. Center; sec. Little Flock Planning Commn.; publicity chmn. S. Central region Nat. Affiliation for Literacy Advance, 1977-78. Recipient Thanks badge Midland Girl Scout Assn., 1948. Mem. N.E.A. (del. conv. 1965), P.T.A. (life), Future Homemakers Am. (life), Ark. Assn. Public Continuing and Adult Edn. (state pres. 1980), S.Central Assn. Lifelong Learning (sec. 1981), Benton County Hist. Soc. (sec. 1981—), Internat. Reading Assn. (honored for services in the promotion of literacy 1985), Delta Kappa Gamma. Episcopalian. Clubs: Altrusa (pres.), Apple Spur Community (both Rogers). Home: Route 2 Rogers AR 72756

SEARS, ROBERT FREDERICK, JR., physics educator; b. Bowling Green, Ky., June 13, 1941; s. Robert Frederick and Virginia Ruth (Buchanan) S.; m. Martha Ann Snyder, June 12, 1965; children—Tekla Suzanne, Derek Jonathan, Amanda Elaine. Student Western Ky. State U., 1959-62; B.A., Centre Coll. Ky., 1963; Ph.D., U. Colo., 1968. Teaching asst. dept. physics U. Colo., Boulder, 1963-64, research asst., 1964-68; asst. prof. physics Austin Peay State U., Clarksville, Tenn., 1968-71, assoc. prof., 1971-78, prof., 1978—, chmn. dept. physics, 1977—. Author: Energy Environment Simulator Training Package, 1981. Mem. Am. Assn. Physics Tchrs. (chmn. sect. reps. 1983—, Tenn. sect. rep. 1977—). Democrat. Baptist. Lodge: Civitan (pres. local club 1980-81). Avocation: gardening. Home: 500 B Peterson Ln Clarksville TN 37040 Office: Austin Peay State U PO Box 4608 Clarksville TN 37044

SEATON, DOUGLASS, music educator, researcher; b. Balt., June 8, 1950; s. Ronald Stuart and Edith (Bender) S.; m. Gayle Ellen Saunders, June 9, 1972. Mus.B., Coll. of Wooster, 1971; M.A., Columbia U., 1973, M.Philosophy, 1974, Ph.D., 1977. Editor-in-chief Current Musicology, N.Y.C., 1977-78; asst. prof. Fla. State U., Tallahassee, 1978-83, assoc. prof. music, 1983—; vis. asst. prof. Yeshiva U., N.Y.C., 1977-78; cons. Prentice Hall, Englewood Cliffs, N.J., 1980—, Wadsworth Pub., Belmont, Calif., 1984, Schirmer Books, N.Y.C., 1984, Holt, Rinehart & Winston, N.Y.C., 1980-83. Contbr. articles to profl. jours. Mem. Am. Musicological Soc., Sonneck Soc., Coll. Music Soc. (pres. So. chapt. 1982-83), Southeastern 19th-Century Studies Assn., Southeastern Am. Soc. 18th-Century Studies. Democrat. Presbyterian. Avocation: tennis. Home: 2613 Faversham Dr Tallahassee FL 32303 Office: Fla State U Sch Music Tallahassee FL 32306-2098

SEATZ, LLOYD FRANK, plant and soil science educator; b. Winchester, Idaho, June 2, 1919; s. William Frank and Emma Lou (Hyder) S.; m. Dorothy Jane Whittle, Aug. 12, 1949; 1 son, William Lloyd. B.S., U. Idaho, 1940; M.S., U. Tenn.-Knoxville, 1941; postgrad. N.C. State U., 1941-42, Ph.D., 1949. Asst. prof. U. Tenn., Knoxville, 1947-49, assoc. prof., 1949-55, prof., 1955-61, prof. and dept. head, 1961—, Clyde B. Austin Disting. Prof. Agr., 1968—; agronomist and asst. br. chief TVA, 1953-55. Elder, Presbyterian Church. Served with AUS, 1942-46. Recipient citation for extraordinary service U. Tenn., 1979. Fellow Am. Soc. Agronomy, Soil Sci. Soc. Am.; mem. Internat. Soc. Soil Sci., Sigma Xi, Phi Kappa Phi, Gamma Sigma Delta, Omicron Delta Kappa, Phi Eta Sigma, Alpha Zeta. Contbr. tech. papers to jours. in field. Home: 9729 Tunbridge Ln Knoxville TN 37922 Office: PO Box 1071 Knoxville TN 39701

SEAY, FRANK H., federal judge; b. Shawnee, Okla., Sept. 5, 1938; s. Frank and Wilma Lynn S.; student So. Meth. U., 1956-57; B.A., U. Okla., 1960. LL.B., 1963; m. Janet Gayle Seay, June 2, 1962; children—Trudy Alice, Laura Lynn. Admitted to Okla. bar, 1963; atty. Seminole County, 1963-66; asst. dist. atty., 1967-68; assoc. dist. judge, 1969; judge Okla. Dist. Ct. 22, 1975-79, chief judge; now chief judge U.S. Dist. Ct. Eastern Dist. Okla. Mem. Am. Bar Assn., Okla. Bar Assn., Seminole County Bar Assn. Democrat. Clubs: Masons, Elks. Lions. Office: PO Box 828 Muskogee OK 74401*

SEAY, HARRY LAUDERDALE, III, lawyer; b. Dallas, Dec. 16, 1937; s. Harry Lauderdale and Nancy (Boggess) S.; m. Joan Garratt, Dec. 11, 1965; children—Elizabeth Garratt, Katherine Lauderdale. B.A., Princeton U., 1959; LL.B., Yale U., 1964. Bar: Okla. 1965. Atty. U.S. Dept. Justice, Washington, 1964-66; assoc. Doerner, Stuart, et al, Tulsa, 1966-70; shareholder Hall, Estill, et al, Tulsa, 1970-83; sole practice, Tulsa, 1984—; lectr. on law and soc. U. Tulsa, 1984. Bd. dirs. Holland Hall Sch., Tulsa, 1976-82, Okla. Arts Inst., 1983—, Concertime, Tulsa, 1976—, Planned Parenthood Northeastern Okla., Tulsa, 1973-79, 84—, Tulsa Met. Ministry, 1984—. Served to lt. (j.g.) USNR, 1959-61. Mem. ABA, Okla. Bar Assn., Tulsa County Bar Assn. (chmn. publs. com., exec. com. 1980-82, 84-85). Democrat. Unitarian. Clubs: Southern Hills, Tulsa. Avocations: skiing; gardening. Home: 2154 E 32d Pl Tulsa OK 74105 Office: 320 S Boston Bldg Suite 714 Tulsa OK 74103

SEBASTIAN, MICHAEL JAMES, manufacturing company executive; b. Chgo., 1930; married. B.S.M.E., Santa Clara U., 1950; grad. advanced mgmt. program Harvard U., 1972. Div. mgr. bearing div. FMC Corp., 1953-77; pres. Rotek, 1977-78; v.p., gen. mgr.-rotary machine div. Gardner-Denver Co., 1978-79; pres. Cooper petroleum and exploration equipment group Cooper Industries Inc., 1979-80, corp. v.p.-ops., Houston, 1980-82, exec. v.p. ops. for compression and drilling equipment, 1982-85, exec. v.p., 1985—. Office: Cooper Industries Inc PO Box 4446 Houston TX 77210

SEBEL, MAY L., legal administrator; b. Dallas, Dec. 7, 1936; d. Milton J. Loeb and Helen A. (Pearlstone) Loeb; children—Lee, Lauren. B.A. in Religion, Northwestern U., 1960; postgrad. in liberal arts So. Meth. U., 1969-71. Owner Innovations, Dallas, 1972-73; pres. G.M. Mart Personnel Service, Inc., Dallas, 1972-73; showroom mgr. Nat. Ekelman & Assocs., Dallas, 1972-76; asst. v.p. customer relations, dir. export sales The Lorch Co., Dallas, 1976-81; asst. dir. adminstrn. Thompson & Knight, Dallas, 1981-84; adminstr. Maxwell, Godwin & Carlton, Dallas, 1984—. Mem. Fashion Group Inc., Assn. Legal Adminstrs.; assoc. mem. ABA. Jewish. Club: Brookhaven Country (Dallas). Office: Maxwell Godwin & Carlton 3300 Interfirst Plaza Dallas TX 75202

SEBRING, MARJORIE MARIE ALLISON, home furnishings company executive; Burnsville, N.C., Oct. 8, 1924; d. James William and Mary Will (Ramsey) Allison Shockey; student Mars Hill Coll., 1943, Home Decorators Sch. Design, N.Y.C., 1948, Wayne State U., 1953; cert. home furnishings rep. U. Va., 1982; 1 dau., Patricia Louise Banner Krohn. Dir. decorating div. Robinson Furniture, Detroit, 1949-57; head buyer Tyner Hi-Way House, Ypsilanti, Mich., 1957-63; head buyer Town and Country, Dearborn, Mich., 1963-66; instr. Nat. Carpet Inst., 1963-65; owner Adams House, Inc., Plymouth, Mich., 1966-72; exec. v.p. mktg. and sales, regional sales and mktg. mgr. Triangle Industries, Los Angeles, 1972—; co-owner Markham-Sebring, Inc., St. Petersburg, Fla., 1983—; dir. contract div. Kane Furniture, 1984-85; co-owner Accessories, Etc., 1985—; rep. at large Heritage Lakes, U.S. Homes. Mem. Presdl. Task Force. Recipient nat. sales awards, recognition for work with youth and aged. Mem. Internat. Home Furnishings Assn., Fla. Home Furnishings Rep. Assn. (officer), Fla. Furniture Dealers Assn., USCG Aux., Nat. Audubon Soc., Internat. Platform Assn. Republican. Contbr. creative display to Better Homes and Gardens, 1957-64. Home: 2601-3 Grist Mill Circle New Port Richey FL 33552

SECHREST, THOMAS LEE, government official; b. Jacksonville, Fla., Jan. 8, 1949; s. Tracy Alvin Lee and Ann Elizabeth (Morrisey) S. B.A., Fla. State U., 1971, M.S., 1973. Television producer-dir. State of Fla., Tallahassee, 1973-76; ind. TV producer, Atlanta, 1976-78; tng. specialist Employment and Tng. Adminstrn., U.S. Dept. Labor, Atlanta, 1978-83; tng. dir. Occupational Safety and Health Adminstrn., Atlanta, 1983—; ind. cons., Atlanta, 1980—; co-writer tng. design Mgmt. Consultraining Co., Fayetteville, Ga., 1983—. Contbr. chpt. to book, articles to profl. jours. Recipient Meritorious Service award for TV programming Nat. Apprenticeship Program, 1976, disting. Achievement award for tng. design, 1985. Mem. Ind. Media Artists Ga., Am. Soc. for Tng. and Devel., Soc. Govt. Meeting Planners, Atlanta Bus. and Profl. Guild, Virginia-Highland Civic Assn., Beta Theta Pi (Chub Rich scholar 1971). Club: Atlanta Venture Sports (bd. dirs. 1977-82, pres. 1981). Avocations: home remodeling; all-terrain bicycling; piano. Home: 701 Park Dr NE Atlanta GA 30306

SECREST, VICKIE LYNN, nurse, hospital administrator; b. Wheeling, W.Va., Aug. 6, 1954; d. Clyde Allen and Loretta Marlene (Hopkins) S. B.S.N., U. Ky., 1976; M.S., Ohio State U., 1979. R.N., Ky., Ohio, La. Head nurse Mercy Hosp., Portsmouth, Ohio, 1978; nurse coordinator VA Med. Ctr., Lexington, Ky., 1979-81, asst. chief nurse trainee, 1981-83; asst. chief nursing service VA Med. Ctr., Shreveport, La., 1983-84; assoc. chief nursing service VA Med. Ctr., North Little Rock, Ark., 1984—. Vol. ARC, Portsmouth, 1976-78; mem. Pax Christi, Lexington and Sport, La., 1980-84; bd. dirs. Parish Council, Shreveport, 1983-84; mem., speaker Shreveport Lupus Found., 1984. Mem. Am. Soc. Nursing Service Adminstrs., Ohio State U. Alumni Assn., Nat. League for Nursing, Sigma Theta Tau. Roman Catholic. Club: Newman Ctr. (Lexington). Avocations: creative writing; reading; needlepoint; walking. Office: VA Med Ctr North Little Rock Div 4300 W 7th St Little Rock AR 72205

SEDGWICK, ALEXANDER, historian, educator; b. Boston, June 8, 1930; s. William Ellery and Sarah (Cabot) S.; m. Charlene Mary Maute, June 24, 1961; children—Catherine Maria, Alexander Cameron. B.A., Harvard U., 1952, Ph.D. in History, 1963. Asst. prof. history Dartmouth Coll., 1962-63; asst. prof. U. Va., Charlottesville, 1963-66, assoc. prof., 1966-74, prof., 1974—, chmn. history dept., 1979-85, dean Coll. Arts and Scis., 1985—; mem. adv. screening com. in history Sr. Fulbright Awards Council for Internat. Exchange of Scholars. Served with AUS, 1952-54. Fulbright fellow, 1960-62; recipient Am. Council Learned Socs. grant-in-aid, 1967-78, Am. Philos. Soc. grant-in-aid, 1971. Mem. AAUP (nat. council 1976-79), Soc. French Hist. Studies (sec. 1979-83, pres. 1983-84), Am. Hist. Assn. Author: The Ralliement in French Politics 1890-98, 1965; The Third French Republic, 1870-1914, 1968; Jansenism in Seventeenth Century France, Voices in the Wilderness, 1977; contbg. author Church, State and Society under the Bourbon Kings of France, 1982. Home: 1409 Rugby Rd Charlottesville VA 22903 Office: U Va Dept History Randall Hall Charlottesville VA 22903

SEDKI, SABAH SAM, accounting educator; b. Kirkuk, Iraq, July 1, 1943; came to U.S., 1964; s. Sedki S. and Nadima (Saleh) S.; m. Deborah Jean Joyner, July 16, 1982; children—Laila Rene, Alia Joy. B.A., U. Baghdad, 1963; M.B.A., Ft. Hays Kans. State U., 1967; Ph.D., U. No. Colo., 1973. Sr. acct. Parkview, Inc., Kansas City, Mo., 1967-69; asst. prof. Dakota State Coll., Madison, S.D., 1969-74; asst. prof. U. Wis.-Eau Claire, 1974-75; asst. dean Eastern Ill. U., Charleston, 1975-78; assoc. prof. bus. U. Mont., Great Falls, 1978-81; chmn. dept. acctg. St. Mary's U., San Antonio, Tex., 1981—; acct., tax cons. J. Woloszyn, Architect, Great Falls, 1979-81. Mem. Am. Acctg. Assn. (program chmn. southwestern region 1983—, dir., 1983—, now v.p.), Nat. Assn. Accts. (manuscript dir. 1983—), Southwestern Fedn. Adminstrv. Disciplines (dir. 1983—). Republican. Lodge: Rotary. Author articles. Office: Saint Mary's Univ 1 Camino Santa Maria San Antonio TX 78284

SEDLER, MYRNA WILLIAMS, pharmacist, hospital pharmacy executive; b. Rochester, N.Y., Aug. 23, 1930; d. Roger Vincent and Ruth (Leavens) Williams; m. Raphael M. Sedler, May 20, 1955 (div. May 1973); children—Leslie Ann, Herbert B., Jennifer Marleah. B.S. in Pharmacy, U. Buffalo, 1952; M.P.A., Nova U., 1981. Registered pharmacist, N.Y., Fla. Staff pharmacist Strong Meml. Hosp., Rochester, 1952-55; community pharmacist Miami Springs (Fla.) Pharmacy, 1960-63; co-owner, pharmacist Franjo Pharmacy, Miami, Fla., 1963-73; staff pharmacist Jackson Meml. Hosp., Miami, 1973-75, supr. controlled substances, 1975-78, pharmacy mgr., 1978, supr. ambulatory pharmacy, 1978-79, supr. Inst. Rehab. Pharmacy, 1979-81, supr. decentralized pharmacy, 1981-84, pharmacy quality circle facilitator, 1982—, cons. pharmacist, 1974-86; mem. Speakers Bur., Pharmacy Assn., Miami, 1963; intern preceptor U. Fla. Coll. Pharmacy, Miami, 1982-84. Mem. bd. Miami Dance Theatre Ballet Co., 1982, founding pres., 1982-83; treas. Howard Drive Elem. PTA, Miami, 1970-71. Mem. S.E. Fla. Soc. Hosp. Pharmacists (treas. 1978-79), Sigma Kappa. Home: 8502 SW 103rd Ave Miami FL 33173 Office: Univ of Miami/Jackson Meml Med Center 1611 NW 12th Ave Miami FL 33136

SEEBASS, TILMAN, musicologist; b. Basel, Switzerland, Sept. 8, 1939; came to U.S. 1977; s. Adolf Ludwig and Julie (Gaupp) S.; m. Marie Elisabeth Mischler, Mar. 23, 1968; children—Felicitas Anne Julie, Valentin Donatus Georg. Gymnasium, Basel, 1959; Ph.D., Basel U., 1970. Asst. U. Basel, 1967-70; research fellow Swiss Nat. Funds, Switzerland, 1970-75; mng. dir. Haus der Buecher, Basel, 1975-77; asst. prof. Duke U., Durham, N.C., 1977-79, assoc. prof., 1979—. Author: The Representation of Music and the Illustration of the Book of Psalms, (2 vols.), 1973, Musical Autographs in Basel, 1975. Editor: International Yearbook of Musical Iconography, 1981, Imago Musicae, vol. 1, 1984—. Author: (with others) The musical manuscripts of the Paul Sacher Collection, 1976, The Music of Lombok, 1976. Contbr. articles to profl. jours. Field Research grantee Swiss Nat. Funds, 1972-73, travel grantee Am. Council Learned Socs., Duke Research Council, M.D. Biddle Found., 1981, 82. Office: Dept of Music Duke U 6695 College Station Durham NC 27708

SEED, PATRICIA, historian, educator; b. Balt., Sept. 20, 1949; d. John Cathro and Pauline (Sullivan) S.; m. George E. Marcus, June 22, 1984. B.A., Fordham U., 1971; M.A., U. Tex., 1975; Ph.D., U. Wis., 1980. Lectr. Ohio U., Athens, 1979; asst. prof. Coll. Charleston, S.C., 1980-82; asst. prof. history Rice U., Houston, 1982—; vis. researcher Nat. Anthropology Inst., Mex., 1976-78. Contbr. articles to profl. jours. Fellow Tinker Found, 1984, NEH, 1981, Social Sci. Research Council, 1976-78, Fulbright Found., 1976-77. Mem. Am. Hist. Soc., Latin Am. Studies Assn., Conf. Latin Am. History. Avocations: ballet; modern dance. Office: Rice U PO Box 1892 Houston TX 77251

SEEGAR, CHARLON IONE, hospital social worker, psycho therapist, educator; b. Denver, May 13, 1936; d. Wilner Hopson and Cordelia Ione (Lipham) S.; A.B., LaGrange Coll., 1959; M.S.W., U. N.C., Chapel Hill, 1964. Social worker Am. Nat. Red Cross Service to Mil. Hosps., Ft. Jackson, S.C., 1959-61, Maxwell AFB Hosp., Ala., 1962-63, Ft. Bragg Army Hosp., N.C., 1964-65, U.S. Army Hosp., Frankfurt Am Main, Germany, 1965-67, Charleston (S.C.) Naval Hosp., 1967; family planning cons. Dept. Family and Children Services, State of Ga., 1967-69; chief social worker maternal and infant care project, family planning project dept. ob-gyn Med. Coll. Ga., 1969-80, asst. prof., 1980—, social scientist, 1980—, coordinator outpatient div., 1980—; cons. community hosps. and nursing homes, 1975—; adj. instr. Sch. Social Work, U. Ga., 1983— lectr. in field. Treas., SCLC, Augusta, Ga., 1969-73. Mem. Nat. Assn. Social Workers (dir. 1969-75), Planned Parenthood E. Central Ga. (dir. 1975-80), Mental Health Assn. Ga., Mental Health Assn. Augusta, Ga. Conf. Social Welfare, Nat. Assn. Female Execs., Epilepsy Assn. Ga., Research Orgn., AAUW, LWF. Home: 5 Lakeshore Loop August GA 30904 Office: 1515 Pope Ave Dept Psychiatry Med Coll Ga Augusta GA 30912

SEEGMILLER, RAY REUBEN, machinery manufacturing company executive; b. Dysart, Iowa, 1935; married. B.S., Drake U. Sr. systems analyst Arthur Andersen & Co., 1957-61; div. controller Southwest Forest Industries, 1963-68; fin. analyst Motorola Inc., 1968-69; with Marathon Mfg. Co., Houston, 1969—, controller, 1972-73, v.p., fin. officer, 1973-78, v.p., treas., 1978-79, exec. v.p., chief fin. officer, from 1979, now exec. v.p., also dir. Served with U.S. Army, 1957-63. Office: Marathon Mfg Co 600 Jefferson Houston TX 77208*

SEERDEN, BETTY MARLENE, mfg. co. exec.; b. Old Gulf, Tex., Aug. 30, 1932; d. Lenon Earl and Josie Margaret (Seerden) Mason; student public schs., Bay City, Tex.; m. Doyle A. Bridges, Jr., May 16, 1951; children—Pamela A. Bridges Theis, Michael Alan, Patrick Lee; m. H. Murray Seerden, Mar. 5, 1975. Bookkeeper, B.F. Goodrich, Beaumont and Bay City, Tex., 1953-54, Pepsi Cola Co., Baton Rouge, 1966-67; with Bay City Newspapers, 1965—, bus. mgr., 1972—, officer, 1981—. Presbyterian. Clubs: Fraternal Order of Eagles Aux. (pres. 1978-79, trustee and v.p. 1981—), Matagorda County Genealogical Soc. (historian 1981—). Home: 1613 Highland Dr Bay City TX 77414 Office: PO Box 1551 Bay City TX 77414

SEGAL, MARILYN MAILMAN, psychologist, developmental psychology educator; b. Utica, N.Y., Aug. 9, 1927; d. Abraham and Alice (Lyons) Mailman; children—Betty, Wendy, Richard, Patti, Debbie. B.A., Wellesley Coll., 1948; B.S., McGill U., 1949; Ph.D., Nova U., 1970. Social worker Floating Hosp., Boston, 1950-51; dir. Preschool of Hollywood, Fla., 1955-60, Univ. Sch., Fort Lauderdale, Fla., 1960-62; prof. devel. psychology Nova U., Fort Lauderdale, 1962—; dir. Nova Univ. Family Ctr., Fort Lauderdale, 19890—; trustee U. Miami, Fla., 1970—; chmn. A.L. Mailman Family Found. Author: Run Away Little Girl, 1975; Social Competence, 1977; Play and Learn, 1978; Just Pretending, 1981; Making Friends, 1982; All About Child Care, 1983; Your Child at Play: Birth to One, One to Two, Two to Three, 1985; Play Together, Grow Together, 1985. Chmn. nat. vis. com. Sch. Nursing, U. Miami, 1982—. Recipient Chief award Ind. Colls. and Univs., 1982-83; named Woman of Yr., Fort Lauderdale Bus. and Profl. Women's Club, 1981-82; Woman of Yr., Brandeis U. Nat. Woman's Commn., 1982; Citizen of Yr., Hollywood Civitan Club, 1978. Mem. Am. Psychol. Assn., Soc. Research in Child Devel., Delta Kappa Gamma. Democrat. Jewish. Home: 919 S South Lake Dr Hollywood FL 33019 Office: Nova Univ Family Ctr 3301 College Ave Fort Lauderdale FL 33314

SEGAL, SHIRLEY ROSLYN, vocational rehabilitation counselor, psychotherapist; b. N.Y.C., July 31, 1927; d. Lester J. and Alice (Newhouse) Klawber; m. Paul Manuel Segal, Apr. 4, 1954; children—Charles Lawrence, Brad Marshall. A.A., Manatee Community Coll., 1974; M.A., U. South Fla., 1982. Cert. rehab. counselor. Counselor, Womens Ctr. and Doctors Hosp., Sarasota, Fla., 1983-84, alcohol counselor, 1984; rehab. vocational counselor Fla. Dept. Health and Rehab., Sarasota, 1984—. Mem. Republican Com. Dist. 32, Sarasota, 1984—. Mem. Am. Assn. Counseling and Devel., Am. Mental Health Counselors Assn. Avocations: Scuba diving; sailing; tennis; singing. Home: 1458 Palmwood Dr Sarasota FL 33582 Office: Vocational Rehab 1864 17th St Sarasota FL 33580

SEGERS, HOUSTON RANDOLPH, sales, educational and motivational materials company executive, income tax consultant, clergyman; b. Atlanta, Aug. 2, 1941; s. Henry Tolbert and Mary Magdalene (Gaff) S.; m. Betty Ruth Bamberg, June 16, 1961; 1 dau., Lenora Denise. Student Chipola Jr. Coll., 1960; student Nat. Tax Tng. Sch., 1969, Southeastern Pentecostal Bible Sch., 1970. Ins. agt. Ind. Life, Quincy, Fla., 1961-62; job requisitioner Food Machinery, Lakeland, Fla., 1962-63; night watchman Fla. State Hosp., Chattahoochee, 1963-65; prodn. mgr. Coca Cola Bottling Co., Marianna, Fla., 1965-83; owner H.R. Segers Tax Cons., Sneads, Fla., 1970—; owner, pres. Possibilities Unltd., Sneads, Fla., 1983—; ordained to ministry Pentecostal Ch. of God, 1974; pastor Little Rocky Tabernacle, Marianna, Fla., 1972-74; corp. sec., treas. Ga. Dist. Pentecostal Ch. of God, Junction City, Ga., 1975—. Mem. East Jackson County Ministerial Assn. (sec., treas. 1983—). Democrat. Home: Davis St Sneads FL 32460 Office: Possibilities Unlimited Davis St Sneads FL 32460

SEGERSON, EDWARD CARMACK, JR., reproductive physiologist, educator, researcher, consultant; b. Alexandria, La., June 5, 1943; s. Edward Carmack and Anne Rose (Foppiano) S.; m. Lucy Jean Ford, Mar. 19, 1976; 1 dau., Jennifer Ann. B.S., Memphis State U., 1966, M.S., 1972; Ph.D., N.C. State U., 1975. Formulation chemist Chemform Chem. Co., Memphis, 1967-70; postdoctoral research assoc. Ohio Agr. Research and Devel. Ctr., Wooster, 1975-77; research scientist, lectr., assoc. prof. dept. animal sci. N.C. Agr. and Tech. U., Greensboro, 1977—; cons. in livestock reprodn.; mem. So. region Reproductive Physiology Research Group; seminar speaker livestock extension meetings N.C., Va. Vol. probation aide, 1975-77; vol. firefighter, McLeansville, 1978-82; asst. chief. Kimesville Vol. Fire Dept., 1982—; com. mem. Kimesville Community Watch Program, 1982—. KBJ Ranch fellow, 1977; Coop. State Research Service U.S. Dept. Agr. grantee, 1977—; NIH grantee, 1979. Mem. Am. Soc. Animal Sci., Inst. Nutrition, Soc. for the Study of Reprodn., AAAS, Sigma Xi, Gamma Sigma Delta. Democrat. Roman Catholic. Contbr. articles to profl. jours. Home: 6518 Dusty Rd Liberty NC 27298 Office: N C Agr & Tech U 101 Animal Sci Bldg Greensboro NC 27411

SEGUINOT DE MENDEZ, ROSA, English educator; b. Anasco, P.R., Aug. 16, 1944; d. Ramon and Natividad (Montes) Sequinot; m. Victor J. Mendez, June 14, 1969; children—Vanessa, Michelle. B.A., Catholic U., Ponce, P.R., 1967, M.Ed., 1974. Cert. tchr., P.R. English tchr. Dept. of Instrn., Ponce, 1967-74; English instr. Ponce Technol. Coll., U. P.R., 1974-85, mem. Acad. Senate, 1979-81, mem. personnel com., 1982—. Mem. Assn. Tchrs. of Tech. Writing, Am. Bus. Communication Assn., Assn. Caguax Villa Taina Resort (pres. women's assn., 1984—), Phi Delta Kappa. Club: Lioness (Ponce). Avocation: reading. Home: F-B-13 Urb Jacaranda Ponce PR 00731 Office: Ponce Technol U Coll Ponce PR 00732

SEGURA, NAIDA SYLVIA, school counselor; b. Kingsville, Tex., May 31, 1943; d. Edmundo Leyva and Guadalupe (Gonzalez) Garcia; m. Luis Mendias Segura (dec. Dec. 1983); children—Elvia T., Orlando R. B.A. in English, Incarnate Word Coll., 1965; tchr. certification, St. Mary's U., 1968, M.A., 1980. Lic. profl. sch. counselor Tex. Tchr. English, Southwest Middle Sch., San Antonio, 1965-68; tchr. English and Spanish, Lakeside High Sch., Atlanta, 1968-69; English tchr. Southwest High Sch., San Antonio, 1970-78, Pease Middle Sch., San Antonio, 1978-80; elem. sch. counselor Northside Ind. Sch. Dist., San Antonio, 1980—; state advisor Future Tchrs. Am., San Antonio, 1974-75; counselor, cons. Sunshine Cottage Sch. Hearing Impaired, 1984—; sch. counselor Dolores B. Linton Elem. Sch., 1980—. Speaker Hispanic Women's Conf., San Antonio, 1984, Fed. Program Parents, San Antonio, 1982; judge U. Tex. Prose Reading, San Antonio, 1985, Harlandale Ind. Sch. Dist. Festival Cultural Prose Reading, San Antonio, 1985; 1st v.p. Linton Elem. Sch. PTA, 1985-86. Named Tchr. of Yr., Southwest Educators Assn., 1975, Outstanding Educator, Tex. Tchrs. Assn. 1976; Outstanding Educator Pease Middle Sch. 1979, Tchr. of Yr., 1979; recipient Outstanding Achievement award Northside Ind. Sch. Dist., 1984; Inst. Coop. Ibero-Am. scholar, Madrid, 1984. Mem. Southwest Personnel and Guidance Assn., Tex. Personnel and Guidance Assn., S.W. Educators Assn. (pres. 1974-75), Am. Assn. Counseling and Devel., Career Counselors Tex., Northside Counselors, Assn., United Teaching Profession, NEA, Tex. State Tchrs. Assn., San Antonio Area Women Deans, Adminstrs. and Counselors, Mexican Am. C. of C. San Antonio. Democrat. Roman Catholic. Home: 1422 E Sunshine Dr San Antonio TX 78228 Office: Dolores B Linton Elem Sch 2103 Oakhill Rd San Antonio TX 78238

SEHN, JAMES THOMAS, urological surgeon; b. Detroit, July 26, 1945; s. Francis James and Celestine (Fredericks) S.; m. Christine Calta, June 10, 1972; 1 child, Alexander James. A.B., Sacred Heart Sem., Detroit, 1967; M.D., Georgetown U., 1972; M.Sc., Oxford U., England, 1979. Diplomat Am. Bd. Urology. Intern Univ. Hosp., Ann Arbor, Mich., 1972-73; resident Yale-New Haven Hosp., 1974-78; postdoctoral fellow Yale U., 1975-76, instr., 1976-78; attending physician Prince William Hosp., Manassas, Va., 1979—, chief of surgery, 1982-83. Contbr. articles to profl. publs. Research fellow NIH, 1975. Fellow ACS; mem. Am. Urol. Assn., Alpha Omega Alpha. Roman Catholic. Club: Oxford Soc. Home: Wootton House Middleburg VA 22117 Office: Prince William Hosp 9580 Surveyor Ct Manassas VA 22110

SEHORN, MARSHALL ESTUS, music industry executive; songwriter; b. Concord, N.C., June 25, 1934; s. William Thomas and Bertha (Mesmer) S.; m. Barbara Ann Darcy, May 11, 1934. B.S. in Agr., N.C. State Coll., 1957; B.A. in Music, Belmont Coll., 1981, Council Devel. of French in La., 1983. Owner, operator comml. farm, Concord, 1957-58; producer, co-owner Fury/Fire Records, N.Y.C., 1958-63; producer EMI, London, 1963-64; pres., co-owner Marsaint/Sansu Enterprises, New Orleans, 1965—; sec., co-owner Sea-Saint Studio, New Orleans, 1972—; pres. Jefferson Jazz, New Orleans, 1980—. Producer: (recording) Kansas City (gold record 1959), 1959; co-producer: (recording) Lady Marmalade (gold record 1974), 1974; pub.: (song) Southern Nights (Broadcast Music, Inc. award 1977), 1975; exec. producer: (album) Elvis Live at La. Hayride, 1983. Presdl. appointee Civil Rights Com., Washington, 1961; mem. NAACP, New Orleans, 1961—; gov.'s appointee La. Music Commn., Baton Rouge, 1981—; presdl. appointee Anti-Piracy Commn., Washington, 1981-85. Named Record Man of Yr., Am. Record Mfg. and Distbrs. Assn., 1961, Producer of Yr., 1961; recipient Outstanding Service award Gov. of La., 1979, 82; Outstanding Music Contbn. award Mayor of New Orleans, 1982. Mem. Broadcast Music Inc., Am. Songwriters Assn. (cons., Merit award), Am. Fedn. Musicians, Recording Engrs. Assn., New Orleans C. of C., Ducks Unltd. (Slidell, La.). Republican. Methodist. Clubs: Bass Anglers Am. (New Orleans) (life). Avocations: boating; fishing; songwriting; hunting; art collecting. Home: 10136 Idlewood Pl River Ridge LA 70123 Office: Sea-Saint Recording Studio 3809 Clematis Ave New Orleans LA 70122

SEIBEL, GEORGE HENRY, JR., retired ammunition specialist; b. Centralia, Ill., Apr. 21, 1921; s. George Henry and Marie Sophia (Johnson) S.; student Greer Coll., Chgo., 1939-41, also numerous mil. schs.; m. Estelle Lucille Gulley, Oct. 24, 1948; children—Lorita Joeann, Georgeania Marie, Clifford George, Henry Curtis. Enlisted U.S. Army Air Corps, 1939, advanced to sgt. U.S. Air Force, 1954; ret., 1962; various positions in county and state govt., 1962-66; civilian with U.S. Army, 1966—, surveillance insp. ammunition Blue Grass Army Depot, Richmond, Ky., 1971-73, chief chem. def. team Anniston (Ala.) Army Depot, 1973-79; chief surveillance 193d Inf. Brigade and So. Command, Panama, 1979-81; ret. 1982; cons. in field. Mem. bd. Valier (Ill.) High Sch., 1963-64, Valier Grade Sch., 1963-64; city water and road commr., Valier, 1964. Decorated numerous area ribbons, letters of appreciation and commendation. Mem. Pearl Harbor Survivors Assn. (life), Am. Def. Preparedness Assn., Am. Security Council (nat. adv. bd.), USAF Sgts. Assn., Nat. Hist. Soc., Early Am. Soc., AIAA, Am. Fedn. Govt. Employees. Clubs: USAF Non-Commnd. Officers, Elks. Inventor electronics devices. Home: 607 Briarwood Ave Oak Ridge Estates Eastaboga AL 36260

SEIDEL, ANDREW DAVID, urban affairs educator; b. N.Y.C., Dec. 15, 1949; s. Jacob Carl and Essie (Jablon) S. L.Archt., Royal Danish Acad., 1971; B.Arch., Pratt Inst., 1972; M.C.P., Harvard U., 1974; Ph.D., U. Mich., 1980. Lic. real estate broker. Instr., Harvard U., Cambridge, Mass., 1974-75; asst. prof. SUNY-Buffalo, 1976-80; assoc. prof. urban affairs U. Tex.-Arlington, 1980—; dir. UNESCO Man and the Biosphere Program, N.Y.C., 1983—. Editor-in-chief Jour. Archtl. and Planning Research, 1980—. Contbr. articles to profl. jours. Author: Property Damage in Schools, 1974 (Progressive Architecture award), 1974; Microcomputers in Local Government, 1985. Cons. Dallas Housing Authority, others. Nat. Endowment Arts fellow; Nat. Assn. Schs. Pub. Affairs and Adminstrn. fellow, 1982-83; others. Mem. Environ. Design Research Assn. (dir. 1979-82), Am. Planning Assn., AAAS, Internat. Assn. Applied Psychology, People and Phys. Environ. Research Assn. (Australia). Jewish. Avocations: computers; camping; canoeing; rafting. Home: 3812 Hastings Ct Arlington TX 76013 Office: U Tex 544 University Hall Arlington TX 76019

SEIDEMAN, CHARLES HENRY, financial company executive; b. West Bend, Wis., June 18, 1927; s. Ray F. and Clara S. (Gerner) S.; m. Hertha Krueger, Oct. 6, 1945; children—Sandra K., Steven C., David L., Dean S., D. Mark. B.S. in Edn., U. Nebr.-Omaha, 1965; M.B.A., George Washington U., 1974. Commd. 2d lt. U.S. Army, 1949, advanced through grades to col., 1969; F.A. and procurement officer; service in Europe, Korea, Thailand; ret., 1975; propr. Capital Mgmt. Cons., Austin, Tex., 1975—; chmn. bd. Capital City Leasing, Inc., Austin, 1979—, Capital City Fin. Services, Inc., Austin, 1983—; pres. Capital Concrete Inc., Houston. Decorated Legion of Merit (3), Bronze Star, Meritorious Service medal. Mem. Nat. Contract Mgmt. Assn., Assn. Govtl. Leasing and Fin., Western Assn. Equipment Lessors. Republican. Presbyterian. Lodge: North Austin Rotary. Home: 11109 Spicewood Club Dr Austin TX 78750 Office: 4901 Spicewood Springs Rd Austin TX 78559

SEIDENSTICKER, ROBERT BEACH, tobacco company executive; b. N.Y.C., July 28, 1929; s. Richard Frank and Mildred (Beckwith) S.; m. Verna Williams, June 9, 1951; children—Robert Beach, Sarah Elizabeth. B.S., U. Md., 1955. Mng. dir. internat. ops. Larus & Bros. Co., Inc., Richmond, Va., 1956-68; area dir. Philip Morris Internat., Lausanne, Switzerland, 1968-71; sr. v.p. Rothmans of London, Inc., Richmond, 1971-73; pres. Liggett & Meyers, Internat., Durham, N.C., 1974-78; group v.p. tobacco cos. GrandMet U.S.A., Inc., Owensboro, Ky., 1978—; dir. Durham region N.C. Nat. Bank, 1977—; dir., mem. exec. com. Tobacco Inst., Washington, 1978—; dir. Smokeless Tobacco Council, 1981-84; dir. Owensboro Nat. Bank. Vice pres. N.C. World Trade Assn., Raleigh, 1977; trustee Ky. Wesleyan Coll., 1984. Mem. Am. Mgmt. Assn., Nat. Assn. Mfrs., Tobacco Mchts. Assn. Am. (pres. 1981-82), Durham C. of C. (bd. dirs. 1978). Republican. Clubs: Hope Valley Country, Owensboro Country. Home: 32 Stone Creek Park Owensboro KY 42301 Office: PO Box 986 Owensboro KY 42301

SEIFER, RONALD LESLIE, psychologist; b. Liberty, N.Y., Oct. 23, 1942; s. Leon and Pearl (Treibitz) S.; m. Gail Sandra Eagerman, May 29, 1967; children—David Marc, Robert Eric. B.A., Queens Coll., 1964; M.A., Northeastern U., 1967; Ph.D., U. Miami, 1971. Lic. psychologist, Fla., N.Y. Intern psychologist Albert Einstein Coll. Medicine, Bronx, N.Y., 1968-69; psychologist St. Vincent's Hosp., Harrison, N.Y., 1969-71; supervising psychologist Saratoga County Mental Health Ctr., Saratoga Springs, N.Y., 1971-76; psychologist Brevard County Mental Health Ctr., Melbourne, Fla., 1976-79; pvt. practice clin. psychology, Melbourne, 1978—; assoc. med. staff Holmes Regional Med. Ctr., Melbourne, 1979—; Mem. adv. com. exceptional edn. Brevard County Sch. Bd., Rockledge, Fla., 1980—; coach Satellite Beach Little League, Fla., 1981—; asst. coach Youth Soccer Assn., Satellite Beach, 1981—. Research fellow Northeastern U., 1964-66. Mem. Am. Psychol. Assn., Am. Soc. Clin. Hypnosis, N.Am. Soc. Psychology of Sport and Phys. Activity, Brevard County Psychol. Assn. (pres. 1979-80). Avocations: gardening, fishing. Office: Melbourne Psychiatry 1317 S Oak St Melbourne FL 32901

SEIGLER, AUBREY BELMONT, labor relations exec.; b. Hawthorne, Fla., Oct. 16, 1921; s. James Gardnier and Bertha Mable (Davis) S.; grad. Carlisle Mil. Sch., Bamberg, S.C. Locomotive engr. Seaboard Railroad, Wildwood, Fla., 1941; with Seaboard Air Line Ry., 1941—, chmn. legis. bd., 1969—; vice chmn. bd. appeals Brotherhood of Locomotive Engrs., Cleve., from 1971, now chmn. bd. appeals. Served with AUS, 1942-45; CBI. Named Ky. Col., Ark. Traveler, Lt. Col., Ala. State Militia. Mem. S.E. Assn. Locomotive Engrs., Southeastern Meeting Assn. Democrat. Baptist. Mason (Shriner, 32 deg.), Elk.

SEIGLER, ELIZABETH MIDDLETON, counselor; b. Athens, Ga., Aug. 18, 1928; d. Robert Meriwether and Marie (Davis) Middleton; m. Charles Judson, Aug. 24, 1955; children—Mary Seigler Sullivan, Charles Middleton. B.S.Ed., U. Ga., 1949; M.Ed., 1955; Ed.S., Ga. State U., 1976. Tchr., coach Talbot County High Sch., Talbotton, Ga., 1949-50; tchr. Atlanta Public Schs., 1950-60, counselor, 1960—. Mem. Atlanta Sch. Counselors Assn., Am. Sch. Counselors Assn., Ga. Sch. Counselors Assn., Am. Assn. Counseling and Devel., Delta Kappa Gamma, Alpha Lambda Delta, Kappa Delta Pi. Baptist. Avocations: gardening; camping.

SEIGLER, MICHAEL EDWARD, lawyer; b. Tallahassee, Oct. 14, 1948; s. Claude Milo and Roberta Bradford (Whitfield) S.; m. Janet Cummings, Feb. 19, 1971; children—Kelly Elizabeth, Megan Whitfield. A.A., Lake Sumter Community Coll., 1968; B.S., Fla. State U., 1970, M.S., 1974; J.D., Atlanta Law Sch., 1980. Bar: Ga. Cert. tchr., librarian. Tchr., Sumter Correctional Inst., Bushnell, Fla., 1970-73; asst. library dir. Leesburg Pub. Library (Fla.), 1974-75, library dir., 1975-77; library dir. Atlanta Law Sch., 1979-81; atty. Brooks & Brock, Marietta, Ga., 1981-83; librarian Port Charlotte Pub. Library (Fla.), 1983-84; assoc. Brooks & Brock, Marietta, Ga., 1985, Brock & Barr, Marietta, 1985—; judge pro hac vice State Ct. Cobb County, 1986. Contbr. articles to jours. Vol. worker ACLU, Atlanta, 1979; mem. Fla. State U. Library Com., Tallahassee, 1974, Children's Program Com., Port Charlotte, 1983, Port Charlotte Cultural Ctr. Adv. Com., 1984—; mem. Cobb County Democratic Exec. Com., 1986; mem. jud. council Young Dems. Ga., 1986—; mem. exec. com. Cobb Christmas, 1986-87. Named Tchr. of Yr., Sumter Correctional Inst., 1973. Mem. Nat. Library Assn. (com. chmn. 1975-76), Fla. Library Assn. (caucus chmn. 1976-77), ABA, Atlanta Bar Assn., Fla. State U. Alumni Assn. (life), Atlanta Law Sch. Alumni Assn. (treas. 1986-87), Mensa. Episcopalian. Lodges: Masons, Shriners. Home: 2027 Palace Dr Smyrna GA 30080 Office: Brock & Barr 30 S Park Sq Marietta GA 30060

SEILER, ROBERT CHARLES, geologist; b. North Tonawanda, N.Y., Nov. 29, 1941; s. Robert Carl and Evelyn Lillian (Krupp) S.; m. Jean Ruth Chase, Sept. 21, 1963; children—Michael, Eric. B.A., SUNY-Buffalo, 1969, M.A., 1970. Geologist, Atlantic Richfield Co., Dallas, 1970-73, Jakarta, Indonesia, 1973-76, Tulsa, 1976-81; regional exploration mgr. Omni Exploration, Radnor, Pa., 1981-82; dist. geologist Santa Fe Energy Co., Tulsa, 1982-84, exploration mgr., 1984-86, dist. geologist, 1986—. Served with USAF, 1961-65. Mem. Am. Assn. Petroleum Geologists (cert.). Republican. Lutheran. Avocations: golf; fishing. Home: 101 W Winston Ct Broken Arrow OK 74011 Office: Santa Fe Energy Co 1 W 3d St Tulsa OK 74103

SEITH, ROBERT THEODORE, management consultant; b. Racine, Wis., Aug. 12, 1926; s. Theodore Lewis and Ruth (Cleaver) S.; B.S. in Chem. Engring., Purdue U., 1949; cert. mgmt. cons. Inst. Mgmt. Cons.; m. Ruth Marilyn Sievert, Oct. 12, 1946; children—Michael Robert, Deborah Lynn, Elizabeth Jane. With Mosinee Paper Mills Co. (Wis.), 1949-69, successively research chemist, dir. product devel., sales mgr., 1957-61, v.p. marketing, 1961-69, exec. v.p. Celluponic System, Inc., 1962-69; v.p. marketing, paper div. Gulf States Paper Corp., 1969-77; mgmt. cons., 1977—; dir. Bag West Paper Co., 1965-69; dir. Shuld Mfg. Co. Active Children's Service Soc. Wis., Wis. Assn. for Mental Health. Co-chmn. Republican party Marathon County, 1953. Served with AUS, 1944-46. Mem. Def. Supply Assn. (dir., past pres. Midwest), Salesmens Assn. Paper Industry (v.p. Wis. div. 1962-63, nat. pres. 1966—), Am. Paper Inst. (bd. govs.), Am. Legion, Bleached Converting Assn. (dir.), Kraft Paper Assn. (exec. com. 1960, mem. research and devel. com.), Ala. World Trade Assn., Assn. Mgmt. Cons., Am. Legion, Sigma Phi Epsilon. Lutheran. Mason, Lion (pres. 1953-54). Author various articles profl. jours. Patentee in field. Home: 808 Indian Hills Dr Tuscaloosa AL 35401 Office: 512-514 Alabama Federal Bldg Tuscaloosa AL 35401

SEITHER, FRANCES GARDNER, nursing education administrator; b. Gerlaw, Ill., Mar. 4, 1924; d. Wilbur L. and Evelyn Gardner; m. Curtis C. Luffman; children—John Seither, Deborah Sharp, Richard Seither. B.S., U. Md.-Balt., 1965, M.S., 1968; Ph.D., U. Md.-College Park, 1971. Coordinator child psychology Sch. Nursing, U. Md., Balt., 1971-72, coordinator grad. program, 1972-74; asst. dean grad. studies Sch. Nursing, U. Mo., Columbia, 1974-78; dean Coll. Nursing and Health Services, Radford U., Va., 1978—; bd. mem. Radford U. Found., 1983-85. Contbr. articles to books and jours. City planning commn. City of Radford. Mem. Am. Nurses Assn., Nat. League for Nursing, Va. League for Nursing (treas. 1982-84), Sigma Theta Tau, Phi Kappa Phi. Presbyterian. Home: Route 1 Box 466A Radford VA 24141 Office: Dean of Nursing Radford U University Station Radford VA 24142

SEKADLO, ROGER GEORGE, airport manager; b. Two Rivers, Wis., Dec. 14, 1924; s. George Frank and Linda Marie (Arneman) S.; student U. Wis., 1946-48; B.S., Purdue U., 1951; m. Caron Marie Cockerham, Dec. 31, 1983; children by previous marriage—Steven, Penny, Nancy. Pilot, Purdue Aeros. Corp., West Lafayette, Ind., 1951; mgr. Municipal Airport Authority, Erie, Pa., 1951-57; airport dir. Milwaukee County, Wis., 1957-61; aviation dir. City Fort Worth, 1961-67; exec. dir., mgr. Greensboro-High Point Airport Authority,

Greensboro, N.C., 1967—. Instr. airport mgmt. Guilford Tech. Inst., Jamestown, N.C., 1971-72. Served as pilot USAAF, 1943-46. Decorated Bronze Star. Mem. Airport Operators Council Internat. (dir. 1971-75), Am. Assn. Airport Execs. (dir. 1966-69, 73-78, pres. 1978-79, pres. S.E. chpt., 1984-85). Lutheran. Elk, Rotarian (dir. 1976-79). Home: 3107 Robinhood Dr Greensboro NC 27408 Office: Box 8113 Greensboro NC 27419

SELBST, KENNETH ROBERT, physician; b. Phila., June 15, 1949; s. Sidney Zigmund and Sophie (Singer) S.; m. Arlene Ina Adler, Aug. 20, 1977; children—Daniel, Brian, Jonathan. B.A., Temple U., 1970; M.D., NYU, 1974. Diplomate Am. Bd. Ob-Gyn. Intern, Jackson Meml. Hosp., Miami, Fla., 1974-75, resident, 1975-78; clin. instr. ob-gyn U. Miami Sch. Medicine, 1979—; practice medicine specializing in ob-gyn, Broward County, Fla., 1978—; mem. staff Broward Gen. Med. Ctr., Pembroke Pines Gen. Hosp., Humana Hosp., Bennett, Plantation Gen. Hosp., Jackson Meml. Hosp. Fellow Am. Coll. Obstetricians and Gynecologists; mem. AMA, Fla. Med. Assn., Broward County Med. Assn., Ft. Lauderdale Ob-Gyn Soc., William A. Little Ob-Gyn Soc. Office: 2301 N University Dr Suite 202 Pembroke Pines FL 33024

SELBY, JOHN HORACE, surgeon; b. Springfield, Mass., Nov. 11, 1919; s. Howard Williams and Ethel (Wagg) S.; A.B., Dartmouth Coll., 1941; M.D., Boston U., 1944; postgrad. U. Pa., 1948; children (by previous marriage) John H., Susan, Sherrill, Lucinda; m. 2d, Carolyn Symes, Feb. 14, 1970. Intern Mary Hitchcock Meml. Hosp., Hanover, N.H., 1944-45; resident New Eng. Deaconess Hosp., 1945-46, Portsmouth Naval Hosp., 1946-48, Mass. Meml. Hosp., 1949-50, Boston City Hosp., 1950-51 (all Boston), practice medicine, specializing in thoracic surgery, Lubbock, Tex., 1952—; chief thoracic surgery Meth. Hosp., Lubbock, 1964-73, 77-79, chief surgery, 1954-56, 64-65; chief of staff St. Mary's Hosp., Lubbock, 1973, chief surgery, 1970; chief surgery Univ. Hosp., 1973; active staff Meth. Hosp., St. Mary's, Health Scis. Center; courtesy staff Highland Hosp., med. dir., 1985—; hon. staff West Tex. Hosp.; cons. staff South Park Hosp., Meml., Seminole, Mercy, Slaton, Cook Meml., Levelland hosps.; regional med. dir. Tex. Med. Found., 1986; chmn. bd. South Plains Health Systems, 1975-81; mem. Statewide Health Coordinating Council, 1977-85, exec. com., 1979; clin. prof. surgery Tex. Tech. Med. Sch., 1975—; mem. adv. com. Lubbock County Hosp. Dist. Bd., 1979; trustee, med. dir. All Am. Security Life Ins. Co., 1954-55. Bd. dirs. Tex. Tb Assn., pres., 1967-68; bd. dirs. Lubbock Community Planning Council, 1954-56; chmn. adv. bd. Salvation Army, 1956-57; bd. dirs. Inst. for Internat. Research and Devel.; bd. dirs. Lubbock Area Found., 1983—, treas., 1985. Diplomate Am. Bd. Thoracic Surgery, Am. Bd. Surgery. Fellow A.C.S., Am. Coll. Chest Physicians, Internat. Coll. Surgeons, Internat. Acad. Medicine, Southwestern Surg. Coll.; mem. So. Thoracic Surgery Assn., S.W. Surg. Conf., Am. Thoracic Soc., Tex. Trudeau Soc. (pres. 1959-60), Lubbock-Crosby-Garza County Med. Soc. (pres. 1984), Panhandle S-Plains Med. Soc., Tex. Med. Assn. (ho. of dels. 1979—, com. on health planning 1979-83, council on socioecons. 1983—), AMA, Am. Cancer Soc. (dir. Tex. div. 1961-63), South Plains Heart Assn. (pres. 1957), Lubbock County Tb Assn. (pres. 1959-60). Club: Rotary Internat. (pres. Lubbock 1980-81, dist. gov.'s rep. 1981-82, gov. nominee 1982-83, gov. 1983-84). Home: Park Tower 1617 27th St Lubbock TX 79405 Office: 4809 University St Suite 201 Lubbock TX 79413

SELBY, MILTON EUGENE, retail grocery store manager; b. Cherry, N.C., Nov. 30, 1931; s. Beegie and Zular Virginia (Baum) S. m. Grecia Marva Hickman, July 12, 1963 (div. Nov. 1976); children—Bridget Eileen, Ericka Eugenia. A.A., Norfolk State U., 1952; postgrad. U. Wash., 1964-68, SUNY-Albany, 1982. Sales rep., sales supr. Life Circulation Co., Inc., Seattle, 1958-66; prodn. controller comml. airplane div. Boeing Airplane Co., Seattle, 1966-70; self-employed ins. broker, Virginia Beach, Va., 1970-75; convenience store night mgr. Southland Corp., Norfolk, Va., 1971-73; personnel dir. Blvd. Supermarkets, Chesapeake, Va., 1973-82; prodn. controller power plant div. Naval Air Rework Facility, Naval Air Sta., Norfolk, Va., 1978-83; mgr. Cavalier Foods, Suffolk, Va., 1983—; pres. Deep Creek Co., Inc., Virginia Beach, 1981—. Advisor, Jr. Achievement, Norfolk, 1982. Mem. Nat. Assn. Self-Employed. Office: Cavalier Foods 900 W Washington St Suffolk VA 23434

SELBY, NANCY ANN, educational administrator; b. South Bend, Ind., Sept. 15, 1935; d. Cletus F. and Mildred (Mauck) Chizek; m. David Keith Selby, June 22, 1957; children—Pamela Ann, Katherine Jean, Susan Louise, Elizabeth Ellen. B.S., Miami U., Oxford, Ohio, 1957. Mktg. dir. Verbal Communication, Dallas, 1972-79; pres. Spine Edn. Ctr., Dallas, 1979—; adv. dir. Greater Dallas Safety Council, 1985—. Author: Care for Your Back, 1983. Mem. Am. Soc. Safety Engrs. (treas. 1985, chpt. membership chair 1984—), Tex. Safety Assn. (dir. 1985—, faculty 1981—), Am. Soc. Tng. and Devel. Pi Beta Phi. Episcopalian. Republican. Club: Royal Oaks Country (Dallas). Avocations: golf; aerobics; photography; sailing. Office: SpineEdn Ctr 6161 Harry Hines Blvd 312 Dallas TX 75235

SELDON, JAMES RALPH, economics educator; b. Newmarket, Ont., Can., July 4, 1944; came to U.S., 1981; s. James Menzies and Annie May (Coupland) S.; m. Zena Katherine Aronoff, Oct. 19, 1974; May child, James D. B.A. with honours, Carleton U., Ottawa, Ont., 1966; Ph.D., Duke U., 1969. Asst. prof. U. Man., Winnipeg, Can., 1969-76, assoc. prof., 1976-83; assoc. prof. econs. Auburn U., Montgomery, Ala., 1981-83, prof., 1983—; cons. Hosp. Services Commn., Winnipeg, 1970, Consumer & Corp. Affairs, Winnipeg, 1970-71, Provincial Cabinet Planning Com., Winnipeg, 1972, various law firms, Montgomery, 1984—. Author: Microeconomics and the Canadian Economy, 1973, 2d edit., 1983, Macroeconomics and the Canadian Economy, 1973, 2d edit., 1983; also profl. articles. Mem. Am. Econ. Assn., Can. Econs. Assn., So. Econ. Assn., Can. Health Econs. Research Assn., Omicron Delta Epsilon. Clubs: Midland Golf and Country (Ont.); Bonnie Crest Country (Montgomery). Avocations: golf; skiing; philately. Home: 1249 Edgeworth Dr Montgomery AL 36109 Office: School of Bus Auburn U Montgomery AL 36193

SELDON, ZENA ARONOFF, economics educator; b. San Francisco, Dec. 24, 1947; d. Samuel and Edith Elizabeth (Moyer) Aronoff; m. James Ralph Seldon, Oct. 19, 1974; 1 child, James David. B.S., Iowa State U., 1969, M.S., 1971; Ph.D., U. Man., Can., 1979. Instr.-asst. U. Man., 1976-81; asst. prof. Auburn U., Montgomery, Ala., 1981—. Contbr. articles to profl. jours. Active fund raising Heart Fund, Montgomery, 1984-85. Recipient Teaching award Commerce Students Assn., U. Man., 1979-80. Mem. Acad. Mgmt., Am. Econ. Assn., Southwestern Econ. Assn., Southwestern Soc. Sci. Assn. (women's caucus program chair, 1984-85, pres. 1985—), Can. Econ. Assn. Pub. Choice Soc., Am. Soc. Transp. and Logistics, Ala. Acad. Sci., Omicron Delta Epsilon. Club: Bonnie Crest Country (Montgomery). Avocations: golf, skiing. Home: 1249 Edgeworth Dr Montgomery AL 36109 Office: Dept Econs Auburn U Montgomery AL 36193

SELF, JAMES CUTHBERT, textile company executive; b. Greenwood, S.C., Oct. 19, 1919; s. James Cuthbert and Lura (Mathews) S.; m. Virginia Turner, Jan. 24, 1942; children—James Cuthbert, Virginia Preston, William Mathews, Sally Elizabeth. B.S. in Bus. Adminstrn. The Citadel, LL.D., 1961; Dr. Industry (hon.), Lander Coll., 1964; LL.D., U. S.C., 1973; H.H.D., Erskine Coll., 1975. With Greenwood Mills, Inc., 1935—, asst. treas., 1943-49, treas., 1949-55, pres., 1955—; dir. S.C. Nat. Bank. Pres. Self Found., Greenwood; trustee Duke Endowment, Charlotte, N.C.; life mem. bd. trustees Clemson (S.C.) U. Served from 2d lt. to maj. AUS, 1941-46. Mem. S.C. Textile Mfrs. Assn. Columbia, Greenwood C. of C., Am. Textile Mfrs. Inst., N.Y. Cotton Exchange. Methodist. Clubs: Rotary (Greenwood); Metropolitan (N.Y.C.). Home: 1 S Cedar Dr Greenwood SC 29646 Office: Greenwood Mills Inc Drawer 1017 Greenwood SC 29646*

SELIG, OURY LEVY, port executive; b. Galveston, Tex., Sept. 24, 1924; s. Andrew Lionel and Freda (Schreiber) S.; m. Miriam Claire Pozmantier, Aug. 22, 1948; children—Madeline, Debra, Michael, James. B.B.A., U. Tex., 1949; postgrad. U. Tex., 1950, U. Houston, 1953-56. Office mgr. Calif. Cotton Mills, Uniontown, Ala., 1950-51; asst. comptroller J.T. Flagg Knitting Co., Florence, Ala., 1951-52; asst. bus. adminstr. hosps. U. Tex. Med. Br., Galveston, 1952-54; asst. office mgr. H. Kempner, Galveston, 1954; acct. Port Galveston (Tex.), 1954-57, asst. auditor, 1957-64, asst. to gen. mgr., 1964-69, dir. fin. and adminstrn., 1969-74, dep. exec. dir., 1974—; chmn. risk mgmt. com. Am. Assn. Port Authorities; pres. Tex. Water Conservation Assn., 1979-80. Mem. exec. bd. Bay Area council Boy Scouts Am., 1963—; trustee Galveston County Jewish Welfare Assn. Served with USAAF, 1943-46. Recipient Nehemiah Gitelsohn award Alpha Epsilon Pi, 1948; Silver Beaver award Boy Scouts Am., 1968; Shofar award, 1968; Disting. Service award Jaycees, 1968; named Galveston County Father of Yr., 1967. Mem. Galveston C. of C. (past dir.; chmn. govt. affairs com.), Risk and Ins. Mgmt. Soc., Mcpl. Fin. Officers Assn., Pub. Risk and Ins. Mgmt. Assn., Tex. Water Conservation Assn., Nat. Waterways Conf., Gulf Intracoastal Canal Assn. Sierra Club, Galveston Hist. Found. Democrat. Jewish. Lodge: B'nai B'rith. Club: Propeller. Home: 11 Colony Park Circle Galveston TX 77551 Office: 8th Floor Shearn Moody Plaza 123 Rosenberg Galveston TX 77550

SELIGMAN, LINDA HELEN, counselor educator, psychologist; b. Hartford, Conn., Feb. 17, 1944; s. Irving and Florence (Scolnick) Goldberg; m. Eugene Barry Seligman, June 3, 1973 (div. 1978). A.B., Brandeis U., 1966; M.A., Tchrs. Coll., N.Y.C., 1968; Ph.D., Columbia U., 1974. Psychology intern VA Hosp., N.Y.C. and Newark, 1969-73; lectr. Bklyn. Coll., 1973-74; prof. counselor edn. CUNY, S.I., 1974-77; prof. counselor edn. George Mason U., Fairfax, Va., 1977—, assoc. chmn., 1981-85; cons. psychologist Montgomery County Dept. Corrections, Rockville, Md., 1984—, South Md. Hosp., Clinton, 1979-82, Salvation Army, N.Y.C., 1975-77; pvt. practice psychology, Laurel, Md., also Alexandria, Va., 1979—. Author: Assessment in Developmental Career Counseling, 1980; Diagnosis and Treatment Planning in Counseling, 1986. Editor Jour. Am. Mental Health Counseling Assn., 1983—. Contbr. articles to profl. jours. Mem. Am. Psychol. Assn., Am. Assn. Counseling and Devel., Va. Mental Health Counseling Assn. Home: 6114 Lynley Terr Alexandria VA 22310 Office: Dept Edn George Mason U 4400 University Dr Fairfax VA 22030

SELIN, IVAN, computer services company executive; b. N.Y.C., Mar. 11, 1937; s. Saul and Freda (Kuhlman) Selicoff; B.E., Yale U., 1957, M.E., 1958, Ph.D., 1960; Dr. es Sciences, U. Paris, 1962; m. Nina Cantor, June 8, 1957; children—Douglas, Jessica. Research engr. Rand Corp., Santa Monica, Calif., 1960-65; systems analyst Dept. Def., Washington, 1965-67, dep. asst. sec. def., 1967-69, acting asst. sec. for systems analysis, 1969-70; founder, Am. Mgmt. Systems, Inc., Arlington, Va., 1970—; cons. to govt.; lectr. UCLA, 1961-63. Bd. dirs., gov. UN Assn. U.S.; bd. dirs. Greater Washington Research Center. Tennis Patrons Assn., Washington; chmn. mil. econ. adv. panel Dir. CIA. Decorated Disting. Civilian Service medal; Fulbright scholar, 1959-60; Ford Found. grantee, 1952-54. Mem. Council Fgn. Relations, Fed. City Council Washington, Young Pres.' Orgn., IEEE (editor Trans. on Ifo. Theory 1960-65), Sigma Xi, Tau Beta Pi. Club: Yale. Author: Detection Theory, 1964; contbr. articles to profl. jours. Home: 2905 32d St NW Washington DC 20008 Office: 1777 N Kent St Arlington VA 22209

SELL, BETTY MARIE, library director, educator; b. Coplay, Pa., Oct. 31, 1928; d. William Frederick and Margaret Louisa (Wormick) Haas; m. Kenneth D. Sell, Sept. 17, 1949; children—Peter Daniel, Rebecca Anne. B.S., Ursinus Coll., Pa., 1950; M.R.E., Lancaster (Pa.) Theol. Sem., 1953; M.S., Fla. State U., 1967, A.M.L.S., 1976, Ph.D., 1981. Ednl. missionary United Ch. of Christ, Honduras, 1956-65; instr., asst. librarian Fla. State U., Tallahassee, 1966-68; instr., acquisitions librarian Livingston Coll., Salisbury, N.C., 1968-70; asst. prof. library sci. Catawba Coll., Salisbury, 1970-76, assoc. prof., 1976-83, prof., 1983—, library dir., 1970—. Co-author: Divorce in the U.S., Canada and Great Britian (Outstanding Reference Book of 1978 ALA; Choice Book of Yr., Family Relations jour.), 1978; Suicide: A Guide to Reference Sources, 1980; co-editor: (series) Social Problems and Social Issues, 1977-81; contbg. author: Library Effectiveness: State of the Art, 1980. Sec. LWV, Salisbury, 1968-70; nat. treas. Assn. Couples for Marriage Enrichment, 1977-81; v.p. So. chpt. Hist. Soc. Evang. and Ref. Ch., 1971—; pres. Salisbury-Rowan Family Life Council, 1977-79. U.S. Higher Edn. Act fellow, 1975-76. Mem. ALA, Southeastern Library Assn., N.C. Library Assn., Assn. Coll. and Research Libraries, Library Adminstrn. and Mgmt. Assn., Library Research Roundtable, Women Adminstrs. in N.C. Higher Edn., AAUP (state pres. 1983-84), Delta Kappa Gamma, Beta Phi Mu. Democrat. Mem. United Ch. of Christ. Home: Route 9 Box 112 Salisbury NC 28144 Office: 2300 W Innes St Salisbury NC 28144

SELL, KENNETH DANIEL, sociologist, educator; b. Littlestown, Pa., Apr. 29, 1928; s. Stanley Reginald and Mabel O'Dell (Forry) S.; m. Betty Marie Haas, Sept. 17, 1949; children—Peter, Rebecca. B.S., Ursinus Coll., 1950; B.D., Lancaster Theol. Sem., 1954; cert. Escuela de Idiomas, San Jose, Costa Rica, 1957; M.Ed., Pa. State U., 1961; Ph.D., Fla. State U., 1968. Ordained to ministry United Ch. of Christ, 1954. Pastor Trinity Charge, New Bloomfield, Pa., 1954-57; ednl. missionary United Ch. of Christ, San Pedro Sula, Honduras, 1957-65; instr. Fla. State U., 1967-68; assoc. prof. sociology Livingstone Coll., 1968-72; assoc. prof. Catawba Coll., 1968-72, prof. sociology, 1972—, chmn. dept. sociology, social work and anthropology, 1974—. Mem. Am. Sociol. Assn., So. Sociol. Soc., Nat. Council on Family Relations, Groves Conf. on Marriage and Family, Assn. Couples for Marriage Enrichment. Democrat. Club: Elks. Author: (with Betty Sell) Divorce in the United States, Canada, and Great Britain (ALA Outstanding Reference Book Com. selection 1978), 1978; (with David Lester and Betty Sell) Suicide: A Guide to Information Sources, 1980; Divorce in the 70s: A Subject Bibliography, 1981. Home: Route 9 Box 112 Salisbury NC 28144 Office: Catawba Coll Salisbury NC 28144

SELLARS, TONY DEWAYNE, television and radio sportscaster, writer; b. Wichita Falls, Tex., Sept. 2, 1954; s. Robert Kenneth and Blanche Gertrude (Hansard) S. B.A., Okla. Christian Coll., 1974. Lic. broadcaster FCC. Asst. news dir. Sta. KEBC, Oklahoma City, 1974-76; state capitol corr. Sta. KOCO-TV, Oklahoma City, 1976-78, asst. sports dir., 1978-84; sportscaster Sta. KWTV, Oklahoma City, 1984—; pres. State Capitol Broadcast Com., Oklahoma City, 1977-78; elector Heisman Meml. Trophy, N.Y.C., 1982—; mem. selection com. Okla. Sports Hall of Fame, 1985. Newspaper columnist Okla. Jour., 1980—. Contbg. editor Lawton Mag./Texhoma Monthly, 1980-83. Writer, producer video presentations. Del. Okla. Dem. Conv., 1984; vol. fundraiser United Cerebral Palsy, Am. Cancer Soc., Oklahoma City. Recipient Best Radio Broadcast award AP, 1975; award of excellence for sports coverage UPI, 1982. Mem. Am. Sportscasters Assn., Nat. Press Photog. Assn. Avocations: record collecting; athletic activities. Home: 2404 Northwood Ln Edmond OK 73034 Office: Sta KWTV 7401 N Kelley St Oklahoma City OK 73113

SELLEN, ROBERT WALKER, historian, educator; b. Topeka, Oct. 13, 1930; s. Arthur G. and Grace E. (Walker) S.; m. Donna Deck, July 12, 1952. A.B., Washburn U., 1952; A.M. (Danforth fellow), U. Chgo., 1955, Ph.D. (Univ. fellow), 1958. Asst. prof., assoc. prof. history Baker U., Baldwin City, Kans., 1958-64, dept. chmn., 1963-64; assoc. prof. history Ga. State U., Atlanta, 1964-68, prof. 1968—; vis. prof. NYU, 1965, 68, 70; lectr. U. San Marcos, Lima, Peru, 1980. Democratic election judge, 1960. Served to 1st lt. USAF, 1952-54; to capt. Res., 1954-65. Mem. Am. Hist. Assn., Orgn. Am. Historians, Soc. for Historians of Am. Fgn. Relations, AAUP (pres. Kans. conf. 1962-63), World Future Soc. Presbyterian. Co-editor: The Eisenhower Era, 1974; contbr. to Ency. So. History, 1979; contbr. articles to profl. jours. Office: Dept History Ga State U Atlanta GA 30303-3083

SELLERS, CLYDE ADRIAN, geologist; b. Franklin, La., June 12, 1957; s. Emmet Gerard and Beverly M. (Mayard) S.; m. Deborah Dot Hall, Sept. 10, 1983. B.S. magna cum laude, U. S.W. La., 1979. Geologist, Texaco Co., New Orleans, 1979-81, staff geologist, 1981-82, exploration geologist, 1982-85, unit geologist, 1985—. Mem. Am. Assn. Petroleum Geologists, New Orleans Geol. Soc., Phi Kappa Phi. Democrat. Roman Catholic. Lodge: K.C. Avocations: softball; tennis; skiing; swimming; diving. Home: 1804 Kings Row Slidell LA 70461

SELLERS, ROBERT JULIUS, JR., real estate executive; b. Conway, S.C., Dec. 3, 1954; s. Robert Julius and Louise Viola (Brown) S. A.S., Horry Georgetown Tech. Coll., 1975; B.S., Coker Coll., 1978; M.A., Webster Coll., 1981. Salesman Chapin Co., Myrtle Beach, S.C., 1973-77; mgr. Cobraden Lounge, Hartsville, S.C., 1977-78, Holiday Inns of Am., Myrtle Beach, 1978-83; salesman Sands Resort, Myrtle Beach, 1983-84; mgr. Conner Homes Sales Corp., Sumter, S.C., 1984—. Mem. Republican Congl. Com., Washington, 1984-85. Mem. Nat. Assn. Accts. Republican. Baptist. Lodges: Masons, Shriners. Avocations: tennis; water skiing; snow skiing. Home: 23 Deer Manor Condo Sumter SC 29150 Office: Conner Home Sales Corp 2987 Broad St Extension Sumter SC 29150

SELLERS, WILLIAM DAVID, JR., transportation company executive; b. Anniston, Ala., June 13, 1913; s. William David and Yrma (Ivey) S.; m. Virginia Forsyth, Jan. 23, 1937; children—Forsyth Sellers Donald, Mary Sellers Crommelin. B.A., U. Ala., 1934, LL.D. (hon.), 1981. With White Motor Co., Birmingham, Ala., 1934-36; with Pan Am. Petroleum Corp., 1936-41; with Baggett Transp. Co., Birmingham, 1941—, chmn. bd., 1946—; chmn., dir. Tractor-Trailer Equipment Co., Truck Rentals of Ala., Truck Rentals of La., TRA Truck and Trailer Service Co., Inc., TRA Driver Service Co., Gen. Transport, Inc., Interstate Ins. Agy., Jefferson Properties, Inc., Birmingham; chmn. bd. First Ala. Bank of Birmingham; dir. Am. Heritage Life Ins. Co., Jacksonville, Fla., Multimedia, Inc., Greenville, S.C. Trustee, past pres. Crippled Children's Found., Eye Found. Hosp.; mem. exec. com. Boy Scouts. Am. Mem. Ala. Trucking Assn. (H. Chester Webb award 1973), Newcomen Soc. Am. Democrat. Episcopalian. Clubs: Downtown, Birmingham Country, Shoal Creek Country, Monday Morning Quarterback (Birmingham); Grandfather Mountain Country (Linville, N.C.). Lodge: Rotary. Home: 4226 Old Leeds Rd Birmingham AL 35213 Office: Baggett Transportation Co 2 S 32d St Birmingham AL 35233

SELLS, JOYCE GREEN, nurse; b. Pensacola, Fla., Jan. 7, 1946; d. Elbert Paul Green, Jr. and Ellen (Chandler) Green Shryock; m. James Jerry Smothers, Aug. 12, 1961 (div. 1972); children—Sherry, Leigh, Kimberly, James; m. 2d Haskell Lee Sells II, Feb. 7, 1976. Intermittent student Jefferson State Jr. Coll., 1965-73, N.C. State U., 1978—; A.S. in Nursing, Wake Tech. Jr. Coll., 1979-81; cert. respiratory therapy U. Ala., 1974. R.N., N.C. Respiratory therapy technician South Highlands Hosp., Birmingham, Ala., 1974-76, Rex Hosp., Raleigh, N.C., 1976-79; nurse, respiratory therapy technician Wake Med. Ctr., Raleigh, 1980-82, Duke U. Med. Ctr. Hosp., Durham, N.C., 1982—. Active Raleigh chpt. NOW, 1976—, chairperson membership, 1978-79. Served with U.S. Army N.G., 1974-76. Mem. Am. Assn. Respiratory Therapy, N.C. Assn. Respiratory Therapy. Democrat. Contbr. to Am. Poetry Anthology, 1984.

SELLS, SAUL B., psychologist, educator; b. N.Y.C., Jan. 13, 1913; s. Maxwell I. and Dora Sells; m. Helen Frances Roberts, July 2, 1939. A.B., Bklyn. Coll., 1933; Ph.D., Columbia U., 1936; Sc.D. (hon.), Tex. Christian U., 1984. Research asst. Inst. Ednl. Research, Columbia U., N.Y.C., 1934-36, instr. psychology, 1935-37; lectr. psychology Bklyn. Coll., 1936-37; research assoc. Bd. Edn., N.Y.C., 1935-40; research analyst Pub. Work Res., Washington, 1940-41; chief statistician OPA, Washington, 1941-46; asst. to pres. A.B. Frank Co., San Antonio, 1946-48; prof., head dept. mem. psychology USAF Sch. Aerospace Medicine, Randolph AFB, Tex., 1948-58; adj. prof. Trinity U., San Antonio, 1949-55; vis. prof. psychology U. Tex., Austin, 1950-51; prof. psychology Tex. Christian U., Ft. Worth, 1958-62, research prof. psychology, dir. Inst. behavioral Research, 1962-83, research prof. emeritus, 1983—; vis. prof. psycholoy Tex. A&M U., 1984—; cons. in field; pres. IBR Assocs.; cons./reviewer Can. Sci. Council, 1980-81, NSF, 1975—; mng. editor/assoc. editor Multivariate Behavioral Research, 1966—; cons. editor Psychol. Bull., 1955-58, Jour. Clin. Psychology, 1960—, Psychology in the Schs., 1963—, others. Contbr. articles to profl. jours. Chmn., Tarrant County Heart Assn.; mem. Bexar County Mental Health Assn., San Antonio. Recipient Longacre award Aerospace Med. Assn., 1956; Pace Setter award Nat. Inst. on Drug Abuse, 1978, others. Fellow Aerospace Med. Assn., AAAS; mem. Southwestern Psychol. Assn. (pres.), Tex. Psychol. Assn. (pres.), Soc. for Multivariate Exptl. Psychology (pres. 1964), Am. Psychol. Assn. (pres. mil. div.), Am. Astron. Soc., Am. Ednl. Research Assn., Psychometric Soc., Am. Statis. Assn., Soc. for Psychol. Study Social Issues, Sigma Xi. Home: 3850 Overton Park Dr W Fort Worth TX 76109 Office: Tex Christian U PO Box 32902 Fort Worth TX 76129

SELMAN, ROBERT EBERLE, architect; b. Tulsa, Feb. 5, 1947; s. L.B. and Jeannette G. (Eberle) S.; m. Ellen Shepherd, Jan. 29, 1970; children—Christina Elizabeth, Teresa Elaine, Tracy Lykins. B.Arch., Okla. U., 1970. Assoc., Murray Jones Murray, 1978-80; design coordinator Cities Service, 1980-83; pres. RESCOMPANY, Tulsa, 1983—. Chmn. Dist. 18 Greater Tulsa Council, 1980, Precinct 114 Democratic Party, 1985-87. Served as 2d lt. U.S. Army N.G., 1971. Mem. AIA, Constrn. Specifications Inst. (pres. 1982), Sigma Alpha Epsilon. Lodges: Mason (32 deg.), Scottish Rite, Legion of Honor. Home: 5212 S Columbia Pl Tulsa OK 74105 Office: RESCOMPANY 6440 S Lewis #108 Tulsa OK 74136

SELTZER, LINKIE, professional speaker, writer, consultant; b. Dallas, Nov. 22, 1925; d. Nathan A. and Ann (Ravkind) Levine; widowed; children—Adrienne, Cathy Brenda, Robert Michael. Student So. Methodist U., 1943-44, 76, U. Tex., 1944-45. Profl. dancer Starlight Operettas, Dallas, 1943-44; exec. dir. SW region Am. Friends of Hebrew U., Dallas, 1973; prin. Linkie Seltzer and Co., Dallas, 1981—; assoc. bd. dirs. Profl. Success Mgmt., Atlanta, 1984—; exec. dir. Atlas-Galt Fin. Network, Dallas, 1985—; LOVE in Bus. columnist Achievement Mag., 1985—. Producer TV series: Covenant, 1972-73. Campaign chmn. women's div. Jewish Fedn. Dallas, 1970, pres. div., 1972-73; chmn. pub. relations Greater Dallas Community Relations Commn., 1983—. Named Campaigner of Yr., Jewish Fedn. Dallas, 1969. Mem. Nat. Speaker's Assn., Internat. Platform Assn., N. Tex. Speaker's Assn. (chmn. pub. relations 1984), Assn. Humanistic Psychology, The Fashion Group. Democrat. Office: PO Box 741191 Dallas TX 75374

SEMAAN, DICK, professional speaker; b. Houston, Dec. 14, 1934; s. James and Mildred (Smith) S.; m. Alexandra Marcelle Rice, May 3, 1952; children—Patricia Robin, Sheryl Lynn, Julie Dianne, David Rice. B.S., U. Houston, 1958; postgrad. Dallas Theol. Sem., 1960. Formerly engaged in sales, mktg., radio-TV broadcasting and profl. speaking; now pres. Semaan Enterprises, Houston, Great Am. Seminars; also dir. Crown Ministries, Inc., Houston. Tchr. First Bapt. Ch. Houston. Served with U.S. Army, 1954-56. Mem. Nat. Speakers Assn. (award 1980, election chmn. 1983), Greater Houston Speakers Assn. (bd. dirs. 1984), Downtown Houston Christian Bus. Men's Assn. (program chmn. 1976-78). Republican. Baptist.

SEMAN, IRENE SALLY, interior designer; b. Bklyn. NYU, 1943; cert. interior design N.Y. Sch. Interior Design, 1961; postgrad. Miami Dade Coll., Nova U., Broward Community. Owner, pres. Seman & Graham, 1978-82, Irene Seman Interiors, Ft. Lauderdale, Fla., 1964—; cons. interior design, 1979—. Selected to design rooms for Open Design Houses. Talk show guest. Contbr. articles to newspapers. Bd. dirs. Friends for Life, U. Miami Med. Sch. Aux., 1979—; mem. Friends Ft. Lauderdale Mus., 1976—; mem. Miami Art Ctr., Lowe Mus., Brandeis U., City of Hope, Common Cause, Humane Soc. Mem. Nat. Home Fashions League, Nat. Small Bus. Assn., Nat. Assn. Women Bus. Owners, Ctr. for Group Counseling of Orgn. for Rehab. Through Tng., Am. Contract Bridge League, Phi Sigma Sigma Alumni. Democrat. Clubs: Country of Am., Inverrary Country. Avocations: travel, bridge, art collecting, theatre, music, philosophy. Home and Office: 3301 Spanish Moss Terr Lauderhill FL 33319

SEME, DANIEL JAMES, JR., resort developer, operator, consultant; b. Lakewood, N.J., Feb. 3, 1950; s. Daniel James and Norma Gloria (Paget) S.; m. Carol Ann Proctor, Nov. 2, 1974. B.S. in Health, Phys. Edn. and Recreation, Appalachian State U., Boone, 1972. Dir. profl. ski patrol, Sugar Mountain, N.C., 1969-73; owner, operator Hub-Pub Club, Banner Elk, N.C., 1969-73; v.p. mountain ops. Snowshoe Ski Resort (W.Va.), 1973-81; v.p., co-founder Tory Mountain Resorts, Inc., Harmon, W.Va., 1981—; cons. Canaan Valley Resort Park, State of W.Va. Vice pres. Treetop Condo Assn., 1977-81; fire chief Snowshoe Vol. Fire Dept., 1978-81; bd. dirs. local pub. service, 1979-81. Mem. Aircraft Owners and Pilots Assn., W.Va. Ski Area Assn. (v.p.), Nat. Ski Areas Assn., Nat. Wildlife Fedn. Presbyterian. Club: Elkins Pilot's (pres. 1982—). Lodge: Elks (Elkins). Home: RD 3 Willow Bend Elkins WV 26241 Office: Tory Mt Resorts Inc Harmon WV 26270

SEMMENS, JAMES PIKE, obstetrician, gynecologist, educator, former naval officer; b. Milw., Aug. 16, 1919; s. Thomas Perry and Corinne Middleton (Pike) S.; m. Eve Curtis, Oct. 1, 1982; children by previous marriage—James Alan, Michael Paul, Christine Anne, Gregory George, John Patrick; m. 2d, Eve Curtis, Oct. 1, 1982. B.S., Marquette U., 1941, M.D., 1943. Diplomate Am. Bd. Ob-Gyn.; cert. sex therapist. Intern Milw. Hosp., 1943-44; asst. resident in pediatric surgery and pediatrics Milw. Children's Hosp., 1944-45; commd. lt. (j.g.) U.S. Navy, 1943, advanced through grades to capt., 1962; sr. med. officer USS Halsey Powell, 1945-46, Naval Mag., Port Chicago, Calif., 1954-57; vis. clin. instr. ob-gyn. Med. U. S.C., Charleston, Herbert Burwig lectr., 1968; chief of dependents, chief ob-gyn. dept. U.S. Naval Hosp., Charleston, 1957-61, Pensacola, Fla., 1961-63; chief ob-gyn dept. U.S. Naval Hosp., Oakland, Calif., 1963-69; assoc. prof. ob-gyn U. So. Calif. Sch. Medicine, Los Angeles, 1970-71; assoc. clin. prof. ob-gyn U. Calif. Coll. Medicine-Irvine, 1970-71; ret., 1971; assoc. prof. ob-gyn Med. U. S.C., 1971-79, prof. ob-gyn, 1979-83, prof. emeritus, 1983—; cons. in field. Fellow ACS, Am. Coll. Obstetricians and Gynecologists (chmn. armed forces dist. 1968-71; chmn. audio-visual edn. com. 1971-73; mem. edn. in family life com. 1973-76), Am. Acad. Family Physicians (charter); mem. Am. Fertility Soc., Am. Acad. Gen. Practice, AMA, S.C. Med. Soc., Charleston County Med. Soc., Alameda County Gynecol. Soc., San Francisco Gynecol. Soc. (courtesy mem.), S.C. Obstet. and Gynecol. Soc., Wis. Med. Soc., Assn. Mil. Surgeons U.S., Pacific Coast Fertility Soc., Internat. Assn. Psychosomatic Ob-Gyn., Am. Assn. Sex Educators, Counselors and Therapists (pres. 1976-86, chmn. S.C. sect. 1978-81, 83—; chmn. southeastern dist., dir. 1981-83); Phi Sigma. Contbr. numerous articles to med. publs.; producer med. films. Home and office: 3360 Seabrook Island Rd Route 1 John's Island SC 29455

SEMMENS, RAYMOND THOMAS, health care educator, consultant; b. Cornwall, Eng., Apr. 30, 1946; came to U.S., 1951, naturalized, 1965; s. James Thomas and Mary (Rawlings) S.; m. Christina Ann Peabody, Apr. 27, 1974 (div. Mar. 1984); 1 child, James Bennett. A.A., Northwood Inst., Midland, Mich., 1968, B.B.A., 1970; postgrad. U. Evansville, 1977-83. Dir. admissions Northwood Inst., Cedar Hill, Tex., 1970-71, dean of students, West Baden, Ind., 1971-77; edn. coordinator St. Mary's Med. Ctr., Evansville, Ind., 1977-81; corp. dir. tng. Medco Ctrs., Inc., Evansville, 1981-83; dir. edn. wellness Baton Rouge Gen. Med. Ctr., 1983—. Staff exec. dir. Mich. Young Ams. for Freedom, 1966-68, nat. bd. dirs., Washington, 1968-70; chmn. Young Republicans Northwood Inst., 1967-68. Recipient Gold award Am. Heart Assn., 1980; named Hon. Citizen, City of Indpls., 1972. Mem. Am. Soc. Tng. and Devel. (sec. 1983-84), Am. Soc. Health Care Edn. and Tng., Capital Areas Soc. Health Care Edn. and Tng., La. Soc. Health Care Edn. and Tng., Phi Sigma Beta. Methodist. Avocations: politics, travel, golfing, biking. Home: 123 Live Oaks Apt 210 Baton Rouge LA 70806 Office: Baton Rouge Gen Med Ctr 3600 Florida Blvd Baton Rouge LA 70806

SEMMER, JOHN RICHARD, physician; b. Nanticoke, Pa., Nov. 7, 1943; s. Frederick Lewis and Betty Romayne (Thomas) S.; B.A., U. of South, 1965; M.D., U. Tenn., 1968; m. Glenna Butler McMahan, Aug. 20, 1966; 1 dau., Johnna Blythe. Intern U. Tenn. Meml. Hosp., Knoxville, 1969-70, resident obstetrics and gynecology, 1970-73; commd. 1st lt. USAF, 1969, advanced to maj., 1973; chief obstetrics and gynecology, Base Hosp., Blytheville AFB, Ark., 1973-75; pvt. practice medicine specializing in obstetrics and gynecology, Knoxville, 1975-78, 85—; asso. clin. prof. Clin. Edn. Center, U. Tenn. Center for Health Scis., Knoxville, 1975-78, 85—; from asst. prof. to assoc. prof. ob-gyn, dir. E. Tenn. regional perinatal program U. Tenn. Coll. Medicine, Knoxville, 1978-85; pvt. practice obstetrics and gynecology specializing in high-risk pregnancy, Knoxville, 1985—. Bd. visitors U. Tenn. Coll. Nursing, Knoxville. Diplomate Am. Bd. Obstetrics and Gynecology. Fellow Am. Coll. Obstetrics and Gynecology; mem. AMA, So. Med. Assn., Tenn. Med. Assn., Central Assn. Obstetricians and Gynecologists, So. Obstet. and Gynecol. Seminar Inc., East Tenn. Obstet. and Gynecol. Soc., Nat. Perinatal Assn., So. Perinatal Assn., Tenn. Perinatal Assn. (pres. 1982-84), Continental Obstet. and Gynecol. Soc. Am. Assn. Gynecological Laparoscopists, Knoxville Acad. Medicine, U. Tenn. Alumni Assn., U. of South Assn. Alumni, Beta Theta Pi, Phi Chi. Methodist. Contbr. articles to profl. jours. Home: 5304 Whitehorse Rd Knoxville TN 37919 Office: East Tenn Ob-Gyn Assocs St Mary's Clark Tower Suite 805 939 Emerald Ave Knoxville TN 37917

SEMONES, JAMES KING, sociology educator, human resource consultant; b. Bristol, Va., Nov. 10, 1948; s. James Hogue and Nelwyn (King) S.; m. Phyllis Kay Hicks, Apr. 20, 1968. B.S., East Tenn. State U., 1971, M.A., 1972; Ed.D., North Tex. State U., 1983. Instr. sociology Jacksonville State U., Ala., 1972-74, El Paso Community Coll., Tex., 1975-81, San Jacinto Coll., Houston, 1984—; human resource cons. Xerox Corp., Am. Heart Assn.; tng. cons. Gibralter Savings, Irving, Tex., Pub. Service Co. Okla., Tulsa. Author: Introductory Sociology: A Core Text, 1977; (with others) Key Issues in Higher Education and Society, 1983, Adult Education: Theory and Practice, 1984. Editor: (with others) Adult Learning and Program Development, 1983. Contbr. articles to profl. jours. and book chpts. Mem. Profl. Assn. Coll. Educators (pres. 1979-80), Tex. State Tchrs. Assn., NEA, So. Sociol. Soc., Am. Soc. Tng. and Devel., Phi Kappa Phi, Pi Gamma Mu, Alpha Kappa Delta, Phi Delta Kappa. Presbyterian. Avocations: Antiques; art; photography; travel. Home: 7607 Heather Row Houston TX 77044 Office: Div Social Behavioral Scis San Jacinto Coll N Campus 5800 Uvalde Houston TX 77049-4589

SENDELE, DEBORAH DISTEFANO, ophthalmologist; b. Worcester, Mass., Aug. 18, 1950; d. Anthony J. and Helen (Stachelek) DiStefano; m. Robert L. Sendele, 1974. B.A. magna cum laude, Conn. Coll., 1972; M.D., Med. Coll. Wis., 1976. Diplomate Am. Bd. Ophthalmology. Intern, Med. Coll. Wis., Milw., 1976-77, resident, 1977-80; fellow corneal and external disease Harvard U.-Mass. Eye and Ear Infirmary, Boston, 1980-82; chmn. U. Tenn.-Chattanooga, 1982—; med. dir. 12-0 Lions Eye Bank, Chattanooga, 1982—; vis. prof. Conn. Coll. Contbg. editor Cooper Vision, Inc. Bd. dirs. U. Tenn. Coll. Medicine, Chattanooga, 1982—, Retinitis Pigmentosa, Chattanooga, 1982—. Mem. adv. bd. Hamilton County Bd. Edn., Chattanooga, 1982; asst. dir. East Tenn. Eye Bank, Knoxville, 1982; bd. dirs. Retinitis Pigmentosa, Chattanooga, 1982; mem. sci. rev. com. U. Tenn., Chattanooga, 1982. Corneal External Disease fellow Bausch & Lomb, 1980; postdoctoral fellow NIH, 1980-81. Mem. AMA, Women in Medicine Soc., Hamilton County Med. Soc., Am. Acad. Ophthalmology, Phi Beta Kappa. Office: Dept Ophthalmology 979 E 3d St Suite 802 Chattanooga TN 37403

SENGBUSH, LYNN RAE, educator, psychologist; b. Elkhorn, Wis., May 23, 1946; d. Raymond Lynn and Earlene Edith (Vogel) S. B.S. in Nursing, U. Tex., 1969; M.S. in Community Mental Health/Nursing, Boston U., 1973; Ph.D. in Clin. Psychology, U.S. Internat. U., 1982. R.N. Sr. splty. community mental health therapist Ft. Logan Mental Health Ctr., Denver, 1969-71; therapeutic camp counselor Judge Baker Guidance Ctr., Boston, 1972; instr., curriculum developer, clin. supr. dept. nursing St. Anselm's Coll., Manchester, N.H., 1973-74; mental health cons. Lenawee County chpt. Am. Cancer Soc., Birmingham, Mich., 1974-77; asst. prof. U. Mich., Ann Arbor, 1975-77, Point Loma Coll., San Diego, 1977-78, U. Calif.-San Diego, 1978-79; psychol. clin. specialist V.A. Med. Ctr., San Diego, 1978-80; psychologist Ira Grossman, Inc., San Diego, 1982-84; assoc. prof. Tex. Women's U., Dallas, 1984—; program cons. Willow Creek Adolescent Ctr., Arlington, Tex., 1984; psychology intern, post doc. fellow Mercy Hosp., San Diego, 1980-82; mem. research com. Parkland Hosp., Dallas, 1985. Mem. Am. Psychol. Assn., Am. Orthopsychiat. Assn., Oncology Nursing Soc., Am. Nurses Assn., Tex. Nurses Assn., Dallas Psychol. Soc., Dallas Psychoanalytic Soc., Sigma Theta Tau, Beta Beta, Psi Chi. Democrat. Episcopalian. Club: Jr. Woman's (Grand Prairie, Tex.). Avocations: writing, creative dance, swimming, photography. Home: 1209 Plattner Grand Prairie TX 75050 Office: Tex Women's U 1810 Inwood Rd Dallas TX 75235

SENNEMA, DAVID CARL, museum consultant; b. Grand Rapids, Mich., July 6, 1934; s. Carl Edward and Alice Bertha (Bieri) S.; m. Martha Amanda Dixon, Feb. 22, 1958; children—Daniel Ross, Julia Kathryn, Alice Dixon. B.A., Albion Coll., 1956. Mgr., Columbia Music Festival Assn., 1964-67; exec. dir. S.C. Arts Commn., Columbia, 1967-70; assoc. dir. Federal-State Partnership and Spl. Projects programs Nat. Endowment for the Arts, Washington, 1971-73; prof. arts adminstrn., dir. community arts mgmt. program Sangamon State U., Springfield, Ill., 1973-76; dir. S.C. Mus. Commn. Columbia, 1976-85; cons. in field. Mem. adv. panel Nat. Endowment for the Arts Music, 1968-70. Chmn. Springfield Arts Commn., 1975-76. Served with U.S. Army, 1957-58. Mem. Am. Assn. Mus., Am. Assn. State and Local History, Southeastern Mus. Conf., S.C. Fedn. Mus. Lodge: Rotary (chmn. cultural affairs com. 1978-80). Office: PO Box 11296 Columbia SC 29211

SENNETTI, JOHN THOMAS, statistics educator; b. Allentown, Pa., May 24, 1944; s. John Joseph and Linda Carol (DalMaso) S.; m. Suzanne Stevens; children—Jonathan Scott, Suzannah Marie. B.A. in Math., U. Scranton, 1966; M.A. in Math., Bucknell U., 1968; M.Stats., U. Fla., 1969; Ph.D. in Stats., Va. Poly. Inst. and State U., 1973. Instr. Bucknell U., Lewisburg, Pa., 1966-67; asst. prof. Tex. Tech U., Lubbock, 1971-77, assoc. prof. stats. and info. systems, 1977—; pres. Data Support, Lubbock, 1983—; cons. to law firms, 1980—. Mem. editorial bd. Tex. Bus. Mag., 1979. Reviewer statis. jours., 1978-79. Columnist Tex. Bus. Mag., 1979, Lubbock Avalanche Jour., 1978-79. Contbr. articles to statis. and econ. jours. Mem. Am. Statis. Assn., Nat. Assn. Bus. Economists, Inst. Mgmt. Scis. Republican. Roman Catholic. Club: Toastmasters (Lubbock). Avocation: jogging. Home: 3801 39th St Lubbock TX 79413 Office: Info Systems and Quantitative Scis Coll Bus Adminstrn Texas Tech U Box 4320 Lubbock TX 79409

SENTER, LYONEL THOMAS, JR., federal judge; b. Fulton, Miss., July 30, 1933; s. Lyonel Thomas and Eva Lee (Jetton) S.; m. Elizabeth Bartlett Dickson, Oct. 21, 1956; children—John Thomas, Elizabeth Lee, Stuart Dickson. B.S., U. So. Miss., 1956; LL.B., U. Miss., 1959. Bar: Miss. Pros. atty. Monroe County, Aberdeen, Miss., 1960-64; ptnr. Patterson, Senter & King, Aberdeen, 1961-68; U.S. commr. U.S. Dist. Ct. (no. dist.) Miss., Aberdeen, 1966-68, dist. judge, 1980-82, chief judge, 1982—; judge 1st Jud. Dist. Circuit Miss., 1968-80. Co-author: Mississippi Model Jury Instruction, 1977. Mem. Miss. State Bar Assn., First Jud. Dist. Bar Assn., Monroe County Bar Assn., Am. Judicature Soc. Presbyterian. Home: 104 Walters Dr Aberdeen MS 39730 Office: US Dist Ct West Commerce St Aberdeen MS 39730

SENTER, WILLIAM ROBERT, III, priest; b. Chattanooga, Sept. 13, 1935; s. William R. and Virginia (Mack) S.; m. Linda Anne Howard, Feb. 9, 1963; children—Lydia Elizabeth, Matthew Mack. B.S., U. South, 1957; postgrad. U. Chattanooga, 1955, U. Tenn., 1958; B.D., Bexley Hall Div. Sch. Kenyon coll., 1961; M.Div., Bexley Hall/Colgate Rochester/Crozer Theol. Sem., 1973; postgrad. Vanderbilt Div. Sch., 1969-71, Southeastern Sch. Alcohol and Drug Studies, Athens, Ga., 1976. Ordained deacon, 1961, priest, 1962; cert. substance abuse counselor, Tenn. Asst. St. James Ch., Knoxville, Tenn., 1961-63; priest-in-charge St. Columba's Ch., Bristol, Tenn., 1963-68, Epiphany Episc. Ch., Lebanon, Tenn., 1968-84; rector Grace Episc. Ch., Canton, Miss., 1984—; chaplain Camp Allegheny for Girls, Lewisburg, W.Va., 1976; hon. chaplain for a day U.S. Senate, 1976; pres., treas. Senter Sch., Chatanooga, 1973-78. Founder –Hangout–, Lebanon, 1968-71; originator, first chmn. Project Help (free clothing distbn. project), Lebanon, 1970-73; originator, mem. Lebanon-Wilson County Drug Abuse Commn., 1969-71, chmn., 1974-84; incorporater Lebanon-Wilson County Mental Health Ctr., 1972; mem. Wilson County Welfare adv. bd., 1974-84; chmn. Horizons com., mem. exec. com. Wilson County Bicentennial Commn., 1974-76; personnel and mgmt. tng. cons. Cracker Barrel Old Country Stores, Lebanon, 1974-76; mem. Gov.'s Commn. on Alcohol and Drug Abuse, 1972-77, vice chmn. 1975-77; bd. dirs. Lebanon YMCA, 1973-78. Mem. Tenn. Ornithol. Soc. (v.p. 1973-75), Alumni Council U. South, SAR, Nat. Model R.R. Assn., Am. Assn. Arts and Scis., Profl. Alcohol and Drug Counselors Tenn., South and Light Community Theater Co. Lebanon, Delta Tau Delta. Address: Grace Episcopol Church PO Box 252 Canton MS 39046-0252

SENTERFITT, REUBEN ELBY, lawyer, rancher; b. San Saba, Tex., June 18, 1917; s. Reuben Elby and Allie (Beck) S.; m. Patricia Gray Farley, Oct. 3, 1959; children—Shirley Kroeger, Linda Hall, Ronald, James Farley, Melinda Bratton, Barry, Diane. J.D., U. Tex., 1940. Bar: Tex. 1940. Individual practice. San Saba, 1940-47, 56-65, 82—; ptnr. firms, San Saba, 1947-56, 65-82; city atty. City of San Saba, 1955-60; county atty. San Saba County, 1962-63; pres., chmn. bd. Heart O'Tex. Savs. Assn. Chmn. fin. com. Comanche Trial council Boy Scouts Am.; mem. Tex. Ho. of Reps. 1940-55, speaker 1951-55; elder, trustee 1st Presbyn. Ch. Served to lt. (j.g.) USN 1942-45; PTO. Mem. ABA, Tex. Bar Assn., Tex. Bar Found. (grievance com.), San Saba C. of C. (pres. 1964-65). Order of Coif. Clubs: Rotary (pres.), Masons. Home: 1403 W Dry St San Saba TX 76877 Office: 306 E Wallace St San Saba TX 76877

SENZEL, ALAN JOSEPH, analytical chemistry consultant, editor, author; b. Los Angeles, May 26, 1945; s. Bernard and Esther Mildred (Shykin) S.; m. Phyllis Sharon Abt, June 22, 1969; children—Richard Steven, Lisa Beth. B.S. in Chemistry, Calif. State U.-Long Beach, 1967; M.S., UCLA, 1969, Ph.D., 1970. Assoc. editor Am. Chem. Soc., Washington, 1970-74; methods editor Assn. Ofcl. Analytical Chemists, Washington, 1974-78; info. dir. Chem. Industry Inst. Toxicology, Research Triangle Park, N.C., 1978-79; pvt. cons., Raleigh, N.C., 1978—; cons. Engring.-Sci., Durham, N.C. and Fairfax, Va., 1978—, Corning Glass Works, Raleigh, 1979—, Research Triangle Inst., Research Triangle Park, 1983—, Combustion Engring., Chapel Hill, N.C., 1984—; music critic Raleigh News & Observer, 1982—. Editor: Instrumentation in Analytical Chemistry, 1973; Newburger's Manual of Cosmetic Analysis (FDA award 1978), 1977; Safety in the Laboratory (STC award 1985), 1984; assoc. editor: Official Methods of Analysis, 1975. Pres. Congregation Sha'arei Israel, 1981-83. Mem. Soc. Tech. Communication (v.p. 1985—; achievement award 1985). Republican. Jewish. Club: Bridge-Raleigh, Capitol, Vanderbilt. Lodge: B'nai Brith. Avocations: music; tennis; basketball; bridge. Home: 7704 Audubon Dr Raleigh NC 27609

SEPSI, VICTOR JOHN, JR., clinical counseling psychologist; b. Cleve., Apr. 15, 1930; s. Victor J. and Mary J. (Sopko) S.; B.A., Case Western Res. U., 1968; M.Ed., Kent State U., 1969, Ph.D. (Univ. fellow), 1971. Clergyman, four so. chs., 1956-67; staff psychologist, Martinsburg, W.Va., 1971-76; staff psychologist, chief Mental Hygiene Clinic, VA Med. Center, Martinsburg, 1976—; instr. W.Va. U. Grad. Sch. Extension, Shepherd Coll., Shepherdstown, W.Va., 1975—; cons. Pastoral Counseling Service, Martinsburg, 1976—. Served with U.S. Army N.G., 1957-67. Recipient Gen. Aviation Community Service award Zonta Internat., 1965. Mem. Am. Psychol. Assn., Ohio Psychol. Assn., W.Va. Psychol. Assn., Va. Psychol. Assn., Assn. Advancement of Psychology, Am. Soc. Clin. Hypnosis, Am. Assn. Sex Educators, Counselors and Therapists, Am. Assn. Marriage and Family Therapy, Am. Assn. Biofeedback Clinicians. Home: Sulphur Springs Rd PO Box 566 Inwood WV 25428 Office: Vets Adminstrn Martinsburg WV 25401

SERAFIN, DONALD, plastic surgeon; b. N.Y.C., Jan. 18, 1938; s. Stephen Michael and Julia (Sopko) S.; A.B., Duke U., 1960, M.D., 1964; m. Patricia Serafin; children—Allison Elizabeth, Christina Julia. Surg. intern Grady Meml. Hosp., Atlanta, 1964-65; resident in surgery Emory U. Hosp., Atlanta, 1965-69; asst. resident in plastic and reconstructive surgery Duke U. Med. Center, Durham, N.C., 1971-73, chief resident, 1973-74; Christine Kleinert fellow in hand surgery U. Louisville Hosp., 1972-73; practice medicine specializing in plastic surgery, Durham; mem. staff Durham County Gen. Hosp.; asst. prof. plastic, reconstructive and maxillofacial surgery Duke U., 1974-77, assoc. prof., 1977-81, prof., 1981—, dir. plastic surgery research labs., chief div. plastic, reconstructive and maxillofacial surgery. Assoc. editor Jour. Plastic and Reconstructive Surgery, Jour. Reconstructive Microsurgery. Contbr. articles to profl. jours. Served to maj. M.C., USAF, 1969-71. Diplomate Am. Bd. Surgery, Am. Bd. Plastic Surgery. Fellow ACS; mem. Internat. Soc. Reconstructive Microsurgery, Am. Soc. Plastic and Reconstructive Surgeons, Am. Assn. Plastic Surgeons, Am. Burn Assn., AMA, Plastic Surgery Research Council, N.C. Soc. Plastic, Mixillofacial and Reconstructive Surgeons, Southeastern Soc. Plastic and Reconstructive Surgeons, Southeastern Med. Dental Soc., Sigma Xi. Office: Duke University Medical Center PO Box 3372 Durham NC 27710

SERBAN, WILLIAM MICHAEL, librarian, researcher; b. Canton, Ohio, Sept. 28, 1949; s. George Edward and Virginia (Shearer) S.; m. Darlene Brady, May 9, 1979; (div. 1983). B.A. in Polit. Sci., Purdue U., 1967-71, M.A., Ohio U., 1973; M.L.S., U. Pitts., 1978. Head regional documents depository La. Tech U., Ruston, 1978-80; chmn. social sci. dept. U. New Orleans Library, 1980-85. Co-editor: Stained Glass: An Information Guide, 1980, Stained Glass Index 1976-77, 1968; editorial bd. La. Libr. Assn. Bulletin, 1983-85; publ. com. Stained Glass Mag., Bronxville, N.Y., 1980-82; contbr. articles in field to publs. Mem. La. Library Assn. (documents com. chmn. 1981-82) La. Library Assn. (exec. bd. 1982-83, chmn. oral history interest group 1984-85), Southeastern Library Assn., Glass Art Soc., Am. Polit. Sci. Assn., Beta Phi Mu. (nat. scholar 1978). Home: 2148 Selma St New Orleans LA 70122 Office: Polit Sci Dept U New Orleans Library New Orleans LA 70148

SERETEAN, MARTIN B., carpet manufacturing company executive; b. N.Y.C., 1924; married. B.S., Okla. A&M Coll., 1949; M.S., NYU, 1950. With Abraham & Straus Inc., 1950-51, Allied Stores Corp., 1951-53; sales mgr. Katherine Rug Mills, Inc., 1953-56; with Coronet Industries, Inc., Dalton, Ga., 1956—, pres., chief exec. officer, 1962-72, chmn. bd., chief exec. officer, 1972-80, chmn. bd., 1980—; also dir. Office: Coronet Industries Inc Coronet Dr Box 1248 Dalton GA 30720*

SERNA, FRANCISCO JAVIER, civil engineer; b. Mexico City, Dec. 3, 1925; s. Oscar and Belem (Baylor) S.; student Nat. U. Mex., 1941-43; B.S. in Civil Engring., Tex. A&M U., 1947; m. Margarita Cervantes, Aug. 18, 1951; children—Maria Cristina, Francisco Javier. Pres., Constructora Franser S.A., 1956—, Ingenieros y Arquitectos Consultores, 1965—, Aditec SA de CV, 1970—, INARCO S.A., 1972—, INARCO Eduvision, 1973—, Franina SA de CV, 1980—, INARCO Internacional, 1981—, Edificio San Rafael SA, 1981—, San Miguel Chapultepec SA, 1983—, Cerniser SA de CV, 1983—, Serfran S.A., 1984—; lectr. engring. doctorate div. U. Mex., 1960-70; lectr. U. Guanajuato, others; ASCE tech. lectr. Civil Engring. Coll. of Guatemala; cons. Dept. Environment, London, 1963-68; prof. U. Chile, 1967; cons. Fgn. Bldg. Office, Washington, 1976-71, Secretaria de Asentamientos Humanos y Obras Publicas, 1977-80. Coordinator Christian Family Movement, 1960-65; bd. govs. Am. Brit. Cowdray Hosp., Mexico City, 1965—, pres., 1977-78. Mem. Asociacion de Ingenieros y Arquitectos de Mexico, Consejo Mexicano de Gerencia Profesional (pres. 1964), Sociedad Mexicana de Ingenieria Sismica, ASCE (pres. Mex. sect. 1979-81, internat. dir. 1983—). Clubs: University (dir. 1958-60), Industrial. Lodge: Rotary (dir. 1984-85). Author publs. in field. Home: 126-4 F Berenguer Mexico DF Mexico 11000

SERRAL, FREDERICK AMOS, tobacconist; b. Ambler, Pa., Apr. 30, 1922; s. Anthony and Lydia (Saylor) S.; m. Barbara Carrol Elliott, June 28, 1958; children—Amie C., Fred H., Elliott A. Student, Tusculum Coll. Asst. v.p. Austin Co., Inc., Greeneville, Tenn., 1952-56, v.p., 1956-74, sr. v.p., 1974-80, pres., 1980—; pres. U.S. Burley and Dark Leaf Exporters Assn., Lexington, Ky., 1963—. Served with USMC, 1940-46. Decorated Silver Star, Bronze Star; recipient Tusculum Coll. Pioneer award, 1966. Republican. Methodist. Club: Link Hills Country (pres. 1966-67). Home: 112 Indian Hill Trail Greeneville TN 37743 Office: Austin Co Inc Corner Hall and Cutler Sts Greeneville TN 37743*

SERVESON, MARION COMAS, nurse; b. Ojus, Fla., June 13, 1924; d. Reppard Earl and Emma (Davis) Comas; m. Edwin H. Serveson, June 16, 1946; children—Susan, Kathryn, Peter. R.N. diploma Charity Hosp., New Orleans, 1946. R.N., Fla., Calif., N.J. Asst. charge nurse St. Barnabas Hosp., Livingston, N.J., 1970-71; charge nurse St. Anne's Villa, Convent Station, N.J., 1971-74; staff nurse Fla. Home Health Service, Warm Mineral Springs, Fla., 1975-78, med. auditor, Port Charlotte, Fla., 1980-81; patient care planner Home Health of Sarasota (Fla.), 1978-80; edn. coordinator Fawcett Meml. Hosp., Port Charlotte, 1981-83; mem. adviser United Ostomy Assn., Charlotte County, Fla., 1976-83; mem. adv. bd. Diabetic Assn. Charlotte County, 1980-83; chairperson edn. Am. Cancer Soc., Charlotte County, 1980-83. Editor diabetic info. pamphlet, 1982. Recipient cert. of appreciation ARC, Brevard County, Fla., 1960, Am. Heart Assn., Charlotte County, 1979, Am. Cancer Soc., Charlotte County, 1981; Outstanding Vol. plaque Medic Alert, Charlotte County, 1983. Mem. Char-Soto Nurse Continuing Edn. Council, Nat. Assn. Quality Assurance Profls., Southwest Fla. Council Nurse Educators. Democrat.

SERVICE, WILLIS JAMES, engineering company executive; b. Detroit, Oct. 15, 1925; s. Willis James and Martha Lucille (Meno) S.; m. Geraldine Ellen McDowell, Jan. 21, 1947; children—Christine Martha, Ann Marion, Keith Duncan. Ph.B., U. Chgo., 1947; B.S. in Chem. Engring., U. Mich., 1950, M.S. in Chem. Engring., 1951. Registered profl. engr. Tex., La., Md., N.J. Refinery engr., econs. and capital planning, capital budget mgr. Humble Oil & Refining Co. div. Exxon Co. U.S.A., Baytown, Tex., 1951-57; ptnr. Pace Co., 1957-62; sr. v.p. Pace Co. Cons. & Engrs., 1962-85, also dir.; sr. v.p. Pace Cos., also chief tech. officer, sec.-treas., 1972-78; pres. Pace Internat., Inc., 1978-79; sr. v.p. Jacobs Engring. Group Inc., Houston, 1978-85; dir., sr. v.p. Trans Pacific Industries, Inc.; pres. TPI Cons., Inc. mng. dir. Protec (Pty.) Ltd., S. Africa, 1980; dir. N.Am. Resources Corp., Path Corp., Republican precinct chmn. 1952-56; bd. dirs. Water Control and Improvement Dist., Baytown, 1953-57; mem. Pasadena Now, 1981-83. Served to 1st lt. USAAF, 1943-46. U. Chgo. Fellow, 1943-47; U. Mich. Fellow, 1948-51. Mem. Am. Petroleum Inst., Inst. of Petroleum, Am. Inst. Chem. Engrs., Am. Chem. Soc., Can. Soc. Chem. Engring., Chem. Inst. Can., Am. Assn. Cost Engrs., Nat. Assn. Corrosion Engrs., 25-Year Club of Petroleum Industry, Founders Club of Petrochem. Industries, Tau Beta Pi, Phi Lambda Upsilon, Phi Kappa Phi, Phi Gamma Delta. Episcopalian. Clubs: University (Pasadena, Calif.), Houstonian, Petroleum (Houston), Houston City. Researcher thermodynamic properties of freons. Contbr. articles to jours. Patentee petroleum refining. Home: 7518 Del Monte St Houston TX 77063 Office: Trans Pacific Industries Inc 3700 Buffalo Speedway Suite 1000 Houston TX 77098

SERVIN ANDRADE, LUIS ALEJANDRO, statistician, educator; b. Mexico City, June 23, 1942; s. Antonio Servin and Graciela Andrade y Guerrero; m. Adela Abad, Jan. 11, 1971; children—Luis Alejandro, Saul Francisco. Mech. and Elec. Engr., Ingenieria U. Nacional Autonoma de Mexico, 1967; M.Math. Stats., Cienes, Santiago, Chile, 1971. Statistician, Sci. and Tech. Council Mex., Mexico City, 1971-72, Agrl. Sec., Mexico City, 1972-73, Social Security Inst. Mex., 1973—; instr. of survey sampling, continuing edn. Ingenieria Universidad Nacional Autonoma de Mexico, 1978—. Co-author: Introduction al Muestreo, Limusa, Mexico, 1978. Mem. Am. Statis. Assn., Internat. Assn. Survey Statisticians. Roman Catholic. Home: Amores 107 Col del Valle Mexico DF Mexico 03100

SESSIONS, ROGER CARL, osteopathic physician; b. Stamps, Ark., Oct. 4, 1944; s. Darrell Inman and Linda Evelyn (Rogers) S.; m. Sherri Lorene Steward, June 12, 1971 (div. Oct. 1981); 1 child, David Steward. B.S.E., So. Ark. U., 1966; M.S., Henderson State U., 1971; D.O., Tex. Coll. Osteo. Medicine, 1981. Lic. physician, Tex. Asst. coach Tex. High Sch., Texarkana, 1966-67; track coach Atlanta High Sch., Tex., 1967-72; football coach, athletic dir. Northwest High Sch., Justin, Tex., 1972-77; intern Dallas-Ft. Worth Med. Ctr., Grand Prairie, Tex., 1981-82; practice emergency medicine, osteo. medicine, Grapevine, Tex., 1982—; dir. emergency room New Boston Gen. Hosp., Tex., 1984—. Mem. Am. Osteo. Assn., Tex. Osteo. Med. Assn., Am. Coll. Emergency Physicians, Am. Coll. Gen. Practitioners. Avocation: running.

SESSIONS, WILLIAM STEELE, federal judge; b. Ft. Smith, Ark., May 27, 1930; s. William A. and Edith (Steele) S.; Jr.; student U. Kans.; B.A., Baylor U., 1956, LL.B., J.D., 1958; m. Alice June Lewis, Oct. 5, 1952; children—William Lewis, Peter Anderson, Mark Gregory, Sara Anne. Admitted to Tex. bar, 1959, U.S. Dist. Cts. for Tex., Western and No. Dists., U.S. Ct. Appeals, 5th Circuit, U.S. Supreme Ct. bar; practiced in Waco, Tex., 1959-69; chief govt. ops. sect. criminal div. Dept. Justice, 1969-71; U.S. atty. for Western Dist. Tex., 1971-74; judge U.S. Dist. Ct. for Tex. Western Dist., San Antonio, 1974—, chief judge, 1980—; instr. real estate law McLennan Community Coll.; co-chmn. Tex. Fed.-State Law Enforcement Com., 1973; mem. subcom. on profl. proficiency and communications Atty. Gen.'s Adv. Com. of U.S. Attys., 1973-74; bd. dirs. Fed. Jud. Ctr., Washington, 1980-84; mem. implementation com. on admission of attys. to fed. practice Jud. Conf. U.S., 1979-84, chmn. jud. improvement subcom., 1986; mem. subcom. on jud. improvements, com. on ct. adminstrn. Jud. Conf., 1983-85. Mem. Waco City Council, 1969; bd. dirs. Bluebonnet council Girl Scouts U.S.A., 1960-62, Waco YMCA, 1964-69, McLennan County Council on Alcoholism, 1967; troop committeeman Boy Scouts Am., 1964-68, Chevy Chase, Md., 1970; McLennan County crusade chmn. Am. Cancer Soc., 1965-66; chmn. Waco Bd. Adjustment, 1966-67; chmn. lawyers div. United Fund, 1966; mem. com. on wills and bequests Central Tex. Conf. of Meth. Ch., chmn., 1967-68; active various polit. campaigns. Served to 1st lt. USAF, 1951-55; capt. Res. Mem. Am. Judicature Soc. (dir. 1976—, mem. exec. com. 1982-84), State Bar Tex., Fed. Bar Assn. (pres. San Antonio 1974), San Antonio Bar Assn. (dir. 1974-75), Dist. Judges Assn. 5th Circuit (pres. 1982-83), Pi Sigma Alpha, Phi Delta Phi. Republican. Methodist. Office: US Courthouse 655 E Durango Blvd San Antonio TX 78206*

SESSOMS, HANSON DOUGLAS, recreation administration educator; b. Wilmington, N.C., July 18, 1931; s. Hanson and Sadie Earle (Edens) S.; m. Celeste Heatherley, July 26, 1957 (div. July 1967); m. Anne Cummings Lassiter, Apr. 12, 1968; stepchildren—Benjamin I. Payne, Robert A. Payne. A.A., Wilmington Jr. Coll., 1951; B.A., U. N.C., 1953; M.S., U. Ill., 1954; Ph.D., NYU, 1959. Instr. sociology U. N.C., Chapel Hill, 1954-59, asst. prof., 1959-63, assoc. prof., 1963-69, prof. recreation adminstrn., 1969-72, 73—; vis. prof. Tex. A&M U., College Station, 1972-73. Author: Leisure Services, 6th ed., 1984; (with others) Recreation and Special Populations, 1973, 2d edit., 1977; Leadership and Group Dynamics in Recreational Services, 1981. Mem. NRPA/AALR Council on Accreditation, 1983-86, chmn., 1985-86. Recipient Charles K. Brightbill award U. Ill., 1979, Disting. Alumni award NYU, 1986. Mem. Acad. Leisure Scis. (pres. 1984-85), Acad. Park and Recreation Adminstrs., Soc. Park and Recreation Educators (pres. 1968-69), Am. Assn. Leisure and Recreation (J.B. Nash award 1983), N.C. Recreation and Park Soc. (pres. 1983), Nat. Recreation and Park Assn. (trustee 1979-82; Lit. award 1981). Democrat. Methodist. Avocations: photography; travel; native American art. Home: PO Box 1364 Chapel Hill NC 27514 Office: Curriculum in Recreation Adminstrn U NC 207 Pettigrew Hall Chapel Hill NC 27514

SESSUMS, ROBERT EDWIN, JR., loss control representative; b. Dekalb, Miss., Feb. 24, 1951; s. Robert Edwin and Dourthy (Hairston) S.; m. Elisa Lundy, Dec. 10, 1977; children—Melanie Elyse, Robert Edwin III. B.S. in Mech. Engring., Miss. State U., 1974. Enlisted USAF, 1969, advanced through grades to capt., 1985; mgmt. trainee U.S. Steel Corp., Birmingham, Ala., 1974; student pilot to pilot U.S. Air Force, Phoenix, Jackson, Miss., 1974-77; constrn. foreman Taylor Refrigeration, Jackson, 1977-78; loss control rep. U.S.F.&G. Co. Jackson, Miss., 1978—. Mem. N.G. Assn., Am. Soc. Safety Engrs. (pres. Miss. chpt. 1982-83). Republican. Baptist. Club: Employees (pres. 1984—). Avocations: woodworking, fishing, hunting. Home: 235 Shiloh Dr Jackson MS 39212 Office: USF&G Co 143 LeFleurs Square N Jackson MS 39211

SETIAN, LEO, electrical engineering educator; b. Providence, July 22, 1930; s. Zakar and Armenouhi (Toughtarian) S.; m. Sona Krikorian, June 23, 1957; children—Lynn, Ann, Richard, David, Peter. A.B., Brown U., 1955; M.S., U. R.I., 1966; Ph.D., Mont. State U., 1970. Elec. engr., Underwater Sound Lab., New London, Conn., 1957-63; mem. faculty John Brown U., Siloam Springs, Ark., 1970—, assoc. prof. elec. engring., 1976-84, prof., 1985—; cons. Underwater Systems Ctr., New London, summers 1982, 83, 84. Served with AUS, 1955-57. Mem. Am. Sci. Assn., Am. Soc. Engring. Edn. Avocations: Chess; biking. Office: Engring Sch John Brown Univ Siloam Springs AR 72761

SETLIFF, BEN FRED, educational administrator, security consultant; b. Plainview, Tex., Sept. 12, 1948; s. Odell E. and Nettie Jane (Lewis) S. B.S., West Tex. State Coll., 1970; M.Ed., Tex. Tech U., 1982, postgrad., 1982—. Mgr. K&B Sporting Goods, Lubbock, Tex., 1976-80; tchr. Meadow Schs., Tex., 1980-81; tchr., coach Lubbock Schs., 1981-82; asst. prin. Canyon High Sch., Tex., 1982-84; prin. Manor Schs., Tex., 1984—; pvt. investigator Alibates Security, Austin, Tex., 1974—. Mem. Tex. Assn. Secondary Sch. Prins., Assn. Supervision and Curriculum Devel., Phi Delta Kappa. Democrat. Avocations: hunter; competitive shooter. Office: Manor Ind Sch Dist Drawer L Manor TX 78653

SETLIFFE, CHARLES DAVID, hospital administrator; b. Chattanooga, Aug. 11, 1931; s. David Bert and Willie Mae (Fussell) S.; m. Eva Gertrude Holladay, Nov. 17, 1951; children—Charles Vaden, David Scott, Susan Lynn. B.S., U. Chattanooga, 1956; M.Hosp. Adminstrn., Washington U., St. Louis, 1965. Sales rep. Chemetron Corp., Chattanooga, 1956-60; hosp. purchasing agt. Meml. Hosp., Chattanooga, 1960-63; asst. adminstr. Ft. Sanders Presbyn. Hosp., Knoxville, Tenn., 1965-67, Sts. Mary and Elizabeth Hosp., Louisville, 1968-76, adminstr., 1975-81; adminstr., chief exec. officer Wilson Meml. Hosp., N.C., 1981—; dir. Statewide Health Coordinating Council, Ky., 1982-83, Ky. Health Systems Agy.-West, Louisville, 1978-81. Bd. dirs. ARC, Wilson, Wilson Concerts, Inc., 1982—. Served to sgt. USAF, 1951-55. Mem. Ky. Hosp. Assn. (life, bd. dirs. 1976-81), Wilson County C. of C. Republican. Presbyterian. Club: Wilson Country. Lodge: Kiwanis. Avocations: tennis; travel. Home: 1203 Cambridge Rd Wilson NC 27893 Office: Wilson Meml Hosp 1705 S Tarboro St Wilson NC 27893

SETTERFIELD, BARRY PETER, geologist; b. Chingola, Zambia, Mar. 2, 1955; came to U.S., 1984; s. Peter Henry and Eileen Betty (Hobden) S.; B.S. in Geology with honors, U. London, 1976. Geologist, Core Labs. Inc., Dallas, 1977-80; So. Oil Exploration, Johannesburg, S. Africa, 1980-82, Amoco, Houston, 1982—. Mem. Am. Assn. Petroleum Geologists, Petroleum Exploration Soc. Gt. Britain. Mem. Ch. of England. Avocations: photography; swimming; travel. Office: Amoco Prodn Co PO Box 3092 Houston TX 77253

SETZLER, NIKKI GILES, lawyer, state senator; b. Asheville, N.C., Aug. 7, 1945; s. Harry Earl and Verna Leona (Parker) S.; m. Ada Jane Taylor, Aug. 16, 1969; children—Tara Nikole, Jamie Leona, Sabra Taylor, Amber Jane. B.A., U. S.C., 1968, J.D., 1971. Bar: S.C. Practice law, 1971—; mem. S.C. Senate, 1977—, mem. Joint Appropriations Rev. Com.; mem. adv. com. on criminal justice, crime and delinquency, Central Midlands Regional Planning Council; judge Cayce City, S.C., 1974-76; town atty., Springdale, S.C., 1975—. Chmn. Lexington County Legis. Delegation; mem. ch. council Our Saviour Lutheran Ch., 1973-76. Mem. Lexington Jaycees (dir. 1973), Greater West Columbia-Cayce C. of C. (pres. 1975-76). Democrat. Lodge: Lions. *

SEUNG, HONG IL, physician, educator; b. Seoul, Korea, Aug. 3, 1937; came to U.S., 1963; s. Kwang Kyun and Kwang Sil (Sohn) S.; m. Ran Jo Yu, Oct. 9, 1965; children—Lisa, Sharon, Shauna, Mary, Emily. M.D., Seoul Nat. U., 1962. Diplomate Am. Bd. Otolaryngology. Intern, Hosp. of St. Raphael, New Haven, 1963-64; resident in gen. surgery St. Louis U. Group of Hosps., 1964-65, resident in otolaryngology, 1965-68; fellow in otolaryngology Mt. Sinai Hosp. 1968-69; practice medicine specializing in otolaryngology and head and neck surgery and allergy, Wheeling, W.Va., 1969—; vice-chmn. dept. ophthalmology and otolaryngology Wheeling Hosp., 1975—; clin. asst. prof. W.Va. U. Sch. Medicine, Morgantown, 1981—. Fellow ACS; mem. AMA, Am. Acad. Ophthalmology and Otolaryngology, Am. Soc. Ophthalmologic and Otolaryngologic Allergy, So. Med. Assn., W.Va. Med. Assn., W.Va. Acad. Ophthalmology and Otolaryngology, Ohio County Med. Soc. Republican. Presbyterian. Club: Country (Wheeling). Home: 18 Hawthorne Ct Wheeling WV 26003 Office: Profl Bldg 1300 Market St Wheeling WV 26003

SEVUSH, STEVEN, neurologist; b. Bklyn., Nov. 20, 1950; s. David and Norma (Weisman) S.; m. Elaine Marie Giuffrida, July 16, 1972; children—Jeremy, Jennifer Lori. B.S. in Physics, SUNY-Stony Brook, 1971; M.S. in Physics, U. Calif.-Berkeley, 1973; M.D., N.Y. Med. Coll., 1976. Diplomate Am. Bd. Neurology and Psychiatry. Intern Met. Hosp., N.Y.C., 1976-77; resident in neurology Albert Einstein Coll. Medicine, Bronx, N.Y., 1977-80; behavioral neurology fellow U. Fla., Gainesville, 1980-81; asst. prof. neurology U. Miami (Fla.), 1981—, dir. Dementia and Clin. Neurobehavior Ctr., 1982—; staff physician VA Med. Ctr., Miami, 1981—; mem. staff Jackson Meml. Hosp., Miami. Contbr. articles to various publs. Mem. med. adv. bd. Multiple Sclerosis Soc., 1982. NIH fellow, 1981-82; merit rev. grantee VA, 1984—. Mem. Am. Acad. Neurology, Acad. Aphasia, Internat. Neuropsychology Soc., AAAS, Alpha Omega Alpha, Sigma Pi Sigma. Office: Dept of Neurology (D4-5) PO Box 016960 U Miami Sch of Medicine Miami FL 33101

SEWELL, FRANK KASH, physician; b. Jackson, Ky., Feb. 28, 1909; s. Henry Price and Margaret Ann (Kash) S.; m. Carmie Bach, May 21, 1934; children—Frank, Martha Ann. A.B., U. Ky., 1929; M.D., Vanderbilt U., 1933; M.P.H., Johns Hopkins U., 1939. Diplomate Am. Bd. Family Practice. Intern, Davidson County Hosp., Nashville, 1933-34; practice family medicine, Jackson, Ky., 1934-37; cons. TB and epidemiology Ky. Health Dept., 1937-40; mem. staff VA Hosp., Lexington, Ky., 1945-46; gen. practice medicine, Mt. Sterling, Ky., 1946—; mem. staff Mary Chiles Hosp., Mt. Sterling, chief staff, 1950-60, mem. exec. com., 1960—. Health officer, Montgomery County, Ky., 1946-56. Served to col. M.C., AUS, 1940-45; Africa and Middle East. Decorated Legion of Merit. Mem. AMA, Ky. Med. Assn., Am. Assn. Family Physicians, Montgomery County Med. Soc. Democrat. Mem. Ch. Disciples of Christ. Lodges: Kiwanis, Masons, Odd Fellows.

SEWELL, GARY WILSON, drilling company executive; b. El Dorado, Ark., July 19, 1947; s. Wilson Horace and Jewell Marie (LaGrone) S.; B.B.A., S. Ark. U., 1970; m. Becky Cates, Dec. 4, 1981; children—Gary Brandon, Justin Scott. Supr., Shuler Drilling Co., Inc., El Dorado, Ark., 1970-75, v.p., gen. mgr., 1975—; v.p., treas. E.C. Hammond Oil Co., 1980—; dir. First Fed. Savs. and Loan Assn., El Dorado. Bd. dirs. Union County Farm Bur. Mem. Internat. Assn. Oilwell Drilling Contractors. Republican. Methodist. Home: 601 Nolia St El Dorado AR 71730 Office: 3514 W Hillsboro St El Dorado AR 71730

SEWELL, JAMES DAVID, law enforcement administrator, criminal justice researcher and consultant; b. Jacksonville, Fla., Sept. 27, 1950; s. Julian Davis and Alyce Elizabeth (Green) S.; m. Lauren Louise Hafner, Aug. 9, 1985. B.S., Fla. State U., 1971, M.S., 1975, Ph.D., 1980. Officer-lt. Fla. State U. Dept. Pub. Safety, 1973-80; internal insp. Fla. Dept. Law Enforcement, 1980-81, chief criminal intelligence bur., 1981, dep. dir. div. local law enforcement assistance, 1981-82, dep. dir. div. criminal justice info. systems, 1982, dir. mgmt. and planning services, dept hwy. safety and motor vehicles, 1982-86; chief of police City of Gulfport, Fla., 1986—; adj. prof. Sch. Criminology, Fla. State U.; cons. and inservice tng. police mgmt. Pres., bd. dirs. Tallahassee Telephone Counseling/Referral Service, 1985-86; v.p. Tallahassee Rape Crisis Service, bd. dirs., 1978-80. Mem. Soc. Police and Criminal Psychology, Internat. Assn. Campus Law Enforcement Adminstrs., Am. Soc. Pub. Adminstrn., Fla. Police Chiefs Assn., Internat. Law Enforcement Stress Assn. Democrat. Contbr. articles to profl. jours. Home: 817 Kendall Dr Tallahassee FL 32301 Office: Gulfport Police Dept Gulfport FL 33707

SEXAUER, ARWIN F.B. GARELLICK, retired librarian, poet, editor; b. Richford, Vt, Aug. 18, 1921; hon. diploma in arts and letters, Athens, Greece, 1979; D.Litt. (hon.), World U., World Acad. Arts and Letters, 1982; hon. diploma arts and letters Accademia Internazionale, Italy, 1982; m. Charles D. Bashaw, 1942 (dec.); children—Dawn Bashaw Mennucci, Alson C. Bashaw; m. 2d, Jack L. Garelick, 1963 (dec.); m. 3d, Howard T. Sexauer, 1979 (dec.). Asst. librarian Kellogg-Hubbard Library, Montpelier, Vt., 1966-73, head librarian, 1974-76; editor Vt. Odd Fellow mag., 1959-70; v.p. internat. affairs Marquis Scicluna Internat. U. Found., 1984—; author: (book of poetry) No Fanfare, 1953; Remembered Winds, 1963; poems in numerous anthologies; lyricist, monologist.; radio appearances Co-founder Music Mission Inc., 1963; past pres. United Meth. Ch. Women, Franklin County Pomona Grange, PTA; past v.p. Vt. 4-H Council; youth leader 4-H. Recipient numerous awards, including George Washington Honor medals, 1957, 59, 73, ASCAP Popular Panel awards (15), 1967-78, 82, citation, 1982; Richard Rodgers Music Found, award, Grand Ole Opry Trust Fund award, Dr. Arthur Hewitt Meml. award religious poetry, Virgilio-Mantegna medal, 1982; 2 spl. merit citations for poetry, 1982; spl. citation for poetry Internat. Congress Poets, 1982, numerous others. Fellow Internat. Acad. Poets (life), Anglo-Am. Acad. (hon.); mem. Accademia Leonardo da Vinci (diploma di benemerenza, diploma of honor The Glory, poet award, hon. rep.), World Poetry Soc. Intercontinental (disting. service citation, Vt. state rep.), Hellenic Writer's Club (life), Dr. Stella Woodall Poetry Soc. Internat., Calif. Fedn. Chaparral Poets, Poetry Soc. Vt., Gospel Music Assn., ASCAP, Vt. Library Assn., Internat. Press Assn., numerous others. Club: Rebekah (past noble grand). Poems, songs, other artifacts at Gleeson Library, U. San Francisco. Address: Idle Tide Cottage Box 303 Sanibel FL 33957

SEXTON, ANDREW LOUIS, consulting geologist, oil exploration company administrator; b. Lexington, Ky., Nov. 25, 1951; s. Bradley and Virginia (Johnson) S. B.A., Miami U., Oxford, Ohio, 1975. Field supr. Exploration Logging, Houston, 1978-81; v.p. Anadarko Cons., Perryton, Tex., 1981-84, owner, operator Anadarko Logging Service, Booker, Tex., 1984-85. Mem. Am. Assn. Petroleum Geologists, Soc. Petroleum Engrs., Tulsa Geol. Soc., Houston Geol. Soc. Avocations: water sports; camping. Office: Anadarko Logging Service PO Box 75 Perryton TX 79070

SEXTON, DONAL JAMES, JR., history educator, researcher; b. Buffalo, July 13, 1939; s. Donal James and Harriet Ann (Self) S.; m. Margaret Jean Roberts; children—Andrew Michael, Allison Leigh. B.A., Mich. State U., 1963, M.A., 1965; Cert. in Western Civilization, Carnegie-Mellon U., 1966; Ph.D., U. Tenn.-Knoxville, 1976. Prof. history Tusculum Coll., Greeneville, Tenn., 1965—; tchg. asst. history dept. U. Tenn., Knoxville, 1974-75; dir. Horse Creek Oral History Project, Tenn., 1985—. Contbr. articles to profl. jours. McClure fellow U. Tenn., 1973. Mem. Am. Mil. Inst. (Monacdo prize 1984), Orgn. Am. Historians, Am. Soc. Mil. Insignia Collectors (nat. adjutant treas. 1984—), Am. Com. History of Second World War. Presbyterian. Lodge: Moose. Avocations: hiking, gardening, music, collecting military insignia. Office: Tusculum College PO Box 5089 Greeneville TN 37743

SEXTON, HARLEY H., accountant, former hospital administrator; b. Clarksville, Ark., May 4. 1913; s. William Jacob and Dena H. Hudson) S.; attended Henderson State Coll., Arkadelphia, Ark.; m. Nettie Little, June 22, 1940; Co-owner, sec.-treas. wholesale grocery co., Hot Springs, Ark., 1937-57; acct., Hot Springs, 1958-62; asst. dir. Ark. Div. Legis. Audit, Little Rock, 1963-67; chief acct. Henderson State Coll., Arkadelphia, Ark., 1968-69; fiscal adminstr. St. Joseph's Hosp., Hot Springs, 1969-81. C.P.A. Mem. Am. Inst. C.P.A.s, Ark. Soc. C.P.A.s. Methodist (bd. dirs.). Lodge: Masons. Home: 265 Terry Hot Springs AR 71901

SEXTON, IRWIN, librarian; b. Lafayette, Ind., Nov. 7, 1921; s. Orville C. and Mary Della (Hayth) S.; B.S. in Trade and Indsl. Edn., Purdue U., 1949; M.S. in L.S., Western Res. U., 1952; m. Kathryn Segee, Nov. 24, 1950; 1 son, David. Dir., St. Joseph (Mo.) Pub. Library, 1955-57, Oklahoma City Libraries, 1958-60, San Antonio Pub. Library 1961—. Pres., St. Joseph Mental Health Assn., 1957. Served with USAAF, 1942-46. Mem. Am., Tex., Southwestern, Bexar library assns. Author: Industrial Techniques for the School Shop, 1955. Office: 203 S St Mary's St San Antonio TX 78205

SEXTON, JAMES LOYD, bank regulator; b. Pampa, Tex., May 3, 1939; s. James Willard and Irma Lou (Black) S.; m. Wilma Marie Martin, July 16, 1960; children—Sheryl Lynn, Carole Beth. B.B.A., West Tex. State U., 1965; diploma Stonier Grad. Sch. Banking, 1973; grad. Am. Inst. Banking, 1968, 78. Examiner, FDIC, Fort Worth, 1965-71, rev. examiner, Dallas, 1971-75, asst. regional dir., Memphis, 1975-79, regional dir., Phila., 1979-80, assoc. dir. div. banking suprs., Washington, 1980-82, dir. banking suprs., 1982-83; commr. Tex. Banking Dept., Austin, Tex., 1983—. Baptist. Avocations: golf; bridge; chess; reading. Office: Tex Banking Dept 2601 N Lamar St Austin TX 78705

SEYDEL, SCOTT O'SULLIVAN, chemical company executive; b. Atlanta, Mar. 29, 1940; s. John Rutherford and Jane (Reynolds) S.; student Ga. Inst. Tech., 1959-62, Textile Engr.; student U. Ga. Sch. Journalism, 1962-63; student bus. adminstrn. N. Tex. State U., 1963; m. Ruth Clark, Apr. 20, 1985; children—John Rutherford II, Rosina Marie, Lael Elizabeth, Scott O'Sullivan, Howard Clark. With Tex. Textile Mills, Inc., McKinney, 1963-64; personnel dir. Seydel-Woolley & Co., AZS Corp., Atlanta, 1965, public relations dir., 1966, asst. v.p., 1967, asst. exec. v.p., 1968, corp. dir., 1968-70, v.p. diversification, dir. internat. activities, 1969-70; pres. Seydel Cos., Atlanta, 1970—; chmn. Ednl. Solutions, Inc., Atlanta, 1985—; vice chmn. Ednl. Solutions S.C., Inc.; v.p., dir. SICHEM, Ghent, Belgium, 1975—, SICO South Africa, Durben, South Africa, 1975—, SIVEN, S.A., Caracas, Venezuela, 1971—, Quatic So., Inc., Atlanta, 1978-85; dir. Químicas de Centroamerica, Guatemala, Atlanta Overseas, Inc., Seydel Peruana, Lima, Internat. Precision, Inc., Clemson, S.C., Indsl. Precision, Inc., Clemson; chmn. Ednl. Solutions, Inc. Bd. dirs. Coll. Edn., Ga. State U., 1977-85, Coll. of Edn., 1985—, Atlanta Lung Assn.; bd. dirs., mem. exec. com. Triad Ednl. Consortium; chmn. bd. advs. Ga. World Congress Inst., 1981-85; bd. dirs. So. Regional Research Assn., Atlanta Council Internat. Visitors, Mayor Andrew Young's Internat. Task Force. Fellow Am. Assn. Textile Chemists and Colorists; mem. Internat. Council for Textile Technologists (dir. 1957—, sec. 1971—), So. Textile Assn., Atlanta Assn. Internat. Edn. (dir.), U.S. C. of C. (exec. res. com., export council), Atlanta Benedicts (v.p. 1972, dir. 1971-74), Chi Phi. Clubs: Rotary, Atlanta Commerce, Piedmont Driving (Atlanta). Contbr. articles to profl. jours. Home: 2700 Habersham Rd Atlanta GA 30305 Office: 80 Broad St Atlanta GA 30325

SEYDELL, MILDRED, writer, lectr., traveler; b. Atlanta; d. Vasser and Elizabeth Cobb (Rutherford) Woolley; ed. Washington Sem., Atlanta, The Lucy Cobb Inst., Athens, Ga., and Sorbonne, Paris; m. Paul Bernard Seydel (dec.); children—Paul Vasser, John Rutherford; m. 2d, Max Seydell (dec.). Columnist Charleston (W.Va.) Gazette, 1921; rep. Hearst Crime Commn., in Europe, 1926, collecting data for series of articles and interviews; traveled in Belgium and Ireland, 1927, in Balkan States, Hungary, Turkey and Greece, 1929, Sweden, Germany and France, 1931; contributed Talks with Celebrities; made spl. study of liquor regulation in Sweden; traveled through Africa from Capetown to Cairo and into Palestine, 1934; made spl. study of history of diamonds and gold in S. Africa and native customs of Belgian Congo, investigation of activity of Jews in Palestine; adventure in friendship to South Sea Islands, New Zealand and Australia, 1937; Internat. News Service rep. in Germany and Czechoslovakia, 1938, Finland, 1939; corr. U.S. papers; adventures in Europe, 1955, Eng., Wales, 1956; pres. Mildred Seydell Pub. Co. Belgian dir. World Poetry Day. Mem. Ga. Mothers Com.; v.p. Meml. Day Com. Decorated knight Order Leopold (Belgium); recipient 1st Book of Golden Deeds award Roswell Exchange Club, 1978. Mem. Nat. League Am. Pen Women, Internat. Periodic Press (dir. poetry Belgian sect.), Friends of Emory U. Library (hon.), A.G. Rhodes Home (hon.), Beta Sigma Phi (hon.). Clubs: Peony Garden (hon.); American Women's (Brussels). Author: Secret Fathers, 1930; Then I Saw North Carolina, 1936; Chins Up, 1939; Come Along to Belgium, 1969; Keep the Course, 1981. Editor: Poetry Profile of Belgium, 1960. Publisher: Silent Singing (poems); Essays Wise and Otherwise. Mem. adv. bd. Sunshine Mag., Fellowship in Prayer mag. Home: 9530 Scott Rd Route 2 Roswell GA 30076

SEYFRIED, GEORGE GORDON, civil engineer, tax accountant; b. Evanston, Ill., Nov. 11, 1936; s. John Edwin and Susan Jane (Tietgens) S.; m. Christie van Cleve, June 2, 1962 (div. Oct. 1971); 1 son, John Christie; m. 2d, Reni Hannon. B.S. in Civil Engring., U. Colo., 1959, B.S. in Bus. Adminstrn., 1959. Registered profl. engr., Colo. Engr., Sproul Land Co., Colorado Springs, Colo., 1959; engr. FAA, Los Angeles, 1960-62, Denver, 1962-73, Fort Worth, 1973—. Served to 2d lt. U.S. Army, 1959-60. Republican. Episcopalian. Lodge: Elks. Home: PO Box 12626 Fort Worth TX 76116 Office: FAA PO Box 1689 Fort Worth TX 76101

SEYMOUR, CLIFFORD THEODORE, educator; b. Pueblo, Colo., Feb. 23, 1915; s. Matthew Otto and Mattie Aldridge S.; m. Anna Florine McDonnell, July 23, 1948; 1 son, Clifford Theodore. A.A., Pueblo Jr. Coll., 1939; B.S., Va. Union U., 1943; M.S., Ind. U., 1951, Ed.D., 1952. Grad. asst. Ind. U., Bloomington, 1951-53; instr. Grambling (La.) Coll., 1952-55; mem. faculty dept. leisure sci. So. U., Baton Rouge, 1955—, dept. chmn., 1955-83, prof., 1974—, dir. div. health, phys. edn., recreation and dance, 1980—. Chmn. Greater Baton Rouge Council on Aging, 1975-77, 81-83; mem. adv. com. Nat. Park Service, 1979-80; bd. dirs. Capitol Area Agy., 1979-82, Girl Scouts U.S.A., 1980-82, Baton Rouge Mental Health Assn., 1981—; elder Presbyn. Ch. of Scotlandville; chmn. adv. com. Baton Rouge Area Council on Aging, 1983-84. Served with U.S. Army, 1943-46. Recipient Silver Beaver award Boy Scouts Am., 1976. Mem. AAHPERD (v.p. So. dist. recreation sect. 1979, Dist. Fellowship award 1980), La. Assn. Health, Phys. Edn. and Recreation (v.p. recreation sect. 1980), Nat. Parks and Recreation Assn., Nat. Recreation Therapeutic Assn., Soc. Parks and Recreation Educators, Am. Leisure and Recreation Assn. (v.p. 1979), La. Parks and Recreation Assn. (honor award 1982). Office: Dept Leisure and Recreation Services Southern U Baton Rouge LA 70813

SEYMOUR, GEORGE AUSTIN, pipeline company executive; b. Westfield, N.J., Mar. 10, 1926; s. Edward Drullard and Ruth Ellen (Pierce) S.; m. Harriet Virginia Harvie, June 15, 1947 (div.); children—Ruth, Peter, Harriet, Kathryn; m. Pauline Gill, Dec. 29, 1976. B.M.E., Rensselaer Poly. Inst., 1946. Engr. domestic, foreign pipeline constrn. Mobil Corp., Mobil Pipe Line Co., Venezuela, Tex., France, Algeria, 1947-61, with producing mgmt., Venezuela, 1961-66, sr. exec. tech., joint interest pipeline activities, U.S. and Norway, 1966-79, sr. exec. mgmt. of foreign pipeline projects, 1979-85; dir., officer maj. petroleum pipeline cos., 1968-76, 85. Served to lt. USNR, 1943-47, 51-53. Decorated knight Order of Saharan Merit (France), 1961. Mem. Am. Petroleum Inst. Republican. Club: Engineer's (Dallas). Office: PO Box 900 Dallas TX 75221

SEYMOUR, MARTHA DAILEY, nurse, administrator medical surgical nursing; b. Birmingham, Ala., Dec. 10, 1944; d. James Louis and Mae (Williams) Dailey; m. James Franklin Seymour, Mar. 10, 1962; children—Terry, Tracy. A.D., Jefferson State Jr. Coll., 1969; B.S. in Nursing, Samford U., 1981. Staff nurse Baptist Med. Ctr., Birmingham, 1969-71, nursing supr., 1971-77, dir. nursing, 1977—. Mem. Am. Soc. Nursing Service Adminstrs., Am. Nurses Assn. Roman Catholic. Home: 579 Karey Dr Birmingham AL 35215 Office: Baptist Med Ctr 800 Montclair Rd Birmingham AL 35213

SEYMOUR, RAYMOND BENEDICT, chemical engineering educator emeritus, consultant; b. Boston, July 26, 1912; s. Walter A. and Marie E. (Doherty) S.; B.S., U. N.H., 1933, M.S., 1935; Ph.D., State U. Iowa, 1937; postdoctoral Rensselaer Poly. Inst., 1963, U. Utah, 1964; m. Frances B. Horan, Sept. 16, 1936; children—David Ray, Susan (Mrs. Howard Smith), Peter, Phillip Alan. Instr. chemistry U. N.H., 1933-35, U. Iowa, 1935-37; research chemist Goodyear Tire & Rubber Co., Akron, Ohio, 1937-39; chief chemist Atlas Mineral Products div. Electric Storage Battery Co., Mertztown, Pa., 1939-41, exec. v.p., gen. mgr., tech. dir., 1949-54, pres., dir., 1954-55; research group leader Monsanto Co., Dayton, Ohio, 1941-45; dir. research, U. Chattanooga, 1945-48; dir. research Johnson & Johnson, New Brunswick, N.J., 1948-49; pres., tech. dir. Loven Chem. of Calif., 1955-58; pres. Corrosion Resistant Products, Inc., 1956-57; pres., chmn. bd. Alcylite Plastics & Chem. Corp., 1958-60; prof. chemistry, chmn. sci. div. Sul Ross State U., 1959-64; asso. chmn. chemistry dept. U. Houston. 1964-66, coordinator polymer chemistry, 1964-76, asso. prof. chemistry, 1964-69, prof., 1969-76, prof. emeritus, 1976—, asso. dir. research, 1966-68; adj. prof. polymer sci. U. So. Miss., Hattiesburg, 1974-76, distinguished prof., 1976—; cons. edn. AID, U.S. Dept. State, East Pakistan, 1968; mem. execs. res. Dept. Def.; dir. NSF Inst., 1965; Nat. Acad. Scis. vis. prof., Yugoslavia, 1976, Australia, 1977, USSR, 1978, China, 1979. Recipient Western Plastics award, 1960; Teaching Excellence award U. Houston, 1975; Catalyst Excellence in Teaching award Chem. Mfrs. Assn., 1976; So. Chemists award, 1981; elected to Western Plastics Hall of Fame, 1981. Registered profl. engr., Tex., Ohio. Fellow AAAS, Am. Inst. Chemists (Honor Scroll 1980, Chemist Pioneer award 1985), Tex. Acad. Sci.; mem. Am. Inst. Chem. Engrs., Am. Chem. Soc. (Southeastern Tex. Ann. award 1972, So. Chemist award 1982, Charles Herty award 1985), Soc. Plastics Industry, Nat. Assn. Corrosion Engrs., Am. Soc. Oceanography, AAUP, Soc. Plastic Engrs. (internat. edn. award 1982), Plastics Pioneers Assn., Miss. Acad. Sci., Sigma Xi, Phi Kappa Phi, Alpha Chi Sigma, Gamma Sigma Epsilon. Rotarian. Club: Hattiesburg Country. Author: National Paint Dictionary, 3d edit., 1948; Plastics for Corrosion Resistant Applications; 1955; Hot Organic Coatings, 1959; Introduction to Polymer Chemistry, 1971, 79; General Organic Chemistry, 1971; Experimental Organic Chemistry, 1971; Modern Plastics Technology, 1974; Chemistry and You, 1974; Structure-Solubility Relationships in Polymers, 1977; Polymer Chemistry, 1977, 81; Additives for Plastics, Vol. I and II, 1977; Plastic Mortars, Sealants, and Caulking Compounds, 1979; Block Co-polymers, 1981; Polymer Chemistry and Technology (audio course), 1981; Polymer Chemistry: an introduction, 1981; Plastics vs. Corrosives, 1982; History of Polymer Chemistry, 1981; Plastics vs. Solvents, 1981; Ann. Plastic Review 1948—; Property-Structure Relationships in Polymers, 1983; Genesis of Polymer Science, 1983; Conductive Polymers, 1981; Macromolecular Solutions, 1982; History of Polyolefins, 1985; Advances in Polyolefins, 1986; also articles. Patentee in field. Home: 111 Lakeshore Dr Route 10 Hattiesburg MS 39401

SEYMOUR, STEPHANIE KULP, U.S. judge; b. Battle Creek, Mich., Oct. 16, 1940; d. Francis Bruce and Frances Cecelia (Bria) Kulp. B.A. magna cum laude, Smith Coll., 1962; J.D., Harvard U., 1965; m. R. Thomas Seymour, June 10, 1972; children—Bart, Bria, Sara, Anna. Admitted to Okla. bar, 1965; practice of law, Boston, 1965-66, Tulsa, 1966-67, 71-79, Houston, 1968-69; assoc. firm Doerner, Stuart, Saunders, Daniel & Anderson, Tulsa, 1971-75, ptnr., 1975-79; judge U.S. Ct. Appeals 10th Circuit, Tulsa, 1979—; assoc. bar examiner Okla. Bar Assn., 1973-79; trustee Tulsa County Law Library, 1977-78; mem. legal adv. panel Tulsa Task Force on Battered Women, 1971-77. Mem. various task forces Tulsa Human Rights Commn., 1972-76. Mem. ABA, Okla. Bar Assn., Tulsa County Bar Assn., Phi Beta Kappa.

SHACKELFORD, GEORGE GREEN, history educator; b. Orange, Va., Dec. 17, 1920; s. Virginius Randolph and Peachy Gascoigne (Lyne) S.; B.A., U. Va., 1943; M.A., U. Va., 1948, Ph.D., 1955; postgrad. Columbia U., 1949-51; cert. Attingham (Eng.), 1957; m. Grace Howard McConnell, June 9, 1962. Asst. prof. history Birmingham (Ala.) So. Coll., 1948-49; research fellow Va. Hist. Soc., Richmond, 1951-53; instr. Va. Poly. Inst. and State U., Blacksburg, 1954-55, asst. prof. history, 1955-58, assoc. prof., 1958-68, prof., 1968—; cons. hist. mgmt. Westmoreland Davis Meml. Found., Leesburg, Va., 1967-73, 77—. Mem. Va. Comm. on Bicentenial of U.S. Constitution, 1985—. Recipient Historic Preservation award of Va. soc. Am. Inst. Architects, 1985. Served to lt. USNR, 1943-49. Mem. Am. Hist. Assn., English Speaking Union (pres. SW Va. br. 1979), Nat. Trust Historic Preservation (bd. advs. 1976-79), Assn. Inst. Early Am. History and Culture, Attingham Assos., Assn. Preservation Va. Antiquities (dir. 1960-64, 67-77), Monticello Assn. (pres. 1969-71), So. Hist. Assn., Va. Hist. Assn., Soc. Archtl. History. Democrat. Episcopalian. Clubs: Farmington Country (Charlottesville, Va.); Shenandoah (Roanoke, Va.); Univ. (Blacksburg, Va.). Editor: Monticello Assn. Collected Papers, Vol. I, 1965, Vol. 2, 1984; co-editor Va. Social Sci. Jour., 1967-68; contbr. articles in field to profl. jours. Home: Box 219 301 Wall St Blacksburg VA 24060 Office: Dept History Va Poly Inst and State U Blacksburg VA 24061

SHADDIX, LINDA PARSONS, counselor, educator; b. Epps, Ala., Aug. 7, 1946; d. Selburn Weir and Anne Ruth (McCray) P.; m. Robert Leroy Shaddix, Jan. 23, 1965; children—Stacey Renee, Holley Lynn. B.S. in Elem. Edn., U. Ala., 1975; M.Ed., U. Cin., 1980. Orientation asst. U. Cin., 1975-77, teaching asst., 1977-78; counselor Warren Yazoo Mental Health Vicksburg, Miss., 1978-81, Nordal Clinic, P.A., Vicksburg, 1981-82, Personal Growth Ctr.,

Vicksburg, 1982-83, U. N.C., Wilmington, 1983—; coordinator Services for Handicapped Students, Wilmington, 1984—. Mem. Task Force Against Family Violence, Wilmington, 1983-85, Council on Status of Women, Wilmington, 1984-85. Mem. Assn. on Handicap Services in Postsecondary Edn., Am. Assn. Mental Health Counselors, Am. Coll. Personnel Assn. Democrat. Roman Catholic. Lodge: Eastern Star. Avocation: sailing. Home: 811 Greenbriar Rd Wilmington NC 28403 Office: U NC Wilmington NC 28403

SHADE, RONALD HERBERT, information developer; b. Cleve., Apr. 18, 1942; s. Raymond Herbert and Rita Marie (Miller) S.; m. Temmie Lois Shade, July 22, 1978; children—Stacey Elizabeth, Stephanie Gabrielle. B.B.A., U. Houston, 1971; M.L.S., N. Tex. State U., 1983. Bldg. ops. coordinator U. Houston, 1968-73; info. developer IBM Corp., Dallas, 1967-68, 73—. Served with USAF, 1959-67. Mem. Am. Soc. Info. Sci., ALA, Spl. Library Assn., Beta Phi Mu. Roman Catholic. Home: 717 Jannie St Denton TX 76201 Office: IBM Corp 220 Las Colinas Blvd Irving TX 75039

SHADOAN, WILLIAM LEWIS, circuit judge; b. Galesburg, Ill., July 12, 1931; s. William Parker and Hortense (Lewis) S.; m. Katherine E. Shadoan; children—Ann-Wayne Harlan, Kate, Tom. B.S., U. Ky., 1955; J.D., U. Louisville, 1961. Bar: Ky. 1961, U.S. Dist. Ct. (we. dist.) Ky. 1961. City atty., Wickliffe, Ky., 1963-65; county atty. Ballard County, Ky., 1967-79; circuit judge 1st Jud. Dist., Wickliffe, Ky., 1984—. Chmn., Ballard County Democratic Party, 1963; trustee Methodist Ch., Wickliffe, 1961-84; adviser Selective Service, Paducah, Ky., 1968; chmn. Wickliffe C. of C., 1967-71; mem. exec. com. Ky. Hist. Soc., Frankfort. Named assoc. justice Ky. Supreme Ct., 1984. Served to capt. U.S. Army, 1955-59. Mem. Ky. Health Systems Assn. (vice chmn. 1976-82), ABA, Ky. Bar, Assn. Trial Lawyers Am., Ky. County Ofcls. Bd. (chmn. 1976-80), Miss. River Commn. (chmn. 1976-83), Ky. County Attys. Assn. (pres. 1966-77), First Dist. Bar Assn. (pres.). Lodges: Mason (Wickliffe); Shriners (Madisonville, Ky.); Order of Eastern Star, Elks. Home: Route 2 Wickliffe KY 42087 Office: Ballard Courthouse 4th St Wickliffe KY 42087

SHADOMY, SMITH, microbiology and chemotherapeutics educator; b. Denver, Aug. 29, 1931; s. Henry Kesler and Helen Budd (Dart) Kesler; m. Helen Jean Mills, Jan. 22, 1956; children—Barbara Louise, Sean Vincent. B.A. in Bacteriology, UCLA, 1955; Ph.D. in Microbiology, 1963. Registered spl. microbiologist. Research microbiologist Walter Reed Army Inst. Research, Washington, 1963-65; asst. prof. medicine Med. Coll. Va., Richmond, 1965-67; assoc. prof. medicine and microbiology Va. Commonwealth U., Richmond, 1967-77, prof. medicine and microbiology, 1977-82, prof. medicine and pathology, prof. microbiology and immunology, 1982—; cons. various pharm. firms on antifungal chemotherapy. Founding mem., past pres. Richmond Montessori Sch. PTA, 1975-77. Served to 1st lt. USAR, 1956; to capt. AUS, 1963-65; col. USAR, 1979. Mem. Am. Soc. Microbiology, Infectious Disease Soc. Am., Med. Mycol. Soc. Ams. (Meridian award 1986), Brit. Soc. Mycopathology (hon.), Internat. Soc. Human and Animal Mycology, Nat. Rifle Assn. Contbr. chpts. to books, articles to profl. jours. Office: PO Box 38 MCV Sta Med Coll Va Va Commonwealth U Richmond VA 23298

SHAFER, BARBARA HOUGH, educator; b. Ft. Myers, Fla., Apr. 16, 1928; d. Wendell M. and Jeannette (Carmichael) Hough; m. Robert T. Shafer, Jr., Dec. 27, 1950; children—Richard, Janet, Charles. B.A., Coll. Wooster, 1950; M.A., U. South Fla., 1982. Tchr., Wooster High Sch. (Ohio), 1950-51; tchr. Ft. Myers High Sch. (Fla.), 1951-53, tchr., coordinator girls sports, 1969—, volleyball/basketball coach, 1969—; tchr. Withrow High Sch. (Cin.), 1953-55, Bishop Verot High Sch., Ft. Myers, 1955-59. Vol. ARC, 1970—; mem. steering com. for girls sports State of Fla., 1974-76, Lee County steering com. for girls sports, 1974-76. Republican. Presbyterian. Home: 2704 Shriver Dr Fort Myers FL 33901 Office: Fort Myers High Sch Cortez Blvd Fort Myers FL 39901

SHAFER, DIANE ELAIN, orthopaedic surgeon; b. Oil City, Pa., Apr. 30, 1952; d. Lawrence Archie and Sara Ann (Dickinson) S.; 1 child, Sara Teresa. B.S., Pa. State U., 1972; M.D., Temple U., 1975. Intern, Hamot Med. Ctr., Erie, Pa., 1975-76, resident in orthopedic surgery, 1976-78; resident in orthopedic surgery Pa. State Hershey Med. Ctr., Hershey, Pa., 1978-80; pvt. practice medicine specializing in orthopedic surgery, Williamson, W.Va., 1980—; med. dir. dept. phys. medicine Williamson Appalachian Regional Hosp., 1980—; attending physician orthopaedic surgery Williamson Meml. Hosp., 1980—, Paul B. Hall Med. Ctr., Highlands Regional Med. Ctr., Prestonsburg, Ky.; ptnr. Lock, Stock and Barrel Restaurant; hammered dulcimer player Bluegrass group Ind. Mountaineers. Chairperson adv. bd. Salvation Army, 1982—; pres., bd. dirs. Tug Valley Recovery Shelter, 1980—; founder Domestic Violence Ctr. Mem. AMA, W.Va. Med. Assn. (counselor, del. 1980—), Ky. Med. Assn., Pike County Med. Assn., Mingo County Med. Soc. (sec.-treas.), Am. Back Soc. (bd. dirs.), Am. Acad. Neurologic and Orthopaedic Surgery (diplomate). Republican. Presbyterian. Home: Box 27 Turkey Creek KY 41570 Office: Box 749 Williamson WV 25661

SHAFER, HELEN LOUISE, school administrator; b. Athens, Tex., July 14, 1930; d. Horace Scott and Willouise (Low) Barron; m. Harvey Lee Shafer, Apr. 30, 1949; children—Julie Louise Shafer Kollhoff, Janet Lynn Shafer Boyanton, Edwin Scott. B.A. in Zoology and Bacteriology, U. Tex., 1950; M.A. in Biology, So. Meth. U., 1972; postgrad. North Tex. State U., 1977-79. Cert. tchr., adminstr., Tex. Tchr. biology and physics Adamson High Sch. Dallas Ind. Sch. Dist., 1967-68, sci. instructional specialist, 1976-78, adminstrv. planner Sci./Tech. High, 1978-80, dean instrn. Bus. Mgmt. Ctr., 1980-82, prin. Sci./Engring. Magnet Sch., 1982—; cons. edn. task force Dallas C. of C., 1978-80. Author: (with Walt Elliot) Career-Oriented Pre-Technical Physics, 1973-75. Ruling elder Wynnewood Presbyterian Ch., Dallas, 1979-81, 84—, chmn. Christian Edn., 1979-81, chom. commitment com., 1984—. Recipient award Excellence in Teaching Perot Found., 1975; NSF grantee, 1969-72, 79. Mem. Nat. Sci. Tchrs. Assn., AAAS, Tex. Assn. Secondary Sch. Prins., Nat. Sci. Suprs. Assn., Am. Assn. Physics Tchrs., N.Y. Acad. Scis., Am. Assn. Curriculum and Supervision, Dallas Sch. Adminstrs. Assn., Tex. Sci. Suprs. Assn., Mensa, Phi Delta Kappa. Avocations: gardening; travel. Home: 1536 Bilco St Dallas TX 75232 Office: Sci/Engring Magnet Sch 3700 Ross Ave Dallas TX 75204

SHAFFER, ANITA MOHRLAND, counselor; b. Racine, Wis., Apr. 5, 1939; d. Milton Arthur and Gudrun Amanda (Sundvoll) Stoffel; m. Ralph Otis Shankle, June 18, 1983 (dec. 1985); stepchildren—Gary Shankle, Kim Perkins. B.S., U. Wis.-Madison, 1961, postgrad., 1962; M.Ed., U. Wash., Seattle, 1966; postgrad. Ariz. State U., 1971-76. Elem. tchr. Racine Unified Sch. Dist., 1961-63; Edmonds Sch. Dist., Alderwood Manor, Wash., 1963-70; tchr. acad. and spl. edn. Ariz. Dept. Corrections, Phoenix, 1971-77, community liaison, 1975-77; spl. edn. tchr. Pasadena Ind. Sch. Dist., Tex., 1977-78, spl. edn. counselor, 1978—. Mem., patron Bay Area Chorus, Houston, 1982—; mem. Clear Lake Symphony, Houston, 1985—; patron Mus. Fine Arts, Houston, 1981—; nat. assoc. Smithsonian Inst., Washington, 1982—. Mem. Internat. Acad. Profl. Counseling and Psychotherapy (diplomate), Am. Assn. Counseling and Devel., Am. Mental Health Counselors Assn., Am. Sch. Counselors Assn., AAUW, Wis. Alumni Assn., Norwegian Soc. Tex., Tex. Assn. Counseling and Devel., Pi Lambda Theta, Beta Sigma Phi. Republican. Avocations: violinist; singer; art; reading; handicrafts. Home: 260 El Dorado Blvd Apt H801 Webster TX 77598 Office: Pasadena Ind Sch Dist 3010 Bay Shore Dr Pasadena TX 77502

SHAFFER, DAVID REED, psychology educator; b. Watsonville, Calif., Feb. 4, 1946; s. Duboise Herbert and Gerrie Doris (Cadieux) S.; m. Garnett Stokes, June 6, 1981. B.A., Humboldt State U., 1967, M.A., 1968; Ph.D., Kent State U., 1972. Asst. prof. psychology Kent State U., Ohio, 1972-73; asst. prof. U. Ga., Athens, 1973-76, assoc. prof., 1976-82, prof., 1982—, head devel. psychology program, 1982—. Author: Social and Personality Development, 1979; Developmental Psychology, 1985. Assoc. editor Personality and Social Psychology Bull., 1975-77, Jour. Personality and Social Psychology, 1978-79, Jour. Personality, 1981—. Contbr. articles to profl. jours. Served with USMCR, 1970-72. NIH grantee, 1974, 75; named Disting. Alumnus, Humboldt State U., 1983. Mem. Am. Psychol. Assn., Soc. Research in Child Devel., Soc. Exptl. Social Psychologists, Southeastern Psychol. Assn. Democrat. Avocations: hiking, sport fishing. Home: 249 Ansley Dr Athens GA 30605 Office: U Ga Dept Psychology Athens GA 30605

SHAFFER, JEANNE ELLISON, college administrator; b. Knoxville, Tenn., May 25, 1925; d. James Harold Butcher and Dorothy Maude (Ellison) Black; m. Loran O. Shaffer, June 14, 1944 (dec.); children—Jeanette Shaffer Sowman, Beverly Shaffer Bean, Madolyn Shaffer Griffen, Larry, Malinda. A.A., Stephens Coll., 1944; B.M., Samford U., 1954; M.M., Birmingham So. Coll., 1958; Ph.D., George Peabody Coll., 1970. Assoc. prof. Union U., Jackson, Tenn., 1970-71; head fine arts interdisciplinary Fisk U., Nashville, 1972-73; head div. fine arts Judson Coll., Marion, Ala., 1973-76; head dept. visual and performing arts Huntingdon Coll., Montgomery, Ala., 1976—. Weekly columnist Jour. Montgomery Advertiser, 1977—; Editor: O Praise the Lord All Ye Nations (Alessandro Scarlatti), 1973. Composer religious anthems, art songs, chamber music. Advisor, Montgomery Jr. League, 1977-78; organist, choirmaster Baptist and Episcopalian Chs., Tenn., Mo., Ala., and Ill., 1944—; soprano soloist Temple Beth Or, Montgomery, 1980—; sec.-treas. Montgomery Performing Arts Co., 1978—; v.p. Sch. Fine Arts, Inc., 1985—. Recipient Composition 1st place award Birmingham Festival Arts, 1954, 59, 61; named Outstanding Alumnus of Yr., Stephens Coll., 1958; Meritt award Ala. State Council Arts, 1980; grantee NDEA, 1967, Nat. Endowment for Humanities, 1984. Mem. Assn. Ala. Coll. Music Adminstrs. (pres. 1979-81), Am. Guild Organists, Nat. Assn. Tchrs. Singing, Am. Choral Dirs. Assn., Am. Women Composers, Southeastern Composers League (sec. 1974-76). Home: 3124 Woodley Terr Montgomery AL 36106 Office: Huntingdon Coll 1500 E Fairview Ave Montgomery AL 36106

SHAFFER, KAY L., educational administrator; b. Warren, Ohio, May 6, 1939; d. Robert G. and Nina L. (Webb) Nagel; m. Richard G. Shaffer, June 12, 1959; children—Nina Marie Stubbs, Scott Robert. B.S. magna cum laude, U. Utah, 1963; M.S., Ga. State U., 1979. Bookkeeper, State Bank of Provo (Utah), 1958-59; adminstrv. asst. U. Utah, Salt Lake City, 1959-62; acctg. asst. N.W. Ga. council Girl Scouts U.S.A., Atlanta, 1976-78; adminstrv. coordinator Ga. Career Info. Ctr., Ga. State U., Atlanta, 1979, asst. dir., 1979—, adj. instr. urban studies and vol. adminstrn., 1980—. Vol. adminstr., youth leader, tchr. Army post chapels and civilian congregations, Army Community Service, Officers' Wives Clubs, Girl Scouts U.S.A., Germany, Ariz., Ind., Ga., 1963-78; com. mem. N.W. Ga. council Girl Scouts U.S.A., Atlanta, 1974—; mem. Community Relations Commn. East Point (Ga.), 1980-81; v.p. support services, bd. dirs. Jesse Draper Boys Club, College Park, Ga., 1984—; cons. Southeast Regional Manpower Devel. Com., Boys Clubs Am., 1984—. Recipient appreciation plaque, N.W. Ga. Girl Scout Council, 1975, appreciation cert. Boys Clubs of Met. Atlanta, 1984. Mem. Am. Humanics Alumni Assn. (cert. youth agy. profl.), Assn. Voluntary Action Scholars, Urban Affairs Assn., Ga. State U. Woman's Network, Am. Sociol. Assn., So. Sociol. Soc., Am. Humanics Alumni Assn. (v.p. Southeastern region 1983—), Atlanta Women's Network, Am. Soc. Tng. and Devel., Phi Kappa Phi, Beta Gamma Sigma, Alpha Kappa Delta, Alpha Lambda Delta, Alpha Phi. . Presbyterian. Author: Girl Scouting & You, 1976; (with others) Job Expectations of College Students, 1979; (with Mary Jane Armstrong) Collaboration Among Youth Agencies, 1979; (with others) God Loves Me, 1979. Office: Ga Career Info Ctr Ga State U Box 1028 Univ Plaza Atlanta GA 30303

SHAFFER, MARTIN, wholesale executive; b. Clarksburg, W.Va., May 11, 1950; s. Shirley James and Francis Josephine (Fahey) S.; m. Victoria Ann Finamore, Sept. 17, 1971; children—Gena, Martin, Alexander. B.S. in Bus. Adminstrn., 1976, M.B.A., 1976; postgrad. in mktg., Cornell U., 1981. Treas. Am. Vending Co., Clarksburg, 1973-83; pres. B.F. Splty. Co., Anmoore, W.Va., 1979—, also chief exec. officer; treas. Clarksburg Enterprises, Am. Amusements; dir. Am. Sales & Concessions. Mem. Senate Adv. Com. on Small Bus.; vice chmn. Harrison County Democratic Com. Named Ky. col., 1978; Young Dem. of Yr., W.Va. Young Dems., 1978; W.Va. Ambassador of Goodwill, 1979; Tobacco Distbr. of Yr., W.Va. Wholesalers Assn., 1982. Mem. W.Va. Wholesalers Assn. (v.p.), Nat. Assn. Tobacco Distbrs., Nat. Automatic Merchandisers Assn., Nat. Candy Wholesalers Assn., Nat. Assn. Concessionaires, Music Operators Am., W.Va. Coalition Small Bus. Roman Catholic. Lodges: KC, Moose. Home: 215 Webster St Clarksburg WV 26301 Office: PO Box 288 Anmoore WV 26323

SHAFFER, SHIRLEY JEAN ANDERSON, publishing company executive; b. Chgo., Sept. 23, 1925; d. Edwin W. and Marie G. (Nelson) A.; student Pan Am. U., 1943; gen. bus. diploma Durhams Jr. Bus. Coll., 1944; student Northwestern U., 1946-49; m. Lester E. Shaffer, Nov. 5, 1949 (div. 1964); children—Bonnie, Larry, Steven, Scott, Leslie. Owner, operator Grefan Kennels, Norridge, Ill., 1955-64; editorial asst. Peacock Bus. Press, Park Ridge, Ill., 1963-67; sales/service coordinator Goodyear Chem. div. Goodyear Co., Elk Grove, Ill., 1967-68; dir. sales rep., various companies, 1968-73; v.p. Mid Am. Investments, Dallas, 1973-74; credit and collection mgr. Boehringer Mannheim Diagnostics, Inc. (formerly Hycel, Inc.), Houston, 1974-80, mgr. corp. purchasing, 1980-82; editor Key Mag—This Month in San Antonio, 1983—. Mem. Nat. Conservative Polit. Action Com., The Conservative Caucus; mem. state adv. bd. Presdl. candidate Congressman Phillip M. Crane, 1979-80. Mem. Nat. Assn. Credit Mgmt., Tex. Assn. Credit Mgmt., Houston Assn. Credit Mgmt., Greater San Antonio C. of C., Nat. Assn. Credit Mgmt. of Tex., Inc. San Antonio Hotel and Motel Assn. (bd. dirs. 1986-87), Tex. Restaurant Assn. (San Antonio chpt.), Am. Kennel Club, Phi Gamma Nu. Republican. Methodist. Home: PO Box 290639 San Antonio TX 78280 Office: 700 N St Mary's 14th Floor San Antonio TX 78205

SHAFFNER, RANDOLPH PRESTON, bookstore owner, author; b. Winston-Salem, N.C., Jan. 17, 1940; s. Emil Nathaniel and Anna Jackson (Preston) S.; m. Margaret Farmer Rhodes; children—Eric Randolph, Edward David, Joseph Andrew, Thomas Matthew. Student, Davidson Coll., 1958-60; B.A. in English, U. N.C., 1962; M.A. in Comparative Lit., 1969, Ph.D., 1973. Tchr. U.S. Peace Corps, Chiengrai, Thailand, 1963-65, St. Christopher's Sch., Richmond, Va., 1969-71, Fairfield U., Conn., 1973-78; editor John F. Blair, Pub., Winston-Salem, 1965-68; bookseller Cycano's Bookshop, Highlands, N.C., 1978—. Author: Apprenticeship Novel, 1984. Chmn. ARC Disaster Services, Fairfield, 1974-78, Zoning Bd. of Adjustment, Highlands, 1981-83, 85—; chaperon Am. Inst. for Fgn. Study, Grenoble, France, 1970. Goethe Inst. scholar, German Embassy, Munich, Fed. Rep. Germany, 1965. Mem. Internat. Comparative Lit. Assn., Am. Comparative Lit. Assn., Am. Booksellers Assn., MLA, Highlands Biol. Found. Democrat. Moravian. Avocations: construction; reading; traveling; hiking; camping. Home: Hickory St Highlands NC 28741 Office: Cyrano's Bookshop Main St Highlands NC 28741

SHAFTMAN, FREDRICK KRISCH, telephone communication executive, lawyer; b. Roanoke, Va., Apr. 9, 1948; s. Sydney and Rosalie (Krisch) S.; B.S. in Bus. Adminstrn., U. Ala., 1970, J.D., 1973; m. Diane Hasson, Dec. 27, 1970; children—Stephanie, Emily. Bar: Va. 1973. Gen. counsel Universal Communication Systems, Inc., Roanoke, 1973-74, v.p., gen. counsel, 1974-79, pres., dir. 1979-84, chief exec. officer, 1984—; v.p. Am. Motor Inns, Inc. Bd. dirs. United Way of Roanoke Valley, Roanoke Mill Mountain Zoo; trustee North Cross Country Day Sch., Roanoke, Roanoke Valley Sci. Mus. Recipient Pres.'s Disting. Service award N.Am. Telecommunication Assn., 1985. Mem. N.Am. Telephone Assn. (dir.), Western Va. Better Bus. Bur. (dir.), ABA, Va. State Bar Assn. Club: Rotary. Office: 1401 Municipal Rd Roanoke VA 24012

SHAHNASARIAN, MICHAEL, career development specialist; b. Chgo., Sept. 27, 1957; s. Edward and Michelle Shahnasarian; m. Jean Marie Saharian, July 3, 1982. B.A. in Psychology, Ind. U., 1979; M.S., Tex. A&M U., 1981; Ph.D. in Counseling Psychology and Human Systems, Fla. State U., 1985. Correctional counselor Joliet Correctional Ctr., Ill., 1981-82; instr. Fla. State U., Tallahassee, 1982-85; career devel. specialist, Tallahassee, 1983—; career devel. cons. to state, law, and pvt. industry orgns., 1983—. Contbr. articles to profl. publs. Research asst. W.K. Kellogg Found., 1983-85. Fellow Am. Bd. Vocat. Experts; mem. Am. Soc. Tng. and Devel., Am. Assn. for Counseling and Devel. Armenian Apostolic. Home: 3732 Sutor Ct Tallahassee FL 32301

SHAMBAUGH, IRVIN CALVIN, JR., aptitude test firm executive; b. Harrisburg, Pa., June 7, 1943; s. Irvin Calvin and Viola Mary (Diebler) S.; m. Amy Willcox, Jan. 3, 1975. B.S. in Geol. Sci., Pa. State U., 1964; postgrad. MIT, 1964-65, Tex. Christian U., Ft. Worth, 1974-76, East. Tex. State U., 1976-78. Research coordinator Johnson O'Connor Research Found., Ft. Worth, 1965-76; pres., chief scientist Aptitude Inventory Measurement Service, Dallas, 1976—. Co-author: AIMS Information About Aptitudes, 1979; co-author, editor: You and Your Aptitudes, 1983; author: Test Manual for Selected AIMS Worksamples, 1986. Contbr. numerous reports and research bulls. to profl. pubs. Developer AIMS test battery, 1976. Served with USMC, 1966-68. Mem. Am. Assn. Counseling and Devel., Assn. Measurement in Edn. and Guidance, Am. Psychol. Assn. (affiliate) Nat. Council Measurement in Edn., AAAS, Nat. Assn. Coll. Admissions Counselors, Nat. Assn. Test Dirs. Home: 934 Westbrook Dr Garland TX 75043 Office: Aptitude Inventory Measurement Service Suite B 2506 McKinney Ave Dallas TX 75201

SHAMBURGER, (ALICE) PAGE, author; b. Aberdeen, N.C.; d. Frank Dudley and Alice (Page) S.; grad. St. Mary's Sch. and Jr. Coll., 1945, Marjorie Webster Coll., 1947. Roving editor Am. Aviation mag., 1949-51; script writer Sta. WHUC, 1951-53; Eastern editor Cross Country News, 1954-67, contbg. editor Air Progress, 1966-74; editor So. Aviation Times, 1975-76; mem. Woman's Adv. Com. on Aviation, 1964-68; mem. aviation div. N.C. Emergency Transp. Task Force, 1966-67; pres., owner Page Travel Agy., Inc. Sec., Mid-South Horse Show Assn.; asst. sec. Moore County Hounds. Recipient commendations N.C. Gov., 1967-68, USAF Tactical Command, 1966; Doris Mullen Meml. Scholarship for helicopter tng., 1969, Lady Hay Drummond-Hay award, 1971. Mem. Aviation/Space Writers Assn., 99s-Internat. Orgn. Lic. Woman Pilots, Aircraft Owners and Pilots Assn., Wingfoot Lighter-than-air Soc., Southeastern Aviation Trades Assn., 99's (gov. S.E. sect. and mem. exec. bd. 1969-70, 71, curator mus. 1969-76), Univ. Aviation Assn. (dir.), Nat. Intercoll. Flying Assn. (adv. bd.), Whirly-Girl 142. Democrat. Methodist. Author: Tracks across the Sky, 1964; Classic Monoplanes, 1966; co-author: Command the Horizon, 1968; World War I Aces and Planes, 1968; Summon the Stars (best non-fiction aviation book 1970 Aviation Space Writers Assn.), 1970; The Curtiss Hawks, 1972. Contbr. articles to profl. publs. Address: 500 Carolina St Aberdeen NC 28315

SHANE, ROBERT, financial company executive; b. Chgo., May 9, 1953; s. Raymond and Francine (Grossman) S. A.A., Miami Dade Jr. Coll., 1972; B.A., Fla. Internat. U., 1974. Pres. Trans Leasing of Fla., Fort Lauderdale, 1976-77; v.p., co-founder Assoc. Leasing Internat. Corp., Fort Lauderdale, 1977—; pres., dir. Assoc. Fin. Internat. Corp., Fort Lauderdale, 1977—; v.p., dir. Assoc. Mortgage Internat. Corp., Fort Lauderdale, 1980—. Contbr. articles to profl. jours. Pres., Manors of Inverrary Condo Assn., Lauderhill, Fla., 1978-79; v.p. San Simeon Homeowners Assn., Boca Raton, Fla., 1984—. Mem. Nat. Psoriasis Found., Milestone Auto Soc., Fort Lauderdale Broward County C. of C., Internat. Machine Tool Assn. (assoc.), Graphic Arts & Printing Soc. (assoc.), Radiol. Soc. N. Am. (assoc.). Clubs: Rolls Royce Owners, Cadillac LaSalle, Woodlands Country. Lodge: B'nai B'rith. Avocations: collecting and restoring classic cars; boating; golf. Office: Assoc Leasing Internat Corp Presidential Plaza 4699 N State Rd 7 Fort Lauderdale FL 33319

SHANE, RONALD, financial company executive; b. Chgo., May 9, 1953; s. Raymond and Francine (Grossman) S. A.A., Miami Dade Jr. Coll., 1972; B.A., Fla. Internat. U., 1974. Assoc. prof. English dept. community coll. studies program Miami Dade Jr. Coll., Fla., 1971, 72; v.p. Trans Leasing Fla., Ft. Lauderdale, 1976-77; pres., co-founder Associated Leasing Internat. Corp., Fort Lauderdale, 1977—; v.p., dir. Associated Fin. Internat. Corp., Ft. Lauderdale, 1977—, Associated Mortgage Internat. Corp., Fort Lauderdale, 1980—. Contbr. articles to fin. trade jours. Sec., bd. dirs. Manors of Inverrary Condo Assn., Lauderhill, Fla., 1978-79; mem. archtl. com. San Simeon Homeowners Assn., Boca Raton, Fla., 1984—. Mem. Internat. Machine Tool Assn. (assoc.), Graphic Arts and Printing Soc. (assoc.), Radiol. Soc. N.Am. (assoc.). Nat. Psoraisis Found. Clubs: Nat. and Local Rolls Royce Owners; Woodlands Country (Tamarac, Fla.). Lodge: B'nai Brith. Avocations: collecting and restoring classic cars; power boating; golf; coin collecting; travel. Office: Associated Leasing Internat Corp Presidential Plaza 4699 N State Rd 7 Fort Lauderdale FL 33319

SHANK, CLARE BROWN WILLIAMS, former Republican party executive; b. Syracuse, N.Y., Sept. 19, 1909; d. Curtiss Crofoot and Clara Irene (Shoudy) Brown; B.Oral English, Syracuse U., 1931; m. Frank E. Williams, Feb. 18, 1940 (dec. Feb. 1957); m. Seth Carl Shank, Dec. 28, 1963 (dec. Jan. 1977). Tchr., 1931-33; merchandising exec., 1933-42; Pinellas County mem. Rep. State Com., 1954-58; life mem. Pinellas County Rep. Exec. Com.; exec. com. Fla. Rep. Com., 1954-64; mem. exec. com. Rep. Nat. Com., 1956-64, asst. chmn. and dir. women's activities, 1958-64; alt., mem. exec. arrangements com. Rep. Nat. Conv. (1st woman to preside over any nat. polit. conv.), 1960; alt., program and arrangement coms. Rep. Nat. Conv., 1964; pres. St. Petersburg Women's Rep. Club, 1955-57. Mem. Def. Adv. Com. on Women in Services, 1959-65; trustee St. Petersburg Housing Authority, 1976-82. Recipient George Arents medal Syracuse U., 1959; citation for patriotic civilian service 5th U.S. Army and Dept. Def. Mem. AAUW, Gen. Fedn. Women's Clubs, DAR, Colonial Dames 17th Century, Fla. Fedn. Women's Clubs (dist. pres. 1976-78), Zeta Phi Eta, Pi Beta Phi (nat. officer 1945-48). Methodist. Clubs: Woman's (pres. 1974-76), Yacht (St. Petersburg). Home: 1120 North Shore Dr NE Apt 901 Saint Petersburg FL 33701

SHANKLE, PERRY, wholesale merchant; b. Paris, Tenn., June 22, 1903; s. David Green and Ada (Childs) S.; m. Alice Stratton, Oct. 20, 1931; children—Alice, Perry (dec.). Student Bowling Green Bus. U., 1922-23. With Nat. Cash Register, 1928-29; prin. organizer Hom-Ond Food Stores, Bird-Shankle Co., wholesale grocers, San Antonio, 1931-47; prin. owner, chmn. bd., chief exec. officer Perry Shankle Co., San Antonio, 1947—. Pres., San Antonio Livestock Exposition, 1949, 50. Mem. Westinghouse and Distbrs. Assn. (pres. 1964-65), Am. Quarter Horse Assn. (dir. 1982-83), San Antonio C. of C. (pres. 1946). Republican. Methodist. Club: San Antonio Country. Home: 140 Patterson Ave Unit No 402 San Antonio TX 78209 Office: 1801 S Flores St San Antonio TX 78204

SHANKLIN, JAMES GORDON, lawyer; b. Elkton, Ky., Dec. 10, 1909; s. William S. and Eva (Jones) S.; B.A., Vanderbilt U., 1932, LL.B., 1934; m. Emily Shacklett, July 15, 1933; children—Elizabeth Eve, William Samuel. Agt. FBI, W.Va., 1943-44, N.Y.C., 1944-46, supr., 1946-47, hdqrs. Washington, 1947-51, asst. spl. agt. in charge Mobile, Ala., 1951-53, spl. agt. in charge 1953-55, Pitts., 1955-56, insp. hdqrs., Washington, 1956-58, spl. agt. in charge El Paso, Tex., 1958-59, Honolulu, 1959-63, Dallas, 1963-75; admitted to Tex. bar, 1975; mem. firm Johnson, Shanklin, Billings & Porter, Dallas, 1975-84; sole practice, 1984—; lectr. police acads.; admitted to Tenn. bar, 1934. Mem. Tenn., Fed., Tex., Dallas bar assns., E. Tex. Police Assn., Soc. Former Spl. Agts. FBI, Kappa Sigma. Baptist. Clubs: Chaparral, Insurance, Masons. Home: 6023 Del Norte St Dallas TX 75225

SHANKS, FRED RHEMES, optometrist; b. Waverly, Tenn., Aug. 9, 1949; s. Ken and Margaret (Boone) S.; m. Donna Denney, Nov. 23, 1968; children—Brandon, Bradley. B.S., So. Coll. Optometry, 1974; O.D., 1974. Optometrist in gen. practice, Dickson, Tenn., 1974—. Chmn., Children's Hosp. Drive, Dickson County. Mem. Am. Optometry Assn., Mid Tenn. Optometry Assn. (past pres.), Tenn. Optometry Assn. Methodist. Lodge: Kiwanis (past pres.). Home: 218 Druid Hills Dickson TN 37055

SHANKS, STEPHEN RAY, engineer; b. San Antonio, Tex., Nov. 1, 1956; s. Leroy and Jane Adams (Coats) S.; m. Vickie Lynn Morrow, Aug. 6, 1977; 1 dau., Erin Monette. Student pub. schs., Corpus Christi, Tex. Engring. technician Gulf Coast Testing Lab., Inc., Corpus Christi, part-time, 1971-75, full-time, 1975-78; br. mgr., quality control adminstr. Shilstone Engring. Testing Lab. div. Profl. Service Industries, Ft. Bend County, 1978—. Mem. ASTM, Am. Concrete Inst., Am. Mgmt. Assn., Am. Welding Soc., Constrn. Specifications Inst. Democrat. Episcopalian. Lodge: Rotary. Author: Procedures and Techniques for Construction Materials Testing, 1978; Inspection and Testing of Asphaltic Concrete, 1979; Concrete Barges: Construction and Repair Techniques, 1984. Editor: (lit. mag.) Viva! 1975; contbr. article to profl. jour. Office: 13308 Redfish Ln Suite 101 Stafford TX 77477

SHANNON, DAVID THOMAS, academic administrator; b. Richmond, Va., Sept. 26, 1933; s. Charles Lee and Phyllis Gary S.; m. Averett Yvonne Powell, June 15, 1957; children—Vernitia Averett, Davine Belinda, David Thomas. B.A., Va. Union U., 1954, B.D. summa cum laude, 1957; S.T.M., Oberlin Grad. Sch. Theology, 1959; D.Min., Vanderbilt U., 1974; Ph.D., U. Pitts., 1975. Ordained to ministry Baptist Ch., 1957. Pastor, Fair Oaks (Va.) Bapt. Ch., 1954-57; student asst. Antioch Bapt. Ch., Cleve., 1957-59; grad. asst. Oberlin Grad. Sch. Theology, 1958-59; univ. pastor Va. Union U., 1960-61, lectr. humanities and history, 1959-69; pastor Ebenezer Bapt. Ch., Richmond, Va., 1960-69; vis. lectr. O.T. studies Howard U., 1968; eastern dir. Christian Higher Edn. Services, Am. Bapt. Bd. Edn. and Publs., 1969-71; vis. prof. St. Mary's Sem. urban tng. program, Cleve., 1969-72; assoc. prof. religion, dir. minority studies Bucknell U., Lewisburg, Pa., 1971-72; dean faculty Pitts. Theol. Sem., 1972-79; Bibl. scholar Hartford Sem. Found. (Conn.), 1979; pres. Va. Union U., Richmond, 1979-85, v.p. acad. services, dean of faculty, 1985; mem. Commn. on Accreditation, Assn. Theol. Schs., Urban Tng. of Atlanta; dir. Sovran Bank, Richmond; chmn. Baptist World Alliance conversations with Roman Catholic Secretariat for Promotion of Christian Unity. Mem. Wards Scholarship com. Philip Morris Scholarship Selection Com. Named Man of Yr.,

NCCJ, 1981; scholar/theologian Am. Bapt. Chs. U.S.A., 1981-82; Disting. Alumnus, U. Pitts., 1981; Civic award Richmond Urban League, 1985, B'nai B'rith, 1985; Spl. Citation, Norfolk State U., 1985; Disting. Service award United Negro Coll. Fund. Mem. Am. Assn. Higher Edn. (hon.), Am. Acad. Religion, Soc. Bibl. Lit., Soc. Study of Black Religion, Alpha Kappa Mu, Phi Beta Sigma. Baptist. Author: Studies in the Life and Works of Paul, 1961; The Old Testament Experience of Faith, 1977; contbr. articles to profl. jours. Home: 3640 Rolling Green Ridge SW Atlanta GA 30331 Office: 671 Beckwith St SW Atlanta GA 30314

SHANNON, EDGAR FINLEY, JR., English language educator; b. Lexington, Va., June 4, 1918; s. Edgar Finley and Eleanor (Duncan) S.; m. Eleanor H. Bosworth, Feb. 11, 1956; children—Eleanor, Elizabeth, Lois, Susan, Virginia. A.B., Washington and Lee U., 1939, Litt.D., 1959; A.M., Duke U., 1941, Harvard U., 1947; Rhodes scholar, Merton Coll., Oxford, 1947-50; D. Phil., Oxford U., 1949; LL.D., Rhodes Coll., 1960, Duke U., 1964, Hampden-Sydney Coll., 1971; H.H.D., Wake Forest U., 1964; D.H.L., Thomas Jefferson U., Phila., 1967, U. Hartford, 1981, Ohio State U., 1981; Litt.D., Centre Coll., 1968, Coll. William and Mary, 1973; L.H.D., Bridgewater Coll., 1970. Assoc. prof. naval sci. and tactics Harvard U., Cambridge, Mass., 1946, instr. English, 1950-52, asst. prof., 1952-56; assoc. prof. English, U. Va., Charlottesville, 1956-59, prof., 1959-74, pres., 1959-74, Commonwealth prof. English, 1974-86, Linden Kent Meml. prof. English, 1986—; chmn. dept. English, 1980-81; mem. state and dist. selection coms. Rhodes scholars; pres. Council So. Univs., 1962-64, 71-72; pres. State Univs. Assn., 1963-64; mem. exec. com. Nat. Assn. State Univs. and Land-Grant Colls., 1964-67, chmn. exec. com., 1966-67, pres., 1965-66; mem. So. Regional Edn. Bd., 1963-71; bd. govs. Nat. Commn. on Accrediting, 1961-67. Mem. U.S. Nat. Commn. for UNESCO, 1966-67, Pres.'s Commn. on CIA Activities within U.S., 1975; bd. visitors U.S. Naval Acad., 1962-64, USAF Acad., 1965-67; bd. cons. Nat. War Coll., 1968-71; bd. dirs. Am. Council on Edn., 1967-70, vice chmn., 1971-72; trustee Thomas Jefferson Meml. Found., 1973—, pres., 1980-83; trustee Washington and Lee U., 1973-85, Darlington Sch., 1966-76, Mariners Mus., 1966-75, Colonial Williamsburg Found., 1975—; chmn. Va. Found. Humanities and Pub. Policy, 1973-79; v.p. Oceanic Edn. Found., 1968-83; bd. adminstrs. Va. Inst. Marine Sci., 1963-71; mem. council White Burkett Miller Ctr. for Pub. Affairs, 1975—; mem. of Va. Gov.'s Task Force on Sci. and Tech., 1982-83; mem. overseer's com. to visit dept. English, Harvard U., 1985—. Served to lt. comdr. USNR, 1941-46; to capt. USNR, 1947-72. Decorated Bronze Star, Meritorious Service medal; named Disting. Eagle Scout, 1973; recipient Disting. Service award Va. State C. of C., 1969; medallion of honor Virginians of Md., 1964; Thomas Jefferson award U. Va., 1965; Algernon Sydney Sullivan award Washington and Lee U., 1939, U. Va., 1975; Jackson Davis award Va. chpt. AAUP, 1977; Guggenheim fellow, 1953-54; Fulbright research fellow, Eng., 1953-54. Mem. Assn. Va. Colls. (pres. 1969-70), Tennyson Soc. (hon. v.p. 1960—), Raven Soc., Signet Soc., Jefferson Soc., MLA, Soc. of Cincinnati, Phi Beta Kappa (senator 1967-85, vis. scholar 1976-77, v.p. 1976-79, pres. 1979-82), Omicron Delta Kappa (Laurel Crowned Circle award 1980), Phi Eta Sigma, Beta Theta Pi. Presbyterian. Clubs: Authors (London); Century Assn.; University (N.Y.C.). Author: Tennyson and the Reviewers, 1952; editor: (with Cecil Y. Lang) The Letters of Alfred Lord Tennyson, I, 1981; contbr. articles to various jour. Home: 1925 Blue Ridge Rd Charlottesville VA 22903 Office: 201 Wilson Hall U Va Charlottesville VA 22903

SHANNON, JOHN SANFORD, railway executive, lawyer; b. Tampa, Fla., Feb. 8, 1931; s. George Thomas and Ruth Evangeline (Garrett) S.; m. Elizabeth Howe, Sept. 22, 1962; children—Scott Howe, Elizabeth Garrett, Sandra Denison. A.B., Roanoke Coll., 1952; J.D., U. Va., 1955; Bar: Va. 1955. Assoc., Hunton Williams Gay Powell & Gibson, Richmond, Va., 1955-56; solicitor Norfolk & Western Ry., Roanoke, Va., 1956-60, asst. gen. solicitor, 1960-64, gen. atty., 1964-65, gen. solicitor, 1965-68, gen. counsel, 1968-69, v.p. law, 1969-80, sr. v.p. law, 1980-82; exec. v.p. law Norfolk So. Corp. (Va.), 1982—; dir. Norfolk and Western Ry., Co., So. Ry. Co., Pocahontas Land Corp., Va. Holding Corp., Wabash R.R. Co., Wheeling and Lake Erie Ry. Co. Trustee Roanoke Coll., Salem, Va., chmn. exec. com., 1979-82; trustee Chrysler Mus., Norfolk; chancellor Episcopal Diocese Southwestern Va., 1974-82; pres., trustee N. Cross Sch., Roanoke, 1973-82. Mem. ABA, Va. Bar Assn., Norfolk and Portsmouth Bar Assn., Order of the Coif, Sigma Chi, Omicron Delta Kappa, Phi Delta Phi. Clubs: Harbor, Norfolk Yacht and Country; Shenandoah, Roanoke Country; Met. (Washington). Home: 7633 Argyle Ave Norfolk VA 23505 Office: 1 Commercial Pl Norfolk VA 23510

SHANNON, ROBERT MCDONALD, architect, planner; b. Bristol, Va., Oct. 2, 1917; s. Robert McDonald and Helen Izetta (Coyner) S.; B.S., Va. Poly. Inst. and State U., 1939, M.S., 1940; postgrad. Woodrow Wilson Sch., Princeton U., 1949-50, Ohio State U., 1954-56; m. Anne MacGowan, June 20, 1953 (div. May 1964); children—Christopher, Alexandra, Nicholas. With U.S. Army C.E., 1940-61, comdg. officer 109th Engr. Bn., Mannheim, Germany; adviser Chinese Chief of Engrs., Taiwan; engr. N.Y. Engr. Dist.; dir. community shelter planning Hays, Seay, Mattern & Mattern, Roanoke, Va., 1961-63; dir. Roanoke Valley Regional Planning Commn., Roanoke, 1964-68; exec. dir. Fifth Planning Dist. Commonwealth of Va., 1969-72; asst. planning and constrn. Va. Commonwealth U., Richmond, 1973-; asst. prof. Ohio State U., 1953-56; instr. U. Md. Far East, 1958, U. Va. Roanoke Center, 1962-65. Mem. com. Roanoke Valley Museum, 1970-73; U.S. observer UN Interregional Seminar, Madrid, Spain, 1970. Bd. dirs. Va. Citizens Planning Assn. Decorated Bronze Star. Registered architect, Va. Mem. AIA, Am. Inst. Cert. Planners, Assn., Tau Beta Pi. Author: (geneology) Frontier Shannon Families, 1985. Author met. area planning studies. Home: 58 Garden Dr Alexandria VA 22304

SHANTHARAM, VANGHIBHURAM VENKATA, nephrologist; b. Madras, India, Dec. 3, 1945; came to U.S., 1970; s. Vanghibhuram V. and Padma (Seshachari) S.; m. Poornima Rangaswamy, May 20, 1976. B.Sc. in Chemistry, U. Madra (India), 1962; M.B.B.S., U. Madras, 1967. Diplomate Am. Bd. Internal Medicine, Am. Bd. Nephrology. Chief resident internal medicine Bridgeport Hosp. (Conn.), 1973-74; postdoctoral fellow in nephrology U. Wash., Seattle, 1975-77; asst. prof. medicine and nephrology, 1977-80; cons. nephrologist St. Vincent's Hosp., Jacksonville, Fla., 1980—; asst. prof. medicine U. Calif.-Davis Med. Ctr., 1977-80, Bapt. Med. Ctr., 1980—, Meml. Med. Ctr., Jacksonville, 1980—. Recipient Cochin Maharaja prize, 1964; Kannuswamy prize, 1965; Dinker Rao Meml. Endowment scholar, 1966; Jewish Hosp. and Med. Ctr. Clin. Soc. award, 1971. Fellow Royal Coll. Medicine Can.; mem. ACP, Am. Fedn. Clin. Research, N.Y. Acad. Sci., Nat. Kidney Found., Internat. Soc. Nephrology, Am. Soc. Nephrology. Club: Summerhouse Beach and Racquet. Contbr. articles to profl. jours. and books. Office: 1820 Barrs St Suite 752 Jacksonville FL 32204

SHAPIRO, ARNOLD, psychologist; b. N.Y.C., Mar. 6, 1929; s. Irving and Stella (Goldstein) S.; m. Adele Alperin, Aug. 23, 1958; children—Ira, Beth. B.A. in Psychology, Hunter Coll., 1962; M.S. in Clin. Psychology, Purdue U., 1965, Ph.D., 1968. Lic. psychologist, N.C. Psychologist Rohrer, Hibler & Replogle, Chgo., 1968-72; pvt. practice, Charlotte, N.C., 1972-85, Boca Raton, Fla., 1985—; cons. N.C. Dept. Correction, various businesses, industries, state and fed. law enforcement agencies. Fellow Internat. Soc. Personality Assessment; mem. Am. Psychol. Assn. (Cattell Fund award 1968), Am. Soc. Clin. Hypnosis (Milton H. Erickson prize 1983). Office: Palm Beach Psychol Services Inc Palmetto Park Rd C Boca Raton FL 33432

SHAPIRO, EDWARD MURAY, dermatologist; b. Denver, Oct. 6, 1924; s. Isador Benjamin and Sara (Berezin) S.; student U. Colo., 1941-43; A.B. with honors, U. Tex., 1948, M.D., 1952; m. Ruth Young, Oct. 14, 1944; children—Adrian Michael, Stefanie Ann. Intern, Jefferson Coll. Medicine Hosp., Phila., 1952-53; resident in dermatology U. Tex. Med. Br., Galveston, 1953-55; resident in dermatology Henry Ford Hosp., Detroit, 1955-56, asso. in dermatology div. dermatology, 1956-57; clin. instr. dermatology Baylor U. Coll. Medicine, Houston, 1957-68, asst. clin. prof., 1968—; staff Jefferson Davis Hosp., Houston, 1958—; attending staff Pasadena (Tex.) Gen. Hosp., 1958—, Pasadena Bayshore Hosp., 1962—, Southmore Hosp., Pasadena, 1958—. Served with USAAF, 1943-46. Henry J. N. Taub research grantee, 1958-60; diplomate Am. Bd. Dermatology. Fellow Am. Acad. Dermatology; mem. AMA, Tex. Med. Assn., Harris County Med. Assn. (dir. 1968-69), S.E. Br. Med. Assn., Houston Dermatology Assn., Houston Art League, Gulf Coast Art Soc., Am. Physicians Art Assn. Jewish. Clubs: B'nai B'rith, Rotary. Contbr. articles in field to med. jours. Home: 2101 S Houston Rd Pasadena TX 77502 Office: 1020 S Tatar St Pasadena TX 77506

SHAPIRO, LEE TOBEY, planetarium administrator, astronomer; b. Chgo., Dec. 12, 1943; s. Sydney Harold and Ruth Iva (Levin) S.; m. Linda Susan Goldman, Aug. 16, 1970; children—Steven Robert, Aaron Edward. B.S. in Physics, Carnegie Inst. Tech., 1966; M.S. in Astronomy, Northwestern U., 1968, Ph.D., 1974. Lectr., Adler Planetarium, Chgo., 1967-74; asst. prof. astronomy Mich. State U., East Lansing, 1974-79, assoc. prof., 1979-82; dir. Abrams Planetarium, 1974-82; dir. Morehead Planetarium U. N.C.-Chapel Hill, 1982—, adj. assoc. prof., 1983—. Fellow Royal Astron. Soc.; mem. Am. Astron. Soc., Am. Assn. Mus., Internat. Planetarium Soc., Great Lakes Planetarium Assn. (pres. 1980). Jewish. Office: Morehead Planetarium Univ NC East Franklin St Chapel Hill NC 27514

SHAPIRO, MARTIN M., psychology professor, lawyer; b. N.Y.C., Dec. 29, 1934; s. Carl and Sadie (Frankel) S.; m. Marlene Lipman, June 19, 1955 (div.); children—Beth Levine, Steven Shapiro. A.B., Yale U., 1955; Ph.D., Ind. U., 1959; J.D., Emory U., 1980. Bar: Ga. 1981. Psychology prof. U. Houston, Tex., 1960-64, Baylor Coll. Medicine, Houston, 1963-64, Emory U., Atlanta, 1964—; sole practice law, Atlanta, 1981—; cons. Golden Rule Ins. Co., Indpls., 1980—; ACLU, 1980—; NAACP Legal Def. Fund, N.Y.C., 1980—; EEOC, Washington, 1980—. Post-doctoral Research fellow USPHS, 1959; Hon. Research fellow Univ. Coll. London, 1971. Mem. ABA, Am. Psychol. Assn., State Bar Ga., Psychonomic Soc. Jewish. Avocation: stained glass crafting. Office: Emory Univ Psychology Dept Atlanta GA also 11 Piedmont Ctr Suite 108 Altanta GA 30305

SHAPIRO, THEODORE ALLEN, transportation company executive; b. Paterson, N.J., June 13, 1939; s. Morris Leonard and Sarah (Schwartz) S.; m. Arlene F. Simon, Feb. 21, 1963; children—Stephanie Lynn, Stacy Leigh. B.B.A., Tex. A&M U., 1964. Vice pres. southeast region, WTC Air Freight, East Point, Ga., 1971-75; v.p. sales Carolina Cartage Co., College Park, Ga., 1975-78; pres. Parts Motor Lines, College Park, 1978—, Any Time Service, College Park, 1980—. Served with USN, 1957-60. Mem. Atlanta Air Cargo Assn. (dir. 1983), Local Air Cargo Com. of Schedules Airlines. Jewish. Clubs: Ga. Cattleman (Coweta County, Ga.); A.Q.H.A. (Atlanta). Lodge: Mason. Office: Any Time Service Co 1638 E Vesta Ave College Park GA 30337

SHAPIRO, WILLIAM, cardiologist, educator; b. Newark, N.J., Dec. 8, 1927; s. Aaron and Celia (Rossman) S.; B.A., Duke Univ., 1947, M.A., 1948, M.D., 1954; m. Olive May Derry, Sept. 22, 1951 (dec. 1982); children—Gordon Marc, Joan Celia, Robin Derry. Intern, Mt. Sinai Hosp., N.Y.C., 1954-55; resident Duke Hosp., Durham, N.C., 1955-58; instr. Med. Coll. Va., Richmond, 1960-62, asst. prof., 1962-65, SW Med. Sch., Dallas, 1965-68, asso. prof., 1968-79, prof., 1979—; chief Cardiovascular Sect., Dallas VA Med. Center, 1968-81, dir. automated ECG services, Med. Service, 1981—. Served with M.C., USN, 1958-60. Diplomate Nat. Bd. Med. Examiners, Am. Bd. Internal Medicine. Fellow Am. Coll. Cardiology, Am. Heart Assn. Council on Clin. Cardiology, ACP, Am. Coll. Angiology; mem. Am. Heart Assn. Stroke Council, Alpha Omega Alpha. Contbr. articles in field to profl. jours. Office: 4500 S Lancaster Dallas TX 75216

SHARER, ARCH WILSON, biology educator; b. Dayton, Ohio, Sept. 19, 1919; s. William R. and Margaret P. (Roller) S.; m. Ann Roddie, Sept. 4, 1941; children—Bruce, Douglas, Susan. B.S., Ohio State U., 1943; M.S., U. Mich., 1948, Ph.D., 1959. Instr. U. Fla., Tallahassee, 1950-53, Lake Forest Coll., Ill, 1953-56, United Educators, Lake Forest, 1956-58; instr. Duke U., Durham, N.C., 1958-60; asst. prof., assoc. prof. then prof. biology N.C. Wesleyan Coll., Rocky Mount, 1960—. Mem. Rocky Mount Energy Adv. Com., 1978—, vice-chmn., 1984-85. Mem. Am. Inst. Biol. Scis., Am. Archaeol. Soc., N.C. Acad. Scis., Nature Conservancy. Democrat. Avocations: photography, paleontology. Home: 623 Sycamore St Rocky Mount NC 27801 Office: NC Wesleyan Coll Rocky Mount NC 27801

SHARETT, ALAN RICHARD, lawyer; b. Hammond, Ind., Apr. 15, 1943; s. Henry S. and Frances (Givel) Smulevitz; divorced, children—Lauren Ruth, Charles Daniel. Student Ind. U., 1962-65; J.D., DePaul U., 1968. Bar: N.Y. 1975, Ind. 1969, U.S. Ct. Appeals (2d cir.) 1975, U.S. Ct. Appeals (7th cir.) 1974, U.S. Supreme Ct. 1973. Assoc. Call, Call, Borns & Theodoros, Gary, Ind., 1969-71; judge pro tem Gary City Ct., 1970-71; environ. dep. prosecutor 31st Jud. Circuit, Lake County, Ind., 1971-75; mem. Cohan, Cohan & Smulevitz, 1971-75; judge pro tem Superior Ct., Lake County, Ind., 1971-75; professorial dir. NYU Pub. Liability Inst., N.Y.C., 1975-76; asst. atty. gen. N.Y. State, N.Y.C., 1976-78; sole practice, Flushing, N.Y., 1980-82, Miami Beach, Fla., 1982—. Chmn. lawyers panel for No. Ind., ACLU, 1969-71. Recipient Honors award in medicolegal litigation Law-Sci. Acad. Am., 1967. Mem. ABA, Assn. Bar City N.Y., N.Y. County Lawyers Assn. (com. on fed. cts. 1977-82), Am. Judicature Soc., Assn. Trial Lawyers Am., Nat. Dist. Attys. Assn. (environ. protection com. 1972-75), N.Y. State Trial Lawyers Assn., N.Y. State Bar Assn., Ind. State Bar Assn., Queens County Bar Assn., Am. Acad. Poets. Democrat. Contbr. articles to profl. jours. Address: B1418-2371 Collins Ave Miami Beach FL 33139

SHARF, ELLEN BETH, financial planner; b. Newport News, Va., May 25, 1959; d. Burt A. and Daralie (Siegel) S. B.S. in Commerce, U. Va., 1982. Fin. Planning assoc. NCNB Nat. Bank, Charlotte, 1982-83; trust officer, certified fin. planner, Wachovia Bank & Trust Co., Winston-Salem, N.C., 1983—. Contbr. articles to profl. jours. Host family N.C. Sch. for Performing Arts, Winston-Salem, N.C., 1984—; participant Charlotte C. of C. Community Leadership Sch., 1983; fund raiser United Way, Arts Council; Am. Heart Assn., 1982—. Recipient Good Citizens award DAR, 1977; Disting. Youth award Civil Service Dept. Army, 1978-81; William B. Harman awards 1982. Mem. Internat. Assn. Fin. Planning (exec. sec., bd. dirs. 1985—), Inst. Cert. Fin. Planners, Fin. Profl. Adv. Panel, AAUW, Nat. Assn. Accts. (assoc. dir. 1983). Democrat. Jewish. Home: 141 Dalewood Dr # 5 Winston-Salem NC 27104 Office: Wachovia Bank & Trust Co 301 N Main St Winston-Salem NC 27150

SHARFMAN, HERBERT, judge; b. Northampton, Pa., July 29, 1909; s. Meyer and Minnie (Caplan) S.; m. Dorothy Muriel Cohen, Feb. 8, 1932; children—Richard M., Jo-Ellen Crews. A.B., U. Pa., 1930; LL.B., Columbia U., 1933. Bar: Pa. 1933, U.S. Dist. Ct. (ea. dist.) Pa. 1935, U.S. Supreme Ct., 1945. Sole practice, Lehigh and Northampton Counties, Pa., 1933-44; atty.-adv. pub. utilities br. OPA, Washington, 1944-46, FCC, Washington, 1946-52; adminstrv. law judge FCC, Washington, 1952-74, Postal Rate Commn. Washington, 1974-76, part-time adminstrv. law judge, 1976—. Mem. ABA, Pa. State Bar Assn., Lehigh County Bar Assn. Jewish. Home: 162 W Center Ave Sebring FL 33870

SHARMA, INDER JEET, data executive, statistical consultant; b. Amritsar, India, May 24, 1950; came to U.S., 1976; s. Lal Chand and Rattan Devi (Dropdi) S.; m. Anuj Sharma, July 31, 1976; children—Rishi Sharma, Nitin Sharma. M.P.H., U. Okla., 1984, M.S., 1980; M.Sc., Meerut U. India, 1972. Statistician, Okla. Med. Research Found., Oklahoma City, 1980-83, statis. cons., 1984—; from programmer to data mgr. U. Okla. Health Services Ctr., Oklahoma City, 1984—, mem. acad. appeals com., 1984. Contbr. articles to profl. jours. Mem. Am. Statis. Assn., Okla. Am. Statis. Assn., Okla. Pub. Health Assn. Home: 2908 N Vermont Oklahoma City OK 73107 Office: 800 Rogers Bldg Oklahoma City OK

SHARP, ALICE ELIZABETH, management consultant; b. Miami; d. Raymond B. and Willie Mae S.; B.S., U. Corpus Christi, 1959; M.A., U. Tex., Austin, 1961; Ph.D., Walden U., 1979. Tchr., marine sci. coordinator Corpus Christi Ind. Sch. Dist., 1961-66; mem. faculty Tarrant County Jr. Coll., Ft. Worth, 1967-69, also Del Mar Coll., Corpus Christi; dir. edn. Spohn Hosp., Corpus Christi, 1969-71; dir. edn. Maine Med. Center, Portland, 1971-76; regional edn. dir. AMI, Houston, 1976-81; owner, prin. MERS, cons. and tng. service, Fort Worth, 1980—. Robert Welch Found. fellow, 1959-60. Mem. Houston C. of C., Am. Soc. Tng. Devel., Assn. Ednl. Communications Technology, Adult Edn. Assn., Am. Mgmt. Assn., Phi Sigma. Presbyterian. Contbr. articles to profl. jours.

SHARP, BOBBY HUEL, university administrator, consumer economics educator; b. Somerville, Ala., Feb. 4, 1951; s. Huel D. and Gladys E. (Whitten) S.; m. Sharon Annette Andrews, Dec. 26, 1972; 1 child, Lindley Colin. B.A. in Philosophy, Birmingham-So. Coll., 1972; M.Div. in Pastoral Counseling, Duke U., 1975; M.S. in Consumer Econs., U. Ky., 1977; Ph.D., Va. Tech. U., 1980. Grad. asst. U. Ky., Lexington, 1975-77, Va. Tech. U., Blacksburg, 1977-80; asst. prof. Miss. U. for Women, Columbus, 1980-84; dir. instl. research, 1982-84; assoc. dir. univ. planning and instl. research U. Miss., University, 1984—. Author: Books Consumerists Should Know About, 1980. Am. Council Life Ins. fellow, 1979. Mem. Assn. Instl. Research, Am. Econ. Assn., Am. Council Consumer Interests, So. Assn. Instl. Research, Phi Beta Kappa, Phi Kappa Phi, Omicron Delta Kappa. Methodist. Avocations: microcomputers; table tennis. Office: Univ Planning and Instl Research University MS 38677

SHARP, GEORGE KENDALL, U.S. district judge; b. Chgo., Dec. 30, 1934; s. Edward S. and Florence S.; m. Mary Bray; children—Florence Kendall, Julia Manger. B.A., Yale U., 1957; J.D., U. Va., 1963. Bar: Fla. 1963. Atty. Sharp, Johnston & Brown, Vero Beach, Fla., 1963-78; pub. defender 19th Circuit, 1964-68; sch. bd. atty. Indian River County, Fla., 1968-79; judge 19th Circuit Ct., Vero Beach, 1978-83; judge U.S. Dist. Ct. for Middle Fla., Orlando, 1983—. Office: 611 US Courthouse 80 N Hughey Ave Orlando FL 32801*

SHARP, HORACE RUEBEN, JR., optometrist; b. Kingsville, Tex., May 7, 1948; s. Horace Rueben and Lillian C. (Terrell) S.; A.S., Wharton County Jr. Coll., 1969; B.S., U. Houston, 1972, O.D., 1973; m. Beverly Ann Roesler, May 13, 1972; children—Michael Jason, Kerri Renee. Ordained minister Full Gospel Ch. Pvt. practice optometry, Cameron, Tex., 1975—; pastor Cameron Faith Fellowship; headmaster Cameron Christian Acad. Served to lt., USNR, 1973-75. Mem. Heart of Tex. Optometric Assn. (past v.p.), Tex. Optometric Assn., Am. Optometric Assn., Full Gospel Bus. Men's Fellowship Internat. (past sec., past pres.). Club: Rotary (past dir.). Home: Route 1 Box 97 Cameron TX 76520 Office: 204 N Fannin St Cameron TX 76520

SHARP, JOHN, state senator, Realtor; b. July 28, 1950. B.A., Tex. A&M U.; M.P.A., Southwest Tex. State. Mem. Tex. Ho. of Reps., 1979-82, mem. econ. devel., intergovtl. relations, and health and human resources coms.; now mem. Tex. Senate. Democrat. Office: Tex Senate PO Box 12068 Austin TX 78711

SHARP, JOHN BUCKNER, JR., forester, educator; b. Maynardville, Tenn., Nov. 5, 1920; s. John Buckner and Daicy Dora Sharp; m. Helen Anderson, Aug. 30, 1949; children—Nancy, Paul, Mary Jean. B.S., in Agr., U. Tenn., 1943, M.S. in Agronomy, 1945; forestry tng. N.C. State U., 1945-46; M.F. in Forest Soils, Duke U., 1947; Ph.D. in Agrl. Econs., Harvard U., 1952. Dist. extension forester U. Tenn., Knoxville, 1947-49, asst. extension forester, 1952-59, state extension forester, 1959-77, prof. forestry, 1977—. Served with USAF, World War II. Harvard U. Grad. Sch. Pub. Adminstrn. Carnegie Corp. fellow, 2 yrs. Mem. Gamma Sigma Delta (U. Tenn. chpt. charter), Xi Sigma Pi (Alpha Kappa chpt.). Contbr. to profl. publs.; patentee in field. Home: 5025 Mountain Crest Dr Knoxville TN 37918 Office: U Tenn 244 Plant Science Bldg Knoxville TN 37901

SHARP, ROLAND PAUL, SR., osteopathic physician and surgeon; b. Frost, W.Va., Dec. 30, 1907; s. Aaron Abraham and Odessa Paul (Jordan) S.; m. Opal Price, Aug. 10, 1931 (dec. Apr. 1978); 1 child, Roland Paul, Jr. (dec.); m. Thelma Lee Kincaid, July 16, 1979. A.B., Concord Coll., Athens, W.Va., 1936; M.S., W.Va. U., 1939; D.O., Kirksville Coll., Mo., 1943. Lic. osteo. physician. Tchr., Pub. Schs., Pocahontas County, W.Va., 1926-28, 30-38; faculty Kirksville Coll. Medicine, 1940-44; indsl. medicine United Mine Workers Am., Mullins. W.Va., 1945-62; gen. practice medicine Green Bank, W.Va., 1962-73; 78—; exec. dean W.Va. Sch. Osteo. Medicine, Lewisburg, 1973-74, pres., 1974-78, adj. prof. gen. practice, 1980—; dir. Concord College Found., Athens, W.Va. Sch. Osteo. Medicine Found., Lewisburg; breeder registered Polled Hereford cattle, 1954—. Mem. W.Va. State Bd. Health, Charleston, 1981—. Roland P. Sharp award named in his honor W.Va. Sch. Osteo. Medicine, 1974. Mem. W.Va. Soc. Osteo. Medicine (named Gen. Practitioner of Yr. 1971, Disting. Service cert. 1976, pres. 1953), Am. Osteo. Assn., Am. Assn. Colls. Osteo. Medicine (bd. govs. 1974-78), Soc. Osteo. Medicine Assn. (George W. Northup award 1979), Health Systems Agy. W.Va. (bd. dirs. 1979-82), W.Va. Bd. Osteo. Examiners (sec. 1952-72), W.Va. Polled Hereford Assn. (bd. dirs. 1982—), Concord Coll. Alumni Assn. (pres. 1952). Republican. Presbyterian. Lodges: Masons, Rotary (pres. 1952). Avocations: farming, music, fishing. Office: Hwy 92 Green Bank WV 24944

SHARP, SHARON ANNETTE ANDREWS, writer, family life educator; b. Birmingham, Ala., Dec. 26, 1952; d. Joseph W. and Ann L. (Steele) Andrews; m. Bobby Huel, Dec. 26, 1972; 1 child, Lindley Colin. B.A. in English, Duke U., 1972-74; M.S. in Human Devel. and Family Relations, U. Ky., 1977; Ph.D., in Family Studies, Va. Tech., 1980. Grad. asst. U. Ky., Lexington, 1975-77; grad. asst. Va. Tech., Blacksburg, 1977-79, health edn. coordinator, 1979-80; asst. prof. Miss. U. for Women, Columbus, Miss., 1980-84; writer, cons., Oxford, Miss., 1984—; free-lance copy editor Macmillan Publs., N.Y.C., 1985—; cons. N.E. Miss. Planning and Devel. Dist., Booneville, 1985; researcher, writer, copy editor Ctr. for Study of So. Culture, U. Miss., 1985—. Grad. fellow U. Ky., Lexington, 1976-77. Mem. Am. Sociol. Assn., Nat. Council on Family Relations, Am. Pub. Health Assn., Nat. Family Life Edn. Network, So. Sociol. Soc., Southeastern Council on Family Relations (chmn. edn. sect. 1984-85, sec. and newsletter editor 1985-87), Miss. Council on Family Relations (pres. 1984-85, counselor 1985-86), Phi Beta Kappa, Phi Kappa Phi. Office: PO Box 924 University MS 38677

SHARP, THOMAS SIMPSON, fundraising executive; b. Hammond, La., Nov. 30, 1944; s. Wiley Howard and Melanie Louise (Ledet) S.; m. Norma Hilbert, June 7, 1980. B.S., La. State U., 1967; B.M.E., S. La. U., 1971, M.Ed., 1973. Tchr., Holy Ghost Cath. Sch., 1968-70, 71-72; owner Lafayette Electronics, 1973-79; treas. Musike Squire Ltd., Hammond, 1979—; mgr. Columbia Theatre, Hammond, 1979; mng. exec. Cutting-Pike Investment Corp., 1979-82; asst. registrar Southeastern La. U., 1982-83, exec. dir. devel. found., 1983—; sec. bd. Centerville Land Co. Choir dir. 1st Christian Ch., Hammond, 1972-79; pres. Columbia Theatre Players, 1976-78, exec. bd., 1978—, bd. dirs., 1978-80; mem. Hammond Arts Council, 1978-79; regional bd. dirs. Baton Rouge Symphony Orch. Mem. Am. Guild Organists, Am. Film Inst., Downtown Mchts. Assn., Hammond Hist. Dist. Assn., Miklos Rozsa Soc., Max Sternei Soc., Film Music Collection, Shakespeare Soc. of New Orleans, Phi Mu Alpha Sinfonia, Delta Tau Delta (pres. So. div., chpt. adv.) Order of Omega (charter). Republican. Roman Catholic. Clubs: Rotary (pres.) (Hammond); Empire (New Orleans). Home: 23 Darrell Dr Hammond LA 70401 Office: PO Box 1672 Hammond LA 70404

SHARP, WILLIAM WHEELER, geologist; b. Shreveport, La., Oct. 9, 1923; s. William Wheeler and Jennie V. (Benson) S.; m. Rubylin Slaughter, Aug. 15, 1958; children—Staci Lynn, Kimberly Cecile. B.S. in Geology, U. Tex.-Austin, 1950, M.A., 1951. Party chief geol. surface party Exxon Creole Petroleum Corp., Caracas, Venezuela, 1951-57; sr. research geologist, dist. devel. geologist, research assoc. and expert geol. witness ARCO, 1957-85. Author geologic publs. Past dir., past chmn. U.S. Tennis Assn. tournaments, Lafayette; pres. Lafayette Tennis Adv. Com., 1972. Served as sgt. USAF, 1943-46, PTO. La. State doubles champion U.S. Tennis Assn., 1970-75; champion Tex.-Ark.-La., Gulf Coast Assn. Geol Soc., Gulf Coast Oilmen's, So. Oilmen's tennis tournaments. Mem. Dallas Geol. Soc., Lafayette Geol. Soc. (dir. 1973-74), Houston Geol. Soc., Am. Assn. Petroleum Geologists, Ft. Worth Geol. Soc. Republican. Methodist. Avocations: sports; music; outdoors; horses.

SHARPE, CHRISTINE PATRICIA, university dean, nurse; b. Independence, Kans., Apr. 9, 1949; d. Loyce C. and Hortense (Reeves) Patrick; m. Edward W. Browne, Sept. 16, 1952 (div.); children—Pamela, Karen, Edward; m. Alfred J. Sharpe, Apr. 16, 1971. A.A., Independence Community Coll., 1949; B.S. in Nursing, Meharry Med. Coll., 1952; M.Nursing, Vanderbilt U., 1979, also postgrad. R.N., Tenn. Dir. day care, handicapped Pub. Health, Nashville, 1960-65; with Dept. Pub. Health, Nashville, 1965-70; dir. nursing project Tenn. State U., Nashville, 1970-75, assoc. prof. nursing, 1976—, dean Sch. of Nursing, 1985—. Author handbooks. Mem. Meharry Governing Bd., Nashville, 1985. Named Outstanding Teacher in Nursing, Tenn. State U., 1978. Mem. Nat. League for Nursing, Meharry Nat. Alumni, Delta Sigma Theta, Chi Eta Phi. Club: Joy of Living (pres. 1984-85) (Nashville). Avocations: fishing; bridge; reading.

SHARPE, ELLIOTT LOUIS, electronics company executive; b. Chgo., Nov. 30, 1942; s. Rubin and Gertrude (Gans) S.; m. Merle Sharon Stolar, Aug. 28, 1966; 1 dau., Cynthia Elizabeth. Student U. Wis., 1959-61; B.S.B.A., Milton Coll., 1963; M.B.A., Northwestern U., 1965. With Armour & Co., 1965-74, 78-80, v.p. adminstrn., Phoenix, 1978-80; dir. mktg. Armour-Dial Co., Phoenix, 1974-78; exec. v.p. Armour Processed Meat Co., Phoenix, 1980-81; pres., chief exec. officer, treas. Metretek, Inc., Melbourne, Fla., 1981—; chmn.

long range planning task force FIT Corp. Office: Metretek Inc 4450 Enterprise Ct Melbourne FL 32935

SHARPE, LEON EDWARD, lawyer; b. Kendall, Fla., Oct. 2, 1952; s. Joe Edward and Dorothy Mae (Saunders) S.; m. Esther Wyllie, Aug. 16, 1975; children—Rashad D., Aaron I., Adam P. B.A., Harvard U., 1974; J.D. cum laude, Columbia U., 1977. Bar: Fla. 1978, U.S. Dist. Ct. (so. dist.) Fla. 1978, U.S. Ct. Appeals (5th cir.) 1978, U.S. Ct. Appeals (11th cir.), U.S. Supreme Ct. Assoc. firm Frates, Floyd Pearson, Stewart, Richman & Greer, P.A., Miami, Fla., 1977-80, Hall & Hauser, P.A., Miami, 1980-81; ptnr. firm McGhee & Sharpe, Miami, 1981-84, Leon E. Sharpe, P.A., 1985—; legal cons. NAACP Urban Affairs Office, Miami, 1982, regional dir. Police Violence Project, Miami, 1981-82. Author booklet: Miami Model City Expo, 1974; contbg. author: NAACP Police Violence, 1982. Dir., treas. Dade Employment and Econ. Devel. Corp., 1982—; bd. dirs. Legal Service of Greater Miami, Inc., 1981-83; dir. Operation PUSH, Miami, 1982. Alexander H. White scholar, Harvard U., 1970-74; recipient Super Achiever's award Boy Scouts Am., 1982. Mem. ABA, Fla. Bar (rules of evidence com.), Nat. Bar Assn., Dade County Bar Assn., Assn. Trial Lawyers Am., Dade County Black Lawyers Assn. Democrat. Roman Catholic. Home: 10671 SW 137th St Miami FL 33176 Office: Leon E Sharpe PA 4770 Biscayne Blvd Suite 970 Miami FL 33137

SHARPE, MARY EVELYN, state insurance department administrator; b. Columbia, S.C., Oct. 14, 1927; d. Burnell Nicholas and Annie M. (Hill) Bolton; m. Jack Dillard Sharpe, Sept. 1, 1950. Student U. S.C.-Columbia, 1967-69, Ins. Inst. Am., Malvern, Pa., 1970. Automobile underwriter USF&G, Columbia, 1953-61; supr. Dept. Ins. State of S.C., Columbia, 1961-74, ins. analyst II, 1974-79, ins. analyst III, 1980—, asst. dir. automobile rating, property and casualty div., 1982—. Tchr. Sunday Sch., Ebeneezer Luth. Ch., Columbia, 1966-70. Mem. Nat. Assn. Ins. Women (cert. profl. ins. woman, dir. Region III 1980-81, mem. nat. exec. bd. 1980-81, 83-84, nat. legis. chmn. 1983-84, chmn. nat. nominating com. nat. conv. 1985, T.J. Mims award of excellence for outstanding service to region III, 1985), Columbia Assn. Ins. Women (editor bull. 1958, sec. 1959, pres. 1961, 75-76, 76-77, mem. exec. bd. 1977-78, Columbia Ins. Woman of Yr. award 1973, 77, 82), Santee Assn. Ins. Women (hon.). Lodges: Dau. of the Nile, Arabi. Home: 302 Beverly Dr West Columbia SC 29169 Office: SC Dept Ins 2711 Middleburg Dr Columbia SC 29204

SHARPE, MEREDITH MAX, orthodontist, educator; b. Frederick, Okla., Dec. 13, 1924; s. Howard D. and Genevieve (Holmes) S.; children—Janet Ruth Sharpe Lonvick, Linda Sue; m. Cynthia Potts Corbin, Oct. 19, 1977. Student U. Okla., 1942-43, 47-51; D.D.S., Baylor U., 1955; M.S., U. Tex.-Houston, 1968; M.S. in Edn., Jackson State U., 1983. Pvt. practice dentistry for children, Lubbock, Tex., 1955-66; pvt. practice orthodontics, Houston, 1968-80; clin. prof. U. Tex. Dental Sch., Houston, 1968-80; assoc. prof. U. Miss. Sch. Dentistry, Jackson, 1980-82, chmn. orthodontics, 1982—. Contbr. articles to profl. jours. Bd. govs. Jackson Symphony Orch., 1980-83. Served to 2d lt. USAAC, 1943-46. Mem. Tex. Soc. Dentistry for Children (pres. 1958-59), Southwestern Soc. Pedodontists, So. Soc. Orthodontists, Miss. Dental Assn., ADA, Am. Assn. Dental Schs., Phi Kappa Phi. Republican. Episcopalian. Avocation: golf. Home: 3540 Hawthorne Dr Jackson MS 39216 Office: U Miss Sch Dept Orthodontics and Pediatric Dentistry Jackson MS 39216

SHARPE, THOMAS ROBERTS, health service research administrator, educator; b. Milw., Nov. 25, 1944; s. Joseph William and Elizabeth Maryalice (Roberts) S.; m. Rebecca E. Dutton, Dec. 21, 1969 (div. Nov. 1981); m. 2d, Margaret N. Hughes, Aug. 20, 1983; 1 dau., Heather Neale. B.S. in Pharmacy, U. Ill., 1970; M.S. in Health Care Adminstrn., U. Miss., 1973, Ph.D. in Health Care Adminstrn., 1975. Asst. prof. U. Miss. Sch. Pharmacy Research Inst. Pharm. Scis., University, 1974-80, assoc. prof., 1980—, asst. dir. health services research, 1974-81, assoc. dir., 1981—; research cons. Miss. Dept. Health, 1976-80, North Miss. Med. Ctr., 1980—. Author numerous research articles and papers. Am. Found. Pharm. Edn. Charles R. Walgreen fellow, 1972-74. Mem. Am. Pharm. Assn. (ho. of dels. 1975), Am. Pub. Health Assn., Am. Soc. Hosp. Pharmacists, Nat. Rural Primary Care Assn. (bd. dirs.), Miss. Primary Health Care Assn. (sec. 1981-83), Kappa Psi, Phi Kappa Phi, Alpha Kappa Delta. Club: Rotary (Oxford, Miss.). Office: U Miss Research Inst of Pharm Scis University MS 38677

SHARRAR, GLORIA KRIZMANICH, business communications, information management consultant; b. Alexandria, Va., Aug. 12, 1948; d. Joseph and Marie (Voithofer) Krizmanich; m. David Lloyd Sharrar, Feb. 14, 1968; children—Katherine, David. B.A., U. Tenn.-Knoxville, 1978, M.L.I.S., 1982. Free lance writer and editor, Knoxville and Washington, 1968—; owner Reading Habit Bookstore, Knoxville, 1981-82, Sharrar Bus. Cons. Services, Knoxville, 1977—; tng. cons. Tenn. Dept. Personnel, 1983—, N.Am. Phillips Corp., 1983—, So. Social Soc. Contbr. articles to periodicals; contbr. poems to nat., internat. library mags. Bd. dirs. Church Street UMC Day Care Ctr., Knoxville, 1983. Nat. Endowment Arts grantee, 1976; 1st place for serious verse nat. competition Fed. Poets, 1970. Mem. ALA, Tenn. Library Assn., Tenn. Lit. Arts Assn. Methodist. Home: 1219 Upland Ave Greenville TN 37743

SHARROCK, ROY GENE, geologist, oil company executive; b. Moran, Tex., Sept. 17, 1933; s. William Roy and Marie (Kruger) S.; m. Geneva Maryanna Bernstein, May 27, 1961; 1 child, Jenny Gene. B.S. in Petroleum Geology, Tex. Tech U., 1955. Registered petroleum geologist. Geologist Duval Corp., Midland, Pecos, Tex., 1967-74, So. Union Gas Co., Dallas, 1974-77; chief geologist So. Union Exploration Co., Dallas, 1977-79, v.p., chief geologist, 1979-84, sr. v.p., chief geologist, 1984—. Author: San Ysidro Gas Storage Unit, 1978. Chmn. bd. edn. Bethel Lutheran Ch. Sch., Dallas, 1975-77; elder Bethel Luth. Ch., Dallas, 1982-84. Served with U.S. Army, 1955-57. Mem. Am. Assn. Petroleum Geologists, Am. Inst. Profl. Geologists, Dallas, Geol. Soc., West Tex. Geol. Soc. Lutheran. Clubs: Dallas Petroleum, Engineers (Dallas). Office: So Union Exploration Co 1217 Main St Suite 400 Dallas TX 75201

SHARUM, MONICA MARIE MARTIN, nurse; b. Paris, Ark., May 11, 1956; d. Gerald Theodore and Anne Albertine (Stehle) Martin; m. John Edward Sharum, Feb. 25, 1984. A.A.S., Westark Community Coll., 1976. R.N., Ark. Asst. team leader St. Edward Mercy Med. Ctr., Ft. Smith, Ark., 1976-78, 3-11 team leader surg. ICU, 1978-81, 3-11 nursing service supr., 1981—; instr. basic CPR, 1978—. Mem. Am. Assn. Critical Care Nurses. Roman Catholic.

SHAUBERGER, MARY LOUISE FRANKLIN, home economist; b. Grand Cane, La., Mar. 1, 1930; d. Bernard Arvil and Corrie Lee (Abington) Franklin; B.S., La. Tech. U., 1951; postgrad. N.E. La. U., summers 1963-65; M.S., La. State U., 1973; m. Mial Jennings Shauberger, June 15, 1952 (dec.); children—Rebecca Louise Shauberger Turner, Mial Jennings III, Gale Franklin (dec.), Sally Elaine Shauberger Rivers. Asst. home demonstration agt. La. Coop. Extension Service, Donaldsonville, 1951-52, asst. home economist, Tallulah, 1966-69, home economist, Coushatta, 1969—; parish chmn. Red River Parish Extension Office, 1982—; elem. tchr. Madison Parish Schs., Tallulah, La., 1962-66; dietary cons. Red River Parish Council on Aging; adviser Red River Parish Fair Assn., Red River Parish Extension Homemakers Council. Dress chmn. Red River Parish Centennial Com., 1971; vol. worker Cystic Fibrosis Bike-a-thon, 1976-78, Red River Parish Blood Drive, 1977-85; mem. Red River Parish Emergency Med. Services Com., 1980; mem. Red River Parish Rural Infant Health Com., 1980-81. Recipient La. Extension Communication award, 1977, 81. Mem. Nat. Assn. Extension Home Economists (Disting. Service awards 1981), La. Assn. Extension Home Economists, La. Tech. U. Home Econs. Found., Am. Home Econs. Assn., La. Home Econs. Assn., Am. Diabetes Assn., DeSoto Parish Hist. Soc., Pilot Internat., Epsilon Sigma Phi. Democrat. Mem. Ch. of Christ. Home: PO Box 616 Ashland Rd Coushatta LA 71019 Office: Adminstrn Bldg PO Drawer E Red Oak Rd Coushatta LA 71019

SHAUNNESSY, GEORGE DANIEL, medical company executive; b. Joliet, Ill., Apr. 15, 1948; s. Daniel Joseph and Florence Elizabeth (Dunfee) S.; m. Martha Ann Waibel, Sept. 20, 1975; children—Katherine Erin, Daniel Joseph, Ellen Frances. B.S. in Indsl. Adminstrn., St. Louis U., 1970; M.H.A., Xavier U., Cin., 1973. With Hosp. Affiliates Internat., Inc., Nashville, 1973-80, regional dir., Miami, 1977-78, v.p. subs. Hosp. Affiliates Mgmt. Corp., 1978-79, v.p. hosp. ops. Southeast Group, Atlanta, 1979-80; v.p. hosp. ops. Charter Med. Corp., Macon, Ga., 1980—, trustee, officer or dir. numerous hosps. Home: 4622 Saint Anne Ct Macon GA 31210 Office: Charter Med Corp 577 Mulberry St Macon GA 31298

SHAVER, EDWARDS BOONE, telephone company executive; b. Louisville, Nov. 24, 1948; s. John Mebane and Martha Perkins (Boone) S.; m. Sharon Ann Smith, Apr. 19, 1980; children—Carrie Anne, Katherine Leigh, Martha Boone, Edwards Boone, Jr. B.S. in Indsl. Mgmt., Ga. Inst. Tech., 1970; M.B.A., Ga. State U., 1984. Supr. traffic staff So. Bell, Savannah, Ga., 1975-76, mgr., Valdosta, Ga., 1976-77, Dublin, Ga., 1977-78, Savannah, 1978-79, ops. mgr., Atlanta, 1980-85, ops. mgr. labor relations and benefits, 1985—; asst. mgr. AT&T, Basking Ridge, N.J., 1979-80. Bd. dirs. DeKalb unit Am. Cancer Soc., Atlanta, 1983—, v.p., 1984-85, pres. elect, 1985-86, pres., 1986-87; div. chmn. Met. United Way, Atlanta, 1982, sect. chmn., 1985; pres. Parkside Homes Assn., Roswell, Ga., 1981; chmn. Laurens County Christmas Seal Drive, Dublin, 1978. Mem. Am. Mgmt. Assn., Sandy Springs C. of C., North Fulton C. of C. (bd. dirs.), Gwinnett County C. of C., DeKalb County C. of C., Buckhead Bus. Assn. Republican. Methodist. Club: Horseshoe Bend Country. Lodges: Rotary, Elks. Home: 220 River Landing Dr Roswell GA 30076 Office: So Bell 349-100 Perimeter Ctr Pl Atlanta GA 30346

SHAW, ALAN BOSWORTH, geologist; b. Englewood, N.J., Mar. 28, 1922; s. Carroll Harper and Natalie Frederique (Howe) S.; m. Marian Tavenner Stoll, Mar. 11, 1954 (dec. 1981); m. Mary Elizabeth Merrem, Sept. 3, 1982. A.B. magna cum laude, Harvard U., 1946, A.M., 1949, Ph.D., 1949. Asst. prof. geology U. Wyo., Laramie, 1949-55; area paleontologist Shell Oil Co., Denver, 1955-60; research sect. supr. Amoco Prodn. Co., Tulsa, 1961-68, cons. geologist, Denver, 1968-76, chief geologist, Chgo., 1977-81, research cons., Tulsa, 1981—; Author: Time in Stratigraphy, 1964. Served to 1st lt. USAAF, 1943-45, ETO. Mem. Paleontol. Soc. (pres. 1968), Soc. Econ. Paleontologists and Mineralogists, Am. Assn. Petroleum Geologists, Paleontol. Assn., Rocky Mountain Assn. Geologists. Republican. Avocation: Byzantine numismatics. Office: Amoco Prodn Research Ctr PO Box 3385 Tulsa OK 74102

SHAW, ALLAN GREGORY, executive search consultant; b. Cleve., Apr. 2, 1940; s. Allan K. and Sara E. (Williams) S.; children—Brett Allan, Christopher David; m. 2d, Geraldine Anne Dunkley, Dec. 31, 1973; stepchildren—Paul, Mark, Jason. B.S. in Bus., Northwestern U., 1963. Sales mgr. White Consol. Industries, Cleve., 1963-73; div. sales mgr. Avon Products, Inc., Kansas City, Mo., 1973-77; exec. v.p. Mgmt. Recruiters Dallas, 1977-80; pres., gen. mgr. Mgmt. Recruiters Nashville, 1980—. Mem. Tenn. Pvt. Employment Agy. Bd., 1983. Mem. Tenn. Assn. Human Resource Cons., Sales and Mktg. Execs., Brentwood C. of C. (dir. 1982—, Mem. of Yr. 1983), Nashville C. of C. (small bus. com.). Methodist. Clubs: Brentwood Country, Maryland Farms Racquet and Country, Nashville Exchange.

SHAW, BRIAN ROBERT, exploration geologist; b. Detroit, Dec. 13, 1950; s. George and Nathalie (Kitay) Shaw Bowsman; m. Lewise Ann Wilson; children—Brian James, George Stephen. B.Sc., Western Mich. U., 1973; M.Sc., U. Mich., 1975; Ph.D., Syracuse U., 1978. Petroleum geologist Amoco Prodn. Co., Houston, 1975-80; chief geologist Samson Resources, Houston, 1980-82; staff explorationist Monsanto Oil Co., Houston, 1982—; adj. prof. Onondaga Community Coll., N.Y., 1975-77; mem. bd. dept. geology Western Mich. U., Kalamazoo, 1982—. Author: Geomathematical and Petrophysical Studies, 1979; Quantitative Stratigraphic Correlation, 1982; contbr. articles to profl. jours. Am. Assn. Petroleum Geologists grantee, 1977. Mem. Am. Assn. Petroleum Geologists, Soc. Econ. Paleontologists and Mineralogists, Geol. Soc. Am., AAAS. Presbyterian. Club: Ciudad (Houston). Office: Monsanto Oil Co 5051 Westheimer St Suite 1300 Houston TX 77056

SHAW, ELMER CARL, dentist; b. Topeka, Kans., Dec. 24, 1948; s. Elmer Carl and Dorothy (Steele) S.; m. Deborah Lee Brown, Dec. 15, 1968; children—Amy Catherine, Amber Leigh. B.A. in Biology, Ga. Coll., Milledgeville, 1971, B.A. in Chemistry, 1972; D.M.D., Med. Coll. Ga., 1975. Dentist, State Hosp., Milledgeville, 1975-76; gen. practice dentistry, Warner Robins, Ga., 1976—. Sponsor Warner Robins Little League, 1979—, Ga. Spl. Olympics, Warner Robins, 1979—. Mem. ADA, Ga. Dental Assn., Central Dist. Assn., Warner Robins Dental Assn. Baptist. Lodge: Moose. Avocations: golf, bowling, hunting, fishing. Home: 108 Oak St Warner Robins GA 31093 Office: Dr E Carl Shaw 100 Hospital Dr Warner Robins GA 31093

SHAW, EUGENE CLAY, JR., congressman; b. Miami, Fla., Apr. 11, 1939; s. Eugene Clay and Rita (Walker) S.; B.A., Stetson U., 1961, J.D., 1966; M.S., U. Ala., 1963; m. Emilie Costar; children—Clay, Mimi, Jennifer, Jacy. Bar: Fla. 1966; C.P.A. Practice law, Fort Lauderdale, Fla., 1967-80; chief prosecutor, Ft. Lauderdale, 1968-69; assoc. mcpl. judge, Ft. Lauderdale, 1969-71; mayor, commr., Ft. Lauderdale, 1972-80; mem. U.S. Ho. of Reps., 1981—. Mem. Nat. Conf. Republican Mayors (past pres.), U.S. Conf. Mayors (mem. exec. com.). Republican. Roman Catholic. Office: 322 Cannon House Office Bldg Washington DC 20515

SHAW, GARTH ANTHONY, import/export company executive, farmer; b. Kingston, Jamaica, Apr. 17, 1956; came to U.S., 1980; s. Leslie Herbert and Enid Mae (Henriques) S.; m. Nerissa Sharon, July 17, 1982; 1 son, Ryan Craig. Student Miami-Dade North Coll., 1981—. Officer Can. Imperial Bank of Commerce, Kingston, Jamaica, 1977-80; v.p. Am. Trading Co., Miami, Fla., 1980—, also dir.; v.p. Lombardo Farms, Kingston, 1980—, also dir.; dir. Reliable Trading Corp., Kingston. Roman Catholic. Home: 11440 SW 203d St Miami FL 33189

SHAW, GEORGE PHILIP (PHIL), hospital administrator; b. Porterdale, Ga., Mar. 16, 1950; s. M. B. and Lucille (Ivey) S.; m. Baxter Pratt, June 15, 1968; children—Susan Ivey, William Matthew. B.S. in Bus. Adminstrn., U. Tenn.-Knoxville, 1974. Auditor, Blue Cross/Blue Shield, Nashville, 1975-77; reimbursement acct. Am. Med. Internat., Atlanta, 1977-79; asst. adminstr. Glenn R. Frye Hosp., Hickory, N.C., 1979-82; exec. dir. Central Carolina Hosp., Sanford, N.C., 1982—. Bd. dirs. Lee County United Way, 1983—, Lee County Heart Assn., 1983-84; dist. mem. Occoneechee council Boy Scouts Am., 1983, 84, 85. Served with USAF, 1971-74. Mem. Fedn. Am. Hosps. (bd. dirs. 1983-84), N.C. Hosp. Assn. Clubs: Rotary, Elks. Avocations: Golf; fishing; winter skiing; basketball. Home: PO Box 553 Sanford NC 27330 Office: Central Carolina Hosp Sanford NC 27330

SHAW, JAMES GARY, architect; b. Cleburne, Tex., Nov. 4, 1938; s. Charlie Bigham and Laura Evelyn (Stanley) S.; m. Sandra Jean Fletcher, Sept. 2, 1958; children—Kerri Dawn, Laura Danell, Kristen Leanne. Registered architect, Tex., Okla., La. Prin., J. Gary Shaw & Assocs., Cleburne, Tex., 1969—; dir. Interfirst Bank, Cleburne, Tex., 1985; mem. Nat. Council Architects Registration Bd., 1972. Baptist. Lodge: Rotary. Home: 1622 Ivy Ct Cleburne TX 76031 Office: J Gary Shaw & Assocs 1638 W Henderson Cleburne TX 76031

SHAW, JEANNE OSBORNE, editor, poet; b. Stone Mountain, Ga., June 1, 1920; d. Virgil Waite and Daisy Hampton (Scruggs) Osborne; B.A., Agnes Scott Coll., 1942; m. Harry B. Shaw, Dec. 10, 1982; children—Robert Allan Gibbs, Marilyn Osborne Gibbs. Mem. editorial staff Atlanta Constitution, 1942; feature writer New London (Conn.) Day, 1943; book reviewer Atlanta Constitution, 1940-42, Atlanta Jour., 1945-48; poetry editor Banner Press, Emory U., 1957-59; book editor Georgia Mag., Decatur, 1957-73. Pres., Newton class Druid Hills Baptist Ch., 1973-74. Recipient Robert Martin, Burke, Otto, in praise of poetry awards N.Y. Poetry Forum, 1973, 79, 81; Westbrook award Ky. Poetry Soc., 1976; Ariz. award Nat. Fedn. State Poetry Socs., 1981. Mem. Ga. Writers Assn. (lit. achievement award 1971), Poetry Soc. Ga. (John Clare prize 1955, Katharine H. Strong prize 1975, Eunice Thomson prize 1976, Jimmy Williamson prize 1977, Capt. Frank Spencer award 1985), Atlanta Writers Club (pres. 1949-50, named Aurelia Austin Writer of Year in poetry 1971), Phi Beta Kappa. Author: The Other Side of the Water (Author of Year in Poetry award Dixie Council of Authors and Journalists), 1970; Unravelling Yarn, 1979; co-author: Noel! Poems of Christmas, 1979; author: Faithbuilders, 1982-84; contbr. poems to mags. Home: 809 Pinetree Dr Decatur GA 30030

SHAW, JOHN GUY (JACK), computer software company executive, consultant; b. East Cleveland, Ohio, Mar. 16, 1950; s. Richard Joseph and Carlla (Ramsey) S.; m. Deborah Ruth Riecke, Feb. 15, 1986; children—Ryan Benjamin, Robyn Allyson. B.S., Yale U., 1971; M.B.A., Northwestern U., 1976. Produce ops. engr. Chiquita Brands, Chgo., 1972-73; treasury planner Esmark, Chgo., 1974-76; market planner Baxter Travenol Labs., Deerfield, Ill., 1976-77; corp. cash mgr. Martin Oil Service, Alsip, Ill., 1977-79; product planning mgr. Mgmt. Sci. Am., Inc., Atlanta, 1979-86; founder, pres. Electronic Cash Mgmt., Inc., Marietta, Ga., 1985—. Contbr. articles to profl. jours. Bd. dirs. Chimney Lakes Homeowners Assn., Roswell, Ga., 1985. Mem. Electronic Bus. Data Interchange (exec. com. Accredited Standards Com. X12 1984—), Nat. Corp. Cash Mgmt. Assn., Automotive Ind. Action Group, Nat. Assn. Credit Mgmt., Nat. Assn. Purchasing Mgmt. Avocations: tennis; skiing; wine tasting; gourmet dining. Home: 401 Riverview Dr SE Marietta GA 30067 Office: Electronic Cash Mgmt Inc 401 Riverview Dr Marietta GA 30067

SHAW, JOHN MALACH, fed. judge; b. Beaumont, Tex., Nov. 14, 1931; s. John Virgil Shaw and Ethel (Malach) Newstadt; student Tulane U., 1949-50; B.S. with spl. attainments in Commerce, Washington and Lee U., 1953; LL.B., J.D., La. State U., 1956; m. Glenda Ledoux, Nov. 11, 1970; children—John Lewis, Stacy Anne. Admitted to La. bar, 1956; partner firm Lewis and Lewis, Opelousas, La., 1958-79; U.S. dist. judge, Western Dist. La., Opelousas, 1979—. Govt. appeal agt. Local Bd. 60, La., 1965-72. Served with U.S. Army, 1956-58. Recipient Presdl. cert. of appreciation for services as appeal agt. Mem. Fifth Circuit Dist. Judges Assn., Opelousas C. of C. (pres., 1966). Democrat. Methodist. Club: Kiwanis. Mem. La. Law Rev., 1954-56, asso. editor, 1955-56, author articles, 1954-56. Office: 3d Floor Federal Bldg Union St Opelousas LA 70570

SHAW, LACY BORDELON, optometrist; b. Alexandria, La., Sept. 9, 1946; s. Roger Falconer Shaw and Jane Sterkx (Bordelon) Shaw Ormsby; m. Christie Ann Smith, Nov. 18, 1972 (div. June 1976). B.S., U. Houston, 1970, O.D., 1972. Practice optometry, Alexandria, 1972-81; pvt. practice optometry, Tioga, La., 1974—, Alexandria, 1981—; cons. Hydrocurve, San Diego, 1976-77, Wesley-Jessen, Chgo., 1984, 85; adj. prof. So. Coll. Optometry, Memphis, 1983, 84, 85. Coach Kiwanis Little League, Alexandria, 1975, Menard High Swim Team, Alexandria, 1974-78; mem. adv. panel CIBA Vision Care, 1983. Mem. Am. Optometric Assn. (mem. contact lens sect.), Heart of Am. Contact Lens Congress, La. Assn. Optometrists (bd. dirs.), New Orleans Contact Lens Soc. Republican. Roman Catholic. Club: Courtyard (Alexandria, La.). Avocations: flying; snow skiing; swimming. Lodge: Kiwanis (v.p. 1985). Office: Eye Care Ctrs 5615 Jackson St Extension Alexandria LA 71303 also Eye Care Ctr 5504 Shreveport Hwy PO Box 1008 Tioga LA 71477

SHAW, MARTIN, civil engineer; b. N.Y.C., Feb. 12, 1951; s. Phil and Clara (Rappaport) S. B.C.E., CCNY, 1974; M.S.C.E., Poly. Inst. N.Y., 1982. Registered profl. engr., N.Y., Va. Asst. to surveying prof. CCNY, 1974; structural designer Frederic R. Harris, Inc., cons. engrs., 1974-75; civil engr. U.S. Army C.E., N.Y. dist., 1976-79; engr. Dept. Energy/Fed. Energy Regulatory Commn., 1979-80; gen. engr. Hdqrs. U.S. Army Materiel Devel. and Readiness Command, Alexandria, Va., 1980-83; lectr. No. Va. Community Coll., Annandale (Va.) Campus, 1980-82; gen. engr. U.S. Army C.E., Facility Engrng. Support Agy., Fort Belvoir, Va., 1983—. Vol., Fairfax County Hist. Preservation, A.R.C. Mem. ASCE, Soc. Am. Mil. Engrs. Home: 9857 Hagel Circle Lorton VA 22079 Office: US Army Facility Engrng Support Agy Bldg 358 Fort Belvoir VA 22060

SHAW, TIMOTHY FRANK, computer technology executive; b. Newport News, Va., Apr. 30, 1953; s. Frank Bernard and Vera Regis (Fitzpatrick) S.; m. Gayle Marie Boyle, June 15, 1974; 1 dau., Elizabeth. B.A., U. Va., 1975; M.S., Johns Hopkins U., 1979. Mathematician, computer systems analyst Nat. Security Agy., Md., 1975-77; systems engr. Computer Network Corp., Washington, 1977-78; systems analyst Viar & Co., Inc., Alexandria, Va., 1978-80; v.p. Viar & Co., Inc., Alexandria, 1980—. Lincoln Found. scholar, 1971-75. Mem. Assn. Computing Machinery. Democrat. Roman Catholic. Club: Lions (v.p. 1982-83, pres. 1984-85). Office: 300 N Lee St Alexandria VA 22314

SHAW, W. PRESTON, educational administrator; b. Terrell, Tex., Feb. 28, 1940; s. Levi Charles and Alma (Kennedy) S.; m. Willie Mae Sinegal, Mar. 10, 1962; children—Tarus Preston, Yolanda Michelle. B.S. in Pre-Medicine, Huston Tillotson Coll., 1962; B.A. in Secondary Edn. Sci., U. Austin, 1953; M.S. in Biology, Tex. Christian U., 1970; M.A. in Pub. Sch. Adminstrn., U. Houston, 1973. Nat. park ranger U.S. Dept. Interior, Yellowstone, Wyo., 1962-63; tchr. sci. Ardmore High Sch., Okla., 1963-64; head sci. dept. Lincoln Jr. High Sch., Beaumont, Tex., 1964-70, asst. prin., 1970-73; prin. G.W. Carver Elem. Sch., Beaumont, 1973-75, Beaumont-Charlton-Pollard, Beaumont, 1975—. Mem. Planning Bd. Adjustment, City Council, Beaumont Planning and Zoning Bd., 1974—; active Melton YMCA, Beaumont. Named Outstanding Adminstr., Beaumont Sch. Dist., 1974-75. Mem. Sabine Sch. Bd. Assn. (treas. 1972), Omega Psi Phi (pres. 1970-74, Omega Man of Yr. 1974, 82, Citizen of Yr. 1982). Democrat. Baptist. Lodge: Lions (bd. dirs.). Avocations: bowling; tennis; racketball; dance; basketball. Home: 4630 Corley St Beaumont TX 77707 Office: Beaumont-Charlton-Polland High Sch 88 Royal Purple Dr 88 Roy Beaumont TX 77707

SHAW, WILLIAM JAMES, psychologist; b. Newark, Mar. 11, 1947; s. William Joseph and Ruth Rita (Spratt) S.; B.A., Iona Coll., 1968; M.A., Fairfield U., 1975; Psy.D. in Psychology, Baylor U., 1976; m. Catherine G. Jarvis, Aug. 17, 1975. Tchr., coach Iona Grammar Sch., New Rochelle, N.Y., 1968-71, Bergen Cath. High Sch., Oradell, N.J., 1971-72; intern U. Okla. Health Scis. Center, Oklahoma City, 1975-76; clin. instr. dept. psychiatry and behavioral scis., 1979-81; pvt. practice clin. psychology Okla. Psychol. and Ednl. Center, Oklahoma City, 1976-78; asso. in criminal justice Oklahoma City U., 1980-81; clin. psychologist adolescent medicine Okla. Children's Meml. Hosp., Oklahoma City, 1981—; dir. psychol. services Okla. Dept. Corrections, 1978-81, also chief psychologist, 1978-81; adj. asst. prof. edn. U. Okla., Norman, 1977-78, asst. prof. psychiatry and behavioral scis., clin. asst. prof. pediatrics Health Scis. Center, 1981—; vice chmn. Okla. State Bd. Examiners of Psychologists, 1980—, chmn., 1981-82. Vol., July-O-Rama Day Camp for Underprivileged Children, New Rochelle, 1966-69, breast cancer rehab. guidelines com. Okla. Med. Research Found., Oklahoma City, 1976-77. Recipient Grant award U.S. Dept. Justice, 1979; N.J. State scholar, 1964; cert. tchr., N.Y.; lic. psychologist, Okla. Diplomate Am. Acad. Behavioral Medicine. Mem. Am. Psychol. Assn. (Disting. Public Service award 1980), Okla. Psychol. Assn., Southwestern Psychol. Assn., Soc. Adolescent Medicine, Soc. Behavioral Medicine. Democrat. Roman Catholic. Contbr. articles to psychol. jours. and books. Home: 2720 NW 58th Pl Oklahoma City OK 73112 Office: U Okla Health Scis Center Dept Psychiatry Box 26901 Oklahoma City OK 73190

SHEA, DAVID BRADLEY, real estate executive/syndicator; b. Vallejo, Calif., Oct. 18, 1946; s. Robert Bradley and Shirley (Hooker) S. B.S. in Commerce, U. Va., 1972. C.P.A. Sr. cons. Ernst & Whinney, C.P.A.s, Richmond, Va., 1972-79; treas. Goodloe-Wagner, Inc., Richmond, 1979-82; controller Area Corp., Richmond, 1983-85; pres. Shea Co., Inc., 1985—. Served with U.S. Army, 1967-69. Mem. Real Estate Securities Inst. (v.p. 1983-85, pres. 1985—). Home: 2221 Hanover Ave Richmond VA 23220 Office: Shea Co Inc 1001 E Main St Suite 1012 Richmond VA 23219

SHEA, JOHN DANIEL, dentist; b. New Orleans, Sept. 19, 1933; s. John Charles and Elise Josephine (Jansen) S.; m. Linda Anne Robinett, July 21, 1956; children—John William, Lisa, Patricia, Michael, Daniel, Kathleen. D.D.S., Loyola U., 1957. Gen. practice dentistry, New Orleans, 1959—; table clinician New Orleans Dental Conf., 1967, Miss. State Dental Assn. Ann. meeting, 1967, Chgo. Mid-Winter Dental Meeting, 1968; clinician New Orleans Dental Assn., New Orleans Dental Hygienists Assn., 1966, New Orleans Dental Assts. Soc., 1966; dental sch. rep. Loyola U. Alumni Adv. Bd., 1967-68, 82-84; mem. La. State Bd. Dentistry, 1970-76, pres., 1973-74. Chmn. dental div. United Way, New Orleans, 1965, 78; treas. cub scout troop 55 Boy Scouts Am., 1967-69; v.p. Mercy Acad. Parents Club, New Orleans, 1975-76; usher Holy Name of Jesus Ch., New Orleans, 1975—. Served as capt. USAFR, 1957-59. Fellow Acad. Gen. Dentistry, Internat. Coll. Dentists; mem. Pierre Fauchard Acad., New Orleans Dental Assn. (pres. 1985-86, council on ins. 1978—), La. Dental Assn. (council on ins. 1978—, ADA, C. Edmund Kells Dental Study Club (chmn. 1966), C. Victor Vignes Dental Soc., Alpha Sigma Nu, Omicron Kappa Upsilon. Republican. Roman Catholic. Clubs: Cactus, Anniversary Study. Avocations: tennis; fishing; water skiing; boating. Home: 6031 S Robertson St New Orleans LA 70118 Office: 4638 S Claiborne Ave New Orleans LA 70125

SHEADEL, JAMES BENJAMIN, rehabilitation administrator; b. Barberton, Ohio, Apr. 24, 1946; s. John Magley and Kathryn Marie (Fries) S.; m. Cheryl Ann Price, Mar. 19, 1971; children—John Robert, Sara Elizabeth. B.A., Westminster Coll., New Wilmington, Pa., 1968; M.Ed., N.C. State U., 1979. Rehab. counselor N.C. Services for Blind, Raleigh, 1975-83; dir. patient support counseling service Duke U. Eye Ctr., Durham, N.C., 1983—; cons.

Voices Project, Durham, 1985; mem. adv. council Durham Retired Sr. Vol. Program, 1985; co-author tng. programs. Mem. Farmington Woods PTA, Cary, N.C., 1983—; asst. coach Pioneers I soccer team, Cary, 1984—; mem. Christian unity work area White Plains United Methodist Ch., Cary, 1984—; chmn. schs. com. MacDonald Woods Homeowners Assn., Cary, 1984—. Grantee Kate B. Reynolds Health Care Trust, 1984. Mem. Triangle Assn. for Visually Impaired (charter), Nat. Rehab. Assn., Am. Assn. Counseling and Devel. Democrat. Avocations: landscaping, photography, hiking, bicycling, reading. Office: Duke U Eye Ctr Box 3802 Erwin Rd Durham NC 27710

SHEAHAN, ROBERT EMMETT, lawyer; b. Chgo., May 20, 1942; s. Robert E. and Lola (Moore) S.; B.A., Ill. Wesleyan U., 1964; J.D., Duke U., 1967; M.B.A., U. Chgo., 1970. Admitted to Ill. bar, 1967, U.S. Supreme Ct. bar, 1971, La. bar, 1975, N.C. bar, 1978, D.C. Circuit Ct. Appeal bars; trial atty. NLRB, Milw. and New Orleans, 1970-75; mem. firm Jones, Walker, Waechter, Poitevent, Carrere & Denegre, New Orleans, 1976-78; mgmt. labor atty. in pvt. practice, High Point, N.C., 1978—. Bd. dirs. High Point United Way. Mem. High Point C. of C., Congressional Action Com., Ill. Bar Assn., N.C. Bar Assn., Am. Bar Assn. (developing labor law com.), Phi Delta Phi. Republican. Roman Catholic. Author: Drug Abuse in the Workplace-An Action Handbook; contbg. author: Developing Labor Law, 1975—. Office: PO Box 29 High Point NC 27261

SHEALY, ARTHUR LISTON, JR., banker; b. Gainesville, Fla., July 3, 1922; s. Arthur Liston and Bonnie Estelle (Lester) S.; m. Mary Julia Bailey, Sept. 10, 1949; 1 child, Julia Ellen. B.S. in Bus. Adminstrn., U. Fla., 1944. C.P.A., Fla. Staff acct. Russel S. Bogue, C.P.A., Tampa, Fla., 1946-48; auditor U. Fla., 1948-50; in charge Jacksonville, Fla., office Ring, Mahoney & Arner, C.P.A.s, 1950-69, ptnr., 1958-69; ptnr. in charge Jacksonville office Coopers & Lybrand, C.P.A.s, 1969-73; exec. pres., controller Barnett Banks of Fla., Inc., Jacksonville, 1973—. Pres. Greater Jacksonville Fair Assn., 1977-79. Served to 1st lt. U.S. Army, 1943-46. Mem. Am. Inst. C.P.A.s (council 1970-73), Fla. Inst. C.P.A.s (pres. 1965), Fin. Exec. Inst., Phi Delta Theta. Presbyterian. Clubs: River, Fla. Yacht, Kiwanis (pres. Jacksonville 1961, dist. lt. gov. Fla. Dist. 1971). Office: 100 Laura St Jacksonville FL 32202

SHEALY, DAVID LEE, physicist, educator; b. Newberry, S.C., Sept. 16, 1944; s. William Elmer and Elizabeth (Plaxico) S.; m. Elaine Wohlford, June 17, 1969; children—Bridget McGill, David McElwee. B.S., U. Ga., 1966, Ph.D., 1973. Prof., chmn. dept. physics, U. Ala.-Birmingham, 1984—; cons. Motorola, Phoenix, 1978—, Jet Propulsion Lab., Pasadena, Calif., 1980-82. Contbr. articles to profl. jours. Faculty fellow NASA, ASEE, 1980, 81; recipient Silver Quill and Publ. award Motorola, 1982, 83, research paper award Ala. Sect. IEEE, 1984. Mem. Am. Assn. Physics Tchrs., Am. Physical Soc., Optical Soc. Am., Acoustical Soc. Am., N.Y. Acad. Sci. Republican. Methodist. Avocations: running. Home: 2337 Morning Star Dr Birmingham AL 35216 Office: U Ala at Birmingham 1401 9th Ave South Birmingham AL 35294

SHEALY, RYAN C., lawyer, state senator; b. Lexington County, S.C., Dec. 9, 1923; s. Thomas C. and Una Lee (Fink) S.; J.D., U. S.C.; m. Elsie Porth, June 15, 1947; children—Sherry Lynn, Rodney, Christy Lane, Shawn, Lorri. Asst. U.S. atty., 1969-74; practice law, Lexington, S.C.; mem. S.C. Ho. of Reps., 1955-64, 67-68; now mem. S.C. Senate. Served with USN, 1942-47. Republican. Office: 125 Stoney Brook Ln Lexington SC 29072*

SHEARER, JAMES ELTON, interior designer; b. Snyder, Tex., Dec. 8, 1945; s. Elton M. and Bernice Marie (Birdwell) S.; m. Elaine Sternberg; children—Joell Lynnette, Holly Leigh, Anna Wynn. B.S., Angelo State U., San Angelo, Tex. Designer, Charles Crawford & Assocs., San Angelo, 1966-68; designer, ptnr. Crawford & Shearer, Inc., San Angelo, 1970-72; staff designer Mildred English, Inc., San Antonio, 1972-75; owner, designer Jim Shearer Inc., San Antonio, 1975—. Bd. dirs. Children's Organ Transplant Assn. San Antonio; mem. Friends of Mc Nay Art Inst. Served with USN, 1968-70. Mem. Am. Soc. Interior Designers, San Antonio C. of C., U.S. C. of C. Republican. Baptist. Address: 15667 San Pedro San Antonio TX 78232

SHEARER, ROSS STERLING, consultant, retired government official; b. Houston, Mar. 25, 1911; s. Thomas William and Hannah (Hutton) S.; m. Elizabeth Ann Rees, Apr. 16, 1938; children—Ross Sterling, Jr., Rees Rucker. Student George Washington U., 1928-31, U. Tex., 1931-34; LL.B., South Tex. Sch. of Law, 1937. Bar: Tex. 1937, U.S. Supreme Ct. 1951. With Tex. Employment Commn., Austin, 1936-41; adminstrv. analyst Social Security Bd., Washington, 1941-42; prin. budget examiner Bur. Budget, Exec. Office of Pres., Washington, 1942-51; acting adminstr. and asst. adminstr. Econ. Stblzn. Agy., Washington, 1951-53; asst. dir. orgn. and personnel AEC, Washington, 1953-61; planning officer U.S. Dept. Commerce, Washington, 1961-63; dir. fin. and mgmt. services, asst. manpower adminstr. U.S. Dept. Labor, Washington, 1963-74; cons., Arlington, Va., 1975—; sec. Pres.'s Nat. Labor Mgmt. Conf., 1945-46; cons. Ind. U., Bloomington for pub. service tng. at Thomassat U., Bangkok, Thailand, 1959; mem. Fgn. Service Selection Bds., Washington, 1965, 68; clk. Com. for Cts. of Justice, Ho. of Dels., Va. Gen. Assembly, Richmond, 1975-79; cons., field rep. Nat. Council Sr. Citizens, Washington, 1975-81. Trustee U. Richmond, 1951-55; investigator appropriations com. U.S. Ho. of Reps., Washington, 1963; bd. dirs., com. mem. Nat. Capital Area United Way, 1967—; chmn. Arlington United Way, 1969-71; treas. For Love of Children, Washington, 1974-80. Mem. Am. Polit. Sci. Assn., State Bar Tex., Kappa Sigma. Democrat. Baptist. Club: Washington Golf and Country (Arlington). Home: 3125 N Abingdon St Arlington VA 22207

SHECHTEL, STEPHEN ALEXANDER, mortgage banking executive, financial consultant; b. Washington, Mar. 8, 1954; s. Herman J. and R. Maxine (Firtag) S.; m. Deborah C. Seidel, July 2, 1978. B.S., U. Md., 1975. C.P.A., 1982-85; Fin. cons. M.B.A. of Washington, Rockville, Md., 1976-79; asst. v.p. J.T. Barnes, Washington, 1979-80; pres. Chesapeake Mortgage Corp., Silver Spring, Md., 1980-82; sr. v.p. Lincoln Fin. Corp., Clearwater, Fla., 1982-85; v.p. lending Life Savings and Loan, Clearwater, Fla., 1985—; dir. First Bankers Fin. Services, Inc., Ocean Atlantic Corp.; lectr. local county community coll. Active Belleair Beach (Fla.) Civic Assn. Recipient cert. of appreciation Suburban Md. Homebuilders Assn., 1981. Mem. Mortgage Bankers Assn. Am., Fla. Mortgage Brokers Assn., Fla. Homebuilders Assn., So. Ariz. Homebuilders Assn., Clearwater C. of C. Jewish. Club: Sertoma. Lodge: Masons, Shriners. Office: US Hwy 19N Clearwater FL 33568

SHEDLER, LEONARD, physician; b. N.Y.C., Apr. 19, 1932; m. Geraldine Renee Schulman; children—Alan, Mark, Howard. B.S. in Pharmacy, Fordham U., 1954; D.O., Chgo. Coll. Osteo. Medicine, 1958. Diplomate Am. Osteo. Bd. Gen. Practice. Intern, Bay View Hosp., Bay Village, Ohio, 1958-59; police surgeon, Paramus, N.J., 1960-70; dir. med. edn. Sun Coast Hosp., Largo, Fla., 1976—; med. dir. St. Petersburg Jr. Coll., 1981-84, Pinellas County Emergency Med. Services, 1983-84, Jacaranda Manor Nursing Home, St. Petersburg, 1974—; teaching staff Sun Coast Hosp.; assoc. prof. clin. medicine W. Va. Sch. Osteo. Medicine; clin. assoc. prof. dept. community medicine Southeastern Coll. Osteo. Medicine; adj. clin. faculty Okla. Coll. Osteo. Medicine and Surgery; adj. clin. assoc. prof. dept. family practice N.Y. Coll. Osteo. Medicine; adj. faculty Coll. Osteo Medicine and Surgery, Des Moines. Sec.-treas. Pinellas County Profl. Standards Rev. Orgn., 1979-81. Mem. Bergen County Soc. Osteo. Physicians and Surgeons (pres. 1964), Pinellas County Osteo. Med. Soc. (pres. 1977-79), Fla. Osteo. Med. Assn., Am. Osteo. Assn., Am. Coll. Emergency Physicians, Am. Coll. Utilization Rev. Physicians, Acad. Osteo. Dirs. Med. Edn., Am. Coll. Gen. Practitioners Osteo. Medicine and Surgery, So. Med. Assn. Address: 13299 87th Pl N Seminole FL 33542

SHEEDER, WILLIAM BENJAMIN, university dean; b. Elmira, N.Y., Jan. 21, 1938; s. Fred and Amy Sheeder; A.B. in Philosophy, Ottawa (Kans.) U., 1960; M.A. in Human Relations, Ohio U., Athens, 1966; children—Lynn, Traci. Mem. faculty Ohio U., 1961-65, asso. dir. Baker U. Center, 1962-64, asst. to dean Coll. Arts and Scis., 1964-66; mem. adminstrn. U. Miami, Coral Gables, Fla., 1966—, dir. student activities Student Union, 1968-73, v.p., sec. Univ. Rathskeller, Inc., 1972—, asst. v.p. student affairs, 1973—, dean students, 1976—; pres. Sheeder Enterprises, Inc., 1982—. Active Dade County Wesley Found., treas., 1971-73, chmn. bd. dirs., 1973-77; mem. work area higher edn. and campus ministry Fla. conf. Council Ministries, United Methodist Ch., 1976-80, 81—. Mem. Assn. Coll. Unions (enrichment chmn. 1975), Nat. Assn. Student Personnel Adminstrs., Nat. Orientation Dirs. Assn., Am. Assn. Higher Edn., Am. Personnel and Guidance Assn., Am. Coll. Personnel Assn., Sigma Alpha, Omicron Delta Kappa, Phi Delta Kappa, Phi Kappa Epsilon, Omega, Phi Mu Alpha, Zeta Beta Tau (adj. brother 1971—). Author articles. Address: Office Dean Students Univ Miami Coral Gables FL 33124

SHEEGOG, JAMES FLEMING, pharmaceutical company executive; b. Jacksonville, N.C., Oct. 19, 1955; s. Robert McCormick and Elizabeth (Tisdale) S.; m. Deborah Stallard, Apr. 25, 1981. B.A. in Criminal Justice systems, U. N.C.-Wilmington, 1973-77; M.S.W., U. N.C.-Chapel Hill, 1978-80. Case mgr. New Hanover Dept. Social Services, Wilmington, 1980-81, tng. specialist, 1981-83; spl. projects dir. Burroughs Wellcome Co., Research Triangle Park, N.C. 1983—; ptnr. Cape Fear Cons. Inc., Wilmington, 1981—. Author: Implementing a Client Outcome Monitoring System, 1984. Recipient Excellence award Burroughs Wellcome Co., 1985. Mem. Nat. Assn. Social Workers, Am. Soc. Tng. and Devel., Acad. Cert. Social Workers. Democrat. Presbyterian. Avocations: Arabian horse training, surfing, computer systems development. Home: 301 Carol St Carrboro NC 27510 Office: Buroughs Wellcome 3030 Cornwallis Rd Research Triangle Park NC 27709

SHEEHAN, AUGUST (GUS), state senator, lawyer; b. Apr. 28, 1917; s. Gus and Louise (Barkhau) S., Sr.; m. Mary Catherine Welp, 1950; children—Joyce Ann Sheehan Vogelpohl, Janet Marie Sheehan Cardiviola, Patricia Mary, Martin Joseph. Grad. Xavier U.; LL.B., Chase Law Sch.; J.D., Salmon P. Chase Coll. Law, 1968. Mem. Ky. Ho. of Reps., 1950-52, 63-66; mem. Ky. Senate, Frankfurt, 1972—; atty.-at-law; pub. News Enterprise, Ky. Mem. Kenton County Democratic Club. Mem. VFW. Clubs: Crusaders, United Travelers Comml. Lodge: KC. Office: Ky Senate State Capitol Frankfurt KY 40601*

SHEEHY, THOMAS WILLIAM, airline pilot; b. Baton Rouge, May 19, 1943; s. John Daniel and Nell Jane (Casey) S.; m. Constance Lynn Sheehy, June 20, 1964; children—Patrick, Daniel. Student U. Fla., 1962, U. Miami, 1963-64. Pilot, Hal DuPont Inc., Miami, Fla., 1965-66; pilot, capt. Delta Airlines, Miami, 1966—, capt., 1978—, check airman, 1983—. Contbr. articles to profl. jours. Named Rookie of Yr., Unltd. Hydroplanes, 1971. Mem. Airline Pilots Assn., Am. Power Boat Assn., Internat. Motor Sports Assn., Emerald Soc. Roman Catholic. Clubs: U. Miami Touchdown (agt. Operation Scholarship 1980—), Fla. Inboard Racing (commodore). Address: 15620 SW 77 Ct Miami FL 33157

SHEERIN, GERALD VINCENT, training consultant, writer; b. N.Y.C., Nov. 11, 1917; s. James Patrick and Mary Agnes (Campbell) S. Grad. cert. with honors, New England Sch. Art, 1950. Ednl. adminstr. SUNY-New Paltz, 1945-47; trainer U.S. Nat. Park Service, Harpers Ferry, W.Va., 1969-83; tng. cons., 1983—. Contbr. articles to fire service jours. Editor: Nat. Park Service Training Methods Manual. Served as 2d lt. U.S. Army, 1942-44. Mem. Soc. Tng. and Devel., Am. Assn. Adult Edn. (founding), Park Rangers Assn., Am. Soc. Interpretive Naturalists. Republican. Avocations: reading; writing. Home: Madison St Bolivar WV 25425 Office: PO Box 747 Harpers Ferry WV 25425

SHEETS, THOMAS JACKSON, research laboratory administrator, educator; b. Asheville, N.C., Dec. 11, 1926; s. Oliver Dewey and Sue (Pittillo) S.; m. Marie Rooks, May 17, 1952; children—Susan, Nancy. B.S., N.C. State Coll., 1951, M.S. in Agronomy, 1954; Ph.D., in Plant Physiology, U. Calif.-Davis, 1959. Research asst. dept. agronomy N.C. State Coll., Raleigh, 1951-54; research agronomist U.S. Dept. Agr., Davis, Calif., 1954-59; research plant physiologist, Stoneville, Miss., 1959-60, research plant physiologist, leader pesticide investigations-behavior in soils, Beltsville, Md., 1961-65; assoc. prof. entomology and crop sci. N.C. State U., Raleigh, 1965-69, prof. entomology, crop sci. and hort. sci., 1969—, dir. Pesticide Residue Research Lab., 1979—. Served with U.S. Army, 1944-46. Fellow Weed Sci. Soc. Am. (v.p. 1980, pres.-elect 1981, pres. 1982); mem. Internat. Weed Sci. Soc. (life), So. Weed Sci. Soc., N.C. Weed Sci. Soc., Council for Agrl. Sci. and Technology, N.C. Acad. Sci., Pesticide Assn. N.C., N.C. Entomol. Soc., Sigma Xi, Phi Kappa Phi, Alpha Gamma Rho. Democrat. Methodist. Editor: Weed Science, 1971-73; (with David Pimentel) Pesticides-Contemporary Roles in Agriculture, Health, and the Environment, 1979. Home: 1518 Delmont Dr Raleigh NC 27606 Office: 3709 Hillsborough St Raleigh NC 27607

SHEFF, HONEY A., clinical psychologist, educator; b. Bklyn., Nov. 24, 1954; d. Herbert Jack and Helene Ida (Sussman) Mendelson; m. Michael Robert Sheff, May 30, 1976; B.A. summa cum laude, Queens Coll., CUNY, 1975; M.A., SUNY-Stony Brook, 1978, Ph.D., 1981. Lic. psychologist. Clin. psychologist Callier Ctr. for Communication Disorders, U. Tex., Dallas, 1981-83; pvt. practice clin. psychology, cons., Dallas, 1983—; TV, radio appearances, Dallas, 1983—; lectr. U. Tex., Dallas, 1982—; clin. instr. psychology, dept. psychiatry U. Tex. Health Sci. Ctr. Southwestern Med. Sch., Dallas, 1983—; guest lectr. dept. emergency med. services U. Tex. Health Sci., Southwestern Med. Sch., Dallas, 1985—, also cons. research project dept. psychiatry cons. psychologist McKinney Job Corps Ctr., Tex., 1984—; presenter, workshop leader, tng. on family violence, Tex., N.Y. and N.H., 1977—. Chmn. Dallas County Mental Health-Mental Retardation Ctr. task force to rev. services to children and adolescents, 1985; founding mem. Parents Helping Parents Task Force, 1982-85; project designer Adolescent Mental Health Needs Dallas County, 1984; co-author jour. article, paper for profl. conf. (now chpt. in book). Charter mem. Parker Vol. Fire Dept., Tex., 1982—, sec.-treas., 1983-85. Recipient Robert S. Woodworth medal for excellence in psychology, Queens Coll., CUNY, 1975; commendation dept. psychology SUNY-Stony Brook, 1977. Mem. Am. Psychol. Assn., Tex. Psychol. Assn., Dallas Psychol. Assn. (pub. forum 1984), Mental Health Assn. Dallas County (mem., chmn. coms., award 1985), Nat. Council Family Relations, Tex. Council Family Violence, Internat. Soc. Prevention Child Abuse and Neglect, Dallas C. of C., Phi Beta Kappa. Democrat. Jewish. Avocations: Horseback riding; knitting and needlepoint; reading. Office: 13601 Preston Rd Suite 517E Dallas TX 75240

SHEIL, WILLIAM BERNARD, retail co. exec.; b. Chgo., Dec. 10, 1930, s. William L. and Mary A. (Foley) S.; m. Nell Leonard, Dec. 28, 1957; 3 children. B.A. in Journalism, Tulsa U., 1954; M.A. in Journalism, Marquette U., 1961. Sports dir. KWGS and KOTV, 1950-54, WREX-TV, Rockford, Ill., 1957-59, WITI, Milw., 1959-61; with advt./pub. relations dept., Boeing Co., Seattle, 1961-63; with Boeing, Huntsville, Ala., 1963—; pub. relations mgr. Harris Corp., Cleve., 1969-71; dir. N.W. Ayer Internat., 1971-76; dir. corporate fin. relations Harvey Hubbell, Inc., Conn., 1976-79; exec. dir. employee communications program Gordon Jewelry Corp., Houston, 1979—. Pres. Cape Kennedy Pub. Relations Assn.; chmn. Apollo Contractors Information Center; Mem. Greater Houston Convention and Visitors Council. Served to lt. (j.g.) USNR, 1954-56. Mem. Nat. Investor Relations Inst. Office: 820 Fannin St Houston TX 77002

SHEINBEIN, MARC L., psychologist; b. Oklahoma City, Dec. 11, 1945; s. Isadore and Gloria G. (Davis) S.; divorced; children—Amy Michelle, David Benjamin; m. Andrea Riff, Nov. 30, 1980. B.A., Vanderbilt U., 1967; M.A., U. Tenn., 1969, Ph.D., 1972. Lic. psychologist, Tex. Intern U. Okla. Med. Sch., Oklahoma City, 1971-72; chief psychologist Children's Med. Ctr., Dallas, 1972-75; asst. prof. U. Tex. Health Scis. Ctr., Dallas, 1972-75; pvt. practice psychology, Dallas, 1973—. Contbr. articles to profl. jours., also chpts. to books in field. Bd. dirs. Temple Emanuel Brotherhood, Dallas, 1973-75. Recipient Southwest Psychol. Pubs. prize, 1973. Mem. Am. Psychol. Assn., Dallas Psychol. Assn., Am. Assn. Marriage and Family Therapists, Dallas Assn. Marriage and Family Therapists, Nat. Registry Health Care Providers, Internat. Mensa. Jewish. Avocations: sailing; bicycling; photography; reading; cooking. Home: 8734 Clover Meadow Dallas TX 75243 Office: 4225 LBJ Freeway Suite 276 Dallas TX 75234

SHELBURNE, ROBERT CRAIG, physician, dermatologist; b. Montgomery County, Va., Oct. 6, 1912; s. Nathaniel Burwell and Lavinia (Harvey) Shelburne; m. Louise Hesson, Sept. 15, 1948; children—Anne Pettus, Robert Craig, Jr., Frances Burwell. A.B., Lynchburg Coll., 1934; M.S. in Organic Chemistry, U. Tenn., 1938; M.D., Med. Coll. Va., 1944. Tchr. chemistry and physics in high sch., then associated with FDA, New Orleans; gen. practice medicine, Lynchburg, Va., 1947-49; practice medicine specializing in dermatology, Asheville, N.C., 1949—. Served with M.C., U.S. Army, 1945-47. Mem. AMA, Buncombe County Med. Soc., Alpha Kappa Kappa., SAR. Democrat. Presbyterian.

SHELBY, JAMES STANFORD, cardiovascular surgeon; b. Ringgold, La., June 15, 1934; s. Jesse Audrey and Mable (Martin) S.; student La. Tech. U., 1952-54; M.D., La. State U., 1958; m. Susan Rainey, July 15, 1967; children—Bryan Christian, Christopher Linden. Intern, Charity Hosp. La., New Orleans, 1958-59, resident surgery and thoracic surgery, 1959-65; fellow cardiovascular surgery Baylor U. Coll. Medicine, Houston, 1965-66; practice medicine specializing in cardiovascular surgery, Shreveport, La., 1967—; mem. staff Schumpert Med. Center, Highland Hosp.; asso. prof. surgery La. State U. Sch. Medicine, Shreveport, 1967—. Served with M.C., AUS, 1961-62. Diplomate Am. Bd. Surgery, Am. Bd. Thoracic Surgery. Mem. Am. Coll. Cardiology, AMA, Soc. Thoracic Surgeons, Am. Heart Assn., Southeastern Surg. Congress, So. Thoracic Surg. Assn. Home: 6003 East Ridge Shreveport LA 71106 Office: 865 Margaret Pl Suite 317 Shreveport LA 71101

SHELBY, RICHARD CRAIG, congressman; b. Birmingham, Ala., May 6, 1934; s. O.H. and Alice L. (Skinner) S.; A.B., U. Ala., 1957, LL.B., 1963; m. Annette Nevin, June 11, 1960; children—Richard Craig, Claude Nevin. Admitted to Ala. bar, 1961; law clk. Supreme Ct. Ala., 1961-62; practiced law, Tuscaloosa, Ala., 1963-79; mem. 96th-98th Congresses from 7th Dist. Ala.; mem. Ala. Senate, 1970-78; prosecutor City of Tuscaloosa, 1964-70; spl. asst. atty. gen. State of Ala., 1969-70; U.S. magistrate No. Dist. Ala., Western div., 1966-70. Pres., Tuscaloosa County Mental Health Assn. Mem. Am. Bar Assn., Ala. Bar Assn., D.C. Bar Assn., Tuscaloosa County Bar Assn. Democrat. Presbyterian. Club: Exchange (Tuscaloosa). Office: 1705 Longworth House Office Bldg Washington DC 20515

SHELDON, DOUGLAS GEORGE, radio station executive; b. Dallas, Oct. 5, 1959; s. Roy George Sheldon and Liane (Long) Sheldon Chapman. B.S., Washington and Lee U., 1982. Cons. Reynolds-Penland, Dallas, 1980, Billye Little & Assocs., Dallas, 1981; credit analyst Republic Bank Dallas, 1982-83; account exec. Sta. KIXK, Dallas, 1984—; pres. Magnolia Plantation Assn., Dallas, 1983—. Vice-chmn. FuturDallas, 1983-84; fund raiser Maureen Connolly Brinker Found., 1982-84, St. Mark's Sch. Tex., 1983-84. Home: 3315 Reagan Dallas TX 75219 Office: Sta. KIXK 8235 Douglas Suite 300 Dallas TX 75225

SHELDON, LARRY COLE, computer company executive, instructional designer, project manager, sales consultant; b. McAllen, Tex., Oct. 15, 1939; s. Edwin Lawrence Sheldon and Mildred Louise (Cole) Smith Student U. Tex.-Austin, 1960; B.A. with honors, Baylor U., 1961. Cert. Data Processing Mgmt. Assn. With IBM, 1965—, staff programmer, Washington, 1965-69, project mgr. contracted to U.S. Army Intelligence, Heidelberg, Germany, 1969-70, devel. mgr., Washington, 1970-73, bus. devel. mgr. data processing services, IBM Can. Ltd., Montreal, Que., Can., 1973-76, adv. mktg. support cons., Burlington, Vt., 1976-81, sr. instr., curriculum cons., Dallas, 1981-82, sr. curriculum devel. project mgr., Irving, Tex., 1982—, mem. IBM mktg. edn. curriculum rev. com.; condr. project mgmt. seminars and workshops, Europe, Japan, Australia, Mex. Active Dallas Mus. Fine Arts, Dallas Hist. Preservation League, Dallas Symphony. Served to lt. USN, 1962-65. Recipient IBM Vice Pres.'s award, 1974, IBM Ednl. Devel. award, 1982, IBM Curriculum Devel. award, 1983; Preservation Patrons award Flynn Theatre for Performing Arts, Burlington, 1981. Mem. Am. Soc. Tng. and Devel., Alpha Chi, Gamma Mu. Republican. Roman Catholic. Regular quar. reviewer Science Books and Films for AAAS; contbr. articles to IBM Tech. Info. Exchange. Office: IBM Corp 5601 Executive Dr Suite 7033 Irving TX 75062

SHELDON, LEE NELSON, periodontist; b. Springfield, Mass., July 7, 1950; s. Julian William and Sonnee (Goldart) S.; m. Eleanor Sue Pritzker, Apr. 14, 1973; children—Daniel, Stephanie, Matthew. B.A. in Biology, Clark U., 1972; D.M.D., Tufts U., 1975; postgrad. cert. in periodontics U. Conn., 1980; also other postgrad. courses in pain therapeutics. Resident in gen. practice Reynolds Army Hosp., Fort Sill, Okla., 1975-76; staff periodontist U.S. Army War Coll., Carlisle Barracks, Pa., 1976-78; practice dentistry specializing in periodontics, Melbourne, Fla., 1980—; mem. dental staff Holmes Regional Med. Ctr., 1981—, dept. chmn., mem. exec. bd., 1983-84. Vice pres. Temple Beth Sholom, Satellite Beach, Fla., 1984—. Served as capt. U.S. Army, 1975-78. Mem. Am. Acad. Periodontology, Fla. Soc. Periodontists, Brevard County Dental Soc., Fla. Dental Assn., ADA. Lodge: B'nai B'rith. Avocations: tennis; golf. Home: 170 Sherwood Ave Satellite Beach FL 32937 Office: 2223 Sarno Rd Melbourne FL 32935

SHELL, BERNARD RAY, auditor, accountant; b. Shell Creek, Tenn., June 17, 1925; s. Harvey and Maida (Tucker) S.; m. Doris Ann Reynolds, Jan. 29, 1959; children—Terri Ann Osborne, Robin Osborne Shell. B.S. in Bus. Adminstrn., East Tenn. State U., 1948, postgrad., 1950-52; postgrad. Ala. A&M U., 1972-74; grad. U.S. Army War Coll., 1977. Cert. internal auditor Inst. Internal Auditors. Sr. acct., office mgr. Pet Dairy Products Co., 1948-54; auditor U.S. Army Audit Agy., southeastern U.S., Europe, C.Z., 1955-69; chief internal rev. and audit compliance div. U.S. Army Safeguard Logistics Command, 1969-73, chief internal rev. office U.S. Army Forces Command, Ft. McPherson, Ga., 1974—. Served with U.S. Army, 1943-45. Decorated Purple Heart, Bronze Star, Combat Infantryman's badge. Mem. Inst. Internal Auditors, Assn. Govt. Accts., Am. Soc. Mil. Comptrollers, Assn. U.S. Army, Army War Coll. Alumni Assn., Hon. Order Ky. Cols., VFW, Am. Legion. Home: 3946 Pinehurst Pl Decatur GA 30034 Office: Hdqrs US Army Forces Command ATTN: AFCO-IR (Mr Shell) Fort McPherson GA 30330

SHELL, LOUIS CALVIN, lawyer; b. DeWitt, Va., Dec. 8, 1925; s. Roger LaFayette and Susie (Hill) S.; B.A., U. Va., 1946, LL.B., 1947; m. Barbara Marie Pamplin, Aug. 5, 1950; children—Pamela Temple, Patricia Ann. Admitted to Va. bar, 1947; asso. White, Hamilton, Wyche & Shell, Petersburg, Va., 1948-51, partner, 1951—, chief trial counsel, 1960—. Pres., Petersburg (Va.) Tb Assn., 1951; pres., Am. Cancer Soc., Petersburg, Va. chpt., 1952. Vice-mayor, City of Petersburg, Va., 1959-60, mem. council, 1957-60; campaign chmn. Senator William B. Spong, Petersburg, Va., 1966, 72; chmn. City Electoral Bd., 1952-55. Recipient award Jr. C. of C., 1956. Mem. Am. Coll. Trial Lawyers, Am. Judicature Soc., Am., Petersburg (pres. 1963) bar assns., Va. State Bar (mem. council 1972-75). Democrat. Methodist. (trustee 1968—). Kiwanian. Home: 1612 E Tuckahoe Saint Petersburg VA 23805 Office: 20 E Tabb Saint Petersburg VA 23803

SHELLEY, DONALD WINBURN, ophthalmologist; b. Kingstree, S.C., Aug. 10, 1946; s. John Carroll and Annette (Wells) S.; m. Susan Rachel Kerns, Apr. 11, 1970; children—Laura Ashley, Brian Wells, Amy Elizabeth. B.S., Clemson Univ., 1967; M.D., Bowman Gray Sch. Medicine, 1971. Diplomate Am. Bd. Ophthalmology. Practice medicine specializing in ophthalmology, Greenville, S.C., 1975—; chmn. dept. ophthalmology Greenville Hosp. System, 1981-83; pres. Med. Coll. Ga. Ophthalmology Alumni, Augusta, 1983—. Bd. dirs. Nat. Soc. to Prevent Blindness, Greenville, 1984—. Mem. Greenville County Med. Soc., S.C. Med. Assn., AMA, S.C. Soc. Ophthalmology, Am. Acad. Ophthalmology, Am. Intraocular Implant Soc., Baptist. Avocations: golf, landscape gardening. Home: 59 Forest Ln Greenville SC 29605 Office: 50 Bear Dr Greenville SC 29605

SHELLEY, JAMES HERBERT, lawyer, paper products company executive; b. Columbia, S.C., Oct. 12, 1943; s. William H. and Elizabeth G. (Garner) S.; m. Waring Patricia Knight, Apr. 1, 1969; children—Joy Patricia, Susan Elizabeth. B.A. in English, U. of S.C., 1965, J.D., 1968. Bar: S.C. 1968. With Sonoco Products Co., Hartsville, S.C., 1969—, indsl. devel. coordinator, 1969-70, indsl. relations rep., 1970-71, dir. indsl. relations, 1971-78, corp. dir. indsl. relations and personnel, 1978-80, staff v.p. personnel and indsl. relations, 1980—. Bd. dirs. Pee Dee Mental Health, vice chmn., 1977-80; vice chmn. Hartsville YMCA project, 1983-86. Served to sgt. 1st class USAR, 1968-73. Recipient Outstanding Drill Sgt. award, 1970. Mem. S.C. Bar Assn. (sec./treas. employment and labor law sect.), ABA (labor law sect.). Methodist. Clubs: Hartsville (S.C.) Country, Prestwood (Hartsville). Home: 219 Park Ave Hartsville SC 29550 Office: Sonoco Products Co North 2d St Hartsville SC 29550

SHELLHASE, FERN KLECKNER, statistician, rehabilitation counselor; b. Jewell County, Kans., July 13, 1925; d. Glenn Homer and Lizzie (Rhoads) Kleckner; m. Leslie John Shellhase, June 6, 1948; children—Jeremy Clayton, Joel Kleckner. Student U. Md.-College Park, 1959-63; B.A., Incarnate Ward Coll., 1966; M.A., U. Ala., 1970. Exec. sec. United Biscuit Co., Omaha, 1944-50; tech. writer Environ. Scis. Service Adminstrn., Rockville, Md., 1966-68, rehab. researcher Spain Rehab. Ctr., Birmingham, Ala., 1970-71; statistician Mental Health Dept., Tuscaloosa, Ala., 1971—. Contbr. articles to profl. jours. and chpt. to book. Mem. L.W.V., Defenders of Wildlife, Nat. Internat. Wildlife, Greenpeace, Mem. Am. Statis. Assn. Home: 3823 Somerset

Pl Tuscaloosa AL 35405 Office: Partlow State Sch and Hosp PO Box 1730 Tuscaloosa AL 35403

SHELLMAN, ROBERT MICHAEL, oil and gas company executive, independent producer; b. Victoria, Tex., Aug. 27, 1951; s. Robert C. and Jeannine M. (Schroeder) S.; m. Carolyn Jane Eubanks, May 13, 1978; 1 child, Alison Blythe. Student Southwestern Tex. State U., 1969-73. Vice pres. Shellman Drilling Co., Flatonia, Tex., 1969-71, pres., 1981-82; pres. Shellman Constrn. Co., San Marcos, Tex., 1974-80; pres., C.E.O. MCA Petroleum Corp., San Marcos, 1983—. Bd. dirs. Parks & Recreation City of San Marcos, 1981-82. Mem. Am. Assn. Petroleum Geologists, Soc. Petroleum Engrs., South Tex. Geol. Soc., Am. Petroleum Inst., Tex. Mid Continent Oil and Gas Assn., Gulf Coast Conservation Assn. Republican. Methodist. Clubs: U.S. Tennis Assn.; Petroleum (San Antonio). Avocations: tennis; hunting; fishing. Home: 127 Mountain Dr San Marcos TX 78666 Office: MCA Petroleum Corp 1205 Hwy 123 Suite 200 San Marcos TX 78666

SHELNUTT, ROBERT CURTIS, manufacturing company administrator; b. Shawmut, Ala., Sept. 2, 1928; s. Curtis Lee and Odell (Campbell) S.; B.S. in Chemistry, U. Ga., 1954; M.B.A., Pepperdine U., 1981; m. Faye Mahan; children—Robert Curtis, Susan Elaine. With Am. Enka Co., Lowland, Tenn., 1954-79, gen. tech. supr. chem., spinning and finishing depts., 1969-71, tech. mgr. rayon filament plant, 1971-75, tech. mgr. rayon staple plant, 1975-76, energy and devel. mgr. rayon staple plant, 1976-77, energy and devel., mgr. Tenn. ops., 1977-79; gen. mgr. chem. ops. Chatsworth div. Organon Teknika Corp., Chatsworth, Calif., 1979-81, dir. mfg. and chem. engring. research and devel., Oklahoma City, 1981-82, dir. quality assurance and chem. activities, 1982—. Served with USAF, 1946-49. Mem. Am. Chem. Soc., Am. Mgmt. Assn. Republican. Baptist. Clubs: Masons, Shriners. Home: 9105 Pebble Ln Oklahoma City OK 73132 Office: 5300 S Portland Oklahoma City OK 73119

SHELTON, BETTY JANE, nursing administrator; b. Gate City, Va., Sept. 7, 1943; d. James Andrew and Martha Jane (Ford) S.; m. Robert Leonard Hickman, Apr. 1, 1967 (div. Jan. 1971). B.S., U. Tenn., 1978, M.S., 1979. Cert. nursing adminstr., La. Asst. dir. nursing Chester County Hosp., S.C., 1980-81; dir. nursing Chester County Nursing Ctr., 1981, Jenkins Clin. Hosp., Ky., 1981-82; nursing adminstr. St. Anne Gen. Hosp., Raceland, La., 1982—. Mem. La. State Nurses Assn., Am. Nurses Assn., La. Hosp. Assn. Nursing Adminstrs. Club: Pilot (v.p.). Avocations: swimming; needlework.

SHELTON, CHARLES RICHARD, safety engineer; b. Nashville, Sept. 20, 1946; s. William Hatch and Aleda Marie Shelton; m. Elenda Ann Akins, June 19, 1973; children—Gregory Scott, Katrina Elizabeth, Kimberlea Suzanne. B.S. in Indsl. Tech., Tenn. Tech. U., 1974. Underwriting surveyor Chubb & Son, Tampa, Fla., 1974-77; loss control rep. Reliance Ins. Co., Tampa, 1977-83; loss control supr. Square D Co., Clearwater, Fla., 1984—, safety dir., Lexington, Ky., 1984—. Served with USN, 1966-70. Mem. Am. Soc. Safety Engrs. (pres. West Fla. chpt. 1977-78), Nat. Mgmt. Assn. Office: Square D Co 1601 Mercer Rd Lexington KY 40511

SHELTON, GAYLE COCHRANE, JR., government official; b. Clarksdale, Miss., Aug. 11, 1918; s. Gayle Cochrane and Marguerite Perryman (Brown) S.; B.A., La. State U., 1940; LL.B., Georgetown U., 1942. Spl. agt. FBI, 1940-47; pres. Pacific Wholesale Corp., Agana, Guam, 1947-62; also Am. Overseas Sales Corp., San Francisco, 1957-62; dir. dist. office U.S. Dept. Commerce, Birmingham, Ala., 1962-78, area dir., 1978—; Southeastern regional export mktg. mgr. Office Field Ops., Domestic and Internat. Bus. Adminstrn., Washington, 1972, acting asst. dir., 1973-74, spl. asst. to dir. Office Bus. Services, Washington, 1971; regional mng. dir. U.S. and Fgn. Comml. Service, Internat. Trade Adminstrn., 1981, chief of staff, 1982-84; guest lectr. OFO Inst., U.S. Dept. Commerce, 1973-74, U. Ala., Birmingham, 1965; speaker U.S. Fgn. Service Comml. Officers Conf., 1978; exec. sec. Southwestern area Nat. Def. Exec. Res., 1964-74; dir. U.S. Trade Mission on Water Pollution, Belgium and Luxembourg, 1976; dir. U.S. Trade Mission on Mining and Mining Related Equipment, Greece and Turkey, 1977; exec. sec. Ala.-Miss. Dist. Export Council, 1971—. Vice pres. Birmingham Festival of Arts, 1972. Named Ala. World Trade man of year, 1972; recipient medals and awards for achievement U.S. Dept. Commerce, 1967, Gold award for disting. achievement, 1981. Mem. Assn. Internationale des Etudiants on Sciences Economiques et Commerciales, Birmingham Area C. of C., Ala. World Trade Assn. (pres. 1974-77), Am. Mgmt. Assn., Am. Soc. Internat. Execs. Club: Relay House (Birmingham). Contbr. articles to trade and profl. jours. Home: 3308 Cliff Rd Birmingham AL 35205 Office: Suite 200 908 S 20th St Birmingham AL 35205

SHELTON, JAMES KENNETH, counselor educator; b. Danville, Va., Apr. 14, 1939; s. James Oliver and Effie Mae Shelton; m. Rose Lee McMullen, Jan. 20, 1960; children—James Kenneth, Angela Lynn. B.S., Appalachian State U., Boone, N.C., 1962; M.S., Radford Coll. (Va.), 1969; Fd.D., Va. Poly. Inst. and State U., Blacksburg, 1974. Tchr., counselor, coach Roanoke County Schs. (Va.), 1962-70; assoc. prof. counselor edn., wrestling coach The Citadel, Charleston, S.C., 1970—; coordinator S.C. Helping Professions Workshop; chmn. support services in instructional devel. Charleston Higher Edn. Consortium; mem. adv. bd. Ednl. Opportunity Ctr. Pub. mem. Palmetto-Low Country Health Systems Agy. Citadel Devel. Found. grantee, 1979—; Gen. Electric Found. grantee, 1979; recipient Pres.'s award S.C. Vocat. Guidance Assn., 1979; Service award State of S.C., 1982. Mem. NEA (life), Am. Assn. for Counseling and Devel., S.C. Personnel and Guidance Assn. (exec. bd.), S.C. Mental Health Assn., S.C. Psychol. Assn., S.C. Vocat. Guidance Assn. Republican. Methodist. Contbr. articles to profl. jours. Office: The Citadel Charleston SC 29409

SHELTON, JAMES OGLESBY, bookseller; b. Birmingham, Ala., Nov. 6, 1946; s. Joseph Oglesby and Mary Florence (McNutt) S.; m. Vivian John Varsellona, Aug. 28, 1981 (div. 1985). B.A., Livingston U., 1969; M.L.S., Fla. State U., 1974. Tchr., Marion Inst., Ala., 1969-70; reference librarian Tampa Pub. Library, Fla., 1971-78, Plant City Pub. Library, Fla., 1978-79; retail bookseller Hyde Park Bookshop, Tampa, 1979—. Bd. dirs. Konglomerati Found., 1984-85. Mem. Fla. Antiquarian Booksellers Assn. (pres. 1983-85, treas. 1981-83), Fla. Bibliophile Soc. (pres. 1984-85). Democrat. Avocations: tennis; writing; reading; book collecting. Office: Hyde Park Book Shop 1109 Swann Ave Tampa FL 33606

SHELTON, JOHN ALTON, educational administrator; b. Pisgah, Ala., Feb. 6, 1936; s. Harvey M. and Hattie (Johnston) S.; m. Margaret Sullivan, June 1, 1960; children—Tina, John Alton. B.S., Jacksonville State U., 1957; M.S., U. Ala., 1962, Ed.D., 1968. Prin., Ala. Pub. Schs., 1957-68, supt. schs., 1968-74; adminstr. Ala. Dept. Edn., Montgomery, 1974—. Mem. Kappa Phi Kappa. Office: Alabama Dept of Edn 501 Dexter Ave Montgomery AL 36104

SHELTON, KARL MASON, banker; b. Lincolnton, N.C., June 8, 1933; s. Karl and Annie (Grace) S.; m. Deloris Hundley, May 8, 1954; children—Melanie Dwain, Leslie Elaine, Kevin Karl. Grad., Am. Inst. Banking, 1960, Carolinas Sch. Banking, 1963, Stonier Grad. Sch. Banking, 1967. Vice pres. N.C. Nat. Bank, Charlotte, 1954-71; sr. v.p., treas. Seattle-First Nat. Bank, 1971-79; pres. Citizens Fidelity Corp., Louisville, 1979-82; exec. v.p. Southeast Bank, N.A., Miami, Fla., 1982—. Contbg. editor: Bankers Handbook, 1978. Served with AUS, 1952-54. Mem. Am. Bankers Assn., Am. Inst. Banking. Methodist. Office: 1 SE Fin Ctr Miami FL 33131

SHELTON, LARRY BRANDON, apparel company executive; b. Paducah, Ky., Aug. 4, 1934; s. Brandon and Annabelle (Jones) S.; m. Lura Jane Peyton, Aug. 26, 1955; children—Tracey Jean, Ted Peyton. B.S. in Commerce, Bowling Green Coll. Commerce, 1956. C.P.A., Tenn. With Genesco Inc., Nashville, 1956—, sr. internal auditor, 1961, spl. fin. asst. exec. dept., 1962-62, v.p. Eastern control office, 1962-69, v.p. central control, 1969, sec., 1973-75, vice chmn., 1975-77, exec. v.p., 1977—. Mem. Am. Inst. C.P.A.s, Tenn. Soc. C.P.A.s. Methodist. Home: 1809 Laurel Ridge Dr Nashville TN 37215 Office: Genesco Inc Genesco Park Nashville TN 37202*

SHELTON, LEWIS ROSS, III, biology educator, consultant; b. Natchez, Miss., May 1, 1942; s. Lewis Ross and Thelma Louise (Newman) S.; m. Gwendolyn Barr Cooper, July 27, 1962; 1 son, Mark Newman. B.S. in Bus., Miss. State U., 1964, M.B.A., 1966, M.S. in Wildlife Biology, 1969; Ph.D. in Wildlife Biology, Colo. State U., 1978. Cert. wildlife biologist. Grad. research asst. dept. fishery and wildlife biology Colo. State U., 1969-71; extension wildlife specialist Miss. State U., State College, 1971-83, now assoc. prof. wildlife biology and dir. W.E. Walker Wildlife Conservation Found. Recipient Merit award Miss. Wildlife Fedn., 1981; NDEA fellow, 1966-69. Mem. Delta Wildlife Council, Miss. Forestry Assn., Nat. Wildlife Refuge Assn., Miss. Wildlife Fedn. (pres.), Wildlife Soc. (sect. pres. 1982-83), AAAS, Outdoor Writers Assn. Am., Soc. Am. Foresters, Epsilon Sigma Phi, Sigma Xi. Republican. Baptist. Club: OKTOC Community (Starkville, Miss.). Contbr. articles to tech. publs.

SHELTON, RAYMOND, educational administrator. Supt. of schs. Hillsborough County, Fla. Office PO Box 3408 Tampa FL 33601*

SHELTON, SARA VALENA, state representative, retired educator; b. Union County, S.C., July 29, 1919; d. Jeremiah Morgan and Mary Lucile (Sims) Beatty; m. LeRoy Anthony Shelton, May 5, 1944; 1 child, Sara Valena Shelton Boggs. B.S., Benedict Coll., 1940; M.Ed., Furman U., 1968, cert. elem. tchr. specialist, 1973; postgrad. Atlanta U., 1944, Columbia U., 1951. Mem. S.C. Ho. of Reps., 1985—; mem. Joint Legis. Com. to Study Problems of Drug and Alcohol Abuse, 1983—, Adv. Com. on Intergovernmental Relations, 1984—, Joint Legis. Com. on Cultural Affairs, 1985. Sec. Greenville County Democratic Com., 1984—. Mem. Dem. Women Greenville County (sec. 1983-84).

SHEMWELL, RONALD EUGENE, obstetrician, gynecologist; b. Shreveport, La., Nov. 2, 1935; s. Joseph Carlton and Mildred Elizabeth (Stoddard) S.; B.S., Centenary Coll., 1957; M.D., La. State U., 1962; m. Virginia Catherine Cage, Nov. 23, 1960; children—Melanie Catherine, Ronald Eugene, David Clayton, Margaret Claire. Intern, Confederate Meml. Hosp., Shreveport, 1962-63; gen. practice resident E. A. Conway Hosp., Monroe, La., 1965-66; fellow ob-gyn Ochsner Clinic, New Orleans, 1966-69, staff physician, 1969-71; practice medicine specializing in ob-gyn, Monroe, La., 1971—; head residency tng. dept. ob-gyn E. A. Conway Meml. Hosp., Monroe, La., 1971-79, acting chief Ob-gyn, 1979-81; clin. prof. La. State U. Sch. Medicine, Shreveport, 1979—. Served with M.C., AUS, 1963-65. Diplomate Am. Bd. Ob-Gyn. Mem. Am. Coll. Obstetricians and Gynecologists, ACS, Am. Fertility Soc., Southeastern Gynecol. Soc., So., La. State med. assns., Ouachita Parish Med. Soc., Central Assn. Obstetricians and Gynecologists, Am. Assn. Gynecologic Laparoscopists. Contbr. articles to profl. jours. Home: Route 4 Box 480 West Monroe LA 71291 Office: 313 Wood St Monroe LA 71201

SHENASSA, EDWARD W., real estate company executive; b. Boca Raton, Feb. 6, 1948; s. George Allen and Frances Mary (Jordan) S.; m. Olivia Anderson, Oct. 12, 1973; children—Gordon, Jeanne, Jennifer. B.A., Fla. State U., 1970, M.S. in Mgmt., 1975. Bookkeeper Kuhn and Eberhart Acctg. Service, Tallahassee, 1975-78; acct. Price Waterhouse & Co., Miami, Fla., 1978-81; v.p. Werik Real Estate Co., Coral Gables, Fla., 1981—, also dir. Served with U.S. Army, 1970-73. Mem. Am. Acctg. Assn., NAREB, Coral Gables Real Estate Assn., Beta Theta Pi. Democrat. Episcopalian. Club: Coral Gables Yacht. Lodges: Lions, Rotary. Office: Werik Real Estate Co 159 Madeira St Coral Gables FL 33134

SHEPARD, CHARLES VIRGIL, human resource executive; b. Springfield, Ill., Nov. 14, 1940; s. Charles Woodrow and Catherine Elizabeth (Vlakovich) S.; B.A. in Bus. Adminstrn. and Econs., 1962; postgrad. U. Ill., Urbana, 1966-72; M.B.A., Sangamon State U., 1972; m. Judy A. Wells; children—Cynthia Lynn, Kimberly Lynn. With Allis-Chalmers Corp., Springfield, 1962-73, supr. employee benefits, 1962-67, adminstrv. asst., 1967-68, mgr. personnel services, 1968-70, mgr. orgn. planning and devel., 1970-72, mgr. indsl. relations, 1972-73; mem. corp. indsl. relations staff Rockwell Internat. Corp., Dallas, 1973, dir. indsl. relations, 1973-74, group dir. personnel, 1974-76, v.p. personnel, 1976-77, staff v.p. electronics personnel, 1977-78, corp. staff v.p. employee relations, 1978-80, v.p. human resources Gen. Industries, 1980-81, v.p. human resources, from 1981, now v.p. personnel, govt. affairs and communications. Mem. Adv. Council Amigos de Ser, 1976—; mem. adv. bd. Richland Coll., 1975-76; bd. dirs. Jr. Achievement, 1981—, Dallas Theater Center, Pitts. Public Theatre, 1979—, Dallas Opera, 1982—, TACA, 1982, Boy Scouts Am., 1982—. Mem. Electronic Industries Assn. (indsl. relations council), Am. Soc. Personnel Adminstrn., Dallas C. of C. (dir. 1974-76). Republican. Methodist. Club: Masons. Home: 6122 Warm Mist Lane Dallas TX 75248 Office: Rockwell Internat Dallas TX 75207

SHEPHERD, DONALD RAY, pathologist; b. Pampa, Tex., Sept. 7, 1935; s. Ray Browden and Lillie Lorene (Moore) S.; B.S. cum laude, Austin Coll., 1958; M.D., U. Tex., Dallas, 1962; m. Elizabeth Day Poole, June 6, 1958; children—Lisa, Stephanie, Leslie, Don Poole. Intern, Univ. Hosp., Little Rock, 1962-63; gen. practice medicine, Bay City, Tex., 1965-66; resident in pathology Hermann Hosp., Houston, 1966-68, Baylor U. Med. Center, Dallas, 1968-70; asst. pathologist Harris Hosp., Ft. Worth, 1970-71; chief pathology, dir. labs. Leggett Meml. Hosp., Cleveland, Tex., 1982—; pathologist, pres. Donald R. Shepherd M.D., P.A., Conroe, 1973—; pres. Profl. Labs., Inc., Houston, 1973-82. Bd. dirs. Am. Cancer Soc. Served as capt. M.C., U.S. Army, 1963-65. Decorated Army Commendation medal; diplomate Am. Bd. Pathology; Am. Cancer Soc. grantee, 1970-71. Fellow Am. Coll. Pathologists, Am. Soc. Clin. Pathologists; mem. Tex. Soc. Pathologists (del.), Tex. Med. Assn., AMA, Montgomery County Med. Soc., Phi Chi. Republican. Presbyterian. Home: 140 Brandon Rd Conroe TX 77302 Office: 704 Longmire Conroe TX 77304

SHEPHERD, JUDY CARLILE, retired government official; b. Kansas City, Mo.; d. John Mercer and Mary Almeda (Chapin) Ellis; student Okla. State U., Tulsa U.; B.A., Am. U., Washington, 1960; m. Joseph Elbert Shepherd; 1 son, John Philip Carlile. Chief probation officer Tulsa County Ct., 1947-50; real estate broker United Farm Agy., 1952-58; bldg. fund campaign mgr. AAUW, Washington, 1958-59; govt. and public relations ofcl. Nat. Counsel Assos., Washington, 1959-61; congressional liaison Dept. Agr., Washington, 1961-65; public info. officer OEO, 1965-70, spl. asst. to dep. dir. ops. Head Start, elderly, Indian and migrant programs, 1970-73; dir. public relations Nat. Assn. Social Workers, Washington, 1973-74; social sci. analyst Congressional Research Service, Library of Congress, Washington, 1976-85 Pres. bd. govs. Agr. Symphony Orch., 1961-64; bd. dirs. ARC, Boy Scouts Am., 1948-50; bd. dirs. Little Theatre, 1956-57. Recipient 1st place Fed. Editors Blue Pencil award, 1967; cert. humanist counselor. Mem. Nat. Press Club, Public Relations Soc. Am., Nat. Assn. Govt. Communicators, Am. Humanist Assn., Assn. Humanistic Psychology, Am. U. Alumni Assn., Okla. State Soc., Ark. State Soc., Mo. State Soc., Library Congress Profl. Assn., Am. Soc. Access Profls. (charter), Humanist Assn. Nat. Capital Area (pres. 1977-78), Nat. Congress Am. Indians, DAR. Club: Woman's Nat Democratic. Coordinator, Am. Discovers Indian Art exhibit, Smithsonian Instn., 1967. Author: Statutory History of United States Capitol Police Force, 6 vols., U.S. Ho. Com. Print. Home: 2365 N Oakland St Arlington VA 22207

SHEPHERD, LINDA PACE, nursing education administrator; b. Toxey, Ala., Jan. 18, 1951; Raymond Lee Pace and Zaylee (Sims) Harris; m. Darryl D. Shepherd, June 4, 1974; children—Darryl D., Jr., Michelle. B.S.N., Dillard U., 1973; M.S.N., U. Ala., 1979. Instr. nursing Mobile Infirmary-Mobile Coll., Ala., 1974-80; dir., instr. S. D. Bishop State Jr. Coll., Mobile, 1980—. Mem. Nat. League Nursing, Am. Nurses Assn., Health Edn. Media Assn., NEA, So. Council on Collegiate Edn. for Nurses, Ala. Edn. Assn., Ala. Assn. Jr. Community Colls., Ala. State Nurses' Assn., Ala. League Nursing, Mobile County Nurses' Soc. Baptist. Club: Wives of Alpha (Mobile). Avocation: singing. Office: Dept Nursing SD Bishop State Jr Coll 351 N Broad St Mobile AL 36690

SHEPHERD, MARK, JR., electronics company executive; b. Dallas, Jan. 18, 1923; s. Mark and Louisa Florence (Daniell) S.; B.S. in Elec. Engring., So. Meth. U., 1942; M.S. in Elec. Engring., U. Ill. at Urbana, 1947; m. Mary Alice Murchland, Dec. 21, 1945; children—Debra Aline (Mrs. Rowland K. Robinson), MaryKay Theresa, Marc Blaine. With Gen. Electric Co., 1942-43, Farnsworth TV and Radio Corp., 1947-48; with Tex. Instruments Inc., Dallas, 1948—, v.p., gen. mgr. semicondr.-components div., 1955-61, exec. v.p. co., 1961-66, pres., 1967-76, chief exec. officer, 1969-84, chmn. bd., 1976—, also dir.; dir. RepublicBank Corp., U.S. Steel Corp.; mem. Internat. council Morgan Guaranty Trust Co. Mem. U.S. Japan Bus. Council; nat. bd. Com. on Present Danger; adv. council Am. Ditchley Found.; bd. govs., trustee So. Meth. U.; trustee, councillor Conf. Bd.; trustee Com. for Econ. Devel., Am. Enterprise Inst. Pub. Policy Research. Served to lt. (j.g.) USNR, 1943-46. Registered profl. engr., Tex. Fellow IEEE; mem. Soc. Exploration Geophysicists, Newcomen Soc., Council on Fgn. Relations, U.S. Council Internat. Bus. (trustee), Tex. Sci. and Tech. Council, Bus. Council, Dallas Citizens Council, Nat. Acad. Engring., Horatio Alger Assn. Disting. Ams. Inc., Sigma Xi, Eta Kappa Nu. Office: PO Box 225474 MS 236 Dallas TX 75265

SHEPPARD, ALBERT EDWARD, architect; b. Mexico City, Mexico, Sept. 21, 1910; s. William Henry and Lillian Bedell (Endweiss) S.; came to U.S., 1919, naturalized, 1942; student San Antonio Jr. Coll., 1929-30; B.A., U. Tex., 1935; m. Reba May Masterson, Mar. 30, 1940; children—Albert Edward, Anthony Dallam, Michael Masterson. Draftsman, City Water Bd., San Antonio, 1930-33, U. Tex. Extension, Austin, 1933-35, Houston Ind. Sch., 1935-36; architect State Bd. Control, Houston, 1936-37; landscape architect Fleming & Sheppard, Houston, 1937-42; architect Brown Shipbldg., Houston, 1942-46; architect Brown & Root, Houston, 1946-56, mng. architect, 1956-75, cons. 1975-82; pres. Sheppard Cons. Inc., 1982—. Mem. Sch. Architecture Found. adv. council U. Tex., 1974-76, chmn. dean's council, 1974-76. Mem. A.I.A., Tex. Soc. Architects. Clubs: Racquet, YMCA Health (Houston). Prin. archtl. works include Manned Spacecraft Center, Houston, Margaret Root Brown Coll., Rice U., Herman Brown Cardiovascular Research Center, Houston, Goodwill Industries Oeland Meml. Chapel, Houston, Brown & Root Internat. Hdqrs. Complex, Houston. Home: 306 W Cowan St Houston TX 77007 Office: 4100 Clinton Dr Houston TX 77001

SHEPPARD, LOUIS CLARKE, biomedical engineering educator; b. Pine Bluff, Ark., May 28, 1933; s. Ellis Allen and Louise (Clarke) S.; m. Nancy Louise Mayer, Feb. 8, 1958; children—David, Susan, Lisa. B.S. in Chem. Engring., U. Ark., 1957; Ph.D. in Elec. Engring., U. London, 1976. Registered profl. engr., Ala. Devel. staff supr. Diamond Alkali Co., Deer Park, Tex., 1957-63; staff engr. IBM, Rochester, Minn., 1963-66; assoc. prof. surgery dept. U. Ala.-Birmingham, 1966—, sr. scientist Cystic Fibrosis Research Ctr., 1981—, prof., chmn. biomed. engring. dept., 1979—; mem. med. adv. bd. Hewlett Packard, 1980-84; cons. IMED Corp.; dir. FBK Internat.; pres. S.E.A. Corp.; mem. editorial bd. Med. Progress Through Tech., Springer-Verlag, Berlin; cons. Nat. Heart, Lung and Blood Inst. Bd. dirs. Birmingham Met. Devel. Bd. Served with AUS, 1958-66. Recipient Ayerton Premium award IEE (U.K.), 1984. Mem. N.Y. Acad. Scis., Brit. Computer Soc., Assn. for Computing Machinery, Nat. Soc. Profl. Engrs., Cardiovascular System Dynamics, Biomed. Engring. Soc. (dir.), IEEE, Am. Inst. Chem. Engrs., Blue Key, Sigma Xi, Tau Beta Pi, Alpha Pi Mu, Theta Tau. Club St. Andrews Soc. of Middle South. Contbr. abstracts, chpts. to books; patentee method and system for estimation of arterial pressure. Home: 3644 Shamley Dr Birmingham AL 35223 Office: BME Dept 256 Engr U Ala University Sta Birmingham AL 35294

SHEPPARD, WILLIAM VERNON, transportation engineer; b. Harlan, Ky., Apr. 18, 1941; s. Vernon L. and Margaret M. (Montgomery) S.; B.C.E., The Citadel, 1964; m. Gaye H. Lott, June 20, 1964; children—W. Kevin, Candice Gaye. Hwy. engr. Howard, Needles, Tammen & Bergendoff, Kansas City, Mo., 1964-65; hwy. engr. Wilbur Smith & Assos., Columbia, S.C., 1967-68, office mgr., Cin., 1968-69, prin. engr., N.Y.C., 1970, asso., Los Angeles, 1971-73, regional v.p., 1973-78, Columbia, 1970-80; v.p. transp. Post Buckley Schuh & Jernigan, Inc., Columbia, 1981—; guest lectr. U. So. Calif. Sch. Architecture and Urban Planning, 1976-77. Served to capt. U.S. Army, 1965-67. Decorated AEM medal. Registered profl. engr., Pa., Calif. Mem. ASCE, Inst. Transp. Engrs., Nat. Soc. Profl. Engrs. Republican. Roman Catholic. Contbr. articles on transp. engring. to profl. publs. Home: 125 Old Woodlands Rd Columbia SC 29209 Office: 1301 Gervais St Columbia SC 29202

SHEPPERD, JOHN BEN, insurance, banking and petroleum company consultant; b. Gladwater, Tex., Oct. 19, 1915; s. Alfred Fulton and Berthal (Phillips) S.; LL.B., U. Tex., 1941; LL.D. (hon.), North Tex. State Coll., 1951, Chapman Christian Coll., Los Angeles, 1953, Southwestern U., 1955; m. Mamie Strieber, Oct. 6, 1938; children—Alfred Lewis, John Ben, Marianne and Suzanne (twins). Bar: Tex. 1941. Sec. state State of Tex., 1950-52, atty. gen., 1952-56; dir. Tex. Commerce Bank-Odessa, First State Bank-Gladewater, Blue Cross-Blue Shield Ins. Co.-Dallas; ptnr. Shepperd and Meacham, Pub. Relations Cons.; ptnr. Shepperd and Rodman, Attys. Former mem., chmn. Tex. Econ. Devel. Commn., Tex. Hist. Commn., Tex. Arts Commn.; mem. Tex. State Library and Archives Commn.; pres. Tex. Jaycees 1941, U.S. Jaycees, 1947, U.S. Jaycees Found., 1984. Mem. Nat. Assn. Attys. Gen. (pres. 1956), West Tex. C. of C. (pres. 1966). Democrat. Mem. Christian Ch. Author: The President's Guide to Club and Organizations Management and Meetings. Home: 3107 Windsor Dr Odessa TX 79762 Office: 1208 Tex Commerce Bank Bldg Odessa TX 79761

SHEPS, CECIL GEORGE, physician, educator; b. Winnipeg, Man., Can., July 24, 1913; s. George and Polly (Lirenman) S.; came to U.S., 1946, naturalized, 1956; m. Ann Shepherd, Aug. 24, 1973; 1 son, Samuel B. M.D., U. Man., 1936, D.Sc. (hon.), 1985; M.P.H., Yale U., 1947; D. Sc. (hon.), Chgo. Med. Sch., 1970; Ph.D. (hon.), Ben Gurion U. of Negev, 1983. Intern St. Joseph's Gen. Hosp., Winnipeg, Man., Can.; resident Corbett Gen. Hosp., Stourbridge, Eng., Queen Mary's Hosp. for East End, London, Camp Osborne Mil. Hosp., Can.; gen. dir. Beth Israel Hosp., 1953-60; clin. prof. preventive medicine Harvard Med. Sch., Boston, 1953-60; prof. med. and hosp. adminstrn. U. Pitts. Grad. Sch. Pub. Health, 1960-65; gen. dir. Beth Israel Med. Ctr., 1965-68; prof. community medicine Mt. Sinai Sch. Medicine, N.Y.C., 1965-68; dir. Health Services Research Ctr., U. N.C., 1969-71; vice chancellor health scis. U. N.C., 1971-76, prof. social medicine, 1968-80, Taylor Grandy disting. prof. social medicine, 1980—; cons. Med. Affairs Welfare Adminstrn., HEW, 1964-67, Robert Wood Johnson Found., Maurice Falk Found., Milbank Meml. Fund. Served to capt. Royal Can. Army Med. Corp, 1943-46. Recipient Can. Pub. Health Assn. Miles award. Mem. Am. Pub. Health Assn. (exec. bd.), Council Social Work Edn., Nat. Library Medicine (bd. regents), Inst. Medicine, Nat. Acad. Scis. Author, editor med. and health care books. Home: 1304 Arboretum Dr Chapel Hill NC 27514 Office: U North Carolina Chase Hall 132A Chapel Hill NC 27514

SHER, F. PATRICK, retail corporation executive; b. Phila., Sept. 21, 1940; s. Frank A. and Elizabeth C. (McGee) S.; m. Barbara Anne Daniels, Feb. 23, 1963; children—Michelle, Tara, Colleen, Kathleen, Patrick. Student U.S. Air Force Acad., 1958-60, Villanova U., 1960-61. Operating mgr. Sears Roebuck & Co., Md., Va., D.C. area, 1962-76; chief exec. officer Lindsley, Inc., Evans Products Co., Miami, Fla., 1976-82; pres., founder HomeOwners Warehouse, Inc., Margate, Fla., 1982—. Roman Catholic. Office: HomeOwners Warehouse Inc 550 North State Rd & Margate FL 33063

SHERAR, JOSEPH WILLIAM, insurance broker, investor; b. Fresno, Calif., Sept. 27, 1930; s. Joseph William Garland and Verna Irene (Kneeland) S.; B.S., U.S. Naval Acad., 1952; J.D., Loyola U., New Orleans, 1965; m. Nancy Barr Gooch, Nov. 6, 1954; children—Deirdra Clarisse, William Gooch, David Kneeland, Lynne Fox. Commd. ensign U.S. Navy, 1952, advanced through grades to lt., 1958; destoyer officer, 1952-53; naval aviator, 1954; landing signal officer, 1956-57; aide to Vice Adm. James Thatch, Com Huk Lant, 1958; flight instr. Saufley Naval Air Sta., Pensacola, Fla., 1958; ret., 1965; trainee Marine Office Am., 1958-59; marine broker Hardin and Ferguson, 1959-61; radar instr. U.S. Maritime Adminstrn., New Orleans, 1961-62; chmn. Ingram-Armistead & Co. SPA, Milan, Italy, 1976-78, Corroon & Black, Inc., New Orleans, 1979; pres. Sherar, Cook & Gardner, Inc., Metairie, La., 1979-86, Sailing Sales Inc., New Orleans, 1972-84, Cathay Trading Corp., 1981—, Altair Ins. Co. Ltd., 1981-84; mng. partner Severn Assos., 1981—; lectr. and seminar chmn. in field; underwriting mem. Lloyd's of London. Edn. chmn. YPO, Rio de Janeiro, Brazil; trustee U.S. Naval Acad. Sailing Found. Inc.; chmn. Fales adv. com. U.S. Naval Acad.; chmn. aviation com. C. of C. New Orleans, 1975-79. Mem. Young Pres.'s Orgn. (chmn. La. chpt. 1978-79), U.S. Naval Acad. Alumni Assn. (pres. New Orleans chpt. 1963), SAR, Colonial Wars Soc. La. (treas. 1978-79), Delta Theta Phi (life mem.). Clubs: Cruising Am., Royal Ocean Racing London (life), Naval Acad. Sailing Squadron (life), Storm Trysail, N.Y. Yacht, So. Yacht, Lloyd's Yacht, The Corinthians, Essex (pres. 1971-72), Bienville. Contbr. articles to profl. jours. Office: 2325 Severn Ave Metairie LA 70001

SHERIDAN, ANDREW JAMES, III, ophthalmologist; b. Washington, Aug. 19, 1944; s. Andrew J. and Mildred (Stohlman) S.; m. Carol Dinkelacker, Oct. 23, 1971; children—Elizabeth, Margaret. A.B., Villanova U., 1966; M.D., Georgetown U., 1970. Diplomate Am. Bd. Ophthalmology. Intern Nassau County Med. Ctr., N.Y., 1970-71, resident in ophthalmology, 1973-76; practice medicine specializing in ophthalmology Eye Assocs., Arlington, Va., 1976—; chief of ophthalmology Arlington Hosp., 1980-84; clin. instr. ophthalmology Georgetown U., 1982—; lectr. in field. Bd. dirs. Va. Med. Polit. Action Com.,

1985. Served to lt. comdr. USPHS, 1971-73. Fellow ACS, Am. Acad. Ophthalmology; mem. Am. Intra-Ocular Implant Soc., Va. Soc. Ophthalmology, AMA, Med. Soc. Va., Arlington County Med. Soc., Brent Soc. Republican. Roman Catholic. Lodge: Lions. Office: Sheridan Eye Assocs 1715 N George Mason Dr #206 Arlington VA 22205

SHERIDAN, ROGER WILLIAMS, civil engineer; b. Dallas, Jan. 26, 1921; s. Lawrence V. and Grace E. (Emmel) S.; student Purdue U., 1940-42, U.S. Mil. Acad., 1942, U. Utah, 1946-50; B.S. in Civil Engring., Westminster Coll., 1955; m. Shirley Parsons, June 12, 1944; children—Kathleen Sheridan Farber, Richard Parsons, Margaret Grace Sheridan Cartledge, Susan Fisher Sheridan Johnston, Sherrie Ann Sheridan Meriwether, Charles Lawrence. Field engr. L.V. Sheridan, Los Alamos, 1948-52; pres., dir. Met. Engrs., Inc., 1952-56; gen. supt. Utah Constrn. Co. (Peru), project mgr. Kaiser Engrs., Volta River Project (Ghana), 1959-61; v.p. constrn. Homesmith, Inc., 1963-64; dir. engring. Khuzestan Water & Power, 1964-67; mgr. constrn. S.-E. Asia, Philco-Ford, 1967-68; asst. v.p., project mgr. Boise-Cascade Corp., 1968-70; v.p. Realtec, Inc., 1970-72; exec. v.p. Metro Surveying & Engring. Co., 1972-73; v.p. gen. mgr. Eastern Pa. Marine Properties, Inc.; exec. v.p. Drums, Inc.; v.p. Lake of Four Seasons, Inc., Acqua Constrn. Co., 1973-74; regional mgr. Envirotech Systems Inc., 1974-75; dir. project ops. Grumman Ecosystems Corp., Bethpage, N.Y., 1975, also Archirodon Group, Athens, Greece; v.p., dir. Delphcon Builders Inc. (Archirodon Group); v.p. Dephinance Devel. Corp.; cons. civil engring. Served to capt. C.E., AUS, World War II; ETO. Decorated Purple Heart, Bronze Star medal. Registered profl. engr., Ga., Ala., N.C., S.C., Fla., Pa., Utah, N.J., Tex., Ind., Ariz., Colo., Wyo., Nev., Okla., Cal. Fellow Am. Soc. C.E., Beavers. Episcopalian. Elk. Office: PO Box 1920 Covington GA 30209

SHERIFF, HILLA, physician; b. Easley, S.C., May 29, 1903; d. John Washington and Mary Lenora (Smith) Sheriff; student Coll. of Charleston (S.C.): 1920-22, D.Humanities (hon.), 1985; M.D., Med. U. of S.C., Charleston, 1926; M.P.H., Harvard U., 1937; H.H.D., Coll. Charleston, 1985; m. George Henry Zerbst, July 10, 1940. Intern, Hosp. of Woman's Med. Coll., Phila., 1926-27, Children's Hosp., Washington, 1928-29, Willard Parker Contagious Disease Hosp., N.Y.C., 1929; practice pediatrics, Spartanburg, S.C., 1929-33; dir. Spartanburg County Health Dept., 1933-40; med. staff Spartanburg Gen. Hosp., med. dir. Am. Women's Hosp. Units in Spartanburg and Greenville Counties, S.C., 1931-36; med. dir. research study in Spartanburg County for Milbank Meml. Fund, N.Y.C., 1935-39; asst. dir. div. maternal and child health Dept. Health and Environ. Control, State of S.C., Columbia, 1940-41, dir., 1941—, chief bur. community health services, asst. state health officer, 1968-74, dep. commr. personal health services, past dir. crippled children's services; clin. prof. pediatrics Med. U. S.C., 1972—, U. S.C. Sch. Medicine; clin. prof. preventive medicine and community health U. S.C. Sch. Medicine. Mem. S.C. State Youth Conservation Com., chmn. health and med. care sub com.; rep. from S.C. to White House Conf., 1940, 50, 60; mem. State Adv. Com. on Adult Edn., 1947. Mem. S.C. Council for Handicapped Children, Gov.'s Interagy. Council on Mental Retardation Planning; chmn. S.C. State Nutrition Com.; bd. dirs. Winthrop Coll. Found., Rock Hill, S.C. Recipient meritorious award S.C. Mental Health Assn., 1972, spl. pioneer award; Outstanding State Employee award S.C. State Employees Assn., 1974; award S.C. Hosp. Assn., 1975; William Weston Disting. Service award U. S.C. Dept. Pediatrics, 1983; named to Order of Palmetto, Gov. of S.C. Diplomate Am. Bd. Preventive Medicine. Fellow Am. Public Health Assn. (council mem. maternal and child health sect., Ross award 1969), Am. Acad. Pediatrics (chpt. pres. 1972), Assn. State Maternal and Child Health and Crippled Children's Dirs. (pres. 1960-62), Am. Assn. Public Health Physicians, Columbia Med. Soc. (v.p. 1962), Am. Med. Women's Assn. (2d v.p. 1946), Am. So., S.C. med. assns., S.C. Public Health Assn., (pres. 1947), Pan Am. Med. Women's Alliance, S.C. Obstet.. and Gynecol. Soc. (hon. mem.), S.C. Pediatric Soc. (sec.-treas. 1941-46, pres. 1972-73), S.C. Mental and Social Hygiene Soc. (pres. 1948-49), S.C. Thoracic Soc., S.C. Conf. Social Work, Delta Kappa Gamma, Alpha Epsilon Iota. Episcopalian. Clubs: S.C. Fedn. of Women's, Business and Professional Women's (charter mem. Spartanburg club), Survey (Columbia, S.C.); Harvard of S.C. (sec.-treas. 1977-79). Home: 807 Hampton Hill Dr Columbia SC 29209

SHERIFF, JIMMY DON, accounting educator; b. Greenville, S.C., Dec. 8, 1940; s. James Donald and Gladys Ellie (Chapman) S.; B.A., Central Wesleyan Coll., 1964; M.B.A., U. Ga., 1970, Ph.D., 1976; m. Gwen Anne Campbell, Aug. 31, 1969. Accountant, Maremont Corp., Greenville, 1965-68; instr. U. Ga., Athens, 1970-73; asst. prof. Presbyn. Coll., Clinton, S.C., 1973-74; prof. Clemson (S.C.) U., 1974—. Chmn. Pickens County Aeros. Commn., 1980—. Served as 1st lt. U.S. Army, 1964; lt. col. USNG. Mem. Nat. Assn. Accts. (Most Valuable Mem. 1978, dir. 1975—, pres. Anderson area 1979-80, nat. dir. 1984-86), Am. Acctg. Assn. (doctoral consortium fellow 1972), Acad. Sci., Acad. Acctg. Historians, Nat. Council Govtl. Accounting, AAUP, S.C. Assn. Acctg. Instrs. (pres. 1974-75), Central Wesleyan Coll. Alumni Assn. (pres. 1970-72), Beta Gamma Sigma, Beta Alpha Psi, Sigma Iota Epsilon. Baptist. Clubs: Lions (pres.), Masons, Shriners. Author: Attitudes Toward Current Values, 1976. Home: Route 4Box 232 Old Shirley Rd Central SC 29630 Office: Sch Accountancy Sirrine Hall Clemson U Clemson SC 29634

SHERIFF, RICHARD ALFRED, pharmacist, chemical company executive; b. Indpls., May 16, 1950; s. Alfred P. and Margaret E.S.; m. Karen Skelton, June 8, 1974; children—Megan Margaret, Timothy Alfred. B.S. in Pharmacy, Purdue U., 1974. Pharmacist, Hook Drugs, Indpls., 1974-75, Ohio State U. Hosp. Nuclear Pharmacy, Columbus, 1975-76; pharmacist Nuclear Pharmacy, Inc., Houston, 1977; mgr. Birmingham, Ala., 1977-80; gen. mgr. Nuclear Medicine Pharmacy, Inc., Columbus, Ga., 1980-83; mgr. diagnostic imaging services Mallinckrodt, Inc., Houston, 1983-84, Dallas, 1984—; adj. prof. Samford U., 1978-80. Contbr. articles to profl. jours. Mem. Am. Pharm. Assn., Acad. Pharmacy Practice, Soc. Nuclear Medicine, Ga. Pharm. Assn., Delta Tau Delta. Republican. Presbyterian. Avocation: swimming; golf. Home: 2705 Magnolia Dr Irving TX 75062 Office: Mallinckrodt Inc 1212 Dolton Suite 307 Dallas TX 75207

SHERIN, ROBERT MORRIS, computer company executive; b. Boston, Apr. 17, 1939; s. Marcus Leon and Sarah (Burwen) S.; student Johns Hopkins, 1958-60, Emerson Coll., 1960-62; m. Joyce Norris; children—David Daniel, Susan Jenifer. Copywriter, announcer radio sta. WNBP, Newburyport, Mass., 1960-62; planneranalyst Eastern Airline, Inc., Miami, Fla., 1965-68; pres. So. Computing Services, Inc., Miami, 1968—, So. List Co., cons. software sales and service for numerous cos.; speaker state taxation of data processing; founding mem. Software Commn. for Issues of the 80's, expert witness on computer issues in ct. cases. Served with AUS, 1962-65. Mem. Data Processing Mgmt. Assn. (newsletter editor 1971-72, publicity chmn. 1975, non-jud. legis. adv. 1977—), Fla. Direct Mktg. Assn., Greater Miami C. of C. Contbr. articles on data processing and high tech. to profl. publs. Contbg. editor ICP Software Publs. Home and office: 15805 SW 101 Ave Miami FL 33157

SHERMAN, CHARLES PATRICK, farm equipment company executive, city official; b. Corsicana, Tex., Mar. 18, 1955; s. Jack Grover and Barbara (Byrd) S.; m. Robin Melinda Frisby, Dec. 31, 1980. B.B.A., So. Methodist U., 1977; M. Pub. Adminstrn., 1978. Vice pres., sec., treas. Corsicana Grader Farm Equip. Co., Corsicana, 1979—; mayor pro-tem City of Corsicana, 1985—, city commr., 1983-85. Author sports column (2d Place award Tex. Interstate Press Assn.), 1973. Chmn. Corsicana Heart Fund, 1980; mem. zoning bd. City of Corsicana, 1981-83; asst. dir. Dallas Democrats, 1978; regional dir. Am. Heart Assn., Houston, 1979. Named Hon. Ky. Col., State Ky., 1976, Hon. Adm. Tex. Navy, 1978. Mem. Direct Mktg. Assn., N. Central Tex. Council Govts (del., rep. 1985—), Tex. Mcpl. League, Corsicana C. of C. (bd. dirs. 1980-83), Ducks Unltd. Conservative Democrat. Episcopalian. Lodge: Rotary. Avocations: golf; hunting; mystery novels. Home: 2205 Dartmouth Corsicana TX 75110 Office: Corsicana Grader Co Box 1699 Corsicana TX 75110

SHERMAN, CORNELIUS WRIGHT, junior high school principal; b. Staunton, Va., July 26, 1934; s. Cornelius R. and Marie (Wright) S.; m. Shirley Claxton, June 16, 1957 (dec. Nov. 1982); children—Rodney Brian, Nicole Marie. B.S., Hampton U., 1956, M.A., 1965. Sci. tchr. Culpeper Sch. Div., Va., 1956-57; tchr. biology Albany Sch. Div., Ga., 1959-61; tchr., counselor Hampton Sch. Div., Va., 1961-66, asst. prin., 1966-80, prin., 1980—; instr. edn. Hampton U., 1968. Mem. Juvenile and Domestic Ct. Adv. com., Hampton, 1981—. Served with U.S. Army, 1957-59. Recipient cert. Nat. Spl. Olympics, 1980, Hampton Tchrs. Assn., Va. Edn. Assn., 1969. Mem. Va. State PTA (hon.), Va. Assn. Secondary Sch. Prins., Nat. Assn. Secondary Sch. Prins., Nat. Middle Sch. Assn. Baptist. Home: 2619 Winona Dr Hampton VA 23661 Office: Spratley Jr High Sch 339 Woodland Rd Hampton VA 23669

SHERMAN, EDWARD FRANCIS, lawyer, educator; b. El Paso, Tex., July 5, 1937; s. Raphael Eugene and Mary (Stedmond) S.; m. Alice Theresa Hammer, Feb. 23, 1963; children—Edward F. Jr., Paul. A.B., Georgetown U., 1959; M.A., U. Tex.-El Paso, 1962, 67; LL.B., Harvard U., 1962. S.J.D., 1981. Bar: Tex. 1962, Ind. 1976. Aide to gov. Nev., state govt. fellow, Carson City, 1962; law clk. to U.S. dist. judge Western dist. Tex., El Paso, 1963; ptnr. firm Mayfield, Broaddus & Perrenot, El Paso, 1963-65; teaching fellow Harvard Law Sch., Cambridge, Mass., 1967-69; prof. Ind. U. Sch. Law, Bloomington, 1969-77; Angus G. Wynne prof. law, U. Tex., Austin, 1977—; counsel Travis County Jail Litigation, 1981-83, Tex. County Jail Litigation, 1978—. Served to capt. U.S. Army, 1965-67, lt. col. Res. Fulbright lectr. in law Trinity Coll., Dublin, Ireland, 1973-74; Am. Bar Found., fellow, 1975-76. Mem. ABA, Am. Soc. Legal History, ACLU (participating atty., bd. dirs.), Tex. State Bar Assn. (chmn. pattern jury charge com. 1984—). Co-author: The Military in American Society, 1979; Complex Litigation, 1985. Home: 2622 Wooldridge Dr Austin TX 78703 Office: U Tex Sch Law Austin TX 78705

SHERMAN, GORDON RAE, computer science educator; b. Menomenee, Mich., Feb. 24, 1928; s. Gordon E. and Myrtle H. (Evenson) S.; m. Lois E. Miller, July 3, 1951; children—Karen Rae, Gordon Thorstein. B.S., Iowa State U., 1953; M.S., Stanford U., 1954; Ph.D., Purdue U., 1960. Instr. math. and research assoc. Statis and Computational Lab., Purdue U., Lafayette, Ind., 1956-60; dir. Computing Ctr., U. Tenn., Knoxville, 1960—, prof. computer sci., 1960—; program dir. techniques and systems Office of Computing Activities, NSF, 1971-72; chmn. membership com. EDUCOM Council, 1983-85. Served with USAF, 1946-49, 50-51. Recipient Chancellor's citation U. Tenn., 1983; NSF grantee, 1974. Fellow Brit. Computer Soc.; mem. Am. Statis. Assn., Assn. for Computing Machinery, Dta Processing Mgmt. Assn. (internat. computer sci. Man of Yr. award S.E. Region VIII, 1973; Profl. of Yr. Region VIII 1979), Ops. Research Soc. Am., Soc. for Indsl. and Applied Math., Sigma Xi, Phi Kappa Phi. Republican. Lutheran. Contbr. articles on computer sci. to profl. jours. Home: 301 Cheshire Dr Apt 105 Knoxville TN 37916 Office: 209 Stokely Mgmt Center U Tenn Knoxville TN 37996

SHERMAN, JEROME NATHANIEL, clinical psychologist; b. Everett, Mass., Nov. 13, 1936; s. Abraham and Anna (Grunberg) S.; m. Ruth Goldberger, Aug. 26, 1962; children—Marc, Scott, Rhonda. B.A., Harvard U., 1958; M.A., Boston U., 1964; Ph.D., U. Houston, 1968. Lic. clin. psychologist, Tex. Instr. psychology Houston Community Coll., 1972-74; assoc. prof. U. Houston/Downtown Coll., 1974-82; dir. Sherman Psychology Clinic, Houston, 1972—; guest lectr. Baylor Coll. Medicine, U. Tex. Med. Sch., Houston; mem. med. team Good Morning Houston program Sta. ABC-TV, Houston. Bd. dirs. Contra Costa County Mental Health Assn. (Calif.), 1969-72; trustee Planned Parenthood Assn. Houston and Southeast Tex., 1974-80. Recipient Disting. Service award Mental Health Assn. Contra Costa County, 1972; appreciation award U. Houston/Downtown Coll., 1982, Path Seekers Inc., 1982. Mem. Am. Assn. Sex Educators, Counselors and Therapists (cert.), Acad. Psychologists in Marital, Sexual and Family Therapy, Houston Psychol. Assn., Tex. Psychol. Assn., Am. Psychol. Assn. Clubs: April Sound Country (Conroe, Tex.); Nottingham Forest (Houston). Home: 14811 Cindywood Dr Houston TX 77079 Office: 909 Frostwood St Suite 133 Houston TX 77024

SHERMAN, JOHN HARVEY, JR., engineering physicist; b. Roanoke, Va., Aug. 12, 1918; s. John Harvey and Mary (Stephens) S.; student Oberlin Coll., 1936-37; A.B., U. Tampa, 1940; M.S., Lehigh U., 1947; postgrad. Cornell U., 1940-41, N.C. State Coll., 1950-51; m. Marie Louise Weill, Mar. 31, 1943; children—Mary Esther (Mrs. Howard J. Ramagli, Jr.), Ida Leah Cole. Optician Spencer Lens Co., Buffalo, 1941-42; asst. prof. elec. engring. N.C. State Coll., 1947-50; engr. Gen. Electric Co., Syracuse, N.Y. and Lynchburg, Va., 1951-80, quartz crystal engr., 1953-80, tech. leader quartz crystal design, 1957-80; cons. to quartz crystal industry, 1980—; mem. Electronic Industries Assn. Working Group P5.4, 1960-80, chmn., 1970-79. Founder Lynchburg Fine Arts Symphony Orch., 1965; bd. dirs. Lynchburg Community Concert Assn., 1968—, pres., 1970-75. Mem. IEEE (sr. life), Elfun Soc., Sigma Xi, Eta Kappa Nu. Unitarian.

SHERMAN, NATHAN, physician; b. Tel Aviv, Aug. 6, 1951; s. Samuel and Stefania (Nirenberg) S.; m. Rebecca Ann Seyler, May 26, 1978; children—Joanna Renee, Sarah Michelle. A.B., Rutgers U., 1972, M.D., 1978. Diplomate Am. Bd. Pathology, Nat. Bd. Med. Examiners. Pediatrics resident U. Med. and Dentistry N.J.-Rutgers Med. Sch., Piscataway, N.J., 1978-79, pathology resident, 1979-83; assoc. pathologist Doctors Hosp. of Prince Georges County, Lanham, Md., 1983-85, Greater Laurel-Beltsville Hosp., Laurel, Md., 1985—. Fellow Coll. Am. Pathologists, Am. Soc. Clin. Pathologists; mem. AMA, Med. and Chirurg. Soc. Md., Washington Soc. Pathologists, Fairfax County Med. Soc., Prince Georges County Med. Soc., Med. Soc. Va. AAAS, Phi Delta Epsilon. Avocations: tennis, sailing, swimming, guitar. Home: 11064 Thrush Ridge Rd Reston VA 22091 Office: Dept Pathology Greater Laurel Beltsville Hosp 7100 Contee Rd Laurel MD 20707

SHERMAN, RICHARD BEATTY, history educator; b. Somerville, Mass., Nov. 16, 1929; s. James Beatty and Hilda Louise (Ford) S.; m. Hanni Fey, June 13, 1952; children—Linda Caroline, Alan Theodore. A.B., Harvard U., 1951, Ph.D., 1959; M.A., U. Pa., 1952. Instr. history Pa. State U., State College, 1957-60; asst. prof. Coll. of William and Mary, Williamsburg, Va., 1960-65, assoc. prof., 1965-70, prof. 1970—; Fulbright prof. Am. history U. Stockholm, 1966-67. Served with U.S. Army, 1952-54. Am. Philos. Soc. grantee, 1964, 66; faculty research grantee, Coll. of William and Mary, 1962, 63, 65, 80. Mem. AAUP, Am. Hist. Assn., Assn. Am. Historians, Phi Beta Kappa. Democrat. Author: The Negro and the City, 1970; The Republican Party and Black America, 1973; contbr. articles to profl. jours. Home: 205 Matoaka Ct Williamsburg VA 23185 Office: Dept History College of William and Mary Williamsburg VA 23185

SHERMAN, ROGER, economics educator; b. Jamestown, N.Y., Sept. 10, 1930; s. Claire B. and Margaret G. (Burke) S.; m. Charlotte Ann Murphy, Apr. 4, 1953; children—C. Randall, Thomas A. B.S., Grove City Coll., 1952; M.B.A., Harvard U., 1959; M.S., Carnegie-Mellon U., 1965, Ph.D., 1966. Mgr. of mfg. control IBM Corp., N.Y.C., 1959-62; from asst. prof. to prof. U. Va., Charlottesville, 1965—, chmn. dept. econs., 1982—; cons. in field. Author: Oligopoly, 1972; The Economics of Industry, 1974; Antitrust Policies and Issues, 1978. Editor: Perspectives on Postal Service Issues, 1980. Bd. dirs. McGuffey Art Ctr., Charlottesville, 1985. Served to lt. USNR, 1952-56. Mem. Am. Econ. Assn., So. Econ. Assn. (mem. exec. com. 1982-84). Home: 1858 Field Rd Charlottesville VA 22903 Office: U Va Rouss Hall Charlottesville VA 22901

SHERMAN, ROGER JOE, public relations consultant; b. Roswell, N.Mex., Nov. 21, 1934; s. Roger Bennett and Bessie Lorena (Atkinson) S.; m. Judith Ann Renard, Apr. 17, 1957; children—Mark Alan, Kathleen Ann. B.S. in Journalism, So. Methodist U., Dallas, 1957, M.A. in English, 1969. Staff writer Dallas Times Herald, 1957-64; dir. info., then dir. info. services So. Meth. U., 1964-78; v.p. public relations Assos. Corp. N. Am., 1978-80; public relations and mktg. cons., Dallas, 1980—. Author: Pastor of the Range, 1985. A Biography of a Southwestern Missionary, 1985. Recipient Journalism award Tex. State Bar, 1962, Nat. Case Study award Am. Coll. Public Relations Assn., 1973. Mem. Public Relations Soc. Am. Republican. Presbyterian. Home: 9860 Elmcrest Dr Dallas TX 75238 Office: 3200 Irving Blvd Dallas TX 75247

SHERMAN, SAUL NORMAN, chiropractor; b. Newark, Aug. 10, 1923; s. Harry and Regina Meryl (Schnall) S.; m. Elaine Levine, Mar. 5, 1950; children—Ruth, Hildy, Cynthia, Mark. B.A., Upsala Coll., 1949; grad. Chiropractic Inst. N.Y., 1957. Diplomate Nat. Bd. Chiropractic Examiners. Resident, Clinic Chiropractic Inst. N.Y.C.; gen. practice chiropractic, 1957—; dir. Livingston Chiropractic Ctr. (N.J.), 1957-78; exec. dir. Family Chiropractors Clinics Fla., Juno Beach, 1978—, Family Chiropractors Multiple Offices, 1978—. County coroner Essex County (N.J.), 1961-65. Served with U.S. Army, World War II. Decorated Bronze Star, Croix de Guerre; recipient Meritorious Achievement award Garden State Chiropractic Soc., 1973. Fellow Royal Soc. Health; mem. Fla. Chiropractic Council (pres. 1981-82), Brit. Guild Drugless Physicians, Fedn. Chiropractic Orgns. Club: Jupiter Inlet Fishing. Lodge: Masons. Editor Chiropractic Health Tracts, 1961-64, Jour. Chiropractics, 1968-69; contbr. articles to profl. jours. Office: 112 US Hwy 1 Juno Beach FL 33408

SHERMAN, WILLIAM EURASTI, lawyer; b. Tampa, Fla., Apr. 28, 1927; s. William Eurasti and Maryetta (Abbott) S.; B.A., U. Fla., 1950, J.D., 1953; m. Frances Rogers, 1950 (div. 1973); children—William Eurasti II, Valerie Ann; m. Vicki Lynn Peterson, June 9, 1974. Bar: Fla. 1953. Spl. asst. to atty. gen. Fla., Tallahassee, 1953; assoc. Francis P. Whitehair, DeLand, Fla., 1954-57; practiced in DeLand, 1958—; mem. firm Hall, Sweeney & Godbee, 1958-59, Hull, Landis, Graham & French, 1960-66, Landis, Graham, French, Husfeld and Sherman, 1966-69, Landis, Graham, French, Husfeld, Sherman & Ford, P.A., 1969—. Mem. Volusia County Charter Study Commn., 1969-71, Volusia County Charter Rev. Commn., 1975; mem. nominating commn. 5th Dist. Ct. Appeals, 1979, 82. Bd. dirs. Internat. Music Festivals, Inc., 1969-71, Montreat (N.C.)-Anderson Coll., 1961-71, Mountain Retreat Assn., 1961-71. Served with Signal Corps, U.S. Army, World War II. Mem. Fla. Bar (gov. 1970-76, chmn. legis. com. 1973-76, exec. com. real property probate and trust sect. 1972—, dir. probate guardianship and trust law div. 1981-83, chmn.-elect 1983, mem. Uniform Probate Code Study Commn.; mem. Marketable Record Title Act Commn. 1984-85), ABA, Volusia County Bar Assn. (pres. 1969-70, MRTA Commn. 1985-86, chmn. estate planning and probate cert. com.), DeLand C. of C. (v.p. 1970-71), Phi Delta Phi, Pi Kappa Alpha, Alpha Delta Sigma. Democrat. Presbyterian (elder). Clubs: Rotary, Halifax. Home: PO Box 48 DeLand FL 32721 Office: 145 E Rich Ave DeLand FL 32721 also 543 S Ridgewood Ave Daytona Beach FL 32014

SHERNOCK, STANLEY KENT, sociologist, criminologist, educator, researcher; b. San Francisco, Aug. 18, 1947; s. Morris and Ada Claire (Alpine) S.; m. Merry Kay Rodenborg, Aug. 20, 1969; children—Mirra Karin-Ada, Britt Morris. B.A., U. Calif.-Berkeley, 1968; M.A., Ind. U., 1971; Ph.D., U. Va., 1979. Instr. sociology Clemson U., S.C., 1971-73; asst. prof. sociology and criminal justice U. Wis.-Superior, 1978-82; asst. prof. sociology and criminal justice Nicholls State U., Thibodaux, La., 1982—; staff cons. Office Criminal Justice Community Assistance, U. Wis.-Eau Claire, 1978-79. Contbr. articles to profl. jours. NIMH fellow, 1970-71; Nat. Def. Fgn. Lang. fellow, 1977-78; Nicholls State U. Research Council grantee, 1982. recipient Nat. Endowment Humanities Summer Research stipend, 1980; Max H. Lavine Annual award U. Wis.-Superior, 1982. Mem. La. Assn. Criminal Justice Educators (chair curriculum com. 1984—), Am. Sociol. Assn., Am. Soc. Criminology, Acad. Criminal Justice Scis., Soc. Study Social Problems. Democrat. Jewish. Avocations: study of international affairs; basketball; ping pong; tennis; hiking; travel. Home: 301 Thoroughbred Park Dr Thibodaux LA 70301 Office: Nicholls State U PO Box 2089 Thibodaux LA 70310

SHERRARD, JOSEPH HOLMES, civil engineering educator, researcher; b. Waynesboro, Va., June 12, 1942; s. Joseph Holmes and Anne Louise (Gleason) S.; m. Frances Anne Coulter, Sept. 5, 1964; children—Stephanie Francesca, Joseph Holmes. B.S., Va. Mil. Inst., 1964; M.S., Calif. State U.-Sacramento, 1969; Ph.D., U. Calif.-Davis, 1971. Registered profl. engr., Okla. Jr. civil engr. Calif. Div. Hwys., Marysville, 1964-65; postdoctoral fellow Cornell U., Ithaca, N.Y., 1971-72; asst. prof. civil engring. Okla. State U., Stillwater, 1972-74; assoc. prof. Va. Poly. Inst. and State U., Blacksburg, 1974-82, prof., 1982—. Editor Civil Engring. for Practicing and Design Engrs. jour., 1982—; Jour. Indsl. Pollution Control, 1985—. Served to capt. U.S. Army, 1965-67; Korea. Fulbright fellow, Ecuador, 1980. Mem. ASCE, Water Pollution Control Fedn., Am. Water Works Assn. Avocations: reading; golf; racquetball. Home: 811 Cherrywood Rd Salem VA 24153 Office: Va Poly Inst and State U Dept Civil Engring Blacksburg VA 24061

SHERRICK, DANIEL NOAH, building materials and manufacturing holding company executive; b. Greenup, Ill., Mar. 28, 1929; s. Conrad D. and Helen Lorene (Neeley) S.; B.S. Ed., Eastern Ill. U., 1956; m. Dora Ann Moore, Aug. 11, 1957; children—Renata Ann, Sherrie Dee. Owner, mgr. Midwest Ins. Agy., Greenup, Ill., 1956-60; supt. agys. Midwest Life Ins. Co., Lincoln, Nebr., 1960-62; asst. v.p. Gulf Life Ins. Co., Jacksonville, Fla., 1962-71; pres. Bank of Carbondale (Ill.), 1971-74; pres. Prescription Learning Corp., Springfield, Ill., 1974-76; exec. v.p. Imperial Industries, Inc., Hialeah, Fla., 1976—, also dir. Pres., Alderman Park Civic Assn., Jaskconville, 1968, Heritage Hills Homeowners Assn., Carbondale, 1973. Served as sgt. USAF, 1948-52; Korea. Mem. Am. Legion (past comdr.), VFW. Conglist. Clubs: Elks, Masons. Home: 14420 Lake Candlewood Ct Miami Lakes FL 33014 Office: 15105 NW 77th Ave Miami Lakes FL 33014

SHERWOOD, CONNIE PRIVETT, nursing eduator; b. Trout Dale, Va., Oct. 24, 1947; d. Charlie Arvel and Loraine Thelma (Testerman) Privett; m. Arthur Lee Sherwood; children—Sharmane Lee, Arthur Lee. B.S. in Nursing, Berea Coll., 1971; M.S. in Nursing, Med. Coll. Va., 1977. R.N., Va. Staff nurse ICU-CCU, Smyth County Community Med. Ctr., Marion, Va., 1971; psychiat. staff nurse Southwestern State Hosp., Marion, 1972-73, psychiat. head nurse, 1973-74; instr. nursing Va. Highlands Community Coll., 1976-80, asst. prof. nursing, 1980—. Mem. Am. Nurses Assn., Va. Nurses Assn., Va. Soc. Profl. Nurses (charter), Assn. Critical Care Nurses, Nat. League Nursing, Va. Council Assoc. Degree Nursing Edn. Baptist. Lodge: Order Eastern Star (conductress 1984—). Home: Route 5 Box 337C Marion VA 24354 Office: Va Highlands Community Coll Abingdon VA 24210

SHERWOOD, ROGER WILLIAM, dentist; b. New Orleans, Apr. 16, 1948; s. Charles Wesley Sherwood and Mary Lenor (Cook) Haase; m. Suzanne Kay Rinardo, June 19, 1971; children—Jonathan William, Chandler Adams. B.S., La. State U., 1971, D.D.S., 1976. Practice dentistry, New Orleans, 1976—. Mem. ADA, La. Dental Assn., Acad. Gen. Dentistry, New Orleans Dental Assn. (peer rev. com.), Postgrad. Seminar New Orleans (pres. 1981). Methodist.

SHEVACK, NOEL HARRIS, technical institute administrator; b. N.Y.C., Apr. 26, 1931; s. George Fred and Josephine Ruth (Giovannette) S.; m. Arline S. Krimko, June 15, 1956; children—Gail, Gloria. B.S. in Marine Engring., N.Y. State Maritime Coll., 1953; M.S. in Mech. Engring., Stevens Inst. Tech., 1957; M.S. in Edn., SUNY-Albany, 1979. Sr. engr. Gen. Electric Co., Schenectady, N.Y., 1957-82, mng. engr. Knolls Atomic Power Lab., Schenectady, 1963-82; sr. recruiting cons., Lendman Assoc., West Palm Beach, Fla. 1982-84; acad. dean New Eng. Inst. Tech., West Palm Beach, 1984-85. Served to lt. USN, 1955-57. Mem. Am. Soc. Tng. and Devel., Am. Vocat. Assn. Avocations: model building; basketball; swimming; hi-fi. Office: New England Inst Tech 1126 53rd Ct West Palm Beach FL 33407

SHEWMAKER, JACK CLIFFORD, discount store chain executive, rancher; b. Buffalo, Mo., Mar. 14, 1938; s. Clifford Verl and Pansy Louise (Brackley) S.; m. Melba June Prosser, Mar. 16, 1958; children—Daniel, Shari Shewmaker Steiger, Emily. Student Ga. Tech. Inst.; Litt.D., Southwest Bapt. U., 1985. Dist. mgr. new store openings Wal-Mart Stores, Inc., Bentonville, Ark., 1970-73, v.p. security, 1973-74, v.p. store ops., 1974-76, exec. v.p., 1976-78, pres., chief operating officer, 1978-84, vice chmn., chief fin. officer, 1984—, dir., 1977—; dir. Lowe's Cos. Inc. Trustee Drury Coll., Springfield, Mo.; active Westarc council Boy Scouts Am.; chmn. bd. students Free Enterprise, Inc., 1985. Named Discount Retailer of Yr., Chgo. Mem. Nat. Mass Retailing Inst. (bd. dirs., exec. and conv. coms.). Republican. So. Baptist. Avocations: hunting; fishing. Office: Wal-Mart Stores Inc 702 SW Eighth St Bentonville AR 72716

SHIELDS, L(ORAN) DONALD, university president; b. San Diego, Sept. 18, 1936; s. Clifford L. and Malta S.; m. Patricia Ann Baldwin, Sept. 1, 1957; children—Ronald, Steven, Cynthia, Laurie. B.A., U. Calif. at Riverside, 1959; postgrad. (grad. asst. teaching fellow), U. Ill., 1959, U. So. Calif., 1959, U. Calif. at Los Angeles, 1959; Ph.D. (duPont teaching fellow), U. Calif. at Los Angeles, 1964. Asst. prof. chemistry Calif. State U., Fullerton, 1963-66, asso. prof., 1966-67, prof., 1967—, v.p. for adminstrn., 1967-70, acting pres., 1970-71, pres., 1971-80, So. Meth. U., Dallas, 1980—; vis. prof. chemistry UCLA, summers, 1964-67; Cons. NSF, 1970—; mem. Nat. Sci. Bd., 1974-80; bd. dirs. Research Corp., 1983-86, Tex. Community Bank-Dallas. Author: Analytical Methods of Organic and Biochemistry, 1968, 76, Modern Methods of Chemical Analysis, 1968, 2d edit., 1976; Contbr. articles to profl. jours. Trustee Nat. Commn. Coop. Edn., 1977—. Recipient Calif. State Legislature Distinguished Teaching award, 1965; named one of Five Outstanding Young Men Calif. Jr. C. of C., 1971; du Pont fellow, 1961-62. Mem. AAAS, Am. Chem. Soc., Am. Coll. Pub. Relations Assn., Am. Inst. Chemists (Honor Scroll award 1980), Orange County C. of C., Tex. Lyceum, Dallas Assembly, Town Hall Calif., Sigma Xi, Phi Lambda Upsilon. Office: So Meth U Dallas TX 75275

SHIELDS, LOYAL MACK, commercial printing shop executive; b. Ringgold, Ga., Sept. 16, 1938; s. James Steward and Hattie Jane (Rinehart) S.; m. Zella

E. Kibble, Jan. 28, 1967; m. Doris Faye Stoker, Feb. 28, 1955 (div. 1966); children—Phillip T., Tonya Kay. Student Aiken Vocat. Sch., 1972-73. Pressman apprentice Standard Packaging Box Co., Louisville, 1957-61; pressman Rock City Box, Chattanooga, 1962-67, Rock-Tenn., Inc., Augusta, Ga., 1968-74, The Mountain Press, Gatlinburg, Tenn., 1974-80; owner, mgr. Sevier Printing, Inc., Pigeon Forge, Tenn., 1980—. Republican. Lodge: Mountain Star. Home: Route 1 Millican Creek Rd Sevierville TN 37862 Office: Sevier Printing Inc 120 Ore Bank Rd Pigeon Forge TN 37863

SHIELDS, MARY VIRGINIA, nurse; b. Lauderdale, Miss., Oct. 28, 1926; d. Luther and Virginia (Grady) Lummus; m. Walter J. Shields, Aug. 9, 1947; children—Jerry. Diploma in nursing Anderson Infirmary, Meridian, Miss., 1947. R.N., Miss. Operating room scrub nurse F.G. Riley Hosp., Meridian, 1950-77, supr. operating room, 1977—. Mem. Miss. Nurses Assn., Am. Nurses Assn., Am. Operating Nurses Assn. Republican. Baptist. Club: Normandal Garden (past pres.) (Meridian). Avocations: gardener; travelling. Home: 4708 13th St Meridian MS 39301 Office: F G Riley Hosp 1102 21st Ave Meridian MS 39301

SHIELDS, PATRICK EDWARD, geologist; b. Fort Smith, Ark., Mar. 10, 1958; s. John Patrick and Jean Marie (Baldner) S. B.S. in Geology, U. Ark., 1982. Sample analyst Profl. Well Logging, Oklahoma City, Okla., 1982; petroleum geologist John P. Shields Co., Fort Smith, Ark., 1982-83, Weiser-Brown Oil Co., Fort Smith, 1983—. Mem. Am. Assn. Petroleum Geologists, Fort Smith Geol. Soc. Club: Town. Avocations: hunting, fishing, racquetball, camping.

SHIELDS, WANDA LOU, college administrator; b. Ft. Worth, Sept. 13, 1940; d. B. Rex and Chrystle O. (Riddle) S.; m. Melvin David Holtzclaw, Dec. 27, 1966 (div. June 1969). B.S., Tex. Women' U., 1962, M.A., 1968; Ed.D., U. Houston, 1978. Tchr., Houston Ind. Sch. Dist., 1962-73, program cons., 1973-75, asst. dir., 1975-78, personnel coordinator, 1978-81, prin. intern, 1980-81; assoc. dean Houston Baptist U., 1981, assoc. dean and dir. M.Ed. and M.A. in Psychology programs, 1981—; cons.; guest lectr. Bd. dirs. SeaArama Marineworld; trustee Northwest Acad. Named Faculty Woman of Year Houston Bapt. U., 1982. Mem. Tex. Soc. Coll. Tchrs. Edn., Houston Prins. Assn., Phi Delta Kappa, Kappa Delta Pi. Baptist. Club: Maplewood Civic. Contbr. to Human Sexuality (James L. McCary), 1968. Office: Houston Bapt U 7502 Fondren Rd Houston TX 77074

SHIELDS, WAYNE SCOTT, law enforcement administrator; b. Martinsville, Va., July 13, 1939; s. Lazarus and Cynthia (Payne) S.; m. Mildred Delores Angle, Sept. 16, 1960; children—Michelle Shields Lewis, Karen Yvonne. Student U. Va., Va. Commonwealth U., Richard Bland Coll., U. Md., U. Ga., FBI Acad. Patrolman Bur. of Police, Petersburg, Va., 1962-65, sgt., 1965-69, lt., 1969-72, capt., 1972-77, acting chief, 1977-78; chief of police Police Dept., Blackstone, Va., 1980—. Chmn. Nottoway County Salvation Army, 1984-85. Recipient Outstanding Achievement award Am. Legion, 1965; Outstanding Law Enforcement Officer of Yr. award Petersburg Jaycees, 1971; Firearms Revolver Expert award FBI, 1974. Mem. Va. Assn. Chief's of Police, Piedmont Law Enforcement Assn. (sec. 1982, v.p. 1983, pres. 1984), FBI Nat. Acad. Assn. Methodist. Clubs: St. Marks Hunt; Southside Equestrian. Avocations: archery; hunting; fishing; riding and showing horses; farming. Home: Route 1 Box 83 Wilsons VA 23894 Office: Police Dept 101 W Elm St Blackstone VA 23824

SHIELS, JAMES HENRY, JR., advertising and industrial art company executive; b. Dallas, Feb. 19, 1930; s. James Henry and Mary (Robbins) S.; B.A., So. Methodist U., 1957; m. Gay Nell Steelmen, June 28, 1957; 1 son, James Henry, III. Staff artist, sales rep., 1956-58; owner, art dir. Henry Shiels Indsl. and Advt. Art Studio, Dallas, 1958—. Vice pres., vice chmn. bd. Mary Shiels Hosp., 1966-74, chmn. bd. dirs., 1974—. Served to 1st lt. USAF, 1952-56; capt. USAF Res., 1960-65. Mem. Nat. Soc. Art Dirs., Dallas-Ft. Worth Art Dirs. Club, Dallas Soc. Visual Communications (dir.). Presbyn. Home: 2905 Purdue Dallas TX 75225 Office: 3402 Oak Grove Suite 204A Dallas TX 75204

SHIFLET, STEPHEN MICHAEL, controller; b. Roanoke, Va., Feb. 27, 1950; s. William Ray and Florence Rachael (Williams) S.; m. Mary Nancy Sutorowski, Jan. 19, 1980; 1 son: Slade Ramsey. A.A., Lake City Community Coll., 1971; B.A., U. West Fla., 1974; M.B.A., Emory U., 1982. Staff auditor Price Waterhouse & Co., Tampa, Fla., 1974-77; corp. auditor J. Ray McDermott & Co., New Orleans, 1977-78; asst. controller Apollo Fuels, Middlesboro, Ky., 1978-79; controller, officer EKA Chems., Inc., Atlanta, 1979—; treas. M.D. Iggesund Inc., 1985—; controller Procomp, 1986—. Vol. for corp. contbns. March of Dimes, Atlanta, 1983. Served with Va. and Fla. N.G., 1970-76. Mem. Delta Sigma Pi. Republican. Home: 212 Bolling Rd Atlanta GA 30305 Office: 2161 Newmarket Pkwy Suite 162 Marietta GA 30067

SHIFTER, MICHAEL EVAN, sociologist, program administrator; b. N.Y.C., Apr. 11, 1955; s. Jerome Paul and Joan Sue (Cooper) S. B.A., summa cum laude, Oberlin Coll., 1977; M.A., Harvard U., 1982. Teaching fellow Harvard U., Cambridge, Mass., 1979-82; cons. Harvard Inst. for Internat. Devel., Cambridge, 1981-82; staff assoc. Woodrow Wilson Internat. Ctr. for Scholars, Washington, 1982-84; program officer Inter-Am. Found., Rosslyn, Va., 1984—; project cons. Found. Am. Communications, Washington, 1983; lectr. Foreign Service Inst., Rosslyn, 1983, 84, 85, Bus. Council for Internat. Understanding, Washington, 1984. Mem. Latin Am. Studies Assn., Am. Sociol. Assn., Phi Beta Kappa, Sigma Xi. Avocations: basketball; raquetball; Irish folk music. Home: 2525 N 10th St Apt 513 Arlington VA Office: Inter-Am Found 1515 Wilson Blvd Rosslyn VA 22209

SHILESKY, DONALD MARK, environmental engineer; b. Akron, Ohio, July 4, 1942; s. Ben Fred and Rose (Pollock) S.; B.S. in Biology, U. Cin., 1964, M.S. in Civil and Environ. Engring., 1966; D.Sc. (fellow), Washington U., 1973; m. Eileen Theresa Nevole, Jan. 25, 1969; children—David Mark, Michael S. Research asst., applied sci. div. Litton Industries, Mpls., 1969-70, mem. sr. tech. staff, Camarillo, Calif., 1970-71; program dir. East-West Gateway Coordinating Council, St. Louis, 1971-73; tech. coordinator Browning-Ferris Industries, Inc., Houston, 1973-75; dir. civil systems Waste Mgmt. Inc., Oak Brook, Ill., 1975-76; mgr. environ. studies Engring. Science, McLean, Va., 1976-77; v.p., dir. SCS Engrs., Reston, Va., 1977-80; mgr. Eastern ops. Harding Lawson Assocs., McLean, Va., 1980-81; mgr. tech. ops. Hazardous Materials Tech. Ctr., Dynamac Corp., 1981-84; pres. Assocs. for Clean Environment; chmn. bd. Hazardous Waste Info. Service; exec. dir Assn. Small Chem. and Indsl. Mfrs., 1984—. Recipient Project of the Year award Camarillo Jaycees, 1970; USPHS grantee, 1966-67. Mem. ASCE (solid waste mgmt. com. 1975-76, chmn. profl. coordinating com. 1978-79), Nat. Solid Wastes Mgmt. (chmn. chem. waste com. 1974-76), Sigma Xi. Mem. editorial adv. bd. Sludge mag.; contbr. articles on solid waste mgmt. and hazardous waste mgmt. to profl. jours. Home: 10403 Pearl St Fairfax VA 22032 Office: PO Box 2383 Fairfax VA 22031

SHILLING, LOUIS, psychologist, educator; b. Balt., Jan. 28, 1929; s. Louis Edwin and Isabell Regina (Toston) S.; m. Catherine Small, July 27, 1968; 1 child, Andrew John. B.A., Marist Coll., 1955; Ed.M., U. Ga., 1968, Ph.D., 1970. Lic. psychologist, profl. counselor, Tex. Asst. to assoc. prof. Atlanta U., 1970-75; assoc. prof. dept. counselor edn. Tex. Woman's U., Denton, 1976-83, prof., 1983—; pvt. practice psychology, Denton, 1982-84, dir. North Tex. Psychol. Services, Carrollton, 1984-85. Author: Perspectives on Counseling Theories, 1984. Served with USN, 1947-51. Mem. Am. Psychol. Assn., Am. Assn. Counseling and Devel., Tex. Assn. Talented and Gifted. Democrat.

SHILLINGBURG, HERBERT THOMPSON, JR., dental educator; b. Ganado, Ariz., Mar. 21, 1938; s. Herbert Thompson and Stefi Marie (Schuster) S.; m. Constance Joanne Murphy, June 11, 1960; children—Lisa Grace, Leslie Susan, Lara Stephanie. Student U. N.Mex., 1955-58, 65-66; D.D.S., U. So. Calif., 1962. Gen. practice dentistry, Albuquerque, 1964-67; asst. prof. fixed prosthodontics sect. UCLA Sch. Dentistry, 1967-70, chmn. 1970-72; chmn. dept. fixed prosthodontics U. Okla. Coll. Dentistry, Oklahoma City, 1972—, David Ross Boyd Disting. prof., 1983; cons. VA Hosp., Muskogee, Okla., 1975—, Oklahoma City, 1977—, U.S. Army Dental Activity, Ft. Knox, Ky., 1980—. Author: Preparations for Cast Gold Restorations, 1972; Fundamentals of Fixed Prosthodontics, 1976, 2d edit., 1981; Guide to Occlusal Waxing, 1979, 2d edit., 1984; Restoration of the Endodontically Treated Tooth, 1982. Co-editor Quintessence of Dental Technology, 1984—. Served to capt. U.S. Army, 1962-64. Recipient award for Teaching Excellence, UCLA Sch. Dentistry, 1973, U. Okla. Coll. Dentistry, 1976, 78, 82. Fellow Am. Coll. Dentists; mem. ADA, Acad. Operative Dentistry, Am. Acad. Crown and Bridge Prosthodontics, Okla. State Dental Assn., Internat. Assn. Dental Research, Okla. Soc. Prosthodontists (assoc.), Omicron Kappa Upsilon. Republican. Episcopalian. Avocations: travel, photography. Home: 6313 NW 84th Pl Oklahoma City OK 73132 Office: U Okla Coll Dentistry PO Box 26091 Oklahoma City OK 73190

SHIM, YOUNG SOON, physician; b. Seoul, Korea, Dec. 16, 1946; d. Hyun and Kui (Ko) Kim; m. Jaimoon Marcus Shim, Feb. 21, 1972. M.D., Ewha U., 1972. Diplomate Am. Bd. Internal Medicine. Physician, Med. Specialist of Hopewell (Va.), 1979—. Mem. ACP, AMA. Presbyterian. Office: Med Specialist of Hopewell 602 N 6th Ave Hopewell VA 23860

SHIPEKY, RUDOLPH LOUIS, engineering manager; b. N.Y.C., Jan. 29, 1936; s. Louis and Anna (Toth) S.; m. Cecilia Mary Molyneux, Oct. 7, 1979. B.M.E., CUNY, 1963; M.S. in Indsl. Engring., Columbia U., 1967. Project engr. Western Electric Co., N.Y.C., 1959-64, turnkey project mgr., Newark, 1965-67, engring. pricing mgr., N.Y.C., 1967-77; engring. mgr. AT&T Co., Basking Ridge, N.J., 1977-81; engring. mgr. AT&T Technologies Inc., Burlington, N.C., 1981-84, product engring. mgr., 1985—; asst. to chief of staff Hdqrs. Tactical Info. Systems Div., Langley AFB, Va., 1983—; N.C. admissions rep. USAF Acad., 1983—. Pres. Telephone Pioneers Am., Burlington, 1984-85. Served to col. USAFR, 1958—. Decorated Air Force Commendation medal. Mem. ASME, Am. Soc. Safety Engrs., Air Force Assn., Armed Forces Communications Electronics Assn., Air Force Sgts. Assn. Office: AT&T Technologies Inc 204 Graham-Hopedale Rd Burlington NC 27215

SHIPLEY, MARY GAY, book store executive; b. Blytheville, Ark., Mar. 8, 1944; d. R.A. and Mary Blanche (Gay) Nelson; m. Paul Larsen Shipley, July 31, 1966. B.A. in Math., Fla. So. Coll., 1966; M.S. in Math., Ark. State U., 1973. Tchr., Gosnell Schs., Ark., 1968-71, Blytheville Schs., 1971-77, Miss. County Community Coll., Blytheville, 1976-80, U. Ark., Park College, Blytheville, 1976-82; pres. The Book Rack, Inc., Blytheville, 1976—; in service trainer State Dept. Edn., Ark., 1972-77; women's leadership tng. team Ark. Edn. Assn., 1975-77; math cons. Blytheville Schs. Creator: outdoor arts festival Springtime on the Mall, 1980, outdoor st. festival Chickasaw Chili Cookoff, 1980, book review series Brown Bagging with Books, 1980. Commr., Ritz Civic Ctr., Blytheville, 1981—; bd. dirs., treas. Blytheville Fine Arts Council, 1983—; crusade chair Am. Cancer Soc., Blytheville, 1984-85; county coordinator Ark. Sesquicentennial, Miss. County, 1984-86. Travelship AAUW, 1972; Scottish Rite Mason scholar, 1972-73; Named Ark. Vol. Gov.'s Office, 1982. Mem. Mid-South Booksellers (pres. 1983—), Am. Booksellers Assn. (bd. 1985-88), Blytheville C. of C. (bd. dirs. 1983, 84), P.E.O. (treas. 1978—), DAR. Episcopalian. Avocations: reading; travel; needlework. Home: 1200 W Walnut Blytheville AR 72315 Office: The Book Rack Inc 316 W Main Blytheville AR 72315

SHIPLEY, ROBERT HOPKINS, psychologist; b. Kalamazoo, Apr. 11, 1945; s. Robert and Jean (Hopkins) S.; children—Kimra, Jennifer. B.S. in Psychology, Mich. State U., 1967; Ph.D. in Clin. Psychology, U. Iowa, 1972. Lic. psychologist, N.C. Staff psychologist Mid Mo. Mental Health Ctr., Columbia, 1972-74, dir. psychology, 1974-77; staff psychologists VA Med. Ctr., Durham, N.C., 1977-80, chief psychology, 1980—; assoc. prof. psychiatry Duke U., Durham, 1980—, dir. Quit Smoking Clinic, 1977—; pres. J.B. Press, Durham, 1985—. Author: Flooding and Implosive Therapy, 1983, Quit Smart; A Guide to Freedom from Cigarettes, 1985. Contbr. articles to profl. jours. Mem. Am. Psychol. Assn., Assn. for Advancement Behavior Therapy, Soc. Behavioral Medicine, Sigma Xi. Avocations: tennis; gardening. Home: Rt 7 Box 274 Durham NC 27707 Office: VA Med Center 116B Durham NC 27705

SHIPMAN, ROSS LOVELACE, geologist, petroleum executive; b. Jackson, Miss., Nov. 20, 1926; s. William Smylie and Jeanette Scott (Lovelace) S.; B.A., U. Miss., 1950, postgrad., 1950; m. Lois Ann Pegrim, June 6, 1948; 1 dau., Leigh Smylie Shipman Anderson. Geologist, Humble Oil & Refining Co., West Tex., 1950-55; petroleum cons., Midland, Tex., 1955-60; petroleum cons., Corpus Christi, 1960-67; asst. exec. dir. Am. Geol. Inst., Washington, 1967-70; assoc. dir. U. Tex. Marine Sci. Inst., Austin, 1971-79; assoc. v.p. research U. Tex., Austin, 1979-84; pres., chief exec. officer Live Oak Energy, Inc., Austin, 1985—. Mem. Tex. Coastal and Marine Council, 1979-85. Served with AUS, 1944-46. Cert. petroleum geologist. Fellow Geol. Soc. Am., Geol. Soc. London; mem. Am. Inst. Profl. Geologists (pres. Tex. sect. 1974, nat. editor 1975-76), Soc. Prof. Earth Sci. Episcopalian. Home: 1803 Great Oaks Dr Round Rock TX 78681 Office: 708 Colorado St Suite 201 Austin TX 78701

SHIPP, VICTOR RAY, retired business executive; b. Oklahoma City, Nov. 22, 1921; s. Ray and Pauline (Ballensky) S.; student public schs., Oklahoma City; m. Wilma Fay Scott, Sept. 27, 1948; children—Donald Ray, Mrs. Gerhardt A. Kratschmann, Mrs. James M. Butler, Jr. Owner, founder Star Printing Co., Oklahoma City, to 1942, Victor R. Shipp Co., 1945-49; sales engr. Am. Type Founders, Inc., 1949; prodn. engr. So. Calif. Newspaper Prodn. Com., to 1954; gen. mgr. Southwestern Press, Ft. Smith, Ark., 1954-59; mgmt. cons. engr., Greenville, S.C., 1959, then in Wichita Falls, Tex.; founder, chief operating officer Vic Shipp Typography, Inc., Oklahoma City, 1961-73; former sec. Creative Printers Am.; pub. Ad Galley newsletter, 10 years; profl. model; charter airline pilot. Mem. nat. adv. bd. Am. Security Council; charter mem. Republican Presdl. Task Force; mem. Rep. Congl. Com., Rep. Nat. Com., Rep. Senatorial Com. Served to capt. USAAF, 1942-45; with Res., to 1963. Decorated D.F.C., Air medal; recipient awards in field. Republican. Club: U.S. Senatorial. Home: 625 NW 19 St Oklahoma City OK 73103

SHIREK, JOHN RICHARD, savings and loan executive; b. Bismarck, N.D., Feb. 5, 1926; s. James Max and Anna Agatha (Lala) S.; student U. Minn., 1944-46; B.S. with honors, Rollins Coll., 1978; m. Ruth Martha Lietz, Sept. 22, 1950; children—Barbara Jo (Mrs. James A. Fowler), Jon Richard, Kenneth Edward. Sports editor Bismarck Tribune, 1943-44; with Gate City Savs. and Loan Assn., Fargo, N.D., 1947-65, v.p., dir., 1960-65; exec. v.p., dir. 1st Fed. Savs. and Loan Assn., Melbourne, Fla., 1966-70; pres., dir. 1st Fed. Savs. and Loan Assn., Cocoa, Fla., 1970-82; exec. v.p., dir. The First, F.A. (formerly First Fed. Savs. & Loan Assn. Orlando), 1982—; dir. Fin. Transaction Systems, Inc., Magnolia Service Corp., First of Cocoa Service Corp., Magnolia Realty, Inc. Chmn., dir. United Fund, Fargo, 1962-65; dir., exec bd. mem. Boy Scouts Am., 1960-70, bd. dirs. Central Fla. Council, 1986—. founding bd. assocs. Fla. Inst. Tech., pres., 1968; trustee Savs. and Loan Found., 1980-84; mem. adv. bd. Brevard Art Center and Mus., 1980-82; trustee Montreat Assn., Presbyn. Ch. U.S., 1980, 81; founding chmn. devel. council Holmes Regional Med. Center, Melbourne, bd. dirs., 1980-82; bd. dirs. Fla. Savs. and Loan Investment Group, Inc., 1980, Orlando Regional Med. Ctr. Found., 1982-85; mem. Mayor's Task Force on Housing, 1983-84; moderator St. Johns Presbytery, 1979, chmn. coordinating council, 1980, 81; moderator Synod of Fla., 1983. Served to lt. (j.g.) USNR, World War II. Mem. Fla. Savs. and Loan League (past dir.), Fla. Savs. and Loan Services (past dir.), Savs. and Loan Found. (state membership chmn. 1976), Fla. Savs. and Loan Polit. Action Com. (dir. 1976-82), U.S. Savs. and Loan League (chmn. advt. and pub. relations com. 1969-70), Downtown Melbourne Assn. (past pres.), Orlando C. of C., Beta Theta Pi, Omicron Delta Epsilon. Republican. Clubs: , Rio Pinar Country, University, Citrus, Rotary (Orlando, Fla.); Country of Brevard; Masons, Shriners, Elks, Cocoa Rotary (pres. 1979). Office: 145 S Magnolia Orlando FL 32802

SHIRLEY, PRESTON, lawyer; b. Ft. Worth, Nov. 14, 1912; s. James Preston and Nevra (Boykin) S.; student Tex. Christian U., 1928-30; LL.B., U. Tex., 1933; m. Elizabeth Hodgson, Nov. 13, 1936; children—Susan Shirley Eckel, Carolyn Shirley Wimberly, Sarah Shirley White. Bar: Tex. 1933, Calif. Ptnr., Boykin, Ray & Shirley, Ft. Worth, 1933-36; asso. prof. law U. Tex., Austin, 1936-40; ptnr. Kelley & Looney, Edinburg, Tex., 1940-41, Holloway, Hudson & Shirley, Ft. Worth, 1945-47, Mills, Shirley, McMicken & Eckel, Galveston, Tex., 1947—; dir. InterFirst Bank Galveston, N.A. (formerly First Hutchings-Sealy Nat. Bank), mem. exec. com., 1967—, chmn. bd., 1974-80, sr. chmn. bd., 1980—; dir. Am. Indemnity Fin. Corp., Galveston, Am. Indemnity Co., Am. Fire & Indemnity Co., Tex. Gen. Indemnity Co., Galveston Corp. Mem. U. Tex. Devel. Bd., Austin, chmn., 1965-66, 66-67; mem. devel. bd. U. Tex. Med. Br., Galveston, 1967—; pres. First Bapt. Found., Galveston; chmn. Galveston Charter Rev. Commn., 1968, 72, mem., 74, 1970; mem. Planning Commn. City of Galveston, 1961-69, Tex. Constl. Revision Commn., 1973—, Gov.'s Task Force on Higher Edn., 1981; bd. dirs., exec. v.p. Sealy & Smith Found. for John-Sealy Hosp., Galveston; bd. dirs. U. Tex. Found., Pres., 1970-72; life trustee, pres. U. Tex. Law Sch. Found.; trustee Mary Hardin Baylor Coll., Belton, Tex., 1974-78. Served from 2d lt. to lt. col., AUS, 1942-45; CBI. Named Disting. Alumnus, U. Tex., 1982, U. Tex. Law Sch., 1985. Fellow Am. Coll. Trial Lawyers, Am. Coll. Probate Counsel, Am. Bar Found., Tex. Bar Found. (50-Yr. Outstanding Lawyer award 1983); mem. Tex. Assn. Def. Counsel (pres. 1963-64), Galveston County Bar Assn. (pres. 1954-55), ABA, State Bar Tex. (com. adminstrn. justice 1952-72), Internat. Assn. Ins. Counsel, Assn. Ins. Attys., Order of Coif, Phi Delta Phi, Phi Kappa Psi. Club: Galveston Arty. Author: Texas Pattern Jury Charges, vols. 1 and 2, 1969. Home: 4602 Sherman Blvd Galveston TX 77550 Office: 700 InterFirst Bank Bldg Galveston TX 77550

SHIVELY, JOE E., state education official; b. Plymouth, Ind., Mar. 3, 1945; s. Claude Russell and Geneva Jane (Baer) S.; m. Linda Kay Davis, Apr. 13, 1963; children—Mark Allen, Brenda Elaine. B.S., Purdue U., 1967, M.S., 1968, Ph.D., 1970. Cert. math. and chemistry tchr., W.Va. Instr., Purdue U., 1970; asst. prof. math. So. Ill. U.-Carbondale, 1970-73; eval. specialist CEMREL, Carbondale, 1970-73; asst. prof. edn. Coll. Grad. Studies, Institute, W.Va., 1974; dir. research and devel. Appalachia Ednl. Lab., Charleston, W.Va., 1973-84; dir. testing W.Va. Dept. Edn., Charleston, 1984—; cons. Ala. A&M U., Huntsville, 1978; workshop trainer U.S. V.I. Schs., 1981. Contbr. articles to ednl. jours. Disney Found. scholar Purdue U., 1963-67; named Ky. Col., 1979, lt. col., a.d.c. to gov. Ala., 1983. Mem. Am. Ednl. Research Assn., Am. Psychol. Assn., Nat. Council on Measurement in Edn., Assn. for Ednl. Data Systems, Evaluation Network, Kappa Delta Pi, Phi Delta Kappa. Democrat. Club: Kanawha Valley Civitan (bd. dirs. 1982-83, 85—) (Charleston). Avocations: golf, basketball. Home: 513 Dabney Dr Charleston WV 25314 Office: West Va Dept of Edn Capitol Complex 6 B-057 Charleston WV 25305

SHIVELY, ROBERT WARREN, management educator; b. Concord, N.H., June 15, 1932; s. Robert C. and Audrey P. (Smith)S.; m. Virginia A. Kenyon, June 26, 1954 (div.); children—Heather Shively Austin, Robert Warren, Jr., Selinda Shively Chiquoine; m. 2d Frances Hughes, Mar. 25, 1978. B.A., Colgate U., 1954; Ed.M., Harvard U., 1962; Ph.D., Cornell U., 1972. Tchr. Deerfield (Mass.) Acad., 1956-61; assoc. dir. fin. aid, Cornell U., Ithaca, N.Y., 1961-63, dir. admissions, student affairs, grad. sch. bus., pub. adminstrn., 1963-67; assoc. dean, Babcock Grad. Sch. Mgmt., Wake Forest U., Winston Salem, N.C., 1970-74, assoc. prof., 1974-80, dean, prof., 1982; dir. sch. bus. pub. adminstrn., U. Puget Sound, Tacoma, 1980-81. Served with USAF, 1954-56. Mem. Acad. Mgmt.; Phi Beta Kappa. Democrat. Club: Twin City (Winston-Salem). Lodge: Rotary (Winston-Salem). Contbr. articles to profl. jours. Home: 160 Idlewilde Dr Winston Salem NC 27106 Office: Babcock Grad Sch Mgmt Wake Forest Univ Box 7659 Reynolda Station Winston Salem NC 27109

SHIVER, DENNIS KEVIN, computer consulting company executive; b. Bethesda, Md., Oct. 18, 1953; s. George Washington and Phyllis Rae (Windle) S.; m. Doris Hallford, Sept. 23, 1977 (div. 1982). Student DeKalb Community Coll., 1970-72, U. Ga., 1972-73; B.S., Augusta Coll., 1976. Cert. data processor, systems profl. Programmer, United Way Am., Alexandria, Va., 1979; lead programmer Mutual Broadcasting System, Arlington, Va., 1979-81; computer cons., Alexandria, 1980-83, 85; mgr. programming ARC, Alexandria, 1983-84; co-owner, operator Apex Consulting, Inc., Alexandria, 1985—. Mem. Assn. for Computing Machinery. Methodist. Avocations: amateur zoologist; boating; reading; sports cars.

SHIVER, MOLLY TYUS, personnel director; b. Milner, Ga., Oct. 27, 1939; d. James Drewery and Wynona Alice (Bevil) Tyus; m. James Thomas Shiver, July 1, 1958; children: Wanda Lea, Patricia Ann. Student Gordon Jr. Coll., 1976-78. Regional sales mgr. Sarah Coventry, Newark, N.Y., 1972-79; seante staff State of Ga., Atlanta, 1980; v.p. sales Jennifer Lynn Ltd., Atlanta, 1980-81; dir. personnel A.L. Williams, Atlanta, 1981—. Treas., bd. dirs. Assn. Retarded Citizens, Barnesville, Ga., 1975-78. Democrat. Baptist. Clubs: Barnesville Bus. and Profl. Woman's (pres. 1976), Barnesville Womens (pres. 1977). Home: Route 1 Milner GA 30257

SHOCKEY, LESLIE KAY, chemical company advertising executive; b. Dayton, Ohio, Apr. 20, 1958; d. Robert Drexel and Wanda (Dunn) S. B.S. in Agr., U. Tenn.-Martin, 1980. Vice pres.-treas. Ida Inc., 1979—; with Drexel Chem. Co., Memphis, 1980—, labeling specialist, advt. mgr., 1980—. Active Memphis In May Festival, 1984-85. Mem. Nat. Agri. Mktg. Assn. (chmn. membership 1984-86, Nat. Recognition award 1985), Mid South Exporters Roundtable, Import-Exporters Club, Alpha Delta Pi Alumni. Republican. Baptist. Home: 1618 W Massey Rd Memphis TN 38119 Office: Drexel Chem Co 2487 Pennsylvania St Memphis TN 38109

SHOCKEY, THOMAS EDWARD, real estate executive, engineer; b. San Antonio, Aug. 17, 1926; s. Verlie Draper and Margaret Ruth (Shuford) S.; B.S. (Davidson fellow Tau Beta Pi), Tex. A&M U., 1950; postgrad. St. Mary's U., 1964, San Antonio Coll., 1972, Pacific Western U., 1981; m. Jacqueline McPherson. June 4, 1949; children—Cheryl Ann, Jocelyn Marie, Valerie Jean. With Petty Geophys. Survey, summers 1947-49, J.E. Ingram Equipment Co., 1950-51; co-owner, archtl. engr., realtor Moffett Lumber Co., Inc., San Antonio, 1952-76; cons. gen. contracting, gen. real estate, 1944—, retailer wholesale bldg. material, 1951—, v.p., 1959—; real estate counselor, appraiser, 1972—; real estate appraiser Gill Appraisal Service, San Antonio, 1977—; comml. loan appraiser, underwriter, analyst Gill Savs. Assn., Gill Cos., San Antonio, 1979; chief appraiser, underwriter, architect, engr., insp. Gill Cos., 1981, v.p., 1981—. Served with inf. Signal Corps, U.S. Army, 1944-46; ETO. Mem. San Antonio C. of C., Nat. Lumber Dealers, Nat. Home Builders, Nat. Real Estate Bd.. Nat. Inst. Real Estate Brokers, Internat. Soc. Real Estate Appraisers, Tex. Assn. Real Estate Insps., Real Estate Appraisers Tex., Nat. Assn. Rev. Appraisers and Mortgage Underwriters, Internat. Inst. Valuers. Home: Star Route Box 87 Mico TX 78056 Office: Gill Companies 615 Soledad PO Box 599 San Antonio TX 78292

SHOCKLEY-SMITH, CAROL FRANCES, psychotherapist; b. Atlanta, Nov. 24, 1948; d. Robert Thomas and Frances Lavada (Scrivner) Shockley; m. Robb Carl Smith, Dec. 14, 1983. B.A., Ga. State U., 1974, M.Ed., 1976; postgrad., U. Ga., 1982—. Cert. in gerontology. Counselor Rape Crisis Ctr., Atlanta, 1979-80; emergency mental health clinician Gwinnett Med. Ctr., Lawrenceville, Ga., 1980—; pvt. practice psychotherapy, Atlanta, 1980—. Leader Alzheimer's Disease Support Group, Athens, Ga., 1984; vol. Reminiscence Group for Elderly, Athens, 1984, 85; vol. counselor Rape Crisis Ctr., Atlanta, 1979; vol. Ga. Mental Health Inst., Atlanta, 1972. Recipient Meritorious service award Beta Gamma Sigma, 1975. Mem. Am. Psychol. Assn., Am. Assn. Counseling and Devel., Sigma Phi Omega, Psi Chi. Avocations: astronomy; archaeology; music; travel.

SHOEMAKER, DON(ALD CLEAVENGER), editor; b. Montreal, Que., Can., Dec. 6, 1912 (parents Am. citizens); s. Richard Samuel and Alberta (Stone) S.; A.B., U. of N.C., 1934; Litt.D., Hollywood Coll.; m. Lyal Reynolds, Oct. 30, 1937 (dec. July 1968); children—Elizabeth Shoemaker Danziger; m. 2d, Suzanne Statler, Aug. 2, 1969; 1 dau., Charlotte. Telegraph editor, Greensboro (N.C.) Record, 1934-37, Asheville (N.C.) Times, 1937-41; asso. editor, Asheville Citizen, 1941-47, editor, 1947-55; exec. dir. So. Edn. Reporting Service, 1955-58; editor, editorial page The Miami Herald, 1958-62, editor, 1962-78, sr. editor, 1978—; columnist Knight-Ridder Newspapers, 1978—. Sec. Fla. World's Fair Authority; mem. Orange Bowl Com., dir., Fla. Bicentennial Commn.; past vice chmn. Fla. Council of 100; chmn. N.C. Conf. Editorial Writers, 1951-52; pres. Buncombe County Community Chest, 1951; chmn., Miami Com. on Fgn. Relations; mem. N.Y. Council on Fgn. Relations; chmn. Dade Coordinating Council, 1974-75; chmn., Fla. region NCCJ, also nat. trustee; trustee, U. Miami, Mus. of Sci.; trustee, chmn. adv. council Fla. Meml. Coll.; trustee United Way Dade County, pres., 1976, chmn. bd., 1977; dir., chief U.S. del. United Way Internat., Hong Kong, 1977; chmn. Fla. Profl. Tchr. Task Force; mem. Fla. Edn. Council, Fla. Task Force on Student Assessment; bd. dirs. Met. Art Mus.; founder Miami Center for Fine Arts. Recipient Silver medallion award, NCCJ, 1970, medal of merit, The Asheville Sch., Diamond Jubilee award Nat. Jewish Hosp., 1974; Disting. Eagle Scout award, 1978. Mem. Inter-Am. Press Assn., Asociacion de Amigos del Pais (Guatemala), Internat. Press Inst., Am. Soc. Newspaper Editors, Order of Golden Fleece (U. N.C.), Newcomen Soc., Pi Kappa Alpha, Sigma Delta Chi. Episcopalian. Clubs: Bath, Miami, Standard (Miami); Palm Bay. Editor: Henry George: Citizen of the World (by Anna George de Mille), 1950; Middle East Journey; The Case of the Lively Ghost, 1957; With All Deliberate Speed, 1957; Spanish Diary, 1974. Contbr. to mags. and encys. Home: 617 Sabal Palm Rd

Bay Point Miami FL 33137 Office: Knight Ridder Newspapers Inc 1 Herald Plaza Miami FL

SHOEMAKER, JOHN FREDERICK, photographer, media consultant; b. Bloomington, Ind., Dec. 5, 1946; s. John Charles and Genivieve Grace (Skinner) S.; m. Judith Ellyne Smith, Apr. 30, 1965 (div. 1976); 1 child, Kristine Lee; m. Karen Diane Lawson, Feb. 4, 1981. A.A., Trident Coll., 1982; student in history Coll. of Charleston, 1982-85. Vice-pres. Marine Contract Labor, Charleston, S.C., 1980-83; mng. editor Meteor Newspaper, Charleston, 1983-84, editor, 1984-85; pres. John F. Shoemaker Photography, Charleston, 1985—; photo cons. Coll. of Charleston Yearbook, 1983-84, photo technician, 1984-85, editorial cons. publs. bd., 1983-85; sr. photographer Comet Yearbook, Charleston, 1984-85. Photographer book: The Comet (outstanding photographic contbn. award 1985), 1985; Faces of Charleston, 1985; also action photo series and portrait photo series. Active Hollings for Pres. Com., Charleston, 1984, Danials for Gov., Charleston, 1985. Recipient 2d place prize Am. Scholastic Press Assn., 1984, 1st place with spl. merit, 1985, outstanding editorial award, 1985. Mem. S.C. Press Assn. (hon. mention award 1984), Am. Scholastic Press Assn., Charleston Publs. Bd. Democrat. Methodist. Club: Charleston Photographic Soc. Office: John F Shoemaker Photography 380 Waltham St Port Charlotte FL 33952

SHOENIGHT, PAULINE ALOISE SOUERS, author; b. Bridgeport, Ill., Nov. 20, 1914; d. William Fitch and Carrie (Milhouse) Souers; B.Ed., Eastern Ill. U., 1937; m. James Richard Tracy, Sept. 18, 1946 (dec. Aug. 1, 1972); m. 2d, Hurley F. Shoenight, June 25, 1976. Mem. P.E.O. Sisterhood, Am. Poets Fellowship Soc. (hon. life), Eastern Ill. Alumni Assn. (life), Ill. (charter), Ala. State poetry socs., Foley Extension Homemakers Club, Am. Poetry League, Christian Writers League Am., Acad. Am. Poets, Nat. Audubon Soc., Pensters, Nat. Geog. Soc., Nat. Ret. Tchrs. Assn., Friends of Libraries of U. Mo. Columbia (life), Baldwin Heritage Mus. Assocs. Inc. (life time charter). Republican. Baptist. Clubs: Baldwin Sr. Travelers. Pleasure Island Sr. Citizens (charter). Author: His Handiwork, 1954; Memory is a Poet, 1964; The Silken Web, 1965; A Merry Heart, 1966; In Two or Three Tomorrows, 1968; All Flesh is Grass, 1971; Beyond the Edge, 1973. Address: Route 3 Box 1107 Foley AL 36535

SHOFFNER, THOMAS PHILIP, pharmacist; b. Greensboro, N.C., Dec. 27, 1951; s. John Thomas and Lorena (Garrett) S.; m. Sondra Louise Chambers, June 15, 1978 (div. 1982). B.S. in Pharmacy, U. N.C., 1975. Staff pharmacist No. Hosp. Surry County, Mt. Airy, N.C., 1975-77; pharmacist The Owen Co., Houston, 1977—, dir. profl. resources, 1982-85. Mem. Am. Pharm. Assn., Am. Soc. Hosp. Pharmacists, Tex. Soc. Hosp. Pharmacists, N.C. Pharm. Assn. Republican. Baptist. Avocations: running; knife collecting; reading. Home: 10805 Benbrook Dr Dallas TX 75228 Office: The Owen Co 9800 Centre Pkwy Suite 1100 Houston TX 75237

SHOFNER, JERRELL HARRIS, history educator; b. Haslet, Tex., Jan. 30, 1929; s. Homer Harris Shofner and Dora Mae (Taylor) Stephens; m. Catherine Helen Stefonetti, Aug. 27, 1955 (div.); m. Shirley Anne Hazlett, Oct. 3, 1981; children—Charles, Michele. B.S., Fla. State U., 1960, M.S., 1961, Ph.D., 1963. Asst. prof. history Ga. So. Coll., Statesboro, 1963-64, Tex. Woman's U., Denton, 1964-67, U. Fla.-Gainesville, 1967-68, Fla. State U., Tallahassee, 1968-72; prof. history, chmn. dept. U. Central Fla., Orlando, 1972—. Author: Nor Is It Over Yet, 1974; History of Jefferson County, 1976; Daniel Ladd, 1978; Orlando: City Beautiful, 1984; History of Jackson County, 1985. Recipient Weyerhauser prize Forest Hist. Soc., 1975. Mem. So. Hist. Assn., Fla. Hist. Soc. (Rembert W. Patrick prize, 1974, 76, Arthur W. Thompson prize 1966, 68, 76, 78, 79), Phi Beta Kappa. Democrat. Home: 202 S Hampton Ave Orlando FL 32803 Office: Dept History U Central Fla PO Box 25000 Orlando FL 32816

SHOJI, HIROMU, orthopedic surgeon, educator; b. Chiba-Ken, Japan; grad. Coll. Gen. Edn., 1959, U. Tokyo, grad. Faculty of Medicine, 1964. Intern, U. Tokyo Hosp., 1964-65, resident in orthopedic surgery, 1965-67; resident in surgery Bklyn. Cumberland Med. Center, 1967-68, N.Y. U. Med. Center, 1968-69; bone tumor clinic fellow Meml. Sloan-Kettering Med. Center, N.Y.C., 1969-70; orthopedic fellow Hosp. for Spl. Surgery, N.Y.C., 1971-72; resident orthopedic surgery Bowman Gray Med. Sch., Winston-Salem, N.C., 1973-74; practice medicine specializing in orthopedic surgery, New Orleans, 1976—; mem. staff Charity Hosp., Hotel Dieu Hosp., Children's Hosp., Jo Ellem Smith Meml. Hosp., Mercy Hosp.; assoc. prof. dept. orthopedic surgery La. State U. Med. Center, 1976-80, prof., 1980—; asst. prof. dept. orthopedic surgery U. Calif., Davis, 1974-76; civilian cons. David Grant Meml. Hosp., Travis AFB, Calif., 1974-76. Diplomate Am. Bd. Orthopedic Surgery (examiner). Mem. Am. Acad. Orthopedic Surgeons, Japanese Orthopedic Assn., Orthopedic Research Soc., Japanese Soc. for Connective Tissue Research, Japanese Rehab. Assn., La. State Med. Soc., Am. Orthopedic Assn., La. Orthopedic Assn., So. Med. Assn., AMA, Nat. Acad. Sci., Am. Rheumatism Assn., Internat. Soc. for Orthopedics and Traumatology. Contbr. numerous articles on orthopedic surgery to med. jours.; patentee orthopedic devices. Office: 1542 Tulane Ave New Orleans LA 70112

SHOLARS, MICHAEL WAYNE, exploration geologist; b. Crockett, Tex.; s. Jack Wayne and June Lee (Gibson) S.; m. Dianna Dee McGee, Sept. 10, 1976; children—Kimberly Lynn, Sherman Wayne. B.S., U. Houston, 1977. Geologist, Indexgeo and Assocs., Houston, 1978-80, Ada Exco, Houston, 1980-82; geologist, geophysicist Mark Producing Co., Houston, 1982-83, Ballard Exploration Co., Houston, 1983-84, Bechtel Exploration Co., Houston, 1984—; cons. in field. Served with USN, 1969-73, Vietnam. Recipient Presdl. Sports award Pres. Carter, 1980. Mem. Soc. Profl. Well Log Analysts, Am. Assn. Petroleum Geologists, Houston Geol. Soc. Republican. Avocations: diving, shooting. Home: 6985 Ashburn St Houston TX 77061 Office: Bechtel Exploration 3050 S Post Oak St Suite 1740 Houston TX 77056

SHOLTESS, CALVIN DORREL, manufacturing company executive; b. Longdale, Okla., Jan. 10, 1926; s. Verden D. and Harriet Opal S.; m. Frances L. Moreno, Aug. 8, 1947; children—Diana, Janet, Debra, Denise. B.S.M.E., U. Tex., 1950. with Hughes Tool Co., successively v.p. indsl. products sales, Dallas, sr. v.p. Europe, Middle East, Africa ops., London, div. pres., chief exec. officer Hughes Tool div., Houston, corp. exec. v.p., dir. Served to lt. USNR, 1943-46. Recipient Disting. Grad. award U. Tex., 1984. Mem. Am. Petroleum Inst., Am. Soc. Metals, Ind. Petroleum Assn., Internat. Assn. Drilling Contracts, Houston Engring. and Sci. Soc., Petroleum Equipment Suppliers Assn., Can. Inst. Mining and Metallurgy, NOMADS, Houston C. of C. Methodist. Clubs: Petroleum, Houston, Warick, Rotary, Brae-Burn; Chaparral (Dallas). Office: 6500 Texas Commerce Tower Houston TX 77002*

SHOMO, SARAH JANE, educator, small business owner; b. Harrisonburg, Va., Apr. 11, 1956; d. James Evell and Allie Lou Etta (Hoskins) S. B.S. with distinction in Geology, James Madison U., 1978; M.S., U. N.C., 1982. Field geologist Champlin Petroleum Co., Jackson, Miss., 1981; instr. geology James Madison U., Harrisonburg, Va., 1980-82; owner, mgr. Ceramics n' Things, Harrisonburg, 1983—; instr. earth scis. Spotswood High Sch., Penn Laird, Va., 1984—. Instr. ceramics Va. Mennonite Retirement Community, Harrisonburg, 1983—. Recipient Leadership award Harrisonburg Daily News-Record, 1974; teaching fellow, U. N.C., 1979-80; named Outstanding Young Women of Am., 1984. Methodist. Home: Route 1 Box 152 Keezletown VA 22832 Office: Ceramics n' Things 20 W Johnson St Harrisonburg VA 22801

SHONKWILER, RONALD WESLEY, mathematician, educator; b. Chgo., Feb. 20, 1942; s. George Wesley and Mary (Cauble) S.; m. Cynthia Jeness. B.S., Calif. State Poly. U., 1964; M.S., U. Colo., 1967, Ph.D., 1970. Aero. engr. U.S. Naval Ordnance Lab., Corona, Calif., 1964-66; teaching assoc. U. Colo., Boulder, 1964-70; asst. prof. math. Ga. Inst. Tech., Atlanta, 1970-76, assoc. prof., 1976—. Scoutmaster, Atlanta council Boy Scouts Am., 1971-75. Mem. Am. Math. Soc., Soc. Math. Biology. Home: 329 Robinhood Rd Atlanta GA 30309 Office: Ga Inst Tech Dept Math Atlanta GA 30332

SHOOB, MARVIN H., judge; b. Walterboro, S.C., Feb. 23, 1923; s. Michael Louis and Lena (Steinberg) S.; m. Janice Paradies, Nov. 14, 1979; children—Michael, Wendy. J.D., U. Ga., 1948. Bar: Ga. 1948. Ptnr., Brown & Shobb, Atlanta, 1949-55, Phillips, Johnson & Shoob, Atlanta, 1955-56, Shoob, McLain & Merritt, Atlanta, 1956-79; judge U.S. Dist. Ct., Atlanta, 1979—; chmn. Juvenile Ct. Com., 1964-70; mem. Ga. State Bar Grievance Tribunal, 1975-79; chmn. Ga. State Bar Fed. Legislation Com., 1977-79; guest lectr. Continuing Legal Edn., Athens, Ga., 1975-77. Chmn. 5th Dist. Democratic Exec. Com., 1974-76. Mem. Phi Eta Sigma, Phi Kappa Phi. Jewish. Office: US District Court 1921 U S Courthouse 75 Spring St SW Atlanta GA 30303

SHOOK, CAROLINE STUART, training and education program coordinator, consultant; b. Portsmouth, Va., Oct. 1, 1953; d. Clifton Augustus and Frances Caroline (Chesson) S. B.S., Va. Poly. Inst. and State U., 1975, M.A., 1976, postgrad., 1983—. Cert. tchr., Va. Sci. tchr. Roanoke Co. Schs., Salem, Va., 1976-77; edn. specialist Marine Corps Inst., Washington, 1977-80, Comptroller of Currency, Washington, 1980-81; cons. Alexandria, Va., 1981—; tng. and edn. coordinator Fed. Emergency Mgmt. Agy., Washington, 1981-85; employee devel. specialist Dept. of Def., 1986—; v.p. Class Acts, Inc., Alexandria, 1982—. Vol. Partnerships in Edn. Program. Mem. Am. Soc. for Tng. and Devel., Phi Delta Kappa. Democrat. Roman Catholic. Office: Dept of Def Office Insp Gen Personnel Pentagon Arlington VA 22202

SHOOK, HAROLD GRAHAM, career, management consultant; b. Portland, Oreg., Apr. 25, 1920; s. Harold Edgar and Nellie Blanche (Graham) S.; A.A., San Francisco Jr. Coll., 1940; B.A., U. Calif.-Berkeley, 1955; M.A. in Internat. Affairs, George Washington U., 1967; m. Rae B. Mayfield, Feb. 13, 1943 (dec. Apr. 1972); children—Stephen J., Michael G., David C., William M.; m. Marilyn J. Berger, Nov. 11, 1972. Commd. 2d lt. U.S. Air Force, 1941, advanced through grades to col., 1956; comdr. fighter squadrons, group Wing and Air Div., 1944-66; combat tour, Europe, 1944, Korea, 1953-54; commdr. USAF Instrument Instr. Pilot. Sch., 1949-52; staff officer USAF Hdqrs. and Joint Chiefs of Staff, 1957-60; ret., 1968; asso., research dir. Internat. Research Inst., McLean, Va., 1968-78; v.p. Crystal Mgmt. Services, McLean, 1968-76; pres. Life Mgmt. Services, Inc., McLean, 1976—; mgmt. devel. and career cons.; cons. to govt. and bus. Mem. Republican Nat. Com. Decorated Legion of Merit, D.F.C., Air medal with 18 oak leaf clusters (U.S.); Fourragère (Belgium); Croix de Guerre (France). Mem. Am. Soc. Tng. and Devel., World Future Soc., Am. Mgmt. Assn., Air Force Assn. Republican (mem. Nat. Com.). Episcopalian. Club: Masons. Editorial bd. Ency. Phys. Sci. and Tech. Home: McLean House Apt 1020 6800 Fleetwood Rd McLean VA 22101 Office: 6825 Redmond Dr McLean VA 22101

SHOPTAW, MARILEE SUE, hospital nursing administrator; b. Rolla, Mo., Jan. 13, 1937; d. Howard Mathew and Opal Irene (Swanner) S. B.S.N., Vanderbilt U., 1960; M.B.A., Miss. Coll., 1982. Adminstrv. supr. Methodist Hosp., Houston, 1964-71; nursing dir. area II, Cleve. Clinic, 1971-77; dir. nursing Miss. Baptist Med. Ctr., Jackson, 1977—. Active Miss. affiliate Am. Heart Assn., Jackson, 1977—. Named to Outstanding Young Women Am., U.S. Jaycees, 1972. Mem. Miss. Nurses Assn. (chmn. coms. 1977—), Am. Nurses Assn. (cert. advanced nursing adminstr.), Miss. Hosp. Assn. Soc. Nursing Service Adminstrs. (bd. dirs. 1982—), Am. Hosp. Assn. Soc. Nursing Service Adminstrs., Alpha Omicron Pi Alumnae Assn. Republican. Presbyterian. Avocations: piano; flute; swimming; pro football. Home: 5846 Club View Dr Jackson MS 39211 Office: Miss Bapt Med Ctr 1225 N State St Jackson MS 39202

SHORE, BETTY JOYCE, constrn. co. exec.; b. Hood County, Tex., Aug. 31, 1936; d. L.B. and Mirom Allen (Fairman) Collins; student Del Mar Jr. Coll., 1968-69; m. Edward Earl Shore, Oct. 5, 1963; children—Desiree Babet, Scott Holiday, Jeanne Annette, Walter Joachim, Erich Edward. Bookkeeper, Hoffpower Anderson Co., Ft. Worth, 1960-62; cost acct. R.W. Gibbins Inc., Ft. Worth, 1963-65; office mgr. Orval Hall Excavating Inc., Ft. Worth, 1965-73; v.p. M.A. Vinson Constrn. Co., Inc., Ft. Worth, 1973—. Mem. Nat. Assn. Women in Constrn. (pres. Ft. Worth chpt.). Democrat. Roman Catholic. Home: 4701 Williams Spring Rd Fort Worth TX 76135 Office: 6910 Midway Rd PO Box 18520 Fort Worth TX 76118

SHORT, BYRON ELLIOTT, educator; b. Putnam, Tex., Dec. 29, 1901; s. Samuel W. and Florence Gertrude (Sublett) S.; B.S., U. Tex., 1926, M.S., 1930; M.M.E., Cornell U., 1936, Ph.D., 1939; m. Mary Jo Fitzgerald, June 1, 1937; children—Mary Aileen (Mrs. James L. Gauntt), Byron Elliott, Jr. Cadet engr. Tex Co., summers 1926-27, mech. engr., summers 1928-30, instr. U. Tex., 1926-29, asst. prof., 1929-36, charge heat-power, fluid mechanics lab. 1930-65, mech. engr., summers 1932-36, 40, asso. prof., 1936-39, prof. mech. engring., 1939-73, prof. emeritus, 1973—, chmn. dept., 1945-47, 51-53, acting dean Coll. Engring., 1948-49; teaching fellow Cornell U., 1935-36; cons. Oak Ridge Nat. Lab., research participant, 1956, 57. Fellow ASME (life, chmn. Tex. sect. 1938-39, mem. heat transfer and power test code com.); mem. ASHRAE (life, asso. editor Databook 1953, 55), Am. Soc. Engring. Edn., SAR, Huguenot Soc. Tex. (state pres. 1983-85), Sigma Xi, Tau Beta Pi, Phi Kappa Phi, Pi Tau Sigma. Clubs: Masons (33 deg.), KT, Shriners. Author: Flow, Measurement and Pumping of Fluids, 1934; Engineering Thermodynamics (with H.L. Kent, B.F. Treat), 1953; Pressure Enthalpy Charts (with H.L. Kent and H.A. Walls), 1970. Editor: Design Volume, Am. Soc. Refrigerating Engrs. Databook, 10th edit. Contbr. articles to engring. jours. Home: 502 E 32d St Austin TX 78705

SHORT, JOHN NYE, political science educator; b. Gilberton, Pa., Sept. 4, 1948; s. John Clark and Martha Mae (Nye) S.; m. Caryn Elyse Cleveland, Dec. 8, 1950; children—Jefferson, Tiffany, Meghann. B.A., Pa. State U., 1970; M.A., SUNY-Albany, 1971; D. of Arts, Lehigh U., 1977. Lectr. Texas A & M U., College Station, 1975-77; asst. prof. U. Ark.-Monticello, 1977-82, assoc. prof., head dept. social and behavioral scis., 1982—. Grantee Nat. Endowment Humanities 1982-84; recipient Danforth Coll. Project Fund award, 1982, Danforth Assoc., Danforth Found., 1981-86. Mem. Am. Polit. Sci. Assn., Ark. Polit. Sci. Assn., ACLU. Democrat. Methodist. Avocations: community theater; movies. Home: 441 Meadowview Monticello AR 71655 Office: U Ark-Monticello Dept Social and Behavioral Scis Monticello AR 71655

SHORT, PAULA MYRICK, educator; b. Pinehurst, N.C., Feb. 25, 1945; d. John Howard and Ruby Pauline (Fields) Myrick; B.A., U. N.C., Greensboro, 1967, M.Ed., 1970; Ph.D., U. N.C., Chapel Hill, 1983; m. Rick Jay Short, Feb. 2, 1980; children—Jeffrey Brent, John Ryan, Rick Jay. Tchr., Greensboro (N.C.) City Schs., 1967-68, Orange County Schs., Hillsborough, N.C., 1968-69; media coordinator Alamance County Schs., Mebane, N.C., 1970-71; tchr. Neal Jr. High Sch., Durham, N.C., 1971-74, Chewning Jr. High Sch., Durham, 1977-79; system level supr. Chapel Hill-Carrboro City Schs., Chapel Hill, N.C., 1979-80; edni. cons. div. ednl. media N.C. Dept. Public Instrn., Raleigh, 1980-82; research asst. Southeastern Regional Council Ednl. Improvement, Research Triangle Park, N.C., 1982-83; co-prin. investigator research grant on discipline, 1983-85; asst. prof. ednl. adminstrn. and supervision Tex. Woman's U., 1984—. Chmn. day care com. Chapel Hill Service League, 1977-78. Delta Kappa Gamma state scholar 1982. Mem. N.C. Assn. Sch. Librarians (state pres. 1981—), Assn. Supervision and Curriculum Devel., N.C. Assn. Sch. Adminstrs., N.C. Media Council (pres. 1982), Delta Kappa Gamma, Pi Lambda Theta, Phi Delta Kappa, Methodist. Home: 1701 Gentilly Dr Shreveport LA 71105

SHORT, R. E., JR., rice and soybean processing company executive; b. 1928; married. Vice chmn. bd. Riceland Foods, Inc., Stuttgart, Ark., from 1972, now chmn. bd., dir.; chmn. Ark. Rice Growers Coop. Assn. Office: Riceland Foods Inc 2120 Park Ave Stuttgart AR 72160*

SHORTAL, TERENCE MICHAEL, systems company executive; b. St. Louis, Oct. 13, 1937; s. Harold Leo and Catherine Margaret S.; B.S. in Elec. Engring., U. Mo., 1961; M.S., U.S. Naval Postgrad. Sch., 1966; grad. program execs., Carnegie-Mellon U., 1979; m. Linda Margaret Elias, May 29, 1965; children—Jennifer Meer, Bradley Alexander. Commd. ensign U.S. Navy, 1961, advanced through grades to capt., 1980; service in Vietnam; asst. officer in charge Engring. Duty Officer Sch., Vallejo, Calif., 1974-77; ship engring. mgr. AEGIS shipbldg. project Naval Sea Systems Command, Washington, 1977-79, tech. dir. DDGX Project, 1979-81; ret., 1981; v.p., dir. Kastle Systems Inc., 1981—. Trustee Cathedral Choral Soc., Washington; mem. of vestry St. John's Episcopal Ch., McLean, Va.; bd. dirs. Langley Sch., McLean. Decorated Meritorious Service medal (2), Navy Commendation medal (2). Mem. Am. Soc. Naval Engrs. (Flagship Sect. award 1979), IEEE (br. award 1961), Assn. Energy Engrs., Sigma Xi, Phi Kappa Theta. Club: Langley (McLean, Va.). Home: 858 Canal Dr McLean VA 22102 Office: 1501 Wilson Blvd Arlington VA 22209

SHORTER, EDWARD SWIFT, artist, museum dir. emeritus; b. Columbus, Ga., July 2, 1902; s. Dr. James Hargraves and Elizabeth (Swift) S.; A.B., Mercer U., 1924; student Corcoran Sch. Art, 1924-28, Boston Museum Sch., 1925, Fontainebleau (France), with Andre Lhote (Paris), Wayman Adams, Hugh Breckenridge; LL.D., Mercer U., 1971; m. Mildred Watts, Oct. 3, 1953. Mem. staff Corcoran Sch. Art, 1930; exec. dir., also instr. art Columbus Mus. Arts and Crafts, 1952-70; now cons. in the arts Columbus Mus. and Hist. Columbus Found.; past lectr. U. Ga. Extension; represented in museums in cities throughout U.S., including: Atlanta, Montgomery, Macon, Columbus, Savannah (all Ga.), N.Y.C., Washington, New Orleans, Waco (Tex.), Ft. Hays (Kans.). Former trustee Boys' Club, Shorter Coll.; trustee Symphony Orch., Ga. Mus. Art (Athens), Ga. Hist. and Fine Arts Commn.; former bd. dirs. Atlanta Art Inst., Columbus Symphony, Brookstone Sch.; bd. dirs. Historic Columbus Found. Corcoran Art scholar, Paris, 1931; recipient Algenon Sydney Sullivan award Mercer U., Distinguished Alumnus award, 1977; Gari Melchers medal Artists Fellowship Inc. Mem. Shorter Coll. Hall of Fame. Mem. S.E. Art Mus. Dirs. Assn. (past dir.), Assn. Am. Museums (trustee), Am. Fedn. Arts, Ga. Hist. Soc., Artists Equity Assn., Am. Artists Profl. League, Nat. Art Club, Nat. Audubon Soc., Sigma Alpha Epsilon. Baptist. Clubs: Green Island Country, Big Eddy, Candun; Salamagundi (N.Y.C.). Home: 6001 Green Island Dr Columbus GA 31904 Office: 1251 Wynnton Rd Columbus GA 31906

SHORTER, WALTER WYATT, forest products company executive; b. 1932; B.S. in Chemistry, Va. Mil. Inst., 1953; M.S. in Pulp and Paper Tech., U. Maine, 1957; married. With Union Camp Corp., 1957-78, v.p., resident mgr., until 1978; pres. Mac Millan Bloedel Inc., Pine Hill, Ala., 1978—, also dir.; dir. First Ala. Bank of Montgomery, First Ala. Bancshares, Inc., Jenkins Brick Co., Fourdrinier Kraft Bd. Group. Bd. visitors Duke U. Sch. Forestry. Served to capt. USMC, 1953-58. Mem. Paper Industry Mgmt. Assn. (past pres., now trustee), Ala. C. of C. (past pres., now trustee), Am. Paper Inst. (dir.). Office: Mac Millan Bloedel Inc Hwy 10 Pine Hill AL 36769

SHOSS, SAMUEL, ophthalmologist, educator; b. Houston, Aug. 2, 1937; s. Max and Becky (Applebaum) S.; m. Karen Marilyn Kohner, June 29, 1963; children—Ronald M., Ricki Jeanette, Robert L. M.D., Tulane U., 1962. Diplomate Am. Bd. Ophthalmology. Intern, Univ. Hosp., Cleve., 1962-63; surgeon USPHS, Washington, 1963-65; resident Baylor Coll. Med. Sch., 1965-68; practice medicine specializing in ophthalmology, Houston, 1968—; clin. asst. prof. Baylor Med. Sch., Houston, 1968—. Mem. Houston Ophthal. Soc., Tex. Ophthal. Soc., Tex. Med. Assn., Am. Intraocular and Implant Soc., Alpha Omega Alpha; fellow Am. Acad. Ophthalmology. Office: 2616 South Loop W #320 Houston TX 77054

SHOTLAND, LAWRENCE MARTIN, geophysicist; b. Bridgeport, Conn., June 13, 1947; s. Edwin and Marianne (Hess) S. B.A. in Psychology, Math., Johns Hopkins U., 1970; tchr. certificate U. No. Colo., 1972; M.S. in Geology, Geophysics, U. Houston, 1983. Exploration technologist Amoco Prodn., Houston, 1978-79; analyst GeoQuest, Houston, 1979-80; sr. analyst Seismograph Service Corp., Casper, Wy., 1980-81; geophysicist Prakla Seismos, Houston, 1982-83, Arco Exploration, Dallas, 1983-85; ind. cons., 1985—. Bd. dirs. Tourette Syndrome Assn., Dallas, 1985—. Recipient Cert. Merit Wash. Acad. Scis., 1965. Mem. Soc. Exploration Geophysicists (assoc.), Am. Assn. Petroleum Geologists, Dallas Geophysical Soc., Geophysical Soc. Houston, Houston Geol. Soc. Avocations: camping, hiking. Home: 418 E Indian Spring Dr Silver Spring MD 20901 Office: PO Box 22262 Houston TX 77227

SHOTZ, FREDERICK ARTHUR, clinical psychotherapist; b. Phila., Jan. 29, 1949; s. Stanley and Suzanne Helen (Wolf) S.; m. Linda Susan Fleischman, Sept. 18, 1973. B.A. in Psychology and Biology, LaSalle Coll., 1971; M.S. summa cum laude in Psychology, Nova U., 1975; Ph.D. in Clin. Psychology, Calif. Coast U., 1983. Founder, trainer, crisis counselor HELP of Phila., 1969-70; crisis counselor Contact Counseling Ctr., Charlotte, N.C., 1971-72; assoc. dir., dir. tng. Miami (Fla.) Crisis Ctr. Switchboard, 1972-73; psychotherapist, clin. dir. Counseling Assocs., Plantation, Fla., 1975—; adj. prof. U. Miami, 1983—; radio commentator. Author: A Comprehensive Training Manual for Telephone Crisis Counselors, 1973. Donor Palm Beach Festival Arts, Broward Art Guild; lectr. Broward Community Coll. Pa. Acad. scholar, 1966-70, Walton Found. scholar, 1966-67; United Methodist Ch. fellow, 1972; recipient Phila. Good Samaritan award, 1968, Internat. Youth in Achievement award, 1981. Mem. Fla. Assn. Psychologists, Psychotherapists and Counselors (exec. sec.), Inst. Creative Art Therapies (bd. dirs.) Fla. Sunset Psychol. Assn. (chmn. bd. dirs.), Am. Personnel and Guidance Assn., Assn. Humanistic Psychology; Am. Assn. Counselor Edn. and Supervision, Sex Edn. and Info. Council U.S. Democrat. Jewish. Office: 7420 NW 5th St Suite 102 Plantation FL 33317

SHOTZ, LINDA FLEISCHMAN, clinical psychotherapist; b. Asbury Park, N.J., Aug. 16, 1949; d. Erwin Lewis and Ruth (Koegel) Fleischman; m. Frederick A. Shotz, Sept. 18, 1973. A.A., Miami Dade Jr. Coll., 1969; B.A. cum laude, U. Fla., 1971; M.S. summa cum laude, Nova U., 1975; Ph.D., Calif. Coast U., 1985. Social worker Div. Family Services, Miami, Fla., 1971-73; clin. psychotherapist Counseling Assocs., Davie, Fla., 1974—; exec. dir. Intimacy Disorders Found., Inc., Davie, 1983—; clin. dir. Family and Divorce Mediation Ctr. Davie, 1983—; registered art, sex and child therapist, 1975—. Author: (with others) Training Crisis Counselors. Fellow Menninger Found., 1983, Am. U., Washington, 1985. Fellow Internat. Council Sex Edn. and Counseling; mem. Am. Assn. Sex Educators, Counselors, and Therapists, Soc. for Sci. Study of Sex, Am. Assn. Counseling and Devel., Am. Assn. of Artists-Therapists, Am. Art Therapy Assn. Avocations: photography, drawing, painting, sculpture. Office: Counseling Assocs 4801 S University Dr Davie FL 33328

SHOUMATE, BELFORD WASHINGTON, architect; b. Aberdeen, Ohio, June 5, 1903; s. William Francis and Lora Dean (Insko) S.; m. Beatrice Stanford Owens, Aug. 18, 1937; children—William Stanford, Thomas Stanford. B. Arch., U. Pa., 1929. Registered architect, Fla. Owner, prin. Belford Shoumate Architect and Assocs., Palm Beach, Fla., 1937—; AIA appointee Nat. Preservation Hist. Bldgs. Mem. Palm Beach Civic Assn.; participant landmark and preservation activities. Recipient Efficiency award Army Civilian Dept. Engring., 1941-43. Mem. Beta Theta Pi Alumni Club. Democrat. Episcopalian. Avocations: antique cars; sailing; photography; old houses. Home and Office: 222 Phipps Plaza Palm Beach FL 33480

SHOWAH, LINDA CASTLEBERRY, insurance company adminstr.; b. Corpus Christi, Dec. 24, 1952; d. Charles King and Barbara Jean (Kinney) Castleberry; m. Joseph Showah; children—Jeffrey Brian, Justin Bradley. B.A. in English cum laude, Belhaven Coll., 1976. Edn. adminstr. So. Farm Bur. Life Ins. Co., Jackson, Miss., 1976-79, supr., 1979-80, mgr. edn., 1980—. Neighborhood chmn. Am. Cancer Soc., 1985, Easter Seals, 1983. Mem. Am. Soc. Tng. and Devel. (pres. 1984-85, awards chmn. 1985—, program chmn. 1983-84). Republican. Baptist. Avocations: tennis; needlework; reading. Home: 6112 Woodhaven Rd Jackson MS 39206 Office: So Farm Bur Life Ins 1401 Livingston Ln Jackson MS 39213

SHOWALTER, JERRY NEWBERN, bookseller; b. Danville, Va., Sept. 21, 1940; s. Samuel James and Muriel Harriet (Newbern) S. B.A., U. Va., 1964. Tchr., Greene County pub. schs., Stanardsville, Va., 1964-67; dir. Newcomb Hall Bookstore, U. Va., Charlottesville, 1967—; mem. adv. bd. Ctr. for the Book, Library of Congress, Washington, 1980—. Editor (with others) A Handbook on Bookselling, 1980. Contbr. articles to profl. jours. Mem. Am. Booksellers Assn. (bd. dirs. 1976-85, treas. 1982-84), Va. Coll. Stores Assn. (pres. 1976, judge for book award 1982-85), Nat. Assn. Coll. Stores (chmn. gen. book com. 1981-86). Presbyterian. Avocation: rare book collector. Home: PO Box 84 Ivy VA 22945 Office: Newcomb Hall Bookstore U Va Charlottesville VA 22901

SHOWER, ROBERT WESLEY, business executive; b. Harvey, Ill., Sept. 5, 1937; s. Glenn Wesley and Chrissie Irene (Ford) S.; B.S., U. Tulsa, 1960; P.M.D., Harvard Business Sch., 1972; m. Sandra Marie Stough, June 27, 1959; children—David Wesley, Lynece Marie. Sr. auditor Arthur Andersen & Co., Tulsa, 1960-64; with The Williams Cos., Tulsa, 1964—, asst. v.p., 1968-69, v.p. adminstrn., 1969-71, v.p., treas., 1971, v.p. fin. 1971-73, sr. v.p. fin., 1973-77, exec. v.p. fin. and adminstrn., dir., 1977—. Bd. dirs. Jr. Achievement of Greater Tulsa, Magic Empire council Girl Scouts U.S.; trustee River Parks Authority. Mem. Am. Inst. C.P.A.s, Okla. Soc. C.P.A.s, Fin. Execs. Inst., Am. Petroleum Inst., Lambda Chi Alpha, Delta Sigma Pi. Club: Southern Hills Country (Tulsa). Home: 8757 S Richmond St Tulsa OK 74137 Office: One Williams Center Tulsa OK 74172

SHOWS, CLARENCE OLIVER, dentist; b. nr. Brantley, Ala., Oct. 17, 1920; s. John Oliver and Cora (Nichols) S.; student Wis. State Coll., 1946-47; D.D.S., Northwestern U., 1951; m. Rachel LaRene Price, July 24, 1943; children—Toni Cherie, Kristin Clare Shows Ball, Bradley Scott, Gregory Norman, Jeffery

Ryan. Individual practice dentistry, Valparaiso, Fla., 1951-53, Pensacola, 1953—. Mem. Pensacola Art Assn.; past pres. Escambia County unit Am. Cancer Soc., now bd. dirs. Fla. unit, also hon. life mem.; mem. Eagle Scout Bd. Rev., Escambia County. Served with USCG, 1939-46. Fellow Royal Soc. Health, Internat. Coll. Dentists, Internat. Acad. Gen. Dentistry, Am. Coll. Dentists; mem. Am. Acad. Gen. Dentistry (master, past pres. Fla. unit), Internat. Orthodontic Assn., Internat. Acad. Preventive Medicine, Am. Orthodontic Soc., Gulf Breeze C. of C. (past pres.), Fla. Soc. Dentistry for Children (past pres.), Acad. Gen. Dentistry, ADA, AAAS, Am. Profl. Practice Assn., L.D. Pankey Dental Found., Fedn. Dental Internat., Am. Assn. Clin. Hypnosis, Northwestern U. Alumni Assn., Navy League (life), G.V. Black Soc. (life), Pensacola Jr. Coll. Found. (life), Psi Omega. Democrat. Presbyterian (elder). Clubs: Masons, Shriners, Jesters, Elks; Pensacola (pres.), Exchange. Home: 516 Navy Cove Blvd Gulf Breeze FL 32561 Office: 3090 Navy Blvd Pensacola FL 32505

SHRECK, DWIGHT C., optometrist; b. Thomas, Okla., Nov. 28, 1956; s. Leo and Sylvia (Jackson) S. D. in optometry, So. Coll. Optometry, 1982. Practice optometry, Weatherford, Okla., 1982—. Mem. Western Okla. Optometric Soc., Am. Optometric Assn., Nat. Fedn. Independent Bus., Weatherford C. of C., Phi Theta Upsilon. Democrat. Mem. Assembly of God. Lodge: Kiwanis. Avocations: water skiing; horseback riding; leathercraft; auto restoration. Office: Dr Dwight C Shreck 1104 E Main Box 829 Weatherford OK 73096

SHRIVER, GREGORY B., designer and builder theatrical equipment and production studios, audio engineer, consultant; b. Norfolk, Va., June 28, 1954; s. Donald Woods and Peggy Ann (Leu) S.; m. Bonnie Lynn Klipple, July 3, 1973; children—Joyce Gwendolyn, Nicholas Dimitri. Research asst. dept. anthropology N.C. State U., 1970, asst., tech. dir. student drama program, 1971-73; media asst. cultural arts div. N.C. Dept. Pub. Instrn., 1971; various indsl. positions 1973; designer, audio engr., constrn. mgr. Stage & Studio Constrn. Services, Raleigh, N.C., 1973—, now chief exec. officer; lectr. 61st Audio Engring. Soc. N.Y.C. Conv., 1978, New Music Conv., 1982. Prin. works include (audio studios) The Basement, N.Y.C., The Big Apple, N.Y.C., Greene St. Rec. Ltd., N.Y.C., others; (video and film shoots) The Phillip Glass Ensemble at Sadler's Wells Theatre, London, The Sammy Kahn Spl. Concord Inn, N.Y.C.; (concert tours and prodns.) The Phillip Glass Ensemble, U.S.A. and Europe, 1975-82, Harry Belefonte European Tour, 1977, Mike Oldfield Tour Europe, 1979; (opera and dramatic theatre) Einstein on the Beach European Tour, 1975, E.O.B. at the Met, N.Y.C., 1973; various nightclubs and halls in N.Y.C. and Raleigh; (theatre and concert halls) The Met. Opera, Lincoln Ctr., N.Y.C., numerous other in U.S.A., The Astoria Theatre, Royal Festival Hall, London, Pavillion de Baltard, Threatre de Champs de Elysees, Paris, numerous others throughout Europe. Mem. Audio Engring. Soc. Democrat. Presbyterian. Avocations: Sound systems; gardening; reading. Office: Stage & Studio Construction Services 212 E Franklin St Raleigh NC 27604

SHROADS-SCHULTZ, CRYSTAL VIRGINIA, science educator; b. Joliet, Ill., Mar. 21, 1949; d. William Myron and Ada (Baldus) Shroads; m. Edward Anson Schultz, Aug. 13, 1977. B.S. in Biology, U. Miami, 1971, M.S. in Biology, 1974. Teaching asst. biology U. Miami, Coral Gables, Fla., 1971-72, 1972-73; tchr. marine biology Gulliver Acad., Coral Gables, 1973—, head sci. dept., 1980—; sec., treas. Tri-Beta Biol. Hon. Soc., 1970-71. Mem. Internat. Oceanographic Found., Tropical Audubon, Internat. Wildlife. Republican. Lutheran. Home: 241 Buttonwood Dr Key Biscayne FL 33149 Office: Gulliver Acad Inc 12595 Red Rd Coral Gables FL 33156

SHROYER, PATRICIA FAYE, financial planner; b. Hollidaysburg, Pa., Mar. 24, 1938; d. John Jacob and Mabel Kathryn (Lafferty) S.; m. Joseph Fletcher Walls, III, June 18, 1960 (div. Apr. 1964). Student Pa. State U., 1960; B.A., Temple U., 1967; postgrad. Drexel U., 1968, U. Minn., 1970, Tallahassee Community Coll., 1975, Fla. A&M U., 1976. Real estate broker, Tex.; agt. IRS. Tax shelter specialist Travelers Ins. Co., Balt., 1977; equity sales supr. Lincoln Nat. Sales Corp., Camp Hill, Pa., 1978; sales cons. U.S. Home, Inc., Houston, 1979-81; sales cons. Stuckey Home, Inc., Houston, 1981, Pre-paid Legal Services, Inc.; fin. planning cons., Houston, 1982—; data processing cons., polit. candidates, 1981—. Bus. and Profl. Women's scholar, 1975. Mem. Internat. Assn. Fin. Planners, Data Processing Mgmt. Assn., Nat. Women's Polit. Caucus, Nat. Assn. Enrolled Agts., Mensa. Home: 8517 Hearth Dr Houston TX 77054

SHRUM, WESLEY MONROE, JR., sociology educator; b. Okmulgee, Okla., Dec. 27, 1953; s. Wesley Monroe and Kathryn Ann (Pitts) S. B.A. in Philosophy, English and Sociology, U. Kans.-Lawrence, 1977; M.A. in Sociology, Princeton U., 1980, Ph.D., 1982. Asst. prof. sociology La. State U., Baton Rouge, 1982—. Author: Organized Technology, 1985. Contbr. articles to profl. publs. Mem. Am. Sociol. Assn., So. Sociol. Assn., Soc. for Social Studies of Sci., Internat. Network for Social Network Analysts. Home: 415 W Parker 17 Baton Rouge LA 70808 Office: La State U Dept Sociology Baton Rouge LA 70803

SHUB, HARVEY ALLEN, surgeon; b. Bklyn., Oct. 28, 1942; s. Irving and Sara (Levin) S.; m. Susan Jayne Smith, Dec. 26, 1970; children—Carolyn, Todd. Student, NYU, 1960-61, 1964-65; B.S. in Zoology, Physics, U. Miami, 1964; M.D., U. Rome, Italy, 1971. Diplomate Am. Bd. Colon and Rectal Surgery. Intern, Beth Israel Med. Ctr., N.Y.C., 1971-72, resident in surgery, 1972-76; fellow in colon and rectal surgery, Muhlenberg Hosp., Plainfield, N.J., 1976-77; practice medicine specializing in colon and rectal surgery, Orlando, Fla., 1977—; mem. staff Fla. Hosp., Winter Park Meml. Hosp., Orlando Regional Med. Ctr., Lucerne Gen. Hosp., South Seminole Community Hosp.; clin. asst. prof. dept. family medicine U. South Fla., Tampa, 1982—. Chmn. pub. edn. com. Am. Cancer Soc. Orange County 1982—. Served to capt. M.C., USAR, 1971-77. Recipient Physician's Recognition award, AMA, 1976, 79, 81, 83. Fellow ACS, Am. Soc. Colon and Rectal Surgeons, Internat. Coll. Surgeons, Southeastern Surg. Congress; mem. AMA, Fla. Med. Assn. (council splty. medicine), Orange County Med. Assn., Piedmont Soc. Colon and Rectal Surgeons, Orange County Ostomy Assn. (med. adviser), Fla. Soc. Colon and Rectal Surgeons (sec.-treas. 1980-82, pres. 1983-84), Internat. Soc. U. Colon and Rectal Surgeons, Am. Soc. Gastrointestinal Enodoscopy, Internat. Soc. Univ. Colon and Rectal Surgeons, Am. Soc. Laser Medicine and Surgery, Soc. Am. Gastrointestinal Endoscopic Surgeons. Consulting editor Jour. Fla. Med. Assn.; contbr. articles to profl. jours. Home: 1224 Roxboro Rd Longwood FL 32750 Office: 308 Groveland St Orlando FL 32804

SHUBERT, BETH COHEN, social worker; b. Greencastle, Ind., Aug. 5, 1941; d. Louis David and Tina (Simon) Cohen; A.B., Oberlin Coll., 1962; M.S.W., U. Pitts., 1964; children—Nina, Jeffrey, Adam. Social worker Dorothea Dix Hosp., 1965, N.C. Correctional Center for Women, 1965-67; supr. Durham County Dept. Social Services, 1968-69; chief social worker Durham Rehab. Center, 1970-71; supr. field U. N.C. Sch. Social Work, Chapel Hill, 1970-71; dir. Child Abuse Prevention Program, Durham, N.C., 1976-79; family therapist Vance, Warren, Franklin, Granville Mental Health Program, Henderson, N.C., 1979-84; asst. pediatrics, social work edu. pediatric pulmonary ctr. U. Fla. Coll. Medicine, 1984—; adj. asst. prof. social work Fla. State U., 1984—; cons. N.C. Justice Acad., 1977-79. Mem. legis. task force Child Abuse and Neglect, State N.C., 1977-79; mem. bd. Triangle N.C. Multiple Sclerosis Found., 1970-74. Mem. Acad. Cert. Social Workers, Nat. Assn. Social Workers. Democrat. Jewish. Home: 2630 NW 47th Place Gainesville FL 32605 Office: Pediatric Pulmonary Ctr U Fla Coll Medicine Box J-296 JHMHC Gainesville FL 32610

SHUCK, RONALD MICHAEL, reservoir engineer, consultant; b. Albany, N.Y., Jan. 17, 1949; s. Richard Donald and Patricia Marjorie (Page) S.; m. Diane Breckeen, Aug. 23, 1973; 1 child, Amanda Elizabeth. B.S. in Biology, U. Tex.-Arlington, 1973; B.S. in Chem. Engring., U. Houston, 1977. Registered profl. engr., Tex. Reservoir engr. Exxon Co. U.S.A., Houston, 1977-79, Esso Middle East, Dharhran, Saudi Arabia, 1981-83; reservoir engr. DeGolyer & MacNaughton, Dallas, 1979-81, 83—, v.p., 1983—. Mem. Soc. Petroleum Engrs. (vice chmn. 1981-82), Am. Assn. Petroleum Geologists (assoc. mem.), Petroleum Engrs. Club (mem. scholarship com. 1983—). Republican. Club: Big —D— Little Birds (Dallas). Avocations: restoration, collection of classic Thunderbirds; water skiing; competitive running; triathlon. Home: 3840 Nantucket Dr Plano TX 75023 Office: DeGolyer & MacNaughton 400 One Energy Square Dallas TX 75206

SHUEY, THEODORE GEORGE, JR., insurance agency executive; b. Roanoke, Va., July 4, 1947; s. Theodore George and Mary Ellen (Long) S.; B.A. in History, Bridgewater Coll., 1969; M.Ed. (tuition grant), U. Va., 1974; m. Judith Hazel Lewis, June 21, 1969; children—Ellen Lewis, Theodore George III. Tchr., New Hope (Va.) Elementary Sch., 1969-73; asst. prin. Hugh Cassell Elementary Sch., Waynesboro, Va., 1973-74; asst. prin., tchr. New Hope Elementary Sch., 1974-77; pres. Cabinet Craft of Va., Inc., Staunton, 1978-80, Shenandoah Bldg. & Remodeling, Inc., 1979-80, Ted Shuey Enterprises, Inc., 1978—, Shuey Agy., Inc., 1980—. Res. policeman City of Staunton, Va., 1969-75. Served to capt. U.S. Army N.G., 1970—. Decorated Bronze Star, Army Commendation medal with oakleaf cluster, others. Mem. Augusta County, Va., Nat. edn. assns., N.C. Exec. Dirs. Assn., Nat. Security Council, Va. N.G. Assn. (pres., ins. adminstr. 1979—, Meritorious Service citation, Past President's award) N.G. Assn. U.S., Am. Def. Preparedness Assn., Phi Delta Kappa. Republican. Lutheran. Home: 511 Willoughby Ln Staunton VA 24401 Office: Middle River Dr Verona VA 24482

SHUFELT, BRIAN LEIGH, dentist; b. Aurora, Ill., Dec. 21, 1947; s. William Henry and Francis Irene (Weigerding) S.; m. Patricia Ann McQuaid, Aug. 9, 1975; children—Jennifer, Alyson, Sarah. B.S., Aurora U., 1968; B.S. in Dentistry, U. Ill.-Chgo., 1970, D.D.S., 1972. Dentist, Driscoll Found., Robstown, Tex., 1974-75; Corpus Christi State Sch., Tex., 1975-78; gen. practice dentistry, Corpus Christi, 1975—; cons. Corpus Christi State Sch., 1978—. Mem. council St. Marks Lutheran Ch., Corpus Christi, 1979—; adminstr. Dental Emergency Exchange, Corpus Christi, 1981—; nation chief YMCA Indian Guides/Princess, Corpus Christi, 1984-85; v.p. Corpus Christi Country Club Homeowners, 1984-85, pres., 1985—. Recipient Outstanding Service award Corpus Christi Sch. Dist., 1981; Leadership Corpus Christi award Corpus Christi C. of C., 1985. Mem. Nueces Valley Dental Assn. (chmn. dental health com. 1979-82, Meritorious Service award 1982), Tex. Dental Assn., ADA, Delta Sigma Delta (social chmn. 1970-72), Sigma Phi Alpha (hon.). Republican. Lutheran. Club: Corpus Christi Country. Lodge: Lions. Avocations: tennis; swimming. Home: 4817 Augusta Circle Corpus Christi TX 78413 Office: 5622 Everhart Rd Corpus Christi TX 78411

SHUFF, THOMAS KILBY, III, data processing manager and consultant; b. Georgetown, Ky., Jan. 16, 1934; s. Thomas Kilby, Jr. and Mary McPherson (Matthews) S.; m. Janice Sue Gierman, Jan. 6, 1958; children—Thomas Kilby IV, Matthew L., Susan D., Karen Shuff Sampson. B.S., U.S. Mil. Acad., 1957. Foreman Ind. Bell Telephone Co., Muncie, 1961-63; transmission engr. So. Bell Tel.&Tel., Jacksonville, Fla., 1963-66; dir. mgmt. systems dept. U. Ky. Hosp., Lexington, 1968-72; pres. Shuff, Little & Assocs., Georgetown, 1972; with Commonwealth of Ky., Frankfort, 1972—, successively mgmt. systems and services dir., mgmt. info. systems asst. mgr., adminstrv. asst. mgr., data processing supr. III, supr. Info. Ctr., state usertng. coordinator Dept. Info. Systems, 1972—; data processing cons. and educator. Mem. Scott County Bd. Edn., 1972-76. Served to 1st lt. U.S. Army, 1957-61; to lt. col. USAR, 1982. Decorated Army Commendation medal, Meritorious Service medal, 1984; recipient spoke award Jacksonville Beach Jr. C. of C., 1966. Republican. Mem. Christian Ch. (deacon). Lodge: Scott County Kiwanis (v.P.). Home: 451 E Main St Georgetown KY 40324 Office: Ky Dept Info Systems 600A Texan Trail Frankfort KY 40601

SHUKLA, VIJAI, petroleum geologist; b. Lucknow, India, Jan. 1, 1950; s. Shri Krishna and Shail (Trivedi) S.; m. Lee Wolpin, June 25, 1978. B.Sc., Lucknow U., 1972, M.Sc., 1973; M.A., Princeton U., 1976; Ph.D., Rensselaer Poly Inst., 1980. Sr. geologist Texaco Research, Houston, 1980—. Mem. Am. Assn. Petroleum Geologists, Soc. Econ. Paleontologists and Mineralogists, Internat. Assn. Sedimentologists, Geol. Soc. Am. Avocations: reading, music, martial arts. Office: Texaco Houston Research Ctr 3901 Briarpark St Houston TX 77054

SHUKOVSKY, LEONARD JAY, physician; b. N.Y.C., Sept. 7, 1942; s. Norman and Florence (Spritzer) S.; m. Nora S. Kanton, June 7, 1966; children—Samuel N., Mark A., Adam. A.B., Dartmouth Coll., 1963; M.D., Columbia U., 1967. Diplomate Am. Bd. Radiology, Nat. Bd. Med. Examiners; lic. physician, Calif., Tex., Fla. Intern, Thomas Jefferson U. Hosp., Phila., 1967-68; fellow in radiotherapy U. Tex., M.D. Anderson Hosp. & Tumor Inst., Houston, 1968-71; asst. chief div. radiotherapy, dept. radiology Walter Reed Gen. Hosp., Washington, 1971-72, chief div. radiotherapy, 1972-73; asst. prof. radiotherapy U. Tex., M.D. Anderson Hosp. & Tumor Inst., 1973-75; clin. asst. prof. radiotherapy U. South Fla., Tampa, 1975-77, clin. assoc. prof., 1977—; radiotherapist Fred J. Woods Radiation Therapy Ctr., St. Joseph's Hosp., Tampa, 1975—. Served to maj. U.S. Army, 1971-73. Recipient Ann. Research award U. Tex./M.D. Anderson Hosp. & Tumor Inst., 1971. Mem. Am. Coll. Radiology, Am. Radium Soc., Am. Soc. Therapeutic Radiologists, Radiol. Soc. N.Am., AMA, Tex. Radiol. Soc., Fla. Radiol. Soc., Fla. Med. Assn., Hillsborough County Med. Soc. Assoc. editor Internat. Jour. Radiation Oncology, Biology, Physics, 1975-80; contbr. articles to profl. jours. Home: 84 Martinique Ave Tampa FL 33606 Office: 3001 W Buffalo Ave Tampa FL 33607

SHULA, DON FRANCIS, professional football coach; b. Grand River, Ohio, Jan. 4, 1930; s. Dan and Mary (Miller) S.; m. Dorothy Bartish, July 19, 1958; children—David, Donna, Sharon, Anne, Michael. B.S., John Carroll U., Cleve., 1951, H.H.D., 1972; M.A., Western Res. U., 1953; Sc.D., Biscayne Coll., 1974. Profl. football player Cleve. Browns, 1951-52, Balt. Colts, 1953-56, Washington Redskins, 1957; asst. coach U. Va., 1958, U. Ky., 1959, Detroit Lions, 1960-62; head coach Baltimore Colts, 1963-69; head coach, v.p. Miami (Fla.) Dolphins, 1970—. Author: The Winning Edge, 1972. Fla. crusade chmn. Nat. Cancer Soc., 1975; co-chmn. Jerry Lewis March Against Dystrophy, 1975; nat. bd. dirs. Jesuit Program for Living and Learning, 1976; mem. nat. sports com. Multiple Sclerosis Soc., Muscular Dystrophy Assn.; bd. dirs. Heart Assn. Greater Miami; hon. chmn. Belen Jesuit Intercultural Fund Campaign to Build Sch. Served with Ohio N.G., 1952. Recipient Coach of Yr. awards, 1964, 70, 71, 72; named Balt. Colts Silver Anniversary Coach, 1977; Coach of Decade Pro Football Hall of Fame, 1980; recipient Brotherhood award Fla. region NCCJ, 1977, Light of Flames Leadership award Barry Coll., 1977. Roman Catholic. Coached 6 superbowl teams, winner, 1972, 73; overall coaching percentage, .737. Office: care Miami Dolphins 3550 Biscayne Blvd Miami FL 33137*

SHULKIN, CARLTON ROGER, bioresearch company executive; b. Sioux City, Iowa, Jan. 29, 1935; s. Samuel Hyman and Faye (Pearlman) S.; B.A., U. Okla., 1956; m. Marlene B. Raskin, Aug. 7, 1955; children—Marsha Jan, David Ross. With Tex. Instruments, Inc., Staford, Tex., 1969-71; sales mgr. for imported car dealership, Houston, 1971-75; owner Sivad of Tex., Houston, 1975—, distbr. Sivad BioResearch Co., Inc., 1975—; nutritional cons., 1975—. Served to maj., arty. U.S. Army, 1957-69. Decorated Bronze Star medal with 3 oak leaf clusters. Fellow Am. Council Applied Clin. Nutrition; asso. mem. Internat. Coll. Applied Nutrition. Republican. Jewish. Mem. People to People Del. to Orient and Peoples Republic of China, 1981. Home: 20214 Brondesbury Katy TX 77450 Office: Sivad of Tex PO Box 277 Barker TX 77413

SHULKO, PATSY LEE, dietitian, consultant; b. Indpls., Sept. 24, 1934; B.S., Mich. State U., 1956, M.A., 1970; m. Richard M. Shulko, Aug. 4, 1973; 1 son, Gregory. Asst. prof. Med. Coll. Ga., Augusta, 1972-82; dietary cons., 1982—; corp. dietitian Beverly Enterprises. Mem. Am. Dietetic Assn., Ga. Dietetic Assn., Augusta Dietetic Assn., Am. Home Econ. Assn., Ga. Heart Assn., Ga. Nutrition Council, Soc. Nutrition Edn., Nutrition Today Soc. (charter), AAUP, AAUW, Omicron Nu, Pi Beta Phi. Clubs: Houndslake Country, Racquet. Home: 425 Waverly Dr Augusta GA 30909 Office: Med Coll Ga Sch Nursing Augusta GA 30902

SHULMAN, WARREN SCOTT, lawyer; photofinishing company executive; b. St. Petersburg, Fla., Oct. 8, 1942; s. Arnold and Mary Frances (Johnson) S.; m. Stella Esther Thompson, Sept. 6, 1980; 1 son, Zachary; children by previous marriage—Dedee, Robert, Allison. B.B.A., U. Ga., 1964, J.D., 1966. Bar: Ga. 1965. Assoc. Shulman & Alembik, Atlanta, 1966-67; staff officer CIA, 1967-72; ptnr. Shulman, Shulman & Bauer, Atlanta, 1972-77, Shulman, Bauer, Deitch, Raines & Hester, Atlanta, 1977-79, Stolz & Shulman, Atlanta, 1979—; instr. Atlanta Law Sch., 1973-74; pres., chmn. bd. Colonial Hospitality Mgmt. Corp., Colonial Equities, Inc. Candidate for mayor of Atlanta, 1981; dist. chmn. Fulton County Republican party, 1982; mem. bus. and industry com. Atlanta Clean City Commn., 1981-82; mem. So. Ctr. for Internat. Studies, 1979-81; trustee Congregation Beth Jacob, Atlanta, 1976-79; bd. dirs. Atlanta Jewish Welfare Fedn., 1980-82. Mem. Atlanta C. of C. (internat. relations task force 1977-80), Am. Soc. Writers on Legal Subjects, ABA, Ga. Bar Assn., Atlanta Bar Assn., Assn. Trial Lawyers Am., Ga. Assn. Trial Lawyers, Am. Judicature Soc., Lawyers Club Atlanta, Assn. Profl. Color Labs. Clubs: Atlanta City, Men's ORT of Atlanta, B'nai B'rith. Author: Georgia Practice and Procedure, 1975, also supplements; contbr. articles to legal jours. Home: 2015 Springdale Dr Columbus GA 31906 Office: 1017 Virginia St Columbus GA 31902

SHULTS, HENRY C., JR., geologist, consultant; b. Vinita, Okla., July 31, 1947; s. Henry C., Sr. and Beatrice Hedwig (Phillips) S.; m. Lyle Ann Paulsen, Feb. 16, 1980; children—Henry C., III, Gwendolin Kay. B.S., Okla. State U., 1983. Joined U.S. Air Force, 1966, advanced through grades to staff sgt., resigned, 1980; geologist, Grand Resources, Tulsa, 1983-84; self-employed geologist, Tulsa, 1984—. Mem. Am. Assn. of Petroleum Geologists. Democrat. Episcopalian. Avocations: hunting; fishing. Home: Box 627 164 Granada Dr Mannford OK 74044

SHULTZ, CATHLEEN MICHAELE, nursing educator, college administrator; b. E. Liverpool, Ohio, June 23, 1946; d. Charles Wilbur and Lenora Agnes (Cottrill) G.; m. James Herbert Smith, Mar. 17, 1967 (dec. 1979); m. Sam Laurence Shultz, Sept. 10, 1983. B.S. in Nursing, U. S.C., 1974; M.N. in Nursing, Emory U., 1976; Ph.D., Vanderbilt U., 1983. Nursing instr. Holzer Hosp. Sch. Nursing, Gallipolis, Ohio, 1968-69, King's Daus. Hosp. Sch. Nursing, Ashland Ky., 1969-71, Dayton Mental Health Ctr., Ohio, 1971-72, Ga. Bapt. Hosp., Atlanta, 1974-75; asst. prof. nursing Harding U., Searcy, Ark., 1976-81, assoc. prof. nursing, 1981—, chmn. dept. nursing, 1977-79, div. chmn., 1978-79, dean Sch. of Nursing, 1979—; cons. in field. Mem. Am. Nurses Assn. (nat. sub-com. 1975), Ark. State Nurses' Assn. (pres. 1980-82; Appreciation Plaque and Gift, 1982), Nat. League Nursing, Vis. Nurse Assn., Ark.'s Deans' Assn., Sigma Theta Tau, Epsilon Omicron, Chi Lambda Chi, Phi Delta Kappa. Church of Christ. Office: Harding U Box 918 Searcy AR 72143

SHULTZ, WILLIAM EUGENE, university administrator; b. Birmingham, Ala., July 1, 1932; s. John William and Dora Lucille (Galloway) S.; m. Vera Elsie Ryde, July 19, 1962; 1 son, John A. B.S.B.A. in Acctg., U. Fla., 1954; M.B.A., U. Mich., 1965; J.D., U. Miss., 1978. Bar: Miss. 1978. Jr. acct. Purvis, Gray & Powers, C.P.A.s, Gainseville, Fla., 1954; commd. ensign U.S. Navy, 1954, advanced through grades to comdr., 1968; supply corps officer, various locations, 1954-57, 58-75; ret., 1975; jr. acct. M.S. Cooley, C.P.A., Athens, Ga., 1957-58; sole practice law, Columbus, Miss., 1978-83; bus. mgr. Cumberland U., Lebanon, Tenn., 1983-84, chmn. bus. div., 1984—. Treas. Lowndes County Republican Party, Miss., 1979-82; vice chmn. Reagan for Pres., Lowndes County, 1980. Mem. So. Mgmt. Assn., Am. Legion. Methodist. Lodge: Masons. Avocation: water skiing. Office: Cumberland U S Greenwood St Lebanon TN 37087

SHUMAKER, WILLIAM RUTLEDGE, optometrist; b. Bristol, Tenn., Mar. 18, 1954; s. Donald Wilson and Mona Irene (Barb) S. Student U. Tenn., 1972, East Tenn. State U., 1973-75; Dr. Optometry, So. Coll. of Optometry, Memphis, 1979. Lic. optometrist, Tenn., Va. Asst. to pres. Barb and Shumaker, Inc., 1970-78; intern USPHS, Gallup, N.Mex., 1979; sole practice optometry, Bristol, 1979—. Advisor spl. edn. com., Bristol Sch. Bd., 1983-84. Mem. Am. Optometric Assn., Tenn. Optometric Assn., Republican. Methodist. Lodge: Lions. Avocations: Little League Coach; golf; tennis. Home: 311 Midway St Bristol TN 37620 Office: 300 North St Bristol TN 37620

SHUMARD, DENNIS MICHAEL, manufacturing company executive; b. Jackson, Mich., July 14, 1945; s. James W. and Helen Margaret (Clark) S.; m. Di Anne Kathlen McLain; 1 son, Denis Martin. B.S. in Indsl. Engring., Allied Inst. Tech., 1968. Prodn. control scheduler Gulf & Western Taylor Forge, Memphis, 1966-68, customer service supr., 1968-70, mgr. expediting, 1970-71, prodn. control mgr., 1971-72, shipping and warehouse mgr., 1972-77, shop mgr., 1977-78, mfg. mgr., 1978—; cons. Mem. Park Commn., City of Addison (Ill.), 1974. Mem. Am. Soc. Indsl. Engrs. Roman Catholic. Home: 2368 Brachton Germantown TN 38138

SHURGER, ROY FULLER, JR., x-ray component manufacturing company sales executive; b. Ithaca, N.Y., Jan. 12, 1932; s. Roy Fuller and Laura Anita (Drouin) S.; m. Irene Stasia Kudla, Mar. 2, 1957 (div. Feb. 1974); children—Roy Fuller III, Paula Ann, Karl Richard, Sharon Ellen, Karen Marie; m. 2d, Brenda P. Dixon, Mar. 11, 1974. Student numerous mgmt. and radiologic tech. profl. courses. Student radiologic technologist Colony Hosp., Norfolk, Mass., 1952-53, staff radiologic technologist, 1953-55; staff radiologic technologist Mass. Gen. Hosp., Boston, 1955-56, asst. chief technologist, 1962-66, coordinator/instr. Sch. Radiologic Tech., 1964-66; staff radiologic technologist Central Hosp., Somerville, Mass., 1956-57; chief radiologic technologist Whidden Meml. Hosp., Everett, Mass., 1957-62, first aid instr. Sch. Nursing, 1957-62; adminstrv. asst. dept. radiology Greater Southeast Community Hosp. (formerly Morris Cafritz Meml. Hosp.), Washington, 1966-72; founder, tech. dir. Paul Himmelfarb Sch. Radiologic Tech., 1967-72; adminstrv. coordinator dept. radiology Sibley Meml. Hosp., Washington, 1972-75; tech. dir. dept. radiology tng. program Univ. Hosp., Jacksonville, Fla., 1975-77; sales assoc. United Bus. Investments, Jacksonville, 1977-78; chief radiologic technologist Touro Infirmary, New Orleans, 1978-79; salesman Metairie Ford (La.), 1979, Dan Quirk Ford Co., Slidell, La., 1979-80; regional mgr. Machlett Labs., Inc., Slidell, 1980—; instr. in radiologic tech. Northeastern U., 1964-66. Active ARC, Lynn, 1959-65, Rosedale Burton-Knolls Citizens Assn., Oxon Hill, Md., 1966-68, PTA, 1967-69, Boy Scouts Am., 1967-71. Mem. Am. Registry Radiologic Technologists, La. Realtors Assn., Designer award-winning exhibits, 1965. Home and Office: 383 Cumberland St Slidell LA 70458

SHURLING, ANNE MARLOWE, psychology educator, consultant; b. Lexington, Ky., Jan. 25, 1947; d. Charles Franklin and Margaret Helen (Crossfield) Marlowe; m. Thomas Lennard Shurling, June 25, 1982; 1 child, Jayne-Margaret. B.M., U. Ky., 1969, Ph.D., 1979; M.S., Fla. State U., 1970. Lic. counseling psychologist, Ky. Asst. dir. student activities Eastern Ky. U., Richmond, 1971-73; mental health specialist Ky. Dept. for Human Resources, Frankfort, 1973-76; personnel research analyst IBM, Lexington, Ky., 1976-79, sr. assoc. instr., 1979-81; asst. v.p. C & S Georgia Corp., Atlanta, 1981-82; prof. psychology Transylvania U., Lexington, 1982—; staff psychologist Anxiety Mgmt. Ctr., Lexington, 1984—; cons. and guest presenter to various groups. Author: Greek Membership: Its Impact on the Value Orientations and Moral Development of College Freshmen, 1979. Contbr. articles in field of psychology to profl. jours. Bd. dirs. Inst. for Social Change, Lexington, 1979—. Mem. Am. Psychol. Assn., Ky. Psychol. Assn., AAUW, Phi Delta Kappa. Republican. Mem. Christian Ch. (Disciples of Christ). Avocations: gardening; music; cooking. Home: 326 Curtin Dr Lexington KY 40503 Office: Transylvania U Lexington KY 40508

SHURN, PETER JOSEPH, III, lawyer; b. Queens, N.Y., Aug. 30, 1946; s. Peter J. and Vivienne (Tagliarino) S.; B.S. in Elec. Engring. magna cum laude, Poly. Inst. Bklyn., 1974; J.D. magna cum laude, New Eng. Sch. Law, 1977; LL.M. in Patent and Trade Regulation Law, George Washington U., 1981; children—Steven Douglas, Vanessa Leigh, David Michael. Admitted to N.C. bar, 1977, Va. bar, 1979, Tex. bar, 1982; assoc. firm Burns, Doane, Swecker & Mathis, Alexandria, Va., 1978-80, Arnold, White & Durkee, Houston, 1981—; adj. prof. South Tex. Coll. Law, 1984—; tech. advisor to judge U.S. Ct. Appeals, Fed. Cir., 1980-81; individual practice law, Raleigh, N.C., 1977-78; research scientist GTE Labs., 1965-77. Served with AUS, 1966-68. Mem. IEEE, Am. Bar Assn., N.C. State Bar Assn., Va. State Bar Assn., Tex. Bar Assn., Assn. Trial Lawyers Am., Am. Patent Law Assn., Houston Patent Law Assn., Sigma Xi. Tech. editor New Eng. Law Rev., 1975-77. Office: Arnold White & Durkee PO Box 4433 Houston TX 77210

SHUSTER, HARVEY L., financial consultant; b. Washington, Oct. 5, 1945; s. Samuel and Dora Shuster; B.S., Temple U., 1968; M.B.A., Drexel U., 1970; m. Joan Schildkaut, Apr. 5, 1970; 1 dau., Heather. With Coopers & Lybrand, 1970-73; asst. treas. Amicor Inc., 1973-78; controller, treas. Peachtree Software, Inc., then cons. to exec. v.p. Mgmt. Sci. Am., Inc., Atlanta, 1979-83; pres. Solid Software, Inc., 1983—. Served to 1t lt. U.S. Army; Vietnam. Decorated Bronze Star. C.P.A., Pa., Ga. Mem. Am. Inst. C.P.A.s (computer com.), Ga. Soc. C.P.A.s (com. on relationships with educators and C.P.A.s in industry), Beta Gamma, Beta Alpha Psi. Home: 9365 Northlake Dr Roswell GA 30676 Office: 2625 Cumberland Pkwy Suite 250 Atlanta GA 30339

SHUSTERMAN, NATHAN, life underwriter, financial consultant; b. Montreal, Que., Can., Aug. 27, 1927; came to U.S., 1950; s. Aaron and Annie (Nulman) S.; m. Norman Thalblum, Jan. 1950; children—Mark D., Claudia S. Student, Sir George Williams Coll., Montreal, 1944-47. C.L.U., chartered fin.

cons., Am. Coll. Retailing mgr. Jefferson Stores, Miami, Fla., 1950-65; gen. agt. Protective Life Ins. Co., Miami, 1965—, also chmn. agts. adv. com.; fin. and estate planning cons.; pres. Am. Fin. Counseling Corp., Miami; instr. in estate and tax planning Am. Coll. Life Underwriters, Bryn Mawr, Pa., 1972—, U. Miami, Coral Gables, Fla., 1972—. Named Man of Yr., Gen. Agts. and Mgrs. Assn., Miami, 1965, 66, 67. Mem. Million Dollar Round Table (life), Top of Table, Assn. Advanced Life Underwriting, Am. Soc. C.L.U.s (pres. Miami chpt.), Nat. Assn. Life Underwriters. Club: Optimists (pres. 1971) (North Miami Beach, Fla.). Lodges: Masons, Shriners; B'nai B'rith (pres. 1950) (Miami). Home: 2320 NE 196th St North Miami Beach FL 33180 Office: Am Fin Counseling Corp 16121 NE 18th Ave North Miami Beach FL 33162

SHYERS, LARRY EDWARD, mental health counselor, educator; b. Middletown, Ohio, Aug. 16, 1948; s. Edward and Ruth Evelyn (Davis) S.; m. Linda Faye Shearon, July 31, 1970; children—Jami Lynn, Karen Lindsey. B.A., David Lipscomb Coll., Nashville, 1970; M.A., Stetson U., DeLand, Fla., 1973; M.Ed., U. Central Fla., 1981; postgrad. U. Fla., 1981-85. Lic. mental health counselor, Fla.; nat. cert. counselor. Ordained to ministry non-denominational Ch. of Christ, 1969; minister Ch. of Christ, Ocala, Fla., 1970-75, Mt. Dora, Fla., 1975-80; tchr. Christian Home and Bible Sch., Mt. Dora, 1970-77, dir. guidance, 1977—; pvt. practice family counselor, Eustis, Fla., 1980—; mem. individual manpower tng. system bd. Vocat.-Tech. Sch., Eustis, 1984—; adj. prof. psychology St. Leo Coll., 1985—; mem. adv. bd. U.S. Achievement Bd., 1983—; cons. in field. Dir. edn. Mt. Dora Ch. of Christ, 1983—. Mem. Fla. Mental Health Counselors Assn. (chmn. award and profl. devel. coms. 1985, chmn. govt. relations com.),), Am. Assn. Counseling and Devel., Am. Mental Health Counselors Assn., Am. Sch. Counselors Assn., Am. Assn. Profl. Hypnotherapists, Internat. Acad. Profl. Counselors and Psychotherapists, Mount Dora C. of C. (mem. youth com. 1984), Kappa Delta Pi, Pi Lambda Theta, Chi Sigma Iota. Republican. Lodge: Kiwanis. Avocations: amateur radio, target shooting. Office: 421 N Bay St Eustis FL 32726

SHYVER, ROBERT BURNELL, aluminum company manager; b. Richlands, N.C., Oct. 2, 1942; s. Larry M. and Jessie (Banks) S.; m. Dee Smith, June 16, 1962; children—Robert, Brian. Student pub. schs., Millersville, Pa. Cold rolling foreman Howmet Aluminum Co., Lancaster, Pa., 1970-74, finishing foreman, 1974-77, finishing supt., 1977-79, finishing mgr., 1979-81, prodn. mgr., Hawesville, Ky., 1981-83; prodn. mgr. Alumax Aluminum Co., Hawesville, 1983—, plant mgr., 1986—. Author tng. manuals, slide presentation. Mem. Fabricating Mfrs. Assn. (outstanding contbn. to edn. award 1984), Ohio Valley Mgmt. Assn., ASME (tech. com. 1982—), Aluminum Assn. (slitting com. 1982—). Democrat. Baptist. Home: 3125 Brent Gray Trace Owensboro KY 42301 Office: Alumax Aluminum PO Box 519 Hawesville KY 42348

SIAS, RICHARD L., fuel company executive. B.A., U. Kans., 1951, LL.D., 1954; M.A. in Spanish Lit., Nat. U. Mex., 1952. With Continental Oil Co., 1954-66; v.p. exploration An-Son Corp., 1966-71; v.p. Mustang Prodn. Co., wholly-owned subs. of Mustang Fuel Corp., Oklahoma City, 1971-73, pres., from 1973, former group v.p. prodn. Mustang Fuel Corp., now vice chmn. bd. dirs. Pres. Okla. Symphony Found.; past pres. bd. dirs. Okla. Symphony; pres. Allied Arts Found.; bd. dirs. Am. Symphony Orch. League, Mid-Am. Arts Alliance, Cimarron Circuit Opera Co., Okla. Mus. Art. Office: Mustang Fuel Corp 1166 First Nat Ctr E Oklahoma City OK 73102*

SIAWELESKI, THEODORE, land planner; b. Bayonne, N.J., Oct. 19, 1954; s. Theodore John and Mary Ann (Zgola) S. B.S. in Architecture, Ohio State U., 1976. Planner, Vernon G. Henry & Assocs. Inc., Houston, 1977-81; sr. assoc. Northrup Assocs., Houston, 1981—. Trustee Houston Jaycee Urban Devel. Found., 1981-82. Mem. Am. Planning Assn. (asst. dir. Houston sect. 1985), Am. Inst. Cert. Planners, Urban Land Inst. (assoc.). Republican. Roman Catholic. Office: Northrup Assocs 4101 Greenbriar Suite 305 Houston TX 77098

SIBLEY, JAMES ASHLEY, JR., educator; b. Shreveport, La., Oct. 21, 1916; s. James Ashley and Lucian Katherine (Hammond) S.; B.A., Centenary Coll., 1940, postgrad., 1941-53; M.Ed., La. State U., 1963; m. Zilda Pickett, Feb. 7, 1957 (dec. Jan. 4, 30 1961); m. Anna May Switzer, Feb. 1, 1963 (dec. Mar. 1975). Asst. mgr. Sibley's Hardware and Variety Stores, 1935-41; farmer, Shreveport, 1941-45; tchr. sci., phys. edn. supr. Lab. Sch., Centenary Coll., Shreveport, 1941-42; tchr. pub. schs., Shreveport, 1942-44, Baton Rouge, 1958-71; dir. VITAL Career Info. Center, La. Dept. Edn., Baton Rouge, 1971-76; dir. Grindstone Bluff Mus. and Environ. Edn. Center, La. Landmark, Shreveport, 1976—; ednl. cons., 1976—; lectr. archaeology Centenary Coll.; tchr. archaeology, acad. internship program Caddo Parish Schs.; personnel technician, examiner La. Civil Service Dept., Baton Rouge, 1944-48; employment counselor, test technician La. Employment Service, Shreveport, 1948-57; ednl. cons. Gulf S. Research Inst.; coordinator cultural resources Unit Project for humanities East Baton Rouge Parish Sch. Bd.; coordinator La. Arts and Sci. Center Planning Project, East Baton Rouge Parish Schs. Mem. econ. council East Baton Rouge Parish Sch. Bd., 1963-64; cons. sect. elementary sci. and social studies Assn. Childhood Edn. Internat., 1963-64; exec. asst. region 7, La. Jr. Acad. Scis., 1963-64, La. Social Studies Fair, 1972-76; adviser La. Indian edn. sect. Nat. Conf. on Employment Am. Indian; cons. La. Indian Cultural Heritage Ednl. Enrichment Program, 1975, La. studies project Caddo Parish Sch. Bd., 1981. Past mem. bd. dirs. Found. for Hist. La. Co-founder, sponsor Jr. Archeol. Soc., Inc., Meml. Mus. and Library Fund; donor site for Ch. of Holy Cross Mission Retreat Ctr.-Research Ctr., 1985. Recipient Merit award for outstanding service to public La. chpt. Internat. Assn. Personnel in Employment Security, 1952; La. Historic Preservation award; La. Gov.'s award service to archeology, 1982; Patron Gold Tag award Shreveport Theater Art's Guild, 1984-85. Mem. Nat. Social Studies Council (pres. East Baton Rouge Parish chpt. 1964-65), Assn. Supervision and Curriculum Devel., La. Hist. Soc., La. Geneal. and Hist. Soc., Am., La. (exec. com., bd. 1972-73) personnel and guidance assns., Nat. Vocat. Guidance Assn., (del.), La. Guidance Assn., Nat. Sci. Tchrs. Assn., Archeol. Inst. Am., Soc. for Am. Archeology, La. Acad. La. Tchrs. Assn., La. Sch. Counselors Assn., Soc. Hist. Archaeology, La., La. Sci. tchrs. assns., Am. Assn. Museums, La. Vocat. Guidance Assn. (pres. 1971-73), Nat. Trust for Hist. Preservation, Am. Anthrop. Assn., Nat., La., ret. tchrs. assns., La. Hist. Assn. No. La. Assn. (charter, past pres.), Ark., Okla., La. (past dir.), Tex. archeol. socs., Historic Preservation Shreveport, Am. Mus. Natural History, Am. Folklore Soc., Smithsonian Assos., Nat., La. wildlife fedns., Nat., La. recreation and park assns., Phi Delta Kappa, Psi Chi (charter mem. L.S.U. chpt.). Episcopalian (past treas. and vestryman). Author: Louisiana's Ancients of Man, 1967; The Junior Archeological Society, 1967; Geology of Baton Rouge and Surrounding S.E. La. Area, 1972; Grindstone Bluff, Sibleyshire, La. Landmark, 1975, others. Editor: Cultural Heritage of East Baton Rouge Parish, 1969; Handbook of Vital Career Information Center; The Development and Use of Behavioral Objectives, 1970; Cultural Heritage of Old Revenue Plantation, Carville, La., 1975. Contbr. articles to profl. publs. Address: PO Box 7965 Shreveport LA 71107

SIBLEY, MARK ANDERSON, ophthalmologist; b. Daytona Beach, Fla., Sept. 15, 1950; s. John Rheney and Alyce K. (McDonald) S.; m. Sue Ellen White, Jan. 27, 1978; children—Paul Anderson, Laura Katherine. A.A., Daytona Beach Jr. Coll., 1970; B.A., U. Fla., 1972; M.D., Meharry Med. Coll., Nashville, 1976. Diplomate Nat. Bd. Med. Examiners, Am. Bd. Ophthalmology. Intern, Orlando Regional Med. Ctr., Fla., 1976-77; resident U. Ala., 1977-80; fellow Eye Found. Hosp., Birmingham, Ala., 1980; ophthalmologist Suncoast Med. Clinic, St. Petersburg, Fla., 1980—; chief med. staff Sunbay Hosp., 1983-85, staff ophthalmologist, 1980—; mem. staff Bayfront Hosp., 1980—, St. Anthony's Hosp., 1980—; asst. clin. prof. U. South Fla., Tampa, 1982—. Contbr. articles to profl. jours. Med. advisor Fla. Soc. Prevent Blindness, Tampa, 1981—; mem. Physician Edn. Network, St. Petersburg, 1981—; bd. dirs. Am. Diabetes Assn., Pinellas County, Fla., 1982—; bd. dirs. Suncoast Med. Clinic, 1984—, also mem. exec. com. Recipient Blue Key award U. Fla., 1970, Physician Recognition, AMA, 1982, 85. Fellow Am. Acad. Ophthalmology; mem. Fla. Soc. Ophthalmology (pub. relations com. 1981—), Am. Soc. Contemporary Ophthalmology (Cert. Advanced Studies award 1982, 85), Fla. Med. Soc., Am. Intraocular Implant Soc. Republican. Roman Catholic. Avocations: biking; fishing. Office: Suncoast Med Clinic 700 6th St S Saint Petersburg FL 33701

SIBLEY, STUART F., real estate developer; b. Miami, Fla., Aug. 8, 1946; s. Richard M. Franken and Marshall H. (Harbeson) F.; m. Harper Sibley, Dec. 14, 1970; 1 son, Benjamin Rush. B.A., U. Miami, 1968, M.A., 1970. Vice pres. Boca Grande Club (Fla.), 1978—; dir. Erosion Masters, Inc. Bd. dirs. Fla. Bd. Landscape Architects, 1980—; trustee Trinity Episcopal Sch., 1985—. Mem. Monumental Brass Soc. (Eng.). Office: Boca Grande Club Boca Grande FL

SIBLEY, WILLIAM ARTHUR, educator, school administrator; b. Ft. Worth, Nov. 22, 1932; s. William F. and Sada R. Sibley; m. Joyce Gregory, Dec. 21, 1957; children—Timothy, Lauren, Steve. B.S. in Physics, U. Okla., 1956, M.S. in Physics, 1958, Ph.D. in Physics, 1960. Research assoc. Kernforschungsanlange, Julich and Inst. for Metal Physics, Tech. U. Aachen (W.Ger.), 1960-61; head non-metals sect. Solid State div. Oak Ridge (Tenn.) Nat. Lab., 1961-70; head dept. physics Okla. State U., Stillwater, 1970-76, dir. research and grad. studies, 1974-76, dir. sch. phys. and earth scis., 1976-78, asst. v.p. research, 1978—; cons. materials sci.; adv. coms. NSF, Nat. Acad. Scis. Mem. Stillwater Indsl. Found. Com.; bd. dirs. Oak Ridge Assoc. Univs., 1982—. Served with U.S. Army; Korea. Recipient Mid-Am. State U. Assn. Disting. Lectr. award, 1978; NSF grantee, 1971—; NATO grantee, 1971-75; Dept. Def. grantee, 1971—, AEC grantee, 1971-73. Fellow Am. Phys. Soc.; mem. Sigma Xi. Democrat. Baptist. Contbr. chpts. to books, numerous articles to profl. jours.

SICA, AURELIO JOSEPH, advertising executive; b. Bklyn., May 13, 1945; s. Joseph and Theresa (Tardio) S.; m. Rosalind Marie, June 16, 1967 (div. Mar. 1974); 1 dau., Vanessa Dawn; m. Nancy Allison Simons, Apr. 16, 1976; children—Amanda Laurel, Victoria Jenna. Student Sch. of Visual Arts, N.Y.C., 1964, 65, 66. Asst. art dir. Redbook Mag., N.Y.C., 1964-65, Shaller-Rubin, N.Y.C., 1966-67; art dir. TV prodn. Campbell-Ewald, N.Y.C., 1968-69, Ogilvy & Mather, N.Y.C., 1973-74; co-creative dir. Vladimir & Evans, Miami, Fla., 1973-74; pres. Aurelio & Friends, Miami, Fla., 1975—; chmn. Miami Advt. Fedn. "Addy Awards", 1975-76. Recipient numerous awards in advt. including: Gold award N.Y. Art Dirs. Club, 1968, 69; award Am. Inst. Graphic Arts, 1968, 69; Rizzoli Europa, Rizzoli Pubs., 1969; also various "Addy's—, 1968-81. Mem. Advt. Fedn. Democrat. Roman Catholic.

SICHEL, BARBARA ELIZABETH, shopping center representative, theatrical consultant; b. Tampa, Fla., Jan. 17, 1917; d. Stedman Wadsworth and Margaret-Mae Ellis (Bailey) Jackson; m. Harry George Sichel, Jan. 14, 1939; 1 dau., Margaret Lee. B.A., Universidad de Buenos Aires, 1936; student, Bellas Artes Sch., 1934-38. Lic. real estate salesman, Fla. Producer, dir. Playhouse in the Park, Toledo, 1961-66; dir. Christian edn. Zion United Meth. Ch., Toledo, 1966-68; adult program dir. YWCA, Toledo, 1968-70; dir. Nationwide Coll. of Commerce, Columbus, Ohio, 1970-71; producer, dir. Columbus Gallery, 1971; acct. Preferred Title Co., Columbus, 1971-72; dir. fin. Capital U., Columbus, 1972-75; dir. Nationwide Beauty Acad., Columbus, 1975-76; controller Mor-Bee Enterprises, Inc., Orlando, Fla., 1977-81; prodn. and script con. Doral Chenoweth Prodns., Columbus, 1977-81; rep. for shopping ctr. sales and acquisitions, Morbitzer Group, Inc., Winter Park, Fla., 1983—. Mem. Internat. Council Shopping Ctrs. Democrat. Episcopalian. Playwright: The End of the Ice Age, 1967; A Kind of Unity, 1966; mng. editor: The Clarion, 1964-66. Office: Morbitzer Group Inc 2950 Aloma Ave Suite 404 Winter Park FL 32793

SICK, WILLIAM NORMAN, JR., electronics company executive; b. Houston, Apr. 20, 1935; s. William Norman and Gladys Phylena (Armstrong) S.; m. Stephanie Anne Williams, Sept. 14, 1963; children—Jill Melanie, David Louis. B.A., Rice U., 1957, B.S.E.E., 1958. With Tex. Instruments Inc., Dallas, Washington, Phila., 1958-70; pres. Tex. Instruments Asia Ltd., Tokyo, 1971-74, asst. v.p. strategic devel., gen. mgr. metals and controls Europe, parent co., Dallas, 1974-77; pres. Tex. Instruments Internat. Trade Corp., Dallas, 1977, v.p., group mgr. materials and elec. products parent co., Attleboro, Mass., 1977-80, v.p., group mgr. consumer products, Dallas, 1980-82, exec. v.p., group mgr. semicondr. products, 1982—; guest lectr. Sophia U., Tokyo, 1973; dir. Tex Instruments Semiconduttori Italia S.P.A. Contbr. articles to profl. jours. Chmn. bd. dirs. Fairhill Sch., Dallas. Recipient Francis award Rice U., 1956. Mem. Japan Am. Soc., IEEE, Sigma Xi, Tau Beta Pi, Sigma Tau. Episcopalian. Club: Bent Tree (Dallas). Office: 13500 N Central Expressway Dallas TX*

SICKEL, GEORGE WILLIAM, pathologist; b. Chester, Pa., Feb. 21, 1926; s. George Benson and Nelle Ione (Bittinger) S.; A.B., Dartmouth Coll., 1950; M.D., Temple U., 1954; m. Ruth Evelyn Bell, Sept. 29, 1956; 1 dau., Evelyn Ann. Cert. infection control. Intern, Chester Hosp., 1954-56, resident in pathology, 1956-58; resident in pathology, Wilmington, Del., 1958-59, Phila., 1959-61; dir. labs. Stanly County Hosp., Albemarle, N.C., 1961-63, Springfield (Ohio) Community Hosp., 1963-66, John Peter Smith Hosp., Ft. Worth, 1966-76; mem. firm Severance & Assos., San Antonio, 1976-77; asso. pathologist Mercy Health Center, Oklahoma City, 1977-79; asst. clin. prof. pathology Southwestern Med. Sch., Dallas, 1966-76; pres. G. William Sickel & Assos., 1974-75; asso. Pathology and Nuclear Med. Assos., Baton Rouge, 1979—. Vestryman, fin. com. Episcopal Parish, Ft. Worth. Served with USNR, 1943-46; PTO. Diplomate Am. Bd. Pathology. Fellow Am. Soc. Clin. Pathologists, Coll. Am. Pathologists; mem. AMA (Physicians Recognition award), So. Med. Assn., Am. Soc. Microbiology, La., East Baton Rouge Parish med. socs. Home: 12047 Oakhaven Way Baton Rouge LA 70810 Office: 5000 Hennessy Blvd Baton Rouge LA 70809

SIDDONS, JAMES, educator, musicologist; b. Narsarssuaq, Greenland, Nov. 1, 1948; s. James Claudius Siddons, Jr., and Willie Belle (Durham) Cox; m. Joyce Lorraine Garbee, July 2, 1977. B.Mus., N.Tex. State U., 1970, postgrad. 1971-72, 74-76, Ph.D., 1983; M.Mus., King's Coll. U. London, 1971. Asst. prof. Liberty U., Lynchburg, Va., 1976-78, assoc. prof., 1978—, chmn. dept. music and art, 1984—. Author: Japan Section, Directory of Music Research Libraries, 1979. Contbr. articles to publs. in field. Research scholar Ministry of Edn. Govt. of Japan, Tokyo U. Arts, 1972-74; Nat. Endowment Humanities summer scholar, 1978, 82, 85. Mem. Am. Musicol. Soc., Internat. Musicol. Soc., Music Library Assn. Am., Soc. for Asian Music, Am. Soc. for Jewish Music, Pi Kappa Lambda. Baptist. Home: 106 Connecticut Ave Lynchburg VA 24502 Office: Dept Music and Art Liberty U Candler's Mountain Rd Lynchburg VA 24506

SIDES, KERMIT FRANKLIN, furniture manufacturing company executive; b. Lee County, Miss., Feb. 13, 1932; s. Robert Franklin and Francis Jet (Cox) S.; grad. high sch., Wheeler, Miss.; m. Edna E. Heavener, Aug. 1, 1953; children—Connie Ann, Timothy Franklin. Mfg. supr. Futorian Mfg. Co., New Albany and Okolona, Miss., 1953-69; v.p. mfg., gen. mgr. Action Industries, Verona, Miss., 1969-79; exec. v.p., sec., treas. PeopLounger Inc., Nettleton, Miss., 1979—, also dir. Indsl. chmn. Lee United Neighbors div. United Way, Tupelo, Miss., 1969-73; dir. United Way of Greater Lee County. co-founder peopLoungers, 1979. Recipient award for Outstanding Contbn. to Appearance of City, 1981. Northeast Miss. Community Relations Assn. (dir. sec., treas.). Baptist. Home: 53 St Andrews Circle Belden MS 38826 Office: PO Drawer 429 Nettleton MS 38858

SIDHU, SURJIT S., research economist, agricultural economic development consultant; b. Village Malla, Ludhiana, Punjab, India, Nov. 8, 1930; s. Isher S. and Sant Kaur (Dhaliwal) S.; came to U.S., 1964, naturalized, 1978; m. Pritam Grewal, May 8, 1954 (div.); children—Bhupinder S., Preetmohinder S.; m. 2d, Sachiko Yamashita, Sept. 10, 1976 B.S. in Agr., Punjab U., 1952; M.S. in Agrl. Econs., Utah State U., 1966; Ph.D. in Agrl. and Applied Econs., U. Minn., 1972. Agrl. officer Punjab State Govt., India, 1952-62; farm mgmt. specialist U.S. AID, Punjab, 1962-64; research asst. Utah State U., Logan, 1965-66; research asst. U. Minn., St. Paul, 1966-72, research assoc., 1972-73, asst. prof., 1973-76; sr. lectr. U. Dar EsSalaam, Tanzania, East Africa, 1973-76, dir. grad. research and teaching in econs., 1974-76; economist Internat. Fertilizer Devel. Ctr., Muscle Shoals, Ala., 1976—; research tchr., cons. in agrl. and economic devel. of developing countries. Mem. exec. com. Southeastern Sikh Religious Soc., 1983. Mem. Am. Agrl. Econs. Assn., Am. Econs. Assn., Indian Soc. Agrl. Econs., Internat. Agrl. Econs. Assn., Punjab Agrl. Univ. Alumni Assn. N. Am. (pres. 1983). Club: Florence Golf and Country. Contbr. articles to profl. jours. Office: PO Box 2040 Muscle Shoals AL 35660

SIEBEL, MATHIAS PAUL, engineer, government executive; b. Witten, Germany, Mar. 6, 1924; came to U.S., 1957, naturalized, 1962; s. Franz and Marie Luise (Polaczek) S.; m. Katherine Elizabeth Jente, May 27, 1960. B.S. in Engring., U. Bristol, Eng., 1949, Ph.D. in Engring., 1952. Cert. profl. engr., N.Y. Research assoc. Columbia U., N.Y.C., 1958-59; mgr. pressure equipment Pall Corp., Glen Cove, N.Y., 1959-64; v.p. ops. RDI, Westbury, N.Y., 1964-65; dir. Mfg. Engring. Lab., NASA Marshall Space Flight Ctr., Huntsville, Ala., 1965-74, mem. sci. staff, 1974-79; mgr. NASA Michoud Assembly Facility NASA, New Orleans, 1979—. Contbr. articles to profl. jours. Patentee in field. Home: 5204 Janice Ave Kenner LA 70065 Office: NASA Michoud Assembly Facility 13800 Old Gentilly Hwy New Orleans LA 70129

SIEGEL, CLIFFORD MYRON, electrical engineer, educator; b. Apple River, Ill., Apr. 15, 1921; s. Harvey Wilhelm and Elizabeth Annie (Schuler) S.; m. Marion Elizabeth Watson, May 25, 1946; children—Wayne, Dale, Mark, Connie. B.E.E., Marquette U., 1947; M.S., U. N.H., 1949; Ph.D. in Elec. Engring, U. Wis., 1951. Instr. in elec. engring. U. N.H., Durham, 1947-49; asst. prof. elec. engring. U. Va., Charlottesville, 1951-52, assoc. prof., 1952-62, prof., 1962—, acting dept. chmn., 1967-69. Served to 1st lt. USAAF, 1943-46. Mem. Am. Soc. Engring. Edn., IEEE, Tau Beta Pi, Eta Kappa Nu. Presbyterian. Patentee 2 electronic circuits. Home: 2503 Hillwood Pl Charlottesville VA 22901 Office: Thornton Hall U Va Charlottesville VA 22901

SIEGEL, HAROLD JULIAN, physicist, consultant; b. Ft. Collins, Colo., Sept. 6, 1934; s. Julian and Ida (Silverman) S.; m. Beverly Ann Tucker, Oct. 3, 1962 (div. 1969); children—Harold J., Jr., Katherine L. Student Colo. State U., 1942-50, Ga. Inst. Tech., 1952-56. Mgr., engr. Philips electronics Inst., Atlanta, 1963-70; engr. Process Equipment Co., Atlanta, 1973; cons. Unified Systems, Atlanta, 1973-75, Pensacola, Fla., 1981—; cons., mem. staff Fla. State U., Tallahassee, Fla., 1976-81; tech. specialist Bausch & Lomb, Atlanta, 1963; customer engr. IBM, Atlanta, 1960-62; sales and design engr. RMS Gen. Electric Co., Atlanta, 1959-60; computer engr. Vitro Weapons Inc., Eglin AFB, Fla., 1958-59. Patentee in field; exhibited sculpture one-man show, 1981. Activist-litigant to U.S. Supreme Ct., 1981. Served with USN, 1956-58. Nominated poet laureate Fla. Sec. State 1980; named Engr. of Yr., Philips Electronic Inst., 1968; Mem. Soc. Applied Spectrascopy, Electron Microscope Soc. Am., Am. Chem. Soc., Sigma Xi.

SIEGEL, LAWRENCE IVER, real estate devel. co. exec.; b. Cleve., Aug. 19, 1925; s. Edward I. and Mary (Mentz) S.; B.B.A., Western Res. U., 1949, LL.B., 1952; m. Joyce Reske, Nov. 4, 1950; children—Leslie, Diane, Frederic, Edward. Pres., Lawrence I. Siegel Co., Baton Rouge, 1980—; chmn. bd. Lisscorp. Inc. Bd. dirs. Tara High Sch. Backers, Baton Rouge, Community Concerts Assn., New Orleans; Cub Scout master, 1967-68. Served with inf. U.S. Army, 1943-46; ETO, PTO. Col. on Staff of gov. La. Mem. Internat. Council Shopping Centers, Mortgage Bankers Assn. Am., Am. Bankers Assn. Club: Kiwanis. Office: 10455 Jefferson Baton Rouge LA 70809

SIEGEL, MARK JORDAN, lawyer; b. Dallas, Feb. 22, 1949; s. Jack H. and Zelda (Sikora) S. B.S. in Psychology, North Tex. State U., 1972; J.D., Southwest Tex. Coll. Law, 1977. Bar: Tex. 1977. Sole practice, Dallas, 1977—. Mem. Tex. Trial Lawyers Assn., Dallas Trial Lawyers Assn., Assn. Trial Lawyers Am. Office: 3611 Fairmount St Dallas TX 75219

SIEGEL, RONNIE SWIRE, landscape architect, artist; b. N.Y.C., Feb. 27, 1953; d. Irving and Roslyn (Potisman) Swire; m. Peter Howard Siegel, July 4, 1976. B.A. cum laude, Colgate U., 1975; M. Landscape Arch., U. Pa., 1978. Lic. landscape architect, N.Y. Landscape architect Arnold Assocs., Princeton, N.J., 1977, Edward Gaudy, South Nyack, N.Y., 1978; cons. Central Park Task Force, N.Y.C., 1979; landscape architect Vreeland & Guerriero, P.C., N.Y.C., 1979-81, Haines Lundberg Waehler, N.Y.C., 1981-82; prin. Swire Siegel, Charlottesville, Va., and Upper Grandview, N.Y., 1982—. Group shows Colgate U., Hamilton, N.Y., 1972, 74, U. Pa. Grad. Sch. Fine Arts, Phila., 1977, Met. Mus. Art, N.Y.C., 1981, Harvard U. Grad. Sch. Design, Cambridge, 1983; prin. works include North Ave. Park, N.Y.C., P.S. 52 playground, S.I., Frank Frontera Park, Queens, N.Y., N.J. Ave. Park, Bklyn. Recipient 2d prize in nat. crushed stone quarry design competition Nat. Assn. Crushed Stone, 1978. Mem. Am. Soc. Landscape Architects, Nat. Trust Hist. Preservation. Avocations: painting; photography; travel; tennis; swimming; nature study. Office: Swire Siegel 801-B E High St Charlottesville VA 22901

SIEGELMAN, DON EUGENE, state official; b. 1946; B.A., U. Ala.; J.D., Georgetown U., 1972; postgrad. Oxford (Eng.) U., 1972-73. Bar: Ala. 1972. Assoc. Robert S. Vance Law Firm, Birmingham, 1973-78; exec. dir., gen. counsel Ala. Democratic Exec. Com., 1973-78; sec. and coordinator Ala. Election Law Commn., 1974-77; sec. of state State of Ala., Montgomery, 1979—; mem. Nat. Commn. on Party Accountibility, 1980-84. Mem. Nat. Assn. Secs. of State (chmn. nat. voter edn. project 1983-84). Office: Sec of State State Capitol Montgomery AL 36130

SIEGFRIED, IVA HUMPHREY, nurse, educator; b. Benton, Ky., Aug. 11, 1956; d. Adorn Hyatt and Dorothy J. (Reeves) Humphrey; m. Bradley Kent Siegfried, July 29, 1978. Diploma in nursing Bapt. Meml. Hosp. Sch. Nursing, 1977; B.S.N., U. Tenn.-Chattanooga, 1982. Cert. critical care nurse. Intensive care staff nurse/charge nurse Bapt. Meml. Hosp., Memphis, 1977-78; intensive care/coronary care asst. head nurse Morristown (Tenn.)-Hamblan Hosp., 1978-79; coronary and intensive care charge nurse, supr. J. Hutcheson Meml. Tri-County Hosp., Chattanooga, 1980-82; nursing instr. Erlanger Sch. Nursing, Chattanooga, 1982-83, clin. specialist, 1983—; CPR instr. ARC, Chattanooga, 1982—. Mem. Am. Nurses Assn., Tenn. Nurses Assn., Nat. League Nursing, Chattanooga League Nursing, Am. Assn. Critical Care Nurses, Sigma Theta Tau. Baptist. Club: Fellowship Bapt. Home: 115 Terri Ln Chickamauga GA 30707 Office: Erlanger Med Center 975 E 3rd St Chattanooga TN 37403

SIEGLER, HOWARD MATTHEW, physician; b. N.Y.C., May 26, 1932; s. Samuel Lewis and Shirley Kendall (Matthews) S.; B.S. in Biochemistry, Hofstra U., 1952; postgrad. Yale U., 1954; M.B., Ch.B., St. Andrews U., 1958; M.D., N.Y. Med. Coll., 1965; m. Toinette Andrau, Dec. 1, 1953; children—Samuel Lewis, Karel Lynn, Jacqueline Andrau, Todd Bradford. Intern, N.Y. U. Med. Center, N.Y.C., 1965, New Rochelle (N.Y.) Hosp., 1966-67; asst. to dean U. Tex. Southwestern Med. Sch., Dallas, 1967-68; sr. fellow dept. phys. medicine Baylor Coll. Medicine, Houston, 1968-69; resident family practice program Meml. Baptist Hosp., 1971; gen. practice medicine, Houston, 1971, 72—; clin. fellow ob-gyn St. Lukes Episcopal Hosp., Houston, 1971-72; mem. staff Tex. Children's, St. Joseph, Center Pavilion, St. Luke's Episc. hosps., St. Anthony's Med. Center (all Houston); co-chmn. Muscular Dystrophy Soc., 1964-65; med. cons. Home Health Care Am.; dir., sr. cons. Houston Comprehensive Gen. Practice Clinic, Tex. Med. Ctr.; cons. div. disability determination Tex. Rehab. Commn., 1973; hon. v.p. St. Louis U. Active Assn. to Help Retarded Children; chmn. sr. div. Protestant Charities N.Y., 1964-65; trustee Huston-Tillotson Coll., Spencer Home for Boys; Rice asso. Rice U.; patron Houston Symphony, Houston Grand Opera, Houston Ballet, Mus. Fine Arts, Friends of Med. Center Library; asso. trustee The Kinkaid Sch.; col., a.d.c. Gov.'s staff, Tenn., Miss., La., 1971; lt. col., a.d.c. Gov.'s staff Ala., 1971. Appointed adm. Tex. Navy, 1973, Ark. Traveler, 1973. Served to maj. 36th Airborne Battery, Tex. Air N.G., ret.; now maj. 4005th Army Hosp. Unit USAR. Fellow Royal Soc. Health, Royal Soc. Medicine; mem. Am. Fertility Soc., Am. Geriatric Soc., AAAS, N.Y. Acad. Scis. (life), Australasian Coll. Biomed. Scientists, Am. Diabetes Assn., Internat. Soc. Cardiology (citation 1978), Am. Social Health Assn., S.W. Sci. Forum, Am. Soc. Bariatrics, Christian Med. Soc., Tex. Med. Assn., So. Med. Assn., Harris County Med. Soc., Am. Med. Soc. Alcoholism, Am. Assn. Gynecol. Laparoscopists, Am. Soc. Contemporary Medicine and Surgery, Tex. Acad. Family Physicians, Alumni Assn. Bellevue-N.Y. U. Med. Center (charter), Denton A. Cooley Cardiovascular Surg. Soc., Internat. Acad. Preventive Medicine, Tex. Assn. Disability Examiners, AMA, Am. Coll. Gen. Practice, Internat. Platform Assn., Phi Chi (chancellor 1963). Episcopalian. Home: 1 Longfellow Ln Houston TX 77005 Office: Suite 1020 Hermann Profl Bldg 6410 Fannin St Houston TX 77025

SIEH, MAURINE KAY, nurse; b. Leon, Iowa, Sept. 28, 1950; d. Vernon Charles and Dorothy Maxine (Akes) Dobson; B.S. in Nursing, N.E. Mo. State U., 1972; cert. childbirth educator, m. Robert Hans Sieh, Nov. 18, 1972; children—Robert Carter, Jennifer Clarissa. Charge nurse psychiat. unit St. John's Hosp., Springfield, Mo., 1972-74; public health nurse Will County Health Dept., Joliet, Ill., 1974-75; unit nurse Mental Health Inst. Mentally Retarded Children, Part Forest, Ill., 1977-79; instr. Lamaze method childbirth, Park Forest, 1977-81; psychiat. nurse, chmn. nurse practice and standards com. Menninger Found., Topeka, 1981; nurse neuro-neurosurg. unit Univ. Med. Center, Jackson, Miss., from 1981, now staff ob/gyn Outpatient Clinic. Mem. Am. Soc. Psychoprophylaxis in Obstetrics, Internat. Childbirth Edn. Assn., Nat. League Nursing, Nat. Audubon Soc., Nature Conservancy, Smithsonian Instn., AAUW. Mem. Brethren Ch. Home: 4953 Oak Leaf Dr Jackson MS 39212

SIEMON, JOYCE MARILYN, lawyer, writer; b. Bridgeport, Conn., Dec. 4, 1944; d. George Lewis and Rita (Siegel) Nissenson; 1 dau., Alyssa Karen. B.A.

in English, Carnegie Inst. Tech., 1966; J.D. with high honors, Fla. State U., 1980. Bar: Fla. Instr. legal writing and research Coll. Law Fla. State U., Tallahassee, 1979-80; intern. Fla. Supreme Ct., 1980; law clk. Office Gen. Counsel, Fla. Dept. Gen. Services, Tallahassee, 1980; assoc. Young, Stern & Tannenbaum, P.A., North Miami Beach, Fla., 1981, Greenberg, Traurig, Askew, Hoffman, Lipoff, Quentel & Wolff, P.A., Miami, Fla., 1981-82, Hornsby & Whisenand, Miami, 1982-85; sole practice, North Miami Beach, 1985—; tech. writer, Computer Sci. Research Center Carnegie Inst. Tech., Pitts., 1965-67; tchr., Leesville Jr. High Sch. (La.), 1967-68, Leesville State Sch., 1968; mag. editor VanTrump, Zeigler and Shane, Pitts., 1969; news editor Pitts. Press, 1970; staff writer Dade County Pub. Safety Dept., Miami, 1971-75; reporter North Dade Jour., Miami, 1977; freelance writer, 1977—. Editor: Lawrenceville: A Short History, 1969; author weekly humor column Siemon Says, North Date Jour., 1977; author employee manual, advt. brochures, newspaper articles and ads, book revs.; author, editor, contbr. articles to legal and non-legal publs. Dade County coordinator Network, 1983; corr. sec. Democratic Club of North Dade. Mem. ABA, Fla. Bar (various coms.), Am. Judicature Soc., Dade County Bar Assn., Order of Coif, Phi Alpha Delta. Jewish. Office: Senator Bldg 13899 Biscayne Blvd North Miami Beach FL 33181

SIERRA, LINDA JIMENEZ, dentist; b. McAllen, Tex., Apr. 26, 1949; d. Luis and Alicia (Flores) Jimenez; m. Angel Sierra, Oct. 2, 1971; children—Louis, Tommy, Andrew. A.A., Del Mar Jr. Coll., Corpus Christi, 1969; B.A., U. Tex., 1971; D.D.S., U. Tex.-Houston, 1978. Chair dental staff Humana Southmore Hosp., Pasadena, Tex., 1983-84; vice-chair dental staff Bayshore Hosp., Pasadena, 1985-86, chmn., 1986—. Mem. ADA, Tex. Dental Assn., Houston Dental Soc., Pasadena C. of C. Roman Catholic. Avocations: gardening; bicycling; aerobics. Office: 4221 Vista Rd Pasadena TX 77504

SIESHOLTZ, HERBERT WILLIAM, laboratory administrator; b. Newark, June 21, 1915; s. David and Betty S.; m. Minnie Yenkinson, Oct. 1, 1943; children—Sara, Stephen, Jerome, Robert. B.Ch.E., Cooper Union Inst. Tech., 1938. Chemist, Witco Chem. Co., N.Y.C. and Chgo., 1938-48; project engr. U.S. Ordnance Dept. Paint Lab., Aberdeen Proving Ground, Md., 1948-52; tech. dir. Crown Paint Inc., Hialeah, Fla., 1953-76; dir. Flamingo Research Labs. Inc., North Miami Beach, Fla., 1976—. Served to maj. U.S. Army, 1941-45; ETO. Mem. Am. Chem. Soc., Fedn. Socs. Coatings Tech., So. Soc. Coatings Tech., Engring. Honor Soc. Jewish. Office: Flamingo Research Labs Inc PO Box 600145 North Miami Beach FL 33160

SIESS, CHARLES P., JR., manufacturing company executive; b. Lake Charles, La., Jan. 28, 1927; m. Jean Muchard, Sept. 27, 1979; children by previous marriage—Charles P. III, S. Kurt. B.S. in Chem. Engring., La. State U., 1948. With Petrolite Corp., St. Louis, 1948-68, v.p., gen. mgr., until 1968; with Energy Services Assocs., (acquired by APCO Oil Corp.), 1968-69; exec. v.p. APCO Corp., Houston, 1969-72, pres., chief exec. officer, 1972-75; pres. Marathon Mfg. Co., Houston, 1976-80, pres., chief exec. officer, 1981—; dir. Penn Central Corp., Camco, Inc. Mem. AIME, Nat. Assn. Corrosion Engrs., Nat. Oil Equipment Mfrs. and Delegates Soc., Nat. Petroleum Refiners Assn. (past dir.), Am. Petroleum Inst. (past dir.), Nat. Ocean Industries Assn. (exec. com.). Avocations: boating, fishing, golf. Office: Marathon Mfg Co 600 Jefferson St 1900 Marathon Bldg Houston TX 77002

SIGEL, MARSHALL E., lawyer, financial consultant; b. Hartford, Conn., Nov. 25, 1941; s. Paul and Bessie (Somer) S.; B.S., U. Pa., 1963; J.D., U. Miami, 1982, LL.M. in Taxation, 1983. Exec. v.p. Advo-System, Inc., Hartford, 1963-69; pres. Ad-Lists, Inc., Hartford, 1963-69, Ad-Type Corp., Hartford, 1962-69, Advo-System div. KMS Industries, Inc., Hartford, 1969-72; dir. Boca Raton First Nat. Bank. Clubs: Tower, Boca Raton Hotel, Boca West. Home: PO Box 273408 Boca Raton FL 33427 Office: 2210 One Financial Plaza Fort Lauderdale FL 33394

SIGLER, KATHIE SUZANNE, college dean, author; b. Detroit, Apr. 19, 1944; d. Georgianna (McNae) Stringer; 1 child, Patrick W. Gettings. B.S., Wayne State U., 1967, M. Ed., 1968; Ed.D., Nova U., 1977. Exec. sec. Gen. Motors Corp., Detroit, 1964-67; faculty Cousino High Sch., Warren, Mich., 1967-69; various positions Miami-Dade Community Coll., Fla., 1969-82, dean adminstrn., 1981—; cons. higher edn. instn., pub. cos. Author: Reference Manual for OFfice Personnel, 1981; Reference Manual for Medical Office Personnel, 1986, others; computer software packages. Recipient Cert. Appreciation Fla. Assn. Community Colls., Cert. Appreciation March of Dimes, 1979, Nat. CETA Builders award; Dr. Kathie Sigler Day proclaimed Metro Dade County Oct. 11, 1984, Dr. Kathie Sigler and Paella '84 Day proclaimed City of Miami Oct. 11, 1984. Mem. Nat. Bus. Edn. Assn. So. Bus. Edn. Assn. Fla. Bus. Edn. Assn. Am. Vocat. Assn., Fla. Vocat. Assn., Fla. Assn. Community Colls., Dade County Bus. Edn. Assn., Am. Assn. Community and Jr. Colls., Women in Am. Community and Jr. Colls., Greater Miami C. of C., Leadership Miami Alumni Assn., Am. Heart Assn., Delta Pi Epsilon. Avocation: computer software.

SIGMUND, ARTHUR WILLIAM, JR., insurance agency executive, financial planner, consultant; b. Evanston, Ill., Apr. 18, 1951; s. Arthur William Sr. and Ruth (Christophersen) S.; m. Dorotheanna Sisson, Aug. 18, 1973; children—Arthur William, III, Stephen Lake. B.S., Ga. Inst. Tech., 1973. C.L.U.; chartered fin. cons. Agent Prudential Ins. Co., Atlanta, 1973-77, devel. mgr., 1977-81; pres. Sigmund & Assocs., Inc., Atlanta, 1980—; chief exec. officer Preferred Fin. Planners, Atlanta, 1985; cons. Gwinnet County, Lawrenceville, Ga., 1985. Pres. Yellow Jacket Club Ga. Tech., 1981. Mem. Chartered Life Underwriters, Chartered Fin. Cons., Atlanta Assn. Life Underwriters (mem. ethics com.), Internat. Assn. Fin. Planners. Republican. Baptist. Lodges: Kiwanis, Masons. Avocations: coaching youth football. Office: Sigmund & Assocs Heritage Bank Bldg 910 Holcomb Bridge Rd Roswell GA 30076

SIKES, ALAN LEE, developmental-behavioral optometrist; b. Meadville, Pa.; s. Robert and Mary (Lang) S. B.A., Edinboro State Coll., 1967; O.D., Pa. Coll. Optometry, 1971. Practice optometry specializing in developmental-behavioral optometry, Burke, Va., 1974—. Served to capt. M.C., U.S. Army, 1971-73. Mem. Optometric Extension Program, Va. Optometric Assn. (learning disorders com. 1980), No. Va. Optometric Assn., Am. Optometric Assn., Coll. Optometrists in Vision Devel. Home: 7708 Harwood Pl Springfield VA 22152 Office: Burke Profl Ctr 8985 Hersand Dr Burke VA 22015

SIKORA, EUGENE STANLEY, engineer; b. Duquesne, Pa., July 21, 1924; s. Adam Joseph and Helen (Pietrowska) S.; student Okla. Bapt. U., 1943-44; B.S. in Indsl. Engring., U. Pitts., 1949; C.E., Carnegie Inst. Tech., 1951; m. Corinne Mary Coliane, Sept. 7, 1946; children—Karyn Ann, Leslie Ann. Bridge design engr. Gannett, Fleming, Corddry & Carpenter, Pitts., 1949-50; structural designer Rust Engring. Co., Pitts., 1950-51, chief field engr., 1951-52, asst. project engr.; project engr. Frank E. Murphy & Assos., Bartow, Fla., 1952-55; v.p. Wellman-Lord Engring. Co., Lakeland, Fla., 1955-61; pres. Gulf Design Co., Lakeland, 1961-74, chmn. Lakeland Constrn., 1974-85; pres. Witcher Creek Coal Co., Belle, W.Va., 1979—; ptnr. Gulf Atlantic Mgmt. Assocs., Lakeland, Maingatea Mall Assocs., 1985—; chmn. Horizon Constrn. & Devel. Inc., 1985—; dir. Eldorado Resources Corp., Reno. Bd. dirs. Polk County Mus. Served with USAAF, 1943-45. Mem. Nat. Soc. Profl. Engrs., Am. Inst. Mining, Metall. and Petroleum Engrs., Am. Mgmt. Assn., Am. Inst. Chem. Engrs., Am. Inst. Indsl. Engrs., Fla. Engring. Soc., Lakeland C. of C. (dir.). Democrat. Episcopalian. Home: 1400 Seville Pl Lakeland FL 33803 Office: One Lone Palm Pl Lakeland FL 33801

SILAS, CECIL JESSE, petroleum company executive; b. Miami, Fla., Apr. 15, 1932; s. David Edward and Hilda Videll (Carver) S.; m. Theodosea Hejda, Nov. 27, 1965; children—Karla, Peter, Michael, James. B.S. in Chem. Engring., Ga. Inst. Tech., 1954. With Phillips Petroleum Co., 1953—, pres. Phillips Petroleum Co. Europe-Africa, Brussels, 1968-74; mng. dir. NRG Europe/Africa, London, 1974-76; v.p. NRG Gas and Gas Liquids, Bartlesville, Okla., 1976-78, sr. v.p., 1978-80, exec. v.p., 1980-82, pres., chief operating officer, dir., chmn. exec. com., 1982—; dir. 1st Nat. Bank in Bartlesville, 1st Nat. Bank & Trust Co. Tulsa. Bd. dirs. Am. Petroleum Inst., Inst. Gas Tech., U.S. Nat. Com. World Energy Conf., Nat. Jr. Achievement, Blue Stem Regional Med. Devel. Found., Okla. Med. Research Found.; mem. nat. adv. bd. Ga. Inst. Tech.; trustee Ga. Tech. Found. Served to 1st lt. Chem. Corps, U.S. Army, 1954-56. Decorated comdr. Order St. Olav (Norway). Mem. Am. Mgmt. Assn., Natural Gas Men Okla., Am. Petroleum Inst. (bd. dirs.). Club: Bartlesville Rotary. Home: 2400 Terrace Dr Bartlesville OK 74006 Office: 18 Phillips Bldg Bartlesville OK 74004

SILBER, NORMAN JULES, lawyer; b. Tampa, Fla., Apr. 18, 1945; s. Abe and Mildred (Hirsch) S.; m. Linda Geraldine Hirsch, June 10, 1979; 1 son, Michael Hirsch. B.A., Tulane U., 1967, J.D., 1969; postgrad. NYU Grad. Sch. Bus. Adminstrn., 1970-72. Bar: Fla. 1970, U.S. Dist. Ct. (so. dist. Fla.) 1975, U.S. Tax Ct. 1975, U.S. Ct. Appeals (5th cir.) 1975, U.S. Ct. Appeals (11th cir.) 1981. With legal dept. Fiduciary Trust Co. N.Y., N.Y.C., 1969-72, asst. trust officer, 1971-72; exec. v.p. I.R.E. Fin. Corp., Miami, Fla., 1972-76; mng. atty. Norman J. Silber, P.A., Miami, 1973-85; ptnr. McDermott, Will & Emery. Mem. ABA, Fla. Bar (chmn. 11th jud. cir. grievance com. I 1982-84), Dade County Bar Assn., Am. Judicature Soc., Assn. Trial Lawyers Am., Acad. Fla. Trial Lawyers. Republican. Jewish. Club: Standard (Miami). Home: 1232 Palermo Ave Coral Gables FL 33134 Office: 700 Brickell Ave Miami FL 33131

SILBERMAN, LOUIS Z., geologist; b. Wilmington, Del., Aug. 31, 1951; s. Jay W. and Rita (Kunin) S. B.S., U. Del., 1973; M.S., Fla. State U., 1979. Prodn. supr. Arkal Plastics, Bet Zera, Israel, 1973-75; mgmt. trainee J. Byrons Co., Miami, Fla., 1976-77; asst. dept. store mgr., West Palm Beach, Fla., 1977; geologist Exxon Co., U.S.A., Lafayette, La., 1979-81, sr. geologist, New Orleans, 1981-83, supervisory geologist, 1983-85, exploration geologist, 1985—. Contbr. articles to profl. jours. Mem. Am. Assn. Petroleum Geologists, New Orleans Geol. Soc. Avocations: Scuba diving; sailing; fishing; photography; camping. Office: Exxon Co U S A Eastern Div PO Box 61812 New Orleans LA 70161

SILBERMAN, MORTON SELIG, university veterinarian; b. N.Y.C., July 12, 1933; s. Louis Mann and Pauline (Alper) S.; m. Donna Mae Olsen, June 20, 1959; 1 dau., Suzanne Dee. A.S., L.I. Agrl. and Tech. Inst., 1954; B.S., U. Ga., 1958, D.V.M., 1968; student U. Minn., 1958-61. Entomologist, Ft. Valley, Ga., 1962; tchr. Forest Park (Ga.) Schs., 1962-63; field research Ga. Poultry Improvement Assn., 1964-68; pvt. practice veterinary medicine, Miami, Fla., 1968-69; cons. veterinarian Feedlots and Livestock in S.E., 1970-75, Lion Country Safari, 1971-76, White Oak Plantation, 1982—, N.Y. Zool. Park, 1976—; univ. veterinarian Emory U., 1976—; asst. prof. pathology, 1983—, mem. faculty Grad. Sch. Arts and Sci., 1977—, assoc. prof. pathology, 1983—; adj. prof. surgery Auburn U., 1983—. Served with AUS, 1954-56. Mem. AVMA, Ga. Vet. Med. Assn., S. Ga. Vet. Med. Assn., Greater Atlanta Vet. Med. Assn., Am. Assn. Zoo Veterinarians (exec. sec., past dir.), Acad. Vet. Consultants (past dir.), Am. Assn. Bovine Practitioners, U.S. Animal Health Assn. (exec. bd., chmn. zool. ops. com., others), Am. Assn. Animal Welfare Veterinarians, Am. Assn. Lab. Animal Practitioners, Southeastern Assn. Lab. Animal Sci. (past pres.), Am. Assn. Lab. Animal Sci., N.Y. Acad. Scis., Sigma Xi, Phi Kappa Phi, Phi Sigma. Contbr. articles to profl. jours. Office: Emory U Office U Veterinarian Drawer TT Atlanta GA 30322

SILBERMAN, STEPHEN LAWRENCE, dental educator, rare book dealer, publisher; b. Bklyn., Nov. 2, 1940; s. Paul B. and Anne (Frank) S.; m. Bernice Susan Spiegel, June 10, 1962; children—Gary Keith, Amy Lee, Jodi Beth. D.M.D., Tufts U., 1963; M.P.H., Harvard U., 1973, Dr. P.H., 1975. Dentist pvt. practice, Lake Grove, N.Y., 1965-72; staff Harvard U. Sch. Dental Medicine, Boston, 1972-75; prof. U. Miss. Sch. Dentistry, Jackson, 1975—; cons. Dept. Health and Human Services, Atlanta, 1975—. Editor: Problem Oriented Approach to Community Dentistry, 1980; also articles. Bd. dirs. Good Samaritan Ctr., Jackson, 1975—, Operation Shoestring, Jackson, 1975-85; dir., v.p. Three Village Jaycees, Stony Brook, N.Y., 1966-68; pres. Citizens for Nuclear Weapons Freeze, Jackson, 1984-85. Served to capt. USAF, 1963-65. Recipient USPHS fellow, 1972-75; award of Distinction Miss. Heart Assn. Fellow Acad. Gen. Dentistry; mem. ADA, Am. Pub. Health Assn. (com. chmn.), Am. Assn. Dental Schs. (del.), Am. Assn. Pub. Health Dentistry. Jewish. Avocations: book collecting; book publishing; art collecting; reading. Home: 5005 Meadow Oaks Park Dr Jackson MS 39211 Office: U Miss Sch Dentistry 2500 N State St Jackson MS 39216

SILCOX, GORDON BRUCE, recruiting consulting company executive; b. Takoma Park, Md., May 11, 1938; s. Walter Bruce and Ruth May (Davis) S.; A.B., Princeton U., 1960; M.B.A., U. Pa., 1965; m. Judith Andrea Smith, Mar. 7, 1970; children—Andrea Davis, Jessica Lyn. Trust investment officer Am. Security Bank, Washington, 1965-69; v.p., trust investment officer, head trust investment div. First Am. Bank of Washington, N.A., 1969-77; v.p., prin. Paul Stafford Assocs., Ltd., Washington, 1977-83; v.p., mgr. MSL Internat., Ltd., Washington, 1983—; sr. v.p. Golembel MSL Mgmt. Selection Cons., Washington, 1985—. Treas., Princeton Class of 1960, 1975-80, v.p., 1980-85. Served to lt. (j.g.) USN, 1960-63. Methodist. Clubs: Wharton Sch. (sec. 1980-81), University (Washington); Princeton (treas. Washington 1972-74) (Washington and N.Y.C.); Montclair (Va.) Country. Home: 3811 Dalebrook Dr Dumfries VA 22026 Office: MSL Internat Ltd 1110 Vermont Ave NW Suite 710 Washington DC 20005

SILER, EUGENE EDWARD, JR., judge; b. Williamsburg, Ky., Oct. 19, 1936; s. Eugene Edward and Lowell (Jones) S.; B.A. cum laude, Vanderbilt U., 1958; LL.B., U. Va., 1962; LL.M., Georgetown U., 1964; m. Christy Dyanne Minnich, Oct. 18, 1969; children—Eugene Edward, Adam Troy. Admitted to Ky. bar, 1963; individual practice law, Williamsburg, 1964-65; atty. Whitley County, Ky., 1965-70; U.S. atty. Eastern Dist. Ky., Lexington, 1970-75, judge U.S. Dist. Ct., Eastern and Western Dists. Ky., 1975—. Campaign co-chmn. Congressman Tim L. Carter, 1966; 5th Congl. Dist. campaign co-chmn. U.S. Senator J.S. Cooper, 1966; trustee Cumberland Coll., Williamsburg, 1965-73, 81—. Served with USNR, 1958-60. E. Barrett Prettyman fellow, 1963-64; recipient medal Freedom's Found., 1968. Mem. Fed., Ky., D.C. bar assns., Va. State Bar. Republican. Baptist. Club: Optimists (pres. Williamsburg 1969). Home: Route 3 Box 259 Williamsburg KY 40769 Office: US Courthouse Room 207 London KY 40741

SILLS, THOMAS WIETT, education educator, administrator; b. Bardwell, Tex., Jan. 24, 1930; s. Tom W. and Evelyn (Phillips) S.; m. Doris Elizabeth Alsmeyer, June 5, 1954; children—Thomas, III, Russell, Evelyn Sue, James. A.S., Murray State Sch. Agr., 1948; A.B., E. Central State U., 1950; Ed.M., Eastern Ky. State U., 1954; Ed.D., U. No. Colo., 1960. Tchr., Chapman Ranch, Tex., 1950-51; tchr., prin. Corpus Christi Pub. Schs., Tex., 1953-61; asst. prof., then assoc. prof. edn. No. Ariz. U., Flagstaff, 1961-64; dean, prof. Sch. Edn., W. Ga. Coll., Carrollton, 1964-80; prof. edn., chmn. dept. Francis Marion Coll., Florence, S.C., 1980—; Chmn. Carroll County Democrats, Ga., 1972-76. Served with U.S. Army, 1951-53. Recipient Disting. Hon. Alumnus award W. Ga. Coll., 1981. Mem. Assn. for Supervision Curriculum Devel. (pres. 1973-74, bd. dirs. 1970-76), Am. Assn. Colls. for Tchr. Edn. (instl. rep. pres. 1974-76), S.C. Council Edn. Deans (chmn. 1982-84), Assn. for Humanistic Edn. (bd. dirs.), Assn. Child Edn. Internat. (pubs. bd. 1968-74), Phi Delta Kappa (pres. 1963-64, Leadership award 1976). Home: 1332 Madison Ave Florence SC 29501 Office: Francis Marion Coll Florence SC 29601

SILVA, JORGE ALBERT, sales/marketing executive; b. Manizales, Colombia, Aug. 1, 1942; came to U.S., 1961, naturalized, 1970; s. Harold and Ofelia Silva. A.S., Monterey Peninsula Coll., 1964; B.S., San Francisco State Coll., 1966; M.B.A., U. Tenn., 1971. Product mgr. Johnson & Johnson Cali, Colombia, 1971-74; sales rep. Hiram Walker, Bogota, 1974-75, area mgr. Colombia, Ecuador, 1975-78, S.Am. West Coast, ABC Islands, Miami, Fla., 1982-83, mktg. mgr. Latin Am. div., 1982-83, mktg. sales mgr. West Coast, Miami, 1983—; mktg. cons. Mem. Colombian Vol. Police Group, 1978-82. Mem. The Group of Mktg. Bogota. Home: 6839 SW 114 Pl Apt D Miami FL 33173 Office: 825 S Bayshore Dr Suite 1144 Miami FL 33131

SILVER, BEVERLY PLEASANTS, biological sciences educator; b. Washington, Jan. 10, 1935; d. Joseph Cameron and Virginia (Bagby) Pleasants; 1 dau., Lauren R. Silver. B.S., Madison Coll., 1957; M.S., La. State U., 1960; postgrad. U. Tex., 1960-61, Syracuse U., 1964-65; Ph.D., SUNY Coll. Environ. Sci. and Forestry, 1973. Instr. Richard Bland Coll., Petersburg, Va., 1961-62; instr. James Madison U., Harrisonburg, Va., 1962-64, asst. prof., 1964-76, assoc. prof. biology, 1976—. Bd. dirs. Va. Skyline council Girl Scouts U.S.A., 1981-85. Mem. AAUP, LWV, Sigma Xi, Delta Kappa Gamma. Presbyterian. Office: Dept Biology James Madison U Harrisonburg VA 22807

SILVER, LAWRENCE ALAN, marketing executive; b. New Haven, Sept. 5, 1943; s. Herman B. and Marcia (Azersky) S.; m. Deena Rae Rosenberg, Feb. 26, 1967; children—Cheryl Ann, Elyse Stephanie, Marc Aaron. B.S. in Journalism, Boston U., 1965, M.S., 1966. Reporter, New Haven Register, 1960-66; freelance writer, Boston, 1964-66; dir. pub. relations Spear & Staff, Inc., Babson Park, Mass., 1966-69; pres. Silver Assocs. Pub. Relations & Advt., Holliston, Mass., 1970-82; pres. RJ Communication, Inc., St. Petersburg, Fla., 1982—; v.p. mktg. services Raymond, James & Assocs., Inc., St. Petersburg, 1982—; v.p. investor relations Raymond James Fin., Inc., St. Petersburg, 1983—; instr. journalism Framingham (Mass.) State Coll., 1974-80. Mem. Holliston Bylaw Study Com., 1978-82; founding pres. Temple Beth Torah, Holliston, 1972-73; bd. dirs. Temple Ahavat Shalom Men's Club, Palm Harbor, 1983-84; trustee Temple Ahavat Shalom, 1985—; pres. Temple Aharat Shalom Brotherhood, 1985—; founding bd. dirs. Jewish Community Ctr. of Greater Framingham, 1969-72. Served with U.S. Army, 1967-69. Mem. Securities Industry Assn. (pub. info. com. 1985—), St. Petersburg C. of C., Boston U. Nat. Alumni Council, Sigma Delta Chi. Assoc. editor Venture Capital Jour., 1978-82. Home: 795 Village Way Palm Harbor FL 33563 Office: Raymond James Ctr 1400 66th St St Petersburg FL 33710

SILVER, RICHARD ABRAHAM, hospital administrator; b. Boston, Nov. 21, 1922; s. Samuel and Sylvia Lena S.; A.B., Boston U., 1943; LL.B., George Washington U., 1955, M.S.P.A., 1966; m. Janice Backer Lavien, June 10, 1948; children—Gary Neil, Ronald Howard, Scott Hugh. Personnel asst. VA, Boston, 1946-50; personnel officer VA, Washington, 1950-71; asst. dir. VA Med. Ctr., East Orange, N.J., 1973-74; dir. VA Med. Ctr., Northampton, Mass., 1974-76, VA Med. Ctr., Brockton, Mass., 1976-79, James A. Haley VA Hosp., Tampa, Fla., 1979—; lectr. U. S.Fla. Sch. Medicine, 1979—. Served as capt. U.S. Army, 1943-46. Mem. Am. Hosp. Assn., Am. Coll. Hosp. Adminstrs., Assn. Am. Med. Colls. (mem. council teaching hosps.), Fla. Gulf Health Systems Agy. (bd. dirs.), Phi Beta Kappa, Alpha Epsilon Pi. Jewish. Office: James A Haley Vets Hosp Bruce Downs Blvd Tampa FL 33612

SILVER, ROY SILVER, sociologist, educator; b. N.Y.C., Oct. 26, 1950; s. Oscar and Stella S. B.A., U. Toledo, 1972; M.A., Queens Coll., 1975; Ph.D., U. Toledo, 1982. Grad. teaching asst. U. Toledo, 1976-80; asst. prof. sociology Union Coll., Barbourville, Ky., 1980-84; spl. project coordinator U. Ky., Lexington, 1984—. Editor: Looking Back: Poems From the Pen of Nellie Hibbard, 1984. Contbr. book revs. to profl. jours. Bd. dirs. Mexican Am. Youth Assn., Toledo, 1978-79; exec. dir. No. Heights Community Devel. Corp., Toledo, 1979-80; bd. dirs. Cumberland Valley Womens Shelter, Barbourville, Ky., 1983. James Still fellow Andrew W. Mellon Found. of N.Y., 1982. Mem. Am. Ednl. Studies Assn., So. Sociol. Assn., Am. Sociol. Assn. Avocations: photography, sports. Home: 537 N Broadway Lexington KY 40508 Office: The Appalachian Ctr Univ Ky 641 S Limestone St Lexington KY 40506

SILVERBERG, JAMES MAYER, university administrator, educator management; b. Thibodaux, La., Nov. 11, 1948; s. Joseph Nathan and Mary Elizabeth (Mayer) Silverberg; m. Katherine Dozier, Aug. 29, 1970; children—Ann Mayer, Jessica Mary. B.A., La. State U., 1970; M.B.A., Nicholls State U., 1978. City reporter Daily Comet Newspaper, Thibodaux, 1968-70, 71; pub. relations dir. Nicholls State U., Thibodaux, 1971—. Chmn. pub. relations com. Thibodaux Rotary Club, 1982, rotaract com., 1983, So. La. Econ. Council Tourism Com., 1984-85. Served to 2d lt. U.S. Army, 1970-71; with La. Army NG, 1978—. Mem. La. Press Assn., La. Higher Edn. Pub. Relations Assn., Council Advancement and Support Edn. (treas. 1982-85). Democrat. Jewish. Club: Bayou Country (bd. dirs. 1985). Avocations: golf; swimming; jogging. Office: Nicholls State U PO Box 2033 Thibodaux LA 70310

SILVERMAN, ELAINE ROSLYN, educator; b. Washington, Aug. 28, 1941; d. Mark and Rebecca (Leopold) S. B.S. in Edn., Temple U., 1963; Ed.M., George Mason U., 1977. Cert. tchr., Va. Group leader Dixon House, Phila., 1962; tchr. Hammond High Sch., Alexandria, Va., 1963-65, T.C. Williams High Sch., Alexandria, 1965—. Participant Alexandria City Democratic Mass Meeting for Presdl. Nomination, 1984. Mem. Va. Edn. Assn., Alexandria Edn. Assn., NEA, Nat. Council for Social Studies, Va. Council for Social Studies. Jewish. Avocation: reading in area of history of English monarchy. Office: T C Williams High Sch 3330 King St Alexandria VA 22311

SILVERMAN, FRED JAY, urban transportation planner; b. N.Y.C., July 5, 1947; s. Irving and Edith (Koslowsky) S. B.City Planning, U. Va., 1970; M.A., U. No. Colo., 1972. Community planner Va. Gov.'s Office, Richmond, 1970-72; sr. planner Metro Atlanta Transit Authority, 1973-74; chief policy planning Met. Dade County, Miami, Fla., 1974-83; dir. transp. planning Barton Aschman Assocs., Tampa, Fla., 1983—. Co-editor: The Case for Rail Transit, 1977. Contbr. articles to profl. jours. Mem. U. Va. Alumni Soc., Fla. Transit Assn. (v.p. 1982-83, dir. policy com. 1984—), Sigma Alpha Mu, Beta Psi. Avocations: photography; reading; music. Office: Barton Aschman Assocs 2901 W Busch Blvd Suite 1010 Tampa FL 33629

SILVERMAN, MARVIN, school psychologist; b. Bklyn., July 21, 1949; s. Hyman and Betty (Cohen) S.; B.A., St. John's U., 1971; M.S., L.I. U., 1972; Ed.D., Nova U., 1980; adopted children—Peter, Victor. Elem. sch. counselor, Monroe County, Fla., 1973-74; co-host Baby Jane Show, WKID-TV., Ft. Lauderdale, Fla., 1976; lectr. psychology Barry Coll., Miami Shores, Fla., 1978-79; elem. sch. counselor, Miami, Fla., 1974—; mental health counselor in pvt. practice, 1979—; adj. prof. edn. Nova U., Ft. Lauderdale, 1977-78. Pres. Universal Aid for Children Inc. Recipient Fla. Little Red Sch. House award, 1974. Mem. Am. Personnel and Guidance Assn., Am. Psychol. Assn., Fla. Personnel and Guidance Assn., Nat. Assn. for Gifted Children. Jewish. Author: (with others) State of Florida Elementary School Guidance Handbook, 1978, Elementary Guidance Outlook, 1975; How to Handle Problem Behaviors In School, 1980; contbr. articles to profl. jours. Home: 2301 N University Dr Apt 207 Pembroke Pines FL 33024 Office: 995 N Miami Beach Blvd Miami FL 33162

SILVERMAN, SHERLEY SHER, artist; b. Maywood, Ill., Jan. 20, 1909; d. Adam and Elizabeth (Portnoy) Sher; student U. Ill., 1927-28, Chgo. Acad. Fine Arts, 1932-35, pvt. studies; m. I.J. Silverman, Oct. 27, 1928; 1 son, Bernard W. Exhibited in one-man shows in Thor Gallery, Louisville, 1967, Covenant Club, Chgo., 1968, B'nai B'rith Exhbn. Hall, Washington, 1969; exhibited in group shows Salon Internat. de Charleroi, Belgium, 1968, Dibuix Premi Internat. Joan Miro, Barcelona, Spain, 1970-73, Galleria D'Arte La Scala, Di Firenze, 1971, Gallery Benhur Sanchez, Bogota, Colombia, Barry Cleaving, N.Z.; represented in permanent collection B'nai B'rith Hdqrs., Washington, pvt. collections. Recipient Internat. medal Honor, Internat. Centro Studi E. Scambi, 1971; Acad. Internat. Leonardo Da Vinci, 1971; Honoris Causa Silver medal Acad. Internat., Campanella, 1972; Gold medal Recognition and Bronze plaque La Scala Gallery, Florence, Italy, 1972; certificate Merit Internat. Dictionary, 1973; diploma of honor Internat Great Prize. Mem. N. Shore Art League, Internat. Arts Guild (comdr. 1965—), Suburban Fine Art League, Com. Gold Coast Art Fair, U.S. Com. Internat. Centro Studi E. Scambi, Acad. Internat. Leonardo De Vinci, Mid-Am. Art Assn. (pres. 1969-71, recipient award Recognition), Acad. Internat. Home and Studio: 9929 SW 16th St Quincy Park Pembroke Pines FL 33024

SILVERMAN, STANLEY EVERET, statistician; b. Miami, Fla., July 29, 1941; s. Harry and Lillian (Friedman) S.; m. Thelma L. Estrada, May 10, 1969; children—David J., Michael H. Student Miami Dade Coll., 1964-66. Lic. real estate salesman, Fla.; notary public. Night mgr. Maisson Hotel Corp., Miami Beach, Fla., 1964-69; statistician Am. Express Travel Related Services, Fort Lauderdale, Fla., 1969—; pres. Jomast Investment Club. Vice-pres. Plantation Pines Assn., 1983-84, 85. Served with U.S. Army, 1963-64. Mem. Am. Soc. Quality Control, Am. Statis. Assn. Home: 469 N Pine Island Rd Apt B-108 Plantation FL 33324

SILVERS, MORGAN DOUGHERTY, podiatrist; b. Piqua, Ohio, Mar. 29, 1942; s. Florent Morgan and Evelyn Mae (Dougherty) S.; m. Karen Cajka, Sept. 20, 1969; children—Kara Laurice, Morgan William. B.S. in Pharmacy, Ohio No. U., 1960; D.P.M., Ohio Coll. Podiatric Medicine, Diplomate Am. Coll. Podiatric Surgery. Pharmacist, Crosby Drug Store, Piqua, Ohio, 1965-66; chief pharmacist Piqua Meml. Hosp., 1966-67; pharmacist Ohio State U. Hosp., Columbus, 1967-69; sales rep. Eli Lily Drug Co., 1969-73; pvt. practice podiatrist, Talladega and Arriston, Ala., 1978—. Paul Harris fellow, Rotary Club Internat., 1982. Mem. Am. Podiatry Assn., Ala. Podiatric Assn. (pres. 1982), Am. Coll. Sports Medicine, Am. Coll. Ambulatory Foot Surgeons, Am. Coll. Hospi Podiatrists, Ala. Archaeology Soc., Ohio Archaeology Soc., Full Gospel Bus. Club. Club: Talladega Rotary. Home: RD 1 Box 511 Godsden AL 35190 Office: 103 Medical Office Pk Talladega AL 36150

SILVERSTEIN, MARTIN BARRY, orthopedic surgeon; b. Phila., Sept. 1, 1942; s. Edward and Libby S.; m. Molly Ann McCabe, Mar. 28, 1981; children—Romy, Elliot. A.B. in Sci., Temple U., 1963, M.D., 1967. Diplomate

Am. Bd. Orthopedic Surgeons. Intern, U. Pa. Service Phila. Gen. Hosp., 1967-68, resident in gen. surgery, 1968-69; orthopedic resident, Temple U. Hosp., Phila., 1971-74; pediatric orthopedic resident, Shriner's Hosp. for Crippled Children, Phila., 1972-73; practice medicine specializing in orthopedic surgery, Ft. Lauderdale, Fla.; active med. staff orthopedic surgery: Fla. Med. Center, Ft. Lauderdale, Plantation Gen. Hosp. (Fla.), Bennett Community Hosp., Plantation. Served with USN, 1969-71. Fellow Am. Acad. Orthopedic Surgeons, ACS, Internat. Coll. Surgeons; mem. AMA, Fla. Med. Assn., Broward County Med. Assn., Fla. Orthopedic Soc., Broward County Orthopedic Soc., Eastern Orthopedic Assn. Jewish. Author articles in field. Office: 4850 W Oakland Park Blvd Lauderdale Lakes FL 33313

SIMARD, HOUSTON HERBERT, manufacturing company executive; b. Fort Smith, Ark., Aug. 27, 1930; s. Joseph George and Vera Beatrice (Jackson) S.; student Ark. Poly. Inst., Russellville, 1948; m. Cogene Diffee Simard, Sept. 1, 1984; children—Rodney Joe, Timothy Vick. Vice-pres. Jackson's Furniture, Inc., Fort Smith, 1947-65; salesman Pratt & Lambert, Inc., Kansas City, Mo., 1965-69; sales mgr. Belwood, Inc. (formerly Belwood div. U.S. Industries), Ackerman, Miss., 1969-70, v.p. mktg., 1970-72, exec. v.p., 1972-74, pres., 1974-86, chmn., pres., 1986—. Served with AUS, 1947-48, 50-51. Mem. Nat. Kitchen Cabinet Assn. (chmn. standards com. 1981-83, dir. 1981—). Republican. Lutheran. Home: 2915 Oakleigh Ln Germantown TN 38138 Office: Belwood Inc PO Drawer A Hwy 15 S Ackerman MS 39735

SIMBERLOFF, DANIEL, biologist, educator; b. Easton, Pa., Apr. 7, 1942; s. Isaac and Ruth (Koplowitz) S. A.B., Harvard U., 1964; Ph.D., 1969. Asst. prof. biology Fla. State U., Tallahassee, 1968-73, assoc. prof., 1973-78, prof., 1978—; vis. prof. U. Mich., 1974, U. Minn., 1980, Hebrew U., Jerusalem, 1984. Contbr. articles to sci. jours. Editor Jour. Biogeography, 1974—. Co-editor: Ecological Communities: Conceptual Issues and the Evidence, 1984. Recipient Developing Scholar award Fla. State U., 1977; Rector's medal U. Helsinki, Finland, 1983. Mem. Ecol. Soc. Am. (Mercer award 1971), Am. Soc. Naturalists, Soc. for Study Evolution, Brit. Ecol. Soc., Soc. for Systematic Zoology. Jewish. Home: 3025 Echo Point Ln Tallahassee FL 32304 Office: Dept Biol Sci Fla State U Tallahassee FL 32306

SIMEL, PAUL JOSEPH, ophthalmologist; b. N.Y.C., Mar. 7, 1930; s. Abraham and Esta (Schwarz) S.; m. Faye Holland, Apr. 14, 1968; children—David, Bruce, Dana, Mark Pace. A.B., Dartmouth Coll., 1951; M.D., Boston U., 1955; postgrad. Yale U., 1959. Diplomate Am. Bd. Ophthalmology. Practice medicine specializing in ophthalmology, Greensboro, N.C., 1955—; vis. eye surgeon Orbis project, N.Y.C., Houston, 1983—. Fellow Am. Acad. Ophthalmology, ACS; mem. Am. Intraocular Implant Soc., Am. Soc. Contemporary Ophthalmologists, Keratorefractive Soc. Club: Starmount Forest (Greensboro). Avocations: tennis; aviation. Home: 16-C Fountain Manor Dr Greensboro NC 27405 Office: Simel Surgical Eye Assocs 111 W Wendover Ave Greensboro NC 27401

SIMITSES, GEORGE JOHN, engineering educator, consultant; b. Athens, Greece, July 31, 1932; came to U.S., 1951, naturalized, 1963; s. John G. and Vasilike (Goutoufas) S.; m. Nena Athena Economy, Sept. 11, 1960; children—John G., William G., Alexandra G. B.S. in Aerospace Engring., Ga. Tech. Inst., 1955, M.S. in Aerospace Engring., 1956; Ph.D. in Aeros. and Astrosci. Stanford U., 1965. From instr. to prof. engring. Ga. Tech. Inst., Atlanta, 1956—; cons. Lockheed-Georgia Co., Marietta, Ga., 1965-70, King & Gavaris Engrs., N.Y.C., 1977-79, Ga. Power Co., Atlanta, 1971-72. Author: Stability of Elastic Structures, 1976. Contbr. chpts. to books, articles to profl. jours. Community rep. Am. Hellenic Inst., Washington, 1976—; del. Ga. State Democratic Conv., Macon, 1969. Fellow AIA (assoc.; various coms. 1974—); mem. ASME (coms. 1976—), Am. Acad. Mechanics, Hellenic Soc. of Theoretical and Applied Mechanics (founding mem.), AHEPA (v.p. chpt. 1978-79, coms. 1975—), Sigma Xi (Sustained Research award 1980, Best Paper award 1985). Home: 1389 Spalding Dr NE Atlanta GA 30338 Office: Ga Inst Tech 225 North Ave SW Atlanta GA 30332

SIMMONS, BARRY DAVID, dentist; b. Atlanta, Jan. 7, 1937; s. Perry and Vivian Hannah (Folkman) S. D.D.S., Emory U., 1963. Pvt. practice dentistry, Athens, Ga., 1963—; pres. Dental Health Internat., Athens, 1973—; vis. lectr. Harvard Sch. Dental Medicine, 1974-76. Served with U.S. Army, 1956-59. Named Young Man of Yr., Athens Jaycees, 1971; One of Ga.'s Five Outstanding Young Men, Ga. Jaycees, 1971; One of Ten Outstanding Young Men in Am., U.S. Jaycees, Indpls., 1971. Mem. ADA, Ga. Dental Assn., Eastern Dist. Dental Soc., Delta Sigma Delta. Jewish. Avocations: sailing; collector of vintage sportscars. Home: 847 S Milledge Ave Athens GA 30605 Office: 847 S Milledge Ave Athens GA 30605

SIMMONS, CARMEN, college bookstore executive; b. Jones County, Miss., Apr. 28, 1922; d. Buford Elmer and Ella Emily (Morgan) Delk; m. Robert Floyd Simmons, Apr. 10, 1942; children—Emily Elizabeth, Robert Delk. Student, William Carey Coll. With Fowler Butane Gas Co., 1951-56, Citizens Bank of Hattiesburg, Miss., 1956-62, William Carey Bookstore & Post Office, Hattiesburg, 1962-84; mgr. William Carey Bookstore, Hattiesburg, 1984—. Mem. Bus. & Profl. Women Orgn., Miss. Assn. College Stores (pres. 1982, dir. 1983). Republican. Baptist. Lodge: Order Eastern Star. Avocations: cooking; needlework; gardening; sewing. Home: 707 N 31st Ave Hattiesburg MS 39401 Office: William Carey College Bookstore Hattiesburg MS 39401

SIMMONS, FLOYD EDWIN, JR., educational administrator; b. Memphis, June 3, 1945; s. Floyd Edwin and Joy (Aiken) S., Sr.; m. Barbara Joyce Langseth, July 6, 1968; children—Jonathan Seth, Rachel Kay. Student, Northwestern Coll., Mpls., 1964-67; B.A., Tabor Coll., Hillsboro, Kans., 1967-68; M.Div., Bethel Sem., St. Paul, 1972; M.B.A., U. Tenn.-Chattanooga, 1981. Mech. staff mgr. Billy Graham Assn., Mpls., 1965-71; prodn. mgr. Central Mailing, Mpls., 1971-73; phys. plant dir. Convenant Coll., Lookout Mountain, Tenn., 1973-80, v.p. bus. and fin., 1980—; cons. King Coll., Bristol, Tenn., 1982. Deacon, First Presbyterian Ch., Chattanooga, 1981—; coordinator United Fund, Convenant Coll., 1980-83. Mem. Nat. Assn. Coll. and Univ. Bus. Officers, So. Assn. Coll. and Univ. Bus. Officers, Assn. Bus. Adminstrs. of Christian Colls.

SIMMONS, FRANK DUNCAN, newspaper editor; b. Morgan County, Ala., Apr. 13, 1934; s. Paul Langford and Lucy Carmen (Griffin) S.; m. Carolyn Ann Dewey, July 2, 1960; children—Cary Lynn, Christopher Allen. B.A. in Econs., Coll. William and Mary, 1959. Reporter, Newport News (Va.) Times-Herald, 1960-63, copy editor, 1964-67, wire editor, 1967-72, mng. editor, 1972-81; reporter The Virginian-Pilot, Norfolk, 1963-64; exec. editor Newport News Daily Press/Times-Herald, 1981—. Served to sgt. USAF, 1951-55; Korea. Mem. Va. Press Assn. (pres. 1982-83), Va. UPI Adv. Bd. (chmn. 1981-82), Va. AP Newspapers (chmn. 1978-79). Lodge: Kiwanis. Office: Daily Press Inc 7505 Warwick Blvd Newport News VA 23607

SIMMONS, FREDERIC RUDOLPH, pediatrician; b. Balt., Apr. 19, 1921; s. Frederic Rudolph and Jessie Agnes (Smith) S.; m. Vera Caldwell, June 24, 1950; children—Mary R., Carol E., Frederic Rudolph, James W., Josephe, Michael T. B.S., Loyola Coll., Balt., 1946; M.D., U. Md., 1950. Diplomate Am. Bd. Pediatrics. Rotating intern Walter Reed Army Hosp., Washington, 1950-51; resident pediatrics Johns Hopkins Hosp., Balt., 1951-53; practice medicine specializing in pediatrics, Daytona Beach, Fla., 1956—; mem. med. staff Halifax Hosp. Med. Center, Daytona Beach, 1956—. Served to maj. USAAF, 1942-45, 50-56. Decorated Air medal with 2 oak leaf clusters, Purple Heart. Mem. AMA, Am. Acad. Pediatrics, Fla. Med. Assn., Alpha Omega Alpha. Republican. Roman Catholic. Office: 135 Broadway Daytona Beach FL 32018

SIMMONS, GILBERT LARRY, dentist; b. Orange, Tex., Nov. 25, 1936; s. Raford Gilbert and Linadine (Smith) S.; B.S., Baylor U., 1959, D.D.S., 1962; m. Mary Sue Dillard, Aug. 31, 1957; children—Stanley A., Steven R., Wade A. Pvt. practice gen. dentistry, Denton, Tex., 1964—. Chmn. planning zoning commn. City of Argyle (Tex.), 1975-78. Served as dental officer USN, 1962-64. Licensed dentist, Tex. Mem. Denton County Dental Soc. (pres. 1971-72), Am., Tex. dental assns., Am. Soc. for Preventive Dentistry, Am. Acad. Gen. Dentistry, Denton C. of C. (dir. 1969-70), Am. Heart Assn. (dir. 1967-69). Baptist (deacon). Clubs: Denton Rotary (dir. 1970-71), Masons, Scottish Rite. Home: 2316 Georgetown Denton TX 76201 Office: 1002 N Elm St Denton TX 76201

SIMMONS, HOMER FISCHER, JR., petroleum geologist, consultant; b. Whittier, Calif., Nov. 12, 1923; s. Homer Fischer and Agnes Jane (Smith) S.; m. Betty Jane Porter, July 29, 1943; 1 child, Pamela Sue Blodgett. A.A., Pasadena Jr. Coll., 1947; B.A., Pomona Coll., 1949. Cert. petroleum geologist. Geologist, various managerial positions Shell Oil Co., Midcontinent, Wichita Falls, Tex., 1949-57, Gulf Coast La. and Tex., 1957-77, head office, N.Y.C., 1963-64; geologist N.A.M., Assen, Nederland, 1971-73; practicing cons. Gulf Coast, Slidell, La. and Monteagle, Tenn., 1977—. Served to sgt. U.S. Army, 1943-46, CBI. Mem. Am. Assn. Petroleum Geologists, Soc. Ind. Profl. Earth Scis. Republican. Avocation: genealogy. Home and Office: PO Box 546 Monteagle TN 37356

SIMMONS, JOELLEN FLORES, state agency administrator; b. Ft. Gulik, Panama, Nov. 12, 1947; d. Joe Bruton and Betsy Ann (Draina) F.; m. Ron Simmons, June 18, 1977; children—Jimmy and Johnny (twins). B.S. in Spl. Edn., Tex. Womens U., 1970; M. Spl. Edn./Psychology, Tex. Tech. U., Lubbock, 1973; postgrad. U. Tex., 1976-78. Spl. educator Andrews Ind. Sch. Dist., Andrews, Tex., 1970-74; cons., program specialist Tex. Edn. Agy., Austin, 1974-83; exec. dir. Tex. Planning Council-Developmental Disabilities Program, Austin, 1983-85; asst. commr. sprl. programs Tex. Rehab. Agy., Austin, 1985—; adminstr. spl. edn. Gulf Coast Council Edn. Region IV, Houston, 1982; state agy. fiscal monitor Tex. Edn. Agy., Austin, 1980-83; state agy. liaison Gov.'s Commn. on Women, Austin, 1984-85; fed. grant reviewer Dept. Health and Human Services, Washington, 1985, 86. Co-author, editor Highlights, 1983-85. Contbr. articles to autism to profl. jours. State agy. rep. Tex. Edn. Agy., Gov.'s Planning Council, Austin, 1975-79. Recipient recognition Gov. State Agy. Women, Austin, 1985. Mem. Nat. Assn. Developmental Disabilities (del. 1983-85), Nat. Assn. Rehab. Dirs., Tex. Council Children Behavior Disorders (pres., recognition award 1982), Council for Exceptional Children, Exec. Women in Govt. Roman Catholic. Office: Tex Rehab Agy 118 E Riverside St Austin TX 78704

SIMMONS, JOSEPH PAUL, geologist; b. Highland, Ind., Aug. 31, 1958; s. John David and Josephine Francis (Zralka) S. B.S. in Geology, Harvard U., 1980; M.S. in Indsl. Adminstrn., Purdue U., 1984; postgrad. U. Ill., 1980, U. Houston, 1982-83, U. S.W. La., 1984. Geologist, Cities Service, Tulsa, 1981-82, exploration geophysicist, Houston, 1982-83; oil and gas prodn. and ops. mgmt. Kerr-McGee, Lafayette, La., 1984—. Mem. Am. Assn. Petroleum Geologists, Soc. Exploration Geophysicists, Soc. Petroleum Engrs. Roman Catholic. Avocations: Tae Kwon Do, local fine arts. Office: Kerr-McGee Corp PO Box 54028 Lafayette LA 70505

SIMMONS, KENNETH BOYD, JR., landscape architect; b. Columbia, S.C., Jan. 8, 1947; s. Kenneth Boyd and Katharine B. (Farinholt) S. B.S. in Ornamental Horticulture, Clemson U., 1969; M. Landscape Architecture, U. Ga., 1972. Registered landscape architect, S.C., Fla., Va., Ky. Draftsman, Office of William Beery, Athens, 1971; park planner S.C. Dept. Parks, Recreation and Tourism, 1972-73; landscape architect Kenneth B. Simmons Assocs., Columbia, S.C., 1973-76, ptnr., 1976—; teaching asst. Sch. Environ. Design U. Ga., Athens, 1972. Mem. S.C. Landscape Archtl. Registration Bds. (chmn. 1977-78), U. Ga. Sch. Environ. Design Alumni Assn. (past pres.), Nat. Council Landscape Archtl. Registration Bds. (past pres.), Am. Soc. Landscape Architects (S.C. trustee), Landscape Architects Registration Bd. Found. (pres. 1982-83), Interprofl. Council on Registration (v.p. 1982-83). Roman Catholic. Clubs: Summit, Bankers Trust Tower (Columbia), Met. Bus. Home: 106 S Pickens St Columbia SC 29205 Office: 3135 Millwood Ave Columbia SC 29205

SIMMONS, MICHAEL DAN, orthodontist; b. Denver, Nov. 18, 1943; s. Carl Wade and Dorothy Maxine (Fitzwater) Simmons Baker; m. Margarita Emma Nichols, Aug. 11, 1970; children—Elizabeth, Tamara. Student, Adams State Coll., 1964; D.D.S., Northwestern U., 1968; M.S., Ohio State U., 1974; cert. in orthodontics, 1974. Practice dentistry specializing in orthodontics, Phoenix, 1974-77; asst. prof. Med. Coll. Ga., Augusta, 1977-80; practice dentistry specializing in orthodontics, Statesville, N.C., 1980—; cons. in field; coordinator clinic Grad. Orthodontic Clinic, Augusta, 1977-80. Contbr. articles to profl. jours. Pres., chmn. Iredell County Health Dept. Adv. Bd., Statesville, 1983-85. Served to lt. comdr. USN, 1968-72. Grantee NIH, 1978-79, Med. Coll. Ga., 1979. Mem. ADA, N.C. Dental Assn., Iredell County Dental Soc., (pres. 1984-85), Am. Assn. Orthodontists, So. Soc. Orthodontists, Am. Cleft Palate Assn., Dental Ariz. Dental Soc. (chmn. publicity 1976), Statesville C. of C. Republican. Episcopalian. Lodge: Rotary. Avocations: snow skiing; tennis; golf. Office: PO Box 1141 Statesville NC 28677

SIMMONS, RICHARD MORGAN, JR., furniture manufacturing company executive; b. Martinsville, Va., Sept. 28, 1926; s. Richard Morgan and Margaret (Sydnor) S.; student Va. Mil. Inst., 1944; B.A., U. Va., 1948; m. Louise Henry Acker, Oct. 9, 1948; children—Catherine, Lee, Morgan, Elizabeth, Louise. With Am. Furniture Co., Inc., Martinsville, Va., 1948—, pres., chief exec. officer, 1961-74, chmn. bd., pres., 1974—; dir. Dibrell Bros., Piedmont Trust Bank, Renfro Co., Tultex Corp., Warren Trucking Co. Served with U.S. Mcht. Marine, 1945. Mem. So. Furniture Mfrs. Assn., Furniture Factories Mktg. Assn. Episcopalian. Office: PO Box 5071 Martinsville VA 24112

SIMMONS, ROBERT BURNS, history and political science educator; b. Gadsden, Ala., Dec. 27, 1937; s. Bruns Hunter and Grace Barbara (Armstrong) S.; B.S. in Chemistry, U. Ala., 1961; B.A. in Biology and History (Woodrow Wilson fellow), Athens State Coll., 1968, M.A. in Teaching, 1969; Ed.S. (Coll. Scholar), George Peabody Coll., 1976; M.A.S., U. Ala., 1978; m. Eleanor Conner, Nov. 11, 1959 (dec.); children—Kathleen D., Mary Ellen; m. 2d, Regina Hunter, July 31, 1981. Quality control chem. lab. supr. Goodyear Tire & Rubber Co., Gadsden, Ala., 1961-65; sect. leader, research and devel. chem. labs. Thiokel Chem. Corp., Redstone Arsenal, Huntsville, Ala., 1966-69; prof. history, polit. sci. and mgmt. John C. Calhoun State Community Coll., Decatur, Ala., 1969—, asst. coordinator instl. devel. grant, 1983-84; asst. acad. dean Vol. State Community Coll., Gallatin, Tenn., 1974. Chmn. coms. Decatur Band Boosters; program com. coordinator Congressman James Martin of Ala.; mem. acad. affairs com. Commn. on Instl. Self Study. U.S. Office Edn. grantee, 1970-71. Mem. Am. Hist. Assn., So. Hist. Assn., Ala. Hist. Assn., Am. Assn. Higher Edn., Ala. Edn. Assn., Am. Chem. Soc., Archaeol. Inst. Am., Community Coll. Humanists Assn., Decatur C. of C., Beta Beta Beta, Phi Delta Kappa. Republican. Baptist. Club: Burningtree Country. Patentee missile propellants. Home: 2307 Burningtree Dr Decatur AL 35603 Office: Harris Bldg Calhoun Community Coll PO Box 2216 Decatur AL 35602

SIMMONS, SAMUEL WILLIAM, retired public health official; b. Benton County, Miss., June 5, 1907; s. Britt L. and Ida E. (Pegram) S.; B.Sc. with honors, Miss. State U., 1931; A.M., George Washington U., 1934; Ph.D., Iowa State U., 1938; m. Lois Grantham, Aug. 5, 1928; children—Samuel William, Grant P. With U.S. Dept. Agr., Bur. Entomology, 1931-44; with USPHS, 1944-71, dir. Carter Meml. Lab., 1944-47; chief tech. devel. br., 1947-53, chief tech. br. communicable disease center 1953-66; chief pesticides program Nat. Ctr. Disease Control, Atlanta, 1966-68; dir. div. pesticide community studies FDA, 1968-71; dir. div. pesticide community studies EPA, 1971-72, ret.; vis. lectr. tropical pub. health Harvard U., 1952-67; asso. preventive medicine and community health Emory U., 1957-72; USPHS rep. Fed. Com. on Pest Control. Recipient Alumni Achievement award George Washington U., 1946, Alumni Centennial Citation award Iowa State U., 1958, Distinguished Service medal USPHS, 1965, William Crawford Gorgas medal Assn. Mil. Surgeons U.S., 1968, Distinguished Career award EPA, 1972. Hon. cons. Army Med. Library, 1940-53; adv. bd. Inst. Agrl. Medicine, U. Iowa Sch. Medicine, U.S.-Japan Com. on Sci. Cooperation. Diplomate Am. Bd. Microbiology. Fellow Am. Soc. Tropical Medicine and Hygiene (councilor 1953), Chem. Spltys. Mfrs. Assns. (interdpl. com. pest control, subcom. vector control inter-agy. com. water resources, chmn. 1964-66), U.S.-Mex. Border Health Assn., WHO (chmn. com. on pesticides 1951, 56, 57), AMA (com. on insecticides 1950-59, com. on toxicology 1960), Research Soc. Am., Entomol. Soc. Am., Nat. Malaria Soc. (sec.-treas. 1951), Nat. Environ. Health Assn., Agrl. Research Inst., Am. Mosquito Control Assn., Armed Forces Pest Control Bd., Nat. Research Council, Nat. Assn. Watch and Clock Collectors (fellow, nat. dir. 1979-83, mem. awards com.), Sigma Xi, Phi Kappa Phi, Gamma Sigma Delta, Los Hidalgos. Contbr. articles to profl. jours.; editor and co-author: The Insecticide DDT and Its Significance, vol. II; contbr. to Human and Veterinary Medicine, 1959; author: Descendants of John Simmons of North Carolina, 1760, 1979; The Pegrams of Virginia and Descendants, 1688-84, 1985. Home: 2050 Blackfox Dr NE Atlanta GA 30345

SIMMONS, SUSAN ANNETTE, business analysis, economics educator; b. Pascagoula, Miss., Apr. 12, 1947; d. Emmitt Leroy and Margie Marie (Coker) S. B.S., Miss. State Coll. for Women, 1969; M.B.A., Miss. State U., 1970; Ph.D., U. Miss., 1976. Asst. prof. Eastern Ky. U., 1976-78, U. Southwestern La., Lafayette, 1978-80; assoc. prof. U. Iowa, Iowa City, 1980-83; asst. prof. Sam Houston State U., Huntsville, Tex., 1983—. Contbr. articles to profl. jours. Editor Jour. Bus. Strategies, 1985; memb. bd. editors Midsouth Jour. Econs., 1979—. Mem. Am. Econ. Assn., S.E. Am. Inst. for Decision Scis. (v.p. student liaison 1978-79, sec. 1979-81, council 1981—), Midsouth Acad. Economists, So. Econ. Assn., Phi Kappa Phi, Omicron Delta Epsilon, Kappa Epsilon (assoc.). Baptist. Office: Sam Houston State U Huntsville TX 77341

SIMMONS, THOMAS WILLIAM, teacher educator; b. Atlanta, Mar. 17, 1921; s. Arbie and Annie Lee (Darden) S.; m. Lillian Reed, May 26, 1951; 1 son, Reginald Fitzgerald. B.S., Tuskegee Inst., 1944; M.Ed., U. Ill., 1954; profl. diploma Columbia U., 1963; Ed.D., U. S.D., 1976. Instr. garment making St. John Vocat. Inst., Lake Charles, La., 1948-49, Govt. St. Tng. Sch., Baton Rouge, 1949-53; asst. prof. history Miles Coll., Birmingham, Ala., 1955-56; instr. edn. Benedict Coll., Columbia, S.C., 1957-60, asst. prof. edn., 1961-76, assoc. prof. ednl. psychology, 1976, chmn. div. edn. St. Augustine's Coll., Raleigh, N.C., 1980—. Mem. profl. rev. com. N.C. State Dept. Pub. Instrn.; trustee Oberlin Bapt. Ch., also mem. Number I Club. Mem. NAACP, YMCA, Southeastern Psychol. Assn., NEA, N.C. Assn. Educators, Am. Psychol. Assn., Kappa Delta Pi, Phi Delta Kappa, Omega Psi Phi. Contbr. articles to profl. jours. Home: 1522 Ben Lloyd Dr Raleigh NC 27604 Office: St Augustine's Coll 1315 Oakwood Ave Raleigh NC 27611

SIMMONS, WILLIAM ISAAC, retired dentist; b. Waco, Tex., Feb. 14, 1924; s. Jared Claude and Blanche (Schwarz) S.; D.D.S., Loyola U., New Orleans, 1946; cert. in orthodontics U. Pa., 1950; m. Evelyn Kottle, June 11, 1967; children—Jared Claude, Walter Neil, Gina Denise, Nancy Dayan, Dylan Sara. Tchr., U. Tex. Dental Sch., 1951; individual practice dentistry, specializing in orthodontics, Shreveport, La., 1951-85, ret. Served with USAF, 1946-48. Mem. ADA (v.p. 4th Dist.), Am. Orthodontic Soc., Royal Soc. Health. Jewish. Clubs: Masons, University (Shreveport); Barksdale Air Force Officers.

SIMMONS, WILLIAM WYNN, data processing executive; b. Johnsonville, S.C., Apr. 10, 1935; s. Durant Joseph and St. Clair (Floyd) S.; m. Dorothy Ann Carey, Nov. 7, 1958; children—Kelly Wynne Melton, William Robert, Michael Jay. B.S., Colo. State U., 1968; M.B.A., Auburn U., 1980. Commd. 2d lt. U.S. Air Force, 1956, advanced through grades to col., 1977; navigator, 1956-58; pilot, 1960-68; squadron comdr., 1969-72; asst. dir. logistics, 1973-75; div. chief Maintenance Systems div., Air Force Data Systems Design Ctr., 1975-80; ret., 1980; mgr. software transition group Planning Research Corp., Jacksonville, Fla., 1980-82, mgr. product assurance group, 1982-83, dir. quality assurance, govt. info. systems McLean, Va., 1983-84; project mgr. Sterling Systems Inc., Harrisburg, Pa., 1984-85, gen. mgr., McLean, 1985—. Mem. Air Force Assn., Ret. Officers Assn., Am. Mgmt. Assn. Republican. Home: 1907 Autumn Chase Ct Falls Church VA 22043 Office: 1500 Planning Research Dr McLean VA 22102

SIMMS, LEROY ALANSON, newspaper executive; b. Emelle, Ala., Sept. 17, 1905; s. John Thomas and Minnie Epes (Thomas) S.; m. Virginia Hammill, June 30, 1926 (dec.); m. Martha Alice Holliman, May 17, 1969; 1 dau., Lucie Grey Simms Grubbs (dec.). Student, U. Ill., 1924-25; L.H.D. (hon.), U. Ala., 1982. Reporter, Birmingham (Ala.) News, 1924-26; Reporter Tampa (Fla.) Morning Tribune, 1926-27; city editor Birmingham Post, 1927-28, mng. editor, 1929-31; asst. editor Newspaper Enterprise Assn., Cleve., 1931-32; day editor AP, Birmingham bur., 1933-38, Ala. corr., 1938-58; mng. editor Birmingham News, 1959-61; editor Huntsville (Ala.) Times, 1961—, v.p., dir., 1963—, pub., 1964—; Dir. Huntsville Indsl. Expansion Com., 1966—, v.p., 1966-70, pres., 1970-71. Author: Road to War: Alabama Leaves the Union, 1960. Mem. Am., So. newspaper pubs. assns., Ala. Press Assn. (dir. 1964-66), Ala. A.P. Assn. (pres. 1965-66), Am. Soc. Newspaper Editors, Sigma Delta Chi (chmn. Ala. 1960), Theta Chi. Clubs: Rotarian, Huntsville Country, Valley Hills Country. Home: 1 Cruse Alley SE Huntsville AL 35801 Office: Huntsville Times Memorial Pkwy Huntsville AL 35807*

SIMMS, ROBERT D., justice Supreme Court Oklahoma; b. Tulsa, Feb. 6, 1926; s. Matthew Scott and Bessie L. (Moore) S.; m. Patricia C., Feb. 16, 1950; 1 son, Robert D. Student, Milligan Coll., Phillips U.; LL.B., U. Tulsa. Bar: Okla. 1950. Practiced law, Sand Springs, Okla., from 1950, asst. county atty., Tulsa County, 1953-54; chief prosecutor County Atty.'s Office, 1955-58, county atty., 1958-62; judge Okla. Dist. Ct., Dist. 14, 1962-71, Okla. Ct. Criminal Appeals, 1971-72; justice Okla. Supreme Ct., 1972—, now vice-chief justice; mem. Okla. Crime Commn. Mem. Gov.'s Spl. Com. on Drug Abuse, 1970; sponsor and coach Pee-Wee Baseball. Served with USN, 1943-46. Mem. Tulsa County Bar Assn., Okla. Bar Assn. (chmn. dist. atty. sect. 1959). Office: Supreme Ct Okla 202 State Capitol Bldg Oklahoma City OK 73105*

SIMON, DONNITA MARIE, nurse; b. Paducah, Ky., Aug. 28, 1946; d. Howard Woodrow and Berthal Marie (Southwell) Ivey; m. Steven Paul Simon, June 25, 1966; children—Annmarie Eileen, Sean Paul. Diploma in Nursing, Hurley Med. Ctr., 1968. Staff nurse Mercy Hosp., Jackson, Mich., 1964-76, staff nurse operating room, 1969-75, asst. head nurse, 1975-76; staff nurse operating room Venice Hosp., Venice, Fla., 1976-82, head nurse, 1982-83, staff nurse operating room, 1983—; cons. Mercy Hosp., Jackson, Mich., 1967. Mem. Student Nurses Assn. (v.p. 1961), Assn. Operating Room Nurses (pres. 1982-83, bd. dirs. 1983-84). Democrat. Episcopalian. Home: 1548 Crest Dr Englewood FL 33533

SIMON, HENRY GERSON, pediatrician; b. New Orleans, June 18, 1926; s. Alvin Barry and Lucile Marie (Hodgson) S.; m. Elsa Clare Metzger, Sept. 20, 1953 (div. 1963); children—Elsa Gaskell, Harriet, Leah; m. Karola Manzke Waterson, Mar. 19, 1981. B.S., Tulane U., 1945, M.D., 1948. Diplomate Am. Bd. Pediatrics. Intern, Charity Hosp., New Orleans, 1948-49; resident in pediatrics St. Christopher Hosp. for Children-Temple U. Sch. Medicine, Phila., 1949-51; pvt. practice medicine specializing in pediatrics, New Orleans, 1951—; sr. ptnr. Diaz-Simon-Stone-Bellard Pediatric Clinic, New Orleans, 1957—; chief pediatrics Touro Infirmary, New Orleans, 1981—; pres. med. staff Children's Hosp., New Orleans, 1975-77; cons. pediatrician Coliseum Med. Center, 1979—, de Paul Hosp., 1978— (both New Orleans); clin. prof. pediatrics Tulane U. Founder, Edn. and Research Treatment Ctr., New Orleans, 1968, pres., 1970-71; pres. adv. bd. New Orleans Juvenile Ct., 1966-67; bd. dirs. Family Service Soc., New Orleans, 1964-68. Mem. La. State Med. Soc. (Walter Reed Meml. award 1948), Orleans Parish Pediatric Soc., La. State Pediatric Soc., Am. Acad. Pediatrics. Democrat. Jewish. Club: River Center Tennis (New Orleans). Home: 7811 Green St New Orleans LA 70118 Office: 1523 Antonine St New Orleans LA 70115

SIMON, H(UEY) PAUL, lawyer; b. Lafayette, La., Oct. 19, 1923; s. Jules and Ida (Rogere) S.; B.S., U. Southwestern La., 1943; J.D., Tulane U., 1947; m. Carolyn Perkins, Aug. 6, 1949; 1 son, John Clark. Admitted to La. bar, 1947, since practiced in New Orleans; asst. prof. advanced acctg. U. Southwestern La., 1944-45; principal in C.P.A. firm Haskins & Sells, New Orleans, 1945-57; gen. ptnr. law firm Deutsch, Kerrigan & Stiles, New Orleans, 1957-79; founding sr. partner law firm Simon, Peragine, Smith & Redfearn, 1979—. C.P.A., La. Mem. Am. Judicature Soc., Internat. Bar Assn., (com. on securities issues and trading 1970—), Inter-Am. Bar Assn., Am. Bar Assn. (ct. procedure com. of tax sect. 1958—), La. Bar Assn. (com. legislation and adminstrv. practice 1966—), New Orleans Bar Assn., Am. Inst. C.P.A.s, New Orleans Assn. Notaries, Soc. La. C.P.A.s, C. of C. (council 1952-66), Met. Area Com., Met. Crime Comm., Council for a Better La., Bur. Govtl. Research, New Orleans Bd. Trade, Pub. Affairs Research Council, Tulane Tax Inst. (program com 1960—), La. Tax Conf. (program com. 1968-72), N.Y. U. Tax Conf.-New Orleans (co-chmn. 1976), Am. Assn. Atty.-C.P.A.s, Internat. Platform Assn., Tulane Alumni Assn., Phi Delta Phi (past pres. New Orleans chpt.), Sigma Pi Alpha. Roman Catholic. Clubs: Young Men's Business (legislation com.), Press, Toastmasters Internat., New Orleans Country, Petroleum, City (New Orleans); Internat. House (dir. 1976-79, 82-85); World Trade Ctr. of New Orleans (dir. fin. com. 1985—); Pendennis. Author: Louisiana Income Tax Law, 1956; Changes Effected by the Louisiana Trust Code, 1965; Gifts to Minors And the Parent's Obligation of Support, 1968; Deductions—Business or Hobby, 1975; Role of Attorney in IRS Tax Return Examination, 1978; asso. editor La. C.P.A., 1956-60; mem. bd. editors Tulane Law Rev., 1945-46. Home:

6075 Canal Blvd New Orleans LA 70124 Office: 30th Floor Energy Ctr New Orleans LA 70169

SIMON, JAMES LOWELL, lawyer; b. Princeton, Ill., Nov. 8, 1944; s. K. Lowell and Elizabeth Ann (Unholz) S.; m. Deborah Ann Wolf, Dec. 27, 1966; children—Heather Lyn, Brandon James. Student, U. Ill., 1962-63; J.D. with honors, 1975; B.S.E.E. magna cum laude, Bradley U., 1967. Bar: Fla. 1975, U.S. Dist. Ct. (mid. dist.) Fla. 1976, U.S. Ct. Appeals (11th cir.) 1981, U.S. Patent Office 1983. Engineer Pan Am. World Airways, Cape Kennedy, Fla., 1967-68; assoc. Akerman, Senterfitt & Eidson, Orlando, Fla., 1975-80; ptnr. Bogin, Munns, Munns & Simon, Orlando, 1980—. Active Seminole County Sch. Adv. Council, Fla., 1981—, Forest City Local Sch. Adv. Com., Altamonte Springs, Fla., 1981-84, Code Enforcement Bd., Altamonte Springs, 1983-84, Central Bus. Dist. Study com., Altamonte Springs, 1983-85, Council of '76 of Republican Party, Seminole County, 1982—. Served to capt. USAF, 1968-72. Named Outstanding Young Men Am. 1981. Mem. ABA, Orange County Bar Assn. (jud. relations com. 1982-83, fee arbitration com. 1983—), Phi Kappa Phi, Tau Beta Pi, Sigma Tau, Eta Kappa Nu. Republican. Mormon. Home: 620 Longmeadow Circle Longwood FL 32779 Office: Bogin Munns Munns & Simon Suite 1001 250 N Orange Ave PO Box 2807 Orlando FL 32802

SIMON, JIMMY LOUIS, pediatrician, educator; b. San Francisco, Dec. 27, 1930; s. Sylvian L. and Hilda (Netter) S.; m. Marilyn Wachter, June 21, 1953. A.B., U. Calif.-Berkeley, 1952; M.D., U. Calif.-San Francisco, 1955. Intern, U. Calif.-San Francisco, 1955-56; resident in pediatrics Grace-New Haven Hosp., 1956-57; sr. asst. resident Boston Children's Hosp., 1957-58; practice medicine specializing in pediatrics, Okla., 1960-64, Galveston, Tex., 1966-74, Winston-Salem, N.C., 1974—; instr., asst. prof. pediatrics U. Okla. Med. Ctr., 1960-64; assoc. prof. pediatrics U. Tex. Med. Br., Galveston, 1966-72, prof. pediatrics, 1972-74; prof., chmn. dept. pediatrics Bowman Gray Sch. Medicine, Winston-Salem, N.C., 1974—. Served with USAF, 1958-60. Mem. So. Soc. Pediatric Research, Ambulatory Pediatric Assn., Am. Pediatric Soc., Am. Acad. Pediatrics, Phi Beta Kappa, Alpha Omega Alpha. Contbr. articles to med. jours. Office: 300 S Hawthorne Rd Winston-Salem NC 27103

SIMON, JOHN PAUL, field safety engr.; b. Franklin, N.J., June 13, 1938; s. John Paul and Anna (Huss) S.; student South Oklahoma City Jr. Coll., Community Coll. of Air Force; m. Lesley Veronica Simon, Nov. 7, 1959; children—Paul, Lori. Enlisted U.S. Air Force, 1955, advanced to master sgt., ret., 1975; instr. South Oklahoma City Jr. Coll., 1975-77; field safety engr. Dresser Industries, Inc., Oklahoma City, 1978—. Decorated D.S.M., Bronze Star, Commendation medal; cert. hazard control mgr. Mem. Am. Soc. Safety Engrs., Vets. of Safety, Assn. Fed. Safety and Health Profls. Democrat. Presbyterian. Club: Masons. Home: 8501 Candlewood St Apt 101 Oklahoma City OK 73132 Office: Dresser Industries Inc Magcobar Group One Grand Park 777 NW Grand Oklahoma City OK 73118

SIMON, JUDITH CANFIELD, business educator; b. Tulsa, Nov. 2, 1939; d. Ira and Billie (Reed) Canfield; 1 child, Gregory. B.S., Okla. State U., 1961, Ed.D., 1976; M.B.A., West Tex. State U., 1969. Sec. Cabot Corp., Pampa, Tex., 1961-67; bus. tchr., chmn. dept. Pampa High Sch., Tex., 1967-74; assoc. prof. dept. office adminstrn. Memphis State U., 1975—; cons. office mgmt. to various orgns. Mem. NEA, Am. Bus. Communications Assn., United Teaching Profession (pres. Memphis State unit 1982-83), Tenn. Bus. Edn. Assn. (exec. bd. 1985—). Office: Dept Office Adminstrn Memphis State U Memphis TN 38152

SIMON, KARLON ROY, geologist; b. Abbeville, La., Nov. 27, 1952; s. Roy Joseph and Merina Marie (Dubois) S.; m. Marcia Lachaussee, June 8, 1974; 1 child, Karl Anthony. B.S., La. State U., 1973. Area ops. geologist Gulf Oil Corp., Morgan City, La., 1973-80, Lafayette, La., 1980-81, sr. staff ops. geologist, Houston, 1981—. Mem. Soc. Petroleum Engrs., Am. Assn. Petroleum Geologists (cert.), Republican. Roman Catholic. Home: 7421 NW 115th St Oklahoma City OK 73132 Office: Chevron USA Oklahoma City OK

SIMON, LORENA COTTS (MRS. SAMUEL C. SIMON), music tchr., poet; b. Sherman, Tex., Jan. 16, 1897; d. George Godfrey and Willie (Jones) Cotts; student Am. Conservatory, summer 1938, Julliard Music Sch., summer 1939; diploma Sherwood Music Sch., 1941; D. Lit. Leadership, Internat. Acad. Leadership, Philippines, 1967; Mus.D., St. Olav's Acad., Sweden, 1969; L.H.D., None Pontifical Acad.; m. Samuel C. Simon, Nov. 6, 1918 (dec.). Tchr. violin, piano, theory and harmony, Port Arthur, Tex., 1919—; organizer, dir. Schubert's Violin Choir, Port Arthur, 1919-55; judge Internat. Poetry Peace Award Contest, 1965; works of poetry in Internat. Poetry Archives, Manchester Central Library, Eng., 1965. Named Poet Laureate of Tex., 1961; Poet Laureate of Magnolia Dist., 1962-64; Poet Laureate of Port Arthur, 1962—; recipient gold plaque Tex. Fedn. Women's Club, 1962, spl. award 1st place in poetry and music Tex. heritage dept., 1963, spl. award in music and fine arts and outstanding service awards, 1965; 1st place in poetry, 1966; Medal of Honor and Diploma of Merit, Centro Studi Scambi Internat., Rome, 1965, Silver, Gold medals of merit, 1967, diploma of merit, 1966, 67; Hon. Poet Laureate-Musician, United Poets Laureate Internat., 1966, Karte of award, 1968, Hon. Internat. Catholic Poet Laureate, 1968, also Silver Laurel Health; Contemporary Internat. Poet Hall of Fame, 1968; honored by Tex. Senate and Ho. of Reps., 1967; crowned Cath. Poet Laureate of World (life), 1969; inducted into Knights and Ladies of Holy Sepulchre, Pope John II, 1982, L.C.H.C., 1986; decorated Equestrian Order Holy Sepulchre of Jerusalem; named Cath. Lady of Humanity. Mem. Internat. Platform Assn., Nat., Tex. press women's assns., Nat. Council Cath. Women, Nat. Guild Piano Tchrs. (charter mem.; adjudicator), Am. Coll. Musicians (adjudicator), Am. Poetry League, Poets Soc. Tex. (counselor 1967—, critic judge), Am. Poets Fellowship Soc. Corp., U.S., UN Assn.-U.S.A., Alpha Delta Kappa. Clubs: Writers' (pres. 1963-64), Symphony. Author: The Golden Key, 1958; From My Heart (1st place award Ann. Poetry Writers Contest of Tex. Press Women's Assn. 1961), 1959; Children's Story Hour (1st place award Nat. Fedn. Press Women's Ann. Writers' Contest 1962), 1960; In Music Land, 1965; That Blessed Night, 1966. Songs pub. include Live Expectantly, 1962, In Search for Growth, 1963, Freedom's Light, 1963, What Can I Do for Jesus, 1963, Adoration, 1985, Prelude, 1985, At Evening Time, 1985, Adoration, 1986, Prelude, 1986, At Evening Time, 1986. Donor funds for constrn. of 9 churches in Africa including Holy Cross Ch., Imaculate Conception Ch., Sacred Heart Ch., Christ the King Ch., Ch. of the Infant Jesus. Address: 411 5th Ave Port Arthur TX 77640

SIMON, RICHARD BRUCE, ophthalmologist; b. Cleve., Sept. 10, 1950. B.S., U. Fla., 1972; M.D., U. Miami, 1976. Diplomate Nat. Bd. Med. Examiners, Am. Bd. Ophthalmology. Intern, Mt. Sinai Hosp., Cleve., 1976-77; resident Washington Hosp. Ctr., 1978-81; fellow pediatric ophthalmology Children's Hosp., Washington, 1981-82; practice medicine specializing in ophthalmology Coral Gables Eye Assn., Fla., 1983—. Fellow Am. Acad. Ophthalmology, Am. Assn. Pediatric Ophthalmology; mem. AMA, Fla. Med. Assn., Dade County Med. Assn. Office: 1516 Venera Ave Coral Gables FL 33146 also 8955 SW 87th Ct Suite 203 Miami Fla 33176

SIMON, ROY MICHAEL, architect; b. Delray Beach, Fla., Oct. 24, 1930; s. Alexander Abraham and Linda Helen (Zaine) S.; m. Mary Elizabeth Wilder, July 29, 1961; children—Roy Michael, Laura Lee, John Christopher. B.S., Ga. Inst. Tech., 1952, B.Arch., 1953. Registered architect, Fla., Ga., N.C., S.C. Pvt. practice architecture, Delray Beach, 1959—. Bd. dirs. Delray Beach Community Chest, 1959-68; trustee Delray Beach Hist. Soc., 1977—, pres., 1979, 84; mem. Delray Beach Bd. Adjustments, Delray Beach Planning and Zoning Bd., Delray Beach Community Appearance Bd., Delray Beach Code Enforcement Bd., Bldg. Bd. Appeals. Served to capt. USAF, 1954-56. Recipient U.S. Jaycee Disting. Service award, 1962, 1965, Jaycee of Yr. award, 1961, 63. Mem. AIA, Fla. Assn. Architects (Architect Community Service award 1971), Delray Beach C. of C. (dir. 1959-74, pres. 1964, 68), Sigma Phi Epsilon. Lodge: Lions (dir. 1957-67, 82-84, pres. 1965-66). Compiler, editor: Materials and Labor Estimator for the Entire Building Industry, 2d edit., 1977. Home: 201 NW 11th St Delray Beach FL 33444 Office: 100 NE 5th Ave Delray Beach FL 33444

SIMONAITIS, RICHARD AMBROSE, chemist; b. Chgo., Dec. 7, 1930; s. George Peter and Sofija Constance (Woijkiewicz) S.; m. Vera Sandra Hall, Sept. 17, 1960; children—Steven, Rachel, Laura. Student Loyola U., Chgo., 1948-50; B.S., U. Ill., 1952; postgrad. Ohio State U., 1952-55, M.S., 1957, Ph.D., 1962. Chemist, Aerojet-Gen. Corp., Nimbus, Calif., 1962-64; research chemist Gulf Oil Corp., Merriam, Kans., 1964-66; analytical chemist Gen. Electric Co., Liverpool, N.Y., 1966-69; research chemist Agrl. Research Service, U.S. Dept. Agr., Savannah, Ga., 1970—; abstractor Chem. Abstracts Co. Bd. dirs. Savannah council Girl Scouts U.S.A., 1978-84, exec. com., 1980-84, neighborhood chmn. Oleander Neighborhood, 1980—; booth chmn. Night in Old Savannah Ethnic Festival, 1977—; usher Nativity of Our Lord Ch., 1974—, capt. ushers, 1977—, sec. Men's Club, 1976, Sunday sch. tchr., 1977-81; bd. dirs. Savannah Young People's Theater, 1980-85, treas., 1983-85. Served with U.S. Army, 1955-56. Mem. Am. Chem. Soc. (exec. com. 1979-83, disting. contbn. plaque, 1978, cert. recognition Chem. Abstract Service 1975), Entomol. Soc. Am., Research Soc. Am., Ga. Entomol. Soc., Assn. Ofcl. Analytical Chemists, ASTM, Chem. Analysts Central N.Y., Wilmington Island Pleasure and Improvement Assn. (treas. 1975—), Tybee Light Power Squadron. Sigma Xi, Phi Lambda Upsilon. Roman Catholic. Lodge: K.C. Contbr. numerous articles to sci. jours. Office: Agrl Research Service US Dept Agr 3401 Edwin St PO Box 22909 Savannah GA 31403

SIMONDS, CHARLES HENRY, geologist; b. San Francisco, June 6, 1945; s. Henry Farrow and Joyce (Webster) S.; m. Jenis Lee Stockman, Aug. 17, 1969; children—Jennifer Ann, Scott Webster. B.S. in Geology, Stanford U., 1967; M.S., U. Ill., 1969, Ph.D., 1971. Postdoctoral fellow Lunar Sci. Inst., Houston, 1971-73, staff scientist, 1973-78; mgr. lunar curatorial lab. Northrop Services Inc., Houston, 1978-81; geologist Tex. Eastern, Houston, 1981, Energy Reserves Group, Houston, 1981—; mem. lunar sample analysis planning team NASA, Houston, 1974-78. Mem. Geol. Soc. Am., Am. Geophys. Union, Am. Assn. Petroleum Geologists, Soc. Profl. Well Log Analysts, Soc. Petroleum Engrs. Club: Seabrook Sailing (Tex.) (race gov. 1984). Avocation: racing sailboats. Home: 17919 St Cloud Dr Houston TX 77062 Office: BHP Petroleum (Americas) 12700 Northborough Suite 400 Houston TX 77067

SIMONDS, JOHN ORMSBEE, landscape architect; b. Jamestown, N.D., Mar. 11, 1913; s. Guy Wallace and Marguerite Lois (Ormsbee) S.; m. Marjorie C. Todd, May 1, 1943; children—Taye Anne, John Todd, Polly Jean, Leslie C. Todd. B.S., Mich. State U., 1935, Sc.D. (hon.), 1968; M. Landscape Arch. (scholar 1936-37, Eugene Dodd medal), Harvard U., 1939. Landscape architect Mich. Dept. Parks, 1935-36; ptnr. Simonds and Simonds, Pitts., 1939-70, Collins, Simonds and Simonds, Washington, 1952-70, The Environ. Planning and Design Partnership, Pitts., also Miami Lakes, 1970-82, emeritus, 1983—; lectr., vis. critic urban and regional planning Carnegie-Mellon U., 1955-67; vis. critic Grad. Sch. Planning, also Sch. Arch., Yale U., 1961-62; cons. Chgo. Central Area Com., 1962, Allegheny County Dept. Regional Parks, 1961-74, Allegheny County Housing Authority, 1960; U.S. cons. community planning Inter-Am. Housing and Planning Ctr., Bogotá, Colombia, 1960-61; mem. jury Am. Acad. Rome, 1963, 65, 66, 69; mem. Nat. Adv. Com. on Hwy. Beautification; chmn. panel on parks and open space White House Conf. on Natural Beauty; mem. Interprofl. Commn. on Environ. Design, Joint Com. on Nat. Capital; mem. urban hwy. adv. bd. U.S. Bur. Pub. Rds., 1965-68; mem. landscape arch. adv. panel C.E., 1968-71, Pres.'s Task Force on Resources and Environment, 1968-70; mem. design adv. panel Operation Breakthrough, HUD, 1970-71; mem. Mid-Atlantic regional adv. bd. Nat. Park Service, 1976-78; assoc. trustee U. Pa., 1962-66, mem. bd. fine arts, 1962-66; chmn. joint com. planning Carnegie-Mellon U. and U. Pitts., 1959-60; overseer's vis. com. Harvard Grad. Sch. Design, 1962-68, exec. council alumni assn., 1960-63; adv. com. Sch. Design, N.C. State U., 1965-67; mem. Fla. Gov.'s Task Force on Natural Resources, 1979-80. Author: Landscape Architecture, The Shaping of Man's Natural Environment, 1961, 1983; Earthscape, A Manual of Environmental Planning, 1978. Editor: Virginia's Common Wealth, 1965; The Freeway in the City, 1968. Bd. dirs. Hubbard Ednl. Trust, 1974—; bd. govs. Pitts. Plan for Arts. Recipient citation Top Men of Yr. Engring. News-Record, 1973, Charles L. Hutchinson medal Chgo. Hort. Soc. Fellow Am. Soc. Landscape Architects (mem. exec. com. 1959-67, pres. 1963-65, pres. found. 1966-68, recipient ASLA medal 1973), Royal Soc. Arts of Great Britain; mem. NAD (assoc.), Urban Land Inst., Nat. Assn. Housing Ofcls., Archtl. League N.Y., Royal Town Planning Inst. (hon. corr.). Presbyterian (ruling elder). Clubs: Harvard, Yale, Princeton (Pitts.).

SIMONS, JAMES ANTHONY, petroleum geologist, reservoir engineer; b. Casper, Wyo., Jan. 30, 1920; s. James Hobart and Ethyl Cleo (Whitaker) S.; m. Doris Marie Peterson, June 10, 1939; 1 child, Priscilla Marie. B.S. in Geology, U. Tulsa, 1943. Registered petroleum geologist, Tex. Subsurface geologist Esso-Standard Oil N.J., various overseas posts, 1943-56; reservoir engr. Libyan Am. Oil., Benghazi, Libya, 1959-65; v.p., tech. Grace Petroleum, Tripoli, Libya, 1965-74; exploration mgr. Norwegian Oil Co., Oslo, 1974-76; valuation engr. U.S. Treas. Dept., Dallas, 1979—. Mem. Geol. Soc. Am., Am. Assn. Petroleum Geologists, Soc. Petroleum Engrs. Roman Catholic. Avocations: history, cooking, gunsmithing. Home: 7314 Walling Ln Dallas TX 75231

SIMPSON, ANNE MARION, retail store manager; b. London, July 5, 1939; came to U.S., 1968; d. Andrew and Mary (O'Keefe) Ward; m. Andrew Gordon Simpson, Aug. 11, 1962 (div. 1981); children—Fiona Judith, Andrew Iain. B.A. with honors, U. London; grad. diploma personnel mgmt. Napier Coll., Scotland, 1978. Exec. trainee, staff mgr. Marks & Spencer, U.K., 1962-64; employment interviewer Sterling Electronics, Houston, 1974; employment mgr. Park Plaza Hosp., Houston, 1975-76; personnel adminstr., asst. mng. dir. Lord & Taylor, Houston, 1978-82; asst. mng. dir., then mng. dir. Abercrombie & Fitch, Houston, 1982-83; mng. dir. Front Row, Houston, 1983—. Address: 2811 Bernadette St Houston TX 77043

SIMPSON, CHARLES WILLIAM, safety engineer; b. Lesage, W.Va., Jan. 12, 1934; s. Carl and Bertha Lillian (Woodrum) S.; m. Verna Winona Cooper, Apr. 7, 1956; children—William Mark, Jon Kelly. B.S. in Engring., Marshall Coll., 1956. Bldg. contractor Simpson Builders, Huntington, W.Va., 1958-61; insp. Huntington Alloys, Huntington, 1961-63, quality control technician, 1963-71, asst. safety coordinator, 1971-76, safety engr. advanced, 1976—; bd. dirs. W.Va. chpt. Nat. Safety Council, Charleston, 1982—; mem. adv. bd. Marshall U. Fire Sch., 1981—. Served as 2d lt. U.S. Army, 1956-58. Mem. W.Va. Safety Council Inc. (pres.), Am. Soc. Safety Engrs. (Safety Profl. of Yr. 1983), Nat. Safety Council Metals Com., W.Va. Mfrs. Assn. (safety com. 1976—). Republican. Baptist. Avocations: automobile customizing; mechanics; welding; carpentry, farming. Home: 6807 Big Seven Mile Rd Lesage WV 25537 Office: Huntington Alloys Box 1958 Guyan River Rd Huntington WV 25720

SIMPSON, CHRISTOPHER DALE, accountant; b. Boston, Mar. 13, 1941; s. Raymond Dale and Anne Ide (Brown) S.; m. Dorothy Simonsen, Apr. 15, 1967; children—Michael, Mark, Matthew. B.S. in Acctg., Bob Jones U., 1963; grad. summer exec. devel. program U. So. Calif., 1982. C.P.A., N.J., N.Y., Tex. With Price Waterhouse, N.Y.C., London, Dallas, 1963—, ptnr., 1975—; mem. acctg. adv. council Tex. Tech U., Lubbock, 1978-81; chmn. adv. bd., dept. acctg. and info. systems N. Tex. State U., 1978-81. Bd. dirs. Dallas Theater Center. Served with U.S. N.G., 1964-70. Recipient Alumni citation Bob Jones U., 1977. Mem. Am. Inst. C.P.A.s, Tex. Soc. C.P.A.s, Pilgrims of U.S., Dallas C. of C., Dallas Council on World Affairs (dir.), Am. Tract Soc. (dir., treas.). Republican. Clubs: City, Northwood Country (Dallas). Contbg. editor: Guide to Accounting Controls-Establishing, Evaluating and Monitoring Control Systems, 1979. Office: 1400 First City Ctr Dallas TX 75201

SIMPSON, DANIEL REID, lawyer; b. Glen Alpine, N.C., Feb. 20, 1927; s. James Reid and Margaret Ethel (Newton) S.; m. Mary Leonard, Sept. 16, 1951; children—Mary Alma Simpson Beyer, James Reid II, Ethel Barie. B.S., Wake Forest U., 1949, B.Laws, 1951. Ptnr. Simpson, Aycock, Beyer & Simpson, P.A., Morganton, N.C., 1951—; judge Burke County Dist. Criminal Ct., Morganton, 1950's. Mayor, councilman Town of Glen Alpine, 1950's; rep. N.C. Gen. Assembly, Raleigh, 1957, 61-63, senator, 1985—; chmn. N.C. Young Republican Club, Morganton. Served with U.S. Army, 1944-47, PTO. Mem. ABA, N.C. Bar Assn., Burke County Bar Assn. Methodist. Lodge: Masons (Master 1956-57). Office: Simpson Aycock Beyer & Simpson PA 204 E McDowell St Morganton NC 28655

SIMPSON, GAREY LAMBERT, geologist; b. Savannah, Ga., Nov. 12, 1951; s. John Ely and Marjorie (McKinnon) S.; m. Cynthia Diane Duke, Sept. 10, 1977; 1 child, Katherine Diane. B.S. in Geology, Ga. So. U., 1975; M.S., San Jose State U., 1978. Registered profl. geologist, Ga. Geologist, U.S. Geol. Survey, Menlo Park, Calif., 1976-79; sr. explorationist Cities Service Oil Co., Houston, 1979-81; sr. geologist Elf Aquitaine Oil Co., Houston, 1981-82; prof. U. Houston, 1983-84; project geologist Soil and Material Engrs., Inc., Atlanta, 1985—. Contbr. articles to profl. jours. Mem. Am. Assn. Petroleum Geologists, Houston Geol. Soc., Alaska Geol. Soc., No. Calif. Geol. Soc. Avocations: sailing; cycling; woodcrafting; landscape architecture. Office: Soil and Material Engrs Inc 3300 Marjan Dr Atlanta GA 30340

SIMPSON, H. RICHARD (DICK), auto dealer; b. Akron, Ohio, Oct. 10, 1930; s. Bert M. and Violet K. (Mathias) S.; m. Joan Rose Marshall, Mar. 22, 1970; children—Carla Sue, Barry Nelson, Richard Drew, Catherine, Irene Elizabeth, Student, U. Akron, 1949-50; B.S., U. Md., 1955. Mgr. Tex. Gen. Motors Corp., Detroit, 1959-62; pres. Friendly Pontiac, Friendly Toyota, Derrick Chrysler, Simpson Oil Corp., Corp. S., Dick Tiger Homes, Austin, 1962-85. Served to lt. col. USAF, 1953-75; Korea. Decorated D.F.C., Air Medal. Mem. Soc. Automotive Engrs., Res. Officers Assn. Methodist. Clubs: Horse Bay Yacht, Horse Bay Country. Lodges: Rotary, Masons. Office: Dessau Park 508 E Dessau Rd Austin TX 78753

SIMPSON, IDA HARPER, sociology educator; b. Pansey, Ala., June 9, 1928; d. A.H. and Smithie Mae (Croom) H.; m. Richard L. Simpson, July 11, 1955; children—Robert D. and Frank D. (twins). A.B., U. Ala., 1949, M.A., 1951; Ph.D., U. N.C., 1956. Instr., Coll. William and Mary, 1954-55; research fellow social research sect. U. N.C., Chapel Hill, 1955-56; instr. Pa. State U., University Park, 1956-57, U. Ill., Chgo., 1957-58; from research asst. to asst. prof. Duke U., Durham, N.C., 1958-63; from assoc. prof. to prof. sociology, 1971—. Author: From Student to Nurse, 1979; also books and articles on sociology, 1952—. Editor: Rose Monograph Series, 1974-77; co-editor Research in Sociology of Work series, 1980—. Fellow Am. Sociol. Soc. (mem. publ. com. 1974-77, nominations com. 1979-80, com. on coms. 1984-85), So. Sociol. Soc. (mem. exec. com. 1976-79, v.p. 1983). Home: 604 Brookview Rd Chapel Hill NC 27514 Office: Dept of Sociology Duke U Durham NC 27706

SIMPSON, JOHN NOEL, hospital administrator; b. Durham, N.C., Feb. 27, 1936; s. William Hays and Lucile (McNab) S.; B.A., Duke U., 1957; M.H.A., Med. Coll. Va., 1959; m. Virginia Marshall, June 27, 1959; children—John Noel, William Marshall. Asso. adminstr. Riverside Hosp., Newport News, 1962-70; asso. adminstr. Richmond (Va.) Meml. Hosp., 1970-74, sr. v.p. and adminstr., 1974-77, exec. v.p., 1977-80, pres., 1980-85; pres. Health Corp. of Va., 1985—; chmn. Va. Hosp. Ins. Reciprocal, 1977-79; vice chmn. Sun Health, Inc., 1984-85, chmn., 1985—; dir. Va. Hosp. Rate Rev. Program, 1982—; mem. Bus./Medicine Health Coalition, 1982. Bd. dirs. Sun Alliance, 1980-82; vice-chmn. Richmond Area Health Care Coalition, 1983-84; mem. exec. com. Instructive Vis. Nurse Assn., 1983-84; pres. Health Corp. Va., 1982—. Served with M.S.C., U.S. Army, 1959-62. Recipient Edgar C. Hayhow award, Am. Coll. Hosp. Adminstrs., 1976. Fellow Am. Coll. Hosp. Adminstrs. (regent state of Va. 1976-82), Va. Hosp. Assn. (dir. 1974-83, sec. treas. 1982-83, chmn. 1984-85), Richmond Met. C. of C. (bd. dirs. 1983—). Republican. Presbyterian. Club: Rotary (v.p. 1969-70). Contbr. articles in field to profl. jours. Home: 1503 Willingham Rd Richmond VA 23233 Office: 1300 Westwood Ave Richmond VA 23227

SIMPSON, JOSEPH GEORGE, compressor manufacturing company executive; b. Monroe, La., Nov. 16, 1945; s. Joe Hall and Mildred Elizabeth (Gillespie) S.; m. Mary Frances Dupuis, May 29, 1970; 1 child, Jamie Joseph. B.S. in Bus. Adminstrn., Nicholls State U., 1972; postgrad. U. South Ala., 1978-80, Faulkner State Jr. Coll., 1981—. Asst. personnel mgr. Universal Services, Inc., New Orleans, 1972, personnel mgr., 1972-77; employment-tng. coordinator Internat. Systems, Mobile, Ala., 1977-78, personnel supt., 1978-80; personnel mgr. Quincy Compressor div. Colt Industries, Bay Minette, Ala., 1980—; mem. Pvt. Industry Council for Ala. Gov.'s Unified Tng. Area Job Tng. Partnership Act 1983, 1983—. Mem., officer La. wing CAP, 1963-65. Served with USN, 1965-67, Vietnam. Named Outstanding Chmn., Mobile Jaycees, 1980. Mem. Am. Soc. Personnel Adminstrn., Internat. Assn. Quality Circles, Am. Soc. Tng. and Devel., Mobile Personnel Assn., Bay Minette C. of C. Republican. Roman Catholic. Lodge: Optimist (pres. Bay Minette 1984—). Avocations: computer; swimming; camping; landscaping. Home: 1650 Fernbrook Dr Mobile AL 36605 Office: Quincy Compressor Div Colt Industries 7th and Dobson Ave Bay Minette AL 36507

SIMPSON, PAULA GAIL, hotel executive; b. Lone Oak, Tex., July 24, 1938; d. J.P. Jr. and Cloyce (Bellamy) Bowen; children—Steven Dale, Nancy Gail McCormack Breeden; m. Darrel Craig Simpson, June 24, 1982. B.S. in Bus. Adminstrn., So. Meth. U., 1972; grad. Holiday Inn U., 1980, Dale Carnegie, 1983; Cert. in Hotel Adminstrn., Ednl., Inst., East Lansing, Mich., 1984. Formerly sec. with various orgns.; front desk mgr. Holiday Inn, Greenville, Tex., 1979; gen. mgr. Holiday Inn, Ada, Okla., 1979-85; owner Trails Motel, 1986—; grad. asst. Dale Carnegie, Ada, 1984. Dir. little theatre prodns. Mem. Ada Arts and Humanities Com., 1982-84, pres., 1984; mem. Ada Rodeo Com., 1984-85, sec., 1984-85; bd. dirs. Ada Community Theatre, 1982. Recipient cert. appreciation Boy Scouts Am., 1981; spl. citation State of Okla., 1982; cert. mgmt. excellence Holiday Inn, 1983, Holiday Inn Staff, 1984. Mem. Ada C. of C. (chmn. recreation and tourism com. 1983-84). Republican. Episcopalian. Lodge: Soroptimists. Avocations: stained glass; sailing. Home: 811 Maple Ada OK 74820 Office: Trails Motel 1115 N Broadway Ada OK 74820

SIMPSON, RICHARD LEE, sociologist, educator; b. Washington, Feb. 2, 1929; s. Donald Dake and Lottie (Lee) S.; m. Ida Ann Harper, July 10, 1955; children—Robert Donald, Frank Daniel. A.B., U.N.C., 1950; M.A., Cornell U., 1952; Ph.D., U.N.C., 1956. Instr. sociology Pa. State U., University Park, 1956-57; asst. prof. sociology Northwestern U., Evanston, Ill., 1957-58; asst. prof. sociology U.N.C., Chapel Hill, 1958-61, assoc. prof. sociology, 1961-65, prof. sociology, 1965-80, Kenan prof. sociology, 1980— acting dir. Inst. Research in Social Sci., 1966-67; cons. editor Charles E. Merrill Pub. Co., 1967-71. Mem. So. Sociol. Soc. (pres. 1971-72), Am. Sociol. Assn., Sociol. Research Assn. Methodist. Author: Attendants in American Mental Hospitals, 1960; editor: Social Organization and Behavior, 1964; Social Forces, 1969-72, 83—; editor, contbr. Institutions and Social Exchange, 1972, Research in Sociology of Work, Vol. 1, 1981, Vol. 2, 1983, Vol. 3, 1985; also numerous jour. articles. Home: 604 Brookview Rd Chapel Hill NC 27514 Office: U North Carolina Dept Sociology Hamilton Hall 070A Chapel Hill NC 27514

SIMPSON, ROBERT JAMES, education law educator, consultant; b. Wyandotte, Mich., Aug. 27, 1928; s. Thomas and Gladys Norene (Cady) S.; m. Delores Evelyn Yost; children—Susan, Melissa, Roberta, James, July. A.B., Eastern Mich. U., 1949; M.S., U. Mich., 1952; Ed.D., Wayne State U., 1961. Cert. elem., secondary tchr., adminstr., Mich. Tchr. Garden City pub. schs., Mich., 1949-52, asst. supt., 1952-57; supt. St. Clair pub. schs., Mich., 1957-60; from asst. prof. to prof. Miami U., Oxford, Ohio, 1961-70; prof. edn. law, chmn. dept. U. Miami, Coral Gables, Fla., 1970—; instr. Wayne State U., Detroit, 1960-61; vis. prof. U. Hawaii, Honolulu, 1963-64. Author: (series) Education and the Law Ohio, Hawaii, Colorado, Tennessee, 1963-70. Author, columnist Sch. Law Newsletter Jour., 1970—. (Sch. Law Prof. Yr. award 1980). Recipient Disting. Service award U. Miami Alumni Assn., 1984. Mem. Nat. Orgn. Legal Profs. Edn. (dir. 1972-76), Assn. for Advancement Internat. Edn. (law columnist), NEA (life), Phi Delta Kappa. Avocations: tennis; bridge. Home: 5120 SW 92d Ave Miami FL 33165 Office: U Miami Sch Edn Allied Professions Dept Ednl Psychol Studies Box 248065 Coral Gables FL 33124

SIMPSON, SUE CAMPBELL, optometrist; b. Houston, May 5, 1956; d. M.O. and Virginia G. (Justiss) Campbell; m. Don G. Simpson, Nov. 29, 1980. B.S. in Biology, Sam Houston State U., 1978; B.S. in Optometry, U. Houston, 1980, D.Optometry, 1982. Pvt. practice optometry, Waco, Tex., 1982—; owner Eye Care Ctr., Bryan, Tex., 1984—. Mem. Am. Optometric Assn., Tex. Assn. Optometrists, Heart of Tex. Optometrist Assn. Republican. Home: Route 5 Box 501 Bryan TX 77803 Office: Eye Care Ctr 3201 Texas Ave Bryan TX 77802

SIMPSON, THOMAS ALEXANDER, mining engineering educator, researcher, consultant; b. Adams, Mass., Oct. 23, 1925; s. Ernest Cleveland and Mabelle (Blaser) S.; m. Susie Pearce Pradat, July 17, 1954; children—Thomas A. Jr., Walter Edward. Student Colby Coll., 1947; B.S. in Mining Engring., Mo. Sch. Mines, 1951; M.S. in Geology, U. Ala., 1959; hon. degree engr. mines, U. Mo., 1965. Mining engr. and hydrogeologist U.S. Geol. Survey, Tuscaloosa and Bessemer, Ala., 1953-59, asst. mining hydrology sect., Washington and Wilkes-Barre, Pa., 1959-61; chief geologist and asst. state geologist Geol. Survey of Ala., Tuscaloosa, 1961-75; lectr. dept. geology and geography U. Ala., Tuscaloosa, 1966-75, assoc. prof. mineral engring., 1975—; commr. Ala. Surface Mining Commn. Served with USMCR, 1943-46, 1st lt. USMCR, 1951-52. Recipient Tchr. of Yr. award U. Ala., 1982. Fellow Geol. Soc. Am., Assn. Engring. Geologists; mem. Am. Inst. Profl. Geologists, AIME, Am. Assn. Petroleum Geologists, Soc. Explosive Engrs., Sigma Xi, Sigma Gamma Epsilon. Republican. Episcopalian. Contbr. articles to profl. jours. Home: 72 Vestavia Hills Northport AL 35476 Office: Dept Mineral Engring U Ala PO Box 1468 Tuscaloosa AL 35486

SIMPSON, WADE BLAND, oil co. exec.; b. Big Spring, Tex., Sept. 11, 1937; s. James Bland Simpson and Clara Modesta Stokes; B.A., Tex. Christian U., 1959, B.S., 1959; student U. Tex., 1964-66. Pres. Regalos, Inc., Austin, Tex., 1965-72; asso. Taylor Realtors, Austin, 1972-74; partner Simpson-Mann Oil Producers, San Angelo, Tex., 1974—; v.p. Modesta's Inc., Big Spring, 1962-77; sr. partner MWA Oil and Gas Co., San Angelo, Tex., 1975-77; v.p. Mann-Simpson Inc., Trustee Episcopalian Diocese, Amarillo, 1977; mem. bd. devel. Tex. Christian U., 1962; treas. Concho Valley Fine Arts Council, 1981; v.p. San Angelo Fine Arts Mus., 1981; bd. dirs., joint venture chmn. West Tex. Rehab. Center, 1980-82; founder San Angelo Found., 1982—. Served with USAF, 1960. Mem. Tex. Ind. Producers and Royalty Owners Assn., W. Tex. Geol. Soc., San Angelo Geol. Soc., Ind. Landman's Assn. Episcopalian. Home: 911 Live Oak St San Angelo TX 76903 Office: PO Box 289 San Angelo TX 76902

SIMPSON, WALTER WILLIS, III, utility company executive; b. Meridian, Miss., Dec. 28, 1950; s. Walter W., Jr. and Ann (Anderson) S.; m. Elizabeth Brown, Apr. 4, 1976. B. Indusl. Engring., Ga. Inst. Tech., 1972; M.B.A., Duke U., 1974. With Carolina Power & Light Co., Raleigh, N.C., 1974—, asst. budget dir., 1974-75, budget dir., 1975-77, dir. fin. planning, 1977-79, mgr. fin. planning, 1979-82, mgr. mgmt. services, 1982—. Past trustee Wake Opportunities Inc.; past mem. exec. com. Duke U. Ann. Fund, past bd. dirs. Alumni Assn., past pres. Duke Bus. Sch. Alumni Assn. Mem. Assn. Internal Mgmt. Cons., Am. Inst. Indsl. Engrs., Southeastern Electric Exchange (chmn. performance sect.). Home: 10509 Whitestone Rd Raleigh NC 27609 Office: Carolina Power & Light Co PO Box 1551 Raleigh NC 27602

SIMPSON, WILLIAM SHAW, III, construction company executive, conservationist; b. Anderson, S.C., Oct. 13, 1940; s. William Shaw and Varina Clinkscales (Ligon) S.; m. Shim C. Simpson, July 28, 1964; children—Suzanne, William Shaw. B.S. in Horticulture, Clemson U., 1962. Supr. Burlington Industries, Mooresville, N.C., 1966-68; research scientist Lipton Tea Co., Charleston, S.C., 1968-73; v.p., gen. mgr. Sanders Bros. Constrn. Co., North Charleston, S.C., 1973—. Patentee in field. Chmn. state adv. council on erosion and sediment reduction, Columbia, S.C., 1984—; commr. Charleston Conservation Dist., 1981—; chmn. bd. advisers Charlestowne Landing, 1983—. Served to capt. U.S. Army, 1963-66. Mem. S.C. Asphalt Pavement Assn. (v.p. 1984—), Am. Subcontractors Assn. (dir., pres. 1984—), S.C. Assn. Conservation Dists. (pres. 1984—). Presbyterian. Club: James Island Yacht. Home: 813 Robert E Lee Blvd Charleston SC 29412 Office: Sanders Bros Constrn Co Inc 4960 LaCross Rd North Charleston SC 29411

SIMRING, MARVIN, periodontist, consultant, researcher, author, lecturer; b. Bklyn., June 16, 1922; s. Julius Wolf and Fannie (Eisenberg) S.; m. Francine S. Robinson, Dec. 17, 1949; children—Elyse, James, June, Robert. B.A., Bklyn. Coll., 1942; D.D.S., NYU, 1944. Diplomate Am. Bd. Periodontology. Pvt. practice gen. dentistry, Bklyn., 1947-55; practice ltd. periodontics, N.Y.C., 1956-79; clin. prof. and dir. postdoctoral program dept. periodontics NYU, 1947-79; assoc. prof. dept. periodontics U. Fla., Gainesville, 1979-82; cons. VA Hosp., Bklyn., Gainesville, Fla. Active Friends of the Earth, Sierra Club. Served to capt. U.S. Army, 1944-46. Recipient Isidore Hirschfeld prize Northeastern Soc. Periodontists, 1978; Loos prize Achievement in Dental Sci. U. Frankfurt-am-Main, W. Germany, 1980. Mem. ADA, Am. Acad. Periodontology, Northeastern Soc. Periodontists (pres. 1968-70), So. Acad. Periodontology, DAV (comdr. Gator chpt. 1984-85). Jewish. Club: Fla. Exotic Plant (pres. 1984, 86). Author: (with H.L. Ward) Manual of Clinical Periodontics, 1973, 2d edit., 1978; (with S.S. Stahl) Periodontal Surgery, 1976; (with H.L. Ward) Periodontal Point of View, 1973; (with S.S. Sorrin) Practice of Periodontia, 1960; contbr. articles to profl. jours.

SIMS, AUDREY E., educational administrator; b. Altoona, Ala., Jan. 11, 1921; d. Farris S. and Judy Lois (Gilliland) Jackson; widowed; children—Judy Evelyn Sims Waits, Audrey Jane Sims Rickles. B.S., Jacksonville State U., 1965, M.S., 1974. Tchr. Attalla City Sch. System, Ala., 1958-71, elem. prin., 1972-82, middle sch. prin., 1983—. Author: That's The Way It Was, 1984. Mem. Ala. Elem. Prin. Assn., Ala. Secondary Prin. Assn., Nat. Secondary Prin. Assn., Ala. Edn. Assn., Ala. PTA. Avocations: reading; gardening. Home: 921 Edgewood Dr Gadsden AL 35901

SIMS, BENNETT JONES, bishop; b. Greenfield, Mass., Aug. 9, 1920; s. Lewis Raymond and Sarah Cosette (Jones) S.; A.B., Baker U., 1943, L.H.D., 1985; postgrad., Princeton Theol. Sem., 1946-47; B.D., Va. Theol. Sem., 1949, D.D., 1966; D.D., U. of South, 1972; Merrill fellow Harvard, 1964-65; postgrad. Cath. U., 1969-71; m. Beatrice May Wimberly, Sept. 25, 1943; children—Laura (Mrs. John P. Boucher), Grayson, David. Ordained to ministry Protestant Episcopal Ch. as deacon, 1949, priest, 1950; rector Ch. of Redeemer, Balt., 1951-64; dir. continuing edn. Va. Theol. Sem., 1966-72; bishop of Atlanta, 1972-83; vis. prof. theology Emory U., Atlanta, 1980-82, dir. Inst. for Servant Leadership, 1983—; priest-in-charge St. Alban's Ch., Tokyo, 1962; spl. lectr. Diocesan Confs., U.S., overseas, 1969. Trustee U. of South. Served with USNR, 1943-46. Named Young Man of Year, Balt. C. of C., 1953; Distinguished Alumnus of Year, Baker U., 1972. Office: 10 Bishops Hall Emory U Atlanta GA 30322

SIMS, BILL, state senator, business executive; b. Jan. 27, 1932. Grad. Tex. A&M U. Mem. Tex. Senate, mem. edn., intergovtl. relations, natural resources coms., vice chmn. subcom. energy. Democrat. Office: Tex Senate PO Box 12068 Austin TX 78711*

SIMS, BOBBI SHIPP, effectiveness training company executive; b. Brown County, Tex., Jan. 4, 1931; d. Albert Wilson and Gladys (Carruth) Shipp; div.; children—David Joe, Phillip Jay. Grad. in Gen. Bus. Coll., Beaumont, Tex., 1963-64; student U. Houston, 1965, So. Methodist U., 1966. Asst. dir. Chenier Bus. Coll., 1964-72; pres., owner Total Effectiveness Tng. Program, Corpus Christi, 1972—. Author: Making a Difference in Your World, 1984. Named Small Bus. Woman of Yr., YWCA, 1981; recipient Communication award Toastmasters Club, 1982. Mem. Nat. Speakers Assn., Corpus Christi C. of C. (small bus. com. 1982—), Am. Soc. Tng. and Devel., Tex. Soc. Assn. Execs., Exec. Woman Internat. (chmn. philanthropy com. 1985). Avocations: reading, gardening. Office: Total Effectiveness Tng 3454 Santa Fe Corpus Christi TX 78411

SIMS, DEAN STRATTON, public relations executive; b. Herrin, Ill., Sept. 30, 1921; s. Dewey Simon and Mary Viola (Porter) S.; B.A., U. Kans., 1945; m. Mary Rebecca Taylor, May 18, 1945; children—Susan, Jeri, David. Reporter, The Kansas City (Mo.) Star, 1943-45; editor, publicist Kansas City (Mo.) Power & Light Co., 1946-51; public relations mgr. Nat. Mgmt. Assn., Dayton, Ohio, 1951-57; public relations mgr. Marathon Oil Co., Findlay, Ohio, 1959-65; chmn. Public Relations Internat., Ltd., Tulsa, 1965—, chmn. Public Relations Internat. of Tex., Houston, Public Relations Internat. (U.K.) Ltd., London, Public Counselors Assn. Gt. Britain, Public Relations Internat. of Colo. Ltd., Denver. Trustee, U. Kans. William Allen White Found. Mem. Internat. Public Relations Assn., Pub. Relations Cons. Assn. London, Inst. Public Relations, Asociación Mexicana de Relaciones Pblicas, Public Relations Soc. Am., Nat. Press Club, Kansas City Press Club, Exporers Club, English-Speaking Union (pres. Tulsa chpt.), Phi Kappa Psi. Sigma Delta Chi. Episcopalian. Office: 801 S Detroit Ave Tulsa OK 74120

SIMS, DIANA MAE, scientific programmer, technical English educator; b. Cleve.; d. Delbert Charles and Irene Renelva (Sharp) Caulfield; m. Donald McDade Keith, June 4, 1949 (div. 1955); children—Susan Keith Crawford, Sharon Keith Turner, Steven, Shelley Keith Steigerwald; m. Donald Louis Sims, Apr. 18, 1958. B.A., Tex. Woman's U., 1971, M.A., 1972; Ph.D., N.Tex. State U., 1978. Teaching fellow Tex. Woman's U., 1971-72; project dir. seminar in descriptive linguistics N.Tex. State U., 1975, doctoral teaching fellow, 1972-76, cons. adult edn., 1976; instr. Mountain View Coll., 1975-76; lang. analyst Limited English Speaking Ability Project, Tex. Edn. Agy., 1976; cons. Nat. Council Jewish Women, 1977-78; curriculum writer Bell Helicopter-Textron, 1978; cons., instr. tech. English for internat. students Bell Ops. Corp., 1978; instr. Dallas Ind. Sch. Dist., 1976-79; adj. prof. E. Tex. State U., 1979; pres. and dir. English Second-Lang. Learning Ctr., Inc., 1977—; lectr. U. Tex., Arlington, 1981—, adj. prof., 1984—; instr. Tarrant County Jr. Coll., 1976-84; dir., sec. Donald Sims, Inc., 1963-84; sci. programmer, project mgr. DOCSYS Documentation System, Design Automation Dept. Tex. Instruments Inc., Dallas, 1979—; paralegal Leslie Shults, Atty., 1957-70; cons. Harbrace College Handbook, 8th edit., 1977; bd. mem. TEX-TESOL IV, Houston, 1979; presenter profl. workshop, 1977. Author: A Manual of Technical Writings, 1976, rev. edit. 1976; Technical English for Non-Native Students, 1984; contbr. writings to publs. in field, papers to profl. confs. Grad. fellow N.Tex. State U., Tex. Woman's U. Mem. Assn. for Computational Linguistics, S.Central MLA (chmn. gen. linguistics 1980), Linguistic Soc. Am., Am. Dialect Soc., Soc. for Tech. Communication, Conf. Coll. Tchrs. English, Sigma Tau Delta, Kappa Delta Pi, Sigma Kappa, Phi Delta Kappa, Alpha Chi. Home: 4017 Kerr Circle Dallas TX 75234 Office: Tex Instruments PO Box 225474 MS 3668 8390 LBJ Freeway Dallas TX 75265

SIMS, EDWARD VERNER, JR., business and education consultant; b. Tuscaloosa, Ala., Aug. 16, 1955; s. Edward Verner and Juanita (Thomas) S. B.S., New Coll. U. Ala.; 1977, M.A., U. Ala., 1980, Ph.D., 1984. Instr. U. Ala., University, 1980-81; asst. prof. U. Montevallo, Ala., 1981-82; research coordinator Early Childhood Day Care Program, University, 1978-83; cons. Kincaid Assocs., Metairie, La., 1983—. Assoc. editor Ala. Studies Psychology, 1982-83. Contbr. chpt. to book, articles to profl. jours. Chmn. edn. commn. Munholland United Methodist Ch., Metairie, 1985; scoutmaster Black Warrior council Boy Scouts Am., 1982-83; mem. Edn. for New La., Metairie, 1985; mem. Bus. Edn. Partnership Plaquemines Parish C. of C., 1985. Recipient Oliver Lacey award U. Ala., 1982, Outstanding Young Man Am. award Jaycees, 1984, 85. Mem. Soc. Tng. Devel., Assn. for Behavior Analysis, Assn. for Direct instruction, United Meth. Men. Democrat. Avocations: music; choral singing; drawing; camping; running. Office: Kincaid Assocs Inc 3925 N I-10 Service Rd Metairie LA 70002

SIMS, JAMES NATHAN, petroleum geologist; b. Orange, Tex., Jan. 16, 1918; s. James Nathan and Nord (Baker) S.; m. Nelda Fagan, Oct. 24, 1947; children—Gail Sims Shipley, Howard James. B.S. in Geology, U. Houston, 1940. Geologist, Phillips Petroleum Co., Houston, 1941-56; ptnr. Acorn Oil Co., Houston, 1956-64, owner, operator, 1964-74; pvt. practice petroleum geologist, Houston, 1974—. Mem. Am. Assn. Petroleum Geologists (cert.), Am. Inst. Profl. Geologists (cert.), Soc. Ind. Profl. Earth Scientists, Houston Geol. Soc., Houston Assn. Petroleum Landmen, Pioneer Oil Producers Soc. Avocations: fishing; boating. Office: 571 San Jacinto Bldg 911 Walker St Houston TX 77002

SIMS, RILEY V., diversified company executive, 826; b. East St. Louis, Ill., 1903; married. Carpenter, 1924-29; with Burnup & Sims, Inc., Ft. Lauderdale, Fla., 1929—, pres., 1941-76, chmn. bd., 1968—, chief exec. officer, to 1971, also dir.; dir. First Fed. Savs. and Loan Assn., Bessemer Trust. Trustee Palm Beach Atlantic Coll.; bd. dirs. Palm Beach Community Found. Office: Burnup & Sims Inc 1333 University Dr Box 15070 Fort Lauderdale FL 33324*

SIMS, ROBERT MCNEILL, educational administrator, soccer coach; b. Birmingham, Ala., Mar. 25, 1928; s. Edwin Webb and Margaret Pauline (McNeill) S.; B.S., Birmingham-So. Coll., 1950; M.A., U. Ala., 1951; postgrad. U. N.C., U. Denver, Hope Coll., Emory U.; m. Marie Ficklen Newton; children—Robert Clayton, Kevin McNeill, Boyce Griffin. Chemistry tchr. Riverside Mil. Acad., Gainesville, Ga., 1951-52, 54-57, Tuscaloosa (Ala.) High Sch., 1952-54; acad. dean, chmn. sci. dept., head soccer coach Westminster Sch., Atlanta, 1957—; sci. cons. Coll. Bd.; chmn. ACS Adv. Test Com., 1986—; soccer coordinator Ga. High Sch. Assn., 1966—; mem. rules com. Nat. Fedn. State High Sch. Assns.; coach 1st nat. All-Star soccer game, West Point, N.Y., 1984. Mem. choir Peachtree Rd. United Meth. Ch., 1957—, mem. adminstrv. bd., 1978—; mem. adminstrv. bd. Northside YMCA, 1976—. Named Atlanta STAR Tchr., 1963, 68; Nat. Tchr.-of-Yr., DuPont award, 1968; Outstanding Educator, Oglethorpe U., 1976; Nat. Soccer Coach-of-Yr., High Sch. Athletic Coaches Assn., 1975; Southeast Soccer Coach of Yr., Nat. Soccer Coaches Assn., 1981, 83; Ga. High Sch. Soccer Coach of Yr., Ga. Athletic Coaches Assn., 1983. Mem. Am. Chem. Soc. (chmn. Ga. sect. 1970), Am. Inst. Chemists (chmn. Ga. sect. 1972), Assn. Supervision and Curriculum Devel., AAAS, Atlanta Amateur Soccer League (pres. 1982-83), Nat. Soccer Coaches Assn. Am. Democrat. Club: Pine Hills Civic. Office: Westminster Sch 1424 W Paces Ferry Rd NW Atlanta GA 30327

SIMS, ROGER COLEMAN, accountant; b. Taft, Calif., Apr. 27, 1949; s. W.P. and Mary Lou Sims; B.B.A., U. Tex., Austin, 1971; m. Arlene Sims; children—Marjorie Monica, Laura Cameron. Tax accountant Tex. Instruments Inc., Dallas, 1972-74; tax mgr. Kaneb Services, Inc., Houston, 1974-80, v.p., 1980-85; acct., 1985—. C.P.A., Tex. Mem. Am. Inst. C.P.A.s, Tex. Soc. C.P.A.s, Tax Execs. Inst. Republican. Presbyterian. Home: 15303 LaMancha St Houston TX 77083 Office: 10250 Bissonnet Suite 330 Houston TX 77036

SIMS, THOMAS RAY, JR., college counselor; b. Pensacola, Fla., Jan. 28, 1946; s. Thomas Ray and Ann Rose (Geary) S.; m. Kathy Suzanne Phillips, Feb. 27, 1982; children—Brian Geary, Steven Howell. B.S., Troy State U., 1968; Ed.M., U. Ga., 1972; Ed.D. in Human Devel. Counseling, Vanderbilt U., 1986. Cert. counselor; lic. clin. marriage/family therapist./ Dir. edn. Pvt. Ctr., Chattanooga, 1972-73; vocat. rehab. counselor State of Ga., Warm Springs, 1974-76; counseling psychologist, program developer VA, La. and Tenn., 1976-82; asst. prof. psychology Belmont Coll., Nashville, 1982-85; program developer, developmental counselor Prestonsburg Community Coll., Ky., 1985—. Advisor, Parents Anonymous, Prestonsburg, 1985; developer, instr. Parenting Stress, 1983—. Served to 1st lt. Ranger Inf., U.S. Army, 1968-70. Mem. Nat. Assn. Cert. Counselors, Am. Assn. Counseling and Devel., Am. Assn. Marriage and Family Therapists, N.Am. Adlerian Soc. Avocations: art, sculpting. Home: PO Box 1058 Prestonsburg KY 41653 Office: Dept Counseling Prestonsburg Community Coll Prestonsburg KY 41653

SIMUS, JAN BORDERS, marketing executive; b. Tyler, Tex., Nov. 16, 1940; d. Dave S. and Flora O. (Buchanan) Borders; m. Don Washburn, Dec. 6, 1963 (div. Nov. 1979); 1 dau., Genifer Jan; m. John O. Simus, June 23, 1984. B.S., Tex. Christian U., 1963. Buyer, W. C. Stripling Co., Ft. Worth, 1963-66; saleswoman Apparel Mart, Dallas, 1966-70; office mgr. Brants Realtors, Ft. Worth, 1973-79; dir. mktg. Wm. Rigg Inc., Realtors, Ft. Worth, 1979-81; dir. mktg. Colonial-Jetton's, Inc., Ft. Worth; ptnr. Combined Concepts Unltd., 1984—. Active Jr. League Ft. Worth, Conv. and Tourist Bur., Ft. Worth Opera Assn. Mem. Internat. Assn. Bus. Communicators, Sales Mktg. Execs., Restaurant Assn., Advt. Club Ft. Worth, C. of C., Kappa Kappa Gamma. Republican. Presbyterian. Home: 3612 Wren Fort Worth TX 76133 Office: 2828 Sandage Fort Worth TX 76109

SIMUTIS, CATHY LOU, psychologist; b. Mpls., Dec. 5, 1946; d. Walter Stanley and Freda Louise (Ellis) Thompson; m. Leonard Joseph Simutis, Sept. 9, 1967 (div. Nov. 1975); children—Nancy Lynn, David Leonard; m. H. Robert Reynolds, Dec. 14, 1984. B.A., U. Minn., 1968; M.A. in Edn., Va. Poly. Inst., 1974; Ph.D., U. Mo., 1983. Lic. psychologist, Mo. Vocat. counselor Jewish Vocat. Service, St. Paul, 1968-69; dir. career planning placement Radford Coll., Va., 1974-75; youth services specialist Scott County Alcoholism Research Found., Davenport, Iowa, 1976; placement counselor Handicapped Devel. Ctr., Davenport, 1977. Adj. faculty St. Ambrose Coll., Davenport, 1978-79, dir. acad. advising career planning, 1977-79; psychology intern Audie L. Murphy Meml. Vets. Hosp., San Antonio, 1982-83; program therapist Laurelwood Hosp., Woodlands, Tex., 1983-84, unit coordinator, 1984-85; pvt. practice psychology, Conroe, Tex., 1984—. Contbr. articles to profl. jours. Service reviewer United Way, Davenport, 1978; group facilitator Women Ctr.-U. Mo., Columbia, 1981-82. Mem. Am. Group Psychotherapy Assn., Am. Psychol. Assn., Phi Beta Kappa, Phi Kappa Phi, Phi Delta Kappa. Avocations: sailing, pottery. Office: 333 N Rivershire Dr Suite 265 Conroe TX 77304

SINCICH, TERENCE LEIGH, statistics educator; b. Sharon, Pa., July 30, 1953; s. Walter O. and Frances E. (Rogan) S.; m. P. Faith Dummeldinger, Sept. 5, 1981; 1 child, Kara Nicole. B.S. in Math., Grove City Coll., 1975; M.S. in Stats., U. Fla., 1977, Ph.D., 1980. Adj. prof. mgmt. U. Fla., Gainesville, 1980-81, asst. prof. bus. stats., 1981—; sr. statis. cons. Info Tech, Inc., Gainesville, 1980-85. Author: Statistics by Example, 1982; Business Statistics by Example, 1982; (with W. Mendenhall) Statistics for Engineers and Computer Scientists, 1984; (with W. Mendenhall and J.T. McClave) A Second Course in Business Statistics: Regression Analysis, 1985. Named M.B.A. Prof. of Yr., U. Fla. Coll. Bus. Adminstrn., 1982, 83, 84; Grad. Tchr. of Yr., U. Fla. Coll. Liberal Arts and Scis., 1979. Mem. Am. Statis. Assn. Democrat. Avocation: tennis. Home: 4411 NW 65th Terr Gainesville FL 32606 Office: Coll Bus Adminstrn U Fla BUS 315 Gainesville FL 32611

SINCLAIR, DORIS PAULA GIMMESON, nurse, educational administrator; b. Troy, Ohio, Dec. 5, 1932; d. Dwight Paul and Florence Mable (Oller) Gimmeson; m. Robert A. Sinclair, Sr., May 16, 1956; children—Elizabeth Ann Sinclair Biggan, Robert A., Mary Ruth. Cert., Trinity U., San Antonio, 1955; diploma Baptist Meml. Hosp. Sch. Nursing, 1955; B.S.N. cum laude, Incarnate Word Coll., San Antonio, 1968; M.S.N., U. Tex.-San Antonio, 1973-74. R.N., Tex. Office nurse for pvt. practitioner, San Antonio, 1955-57, 59-62; staff nurse Bapt. Meml. Hosp., San Antonio, 1957-59, 63-64; instr. maternal child care nursing Bapt. Meml. Hosp. Sch. Nursing, San Antonio, 1962-63, 68-71, instr. clin. nursing, 1964-66; asst. dir. Bapt. Meml. Hosp. System Sch. Nursing, San Antonio, 1971-72, acting dir., 1972-74, dir., 1974—; mem. Bd. Vocat. Nurse Examiners, State of Tex., Austin, 1978-81; accreditation visitor So. Assn. Colls. and Schs., 1981-82; mem. coordinating bd., nursing edn. adv. com., Tex. Coll. and Univ. System, Austin, 1982-83. Coordinator, Explorer Scout Post 634, San Antonio, 1983—; adv. bd. nurse career program Chicano Health Policy Devel., Inc., San Antonio, 1983—. Recipient Nurse of Yr. award Baptist Meml. Hosp. System, 1973. Mem. Nat. League Nursing (accreditation visitor 1983—, accreditation bd. rev. 1984-87), Tex. League Nursing, Am. Hosp. Assn. Assembly Hosp. Schs. Nursing (nominating com. 1976-78, program com. 1979-80, chmn. program com. 1980-81), Council Deans and Dirs. of Schs. of Profl. Nursing for State of Tex. (chairperson 1978-79), Fedn. for Accessible Nursing Edn. and Licensure, Bapt. Meml. Hosp. System Sch. Nursing Alumni Assn. Methodist. Clubs: San Antonio Coll. Faculty Wives, San Antonio Scottish Soc. Avocations: gourmet cooking; ceramics; swimming. Office: Bapt Meml Hosp System Sch Nursing 111 Dallas St San Antonio TX 78286

SINCLAIR, ROBERT EWALD, physician, educator; b. Columbus, Ohio, Jan. 19, 1924; s. George Albert and Bertha Florence (Ewald) S.; m. Mary Almira Underwood, Mar. 31, 1945; children—Marcia Ann, Bonnie Sue. B.A., Ohio State U., 1948, M.D., 1952. Licensed physician, Ohio, Colo., Ala., Kans. Intern, Mt. Carmel Hosp., Columbus, 1952-53; resident in neurology and psychiatry Columbus State Hosp., 1964-66, chief psychiatric resident adolescent unit, 1965-66; pvt. practice medicine, Columbus, 1953-57, Granville, Ohio, 1957-64; dir. student health service, prof. health edn., team physician Denison U., 1957-64; dir. student health service, prof. health edn., team physician U. Cin., 1966-70; dir. Lafene Student Health Ctr. and U. Hosp., team physician Kans. State U., Manhattan, 1970-80; dir. Russell Student Health Ctr. and Hosp., and prof. medicine U. Ala., University, 1980—; physician Westinghouse Electric Corp., Columbus, 1953-57; asst. zone chief Civilian Def., Columbus, 1954-57; mem. Licking County Bd. Health, Ohio, 1958-59. Bd. dirs. social health com. Cin. and Hamilton County, Ohio, 1967-70, drug abuse and edn. com., 1968-70. Served with USNR, 1943-46. Mem. AMA, Ohio Med. Soc., Kans. Med. Soc., Ala. Med. Soc., Columbus Acad. Medicine, Licking County Med. Soc. (Ohio), Riley County Med. Soc. (Kans.), Tuscaloosa County Med. Soc., Nat. Athletic Trainers Assn., Ohio Coll. Health Assn. (editor Newsletter 1968-70, pres. 1970-71), Central Coll. Health Assn. (pres. 1972-73), So. Coll. Health Assn. (pres. 1986), Delta Tau Delta (faculty advisor), Nu Sigma Nu, Nu Sigma Nu Alumni Assn. (pres. 1953-54). Lodges: Kiwanis, Rotary. Home: 1 Rollingwood Tuscaloosa AL 35406 Office: Russell Student Health Center Univ Ala University AL 35486

SINDEN, TONDA LEA, human resources consultant; b. Ravanna, Ohio, Oct. 22, 1956; d. Harold Charles and Josephine Charolette (Mingo) Sinden; m. Gary Mel Redding, Mar. 31, 1979; 1 child, Briana Rose. B.F.A., U. Ariz., 1978; M.S., Fordham U., 1983. Movement therapist Tucson pub. and pvt. schs., 1977-79, N.Y.C. pvt. schs., 1979-82; career counselor Fordham Law Sch., N.Y.C., 1982-83; acting asst. dir. grad. career devel. Pace U., N.Y.C., 1983-84; cons. human resources, Miami, Fla., 1984—; dance dir. Orme Sch., Ariz., 1983; lectr., instr. summer fine arts program U. Ariz., Tucson, 1980. Author, researcher: Rose Köhli Blaser Sinden, 1982. Contbr. to career devel. manuals, articles to profl. publs. Haldeman scholar, 1976-78; Fordham fellow, 1982-83. Mem. Am. Soc. Tng. and Devel., Am. Assn. Counseling and Devel. Avocations: sailing, swimming, photography. Office: 700 NE 63d St D505 Miami FL 33138

SINDERMANN, ROBERT PAUL, SR., government educator, author, consultant; b. North Adams, Mass., Aug. 16, 1928; s. Carl Joseph and Effie Martha (Packard) S.; m. Rachel Theresa St. Pierre, July 21, 1951; children—Robert Paul, Jr., Lisa Marie. B.A. in Govt., U. Mass., 1958, M.A., 1960; A.B.D., U. Tex., 1967. Cert. secondary edn., Mass. Staff dir. interim com. on pub. jr. colls. Texas Senate, Austin, 1972, staff dir. human resources com., 1973, staff dir. local govt. com., 1974; cons. to pres. S.W. Ctr. Urban Research, Houston, 1974-75; monitoring and eval. specialist Texas Dept. Community Affairs, Austin, 1975-77; assoc. prof. San Antonio Coll., Texas, 1977—; polit. cons., Austin, 1975—. Contbr. articles to profl. jours. Del. to county and state Dem. convs., 1962-84; mem. San Antonio Dem. League, 1981—. Served with U.S. Army, 1951-52. Mem. Southwestern Soc. Sci. Assn., Texas Jr. Coll. Tchrs. Assn. (pres. 1969-70), NEA (life), Am. Fedn. Tchrs. Roman Catholic. Avocations: collegiate and professional sports; politics. Home: 8503 Jamestown Dr Austin TX 78758 Office: San Antonio College Govt Dept 1300 San Pedro PO Box 3800 San Antonio TX 78284

SINEATH, TIMOTHY WAYNE, library and information science educator; b. Jacksonville, Fla., May 21, 1940; s. Holcombe A. and Christine M. (Cook) S.; m. Patricia Ann Greenwood, June 9, 1962; children—Philip Greenwood, Paul Byron. B.A., Fla. State U., 1962, M.S., 1963; Ph.D., U. Ill., 1970. Librarian, U. Ga., Athens, 1963-66; instr. U. Ill., Urbana, 1966-68, doctoral fellow, 1968-70; asst. prof. Simmons Coll., Boston, 1970-76; assoc. prof., 1976-77; prof., dean Coll. Library and Info. Sci., U. Ky., Lexington, 1977—; cons., Boston, 1974-77, Lexington, 1977—; trustee Lexington Pub. Library, 1978—. Contbr. articles to profl. jours. Chmn. advisors ASK-US of ARC, Lexington, 1980—; treas. Actors' Guild Lexington, 1985—. Mem. Am. Soc. for Info. Sci., ALA, Assn. for Library and Info. Sci. Edn. (sec.-treas. 1979-82, 83-84). Home: 3418 Bay Leaf Dr Lexington KY 40502 Office: Coll Library and Info Sci U of Ky Lexington KY 40506

SINGER, AMY, psychologist; b. Miami Beach, Fla., Sept. 8, 1953; d. Harry William and Paula (Rosen) S. Student Miami Dade Community Coll., 1971-72, Parsons Coll., 1972-73; B.A. in Psychology, Hofstra U., 1975, M.A. in Psychology, 1977, Ph.D. in Psychology, 1979. Lic. psychologist, N.Y. Intern, United Cerebral Palsy, Roosevelt, N.Y., 1976-77; intern, program evaluator Suffolk Devel. Ctr., Melville, N.Y., 1977-78; regional coordinator program evaluation L.I. Regional Office of Mental Health, Brentwood, N.Y., 1978-80; chief of psychology SHE Ctr., North Miami, Fla., 1980; pvt. practice clin. and cons. psychology, Miami, Fla., 1978-82; cons. to attys., dir. jury selection services, 1980—; pres. Trial Cons., Inc., 1980—; clin. psychologist SHARE Alcohol Rehab. Program, Hollywood Meml. Hosp. (Fla.), 1980-82; chief drug abuse counselor Concept House, Miami, 1981; cons. psychologist, Floral Park, N.Y., 1978—; therapist, cons. to Audrey Sarner Community Sch. Bd. Dist. 26 Drug Rehab. Ctr., Flushing, N.Y., 1974-76; lectr., asst. prof. Hofstra U., 1976-80; intern supr. grad. program in applied research psychology, L.I. Regional Office, 1979-80; adj. faculty Fla. Internat. U., Bay Vista Campus, North Miami, 1980—; Vol., lectr. Jewish Community Ctr. So. Fla.; active NOW. Mem. Am. Psychol. Assn., Psi Chi, Lambda Nu. Club: Miami Ski. Co-author workbook in field, 1978. Home: 21280 NE 23d Ave North Miami FL 33180 Office: 3050 Biscayne Blvd Suite 901 Miami FL 33137

SINGER, MARC GEOFFREY, business educator, management consultant; b. Bklyn., Mar. 2, 1947; s. Harry and Elsa (Vinik) S.; m. Ellen Rita Newerstein, June 29, 1968; children—Jennifer, Adam. B.B.A., CCNY, 1968; M.B.A., Baruch Coll., 1971; Ph.D., U. Tenn., 1973. Lic. profl. counselor, Va. Sr. ptnr. Sindur Humanistics Mgmt. Cons., Harrisonburg, Va., 1979—, also pres. Emadjen Mgmt. Cons., Harrisonburg, 1975—; asst. prof. mgmt. James Madison U., Harrisonburg, from 1973, now prof. personnel and labor relations; cons. to bus. and govtl. orgns. Recipient Ward medal CCNY, 1968. Mem. Acad. Mgmt., Am. Personnel and Guidance Assn., Omicron Delta Kappa, Psi Chi, Phi Chi Theta. Lodge: Rotary. Contbr. numerous articles on personnel, labor relations and transp. to profl. jours. Office: James Madison University Harrisonburg VA 22807

SINGER, MARCIA KAY, pharmacist; b. Canton, Ohio, Jan. 21, 1955; d. Harry W. and Elizabeth A. Singer. B.S. in Pharmacy, Ohio State U., 1978. Pharmacist Eckerd Drugs, Clearwater, Fla., 1978-83; chief pharmacist Cigna Healthplan, Clearwater, 1983—. Mem. Fla. Pharmacy Assn. Republican. Presbyterian. Avocations: scuba diving; windsurfing. Home: 14950 Gulf Blvd 1003 Madeira Beach FL 33708 Office: Cigna Healthplan Pharmacy 1417 S Belcher Rd Clearwater FL 33546

SINGER, RICHARD JAY, periodontist; b. Lynn, Mass., Sept. 27, 1949; s. Louis and Alice (Lowe) S.; m. Susan Fran Kessel, May 28, 1978; children—Justin, Adam, Courtney. B.Sc., McGill U., Montreal, Que., Can., 1970; D.D.S.,

U. Md., 1974; specialty cert. Tufts U., 1979. Diplomate Am. Bd. Periodontology. Pvt. practice periodontology, Hollywood, Fla., 1982—. Served to lt. comdr. USN, 1979-82. Mem. ADA, Am. Acad. Periodontology, Fla. Dental Assn., Fla. Soc. Periodontology, East Coast Dist. Dental Assn. Office: 3911 Hollywood Blvd Hollywood FL 33021

SINGER, ROBERT NORMAN, educator; b. Bklyn., Sept. 27, 1936; s. Abraham and Ann (Norman) Singer; B.S., Bklyn. Coll., 1961; M.S., Pa. State U., 1962; Ph.D., Ohio State U., 1964; m. Beverly Singer; children—Richard, Bonni Jill. Instr. phys. edn. Ohio State U., Columbus, 1963-64, asst. prof., 1964-65; asst. prof. Ill. State U., Normal, 1965-67, dir. motor learning lab., 1965-69, asso. prof., 1968-69, asst. dean. Coll. Applied Sci. and Tech., 1967-69; dir. motor learning lab., assoc. prof. Mich. State U., East Lansing, 1969-70; prof. Fla. State U., Tallahassee, 1970—, dir. motor learning lab., 1970-72, dir. div. human performance, 1972-75, dir. Motor Behavior Center, 1975-83, asst. dean Coll. Edn., 84—; cons. editor Holt, Rinehart and Winston, N.Y.C., 1971-77; lectr. U.S., Asia, S.Am., Africa, Australia and Europe; cons. in field. Coordinator sport psychology, sports medicine council U.S. Olympic Com. Served with U.S. Army, 1955-58. Mem. Am. Ednl. Research Assn., AAHPER, N.Am. Soc. Sport Psychology and Phys. Activity, Internat. Soc. Sport Psychology (pres. 1985—). Author: Motor Learning and Human Performance, 1968, 75, 80; Coaching, Athletics, and Psychology, 1972; Physical Education, 1972; Teaching Physical Education, 1974, 80; Laboratory and Field Experiments in Motor Learning, 1975; Myths and Truths in Sports Psychology, 1975; editor: Readings in Motor Learning, 1972; The Psychomotor Domain, 1972; Foundations of Physical Education, 1976; The Learning of Motor Skills, 1982; Sustaining Motivation in Sport, 1984; Peak Performance award, 1986; editor Completed Research in Health, Phys. Edn., and Recreation, 1986-74; mem. editorial bd. Research Quar., 1968-83, Jour. Motor Behavior, 1968-81, Jour. Sport Psychology, 1979—, Physician and Sportsmedicine, 1979—; contbr. articles to anthologies and profl. jours. Home: 4503 Andrew Jackson Way Tallahassee FL 32303 Office: 106 Montgomery Gym Fla State U Tallahassee FL 32306

SINGER, RONALD F., financial economy educator, researcher; b. N.Y.C., Aug. 7, 1943; s. Jack and Lee (Gitelson) S.; m. Jeanne Miller; children—Gregory, Paul. B.S., Cornell U., 1965; M.B.A., Mich. State U., 1969, Ph.D., 1975. Lectr. CUNY, 1970-75, asst. prof., 1975; asst. prof. NYU, 1976-80, assoc. prof., 1981-82, U. Houston, 1982—; research analyst U.S. V.I. Dept. Commerce, 1969; research asst. Nigerian Rural Devel. Com. Contbr. articles to profl. jours. Mich. State U. fellow, 1975. Mem. Am. Fin. Assn. (proceedings editor 1981-83), Am. Econ. Assn., Western Fin. Assn. Office: U Houston 4800 Calhoun Houston TX 77004

SINGH, AMARJIT, political science educator; b. Montgomery, Pakistan, Aug. 5, 1935; came to U.S., 1961, naturalized, 1969; s. Balwant and Sant (Kaur) S.; m. Susan Andress, Dec. 12, 1965 (div. Apr. 1972); 1 child, Ravinder Sher; m. Deepa Luthera, Nov. 19, 1978; 1 child, Remmi Sant-Kaur. B.A., Punjab U., India, 1956; LL.B., Delhi U., India, 1959; M.Internat. Studies, Claremont Grad. Sch., 1964, Ph.D., 1968. Prof. Benedict Coll., Columbia, S.C., 1966-68; assoc. prof. N.C. A&T State U., Greensboro, 1968-84, prof., 1984—, chmn. dept. polit. sci., 1981—. Treas. Atlantic Coast Sikh Assn., Durham, 1984—. U.S. Dept. Edn. grantee 1982-84, 1984-85. Mem. Am. Polit. Sci. Assn., So. Polit. Assn., N.C. Polit. Sci. Assn. (exec. com. 1982—). Democrat. Sikh. Avocations: gardening, video-taping. Home: 802 Montrose Greensboro NC 27410 Office: NC A&T State U 1601 E Market St Greensboro NC 27411

SINGH, MAHENDRA PRATAP, electrical equipment manufacturing company executive; b. Allahabad, India, Aug. 23, 1950; s. Rajendra Prasad and Shanti Singh; m. Usha Rani Singh, July 16, 1977; children—Niharika, Namita, Deepti. B.S, Indian Inst. Tech., Kanpur, 1971; M.S., Case Western Res. U., 1974; M.B.A., U. Ill., 1976. Registered profl. engr., Wis. Research asst. Case Western Res. U., Cleve., 1971-73; research asst. dept. econs., survey research lab. U. Ill.-Champaign, 1974-75; mgr. application engring. AFL Industries, West Chicago, Ill., 1976-79; product mgr. Dana Corp., Elgin, Ill., 1979-80, Reliance Electric Co., Greenville, S.C., 1980—. Contbr. numerous articles to profl. lit.; patentee control for variable speed drives. NASA research grantee, 1972-73; EPA research grantee, 1974. Mem. ASHRAE, ASME, Am. Mktg. Assn., Mensa. Club: Toastmasters (pres.). Home: 814 Plantation Dr Simpsonville SC 29681 Office: Reliance Electric Co PO Box 499 Greenville SC 29602

SINGH, RANA PRATAP, statistician, consultant; b. Varanasi, India, Aug. 15, 1943; came to U.S., 1970, naturalized, 1979; s. Lalla and Shahjadi (Devi) S.; m. Kanak Lata, July 6, 1973; children—Amit Kumar, Rachna. B.Sc. with honors, Banaras Hindu U. (India), 1962, M.Sc. in Stats., 1964; M.Sc. in Math., U. Windsor (Can.), 1969, Ph.D. in Stats., 1972. Statistician, Va. State U., Petersburg, 1972—; cons. Allied Chem., Hopewell, Va., 1982-84; system analyst, programmer U.S. Army, Fort Lee, Va., 1984. Recipient Minority Access to Research Careers award NIH, 1979-84. Mem. Issue Inc., Am. Statis. Assn., India Assn. Va. (pres. 1985), Beta Kappa Chi (sec. 1985), Sigma Xi, Kappa Mu Epsilon. Avocations: computers; swimming. Home: 5044 Nantucket Ct Colonial Heights VA 23834 Office: Va State U Math Dept Petersburg VA 23803

SINGH, RANBIR (RON), architect, designer, urban planner; b. Gohana, India, Apr. 1, 1949; came to U.S., 1971, naturalized, 1981; s. Ram Narain and Kapoori Devi (Bansal) Gupta; m. Chitra Mittal Singh, June 10, 1975; children—Avni, Neil Amber. B.Arch. with honors, Indian Inst. Tech., Kharagpur, 1970; postgrad. Carnegie-Mellon U., Pitts., 1971-73. Registered architect, Fla. Designer, Sthapatya Kendra, Baroda, India, 1969-71; project mgr. Connell Assoc. Inc., Miami, 1973-80; assoc. Wolfberg Alvarez Taracido & Assocs., Miami, 1980-82; pres. Singh Assocs. Inc., Miami, 1982—; vis. prof. architecture U. Miami, 1975-80; cons. architect US VA, Miami, 1982—; cons. computer US Gen. Services Adminstrn., Washington, 1983—, Kansas City, 1984—; speaker in field of computer application; cons. systems furniture Def. Supply Service, Pentagon, 1985—; archtl. cons. U.S. Coast Guard, Norfolk, Va. and Miami, Fla., 1985—. Chief advisor Jr. Achievement Greater Miami, 1975-76; pres. Fla. chpt. Assn. Asian Indians in Am., Miami, 1981. Heinz Grad. fellow, 1972; recipient Silver medal Indian Inst. Tech., 1971. Mem. AIA (Reynolds Aluminum award 1972, 73; mem. nat. com. computers in architecture 1982-83). Republican. Hindu. Home: 8900 SW 62d Ct Miami FL 33156 Office: Singh Assocs Inc 10115 Sunset Dr Miami FL 33173

SINGH, SOHAN, civil engineering educator, researcher; b. Delhi, India, Mar. 15, 1953; came to U.S., 1977; s. Kehar and Gurcharan (Kaur) S. Ph.D., Rensselaer Poly. Inst., 1982. Structural engr. Gammon India Ltd., 1974-75, Desein Pvt. Ltd., 1975; research asst. Rensselaer Poly. Inst., Troy, N.Y., 1977-82; asst. prof. civil engring. U. Miami, Coral Gables, Fla., 1982—. Mem. ASCE (assoc.), Am. Soc. Engring. Edn., Sigma Xi, Chi Epsilon. Sikh. Contbr. articles to profl. publs.

SINGLETARY, ALVIN D., lawyer; b. New Orleans, Sept. 27, 1942; s. Alvin E. and Alice (Pastoret) S.; m. Judy Louise Singletary, Dec. 3, 1983; 1 child, Shane David. B.A., La. State U., 1964; J.D., Loyola U., New Orleans, 1969. Bar: La. 1969, U.S. Dist. Ct. (ea. dist.) La. 1972, U.S. Ct. Appeals (5th cir.) 1972, U.S. Supreme Ct. 1978, U.S. Ct. Appeals (11th cir.) 1981, U.S. Ct. Internat. Trade 1981, U.S. Ct. Customs and Patent Appeals 1982. Instr. Delgado Coll., New Orleans, 1976-77; sole practice, Slidell, La., 1970—; sec.-treas. St. Tammany Pub. Trust Fin. Authority, Slidell, 1978—. Councilman-at-large City of Slidell, 1978—; mem. Democratic State Central Com., 1978-82; del. La. Constl. Conv., 1972-73; mayor City of Slidell, 1985. Mem. Delta Theta Phi. Baptist. Office: PO Box 1158 Slidell LA 70459

SINGLETARY, OTIS ARNOLD, JR., university president; b. Gulfport, Miss., Oct. 31, 1921; s. Otis Arnold and May Charlotte (Walker) S.; B.A., Millsaps Coll., 1947; M.A., La. State U., 1949, Ph.D., 1954; m. Gloria Walton, June 6, 1944; children—Bonnie, Scot, Kendall Ann. Mem. faculty U. Tex., 1954-61, prof. history, 1960-61, asso. dean arts and scis., 1956-59, asst. to pres., 1960-61; chancellor U. N.C. at Greensboro, 1961-66; v.p. Am. Council on Edn., Washington, 1966-68; dir. Job Corps, Office Econ. Opportunity, Washington, 1964-65; exec. vice chancellor acad. affairs U. Tex. System, 1968-69; pres. U. Ky., Lexington, 1969—; dir. Anchor Hocking Corp., Dana Corp., Howell Corp. Regional chmn. Woodrow Wilson Nat. Fellowship Found., 1959-61; chmn. N.C. Rhodes Scholarship Com., 1964-66, chmn. Ky. com., 1970-71, 73, 74-77, 80-81, 84-85; chmn. hist. adv. com. Dept. of Army, 1972-80; bd. dirs. Am. Assn. Higher Edn., 1969-72, Ednl. Change Inc., 1968—, Inst. Services to Edn., 1969—, So. Regional Edn. Bd., 1970—, bd. visitors Air U., Maxwell AFB, 1973-76. Served with USNR, 1943-46, 51-54; comdr. Res. Recipient Scarborough Teaching Excellence award U. Tex., 1958, Students Assn. Teaching Excellence award, 1958, 59; Carnegie Corp. grantee, 1961. Mem. Am., So. hist. assns., Am. Mil. Inst. (Moncado Book Fund award 1954), Phi Beta Kappa (mem. senate 1977—, v.p. 1985—), Phi Alpha Theta, Omicron Delta Kappa, Pi Kappa Alpha. Democrat. Methodist. Author: Negro Militia and the Reconstruction, 1957; The Mexican War, 1960; American Universities and Colleges, 1968. Office: U Key Lexington KY 40506

SINGLETON, ANNA CONVERSE EVANS, sociologist, cosmetologist; b. Napoleonville, La., Dec. 20, 1941; d. James and Velma (Joseph) Converse; B.A., So. U., 1970; M.A., Howard U., 1973; grad. Advanced Non-Commd. Officer course, 1981, La. Army N.G. Mil. Acad. Cosmetician, Magee's Beauty Salon, New Orleans, 1962-78; sec., counselor Howard U. Dept. Sociology, Washington, 1971-73; sociologist So. U., Baton Rouge, 1974-77; instr. cosmetology B.T. Washington Sr. High Sch., New Orleans, 1977—; public housing instr. and cons.; planning and operations specialist. Served with AUS, 1977. Cert. in vocat. edn, cosmetic therapy for tchrs; decorated Commendation Medal, La. N.G., Army Commendation medal; recipient La. Gen. Excellence medal. Mem. Am. Vocat. Assn., La. Vocat. Assn., Trade and Indsl. Assn., La. Assn. Educators, Am. Sociol. Assn., Non-Commd. Officers Assn., AAUP, Alpha Kappa Delta. Democrat. Baptist. Author: Behavioral Perspective of Housing Management, 1976; Human Relations: A Study of the Socio-Psychological Effects of Occupancy Patterns of Four New Orleans Housing Projects, 1975. Home: 7225 Chef Ment Hwy New Orleans LA 70126 Office: 1201 S Roman St New Orleans LA 70125

SINGLETON, BERNARD, medical mycologist; b. New Orleans, Aug. 30, 1956; s. Ernest and Evelyn S. B.S., Dillard U., 1980; M.S., Tuskegee Inst., 1982, postgrad. Sch. Vet. Medicine, 1982—. Spl. research asst. Dillard U., New Orleans, 1977-80; vet. asst. Lakeview Vet. Hosp., New Orleans, 1978-80; microbiology lab. instr. Tuskegee Inst. (Ala.), 1982-83, med. and animal mycol. researcher, 1983—. Vice pres. New Orleans chpt. ARC, 1974-75; vol. worker New Orleans Pub. Schs., 1974-75; pres. youth dept. New Birth Baptist Ch., New Orleans, 1970-80; pres. Freedman Bapt. Gen. Assn. Youth Dept., 1979-80; nat. rep. Fgn. Mission, Nat. Bapt. Conv. Am.; vol. coach Little League Baseball. Served to 1st lt. U.S. Army Res., 1980—. Army scholar, 1975; Am. Found. Negro Affairs scholar, 1980; NSF grantee, 1981; Edmond Found. scholar; Bill Raskob Found. scholar; recipient Army Mil. History award, 1978. Mem. Am. Soc. Microbiology, Sigma Xi, Beta Kappa Chi. Democrat. Home: 306 Bruce St Tuskegee AL 36088 Office: Tuskegee Inst Sch Vet Medicine Tuskegee Institute AL 36088

SINGLETON, GEORGE LIGHTFOOT, medical center administrator; b. Montgomery, Ala., Sept. 4, 1939; s. Bennett Powell and Mildred Belle (Gillis) S.; m. Alice Newell Brooks, Apr. 28, 1979; children—Sara Brooks, Susanna Gillis, Rebecca Powell. B.A., U. Ala., 1962; M.B.A., U. Tenn.-Nashville, 1975. Dir. research and stats. Tenn. Dept. Employment Sec., Nashville, 1971-72; budget dir. Tenn Dept. Mental Health, Nashville, 1972-76; sr. outlay budget analyst USPHS, Rockville, Md., 1976-78; chief programming, fin. planning VA, Washington, 1978-80; adminstrn. officer VA Med. Ctr., Birmingham, Ala., 1980—. Founding bd. dirs. Chuck Colson Prison Ministry Ala. Served to capt. USAF, 1963-67. Clk. of session Mountain Brook Presbyn. Ch., Birmingham, 1981-83. Mem. Am. Econ. Assn., Res. Officers Assn., Air Force Assn., DAV, Am. Legion. Lodge: Masons. Home: 2509 Matzek Rd Birmingham AL 35226

SINGLETON, JOHN VIRGIL, JR., judge; b. Kaufman, Tex., Mar. 20, 1918; s. John Virgil and Jennie (Shelton) S.; B.A. U. Tex. Law Sch., 1942; m. Jane Guilford Tully, Apr. 18, 1953. Bar: Tex. 1942. Mem. firm Fulbright & Jaworski, 1953-57; partner Bates, Riggs & Singleton, 1953-57, Bell & Singleton, 1957-61, Barrow, Bland, Rehmet & Singleton, 1962-66; judge U.S. Dist. Ct. So. Dist. Tex., 1966—, chief judge, 1979—; pres. Houston Jr. Bar Assn., 1952-53; co-chmn. 5th circuit dist. judges div. Jud. Conf. U.S., 1969, chmn., 1970, chmn. legis. com., dist. rep., 1980-83, chmn. dist. judge reps., 1980-83. Mem. Tex. Depository Bd., 1963-66. Co-chmn. Harris County Lyndon B. Johnson for Pres. Com., 1960-61; del.-at-large Democratic Nat. Conv., 1956, 60, 64; regional coordinator 7-state area Dem. Nat. Com., Lyndon B. Johnson-Hubert Humphrey Campaign for Pres., 1964; mem. exec. com., chmn. fin. com. Tex. Dem. Com., 1962-66; former bd. dirs. Houston Speech and Hearing Center, trustee Houston Legal Found.; mem. chancellor's council U. Tex. Served to lt. comdr. USNR, 1942-46. Mem. Am., Houston (v.p. 1956-57, editor Houston Lawyer 1954-55) bar assns., Tex. State Bar (chmn. grievance com. for Harris County 1963-66, dir. 1965-66, ex-officio bd. dirs.), U. Tex. Ex.-Students Assn. (life mem., pres. Houston 1961-62, mem. exec. com., chmn. scholarship com.), Fed. Judges Assn. (dir.), Cowboys (foreman, straw boss), Delta Tau Delta (pres. 1940-41), Phi Alpha Delta. Episcopalian. Rotarian. Club: Lakeside Country (past sec., dir.) (Houston). Home: 221 Sage Rd Houston TX 77056 Office: Rm 11144 US Courthouse 515 Rusk St Houston TX 77002

SINHA, RAVINDRA PRASAD, petroleum geologist; b. Patna, India; Dec. 14, 1938; came to U.S., 1978, naturalized, 1985; s. Sidheshwari Prasad and Shyam (Dulari) S.; m. Asha Sinha Nigam, May 16, 1965; children—Alok, Anuj. B.Sc. with honors, Patna, U., 1959, M.Sc., 1961; Ph.D., Dalhousie U., 1970. Registered profl. engr., Alta. Geologist, McGill & Assocs., Toronto, Ont., Can., 1969-71, Baron Oil Co., Calgary, Alta., Can., 1973; ops. geologist Syncrude, Ft. McMurray, Alta., 1974-78; research assoc. U.S. Dept. Energy, Carbondale, Ill., 1979; asst. prof. Elizabeth City State U., N.C., 1978-80; staff geologist Amoco Prodn. Co., Houston, 1980—; tech. adv. UN, 1970. Contbr. articles to profl. jours.; lectr. Recipient Gold Medal Patna U., 1961; Dalhousie U. scholar, 1966-69. Fellow Geol. Assn. Can.; mem. Assn. Profl. Engrs., Am. Assn. Petroleum Geologists, others. Avocations: photography; tennis; badminton; cycling. Home: 3706 Riverwood Park Dr Kingwood TX 77345 Office: Amoco 501 Westlake Park Blvd Houston TX 77253

SINK, JOHN DAVIS, educational administrator, scientist; b. Homer City, Pa., Dec. 19, 1934; s. Aaron Tinsman and Louella Bell (Davis) S.; m. Nancy Lee Hile, Nov. 9, 1956 (dec. Aug. 31, 1961); m. Claire Kaye Huschka, June 13, 1964; children—Kara Joan, Karl John. B.S. in Animal/Vet. Sci., Pa. State U., 1956, M.S. in Biophysics/Animal Sci., 1960, Ph.D. in Biochemistry and Animal Sci., 1962; Ed.D. in Higher Edn., U. Pitts., 1986. Administrv. officer, spl. asst. to sec. agr. State of Pa., Harrisburg, 1962; prof., group leader dept. food, dairy and animal sci. Inst. Policy Research and Evaluation, Pa. State U., University Park, 1962-79; joint planning and evaluation staff officer Sci. and Edn. Adminstrn., U.S. Dept. Agr., Washington, 1979-80; prof., chmn. intercollegiate program food sci. and nutrition, interdivisional program agrl. biochemistry and div. animal and vet. scis. W.Va. U., Morgantown, 1980-85; exec. asst., naval rep. to gov. and adj. gen. State W.Va., Charleston, 1981-84; cons. Allied Mills, Inc., Am. Air Lines, Am. Home Foods, Inc., Apollo Analytical Labs., Armour Food Co., Atlas Chem. Industries, others. Author: The Control of Metabolism, 1974. Contbr. numerous articles to profl. publs. Mem. nat. adv. bd. Am. Security Council, 1981—; mem. nat. adv. council Nat. Commn. Higher Edn. Issues, 1980-82; pres. Collegian, Inc., 1971-72; bd. dirs. W.Va. Cattleman's Assn., 1981-83, W.Va. Poultry Assn., 1980-83, Pembroke Welsh Corgi Club Am., 1980-83, Penn State Stockmen's Club, 1969-71. Served to capt. USNR, 1956—. Decorated Army Commendation medal, Armed Forces Res. medal, others; recipient Nat. Merit Trophy award Nat. Block & Bridle Club, 1956; Pa. Meat Packers Assn. scholar, 1958-62; hon. fellow in biochemistry U. Wis., 1965-65; NSF postdoctoral fellow, 1964-65; Darbaker prize Pa. Acad. Sci., 1967. Fellow Am. Inst. Chemists, AAAS, Inst. Food Technologists; mem. Am. Meat Sci. Assn. (pres. 1974-75), Pa. Air N.G. Armory (trustee 1968-80), Pa. Acad. Sci., U.S. Naval Inst., Naval Res. Assn., Navy League U.S., Res. Officers Assn., Armed Forces Communications and Electronics Assn., Am. Assn. Higher Edn., Am. Assn. Univ. Adminstrs., Am. Chem. Soc., Biophys. Soc., Am. Soc. Animal Sci., Inst. Food Technologists, Soc. Research Adminstrs., Alpha Zeta, Omicron Delta Kappa, Gamma Sigma Delta, Sigma Xi, Phi Lambda Upsilon, Gamma Alpha, Phi Tau Sigma, Phi Sigma, Phi Delta Kappa. Democrat. Methodist. Clubs: Penn State Stockmen's (dir. 1969-71). Home: PO Box 4275 Morgantown WV 26504 Office: PO Box 6108 WVA U Morgantown WV 26506

SINNEMAKI, ULLA ULPUKKA, nurse, educator; b. Antrea, Finland, Sept. 11, 1928; came to U.S., 1963, naturalized, 1969; d. Otto William and Kaisa Viola (Jappinen) Spjut; B.A., NYU, 1972; B.S., SUNY, Stony Brook, 1976; M.Ed., McNeese State U., Lake Charles, La., 1978, Ed.S., 1979, M.Ed., 1981; m. Maunu M. J. Sinnemaki, June 12, 1949 (dissolved Feb. 1968); children—Markku Taneli, Sirkka Astrid. Public sch. tchr., prin., Finland, 1948-50, 56-61; operating room asst. St. Charles Meml. Hosp., Port Jefferson, N.Y., 1965-72; field interviewer U.S. Bur. Census, N.Y.C., 1973-75; staff nurse Lake Charles Meml. Hosp., 1976-77; head nurse South Cameron Meml. Hosp., Creole, La., 1977-80, dir. nursing, 1981-84; staff nurse Humana Hosp., Oakdale, 1984—; tchr. adult and continuing edn. Active local Girl Scouts Finland, 1962-63. Recipient Am. Sch. award, 1966-67, Ettinger award NYU, 1970-72. R.N., N.Y. State; teaching cert., sch. media specialist State of N.Y. Mem. Nat. League Nursing, Am. Nurses Assn., Assn. Ednl. Communications and Tech., Assn. Supervision and Curriculum Devel., AAUP, Health Media Assn., ACLU, Am. Mgmt. Assn., Assn. M.B.A. Execs., Nat. Assn. Female Execs., Nat. League Women, Internat. Platform Assn., Coll. Art Assn. Am., Suomi Soc. Author poetry; translator from English to Finnish. Home and Office: 332 W State St Lake Charles LA 70605

SINNI, BARBARA JANE, nurse; b. Bklyn., Aug. 22, 1943; d. Francis Xavier and Jane Leverich (VanSchaick) Keller; m. Eugene Francis Farabaugh, Apr. 21, 1965 (div. 1972); 1 son, Robert Matthew Farabaugh; m. 2d, Paul John Sinni, Dec. 15, 1973; 1 dau., Kristina Joy. B.S.N., Syracuse U., 1964; cert. Nursing Edn., SUNY-Stony Brook, 1968; M.S.N., Hunter Coll., CUNY, 1979. R.N., N.Y., Fla.; advanced registered nurse practitioner, Fla. Asst. head nurse outpatient clinics East Orange (N.J.) Gen. Hosp., 1965; charge nurse medicine and surgery Clara Maas Gen. Hosp., Belleville, N.J., 1966; instr. nursing L.A. Wilson Tech. Inst., Lindenhurst, N.Y., 1966-68; sch. nurse, tchr. West Babylon (N.Y.) Sch. Dist., 1968-71; clin. instr. med.-surg. nursing Southampton Hosp., Riverhead, N.Y., 1971; nurse unit adminstr. psychiatry Northport VA Med. Ctr. (N.Y.), 1971-72, community health nurse satellite clinics, 1973, clin. inservice coordinator, nurse, 1973-74, instr. phys. assessment, 1971-79, clin. preceptor, 1971-79, cons. to assoc. chief of staff/dean clin. campus SUNY, 1974-78; nurse practitioner Brookhaven Meml. Hosp., East Patchogue, N.Y., 1976-77; dir. nursing services Patchogue Nursing Ctr., 1979-80; assoc. dir. nursing services Bayonet Point-Hudson Regional Med. Ctr., Hudson, Fla., 1981; instr. Pasco-Hernando Community Coll., New Port Richey, Fla., 1981-83; head nurse, nurse practitioner ambulatory care dept. VA Med. Ctr., Bay Pines, Fla., 1983—; adj. prof. C.W. Post U., Greenvale, N.Y., 1973-76; cons. Community Hosp., New Port Richey, Fla. Vol. Am. Cancer Soc., L.I. div.; pres. Bellport Beach Property Owners Assn., 1977-80. Served to lt. Nurse Corps, U.S. Army, 1963-65. Scholar, Syracuse U., Hunter Coll. Mem. Fla. Nurses Assn., Am. Fedn. Bus. and Profl. Women, Mensa, Delta Gamma, Sigma Theta Tau. Republican. Roman Catholic. Lodge: Ladies of Elks. Contbr., Guide to Patient Evaluation.

SINNINGER, DWIGHT VIRGIL, research engr.; b. Bourbon, Ind., Dec. 29, 1901; s. Norman E. and Myra (Huff) S.; student Armour Inst., 1928, U. Chgo., 1942, Northwestern, 1943; m. Coyla Annetta Annis, Mar. 1, 1929; m. Charlotte M. Lenz, Jan. 21, 1983. Electronics research engr. Johnson Labs., Chgo., 1935-42; chief engr. Pathfinder Radio Corp., 1943-44, Rowe Engring. Corp., 1945-48; Hupp Electronics Co. div. Hupp Corp., 1948-61; dir. research Pioneer Electric & Research Corp., Forest Park, Ill., 1961-65, Senn Custom, Inc., Forest Park and San Antonio, 1967—; dir. Rowe Engring. Corp. Registered profl. engr., Ill. Mem. IEEE, Instrument Soc. Am., Armed Forces Communications Assn. Holder several U.S. patents. Address: PO Box 982 Kerrville TX 78028

SINTZ, EDWARD FRANCIS, librarian; b. New Trenton, Ind., Feb. 6, 1924; s. John and Edith E. (Rudicil) S.; B.A., U. Kans., 1950; M.A. in L.S., U. Denver, 1954; M.S. in Pub. Adminstrn., U. Mo., 1965; m. Donna Norris, Apr. 12, 1952; children—Ann Kristin, Lesley Elizabeth, Julie Melinda. With Kansas City (Mo.) Pub. Library, 1954-66, asst. dir., 1964-66; assoc. librarian St. Louis Pub. Library, 1966-68; dir. pub. libraries, Miami, Fla., 1968—; instr. Washington U., St. Louis, 1966-67; library surveyor for Mo. State Library, 1967-68; library bldg. Cons. Monroe County, Fla., 1980, Lee County, Fla., 1984. Served with USAAF, 1942-45. Mem. ALA, Fla. Library Assn. (pres. 1975-76), Southeastern Library Assn. Lodge: Kiwanis. Editor Mo. Library Assn. Quar., 1956-58. Home: 5730 SW 56th Terr Miami FL 33143 Office: 1 Biscayne Blvd Miami FL 33132

SIPIORA, LEONARD PAUL, museum director; b. Lawrence, Mass., Sept. 1, 1934; s. Walter and Agnes S.; m. Sandra Joyce Coon, 1962; children—Alexandra, Erika. A.B. cum laude, U. Mich., 1955, M.A., 1956. Dir. museums, City of El Paso, Tex., 1967—; co-founder, pres. El Paso Arts Council, 1969-71; sec.-treas. El Paso Council Internat. Visitors, 1968-71; trustee El Paso Mus. Art; bd. dirs. Tex. Com. Humanities, Assn. Southwestern Humanities Council; adv. bd. S.W. Arts Found. Bd. dirs. Community Concert Assn. El Paso, El Paso Symphony Orch., El Paso Hist. Soc. Mem. Assn. Mus. Dirs., Mountain Plains Mus. Assn. (pres. 1978-79), Tex. Assn. Museums (pres. 1977-79), Kappa Pi. Republican. Lutheran. Home: 1012 E Blanchard St El Paso TX 79902 Office: 1211 Montana Ave El Paso TX 79902

SIRCHIA, RAYMOND JOSEPH, business exec.; b. Bklyn., Feb. 4, 1941; s. Joseph and Mary A. (Burruso) S.; student N.Y. U., 1965, So. Meth. U., 1969-70; diploma Elkins Inst., 1971; student El Centro Coll., 1971-73, U. Tex., 1980-81; m. Carol Ann Kohler, Apr. 22, 1961; children—Linda Marie, Gary Thomas, Michelle Leigh. Sr. draftsman Pan Am. Airways, Jamaica, N.Y., 1962-65; contract aerospace designer Boeing Aircraft, Seattle, Gen. Dynamics, Ft. Worth, Grumman Aircraft, Bethpage, N.Y., 1965-67; environ. test engr. Grumman Aircraft, Bethpage, 1967-68; design engr. L.T.V. Corp., Grand Prairie, Tex., 1968, Aquatronics, Inc., Dallas, 1968-69, project engr., mgr., 1969-70; dir. ops., 1970-73; gen. partner Titan Internat. Co., Dallas, 1973-74; designer Rockwell Internat., Collins Radio Group, Richardson, Tex., 1974-75; dir. environ. services ServiceMaster Mgmt. Services Corp., Longview, Tex., 1975-79, regional ops. mgr. S.W. div., 1979-81, S.W. div. dir. plant ops. and maintenance, 1981—; owner Drafting and Design Service, 1977—. Chmn., Longview United Fund Campaign, 1977-78; coach Longview YMCA soccer team. Served with USAF, 1958-62. Recipient Excellence award ServiceMaster Mgmt. Services Corp, 1976, 78; Leadership award Longview United Fund, 1978. Mem. Am. Soc. Hosp. Engrs., Nat. Fire Protection Assn. Baptist. Office: ServiceMaster Mgmt Services Corp 4255 LBJ & Midway Dallas TX 75234

SIRGO, HENRY BARBIER, political science educator; b. New Orleans, s. George Louis and Noemie Germaine (Barbier) S. B.A., U. New Orleans, 1972; M.S., Fla. State U., 1973, Ph.D., 1976. Asst. prof. McNeese State U., Lake Charles, La., 1976—, assoc. prof. polit. sci., 1982—. Contbr. articles to profl. jours. Def. resource person LWV, Lake Charles, 1983; regulation resource person Council Better La., 1977; active in Calsasieu League Environ. Action Now, 1983—. Grantee NEH, 1983, Harry S. Truman Library, 1984, NSF, 1978, 79. Mem. Am. Polit. Sci. Assn., La. Polit. Assn. (pres. 1984—), Am. Soc. Pub. Adminstrn., La. Soc. Pub. Adminstrn., Pi Sigma Alpha. Democrat. Roman Catholic. Clubs: Lake Charles Cyclists, Lake Charles Yacht. Avocations: scuba, weightlifting, running, sailing, bicycling. Office: McNeese State U Dept Social Scis Lake Charles LA 70609

SIRGY, M(AGDY) JOSEPH, marketing science educator, consultant; b. Cairo, Egypt, May 31, 1952; came to U.S., 1960, naturalized, 1972; s. Joseph Ibrahim and Odette Mikhail (Hosni) S.; m. Karen Sue Cornet, Nov. 13, 1972; children—Melissa Jane, Danielle Odette. B.A., U. Calif., 1974; M.A., Calif. State U., 1977; Ph.D., U. Mass., 1979. Asst. prof. mktg. Va. Tech. U., 1979-85, assoc. prof., 1985—; ptnr. S & S Assocs., Greensboro, N.C. and Blacksburg, Va., 1983—. Author: Social Cognition and Consumer Behavior, 1983; Marketing as Social Behavior: A General Systems Theory, 1984; Self-Congruity: A New Theory of Personality and Cybernetics, 1985. Served with U.S. Army, 1971-73. Mem. Am. Psychol. Assn., Acad. Mktg. Sci., Assn. Consumers Research, Soc. Gen. Systems Research. Home: 2102 Birch Leaf Ln Blacksburg VA 24060 Office: Va Tech Mktg Dept Blacksburg VA 24061

SISISKY, NORMAN, congressman, soft drink bottler; b. Balt., June 9, 1927; m. Rhoda Brown, June 12, 1949; children—Mark B., Terry R., Richard L., Stuart J. B.S. in Bus. Adminstrn., Va. Commonwealth U., 1949; LL.D. (hon.), Va. State U. Pres., owner Pepsi-Cola Bottling Co. of Petersburg, Inc.; pres., dir. Lee Distbg. Co., Inc., Petersburg, Rhonor Corp.; pres. Belfield Land, Inc., Petersburg; mem. Va. Gen. Assembly, Richmond, 1974-82, 98th Congress from Va.; dir. Bank of Va., Richmond. Pres. Appomattox Indls. Devel. Corp.; bd. visitors Va. State U.; commr. Petersburg Hosp. Authority; trustee Va. State Coll. Found.; bd. dirs. Southside Va. Emergency Crew and Community Resource Devel. Bd. Served with USN, 1945-46. Recipient Outstanding Service award Va. Early Childhood and edn. Assn., 1978. Mem. Nat. Soft Drink Assn. (chmn. bd. 1981-82), Petersburg C. of C. Office: Room 426 Cannon House Office Bldg Washington DC 20515*

SISNEY, SHERLEEN SUE, educator; b. Stillwater, Okla., Oct. 19, 1946; m. Lee Sisney, June 11, 1969; 1 child, Shara Lee. B.S. in Secondary Edn., Okla. State U., 1968; M.Ed., U. Louisville, 1975. Tchr. Merrill Jr. High Sch., Denver, 1968-69, Monterey High Sch., Calif., 1969-71, Ballard High Sch., Louisville, 1971—; mem. pub.'s adv. council Quantum Communications, Inc.; dir. New Foundations in Edn., 1984—; mem. adv. council tchr. and edn. div. Met. Life Found.; mem. Gov.'s Council on Edn. Reform, Joint Council Econ. Edn.; mem. task force social studies Ky. Dept. Edn. Mem. Okla. State U. Centennial Adv. Commn., Jr. League Louisville. Named Nat. Tchr. of Yr., 1984. Mem. Ky. Edn. Assn. (Outstanding Tchr. 1979-80), Phi Delta Kappa, others. Home: 8002 Montero Ct Prospect KY 40059

SISSELMAN, MURRAY, educator, union executive; b. N.Y.C., Jan. 10, 1930; B.Ed., U. Miami; M.S., Ed.S., Nova U.; m. Ludmila Sisselman; children—David, Helen, Jagger. Classroom tchr., Dade County, Fla., 1956—; v.p. Fla. Am. Fedn. Tchrs. AFL-CIO, 1974, pres. United Tchrs. Dade local Am. Fedn. Tchrs., 1974, AFL-CIO, 1975—; v.p. Fla. Edn. Assn./United; mem. exec. bd. South Fla., AFL-CIO, 1977-78, 85-86. Mem. Dade Democratic exec. com., 1971-74; patron Hist. Assn. So. Fla.; mem. com. juvenile health needs Mental Health Bd. Dade County; mem. com. on edn. Third Century U.S.A.; mem. nat. exec. bd. Jewish Labor Com., 1977—; mem. rules com. Dem. exec. com. Fla.; committeeman Fla. Dem. State Com., 1985-86; mem. citizens adv. com. Fla. Dept. Health and Rehab. Services; mem. Dade County Bd. Rules and Appeals, 1975-77, Dade County Zoning Appeals Bd.; trustee City of Hope Pilot Med. Center, 1979—; ednl. dir. Temple Sinai of North Dade, 1966-71; religious sch. prin. Temple Emanu-El, Ft. Lauderdale, Fla., 1971-72. Served with U.S. Army, 1954-56. Recipient Personal Service award C. of C. North Miami Beach (Fla.); Cert. of Appreciation, Nat. Police Officers Assn., Am. Judges Assn., Fla. Edn. Assn./United. Mem. Nat. Congress Parents and Tchrs. (hon. life), Fla. Congress Parents and Tchrs. (hon. life), VFW (citation), Dade County Classroom Tchrs. Assn. (acting pres.), Fla. Edn. Assn. (dir., chmn. legis. com.), Nat. Hist. Soc. (founding assn.), Nat. Assn. Temple Educators, USS Constitution Museum Found. (charter), Alpha Phi Omega (past officer), Sigma Alpha Mu (past pres.), Pi Sigma Rho, Phi Delta Kappa, Kappa Delta Pi. Clubs: Elks, Masons. Office: 2929 SW 3d Ave Miami FL 33129

SISSON, THOMAS EDWIN (PETE), lawyer, development company executive; b. Memphis, Aug. 28, 1927; s. Thomas Andrew and Dora (Butler) S.; m. Jewel Omega Hipps, Oct. 25, 1953; children—Thomas Edwin Jr., Judy Sisson Wimbs, Jerry Allan, Debbie Sisson Dees, Ginger Sisson Hamlet, Larry William, Steve Herbert. B.S., Memphis State U., 1950; LL.B., U. Memphis, 1961. Bar: Tenn. Commr., Dept. of Public Works, Memphis, 1964-68; ptnr. Sisson and Sisson, Memphis, 1968—; mem. Shelby County Bd. Commrs., Shelby County, Tenn., 1976—; pres. TESCO Devel., Inc., Memphis, 1981—. Campaign chmn. Girl Scouts U.S.A., Memphis, 1967-68; pres. Memphis Jr. C. of C., 1958-59. Recipient Perry Pipkin Jr. award Memphis Jr. C. of C., 1957-58; named Boss of Yr. Memphis chpt. Am. Bus. Women Assn., 1965. Mem. Memphis Bar Assn., Shelby County Bar Assn., Tenn. Bar Assn., ABA. Republican. Office: Sisson and Sisson Law Firm 5350 Poplar Ave Suite 415 Memphis TN 38119

SIT, HONG CHAN, minister; b. St. Louis, Nov. 25, 1921; s. Gan and Ying Foon (Wong) S.; m. Amy Wang, June 16, 1949; children—David, Daniel, Estelle Joy, Mary. B.S. summa cum laude, U. Ill., 1943; B.D., Faith Theol. Sem., 1950, S.T.M., 1950; Th.D., No. Bapt. Theol. Sem., 1957. Ordained to ministry Blue Church, Springfield, Pa., 1950. Missionary China Intern Varsity Fellowship, Shanghai, 1947; pastor Chinese Evang. Ch., N.Y.C., 1950-51, Chinese Bapt. Ch., Houston, 1953-56, Grace Chapel, 1956—. Pres. Chinese Fgn. Missionary Union, 1974—, Chinese Full Gospel Fellowship Internat., Hong Kong, 1983—. Author: Your Next Step With Jesus, 1977. Contbr. articles to profl. jours. Mem. Phi Beta Kappa, Phi Lambda Upsilon. Office: Grace Chapel 1055 Bingle Rd Houston TX 77055

SITELMAN, ARTHUR, pathologist; b. Phila., Aug. 21, 1951; s. Samuel and Golda (Podolnick) S. B.S., Pa. State U., 1973; M.D., Jefferson Med. Coll., 1975. Diplomate Am. Bd. Pathology. Resident anatomic and clin. pathology Upstate Med. Ctr., Syracuse, N.Y., 1975-78; resident and chief resident anatomic and clin. pathology NYU Med. Ctr., N.Y.C., 1978-80; pathologist, med. dir Lab. Hematology and Blood Bank, St. Elizabeth Med. Ctr., Covington and Edgewood, Ky., 1980—; med. adv. bd. Hoxworth Blood Ctr., Cin., 1981—; clin. instr. pathology U. Cin. Med. Ctr., 1982—. Mem. leadership council, Jewish Fedn. Cin., 1982—. Mem. Coll. Am. Pathologists (lab. accreditation inspector), Am. Soc. Clin. Pathologists, AMA (Physicians Recognition award 1978-81, 81-84, 84-87), Internat. Assn. Pathology, Internat. Soc. Blood Transfusion, N.Y. Acad. Scis., Assn. Clin. Scientists. Jewish. Office: 401 E 20th St Covington KY 41014

SITTER, C. R., oil company executive. Exec. v.p. Exxon Co., U.S.A., Houston. Office: Exxon Co USA 800 Bell Ave Houston TX 77002*

SITTON, CLAUDE FOX, newspaper editor; b. Emory, Ga., Dec. 4, 1925; s. Claude B. and Pauline (Fox) S.; A.B., Emory U., 1949; m. Eva McLaurin Whetstone, June 5, 1953; children—Lauren Lea, Clinton, Suzanna, McLaurin. Reporter, Internat. News Service, 1949-50; with U.P., 1950-55, writer-editor, N.Y.C., 1952-55; information officer USIA, 1955-57; mem. staff N.Y. Times, 1957-68, nat. news dir., 1964-68; editorial dir. The News and Observer Pub. Co., Raleigh, N.C., 1968—, dir., 1969, v.p., 1970—, editor News and Observer, 1970—. Served USNR, 1943-46. Mem. Am. Soc. Newspaper Editors (dir. 1977—), Sigma Delta Chi. Presbyn. Clubs: Watauga, Kiwanis. Office: News and Observer 215 S McDowell St Raleigh NC 27602

SIZELER, I. WILLIAM, architect; b. New Orleans, Oct. 1, 1939; s. A. Louis and Helen (Lebow) S.; m. Jane Levy, Aug. 12, 1962; children—Katherine, Elizabeth, Deborah. B.A. magna cum laude, Brandeis U., 1961; M.Arch. with honors, U. Pa., 1965. Lic. architect, La. Assoc. architect August Perez & Assocs., New Orleans, 1966-72; ptnr. Sizeler & Muller, New Orleans, 1973-79; pres. I. William Sizeler & Assocs., New Orleans, 1979—; mem. div. bd. 1st Met. Bank, Metairie, La., 1983-84. Mem. pres.'s council Brandeis U., 1980—; sec. bd. dirs. Metairie Park Country Day Sch., Metairie, 1982—, bd. dirs., 1979—. Recipient So. Region award Illuminating Engring. Soc., 1967; Merit cert. Vieux Carre Commn., New Orleans, 1979. Mem. AIA (chpt. bd. dirs. 1974-76, chpt. exec. com. 1974-77), La. Architects Assn. Avocations: tennis, swimming. Home: 3039 Octavia St New Orleans LA 70125 Office: I William Sizeler & Assocs 300 Lafayette Mall Suite 200 New Orleans LA 70130

SIZEMORE, T(HOMAS) C(URTIS), newspaper executive; b. Ashers Fork, Ky., Mar. 8, 1921; s. Carlo L. and Allie (Jackson) S.; B.S., Union Coll., Barbourville, Ky., 1952; LL.D. (hon.), London Inst. Applied Research, 1973; m. Patricia A. Hamlin, Dec. 24, 1941 (div.); 1 son, Timothy Curtis (dec.). Owner, Times, Jamestown, Tenn., 1961-63, Leslie County News, Hyden, Ky., 1963-65; owner People's Jour., Booneville, Ky., 1965-76, pres., pub., 1966—; sheriff Clay County (Ky.), Manchester, 1958-61; ordained minister, Bapt. Ch. Pres. S.E. Ky. Homecoming Festival, 1966-74. Served to col. U.S. Army, 1943-45; PTO. Named Outstanding Leader of Achievement, Bicentennial Yr. Hist. Soc., Raleigh, N.C., 1970, Kentuckian of Yr. Mem. Nat. Hist. Assn., U.S. Air Force Assn., Am. Legion (chaplain) Ky. Press Assn., Nat. Newspaper Assn. Republican. Baptist. Clubs: VFW (comdr. Owsley Post 1970-73). Office: Mt View Hts Apt 111 Box 432 Manchester KY 40962

SJOGREN, KENNETH ANDREW, agronomist, farmer, seed dealer; b. Plainview, Tex., Jan. 19, 1951; s. Carl Stanford and Katherine Anna (Nafzger) S.; B.S., Tex. Tech. U., 1973; m. Charlotte Kay Sammann, May 18, 1974; children—Jennifer Nichole, Seth Eric, Tiffany Aija. Farmer, Olton, Tex., 1973-76, Plainview, Tex., 1977—; Tex. cert. comml. pesticide applicator, 1978—; dealer Northrup King Seed, Plainview, 1977—, Bluff Farmers Crop Ins., 1983—. Mem. Doanes County Wide Farm Panel, 1977—, Founders of Plainview Community Concerts, 1982-84; sustaining mem. Plainview Community Concerts, 1980—; bd. dirs. Symphony of Llano Estacdo; elder Luth. Ch., 1979-81, Sunday sch. tchr., 1977-83, area zone youth councilor, 1980-81. A.W. Young agronomy scholar, 1984-85. Mem. Council Agr. Sci. and Tech., Am. Soc. Agronomy, Crop Sci. Soc. Am., Soil Sci. Soc. Am., Am. Phytopathol. Soc., Nat. Rifle Assn. (life). Lutheran. Club: Tex. Tech. Century. Address: Route 2 Plainview TX 79072

SJOSTEDT-SWEET, CARLOS WILLIAM, investment company executive; b. Rio de Janiero, Brazil, June 9, 1952; came to U.S., 1977; s. William Beck and Astri Annmari (Sjostedt) S.; m. Iris Baren, Aug. 1975; 1 son, Alexandre Baren. B.B.A., U. Miami, 1975. Econs. analyst Exxon Corp., Rio de Janiero, 1975-77; credit officer 1st Nat. Bank of Boston, 1977-81; comml. loan officer Bank of Boston Internat. South, Miami, 1982; chmn. bd. SSI Investment Corp., Miami, 1982—; dir. Rosalta S.A., Rio de Janeiro. Mem. Brazilian-Am. C. of C., Am. Assn. Ind. Investors. Republican. Home: 7080 SW 107th Terr Miami FL 33156 Office: SSI Investment Corp Box 01-5538 Miami FL 33101

SKAFF, JOHN EDWARD, engring. services co. exec.; b. Madison, W.Va., Aug. 17, 1956; s. Paul Richard and Virginia Lee (Haddad) S.; B.B.A., Marshall U., 1978; postgrad. W.Va. Coll., 1982—. Mktg. rep. Schlitz Breweries, Brisbin Distbrs., Huntington, W.Va., 1976-78; mgr. contract services Midwest Tech. Inc., St. Albans, W.Va., 1978—. Advisor, W.Va. Jr. Achievement, 1981-83. Mem. Alpha Kappa Psi (past pres.). Home: 871 Carroll Rd Charleston WV 25314 Office: 2 Smiley Dr Saint Albans WV 25177

SKALKO, RICHARD GALLANT, anatomist, educator; b. Providence, Apr. 10, 1936; s. Francis Charles and Emilie Margaret (Gallant) S.; m. Louise Marie Luchetti (div. 1982); m. Priscilla Ann Brown, 1985; children—Patricia, Margaret, Christine. A.B., Providence Coll., 1957; M.S., St. John's U., 1959; Ph.D., U. Fla., 1963. Instr. anatomy Cornell U. Med. Coll., 1963-66, asst. prof., 1966-67; asst. prof. anatomy La. State U. Med. Ctr., New Orleans, 1967-69, assoc. prof., 1969-70; dir. Embryology Lab., Birth Defects Inst., N.Y. State Health Dept., Albany, 1970-77; assoc. prof. anatomy and toxicology Albany Med. Coll., 1970-76, prof., 1976-77; prof. anatomy East Tenn. State U. Coll. Medicine, Johnson City, 1977—, chmn. dept., 1977—; mem. sci. adv. bd. NCTR, FDA, 1976-79; vis. prof. Institut fur Toxikologie und Embryonalpharmakologie, Freie U., Berlin, 1978; mem. toxicology study sect. NIH. Mem. Am. Assn. Anatomists, Teratology Soc., Soc. Devel. Biology, European Teratology Soc., So. Soc. Anatomists (pres. 1982-83). Democrat. Roman Catholic. Author: Basic Concepts in Teratology, 1985; editor: Heredity and Society, 1973; Congenital Defects, 1974. Home: 3302 Pine Timbers Dr Johnson City TN 37601 Office: Dept Anatomy Box 19960A East Tenn State U Johnson City TN 37614

SKANDALAKIS, JOHN E., state university system official. Chmn. bd. regents Univ. System Ga., Atlanta. Office: Univ System Ga 244 Washington St SW Atlanta GA 30334*

SKARPNESS, BRADLEY OWEN, statistics educator; b. Glenwood, Minn., June 15, 1951; s. Norman Lyle and Marlene Ann (Johnson) S.; m. Debbie Ann Woll, June 15, 1985; 1 child, Erika. B.S., Columbus Coll., 1973, M.S., U. Ark., 1976, Ph.D., Iowa State U., 1981. Asst. prof. stats. Va. Poly. Inst. and State U., Blacksburg, 1981—. Contbr. articles to profl. jours. Mem. Am. Statis. Assn., Inst. Indsl. Engrs. (assoc.), Mu Sigma Rho, Pi Mu Epsilon. Democrat. Lutheran. Avocations: hunting; fishing; hiking. Home: Rt 1 Box 341C Blacksburg VA 24060 Office: Va Poly Inst and State U Dept Stats Blacksburg VA 24061

SKEEN, JAMES NORMAN, corporate executive, museum planner; b. Knoxville, Tenn., Feb. 23, 1942; s. William Hugh and Betty Ruth (Simmons) S.; m. Marianne Louise Jefferson, Feb. 5, 1966. B.S., Maryville Coll., 1964; M.S., U. Ga., 1966; Ph.D., 1969. Asst. prof. biology Atlanta Bapt. Coll., 1969-70, acting chmn. biology, 1970-71; temporary instr. biology Brenau Coll., 1972; ecologist Fernbank Sci. Ctr., Atlanta, 1972-85; assoc. dir. Fernbank, Inc., 1985—; adj. assoc. prof. biology Emory U., 1978—; bd. sci. advisors Marshall Forest, Rome, Ga. Ga. Dept. Edn. grantee, 1974; Dept. Energy grantee, 1978-79; NSF grantee, 1980. Mem. Torrey Bot. Club, So. Appalachian Bot. Club, Tenn. Acad. Sci., Ga. Acad. Sci., Southeastern Mus. Conf., Am. Assn. Mus. Contbr. numerous articles to sci. jours. Home: 553 N Superior Ave Decatur GA 30033 Office: 1788 Ponce de Leon Ave Atlanta GA 30307

SKEFOS, HARRY JERRY, lawyer; b. Memphis, Mar. 12, 1951; s. Jerry and Katherine (Fillon) S.; m. Catherine Hetos, June 21, 1975; 1 child, Chrystan Maria. B.S. in Econs., U. Pa., 1973, M.S. in Acctg., 1973; J.D., George Washington U., 1976. Bar: Tenn. 1976, U.S. Dist. Ct. Tenn. 1981, U.S. Tax Ct. 1983. Chmn. bd. Consol. Poultry & Egg Co., Inc., Memphis, 1976-84, Omega Properties, Inc., Gas 'N Go, Inc., Memphis, 1976—; assoc. Martin, Tate, Morrow & Marston, Memphis, 1979—; instr. acctg. Community Wharton Edn. Program, 1972-73; Nat. councilman Greek Orthodox Youth Am., 1972-73; charter mem. Memphis Youth Symphony, 1972; mem. Memphis Symphony Chorus, 1979-80; bd. dirs. Annunciation Greek Orthodox Ch., 1980—. Served with U.S. Army ROTC, 1970-73. Mem. Memphis and Shelby County Bar Assn., ABA, Tenn. Bar Assn., U. Pa. Alumni Assn. (recruitment com.), Beta Alpha Psi. Office: Falls Bldg 11th Floor Memphis TN 38103

SKELTON, DOROTHY GENEVA SIMMONS (MRS. JOHN WILLIAM SKELTON), artist, educator; b. Woodland, Calif.; d. Jack Elijah and Helen Anna (Siebe) Simmons; B.A., U. Calif., 1940, M.A., 1943; m. John William Skelton, July 16, 1941. Sr. research analyst War Dept., Gen. Staff, M.I. Div. G-2, Washington, 1944-45; vol. researcher, monuments, fine arts and archives sect. Restitution Br., Office Mil. Govt. for Hesse, Wiesbaden, Germany, 1947-48; vol. art tchr. German children, Bad Nauheim, Germany, 1947-48; art educator, lectr. Dayton (Ohio) Art Inst., 1955; art educator Lincoln Sch., Dayton, 1956-60; instr. art edn. U. Va. Sch. Continuing Edn., Charlottesville, 1962-75; researcher in genealogy; exhibited in group shows, Calif., Colo., Ohio, Washington and Va.; represented in permanent collections: Madison Hall, Charlottesville, Madison Center (Va.). Mem. Nat. League Am. Pen Women, Am. Assn. Museums, Coll. Art Assn. Am., Nat. Soc. Arts and Letters, Inst. Study of Art in Edn., Dayton Soc. Painters and Sculptors, Va. Mus. Fine Arts, Calif. Alumni Assn., AAUW. Republican. Methodist. Clubs: Army Navy Country, Air Force Officers Wives, Lake of the Woods (Va.) Golf and Country. Author: The Squire Simmons Family 1746-1986, 1986. Chief collaborator: John Skelton of Georgia, 1969. Address: Lotos Lakes Brightwood VA 22715

SKELTON, HOWARD CLIFTON, marketing executive; b. Birmingham, Ala., Mar. 6, 1932; s. Howard C. and Sarah Ethel (Holmes) S.; B.S., Auburn U., 1955; m. Winifred Harriet Karger, May 19, 1962; 1 dau., Susan Lynn. Copywriter, Rich's, Inc., Atlanta, 1955-59, Ga. Power Co., Atlanta, 1959-61; dir. advt. and sales promotion Callaway Mills, Inc., LaGrange, Ga., 1961-65, Thomasville Furniture Industries (N.C.), 1965-66; v.p. in charge fashion and textiles Gaynor & Ducas, N.Y.C., 1966-70; dir. communications Collins & Aikman, N.Y.C., 1970-73; exec. v.p. Marketplace, Inc., Atlanta, 1973-74; v.p. mktg. and communications Internat. City Corp., Atlanta, 1974-75; pres. Howard Skelton Assocs., Atlanta, 1976-84, Sarasota, Fla., 1984—. Mem. adv. bd. Salvation Army, United Way. Served with Signal Corps, AUS, 1956-58. Recipient Danforth Found. award, 1950. Mem. Sarasota-Bradenton-Venice Advt. Fedn. (bd. dirs.), Sarasota C. of C., Atlanta Conv. and Visitors Bur., Omicron Delta Kappa, Lambda Chi Alpha, Sigma Delta Chi. Home: 708 Garfield Dr Sarasota FL 33577 Office: 950 S Tamiami Trail Suite 207 Sarasota FL 33577

SKELTON, JOHN GOSS, JR., psychologist; b. Columbus, Ga.; s. John Goss and Willie Mae (Langford) S.; B.A., Emory U., 1950; M.Ed., Our Lady of Lake U., 1964; Ph.D., Tex. Tech. U., 1967. Positions with advt. agy., newspaper, trade assn., 1950-63; staff psychologist San Antonio State Hosp., 1963; resident in clin. psychology U. Tex. Med. Br., Galveston, 1966-67; dir., clin. psychologist Psychol. Services Clinic, Harlingen, Tex., 1967-68; clin. psychologist Santa Rosa Med. Center, San Antonio, 1968-71; pvt. practice clin. psychology San Antonio, 1971—; chmn. dept. psychology Park North Gen. Hosp., San Antonio, 1971-83; clin. asst. prof. U. Tex. Health Sci. Center, San Antonio, 1971-78; cons. S.W. Ind. Sch. Dist. San Antonio, 1974—, Brookwood Recovery Ctr., San Antonio; instr. Our Lady of Lake U., San Antonio, summers 1968-71, Tex. Tech U., summer 1967. Pres., Vis. Nurses Assn. Bexar County, 1976-77; bd. dirs. Halfway House San Antonio, 1964-65, Mental Health Assn. Bexar County, 1969-75; dir. steering com. San Antonio Area Crisis Center, 1971-74. Served with USN, 1945-46. Vocat. Rehab. fellow, 1965-67. Mem. Am. Psychol. Assn., Bexar County Psychol. Assn. (pres. 1970-71), Assn. Children with Learning Disabilities Tex., Tex. Psychol. Assn., Soc. Behavioral Medicine, San Antonio Mus. Assn. Episcopalian. Office: 7950 Floyd Curl Dr Suite 701 San Antonio TX 78229

SKELTON, STEVEN, researcher; b. Greenville, S.C., Mar. 18, 1949. Student John B. Stetson U., 1967-69; B.A. in English, U. S.C., 1972. Caseworker, Richland County Dept. Social Services, 1973-74; youth counselor John G. Richards Sch. Boys, 1974; clin. counselor Pee Dee Mental Health Ctr., Florence, S.C., 1974-76; instr. Florence-Darlington Tech. Coll., Florence, S.C., 1975-76; grad. asst. Univ. Affiliated Facilities, Ctr. for Devel. Disabilities U. S.C., 1976-77; mental health asst. Richland Meml. Hosp., 1978; research technician Teepak, Inc., 1978-80; mgr. B. Dalton Bookseller, 1980-82; composition specialist State Printing Co., 1982-84; research assoc. Coll. Applied Profl. Scis. U. S.C., Columbia, 1985—; dir. The Crown Agy., editing, research and cons. services, 1985—; coordinator and co-trainer goal planning workshop Pee Dee Mental Health Ctr., co-trainer psychodrama workshop; coordinator in-house workshop on standards and specifications Teepak. Co-author student workbook and tchr.'s manual for children's series. Contbr. articles to profl. jours.; cited in acknowledgments of numerous publs.; editorial asst. Fitzgerald/Hemingway Ann., 1970, 71. Editor: Univ. Affiliated Facilities Tng. Manual, 1977. Co-founder karate class YMCA, Greenwood, S.C., 1967; charter mem., mem. exec. com. Columbia Adlerian Soc., 1973; sec., treas. Florence County Human Services Assn., 1975-76; leader parent edn. groups Unitarian-Universalist Fellowship, Irmo Middle Jr. Sch., 1974; speaker on topic of child-raising to parent groups of Head Start, Florence, 1975-76; chmn. religious edn. com. Unitarian-Universalist Fellowship, 1978-79; bd. dirs. Gt. Works Found., 1985—. Mem. Columbia Film Soc., Christ Unity of Columbia, Mensa.

SKIDMORE, EDGAR STEWART, writing instrument company executive; b. Havana, Cuba, Oct. 10, 1916; s. Edgar Hamilton and Kathryn Louise (Adams) S.; m. Marjorie Jean Montgomery, May 25, 1943 (dec. 1981); children—Montgomery Skidmore, Shelby Skidmore Woodard; m. Genevieve Morrow Bohlman, Dec. 30, 1982. B.B.A., U. Tex., 1938. With Parker Pen Co., San Antonio, 1939-40, mgr. Parker Mexicana, 1946-57, v.p. Latin Am. ops., 1957-79; pres. Skidmore & Assocs., San Antonio, 1979—. Served to lt. USN, 1940-45; ATO, ETO. Decorated Navy Commendation medal. Mem. Kappa Alpha. Republican. Episcopalian. Clubs: Houston Country, Riverhill. Lodges: Masons, Shriners, KT. Contbr. articles to profl. jours. Home: 3203 Avalon Pl Houston TX 77019 Office: PO Box 22711 Houston TX 77227

SKINNER, CHARLES GORDON, chemist, educator; b. Dallas, Apr. 23, 1923; s. Charles Grady and Benona Pricilla (Skiles) S.; B.S., N. Tex. State U., 1943, M.S., 1947; Ph.D., U. Tex., Austin, 1953; m. Lilly Ruth Brown, Apr. 4, 1944; children—Robert Gordon, Gary Wayne. Eli Lilly postdoctoral fellow, 1953; chemist Clayton Found. Biochemistry Inst., Austin, 1954-64; prof. chemistry N. Tex. State U., Denton, 1964—, chmn. dept., 1969-75, chmn. dept. basic health sci., 1975—, asst. dean basic scis. Tex. Coll. Osteopathic Medicine, 1975-80. Served with U.S. Army, 1944-46. Recipient numerous NIH grants, NSF grants. Mem. Am. Chem. Soc. (councilor Dallas-Ft Worth sect.), Am. Soc. Biol. Chemistry, Am. Inst. Chemists, Am. Soc. Plant Physiology, Tex. Acad. Sci., Sigma Xi, Alpha Chi Sigma, Phi Lambda Upsilon. Contbr. articles to profl. jours; patentee in field. Office: North Texas State U Denton TX 76203

SKINNER, HUBERT C., geology and paleontology educator, consultant, researcher; b. Tulsa, Okla., Oct. 3, 1929; s. Orlo C. and Onamae (Hood) S.; m. Judith Miller, Dec. 27, 1958 (dec. 1976); children—Susan Ann, Sharon Lynn, Kathryn Louise. B.S. in Geology, U. Okla., 1951, M.S., 1953, Ph.D., 1954. Chief paleontologist Texaco, Inc., New Orleans, 1954-57; assoc. prof. Tulane U., New Orleans, 1957-62, prof. geology, paleontology, 1962—, editor Tulane Studies in Geology Paleontology, 1962—. Author: Gulf Coast Stratigraphic Correlation, 1972; United States Cancellations: 1845-1869, 1980; (with others) Two Hundred Years of Geology in America, 1979 (Outstanding Book in Am. 1981). Editor: Charles Lyell on North American Geology, 1977; Jules Marcou on the Taconic System in North America, 1977. Served to 1st lt. USAFR, 1951-58. Recipient Walter McCoy award Am. Philatelic Congress, 1977, August Dietz award Confederate Stamp Alliance, 1979, Internat. Gold medal Interphil, 1976, Internat. Gold medal London Stampex, 1980, Internat. Gold medal CAPEX, 1978. Fellow Geol. Soc. Am. (chmn. history of geology div. 1984), Geol. Soc. London; mem. Soc. Econ. Paleontologist Mineralogists (nat. council 1966-67, (pres. Gulf Coast sect. 1966-67), La. Landmarks Soc., New Orleans Mus. Art, La. State Mus. Democrat. Methodist. Avocations: postal history; philatelic writing; research. Office: Dept Geology Tulane U New Orleans LA 70118

SKINNER, LARRY WARD, chemical manufacturing company executive; b. Savannah, Ga., Sept. 15, 1942; s. Ward Jones and Thelma Roach (McDonald) S.; A.A., Truett McConnell Coll., 1966; B.S., Piedmont Coll., 1968; m. Marjorie Lynn Waters, Dec. 24, 1973 (div. 1983); children—Randal Lawrence, William Pool, Christopher Scott, Ceryl, Larry Ward II, Mary Ella. Fireman, U.S.S. Pierce, U.S. Coast and Geodetic Survey, Savannah, 1963-65; tchr. Jasper County Bd. Edn., 1968-69; prin. Patrick Henry Acad., Savannah, 1969-70, Southside Elem. Sch., Savannah, 1970-71, Nova Acads., Savannah, 1971-72; pres., chmn. bd. Hedgetree Chem. Mfg., Inc., Savannah, 1972—; co-founder, owner Pharms. of Am., Inc.; chem. cons. Hon. mem. Women's Soc. Christian Service, DAR; host family, area rep. Am.-Scandinavian Student Exchange Program. Recipient award for heroism, Hunter Army Air Field, 1969. Mem. Ga. Hist. Soc. Methodist. Clubs: Masons, Shriners, Eastern Star. Composer, writer, pub.; research and devel. of dispensing systems for coal dust in exporting, Solution to suppress coal dust, liquid organic cleaning concentrate. Home: 7 Skinners Pl Savannah GA 31406 Office: 119 Prosperity Dr Savannah GA 31408

SKINNER, L(INDA) MAUREEN, educational consultant; b. Nashville, July 29, 1947; d. James R. and Ann Ruth (Sanders) Martin; children—Jamie Elizabeth, Douglas Edward. B.A., Fla. State U., 1969, M.L.S., 1970. Media specialist Leon County Schs., Tallahassee, Fla., 1970-80; edml. cons. Fla. Dept. Edn., Tallahassee, 1980—. Mem. editorial bd. Sch. Library Media Quar. Mem. ALA, Nat. Assn. State Ednl. Media Profls., Am. Assn. Sch. Librarians, Assn. Ednl. Communications and Tech., Fla. Library Assn., Fla. Assn. for Media Edn. (sec. 1985—). Home: 2015 Trescott Dr Tallahassee FL 32312 Office: Fla Dept Edn Knott Bldg Tallahassee FL 32301

SKINNER, ROBERT GORDON, librarian, educator; b. Austin, Tex., Jan. 9, 1948; s. Charles Gordon and Lilly Ruth (Brown) S.; m. Cheryl Gayle Noden, Aug. 24, 1973. B.A., North Tex. State U., 1974, M.L.S., 1977. Record librarian Harvard U., Cambridge, Mass., 1978-79; music and fine arts librarian So. Meth. U., Dallas, 1980—, adj. prof. music history, 1982—. Contbr. articles to profl. jours. Reviewer reference books, 1980—. So. Meth. U. grantee, 1983. Mem. Am. Musicol. Soc., Music Library Assn., Tex. Chpt. Music Library Assn. (chmn. various coms.). Avocation: microcomputers. Home: 10625 Northboro St Dallas TX 75230 Office: So Meth U Library Owen Arts Ctr Dallas TX 75275

SKLENAR, HERBERT ANTHONY, diversified products manufacturing company executive; b. Omaha, June 7, 1931; s. Michael Joseph and Alice Madeline (Spicka) S.; m. Eleanor L. Vincenz, Sept. 15, 1956; children—Susan Allison, Patricia Irene. B.S. in Bus. Adminstrn. summa cum laude, U. Nebr.-Omaha, 1952; M.B.A., Harvard U., 1954. Vice-pres., comptroller Parkersburg-Aetna Corp. (W.Va.), 1956-63; v.p. Marmac Corp., Parkersburg, 1963-66, also dir.; mgr. fin. control Boise Cascade Corp. (Idaho), 1966-67; exec. v.p. fin. and adminstrn., sec. Cudahy Co., Phoenix, 1967-72; exec. v.p., chief adminstrv. officer Vulcan Materials Co., Birmingham, Ala., 1972-85, pres., chief operating officer, 1985—, also dir.; mem. So. adv. bd. Allendale Mut. Ins. Co.; mem. task force on conceptual framework project funds flows and liquidity Fin. Acctg. Standards Bd., 1979-81. Author: (with others) The Automatic Factory: A Critical Examination, 1955. Met. bd. dirs. YMCA, Birmingham; mem. adv. bd. Sch. Bus., Samford U. Served with U.S. Army, 1954-56. Recipient Elizah Watts Sells award Am. Inst. C.P.A.s, 1965; Alumni Achievement award U. Nebr.-Omaha, 1977. C.P.A., W.Va. Mem. Am. Inst. C.P.A.s, Fin. Execs. Inst., Nat. Assn. Accts., Phi Kappa Phi, Omicron Delta Kappa, Phi Eta Sigma, Delta Sigma Pi. Republican. Presbyterian. Clubs: The Club, Wall St., Mountain Brook Racquet and Swim. Home: 3908 Knollwood Dr Birmingham AL 35243 Office: One Metroplex Dr Birmingham AL 35209*

SKOCIK, E(DITH) M(AE) REGINA, clinical psychologist, forensic consultant, researcher; b. Paris, Aug. 3, 1929; came to U.S., 1947, naturalized, 1953; d. Berl Vogelfang and Lucienne (DeBuquet) Hettema; m. Frank Skocik, Apr. 1967 (dec. Jan. 1979). Lic. psychologist, Mo., Kans. Spl. edn. coordinator, psychologist Hickman Sch. Dist., Mills, Mo., 1960-63; chief psychologist State Inst., Winfield, Kans., 1963-67; dir. psychiatric services Dept. Pub. Health, Port-au-Prince, Haiti, 1972-82; counselor III, research coordinator Fla. Dept. Corrections, Lantana Correctional Inst., 1982—; spl. edn. cons. Program Devel., Kans., 1962; cons. Mental Health Program Devel., Port-au-Prince, 1967. Author: Special Education Curriculum Guide, 1962; Sharks Around Us, 1973. Mem. Am. Psychol. Assn., Am. Assn. Mental Deficiency, Am. Inst. Hypnosis (cert.), Am. Correctional Assn., Am. Assn. Correctional Psychologists, N.Y. Acad. Scis. Republican. Jewish. Avocations: scuba diving; cultural anthropology. Home: 8086 Ambach Way Lantana FL 33462

SKVORETZ, JOHN VINCENT, sociologist, educator; b. Allentown, Pa., Sept. 8, 1947; s. John Vincent and Ruth Elizabeth (Heffelfinger) S.; m. Sharon Louise Anthony, Aug. 31, 1968; children—Jonathan, Christopher, Matthew. B.A. in Sociology, Lehigh U., 1969, B.A. in Math., 1969; Ph.D. in Sociology, U. Pitts., 1976. Assoc. prof. sociology U. S.C., Columbia, 1980—, chmn. dept. sociology, 1984—. Assoc. editor Social Forces, 1984—. Contbr. articles to profl. jours. NSF fellow, 1970-73. Mem. Am. Sociol. Assn., So. Sociol. Soc., Phi Beta Kappa. Democrat. Office: U SC Dept Sociology Columbia SC 29208

SLADE, BONNIE BATTER, clinical psychologist; b. New Haven, Mar. 27, 1951; d. Irwin Levian and Sara (Glass) Batter; m. Jon Jeffrey Slade; 1 child, Jennifer. A.B., Vassar Coll., 1972; Ph.D., U. Calif.-Davis, 1979. Lic. psychologist, Fla. Instr. early childhood edn. Yale U., New Haven, 1974-75, asst. prof., 1979-81; asst. prof. Fla. Inst. Tech., Melbourne, 1981-82; pvt. practice psychology, Palm Bay, Fla., 1982—. Contbr. articles to profl. jours. and chpt. to book. Regents fellow State of Calif., 1977, Chancellors fellow, 1978. Mem. Am. Psychol. Assn., Soc. For Research in Child Devel., Brevard County Psychol. Assn. Avocations: tennis; reading; swimming. Office: 1520 Bottlebrush Dr Suite A2 Palm Beach FL 32905

SLANEY-DAVIS, ALICE JEAN, Realtor; b. Philipsburg, Pa., Dec. 10, 1932; d. Wesley Gray and Margaret Maria (Flegal) Woodring; m. James D. Slaney, Apr. 18, 1953 (div. 1973); children—Scott Gair, Lynn Gay, 1 step-son Thomas J.; m. H. Richard Davis, Dec. 31, 1982; stepsons—Scott Davis, Rich Davis. Student Thompson Coll., York, Pa., 1950-51. Sales mgr. Lillian Harris, Realtors, Richardson, Tex., 1971-75; sales assoc. Paula Stringer, Realtors, Richardson, 75-77, v.p., mgr. Preston Center office, 1977-79; v.p., mgr. Merrill Lynch Realty, Dallas, 1979-81, v.p., mgr. Promenade South office, Richardson, Tex., 1981—. Mem. Greater Dallas Bd. Realtors, Tex. Assn. Realtors. Republican. Methodist.

SLATINSKY, JOHANNE MARIE, psychotherapist; b. Sorel, Que., Can., Mar. 23, 1954; came to U.S., 1967; d. Claude N. and Charlotte E. (Simard) Boutin; m. Daniel A. Slatinsky, June 18, 1982; children—Sean, Noah; m. Carl N. Volk, May 28, 1978 (div. 1981). B.A., U. Mich., 1975; M.S., Eastern Mich. U., 1980. Lic. psychologist, Mich. Intake worker Planned Parenthood, Ann Arbor, Mich., 1977-78; psychotherapist Community Mental Health, Washtenaw County, Mich., 1980; psychotherapist, intake worker Huron Valley Inst., Dexter, Mich., 1980-82; psychotherapist Spectrum Counseling, Ypsilanti, Mich., 1982-85, dir., psychotherapist, Roswell, Ga., 1985—; cons. Social Security Adminstrn., Lansing, Mich., 1980-85. Mem. Am. Personnel and Guidance Assn., Am. Psychol. Assn. (assoc.). Avocations: aerobics; skiing. Home: 315 Hembree Forest Circle Roswell GA 30076 Office: Spectrum Counseling Services Inc 45 W Crossville Rd Suite 514 Roswell GA 30075

SLATT, ROGER MALCOLM, petroleum geologist; b. San Francisco, July 5, 1941; s. Earl and Helen (Nacht) S.; m. Lyn Braley, Aug. 13, 1964 (div. 1983); children—Andrew Martin, Thomas Wayne. A.A., San Francisco City Coll., 1961; B.A., Calif. State U.-San Jose, 1965; M.S., U. Alaska, 1967, Ph.D., 1970. Assoc. prof. geology Meml. U., Nfld., Can., 1970-76; vis. asst. prof. geology Ariz. State U., Tempe, 1976-78; sr. research geologist Atlantic Richfield Co., Dallas, 1978-80; stratigraphy research mgr. Cities Service Exploration Prodn Research, Tulsa, 1980-83; dir. reservoir evaluation Arco Exploration Tech., Plano, Tex., 1983—. Contbr. articles to profl. jours. NSF trainee, 1970; Ethan Allen scholar, 1965; fellow NDEA, 1968, Pan Am. Petroleum Found., 1970. Mem. Soc. Econ. Paleontologists and Mineralogists (research com. 1983—), Am. Assn. Petroleum Geologists (research com. 1981—). Home: 2200 W Park Blvd 1602 Plano TX 75075 Office: Arco Exploration and Tech 2300 W Plano Pkwy Plano TX 75075

SLATTERY, SANDRA LEE, college advisor; b. Chgo., July 29, 1946; d. Melvin Henry and Murl Irene (Rodgers) Wichert; m. Dennis Patrick Slattery, Mar. 23, 1968; children—Matthew Damian, Stephen Benedict. Student Miami U., Oxford, Ohio, Kent State U., So. Meth. U. Tchr. Jr. High Sch., Lorain, Ohio, 1971-73; asst. dir. U. Dallas, Rome, 1976-78, internat. advisor, Dallas, 1978-81, So. Meth. U., Dallas, 1981—; asst. dir. Japan Exchange Program, Dallas, 1985—; dir. Internat. Office So. Meth. U. Recipient Chaplains Service award So. Meth. U., 1982; Taiwan Ednl. Tour award Cultural Office, Washington, 1981. Mem. Nat. Assn. Fgn. Student Affairs Am. Coll. Personnel Assn. (bd. dirs. 1983-85), Soc. Intercultural Edn. Tng. and Research. Roman Catholic. Club: So. Methodist Women's. Avocations: foreign affairs; cross cultural activities. Home: 2704 Peach Tree Ln Irving TX 75062 Office: So Meth U PO Box 381 Dallas TX 75062

SLAUGHTER, ANNE TURRIFF, retail executive, real estate agent; b. Denver, Jan. 5, 1944; d. James Austin and Janice (Lindsay) Turriff; m. Peter Randolph Slaughter, Jr., Mar. 1971. Student U. Okla., 1962-63; B.A., So. Methodist U., 1966. Lic. real estate agt., Tex. Owner, pres., Pipe 'n Pouch, Ltd., Co., Dallas, 1981—. Docent, Mus. Natural Hist., Los Angeles, 1971-73, Nelson Atkins Art Mus., Kansas City, Mo., 1973-76, Dallas Mus. Fine Arts, 1978-81; bd. dirs. Women's Com., Dallas Ballet, Friends of Ctr. Pastoral Care and Family Counseling; adminstr. Sch. Spirituality, Episcopal Renewal Ctr. Mem. So. Meml. Assn., Innovators of Dallas Symphony Orch., Wadley Guild Dallas. Clubs: Cotillion, Slipper, Royal Oaks Country (Dallas). Home: 3635 Amherst St Dallas TX 75225

SLAUGHTER, DANIEL FRENCH, JR., congressman; b. Culpeper, Va., May 20, 1925; s. Daniel French and Caroline (Strother) S.; m. Kathleen Rowe, Jan. 27, 1951; children—Daniel French, Kathleen Slaughter Frey. Student Va. Mil. Inst., 1942-43; B.A., U. Va., 1949, LL.B., 1953. Bar: Va. 1953. Ptnr. firm Button, Slaughter, Yeaman & Morton, Culpeper, Va., 1958-84; mem. House of Dels., Gen. Assembly of Va., Richmond, 1958-78; mem. U.S. Ho. of Reps. from 7th Dist. of Va., 1984—. Served with U.S. Army, 1943-47; ETO. Decorated Purple Heart. Mem. Va. State Bar. Republican. Episcopalian. Office: US House of Reps 319 Cannon House Office Bldg Washington DC 20515

SLAUGHTER, FREEMAN CLUFF, dentist; b. Estes, Miss., Dec. 30, 1926; s. William Cluff and Vay (Fox) S.; student Wake Forest Coll., 1944; student Emory U., 1946-47, D.D.S., 1951; m. Genevieve Anne Parks, July 30, 1948; children—Mary Anne, Thomas Freeman, James Hugh. Practice gen. dentistry, Kannapolis, N.C., 1951—; mem. N.C. Bd. Dental Examiners, 1966-75, pres., 1968-69, sec.-treas., 1971-74; chief dental staff Cabarrus Meml. Hosp., Concord, N.C., 1965-66, 75; mem. N.C. Adv. Com. for Edn. Dental Aux. Personnel-N.C. State Bd. Edn., 1967-70; adviser dental asst. program Rowan Tech. Inst., 1973—. Trustee N.C. Symphony Soc., 1962-68, pres. Kannapolis chpt., 1961; mem. Cabarrus County Bd. Health, 1977-83, chmn., 1981-83, acting health dir., 1981; vice chmn. Kannapolis Charter Commn., 1983-84; mem. City Council Kannapolis, 1983-84; mayor pro tem Kannapolis, 1984-85; active Boy Scouts Am., Eagle scout with silver palm. Served with USNR, 1944-46; ETO, MTO. Recipient Kanapolis Citizen of Yr. award, 1982. Lic. real estate broker. Fellow Am. Coll. Dentists; mem. Am. Legion, Kannapolis Jr. C. of C. (v.p. 1952), Toastmasters Internat. (pres. Kannapolis 1963-64), ADA, Am. Assn. Dental Examiners (Dentist Citizen of Year 1975; v.p. 1977-79), So. Conf. Dental Deans and Examiners (v.p. 1969), N.C. Dental Soc. (resolution of commendation 1975), N.C. Dental Soc. Anesthesiology (pres. 1964), Southeastern Acad. Prosthodontics, So. Acad. Oral Surgery, Am. Soc. Dentistry for Children (pres. N.C. unit 1957), Internat. Assn. Dental Research, Cabarrus County Dental Soc. (pres. 1953-54, 63-64, 69), N.C. Assn. Professions (dir. 1976-80), Omicron Kappa Upsilon, Alpha Epsilon Upsilon. Clubs: Masons, Shriners, Kannapolis Music (pres. 1962-63), Rotary (dir. 1977-80). Office: Professional Bldg Kannapolis NC 28081

SLAUGHTER, LURLINE EDDY, artist; b. Silver City, Miss., June 19, 1919; d. Gilbert Emmings and Lurline Elizabeth (Heidelberg) Eddy; m. James Fant Slaughter, Jan. 27, 1946; children—Beverly Slaughter Lowery, Anne Lumbley Slaughter Towles. B.S. in Bus., Miss. U. for Women, 1939; student art workshops. Tchr., Silver City High Sch., Miss., 1939-41; with VA, Washington, 1941-42; free-lance artist, Silver City, 1959—; bd. dirs. Miss. Art Colony, Utica, 1963—. Exhibited group shows U.S. Fine Arts Registry, N.Y.C. (Outstanding Artist award 1966), 1966; McComb Arts Festival, Miss. (Best in Show 1967, 75); So. Contemporary Art Festival, Greenville, Miss. (Best in Show 1966); Acapulco Ann. Hilton Hotel, Mex. (Best in show 1979); World's Fair Miss. Pavillion, New Orleans, 1984. Artist Gulf South Gallery, McComb, McCartys Gallerys, Merigold, Miss., Monteagle, Tenn. Sunday sch. tchr. Methodist Ch., Silver City, 1957-61; pres. PTA, Silver City, 1964-65; mem. Miss. Mus. Art, Jackson, Jackson Mcpl. Gallery, Miss. Inst. Arts and Letters. Served as lt. USNR, 1942-45. Club: Humphreys Country (Belzoni, Miss.). Avocation: tennis. Home: Seldom Seen Plantation Silver City MS 39166

SLAUGHTER, RICHARD AUBREY, III, clinical psychologist, educator, consultant; b. Richmond, Va., Jan. 29, 1952; s. Richard Aubrey Jr. and Virginia Burns (Weston) S. B.S., Western Ill. U., 1976; M.A., Redford U., 1980; Psy.D., Fla. Inst. Tech., 1983. Lic. psychologist, Tex. Counselor Alpha, Melbourne, Fla., 1981, Brevard County Mental Health, Rockford, Fla., 1980-82; clin. psychology intern Nueces County Mental Health, Corpus Christi, 1982-83; clin. psychologist Wichita Falls State Hosp., Tex., 1983—; cons. Cooke County Mental Health Ctr., Gainesville, Tex., 1985—; prof. psychology Vernon Regional Coll., Tex., 1985—; ptnr. Wichita Falls Psychol. Services, 1986—; chmn. qualitative peer rev. Wichita Falls State Hosp., 1983—. Mem. Am. Psychol. Assn., Mental Health Assn. Home: 5041 Lindale St Wichita Falls TX 76310 Office: Wichita Falls State Hosp Box 300 Wichita Falls TX 76327

SLAUGHTER, ROBERT IRA, loss control manager; b. Lafayette, Ind., July 7, 1938; s. Robert Walter and Dorothy Lucille (Wilson) S.; m. Carole Lou Carder, Nov. 27, 1965; children—Kristen Gae, William Grant. B.S. in Indsl. Edn., Purdue U., 1965. Registered profl. safety engr., Calif.; cert. safety profl.; accredited safety auditor. Personnel mgr. Sterling Brewers, Inc., Evansville, Ind., 1965-67, Central Inds., Inc., Evansville, 1967; corp. safety dir. Fansteel Inc., North Chicago, Ill., 1967-68; corp. safety and OSHA supr. CBI Industries, Inc., Oak Brook, Ill., 1968-77; mgr. loss control The Western Co. N.Am., Ft. Worth, 1977—. Mem. Petroleum Equipment Suppliers Assn. (chmn. service co. safety com. 1982—), Nat. Safety Council (petroleum sect. exec. com. 1977—, asst. editor metals sect. newsletter 1975, author metals sect. newsletter 1974, petroleum sect. newsletter 1982, 84), Am. Soc. Safety Engrs. Republican. Methodist. Avocations: reading, gardening. Home: 5400 Summit Ridge Trail Arlington TX 76017 Office: The Western Co of N Am 6100 Western Place Ft Worth TX 76107

SLAVEN, BETTYE DEJON, psychotherapist; b. New Orleans, Sept. 27, 1946; d. Edward William and Bettye (Ray) DeJ.; m. Richard W. Slaven, Nov. 28, 1968; children—Kelly DeJon Slaven, Richard Daniel. B.A., Tex. Tech U., 1969; M.A., U. Houston, 1974; postgrad. N. Tex. State U., 1974-76. Lic. counselor, Tex. Tchr. Richardson Ind. Sch. Dist., Tex., 1970-71, 73-74, Somerville Pub. Schs., Mass., 1971-72, Trinity Episcopal Sch., New Orleans, 1972-73; with Goals for Dallas-Devel., 1975—; pvt. practice psychotherapy, Dallas, 1979—. Bd. dirs. Way Back House-Vol. Psychol. Assistance, 1979—; founder, project chmn. Women's Way Back House, 1979; pres. living bible class Highland Park Methodist Ch., Dallas, 1982; city chmn. Dallas Area Rapid Transit, 1983; pub. affairs chmn. Jr. League Dallas, 1984, research and devel. chmn., 1985-86, community v.p., 1986-87. Mem. Am. Assn. Marriage and Family Therapy, Dallas Psychol. Assn. Avocations: sailing; swimming; reading.

SLAVENS, GEORGE EVERETT, history educator; b. Kansas City, Kans., Oct. 3, 1931; s. Ralph Westmeyer; m. Beverly Ann McGuire, Oct. 25, 1975; children—Margaret Elizabeth, Douglas E., Rebecca Ann. A.B., U. Mo., 1955, A.M., 1957, Ph.D., 1969. Instr. Sch. of Ozarks, Branson, Mo., 1957-59; prof. history Ouachita Baptist U., Arkadelphia, Ark., 1961—. Mem. Orgn. Am. Historians, Ark. Assn. Coll. History Tchrs. (pres. 1985—), Ark. Hist. Assn., AAUP. Democrat. Presbyterian. Home: 320 N 9th St Arkadelphia AR 71923 Office: Ouachita Bapt U Box 3715 Arkadelphia AR 71923

SLAVIN, ARTHUR JOSEPH, humanities educator; b. N.Y.C., Feb. 15, 1933; s. David and Mildred (Eisner) S.; m. Camille LeBlanc, June 19, 1954 (div. 1966); children—Ruth, Aaron, Rebecca, Laura; m. Inger-Johanne Espe, Nov. 30, 1968; 1 dau., Solveig. Student NYU, 1950-51; B.A. summa cum laude, La. State U., 1958; Ph.D., U. N.C., 1961. Asst. prof. Bucknell U., 1961-65; assoc. prof. UCLA, 1965-70, prof., 1971-73; Justus Bier disting. prof. humanities and history U. Louisville, 1977—, dean arts and scis., 1974-77; cons. NEH. Author: Henry VIII and English Reformation, 1965; Politics and Profit, 1966; Humanism and Reform, 1968; Thomas Cromwell; Letters, 1969; The Way of the West, 3 vols., 1971-74; Tudor Men and Institutions, 1972; The Precarious Balance, 1973; The Tudor Age and Beyond, 1986. Contbr. numerous articles to profl. jours. Served with USAF, 1951-55. Woodrow Wilson fellow, 1958-59; Folger Library fellow, 1964, 70-71; Guggenheim fellow, 1967-68; NEH fellow, 1980-81. Fellow Royal Hist. Soc.; mem. Am. Soc. Reformation Research, Renaissance Soc. Am., N.Am. Conf. Brit. Studies. Democrat. Jewish.

SLAVIN, HILARY BERNARD, psychologist, neuropsychologist; b. Bklyn., Aug. 22, 1948; s. Louis and Betty (Fleischer) S. B.A., Bklyn. Coll., 1969; M.A., Clark U., 1974; Psy.D., Fla. Inst. Tech., 1983. Lic. psychologist, Ga. Staff psychologist Taunton Community Mental Health Program, Mass., 1976-79; clin. child psychologist Taunton Area Assocs. for Human Services, 1979-80; psychologist trainee Brevard County Mental Health Ctr., Melbourne, Fla., 1981; clin. psychology intern Atlanta VA Med. Ctr., 1982-83; psychologist Ga. Mental Health Inst., Atlanta, 1983—; pvt. practice clin. psychology, Atlanta, 1984—. Clark U. fellow, 1969-70, 71-73. Mem. Southeastern Psychol. Assn., Ga. Psychol. Assn., Am. Psychol. Assn. Jewish. Avocations: photography, hiking, reading. Home: 327 Hillcrest Ave Decatur GA 30030 Office: Ga Mental Health Inst 1256 Briarcliff Rd NE Atlanta GA 30306 also 120 Ralph McGill Blvd Suite 820 Atlanta GA 30308

SLAVIN, SIDNEY HAROLD, optometrist; b. Petersburg, Va., June 9, 1937; s. Nelson N. and Annie (Krell) S.; m. Judith Bensky, Jan. 5, 1964; children—Melanie, Mitchell, Diana, Avi. B.A. in Exptl. Psychology, U. Va., 1959; O.D., So. Coll. Optometry, 1963. Registered optometrist, Va. Research optometrist Designs for Vision, N.Y.C., 1963-64; practice assoc. Dr. Martin Rosenbloom, Richmond, Va., 1964-68; gen. practice optometry, Richmond, 1968—; pres. Va. Vision Services, Richmond, 1977-79; lectr. various colls. nationwide, 1966—. Contbr. chpt. to textbook, articles to profl. jours. Patentee in field. Recipient Pres.'s award West End Jaycees, 1967, awards for service Henrico Juvenile Cts., Richmond Juvenile Cts. Va. Optometric Assn. Fellow Coll. Optometrists in Vision Devel.; mem. Am. Optometric Assns., Va. Optometric Assn., Optometric Extension Program (clin. assoc.). Jewish. Lodges: Rotary (pres.), Masons, Shriners, B'nai Brith. Avocations: research; art; reading. Home: 9505 Carterwood Rd Richmond VA 23229 Office: 4883 Finlay St Richmond VA 23231

SLAWSON, BOBBY JOE, restaurant executive; b. Jacksonville, Tex., Apr. 19, 1939; s. Harvey E. and Eva (Hammonds) S.; student Baylor U., 1958-59; A.A., Lon Morris Coll., 1960; B.B.A., Sam Houston State U., 1962; M.B.A., So. Meth. U., 1971; m. Harriet N. Whigham, Sept. 1, 1961; children—Steven Edward, Susan Eleanor. Fin., cost, budget and acctg. mgr. Tex. Instruments, Dallas, 1965-71; controller Taylor Pub. Co., Dallas, 1971-76; chief fin. officer Bonanza Internat., Inc., Dallas, 1976-78; pres., chief exec. officer Steaks Renowned, Inc., 1978-81; chief acctg. officer, v.p. Showbiz Pizza Time, Inc., 1982—. Served to lt. USAF, 1965-68. C.P.A., Tex. Mem. Am. Inst. C.P.A.'s, Tex. Soc. C.P.A.'s. Home: 1914 Shari Ln Garland TX 75043 Office: 4441 Airport Freeway Irving TX

SLAYTON, PAUL CHARLES, JR., English education educator, consultant; b. Walnut Ridge, Ark., July 28, 1930; s. Paul C. and Guthrie Mae (Meadows) S.; m. Ann Shackelford, July 25, 1951; children—Paul Charles, Roderic Howard. B.S., U. Va., 1956, M.S., 1959, Ed.D., 1969. Tchr. English pub. schs., Fairfax County, Va., 1956-57; prin. pub. schs., Orange County, Va., 1957-60; prin., dir. adult edn. pub. schs., Charlottesville, Va., 1961-64; asst. prof. English edn. Mary Washington Coll., Fredericksburg, Va., 1966-69, assoc. prof., 1969-74, prof., 1974—, chmn. dept. edn., 1968—, dir. pub. edn. services, 1978—; cons. Va. State Dept. Edn., 1968-71, Lee County schs., Hampton City schs., Spotsylvania County schs.; vis. prof. U. Va. Sch. Edn., summers, 1966, 67, 70, 76, 81. Del., Jefferson Meeting on Constn., 1984. Co-author: Virginia: 1830 to the Present, 1984; Virginia History and Government, 1985. Contbr. articles and stories to profl. jours. Served with USAF, 1947-53. Va. Found. Humanities grantee, 1975, 76. Mem. Nat. Council Tchrs. English (dir. 1968-70, com. against censorship), Va. Assn. Tchrs. English (pres. 1969-70, chmn. com. against censorship), Phi Delta Kappa (pres. Beta chpt. 1965-66), Kappa Delta Pi. Home: PO Box 234 Spotsylvania VA 22553 Office: Mary Washington Coll DuPont 201 Fredericksburg VA 22401

SLEDD, HOWARD RONALD, electrical contracting firm executive; b. Richmond, Va., May 8, 1941; s. Thomas Charles and Olive Pearl (Butler) S.; m. Frances Pearl Johnson, Apr. 23, 1960; children—Howard Ronald, Jr., Carrie, Frances, Melissa, Kathryn. Area mgr. H.P. Foley, Charlottesville, Va., 1969-73, br. mgr., Memphis, 1973-78; pres. H.R. Sledd, Millington, Tenn., 1978—. Trustee Pension benefit Internat. Brotherhood Elec. Workers-Nat. Elec. Contractors Assn., 1980—. Served with U.S. Navy, 1960. Mem. Nat. Elec. Contractors Assn. Jehovah Witness. Club: Woodstock Hills Country (Millington). Office: 5948 Hiway 51N Millington TN 38053

SLEDD, JAMES HINTON, English educator; b. Atlanta, Dec. 5, 1914; s. Andrew and Anne Florence (Candler) S.; m. Joan Webb, July 16, 1939; children—Andrew, Robert, James, John, Anne. B.A., Emory U., 1936; B.A., Oxford U., 1939; Ph.D., U. Tex., Austin, 1947. Mem. faculty U. Chgo., 1945-46, 48-56; asst. prof. Duke U., 1946-48; assoc. prof. English, U. Calif.-Berkeley, 1956-59; prof. English, U. Ceylon, Peradeniya, 1959-60; prof. Northwestern U., Evanston, Ill., 1960-64; prof. U. Tex., Austin, 1964-85. Founding mem. and 1st pres. The Whole Child Found. Rhodes scholar, 1936-39; Ford Found. grantee, 1951-52; Rockefeller Found. grantee, 1952-53; Guggenheim fellow, 1953-54. Mem. Linguistic Soc., Nat. Council Tchrs. English. Author: (with Gwin Kolb) Dr. Johnson's Dictionary, 1955; A Short Introduction to English Grammar, 1959; (with Wilma Ebbitt) Dictionaries and THAT Dictionary, 1962; contbr. articles to profl. jours. Home: 3704 Gilbert St Austin TX 78703 Office: Calhoun Hall 218 U Tex Austin TX 78712

SLEDGE, JAMES SCOTT, lawyer; b. Gadsden, Ala., July 20, 1947; s. L. Lee and Kathryn (Privott) S.; m. Joan Nichols, Dec. 27, 1969; children—Joanna Scott, Dorothy Privott. B.A., Auburn U., 1969; J.D., U. Ala., 1974. Bar: Ala. 1974, U.S. Ct. Appeals (5th cir.) 1975, U.S. Ct. Appeals (11th cir.) 1981. Ptnr. Inzer, Suttle, Swann & Stivender, P.A., Gadsden, 1974—; mcpl. judge, Gadsden, 1975—; instr. U. Ala., Gadsden, 1975-77. Lay minister, vestryman Holy Comforter Episc. Ch., Gadsden, 1976—; incorporator Episc. Day Sch., Gadsden, 1976, Kyle Home for Devel. Disadvantaged, Gadsden, 1979; county coordinator U.S. Senator Howell Heflin, Etowah County, Ala., 1978, 84; mem. Etowah County Democratic Exec. Com., 1985—; founder Gadsden Cultural Arts Found., 1983; bd. dirs. Salvation Army, 1984—; actor regional theatres. Served to capt. U.S. Army, 1969-71, Vietnam. Decorated Bronze Star; Legion of Honor (Vietnam); Mem. Ala. State Bar (charter mem. bankruptcy sect., vice chmn. 1984, regional liaison bankruptcy bench and bar 1984), Phi Kappa Phi, Phi Eta Sigma. Democrat. Lodge: Kiwanis (bd. dirs. 1981-84). Home: 435 Turrentine Ave Gadsden AL 35901 Office: Inzer Suttle Swann & Stivender PA 601 Broad St Gadsden AL 35901

SLEDGE, ROBERT WATSON, history educator; b. Brownsville, Tex., Sept. 14, 1932; s. Robert Lee and Peggy (Watson) S.; m. Marjorie Stout, Aug. 14, 1956; children—Margaret Ann, Robert Lee II. B.S., Southwestern U., 1953, B.A., 1956; B.D., So. Meth. U., 1960; M.A., U. Tex.-Austin, 1964, Ph.D., 1972. Pastor Buda Methodist Ch., Tex., 1960-63; instr. history Nebr. Wesleyan U., Lincoln, 1963-64; prof. history McMurry Coll., Abilene, Tex., 1964—; vis. prof. Pan Am. U., Edinburg, Tex., 1974, 76; instr. pastors sch. So. Meth. U., Dallas, 1977-80, 84—. Author: Hands on the Ark (Jesse Lee prize 1972), 1975; The Methodist Excitement in Texas, 1984; also articles. Precinct chmn. Democratic Party, Taylor County, 1980—; mem. gen. commn. archives and history United Meth. Ch. Served with U.S. Army, 1953-55. Mem. South Central Jurisdiction Com. Archives and History (chmn. 1984-88), Alpha Chi (nat. pres. 1983-87). Methodist. Avocations: tennis; hiking. Home: 4917C Greenslope Abilene TX 79606 Office: McMurry Coll Abilene TX 79697

SLEEMAN, WILLIAM CLIFFORD, JR., aerospace technologist; b. Birmingham, Ala., June 29, 1923; s. William Clifford and Olive Mae (Watson) S.; student Birmingham-So. Coll., 1940-42; B.S. in Aero. Engring., U. Ala., 1944; m. Mary Frances Mikell, Apr. 12, 1947; children—William Clifford III, Richard McDonald, Melanie Frances. Aero. engr. NACA/NASA Langley Research Center, Hampton, Va., 1944-52, aero. research engr., 1952-62, aerospace engr., 1962-67, aerospace technologist, 1967-81, head flexible wing sect., 1967-73, ret., 1981, disting. research asso., 1981—. Singer in prin. roles, chorus Peninsula Civic Opera Co., Newport News, Va. 1955-65. Choir dir. Hidenwood Presbyterian Ch., Newport News, 1956-76, elder, 1967-75, 79-82. Recipient Achievements awards NASA, 1968-70. Asso. fellow Am. Inst. Aeros. and Astronautics; mem. Engrs.' Club of Va. Peninsula (treas. 1963-64). Club: Warwick Yacht and Country (Newport News). Contbr. articles to profl. jours. Home: 207 Mistletoe Dr Newport News VA 23606 Office: NASA Langley Research Center Hampton VA 23665

SLEEPER, DWIGHT WILLIAM, JR., insurance agency executive; b. Sharon, Mass., July 17, 1915; s. Dwight William and Glenna May S.; m. Joan King, Sept. 1, 1939; children—William Earl, Glenna Sleeper Wester. Student, U. Tex., 1935-38. Ins. cons., Dallas, 1938-42; br. mgr. Ins. Co. N.Am., Cleve., 1942-52; ptnr. Lake Morrison Agy., 1952-62; owner, ptnr., pres. Sleeper Sewell & Co., Dallas, 1962-82, chmn. bd., 1962—. Served with USAF, 1943-49. Named Dallas Ins. Man of Yr., Dallas Assn. Ins. Agts., 1974; Tex. Ins. Man of Yr., Ind. Ins. Agts. of Tex., 1977. Mem. Ind. Ins. Agts. Am., Ind. Ins. Agts. Dallas. Christian Scientist. Office: PO Box 8145 Dallas TX 75205

SLEMP, MITCHELL G., vocational educator; b. Oklahoma City, Oct. 8, 1947; s. Elmo M. and Carrie Edith (Scarlett) S.; m. Pamela Grinstead, June 28, 1969 (div. June, 1981); 1 son, Scott Aaron. M.Ed. cum laude, Central State U., Edmond, Okla., 1979; postgrad. Okla. State U., 1979-80, U. Okla., 1980—. Owner, operator Holiday Pro Shop & Bowling Supply, Oklahoma City, 1970-72; tool and diemaker Western Electric Co., Inc., Oklahoma City, 1966-74; pvt. pilot ground sch. instr. Mid-Am. Vo-Tech Sch., Wayne, Okla., 1974-80, instr. machine shop, 1974—, supr. short-term adult night classes, 1980—. Named Outstanding Trade and Indsl. Educator, U.S. Jaycees, 1983. Mem. Am. Vocat. Assn., Okla. Vocat. Assn. (Educator 1983) Nat. Assn. Trade and Indsl. Instrs., Trade and Indsl. Edn. Assn., Vocat. Indsl. Clubs Am., Iota Lambda Sigma. Club: Sooner Aero (Oklahoma City). Office: Mid-Am Vo-Tech Sch Hwy 59 and I-35 Wayne OK 73095

SLETTEN, SHIRLEY FAYE, nurse; b. Underwood, N.D., Jan. 5, 1938; d. John E. and Tillie (Blotter) Eslinger; m. LeRoy Harold Sletten, Nov. 8, 1958; children—Lori K., Melanie F. Diploma, Trinity Sch. Nursing, 1958. R.N., N.D. Operating room staff nurse Trinity Hosp., Minot, N.D., 1958-61; head nurse operating room Bennett Clarkson Hosp., Rapid City, S.D., 1961-71; geriatric clin. specialist VA Med. Ctr., Hot Springs, S.D., 1971-77; staff nurse med./surgery VA Med Ctr., Fayetteville, Ark., 1977-79, head nurse operating room, 1979—; operating room nurse day local career devel. U. Ark., Fayetteville, 1984. Recipient Operating Room Nursing Performance award VA Med. Ctr., 1975, 80, 83. Mem. Assn. Operating Room Nurses (local chpt., bylaws com. 1984, nominating com. 1985, bd. dirs. 1985, alt. del. to nat. conv. 1985). Club: Bus. and Profl. Women (sec. 1978-79) (Siloam Springs, Ark.). Avocations: piano; reading; camping. Home: 802 Gail St Springdale AR 72764

SLICKER, MICHAEL FRANK, antiquarian book dealer, publisher, consultant; b. St. Petersburg, Fla., Sept. 1, 1948; s. Melvin F. and Elsie Louise (Sellers) S.; m. Virginia Atkinson, Mar. 25, 1975 (div. Jan. 1979); m. Catherine McWhirter, May 9, 1980; children—Rodney J. MacKinnon, Sarah C., Michael T. A.B. in Psychology, U. Calif.-Davis, 1971; postgrad. Ga. State U., 1972. Jr. ptnr. Affinity Book Warehouse, Sacramento, 1973-75; assoc. Argus Books, Sacramento, 1975-77; propr., operator Lighthouse Books, St. Petersburg, 1977—; gen. ptnr. Little Bayou Press, St. Petersburg, 1982—. Contbr. articles to profl. publs. Mem. Internat. League Antiquarian Booksellers, Antiquarian Booksellers Assn. Am., Fla Antiquarian Booksellers Assn. (founder, pres. 1979-83, bd. dirs. 1983-85), Fla. Hist. Soc. (bd. dirs. 1984—). Office: Lighthouse Books 1735 1st Ave N Saint Petersburg FL 33713

SLIGAR, STEVEN ROSS, deafness rehabilitation administrator; b. Kansas City, Mo., Sept. 9, 1950; s. Glenn William and Fern Lucille (Smith) S.; m. Patricia Ann Gunsten, Aug. 18, 1972 (div. Mar. 1985); children—Erin Christi, Brandon Thomas. B.A., W. Ga. Coll., 1972; M.Ed., Auburn U., 1975. Vocat. evaluator Rehab. Ctr. for Deaf, Cave Spring, Ga., 1972-77; vocat. evaluator Southwest Ctr. for Hearing Impaired, San Antonio, 1977-79, dir., 1980—; instr. San Antonio Coll. 1979—; cons. Helen Keller Nat. Ctr., L.I., 1984—, Regional Rehab. Exchange, Austin, Tex., 1984—. Co-author: Deaf Evaluation and Adjustment Feasibility, 1977; Vocational Evaluation of Hearing Impaired Persons, 1983. Adviser, San Antonio Council Advancement Services for the Deaf, San Antonio, 1980-84. Mem. Am. Deafness and Rehab. Assn. (pres. 1985—), Nat. rehab. Assn., Vocat. Evaluation and Work Adjustment Assn. Lutheran. Avocations: Reading; swimming; hiking; writing. Home: 9546

Stillforest St San Antonio TX 78250 Office: Southwest Ctr for Hearing Impaired 6487 Whitby Rd San Antonio TX 78240

SLIGER, BERNARD FRANCIS, univ. pres., economist; b. Sept. 30, 1924; B.A., Mich. State U., 1949, M.A., 1950, Ph.D., 1955; m. 1945; children—Nan, Paul, Greta, Sten. Tchr., Interior Twp. (Mich.) High Sch., 1947-48; asst. prof. econs. La. State U., 1953-56;, asso. prof., 1956-61, prof., 1961-69, head dept. econs., 1961-65, dean acad. affairs, 1965-68, vice-chancellor, 1968-69; exec. dir. La. Coordinating Council for Higher Edn., Baton Rouge, 1969-72; prof. econs. Fla. State U., 1972—, exec. v.p., 1972-73, exec. v.p., chief acad. officer, 1973-76, exec. v.p., interim pres., 1976-77, pres., 1977—; vis. asst. prof. Mich. State U., 1955, vis. prof., 1961, vis. lectr., 1961; fellow U. Minn., 1962; mem., chief cons. to Gov. La's. Tax Study Com., 1968; commr. of adminstrn., chief budget officer State of La., 1968-69. Served with U.S. Army, 1943-46. Mem. Am. Econs. Assn., Nat. Tax Assn., Omicron Delta Kappa, Phi Kappa Phi, Alpha Kappa Psi. Author: (with Ansel M. Sharp) Public Finance, 1970. Office: Office of Pres Fla State U Tallahassee FL 32306

SLIMMER, VIRGINIA MCKINLEY, home economist; b. Mullinville, Kans., June 21, 1932; d. John W. and Virga (Pridy) McKinley; B.S., Fort Hays State U., 1969; M.S., Kans. State U., 1970; Ed.S., Fort Hays State U., 1977; Ph.D., Iowa State U., 1981; m. Myrl D. Slimmer, Nov. 26, 1950; children—Jackie Slimmer Langholz, Kathy, Bruce. Co owner, mgr. ranch, Plainville, Kans., 1962—; instr. Fort Hays State U., 1970-71; tchr. vocat. home econs. Plainville (Kans.) High Sch., 1972-74; tchr. Hays (Kans.) Sr. High Sch., 1975-79; asst. alumni dir. Fort Hays State U., 1977-79; adminstrv. asst. to dean Coll. Home Econs., asst. prof. clothing, textiles and interior design Kans. State U., Manhattan, 1981-82; asso. prof., chairperson dept. home econs. Murray (Ky.) State U., 1982—. Mem. Ellis County Exec. Bd., 1954-75; sec. bd. Ellis County Fair, 1974-75; leader 4-H Club, 1962-79; bd. dirs. Ellis County Cancer Soc., 1955-73. Kans. Home Econs. Assn. scholar, 1971-72. Mem. Am. Assn. Higher Edn., Kans. State U. Alumni Assn., Iowa State U. Alumni Assn., Am. Home Econs. Assn., AAUW, Kappa Omicron Phi, Phi Delta Gamma, Phi Kappa Phi, Phi Delta Kappa. Republican. Methodist. Contbr. articles to profl. jours. Office: Dept Home Econs Murray State U Murray KY

SLINE, MELVIN RICHARD, microcomputer consultant, construction company administrator; b. Houston, Tex., Apr. 29, 1947; s. Louis Leonard and Eva (Sussman) S.; m. Royce Ann Goodman, June 17, 1967; 1 son, Daniel Bryan. B.S. in Chem. Engring., MIT, 1969, postgrad. in chem. engring., 1969-70; postgrad. La. State U., 1973-75. Estimator Sline Indsl. Painters, Houston, Tex., 1970-72, project engr., 1973-74, safety dir., 1970-75, project mgr., 1975-79, mgr. Tex. products, 1980-81, v.p. adminstrn., 1982-85, quality assurance mgr., 1976-85; pres. Microcomputer Specialists, Houston, 1983—. Mem. Ind. Computer Cons. Assn. Office: 6009 Richmond Suite 108 Houston TX 77057

SLINKER, JON JACOB, manufacturing engineer; b. Lamar, Mo., Feb. 28, 1949; s. Robert K. and Ruth Pauline S.; B.S. in Engring., U. Nev., 1975; postgrad. Tulsa U., 1980—; m. Janice C. Osborne, Aug. 18, 1973; children—Erica Anne, Jon Jacob II. With Waterloo (Iowa) tractor works John Deere, 1976-79, mfg. project engr., drive train assembly layout and devel., 1979; sr. process engr., capital resources mgr. Unit Rig & Equipment Co., Tulsa, 1979-80; mgr. plant engring. I.H. Okla., 1980-81; now mgr. mfg. engring. Preway Industries Inc., Paragould, Ark. Served with USAF, 1968-72. Registered profl. engr., Okla., Ark. Mem. Nat. Soc. Profl. Engrs. (v.p. East chpt.), Soc. Mfg. Engrs. Office: Preway Industries Inc Route 1 Box 1A Paragould AR 72450

SLOAN, ALBERT FRAZIER, food products corporation executive; b. Charlotte, N.C., 1929; married. Grad., Presbyn. Coll., 1955, U. N.C., 1969. With Lance Inc., Charlotte, 1955—, exec. v.p., 1967-73, pres., 1973—, chmn. bd., 1976—, also dir.; dir. Dr. Pepper Co., NCNB Corp., PCA Internat. Inc. Office: Lance Inc Pineville Rd Box 2389 Charlotte NC 28201*

SLOAN, DENNIS BRICE, educator; b. Statesville, N.C., Dec. 21, 1931; s. Riley Newman and Pearl Amanda (Jordan) S.; m. Mary Laverne Goodwin, July 25, 1953; children—Steven Brice, Phillip James. B.S., Lenoir Rhyne Coll., 1958; M.A., Appalachian State U., 1963; postgrad. U. N.C., 1970, Duke U., 1971, N.C. State U., 1972. High sch. instr. Iredell County, Harmony, N.C., 1958-63; bus. instr. Mitchell Community Coll., Statesville, 1963—, also chmn. bus. div.; cons., Statesville, 1958—. Democrat. Methodist. Avocations: fishing; camping; motorcycling; sports. Home: 121 Ridgeway Ave Statesville NC 28677 Office: Mitchell Community Coll W Broad St Statesville NC 28677

SLOAN, JAMES PARK, emeritus political science educator; b. Clinton, S.C., Oct. 2, 1916; s. Eugene Blakely and Janie Pressly (Lindsay) S.; B.A., Erskine Coll., 1937; M.A., Tulane U., 1938; m. Alice Catherine Gaines, June 26, 1941; children—James Park, Edwin Gaines. Tchr. econs., govt., sociology and English, Ga. Mil. Acad., College Park, 1938-39; tchr. history, govt. Clinton (S.C.) High Sch., 1939-41; asst. to chmn. S.C. Def. Council, Clinton, 1941-42; paymaster Joanna Mills Co. (S.C.), 1942, personnel dir., 1946-58, dir. indsl. pub. relations, 1958-64; editor co. monthly mag. The Joanna Way, 1950-64; asst. prof. polit. sci. Coll. of Charleston (S.C.), 1964-67; instr. polit. sci. Spartanburg regional campus U. S.C., 1967-70, 73—, asst. prof., 1970-79, asst. prof. emeritus, 1978—, dir. acad. affairs, 1970-73, editor instl. self-study report to So. Assn. Colls. and Schs., 1969. Mem. adv. council S.C. Employment Security Commn., 1955—; mem. planning bd. S.C. Accident Prevention Conf., 1954-57; mem. nat. com. to promote brotherhood week NCCJ, 1961; mem. U.S. savs. bonds nat. adv. com., 1961-62; mem. edn. task force Model Cities Program, City of Spartanburg, 1971-72; mem. long-range planning com. City of Spartanburg, 1970-73; vice chmn. Laurens County S.C. Heart Assn., 1953-64; mem. Laurens County Tri-Centennial Com., 1970; vice chmn. Laurens County chpt. Am. Cancer Soc., 1956-64, exec. dir. Joanna Community Chest, 1950-64; mem. standing com. on communications Asso. Reformed Presbyn. Synod, 1970-72, chmn. standing com. on publs., 1973-75, mem. standing com. on hist. concerns, 1979—; mem. Laurens County Bd. Election Commrs., 1970—, now chmn.; mem. adv. council S.C. dist. SBA, 1974-80; del. Current Strategy Forum, U.S. Naval War Coll., Newport, R.I., 1975; chmn. Clinton City Am. Revolution Bicentennial Com., 1975-76; mem. S.C. Ho. of Reps., 1940-42; mem. Clinton City Council, 1954-60, mayor pro tem, 1958-60; chmn. fin. com., mem. Clinton City Employee Appeal Bd., 1973—, Clinton City Mgr. Adv. Com., 1973—; mem. 3 citizen search coms. to recomend city mgrs. for Clinton; del. Nat. Dem. Conv., 1956; del. S.C. Dem. Conv., 1942, 46, 48, 52, 54, 56, 60; mem. Laurens County Dem. Exec. Com., 1950-60, chmn., 1948-50; county chmn. S. Carolinians for Ind. Electors, 1956; del. S.C. Republican Conv., 1968, 70, 72, 74, 78, 80; chmn. Laurens County Rep. Conv., 1972; trustee Erskine Coll., 1949-53, Joanna Found., 1955-66; trustee John de la Howe Sch., 1975—, sec., 1976—; bd. dirs. Clinton-Newberry Natural Gas Authority, 1954-60. Served from apprentice seaman to lt. USNR, 1942-46; ETO, PTO. Recipient George Washington Honor medal Freedoms Found., 1963; named Disting. Tchr. of Year, U. S.C., Spartanburg, 1975, hon. mem. Student Govt. Assn., 1977, hon. crewman USS Mount Baker. Mem. South Caroliniana Soc., Am. Assn. Indsl. Editors (dir. 1950, 58-60, pres. 1960-61), So., S.C. polit. sci. assns., U.S. Naval Inst., Laurens County Hist. Soc. (charter), Omicron Delta Kappa. Mem. Asso. Ref. Presbyn. Ch. (ruling elder, 1947-70, life ruling elder 1971, trustee 1974—, clk. of session 1985—, supt. Sunday sch. 1939-60, now tchr. men's class). Club: Piedmont (Spartanburg). Author: A History of the Providence Associate Reformed Presbyterian Church, 1977; assoc. editor: The Scrapbook, History of Laurens County, 1982; contbr. articles to trade jours., religious and hist. publs. newspapers. Home: 208 Young Dr Clinton SC 29325 Office: U SC Spartanburg SC 29303

SLOAN, MARY JEAN, media specialist; b. Lakeland, Fla., Nov. 29, 1927; d. Marion Wilder and Elba (Jinks) Sloan. B.S., Peabody Coll., Nashville, 1949; M.L.S., Atlanta U., 1978, S.L.S., 1980. Cert. library media specialist. Music dir. Pinecrest Sch., Tampa, Fla., 1949-50, Polk County Schs., Bartow, Fla., 1950-54; pvt. music tchr. Lakeland, 1954-58; tchr. Clayton County Schs., Jonesboro Ga., 1958-59; media specialist Eastualley Sch., Marietta, Ga., 1959—; coordinator conf. Ga. Library Media Dept., Jekyll Island, 1982-83, sec., Atlanta, 1982-83, com. chmn. ethnic conf., Atlanta, 1978, pres., 1984-85, state pres., 1985-86. Contbr. to bibliographies. Mem. ALA (del. 1984, 85), NEA, Southeastern Library Assn., Am. Assn. Sch. Librarians, Soc. Sch. Librarians Internat., Ga. Assn. Educators (polit. action com. 1983), Beta Phi Mu. Republican. Methodist. Home: 797 Yorkshire Rd NE Atlanta GA 30306 Office: Eastvalley Elem Sch 2570 Lower Roswell Rd Marietta GA 30067

SLOAN, STANLEY, management consultant; b. Phila., Jan. 7, 1943; s. Jack and Betty Sloan; m. Sarah Meszar, May 25, 1980; 1 child, Rebecca. A.B., Temple U., 1964; M.S., Kans. State U., 1966; Ph.D., U. Wis.-Madison, 1969. Assoc. The Hay Group, Dallas, 1969-71, prin., Atlanta, 1974-78, sr. prin., 1978—; dir. human resources Pizza Hut, Inc., Wichita, Kans., 1972-74. Contbr. articles to profl. jours. Officer various community bds., Atlanta, 1979—. Mem. Indsl. Relations Research Assn., Wis. Indsl. Relations Alumni Assn. (exec. bd.), Am. Soc. Personnel Adminstrn., Am. Psychol. Assn., Acad. Mgmt. Avocation: jogging. Home: 1474 Stephens Dr NE Atlanta GA 30329 Office: The Hay Group Suite 250 Palisades II 5901-B Peachtree-Dunwoody Rd NE Atlanta GA 30328

SLOAN, THOMAS MENZIES, investment counselor; b. San Angelo, Tex., Apr. 16, 1933; s. Thomas Nettleton and Mary Frances (Menzies) S.; m. Mary Ann McRae, Aug. 31, 1956; children—Thomas McRae, Mary Katherine. B.B.A., U. Tex., Austin, 1958. Investment counselor, Shearson/Am. Express, Midland, Tex., 1959—, now sr. v.p. investment. Mem. City Council Midland, 1978-83, mayor pro tem, 1980-81; mem. adv. bd. Hospice of Midland. Episcopalian. Club: Racquet (Midland).

SLOCUM, ELLIOTT LEROY, accountant; b. Monroe, La., Dec. 27, 1940; s. Oliver Norwood and Estelle (Malone) S.; B.S., La. Tech. U., 1962; M.A., U. Mo., 1963, Ph.D., 1972; m. Lois Ileane Twyford, June 4, 1964; children—Christopher Elliott, Brian Norwood. Asst. instr. acctg. U. Mo., 1962-64, 65-66; staffman, faculty intern Arthur Andersen & Co., C.P.A.s, St. Louis, 1964-65; instr. Central Methodist Coll., Fayette, Mo., 1966; asso. prof. acctg., Ga. State U., Atlanta, 1966—. Active local Boy Scouts Am. Mem. Nat. Assn. Accts. (pres. Atlanta Central chpt. 1974-75, 1st v.p. Dixie council 1982-83, pres. council, 1983-84, nat. dir. 1978-80; W.J. Carter trophy Atlanta Central chpt. 1976-77, 81-82, cert. merit 1977), Acad. Acctg. Historians (assoc. dir. Acctg. History Research Ctr.), Am. Acctg. Assn., Ga. Assn. Acctg. Instrs., Stuart Cameron McLeod Soc., Phi Kappa Phi (chpt. treas. 1974-84), Beta Alpha Psi (chpt. adv. 1973-75), Delta Sigma Pi. Democrat. Baptist. Author articles in field. Office: Sch Accountancy Ga State U Univ Plaza Atlanta GA 30303

SLOCUM, GEORGE SIGMAN, energy company executive; b. East Orange, N.J., Sept. 9, 1940; s. Arthur Fonda and Jane Borier (Sigman) S.; m. Priscilla McConnell Hinebauch, June 11, 1966; children—Priscilla, David, Andrew. B.A. in Econs., Cornell U., 1962, M.B.A., 1967. Mgmt. trainee, Richardson-Merrell, Inc., 1962; v.p. Citibank, N.A., N.Y.C., 1967-78; pres., chief operating officer, dir. Transco Energy Co., Houston, 1978—; dir. Tex. Commerce Bank-Houston. Mem. council Cornell U. Served to 1st lt. U.S. Army, 1963-65. Decorated D.S.M. Mem. Am. Gas Assn. (dir.), Interstate Natural Gas Assn. (chmn. fin. com.), Fin. Execs. Inst., Soc. Performing Arts of Houston (pres.). Presbyterian. Clubs: University, Petroleum, Racquet (Houston). Home: 151 Hickory Ridge Ct Houston TX 77024 Office: 2800 Post Oak Blvd Houston TX 77056

SLOCUM, LOIS ILEANE, nurse; b. Jacksonville, Ill., Nov. 16, 1942; d. Carl Raymond Twyford and Mary Eloise (Grider) Walker; m. Elliott Leroy Slocum, June 4, 1964; children—Christopher Elliott, Brian Norwood. Diploma, Passavant Meml. Hosp., Jacksonville, 1963; B.S. in Nursing, Brenau Hall Sch. Nursing, Gainesville, Ga., 1983. R.N., Ga.; cert. nurse adminstr. Am. Nurses Assn. Staff nurse Boone County Hosp., Columbia, Mo., 1963-66, Dekalb Gen. Hosp., Decatur, Ga., 1966-69; staff nurse Doctors' Hosp., Tucker, Ga., 1969-77, clin. supr., 1977-83; clin. supr. Humana Hosp. Gwinnett, Snellville, Ga., 1983—. Merit badge counselor Troop 648, Boy Scouts Am., Norcross, Ga., 1979—. Mem. Am. Nurses Assn., Nursing Honor Soc. Brenau Hall Sch. Nursing. Republican. Baptist. Home: 921 Rockbridge Rd Norcross GA 30093 Office: Gwinnett Community Hosp 2160 Fountain Dr Snellville GA 30278

SLOCUM, RICHARD EARL, fine arts educator; b. Beloit, Kans., Dec. 31, 1941; s. Calvin Ernest and Mary Edith (Settles) S.; m. Mary Pamela Sauter, Dec. 20, 1972; children—Samuel Emil, Joseph Michael. B.A. in Speech and Drama, Oklahoma City U., 1963; M.A. in Playwrighting, Trinity U., 1967. Resident co. mem. Dallas Theatre, 1966; designer Trinity U., 1967; actor Repertory Theatre Am., Hollywood, Calif., 1968; prof. fine arts Our Lady of the Lake, San Antonio, Tex., 1968—, Moody prof., 1983. Dir. 24th St. Experiment, Playwright Avocation: Proposin, 1983, others. Wurlitzer Found. grantee, 1965. Democrat. Episcopalian. Avocation: Chinese cooking. Home: 1434 W Rosewood St San Antonio TX 78201 Office: Out Lady of the Lake U 411 SW 24th St San Antonio TX 78285

SLODOWSKI, THOMAS RAYMOND, exploration geologist; b. Jersey City, Dec. 21, 1926; s. Raymond and Victoria (Siwak) S.; m. Patricia C. Lang, Sept. 13, 1952 (div. 1975); children—Vickie Lynn, Kathryn Ann. B.S. in Geology, Calif. Inst. Tech., 1953; Ph.D. in Geology, Princeton U., 1956. Geologist, Am. Overseas Petroleum, Tripoli, Libya, 1956-60, regional geologist, Madrid, Spain, 1960-74, 1966-68, staff geologist, The Hague, Holland, 1965; sr. regional geologist Standard Oil Calif., Bakersfield, 1969-72; sr. exploration geologist Union Oil Co. Calif., Los Angeles, 1973-79; sr. staff explorationist Tex. Eastern Corp., Houston, 1980—. Served with U.S. Army, 1945-46. Princeton U. fellow, 1955-56. Fellow Geol. Soc. Am.; mem. Am. Assn. Petroleum Geologists, Houston Geol. Soc. Republican. Roman Catholic. Home: 2660 Marilee Ln Apt A62 Houston TX 77057 Office: 1221 McKinney Houston TX 77252

SLOTKIN, ALAN R., English educator; b. Bklyn., Nov. 7, 1943; s. Mark and Lee (Tuckman) S. A.B., U. Miami, 1965; M.A., U. S.C., 1969, Ph.D., 1970. Asst. prof. Tenn. Tech. U., Cookeville, 1970-76, assoc. prof., 1976-81, prof. English, 1982—. Editor Tenn. Linguistics Jour., 1982—. Contbr. articles to profl. jours. NDEA fellow, 1965, NSF fellow, 1967-70. Mem. S.E. Conf. Linguistics, South Atlantic Modern Language Assn., Linguistic Soc. Am., Am. Dialect Soc. (mem. com. usage 1983-85), Tenn. Conf. Linguistics (sec., treas. 1982—). Democrat. Avocations: stamp collecting; travel. Home: Route 5 Box 308A Cookeville TN 38501 Office: Tenn Tech U English Dept Box 5053 Cookeville TN 38505

SLOWIK, RICHARD ANDREW, air force officer; b. Detroit, Sept. 9, 1939; s. Louis Stanley and Mary Jean (Zaucha) S.; m. Patricia Anne Lincoln; 1 stepchild, Amber Dawn. B.S., U.S. Air Force Acad., 1963; B.S. in Bus. Adminstrn., No. Mich. U., 1967; LL.B., LaSalle Extension U., 1969; M.B.A., Fla. Tech. U., 1972; M.S. in Adminstrn., Ga. Coll., 1979; M.A., Georgetown U., 1983. Commd. 1st lt. U.S. Air Force, 1963, advanced through grades to lt. col.; pilot Craig AFB, Ala., 1963-64, Sawyer AFB, Mich., 1964-68; forward air controller Pacific Air Forces, South Vietnam, 1968-69; pilot SAC, McCoy AFB, Fla., 1969-71; asst. prof. aerospace studies Va. Poly. Inst. and State U., Blacksburg, 1972-76; br. chief current ops. br. Robins AFB, Ga., 1976-80; asst. dep. chief ops. group Hdqrs. Air Force, Pentagon, Washington, 1980-82; Western Hemisphere and Pacific Area desk officer Nat. Mil. Command Center, Pentagon, Washington, 1982-83; mil. rep. Ops. Ctr., Dept. State, Washington, 1983-85; ops. officer 97th Bombardment Wing, Blytheville AFB, Ark., 1985—. Group ops. officer CAP, Marquette, Mich., 1967-68, Orlando, Fla., 1970-72, sr. programs officer, Blacksburg, 1972-76, Warner Robins, Ga., 1976-80, wing plans and programs officer, Washington, 1980—. Decorated 10 Air medals, 2 Meritorious Service medals, 2 Commendation medals, Cross of Gallantry with Palm, others; recipient Presdl. Medal of Merit, Presdl. Achievement award. Mem. Acad. of Mgmt., Air Force Assn., Am. Numis. Assn., Internat. Platform Assn., Mil. Order World Wars, World Affairs Council, Smithsonian Instn. (resident asso.), Washington Performing Arts Assn., Am. Def. Preparedness Assn., Am. Security Council, Order of Daedalians. Roman Catholic. Home: 1708 N Broadway Blytheville AR 72315 Office: 19BMW/DOTO Blytheville AFB AR 72317

SLY, DAVID FRANK, sociology educator; b. Saginaw, Mich., June 29, 1944; s. Frank W. and Clara F. (Menzel) S.; m. Janice Snyder, June 25, 1966; children—Tanner Sven, Abbygail Lyn. B.A., Central Mich. U., 1966; M.A., Brown U., 1968, Ph.D., 1970. From asst. prof. to prof. sociology Fla. State U., Tallahassee, 1970—, dir. Ctr. for Study of Population, 1980—; population affairs officer UN, 1972-73; research assoc. Internat. Union for Sci. Study of Population, Liege, Belgium, 1973-76; prof. demography U. Nairobi (Kenya), 1978—. Grantee NIH, NSF, Dept. Transp., UN, Ford Found., Rockefeller Found., Hewlett Found. Mem. Population Assn. Am., Am. Sociol. Assn., So. Regional Demographic Group. Democrat. Contbr. articles on sociology to profl. jours. Home: 3606 N Meridian Rd Tallahassee FL 32312 Office: Center for Study of Population Fla State U Tallahassee FL 32306

SMADI, AHMAD ABDEL-MAJID, counselor, researcher, writer; b. Nuaimeh, Jordan, Dec. 26, 1953; came to U.S., 1980; s. Abdel-Majid Abder-Rahman and Faudah (Abdel-Majid) S.; m. Inshirah Mohmad, June 17, 1983; 1 child, Judy. B.A., U. Jordan, 1977; M.A., Tex. So. U., 1982; postgrad. North Tex. State U., 1986—. Writer The Journalist, Amman, Jordan, 1974-77; journalist The News, Amman, 1977-78; researcher U. Jordan, Amman, 1977-78; tchr., counselor Ministry of Edn., Amman, 1978-80; co-psychologist St. Joseph Hosp., Houston, 1981-82. Ministry of Edn. scholar, Amman, 1973-77. Mem. Am. Assn. Counseling and Devel., Tex. Assn. Counseling and Devel. Avocations: reading; sports; travel; writing. Home: 612 Londonderry #103 Denton TX 76205

SMAISTRLA, JEAN ANN, family therapist; b. South Gate, Calif., Oct. 12, 1936; d. Benjamin J. and Janet (Pollock) Craig; m. Charles J. Smaistrla, July 12, 1958; children—Amy Jean, Ben, John. B.B.A. in Mktg., Lamar U., 1958; elec. edn. cert. Tex. Wesleyan Coll., 1963; M.Ed. in Counseling, Tex. Christian U., 1975. Tchr. Houston Ind. Schs., 1958-61, Arlington Ind. Schs., Tex., 1961-72; counselor, therapist Arlington Counseling and Cons. Ctr., 1983-85; family therapist Willow Creek Adolescent Ctr., Arlington, 1985—; owner, founder Adolescent Services Arlington, 1981-85; cons. Charles J. Smaistrla, D.D.S., Arlington, 1978-85. Vice chmn. bd. Arlington Community Hosp., 1981-85; life mem. PTA; bd. dirs. Arlington Art Assn., 1981-85, Ctr. for Well-Being, 1985. Mem. Am. Assn. Marriage and Family Therapy, Tarrant County Assn. Marriage and Family Therapy, North Central Tex. Assn. Counseling and Devel., Am. Assn. Counseling and Devel., Alpha Delta Pi. Republican. Roman Catholic. Clubs: Jr. League Arlington, Arlington Women's. Avocations: Sailing; sewing; doll collecting.

SMALL, ALDEN THOMAS, judge; b. Columbia, S.C., Oct. 4, 1943; s. Alden Killin and Shirley Edna (Eldridge) S.; m. Judy Jo Worley, June 25, 1966; children—Benjamin, Jane. A.B., Duke U., 1965; J.D., Wake Forest U., 1969. Bar: N.C. 1969. Asst. v.p. First Union Corp., Greensboro, N.C., 1969-72, v.p., assoc. gen. counsel, Raleigh, N.C., 1973-82; assoc. dir., gen. counsel Community Enterprise Devel. Corp. Alaska, Anchorage, 1972-73; bankruptcy judge eastern dist. N.C., Raleigh, 1982—; adj. prof. law Campbell U., Buies Creek, N.C., 1980-82; mem. faculty Nat. Comml. Lending Sch., 1980-82; cons. Nat. Coalition Bankruptcy Reform, 1981-82. Author handbook on consumer bankruptcy. Contbr. articles to profl. jours. Mem. N.C. Bar Assn. (council 1979-81), ABA, Kappa Sigma, Phi Alpha Delta. Republican. Lodge: Lions. Office: US Bankruptcy Ct PO Box 2747 Raleigh NC 27602

SMALL, AUDREY EILEEN, student nurse; b. Ponca City, Okla., Jan. 19, 1951; d. Ernest J. and Audrey (Pitts) Glaser; m. Herbert LeRoy Small, Nov. 20, 1968; children—Shea Marie, Herbert Ernest, Casey Leroy, Brett Joseph. Student San Sacinto Coll.; grad. Realtors Inst., Okla. Broker real estate Golden Rule Agy., Ponca City, Okla., 1973-80; student nurse San Sacinto Coll., Pasadena, Tex., 1981—. Recipient scholarship Good Samaritan Found., Houston, 1981. Mem. Ponca City Bd. Realtors, Phi Theta Kappa, Delta Rho. Republican. Roman Catholic. Club: Falcon Boosters (dir. 1982-83). Author: Norton and the Night Monster, 1980.

SMALL, DARIS LEE, nursing educator, consultant; b. Martinsburg, W.Va., Apr. 12, 1929; d. Orman and Hester (Hardy) B.; m. Richard Eugene Small, Sept. 5, 1946; 1 child, Richard Scott. R.N., Kings Daus. Hosp. Sch. Nursing, 1964; B.S., Shepherd Coll., 1970; postgrad. U. Madison, 1973; Ed.D., W.Va., U., 1985. Staff nurse Kings Daus. Hosp., Martinsburg, 1964-65, instr., 1965-72; instr. nursing Shenandoah Coll., Winchester, Va., 1972-74, chmn. allied health, 1974-83, dean Sch. Nursing and Health Professions, 1983—; dir. Lord Fairfax Sub Area Health Dist., Winchester, 1978—; Adv. com. S.S. Nursing Home, Winchester, 1980—, Radiology Sch. Winchester Med. Ctr., 1980—. Author: Nursing Faculty Workloads, 1955. Chmn. scholar. commn. Va. Gen. Assembly, Richmond, 1983-85; vol. Project Hope, Millwood, Va., 1985—. Mem. Va. Council Assocs. Degree Nurses Edn. (pres. 1982-84), Va. Assn. Colls. Nursing, Nat. League for Nursing, Am. Nurses Assn. Avocations: tennis; golf; reading; needlework. Home: Route 6 Box 354 Martinsburg WV 25401 Office: Shenandoah Coll and Conservatory 203 S Cameron St Winchester VA 22601

SMALL, ROBERT SCOTT, textile company executive; b. Charleston, S.C., July 18, 1915; s. Robert Scott and Louise (Johnson) S.; m. Sallie Tyler, June 17, 1938; children—Sallie Small Johnson, Robert Scott, Oscar Johnson, Charles Innes, Elizabeth Johnson. B.S., Coll. Charleston, 1936; LL.D., Clemson U., 1964, Furman U., 1968, Coll. Charleston, 1970. Mgr. S.C. Nat. Bank, Pickens, 1936-38, asst. mgr., Greenville, 1938-41, cashier, trust officer, 1941-47, now dir., Charleston; pres., treas. Ottaray Textiles, Inc., Anderson, S.C., Haynsworth Mills, Anderson, 1947-51; v.p., dir. Woodside Mills, Greenville, S.C., 1951-58, pres., 1958-66; chief exec. officer, treas., dir.; pres., chief exec. officer Dan River Mills, Inc., 1966-77, chmn., chief exec. officer, from 1977; dir. So. Bell Tel. & Tel., Liberty Corp., Greenville, Piedmont Natural Gas Co., Charlotte, N.C., Textile Hall Corp., Greenville, Dan River Mills, Inc. Campaign mgr. United Fund, 1957; Trustee, chmn. Greenville Gen. Hosp., 1960-66, Coll. Charleston, 1960-66; trustee J.E. Sirrine Found.; adv. com. Furman U.; fin. com. Episcopal Ch. Home for Children. Mem. Am. Textile Mfrs. Assn. (past pres.), S.C. Textile Mfrs. Assn. (pres. 1963). Clubs: Green Valley Country (pres. 1961), Cotillion (sr. com. 1960-62), Greenville Country, Poinsett (all Greenville); Carolina Yacht (Charleston). Office: PO Box 6126 107 Frederick St Greenville SC 29606*

SMALLEY, LEE ALAN, ophthalmologist; b. Berkeley, Calif., Feb. 27, 1947; s. Wayne Leroy and Ruth (Eagleson) S.; m. Linda Burrus, July 19, 1968; children—Carrie Beth, Chad Carlton. B.S., U. Tenn., 1969, M.D., Memphis, 1972. Diplomate Am. Bd. Ophthalmology. Resident, U. Ariz., 1976; staff ophthalmologist Methodist Med. Ctr., Oak Ridge, 1977—, chief of staff, 1985—. Fellow Am. Acad. Ophthalmology, Am. Bd. Ophthalmology. Office: 988 Oak Ridge Turnpike 370 Oak Ridge TN 37830

SMART, GROVER CLEVELAND, JR., nematology educator, researcher; b. Stuart, Va., Nov. 6, 1929; s. Grover Cleveland and Goldie Mae (Williams) S.; m. Patricia Ann Fowler, Aug. 24, 1957; children—Jeffrey Hilton, Gregory Stuart. B.A., U. Va., 1952, M.A., 1957; Ph.D., U. Wis., 1960. Asst. prof. Va. Poly. Inst., Holland, 1960-64; asst. prof. U. Fla., Gainesville, 1964-67, assoc. prof., 1967-73, prof., 1973—, asst. chmn. dept. entomology and nematology, 1976-79, acting chmn., 1979-80. Served with U.S. Army, 1953-56. NSF grantee, 1957; U.S. Dept. Agr. grantee, 1965-68, 83-86; Ctr. for Aquatic Weeds, U. Fla. grantee, 1983-86. Mem. Soc. Nematologists, Orgn. Tropical Am. Nematologists, European Soc. Nematologists, Helminthological Soc. Washington, Am. Inst. Biol. Scis., Fla. State Hort. Soc., Soil and Crop Sci. Soc. Fla., Sigma Xi, Gamma Sigma Delta. Methodist. Contbr. articles to profl. jours. Home: 804 NW 36th Dr Gainesville FL 32605 Office: Entomology and Nematology Dept U Fla Bldg 78 Gainesville FL 32611

SMART, LINDA LOUISE, geologist, consultant; b. Amarillo, Tex., Apr. 23, 1951; d. Wesley Lee and Thresea Inez (Milford) Mitchell; m. Emmett L. Smart, Dec. 17, 1976; 1 child, Tammy Lorraine. B.B.S. in Edn., West Tex. State U., 1978, B.B.S. in Geology, 1981. Tchr. Boy's Ranch High Sch., Tex., 1979, Bonham Jr. High Sch., Amarillo, 1979-80; geologist Scarth Oil and Gas Co., Amarillo, 1981-84; ind. geologist, Amarillo, 1984—; cons. geologist CAG Petroleum, Dallas, 1984—, Harding Exploration, Wichita Falls, Tex., 1984—, Farrex, Inc., Richardson, Tex., 1984—, Dallas Energy Devel., 1984—. Vol. Am. Cancer Soc., Amarillo, 1984. Mem. Am. Assn. Petroleum Geologists (assoc.), Panhandle Geol. Soc., Amarillo C. of C. Republican. Baptist. Lodge: Order of Eastern Star (chaplin 1982, conductress 1984). Avocations: reading; fishing; skiing; needlework; ceramics. Home and Office: 6792 Thicket Hill Ct Florence KY 41042

SMART, TERRY LEE, history educator; b. Waxahachie, Tex., Apr. 11, 1935; s. Irvin L. and Marion C. (Cook) S.; m. Bridget E. Grover, June 21, 1958; children—Terence B., Maryjane G., Christopher E. B.A., Ind. U., 1957; M.A., U. Houston, 1965; Ph.D., U. Kansas, 1968. Tchr. social studies, curriculum writer pub. schs., Houston, 1960-64; asst. instr., U. Kans., Lawrence, 1964-65; asst. prof. history, Trinity U., San Antonio, Tex., 1967-71, assoc. prof., 1971-80, prof., 1980—, chmn. dept. history, 1981—. Served to capt. USAR, 1958-66. Mem. Am. Hist. Assn., Nat. Council Social Studies, Tex. Assn. Advancement of History. Co-author: People and Our World: A Study of World History, 1977, 81, 83; Fundamentals of the American Free Enterprise System, 1977; American Government, 1980, 83; Civics: Citizens & Society, 1980, 83; Essentials of Economics and Free Enterprise, 1982. Home: 1025 Canterbury Hill San Antonio TX 78209 Office: Trinity Univ Box 59 San Antonio TX 78284

SMARTT, JOHN MADISON, lawyer; b. Smartt, Tenn., Feb. 24, 1919; s. Robert White and Sarah Alma (Roggli) S.; B.S., U. Tenn., 1942, J.D., 1948; m. Harriet Chapin, June 9, 1943; children—John Madison, Jane (Mrs. Roy D. Stroud), Douglas D., Robert W., III. Admitted to Tenn. bar. 1948; since practiced in McMinnville; dir. alumni affairs U. Tenn., Knoxville, 1948-69; mem. firm Fowler, Rowntree, Fowler & Robertson, Knoxville, 1969-83; of counsel Ambrose, Wilson & Grimm, Knoxville, 1983—; life mem. 6th Circuit Jud. Conf. Served to capt. AUS, 1942-46; lt. col. Res. Mem. Phi Delta Phi. Democrat. Presbyterian (mem. session 1970-73). Club: Kiwanis. Home: 4603 Holston Hills Rd Knoxville TN 37914 Office: 9th Floor Valley Fidelity Bank Bldg Knoxville TN 37902

SMELSER, DANIEL RICHARD, music educator, conductor, recorder soloist; b. Neosho, Mo., Oct. 19, 1944; s. Harold Richard and Hazel (Walker) S.; m. Rebecca Susan Rhea, June 10, 1967; 1 child, Judith Allegra. B.Mus., Okla. Bapt. U., 1967, M.Mus., New Eng. Conservatory, 1969. French horn player Oklahoma City Symphony, 1966-67; mus. dir. Arlington Friends of Drama, Mass., 1970; instr. French horn, theory Weston Schs., Mass., 1967-73; condr. Nashua Choral Soc., N.H., 1969-73; dir. instrumental music Brewton-Parker Coll., Mt. Vernon, Ga., 1973—; instr. Am. Recorder Soc. workshops; soloist recorder Ga. Pub. TV, Atlanta. Condr. Vidalia Community Chorus, 1974—. Mem. Coll. Music Soc., Coll. Band Dirs. Nat. Assn., Nat. Assn. Choral Condrs., Am. Recorder Soc., Am. Radio Relay League. Avocations: tennis; amateur radio; photography; travel. Office: Brewton-Parker Coll College Ave Mount Vernon GA 30445

SMIALEK, WILLIAM, musicologist; b. Fall River, Mass., June 9, 1952; s. Jacob Joseph and Amelia Mary (Skrzypiec) S.; m. Molly McCoy, Dec. 30, 1978; 1 child, Andrew Jacob. B. Mus., U. R.I., 1974; M. Mus., No. Tex. State U., 1976, Ph.D., 1981. Coordinator of fine arts, asst. prof. music Jarvis Christian Coll., Hawkins, Tex., 1981—; pvt. music instr., Tyler, Tex., 1980—. Author: The Symphony in Poland, 1982. Bd. dirs. Tyler Civic Chorale, 1981—; ch. musician Christ Episcopal Ch., Tyler, 1983—. Fulbright scholar, 1979-80; Kosciuszko Found. grantee, 1978, 80. Mem. Am. Musicol. Soc., Coll. Music Soc., Music Library Assn., Polish Inst. of Arts and Scis. Home: 2917 Tanglewood Dr Tyler TX 75701 Office: Jarvis Christian Coll Drawer G Hawkins TX 75765

SMILEY, JOSEPH ELBERT, JR., evaluation engineer, librarian; b. Cin., Dec. 21, 1922; s. Joseph Elbert and Esther Marie (Lentz) S.; m. Leona Caroline Besenfelder, Aug. 23, 1953; 1 dau., Mary Susan Smiley Liuzzi. A.A., Edison Community Coll., 1978; B.A., U. S. Fla., 1981, M.A., 1983. Expediter VA, Miami, Fla., 1948-51, analyzer, 1953; evaluation engr. photographic equipment, CIA, Washington, 1953-75. Second v.p. pub. relations Country Club Estates Assn. Lehigh Acres, Inc., 1981-84, pres., 1984—; coordinator, acting zone capt. Lehigh Acres Emergency Preparedness Com., 1983-84, chmn., 1984—. Served with U.S. Army, 1942-45, with USAF, 1951-52. Recipient commendation ribbon USAF, 1951; cert. of merit CIA, 1974, certs. of appreciation, 1975, 1981; letter of congratulations Gerald R. Ford, CIA, 1975. Mem. ALA, Fla. Library Assn., Fla. Assn. Realtors, Phi Theta Kappa, Kappa Delta Pi, Phi Kappa Phi, Beta Phi Mu. Republican. Roman Catholic. Club: KC. Home: 306 Dania St Lehigh Acres FL 33936

SMILLIE, THOMSON JOHN, opera producer; b. Glasgow, Scotland, Sept. 29, 1942; s. John Baird and Mary (Thomson) S.; m. Anne Ivy Pringle, July 14, 1965; children—Jane, Jonathan, Julia, David. M.A., Glasgow U., 1963. Dir. pub. relations Scottish Opera, 1966-78; artistic dir. Wexford Festival (Ireland), 1973-78; gen. mgr. Opera Co. Boston, 1978-80; gen. dir. Ky. Opera, Louisville, 1981—; v.p. So. Opera Conf., 1982—. Contbr. articles to various publs. Home: 6328 Upper River Rd Harrod's Creek KY 40027

SMILOR, RAYMOND WESLEY, business educator; b. Cleve., May 17, 1947; s. Francis W. and Maureen P. Smilor; m. Judy A. Zahniser, Aug. 29, 1969; children—Matthew W., Kevin R. B.A., St. Edward's U., Austin, Tex., 1969; M.A., U. Tex.-Austin, 1972, Ph.D., 1978. Tchr., Tex. Sch. Deaf and Austin Inc. Sch. Dist., 1969-74; research fellow NSF Inst. for Computing Sci., U. Tex., 1978-79, project dir. IC2 Inst., 1979-83, asst. dir., 1983-84, assoc. dir., 1984—; lectr. dept. mgmt. and mktg., 1980—; pres. Mgmt. Strategies Group, 1984—; chmn. High Mark Internat., 1986—. Bd. dirs. Tex. Lyceum Assn., Laguna Gloria Art Mus., Resources for Future fellow, 1976-77. Mem. Tex. Econ. and Demographic Assn. Bd. dirs., editor-in-chief Jour. High Technology Marketing; editor: Regional/Territorial Planning and Development, 1981; Economic Growth and Planning; Regional and National Perspectives, 1982; Small Business and Entrepreneurial Spirit, 1983; Corporate Creativity, 1984; co-author: Financing and Managing Fast Growth Companies, 1985; The New Business Incubator, 1986; co-editor: Improving U.S. Energy Security, 1985, Art and Science of Entrepreneurship, 1986. Contbr. articles to profl. jours. Office: 2815 San Gabriel Austin TX 78705

SMITH, ALBERT K., corporate executive; b. 1910; married. Joined Big Three Industries Inc., 1928, v.p., 1956-64, pres., 1964—, now co-chmn., also dir. Office: 3535 W 12th St Box 3047 Houston TX 77008*

SMITH, ALBERT KEENE, hospital administrator; b. Aiktin, Minn., July 7, 1924; s. Albert Keene and Margurite (Carr) S.; m. Eddyth Jean Rosenberg, Nov. 28, 1947; children—Marc David, Laurel Jean. B.A., U. N.D., 1949; M.H.A., Northwestern U., 1955. Hosp. adminstr. Gen. Hosps., 1949-51; exec. officer Health Dept., Pago Pago, Samoa, 1951-53; dir. postgrad. in med. edn. U. Nebr., Omaha, 1953-54; adminstr. Ill. Dept. Mental Health/Mental Retardation, Dixon, Alton, 1955-81; supt. Big Spring State Hosp., Tex., 1981—. Lay reader St. Mary's Episc. Ch., Big Spring, 1982—, vestryman, 1982—. Served to master sgt. U.S. Army, 1942-45; ETO. Mem. Assn. Mental Health Adminstrs. (cert., bd. govs. 1977—). Avocations: boating; gardening; fishing.

SMITH, ALEXANDER B., III, hospital administrator, consultant; b. San Angelo, Tex., Apr. 22, 1947; s. Alexander B. and Phyllis (Higgins) S. B.B.A., U. Tex., 1973; M.H.A., Trinity U., 1975. Adminstrv. resident Brackenridge Hosp., Austin, Tex., 1974-75; asst. adminstr. Med. Ctr. Hosp., Odessa, Tex., 1975-77; adminstr. Doctors Hosp., Santa Ana, Calif., 1977-78, El Centro Community Hosp., Calif., 1978-81; exec. dir. Tenebonne Gen. Med. Ctr., Houma, La., 1981—; mem. Metro Hosp. Council, New Orleans, 1982—; pres. Imperial Valley Blood Bank, El Centro, 1979-80; bd. dirs. Hosp. Council San Diego, 1979-81. Mem. Friends of the Library, 1985, Museum Found., Houma, 1985. Recipient Disting. Service award El Centro Community Hosp. Mem. Am. Coll. Hosp. Adminstrs., Am. Hosp. Assn., La. Hosp. Assn., Tex. Hosp. Assn., Houma-Terrebonne C. of C. Roman Catholic. Lodge: Rotary. Home: 218 Crescent Ct Houma LA 70360 Office: Terrebonne Gen Med Ctr 936 E Main St Houma LA 70360

SMITH, ALLAN HERBISON, management consultant, author; b. Buffalo, N.Y., Dec. 3, 1929; s. Eugene Franklin and Vera Bessie (Herbison) S.; m. Judith Louise Robbins, May 27, 1960; children—Bryan, Kimberly, Robin, Paul, Bradley. B.S. in Pharmacy, U. Buffalo, 1951; M.B.A., Ph.D., Calif. Coast U., 1985. Leader Allan Smith Orch., Kenmore, N.Y., 1942-51; chief exec. officer Smith Pharmacies, Buffalo, 1951-78; pres. Rexall Internat., Los Angeles, 1969-71; dir. Leader Drug, Buffalo, 1975-77; dir. Acad. Continuing Edn., West Palm Beach, Fla., 1978—; pres. Success Group, West Palm Beach; instr. Palm Beach Jr. Coll.; instr. Dale Carnegie courses, Buffalo, West Palm Beach, 1969-81; newsletter pub. Author: How to Compete with Chains, 1979; Teenage Guide to Success, 1983; Sewing for Profits, 1984; How to Sell Your Homemade Creation, 1985; contbr. articles to profl. publs. Bd. dirs. Del Nursing Home, 1962-69, LaFayette Hosp., Buffalo, 1969-78; pres. Buffalo Businessmen, 1969-71; founder West Side Drug Abuse Ctr., Buffalo, 1968, Buffalo West Side Civic Ctr., 1969. Served to capt. AUS, 1951-58. Recipient Merck Chem. Corp. award, 1951, Eli Lilly trophy, 1977; name Buffalo Outstanding Citizen, 1970. Mem. Erie County Pharm. Assn. (bd. dirs. 1975-77), Kappa Psi (treas. 1949-51, Man of Yr. 1966). Republican. Presbyterian. Club: Rotary (West Palm Beach). Lodges: Masons, Elks, Shriners. Address: 8084 Nashua Dr Lake Park FL

SMITH, AMOS MICHAEL, mechanical contractor executive; b. Opalocka, Fla., Jan. 24, 1951; s. Amos Morgan and Sue (Greer) S.; m. Sharon D. Smith, Mar. 16, 1973; children—Michael Bradley, Sean Duncan, James Nathan. A.S.B.A., Tri-County Coll., 1978. Asst. mgr. Security Fin., Greenville, S.C., 1969-70; mechanic technician Smith Heating & Air Conditioning, Easley, S.C., 1970-71, service technician, 1971-73, v.p., 1973-80, sr. v.p., 1980—. Chmn. bldg. and grounds Brushy Creek Bapt. Ch., Easley, S.C., 1981-83, chmn. deacons, 1983, vice-chmn. long range, 1982-83. Mem. ASHRAE, Mech. Contractors Assn., Assoc. Gen. Contractors. Republican. Baptist. Lodges: Kiwanis, Masons. Office: Smith Heating & Air Conditioning Inc PO Box 401 Easley SC 29640

SMITH, ANDERSON DODD, psychologist; b. Richmond, Va., May 3, 1944; s. John Edward and Nancy (Dodd) S.; B.A., Washington and Lee U., Lexington, Va., 1966; M.A., U. Va., 1969, Ph.D. in Exptl. Psychology (Francis DuPont fellow), 1970; m. Glenna Ellen Bevell, Aug. 13, 1966; children—Nancy Taylor, Leigh-Ellen Anderson. Research and teaching asst. U. Va., 1966-70; mem. faculty Ga. Inst. Tech., Atlanta, 1970—, prof. psychology, 1980—; affiliate scientist Yerkes Regional Primate Center. Vice chmn. Atlanta Neighborhood Planning Unit; bd. dirs. Collier Hills Civic Assn.; vestryman St. Anne's Episcopal Ch., Atlanta. Recipient Outstanding Tchr. award Ga. Inst. Tech., 1975; Monie Ferst Sustained Research award Sigma Xi, 1982; grantee NIH, 1972—, NIMH, 1978-79, 80-81. Fellow Am. Psychol. Assn. (chmn. program and edn. coms. div. 20), Gerontol. Soc.; mem. Psychonomic Soc., Southeastern Psychol. Assn., Sigma Xi, Phi Kappa Phi (past chpt. pres.). Asso. editor: Aging in the 1980's, 1980; editor psychol. scis. Jour. Gerontology, 1980—. Contbr. articles to profl. publs. Home: 717 Channing Dr NW Atlanta GA 30318 Office: Sch Psychology Ga Inst Tech Atlanta GA 30332

SMITH, ANN TURNHAM, vocational education specialist, administrative consultant, researcher; b. Lanett, Ala., Oct. 19, 1937; d. J.C. and Elsie (Thompson) Turnham; m. George Smith (div. 1984). B.A., Samford U., 1959; M.A., Troy State U., 1974. Dir. vocat. edn. Elmore County Bd. Edn., Wetumpka, Ala., 1973-77; vocat. equity coordinator, state displaced homemaker coordinator State Dept. Edn., Montgomery, Ala., 1977—; cons. in field. Contbr. articles to profl. jours. Bd. dirs. Autauga, Elmore and Montgomery Consortium, 1976, 77; chmn. So. Women in Partnership for Equity, 1983, 84; legis. rep. Ala. Edn. Assn.; tech. assistance cons. Ohio State U., Nat. Ctr. Vocat. Edn.; active Ala. Women's Campaign Fund, Women's Prison Tchr. Mem. Ala. Vocat. Assn., Am. Vocat. Assn., Ala. Council Local Vocat. Adminstrs., Vocat. Edn. Equity Council, NEA, Ala. Edn. Assn., Am. Bus. Women's Assn., Ala. Coalition Women and Girls in Edn., Nat. Assn. Exec. Females, AAUW, Ala. Assn. Women Deans, Adminstrs., and Counselors, Older Women's League, Am. Soc. Pub. Adminstrs. Home: 2076 Teresa St Montgomery AL 36107 Office: Ala Dept Edn 810 State Office Bldg Montgomery AL 36130

SMITH, ASHLEY SCOTT, interior designer; b. New Orleans, Apr. 4, 1943; d. Nauman Steele and Blanche (Hammond) S.; m. J. Emmett Smith, Oct. 10, 1965 (div. Sept. 1983); 1 son, Ashton Emmett. Student La. State U., 1965, U. Florence (Italy), 1965-66. Profl. runway and photographic model Kim Dawson Agy., Dallas, 1967-70; comml. interior designer Enloe, Murray and Summers, Dallas, 1982—. Bd. dirs. TACA, Dallas; bd. dirs., chmn. Cattle Baron's Ball, Am. Cancer Soc., 1982; bd. dirs. Children's Arts and Ideas Found., Dallas Opera, Susan G. Komen Found., St. Michael Sch., Greater Dallas area Am. Cancer Soc. Republican. Episcopalian. Home: 5909 Luther Ln Dallas TX 75225 Office: 2201 Laws St Dallas TX 75202

SMITH, AUSTIN, retired pharmaceutical company executive, consultant; b. Belleville, Ont., Can., Nov. 25, 1912; came to U.S., 1939, naturalized, 1943; s. Wilfred and Keitha Smith; m. Eve Underwood, Apr. 13; 1 son, Craig Lance. M.D., C.M., Queens U., 1938, M.Sc. in Medicine, 1940; 5 hon. degrees. Editor Jour. AMA, Chgo., 1949-58; pres. Pharm. Mfrs. Assn., Washington, 1959-66; chmn. bd., chief exec. officer Parke-Davis Co., Detroit, 1966-72; cons. in field. Author books; contbr. numerous papers to various profl. jours. Address: PO Box 06679 Fort Myers FL 33906

SMITH, BAKER ARMSTRONG, construction company executive, lawyer; b. Brunswick, Ga., Oct. 3, 1947; s. William Armstrong and Priscilla (Baker) S.; m. Deborah Elizabeth Ellis, Nov. 13, 1982; children—Ellis Armstrong, Elizabeth Anne. B.S., U.S. Naval Acad., 1969; M.B.A., Northeastern U., 1975; J.D. cum laude, Suffolk U., 1977; LL.M. in Labor, Georgetown U., 1981. Bar: Ga. 1977, D.C. 1978, U.S. Supreme Ct. 1980. Commd. ensign U.S. Navy, 1969, advanced through grades to lt., 1974; exec. dir., founder The Center on Nat. Labor Policy, Inc., North Springfield, Va., 1977-81; asst. to Sec., dir. labor relations U.S. Dept. HUD, Washington, 1981-83; exec. v.p. U.S. Bus. and Indsl. Council, Nashville, 1983-84; pres. Am. Quality Builders, Inc., Nashville, 1984—; sec., founder U.S. Constitutional Rights Legal Def. Fund, Inc., Nashville, 1983—; trustee Leadership Inst., Springfield, Va., 1978—; gov. Council for Nat. Policy, Washington, 1981—; mem. Civil Rights Reviewing Authority U.S. Dept. Edn., Washington, 1984—; transition team leader Office of the Pres.-Elect of the U.S., NLRB, Occupational Safety and Health Review Commn., Fed. Mediation and Conciliation Service, Nat. Mediation Bd., Fed. Labor Relations Authority, Washington, 1980-81; instr. law, faculty sec. No. Va. Law Sch., Alexandria, Va., 1980-83; instr. law D.C. Law Sch., Washington, 1978-80. Contbr. articles to profl. jours.; contbg. author: Mandate for Leadership, 1981. Served to lt. USN, 1969-74. Mem. St. George's House, Windsor Castle (assoc.), ABA (Nat. Law Day chmn. 1976-77, Silver Key award 1977), Phila. Soc., U.S. Supreme Ct. Hist. Soc., Beta Gamma Sigma. Republican. Presbyterian. Club: Capitol Hill (Washington). Office: Am Quality Builders Inc 2119 24th Ave N Nashville TN 37208

SMITH, BARBARA ANN, accountant; b. Dallas, May 6, 1935; d. George Jefferson and Ina Pearl (Nowlin) Gardner; Asso. Mid. Mgmt., Mountain View Jr. Coll., 1975; div.; children—Cynthia Marie Dixon, Robert Lee Dixon. Asst. cashier U.S. Rubber Co., Dallas, 1954-57; sec.-treas. Am. Graphics Co., Dallas, 1974-79; pres. Am. Way Credit Union, Dallas, 1974-76; sec.-treas. Am. Legal Printing Co., Dallas, 1964-79, Abco Inc., Dallas, 1964-79, Am. Poster & Printing Co., Dallas, 1964-79; asst. sec.-treas. Am. Equity Press Inc., Dallas, 1974-79; partner MS Services, Dallas, 1979—. Home: 3515 Brown 109 Dallas TX 75219 Office: Wimbledon Pl Suite 109 Dallas TX 75219

SMITH, BARTON A., economics educator; b. Portland, Oreg., May 4, 1944; s. Kenneth Alan and Natalie Ann S.; m. Wendy J. Sabey, Sept. 9, 1968; children—Michael, Kelly, Jefferson, Matthew, Katherine. B.A., Brigham Young U., 1969; M.A., U. Chgo., 1971, Ph.D., 1974. Asst. prof. U. Houston, 1973-80, assoc. prof. econs., 1980—, dir. Ctr. for Pub. Policy, 1984—; vis. prof. Brigham Young U., Provo, Utah, 1982-83. Mem. Am. Econ. Assn., Western Econ. Assn., So. Econ. Assn. Mormon. Home: 11719 Glenway Dr Houston TX 77070 Office: Ctr for Pub Policy U Houston Houston TX 77004

SMITH, BESSIE SHEFFIELD, counselor educator; b. Birmingham, Ala., July 11, 1945; d. Jesse Fred and Clara Verdell (Whitehead) Sheffield; m. Howard Michael Smith, Dec. 23, 1970; 1 child, Rishona Aleeza. B.S., Tuskegee Inst., 1969, Ed.M., 1970; postgrad. Morehead State U., 1972-73; Ed.S., U. Ala.-Birmingham, 1977; Ed.D., Tex. So. U., 1983. Lic. profl. counselor, Tex.; nat. cert. counselor. Counselor Alexander City State Jr. Coll., Ala., 1970-72; counselor, tutor coordinator Morehead State U., Ky., 1972-73, Tex. So. U., Houston, 1978; counselor, instr. Prairie View A&M U., Tex., 1976-78, counselor, asst. prof., 1979-81; assoc. dir. student affairs, 1983-84, dir. univ. counseling, 1984—; residence counselor YWCA, Birmingham, 1974-75; tchr. math. Scarborough Sr. High Sch., Houston, 1981-83. Mem. Am. Assn. for Counseling Devel., Am. Coll. Personnel Assn., Assn. for Counselor Edn. Suprs., Am. Mental Health Counselors Assn., Assn. for Non-White Concerns Personnel Guidance, Top Ladies of Distinction, Phi Delta Kappa, Phi Eta Sigma, Delta Sigma Theta. Democrat. Methodist. Club: Jack and Jill (Spring, Tex.). Avocations: reading; fashions and designs; floral arrangement; interior decorating. Office: Prairie View A&M U PO Box 2662 Prairie View TX 77446

SMITH, BETTY LEE, international conference planner, consultant; b. Mount Airy, N.C., Oct. 26, 1938; d. Robert Otis and Edna Onedia (Harman) Smith. B.A. in English, Longwood Coll., 1959; M.R.E., So. Baptist Theol. Sem., 1962. Dir. religious activities Va. Intermont Coll., Bristol, Va., 1961-66; asst. sec. for conf. and youth work, 1st woman exec. Baptist World Alliance, Washington, 1966-81; dir. confs. Am. Soc. Tng. and Devel., Washington, 1981-82; corp. meeting planner Mars, Inc., McLean, Va., 1983—. Vol. Bristol Community Hosp., Va., 1964-66, Alexandria Hosp., 1967. Mem. Prost-Profl. Women in Travel (treas. 1979), Pacific Area Travel Assn., Washington Soc. Assn. Execs., Meeting Planners Internat. Baptist. Avocations: music; oil painting; reading; travel; swimming. Home: 5055 Seminary Rd Apt 333 Alexandria VA 22311

SMITH, BOBBY LEE, school principal; b. Henderson, Tex., July 3, 1935; s. Guy L. and Ida M. (Ward) S.; m. Patricia Aline Keen, Oct. 22, 1957 (div.); children—Deborah J., Mark Lee, Todd Ray; m. Donna Kay Kincaid, June 2, 1972. A.A., Del Mar Coll.; B.S., M.S., Tex. A&I U.; M.S., Corpus Christi State U. Cert. provisional tchr. social studies, mid-mgmt, supt., Tex. Tchr. Corpus Christi Ind. Sch. Dist., 1960-64; instr. in govt. Howard Coll., Big Spring, Tex., 1964-70, chmn. dept. social sci., 1970-80; tchr. Port Aransas Ind. Sch. Dist., Tex., 1980-81, prin. high sch., 1981—; ednl. cons. Goals for Big Spring, 1973-74; dir. Fed. Program County and Local Employees, West Tex., 1974-75. Author filmstrip series: Our National Heritage, 1976. Mem. sch. bd. St. Mary's Episcopal Sch., Big Spring, 1966. Served with USAF, 1954-58. Recipient Outstanding award Howard County Bicentennial, 1976. Mem. Phi Alpha Theta. Democrat. Avocations: golf; fishing; motorcycle riding. Home: 400 Dolphin Ln PO Box 212 Port Aransas TX 78373 Office: Port Aransas High Sch PO Box 1297 Port Aransas TX 79873

SMITH, BRIAN BETHEA, architect, development coordinator; b. Orangeburg, S.C., Dec. 29, 1954; s. Hugh Elmore and Martha Elizabeth (Meares) S.; B.A. in Architecture, Clemson U., 1977; M.A. in Architecture and Real Estate Devel., Ga. Inst. Tech., 1979. Registered architect, Ga. Architect Thompson, Ventulett & Stainback, Atlanta, 1979-81; architect, project mgr. Niles Bolton Assocs. Inc., Atlanta, 1981—. Contbr. Piedmont Arts Festival, 1983—; active Theater League Am., 1984—. Mem. AIA, Urban Land Inst., Phi Eta Sigma, Tau Sigma Delta, Sigma Nu. Avocations: skiing; sailing; travel. Home: 992 Magill Pk NE Atlanta GA 30309 Office: Niles Bolton Assocs Inc 3166 Mathieson Dr Atlanta GA 30305

SMITH, BRYANT MORGAN, real estate broker, consultant; b. Carrollton, Ga., June 16, 1902; s. Elisha Morgan and Ade (Hughie) S.; m. Sarah Brundage, July 29, 1923; children—Bryant Morgan, Luke Brundage. LL.B., Winder Law Sch., 1933. Bar: Ga. 1933. Dep. clk. Carroll County, Carrollton, Ga., 1920-32; sec. E.M. Owen, 4th Congl. Dist. Ga., Washington, 1933; atty. John Hancock Mut. Life, Athens, Ga., 1934-46; owner, mgr. Nat. Parts Warehouse, Forest Park, Ga., 1946-72; broker North Point Realty, Inc., Atlanta, 1972—. Mem. sch. bd. Athens High Sch., 1945-49; atty. Nat. Lawyers Club, Washington, 1978. Served to 2d lt. USAR, 1922-26. Democrat. Baptist. Lodge: Masons (master; comdr. Hebrew Command), Rotary. Home: 350 Carpenter Dr NE Apt 920 Atlanta GA 30328 Office: North Point Realty Inc 4126 Pleasantdale Rd Suite B-207 Doraville GA 30341

SMITH, CAMERON OUTCALT, oil company executive; b. Calgary, Alta., Can., July 29, 1950; came to U.S., 1956, naturalized, 1968; s. William Francis and Jane (Buckley) S.; m. Liza Vann, Oct. 10, 1976. A.B. in Art History summa cum laude, Princeton U., 1972; M.S. in Geology, Pa. State U., 1975. Geologist, then pres. The Catawba Corp., N.Y.C., 1973—; exec. v.p., then pres. Taconic Petroleum Corp., Tulsa, 1978—; pres. Riga Oil Co., Tulsa, 1985—; dir. Borealis Exploration Ltd., Calgary, 1978—. Trustee Indian Mountain Sch., Lakeville, Conn., 1976-80. Mem. Tulsa Geol. Soc., Am. Assn. Petroleum Geologists, Petroleum Exploration Soc. N.Y., Phi Beta Kappa. Republican. Episcopalian. Clubs: Tulsa; Union League (gov. 1976-81). Avocations: golf; soccer; racquet sports; book collecting. Office: Taconic Petroleum Corp The Skelly 23 W 4th St Suite 410 Tulsa OK 74103

SMITH, CASON CONRAD, dermatologist; b. Augusta, Ga., Feb. 3, 1920; s. Walter Cason and Violet Marie (Knapp) S.; m. Jean Celeste Rae, June 29, 1942; children—C. Conrad Jr., Gail, Stephen, Barry, Joel. B.S., U. Ga., 1940; M.D., Med. Coll. of Ga., 1943; M.Sc. in Dermatology, NYU, 1953. Diplomate Am. Bd. Dermatology. Intern Univ. Hosp., Augusta, Ga., 1943-44; resident and fellow skin and cancer unit NYU and Bellevue Med. Ctr., N.Y.C., 1950-53; gen. practice medicine, Chester, S.C., 1946-50; practice medicine specializing in dermatology, Augusta, 1953—; cons. dermatologist Univ. Hosp., St. Joseph Hosp., Humana Hosp., Augusta; clin. prof. dermatology Med. Coll. Ga., Augusta. Contbr. articles to profl. jours., chpts. to books. Served to capt. M.C., U.S. Army, 1944-46. Fellow Am. Acad. Dermatology; mem. N.Y. Acad. Scis., Ga. Soc. Dermatologists (pres. 1964-67), Southeastern Dermatol. Assn. (v.p. 1981, bd. dirs. 1982-85), AMA, So. Med. Assn., Ga. Med. Assn., Richmond County Med. Soc. Presbyterian. Clubs: Augusta Country; Savannah River Hunting (Jackson, S.C.). Lodge: Elks. Avocations: hunting; fishing; antique weapons collecting. Home: 3201 Huxley Dr Augusta GA 30909 Office: 1345 Druid Park Ave Augusta GA 30904

SMITH, CHARLES CLINTON, osteopathic physician; b. Monroe, La., Nov. 19, 1940; s. Charles Clinton and Lennie Pearl (Stansberry) S.; m. Linda Holmes, Aug. 5, 1967; children—Katherine, Charles, Robert. B.A., Ark. Coll., 1960; Ph.D., U. Okla., 1970; D.O., Okla. Coll. Osteo. Medicine, 1979. Assoc. prof. biology N.E. Okla. State U., Tahlequah, 1967-76; intern Kirksville Health Ctr., Mo., 1979-80; gen. practice medicine, Wewoka, Okla., 1980—. Elder, Presbyn. Ch., Wewoka, 1981—. NDEA fellow, 1961-64. Mem. Hughes-Seminole County Med. Soc., Okla. Osteo. Assn., Am. Osteo. Assn., Am. Coll. Osteo. Physicians, Am. Coll. Gen. Practitioners, Wewoka C. of C. Lodge: Lions. Home: 501 S Okfuskee St Wewoka OK 74884 Office: Wewoka Family Clinic Inc PO Box 480 Wewoka OK 74884

SMITH, CHARLES EDWARD, electrical engineering educator; b. Clayton, Ala., June 8, 1934; s. Roy L. and Emma E. (Boyd) S.; m. Evelyn Juanita Blow, July 1, 1960; children—Charles E., Jr., Steven A., Gary L. B.E.E., Auburn U., 1959, M.S., 1963, Ph.D., 1968. Research engr. Auburn U., Ala., 1959-68; asst. prof. dept. elec. engring. U. Miss., University, 1968-69, assoc. prof., 1969-74, assoc. prof., chmn. dept. elec. engring., 1975-76, prof., chmn. dept. elec. engring., 1977—. Contbr. articles to profl. jours. Served with USAR, 1953-65. Named Outstanding Engring. Tchr. U. Miss. Alumni Engring., 1970-71, Outstanding Faculty Mem., 1980-81. Mem. IEEE (sr.), Ala. Acad. Sci., Am. Soc. Engring. Edn., Sigma Xi (pres. U. Miss. chpt. 1976-77), Tau Beta Pi, Eta Kappa Nu, Phi Kappa Phi (exec. com. U. Miss. chpt. 1985). Baptist. Lodge: Kiwanis (v.p., pres. 1975-77). Office: Dept Elec Engring U Miss University MS 38677

SMITH, CHARLES EDWARD, university administrator; b. White County, Tenn., May 19, 1939; s. Cecil Edward and Christine (Newsome) S.; m. Shawna Lea Hickerson, Dec. 15, 1962; children—Chip, Tandy. B.S. in Journalism, U. Tenn., 1961; M.A. in English, George Peabody Coll., Nashville, 1966; Ph.D. in Higher Edn., George Peabody Coll., Nashville, 1976. Editor Sparta Expositor, Tenn., 1961-63; mng. editor Putnam County Herald-Cookeville Citizen, Cookeville, Tenn., 1963-64; asst. news editor Nashville Tennessean, 1964-67; news bur. dir. U. Tenn., Knoxville, 1967-68, pub. relations dir., 1968-71, exec. asst. to chancellor, 1971-73; exec. asst. to pres. U. Tenn. System, Knoxville, 1973-75; chancellor U. Tenn., Nashville, 1975-79; v.p. pub. service U. Tenn. System; editor Nashville Banner, 1979-80; chancellor U. Tenn., Martin, 1980-85, v.p. adminstrn., 1986—. Contbr. articles to profl. jours. Mem., 1st v.p. Ensworth Sch. Bd., Nashville, 1976-79; bd. dirs. Nashville Better Bus. Bur., 1976-79; mem. founder com. Tennesseans for Better Schs., 1983-84; chmn. W. Tenn. Job Conf., 1983-84; chmn. Weakley County Edn. Task Force, 1984-85. Recipient Single Best Editorial award Tenn. Press Assn., 1962; Fulbright fellow, 1980. Mem. Gulf South Ahtletic Conf. (pres. 1982-84), Council Advancement and Support Edn., Am. Assn. State Colls. and Univs. (com. on internat. programs 1982-84, com. on undergrad. edn. 1984-85), Phi Kappa Phi. Democrat. Mem. Ch. of Christ. Home: 1212 Ryan Pl Knoxville TN 37919 Office: Univ Tenn Office of Vice Pres Knoxville TN 37996

SMITH, CHARLES EDWARD, business executive; b. Charlotte, N.C., May 2, 1956; s. William Gary and Peggy (Crowley) W.; married. B.S., Clemson U., 1978. Sales and service rep. Tamper, Inc., Columbia, S.C., 1978-80, tech. writer advt., 1980-81, contract rep., 1981-83, new products mgr., 1983—. Mem. Am. Mgmt. Assn. Republican. Methodist. Home: 324 Lambeth Ct Columbia SC 29210 Office: 2401 Edmund Rd West Columbia SC 29169

SMITH, CHARLES EUGENE, biomathematician; b. Atlanta, June 22, 1950; s. Willie Eugene and Lillian Dorothy (Bates) S.; m. Ai Li Lee, Aug. 30, 1975; 1 child, Tara. B.S. in Physics, MIT, 1972; M.S. in Theoretical Biology, U. Chgo., 1973, Ph.D. in Biophysics and Theoretical Biology, 1979. Cardiometrician postdoctoral fellow Med. U. of S.C., Charleston, 1979-80, asst. prof., 1980-83, co-dir. cardiometrician scientist tng. program, 1981-82; asst. prof. N.C. State U., Raleigh, 1983—. Contbr. articles to profl. jours. Mem. Am. Statis. Assn., Biometric Soc., IEEE, Acoustical Soc. Am., Soc. Math. Biology. Office: Dept Stats NC State U Box 8203 Raleigh NC 27695-8203

SMITH, CHARLES LLOYD, nursing administrator; b. Fayette City, Pa., Sept. 25, 1940; s. Lester Elwood and Jane Elizabeth (Duncan) S.; m. Carol Ann Thompson, June 30, 1962; children—Timothy Lloyd, Todd Lewis. R.N., Sharon General Hosp., Pa., 1965; B.S. in Nursing, Med. Coll. Ga., 1978; M.S.

in Nursing, U. Ala., 1982. R.N., Ga., Pa. Commd. 2d lt. U.S. Army, 1966, advanced through grades to lt. col., 1982; operating room supr. Fox Army Community Hosp., Redstone, Ala., 1978-82, Darnall Army Hosp., Ft. Hood, Tex., 1982-84; dir. surg. services Athens Gen. Hosp., Ga., 1984—. Contbr. chpts. to books. Football coach Youth Activities, Camp Drake, Japan, 1968, baseball, football commr., Ft. Sam Houston, 1974-77; softball coach U.S. Army, 1969-84. Decorated Nat. Def. Service medal, Meritorious Service medal (2), Army Commendation medal. Mem. Assn. Operating Room Nurses, Sigma Theta Tau. Democrat. Avocations: golfing; bowling; softball. Home: 1031 Kings Rd Watkinsville GA 30677 Office: Athens Gen Hosp 1199 Prince Ave Athens GA 30613

SMITH, CHARLES MADISON, automotive and power equipment manufacturing company sales manager; b. Miami, Fla., Feb. 10, 1948; s. Charles M. and Geneva A. (Yarborough) S.; m. Linda Louise Edwards, May 15, 1969 (div. 1973); 1 child, Christine Lynn; m. Carol Jean Schulten, July 14, 1981; children—Robert Scott, Sherry Jean. B.S. in Journalism, U. Miami, 1970. Gen. mgr. Gables Honda, Coral Gables, Fla., 1970-71, Action Honda, Sanford, Fla., 1971-74; service dir. Holler Honda, Winter Park, Fla., 1974-77; sales mgr. Vespa of Am., Brisbane, Calif., 1977-78; dist. sales mgr. Am. Honda, Orlando, Fla., 1978-79, sales mgr. S.E. region, Alpharetta, Ga., 1979—. Mem. Orange County Sch. Bd., Orlando, 1975—, Big Bros., Atlanta, 1979-84; chmn. bd. 9, Selective Service System, Atlanta, 1982—; pres. Cystic Fibrosis Found., Atlanta, 1983-86. U. Miami scholar, 1966-68. Mem. Am. Mgmt. Assn., Am. Mktg. Assn., Nat. Engine Service Dealers Assn. Republican. Baptist (evangelist, minister). Avocations: Computer programming; fishing; bowling; golf; tennis; camping. Home: 1049 Pine Grove Dr Alpharetta GA 30201 Office: Am Honda Motor Co Inc 1500 Morrison Pkwy Alpharetta GA 30201

SMITH, CHARLOTTE GEORGE, physiologist, hypnotherapist; b. Cin., Aug. 26, 1938; d. Karl Franklin and Thelma Alena Smith; B.S. in Zoology, U. Ill., Urbana, 1960, M.S. in Physiology, 1961. Physiologist, NASA-Johnson Space Center, 1962—; dir. Independence Inst., 1980—; cons. in hypnotherapy and rehab. Recipient NASA Apollo Achievement award, 1969, Petticoat Pilot Achievement award, 1967; lic. pilot. Asso. fellow Aerospace Med. Assn.; mem. AAAS, Found. Sci. and Handicapped. Am. Soc. Profl. Hypnologists, Houston Profl. Hypnotists Assn., Nat. Assn. Female Execs. Office: NASA-Johnson Space Center Houston TX 77058

SMITH, CHARLOTTE REED, music theory educator; b. Eubank, Ky., Sept. 15, 1921; d. Joseph Lumpkin and Cornelia Elizabeth (Spencer) Reed; m. Walter Lindsay Smith, Aug. 24, 1949; children—Walter Lindsay IV, Elizabeth Reed. B.A., Tift Coll., 1941; M.A., Eastman Sch. Music, 1946. Instr. Okla. Bapt. U., Shawnee, 1942-43; asst. prof. Washburn U., Topeka, 1946-48; prof. Furman U., Greenville, S.C., 1948—. Editor: Orlando di Lasso-Seven Penitential Psalms with Two Laudate Psalms, 1983. Recipient Meritorious Tchr. award Furman U., 1974; NEH award, 1979. Mem. Am. Musicol. Soc., Soc. Music Theory. Republican. Baptist. Clubs: Music (jr. composition adjudicator 1978-83), Thursday Afternoon Literary (sec. 1983-85). Avocation: gardening. Office: Furman U Poinsett Hwy Greenville SC 29613

SMITH, CHRISTINA LEE, educator; b. San Francisco, Dec. 26, 1947; d. Ray Carden and Doris Maxine (Campbell) S. B.S., Central State U., 1970; M.A., U. No. Colo., 1976. Dir. athletics Woman's U. Okla., Norma, 1971-73; asst. dir. safety ARC, Tulsa, 1973-75; volleyball coach Lake Forest Coll., Ill., 1976-78; tchr. phys. edn., coach tennis Holland Hall Schs., Tulsa, 1978—. Contbr. articles to profl. jours. Aquatics instr.-trainer ARC, Tulsa, 1983, youth services sponsor, 1983-84, chpt. chmn., Waukegan, Ill., 1976-78. Recipient Humanity award ARC, 1976; Achievement medal USAR, 1983. Mem. Okla. Assn. Health, Phys. Edn., Recreation and Dance (dir., exec. sec. 1980-83), AAHPERD, Delta Psi Kappa (chpt. pres. 1979-80). Republican. Methodist. Club: Tulsa So. Tennis. Home: 7162 S Erie Ave Apt 2214 Tulsa OK 74136 Office: Holland Hall Schs 5666 E 81st St Tulsa OK 74136

SMITH, CLYDE GAYLON, obstetrician/gynecologist; b. Caraway, Ark., Nov. 9, 1945; s. William Harry and Thelma Lee (Johnson) S.; m. Deanna Sue Holland, July 22, 1967; children—Craig, Keith. B.S., Harding U., 1967; M.D., U. Tenn., 1971. Diplomate Am. Bd. Ob-Gyn. Intern, Meth. Hosp., Memphis, 1972; resident in ob-gyn City of Memphis Hosp., 1973, Meth. Hosp., Memphis, 1974-75; practice medicine, specializing in obstetrics and gynecology, Memphis, 1976—; lectr. dept. nursing Meth. Hosp., 1976-82, Bapt. Meml. Hosp., 1983—; staff Bapt. East Hosp., Memphis, 1981—; clin. instr. dept. ob-gyn U. Tenn. Ctr. Health Scis., Memphis, 1977—. Mem. devel. council Harding U., Searcy, Ark., 1975—, Harding Acad., Memphis, 1981—; adv. bd. Heartbeat, 1982, campaign div. chmn., 1981; sponsoring com., rev. editor Upreach, 1982—. Recipient AMA Physician Recognition award, 1976, 79, 82, 85. Fellow ACS, Am. Coll. Obstetricians and Gynecologists (Recognition award 1976, 79, 82, 85); mem. AMA, Tenn. Med. Soc., Memphis Shelby County Med. Soc., Soc. Obstetrical Anesthesia and Perinatology, Am. Fertility Soc., Am. Assn. Region Anesthesia, Nat. Perinatology Soc., So. Perinatal Soc., Memphis Obstetrical and Gynecol. Soc., Tenn. Obstetrical and Gynecol. Soc., Am. Assn. Gynecol. Laparoscopists. Mem. Ch. of Christ (deacon). Contbr. articles to profl. jours.; rev. editor Practical Gastroenterology, 1979—, Upreach, 1981—. Home: 174 Grove Park Memphis TN 38117 Office: 6266 Poplar St Memphis TN 38119

SMITH, CONNIE KAY, educational counselor; b. Pittsburg, Kans., Mar. 21, 1951; d. Robert Norman and Gertrude (Ellis) Sackett; m. Darrel Regan Ratliff, June 21, 1969 (div. 1979); m. Lee Roy Smith, Feb. 2, 1984; 1 stepchild, Jason Todd. B.A. in Edn., Northeastern State U., 1973, M.A. in Edn., 1976. Legal sec. Durrett & Johnson, Tahlequah, Okla., 1971-73; spl. edn. tchr. Watts Pub. Schs., Okla., 1976-78, Cherokee County Supt., Tahlequah, 1978-79; counselor Coweta Pub. Schs., Okla., 1979—. Active Learning Disabilities Camp, Northeastern State U., 1979, 85, Spl. Olympics, Okla., 1976, 85, 86, smoke alarm program Am. Lung Assn., Tulsa, 1984. Recipient 5 Yr. Service award Coweta Pub. Schs., 1984. Mem. Nat. Realtors Assn. Okla., NEA, Coweta Edn. Assn., Am. Assn. Counseling and Devel., Okla. Sch. Counselor Assn., Am. Sch. Counselor Assn. Avocations: antiques; decorating; skiing; boating; reading. Home: 6808 S 5th Ave Broken Arrow OK 74011 Office: Coweta Pub Schs 302 N Broadway Coweta OK 74429

SMITH, CRAIG WYATT, psychologist, educator; b. Bakersfield, Calif., Sept. 5, 1952; s. Wayne Lincoln and Joyce (Wyatt) S.; m. Nancy Kim Worley, Feb. 14, 1974; children—Zachary, Maggie, Jacqueline. B.S., Utah State U., 1976; M.S., U. Ariz., 1977; Ph.D., Brigham Young U., 1980. Pres. Family Devel. Resources, Phoenix, 1980-84; asst. prof. marriage and family therapy, Auburn U., Ala., 1984—. Contbr. articles to profl. jours. Cons. Ariz. Gov.'s Task Force on Marriage and the Family, 1978. Mem. Am. Assn. for Marriage and Family Therapy (clin. mem.), Ala. Assn. for Marriage and Family Therapy (1st v.p. 1985—), Am. Psychol. Assn., Nat. Council on Family Relations, Psi Chi. Republican. Mormon. Office: Dept of Family and Child Devel Auburn U Auburn AL 36849

SMITH, CURTIS HENRY, pharmacist, clinical instructor; b. Reedville, Va., Aug. 12, 1952; s. Orrie Lee and Easter Marie (Deihl) S.; m. Marilyn Rose Bowles, Aug. 13, 1977. A.A. in Chemistry, Ferrum Coll., 1972; B.S. in Pharmacy, Med. Coll. Va., 1975. Registered pharmacist, Va. Chief pharmacist Rappahannock Gen. Hosp., Kilmarnock, Va., 1977—; clin. investigator Nat. Cancer Inst., Rappahannock Gen. Hosp., 1981—; mem. clin. faculty Va. Commonwealth U.-Med. Coll. Va., Richmond, 1981—. Bd. dirs. Bethany United Meth. Ch. Recipient Merck award Va. Commonwealth U.-Med. Coll. Va. Clin. Pharm. Sch. faculty, 1975. Mem. Chesapeake Pharm. Assn. (pres. 1980-82), Va. Soc. Hosp. Pharmacists, Va. Pharm. Assn. (state council rep. 1981). Republican. Methodist. Club: Indian Creek Yacht and Country. Lodge: Masons (sr. warden 1986). Avocations: snow skiing; tennis; golf. Home: Route 1 Box 3333 Hatton Ave Kilmarnock VA 22482 Office: Pharmacy Dept Rappahannock Gen Hosp PO Box 1449 Harris Dr Kilmarnock VA 22482

SMITH, DALLAS PAUL, training specialist; b. Tyler, Tex., Dec. 8, 1946; s. Dallas Coy and Ruby Neil (Lunsford) S.; m. Janice Lorraine Emerson, Feb. 1, 1969. B.B.A. in Mgmt., Tex. A&M U., 1969. Residential heating specialist Tex. Power & Light Co., Palestine and Tyler, 1970-75, heating and cooling specialist, Tyler, 1975-79; tng. specialist Tex. Utilities Generating Co., Athens, 1979-81, personnel rep., Fairfield, 1981-83, tng. specialist, Dallas, 1983—. Sunday sch. tchr. Baptist Ch. Mem. Am. Soc. Tng. and Devel. (pres. East Tex. chpt. 1986). Republican. Avocations: fishing, softball, basketball. Home: 701 Village Green Rockwall TX 75087 Office: Texas Utilities Generating Co 400 N Olive St Dallas TX 75201

SMITH, DAN MILLARD, advertising and marketing firm executive; b. Oklahoma City, Apr. 28, 1943; s. Jim Dewey and Virginia Lee (Rice) S.; children—James Kevin, Jeffrey Lee. Student, N.Mex. State U., 1961-68. Sports dir. Sta. KOBE, Las Cruces, N.Mex., 1966-70, Sta. KGGM-TV, Albuquerque, 1970-76; v.p. Competitive Edge Advt. Co., Chgo., 1976-78; pres. Smith/Tarter & Co., Amarillo, Tex., 1978—. Bd. dirs. Cystic Fibrosis Found., Albuquerque, 1973-76, All Faith's Receiving Home, 1974-76; deacon Paramount Terr. Christian Ch., Amarillo, 1983. Named N.Mex. Sportscaster of Yr., N.Mex. Broadcasters Assn., 1969-74, Nat. Sportscasters and Writers Assn., 1972. Mem. Am. Assn. Advt. Agys., Am. Advt. Fedn. Republican. Office: Smith/Tarter & Co PO Box 30818 Amarillo TX 79120

SMITH, DAVID ALEXANDER, mathematics educator, researcher, consultant, writer; b. N.Y.C., Jan. 6, 1938; s. Joshua Avery and Elma Carlotta (Clark) S.; m. Dorothy Elizabeth Ross, Mar. 30, 1958; children—David II, Charles, Scott, Cynthia. B.S., Trinity Coll., 1958; Ph.D., Yale U., 1963. Asst. prof. Duke U., Durham, N.C., 1962-68, assoc. prof. math., 1968—; vis. assoc. prof. Case Western Res. U., Cleve., 1975-76; vis. prof. Benedict Coll., Columbia, S.C., 1984-86; Calculus project advisor D.C. Heath Co., Lexington, Mass., 1976-79. Author: Interface: Calculus and the Computer, 1st edit., 1976, 2d edit., 1984. Author instructional software packages. Assoc. editor Mathematics Mag., 1981-85, Coll. Math. Jour., 1986—; series editor Conduit, Iowa City, 1975—; cons. editor Saunders Coll. Publ., 1983—. Contbr. articles to profl. jours. United Negro Coll. Fund scholar at large, 1984. Mem. Math. Assn. Am. (Carl B. Allendoerfer award 1977), Am. Math. Soc., Soc. Indsl. and Applied Math., AAUP, AAAS. Avocation: microcomputers. Home: 1823 Glenwood Rd Columbia SC 29204 Office: Benedict Coll Box 253 Columbia SC 29204

SMITH, DAVID R., federal government official, lawyer; b. Cin., Aug. 3, 1947; s. Roy E. and Ann E. (Jung) S.; m. Jeanne M. Archer, June 3, 1978; children—Gregory, Laura. B.S. in Bus. Adminstrn., Ohio State U., 1969; J.D., U. Cin., 1974. Bar: Ohio, N.Y., Fla. Asst. dist. counsel IRS, Miami, Fla., 1981—, atty. IRS, Buffalo, Miami, 1974-81; lectr. tax litigation seminar Fla. Bar Programs, Tallahassee, 1982. Served with AUS, 1970-72. Evans Scholar Found., Western Golf Assn. scholar, Chgo., 1965. Mem. ABA, Fla. Bar Assn. Presbyterian. Home: 14390 SW 73d Ct Miami FL 33158 Office: IRS 51 SW 1st Ave Miami FL 33130

SMITH, DAVID REID, pharmaceutical sales representative; b. Spartanburg, S.C., Feb. 15, 1954; s. Boyce Luther and Doris Ellen (Alverson) S.; m. Jan Corley, May 29, 1982; 1 son, Zachary David. B.S. in Pharmacy, U. S.C., 1976. Registered pharmacist, S.C. Staff pharmacist Self Meml. Hosp., Greenwood, S.C., 1976-81; sales rep. Eli Lilly & Co., Myrtle Beach, S.C., 1981-83, splty. sales rep., Little Rock, Ark., 1983—. Mem. S.C. Pharm. Assn. (v.p. 1981-82), 8th Dist. Pharm. Assn. (treas. 1981-83), Kappa Psi (regent 1976). Baptist.

SMITH, DAWN ELLEN, nurse; b. Youngstown, Ohio, Sept. 13, 1955; d. John Ronald and Carol Ann (Fanson) Smith. Student Barry U., 1973-75; B.S.N., Vanderbilt U., 1978; postgrad. Emory U., 1983—. Staff nurse Ga. Bapt. Hosp., Atlanta, 1978; staff nurse Protem, Atlanta, 1978-79, dir. nursing, 1979-80; staff nurse telemetry Crawford West Long Hosp., Atlanta, 1980-81; cardiovascular staff nurse Emory U. Hosp., Atlanta, 1981-83, cardiology staff nurse, 1983-84; ICU-CCU nurse Humana Gwinnett Community Hosp., Snellville, Ga., 1984-85; customer service rep. Adler Instruments Co., 1985—. Mem. Am. Assn. Critical Care Nurses, Gamma Phi Beta, Panhellenic Soc. (sec. Nashville 1976-77). Office: Adler Instruments Co Norcross GA

SMITH, DEAN EDWARDS, basketball coach; b. Emporia, Kans., Feb. 28, 1931; s. Alfred Dillon and Vesta Marie (Edwards) S.; m. Linnea Weblemoe, May 21, 1976; children—Sharon, Sandy, Scott, Kristen, Kelly. B.S. in Math. and Phys. Edn. U. Kans., 1953. Asst. basketball coach U.S. Air Force Acad., 1955-58; asst. basketball coach U. N.C., 1958-61, head basketball coach, 1961—; mem. U.S. and Canadian Basketball Rules Com., 1967-73; U.S. basketball coach Olympics, Montreal, Que., Can., 1976; lectr. basketball clinics, Germany, Italy. Served with USAF, 1954-58. Named Coach of Year Atlantic Coast Conf., 1967, 1968, 1971, 1976, 1977, 79, Nat. Basketball Coach of Year, 1977, Nat. Coach of Yr. U.S. Basketball Writers, 1979, Naismith Basketball Hall of Fame, 1982. Mem. Nat. Assn. Basketball Coaches (Nat. Basketball Coach of Year 1976, dir. 1972—, pres. 1981-82), Fellowship Christian Athletes (dir. 1965-70). Baptist. Office: PO Box 2126 Chapel Hill NC 27514*

SMITH, DENNIS MARTIN, physician, biostatistical consultant; b. Buffalo, Feb. 27, 1954; s. Adolph and Virginia Marie (Szwejda) S. B.A. in Econs. and Stats., SUNY-Buffalo, 1976, M.D., 1980; M.A. in Stats., U. Rochester, 1983; postgrad. pub. health Columbia U., 1983—. Grad. research asst. dept. stats. U. Rochester, N.Y., 1976-77; surg. resident Millard Fillmore Hosp., Buffalo, 1981-82; clin. and research assoc. L. Maxwell Lockie, M.D., Buffalo, 1980-85; gen. practice medicine, Buffalo and Atlanta, 1983—; vis. scientist agent orange projects Ctr. for Disease Control, 1983—; biostatis. cons. in arthritis research, Buffalo, 1980-85. Contbr. articles to profl. jours. Co-author musical plays including Drood, Safety Zone, Thorn of Anxiety. Mem. Am. Rheumatism Assn., Am. Statis. Assn., Biometric Soc., Am. Coll. Sports Medicine, Med. Assn. of Ga., Med. Assn. of Atlanta, Soc. for Clin. Trials, Soc. Med. Decision Making, Dramatists Guild, Authors League of Am., Ga. Thoroughbred Owners and Breeders Assn. Clubs: Atlanta Polo. Republican. Roman Catholic. Avocations: equitation; polo; statistical analysis of racing equines. Home: 3442-S North Druid Hills Rd Decatur GA 30033 Office: Agent Orange Projects Ctrs for Disease Control C-25 Atlanta GA 30333

SMITH, DEUEL COILY, JR., former wood products company official; b. Muskogee, Okla., Feb. 19, 1943; s. Deuel Coily and Jewell G. (Burkett) S.; m. Sharon Jean Mann, Dec. 3, 1960; 1 dau., Rebekah. B.A. in Sociology, N.E. La. U., 1967, M.A. in Criminal Justice, 1981. With Troop F, La. State Police, 1964-66; with Monroe (La.) Police Dept., 1966-69, Gov.'s Commn. on Law Enforcement, 1969-70; spl. agt. FBI, 1970-76; security cons. to bus. and industry, 1976-78; security mgr. Mid-Continent Wood Products Mfg. div. Ga.-Pacific Corp., Crossett, Ark., 1978-85; seminarian Episcopal Theol. Sem. of the S.W., Austin, Tex., 1985—; lectr. corporate security mgmt. Ind. U., 1979-82. Vestryman, sr. warden, St. Mark's Episcopal Ch., Crossett, 1979-81. Served as M.P., U.S. Army, 1961-64. Mem. Am. Soc. Indsl. Security (charter mem. Ark.; cert. protection profl.), Internat. Assn. Chiefs of Police. Republican. Clubs: Rotary (Crossett); Masons; Shriners (Monroe, La.). Home: 8311 Stillwood Ln Austin TX 78758 Office: PO Box 2247 606 Rathervue Pl Austin TX 78758

SMITH, DONALD ALAN, advertising executive; b. Newark, Ohio, Dec. 4, 1934; s. Brooks and Ella (Jaeger) S.; B.F.A., U. Ga., 1956; children—Kirk Martin, Angela. Div. designer Dairypak, Athens, Ga., 1957—; owner The Adsmith, Athens, 1960—; design cons. Athens Daily News, Athens Banner Herald, 1965-78, Athens Observer, 1979, Ga. Outdoor Advt., 1963—, Athens Tempo mag., 1979; art dir. Athens mag., 1968-73. Served with U.S. Army, 1957-58. Recipient Design award Internat. Paper Co., 1970; 1st place awards Inst. Outdoor Advt., 1970; awards of excellence Deep South Advt. Show, 1971, 72; Gold Medal award Ga./Ala. Newspaper Advt. Execs. Assn., 1971; awards of excellence So. Creativity Show, 1972, 73, 79, merit awards, 1980, gold award, 1981, 3 merit awards, 1981; award Ga. Press Assn., 1975, Best of Show award, 1981; 1st place award So. Classified Advt. Mgrs., 1978; Outstanding Service award Ga. div. Am. Cancer Soc., 1980; Ga. Press award, 1981; 2d pl. Addy award, 1982; Archie awards, 1983, 84, 85; Am. Advt. Silver Medal award, 1983; citation Ga. Ho. of Reps., 1983, also others. Mem. Am. Advt. Fedn., Athens Ad Club (pres. 1983-84), Atlanta Advt. Club (Phoenix awards 1970, 74), Athens Area C. of C. (pub. realtions chmn. 1965-70, Outstanding Service award 1965-66, ambassador of yr. 1983-84, community service award in arts 1986), Phi Beta Kappa, Phi Kappa Phi. Presbyterian. Home: 4 Tangelwood Ct Athens GA 30606

SMITH, DONALD ALBERT, college administrator; b. Yonkers, N.Y., Nov. 19, 1931; s. Albert Henry and Ruth Isabelle (Joudrey) S.; m. Barbara Eleanor Atkeson, Dec. 28, 1957; children—Jean Marie, Carolyn Rene, David Andrew. B.A., Columbia U., 1953, M.A., Tchrs. Coll., Columbia U., 1959, Ed.D., 1965; M.Div., Union Theol. Sem., 1956. Asst. to registrar Tchrs. Coll. Columbia U., N.Y.C., 1957-58, assoc. dir. placement Grad. Sch. Bus., 1958-60; assoc. dean of students Alderson-Broaddus Coll., Philippi, W.Va., 1960-64, assoc. dean for experiential edn., 1964-77, v.p. coll. relations and devel., 1977-85, dir. coll. relations and publs., 1985—; cons. experiental edn. Contbr. articles on arctic exploration and experiential edn. to publs. Chmn. Republican Party Barbour County, W.Va., 1964-68; sec.-treas. Barbour County Parks and Recreation Commn., 1970—; chmn. bd. fin., former moderator Philippi Bapt. Ch., 1960—. Recipient George William Curtis medal for pub. speaking, Columbia U., 1953; Danforth Assoc., Alderson-Broaddus Coll., 1961-63. Mem. Council for Advancement and Support of Edn., Pub. Relations Assn. of Am. Bapt. Chs. USA, Nat. Coop. Edn. Assn. (v.p. 1974-75), Middle Atlantic Placement Assn. (v.p. 1974-75), Student Personnel Adminstrs. W.Va. Colls. and Univs. (pres. 1964-65), W.Va. Assn. Colls. (bd. dirs. 1966-67), N.Am. Assn. Ventriloquists, W.Va. C. of C. (vice chmn. edn. com. 1980—), W.Va. Council on Econ. Edn. (bd. dirs. 1980—), Sigma Chi. Clubs: Lions (pres. Philippi 1967, sec. Dist. 29-I 1967), Order Ky. Cols. Home and Office: Box 277 Alderson-Broaddus Coll Philippi WV 26416

SMITH, DONALD VAUGHAN, publisher; b. Pascagoula, Miss., Dec. 4, 1954; s. Arthur V. and Doris (Megehee) S. B.Engring., U. Miss., 1978. Supr. shipping dept. PPG Industries, Inc., Lake Charles, La., 1978-81; compiler, editor, pub. The Columns of Arthur V. Smith, 1981-82; founder, pub., editor So. Style mag., Pascagoula, 1982—; profl. lounge singer, 1975—. Officer, CAP, 1981—. Mem. C. of C. Presbyterian. Contbr. articles to profl. jours.; editor Ole Miss Engr., 1975-77. Home: 3003 Pascagoula St Pascagoula MS 39567 Office: PO Box 955 Pascagoula MS 39567

SMITH, DOROTHY BRAND, librarian; b. Beaumont, Tex., Oct. 4, 1922; d. Robert and Lula (Jones) Brand; m. William E. Smith, June 15, 1941; children—Wilson B., Lurinda. B.S. in Social Sci., Lamar U., 1954; M.L.S., U. Tex., 1971. Tchr., Beaumont Ind. Sch. Dist., 1954-62; tchr. Austin Ind. Sch. Dist. (Tex.), 1962-66; librarian, 1966—; cons. Edn. Service Center, Austin, 1974, 83; workshop leader Austin Ind. Schs., 1980. Recipient Siddie Joe Johnson award Children's Roundtable of Tex. Library Assn., 1984. Mem. ALA, Tex. Library Assn. (life), Tex. State Tchrs. Assn. (life), AAUW, Delta Kappa Gamma, Phi Delta Kappa. Presbyterian. Home: 6108 Mountainclimb Dr Austin TX 78731 Office: K Cook Sch 1511 Cripple Creek Dr Austin TX 78758

SMITH, DUDLEY, former trade assn. exec., sugar cons., author; b. Campbellsville, Ky., Dec. 6, 1904; s. Herbert G. and Addie (Feather) S.; B.S., U. Ky., 1931; postgrad. U.S. Dept. Agr. Grad. Sch., 1931-35; m. Verta Enid Templeton, June 9, 1935; children—Mary Lou Smith Brown, Dudley T., Elizabeth Smith Jones. Tobacco mktg. and program specialist U. Ky., 1929-31, U.S. Govt., 1931-36; ofcl. Washington and San Juan (P.R.) offices Assn. Sugar Producers P.R., 1936-72, v.p., 1941-72; tobacco and livestock farmer, Mitchellville, Md., 1941-68; internat. cons. sugar and tobacco, 1940—; exec. sec. Sugar Equipment and Services Exporters Assn., 1976-80; mem., ofcl. various Md. agrl. orgns., 1947-69; chmn. Nat. Sugar Research and Mktg. Adv. Com., 1951-58; mem. Nat. Tobacco Industry Adv. Com., 1963-65, Nat. Tobacco Research Adv. Com., 1964-66. Mem. Internat., P.R., Am., sugar technologists assns., Alpha Gamma Rho, Alpha Zeta. Democrat. Methodist. Club: Sarasota U. Lodges: Masons, Rotary. Author: Cane Sugar World, 1977; editor Sugar y Azucar Yearbook, 1971-77. Home: 1 Benjamin Franklin Dr Sarasota FL 33577 Office: 582 S Washington Dr Sarasota FL 33577

SMITH, DWIGHT PHELAN, public relations agency executive; b. St. Paul, June 7, 1945; s. William M. and Anne Warren (Stringer) S.; B.A., So. Methodist U., 1967; children—Anne Blair, McNeil Stringer. Journalist, UPI, 1967, 69; communications dir. Met. Dallas, Nat. Alliance Businessmen, 1972; dir. corp. communications Hydrometals, Inc., Dallas, 1972-76; account exec., then v.p. Hill and Knowlton, Inc., Dallas, 1976-79, sr. v.p., mgr., 1979—, mgr. S.W. region, 1984—. Trustee, Cath. Found. Dallas, 1980—; vice chmn. Dallas Transit Bd., 1975-77; mem. bd. Lone Star Transp. Authority, 1979-80. Served to lt. (j.g.) USN, 1967-69. Mem. Public Relations Soc. An., Nat. Investor Relations Inst., Dallas Advt. League. Republican. Home: 4592 Belfort St Dallas TX 75205 Office: 1500 One Dallas Centre Dallas TX 75201

SMITH, E. CARLYLE, JR., architect, civil engineer, state legislator; b. Grand Prairie, Tex., Mar. 12, 1939; s. E. Carlyle and Phyllis (Matlock) S.; m. Ouida Marie Daugherty, Sept. 15, 1962. B.Arch., B.S. in Civil Enging., Tex. Tech U., 1963. Draftsman Smith & Warder, Architects and Engrs. (became Smith & Warder, Inc., Architects & Engrs. 1978), Grand Prairie, 1963-66, prin., 1966-78, pres., 1978—; mem. Tex. Ho. of Reps., Austin, 1975—; dir. Republic Bank, Grand Prairie. Served with Air N.G., 1963-69. Recipient award for residential archtl. design Tex. Forestry Assn., 1982; named Disting. Engr., Tex. Tech U. Dept. Engring., 1983. Mem. AIA, Tex. Soc. Architects, AIA (Dallas chpt.), Grand Prairie C. of C. (pres. 1970, Citizen of Yr. 1968). Lodges: Rotary (bd. dirs. local lodge 1968-70, local pres. elect 1985—), Masons (master 1971-72, dist. dep. grand master 1985).

SMITH, E. KEITH, import and manufacturing representative, antique dealer; b. Comanche, Okla., May 27, 1940; s. Wilbert C. and Thelma Mae (Davis) S. B.A., U. Okla., 1962. Dir., Central Okla. Govts., Oklahoma City, 1964-66; ptnr. Crissman-Smith, Ltd., Dallas, 1973-78; pres. Keith Smith, Ltd., Dallas, 1973—; exec. v.p. TAITU, Dallas, 1973—. Exec. dir. Democratic Party, Oklahoma City, 1979-83; bd. dirs. Atlanta Merchandise Mart, 1962-68; bd. assocs. U. Okla.-Norman, 1979-83. Served with USAFR, 1962-68. Mem. Gift and Decorative Accessories, Nat. China-Tabletop Orgn., C. of C. Methodist. Office: 2999 Dallas Trade Mart Dallas TX 75207

SMITH, EDWARD EARL, educational administrator; b. New Castle, Pa., Feb. 11, 1926; s. Edward R. and Naomi (Williams) S.; m. Alma Mae Faircloth, July 19, 1955 (dec. 1978); children—Deborah Lee, Edward Randolph; m. Letha Jean Lawson, June 15, 1979. B.S., Youngstown State U., 1948; M.S., U. Utah, 1968; M.A., U. Okla., 1972, Ph.D., 1979. Commd. 2d lt., U.S. Marine Corps, 1948, advanced through grades to lt. col., 1971, ret., 1971; supr. tng. Okla. Ctr. Continuing Edn., U. Okla., Lawton, 1971-76; program dir. Mgmt. Tng. Ctr., Rose State Coll., Midwest City, Okla., 1977—; cons. in field. Served with USAAF, 1943-45. Decorated Bronze Star with V, Navy Commendation medal, Air medal. Lodges: Mason (32 deg.), Shriners. Home: 15284 Falcon Way Rd Choctaw OK 73020 Office: Mgmt Tng Center Rose State Coll Midwest City OK 73110

SMITH, EDWARD LEE, educational administrator; b. Harrisonburg, Va., Oct. 1, 1946; s. Grattan Addison and Mary Alice (Hess) S.; m. Betty M. Starr, June 11, 1968; children—Daniel Addison, Amy Elizabeth, Andrew Grattan. B.S., Appalachian State U., 1968; M.Ed., U. Va., 1974. Tchr. Watauga County Schs., Boone, N.C., 1968-70, Harrisonburg City Schs., 1971-73; adminstr. Rockingham County Schs., Harrisonburg, 1974—; prin. Spotswood High Sch., Penn Laird, Va., 1984—. Bd. dirs. Am. Heart Assn., Harrisonburg, 1980—. Mem. Nat. Assn. Secondary Sch. Prins., Phi Delta Kappa. Mem. Brethren Ch. Club: Ruritan Nat. Lodge: Elks. Avocations: tennis; jogging. Office: Spotswood High Sch Penn Laird VA 22846

SMITH, EDWARD O'DELL, social sciences educator, minister; b. Bristol, Tenn., Mar. 22, 1929; s. Haskell V. and Eva M. (O'Dell) S.; m. Patricia Spencer Rees, Sept. 1, 1955; children—Mimi, Mark, Josh, Sean, Carrie. A.B., Emory and Henry Coll., 1951; M.Div., Union Theol. Sem., 1958. Ordained to ministry Presbyn. Ch. U.S.A., 1958. Missionary to Brazil, 1958-62; pastor 1st Presbyn. Ch., Jefferson City, Tenn., 1962-68; dean students Lees-McRae Coll., Banner Elk, N.C., 1968-80, chmn. div. social scis., 1980—. Chmn. Town Planning Bd., Banner Elk, 1978-80; trustee Cannon Meml. Hosp., Banner Elk, 1984—. Served with U.S. Army, 1951-54. Home: Box 296 Banner Elk NC 78604 Office: Dept Social Sci Lees-McRae Coll Banner Elk NC 28604

SMITH, EDWARD THOMPSON, JR., dentist; b. Goldsboro, N.C., Dec. 23, 1950; s. Edward Thompson and Rebecca (Cozart) S.; m. Janet Memory Johnson, Aug. 9, 1975; children—Wingate Thompson. B.S., Wake Forest U., 1973; D.D.S., U. N.C., 1977. Resident Balt. City Hosps., 1977-78; assoc. Thomas A. Whicker D.D.S., P.A., Thomasville, N.C., 1978-79; v.p., sec. Whicker & Smith, D.D.S., P.A., Thomasville, 1979—. Asst. scoutmaster Boy Scouts Am., Thomasville, 1980—; chmn. work area on missions Meml. United Meth. Ch., Thomasville, 1981—; bd. dirs. Thomasville Area United Way, 1983-85, Mental Health Assn. Davidson County, Lexington, N.C., 1984-86. Recipient Disting. Service award Thomasville Jaycees, 1983. Mem. ADA, Acad. Gen. Dentistry (fellowship 1984), N.C. Dental Soc., 2d Dist. Dental Soc., Davidson County Dental Soc., Pierre Fauchard Acad. Lodge: Rotary. Home: 300 Skiles Heights Thomasville NC 27360 Office: Whicker and Smith 210 Arthur Dr Thomasville NC 27360

SMITH, EDWARD VANCE, III, lawyer; b. Dallas, May 24, 1937; s. Edward Vance, Jr. and Helen Louetta (Pitts) S. B.A., North Tex. State U., 1960; J.D., So. Meth. U., 1963. Bar: Tex. 1963, U.S. Dist. Ct. (no. dist.) Tex. 1965, U.S. Ct. Appeals (5th cir.) 1974, U.S. Dist. Ct. (ea. dist.) Tex. 1981. Ptnr. Taylor & Mizell, Dallas, 1970—, dir., officer. Bd. regents North Tex. State U., 1978-79; runner Olympic Torch Relay, 1984. Recipient Outstanding Alumni Service award North Tex. State U., 1974; named North Tex. State U. Alumnus of Yr., Kappa Sigma, 1979. Fellow Am. Coll. Probate Counsel; mem. Tex. State Bar (speaker, author advanced family law course 1981, advanced estate planning and probate course 1982, course dir. 1981). Presbyterian. Author, lectr., 1979, 80, 84. Office: 3000 Lincoln Plaza Suite LB-5 500 N Akard Dallas TX 75201

SMITH, EMILY GUTHRIE, artist; b. Fort Worth, July 8, 1909; d. William Craton and Lillian (Fakes) Guthrie; m. Tolbert C. Smith, Apr. 15, 1932 (dec. Nov. 1978); children—Van Zandt II, Grace Clifton Smith Smith. Student Tex. Woman's U., 1927-29, Art Students League, N.Y.C., summer 1931; B.A., Okla. U., 1931. Instr. Fort Worth Mus. Fine Arts, 1955-70, Toas Inst. Creative Orientation, Taos, N.Mex., 1956-58; instr. various art workshops, Taos, Ruidoso and Las Vegas, N.Mex. One-woman shows: Fifth Ave. Gallery, Ft. Worth, 1960, 62, Carlin Galleries, Ft. Worth, 1963, 71, 74, 80, 83, 85, Wichita Falls Mus. Fine Arts, 1970, (retrospective) Ft. Worth Mus. Fine Arts, 1966; group shows include Diamond M Museum, Snyder, Tex., L & L Galleries, Longview, Tex.; represented in permanent collections Dallas Mus. Fine Arts, Ft. Worth Mus. Fine Arts, U. Tex., Arlington, Mus. of Texas Tech U.; works include numerous portraits, murals. Recipient awards Longview Mus. Invitational, Tex., 1961-72, Dallas Mus. Fine Arts Tex. Anns., 1963—. Mem. Pastel Soc. Am. (judge 1983, awards 1978-84, Hall of Fame 1984), Fort Worth Mus. Art, Dallas Art Mus., Met. Mus. Art, Nat. Soc. Lit. and the Arts, Jr. League Fort Worth, Kappa Alpha Theta. Republican. Presbyterian. Avocation: photography. Home: 408 Crestwood Dr Fort Worth TX 76107

SMITH, EUGENE WILSON, university president; b. Forrest City, Ark., June 10, 1930; s. Milton Samuel and Frank Leslie (Wilson) S.; m. Rebecca Ann Slaughter, May 27, 1956; children—Lucinda Ann Smith McDaniel, Bradley Eugene. B.A., Ark. State U., 1952; M.Ed., U. Miss., 1955, Ed.D., 1958. From instr. to prof. Ark. State U., State University, 1958—, asst. to pres., 1959-68, v.p. adminstrn., 1968-71, dean grad. sch., 1971-84, sr. v.p., 1980-84, pres., 1984—. Alderman, City of Jonesboro, Ark., 1982-84; pres. Jonesboro Indsl. Devel. Corp., 1983—. Served to 1st lt. U.S. Army, 1952-54. Mem. Jonesboro C. of C. (pres. 1982-83), Phi Kappa Phi, Phi Delta Kappa, Kappa Delta Pi. Lodge: Rotary (pres. 1974-75). Avocations: golf; fishing. Home: 1503 E Nettleton Ave Jonesboro AR 72401 Office: Office of Pres Ark State U State University AR 72467

SMITH, FLAVIOUS JOSEPH, university administrator; b. Silver Point, Tenn., Aug. 19, 1929; s. Johnnie Haskell and Lucy Avo (Thomas) S.; m. Mary June McMurtry, May 5, 1954; children—Rene Jean, Flavious Joseph Jr., Bradley Lee. B.S., Tenn. Tech. U., Cookeville, 1952; M.A., G. Peabody Coll., 1957, Ed.D., 1962. Fellow Peabody Coll., Nashville, 1957-58; coach, instr. Cumberland Coll., Lebanon, Tenn., 1959-60, Shepherds Coll., Shepherds Town, W.Va., 1960-61, Millsap Coll., Jackson, Miss., 1961-62; chmn. dept. health and phys. edn. Tenn. Tech. U., 1962—. Author: Enduring Memories, 1985. Served to 1st lt. U.S. Army, 1954-57. Mem. Tenn. Edn. Assn. NEA, Tenn. Assn. Health, Phys. Edn., Recreation and Dance (pres. 1970-71), Am. Assn. Health, Phys. Edn. and Recreation. Methodist. Avocations: farming; hunting; fishing; writing; reading. Home: Route 5 Box 312 Longview Cookeville TN 38501 Office: Dept Health and Phys Edn Box 5043 Tenn Tech U Cookeville TN 38505

SMITH, FRANCIS COLZEY, director pharmaceutical services; b. Bristol, Va., Aug. 31, 1928; s. Francis Ogden and Martha Prier (Colzey) S.; m. Rosemary Prickett, Dec. 22, 1851 (div. 1964); children—Francis C. Jr., Patricia Louise, William Sidney; m. Linda Sue Daniel, Dec. 30, 1964. B.S. in Pharmacy, Auburn U., 1952. Pharmacist Leeth Apothecary, Cullman, Ala., 1953-54; pharm. rep. Lederle Labs., Pearl River, N.Y., 1954-55; pharmacist, owner Med. Arts Apothecary, Cullman, 1955-64; pharmacist Midway Drug, Grundy, Va., 1964-71, Citizen Drug, Clintwood, Va., 1971-74, owner, Norton Pharmacy, Va., 1971-81; dir. pharmacy Russell County Med. Ctr., Lebanon, Va., 1981—. Served to 1st lt. U.S. Army, 1946-48, 52-53. Mem. Am. Soc. Hosp. Pharmacists, Va. Soc. Hosp. Pharmacists. Avocation: golf. Home: 1 Circle Dr Wise VA 24293 Office: Russell County Med Ctr Carroll & Tate Sts Lebanon VA 24293

SMITH, FREDERICK PAUL, forensic science educator, consultant; b. Pitts., June 14, 1951; s. Donald Fred and Dorothy Dayle (Cuddy) S.; m. Deborah Jayne Brown, May 29, 1982; children—Madeline Claire, Charles Paul. Student NYU, 1969-70; B.A., Antioch Coll., 1974; M.S., U. Pitts., 1976, Ph.D., 1978. Research asst. scientist U. Pitts., 1977-78; dir. criminalistics Office Chief Med. Examiner, N.Y.C., 1979; asst. prof. U. Ala., Birmingham, 1979-82, assoc. prof. forensic sci., 1982—, dir. forensic sci., 1981—; pres. Frederick P. Smith & Assocs., Inc., Birmingham, 1982—; mem. adv. bd. Wallace State Coll., Cullman, Ala., 1982—; cons. in field. Contbr. articles to profl. jours. Scholar Commonwealth of Pa., 1969-74, NYU, 1969, Antioch Coll., 1970-74. Mem. Am. Chem. Soc., Internat. Assn. Identification, Am. Acad. Forensic Scis., Sigma Xi, Phi Lambda Upsilon. Avocations: sailing; music. Office: U Ala Criminalistics Lab Birmingham AL 35294

SMITH, FREDERICK WALLACE, transportation company executive; b. Marks, Miss., Aug. 11, 1944; s. Frederick C. S.; m. Dianne Davis. Grad., Yale U., 1966. Cert. comml. pilot. Founder, chmn. bd., chief exec. officer Fed. Express Corp., Memphis, 1972—. Served with USMC, 1966-70. Office: PO Box 727 Memphis TN 38194*

SMITH, FURMAN MASON, optometrist; b. Columbia, S.C., Aug. 19, 1949; s. J. Lewis and Aline H. (Mason) S.; m. Elizabeth Ann Gay, Aug. 25, 1973; children—Matthew Mason, Parker Madison. B.S. in Biology, The Citadel, 1971, M.B.A., 1985; O.D., So. Coll. Optometry, 1976. Diplomate Nat. Bd. Optometry. Lic. optometrist, S.C., Ga., Tenn., Ohio. Assoc. Drs. Scarborough, Lopanik & Smith, Charleston, S.C., 1980-81; practice optometry Family Vision Care, Mt. Pleasant, S.C., 1981—, pres., 1983—; clin. investigator Allergan Pharms., Irvine, Calif., 1981—; sec., bd. dirs. Southeastern Vision Service Plan, Norcross, Ga., 1982—. Chmn. planning bd. Trident United Way, Charleston, 1985; bd. dirs. Carolina Lowcountry ARC, Charleston, 1985. Served to capt. USAF, 1976-79. Bausch & Lomb fellow, 1975; recipient Outstanding Clinician award Bausch & Lomb, 1976. Mem. Trident C. of C. (East Cooper steering council 1982—, Small Businessperson of Quarter 1985, chmn. bus. dialog com. 1984), Am. Optometric Assn., S.C. Optometric Assn., Coastal Carolina Optometric Assn. (pres. 1984—). Episcopalian. Clubs: Carolina Yacht, Optimist. Lodge: Rotary. Home: 1198 Ambling Way Mount Pleasant SC 29464 Office: Family Vision Care 1035 Hwy 17 By-Pass Mount Pleasant SC 29464

SMITH, G. ARTHUR, JR., communications company executive; b. New Orleans, Mar. 12, 1935; s. Guerdon Arthur and Freddie Olivia (Hyde) S.; m. Darlene Wayve Rash, Dec. 25, 1958; children—Stephen Guerdon, Lauren Elizabeth, Stuart Arthur, Andrew Wade. B.B.A., Tulane U., 1957. With Ochsner Found. Hosp., New Orleans, 1958-62; br. mgr. community relations Xerox Corp., Dallas, 1962-67; asst. v.p. for univ. devel. Tulane U., New Orleans, 1968-72; prin., exec. v.p. Performance Communications Inc., N.Y.C., Los Angeles and Paris, 1972—; pres. Visual Image Programs, Inc., Gretna, Va., 1980—; cons. in field. Author: (with Thomas J. Deegan and Merrill Gerstner) Sales Meetings That Sell, 1973. Editor, devel. assoc.: (with Peter Binney) Meeting and Management Techniques, 1979. Recipient Balanced Mgmt. award IBM-World Trade, 1975, Pres.'s award Tulane U., 1977. Democrat. Episcopalian. Avocations: music, antique furniture, philately, numismatics, western philosophy. Office: Visual Image Programs Inc 671-B Whitney Ave Gretna LA 70053

SMITH, GARY DICKENS, personnel executive; b. Brookhaven, Miss., Sept. 9, 1944; s. Emmett Burnell and Dana Pauline (Dickens) S.; B.S. in Psychology, U. So. Miss., 1966. Regional payroll and employee benefits mgr. Great A & P Tea Co., Inc., New Orleans, 1977-80, regional claims mgr., 1976-77, dir. personnel, 1975-76, asst. personnel dir., 1968-75; payroll and personnel supr. Tulane U., New Orleans, 1980; regional dir. human resources Fleming Cos., Inc., Dothan, Ala., 1980—. Active United Way; chmn. adv. bd. Distributive Edn., New Orleans pub. schs.; mem. indsl. adv. com. S.E. Ala. Rehab. Ctr. Mem. Am. Soc. Personnel Adminstrn., Wiregrass Personnel Assn., Dothan-Houston County Personnel Mgrs. Com., Dothan-Houston County C. of C. Democrat. Baptist. Home: 1705 Briarwood Dr Dothan AL 36303 Office: 3119 Ross Clark Circle NW Dothan AL 36303

SMITH, GEORGE DEE, retired tobacco company executive, bank executive; b. Winston-Salem, N.C., Nov. 23, 1929; s. George Franklin and Vera Virginia (Hilton) S.; m. Jeannine Rose Meacham, May 23, 1953; 1 dau., Dee Ann. A.B., U. N.C., 1951. With R.J. Reynolds Tobacco Co., 1955—, dir., comptroller, 1970—, v.p., 1972, sr. v.p., 1973—; chmn., chief exec. officer Macdonald Tobacco Inc., Montreal, Que., Can., 1974-76; pres., chief operating officer R.J. Reynolds Tobacco Internat., Inc., 1976-80; sr. v.p. R.J. Reynolds Tobacco Co., 1980-81, exec. v.p., 1981-85, retired; pres., chief exec. officer 1st Home Fed., 1986—; dir. 1st Union Nat. Bank, Hunter Pub. Co., Carolina Medicorp, Inc. Bd. dirs. Moravian Home, Inc., Excellence Fund of U. N.C., Greensboro, United Way of Forsyth County; trustee Old Salem, Inc.; mem. bus. adv. council Western Carolina U.; trustee U. N.C., Greensboro. Served to lt. USNR, 1951-55. Mem. Greater Winston-Salem C. of C. (dir., 1st v.p.). Home: 317 Sherwood Forest Rd Winston-Salem NC 27104 Office: 1st Home Fed PO Box 26400 Greensboro NC 27420

SMITH, GEORGE DUFFIELD, JR., lawyer; b. Dallas, Dec. 23, 1930; s. G. Duffield and Gladys (Cassle) S.; m. Ann L. Suggs, Aug. 29, 1956; children—Jeanie, Christina, Duffield. B.S. in Bus. Adminstrn., U. N.C.-Chapel Hill, 1952; LL.B., So. Meth. U., 1957. Bar: Tex. 1957, U.S. Dist. Ct. (no. and ea. dists.) Tex. 1960, U.S. Ct. Appeals (5th and 10th cirs.) 1983. Assoc. Lyne, Blanchett & Smith, Dallas, 1957-60, Touchstone, Bernays & Johnson, Dallas, 1960-65; ptnr. Gardere, Porter & DeHay, Dallas, 1965-79, Gardere & Wynne, Dallas, 1979—; instr. Internat. Assn. Ins. Counsel Trial Acad., 1982. Elder, Highland Park Presbyn. Ch., Dallas; pres. Shakespeare Festival, Dallas, 1976; bd. dirs. Hope Cottage, Dallas, Ctr. Pastoral Care & Counseling, 1979-81. Served to capt. USAF, 56. Mem. ABA, Tex. Bar Assn., Dallas Bar Assn., Tex. Assn. Def. Counsel (pres.), Def. Research Inst. (regional v.p. 1980-83, dir. 1983-86, v.p. pub. relations 1986), State Bar Tex. (bd. dirs. 1985—), Tex. Bar Found., Internat. Assn. Ins. Counsel, Am. Bd. Trial Advocates, Trial Attys. Assn. Am. Republican. Club: Brook Hollow Golf (Dallas). Office: Diamond Shamrock Tower Suite 1500 Dallas TX 75201

SMITH, GEORGE NORVELL, physician; b. Del Rio, Tex., Oct. 13, 1947; s. Weldon Arch Smith and Angeline Kate (Patrick) Hill; m. Jean Louise Hockett, July 29, 1972; children—Michelle Renee, Heather Diane, Brian Eugene, Kevin Wayne. B.S., U. Tex.-El Paso, 1970; D.O., Kansas City Coll., 1974. Intern Lakeside Hosp., Kansas City, Mo., 1974-75; family practitioner West Med. and Surg. Clinic, West, Tex., 1975—; clin. assoc. prof. Tex. Coll. Osteo. Medicine, Ft. Worth, 1982—; med. dir. West Rest Haven, 1976—. Bd. dirs. West United Meth. Ch., 1980—, council of ministries, 1980—; team physician West Pub. Schs., 1975—. Mem. Am. Osteo. Assn., Tex. Osteo. Med. Assn., Am. Coll. Osteo. Gen. Practitioners, Kansas City Coll. Osteo. Medicine Alumni Assn. (pres. 1982), West C. of C. Club: Sokol Gymnastics Assn. West (pres. 1982-84). Lodge: Kiwanis. Avocations: gymnastics; sports medicine; volleyball. Home: 1211 N Davis West TX 76691 Office: West Med and Surgical Clinic 500 Meadow West TX 76691-1099

SMITH, GEORGE ROSE, justice Ark. Supreme Ct.; b. Little Rock, July 26, 1911; s. Hay Watson and Jessie Alice (Rose) S.; student Washington and Lee U., 1928-31; LL.B., U. Ark., 1933; m. Peg Newton, Dec. 3, 1938; 1 dau., Laurinda Hempstead. Admitted to Ark. bar, 1933; practiced in Little Rock, 1933-49; mem. firm Rose, Dobyns, Meek & House; asso. justice Ark. Supreme Ct., 1949—, also mem. com. jury instrns. Served to maj. AUS, 1942-46. Mem. Ark. Bar Assn., Inst. Jud. Adminstrn., Sigma Alpha Epsilon, Phi Delta Phi. Author: Arkansas Annotations to Restatement of Trusts, 1938; Arkansas Mining and Mineral Law, 1942; A Primer of Opinion Writing, 1967. Home: 2 Cantrell Rd Little Rock AR 72207

SMITH, GEORGE THORNEWELL, state supreme court justice; b. Camilla, Ga., Oct. 15, 1916; s. George C. and Rosa (Gray) S.; student Abraham Baldwin Agrl. Coll., 1940; LL.B., U. Ga., 1948; m. Eloise Taylor, Sept. 1, 1943. Admitted to Ga. bar, 1947; practiced in Cairo, Ga., from 1947; atty. City of Cairo, 1949-58, Grady County, Ga., 1950-59; solicitor Cairo City Ct., 1951-59; mem. Ga. Ho. of Reps., 1959-67, speaker, 1963-67; lt. gov. State of Ga., 1967-71; atty. City of East Point (Ga.), 1973-76; judge Ga. Ct. Appeals, Atlanta, 1976-80; assoc. justice Ga. Supreme Ct., Atlanta, 1980—; mem. exec. com. Appellate Judges Conf., 1981—. Bd. dirs. Nat. Arthritis Found. Served to lt. comdr. USN, 1940-45. Mem. ABA, State Bar Ga., Cobb County Bar Assn., Am. Legion, VFW. Democrat. Baptist. Clubs: Kiwanis, Moose. First person in Ga. history to be elected to all three brs. of govt. Office: Supreme Ct Judicial Bldg Atlanta GA 30334

SMITH, GEORGE WILLIAM, safety engineer; b. Tarentum, Pa., Aug. 1, 1937; s. Charles James and Edith L. (Johnson) S.; m. Sylvia P. Grove, Aug. 27, 1966; children—Amber, Caroline, Melessia. B.S., Pa. State U., 1964; B.S. in Aero. Engring., Embry-Riddle Aero. U., 1969. Registered profl. engr., N.C.; cert. safety profl. Jr. research pharmacologist Norwich Pharmacal Co., 1964-65; electronic technician Naval Ordinance Research Lab., Pa. State U., 1965-66; test engr. United Aircraft Research Labs., Hartford, Conn., 1969-70; safety engr. Aetna Life & Casualty Co., Hartford, 1970-71; safety and fire protection engr. Indsl. Risk Insurers, Charlotte, N.C., 1971-79; safety engr. McNeary Ins. Cons. Service, Charlotte, 1979-83; instr. fire protection Central Piedmont Community Coll., Charlotte, 1983-85; product safety engr., dir. staff engr. Bush Hog Implement div. Allied Products Corp., Selma, Ala., 1985—. Served with USN, 1956-60. Mem. Am. Soc. Safety Engrs., Am. Soc. Agrl. Engrs. Avocations: flying; fishing; painting. Office: Bush Hog Implement Div PO Box 1039 Selma AL 36701

SMITH, GERALD BUELL, airline captain, real estate broker; b. Stockton, Calif., June 15, 1938; s. Manuel Lawrence and Phyllis Gwendolyn (Austin) S.; m. Carolyn Louise Freeman, Dec. 19, 1967 (div. Apr. 1975); children—Jess, Brett, Blair. Student, San Diego City Coll., 1962, Southwestern Coll., 1963-64; grad., Tex. Realtors Inst., 1971; B.C.A. magna cum laude, Dallas Bapt. Coll., 1982; postgrad., U. Dallas, 1982-83. Enlisted U.S. Navy, 1955, advanced through grades to lt. comdr., 1965; officer, pilot, instr. U.S. Navy, 1955-65; capt. Delta Air Lines, Dallas, 1965—; real estate broker, Irving, 1973—. Bd. dirs. Irving Community Concert Assn., 1978-80. Named Disting. Toastmaster Toastmasters Internat. 1981, Toastmaster of Yr., Dist. 25 Toastmasters 1978. Mem. Irving C. of C. (dir. 1973-78), Airplane Pilots Assn., Nat. Speakers Assn., Internat. Platform Assn., Jaycees, Mensa, Tex. Assn. Realtors. Republican. Lodge: Toastmasters (pres. 1976-77, gov. dist. 1979-80). Avocations: theater organ; coin collecting; sailing; fishing; hunting. Office: PO Box 153003 Irving TX 75015

SMITH, GERALD H., bank holding company executive. Pres., chief exec. officer Allied Bancshares, Inc. Office: 1000 Louisiana Houston TX 77002*

SMITH, GLENN ALVIN, hospital administrator; b. Forest Hills, Ky., Feb. 19, 1946; s. Willie Lawson and Ethel (Blackburn) S.; m. Sharon Frances Skidmore, June 29, 1969; children—Robert Glenn, Paul David, Kate Marie, Matthew Holden. B.S. in Bus. Adminstrn., Berea Coll., 1969. Administrv. asst. Appalachian Regional Hosp., Whiteburg, Ky., 1969-73; program administr. Mountain Comprehensive Health, Hazard, Ky., 1973-76, Indian Mountain Health, Williamsburg, Ky., 1976-77; adminstr. J.G. Ford Meml. Hosp., Georgetown, Ky., 1977-82; chief exec. officer Scott Gen. Hosp., Georgetown, 1982—, sec. bd., 1982—. Bd. dirs., sec., treas. Scott County Jr. Pro Basketball, Georgetown, 1980-82. Mem. Ky. Hosp. Assn. (council 1977—), Bluegrass Hosp. Dist., Lexington Hosp. Council. Democrat. Baptist. Avocations: hunting, fishing, camping, woodworking. Office: Scott Gen Hosp 1140 Lexington Rd Georgetown KY 40324

SMITH, GRANT WARREN, II, physical sciences educator, university official; b. Kansas City, Mo., Jan. 21, 1941; m. Constance M. Krambeer, 1962; 1 son, Grant Warren III. B.A., Grinnell Coll., 1962; Ph.D. (NIH fellow), Cornell U., 1966, postgrad. (DuPont fellow), 1967. Asst. prof. chemistry Cornell U., Ithaca, N.Y., 1966-68, vis. prof., Am. Council on Edn. fellow, 1973-74; head, dept. chemistry and chem. engring. U. Alaska, Fairbanks, 1968-73, pres. univ. assembly, 1976-77; assoc. prof., 1968-77, prof., 1977-78; prof. phys. scis. U. Houston-Clear Lake, 1979-84, dean Sch. Scis. and Techs., 1979-83, spl. asst. to provost, 1984; v.p. for acad. affairs Southeastern La. U., Hammond, 1984—. Bd. dirs. Houston Area Research Ctr., 1982-83; violinist, pres. exec. bd. Clear Lake Symphony, 1980-84. Fellow Explorers Club; mem. Am. Assn. Higher Edn., Am. Assn. Univ. Adminstrs. (dir. 1982-85), AAUP, AAAS, Am. Chem. Soc., Royal Soc. Chemistry (London), Campus Safety Assn., Soc. Econ. Botany, Am. Soc. Pharmacognosy, Ethnopharmacology Soc., Nat. Speleological Soc., Am. Spelean History Assn., Arctic Inst. N.Am., Am. Polar Soc., Sigma Xi, Phi Kappa Phi. Lodge: Rotary. Office: Southeastern La U Box 768 University Station Hammond LA 70402

SMITH, GUY LINCOLN, III, zoological park executive; b. Johnson City, Tenn., Mar. 4, 1922; s. Guy L. and Thelma (McNab) S.; m. Laura Orr, Oct. 9, 1946; children—Guy Lincoln, Marie L. Smith Camors, Christopher Zachary. Student U. Tenn., 1940-41. Sales mgr. Sta. WKGN, 1953-61; gen. sales mgr. Sta. WTVK-TV, 1965-74; pres. Nelson-Chessman Advt. and Mktg. Agy., Knoxville, Tenn., 1962-64; acting zoo dir. Knoxville Zool. Park, 1971-74, exec. dir., 1974—; bds. dirs. Kaosiung City Zoo, 1976, City of Taipei New Zoo, 1976. Author: A House for Joshua, 1984. Bd. dirs. Knoxville Internat. Trade Mart, 1974-80; founder, bd. dirs. Knoxville Siser City Program; bd. dirs. Tenn. Valley Fair. Served to lt. USAAF, 1943-45. Recipient Community Service award, Knoxville C. of C., 1973, Exemplary Achievement Commendation, Sister Cities Internat., 1981; named hon. citizen City of Kaohsiung, 1976. Profl. fellow Am. Assn. Zool. Parks and Aquariums (internat. studbook keeper for Indian Lion, species coordinator Species Survival Plan for Indian Lion); mem. Internat. Union for Conservation of Nature and Natural Resources Cat Specialists Group, Kappa Sigma. Republican. Roman Catholic. Office: 3333 Woodbine Ave PO Box 6040 Knoxville TN 37914

SMITH, HAMPDEN HARRISON, III, journalism educator, journalism consultant; b. Lynchburg, Va., Sept. 11, 1940; s. Hampden Harrison Jr. and Katharine Greenway (Russell) S.; m. Aine Marguerite Peterson, Aug. 30, 1964; children—Katharine Enid, H. Harrison IV. B.A., Randolph-Macon Coll., 1962; M.A., Boston U., 1967; postgrad. U. Va., 1975-78. Nat. fgn. news editor News Leader, Richmond, Va., 1968-71, asst. city editor, 1971-74; asst. prof. journalism Washington and Lee U., Lexington, Va., 1974-81, assoc. prof., 1981—; speaker, cons. newspaper assns. and cos. Contbr. articles to profl. jours. and mags. Pres. United Way Lexington-Rockbridge County, Va., 1983—. Mem. Soc. Profl. Journalists, Am. Polit. Sci. Assn., Assn. Edn. Journalism and Mass Communications. Episcopalian. Home: 304 S Jefferson St Lexington VA 24450 Office: Washington and Lee U Dept Journalism and Communications Lexington VA 24450

SMITH, HAROLD COLBY, retired graphic arts executive; b. Clifton, Ill., Aug. 28, 1903; s. Weldon Charles and Alice Mary (Colby) S.; m. Maude Adams, May 9, 1930; children—Lewis Adams, Carolyn Colby (Mrs. Kent Chambers Davies), Miriam Goodale. A.B., U. Ill., 1927. With advt. dept. Chgo. Tribune, 1927-30; with J.J. Little & Ives, N.Y.C., 1930-31; with Colonial Press, Inc., Clinton, Mass., 1931-73, pres., dir., 1937-72; pres., dir. C.H. Simonds Co., 1943-61, Colonial Offset, Inc., Clinton, 1961-68; v.p., dir. Victoreen Leece Neville, Inc., Cleve., 1967-73; treas., dir., exec. com. Rex. Corp., West Acton, Mass., 1955-59; cons. Am. Enka Corp., Ashville, N.C., 1957-67; dir., treas. Nashoba Engring. Co., Inc., Gilbert Harold, Inc.; mem. adv. com. Worcester County Nat. Bank, 1962-68; dir. Freeman, Cooper & Co., San Francisco, Colorcon, Inc., West Point, Pa., 1972-78. Mem. fin. bd. Town of Concord, 1950-57, bd. selectmen, 1957-61, chmn., 1958-61; trustee Clinton Hosp. Assn., 1948-70, v.p., 1950-70; trustee Mus. of Sci., Miami, Fla., 1973-78; mem. Nat. Def. Exec. Res., 1959—. Served as pvt. Q.M.C., U.S. Army (at age 14), 1918-19, Bordeaux, France. Mem. Asso. Industries Mass. (dir. 1960-70), Am. Inst. Graphic Arts, Worcester Metal Trades Assn. (dir. 1947-49), Soc. Colonial Wars, Soc. of Cincinnati, SAR, Phi Kappa Sigma. Republican. Clubs: Rotary (hon.) (Clinton); Social Circle, Concord Country (Concord, Mass.); Hyannisport (Mass.); Bass River Yacht (gov. 1961-65); Key Biscayne Yacht (Fla.) Home: 1045 Mariner Dr Key Biscayne FL 33149

SMITH, HARRY K., diversified company executive; b. Pitts., 1911; married. Pres. Big Three Industries Inc. (formerly Big Three Indsl. Gas & Equipment Co. and predecessors), Houston, 1956-64, chmn. bd., chief exec. officer, 1964—, also dir.; ptnr. Smith Mining & Exploration Co.; dir. Lincoln Electric Co., Tex. Commerce Bancshares. Gov. adviser William Marsh Rice U.; trustee Lake Erie Coll. Office: Big Three Industries Inc 3535 W 12th St Houston TX 77253*

SMITH, HARWELL FITZHUGH, clinical psychologist; b. Heidelberg, Germany, Nov. 1, 1951; came to U.S., 1952; s. Harwell Fitzhugh and Louise Mae (Hocking) S.; m. Marthanne Olivia Manion, June 11, 1977; 1 child, Hayley Manion. B.S., U. Tenn., 1973, M.A., 1976, Ph.D., 1978. Lic. psychologist, Ky. Clin. psychologist Foothills Mental Health Program, Lenoir, N.C., 1978-81; program dir. Eastern State Hosp., Lexington, Ky., 1982-85; pvt. practice clin. psychology, Lexington, 1985—. Mem. Am. Psychol. Assn., Southeastern Psychol. Assn., Ky. Psychol. Assn. Democrat. Home: 1639 Duntreath Dr Lexington KY 40504 Office: 1517 Nicholasville Rd Lexington KY 40503

SMITH, HENRY LEROY, educational administrator; b. Mt. Holly, N.C., July 25, 1931; s. Henry L. and Jennie M. (Hill) S.; A.B., Lenoir Rhyne Coll., 1967; Ed.M., U. Va., 1962, Ed.D., 1967; m. La Vonne Elaine Stroupe, Nov. 12, 1955; children—Preston Browning, Robin Elaine. Tchr. elem. and secondary levels N.C. public schs., 1955-60; dir. spl. edn. Lynchburg (Va.) public schs., 1961-66, Charlotte-Mecklenburg (N.C.) public schs., 1966-69; sr. state plan officer Bur. Edn. for Handicapped, U.S. Office Edn., Washington, 1969-73; chmn. spl. edn. dept. Auburn (Ala.) U., 1973-76; dir. internat. programs Latin Am. and Africa, Goodwill Industries Am., Bethesda, Md., 1976-77; asst. state supt. edn. La. State Dept. Edn., Baton Rouge, 1976—; cons. to numerous local public sch. systems in various states, 1966-79, state edn. agys., 1967-79; mem. profl. adv. com. Epilepsy Found. Am., 1981; lectr. various colls. and univs., 1963-79; mem. faculty U. Va., 1963-66, Lynchburg Coll., 1965. Mem. Mental Health Bd., State of Va., 1964-66, N.C., 1968-69; pres. Lynchburg Mental Health Assn., 1964-66, Lynchburg Sheltered Workshop, Inc., 1965-66, Charlotte Mental Health Assn., 1968, Charlotte Assn. Ret. Citizens, 1969, Auburn Mental Health Assn., 1975; chmn. (N.C.) Gov.'s Study Commn. Spl. Edn., 1969; mem. La. Gov.'s Commn. on the Deaf, 1981. Served with USN, 1947-49. Recipient Disting. Public Service award La. Assn. Ret. Citizens, 1977, Man of the Year award, City of Lynchburg, 1966, W. Kuhn Barnett award, 1967; Disting. Service award La. Assn. Gifted/Talented, 1979; Educator of Year, Phi Delta Kappa, 1979, Gov.'s Cup, La. Assn. Retarded Citizens, 1980. Fellow Am. Assn. Mental Deficiency; mem. Internat. Council for Exceptional Children (gov.-at-large 1978—, 1st v.p. 1980-81, pres.-elect 1981-82), NEA, La. Assn. Educators, Phi Delta Kappa, Kappa Delta Pi. Baptist. Clubs: Lions, Rotary. Home: 1256 Kenilworth Pkwy Baton Rouge LA 70808 Office: Box 44064 La State Dept Edn Baton Rouge LA 70804

SMITH, HILARY HERBERT, economist; b. Washington, Jan. 11, 1947; s. Jay and Eleanor Louise (West) S.; m. Julianne Hope Wendt, Jan. 7, 1978; children—Cooper, Martin. B.S. in Mech. Engring., Va. Polytech. Inst., 1971; B.A. in Econs., Am. U., 1975; M.A. in Econs., Georgetown U., 1979; Ph.D. in Econs., Iowa State U., 1982. Mech. engr. U.S. Navy Naval Ship Engring. Ctr., Washington, 1971-79; economist Fed. Res. Bank Dallas, 1982—. Mem. Am. Econ. Assn., Am. Agrl. Econ. Assn., Western Agrl. Econ. Assn., So. Agrl. Assn. Democrat. Episcopalian. Avocations: automobiles; gardening. Office: Research Dept Fed Reserve Bank of Dallas 400 South Akard St Dallas TX 75222

SMITH, HORACE CARROLL, lawyer, state senator; b. Gray Court, S.C., June 11, 1922; s. John H. and Josie A. (Kesler) S.; grad. Spartanburg Jr. Coll., 1940; B.S., Wofford Coll., 1942; postgrad. Duke U. Law Sch., 1946-48; m. Dorothy Williams, July 21, 1942. Mem. firm Whiteside, Smith, Jones & Duncan, Spartanburg, S.C.; county solicitor, 1960-66; mem. S.C. Ho. of Reps., 1951-56, 59-60, S.C. Senate, 1967—. Trustee, S.C. Baptist Found.; deacon Fernwood Bapt. Ch.; pres. Carolina-Piedmont Found. Served with USAAF, 1942-45. Mem. S.C. Bar Assn., County Bar Assn. (past pres.). Democrat. Clubs: Lions, Masons, Shriners. Office: 220 N Church St Box 1144 Spartanburg SC 29301*

SMITH, HOWARD ROSS, educator, researcher, consultant; b. Des Moines, July 6, 1917; s. John Truman and Miriam Sylvia (Ross) S.; m. Gwendolyn Thomas Collins, Feb. 20, 1943; children—David, Janet, Richard. A.B., Simpson Coll., 1938; M.A., La. State U., 1940, Ph.D., 1945. Instr. La. State U., Baton Rouge, 1940-43; economist War Prodn. Bd., Washington, 1943-46; assoc. prof. U. Ga., Athens, 1946-49, prof., 1949—, dept. head, 1963-76. Rockefeller Found. fellow, 1948-49; recipient Ford Found. award, Egypt, 1961-63; Fulbright award, Columbia, 1973. Mem. Acad. Mgmt. Democrat. Presbyterian. Author: Economic History of U.S., 1955; Government and Business, 1958; Democracy and Public Interest, 1960; The Capitalist Imperative, 1975; Management, 1980. Home: 382 Westview Ave Athens GA 30606 Office: U Ga Athens GA 30602

SMITH, HUGH EDWARD, JR., engineer, consultant; b. Atlanta, Aug. 6, 1935; s. Hugh Edward and Eunice (Scheff) S.; m. Eleanor Wilson, Sept. 9, 1956; children—Lynda Elaine, Diane Evelyn, Kathryn Ellen. B. Indsl. Engring., Ga. Inst. Tech., Atlanta, 1961; postgrad. Ga. State U.-Atlanta, 1983—. Registered profl. engr., Ga. Program mgr. NASA Contracts, Marietta, Ga., 1977; flight test dir. Lockheed-Ga. Co., Marietta, 1978—, staff engr., 1980-82, 83—; pres. Tele-Gard, Inc., Smyrna, Ga., 1975—; cons. Meridian Capital Co., N.Y.C., 1982, Miss. State U., Starkville, 1982. Contbr. articles to profl. jours. Coach, Little League, Atlanta, 1974-76; pres. ch. class Sandy Springs Meth. Ch., Atlanta, 1975. Served with U.S. Army, 1959. Recipient Disclosure of Invention award Lockheed-Ga. Co., 1980. Mem. Soc. Flight Test Engrs. (pres. Southeastern chpt. 1982, dir. 1983), Soc. Profl. Engrs. (sec. Sandy Springs chpt. 1975), Ga. Tech. Alumni Assn., Soaring Soc. Am. Home: 6490 Arlington Dr Dunwoody GA 30338

SMITH, HUNTINGTON FRANK, JR., judge, retired federal law enforcement officer; b. Kingston, Pa., Mar. 22, 1931; s. Huntington Frank and Mabel (Pugh) S.; m. Ann Moss, June 28, 1958; children—Cynthia Ann, Matthew Huntington, Andrew Moss. Student Capitol Radio Engring. Inst., 1950-52, U. Md., 1960. Law enforcement officer Met. Police, Washington, 1954-55, U.S. Secret Service, 1955-57, U.S. Dept. Interior, 1957-70; magistrate judge Morgan County, Berkeley Springs, W.Va., 1978—. Trustee Harmony Hall Elem. Sch., Fort Washington, Md., 1963; scoutmaster Shenandoah council Boy Scouts Am., 1974; mgr., coach Little League Baseball, Berkeley Springs, 1976. Served with USN, 1952-53, Korea. Recipient Excellence of Service award U.S. Dept. Interior, 1968; named Ambassador of Goodwill, Sec. of State, Charleston, W.Va., 1981, Mountaineer Millionaire, Treas. W.Va., 1985. Mem. Am. Judges Assn., Counseling Service (chmn. 1983-85), Cherry River Navy (adm.). Democrat. Lodges: Rotary (pres. 1984-85), Masons. Office: Morgan County Courthouse Fairfax St Berkeley Springs WV 25411

SMITH, JACK C., association executive. Pres., Roanoke C of C, Va. Office: Roanoke C of C 14 W Kirk Ave Roanoke VA 24011*

SMITH, JACK CARL, publisher; b. Cleve., Sept. 11, 1928; s. John Carl and Florence Agnes (O'Rourke) S.; m. Nannette June Boyd, Dec. 1, 1962; 1 dau., Colleen Wentworth. Student, Baldwin Wallace Coll., 1948-51, postgrad., 1958; B.A., Ohio U., 1954. Rep. Flying Tiger Line, Inc., Los Angeles, 1958-61; prin. Pub. Rep. bus., Cleve., 1961-64; pub. Penton/IPC, Inc., Cleve., 1964—; dir. Central Cleve. Corp., Nat. Distbn. Terminals. Served with USAF, 1954-58. Mem. Am. Mgmt. Assn., Material Handling Inst., Am. Trucking Assn., Nat. Council Phys. Distbn. Mgmt., Family Motor Coach Assn., Recreation Vehicle Industry Assn., Am. Bus. Press, Mag. Pubs. Assn., Sigma Xi., Sigma Chi. Club: Wings (N.Y.C.).

SMITH, JACKSON STOCKS, III, advertising executive; b. Charlotte, N.C., Sept. 9, 1946; s. Jackson Stocks and Ethel Vara (Brady) S.; B.S., Auburn U., 1968; M.B.A., U. Ga., 1969; m. Dorothy Elizabeth Crutsinger, Aug. 3, 1978; children—Stacey, Katherine, Shelby. Sales rep. Scott Paper Co., Atlanta, 1969-70, sr. sales rep., Jacksonville, Fla., 1970-71; advt. mgr. Internat. Dairy Queen, Inc., Mpls., 1971-74; pres. Jackson Smith Advt., Inc., Atlanta, 1974-85; exec. v.p. Barrett Smith Vargas Zeeman Inc., Atlanta, 1985—. Episcopalian. Clubs: Cherokee Town and Country, Atlanta Auburn. Home: 5350 N Powers Ferry Rd Atlanta GA 30327 Office: 6540 Powers Ferry Rd Suite 150 Atlanta GA 30339

SMITH, JAMES ALTON, organization administrator, counselor; b. Corpus Christi, May 28, 1942; s. Hugh Alton and Alice Marie (Vaughn) S.; m. Sarah Ann Wiatt, Feb. 9, 1974; children—James Wiatt, Susan Marie, Stephen Alton. B.A. in Psychology, Covenant Coll., 1969; M.Ed. in Counseling, West Ga. Coll., 1972; D.Min. in Family Counseling, Luther Rice Sem., 1984. Lic. profl. counselor, Ga. Counselor, Ga. Dept. Offender Rehab., Valdosta, 1972-74; family counselor, Huntsville, Ala., 1974-78; family seminar dir. Presbyn. Evangelistic Fellowship, Atlanta, 1975-78; area dir. Christian Broadcasting Network 700 Club, Atlanta, 1978-84; founding dir. Inst. Bibl. Therapy, Huntsville, 1984—; asst. prof. Atlanta Sch. Bibl. Studies, 1978-84; dir. counseling Ingleside Presbyn. Ch., Atlanta, 1978-84. Served with USNR, 1960-66. Mem. Assn. Christian Clin. Counselors (diplomate 1982), Am. Mental Health Counselors Asns., Am. Assn. for Counseling and Devel. Republican. Pentecostal. Lodge: Lions. Avocations: performing with auto-harp; jogging; marathons. Home: 1949 Litle Cove Rd Brownsboro AL 35471 Office: Inst Bibl Therapy 115 Longwood SW Huntsville AL 35801

SMITH, JAMES DRAYTON, JR., dentist; b. Birmingham, Ala., Mar. 8, 1944; s. James Drayton and Vernzola (McCarley) S.; m. Sharon Scarbrough, June 4, 1966; children—James Drayton III, Charles Benjamin. B.S. in Indsl. Mgmt., Auburn U., 1967; B.S., U. Ala.-Birmingham, 1980, D.M.D., 1984. Sales engr. Ala. Power Co., Birmingham, 1967-71, Dixie Indsl. Co., Birmingham, 1971-78; pvt. practice gen. dentistry, Birmingham, 1984—. Recipient Alumni Leadership award U. Ala., 1984. Mem. ADA, Birmingham Dist. Dental Soc., Acad. Gen. Dentistry, Ala. Dental Assn. (student leadership award 1984). Republican. Presbyterian. Home: 4604 Five Oaks Circle Birmingham AL 35243 Office: 4505 Valleydale Rd Birmingham AL 35243

SMITH, JAMES LAMARR, printer, museum curator; b. Fort Towson, Okla., Feb. 26, 1916; s. Lamar Thomas and Anna Maude (Spears) S.; m. Elizabeth Ann Alford, July 8, 1968; children—Cynthia Smith Brown, LaDell, LaMarr Jr. Student pub. schs., Fort Towson. Owner, operator Meml. Indian Mus., Broken Bow, Okla., 1962—; printer McCurtain Gazette, Idabel, Okla., part-time 1953—. Contbr. to Poets of Am., 1940. Active Oak Grove Baptist Ch., Broken Bow, 1953—. Democrat. Avocations: hunting; painting; archeology. Home and Office: PO Box 483 Broken Bow OK 74728

SMITH, JAMES P., lawyer, state senator; b. Texarkana, Ark., Oct. 17, 1950; s. T.P. and Frances (Dollarhyde) S. B.A., U. Ala., 1973, J.D., 1976. Bar: Ala. 1976. Assoc., Ford, Caldwell, Ford & Payne, Huntsville, 1976-78; ptnr. Harrison and Smith, Huntsville, 1978-83, Smith and Stevens, Huntsville, 1983-84, Smith and Waldrop, 1984—. Nat. v.p. Young Democrats, 1973-75; mem. Ala. Ho. of Reps., 1978-82, Ala. State Senate, 1982-86. Recipient Nat. Comdr.'s award DAV, 1982; Legis. Crime Fighting award Ala. Dist. Attys. Assn., 1982; Good Govt. award U. Ala.-Huntsville, 1983. Mem. Ala. Bar Assn., Order of Coif. Club: Jaycees. Home: 1820 Carson Ln Huntsville AL 35805 Office: Smith and Waldrop Attys 108-A S Side Sq Huntsville AL 35801

SMITH, JAMES RALPH, plastic surgeon; b. Lowell, Ark., July 11, 1927; s. James Harrison and Canda S.; m. Sally Tow, Sept. 4, 1949; children—Chris, Canda, Ralph. B.S., U. Ark., 1948; M.D., U. Ark., 1952. Diplomate Am. Bd. Surgery, Am. Bd. Plastic Surgery. Intern, Harris Hosp., Ft. Worth, 1952-53; resident in surgery U. Tex. Med. Br. Hosps., Galveston, 1954-59; practice medicine specializing in plastic surgery, San Antonio, 1964—; mem. staff So. Meth. Hosp., St. Luke Hosp., San Antonio; prof. plastic surgery U. Tex.-San Antonio, 1967-71; instr. U. Tex. Med. Br.-Galveston, 1970—. Served to maj. M.C., USAF, 1956-64. Mem. AMA, Am. Soc. Plastic and Reconstructive Surgery, Fellowship Christian Athletes. Democrat. Baptist. Club: Oak Hills Country.

SMITH, J(AMES) ROY, educator; b. Washington, Ga., Sept. 13, 1936; s. James Roy and Nellie Irene (Mansfield) S.; A.B., Mercer U., 1956; postgrad. Brown U., 1956-57, Oxford (Eng.) U., 1963. Public sch. tchr., Cranston, R.I., 1957-58, Charleston, S.C., 1962-64, 76-79, Atlanta, 1964-76; tchr. English dept. Berkeley High Sch., Moncks Corner, S.C., 1979—. Served to lt. j.g. USNR, 1959-62. English Speaking Union study grantee, 1963—. Mem. Sons and Daus. of Pilgrims (gov. Ga. br. 1975-76, hon. life gov. 1976), SAR (sec.-treas. S.C. soc. 1980-81, Silver Good Citizenship award Ga. soc. 1972), Sons of Revolution, Soc. 2d War with Gt. Britain, S.C. Hist. Soc., Kappa Phi Kappa. Republican. Episcopalian. Home: 110 Coming St Charleston SC 29403

SMITH, JAMES RUSSELL, city official; b. Memphis, Mar. 25, 1931; s. James P. and Marguerite (Morris) S.; m. Lela Ann Howard, Mar. 25, 1949; children—James Russell, Steven Howard. Grad. high sch. With Memphis Fire Dept., 1950-85, dep. chief, 1976-81, dir., 1981-85; chief Germantown Fire Dept., 1985—. Fire rep. Shelby United Neighbors, Memphis, 1970, Memphis Goodfellows, 1981-83, Handicapt, Inc., Memphis, 1981-85. Recipient cert. of appreciation U.S. Secret Service, 1984, 85; Pub. Service award Cotton Carnival Assn., 1983. Mem. Internat. Soc. Fire Service Instrs., Internat. Assn. Fire Chiefs, Southeastern Assn. Fire Chiefs, Tenn. Assn. Fire Chiefs, Shelby County Assn. Fire Chiefs, Met. Fire Chiefs Internat. Assn. Methodist. Lodges: Masons, Shriners, Moose. Avocation: jogging. Home: 8871 E Shelby Dr Memphis TN 38115 Office: 7766 Farmington Blvd Germantown TN 38138

SMITH, JANIE WILKINS, educator; b. Columbia, La., Apr. 5, 1930; d. James Climent and Hester (Bibb) Wilkins; B.A., La. Tech. U., 1951; postgrad. Fla. State U., 1962-70; U. Fla., 1962-63, U. South Fla., 1963-64; m. Thomas L. Smith, Nov. 3, 1950 (div.); children—Linda Karen, Thomas, Jr., Eric Andrew. English librarian Morehouse Parish Sch. Bd., Bastrop, La., 1951-52, Union Parish Sch. Bd., Farmerville, La., 1952-56, East Carroll Parish Sch. Bd., Lake Providence, La., 1957-60, Union Parish Schs., Farmerville, 1970-75, Ouachita Parish Schs., Monroe, La., 1976-79; ref. librarian Ouachita Parish Public Library, 1960-62; librarian lang. arts Brevard County Bd. Public Instrn., Titusville, Fla., 1962-70; info. specialist Columbian Chems. Co., Swartz, La., 1980-83; tchr. English, West Orange High Sch., Winter Garden, Fla., 1983—. Mem. AAUW (membership com.), Fla. Council Tchrs. English, Fla. Edn. Assn., Spl. Library Assn., Nat. Library Assn. Methodist. Home: 409 Birchwood Dr Monroe LA 71203 Office: East Union Acad Marion LA

SMITH, JARRELL MCRAE, psychologist; b. Americus, Ga., Nov. 28, 1946; s. Alma Jackson and Carolyn Jewel (McRae) S.; m. Karen Frances Gregory, Mar. 4, 1979. B.A., Ga. So. Coll., 1968; M.A., Ball State U., 1973; Ph.D., U. S.C., 1980. Psychologist Crafts-Farrow Hosp., Columbia, S.C., 1973-76; project developer S.C. Dept. Mental Health, Columbia, 1976-78; psychologist S.C. Dept. Youth Services, Columbia, 1978-82; dir. instl. psychology, 1982-85, asst. commr. for treatment services, 1985—. Author: Manual for Classification of Delinquents, 1979. Served with USAF, 1969-72. Mem. Am. Psychol. Assn., Am. Assn. Group Psychotherapy, Am. Correctional Assn. Club: Rotary. Avocations: gardening; home computers; jogging; cocker spaniels. Home: 140 Hartwood Circle Columbia SC 29210 Office: Asst Commr SC Dept Youth Services PO Box 7367 Columbia SC 29202

SMITH, JEAN CAROL, basketball coach, physical education educator; b. Dunn, N.C., Apr. 5, 1943; d. Iva Neighbors Whittenton. B.S., East Carolina U., 1964; M.A.Ed., Western Carolina U., 1968; Ed.D., U. N.C.-Greensboro, 1977. Tchr., coach Henderson City Schs. (N.C.), 1964-67, Erskine Coll., Due West, S.C., 1968-70; tchr., coach Longwood Coll., Farmville, Va., 1970-75; tchr., coach Murray State U. (Ky.), 1977-84, head basketball coach, 1977—. Recipient Alumni Disting. Service award Longwood Coll. Mem. AAUP, AAHPERD, Women's Assn. Basketball Coaches. Democrat. Baptist. Home: 1326 Diuguid Dr Murray KY 42071 Office: Murray State U Dept HPER Murray KY 42071

SMITH, JEFFREY MICHAEL, lawyer; b. Mpls., July 9, 1947; s. Philip and Gertrude E. (Miller) S.; 1 son, Brandon Michael. B.A. summa cum laude, U. Minn., 1970; student U. Malaya, 1967-68; J.D. magna cum laude, U. Minn., 1973. Bar: Ga. 1973. Assoc. Powell, Goldstein, Frazier & Murphy, 1973-76; ptnr. Rogers & Hardin, 1976-79, Bondurant, Stephenson & Smith, Atlanta, 1979-85, Arnall Golden & Gregory, 1985—; vis. lectr. Duke U., 1976-77, 79-80, 86; adj. prof. Emory U.; lectr. Vanderbilt U., 1977-82. Bd. visitors U. Minn. Law Sch., 1976-82. Mem. ABA (vice chmn. com. profl. officers and dirs. liability law 1979-83, chmn. 1983-84, vice chmn. com. profl. liability 1980-82, mem. standing com. lawyer's profl. liability 1981-85, chmn. 1985-86), State Bar of Ga. (chmn. profl. liability and ins. com. 1978—, trustee Inst. of Continuing Legal Edn. in Ga. 1979-80), Order of Coif, Phi Beta Kappa. Office: 55 Park Place 4th Floor Atlanta GA 30335

SMITH, JEROME HAZEN, pathologist; b. Omaha, Oct. 9, 1936; s. Hazen Dow and Helen Kellogg (Hewitt) S.; B.S. in Medicine, U. Nebr., 1960, M.D., 1963, M.S. in Anatomy, 1962; M.Sc.Hyg. in Tropical Public Health, Harvard U., 1969; m. Marilyn Kay Stauber, 1961; children—Nathaniel Hazen, Kathryn Hewitt, Andrew Kellogg. Rotating intern Mpls.-Hennepin County Gen. Hosp., 1963-64; from jr. asst. resident in pathology to chief resident in clin. pathology Peter Bent Brigham Hosp., Boston, 1964-72, asso. pathologist, 1973; from research fellow in pathology to instr. Harvard U. Med. Sch., 1964-73; pathologist, head dept. Inst. Med. Evangelique, Kimpese, Congo, 1968; chief autopsy service Inst. Tropical Medicine, Hosp. Mama Yemo, Fomeco, Kinshasa, Zaire, 1973-74, med. dir. anatomic pathology, 1974; asst. prof. U. Ariz. Med. Sch., Tucson, also dir. anatomic pathology and microbiology Tucson VA Hosp., 1975-76; mem. faculty U. Tex. Med. Br., Galveston, 1976—, prof. pathology, 1979—, dir. autopsy service, 1977—, dir. clin. parasitology lab., 1977—, asso. prof. Grad. Sch., 1978—; cons. Shriners Burn Inst., Galveston, 1980—. Served as officer M.C., USNR, 1969-71. Recipient Avalon Tuition award, 1961; NSF fellow, 1959; Poynter fellow, 1960; USPHS trainee, 1961, 68-69; diplomate Am. Bd. Pathology. Mem. Am. Soc. Clin. Pathologists, Internat. Acad. Pathologists, Am. Soc. Parasitologists, Am. Soc. Tropical Medicine and Hygiene, Am. Assn. Pathologists, N.Y. Acad. Scis., Tex. Med. Assn., Tex. Soc. Pathologists, Tex. Soc. Infectious Diseases, Galveston County Med. Soc., Royal Soc. Tropical Medicine and Hygiene, Sigma Xi. Republican. Contbr. numerous articles to med. jours. Home: 3731 Manor Ln Dickinson TX 77539 Office: Dept Pathology (K-101) U Tex Med Br Galveston TX 77550

SMITH, JERRY LEE, state senator; b. Muskogee, Okla., Dec. 6, 1943; s. Hollis C. and Eulema M. (Hall) S.; B.A., Okla. State U., 1967; J.D., U. Tulsa, 1970; m. Sally Howe. Admitted to Okla. bar, 1971; mem. firm Frazier and Dyer, Tulsa, 1972-80, firm Frazier, Smith and Farris, 1980-81, Frazier and Smith, 1981-83, Frazier, Smith, Underwood & Cates, 1983—; mem. Okla. Ho. of Reps., 1972-80; mem. Okla. Senate, 1980—, minority whip, 1982—; mem. Am. Legis. Exchange Council. Mem. Okla., Tulsa County bar assns., Okla. Trial Lawyers Assn., Nat. Republican Legislators Assn., Phi Delta Phi. Office: 1424 Terrace Dr Tulsa OK 74104

SMITH, JIM, state official, lawyer; b. Jacksonville, Fla., May 25, 1940; s. John Albert and Fannie Elizabeth (West) S.; m. Carole Ann Clark, Dec. 29, 1962; children—Kathryn Elizabeth, Robert Scott, James Clark. B.A. in Govt. and Bus. Adminstrn., Fla. State U., 1962; J.D., Stetson U., 1967. Bar: Fla. 1967. Sole practice, Tallahassee, 1967; exec. asst. to sec. of state, dept. sec. of state Fla., 1967-70; exec. asst. to lt. gov. dep. sec. commerce, sr. staff asst. to gov. Fla., Tallahassee, 1970-72; ptnr. Smith, Young & Blue, Tallahassee, 1972-77; atty. gen. State of Fla., Tallahassee, 1978-82, 82—. Mem. adv. bd. Nat. Fedn. of Parents for Drug Free Youth; chmn. Gov.'s Adv. Com. on Corrections. Served to capt. USAR, 1962-64. Recipient Furtherance of Justice award, 1980; Pub. Service award U.S. Atty. Gen., 1980; named Conservationist of Yr., Fla. Audubon Soc., 1981. Mem. ABA (criminal law com.). Democrat. Methodist. Lodges: Northside Rotary. Masons (Tallahassee). Office: Dept Legal Affairs The Capitol Tallahassee FL 32301

SMITH, JIM RAY, realtor, former professional football player; b. West Columbia, Tex., Feb. 27, 1932; s. William G. and Laura A. (Brown) S.; B.B.A., Baylor U., 1957; m. Paula M. Braden, Apr. 2, 1955; children—James Ray, Paul Braden, Ripple Alicia. Mem. Cleve. Browns Football Club, 1956-62, Dallas Cowboys Football Club, 1963-64; owner Jim Ray Smith & Co., comml. and indsl. realty, Dallas, 1965—; dir. Interfirst Bank, Addison; mem. Dallas Equalization Bd., 1972-73. Vice chmn. realtors sect. com. gifts, trusts and bequests Wadley Insts. Molecular Medicine, Dallas, 1973—; bd. dirs. Baylor U. Stadium Corp.; pres. Cotton Bowl Athletic Assn. Served with AUS, 1955-56. Named to High Sch. All-Star Football Game, 1950, All S.W. Conf. Baylor U., 1953, 54, Coll. All-Star Football Team Chgo. News, 1955, Browns All-Time All-Star Team, 1962, play in Pro-Bowl Los Angeles Times, 1958, 59, 60, 61, 62, Baylor U. Hall of Fame, 1968; named Lineman of Week, UP and AP, 1953, All Am. Baylor U., 1953, All Pro Cleve. Browns, 1958, 59, 60, 61, 62. Mem. Dallas Bd. Realtors, Tex., Nat. assns. realtors, Ex-student Assn. Baylor U. Hankamer Sch. Bus. (pres. 1973), Baylor B Assn., Baylor Letterman's Assn. (pres.), Baylor Alumni Assn., Baylor Bear Club, Fellowship Christian Athletes (pres. chpt. 1969), Bill Glass Evangelistic Assn. (treas. 1971, dir.), NFL Alumni Assn. (past pres. Dallas chpt.), Baylor Lettermans Assn. (pres.), Salesmanship Club Dallas (dir. 1976). Baptist (deacon). Club: Bent Tree Country. Home: 7049 Cliffbrook St Dallas TX 75240 Office: PO Box 182 Addison TX 75001

SMITH, JOAN TRUEHILL, public health program director; b. New Orleans, Sept. 21, 1941; d. Marshall and Elizabeth (May) Truehill; B.S., La. State U., 1964; postgrad. IBM, 1968, Tulane U., 1969, Upjohn Inst., 1970, Delgado Coll., 1970; M.P.H., Tulane U., 1978; cert. of supervisory techniques, La.; m. William O. Smith, June 8, 1963; children—Frank, Angela, Treena, Crystal. Tchr. Orleans Parish Sch. Bd., New Orleans, 1964; nurse's asst. Total Community Action, New Orleans, 1966, recreational supr., 1966-67; clk. Family Planning, Inc., New Orleans, 1967, asst. records analyst, 1967-68, data processing supr., 1968-71, mgr. computer ops., 1971-72; asst. to dep. dir. Family Health Found., New Orleans, 1972-73, grants mgr., 1973-74, program coordinator, 1974; exec. asst. La. Family Planning Program, La. State Dept. Health and Human Resources, New Orleans, 1974-76, dir. family planning Office Health Services and Environ. Quality Family Planning Program, New Orleans, 1976—. Recipient Family Planning award Fed. Women's Program New Orleans, 1970. Mem. Nat. Assn. Exec. Females, Am. Public Health Assn., La. Public Health Assn., NAACP, Nat. Family Planning and Reproductive Health Assn. (bd. dirs.), Nat. Council Negro Women. Epsilon Sigma, Tau Gamma Delta (pres. La. charter chpt.). Baptist. Home: 153 Louisiana St Westwego LA 70094 Office: 325 Loyola Ave New Orleans LA 70112

SMITH, JODY BRANT, educator; b. Macon, Ga., May 7, 1943; s. Jody Bass and Gladys Irene (Patterson) S.; A.B., Mercer U., 1965; M.A., U. Miami, 1969, postgrad., 1970; m. Deborah Faye Everett, Aug. 20, 1971 (div. 1978); children—Heather Deborah, Jody Brant II; m. Germana D. Teixeira, Nov. 10, 1981. Asst. prof. philosophy and humanities Pensacola Jr. Coll., 1970-81, assoc. prof., 1981—; pres. Pyrrho Press, Inc., Gulf Breeze, Fla., 1974-77; pres. Image of Guadalupe Research Project, Inc., 1979-82; invited reader Indian Philos. Congress, New Delhi, 1975. Bd. dirs. Pensacola Right to Life, Inc., 1973-76, Fla. State Right to Life Com., Inc., 1974-75; provider written testimony U.S. Ho. of Reps. and U.S. Senate coms., 1975, 76, 83. Fla. Endowment for Humanities grantee, 1974. Fellow Am. Soc. Psychical Research; mem. Cath. Philos. Assn., Psychical Research Found., Beta Beta Beta. Co-author: The Tilma—An Infrared Study, 1981; author: Guadalupan Studies, 1982; The Image of Guadalupe, 1983; The Guadalupe Madonna, 1983, rev. edit., 1985; contbr. articles to profl. jours. Home: 1503 E Lakeview Ave Pensacola FL 32503 Office: 1000 College Blvd Pensacola FL 32504

SMITH, JOEL SHERLON, pharmacologist, consultant; b. Waycross, Ga., July 25, 1953; s. Jack Palmer and Dorothy (Sarvis) S.; m. Mary George Chiotellis, May 22, 1982. B.S. in Pharmacy, U. Ga., 1976; Ph.D. in Pharmacology, Med. Coll. Ga., 1981. Registered pharmacist, Ga., Ala. Staff pharmacist St. Joseph's Hosp., Augusta, Ga., 1977-81; community pharmacist Eastern Valley Drugs, Bessemer, Ala., 1981-82; postdoctoral research fellow Univ. Ala., Birmingham, 1981-83; mgr. sci., tech. affairs Hoechst-Roussel Pharms., Inc., Atlanta, 1983—. Served with Ga. Air N.G., 1972-78. Recipient Sigma Xi Research award, 1981. Mem. Am. Pharm. Assn., Am. Assn. Hosp. Pharmacists, N.Y. Acad. Scis., Phi Delta Chi, Sigma Xi. Baptist. Contbr. articles to sci. jours.

SMITH, JOHN MARVIN, III, surgeon, educator; b. San Antonio, July 31, 1947; s. John M. and Jane (Jordan) S.; m. Jill Jones, Aug. 1, 1981. M.D., Tulane U., 1972. Diplomate Am. Bd. Surgery, Am. Bd. Thoracic Surgery. Intern, U. Tex. Southwest Med. Sch., Dallas, 1972-73; resident in surgery U. Tex., San Antonio, 1973-77, resident in thoracic and cardiovascular surgery Tex. Heart Inst., Houston, 1977-79; practice medicine specializing in cardiovascular and thoracic surgery, San Antonio, 1979—; mem. Staff Bapt. Med. Ctr., S.W. Tex. Meth. Hosp., Santa Rosa Med. Center, Met. Hosp., Nix Meml. Hosp.; clin. asst. prof. surgery U. Tex. Health Sci. Ctr., San Antonio, 1979—. Contbr. articles to profl. jours. Bd. mgrs. Bexar County Hosp. Dist. Served to maj. USAF, 1979-81. Fellow Am. Coll. Cardiology, ACP; mem. AMA, Tex. Med. Assn., Bexar County Med. Soc., Denton A. Cooley Cardiovascular Surg. Soc., Cooley Hands, J. Bradley Aust Surg. Soc., Soc. Air Force Clin. Surgeons, San Antonio Surg. Soc., San Antonio Cardiology Soc., So. Thoracic Surg. Assn., Tex. Hist. Soc., Sigma Alpha Epsilon, Nu Sigma Nu. Episcopalian. Clubs: San Antonio Country, The Argyle, Giraud, Order Alamo, German, Christmas Cotillion, Sons Republic Tex., San Antonio Gun. Home: 204 Zambrano San Antonio TX 78209 Office: 7711 Louis Pasteur St #510 San Antonio TX 78229

SMITH, JOHN RICHARD, railroad executive; b. Appalachia, Va., Jan. 24, 1927; s. Robert Clarence and Mary Lettitia (Mullins) S.; m. Betty Jane Humbert, Mar. 26, 1947; children—Margaret Lettitia Smith Kibler, John Richard, Mary Jane Smith Wardlow. Student Hiwassie Coll., 1950-52; B.A., Lincoln Meml. U., 1954. Tchr., football/basketball coach Big Stone Gap High Sch. (Va.), 1954-55, St. Paul High Sch. (Va.), 1955-56, Handley High Sch., Winchester, Va., 1957-60; with So. R.R. Co., Appalachia, Va., 1960—, supt. safety, Somerset, Ky., 1972—. Served with USN, 1944-46. Decorated Bronze Stars. Mem. Nat. Safety Council, Ky. Peace Officer Assn. Democrat. Methodist. Club: Optimist. Home: 315 Sioux Trail Somerset KY 42501

SMITH, JOSEPH FRANCIS, JR., insurance company executive; b. Union City, N.J., Apr. 2, 1943; s. Joseph F. and Irma A. (Holtgrave) S.; m. Carole A. Smyth, June 26, 1965; children—Karen J., Beverly L., Leigh A. B.S., Fordham U., 1965. Tchr., coach St. Rose High Sch., Belmar, N.J., 1965-78; br. mgr. Met. Ins. Co., Hollywood, Fla., 1979—. Fellow Nat. Assn. Life Underwriters, Gen. Agy. Mgrs. Assn. Democrat. Roman Catholic. Clubs: Lauderdale Lakes Athletic, Point Pleasant Jaycees. Home: 3300 NW 40th Ct Lauderdale Lakes FL 33309 Office: 4601 Sheridan St Hollywood FL 33321

SMITH, JOY ESTELLE, retired educator; b. Antlers, Okla., Dec. 17, 1915; d. Barney and Eula (Chapman) S. B.S. in Home Econs., Okla. State U., 1945; M.S., U. Houston, 1962; postgrad. Tex. Woman's U., 1962-73, also Okla. State U. Cert. tchr., Okla., Calif. Classroom tchr. various schs., Okla., Calif., Tex., 1945-1963; dean women, head home econ. dept. Panhandle State U., Goodwell, Okla., 1963-67; asst. prof., head home econs. dept. Wharton County Jr. Coll., Tex., 1967-77; ret. Co-chmn. Atoka County Dem. Party, Okla., 1981-83, 85-87, del. to dist. and state convs., 1981, 83, 85; pres. Gen. Fedn. of Women's Clubs, Atoka, 1984-86, dist. chmn. prevention of child abuse, 1984-86. Recipient Cert. of Appreciation, U.S. Dem. Senatorial Campaign Com., 1984. Mem. Tex. Ret. Tchrs. Assn., Nat. Ret. Tchrs. Assn., Nat. Ret. Persons Assn., Southeast Okla. Garden Clubs (chmn. dist. program and yearbook com. 1985-87), Yellow Rose Garden Club (rec. sec. 1983-87). Presbyterian. Avocations: bridge; travel; gardening; reading; interior design. Home: PO Box 414 Atoka OK 74525

SMITH, JUDITH PELHAM, hospital administrator; b. Bristol, Conn., July 23, 1945; d. Marvin Curtis and Muriel (Chodos) Pelham; m. Hubert Lipscomb Smith, Jan. 27, 1968. B.A., Smith Coll., 1967; M.P.A., Harvard U., 1975. Various govt. positions, 1968-72; prin. analyst Urban Systems, Cambridge, Mass., 1972-73; dir. devel. and planning Roxbury Dental and Med. Group, Boston, 1975-76; asst. to dir. gen. med. and ambulatory care Peter Bent Brigham Hosp., Boston, 1976-77, asst. dir. ambulatory care, 1977-79; asst. v.p. Brigham & Women's Hosp., Boston, 1980-81; dir. planning and mktg. Seton Med. Ctr., Austin, Tex., 1981-82, pres., 1982—; cons. Robert W. Johnson Found., Princeton, N.J., 1980-81. Trustee A. Shivers Radiation Therapy Ctr., Austin, 1982—, Marywood Maternity and Adoption Agy., Austin, 1982—; bd. dirs. Seton Fund, Austin, 1982—, League House, Austin, 1982—, Tex. Conf. Catholic Health Facilities, 1985—, HOSPAC, 1986—. Contbr. articles to publs. Charter mem. Leadership Tex., Austin, 1983; mem. Gov.'s Job Tng. Coordinating Council, Austin, 1983-84, U. Tex. Social Work Found. Adv. Council, Austin, 1983-86. Mem. Am. Hosp. Assn., Tex. Hosp. Assn., Tex. Hosp. Assn. Council on Adminstrv. Practice Com. on Major Vol. Hosps., Coll. Health Care Execs. (nominee), Austin C. of C. (dir. 1983-85). Office: Seton Med Center 1201 W 38th St Austin TX 78705

SMITH, KATHRYN MUNDY, psychometrist; b. St. Albans, N.Y., May 16, 1951; d. Stuart Springer and Jean (Murray) S. B.A., Fairleigh U., 1972; M.A., SUNY, 1976. Vocat. evaluator Hilltop Industries, Mt. Morris, N.Y., 1976-78; psychometrist Brauner Psychiat. Inst., Smyrna, Ga., 1979-80, Ctr. for Interpersonal Studies, Smyrna, 1980—. Fellow Am. Psychol. Assn., Ga. Psychol. Assn. Home: 922 Myrtle St Apt 4 Atlanta GA 30309 Office: Ctr for Interpersonal Studies 3188 Atlanta St Smyrna GA 30080

SMITH, KENNETH EDWARD, clergyman, pastoral psychotherapist; b. Columbia, S.C., July 5, 1949; s. Edward Dubose and Daphene (Shell) S.; m. Donna Lynn Morgan, June 10, 1972; children—Alison Elizabeth, Ashley Morgan. B.A., Wofford Coll., Spartanburg, S.C., 1971; M.Div., Yale U., 1974; D.Min., Vanderbilt U., 1975; postdoctorial student Duke U., 1980. Ordained elder S.C. Conf. United Meth. Ch., 1976; assoc. minister Bethel United Meth. Ch., Spartanburg, 1976-77, minister Lake View Charge (S.C.), 1977-81; dir. Grand Strand Pastoral Counseling Service, Myrtle Beach, S.C., 1981—; adj. prof. religion and philosophy St. Leo's Coll.; cons. in field. Bd. dirs. Myrtle

Beach Family YMCA, 1983—, Leadership Grand Strand, 1983. Mem. Am. Assn. Pastoral Counselors, Am. Assn. Marriage and Family Therapists, Am. Assn. Sex. Educators, Counselors and Therapists. Democrat. Clubs: Dunes Golf and Tennis (Myrtle Beach); Grand Strand Sertoma; Chicora Rotary. Home: 13 Elizabeth Ln Myrtle Beach SC 29577 Office: PO Box 2967 Myrtle Beach SC 29578

SMITH, KENNETH JOSEPH, sociology educator; b. Buffalo, Mar. 10, 1937; s. Kenneth Edward and Dorothy (Brenn) S. children—Sean, Kevin, Conor. A.B., U. Dayton, 1959; M.A., Ohio State U., 1961; Ph.D., Duke U., 1970. Assoc. prof. sociology U. Miami, Coral Gables, 1965—. Home: 5595 SW 80th St South Miami FL 33143 Office: U Miami Coral Gables FL 33124

SMITH, KENNETH Y(EOMAN), architectural engineering educator and administrator, architectural consultant; b. Liberty, S.C., Dec. 28, 1923; s. Jesse E. and Kate A. Smith; m. Eloise Peeples, Feb. 19, 1952; children—Kaye Grant, Kenneth Y., Jayne Eloise. B.S. in Arch., Clemson U., 1953; postgrad. Furman U., 1972-73, U. S.C.-Spartanburg, 1977-78. Dist. engr. Am. Oil Co., Jacksonville, Fla., 1958-62; assoc. architect Townes Assocs., Architects, Greenville, S.C., 1962-64; faculty Greenville Tech. Coll., 1964—, dept. head archtl. engring. tech., 1983—, past chmn. Faculty Senate and Faculty Adv. Council; archtl. cons., site planner. Hon. mem. Humane Soc. Pickens County, S.C.; mem. Pickens County Art Assn. Served with C.E., U.S. Army, 1942-46. Mem. Am. Soc. Engring. Edn., S.C. Edn. Assn., S.C. State Employees Assn. Democrat. Baptist. Lodge: Masons. Author self-instructional books in field; qualified fallout shelter analyst, Dept. Def., Office Civil Def.

SMITH, KENNITH LEO, artist, educator; b. Ralls, Tex., July 20, 1941; s. Leonard Henry and Christeene (Lowrance) S.; m. Gayle Enloe, Aug. 14, 1965 (div. Feb. 1981); 1 dau., Stephanie. B.S., Tex. Tech U., 1966, M.S., 1971. Cert. tchr., Tex. One man shows: Lubbock Art Assn., 1979, Southwestern Med. Sch., 1982, Irving Art Assn., 1982, Artisans Gallery, Houston, 1982, Artisan's Studio, Dallas, 1983; group shows include: Am. Watercolor Soc., 1978, Lubbock Art Assn., 1978, Artist Workshop, Lubbock, 1979, Artisan's Studio, Dallas, 1980, 81, 82, 83, 84, 85, D'Art Dallas, 1983, 84, 85, Dallas Arts Dist., 1983; represented in permanent collections: Mus. of Tex. Tech U., Mus. of S.W., Sohio Oil Co., Furr's Inc., Tex. State Savs., Tex. Bank Dallas; head dept. art Mackenzie Jr. High Sch., Lubbock, 1966-70; head dept. art Dunbar-Struggs High Sch., Lubbock, 1970-80; owner Artisan's Studio, Dallas, 1980—; tchr. Brookhaven Coll., Dallas, 1981-82; drawing instr. Art Inst. Dallas, 1983—; curriculum developer State of Tex., 1975-80. Mem. Parks and Recreation Com., Lubbock, 1975-78. Recipient Best of Show award Tex. Tech. Mus., 1978; Merit award Tex. Fine Arts, 1983; Best of Show award Mus. Natural History Dallas, 1983, also Tex. Fine Arts Dallas region show, 1983; Grumbacher award, Bud Briggs award, Dick Blick-Northlight award Southwestern Watercolor Soc., 1985, others. Mem. West Tex. Watercolor Soc. (pres. 1978-79), Western Fedn. Watercolor Socs. (pres. 1979-80, merit award 1979), Tex. Watercolor Soc. (purchase award 1982), Southwestern Water Color Soc. (award 1983), Am. Watercolor Soc. Methodist. Club: Tex. Fine Arts (dir. 1975-79). Author: Art Guide, 1977.

SMITH, LANTY L(LOYD), lawyer textile manufacturing company executive; b. Sherrodsville, Ohio, Dec. 11, 1942; s. Lloyd H. and Ellen Ruth (Newell) S.; B.S. with honors in Mathematics, Wittenberg U., Springfield, Ohio, 1964; LL.B. with honors, Duke U., 1967; m. Margaret Hays Chandler, June 11, 1966; children—Abigail Lamoreaux, Margaret Ellen, Amanda Prescott. Admitted to Ohio bar, 1967; assoc. firm Jones, Day, Cockley & Reavis, Cleve., 1967-68, 69-73; partner firm Jones, Day, Reavis & Pogue, Cleve., 1974-77; exec. v.p., Burlington Industries, Inc., Greensboro, N.C., 1977—. Mem. bd. visitors Duke U. Sch. Law; nat. adv. council Wittenberg U.; mem. adv. council sch. Bus. and Econs. U. N.C.-Greensboro; trustee N.C. Ctr. for Pub. Policy Research. Served with Office Gen. Counsel, USN, 1968-69. Mem. Am. Bar Assn. Episcopalian. Home: 1401 Westridge Rd Greensboro NC 27410 Office: 3330 W Friendly Rd Greensboro NC 27410

SMITH, LARRY IRA, lawyer; b. Augusta, Ga., Dec. 18, 1950; s. John Milledge and Estelle Julia (Barnard) S.; m. Jo Ann Priest, Aug. 5, 1972; children—Brooke Estelle, Barclay Gerald. B.A., Augusta Coll., 1974; J.D., U. Ga., 1977. Bar: Ga. 1977, U.S. Dist. Ct. (so. dist.) Ga. 1978, U.S. Ct. Appeals (5th cir.) 1978, U.S. Ct. Appeals (11th cir.) 1981. Assoc. Fleming & Blanchard, Augusta, Ga., 1977-82; ptnr. Paine, Dalis, Smith & McElreath, Augusta, 1982—; city ct. judge, Grovetown, Ga., 1982—; dir. RETAC, Inc., Augusta. Mem. Com. to Elect Sam Sibley D.A., Augusta, 1980, Com. to Re-elect Sam Sibley, Augusta, 1984, Com. to Elect Hardy Gregory, Supreme Ct., Augusta, 1983. Served with USMC, 1970-71. Mem. ABA, Assn. Trial Lawyers Am., State Bar Ga., Ga. Trial Lawyers Assn., Augusta Bar Assn., Augusta Area Trial Lawyers Assn. Presbyterian. Clubs: Augusta Athletic, Augusta Country. Home: 75 Conifer Circle E Augusta GA 30909 Office: Paine Dalis Smith & McElreath 454 Greene St Augusta GA 30901

SMITH, LAWRENCE JACK, congressman; b. N.Y.C., Apr. 25, 1941; s. Martin and Myra (Bank) S.; m. Sheila Smith, July 7, 1962; children—Grant, Lauren. Student, NYU; J.D., Bklyn. Law Sch. Chmn. City of Hollywood Planning and Zoning Bd., 1975-78; mem. Fla. Ho. of Reps., 1978-82, 98th Congress from Fla.; mem. adv. bd. Transflorida Bank, 1980—. Pres. Stirling Elem. Sch. PTA, Hollywood Fla., 1975-76; mem. Democratic Exec. Com. Broward County, Fla., 1972—. Named Man of Yr. Jewish Nat. Fund, Civitan Internat., 1982, Friend of Edn. Classroom Tchrs. Assn., 1980-81. Mem. South Broward Bar Assn. (pres.). Jewish. Lodges: Optimists; B'nai B'rith. Home: 3511 N 52d Ave Hollywood FL 33021

SMITH, LAWRENCE LEIGHTON, conductor; b. Portland, Oreg., Apr. 8, 1936; s. Lawrence Keller and Bonita Evelyn (Wood) S.; m. Kathleen Dale, June 4, 1976; 1 dau., Laura; children by previous marriage—Kevin, Gregory; stepchildren—Kristine, John. B.S. cum laude, Portland State Coll., 1956; grad. magna cum laude, Mannes Coll. Music, N.Y.C., 1959. Mem. faculty Mannes Coll. Music, 1959-62; prof. piano Boston U., 1963-64; asst. condr. Met. Opera, 1964-67; mem. faculty Curtis Inst., Phila., 1968-69, Calif. Inst. Arts, 1970-72, U. Tex., 1962-63; prin. guest condr. Phoenix Symphony, 1970-73; music dir., condr. Austin (Tex.) Symphony, 1971-72, Oreg. Symphony, Portland, 1973-80; music dir. San Antonio Symphony, 1980-85; pres., music dir. Louisville Orch., 1983—, Music Acad. of West, 1985—; guest condr. N.Y. Philharm., Los Angeles Philharm., Tulsa Philharm., Winnipeg Orch. (Man., Can.), Minn. Orch., Cin. Symphony, St. Louis Symphony. Recipient 1st prize Met. Internat. Condrs. competition, 1964. Mem. Am. Fedn. Musicians, Mensa. Buddhist.

SMITH, LEE ANDERSON, petroleum exploration geologist; b. Wichita Falls, Tex., Mar. 9, 1927; s. Robert Lee and Clara Jeanette (Stulce) S.; m. Elizabeth Miremont, Mar. 21, 1958; 1 child, Christopher (dec.). B.A., Tex. Christian U., 1957, M.A., 1959; Ph.D., Stanford, U., 1962. Sr. staff geologist Monsanto Chem. Co., Houston, 1962-64; research assoc. Exxon Prodn. Research, Houston, 1964-81; dir. research Esso France, Bordeaux, 1973-77; geology chmn. Tex. Christian U., Fort Worth, 1981-84; sr. cons. Amerada Hess Corp., Houston, 1984—; dir. Inst. for Tertiary and Quaternary Research, Nebr. Acad. Sci. Vol. editor: Sepm Symposium on Calcareous Nannofossils, 1973. Lead palgontologist: (book) Deep sea Drilling Project Leg X, 1973. Precinct chmn. Houston Ind. Sch. Bd. Race, Houston, 1970. Served to sgt. USMC, 1943-53, PTO. NSF fellow; Socony-Mobil scholar Stanford U., 1960-61. Mem. Am. Assn. Petroleum Geologists, Geol. Soc. Am., Soc. Econ. Paleontologists and Mineralogists, AAAS, Smithsonian Inst., Sigma Xi. Democrat. Baptist. Avocations: philately, art history, writing. Home: 2739 Centenary Houston TX 77005 Office: Amerada Hess Corp 1200 Milam 7th Floor Houston TX 77002

SMITH, LEROY WILLIAM, oil company executive, geologist; b. Standish, Mich., May 12, 1941; s. Connor Dart and Alice Amelia (Tennant) S.; m. Helen Jane Frier, June 24, 1964; children—Craig D., Emily K. B.S. in Geology Mich. State U., 1962, M.S. in Geology, 1967; student computer system tng. Tulane U., 1968-70. Cert. petroleum geologist, geol. scientist. Exploration geologist La. Land & Exploration, Houston, 1972-76; dir. exploration C&K Petroleum, Houston, 1976-78, v.p. exploration, 1979-80; exec. v.p. Consol. Resources of Am., Houston, 1980—; pres. Consol. So. Corp., Houston, 1983—; dir. Consol. Resources Am., Inc., Cin. Asst. editor Gulf Coast Geology bibliography, 1970. Bd. dirs. Trailwood Village Community Assn., Kingwood, Tex., 1982-85, Kingwood Service Assn., 1982-83; vestryman Episcopal Ch. of the Good Shepherd, Kingwood, 1983—; treas. Trailwood Village Community Assn., 1975-77. Served as 2d lt. USN, 1962-65. Mem. Am. Assn. Petroleum Geologists, Houston Geol. Soc., Soc. Econ. Paleontologists and Mineralogists. Office: Consol So Corp 3838 North Belt East Houston TX 77032

SMITH, LEWIS ALAN, surgeon, educator; b. Atlanta, Aug. 9, 1946; s. Laurin G. and Mary Alice (Boggs) S.; m. Lavonne Elaine Brown, Apr. 3, 1979; children—Allison, Cheryl, Derek, Alana. B.S., U. Fla., 1968; M.D., U. Miami, 1972. Diplomate Am. Bd. Surgery. Intern, Univ. Hosp., Jacksonville, Fla., 1972-73; resident in surgery Jacksonville Health Edn. Program, Jacksonville, 1974-78; practice medicine specializing in gen. surgery, Jacksonville, 1978—; clin. asst. prof. surgery U. Fla., Jacksonville, 1978—. Served to lt. USNR, 1971-73. Mem. ACS, S.E. Surg. Congress, Fla. Assn. Gen. Surgery. Office: 3636 University Blvd S Suite C-1 Jacksonville FL 32216

SMITH, LEWIS LAWRENCE, economist; b. Phila., Dec. 19, 1933; s. Lawrence M.C. and Eleanor (Houston) S.; m. Trinita Muniz-Burogs, June 8, 1957; children—Clemson L., Stanley H., Sarah E., C. Rebecca. A.B. magna cum laude, Harvard U., 1954, M.B.A., 1958. Economist Commonwealth Oil Refining Co., San Juan, P.R., 1966-71; chief economist Econ. Devel. Adminstrn. P.R., San Juan, 1971-76; pvt. practice as cons. economist, San Juan, 1977—. Served with USAF, 1954-56. Mem. Am. Econ. Assn., Asociacion de Economistas de Puerto Rico, Nat. Assn. Bus. Economists, Sociedad Interamericana de Planificacion, Carribean Aquaculture Soc., Nat. Economists Club, P.R. C. of C. (council advs. 1984—). Office: Hacienda de Trinitarias Apdo 25028 Rio Piedras PR 00928-5028

SMITH, LINDA BRUNTON, psychology educator; b. Louisville, Feb. 13, 1957; d. William Raymond and Doris Jean (Zehnder) B.; m. Dean Scott Smith, Aug. 27, 1983. B.S. in Psychology, Eastern Ky. U., 1979, M.A., 1981. Instr. psychology Columbia State Community Coll., Columbia, Tenn., 1981—. Contbr. articles to profl. jours. Mem. AAUW, Am. Psychol. Assn., Middle Tenn. Psychol. Assn., Tenn. Psychol. Assn. Democrat. Avocations: flower arranging; sewing. Home: Milton Fox Rd Franklin TN 37064 Office: Columbia State Community Coll Hampshire Pike Columbia TN 38401

SMITH, LINDA LEA, university counselor; b. Wichita, Kans., June 18, 1958; d. Clifford Allen and Myrtle Elizabeth (Hoyne) S. B.S., Ball State U., 1981; M.S., Northwest Mo. State U., 1984. Counselor, Julia Jameson Health Camp for Children, Inc., Indpls., 1979, program dir., 1980; mem. student staff Ball State U., Muncie, Ind., 1979-81; hall dir. Northwest Mo. State U., Maryville, 1981-84; counselor Ark. State U., Jonesboro, 1984—, advisor Residence Hall Assn., Hall Council, Kays Hall, Hall Council-University Hall, Kays Hall Jud. Bd. Mem. Ark. Coll. and Personnel Assn. Democrat. Methodist. Clubs: Jonesboro Women of Today, Methodist Singles (mem. planning com.) (Jonesboro, Ark.). Avocations: swimming; weight lifting. Office: Arkansas State U PO Box 119 Student Affairs Jonesboro AR 72403

SMITH, LORETTE, ednl. adminstr.; b. Isola, Miss.; d. Ruble L. and Bertha Hoke; B.A., Greenville Coll., 1956; postgrad. Butler U., 1958, Ind. U., 1959; M.A., Fla. Atlantic U., 1969; Ed.D., Nova U., 1979; m. John Smith, Oct. 27, 1960; children—Leah Michelle, Eileen Monna. Tchr., Indpls. Public Sch. System, 1956-57, 60-63; tchr. Broward County Sch. System, Ft. Lauderdale, Fla., 1963-72, curriculum specialist, 1972-73, prin. Westchester Elem. Sch., Coral Springs, 1973—. Bd. govs. Nova U., 1975—, sec., 1978, acting chmn., 1980, vice chmn., 1981-82, pres. Drill Team Parents Assn., 1980-81; chmn. Coral Springs Cultural Soc., 1981-82; mem. grants rev. com. Tourist Devel. Council, 1981-82; mem. Consumer Protection Bd., 1981-82. Named Outstanding Woman of Yr. in Edn., Women in Communications, 1979; Little Red Sch. House award, 1978, 80. Mem. Nat. Assn. Elem. Sch. Prins., Am. Assn. Sch. Adminstrs., Broward Assn. Elem. Sch. Prins., Fla. Assn. Sch. Adminstrs., North Area Elem. Prins. (chmn. 1979-81), Phi Delta Kappa, Delta Kappa Gamma. Club: Zonta. Office: 12405 Royal Palm Blvd Coral Springs FL 33065

SMITH, LOUISE EDWARDS, school counselor; b. Fayetteville, Ark., Sept. 12, 1926; d. William Sidney and Nora (Oyler) Edwards; m. Paul E. Smith, Aug. 13, 1942 (dec. May 1982); children—Ronald Eugene, Donald Edward, Paul Eugene Jr. B.A., U. Tulsa, 1957, M.A., Calif. State U.-Long Beach, 1966; diploma in sch. counseling Okla. State U., 1972. Tchr. Tulsa Pub. Schs., 1957-63; counselor Cleveland Schs., Okla., 1965-66, Tulsa Pub. Schs., 1966—. Adv. Bd. Latch Key Children, Tulsa, 1984; sec. Okla. Elem. Counselors, Oklahoma City, 1968-69; chmn. precinct Democratic Party, Cleve., Okla., 1982. Mem. NEA, Okla. Edn. Assn., Tulsa Edn. Assn., Am. Assn. Counseling and Devel. (del. 1972-74), Okla. Sch. Counselors Assn. (pres. 1972-73), Tulsa Assn. Counseling and Devel. (pres. 1984—), Keystone Colony Property Owners Assn. (Sec. 1984-85), Kappa Delta Phi, Phi Alpha Theta, Pi Gamma Mu. Baptist. Avocations: singing; piano; water sports; bridge; canasta. Home: Route 1 Box 130 Cleveland OK 74020 Office: Roosevelt Sch 1202 W Easton St Tulsa OK 74020

SMITH, MAE MULHERIN, business educator; b. Augusta, Ga., June 21, 1945; s. Anthony Thomas and Alice Mae (Cartledge) M.; m. Roy Stanley Smith, Mar. 16, 1980. B.S., Augusta Coll., 1967; M.A., U. Ga., 1970, Ph.D., 1978. Statistician S.C. Dept. Edn., Columbia, 1971-73; tchr. North Augusta Jr. High, S.C., 1973-74; statistician EPA, Athens, Ga., 1975-76; instr. U. Ga., Athens, 1976-77; asst. prof. Ga. Coll., Milledgeville, Ga., 1977-82, assoc. prof. bus., 1982—. Mem. Milledgeville C. of C., Am. Statis. Assn., (Atlanta chpt. treas. 1976-78), Delta Sigma Pi (faculty advisor 1979—). Avocations: swimming; water skiing. Home: 103 Pecan Cove SE Eatonton GA 31024 Office: Ga Coll Sch Bus Milledgeville GA 31061

SMITH, MARILYN JOAN, educational administrator; b. Pitts., May 29, 1938; s. Joseph Edwards and Mary Elizabeth (Dolan) Lewis; B.S., U. Houston, 1959, M.A., 1962; M.S., U. Tex., Dallas, 1980; children—Joseph Lewis, Jefferson Lee, Robert Christopher. Therapist Houston Speech and Hearing Center, 1960-62; dir. Spl. Care Sch., Dallas, 1964-68; dir. edn. and day care service Dallas County Mental Health and Mental Retardation Center, 1968-70; program dir. Children, Inc., Dallas, 1970-72, Angels, Inc., Dallas, 1971-76; pres. Package Deal, Inc., 1977—; exec. dir. Creative Children's Center, 1977-82; ednl. writer Internat. House Publs. Instr. community service div. El Centro Jr. Coll., Dallas, 1968-78; faculty Richland Community Coll., 1975-78. Mem. Adv. Bd. Helping Hand Sch., Irving, Tex., 1969-78; human services adv. com. Eastfield Coll., 1975-77. Mem. Am. Assn. Mental Deficiency, Council for Exceptional Children, Gamma Phi Beta. Home: 15931 Long Vista Dallas TX 75248 Office: 14902 Preston Rd Suite 212-075 Dallas TX 75240

SMITH, MARILYN VIOLA, metaphysician, minister; b. Astoria, L.I., N.Y., Aug. 25, 1934; d. Bernard P. and DeRetta (Williamson) S.; B.S., U. Tex., 1955; grad. Esoteric Philosophy Center, Houston, 1984. m. Charles Stoneberg, June 28, 1958 (dec. Apr. 1968); m. Jon E. Curtis, Mar. 28, 1969 (div. May 1975); m. Charles Marchand, Aug. 21, 1981 (div. Oct. 1983). Ordained Minister, 1982. Pharmacist, Med. Arts Pharmacy, San Antonio, 1955-56, Northside Drug, San Antonio, 1956-58; pharmacist Jones Apothecary, Houston, 1958-68, 73-83; pharmacist Madings Drugs, 1968-69, Phillips Pharmacy, 1968-70, Gloyer's Pharmacy, 1969-73, Fed-Mart Pharmacy, Pasadena, Tex., 1970-72, Walgreen's, Houston, 1983—; founder Ctr. Metaphys. Studies, 1983, head creative manifestation of soul power, lectr. Esoteric Philosophy Center; tchr. New Age Chs., other orgns. flight instr. Barstow Aviation, Houston, 1962, free lance, 1962-64, Consol. Aero, Houston, 1967-68; participant Powder Puff Derby, 1960, Internat. Air Race, 1962, All Women's Internat. Air Race, 1964, other races; mem. 1st Women's Nat. Pylon Racing Team, 1967-71. Mem. Tex. Aviation Assn. (sec.-treas. 1962-64), Petticoat Pilots (pres. 1964-65), 99's (pres. Houston 1966-68), Aircraft Owners and Pilots Assn., Nat. Assn. Flight Instrs., Houston Metaphys. Council, Animal Behavior Soc., NOW, Tex. and Harris County Womens Polit. Caucus. Home: 22414 Lakeway Dr Spring TX 77373 Office: 10826 North Freeway Houston TX 77037

SMITH, MARK EVAN, geologist; b. Fort Worth, Aug. 1, 1956; s. Theron Lavon and Barbara Jean (Harvison) S. A.A., Tarrant County Jr. Coll., 1977; B.S., U. Tex., Arlington, 1979. Geologist, Dynamic Prodn., Inc., Fort Worth, 1979-81; chief geologist RAW Energy Corp., Weatherford, Tex., 1981-84; pres. M.E. Smith Co., Fort Worth, 1984-85; pres. M.E. Exploration Inc., Fort Worth, 1985; geologist, ptnr. Cayce Enterprises, Fort Worth, 1984—. Mem. Am. Assn. Petroleum Geologists, Soc. Econ. Paleontologists and Mineralogists, Soc. Exploration Geophysicists, Fort Worth Geol. So., Kans. Geol. Soc. Republican. Mem. Ch. of Disciples of Christ. Avocations: Scuba diving; antique collecting. Office: Cayce Enterprises 2413 E Loop 820 N Fort Worth TX 76118

SMITH, M(ARSHALL) LEE, publisher, political commentator, lawyer; b. Johnson City, Tenn., Sept. 5, 1942; s. William J. and Ruth (Marshall) S.; m. Billie Ann Gloth, Jan. 31, 1970; children—Connie, Marshall, Lily. B.A., Vanderbilt U., 1964, J.D., 1967. Bar: Tenn. 1967. Clk., U.S. Dist. Judge, Nashville, 1967-68; legis. asst. Senator Howard Baker, Washington, 1968-70; exec. asst. Gov. Winfield Dunn State of Tenn., Nashville, 1971-75; owner M. Lee Smith Publishers & Printers, Nashville, 1975—; commentator Sta. WSMV-TV, Nashville, 1984—. Columnist Tenn. newspapers, 1975—. Mem. Tenn. Bar Assn., Nashville Bar Assn., Newsletter Assn. Am., Nashville Area C. of C. Presbyterian. Club: Nashville City. Lodge: Rotary. Home: 6417 Worchester Dr Nashville TN 37221 Office: M Lee Smith Publishers & Printers PO Box 2678 Arcade Sta 162 4th Ave N Nashville TN 37219

SMITH, MARVETTE THOMAS, college administrator; b. Montgomery, Ala., Jan. 27, 1953; d. Robert Marvin and Bernice Johnetta (Morgan), Thomas; m. Richard E. Cobb, May 7, 1971 (div. 1982); 1 child, Janel Bernice; m. Charlie M. Smith, Mar. 27, 1982. B.S., Austin Peay State U., 1978; M.S., Murray State U., 1980; Ed.D., Vanderbilt U., 1984. Grad. asst. Vanderbilt U., Nashville, 1981; spl. edn. instr. Northwest High Sch., Clarksville, Tenn., 1979-83; counselor La. State U. Eunice, 1984, acting dir. spl. services and devel., 1984-85, dir. student spl. service, 1985—. Mem. Am. Assn. Counseling and Devel., S.W. Assn. Student Assistance Programs, Nat. Assn. Female Execs., Nat. Assn. Univ. Women, La. Assn. Student Assistance Programs (congl. team 1985), La. Assn. Devel. Edn. (exec. council 1985), Delta Sigma Theta (pres. 1982-83). Democrat. Club: Socialite (Eunice). Avocations: travel; tennis; reading. Office: La State U Eunice PO Box 1129 Eunice LA 70535

SMITH, MENDEL WALLACE, II, clinical pharmacist, consultant; b. Gulfport, Miss., Dec. 14, 1946; s. Mendel Wallace and Ola Gene (Warden) S.; m. Evelyn Ann Dunnaway, June 10, 1967; 1 dau., Heidi Ann. B.S. in Pharmacy, U. Miss., 1972; B.S. in Biology, U. So. Miss., 1969; D.Pharmacy, Mercer U., 1984. Lic. pharmacist, Miss., Va., N.C. Staff pharmacist Singing River Hosp., Pascagoula, Miss., 1972-74; retail pharmacy ptnr., mgr. Stan's Pharmacy, North Biloxi, Miss., 1974-76; asst. dir. Gulf Coast Community Hosp., Biloxi, Miss., 1976-77, dir. pharmacy, 1977-83; dir. clin. pharmacy Pulaski Community Hosp., Va., 1984-85; pharmacist, mgr. Jefferson Drug Co., N.C., 1985—; clin. cons. in pharmacokinetics, metabolic support, family practice Jefferson Drug Co., 1984—. Research, author Aminoglycoside Monitoring and Therapy: Comparison of Pharmacokinetic Service to Staff Physicians, 1984. Recipient Disting. Service award as dir. pharmacy Gulf Coast Community Hosp., 1982. Mem. Am. Soc. Hosp. Pharmacists, Miss. Soc. Hosp. Pharmacists, Ga. Soc. Hosp. Pharmacists, N.C. Soc. Hosp. Pharmacists, Am. Pharm. Assn., Am. Soc. Retail Pharmacists, New Orleans Mycological Soc., Nat. Wildlife Fedn., Miss. Native Plant Soc., Nat. Barrier Islands Protection Soc., Am. Motorcyclist Assn., Gulf Coast Orchid Soc. Republican. Methodist. Avocations: botany; mycology; natural sciences, motorcycle competition; sailing; wood carving. Home: Route 1 Box 51 Warrensville NC 28693 Office: Jefferson Drug Co PO Box 155 Jefferson NC 28640

SMITH, MICAH PEARCE, JR., advertising executive; b. Norman, Okla., Nov. 13, 1916; s. Micah Pearce and Julia Maud (Beeler) S.; m. Viola Sarajane Hatfield, June 1, 1946; children—Julia Annette, Carla Marie. Student U. Okla., 1936-41, corr. student, 1941-78. Dir. advt. Clinton Daily News (Okla.), 1946-53; dir. advt. Great Bend Daily Tribune (Kans.), 1953-55; ptnr., exec. v.p., gen. mgr. Indsl. Printing Inc., Oklahoma City, 1956-57; dir. advt. Daily Ardmoreite, Ardmore, Okla., 1958; dir. advt. Norman Transcript (Okla.), 1959-60; editor, pub. North Star, Oklahoma City, 1961; ptnr., exec. v.p. Gelders, Holderby & Smith, Inc., Oklahoma City, 1961-73; editor Chickasaw Times, Norman, 1970-78; fuels allocation officer State of Okla., 1973-80; chmn., pres., mgr. Media Mktg. Assocs., Inc., Oklahoma City, 1981—. Author syndicated newspaper TV column. Sec. Ruling Council of Chickasaw Indian Tribe, Ada, Okla., 1971-79; coordinator gov. campaign State of Okla., 1969-70. Served with Aviation Cadets, 1941. Recipient Blue Ribbon awards Okla. Press Assn.; Blue Ribbon award Nat. Dairy Council. Mem. Okla. Advt. Mgrs. Assn. (pres.). Presbyterian. Home: 1525 Melrose Dr Norman OK 73069 Office: 1525 Melrose Dr Nofrman OK 73069

SMITH, MICHAEL ALEXIS, petroleum geologist; b. Boston, Nov. 8, 1944; s. Albert Charles and Nina (Gronstrand) S.; m. Nancy Laura Wilson, Dec. 19, 1971; 1 child, Christine Lara. B.S., U. Mich., 1966; M.S., U. Kans., 1969; Ph.D., U. Tex., 1975. Marine geologist U.S. Geol. Survey, Washington, 1966-68, petroleum geologist, 1975-81, geochemist, 1976-81; research geochemist Getty Oil Co., Houston, 1981-83, supr. basin evaluation, 1983-84; research assoc. Texaco Inc., Houston, 1984—. Contbr. articles to profl. jours. Fellow Geol. Soc. Am.; mem. Am. Assn. Petroleum Geologists, Am. Geophys. Union, AAAS, Assn. Petroleum Geochem. Explorationists, Geochem. Soc., Internat. Assn. Geochemistry and Cosmochemistry, Houston Geol. Soc., Rocky Mountain Assn. Geologists, Soc. Organic Petrology (founding mem.). Avocations: music; running. Home: 1123 Shillington Dr Katy TX 77450 Office: Texaco Research Ctr 3901 Briarpark Houston TX 77042

SMITH, MICHAEL ARTHUR, police chief; b. Des Moines, Oct. 30, 1951; s. Robert Lee and Betty Ann (Henry) S.; m. Wanda Elaine Todd, Aug. 22, 1980; children—Melissa, Deanna, Dana, Brandy; m. Rebecca Jean Still, Dec. 7, 1973 (div. 1979). Student N. Tex. State U., 1969-70, El Centro Jr. Coll., Dallas, 1970-72, South Plains Coll., 1981-85. Lic. peace officer, Tex. Patrolman, Univ. Police Dept., Lubbock, Tex., 1980-81; chief of police Sundown Police Dept., Tex., 1981-84, Littlefield Police Dept., Tex., 1984—; advisor S. Plains Assn. Govts. Tng. Bd., Lubbock, 1984—; tng. advisor South Plains Coll., Levelland, Tex., 1984—, instr., 1983-85. Dist. commr. (George White dist. council Boy Scouts Am., 1984-85; mem. regional bd. dirs. ARC, 1984—, instr., 1984-85; bd. dirs. Salvation Army, Littlefield, 1984—. Recipient Outstanding Community Service award South Plains Coll., 1983, Outstanding Service award ARC, 1985, Outstanding Instr. award South Plains Assn. Govts., Lubbock, 1984, 85. Mem. Tex. Police Chiefs Assn., Nat. Assn. Chiefs Police, South Plains of Tex. Chiefs of Police (sec.-treas.), Tex. Narcotic Officers Assn. Baptist. Club: Rotary. Avocations: hunting, outdoor sports. Home: 511 E 13th St Littlefield TX 79339 Office: PO Box 1267 100 W 6th St Littlefield TX 79339

SMITH, MICHAEL WESTON, geologist, consultant; b. St. Albans, Vt., Jan. 18, 1955; s. George Weston and Betty Ann (Hildebrand) S.; m. Wynona Kay Latta, May 21, 1977. B.S. in Geology, Oceanography, Purdue U., 1977. Geologist, Herbert G. Davis, Inc., Oklahoma City, 1978-81; sr. geologist Phoenix Resources, Oklahoma City, 1981-82, F.C.D. Oil, Oklahoma City, 1982-83; owner, operator Condor Investments, Oklahoma City, 1983—; pres. Reconnaissance Magnetics, Inc., Oklahoma City, 1983—. Mem. Am. Assn. Petroleum Geologists, Rocky Mountain Assn. Geologists, Wyo. Geol. Soc., Four Corners Geol. Soc., Okla. Geol. Soc. Club: Hall of Fame Tip. Avocations: scuba diving; travel; camping; flying; golf. Home: 10929 Blue Fox Dr Edmond OK 73034 Office: Condor Investments 1600 E 19th Suite 203 Edmond OK 73034

SMITH, MICHAEL WILLIAM, steel corporation safety executive; b. Clarksville, Tenn., Jan. 27, 1947; s. Burch Lee and Mary Patrice (Kilpatrick) S.; m. Marie-Dominique Beauvalet, Apr. 2, 1970; children—Christopher, Nicholas. B.S., Peabody Coll., 1977, M.S., 1978. Cert. safety exec.; cert. hazard control mgr. Mental therapist DeDe Wallace Community Mental Health, Nashville, 1978-80; loss prevention rep. Liberty Mut. Ins. Co., Memphis, 1980-81; dir. safety, personnel Fischer Steel Corp., Memphis, 1981—. Served with USAF, 1967-74. Grantee NIMH, 1977, Biomed. Research Support, 1978, HEW, 1978. Mem. Am. Soc. Safety Engrs. (v.p. 1984, pres. 1985 W. Tenn. Chpt.), Nat. Fire Prevention Assn. Republican. Presbyterian. Avocations: photography; canoeing; sailing; gardening. Office: Fischer Steel Corp 3347 Pearson Rd Memphis TN 38118

SMITH, MILLARD GAMBRELL, JR., educational administrator, cattle rancher; b. Birmingham, Ala., Sept. 14, 1928; s. Millard G. and Cornelia

(Matthews) S.; m. Doris Jean Hamby, Feb. 7, 1968; 1 child, Michelle Renae. Student U. Ala., 1946-48; B.B.A. in Pre-Law, Huntingdon Coll., 1951; postgrad. Clemson U., 1971-81, U. S.C., 1982-83. Dir., coordinator Summer Youth Programs Starr, S.C. Sch. Dist. 3, S.C., 1976-82; dir. pre-vocat. edn., 1969-82; exec. sec., supt. schs. Anderson County Bd. Edn., S.C., 1982—. Exec. committeeman Anderson County Democratic Party S.C., 1974—; del. state conv. Dem. Party S.C., Cola, 1982—. Recipient Outstanding Contbn. to Edn. award Anderson County Bd. Edn., 1982. Mem. S.C. Edn. Assn., S.C. Vocat. Edn. Assn. (state pres. 1976-81), Anderson County Tchrs. Fed. Credit Union (pres. 1982-85). S.C. Prevocat. Tchrs. Assn. (state pres. 1976-81, life mem., Outstanding Leadership award 1982-83), Piedmont Credit Union Assn., Santa Gertrudis Breeders Internat., Am. Quarter Horses Assn., Alpha Tau Omega. Methodist. Club: Donalds Grange (S.C.). Lodge: Rotary. Avocations: sports; hunting; fishing; horses. Home: Route 2 Box 63 Smith Rd Starr SC 29684 Office: Anderson County Dept Edn 402 Bleckley St Anderson SC 29621

SMITH, NAN SHELLEY, art educator, sculptor; b. Phila., Nov. 10, 1952; d. Frank Smith and Rosalyn Schaeffer; B.F.A., Tyler Sch. Art Temple U., 1974; M.F.A., Ohio State U., 1977. Grad. teaching assoc. Ohio State U., Columbus, 1974-77; vis. instr. U. Ill., Champaign, 1977-79; assoc. prof. U. Fla., Gainesville, 1979—; co-chmn. vis. arts com. U. Fla., Gainesville, 1981—, chmn. publicity com., 1983-85. One woman shows include Valencia Community Coll. North Gallery, Orlando, Fla., 1985, The McQuade Gallery, North Andover, Mass., 1984, The Shillard-Smith Gallery, Clearwater-Belleair, Fla., 1983, The Sampson Gallery, Deland, Fla., 1983, The University Gallery, Gainesville, Fla., 1981. Community rep. Leukemia Soc. Am., Gainesville, 1983-84. Recipient Nathan Margolis award Tyler Sch. Art, 1974; Edith Fergus Material Fund grantee Ohio State U., 1977, Ford Found. grantee Ohio State U., 1977, Ford Found. Faculty grantee U. Ill., 1977, 1978, Grad. Faculty Research grantee U. Fla., 1980, 1983-84; Individual Artists fellowship Dept. of State and Fine Arts Council Fla., 1980-81. Mem. Internat. Sculpture Ctr., Internat. Platform Assn., Nat. Council Edn. Ceramic Arts, Coll. Art Assn., Fla. Craftsman. Democrat. Jewish. Clubs: Internat., Folk Dance. Home: 4409 NW 27th Terr Gainesville FL 32605 Office: Dept Art U Fla 302 FAC Gainesville FL 32611

SMITH, NELL WHITLEY, state senator; b. Washington, N.C., Nov. 12, 1929; d. Arthur H. and Alice (Whitley) S.; m. Harris Page Smith, Apr. 18, 1952 (dec.); children—Sam, Susan, Hugh, Phyllis. Student Salem Coll., 1947-48; B.S., U. N.C., 1951. Owner, mgr. The House Antiques and Gifts; tchr. sci. Easley Pub. Schs., 6 yrs.; mem. S.C. Senate, 1981—. Mem. Pickens County Art Com. Bd., 1976-80, bd. dirs. Pickens County Library, 1975-78, Home Health Care, 1977-79; pres. Palmetto Cabinet, 1977-78. Democrat. Presbyterian. Club: Easley Book. Office: 512 Gressette Bldg Columbia SC 29202*

SMITH, NICHOLAS PETER, exploration geologist; b. New Orleans, Feb. 9, 1949; s. Lucas James and Theresa Mary (Mule) Bacino; m. Mary Ilene Hannon, Oct. 22, 1976; children—Kyle Ryan, Kristen Anne, Kara Michelle. B.S., U. New Orleans, 1971, M.S., 1974. Cert. petroleum geologist. Assoc. U. New Orleans, 1971-72; geologist U.S. Geol. Survey, New Orleans, 1974-80; exploration geologist Superior Oil Co., New Orleans, 1980-84; exploration supr. Mobil Oil Corp., Lafayette, La., 1984—. Mem. Am. Assn. Petroleum Geologists, Lafayette Geol. Soc., Lafayette Geophys. Soc. Republican. Roman Catholic. Lodge: Elks. Avocations: sports; woodworking; crafts. Office: Mobil Oil Corp 3861 Ambassador Caffery Lafayette LA 70505

SMITH, ORLANDO FLYE, architectural, engineering and planning firm executive; b. Santa Maria, Colombia, Apr. 15, 1932 (parents Am. citizens); s. John Palmer, Jr. and Eva Victoria (Flye) S.; B.S. in Civil Engring., Clemson (S.C.) U., 1954; M.S., in Engring., Ariz. State U., 1967; m. Mary Ann Maner Sams, Apr. 10, 1955; children—Orlando Flye, Evita Victoria. Commd. 2d lt. USAF, 1954, advanced through grades to lt. col., 1978; service in Vietnam, flew 266 combat missions; chief ops. and planning Hdqrs. USAF, Washington, 1973-78, ret., 1978; v.p., asst. mgr. VTN Inc., Charleston, W.Va., 1978-82; v.p., gen. mgr. Lindbergh & Assocs., Charleston, S.C.; adj. prof. The Citadel Coll.; adv. com. Air Force Inst. Tech. Decorated D.F.C. with one oak leaf cluster, Air medal with 5 oak leaf clusters, Purple Heart, Air Force Meritorious medal with 3 oak leaf clusters; Vietnam Cross Gallantry with 2 palms; recipient A.M. Minton award Air Force C.E.-Air Force Assn., 1977. Mem. Am. Inst. Plant Engrs., Soc. Am. Mil. Engrs. (pres. 1969-71), Am. Public Works Assn., ASCE, Nat. Soc. Profl. Engrs., Am. Water Works Assn., Am. Fedn. Pollution Control, Soc. USAF Fighter Pilots Assn., Ranch Hand Assn. Republican. Episcopalian. Office: 100 Kanawha Blvd Charleston WV 25302

SMITH, PATRICIA ALDEN, real estate company executive; b. Warren, Ohio, Aug. 22, 1938; d. Ennels George Alden and Genevere (Hutchinson) Umsted; divorced; children—Kilby Page IV, Stacy Alden. Student Sophie Newcomb Coll., 1955-57; Realtor Nat. Mktg. Inst., U. S.C., 1979-81. Sales assoc. Johnson & Johnson, Old Bethpage, N.Y., 1963-67, Real Estate Service, Greenville, S.C., 1972-74; sales mgr. Phillip T. Bradley Realtors, Greenville, 1974-79; sales mgr., dir. corp. sales Goldsmith Realtors, Greenville, 1979-84; pres. Patt Smith Realty Inc., Greenville, 1984—; dir. Multiple Listing Service, Greenville. Mem. pres.'s adv. bd. Winthrop Coll., Rockhill, S.C., 1984-85. Recipient Million Dollar Club award Greenville Bd. Realtors, 1983, 84, 85. Mem. Nat. Assn. Realtors (com. fed. campaigns 1982-83), S.C. Assn. Realtors, (dir. 1980-83, chmn. state polit. affairs com. 1981-82), 300 for Greenville Assn., Greenville C. of C. (exec. com. 1984-85, polit. affairs com. 1980-85, chmn. awards and recognitions 1984-85). Republican. Home: 22 Jamestown Dr Greenville SC 29615 Office: Patt Smith Realty Inc 49 Greenland Dr Greenville SC 29615

SMITH, PATRICIA LEE, research mathematician; b. Houston, Sept. 16, 1946; d. Harold Edwin and Gwendolyn (Cribbs) Murphree; m. Philip W. Smith, June 6, 1969; children—Alexis, Jessica. Student U. Nantes, France, 1966-67; B.A., Southwestern U., Georgetown, Tex., 1968; M.S., Purdue U., 1970; Ph.D., Tex. A&M U., 1975. Schedule dep. instr. Purdue U., 1970-72; asst. prof. Tex. A&M U., 1976-79; vis. prof. U. Alta., Edmonton, Can., 1979; asst. prof. Old Dominion U., Norfolk, Va., 1980-82; site mgr. Computer Dynamics, Inc., Virginia Beach, Va., 1982—. Mem. Am. Statis. Assn. (v.p. 1978-79, sec. 1981-82). Home: 1326 Beaujolais Houston TX 77077 Office: Shell Devel Co PO Box 1380 Houston TX 77251

SMITH, PATSY JUANITA, cosmetics company executive, claims adjustor; b. Dallas, Aug. 3, 1939; d. Roland Murl and Ruby Esther (Whiteside) Stephens; m. Jerry Arlin Kerby, June 7, 1957 (div. Nov. 1971); children—Timmy Wayne, Pamela Anita; m. 2d, Charles Albert Smith, June 17, 1977. Student, Ins. Inst., Dale Carnegie Sch. Claims adjuster Crum & Forster, Dallas, 1967-77, Atlantic Mut. Co., Dallas, 1978-79, Am. States Ins. Co., Dallas, 1979-81, Trinity Adjusting Co., Dallas, 1981-83; beauty cons. Mary Kay Cosmetics, Dallas, 1980-83, sales dir., 1983—. Precinct chmn. Democratic party, Dallas, 1981, election judge, 1981, 82. Named Queen of Sales, Rachel Tarbet unit Mary Kay Cosmetics, 1982, Queen of Recruiting, 1982. Mem. Ins. Women of Dallas (Claimswoman of Year 1979, 80, pres. 1981-82), Am. Bus. Women Assn. (sec. 1980). Home: 7222 Winedale St Dallas TX 75231

SMITH, PAUL EDMUND, JR., educator; b. Northampton, Mass., Feb. 6, 1927; s. Paul Edmund and Mary Jane (Murphy) S.; B.A., U. Mass., 1948; postgrad. Harvard U., 1948-49; M.A., Boston U., 1957; B.D., Columbia Theol. Sem., 1957, M.Div., 1971; postgrad. U. N.C., 1967-68. Instr. Latin and French, Chester (Vt.) High Sch., 1949-53, Loris (S.C.) High Sch., 1953-54; lectr. history U. Ga., Albany, 1957-59; instr. Latin, Rocky Mount (Va.) High Sch., 1959-61; minister Henderson Presbyn. Ch., Albany, 1957-59, Rocky Mount (Va.) Presbyn. Ch., 1959-64; asst. prof. religion Ferrum (Va.) Coll., 1961-68; vis. lectr. history John Tyler Community Coll., Chester, Va., 1968-69; instr. philosophy and religion Richard Bland Coll., Petersburg, Va., 1968-71, asst. prof., 1971-76, asso. prof., 1976—, chmn. dept., 1971—. Mem. Am. Hist. Assn., Fincastle Presbytery. Democrat. Presbyterian. Office: Commerce Hall Richard Bland Coll Petersburg VA 23805

SMITH, PETER FREDRIC, architect; b. Cin., Apr. 6, 1948; s. C. Arden and Billie J. (Beidler) S. B.A., Wesleyan U., 1970; M.Arch., U. Pa., 1973. Prin., Peter F. Smith, Nantucket, Mass., 1974-75; intern architect Morehouse & Chesley, Architects, Lexington, Mass., 1976. Benjamin Thompson & Assocs., Cambridge, Mass., 1977-78; prin. Peter Smith AIA, Nantucket, 1978-80; sales rep. The Ryland Group, Inc., 1981-82; prin. Peter Smith, AIA, The Woodlands, Tex., 1983—. Dales Traveling fellow, 1971. Mem. AIA. Address: 36 S Brook Pebble Ct The Woodlands TX 77380

SMITH, R. J., JR., oil company executive; b. Big Spring, Tex., Sept. 9, 1930; s. R. J. and Myrtle (O'Quinn) S.; m. Sarah Sue Holmes, Sept. 8, 1950 (div. 1962); children—Molly Smith Frank, Cassie Smith Bichler; m. 2d, Sandra Ann Schroeder, Jan. 21, 1971. Student, Abilene Christian U., 1948-50, So. Methodist U., 1951-52, Goethe U., Frankfurt, Germany, 1953-54; LL.D., Northwood Inst., 1983. Aero. engr. Chance-Vought Aircraft, Dallas, 1951-52; ind. oil operator, Dallas, 1960-62; ops. chief Leland Fikes, Dallas, 1963-66; owner, operator Texon Petroleum Corp (sold to Exxon USA 1983), Dallas, 1967-83; owner, pres. Cheyenne Petroleum Corp., Dallas, 1967—. Bd. dirs. Effie and Wofford Cain Found., Dallas, 1979—; trustee Northwood Inst., West Baden, Ind., Midland, Mich. and Dallas, 1968—. Mem. Tex. Ind. Producers and Royalty Owners, Ind. Producers Assn. Am. Mid-Continent Producers Assn., N.Mex. Ind. Producers Assn. Republican. Clubs: Preston Trail Golf, Dallas Gun, Oak Cliff Country, University, Quadrant, Bent Tree Country (all Tex.); Del Mar Turf (Calif.). Office: Texan Petroleum Corporation 2626 Cole Ave Suite 603 LB63 Dallas TX 75204

SMITH, RANDOLPH RELIHAN, plastic surgeon; b. Augusta, Ga., Apr. 13, 1944; s. Lester Vernon and Maxine (Relihan) S.; B.S., Clemson U., 1966; M.D., Coll. Ga., 1970; m. Becky Jo Hardy; children—Katherine, Randolph, Rebecca. Intern, Bowman Gray Sch. Medicine, Winston-Salem, N.C., 1970-71; resident in surgery and otolaryngology Duke U., Durham, N.C., 1971-75; resident in plastic and reconstructive surgery Med. Coll. Ga., 1975-77; Christine Kleinert fellow in hand surgery U. Louisville, 1977; attending physician Univ. Hosp., Augusta, Ga., 1977—; asst. clin. prof. plastic surgery Med. Coll. Ga., 1978—. Bd. dirs. Augusta Opera Assn., Planned Parenthood. Served to maj. M.C., U.S. Army, 1971-77. Diplomate Am. Bd. Otolaryngology, Am. Bd. Plastic Surgery. Fellow Am. Acad. Otolaryngology, A.C.S.; mem. Am. Soc. Plastic and Reconstructive Surgeons, Am. Soc. Aesthetic Plastic Surgery, Ga. Soc. Plastic and Reconstructive Surgeons, Southeastern Soc. Plastic and Reconstructive Surgeons. Episcopalian. Clubs: Exchange, Augusta Symphony League. Contbr. articles in field to profl. jours. Office: Suite 2F University Hospital 820 Saint Sebastian Way Augusta GA 30902

SMITH, RANKIN MCEACHERN, insurance company executive, professional football team executive; b. Atlanta, Oct. 29, 1925; (married); 5 children. Ed., Emory U., U. Fla., U. Ga. With Life Ins. Co. of Ga., 1943—, agy. asst. v.p., 1954, corp. sec., 1954-57, agy. v.p., 1957-63, exec. v.p., 1963-68, sr. v.p., 1968-70, pres., chief exec. officer, from 1970; later chmn., now dir.; owner Atlanta Falcons football team, 1965—, past pres., now chmn. bd.; dir. Greyhound, Inc., Trust Co. Ga. Assos. Div. chmn. United Way, Atlanta, 1973-74; Ga. sightsaving chmn. Nat. Soc. for Prevention Blindness, 1973-74; mem. exec. com. Central Atlanta Progress, Inc.; mem. exec. bd. Atlanta Area Council Boy Scouts Am.; Bd. dirs. Better Bus. Bur. Atlanta; trustee U. Ga. Found., Reinhardt Coll., Waleska, Ga., Lovett Sch., Atlanta. Mem. Atlanta C. of C., Commerce Club, Chi Pi. Methodist. Clubs: Capitol City (gov.), Piedmont Driving. Lodges: Masons; Shriners; Rotary. Office: care Atlanta Falcons I-85 and Suwanee Rd Suwanee GA 30174*

SMITH, RAYMOND KERMIT, former educational administrator; b. Hahnville, La., July 6, 1915; married, 2 children. B.A., Xavier U., 1946, M.A. in Adminstrn. and Supervision, 1951; postgrad. in reading No. Mich. U., 1962, La. State U., 1965-66, Loyola U., New Orleans, 1966-68, Internat. Grade Sch., New Orleans, 1973. Tchr.-prin. St. Charles Parish Schs., Luling, La., 1937-42, supr. instrn., 1942-79, asst. supt. instrn., 1979-81; ret., 1981; instr. reading Loyola U., New Orleans, part-time, 1968-75. Pres., United Givers Fund St. Charles Parish, 1971-72; v.p. Bayou-River Health Planning Council, 1974-77, pres., 1977—; pres. New Orleans/Bayou River Health Systems Agy., 1978, St. Charles Parish Cancer Soc., charter mem. St. Charles Toy and Gift Fund; chmn. bd. commrs. St. Charles Hosp., Luling; lector, commentator, mem. parish council Holy Rosary Ch., Hahnville. Recipient citation for directing 10 years of Head Start, Sec. HEW. Mem. NEA. Clubs: Famous G Social of New Orleans (v.p.); K.C., West St. Charles Rotary. Contbr. articles to profl. jours. Home: 104 Gum St PO Box 70 Hahnville LA 70057 Office: Sch Bd Office Box 46 Luling LA 70070

SMITH, REGINALD BRIAN FURNESS, anesthesiologist; b. Warrington, Eng., Feb. 7, 1931; s. Reginald and Betty (Bell) S.; came to U.S., 1962, naturalized, 1967; M.B., B.S., U. London (Eng.), 1955; m. Margarete Groppe, July 18, 1963; children—Corinne, Malcolm. Intern, Poole Gen. Hosp., Dorset, Eng., 1955-56; rotating intern Wilson Meml. Hosp., Johnson City, N.Y., 1962-63; resident anesthesiology Med. Coll. Va., Richmond, 1963-64, U. Pitts., 1964-65; clin. instr. U. Pitts., 1965-66, asst. prof., 1969-71, asso. clin. prof., 1971-74, prof., 1974-78, vice chmn. dept. anesthesiology, 1974-77, acting chmn., 1977-78; prof. and chmn. anesthesiology U. Tex., San Antonio, 1978—; dir. anesthesiology Eye and Ear Hosp., Pitts., 1971-76; anesthesiologist in chief Presbyn.-Univ. Hosp., Pitts., 1976-78. Served to capt. Royal Army Med. Corps, 1957-59. Diplomate Am. Bd. Anesthesiology. Fellow Am. Coll. Anesthesiology, Am. Coll. Medicine, ACP, Am. Coll. Chest Physicians; mem. Internat. Anesthesia Research Soc., Am. Soc. Anesthesiologists, Western Pa. Soc. Anesthesiologists (pres. 1974-75). Editor: International Ophthalmology Clinics, 1973; International Anesthesiology Clinics, 1983; contbr. articles to profl. jours. Office: 7703 Floyd Curl Dr San Antonio TX 78284

SMITH, RICHARD ELLIS, psychologist; b. Baraboo, Wis., Feb. 22, 1948; s. James Ellis and Carmen Mae (Carpenter) S.; student So. Meth. U., 1966-68; B.S., N. Tex. State U., 1970, M.S., 1971; m. Jean Wright, Aug. 27, 1969; children—Hilary, W. Travis. Child care worker Shady Brook Sch., Richardson, Tex., 1969-70; research asst. North Tex. State U., Denton, 1970-71; counselor intern U.S. Dept. Justice, Fed. Bur. Prisons, Seagoville, Tex., 1971; elem. tchr., Plano, Tex., 1972-73; cons. on spl. projects, asso. sch. psychologist Edn. Service Center, Region 10, Richardson, Tex., 1973-76; research asso. U. Tex., Dallas, 1976-77; coordinator of appraisal Collin County Coop. Spl. Services, Wylie, Tex., 1977-81; pvt. practice ednl. cons., Plano, Tex., 1981—. Mem. Nat. Assn. Sch. Psychologists, Am. Psychol. Assn., Tex. Psychol. Assn., Psi Chi. Home and office: 3808 Deep Valley Trail Plano TX 75023

SMITH, RICHARD STOWERS, investment banker, rancher; b. San Antonio, July 20, 1934; s. Luther Stevens and Hazel (Stowers) S.; B.A., Yale U., 1955; m. Josephine McRae Powell, Jan. 13, 1962; children—Elliott Stowers, Quincy McRae. Asso. investment banking Lazard Freres Co., N.Y.C., 1958-63; v.p., dir. Russ Co., San Antonio, 1964; v.p., dir. N.Y. Securities Co. Inc., 1965-72; sr. v.p., dir. Rotan Mosle Inc., Houston, 1973-84; pres. Allied Capital Co., 1984—; mng. ptnr. Stowers Ranch Co., 1967—; former dir. Mesa Petroleum Co., Chesapeake Industries, Stowers Furniture Co., David M. Lea, Chesterfield Land & Timber Corp., Thomson Industries Ltd., Rocky Mountain Exploration Co., Verna Corp., Dreco Energy Services Ltd. Former bd. dirs. Houston Ballet; pres., former bd. dirs. Houston Child Guidance Center; trustee Contemporary Arts Mus. Republican. Episcopalian. Clubs: River, Union, Downtown Assn. (N.Y.C.); Port Bay Hunting and Fishing (Rockport, Tex.); Tex. Corinthian Yacht (Kema); Argyle (San Antonio); Coronado, Bayou (Houston). Home: 2233 Troon Rd Houston TX 77019 Office: Allied Bank Plaza PO Box 3326 Houston TX 77253

SMITH, RICHARD TRAVIS, grocery store manager; b. Beaufort, N.C., July 4, 1925; s. Carl and Aleta (Mason) S.; m. Valeria Mae Lawrence, Oct. 15, 1949; children—Joyce, Aleta, Richard. Student pub. schs., Beaufort. With Colonial Stores, Beaufort, 1944-80, store mgr., 1954-80; gen. mgr. The Grand Union Co., Beaufort, 1980—. Bd. dirs. N.C. State Bd. Social Services, Raleigh, 1973-77; bd. dirs. Carteret County Fed. Credit Union, Beaufort, 1984—. Recipient Order of Long Leaf Pine, gov. of N.C., 1974; Service award, Grand Union Co., 1984. Mem. Beaufort Sq. Mcht. Assn. (pres. 1982-84). Republican. Baptist. Lodges: Odd Fellow, Masons. Avocations: woodworking; fishing. Home: 116 Gordon St Beaufort NC 28516 Office: Grand Union Co Hwy 70 E Beaufort NC 28516

SMITH, ROBERT JOHN, cartographer; b. Abington, Pa., Jan. 20, 1949; s. Robert J. and Rose (Skoczalek) S.; m. Nina Maria Geiken, Nov. 18, 1972; children—Cara Ann, Rachel Marie. B.A., U. Md., 1972. Cartographer, Soil Conservation Service, Dept. Agr., Washington, 1972-78, asst. head cartographic staff Nat. Tech. Service Ctr., Ft. Worth, 1978-82, asst. head east sect., 1982-83, asst. head ops., 1983—. Mem. Am. Congress of Surveying and Mapping. Democrat. Roman Catholic. Office: Nat Cartographic Ctr PO Box 6567 Fort Worth TX 76115

SMITH, ROBERT JOHN, loss prevention manager; b. Bronx, N.Y., Dec. 27, 1944; s. Gilbert P. and Fannie R. S.; m. Patricia Marie Brady, Aug. 10, 1968; children—Kimberly Marie, Robert Joseph. Student, Westchester County (N.Y.) Police Acad., 1968; A.S. with honors, Hillsborough Community Coll., 1983. Patrolman, City of White Plains Police Dept. (N.Y.), 1967-72; investigator Lindsley, Inc., West Coast office, Tampa, Fla., 1972-73, sr. investigator, 1973-75, asst. dir. security, 1975-84, loss prevention mgr., 1984—. Served with USMC, 1962-66. Mem. Am. Soc. Indsl. Security (attendance chmn. 1980, program chmn. 1981, Charles Knight award 1980), Am. Soc. Safety Engrs. Home: 2348 Willow Tree Trail Clearwater FL 33575

SMITH, ROBERT JOSEPH SCHORP, corporation executive, geologist; b. Pearsall, Tex., Oct. 18, 1926; s. Walter Frank and Ida Helen (Schorp) S.; m. Cynthia Lou Bingman, Nov. 3, 1962; children—Robert Boyd Bingman, Harriett Mandena, Helen Marie. B.S., U. Okla., 1950. Cert. geologist. Geologist Standard Oil. of Calif., Tex., 1951-73; pres. Santa Maria Internat. Corp., Houston, 1973—; dir. First Nat. Bank of Bellaire, Houston. Active The One Hundred Club of Houston. Served with USAAF, 1945-46; ETO. Mem. Am. Inst. Profl. Geologists, Am. Assn. Petroleum Geologists, Houston Geol. Soc., Sons Republic of Tex. Republican. Roman Catholic. Club: The Houstonian. Office: Santa Maria Internat Corp 3603 Westcenter Dr #100 Houston TX 77042

SMITH, ROBERT LEO, ecologist, wildlife biologist, educator; b. Brookville, Pa., Mar. 23, 1925; s. Leo F. and Josephine Elizabeth (Ferguson) S.; m. Alice Elizabeth Casey, Nov. 15, 1952; children—Robert Leo, Thomas Michael, Pauline Ann, Maureen Elizabeth. B.S., Pa. State U., 1949, M.S., 1954; Ph.D., Cornell U., 1956. Asst. prof. biology SUNY-Plattsburgh, 1956-58; prof. wildlife ecology W.Va. U., Morgantown, 1958—; cons. in ecology to publs. and govt. Author: Ecology and Field Biology, 3d edit., 1980; The Ecology of Man: An Ecosystem Approach, 1976, 2d edit. Russian translation; Elements of Ecology, 2d edit., 1986; mem. adv. bd., contbr. Funk and Wagnalls Ency.; contbr. to Ency. Brit., World Book Ency., also var. ecology books and jours. Served with AUS, 1950-52. Mem. Ecol. Soc. Am., Am. Ornithologists Union, Wildlife Soc., Am. Soc. Mammalogists, AAAS, Am. Inst. Biol. Scis., Wilson Ornithol. Soc., Cooper Ornith. Soc., Sigma Xi. Republican. Roman Catholic. Home: Route 7 Box 660 Morgantown WV 26505 Office: West Virginia U Division Forestry PO Box 6125 Morgantown WV 16506

SMITH, ROBERT MARVIN, professional services executive; b. Hodge, Mo., Jan. 18, 1940; s. Robert Lunsford and Laura Eloyse (Walters) S.; m. Phyllis Ann Phipps, Jan. 26, 1962; children—Lisa Ann, Jennifer Lee. B.S. in Applied Math., U. Mo.-Rolla, 1963, M.S. in Applied Math., 1964, Ph.D. in Math. Stats., 1975. Engr. dynamics group Douglas Aircraft Co., 1965-67, Gen. Dynamics, Ft. Worth, 1967-70; tchr. U. Mo., Rolla, 1970-73, 74-75; statistician, safety researcher Ford Motor Co., 1973-74; analyst, mgr., marketeer The BDM Corp., Albuquerque and Huntsville, Ala., 1975—. Papers presented to various symposiums; contbr. articles to profl. jours. Mem. Am. Statis. Assn., Am. Def. Preparedness Assn., Mil. Ops. Research Soc. (assoc.), Internat. Test and Evaluation Assn. (chpt. program chmn. 1984—). Lutheran. Avocation: raising Paso Fino horses. Home: Rt 2 Box 629A Somerville AL 35670 Office: The BDM Corp 2227 Drake Ave Huntsville AL 35805

SMITH, ROBERT ROYCE, oil and gas operator, real estate developer, bank executive; b. Rule, Tex., July 19, 1928; s. Joseph Bunyan and Ima (Spurlin) S.; m. Claudia Townsend, Dec. 21, 1975; children—Rebecca, Kathy, Joey. B.S., Tex. A&M U., 1949. Lab asst. Core Labs., Midland, Tex., 1953; landman Monsanto Co., Midland, 1953-58; landman Burford & Sams, Midland, 1958-60; ind. landman, Midland, 1960-77; exec. asst. Clayton W. Williams, Jr., Midland, 1977—; exec. v.p., dir. ClayDesta Corp., Midland, 1981—; dir., organizer ClayDesta Nat. Bank, 1982—, cons., 1983—; v.p., dir. ClayDesta Regional Med. Ctr., 1985—; bd. govs. Plaza Club, Midland, 1983—. Served to 1st lt. U.S. Army, 1951-53. Mem. Tex. A&M U. Ex-Students Assn. Republican. Avocations: photography. Office: 6 Desta Dr Suite 3333 Midland TX 79705

SMITH, ROBERT SIDNEY, business executive; b. Charlotte, N.C., Feb. 26, 1945; s. Edward Mason and Virginia Irene Smith; m. Lynn Little. A.B. in Econs. and Bus. Adminstrn., Wofford Coll., Spartanburg, S.C., 1967. With mktg. dept. Humble Oil & Refining Co., 1971-72; v.p. Nat. Assn. Hosiery Mfrs., Charlotte, 1972-78, sr. v.p., 1978-82, pres., chief exec. officer, 1982—; partner, v.p. Green, Smith & Crockett Inc., 1978-82; cons. in field. Chmn. research com. Mecklenburg County Republican Party, 1977-78; sect. chmn. Charlotte United Way; pres. Charlotte Area Alumni Club Wofford Coll., 1977; chmn. bd. dirs. Leadership Charlotte Program, 1980-81; bd. dirs. Nat. Alumni Assn. Wofford Coll.; bd. dirs. U.S. Apparel Council, treas., 1982—; mem. industry sector adv. com. on textile for U.S. spl. trade rep. U.S. Dept. Commerce, also mem. mgmt. labor textile adv. com.; mem. City Zoning Bd. Adjustment, Charlotte. Served to capt. USMC, 1967-70; Vietnam. Decorated Purple Heart; Vietnamese Cross Gallantry. Mem. Am. Statis. Assn., Textile Analysts Club N.Y.C., Am. Inst. Econ. Research, Charlotte Textile Club, DAV, Mil. Order Purple Heart, Sigma Alpha Epsilon (pres. Charlotte area alumni club 1980-81). Presbyterian. Home: 4733 Truscott Rd Matthews NC 28105 Office: 477 S Sharon Amity Rd Charlotte NC 28211

SMITH, RODNEY WIKE, engineering company executive; b. Havre de Grace, Md., July 29, 1944; s. Marshall Thomas and Ellen Nora (Wike) S.; B.S., Va. Poly. Inst. and State U., 1972; m. Mary Katherine Trent, Dec. 20, 1967; children—Scott Walker, Craig Duncan. Project engr. Hercules, Inc., Radford, Va., 1967-72; planning engr. Va. state Water Control Bd., Richmond, 1972; project mgr. Central Shenandoah Planning Dist. Commn., Staunton, 1972-76; v.p., br. office mgr. Patton, Harris, Rust & Assocs., Bridgewater, Va., 1976-82, prin. in charge office Buchanan, W.Va., 1980-82; sr. v.p. Copper & Smith, P.C., Harrisonburg, Va., 1982—. Contbr. articles to profl. jours. Registered profl. engr., Va., W.Va. Named Exec. of Yr., Profl. Secs. Internat. Mem. Nat. Soc. Profl. Engrs., Water Pollution Control Fedn., Am. Water Works Assn., Nat. Water Well Assn. Republican. Lutheran. Home: Rt-5 Box 128 E Staunton VA 24401 Office: 1041 S High St Harrisonburg VA 22801

SMITH, RONNIE LEW, music educator, tennis professional; b. Amarillo, Tex., Feb. 2, 1936; s. Terry G. and Velma R. (Shaw) S.; m. E. Joyce Earley, Apr. 4, 1958; children—Terry Don, Ron Earley. B. Music Edn., West Tex. State U., 1958; M. Ch. Music, Southwestern Bapt. Sem., 1961, D. Musical Arts, 1969. Minister music Wyatt Park Bapt. Ch., St. Joseph, Mo., 1961-63; choral dir., tennis coach Carter-Riverside High Sch., Ft. Worth, 1965-66; gen. music tchr. Charles E. Nash Elem. Sch., Ft. Worth, 1966-68; chmn. music dept. Lincoln Meml. U., Harrogate, Tenn., 1969-71, Campbellsville Coll., Ky., 1971-81, Palm Beach Atlantic Coll., Fla., 1981—; adjudicator Ch. Music Festivals, Tex., Tenn., Ohio, Ky. Fla., 1958—, Sch. Music Contests, Ky., Tenn., Fla., 1971—; tchr. Ridgecrest Music Week., N.C., 1977; pres. Gold Coast handbell Guild, West Palm Beach, Fla., 1984-86. Author: Grove's Dictionary Music and Musicians, 1980; Grove's Dictionary of American Music. Mem. So. Baptist Ch. Music Conf., Hymn Soc. Am., Coll. Music Soc., Am. Guild English Handbell Ringers, Music Educators Nat. Conf., U.S. Tennis Assn. Home: 324 Edgewood Dr West Palm Beach FL 33405 Office: Palm Beach Atlantic Coll 1101 S Olive Ave West Palm Beach FL 33401

SMITH, RUBY LUCILLE, retired librarian; b. Nobob, Ky., Sept. 19, 1917; d. James Ira and Myrtie Olive (Crabtree) Jones; A.B., Western Ky. State Tchrs. Coll., 1943, M.A., 1966; m. Kenneth Cornelius Smith, Dec. 25, 1946; children—Kenneth Cornelius, Corma Ann. Tchr. rural schs., Barren County, Ky., 1941-42; tchr. secondary sch. English, librarian Temple Hill Consol. Sch., Glasgow, Ky., 1943-47, 49-51, 53-56, sch. librarian, 1956-83, ret., 1983. Sec. Barren County Cancer Soc., 1968-70, Barren County Fair Bd., 1969-70; leader 4-H Club, 1957-72, mem. council Barren County. Trustee Mary Wood Weldon Meml. Library, 1964—; trustee Barren County Pub. Library, 1969—, sec., 1969—. Mem. NEA (life), Ky. Edn. Assn., Ky. Assn. Sch. Librarians (sec. 1970-71), 3d Dist. Library Assn. (pres. 1964, 66), Barren County Edn. Assn. (pres. 1960-62), Ky. Audio Visual Assn., Glasgow-Barren County Ret. Tchrs. Assn. (pres. 1984—), Monroe Assn. Woman's Missionary Union (dir. 1968-72, 79-81), Monroe Assn. Baptists (library dir. 1972—), Delta Kappa Gamma (corr. sec. 1982-84). Republican. Home: Route 1 Box 65 Summer Shade KY 42166

SMITH, RUSH HENRY, vocational administrator; b. Palestine, Tex., Apr. 27, 1937; s. Rush and Elenora (Kitcher) S.; m. Eva Pauline Haley, Aug. 17, 1957; children—Michael, Sheryl, Angela. B.S., Sam Houston State U., 1959; M.Theology, So. Meth. U., 1965. Instr., N.T., El Paso, 1965-70; mktg. and distributive edn. tchr. Port Arthur (Tex.) Ind. Sch. Dist., 1970-71; regional tng. mgr. McDonald's Systems, Inc., Dallas, 1971-75; vocat. tchr./counselor Palestine (Tex.) Ind. Sch. Dist., 1975-80; vocat. adminstr. Spring Ind. Sch. Dist., Houston, 1980—; cons. Gulf Coast Counselors Assn.; instr. bus. Henderson County Jr. Coll., 1977-80. Mem. City Council, Palestine, 1980; mem. Tex. State Com. for Implementation of Career Edn., 1980-81; mem. Task Force for Articulation of Secondary and Post Secondary Vocat. Edn., 1982-83. Mem. Tex. Vocat. Adminstrs. Assn., Am. Vocat. Assn., Tex. Vocat. Guidance Assn. Methodist. Lodge: Masons. Office: 16717 Ella St Houston TX 77090

SMITH, RUTH GREEN, nursing administrator; b. Bellwood, Pa., Oct. 3, 1927; d. Paul Martin and Mildred Lois (Fuoss) Green; m. Robert Wayne Smith, Dec. 29, 1950; children—Brenda Smith Gross, Betty Jo Smith McCorkle. R.N., Hahnemann Hosp., 1949. Nurse Hahnemann Hosp., Phila., 1949-50, Providence Hosp., Washington, 1950-52, Dr. Donald B. Koonce, Wilmington, N.C., 1954-60, Cape Fear Meml. Hosp., Wilmington, 1960—, dir. surg. service dept. Mem. Assn. Operating Room Nurses (pres. Southeastern sect. 1981-83). Avocations: sewing; knitting; cross stitch. Home: 3909 Evergreen Dr Wilmington NC 28403 Office: Cape Fear Meml Hosp 5301 Wrightsville Ave Wilmington NC 28403

SMITH, S. JAY, statistician; b. Moultrie, Ga., Sept. 8, 1943; s. S. J. and Nina (Treadaway) S.; m. V. Anne Guice; 1 child, Katharine. B.S. in Math., U. Ga., 1965, M.S. in Stats., 1972; M.S. in Info. Sci., Ga. State U., 1980. Dir. labor research Ga. Dept. Labor, Atlanta, 1972-74; statistician Ctrs. for Disease Control, Atlanta, 1974—. Contbr. articles to profl. jours. Served to capt. USAF, 1967-71. Mem. Am. Statis. Assn. (pres. Atlanta chpt. 1975-76), AAAS, Internat. Union of Immunol. Socs. (vice-chmn. biometrics subcom.), Coll. Am. Pathologists (com. serum proteins standardization), Sigma Xi, Upsilon Pi Epsilon. Avocation: sailing. Home: 5231 Chamblee-Dunwoody Rd Dunwoody GA 30338 Office: Ctrs for Disease Control Atlanta GA 30333

SMITH, SAM L., project engineering supervisor; b. Marion, Ill., Sept. 3, 1940; s. Samuel P. and Ovalee K. (Harvey) S.; m. Glatha M. Stroup, Mar. 30, 1963; children—Deneen, Eric, Andrea. B.S.M.E., Mo. Sch. Mines, 1963. Registered profl. engr., Colo., Ky. Engr., Olin Inc., Marion, Ill., 1963-69, Central Tech. Inc., Herrin, Ill., 1969-70; sr. engr. Nat. Southwire Aluminum, Hawesville, Ky., 1970-72, sr. engr., new plant design and start-up, 1972-75, chief engr. pilot plant, new plant design and start up for alumina prodn. from alt. source, 1975—, adv., instr. maintenance mechanic tng. program, 1977—. Mem. Nat. Soc. Profl. Engrs., ASME, Ohio Valley Mgmt. Club. Baptist. Lodge: Masons (Marion). Patentee in field. Home: 1318 Woodmere Ln Owensboro KY 42301 Office: Nat Southwire Aluminum PO Box 500 Hawesville KY 42348

SMITH, SARAH KIM HUEY, aviation company executive, training and development administrator, consultant; b. Wichita Falls, Tex., Nov. 5, 1952; d. John Thomas Huey and Dovie Maurine (Nash) Huey Murphy; m. Robert Lynn Smith, Apr. 22, 1982. B.A. summa cum laude, Midwestern State U., 1975; M.A., Tex. Tech U., 1976. Prodn. coordinator Tex. Instruments, Inc., Lubbock, Tex., 1976-77, tng. mgr., 1977-80, br. tng. mgr., 1980-82; sr. cons. Action Systems, Inc., Dallas, 1982-84; tng. mgr. Aviall, Inc., Dallas, 1984—; presentor seminars, papers at convs. Vol. tchr. Operation L.I.F.T. (Literacy Instrn. for Texans), Dallas, 1983-84. Tex. Tech U. grad. asst., 1975-76. Mem. Am. Soc. Tng. and Devel., Nat. Assn. Female Execs., Alpha Chi Omega, Alpha Psi Omega. Democrat. Avocations: running; redoing older homes. Home: 10020 Trailpine Dr Dallas TX 75238 Office: Aviall Inc 7555 Lemmon Ave PO Box 7086 Dallas TX 75209-0086

SMITH, SHERMAN N., III, lawyer; b. Vero Beach, Fla., Feb. 22, 1946; s. Sherman N. and Olive (Heath) S.; m. Melodee Ann Moore, Dec. 30, 1978; B.A., Fla. Presbyterian Coll., 1968; J.D., U. Fla., 1970. Bar Fla. 1971, U.S. Dist. Ct. (so. dist.) Fla. 1973, U.S. Ct. Appeals (5th cir.) 1973, U.S. Ct. Appeals (11th cir.) 1981. Ptnr. Smith Heath Smith & O'Haire, Vero Beach, Fla., 1971-79; sole practice, Vero Beach, 1980-82, ptnr. Reed Smith Shaw & McClay, Vero Beach, 1982-85; chmn. 19th Jud. Cir. of Fla. Grievance Com., 1982-83. Mem. ABA, Fla. Bar, Acad. Fla. Trial Lawyers, Indian River County Bar Assn. (pres. 1983). Democrat Club: Vero Beach Country. General practice, State civil litigation. Probate. Office: 886 Dahlia Ln Vero Beach FL 32963

SMITH, SHERWOOD HUBBARD, JR., utilities executive; b. Jacksonville, Fla., Sept. 1, 1934; s. Sherwood Hubbard and Catherine Gertrude (Milliken) S.; m. Eva Hackney Hargrave, July 20, 1957; children—Marlin Hamilton, Cameron Hargrave, Eva Hackney. A.B., U. N.C., 1956, J.D., 1960. Bar: N.C. 1960. Assoc. Lassiter, Moore & Van Allen, Charlotte, 1960-62; partner Joyner & Howison, Raleigh, 1963-65; asso. gen. counsel Carolina Power & Light Co., Raleigh, 1965-70, sr. v.p., gen. counsel, 1971-74, exec. v.p., 1974-76, pres., 1976—, chmn., 1980—, also dir.; bd. dirs. Am. Nuclear Energy Council, 1980—, Atomic Indsl. Forum, Inc.; dir. Edison Electric Inst., 1981—, U.S. Com. on Energy Awareness, Southeastern Electric Exchange, Hackney Bros. Body Co., Wilson, N.C., Wachovia Bank & Trust Co., Durham Life Ins. Co., Durham Corp.; sec.-treas., dir. Southeastern Electric Reliability Council. Chmn. Raleigh Civic Center Authority, 1973-77; vice chmn. Morehead Scholar Central Selection Com., U. N.C., 1970—; mem. Gov.'s Efficiency Study Commn., 1973, N.C. Council Mgmt. and Devel.; bd. dirs. Bus. Found. N.C., 1977—, sec., 1977-81, pres., 1981—; trustee Z. Smith Reynolds Found., 1978—, Ind. Coll. Fund N.C.; chmn. bd. dirs. N.C. Heart Assn., 1971-74; bd. dirs. United Fund Wake County; bd. dirs., exec. com., 2d vice chmn. N.C. Citizens for Bus. and Industry; bd. dirs. Research Triangle. Found. of N.C.; bd. dirs. U.S. nat. com. World Energy Conf.; vice-chmn., bd. dirs. Microelectronics Center of N.C., 1980—; vice chmn. trustees Rex Hosp.; mem. Pres.'s Council for Internat. Youth Exchange; mem. nat. corps. com. United Negro Coll. Fund. Served as ensign USN, 1956-57. Mem. Greater Raleigh C. of C. (pres. 1979), Am. Nuclear Soc., U.S. C. of C. (energy com.), Phi Beta Kappa. Office: PO Box 1551 Raleigh NC 27602*

SMITH, SHIRLEY ANN LIVELY, university administrator, counselor; b. Dallas, Aug. 2, 1934; d. Richard Price and Elsie Mae (Keathley) Lively; children—Richard Whitfield. Student Tex. Christian U., 1952; B.S., U. Tex., 1955; M.A., So. Methodist U., 1967. Cert. profl. elem. tchr., Tex.; cert. profl. secondary tchr., Tex.; cert. profl. counselor, Tex.; lic. prof. counselor, Tex. Tchr. jr. and sr. high Dallas Ind. Sch. Dist., 1956-58, 62-65, guidance counselor, 1965-67, dir. Gen. Ednl. Devel. testing, 1979-85; elem. tchr. Midland Ind. Sch. Dist., Tex., 1958-62; mem. faculty, dept. edn. So. Methodist U., Dallas, 1967-68, part-time, 1969, 72, 75, 79-83, assoc. dir. Master Liberal Arts degree program, 1983—, Coll. Prep. Inst., 1985—; testing workshop presenter Dallas Ind. Sch. Dist., 1969, 80, 82; cons., asst. auditor Ednl. Testing Service, Dallas, 1979-82; homebound tchr. Highland Park Ind. Sch. Dist., Dallas, part-time 1982-83. Vol., Republican Party, Dallas, 1972-73; mem. parent and family life bd. PTA, Dallas, 1977-78; vol. task force Dallas Ind. Sch. Dist., 1980, 81, 82. Recipient Merit Tchr. award Sch. Bd. Midland Ind. Sch. Dist., 1960-61. Mem. Am. Assn. Counseling and Devel., Am. Assn. Measurement and Evaluation in Counseling and Devel., Tex. Mental Health Counselors Assn. (treas. 1984-85, membership chmn. 1985-86), Tex. Assn. Measurement and Evaluation in Counseling and Devel., North Central Tex. Assn. Counseling and Devel., Zeta Tau Alpha (chmn. charity bazaar 1972, 73, v.p. programs 1973-74). Methodist. Club: Charity for Singles (pres. 1960-61). Avocations: reading; sewing; ceramics; knitting. Office: So Methodist U PO Box 253 Dallas TX 75275

SMITH, STEPHEN EARLE, construction company executive; b. Dallas, Oct. 7, 1947; s. Alpha Durward and Oma (Mettauer) S.; m. Susan Kay Krueger, Apr. 5, 1975; children—Edward Stuart, Stephanie Krueger. B.S. in Architecture, Tex. A&M U., 1971. Architect, Kirby-Mayer & Assocs., Dallas, 1971-73, Brooks & Orendain Inc., Dallas, 1973, Thomas E. Stanley, Dallas, 1973-75; project mgr. J.L. Williams & Co., Dallas, 1975-77; project mgr. Butcher & Sweeney Constrn. Co., Ft. Worth, 1977-85, v.p. Butcher & Sweeney Constrn. Co., Lydick & Adams, Inc., 1985—. Mem. Associated Gen. Contractors Am. Republican. Methodist. Club: Optimist. Home: 5309 Wagon Track Ct Fort Worth TX 76132 Office: Butcher & Sweeney Constrn Co Lydick & Adams Inc 1633 Rogers Rd Fort Worth TX 76107

SMITH, SUSAN ANN, nursing administrator; b. Newport, Ark., Mar. 24, 1953; d. Thomas Vernon and Helen (Huie) Wise; m. David Bruce Smith; children—Bryan, Chad. B.S.N., U. Central Ark., 1975; now postgrad. in nursing. Cert. intravenous therapist, Ark. Office nurse Smith Clinic, Bradford, Ark., 1975-76; team leader psychiatry Bapt. Med. Ctr., Little Rock, 1976-78, instr. Sch. Practical Nursing, 1978-79; infection control nurse Central Ark. Gen. Hosp., Searcy, 1979-81, tng. and devel. coordinator, 1981—. Mem. Gamma Beta Phi, Sigma Theta Tau. Republican. Baptist. Avocations: crocheting; counted cross stitching; water sports; family activities. Home: PO Box 116 Searcy AR 72143

SMITH, TAD RANDOLPH, lawyer; b. El Paso, July 20, 1928; s. Eugene Rufus and Dorothy (Derrick) S.; B.B.A., U. Tex., 1952, LL.B., 1951; m. JoAnn Wilson, Aug. 24, 1949; children—Laura, Derrick, Cameron Ann. Admitted to Tex. bar, 1951; asso. firm Kemp, Smith, White, Duncan & Hammond, El Paso, 1951, partner, 1952—; dir. El Paso Electric Co., State Nat. Bank El Paso, Property Trust Am. Active United Way of El Paso, NCCJ. Recipient Humanitarian award El Paso chpt. NCCJ. Mem. Am. Bar Assn., State Bar Tex., El Paso Bar Assn. (pres. 1971-72), El Paso C. of C. (dir. 1979-82). Republican. Methodist. Home: 1202 Thunderbird El Paso TX 79912 Office: 2000 State Nat Plaza El Paso TX 79901

SMITH, TERRENCE JOHN, financial services company executive; b. N.Y.C., Apr. 29, 1940; s. John Frances and Florence May (Foster) S.; m. Eileen Jane Malone, June 10, 1967; children—Matthew, Daniel, Deborah. B.S. with honors in Computer Sci., NYU, 1971; M.B.A., Fairleigh Dickinson U., 1976. Mgr., Equitable Life Ins. Co., N.Y.C., 1958-70; mgr. data ctr., dir. corp. info. services Schering Plough, N.J., 1971-79; v.p. tech. services Am. Express, N.Y.C., 1979-80, v.p. data processing, Ft. Lauderdale, 1981-84, sr. v.p. ops., 1984—. Served with USCGR, 1963-70. Mem. Beta Gamma Sigma, Delta Pi Sigma. Home: 1901 SW 67th Ave Plantation FL 33317 Office: 777 American Expressway Fort Lauderdale FL 33337

SMITH, TERRY RANDALL, accounting firm executive; b. Monahans, Tex., Aug. 9, 1950; s. John Jackson and Ocil Lorene (Burch) S.; m. Frances Catherine Green, Nov. 21, 1971 (div. Apr. 1977); m. Florence Joan Gurley, Sept. 16, 1978; 1 child, James Cassidy. B.B.A., Sul Ross State U., 1973. C.P.A., Tex. Asst. instr. Sul Ross State U., Alpine, Tex., 1972-73; staff acct. Hoyer & Hardisty C.P.A.s, Monahans, 1974-81, ptnr. Hoyer, Hardisty, Kelley, Smith & Welch, C.P.A.s, Monahans, 1981—. Coach Monahans Freshman Div. Baseball, 1982-84; sec. Crime Stoppers Anonymous, Monahans, 1983-85. Mem. Am. Inst. C.P.A.s, Tex. Soc. C.P.A.S, Permian Basin Soc. C.P.A.s. (dir.-at-large 1982-83). Republican. Baptist. Lodge: Lions (bd. dirs. 1982-84, pres. 1984-85, zone chmn. 1985—). Avocations: golf; hunting; yard work. Home: 1204 S Murray Monahans TX 79756 Office: Hoyer Hardisty Kelley Smith & Welch 300 S Main St PO Box 640 Monahans TX 79756

SMITH, THOMAS EARLE, JR., lawyer, state senator; b. Oxford, N.C., July 22, 1938; s. Thomas Earle and Margaret Louise (Osterhout) S.; A.B., Davidson Coll., 1960; J.D., U. S.C., 1963; m. Elizabeth Eulalia Munn, June 23, 1962; children—Mary Dresden, Amy Louise. Admitted to S.C. Bar Assn., 1963; mem. firm James P. Mozingo, 1963-65; individual practice law, Pamplico, S.C., 1965-73; partner firm Nettles, Smith, Turbeville and Reddeck, Pamplico, 1973-79; sole practice law, 1979—; dir. Pamplico Bank and Trust Co., Johnsonville (S.C.) State Bank; partner Ind. Warehouse, Pamplico, 1972—; mem. S.C. Ho. of Reps., 1966-72; mem. S.C. Senate, 1973—. Recipient Outstanding Legislator award S.C. Council Exceptional Children 1976; Senate of Year award S.C. Assn. Retarded Citizens, 1975; Legislator of year award S.C. Young Democrats, 1979. Mem. ABA, S.C. Bar Assn. Democrat. Methodist. Clubs: Lions, Masons, Shriners. Office: 100 Walnut St Pamplico SC 29583

SMITH, THOMAS ERROL, tobacco company executive; b. Mansfield, Ohio, Dec. 8, 1941; s. Homer William and Margaret (Piper) S.; m. Mary Constance Castle, Nov. 25, 1966; children—Thomas Travis, Kelly Cheri. B.S. in Bus. Fin. and Acctg., Eastern Ky. U., 1964; M.S.B.E. in Fin. and Computer Sci., U. N.C., 1973. Vice pres. fin. and adminstrn., chief fin. officer R.J. Reynolds Tobacco P.R./Caribbean, 1979-82, v.p. fin. area III, Latin Am./Caribbean Hdqrs., Miami, Fla., 1982—. Coach youth football, baseball and basketball. Served with USMC, 1963-64. Republican. Clubs: Masons, Shriners. Office: 8325 NW 53d St Suite 101 Miami FL 33166

SMITH, THOMAS LUTHER, educational administrator; b. Gatesville, N.C., Jan. 11, 1943; s. John Lee and Genevieve (Brown) S.; A.A., Chowan Coll., 1963; B.S., Atlantic Christian Coll., 1965; M.A., Appalachian State U., 1975; Edn. Specialist, 1976. Tchr., Nansemond County Schs., Suffolk, Va., 1965-66, Suffolk (Va.) City Schs., 1966-69; asst. prin. Wake County Schs., Raleigh, N.C., 1969-70; headmaster St. Timothy's Sch., Raleigh, 1970-73, Father G.B.S. Hale High Sch., Raleigh, 1973-75; prin. Brunswick County Schs., Lawrenceville, Va., 1975—, adult edn. tchr., 1976-78, adult edn. supr., 1978—, chief examiner GED, 1981—; instr. Southside Va. Community Coll., Alberta, Va., 1979-81. Mem. Va. Assn. Elem. Sch. Prins., Nat. Assn. Elem. Sch. Prins. Nat. Community Edn. Assn., Am. Assn. Adult and Continuing Edn., Adult Edn. Assn. Va., Va. Jaycees, Playmakers, Phi Delta Kappa, Alpha Sigma Phi. Democrat. Episcopalian. Lodges: Rotary, Lions, Masons, Shriners, Moose. Home: 527 Chaptice Rd PO Box 812 South Hill VA 23970 Office: Red Oak Elementary Sch Route 1 Box 300 Alberta VA 23821

SMITH, THOMAS RALPH, mathematics educator; b. Moselle, Miss., Mar. 21, 1933; s. Jay B. and Oliva Ruth (Partridge) S.; m. Sybil Christian Smith, May 31, 1962; 1 child, Anne Renee Grierson. B.S., La. Coll., 1959; M.S., U. So. Miss., 1963. High sch. tchr. Jones Country System, Laurel, Miss., 1960-62; instr. Decater Jr. Coll., Miss., 1962-63; high sch. prin. Jackson County System, Pascagoula, Miss., 1963-65; chmn. math. dept. Miss. Gulf Coast Jr. Coll., Gautier, 1965—. Served as sgt. USMC, 1954-57. Mem. Nat. Council Tchrs. Math., Am. Soc. 2-Year Coll. Math. (Miss. rep.), Miss. Tchrs. Coll. Math. (pres. 1984-85), NEA, Miss. Assn. Educators, Phi Delta Kappa. Baptist. Club: Gideon (Pascagoula) (v.p.). Lodge: Rotary (bd. dirs. Gautier). Avocations: gardening; golf. Home: 1816 Anders Rd Gautier MS 39553

SMITH, TIMOTHY DONNELL, mortgage banker; b. Atlanta, Apr. 12, 1944; s. Claude Hampton and Billie Lee (Hall) Smith; m. Charlotte Whaley, May 24, 1975; children—Timothy Donnell, James Townsend. B.A. in Journalism, U. Ga., 1970, B.B.A., 1971. Sr. v.p., prodn. mgr. Scott Hudgens Mortgage Inc., Atlanta, 1977-81; v.p., regional mgr. Arvida Mortgage Co., Atlanta, 1981-84, v.p. residential prodn., Clearwater, Fla., 1984—. Mem. Mortgage Bankers Assn. of Ga. (sec.-treas. 1983—), Atlanta Mortgage Bankers Assn. (pres. 1983-84). Club: Atlanta Athletic (Duluth, Ga.). Office: Arvida Mortgage Co 1307 US Hwy 19 S Clearwater FL 33546

SMITH, WALTER S., federal judge; b. Marlin, Tex., Oct. 26, 1940; s. Walter S. and Mary Elizabeth Smith; children—Debra Elizabeth, Susan Kay. B.A., Baylor U., 1964, J.D., 1966. Assoc., Dunnam & Dunnam, Waco, Tex., 1966-69, Wallace & Smith, Waco, 1969-78, Haley, Fulbright, Waco, 1978-80; judge Tex. Dist. Ct., Waco, 1980-83; U.S. magistrate, Western Tex., 1983-84; judge U.S. Dist. Ct. (we. dist.) Tex., Waco, 1984—. Office: PO Box 1906 Waco TX 76703*

SMITH, WANDA BILLINGSLEA, realtor; b. Augusta, Ark., Nov. 1, 1923; d. Eugene Lewis and Berniece (Garrison) Williamson; m. Claude Edgar McCreight, Jr., July 21, 1945 (div. 1962); children—William Richard, Claudia, Cindy; m. 2d, Clay Blevins Yoe, Jr., Jan. 5, 1965 (dec. 1967); m. 3d, Rex Alan Smith, Oct. 3, 1980. B.A., Henderson State U., 1945; postgrad. U. Ark., 1962-63, 1979-80. Tchr. Am. Sch. Belem, Para, Brazil, 1959-62, Fayetteville (Ark.) High Sch., 1962-65; owner, mgr. Clay Yoe Devel. Co., Fayetteville, 1967-79; co-owner, sec., bd. dirs. Billingslea & Kirby, Inc., Nu-Tech., Inc., 1969-71; realtor Schultz & Taylor, Inc., Fayetteville, 1973-76; adminstrv. asst. to E. G. Bradberry, Fayetteville, 1977-79; sec. bd. B & B Resources, Inc., Continental Ozark, Inc., Fayetteville, Ark., 1977-79. Realtor Al Hughes Agy., Fayetteville, 1976—; editorial asst. to writers, Fayetteville, 1974—. Bd. dirs. P.T.A., Ft. Worth, 1956-58; sec. bd. Am. Sch. Belem, Para, Brazil, 1960-61. Mem. Ark. Realtors Assn., Nat. Assn. Realtors. Republican. Episcopalian. Home: 208 N East St Fayetteville AR 72701 Office: Al Hughes Agy 1765 N College Ave Fayetteville AR 72701

SMITH, WARREN THOMAS, clergyman, educator; b. Knoxville, Tenn., Oct. 20, 1923; s. Warren T. and Lola May (Jones) S.; m. Barbara Ann Sullards, Dec. 27, 1949; 1 child, James Warren. Student Maryville Coll., 1942-43; B.A., Ohio Wesleyan U., 1945; B.D., Emory U., 1948, postgrad., 1974-75; Ph.D., Boston U., 1953; D.D., Lincoln Meml. U., 1958. Ordained deacon Methodist Ch., 1947, elder, 1949; full connection N. Ga. Ann. Conf., 1951. Pastor, Waldo Meth. Ch. (Ohio), 1944-45, Howard Ave. Meth. Ch., Dorchester, Mass., 1949-50; assoc. pastor Peachtree Rd. Meth. Ch., Atlanta, 1950-53; pastor Sharp Meml. Meth. Ch., dir. religious life, head dept. religion Young Harris Coll., 1953-57; pastor Trinity Meth. Ch., Atlanta, 1957-60; mem. staff Bd. edn. Meth. Ch., 1960-64; pastor Young Harris Meml. Ch., Athens, Ga., 1964-66, N. Decatur Meth. Ch., 1966-68; sr. pastor First United Meth. Ch., College Park, Ga., 1968-74; asst. prof. ch. history Interdenominational Theol. Ctr., Atlanta, 1974-79, assoc. prof., 1979-84, prof., chmn. dept., 1984—; interpreter for Meth. Bicentennial, N. Ga., 1980-84. Author: Thomas Coke, Foreign Minister of Methodism, 1959; Heralds of Christ, 1963; Selections form the Writings of Thomas Coke, 1966; At Christmas, 1969; Preludes: Georgia, Methodism, The American Revolution, 1976; And the Play Goes On: Characters in the Biblical Drama, 1980; Augustine: His Life and Thought, 1980; Harry Hosier: Circuit Rider, 1981; 1784 I Remember the Christmas Conference, 1983; Journey in Faith, 1984; John Wesley and Slavery, 1986; contbr. articles to religious jours. Nat. Endowment for Humanities grantee, 1969. Mem. Am. Soc. Ch. History, Wesley Hist. Soc. (Eng.), Am. Hist. Assn., Southeastern Jurisdiction Hist. Soc., North Ga. Hist. Soc., World Meth. Hist. Soc., Theta Phi, Omicron Delta Kappa, Delta Tau Delta. Office: 671 Beckwith St SW Atlanta GA 30314

SMITH, WAYNE DONALD, estimating engineer; b. Bellevue, Pa., July 26, 1942; s. Joseph Wylie and Hazel (Willoughby) S.; m. Patricia C. Wagner, Nov. 24, 1966; children—Daniel W., Michele E., Maureen C. Grad. in Design Tech., Pa. State U., 1968. Registered profl. estimator; lic. gen. contractor, Fla. Estimator, field engr. Mc Donough Constrn. Co., Atlanta, 1968-74, Gene McKee Constrn. Co., Atlanta, 1974-75; senior estimator Helton Constrn. Co., Atlanta, 1975-76; project mgr. Banks Constrn. Co., Atlanta, 1976-77; project engr. Hensel Phelps, Atlanta, 1977-79; lead estimator Transit Products Co., Atlanta, 1979-83; sr. civil estimator Parsons, Brinckerhoff, Tudor, Atlanta, 1983—. Pres. St. Thomas More PTA, Decatur, Ga., 1977; active mem. Inman Park Restoration Assn., recipient Community Service award, 1976; bd. dirs. Gail Theater, Atlanta; founder, bd. dirs. Atlanta Edgewood Railway Co. Served with U.S. Army, 1960-63. Mem. Am. Soc. Profl. Estimators (pres. Atlanta chpt. 1983-84). Roman Catholic. Club: Toastmasters (Atlanta). Home: 80 Spruce St NE Atlanta GA 30307

SMITH, WAYNE L., banker; b. Monmouth, Ill., Aug. 7, 1936; s. Galen and Mary Kathryn (Angel) S.; m. Janet E. Gray, Mar. 17, 1956; 4 children. B.S. in Acctg., U. Cin., 1969; grad. cert. in banking U. Wis.-Madison, 1969; cert. comml. lending U. Okla., 1971. With Central Bank & Trust Co., Lexington, Ky., 1975—, pres., 1976—; former lectr. Cuyahoga Community Coll., Cleve.; lectr. U. Wis. Postgrad. Sch. Banking; thesis examiner Stonier Grad. Sch. Banking, Rutgers U., 1971—. Bd. regents Nat. Comml. Lending Sch., U. Okla., 1972-79; bd. dirs. United Way of the Bluegrass, Lexington, 1976—, pres., 1981, 82, chmn. 1978 campaign; bd. dirs. Jr. Achievement of the Bluegrass, Lexington, 1978—, pres., 1982-83; bd. dirs. Triangle Park Found., Lexington, 1981—; bd. dirs. Lexington Arts Council, 1981—, pres., 1983-84; state fin. chair Jim Bunning for Gov. Ky., 1983. Mem. Am. Inst. Banking (past chpt. bd. govs.), Nat. Comml. Lending Sch. Alumni Assn. (past chpt. pres.), Am. Bankers Assn. (past exec. com. of comml. lending div.; past edn. com. nat.), Lexington Area C. of C. (dir., chmn.-elect). Home: 973 Turkey Foot Rd Lexington KY 40502 Office: Kinkaid Towers Lexington KY 40507

SMITH, WILLIAM CHARLES, II, optometrist; b. Blairsville, Pa., July 23, 1953; s. William Charles and Dorothy Marie (Bell) S.; m. Kathleen Toohey, June 18, 1977; children—Jessica, Billy. B.S. cum laude, St. Vincent Coll., 1975; O.D., Ill. Coll., 1979. Optometrist, prin. Wm. C. Smith O.D., P.C., Murfreesboro, Tenn., 1980—. Recipient Cert. of Appreciation, ARC, 1982, 83, 84, 85. Mem. Murfreesboro Jaycees (community devel. v.p. 1984—), Middle Tenn. Optometric Soc. (sec.-treas. 1984—), Tenn. Optometric Soc., Am. Optometric Soc., S.E. Council Optometrists. Democrat. Roman Catholic. Lodges: K.C. (grand knight 1984—, Knight of Yr. award 1983, 84), Lions (sec. 1984—), Moose. Avocations: golfing; racquetball; water skiing; stamp collecting. Home: 1404 Stonewall Blvd Murfreesboro TN 37130 Office: 102 E College St Murfreesboro TN 37130

SMITH, WILLIAM EDWARD, furniture manufacturing company executive; b. Kevil, Ky., June 15, 1922; s. William Gobel and Grace (Hatler) S.; m. Patricia Sprecher Torson, June 20, 1954 (div. June 1964); children—William Edward, Matthew Tory; m. Laura Poe Ervin, Nov. 27, 1969. B.S., Harvard U., 1944. With sales dept. Heritage Henredon Furniture Co., High Point, N.C., 1947-49, sales rep., Chgo., 1949-56; sales mgr. Henredon Furniture Industries, Inc., Morganton, N.C., 1957-77, pres., chief exec. officer, Morgantown, N.C., 1977—. Served to 1st lt. F.A., U.S. Army, 1943-46; ETO. Democrat. Presbyterian. Office: Henredon Furniture Industries Inc PO Box 70 Morganton NC 28655*

SMITH, WILLIAM JACOB, II, bank examiner; b. Huntington, W. Va., May 15, 1946; s. William Jacob and Opal (Cyrus) S.; student Ohio State U., 1964-65; B.B.A., Morehead State U., 1969; certificate Am. Inst. Banking, 1973; grad. Stonier Grad. Sch. Banking, Rutgers U., 1980; m. Patricia Rose Ball, June 16, 1973; children—Stephanie Suzanne, William Jacob III, Matthew Arnold. Law enforcement officer Village of Chesapeake (Ohio), 1967-69; trainee examiner FDIC, Columbus, 1969-70, jr. asst. examiner, 1970-71, sr. asst. examiner, 1971-73, examiner, 1974-78, bank examiner (EDP), 1978-84, field office supr., 1984—; EDP instr. FDIC Tng. Center, Arlington, Va. Mem. Chesapeake Vol. Fire Dept., 1959-70. Republican. Baptist. Lodge: Masons. Home: 3245 Carriage Ln Lexington KY 40502 Office: Suite 2600 One Nationwide Plaza Columbus OH 43215

SMITH, WILLIAM JOSEPH, gas company executive; b. McComb, Miss., Feb. 18, 1927; s. Howard C. and Tinie Maureen (Thompson) S.; m. Rosemary Jones, Aug. 14, 1946; children—William Carl, David Anderson, Thomas Joseph, Sam Jones, Jeffrey Luther. Student, Edinburg Jr. Coll., 1946-47; B.S.E.E., Tex. A&M U., 1949. Prodn. supr. Tex. Electric Service Co., Ft. Worth, 1949-56; utilities systems engr. Gen. Electric Co., Cin., 1956-57; power engr. Dow Chem. Co., 1957-58; project engr. Barnard & Burk Pipeline Engrs., 1958-59; pres. Fla. Gas Transmission Co., Winter Park, 1959—. Served with USN, 1945-46. Mem. Fla. Natural Gas Assn., So. Natural Gas Assn. (dir.), Am. Gas Assn. Republican. Episcopalian. Office: PO Box 44 Winter Park FL 32790*

SMITH, WILLIAM LEWIS, editor, editorial consultant; b. Bklyn., Apr. 22, 1929; s. James Austin and Doris Emeline (Loomis) S.; m. Janet McNicoll Hawkins, May 28, 1961; children—Heather, William Lewis, Austin McNicoll. A.B., Colgate U., 1952. Asst. makeup editor N.Y. Times, 1955-56; asst. editor Businessweek, 1956-58; pub. editor Pa. State U. Press, State College, 1959-61; corr. Bus. Week, Washington, 1961-69; assoc. editor U.S. News and World Report, Washington, 1969-71; editor Transport Topics, Washington, 1977—. Columnist various newspapers and mags. Contbr. articles on wine and food, golf, and skiing to publs. Mem. Nat. Alliance Businessmen (dir. pub. relations, 1969). Club: Nat. Press (Washington). Home: 1544 Hunting Ave McLean VA 22102 Office: Transport Topics 2200 Mill Rd Alexandria VA 22314

SMITH, WILLIAM LLOYD, engineer; b. Asheville, N.C., May 27, 1957; s. J. Lloyd and Betty Edna (Robinson) S.; m. Royanna Hall, Aug. 5, 1978; children—Leslie Erin, Lauren Elizabeth. B.S. magna cum laude, N.C. State U., 1979. Registered profl. engr., N.C. Engr., So. Bell Telephone Co., Asheville, 1979-81, mgr. engring., 1981—. Recipient Outstanding Sr. award Assn. Gen. Contractors, 1979. Mem. Nat. Soc. Profl. Engrs., ASCE, Profl. Engrs. Soc. N.C., Tau Beta Pi, Chi Epsilon. Office: Southern Bell Telephone Co 1100 E Wendover Ave Greensboro NC 27405

SMITH, WILLIAM MILTON, bishop; b. Stockton, Ala., Dec. 18, 1918; s. George and Elizabeth Smith; ed. Ala. State U., Tuskegee Inst., Livinstone Coll., Hool Sem., So. Meth. U., Perkins Sch. Theology; m. Ida M. Anderson, Jan. 19, 1935; 1 dau., Eula C. Goole. Ordained to ministry African Methodist Episcopal Zion Ch.; minister various chs.; bishop African Meth. Episcopal Zion Ch., Buffalo, from 1960; now sr. bishop, Mobile, Ala. Trustee, Ala. State U., 1980. Recipient award Ebony mag., 1980. Republican. Office: African Meth Episcopal Zion Ch 3753 Springhill Ave Mobile AL 36608

SMITH, WILLIAM PRESTON, JR., employee development and training specialist; b. Salisbury, Md., Mar. 26, 1948; s. William and Buelah Mae (Barkley) S.; m. Karen Elaine White, May 19, 1984; 1 child, William Preston III. B.S., Hampton U., 1970; postgrad. Humanities Inst., Ind. U., summer 1972, Journalism Inst., Yale U., 1970; doctoral candidate Emory U., 1974-78, George Washington U., 1984—. Staff program dir. Urban Youth Core, Hartford, Conn., summer 1969; reporter intern Hartford Courant, 1970; English tchr. Norwalk High Sch., Conn., 1970-74; instr. Morehouse Coll., Atlanta, 1976-78, dir. Afro-Am. studies, 1976-78; instr. humanities Atlanta U., summer 1978, Drexel U., Phila., 1979-80; equal employment opportunity specialist Aviation Supply Office, Phila., 1979-80; equal opportunity and human resource mgmt. specialist Navy Dept., Arlington, Va., 1980-82; human resource mgmt. specialist Naval Civilian Personnel Command, Arlington, 1982-83, employee devel. specialist, 1983-85; tng. mgr. Office of Insp. Gen., EPA Hdqrs., 1985—; human resource mgmt. and communications cons., Washington, 1980—. Contbr. articles to profl. jours. Mem. Big Bros. Am., Washington, 1983—. Served with USAR, 1970-76. Recipient Outstanding Service citation, Afro-Am. Educators Am., Conn., 1974; fellow NEH, 1974-77, Lilly Found., 1972; Rockefeller Found. grantee, 1979. Mem. Am. Soc. Tng. and Devel., Blacks in Govt., Nat. Urban League, Am. Mgmt. Assn., Sigma Tau Delta.

SMITH, WILLIAM RAY, chiropractor; b. Huntington, W.Va., Nov. 10, 1949; s. Morris Harvey and Nancy Jo (Dray) S.; m. Jane Ellen Mills, June 26, 1971; children—Julie Lauren, Sarah Ann. Student, Marshal U., 1967-70; D. Chiropractic, Palmer Coll. Chiropractic, 1974. Diplomate Nat. Bd. Chiropractic Examiners, W.Va. Bd. Chiropractic Examiners. Chiropractor, Huntington (W.Va.) Chiropractic Clinic, 1974, Dunbar, W.Va., 1974—; mem. adv. council Workmen's Compensation Fund, 1982—; lectr., tchr. to state health agys., ins. cos., civic and ch. groups and schs. on chiropractic. Bd. dirs. Revival Crusade, Charleston, W.Va.; mem. Dunbar (W.Va.) Civil Service Fire Works Commn., 1974. Served with U.S. Army, 1970-71. Mem. Am. Chiropractic Assn. (del., W.Va. dir. polit. action com.), Council on Chiropractic Nutrition, Council on Roetgenology, W.Va. Chiropractic Soc. (pres. 1979-81, sec.-treas. 1981-83, bd. dirs. 1976, 83), Palmer Coll. Alumni Assn. (pres.). Democrat. Baptist. Club: Kiwanis (Dunbar, W.Va.). Home: 147 Maplewood Estates Scott Depot WV 25560 Office: 100 Dunbar Office Park Dunbar WV 25064

SMITH, WILLIAM ROBERT, clergyman, writer; b. Evansville, Ind., June 3, 1935; s. William Claude and Mary Lee (Toombs) S.; m. Josephine Freudt; children—Mary William Robert, Raymond. B.S. with honors, East Tenn. State U., 1958; B.D., Southwestern Baptist Theol. Sem., Ft. Worth, 1966, M.Div., 1967; D.Min., Union Theol. Sem., Richmond, Va., 1975. Ordained to ministry So. Bapt. Ch., 1956. Pastor Thalia Lynn Bapt. Ch., Virginia Beach, Va., 1960-63, Morningside Bapt. Ch., Savannah, Ga., 1967-71, Chamberlayne Bapt. Ch., Richmond, Va., 1971-81, Terry Parker Bapt. Ch., Jacksonville, Fla., 1981-82, 1st Bapt. Ch., South Miami, Fla., 1982—; pres. Norfolk (Va.) Bapt. Pastor's Conf. 1961, Savannah Bapt. Pastor's Conf., 1970, Chatham Clergy Conf., Savannah, 1970; v.p. Miami Bapt. Pastor's Conf. (Fla.), 1983; moderator Miami Bapt. Assn., 1984. Author: Our Unfinished Revolution, 1976; contbr. numerous articles to denominational and other religious and secular publs. Mem. Community Health Planning Agy., Savannah, 1969-70; mem. Savannah Mayor's Com. on Drug Abuse, 1970; chmn. The Ctr., Savannah, 1970; bd. dirs. Jacksonville Blood Bank, 1981-82. Recipient Bicentennial Preaching award Va. Bapt. Bd., 1976, also numerous awards for civic work. Home: 17821 SW 78th Ave Miami FL 33157 Office: First Bapt Ch 6767 Sunset Dr Miami FL 33157

SMITH, WILLIAM ROBERT, francise executive; b. Louisville, Feb. 13, 1926; s. William H. and Flora (Gamage) S.; student parochial schs., Louisville; m. Rena V. Parker, Sept. 8, 1973; children—Steve, Marcia, Diane, Douglas, Gregory, Janet, Karen. With Ky. Retail Food Dealers Assn., Louisville, 1947-64; pres., owner Marmi, Inc., doing bus. as H&R Block Louisville, 1959—; chmn. bd. Brewer-Smith Fin. Planners, 1983—; pres. Advanced Advt. Treas. Jr. Achievement KYANA, 1980-81, now bd. dirs.; mem. U.S. Congl. Adv. Bd. Served with USN, 1945-46. Mem. Louisville Sales Club (founder), President's Soc. Bellarmine Coll., Sales and Mktg. Execs. (dir. 1978), Block Franchise Assn. (sec. 1975-83), Assoc. Industries Ky., Louisville C. of C., Ky. C. of C., Food Industries Assn. Execs. (sec. 1960-61), Entrepreneur Soc. (founder, pres. 1984—), Productivity Internat., Am. Soc. Tng. and Devel. Democrat. Roman Catholic. Lodge: Optomists. Club: Advertising of Louisville. Office: 1359 S 3d St Louisville KY 40208

SMITH, WILLIAM T., petroleum and natural gas company executive; b. 1924; married. B.S. in Geology, U. Mich., M.S., 1948. Vice pres., div. mgr. Standard Oil & Gas Co., 1948-75; exec. v.p. Amoco Prodn. Co., 1975; pres. Champlin Petroleum Co., Ft. Worth, 1975—, also dir.; dir. Union Pacific Corp., First United Bankcard Corp., Tandy Corp. Office: Champlin Petroleum Co 5301 Camp Bowie Blvd Box 9365 Fort Worth TX 76107*

SMITH, WILLIAM WALTER, naval officer, optometrist; b. Bellows Falls, Vt., Feb. 6, 1945; s. Walter Henry and Bradleigh (Washburn) S.; m. Hazel Anne Fancy, June 1967 (div. 1976); children—Scott William, Mark Allen; m. Theresa Colleen Medley, July 2, 1977; 1 child, Andrew Thomas. Student, U. Vt., 1962; B.S., Mass. Coll. Optometry, 1967, O.D., 1967. Commd. lt. (j.g.) U.S. Navy, 1967, advanced through grades to capt., 1985; clin. optometrist U.S. Naval Hosp., St. Albans, N.Y., 1967-69; safety vision officer Naval Air Sta., Pensacola, Fla., 1969-70; chief of optometry U.S. Naval Hosp., Yokosuka, Japan, 1970-74, Bremerton, Wash., 1974-80; exec. officer Naval Ophthalmic Support and Tng. Activity, Naval Weapons Sta., Yorktown, Va., 1980—; tng. officer Naval Opticians Sch., Naval Weapons Sta., 1980-84; clin. optometrist Bd. Med. Clinic, Naval Weapons Sta., 1980—; mem. curriculum rev. bd. Thomas Nelson Community Coll., Newport News, Va., 1980—; mem. com. Am. Nat. Standards Inst., N.Y.C., 1981—. Fellow Am. Acad. Optometry; mem. Armed Forces Optometric Soc., Am. Med. Surgeons U.S. Republican. Club: Naval Weapons Sta. Golf Assn. Lodge: Elks. Avocations: golf; hunting; fishing; gourmet cooking. Home: Box 98 Naval Weapons Sta Yorktown VA 23691 Office: Naval Ophthalmic Support and Tng Activity Naval Weapons Sta Yorktown VA 23691

SMITH, WILLIE TESREAU, JR., judge, lawyer; b. Sumter, S.C., Jan. 17, 1920; s. Willie T. and Mary (Moore) S.; student Benedict Coll., 1937-40; A.B., Johnson C. Smith U., 1947; LL.B., S.C. State Coll., 1954, J.D., 1976; m. Anna Marie Clark, June 9, 1955; 1 son, Willie Tesreau, III. Admitted to S.C. bar, 1954; began gen. practice, Greenville, 1954; past exec. dir. Legal Services Agy. Greenville County, Inc.; state family ct. judge 13th Jud. Circuit S.C., 1977—. Mem. adv. bd. Greenville Tech. Edn. Center Adult Edn. Program and Para-Legal Program; past bd. dirs. Greenville Urban League; past trustee Greenville County Sch. Dist. Served with AUS, 1942-45, USAF, 1949-52. Mem. Am., Nat. (jud. council), S.C., Greenville County bar assns., Southeastern Lawyers Assn., Nat. Council Juvenile and Family Ct. Judges, Am. Legion, Greater Greenville C. of C. (past dir.), Phillis Wheatley Assn. (dir.), NAACP, Omega Psi Phi. Presbyterian (past chmn. bd. trustees Fairfield-McClelland Presbytery). Clubs: Masons, Shriners, Rotary. Home: 601 Jacob Rd Greenville SC 29605 Office: County Office Bldg S Main St PO Box 757 Greenville SC 29602

SMITHERMAN, HOWARD O'NEAL, psychologist, researcher; b. Clanton, Ala., Jan. 21, 1949; s. Adolph Howard and Willie Mae (Emfinger) S.; m. Sandra Kay Hayes, Apr. 9, 1971; 1 child, Katie. B.S. in Psychology, U. Ala.-Tuscaloosa, 1971, M.A. in Sociology, 1973, Ph.D. in Ednl. Psychology, 1977. Research assoc. U. Ala., Tuscaloosa, 1975-78, statis. research analyst Chancellor's office, 1984—; research assoc. Va. Community Colls., Richmond, 1979-80; community psychologist Dept. Mental Health, Tuscaloosa, 1980-81, dir. community services, 1981-84. Author: Handbook of Scales in C & D, 1983. Contbr. articles to profl. jours. Recipient Research award Ctr. for Study of Aging. Mem. Am. Psychol. Assn., Ala. Psychol. Assn., Assoc. Instl. Research. Club: MicroComputer Users Group (Tuscaloosa). Home: 100 Heritage Hills Tuscaloosa AL 35401 Office: Univ Ala System 401 Queen City Ave Tuscaloosa AL 35401

SMITHGALL, CHARLES AUGUSTUS, III, broadcasting executive; b. Atlanta, July 19, 1942; s. Charles Augustus and Celestia (Bailey) S.; m. Sally Griffitts, Sept. 5, 1970; children—Charles, Meghan Griffitts. B.S., Ga. Inst. Tech., 1965; student Wharton Sch., 1966, Colo. State U., 1970, Harvard Bus. Sch., 1975. Vice pres. Holder Constrn. Co., Atlanta, 1970-75, Chattanooga Cable TV Co., 1976-78, Southmedia Co., Atlanta, 1978-79; sales exec. Turner Broadcasting System, Atlanta, 1979-81; pres. WCNN Radio, Atlanta, 1981—. Area chmn. United Way, Atlanta, 1974-75; chmn. Big Heart Award Banquet, Atlanta, 1981—. Served to 1st lt. U.S. Army, 1968-70. Mem. Atlanta C. of C. (membership com. 1973-74), Ga. Tech. Alumni Assn. (trustee 1981—). Clubs: Piedmont Driving (Atlanta); Harvard Business School Alumni. Home: 2866 Wyngate NW Atlanta GA 30305

SMOAKE, PATRICIA PRIDEMORE, communications executive; b. Union, S.C., Nov. 18, 1954; d. Carson Jack and Mary Nell (Liner) Pridemore; m. James Gregory Smoake, Dec. 29, 1973. B.A. in Journalism summa cum laude, U. S.C., 1976. Asst. to exec. v.p. S.C. Hosp. Assn., West Columbia, 1976-77, coordinator legis. and govtl. affairs, 1977-79, v.p. for govt. relations activities, 1979-82, v.p. communications, 1982-84, v.p. pub. relations, 1984—. Mem. Pub. Relations Soc. Am., Carolinas Hosp. Pub. Relations Soc., Phi Beta Kappa, Kappa Tau Alpha. Lutheran. Home: 110 Sweetgum Dr Cayce SC 29033 Office: 101 Medical Circle West Columbia SC 29169

SMOCK, CAROLYN DIANE, lawyer; b. Iowa City, Dec. 18, 1953; d. Charles D. and Bette J. (Stum) S.; m. Bradford W. Wyche, July 1, 1978; 1 child, Charles Denby Smock. B.A., U. Ga., 1974; J.D., U. Va., 1979. Bar: S.C. 1980, U.S. Dist. Ct. S.C. 1980, U.S. Ct. Appeals (4th cir.) 1980. Assoc. Riley & Riley, Greenville, S.C., 1980-82; ptnr. Yarborough, Moore & Smock, Greenville, 1982—. Editor, co-author: Your Legal Rights as a Woman-A Handbook for Virginians, 1979. Bd. dirs. YWCA, 1980-82, Met. Arts Council, 1981-83, Greater Greenville C. of C., 1984—, Greenville Events, Inc., 1983—, Conv. and Visitors Bur., 1984—, Greenville Urban League, 1983—; fin. chmn. Greenville County Democratic Party, 1984—, S.C. Arts Commn., 1985—, S.C. Water Law Rev. Com., 1984. Recipient Outstanding Young Woman of Am. award 1981; Young Career Woman award Bus. and Profl. Women, 1982; Career Woman of Yr. award Zonta, 1984. Mem. S.C. Bar Assn. (exec. council young lawyers div. 1983—), Greenville County Bar Assn. (exec. com. 1982-83), Greenville Profl. Women's Forum (com. chmn.), S.C. Lawyers for Arts (dir. 1980—), ABA (vice chmn. lawyers and arts com. 1985-86). Democrat. Unitarian. Club: Commerce (gov. 1983—). Office: Yarborough Moore & Smock PO Box 10023 Greenville SC 29603

SMOOK, JOHN T., manufacturing company executive; b. Detroit, Oct. 28, 1927; s. Theo and Mary (O'Donnell) S.; student Westminster Coll., 1947-48, U. Utah, 1949-50; m. Hope van der Smissen, Jan. 21, 1951 (div.); children—Ted, Jim, Cindy, Pam, Pat, Jeannette; m. Barbara Quinn, Feb. 2, 1983. Founder, pres. Kosmo Corp., Glen Allen, Va., 1954—; founder, pres. Internat. Security Vault Systems Inc., Glen Allen, 1982—; v.p. Micromedia TV Cable, Glen Allen, 1983; sec. Mid-Atlantic Ins. Underwriters, Richmond, Va., 1981. Served with USN, 1946, U.S. Army, 1950-53. Mem. Va. Campground Owners Assn., Soc. Mfg. Engrs., Va. Mfg. Housing Assn., Internat. Meditation Soc. (adv. bd. Greater Richmond area). Clubs: Richmond Ski, Underseas Explorers, Confrere. Home: Route 4 Box 250 Glen Allen VA 23060 Office: 24100 Washington Hwy Glen Allen VA 23060

SMOTHERMAN, RICHARD STANLEY, educational administrator; b. Baxter Springs, Kans., Feb. 15, 1942; s. Golden R. and Ina M. Smotherman; m. Gloria Gayle Lee, Aug. 13, 1966; 1 child, Shannon Annette. Student U. Tulsa, 1960-61; B.A., in English and Speech, S.W. Baptist Coll., 1966; student U. Tex.-Arlington, summers 1965-67; M.S. in Ednl. Adminstrn. and Supervision, U. Tenn.-Knoxville, 1975. Tchr., football coach Lee Jr. High Sch., Grand Prairie, Tex., 1966-69; head football coach, athletic dir. Fayette-Ware High Sch., Somerville, Tenn., 1970-73; tchr., football coach Halls Middle Sch., Knoxville, 1973-75; asst. prin., athletic dir. Cocke County High Sch., Newport, Tenn., 1975-77; asst. prin. Morristown East High Sch., Tenn., 1977-79; prin. Lenoir City High Sch., Tenn., 1979-82, Cherokee High Sch., Rogersville, Tenn., 1982-85; asst. prin. McKinney High Sch., Tex., 1985—. Pres. Optimist Club, Brownwood, Tex., 1969; v.p. Jaycees, Somerville, 1970-72; active Exchange Club, Morristown, 1977-79, charter mem., Rogersville. Recipient Outstanding Young Men of Am. award Jaycees, 1972; Tenn. Secondary Sch. Prins. fellow U. Tenn., 1981. Mem. Nat. Assn. Secondary Sch. Prins., Tenn. Assn. Secondary Sch. Prins., NEA, Tenn. Edn. Assn., East Tenn. Edn. Assn., Tenn. Athletic Coaches Assn., Mid-Atlantic Conf. (pres. 1977), Intermountain Athletic Conf. Baptist. Avocations: reading; tennis; golf; softball; amateur theater. Home: 123 Wilson Creek Blvd McKinney TX 75069 Office: McKinney High Sch 2000 Rollins St McKinney TX 75069

SMOTHERS, CARL LEE, marketing executive; b. Lawton, Okla., July 15, 1940; s. Loyd and Patricia Emma (Hogue) S.; B.S. (War Orphan scholar), West Coast U., 1967; M.S. (Hughes fellow), Calif. State U., 1973; m. Regina Louise Ellis, Nov. 19, 1977. Tech. staff asst., tech. dir. Hughes Aircraft Co., Fullerton, Calif., 1963-77; Surtass program mgr., engrng. mgr. Hydrosci., Inc., Dallas, 1977-80; chmn. bd. Davro Service Corp., Dallas, 1979-80; dir. research and devel. Seismic Engrng. Co., Dallas, 1980-82; mgr. marine programs Geophys. Services, Inc., Dallas, 1982-86; mktg. mgr. Tex. Instruments, Inc., McKinney, 1986—; instr. engrng. Fullerton Coll., 1968. Served with USNR, 1958-61. Registered profl. engr., Tex. Mem. Soc. Exploration Geophysicists. Republican. Baptist. Contbr.: Introduction to Air Defense Systems, 1971. Patentee optical hydrophone and computer ballasting methods. Home: 1600 Hartford Dr Carrollton TX 75007 Office: Tex Instruments Inc 2501 W University McKinney TX

SMULIAN, BETTY RHODA, lighting fixture manufacturing company executive; b. Phila., Jan. 18, 1928; d. Samuel B. and Anna G. (Seltzer) Forman; m. James Smulian, Apr. 8, 1951; children—Robert Drew, John Carter. B.F.A., U. Pa.-Phila., 1949. Store designer Gimbel Bros., Phila., 1949-51; engrng. dredge designer Ellicott Machine Corp., Balt., 1951-56; co-owner, chmn. Trimble House Corp., Norcross, Ga., 1963—; mem. Gov.'s Commn. on Pvt. Initiative, Atlanta, 1983; dir. 1st Ga. Bank, Atlanta. Bd. dirs. NCCJ, Atlanta, 1982—; bd. sponsors Atlanta Women's Network, Atlanta, 1982—; v.p. Am. Jewish Com., Atlanta, 1983—; bd. dirs. Jr. Achievement of Atlanta, 1983—; bd. councillors Gerontology Ctr. Ga. State U., 1983—, mem. adv. council Coll. Bus. Adminstrn., 1983. Ga. World Congress Inst. Internat. Bus. fellow, 1984. Mem. Allied Bd. Trade, Bus. Council Ga. (dir. 1982—), Com. 200, Nat. Orgn. Leading Women in Bus., Women Bus. Owners Atlanta (dir., v.p., pres. 1984-85). Club: Women's Commerce (founder, dir. 1981-83) (Atlanta). Office: Trimble House Corp 4658 Old Peachtree Rd Norcross GA 30071

SNAPP, ELIZABETH, educator, librarian; b. Lubbock, Tex., Mar. 31, 1937; d. William James and Louise (Lanham) Mitchell; B.A. magna cum laude, N. Tex. State U., Denton, 1968, M.L.S., 1969, M.A., 1977; m. Harry Franklin Snapp, June 1, 1956. Asst. to archivist Archive of New Orleans Jazz, Tulane U., 1960-63; catalog librarian Tex. Woman's U., Denton, 1969-71, head acquisitions dept., 1971-74, coordinator readers services, 1974-77, asst. to dean Grad. Sch., 1977-79, instr. library sci., 1977—, acting univ. librarian, 1979-82, dir. libraries, 1982—; mem. adv. com. for library formula Coordinating Bd. Tex. Coll. and Univ. System. Co-sponsor Irish Lecture Series, Denton, 1968, 70, 73, 78; sec. Denton County Democratic Caucus, 1970. Nat. Endowment for Humanities grantee. Mem. ALA (standards com. 1983-85), Southwestern, Tex. (Dist. VII chmn. 1985—) library assns., Women's Collecting Group (chmn. ad hoc com. 1984—), AAUW (legis. br. chmn. 1973-74, br. pres. 1979-81), So. Conf. Brit. Studies, AAUP, Tex. Assn. Coll. Tchrs. (pres. Tex. Woman's U. chpt. 1976-77), Woman's Shakespeare Club (pres. 1967-69), Beta Phi Mu (chpt. pres. 1976-78, pres. nat. adv. assembly 1979-80, nat. dir. 1981—), Alpha Chi, Alpha Lambda Sigma (pres. 1970-71), Pi Delta Phi. Episcopalian (directress altar guild 1966-68, 73-76). Club: Soroptimist (v.p. 1985—) (Denton). Asst. editor Tex. Academe, 1973-76; co-editor Bull. Women's History Sources, 1985—; book reviewer Library Resources and Tech. Services, 1973—; contbg. author: Women in Special Collections, 1985. Contbr. articles to profl. jours. Home: 1904 North Lake Trail Denton TX 76201 Office: PO Box 24093 TWU Sta Denton TX 76204

SNAPP, HARRY FRANKLIN, historian; b. Bryan, Tex., Oct. 15, 1930; s. H.F. and Ethel (Manning) S.; B.A., Baylor U., 1952, M.A., 1953; Ph.D., Tulane U., 1963; m. Elizabeth Mitchell, June 1, 1956. Instr., U. Coll. Tulane U., 1960-62; asst. prof. history Wofford Coll., 1963-64; asst. prof. history North Tex. State U., Denton, 1964-69, asso. prof., 1969—. Editor Brit. Studies Mercury, 1970—, Tex. Academe, 1973-76; contbr. articles to profl. jours. Mem. Friends of Winchester Cathedral, Am. Com. for Irish Studies; mem. adv. com. on acad. freedom and tenure policy, coordinating bd. Tex. Coll. and Univ. System. Recipient North Tex. State U. Faculty Research award, 1966, 67. Mem. AAUP (pres. North Tex. chpt. 1968-69, pres. Southwestern regional conf. 1971-72, pres. Tex. conf. 1974-76, nat. council 1976—), So. Conf. Brit. Studies (sec.-treas.), Am., So. hist. assns., Hist. Assn. (London), Library Research Round Table, Library History Round Table, Northamptonshire Record Soc., Butler Soc. (Ireland), Econ. History Soc., Ch. Hist. Soc., Tulane U. Alumni Assn., Alpha Chi. Episcopalian. Editor Brit. Studies Mercury, 1970—, Tex. Academe, 1973-76; contbr. articles to profl. jours. Home: 1904 N Lake Trail Denton TX 76201 Office: PO Box 5184 Denton TX 76203

SNEAD, CHARLES WILLIAM, JR., accountant, educator; b. Danville, Va., Jan. 27, 1951; s. Charles William and Sarah Elizabeth (Blalock) S.; m. Kary Murphy, Sept. 25, 1971; children—Charles William, Melissa Mallory. B.B.A., Delta State U., 32 1975, postgrad., 1975-76; postgrad. Miss. State U., 1975. C.P.A. Sr. acct. Franklin Turner & Carnathan, C.P.A.s, Birmingham, Ala., 1975-76, Manning, Perkinson, Floyd & Co., C.P.A.s, Danville, 1976-80; prin. Charles W. Snead Jr., C.P.A., Danville, 1980-82; ptnr. Smith & Snead, C.P.A.s, Danville, 1982—; adj. prof. acctg., taxation Avrett Coll., Danville, 1976-80; instr. acctg. Va. Community Coll. System, Danville, 1980-83. Active Big Bros.-Big Sisters, 1980-84, Mental Health Assn., 1981-84; adv. com. to bus. div. Va. Community Coll. System, 1981-84. Recipient Danville Jaycees, Commitment award, 1980. Mem. Danville Estate Planning Council, Am. Inst. C.P.A.s, Va. and N.C. Soc. C.P.A.s, Am. Assn. Accts., Danville C. of C. Baptist. Club: Tuscarora Country (Danville). Lodges: Lions, Sertoma (Danville). Author: Individual Financial Planning; Registration of Charitable Organizations. Home: 257 Crosland Ave Danville VA 24541 Office: PO Box 498 Danville VA 24543

SNEAD, CLAUDE BARTLEY, III, college counselor, administrator; b. Atlanta, May 17, 1944; s. Claude B. and Doris (Johnson) S.; m. Antoinette L. Gayman, June 21, 1971; children—Bart, Tonya, Jenny, Autumn, Dustin, Robyn. B.A., Augusta Coll., 1975; M.A., U. No. Iowa, 1982. Acting registrar Augusta Coll., Ga., 1981, admissions counselor, 1978—. Vice pres. Montclair Bd. Govs., Augusta, 1984—. Served to capt. U.S. Army, 1965-71, Vietnam. Mem. Am. Assn. for Counseling Devel., DAV, Am. Coll. Personnel Assn. Democrat. Baptist. Home: 3303 Crane Ferry Rd Augusta GA 30907 Augusta Coll 2500 Walton Way Augusta GA 30910

SNEDEN, JOHN AITKEN, JR., arts administrator; b. Englewood, N.J., Apr. 19, 1936; s. John Aitken and Jean (Mackey) S.; m. Julia Carolyn Brown, Nov. 11, 1965; children—John Aitken, III, William Mackey, Robert Chandler. B.A., U. N.C., 1958, M.A., 1960. Dir. theatre Davidson Coll., N.C., 1961-62; head theatre design program East Carolina U., Greenville, N.C., 1962-70; dean Sch. Design and Prodn., N.C. Sch. Arts, Winston-Salem, 1970—; theatrical designer Cape Playhouse, Dennis-on-Cape-Cod, Mass., 1963; resident designer East Carolina Summer Theatre, 1964-70; designer N.C. Shakespeare Festival, High Point, N.C., 1977. Designer theatrical scenes for various colls. and theatrical cos. Recipient Carolina Playmakers Alumnal award U. N.C., 1972. Mem. Am. Theatre Assn., U.S. Inst. for Theatre Tech., League Profl. Theatre Tng. Programs, Phi Beta Kappa. Presbyterian. Avocations: Home renovation, family research, singing. Home: 1806 Sussex Ln Winston-Salem NC 27104 Office: NC Sch Arts Sch Design and Prodn Winston-Salem NC 27107

SNELL, MARY KAY HOLMES, librarian, researcher; b. Sayre, Okla., Aug. 13, 1936; d. William Franklin and Ernestine Elizabeth (Reynolds) Holmes; m. Virgil Lee Snell, Nov. 25, 1955; children—Benjamin Franklin, Katherine Elizabeth. B.S., U. Tex., 1973, M.L.S., 1976. Librarian I, Tex. State Library, Austin, 1974-77; head reference and adult services Amarillo Pub. Library, Tex., 1977-79, asst. city librarian, 1979-81, city librarian, 1981—; dir. Tex. Panhandle Library System, Amarillo, 1981—; chmn. Harrington Library Consortium, Amarillo, 1984—; mem. council Library Services and Constrn. Act Adv. Council Tex., 1985—. Bd. dirs. Tex. Archival Network, Amarillo, 1984—, Amarillo Area Literacy Council, 1984—. Mem. ALA, Tex. Library Assn., Phi Beta Kappa, Phi Kappa Phi. Methodist. Avocation: historical and genealogical research. Office: Amarillo Pub Library 413 E 4th St Amarillo TX 79101

SNELL, WILLIAM ROBERT, educator; b. Birmingham, Ala., Oct. 16, 1930; s. Eugene B. and Cora A. (Hirschy) S.; m. Cora Mae Ricuey, Aug. 27, 1956 (div. 1961); children—William R., Jr., Mark E.; m. Janet Elizabeth Warren, Sept. 2, 1963; children—Stephen Michael, Jeffrey Alan. B.S., Samford U., 1952; B.D., So. Sem., 1956, Th.M., 1957; M.A., Samford U., 1967; Ph.D., U. Ala., 1973. Asst. pastor 1st Baptist Ch., Talladege, Ala., 1957-59; pastor Camp Hill Bapt. Ch., 1959-61; tchr. Weogufka, High Sch., Ala., 1961-62, Mountain Brook Jr. High, Birmingham, 1964-66, Mountain Brook High Sch., 1966-67, Lee Coll., Cleveland, Tenn., 1970—; instr. Samford U., Birmingham, 1962-64. Editor: Hard Times Remembered, 1983. Contbr. articles to hist. jours. City historian City of Cleveland, 1982. R.J. Reynolds Tobacco Co. fellow, 1966. Mem. Orgn. Am. Historians, So. Hist. Assn., East Tenn. Hist. Soc., Bradley County Hist. Soc. (pres. 1978-79), Ala. Hist. Assn. Democrat. Avocation: book collecting. Home: 3765 Hillsdale Dr NE Cleveland TN 37311-3039 Office: Lee Coll N Ocoee St Cleveland TN 37311

SNELLING, GEORGE ARTHUR, banker; b. St. Petersburg, Fla., June 27, 1929; s. William Henry and Eula Hall S.; B.S.B.A., U. Fla., 1951; m. Carolyn Shiver, Mar. 3, 1963; children—George, John S. Partner, Smoak, Davis, Nixon & Snelling, C.P.A.'s, Jacksonville, Orlando, Fla., 1956-66; v.p. planning Barnett Banks of Fla., Jacksonville, 1966-76; exec. v.p. 1st Bancshares of Fla., Boca Raton, 1976-78; exec. v.p. Fla. Nat. Banks of Fla., Jacksonville, 1979-80; sr. v.p. corp. devel. Sun Banks of Fla., Orlando, 1981—; dir. Served with USAF, 1951-55. Mem. Am. Inst. C.P.A.'s, Assn. Bank Holding Cos., Fla. Bankers Assn. Democrat. Methodist. Home: 1133 Bryn Mawr St Orlando FL 32804 Office: PO Box 2848 Orlando FL 32801

SNELLINGS, ELEANOR CRAIG, economics educator; b. Laurinburg, N.C., Nov. 3, 1926; d. Carl Brackett and Eleanor (Johnston) Craig; m. Henry L. Snellings Jr., Oct. 1, 1960 (dec. 1970); 1 child, Hill. B.A., U. N.C., 1947, M.A., 1950; Ph.D., Duke U., 1959. Instr. U. Ark., Fayetteville, 1948-49, U. N.C.-Greensboro, 1949-56; research assoc. Fed. Res. Bank of Richmond, Va., 1956-58, assoc. economist, 1959-60, economist, 1960-62; adj. faculty Va. Commonwealth U., Richmond, 1962-68, assoc. prof. econs., 1968—; econ. dir. South River Assn., Greensboro, 1974-77. Grantee So. Fellowships Fund, 1954, So. Bus. Adminstrn. Assn., 1981-82. Mem. Am. Econ. Assn., So. Econ. Assn., Indsl. Orgn. Soc., Atlantic Econ. Soc., Va. Assn. Economists (v.p. 1980-81). Presbyterian. Home: 4607 King William Rd Richmond VA 23225 Office: Va Commonwealth U 901 W Franklin St Richmond VA 23284

SNIDER, HELEN KAYE, mutual fund portfolio manager; b. Louisville, Mar. 19, 1954; d. Elmer B. and Frances (Blake) S.; m. Reece Bennett DeBerry, III, Mar. 11, 1978. B.A., Bellarmine Coll., 1973; M.B.A., U. Louisville, 1978. Tax acct. Capital Holding Corp., Louisville, 1978-80, investment analyst, 1980-82; v.p. First Nat. Bank in Palm Beach, Fla., 1982-84; portfolio mgr. ABT Security Income Fund, Palm Beach, 1983—; v.p. Palm Beach Capital Mgmt., 1984—. Mem. Fin. Analysts Fedn., Fin. Analysts Soc. South Fla., Nat. Option and Futures Soc. (dir. 1985); S.E. Option and Futures Soc. (pres. 1985-86). Avocations: teaching English as 2d language. Home: PO Box 2227 Palm Beach FL 33480 Office: Palm Beach Capital Mgmt 151 Royal Palm Way Palm Beach FL 33480

SNIDER, JAMES HENRY, educator, photographer; b. Franklin, Ky., Feb. 27, 1953; s. Douglas Brundage and Jewette Pearl (Steele) S. Student Georgetown U., 1973; B.S., Western Ky. U., 1975, M.A., 1977; postgrad. Vanderbilt U., 1981—. Staff organist Franklin (Ky.) Presbyn. Ch., 1971-76, 79; intern Office U.S. Senator Marlow W. Cook, Washington, 1973; intern Barren River Area Devel. Dist., Bowling Green, Ky., 1973-75; photographer Office Pub. Relations, Western Ky. U., Bowling Green, 1973-75; self-employed photographer, Franklin, Ky., 1970—; substitute tchr. Simpson, Warren, Logan County, Bowling Green Ind. (Ky.) Bds. Edn., 1976-83, tchr. Alvaton Elementary Sch. (Ky.), 1983—. Commr., Simpson County Bd. Elections; edn. chmn. Simpson County chpt. Am. Cancer Soc., vol. umpire Little League Baseball; basketball commr. Ch. League; project leader, judge 4-H; deacon, youth leader, Bible tchr. First Bapt. Ch. Recipient Key to the City of Franklin (Ky.), 1978; named Ky. Col. Mem. NEA, Ky. Edn. Assn., Ky. Hist. Soc., Ky. Council for Social Studies, Ky. Council Tchrs. Math., Nat. Council Tchrs. Math., Ky. Assn. Gifted Edn., Warren County Assn. Gifted Edn.; PTA, Ky. Hist. Soc., Simpson County Hist. Soc. (v.p., pres.), Gamma Beta Phi Alumni Assn. Republican. Baptist. Co-author: Franklin and Simpson County: A Picture of Progress-1819-1975, 1976, Franklin and Simpson County: Reflections of 1976 and a Supplement to a Picture of Progress-1819-1975, 1977.

SNIDER, JAMES RHODES, radiologist, educator; b. Pawnee, Okla., May 16, 1931; s. John Henry and Gladys Opal (Rhodes) S.; B.S., U. Okla., 1953,

M.D., 1956; m. Lynadell Vivion, Dec. 27, 1954; children—Jon, Jan. Intern, Edward Meyer Meml. Hosp., Buffalo, 1956-57; resident radiology U. Okla. Med. Center, 1959-62; radiologist Holt-Krock Clinic and Sparks Regional Med. Center, Ft. Smith, Ark., 1962—; clin. asst. prof. radiology U. Ark. Med. Center, Little Rock, 1976—; cons. USPHS Hosp., Talihina, Okla., 1962—; dir. Fairfield Communities Inc., Little Rock. Mem. Ark. Bd. Public Welfare, 1969-71; bd. dirs. U. Okla. Assn., 1967-70, U. Okla. Alumni Devel. Fund, 1970-74; bd. visitors U. Okla., 1976-79. Served to lt. comdr. USNR, 1957-62. Mem. Am. Coll. Radiology, Radiol. Soc. N.Am., AMA, Am. Roentgen Ray Soc., Phi Beta Kappa, Beta Theta Pi, Alpha Epsilon Delta. Republican. Baptist. Club: Hardscrabble Country. Asso. editor Computerized Tomography, 1976—. Home: 5814 Cliff Dr Fort Smith AR 72901 Office: 1500 Dodson St Fort Smith AR 72901

SNODDERLY, KAREN WEBSTER, programmer/analyst; b. Knoxville, Tenn., July 16, 1951; d. John Arthur and Martha Elizabeth (Armstrong) Webster; B.S. in Bus. Adminstrn., Carson-Newman Coll., 1971; post-grad. U. Tenn., 1977; 1 dau., Rachel Hope. Data control clk. U. Tenn., Knoxville, 1974, research asst., 1974-75, mgr. student info., 1975-79, dir. data analysis, 1979-82, mem. fin. aid and admission system design team, 1979-80, cons. Analytical and Data Services, 1983—. Vice chmn. Friends of Strawberry Plains (Tenn.) Library, 1978; vice chmn. bd. dirs. Knoxville Rape Crisis Center, 1982, now coordinator vols. Mem. Am. Bus. Women's Assn. (Mem. of Month award 1981), Coll. and Univ. Machine Records Conf., Phi Chi Theta. Compiler-editor U. Tenn. Ann. Report Info. Requests, 1979-81. Home: PO Box 344 Jefferson City TN 37760 Office: P225 Andy Holt Tower Knoxville TN 37916

SNODDERLY, LOUISE DAVIS, librarian; b. Polk County, Oreg., Feb. 1, 1925; d. Charles Benjamin Franklin and Grace L. (Cassady) Davis; m. Charles Hugh Snodderly, May 19, 1949; 1 son, Lynn Jerome. B.S., E. Tenn. State U., 1946; M.S., U. Tenn., 1962, postgrad., 1979, 82. Tchr., girls' coach Rush Strong High Sch., Strawberry Plains, Tenn., 1946-49, librarian, 1954-62; tchr., girls' coach Cosby High Sch., Tenn., 1949-50; tchr., librarian Maury High Sch., Dandridge, Tenn., 1951-54; cataloger City of Knoxville, Tenn., 1962-67; periodicals librarian Carson-Newman Coll., Jefferson City, Tenn., 1967—; cons. Jefferson County Librarians, Tenn., 1976—. Sch. commr. Jefferson County, 1976—; com. woman Nat. Fedn. Republican Women, Jefferson County, 1976—. Mem. ALA, Southeastern Library Assn., Tenn. Library Assn., Am. Sch. Bd. Assn., Tenn. Library Assn., NEA, PTA, Pi Lambda Theta. Baptist. Club: Women's Faculty. Lodge: Order Eastern Star. Home: Route 3 Box 420 Strawberry Plains TN 37871

SNOOK, JOHN MCCLURE, telephone co. exec.; b. Toledo, May 31, 1917; s. Ward H. and Grace (McClure) S.; student Ohio State U., 1936-43. Instr. history, fine arts and scis. Ohio State U., Columbus; exec. v.p. Gulf Telephone Co., Foley, Ala., 1955-71, pres., 1971—. Chmn., Baldwin Sesquicentennial, 1969; mem. Baldwin County Bicentennial Commn.; pageant chmn., dir. Ft. Morgan Bicentennial Program, 1976; mem. hon. staff Gov. Ala., 1967—; past pres. Friends of Library Assn.; asso. sponsor Gulf Shores Mardi Gras Assn. Hon. a.d.c. lt. col. Ala.; hon. Ala. state trooper; recipient Citizen of Year award Gulf Shores, 1956-57. Mem. Ala.-Miss. Ind. Telephone Assn. (past pres.), Nat. Rifle Assn. (life), Am. Ordnance Assn., South Baldwin C. of C., Delaware County, Baldwin County hist. assns., Defiance and Williams' Hist. Soc., Am. Mus. Nat. History Assn., Nat. Hist. Soc., Nat. Wildlife Fedn., Clan McLeod Soc., Smithsonian Assn., Am. Heritage Soc., Nat. Fedn. Blind, Ohio State Alumni Assn., Ala. Ind. Telephone Assn., Telephone Pioneers, Ind. Pioneers, Gulf Coast Gun Collectors Assn. (hon. life). Clubs: Lions (past pres.), Kiwanis (past pres.; asst. chmn. ann. Christmas Party and Parade). Office: Gulf Telephone Co Box 670 Foley AL 36535

SNOW, AUBURN LEE, training consultant; b. Moscow, Ky., Jan. 29, 1937; s. William Auburn and Evelyn Monette (Campbell) S.; student Bethel Coll., Hopkinsville, Ky., 1958-60; B.A. in Speech Communications, Oklahoma City U., 1965; m. Janice Sue Stinson, May 10, 1960; children—Mark, Susan, Dee, Christopher, Philip. Newsman, Sta. WKY, Oklahoma City, 1962-66; reporter, anchorman KWTV-TV, Oklahoma City, 1966-67; sales mgr. Xerox Corp., Tampa, Fla., 1967-71, dist. mgr. Xerox Learning Systems, Tampa, 1972-77; pres. Mgmt. Leadership Services, Inc., Tampa, 1971-72; prin. A. Lee Snow Assocs., Tampa, 1977—; sales tng. cons. to major newspapers. Served with U.S. Army, 1961-62. Recipient various awards Xerox Corp. Mem. Am. Soc. Tng. and Devel., Sales and Mktg. Execs. Internat., Internat. Newspaper Advt. and Mktg. Execs. Assn. Republican. Methodist. Author: In Search of Excellence (sales tng. program), 1978. Home and office: 12720 Carte Dr Tampa FL 33618

SNOWDEN, CHARLES DURKEE, JR., educator; b. Cin., Aug. 7, 1944; s. Charles Durkee and Charlotte Candee (White) S.; m. Patricia Rawlings Parrish, June 11, 1966; children—Charles Durkee, Mary Rawlings, William Herron Cameron. B.A., U. South, 1966; M.A., U. Del., 1973. Master, St. Andrew's Sch., Middleton, Del., 1966-73; asst. headmaster St. Pauls Episcopal Sch., Mobile, Ala., 1973—. Vice chmn. ann. campaign United Way of Mobile County, 1978-83, 85; chmn. bd. St. Mary's Home, Mobile, 1981—; chmn. nominating com. Deep South Council Girl Scouts U.S.A., Mobile, 1980-84, 2d v.p. bd. dirs.; mem. Archbishop's Fedn. Cath. Social Services. St. Andrew's fellow, 1966; recipient Leadership Mobile, United Way of Mobile County, 1976. Mem. Mid-South Assn. Ind. Schs. (div. chmn. 1980-81), So. Assn. Colls. and Schs. (chmn. vis. com. 1983-84). Republican. Clubs: Leadership Mobile Alumni Assn. (chmn. by-laws 1981—), Sewanee. Lodge: Lions (bd. dirs.; Tail Twister). Home: 123 Provident Ln Mobile AL 36608 Office: St Pauls Episcopal Sch 161 Dogwood Ln Mobile AL 36690

SNYDER, ADELAIDE R., university official; b. Rochester, N.Y., Nov. 9, 1925; d. I.S. and Cecilia (Richardson) S.; m. Joseph, Dec. 23, 1944; children—Richard, Florence. B.A., Kent State U., 1944, M.A., 1950; postgrad. Mich. State U., 1944-45. Mem. faculty Youngstown (Ohio) Coll., 1950's, prod./hostess Sta. WFMJ-TV, Youngstown, 1955-59; relocation dir. City of Youngstown, 1957-59; dir. admissions and publs. Miami (Fla.)-Dade County Community Coll., 1960-62; v.p. Fla. Atlantic U., Boca Raton, 1962—. Founding mem. Music Guild Boca Raton, 1983; chmn. allocations com. United Way, Boca Raton, 1983, bd. dirs., 1983—; bd. dirs., mem. adv. bd. Palm Glades council Girl Scouts U.S.A., 1983—; bd. dirs. Planned Parenthood. Named Woman of Yr., Soroptimists Internat., 1984; recipient Outstanding Alumni award Fla. Atlantic U., 1985; Grad. fellow Mich. State U., 1944. Mem. Fla. Pub. Relations Assn., Women in Communications, AAUW, Nat. League for Arts and Letters, English Speaking Union (founding mem. Boca Raton chpt.). Home: 1334 SW 14th St Boca Raton FL 33432 Office: Fla Atlantic U Boca Raton FL 33431

SNYDER, CHESTER HARTRANST, JR., engineer; b. Mt. Carmel, Pa., Jan. 15, 1943; s. Chester H. and Roma May (Haas) S.; children—Martin Douglas, Amy Dawn, Lorraine Dara. Student Harrisburg Area Community Coll., 1966-70; B.B.A., Ga. State U., 1981. Electronics technician Reeves-Hoffman, Carlisle, Pa., 1964; maintenance supr. Ralston Purina Co., St. Louis, 1964-76, Joseph Schlitz Brewing Co., Winston-Salem, N.C., 1976-78, Keebler Co., Atlanta, 1978-80; maintenance supt. ABS of Atlanta, 1980-82; new projects mgr. A.B.S., Inc., Atlanta, 1982—; instr. Ga. Assn. Power Engring., Atlanta, 1979—, Atlanta Area Tech., Power Plant Tech., 1979—; engring. cons. Affiliated Bldg. Services, Inc., 1982—, new projects mgr., 1982—. Served with USAF, 1960-64. Mem. Ga. State Assn. Power Engrs. (examining engr. 1975—, chief engr. 1974, state pres. 1984, William B. Hicks award 1983), Soc. Am. Mil. Engrs. Lutheran. Home: 317 Lucan Way Riverdale GA 30274 Office: Affiliated Bldg Services Inc 1745 Phoenix Blvd Atlanta GA 30349

SNYDER, HOWARD DARRELL, telecommunications safety manager, safety educator consultant; b. North Liberty, Ind., June 6, 1944; s. Harold Earl and Helen Marie (Kaser) S.; m. Noreen Ann Brink, Sept. 14, 1963; children—Rachel, Sarah, Howard Darrell, Ruth. B.A. in Edn., Marion Coll., 1967. Cert. advanced safety, Nat. Safety Council. Tchr. secondary schs. Benzie County Central Schs., Benzonia, Mich., 1969-74; service supr. United Telecommunications, Avon Park, Fla., 1978-79, plant instr., Ft. Myers, Fla., 1979-81, transmission and protection engr., 1981-83, div. safety mgr., 1983—; various craft positions United Telephone of Fla., 1974-78. Pres. bd. dirs. S.W. Fla. Safety Council, 1985—S.W. Fla. Counterattack Sch., 1984—; bd. dirs. Lee County chpt. ARC, Ft. Myers, 1983—. NSF study grantee, 1972. Mem. Am. Soc. Safety Engrs. Republican. Baptist. Avocations: Tennis; woodworking. Office: United Telephone Fla 1520 Lee St Fort Myers FL 33902

SNYDER, JOSEPH JOHN, author, lecturer, prehistorian; b. Washington, Aug. 27, 1946; s. Joseph John and Amy Josephine (Hamilton) S.; m. Sally Hale Walker, July 4, 1973; children—Lauren Elizabeth, Brian Joseph Seth. B.A. in Anthropology, George Washington U., 1968; M.A. in Anthropology, U. N.Mex., 1973. With U.S. CSC, Washington, 1974-77; editor, writer U.S. Nat. Park Service, Harpers Ferry, W.Va., 1977-81; cons. editor Early Man mag., Evanston, Ill., 1978-83; freelance writer, 1981—; lectr. Maya archaeology Norwegian-Caribbean Lines, Miami, Fla., 1982; cons. mus. design. Chmn. parks com. Neighborhood Planning Adv. Group, Croydon Park, Rockville, Md., 1980-81. Served with U.S. Army, 1970-71; Vietnam. Decorated Bronze Star. Mem. Washington Ind. Writers, Soc. Am. Archaeology, Council Md. Archaeology, Hakluyt Soc., Am. Com. for AdvancementStudy of Petroglyphs and Pictographs (exec. sec. 1980—, editor Jour. Rock Art). Democrat. Contbr. articles to popular mags. Home: 1100 Washington St Harpers Ferry WV 25425 Office: PO Box 260 Harpers Ferry WV 25425

SNYDER, KAROLYN JOHNSON, educator; b. Mpls., Mar. 2, 1938; d. Wade L. and Helen A. Johnson; B.A., Wheaton (Ill.) Coll., 1960; M.Ed., Temple U., Phila., 1965; Ed.D., Tex. Tech. U., 1977; m. T. Richard Snyder, Aug. 22, 1959; 1 dau., Kristen Michelle; m. 2d, Robert H. Anderson, Jan. 26, 1979. Tchr. public schs., N.J. and Pa., also Am. Sch., Rio de Janeiro, Brazil, 1959-68; founder, adminstr. Project Learn, elem. schs., Phila., 1968-71; unit leader, house leader E. Windsor regional schs., Hightstown, N.J., 1972-75; part-time instr. Tex. Tech. U., 1975-76; v.p., programs adminstr. Pedamorphosis, Inc., Lubbock, Tex., 1977—; cons., trainer in field. Mem. Am. Assn. Sch. Adminstrs., Assn. Supervision and Curriculum Devel., Am. Ednl. Research Assn., Am. Assn. Tng. and Devel., Council Profs. Instructional Supervision, Nat. Assn. Elem. Prins., Nat. Assn. Secondary Sch. Prins., Phi Delta Kappa. Author articles in field, 5-part tng. program in instructional leadership for prins. Home: 5414 20th St Lubbock TX 79407 Office: 1220 Broadway Suite 605 Lubbock TX 79401

SNYDER, LOIS DE ORSEY, public relations exec.; b. Whitinsville, Mass., Aug. 12, 1929; d. Francis X. and Germaine Gagnon De Orsey; A.B., Lenoir-Rhyne Coll., 1953; postgrad. Duke U., 1953-56; m. Harry M. Snyder, Jr. (dec. 1974); children—Stephen De Orsey, Melissa Anne. French tchr. Lenoir-Rhyne Coll., 1952-53; tchr. English, speech and drama Hickory (N.C.) High Sch., 1953-54; dir. public relations Hickory Furniture Mart, 1979-81; pvt. practice public relations, Hickory, 1981—. Pres., Hickory Dyslexia Found., Catawba County Arts Council, Hickory Landmarks Soc., ARC, Catawba County Mental Health Assn., N.C. Cerebral Palsy Assn. Recipient Outstanding Service award N.C. Assn. Cerebral Palsy, 1965. Mem. Catawba County Execs. Club, Internat. Platform Assn., Catawba County C. of C. (dir.), Lenoir-Rhyne Coll. Alumni Assn. (pres.), Alpha Psi Omega. Republican. Home: Rt 10 Box 684 Hickory NC 28601 also: 1725 5th St Dr NW Hickory NC 28601

SNYDER, MARION GENE, congressman; b. Louisville, Jan. 26, 1928; s. M.G. and Lois (Berg) S.; 1 child, Mark; m. Patricia C. Robertson, Apr. 10, 1973; 3 step-children. J.D., U. Louisville, 1951; LL.B. cum laude, Jefferson Sch. Law, Louisville, 1951. Bar: Ky. 1950, D.C. 1970. Lawyer, farmer, Louisville, 1957—; city atty., Jeffersontown, 1953-57; magistrate 1st Dist. Jefferson County, 1957-61; real estate broker, 1949—; mem. 88th U.S. Congress from 3d Dist. Ky., 90th-99th congresses from 4th dist. Ky. Vice pres. Ky. Magistrates and Commrs., 1958, Jeffersontown Civic Ctr., 1953-54; pres. Lincoln Republican Club Ky., 1960-61, 1st Magisterial Dist. Rep. Club, 1955-57. Mem. Ky. Bar Assn., Louisville Bar Assn., D.C. Bar Assn., Ky. Farm Bur., Louisville Bd. Realtors, Kenton-Boone Bd. Realtors. Club: Optimists. Lodges: Lions, Masons, Shriners. Offices: US House of Reps Washington DC 20515 also Fed Bldg Covington KY*

SNYDER, MARK EVAN, management consultant, engineer; b. Wichita, Kans., Jan. 23, 1951; s. Alan Howard and Dorothea (Jones) S. B.S., U. Tex. at Arlington, 1974, M.S., 1977. Registered profl. engr.; cert. mgmt. cons. Planning analyst Fed. Res. Bank Dallas, 1974-77; asst. to v.p. sales Qwip Systems, Dallas, 1977; electronic funds transfer dir. Tex. Credit Union League, Dallas, 1977-79; v.p. ops. and devel. Real Save Inc., Dallas, 1979-81; mgmt. cons. Lifson, Herrmann, Blackmarr & Harris, Dallas, 1979-82; ptnr. B.R. Blackmarr & Assocs., 1982—; cons. S.W.D. Machines, Ft. Worth, Earl Carver & Assocs. Mem. Am. Inst. Indsl. Engrs. (sr.), Planning Execs. Inst., Soc. Ins. Research, Tex. Soc. Profl. Engrs., Epsilon Nu Gamma, Alpha Pi Mu. Republican. Presbyterian. Home: 2311 Fall River Arlington TX 76006 Office: One Turtle Creek Village Suite 606 Dallas TX 75219

SNYDER, RALPH EUGENE, physician, medical director; b. Herkimer, N.Y., Apr. 13, 1922; s. Ralph Gordon and Grace Bush (Hollingsworth) S.; m. Jacqueline Beekman Tallman, Oct. 4, 1952; children—Ralph Gordon, Victoria Beekman. A.B. Harvard U., 1943; M.D., N.Y. Med. Coll., 1950. Diplomate Nat. Bd. Med. Examiners. Intern, Flower and Fifth Ave. Hosps., N.Y.C., 1950-51; asst. dean N.Y. Med. Coll., Flower and Fifth Ave. Hosps., Met. Hosp. Center, 1951-53, exec. dean, 1953-54, dean, 1954-57, dean and chief exec. officer, 1957-59, pres., dean, 1959-66; dir. profl. relations Merck, Sharp & Dohme, West Point, Pa., 1967-77; civilian med. officer Womack Army Hosp., Ft. Bragg, N.C., part time 1977-78; pvt. practice, Aberdeen, N.C., 1979—; med. dir. Med. Rev. N.C., 1985—; mem. staffs Moore Meml. Hosp., Pinehurst, N.C., 1979—, St. Joseph of Pines Hosp., Southern Pines, N.C., 1979—; bd. dirs. North Penn Hosp., Lansdale, Pa., 1968-70; chmn. deans' com. N.Y. VA Hosps., 1957-59; med. council Bd. Regents, State of N.Y., 1953-66; cons. surgeon gen. U.S. Army, 1959-67. Contbr. med. articles to profl. jours. Recipient Interfaith medal Interfaith Movement, Inc. N.Y., 1965; Bronze medal City of N.Y., 1965, Appreciation citation, 1968; Merit award Am. Acad. Family Physicians, 1976; Max Cheplove Silver medal Erie County chpt. N.Y. State Acad. Family Physicians, 1980. Fellow ACP; hon. fellow Internat. Coll. Surgeons, Am. Coll. Gastroenterology; mem. Nat. Pharm. Council, Health Care Exhibitors Assn. (treas. 1975-76), Am. Assn. Med. Assts. (hon.), Alpha Omega Alpha. Clubs: Country of N.C. (Pinehurst); N.Y. Athletic. Home: 378A Pine Ridge Dr Whispering Pines NC 28327 Office: 1902C N Sandhills Blvd Aberdeen NC 28315 also 1101 Schaub Dr Box 37309 Raleigh NC 27627

SNYDER, STEVEN ROBERT, computer company executive; b. Jackson, Mich., June 10, 1953; s. Robert Earl and Juan Marie (Ewing) S.; m. Donna Louise Sayre, July 11, 1975; 1 dau., Heather Leigh Anne. Student elec. engring. Western Mich. U., 1971-73. Jr. design engr. Data Plus, 1978-79; service mgr. Computer Plus, 1979-80; pres. AIC Inc., Arlington, Va., 1980—; cons. micro-computer field. Served with USN, 1973-76. Mem. Internat. Assn. Cromenco Users (charter), U.S. C. of C., Planetary Soc., Nat. Acad. Scis., Cousteau Soc., DAV, Greater Washington CP/M Users Group, Molecular Users Group. Implemented various operating systems for micro-computers. Office: 8197-K Backlick Rd Lorton VA 22079

SNYDER, THOMAS DANIEL, retired electronics engineer, consultant; b. Phila., Aug. 30, 1925; s. Thomas Daniel and Edith May (Lees) S.; Asso. in Applied Sci. in Radio and TV Tech., Milw. Sch. Engring., 1951; m. Mary Ann Wilson, Aug. 28, 1954; children—Thomas Daniel, Ellen Mary, John W. Foreman Prime Mfg. Co., Milw., 1951; with engring. dept. No. Light Co., Milw., 1951-52; communications clk. fgn. service U.S. Dept. State, 1952-55; electronics engr. U.S. Dept. Def., Warrenton, Va., 1955-85; staff cons. Am. Elect. Labs. Cons. accoustics and magnetics govt. agys., 1964—; lectr. metric conversion; participant Solid States Application Conf., Fla. Atlanta U., 1971; participant profl. seminars Mass. Inst. Tech., 1962, 64, 66, Columbia, 1963, Pa. State U., 1967, U. Wis., 1969. Pres., PTA, Fairfax, Va., 1971, county rep., 1972. Served with USNR, 1943-46; PTO. Recipient Meritorious award for outstanding design in electronics equipment, U.S. Govt., 1969. Mem. AAAS, IEEE, Optical Soc. Am., Metric Assn., Am. Nat. Metric Council, Am. Legion, Cath. War Vets. (adj. 1964-67). Roman Catholic. Contbr. articles to profl. jours. Patentee in field. Home: 4246 Worcester Dr Fairfax VA 22030 Office: 2922 Telestar Ct Falls Church VA 22042

SNYDER, WARREN WILSON, management company executive, management consultant; b. Louisville, Aug. 8, 1945; s. Woodrow Wilson and Glenna Marie (Minor) S.; m. Donna Marie Farnham, July 17, 1971. B.Indsl. Design, Syracuse U., 1968; M.B.A., Old Dominion U., 1980. Graphics supr. planning and program devel. Norfolk (Va.). Redevel. Housing Authority, 1973-75; program mgr. Cerberonics, Inc., Alexandria, Va., 1975-78; v.p. ops. Atlantic DALFI, Inc., Norfolk, Va., 1978—, dir., San Diego, 1979—. Served to capt. USAF, 1968-73. Mem. Indsl. Design Soc. Am., Nat. Contract Mgrs. Assn., Alpha Xi Alpha. Home: 1364 Marshall Ln Virginia Beach VA 23455 Office: DALFI Inc 2125 Smith Ave Suite 202 Chesapeake VA 23320

SNYDER, WILLIAM JUNIOR, hospital management consultant; b. Meyersdale, Pa., Apr. 6, 1926; s. William Roy and Fannie (Miller) S.; m. Anna Philip, Aug. 23, 1947; children—Robbyn, Cheryl, Carol. Student, Bethany (W.Va.) Coll., 1943-44, U. N.C., 1944-45, Harvard U., 1945, George Washington U., 1948-49; M.S. in Mgmt., U.S. Naval Postgrad. Sch., 1964. Commd. ensign U.S. Navy, 1945, advanced through grades to comdr., 1963; chief acct., Luke AFB, 1954-55; comdr. Supply Corps, 1955-70; ret., 1970; coordinator mgmt. Supervision Program, San Jose, Calif., 1970-71; assoc. prof. W.Va. U. and Frostburg State Tchrs. Coll. (Md.), 1971-72; materiel mgr. Univ. Hosps. Cleve., 1973—; cons., Sebring, Fla., 1982—; instr. Case Western Res. U., Cuyahoga Community Coll. Pres., Indian Wells Valley Council for Retarded Children, 1965-67; mem. Speakers Bur., Potomac State Coll. of W.Va. U., 1971-72. Decorated Joint Services Commendation medal; cert. jr. coll. tchr., Calif., Ariz. Mem. Am. Soc. Hosp. Purchasing and Materiel Mgmt., N.E. Ohio Soc. Health Care Materiel Mgmt. (past pres.), Internat. Material Mgmt. Soc. (cert. profl. in health care material mgmt.), Ret. Officers Assn. Clubs: Spring Lake Golf and Country. Lodge: Elks. Author: Bookkeeping for the Small Businessman, 1969; (with Bruce Moritz) Four Functions of Management, 1970. Home: 7155 Parkwood St Sebring FL 33870

SOAPER, ROBERT CALLAWAY, III, chemical company executive, independent oil producer; b. Henderson, Ky., June 6, 1932; s. Robert Callaway and Edith (Wilson) S.; m. Barbara Joan Shaver, Dec. 28, 1959; children—Susan Pringle, Robert Callaway IV. Student U. Ky., 1950-52, 56-57. With Soaper Oil Co., Henderson, 1960—, pres. 1965—; pres. Soaper Chem. Co., Henderson, 1965—. Served to 1st class petty officer USCG, 1952-56. Mem. Ind. Petroleum Assn. Am. (regional bd. dirs. 1983-85), Ky. Oil and Gas Assn. (pres. 1982-84), Ill. Oil and Gas Assn., Tenn. Oil and Gas Assn., Mich. Oil and Gas Assn., Indiana Oil and Gas Assn. Republican. Episcopalian. Office: Soaper Chem Co Inc PO Box 215 Henderson KY 42420

SOBEL, DAVID L., lawyer; b. Tulsa, Dec. 18, 1946; s. S. L. and Lucille (Miller) S; m. Judy Applebaum, Aug. 25, 1968; children—Lisa Diane, Amanda Beth, Laura Rose. B.B.A., U. Okla., 1965; J.D., Cumberland Sch. Law, 1972. Bar: Okla. 1972, U.S. Dist. Ct. (no. dist.) Okla., 1973, U.S. Dist. Ct. (we. dist.) Okla. 1974, U.S. Ct. Appeals (10th cir.) 1981, U.S. Supreme Ct. 1976. Assoc., Dyer, Powers & Marsh, Tulsa, 1972-75; sole practice, Tulsa, 1975-76, 82—; ptnr. Sobel, Moran, Lysiak & Harral, 1976-82. Mem. Faculty Tulsa Jr. Coll., 1982-83. Mem. Assn. Trial Lawyers Am., ABA, Okla. Bar Assn., Tulsa County Bar Assn. (chmn. pub. info. com., cdnl. com. 1984-85). Home: 1388 E 26th Pl Tulsa OK 74114 Office: 2642 E 21st St Suite 240 Tulsa OK 74114

SOBEL, SUZANNE BARBARA, clinical psychologist; b. Bklyn.; d. Albert E. and Jeannette (Schneider) S.; student Clark U., 1960-62; B.A., Adelphi U., 1964, M.A., 1966; Ph.D., U. Tenn., 1971. Psychologist, Orleans (La.) Parish Sch. Bd., 1971-72; asst. prof. Dillard U., 1972-73; clin. psychologist D.C. Children's Center, 1973-75; research clin. psychologist Mental Health Study Center, Nat. Inst. Mental Health, Adelphi, Md., 1975-79; lectr. Univ. Coll., U. Md., 1975-79; pvt. practice clin. psychology, Washington, 1975-80, Indian Harbor Beach, 1980-82, Satellite Beach, Fla., 1982—; asso. dean acad. affairs, prof. psychology Sch. Profl. Psychology, Fla. Inst. Tech., 1980-82; civil rights coordinator Alcohol, Drug Abuse and Mental Health Adminstrn., HEW, Rockville, Md., 1979—; cons. clin. psychologist Children's Brain Research Center, 1976—. Public mem. D.C. Criminal Justice Coordinating Bd., 1977-78; mem. President's Commn. on Mental Health, 1977-78; mem. female offender and female juvenile offender coms. D.C. Commn. on Women, 1976. Fellow Am. Orthopsychiat. Assn., Am. Psychol. Assn. (pres. div. child and youth services 1980-81, sec. div. psychotherapy 1981-84); mem. Southeastern Psychol. Assn., Soc. Pediatric Psychology, Am. Psychology Law Soc., Am. Soc. Correctional Psychologists, NOW, Nat. Assn. Female Execs., ORT. Mem. editorial bd. Jour. Clin. Child Psychology, 1976—, Jour. Early Adolescence, 1981—, Psychotherapy in Pvt. Practice, 1983—; cons. editor Prof. Psychology, 1979—; editorial cons. Am. Psychologist, 1976—; cons. editor Psychotherapy: Theory, Research and Practice 1980—. Contbr. articles to profl. jours. Home: 238 Harbor Dr East Indian Harbor Beach FL 32937 Office: 1290 Hwy A1A Suite 103B Satellite Beach FL 32937

SOBER, GARY LYNN, environmental educator, consultant; b. Oklahoma City, Oct. 12, 1947; s. Willard Orlo and Olene Della (Wells) S.; m. Debra Evonne Jordan, May 24, 1980; children—Kara Kristine, Jeffrey Lynn, Kimberly Dyan. BS., Okla. State U.-Stillwater, 1970. Cert. water operator, Okla., Tex.; cert. wastewater operator, Okla., Tex.; registered profl. sanitarian, Okla., Tex. Research asst. Ozark Fisheries, Stoutland, Mo., 1970-71; sanitarian Garfield County Dept. Health, Enid, Okla., 1974-76; health specialist II Okla. Health Dept., Oklahoma City, 1976-80; cons., co-owner Enviro-O-Spec, Inc., Austin, Tex., 1981—; environ. trainer, owner Environ. Tng. and Devel. Service, Austin, 1980—; advisor, cons. Emergency Tech. Response Team State of Okla., Oklahoma City, 1978-80; advisor, com. mem. Pub. Water Supply Operational Regulations com. State of Okla., 1978-80. Recipient Outstanding Service award Jaycees, 1976; Young Man of the Yr. award Capitol Area Assn., 1982. Mem. Am. Water Works Assn., Water Pollution Control Fedn., Nat. Environ. Tng. Assn., Tex. Water Utilities Assn., Capital Area Utilities Assn. (pres. 1983—), Soc. Profl. Sanitarians, Okla. Water Assn., Jaycees (social chmn. 1975-76, athletic dir. 1975-76). Republican. Methodist. Lodge: Kiwanis. Author textbooks including: Basic Water, 1981, Basic Wastewater, 1981, Advanced Water, 1981, Advanced Wastewater, 1981. Office: Environmental Training and Development Service PO Box 10257 Austin TX 78766

SOBERANO, RAWLEIN GAMBOA, college dean, social sciences educator; b. Bacolod, Philippines, Apr. 19, 1941; s. Leopoldo and Azela Gamboa; B.A., St. Vincent's Coll. (Philippines), 1962; M.A. in Sociology, St. John's U., 1970, M.A. in Asian History, 1971, Ph.D., 1974; m. Theresa Jane Zilles, Nov. 25, 1972; children—Leilani, David, Deborah. Lectr. adult edn. program Diocese of Bklyn., 1968-70; instr. Asian studies St. John's U., 1970-71; instr. social scis. Molloy Coll., Rockville Centre, N.Y., also lectr. sociology Nassau Community Coll., Garden City, N.Y., 1973-74; asst. prof. social scis. Our Lady of Holy Cross Coll., New Orleans, 1977-80, assoc. prof., dean continuing edn. 1980—; presdl. appointee Nat. Adv. Council on Adult Edn., chmn., 1982-84; spl. asst. to dep. asst. sec. student fin. aid, also exec. dir. nat. adv. bd. on internat. edn. programs U.S. Dept. Edn. Recipient cert. of merit Mayor of New Orleans, 1977, Dept. of Commerce Bur. of Census, 1980; Disting. Service award Nat. Assn. Asian and Pacific Am. Educators, 1981; named Outstanding Citizen, City of New Orleans, 1984. Mem. Assn. Asian Studies, Asia Soc., Soc. Higher Edn., Assn. Continuing Higher Edn., La. Assn. Continuing Higher Edn. (dir. at large), Nat. Assn. Asian and Pacific Am. Educators, Orgn. Am. Historians, Am. Hist. Rev., Acad. Polit. Sci., Inter-Am. Soc., Blue Key, Phi Delta Kappa. Contbr. articles to profl. jours.

SOBEY, EDWIN J. C., museum director, oceanographer, consultant; b. Phila., Apr. 7, 1948; s. Edwin J. and Helen (Chapin) S.; m. Barbara Lee, May 9, 1970; children—Ted Woodall, Andrew Chapin. B.S., U. Richmond (Va.), 1969; M.S., Oreg. State U., 1974, Ph.D., 1977. Research scientist Sci. Applications, Inc., Boulder, Colo., 1977-79, div. mgr., 1979-81; exec. dir. Sci. Mus., West Palm Beach, Fla., 1981—. Alumni v.p. Leadership Palm Beach County; mem. County Commn. Com. on Artificial Reefs; expdn. leader Expdn. Tng. Inst., S.E. Alaska, 1980; mem. U.S. Antarctic Research Program, 1974. Author: Complete Circuit Training Guide, 1980; Strength Training Book, 1981; (with others) Aerobic Weight Training Book, 1982. Founder, bd. dirs. Visually Impaired Sports Program, Boulder, 1978-81; fitness instr. YMCA Boulder, 1977-81; convener 1st Nat. Conf. Sports for the Blind, 1979. Served to lt. USN, 1970-73. Fellow Explorers Club; mem. Marine Tech. Soc. (sect. chmn. 1982-84), Coral Reef Soc. (chpt. pres. 1982—). Home: 2728 Starwood Circle West Palm Beach FL 33406 Office: 4801 Dreher Trail West Palm Beach FL 33405

SOGARD, LANORE IRENE, state education agency official; b.Chgo., Mar. 12, 1932; d. Walter H. and Edith B. (Peterson) S. B.S., Iowa State U., 1955; M.S., Kans. State U., 1961; Ph.D., U. Wis., 1972. Cert. elem. tchr., Wis. Tchr., Child Care Ctr., Inc., Milw., 1955-57; instr. home econs., dir. nursery sch. La. Coll., Pineville, 1957-59; instr. psychology, dir. Child Study Ctr., Lindenwood Coll., St. Charles, Mo., 1960-62; asst. prof., dir. Child Study Ctr., Simmons Coll., Boston, 1962-66; asst. prof. child devel./family life Stout State U., Menomonie, Wis., 1967-71; coordinator county accreditation and child devel. W.Va. Dept. Edn., Charleston, 1972—; cons. Mass. Dept. Edn., Boston,

1962-66, Head Start, Mass., Wis., W.Va., 1965—; mem. regional adv. bd. Head Start, 1984—; Title 1 supr. Cassanovia Schs., Cassanovia, Wis., 1971-72; cons. task force Appalachia Edn. Lab., Charleston, 1972—. Author: Child Assessment System, 1980-85, slide and tape show The Best for Our Children, 1980. E.B. Fred fellow U. Wis., 1980. Mem. Am. Soc. Tng. and Devel., Phi Delta Kappa (sec. 1982-83, 84-85). Democrat. Lutheran. Club: Soroptimist Internat. of Charleston (dir. 1978-80, treas. 1980-82, pres. 1985—). Home: 941 Hazelwood Ave Charleston WV 25302 Office: W Va Dept Edn Capitol Complex Bldg 6 Charleston WV 25305

SOLES, WILLIAM ROGER, insurance company executive; b. Whiteville, N.C., Sept. 16, 1920; s. John William and Margaret (Watts) S.; B.S. in Commerce, U. N.C., 1947, postgrad., 1956; m. Majelle Marrene Morris, Sept. 22, 1956; children—William Roger, Majelle Janette. With Jefferson Standard Life Ins. Co., Greensboro, N.C., 1947—, v.p., mgr. securities dept., 1962-64, asst. to pres., 1964-66, exec. v.p., mgr. securities dept., 1966, now pres., also dir.; pres., dir. Jefferson-Pilot Corp.; chmn. bd. Jefferson-Pilot Fire & Casualty Co., Jefferson-Pilot Title Ins. Co.; dir. Pilot Life Ins. Co., Jefferson-Pilot Communications Co. Va., Piedmont Natural Gas Co., NCNB Corp., N.C. Nat. Bank. Chmn. bd. trustees High Point Coll., Wesley Long Community Hosp.; past chmn. Ind. Coll. Fund N.C.; past pres. Bus. Found. N.C.; past chmn. N.C. Citizens Assn.; bd. dirs. N.C. Ins. Edn. Found., Inc. Served with USAAF, 1941-45. Mem. Am. Council Life Ins. (past chmn., dir.), N.C. Council Mgmt. and Devel., Beta Gamma Sigma. Club: Greensboro Country. Home: 604 Kimberly Dr Greensboro NC 27408 Office: PO Box 21008 Greensboro NC 27420

SOLIS, RONNIE WILLIAM, banker; b. New Orleans, Jan. 3, 1944; s. William Harry and Jessie Mildred (Schmidt) S.; m. Elayne Weber, Oct. 19, 1968; children—Laura Elayne, Mark William, Paul Michael. A.A., Delgado Jr. Coll., 1965; B.A., Southwestern La. U., 1968; M.B.A., Loyola U., New Orleans, 1973; grad. Midsouth Exec. Devel. Program, La. State U., 1976. Sr. acct. Fed. Land Bank, New Orleans, 1970-72, chief acct., 1972-73, asst. treas., 1973-77, asst. v.p., 1977-78, treas., 1978-79, v.p., treas., 1979—. Served with U.S. Army, 1964-70. Recipient Emergency Service award La. Army N.G., 1964. Democrat. Roman Catholic. Lodge: Kiwanis (treas. 1973) (New Orleans). Home: 1317 Giuffrias Ave Metairie LA 70001 Office: Fed Land Bank New Orleans PO Box 50590 New Orleans LA 70150

SOLIS, YOLANDA C(UELLAR), foreign language educator, consultant; b. San Antonio, Mar. 10, 1948; d. Cruz, Sr., and Trinidad Olga (Cuellar) S. A.A., San Antonio Coll., 1969; B.A., Southwest Tex. State U., 1971. Cert. secondary tchr. Tchr. San Antonio Ind. Sch. Dist., 1971—, fgn. lang. tchr. Sam Houston High Sch., 1971—, tennis coach, 1979-82, cheerleader sponsor, 1983; lang. cons. Mex. Am. Cultural Ctr., San Antonio, 1974—. Mem. Assn. Tex. Profl. Educators. Democrat. Roman Catholic. Office: San Antonio Ind Sch Dist 141 Lavaca San Antonio TX 78207

SOLIZ, JOSEPH GUY, lawyer; b. Corpus Christi, Tex., June 25, 1954; s. Oscar and Ola Mae (Trammell) S.; B.A. with highest honors, S.W. Tex. State U., 1976; J.D., Harvard U., 1979; m. Juanita Solis, June 3, 1978. Bar: Tex. 1979, U.S. Ct. Appeals (5th and 11th cirs.), U.S. Dist. Ct. (no. dist.) Tex. atty. Gulf Oil Corp., Houston, 1979-81; ptnr. firm Chamberlain, Hrdlicka, White, Johnson & Williams, Houston, 1981—. Mem. Am. Bar Assn., State Bar Tex., Houston Bar Assn., Houston Young Lawyers Assn., Internat. Bar Assn., Delta Tau Kappa, Alpha Chi, Pi Gamma Mu. Democrat. Roman Catholic. Home: 9406 Beverly Hill Houston TX 77063 Office: 1400 Citicorp Ctr 1200 Smith St Houston TX 77002

SOLIZ, MANUEL, real estate investment consultant; b. San Antonio, Sept. 30, 1946; s. Manuel A. and Manuela S. Soliz; B.A., Tex. A&I U., 1970; m. Raquel Aleman, June 24, 1972; childen—Manuel III, Marco Antonio. Research analyst, program specialist Interstate Research Assos., Washington, 1971-73; dir. prepaid services El Valley Community Health Plan, Harlingen, Tex., 1973-76; exec. dir. Rio Grande Fedn. of Health Centers, Inc., San Antonio, 1976-79; health systems cons., San Antonio, 1979—; mem. Nat. Adv. Com. on Nat. Health Ins. Issues, 1977—. Mem. Am. Public Health Assn., Am. Acad. Health Adminstrn., Am. Mgmt. Assn., Forum of Nat. Hispanic Orgn., Am. Heart Assn., Regional Assn. for Non Profit Community Health Orgns. (mem. exec. com.), U.S. Mexican Border Public Health Assn., Tex. Health Maintenance Orgns. Assn., Tex. State Health Coalition, AAAS, Assn. Med. Rehab. Dirs. and Coordinators, Nat. Bd. Realtors, Tex. Assn. Realtors, San Antonio Bd. Realtors, League United Latin Am. Citizens. Democrat. Roman Catholic. Home and Office: 6243 IH 10W San Antonio TX 78201

SOLKOFF, JEROME IRA, lawyer, consultant, lecturer; b. Rochester, N.Y., Feb. 15, 1939; s. Samuel and Dorothy (Krovetz) S.; m. Doreen Hurwitz, Aug. 11, 1963; children—Scott Michael, Anne Lynn. B.S., Sch. Indsl. and Labor Relations, Cornell U., 1961; J.D., U. Buffalo, 1964. Bar: N.Y. 1965, U.S. Dist. Ct. (we. dist.) N.Y. 1965, Fla. 1974. Assoc. Nusbaum, Tarricone, Weltman, Bilgore & Silver, Rochester, N.Y., 1964-66, Mousaw, Vigdor, Reeves, Heilbronner & Kroll, Rochester, 1966-70; sr. mcpl. atty. Urban Renewal Agy., Rochester, 1970-73; sole practice, Rochester, 1970-73; chief legal counsel Arlen Realty Mgmt., Inc., Miami, Fla., 1973-75; assoc. Britton, Cohen, Kaufman, Benson & Schantz, Miami, 1975-76; chief legal counsel First Mortgage Investors, Miami Beach, Fla., 1976-79; ptnr. Cassel & Cassel, P.A., Miami, 1979-82; sole practice, Deerfield Beach, Fla., 1982—; lectr. on fgn. investment practices in U.S., Eng., 1981, 82, 83, Montreal, Can., 1981. Dir., 1st v.p. Fla. Creative Sci. and Tech. Center, Inc., 1982—; dir. Jewish Community Centers of South Broward, Fla., 1979—, Temple Solel, Hollywood, 1978—. Mem. ABA (sects. real property, trust and probate law), Fla. Bar (sects. real property law and internat. law). Club: Masons (Rochester). Author: Fundamentals of Foreign Investing in American Real Estate and Businesses, 1981, Checklist of N.Y. Mortgage Foreclosure Procedures, 1970, History of Municipal Employee Unions, 1964.

SOLOMON, GARY STUART, psychologist; b. Charleston, S.C., Dec. 23, 1952; s. A. Melvin and Rita E. (Ness) S. B.A., U. Ga., 1974; M.S., Miss. State U., 1975; Ph.D., Tex. Tech U., 1983. Lic. psychologist, Tenn. Psychologist, S.C. State Hosp., Columbia, 1976; dir. Brunswick Mental Health Ctr., Lawrenceville, Va., 1976-78; staff psychologist Lubbock Mental Health Ctr., Tex., 1981-82; asst. prof. SUNY-Albany, 1983-84; chief psychologist Columbia Mental Health Ctr., Tenn., 1984-85; practicing psychologist, Nashville, 1984—, Columbia, 1985—; cons. Lubbock pub. schs., 1980-82, Behavior Mgmt. Cons., Nashville, 1982-83, Albany VA Med. Ctr., 1983-84, Rebound Head Trauma Ctr., Gallatin, Tenn., 1985—. Contbr. articles to profl. jours., chpt. to book. Recipient Horace Russell prize U. Ga., 1974; Chair's scholar Tex. Tech U., 1982. Mem. Am. Psychol. Assn., Internat. Neuropsychol. Soc., Nat. Acad. Neuropsychologists (assoc.), Tenn. Psychol. Assn., Southeastern Psychol. Assn. Home: 1219 Trotwood Ave Columbia TN 38401 Office: 1300 Hatcher Ln Columbia TN 38401

SOLOMON, LEON J., business administrator; b. Kansas City, Mo., Feb. 1, 1946; s. Maurice David and Betty (Mallin) S.; m. Carol Sue Miller, Dec. 13, 1970; children. Student, U. Mo., 1964-66; B.S., SUNY; postgrad. U. Ill.; M.B.A., Columbia Pacific U., Ph.D.; postgrad. Nova U., La. State U. Mgmt. services devel. Zale Jewelry Corp., Dallas, 1968-70; regional gen. mgr. Midwest div. retail ops. Gordon Jewelry Corp., Houston, 1970-75; pres. JMS, Inc., Kansas City, Mo., 1975-80; mktg. dir., gen. mgr. estate div. David R. Balogh, Inc., Fort Lauderdale, Fla., 1980—. Bd. dirs. Broward Jewish Fedn. Recipient Citizenship award B'nai B'rith; Leadership award Fla. Jewish Fedns.; Sales Devel. award Bulova Watch Corp., 1978. Mem. Am. Mgmt. Assn., Sales Mktg. and Mgmt. Assn., Gemological Inst. Am., Nat. Assn. Appraisers, U.S. C. of C., U.S. Jaycees (bd. dirs.). Democrat. Jewish. Clubs: Inverrary Country; Fort Lauderdale Roadrunners. Author: Entrepreneurialism-The Motivation of Business, 1983. Office: 5558 W Oakland Park Blvd Fort Lauderdale FL 33313

SOLOMON, LOUIS BERNARD, social service agency executive; b. Indpls., Dec. 31, 1939; s. Harry and Dorothy (Gavin) S.; m. Marlene Paula Bromberg, Aug. 24, 1970; children—Mindy Jo, Amy Jo. B.S. in Recreation, Ind. U., 1964; Cert. Jewish Communal Studies, Hebrew Union Coll.-Jewish Inst. Religion, 1972. Health/phys. edn. dir. Jewish Community Ctr., Troy, N.Y., 1967-69; asst. dir. United Jewish Fund and Council, St. Paul, 1969-73; exec. dir. Jewish Fedn. Pinellas County, St. Petersburg, Fla., 1973-75, Jewish Fedn. of Omaha, 1975-82; exec. v.p. Jewish Welfare Fedn., Indpls., 1982-84, Jacksonville Jewish Fedn., Fla., 1984—. Mem. Civic Round Table, Jacksonville, 1985. Mem. Assn. Jewish Community Orgn. Personnel (pres. 1983-85). Democrat. Jewish. Lodge: B'nai B'rith. Avocations: racquetball; golf. Home: 2248 Cheryl Dr Jacksonville FL 32217 Office: Jacksonville Jewish Fedn 10829 Old St Augustine Rd Jacksonville FL 32223

SOLOMON, MARVIN, lawyer; b. Tampa, Fla., Dec. 18, 1933; s. Rudolph and Isabel Ruth (Moed) S.; B.S., B.A., U. Fla., 1955, J.D., 1960; m. Karen Marie Melich, Oct. 23, 1965; children—Elise A., Robert B. Admitted to Fla. bar, 1961; pres. firm Marvin Solomon, Tampa, 1974—. Bd. dirs. Fla. Orch. Served with U.S. Army, 1955-57. Mem. Comml. Law League Am., U. South Fla. Pres.' Council, Am. Judicature Soc., Pi Lambda Phi, Phi Alpha Delta. Democrat. Jewish. Club: Masons. Home: 4926 W Bay Way Dr Tampa FL 33629 Office: 1702 N Florida Ave Tampa FL 33602

SOLOMON, RICHARD BENJAMIN, architectural and engineering company executive; b. S.I., N.Y., Sept. 3, 1942; s. Irving and Lillian Ray (Sheld) S.; B.A., U. Miami, 1968; m. Barbara Hoberman, Nov. 7, 1965; children—Martin Bradley, Daniel Louis. Specification writer T Trip Russell Assos., Miami, Fla., 1962-70; v.p., prin. Greenleaf/Telesca, Planners, Engrs., Architects, Inc., 1970-83; v.p., prin. APEC Cons., Inc., Architects, Planners, Engrs., Cost Cons., 1983—; instr. Miami Dade Community Coll., 1973; guest lectr. Fla. Internat. U., 1976—. Pres., Kendale Homeowners Assn., 1974. Served with USNR, 1963-65. Recipient various prizes Nat. Specifications Competition, 1970-74. Fellow Constrn. Specifications Inst. (nat. dir. 1977-79, v.p. 1983-84, pres. 1985-86, pres. Greater Miami chpt. 1972-73, Ben John Small Meml. award 1975, J. Norman Hunter Meml. award 1980). Home: 10000 SW 102d Ave Rd Miami FL 33176 Office: 2780 SW Douglas Rd Miami FL 33133

SOLOMONSON, CHARLES D., motel chain executive; b. 1930; m. Sarah B. Auer, 1952; children—Katherine M., Charles W. B.S., Columbia U., 1954; M.B.A., Harvard U., 1956. With Denver Union Stock Yard Co., 1956-60; sec., asst. treas. G. D. Searle & Co., 1960-68; with Jos. Schlitz Brewing Co., 1968-69, treas., 1968-69; v.p. fin. Fairmont Food Co., Omaha, 1969-73, pres., 1973-74, dir., 1972-75; v.p. fin., treas. Hobart Corp., Troy, Ohio, 1975-77, v.p. fin. and Adminstrn., dir., 1977-79; sr. v.p., chief fin. officer Holiday Inns, Inc., Memphis, 1979, dir., 1980—, exec. v.p., chief fin. and adminstrv. officer, 1981—; dir. Protection Mut. Ins. Co., 1970-82, Mut. of Omaha, 1973-80, Commerce Union Bank of Memphis, 1984—. Trustee Nebr. Meth. Hosp., 1973-75, Miami Valley Hosp., Dayton, Ohio, 1977-79, WKNO-TV-FM, Memphis, 1983—, Dixon Gallery & Gardens, 1985—; bd. dirs. Memphis Orchestral Soc., 1983—, Econ. Club of Memphis, 1985—. Mem. Indsl. Real Estate Financing Adv. Council and Fin. Execs. Inst. Episcopalian. Home: 2012 Farmington Bend Germantown TN 38138 Office: Holiday Corp 1023 Cherry Rd Memphis TN 38117

SOLOWSKY, JAY HOWARD, lawyer; b. N.Y.C., Dec. 22, 1951; s. George and Jean (Rosenberg) S.; m. Ellen Goldberg, July 18, 1976; 1 child, Leah. B.A. cum laude, U. Mass., 1975; J.D. cum laude, U. Miami, 1979. Bar: Fla. 1979, U.S. Dist. Ct. (so. dist.) Fla. 1979, U.S. Ct. Appeals (11th cir.) 1983. Assoc. Martin Engels, P.A., Miami, Fla., 1979-81; ptnr. Engels & Solowsky, P.A., Miami, 1981-82, Wallace, Engels, Pertnoy & Solowsky, Miami, 1982-84, Solowsky & Allen, P.A., Miami, 1984—; adj. prof. U. Miami Sch. Law, Coral Gables, 1982—, Fla. Internat. U., Miami, 1983—; chmn. Moot Ct. Bd. U. Miami Sch. Law, 1978-79. Contbr. articles to profl. jours. Mem. Dade County Bar Assn. (Disting. Service award 1983, 84), Fla. Bar, Fed. Bar Assn., Assn. Trial Lawyers Am., Bar and Gavel, Phi Delta Phi (Province Grad. of Yr. 1979). Republican. Office: One Datran Ctr Suite 1406 9100 S Dadeland Blvd Miami FL 33156

SOLZMAN, NATHAN JEROME, accountant; b. Greenville, Ky., May 25, 1951; s. Irving Daniel and Ruth (Cohen) S.; m. Sheri Diane Goldberg, July 31, 1977; 1 child, Daniel Eric. B.S., U. Ky.-Lexington, 1973. C.P.A., Ky. Staff acct. U.S. Army Audit Agy., East Central Dist., Md., 1973-74; Ky. auditor pub. accounts, county auditor, Frankfort, Ky., 1974-78; sr. staff acct. Welenken, Himmelfarb & Co., Louisville, Ky., 1978—. Mem. Assn. Govt. Accts. (treas. Central Ky. chpt. 1982-83), Ky. Soc. C.P.A.s (state and local taxation com. 1982-83), Am. Inst. C.P.A.s, Zeta Beta Tau. Democrat. Jewish. Office: 730 W Market St Suite 200 Louisville KY 40202

SOMAYAJULU, GOLLAKOTA RAAM, research scientist; b. Pithapuram, Andhra, India, July 15, 1928; came to U.S., 1958, naturalized, 1981; s. Venkat Ramiah and Veera Bhadra (Kambhampati) Gollakota; m. Ramana Venkata Sripada, June 7, 1957 (div. 1981); 1 child, Ramgopal Venkat Gollakota. B.S., Andhra U., Waltair, Andhra, India, 1949; M.S., Banaras Hindu U., India, 1952; Ph.D., Jadavpur U., Calcutta, India, 1960. Research assoc. U. N.C., Chapel Hill, 1958-60; U. Calif., Berkeley, 1960-62; sci. officer Osmania U., Hyderabad, Andhra, India, 1962-64; research metallurgist U. Calif., Berkeley, 1966-69; sr. chem. physicist Tex. A&M U., College Station, 1970—. Author: Cyclic Universe, 1969; (with others) Nonaqueous Titration, 1954. Contbr. sci. articles to profl. jours. Mem. Linguistic Soc. Am., N.Y. Acad. Scis. Democrat. Hindu. Avocations: epigraphy; philosophy; astrology; stargazing. Office: Tex A&M U College Station TX 77843

SOMERVILLE, PAUL NOBLE, statistics educator; b. Vulcan, Alta., Can., May 7, 1925; s. Bert Noble and Simone Marie (Deroussiaux) S.; m. Sheila Doreen Bell, Dec. 11, 1954; children—Deborah, David. B.Sc., U. Alta., 1949; Ph.D. in Stats., U. N.C., 1953. Tchr., Can., 1942-44; assoc. prof. stats. Va. Poly. Inst., and assoc. statsitician Extension Service Agr. Expt. Sta., 1953-55; vis. prof. math. Am. U., 1955-57; asst. project dir. C-E-I-R Inc., Ariz., 1958-61, mgr. Utah office, 1961-62; mgr. tech. evaluation RCA Corp., Cocoa Beach, Fla., 1962-72; assoc. prof., U. Central Fla., 1972-79, prof. stats., 1979—; guest scientist Nat. Bur. Standards, 1955-57; lectr. U. Ariz., 1958-61, Brigham Young U., 1962; chmn. math. dept. Fla. Inst. Tech., 1963-72; adj. prof. U. Fla., Genesys, 1968-72. Served with Can. Army, 1944-45. Mem. Am. Stats. Assn., Am. Meteorol. Soc., Internat. Assn. Statis. Computing, Bernouilli Soc. Probability and Stats. Contbr. articles to profl. jours. Office: Dept Statistics U Central Fla Orlando FL 32816

SOMERVILLE, WILLIAM GLASSELL, JR., lawyer; b. Memphis, July 27, 1933; s. William Glassell and Hilda (Deeth) S.; m. Mary Hateley Quincey, June 13, 1959; children—William Glassell, John Quincey, Mary Campbell, Sarah Guerrant. A.B., Princeton U., 1955; LL.B., U. Va., 1961. Bar: Ala. 1961, U.S. Ct. Appeals (5th cir.) 1963, U.S. Supreme Ct. 1964, U.S. Ct. Appeals (8th cir.) 1968. Law clk. to chief judge U.S. Dist. Ct. (no. dist.) Ala., 1961-63; assoc. Lange, Simpson, Robinson & Somerville, Birmingham, Ala., 1963-66, ptnr., 1966—; mem. supreme ct. adv. com. on rules of Ala. appellate procedure, 1972-77; mem. standing com. on Ala. rules of appellate procedure, 1979—. Served with CIC, U.S. Army, 1955-58. Mem. ABA, Ala. Bar Assn., Am. Judicature Soc. Clubs: Ivy (Princeton), Birmingham Country. Lodge: Rotary. Office: Suite 1700 F A B Bldg Birmingham AL 35203

SOMMERFIELD, ELISSA BERWALD, English language educator; b. Dallas; d. Elihu Edward and Ann Shirley (Meltz) Berwald; m. Frank Edgar Sommerfield, Feb. 23, 1961; children—Frank Edgar, John. B.A. summa cum laude, Tex. U.; M.A., So. Meth. U. Instr. English, So. Meth. U., Dallas, Dallas Community Coll.; tutor in English, 1961—; freelance writer; copywriter Bloom's Advt.; dir. verbal and math. skills seminar, SAT preparation courses, 1975—, study skills seminar. Co-author: PSAT-SAT Multimedia Guide and Study Skills Guide: A Survivor's Manual. Mem. Assn. Coll. Counselors Am., Nat. Conf. Coll. English Tchrs., Phi Beta Kappa. Jewish. Home: 9636 Hollow Way Dallas TX 75220

SOMMERVILLE, MARGARET JEAN LOSEKE, physician; b. Columbus, Nebr., Feb. 21, 1925; d. Edward G. and Emma C. (Luers) Loseke; m. James J. Sommerville, Nov. 6, 1954; children—Jean, Ann, Peggy. B.A., M.D., U. Iowa. Diplomate Am. Acad. Family Practice. Intern, Kings Coll. Hosp., Bklyn., 1951-53; individual practice, specializing in family medicine, Strawberry Point, Iowa, 1953-55, Des Moines, 1955, White Plains and Port Chester, N.Y., 1956-59, Atlanta, 1959—; mem. wellness com. Northside Hosp., Atlanta. Mem. Nu Sigma Phi. Republican. Lutheran. Office: 90 W Wieuca Rd NE Atlanta GA 30342

SONJU, NORM, professional basketball team executive; b. 1938; m. Carole; 3 children. B.A., Grinnell Coll., 1960; M.B.A., U. Chgo., 1967. With Service-Master Industries, Downers Grove, Ill., 1967-76; pres., gen. mgr. Buffalo Braves, NBA, 1976-78; v.p., gen. mgr. Dallas Mavericks, NBA, 1980—. Office: Dallas Mavericks Reunion Arena 777 Sports St Dallas TX 75207

SOOY, WILLIAM RAY, electrical engineer, consultant; b. Vineland, N.J., Jan. 12, 1951; s. Edward Leinau and Alice Elizabeth (Franklin) S.; m. Jean Marie Sooy, Sept. 17, 1976; 1 dau., Jennifer. B.S. in E.E., U. Miami, 1973, M.S., 1977. Registered profl. engr., Fla. Engr., Fla. Power and Light, Miami, 1973-80, sr. engr., 1981—; engr. Harris Corp., Melbourne, Fla., 1980-81. Mem. IEEE, Eta Kappa Nu. Republican. Presbyterian. Home: 14500 SW 95th Ave Miami FL 33176 Office: Fla Power and Light 9250 Flagler GE Miami FL 33152

SORRELLS, AUDREY HANNAH, educational counselor; b. Cedartown, Ga., Oct. 14, 1938; d. Ralph Bunyan and Audrey Bonnie (Terry) Hannah; m. Jerry Howell, June 25, 1961. A.B. in English, Tift Coll., 1960; M.S. in Counseling, Nova U., 1980. Tchr. Miami Springs (Fla.) Jr. High Sch., 1960-71; tchr. Hialeah (Fla.)-Miami Lakes Sr. High Sch., 1971-80, secondary counselor, 1980—, also intern dir., 1973; co-chmn. North Area Counseling, Hialeah, 1983-84; cons. textbook World of Communications, 1974. Sponsor Christian Children's Fund, 1970-84; mem. Miami Lakes Civic Assn., 1981—, Hialeah-Miami Lakes Booster Assn., 1971—. Recipient Tchr. of Yr. award Hialeah-Miami Lakes Sr. High Sch., 1974, 75, 77, Hialeah Women's Club, 1974; Most Dedicated Tchr. award, 1980. Mem. Am. Assn. for Counseling and Devel., Fla. Personnel and Guidance Assn., Dade County Personnel and Guidance Assn., United Tchrs. of Dade, Fla. Sch. Counselors Assn., Women Sports Found., Delta Kappa Gamma, Alpha Psi Omega. Democrat. Baptist. Home: 2328 SE 19th Circle Ocala FL 32671 Office: Hialeah Miami Lakes Sr High Sch 7977 W 12th Ave Hialeah FL 33014

SORRELLS, BOBBY GENE, real estate appraiser, consultant; b. East Point, Ga., Apr. 26, 1934; s. James Clifford and Bernice U. (Moore) S.; m. Dorothy Sue Landrum, Mar. 1, 1955; children—Sharon, Danny, Renee. Student Ga. Tech. U. Paint and plastics specialist Lockheed Aircraft, Marietta, Ga., 1955-59; spl. agt. So. Ry. System, Atlanta, 1959-69; real estate appraiser, cons. Bob Sorrells & Assocs., Atlanta, 1969—. Served to cpl. AUS, 1953-55; Korea. Mem. Nat. Assn. Ind. Fee Appraisers (v.p. 1982-83), Cert. Rev. Appraisers Assn., Old Nat. Bus. and Profl. Assn. (pres. 1974-75). Clubs: Airport Optimist College Park, Ga.); Lodge: Masons. Home: 2665 Dunmoreland Terr College Park GA 30349 Office: Bob Sorrells & Associates Inc 6585 Church St Riverdale GA 30274

SORRELLS, JAMES GORMAN, energy company exploration geologist; b. Linden, Tex., June 1, 1950; s. James Norman and Kathryn Faye (Fountain) S.; m. Virginia Ruth Dibble, Aug. 17, 1968; children—James Tracy, Wesley Jay. A.S., Kilgore Coll., 1974; B.S., U. Tex.-Arlington, 1976. Geologist, Cavalla Energy Exploration, Houston, 1976-77, Realitos Energy Corp., Houston, 1977-81, Phylko Energy Corp., Houston, 1981—. Cub master Sam Houston Area council Boy Scouts Am., 1980; sponsor Alief Little League, Houston, 1981-85, Alief Youth Assn., Houston, 1984. Served with USAF, 1968-72. Mem. Am. Assn. Petroleum Geologists, Houston Geol. Soc. Republican. Baptist. Home: 3311 Ashford Park Dr Houston TX 77082 Office: Phylko Energy Corp 5701 Woodway 312 Houston TX 77057

SORRELLS, RONALD EUGENE, computer scientist; b. Macon, Ga., May 24, 1954; s. Eugene Clarence and Irene Martha (Lawrence) S.; m. Cheryl Lynn DeLaurier, Mar. 27, 1982. B.S. with honors, Ga. Inst. Tech. Asst. analyst Ga. Power Co., Atlanta, 1978-80; analyst Southwire Co., Carrolton, Ga., 1980-81; scientist U.S. Def. Dept., Warner Robins, Ga., 1981-82; computer scientist WM Labs, Macon, Ga., 1982—. Mem. Beta Gamma Sigma, Eta Kappa Nu. Baptist. Home: 2297 New Clinton Rd Macon GA 31201 Office: PO Box 6401 Macon GA 31208

SORRIER, ISABEL LANE, librarian; b. Statesboro, Ga., Aug. 13, 1917; d. Brooks Blitch and Caroline Viola (Moore) Sorrier; B.S., Ga. So. Coll., 1938; postgrad. U. Ga., 1940; B.S., George Peabody Coll., 1942. Intern, Warder Pub. Library, Springfield, Ohio, 1942; librarian Homerville (Ga.) High Sch., 1939-41; head librarian Waycross (Ga.) Pub. Library, 1942; librarian Newnan (Ga.) High Sch., 1943; dir. Statesboro (Ga.) Regional Library, 1944—; mem. library adv. com. bldg. constrn. Ga. Dept. Edn., mem. book selection com. Sec. chpt. ARC, 1945-48; mem. library services and constrn. Act Adv. Council, 1976—. Named Boss of Yr., Am. Bus. Women's Assn., 1980. Mem. ALA, S.E., Ga. (exec. bd. 1960, chmn. sect. 1960-62) library assns., Ga. Edn. Assn., Bus. and Profl. Women's Club (treas. 1950-52). Presbyterian. Home: 112 Park Ave Statesboro GA 30485 Office: 124 S Main St Statesboro GA 30458

SOTO, RAFAEL AVELINO, physician; b. Cienfuegos, Cuba, Dec. 9, 1936; came to U.S., 1974; s. Jose Antonio and Emilia (Hernandez) S.; m. Maria Teresa Rios, July 28, 1962; children—Emilia Maria, Lourdes. B.S., Maristas Sch., 1954; M.D., U. Havana, 1963. Intern Calixto Garcia Hosp., Havana, 1962; resident Gen. Hosp. of Cienfuegos (Cuba); surgeon Cuba, 1963-74; practice medicine specializing in family practice; gov., mem. staff South Shore Hosp., Miami Beach, Fla.; gen. physician Soto Med. Ctr. Miami Beach, Fla., 1980—. Mem. Cuban Med. Coll., Dade County Med. Assn., AMA, Am. Geriatrics Soc., Am. Coll. Gen. Practice. Republican. Roman Catholic.

SOTOMAYOR-VICÉNS, EDUARDO, health services adminstr.; b. Rio Piedras, P.R., Oct. 6, 1948; s. Eduardo and Rafaela (Sotomayor) S.; B.S., U. P.R., 1970, M.S. in Health Services Adminstrn., 1972; m. Ada M. Mena, Dec. 20, 1969; children—Eduardo D., Ada E., Ricardo J. Adminstr. emergency med. services San Juan Health Dept., P.R., 1972-75, State Dept. Health, 1975-76; dep. adminstr. Oncologic Hosp., Dr. J. Gonzalez Martinez, P.R., 1976-78; dir. med. services Intercontinental Life Ins. Co., P.R., 1978-80; v.p. South Continental Ins. Agy., P.R., 1980-81; pres. Health Plans Mgmt. Con. Inc., Hato Rey, P.R., 1981—; pres. Health Care Inc., 1983—, Health Professions Devel. Ctr. Inc., 1985—; instr. Sacred Heart Jr. Coll., 1971-73. Pres. Cancer Telethon Organizing Com., Served with USAR, 1970—. Mem. P.R. Assn. of Hosp. Adminstrs. (presdl. award 1977-78; pres. 1979-80), P.R. Profls. Assn. (pres. 1982-83), Hosp. Fin. Mgmt. Assn. (P.R. chpt.), Am. Coll. Hosp. Adminstrn. Roman Catholic. Club: San Juan Lions (sec. 1983-84). Home: German Moyer 397 Hato Rey PR 00918 Office: Padre Las Casas 113 Hato Rey PR 00918

SOTO-MUÑOZ, MANUEL, painter; b. Caguas, P.R., Jan. 20, 1913; s. Manuel Soto and Elisa Muñoz; student Art Students League N.Y., 1947-51; m. Clara Hernández, Sept. 3, 1948; 1 child, Angel Manuel. Draftsman, P.R. Water Resources Authority, San Juan, 1937-47; artist Art Award Co., Inc., Bklyn., 1950-62; art dir. La Milagrosa mag., San Juan, 1962-65; art instr. extension div. U. P.R., Rio Piedrás, 1962-64; art instr., Rio Piedras, 1960-78. Exhibited in group shows Keane Mason Gallery, N.Y.C., 1982, Gallery II-RSVP, Charlottesville, Va., 1983, 1st Presbyn. Ch., Wheaton, Ill., 1983, Internat. Small Fine Arts Exhbn., Atlanta, 1984, Pinnacle Gallery, Rochester, N.Y., 1984, F.A.C.E.T., Taos, N.Mex., 1984, Ariel Gallery, N.Y.C., 1985, Chimerical Gregg Art Gallery, La Puente, Calif., 1986 (Spl. award). Served with U.S. Army, 1942-45. Recipient award of merit Fla. So. Coll., 1958; prize Art Students League N.Y., 1950; 1st prize Salón Arte Sacro de P.R., Aguadilla Art Center, 1979. Mem. Artists Equity Assn., Long Beach Art Assn. (N.Y.), Internat. Soc. Artists, Art Students League N.Y. (life), Nat. Soc. Painters in Casein and Acrylic (asso.), Am. Biog. Research Assn. Roman Catholic. Club: Exchange (v.p. 1968-70) (Bayamón Sur, Bayamón P.R.). Artist practicing and teaching Art Form of Painting, 1960-86. Home and Office: 1605 Indo St El Cerezal Rio Piedras PR 00926

SOTTILE, JOHN HOOKS, mining and electrical construction company executive; b. Miami, Fla., Nov. 29, 1947; s. James and Ethel Brundage (Hooks) S.; m. Ann Grubbs; children—Sara Elaine, Rachel Ethel, John Nicholas. B.S., U. Miami, 1971. Vice-pres., dir. Lake Byrd Citrus Packing Co., 1967—, Citrus Growers Fla. Inc., 1967—, Indian River Orange Groves, 1967-69, Fla. Orange Growers Inc., 1967—; pres., dir. 65 E NASA Corp., 1977-80; dir. Valencia Center, Inc., 1974—; exec. asst. The Goldfield Corp., Melbourne, Fla., 1971-76, asst. to pres., 1976-83, v.p., 1983, pres., 1983—; pres., dir. No. Goldfield Investments Ltd. Inc., Black Range Mining Corp., U.S. Treasury Mining Co., San Pedro Mining Corp., Fla. Transport Corp.; v.p., dir. Power Corp. Am., S.E. Power Corp.; pres., dir. Contractors Leasing Corp., Goldfield Consol. Mines Co., Detrital Valley Salt Co. Democrat. Roman Catholic. Club: Eau Gallie Yacht. Home: 2324 Brookside Way Indialantic FL 32903 Office: 100 Rialto Pl Suite 500 Melbourne FL 32901

SOUDEK, MILOS, refining company executive; b. Brno, Czechoslovakia, June 17, 1932; came to U.S., 1979; s. Jan and Marie (Behringerova) S.; m. Vera Ludmilla Svatkova, Feb. 21, 1953; children—Milos, Ales. B.S. in Chem. Engring. summa cum laude, Mil. High Tech. Acad., Brno, 1956. From process engr. to chief process engr. Chemoprojekt, Brno, 1956-66; cons. Iraqi Ministry Oil, Baghdad, 1966-68; from sr. process engr. to div. mgr. M.W. Kellogg, Houston, 1979, Kellogg Internat. Corp., London, 1969-78; process design dept. mgr. Bechtel, Houston, 1980; v.p. refining engring. Coastal Corp., Houston, 1981—. Fellow Brit. Inst. Chem. Engring.; mem. Am. Inst. Chem. Engrs. Contbr. articles to profl. jours.

SOUDER, HERSHEL RAY, information systems educator; b. Cin., July 8, 1944; s. William August and Luella (Lanter) Goering; m. Jean Horton, Jan. 14, 1978. B.B.A., U. Cin., 1972, M.B.A., 1973, Ph.D., 1983. Exec., Complete Systems, Inc., Cin., 1973-77, Visionnaire, Inc., Cin., 1977-81, R3M, Inc., Cin., 1978-79; prof. No. Ky. U., Highland Heights, 1981—; cons. computer systems design; dir. Robinson, Mitchell and Assocs. Served with U.S. Army, 1964-69. Decorated Purple Heart, Bronze Star. Grantee in field. Mem. Acad. Mgmt., Am. Prodn. and Inventory Control Soc., Am. Soc. Info. Sci., Am. Inst. Indsl. Engrs., Data Processing Mgmt. Assn., Am. Inst. for Decision Scis., Literary Guild. Republican. Presbyterian. Author: Simple Linear and Multiple Regressions Analysis, 1982. Contbr. articles on info. scis. to profl. jours.

SOUDERS, BRUCE CHESTER, clergyman, humanities educator; b. Richland, Pa., Dec. 27, 1920; s. Ray Levan and Sue (Hartman) S.; B.A., Lebanon Valley Coll., 1944; M.Div., United Theol. Sem., 1947; M.A., Columbia U., 1953; student Luth. Theol. Sem., Gettysburg, Pa., 1953-66, James Madison U., 1967-69; m. Patricia Marie Bartels, Aug. 18, 1945; 1 son, Gregory Allen. Ordained to ministry, United Meth. Ch., 1947; instr. Lebanon Valley Coll., 1947-49; pastor Neidig Meml. United Meth. Ch., Oberlin, Pa., 1949-57; instr. Lebanon Valley Coll. Extension Program, Harrisburg, Pa., 1957-66; dir. public relations, 1957-65, dir. publs., 1965-66; mem. staff Shenandoah Coll. and Conservatory of Music, 1966—, chmn. English dept., 1966-73, chmn. arts and scis. faculty, 1972-84, prof. English, 1975-80, prof. English and humanities, 1980-84, coll. historian, prof. humanities, 1984—; resident fellow Va. Ctr. for Creative Arts, 1983; lectr., judge poetry contests; panelist Nat. Endowment for the Humanities. Recipient Honor medal Freedom Found., 1951; Nat. Endowment for Humanities fellow, 1971; faculty devel. grantee Shenandoah Coll., 1983, 85; citation LeGanon Valley Coll. Alumni Assn., 1969. Mem. Hist. Soc. Winchester and Frederick County, Preservation of Hist. Winchester Assn., Winchester-Frederick County Ministerial Assn., MLA, Nat. Council Tchrs. English, So. Humanities Conf. (exec. com. 1981-84), Blue Ridge chpt. Va. Mus. Fine Arts (pres. 1974-76), Poetry Soc. Va. (contest chmn. 1976, 77, v.p. 1981-84, pres. 1984—), Poetry Soc. Am., Shenandoah Valley Writers Guild, Smithsonian Assocs., Va. Conf. Hist. Soc. United Meth. Ch. (Evang. United Brethren historian). Author: To A Student Dying Young and Other Poems, 1978; editor: Lebanon Valley Coll. Alumni Rev., 1957-66; Lebanon Valley College: A Centennial History 1866-1966, 1966; editorial advisor, contbr. Ency. World Methodism, 1974; mem. editorial com. 200 years of Methodism in Virginia, 1982—, Virginia United Methodist Heritage; contbr. poetry, articles and book revs. to jours. and religious publs. Home: 1625 Stafford Dr Winchester VA 22601 Office: Shenandoah Coll and Conservatory of Music College Dr Winchester VA 22601

SOUSOULAS, JAMES GEORGE, dentist; b. Memphis, May 29, 1928; s. Frank George and Mary (Pappademitriou) S.; m. Sophie Makris, June 20, 1954; children—Stephanie Marie, George James. B.S., Memphis State U., 1950; D.D.S., U. Tenn., 1954. Gen. practice dentistry, Memphis, 1957—; assoc. prof. U. Tenn., 1961-76. Served to capt. USAF, 1955-57. Home: 4585 Walnut Grove Rd Memphis TN 38117 Office: Dental Clinic 555 Perkins Extd Suite 309 Memphis TN 38117

SOUTH, DWALIA SHERREE, physician, writer; b. Ripley, Miss., Apr. 23, 1955; d. Terry Vance and Velma Overa (McCown) S.; m. Chard Williams, Nov. 24, 1979; 1 son, Chard Jesse Williams. A.A., Northeast Miss. Jr. Coll., 1975; B.S. in Biology and Psychology, Blue Mountain Coll., 1976; M.D., U. Miss., 1980. Resident physician U. Tenn. Family Practice, Jackson, 1980-81; family physician Ripley Med. Clinic, P.A. (Miss.), 1981—; vice-chief of staff Tippah County Hosp., Ripley, 1984—; mem. med. staff Ripley Manor Nursing Home, 1981—, Resthaven Nursing Home; Ripley Med. Clinic, P.A., 1981—; emergency physician coordinator Tippah County Hosp.; lectr. Scholarship judge Walmart Found., 1983. Recipient Achievement award Miss. Coll. Press Assn., 1975. Affiliate mem. Am. Acad. Family Practice; mem. Miss. Acad. Family Physicians, Tenn. Acad. Family Physicians, AMA, So. Med. Assn., Miss. Med. Assn., N. Miss. Med. Soc. (pres.), Tippah County Med. Soc. (pres.), Phi Theta Kappa. Republican. Baptist. Illustrator: Instant Skiing, 1975; contbr. articles to newspaper.

SOUTHERLIN, TAMMY JONES, retail sales official; b. Anderson, S.C., Sept. 26, 1959; d. R.C. and Ander Kate (Vassar) Jones; m. Michael William Southerlin, June 30, 1979; 1 dau., Ashley Michele. Student Furman U., 1977—. Office mgr. Carolina Auto Parts Co., Mauldin, 1978-82; retail sales coordinator Friddle-Young & Roberts, Greenville, S.C., 1984—; pvt. vocal coach. Pres. chancel choir Mauldin United Methodist Ch., 1980—, dir. pre-sch. choir, 1980—, dir. music, 1985; soloist Mauldin Community Choir, 1984; actress, soloist Greenville Little Theater, 1983-85; soloist, dance capt. Greenville Savoyards, 1985; local pageant entertainer and judge. Club: Mauldin Music. Avocations: dance; music; theatre. Office: Friddle-Young & Roberts Inc 1 Wedd Rd Greenville SC 29606

SOUTHERN, PAUL MORRIS, JR., physician, educator; b. Ft. Worth, June 26, 1932; s. Paul Morris and Margaret M. (Moore) S.; B.S., Abilene Christian Coll., 1953; M.D., U. Tex., 1959; children by previous marriage—Sheryl Ann, Mark Lee. Intern, Parkland Meml. Hosp., Dallas, 1959-60, resident, 1960-62; research fellow infectious diseases U. Tex. Southwestern Med. Sch., Dallas, 1962-63, 66-68; practice medicine, specializing in internal medicine, Irving, Tex., 1963-66; asst. prof. internal medicine U. Tex. Southwestern Med. Sch., Dallas, 1968-71, asso. prof. pathology and internal medicine, 1973-81, prof., 1981—; asst. prof. lab. medicine Washington U. Sch. Medicine, St. Louis, 1971-73; dir. clin. microbiology Parkland Meml. Hosp., Dallas, 1973—; vis. prof. dept. microbiology St. Thomas's Hosp. Med. Sch., London, 1980-81, Kuwait U. Faculty Medicine, 1981, 82. Diplomate Am. Bd. Internal Medicine, Am. Bd. Infectious Diseases, Am. Bd. Pathology. Fellow A.C.P.; mem. Tex. Soc. Clin. Microbiology (pres. 1974-76), Acad. Clin. Lab. Physicians and Scientists, Am. Soc. Microbiology, Infectious Diseases Soc. Am., Tex. Infectious Diseases Soc. (pres. 1983-84), Am. Soc. Clin. Pathologists, So. Soc. Clin. Investigation, Am. Fedn. Clin. Research, Alpha Omega Alpha. Contbr. articles to profl. jours. Home: 257 Creekwood Lancaster TX 75146 Office: 5323 Harry Hines Blvd Dallas TX 75235

SOUTH-PAUL, JEANNETTE ELIZABETH, physician; b. Greensboro, Ala., Aug. 14, 1953; d. Carl Harold and Iris Ciceretta S.; m. Michael David Paul, Sept. 25, 1982; 1 child, Augustine H. G. B.S., U. Pa., 1975; M.D., U. Pitts., 1979. Diplomate Am. Acad. Family Practice. Research asst. Clin. Research Ctr., Phila. Gen. Hosp., 1971-75; commd. capt. M.C., U.S. Army, 1979; intern D.D. Eisenhower Army Med. Ctr., Ft. Gordon, Ga., 1979-80, resident in family practice, 1980-82, mem. staff and faculty family practice residency, 1982—; asst. clin. prof. family medicine Med. Coll. Ga., Augusta, 1983—; faculty devel. fellow U. N.C., Chapel Hill, 1983-84. Fellow Am. Acad. Family Physicians (women in medicine com. 1985—); mem. Uniformed Services Acad. Family Practice (research award 1982), Am. Soc. Clin. Pathologists, Stoney Med./Dental/Pharm. Soc., Officers' Christian Fellowship. Office: Dept Family Practice DD D Eisenhower Army Med Ctr Fort Gordon GA 30905

SOUTHWELL, JOSEPH RAY, JR., computer cons.; b. Oklahoma City, Nov. 20, 1952; s. Joseph Ray and Grace Elizabeth S.; B.S., Okla. State U., 1979; m. Deborah Ann DeShazo, Aug. 20, 1978. Founder, pres. Freelance Computer Programming, Inc., Oklahoma City, 1977-83; pres. Inc. Freelance Data Centers, Inc., Oklahoma City, 1978-83; founder, pres. Tariff Data Systems, 1983—; TCG, Inc.; v.p. Synthetic Lubricants, Inc.; dir. info. processing Mktg. Concepts. Treas. King's Acad. Found. Office: 2912 Classen Blvd Oklahoma City OK 73106

SOUTHWORTH, LOIS GILL, educator, psychologist; b. Atoka, Okla., July 21, 1915; d. James Hugh and Lois Elizabeth (McCuiston) Gill; B.S., NE Okla. State U., 1934; Ed.S., U. Tenn., 1973; lic. psychol. examiner m. James Larry Southworth, Feb. 29, 1936 (dec.); children—John Scott, Bruce Alan. Tchr., Strayer Coll., Washington, 1938-39, Ballard Sch., N.Y.C., 1939-45; pvt. practice psychology, Knoxville, Tenn., 1964-68; asst. prof. dept. child and family studies, U. Tenn., Knoxville, 1967—, researcher Appalachian Children and Families. Active Knoxville Symphony Assn., Dulin Art Gallery Assn., Women's Center of Knoxville, Children's Internat. Village, Common Cause. Lic. psychol. examiner, Tenn. Mem. AAUP, AAUW, Am. Psychol. Assn., Nat. Assn. Psychology in the Schs., Nat. Assn. of Disability Examiners, Nat. Assn. of Children with Learning Disabilities, LWV, NOW, Pi Lambda Theta, Phi Delta Kappa. Democrat. Unitarian. Club: Women's Aux. of Knoxville Acad. Medicine. Author: Screening and Evaluating the Young Child—A Handbook of Instruments to Use from Infancy to Six Years, 1980; contbr. articles in field to profl. jours. Home: 921 Kenesaw Ave Knoxville TN 37919 Office: Dept Child and Family Studies U Tenn Knoxville TN 37916

SOWA, PHILLIP EDWARD, medical center administrator; b. Pawtucket, R.I., May 26, 1947; s. Edward Phillip and Isabelle Anne (Goidz) S.; children—J. Spence, Lindsay Anne. B.S., St. Louis U., 1969, M.S. in Hosp. and Health Care Adminstrn., 1973. Asst. adminstr. Jefferson Meml. Hosp., Festus, Mo., 1973, St. Francis Med. Ctr., Cape Girardeau, Mo., 1973-74, assoc. administr., 1974-77; exec. v.p. Earl L. Meyer Assn., Reston, Va., 1977-78; asst. exec. dir. ops. Univ. Hosp., Louisville, 1978-82; pres. Regional Med. Ctr., Memphis, 1982—; bd. dirs. Health Resource Devel. Corp., Memphis; mem. Gov.'s Com. on Health, 1984—, Gov.'s Com. on Medicaid, 1984—; adj. asst. prof. U. Ala., Birmingham, 1984—; lectr. Memphis State U., 1982—, U. Tenn. Sch. Allied Health Scis., 1982—. Mem. Memphis Agys. Serving the Homeless, 1984—; bd. dirs. Memphis Urban League. Mem. Am. Coll. Hosp. Adminstrs., Am. Hosp. Assn., Am. Acad. Med. Administrs., Nat. Assn. Pub. Hosps. (bd. dirs.). Roman Catholic. Lodge: Kiwanis. Avocations: golf; racquet sports; jogging; music. Home: 885 S Yates St Memphis TN 38119 Office: Regional Med Ctr at Memphis 877 Jefferson Memphis TN 38103

SOWA, WALTER D., educator, lawyer; b. McKeesport, Pa., Jan. 17, 1907; s. Peter and Anna (Jankowska) S.; A.B., U. Pitts., 1928, Litt.M., 1940; J.D., Duquesne U., 1933; m. Eva Ingersoll Long, Apr. 4, 1942; children—Peter William, Thomas Michael. Tchr. elementary sch., Alliquippa, Pa., 1928-30, high sch., Pa., 1930-42; probation officer Juvenile Ct., Allegheny County, Pa., 1940-41; joined U.S. Army, 1942, advanced through grades to lt. col., 1962; acad. coordinator Baylor U., 1943-44, Tex. A. and M. Coll., 1944-46; judge adv. Korea Base Command, 1946-48; at Pa. State Coll., 1948-50; asst. judge adv. X Corps, Korea, 1950-51; sec. gen. staff X Corps, 1951-52; chief contracting div. Hdqrs. 3d Army, 1952-56; legal assistance adviser, 1956-60; trial observer-lawyer, 1960-62, ret., 1962; prof. criminal law Cumberland Law Sch. Howard Coll., Birmingham, Ala., 1963—; prof. criminal law and evidence Samford U., Birmingham, 1963-77, adj. prof. law, 1977—. Decorated Bronze Star. Mem. Am., Ga., Ala. bar assns., Pa. Edn. Assn. Methodist. Mason. Home: 2121 16th Ave S Birmingham AL 35205

SOWELL, VIRGINIA MURRAY, educator; b. Presidio, Tex., Mar. 23, 1931; d. Marshall Bishop and Mary Alice (Daniel) Murray; B.A., Sam Houston State U., 1951; M.A., Trinity U., 1955-57; Ph.D., U. Tex., Austin, 1975; children—John, Paul. Secondary English tchr. San Antonio Ind. Sch. Dist., 1952-53, elem. spl. edn. tchr., 1955-58; instr. edn. San Antonio Coll., part-time 1961-66, asst. to asso. prof. reading, 1969-76; asst. prof. Tex. Tech U., Lubbock, 1976—, assoc. prof. spl. edn., 1980-86, prof., 1986—, asst. v.p. acad. affairs, 1984—, pres. faculty senate, 1982-83. Cons. editor Edn. of Visually Handicapped. Mem. adv. bd. Tex. Sch. for Blind, 1980-86, chmn. 1986-89, Devel. Edn. from Birth through Two, Lubbock, 1978—. Hogg Found. grantee, 1974-75, Fed. Personnel Perparation grantee, 1977—. Mem. Council for Exceptional Children (gov. 1982-85), Council for Learning Disorders (pres. Tex. div. 1979-80), Am. Assn. for Edn. Severely/Profoundly Handicapped, Assn. for Children with Learning Disabilities, Internat. Reading Assn., Tex. Council Exceptional Children (treas. 1982-86), Assn. for Edn. Visually Handicapped (pres. South Central region 1984—), Am. Ednl. Research Assn., Assn. for Supervision and Curriculum Devel., Tex. Assn. Coll. Tchrs., AAUP, Phi Delta Kappa, Zeta Tau Alpha, Delta Kappa Gamma. Contbr. articles in field to profl. jours. Home: 4610 28th St Lubbock TX 79410 Office: Office Acad Affairs Tex Tech U Lubbock TX 79409

SOWELL, W. R. (BILL), aviation company executive; b. Chipley, Fla., Nov. 8, 1920; s. Claude Tee and Eunice (Richardson) S.; student Centenary Coll., 1940-42; grad. Norton Bus. Coll., Shreveport, La., 1942; m. Nadine Martin, Sept. 1942 (div. Feb. 1971); children—J. Donald, Doris Dianne Sowell Preston, Deborah K., Sheri Denise. Owner, pres. Panama Airways, Inc., Panama City, Fla., 1946-53; pilot instr., flying supr. So. Airways, Bainbridge, Ga., 1950-53; founder, prin. owner, chmn. bd. pilot, instr. Sowell Aviation Co., Inc., Panama City, 1954—; chmn. bd. Sowell Aircraft Service, Inc., Panama City, 1964—; founder, pres., owner Pensacola (Fla.) Aviation Inc., 1964-72; pres., co-owner Sowell Rent-A-Car, Inc., Panama City; airplane and instrument pilot examiner FAA, 1946-79; mem. Panama City Airport Bd., 1959-61, chmn., 1959-61; mem. Fla. Gov.'s Aviation Com., 1972—, chmn., 1977-79. Served with AC, AUS, 1940-45. Mem. Airplane Owners and Pilots Assn., Quiet Birdmen, Nat. Aviation Transp. Assn., Fla. Aviation Trades Assn. (pres. 1970-72, dir.) Bay County C. of C. (dir. 1956-66, chmn. aviation com. 1962-63). Baptist. Clubs: Rotary, Masons, Shriners, Elks. Home: 3037 W 30th Ct Panama City FL 32405 Office: Panama City Bay County Municipal Airport Panama City FL 32405

SOWERS, DAVID KENT, food company executive; b. Biloxi, Miss., Sept. 13, 1952; s. Bill David and Shelma Rose (Henderson) S.; m. Lorraine Joan Gassmann, Jan. 10, 1976; children—Justin Alan, Jenny Elizabeth, Jillian Alicia. B.B.A., Okla. U., 1974, M.B.A., 1976. Pres. LoriLea Candies, Ltd., Norman, Okla., 1977-80; asst. controller Trice Electronics, Oklahoma City, 1980-81; ops. mgr. L.D. Jones Food Co., Oklahoma City, 1981-85, Carlstrom Foods, St. Louis, 1985—. Mem. Cleveland County Geneal. Soc. (v.p. 1983-84). Republican. Methodist. Club: 1889er Soc. (Oklahoma City). Avocations: stained glass; woodworking; boating. Home: 1918 Oakhollow Dr Norman OK 73071 Office: Carlstrom Foods 5500 S Walker Oklahoma City OK 73109

SOZA, WILLIAM, accountant; b. Shafter, Tex., Apr. 14, 1936; s. Manuel G. and Rebecca (Velasco) S.; B.B.A., U. Tex. at Austin, 1960; m. Susan P. Eddy, Nov. 20, 1965; children—Stephanie, Mary Elizabeth. Sr. accountant Main Hurdman, Washington, 1964-67; mgr. audits and taxes NUS Corp., Rockville, Md., 1967-69; pvt. practice pub. accounting, Falls Church, Va., 1969-73; prin. Soza & Co., Ltd., C.P.A.'s, Falls Church, 1973—. Mem. adv. bd. Fairfax County Corps, Salvation Army, 1970-84, chmn., 1983-84. Served with AUS, 1962. Mem. Va. Soc. C.P.A.s, Am. Inst. C.P.A.s, Ibero-Am. C. of C. (bd. dirs. 1981-84), Greater Falls Church C. of C. (dir., 1st v.p. 1983-85), Am. Assn. Hispanic C.P.A.s (bd. dirs. 1983-85). Roman Catholic. Clubs: Touchdown (Washington); Annandale (Va.) Rotary (dir. 1973-75), Tysons Corner (Va.) Rotary (dir., treas. 1983—). Home: 2307 Locust Ridge Ct Falls Church VA 22046 Office: 803 W Broad St Falls Church VA 22046

SPACCARELLI, THOMAS DEAN, foreign language educator; b. Chgo., Sept. 25, 1947; s. Thomas and Marie (Dean) S.; m. Rose Marie Kundanis, July 11, 1970 (div. 1980). A.B., U. Ill.-Chgo., 1969, M.A., U. Wis., 1971, Ph.D., 1975. Lectr. U. Ill.-Chgo., 1973-74; asst. prof. Spanish, U. of the South, Sewanee, Tenn., 1974-84, assoc. prof., 1982—, acting chmn., 1984. Active Sewanee Peace Fellowship. N.Am. Joint Com. for Ednl. and Cultural Affairs grantee, 1980-81; Mellon faculty grantee, 1981. Mem. Am. Assn. Tchrs. of Spanish and Portuguese. Mem. Democratic Socialist Party. Quaker. Assoc. editor: Complete Concordances and Texts of the Fourteenth-Century Aragonese Manuscripts of Juan Fernandez de Heredia, 1982.

SPACH, JULE CHRISTIAN, church executive; b. Winston-Salem, N.C., Dec. 21, 1923; s. Jule Christian and Margaret Stockton (Coyner) S.; student Va. Mil. Inst., 1942-43; B.S. in Chem. Engring., Ga. Inst. Tech., 1949; postgrad. Union Theol. Sem., Richmond, Va., 1951-52, Duke U., 1955-56; M.A. in Ednl. Adminstrn., U. N.C., Greensboro, 1976; L.H.D. (hon.), Stillman Coll., Tuscaloosa, Ala., 1977; Litt.D. (hon.), Belhaven Coll., Jackson, Miss., 1977; LL.D. (hon.), King Coll., Bristol, Tenn., 1977; m. Nancy Clendenin, Sept. 18, 1948; children—Nancy Lynn Lane, Margaret Cunningham, Ann Thomerson, Cecelia Welborn, Robert. Salesman, Mengle Corp. subs. Internat. Container Corp., Winston-Salem, 1950-52; prof. scis., athletic dir. Quinze de Novembro Coll., Garanhuns, Pernanbuco, Brazil, 1952-56, pres., 1956-64; edn. dir. Cruzada ABC-Recife, Pernanbuco, 1965-70, pres., 1969-70; exec. sec. Parliamentary Christian Leadership, Brasilia, Fed. Dist., Brazil, 1970-73; exec. dir. Presbyn. Mission in Brazil, Campinas, São Paulo, 1973-75; moderator Gen. Assembly of Presbyn. Ch. in U.S., Atlanta, 1976-77; exec. dir. Triad United Methodist Home, Inc., Winston-Salem, 1977—; mem. bd. visitors Montreat Anderson Coll.; bd. dirs. Forsyth Council for Older Adults. Trustee King Coll., Bristol; bd. dirs. Sr. Services, William Black Lodge; bd. dirs. Lee's McRae Coll., Covenant Fellowship of Presbyterians, William Black Lodge, Sr. Services, Winston-Salem, Leadership Winston-Salem; bd. dirs. Instituto Gammon, Presbyn. Ch. U.S. Served with USAAF, 1943-45. Decorated Purple Heart. Republican. Clubs: Lions (Brazil); Rotary (Winston-Salem). Home: 444 Anita Dr Winston-Salem NC 27104 Office: Triad United Methodist Home 1240 Arbor Rd Winston-Salem NC 27104

SPAHICH, EKREM (ECK), journalist, realtor; b. Tuzla, Bosnia, Croatia, Jan. 15, 1945; came to U.S., 1960, naturalized, 1966; s. Mo and Devleta H. (Aliefendic) S.; B.A. in Journalism, West Tex. State U., 1969, postgrad., 1972-82; m. Helen Sue Reid, Apr. 20, 1973; children—Michael, Holly. Public info. officer Borger unit Tex. Army N.G., 1972-73; corr. AP wire service, Dallas, 1972—; area corr. Amarillo (Tex.) Daily News and Globe-Times, Sta. KGNC and KVII-TV, Amarillo, 1972-79; reporter Borger (Tex.) News-Herald, 1972-78, asst. editor, 1978-79, editor, 1979-82; bd. dirs. Borger Satellite Workshop Center, 1977—. Publicity dir. Hutchinson County Hist. Commn., 1975—; mem. Hutchinson County Sch. Bd., 78. Served with U.S. Army, 1969-71. Decorated Bronze Star; named outstanding com. chmn., Tex. Hist. Commn., 1978, Tex. Hist. Found., Kerrville, 1979. Mem. Panhandle Press Assn. (dir. 1980-82), VFW, Am. Legion, Sigma Delta Chi. Methodist. Clubs: Borger Soccer Assn. (founding pres., 1978), Croatian Philatelic and Numismatic Soc. (founder, exec. dir.), Order DeMolay (adv. council Borger chpt. 1977-81; various awards). Researcher Croatian history, philately and numismatism. Home: 1512 Lancelot Borger TX 79007

SPAIN, FRANK EDWARD, retired lawyer; b. Memphis, Oct. 11, 1891; s. John Batt Kennedy and Ida (Lockard) S.; m. Margaret Cameron, July 21, 1917 (dec. 1971); children—Margaret C. Spain McDonald, Frances Spain Hodges (dec.); m. Nettie Elizabeth Edwards, 1974. A.B., So. U. (now Birmingham-So.), 1910, LL.D. (hon.), 1955; LL.B., U. Ala., 1913, LL.D. (hon.), 1962. Bar: Ala. 1913. Asst. city atty. Birmingham (Ala.), 1917; ptnr. Spain, Gillon, Riley, Tate & Etheredge, Birmingham, to 1980; dir. emeritus Liberty Nat. Life Ins. Co.; former gen. counsel U.S. Fidelity and Guaranty Co.; former sec., dir. Odum Bowers and White Corp. Food adminstr. for Jefferson County, 1917; fair price commr. for Ala., 1919; chmn. Housing Authority of Birmingham Dist., 1938-43; chmn. Ala. Assn. Housing Authorities, 1938-43; appeal chmn. Jefferson County Community and War Chest Drive, 1943, Ala. War Chest, 1945; pres. Community Chest of Birmingham, 1946-47; mem. State Adv. Council Constrn. Mental Retardation Facilities; mem. Coll. Electors, NYU Hall of Fame of Gt. Ams.; past dir. U. Ala. Med. Ctr. Found., Ala. Soc. Crippled Children and Adults, Eye Found.; mem. Guy E. Snavely So., Birmingham So. Coll.; adv. bd. Cumberland Law Sch.; trustee Birmingham-So. Coll.; hon. mem. pres.'s council U. Ala. Served to 2d lt. arty. U.S. Army, 1918. Decorated chevalier Legion of Honor (France); recipient Gorgas award Ala. Med. Assn., 1964; named to Ala. Acad. of Honor, 1973, Ala. Bus. Hall of Fame, 1980; inducted into Birmingham Gallery of Disting. Citizens, 1983. Mem. Ala. Motorists Assn. (pres. 1930-41), ABA (chmn. ins. sect. 1944-46), Ala. State Bar Assn., Birmingham Bar Assn. (Man of Yr. nominee 1973), Assn. Life Ins. Counsel, Am. Life Conv. (past chmn. legal sect.), Phi Beta Kappa, Sigma Alpha Epsilon, Omicron Delta Kappa. Democrat. Episcopalian. Clubs: Mountain Brook, The Club, Relay House (Birmingham); Lakeview Country (Greensboro, Ala.); North River Yacht (Tuscaloosa, Ala.). Lodge: Rotary (pres. 1942-43, nat. pres. 1951-52). Home: Medley PO Box 400 Greensboro AL 36744 also Park Tower Birmingham AL 35205

SPAIN, NETTIE EDWARDS, civic worker; b. Alexandria, La., Oct. 9, 1918; d. John Henry and Sallie Tamson (Donald) Edwards; student Alexandria Bus. Coll., 1936-37, Birmingham-Southern Coll., 1958-59, Nat. Tng. Inst., United Community Funds and Councils Am., 1965-66; m. Frank E. Spain, May 18, 1974. Reporter, Alexandria Daily Town Talk, 1942-45; staff writer Brimingham (Ala.) Post, 1945-49; pub. relations dir. Community Chest, Birmingham, 1949-53; dir. info. services Pa. United Fund, Phila., 1953-55; asst. exec. dir. Ala. Assn. for Mental Health, Birmingham, 1956-57; pub. relations dir. United Appeal, Birmingham, 1958-68, asst. exec. dir., 1968-71; asst. to pres. for devel. U. Ala., Birmingham, 1971-74, acting dir., 1975. Mem. pub. relations com. Ala. Heart Assn., 1972-73; bd. dirs. Hale County chpt. ARC, Norton Center for Continuing Edn. in Bus. Birmingham-So. Coll.; mem. exec. com., past trustee Kate Duncan Smith DAR Sch., Grant, Ala., 1981-82, Hist. Magnolia Grove Found.; charter mem. bd. dirs. Birmingham Children's Theater; bd. dirs., chmn. house com. Children's Aid Soc., 1971-79, v.p., 1976-77, 81-84; bd. dirs. Jefferson-Shelby Lung Assn., 1972-75, Vol. Bur. of Greater Birmingham, 1972-77; mem. community adv. com. Jr. League, 1974-75; adv. bd. dirs. Historic Hale County Preservation Soc.; mem. adv. com. Internat. Friendship program U. Ala., Birmingham, 1974-79, hon. mem. pres.'s council, mem. Med. Ctr. Adv. Council; mem. presdl. adv. com. Marion Mil. Inst. Recipient 1st place awards Nat. Photos for Fedn., 1966-67; citation Pa. United Fund, 1955, citation for service Jefferson-Shelby Lung Assn., 1975, citation Ala. Heart Assn., 1974; award of merit Ala. Hist. Commn., 1977; Disting. Service citation Vol. Bur. Greater Birmingham, 1977. Benjamin Franklin fellow Royal Soc. Arts, London, U.S.A.; mem. Nat. Pub. Relations Council of Health and Welfare Services (dir. 1967-69), Women's Com. of 100 (sustaining mem.), Progress Study Club, Greater Birmingham Arts Alliance, Hale County Library (dir.), Met. Opera Guild, Birmingham Opera Guild, English Speaking Union, Cauldron Club, Pub. Relations Council Ala. (hon. life), Colonial Dames Am., DAR (registrar Choctaw chpt.), Ala. Burgess, First Families of Va., Nat. Trust for Hist. Preservation, Guy E. Snavely Soc. Birmingham-So. Coll., Hist. Hale County Preservation Soc., Ala. Hist. Assn., Hale County Hist. Soc. Episcopalian. Clubs: Lakeview Country (Greensboro, Ala.); Mountain Brook Country (Birmingham); North River Yacht (Tuscaloosa, Ala.). Home: Medley PO Box 400 Greensboro AL 36744 also 801 Park Tower Birmingham AL 35205

SPAMPINATO, FRANK ONOFRIO, investment banker; b. N.Y.C., Nov. 16, 1944; s. Onofrio T. and Josephine (Gerbino) S.; m. Patricia Ann Frick, Jan. 28, 1966 (div. 1976); 1 son, Frank Thomas; m. Charlene L. Barrie, Aug. 28, 1977. B.S., CUNY, 1967; postgrad. Fla. Atlantic U., 1981—. Pvt. pilot, FAA, 1976; cert. scuba diver, Nat. Assn. Scuba Diving Schs., 1974. Ops. officer Chase Manhattan Bank N.A., N.Y.C., 1965-72; ptnr. Out Island Yachts, Inc., Miami, Fla., 1973-78; dir. Essex Trading, Ltd., Ft. Lauderdale, Fla., 1983; v.p., controller Marcus, Stowell & Beye Cos., Ft. Lauderdale, 1979-83; v.p., controller, prin. A.F. Best Securities Inc., Ft. Lauderdale, 1984—; chief exec. officer, dir. Essex Trading Ltd., Ft. Lauderdale, 1983-85; sr. v.p., chief operating officer, dir., prin. A.F. Best Securities, Inc. Ft. Lauderdale, 1984—; cons. commodities, stocks and bonds to various cos., 1979—; cons. marine geologist/geophysics Bahamas Antiquities Inst., 1975-76. Club: Miami Yacht. Author: Inundation, 1978. Office: Inverrary Fin Centre 3810 Inverrary Blvd Suite 402 Ft Lauderdale FL 33319

SPANGENBERG, DOROTHY BRESLIN, biology educator; b. Galveston, Tex., Aug. 31, 1931; d. William Aloysius and Louise Margaret (Poole) Breslin; m. Ronald Wesley Spangenberg, May 31, 1958; 1 dau., Laurel Jane. B.A., U. Tex., 1956, M.A., 1958, Ph.D., 1960. Research assoc. U. Ark. Med. Center, Little Rock, 1962-65; assoc. prof. Little Rock U., 1965-66; research scholar Ind. U., 1966-69; assoc. prof. U. Louisville sch. Dentistry, 1970-72, vis. assoc. prof. U. Colo., Boulder, 1972-77; assoc. prof. Eastern Va. Med. Sch., Norfolk, 1977-82, research prof., 1982—. Grantee, NSF, 1964-66, NIH 1966-79, Child Health and Human Devel. 1966-76, U.S. Dept. Energy, 1977-82, NASA, 1984. Mem. Am. Soc. Zoologists, Am. Soc. Cell Biologists, Electron Microscopy Soc. Am., AAAS, Am. Soc. Gravity and Space Biology, N.Y. Acad. Scis., Sigma Xi. Episcopalian. Contbr. articles to profl. jours. Home: 6085 River Crescent Norfolk VA 23505 Office: Eastern Va Med Sch Norfolk VA 23501

SPANGLER, DAVID WADE, hospital administrator; b. Charleston, W.Va., Dec. 30, 1942; s. Robert Dale and Helen (Akrom) S.; m. Ann Salter, Dec. 21, 1965; children—Matthew, Leigh. Student Ohio U., 1961-63; B.S. in Pharmacy, Samford U., 1966; M.H.A., Med. Coll. Va., 1970. Pharmacist, mgr. People's Drug Co., South Boston, Va., 1972-78; asst. adminstr. Halifax Hosp., South Boston, 1978-82; adminstr. Blue Ridge Hosp. System, Spruce Pine, N.C., 1982—. Bd. dirs. United Way, Spruce Pine, 1983—. Mem. Am. Coll. Hosp. Adminstrs. Methodist. Lodge: Kiwanis. Avocations: Jogging; tennis; golf; hiking. Home: 201 Balsam Ave Spruce Pine NC 28777 Office: Blue Ridge Hosp System PO Box 9 Spruce Pine NC 28777

SPANN, GEORGE WILLIAM, management consultant; b. Cuthbert, Ga., July 21, 1946; s. Glinn Linwood and Mary Grace (Hiller) S.; B.S. in Physics with honors, Ga. Inst. Tech., 1968, M.S., 1970, M.S. in Indsl. Mgmt., 1973; m. Laura Jeanne Nason, June 10, 1967; children—Tanya Lynne, Stephen William. Engr., Martin Marietta Corp., Orlando, Fla., 1968-70; research scientist Engring. Expt. Sta., Ga. Inst. Tech., 1970-75; v.p., dir. Metrics, Inc., mgmt. and engring. cons., Atlanta, 1973-78, pres., dir., 1978—; v.p., dir. Exec. Data Systems, Inc., 1980—; mem. com. on practical applications of remote sensing from satellites Space Applicators Bd., NRC; mem. Ga. Energy Policy Council, Ga. Metrication Council, NASA applications survey group for Landsat follow-on; market research cons. NOAA, NASA, pvt. cos. Regents scholar, 1964. Mem. Am. Soc. Photogrammetry, Urban and Regional Info. Systems Assn., Atlanta Jaycees, Tau Beta Pi, Phi Kappa Phi, Sigma Pi Sigma. Author papers, reports. Home: 3475 Clubland Dr Marietta GA 30067 Office: 1845 The Exchange Suite 140 Atlanta GA 30339

SPANN, JAMES DOUGLAS, hospital administrator; b. Haslam, Tex., Jan. 14, 1941; s. Edward Dorsey and Mildred Emily (Parish) S.; m. Eva Ann Margiotta, July 29, 1961; children—Gina Spann-Jones, Maria Emily, James Nicholas. Registered med. technologist and radiography technologist So. Coll. Med. Tech., 1960; M.T. and R.T. in Hosp. Adminstrn., Trinity U., San Antonio, 1972; grad. in Nursing Home Adminstrn., U. Tex., 1978. Adminstr. Huntsville Meml. Hosp.-Hosp. Corp. Am., Tex., 1973-77, Christian Home for Aged-Unicare Health Services, Houston, 1978-81, Pleasant Hill Gen. Hosp., La., 1981—; bd. dirs. Joe Davis Sch. Nursing, Huntsville, 1973-77, Brazos Valley Health Devel. Council, Bryan, Tex., 1969-73. Vice pres. Battle of Pleasant Hill, Inc., 1983—. Served with U.S. Army, 1963-69. Mem. Am. Hosp. Assn., Tex. Hosp. Assn., La. Hosp. Assn., Tex. Soc. Med. Technologists. Democrat. Roman Catholic.

SPANN, RONALD THOMAS, lawyer; b. Chgo., Aug. 27, 1949; s. Daniel Anthony and Lorraine Marie (Gervasio) S. Student Sophia U., Tokyo, 1969; A.B., St. Mary's Coll., Rome, 1970; postgrad. U. Notre Dame, 1971, Fordham Law Sch. Inst. State and Law, Warsaw, Poland, 1976, Trinity Coll., Cambridge U., 1976; J.D., John Marshall Law Sch., Chgo., 1977; diploma internat. trade law. Bar: Ill., 1977, D.C., 1980, U.S. Dist. Ct. (no. dist.) Ill., U.S. Ct. Appeals (7th cir.), N.Y. 1984, Fla. 1984, U.S. Dist. Ct. (so. dist.) Fla., U.S. Supreme Ct.; lic. real estate and mortgage broker. Solicitor, U.S. Dept. Labor; trial atty. EEOC; law clk. to chief judge U.S. Dist. Ct. for No. Dist. Ill.; assoc. Baker & McKenzie, Chgo.; ptnr. firm Newman & Spann, Chgo.; mng. ptnr. Beck, Spann, Bernstein, P.A., Fort Lauderdale, Tampa and Miami, Fla.; pres. U.S. Arbitration and Mediation (S.E.), Inc.; sec., corp. counsel Trans-Communications, Inc., Barter Ctr., Internat. Devel. Corp., CoIlnnes Co. trial counsel Fedn. for Am. Immigration Reform; pres. AMERI-TRUST, Inc.; pres. Internat. Barter Exchange, Inc.; sec.-treas. Global Funding; prof. Internat. Career Inst., Ft. Lauderdale, Fla.; dir. TBM/USA, Inc., Lawyer's Trust. real estate rehabilitator. Bd. dirs. Edgewater Community Council, Advs. for Human Dignity, Advs. for Human Rights; corr. Amnesty Internat., U.S.A. Mem. ABA (chmn. internat. human rights com.), Ill. Bar Assn., D.C. Bar Assn., N.Y. Bar Assn., Chgo. Bar Assn., Fed. Bar Assn. (bd. dirs. Chgo. chpt., chmn. internat. human rights com.), Assn. Trial Lawyers Am., Christian Legal Soc., Lawyers in Mensa, Fla. Bar Assn., Broward County Bar Assn., Nat. Assn. Realtors, Ft. Lauderdale Bd. Realtors (lawyers com.). Club: Dolphin Dem. (dir.). Office: 607 E Las Olas Blvd Fort Lauderdale FL 33301 also 3550 Biscayne Blvd Miami FL also 180 S. LaSalle Chicago IL 60604 also 253 W 72d St New York NY 10023

SPARKS, MEREDITH PLEASANT (MRS. WILLIAM J. SPARKS), lawyer; b. Palestine, Ill.; d. John L. and Laura (Bicknell) Pleasant; A.B. with distinction, Ind. U., 1927, A.M., 1928; Ph.D., U. Ill., 1936; J.D., Rutgers U., 1958; m. William J. Sparks, Dec. 31, 1930 (dec.); children—Ruth Sparks Foster, Katherine Sparks Crowl, Charles, John. Tchr. chemistry Rochester (Ind.) High Sch., 1928-29; chemist DuPont Co., Niagara Falls, N.Y., 1929-34, Northam Warren Co., N.Y.C., 1939; chem. patent agt. Am. Cyanamid Co., Bound Brook N.J., 1941-46; bars: Fla. 1958, U.S. Ct. Appeals (fed. cir.), U.S. Dist. Ct. (so. dist.) Fla., U.S. Supreme Ct.; patent agt., 1946-58; patent atty., 1958—; pres. Sparks Innovators, Inc., 1979-84. Mem. nat. bd. Med. Coll. Pa. Mem. Assn. Ind. U. Chemists (pres. 1950-51), Internat., Am., Fla., Coral Gables bar assns., Am., N.J., South Fla. patent law assns., Internat. Patent and Trademark Assn., Am. Chem. Soc., Nat. Assn. Women Lawyers (pres.), AAUW, U. Ill. Pres. Council (life), Phi Beta Kappa (Homecoming honoree 1984), Sigma Xi, Kappa Delta. Club: Zonta, Riviera Country (Coral Gables). Contbr. articles to profl. jours. Patentee in field. Address: 5129 Granada Blvd Coral Gables FL 33146 Office: The Law Center 370 Minorca Ave Coral Gables FL 33134

SPARKS, RANDAL PAUL, osteopathic physician; b. Dallas, Aug. 31, 1947; s. Sherman Paul and Billie June (Wester) S.; m. Linda Ann Edwards, Jan. 21, 1970; children—Leigha, Terra, Billy. B.S., East Tex. State U., 1969; D.O., Kirksville Coll. Osteo. Medicine, 1973. Staff physician Rockwall Family Health Ctr., Tex., 1977—; assoc. prof. Tex. Coll. of Osteo. Medicine, Ft. Worth, 1981—. County health officer Rockwall County, 1977—; trustee Rockwall Sch. Bd., 1981—; dir. Disaster Preparedness Program, Rockwall, 1984. Served to major USAF, 1972-77. Mem. Am. Coll. Emergency Physicians, Am. Osteo. Assn., Aerospace Med. Assn. Republican. Methodist. Avocations: skiing; racquetball. Office: Rockwall Family Health Ctr 103 N 1st St Rockwall TX 75087

SPARLING, GEORGE BRYANT, helicopter company executive; b. St. Louis, Aug. 31, 1945; s. George Henry and Dorothy Dean (Charlwood) S.; B.S. in Aerospace Engring., U. Tex., Arlington, 1968, postgrad., 1968—; m. Sherry Ann Jones, Nov. 16, 1974; children—Irene Margaret, Jessica Ann. Design engr. Ling Temco Vought Aerospace Co., Dallas, 1968-72; research engr. Bell Helicopter Co., Fort Worth, 1972-79; project engr. Aerospatiale Helicopter Corp., Grand Prairie, Tex., 1979-80, chief of airframe, SRR, 1981-84, mgr. vehicle systems, 1984—; pres. Sparling Enterprises, Aircraft Modification & Customizing, Arlington, Tex., 1972—. Instr., Tex. Vol. Hunter Safety Program, 1972-82, Operation Orphans, Tex., 1968-72; mem. aerospace engring. curriculum adv. bd. U. Tex. at Arlington. NSF grantee, 1968; registered profl. engr.; certified res. police officer; named Res. Police Officer of the Yr., 1982. Mem. Am. Helicopter Soc., Nat., Tex. socs. profl. engrs., Soc. Automotive Engrs., Internat. Aerobatic Club, Aerobatic Club Am., Exptl. Aircraft Assn., Nat. Rifle Assn., Mensa, Tau Beta Pi. Episcopalian. Club: Arlington Sportsman's. Home: 2615 Kingston St Arlington TX 76015 Office: 2701 Forum Dr Grand Prairie TX 75053

SPATZER, SAMUEL MARK, lawyer; b. Washington, Aug. 15, 1947; d. David and Ethel (Brint) S.; m. Susan Stamler, July 21, 1976; children—Barry, Eric. B.B.A., U. Miami-Fla., 1969, J.D., 1972. Bar: Fla. 1972. Sole practice, Miami, Fla., 1972—; lectr. Mem. Fla. Bar Assn., Am. Trial Lawyer's Assn., Fla. Trial Lawyers Assn., Dade County Bar Assn., ABA, Democrat. Jewish. Office: 4601 Ponce DeLeon Blvd Suite 310 Coral Gables FL 33146

SPEAKS, ALTON JERRY, agricultural leasing company executive; b. Yazoo City, Miss., Jan. 17, 1942; s. Travis Griffin and Mary (Crutchfield) S.; m. Jan Ann Shepherd, Nov. 23, 1967. B.S., Miss. Coll., 1967. Mgmt. trainee, asst. credit mgr. Ralston Purina Co., Gainesville, Ga. and Nashville, 1967-70; credit mgr., adminstrv. mgr. Cargill, Inc., Memphis, 1970-76; regional credit mgr. Internat. Multi Foods, Inc., Mpls., 1976-79; pres., co-owner Consol. Agri Leasing Inc., Memphis, 1979—. Republican. Methodist. Clubs: Ridgeway Country, Summit, Masons, Moose, Shriners. Office: 6584 Poplar Ave Suite 480 Memphis TN 38138

SPEAKS, RUBEN LEE, bishop; b. Lake Providence, La., Jan. 8, 1920; s. Benjamin and Jessie Bell (Nichols) S.; m. Janie Angeline Griffin, Aug. 31, 1947; children—Robert Bernard, Joan Cordelia, Faith Elizabeth. A.B., Drake U., 1946; M.Div., Drew Theol. Sem., 1949; S.T.M., Temple U., 1952; postgrad., Div. Sch., Duke U., 1961; D.D., Hood Theol. Sem., 1972. Ordained deacon Christian Ch., 1942; elder African Methodist Episcopal Zion Ch., 1947; minister St. Thomas A.M.E. Zion Ch., Somerville, N.J., 1947, Wallace Chapel A.M.E. Zion Ch., Summit, N.J., 1948-50, Varick A.M.E. Zion Ch., Phila., 1950-56, St. Mark A.M.E. Zion Ch., Durham, N.C., 1956-64, 1st A.M.E. Zion Ch., Bklyn., 1964-72; bishop 10th Episcopal Area, Roosevelt, N.Y., 1972—. Author: Higher Catechism for Ministers and Laymen, 1966. The Minister and His Task, 1968, The Church and Black Liberation, 1972. Bd. dirs. Durham Com. on Negro Affairs, 1958-63, N.Y. Urban League, 1967-72; trustee Lincoln Hosp., Durham; chmn. exec. com. NAACP, 1958-63. Recipient Citizens award City of Durham, 1964, Meritorious Service award N.Y. Urban League, 1968. Mem. Nat. Acad. Sci. and Religion. *

SPEARMAN, DAVID HAGOOD, veterinarian; b. Greenville, S.C., Nov. 16, 1932; s. David Ralph and Elizabeth (Hagood) S.; student Clemson Coll., 1950-52, B.S., 1975; D.V.M., U. Ga., 1956; m. Patsy Lee Cordle, Dec. 18, 1954; children—Kathleen Elizabeth, David Hagood. With Cleveland Park Animal Hosp., Greenville, 1956-57; individual practice vet. medicine, Easley, S.C., 1957—. Mem. S.C. State Bd. Vet. Examiners, 1982—. Mem. Pickens County Planning and Devel. Bd., 1972—; pres. Northside Parent-Tchr. Orgn., 1965-67; mem. adv. bd. vet. technicians program Tri-County Tech., 1975-76; mem. admissions com. Vet. Coll., U. Ga., 1975; mem. adv. com. Pre-Vet Club, Clemson U.; chmn. Easley Zoning Bd., 1980-83. Mem. AVMA, Blue Ridge Veterinary Med. Assn. (founder, pres., sec.), S.C. Assn. Veterinarians (pres. 1974-75, publicity chmn. 1975—, Veterinarian of Yr. 1985), Am. Animal Hosp. Assn. (assoc.), Pickens County Horse, Cattle, and Fair Assn. (pres.), Jr. C. of C. (past officer, Key Man award 1959), Trout Unltd. (state dir.), Pickens County Foxhunters Assn., Clemson U. Lettermen Assn., Easley Boosters Club, Easley C. of C., World Wildlife Fund, Nat. Wildlife Fedn., Pickens County Hist. Soc., Pendelton Farmers Soc. Alpha Psi, Alpha Zeta. Presbyterian (deacon, youth leader 1972-74, chmn. orgn. com. 1973-75, 83-85). Club: Lions (pres., internat. del. 1971, 73). Home: Burdine Springs 505 Asbury Circle PO Box 327 Easley SC 29640 Office: 447 By Pass 123 Easley SC 29640

SPEARMAN, LEONARD H. O., university president. Pres. Tex. So. U., Houston. Office: Office of Pres Tex So U 3201 Wheeler Ave Houston TX 77004*

SPEARMAN, MICHAEL FRANCIS, fleet administrator; b. Bklyn., Mar. 12, 1940; s. Francis Joseph and Mary Elizabeth (Knowell) S.; m. Alberta Hipson, June 8, 1962; children—Darlene, William, Douglas, Stephen. Ed. Georgetown U. Owner, Cold Spring Service, Cold Springs Harbor, N.Y., 1965-71; v.p. Sound Systems/Lafayette Radio, Miami, Fla., 1971-73; maintenance mgr. I.W. Assocs., Ft. Lauderdale, Fla., 1973-74; fleet ops. mgr. Hertz Corp., Miami, 1974-78; shop mgr. Palm Peterbilt, Hollywood, Fla., 1978-80; fleet dir. Gen. Cinema Corp., Miami, 1980—; mem. Nat. Com. Motor Fleet Supervision Tng.; fleet cons. Capt., Halesite (N.Y.) Vol. Fire Dept., 1959-71. Mem. Soc. Fleet Suprs., Fla. Trucking Assn. Lutheran. Lodge: Elks. Home: 7813 Normandy St Miramar FL 33023 Office: Pepsi Cola of Miami G.C.C. Beverages 7777 NW 41 St Miami FL 33166

SPEARMAN, PATSY CORDLE, real estate broker; b. Richmond, Va., Aug. 23, 1934; d. Lee Pierce and Kathleen Jeanette (Munn) Cordle; A.A., Coll. William and Mary, Richmond, 1952; student U. Ga., 1953-54; grad. Realtors Inst., 1979; cert. residential specialist, 1985; m. David Hagood Spearman, Dec. 18, 1954; children—Kathleen Elizabeth, David Hagood. Copywriter, Cabell Eanes Advt. Agy., Richmond, 1952; clk. athletic dept. U. Ga., Athens, 1954-55; real estate saleswoman Merrill Lynch Real Estate, C. Dan Joyner & Co., Inc., Greenville, S.C., 1978—. Pres. Women of the Ch.; Presbyn. Ch., 1960-61, youth leader, 1972-74. Recipient numerous awards for obtaining eye bank donors Lions Club and S.C. Eye Bank. Mem. Nat. Assn. Realtors, Real Estate Securities and Syndication Inst., S.C. Assn. Realtors, Greenville Bd. Realtors (chmn. membership com. 1983), Pickens County Bd. Realtors, Women's Council of Realtors, Million Dollar Club (charter), S.C. Vet. Aux. (treas. 1984-86). Club: Better Homes (Easley). Home: 505 Asbury Circle Burdine Springs Easley SC 29640 Office: 745 N Pleasantburg Dr Greenville SC 29606

SPEARS, BOBBYE DORRIS BELL, lawyer; b. Watertown, Tenn., Dec. 11, 1932; d. Albert M. and Pauline (Adamson) Bell; m. A. Barry Spears, June 10, 1950 (div. 1957); 1 dau., Susan Spears Alsup. B.S., Tenn. Poly. U., Cookeville, 1954; J.D., U. Tenn.-Knoxville, 1961. Bar: Tenn. 1962. Trial atty. U.S. Dept. Labor, Nashville, 1962-69, asst. counsel for trial litigation, Washington, 1969-71, counsel for adminstrn. legal services, 1971-73, dep. assoc. solicitor of labor, 1973-75, assoc. solicitor, 1975-76, regional solicitor, Atlanta, 1976—. Home: 4424 Paces Battle NW Atlanta GA 30327 Office: Office of the Solicitor 1371 Peachtree St NE Atlanta GA 30309

SPEARS, FRANKLIN SCOTT, state supreme court justice; b. San Antonio, Aug. 20, 1931; s. Jacob Franklin and Lois Harkey S.; student So. Meth. U., 1948-50; B.B.A., U. Tex., 1954, J.D., 1954; m. Rebecca Errington, Dec. 3, 1977; children by previous marriage—Franklin Scott, Carleton Blaise, John Adrian. Bar: Tex. 1954. Practice law, San Antonio, from 1954; judge 57th Dist. Ct., San Antonio, 1968-78; justice Tex. Supreme Ct., 1978—; mem. Tex. Ho. of Reps., 1958-61; mem. Tex. Senate, 1961-67. Office: PO Box 12248 Capitol Sta Austin TX 78711

SPEARS, JEFFREY BRENT, pharmacist; b. Cin., Nov. 17, 1952; s. John D. and Dolores L. (Kalins) S.; m. Mary E. Lehrter, Mar. 22, 1974; children—Brian, Linnea, Matthew, Michael. B.S., U. Cin., 1975, Pharm. D., 1977. Resident in hosp. pharmacy Cin. Gen. Hosp., 1975-77; clin. pharmacist Mercy Hosp., Des Moines, 1977-78; asst. clin. prof. pharmacy Drake U., Des Moines, 1977-78; asst. adminstr. clin. pharmacy services Jackson Meml. Hosp., Miami, Fla., 1979-80, chief clin. pharmacy services, 1980-82; mgr. pharmacy clin. services Dynamic Control div. Travenol Labs., Inc., Longwood, Fla., 1983—; lectr. in field; pharmacy cons. Dynamic Control Corp., Miami. Bd. dirs. Am. Lung Assn. of Dade-Monroe, 1980—, sec. bd., 1982-83; mem. music ministry St. Stephen Cath. Community, Winter Springs, Fla. Mem. Am. Soc. Hosp. Pharmacists, Fla. Soc. Hosp. Pharmacists (bd. dirs., sec. central dist.), Am. Mgmt. Assn., Spl. Interest Groups on Adult Clin. Pharmacy, Clin. Pharmacokinetics. Roman Catholic. Co-author chpt. on hypnotics in Quick Reference to Clinical Toxicology, 1980. Home: 1008 Chokecherry Dr Winter Springs FL 32708 Office: 587 E Sanlando Springs Rd Longwood FL 32750

SPECK, DAVID GEORGE, investment executive; b. N.Y.C., Sept. 12, 1945; s. George and Doris Jean (de Ford) S.; m. Suzanne Stotter Kratzok, Oct. 5, 1968; children—Elizabeth Doris, Jonathan Samuel. Student U. Va., 1963-65; B.A., George Washington U., 1967, M.A., 1968, Ed.D., 1973. Various adminstrv. and teaching positions George Washington U., Washington, 1967-76; exec. asst. to dir. Office Fed. Contract Compliance, U.S. Dept. Labor, Washington, 1976-77; ind. cons., Alexandria, Va., 1977-82; sr. v.p., dir. tng. and recruitment Johnston, Lemon & Co., Inc., Washington and Alexandria, 1982—; moderator weekly news analysis panel show on cable TV, 1982—. Fin. columnist Alexandria Gazette, 1984—. Mem. Va. Ho. of Dels., 1979-82; bd. dirs. Alexandria Hosp., 1982—; trustee Robert S. Rixse Found., Alexandria, 1984—. Republican. Jewish. Office: Johnston Lemon & Co Inc 277 S Washington St Alexandria VA 22314

SPECTOR, MICHAEL JOSEPH, recording co. exec.; b. N.Y.C., Feb. 13, 1947; s. Martin Wilson and Dorothy (Miller) S.; B.S., Washington and Lee U., 1968; m. Margaret Dickson, Sept. 14, 1977. Research chemist Am. Viscose, Phila., 1968-69; pres. MJS Entertainment Corp., Miami, Fla., 1970—, also MJS Internat., Inc.; dir. Plaza Bank of Miami, 1980-83; partner Old Town Key West Devel. Ltd. (Fla.), 1977—; pres. MJS Entertainment of Can. Inc., Toronto, Ont., Margo Farms, MJS Prodns., Inc., N.Y.C.; dir. JBJ Inc. Bd. dirs. Goodwill Industries So. Fla., v.p. fin., 1980. Served with AUS, 1969-70. Recipient Robert E. Lee research grant Washington and Lee U., 1967-68. Mem. Nat. Assn. Record Merchandisers (dir. Nova div., chmn. one-stop distbn. com. 1982-83), Country Music Assn., Delta Tau Delta. Clubs: Met., Grove Isle, Bankers, Standard (Miami); Ocean Reef (Key Largo, Fla.). Patentee synthetic stretching process. Office: PO Box 52-3725 Miami FL 33152

SPECTOR, MYRON, orthopedics/biomedical engineering educator, researcher, consultant; b. Pitts., Apr. 29, 1945; s. Morris and Bernetta (Swiss) S.; m. Joanne Freedman, Nov. 18, 1967; children—Jonathan Michael, Daniel Todd. B.S. in Civil Engring., Carnegie Mellon U., Pitts. 1967, M.S. in Civil Engring., 1969, Ph.D. in Biomed. Engring., 1971. Asst. prof. bioengring. Clemson U., 1972-74; assoc. prof. biology and phys. sci. Med. U. S.C., Charleston, 1975-76, prof., 1977-81; prof. orthopaedics Emory U., Atlanta, 1982—, assoc. prof. pathology, 1982—; prin. research engr. Ga. Inst. Tech., 1982—; cons. Union Carbide Corp., Richards Med. Co., Inc. Recipient Nat. Inst. Health Research Career Devel. award, 1979-83; NASA-ASEE Summer Faculty fellow, 1972-73. Mem. AAAS, Soc. Biomaterials, Orthopaedic Research Soc., Internat. Assn. Dental Research, Sigma Xi. Contbr. articles to profl. jours.; patentee in field. Office: 69 Butler St Room 402 Atlanta GA 30303

SPELL, ARVIN FRANCIS, III, accountant; b. Waycross, Ga., Aug. 12, 1939; s. Arvin Francis, Jr. and Ulma (Johnson) S.; m. Judith Ann Brister, June 10, 1967 (div. Mar. 1982); children—Lara Chante, Arvin Francis IV. B.A. in Econs., Mercer U., 1961; postgrad. Ga. State U., 1971. Tchr. Jeff Davis County Schs., Hazelhurst, Ga., 1961-65; acct. Ralph Birdsong firm, Atlanta, 1965-70; John R. McNair, C.P.A., Atlanta, 1970-72; acct., owner Spell & Gambrell, P.C., C.P.A.s, Atlanta, 1972—. Organizer, past bd. dirs. Amaranth Diabetic Found. Mem. Am. Inst. C.P.A.s, Ga. Soc. C.P.A.s. Republican. Episcopalian. Lodges: Masons (32d deg.), Order Eastern Star (past royal patron), Order White Shrine (past watchman), Order Amaranth (past supreme royal patron, supreme council). Avocation: antique collecting. Home: 1228 Wood Circle Atlanta GA 30324 Office: Spell & Gambrell PC CPAs 2470 Cheshire Bridge Rd Suite 102 Atlanta GA 30324

SPELLACY, JOHN FREDERICK, lawyer; b. Steubenville, Ohio, Mar. 24, 1930; s. Joseph Roland and Thelma Fay (Stone) S.; m. Martha Jane Manning June 18, 1955; children—Joseph, James, John, Lawrence. Ph.B., Loyola Coll. Balt., 1952; LL.D., U. Miami (Fla.) 1958. Bar: Fla. 1960, U.S. Dist. Ct. (so. dist.) Fla. 1961. Ptnr., Kirsch & Spellacym Fort Lauderdale, Fla., 1958-69, DiGiulian, Spellacy, Ft. Lauderdale, 1969-83, Spellacy & McFann, Ft. Lauderdale, 1983—; municipal judge City of Plantation, Fla., 1971-75. Mem. City Council, Plantation, 1962-71; mem. Broward Sheriffs Adv. Council. Served to capt. USMC, 1952-54. Fellow Fla. Trial Lawyers Assn.; mem. Am. Arbitration Assn., ABA, Fed. Bar Assn., Fla. Bar, Assn. Trial Lawyers Am., Am. Judicature Soc., Broward County Mcpl. Judges Assn. (pres. 1974-75), Broward County. Trial Lawyers Assn. (pres. 1978-79). Democrat. Roman Catholic. Club: Civitan (v.p. Plantation 1965-70). Lodge: Elks. Home: 1313 Ponce de Leon Dr Fort Lauderdale FL 33316 Office: Spellacy & McFann 888 SE 3d Ave Fort Lauderdale FL 33316

SPELLMAN, EUGENE PAUL, judge; b. N.Y.C., Sept. 16, 1930; s. Michael Francis and Mary Elizabeth (Loftus) S.; A.A., U. Fla., 1951, B.A., 1953, LL.B., 1955, J.D., 1967; D.H.L., Biscayne Coll., 1977; m. Roberta J. Recht, July 16, 1959; children—James Kevin, Michael Patrick. Admitted to Fla. bar, 1956; research aide to chief judge 3d Dist. Ct. Appeals, Miami, Fla., 1957-58; asst. atty. gen. Criminal Appeals Div., Tallahassee, 1958-59, 60-61; asst. state atty. Dade County (Fla.), also head Rackets and Frauds div., 1959-61; apptd. spl. prosecutor Judge Curtis E. Chillingsworth murder case by Govs. Leroy Collins and Farris Bryant, 1969-70; apptd. spl. asst. atty. gen., 1969-70; gen counsel Biscayne Coll., 1970-80; judge U.S. Dist. Ct., Miami, 1980—. Chmn., Fla. Council for Blind, 1963-65; pres. Southeastern Inst. Human Devel., 1977; bd. dirs. Marian Center Inc.; mem. South Miami Hosp. Found. Hon. mem. Order St. Augustine, Rome; recipient Outstanding Achievement award Fla. Assn. Rehab. Facilities. Mem. Am., Fla., Dade County bar assns., Am., Fla. trial lawyers assns., Supreme Ct. Hist. Soc., Am. Judicature Soc., Dade County Assn. Retarded Citizens, Fla. Assn. Rehab. Facilities. Democrat. Roman Catholic. Clubs: Two Hundred, Miami Bankers. Office: US Courthouse 300 NE 1st Ave PO Box 013170 Miami FL 33101*

SPENCE, FLOYD DAVIDSON, congressman; b. Columbia, S.C., Apr. 9, 1928; s. James Wilson and Addie (Lucas) S.; A.B., U.S.C., 1952, J.D., 1956; m. Lula Hancock Drake, Dec. 22, 1952 (dec.); children—David, Zack, Benjamin, Caldwell. Admitted to S.C. bar, 1956; ptnr. firm Callison and Spence, West Columbia, 1956—; mem. S.C. Ho. Reps., 1956-62; mem. S.C. Senate, 1966-70, minority leader, 1966-70, chmn. joint internal security com., 1969; mem. 92d-98th Congresses from S.C.; mem. Com. on Standards Ofcl. Conduct, Armed Services Com. Past chmn. Ridge dist., also Granby dist. Boy Scouts Am., former scoutmaster, also exec. bd. S.C. council; chmn. Lexington County Mental Health Assn., 1959; mem. exec. com. bd. dirs. Mid-Carolina Mental Health Assn., 1970. Served to capt. USNR. Mem. Am. Legion (mem. counter-subversive activities com. 1966, 67), VFW, Res. Officers Assn., Navy League, Columbia Carillon (dir. 1966-70), West Columbia-Cayce, Lexington, S.C. chambers commerce. Lutheran. Contbr. articles on communism to profl. jours.; lectr. in field. Home: Box 869 Lexington SC 29072 Office: 1916 Assembly St Columbia SC 29201

SPENCE, MICHAEL STUART, writer, editor; b. Charlottesville, Va., Dec. 14, 1952; s. George David and Anne Seitz (Landauer) S.; m. Ramona Louise Eckert, Apr. 25, 1981. A.B., Princeton U., 1974; M.Div., Grace Theol. Sem., 1979, Th.M., 1982. Graphic designer pvt. practice, Kennett, Mo., and Winona Lake, Ind., 1975-85; typesetter and paste-up, Eisenbrauns, Winona Lake, 1979-82; Bible editor and project coordinator Thomas Nelson Pubs., Nashville, 1982-85; free lance writer-editor, Nashville, 1985—. Designer logo for Princeton Evang. Fellowship, 1976, mag. cover and logo Grace Theol. Jour., 1980, logo for Nashville Youth Fellowship, 1985; co-editor The Christian Life Bible, 1985; contbr. articles to jours. Active Gideons Internat., 1984-85. Republican. Presbyterian. Avocations: singing; reading; computer programming. Home: 3818 Moss Rose Dr Nashville TN 37216

SPENCER, ALEXANDER BURKE, geologist; b. San Antonio, Dec. 28, 1932; s. Alexander Burke and Josephine Martha (Frost) S.; children—Rachel Elizabeth, John Randolph. B.S., Tex. Western Coll., 1955; M.S., U. Okla., 1961; Ph.D., U. Tex., 1966. Asst. prof. Carnegie Inst. Tech., Pitts., 1965-67; research geologist Mobil Research & Devel., Dallas, 1967-71; sr. research geologist, 1971-73, tech. service coordinator, 1973-75; sr. staff geologist Mobil Oil Libya, Tripoli, 1975-77, Mobil Exploration, Dallas, 1977-81; exploration supr. Australasia, Dallas, 1981—. Contbr. articles to profl. jours. Served to 1st lt. U.S. Army, 1955-57. Mem. Am. Assn. Petroleum Geologists, Soc. Exploration Geophysicists, Soc. Economic Paleontologists and Mineralogists, Soc. Cincinnati, Sigma Xi.

SPENCER, FREDERICK STRAWN, lawyer; b. El Dorado, Ark., May 28, 1947; s. James Victor and Mary Margaret (Strawn) S.; m. Coralee Faith Eck, Aug. 6, 1971; 1 child, Sarah Faith. B.S.B.A., U. Ark., 1970, J.D., 1975. Bar: Ark. 1975, U.S. Dist. Ct. (ea. and we. dists.) Ark. 1975, U.S. Ct. Appeals (8th cir.) 1975, U.S. Supreme Ct. 1981. Sole practice, Mountain Home, Ark., 1975—; dir., atty. Ark. Inst. Theology, Fayetteville, 1984—; lectr. in law. Author: (video) Principles of SSA Claims, Dir., atty., Johnson Brothers Youth Ranch, Bruno, Ark., 1981—; pres., founder Ark. Injured Worker's Assn., 1982-84, mem. exec. com. 1985—; dir., atty., Christian Broadcasting Group, Mountain Home, Ark., 1983—; witness U.S. Congress, 1984. Winner Environ. Law Essay Contest Am. Trial Lawyers Assn. 1974; mem. ABA, Ark. Bar Assn. (Reaching Out to Serve award 1983), Baxter County Bar Assn. (sec. 1977-78). Mem. Mountain Home Bible Ch. Clubs: Racquet, Athletic (Mountain Home). Home: Route 6 Box 431 Robinson Point Mountain Home AR 72653 Office: 409 E 6th St Mountain Home AR 72653

SPENCER, JESSE GARNET, chemistry educator; b. Farmville, N.C., Apr. 10, 1935; s. Jesse Garnet and Frances (Joyner) S.; m. Jeanne Thomas, June 15, 1973; children—Jennifer, Jesse, Frances. B.S., U. N.C., 1957; M.S., U. Va., 1959, Ph.D., 1962; postgrad. U. N.C., 1962. Asst. prof. U. Charleston (W.Va.), 1962-66, assoc. prof., 1966-68, prof. chemistry, 1968-84, chmn. div. health services, 1977-79, head med. lab. tech., 1975-79, head chemistry, 1965-80, catalog editor, 1979-84, dir. computer services and records, 1981-84, dean arts and scis., 1982-83; prof. chemistry, head dept. Valdosta State Coll., Ga., 1984—. Mem. Am. Chem. Soc., Ga. Acad. Sci., Sigma Xi, Phi Beta Kappa. Democrat. Presbyterian. Home: 2112 Westfield Ave Valdosta GA 31602-2120 Office: Valdosta State Coll Nevins Hall Valdosta GA 31698

SPENCER, MARY MILLER, civic worker, club woman; b. Comanche, Tex., May 25, 1924; d. Aaron Gaynor and Alma (Grissom) Miller; B.S., North Tex. State U., 1943; 1 dau., Mara Lynn. Cafeteria dir. Mercedes (Tex.) Pub. Schs., 1943-46; home economist coordinator All-Orange Dessert Contest, Fla. Citrus Commn., Lakeland, 1959-62, 64; children's services worker Fla. Div. Family Services, Lakeland, 1969-70, social worker, 1970-80, Fla. Health and Rehab. Services, Overpayment, Fraud and Recoupment Unit, lead worker, pub. assistance eligibility specialist II, 1981-82, pub. assistance specialist IV, 1984—; tchr. purchasing sch. lunch dept. Fla. Dept. Edn., 1960. Clothing judge Polk County (Fla.) Youth Fair, 1951-68, Polk County Federated Women's Clubs, 1964-66; pres. Dixieland Elementary Sch. PTA, 1955-57, Polk County Council PTA's, 1958-60; dist. 7. Fla. Congress Parents and Tchrs., 1961-63; chmn. pub. edn. com. Polk County unit Am. Cancer Soc., 1959-60, bd. dirs., 1962-72; charter mem., bd. dirs. Lakeland YMCA; sec. Greater Lakeland Community Nursing Council, 1965-69; trustee, vice chmn. Polk County Eye Clinic, 1962-64, pres., 1964-82; bd. dirs. Polk County Scholarship and Loan Fund, Inc.; mem. exec. com. West Polk County (Fla.) Community Welfare Council, 1960-62, 65-68; mem. budget and audit com. Greater Lakeland United Fund,

1960-62; mem. adv. bd. Polk County Juvenile and Domestic Relations Ct., 1960-69,; mem. exec. com. Sun Coast Health Council, 1968-72, vol., disaster res. social worker ARC, 1970—; mem. Fla. Health and Welfare Council, 1970-73, Polk County Mental Health Assn., 1970—. Sec. bd. dirs. Fla. West Coast Ednl. Television, 1960-82. Mem. Fla. Congress Parents and Tchrs. (hon. life, pub. relations chmn. 1962-66.), Fla. Assn. Health and Social Services, Fla. Pub. Health Assn., Nat. Welfare Fraud Assn., Alumni Assn. North Tex. State U. Democrat. Methodist. Mem. Order Eastern Star. Home: 535 W Beacon Rd Lakeland FL 33803 Office: PO Box 2161 Lakeland FL 33806

SPENCER, NATHANIEL ROSCOE, surgeon; b. Balt., Nov. 16, 1916; s. Roscoe Roy and Mary Garland (Grasty) S.; m. Barrie Mae Walsworth, Oct. 23, 1943; children—Barrie Elaine, Nathaniel Walsworth, Douglas Wilson. A.B., George Washington U., 1938; M.D., U. Tex., 1942. Diplomate Am. Bd. Surgery. Intern, Walter Reed Gen. Hosp., Washington, 1943; resident in surgery Brooke Gen. Hosp., San Antonio, 1948; chief ob-gyn, Fort Benning, Ga., 1949-50; teaching fellow Tulane U., New Orleans, 1951-53; sr. surgeon VA Hosp., Jackson, Miss., 1954-57; pvt. practice surgery, Monroe, La., 1957—; aviation med. examiner FAA, 1964—. Served to maj. U.S. Army, 1943-51. Fellow Am. Soc. Abdominal Surgery (pres. south central sect. 1969); mem. Ouachita Med. Soc. (sec. 1965-66), La. State Med. Soc. (cancer commn. 1965-69), AMA (Physicians Recognition award 1979-84), Clin. Congress Abdominal Surgeons (testimonial appreciation 1965), La. Surg. Assn., Italo-Am. Med. Assn., Civil Aviation Med. Assn., So. Med. Assn. Home: 2211 Dogwood Dr Monroe LA 71201 Office: 900 Jackson St Monroe LA 71201

SPENCER, ROGER FELIX, psychiatrist, psychoanalyst, medical educator; b. Vienna, Austria, Apr. 19, 1934; s. Eugene S. Spitzer and Santa (Kurz) Spitzer; m. Barbara Ann Houser, Aug. 18, 1958; children—Geoffrey, Jennifer, Rebecca. B.S., Yale Coll., 1956; M.D., Harvard Med. Sch., 1959. Diplomate Am. Bd. Psychiatry. Intern, N.C. Meml. Hosp., Chapel Hill, 1959-60, resident in psychiatry, 1960-63; instr. U. N.C. Sch. Medicine, 1963-66, asst. prof., 1966-69, assoc. prof., 1969-76, prof., 1976—, dir. of liaison and cons., 1967-77, dir. out patient psychiatry, 1977—; cons. VA, Fayetteville. Recipient Career Tchr. award NIMH, 1965-67. Mem. Am. Psychiat. Assn., Am. Psychosomatic Soc., Am. Psychoanalytic Assn., AAAS, AMA, N.C. Psychiat. Soc., N.C. Neuropsychiat. Assn. Club: Chapel Hill Tennis. Contbr. articles to profl. jours. Office: 201 S Wing NC Meml Hosp Chapel Hill NC 27514

SPENCER, W. THOMAS, lawyer; b. Crawfordsville, Ind., Aug. 6, 1928; s. Walter White and Jean Anna (Springer) S.; m. Patricia Audrey Raia, Mar. 30, 1974; children—Thomas Alfred, Jamie Raia. Student Wabash Coll., Crawfordsville, 1946-47; A.B., U. Miami-Coral Gables, 1950, J.D., 1956. Bar: Fla. 1956, U.S. Dist. Ct. (so. dist.) Fla. 1957, U.S. Dist. Ct. (no. dist.) Fla. 1963, U.S. Ct. Appeals (11th cir.) 1981, U. S. Supreme Ct. 1984; cert. civil trial atty. Assoc., Dean, Adams & Fischer, Miami, 1957-63; ptnr. Spencer & Taylor, Miami, 1963-81, Spencer, Taylor & Homer, Miami, 1982-84, Spencer & Taylor, 1984—; mem. Fla. Ho. Reps., 1963-66; mem. Fla. Senate, 1966-68. Served to lt. USNR, 1952-55. Mem. ABA, Dade County Bar Assn., Am. Judicature Soc., Def. Research Inst., Fla. Def. Lawyers Assn. Democrat. Methodist. Clubs: Riviera Country, Coral Gables Country (Coral Gables); Bath (Miami Beach, Fla.). Home: 4520 Santa Maria St Coral Gables FL 33146 Office: 1107 Biscayne Bldg 19 W Flagler St Miami FL 33130

SPENCER, WARREN FRANK, historian, educator; b. Swan Quarter, N.C., Jan. 27, 1923; s. Carroll Baxter and Lucille Gertrude (Mann) S.; student George Washington U., 1942, U. Fla., 1942-43; B.S.S. cum laude, Georgetown U., 1947; M.A., U. Pa., 1949, Ph.D., 1955; m. Elizabeth Jolanda Toth, Sept. 6, 1947; children—Lucille Mann, Carroll Baxter. Instr. history Salem Coll., Winston-Salem, N.C., 1950-53, asst. prof., 1953-56; asst. prof. Old Dominion U., Norfolk, Va., 1956-57, assoc. prof., 1957-61, prof., 1961-67, chmn. div. social studies and dept. history, 1961-67; prof. history U. Ga., Athens, 1967—, Sandy Beaver teaching prof. history, 1978-82. Served with AUS, 1943-45. Vis. scholar, Duke, 1952; Am. Philos. Soc. fellow, 1958, 70, 75; recipient 1st ann. Faculty award Old Dominion U., 1961-62; Best History Book Published in 1970 award Phi Alpha Theta, 1971; named Outstanding Honors Tchr., U. Ga., Athens, 1977, 85, recipient creative research award, 1984. Mem. Am. Hist. Assn., So. Hist. Assn. (chmn. European History sect. program com. 1970), Ga. Assn. Historians (pres. 1979-80), Soc. French Hist. Studies, Phi Alpha Theta. Democrat. Episcopalian. Co-founder, pres. Norfolk Hist. Soc., 1966-67. Author: (with Lynn M. Case) The United States and France: Civil War Diplomacy, 1970; The Confederate Navy in Europe, 1983. Contbr. to profl. jours. Office: Dept History U Georgia Athens GA 30602

SPENCER, WILLIAM MICAJAH, III, science research company executive; b. Birmingham, Ala., Dec. 10, 1920; s. William Micajah and Margaret Woodward (Evins) S.; B.S., U. South, 1941; postgrad. Grad. Sch. Bus. Adminstrn., Harvard U., 1947; m. Evalina Sommerville Brown, Sept. 28, 1946; children—Murray Brown Spencer South, Margaret Anne Spencer Smith. Vice pres. Owen-Richards Co. (name changed to Motion Industries, Inc. 1972), Birmingham, 1946-52, pres., 1952-72, chmn. bd., 1972-84; chmn. Molecular Engring. Assocs., Birmingham, 1984—; dir. Genuine Parts Co., Atlanta, AmSouth Bank, AmSouth Bancorp., Ala. Gt. So. Ry., Mead Corp., Healthcare Services Am., Robertson Banking Co., ALTEC, Inc. Pres., Birmingham C. of C., 1963-64, Birmingham Festival of Arts, 1964-65, Bapt. Med. Center Found., Birmingham, Ala. Safety Council, 1979-80. Served to capt. USMC, 1942-46. Decorated Bronze Star. Mem. Blue Key, Phi Beta Kappa, Omega Delta Kappa. Episcopalian. Home: 3035 Briarcliff Rd Birmingham AL 35223 Office: 2001 Park Pl Suite 1040 Birmingham AL 35203

SPERLAZZA, JAMES ANTHONY, medical sales company executive; b. Meriden, Conn., Oct. 17, 1948; s. Santino B. and Nancy Ann (Corbet) S.; m. Geraldine Ann Panella, Apr. 6, 1968 (div. 1969); m. Patricia Ann Lavezzo, June 16, 1978; children—Tony, Danny, Kelly; 1 dau. by previous marriage—Gina. Student Yale U., 1966-68. Owner, mgr. County Farms, Meriden, 1969-72; regional mgr. Red Hen Restaurants, New Canaan, Conn., 1968-70; sales cons. Mgmt. Recruiters, Alexandria, Va., 1972-76; sales mgr. Sonicaid Med. Co., Fredericksburg, Va., 1976-78; pres. Clin. Diagnostic Instruments Inc., distbr. for Diasonics, Inc., Winchester, Va., 1978—; cons. Diasonics, Inc., Milpitas, Calif.; cons. Bowman Gray Med. Sch., 1978-81. Served with AUS, 1968. Mem. Winchester C. of C., Health Care Exhibitors Assn. Home: Box 2718 Winchester VA 22601 Office: 136 S Cameron St Winchester VA 22601

SPERO, MITCHELL E., psychologist; b. Phila., Jan. 9, 1958; s. Jerome B. and Vero O. (Lieberman) S.; m. Dawn L. Bittle, June 27, 1981. B.S. in Psychology, U. Pitts., 1979; M.S.Ed., U. Miami, 1981; postgrad. in psychology Nova U., 1982—. Psychometrist Highland Park Gen. Hosp., Miami, Fla., 1981-82; psychology instr. Ft. Lauderdale Coll., 1981, Ft. Lauderdale Adult Edn. Program, 1983-84; youth intervention coordinator Centre for Counseling and Edn., Miami, 1981-82; assoc. Marvin Fredman, Ph.D., P.A., Ctr. for Psychol. Services, Lauderhill, Fla., 1983—; cons. S. Fla. Psychiat. Assn., Miami, 1983-85; clin. psychology doctoral intern N.W. Dade Community Mental Health Ctr., Hialeah, Fla., 1985—; ptnr. COR Counseling Ctr., Miami, 1982. Sunday Sch. tchr. Temple Beth Israel, Pitts., 1978-79; vol. Dade County Halfway House for Boys, Miami, 1979. Mem. Am. Assn. for Counseling and Devel., Am. Psychol. Assn. (student mem.), Mental Health Assn. Broward County (cert. appreciation 1984), U. Pitts. Varsity Letter Club, U. Pitts. Club S. Fla., Nat. Humane Edn. Soc., Phi Kappa Phi. Democrat. Jewish. Lodge: Fraternal Order Police. Avocations: gymnastics, guitar, woodworking, swimming. Office: Marvin Fredman PhD PA Ctr for Psychol Services 5950 W Oakland Park Blvd Suite 205 Lauderhill FL 33313

SPETSERIS, JERRY JOHN, explorationist; b. El Paso, Tex., Aug. 27, 1954; s. John Jerry Spetseris and Elaine Diane (Liatti) Carr; m. Martha Marie Manning, Apr. 26, 1980; children—John Jerry, Alexander Michael. B.S., Ohio U., 1976; M.S., U. Houston, 1986. Area geophysicist Arco Oil & Gas Co., Houston, 1978-85; ind. petroleum explorationist, 1985—. Vol., Progressive Amateur Boxing Assn., Houston, 1981—. Mem. Am. Assn. Petroleum Geologists, Soc. Exploration Geophysicists, Soc. Econ. Paleontologists and Mineralogists, Houston Geol. Soc. Methodist. Home: 11903 Hillbrook Dr Houston TX 77077 Office: 11903 Hillbrook Dr Houston TX 77070

SPEYRER, JUDE, bishop; b. Leonville, La., Apr. 14, 1929. Student St. Joseph Sem., Covington, La., Notre Dame Sem., New Orleans, Gregorian U., Rome, U. Fribourg, Switzerland. Ordained priest Roman Catholic Ch., 1953. First Bishop of Lake Charles, La., 1980—. Address: Roman Catholic Ch Chancery Office Weber Office Bldg PO Box 3223 Lake Charles LA 70602*

SPICER, CARLTON REVERE, JR., educational administrator; b. Gauley Bridge, W.Va., Oct. 23, 1944; s. Carlton R. and Grace Marie (Kincaid) S.; m. Rebekah Kay Thompson, June 19, 1982; children—Johna Leigh, Catherine Grace, Carlton R., III. B.A., Glenville State Coll., 1968; M.A., W.Va. U., 1978; postgrad. W.Va. U. and W.Va. Coll. Grad. Studies, 1978—. Pub. health inspector W.Va. Dept. Health, Charleston, 1968; tchr., coach Gauley Bridge High Sch., W.Va., 1968-75; asst. prin. Fayetteville High Sch., W.Va., 1975-78; prin. Fayetteville Middle Sch., 1978—; chmn. eval. teams North Central Assn. W.Va. Schs., 1978—; instr. community edn. program W.Va. Inst. Tech., Montgomery, 1981-83; dean camping for high sch. and coll. students W.Va. Baptist Youth Camps, Cowen, W.Va., 1979-80. Pres. Upper Kanawha Valley Little League, Gauley Bridge, 1981; dir. Upper Kanawha Valley Assn. Am. Bapt. Youth, Charleston, W.Va., 1980. Mem. Nat. Assn. Secondary Sch. Prins., W.Va. Assn. Secondary Sch. Prins., W. Va. Assn. Middle Sch. Prins., Fayette County Prins. Assn. Democrat. Baptist. Home: Box 1160 Crab Orchard WV 25827-1160 Office: Fayetteville Middle Sch 135 High St Fayetteville WV 25840

SPICER, STANLEY RUSSELL, diversified conglomerate executive, geological consultant; b. Tulsa, Mar. 26, 1946; s. Russell Jay and Betsy Ross (Wilkerson) S.; m. Doris Lee Ennis, Dec. 23, 1964; children—Christopher Stanley, Natalie Doris, Meredith Michelle. B.S., Ark. Tech. U., 1968; M.S., Kent State U., 1970; Ph.D., Tulsa U., 1980; Ph.D. (hon.), Pacific Western U., 1984. Registered profl. geologist. Assoc. prof. Ark. Tech. U., Russellville, 1970-75; geologist Ashland Oil Co., Fort Smith, Ark., 1975-77; founder, pres., chief exec. officer Spicer Petroleum Cons., Inc., Tulsa, 1977—; research geologist Cities Service Co., Tulsa, 1977-80; pres. 2-S Investment Corp., Tulsa, 1977—, Combined Investments Corp., Ponca City, 1982—; founder, chief exec. officer, gen. mgr. Indeco, Inc., Tulsa, 1978—; chmn., Chief exec. officer Far Star Exploration, Inc., Tulsa, 1979—; exec. v.p., gen. mgr. Daystar Energy, Inc., Tulsa, 1979—; sr. geologist Amerada Hess Corp., Tulsa, 1980-82; pres., gen. mgr. S&M Drilling, Inc., Tulsa, 1980—; dir. sr. v.p. Morning Star Energy Corp., Tulsa, 1980—; dir. chief geologist U.S. Exploration, Inc., Tulsa, 1980—; chmn. chief exec. officer Bright Star Exploration, Inc., Tulsa, 1981—; chief geologist Bird Creek Oil Co., Inc., Tulsa, 1982-84; exploration mgr. Okla. Drill Corp., Tulsa, 1982—; chief exec. officer, pres. U.S. Oil and Gas Corp., Tulsa, 1982—; chief geologist Fenix & Scisson, Inc., Tulsa, 1984—; vis. instr. Kent State U., Ohio, 1970, U. Okla., Norman, 1975, Westark Coll., Fort Smith, Ark., 1977; adj. prof. U. Tulsa, 1979-81; ptnr. Dixie Drilling Ventures, Inc., Fort Smith, 1981—; cons. in field; dir. Apache Resources, Inc., Tulsa, Tri-Star Exploration, Inc., Ponca City, Okla., Agape Petroleum Corp., Oklahoma City, Tri-State Prodn. Corp., Tulsa, East Okla. Gas Corp., Tulsa. Author: Stratigraphy and Faunal Succession of the Jones Sink Area, Meade County, Kansas, 1970; Annotated Analysis of Dolomitization and Stable Isotopes in Dolomite, 1978; The Abo Trend of Western Texas, 1983; Nontraditional Permeability Pathways, 1984; numerous other tech. publs. Editor: Carbonate Techniques Manual. Rep. Quorum Ct., Ark., 1970-76; county chmn. Lt. Gov. Campaign, Pope County, Ark., 1974; bd. dirs. Quapaw, Westark, Indian Nations councils Boy Scouts Am., 1974-82; state v.p. U.S. Jr. C. of C., 1974-75; mem. Kansas Sports Fedn., 1976-78, Okla. Soccer Assn., 1978—, Green Country Soccer Assn., Okla., 1978—, Republican Com., Tulsa, 1978—. Grantee Sigma Xi, NSF, 1970; recipient Plaque for Outstanding Service, Russellville, Ark., 1974, Plaque for Appreciation award Ark. Tech. U., Russellville, 1974, Ark. Outstanding Young Man award Ark. Jaycees, 1975, Ark. Outstanding Educator award Ark. Edn. Assn., 1975, Disting. Service award Russellville, 1975, Presdl. award of Honor, Pres. of U.S., 1975, Outstanding Young Educator award, Pope County, 1975, numerous awards Lions Club, Boy Scouts Am., U.S. Jr. C. of C. Mem. Am. Assn. Petroleum Geologists, Soc. Econ. Paleontologists and Mineralogists, Mensa Soc., NAM, Paleontol. Soc., Assn. Engring. Geologists, Nat. Council Petroleum Producers, Internat. Assn. Drilling Contractors, Assn. Oil Well Servicing Contractors, Soc. Profl. Well Log Analysts, Gulf Coast Assn. Geol. Socs., Nat. Crime Prevention Council, West Tex. Geol. Soc., Sigma Gamma Epsilon, Phi Delta Kappa, others. Clubs: Tulsa Petroleum, East Tulsa Soccer (treas. 1983-84). Avocations: spelunking; rapelling; gemology.

SPIELBERGER, CHARLES DONALD, psychology educator, behavioral medicine, clinical and community psychology administrator; b. Atlanta, Mar. 28, 1927; s. A.R. and Eleanor (Wachman) S.; m. Carol M. Lee, June 2, 1971. B.S., Ga. Tech. 1949; B.A., U. Iowa, 1951, M.A., 1953, Ph.D., 1954. Cert. psychologist, Fla. Asst. prof. med. psychology Duke U., Durham, N.C., 1955-58, from asst. prof. to assoc. prof. psychology, 1955-63; prof. psychology Vanderbilt U., Nashville, 1963-66; tng. specialist in psychology NIMH, Bethesda, Md., 1965-67; prof. psychology Fla. State U., Tallahassee, 1967-72; prof. psychology U. South Fla., Tampa, 1972—, disting. Univ. prof., 1985—; fellow Netherlands Inst. for Advanced Study, Wassenaar, 1979-80; cons. FAA, NIMH, VA, USAF, others. Author: Understanding Stress and Anxiety, 1979. Editor: Stress and Anxiety, 1975-85. Gen. editor: Centennial Psychology Series, 1979—. Served with USNR, 1945-79. Named Disting. scholar U. S. Fla., 1973; Disting. Sci. Contbr., Fla. Psychol. Assn., 1977; Outstanding Faculty Researcher U. South Fla., 1985. Fellow Am. Psychol. Assn. (pres. div. community psychology 1972-73); mem. Southeastern Psychol. Assn. (pres. 1975-76), Internat. Council Psychologists (pres. 1986—), Psi Chi (nat. pres. 1980-83). Home: 11313 Carrollwood Dr Tampa FL 33618 Office: Dept Psychology U South Fla Tampa FL 33620

SPIELBERGER, RONALD EDWARD, journalism and advertising educator; b. Memphis, Aug. 27, 1941; s. Joseph Harry and Ethel Pamela (Sharp) S.; m. Deborah Rose Parham, Aug. 18, 1975; 1 child, Robin Ashely Rose. B.S., Memphis State U., 1959-63; M.A., Ohio State U., 1965, postgrad., 1972; postgrad. U. Colo., 1967. Asst. dir. pub. relations Ohio Dept. Liquor Control, Columbus, 1964-65; instr. Jacksonville State U., Ala., 1965-68; assoc. prof. journalism Memphis State U., 1968—; bus. mgr. Coll. Media Review, Memphis, 1978-80; pub. relations cons. E.I. DuPont, Memphis, 1980-82. Contbr. articles to profl. jours. NSF fellow 1972; Direct Mail Assn. fellow, 1974. Mem. Memphis Advt. Fedn. (bd. dirs. 1979—), Coll. Media Advisers (bd. dirs. 1978—), Sigma Delta Chi. Baptist. Avocations: photography; gardening; fishing. Home: 2746 Green Mill Dr Memphis TN 38119 Office: Dept Journalism Memphis State U Veterans Ave Memphis TN 38152

SPIEWAK, IRVING, nuclear and energy scientist, consultant; b. Bklyn., Jan. 5, 1928; s. Meyer and Ethel (Teichteil) S.; m. Mary Elma Bryan, July 19, 1952; children—Alan Richard, Jonathan Andrew, Leah. B.S. in Chem. Engring., Cooper Union, 1947; M.S. in Chem. Engring., MIT, 1949. Registered profl. engr., Tenn. Staff mem. Oak Ridge Nat. Lab., 1949-83, cons., dir. nuclear energy assessments; Mellon fellow Inst. Energy Analysis, Oak Ridge, 1983—. Bd. dirs. Anderson County, Tenn. Schs., 1967-78, chmn.; concert master Oak Ridge Symphony. Mem. Am. Nuclear Soc., Am. Inst. Chem. Engrs., Sigma Xi. Jewish. Contbr. articles to profl. jours. Home: 712 S Main St Clinton TN 37716 Office: Inst Energy Analysis PO Box 117 Oak Ridge TN 37830

SPILMAN, ROBERT HENKEL, furniture manufacturing company executive; b. Knoxville, Tenn., Sept. 27, 1927; s. Robert R. and Lila (Henkel) S.; 1953. m. Jane Bassett, Apr. 2, 1955; children—Robert Henkel, Virginia Sale, Vance H. B.S. in Textiles, N.C. State Coll., 1950; student NYU Grad. Sch. Commerce, 1953. With Bassett Industries, 1957—, pres., 1966—, chmn. bd., 1982—, chief exec. officer, 1979—, also dir.; dir. Jefferson-Pilot Corp., Libbey-Owens-Ford Co., Blue Ridge Hardware, NCNB Corp., So. Furniture Expn. Bldg., Inc.; mem. Va. adv. bd. Liberty Mut. Trustee W.M. Bassett Community Center; chmn. Va. Port Authority; bd. visitors Va. Mil. Inst.; mem. Va. Gov.'s Econ. Adv. Council. Served to lt. airborne inf. AUS, World War II, Korea. Mem. So. Furniture Mfrs. Assn. (pres. 1970 chmn. bd. 1971), Va. Mfrs. Assn. (dir.). Home: Bassett VA 24055 Office: Bassett Furniture Industries Bassett VA 24055

SPINING, BONNIE CLARK, copy service executive; b. Asheville, N.C., Jan. 21, 1954; d. Edward Louis and Mary (Koval) Clark; m. Richard Wilson Spining, July 31, 1976. B. Social Welfare, E. Tenn. State U., 1976. Probation officer Anderson County Sch. System, Clinton, Tenn., 1976-77; field coordinator E. Tenn. Human Resource Agy., Knoxville, 1977-80; owner, mgr. Clark's Copy Service Inc., Oak Ridge, 1980—. Bd. dirs. United Way Anderson County, 1984-87. Mem. Oak Ridge C. of C. (small bus. council, membership com.). Democrat. Baptist. Office: Clark's Copy Service Inc 965 Oak Ridge Turnpike Oak Ridge TN 37830

SPINKS, DAVID WAYNE, osteopathic physician; b. Pasadena, Tex., Sept. 20, 1952; s. Victor Eugene and Evelyn Ollie (Lubojasky) S.; m. Kathleen Denise Mason, Aug. 18, 1973; children—Damon, Dustin, Devin. B.S. magna cum laude, Tex. A&M U., 1975; D.O., Tex. Coll. Osteo. Medicine-North Tex. State U., 1979. Intern Okla. Osteo. Hosp., Tulsa, 1979-80; practice osteo. family medicine Deer Park Clinic, Tex., 1980-82; ptnr., physician San Augustine Family Medicine Clinic, Deer Park, 1982—; ptnr. M & S Properties, Deer Park, 1984—, Thoroughbred Quarter Horse, Ft. Worth, 1984—; stockholder S.E. Med. Services, Pasadena, Tex., 1984—; mem. Pasadena Cons., Tex., 1982—; dir. S.E. Ednl. Investment Inc., Deer Park, Gulf Coast Entertainment Group, Inc., Deer Park; pres. Club Investment, Inc., Deer Park; co-owner Physicians Weight Reduction Ctr., Deer Park, 1985—; ptnr. Ct. Assocs., Pasadena, 1985. Mem. AMA, Tex. Med. Assn., Am. Osteo. Assn., Tex. Osteo. Med. Assn., Harris County Med. Soc., Harris County Osteo. Med. Soc., Phi Eta Sigma, Psi Chi, Phi Kappa Phi, Sigma Sigma Phi. Republican. Baptist. Clubs: Optimist, Atlas. Avocations: travel; skiing; jogging; weight lifting. Home: 6842 Cedar Lawn Circle Pasadena TX 77505 Office: San Augustine Family Medicine Clini 321 W San Augustine St Deer Park TX 77535

SPINKS, NELDA HUGHES, educator; b. Ruston, La., Sept. 3, 1928; d. Willie B. and Elizabeth Hughes; m. Wyman Allison Spinks, June 12, 1948; 1 son, Hugh Allison. B.A., La. Tech. U.; M.Ed., U. Southwestern La.; Ed.D., La. State U. Cert. tchr., La. Instr. Acadia Baptist Acad., Eunice, La., 1954-63, Lafayette Parish Sch. Bd., 1963-67; asst. prof. U. Southwestern La., Lafayette, 1967-73, 75—. Author: A Study of the Educational Needs of Potential Office Managers, 1974. Contbr. articles to mags. Mem. Am. Bus. Communication Assn., Am. Mgmt. Assn. Nat. Collegiate Assn. for Secs. (sponsor), Lafayette C. of C. (edn. com. 1977), Kappa Delta Pi, Omicron Delta Epsilon, Phi Delta Kappa. Avocations: needlework, sports, reading. Home: 218 Brentwood Blvd Lafayette LA 70503 Office: U Southwestern La PO Box 41503 Lafayette LA 70504

SPITZ, HUGO MAX, lawyer; b. Richmond, Va., Aug. 17, 1927, s. Jacob Gustav and Clara (Herzfeld) S.; m. Barbara Steinberg, June 22, 1952; children—Jack Gray, Jill Ann Levy, Sally. A.A., U. Fla., 1948, B.Laws, 1951, J.D., 1967. Bar: Fla. 1951, S.C., 1955, U.S. Dist. Ct. (so. dist.) Fla. 1951, U.S. Dist. Ct. (ea. dist.) S.C. 1956, U.S. Ct. Appeals (4th cir.) 1957. Asst. atty. gen. State of Fla., Tallahassee, 1951; assoc. Williams, Salomon & Katz, Miami, Fla., 1951-54, Steinberg & Levkoff, Charleston, S.C., 1954-57; sr. ptnr. Steinberg, Levkoff, Spitz & Goldberg, Charleston, 1957—; lectr. S.C. Trial Lawyers Assn., Columbia, 1958—, S.C. U. Sch. Law, Columbia, 1975, S.C. Bar Assn., 1955—. Assoc. mcpl. judge Charleston, 1972-74, mcpl. judge, 1974-76; commr. Charleston County Substance Abuse Commn., 1976-79; bd. govs. S.C. Patient's Compensation Fund, Columbia, 1978-89; chmn. bd. dirs. Franklin C. Fetter Health Ctr., Charleston, 1977-78; pres. Synagogue Emanu-El, 1969-71. Served with USN, 1945-46. S.C. Bar Assn. fellow, 1979; U. S.C. Ednl. Found. fellow, 1981. Mem. ABA, S.C. Trial Lawyers Assn. (pres. 1985-86), S.C. Claimants' Attys. for Worker's Compensation, S.C. Worker's Compensation Ednl. Assn. (bd. dirs. 1978—), Am. Judicature Soc., Am. Trial Lawyers Assn., Nat. Rehab. Assn., Nat. Orgn. Social Security Claimants' Reps. S.C. Bar (chmn. trial and appellate sect. 1982-83; ho. of dels. 1984-85), So. Assn. Workmen's Compensation Adminstrs., Democrat. Jewish. Clubs: Hebrew Benevolent Soc. (pres. 1974-75), Jewish Community Ctr. (v.p. 1972-74) (Charleston). Home: 337 Confederate Circle Charleston SC 29407 Office: Steinberg Levkoff Spitz & Goldberg PO Box 9 Charleston SC 29402

SPITZLI, DONALD HAWKES, JR., lawyer; b. Newark, Mar. 19, 1934; s. Donald Hawkes and Beatrice (Banister) S.; m. Rita Anne Angell, June 17, 1956 (div. 1979); children—Donald Hawkes III, Peter Gilbert; m. 2d, Jacqueline Anne Lilley, Mar. 3, 1979; children—Lori Anne, Seth Armstrong. A.B., Dartmouth Coll., 1956; LL.B., U. Va., LL.D., 1963. Bar: Va. 1963. Assoc. firm Willcox, Savage, Lawrence, Dickson & Spindle, Norfolk, Va., 1964-67, 68-70, ptnr., 1971-77; atty. Eastman Kodak Co., Rochester, N.Y., 1967-68; pres. Marine Hydraulics Internat., Inc., Chesapeake, Va., 1978-80; sole practice law, Virginia Beach, Va., 1980—; pres. Chieftain Motor Inn, Inc., Hanover, N.H., 1980—; gen. counsel Nat. Energy Jour., Chesapeake, 1981-84. Served to comdr. USNR, 1956-70. Mem. ABA, Va. Bar Assn., Phi Alpha Delta, Pi Delta Epsilon. Episcopalian. Clubs: Dartmouth, Yale (N.Y.C.). Office: 2840 S Lynnhaven Rd Virginia Beach VA 23452

SPIVEY, ED L., clergyman; b. Rusk, Tex., Oct. 12, 1933; s. Verner and Eddie (Sherman) S.; m. Ann Claudette Ray, May 26, 1956; children—Kevin, Sandra. Student Rice U., 1951-52; B.A., Baylor U., 1955; M.Div., Southwestern Bapt. Theol. Sem., 1959. Ordained to ministry Baptist Ch., 1959. Pastor First Bapt. Ch., Flomot, Tex., 1959-61, First Bapt. Ch., Lefors, Tex., 1961-68, Eden Hills Bapt. Ch., Wichita Falls, Tex., 1968-71, First Bapt. Ch., Mexia, Tex., 1971-82, Quail Valley Bapt. Ch., Missouri City, Tex., 1982—; moderator Palo Duro Bapt. Assn., Pampa, Tex., 1965-67, Wichita Bapt. Assn., Wichita Falls, Tex., 1970-71, Bi-Stone Bapt. Assn., Mexia Tex., 1974-75. Contbr. articles to profl. jours. Chaplain, City Council, Mexia, Tex., 1972-82; commr. Planning and Zoning Commn., Missouri City, Tex., 1982—; trustee U. Mary Hardin Baylor, Belton, Tex., 1975-84; bd. dirs. Ft. Bend Texans War on Drugs, 1983—, Ft. Bend Am. Cancer Soc., 1984—. Mem. Tri-Cities Ministers Fellowship (chmn. 1983—). Lodge: Lions (tailtwister 1972-79, v.p.). Avocations: travel; sports; family activities. Office: Quail Valley Baptist Ch 2723 Kingsbrook St Missouri City TX 77459

SPOFFORD, JO ANN, nurse; b. Council Grove, Kans., Oct. 2, 1945; d. Alfred Brackston and Tenella (Brown) Smith; m. Carl Edward Spofford, Feb. 14, 1970; 1 dau., Shannon Christina. Diploma, W.A. Candler Sch. Nursing, Savannah, Ga., 1966; student Armstrong State Coll., 1963-64, Century U., 1984, Purdue U., 1982. R.N. Staff nurse, various hosps., Savannah, 1966-75; head nurse post anesthesia recovery McAllen Methodist Hosp., Tex., 1975-78, Glynn-Brunswick Hosp., Brunswick, Ga., 1978-79; mgr. central service Candler Gen. Hosp., 1981. Bd. dirs. Candler Gen. Fed. Credit Union, Savannah, 1984—. Recipient Pacer award Ga. Hosp. Assn., 1982. Mem. Coastal Empire Soc. for Hosp. Central Service Personnel (pres. 1983—), Am. Soc. Hosp. Service Personnel, Assn. Advancement Med. Instrumentation. Baptist. Avocation: cooking. Home: 114 E 48th St Savannah GA 31405 Office: Candler Gen Hosp 5353 Reynolds St Savannah GA 31405

SPRADLEY, DON DELOY, real estate broker; b. Kern County, Calif., Dec. 8, 1934; s. Clyde Anderson Spradley and Veda Latan (Ellis) Spradley Quade; B.S., Kans. State COll., 1961; postgrad. La Salle Extension U., 1965-68. With Farmers Ins. Group, 1962-65, MFA Mut. Ins. Cos., Columbia, Mo., 1965-72, Medallion Ins. Co., Kansas City, Mo., 1972-74. Owner, pres., broker Olive Branch Realty, Arlington, Tex., 1975—. Lic. real estate broker, lic. ins. adjuster, Tex. Mem. Nat. Assn. Realtors, Tex. Claims Assn., Tex. Assn. Realtors, Arlington Bd. Realtors. Democrat. Baptist. Club: Kiwanis (pres.) (Arlington). Home: 1411 Waggoner Dr Arlington TX 76013 Office: 2417 W Park Row Suite 204 Arlington TX 76013

SPRAGUE, CHARLES CAMERON, college president; b. Dallas, Nov. 14, 1916; s. George Able and Minna (Schwartz) S.; B.B.A., B.S., D.Sc., So. Meth. U., D.Sc. (hon.), 1966; M.D., U. Tex., 1943; m. Margaret Frederica Dickson, Sept. 7, 1943; 1 dau., Cynthia Cameron. Intern, U.S. Naval Med. Center, Bethesda, Md., 1943-44; resident Charity Hosp., New Orleans, 1947-48, Tulane U. Med. Sch., 1948-50; Commonwealth research fellow in hematology Washington U. Sch. Medicine, St. Louis, also Oxford (Eng.) U., 1950-52; mem. faculty Med. Sch. Tulane U., 1952-67, prof. medicine, 1959-67, dean Sch. Medicine, 1963-67; prof., dean U. Tex. Southwestern Med. Sch., Dallas, 1967-72; pres. U. Tex. Health Sci. Center, Dallas, 1972—. Mem. Nat. Adv. Council, 1966-70; mem. adv. com. to dir. NIH, 1973—; chmn. Gov.'s Task Force Health Manpower, 1981; chmn. Gov.'s Med. Edn. Mgmt. Effectiveness Com.; chmn. allied health edn. adv. com., coordinating bd. Tex. Coll. and Univ. System. Served with USN, 1943-47. Recipient Ashbel Smith Distinguished Alumnus award U. Tex. Med. Br., 1967; Distinguished Alumnus award So. Meth. U., 1965; recipient Sports Illustrated Silver Anniversary award, 1963. Mem. Assn. Am. Med. Colls. (chmn. council deans 1970, chmn. exec. council and assembly 1972-73), Assn. Acad. Health Ctrs. (bd. dirs. 1983—, chmn. 1985-86), Am. Soc. Hematology (pres. 1968). Office: U Tex Health Sci Center 5323 Harry Hines Blvd Dallas TX 75235

SPRAGUE, JAMES DARRELL, construction company executive, safety consultant; b. Panhandle, Tex., July 8, 1933; s. Fred Irvan and Delia May (Hodges) S.; m. JoAnna Ives, Sept. 5, 1956; children—Kathy Ann, Kristi Dawn, James Jr., John G. B.S., Okla. U., 1956, M.A., 1972. Supr. Central State Hosp., Norman, Okla., 1954-56; commd. officer U.S. Army, 1957, advanced through ranks to lt. col., retired, 1977; corp. safety dir. Campbell Taggart, Dallas, 1976-77; supt. tng. Kerr-McGee Corp., Gallup, N. Mex., 1977-79; mgr.

ops. and safety Associated Gen. Contractors, Dallas, 1979—. Mem. System Safety Soc., Am. Soc. Safety Engrs., ASTM, Nat. Safety Council (exec. com.), Tex. Safety Assn. (chmn. assns. com. 1980—). Republican. Baptist. Avocations: camping; fishing; carpentry. Home: 4070 Creekdale Dr Dallas TX 75229 Office: Associated Gen Contractors 10210 Monroe Dr Dallas TX 75229

SPRAGUE, WILLIAM WALLACE, JR., foods corporation executive; b. Savannah, Ga., Nov. 11, 1926; s. William Wallace and Mary (Crowther) S.; m. Elizabeth Louise Carr, Oct. 3, 1953; children—Courtney and Lauren Duane, William Wallace, Elizabeth Louise. B.S. in Mech. Engring., Yale U., 1950. With Savannah Foods & Industries, Inc., 1952—, salesman, 1952-59, mgr. indsl. products, 1959, asst. sec., 1959-61, sec., 1961-62, v.p., 1962-72, pres., chief exec. officer, 1972—; dir. Savannah Foods, Everglades Sugar Refinery, U.S. Sugar Corp., Adeline Sugar Factory Co., Ltd., Atlantic Towing, C&S Nat. Bank of Ga., C&S Nat. Bank Savannah. Active U. Ga. Pres. Club. Served with USN, 1945-46. Mem. Sugar Assn. (bd. dirs.), Ga. Bus. and Industry Assn. (bd. govs.), World Sugar Research Orgn., (chmn.), Grocery Mfrs. Am. (dirs.), NAM (dir.). Clubs: Oglethorpe, Century, Cotillion, Carolina Plantation Soc., Yale Club of N.Y.C., St. Andrew's Soc. Home: PO Box 339 Savannah GA 31402 Office: PO Box 339 Savannah GA 31402

SPRAKER, HAROLD STEPHEN, mathematics and computer science educator; b. Cedar Bluff, Va., May 13, 1929; s. Stephen M. and Cynthia Polly (Cook) S.; m. Betty Jean Conley, Oct. 2, 1954; children—John Stephen, Mark Conley. B.S., Roanoke Coll., 1950; Ed.M., U. Va., 1955, cert. of advanced grad. study, 1959, Ed.D., 1960. Asst. prin., tchr. math. Richlands High Sch., Va., 1953-57; research asst., assoc. U. Va., Charlottesville, 1958-60, instr. extension div., 1959-60; prof. math. Middle Tenn. State U., Murfreesboro, 1960-67, chmn. dept. math., computer sci., 1967—. Served with U.S. Army, 1951-53. Recipient Outstanding Tchr. award Middle Tenn. State U., 1967; NSF grantee, 1957-58. Mem. Nat. Council Tchrs. Math., Tenn. Math. Tchrs. Assn. (statistician), Math. Assn. Am., Pi Mu Epsilon. Lutheran. Avocations: camping; photography; gardening; traveling; reading. Home: Route 6 Box 380 Elam Rd Murfreesboro TN 37130 Office: Middle Tenn State U Dept Math Computer Sci Murfreesboro TN 37132

SPRATT, JOHN MCKEE, JR., congressman, lawyer; b. Charlotte, N.C., Nov. 1, 1942; s. John McKee and Jane Love (Bratton) S.; m. Jane Stacy, May 31, 1968; children—Susan Elizabeth, Sarah Stacy, Catherine Bratton. A.B., Davidson Coll., 1964; M.A., Corpus Christi Co., Oxford U., 1966; LL.B., Yale U., 1969. Ops. analyst Office of Asst. Sec. of Def., 1969-71; ptnr. Spratt, McKeown & Spratt, Mork, S.C., 1971-83; pres. Bank of Ft. Mill, S.C., 1973-82; mem. 98th Congress, S.C.; former dir. Bank of York; pres. Spratt Ins. Agy., Ft. Mill, 1973-82. Chmn. bd. trustees Divine Saviour Hosp., York, 1980-82; bd. dirs. Piedmont Legal Services, Inc., 1978-82; bd. visitors Davidson Coll., 1978-80; chmn. bd. visitors Winthrop Coll., 1976. Served to capt. JAGC, U.S. Army, 1969-71. Mem. S.C. Bar Assn. (ho. of dels.), ABA. Democrat. Presbyterian. Home: 233 Kings Mountain St York SC 29745 Office: 1118 Longworth Bldg Washington DC 20515

SPRATT, JOHN STRICKLIN, surgeon, educator, researcher; b. San Angelo, Tex., Jan. 3, 1929; s. John Stricklin and Nannie Lee (Morgan) S.; m. Beverly Jane Winfiele, Dec. 27, 1951; children—John Arthur, Shelley Winfiele, Robert Stricklin. A.S., U. Tex.-Arlington, 1947; B.S. with high honors, So. Methodist U., 1949; M.D., U. Tex.-Dallas, 1952; M.S.P.H., U. Mo., 1970; postgrad. Washington U., St. Louis, 1961. Asst. in physiology Southwestern Med. Sch., U. Tex., Dallas, 1952; intern, Barnes Hosp., Washington U., St. Louis, 1952-53, asst. resident in surgery, 1955-57, resident, Am. Cancer Soc. fellow in surgery, 1958-59; USPHS Cancer Research fellow in radiotherapy and surgery Mallinckrodt Inst. Radiology, St. Louis, 1957-58, chief resident, 1958-59; mem. surg. faculty Washington U., 1952-76; chief surgeon Ellis Fischel State Cancer Hosp., Columbia, Mo., 1961-76; practice medicine specializing in surgery, Louisville, 1976—; mem. staffs Humana Hosp., Norton-Kosair Children's Hosp., VA Hosp., Louisville, Bapt. Hosps. of Louisville; prof. surgery U. Mo.-Columbia, 1961-76; prof. surgery U. Louisville, 1976—, prof. community health, head div. health systems, 1980—. Contbr. numerous articles in cancer, surgery and med. edn. fields to sci. publs. Mem. editorial bd. Cancer mag., Am. Jour. Surgery, Jour. Surg. Oncology. Editor, editor-in-chief Louisville Medicine mag., 1979-82. Served to capt. USNR, 1953—. Grantee Nat. Cancer Inst., Am. Cancer Soc. Fellow ACS; mem. Am. Surg. Assn., Soc. Surg. Oncology, Res. Officers Assn., Alpha Omega Alpha. Democrat. Baptist. Club: Cosmos (Washington). Lodge: Rotary. Home: 2206 Bell Tavern Ct Louisville KY 40207 Office: 529 S Jackson St Louisville KY 40202

SPRAY, PAUL, surgeon; b. Wilkinsburg, Pa., Apr. 9, 1921; s. Lester E. and Phoebe Gertrude (Hull) S.; B.S., U. Pitts., 1942; M.D., George Washington U., 1944; M.S., U. Minn., 1950; m. Mary Louise Conover, Nov. 28, 1943; children—David C., Thomas L., Mary Lynn (Mrs. Thomas Branham). Intern, U.S. Marine Hosp., S.I., 1944-45; resident Mayo Found., Rochester, Minn., 1945-46, 48-50; practice medicine specializing in orthopedic surgery, Oak Ridge, 1950—; mem. staff Oak Ridge Hosp., E. Tenn. Meml., East Tenn. Baptist, Park West hosps., Knoxville, Harriman (Tenn.) Hosp., Chamberlain Meml. Hosp., Rockwood, Tenn.; cons., Daniel Arthur Rehab. Center, Oak Ridge Associated Univs.; vol. vis. cons., CARE Medico, Jordan, 1959, Nigeria, 1962, 65, Algeria, 1963, Afghanistan, 1970, Bangladesh, 1975, 77, 79, Peru, 1980, U. Ghana, 1982; AMA voluntary physician, Vietnam, 1967, 72; vis. assoc. prof. U. Nairobi, 1973; mem. teaching team of Internat. Coll. Surgeons to Khartoum, vis. prof. orthopedic surgery U. Khartoum, 1976; hon. prof. San Luis Gonzaga U., Ica, Peru; AmDoc vol. cons., U. Biafra Teaching Hosp., 1969; sec. orthopedics overseas div. CARE Medico, 1971-76, sec. medico adv. bd., 1974-76, vice chmn., 1976, chmn., 1977-79, v.p. CARE, Inc., 1977-79, pub. mem. care bd., 1980—; chmn. Orthopedics Overseas, Inc., 1982-86, treas., 1986—; mem. U.S. organizing com. 1st Internat. Acad. Symposium on Orthopedics, Tianjin, China, 1983. Vice pres. Anderson County Health Council, 1975, pres., 1976-77; pres. health commn. Council So. Mountains, 1958-65, sec. bd., 1965-66; Tenn. pres. UN Assn., 1966-67; vice chmn. bd. Camelot Care Center Tenn., 1979-82, chmn., 1982—. Mem. editorial bd. Contemporary Orthopedics, 1984—. Served to capt. AUS, 1946-48. Recipient various humanitarian awards; Sertoma Service to Mankind award, 1967; Freedom citation Sertoma, 1978; Medico Disting. Service award, 1980. 1st ann. Vocat. Service award Oak Ridge Rotary Club, 1979; diplomate Am. Bd. Orthopedic Surgery. Fellow ACS (mem. trauma com. Tenn. chpt. 1983—); Internat. Coll. Surgeons (Tenn. regent 1976-80, bd. councillors 1980-84, hon. chmn. bd. trustees 1981-83, trustee 1983-84, v.p. U.S. sect. 1982-83, mem. Surg. teams com. 1983—); mem. Société International Chirurgie Orthopedique et de Traumatologie, Western Pacific Orthopedic Assn., Orthopedic Letters Club, Am. Fracture Assn., Am. Acad. Orthopedic Surgeons (mem. com. on injuries 1980-86), AMA (Humanitarian Service award 1967, 72), Am. Assn. Vol. Physicians (pres. 1977-78), Tenn. Med. Assn. (com. on emergency med. services 1978—), Alumni and Friends of Medico (pres. 1975-77), Indonesian Orthopedic Soc. (hon.), Peru Acad. Surgery (corr.), Peruvian Soc. Orthopedic Surgery and Traumatology (corr.). Quaker. Club: Lions (Humanitarian award 1968, Ambassador of Goodwill award 1979). Home: 507 Delaware Ave Oak Ridge TN 37830 Office: 145 E Vance Rd Oak Ridge TN 37830

SPREHE, DANIEL JOSEPH, psychiatrist, medical educator; b. Oklahoma City, Feb. 21, 1932; s. Francis L. and Stella S. B.S., U. Okla., 1953, M.D., 1957. Diplomate Am. Bd. Psychiatry and Neurology (examiner 1980—), Am. Bd. Forensic Psychiatry. Intern, Charity Hosp. La., New Orleans, 1957-58; resident in psychiatry Tulane U., Sch. Medicine, New Orleans, 1963-66; research cons. East La. State Hosp., Tulane Research Unit, Jackson, 1963-64; clin. asst. prof. psychiatry Tulane U. Med. Sch. 1964-66; clin. dir. Southeast La. Hosp., Mandeville, 1965-66; med. dir. Matairie (La.) Mental Health Clinic, 1965-66; chmn. Mental Health Div., Community Welfare Council, Jefferson Parish, La., New Orleans 1965-66; med. dir. New Orleans Mental Health Ctr., 1966; clin. asst. prof. U. South Fla., Coll. Medicine, Tampa, 1971-77, clin. assoc. prof., 1977—, chief sect. forensic psychiatry, 1978—; mem. staff Tampa Gen. Hosp., St. Joseph's Hosp., Meml. Hosp.; cons., lectr. in field. Served with USAF, 1957-61; spl. USAFR, 1961-64. Fellow Am. Psychiat. Assn.; mem. AMA, Am. Group Psychotherapy Assn., Am. Acad. Psychiatry and Law (family law task force), Am. Acad. Forensic Scis., Fla. Med. Assn., Fla. Psychiat. Soc. (pres.), Fla. Acad. Forensic Psychiatry (pres.), Hillsborough County Med. Assn. (com. mem. bd. censors), Southeast Group Psychotherapy Assn., Tampa Psychiat. Assn. (pres. 1976-77), Pan Am. Psychiat. Assn., So. Psychiat. Assn. Contbr. numerous papers to profl. jours. Address: 800 W Buffalo Ave Suite 4 Tampa FL 33603

SPREHN, BRIAN DIETRICH, communications company systems executive; b. Washington, Feb. 2, 1949; s. George Warren and Charlotte Elizabeth (Austin) S.; m. Mary Jenney, June 1968 (div. Dec. 1971); 1 dau., Mindi Gwendolyn; m. 2d, Regenia Carder, Nov. 11, 1978; children—Melanie Marie, Kristen Charlotte. Student Manatee Jr. Coll., 1967-68, Dekalb Community Coll., 1980-81. Repair technician Gen. Telephone of Fla., Sarasota, 1971-72; with So. Bell Telephone and Telegraph Co., Atlanta, 1972—, engr., 1978-79, data systems adminstr., 1979—. Served with U.S. Army, 1969-70. Decorated Bronze Star, Army Commendation medal, Air medal. Mem. Exptl. Aircraft Assn., Exptl. Aircraft Assn. Ultralight Assn. Developer computer user courses. Home: 4771 Vermack Rd Dunwoody GA 30338 Office: 675 W Peachtree St Atlanta GA 30375

SPRENGER, THOMAS ROBERT, orthopedic surgeon; b. Seymour, Ind., Aug. 22, 1931; s. Robert D. and Margaret Sprenger; B.S., Marshall U., 1975; M.D., Ind. U., 1956; grad. U.S. Army War Coll., 1975, U.S. Army Command and Gen. Staff Coll., 1970; m. Justine Gambill Stinson, June 24, 1956; children—Rebecca Lee, Michael Thomas. Diplomate Am. Bd. Orthopedic Surgery. Intern St. Vincent's Hosp., Indpls., 1956-57; resident in orthopedic surgery Indpls. Gen. Hosp., 1957-58, Riley Children's Hosp. Ind. U., 1958-59, VA Hosp., New Orleans, 1959-60, Tampa Gen. Hosp., 1960; practice medicine specializing in orthopedic surgery, Bradenton, Fla., 1961—; orthopedic surgeon Pitts. Pirates, Bradenton, 1969—; sr. attending orthopedic surgeon Manatee Meml. Hosp., Bradenton, 1961—, chief of staff, 1967; sr. attending orthopedic surgeon L.W. Blake Meml. Hosp., Bradenton, 1973—, trustee, 1970—, sec. bd., 1970-80, vice chmn. bd., 1980-81, chmn. bd., 1982-84. Pres., Gulfcoast chpt. Nat. Arthritis Found., 1965, 82—; mem. Bd. Pub. Instrn. Manatee County, 1966-71, chmn., 1967-69; mem. exec. com. Bishop Mus. and Planetarium, 1967-69; founding mem. Health Systems Agy. Manatee County, 1968, mem., 1968-79. Col. Army NG, 1956—. Mem. Pres.'s Council, U. South Fla., 1981. Mem. Am. Acad. Orthopedic Surgeons, ACS, Internat. Coll. Surgeons, Assn. Mil. Surgeons U.S., Am. Fracture Assn., Orthopedics Letters Club, Fla. Orthopedics Letters Club, Fla. Orthopedic Soc. (chmn. membership 1982—), Fla. Med. Soc., So. Orthopedic Assn., AMA, So. Med. Assn., Manatee County Med. Soc., Eastern Orthopedic Assn., Soc. Med. Cons. to Armed Forces, N.G. Officers Assn. Fla. (pres. 1980-81), Phi Eta Sigma, Alpha Epsilon Delta. Presbyterian. Contbr. articles to profl. jours. Home: 8221 DeSoto Memorial Hwy NW Bradenton FL 33529 Office: 2101 61st St W Bradenton FL 33529

SPRIGGS, CHARLES KENNETH, architect; b. Washington, July 12, 1946; s. Kahl Kenneth and Rosa Nell (Booth) S.; B.A., Princeton U., 1968; M.Arch., Harvard U., 1971; certificate in project mgmt. Air Force Inst. Tech., 1972. Transp. planner C.E. Maguire, Inc., Waltham, Mass., 1971; design mgr. Sea Pines Co., Hilton Head Island, S.C., 1973-75; architect, corp. sec. Maddox & Assos., P.C., Savannah, Ga., 1975-77; pres. Spriggs & Wilkes, P.C., Savannah, 1979-83; pres. The Spriggs Group, P.C., Savannah, 1983—; mem. Nat. Com. Architecture for Justice, 1978—; project dir. Art in Pub. Places Program, Chatham County, Ga., 1977-78; bd. dirs. Collaborative Resources Internat., Inc., Savannah, 1979-84. Bd. trustees mem., archtl. cons. Telfair Acad. of Arts and Scis., Savannah, 1977—; mem. Leadership Savannah, 1977-78. Served to capt. Civil Engring. Squadron, USAF, 1971-73. Registered architect, Ga., S.C., Md., Fla., Tenn.; certificate, Nat. Council of Archtl. Registration Bds. Mem. AIA, (pres. South Ga. chpt. 1984), Nat. Trust for Historic Preservation, Assn. for Preservation Tech., Historic Savannah, Ga. Conservancy. Clubs: Harvard Club of Washington, D.C., Harvard Club of Atlanta, Princeton Club of N.Y.C., Savannah Golf, Columbia Country (Chevy Chase, Md.). Author documentary: Patterns of Change, The Evolution of a Courthouse, 1978; archtl. works include: Chatham County Courthouse, Savannah, 1977; Residence for Officials from Kuwait, Kiawah Island, S.C., 1975; Flight Ops. Center, Dobbins AFB, Ga., 1985. Home: PO Box 10062 Savannah GA 31412 Office: PO Box 10062 Savannah GA 31412

SPRING, BONNIE JOAN, psychology educator, researcher; b. Hackensack, N.J., Oct. 9, 1949; d. John Edwin and Sonja Joan (Litwinowich) S.; m. Ronald Terrazas, Oct. 21, 1979 (div. 1981). B.A., Bucknell U., 1971; M.A., Harvard U., 1975, Ph.D., 1977. Lic. psychologist, Mass. Research scientist Biometrics Research, N.Y.C., 1975-78; instr. psychology Harvard U., Cambridge, Mass., 1977, asst. prof., 1977-82, assoc. prof., 1982-84; prof. Tex. Tech U., Lubbock, 1984—; lectr. psychiatry Columbia Coll. Physicians and Surgeons, N.Y.C., 1979—; vis. lectr. nutrition MIT, Cambridge, 1979-80; staff psychologist Mass. Mental Health, Boston, 1981-84; research assoc. prof. psychiatry U. Md. Med. Sch., Balt., 1984—. Editor: Attention in Schizophrenia, 1979. Contbr. articles to profl. jours. Mem. Harvard U. Commn. on Status of Women, Cambridge, 1979-81; panel mem. com. on nat. needs for behavioral research personnel Inst. of Medicine, Nat. Acad. Scis., Washington, 1984—. Nutrition grantee Ctr. for Brain Scis., 1980-81, Ford Found., 1981-82; Cognition grantee Kali-Duphar Labs., 1982—; Schizophrenia grantee NIMH, 1980-84. Fellow Am. Psychol. Assn.; mem. AAAS, Am. Psychopathol. Assn., Am. Coll. Neuropsychopharmacology, Sigma Xi. Avocations: swimming, international travel. Office: Dept Psychology Tex Tech U PO Box 4100 Lubbock TX 79409

SPRING, DONALD JACOB, aerospace engineer, educator; b. Aurora, Ill., Mar. 5, 1931; s. Jacob Peter and Leona Ann (Babcock) Lies Spring; m. Patty Cleone Ballard, Aug. 6, 1951; children—Cherilynn, Venita, Jason. B.A.E., Auburn U., 1956, M.S.A.E., 1964; Ph.D., U. Ill., 1972. Registered profl. engr., Ala. Engr., Convair, Gen. Dynamics, Fort Worth, 1957-58; project engr. ARO, Inc., Tullahoma, Tenn., 1958-61; research engr. Army Missile Command, Redstone Arsenal, Ala., 1961-82; supervisory engr., 1982-85; mem. engring. adv. com. Auburn U., Ala., 1977—. Contbg. author: Aerodynamics of Base Combustion, 1974. Contbr. articles to profl. jours. Pres. Agape of N. Ala., Huntsville, 1984; bd. dirs. Madison Acad., Huntsville, 1984—. Served with USAF, 1948-54. Named Outstanding Alumni, Sigma Gamma Tau, 1980. Assoc. fellow AIAA (dir. 1972-77, tech. com. 1975-83, Oberth award 1984), Pi Tau Sigma. Mem. Ch. of Christ. Avocations: golf; Little League coaching. Home: 2103 Harris Rd Huntsville AL 35810 Office: US Army Missile Command AMSMI-RD-SS-SO Redstone Arsenal AL 35898-5252

SPRINGBORN, BRUCE ALAN, consultant, educator; b. Geneva, Ill., Nov. 21, 1936; s. Carl Frederick and Mabel Nellie (Lintner) S.; m. Rosemary Kelly, Dec. 19, 1964. B.A., Northwestern U., 1958, A.M., 1959; Ph.D., U. Mich., 1963. Cons. A.T. Kearney, Chgo., 1968-70; dir. personnel R.R. Donnelley & Sons, Chgo., 1970-74; dir. orgn. devel. Quaker Oats, Chgo., 1974-77; v.p. Marshall Field & Co., Chgo., 1977-79; ptnr. Kelly/Springborn Assocs. Inc., Lakeland, Fla., 1977—; pres. Highlands Future, Inc., Lakeland, 1983—; adj. prof. Fla. So. Coll., Lakeland, 1981—; dir. Child and Family Services, Chgo., 1977-79; mem. adv. council Northwestern U., Chgo., 1972-74. Contbr. articles to profl. jours. USPHS scholar, U. Mich., 1960-62; Rackham Grad. Sch. grantee, U. Mich., 1962. Mem. Am. Psychol. Assn. Home: 2834 Elizabeth Pl Lakeland FL 33803

SPRINGER, JACK G., association executive; b. Norman, Okla., Sept. 11, 1926; s. Charles S. and Mary A. (Goff) S.; m. Doris M. Lebow, Apr. 14, 1945; children—Carol Springer Power, Sheryl Springer Snesko, Jane, Cynthia Springer Downs. B.S., U. Okla., 1950. With Pauls Valley (Okla.) C. of C., 1950-51, Seminole (Okla.) C. of C., 1951-53; Bryan-Coll. Station (Tex.) C. of C., 1953-61, Galveston (Tex.) C. of C., 1961-63, W. Tex. Regional C. of C., 1963-71; exec. v.p. Okla. State C. of C., Oklahoma City, 1971—. Served with U.S. Army, 1944-46. Mem. Assn. Am. C. of C. Execs., Okla. C. of C. Execs. (dir.), Council State Chambers Commerce (past (pres., mem. exec. com.), U.S. C. of C. (c. of c. com.). Home: 6224 NW 85th St Oklahoma City OK 73132 Office: 4020 N Lincoln Blvd Oklahoma City OK 73105

SPRINGER, JACK HENDERSON, municipal agency administrator; b. Sistersville, W.Va., Apr. 22, 1917; s. A.G. and Joberta (Henderson) S.; B.S., W.Va. U., 1941, M.S., 1949; m. Wanda Attice Davis, June 7, 1952; children—Jack Henderson, Marjo Springer Poole. Coach, comdt. Fishburne Mil. Sch., Waynesboro, Va., 1946-48; coach Manchester (Va.) High Sch. and Galax (Va.) High Sch., 1948-54; dir. recreation Statesville (N.C.) Recreation Dept., 1954-82. Past nat. bd. dirs. Babe Ruth Baseball Inc.; past pres. Iredell County Cancer Assn.; pres. Carolina Dogwood Festival 1972-73. Served to maj. U.S. Army, 1941-46; ETO. Decorated Bronze Star, Army Commendation medal. Mem. Nat. Recreation and Park Assn., N.C. Recreation and Park Soc. (past v.p., fellow award, Meritorious Service plaque 1981), Am. Assn. Ret. Persons, W.Va. U. Alumni Assn. (life), N.C. Sr. Citizens Clubs (chmn. 1975-76), Nat. Horseshoe Pitchers Assn. (sec.-treas. N.C. 1979—, nat. youth chmn. 1981—; spl. award plaque 1979), Am. Legion (Va. state vice comdr.), 40 and 8, VFW, DAV (life), Sigma Chi (life). Democrat. Baptist. Clubs: Masons, Shriners. Home: 925 Henkel Rd Statesville NC 28677 Office: Statesville Recreation Dept 432 W Bell St Statesville NC 28677

SPRINGER, MELVIN DALE, industrial engineering educator; b. Saybrook, Ill., Sept. 12, 1918; s. David Valentine and Lena A. (Birkey) S.; m. Wilma Irene Nelson, Aug. 7, 1948; 1 dau., Beth Ann. B.S., U. Ill., 1940, M.S., 1941, Ph.D., 1947. Asst. prof. math. stats. Mich. State U., East Lansing, 1948-50; math. statistician U.S. Naval Ordnance Plant, Indpls., 1950-56; sr. ops. analyst Tech. Ops., Inc., Ft. Monroe, Va., 1956-59; systems ops. analyst Gen. Motors Aerospace Research Labs., Santa Barbara, Calif., 1959-67; dir. reliability research A.C. Electronics div. Gen. Motors Corp., Milw., 1967-68; prof. indsl. engring. U. Ark., Fayetteville, 1968—. Served with USN, 1944-46. Mem. Am. Statis. Assn., Am. Inst. Indsl. Engrs., Soc. Indsl. and Applied Math., Math. Assn. Am. Republican. Baptist. Author: The Algebra of Random Variables, 1979; contbr. articles to profl. jours. Home: 805 Crestwood St Springdale AR 72764 Office: Indsl Engring Dept U Ark Fayetteville AR 72701

SPRINKLE, ROBERT LEE, JR., podiatrist; b. Winston-Salem, N.C., July 13, 1932; s. Robert Lee and Elton Elizabeth Sprinkle; children—Robert, Karen, Ralph, Richard, Roy, Randy, Drouin. Student Salem Coll., 1952; B.S., Ohio Coll. Podiatry, 1956; D.P.M., Pa. Coll. Podiatry, 1970. Pvt. practice podiatry, Winston-Salem, 1957—; chmn. N.C. Bd. Podiatry Examiners, 1968-74. Chmn. Mayor's Com. on Hiring the Handicapped, 1963-64; commr. Old Hickory council Boy Scouts Am., 1970-71, v.p., 1973-74, Silver Beaver award, 1969; pres. St. Leo's Parochial Sch. PTA, 1969-70; dir. Half Way House, 1965-66; chmn. Bishop McGuiness PTA, 1976. Paul Harris fellow Rotary Internat., 1971-72; grantee Schering, Inc., 1972-74; recipient St. George medal, 1971. Mem. Am. Podiatry Assn., N.C. Podiatry Assn. (past pres.), Piedmont Podiatry Assn., Am. Pub. Health Assn., Internat. Analgesia Soc. Democrat. Roman Catholic. Clubs: Forsyth Country, Twin City, Stratford Rotary (pres. 1971-72, dist. gov. 1976-77) Ardmore Community. Home: 1930 Swaim Rd Winston-Salem NC 27107 Office: PO Box 5442 2240 Cloverdale Ave Profl Bldg Suite 216 Winston-Salem NC 27113

SPROAT, JOHN GERALD, historian, educator; b. Los Angeles, Apr. 1, 1921; s. John Gerald and Grace (Elwell) Drummond S.; B.A., San Jose State Coll., 1950; M.A., U. Calif., Berkeley, 1952, Ph.D., 1959; m. Ruth Christensen, Mar. 18, 1967; 1 dau. by previous marriage, Barbara. Instr., Mich. State U., 1956-57; asst. prof. Williams Coll., 1957-63; prof. Lake Forest (Ill.) Coll., 1963-74; prof. history U. S.C., Columbia, 1974—, chmn. dept., 1974-83; Fulbright prof. Hamburg (Germany) U., 1961-62; vis. fellow Cambridge (Eng.) U., 1970; vis. prof. U. Calif., Berkeley, 1972; Fulbright prof. U. Munich (Germany), 1982; mem. S.C. Commn. Archives and History, 1974-83, chmn., 1979-83; mem. S.C. Bd. Rev. Hist. Places, 1974—, chmn., 1978-83. Pres., trustee Columbia Mus. Art. Served with USAAF, 1941-45. Nat. Endowment Humanities grantee, 1976, 77, 79, 85-86; Shell Found. grantee, 1967, 70, 73; Lilly Endowment grantee, 1966-67. Mem. Am. Hist. Assn., Orgn. Am. Historians, So. Hist. Assn., Nat. Trust Hist. Preservation. Episcopalian. Clubs: Palmetto (Columbia); Caxton (Chgo.). Author: The Best Men: Liberal Reformers in the Gilded Age, 1968; (with others) The Shaping of America, 1972; contbr. chpts. to books; exec. producer A Bond of Iron, S.C. ETV, 1979. Home: 1686 Woodlake Dr Columbia SC 29206 Office: Dept History U South Carolina Columbia SC 29208

SPROUSE, JAMES MARSHALL, federal judge; b. Williamson, W.Va., Dec. 3, 1923; s. James and Garnet (Lawson) S.; grad. St. Bonaventure (N.Y.) U., 1947; LL.B., Columbia U., 1949; postgrad. in internat. law U. Bordeaux (France), 1950; m. June Dolores Burt, Sept. 25, 1952; children—Tracy Sprouse Ferguson, Jeffrey Marshall, Andrew Michael, Sherry Lee, Shelly Lynn. Admitted to W.Va. bar; agt. CIA, 1952-57; pvt. practice, W.Va., 1957-73, 75-79, asst. atty. gen. State of W.Va., 1949; justice W.Va. Supreme Ct. Appeals, 1972-75; judge U.S. Circuit Ct. Appeals 4th Circuit, Charleston, 1979—. Served with AUS, 1942-45. Fulbright scholar. Mem. ABA, W.Va. State Bar, W.Va. Bar Assn., W.Va. Trial Lawyers Assn., Kanawha County Bar Assn., VFW, Am. Legion. Democrat. Presbyterian. Clubs: Shriners. Aheppa. Home: Union WV 24983 Office: 122 N Court St Lewisburg WV 24901

SPURILL, HOWARD VERNON, clergyman, college official; b. South Norfolk, Va., Dec. 27, 1919; s. Veron B. and Mabel E. (Kirby) S.; m. Daisy Lee Singleton, Dec. 11, 1943; 1 child, Ruth Elaine, B.S., Valley Forge Christian Coll., 1977; M.Div., Luther Rice Sem., 1978, D.Min., 1980. Ordained to ministry Assemblies of God Ch., 1953. Auditor, U.S. Navy, Little Creek, Va., 1945-50; pastor Elk Garden, W.Va., 1950-52, Emporia, Va., 1952-57, Manassas, Va., 1957-69, dist. sec., treas., 1968-74; pastor, Silver Springs, Md., 1974-79; dist. supt. Potomac Dist. Council, Assemblies of God Ch., 1979—; pres. Valley Forge Christian Coll., 1982; chmn. bd. regents, 1968—; pres. Prince William County Ministerial Assn., 1966-68. Served with U.S. Army, 1937-45. Author: Deacon Servant to God and Man, 1980. Home: 4371 Harvester Farm Ln Fairfax VA 22032 Office: PO Box 518 Fairfax VA 22030

SPURLIN, CHARLES DENNIS, history educator; b. Franklin, Tex., Aug. 4, 1932; s. Robert Jerry and Effie Mae (Freeman) S.; m. Patricia Agnes Liston, Nov. 26, 1953; children—Cynthia Ann, Debra Sue, Charles Dennis, Preston David, Steven Michael. B.A., Tex. Tech Coll., 1956; M.A., Sam Houston State U., 1961. Teaching asst. Sam Houston State U., Huntsville, Tex., 1960-61; instr. history and govt. Victoria Coll., Tex., 1961-76, chmn. dept. social scis., 1976—. Author: West of the Mississippi with Waller's 13th Texas Cavalry Bn., CSA, 1971 (Jefferson Davis medal 1982); Historic Preservation Study and Plan: City of Victoria, Texas, 1980. Compiler (book) Texas Veterans in the Mexican War, 1984. Contbr. articles to profl. jours. Active local athletic orgns.; mem. steering com. S.W. Tex. State U. Parents' Club., 1980-81. Served to staff sgt. U.S. Army, 1951-54, Korea. Mem. South Tex. Social Studies Assn. (pres. 1983—), Tex. State Hist. Assn., Soc. Historians of Early Am. Republic, South Tex. Hist. Assn., Victoria County Hist. Commn. Democrat. Baptist. Lodge: Masons. Home: 2106 E Mistletoe Victoria TX 77901 Office: Victoria Coll 2200 E Red River Victoria TX 77901

SQUIRE, MATTIE LUE, educator; b. Goshen, Ala., Jan. 1, 1925; d. Brunie and Bertha M. (Smith) Sconions; m. Robert L. Squire, July 31, 1940; children—Barbara L., Madelyn C., Linda A., Robert L. A.A., Miami Dade Coll., 1970; B.S., Fla. Internat. U., 1973, M.S., 1974. Sch. lunch cashier, maid Dade County Pub. Schs., Miami, Fla., 1957-64, tchr.'s aide, 1964-69, tchr. asst., 1969-73, tchr., 1973—; mgr. New Century Reading Lab., 1975-76, mgr. Title I Reading Lab., 1976-79. Chmn. Miami Women's Com. of 100, 1980; bd. dirs. Brownsville Neighborhood Civic Assn., Miami, 1975; founder Back to Coll. Brunch, Miami, 1960; founder Israel Bethel P.B. Ch. Scholarship Fund, Miami, 1980, also Sunday Sch. tchr., 1942—. Recipient Cert. of Achievement, Fla. Internat. U., Miami, 1974. Mem. AAUW, Fla. Fedn. Bus. and Prof. Women's Clubs, Dade Fedn. Bus. and Profl. Women's Clubs (Woman of Yr. 1981), Fla. State Reading Council, Epsilon Tau Lambda.

SQUIRES, JAMES RALPH, constrn. co. exec.; b. Dillon, S.C., Jan. 2, 1940; s. William Guilford and Ruby Alice (Whittington) S.; student public schs., Charlotte, N.C.; m. Ann Newton, Apr. 17, 1965; children—Samuel Guilford, James Drew. With Squires Constrn. Co., 1959-62; pres. SBS Builders, Inc., Charlotte, 1968-70; pres. Ralph Squires Homes, Charlotte, 1970—, Squires & Assos., Realtors, 1975—, JRS Enterprises, Inc., 1976—. Mem. Charlotte Tree Commn., 1977; bd. dirs. Athletic Found. U. N.C., Charlotte, 1979, Providence Day Sch., 1981-84, Better Bus. Bur., 1983; appointee pub. mem. N.C. State Bar; pres. Metrolina Home Owners, 1982, bd. dirs., 1983; bd. govs. Polit. Action Com for Building Industry. Recipient Profile award N.C. Blue Cross/Blue Shield, 1974, Albert Gallatin merit cert., 1974. Mem. Charlotte Homebuilders Assn. (pres. 1974), N.C. Home Builders Assn. (v.p. 1975), Nat. Homebuilders Assn., Charlotte Bd. Realtors. Republican. Baptist. Club: Charlotte Athletic. Home: 736 Sardis Ln Charlotte NC 28211 Office: 6809 Orchard Ridge Dr Charlotte NC 28212

SRIGLEY-SEITSINGER, GRETCHEN HEDGES, hospital administrator; b. Ashville, Ohio, Apr. 11, 1919; d. Richard Harrison and Sarah Anne (Millar) Hedges; m. Robert Sprague Srigley, Nov. 14, 1943 (dec. 1973); children—Robert, Pamela, Penelope; m. Ralph Emerson Seitsinger, Jan. 27, 1984; stepchildren—Eddie, Jean, Patsy, Richard, Carol. B.S., Ohio State U., 1940; M.B.A., Central State U., Edmond, Okla., 1979, M.Ed., 1980. Head bacteriologist Children's Hosp., Columbus, Ohio, 1939-43; owner Srigley Labs., Columbus, 1943-45; ptnr. Srigley Hosp. and Lab., Hollis, Okla., 1945-72; exec. dir. Maynard McDougall Hosp., Nome, Alaska, 1975-77, Newark Methodist Hosp., El Paso, Tex., 1979—; bd. dirs. Norton Sound Health Corp., Nome,

1976-77. Mem. Am. Coll. Hosp. Adminstrs., Hosp. Council, Wesleyan Hosp. Assn., DAR (regent 1945—), Alpha Zi Delta, Alpha Kappa Delta. Republican. Methodist. Avocations: gardening, serving, golfing. Office: Newark Methodist Hosp-Houchen Community Ctr 1109 E 5th Ave El Paso TX 79901

STAATS, M'LOU BARNETT, nursing educator, researcher; b. Shreveport, La., Oct. 1, 1954; d. Charles Lee and Anne (Runyon) Barnett; m. Thomas E. Staats, July 7, 1978; children—Lauren Malu, Kara Kristyn. B.S. in Nursing, Northwestern State U., Natchitoches, La., 1976; M.S. in Nursing, Tex. State Woman's U., 1981. Head nurse evening shift ICU, Willis-Knighton Hosp., Shreveport, 1976-77; burn clin. nurse specialist La. State U. Med. Ctr., Shreveport, 1981; instr. Northwestern State U. Coll. Nursing, Shreveport, 1981—; research asst. Drs. Psychol. Ctr., 1984—; lectr. in field; clin supr. to nursing students in surg., neurol. and burn ICU's; nursing student's supr. Health Fair. Vol. Services for Aged, 1976-77, ARC, 1983; mem. La. Gov.'s Com. of 1000, 1983. Mem. Grad. Student Assn. Tex. Women's U. (v.p.), Am. Nurses Assn., Am. Burn Assn., Am. Assn. Biofeedback Clinicians, Am. Assn. Critical Care Nurses, La. Biofeedback Soc., Alumni Assn. Northwestern State U. Sigma Theta Tau. Episcopalian. Club: Shreveport Hi-Noon Toastmasters. Contbr. articles to nursing, psychol. and burn jours. Office: Northwestern State U Coll Nursing 1800 Warrington Pl Shreveport LA 71101

STAATS, THOMAS ELWYN, psychologist; b. Marietta, Ohio; s. Percy Anderson and Julia (Bourmorck) S.; m. M'Lou Denise Barnett, July 7, 1978; children—Lauren Malu, Kara Kristyn. B.A. cum laude, Emory U., 1970; M.A., U. Ala., 1972, Ph.D., 1974. Lic. psychologist. Dir., chief psychologist Caddo Parish Diagnostic Ctr., Shreveport, La., 1974-81; exec. dir. Doctors Psychol. Ctr., Shreveport, 1979—; v.p. research and devel. Medicomp, Inc., Shreveport, 1981—, Applied Stress Research Assocs., Shreveport, 1983—; clin. asst. prof. psychology La. State U., Shreveport, 1977—, clin. asst. prof. psychiatry Sch. Medicine, 1980—. Author: Manual For the Stress Vector Analysis Test Series, 1983; Stress Management and Relaxation Training System Handbook. Contbr. articles to profl. jours. Mem. Gov's. Com. of 1000, La., 1979—. U. Ala. Grad. Research Council fellow, 1974. Mem. Am. Psychol. Assn., Biofeedback Soc. Am., Am. Assn. Biofeedback Clinicians, La. Biofeedback Soc., La. Psychol. Assn. Republican. Episcopalian. Avocations: scuba diving; gun collecting; camping; boating; water skiing. Home: 2834 Oak Mont Circle Shreveport LA 71119 Office: Doctors Psychol Ctr 3300 Virginia Ave 2 Shreveport LA 71103

STABLER, JOHN ROBERTS, psychologist, educator; b. New Rochelle, N.Y., Apr. 11, 1932; s. Charles Norman and Elizabeth (Miller) S.; m. Joan Obrist, Oct. 13, 1955; children—Hetty Suzanne, John Michael. B.A., Antioch Coll., 1956; M.A., So. Methodist U., 1958; Ph.D., U. Tex., 1961. Asst. prof. psychology La. State U., Baton Rouge, 1961-68, assoc. prof., 1968-69, dir. Office Child Research, 1963-69; vis. prof. So. U., Baton Rouge, 1964-65; assoc. prof. psychology Ga. State U., Atlanta, 1969—, dir. Office Devel. Research, 1971-76. Served with U.S. Army, 1955-57. Lic. psychologist, Ga. Mem. Am. Psychol. Assn., AAUP, Assn. Gerontology in Higher Edn., Assn. Gen. and Liberal Studies, Adult Edn. Assn. Home: 2072 Clairmont Terr Atlanta GA 30345 Office: Dept Psychology Ga State U Atlanta GA 30303

STACK, CHARLES RICKMAN, lawyer; b. Boston, Sept. 26, 1935; s. John Joseph and Caroline Bernadett (Rickman) S.; m. Barbara Alice Levine, Oct. 12, 1963; children—Caroline K., Kevin C., Constance K. B.S. in Bus. Adminstrn., U. Fla. 1957, J.D., 1960; diplomate Nat. Bd. Trial Advocacy; cert. Fla. Bd. Trial Certification. Bar: Fla. 1960, U.S. dist. ct. (so. dist.) Fla. 1960. Assoc. Macfarlane, Ferguson, Allison & Kelly, Tampa, Fla., 1960-62; ptnr. High, Stack, Lazenby, Bender, Palahach & Lacasa, Miami, Fla., 1962—, sr. ptnr. 1968—; mem., sec. U.S. Dist. Ct. Peer Rev. commn., 1983—; instr. bus. law U. South Fla. 1960-62; instr. comml. law Am. Inst. Banking, Tampa, 1960-62. Chmn. Fla. Jud. Nominations Commn. for 11th Cir., 1970-76; Dade County campaign chmn. Ruebin Askew for Gov., 1970, Steve Clark for Mayor, 1972; mem. Fla. Constn. Revision Com., 1968; chmn. Fla. Corp. Income Tax Com., 1972; mem. Fla. Democratic Conv. Com., 1972; chmn. Fla. Bar Legis. Com. 11th cir., 1978-79; chmn. Dade County Legis. Com., 1978-79; chmn. Fla. Bar Jud. Tenure Commn., 1972-73; mem. City of Miami Downtown Devel. Authority, 1979-82. Roscoe Pound Found. fellow. Mem. ABA (tort and ins. sect.) Fla. Bar, Am. Trial Lawyers Assn., Lawyers for Pub. Justice, Acad. Fla. Trial Lawyers, Tex. Trial Lawyers, Dade County Trial Lawyers, Com. of 100, Dade County Bar Assn., Am. Arbitration Assn., Am. Judicature Soc., Brevard County Bar Assn. Democrat. Episcopalian. Clubs: Univ. (Miami); Riviera Country (Coral Gables, Fla.). Contbr. numerous articles to profl. jours. Home: 11900 SW 67th Ct Miami FL 33156 Office: 3929 Ponce de Leon Blvd Coral Gables FL 33134

STACK, HORACE WAYNE, JR., city official, educator; b. Houston, July 20, 1948; s. Horace Wayne and Marie LaVerne (Odom) S.; m. Thelma Ann Mulvihill, June 18, 1968; 1 child, Christopher Wayne. Student in Engring., U. Houston, 1966-69; student in Fire Protection, San Jacinto Coll., 1979-80. Cert. instr. of firefighters, advanced firefighter, Tex. Engring. designer Schlumberger, Houston, 1968-80; fire chief City of Deer Park, Tex., 1980—; guest instr. Tex. A&M U., 1982—; cons. fire protection program San Jacinto Coll., 1984—. Contbr. articles to fire jours. Recipient Meritorious Service award Am. Legion, 1977; named Outstanding Firefighter, Jaycees, Deer Park, 1980. Mem. Nat. Fire Protection Assn., Tex. State Firemen's Assn., Harris County Firefighters Assn. (pres. 1983—), Internat. Assn. Fire Chiefs, Internat. Soc. Fire Service Instrs. Republican. Methodist. Avocation: Golf. Office: City of Deer Park 1302 Center St Deer Park TX 77536

STACK, SAMUEL FREDERICK, JR., clinical laboratory scientist; b. Greer, S.C., Dec. 27, 1954; s. Samuel Frederick and Mary Evelyn (Bryson) S.; m. Linda Jean Shelley, Aug. 9, 1980; children—Mary Katherine, Ashley Elizabeth. B.A., Furman U., 1977; M.Ed., U. S.C., 1984, postgrad., 1985—. Med. technologist T.R. Wilson Lab., Greenville Hosp. System, S.C., 1978-80, Allen Bennett Hosp., Greer, S.C., 1981—. Mem. Am. Sociol. Assn., Arabian Horse Registry, U.S. Soccer Fedn., SCV, (state officer 1984). Democrat. Baptist. Avocations: playing 5 musical instruments; soccer; tennis; snow skiing; golf; horses. Home: 200 Maplewood Circle Greer SC 29651 Office: Allen Bennett Hosp Meml Dr Greer SC 29651

STACY, DENNIS WILLIAM, architect; b. Council Bluffs, Iowa, Sept. 22, 1945; s. William L. and Mildred Glee (Carlsen) S.; B.Arch., Iowa State U., 1969; postgrad. U. Nebr., Omaha Grad. Coll., 1972; m. Judy Annette Long, Dec. 28, 1968. Designer Troy & Stalder Architects, Omaha, 1967, Architects Assos., Des Moines, 1968-69, Logsdon & Voelter Architects, Temple, Tex., 1970; project architect Roger Schutte & Assocs., Omaha, 1972-73; architect, asso. Robert H. Burgin & Assocs., Council Bluffs, 1973-75, Neil Astle & Assocs., Omaha, 1975-78; owner, prin. Dennis W. Stacy, AIA, Architect, Glenwood, Iowa, 1978-81, Dallas, 1981—. Chmn., Glenwood Zoning Bd. Adjustment, 1979-81; chmn. Mills County Plant Iowa Program, 1979-81; mem. Southwest Iowa Citizen's Adv. Com., Iowa State Dept. Transp., 1977-81; regional screening chmn. Am. Field Service Internat./Intercultural Programs, 1974-79, Iowa-Nebr. rep., 1978-80. Served with U.S. Army, 1969-71. Decorated Nat. Def. Service medal, Vietnam Service medal, Vietnam Campaign medal, Army Commendation medal; recipient Iowa AIA award, 1981; registered architect, Iowa, Tex., Colo., Mo. Mem. AIA, Nat. Council Archtl. Registration Bds., Dallas Mus. Fine Arts, Mus. Modern Art, Kimball Art Mus., The 500 Inc. (Outstanding Mem. 1985). Clubs: Glenwood Optimist (Disting. Service award 1982, pres. 1980-81), Masons. Archtl. works include Davies Amphitheater, 1980; Maher Law Office, 1981; Pizza Factory, 1983; La Fountain Centre Office Bldgs., 1985; The Colonnade Office Bldgs., 1985; Fairview Recreation Ctr., 1984. Home: 4148 Cobblers Ln Dallas TX 75252 Office: 3939 Belt Line Rd Suite 717 Dallas TX 75244

STACY, FORREST FARREL, JR., power company executive; b. Winfield, Kans., Sept. 23, 1941; s. Forrest Farrel and Virginia (Hamm) S.; m. Carolyn Sue Gann, July 8, 1960; children—Christopher Scott, Gregg Wesley. A.A. in Elec. Power, Okla. State U., 1962; M.B.A., Ga. State U., 1982. Project engr. C.H. Guernsey & Co., Oklahoma City, 1962-69, Ulteig Engr., Inc., Mpls., 1969-70; mgr. engring. Central Iowa Power Coop., Marion, 1970-74; gen. mgr. Oglethorpe Power Corp., Atlanta, 1974—; Ga. Rural Electric Coops. rep. People to People del. Republic of China, 1982; chmn. Southeastern Power Resources Commn., 1974—; dir. Advanced Reactor Corp.; stockholders' adv. com. Columbia Bank for Coops. Mem. Nat. G and T Mgrs. Assn. (2d vice chmn.), Nat. Rural Electric Coop. Assn. (chmn. com. on joint ownership, chmn. nat. preference customer com.), Am. Nuclear Soc. Home: 1948 Harbor Oaks Dr Snellville GA 30278 Office: Oglethorpe Power Corp 2100 E Exchange Pl PO Box 1349 Tucker GA 30085

STACY, GALEN DWIGHT, chemical engineer; b. Pittsburg, Kans., Sept. 19, 1934; s. Carl Edward and Faye Victoria (Helms) S.; B.S. in Phys. Scis., Pittsburg State U., 1956; M.S. in Engring., Okla. State U., 1971; m. Nancy Marilyn Wagner, Dec. 22, 1954; children—Galen Charles, David Neil, Douglas Paul. Engr., sr. engr. Phillips Petroleum Co., Bartlesville, Okla., 1962-68; mgr. systems programming and mgr. chem. projects sects. Applied Automation Inc., Bartlesville, 1968-75, dir. process studies br., 1975-76, spl. asst. to mktg. dir., 1976-78, dir. computer applications br., 1978-80, dir. Optrol Products br., 1980-83, mktg. product mgr., 1983-84, dir. mktg. and product planning, 1984—. Served to lt. USN, 1956-62. Registered profl. engr., Calif. Mem. Instrument Soc. Am. (sr.), Am. Inst. Chem. Engrs. Home: 2435 Locust Rd Bartlesville OK 74003 Office: Applied Automation Inc 324 E & A Pawhuska Rd Bartlesville OK 74004

STACY, TED THEODORE, state senator, insurance agency executive; b. Grundy, Va., Mar. 10, 1923; s. Samuel Mathew and Eleventha (Smith) S.; m. Elizabeth Ann Barnette, 1960; 1 son, Larry Ted. A.B.A., Beckley Coll., 1952; B.S., Morris Harvey Coll., 1968; LL.B., LaSalle Extension U., 1969. Owner, mgr. Gen. Ins. Agy., Beckley, W.Va., 1948—; mem. W.Va. Ho. of Dels., 1958-80, W.Va. Senate, 1982—. Served to cpl. U.S. Army, 1940-45, PTO. Democrat. Methodist. Lodges: Shriners, Masons. Office: WVa Senate State Capitol Charleston WV 25305*

STADELMANN, RICHARD WILLIAM, clergyman, educator; b. Lynn, Mass., Dec. 16, 1932; s. William Louis and Olga Ann (Halbich) S.; B.A., Earlham Coll., 1954; M.Div., Yale, 1958; postgrad. Tulane, 1960-65; m. Bonnie Sue Shelton, June 16, 1956 (div. Dec. 1972); children—Marcus Richard, Lowell Shelton, Mary Idell, Kristine Marie; m. 2d, Patricia Annette Perry, June 12, 1976; children—Olga Gertrude, Greta Katryn; stepchildren—Aimee Elizabeth, Lisa Annette. Ordained minister Christian Ch., 1954; minister Bethel Christian Ch., Fountain City, Ind., 1952-54, Perry (Ohio) Christian Ch., 1958-60; instr. Tulane, 1962-63, La. State U., New Orleans, 1963-67; asst. prof. philosophy Tex. A & M U., College Station, 1967—; minister Brenham (Tex.) Christian Ch., 1968-76, Smithville (Tex.) Christian Ch., 1978-80. County chmn. Burleson County Republican party, 1973-74, county vice-chmn. Brazos County, 1974-84. Served with USNR, 1958. Lindemuth scholar, 1950-54; Elk scholar, 1950-54; Am. Legion scholar, 1950-54; Yale U. scholar, 1957-58; Tulane scholar, 1960-65; recipient Downes award, 1958. Mem. AAUP (pres. 1971-72), Am. Philos. Assn., Metaphys. Soc. Am., Soc. Process Studies, Southwestern Philos. Soc., Am. Forensic Assn., Assocs. for Religion and Intellectual Life, Soc. Christian Philosophers, Tau Kappa Alpha. Home: Route 5 Box 57 Brenham TX 77833 Office: Dept Philosophy Tex A & M Univ College Station TX 77843

STADER, WILLIAM EARL, safety engineer; b. Christiansburg, Va., Aug. 17, 1937; s. William Earl and Gillie (Kanode) S.; m. Elayne Snyder, Dec. 17, 1956; children—Gregory Dean, Sandra Renee, Stacy Elayne, William Barry. B.S. in Bus. Adminstrn., Va. Poly. Inst. and State U., 1958. Cert. hazard control mgr. Engr., Factory Ins. Assn., Charlotte, N.C., 1957-66; fire protection specialist Travelers Ins. Co., Charlotte, 1966-72; div. supr. Allstate Ins. Co., Roanoke, Va., 1972-79, Aetna Ins. Co., Roanoke, Va., 1979—. Mem. Am. Soc. Safety Engrs. Democrat. Baptist. Avocations: golf; fishing. Home: 4464 Oleva St Roanoke VA 24017

STAFFELBACH, ANDRE, interior designer; b. Chur, Switzerland, July 24, 1939; came to U.S., 1962; s. Jacob and Anna (Della-Bella) S.; m. Jewel Van Beber, May 24, 1969; children—Anna Lisa, Deon Andre. Apprentice in Interior Design, Chur, 1955-59; Profl. Degree in Interior Architecture, Kunstgewerbeschule, Zurich, Switzerland, 1960-61. Interior architect Sporri Interiors, Zurich, 1960-62; interior designer E.R. Cole, N.Y.C., 1962-63, Town House Interiors, Chgo., 1963-65, Weston's, Dallas, 1965-66; pres. Andre Staffelbach Designs, Dallas, 1966—; cons. Nat. Endowment Arts, Washington, 1976. Served with Swiss Army, 1959-62. Recipient Giants 100 award Interior Design Mag., 1983-85; fellow Inst. Bus. Designers, Chgo., 1977. Mem. Inst. Bus. Designers (nat. pres. 1975-77), Nat. Council Interior Design (council 1981-83, nat. pres. 1984), Am. Soc. Interior Designers. Republican. Avocations: running; snow skiing. Home: 3116 Southwestern St Dallas TX 75225 Office: 2525 Carlisle Dallas TX 75201

STAFFINS, RALPH CALVIN, JR., iron company executive; b. Atlanta, Dec. 13, 1949; s. Ralph Calvin and Gladys Charlene (Morgan) S.; m. Katherine Lee Anderson, Aug. 16, 1980; children—Ralph Calvin III, Gary Christopher. Grad. high sch. Clarkston, Ga., 1967. Vice pres. Artistic Ornamental Iron Co., Inc., Atlanta, 1969—. Lt. col. Gov.'s Staff, State of Ga., 1983—; dep. lt. Sheriff Dekalb County, Ga., 1985. Mem. Nat. Ornamental Miscellaneous Metal Assn., Greater Atlanta Ornamental Iron and Miscellaneous Metal Mfrs. Assn. Democrat. Methodist. Avocations: hunting; fishing. Office: Artistic Ornamental Iron Co Inc 1977 College Ave NE Atlanta GA 30317

STAFFORD, BEVERLY LOUISE, health and physical education educator; b. Cheneyville, La., Jan. 7, 1928; d. William Roland and Ione (Hulsey) S.; B.S., U. Southwestern La., 1950; M.S., La. State U., 1955, Ed.D., 1969. Tchr., coach Avoyeles Parish, Bunkie, La., 1949-52, Rapides Parish, Pineville, La., 1952-56, 58-65; prof. U. Southeastern La., Hammond, 1956-57; dir. womens programs U. So. Miss., Hattiesburg, 1967-72; head dept. health and phys. edn. Nicholls State U., Thibodaux, La., 1972—. Named Outstanding Alumna, U. Southwestern La., 1985. Mem. La. Assn. Health, Phys. Edn., Recreation and Dance (pres. 1965-66, honor award 1977), Am. Alliance Health, Phys. Edn., Recreation and Dance. Democrat. Baptist. Avocations: gardening; fishing; walking; tennis; antique refinishing. Home: 203 Melrose Dr Thibodaux LA 70301 Office: Dept Health and Phys Edn Nicholls State U Thibodaux LA 70301

STAFFORD, DONALD GENE, chemistry educator; b. Valliant, Okla., Oct. 9, 1930; s. Otto Lewis and Rose (Osterdock) S.; m. Jane Wright, July 5, 1951; children—Michael, Robert, Joel. B.S. in Math., U. Okla., 1957; M.S. in Chemistry, Okla. State U., 1961; Ph.D. in Sci., U. Okla., 1969. Prof. chemistry East Central U., Ada, Okla., 1961—; cons. U. Calif.-Berkeley, 1965-67; adj. prof. U. Okla., Norman, 1968-85. Author: Learning Science, 1977; Teaching Science, 1977; Physical Science, 1978; Science: Teaching and Learning, 1978. Contbr. articles to profl. jours. Served to sgt. U.S. Army, 1948-53. Mem. Am. Chem. Soc., Nat. Sci. Tchrs. Assn., Okla. Sci. Tchrs. Assn. (pres. 1972, 80), Sigma Xi. So. Baptist. Lodge: Lions. Home: 2202 Fullview Ada OK 74820 Office: East Central U Ada OK 74820

STAFFORD, JAMES FRANCIS, bishop; b. Balt., July 26, 1932; s. F. Emmett and Mary Dorothy Stafford. Student Loyola Coll., 1950-52; B.A., St. Mary Sem., 1954; S.T.B., S.T.L., Gregorian U., Rome, 1958; M.S.W., Catholic U., 1964; postgrad. Rutgers U. Ctr. for Alcohol Studies, 1963, Mgmt. Inst. U. Wis., 1969, St. Mary's Sem. and U., 1973-75. Spiritual moderator Soc. St. Vincent de Paul, Balt., 1965-76, Ladies of Charity, Balt., 1966-76; dir. Assn. Cath. Charities, Balt., 1966-76; urban vicar Archdiocese of Balt., 1966-76, vicar gen., 1976-83; archdiocesan liaison to Md. Cath. Conf., Balt., 1975-78; Cath. bishop Diocese of Memphis, 1983—. Contbr. articles to profl. jours. Trustee Good Samaritan Hosp., Balt., 1973-76, chmn. com. to study use of bequest funds, 1975—; trustee Balt. Urban coalition, 1970-75, Blue Cross/Md., Inc., 1973-76; bd. dirs. U. Md. Sch. Social Work and Planning, 1973-76. Named Alumni Laureate, Loyola Coll., 1979; recipient Father Kelly Alumni award Loyola High Sch., 1978. Mem. World Methodist Conf./Roman Catholic Dialogue (co-chmn. 1977—), Oriental Orthodox/Roman Catholic Consultation (co-chmn. 1977-85), Lutheran/Roman Catholic Dialogue (co-chmn. 1985—), Nat. Conf. Catholic Bishops (bishops' com. for ecumenical and interreligious affairs 1980, Internat. Synod of Bishops Rome/White House Conf. on Family 1980, adminstrv. bd. 1985). Office: PO Box 41679 Memphis TN 38174

STAFFORD, JAMES POLK, JR., civil engr.; b. Oxford, Miss., Oct. 13, 1918; s. James Polk and Lottie Etoile (Smith) S.; B.S., Miss. State Coll., 1939; M.S., Iowa State Coll., 1940; m. Edna Earle Snyder, May 29, 1941; children—Jeanette Patricia, Pamela Anne, James Polk III. Engr., Soil Conservation Service, U.S. Dept. Agr., 1940, 46; civil engr. office engring. br., constrn. div. U.S. Army Engr. Dist., Vicksburg, Miss., 1947-62, resident engr. DeGray Dam, 1963-72, chief constrn. div., 1973—. Pres., Cooper High Sch. PTA, 1962, Arkadelphia High Sch. Booster Club, 1967, Vicksburg Community Chorus, 1975-76. Served with U.S. Army, 1941-45. Recipient George Marshall Scholastic award Command and Gen. Staff Coll., 1963; Meritorious Service medal U.S. Army Reserve, 1973. Mem. Soc. Am. Mil. Engrs. (Goethals award 1974), ASCE, U.S. Com. on Large Dams. Registered profl. engr., Miss. Methodist. Club: Lions. Home: 326 McAuley Dr Vicksburg MS 39180 Office: PO Box 60 Vicksburg MS 39180

STAFFORD, JOHN FRANK, research corp. exec.; b. Detroit, June 28, 1924; s. Frank Williams and Bessie Edith (Erdmann) S.; A.B., Albion Coll., 1951; postgrad. U. Mainz, Germany, 1962; m. Alice Lucille Dowell, June 4, 1955; children—Frank J., Julie A. Chemist technician U. Ariz., Tucson, 1963-65; chief chemist tertiary treatment project City of Tucson, 1965-70; supr., analytical chemist Los Angeles County San. Dist., 1970-71; facility chemist, lab. supr. Burns & Roe, Inc., Yuma, Ariz., 1972-77, Planning Research Corp., Yuma, 1977-78; lab. supervising chemist water and power U.S. Naval Base, Guantanamo Bay, Cuba, 1978—; mem. task force revision Standard Methods of Analysis for Water and Wastewater, 16th edit., 1980-81. Bd. dirs. Taxpayers Action Group (Ariz.); bd. dirs., treas., Ariz., United Cerebral Palsy, 1965-66; res. detective Sheriff's Dept. Pima County, Ariz., 1965-70. Mem. Water Pollution Control Fedn., Am. Water Works Assn., Nat. Sheriffs Assn., Theta Nu Epsilon. Clubs: Hockenlockers (Petoskey, Mich.); Translator chem. sect. Intersexualitat, 1962. Home: 19731 Redroot Dr Houston TX 77084 Office: PO Box 47 FBPO Norfolk VA 23593

STAFFORD, RICHARD RAYMOND, clinical psychologist, educator; b. Andrews, Tex., July 30, 1948; s. Vernon Cecil and Xantippe (Ramsey) S.; 1 dau. by previous marriage—Tanya Shay. B.A., Tex. Tech U., 1972, Ph.D., 1978; M.Ed., Stephen F. Austin U., 1973. Counselor, Community Ctr., Nacogdoches, Tex., 1973; diagnostician Lubbock (Tex.) Ind. Sch. Dist., 1973-75; instr. reading and study skills Tex. Tech U., Lubbock, 1974-76; counselor Slaton (Tex.) Ind. Sch. Dist., 1974-76; intern, resident in psychology Olin E. Teague VA Ctr., Temple, Tex., 1976-78; dir. Mental Health Ctr., Plainview, Tex., 1978-80; instr. So. Plains Jr. Coll., Plainview, 1978-79; pvt. practice clin. psychology, Plainview, 1979-82; vis. prof. Tex. Tech U., Lubbock, 1979—; asst. chief psychology Big Spring State Hosp., 1982—. Pres., Hale County Council Alcohol Abuse, 1982, treas., 1979-81; mem. adv. bd. Parents Without Ptnrs., 1982; steering com. Plainview Rape Crisis Ctr.; mem. Plainview Civic Theatre, Plainview Community Concerts, Baptist Brotherhood. State of Tex. grantee on Alcoholism, 1973. Mem. Am. Psychol. Assn., Tex. Psychol. Assn., West Tex. Adlerian Soc., N.Am. Soc. Adlerian Psychology, Biofeedback Soc. Am., Am. Soc. Clin. Hypnosis. Baptist. Lodge: Rotary. Home: PO Box 3628 Big Spring TX 79720 Office: 306 W 3d St Big Spring TX 79720

STAFFORD, WILLIAM HENRY, JR., federal judge; b. Masury, Ohio, May 11, 1931; s. William Henry and Frieda Gertrude (Nau) S.; B.S., Temple U., 1953, LL.B., 1956 (J.D., 1968); m. Nancy Marie Helman, July 11, 1959; children—William Henry, Donald Helman, David Harrold. Admitted to Fla. bar, 1961, U.S. Supreme Ct. bar, 1970, U.S. 5th Circuit Ct. Appeals bar, 1969; asso. firm Robinson & Roark, Pensacola, 1961-64; individual practice law, Pensacola, 1964-67; state atty., Pensacola, 1967-69; U.S. atty., Pensacola, 1969-75; U.S. dist. judge No. Dist. Fla., Tallahassee, 1975—, now chief judge; instr. Pensacola Jr. Coll., 1964, 68. Served to lt. (j.g.) USN, 1957-60. Mem. Am., Tallahassee bar assns., Fla. Bar (chmn. fed. funding com., mem. exec. council trial lawyers sect. 1972-75), Soc. Bar First Jud. Circuit Fla., Sigma Phi Epsilon, Phi Delta Phi. Republican. Episcopalian. Clubs: Masons, Shriners, Rotary, Pensacola Yacht. Office: US Courthouse 110 E Park Ave PO Box 1731 Tallahassee FL 32302*

STAGG, LOUIS CHARLES, educator; b. New Orleans, Jan. 3, 1933; s. Louis Anatol and Gladys (Andrews) S.; B.A. in English, La. Coll., 1955; M.A. in English U. Ark., 1957, Ph.D. in English, 1963; m. Mary Casner, June 5, 1959; children—Robert Charles, Helen Marie. Teaching asst. English U. Ark., 1955-59; asst. prof. William Jewell Coll., 1959-60; instr. Stephen F. Austin State U., 1960-62; asst. prof. Memphis State U., 1962-69, assoc. prof., 1969-77, prof., 1977—, dir. English Drama Players, 1968—, chmn. Renaissance Festival, 1986; cons. Nat. Endowment for Humanities, 1975, 76, 78, Ohio State U. Press, summer 1985, U. Jordan, Aman, 1985. Mem. Memphis Oratorio Soc. Chorus, 1969—. Recipient summer stipend Nat. Endowment for Humanities, 1967; Memphis State U. grantee, 1965—; travel grantee to U.S. Library of Congress, summer 1971. Mem. MLA, So. Humanities Conf. (sec.-treas. 1974-76, exec. com. 1976-83, chmn. sect. humanities in pluralistic society 1984), ad hoc com. on crisis in teaching humanities 1977—), Tenn. Philol. Assn. (pres. 1976-77, exec. com. 1977, local arrangements chmn. 1987), Marlowe Soc. Am. (book reviewer 1984, 86), Samuel Beckett Soc., Conf. on Christianity and Lit., Ark. Philol. Assn., Shakespeare Assn. Am. (local arrangements host com. 1985—), Internat. Shakespeare Assn., Medieval and Renaissance Drama Soc., Renaissance Soc. Am., South Central Renaissance Conf. (chmn. nominations 1976, exec. com. 1978-80, program com. 1981-83, chmn. sect. Shakespeare 1981, 16th Century lit. 1982, chmn. local arrangements 1983, symposium on humanism 1984, chmn. Shakespeare sect. 1985), South Central MLA (assoc. editor for English, South Central Bull. 1982-84, nominations com. 1985-86, book reviewer South Central Rev. 1983, 85), South Atlantic MLA, South Central Coll. English Assn. (sec.-treas. 1980-81, v.p. 1981-82, pres. 1982-83, exec. com. 1983—), Patristic Medieval and Renaissance Conf. Middle Atlantic States (sect. chmn. Medieval drama 1977), Am. Theatre Assn. (chmn. sect. combining Brit. lit. and theatre in teaching of drama 1983), AAUP, Phi Beta Kappa (pres. Memphis alumni chpt. 1985-87), Alpha Chi. Democrat. Episcopalian (lay reader 1969—). Author: (with J. Lasley Dameron) Poe's Critical Vocabulary, 1966; author series: Index To The Figurative Language of John Webster's Tragedies, 1967, of Ben Jonson's Tragedies, 1967, of Thomas Heywood's Tragedies, 1967, of George Chapman's Tragedies, 1970, of John Marston's Tragedies, 1970, of Thomas Middleton's Tragedies, 1970, of Cyril Tourneur's Tragedies, 2d edit. all 7 under title Index to the Figurative Language of the Tragedies of Shakespeare's Chief 17th Century Contemporaries 1977), 3d edit., 1982; Index to the Figurative Language of the Tragedies of Shakespeare's Chief 16th Century Contemporaries, 1984; contbr. to Great Writers of the English Language: Dramatists, 1979. Circulation editor Interpretations, 1976-80. Contbr. articles on English drama to profl. jours., publs. on Shakespeare. Home: 5219 Mason Rd Memphis TN 38117 Office: Dept English Memphis State U Memphis TN 38152

STAGG, TOM, judge; b. Shreveport, La., Jan. 19, 1923; s. Thomas Eaton and Beulah (Meyer) S.; B.A., La. State U., 1943, J.D., 1949; m. Margaret Mary O'Brien, Aug. 21, 1946; children—Julie, Margaret Mary. Admitted to La. bar, 1949; with firm Hargrove, Guyton, Van Hook & Hargrove, Shreveport, 1949-53; pvt. practice, Shreveport, 1953-58; sr. partner firm Stagg, Cady & Beard, Shreveport, 1958-74; U.S. dist. judge Western Dist. of La., 1974—, now chief judge. Pres., Abe Meyer Corp., 1960-74, Stagg Investments, Inc., 1964-74; mng. partner Pierremont Mall Shopping Center, 1963-74; v.p. King Hardware Co., 1955-74. Mem. Shreveport Airport Authority, 1967-73, chmn., 1970-73; chmn. Gov.'s Tidelands Adv. Council, 1969-70; del. La. Constl. Conv., 1973-74, chmn. rules com., com. on exec. dept.; mem. Gov.'s Adv. Com. on Offshore Revenues, 1972-74. Active Republican party, 1950-74, del. convs., 1956, 60, 64, 68, 72, mem. Nat. Com. for La., 1964-72, mem. exec. com., 1964-68. Pres., Shreveport Jr. C. of C., 1955-56; v.p. La. Jr. C. of C., 1956-57. Served to capt., inf. AUS, 1943-46; ETO. Decorated Bronze Star, Purple Heart with oak leaf cluster. Mem. Am., La., Shreveport bar assns., Photog. Soc. Am. Home: 4847 Camellia Ln Shreveport LA 71106 Office: US Court House Room 2B15 500 Fannin St Shreveport LA 71101

STAGGERS, HARLEY ORRIN, congressman; b. Keyser, W.Va., Aug. 3, 1907; s. Jacob Kinsey and Frances Winona (Cuberledge) S.; m. Mary Veronica Casey, Oct. 4, 1943; children—Margaret Ann, Mary Katherine, Frances Susan, Elizabeth Ellen, Harley Orrin, Daniel Casey. A.B., Emory and Henry Coll., 1931, LL.D., 1953; postgrad., Duke U., 1935; LL.D., Davis and Elkins Coll., 1969, W.Va. U., W.Va. Wesleyan Coll., 1971. Coach, tchr. sci. Norton High Sch., Va., 1931-33; head coach Potomac State Coll., Keyser, 1933-35; sheriff Mineral County, Keyser, 1937-41; right-of-way agt., Va. dir. Office Govt. Reports Later OWI, 1942; mem. 81st-99th congresses from 2d W.Va. Dist.; ret., 1981. Served as lt. comdr. AC USNR, 1942-46; ATP, PTO. Mem. W.Va. Farm Bur., Am. Legion, VFW, DAV, Amvets. Democrat. Methodist. Lodges: K.P.; Elks; Moose; Lions. Home: Keyser WV 26726

STAGNER, ROBERT ALLEN, research pharmacist; b. Washington, Iowa, Oct. 21, 1955; s. Vernon Gerrard and Eunice Evangeline (Craig) S.; m. Lorraine Marie Bloyer, Nov. 21, 1981; 1 child, Lindsay Yvonne. B.S. in Pharmacy, U. Iowa, 1979. Registered pharmacist, Iowa, N.C. Mgr. Johnson Pharmacy, Forest City, Iowa, 1979; staff pharmacist Clinic Pharmacy, Ames, Iowa, 1979-81; research pharmacist Burroughs Wellcome Co., Greenville, N.C.,

1981—. Contbr. articles to profl. jours. NSF grantee, 1978. Mem. Am. Pharm. Assn., Acad. Pharm. Scis., Boone Story County Pharmacists Assn. (v.p. 1981), Kappa Psi, Rho Chi. Republican. Methodist. Lodge: Masons. Avocations: camping; travel; music; sports. Office: Burroughs Wellcome Co PO Box 1887 Greenville NC 27834

STAHL, LOWELL JOHN, insurance company executive; b. New Brunswick, N.J., Dec. 31, 1933; s. Joseph Nicholas and Esther Elizabeth S.; m. Sharon Doolittle, Mar. 2, 1956; children—Jeffrey Glenn, Denise Cheri. B.S., U. Miami (Fla.), 1955; Ph.D., Century U., 1982. Cert. pilot. Commd. 2d lt. U.S. Air Force, 1955, advanced through grades to col. 1982; pilot, 1956-61; pilot Air Force NG, 1967-72; comdr. Air Force Acad., 1983; comdr. Res. Forces, Patrick AFB, 1983; ins. agt., owner, pres. Arthur Assocs., Inc., Orlando, Fla., 1982—. Decorated Air Force Commendation medal. Mem. Ind. Ins. Agts. Assn., Res. Officers Assn. (Minute Man award 1980), Air Force Assn., Mil. Order World Wars. Republican. Office: PO Box 60580 Orlando FL 32853

STAHL, O(SCAR) GLENN, writer, lecturer; b. Evansville, Ind., Apr. 30, 1910; s. Oscar and Mayme (Wittmer) S.; m. Marie Jane Rueter, June 26, 1934; children—Elaine Marie, Alan G. A.B., U. Evansville, 1931; M.A., U. Wis., 1933; Ph.D., NYU, 1936; LL.D., U. Evansville, 1984. Instr. govt. NYU, 1933-35; personnel officer TVA, 1935-41; with Fed. Security Agy. (later HEW), 1941-51, dir. personnel, 1948-51; with U.S. CSC (now OPM), 1951-69, dir. bur. policies and standards, 1955-69; adj. prof. pub. adminstrn. Am. U., 1949-69; part-time prof. U. Tenn., 1939, Dept. Agr. Grad. Sch., 1941-49; vis. lectr. various univs., U.S. and abroad; lectr. Salzburg Seminar Am. Studies, Austria, 1965; tech. assistance advisor to Venezuela, UN, 1958-59, 72, U.S. rep. UN Conf., Ethiopia, 1964; Ford Found. cons., India, 1968-69, 71, Nepal, 1969, Pakistan, 1974; AID advisor, Pakistan, 1969, 71; U.S. rapporteur Internat. Congress Adminstrv. Scis., Dublin, 1968; U.S. rep. UN Seminar, Tashkent, USSR, 1969; spl. advisor, Fed. Republic Germany, 1971; spl. cons. Pub. Adminstrn. Service, Govtl. Affairs Inst. and Internat. Personnel Mgmt. Assn., 1973-76; dir. Internat. Symposium on Pub. Personnel Adminstrn., Salzburg, 1973, 75. Author: Training Career Public Servants for the City of New York, 1936; Public Personnel Administration, 8th edit., 1983; The Personnel Job of Government Managers, 1971; Frontier Mother, 1979. Editor: Police Personnel Administration, 1974; Improving Public Services, 1979; editor Personnel Adminstrn., 1945-55. Contbr. articles to profl. jours. Mem. Arlington County Sch. Bd., Va., 1948-50; pres. Arlington Com. to Preserve Pub. Schs., 1958-61. Recipient Disting. Service award CSC, 1960; Stockberger award Soc. Personnel Adminstrn., 1962; Career Service award Nat. Civil Service League, 1967; medal of honor U. Evansville, 1981. Mem. Am. Polit. Sci. Assn., Am. Soc. Pub. Adminstrn., (editorial bd. 1955-58), Internat. Inst. Adminstrv. Sci., Internat. Personnel Mgmt. Assn. (hon. life, exec. com. Pub. Personnel Assn. 1951-54, pres. 1965-66, Washington rep. 1971-73), Fed. Exec. and Profl. Assn. (bd. dirs.). Presbyterian. Address: 3600 N Piedmont St Arlington VA 22207

STAHL, RAY EMERSON, freelance writer, public relations cons.; b. Latrobe, Pa., Mar. 24, 1917; s. Curtis E. and Josephine (King) S.; A.B., Bethany Coll., 1938; M.Div., Butler U., 1943; Ed.M., U. Pitts. 1946; postgrad. St. Vincent Coll., 1939. Pitts. Sch. Accountancy, 1939-40, U. Ky., 1955; M.A., Ohio State U., 1969; m. Faith Worrell, Aug. 25, 1941; children—Ellen Josephine (Mrs. Lawrence Carpenter), Ray Emerson. Ordained to ministry Disciples of Christ Ch., 1941; minister Brentwood Christian Ch., Pitts., 1943-46, First Christian Ch., Erwin, Tenn., 1946-50; exec. sec. in charge bus. adminstrn. and pub. relations Milligan Coll., Tenn., 1950-68; dir. pub. relations E. Tenn. State U., Johnson City, 1968-78. Bd. dirs. United Way, ARC, Am. Cancer Soc., Reece Mus., Tipton-Haynes Hist. Assn. Mem. Council for Advancement Small Colls. (chmn. pub. relations 1957-61), Pub. Relations Soc. Am. (accredited), East Tenn. Edn. Assn. (chmn. pub. relations 1968-76), Johnson City C. of C. (dir.), Kappa Alpha, Theta Phi, Kappa Tau Alpha. Republican. Mem. Christian Ch. (elder). Club: Kiwanis (sec.-treas. 1983-84). Author: How to Finance the Local Church, 1953; Six Decades of Progress, 1976; History of Tennessee-Virginia Energy Corporation, 1981; Money, Wealth, the Bible and You, 1983; Johnson City, Tennessee, A Pictorial History, 1983, rev. 2d edit., 1986; contbr. articles to profl. jours. Home: 109 Woodland Rd Johnson City TN 37601

STAHL, ROLAND WALTER, systems engineer; b. Spokane, Wash., Sept. 4, 1938; s. Walter Robert and Elizabeth Foster (Rollo) S.; B.S., Wash. State U., 1960; M.Ed., Am. U., 1970; grad. Armed Forces Staff Coll., 1976; m. Janet Louise Rausch, Oct. 29, 1960; children—Robert E., John C. Commd. 2d lt. U.S. Army, 1960, advanced through grades to lt. col., 1976; service in W. Ger., Korea and Vietnam; ret., 1980; cons. staff mem. def. and intelligence affairs BDM Internat., McLean, Va., 1980-82; mgr. systems engring. dept. Inco, Inc., McLean, Va., 1982-84; systems engr. Computer Scis. Corp., Wallops Island, Va., 1984—. Decorated Bronze Star, Def. Meritorious Service medal, Army Meritorious Service medal with oak leaf cluster, Joint Service Commendation medal, Army Commendation medal with 3 oak leaf clusters. Mem. Assn. U.S. Army, Armed Forces Communications and Electronics Assn., Ret. Officers Assn. Author articles, papers in field. Home: 31 King St Onancock VA 23417 Office: WFF Bldg E-2 Room 300 Wallops Island VA 23337

STAHLECKER, HARLAN GENE, real estate broker; b. Naper, Nebr., Apr. 23, 1934; s. John George and Ester (Juran) S.; m. Vi E. Cain, June 7, 1980; children by previous marriage—Valorie, Vickie; 1 stepdau., Stephanie Alexander. B.S., U. S.D., 1960; postgrad. U. Wyo., 1961-62. Tchr., coach Wood High Sch., S.D., 1954-60; prin., supt., 1961-63; owner, broker United Farm Agy., Nacogdoches, Tex., 1963-68; dir. mktg., v.p. United Farm Agy., Kansas City, Mo., 1968-73; owner, broker Alamo Realty, Nacogdoches, 1973-79, Duke & Assocs., Longview, Tex., 1979—, Nacogdoches, 1986—. Active various charitable orgns. Mem. Nat. Assn. Realtors, Tex. Assn. Realtors, Fin. Mgmt. Assn. of Nat. Honor Soc., C. of C. Republican. Methodist. Clubs: Boosters. Lodges: Lions, Rotary. Home: 1402 LeDuke Blvd Longview TX 75601 Office: Duke and Assocs 606 N Fredonia Longview TX 75601

STAINBACK, GARY JUDSON, educational administrator, school psychologist; b. Raleigh, N.C., Aug. 29, 1952; s. Marvin Justice and Doris Jean (Etheridge) S.; m. Teresa Ann Owens, Aug. 10, 1974; 1 child, Amanda. B.A., East Carolina U., 1975, M.A., 1979, C.A.S., 1979; Ph.D., N.C. State U., 1986. Lic. psychologist. Psychol. asst. Duplin County Mental Health, Kenansville, N.C., 1975-78; sch. psychologist New Bern-Craven County Sch., N.C., 1978-84; program adminstr. Tarboro City Schs., N.C., 1985—; psychol. assoc., New Bern, 1980-85. Mem. Am. Psychol. Assn., Nat. Assn. Sch. Psychologists, N.C. Sch. Psychology Assn. Democrat. Methodist. Avocations: saltwater sportfishing; tennis; softball; basketball. Home: 1506 Circle St Tarboro NC 27886 Office: Tarboro City Schs 308 St Patrick St Tarboro NC 27886-0370

STAKELY, CHARLES AVERETT, lawyer; b. Montgomery, Ala., June 2, 1935; s. Charles A. and Harriotte (Johnston) S.; m. Carolyn Cowan, Nov. 28, 1957; children—Charlie, Frank, Harry, Ben. Student U. Ala., 1953-55, J.D., 1960; student U. Ariz., 1955-57. Bar: Ala. 1960, U.S. Dist Ct. (mid. dist.) Ala., U.S. Ct. Appeals (5th cir.), U.S. Ct. Appeals (11th cir.). Assoc. Rushton, Stakely, Johnston & Garrett, Montgomery, Ala., 1960-65, mem., 1965—, now sr. ptnr.; instr. Jones Law Sch., Montgomery. Chmn. bd. Montgomery YMCA, Montgomery Park and Recreation Dept.; mem. Ala. Securities Commn.; founding mem. Ala. Constl. Commn. Named Man of Year, City of Montgomery, 1975; recipient Disting. Service award, Jaycees, 1972. Mem. ABA, Ala. Bar Assn., Am. Coll. Trial Lawyers, Montgomery County Bar Assn., Ala. Def. Lawyers Assn., Internat. Assn. Ins. Counsel, Am. Soc. Hosp. Attys. Baptist. Contbr. articles to legal jours. Office: Rushton Stakely Johnston & Garrett PO Box 270 Montgomery AL 36195

STAKER, ROBERT JACKSON, federal judge; b. Kermit, W.Va., Feb. 14, 1925; s. Frederick George and Nada (Frazier) S.; student Marshall U., Huntington, W.Va., W.Va. U., Morgantown, U. Ky., Lexington; LL.B. W.Va. U., 1952; m. Sue Blankenship Poore, July 16, 1955; 1 son, Donald Seth; 1 stepson, John Timothy Poore. Admitted to W.Va. bar, 1952; practiced in Williamson, 1952-68; judge Mingo County Circuit Ct., Williamson, 1969-79; U.S. dist. judge So. Dist. W.Va., Huntington, 1979—. Served with USN, 1943-46. Mem. ABA, Am. Judicature Soc., W.Va. Bar Assn., W.Va. State Bar. Democrat. Presbyterian. Office: Old Post Office Bldg 5th Ave PO Box 1570 Huntington WV 25716*

STALCUP, ROBERT JOE, personnel executive; b. Liberal, Kans., Jan. 17, 1946; s. John Chaffin and Helen Charolette (Jones) S.; B.S.E. cum laude in Speech Communication, 1968; M.S. in Mgmt. and Human Relations, Abilene Christian U., 1978; m. Linda Kay Hamer, July 1, 1967; children—Matthew Robert, Erin Elizabeth and Stacie Helen (twins). Advisor to speech and English depts. Kansas City (Kans.) Sch. Dist., 1968-69; interviewer U.S. Steel, Tex. Works, Baytown, 1973-74; tng. specialist oil and gas div. Atlantic Richfield Co., Dallas, 1974-77; coordinator equal opportunity affairs, 1977-78; coordinator equal opportunity affairs corp. hdqrs. ARCO, Los Angeles, 1978-79, mgr. profl. recruitment, 1979-80; corp. dir. equal employment opportunity Occidental Petroleum Corp., Houston, 1980-83, corp. dir. personnel and EEO regulatory affairs, 1983-84; mgr. employee relations Amerada Hess Corp., 1984—. Condr. workshops and seminars; author tng. programs; developer performance appraisal system, affirmative action plan prototype for cos.; mem. Nat. Chem. and Office of Fed. Contract Compliance Programs Liaison Group. Active Republican politics; adult class tchr., zone leader Ch. of Christ; chmn. sub-com. Harris County Employment of Handicapped Com. Served with U.S. Army, 1969-71. Mem. Orgn. Resources Counselors, Equal Opportunity Group, Employment Mgmt. Assn., Houston Personnel Assn., Am. Mgmt. Assn., Am. Soc. Personnel Adminstrn., Equal Employment Adv. Council (vice chmn. affirmative action com.), Alpha Psi Omega, Alpha Chi, Phi Kappa Delta.

STALEY, DAVID CHARLES, computer company executive; b. Chesapeake, Va., Jan. 30, 1957; s. Billy Joe and June C. (Overton) S.; m. Paula Gail Kebbel, June 8, 1984; children—Michelle Ann, Sean William. B.A. magna cum laude in Polit. Sci., Old Dominion U., 1979, M.P.A., 1981. Adminstrv. asst. III, City of Virginia Beach, Va., 1977-82; corp. mgr. employment and safety Stewart Sandwiches Inc., Norfolk, Va., 1982-84; v.p. employee relations and adminstrn. Computer Dynamics, Inc., Virginia Beach, 1984—. Mem. Am. Soc. Personnel Adminstrn., Am. Soc. Safety Engrs. Avocations: softball; football; basketball; tennis; golf. Office: Computer Dynamics 4452 Corporation Ln Virginia Beach VA 23462

STALEY, SAMUEL SORBER, logistician; b. Honolulu, Mar. 4, 1931; s. Samuel Sorber and Pauline Alice (Jones) S.; m. Dorinda Merle Reed, June 29, 1957; children—Clinton, Lisle, Wynne. A.B., Principia Coll., 1952; student Harvard Law Sch., 1952-53, 56-57; A.M., George Washington U., 1962; Ph.D., Am. U., 1971. Supr., Bur. Mgmt. Ctr., Navy Supply, Washington, 1958-60; staff asst. IBRD, Washington, 1961-63; dept. dir. Fleet Assistance Group Pacific, San Diego, 1964-65, head supply systems div., 1966-67, head publs. div., 1968-69, head surface warfare logistics planning office, 1970-73, dept. head tech. data dept., 1973-74; dep. head supply ops. dept., 1975-76, head logistics program dept. Naval Ship Weapons, 1976-82; prof. systems acquisition mgmt. Def. Systems Mgmt. Coll., Fort Belvoir, Va., 1982-83; chief logistician Joint Cruise Missiles Project, Washington, 1983—; instr. mgmt. U. Calif. at Santa Barbara, 1967-68; instr. logistics U.S. Navy, 1971-72. Adminstr., Combined Fed. Campaign, Ventura, 1975. Served with AUS, 1953-56. Recipient Navy Edn. fellowship, 1969-70; Navy Outstanding Performance awards, 1967-69, Sustained Superior Performance awards, 1977, 80, Spl. Act awards, 1981, Exceptional Performance award, 1983. Mem. Am. Soc. Pub. Adminstrn., Soc. Logistics Engrs., Am. Polit. Sci. Assn. Republican. Christian Scientist (reader, chmn. bd.). Editor, contbr. Integrated Logistics Support Handbook, 1969; contbr. articles to profl. jours. Home: 8417 Bluedale Alexandria VA 22308 Office: Joint Cruise Missiles Project Office Arlington VA 22202

STALEY, THOMAS FABIAN, literary critic, educator; b. Pitts., Aug. 13, 1935; s. Fabian Richard and Mary (McNulty) S.; m. Carolyn O'Brien, Sept. 3, 1960; children—Thomas Fabian, Caroline Ann, Mary Elizabeth, Timothy X. B.A., Regis Coll., 1957, D.H.L. (hon.), 1979; M.S., U. Tulsa, 1958; Ph.D., U. Pitts., 1962; Prof. English, U. Tulsa, 1969-76, dean grad. sch., 1969-76, acting v.p. acad. affairs, 1977, Trustees prof. modern lit., 1977—, dean Coll. Arts and Scis., 1981-83, provost, v.p. acad. affairs, 1983—. Mem. NCCJ, 1979—, Com. of 100, 1982—; bd. dirs. Tulsa Philharm. Soc., 1982—, Tulsa Arts Council, 1969—. Am. Council Learned Socs. grant-in-aid, 1980; 82; recipient Fulbright award, Italy, spring 1971; Fulbright research prof., Trieste, Italy, 1966-67; Danforth Assoc., 1962-66, sr. assoc., 1967. Mem. AAUP, MLA, South Central Modern Lang. Assn., Anglo-Irish Studies Assn., Am. Com. Irish Studies, James Joyce Found., Hopkins Soc. Club: Tulsa Tennis. Author: Twentieth-Century Women Novelists, Jean Rhys, A Critical Study, Approaches to Joyce's Portrait, 1976; Ten Essays, Dorothy Richardson, Ulysses: Fifty Years, 1974; Approaches to Ulysses: Ten Essays, 1970; The Shapeless God: Essays on the Modern Novel, 1968; James Joyce's A Portrait of the Artist, 1968; Italo Svevo: Essays on His Work, 1969; Dubliners: A Critical Handbook, 1969; adv. editor Twentieth Century Lit., 1966—; Contbr. articles to profl. jours.

STALKER, KENNETH WALTER, consulting engineer; b. St. John, Kans., Oct. 3, 1918; s. Walter Richard and Bertha (Bissett) S.; B.A., U. Colo., 1941; LL.B., LaSalle U., 1952; m. Eva Leona Teagarden, Feb. 7, 1947. Mfg. engr. Gen. Electric Co., Lynn, Mass., 1950-52; mgr. mfg. engring. and process devel. Aircraft Engring. Group, Gen. Electric Co., Cin., 1952-59, chief cons. engr. process advanced tech., 1965-81; mgr. engring. Goodman Mfg. Co., Chgo., 1959-64; mem. critical material task force Metal Property Council, 1980-81; cons. engr. Pratt & Whitney Aircraft, Spl. Metals Corp.; editorial adv. bd. Nat. Acad. Sci.; lectr. U. Ark. Precinct committeeman Cook County (Ill.) Republican Party, 1962-64; trustee Presbyn. Ch. of Wyoming (Ohio), 1978-81. Recipient managerial award Gen. Electric Co., 1956, William L. Badger Meml. award, 1970, award for outstanding contbns. Pratt & Whitney Aircraft, 1984, 85. Mem. ASME, Soc. Mfg. Engrs., Soc. Automotive Engrs. Clubs: Masons, Shriners. Contbr. articles to trade jours. Patentee in field. Home and office: 500 N Sequoyan Dr Fayetteville AR 72701 also 900 E Indiantown Rd Suite 209 Jupiter FL 33458

STALL, RICHARD BACOT, banker, human resource developer; b. Greenville, S.C., June 22, 1947; s. Ad Newton and Helen (Hunt) S. B.S. in Bus. Adminstrn., Presbyn. Coll., 1969; M.B.A., U. Ga., 1971. Mktg. researcher Henderson Advt., Greenville, S.C., 1971-72; mktg. planner Wachovia Bank & Trust Co., Winston-Salem, N.C., 1973-77, br. mgr., Raleigh, N.C., 1977-81, mgr. retail tng. and staff devel., Winston-Salem, 1981—. Vestryman, St. Anne's Episcopal Ch., Winston-Salem, 1985—; bd. dirs. Women's Shelter of Wake County, Raleigh, 1980-81. Served to capt. USAR, 1969-76. Mem. young adult com. Episcopal Diocese N.C., 1979-80. Mem. Am. Soc. Tng. and Devel., Huguenot Soc. S.C. (life). Avocations: swimming; water skiing; community theatre; travel. Office: Wachovia Bank & Trust Co NA 301 N Main St Winston-Salem NC 27102

STALLARD, CHARLES K., computer educator, instructional design consultant; b. Coeburn, Va., Apr. 6, 1942; s. Charles Kelson and Helen Mercedes (Colyer) S.; m. Loretta Lee Miller, Aug. 13, 1963; 1 child, Julie Elizabeth. B.S. in English Edn., U. Va., 1965, Ed.D. in Instructional Tech., 1970; M.A. in English, East Tenn. State U., 1968. Prin., Hurricane Elem. Sch., Wise, Va., 1965-66; chmn. English dept. Burton High Sch., Norton, Va., 1966-70; instr. U. Va., Charlottesville, 1970-72; assoc. prof. Old Dominion U., Norfolk, Va., 1972-85, coordinator computer edn., 1985—; pres. Va. Council for Computers in Edn., 1982-83; cons. on computer edn. Advanced Tech., Reston, Va., 1984-85, U.S. Navy, 1982-83. Author articles on English edn. and computer edn.; host weekly pub. radio program; Education Outlook, sta. WHRO, Norfolk, 1983—. Mem. Nat. Council Tchrs. English (task force 1982-85), Am. Mgmt. Assn., Va. Assn. Tchrs. English, Phi Delta Kappa. Home: 605 Botetourt Gardens Norfolk VA 23507

STALLER, NATHANIEL RAYMOND, dental surgeon; b. Phila., May 29, 1949; s. Martin and Doris (Greenblatt) S.; m. Barbara Ruth Fleckman, Nov. 9, 1980; 1 child, Carrie Jennifer. B.A., Temple U., 1971; D.D.S., 1975. Intern, Temple U., Phila., 1971-72; practice medicine specializing in dental surgery, Delray Beach, Fla., 1981—; clin. instr., asst. prof. Temple Dental Sch., Phila., 1975-79; mem. med. staff surgery Delray Community Hosp., Delray Beach, 1983—; cons. Am. Heart Assn., West Palm Beach, Fla., 1983—, lectr., 1985; cons. Am. Cancer Soc., West Palm Beach, 1983—. Mem. ADA, Fla. Dental Assn., East Coast Dist. Dental Assn., Acad. Gen. Dentistry, Atlantic Dental Soc. (lectr. 1981—), Alpha Omega. Avocations: reading; music; tennis; golf. Office: 5054 W Atlantic Ave Delray Beach FL 33465

STALLINGS, JESSE DANIEL, logistician; b. Terrell, Tex., Apr. 20, 1915; s. William Thomas and Katherine Lee (Hall) S.; Certified Internat. Inst. Photographic Arts, 1950, Am. Mgmt. Assn., 1973, Inst. Profl. Mgrs., Trinity U., 1976, Rockwell Internat. Schedule Cost Control Systems Program, 1977; m. Toinette Marie Heffington, July 25, 1945; children—Sharon Sue, Michael Daniel, Melissa Marie, Robin Joseph. Stunt man, actor various employers, and locations, 1930-40; surveyor Ky. Nat. Gas Co., Owensboro, 1938; field supt. Municipal Service Co., Henderson, Ky., 1939-40; constrn. supt. Ky. Ice and Storage Co., Henderson, 1948; constrn. mgr. Gulf South Utilities, Lucedale, Miss., 1949-50; mgr. Myres Photo Labs., Dallas, 1950-51; art editor and pub. relations dir. Southwestern Square Dancer Mag., Dallas, 1951-52; supv. State Farm Ins. Co., Dallas, 1952-62; mgr. provisioning dept. Collins Radio Divs., Rockwell Internat., Dallas, 1962-77; logistics cons., Garland, Tex., 1977—; mgr. provisioning dept., sr. logistics engr. Tracor Inc., 1978—; dir. Vector Engring., Buda, Tex. Team leader U.S. Savs. Bond Drive, Dallas, 1975; loaned exec. United Way Fund Drive, 1976; co-organizer, dir., curator 112th Cavalry Mus., 1960-77; asst. to Irving (Tex.) Bicentennial Mus. Com., 1976—. Served as capt. U.S. Army, 1940-47; mem. 112th Cavalry Tex. NG, 1930-40. Decorated Bronze Star, Purple Heart. Recipient Leadership award, North Tex. chpt. Soc. Logistics Engrs., 1974, 75; Patriotic Service award, U.S. Treasury Dept., 1975; letter of commendation Rockwell Internat., 1976; certificate of Appreciation City of Irving Bicentennial Commn., 1976; 112th Cavalry Assn., 1974. Mem. Am. Mgmt. Assn., Soc. Logistics Engrs. (chmn. North Tex. chpt. 1974-75, organizer, chmn. Tex. chpt. 1978-79, mem. dist. bd. advs., President's award for merit 1985), Electronics Industries Assn., Soc. Logistics Engrs. (Tex. dir. 1983—), Internat. Platform Assn., Sheriffs Assn. Tex., Nat. Rifle Assn., U.S. Horse Cavalry Assn., 112th Cavalry Assn. (co-organizer 1957, dir. 1957—, pres. 1959, 71, 72, 73), 1st Cavalry Div. Assn., Ret. Officer Assns., VFW. Mem. Christian Ch. Home: Pet Rock Ranch 15 Country Oaks Dr Buda TX 78610

STALLWORTH, BILLY ED, construction company executive; b. Rosebud, Tex., June 16, 1932; s. Ira and Maudine (Richerson) S.; m. Jackie Wardlaw, Feb. 11, 1957; children—William Wardlaw, Suzanne. B.S. in Archtl. Constrn., Tex. A&M U., 1954. With Brown & Root, Inc., 1973—, v.p., then. sr. v.p., 1974—, group v.p. marine ops., Houston, 1975-82, exec. v.p., 1982—, also dir., mem. exec. com.; pres. Brown & Root Internat. Inc., 1985—. Served with USAF, 1954-56. Mem. Houston Engring. and Sci. Soc. Clubs: Petroleum, Houstonian. Office: Brown & Root Inc PO Box 3 Houston TX 77001*

STALSBY, JACK EVERETT, diversified company executive; b. Conroe, Tex., Aug. 3, 1926; s. James Everett and Elva Christine (Gilchrease) S.; m. Greta Sue Wright, Aug. 3, 1973. B.S. in Econs., U. Houston, 1949. Mgr. div. Conoco, various locations, 1955-67; mgr. wholesale sales Tex. Eastern Transp., Houston, 1967-70; v.p. mktg. The Oil Daily, Houston, 1970-75; prin., pres. Stalsby, Inc., Houston, 1975—; cons., dir. Stalsby Wilson, Houston, 1980—; dir. Stalsby, Inc., Entrust, Inc., Houston, M Bank Meml., Houston. Served to lt. USAF, 1944-46. Republican. Episcopalian. Clubs: Champions Golf, Westlake. Avocations: golf; reading. Office: Stalsby Inc 1035 Dairy Ashford Rd Houston TX 77079

STAMBAUGH, REGINALD JACK, ophthalmologist; b. West Palm Beach, Fla., Jan 1, 1930; s. Gleason Noah and Marjorie (Hilton) S.; A.B., U. Fla., 1952; M.D., U. Miami, 1959; m. Carolyn Stroupe, Nov. 24, 1965; children—Melanie, Joette, Valerie, Reginald Giles. Intern, Grady Meml. Hosp., Atlanta, 1959-60, resident, 1960-64; individual practice medicine specializing in ophthalmology, West Palm Beach, 1963—; chief ophthalmology Good Samaritan Hosp., West Palm Beach, 1966-74; lectr. Bascom Palmer Eye Inst., U. Miami Sch. Medicine, 1964-73; mem. med. adv. bd. Fla. Soc. for Prevention of Blindness, 1972-77, Crippled Children's Soc. of Palm Beach, 1965-82. Bd. dirs. Fla. Med. Polit. Action Com., 1975-81, Palm Beach County Hall of Fame, 1977-80, Health Planning Council, 1979-81; bd. dirs. Found. Med. Care, 1979-82, pres., 1980; mem. vestry Bethesda by the Sea Ch., Palm Beach, 1981—. Served with USAF, 1952-54. Decorated Korean Presdl. citation; diplomate Am. Bd. Ophthalmology, Nat. Bd. Med. Examiners. Mem. Fla., So. med. assns., AMA, Am. Acad. Ophthalmology (bd. councilors 1981—), Am. Assn. Ophthalmology (trustee 1979-81), West Palm Beach C. of C. (bd. dirs. 1981—), Fla. Soc. Ophthalmology (sec.-treas. 1975-77, pres. 1980-81), Palm Beach County Med. Soc. (pres. 1977, trustee 1977—). Democrat. Episcopalian. Clubs: Sailfish of Fla. (bd. govs. 1976-78), Bath and Tennis (Palm Beach). Contbr. numerous articles, papers in field. Home: 272 Queens Ln Palm Beach FL 33480 Office: 2707 N Flagler Dr West Palm Beach FL 33407

STAMM, DAVID THOMAS, manufacturing company executive; b. Alton, Ill., July 20, 1947; s. Russell Albert and Pearlie May (Elliot) S.; m. Rebecca Ann McCann, Jan. 31, 1970; children—Larry, Wade, Alandra, Ryan. Student Lewis and Clark Coll., 1972-74; B.S., Edison State Coll., 1980; postgrad. Fairleigh Dickinson U., 1981—. Engring. rep. Ins. Services Office, St. Louis, 1972-73; loss control engr. Continental Ins. Co., Louisville, 1974-75; supr. dept. accident and loss prevention Aetna Ins. Co., Louisville, 1976; with NL Industries, Inc., 1977—, div. mgr. safety and health Titanium Pigments div., South Amboy, N.J., 1978-79, mgr. safety and health NL Chems., N.Am. ops., Hightstown, N.J., 1979-81, mgr. safety health worldwide ops., 1981-83, plant mgr., Charleston, W.Va., 1983—; lectr. in field. Active Charleston C. of C. and Devel., chmn. legis. com., 1985; active Charleston Renaissance Corp.; chmn. indsl. sect. Fund for Arts in Charleston, 1985. Served with U.S. Army, 1965-68. Decorated Air medal. Mem. Am. Soc. Safety Engrs. (chmn. pub. relations com. N.J. chpt. 1980-81), N.J. Indsl. Safety Com., VFW, Republican. Mormon. Home: 2027 Mt Vernon Rd Hurricane WV 25526 Office: NL Chems PO Box 1467 Charleston WV 25325

STAMM, RICHARD LEROY, business educator, consultant; b. Washington, Kans., Aug. 8, 1938; s. Clarence Henry and Laura Alice (Woodcock) S.; m. Judith Rhea Von Waaden, July 1, 1959; children—Dawn Renae, Dana Kimberly. B.S., Auburn U., 1972; M.S., Kans. State U., 1973; Ph.D., 1976. Enlisted U.S. Army, 1960, advanced through grades to lt. col., 1981; various command and staff assignments through, U.S. and world, 1960-81, cons., 1981—; chmn. mgmt. and bus. div. Am. Tech. U., Killeen, Tex., 1981—. Author, co-author Army tng. manuals and workshop publs. Mem. Acad. Mgmt., Southwest Small Bus. Inst., Southwest Fedn. Adminstrv. Disciplines, Nat. Assn. Trainers and Developers. Republican. Lutheran. Avocations: sports; reading; church; family. Home: Allen Estates 2 Box 3303 Kempner TX 76539 Office: Am Tech U West Hwy 190 PO Box 1416 Killeen TX 76540

STAMM, ROBERT CALVIN, consulting engineer; b. Phila., July 2, 1925; s. William Calvin and Allis Patience (Gill) S.; student Columbia Coll., 1943, Wittenberg U., 1944; B.S.M.E., Columbia U., 1950; m. Esther Elizabeth Smith, Aug. 8, 1953. Project engr. Westvaco Corp., N.Y.C., 1950-56, mgr. design and constrn., 1956-59, engring. group mgr., 1959-69, chief engr., 1969-75, corp. mgr. energy and property conservation, 1975-76; v.p. Brown & Root, Inc., Houston, 1976-82; cons. engr., 1982—. Served with USAAF, 1944-46. Fellow TAPPI (past dir., exec. com.); mem. AAAS, ASME, N.Y. Acad. Scis., Res. Officers Assn., Phi Kappa Psi, Tau Beta Pi. Home and Office: 1643 W Belt Dr S Houston TX 77042 also 139 E 63d St New York NY 10021

STAMPFLI, ROBERT FRANK, educator classics and art history, consultant; b. Nashville, Jan. 16, 1945; s. Ernest and Leitha (Schindler) S. B.A., Vanderbilt U., 1967, Ph.D., 1971. Asst. prof. Tex. Tech U., Lubbock, 1971-73; assoc. prof. Troy State U., Ala., 1973—; cons. Jasmine Hill Gardens, Montgomery, Ala., 1984—. Author: Jasmine Hill: A Little Corner of Greece, 1985; also articles. Woodrow Wilson fellow, 1971. Mem. Classical Assn. Middle West and South, Am. Philol. Assn., Ala. Classical Assn. Episcopalian. Avocations: firearms; hiking. Home: 205 Highland Ave Troy AL 36081 Office: Troy State U Troy AL 36082

STAMPIGLIA, FAUSTO S., religious administrator; b. Rome, Italy; Oct. 7, 1935; came to U.S., 1964; s. Carlo and Antonio (Falciatori) S. Ph.B., Gregorian U., 1957, B.A., M.A., 1961; M.S. in Psychology, Fordham U., 1975; S.T.D., St. Thomas Aquinas U., Rome, 1979. Ordained priest Roman Catholic Ch., 1960. Pastor, St. Ann Ch., N.Y.C., 1972-75, Sacred Heart Ch., Cohoes, N.Y., 1975-77, St. Rita Ch., Cohoes, 1975-77, St. Joseph Ch., Port St. Joe, Fla., 1977-80; episcopal vicar Rural Vicariate, Chipley, Fla., 1980-82; instr. St. Leo Coll., Fla., 1979-85; dir. permanent diaconate Diocese of Pensacola, Fla., 1977-82, Diocese of St. Petersburg, Fla., 1982-85, Diocese of Venice, Fla., 1984-85, Diocese of Corpus Christi, Tex., 1985—. Author: Study of New York City Immigrant Parish, 1979. Contbr. articles to profl. jours. Bd. dirs. 1199 Housing Corp., N.Y.C., 1972-75. Decorated Order of Knights of Holy Sepulcher. Mem. Am. Assn. Counseling and Devel., Assn. for Religious Values in Counseling. Democrat. Lodge: K.C. Avocations: music composition; photography; camping; hunting; reading. Home: PO Box 1899 Corpus Christi TX 78403 Office: Permanent Diaconate Office 1200 Lantana Corpus Christi TX 78407

STAMPS, B. J., educational administrator. Supt. of schs. Amarillo, Tex. Office: 910 W 8th St Amarillo TX 79101*

STAMPS, LEIGHTON ELDERKIN, psychology educator; b. Pitts., Mar. 10, 1947; s. Ranzie Washington and Florence Elderkin (Cromlish) S.; m. Diane Jean Cranisky, May 29, 1971; children—Jason, Lauren, Christopher, Justin. B.A. in Econs., Westminster Coll., 1969; M.A. in Psychology, W.V.A. U., 1972, Ph.D., 1974. Lic. psychologist, La.; cert. sch. psychologist, La. Asst., assoc. prof. psychology U. New Orleans, 1974—, chmn. dept., 1982-84; pvt. practice psychology, La., 1978—. Contbr. articles to profl. jours. Mem. Am. Psychol. Assn., Soc. Psychophysiol. Research (conv. com. 1980-83), La. Psychol. Assn. (chmn. sci. affairs com. 1984). Office: Dept Psychology U New Orleans Lakefront New Orleans LA 70148

STAMPS, THOMAS PATY, lawyer; b. Mineola, N.Y., May 10, 1952; s. George Moreland and Helen Leone (Paty) S.; m. Regina Ruth Thomas, May 23, 1981; 1 dau.: Katherine Camilla. B.A., U. Ill., 1973; M.A., Emory U., J.D., Wake Forest U., 1979. Bar: Ga. 1979, N.C. 1979. Personnel dir. Norman Jaspan, N.Y.C., 1973-74; assoc. Macey & Zusmann, Atlanta, 1979-81; owner Zusmann, Small, Stamps & White PC, Atlanta, 1981—; cons. GMS Cons., Westport, Conn., 1975—; ptnr. Destin Enterprises, Atlanta, 1983—. Chmn. Summer Law Inst., Atlanta, 1981—; mem. Dem. Party of Ga., Atlanta, 1983—; atty. Vol. Lawyers for Arts, Atlanta, 1981-85. Recipient Service award Inst. Continuing Legal Edn., Athens, Ga., 1981. Mem. ABA, Atlanta Bar Assn. (com. chmn. 1981-85), N.C. Bar Assn., Internat. Bar Assn., Hon. Order Ky. Cols., Phi Alpha Delta (justice, Atlanta 1982-83, emeritus 1983). Clubs: Lawyers (Atlanta); West Paces Racquet. Author: Study of a Student, 1973; History of Coca-Cola, 1976. Office: Zusmann Small Stamps & White 2964 Peachtree Rd NW Atlanta GA 30305

STANALAND, WILLIAM WHIT, JR., accountant; b. Benson Junction, Fla., Mar. 15, 1930; s. William Whit and Goldie (Merritt) S.; B.S. in Bus. Adminstrn., U. Fla., 1957, postgrad., 1959; postgrad. Rollins Coll., 1964; m. Norma Lee Ober, June 24, 1961; children—Sherry D., William Whit III, Terence B., Dana Lee; m. 2d, Sandra L. Swann, Dec. 1, 1971. Jr. accountant Pepsi Cola Bottling Co., 1957-58; accountant Wells, Laney, Earlich & Baer, 1958-59, A.J. Mixner, C.P.A., 1961-63; controller Halco Products, Inc., 1959-61; C.P.A., Orlando, Fla., 1963—. Served with USMC, 1948-52. C.P.A., Fla. Mem. Am., Fla. insts. C.P.A.'s, Asso. Builders and Contractors, Associated Gen. Contractors of Mid-Fla., Mortgage Bankers Association, Central Fla. Tax Roundtable; Clubs: Kiwanis, Toastmasters. Home: 441 N Harbor City Blvd Unit C-20 Melbourne FL 32935 Office: 27 E Dale Ave Melbourne FL 32935

STANBACK, WILLARD ARTHUR, mathematics and statistics educator; b. Portsmouth, Va., Oct. 24, 1930; s. Walter Alonzo and Rose Eva (Baker) S.; m. Bessie Irene Alsop, Feb. 1, 1958; children—Willard Alonzo, William Anthony (dec.). B.S. in Math., Va. State U., 1957; Ed.M., Tuskegee Inst., 1960; M.S., Syracuse U., 1977, M.Philosophy, 1979. Instr., Portsmouth pub. schs., 1957-59; asst. prof. math. and stats. Norfolk State U., Va., 1961—; cons. statis. analysis NASA, Hampton, Va., 1981-84. Served with USAF, 1950-54. NSF grantee, 1957, 64, 65; Syracuse U. grad. asst., 1975-81. Mem. Am. Statis. Assn., Math. Assn. Am., Nat. Inst. Sci. Democrat. Baptist. Avocation: photography. Home: 1415 Ellington Sq Portsmouth VA 23701 Office: Norfolk State U Norfolk VA 23504

STANDARD, DAVID MICHAEL, architect; b. Bastrop, La., Mar. 17, 1951; s. Charles Levi and Jeannette S.; m. Maida Thompson, (div. 1981); 1 child, David Edward. B.Arch., La. State U., 1974. Cert., NCARB. Intern in architecture Koetter, Tharp & Cowell, Houston, 1976-79; architect Thompson, Ventulett & Strinback, Atlanta, 1979-80, Surber, Barber & Mooney, Atlanta, 1980-83; assoc. Smallwood, Reynolds, Stewart & Stewart Interiors, Atlanta, 1983—. Display in art competition So. Tower to the Past, 1981. Mem. AIA. Avocations: photography; drawing; carpentry. Office: Smallwood Reynolds Stewart Stewart Interiors 3565 Piedmont Rd Atlanta GA 30305

STANDIFER, HUGH AVERY, computer consultant; b. Johnson County, Tex., Dec. 19, 1932; s. Mynis William and Lucy Kate (Lomax) S.; student Sam Houston State U., 1950, 70-71, U. Tex., Arlington, 1958, Central Tex. Coll., 1971-72, St. Edwards U., 1973; B.S. in Criminal Justice, Am. Tech. U., 1974; m. Bonnie K. Ruschmyer Juergens, Apr. 14, 1979; children by previous marriage—Hugh Marcus, William Herman, Penny Teresa, Patti Christine. Computer programmer Gen. Foods Corp., 1958-64; ops. mgr. Nat. Western Life Ins. Co., Austin, Tex., 1964-67; asst. div. chief for data processing Tex. Dept. Public Safety, Austin, 1967-73; info. systems dir. City of Austin, 1974-84; partner Justan Enterprises, Data Processing Consultation and Services; mem. rev. bd. Public Technology, Inc., 1975-76; instr. Tex. A&M U., 1969-74; mem. textbook selection com. Austin Ind. Sch. Dist., 1975-76, Gov.'s Commn. on Standards and Goals for Tex., 1975-76. Served with AUS, 1955-58. Mem. Met. Info. Exchange (pres. 1980), Govt. Mgmt. Info. Scis., Urban and Regional Info. Systems Assn., Library and Info. Tech. Assn., ALA, Tex. Assn. Govtl. Data Processing Mgrs. (exec. com., chmn. edn. com., v.p. 1981, pres. 1982). Lutheran. Pioneer in use of convict labor for clerical/data preparation activities. Office: PO Box 33160 Austin TX 78764

STANDIFER, JAMES WILLIAM, health, physical education, safety consultant; b. Beaumont, Tex., Oct. 20, 1913; s. Samuel Francis and Zena Zora (Owens) S.; B.S., Tex. A&M U., 1944; M.Ed., U. Tex., Austin, 1945; Ed.D., U. Mich., 1957; m. Lillian Lela Hill, July 22, 1944; 1 child, Jo Lynn. Asst. coach, intramural dir. Lamar Coll., 1940-42; instr. phys. edn., asst. intramurals Tex. A&M U., 1942-43; athletic dir. Austin Recreation Dept., 1944-46; dir. phys. edn., athletic dir. Wharton Coll., 1946-47; dir. recreation Cactus Plant, Phillips Petroleum Co., 1947-52; asst. prof. health and phys. edn. U. Dayton (Ohio), 1956-57; asso. prof. Tex. Christian U., Fort Worth, 1957-60, prof. phys. edn., 1960-79; cons. driver edn. Tex. Edn. Agy., 1971; vis. prof. Sul Ross State U., 1974; ind. cons. driver and traffic safety, Ft. Worth, 1979—. Contbr. articles to profl. jours. Mem. AAHPER, Nat. Coll. Phys. Edn. Assn. for Men and Women, Am. Driver and Traffic Safety Edn. Assn. (bd. dirs., award of merit), AAUP, Am. Coll. Safety Assn., Tex. Driver and Safety Edn. Assn. (bd. dirs., past pres., honor award, award named in his honor), Tex. Assn. Health and Phys. Edn., Tex. Assn. Coll. Tchrs., Ft. Worth Driver Edn. Assn., Phi Delta Kappa. Home: 4404 Wedgmont Circle S Fort Worth TX 76133 Office: Dept Kinesiological Studies Tex Christian U Fort Worth TX 76129

STANGLIN, GERALD MINOR, social science educator; b. Dallas, Apr. 26, 1947; s. John Edward and Edna Mae (Minor) S.; m. Alice Gwynn Gallegly, Aug. 23, 1968; children—Suzanne Marie, Jeffrey Michael. A.A., Christian Coll. Southwest, 1967; B.A. in History, Abilene Christian U., 1969; M.A. in History, North Tex. State U., 1971, postgrad., 1973—. Tchr. Dallas Christian Sch., 1971-73; asst. prof. polit. sci. Abilene Christian U., Garland, Tex., 1973-80; tchr. Berkner High Sch., Richardson, Tex., 1980-82; div. chmn. Cedar Valley Coll., Lancaster, Tex., 1982—; chmn. curriculum study task force Dallas Christian High Sch., Mesquite, Tex., 1981. Mem. bd. edn. Dallas Ind. Sch. Dist., 1977-81; legis. liaison Dallas Sch. Bd., 1978-80; dist. rep. to Congress Nat. Sch. Bds. Assn. Fed. Relations Network, 1977-79; del. Tex. State Dem. Conv., 1976. Recipient Outstanding Christian Service in Edn. award North Dallas chpt. Abilene Christian U. Alumni Assn., 1978; Disting. Alumnus award Dallas Christian Sch., 1977. Mem. Southwestern Social Sci. Assn., Tex. Jr. Coll. Tchrs. Assn., Am. Mgmt. Assn., Phi Alpha Theta. Mem. Ch. of Christ. Avocation: singing. Home: 8347 Foxwood Ln Dallas TX 75217 Office: Cedar Valley Coll 3030 N Dallas Ave Lancaster TX 75134

STANITZKY, CARL ANTHONY, insurance company executive; b. Hearne, Tex., Nov. 10, 1944; s. Charles A. and Mary (McCarty) S.; m. Dorothy Maxine Sullivan, Aug. 13, 1982; children—Tammie, Gregory Lee, Tony. B.A. in Math., Tex. A&M U., 1967, M.B.A., 1969. Vice pres. Tome James Clothiers, Ft. Worth, 1969-75; ins. sales Don Corcey Agy., Ft. Worth, 1975-79; ind. broker Arlington, Tex., 1979-82; v.p. sales Western Fidelity Ins., Arlington, 1982-85; pres. Am. Health Underwriters, Lafayette, La., 1985—. Recipient Outstanding Sales award Sales Mktg. Execs., 1978; Named Top Agt. for Yr. Don Corcey Agy., 1977, 78, 79, Western Casualty Ins. Co., 1983. Mem. Nat. Assn. Health Underwriters (Highest Honors, 1984), Lafayette C. of C. (small bus. council 1985). Republican. Baptist. Avocations: tennis, raquetball, billiards. Home: 117 Clipper Cove Lafayette LA 70508 Office: Am Health Underwriters 5700 Johnston 250 Lafayette LA 70503

STANLEY, BRUCE MCLAREN, lawyer; b. Cleve., May 13, 1948; s. Willard Cyrus and Isabel (Anderson) S.; m. Pamela Soderholm, June 23, 1984. B.A., Coll. William and Mary, 1970; J.D., U. Va., 1974. Bar: Fla. 1974, U.S. Supreme Ct. 1978, U.S. Dist. Ct. (so. dist.) Fla. 1974, U.S. Dist. Ct. (mid. dist.) U.S. Ct. Appeals (5th cir.) 1975, U.S. Ct. Appeals (11th cir.) 1982. Assoc., Bradford, Williams, McKay, Kimbrell, Hamann & Jennings, Miami, Fla., 1974-79; ptnr. Blackwell, Walker, Gray, Powers, Flick, & Hoehl, Miami, 1979-85; assoc. Henderson, Franklin, Starnes & Holt, 1985—. Fla. Bar Assn. (cert. in trial law 1984), Dade County Bar Assn. (bd. dirs. 1982-85), Dade County Def. Bar (bd. dirs. 1980-85), ABA. Presbyterian. Office: 2100 2d St PO Box 280 Fort Myers FL 33902

STANLEY, DAVID WAYNE, engineering executive; b. Houston, June 27, 1949; s. Waymon Bennett and Billie Joe (Coats) S.; m. Sandra Lu Higginbotham, Feb. 28, 1976; children—Michael, Nicholas. B.S. in Petroleum Engring., U. Southwestern La., 1972; M.B.A., Houston Bapt. U., 1983. Petroleum engr. Tenneco, Houston, 1975-79, Mitchell Energy Corp., Houston, 1979-81; engring. mgr. U.S.A., The Royal Bank of Can., Global Energy & Minerals Group, Houston, 1981—; dir. Harvest Drilling Co., Cleveland, Tex. Active Republican Senatorial Com, Washington, 1980, Republican Party Tex., Austin, 1984. Served with U.S. Army, 1972-75. Jr. Petroleum Engring. scholar Chevron Oil Co., 1971; Sr. Petroleum Engring. scholar Pennzoil Oil Co., 1972. Mem. Soc. Petroleum Engrs., Houston Geol. Soc., Am. Assn. Petroleum Geologists. Republican. Baptist. Home: 12119 Great Oak Pl The Woodlands TX 77380 Office: Royal Bank Can 6850 Tex Commerce Tower Houston TX 77002

STANLEY, EDWARD ALEXANDER, geologist; b. N.Y.C., Apr. 7, 1929; s. Frank and Elizabeth (Wolf) S.; m. Elizabeth Ann Allison, June 7, 1958; children—Karen, Scott. B.S., Rutgers U., 1954; M.S., Pa. State U., 1956, Ph.D., 1960. Geologist, Amoco Co., Tulsa, 1960-62; prof. U. Del., 1962-64, U. Ga., 1964-77; adminstr. Indiana U. Pa., 1977-81; supr. Phillips Petroleum Co., Bartlesville, Okla., 1981—; cons. geology, Athens, Ga., 1963-77, Indiana, Pa., 1977-81. Contbr. articles to profl. jours. Served to sgt. USAF, 1947-50. Grantee NSF, 1965-68, Office Water Resources Research, 1965-68, Nat. Acad. Sci., 1968, 73. Fellow AAAS, Geol. Soc. Am.; mem. Am. Assn. Petroleum Geologists, Paleontol. Soc., Sigma Xi. Presbyterian. Avocations: photography; music; firearms. Home: 2601 Regency Rd Bartlesville OK 74006 Office: Phillips Petroleum Co 240 FPB Bartlesville OK 74006

STANLEY, HERMAN PAUL, JR., psychologist, educator; b. Memphis, Oct. 19, 1951; s. Herman Paul and Robbie June (Payne) S.; m. Rebecca Jeanne Williams, Dec. 29, 1978; children—David Paul, Michael Luke. B.A., Mid-South Bible Coll., 1974; M.A. in Religion, Harding Coll., 1977; student Memphis State U., 1975-79; Ph.D., U. Miss., 1983. Lic. psychologist, Tenn., Ark. Coordinator personal services Salvation Army Adult Rehab. Ctr., Memphis, 1977-78; grad. instr. U. Miss., Oxford, 1981-82; alcohol and drug counselor N.E. Community Mental Health Ctr., Memphis, 1978-82, cons., 1983-85; adj. instr. Mid-South Bible Coll., Memphis, 1983-85, asst. prof., chmn. dept. social sci., 1985—; psychologist Christian Psychol. and Ednl. Services, Memphis, 1983—; cons. Meth. Outreach, Inc., 1984-85, Mid-South Hosp., Inc., 1985—. Bd. dirs. Grace House of Memphis, Inc., 1982—; mem. regional adv. planning com. Tenn. Dept. Mental Health and Mental Retardation, Memphis, 1983. Mem. Am. Psychol. Assn., Tenn. Psychol. Assn., Memphis Area Psychol. Assn. Mem. First Evang. Ch. Home: 3310 Guernsey Ave Memphis TN 38122 Office: Christian Psychol and Ednl Services Reddoch Profl Ctr 965 Reddoch Cove Memphis TN 38119

STANLEY, JAMES GORDON, engineering marketing executive, writer; b. Birmingham, Ala., Feb. 13, 1925; s. Joseph Gordon and Amy I. (Crocker) S.; B.S., U. Ala., 1949; m. children—Cynthia Ruth, Pamela Anne, Gordon Bruce, James Alan, Joseph Christopher; m. 2d, Patricia Ann Peuvion, 1969. Instr., Miss. State U. Extension, Jackson, 1956; tech. rep. S.E., Price Brothers Co., Dayton, 1957-59; project mgr., dept. mgr. Brown Engring. Co., Kennedy Space Center, Fla. and Huntsville, Ala., 1959-64; dir. engring., reliability Bendix Launch Support Div., 1964-67; mgr. reliability, systems engr. Dow Chem. Co., Kennedy Space Center, 1967-71, mgr. engring. mktg. Houston, 1971-73, contract research mgr., Midland, Mich., 1973-80, sr. project mgr. Houston, 1980—, assigned as project bus. mgr. Dow/Dept. Energy geothermal project, Lafayette, La., 1981-83; free lance writer. Served to lt. (j.g.) USNR, 1943-66. Recipient Toulmin medal for best article Mil. Engr. Mag., 1980. Mem. Cocoa Beach C. of C., Phi Gamma Delta. Baptist. Club: Elks. Contbg. editor for energy Nat. Def. Mag. Home: 2947 Meadowgrass Ln Houston TX 77082 Office: Dow Chem USA 400 West Belt S Houston TX 77042

STANLEY, JEANIE RICKETTS, political science educator; b. Urbana, Ill., Oct. 9, 1946; d. Marion Masters and Dorthea June (Cox) Ricketts; m. James Howard Stanley, May 6, 1969. B.A. in Polit. Sci., U. Tex., 1968, M.A., 1970, Ph.D., 1981. Instr. polit. sci. Ursuline Acad., Dallas, 1970-71, Kilgore Coll., Tex., 1973-77; asst. prof. U. Tex., Tyler, 1979—. Contbr. chpts. to books, articles to profl. jours. Vice chmn. Tex. State Bd. Examiners of Profl. Counselors, 1984—; committeeman Tex. Democratic Exec. Com., 1982—, del. Nat. Conv., San Francisco, 1984. Fulbright scholar, 1968-69; NDEA fellow, 1970; Earhart Found. fellow, 1980. Mem. Am. Polit. Sci. Assn., Southwestern Polit. Sci. Assn., So. Polit. Sci. Assn. Presbyterian. Home: 1225 Oak Dr Kilgore TX 75662 Office: U Tex 3900 University Blvd Tyler TX 75701

STANLEY, LUTICIOUS BRYAN, JR., mechanical and civil engineer; b. Atlanta, Aug. 26, 1947; s. Luticious Bryan and Frances Aileen (William) S.; B.S., So. Tech. Inst., 1974, 82; postgrad. Ga. State U., 1976-77. Registered profl. engr., Ga. Field engr. Jordan, Jones & Goulding, Inc., Atlanta, 1974-79; project mgr., engr. Mayes, Sudderth & Etheredge, Inc., Atlanta, 1979-82; engr. Westinghouse Electric Corp., Chattanooga, 1982-85, asst. regional projects mgr., Atlanta, 1985—; prin. LBS Enterprises. Served with USAR, 1969-75. Phi Theta Pi scholar, 1968. Mem. ASME. Christian Scientist. Club: Cobb County Lions (Rookie of Year award 1981). Author articles in field. Home: PO Box 5386WSB Gainesville GA 30501 Office: 1299 Northside Dr NW Atlanta GA 30318

STANLEY, NANCY NELL, gerontologist; b. Blum, Tex., Nov. 26, 1924; d. James Harvey and Sadie Pearl (Luton) Stanley; student Southwestern Bapt. Theol. Sem., 1952-53; B.A., U. Mary Hardin-Baylor, 1956; postgrad. in library sci. Va. Commonwealth U., 1960-61; M.A., North Tex. State U., 1982. Dir. religious edn. First Bapt. Ch., Belton, Tex., 1956-57; dir. religious edn. for youth First Bapt. Ch., Brownwood Tex., 1957-58; mgr. library and archives Fgn. Mission Bd., So. Bapt. Conv., Richmond, Va., 1958-80; long-term care adminstr., dir. staff devel. Bapt. Meml. Geriatric Center, San Angelo, Tex., 1981—. Dean women, counselor Bapt. ch. camps in Tex., 1954-58. Mem. ALA, Soc. Am. Archivists, So. Bapt. Hist. Soc., Assn. Nat. Archives, Smithsonian Instn. (asso.), Gerontol. Assn., Alpha Chi, Sigma Tau Delta. Author: Southern Baptist Involvement In Long-Term Care as Mandated by Judeo-Christian Teachings; author tng. manuals; contbr. articles to religious jours. Home: 902 N Main St Apt D 6W San Angelo TX 76902 Office: Bapt Meml Geriatric Center 902 Main St PO Box 5661 San Angelo TX 76902

STANLEY, NORMAN KEITH, chemist; computer consultant; b. Dec. 15, 1956; s. Verne Ray and Sarah Catherine (Smith) S. B.A., U. Tenn.-Chattanooga, 1978. Chemist, Gilman Co., Chattanooga, 1978-80, SCM Glidden, Atlanta, 1980-82; chemist Kimberly Clark Corp., Roswell Ga., 1982—. Treas. Friends of Piedmont Park, Atlanta, 1984; patron High Mus. Art. Experiment in Internat. Living scholar, 1977. Mem. Am. Chem. Soc. Republican. Episcopalian. Home: PO Box 550432 Atlanta GA 30324 Office: Kimberly Clark Corp 1400 Holcomb Bridge Rd Roswell GA 30076

STANSBURY, GILBERT JOHN, oil company executive; b. Port Sulphur, La., Aug. 29, 1941; s. Woodrow Wilson Stansbury and Elsie May (Buras) S.; m. Elizabeth Marie Laura, Aug. 17, 1963; children—Laura, Lisa, Jill. B.A. in Liberal Arts, St. Edwards U., 1963. Policyholders service rep Ins. Co. of N.Am., New Orleans, 1966-70; safety engr. Freeport Sulpur Co., New Orleans, 1970; safety mktg. rep. Hanover Ins. Co., New Orleans, 1970-74; loss control cons. Hartford Ins. Co., New Orleans, 1974-78; mgr. safety and tng. CNG Producing Co., New Orleans, 1978—; chmn. personal floatation devices Gulf Coast Safety and Tng. Group, New Orleans, 1978—, past pres. Bd. dirs. Algiers Point Civic Assn., New Orleans, 1976, Norman Playground Boosters Club, New Orleans, 1984. Mem. Acadania Safety Assn. (bd. dirs. cir. research com. 1985), Am. Soc. Safety Engrs., Am. Soc. Tng. and Devel., Nat. Safety Mgmt. Soc. Democrat. Roman Catholic. Avocations: fishing; water skiing; carpentry. Home: Rt 1 Box 429 Slidell LA 70458 Office: CNG Producing Co Suite 3100 Canal Place 1 New Orleans LA 70114

STANSELL, LELAND EDWIN, JR., lawyer, educator; b. Central, S.C., July 13, 1934; s. Leland Edwin and Hettie Katherine (Hollis) S.; children—James Leland, Susan. B.S., Fla. So. Coll., 1957; LL.B., U. Miami (Fla.), 1961, J.D., 1968. Bar: Fla. 1961. Assoc. Wicker & Smith, Miami, 1961-62, ptnr., 1962-75; sole practice, Miami, 1975—; chmn. Jud. Nominating Commn., Dade County (Fla.), 1983—; adv. council Am. Arbitration Assn., 1975—. Served with U.S. Army, 1957. Mem. U. Miami Law Alumni Assn. (dir., officer, pres. 1968-69), Dade County Bar Assn. (dir. 1969-72, exec. com. 1974-75, pres. 1975-76), Fla. Bar (bd. govs. 1966-70, 70-80), ABA (house of dels. 1982—), Fla. Criminal Def. Attys. Assn. (treas. 1964-66), Fla. Def. Lawyers Assn., Am. Judicature Soc., Fedn. Ins. Counsel, Delta Theta Phi. Clubs: University, Miami Rod and Reel, Coral Reef Yacht, Jockey, American, Bankers. Office: Suite 903 Biscayne Bldg 19 W Flagler St Miami FL 33130

STANSELL, VANCE DALE, psychologist; b. Longview, Tex., Mar. 29, 1948; s. Elton Curtis and Trudy (Smith) S.; m. Mary Jane Whitaker, May 30, 1970; children—Jason Curtis, Kevin Allen. Student Kilgore Coll., 1966-68; B.B.A., U. Tex., 1970; M.A., Stephen F. Austin State U., 1974; Ph.D., U. Okla., 1979. Diplomate Am. Acad. Behavioral Medicine, Internat. Acad. Profl. Counseling and Psychotherapy; cert., lic. psychologist, Tex.; lic. profl. counselor, Tex. Psychol. cons. Evaluation, Research and Tng. Assn., Norman, Okla., 1978-80, part-time psychol. cons., 1980-83; adj. asst. prof. U. Okla., Norman, 1980; v.p., psychologist Double D Affiliates, San Angelo, Tex., 1980-83; pvt. practice psychology, San Angelo, 1984, West Tex. Med. Assocs., San Angelo, 1984—. Contbr. papers to profl. publs. and confs. Mem. Am. Psychol. Assn., Tex. Psychol. Assn., Okla. Psychol. Assn., Soc. Behavioral Medicine, Assn. for Advancement of Behavior Therapy, Psi Chi, Phi Delta Kappa. Avocations: Tennis; golf; backpacking; cross country skiing; sailing; travel, jogging, bicycling. Home: 3306 Shadyhill San Angelo TX 76904 Office: West Tex Med Assocs 3555 Knickerbocker Rd San Angelo TX 76904

STANSFIELD, GEORGE JAMES, librarian, historian; b. Oak Park, Ill., Mar. 8, 1917; s. James Howard and Inez Pearl (Snyder) S.; student MIT, 1934-35; B.S., Harvard U., 1940; postgrad. Am. U., 1940-44, 61-64, M.A., 1983; postgrad. George Washington U., 1965-66; m. Anna Bryant Hill, Oct. 20, 1945; children—Louisa Westcott, James Ross. With Nat. Park Service, 1941-42, Nat. Archives, Washington, 1942-46, World War I Declassification Bd., Dept. Army, 1946-48; with library reference sect. Nat. War Coll., Washington, 1948-61, library dir., 1961-73, historian, 1965-76; historian Nat. Def. U., Washington, 1976-78, chief spl. collection, hist. br., library div., 1978-80; sr. historian DARCOM, Dept. Army, 1980-83; librarian Am. Mil. Inst., 1944-63; mem. Fed. Library Com. Task Force on acquisition of library materials and correlation of fed. library resources, 1965-72. Chmn., Hist. Records Adv. Com. City of Alexandria, 1975—; Recipient Comdr's. award for civilian service Dept. Army, 1980. Fellow Am. Mil. Inst. (life); mem. Nat. War Coll. Alumni Assn. (hon., life), Alexandria Library Co. (pres. 1985—), Spl. Libraries Assn. (chmn. archives com. mil. librarians div. 1966-76), Alexandria Assn. (pres. 1972-73), Soc. Am. Archivists (awards sub-com. chmn. Colonial Dames Scholarships 1981-82), Am. Hist. Assn., Alexandria Hist. Soc. (treas. 1974-76), SAR. Episcopalian. Book rev. editor Mil. Affairs, 1944-46, 50-63; asso. editor, author chpt. Alexandria: A Towne in Transition, 1800-1900, 1977; adv. bd. No. Va. Heritage, 1978—; editorial com. Alexandria History, Vol. I, 1978; contbr. sects. to books, articles to jours., reports, ency. Address: 512 Duke St Alexandria VA 22314

STANSFIELD, JAMES ROSS, commercial photographer; b. Alexandria, Va., July 10, 1950; s. George James and Anna Bryant (Hill) S.; m. Carol Brent McLaughlin, May 7, 1982; 1 son, Brian Ross. B.A., George Mason Coll., 1975. Head photographer Port Packet Newspaper, Alexandria, Va., 1975-80; free lance comml. photographer Alexandria, 1980—. Photographer: pictorial history Pictorial History of Alexandria, 1977; contbr: Alexandria: A town in Transition 1800-1900, 1977. Mem. Art Dirs. Club, Am. Soc. Mag. Photographers. Home: 3187 N Pollard St Arlington VA 22207 Office: 4938 D Eisenhower Ave Studio D Alexandria VA 22304

STANTON, G(ARDNER) KIMMEL, pharmacist, educator; b. Waurika, Okla., July 24, 1942; s. Jake Mack and Syble Emma (Gardner) S.; m. Jymmie Lea Pass, June 29, 1961; children—David Landon, Michael Scott. B.S. in Pharmacy, Okla. U., 1964, M.S., 1966. Lic. pharmacist, Okla., Ark., Tex. Dir. pharmacy St. Edwards Mercy Hosp., Fort Smith, Ark., 1964-65, Norman Regional Hosp., Okla., 1965—; instr. pharmacy Okla. U., Oklahoma City, 1975—, pharmacy program cons. Central Okla. Vocat.-Tech. Adminstrn., Norman, 1976—; instr. pharmacology Norman area Vocat.-Tech. Nursing Program, 1966—. Editor: (hosp. pharmacist column) Okla. Pharmacist, 1973-80; (profl. newsletter) Okla. Soc. Hosp. Pharmacists Lantern, 1965-75. Contbr. articles to profl. jours., poetry to lit. mags. Mem. Okla. Soc. Hosp. Pharmacists (pres. 1970-71, 1978-79; Squibb Leadership award 1970, 79, Geigy Pharmacist award 1971, 79), Am. Soc. Hosp. Pharmacists, Am. Pharm. Assn., Okla. Pharm. Assn. (dist. dir. 1976), Okla. Pharm. Heritage Found., Okla. Pharmacy Alumni Assn. (pres. 1966-67). Office: Norman Regional Hosp Pharmacy 901 N Porter St Norman OK 73071

STANTON, GEORGE DUWE, petroleum geologist; b. Chgo., Mar. 23, 1949; s. John Woolsey and Dorothy May (Duwe) S.; m. Barbara Jeanne Beard, Sept. 1, 1979. B.S., U. Fla., 1971; M.A., U. Tex., 1977. Mgr. geologic projects Bendix Corp., Austin, Tex., 1976-80; cons. petroleum exploration Austin, Corpus Christi, 1980-82; ind. petroleum explorationist Austin, 1982—. Author: Factors Influencing Porosity and Permeability, Wilcox Formation, Karnes, County, Tex., 1977, Uranium Favoribility N. Central Texas and Southwest Oklahoma, 1977. Mem. Am. Assn. Petroleum Geologists (ho. of dels. 1980-82, 85—), Austin Geol. Soc. Avocations: water sports; art collecting. Home: 5305 Turnabout Ln Austin TX 78731 Office: 121 E 8th St Suite 1200 Austin TX 78701

STANTON, GEORGE PATRICK, JR., lawyer; b. Fairmont, W.Va., Nov. 21, 1933; s. George Patrick and Wilma Roberta (Everson) S.; m. Shirley Jean Champ, Sept. 3, 1956; children—George Patrick, Edward Scott. B.S. in Bus. Adminstrn., Fairmont Coll., 1956; M.B.A. in Fin., U. Dayton, 1969; J.D., U. Balt., 1977. Bar: Md. 1978, U.S. Dist. Ct. Md. 1978, W.Va. 1979, U.S. Dist. Ct. (so. dist.) W.Va. 1979, U.S. Dist. Ct. (no. dist.) W.Va. 1980, U.S. Ct. Appeals (4th cir.) 1985.Auditor 1st Nat. Bank Fairmont, 1955-61; asst. cashier S.C. Nat. Bank, Columbia, 1961-64; sr. systems analyst Chase Manhattan Bank, N.Y.C., 1964-65; asst. v.p. Winters Nat. Bank, Dayton, Ohio, 1965-69, Md. Nat. Bank, Balt., 1969-74; v.p. Equitable Trust Co., Balt., 1974-79; gen. ptnr. Stanton & Stanton Attys. at Law, Fairmont, 1979—; staff sect. leader, mem. faculty Sch. for Bank Adminstrn. U. Wis.-Madison, 1978—. Treas. Mountaineer Area council Boy Scouts Am., Fairmont, 1982—; v.p. Three Rivers Coal Festival, Inc., Fairmont, 1984-85, pres., 1985—; mem. adv. bd. Inst. for Living, Fairmont, 1983—. Mem. ABA, Assn. Trial Lawyers Am., Comml. Law League Am., W.Va. State Bar Assn., Marion County Bar Assn., Md. State Bar Assn., W.Va. Trial Lawyers Assn., Marion County C. of C. (bd. dirs. 1983—), Fairmont State Coll. Alumni Assn. (bd. dirs. 1982—). Club: Fairmont Field. Lodges: Rotary, Masons. Home: 2 West Hills Dr Fairmont WV 26554 Office: Stanton & Stanton Suite 707 First National Bank Bldg Fairmont WV 26554

STANTON, JOSHUA JOYNER, JR., agronomist; b. Stantonsburg, N.C., May 27, 1933; s. Joshua Joyner and Mabel Estelle (Wooten) S.; B.S., N.C. State U., 1955; m. Linda Anne Williams, Dec. 23, 1961; children—James E., David W. Asst. small grains breeder Coker's Pedigreed Seed Co., Hartsville, S.C., 1959-65, plant breeder Cotton-Soybean div., 1967-72, dir. soybean research, 1972—; asst. hybrid corn breeder McNair Seed Co., Laurinburg, N.C., 1965-66. Served with AUS, 1956-58. Mem. Am. Soc. Agronomy, Crop Sci. Soc. Am., AAAS, Am. Phytopath. Soc., Am. Soybean Assn., S.C. Soybean Assn. (past pres., dir.), Gamma Sigma Delta. Methodist. Research on soybean cultivars. Home: 222 Holly Dr Hartsville SC 29550 Office: PO Box 340 Hartsville SC 29550

STANTON, RUFUS H., JR., dentist; b. Galveston, Tex., May 27, 1925; s. Rufus H. and Carrie Whitsett (McFadden) S.; m. Janice D. Splane, Apr. 7, 1944; children—Rufus H. III, Deborah Ann Stanton Burke, Robert T. II. B.A., Wiley Coll., 1948; D.D.S., Meharry Med. Coll., 1953. Practice dentistry, Galveston, 1953—; dir. U.S. Nat. Bank, Galveston, Tex. Bd. dirs. Galveston Mcpl. Golf Course, 1963-73; chmn. bd. trustees Reedy Chapel AME Ch., 1979—; mem. integration com. adv. bd. Galveston Ind. Sch. Dist., 1965-70; bd. dirs. St. Vincents House, 1975-80. Served with U.S. Army, 1944-46. Mem. ADA, Nat. Dental Assn., 9th Dist. Dental Soc., Gulf States Dental Assn. (past pres.), Tex. Dental Assn., Charles A. George Dental Soc., Am Legion, Alpha

Phi Alpha. Democrat. Avocations: golf; bicycling. Home: 3615 Ave O Galveston TX 77550 Office: 3617 Ave O Galveston TX 77550

STANTON, VIVIAN BRENNAN (MRS. ERNEST STANTON), retired educator; b. Waterbury, Conn.; d. Francis P. and Josephine (Ryan) Brennan; B.A., Albertus Magnus Coll., 1939; M.S., So. Conn. State Coll., 1962, 6th yr. degree, 1965; postgrad. Columbia U.; m. Ernest Stanton, May 31, 1947; children—Pamela L., Bonita F., Kim Ernest. Tchr. English, history, govt. Milford (Conn.) High Sch., 1940-48; tchr. English, history, fgn. Born Night Sch., New Haven, 1948-54, Simon Lake Sch., Milford, 1960-62; guidance counselor, psychol. examiner Jonathan Law High Sch., Milford, 1962-73, Nat. Honor Soc. adv., 1966-73, mem. Curriculum Councils, Graduation Requirement Council, Gifted Child Com., others, 1940-48, 60-73; guidance dir. Foran High Sch., Milford, 1973-79, career center coordinator, 1976-79, ret., 1979. Active various community drives; mem. exec. bd. Ridge Rd PTA, 1956-59; mem. Parent-Tchr. council Hopkins Grammer Sch., New Haven; mem. Human Relations Council, North Haven, 1967-69; vol., patient rep. surg. waiting rm. Fawcett Meml. Hosp., P.C. Mem. Nat. Assn. Secondary Schs. and Colls. (evaluation com.; chmn. testing com.), AAUW, LWV, Conn. Personnel and Guidance Assn., Conn. Sch. Counselors Assn., Conn. Assn. Sch. Psychol. Personnel, Conn., Milford (pres. 1945-47) edn. assns. Clubs: Univ., Charlotte Harbor Yacht. Home: 704 Westmont Way Greenbriar Sun City Center FL 33570

STAPLER, HARRY BASCOM, journalism educator, publisher; b. N.Y.C., Mar. 10, 1919; s. Henry Bascom and Gertrude (Haupert) S.; m. Lorie Donoho, Aug. 7, 1982. B.A., Coll. Wooster (Ohio), 1950; M.A., Central Mich. U., 1981. Reporter, Daily Record, Wooster, 1940-41, 47-50, also photographer; reporter AP, Detroit, 1950, regional sports editor, 1951-53; sports reporter Detroit News, 1953-58; editor Fostoria Rev. Times (Ohio), 1958-60; bus. reporter Lansing State Jour. (Mich.), 1960-62; pub., editor, founder East Lansing Towne Courier (Mich.), 1962-73, pres., 1966-73; pub., editor, founder Meridian Towne Courier, Okemos, Mich., 1965-73; pub., editor Williamston Enterpise (Mich.), 1966-73; v.p. Suburban Newspapers Mich., 1969-73; instr. journalism Ferris State Coll., 1974-79, dir. journalism program, 1977-79; instr., asst. chmn. Sch. Journalism, Mich. State U., East Lansing, 1979-82; asst. prof. journalism U. Fla.-Gainesville, 1982—; mng. editor Competency Forum, 1977-79. Served with USNR, 1941-46. Recipient John Field Journalism Edn. award Mich. Interscholastic Press Assn., 1973. Mem. Soc. Newspaper Design, Assn. for Edn. in Journalism and Mass Communication. Presbyterian. Author: The Student Journalist and Sportswriting, 1974; Exploring Pro Sports, 1982. Home: 1810-258 NW 23d Blvd Gainesville FL 32605

STAPP, BRUCE MICHAEL, government vocational rehabilitation evaluator; b. Oklahoma City, Dec. 25, 1944; s. Carl Herbert and Willie Lee (Broome) S.; children—Jonathan Michael, Benjamin Matthew. B.B.A., Central State U. Okla., 1973, M.Ed., 1974; postgrad. U. Okla., 1975-78; Ph.D. cand., Calif. Coast U., 1985. Cert. rehab. counselor; lic. profl. counselor, career counselor. Sr. vocat. rehab. counselor Okla. Dept. Human Services, Oklahoma City, 1974-78, sr. vocat. rehab. evaluator, Norman, 1978-80, Oklahoma City, 1980—; cons. in career counseling, Norman, 1984—. Scouting coordinator Boy Scouts Am., 1985. Served with USN, 1965-67; vietnam. Mem. Internat. Acad. Profl., Counseling and Psychotherapy (clin.), Okla. Assn. Counseling and Devel., Okla. Career Devel. Assn., Am. Assn. Counseling and Devel., Nat. Career Devel. Assn., Kappa Delta Pi. Democrat. Baptist. Avocations: Skydiving; scuba diving; snow skiing; water skiing. Home: 1623 Glen Bo Dr Norman OK 73071 Office: Dept Human and Rehab Services 5813 S Robinson St Oklahoma City OK 73109

STAPP, DAVID PHARIS, oil company executive, geologist; b. Lockney, Tex., Sept. 13, 1950; s. Elmer Lee and Betty Juanita (Boutwell) S.; m. Pamela Patricia Baccus, June 7, 1971; children—Aryn Elise, Joshua David. B.S. in Geology, Tex. Tech U., 1973. Stimulation engr. Western Co. N.Am., Snyder, Tex., 1977; sales engr. Champion Chems., Rock Springs, Wyo., 1977-78; mgr. petro-data Core Labs., Dallas, 1978-81; chief geologist Western Continent Oil Co., Dallas, 1981-82; pres., geologist Texcel Exploration, Inc., Lewisville, Tex., 1982—; cons. geologist Sweetgrass Energy, Dallas, 1982-83, Kodiak Energy, Dallas, 1984, Gennoil, Inc., Dallas, 1983—. Mem. Am. Assn. Petroleum Geologists, Engrs. Club Dallas, Dallas Geol. Soc. Mem. Ch. of Christ. Avocations: fishing; hunting; weight lifting. Home: 437 Louise Ln Lewisville TX 75067 Office: Texcel Exploration Inc 2300 Highland Village Suite 530 Lewisville TX 75067

STARBUCK, JOHN EMERSON, landscape architect, contractor; b. Atlanta, Sept. 11, 1944; s. John E. and Elizabeth (Hurt) S.; m. Eloise Maxwell, Aug. 2, 1968. Student Darlington Sch., Rome, Ga., 1963; B.S. in Landscape Architecture, U. Ga., 1969. Registered landscape architect, Ala. Landscape architect, contractor Landscape Services Inc., Birmingham, Ala., 1968-78, landscape architect, prin. J.E. Starbuck, Inc., Birmingham, 1978—. Bd. dirs. Birmingham Zoo. Recipient Honor award Darnell Residence Ala. chpt. Am. Soc. Landscape Architects. Served with U.S. Army, 1969-71. Mem. Am. Soc. Landscape Architects (nat. trustee 1984-87, past pres. Ala. chpt. 1981-82). Republican. Methodist. Clubs: Pine Harbor; Yacht (Cropwell). Lodges: Lions (past pres., treas. Mountain Brook, Ala.). Avocation: sailing. Home: 3349 Brookwood Rd Birmingham AL 35223 Office: JE Starbuck Inc 1037 22d St S Suite 201 Birmingham AL 35205

STARCEVICH, MATTHEW MARK, management consultant; b. Norman, Okla., Apr. 17, 1943; s. Matthew Paul and Clemence Alice (Simon) S.; m. Judith Lynn Kaiser, Jan., 1968; 1 child, Matthew Brett. B.S., Western Ill. U., 1965; M.B.A., No. Ill. U., 1968; Ph.D., U. Okla., 1971. Asst. prof. U. Notre Dame, Ind., 1971-74; mgr. orgn. devel. Phillips Petroleum Co., Bartlesville, Okla., 1974-79; pres. Ctr. for Mgmt. and Orgn. Effect, Bartlesville, 1979—. Author: Introduction to Business Systems, 1979. Editor: OD Proceedings, 1984. Mem. Am. Soc. Tng. and Devel. (exec. com. 1983-85, dir., 1985—), Am. Psychol. Assn. Republican. Roman Catholic. Avocations: hunting, tennis, reading. Home: 1350 Cherokee Hills Ct Bartlesville OK 74006

STARCKE, EDGAR NOLTE, JR., prosthodontist; b. Seguin, Tex., May 28, 1938; s. Edgar Nolte and Gladys Geraldine (Lynch) S.; m. Margie Schwartz, July 22, 1962; children—Barbara Claire, John Christopher. Student Tex. Luth. Coll., 1956-58, U. Tex., 1958-59; D.D.S., U. Tex. Dental Br., Houston, 1963; cert. prosthodontics VA Med. Ctr. and U. Ala. Sch. Dentistry, Birmingham, 1970. Diplomate Am. Bd. Prosthodontics. Gen. practice dentistry, Seguin, 1965-67; staff dentist VA Med. Ctr., Amarillo, Tex., 1967-68; resident in prosthodontics U. Ala. Sch. Dentistry, 1968-70, instr., 1969-70; staff prosthodontist VA Med. Ctr., Atlanta, 1970-72; staff prosthodontist VA Med. Ctr., Houston, 1972-80, dir. prosthodontics residency, 1972—, asst. chief dental services, 1979-80, chief dental service, 1980—; clin. instr. Emory U. Sch. Dentistry, Atlanta, 1970-72; clin. asst. prof. U. Tex. Dental Br., 1973-79, clin. assoc. prof., 1979—. Contbr. articles to profl. jours. Co-developer Oralube saliva substitute. Pres. Spring Shadows Elem. Sch. PTA, Houston, 1983-84. Served as capt. U.S. Army, 1963-65. VA grantee, 1974. Fellow Am. Coll. Prosthodontists; mem. ADA, Fedn. Prosthodontic Orgns., Am. Prosthodontic Soc., Am. Assn. Hosp. Dentists, S.W. Prosthodontic Soc., Psi Omega. Presbyterian. Avocations: art; antiques. Office: Chief Dental Service VA Med Ctr 2002 Holcombe Blvd Houston TX 77211

STARFORD, MARKUS JAY, educational foundation administrator, consultant, author; b. Eastport, Maine, June 23, 1952; s. Benson Myron and Lila Barbara (Gluck) Flanzbaum. B.A. in Human Devel., Antioch U., 1974, spl. edn. degree, 1974; Montessori teaching cert., 1974. Tchr. Montessori of West Los Angeles, Calif., 1971-79; adminstr., tchr. Pines Montessori Sch., Kingwood, Tex., 1979—; exec. dir. Spl. Children's Individualized Learning System, Kingwood, 1977—, program innovator, lectr., 1979—, dir. Atelier, Studio-Children's Art Gallery, 1985—; cons. Am. Montessori Soc., N.Y., 1984—. Author: (tape series) Understanding and Mgmt. of developmentally Delayed Children, 1981. Mem. Nat. Sci. Tchrs. Assn., Tex. Edn. Agy. (supt. 1982—), Nat. Down Syndrome congress (author, contbr. 1982—), Am. Montessori Soc., Young Democratic League. Avocations: international travel; soccer; swimming; computers. Office: SCILS Found 3535 Cedar Knolls Dr Kingwood TX 77339

STARK, KIM DOUGLAS, trade show exhibit builder; b. Kansas City, Kans., Jan. 27, 1958; s. Clarence Daniel and Marjorie Jane (McGinnis) S.; m. Carolyn Elaine Garland, June 6, 1980; children—Angela Rena, Tiffany Leanne. A.A.S., Weatherford Coll., 1978; student So. Meth. U., 1978-80. Writer, Weatherford (Tex.) Democrat, 1976-78; dir. mktg. Display Co. of Dallas, Garland, 1978-80, v.p., 1980-81, pres., 1981-82; pres. Exhibit House, Inc., Dallas, 1982—. Recipient Best Booth award Nat. Office Products Assn., 1983. Mem. Internat. Exhibitors Assn. (membership chmn. 1983—, profl. devel. cert. 1983), Trade Show Bur. Republican. Roman Catholic. Home: 427 Frank Keasler Duncanville TX 75116 Office: Greyhound Exhibit Group Inc 3412 Dilido Rd Dallas TX 75228

STARKE, EDGAR ARLIN, JR., metallurgist, educator; b. Richmond, Va., May 10, 1936; s. Edgar Arlin and Mary Louise (Stein) S.; B.S. in Metall. Engring., Va. Poly. Inst., 1960; M.S., U. Ill., 1961; Ph.D. in Metall. Engring., U. Fla., 1964; m. Donna Lee Frazier, June 10, 1961; children—John Arlin, Karen Lee. Metallurgist, Savannah River Lab., Aiken, S.C., 1961-62; asst. prof. Ga. Inst. Tech., 1964-68, assoc. prof. metallurgy, 1968-72, prof., 1972-82, dir. Fracture and Fatigue Research Lab., 1978-82; Earnest Oglesby prof. materials sci. U. Va., 1983—, dean sch. engring. and applied sci., 1984—. Vis. scientist Oak Ridge (Tenn.) Nat. Lab., 1967, Max-Planck-Institut fur Metallforschung, Stuttgart, Germany, 1971; cons. Bell Tel. Lab., 1973-75, Lockheed Ga. Research Lab., 1965—, Southwire Co., 1967—. Served with AUS, 1954-56. Mem. Am. Soc. Metals (sec. Atlanta chpt. 1974-75), Am. Inst. Mining and Metall. Engrs. (sec.-treas. Ga. chpt. 1965-66, v.p. Ga. chpt. 1967, pres. chpt. 1968, sec. Non-Ferrous Metallurgy com. 1973-74, vice chmn. Non-Ferrous Metallurgy com. 1974-75, chmn. 1976-78, vice chmn. program metal sci.), Sigma Xi (sec. Ga. Inst. Tech. chpt. 1974-75), Tau Beta Pi, Alpha Sigma Mu, Omicron Delta Kappa, Pi Delta Epsilon. Contbr. numerous articles to profl. jours. Home: Route 5 Box 331A Charlottesville VA 22901

STARKEY, RUSSELL BRUCE, JR., utility company executive; b. Lumberport, W.Va., July 20, 1942; s. Russell Bruce and Dorotha Mable (Field) S.; m. Joan McClellan, May 27, 1966; children—Christine, Pamela, Joanne. B.S., Miami U., Oxford, Ohio, 1964; postgrad. U. New Haven, 1972-73, N.C. State U., 1974-75, U.S. Navy Schs., 1964-66, 68. Sr. engr., nuclear generation sect. Carolina Power & Light Co., Raleigh, N.C., 1973-74, sr. engr. ops. quality assurance, 1974, prin. engr., 1974-75, quality assurance supr. Brunswick Steam Electric Plant, Southport, N.C., 1975-76, supt. tech. and adminstrn., 1976, supt. ops. and maintenance, 1976-77, plant mgr. H. B. Robinson Steam Electric Plant, Hartsville, S.C., 1977-83; exec. dir. nuclear ops. Pub. Service, Ind., Marble Hill and New Washington, Ind., 1983-84; mgr. environ. services Carolina Power and Light Co., Raleigh, 1984-85; mgr. nuclear safety and environ. services dept., 1985—. Served with USN, 1964-73. Mem. Am. Nuclear Soc. Home: 1001 Carrington Dr Raleigh NC 27609 Office: Carolina Power & Light Co PO Box 1551 Raleigh NC 27602

STARKOFF, BERNARD JULIUS, publisher; b. Cleve., Aug. 8, 1917; s. Jack and Rea (Aronovitz) S.; m. Florence Friedman, Oct. 14, 1944; children—Jay, Earl, Barbara Starkoff Jones. B.A., U. Cin., 1940; M.H.L., Hebrew Union Coll., 1943. Vice pres. Chem. Rubber Co., Cleve., 1947-62, pres., 1963-73; chmn. bd., pres. CRC Press Inc. successor to Chem. Rubber Co., Boca Raton, Fla., 1973—; mng. ptnr. Staroff Assocs., Boca Raton, 1978—; pres. Superindex, Inc., Boca Raton, 1982—; dir. Imreg Corp., New Orleans. Bd. dirs., bd. regents Coll. of Boca Raton, 1982—; bd. dirs. Found. Fla. Atlantic U., Boca Raton, 1982—, Temple Beth El, Boca Raton, 1981—, United Way, Boca Raton, 1980—. Jewish. Office: CRC Press Inc 2000 Corporate Blvd NW Boca Raton FL 33431*

STARNES, R(ALPH) EMORY, JR., wire and cable development engineer; b. Dalton, Ga., Oct. 12, 1938; s. Ralph Emory and Annie Laura (Wilson) S.; m. Allene Elizabeth Harris, Mar. 28, 1959; children—Chris, Pam. Student Ga. Inst. Tech., 1956-58; A.S., So. Inst. Tech., 1963. Cert. jr. engring. technician. With Kroger Co., Smyrna, Ga., 1958-63, Westinghouse Elevator Co., Atlanta, 1963-68; asst. process engr. Southwire Co., Carrollton, Ga., 1968-70, process engr., 1970-75, sr. process engr., 1975-82, devel. engr., 1982-85, sr. devel. engr., 1985—. Patentee wire and cable related devices and processes. Deacon, Tabernacle Baptist Ch., Carrollton, 1984—. Recipient Disting. Service award Southwire Co., 1976, A.A. Case Tech. Achievement award, 1984, Roger Schoerner Project of Yr. award, 1984. Mem. Soc. Mfg. Engrs. Club: Civitan (sec. 1972-73). Avocation: fishing. Office: Southwire Co Fertilla St Carrollton GA 30119

STARNS, KARL LINDELL, III, pharmacist, administrator; b. Bogalusa, La., May 13, 1955; s. Karl Lindell and Joan Yvone (Bass) S.; m. Lisa Lynn Davis, Jan. 2, 1977 (div. June 1983); 1 child, Circe Brooke; m. Martha Joanne Hernandez, Aug. 26, 1983. B.S., N.E. La. U., 1977. Registered pharmacist. Pharmacist, Starns Pharmacy, Bogalusa, La., 1977-81, Bogalusa Community Med. Ctr., 1978-81, dir., 1981—; cert. preceptor N.E. La.; intern/extern program U. La. Bd. Pharmacy, 1984—. Recipient Key to City, Mayor of Bogalusa, 1983; named Knight of Yr., K.C., Bogalusa, 1983. Mem. La. Pharmacist Assn., La. Soc. Hosp. Pharmacists, Am. Soc. Hosp. Pharmacists, Jaycees. Democrat. Roman Catholic. Lodge: K.C. (grand knight Bogalusa). Avocations: scuba diving; tennis; hunting; piano/guitar; camping; rafting. Home: 1948 Ave F Bogalusa LA 70427 Office: Bogalusa Community Med Ctr 433 Plaza Bogalusa LA 70427

STARR, GEORGE LEON, insurance company executive; b. Norfolk, Va., July 30, 1944; s. George Barton and Celene Estelle (Price) S.; m. Sandra Marie Murr, Oct. 26, 1984; children—Holly Lynne, Christa Carole, Jennipher Michele, Christopher Blaine. B.Music, Samford U., 1966; M.Music, New Orleans Bapt. Theol. Sem., 1968. Ordained to ministry Bapt. Ch., 1970; career agt. Am. Gen. Life Ins., Pensacola, Fla., 1975-78, career mgr., 1978—; owner G. Leon Starr & Assocs., Pensacola, 1978—; instr. Life Underwriters Tng. Council, Pensacola, 1978—. Named Agt. of Year, Am. Gen. Life Ins., 1978. Mem. Pensacola Assn. Life Underwriters (pres. 1982-83), Fla. Assn. Life Underwriters (regional v.p. 1984—), Nat. Assn. Life Underwriters, Gen. Mgrs. Confs. Republican. Methodist. Office: Stonegate Suite 10 7100 Plantation Rd Pensacola FL 32504

STARR, JENNIE SPRING, architectural designer, advertising executive, building contractor; b. Columbus, Ohio, Jan. 7, 1935; d. Ralph Downing and Mary Alice (Gard) Spring; student Columbus Coll. Art and Design, 1960-62, Wittenberg U., 1962-65, Penland Sch. Crafts, 1963, Inst. Irish Studies, 1979; m. John Clark Starr, June 14, 1958; children—Victoria Prince, Cynthia Knickerbocker, Teresa Gaa, Kristi Hodge, Holly Schuler, Tina Ell, Charles, Penny; foster-children—Hans Jurgen Zander, Edward V. Rahal. Art tchr. St. Patrick Sch., 1964-65; exec. sec. Madison County Continuing Med. Edn. Dept. and Madison County Hosp., 1967-71; owner London Internat. Travel, Inc. (Ohio), 1971-73; art dir. Madison County Schs., 1974-75; archtl. designer, art dir. Starr Studios, London, Ohio, 1973-76, Sarasota, Fla., 1976—; coordinator devel. U. Sarasota, 1981-82; lectr; charter mem. Ohio Arts Council; bd. dirs. Madison County Arts Guild, 1975-76; sculptor, works exhibited numerous one-woman shows. News editor Project HOPE, 1973-74; bd. dirs. Quality of Life Found., 1982-85. Recipient Spark Plug award City of London, 1967; hon. Kiwanian. Mem. Contractors Assn. Sarasota, Manatee, Harden and Lee Counties, Women in Constrn., Am. Soc. Profl. Estimators, Women Owners Network, Sarasota Advt. Club, Internat. Platform Assn. Episcopalian. Club: London Country. Garden editor: Madison Press, 1962-67; contbg. editor Madison County History, 1976; editor; Fla. Women's News, 1985; author works Irish history, Irish arts and crafts. Designer U. Sarasota campus, residences. Home: 3654 Dorst Ln Sarasota FL 33583

STARR, JOHN ROBERT, newspaper editor; b. Lake Village, Ark., Dec. 29, 1927; s. John Philip and Thelma Lucille (Russell) S.; B.A., Southwestern U., Memphis, 1952; Ph.D. candidate U. Tenn., 1977-78; m. Norma Jeannette Wilson, Nov. 14, 1948; children—John Phillip, Linda Sharon, Robert Russell. Sports writer Memphis Comml. Appeal, 1952-57; newsman AP, Little Rock, 1957-66, chief of bur., 1966-76; writer-in-residence U. Ark., Little Rock, 1976-77; mng. editor Ark. Democrat, Little Rock, 1978—. Pres., Geyer Springs Community Assn., 1963, 65, 68, 69, 76. Served with AUS, 1946-47, USNR, 1948-53. Named Ark. Journalist, Faculty U. Ark., Little Rock, 1981. Mem. Sigma Delta Chi. Home: 8 Daven Ct Little Rock AR 72209 Office: 121 E Capitol Little Rock AR 72201

STARR, PAUL DOUGLAS, sociologist, educator, social scientist; b. Bismarck, N.D., Aug. 2, 1942; s. Paul Arthur and Evelyn Annette (Freyer) S.; m. Susan Elizabeth Boehme, Aug. 14, 1972; children—Meredith, Kristen. Cert., Universite D' Aix-en-Provence, France, 1963; A.B., U. of the Pacific, 1964; M.A., U. Calif.-Santa Barbara, 1970, Ph.D., 1972. Devel. officer U.S. AID, Washington, 1966-69; lectr. sociology U. Calif.-Santa Barbara, 1971; asst. prof. sociology Am. U. Beirut, Lebanon, 1972-75; from asst. prof. to assoc. prof. Auburn U., Ala., 1975-85; vis. assoc. prof. Am. U. in Cairo, Egypt, 1982-84; prof. sociology, dir. grad. studies Auburn U., Ala., 1985—; vis. fellow Inst. Devel. Studies, U. Sussex, Eng., 1983; vis. scholar Oxford U., Eng., 1984. Author: Crucial Bonds, 1980. Contbr. articles to profl. jours. Intern, Inst. Internat. Edn., N.Y., 1966; alumni counselor Inst. Am. U., Aix-en-Provence, 1977—; mem. rev. com. Nat. Inst. Child Health and Human Devel., Rockville, Md., 1980. Research grantee U. Calif. Regents Fund, 1971-72, Miss.-Ala. Sea Grant Consortium, 1981-82, NIH, 1978-82. Mem. Am. Sociol. Assn., So. Soc. Soc., World Future Soc. Democrat. Club: U. Calif.-Santa Barbara Alumni Assn. (life). Avocations: travel; outdoor recreation. Home: 617 Seminole Auburn AL 36830 Office: Dept Sociology Anthropology and Social Work Auburn U Auburn AL 36849

STARRETT, RICHARD ALTON, social work educator, consultant; b. Toledo, Ohio, Aug. 30, 1942; s. Alton Burton and Thelma Elizabeth (Sherlock) S.; children—Richard Aaron, Timothy Bradford. A.A., UCLA, 1963; B.A., Calif. State U.-Fresno, 1973, M.A., 1977; Ph.D., U. Tex.-Arlington, 1983. Lic. mental health counselor, Calif. Coordinator, Camarillo State Hosp., Calif., 1974-75; instr. Fresno Coll., 1975-77, Moor Park Coll., Calif., 1977-78; asst. prof. U. Tex.-El Paso, 1978-80, research assoc., Arlington, 1980-83; assoc. prof. sociology Sch. Social Work, Barry U., Miami Shores, Fla., 1983—, also dir. alcoholic studies; research cons. Area Office on Aging, Miami, Fla., 1984—, Toledo Hosp., Ohio, 1984—, Urban Studies Inst., Miami, 1983—. Contbr. articles to profl. jours., chpts. to books. Bd. dirs. Area Office Aging, Miami, 1984—, Long Term Care United Way, 1984. Gerontol. Soc. Am. fellow, 1984. Mem. Gerontol. Soc. Am., Am. Sociol. Assn., Council Social Work Edn., Nat. Assn. Social Workers, So. Gerontol. Soc. Democrat. Avocations: camping; hiking; jogging; fishing. Home: 19731 NW 4th Ave North Miami Beach FL 33169 Office: Barry U Sch Social Work 11300 NE 2d Ave Miami Shores FL 33161

STARTZEL, RONALD NORMAN, nursing administrator, cardiopulmonary resuscitation educator; b. Bossier City, La., Oct. 5, 1956; s. Donald Norman and Dorothy (Ford) S. B.S. in Nursing, U. Tex., 1981. Registered nurse, advanced cardiac life support. Relief nurse Med. Personnel Pool, Austin, Tex., 1981-82; nursing supr. Meml. Hosp., Bastrop, Tex., 1982-84; dir. nursing Lockhart Hosp., Inc., Tex., 1984—; CPR instr. Am. Heart Assn., Lockhart, Tex., 1984—, faculty blood pressure awareness task force Tex. affiliate, 1985—, also mem. local council program com. Sec., bd. dirs. Coll. Houses, Inc., Austin, 1979-81; pres. Opsis Coll. House, Austin, 1980-81. Mem. Tex. Nurses Assn., Am. Nurses Assn., Tex. Soc. Hosp. Nursing Service Adminstrs., North Caldwell County Heart Assn. (bd. dirs., v.p. 1984—, program com. chmn. 1984—), Ex Student's Assn. U. Tex. Lodge: Kiwanis. Avocations: professional disc golfer; boating. Home: PO Box 553 Lockhart TX 78644 Office: Lockhart Hosp Inc 901 Bois D'Arc Lockhart TX 78644

STATHAM, BILL R., utility company executive; b. Hubbard, Tex., Feb. 11, 1934; s. Forest William and Gladys Maggie (Armstrong) S.; m. Eleanor Frances Collier, Aug. 11, 1963; children—Shannon Rae, Billy Ray, Forest Ray. B.S., Sam Houston State U., 1958. Lic. real estate broker. With Dallas Power & Light Co., 1958—, mgr. customer service div., 1975-77, exec. asst. to v.p., 1977-79, mgr. econ. devel., 1979-85, mgr. conservation and ecol. devel., 1985—, chmn. polit. action com., 1978—. Mem. The Dallas 40, 1973—; bd. dirs. Greater Dallas Crime Commn., 1981—. Served with AUS, 1958-60. Mem. Dallas Electric Club (sec.-treas.), Dallas C. of C., Dallas Indsl. Developers, Oak Cliff C. of C. Methodist. Lodge: Masons, Shriners. Home: 2652 Beechmont St Dallas TX 75228 Office: 1506 Commerce St Dallas TX 75201

STATON, SUE ANN, nurse; b. New Iberia, La., Sept. 24, 1957; d. James Edward and Marie (Rouly) S. B.S.N., U. Southwestern La., 1981. R.N., La. Nurse aide Dauterive Hosp., New Iberia, 1978-79, nurse aide IV, 1979-81, nurse, 1981—. Grantee Ladies Aux.-Iberia Parish, 1977-78, Pink Ladies Club, 1978, Am. Bus. Women's Assn., 1980. Mem. Am. Bus. Women's Assn. (corr. sec. New Iberia 1980-81, rec. sec. 1981-82, pres. 1982-83, Woman of Yr. 1983). Home: 1308 St Jude Ave New Iberia LA 70560 Office: Dauterive Hosp Inc 600 N Lewis New Iberia LA 70560

STAUBLIN, JUDITH ANN, computer co. mgr.; b. Anderson, Ind., Jan. 17, 1936; d. Leslie Fred and Esta Virginia (Ringo) Wiley; student Ball State U., 1954-55, 69-70, Savs. and Loan Inst., 1962-67, U. Ga., 1974, Wright State U., 1975; children—Juli Jackson, Scott Jackson. Teller, Anderson Fed. Savs. and Loan Assn., Anderson, 1962-64, data processing mgr., 1965-70, loan officer, 1970-72, v.p. systems, 1972-74, fin. systems mktg., 1974-76; fin. dist. mgr. data centers div. NCR Corp., Atlanta, 1977-81, nat. mgr. EFT Services data center div., Dayton, Ohio, 1981-82, fin. dist. mgr. data center div., Atlanta, 1982—. Active United Way. Mem. Am. Savs. and Loan Inst., Fin. Mgrs. Soc., Anderson C. of C. Home: 6115 Woodmont Blvd Norcross GA 30092 Office: NCR Corp 5 Executive Park Atlanta GA 30329

STAUFFER, THOMAS M., educational administrator; b. Harrisburg, Pa.; m. Marion Walker; children—Amity Juliet, Courtney Amanda, Winston Thomas. Student Juniata Coll., 1959-61; B.A. cum laude, Wittenberg U., Ohio, 1963; Cert. in European Politics, Freie U. Berlin, 1964; M.A., Ph.D. in Internat. Studies, U. Denver, 1972. Asst. dean coll. and asst. prof. polit. sci. Keene State Coll., 1968-72; Am. Council Edn. fellow in acad. adminstrn. U. N.H. System, 1971-72; dir. Am. Council Edn. fellows in acad. adminstrn., 1972-76, dir. Office of Leadership Devel. in Higher Edn., 1974-78, dir., v.p. div. external relations Am. Council on Edn., Washington, 1978-82; chancellor and prof. pub. policy U. Houston, Clear Lake, 1982—; vis. assoc. prof. George Washington U.; vis. prof., lectr. Regis Coll., Colo.; asst. prof. polit. sci. Radford Coll., Va.; teaching asst. in internat. relations U. Denver. Contbr. articles to profl. jours, chpts. to books. Vice pres. Clear Lake Econ. Devel. Found., 1985; mem. steering com. Houston Econ. Devel. Council, 1985; chair Houston World Trade Ctr. Task Force, 1985; vice chair Tex. Sci. and Tech. Council, 1985; co-chair edn. sect. Houston United Way Campaign, 1985; mem. Houston Hosp. Council Found., Tex. Council on Econ. Edn., Houston Com. on Fgn. Relations, Inst. Space Commercialization, MIT Enterprise Forum, St. John's Hosp., M. Bank, Clear Lake, Armand Bayou Nature Ctr. Fellow Am. Council on Edn., Am. Leadership Forum, Social Sci. Found., Ford Found.; grantee MacArthur Found., Bus.-Higher Edn. Forum, NSF, U.S. Office Edn., Ford Found., Rockefeller Found., U.S. Civil Service Commn., Lilly Endowment, HEW. Mem. Internat. Studies Assn. (chmn. fed. relations com., governing council, co-chmn. 1978 ann. meeting), Policy Studies Orgn., Asia Soc., Forum Club, Washington Higher Edn. Group, AAAS, Houston and Clear Lake C. of C. (chmn. com. on planning econ. diversification 1983), Council of State and Econ. Devel., Am. Assn. State Colls. and Univs., U.S. Yugoslavian Higher Edn. Com. Home: 15706 Larkfield Dr Houston TX 77059 Office: Office of Chancellor University of Houston Houston TX 77058

STAVINOHA, WILLIAM BERNARD, pharmacology educator, researcher; b. Temple, Tex., June 11, 1928; s. Adolph Alfonse and Lillian Ruby (Schiller) S.; m. Karen Peterson, 1958 (dec. 1965); m. Marilyn Cole, Feb. 8, 1966; children—Shannon, Elena, Rosie, Anna Christa. B.S. in Pharmacy, U. Tex., 1951, Pharm.M., 1954, Ph.D., 1959. Diplomate in Pharmacology and Toxicology. Instr. pharmacology U. Tex. Med. Br., Galveston, 1958-60, asst. prof., 1960; chief pharmacology, toxicology sect. Civil Aeromed. Research Inst., 1960-66, chief toxicology research div., 1966-68; assoc. prof., chief toxicology, dept. pharmacology U. Tex. Health Sci. Ctr., 1968-73, prof., chief toxicology, 1973—. Editor: Microwave Fixation of Labile Metabolites, 1983. contbr. articles to profl. jours. Recipient Disting. Alumnus award U. Tex., 1980. Mem. Soc. Exptl. Biology and Medicine, Soc. Neurochemistry, Brit. Brain Research Assn., Internat. Union Toxicology, Am. Soc. Pharmacology and Exptl. Therapeutics, Rho Chi, Kappa Psi, Sigma Xi. Office: U Tex Health Sci Ctr 7703 Floyd Curl Dr San Antonio TX 78284

STEAD, FREDERICK LEE, geologist, consultant; b. Toledo, Dec. 20, 1923; s. Jay Wheeler and Ona K. (Grunder) S.; m. Betty Ellen Leonard, Feb. 4, 1946; children—Michele Lee Stead Lamar, Patricia Lance Stead Sullivan, Ashley Summers, Frederick Lee. B.A., Coll. of Wooster, 1947, M.A., U. Tex., 1950. Lic. geologist, Calif. Instr. geology U. Tex., Austin, 1948-50; dist. geologist Continental Oil Co., Midland, Tex., 1951-54; div. mgr. Ada Oil Co., Midland, 1954-56; chief geologist McAlester Fuel Co., Magnolia, Ark., 1956-60; cons. geologist Los Angeles and Denver, 1960-77; pres. F.L. Stead and Assocs., Inc., Dallas, 1977—, guest lectr. Ark. State Coll., Magnolia, 1957-58; cons. geologist, Magnolia, 1960-62, Houston, 1965-67, Los Angeles, 1968-70; pres. Gt. Lakes Gas Corp., Dallas, 1963-64, Tri-Coast Petroleum, Inc., Los Angeles, 1970-73, Helmet Petroleum, Denver, 1975-76. Contbr. articles to profl. jours.

Ark. state chmn. Boys Clubs Am., 1965-66, Magnolia pres., 1967; elder Presbyn. Ch.; bd. dirs. Parkland Residential Sch., El Toro, Calif. Served to 2d lt. USAAF, 1943-45. Fellow Geol. Soc. Am.; mem. Am. Assn. Petroleum Geologists, Am. Inst. Profl. Geologists (pres. Calif. sect. 1975, nat. v.p. 1977), Soc. Econ. Paleontologists and Mineralogists, Soc. Mining Engrs. of AIME, Sigma Gamma Epsilon. Republican. Clubs: Petroleum, Energy (Dallas); Petroleum (Denver). Office: FL Stead and Assocs Inc Box 740128 Dallas TX 75374

STEADMAN, DAVID WILTON, museum official; b. Honolulu, Oct. 24, 1936; s. Alva Edgar and Martha (Cooke) S.; m. Kathleen Carroll Reilly, Aug. 1, 1964; children—Alexander Carroll, Kate Montague. B.A., Harvard U., 1960, M.A.T., 1961; M.A., U. Calif.-Berkeley, 1966; Ph.D., Princeton U., 1974. Lectr. Frick Collection, N.Y.C., 1970-71; asst. dir., acting dir., assoc. dir. Princeton U. Art Mus., 1971-73; dir. Galleries Claremont Colls., (Calif.), 1974-80; dir. Chrysler Mus., Norfolk, Va., 1980—; art cons. Archtl. Digest, Los Angeles, 1974-77; research curator Norton Simon Mus., Pasadena, Calif., 1977-80; trustee Art Mus. Assn. Am., 1984—. Author: Graphic Art of Francisco Goya, 1975, Works on Paper 1900-1960, 1977, Abraham van Diepenbeeck, 1982. Chester Dale fellow Nat. Gallery Art, Washington, 1969-70. Mem. Coll. Art Assn., Am. Assn. Mus. Dirs. Episcopalian. Office: Chrysler Mus Olney Rd Norfolk VA 23510

STEADMAN, RICHARD ANDERSON, JR., lawyer; b. Charleston, S.C., Sept. 17, 1954; s. Richard A. and Elizabeth (Barber) S.; m. Sarah Stokes, Aug. 5, 1978. B.A., Wofford Coll., 1976; J.D., U. S.C., 1981. Bar: S.C. 1981, U.S. Dist. Ct. S.C. 1982. Assoc. Willis Fuller, P.A., Charleston, 1981-82; sole practice, Charleston, 1982—; assoc. Lewis, Lewis, Bruce & Truslow, Charleston, 1982—. Dir. East Cooper Lifestyles, Inc., Mt. Pleasant, S.C., 1983-85. Mem. S.C. Bar Assn. (publs. editor Real Estate Lawyer 1982-83), Charleston County Bar Assn., S.C. Trial Lawyers Assn., Assn. Trial Lawyers Am., ABA, Lawyer's Club, Charleston Young Lawyers Club. Lodge: Optimists (bd. dirs. 1984-85, Yearling award 1983). Home: 1476 Short St Mount Pleasant SC 29464 Office: Lewis Lewis Bruce & Truslow PA 4 Carriage Ln Suite 204 Charleston SC 29407

STEARLEY, MILDRED SUTCLIFFE VOLANDT, former foundation executive; b. Ft. Myer, Va., Aug. 3, 1905; d. William Frederick and Mabel Emma (Sutcliffe) Volandt; student George Washington U., 1923-24, 25-28; m. Ralph F. Stearley, Sept. 19, 1931. Elementary tchr. Brent Sch., Baguio, Philippines, 1929-30; staff aide vol. services ARC, also acting chmn., Charlotte, N.C., 1943, staff asst., Washington, 1943-47, Gray Lady vol., Okinawa, 1950-53, Brazil, Ind., 1954; trustee Air Force Village Found., San Antonio, 1975-78, sec. bd., 1975-77; vol. Wilford Hall Med. Center, Lackland AFB, Tex. Mem. adv. bd. Am. Security Council; life mem. Air Force Village Found. Recipient commendation ARC, 1943. Mem. Army Daus., Am. Legion Aux., Army-Navy Club Aux., Smithsonian Instn., San Antonio Museum Assn., P.E.O. (life), Pi Beta Phi. Episcopalian. Clubs: Shakespeare Circle, Ladies Reading (Brazil, Ind.); Lackland Officers Wives, Bright Shawl (San Antonio). Home: 4917 Ravenswood Dr San Antonio TX 78227

STEARNS, E(LIZABETH) CAROLYN, medical administrator; b. Mooresville, Ind., Aug. 16, 1928; d. Gale Able and Ercie Louise (Smith) Rose; grad. high sch.; m. William Joseph Sawyers, Sept. 6, 1946 (div. May 1951); children—William Joseph, Sherry Lou; m. John Pershing Stearns, Oct. 4, 1954 (div. Mar. 1980); 1 son, Dennis Gale. Sec., Lab. Equipment Corp., Mooresville, 1946-49, Hdqrs. 10th Air Force, 1949-50; with VA Hosp., Indpls., 1950-72, adminstrv. asst. to chief med. service, 1966-70, adminstrv. officer med. service, 1970-72; staff asst. med. service VA Hosp., Tampa, 1972-80, adminstrv. officer, 1980—; adminstrv. asst. to chmn. dept. internal medicine U. South Fla. Coll. Medicine, Tampa, 1972—. Mem. bus. edn. adv. com. J. Everett Light Career Center, Indpls., 1969-72. Recipient Cert. of Appreciation, AMVETS, 1971. Mem. Med. Group Mgmt. Assn., Adminstrs. Internal Medicine Assn., Am. Soc. Profl. and Exec. Women, Nat. Notary Assn., Nat. Assn. Female Execs., Hillsborough County Med. Assts. Assn. Office: Dept Internal Medicine 12901 N 30th St Box 19 Tampa FL 33612

STEARNS, SUZANNE ANDERSON, graphic designer, photographer; b. Reading, Pa., May 22, 1944; d. Winthrop and Frances (Prettyman) S.; student Spartanburg Jr. Coll., 1962-63, Atlanta Coll. Art, 1963-66, Ga. State U., 1966-67. Art dir. Atlanta mag., 1969-78; graphics dir. Atlanta newspapers, 1978-80; owner, mgr. Suzanne Anderson and Assoc. Inc., Atlanta, 1980—; tchr. graphics to profls.; speaker on graphics and photography to local colls. and univs.; several one-man shows of photography; exhibited in group art shows. Recipient 45 nat. and internat. awards in graphics and photography. Mem. Am. Soc. Mag. Photographers. Quaker. Home: 1448 N Morningside Dr NE Atlanta GA 30306 Office: 3355 Lenox Rd Suite 200 Atlanta GA 30326

STECKELBERG, DAVID OWEN, mortgage company executive, re-manufacturing company executive, real estate executive; b. Chamberlain, S.D., Nov. 13, 1944; s. Raymond Donald and Madeline (Mayer) S.; m. Linda Marie Cullen, Aug. 12, 1966; children—Kelly Sue, Christine Marie, Amanda Lou. Student, S.D. Sch. Mines, 1962-63; B.S., U. S.D., 1966. C.P.A., Tex. Acct. Peat, Marwick, Mitchell & Co., Davenport, Iowa and San Antonio, 1971-79; treas., chief fin. officer James Avery Craftsman, Kerrville, Tex., 1979-82; v.p. fin. Southeast Exploration Co., Sooner Exploration Co. and Okla. Warrior Drilling Co., Oklahoma City, 1982-83; accountant, mortgage banker Royal Mortgage Co., Kerrville, 1983—; pres. Numericon, Inc., Kerrville, 1983—; gen. ptnr. Indsl.-Tech. Properties, Ltd., Kerrville, 1984—. Mem. Am. Inst. C.P.A.s, Tex. Soc. C.P.A.s, Kerrville Soc. C.P.A.s (edn. com. 1980-82). Republican. Club: Exchange of Kerrville (pres. 1981-82, Tex. dist. dir. for youth camps 1980). Home: Kerrville TX 78028 Office: Royal Mortgage & Investment Co Suite 323 First Nat Bank Bldg Kerrville TX 78028

STEDING, WILLIAM JOHN, broadcasting company executive; b. Lancaster, Calif., Apr. 22, 1957; s. John Reynolds and Frances Elaine (Goodfellow) S.; m. Kathryn Wirran Browell, May 7, 1983; B.A. in Bus. Adminstrn., U. Wash., 1979. Cert. radio mktg. cons. Account exec. Pacific N.W. Bell Co., Seattle, 1979-80, Sta. KIRO-TV, 1980-81; nat. sales mgr. Sta. KIRO/KSEA, Seattle, 1981-82; gen. mgr. Sta. KAAM/KAFM, Dallas, 1982-83, v.p., chief exec. officer, 1983-84; exec. v.p. KAAM, KAFM, KMBZ, KMBR, 1984—; dir. Tex. Commerce Bank-North Dallas. Radio mgr. United Way; bd. dirs. Episcopal Girls Home, Juvenile Diabetes Found. Mem. Assn. Radio Mgrs. Dallas/Ft. Worth (pres.), Assn. Broadcast Execs. Tex., Tex. Assn. Broadcasters, Radio Advt. Bur., Nat. Radio Broadcasters Assn., Nat. Assn. Broadcasters, Clubs: Willow Bend Polo and Hunt, Aerobics Activity Ctr., Variety of Tex. Office: 15851 Dallas Pkwy Suite 1200 Dallas TX 75251

STEDMAN, ROBERT WILLIAM, utility company executive, accountant; b. St. James, Mo., Dec. 5, 1941; s. Raymond Edwin and Augustine Roxie (Dostal) S.; m. Frances Marie Spears, Apr. 24, 1964; 1 child, Robert William. B.B.A. magna cum laude, Memphis State U., 1970. C.P.A., Tenn. Staff acct. Arthur Andersen & Co., Memphis, 1970-72; asst. to sr. v.p. S.C. Electric & Gas Co., Columbia, 1972-73, asst. controller, 1973-80, controller, 1980-83, v.p., controller, 1983—. Served with USN, 1960-69. Mem. Am. Inst. C.P.A.s, Edison Electric Inst. (mem. acctg. mgmt. com., mem. info. systems com.), Southeastern Electric Exchange (mem. acctg. and control sect. 1981—, chmn. 1980-81), Tenn. Soc. C.P.A.s (assoc.), Columbia C. of C. Home: 440 Valley Springs Rd Columbia SC 29223 Office: SC Electric and Gas Co PO Box 764 Palmetto Ctr Main St Columbia SC 29218

STEED, MARY LOU, sociology educator; b. Fremont, Ohio, Mar. 10, 1942; d. Earl Albright and Helen Marguerite (Goetz) Widmer; m. John Griffith Steed, Dec. 19, 1965; 1 child, James Widmer. B.A., Atlantic Christian Coll., 1976; M.A., N.C. Central U., 1978; Ph.D., Duke U., 1981. Vis. lectr. N.C. Central U., Durham, 1978-80; asst. prof. sociology N.C. Wesleyan Coll., Rocky Mount, N.C., 1980—. Contbr. articles to profl. jours. Mem. Am. Sociol. Assn., Soc. Sci. Study Religion, Assn. Sociology Religion, N.C. Sociol. Assn. Democrat. Episcopalian. Avocations: reading, tennis. Home: 1917 W Club Blvd Durham NC 27705 Office: NC Wesleyan Coll College Sta Rocky Mount NC 27801

STEEG, MELBA LAW, legal administrator; b. Mansfield, La., May 4, 1923; d. George Harris and Marie (Tiller) Law; B.A., Northwestern State U., 1944; m. A.L. Shushan, 1950 (dec. 1966); m. 2d, Moise S. Steeg Jr., Nov. 29, 1969; adopted children—Barbara Steeg Midlo, Marion, Robert M. With Shushan Bros. & Co., New Orleans, 1945-49; spl. fashion cons. Gus Mayer Co., New Orleans, 1967-68; legal adminstr. Steeg & O'Connor, New Orleans, 1971—; mgr. Magnolia Shopping Center, Metairie, La., 1979—. Bd. dirs., sec. Nat. Lukemia Found., 1971-74; bd. dirs. So. Eye Bank, 1968-72, 77—, NCCJ, 1983; founder, bd. dirs. Rudolph Ellender Found. for Med. Research, 1967—; bd. dirs., sec. Children's Hosp., 1979-83; bd. dirs., mem. exec. com. Greater New Orleans Tourist and Conv. Commn., 1979—; bd. dirs. Temple Sinai, 1980—, v.p., 1983; trustee New Orleans Mus. Art, 1983—; chmn. aviation com. The Chamber/New Orleans and River Region, 1983—. Mem. Assn. Legal Adminstrs., DAR, UDC. Home: 1503 Valence St New Orleans LA 70115 Office: 1100 Tulane Ave New Orleans LA 70112

STEELE, DAVIS TILLOU, mech. engr.; b. Springfield, Mo., Jan. 10, 1923; s. Davis William and Aliene (Tillou) S.; B.S. in Mech. Engring., U. Mo., Rolla, 1950; m. Frances Eloise Van Schaick, Feb. 23, 1952; children—Michael, Cynthia, Janet, Dan. Engr. and weapons system mgr. Boeing Co., Wichita, Kans., also Seattle, 1954-63; systems support mgr. Bendix Systems Div., Ann Arbor, Mich., 1963-68; v.p. Am. Sentry N. Tex., Fort Worth, 1968-71; pres. Housing Engrs., Inc., Fort Worth, 1971—. Served with USN, 1943-46. Registered profl. engr., Tex. Mem. Am. Engring. Assn. (chpt. sec.). Clubs: Masons, Shriners. Office: 7305 Grapevine Hwy Fort Worth TX 76118

STEELE, GLEN TIDWELL, optometrist, educator; b. Dickson, Tenn., Sept. 14, 1944; s. Glen D. and Alice (Tidwell) S.; m. Cleta Beggs, June 9, 1968; children—Samuel Todd, Stephen Trent. A.A., Martin Coll., 1964; B.S., So. Coll. Optometry, 1969, O.D., 1969. Pvt. practice optometry, Memphis, 1972—; prof. III, So. Coll. Optometry, Memphis, 1969—; chief vision therapy clinic, 1976-81. Vice pres. Keswick East Civic Assn., Memphis, 1984-85; trustee Concord Acad., Memphis, 1983—. Clin. fellow Gesell Inst. Child Devel., New Haven, 1970-71. Fellow Coll. Optometrists in Vision Devel. (S.E. regional dir. 1984—); mem. Optometric Extension Program Found., Am. Optometric Assn., Assn. Children with Learning Disabilities (profl. adv. bd. 1981—), Sports Vision Assn. Am. Democrat. Methodist. Home: 2763 Tangbourne St Memphis TN 38119 Office: So Coll Optometry Memphis TN 38104 also 803 Mt Moriah Rd Memphis TN 38117

STEELE, JACK, chemistry educator; b. Indianapolis, Jan. 22, 1942; s. Dick J. and Dorothy (Grossman) S.; m. Carolyn J. Botts, May 18, 1968; children—M. Craig, Rebecca L., Jeffrey S. A.B., DePauw U., 1964; Ph.D., U. Ky., 1968. Postdoctoral research/teaching intern Wash. State U., Pullman, 1968-70; asst. prof. chemistry Albany (Ga.) State Coll., 1970-75, assoc. prof., 1975-80, prof., 1980—, chmn. chemistry and physics, 1981—; undergrad. lab. asst. gen. and analytical chemistry DePauw U., Greencastle, Ind., 1963-64; grad. teaching asst. in gen. and analytical chemistry U. Ky., Lexington, 1964-66, recitation instr., 1967-68; grad. research asst. NSF, 1967; extra-mural reviewer EPA, 1977-80, NSF, 1978—. Rector scholar DePauw U., 1960-63; Ky. Research Found. doctoral year fellow, 1968; grantee NSF, 1972-73, Minority Schs. Biomed. Support, 1972-77. Mem. Am. Chem. Soc. (congl. sci. counselor, co-founder, chmn. S.W. Ga. subsect., Am. Assn. Clin. Chemistry (clin. chemistry recognition award 1980), Ga. Acad. Scis., Sigma Xi. Office: Dept Natural Sci Albany State Coll Albany GA 31705

STEELE, JAMES EUGENE, ednl. adminstr.; b. South Norfolk, Va.; s. James Edward and Blanche Eugenia (Munden) S.; B.S. in Music Edn., William & Mary Coll., Norfolk, 1961; M.Ed. in Ednl. Adminstrn. and Supervision, Temple U., 1972; Ed.D. in Ednl. Adminstrn., Nova U., 1965. Piccoloist, Norfolk Symphony Orch., 1951-73; dir. choral music Hampton (Va.) City Schs., 1960-65, supr. music, 1965—. Dir. fine arts div. Hampton Assn. Arts Humanities, 1967—. Mem. NEA, Va., Hampton edn. assns., Va. Assn. Sch. Execs., Hampton Instructional Suprs. Assn., Tidewater Regional Suprs., Va. Assn. Sch. Curriculum Devel., Va. Music Suprs. Assn., Va. Music Educators Assn., Music Educators Nat. Conf., Va. Choral Dirs. Assn., Va. Band and Orchestra Dirs. Assn., Va. String Tchrs. Assn. Guest flute soloist Music Tchrs. Assn. Great Britain, 1962. Certified as tchr. supr., Va. Home: 132 Fayton Ave Norfolk VA 23505 Office: 1300 Thomas St Hampton VA 23669

STEEN, JOHN THOMAS, JR., lawyer; b. San Antonio, Dec. 27, 1949; s. John Thomas and Nell (Donnell) S.; m. Ida Louise Clement, May 12, 1979; children—John T., Ida Louise Larkin. A.B., Princeton U., 1971; J.D., U. Tex., 1974. Bar: Tex., 1974. Assoc. Matthews and Branscomb, San Antonio, 1977-82; ptnr. Soules, Cliffe and Reed, San Antonio, 1982-83; sr. v.p., gen. counsel Commerce Savs. Assn., San Antonio, 1983—, also dir.; dir. North Frost Bank, 1982-84, KPAC Radio, 1985—. Vice chmn., trustee Alamo Community Coll. Dist., 1977-82; mem. research and planning council San Antonio, 1978-81, Community Guidance Ctr., 1983-84; pres. San Antonio Acad. Alumni Assn., 1976-77, Princeton Club, 1979-81, San Antonio Performing Arts Assn., 1984; commr. Bexar County, 1982, Fiesta San Antonio, 1982-83; chmn. World Affairs Council of San Antonio, 1984—; gov.'s appointee Tex. Commn. on Economy and Efficiency in State Govt., 1985—; active numerous other civic coms. Served to 1st lt. USAR, 1973-81. Mem. Tex. Bar Assn., San Antonio Bar Assn., Santa Gertrudis Breeders Internat., Tex. and S.W. Cattle Raisers Assn. Clubs: Ivy (Princeton); San Antonio German (pres. 1982-83), Conopus, Order of Alamo, Tex. Cavaliers, San Antonio Country. Presbyterian. Home: 207 Ridgemont Ave San Antonio TX 78209 Office: Commerce Savings Bank 111 Soledad Suite 1300 San Antonio TX 78205

STEEN, WESLEY WILSON, bankruptcy judge; b. Abbeville, La., Feb. 15, 1946; s. John Wesley and Margaret (Chauvin) S.; m. Evelyn Finch, Aug. 29, 1970; children—Anna Frances, John Wesley, Lee Wilson. B.A. in English, U. Va., 1968; J.D., La. State U., 1974. Bar: La. 1974. Assoc. atty. Sanders, Downing, et al, Baton Rouge, 1974-77, ptnr., 1977-80; sole practice law, Baton Rouge, 1980-83; pres., atty. Steen, Rubin, et al, Baton Rouge, 1983-84; bankruptcy judge U.S. Bankruptcy Ct., Middle Dist. La., part time, 1983-84, full time, Baton Rouge, 1984—; mem. La. State Law Inst. Continuous Revision Com., La. Trust Code, 1980—; mem. Baton Rouge Estate and Bus. Planning Council, 1980—, State Bar Com. on Bar Admissions, Baton Rouge, 1981-85; adj. asst. prof. law La. State U., 1979—, So. U. Law Sch., 1981; congl. page U.S. Ho. of Reps., 1963-64. Contbr. articles to profl. jours. Vestryman, St. James Episcopal Ch., 1980-83; bd. dirs. Baton Rouge Symphony Assn., 1976-85, St. James Place, 1985, Cerebral Palsy Ctr., 1981, Baton Rouge Gallery, 1982. Mem. Baton Rouge Bar Assns., La. Bar Assn., Order of Coif, Omicron Delta Kappa. Republican. Episcopalian. Lodge: Rotary. Avocations: jogging; computers. Home: 3155 E Lakeshore Dr Baton Rouge LA 70808 Office: US Bankruptcy Ct Middle Dist La 352 Florida St Rm 301 Baton Rouge LA 70801

STEENSLAND, RONALD PAUL, library administrator; b. Dothan, Ala., Dec. 16, 1946; s. Maurice John and Claire (Folkes) S.; m. Nancy Hollister, Dec. 22, 1970; 1 son, Ronald Paul. B.A., Fla. State U., 1969, M.S., 1970; postgrad. Miami U., 1972, exec. devel. program for library adminstrs. U. Md., 1980. Cert. librarian, Ky. Dir., Davidson County Pub. Library, Lexington, N.C., 1970-73, Hidalgo County Library Systems, McAllen, Tex., 1973-76, Los Alamos County Library, 1976-77, Lexington Pub. Library (Ky.), 1977—; chmn. John Cotton Dana Library Pub. Relations Awards, 1977. Treas. Hidalgo County ARC, 1975. Served with USAR, 1969-70. Recipient United Way Service award. Mem. Res. Officers Assn., Assn. U.S. Army (sec. Bluegrass chpt.), U.S. Chess Fedn., ALA, Ky. Library Assn., Lexington C. of C., Alpha Tau Omega. Democrat. Baptist. Clubs: Lexington Chess; Lafayette and Ionosphere. Lodge: Rotary (sec. Lexington, N.C. 1970-73). Contbr. articles to profl. jours. Office: 251 W 2d St Lexington KY 40507

STEERE, ANNE BULLIVANT, student advisor; b. Phila., July 27, 1921; d. Stuart Lodge and Elizabeth MacCuen (Smith) B.; m. Richard M. H. Harper Jr., Nov. 14, 1942 (div. Oct. 1967); children—Virginia Harper Kliever, Richard M. H. III, Patricia Harper Flint, Stuart Lodge; m. Bruce Middleton Steere, July 5, 1968. B.S. in Sociology, So. Meth. U., 1978, M.Liberal Arts, 1985. Asst. to dir. Harvard Law Sch. Fund, Cambridge, Mass., 1958-68; advisor to older students So. Meth. U., Dallas, 1976-85. Contbr. articles to profl. jours. Trustee, Pine Manor Coll., Chestnut Hill, Mass., 1983—; bd. dirs. Planned Parenthood, Dallas, 1984—. Mem. Alpha Kappa Delta. Episcopalian. Clubs: Chilton (Boston); Jr. League (Dallas). Avocations: reading; needlepoint; sailing. Home: PO Box 660274 Dallas TX 75266-0274 also 1177 N Lake Way Palm Beach FL 33480

STEFFEN, PHILIP DENTON, professional speaker, consultant; b. Chgo., Oct. 14, 1948; s. George Melven and Jean Faye (Cearley) S.; m. Janet Mary Gall, Aug. 31, 1968; children—C.J., Troy. B.S. in Edn., Eastern Ill. U., 1970. Indsl. devel. mgr. Horizon Corp., El Paso, Tex., 1972-73; leasing mgr. Eaton Internat. Corp., Phoenix, 1973; regional mgr. Evelyn Wood Reading, Walnut Creek, Calif., 1974-76; prin. Philip D. Steffen Assocs. Inc., Marietta, Ga., 1976—. Mem. Nat. Speakers Assn. (cert. speaking profl., bd. dirs. 1983-84, Brochure award 1980), Am. Soc. Assn. Execs. (assoc.), Meeting Planners Internat. (supplier mem.), Sales and Mktg. Execs. of Atlanta, Ga. Speakers Assn. (charter), Ga. Soc. Assn. Execs. (assoc.), N.E. Cobb Jaycees, U. Ga. Bulldog Club. Avocations: tennis, reading, photography, Georgia football. Office: Philip D Steffen Assocs Inc 2627 Sandy Plains Rd Suite 201 Marietta GA 30066

STEFFY, JOHN RICHARD, nautical archaeologist, educator; b. Lancaster, Pa., May 1, 1924; s. Milton Grill and Zoe Minerva (Fry) S.; m. Esther Lucille Koch, Oct. 20, 1951; children—David Alan, Loren Craig. Student Pa. Area Coll., Lancaster, 1946-47, Milw. Sch. Engring., 1947-49. Ptnr. M.G. Steffy & Sons, Denver, Pa., 1950-72; ship reconstructor Kyrenia Ship Project, Cyprus, 1972-73, Inst. Nautical Archaeology, College Station, Tex., 1973—; assoc. prof. anthropology, Tex. A&M U., College Station, 1976—; lectr. on ship constrn. Contbr. articles to profl. publs. Sec. Denver Borough Authority, Pa., 1962-72. Served with USN, 1942-45. MacArthur Found. fellow, 1985. Mem. Archaeol. Inst. Am., Soc. Nautical Research, N.Am. Soc. Oceanic History, Republican. Methodist. Lodge: Lions. Office: Inst Nautical Archaeology PO Drawer AU College Station TX 77840

STEG, ADAM-ANTHONY, media relations executive; b. New Orleans, Aug. 6, 1955; s. James Louis and Margret (O'Brien) S. B.A. in Arts and Scis., Syracuse U., 1976. Asst. technician Ortf French TV, Strasbourg, France, 1975-76; studio mgr. Synapse Video Ctr., Syracuse, N.Y., 1974-76; producer Novac Video Prodn., New Orleans, 1977-79; dir. media relations French Cultural Services, New Orleans, 1979—; former dir. Cultural Cable Channel, New Orleans; dir. Media-Louisiane, Lafayette, La. Mem. Ethnic and Cultural Orgn. for Cable TV (sec. 1984), Council for French in La. (dir. media relations 1981—), Nat. Fedn. Local Cable Programmers (dir. internat. exchanges 1985—), Profl. Assn. Diving Instrs.

STEGALL, ROBERT WAYNE, chemical company executive; b. Vernon, Tex., Aug. 26, 1947; s. Robert Clifton and Dorothy Lee (Hollingsworth) S.; m. Jill Baldwin, Oct. 8, 1967; children—Lisa, Michelle, Daniel, Michael. A.A.S., Lamar U., 1977. Cert. safety profl. Trainer, Jefferson Chem. Co., Port Neches, Tex., 1968-77; safety specialist Texaco Chem. Co., Port Neches, 1977-81, sr. safety specialist, 1981—; sr. mem. Texaco Chem. Emergency Response Team, Port Arthur, Tex., 1977—; instr. hazardous materials Lamar U., Beaumont, Tex., 1985—, Tex. A&M U., College Station, 1984; mem. hazardous materials adv. com. Lamar U., 1985. Contbr. photographs to newspapers and mags. Chmn. petrochem. sec. Sunbelt Safety Conf., Beaumont, 1985. Recipient Disting. Pub. Service Medal U.S. Coast Guard, 1985. Mem. Am. Soc. Safety Engrs. (bd. dirs. local chpt. 1983—), Sabine Neches Chiefs Assn. (com. chmn. 1985). Avocations: industrial and sports photography. Home: 6370 Madison Groves TX 77619 Office: Texaco Chem Co PO Box 968 Port Arthur TX 77640

STEGALL, SYDNEY WALLACE, composer, educator; b. Knoxville, Tenn., Dec. 13, 1941; s. Sydney Hugh and Ruth Lynn (Wallace) S. Mus.B., Cin. Coll.-Conservatory, 1964, Mus.M., 1966; postdoctoral studies Emory U., 1978—. Dir. theatrical Martha Bippus Singers, N.Y.C., 1970; pianist Hampton Grease Band, Atlanta, 1971; engr. lighting Concert Systems, Ltd., Monroe, N.C., 1971-72; prin. Sydney W. Stegall, Audio Engr., Atlanta, 1972-79; instr. drama Spelman Coll., Atlanta, 1981-82; specialist media Emory U., Atlanta, 1982—. Composer: (graphic composition) Dappled Fields, No. 2, 1969; (electronic composition) Solidarnosc-Tren, 1981, Whispers, 1982; (multi-media composition) In Rapture, 1985. Morse Found. fellow, 1966-68, Grad. Inst. Liberal Arts fellow Emory U., 1980-81; composer-in-residence grantee Hambidge Ctr., 1979. Mem. Am. Musicological Soc., Coll. Music Soc., Soc. for Ethnomusicology. Avocations: hiking; camping. Office: Grad Inst Liberal Arts Emory U Atlanta GA 30322

STEGE, HARRY, law enforcement official. Chief of police, Tulsa. Office: City Hall 200 Civic Ctr Tulsa OK 74102*

STEGER, WILLIAM MERRITT, judge; b. Dallas, Aug. 22, 1920; s. Merritt and Lottie (Reese) S.; m. Ann Hollandsworth, Feb. 14, 1948; 1 son, Merritt Reed (dec.). Student, Baylor U., 1938-41; LL.B., So. Meth. U., 1950. Bar: Tex. bar 1951. Pvt. practice, Longview, 1951-53; apptd. U.S. dist. atty. Eastern Dist. Tex., 1953-59; mem. firm Wilson, Miller, Spivey & Steger, Tyler, Tex., 1959-70; U.S. dist. judge Eastern Dist. Tex., Tyler, 1970—. Republican candidate for gov. of Tex., 1960; for U.S. Ho. of Reps., 1962; mem. Tex. State Republican Exec. Com., 1966-69; chmn. Tex. State Republican Party, 1969-70. Served as pilot with ranks 2d lt. to capt. USAAF, 1942-47. Mem. Am. Bar Assn., State Bar Tex. Club: Mason (32 deg., Shriner). Home: 801 Meadow Creek Tyler TX 75703 Office: PO Box 1109 Tyler TX 75710

STEHN, LORRAINE STRELNICK, physician; b. Richmond, Ind., Aug. 27, 1950; d. Daniel H. and Eleanor Gayle (Robertson) Strelnick; m. Thomas Veasey Stehn, June 16, 1973; children—Alexander Veasey, Andrew Thomas. B.A., Carleton Coll., 1972; D.O., Coll. Osteo. Medicine and Surgery, 1972. Diplomate Am. Bd. Family Practice. Intern, Pontiac Osteo. Hosp., Mich., 1976-77; vol. med. officer U.S. Peace Corps, Swaziland, 1977-79; resident in family practice St. Mary's Hosp., Port Arthur, Tex., 1980-82; family practice osteo. medicine, Aransas Pass, Tex., 1982—; med. adv. Christian Service Ctr., Aransas Pass, 1983—; chief staff Coastal Bend Hosp., Aransas Pass, 1985—. Recipient Service award Aransas Pass Jr. High 1984. Mem. Am. Acad. Family Practice, Tex. Osteo. Med. Assn. Democrat. Home: 1613 S Saunders Aransas Pass TX 78336

STEIGER, HOWARD PAUL, dermatologist; b. Williamsport, Pa., Nov. 2, 1915; s. Howard L. and Helen E. (Taylor-Ring) S.; m. Elizabeth Butler, Aug. 17, 1940; children—Helen Steiger Kellicut, Louise Steiger Heizer, Edith Steiger Seaman, Howard Paul Jr. B.S., Duke U., 1937, M.D., 1940. Diplomate Am. Bd. Dermatology. Intern, Ga. Bapt. Hosp., Atlanta, 1940, U.S. Marine Hosp., New Orleans, 1940-41; resident U. Pa. Hosp., Phila., 1941-47; practice medicine specializing in dermatology, Charlotte, N.C., 1947—; mem. staff Charlotte Meml. Hosp., Presbyn. Hosp., Mercy Hosp. Served with USPHS, 1940-41, 42-47. Mem. AMA, Am. Acad. Dermatology, N.Am. Clin. Dermatol Soc. Republican. Episcopalian. Clubs: Myers Park Country (Charlotte); Litchfield Country (Pawleys Island, S.C.). Lodges: Mason, Shriners.

STEIGNER, (JOHN) BRUCE, ophthalmologist; b. Phila., Oct. 31, 1942; s. John Mark and Regina (Fillippo) S.; m. Mildred Elizabeth Lally, Sept. 19, 1970; (div. 1983); children—John, Michael, Patrick, Jason; m. Elisabeth Lee Wright, May 25, 1985. B.S., Davidson Coll., 1964; M.D., Med. Coll. S.C., 1968. Diplomate Am. Bd. Ophthalmology. Intern Ochsner Found. Hosp., New Orleans, 1968-69, resident, 1969-72; gen. practice ophthalmology and ophthalmic surgery, Houma, La., 1972—; mem. active staff Terrebonne Gen. Hosp.; mem. cons. staff St. Anne's Gen. Hosp., Raceland, La., Thibodaux Gen. Hosp., La. Contbr. articles to profl. jours. Served to lt. comdr. USNR, 1965-75. Fellow ACS, Am. Acad. Ophthalmology; mem. Soc. Eye Surgeons, Am. Intraocular Implant Soc., Contact Lens Assn. of Ophthalmologists, La. Ophthalmology Assn. (trustee), AMA, Am. Assn. Ophthalmology, Assn. Research in Vision and Ophthalmology, Internat. Glaucoma Congress, Council Med. Staffs, Physicians Edn. Network (founder), LAMPAC (regional dir.), La. State Med. Soc. (del. 1982, 83, 84, 85), Terrebonne Parish Med. Soc. (pres. 1981, 83, 84, 85, 86). Republican. Avocation: target shooting. Home: 217 Wilson Ave Houma LA 70364 Office: 712 Belanger St Houma LA 70360

STEIN, ALVIN, surgeon; b. Paterson, N.J., Oct. 16, 1936; s. David and Minnie (Bochner) S.; B.A., N.Y. U., 1957; M.D., Chgo. Med. Sch., 1961; m. Leona L. Greenbaum, June 22, 1958; children—Eileen Gale, Randy Sue, David. Intern, Hosp. for Joint Diseases, N.Y.C., 1961-62, resident, 1962-63; resident Met. Hosp. and Flower-Fifth Ave. Hosp., N.Y.C., 1963-64, 65-66, Hosp. for Crippled Children, Newark, 1964-65; practice medicine, specializing in orthopedic surgery, Bronx, N.Y., 1966-73, Ft. Lauderdale area, Fla., 1973—; chief Children's Orthopedic Service and Bronx Lebanon Hosp., 1960-73; chief staff Fla. Med. Center, 1974-75; mem. staff Humana Hosp. Bennett, Plantation, Fla., Plantation Gen. Hosp., Univ. Community Hosp., Tamarac, Fla., Cypress Community Hosp., 1973-77, Pompano Beach, Fla.; dir. Pointe Savs. & Loan, Boca Pointe, Fla. Bd. dirs. Miami Hebrew Acad., 1973-81, mem. exec. com. bd., 1975-81; bd. dirs. Moriah Sch., Englewood, N.J., 1968—, Yeshiva Torah Vodaath and Mesifta, Bklyn., 1965—; v.p. Hebrew Acad. Greater Miami, 1977-80. Diplomate Am. Bd. Orthopedic Surgery. Fellow A.C.S., Am. Acad.

Orthopedic Surgeons, Internat. Coll. Surgeons; mem. Fla., Eastern Orthopedic assns., Broward County Orthopedic Soc., Internat. Arthroscopy Soc., Chgo. Med. Sch. Alumni Assn. (nat. exec. com. 1975—, 1st v.p. 1981-85, nat. pres. 1985—). Mason (Shriner). Home: 5220 N 31st Pl Hollywood FL 33021 Office: 8251 W Broward Blvd Fort Lauderdale FL 33324

STEIN, BARBARA LAMBERT, marriage and family therapist; b. Detroit, Feb. 10, 1945; d. Joseph J. and Sylvia (Siegel) Lambert; m. David Joel Stein, Jan. 1, 1967; children—Craig Andrew, Todd Alexander. Student psychology Mich. State U., 1962-64; B.A. in Sociology, Wayne State U., 1966, postgrad. in psychiat. social work, 1972-74; M.S. in Counseling Psychology, Nova U., 1980; student, Art Inst. Ft. Lauderdale, 1985. Vol. abuse and neglect dept. Wayne County Juvenile Ct., Detroit, 1964-65; vol. D.J. Healy Shelter for Children, 1965-67; med. social worker Hutzel Hosp., Detroit, 1967-68; developer neighborhood teen drug program City of West Bloomfield (Mich.), 1970-71; med. social worker Extended Care Facilities, Inc., Birmingham, Mich., 1972-73; vol. group and occupational therapist Henderson Psychiat. Clinic Day Treatment Ctr., Ft. Lauderdale, Fla., 1977-78; pvt. practice family and marital therapy, Deerfield Beach, Fla., 1980-85. Mem. Temple Beth El of Boca Raton (Fla.) Sch. Edn. Bd.; Recipient cert. of Meritorious Achievement, Henderson Psychiat. Clinic Day Treatment Ctr. Mem. Am. Assn. Marriage and Family Therapy (assoc.), Am. Psychol. Assn. (assoc.), Am. Assn. Counseling and Devel., Wayne State U. Alumni Assn., Nova U. Alumni Assn., Orton Dyslexia Soc., Palm Beach Assn. Sch. Psychologists (assoc.), Assn. Children and Adults with Learning Disabilities, South County Jewish Fedn.

STEIN, CARMEN TERESA, psychotherapist; b. Santiago, Chile, Sept. 13, 1956; came to U.S., 1966, naturalized, 1980; d. Robert and Carmen (Baehr) Ferrer; m. Alfred Philip Stein, Oct. 23, 1982; children—Carmen Camille, Candice Melody. B.A., U. Tampa, 1985; M.A., U. South Fla., 1986. Owner, B&D Assocs. Constrn. Co., Junction City, Kans., 1979-81, N.Y. Deli, Fort Riley, Kans., 1980-81; mental health counselor VA Ctr., Tampa, Fla., 1985—. Served with U.S. Army, 1974-79. Named Outstanding Woman of Yr. award Epsilon Sigma Alpha, 1981; recipient Program of Yr. award Beta Sigma Phi, 1980. Mem. Am. Assn. for Counseling and Devel., Psi Chi. Jewish. Office: Discovery the Gestalt and Humanistic Inst 1420 W Busch Blvd Tampa FL 33612

STEIN, JANET WEISSBECKER, optometrist; b. Plainfield, N.J., Apr. 11, 1957; d. Ludwig and Betty (Spitzer) Weissbecker; m. Alan Lewis Stein, June 12, 1983. B.A. with distinction, U. Va., 1979; B.S., Pa. Coll. Optometry, 1980, D.Optometry, 1982. Lic. optometrist, N.J., Va. Optometrist Eye Surgeons of Richmond, Va., 1982-83, Dr. Parker T. May, Sterling, Va., 1983—, Dr. David Harvan, opthalmologist, Manassas, Va., 1983—; practice optometry, Woodbridge, Va., 1983—. Recipient Bernell Clin. Optometry award Pa. Coll. Optometry, 1982. Mem. Am. Optometric Assn., Va. Optometric Assn., No. Va. Optometric Assn. Jewish. Home: 11362 Cromwell Court Woodbridge VA 22192

STEIN, JANICE MARY, technical writer, writing consultant; b. New Orleans, June 27, 1943; d. John V. and Elaine (Veale) May; divorced; children—Jeannine, Scott, Gretchen, Ross; m. Daniel W. Broe, Dec. 31, 1981. A.A., Delgado Community Coll., 1978; B.Liberal Studies, Loyola U., 1984. Support enforcement intake supr. Dist. Atty.'s Office, Jefferson Parish, La., 1979-81; policy and procedure coordinator Touro Infirmary, New Orleans, 1981—; communications cons. Hosp. Med.-Fin. Reviewers Assn., New Orleans, 1984—, Effective Communications Co., New Orleans, 1984—. Author poetry, articles, stories. Editor Prism: A Students' Jour., 1976-78, Roux, 1981-82. Coordinator West Bank Writers' Forum, New Orleans, 1977-79; prin. St. Joseph Ch. Sch. Religion, Gretna, La., 1977-78; bd. dirs. Delgado Coll. Citizen Adv. Bd., New Orleans, 1984—; mem. Women in Mainstream, New Orleans, 1983—. Recipient 2d Place award Nat. Collegiate Poets' Anthology, 1978. Mem. Am. Med. Writers Assn., Assn. for Bus. Communication, Alpha Sigma Lambda. Roman Catholic. Avocations: writing poetry; jogging. Home: 3201 Rue Parc Fontaine 2702 New Orleans LA 70114 Office: Touro Infirmary 1401 Foucher New Orleans LA 70115

STEIN, ROBERT MELVIN, environmental engineer; b. Albany, N.Y., Oct. 27, 1943; s. Samuel and Bessie Stein; m. Lenora Silverstein, Sept. 7, 1969; 1 son, Seth. B.A. in Applied Sci., Memphis State U., 1968, B.E. in Civil Engring., 1969; M.S. in Environ. Engring., Vanderbilt U., 1971. Project engr. Dept. of Transp., State of N.Y., Albany, 1968-70; v.p. AWARE Corp., Nashville, 1970—. Recipient F.W. Kellogg award Memphis State U., 1969. Mem. Am. Water Works Assn., TAPPI, Water Pollution Control Fedn. Home: 6125 Fair Valley Dr Charlotte NC 28220 Office: HDR Corp Box 11257 Charlotte NC 28220

STEIN, STEVEN JEFFREY, industrial psychologist; b. Newark, May 29, 1953; s. Irving Nathan and Esther (Goldman) S.; m. Amy Greene, June 29, 1980; 1 child, Rebecca Leigh. B.A., George Washington U., 1974; M.A., Grad. Faculty, New Sch. for Social Research, 1978; Ph.D., U. Fla., 1981. Cons. psychologist Corp. Stress Control Socs., N.Y.C., 1981; dir. psychol. services Hay Career Cons., N.Y.C., 1981-83; personnel cons. Knight-Ridder Newspapers, Miami, Fla., 1983—. Home: 1000 Quayside Terr Miami FL 33138 Office: Knight-Ridder Newspapers One Herald Plaza Miami FL 33101

STEIN, WILLIAM EDUARD, business administration educator; b. Cleve., June 18, 1946; s. William E. and Florence (Helm) S. B.S., Case Inst. Tech., 1968; M.S., Purdue U., 1970; Ph.D., U. N.C., 1975. Asst. prof. U. Ill.-Chgo., 1974-77; assoc. prof. Tex. Christian U., Fort Worth, 1977-82; assoc. prof. bus. adinstrn. Tex. A&M U., College Station, 1982—. Author: Response Models for Detection of Change, 1977; contbr. articles to profl. jours. Mem. Ops. Research Soc. Am. Home: 2809 Normand Dr College Station TX 77840 Office: Dept Bus Analysis Tex A&M U College Station TX 77843

STEINBERG, EUGENE BARRY, optician, researcher, contact lens specialist, ophthalmic technician, writer; b. Bklyn., Sept. 16, 1953; s. Lester and Hannah (Bailowitz) S.; m. Ilene G. Richards, Oct. 22, 1977; children—Jessica Brittany, Melissa Heather. A.A. with honors, U. Hartford, 1973; B.A. with honors in Psychology, SUNY-Binghamton, 1975; A. Applied Sci. in Ophthalmic Dispensing with honors, N.Y.C. Tech. Coll., 1979. Lic. dispensing optician, Ga., Va., N.Y.; lic. contact lens specialist, N.Y. Apprentice optician Am. Vision Ctr., Bklyn., 1977-78; mgr. Cohens Fashion Optical, Bklyn., 1978-79; chief contact lens fitter Digby Opticians, Atlanta, 1979-80; clin. research coordinator dept. ophthalmology Emory U. Eye Ctr. Prospective Eval. Radial Keratotomy Study Atlanta, 1980—, ophthalmic technician Eye Clinic, 1980—. Contbr. articles to profl. jours. and books. Recipient Disting. Service award Nat. Eye Inst., 1983, Appreciation cert. Binghamton Psychiatric Ctr., 1975. Mem. Opticians Assn. Ga., Atlanta Lawn Tennis Assn., Tau Phi Sigma. Democrat. Jewish. Avocations: guitarist; vocalist; recording artist. Office: Emory U Eye Ctr 1327 Clifton Rd NE Atlanta GA 30322

STEINBERG, FRED ARNOLD, psychologist, consultant, researcher; b. Pitts., Aug. 26, 1949; s. Harold and Elizabeth (Sharpe) S.; m. Marilyn Ann Crouse, Oct. 18, 1980; 1 child, Ashley Lauren. B.A., Pa. State U., 1971; M.Ed., Boston U., 1972; Ph.D., Calif. Sch. Profl. Psychology, 1977. Lic. clin. psychologist, Tenn. Clin. psychologist Linn County Psychiat. Clinic, Cedar Rapids, Iowa, 1977-79; clin. coordinator children and youth services White Haven S.W. Mental Health Ctr., Memphis, 1980-81; coordinator psychol. services IMLADRIS, Inc., Memphis, 1981—; chief exec. officer, clin. dir. Rivendell Clinic, 1985—; pvt. practice clin. psychology, Memphis, 1981—; clin. instr. U. Tenn. Ctr. for Health Scis., Memphis, 1982—; adj. prof. Memphis State U., 1980-86. Cons. editor Jour. of Child and Adolescent Psychotherapy, 1984—. Mem. Am. Psychol. Assn., Nat. Register for Health Service Providers in Psychology. Democrat. Jewish. Avocations: racquetball, jogging, guitar, antique furniture. Home: 9272 Oak Knoll Cove Cordova TN 38018 Office: Rivendell Clinic 210 Jackson St Suite 401 Memphis TN 38105

STEINBERG, JILL ENID, computer sales official; b. Jersey City, Oct. 27, 1955; d. Edwin Jay and Renee Ruth (Kaufman) S. B.A., U. Miami (Fla.), 1979. Salesperson luggage Burdine's, Miami, Fla., 1979-80, asst. mgr. area, 1980-81, commn. sales advanced consumer electronics, 1981-83, computer salesperson, 1983-84, mkgt. rep. computers, 1984-85, asst. mgr. computer dept., 1985—; participant Apple seminar, 1983. Named outstanding salesperson So. Region, Hartmann Luggage, 1980; mem. Burdine's B Club. Mem. AAUW (com.), Nat. Assn. Female Execs., Alpha Kappa Delta, Delta Phi Epsilon. Lodge: Hadassah (life). Home: 15725 SW 88th Ct Miami FL 33157 Office: Burdines Computer Depot 7303 N Kendall Dr Miami FL 33156

STEINBERG, LAIRD DEANN, logistics analyst; b. Kingsville, Tex., Feb. 22, 1961; d. Mitchell and Jeannine Jones (Johnson) S. B.S. in Mgmt., Va. Poly. Tech. Inst. and State U., 1983. Adminstrv. aide Ednl. Film Ctr., Springfield, Va., 1978-80; sec. No. Va. Community Coll., Alexandria, 1980; logistics analyst Gen. Research Corp., McLean, Va., 1983-84; logistics analyst JAYCOR, Alexandria, 1984-85; logistics support, coordinator TRW, McLean, Va., 1985—. Named Outstanding Young Woman of Am., 1984. Mem. Soc. Logistics Engrs. (vice chmn. fin. and adminstrn. 1984-85, vice chmn. ops. 1985-86, Disting. Service award 1985, No. Va. chpt.), Nat. Trust Historic Preservation, Jr. C. of C. (Alexandria), Delta Zeta Alumnae Assn. Presbyterian. Home: 6107 Rockwell Court Burke VA 22015 Office: TRW 7600 Colshire Dr McLean VA 22102

STEINBRENNER, GEORGE MICHAEL, III, shipbuilding company executive, baseball executive; b. Rocky River, Ohio, July 4, 1930; s. Henry G. and Rita (Haley) S.; m. Elizabeth Joan Zieg, May 12, 1956; children—Henry G. III, Jennifer Lynn, Jessica Joan, Harold Zieg. B.A., Williams Coll., 1952; postgrad., Ohio State U., 1954-55. Asst. football coach Northwestern U., 1955, Purdue U., 1956-67; treas. Kinsman Transit Co., Cleve., 1957-63; pres. Kinsman Marine Transit Co., 1963-67, dir., 1965—; pres., chmn. bd. Am. Ship Bldg. Co., Cleve., 1967-78, chmn. bd., 1978—; prin. owner N.Y. Yankees, 1973—; dir. Gt. Lakes Internat. Corp., Gt. Lakes Assos., Cin. Sheet Metal & Roofing Co., Nashville Bridge Co., Nederlander-Steinbrenner Prodns. Mem. Cleve. Little Hoover Com., group chmn., 1966; chmn. Cleve. Urban Coalition; vice chmn. Greater Cleve. Growth Corp., Greater Cleve. Jr. Olympic Found.; Bd. dirs. Greater Cleve. Growth Assn. Served to 1st lt. USAF, 1952-54. Named Outstanding Young Man of Year Ohio Cleve. jr. chambers commerce, 1960; named Chief Town Crier, Cleve., 1968; Man of Yr. Cleve. Press Club, 1968; recipient Acad. Achievement Gold Plate award, Dallas, 1960. Office: 512 Florida Ave Tampa FL 33601*

STEINBUCHEL, MARK JOSEPH, industrial safety engineer; b. Wichita, Kans., Oct. 2, 1949; s. Maximillian Hubert and Patricia (Manley) S.; m. Carla Faye Jansson, June 5, 1969; children—Carla Lara, Cara Nicole. A.A., Wichita State U., 1976; B.S., SUNY-Albany, 1978. Los control engr. USF&G Ins., Wichita, 1976-77; Iowa Nat. Mut., Wichita, 1977-80; mgr. safety and indsl. hygiene Boeing Mil. Airplane Co., Huntsville, Ala., 1980—. Adv. bd. ARC, Wichita, 1984-85. Served to 2d lt. USAR, 1969-79. Mem. Am. Soc. Safety Engrs. (Wichita chpt. pres. 1982-83), Am. Indsl. Hygiene Assn. Republican. Methodist. Avocations: hot air balloons, snow skiing. Home: 2511 Galahad St Huntsville AL 35803 Office: Boeing Mil Airplane Co PO Box 1470 Suite JW-19 Huntsville AL 35807

STEINER, JOSEPH, dentist; b. London, Sept. 20, 1943; s. Rudolph and Marie (Engelstein) S.; m. Renee Sherry Perlowitz, June 22, 1969; children—Michelle Jacqueline, Shara Deborah. B.S., CCNY, 1965; D.D.S., NYU, 1969. Intern N.Y. Polyclinic Hosp., N.Y.C., 1969-70; practice dentistry, Charlotte, N.C., 1972—; dental cons. Equitable Life Assurance Soc., 1977—; attending dentist Charlotte Meml. Hosp., 1972—, vice chief dental service, 1985-86. Vice pres. N.C. Hebrew Acad., Charlotte, 1985; trustee Temple Israel, 1973-82. Served to lt. USN, 1970-72, to comdr. USNR, 1980—. Mem. Am. Assn. Endodontists (assoc.), Charlotte Dental Soc. (program chmn. 1984-85), ADA. Lodge: B'nai B'rith (pres 1977-78; bd. govs. dist. 5, 1980—; N.C. state pres. 1981). Avocations: Marathon running; skiing; stamps; O gauge electric trains. Home: 5415 Pepperdine Dr Charlotte NC 28226 Office: 5200 Park Rd Charlotte NC 28209

STEINFELDT, CECILIA IRENE, museum curator, consultant, researcher; b. Montello, Wis., May 24, 1915; d. Louis Jacob and Evalina Valeska (Erbe) Neuheisel; m. Eric Steinfeldt, Aug. 11, 1939; 1 child, Richard. Student U. Mex., 1933-34, Witte Mus. Sch. Art, 1937-42, San Antonio Art Inst., 1942-43, San Antonio Coll., 1952. Tchr. art Witte Meml. Mus., San Antonio, 1947-60; curator history San Antonio Mus. Assn., 1960-70, curator history and decorative arts, 1970-80, sr. curator, 1980—. Organizer exhbn., co-author book: Early Texas Furniture and Decorative Arts (San Antonio Conservation Soc. award 1974), 1973; The Onderdonks: A Family of Texas Painters (San Antonio Conservation Soc. award 1975), 1975. Organizer exhbn. A Survey of Native Texas Artists, 1978. Author: San Antonio Was: Seen Through a Magic Lantern (San Antonio Conservation Soc. Literary award 1979, Mitchell A. Wilder Silver award Tex. Assn. Mus. 1980), 1978. Author: Texas Folk Art: One Hundred Fifty Years of the Southwestern Tradition, 1981. Contbr. articles to Southwestern Art, Needle Arts, Antiques. Recipient awards San Antonio Conservation Soc., 1969, 71; Am. Assn. State and Local History fellow, 1974; named to San Antonio Women's Hall of Fame, 1984. Mem. Am. Assn. Museums, Tex. Assn. Museums (adv. council 1981—), Tex. Hist. Found., Am. Assn. for State and Local History, Smithsonian Assoc., Costume Soc. Am., San Antonio Mus. Assn., San Antonio Conservation Soc., Inst. Texan Cultures, San Antonio Needlework Guild, Western Library Soc. Episcopalian. Avocation: travel. Office: San Antonio Museum Assn PO Box 2601 3801 Broadway San Antonio TX 78299-2601

STEINGARTEN, KAREN ANN, psychologist; b. N.Y.C., Jan. 25, 1948; d. Robert and Susan Lucy (Ruben) Steingarten. B.A., Syracuse U., 1968; M.S., U. Ga., 1974, Ph.D., 1977. Diplomate Am. Bd. Profl. Neuropsychology. Lic. psychologist, Fla. Psychologist, U.S. Navy, Yokosuka, Japan, 1977-79, Jacksonville, Fla., 1979-82; pvt. practice psychology, Jacksonville, 1982—; neuropsychologist Alzheimers Clinic, Baptist Med. Ctr., Jacksonville, 1984—; chief psychol. services St. Johns River Hosp., Jacksonville, 1982—. Served to lt. USN, 1975-82. Me. Am. Psychol. Assn., Nat. Acad. Neuropsychologists, Internat. Neuropsychol. Soc., Fla. Psychol. Assn. Democrat. Jewish. Avocations: swimming; gardening; bridge; cooking. Office: 3000-11 Hartley Rd Jacksonville FL 32217

STEINHART, RONALD GLEN, banker; b. Beaumont, Tex., June 15, 1940; s. Werner and Marga S.; m. Phyllis Yonet, Feb. 14, 1965; children—David Alan, Kenneth Jason, Barry Joel. B.B.A., U. Tex., 1962, M.B.A., 1963. C.P.A., Tex. Pres., Dallas Bank & Trust Co., 1965-69; chmn. bd. Town North Nat. Bank, Dallas, 1972-75, Dallas/Ft. Worth Airport Bank, 1972-75; pres. Main Street Nat. Bank, Dallas, 1969-77; chmn. bd. Equitable Bank, Dallas, 1979-80; pres. Valley View Bank, Dallas, 1977-80; vice chmn. InterFirst Corp., Dallas, now pres. and chief operating officer, 1980—; prin. rep. Assn. Bank Holding Cos. Mem. Gov.'s Exec. Council for Tex. State Govt. Mgmt. Effectiveness, 1982—; fin. chmn. Transp. Task Force, 1982—; mem. Edwin L. Cox. Sch. Bus. Assoc. Bd., So. Meth. U., 1981—; mem. Coll. of Bus. Adv. Council, U. Tex.-Arlington, 1981—, chmn. exec. bd., 1983; mem. Scout Show, Circle Ten Council, Boy Scouts Am.; chmn. bd. commrs. Dallas Housing Authority, 1981-82; pres. Dallas Assembly, 1980; co-chmn. budget com. United Way; mem. Dallas Citizens Council; bd. dirs. Jewish Welfare Fedn. Found. Served with USAFR, 1958-68. Mem. Tex. Soc. C.P.A.s, Young Pres. Orgn., Assn. Res. City Bankers. Jewish. Office: PO Box 83205 Dallas TX 75283

STEINHAUER, RALEIGH FRED, educator; b. Barada, Nebr., Mar. 30, 1921; s. Jacob and Addie Day (Hurless) S.; B.S., U. Omaha, 1954; M.B.A., U. Mich., 1958; M.A., George Washington U., 1962, D.B.A., 1972; grad. civilian edn. programs USAF Inst. Tech., 1958, USAF War Coll., 1962; m. Doris Elsie Schmeisser, May 20, 1944; children—Carol Alys, Raleigh Fred. Enlisted in USAAC, 1939, commd. 2d lt. U.S. Army Air Force, 1942, advanced through grades to col. U.S. Air Force, 1962; staff logistics officer, Port Newark, N.J., 1942-46; service in Ger., 1946-49; with SAC, 1949-57; chief mgmt. engring. Hdqrs. USAF, Washington, 1958-61; dep. comdr. materiel Tactical Fighter Wing, Tampa, Fla., 1962-63, Bitburg, Ger., 1963-66; mgmt. engring. and manpower div. chief Hdqrs., Washington, 1966-70; ret., 1970; asst. prof. bus. adminstrn. George Mason U., 1972-75, asso. prof., 1975-81, prof. mgmt., 1981—, chmn. mgmt. faculty, 1980-83; cons. to local govts.; mem. Met. Washington Area Council Govts. Purchasing Officers Com., 1970-72; mem. No. Va. Purchasing Officers Council, 1973—. Supt. ch. sch. St. Mark's Lutheran Ch., Springfield, Va., 1960-61. Decorated Legion of Merit, Air Force Commendation medal with 3 oak leaf clusters; named Outstanding USAF War Coll. Grad., 1962. Mem. Acad. Mgmt., So. Mgmt. Assn., Organizational Behavior Teaching Soc. Republican. Lutheran. Clubs: Shriners, Masons. Author: Fundamentals of Business Policy, 1977; contbr. articles to profl. jours. Office: George Mason U Sch Bus Adminstrn Fairfax VA 22030

STEINMAN, JUDITH SANDREA BARR, mental health and career counselor, auditor; b. N.Y.C., Sept. 27, 1928; d. Bertram and Bertha (Marcus) Barr; m. Harry Steinman, Sept. 27, 1953; children—Richard Mark, Robert Jay. Student NYU, 1946-49; A.A., Miami Dade Jr. Coll., 1972; B.S., Fla. Internat. U., 1974; M.S., Barry U., 1979. Cert. mental health counselor, Fla. Buyer, Lerner Shops, N.Y.C., 1947-56; office mgr. Eastern Assocs., Miami, Fla., 1964-74; counselor employment/mental health Fla. Employment Service, Miami, 1974-83; counselor mental health, Miami, 1979—; tax auditor Fla. Unemployment Compensation Tax, Miami, 1983—; lectr. seminars Dade County Sch. System, Miami and Miami Beach, 1980-83; career counselor Vets. Ctr., Miami, 1981-83. Author: Community Career and Training Programs, 1977. Vice pres. PTA, Miami, 1967-69. Mem. Am. Assn. For Counseling and Devel., Fla. Assn. for Counseling and Devel., Barry U. Counseling Assn., Internat. Assn. Personnel in Employment Security, YWCA Women's Network. Office: 2375 NE 195 St Miami FL 33180 also Fla Unemployment Compensation Tax 111 NW 183 St Suite 425 Miami FL 33169

STEINMETZ, DEBORAH SUSAN, interior designer; b. New Orleans, Nov. 29, 1951; d. Donald Frederick and Estelle Margaret (Ulmer) Tossell; B.F.A., La. State U., 1973; m. Robert Steinmetz, Dec. 29, 1973. Interior designer David Grinnell Architect, 1973-75; ind. design cons., Columbus, Ga., 1975-77; designer Dameron-Pierson, New Orleans, 1977-79; v.p. interior design Interior Environments, Inc., New Orleans, 1979-83; prin. Steinmetz & Assocs., New Orleans, 1983—; mem. interior design curriculum com. Dominican Coll., New Orleans, 1981-82; mem. interior design adv. com. Delgado Community Coll., New Orleans, 1982—. Mem. visual arts com. Contemporary Art Center, 1980-81. Mem. Am. Soc. Interior Designers (Presdl. citation; chmn. New Orleans assn. 1980-81, dir. La. chpt. 1982—, newsletter editor La. chpt. 1982, admissions chmn. La. chpt. 1984), Nat. Trust Hist. Preservation, La. Landmarks Soc. Roman Catholic. Home: 2850 Annunciation St New Orleans LA 70115 Office: 225 Baronne St Suite 207 New Orleans LA 70112

STELL, JACKSON RONALD, museum administrator, consultant; b. Russellville, Ala., Aug. 22, 1939; s. William Ramsey and Catherine (Carruth) Stell. B. Interior Design, Auburn U., 1965; postgrad. in interior design U. Ga., 1970; postgrad. in history Auburn U., 1970-72. Interior designer Lamar's, Florence, Ala., 1965-69; hist. house and mus. coordinator Ala. Hist. Commn., Montgomery, 1973—; also cons. Recipient Disting. Service award Garden Club of Ala., 1977. Mem. Soc. Ala. Archivists (bd. dirs. 1981-83), Ala. Mus. Assn., SAR (pres. William Burgess chpt. 1975-77, v.p. Ala. soc. 1975-77, MacArthur award Ala. soc. 1975), St. Andrew's Soc. of Montgomery (bd. dirs. 1984—). Democrat. Avocations: genealogical research; travel. Home: 3128 S Court St Montgomery AL 36105

STELL, WALTER JOSEPH, III, theatre educator, theatrical designer, researcher; b. Charlotte, N.C., Sept. 10, 1936; s. Walter Joseph Jr. and Lillian (Moore) S.; m. Agnes Gertrude David, June 18, 1964; 1 child, Heather Elaine. B.S., East Carolina Coll., 1958; M.A., NYU, 1962; Ph.D., Bowling Green State U., 1975. Lighting designer Man. Theatre Centre, Winnipeg, Can., 1962-63; instr. Richmond Profl. Inst., Va., 1963-66; asst. prof. U. Ga., Athens, 1966-76, assoc. prof., 1976-83, prof. drama, 1983—; chmn. div. fine arts, 1984—; theatrical cons.; mem. fine and applied arts com. Univ. System Adv. Council, Atlanta, 1985—. Author: The Theatre Student: Scenery, 1970; also numerous articles. Assoc. editor So. Theatre, 1976-80. Designer scenery and/or lighting for numerous theatrical prodns., including Oliver! at Alliance Theatre, Atlanta, 1979 (Atlanta Jour. Best Scenic Design for 1979-80), and, most recently, Candide at Balt. Opera, 1984, Jekyll Island Musical Comedy Theatre prodns., Ga., 1985. Mem. sites and facilities needs assessment com. Clarke County Sch. Dist., Ga., 1979-80; vol. Am. Heart Assn., Clarke County, 1984—. Recipient Creative Research medallion U. Ga., 1984, Silver cert. Am. Heart Assn., Clarke County, 1984, Gold cert. Am. Heart Assn., Clarke County, 1985. Mem. U.S. Inst. for Theatre Tech. (sec.-treas. Southeast region 1977-78), Southeastern Theatre Conf., Kappa Delta Pi, Phi Kappa Phi. Methodist. Avocations: photography; drawing and painting; travel. Home: 320 Rivermont Rd Athens GA 30606 Office: Dept Drama U Ga Athens GA 30602

STELLER, ARTHUR WAYNE, superintendent schools; b. Columbus, Ohio, Apr. 12, 1947; s. Fredrick and Bonnie Jean (Clark) S.; m. Deborah Ann Hasselo, Aug. 14, 1981; children—Jonathon, Matthew. B.S. in Elem. Edn., Ohio U., 1969, M.A. in Elem. Sch. Adminstrn., 1970, Ph.D. in Ednl. Adminstrn., 1973. Tchr. Athens (Ohio) City Schs., 1969-71; lang. arts specialist Belpre City (Ohio) Schs., 1971-72, curriculum coordinator, 1971-72; head tchr. summer learning disabilities program South-Western City Schs., Grove City, Ohio, 1973, prin. elem. sch., 1972-76; dir. elem. edn. Beverly (Mass.) Pub. Schs., 1976-78; coordinator spl. projects and systemwide planning Montgomery County Pub. Schs., Rockville, Md., 1978-80; asst. supt. schs. Shaker Heights City (Ohio) Sch. Dist., 1980-83; supt. schs. Mercer County Pub. Schs., Princeton, W.Va., 1983-85; supt. schs. Oklahoma City, 1985—; elem. sch. adminstrn. and supervision Lesley Coll., Cambridge, Mass., 1976-78; adj. arts instr., 1977-78; cons. in field. Mem. adv. bd. Langston U.; mem. community adv. bd. Jr. League, Oklahoma City; bd. govs, Kirkpatrick Ctr.; bd. trustees Omniplex Sci. & Arts Mus.; bd. dirs. Jr. Achievement, Oklahoma City, Last Frontier Council ; mem. Trustees Acad.-Ohio U. Mem. Am. Assn. Sch. Adminstrs., Nat. Assn. Elem. Sch. Prins., Nat. Assn. for Edn. Young Children, Assn. Supervision and Curriculum Devel. (nat. dir. 1983, resolutions com. chmn. 1986-87), Okla. Assn. Sch. Adminstrs., Okla. Assn. Supervision & Curriculum Devel., Okla. State Supts. Adv. Council, Oklahoma City C. of C., South Oklahoma City C. of C., Arts Council of Oklahoma City, Oklahoma City Symphony Audience Devel. & Edn. com. Nat. Soc. Study Edn., Okla. State Fair Bd. Phi Delta Kappa, Kappa Delta Pi, Tau Kappa Epsilon. Methodist. Lodge: Rotary, Author: Educational Planning for Educational Success, 1980; editor Effective Instructional Management, 1983, Implications for Programmatic Excellence and Equity; book rev. editor Jour. for Edn. Communication; cons. ed. Jour. of Curriculum and Supervision; contbr. numerous articles to profl. jours. Home: 217 NW 19th St Oklahoma City OK 73103 Office: 900 N Klein Oklahoma City OK 73106

STELLER, DEBORAH ANN HASSELO, educator; b. Cleve., Nov. 21, 1947; d. Milton John and Sarah Hefner (Valek) Hasselo; B.S., Fla. State U., 1970; M.Ed., Miss. State U., 1973, Ed.D., 1979. Grad. asst. in instl. research Miss. State U., Starkville, 1973-74; elem. sch. tchr., Tampa, Fla., 1970-76, team leader, 1974-76, curriculum specialist, 1976, curriculum intervention specialist, 1976-79, elem. curriculum supr., 1979-81, head tchr. extended sch. year program, summers 1976-79; elem. prin. Nordonia Hills City Schs., Macedonia, Ohio, 1981-83, Mercer County Schs., Princeton, W.Va., 1983-85; asst. prof. U. Okla.; cons. in field. Mem. certification study, Center Econ. Edn., U. So. Fla., 1978; counselor, group leader Judeo-Christian Coalition Clinic, 1979-81; bd. dirs. Palma Ceia United Meth. Ch., 1980-81. Mem. Assn. Supervision and Curriculum Devel. (curriculum com. of 75), Fla. Assn. Supervision and Curriculum Devel., Nat. Council Tchrs. of Math., Internat. Reading Assn., Phi Delta Kappa (life), Kappa Delta Pi (life), Miss. State Alumni Assn., Fla. State Alumni Assn., Chi Omega Alumnae Assn. (treas. Tampa chpt., 1978-80). Home: 217 NW 19th St Oklahoma City OK 73103 Office: U Okla 313 Collings Hall Norman OK 73019

STELTING, CHARLES EDWARD, geologist; b. Clinton, Okla., Jan. 23, 1947; s. Ervin Ray and LaVeta (Byfield) S.; m. Linda Lee Bergman, Aug. 2, 1969; children—Brandy Lynn, Charles Edward II. B.S. in Geology, Tex. A&I U., 1980. Technician, geologist U.S. Geol. Survey, Corpus Christi, 1976-82, Gulf Research and Devel. Co., Houston, 1982-85; research technologist Chevron Oil Field Research, Co., 1985—; interim prof. Del Mar Coll., Corpus Christi, 1982; sedimentologist Deep Sea Drilling Project Leg 96, Miss. Fan, Gulf Mexico, 1983. Author: Seismic Expression of Structural Styles: A Picture and Work Atlas, 1983; Submarine Fans and Related Turbidite Systems, 1985. Served with USN, 1966-70. Mem. Am. Assn. Petroleum Geologists, Soc. Econ. Paleontologists and Mineralogists, Democrat. Avocations: golf, woodworking. Office: Chevron Oil Field Research Co PO Box 36506 Houston TX 77236

STELTMANN, HARRY FREDERICK, aerospace company executive; b. Elizabeth, N.J., Jan. 11, 1943; s. Harry Frederick and Alverna Ruth (Smithman) S.; B.B.A., Hofstra U., 1964; M.B.A., Eastern Mich. U., 1974; m. Mary Jo Pfeiffer, Dec. 23, 1967; children—Joan, Michael, Andrew, Daniel. Plant fin. analyst Ford Motor Co., Saline, Mich., 1969-72, sr. fin. analyst, Rawsonville, Mich., 1972-73; capital investment mgr. Rockwell Internat. Corp., Troy, Mich., 1973-74, plant controller, Allegan, Mich., 1974-76, div. controller suspenion systems, Troy, 1976-77, div. controller, dir. bus. planning plastics, 1977-78, dir. mktg. and bus. planning plastics, 1978-79, group dir. fin.

and bus. planning axle group, 1979-80, dir. ops. hydraulics group, Cheltenham, Eng., 1980-82, dir. ops. U.K. axle ops., London, 1982-83; v.p. fin. and bus. planning Aero Structures div. Avco, Nashville, Tenn., 1983-84; sr. v.p. fin. and materials Aero Structures div. Avco-Textron, Nashville, 1984—. Pres. bd. dirs., chmn. Nashville City Ballet; bd. dirs. Jr. Achievement; chmn. adv. bd. Crisis Intervention Ctr. Served with AUS, 1964-69. Decorated Bronze Star, Purple Heart; Silver Knight award Nat. Mgmt. Assn., 1985. Mem. Nashville C. of C., Nashville Performing Arts Coalition, Fin. Execs. Inst., Machinery and Allied Products Inst., Soc. Automotive Engrs. Methodist. Club: Brentwood Men's Soccer. Lodge: Rotary. Home: 6017 Foxland Dr Brentwood TN 37027

STELZMAN, JAMES STEPHEN, dentist; b. South Charleston, W.Va., Nov. 30, 1946; s. Walter James and Carolyn Grace (Waldon) S.; m. Elizabeth Ann Clark, Mar. 22, 1969 (div. June 1976). D.D.S., U. Tenn.-Memphis, 1971. Dentist, USPHS, Tenn., 1975-76; pvt. practice dentistry, Strawberry Plains, Tenn., 1975-85; clin. practice dentistry, Morristown, Tenn., 1980—. Served to capt. USAF, 1972-75, Japan. Mem. ADA, Acad. Gen. Dentistry, Tenn. Dental Assn., 2d Dist. Dental Assn. Home: 920 Chilhowee Dr Knoxville TN 37914 Office: Morristown Dental Ctr 1748 W Andrew Johnson Hwy Morristown TN 37814

STEM, CARL HERBERT, college dean, business educator; b. Eagleville, Tenn., Jan. 30, 1935; s. Marion Ogilvie and Sara Elizabeth (Jones) S.; m. Linda Marlene Wheeler, Dec. 28, 1963; children—Anna Elizabeth, Susan Kathleen, John Carl, David Leslie. B.A., Vanderbilt U., 1957; A.M., Harvard U., 1960, Ph.D., 1969. Internat. fin. economist, bd. govs. Fed. Res. System, Washington, 1963-70; prof. fin., coordinator dept. fin. Coll. Bus. Adminstrn., Tex. Tech. U., Lubbock, 1970-72, assoc. dean. Coll. Bus. Adminstrn., 1972-73, 74-75, dean, prof. Coll. Bus. Adminstrn., 1975—; sr. econ. advisor, office fgn. direct investments U.S. Dept. Commerce, Washington, 1973-74; con. U.S. Dept. Treasury, Washington, 1974-75; adj. scholar Am. Enterprise Inst., Washington, 1974—; mem. faculty Grad. Sch. Credit and Fin. Mgmt., Lake Success, N.Y., 1974-82. Editor: Eurocurrencies and the International Montary System, 1976. Contbr. articles to profl. jours. Pres., Lubbock Econs. Council, 1973, Tex. Council Coll. Edn. for Bus., 1978-79. Served to capt. U.S. Army, 1961-62. Mem. Am. Assembly Coll. Sch. of Bus. (standards com. 1981-84), Nat. Assn. Bus. Econs., Southwestern Bus. Adminstrn. Assn. (pres. 1983-84), So. Bus. Adminstrn. Assn. (v.p. 1985-86), Phi Beta Kappa, Phi Kappa Phi, Beta Gamma Sigma, Tau Kappa Alpha, Omicron Delta Kappa. Mem. Ch. of Christ. Clubs: Lubbock (v.p. 1985—), University City (Lubbock). Home: 6218 Louisville Dr Lubbock TX 79413 Office: Coll Bus Adminstrn Tex Tech U Lubbock TX 79409

STEMBLER, JOHN HARDWICK, theatre company executive; b. Miami, Fla., Feb. 18, 1913; s. George C. and Harriett Elizabeth (Sligh) S.; m. Katherine Jenkins, July 5, 1941; children—John Hardwick, William Jenkins. J.D., U. Fla., 1937. Bar: Fla. 1937. Mem. firm Carson, Petteway & Stembler, Miami, 1937-41; asst. U.S. atty. So. Dist. Fla., 1941; with Ga. Theatre Co., Atlanta, 1946—, pres., 1954—; past chmn. bd., past chmn. exec. com. Nat. Bank Ga., Atlanta. Trustee Atlanta Music Festival Assn.; bd. dirs. Ga. div. Am. Cancer Soc., 1957—, pres., gen. chmn. edn. funds crusade Fulton County unit, 1956; bd. dirs. Atlanta area council Boy Scouts Am., 1953—, pres., 1959-61. Served as lt. col. USAAF, 1941-46; maj. gen. USAF ret. Decorated Air medal with oak leaf cluster, Legion of Merit. Mem. Nat. Assn. Theatre Owners (past pres., chmn. fin. com.), Motion Picture Theatre Owners and Operators Ga. (v.p., dir.), Phi Delta Phi, Sigma Alpha Epsilon, Fla. Blue Key. Clubs: Capital City, Commerce, Peachtree Golf, Piedmont Driving. Lodge: Rotary. Home: 309 Peachtree Ave NW Atlanta GA 30305 Office: 3445 Peachtree Rd NE Atlanta GA 30326

STEMLER, ARTHUR WHEELER, shipping cases manufacturing company executive; b. Bklyn., June 26, 1923; s. Arthur Ludwig and Dorothy (Wheeler) S.; m. Shirley Ruth Beebe, June 25, 1949; children—Robert D., Bruce S., Carol K. Stemler Strickland. A.B., Conn. Wesleyan U., 1949. Vice pres. farm kitchen brands Jack Isaminger, Dallas, 1949-58; sales mgr., gen. mgr. Atlas Advt., Tampa, Fla., 1958-72; controller Anderson Surg. Supply, Tampa, 1972-77; pres. Viking Cases, St. Petersburg, Fla., 1977—. Served with AUS, 1942-46. Mem. Nat. Audio Visual Assn., Nat. Assn. Musical Mchts., Nat. Assn. Broadcasters, Tampa C. of C. Republican. Methodist (ofcl. bd.). Clubs: Golden Triangle Fishing (pres.), Tampa Yacht and Country. Home: 2901 Wallcraft Ave Tampa FL 33611 Office: 10480 Oak St NE Saint Petersburg FL 33702

STEMPEL, FRANK TAYLOR, financial consultant; b. Los Angeles, Oct. 24, 1941; s. Frank and Jane Arden (Slease) S.; m. Sharon Lloyd Burke, Dec. 19, 1970 (div. Jan. 1982); children—Angela, Leah, James. B.S., U. So. Calif., 1964, M.B.A., 1968. Account rep. J. Walter Thompson, N.Y.C., 1968-70; v.p. Merrill Lynch, N.Y.C., 1970-81, Salomon Bros., Atlanta, 1982-83; region mgr. Arthur D. Little, Atlanta, 1985—. Contbr. articles to popular mags. Mem. young careers group High Mus. of Art, Atlanta, 1982—. Served to 1st lt. USMC, 1964-67, Vietnam. Fellow Fin. Analysts Fedn.; mem. N.Y. Soc. Security Analysts, Atlanta Soc. Fin. Analysts. Republican. Episcopalian. Clubs: Stamford Yacht, N.Y. Athletic. Avocations: sailing, skiing. Home: 52 Chaumont Sq Atlanta GA 30327 Office: Arthur D Little Inc 200 Galleria Pkwy Suite 1290 Atlanta GA 30339

STENHOLM, CHARLES WALTER, congressman; b. Stamford, Tex., Oct. 26, 1938; s. Lambert and Irene Stenholm; B.S. in Agr., Tex. Tech U., 1961, M.S., 1962; m. Cynthia Ann Watson, July 1, 1961; children—Chris, Cary, Courtney. Vocat. agr. tchr., 1962-64; pres. Rolling Plains Cotton Growers, 1964-67; gen. mgr. Stamford Electric Coop., 1967-76; owner, mgr. Stenholm Farms, Stamford, 1969-76; pres. Double S. Farms, Inc., 1976-77; dir. First Nat. Bank Stamford, 1975-78, adv. dir., 1979—; charter trustee Cotton Inc.; pres. Tex. Electric Coop., 1976; v.p. Tex. Fedn. Coops., 1977; mem. Tex. Agr. Stablzn. Com.; mem. 96th-98th congresses from 17th Dist. Tex. Pres. Stamford Little League Baseball, 1977, Stamford United Way, 1974; exec. com. 30th Senatorial Dist. Tex. Democratic Party, 1974; coordinator Conservative Dem. Forum, 1980—. Named Am. Farmer, Future Farmers Am., 1959. Mem. Rolling Plains Cotton Growers (past pres.), Stamford C. of C. (past pres.). Lutheran. Club: Stamford Exchange. Address: 1232 Longworth Bldg Washington DC 20515

STENNIS, JOHN CORNELIUS, senator; b. Kemper County, Miss., Aug. 3, 1901; s. Hampton Howell and Cornelia (Adams) S.; m. Coy Hines, Dec. 24, 1929; children—John Hampton, Margaret Jane (Mrs. Womble). B.S., Miss. State U., 1923; LL.B., U. Va., 1928; LL.D., Millsaps Coll., 1957, U. Wyo., 1962, Miss. Coll., 1969, Belhaven Coll., 1972, William Carey Coll., 1975. Bar: Miss. Practiced in, DeKalb, Miss.; mem. Miss. Ho. of Reps., 1928-32; dist. pros. atty. 16th Jud. Dist., 1931-37; circuit judge, 1937-47; mem. U.S. Senate from Miss., 1947—, mem. armed services com. Active in promotion farm youth tng. programs; state chmn. Miss. 4-H Adv. Council. Mem. Am., Miss. bar assns., Phi Alpha Delta, Phi Beta Kappa, Alpha Chi Rho. Presbyterian (deacon). Lodges: Masons, Lions. Home: DeKalb MS 39328 Office: Russell Bldg US Senate Washington DC 20510*

STENQUIST, CONNIE UNDERWOOD, university administrative manager; b. Goldsboro, N.C., Dec. 20, 1949; d. Luther Rodney and Gouldia (Summerlin) Underwood; m. James Delvin Benton, Jan. 6, 1969 (div.); children—Jason, Jacob; m. 2d Ronald E. Stenquist, July 31, 1976; 1 dau., Brandy. A.A.S. in Bus., Wayne Community Coll., 1974; postgrad. East Carolina U., 1979-80. Sec. Wayne Community Coll., Goldsboro, 1974-75; exhibit coordinator N.C. Assn. Educators, Raleigh, 1975-76; personnel sec. East Carolina U., Greenville, N.C., 1976-78, adminstr. dept. surgery, 1979—; bus. mgr. Stonebranch Prodns., Farmville, N.C., 1983—. Mem. Phi Theta Kappa. Home: RR 2 PO Box 106 Farmville NC 27828 Office: Dept Surgery East Carolina Univ Greenville NC 27834

STENSTROP, ERNEST, architect; b. Chgo., Mar. 29, 1927; s. Carl Peter and Emma Fredericka (Jensen) S.; m. Lois L. Lavelle, May 9, 1953; m. Margaret K. Ewald, Dec. 4, 1971; children—Linda Sue, Leslie Ann, Victoria Kay, Janet. B.A., U. Ill., 1951. Designer, Chgo. Park Dist., 1953-64; designer, project mgr. Lawrence Monberg Assoc., Archtl. Engring. Cons., Kenosha, Wis., 1964-65; project mgr. A.M. Kinney Assoc. Inc., archtl. engring. cons., Skokie, Ill., 1965-68; project mgr. real estate and constrn. div. IBM Corp., Chgo., 1968-77, project mgr. real estate and constrn. div. IBM Corp., Atlanta, 1977—; co-founder, pres. Apparel Care Ctr., Inc., 1984—. Served with U.S. Army, 1945-47. Mem. AIA, Nat. Com. Architects in Industry Lodge: Masons. Archtl. works: Farm in the Zoo, Lincoln Park, Chgo.; Garfield Park Conservatory, Chgo.; Ott Chem. Co. Complex, Muskegon, Mich.; Merrimac Park Fieldhouse, Chgo.; Space Planner for numerous IBM Bldgs., Madison, Wis., Des Moines, South Bend, Ind., Lexington, Ky., Little Rock, Ark., Memphis, Metairie, La., Raleigh, N.C. Lutheran. Home: 455 Hackberry Ln Roswell GA 30076 Office: 2580 Cumberland Pkwy Atlanta GA 30339

STEPHENS, ALONZO THEODORE, history educator; b. St. Petersburg, Fla., Apr. 19, 1919; s. John Wesley and Alice Elizabeth (Dicks) S.; A.B., Fla. A&M U., 1948; M. Letters, U. Pitts., 1951, Ph.D. in History, 1955; m. Dorothy Andrews, Dec. 24, 1950; children—Andrea Katrina, Alonzo T. Tchr. social scis. public schs., St. Petersburg, 1942, Lakeland, Fla., 1948-50; edn. tng. coordinator VA, 1946-47; asst. prof. history Fla. A&M U., 1953-55; assoc. prof. Savannah State Coll., 1955-58; prof. history Tenn. State U., Nashville, 1958-84, prof. emeritus history and geography, 1984—, head dept., 1958-81. Charter mem. Children's Internat. Edn. Ctr., Nashville, 1980; mem. Tenn. Heritage Alliance, 1982-85; chmn. Tenn. Hist. Sites Commn., Nashville, 1983-84. Served with U.S. Army, 1943-46; ETO, PTO. Recipient Disting. Scholar, Writer, and Lit. Critic award Fla. A&M U., 1965; Outstanding Service in Social Scis. award Ind. U., 1970; various other awards for disting. achievements in field; postdoctoral fellow St. Louis U., 1962; African Am. Inst./U.S. Dept. State fellow, U. Cairo and Hebrew U., summer 1964, African countries, summer 1973; Danforth fellow (life appointment), 1970—; travel fellow Am. Hist. Assn./Internat. Econ. History Assn., 1970; Phelps-Stokes Fund and Fisk U. grantee; Recognition award Tenn. Legislature, 1984. Mem. Assn. Social and Behavioral Scientists (pres. 1965, Presdl. Service award 1973), UN Assn. (pres. Tenn. div. 1972-81, pres. Nashville sect. 1968-70), Middle Tenn. Conf. Afro-Am. Historians (pres. 1975-81), So. Hist. Assn., Am. Hist. Assn. (fellow USSR, summer 1970), Assn. Study of Afro-Am. Life and History, Middle East Studies Assn., Am. Polit. Sci. Assn., Tenn. Hist. Sites Commn. (chmn. 1980-81), Commn. Study Orgn. of Peace, African Studies Assn. Democrat. Presbyterian. Editor The Faculty Jour., 1960-80; contbg. editor Quar. Rev. of Higher Edn., 1958-70; contbr. articles to profl. jours., chpts. to books. Office: Dept History and Geography Tenn State U Nashville TN 37203

STEPHENS, BRAD, financial executive; b. Jan. 1, 1951; m. Constance Fiero; children—Jennifer, Lauren, Jeffrey. B.B.A. cum laude in Acctg., Tex. Wesleyan Coll., 1975. C.P.A., Tex. Mem. staff Ft. Worth Nat. Bank, 1973-75, Deloitte, Haskins & Sells, Ft. Worth, 1975-78; v.p. First State Bank, Abilene, Tex., 1978-80, sr. v.p. comml. lending, 1980, exec. v.p., 1980-83, pres. Holding Co., Ind. Bankshares, Inc., 1983-85, pres., 1985—, also dir.; part owner, operator Curtis Mathes Dealership, Abilene and Lubbock, Tex.; ptnr. various comml. real estate devels.; speaker civic clubs. Mem. steering com. Abilene Cultural Affairs Council 'Patron 200', 1982—; crusade chmn. Taylor County Am. Cancer Soc., 1983; fundraising chmn. Big County Kidney Found. USTPA Profl. Tennis Tournament, 1983; chmn. advanced div. Indsl. Found. Drive, 1983-84; bd. dirs. ARC, 1980-82, treas. 1980-82; asst. treas. St. John's Sch., 1983—, YMCA, 1981-82; mem. loan exec., budget and allocation com. United Way, 1980-83, Com. to Re-elect Clements, 1982; charter mem. Leadership Abilene, 1979; del. John Ben Shepherd Leadership Forum, 1985. Named Outstanding Young Abilinian, 1985. Richardson scholar, 1974. Mem. Tex. Soc. C.P.A.s (Abilene chpt.), Am. Inst. C.P.A.s, U.S. Jaycees (pres.'s task force, fin. planning com., fin. aid-safety city, adv. dir. exec. officers 1978-82), Abilene C. of C. (bd. dirs., treas. 1983—), Abilene Jaycees (motivational speaker, instr.). Clubs: Fairway Oaks, Abilene Country, Petroleum.

STEPHENS, CHARLES ANTHON, physician; b. Camden, Tex., Oct. 13, 1925; s. Buford Dured and Carrie (Collins) Stephens; B.A., U. Tex., 1950, M.D., 1954; m. Nancy Raisch, June 25, 1954; children—Deborah, Claudia, Charles Anthon II, Barbara, Jerry. Intern Univ. Hosp., Little Rock, 1954-55; resident U. Tex. Med. Br., Galveston, 1955-58; practice medicine specializing in obstetrics-gynecology, Odessa, Tex., 1958—; mem. staff Med. Center Hosp., chief of staff 1962, chief dept. ob-gyn, 1975-86; mem. staff Odessa Women's and Children's Hosp., chief ob-gyn., 1979-80. Bd. dirs. Odessa Community Chest and United Fund, 1959-60, Ector County Assn. Retarded Children, Midland-Odessa Mental Health-Mental Retardation Bd. Served with USNR, 1943-46. Diplomate Am. Bd. Obstetrics and Gynecology. Fellow Am. Coll. Obstetrics-Gynecology; mem. AMA, Tex. Med. Assn., Ector County Med. Soc., Tex. Obstetrics and Gynecology Soc., Tex. Perinatal Assn., Willard R. Cooke Obstetrics-Gynecology Soc., Pi Kappa Alpha, Phi Chi. Home: 3204 Blossom Lane Odessa TX 79762 Office: 6th and Washington Odessa TX 79761

STEPHENS, DAVID DEWITT, apparel company executive; b. Durham, N.C., Jan. 23, 1944; s. Landrum Arthur and Doris Ann (Smith) S.; m. Harriet Ellen Godfrey, Aug. 13, 1966; children—Jeff D., M. Scott, Kevin D., Angela K. B.S. in Bus., U. S.C., 1967. Asst. to v.p. Colonial Life Co., Columbia, S.C., 1967-68; employment mgr. Mohasco, Bennettsville, S.C., 1968-71; personnel mgr. Owen Electric Steel Co., West Columbia, S.C., 1971-74, Campus Sportswear, Chester, S.C., 1974-77, asst. plant mgr., 1977-78, plant mgr., 1978—; mgmt. instr. Midlands Tech. Coll., Columbia, 1973. Head div. United Way of Chester County, 1981, 82, 83; coach Little League Baseball, Chester, 1977-82, Little League Football, 1978—. Republican. Presbyterian. Lodges: Sertoma (dir. 1982-83, membership chmn. 1983), Rotary (com. chmn. 1983-84) (Chester). Office: Campus Sportswear Co PO Box 189 Chester SC 29706

STEPHENS, ELTON BRYSON, service/manufacturing company executive; b. Clio, Ala., Aug. 4, 1911; s. James Nelson and Clara (Stuckey) S.; m. Alys Varian Robinson, Nov. 28, 1935; children—James Thomas, Jane Stephens Comer, Elton Bryson, Dell Stephens Brooke. B.A., Birmingham-So. Coll., 1932, LL.D., 1977; LL.B., U. Ala., 1936; grad., Advanced Mgmt. Program, Harvard U., 1960. Bar: Ala. bar 1936. Regional dir. Keystone Readers Service, Birmingham, 1937-43; partner, then pres. Mil. Service Co., Inc. (predecessor of EBSCO Industries, Inc.), Birmingham, 1943-58; founder, 1958, since pres., chmn. bd., Birmingham; founder Bank of Southeast, Birmingham, 1970, co-organizer, 1971, dir., chmn. exec. com., 1977—; chmn., dir. R.A. Brown Ins. Agy., Inc., 1966—; chmn. EBSCO Investment Service, Inc., 1959—, Canebsco Subscription Service, Toronto, Ont., Can., 1972—; trustee EBSCO Employees Savs. & Profit Sharing Trust, 1958—. Mem. fin. and investment com., past chmn. bd. trustees, chmn. exec. com. Birmingham-So. Coll.; trustee So. Research Inst.; former pres., chmn. bd. trustee Birmingham Met. YMCA; former chmn., Multi-State Transp. Systems Adv. Bd.; mem. bd., chmn. econ. pension com. Tenn.-Tombigbee Waterway Authority; mem. Ala. Election Law Commn.; exec. com. Future Farmers Am. Ala. Found.; founder Ala. 5% Club. Mem. Alpha Tau Omega (past chmn. nat. found.), Omicron Delta Kappa, Phi Alpha Delta. Methodist. Clubs: Downtown, The Club, Birmingham Press, Relay House (Birmingham); Mountain Brook (Ala.) Country, Santa Rosa (Fla.) Golf. Lodge: Shades Valley Rotary (pres. 1979-80) (Homewood, Ala.) (Paul Harris fellow). Elton B. Stephens Expressway dedicated, 1970, Elton B. Stephens Library dedicated, Clio, 1979. Office: EBSCO Industries Inc atop Double Oak Mountain Birmingham AL 35201-1943*

STEPHENS, GARY LEWIS, air traffic control specialist; b. Atlanta, Aug. 27, 1951; s. Thomas Lewis and Mary Ella (White) S.; m. Deborah Clarissa Mauldin, Oct. 2, 1976. Student DeKalb Coll., 1975; B.S. in Aeros., Embry-Riddle Aero. U., 1980. Reinsurance acctg. mgr. Kennesaw Life, Atlanta, 1971-72; sales rep. Nat. Display, Atlanta, 1972-74; owner, mgr. Ajax Enterprises, Atlanta, 1979-83; air traffic controller FAA, Atlanta, 1981—. Served with U.S. Army, 1976-79. Mem. Fayetteville C. of C. Republican. Methodist. Club: Yaarab Temple (Atlanta). Lodge: Masons. Office: 299 Woolsey Rd Hampton GA 30228

STEPHENS, JOSEPH VIVIAN, engineering consultant; b. Malta, George Cross, Sept. 3, 1925; s. Percy Victor and Maria Stella (Salafia) S.; E.E. diploma City and Guilds of London Inst., 1944; ed. Admiralty Tech. Coll., 1940-44, N.Y. U., 1961-73; m. Anna Luise Katharina Tschanun, Mar. 14, 1953; children—Gabriele Ingwelde, Maria Stella. Engr., naval apprentice Admiralty, London and Malta, 1940-46; elec. fitter, 1946-47; engr. officer Royal Mail Lines Ltd., London, 1948-50; sr. designer draftsman D. Napier & Son Ltd., London, 1950-53; sta. engr. Air Ministry, London, 1953-55; elec. design engr. H.K. Ferguson Co., London, 1955-57; elec. designer Gibbs & Hill, N.Y.C., 1957-58; elec. engr. Vitro Corp. Am., N.Y.C., 1958-61; sr. elec. engr. EBASCO Services, N.Y.C., 1961-66, Bechtel Corp., San Francisco, 1966-67; supervising elec. engr. Gibbs & Hill, N.Y.C., 1967-73; sr. staff mgr. Brown & Root, Houston, 1973-79; dept. mgr. elec. engring. Gilbert/Commonwealth, Jackson, Mich., 1980-81, Bellevue, Wash., 1981-83; engring. cons., 1983—. Served with Royal Fleet Aux. Service, 1947-48. At Malta sta., World War II, civil population award of George Cross for heroism King George VI, 1942. Registered engr. Engrs. Registration Bd. London, Wis., Calif., Pa. Fellow Elec. and Electronics Inc. Engrs. London; mem. IEEE (sr.), Assn. Supervisory and Exec. Engrs. Gt. Britain. Roman Catholic. Contbr. articles on power generation nuclear safety to profl. jours. Home: Route 3 Box 292 Victory Rd Franklin GA 30217

STEPHENS, KENNETH DEAN, JR., communications executive; b. Logan, Utah, Dec. 8, 1942; s. Kenneth Dean and Dorothy Clara (Hoffler) S.; student U. Utah, 1961-63, U. P.R. Grad. Sch. Physics, 1973; m. Julia E. Acevedo, Oct. 11, 1980; children—Trina Ridvan, Nick Jalal. Staff engr. Sta. KLOR-TV, Provo, Utah and Sta. KLRJ-TV, Las Vegas, Nev., 1958-61; chief engr. Sta. KUER-FM, Salt Lake City and Sta. KOET-TV, Ogden, Utah, 1961-63; dir. TV research U. Utah, 1964-67; pres. Electronic Research Corp., Salt Lake City, 1968-71; mgr. Tele-San Juan, Inc, owner Sta. WTSJ-TV, San Juan, P.R., Sta. WPSJ-TV, Ponce, P.R. and Sta. WMGZ-TV, Mayaguez, P.R., 1970-74; pres. Broadcast Devels. Internat., St. Just, P.R., 1974-81; v.p. R&D, Focus Communications, Inc., Brentwood, Tenn., 1981—. Cons., UPI; tech. adv. Universal House of Justice, Baha'i World Center, Haifa, Israel; cons. for UN Sci. activities Baha'i Internat. Community (New York); prof. broadcasting and communications Amoz Gibson Ctr. Lic. 1st class radiotelephone operator FCC. Mem. Am. Wind Energy Assn., Soc. Broadcast Engrs. (cert. sr. broadcast engr.), Internat. Inst. Communications. Baha'i. Patentee video rec., color TV projection, radar glasses for blind, color TV system, TV transmission, TV encryption/decryption system, direct broadcast satellite antenna; developed color TV system used by NASA manned spacecraft. Office: HC02 Box 14765 Arecibo PR 00612

STEPHENS, LOWNDES FREDERICK, journalism educator; b. Frankfort, Ky., Sept. 27, 1945; s. James Willis and Harriet Connally (Barton) S.; m. Sally Lanier Smith, June 15, 1968; children—Sally Randolph, John Brent. B.A. in Econs., U. Ky., 1967, M.A. in Communications, 1969; Ph.D., U. Wis., 1975. Publs. officer Ky. div. Devel. Info., Frankfort, 1968-69; research economist Spindletop Research, Inc., Lexington, Ky., 1969-72; content research writer Ky. Ednl. TV Found., Lexington, 1972; editor Lake Superior project Inst. Environ. Studies, U. Wis.-Madison, 1972-74; dir. Communications Research Ctr., asst. prof. U. N.D., 1974-76; assoc. prof. Coll. Journalism U. S.C., Columbia, 1976—; cons. Dept. Def., Am. Newspaper Pubs. Assn., U.S. Office Edn., CPC Internat.; faculty cons. Army Command and Gen. Staff Coll., 1979—. Nat. Adv. bd., Am. Vets. Com., 1979—; mem. nat. adv. panel George Polk Awards. Served to lt. col. USAR, 1985—. Rockefeller Found. grantee U. Wis., 1972-74. Fellow Inter-U. Seminar Armed Forces and Soc.; mem. Internat. Communication Assn., Assn. Edn. Journalism and Mass Communications (chmn. mass communication and society div. 1986—), Am. Sociol. Assn., Assn. Consumer Research, So. Assn. Pub. Opinion Research, Sigma Delta Chi, Omicron Delta Kappa, Omicron Delta Epsilon, Kappa Tau Alpha. Democrat. Methodist. Editorial bd. World Press Ency., Pub. Relations Quar., Newspaper Research Jour. Contbr. articles to profl. jours. Home: 443 Brookshire Dr Columbia SC 29210 Office: Coll Journalism U SC Columbia SC 29208

STEPHENS, PAUL EUGENE, electronic engineer, consultant; b. Grisemore, Pa., Dec. 15, 1903; s. Arthur Philip and Gertrude Lutman S.; m. Ruby Beth McCoy; children—Edwin Harold, Paul Eugene, Arthur Philip II. B.S. in Elec. Engring., Pa. State U., 1927. High power and voltage engr. Westinghouse Electric Co., 1927-33, engr. in charge lightning investigation, Chilhowee, Tenn., 1929, lightning protection devel. engr., Pitts., 1933; installation engr. lightning generator, St. Louis, 1933; bldg. constrn. Arthur P. Stephens, State College, Pa., 1933-41; with electronic services engring. extension services Pa. State U., University Park, 1941-69; pvt. practice textile designs from cathode rays, cyrstals, kaleidoscopes and computers, St. Petersburg, Fla., 1980—. Pres., sec. Sch. Bd., 1942-48; pres. P.T.A., 1948. Mem. Am. Radio Relay League, Am. Sci. Film Assn., IEEE, Am. Inst. Elec. Engrs., Instrument Soc. Am., Photog. Soc. Am., Soc. Pa. Archeologica. Clubs: Color Slide, Masons, Second Wind Hall of Fame, Shriners. Author: Photo Art Designs, 1965; Art Designs using Cathode Rays, 1968; Conversion of Scientific Photographs to Textile Designs, 1970; Kaleidoscopic Textile Designs, 1971; Textile Designs from Crystals and Kaleidoscopes, 1981; Textile Designs from Computers, 1983.

STEPHENS, ROBERT F., state supreme ct. justice; b. Covington, Ky., Aug. 16, 1927; student Ind. U.; LL.B., U. Ky., 1951. Admitted to Ky. bar, 1951; asst. atty. Fayette County (Ky.), 1964-69; judge Fayette County, 1969-75; atty. gen. Ky., Frankfort, 1976-79; justice Ky. Supreme Ct., 1979—, chief justice, 1982—. Bd. dirs. Nat. Assn. Counties, 1973-75; 1st pres. Ky. Assn. Counties; 1st chmn. Bluegrass Area Devel. Dist. Served with USN, World War II. Named Outstanding County Judge of Ky., 1972. Democrat. Office: State Capitol Frankfort KY 40601

STEPHENS, ROBERT MONROE, petroleum company executive, petroleum consultant; b. Jonesboro, Ill., Dec. 25, 1924; s. Robert Dewey and Lucille Octavia (Hileman) S.; m. Nelwyn Cordell, Jan. 6, 1951. B.S. in Mining Engring., U. Ill., 1948, M.S. in Geology, 1949; postgrad. Northwestern U., 1962, Harvard U., 1968. Registered profl. engr., Tex. Geol. engr. Shell Oil Co., Houston, 1949-52; sr. v.p. Tenneco Oil Co., Houston, 1952-71; pres. Anadarko Prodn. Co., Houston, 1971-77, R.M. Stephens & Assocs., Inc., Houston, 1977—; dir. London Am. Energy, N.V., London. Served to sgt. U.S. Army, 1944-46. Mem. Soc. Petroleum Engrs., Soc. Petroleum Evaluation Engrs., Am. Assn. Petroleum Geologists, Am. Assn. Petroleum Geologists, Inst. Profl. Geologists, Ind. Petroleum Assn. Am., Sigma Xi. Republican. Unitarian. Club: Harvard (Houston). Avocations: tennis; sailing. Home: 5442 Bordley Dr Houston TX 77056 Office: RM Stephens & Assocs Inc 5100 Westheimer Suite 275 Houston TX 77056

STEPHENS, ROBERT OREN, English language educator; b. Corpus Christi, Tex., Oct. 2, 1928; s. Joe Key, Sr., and Mary Emma (Robertson) S.; m. Carey Virginia Jones, Sept. 8, 1956; children—Nancy, Melissa, Robert Allan. Student Del Mar Coll., 1945-47; B.A., Tex. Coll. Arts and Industries, 1949; M.A., U. Tex., 1951, Ph.D., 1958. English tchr. Shiner High Sch., Tex., 1949-50; instr. U. Tex.-Austin, 1957-61; asst. prof. U. N.C.-Greensboro, 1961-66, assoc. prof., 1966-68, prof. English, 1968—, chmn., 1981—, dir. grad. studies in English, 1967-81; vis. asst. prof. Appalachian State U., Boone, N.C., summer 1962, vis. assoc. prof., summer 1967. Author: Hemingway's NonFiction: The Public Voice, 1968; Ernest Hemingway: The Critical Reception, 1977; author articles on Ernest Hemingway, Sarah Kemble Knight, Tex. Oil Folklore, George Washington Cable. Ruling elder Presbyterian Ch., Greensboro, 1965—. Served to lt. USNR, 1951-55. Coop. fellow in humanities, U. N.C.-Duke U., 1965-66. Mem. MLA, South Atlantic MLA, Soc. for Study of So. Lit., Southeastern Am. Studies Assn., Philol. Assn. of the Carolinas, Nat. Council Tchrs. of English. Democrat. Avocations: Tennis; hiking; landscape gardening and design. Home: 1706 Sylvan Rd Greensboro NC 27403 Office: Dept English U NC at Greensboro Greensboro NC 27412

STEPHENS, RUTH ANDERSON, nurse, educator; b. Jacksonville, Fla., Jan. 22, 1933; d. Willie A. and Eliza (Dilligard) Anderson; m. Johnnie James Stephens, Dec. 2, 1956; children—Johnetta, Andrinne. B.S. in Nursing, Fla. A&M U., 1954; M.S., U. N.C., 1965; Ph.D., Emory U., 1982. Staff nurse Brewster Hosp., Jacksonville, 1954-56, instr. Brewster-Duval Sch. Nursing, 1957-62; instr. Duval County Practical Nursing Program, Jacksonville, 1965-66; asst. prof. Fla. A&M U., Tallahassee, 1966-82, assoc. prof., 1982-83, interim dean, 1982; chmn. dept. baccalaureate nursing Alcorn State U., Natchez, Miss., 1983—, prof., 1983—. Bd. dirs. YWCA, 1975-76, program chmn., 1976-77, endowment com. chmn., 1976-77; mem. Duval County adv. com. Health Occupations Edn., 1975-76. Roswell Park Meml. Inst. fellow, Buffalo, 1972—, Am. Cancer Soc.; named Tchr. of Year, Student Nurses Assn., Fla. A&M U., 1970-71, Outstanding Tchr. of Year, Sch. Nursing, 1979-80. Fellow Am. Nurses Assn. (minority fellowship program 1976—); mem. Fla. Nurses Assn., Sigma Theta Tau, Zeta Phi Beta. Democrat. Baptist. Home: PO Box 341 Natchez MS 39120 Office: Dept Nursing Alcorn State U PO Box 1830 Natchez MS 39120

STEPHENS, SIDNEY DEE, chemical manufacturing company executive; b. St. Joseph, Mo., Apr. 26, 1945; s. Lindsay Caldwell and Edith Mae (Thompson) S.; m. Ellen Marie Boeh, June 15, 1968 (div. 1973); m. Elizabeth Ann Harris, Sept. 22, 1973; 1 child, Laura Nicole. B.S., Mo. Western State U., 1971; M.A., U. Houston, 1980. Assoc. urban planner Met. Planning Commn., St. Joseph, Mo., 1967-71; prodn. acctg. assoc. Quaker Oats Co., St. Joseph, 1971-72, office mgr., personnel rep., Rosemont, Ill., 1972-73, employee and community relations mgr., New Brunswick, N.J., 1973-75, Pasadena, Tex., 1975-80; site personnel mgr. ICI Americas, Inc., Pasadena, Tex., 1980—; pvt. mgmt. cons., Houston, 1981—. Contbr. articles to profl. jours. Served with USNR, 1963-65. Mem. Am. Soc. Personnel Adminstrs., Houston Personnel

Assn. (community and govt. affairs com. 1984-85). Republican. Methodist. Home: 16446 Longvale Dr Houston TX 77059 Office: ICI Americas Inc 5757 Underwood Rd Pasadena TX 77507

STEPHENS, WILL BETH DODSON, psychologist, educator; b. Van Horn, Tex., July 14, 1918; d. John Lester and Almeda (Garner) Dodson; m. Jack Howard Stephens, Feb. 18, 1944; children—Jack Howard, Jill Stephens McFarland. B.F.A., U. Tex., 1942, M.Ed., 1958, Ph.D., 1964. Asst. dir., USO, Del Rio, Tex., 1942-45; asst. dir. YWCA, Austin Tex., 1946-47; spl. edn. tchr. pub. schs., Tyler, Tex., 1956-60; research assoc. U. Tex., Austin, 1962-64; research asst. prof. Inst. for Research on Exceptional Children, U. Ill., Urbana, 1965-66; assoc. prof. ednl. psychology Temple U., Phila., 1966-70, prof. spl. edn., 1970-75; head spl. edn. program, U. Tex.-Dallas, 1975-80; dir. Dept. Def. Dependents Schs., Alexandria, Va., 1981—. Mem. Pres.' Com. on Retardation, 1971-78; bd. dirs., past pres. Found. for Exceptional Children; mem. edn. adv. bd. Am. Found. for the Blind, mem. adv. bd. Tex. Easter Seal Soc. Vocat. Rehab. Adminstrn. fellow, U. Geneva (Switzerland), 1964-65. Fellow Am. Psychol. Assn., Pa. Psychol. Assn., Am. Assn. Mental Deficiency (v.p. ednl. div 1977-79), mem. Council for Exceptional Children (past pres. div. mental retardation, chmn. nat. research com.), Nat. Assn. Retarded Children (nat. edn. com.), Jean Piaget Soc., Am. Psychol. Assn., Soc. for Research in Child Devel., Internat. Assn. for Sci. Study of Mental Deficiency, Am. Ednl. Research Assn., DAR. Episcopalian. Editorial bd. Topics in Early Childhood Edn. Contbr articles to profl. jours. Home: 307 Yoakum Pkwy Apt 626 Alexandria VA 22304 Office: Dept Def Dependents Schs 2461 Eisenhower Dr Alexandria VA 22331

STEPHENSON, CHARLES A., music educator; b. Shenandoah, Iowa, Nov. 18, 1922; s. John Sherman and Irene Osborne (McClelland) S.; m. Sue Ann Slaughter, Aug. 14, 1954; children—Gregory Alan, Marc Joel. B.A. in Music, Simpson Coll., 1950; M.A. in Mus., U. Mich., 1952. Instr. music Lon Morris Coll., Jacksonville, Fla., 1953-56; instr. voice U. Wichita, Kans., 1957-58; instr. music Lee Coll., Baytown, Tex., 1959—, chmn. dept. fine arts, 1963—. Served with USAF, 1942-45. Mem. Am. Choral Dirs. Assn., Tex. Assn. Music Schs. (bd. govs. 1982-85). Democrat. Methodist. Avocations: woodworking; reading; gardening; computers. Home: 5409 Louise St Baytown TX 77521 Office: Lee Coll PO Box 818 Baytown TX 77520

STEPHENSON, JAMES BENNETT, state ct. justice; b. Greenup, Ky., Jan. 26, 1916; s. Elmer D. and Emabel (Bennett) S.; A.B., U. Ky., Lexington, 1938, LL.B., 1951; m. Elizabeth Campbell Paddison, June 28, 1941; children—Martha Bennett, Jane Marsh. Admitted to Ky. bar, 1939; practice in Pikeville, Ky., 1940-57; circuit judge Div. I 35th Jud. Dist., Pike County, 1957-73; justice Ky. Ct. Appeals, 1973-75; justice Supreme Ct. Ky., 1975—. 1973—. Mem. Jud. Council Ky., 1959-61. Bd. dirs. Meth. Hosp., Pikeville. Served to capt. USAAF, 1942-45. Mem. Sigma Chi, Phi Delta Phi. Democrat. Methodist (chmn. fin. com. 1955-70; chmn. ofcl. bd. 1971-72; Ky. Conf. Com. on World Service and Fin. 1969-72). Home: 37 Timberlawn Circle Frankfort KY 41601 Office: 239 State Capitol Frankfort KY 40601

STEPHENSON, JOSEPH ELMER, surgeon; b. Pikeville, Ky., Oct. 3, 1917; s. Elmer D'Ester and Emabel (Bennett) S.; A.B., U. Ky., 1939; M.D., U. Louisville, 1942; m. Juanita Jeanice (Polly) Floyd, Dec. 30, 1939; children—Joseph Floyd, John Wesley, James Gibbs Rich. Intern Charity Hosp. La., New Orleans, 1942-43; practice medicine, Elkhorn City, Ky., 1946-51; resident div. grad. medicine Tulane Med. Sch., 1951-54, fellow in gen. surgery Ochsner Found. Hosp. and Clinic, 1951-54; sr. surg. resident Lallie Kemp Charity Hosp., Independence, La., 1954-55; practice medicine specializing in gen. surgery, Ashland, Ky., 1956-83. Served to capt. M.C., USAAF, 1943-46. Diplomate Am. Bd. Surgery. Fellow ACS; mem. Ky. Med. Soc., AMA, Boyd County Med. Soc., Ochsner Surg. Soc., Ky. Hist. Soc. (life), Sigma Chi (life), Alpha Kappa Kappa, Alpha Omega Alpha. Author 2 books. Home: 2726 Cumberland Ave Ashland KY 41101

STEPHENSON, LARRY WAYNE, university administrator, accounting educator; b. Worthington, Ky., Apr. 18, 1940; s. Morris and Lucille (Tackett) S. m. Kay Wheeler, July 13, 1963; children—Kerry Rae Stephenson Logan, Robert Crayton. A.B., Morehead State U., Ky., 1964, A.M. in Edn., 1968, M. Higher Edn., 1976. Tchr., coach Augusta Pub. Schs., Ky., 1964-67; dir. housing Morehead State U., Ky., 1967-76, dean of students, 1976-80, dir. adminstrv. services, 1980—. Mem. Nat. Assn. Student Personnel Advs., Am. Assn. Counseling and Devel. Democrat. Home: 335 Bays Ave Morehead KY 40351 Office: Morehead State U 301 Howell-McDowell Adminstrn Bldg Morehead KY 40351

STEPHENSON, RICHARD MURRELL, clergyman; b. Southampton County, Va., Dec. 1, 1921; s. Edgar Vick and Eleanor (Daughtrey) S.; m. Noralee Mellor, Feb. 1, 1949; children—Vivian, Lee, Richard. B.A., Hampden-Sydney U.; Th.M., So. Bapt. Theol. Sem.; D.D.(hon.), U. Richmond. Ordained minister Baptist Ch., 1944; pastor First Bapt., Ft. Myers, Fla., 1946-50, Columbia Bapt., Falls Church, Va., 1950-68; exec. dir. Bapt. Gen. Assn. Va., Richmond, 1968—. Bd. dirs. local chpt. ARC, local council Boy Scouts Am.; trustee Va. Bapt. Found., So. Bapt. Found., So. Bapt. Theol. Sem.; pres. Assn. Bapt. State Convs. Recipient Algernon Sydney Sullivan medallion, 1943, George Washington medal Freedoms Found., 1964. Club: Country of Va. Home: 8951 Belefonte Rd Richmond Va 23229 Office: Bapt Gen Assn Monument at Willow Lawn Sts PO Box 8568 Richmond VA 23226

STEPHENSON, ROSCOE BOLAR, JR., state supreme court justice; b. Covington, Va., Feb. 22, 1922. A.B., Washington and Lee U., 1943, J.D., 1947, LL.D. (hon.), 1983. Bar: Va. 1947. Ptnr. Stephenson & Stephenson, Covington, 1947-52; commonwealth's atty. Alleghany County, Va., 1952-64; ptnr. Stephenson, Kostel, Watson, Carson and Snyder, Covington, 1964-73; judge 25th Jud. Cir. Ct. Commonwealth Va., Covington, 1973-81; justice Va. Supreme Ct., Richmond, 1981—. Recipient Covington Citizen of Yr. award, 1973, Outstanding Alumni award Covington High Sch., 1973. Fellow Am. Coll. Trial Lawyers; mem. Va. State Bar (council 1969-73), Va. Bar Assn., Va. Trial Lawyers Assn., Order of the Coif. Home: Clearwater Park Covington VA 24426 Office: Va Supreme Ct Supreme Ct Bldg Richmond VA 23219 Office: 214 W Main St Covington VA 24426

STEPHENSON, SAMUEL EDWARD, JR., surgeon; b. Bristol, Tenn., May 16, 1926; s. Samuel Edward and Hazel Beatrice (Walters) S.; m. Dorothea Cole, June 12, 1950 (div.); children—Samuel E. III, William Douglas, Dorothea Louise, Judith Maria; m. 2d, Janet Spotts, May 16, 1970. B.S., U. S.C., 1946; M.D., Vanderbilt U., 1950. Diplomate Am. Bd. Surgery, Am. Bd. Thoracic Surgery. Intern, Butterworth Hosp., Grand Rapids, Mich., 1950-51; resident in surgery Vanderbilt U. Hosp., Nashville, 1951-57, lab. researcher, 1957-65, faculty mem. dept. surgery, 1955-67; chief surgery Duval Med. Ctr., Jacksonville, Fla., 1967-79; chief gen. surgery Bapt. Med. Ctr., Jacksonville, 1979—; med. dir. Lifeflight, 1981—; clin. prof. surgery U. Fla., Gainesville, 1979—. Served with USNR, 1944-45. NIH grantee, 1957-67; recipient Ignacio Barraquer award for excellence in Mott Med. Photography, 1967. Mem. Am. Surg. Assn., So. Surg. Assn., Soc. Univ. Surgeons, ACS, Am. Thoracic Surg. Assn., So. Thoracic Surg. Assn. Republican. Episcopalian. Clubs: University (Jacksonville). Lodge: Masons. Developed first synchronous cardiac pacemaker and electronic control of artificial ventilators. Office: Baptist Pavillion Suite 808 836 Prudential Dr Jacksonville FL 32207

STEPP, MARTHA JANE, pharmacist; b. Harlan, Ky., Jan. 31, 1941; d. Ernest Wendell and Pauline (Lewis) S. B.S. in Pharmacy, Med. Coll. Va. Sch. Pharmacy, 1962. Pharmacist, Creech Drug Store, Harlan, Ky., 1962—. Mem. Ky. Hist. Soc. (cert. pioneer 1975), 1979, Ky. Col., 1963. Solo Cert. award Robert Y. Blakeman, 1975. Mem. S.E. Ky. Pharmacists, Ky. Pharmacists. Assn., Fla. Pharmacy Assn., Am. Pharm. Assn., Alumni Assn. Med. Coll. Va. Republican. Baptist. Club: Harlan Country. Avocations: golf; reading; traveling; genealogy. Home: 411 Mound St Harlan KY 40831 Office: Creech Drug Store 217 Central St Harlan KY 40831

STERLING, JOHN EARL, computer-graphics augmented design and manufacturing executive, electro-mechanical designer; b. Lawton, Okla., Jan. 25, 1955; s. LeRoy Ashby, Jr. and Ruby Mae (Pierce) S. Student U. Houston, 1976, Austin Community Coll., 1977-83. TV technician RCA Services Inc., Houston, 1973-76; line printers group leader Tex. Instruments Inc., Houston and Austin, 1976-77; carpenter, Austin, 1977-78; lead, supr. DeGeest Marine Engring. Co., Austin, 1978-79; draftsman Gifford Drafting and Design, Austin, 1979; design draftsman IBM Corp., Austin, 1979-80, computer-graphics augmented design operator, 1982, 84-85; electro/mech. designer Tracoustics, Austin, 1980; design draftsman Tracor Aerospace div. U.S. Army Eradcom Combat Surveillance in Target Acquisition Lab., Austin, 1980; packaging designer heavy indsl. motor div. Westinghouse Corp., Round Rock, Tex., 1980-82; designer electro/mech. drawings AMI Systems Inc., Austin, 1983; computer-graphics augmented design operator Lockheed Missiles and Space Co., Austin, 1983, engring. design draftsman, 1983-84, electro/mech. computer-graphics augmented designer, 1985—; design draftsman detailer RTS Tech. Services, Austin, 1983. Home: 1103 Pitcairn Dr Pflugerville TX 78660 Office: Lockheed Missiles and Space Co Austin TX 78760

STERLING, ROSS N., U.S. district judge; b. 1931. B.A., U. Tex., 1956, LL.B., 1957. Assoc. Vinson & Elkins, 1958-76; judge U.S. Dist. Ct. for So. Tex., Houston, 1976—. Address: PO Box 61527 Houston TX 77208*

STERLING, THOMAS ARTHUR, risk management services company executive; b. Richmond Twp., Pa., June 2, 1933; s. Thomas and Florence May (Crooks) S.; A.B., Wabash Coll., 1955; postgrad. (Am. Jurisprudence award), Ind. U., 1968; m. Frances Louise Wilson, Apr. 17, 1971; children—Heather, Perry, Kelly, Heidi, Kyle. Feature writer Collinwood Pub. Co., Cleve., 1955-56; mgr. Firestone Tire & Rubber, 1957; claim agent N.Y. Central R.R., 1959-66; negotiator, trial asst. Penn Central Transp. Co., 1967-72; loss control cons. Sentry Ins. Co., Chgo., 1973-77, field risk control supr., Atlanta, 1978-81; casualty account cons. Johnson & Higgins Ga., Inc., 1981-82; v.p., loss control mgr. Fickling & Walker Ins. Services, Inc., Atlanta, 1982-85; regional cons. risk control Crawford & Co., Atlanta, 1985—; owner, pres. Coll. Resource Counselors. Cons. indsl. safety advisor Jr. Achievement, Central Ind. chpt., 1976-78, Cobb County, Ga., 1980-81. Served with U.S. Navy, 1957-61. Cert. safety profl. Mem. Am. Soc. Safety Engrs., Nat. Safety Mgmt. Soc., Assn. Mut. Ins. Engrs., Nat. Ry. Claims Assn., Nat. Fire Protection Assn., Nat. Safety Council, Am. Welding Soc., Ga. Motor Trucking Assn., Lambda Chi Alpha. Methodist. Clubs: DeMolay, Canterbury Country, Planetary Soc. Contbr. poetry and short stories. Home: 3968 Fairington Dr Marietta GA 30066 Office: 5780 Peachtree Dunwoody Rd Suite 300 Atlanta GA 30302

STERN, DUKE NORDLINGER, lawyer, consultant; b. Chgo., Apr. 14, 1942; B.S. in Econs., U. Pa., 1963; postgrad. U. Va., 1964; J.D., Temple U., 1968; M.B.A., U. Mo., 1969; Ph.D., 1972. Bar: Mo. 1969, U.S. Sup. Ct. 1978. Dir. Ctr. for Adminstrn. Legal Systems, Duquesne U., Pitts., 1974-75; exec. dir., gen. counsel W.Va. State Bar, Charleston, 1975-79; pres. Risk & Ins. Services Cons., Inc., St. Petersburg, Fla., 1979-80, Duke Nordlinger Stern & Assocs., Inc., St. Petersburg, 1980—, Duke Nordlinger Stern & Assocs. (U.K.) Ltd., London, 1984—. Pres., W.Va. Legal Services Plan, Inc., 1978-79. Mem. Am. Soc. Assn. Execs. (cert.), Am. Arbitration Assn., Nat. Assn. Corp. Dirs., Am. Judicature Soc., ABA. Author: An Attorney's Guide to Malpractice Liability, 1977; Case in Labor Law, 1977; An Accountant's Guide to Malpractice Liability, 1979; Avoiding Accountant's Malpractice Claims, 1982; Avoiding Legal Malpractice Claims, 1982; A Practical Guide to Preventing Legal Malpractice, 1983. Office: Duke Nordlinger Stern & Assocs Inc 1336 54th Ave NE Saint Petersburg FL 33703

STERN, LARRY NATHAN, political science educator; b. Newark, Ohio, Sept. 17, 1941; s. Morelle E. and Florence E. (Field) S.; m. Teresa G. Metcalf, July 6, 1974; 1 child, Lucas Eric. B.A., Coll. of Wooster, 1962; Ph.D., U. N.C., 1967. Instr. evening coll. U. N.C.-Chapel Hill, 1965-66; asst. prof. Fla. State U., Tallahassee, 1966-71; assoc. prof. Mars Hill Coll., N.C., 1971-78, prof. polit. sci., 1978—, dir. instl. research, 1982—; cons. mil. credit evals. Am. Council on Edn., Washington, 1977—. Author (with others) Interdisciplinary Study of Politics, 1974. Contbr. articles to profl. jours. Mem. exec. com. N.C. Clean, Raleigh, 1984—; chmn. Western N.C. Community Devel. Program, Asheville, 1984—; mem. N.C. Goals and Policies Bd., 1985—; alt. del. Republican Nat. Convention, Miami, 1972; treas. N.C. Fedn. Young Reps., Raleigh, 1973-75; chmn. exec. com. Madison County Reps., Marshall, N.C., 1977-83; trustee N.C. Rep. Bldg. Fund, Raleigh, 1977—. Recipient Barbershopper of Yr. award SPEBSQSA, 1970, Community Devel. Man of Yr. award Madison County Devel. Council, 1982. Mem. N.C. Polit. Sci. Assn. (pres. 1982-83), N.C. Assn. for Instl. Research, Internat. Studies Assn., Assn. for Instl. Research, Am. Polit. Sci. Assn., N. Am. Simulation and Gaming Assn. (v. chmn. bd. dirs. 1981-82), Western N.C. Devel. Assn. (bd. dirs. 19—), UN Assn. (bd. dir. 1983—). Presbyterian. Club: SPEBSQSA (pres. 1978) (Asheville). Home: Crooked St Box 279 Mars Hill NC 28754 Office: Mars Hill Coll Mars Hill NC 28754

STERN, MARK, political science educator; b. Bklyn., Aug. 4, 1945; s. Alexander and Nettie (Sterling) S.; m. Marcia Davidson, Mar. 13, 1972 (div. Mar. 1978); m. Barbara Slater, Sept. 23, 1984; 1 child, Benjamin David. B.A., Bklyn. Coll., 1965; Ph.D., U. Rochester, 1970. Asst. prof. U. Mo.-St. Louis, 1968-72; assoc. prof. U. Central Fla., Orlando, 1972-82, prof., 1983—, pres. United Faculty of Fla., 1978-80, mem. state senate, 1980—. Mem. editorial bd. Choice Mag., 1973—. Contbr. articles to profl. jours. Exec. Com. Democratic County, Seminole County, Fla., 1980-82; pack leader Seminole council Boy Scouts Am., 1983-84. Nat. Endowment Humanities fellow 1977, 81; grantee LBJ Found. 1984, So. Regional Edn. Bd. 1985. Jewish. Home: 1048 Ramsgate Winter Park FL 32792 Office: U Central Fla Dept Polit Sci Orlando FL 32792

STERN, THOMAS NEUTON, physician, educator; b. Memphis, Apr. 22, 1926; s. Neuton Samuel and Beatrice (Wolf) S.; m. Harriet Wise, June 16, 1957; children—Susan, Carol, David. Student Harvard U., 1943-44; M.D., Washington U., St. Louis, 1948. Diplomate Am. Bd. Internal Medicine, Am. Bd. Cardiovascular Disease. Practice medicine specializing in cardiology, Memphis, 1952—; clin. prof. medicine and cardiology U. Tenn.; dir. cardiovascular tng. Baptist Meml. Hosp., Memphis. Mem. Memphis City Schs. Bd. Edn., 1980—, (pres. 1982); pres. Memphis Heart Assn., 1963-64; v.p. Opera Memphis, 1979; v.p. Memphis Arts Council, 1974, 78; mem. nat. exec. com. Am. Jewish Com. Served to capt. USMC, 1953-55. (Fellow) ACP, Am. Coll. Cardiology, Am. Heart Assn. (council on clin. cardiology); mem. Nat. Sch. Bd. Assn. Democrat. Jewish. Author: (with Neuton S. Stern) The Bases of Treatment, 1957; Clinical Examination, 1964; contbr. articles to profl. jours. Office: 910 Madison Ave Suite 608 Memphis TN 38103

STERN, WAYNE BRIAN, specialty chemicals company executive, management consultant; b. New Rochelle, N.Y., Jan. 8, 1948; s. Edward A. Stern and Gertrude (Eger) Lurie; m. Yvonne Eva Segelbaum, Sept. 1, 1968; children—Tiffany Joy, Colette Avi. B.S. in Aerospace Engring., U. Md.-College Park, 1970; M.B.A. in Fin. and Internat. Bus., U. Wash.-Seattle, 1977. Structures design engr. Pratt & Whitney Aircraft, West Palm Beach, Fla., 1970-72; control system engr., system cost analyst, mgr. internat. market research Boeing Co., Seattle, 1973-77; group mgr., v.p. planning and devel. W.R. Grace & Co., N.Y.C. and Troy, Mich., 1977-81; v.p., gen. mgr. Compo Industries, Inc., Cartersville, Ga., 1981—. Recipient Outstanding Research award AIAA, 1970. Mem. Am. Mgmt. Assn., Assn. Corp. Growth, Tau Beta Pi, Sigma Gamma Tau (past v.p.), Pi Mu Epsilon, Omicron Delta Kappa, Beta Gamma Sigma. Republican. Jewish. Home: 745 Old Campus Trail Atlanta GA 30328 Office: Compo Industries Inc 21 River Dr Cartersville GA 30120

STERNBACH, CHARLES ALAN, geoscientist; b. N.Y.C., May 15, 1957; s. Gerald Malcolm and Juliette (Bruchhauser) S.; m. Linda Ann Raine, Aug. 13, 1983. B.A., Columbia U., 1980; M.S., Rensselaer Poly. U., 1981, Ph.D., 1984. Geologist, U.S. Army C.E., Hanover, N.H., 1980, Sun Prodn. Co., Houston, 1981, Tulsa, 1982, Shell Western Exploration and Prodn. Inc., Houston, 1984—; research asst. U.S. Dept. Energy, Rensselaer Poly. Inst., Troy, N.Y., 1981-84. Co-author: Field Guide to the Geology of the Paleozoic, Mesozoic and Tertiary Rocks of New Jersey and the Central Hudson Valley, 1981. Contbr. articles to profl. jours. Mem. Am. Assn. Petroleum Geologists, Soc. Econ. Paleontologists and Mineralogists, Soc. Profl. Well Log Analysts. Avocations: Carbonate and clastic petrology; diagenesis and dolomitization; structural and petroleum geology. Home: 20331 Prince Creek Katy TX 77450 Office: Shell Western Exploration and Petroleum Inc PO Box 991 Houston TX 77450

STERNBERG, DONNA GAIL (WEINTRAUB), retail company executive; b. Little Rock, Dec. 16, 1943; d. Charles Simon and Sadie Frieda (Lulky) Weintraub; m. Hans Joachim Sternberg, Feb. 19, 1967; children—Erich, Julie Ellen, Deborah Ann, Marc Samuel. B.A. cum laude, U. Tex., 1966; postgrad. Columbia U., 1966. Buyer, mgr. Goudchaux's, Inc., Baton Rouge, 1967-76, mdse. mgr., 1976-81, v.p., mdse. mgr. fur dept. Gouchaux/Maison Blanche, 1981—. Founder women's div. Jewish Fedn. Greater Baton Rouge, 1970; chmn. women's div. La. United Jewish Appeal, 1972-74; nat. bd. dirs. women's div. United Jewish Appeal, 1972-76; regent Nat. Fedn. Republican Women; mem. community adv. com. La. State U. Honors Div., Baton Rouge, 1981—; mem. Nat. Commn. on Presdl. Scholars, 1982—; mem. exec. com. Am. Israel Pub. Affairs Com., 1982—; bd. dirs., sec. Louisianians for Am. Security Polit. Action Com., 1983—; co-chmn. Alumni Schs. Com. Princeton U. and Columbia Coll. Alice Stetton fellow, Columbia U. Sch. Internat. Affairs, 1966. Mem. Baton Rouge Phi Beta Kappa Community Assn. (founder 1979, pres. 1979-81), Phi Beta Kappa, Alpha Lambda Delta. Lodge: B'nai B'rith Women (charter pres. and founder Baton Rouge chpt. 1970-72). Office: PO Box 3478 Baton Rouge LA 70821

STETZER, MARTIN CHARLES, oil company executive; b. Pitts., Aug. 10, 1942; s. Charles William and Rita T. (Dietzen) S.; m. Katherine Elizabeth Kilker, Jan. 25, 1969; children—Alec C., Douglas M., Max E. B.M.E., Gen. Motors Inst., 1965; M.A. in Indsl. Adminstrn., Carnegie Mellon U., 1967. Engring. economist Esso Eastern Inc, N.Y.C., 1967-70, various mech. planning projects, purchasing assignments Esso-Singapore, 1970-74, mktg. sr. planner Esso Eastern Inc, Houston, 1974-77, automotive mgr., mktg. planner Esso Australia, Ltd., Sydney, Australia, 1977-80; corporate mgr. purchasing and materials Superior Oil, Houston, 1980-85; sr. v.p. ops. Wilson Supply, Houston, 1985—. Contbr. articles to profl. publs. Grad. Sch. Indsl. Adminstrn. scholar, Carnegie Mellon U., 1965. Mem. Nat. Assn. Purchasing Mgrs., Robot Soc. (Gen. Motors Inst.). Home: 9813 Shadow Wood Dr Houston TX 77080

STEVENS, BARBARA FISHER, nurse; b. Blossburg, Pa., May 24, 1949; d. C. Raymond and F. Betty (Conkl) Fisher; m. James R. Stevens, June 14, 1974. R.N., Hosp. U. Pa., 1970. Operating room staff nurse Hershey Med. Ctr., Pa., 1971-73, Community Med. Ctr., Scranton, Pa., 1973-74, Riverside Hosp., Newport News, Va., 1974-77; head nurse operating room, recovery room Walter Reed Meml. Hosp., Gloucester, Va., 1977—. Mem. Tidewater Assn. Operating Room Nurses. Baptist. Club: Gloucester Choral Soc. Avocations: needle crafts; sewing; swimming. Office: Walter Reed Meml Hosp Route 17 Gloucester VA 23061

STEVENS, BEN DEE, lawyer; b. San Angelo, Tex., Jan. 13, 1942; s. Rex W. and Nettie Marie (Evans) S.; m. Joyce Irene Dymke, June 22, 1964 (div. 1966); children—Mark Richard, Samantha Ann, Andrew Duncan; m. Paula Sue Smith, June 4, 1983; 1 stepchild, Shan Michelle Spear. B.B.A., U. Houston-Clear Lake, 1978; J.D., S. Tex. Coll., 1981. Bar: Tex. 1981, U.S. Tax Ct. 1982, U.S. Dist. Ct. (so. dist.) Tex. 1982, U.S. Ct. Appeals (5th cir.) 1982. Sole practice, Houston, 1981-84; gen. counsel Cantrell & Co., Houston, 1984—. Mem. ABA, Tex. Bar Assn., Houston Bar Assn., Am. Trial Lawyers Assn., Phi Alpha Delta. Republican. Episcopalian. Office: 4204 Bellaire Blvd Suite 204 Houston TX 77025

STEVENS, DONALD KING, aeronautical engineer, nuclear consultant, retired army officer; b. Danville, Ill., Oct. 27, 1920; s. Douglas Franklin and Ida Harriet (King) S.; B.S. with high honors in Ceramic Engring., U. Ill., 1942; M.S. in Aeros. and Guided Missiles, U. So. Calif., 1949; grad. U.S. Army Command and Gen. Staff Coll., 1957, U.S. Army War Coll., 1962; m. Adele Carman de Werff, July 11, 1942; children—Charles August, Anne Louise, Alice Jeanne Stevens Kay. Served with Ill. State Geol. Survey, 1938-40; ceramic engr. Harbison-Walker Refractories Co., Pitts., 1945-46; commd. 1st lt. U.S. Army, 1946, advanced through grades to col., 1963; with Arty. Sch., Fort Bliss, Tex., 1949-52; supr. unit tng. and Nike missile firings, N.Mex., 1953-56; mem. Weapons Systems Evaluation Group, Office Sec. of Def., Washington, 1957-61; comdr. Niagara-Buffalo (N.Y.) Def., 31st Arty. Brigade, Lockport, N.Y., 1963-65; chief Air Def. and Nuclear br. War Plans div. 1965-67, chief strategic forces div. Office Dep. Chief Staff for Mil. Ops., 1967-69; chief spl. weapons plans, J5, U.S. European Command, Ger., 1969-72, ret., 1972; guest lectr. U.S. Mil. Acad. 1958-59; cons. U.S. Army Concepts Analysis Agy., Bethesda, Md., 1973—; cons. on strategy Lulejian & Assocs., Inc., 1974-75; cons. nuclear policy and plans to Office Asst. Sec. of Def., 1975-80, 84—; cons. Sci. Applications, Inc., 1976-78; Asst. camp dir. Piankeshaw Area council Boy Scouts Am., 1937; mem. chancel choir, elder First Christian Ch., Falls Church, Va., 1957-61, 65-69, 72—; elder, trustee Presbyn. Ch., 1963-65. Decorated D.S.M. (Army), Legion of Merit, Bronze Star. Mem. Am. Ceramic Soc., Assn. U.S. Army, U. Ill. Alumni Assn., U. So. Calif. Alumni Assn., Sigma Xi, Sigma Tau, Tau Beta Pi, Phi Kappa Phi, Alpha Phi Omega. Clubs: Rotary, Niagara Falls Country; Ill. (Washington); Terrapin. Contbr. articles to engring. jours.; pioneer in tactics and deployment plans for Army surface-to-air missiles. Address: 5916 5th St N Arlington VA 22203

STEVENS, DONALD MEADE, energy production equipment company executive; b. Lynchburg, Va., May 9, 1947; s. Samuel Meade and Emma Elizabeth (Huff) S.; m. Mary Anne Henry, June 20, 1970. B.S. in Physics, Va. Poly. Inst. and State U., 1969, M.S. in Physics, 1970, Ph.D. in Physics, 1974. NSF undergrad. researcher Va. Poly. Inst. and State U., Blacksburg, 1968-69; research assoc., 1970-74; research asst. Brookhaven Nat. Lab., Upton, N.Y., 1969-70; sr. research engr. Babcock & Wilcox, Lynchburg, Va., 1974-80, group supr., 1980-85, mgr. nondestructive methods and diagnostics, 1985—. Contbr. articles to profl. publs. NSF traineeship, 1972; fellow Gulf Oil Co., 1971. Mem. IEEE, ASME (program chmn. 1985—, chmn. operating com. 1984—, sec. 1983—), Am. Phys. Soc., ASTM. Lodge: Lions. Home: Route 1 Box 164 B Lovingston VA 22949 Office: Babcock & Wilcox PO Box 11165 Lynchburg VA 24506

STEVENS, FREDERICK LECOMPTE, JR., psychologist, mental health administrator; b. Cambridge, Md., Dec. 30, 1945; s. Frederick LeCompte and Fannie (Mowbray) S.; m. Deanna Faye Rebert, June 10, 1967; children—Michael Frederick, Michelle Renee. B.A., U. Md., 1967; M.S., Iowa State U., 1968, Ph.D., 1971; M.H.A., U. Minn., 1984. Cert. mental health adminstr. Field Instr. Sch. Social Welfare, U. Kans., Lawrence, 1972-75; adj. prof. Park Coll. Crown Ctr., Kansas City, Mo., 1975, James Madison U., Harrisonburg, Va., 1977; dir. Massanutten Mental Health Ctr., Harrisonburg, 1975-85; asst. adminstr. Holly Hill Hosp., Raleigh, N.C., 1985—. Bd. dirs. Va. Assn. Mental Health Dirs., 1979-84, MHA, 1976-78; chmn. bd. dirs. Helpline, Leavenworth, Kans., 1974-75; v.p. Muhlenberg Lutheran Ch. Council, Harrisonburg, 1977, pres., 1978-79. Served to capt. Med. Service Corps. U.S. Army, 1969-75. Mem. Assn. Mental Health Adminstrs. (cert.), Am. Psychol. Assn., Va. Assn. Community Service Bds. Avocation: gardening; running; softball; reading. Lodges: Kiwanis, Rotary. Home: 6208 Lewisand Ct Raleigh NC 27609 Office: Holly Hill Hosp 3019 Falstaff Rd Raleigh NC 27610

STEVENS, JOE MILTON, hospital administrator; b. Slaton, Tex., Mar. 18, 1933; s. Joseph Robert Stevens and Vera Marie (Remy) Meester; m. Wanda Lee Breeding, Sept. 21, 1956; children—Vickie, Scott. B.B.A., Tex. Tech U., 1974. Enlisted U.S. Air Force, 1953, advanced through grades to sr. master sgt., 1968; various hosp. adminstrn. positions, Korea, Japan, W.Ger., to 1973; ret., 1973; mgr. arts and crafts Tandy-Am. Handicrafts Co., Little Rock, 1975-76; adminstr. Dublin Hosp., Tex., 1976-79, Meml. Hosp., Gonzales, Tex., 1979—; mem. hosp. licensing adv. council State of Tex., 1980—; dir. Tex. Hosp. Ins. Exchange, Austin, 1979—. Contbr. articles to mags. Mem. Tex. Hosp. Assn. (dist. advisor 1983-85). Avocations: Oil painting; woodworking; fishing. Office: Meml Hosp PO Box 587 Gonzales TX 78629

STEVENS, MARK LESLIE, beverage company executive; b. N.Y.C., Apr. 30, 1941; s. Hy and Edna S.; B.A., U. Pa., 1962, M.B.A., 1964; m. Jacqueline Lee McLaughlin, May 24, 1964; children—Victoria Joyce, Scott Paul. Mem. brand mgmt. staff Gen. Mills Co., Mpls., 1965-69, R.J. Reynolds Co., Winston-Salem, N.C., 1969-72; asst. to pres. Internat. Playtex Co., N.Y.C., 1972-73; v.p. mktg. Gen. Cinema Corp., Miami, Fla., 1973-77, group v.p., 1977, pres. Sunkist Soft Drinks Inc. subs., Atlanta, 1977—. Bd. visitors Oglethorpe U.; bd. dirs. Atlanta Univ. Ctr., Better Bus. Bur.; mem. mgmt. adv. bd. Emory U. Sch. Bus. Mem. Am. Mgmt. Assn., DeKalb C. of C. (dir.). Office: Sunkist Bldg 2600 Century Pkwy Atlanta GA 30345

STEVENS, RICHARD YATES, county official, lawyer; b. Raleigh, N.C., Dec. 12, 1948; s. Floyd L. and Luna (Yates) S.; B.A. in Polit. Sci., U. N.C., 1970, J.D., 1974, M.Pub. Adminstrn., 1978; m. Jere Ann Gilmore, Sept. 13, 1980; children—Charles Andrew, Katherine Elizabeth. Bar: N.C. 1974. Asst. dean men U. N.C.-Chapel Hill, 1970-71, asst. residence dir., 1971-75, asst. Office Student Affairs, 1973-75; sole practice, Chapel Hill, 1974-76; adminstrv. asst. City of Durham (N.C.), 1975-76, budget officer, 1976-78, dir. adminstrn., 1978-79, dir. fin. and program devel., 1979-80; asst. county mgr. Wake County (N.C.), 1980-84, county mgr., 1984—; adj. prof. polit. sci. N.C. State U., 1979-80; coordinator N.C. State Govt. intern program Inst. Govt., summer

1971. Mem. Internat. City Mgmt. Assn., Am. Soc. Pub. Adminstrn., N.C. Bar, N.C. City-County Mgmt. Assn., U. N.C. Pub. Adminstrn. Alumni Assn. (pres. 1977-79, dir. 1982-84), U. N.C. Gen. Alumni Assn. (dir. 1978-80, 83-84, 85—). Democrat. Home: 900 Vickie Dr Cary NC 27511 Office: Wake County Courthouse PO Box 550 Raleigh NC 27602

STEVENSON, BEN, choreographer; b. Portsmouth, Eng., Apr. 4, 1936; came to U.S., 1968; s. Benjamin John and Florence May (Gundry) S.; m. Joan Toastivine, Jan. 6, 1968. Grad., Arts Ednl. Sch., London, 1955. Mem. dance panel Tex. Commn. Arts, 1977. Dancer, Theatre Arts Ballet, London, 1952-54, Sadlers Wells Theatre Ballet, 1955-56, Royal Ballet, 1956-60, London Festival Ballet, 1960-62; appearances in: Wedding in Paris, 1954-55, Music Man, London, 1962-63, Half a Sixpence, also, Boys in Syracuse, London, 1964; prin. dancer, ballet master, London Festival Ballet, 1964-68; artistic dir., Harkness Ballet Youth Dancers, 1968-71; co-dir., Nat. Ballet, Washington, 1971-74; artistic dir., Chgo. Ballet, 1974-75, Houston Ballet, 1976—; prin. ballets choreographed include Three Faces of Eve, 1965, Cast Out, 1966, Sleeping Beauty (full length), 1967, 71, 76, 78, Fervor, 1968, Three Preludes, 1968, Forbidden, 1969, Cinderella (full length), 1969, 71, 73, 74, 76, Bartok Concerto, 1970, Nutcracker (full length), 1972, 76, Symphonetta, 1972, Courant, 1973, Swan Lake (full length), 1977, L, 1978, Britten Pas de Deux, 1979, Four Last Songs, 1979, Space City, 1980, Peer Gynt (full length), 1981. Recipient 1st prize London Choreographic competitions, 1965, 66, 67, 1st prize modern ballet choreography Internat. Ballet Competition, Varna, Bulgaria, 1972, Gold medal for choreography, 1982. Assoc. mem. Royal Acad. Dancing (Adeline Genee Gold medal 1955). Office: Houston Ballet 2615 Colquitt St Houston TX 77098*

STEVENSON, RAY, health care management company executive; b. Marion, Ohio, July 25, 1937; s. Ray and Hazel (Emmelhainz) S.; m. Patricia Parker, June 17, 1960 (div. 1979); children—Jeffrey Parker, Kirk Andrew; m. Alma Burton, July 27, 1980. B.S., Ohio State U., 1959, M.B.A., 1967. Asst. adminstr. Children's Hosp., Columbus, Ohio, 1963-67; adminstr. Martin Meml. Hosp., Mt. Vernon, Ohio, 1967-71; sr. v.p. Hosp. Affiliates, Nashville, 1971-77; exec. v.p. Charles Med. Corp., Macon, Ga., 1977-79, pres., 1979—, dir.; mem. adj. faculty Ohio State U., 1979—; dir. Daniel's Tenn. Smoke, Atlanta, 1981—; chmn. R.S. Investors Inc., Atlanta. Mem. Am. Coll. Hosps., Fedn. Am. Hosps. (dir. 1979-81), Nat. Assn. Psychiat. Hosps. Republican. Episcopalian. Clubs: Idle Hour Country (Macon); Carlton (Chgo.). Office: Charter Medical Corp 577 Mulberry St Macon GA 31298*

STEVENSON, ROBERT JAMES, educational association administrator; b. Oneonta, N.Y., Feb. 2, 1925; s. Charles Robert and Iva (Prindle) S.; children from previous marriage—Kathleen E. Soloway, David B.; m. Florence Glenn Foute, June 9, 1979; 1 stepchild, Donna J. Pugh. B.S., SUNY-Oneonta, 1950; M.A., Columbia U., 1951, Ed.D., 1957. Prof. edn. SUNY-Oneonta, 1963-65; assoc. dir. Nat. Council for Accreditation Tchr. Edn., Washington, 1965-67; dep. chief Tchr. Edn. East Africa, Kampala, Uganda, 1967-68; projects dir. Am. Assn. Coll. Tchr. Edn., Washington, 1968-72; spl. projects coordinator Council for Exceptional Children, Reston, Va., 1972-75; exec. dir. Assn. Tchr. Educators, Reston, 1976—. Served with USCG, 1943-46. Fellow Nat. Acad. Tchr. Edn.; mem. Assn. Supervision and Curriculum Devel., Assn. Tchr. Educators (life). Avocations: reading; gardening; landscaping. Home: PO Box 555 Manassas VA 22110 Office: Assn Tchr Educators 1900 Association Dr Reston VA 22091

STEVENSON, ROBERT LLOYD, construction company executive; b. Lubbock, Tex., Nov. 15, 1951; s. Lloyd Henry and Jamie Louise (Hinson) S.; m. Natalie Rocca, Aug. 2, 1975; children—Lori Christine, Traci Renee. A.A., San Jacinto Coll., 1982; student U. Houston, 1982—. Cert. broker, Tex. Supt. Village Builders subs. Exxon U.S.A., Houston, 1980, purchasing coordinator, 1982—, residential coordinator Friendswood Devel. subs., 1980-82. Democrat. Methodist. Lodge: Masons. Home: 15423 Tadworth Houston TX 77062 Office: Village Builders-Friendswood Devel Co PO Box 2567 Houston TX 77001

STEVENSON, WAYNE L., economist; b. Chgo., May 30, 1945; s. Wendel Adam and Eleanor (Kohler) Allen S.; m. Mary Edna Patterson, Mar. 21, 1970; 1 child: Sarah Marie. B.S., Ripon Coll., Wis., 1967; Ph.D., U. Minn., 1972. Research assoc. Marshall Kaplan, Gans and Kahn Inc., San Francisco, 1966; teaching assoc. U. Minn., Mpls., 1967-71; vis. lectr. Lawrence U., Appleton, Wis., 1971-72; vis. asst. prof. Middlebury Coll., Vt., 1972-73; asst. prof. dept. econs. U. Utah, Salt Lake City, 1973-78; assoc. prof. dept. econs. SUNY-Potsdam, 1978-79; sr. economist Labor and Policy Studies Program, Oak Ridge Associated Universities, 1979-84, program dir. univ. programs div., 1984—; cons. and lectr. in field. Author: Quantitative Analysis in Human Resources Research, 1976; Empirical Aspects of Macroeconomic Theory: Data Set and Problems, 1977; The Lingering Crisis of Youth Unemployment, 1978. Contbr. chpts. to books, articles to profl. jours. Expert witness U.S. House of Reps. Hearings on Energy and Employment, Washington, 1983. NSF fellow, 1968-71; NSF grantee, 1971-72. Mem. Am. Econs. Assn., Nat. Sci. Tchrs. Assn., Midwest Econs. Assn. Home: 1129 W Outer Dr Oak Ridge TN 37830 Office: Oak Ridge Assoc Univs 200 Badger Ave Oak Ridge TN 37831

STEWARD, CHARLES ROBERT, water pollution control co. exec.; b. Bedford, Iowa, Nov. 11, 1935; s. Charles William and Charlotte Winifred (Garwood) S.; B.S.M.E., State U. Iowa, 1959; M.S.B.A., No. Ill. U., 1970; m. Vada Ruth Clymens, Nov. 27, 1953; children—C. Robert II, C. Summer, Clark, Lori, David, Bruce. Design engr. Stanley Cons., Muscatine, Iowa, 1959-63; staff engr. Beloit Corp. (Wis.), 1963-66; project engr., mktg. mgr. Passavant Corp., Birmingham, Ala., 1966-75; founder, pres. Performance Systems, Inc., Birmingham, 1975-81, v.p., dir. mktg., 1981-82; pres. Ridge Group, Inc., Birmingham, 1982—; dir. Beloit Indsl. Service Co., Tech. Trade Corp. Counselor to bishop Ch. of Jesus Christ of Latter-day Saints, 1964-71, stake high counselor, 1973-81. Registered profl. engr., Iowa, Wis. Mem. ASME, Nat. Soc. Profl. Engrs., Ala. Soc. Profl. Engrs., Water Pollution Control Fedn., Nat. Rifle Assn., Theta Tau, Pi Tau Sigma. Contbr. to Industrial Sludge Handling. Office: 4265 1st Ave N Birmingham AL 35206

STEWARD, LARRY GLENN, horticulturist; b. Columbus, Ohio, July 12, 1943; s. Harold E. and Ruth (Campbell) S.; m. Sheryle Ann Adkins, Sept. 11, 1965 (div. Apr. 1971); m. Deanna Eloise Mason, July 10, 1971; 1 child, Michael Glenn; adopted children—Lin Allen, Dennis Edward; child from previous Marriage, Kristina Noelle. B.S.A., Ohio State U., 1966, postgrad., 1967. County 4-H extension agt. Ohio State U., Union County, 1967-68; head landscape div. J.L. Kidwell Landscaping, Inc., Culpeper, Va., 1968-70; asst. dir. landscape U. Va., Charlottesville, 1970—, also exec. sec. com. on Arboretum; cons. landscape maintenance, Charlottesville, 1972—; adj. instr. Piedmont, Va. Community Coll., Charlottesville, 1981—; Scoutmaster, committeeman Boy Scouts Am., 1972—; deacon, 1st Presbyn. Ch., 1979—. Recipient Scouter's Tng. award Boy Scouts Am., 1977. Mem. Piedmont Profl. Grounds Mgrs. (charter), Am. Boxwood Soc. (life), Am. Hort. Soc., Internat. Soc. Arboriculture, Ohio State U. Floriculture/Landscape Horticulture Alumni Assn., Nat. Inst. Parks and Grounds Mgmt., Profl. Grounds Mgmt. Soc., Mcpl. Arborists and Urban Foresters Soc., Pi Alpha Xi, Gamma Sigma Delta. Home: Route 8 Box 314 Riverview Charlottesville VA 22901 Office: Dept Phys Plant Univ Va 575 Alderman Rd Charlottesville VA 22903

STEWARD, SCOTT CHRISTOFFER, consumer products executive, marketing and research executive; b. Eureka, Calif., Mar. 9, 1950; s. Newton Laverne and Elisabeth (Storen) S.; m. Katherine Nancy Boyles, Sept. 23, 1978. B.S. in Systems Engrng., U.S. Naval Acad., 1971; postgrad. Calif. State U., 1974-75. Marketing brand mgr. Procter & Gamble Co., Cin., 1976-81; mktg. dir. Pepsico Inc. (Frito-Lay), Dallas, 1981-83; dir. mktg., dir. research and devel. Internat. Spike, Inc., Lexington, Ky., 1983—. Assoc., Smithsonian Instn., Washington, 1976—; mem. Rep. Nat. Com., Washington, 1984—. Served to lt. USN, 1971-76. Mem. Am. Mgmt. Assn., Am. Horse Show Assn., U.S. Dressage Assn., AAAS. Club: Greenbriar Country (Lexington). Avocations: sailing; equestrian sports; golf. Home: 6050 Richmond Rd Lexington KY 40515 Office: Internat Spike Inc 817 E Third St Lexington KY 40593

STEWART, BURTON GLOYDEN, JR., banker; b. Clayton, N.C., Mar. 14, 1933; s. Burton Gloyden and Evelyn I. (Stallings) S.; A.B., Duke U., 1955; grad. Sch. Banking of South, 1970; exec. program U. N.C., 1975; m. Patricia Taylor, June 16, 1956; children—Burton Gloyden III, H. Taylor. With Allstate Ins. Co., 1957-66, regional sales mgr., Charlotte, N.C., 1964-66; with Branch Banking and Trust Co., Wilson, N.C., 1966—, sr. v.p., mgr. corp. planning and mktg. div., 1972-81, mgr. corp. planning and investor relations, 1981—; dir. Branch Corp., 1974-82; dir. N.C. Payments System, 1980—, v.p., 1983—. Bd. dirs. Wilson Heart Assn., 1968; bd. dirs., treas. Wilson Arts Council, 1969-71; bd. dirs. Wilson United Way, 1974-80, campaign chmn., 1977, pres., 1979; mem. N.C. Gov.'s Efficiency Study Commn., 1985, N.C. Goals and Policy Bd., 1985—. Served as lt. USNR, 1955-57. Mem. Bank Mktg. Assn., Bank Investor Relations Assn. (dir., v.p. 1984-85), Am. Mgmt. Assn., N.C. Bankers Assn. (chmn. mktg. com. 1976). Methodist. Club: Wilson Country. Office: 223 W Nash St Wilson NC 27893

STEWART, CHARLES DONOVAN, designer; b. Texarkana, Ark., July 28, 1945; s. Charles Curtright and Charlene Elizabeth (Griffin) S.; B.B.A., N. Tex. State U., 1968; m. Linda Louise Ingle, Jan. 1, 1966; children—Staci Leigh, James Donovan. Chmn. bd., dir., owner Stewarts' Designers, Inc., Dallas, 1977—. Served to 1st lt. U.S. Army, 1969-72. Decorated Army Commendation medal; recipient Home and Apt. Builders McSam award, 1981. Mem. Home and Apt. Builders Assn., Soc. Grads., Ft. Sill OCS Brigade, Hood's Tex. Brigade Assn. Home: 1847 Hatherly Dr Plano TX 75023 Office: 1200 Commerce Suite 116 Plano TX 75075

STEWART, CHARLES E., energy company executive; b. Kewanee, Ill., 1935; married. B.S., Marquette U., 1957. In indsl. chem. sales Diamond Shamrock Corp., Dallas, 1958-63, asst. product mgr.-electro chem. div., 1963-65, new products mgr., 1965-66, product and mktg. mgr.-electro chem. div., 1967-73, v.p., gen. mgr.-soda products div., 1973-75, v.p., gen. mgr.-process chem. div., 1975-78, corp. v.p.-planning and devel., 1978-80, exec. v.p., unit pres., 1980—. Office: Diamond Shamrock Corp 717 N Harwood St Dallas TX 75201*

STEWART, CLARA WOODARD, advertising executive; b. Mineola, N.Y., May 1, 1952; d. Samuel Woodard and Irene (Colm) S.; B.A. in Broadcasting and Psychology, Mich. State U., 1974; M.A. in Journalism and Communications, U. Fla., 1975. Sales rep. Sta. WSBR, Boca Raton, 1976-77; media dir. Fred Wagenvoord Assoc., Inc., Boca Raton, Fla., 1977-81; v.p., account exec., media dir. Birkenes & Foreman Advt., Boca Raton, 1981—. Bd. dirs. Boca Raton Community Theater, 1977-78, publicity chmn., 1977-78; bd. dirs. United Way Greater Boca Raton, 1979—; pres. Friends of Boca Raton Public Library, 1981—; mem. adv. bd. Boca Raton Symphony Orch., 1983—; mem. Young Pres.'s Council Norton Gallery; treas. Friends of Caldwell Playhouse, 1984—. Mem. B/PAA (treas. Southeast Fla. chpt. 1984—), Women in Communications, Advt. Fedn. Greater Ft. Lauderdale, Mensa (SE regional public relations asst. 1978-80, treas. Palm Beach County 1981-83), Palm Beach County Hist. Soc. (newsletter editor 1980-82), Palm Beach County Geneal. Soc., Am. Film Inst., Nat. Trust Historic Preservation, Phi Kappa Phi. Home: 1755 Forest Hill Blvd Apt 4 West Palm Beach FL 33406 Office: 1388 NW 2d Ave Suite 1 Boca Raton FL 33432

STEWART, D. NEAL, design company executive; b. Bastrop, La., Dec. 6, 1950; s. John William and Annie Mae (Wells) S. B.F.A., La. Tech. U., 1973. Pres., Neal Stewart/Design Assocs., Inc., Dallas, 1984—. Office: Neal Stewart/Design Assocs Inc 1330 HiLine Dr Dallas TX 75207

STEWART, DAVID HUGH, English, speech and theatre arts educator; b. Fort Wayne, Ind., Aug. 12, 1926; s. Carey Hugh and Priscilla (Stauffer) S.; m. Diane Silva, July 25, 1949; children—Marc Silva, Christopher David. B.A., U. Mich., 1947, M.A., 1949, Ph.D., 1959; M.A., cert. Russian Inst., Columbia U., 1954. From instr. to asst. prof. English, Eastern Mich. U., Ypsilanti, 1957-59; asst. prof. U. Alta., Edmonton, Can., 1959-60; from asst. to assoc. prof. U. Mich., Ann Arbor, 1960-67; prof. English, chmn. dept. Idaho State U., Pocatello, 1968-71; prof., chmn. dept. English, Pa. State U., University Park, 1972-74; prof. English, speech and theatre arts head dept. English, speech and theatre arts Tex. A&M U., College Station, Tex., 1975—; cons. to study group Nat. Endowment Humanities, Washington, 1984. Author: M. A. Sholokhov-A Critical Introduction, 1967; co-author: The Wiley Reader, 1976. Pres. Opera and Performing Arts Soc., College Station, 1979, Arts Council of Brazos Valley, Bryan, Tex., 1981; bd. dirs. Allen Acad. Bryan, 1980—. Served with USN, 1944-46. Mem. MLA (del. assembly 1971-74), Nat. Council Tchrs. English (coll. com. 1980-84), Phi Kappa Phi (pres. local chpts. 1967, 72). Presbyterian. Lodge: Elks. Home: 2304 Bristol Bryan TX 77802 Office: Tex A&M U Dept English College Station TX 77843

STEWART, DONALD ANTHONY, clinical psychologist, psychology educator; b. Bronx, N.Y., Mar. 7, 1952; s. Donald Anthony and Margaret Frances (Burke) S.; m. Catherine Louise Pronti, Oct. 22, 1977; children—Meaghan Elizabeth, Timothy Michael. B.S., Fla. Inst. Tech., 1974; M.A., Columbia U., 1975; Psy.D., Fla. Inst. Tech., 1983. Lic. clin. psychologist, Fla. Dir. phys. disability Diagnostic Ctr., Okeechobee, Fla., 1975-76; diagnostician Troywood Sch., Palm Beach, Fla., 1976-78; pres., founder Learning Bound Sch., North Palm Beach, Fla., 1977-78; clin. intern Brevard Mental Health Ctr. and Hosp., Melbourne, Fla., 1982-83; clin. psychologist, Merritt Island, Fla., 1983—; mem. staff Cape Canaveral Hosp.; cons. Child Abuse Team, Brevard County, Fla., 1983—, Diagnostic Reading, Merritt Island, 1983—. Contbr. articles to profl. jours. Cons. Brevard Jr. League, Merritt Island, 1984—; panel mem. WMOD TV program on eating disorders, Melbourne, 1984; guest speaker The Woman's Ctr. Workshops, Melbourne, 1984. Columbia U. fellow, 1974. Mem. Am. Psychol. Assn., Am. Soc. Clin. Hypnosis, Fla. Psychol. Assn., Fla. Soc. Clin. Hypnosis, Southeastern Psychol. Assn., Nat. Register Health Service Providers in Psychology. Republican. Roman Catholic. Avocations: golf, tennis, swimming, writing, art. Home: 2220 Queen Ann St Merritt Island FL 32952 Office: Bernstein O'Halloran & Stewart 2245 N Courtenay St E Merritt Island FL 32953

STEWART, DOROTHY ANNE, research physicist; b. Beach Grove, Ind., June 2, 1937; d. Thomas Edward and Dorothy Anne (Browne) S.; B.S., U. Tampa, 1958; M.S., Fla. State U., 1961, Ph.D., 1966. Tchr. math, sci., high sch., Live Oak, Fla., 1958-59; research physicist U.S. Army Missile Command, Redstone Arsenal, Ala., 1966—. Mem. Am. Meteorol. Soc., Am. Geophys. Union, AAAS, Ala. Acad. Scis., Sigma Xi. Contbr. articles to profl. jours. Home: 5204 Whitesburg Dr Huntsville AL 35802 Office: US Army Missile Command Attn AMSMI-RRA Redstone Arsenal AL 35898

STEWART, DUNCAN EDWIN, artist, educator; b. St. Paul, Sept. 30, 1940; s. John McLeod and Mary (Simonds) Stewart; m. Sue Danley, July 5, 1962; children—Christopher, Duncan, Ian. B.A., San Diego State U., 1967, M.A., 1969; postgrad. Fla. State U., 1974-75. Instr. World Campus Afloat, winter 1969, coordinator art dept., 1973, asst. prof., 1975; asst. prof. U. West Fla., Pensacola, 1975-81, asst. prof. art, dir. art gallery 1977-79; assoc. prof., 1982—; prof. Florence program Fla. State U., fall 1982; one-man shows Ward-Nasse Gallery, N.Y.C., 1976, North Fla. Jr. Coll., 1977, Jefferson Davis Jr. Coll., Brewton, Ala., 1978, VZTOP Gallery, Pensacola, 1981, Jefferson Davis Community Coll., 1982, Fla. State U. Florence Study Ctr., 1982, Mario Villa Gallery, 1985, U. New Orleans, 1986; exhibited in group shows Avery Fisher Hall, Lincoln Ctr., N.Y.C., 1974, Coll. of Mainland, Texas City, Tex., 1974, Lever House, N.Y.C., 1976, Pensacola Jr. Coll., 1977, East Tenn. State U., 1977, El Paso Mus. Art, 1978, Ringling Mus. Art, 1978, Pensacola Jr. Coll., 1979, Arrowmont Sch., 1980, Second Street Gallery, Charleston, Va., 1980, LeMoyne Art Ctr., 1980, Quinlan Art Ctr., Gainesville, Ga., 1980, Valencia Jr. Coll., 1981, Pensacola Mus. Art, 1981, Gulf Coast Community Coll., 1981, Valencia Jr. Coll., 1983. Trustee Pensacola Mus. Art. Ford Venture Fund grantee, 1975; NEH summer seminar, 1975; U. West Fla. summer research grantee, 1978. Mem. Southeast Coll. Arts Assn., Coll. Art Assn. Office: Bldg 50 Room 237 Univ West Fla Pensacola FL 32514

STEWART, DWIGHT CALVERT, philosophy educator; b. Ionia, Mich., Oct. 10, 1930; s. Paul Lemuel and Brite Frances (Beal) S.; m. Jane Hale Howerton, Dec. 28, 1951; children—Carol Jane, Joseph Dwight, Paul Robert. B.A., Culver-Stockton Coll., 1952; M.Div., Drake U., 1955; A.M., Harvard U., 1960; Ph.D., Northwestern U., 1973. Asst. prof., then assoc. prof. religion and philosophy Culver-Stockton Coll., Canton, Mo., 1959-65; asst. prof. religion Boston U., 1968-73; assoc. prof. philosophy Union Coll., Barbourville, Ky., 1974-77, prof., 1977-84, dean undergrad. acad. affairs, 1978-79, dean of faculty, 1979-83, v.p. acad. affairs, 1983-84; dean acad. affairs Midway Coll., Ky., 1984—. Danforth Found. grantee, 1966. Mem. AAUP, Am. Acad. Religion. Contbg. editor publs. in field. Home: 807 Pheasant Lane Versailles KY 40383 Office: Midway Coll Midway KY 40347

STEWART, GEORGE RAY, librarian; b. Birmingham, Ala., Aug. 19, 1944; s. DeWitt and Ann (McCain) S.; m. Nancy Ann Norton, June 5, 1964; children—Steven Ray, Jeffery Alan. B.A., Samford U., Birmingham, 1966, M.A., 1967; M.A., Emory U., 1971. Mem. staff Birmingham Public Library, 1960—, assoc. dir., 1970-76, dir., 1976—. Bd. dirs. Red Mountain Museum, 1972-79; bd. dirs. Indsl. Health Council Birmingham, 1972—, sec., 1979—, pres. bd. dirs., 1982, 83. Mem. ALA, Southeastern Library Assn. (treas. 1985-86), Ala. Library Assn. (scholarship 1968, pres. 1976), Ala. Hist. Assn., Birmingham Hist. Assn., Am. Soc. Pub. Adminstrn. Baptist. Home: 2100 Polk Pl Birmingham AL 35203 Office: 2020 Park Pl Birmingham AL 35203

STEWART, JAMES GARDINER, petroleum geologist and oil operator, consultant; b. Fort Worth, May 18, 1925; s. Thomas C. and Mary (Kendall) S.; children—Linda Kathleen, James Randall, Sterling Scott. B.S. in Petroleum Geology, Tex. Tech. U., 1950. Certified geologist. Roughneck, Rowan Drilling Co., Fort Worth, 1950-51; prodn. geologist G. W. Strake, Houston, 1951-57; mgr. New Idria Mineral & Chem. Co., Calif., Graham, Tex., 1957-60; pvt. practice cons. and ind. geology, Graham, 1960—. Scoutmaster Explorer Post, Boy Scouts Am., Ballinger, Tex., 1952—; leader Royal Ambassadors, 1st Bapt. Ch., Ballinger, 1952. Served with U.S. Army, 1943-46, ETO. Mem. Am. Assn. Petroleum Geologists, Am. Inst. Profl. Geologists, Graham Geol. Soc. Republican. Baptist. Avocations; fishing; outdoor activities. Home: 1410 Brazos St Graham TX 76046 Office: 201 Petroleum Bldg Box 877 601 Elm St Graham TX 76096

STEWART, JAMES RAY, biology and chemistry educator; b. Beeville, Tex., Aug. 5, 1937; s. Preston and Hattie (Ray) S.; married; children—Kelly Diane, Gregory Allen. B.S., North Tex. State U., 1959; M.S. in Biology, U. Ala., 1965; Ph.D. in Biol. Sci., U. Tex., 1969. Postdoctoral fellow U. Tex. Med. Sch., San Antonio, 1970-74; asst. prof. U. Tex.-Tyler, 1974-77, assoc. prof. biology and chemistry, 1977—, chmn. dept. biology, 1980—. Mem. Am. Soc. Microbiology, Phycol. Soc. Am., Tex. Soc. Electron Microscopy, Sigma Xi. Home: Route 1 Box 414 Whitehouse TX 75791 Office: U Tex 3900 University Blvd Tyler TX 75701

STEWART, JAMES RUSH, JR., research oil company executive; b. Orange, Tex., Dec. 28, 1926; s. James Rush and Laura Mae (Harris) S.; m. Elaine Marian Johnson, Dec. 1951; children—Carol Joan, Linda Kay, James R. III, Patricia Ann. B.S. in Chem. Engrng., La. Tech. U., 1950; M. Gas. Tech., M.S., in Chem. Engrng., Ill. Inst. Tech., 1952. Research engr. United Gas Corp., Shreveport, La., 1952-59, sr. research assoc., 1959-68; sr. research assoc. Pennzoil Products Co., Shreveport, 1968-84, mgr. process research, The Woodlands, Tex., 1984—. Patentee in field. Bd. dirs. Shreveport Soc. for Nature Study, 1957-83. Mem. Inst. Chem. Engrs., Am. Chem. Soc., Am. Ornithologists' Union, Cooper Ornithol. Soc., La. Ornithol. Soc. (pres. 1958-59). Republican. Lutheran. Club: Shreveport Petroleum. Avocations: Ornithology, birding, genealogy. Home: 3613 Mosswood Dr Conroe TX 77302 Office: Pennzoil Products Co Box 7569 The Woodlands TX 77387

STEWART, JAMES THOMAS, medicinal chemist, consultant; b. Birmingham, Ala., Dec. 1, 1938; s. William Edmund and Mary (Park) S.; m. Ella Vale Johnson, Aug. 10, 1963; children—Elisa, Cathryn, Sharyn. B.S., Auburn U., 1960, M.S., 1963; Ph.D., U. Mich., 1967. Lic. pharmacist, Ala. Asst. prof. Coll. Pharmacy, U. Ga., Athens, 1963-67, assoc. prof. Coll. Pharmacy, 1968-75, prof. Coll. Pharmacy, 1975—; cons. FDA. Mem. Athens Choral Soc., 1970—; pres. Forest Heights Pool Assn., 1982-84. Recipient Lehn and Fink award, 1960; Am. Found. Pharm. Edn. fellow, 1961-67; Mead-Johnson Research award, 1968; Tchr. of Yr. award, 1978; Chemist of Yr. award, 1978. Mem. Am. Pharm. Assn., Am. Chem. Soc., Ala. Pharm. Assn. (scholarship award 1960). Presbyterian. Author: (with R. Smith) Textbook of Biopharmaceutic Analysis, 1980; contbr. articles to profl. jours.

STEWART, JAMES WILLIAM, electrical engineer; b. Clarksville, Tex., July 23, 1926; s. Virgil Alfred and Effie Marie (Green) S.; m. Betty Gean Sutton, Apr. 24, 1945; children—James E., William W., Charles S. B.S. in E.E., Tex. Tech. U., 1950; M.B.A., Harvard U., 1956; cert. U.S. Army Command & Gen. Staff Coll., 1967. Mgr. bus. planning Ryan Aero. Co., San Diego, 1960-63; mgr. ops., spl. projects E-Systems, Inc., Dallas, 1963—. Sustaining mem. Republican Nat. Com. Served with USN, 1944-46, to maj. U.S. Army, 1950-60. Decorated Bronze Star. Mem. Res. Officers Assn., Second Inf. Div. Assn. (v.p.), Tex. Tech. Elec. Engrng. Assn., Nat. Property Mgmt. Assn., Assn. Old Crows, French Regiment de Corée (hon.), Tau Beta Pi, Phi Eta Sigma, Eta Kappa Nu, Alpha Chi. Republican. Presbyterian. Clubs: Forest Hollow (past pres.), Engrs., Harvard, Harvard Bus. (all Dallas). Address: 9040 Westbriar Dr Dallas TX 75228

STEWART, JEFFREY BAYRD, lawyer, investment banker; b. Chgo., Feb. 6, 1952; s. Bruce A. and Harriet B. Stewart. A.B. magna cum laude (Rufus Choate scholar), Dartmouth Coll., 1974; J.D., Emory U., 1978. Bar: Ga. 1978. Ptnr., Arnall Golden & Gregory, Atlanta, 1978—; co-founder HyTech Med. Investments, Inc., Austin, Tex., 1982. Mem. editorial bd. Emory Law Jour., 1977-78. Mem. ABA, State Bar Ga. Home: 724 Summit N Dr Atlanta GA 30324 Office: Arnall Golden & Gregory 55 Park Pl Atlanta GA 30335

STEWART, JOHN GILMAN, government official; b. Bklyn., Feb. 15, 1935; s. F. Gilman and Winifred Ann (Link) S.; m. Nancy Potter, June 23, 1957; children—Michael Gilman, Cara Jane. B.A., Colgate U., 1957; M.A., U. Chgo., 1959, Ph.D., 1968. Asst. dir. Am. Polit. Sci. Assn., Washington, 1961-62; legis. asst. to Senator Hubert Humphrey, Washington, 1962-65; exec. asst. to v.p. Hubert Humphrey, Washington, 1965-69; dir. communications Democratic Nat. Com., Washington, 1970-73; staff dir. energy subcom. Joint Econ. Com., U.S. Congress, 1974-77; staff dir. Sci. Tech. and Space Subcom., U.S. Senate, Washington, 1977-79; mgr. Office of Planning and Budget, TVA, Knoxville, 1979-82, Office Corp. Adminstrn. and Planning, 1982—; cons. Joint Com. on Congl. Ops., U.S. Congress, Washington, 1973-75; mem. aerospace safety adv. panel NASA, Washington, 1980—. Author: One Last Chance, The Democratic Party, 1974-76, 1974. Contbr. articles on congl. leadership and polit. parties and civil rights to profl. jours. Bd. dirs. Knoxville Opera Co., 1982—. Fellow Inst. Politics, Harvard U., Cambridge, Mass., 1966-67; recipient Disting. Alumnus award U. Chgo., 1973. Mem. Am. Polit. Sci. Assn., Am. Soc. Pub. Adminstrn., Nat. Mgmt. Assn. Democrat. Avocations: gardening, running. Home: 6611 Ridge Rock Ln Knoxville TN 37919 Office: TVA 400 Summit Hill Dr Knoxville TN 37902

STEWART, JON STERLING, architect; b. Abilene, Tex., July 5, 1948; s. Orel Holmes and Martha Evelyn (Akins) S.; m. Teresa Rae Crabtree, Oct. 30, 1970 (div. Aug. 1974); m. Deborah Mathewson, July 7, 1979; children—James Sterling, Kimberly Michelle. B.Arch., U. Tex., 1976. Ptnr., Rayburn-Stewart & Assocs., Architects, Austin, Tex., 1975-77; architect, mgr. John Fitzpatrick, Architect, Austin, 1977-79; project architect Garland & Hilles Architects, El Paso, Tex., 1979-82; prin. architect Condel Architects and Engrs., Inc., El Paso, 1982—. Mem. AIA (sec. El Paso chpt. 1985—), Tex. Soc. Architects. Avocation: camping. Home: 216 Flynn Dr El Paso TX 79932 Office: Condel Architects and Engrs Inc 6080 Surety Dr El Paso TX 79905

STEWART, MARCUS J(EFFERSON), orthopedic surgeon, consultant, educator; b. Whiteville, Tenn., July 13, 1911; s. Marcus Jefferson and Mattie Sue (Crowder) S.; m. Mariette Solvay McDonald, Nov. 3, 1944; children—Mariette E. Stewart Rhodes, Jeanne M. Stewart Jemison, Lee Jurion Stewart Bowen. B.S. cum laude, Milligan Coll., 1933; M.D., U. Tenn., 1938, M.S. in Orthopedic Surgery, 1945. Diplomate Am. Bd. Orthopedic Surgery. (examiner 1952-70). Intern, City of Memphis Hosp., 1938-39; resident in orthopedic surgery Campbell Clinic, Memphis, 1939-41; postgrad. course in fractures U. London, 1942, course in prosthetics UCLA, 1954; clin. asst. dept. orthopedics, U. Tenn. Ctr. Health Scis., Memphis, 1947-49, clin. instr., 1949-51, clin. asst. prof., 1951-58, clin. assoc. prof., 1958-71, prof., 1971—, chmn. med. affairs com., trustee, 1975-81; chief orthopedic sect. VA Med. Ctr., Memphis, 1981—; mem. Council on Sports Medicine U.S. Olympic Com., 1978-84; mem. staff Campbell Clinic, Crippled Children's Hosp. Memphis, 1947-81; mem. staff Bapt. Meml. Hosp., 1947—, chief staff, 1963; mem. staff City of Memphis Hosp., 1947—, bd. dirs., 1971-78; mem. staff Meth. Hosp.; cons. to surgeon gen. U.S. Army, 1947—; active staff cons. LeBonheur Children's Hosp., Memphis, Crittenden Meml. Hosp., West Memphis, Ark.; chmn. Com. of Sports Medicine for Disabled Athletes, 1981—; mem. Pres.'s Com. for Employment of Physically Handicapped, 1959-72; chmn. Gov.'s Com. for Employment of Physically Handicapped, 1959, 1960. Vestryman, St. John's Episcopal Ch., 1966-68, 81-83, sr. warden, 1968; bd. dirs. Les Passees Rehab. Ctr., chmn., 1964-65; trustee U. Tenn., 1970-81, Memphis and Shelby County hosps., 1970-78, Hutchison Sch. for Girls, 1967-70; adv. bd. Am. Phys. Therapy Assn.; chmn. med. com. Memphis Sesquicentennial, 1969; dir. First

Fed. Savs. and Loan Assn., 1965—. Served with M.C. U.S. Army, 1941-46; served to col. USAR, 1947-71. Decorated Legion of Merit. Recipient Disting. Alumnus award Milligan Coll., 1973, U. Tenn. Coll. Medicine, 1976; mem. U. Tenn. Pres.'s Club, 1970—, Milligan Coll. Pres.'s Club, 1972—. Fellow ACS (gov. 1962-64); mem. Am. Orthopedic Assn., Am. Assn. for Surgery of Trauma, Am. Acad. Orthopedic Surgeons (joint com. mil. affairs 1948-70, mem., chmn. coms.), AMA, Am. Orthopedic Foot Soc. (founding), Am. Orthopedic Soc. for Sports Medicine (founding pres. 1977-78), Contemporary Orthopedic Soc. (pres. 1959), Internat. Soc. Orthopedics and Traumatology, Am. Trauma Soc. (founding), Mid-Am. Orthopedic Assn. (founding), So. Med. Soc., Robert Jones Orthopedic Soc. (pres. 1960), Tenn. State Med. Soc., Tenn. State Orthopedic Soc. (pres. 1955), Clin. Orthopedic Soc. (pres. 1958), Memphis Orthopedic Soc. (founding pres. 1976), Brit. Orthopedic Assn. (guest), La. Orthopedic Assn. (hon.), S.C. Orthopedic Assn. (hon.), Memphis and Shelby County Med. Soc., Soc. of Med. Cons. to Armed Forces, U. Tenn. Med. Alumni Assn. (founder, past pres.), Willis C. Campbell Orthopedic Club (founder, pres. 1955, bd. dirs., found. pres. 1965-80), Alpha Omega Alpha. Republican. Clubs: Memphis Country, Rotary (v.p. Memphis 1981-82, pres. 1983-84). Panel mem., speaker, lectr. in field profl. confs.; vis. prof., invited lectr. profl. orgns. and hosps.; contbr. writings to profl. publs. Home: 2909 Garden Ln Memphis TN 38111 Office: 910 Madison Ave Suite 609 Memphis TN 38104

STEWART, MILTON MONROE, JR., designer and builder, executive; b. Jackson, Miss., Nov. 22, 1950; s. Milton Monroe and Virginia (Hansell) S.; m. Carole Huddleston Crump, Dec. 16, 1978; children—Scott, Robert, John. B.A., Memphis State U., Pres., Milton M. Stewart, Inc., Jackson, 1976—. Republican. Episcopalian. Home: 4032 Pinewood Jackson MS 39211 Office: Milton M Stewart Inc 2620 Southerland Dr Jackson MS 39216

STEWART, MURRAY BAKER, lawyer; b. Muskogee, Okla., May 16, 1931; s. Francis and Fannie Penelope (Murray) S.; m. Roseanna Furgason; children—Melinda, Jeffrey, Cheryl. B.A., U. Okla., 1953, LL.B., 1955; postgrad. Georgetown U., 1958-59; C.L.U., Am. Coll., 1980, chartered fin. cons., 1984; fellow Life Mgmt. Inst., 1983. Bar: Okla. 1955, U.S. Tax Ct. 1957, U.S. Supreme Ct. 1958, U.S. Ct. Mil. Appeals 1958. Partner, Stewart & Stewart, Tulsa and Muskogee, Okla., 1955, 62-72; asst. v.p. First Nat. Bank and Trust Co. of Tulsa, 1959-62, 77-78; mem. Hutchins, Stewart, Stewart & Elmore, Tulsa, 1972-77; atty., sr. cons. advanced underwriting Met. Life and affiliated cos., N.Y.C., 1978—. Served to capt. U.S. Army, 1955-59. Mem. ABA, Okla. Bar Assn., Nat. Securities Dealers Assn. (registered gen. securities rep.), Nat. Platform Assn., Employee Benefits Group, Phi Delta Theta. Contbr. articles to legal and ins. and fin. jours. Office: PO Box 500 Tulsa OK 74102

STEWART, OPAL ALLINE, nurse, educator; consultant; b. Chouteau, Okla., June 28, 1924; d. Newton and Lille (Wyatt) Stewart. Diploma, North La. Sch. Nursing, Shreveport, 1947; A.A., Kilgore Coll. (Tex.), 1960; B.S., Stephen F. Austin U., 1966; M.S. East Tex. State U., 1968, Ed.D., 1984. Staff nurse Markham Hosp., Longview, Tex., 1947-53; supr. operating room Laird Hosp., Kilgore, 1953-56; sch. nurse Kilgore Ind. Sch. Dist., 1956-66; dir. health occupations Navarro Coll., Corsicana, Tex., 1966-68; dir. div. nursing Angelina Coll., Lufkin, Tex., 1968-73; chmn. dept. nursing Kilgore Coll., 1973—, also dir. health careers; mem. adv. bd. nursing program U. Tex.-Tyler, 1975—; adviser cardiac rehab. East Tex. Treatment Ctr., Kilgore, 1980-82; edn. com. Am. Cancer Soc., Longview, Tex., 1973-83; bd. dirs. Gregg County Heart Assn., Longview, 1984—. Mem. Am. Nurses' Assn., Dist. 25 Tex. Nurses' Assn. (pres. Tex. group 1976), Tex. State Tchr's Assn. (pres. Kilgore Coll. chpt.; life mem.), Tex. Jr. Coll. Tchrs. Assn., Kilgore Bus. and Profl. Women (past pres.), LWV, Sigma Theta Tau, Phi Delta Kappa. Clubs: Pilot Internat. (Lufkin, Tex.) (past pres.). Home: 2902 Regent Kilgore TX 75662 Office: SP Kilgore Coll Dept Nursing 1100 Broadway Kilgore TX 75662

STEWART, PATRICIA LUCILLE, nurse, army officer; b. Terre Haute, Ind., Dec. 31, 1946; d. Etzell L. and Virginia Pearl (Ripple) S.; diploma, St. Anthony Hosp. Sch. Nursing, 1967; B.S.N., Loretta Heights Coll., 1972; M.Hosp. Adminstrn., Baylor U., 1977. Commd. 2d. lt. Nurse Corps, U.S. Army, 1967, advanced through grades to lt. col., 1979; staff nurse Ft. Bragg Hosp., N.C., 1967-68, Vietnam, 1968-69, resigned, 1969, rejoined service, 1970; head nurse, supr. dept. clinics W. Ger., 1972-74, spl. projects officer dept. nursing Brooke Army Med. Center, Ft. Sam Houston, Tex., 1974-75; nursing methods analyst, computer project officer William Beaumont Army Med. Center, El Paso, Tex., 1977-81; asst. chief dept. nursing Redstone Arsenal, Ala., 1981-82; chief functional br. UCA implementation team Health Services Command, Ft. Sam Houston, Tex., 1982—; evening charge nurse Porter Meml. Hosp., Denver, 1969-70. Decorated Army Achievement medal, Army Commendation medal with two oak leaf clusters, Meritorious Service medal. Mem. Tex. Hosp. Assn., Am. Hosp. Assn. Republican. Baptist. Home: 5837 Archwood San Antonio TX 78239 Office: Hdqrs Health Services Command HSHS-U Fort Sam Houston TX 78234

STEWART, PAUL TAYLOR, school transportation administrator; b. Blacksville, W.Va., May 20, 1918; s. James Richard and Cora Blanche (Johnson) S.; m. Martha Jean McDaniel, Feb. 2, 1944; children—Roger, Donna, Elaine, Janet. Various occupations, W.Va., 1942-57; dir. sch. transp. Monongalia County Schs., Morgantown, W.Va., 1953-66, Nat. Safety Council, Chgo., 1966-73, Kanawha County Schs., Charleston, W.Va., 1973-76; supv. sch. bus driver tng. safety W.Va. Dept. Edn., Charleston, 1976-78, dir. sch. transp., 1978—; mem. edn. and tng. com. Nat. Research Council, Washington, 1985—; cons. in field. Author: Driver Training Program, U.S. Forest Service, 1969. Author Sch. Transp. Supvs. Guide, 1966. Named Adminstr. of Yr., Sch. Bus Fleet Bobit Publs., 1982. Mem. Nat. Assn. State Dirs. Pupil Transp. Services (pres. 1983-85), W.Va. Assn. County Dirs. Sch. Transp. (pres. 1963-64), Nat. Assn. for Pupil Transp. (pres. 1977-78), Nat. Safety Council Motor Transp. Div. (sec. 1980-81), Nat. Safety Council Sch. Transp. Sect., Nat. Safety Council (bd. dirs.). Republican. Mem. Ch. of Christ. Avocations: swimming; golf; visiting the farm. Home: 2043 Oakridge Dr Charleston WV 25311 Office: W Va Dept Edn 1900 Washington St E Charleston WV 25305

STEWART, PETER PAULS, wholesale distribution company executive, religious and educational foundation administrator; b. Kansas City, Mo., May 26, 1920; s. Harry Ewing and Myrtle Marie (Pauls) S.; m. Elizabeth May Exall, July 18, 1942; children—Elizabeth Stewart Wally, Peter Bruce, Alan Gordon, Margaret Catherine, David Exall. B.A. cum laude in Econs., Harvard U., 1942. Asst. mgr. Stoneleigh Hotel, Dallas, 1942; asst. gen. mgr. Tractores Universales, Mexico City, 1948; mgr. Auto Productos, Mexico City, 1949; asst. sales mgr. The Stewart Co., Dallas, 1950-54, pres., 1956—; ptnr. Auto Convoy Co., Dallas, 1950-83; pres., founding dir. Thanks-Giving Sq. Found., Ctr. for World Thanksgiving, Nat. Thanksgiving Commn. City plan commr., 1958-60; past mem. bd. dirs. Dallas Mus. Fine Arts, Dallas Arboretum, Hockaday Sch., Dallas; pres. Dallas Assembly, 1970-71. Served to capt. AUS, 1943-46. Decorated Bronze Star. Recipient Linz award, 1970. Mem. Chief Execs. Orgn., Young Pres.' Orgn. Republican. Episcopalian. Clubs: Brook Hollow Golf, Chaparral, Tower (Dallas). Author: The Spirit of Thanksgiving, 1969; With United Hearts, 1975; The First Thanksgiving of the U.S., 1977; The World Gives Thanks, 1982.

STEWART, PRISCILLA ANN MABIE, art historian, educator; b. Iowa City, Sept. 21, 1926; d. Edward Charles and Grace Frances (Chase) Mabie; B.A., State U. Iowa, 1948; M.A., U. South Fla., 1971; Ed.S., Fla. Atlantic U., 1983; m. Thomas Wilson Stewart, Aug. 28, 1949. Coordinator elem. art Manatee County (Fla.), 1953-59; tchr. art history and photography Manatee Community Coll., 1959—; organizer, dir. Pelican Perch Wild Bird Hosp., Bradenton, 1953-85. Mem. Intertel Soc., Profl. Photographers Am. (edn. div.), Nat. Art Edn. Assn., Fla. Art Edn. Assn., Fla. Ornithol. Soc., Mensa, Sarasota-Manatee Phi Beta Kappa Assn. (pres. 1984-85, 85-86), Phi Beta Kappa, Alpha Xi Delta, Phi Kappa Phi. Republican. Episcopalian. Home: 2705 Riverview Blvd W Bradenton FL 33505 Office: Dept Art Manatee Community Coll Bradenton FL 33507

STEWART, ROBERT DESBROW, JR., lawyer; b. Manchester, N.H., Mar. 26, 1942; s. Robert D. and Ruth E. (Burgess) S.; m. Patricia Ann Byrne, Dec. 3, 1966; children—Kimberly, Robert, Deborah. B.A., U. Okla., 1966, J.D., 1971. Bar: Okla. 1972, U.S. Supreme Ct. 1982. Assoc. Hotsley Epton & Culp, Wewoka, Okla., 1972-73, ptnr., 1973-79; sr. staff counsel Okla. Corp. Commn., Oklahoma City, 1979; gen. counsel, 1979-82; staff atty. Okla. Gas & Electric Co., Oklahoma City, 1983—; instr. U. Okla. Law Center, 1982. Served with U.S. Army, 1966-70, Okla. Army N.G., 1973-85. Decorated Bronze Star, Army Commendation medal. Mem. Okla. Bar Assn., ABA. Democrat. Roman Catholic. Club: Rotary (pres. 1978). Lodge: KC. Author: Overview of Utility Regulation, 1982; A Bankrupt Electric Utility-What If?, 1983. Office: Oklahoma Gas & Electric Co 321 N Harvey St Oklahoma City OK 73101

STEWART, ROBERT H., III, banker, holding company executive; b. Dallas, Dec. 3, 1925; m. Pamela Sue Shelton, Nov. 27, 1976; children by previous marriage—Cynthia, Alice. B.B.A., So. Meth. U., 1949. With Empire State Bank, Dallas, 1949-51; asst. cashier InterFirst Bank of Dallas, 1951, asst. v.p., 1951-53, v.p., 1953-59, sr. v.p., 1959-60, pres., chief exec. officer, 1960-65, chmn. bd., chief exec. officer, 1965, 1983—; chmn. bd., chief exec. officer InterFirst Corp., Dallas, 1972-80, 1984—, chmn. exec. com., 1980-84; dir. PepsiCo Inc., Purchase, N.Y., Atlantic Richfield Co., Los Angeles, Fidelity Union Life Ins. Co., Dallas; past mem. fed. adv. council Fed. Res. System; past mem. Pres.'s Commn. on Fin. Structure and Regulation. Bd. govs. So. Meth. U., Dallas. Served to 1st lt., inf. U.S. Army, 1944-46. Mem. Assn. Res. City Bankers, Conf. Bd. Clubs: Brook Hollow Golf (Dallas); Augusta Nat. Golf (Ga.). Office: InterFirst Corp PO Box 83000 Dallas TX 75283

STEWART, ROBERT WILLIAM, international health care company executive, consultant; b. Niagara Falls, N.Y., May 25, 1947; s. William and Voncile (Wages) S.; m. Carolyn Faye Whitaker, Aug. 1, 1970 (div. Aug. 1975); m. 2d, Leona Veronica Thomasek, July 8, 1983; 1 dau., Stephanie Joanna. A.A., St. Petersburg Jr. Coll., 1970; B.S., U. Ala., 1972. C.P.A., Fla., Calif. Acct. Peat, Marwick, Mitchell & Co., Miami, Fla., 1972-75; sr. cons. Hosp. Affiliates Internat., Inc., Nashville, 1976-79; v.p. Electro Sound, Inc., Virginia Beach, Va., 1979-80, Nat. Med. Enterprises, Inc., Marietta, Ga., 1980—, v.p. acquisitions and devel., 1980—. Served with USMC, 1965-69; Vietnam. Mem. Am. Inst. C.P.A.s., Fla. Inst. C.P.A.s., Calif. Inst. C.P.A.s., Am. Coll. Hosp. Adminstrn., Hosp. Fin. Mgmt. Assn. Republican. Home: 14140 82d Ave N Seminole FL 33542 Office: Nat Med Enterprises Inc 1827 Powers Ferry Rd Bldg 23 Marietta GA 30067

STEWART, ROY ALLEN, opthalmologist; b. Leary, Ga., Dec. 28, 1915; s. John Chesley and Bonnie Mae (Allen) S.; m. Pauline Richter, Apr. 26, 1941; 1 child, Larry Wayne. B.S., Emory U., M.D., 1940. Diplomate Am. Bd. Opthalmology. Intern, Md. Gen. Hosp., Balt., 1940-41; resident Balt. Eye Ear & Throat Hosp., 1941-43; practice medicine specializing in opthalmology, Newton, N.C., 1946—. Served to lt. USN, 1943-46. Mem. Am. Acad. Ophthalmology, N.C. Med. Soc., AMA. Republican. Baptist. Avocations: golf, music, aviation, photography. Home: 211 W 9th St Newton NC 28658 Office: 427 N Main Ave Newton NC 28658

STEWART, SHELLEY ANN, industrial psychologist; b. East Lansing, Mich., Jan. 25, 1951; d. Donald Richard and Adrienne Dubois (Eastman) Hoover; m. Dana Joseph Stewart, June 4, 1982; 1 child, Scott Allen. B.Indsl./Organizational Psychology, San Diego State U., 1979, M.S. with high honors, 1983. Psychology instr. San Diego State U., 1979-80; data analyst San Diego State U. Found., 1978-81; personnel research psychologist Naval Personnel Research Div. Ctr., 1980; supr. pilot tng., asst. supr. maintainer tng. Allen Corp. Am., Lemoore, Calif., 1981-85, site mgr. pilot and maintainer tng., Jacksonville, Fla., 1985—; instr. Chapman Coll., 1983-84; cons. in field. Contbr. articles to profl. jours. Served with U.S. Army, 1974-77. Mem. Am. Soc. Tng. and Devel., Am. Def. Preparedness Assn., Am. Psychol. Assn. (assoc.). Democrat. Presbyterian. Avocations: aerobics; exploring historical sites. Home: 4375 Confederate Point Rd #4A Jacksonville FL 32210

STEWART, STEPHEN HURLEY, university coordinator, health science educator; b. Ironton, Ohio, Oct. 18, 1947; s. Daniel Howard and Nora Frances (Hurley) S.; m. Donna Victoria Ludwig, May 9, 1975; children—Sarah Elizabeth, Joshua Ludwig. B.S. in Health, U. Ky., 1973; M.P.H., U. Okla., 1977, Dr.P.H., 1979. Environ. health supr. Fla. Div. Health, Sarasota, 1973-76; cons. Don Jennings & Assoc., Tulsa, 1976-79; coordinator health sci. James Madison U., Harrisonburg, Va., 1979—; mem. Va. State Health Edn. Adv. com., Richmond, 1984—; cons. in field. Author: Family Health and Human Relations, 1980, First Aid Principles and Practices, 1985. Contbr. articles to profl. publs. Mem. Am. Heart Assn. CPR coms., Harrisonburg, 1980—; local coordinator, com. mem. various local and nat. polit. candidates, Harrisonburg, 1979—. Served to E-5 U.S. Army, 1970-72. Recipient Disting. Service award Nat. Inst. For Foodservice Industry, 1981. Mem. Am. Pub. Health Assn., Am. Sch. Health Assn., Va. Alliance Health, Phys. Edn., Recreation and Dance (health chairperson 1984—). Avocations: tennis, skin diving, reading. Home: 1447 Butler St Harrisonburg VA 22801 Office: James Madison U Box 28 Godwin Hall Harrisonburg VA 22807

STEWART, WALTER SIOUX, JR., auditor; b. Carfax, Va., Mar. 13, 1940; s. Walter Sioux and Louise (Hall) S.; m. Linda K. Lilly, Nov. 10, 1967; children—Jennifer Lynn, Walter Sioux, Samuel Thomas. B.S., East Tenn. State U., 1966; postgrad. U. Tenn., 1976. Chief hosp. acct./budget officer State of Tenn., Greene Valley Hosp., Greeneville, 1967; acct. Magnavox Co., Greeneville, 1970; chief plant acct. Jarl Extrusions, Inc., Elizabethton, Tenn., 1972; supr. comprehensive employment tng. program City of Johnson City (Tenn.), 1975; tchr. Johnson City Vocat. Sch., 1966-76; auditor U.S. Office Personnel Mgmt., Washington, 1977-81; auditor U.S. Dept. HUD, Washington, 1981, Knoxville, Tenn., 1981—. Served with U.S. Army, 1959-62. Mem. Nat. Assn. Accts. (assoc. dir. membership), Assn. Govt. Accts., Hosp. Fin. Mgmt. Assn., Acad. Med. Adminstrs. Baptist. Lodge: Lions. Home: 1804 Hillsboro Ave Johnson City TN 37601 Office: Duty Station Region IV 1111 Northshore Dr Room 306 Knoxville TN 37919

STEWART, WILLIAM HISTASPAS, political science educator, writer; b. Hartselle, Ala., Aug. 20, 1939; s. William Histaspas and Opal Evelyn (Cross) S.; m. Connie Sue Scott, May 12, 1975; 1 son, William Histaspas. B.A., U. Ala., 1960, Ph.D., 1968; M.A., George Washington U., 1961. Asst. prof. polit. sci. The Citadel, Charleston, S.C., 1968-69; asst. prof. U. Ala., 1969-72, assoc. prof., 1972—; cons. in field. Mem. Citizens Forum on Self-Govt./Nat. Mcpl. League; speaker to civic and youth groups. State of Ala. Scottish-Rite fellow, 1960-61; vis. scholar Summer Tng. Program of the Inter-Univ. Consortium for Polit. and Social Research U. Mich., 1981. Mem. Am. Polit. Sci. Assn., Ala. Polit. Sci. Assn., Conf. for Fed. Studies, Pi Sigma Alpha. Republican. Mem. Ch. of Christ. Lodge: Mason. Author: The Alabama Constitutional Commission, 1975; Citizen Participation in Public Administration, 1976; The Tennessee-Tombigbee Waterway, 1971; Concepts of Federalism, 1984. Contbr. articles in field to profl. jours. Office: Drawer I University AL 35486

STICCO, ELMER ANTHONY, manufacturing company executive; b. Yatesville, Pa., Feb. 7, 1925; s. Anthony and Eleanor Sticco; B.S., U. Conn., 1952; m. Gloria Massimo, Sept. 2, 1946; children—Lewis, Alan, Susan. Accountant, Peat, Marwick, Mitchell & Co., C.P.A.'s, 1952-59; with Electronic Specialty Co., 1959-69, exec. v.p., dir., 1969-81; with Internat. Controls Corp., Boca Raton, Fla., 1969-78, exec., v.p., chief operating officer, from 1978, pres., chief exec. officer, dir., 1973—; chmn., chief exec. officer All Am. Industries, Inc., 1973—; chmn., chief exec. officer Datron Systems, Inc. Served with USNR, 1943-46. C.P.A., Conn. Mem. Nat. Assn. Accountants, Am. Mgmt. Assn., Am. Inst. C.P.A.'s, Conn. Soc. C.P.A.'s. Roman Catholic. Club: Boca Raton Hotel. Office: 5499 N Federal Hwy Boca Raton FL 33432

STICE, JAMES EDWARD, engineering educator; b. Fayetteville, Ark., Sept. 19, 1928; s. F. Fenner and Charlotte (Anderson) S.; m. Patricia Ann Stroner, Sept. 22, 1951; children—Susan Emily, James Clayton. B.S., U. Ark., 1949; M.S., Ill. Inst. Tech., 1952, Ph.D., 1963. Registered profl. engr., Ark., Tex. Process engr. Visking Corp., North Little Rock, Ark., 1951-53; chem. engr. Thurston Chem. Co. div. W. R. Grace & Co., Joplin, Mo., 1953-54; asst. prof. chem. engring. U. Ark., 1954-57, assoc. prof., 1962-67, prof., 1967-68; instr. chem. engring. Ill. Inst. Tech., Chgo., 1957-62; dir. Bur. Engring. Teaching, assoc. prof. chem. engring. U. Tex.-Austin, 1968-73, prof. engring. edn. in chem. engring., 1973-85, T. Brockett Hudson prof. chem. engring., 1985—, dir. Center for Teaching Effectiveness, 1973—; summer cons. E. I. duPont de Nemours & Co., Inc., Savannah River Plant, Aiken, S.C., 1955, Humble Oil & Refining Co., Baytown, Tex., 1956, Universal Oil Products Co., Des Plaines, Ill., 1957-58, Phillips Petroleum Co., Bartlesville, Okla., 1963, Ethyl Corp., Baton Rouge, 1965, U. Wis.-Eau Claire, 1970—. Fellow Armour Research Found., 1949-51, NSF Sci. Faculty fellow, 1959-60. Recipient award for excellence in engring. teaching Gen. Dynamics, 1980, award Western Electric, 1981; Chester F. Carlson award for innovation in engring. edn., 1984; co-recipient ISA Jour. award, 1966. Mem. Am. Inst. Chem. Engrs., Am. Soc. Engring. Edn. (bd. dirs. 1983-85), Instrument Soc. Am., Scabbard and Blade, Sigma Xi, Delta Sigma, Sigma Chi, Phi Eta Sigma, Pi Mu Epsilon, Alpha Chi Sigma, Tau Beta Pi, Omicron Delta Kappa, Phi Lambda Upsilon, Phi Kappa Phi. Republican. Presbyterian. Author: (with B. S. Swanson) Electronic Analog Computer Primer, 1965; Computadoras Analogicas Electronicas, 1971; Expansion of Keller Plan Instruction in Engineering and Selected Other Disciplines, 1975. Home: 1503 W 32d St Austin TX 78703

STICK, KLAUS, real estate executive, consultant; b. Bad Bramstedt, Schleswig-Holstein, W.Ger., June 24, 1945; s. Johannes Adolf Stick and Kaethe (Stueben) Vollmer; m. Diane Warren, Oct. 24, 1975 (div. Aug. 1979). Kuchenmeister, Industrie U. Heidelberg, 1973; Diplom Betriebswirt, Hotel Adminstrn. Sch., Heidelberg, 1973; cert. econs. and hotel mgmt., Cornell U., 1974. Gen. mgr. club and food facilities World Trade Ctr., Dallas, 1977-78; mgr. Willow Bend Polo Club, Dallas, 1978-79; v.p. Commerce Club, Dallas, 1980; broker assoc. Henry S. Miller Co., Dallas, 1980-83; pres., owner K. Stick & Assocs., Dallas, 1983—; asst. exec. chef Fairmont Hotel, Dallas, 1974-75; dir. Italian Pavillion, Dallas, 1974-75; gen. mgr. asst. Brennan's Restaurant, Dallas, 1975-76; gen. mgr., exec. chef Raintree Restaurant, Dallas, 1976-77. Guest seminar leader Est Orgn., 1982—; supporter Dallas Symphony and Opera, 1976—. Recipient Gold medal World Chefs Orgn. Culinary Olympics, Frankfurt, W.Ger., 1976. Mem. Union Helvetia, Tex. Club Mgrs. Assn. Republican. Club: Willow Bend. Office: Klaus Stick & Assocs 4553 Westgrove St Dallas TX 75248

STICKLEY, JOHN LEON, textile executive; b. Cambridge, Mass., Sept. 6, 1902; s. Leonard and Annie Hanora (Saint) S.; m. Jennie Williamson McMichael, Apr. 6, 1928; children—John Leon, Georgiana Stickley Meginley, Nancy Stickley Grant. Student Lowell Textile Inst., 1922. So. mgr. William Whitman Co., Inc., 1923-48; pres. John L. Stickley & Co., Charlotte, N.C., 1948-68, chmn., 1968—; chmn. Stickley Textiles, Inc., Textile Assocs., Gemini Ltd.; dir. Engraph, Inc., Camelot Industries, Rossville Yarn Processing Co., Rossville Mills. Past mem. N.C. State Bd. Elections, N.C. Bd. Higher Edn. Served with USNG, 1920-21. Recipient Merit of Honor medals, Peru, 1956, Ecuador, 1957. Republican. Baptist. Clubs: Union League (N.Y.C.); Charlotte City, Myers Park (Charlotte, N.C.). Lodges: Masons, Shriners, Lions (past internat. pres.). Home: 2270 Sharon Ln Charlotte NC 28211 Office: 5672 International Way Providence Sq Box 13589 Charlotte NC 28211

STIDHAM, RONALD, political science educator, researcher; b. Stickleyville, Va., Dec. 10, 1940; s. Cecil and Margaret Pauline (Robinette) S.; m. Mary Lee Vermillion, Mar. 31, 1962 (div. 1974); children—Ronald Anthony, Todd Emerson; m. Laquita Louise Gotcher, Oct. 1, 1976; children—Samuel Austin, Heather Elizabeth. B.S., East Tenn. State U., 1965, M.A., 1970; Ph.D., U. Houston, 1979. Instr., Lamar U., Beaumont, Tex., 1970-78, asst. prof., 1978-83, assoc. prof., 1983—; cons. Nat. Ctr. for State Cts., Williamsburg, Va., summer 1977. Author: (with others) The Federal Courts, 1985. Mem. Am. Polit. Sci. Assn., So. Polit. Sci. Assn., Southwest Social Sci. Assn., Tex. Assn. Coll. Tchrs., Pi Gamma Mu Soc. Democrat. Baptist. Avocations: photography; stained glass. Home: 3936 Broadmoor Dr Beaumont TX 77707 Office: Dept Polit Sci Lamar U PO Box 10030 Beaumont TX 77710

STIEGLITZ, ALBERT BLACKWELL, lawyer; b. Warrenton, Va., May 21, 1936; s. Valentine Henry and Mary (Blackwell) S.; m. Rosemary Jeanne Dommerich, Nov. 11, 1971; children—Albert Blackwell Jr., John Dommerich. Student U. Fla., 1954-1955; B.A., U. Miami, 1958, LL.B., 1964. Bar: Fla. 1964, U.S. Dist. Ct. (so. dist.) Fla. 1964, U.S. Ct. Appeals (5th and 11th cirs.) 1964. Ptnr. Fowler, White, Burnett, Hurley, Banick and Strickroot, Miami, Fla., 1969—. Served to 1st lt. USAF, 1958-61. Mem. ABA, Fla. Bar Assn., Internat. Assn. Ins. Counsel (exec. com. 1981-84), Dade County Def. Bar Assn. (pres. 1978-79), Delta Theta Phi. Republican. Episcopalian. Clubs: Riviera Country (Coral Gables); Com. of 100, Bath (Miami Beach, Fla.); University, Bankers (Miami). Lodge: Rotary. Office: Fowler White Burnett Hurley Banick and Strickroot 5th Floor City Nat Bank Bldg Miami FL 33130

STIFTEL, BRUCE, environmental planning educator; b. Bklyn., Apr. 19, 1954; s. Joseph and Isabelle Claire (Leibowitz) S.; B.S., SUNY, 1975; M.Regional Planning, U. N.C., 1981. Community planner U.S. EPA, Research Triangle Park, N.C., 1977; research assoc. U. N.C., Chapel Hill, 1977-83; asst. prof. Fla. State U., Tallahassee, 1983—. Editor Carolina Planning mag., 1976-77. Contbr. chpts. to books, articles to profl. jours. Mem. Am. Planning Assn., Planners Network. Democrat. Jewish. Office: Florida State U Dept Urban and Regional Planning Tallahassee FL 32306

STILES, DON RAY, state official, corrections consultant; b. Whitesboro, Tex., June 19, 1937; s. A.J. and Rosemary (Burkhalter) S.; m. Charlsie Jean Hite, Feb. 12, 1955 (dec. Jan. 1976); children—Stephen Ray, Bruce Duane; m. Gail Ann Kasuls, Sept. 10, 1977; 1 stepchild, Barton Craig. B.A., East Tex. Bapt. U., 1962; M.A., Sam Houston State U., 1974. Salesman bldg. materials, 1967; owner, operator Stiles Supply Co., Sherman, Tex., 1967-68, Dallas Service Ctr., 1969-72; chief adult probation officer Grayson County, Sherman, Tex., 1966-67; unit supr. Adult Probation Dept., Dallas, 1968-75; parole commr. Tex. Bd. Pardons and Paroles, Austin, 1976-77; exec. dir. Tex. Adult Probation Commn., Austin, 1977—; corrections cons. to various orgns. and agys.; mem. adv. bd. Probation Officer Tng. Inst., Sam Houston State U.; mem. Tex. Criminal Justice Coordinating Council; mem. crime in the streets com. State Bar Tex.; chmn. criminal justice policy devel. com. Criminal Justice Coordinating Council; mem. Nat. Task Force on the Interstate Compact Regulating the Movement of Probationers and Parolees Between States. Mem. Bd. of Zoning Adjustments, City of Grapevine (Tex.), 1970-72, mem. Planning and Zoning Commn., 1972-75. Mem. Nat. Assn. Probation Execs. (pres. 1984—), Am. Corrections Assn. (del. 1978), Am. Probation and Parole Assn. (bd. dirs. 1984—), So. States Corrections Assn., Tex. Corrections Assn. (pres. 1978, bd. dirs. 1976—, Hall of Honor award 1984). Office: Texas Adult Probation Commission 8100 Cameron Rd Austin TX 78753

STILES, G. E. R., business executive; b. Hanover County, Va., Apr. 4, 1932; s. Joseph Clay and Virginia Clay (Robertson) S.; m. Meredith W. Moon, Mar. 24, 1956 (div. Jan. 1982); children—Cameron Clay, Lisa Blair, G.E.R. II; m. Anna V. Wallner, Sept. 8, 1984. B.S., Randolph-Macon Coll., 1954; M.B.A., U. Va., 1959. Sr. v.p. A.H. Robins Co. Inc., Richmond, Va. Chmn. Ashland Town Council, Va., 1968-72; trustee Randolph Macon Coll., Ashland, 1974—. Served with U.S. Army, 1955-57. Republican. Episcopalian. Avocations: sports, bridge, reading. Home: 301 Caroline St Ashland VA 23005 Office: AH Robins Co Inc 1407 Cummings Dr Richmond VA 23220

STILLMAN, J(AMES) DAVID, investment company executive; b. Wilmington, N.C., Feb. 16, 1940; s. Enoch W. and Virginia O. Stillman; m. Norma J. Buie, May 18, 1963; children—Cary Lynn, Connie Elizabeth, Amy Caroline. A.A., U. N.C.-Wilmington, 1961; grad. N.Y. Inst. Fin., 1968; postgrad. Coll. for Fin. Planning, 1979, Wharton Bus. Sch., 1984-85. Cert. fin. planner. Assoc. v.p. Renold Securities, St. Petersburg, Fla., 1968-72, syndicate mgr., 1972-78; assoc. v.p. Dean Witter Reynolds, St. Petersburg, 1978-81, 1st v.p., br. mgr. so. div., 1981—, also chmn. nat. adv. council. Mem. Nat. Assn. Securities Dealers (chmn. divisional adv. council 1974-75), St. Petersburg Stock and Bond Club (dir. 1971), St. Petersburg C. of C. Republican. Baptist. Clubs: St. Petersburg Quarterback, St. Petersburg Sertoma (treas., dir. 1972-73), St. Petersburg Yacht, Seminole Lake Country, Treasure Island Tennis and Yacht, Pres.'s, Rainbow Springs Golf and Country. Home: 6421 3d Palm Point Saint Petersburg Beach FL 33706 Office: 3251 3d Ave N Saint Petersburg FL 33713

STILWELL, ROBIN LISA, family therapist; b. Bklyn., June 28, 1952; d. Edward Osher and Rita Joann (Fabian) Kaye; m. Joseph Tracy Stilwell, Sept. 12, 1976; 1 child, Leah. Student Merrill-Palmer Inst. Child Devel. and Family Life, Detriot, 1972; B.S., SUNY-Oneonta, 1973; M.A., Mich. State U., 1975. Geriatric care technician Fox Hosp. Nursing Home, Oneonta, N.Y., 1973-74; social worker Metro Dade Comprehensive Drug Program, Miami, Fla., 1975-76; social worker Metro Dade Youth and Family Devel., Miami, 1976-81, asst. regional supr., 1981—; pvt. practice marital and family therapist, Miami, 1985—; cons. Planned Parenthood Assn., Oneonta, 1972-74; field supr. Sch. Social Work, Fla. Internat. U., Miami, 1977—. Mem. Am. Assn. Marriage and Family Therapy, Am. Orthopsychiatric Assn., Am. Mental Health Counselors Assn., Phi Upsilon Omicron. Democrat. Jewish. Avocations: ballet; cooking; swimming; sewing. Office: Metro Dade Youth and Family Devel 11025 SW 84th St Miami FL 33173

STIMITS, LYNNE DENISE, educator; b. Port Arthur, Tex., Oct. 11, 1956; d. Ralph Clinton Stimits and Glenda Marie (Neel) Stimits Knippa. B.S.,

Houston Baptist U., 1980. Lic. tchr., Tex.; lic. and cert. athletic trainer. Athletic trainer, tchr. biology/health Conroe Ind. Sch. Dist. (Tex.), 1980—; examiner Tex. Licensure Program, Houston, 1983-84. Mem. Nat. Athletic Trainers Assn., S.W. Athletic Trainers Assn., Fellowship Athletic Trainers, Gulf Coast Athletic Trainers Assn. Republican. Lutheran. Home: 16402 Villa Del Norte Houston TX 77070 Office: McCullough High Sch Conroe Ind Sch Dist 3800 S Panther Creek Dr The Woodlands TX 77380

STINE, EARLE JOHN, JR., physician, radiologist; b. Saginaw, Mich., Feb. 21, 1932; s. Earle John and Ione Genevieve (Best) S.; m. Bernita Evelyn Emerson, Aug. 27, 1954; children—Renee Evelyn, Mark Earle, John Emerson. A.B., Albion Coll., 1954; M.D., Wayne State U., 1958. Diplomate Am. Bd. Radiology. Intern, Bon Secours Hosp., Grosse Pointe, Mich., 1958-59, gen. surgery resident, 1959-61; practice medicine, Pigeon, Mich., 1961-62, Marcus, Iowa, 1962-65, Ida Grove, Iowa, 1965-75; radiology residency U. Iowa, Iowa City, 1975-78; staff radiologist St. Joseph Med. Ctr., Ponca City, Okla., 1978-80; med. dir. radiology Jackson County Meml. Hosp., Altus, Okla., 1980—. Mem. AMA, Am. Coll. Radiology, Radiol. Soc. N.Am. Republican. Methodist. Avocation: weaving. Home: 16 LLL RR3 Altus OK 73521 Office: Diagnostic Imaging Cons 1133 E Maple Altus OK 73521

STINE, GORDAN BERNARD, dental educator and administrator, dentist; b. Charleston, S.C., Feb. 10, 1924; s. Abe Jack and Helen (Pinosky) S.; m. Barbara Berlinsky, Jan. 20, 1951; children—Steven Mark, Robert Jay. B.S. in Chemistry, Coll. of Charleston, 1944; D.D.S., Emory U., 1950. Lic. dentist, Ga., S.C. Assoc. to Dr. William McDowell, Charleston, 1953-54; pvt. practice gen. dentistry, Charleston, 1954—; spl. asst. to pres. Med. U., S.C., Charleston, 1983—, clin. assoc. prof. community dentistry, 1983—, dir. Dental Continuing Edn., 1985—, bd. visitors, 1982, 83, chmn., 1982, chmn. Cultural Projects Council, 1984-85; instr. Trident Tech. Coll., 1981; mem. dental adv. com. Div. Dental Health S.C. State Bd. Health, 1967-68; mem. regional adv. group S.C. Regional Med. Program, 1974-75. Chmn. S.C. Dental Polit. Action Com., 1973-74, 76-84, bd. dirs., 1973-85; bd. dirs. Coastal Carolina Fair Assn., 1957-61, 63-65, pres., 1965, 66; bd. dirs. Charleston Symphony Assn., 1963-68, pres. 1965, mem. pres.' council 1983-84; bd. dirs. Charleston Civic Ballet, 1968, S.C. Art Alliance, 1973-74, Charleston Concert Assn., 1967-73, Charleston Rwy. Hist. Soc., 1967-68; bd. dirs. Coastal Carolina council Boy Scouts Am., 1972, 74, 75, 82, 83, 84, v.p. for programs 1985, 86, adv. com. 1972, 74, 75, 82, 83, 84, 85, chmn. Kiawah Dist. 1982, chmn. coms.; bd. mem. Coll. Prep. Sch., 1963-67, vice chmn. 1964-66; mem. Task Force for Martin Luther King, Jr. Legal Holiday, YMCA of Greater Charleston, 1974-75, Martin King County Wide Birthday Celebration, 1975; founder Charleston Mini Parks, 1969, bd. mem., 1969-71, chmn., 1969, 71; bd. mem. Charleston Pride, 1967-86, chmn., 1973-74, 74-75, 83-85; chmn. dental div. Trident United Way, 1962, 69, bd. mem. 1970-73, 74-76, 78-80, 81-85, community welfare planning council 1967, 68, pres. 1982, exec. com. 1977-79, 81-84, chmn. coms.; chmn. fund raising dental div. Cancer Soc., 1956, 61, 66, 70, 71; chmn. Charleston County Democratic Party, 1968-72; Charleston County councilman 1975-84, chmn. 1979-80; alderman Ward 13 City of Charleston 1971-75; active pub. service coms. including S.C. Assembly on Growth, 1981, Trident Devel. Council 1972, legis. com. S.C. Assn. Counties 1979, 81, 82, Charleston Waterfront Park Adv. Com. 1982-83, Charleston Neighborhood Housing Services Bd. 1984; state senatorial candidate, 1975; vice chmn. Berkeley-Charleston-Dorchester Council of Govts., 1983-84, sec. 1985-86, mem., chmn. coms.; exec. com. Charleston Mus. 1980, bd. mem. 1977-78, steering com. 1978-80; chmn. Charleston Bicentennial Com. 1972-75; bd. mem. Carolina Art Assn. 1978; fund drive chmn. Roper Hosp. 1973; bd. mem. Coastal Fed. Credit Union 1979-80, pres. 1976; exec. com. Greater Charleston Safety Council, 1976-85, v.p., 1986; bd. mem. Trident Area Found., 1977-80, adv. bd., 1981-82; mem. steering com. Charleston campaign United Negro Coll. Fund, 1972, 73; bd. mem. Robert Shaw Boys Ctr., 1975-77, Mil. Services Ctr., 1979-82, Trident 100, 1980-81; chmn. State Health Fair Adv. Bd. for Nat. Health Screening Council, 1984-85; mem. Pres.' Adv. Council Winthrop Coll., 1984-85; mem. extension adv. bd. Clemson U., 1985, 86, chmn. statewide community devel. adv. com., 1985; bd. mem. Hebrew Benevolent Soc., 1968-71, pres., 1970, 71; bd. trustees Congregation Beth Elohim, 1959-64, pres., 1967, 68, Brotherhood pres., 1960; pres. Jewish Welfare Bd., 1970-71, mem. coms.; mem. YMCA. Served with USMC, 1942, with USN, 1945-46, 51-53; served with USNR, 1953-72, with USN Ret. Res. 1971-84. Named Coll. of Charleston Alumnus of Yr., 1966, Community Leader Am., 1968-71; recipient Hettie Rickett Community Devel. award, 1979, award adv. dental bd. Carolina Continental Ins. Co., 1983-84, Gov.'s Order of Palmetto award, 1985. Fellow Royal Soc. Health; mem. ADA, Coastal Dist. Dental Soc. (pres. 1954), Charleston Dental Soc. (pres. 1957-58), Am. Pub. Health Assn., Israel Dental Assn., Pierre Fauchard Acad., S.C. Dental Assn. (pres. 1974-75), Alpha Omega (pres. 1949-50, Disting. Service award 1976-77), Southeastern Alpha Omega Group (pres. 1960-78, charter mem.), Charleston Trident C. of C. (pres. 1972, bd. mem. 1968-74, 80), Tau Epsilon Phi. Clubs: Exchange Club of Charleston (pres. 1962), S.C. State Exchange (bd. dirs. 1965-68). Avocation: Gardening. Home: 2 Beverly Rd Charleston SC 29407 Office: Med Univ SC 171 Ashley Ave Charleston SC 29425

STINNETT, GENE ROSS, optometrist; b. Madisonville, Ky., Jan. 4, 1932; s. George Ross and Nolene (Beard) S.; m. Betty Adair Childers, June 14, 1953; children—Christie Lynn, Kimberly Jean. B.S., So. Coll. Optometry, 1960, D. Optometry, 1960. Gen. practice optometry, Madisonville, 1961—. Mem. Ky. Optometric Assn., Am. Optometric Assn., C. of C. Democrat. Club: Madisonville Country. Lodges: Elks, Lions. Avocations: golf; building. Home: 402 Country Club Ln Madisonville KY 42431 Office: 258 S Main St Madisonville KY 42431

STIPE, GENE, state senator; b. Oct. 21, 1926; LL.B., U. Okla. Mem. Okla. Ho. of Reps., 1949-54, Okla. Senate, 1957—. Office: PO Box 1368 McAlester OK 74502

STITT, VAN JUNIUS, JR., physician; b. Charlotte, N.C., Oct. 14, 1945; s. Van Junius and Cora Lee (Smith) S.; m. Gladys Feely, Nov. 2, 1974; 1 son, Van J. B.S. in Physics cum laude, Johnson C. Smith U., 1971; M.D., U. N.C., 1975. Diplomate Am. Acad. Family Physicians. Intern, Charlotte Meml. Hosp., 1976-75; resident in family practice, 1976-78; assoc. med. dir. Fayetteville Area Health Edn. Ctr. Residency Program, 1980—. Coordinator Boy Scouts Am.; Blue and Gold officer Naval Acad.; physician Spl. Olympics. Served with USAF, 1963-67, USN, 1975-79. Fellow Am. Acad. Family Physicians; mem. AMA, N.C. Acad. Family Physicians, Soc. Tchrs. Family Practice, Am. Geriatric Soc. Democrat. Baptist. Club: Aero. Contbr. articles to profl. jours. Home: 3311 Granville Dr Fayetteville NC 28303 Office: 1601-B Owen Dr PO Box 64699 Fayetteville NC 28306

STITZIEL, GEORGE LEONARD, banker; b. Kansas City, Kans., Oct. 18, 1933; s. William Harley and Gladys Pearl (Harris) S.; m. Helen Lois Meyers; children—Janice Pearl, Linda Susan, Katherine Helene. B.A., U. Mo., 1961, M.A., 1962; J.D., U. Tulsa, 1967. Bar: Okla. 1967. Sr. economist Skelly Oil Co., Tulsa, 1962-67; chief oil analyst Duff Anderson & Clark, Chgo., 1967-71, Eppler, Guerin & Turner, Dallas, 1971-72; sr. investment advisor, portfolio mgr. Republic Bank Dallas, 1972—; chmn. Fin. Analyst Oil Group, Chgo., 1970-71. Served with USN, 1952-57. Mem. Fin. Analysts Fedn., Dallas Assn. Investment Analysts, Nat. Assn. Petroleum Investment Analysts, Okla. Bar Assn. Club: Amex (Dallas). Home: 5410 Del Roy Dr Dallas TX 75229 Office: Republic Bank Dallas PO Box 241 Dallas TX 75221

STOBS, JAMES ROBERT, construction company executive, artist; b. Logan, Iowa, Nov. 30, 1913; s. Matthew and Bonnie (Twiford) S.; B.F.A., U. Fla., 1937; m. Ruby Lee Wentworth, Mar. 5, 1939; children—James Robert II, Barbara Lee (Mrs. Fredrick Merrill Macy), Gayle Anne. Chmn. bd., founder Stobs Bros. Constrn. Co., Miami, Fla., 1937—; sec.-treas. Forming Services, Inc., Miami, 1965—; developer-promoter acreage ltd. partnerships. Built Internat. Oceanographic Found. Planet Ocean, S.C.M. Bldg., Addressograph-Multigraph Dist. Offices, Eastern Air Lines Computer Reservations Center, J.F. Kennedy Meml. Library, Hialeah Sr. High Sch., Palmetto Hosp. (all Miami); Pier House, Mary Immaculata High Sch. and Convent, Key West, Fla., psychotic children's unit J. Hillis Miller Hosp., Gaineville, Fla.; exhibited in group art shows Tri-County Fair, Tampa, Fla., Soc. Four Arts, Palm Beach, Fla., others; exhibited in one-man show Witt's Gallery, 1978; represented by Phyllis Powers Art Gallery, Miami Lakes, Fla.; mem. North Miami Art League Jury, 1976, 77-78, Ann. Dade County Poincianna Art Exhbn., Jury, 1972, 73, others. Mem. Miami Shores (Fla.) Planning Bd., 1950-53; v.p. Progress for Dade County, Inc., 1977-78. Recipient Blue Ribbon, Tri-County Fair, Tampa, 1936, cash prize Soc. Four Arts Exhbn., Palm Beach, 1937, Art award Am. Heritage Bicentennial, 1976, also others. Mem. Asso. Gen. Contractors (Safety award 1968-81, treas. nat. conv. 1952), Internat. Platform Assn., Miami Shores C. of C. (dir. 1976—), Greater Miami C. of C. (legis. action com.), Little River C. of C. (v.p. 1982), Delta Sigma Phi. Republican. Presbyterian (deacon 1961-63). Clubs: Miami Shores Country (chmn. social com. 1979-80), Kiwanis (dir. 1977-82). Home: 429 NE 101st St Miami Shores FL 33138 Office: 7010 NE 4th Ct Miami FL 33138

STOCKARD, ALAN RAY, osteopathic physician; b. Decatur, Tex., Apr. 24, 1949; s. Nolan Ray Stockard and Jackie Marcella (Huse) Beavers; children—Kati Suzette, Jason Alan, Elisabeth Jane. B.S., U. Tex.-Arlington, 1972; D.O., Tex. Coll. Osteo. Medicine, 1976. Intern, Doctors Hosp., Tucker, Ga., 1976-77; gen. practice osteo. medicine, Clarkston, Ga., 1977—; clin. dir. Atlanta Sports Medicine Clinic, Clarkston, 1977—; chief staff Doctors Hosp., Tucker, 1981-82; team physician Ga. Gens. Pro Soccer Team, Stone Mountain, 1982. Team physician DeKalb Coll. baseball, basketball and soccer teams, Ga., 1980—, various high schs., DeKalb County, Gwinnett County, 1981—. Mem. Am. Osteo. Assn., Am. Osteo. Acad. Sports Medicine. Republican. Roman Catholic. Office: Atlanta Sports Medicine Clinic Indian Creek Dr Clarkston GA 30021

STOCKARD, JANET LOUISE, lawyer; b. Beaumont, Tex., July 22, 1948; d. Louis and Louise (Land) S. B.S. with honors, U. Tex., 1970, J.D., 1973. Bar: Tex. 1973. Sole practice, Austin, Tex., 1973—. Vol. dep. registrar for voter registration; supporter Women's Advocacy Project, Rape Crisis Center; mem. City of Austin Parks and Recreation Bd., 1977-79. Named one of Most Noteworthy Austinites of Yr., Austin Homes and Gardens mag., 1983. Mem. State Bar Tex. (charter mem. coll. 1983-84), Travis County Bar Assn., Austin Young Lawyers Assn., Travis County Women Trial Lawyers (founder 1982, pres. 1983), Travis County Women Lawyers Assn. (founder 1976-77, pres. 1977-78), Barton Hills Horseshoe Bend Neighborhood Assn., Austin C. of C., Tex. Women's Polit. Caucus, Austin Women's Polit. Caucus, U. Tex. Ex-Students Assn., Nat. Assn. Women Lawyers, Travis County Democratic Women, NOW, Longhorn Assocs. (charter mem. for excellence in athletics 1983), Better Bus. Bur., Kappa Delta Pi, Pi Sigma Alpha. Roman Catholic. Office: 1209 Nueces Austin TX 78701

STOCKDALE, JOHN ALEXANDER DOUGLAS, physicist, company executive; b. Ipswich, Queensland, Australia, Mar. 15, 1936; came to U.S., 1966; s. Reginald Ian and Catriona Mary (Cameron) S.; m. Helen Margaret Sutton, Mar. 30, 1957; children—Helen, Alexander, Shane, B.S., U. Sydney, 1957, M.S., 1960; Ph.D., U. Tenn., 1969. Research scientist Australian Atomic Energy Commn., Sydney, 1958-66; research staff mem. Oak Ridge Nat. Lab., 1966—; pres. Comstock Inc., Oak Ridge, 1979—; vis. prof. and cons. NYU, N.Y.C., 1975—. Author, co-author jour. articles. John Simon Guggenheim Found. fellow, 1970-71. Mem. Am. Phys. Soc. Avocations: Painting; photography; sailing. Office: Comstock Inc PO Box 199 Oak Ridge TN 37831-0199

STOCKERT, JOHN WAGNER, national park executive; b. Canal Fulton, Ohio, Oct. 6, 1933; s. Ray Maurice and Mary Elizabeth (Wagner) S.; m. Joanne Wallace, June 11, 1964; children—Mary Margaret, Jeanne Elizabeth. B.A., Capital U., 1955. Supervisory park ranger Badlands Nat. Pk., Interior, S.D., 1966-71, Yellowstone Nat. Pk., Wyo., 1971-74, Blue Ridge Pkwy., Asheville, N.C., 1974-78; supt. Moores Creek Nat. Battlefield, Currie, N.C., 1978-85, Ft. Donelson Nat. Battlefield, Dover, Tenn., 1985—; instr. Coll. African Wildlife Mgmt., Tanzania, 1980. Author: (with others) Common Wildflowers of the Grand Canyon, 1967. Editor, pub. booklets: Badlands, Its Life and Landscape, 1969; Wildflowers of No. Plains and Black Hills, 1971; History of Badlands National Monument, 1968. Dist. rep. Am. Field Service, N.C., 1980-84. Served to SP-3 U.S. Army, 1955-57. Recipient Spl. Achievement award Nat. Pk. Service, 1971, 75. Mem. Parks Arts Assn. Inc., Assn. Nat. Park Rangers. Democrat. Lodges: Kiwanis, Rotary. Avocations: wildflower identification; international correspondence; traveling. Home: PO Box F Dover TN 37058-0120 Office: Fort Donelson Nat Battlefield Nat Park Service PO Box F Dover TN 37058-0120

STOCKMAN, BENEVEST ADVARRDS, fin. exec.; b. Jefferson County, Ky., Dec. 29, 1951; s. John A. and Marry V. (Victoria) S.; Ph.D., Stanford U. Owner United Mortgage Co., Eminence, Ky., Sacco Oil Co., Jefferson County, Ky., 1973-74; owner, pres. Stockman Enterprises Inc., Eminence, 1981—; dir. First United Fund, Eminence, Mcht. Brokers Exchange, N.Y.C., 1979—; prof. Stanford (Calif.) U., 1968. Recipient various bus. and fin. awards. Mem. Pres.'s Exec. Exchange, Practising Law Inst., Internat. Bankers, Internat. Mortgage Bankers, Internat. Import/Export, Internat. Stock Exchange, N.Y. Mcht. Exchange. Jewish. Clubs: Young Businessmen's Millionaires, Internat. Fin., No. Hunter, Bow Hunter, No. Yacht, Deer Hunters, Cattlemen's, others. Home: Route 2 Eminence KY 40019 Office: E Elm St Eminence KY 40019

STOCKMEYER, PAUL KELLY, computer scientist, educator; b. Detroit, May 1, 1943; s. Norman Otto and Lillian Ruth (Hitchman) S.; m. Bonita Lee Karels, July 2, 1966; children—Elizabeth Anne, Andrea Lynn. A.B. in Math., Earlham Coll., 1965; M.A., U. Mich., 1966, Ph.D., 1971. Asst. prof. computer sci. Coll. William and Mary, Williamsburg, Va., 1971-77, assoc. prof., 1977—. Contbr. articles to profl. jours., 1970-84. Recipient award for advancement of scholarship Phi Beta Kappa, Williamsburg, 1980. Mem. Am. Math. Soc., Math. Assn. Am., Assn. Computing Machinery. Presbyterian. Home: 206 Kingswood Dr Williamsburg VA 23185 Office: Coll William and Mary Dept Computer Sci Williamsburg VA 23185

STOCKTON, CHARLES KENNETH, safety engineer; b. Moulton, Ala., Feb. 21, 1947; s. William Travis and Virgie Inez (Brooks) S.; m. Cynthia A. Mansfield, June 9, 1972; 1 child, Scott K. Student bus. Pasco-Hernando Coll., 1974-78. Dir. safety and tng. concrete group Fla. Rock Industries, Inc., Jacksonville, 1978—; instr. mine safety and health, 1978—; instr. def. driving Nat. Safety Council, 1984—, instr. CPR Am. Heart Assn., 1982—; instr. ARC, 1980—. Bd. dirs. Hernando County chpt. ARC, 1981. Served with U.S. Army, 1966-69. Mem. Am. Soc. Safety Engrs., Nat. Safety Council, Tampa Safety Council. Lodge: Rotary (pres. elect Brooksville 1984-85). Office: Florida Rock Industries Inc PO Box 4667 Jacksonville FL 32201

STOCKTON, ROBERT LOUIS, physician, surgeon; b. Bethany, Okla., June 12, 1932; s. Frank Howard and Lola Bess (Abbott) S.; B.S., Okla. Central State U., Edmond, 1955; M.D., U. Okla., 1959; m. Sylvia Zoe Davis, Aug. 31, 1957; children—Sheryl Kay, Scott Alan. Intern, Baylor U. Med. Center, Dallas, 1959-60, resident gen. surgery, 1960-61; resident neurol. surgery U. Tex. Health Sci. Ctr., Dallas, 1961-66; practice medicine, specializing in neurol. surgery, Ft. Worth and Waco, Tex., 1966—. Bd. dirs. Waco Municipal Airport, 1976-77. Served to col. M.C. Tex. Army N.G., 1949-83. Diplomate Am. Bd. Neurol. Surgery. Fellow A.C.S.; mem. Am. Assn. Neurol. Surgeons, Congress Neurol. Surgeons, Univ. Assn. Emergency Med. Services, Aerospace Med. Assn., U.S. Army Flight Surgeons Assn., So. Neurosurgeon Soc., Tex. Neurosurgical Soc., Assn. U.S. Mil. Surgeons, AMA, Tex. Med. Assn. (mem. disaster med. care com. 1970-82, chmn. 1979-81), McLennan County Med. Soc. Baptist. Home: 4617 Scottwood St Waco TX 76708 Office: Box 3188 824 N 18th St Waco TX 76707

STODGHILL, RUTH LAUNA, real estate appraiser; b. Beaumont, Tex., Apr. 2, 1944; d. Hayward Olin Stodghill and Hazel Lee (Alford) Stodghill Guinn. B.A., Lamar U., 1966. Staff appraiser Suburban Coastal Mortgage, Houston, 1981; pres. Stodghill and Assocs., Houston, 1982—; cons. VA, Houston, 1983—. Contbr. articles to profl. jours. Chmn. ecology com. Young Republicans, Houston, 1970. Recipient Young Rep. of Month award, 1970. Mem. Soc. Real Estate Appraisers (speakers bur. 1981-82); fellow Internat. Inst. Valuers, Assn. Profl. Mortgage Woman. Clubs: Lamra Ex's Assn., Young Women Arts, Encorps. Home: 4253 Albans St Houston TX 77005 Office: Stodghill and Assocs 6633 Hillcroft #112 Houston TX 70018

STOFFER, GERALD RAY, psychology educator; b. Klamath Falls, Oreg., July 1, 1946; s. Rex V. Stoffer and June I. Stoffer Brown; m. Irene E. Wise, Feb. 1, 1981; children—Kraig, Andrea. M.A. in Psychology, U. Mont., 1971, Ph.D. in Psychology, 1973; M.A. in Human Resources Mgmt., Pepperdine U., 1981; M.B.A., Fla. Inst. Tech., 1982. Asst. prof. psychology Pacific Luth. U., Tacoma, Wash., 1973-78; adj. prof. Columbia Coll., Orlando, Fla., 1983—; bus. psychologist 100% Real Estate, Inc., Orlando, 1983—, Wall St. Realtors, Maitland, Fla., 1983—. Author: (weekly newspaper column) Real Estate Doctor, 1984—. Chmn. Christian Edn., Reorganized Ch. of Jesus Christ of Latter Day Saints, Orlando, 1985. Served to lt. USNR, 1978-83. NDEA fellow, 1970-72. Mem. Nat. Assn. Realtors, Central Fla. Investment Soc., Phi Beta Kappa, Sigma Xi, Phi Kappa Phi, Psi Chi. Republican. Avocation: traveling. Home: 800 S Lake Sybelia Dr Maitland FL 32751 Office: Watt St Realtors 2600 Maitland Ctr Maitland FL 32751

STOKELY, CECIL R., hospital administrator; b. Coolidge, Tex., Sept. 29, 1924; s. Loris Eugene and Callie Alice (Brewer) S.; m. Gladys Lerline Thompson, June 13, 1947; children—Kenneth Wayne, Carolyn Sue. A.A., Kilgore Coll. Registered nurse. Salesman, Nat. Supply, Kilgore, Tex., 1946; adminstr. Humble Oil & Refining Co., various locations in Tex., 1946-65; owner, administr. nursing home, New London, Tex., 1965-79; adminstr. Overton Med. Ctr., Overton, Tex., 1979—; vocat. instr. Panola Jr. Coll., Carthage, Tex., 1971. Com. mem. Rusk County Program Bldg. Co., Henderson, Tex., 1970. Mem. Tex. A&M C. of C. (bd. dirs. 1985). Mem. Ch. of the Nazarene. Avocations: genealogy; music. Home: PO Box 127 New London TX 75682

STOKES, CARL NICHOLAS, lawyer; b. Memphis, Jan. 26, 1907; s. John William and Edith Isabell (Burgess) S.; student Draughton's Bus. Coll., 1929-30; LL.B., U. Memphis, 1933; m. Laverne Judson, Aug. 21, 1930; 1 dau., Vicki Laverne Stokes Koehn. Bar: Tenn. 1934. Mem. Norvell & Monteverde, Memphis, 1934-38; with legal dept. Tenn. Unemployment Compensation Div., 1937-38; clk. City Ct. Memphis, 1938-42, Criminal Cts. Shelby County, 1946-50; judge City Ct. Memphis, 1950-52; mem. Shea & Pierotti, Memphis, 1952-62; v.p., gen. counsel Allen & O'Hara, Inc., Memphis, 1962-72; mem. firm Johnson Grusin Kee & May, P.C., Memphis; dir. 1st Fed. Savs. and Loan Assn. Life mem. adv. bd. Salvation Army, chmn., 1973-75; trustee Shrine Sch. for Handicapped Children; tax atty. Office of Shelby County Trustees. Served to capt., inf. AUS, 1942-46. Recipient award of merit Tenn. Bar Assn., 1958; Americanism award Am. Legion, 1980. Mem. ABA, Tenn., Memphis and Shelby County bar assns., Memphis Estate Planning Council, Memphis Area C. of C. (chmn. welcome com. 1972-73). Mem. Christian Ch. (life elder). Clubs: Masons (33 deg.), KT, Shriners. Kiwanis (pres. 1971-72, lt. gov. 1974-75, T.G. Kirkpatrick Meml. award 1978). Home: 2237 Massey Rd Memphis TN 38119 Office: 5855 Ridge Bend Rd Memphis TN 38119

STOKES, DEE HUNTINGTON, accountant, food products company executive; b. San Antonio, Oct. 1, 1943; s. Aldin Lowell and Wilma Susan (Redwine) S.; B.B.A. in Acctg., U. Tex., Austin, 1966; m. Janet Elaine Longway, June 6, 1970; children—Dee Huntington II, Justin Blair. From jr. acct. to staff acct. Collier, Johnson & Woods, CPAs, Corpus Christi, Tex., 1970-73; v.p., controller Weaver Potato Chip Co., Denver, 1973; partner Stokes Co., San Antonio, 1973-74; fin. analyst Mooney Aircraft Corp., Kerrville, Tex., 1974-75, mgr. acctg., 1975-78; controller Abilene (Tex.) facility Gen. Dynamics, 1978-81; controller Freeze Dry div. Right Away Foods Corp., 1981, gen. mgr. Freeze Dry div., 1981-83, v.p. fin. MRE div., 1983—. Served with USAF, 1966-70; maj. Res. C.P.A. Mem. Am. Inst. C.P.A.s, Tex. Soc. C.P.A.s. So. Baptist. Home: 405 Jonquil McAllen TX 78501 Office: PO Box 55 McAllen TX 78502

STOKES, THOMAS EDWARD, librarian; b. Canton, Ohio, Oct. 17, 1942; s. Thomas Edward and Elsie Mae (Groves) S.; m. Barbara Ann Wise, Aug. 19, 1967; children—Andrew Thomas, Ian Philip. B.A., Malone Coll., 1968; M.Div., Emmanuel Sch. Religion, 1974; M.L.S., George Peabody Coll. for Tchrs., 1974. Ordained to ministry Christian Ch., 1969; youth minister Calvary Evang. United Brethren Ch., Canton, 1966-67; resident counselor Malone Coll., Canton, 1967-69; student union mgr. Milligan Coll. (Tenn.), 1969-74; library asst. George Peabody Coll. for Tchrs., Nashville, 1974-75; librarian, mem. faculty Emmanuel Sch. Religion, Johnson City, Tenn., 1975—, asst. prof., 1979-81, assoc. prof. bibliography and research, 1981—; treas. Chaplaincy Endorsement Commn., Christian Chs. and Chs. of Christ, Johnson City, 1976—. Chaplain, Tenn. Army N.G., 1974—; asst. scoutmaster Boy Scouts Am., Johnson City, 1983—. Served with USNR, 1960-63. Named An Outstanding Young Man of Am., Johnson City Jaycees, 1971. Mem. ALA, Am. Theol. Library Assn., Tenn. Theol. Library Assn. (v.p. pres.-elect 1982-85, pres. 1985-87), Disciples of Christ Hist. Soc. Club: Johnson City Optimist (pres. 1979-80, 81-82, sec.-treas. 1982-83). Office: Emmanuel Sch Religion Route 6 Box 500 Johnson City TN 37601

STOKES, WILLIAM WOODS, education educator; b. Panama City, Fla., May 28, 1932; s. John Edward and Elma (Steen) S.; m. Shirley Connatser, May 4, 1961; children—William Thomas, Lela Shirley. B.A., U. Fla., 1954, M.Ed., 1961, Ed.D., 1963. English tchr. Duval County, Jacksonville, Fla., 1956-58, head dept. English, 1958-60; grad. asst. U. Fla., Gainesville, 1960-63; asst. prof. Tex. A&M U., College Station, 1963-64, chmn. secondary edn., 1964-67; head dept. Armstrong State Coll., Savannah, 1967—. Bd. dirs. Savannah Speech and Hearing Ctr., 1973, Savannah Symphony, 1970. Served in U.S. Army, 1954-56, Japan. Mem. Phi Delta Kappa, Kappa Delta Pi. Democrat. Episcopalian. Lodge: Rotary (Savannah). Avocations: reading; fishing. Office: Armstrong State Coll 11935 Abercorn St Savannah GA 31406-7197

STOLL, FRED MICHAEL, air force officer; b. McKeesport, Pa., Nov. 19, 1951; s. Fred Mathew and Helen Elizabeth (Vehec) S.; m. Joyce Marie Martin, June 12, 1972; 1 child, Mary Ann Elizabeth. A.A., Coll. of Air Force, Sacramento, Calif., 1980; B.S., Embry Riddle Aero. U., Daytona Beach, Fla., 1980, M.B.A., 1983. Joined U.S. Air Force as E-1, 1970, advanced through grades to E-6, 1985; air traffic controller, Miss., Nev., S.C. and Calif., 1973-84; computer programmer analyst Command and Control Systems Office, Tinker Air Force Base, Oklahoma City, 1984—; tchr. Embry-Riddle Aero. U., 1981-84; bus. cons. Small Bus. Adminstrn., No. Calif., 1982-84. Fellow Embry-Riddle Alumnus Assn. Republican. Club: Cobra Booster (No. Calif.) (pres. 1983-84). Avocations: flying; sailing; horseback riding. Office: Command and Control Systems Office Tinker Air Force Base Oklahoma City OK 73145

STOLL, TONI, artist; b. N.Y.C., Nov. 5; d. Leo and Rose (Kamerman) Rosenberg; B.F.A., Syracuse U., 1941; postgrad. Rutgers U.; m. Herbert Stoll, Dec. 31, 1941; children—Joanne Stoll Snyder, Barbara Stoll Law. Tchr. art classes USO, Denver, 1942, Lafayette Sch., Highland Park, N.J., 1953-58; painting instr. New Brunswick (N.J.) Art Center, 1953-69; decorating cons. Feverlight & Stoll Furniture Co., 1959-74; exhibited Nat. Arts Club, N.Y.C., 1961-62, Smithsonian Instn., Washington, 1961-63, Jersey City Mus., 1961-66, Douglas Coll., Rutgers U. Tercentennial, 1964, Fairleigh Dickinson U., Madison, N.J., Fla. Watercolor Soc., 1982, 83, Broward Art Guild, Ft. Lauderdale, 1983, galleries in N.Y.C., Phila., Palm Beach; one-man and group shows, Miami, Hollywood, Ft. Lauderdale, others; represented in permanent collections: New Brunswick Public Library, Jewish Community Center of L.I., Beach Haven, N.J., Public Service Gas & Electric Co., Newark, Terra Bank Bldg., Miami, Ryder Systems Bldg., Miami; numerous pvt. collections; judge art exhibits Roebling-Boehm Art Scholar competition, New Brunswick Area, 1962, Fedn. Women's Clubs, spring, 1964, Cinema Theatre Children's Exhibit, Menlo Park, N.J., 1968-69, Hollywood Guild Members' Show, 1980, 81, 82. Artist liaison chmn. Anshe Emeth Meml. Temple Art Show, 1959-60. Recipient Grumbacher 1st prize best in oils, 1960, 62; 2d prize, honorable mention Am. Artists Profl. League, Drew U., 1962, 64; best in watercolor South River (N.J.) Art Show, 1963; award Gold Coast Watercolor Soc. 5th Ann., 1980, 7th ann., 1982; Grumbacher award, 1986. Mem. Am. Artists Profl. League, Am. Fedn. Arts, Broward Art Guild, Gold Coast Water Color Soc., Fla. Watercolor Soc. (participating mem.), Am. Portrait Soc., Miami Watercolor Soc., Palm Beach Watercolor Soc. Home: 1703 Saint Andrews Rd Hollywood FL 33021

STOLL, WILLIAM HERMANN, realty executive; b. St. Louis, Aug. 7, 1944; s. Gottfried Alois and Mary Elizabeth (Lochrie) S.; m. Elizabeth Anne Stoll, Aug. 5, 1967. B.B.A., U. Ark.-Fayetteville, 1966; M.A. (grad. fellow), U. Tex.-Austin, 1970. Budget examiner Tex. Gov.'s Office, 1967-71; fin. grants adminstr. City Mgrs. Office, Austin, Tex., 1971-73; dir. program devel. Tex. Dept. Community Affairs, 1973-78; gen. mgr. AIS Data Systems, Inc., Austin, 1978-81; pres. Submariner, Inc., Austin, 1981-84; assoc. Manfred Kerschke Realtor, Austin, 1984—; chmn. Southwest Nat. Bank, Austin, 1980-82, also dir., Author digest: Texas Water Plan, 1967. Presiding judge Travis County Election Precinct, Austin, 1976-79; vice chmn. Austin Planning and Zoning Commn., 1976-80; fin. chmn. Travis County Democratic Party, 1977-78; chmn. North Austin Mental Health/Mental Retardation Com., 1975-76; rep. Goals for Austin Tomorrow, 1974-75; chmn. Allandale Neighborhood Assn., 1975-76. Mem. Austin C. of C., Austin Soc. Pub. Adminstrn., Sigma Phi Epsilon. Roman Catholic. Clubs: Kiwanis, Young Men's Bus. Home: 8704 Azalea Trail Austin TX 78759

STOLTZ, JOSEPHINE CARDENAS, real estate developer; b. Del Rio, Tex., Apr. 1, 1936; d. Rudolph and Amelia (Blyth) Cardenas; children—Larry, Jim, Barbara, Suzanne. Student U. Tex., 1970s. Lic. real estate broker, Tex. Real estate sales with various cos., Austin, Tex.; broker JCS Properties, Austin; real estate investor and developer Meisler/Stoltz Investments, Austin, 1978—. Named Hispanic Female of Yr., Mexican Am. Bus. and Profl. Assn., Austin, 1984. Mem. Nat. Assn. Indsl. and Office Parks, Nat. Assn. Corp. Real Estate Execs., Mexican Am. C. of C. Methodist. Avocations: travel; race horses. Home: 1707 Spyglass #49 Austin TX 78746 Office: Meisler/Stoltz 400 W 15th St Suite 1620 Austin TX 78701

STOMPS, WALTER EMERY, artist, educator; b. Hamilton, Ohio, July 13, 1929; s. Walter E. and Eva Rose (Malotte) S. B.F.A., Miami U., Oxford, Ohio, 1952; B.F.A. in Painting, The Sch. Art Inst. Chgo., 1959, M.F.A., 1963; postgrad. Syracuse U., 1962-63. Dir. Middletown Fine Arts Ctr., Ohio, 1961-62; prof. art Coll. of Dayton Art Inst., Ohio, 1963-75, Western Ky. U., Bowling Green, 1975—; work exhibited Evansville Mus. Art and Scis., 1985. Executed mural, Dayton, 1974; designer Bi-Centenial Celebration Print, A Patriots Colors, 1976. Recipient James Nelson Raymond award The Sch. of Art Inst. Chgo., 1959; Mid-Am. Exhbn. Painting, Owensboro Mus. Fine Art, Ky., 1979; Glenmore Distillery purchase award Owensboro Area Mus., 1981; Siegfried Weng purchase award Mid States Exhbn., Evansville Mus. Art and Scis., Ind., 1985. Avocation: Equitation. Office: Western Ky U College Heights Bowling Green KY 42101

STONE, CHARLES HUDSON, county official; b. Madison, Ala., Oct. 30, 1934; s. Roy Landess and Mae (Hudson) S.; m. Carolyn Phillips; children—Ronda Phillips Stone Myrick, Martha Lynn Stone Hewlett, Roy Landess. B.A., Auburn U., 1957. Farmer, Gurley, Ala., 1957-77; commr. Madison County Commn., Brownsboro, Ala., 1977—. Developer automated feeder for calves; inventor cotton duster-sprayer; pioneer mulch planting of soy beans. Chmn. Madison County Bd. Equalization, Madison County Com. for Adequate Rural and Community Fire Protection; vice-chmn. Community Resource Devel. Com.; trustee Madison County Sch. System; mem. steering com. Madison County Bd. Edn.; bd. dirs. Huntsville-Madison County Rural YMCA, Huntsville YMCA, Family Counseling Assn., Madison County Recreation Bd., Girl Scouts North Ala. Inc., Madison County Assn. Mental Health, Rocket City Credit Union, Huntsville-Madison County Clean Community System, Rural Sr. Services, Inc., Huntsville 2,000, Huntsville-Madison County Pub. Library Devel. Council; mem. adminstrv. bd. Gurley Methodist Ch.; mem. Huntsville Mus. Art, Ala. Soc. Crippled Children; mem. law planning com. U. Ala.; mem. Auburn U.-Madison County Com., Madison County Health Council. Named Outstanding Young Farmer Madison County, Outstanding Farmers Am., Outstanding Young Farmer Ala., Outstanding Young Farmer Am.; recipient Loyalty award VFW, Achievement awards Nat. Assn. Counties, 1977-85, others. Mem. Artificial Insemination Assn. (pres.), Assn. County Commns. (pres.), Outstanding Farmers Am., Future Farmers Am. (hon.), Madison County Cattlemen's Assn., New C. of C., Gurley Jaycees, Auburn U. Agrl. Alumni. Democrat. Methodist. Club: Huntsville Racquet. Avocations: fishing; hunting; horse back riding; restoring old log cabins. Office: 4273 Hwy 72E Brownsboro AL 35741

STONE, CHARLES NORMAN, pharmacy and surgical supply company executive, consultant; b. Marion, Ky., May 11, 1923; s. Norman Virgil and Effie (Davis) S.; m. Geneva Faye Twitchell, Nov. 24, 1949; children—Michael Kevin, Debra Diane, Kimberley Faye. B.S., Murray State U., 1948; B.S. in Pharmacy, St. Louis Coll. Pharmacy, 1951. Mgr. Lang Bros. Drug Co., Paducah, Ky., 1951-57, owner, mgr., 1957-72; pres. Stone-Lang Co., Paducah, 1972—; dir. Pharm. Pac K, Frankfort, Ky., 1984—; trustee KPERF Research Found., Frankfort, 1983—. Co-author code of ethics Nat. Hearing Aid Soc., 1983. Chmn. Ky. Bd. Licensing Hearing Aid Dealers, Frankfort, 1972-75, 76-80. Served with USAF, 1943-46. Mem. Ky. Pharmacists Assn. (dir. 1983—), First Dist. Pharmacists Assn. (pres. 1982-83, Pharmacist of Yr.), Nat. Assn. Retail Druggists (mem. steering com. 1985—), Am. Pharm. Assn., Hearing Aid Assn. Ky. (pres. 1978-81, Outstanding Pres.), Optimist Internat. (lt. gov. Ky., W.Va. Dist. 1969, Outstanding Leadership as Pres. 1967, Man of Yr. 1969, life mem.), Ky. Hist. Soc. Baptist. Club: Rolling Hills Country. Lodges: Am. Legion, Kiwanis. Home: 279 Old Orchard Rd Paducah KY 42001 Office: Stone-Lang Co 2620 Broadway Paducah KY 42001

STONE, HUBERT DEAN, journalist; b. Maryville, Tenn., Sept. 23, 1924; s. Archie Hubert and Annie (Cupp) S.; student Maryville Coll., 1942-43; B.A., U. Okla., 1949; m. Agnes Shirley, Sept. 12, 1953 (dec. Mar. 1973); 1 son, Neal Anson. Sunday editor Maryville-Alcoa Daily Times, 1949; mng. editor Maryville-Alcoa Times, 1949-78, editor, 1978—; v.p. Maryville-Alcoa Newspapers, Inc., 1960—; pres. Stonecraft, 1954—. Mem. mayor's adv. com. City of Maryville; mem. air service adv. com. Knoxville Met. Airport Authority; bd. dirs. United Fund of Blount County, 1961-63, 74-76, vice chmn. campaign, 1971-72, campaign chmn., 1973, v.p., 1974, pres., 1975; mem. Leadership Knoxville; vice chmn. Maryville Utilities Bd.; chmn. Blount County Long Range Planning for Sch. Facilities; mem. adv. com. Alternative Ctr. for Learning; chmn. adv. com. Maryville Coll.; bd. dirs. Blount County Historic Trust, Nat. Hillbilly Homecoming Assn., Friendsville Acad., 1968-73, Middle East Tenn. Regional Tourism Group; bd. dirs., treas. Smoky Mountain Passion Play Assn.; adv. bd. Harrison-Chilhowee Bapt. Acad. Served from pvt. to staff sgt. AUS, 1943-45. Decorated Bronze Star; named Outstanding Sr. Man of Blount County, 1970, 77, Ky. Col. Mem. Profl. Photographers of Am., Tenn. Profl. Photographers Assn., Internat. Postcard Distbrs. Assn., Great Smoky Mountains Natural History Assn., Ft. Loudoun Assn., Blount County Arts and Crafts Guild, Tenn. Jaycees (editor Tenn. Vol. 1954-55, life mem., sec.-treas. 1955-56), Jr. Chamber Internat. (senator), Maryville-Alcoa Jaycees (life mem., pres. 1953-54), Blount County (dir. 1980-83, v.p. 1971, 76, pres. 1977), Townsend (dir. 1969-71, 83-85, pres. 1983) chambers commerce, Tenn. Asso. Press News Execs. Assn. (v.p. 1973, pres. 1974), Asso. Press Mng. Editors Assn., Am. Legion, VFW, Chilhowee Bapt. Assn. (chmn. history com.) U. Okla. Alumni Assn. (life mem., pres. E. Tenn. chpt. 1954-55), Sigma Delta Chi (life; dir. E. Tenn. chpt.). Baptist (pres. trustees, deacon, chmn. nominating, evangelism, fin., personnel coms.). Club: Green Meadow Country, Masons, Kiwanis (Alcoa pres. 1969-70). Author articles in field. Home: 1510 Scenic Dr Maryville TN 37801 Office: 307 E Harper Ave Maryville TN 37803

STONE, JAMES HIRAM, oil co. exec.; b. N.Y.C., Dec. 20, 1925; s. Jacob Chauncey and Isabel (Green) S.; B.A., Williams Coll.; postgrad. in geology Tex. A&M U., 1950; children—Suzanne, Andrew, Thomas, Margaret. Owner, operator Stone Oil Corp., New Orleans, 1951—, chmn. bd., chief exec. officer, 1975—; underwriting mem. Lloyds of London; dir. Hibernia Nat. Bank. Bd. dirs. New Orleans Crime Commn., 1976—; mem. Pres.'s Council Tulane U.; trustee Med. Ctr. Served to capt. U.S. Marine Corp, 1943-46. Mem. Ind. Petroleum Assn. Am., New Orleans, Lafayette geol. socs., Ducks Unltd. (life). Republican. Episcopalian. Clubs: Los Angeles Rams Football (dir.), Cin. Country, Queen City (Cin.); Lake Placid (N.Y.); Palm Bay (Miami, Fla.); Keenland (Lexington, Ky.); Petroleum, Plimsoll, New Orleans Country (New Orleans). Home: 711 Bienville St New Orleans LA 70130 Office: Stone Oil Corp Pan Am Life Center Suite 2660 601 Poydras St New Orleans LA 70130

STONE, JESSE NEALAND, JR., university president, lawyer; b. Gibsland, La., June 17, 1924; m. Willie D. Anderson; children—Michael (dec.), Shonda. Grad. So. U., 1946, J.D., 1950. Dean, So. U. Law Sch., Baton Rouge, La., 1971-72; asst. supt. edn. State of La., 1972-74; pres. So. U. System, Baton Rouge, 1974-85; acting chmn. La. Adv. Com. to Pres.'s Cabinet Com. on Edn., 1971-72; assoc. dir. La. Commn. Human Relations, Rights and Responsibilities, 1966-70; interim justice La. State Supreme Ct., 1979; guest speaker various colls. and univs.; conferee and cons. at various seminars. Trustee Ben Johnson Charitable Trust; counsel NAACP, 1950, CORE, 1961-66, SCLC, 1957-66, So. U. Alumni Fedn., 1960-69. Author: Louisiana Report to the White House Conf. on Children and Youth, 1970, numerous articles and reports. Served with AUS, 1943-45. Recipient Anne Brewster Meml. award NAACP, 1964; Omega Man of Yr., 1966; Citizen of Yr. award Omega Psi Phi, 1966; Appreciation award ARC, 1973. Mem. La. Edn. Assn. (Disting. Service award 1969), Baton Rouge Bar Assn., NEA, Shreveport Bar Assn., La. Bar Assn. Office: So Univ and Agrl and Mech Coll So Br PO Baton Rouge LA 70813*

STONE, JOHN AUSTIN, nuclear chemist; b. Paintsville, Ky., Nov. 30, 1935; s. James William and Christine (Austin) S.; m. Helen Reynolds, June 2, 1968; children—Tracye Victoria, Philip Austin, Suzanne Reynolds. B.S. in Chemistry, with highest honors, U. Louisville, 1955; Ph.D., U. Calif.-Berkeley, 1963. Research chemist Savannah River Lab., E.I. duPont de Nemours & Co., Aiken, S.C., 1963-68, staff chemist, 1968-74, research staff chemist, 1974-81, research assoc., 1981—; traveling lectr. Oak Ridge Assoc. Univs., 1964-74. Served with USCG, 1955-57. Recipient Best Paper award Am. Ceramic Soc., 1982. Mem. Am. Phys. Soc., Am. Chem. Soc., Materials Research Soc. (chmn. steering com. Nuclear Waste Symposium 1980-81, chmn. program com. 1984, editor procs. 1985). Episcopalian. Assoc. editor Materials Letters mag., 1983—. Contbr. articles and reports to profl. jours. Home: 2221 Morningside Dr Augusta GA 30904 Office: Savannah River Lab Aiken SC 29808

STONE, LEON, banker; b. Rockdale, Tex., Feb. 27, 1914; s. Harley J. and Ella (Strelsky) S.; student Blinn Coll., Brenham, Tex, 1932, Sul Ross Coll., Alpine, Tex., 1934, U. Tex., 1935, Rutgers U., 1954; m. Bess Northington, Aug. 39, 1939; children—Pebble Stone Moss, Cherry J. Stone Wallin. With Brown & Root, Houston, 1936-37; Guggenheim-Goldsmith, Austin Tex., 1937-38; with Austin Nat. Bank, 1938—, pres., 1963—, also dir.; dean Southwestern Grad. Sch. Banking, So. Meth. U., Dallas; dir. Lockhart (Tex.) State Bank, First State Bank, Burnet, Tex., InterFirst Corp. Dallas; dir., chmn. exec. com. InterFirst Bank Austin, N.A. Vice chmn. Tchr. Retirement System Tex., 1956-77. Bd. dirs. Presbyn. Theol. Sem., 1958—, Mental Health and Mental Retardation Assn. 1965—, Seton Hosp., 1966—. Served to lt. col. U.S. Army, ETO. Named Boss of Yr., Credit Women of Austin, 1966. Mem. Am. Bankers Assn. (regional v.p. 1965—, exec. com., 1966—), Tex. Bankers Assn. (pres. 1973), Am. Inst. Banking (past pres.), Austin C. of C. (pres. 1968), Tex. Taxpayers Assn. (pres.). Clubs: Rotary, Masons, Shriners (Jester). Office: 501 Congress Ave Austin TX 78731

STONE, LEROY ALLEN, clinical psychologist, consultant; b. San Francisco, Sept. 13, 1931; s. George Clifford and Hilda Helen (Zillmer) S.; m. Patricia Joan Snyder, Dec. 27, 1957; 1 child, Erika Deidre. A.A., Santa Rosa Jr. Coll., 1951; A.B., San Jose State U., 1953, M.A., 1954; Ph.D., U. N.D., 1962. Asst. prof. Kans. State U., Manhattan, 1962-64, asst. dir. Student Counseling Ctr., 1962-64; chief research psychologist Mental Health Research Inst., Ft. Steilacoom, Wash., 1964-65; prof. community medicine U. N.D., Grand Forks, 1972-75, prof. psychology, 1965-75; dep. chief psychol. services Nat. Security Agy., Ft. Meade, Md., 1975—; cons. in field; pvt. practice forensic psychology, Harpers Ferry, W.Va., 1977—; pres. bd. dirs. Judgmetrics, Inc., Grand Forks, 1970-75. Author: Psychophysical Scaling Applications with Clinical and Educational Concerns, 1969; Readings in Contemporary Psychophysics and Scaling, 1969. Contbr. articles to profl. jours. Mem. Harpers Ferry Civil War Round Table, 1978—. Served with U.S. Army, 1955-56. Fellow NIMH, USPHS, 1966-68. Mem. Am. Psychol. Assn., Psychonomic Soc. Republican. Avocations: antique glass; print collecting. Home: 1629 Washington St PO Box 395 Harpers Ferry WV 25425 Office: Med Ctr Nat Security Agy 9800 Savage Rd Fort Meade MD 20755

STONE, LORENE HEMPHILL, sociology educator, researcher; b. Marshalltown, Iowa, Nov. 7, 1953; d. Albert Earl and Margaret Ann (Seward) Hemphill; m. Daniel Frost Stone, Dec. 30, 1977. B.S., Iowa State U., 1975; M.A. Wash. State U., 1978, Ph.D., 1980. Asst. prof. Central Mich. U., Mt. Pleasant, 1980-84; asst. prof. sociology Lamar U., Beaumont, Tex., 1984—. Chmn. Women's Aid Service, Mt. Pleasant, Mich., 1981-84. Central Mich. U. research fellow, 1983. Mem. Nat. Council Family Relations, Am. Sociol. Assn. Office: LaMar U Po Box 10026 Beaumont TX 77710

STONE, MARVIN JULES, physician, educator; b. Columbus, Ohio, Aug. 3, 1937; s. Roy J. and Lillian (Bedwinek) S.; student Ohio State U., 1955-58; S.M. in Pathology, U. Chgo., 1962, M.D. with honors, 1963; m. Jill Feinstein, June 29, 1958; children—Nancy Lillian, Robert Howard. Intern ward med. service Barnes Hosp., St. Louis, 1963-64, asst. resident, 1964-65; clin. asso. arthritis and rheumatism br. Nat. Inst. Arthritis and Metabolic Diseases, NIH, Bethesda, Md., 1965-68; resident in medicine, A.C.P. scholar Parkland Meml. Hosp., Dallas, 1968-69; fellow in hematology dept. internal medicine U. Tex. Southwestern Med. Sch., Dallas, 1969-70, instr. dept. internal medicine, 1970-71, asst. prof., 1971-73, asso. prof., 1974-76, clin. prof., 1976—, chmn. biomed. ethics com., 1979-81; adj. prof. biology So. Meth. U., Dallas, 1977—; dir. Charles A. Sammons Cancer Center, chief oncology, dir. immunology, co-dir. div. hematology-oncology Baylor U. Med. Center, Dallas, 1976—; mem. faculty and steering com. immunology grad. program Grad. Sch. Biomed. Scis., U. Tex. Health Sci. Center, Dallas, 1975-76, adj. mem., 1976—; v.p. med. staff Parkland Meml. Hosp., Dallas, 1982; Chmn. com. patient-aid Greater Dallas/Ft. Worth chpt. Leukemia Soc. Am., 1971-76, chmn. med. adv. com. Dallas/Ft. Worth chpt., 1978-80, med. dir. Dallas Met. dist., 1979-80; med. v.p. Dallas unit Am. Cancer Soc., 1977-78, pres., 1978-80. Served with USPHS, 1965-68. Diplomate Am. Bd. Internal Medicine. Named Outstanding Faculty Mem. Dept. Internal Medicine, Baylor U., 1977-78. Fellow A.C.P.; mem. AAAS, Am. Rheumatism Assn., Reticuloendothelial Soc., Am. Assn. Immunologists, AMA, Am. Fedn. Clin. Research, Internat. Soc. Hematology, Am. Soc. Hematology, N.Y. Acad. Scis., Council on Thrombosis, Am. Heart Assn. (established investigator 1970-75), Am. Soc. Clin. Oncology, Am. Assn. Cancer Research, Tex. Med. Assn., Dallas County Med. Soc., Am. Soc. Preventive Oncology, Fedn. Am. Scientists, So. Soc. Clin. Investigation, Phi Beta Kappa, Sigma Xi, Alpha Omega Alpha. Contbr. articles to profl. Jours., chpts. to books. Office: Charles A Sammons Cancer Center Baylor U Med Center 3500 Gaston Ave Dallas TX 75246

STONE, MARVIN LIVINGSTON, oil company executive; b. Oklahoma City, Dec. 22, 1924; s. Earl Livingston and Virginia (Heyser) S.; m. Margaret Ellen Burton, Dec. 24, 1945; children—Lelia Margaret, Martha Ellen, Ann Marie. B.S. in Petroleum Engring., Tex. A&M U., 1950, B.S. in Geol. Engring., 1950. Registered profl. engr., Tex., La. Petroleum engr. John W. Mecon, Houston, 1950-54; asst. drilling supt. Carnes W. Weaver, Houston, 1954-56; gen. supt. U.M. Harrison, Houston, 1956-59; pres. M.L. Stone Drilling Co., Inc., Saratoga, Tex., 1959—; owner M.L. Stone, San Antonio, 1959—. Served to 1st lt. USMCR, 1943-47. Mem. Soc. Petroleum Engrs. of AIME, Am. Assn. Petroleum Geologists, Soc. Profl. Earth Scientists. Republican. Baptist. Avocations: bridge; tennis. Home: PO Box 990 Kerrville TX 78029 Office: ML Stone 10000 IH 110 W Suite 406 San Antonio TX 78230

STONE, MARY ALICE, house products company sales organizer; b. Savannah, Ga., Oct. 27, 1940; d. Melvin Theodore and Alice May (Shaw) Pearson; m. Thomas Lanier Stone, Aug. 14, 1960; children—Thomas Lanier, Jr., Michael A., Vicki Lynn. Bookkeeper, Radix Microelectronics, Tustin, Calif., 1967-69; owner Smart Set Bookkeeping-Employment Agy., Santa Ana, Calif., 1969-72; cons. Princess House Products, Havelock, N.C., 1973-74, unit organizer, 1974-77, area organizer, New Bern, N.C. and Ga., 1977-82, sr. area organizer, Marietta, Ga., 1982—. Philanthropic chmn. Cystic Fibrosis Found., Tustin, Calif., 1971-72; vol. Craven Cherry Point Child Devel. Ctr., Havelock, 1972, Spl. Olympics, Marietta, 1983-84; choir dir. Christ Episcopal Ch., Havelock, 1973; cookie chmn. Craven Country Council Girl Scouts U.S., Recipient #1 Area award Princess House Field, 1980; named to Nat. Area Honor Roll Princess House Inc., 1985. Mem. Nat. Female Execs. Assn., Am. Soc. Profl. Exec. Women, Beta Sigma Phi (Woman of Yr. Havelock chpt. 1973), Beta Sigma Phi Internat. (life, order of Rose Degree 1979). Avocations: Swimming; reading; dancing. Office: Princess House Products PO Box 965065 Marietta GA 30066

STONE, MICHAEL ROBERT, association executive; freelance writer; b. East St. Louis, Ill., May 10, 1951; s. Robert Beckwith and Claire Dean (Kiggins) S.; m. Kristine Lynn Moss, Feb. 4, 1978; children—Leslie Michele, Stephanie Marie. B.J., U. Mo., 1973, B.A., 1974. Editor, Tribune, Fairview Heights, Ill., 1975-77; mng. editor Yelvington Publications, Mascoutah, Ill., 1977; enforcement officer City of Fairview Heights, 1977-81; exec. dir., editor Internat. Assn. Personnel in Employment Security, Frankfort, Ky., 1981—. Mem. Am. Soc. of Assn. Execs. Lodge: Lincoln Trail Optimists (pres. 1980) (Fairview Heights). Avocations: model railroading; water sports; golf. Home: 555 Poa Dr Frankfort KY 40601 Office: IAPES Exec Office 1801 Louisville Rd Frankfort KY 40601

STONE, ROBERT MERSHON, college dean; b. Freeburn, Ky., Apr. 11, 1941; s. Robert Carroll and Erma Lucille (Mershon) S.; m. Patricia Janelle Hall, June 17, 1962; children—Shawna Janelle, Robyne Carole, Scott Patrick. A.A.S., Sandhills Community Coll., Southern Pines, N.C., 1975-77; B.A., Atlantic Christian Coll., 1963; M.Div., Tex. Christian U., 1966; M.Ed., N.C. State U., 1975; Ph.D., Southeastern U., 1981. Ordained to ministry Christian Ch., 1963. Minister, 1st Christian Ch., Winston-Salem, N.C., 1967-68; regional sales mgr. Renn Enterprises, Ltd., Winston-Salem, also Ont., Can., 1968-71; counselor Sandhills Community Coll., 1971-77; exec. dir. Youth Help, Inc., Wilmington, N.C., 1977-83; dean student devel. Catawba Valley Tech. Coll., Hickory, N.C., 1983—; pres. Community Alts. for Youth, N.C., 1982-83. Bd. dirs. Community Arts Council, Southern Pines, 1975-77; commr. Southern Pines Housing Authority, 1975-77; mem. N.C. Gov.'s Task Force on Children and Youth, 1980-81; active Guardian Ad Litem Program, Hickory, 1985—. Mem. Nat. Assn. Student Personnel Adminstrs., N.C. Assn. for Counseling and Devel., N.C. Coll. Personnel Assn., N.C. Student Personnel Assn., Hickory C. of C. (quality of edn. com. 1985—), Greater Hickory Tennis Assn., Catawba Valley Ski Club. Avocations: skiing, whitewater canoeing, flying, golf, other sports. Home: 140 27th Ave Dr NW Hickory NC 28601 Office: Catawba Valley Tech Coll Hwy 64-70 Hickory NC 28601

STONE, ROCKY, school administrator; b. Corona, Calif., Nov. 27, 1952; s. Robert James Stone and Thelma (McGill) Findley; m. Cheryl Leslie Clark, Dec. 24, 1978 (div. 1980); 1 child, Leslie. B.S., Northeastern State U., 1976, M.S., 1984. Tchr., Checotah Schs., Okla., 1976-81; tchr. Kiefer Schs., Okla., 1981-83, prin., 1983—. Democrat. Home: Box 803 Kiefer OK 74041 Office: Kiefer Schs Box 428 Kiefer OK 74041

STONE, TIMOTHY LEROY, architect, consultant; b. Mpls., Nov. 4, 1940; s. Charlton L. and Elizabeth J. (McFarlane) S.; m. Gail L. Johnson, June 23, 1962 (div. Jan. 1979); children—Melanie, Christopher; m. Carol E. Barnett, July 18, 1981. B.A., U. Minn., 1962, B. Architecture, 1964; M. Inst. Planning, 1966. Registered architect, Minn., Fla., N.C., Nat. Council Archtl. Registration Bds. Assoc. prof. U. Minn.-Mpls., 1963-65; assoc. Horan, Hustad Assocs., Mpls., 1965-68, Rapson & Assocs., Mpls., 1968-78, Pink and Assocs., Mpls., 1978-80; prin., chief exec. officer Archtl. Resources Corp., Ft. Myers, Fla., 1980—, also dir. dir. BSW Corp., Ft. Myers. Mem. adv. bd. Minn. Assn. Retarded Citizens, Mpls., 1966; Hennipen County Met. Planning adviser, Mpls., 1979-80; commr. City of Chanhassen Planning Bd., Mpls., 1975-80, City of Chanhassen Human Rights Bd., 1974-75. Mem. AIA (Merit Design award 1974, 75, 76, 77), Nat. Council Archtl. Registration Bd., Constrn. Specifications Inst. Lodge: Kiwanis. Office: Archtl Resources Corp 1500 Royal Palm Sq Blvd Fort Myers FL 33907

STONEBROOK, MARGARET ANN, librarian; b. Sikeston, Mo., Nov. 27, 1929; d. Alphonso and Audrey Elizabeth (Williams) Swaim; m. Richard Eugene Dietz, Apr. 5, 1952 (dec. 1966); children—Heather Dietz Kleinhenz, Brian R., Brent H.; m. Phillip Stanley Stonebrook, June 14, 1970. Student U. Akron, 1947-48; B.S. in Elem. Edn., Rollins Coll., 1979; M.L.S., U. South Fla., 1983. Reservationist, ticket agt. Capital Airlines, Cleve., 1951-52; service rep. Ohio Bell Telephone Co., Akron, 1952-54; social worker Summit County Ct. Domestic Relations, Akron, 1967-73; children's library asst. Eau Gallie Pub. Library, Melbourne, Fla., 1973-78, children's librarian, 1978-83; reference librarian Satellite Beach Pub. Library (Fla.), 1983—; chmn. children's librarians Brevard County (Fla.), 1979. Implemented unique Toddler Time Program in pub. library, 1980-83. Former mem. televised children's program Puppeteers of Am., 1982. Pres., Women's Assn. Oak Hill United Presbyn. Ch., Akron, 1960; deacon Eastminster Presbyn. Ch., Indialantic, Fla., 1981-82, 86—. Contbr. articles to profl. jours. Mem. Fla. Library Assn. (rec. sec. bibliotherapy caucus 1983), Library Assn. Brevard (v.p. 1985-86), ALA, Literacy Council of South Brevard (founder, charter mem. 1984), Beta Phi Mu, Phi Kappa Phi, Zeta Tau Alpha (pres. bd. dirs. 1958-59, historian 1979-82). Republican. Clubs: Solo Parents (pres. 1968-69), Parents Without Ptnrs. (profl. adv. bd. 1970-72). Home: 404 Surf Rd Melbourne Beach FL 32951 Office: Satellite Beach Pub Library 565 Cassia Blvd Satellite Beach FL 32937

STONEHAM, JOHN ANDERSON, investment company executive; b. Atlanta, June 23, 1943; s. Jack Johnston and Elizabeth Watson (Slowe) S.; m. Harriet Higginbotham, June 12, 1976; children—Davitt, Harrison, Elizabeth. B.A., Emory U., 1965; M.B.A., So. Meth. U., 1967. Mem. staff Am. Embassy, London, 1966; portfolio mgr. Great Commonwealth Life Ins. Co., Dallas, 1968-70, Jack J. Stoneham & Co., Dallas, 1970-76; pres. Stoneham Investment Co., Dallas, 1976—; pres. Dallas Cotton Exchange, 1979-80. Bd. dirs. The 500 Inc., 1969; trustee Endowment of the Episcopate Diocese of Dallas, 1976—; bd. dirs. Family Guidance Ctr. Dallas. Mem. Dallas Soc. Fin. Analysts. Episcopalian. Clubs: Brook Hollow Golf, The Dallas, Lansdowne, Solid Comfort Fishing.

STONESIFER, JOSEPH NOVAK, management and administration specialist; b. Oak Park, Ill., Feb. 24, 1914; s. Joseph Bernard and Bessie Sadie (Novak) S.; A.A., Morton Jr. Coll., 1933; B.S., U. Ill., 1936; M.A., George Washington U., 1946; A.B.D. in Adminstrn. and Edn., Am. U., 1973; m. Jean Ann Fisher, Mar. 5, 1955; children—Joseph Novak, John Dewitt, Jean Ann. Wholesale rep. Armour & Co., Chgo., 1932-34; personnel classification analyst CSC, Washington, 1935-38; dir. orgn. U.S. Maritime Commn., 1938-46; dir. personnel U.S. Naval Air Sta., Oahu, Hawaii, 1939-40; dir. adminstrn. Office of Chief Naval Ops. and Office of Sec. Navy, Washington, 1946-50; planning officer Office of Adminstrn., CAA, Washington, 1950-54; moblzn. liaison officer Exec. Office of Pres., Washington, 1954-59; dir. mgmt. studies FAA, Washington, 1959-69; coordinator computer applications Dept. Transp., Washington, 1965-69; dir. orgn. Exec. Office of the Pres., Washington, 1966-68; faculty George Washington U., Washington, 1955-71, asso. prof. bus. and pub. adminstrn., 1969—. Asso. prof. Central Mich. U., 1974-76; propr. Janus Enterprises, cons. on mgmt., Falls Church, Va., 1965—; dir. manpower devel. Fairfax Community Action Program, 1977-79; exec. dir. No. Va. Consortium for Med. Edn., 1979—. Served to lt. comdr. USNR, 1942-46; mem. Res. (ret.). Mem. Am. Assn. Sch. Adminstrs., Am. Soc. Personnel Adminstrn. (accredited), Internat. Personnel Mgmt. Assn., Am. Soc. Public Adminstrn., Soc. for Advancement Mgmt., Am. Psychol. Assn., Am. Assn. for Higher Edn., Am. Assn. Sch. Adminstrs., Am. Ednl. Research Assn., Acad. Mgmt., Am. Polit. Sci. Assn., Beta Beta Tau, Phi Delta Kappa. Club: Toastmasters Internat. (pres. 1950-51). Author: Background and Success of Classification Analysts, 1950; The Executive Officer's Handbook, 1959; Selective Bibliography for Personnel Management, 1960; Conduct of Organization Review Programs, 1969; Regulatory Functions in the Federal Government, 1970; Solving Broad Management Problems, 1975; contbr. articles to profl. jours. Home: 3137 Valley Ln Falls Church VA 22044 Office: Janus Enterprises Falls Church VA 22044

STORIN, EDWARD MICHAEL, editor; b. Providence, Dec. 4, 1929; s. Edmund Aloysius and Evelyn Ruth (O'Brien) S.; B.A., U. Miami, 1951; m. Virginia Mae Robak, Feb. 7, 1953; children—Kathy Lynn, Michael, Robert, Edward. With Miami Herald, 1951—, asst. city editor, 1963-64, night exec. sports editor, 1964-68, exec. sports editor, 1968-77, asst. mng. editor, 1977-83, assoc. mng. editor, 1983—. Served with USNR, 1952-54. Mem. Iron Arrow, Omicron Delta Kappa, Sigma Delta Chi, Sigma Alpha Epsilon. Home: 825 Bella Vista St Coral Gables FL 33156 Office: 1 Herald Plaza Miami FL 33101

STORM, CHRISTOPHER KNOX, real estate developer; m. Amarillo, Tex., Mar. 7, 1951; s. Frank Joseph and Sarah Elizabeth (Knox) S.; m. Julie Catherine Peterson, Nov. 8, 1975; children—Christopher Knox, George Michael, Andrew Murchison. B.B.A., So. Meth. U., 1973. Vice pres. Robert S. Folsom Investments, Dallas, 1972-76; sr. v.p. Vantage Cos., Dallas, 1976-79; exec. v.p. First Southwest Equity Corp., 1979-81; pres. Knox Capital Corp., Amarillo, Tex., 1981—. Mem. Mensa. Republican. Presbyterian. Office: 630 Fisk Bldg Amarillo TX 79101

STORMONT, RICHARD MANSFIELD, hotel executive; b. Chgo., Apr. 4, 1936; s. Daniel Lytle and E. Mildred (Milligan) S.; B.S., Cornell U., 1958; m. Virginia Louellen Walters, Nov. 21, 1959; children—Stacy Lee, Richard Mansfield, John Frederick. Food cost analyst, sales rep. Edgewater Beach Hotel, Chgo., 1957-58, asst. sales mgr. Marriott Motor Hotels, Inc., Washington, 1962-64; dir. sales Marriott Hotel, Atlanta, 1964-68, resident mgr., 1969-71, gen. mgr. Marriott Hotel, Dallas, 1971-73, Phila., 1973-74; gen. mgr., 1974-79, v.p. Marriott Hotels, Washington, 1980-84; pres. Hardin Mgmt. Co., 1979-80; pres. Stormont Cos. Inc., Atlanta, 1984—; Pres., Atlanta Conv. and Visitors Bur., 1975-76, chmn. bd., 1976-77; bd. dirs., exec. com. Central Atlanta Progress, Inc.; bd. dirs. Better Bus. Bur.; mem. exec. council Boy Scouts Am. Served to lt. (j.g.) USNR, 1959-62. Recipient Disting. Salesman of Yr. award Marriott, 1967. Mem. Sales and Mktg. (v.p. 1968, exec. v.p. 1969-70, pres. Atlanta chpt. 1970-71), Atlanta C. of C. (v.p.), Ga. Bus. and Industry Assn. (dir.), Atlanta Hotel-Motel Assn. (pres. 1976-77), Hotel Sales Mgmt. Assn. (past chpt. pres.), Ga. Hospitality and Travel Assn. (founder, dir. 1977-79), Cornell Soc. Hotelmen (pres. Ga. chpt. 1976), Pi Sigma Epsilon, Phi Kappa Psi. Rotarian. Home: 3633 Haddon Hall Rd Atlanta GA 30327 Office: 1160 Old Johnson Ferry Rd Atlanta GA 30319

STORRER, BRADLEY RAY, architect; b. Dearborn, Mich., Oct. 31, 1930; s. Fredrick Ray and Margaret (Pitts) S.; m. Helen Patricia Strieter, Apr. 27, 1957 (div. 1978); children—David Ray, Carolyn Beth, Brian Fredrick. Frank Lloyd Wright Found. fellow, Taliesin fellow U. Mich. Coll. Architecture & Design, Ann Arbor, 1948-49, 1951. Registered architect, Mich., S.C., Miss., Ala.; cert. Nat. Council Archtl. Registration Bds., 1975. Prin., Bradley Ray Storrer/Architect, Dearborn, Mich., 1957-61; ptnr. Schmiedeke & Storrer/Architects, Dearborn, 1961-65; assoc. Smith & Smith Assocs., Royal Oak, Mich., 1965-68; head specifications, research Bertrand Goldberg Assocs., Chgo., 1968-72; dir. prodn. LBC&W, Inc., Columbia, S.C., 1972-76; prin. Bradley Ray Storrer, AIA, Columbia, 1976-78; prin., dir. architecture Assoc. Cons., Ltd., Meridian, Miss., 1978—; pres. Assoc. Cons. Ala., Inc., 1984—; cons. in constrn. documentation, 1976-78; mem. comml. panel Am. Arbitration Assn., 1982—. Mem. LBC&W Fed. Credit Union, Columbia, pres. 1974-75. Recipient Cert. of Appreciation, Dearborn C. of C., 1968. Mem. AIA, Miss. chpt. AIA, Meridian C. of C., Meridian Mfrs. Assn. Ind. Republican. Lodge: Rotary (bd. dirs. 1984—) (Meridian). Archtl. designs include Dr. James R. Adams Residence (Dearborn, Mich.) 1958; First Baptist Ch. of Dearborn, 1963; Central Methodist Ch., Meridian, 1982, Lauderdale County Tng. Ctr. for the Mentally Retarded, 1982. Home: PO Box 3655 Meridian MS 39301 Office: Assoc Cons Ltd PO Box 5654 Meridian MS 39301

STORRS, THOMAS IRWIN, former banker; b. Nashville, Aug. 25, 1918; s. Robert Williamson and Addie Sue (Payne) S.; B.A., U. Va., 1940; M.A., Harvard, 1950, Ph.D., 1955; m. Kitty Stewart Bird, July 19, 1948; children—Thomas, Margaret. With Fed. Res. Bank, Richmond, Va., 1934-60, v.p. charge research, 1957-59, v.p. charge Charlotte br., N.C., 1959-60; exec. v.p. NCNB Nat. Bank, Charlotte, 1960-67, vice chmn. bd. dirs., 1967-69, pres., 1969-73, chmn. bd., 1977-83; pres. NCNB Corp., 1968-73, chmn. bd., 1974-83; dir. Black and Decker Mfg. Co. Pres., Fed. Adv. Council, 1974-75. Trustee, chmn. U. N.C., Charlotte, Davidson (N.C.) Coll. Served to lt. comdr. USNR, 1941-45, 51-52; comdr. Res., ret. Mem. N.C. Citizens Assn. (pres. 1971-72), Assn. Res. City Bankers (pres. 1980-81). Episcopalian. Clubs: Quail Hollow Country, Charlotte Country, Charlotte City. Home: 2633 Richardson Dr Charlotte NC 28211 Office: One NCNB Plaza Charlotte NC 28255

STORY, EDWARD T., JR., oil company executive; b. Hillsboro, Tex., Nov. 7, 1943; s. Edward T. and Mildred Mae (Holland) S.; B.S. in Acctg. cum laude, Trinity U., 1965; M.B.A., U. Tex., 1966; children—Elisabeth Claire, Emily Catherine, Sara Marie. Fin. analyst Esso Eastern Inc., N.Y.C., 1966-68; acctg. mgr. Esso Thailand-Bangkok, 1968-70; asst. controller Esso Standard Sekiyu-Tokyo, Japan, 1970-73; controller Esso Asia Services, Inc., Singapore, 1973-75; refining controller Exxon Co., Houston, 1975-78, exploration and prodn. controller, 1978; v.p. fin., chief fin. officer Superior Oil, Houston, 1979-81; vice chmn. bd., dir. Conquest Exploration Co., Houston, 1981—; dir. Madison Resources Inc. Chmn., Yokohama Internat. Sch. Bd., 1972-73; treas. Superior Oil Polit. Action Com., 1980-81; bd. dirs. Chrysalis Repertory Dance Co. Recipient Wall St. Jour. Scholastic Achievement award, 1965. Mem. Fin. Execs. Inst., Am. Petroleum Inst., Mid-Continent Oil and Gas Assn., Alpha Chi, Phi Kappa Phi, Beta Alpha Psi. Republican. Methodist. Club: Texas. Office: PO Box 4512 Houston TX 77210

STORY, MICHAEL LYNN, geologist, consultant, hydrocarbon mud logger; b. Dallas, Dec. 17, 1946; s. Ernest Benjamin and Frances Earle (Craig) S.; m. Susanna Rosemarie Van Der Waal, July 6, 1972 (div. June 1975); m. Patricia Ann Hart, June 19, 1981; 1 child, William Michael. B.S. in Geology, U. Tex.-Arlington, 1970. Mud engr., logger Baroid, Oklahoma City, 1971-73; mud engr., logger, advanced drilling tech. engr. Baroid Internat., Houston, 1973-77; directional driller BOCO de Venezuela, Cuidad Ojeda, 1977-78; advanced drilling tech. engr., logger Baroid Petroleum Services, Lafayette, La., 1978-81; cons. mud logger Stivers Cons., Inc., Graham, Tex., 1982-84; cons. geologist Diamond S. Enterprises, Eliasville, Tex., 1984—. Mem. Am. Assn. Petroleum Geologists (jr.). Republican. Baptist. Avocations: fishing; camping; casting natal horoscopes. Home and Office: PO Box 615 Eliasville TX 76038

STOTESBERY, WILLIAM DAVID, computer technology corporation executive; b. Pitts., Sept. 30, 1952; s. Thomas J. and Joan (Beegle) S.; m. Mary C. Dudley, Jan. 21, 1975. B.A., Tex. Christian U., 1974; M.Pub.Affairs, U. Tex., 1977. Sr. cons. Peat, Marwick & Mitchell, Austin, Tex., 1977-82; pvt. mgmt. cons., Austin, 1982-83; dir. govt., pub. affairs Microelectronics & Computer Tech. Corp., Austin, 1983—. Contbr. articles to profl. jours. Mem. Austin Community Devel. Commn., 1978-81; exec. com. Leadership Austin, 1983—, curriculum chmn., 1983-84; bd. dirs. Austin Women's Ctr., 1983-85. Office: Microelectronics & Computer Tech Corp 9430 Research Blvd Austin TX 78759

STOUDEMIRE, STERLING A(UBREY), ret. educator; b. Concord, N.C., Sept. 4, 1902; s. Palmer and Frances (Cranford) S.; A.B., U. N.C., 1923, M.A., 1924, Ph.D., 1930; m. Irene Slate, 1925 (dec. 1940); 1 dau., Marian S. (Mrs. James A. Hawkins); m. 2d, Mary Arthur Billups, 1946; 1 son, Sterling Cranford. Instr. Spanish, U. N.C., 1924-30, asst. prof. Spanish, 1930-35; asso. prof. Spanish, 1935-41, prof. Spanish, 1941-73, prof. emeritus, 1973—, head dept. Romance langs., 1949-64. Served as lt. comdr. USNR, 1942-45. Mem. Modern Lang. Assn., S. Atlantic Modern Lang. Assn. (pres. 1962), Am. Assn. Tchrs. Spanish and Portuguese, Am. Name Soc., Phi Gamma Delta. Episcopalian. Author articles on Spanish Romanticism, Italian opera in Spain; author and editor Spanish texts and anthologies. Translator: Oviedo's Natural History of the West Indies, 1959; Christian Doctrine (Pedro de Cordoba), 1970. Home: 712 Gimghoul Rd Chapel Hill NC 27514

STOUDENMIRE, WILLIAM WARD, lawyer; b. Charlotte, N.C., Apr. 8, 1944; s. Sterling and Betty Zane (Scott) S. B.A. in Polit. Sci., Furman U., 1966; J.D., U. S.C., 1970. Bar: Ala. 1970, U.S. Dist. Ct. (so. dist.) Ala. 1970, U.S. Ct. Appeals (5th cir.) 1971, U.S. Supreme Ct. 1973, U.S. Tax Ct. 1982, U.S. Ct. Appeals (11th cir.) 1982, U.S. Ct. Appeals (D.C. cir.) 1982, D.C. bar 1983. Sole practice, Mobile, Ala., 1982—; legal research asst. Select Com. on Crime, U.S. Ho. of Reps., 1969. Mem. Leadership Mobile Adv. Council on Govt., 1982; vice chmn. Mobile County Republican Exec. Com., 1976-81, chmn., 1981-86; mem. Ala. Rep. Exec. Com., 1979—, vice chmn., 1985—. Served with USCGR, 1966-72. Mem. Mobile Bar Assn. (law day com. 1974-78, chmn. 1977, del. young lawyers sect. ABA conv. 1976, 77), Ala. State Bar (law day com. 1975-78, chmn. 1978), ABA (internat. sect. human rights subcom. 1975—, chmn. 1976-79), Internat. Bar Assn., Phi Delta Phi. Episcopalian. Home: 212 C Nack Ln Mobile AL 36608 Office: Dauphin Ctr Office Plaza 2864 Dauphin St Mobile AL 36616

STOUGH, FURMAN CHARLES, bishop; b. Montgomery, Ala., July 11, 1928; s. Furman Charles and Martha Elizabeth (Turnipseed) S.; B.A., U. of South, 1951, B.D., 1955, D.D., 1971; m. Margaret Dargan McCaa, May 12, 1951; 2 children. Ordained priest Episcopal Ch., 1955, rector St. Andrew's Ch., Sylacauga, Ala., St. Mary's Ch., Childersburg, Ala., 1955-59, Grace Ch., Sheffield, Ala., 1959-65; priest in charge All Souls Ch., Machinato, Okinawa, 1965-68; missioner, Ala., 1968-70; rector St. John's Ch., Decatur, Ill., 1970-71; bishop Diocese of Ala., 1971—. Office: 521 20th St Birmingham AL 35203*

STOUGH, JOAN B., palynologist; b. Washington, Feb. 6, 1932; d. Bert Ray and Mary Edith (Carruthers) Stough. B.A., U. Colo., 1954, M.A., 1957. Palynologist, Exxon Products Research, Houston, 1957-67, Bordeaux, France, 1967, Houston, 1968-71; palynologist Exxon Co., USA, Houston, 1972-83, supr. palynology 1984—. Mem. Am. Assn. Stratigraphic Palynologists, Am. Assn. Petroleum Geologists, AAAS, Palaeontol. Assn. Office: Exxon Co USA PO Box 2180 Houston TX 77001

STOUT, BILL A., agricultural engineering educator; b. Grant, Nebr., July 9, 1932; s. Homer and Gertrude (Thornton) S.; m. Rita Lee Hurlburt, June 22, 1951; children—Jo Ellen, Craige. B.S., U. Nebr., 1954; M.S., Mich. State Coll., 1955; Ph.D., Mich. State U., 1959. Registered profl. engr., Mich., Tex. With John Deere Waterloo Tractor Works, Iowa, 1953; mem. faculty Mich. State U., East Lansing, 1954-81, prof. agrl. engring., 1966-81; prof. Tex. A&M U., College Station, 1981—; farm power and machinery specialist FAO, Rome, 1963-64; vis. prof. U. Calif.-Davis, 1969-70, energy research and extension, 1975-79. Contbr. articles to profl. jours. Fellow AAAS, Am. Soc. Agrl. Engrs.; mem. Nat. Soc. Profl. Engrs. Patentee in field. Office: Agrl Engring Dept Tex A&M U College Station TX 77843

STOUT, JOSEPH EARL, state official; b. Lake Charles, La., Apr. 27, 1927; s. Charles Earl and Mabel (Fargue) S.; student U. Tenn., 1960, La. State U., 1965, FBI Nat. Acad., 1967, Tex. A&M U., 1969; m. Dora Elaine Cole, Dec. 8, 1951; 1 child, Martha Jane. Patrolman, Lake Charles (La.) Police Dept., 1948-49, sgt., 1949-53, detective sgt., 1953-56, capt., 1956-65, chief, 1965-74; mem. La. Bd. Parole, 1975—; vice chmn. adv. com. La. State U. Law Enforcement Tng., 1965, coordinator tng., 1980—; mem. Commn. on Law Enforcement Standards and Edn., 1969; mem. La. Commn. Law Enforcement Adminstrn. of Criminal Justice, Com. on Law Enforcement, 1969-71; chmn. Red Carpet Com., 1968. Bd. dirs. S.W. Guidance Council. Recipient recognition certificate of merit Gov. La., 1971, certificate of merit La. State U., 1971, Tourism award Lake Charles Assn. Commerce, 1967, Law Enforcement award Optimist Internat., 1968. Mem. La. Assn. Chiefs Police (pres. 1967-68), La. Peace Officers Assn. (pres. 1970-71), Internat. Assn. Chiefs Police (chmn. membership com. 1966-68), Municipal Police Officers Assn., FBI Nat. Acad. Grads. (3d v.p. La. chpt. 1971-72, pres. La. chpt. 1974), Greater Lake Charles C. of C. Methodist (dir. 1970-72). Rotarian. Club: Buccaneer (dir. 1971-72). Home: 9803 Dwyerwood Ave Baton Rouge LA 70809 Office: Law Enforcement Tng Program Pleasant Hall La State U Baton Rouge LA 70803

STOVALL, C. Y. (BUNNY), oil and gas broker; b. Brownfield, Tex., Jan. 19, 1935; d. Elmer Clay and Bernice Arlene (Donathan) Griffith; student pub. schs., Idalou, Tex.; m. Leland Zane Stovall, June 14, 1953; children—Sabrina D. Stovall Linn, Leighland Shawn. Prodn. mgr., sales mgr. Tex. Mesquite, Mesquite Daily News, 1964-74, prodn. mgr., 1965-74, account exec., 77; mgr. div. Mgmt. Recruiters Dallas, Inc., with Search Group, Lineback Assocs. div., 1977—, v.p. mktg. devel., public relations, ops. and energy ops., 1981—, also dir.; v.p. ops., founder MRDI Mktg. Div., Lineback Assocs., 1980-81; founder, pres. Stovall/Lineback Assocs., 1981-83; founder, propr. C.Y. Stovall, Inc., oil and gas broker, Dallas, 1983; founder, propr. Artemisia Inc., Dallas, 1983—, Zane-Stovall Inc., 1983—; tchr. offset printing. Tchr. Sunday sch. Northridge Baptist Ch., 1961-75, Methodist Ch., 1968-71. Named Nat. S.W. Account Exec. of Yr., 1975-79; recipient Gold Chip All-Time Sales award, 1980, Pres.'s award and mem. Million Dollar Club, 1980, No. 1 Female and Male Sales award, 1980. Accredited account exec. Mem. Bus. Women Dallas. Republican. Club: Order Eastern Star. Home: Route 2 209 N Jobson St Sunnyvale TX 75182 Office: I Energy Sq Suite 1218 Dallas TX 75206

STOVALL, GUY FRANKLIN, JR., investment executive; b. El Campo, Tex., Jan. 13, 1934; s. Guy Franklin and Edith I. Stovall; B.B.A., U. Houston, 1956; m. Kay Kuhn, Feb. 7, 1956; children—Guy Franklin III, Becky, Linda, David, Eric. Trader in oil, land, cattle, rice investments; dir., chmn. bd. 1st Nat. Bank, El Campo, Tex. Trustee Gulf Coast Med. Found., Wharton County Jr. Coll. Found., Tex. Scottish Rite Hosp. for Crippled Children, Dallas, also numerous trusts. Recipient Elk of Yr. award, 1969-70; Comdr.'s award for Pub. Service, U.S. Dept. Army, 1985. Mem. Tex. and Southwestern Cattle Raisers Assn. (dir. 1984). Methodist (trustee 1965-77). Home: El Campo TX 77437 Office: 202 E Jackson St El Campo TX 77437

STOVALL, JAMES THOMAS, III, wood products company executive; b. Athens, Ga., Mar. 14, 1948; s. James Thomas and Isabella (Cox) S.; m. Mildred Stringer, Sept. 17, 1967; children—James Thomas IV, Benjamin Clark. B.S. in Forestry, U. Ga., 1969. Area forester Union Camp Corp., Homerville, Ga., 1970-72; procurement forester Allied Timber Co., Jesup, Ga., 1972-74; pres., chief exec. officer B & M Wood Products Inc., Manor, Ga., 1974—. Sunday sch. tchr. Bapt. Ch., Homerville, 1974—; scoutmaster Boy Scouts Am., Homerville, 1985; mem. Republican Nat. Com., 1985. Mem. Am. Wood Preservers Inst. (exec. com. 1985), Clinch C. of C., NAM, So. Pressure Treaters Assn., So. Forest Products Assn. Club: Exchange (reporter 1974). Lodge: Lions. Avocations: photography; camping; fishing. Home: 603 W Dame Ave Homerville GA 31634 Office: B & M Wood Products Inc Box 176 Manor GA 31550

STOVALL, JOHN CHAILLE, JR., dentist; b. Baton Rouge, La., Jan. 4, 1950; s. John Chaille Sr. and Ruby Pershing (Peyton) S.; m. Charlene Ann Sperling, Apr. 10, 1976; 1 child, Zachary Lane. D.D.S., La. State U., 1976. Gen. practice dentistry, Baton Rouge, 1976—. Mem. Nat. Audubon Soc., Nature Conservancy, Sierra Club, Am. Dental Assn., La. State Dental Assn., East Baton Rouge Parish Dental Assn. Office: 6780 Florida Blvd Baton Rouge LA 70806

STOVALL, RANDALL HOWARD, biology educator; b. Norman, Okla., Feb. 3, 1951; s. Jack W. and Dorothy L. S.; m. L. Laraine Kaminsky, Aug. 12, 1977. B.S., U. Tex.-Arlington, 1973, M.A. in Biology, 1975; Ph.D. in Zoology, Okla. State U., 1982. Grad. teaching asst. biology dept. U. Tex.-Arlington, 1973-75; grad. research asst. U. Tex. Med. Ctr., Houston, 1975-77; instr. biology North Harris County Coll., Houston, 1977-78; grad. teaching asst. zoology dept. Okla. State U., Stillwater, 1978-79; asst. prof. biology N.W. Okla. State U., Alva, 1979-80; adj. biology instr. Pasco-Hernando Community Coll., New Port Richey, Fla., 1980-82; program biologist Environ. Studies Ctr., Hillsborough Community Coll., Tampa, Fla., 1981-82; prof. biology Valencia Community Coll., Orlando, Fla., 1982—. Mem. AAAS, Am. Soc. Ichthyologists and Herpetologists, Soc. for Study Amphibians and Reptiles, Fla. Acad. Sci., League Environ. Educators Fla., Fla. Marine Sci. Edn. Assn., Fla. Assn. Community Colls., Sigma Xi, Phi Sigma. Editor: Proc. 8th Ann. Conf. on Wetlands Restoration and Creation, 1982; contbr. articles to sci. jours. Office: Valencia Community College Orlando FL 32802

STOVER, BONNIE, bank executive; b. Corsicana, Tex., Dec. 19, 1949; d. Virgle Edell and Ruby Juanita Widener; B.S., Tex. Woman's U., 1971; postgrad. U. Tex., Arlington, 1972-73. With First Nat. Bank of Corsicana, 1974—, asst. v.p., 1977-79, v.p., 1979—; dir. Old Reliable Mortgage Co., Inc., Corsicana. Bd. dirs. Camp Fire Inc., Corsicana, 1981; co-chmn. United Fund Residential Dr., Corsicana, 1981, chmn., 1985. Nat. Assn. Bank Women regional scholar, 1979. Mem. Nat. Assn. Bank Women (treas. 1983-84, 2d vice chmn. chpt 1984-85, pres. 1985-86), Mortgage Bankers Assn. Am., Nat. Homebuilders Assn., Tex. Mortgage Bankers Assn., Ambassadors C. of C. (chmn. 1985-86; Pres.'s Cup 1985), Nat. Fedn. Bus. and Profl. Women (dist. dir.). Baptist. Office: 100 N Main Corsicana TX 75110

STOVER, ENOS LOY, environmental engineering consulting company executive; b. Shawnee, Okla., Nov. 19, 1948; s. Euell Lavoy and Geneva Nadine (Laughlin) S.; m. Penelope Susan Crites, May 27, 1972; children—Suzanna Rae, Aaron Lee, Ted Ross. B.S. in Civil Engring., Okla. State U.-Stillwater, 1971, M.S., 1972, Ph.D., 1974. Registered profl. engr., Okla., Pa., Mass. Supr. process devel. Roy F. Weston, Inc., West Chester, Pa., 1974-78; dir. research and devel. Metcalf & Eddy, Inc., Boston, 1978-80; assoc. prof. Okla. State U., Stillwater, 1980-84, prof., 1984—; pres. Stover & Assocs., Stillwater, 1984—. Mem. Water Pollution Control Fedn., Am. Water Works Assn., Internat. Ozone Assn. Author: (with others) The Handbook of Hazardous Waste Management, 1980; contbr. articles to profl. jours. Home: Route 4 Box 666 Stillwater OK 74074 Office: PO Box 2056 Stillwater OK 74076

STOVER, PHIL SHERIDAN, JR., investment consultant; b. Tulsa, Jan. 23, 1926; s. Phil Sheridan and Noma (Smith) S.; student Yale U., 1943-44, Denison U., 1944-45; B.S., U. Pa., 1948. With Nat. Bank Tulsa, 1948-70, v.p., 1956-64, sr. v.p., 1964-65, sr. v.p., cashier, 1965-70; owner Phil Stover & Assocs., Tulsa, 1970—; pres., treas. Tulsalite, Inc., mag. pubs., 1973-79; vice chmn., dir. Tulsa Oiler Baseball Club, 1975—, Springfield (Ill.) Redbirds Baseball Club, 1977-81; pres. Macon (Ga.) Baseball Club, 1980; v.p. Louisville Kent Redbirds Baseball Club, 1982—; ptnr. A Hotel ... The Frenchmen, New Orleans, 1983—. Chmn., Tulsa County chpt. Nat. Found., 1956-59, Tulsa Met. Water Authority, 1961-70; vice chmn. Tulsa Utility Bd., 1957-70; treas. adv. bd. Salvation Army. Served with USNR, 1944-46. Named Okla. Jr. C. of C. Outstanding Young Man, 1954. Republican. Presbyn. Address: University Club Tower 1722 S Carson St Tulsa OK 74119

STOVER, RICHARD STEPHEN, insurance company executive; b. Overton County, Tenn., Sept. 18, 1943; s. Cecil and Clarice Louise (Smith) S.; div., children—Kimberly Anne, Kristie Annette; m. Catherine Lee Dyer, June 4, 1974; 1 child, Micah Lauren. B.S. in Bus. Mgmt., Western Ky. U., 1966. Sales rep., mgr. Southwestern Co., Nashville, 1961-66; tchr., prin. coach Overton County Schs., Livingston, Tenn., 1966-68; rep. group ins. Corroon and Black, Nashville, 1968-69; underwriter, spl. agt. Northwestern Mut., Franklin, Tenn., 1969—. Contbr. articles to profl. jours. Chmn. Williamson County March of Dimes, 1983. Recipient Life Mem. award Million Dollar Round Table, 1970. Mem. Spl. Agts. Assn. (200 Lives Club 1978, 79, 80, 83), Nat. Assn. Life Underwriters (achievement award, nat. quality award), C. of C. Republican. Mem. Ch. of Christ. Avocation: fishing. Home: 75 Creekside Ct Franklin TN 37064 Office: Northwestern Mutual Life 436 A Main St Franklin TN 38064

STOVER, WILLIAM REITZEL, retired educator, condominium cons.; b. Waynesboro, Pa., June 8, 1906; s. Harry Edgar and Antoinette (Reitzel) S.; B.S., Temple U., 1938, Ed.M., 1940; Litt. D., Wagner Coll., 1953; m. Anna Mary Miller, June 5, 1928. Prin. Amon Heights and Jr. High Sch., Pennsauken, N.J., 1928-47, supt., 1947-55; supt. Central Regional High Sch. Dist., Bayville, N.J, 1955-58, Mainland Regional High Sch. Dist., Linwood, 1958-64. Ofcl. local congregation Luth. Ch., 1931—, ofcl. N.J. Synod, 1953-64; mem. commn. on ministry with aging Fla. Synod; instr. Christian edn., 1950—, del. Luth. Ch. Convs., 1952-64; mem. Luth. Laymen's Movement. Troop com. chmn. Boy Scouts Am., 1936-42, mem. bd. review 1941-42; pres. Condominium Assn. and area council, 1970-72; active various civic or charity drives. Bd. dirs. Wagner Coll., Mt. Airy Sem., Phila., S.W. Fla. Retirement Center, Community Mobile Meals. Mem. NEA (life), PTA (life), N.J. Edn. Assn. (pres. 1951-53), Nat., N.J. assns. sch. adminstrs., Assn. Ret. Persons (local pres. 1966-68), Phi Delta Kappa. Lutheran. Mason (Shriner). Author: What You Should Know Before Buying a Condominium, 1972; cross-reference Index of Florida Condominium Laws, ann. Home: 920 Tamiami Trail S Apt 4552 Venice FL 33595

STOWE, CHARLES ROBINSON BEECHER, management consultant, educator; b. Seattle, July 18, 1949; s. David Beecher and Edith Beecher (Andrade) S.; B.A., Vanderbilt U., 1971; M.B.A., U. Dallas, 1975; J.D., U. Houston, 1982. Account exec. Engleman Co., public relations and advt., Dallas, 1974-75; instr. Richland Coll., Dallas, spring 1976; acct. Arthur Andersen & Co., Dallas, 1976-78; part-time public relations cons.; dir. Productive Capital Corp.; gen. partner Productive Capital Assos.; pres. Stowe & Co., mgmt. cons., Dallas, 1978-82; asst. prof. Coll. Bus. Administrn., asst. to pres. Sam Houston State U., Huntsville, Tex., 1982—, dir. Office Free Enterprise and Entrepreneurship, 1984—; mgmt. cons. Trustee, Stowe-Day Found., 1979-82; mem. nat. adv. bd. Young Am.'s Found., 1979—. Served as officer USNR, 1971-74; lt. comdr. Res. Recipient Freedoms Found. award, 1969; Navy Achievement medal, 1973; 2d award Gold Star, 1986; Disting. Service award U. Houston Coll. Law, 1982. Mem. Am. Bar Assn., State Bar Tex., Pub. Relations Soc. Am., U.S. Navy League, Naval Res. Assn., Res. Officers Assn., Sigma Iota Epsilon. Club: Dallas Vanderbilt (pres. 1977-78). Author: CPA Review, 2d-4th edits., 1986, articles; editor Houston Jour. Internat. Law, 1981-82. Home: Box 2676 Huntsville TX 77341

STOWELL, JOHN CHARLES, chemistry educator; b. Passaic, N.J., Sept. 10, 1938; s. Charles and Daisy Clara (Hindle) S.; m. Jane Beverly Myers, Nov. 27, 1964 (div. 1985); children—Sandra, Alan. B.S. in Chemistry, Rutgers U., 1960; Ph.D. in Chemistry, MIT, 1964. Research specialist Minn. Mining and Mfg. Co., St. Paul, 1964-69; NIH postdoctoral fellow Ohio State U., Columbus, 1969-70; prof. chemistry U. New Orleans, 1970—. Author: Carbanions in Organic Synthesis, 1979. Contbr. articles to profl. jours. Vice pres. Grace Lutheran Ch., New Orleans, 1984—. Mem. Am. Chem. Soc. Avocations: canoeing; sailing; microscopy; cooking; photography. Office: Dept Chemistry U New Orleans New Orleans LA 70148

STRAHLE, ROLF GULLMAR, educator, architect; b. Gothenburg, Sweden, May 21, 1919; s. Gunnar W. and Gerda C. (Hedlund) S.; M.Arch., Swedish State Coll. Tech., 1944; postgrad. U. Gothenburg, 1948-49, seismic design course Stanford U., 1977; m. Ivy Soriano de Strahle, Nov. 21, 1956; children—Bjorn Gullmar, Jeanne-Marie Karin. Came to U.S., 1947. Expert, adviser UN Tech. Assistance, Nigeria, Dahomey, 1961, Ethopia, Kenya, 1964-66, Peru, 1969-73, Kuwait and Paris, 1981, Ecuador, 1981, Equatorial Guinea and Vienna, 1982. Chief architect Inst. Urban Housing, San Salvador, El Salvador, C.A., 1950-57; prof. Sch. Architecture, U. El Salvador, 1950-57; cons. architect, design and planning dept. suburbs City Gothenburg, 1957-58; asso. prof. Sch. Architecture, Syracuse U., N.Y., 1958-59; prof. Sch. Architecture Tulane U., New Orleans, 1959-69; now prof. Sch. Architecture U. Southwestern La., Lafayette; adviser, cons. internat. field of housing. Served with Royal Engrs. (Sweden), 1940-44. Mem. Swedish Inst. Architects, AIA, AAUP. Home: 101 Suffolk Ave Ivanhoe Estates Lafayette LA 70508

STRAIGHT, ELSIE HOSKING, retired art librarian, sculptor; b. Moresby, Cumberland, Eng.; Oct. 9, 1914; came to U.S., 1923, naturalized, 1926; d. Thomas E. and Anne (Molyneaux) Hosking; div.; 1 child, Elaine W. Sanders. A.A., Art Inst. Pitts., 1940, N.Y. Sch. Applied Design, 1941; B.A., Roger Williams Coll., 1969; M.L.S., U. R.I., 1974. Librarian, St. Raphael Acad., Pawtucket, R.I., 1960-68, Elmhurst Acad., Portsmouth, R.I., 1968-74; library dir. Ringling Sch. Art and Design, Sarasota, Fla., 1974-81, ret.; cons. U. South Fla., Sarasota, 1981—. Sculpture exhibited Manatee Art League, Bradenton, Fla., 1980-82, 83, 84, Plaza Art Show, Sarasota, 1983, Longboat Key Art Ctr., Sarasota, 1984. Mem. Art Librarian's Soc. (dir. 1980), Art League Manatee County, Longboat Key Art Ctr., Ringling Sch. Art Library Assn. Avocation: writing. Home: 435 Edwards Dr Sarasota FL 33580

STRAIGHT, SUSAN RENEE, pharmacist; b. Fairmont, W.Va., Mar. 28, 1959; d. David Lee and Jacqueline M. (Olesky) S. B.S. in Pharmacy, W.V.A., U., 1982. Registered pharmacist, W.Va. Receptionist, John M. Stiles, O.D., Rivesville, W.Va., 1979; pharmacy intern MVA Clinic, Inc., Fairmont, 1980-82; pharmacist Harbert's Drug Store, Clarksburg, W.Va., 1982; pharmacist Fairmont Gen. Hosp., 1982—, poison prevention week coordinator, 1982—, hosp. newspaper reporter, 1982—, auditor for medication usage, 1982—. Minister of the cup Assumption Catholic Ch., Rivesville, W.Va., 1983-85. Mem. Am. Soc. Hosp. Pharmacists, Am. Pharm. Assn., W.Va. Soc. Hosp. Pharmacists, W.Va. Pharm. Assn. Avocations: snow skiing; athletic events; exercise; crocheting; sewing. Home: Route 1 Box 42 Rivesville WV 26588

STRAIN, PAULA MARY, retired librarian; b. Brooke County, W.Va.; d. Paul Russell and Margaret (Evans) Strain; A.B., Bethany Coll., 1937; B.S., Carnegie Inst. Tech., 1938; student U. Pitts., 1940-41. Asst. librarian Westminster Coll., 1939-40; asst. librarian Carnegie-Ill. Steel Corp., Pitts., 1940-42, librarian, 1942-44; librarian U.S. Naval Photog. Interpretation Center, Washington, 1946-48, liaison and selection officer Library of Congress, 1948-57; sr. research analyst Library of Congress, 1957-60; tech. librarian Electronics Systems Cetner, IBM, Owego, N.Y., 1960-68; head librarian Booz Allen Applied Research, Inc., Bethesda, Md., 1968-70; mgr. info. services MITRE Corp., McLean, Va., 1970-84. Served with USNR, 1944-46. Mem. bd. mgrs. Finger Lakes Trail Conf., 1962-68, pres., 1966-67. Mem. Appalachian Trail Conf. (bd. mgrs. 1979-80), Spl. Libraries Assn. (various offices). Clubs: Potomac Appalachian Trail (council 1957-60, 69-80, pres. 1970-72), Adirondack Mountain. Author articles various periodicals and jours. Home: 118 Monroe St Apt 804 Rockville MD 20850

STRAITON, ARCHIE WAUGH, electrical engineering educator; b. Arlington, Tex., Aug. 27, 1907; s. John and Jeannie Bell (Waugh) S.; m. Esther McDonald, Dec. 28, 1932; children—Janelle Straiton Holman, Carolyn Straiton Erlinger. B.S.E.E., U. Tex., 1929, M.A., 1931, Ph.D., 1939. Staff engr. Bell Telephone Labs., N.Y.C., 1929-30; asst. prof. to prof., head engring. dept. Tex. Coll. Arts and Industries, Kingsville, 1931-43; assoc. prof. elec. engring. U. Tex., Austin, 1943-48, prof., 1948—; dir. Inst. Radio Engrs., 1953-54; mem. U.S.A. nat. com. Sci. Radio Union, 1951-53, 55-58, 65-69. Mem. Austin Energy Conservation Commn., 1974-79, chmn., 1978-79. Fellow IEEE; mem. Nat. Acad. Engring., Sigma Xi, Phi Kappa Phi, Tau Beta Pi, Eta Kappa Nu. Methodist. Lodge: Kiwanis (Austin). Contbr. numerous articles in field to tech. jours. Home: 4212 Far West Blvd Austin TX 78731 Office: Dept Elec Engring U Tex Austin TX 78712

STRANAK, LINN MICHAEL, physical education administrator; b. Murray, Ky., Aug. 12, 1948; s. Michael Walter and Lucy (Linn) S.; m. Judith Ann Munsey, May 12, 1969; children—Michael, John, Sarah. B.S., Union U., 1970; M.S., U. Ky., 1972; D. Arts., Middle Tenn. State U., 1977. Chmn. dept. phys. edn. Montreat Anderson Jr. Coll., N.C., 1973-80, Union U., Jackson, Tenn., 1980—; cons. Saundoers Pub. Co., Calif., 1985. Contbr. articles to profl. jours. Vol., ARC, Jackson, 1980—; bd. dirs. Area XI Spl. Olympics, Jackson, 1981—; youth league dir. Madison County Parks and Recreation, Jackson, 1981—. Mem. Am. Alliance Health Phys. Edn. Recreation and Dance, Tenn. Alliance Health Phys. Edn. Recreation and Dance, Nat. Assn. Intercoll. Athletics, Tenn. Recreation and Parks Assn., Kappa Mu Epsilon. Baptist. Avocations: Yard work; fishing; youth activities; wood working. Home: 48 Reynolds Dr Jackson TN 38305 Office: Union U 45 ByPass Jackson TN 38305

STRANGE, DOUGLAS HART MCKOY, civic worker; b. Wilmington, N.C., Mar. 16, 1929; d. Adair Morey and Katie Reston (Grainger) McKoy; student Hollins Coll., 1946-48; m. Robert Strange, July 16, 1949; children—Robert VI, John Allan, Elizabeth Adair, Katherine Grainger. Fin. chmn. and provisional co-chmn. Knoxville Jr. League; former tchr. Bible class, vestrywoman, pres. ch. women Fox Chapel Episcopal Ch.; former chmn. Fox Chapel House Tour; former chmn. altar guild, mem. worship com. bd. dirs. ch. women, St. John's Episcopal Ch.; altar guild chmn. Diocese of Tenn.; bd. dirs. Dulin Com., Dulin Gallery Art. Recipient cert. of merit Pitts. Heart Fund, 1975, engraved plate Fox Chapel Episcopal Ch., 1976. Mem. Assn. Jr. Leagues Am., Nat. Soc. Colonial Dames Am. (asst. to editor and bus. mgr. newsletter, 1978-79), Knoxville Civic Opera. Republican. Clubs. Cherokee Garden, Nine-o-clock Cotillion, Cherokee Country. Home: 1126 Bordeaux Circle Knoxville TN 37919

STRANGE, VANCE MEDLOCK, surgeon; b. Stamps, Ark., Mar. 4, 1909; s. Luther Thomas and Minnie Mae (Medlock) S.; m. Monda Dunn, May 18, 1939 (dec. Aug. 1971); children—Vance Medlock, Stephen L., Bruce A., Deborah Strange Ward; m. Lydia Babka, Apr. 28, 1974. B.S., Tulane U., 1930, M.D., 1934. Intern, So. Pacific Hosp., San Francisco, 1934-35, resident, 1935-36; city emergency surgeon City of San Francisco, 1936-38, 40-43; pvt. practice medicine specializing in surgery, San Francisco, 1936-71, Stamps, Ark., 1974—; chief med. examiner So. Pacific Co., San Francisco, 1938-40, staff surgeon, 1940-47, chief surgeon, 1957-71; chief surgeon western div. U.S. Steel Co., San Francisco, 1947-57; chmn. adv. council St. Francis Meml. Hosp., San Francisco, 1948. Fellow ACS (emeritus mem.); mem. AMA (emeritus), Ark. Med. Soc. (emeritus), Western Assn. Ry. Surgeons, Tulane Alumni Assn. (pres. Pacific Coast 1949-52, nat. pres. 1960-61), Stamps C. of C. Presbyterian. Lodge: Rotary. Avocations: conservation and forestry; real estate.

STRATTAN, ROBERT DEAN, electrical engineering educator, electromagnetics consultant; b. Newton, Kans., Dec. 7, 1936; s. Kermit McAllister and Willa Norine (Starr) S.; m. Vada May Egy, Jan. 24, 1960; children—Barry, Scott. B.S. in Elec. Engring., Wichita State U., 1958; M.S. in Elec. Engring., Carnegie-Mellon U., 1959, Ph.D. in Elec. Engring., 1962. Registered profl. engr., Okla. Research engr. Boeing Co., Wichita, Kans., 1961-63; tech. staff mem. Rockwell Internat., Tulsa, 1963-68; prof. elec. engring. U. Tulsa, 1968—. Recipient Teetor award Soc. Automotive Engrs., 1982. Sr. mem. IEEE (chmn. Tulsa sect. 1982-83); mem. Nat. Soc. Profl. Engrs. (S.W. region v.p. 1981-83), Okla. Soc. Profl. Engrs. (Tulsa chpt. pres. 1977-78, outstanding engr. award 1977). Republican. Presbyterian. Club: Sports Car of Am. Avocations: sports car road racing; vintage autos; hunting. Office: U Tulsa 600 S College Ave Tulsa OK 74104

STRATTON, EDWARD SAMUEL, JR., interior decorating company executive; b. Waynesboro, Va., Sept. 22, 1945; s. Edward and Emma Lillian (Mantiply) S.; m. Susan Dianne Haynes, Sept. 24, 1972; children—Jane Meredith, Ann Kathryn. A.A., Wingate Jr. Coll., 1966; B.A., High Point Coll., 1968. Owner, operator Cleaners & Tailors, 1968-83, Augusta Interiors, Waynesboro; dir. Souran Bank, Waynesboro. Vice pres. Fall Foliage Festival, Waynesboro 1975-78; 1st, 2d v.p. Waynesboro-East Augusta C. of C., 1975-79; deacon, chmn. diaconate First Baptist Ch., Waynesboro, 1972-76, 80-84; bd. dirs. ARC, 1980—, Econ. Devel. Council of Waynesboro, Stanton and Augusta Counties, 1978—; mem. Planning Council of Waynesboro Sch. Bd., Downtown Devel. Com., Waynesboro; pres. Round Table Club, Waynesboro, 1984-85; trustee Fishman Mil. Sch., Waynesboro, 1982—; chmn. planning com. City of Waynesboro, 1985—; pres. Retail Mchts. Assn., Waynesboro, 1979-80. Named Outstanding Young Man, Waynesboro Jaycees, 1976. Lodge: Waynesboro Rotary (pres. 1977-78). Avocations: art; painting; collecting; tennis. Home: 800 Oak Ave Waynesboro VA 22980 Office: Augusta Interiors 321 Main St Waynesboro VA 22980

STRAUCHS, JOHN JANIS, security systems engineering company executive, consultant; b. Valmiera, Latvia, June 13, 1944; s. Karlis F. and Erika M. (Buks) S.; m. Sharon L. Peruzzi, May 29, 1971; children—Tiffany Yolanda, Karlis William. B.A. in Internat. Relations, Lehigh U., 1970; M.A. in Internat. Affairs, George Washington U., 1975. Staff officer U.S. CIA, Washington, 1970-74; cons. Nat. Sci. Corp., Arlington, Va., 1975-76; pres. Gordian Corp., Occoquan, Va., 1976-79; prin. Gage-Babcock & Assos., Inc., Vienna, Va., 1979-84; pres. Systech Group, Inc., Gt. Falls, Va., 1985—. Bd. dirs. Dranesville Dist. Council, Falls Manor Home Owners Assn., 1982—. Served to capt. USAR, 1964-67. Decorated Bronze Star. Mem. ASTM, (chmn. com.), Am. Soc. Indsl. Security (chmn. com.), Nat. Cargo Security Council (bd. dirs.).

STRAUSS, ALBRECHT BENNO, English educator, editor; b. Berlin, May 17, 1921; came to U.S., 1940; s. Bruno and Bertha (Badt) S.; m. Nancy Grace Barron, July 30, 1978; 1 dau., Rebecca Ilse; stepchildren—Carolyn, Kathryn. Instr. English, Brandeis U., 1951-52; teaching fellow gen. edn. Harvard U., 1952-55; instr. English, Yale U., 1955-59; asst. prof. English, U. Okla., Norman, 1959-60; asst. prof. U. N.C., Chapel Hill, 1960-64, assoc. prof., 1964-70, prof., 1970—. Served with U.S. Army, 1942-46. Recipient Tanner Teaching award U. N.C., 1966; Fulbright fellow, Germany, 1983-84. Mem. MLA, South Atlantic MLA, Am. Soc. Eighteenth-Century Studies (pres. Southeastern group 1980-81), Coll. English Assn., The Johnsonians. Republican. Jewish. Editor, Studies in Philology, 1974-80; sec. editorial com. Yale Edit. of Works of Samuel Johnson, 1975—; contbr. articles to lit. publs. Home: 396 Lake Shore Ln Chapel Hill NC 27514 Office: 401 Greenlaw Bldg U NC Chapel Hill NC 27514

STRAUSS, JEANNE H., technical translator; b. Hamburg, Germany, Mar. 5, 1928; came to U.S., 1948, naturalized, 1954; d. Frederic and Julie S.; B.A., Roosevelt U., 1956; M.A., Loyola U., Chgo., 1960; Ph.D. all but dissertation, U. Wis., Madison, 1968. Legal sec. Montgomery Ward, Chgo., 1957-60; instr. Creighton U., Omaha, 1961-63; teaching asst. U. Wis., Madison, 1964-65; asst. prof. U. Wis., Stevens Point, 1965-69, Western Ill. U., Macomb, 1969-71, U. Wis., Superior, 1973-75; tech. translator Phillips Petroleum Co., Bartlesville, Okla., 1975—. Mem. Am. Assn. Tchrs. French, Am. Assn. Tchrs. Spanish and Portugese, Am. Translators Assn., ASME (affiliate), MLA, Philbrook Art Mus. Republican. Lodge: Toastmasters Internat. Home: PO Box 78 Bartlesville OK 74005

STRAUSS, PATRICIA SHELDON, business executive; b. Greenville, Miss., Feb. 7, 1941; d. Anson Hoisington and Beatrice Everett Sheldon; student Miss. State Coll. for Women, 1958-59; B.A., U. Miss., 1962; m. Willard Louis Ekstrum, Jr., Dec. 17, 1983; 1 child, Anne Michelle. With U. Miss. Med. Center, Jackson, 1965-75, grant coordinator, workshop coordinator, in-house instr., 1975; legal sec., office mgr. Parks & Moss, Houston, 1975-77; adminstrv. asst. 3D/ Internat., Houston, 1977-79, spl. facilities coordinator, 1979-81, assoc. 1980-85, sr. assoc., 1985—; exec. asst., 1981—. Pres., bd. trustees Jackson Ballet Guild; co-founder, trustee Jackson Ballet Guild Sch., 1973-75; mem. Jackson Civic Arts Council, 1971-73; auction co-chmn. Jackson Symphony League, 1967-75. Mem. Exec. Women Internat. Republican. Episcopalian. Club: Univ. (Houston). Office: 1900 W Loop S Suite 2100 Houston TX 77027

STRAUSSER, JEFFREY ALLEN, petroleum geologist; b. Columbus, Ohio, Oct. 10, 1954; s. Richard Thomas and Rose Marie (Zeolla) S.; m. Beth Ann Selewitz, Apr. 8, 1978; 1 child, Katherine Ann. BS., U. Pitts., 1976; M.B.A., U. St. Thomas, 1985. Exploration geologist Equitable Gas Co., Pitts., 1976-78; supervisory geologist Tenneco Inc., Houston, 1978-82; mgr. gas reserves Houston Natural Gas Co., 1982—. Sec., Maplewood Civic Club, Houston, 1985. Mem. Am. Assn. Petroleum Geologists, Internat. Assn. Energy Economists. Republican. Roman Catholic. Club: Houston Triathlon. Avocations: Running; swimming, biking; writing. Home: 5462 Carew St Houston TX 77096 Office: Houston Natural Gas PO Box 1188 Houston TX 77001

STRAWN, DAVID UPDEGRAFF, lawyer; b. DeLand, Fla., May 21, 1936; B.A. in Polit. Sci., U. Fla., 1958, J.D., 1961. Bar: Fla. 1961. Assoc., Akerman, Turnbull, Senterfitt & Eidson, Orlando, Fla., 1961-62; ptnr. Gleason & Strawn, Melbourne, Fla., 1962-67, Strawn and Rumberger, Melbourne, 1967-70, Akerman, Senterfitt and Edison, Orlando, Fla., 1979-83; sole practice, 1983—; judge 18th Jud. Cir. Ct. Fla., Titusville, 1972-78; sheriff, Brevard County (Fla.), 1978-79; vis. professorial lectr. Holland Law Ctr., U. Fla., Gainesville, 1979; mem. faculty Nat. Jud. Coll., U. Nev., 1976—. Bd. dirs. Fla. Endowment for Humanities, 1977-79; v.p. Fla. Tech. U. Found., 1977-79; chmn. bd. dirs. Inst. Study of Trial, U. Central Fla., Orlando, 1978—, adj. prof. communication U. Central Fla., 1979—; chmn. State of Fla. Study Commn. on Alternative Dispute Resolution for the Courts, 1984—. Recipient Disting. Service award Fla. Council Crime and Delinquency, 1977, Sunshine award Soc. Profl. Journalists Central Fla., 1978. Mem. ABA, Fla. Bar Assn., Fla. Bar Found., Brevard County Bar Assn., Seminole County Bar Assn., Orange County Bar Assn., Am. Judicature Soc. (bd. dirs. 1984—). Author: (with R. Buchanan and K. Taylor) Communication Strategies for Trial Attorneys, 1983. Contbr. articles to legal jours. and gen. interest periodicals. Office: PO Box 231 Orlando FL 32802

STRAYER, MICHELE YVONNE ZDINAK, educator; b. Steubenville, Ohio, Apr. 1, 1948; d. Michael and Anne (Yatsco) Zdinak; m. Spencer Lee Strayer, Aug. 15, 1971 (div. Dec. 1978); children—April Michele, Colleen Marie. B.A., West Liberty State Coll., 1969; M.Ed., Johns Hopkins U., 1976; math. endorsement Roanoke Coll., 1985. Tchr., Hancock County Schs., Weirton, W.Va., 1969-70, Balt. County Schs., 1970-77, Roanoke City Schs. (Va.), 1977—, level coordinator, 1978—; facilitator/leader Baltimore County Title I summer sch., 1974-75; facilitator for Project Learning Tree and Project Wild, Va. State Dept. and Roanoke City Schs., 1982-83. Author plays: Ecology Works, 1979; Papertron's Pollution Solution, 1981. Bd. dirs. Southeast Community Edn., Roanoke, 1980-83; vol. coordinator Roanoke City-Virginia Heights, 1983—; mem. lay pastoral com., Roanoke, 1982-83. Mem. NEA, Parents Without Partners. Democrat. Byzantine Catholic. Home: 4035 Kentland Dr Roanoke VA 24018 Office: M and S Prodns 4035 Kentland Dr Roanoke VA 24018

STREETER, JOHN VINTON, public safety administrator, management consultant; b. Mpls., Feb. 3, 1940; s. Dale Robinson and Carmen Camile S.; m. Gloria Jean Zickefoose, Jan. 9, 1976; 1 child, Julie Lynn. A.A. in Pub. Adminstrn., Am. U., 1971, B.S. in Pub. Adminstrn., 1973; postgrad. in behavioral psychology George Washington U., 1975—. Constable in chief, Medicine Lake, Minn., 1960-63; police officer, Alexandria, Va., 1966-72, supr., 1972-74, comdr., 1974-78, dep. chief, 1979, dep. dir. pub. safety, 1979—. Cons. Active Potomac West Trade Assn., Old Town Merchants Assn. Served with U.S. Army, 1962-65. Life mem. Friendship Fire Engine Co., 1973. Mem. Police Mgmt. Assn. (v.p.), Internat. Assn. Chiefs of Police. Republican. Methodist. Club: Mt. Vernon Ice Hockey (Alexandria, Va.). Contbr. articles to jours. in field. Office: 400 N Pitt St Alexandria VA 22314

STREETMAN, CHRISTINE NORMAN, artist; b. Lawton, Okla., Jan. 12, 1903; d. Thomas Fleming and Nancy Kate (Saunders) N.; m. Sam Streetman, Dec. 26, 1926; (dec. Oct. 1983); 1 child, Nancy Kate. Student Tex. Womens U., 1920-21, Rice U., 1923-24; B.S., U. Houston, 1945; postgrad Rice U., 1946-47. Tchr. art, YWCA, Houston, 1930-40; pvt. instr., Houston, 1950-73; lectr. art, Guanajuato, Mexico, 1975-80; owner studio/gallery, Guanajuato, 1973-83; exhibited in group show Tex. Artists, Austin, 1959, Houston Artists (Purchase prize), 1957; represented in permanent collection Houston Mus. Fine Arts. Recipient Bronze medal Cat Fanciers Assn., 1973; gold medals, silver cups Houston Yacht Club. Mem. Houston Art League, Houston Mus. Fine Arts, Cat Fanciers Assn. (yearbook editor). Home: 8951 Breasmont #149 Houston TX 77096

STRELETZKY, KATHRYN DIANE, sales executive; b. Bklyn., July 13, 1957; d. Donald Charles and Eleanor Jean (Galassi) S. B.A. with highest honors, Pa. State U.; postgrad. Coll. William and Mary. Sales exec. Procter & Gamble, Milw., Balt., 1979-81, 3M, Phila., Atlanta, 1982—. Regional coordinator Pa. State U. Alumni Admissions Com., Washington and No. Va., 1984—; treas. Whisperwood Homes Assn., Reston, Va., 1985—. Mem. Cooperating for Growth, Pa. State Alumni Assn. (adv. bd. 1985), Phi Beta Kappa, Phi Kappa Phi. Republican. Roman Catholic. Home: 11269 Silentwood Ln Reston VA 22091

STRETCH, SHIRLEY MARIE, marketing educator; b. Wauneta, Nebr., May 6, 1949; d. Lloyd Ray and Roberta Marie S. B.S., U. Nebr.-Lincoln, 1971; M.S., Kans. State U.-Manhattan, 1972; M.B.A., Ohio State U., 1977, Ph.D., 1982. EPDA fellow Kans. State U., Manhattan, 1971-73; instr. Bowling Green (Ohio) State U., 1973-75; grad. adminstrv. assoc. Univ. Coll., Ohio State U., Columbus, 1976-78, 80; asst. mgr. direct mktg. Ashland, Save-Mart Div., Columbus, 1978-80; asst. prof. merchandising Tex. Tech U., Lubbock, 1980-85, Valdosta State Coll., Ga., 1985—. Nebr. Gov. scholar, 1969. Mem. Am. Mktg. Assn., Southwestern Mktg. Assn., So. Mktg. Assn., Am. Collegiate Retailing Assn., Assn. Coll. Profs. Textiles and Clothing. Republican. Methodist. Clubs: West Tex. Ski, Tex. Twisters Ski (Lubbock). Home: 4604C 55th Dr Lubbock TX 79414

STRICKER, SUSAN POSTON, radiologic technology educator, administrator; b. Mooresville, N.C., Sept. 12, 1941; d. Samuel Lafayette and Margarette Taylor (Johnston) P.; m. Kurt Alan Marwitz, May 12, 1972 (div. 1984); m. Jack Thomas Stricker, 1986. Radiologic Tech., Charlotte Meml. Hosp. and Med. Ctr., 1961; postgrad. Queens Coll., 1984—. Staff tech. Charlotte Meml. Hosp. and Med. Ctr., N.C., 1961-65, supr., 1965-68, instr., 1965-68, edn. dir., 1968—; site vis. Joint Review Com. on Edn. in Radiologic Tech., Chgo., 1983—. Mem. N.C. Soc. Radiologic Techs. (membership award 1976, 80), Am. Registry Radiologic Techs. Republican. Avocations: golf; travel; sewing. Home: 10824 Winterbourne Ct Matthews NC 28105 Office: Charlotte Meml Hosp and Med Ctr PO Box 32861 Charlotte NC 28232

STRICKLAND, BARBARA ROGERS, bookstore manager; b. Brunswick, Ga., June 10, 1944; d. Bernard Harold and Nancy Elizabeth (Odum) Rogers; m. L.J. Jack Strickland, May 4, 1963; children—Brandy, Kevin. Student Ware County Vo-Tec., 1975. Sales rep. Rogers Studio, Douglas, Ga., 1958-63; credit corr. Sears, Roebuck & Co., Atlanta, 1963, Brunswick, Ga., 1964-66; owner, operator Kiddie Acre Playschool, Douglas, 1973-78; bookstore mgr. Abundant Life Book and Gift Shoppe, Margate, Fla., 1980—; phone counselor TBN and Abundant Life, Hollywood, Fla., 1978—; cons. for area bookstores, Fla., 1984—. Leader, Savannah council Girl Scouts Am., 1969-70; mem. Steering com. Abundant Life Christian, Margate, 1985. Mem. Christian Booksellers Assn., Cornerstone Abundant Life Christian Ctr. Republican. Avocations: writing poetry; horseback riding; reading. Office: Abundant Life Christian Bookstore 1500 N State Rd 7 Margate FL 33063

STRICKLAND, BETTY EALEY, educator; b. Edison, Ga., Dec. 20, 1936; s. James and Dorothy (Johnson) Ealey; B.A., Spelman Coll., 1958; M.A., Atlanta U., 1974, Adminstrn. and Supervision, 1980; postgrad. Appalachian State U., W. Ga. State U. Tchr., librarian Calhoun City Bd. Edn. (Ga.), 1958-59; tchr. Fulton County Bd. Edn., Atlanta, 1959-75, tchr. reading, 1975-78, itinerant reading tchr., 1978-79, reading resource tchr., 1979-81, dir. elem. curriculum, 1982—. Mem. membership com. YMCA, 1964; leader Girl Scouts U.S.A., 1964; den mother Boy Scouts Am., 1965-68; vol. Fulton County Emergency Shelter, 1980-81. Mem. So. Assn. Colls. and Schs., NEA, Ga. Assn. Edn., Fulton County Assn. Edn., Assn. Supervision and Curriculum Devel., Met. Council Internat. Reading Assn., Ga. Council Reading, Ga. Assn. Community Edn., Nat. Coalition ESA Title I Parents. Baptist. Club: Toastmistress (treas. 1978-79). Home: 50 Peyton Rd SW Atlanta GA 30311 Office: 768 Cleveland Ave SW Atlanta GA 30315

STRICKLAND, JAMES TRAVIS, oilfield sales engineer, consultant, well log analyst; b. Panama City, Fla., Sept. 17, 1952; s. Thomas Irvin and Ellen Donna (Beatty) S.; m. Sylvia Bea Laney, Aug. 17, 1973 (div. Mar. 1979); m. Doris Marie Culver, July 20, 1979. Student U. Tex., 1970-73. Equipment operator Welex, A. Halliburton Co., Victoria, Tex., 1975-76, field engr., 1976-79; sr. field engr. Gearhart Industries, Inc., Victoria, 1979-81, dist. mgr., San Antonio, 1981-82, Tyler, Tex., 1982-83, sales engr., 1983—; cons. Gearhart Industries, Inc., Victoria, San Antonio and Tyler, 1979—, log analyst, 1979—. Mem. Soc. Profl. Well Log Analysts, Soc. Petroleum Engrs., Am. Assn. Petroleum Geologists, Am. Petroleum Inst., East Tex. Geol. Soc., Soc. Econ. Paleontologists and Mineralogists, Corpus Christi Geol. Soc. Republican. Club: Willow Brook Country (Tyler). Avocations: reading, model airplanes, golf, softball, racquetball, tennis. Home: Three Creeks Estates Route 1 19-B Timbercreek Dr Flint TX 75762 Office: Gearhart Industries Inc Hwy 69 N PO Box 4177 Tyler TX 75712

STRICKLAND, JOSEPH MONROE, lawyer; b. Abbeville, S.C., Sept. 24, 1955; s. Joseph Coolidge and Thomasena (Lee) S.; A.B., Princeton U., 1977; J.D., Vanderbilt U., 1981. Bar: D.C. 1984, S.C. 1985. Second asst. parliamentarian U.S. Senate, 1981-84; law clk. U.S. Dist. Ct., Columbia, S.C., 1984-85; assoc. Nelson, Mullins, Grier & Scarborough, Columbia, 1985—. Served to 2d lt. USAR, 1977-85. Named Outstanding Young Man, Jaycees, 1982. Mem. NAACP. Baptist. Club: Princeton (N.Y.C.). Home: PO Box 7663 Columbia SC 29202 Office: Nelson Mullins Grier & Scarborough 1310 Lady St PO Box 11070 Columbia SC 29211

STRICKLAND, ROBERT, banker; b. Atlanta, May 20, 1927; s. Robert M. and Jessie (Dickey) S.; grad. Marist Coll., 1944; B.S., Davidson Coll., 1948; LL.B., Atlanta Law Sch., 1953; m. Telside Matthews, July 24, 1953; children—Robert Marion, Douglas Watson, William Logan, Walter Dickey. With Trust Co. of Ga., Atlanta, 1948—, v.p., 1959-67, group v.p., 1967, sr. v.p., 1968-72, sr. exec. v.p., 1972-73, pres., 1973—; chmn. bd. dirs. Trust Co. Bank, 1974—; pres. Trust Co. Ga., holding co., 1976—, chmn. bd., 1978—; chmn. bd., dir. SunTrust Banks, Inc., 1984—; dir. Equifax, Inc., Trust Co. Ga. and Trust Co. Bank, Life Ins. Co. Ga., Ga. U.S. Corp., Investment Ctr., Ga. Power Co., Oxford Industries, Inc. Past pres. United Way Met. Atlanta, chmn. 1972 gen. campaign; chmn. finance com., v.p. bd. dirs. Piedmont Hosp.; bd. dirs. Fulton County unit, bd. dirs. Ga. div. Am. Cancer Soc.; trustee emeritus Westminster Schs.; chmn. bd. trustees Emory U.; mem. exec. com., past chmn. Central Atlanta Progress, Inc. Served with AUS, 1950-52. Mem. Assn. Res. City Bankers, Am. (past state v.p.), Ga. (past pres.) bankers assns., Atlanta C. of C., Sigma Alpha Epsilon, Atlanta Arts Alliance (past chmn. bd., trustee, exec. com.). Methodist. Rotarian. Clubs: Piedmont Driving (past pres.), Capital City, Commerce (dir.), Peachtree Golf (Atlanta); Augusta Nat. Golf. Home: 94 Brighton Rd NE Atlanta GA 30309 Office: PO Box 4418 Atlanta GA 30302

STRICKLAND, SANDRA JEAN HEINRICH, nurse; b. Tucson, Sept. 18, 1943; d. Henry and Ada (Schmidt) Heinrich; B.S., U. Tex. Sch. Nursing, 1965; M.S. in Nursing (fellow), U. Md., 1969; D.P.H., U. Tex., 1978; m. William C. Strickland, Aug. 18, 1973; children—William Henry, Angela Lee. Clin. instr. U. Tex. Sch. Nursing, Galveston, 1965-66; staff nurse Hidalgo County Health Dept., Edinburg, Tex., 1966-67; supr. nursing Tex. Dept. Health Tb Control, Austin, 1969-70; instr. St. Luke's Hosp. Sch. Nursing, Houston, 1971-72, Tex. Women's U. Sch. Nursing, Houston and Dallas, 1972-73; dir. nursing Dallas City Health Dept., 1974-80; assoc. prof. community health nursing grad. program Tex. Woman's U., Dallas, 1980—; mem. profl. adv. com. Dallas Vis. Nurse Assn., 1978-83; mem. health adv. bd. Dallas Ind. Sch. Dist.; chmn. nursing and health services Dallas chpt. ARC, 1984—, also bd. dirs. Tex. Public Health Assn. fellow, 1977. Mem. Tex. Public Health Assn., Am. Public Health Assn., Sigma Theta Tau. Methodist. Home: 206 N Willomet Dallas TX 75208 Office: 1810 Inwood Rd Dallas TX 75235

STRICKLAND, THOMAS JOSEPH, artist, painting instructor; b. Keyport, N.J., Dec. 28, 1932; s. Charles Edward and Clementine Maria (Grasso) S. Student Newark Sch. Fine and Indsl. Art, 1951-53, Am. Art Sch., 1955-59, Nation Acad. Sch. Design, 1955-59. One man shows include Hollywood Art Mus., Hollywood, Fla., 1972, Elliott Mus. Martin County Hist. Soc., 1974, Greater Miami C. of C., 1973, St. Vincent Coll., Latrobe, Pa., Salem Coll., Winston-Salem, N.C.; group shows include Grand Prix Internat. De Peinture De Lacotediazur, Cannes, 1971, Am. Painters in Paris, 1975, Butler Inst. Am. Art, Younstown, Ohio, 1963. Served with U.S. Army, 1953-55. Recipient First prize Hollwood Art Mus., 1973; 1st pl. Fine Arts League Annual Show, 1973; Charles Hawthorne Meml. award Nat. Art Club, 1977; First prize Miami Palette Club, 1978. Mem. Pastel Soc. Am., Fla. Pastel Assn., Miami Palette Club. Home: 2595 Taluga Dr Miami FL 33133

STRICKLER, JANIS BROWN, nurse; b. Fall Branch, Tenn., Apr. 12, 1938; d. Edgar George and Wilma Justine (Bacon) Brown; m. Carl Lee Strickler, Dec. 21, 1957; children—Janet Denise, Michael Lee. B.S. in Nursing, East Tenn. State U., 1960; postgrad. in advanced tng.-infection control U. Va., 1978. R.N., Tenn., Va., N.C. Staff nurse Johnson City Med. Ctr., Tenn., 1960-61; instr. psychiat. nursing Dorothea Dix Hosp., Raleigh, N.C., 1961-62; relief nurse supr. Halifax County Hosp., South Boston, Va., 1967-70; alcoholic rehab. head nurse Detoxification Ctr., Kingsport, Tenn., 1971-72; nurse epidemiologist Holston Valley Hosp. and Med. Ctr., Kingsport, 1972—. Co-author: Annals of Internal Medicine, 1979. Author book rev. Am. Jour. of Nursing, 1978. Mem. Smoky Mountain Assn. Practitioners Infection Control, Nat. Orgn. Assn. Practitioners Infection Control. Republican. Baptist. Avocation: needlework. Home: 1229 Malabar Dr Kingsport TN 37660 Office: Holston Valley Hosp and Med Ctr Box 238 Kingsport TN 37662

STRICKROOT, JOHN CARL, lawyer; b. Detroit, Aug. 4, 1932; s. Fred C. and Marguerite I. (Roberts) S.; m. Aimee J. Gross, Jan. 17, 1959; children—John C., Susan Aimee. B.S. in Commerce, U. Notre Dame, 1954; J.D., U. Fla., 1957. Bar: Fla. 1957, Mich. 1957. Lawyer, Nat. Bank of Detroit, 1960-62; assoc. Fowler, White, Burnett, Hurley, Banick & Strickroot, Miami, Fla., 1962—, mng. dir., 1976—, v.p., 1976—. Mem. citizens bd. U. Miami, Coral Gables, 1981—, v.p., 1985—; fund raiser United Way, Miami, 1981—, Leukemia Soc. drive, 1982—; bd. dirs. Exec. Assn. Greater Miami, 1982—, pres., 1984-85. Served to capt. USAF, 1958-60. Mem. Mich. Bar Assn., Fla. Bar Assn., Dade County Bar Assn. Democrat. Roman Catholic. Club: Bankers (Miami); Riviera Country (Coral Gables). Office: Fowler White Burnett Hurley Banick & Strickroot PA 25 W Flagler St Miami FL 33130

STRINGER, DONALD HALL, insurance company executive; b. Brookhaven, Miss., Aug. 13, 1938; s. Flavil Hall and Ella V. (Bowman) S.; B.A., Harding Coll., Searcy, Ark., 1967; m. Betty Lee Cox, Nov. 30, 1973; children—Caroline, Kip, Colleen, Clint. Vice pres. Shannon Supply Co., Clinton, Ark., 1961-65; sci. tchr. Bradford (Ark.) public schs., 1967-68; group rep. Conn. Gen. Life Ins. Co., Houston, 1969-74; regional group mgr. Home Life Ins. Co., New Orleans, 1974-79, Dallas, 1979-82; founder, prin. Stringer & Assocs., ins. brokerage agy., Dallas, 1982—; pres. Cody Mktg., Inc. Mem. pres.'s devel. council Harding Coll., 1974—; mem. Congressman Livingston's ins. and pension adv. com., 1978. Served with U.S. Army, 1959-65. Named Mgr. of Year, Home Life Ins. Co., 1977. Mem. Gen. Agts. and Mgrs. Assn., Life Underwriters Assn., Nat. Health Underwriters Assn., Am. Quarter Horse Assn., Palomino Horse Owners and Breeders Assn., Palomino Horse Assn., Mensa. Republican. Mem. Ch. of Christ. Home: Rt 1 Box 687B Sanger TX 76266 Office: 2735 Villa Creek Dr Suite 100 Dallas TX 75234

STRINGER, JOE ROBERT, bank executive, real estate broker; b. Dallas, Aug. 10, 1955; s. Joe Harold and Eleanor (Andrew) S. B.B.A. in Mktg., Tex. A & M U., College Station, 1978; M.B.A. in Mgmt., U. Dallas, 1983. Lic. real estate broker, ins. rep., Tex. Fin. analyst Amoco Prodn. Co., Odessa, Tex., 1978-79; bond investment v.p. Republic Bank, Dallas, 1979—, speaker exec. tng. program, 1979—; player Tex. Wranglers Semi-pro Football Team, 1980-83. Contbr. articles to profl. jours. Motivational speaker Jr. Achievement, Dallas, 1979—; group organizer United Way of Dallas, 1980; staff mem. Camp Grady Service Staff YMCA, Dallas, 1982; mem. Young Republicans, Dallas, 1983—. Mem. Sigma Iota Epsilon. Baptist. Lodge: Kiwanis Internat. (Dallas). Home: 2424 Old Bullard Rd Tyler TX 75701 Office: Republic Bank Dallas Pacific St and Ervay St Dallas TX 75225

STRINGER, SHARON ANTONIA, psychology educator, researcher; b. Mountain Lakes, N.J., Sept. 8, 1955; d. Arthur Jr. and Regina Mahoney (Holl) S. B.S. cum laude, Georgetown U., 1977; M.S., U. Miami, 1980, Ph.D., 1982. Research asst. dept. pediatrics Georgetown U., Washington, 1975-77, dept. psychology, 1976-77; cons. Nat. Inst. Child Health Human Devel., 1977-78; research asst. dept. pediatrics Mailman Ctr. Child Devel., 1978-80, cons. child protection team, 1980-82; asst. prof. U. New Orleans, 1982—. Office: Dept Psychology Sci Engring Bldg U New Orleans New Orleans LA 70148

STRINGFIELD, CHARLES DAVID, hospital administrator; b. Nashville, May 11, 1939; s. Ernest Jake and Lucille (Lovelace) Stringfield Birthright; m. Ruth Dvorak, Aug. 25, 1962; children—David Fisher, John Lovelace. B.A., Vanderbilt U., 1961; tchr.'s cert. George Peabody Coll., 1962, M.A. in Sch. Adminstrn., 1964; M.A. in Hosp. Adminstrn., Washington U., St. Louis, 1966. Tchr. Sch. Dist. #11, Colorado Springs, Colo., 1962-64; adminstrv. asst., adminstrv. resident Milw. County Instns., 1965-66; exec. dir. Tenn. Nursing Home Assn., Nashville, 1966-67; asst. dir. Tenn. Hosp. Assn., Nashville, 1966-68; adminstrv. dir. Bapt. Hosp., Inc., Nasville, 1968-70, exec. v.p., 1970-82, exec. v.p. and chief exec. officer, 1981-82, pres., 1982—. Fellow Am. Coll. Hosp. Adminstrs.; mem. Hosp. Alliance of Tenn., Inc. (bd. dirs.), Voluntary Hosps. of Am. (bd. dirs.), Am. Hosp. Assn., Am. Nursing Home Assn., Southeastern Hosp. Assn., Mid-Tenn. Eye Bank Found. (governing bd.). Baptist. Lodge: Kiwanis (Nashville). Home: 4320 Esteswood Dr Nashville TN 37215 Office: Baptist Hosp Inc 2000 Church St Nashville TN 37214

STRINGFIELD, SAMUEL COBURN, educational psychologist; b. Waynesville, N.C., Jan. 24, 1949; s. Thomas and Harriet Cutler (Coburn) S. B.A., U. N.C., 1971, M.A.T., 1978; Ph.D., Temple U., 1983. Research asst. Carolina Population Ctr., U. N.C., 1971-72, Therapeutic Presch., Project Early Aid, 1971, 77; research, eval. coordinator O.P.C. Mental Health Ctr., Chapel Hill, N.C., 1978-79; instr. dept. ednl. psychology Temple U., 1979-82; asst. prof. psychology dept. edn. Tulane U., New Orleans, 1982—; cons. in field. Contbr. numerous articles to profl. jours. Mem. Pub. Edn. Task Force, New Orleans, 1983-84. Fellow W.K. Kellogg Found., 1984—, Temple U., 1980-82. Mem. New Orleans Computer Soc. (co-founder 1983), Am. Edn. Research Assn. (pres. elect sch. effectiveness group 1986—), Eval. Network, Am. Psychol. Assn., Assn. Supervision and Curriculum Devel., Southwest Ednl. Research Assn., Boston Computer Soc. Democrat. Methodist. Club: Sierra. Avocations: Backpacking; sailing. Home: 7916 1/2 Maple St New Orleans LA 70118 Office: Dept Edn Tulane U New Orleans LA 70118

STRISCHEK, MARTIN JOSEPH, III, banker, educator; b. Chgo., Sept. 16, 1946; s. Martin Joseph Jr. and Rosalie Elizabeth (Ekstam) S.; m. Cherry Lyn Askins, Aug. 2, 1968 (div. 1972); 1 child, Krystyna Leilani; m. Valerie Gail Kogut, Feb. 16, 1980. B.S., Ohio State U., 1968; M.B.A., U. Hawaii, 1970; diploma Stonier Grad. Sch. Banking, 1981. Staff officer Huntington Nat. Bank, Columbus, Ohio, 1971-73; controller Oahu Interiors, Inc., Honolulu, 1973-75; lectr. econs. Chaminade U., Honolulu, 1975-76; v.p. Commerce Bank, Kansas City, Mo., 1976-81, S.E. Bank, Ft. Lauderdale, Fla., 1981-83; sr. v.p. Barnett Bank, Miami, Fla., 1983—; instr. econs. Rockhurst Coll., Kansas City, 1977-81; instr. fin. analysis Robert Morris Assocs., Phila., 1982—. Contbr. articles on fin. analysis to profl. jours. Mem. adv. bd. Fla. Atlantic U. Sch. Acctg., Boca Raton, 1982—; mem. bd. regents RMA Fla. Sch. Comml. Banking, 1984—; mem. 2000 Com., Coral Springs, Fla., 1983—. Mem. Robert Morris Assocs. (pres. Fla. chpt. 1984—, chmn. Phila. credit quality com. 1984-85, mem. nat. credit div. council), Nat. Assn. Accts. (v.p. Fla. chpt. 1984-85), Nat. Assn. Credit Mgmt. (bd. dirs. South Fla. chpt.). Office: Barnett Bank 800 Brickell Ave Miami FL 33131

STRITE, JACOB JAY MILLER, clergyman; b. Greencastle, Pa., Dec. 19, 1904; s. John Calvin and Daisy Belle (Miller) S.; A.B., Lynchburg Coll., 1930; student Christian Theol. Sem., Indpls., 1933-37; B.D., Lexington Theol. Sem., 1958, Th.M., 1959; m. Anna Irene Eckert Foltz, Aug. 9, 1929 (dec. 1953); children—Georgia Annabelle Strite Flock, Martha Eckert Strite Scull; m. 2d, Clara Belle Fleishman, Oct. 23, 1954. Ordained to ministry Disciples of Christ Ch., 1933; minister North Eastwood Christian Ch., Indpls., 1933-35, Daleville (Ind.) Christian Ch., 1935-44, Corydon (Ind.) Christian Ch., 1945-50, Melrose Christian Ch., Roanoke, Va., 1950-57, Mt. Carmel Christian Ch., Winchester, Ky., 1957-60, Christian Coll. Ga., Athens, Ga., 1960-61 (also counselor, tchr.), Friendship Christian Ch., Athens, 1962-64, minister at large, 1964-69; asso. Bethany Christian Ch., Roanoke, Va., 1969—; mem. council on Christian Unity, Christian Ch. Named Tchr. of Yr., Bethany Christian Ch., 1983. Mem. Disciples of Christ Hist. Soc., Nat. Audubon Soc., Smithsonian Assos., Postal Commemorative Soc., Am. Assn. Ret. Persons, Va. Christian Ministers Conf., Roanoke Valley Ministers Conf., Am. Conservative Union, Nat. Taxpayers Union, Nat. Wildlife Fedn., Automobile Club Va. Republican. Club: Pioneer (Lynchburg Coll.) (dir.). Home: 1678 Springbrook Rd NW Roanoke VA 24017

STROBEL, HOWARD AUSTIN, chemistry educator, researcher; b. Bremerton, Wash., Sept. 5, 1920; s. Franklin Edward and Emma Lena (Scheurer) S.; m. Shirley Lou Holcomb, Aug. 26, 1953; children—Paul Austin, Gary Dent, Linda Susan. B.S., Wash. State U., 1942; Ph.D., Brown U., 1947. Jr. chemist Manhattan Project, Brown U., Providence, 1943-45; instr. Duke U., Durham, N.C., 1948-51, asst. prof., 1951-58, assoc. prof., 1958-64, prof., 1964—, asst. dean Trinity Coll., 1956-64, 72-82, assoc. dean, 1964-66, coordinator of fedns., 1974-82, dean Baldwin Fedn., 1972-75, faculty fellow, 1975-83; researcher/participant Oak Ridge Nat. Lab., 1950; vis. prof. U. Leicester, 1971-72; cons. NSF. Recipient Outstanding Prof. award Duke U., 1969. Mem. Am. Chem. Soc., Royal Soc. Chemistry, Phi Beta Kappa, Sigma Xi. Democrat. Baptist. Author: Chemical Instrumentation, 2d edit., 1973; contbr. numerous articles to profl. jours. Home: 1119 Woodburn Rd Durham NC 27705 Office: Dept Chemistry Duke U Durham NC 27706

STRODE, STEVEN WAYNE, physician; b. Dallas, Jan. 4, 1949; s. Royall Maurice and Maida (Sommerville) S.; B.S., So. Meth. U., 1969; M.D., U. Tex. Southwestern Med. Sch., 1974; m. Peggy Lee O'Neill, Sept. 21, 1974; children—Sean Wayne, Colleen Leigh. Intern, U. Ark. for Med. Scis., Little Rock, 1974-75; resident in family practice U. Ark. for Med. Scis., Little Rock, 1974-77, chief resident in family medicine, 1976-77, asst. prof. dept. family and community medicine, 1978—, also dir. behavioral sci., residency dir. dept. family and community medicine. teaching fellow in family medicine U. Western Ont., London, Can., 1977; practice family medicine, Jacksonville, Ark., 1977, Sherwood, Ark., 1980-84. Diplomate Am. Bd. Family Practice. Mem. Am. Acad. Family Physicians, Ark. Acad. Family Physicians, Soc. Tchrs. Family Medicine, Conf. Family Practice Residents (Ark. del. 1975-76), Phi Beta Kappa, Phi Eta Sigma, Beta Beta Beta. Methodist. Home: 104 Charter Ct Sherwood AR 72116 Office: UAMS Slot 530 Little Rock AR 72205

STRONACH, CAREY ELLIOTT, physicist, educator; b. Boston, Aug. 8, 1940; s. Ralph Howard and Frances Burns (Maynard) S.; B.S., U. Richmond (Va.), 1961; M.S. (duPont fellow 1961-63), U. Va., 1963; Ph.D., Coll. William and Mary, Williamsburg, Va., 1975; m. Joan Alice Louise Venner, Aug. 20, 1966; children—John Maynard, Howard Stanley. Instr. physics Va. State U., Petersburg, 1965-66, asst. prof., 1966-71, 72-76, assoc. prof., 1976-78, 79-80, prof., 1980—, dir. Muon Spin Rotation Research Program, 1977—, dir. Solid State Physics Research Inst., 1983—, radiation safety officer, 1983—; vis. assoc. prof. U. Alta., 1978-79; guest scientist Brookhaven Nat. Lab. Pres., Petersburg area chpt. Va. Council Human Relations, 1965-67; mem. Petersburg Commn. Community Relations Affairs, 1974-77; corr. sec. Petersburg Democratic Com., 1974-77, mem., 1972-78, 79—, vice chmn., 1981-85; mem. Va. Nat. Dems. NSF sci. faculty fellow, 1971-72; NASA summer faculty fellow, 1976. Mem. Am. Phys. Soc., Am. Assn. Physics Tchrs., AAUP (chpt. pres. 1968-70), AAAS, Va. Acad. Sci. (sec. astronomy, math. and physics sect. 1983-84, chmn. 1984-85), Nat. Inst. Sci., Fedn. Am. Scientists, Southeastern Univs. Research Assn. (site selection com. 1980-81, materials sci. com. 1983—, trustee 1983—, sci. and tech. com. 1986—), Los Alamos Meson Physics Facility Users' Group, Phi Beta Kappa, Sigma Xi (chpt. sec. 1977-78, chpt. pres. 1980—), Sigma Pi Sigma, Pi Mu Epsilon. Episcopalian. Club: Richmond Physics. Author papers in field. Home: 2241 Buckner St Petersburg VA 23805 Office: Box 358 Va State U Petersburg VA 23803

STRONG, LINDA JO, oil co. exec.; b. Alba, Tex., Apr. 20, 1941; d. Leonard Leon and Lucy (Earlene) McCollum) Oglesby; ed. Tyler Comml. Coll.; m. Jimmy C. McDonough, Feb. 12, 1960; children—Anna Catherine, Deborah Sue; m. George R. Strong, Mar. 18, 1983. Sec. to trust officer First Nat. Bank Dallas, 1960-64; payroll clk., Woolf & Magee, Inc., Tyler, Tex., 1964-70, acctg. dept., 1970-80, sec., treas., office mgr., 1981—. Named First Lady Desk and Derrick, 1975. Mem. Tyler Desk & Derrick Club Am. Republican. Baptist. Club: Rose Capital Pilot (pres. 1983-84). Home: Rt 4 Box 504 Lindale TX 75771 Office: PO Box 6566 Tyler TX 75703

STRONG, ROBERT ALAN, political science educator, author; b. Balt., May 24, 1948; s. Edwin George and Catherine (Baker) S.; m. Elaine Marie Chisek, Sept. 5, 1976. B.A., Kenyon Coll., 1970; M.A., No. Ill. U., 1977; Ph.D., U. Va., 1980. Vis. fellow U. Coll. Wales, Aberystwyth, 1980-81; research assoc. Miller Ctr., U. Va., Charlottesville, 1981-82; asst. prof. polit. sci. Tulane U., New Orleans, 1982—. Author: Bureaucracy and Statesmanship, 1985. Served to lt. USN, 1970-74. Leverhulme fellow 1980-81, Earhart fellow, 1981-82. Mem. Am. Polit. Sci. Assn., Fgn. Relations Assn. Office: Tulane U Dept Polit Sci New Orleans LA 70118

STROPE, RALPH MORGAN, food company executive; b. Cameron, W.Va., Dec. 19, 1944; s. George Morgan and Mary Myrtle (Haws) S.; B.S. in Math., W.Va., Inst. Tech., 1966; m. Carol Lee Feist, Apr. 24, 1971; children—Steven, Kevin. Indsl. engr. Gen. Foods Corp., Dover, Del., 1969-73, planning and distbn. mgr., White Plains, N.Y., 1973-76, ops. mgr., 1976-80; v.p. ops. King Cola World Corp., N.Y.C., 1980-82; mgr. Kroger Sav-On, div. Kroger Co., Charleston, S.C., 1982-86; sales coordinator Westover Dairy div. Kroger Co., 1986—. Mem. Soc. Soft Drink Technologists, U.S. C. of C., Nat. Rifle Assn. (life). Republican. Clubs: Elks, Masons, Shriners. Home: 7200 Oswego Ct Charlotte NC 28226 Office: 5435 Seventy-Seven Center Dr Charlotte NC 28224

STROUD, ROBERT EDWARD, lawyer; b. Chester, S.C., July 24, 1934; s. Coy Franklin and Leila (Caldwell) S.; A.B., Washington and Lee U., 1956, LL.B., 1959; m. Katherine E. Clark, Apr. 8, 1961; children—Robert Gordon, Margaret Lathan. Admitted to Va. bar, 1959; asso. McGuire, Woods & Battle, Charlottesville, 1959-64, partner 1964—, mem. exec. com., 1977—, head Charlottesville Office, 1977—; lectr. Washington and Lee U., 1957-59; lectr. bus. taxation Grad. Sch. Bus. Adminstrn., U. Va., 1969—; lectr. various legal edn. insts.; adj. prof. corp. law Washington and Lee Law Sch., 1984; Pres. Charlottesville Housing Found., 1968-73; mem. Montreat (N.C.) Mgmt. Council, 1974-77; mem. council Synod of Virginias, Presbyn. Ch. U.S., 1973-77, moderator, 1977-78; mem. Washington and Lee Law Council, 1975-81, pres., 1979-80; trustee Presbyn. Found., 1972-73, Union Theol. Sem., Va., 1983—; mem. gen. exec. bd. Presbyn. Ch. U.S., 1972-73. Served to 2d lt. with AUS, 1957. Mem. ABA, Va. Bar Assn. (vice chmn. bd. govs. bus. law sect. 1981-82), Tax Inst. Am., Am. Judicature Soc., Washington and Lee Law Sch. Assn. (pres. 1979-80), Phi Eta Sigma, Pi Kappa Phi, Omicron Delta Kappa, Phi Delta Phi. Co-author: Buying, Selling and Merging Businesses, 1975. Editor: Advising Small Business Clients, Vol. I, 1978, 82, Vol. II, 1980, 83; editor-in-chief Washington and Lee Law Rev., 1959; contbr. articles to profl. jours. Home: 104 Woodstock Dr Charlottesville VA 22901 Office: PO Box 1219 Charlottesville VA 22902

STROUPE, HENRY SMITH, university dean, history educator; b. Alexis, N.C., June 3, 1914; s. Stephen Morris and Augie Virginia (Lineberger) S.; m. Mary Elizabeth Denham, June 2, 1942; children—Stephen Denham, David Henry. Student Mars Hill Coll., Mars Hill, N.C., 1931-33; B.S., Wake Forest Coll., 1935, M.A., 1937; Ph.D., Duke U., 1942. Mem. faculty Wake Forest U., 1937—, assoc. prof. history, 1949-54, prof., 1954—, chmn. dept. history, 1954-68, dir. evening classes, 1957-61, dir. div. grad. studies, 1961-67, dean Grad. Sch., 1967—; vis. prof. Duke U., 1960. Mem. Civil War Centennial Commn. of State of N.C., 1959-61; mem. N.C. Hwy. Hist. Marker Com., 1971-77. Served to lt. USNR, 1943-46. Recipient Christopher Crittenden Meml. award Lit. and Hist. Assn. N.C., 1982. Mem. So. Hist. Assn., Hist. Soc. N.C., Lit. and Hist. Assn. N.C., Phi Beta Kappa. Democrat. Baptist. Club: Pine Brook (Winston-Salem). Author: The Religious Press in the South Atlantic States, 1802-1865, An Annotated Bibliography with Historical Introduction and Notes, 1956; mem. adv. editorial bd. N.C. Hist. Rev., 1963-69. Home: 2016 Faculty Dr Winston Salem NC 27106 Office: Wake Forest U Winston Salem NC 27109

STRUENSE, RICHARD WAYNE, delivery service administrator; b. East St. Louis, Ill., June 21, 1945; s. Philip J. and Myrtle (Root) S.; m. Sherry Ann Wilson, Jan. 21, 1964; children—Richard Brent, Brian Keith, Brock Ashton. B.S. in Data Processing, Washington U., St. Louis, 1976. With Ralson Purina, Gen. Steel Industries and Scott Paper Co., various locations, 1967-71; support rep. Pet Inc., St. Louis, 1972-76; sr. programmer/analyst Ingalls Shipbuilding Div., Litton Industries, 1976-79, Federal Express, 1979-81; sr. mgr. info. ctr. Federal Express, Memphis, 1981—; pres. CITA Data Services. Bd. dirs. Boy's Town of Memphis, 1983—; pres. Collierville Band Boosters, 1981-82. Mem. Data Processing Mgmt. Assn., Guide Internat. (mgr. info. ctr. project, group mgr. methodologies and futures), Full Gospel Bus. Men's Assn. Republican. Mem. Pentecostal Ch. Club: Sertoma (v.p.).

STRUHL, THEODORE ROOSEVELT, surgeon; b. N.Y.C., Jan. 5, 1917; s. Samuel and Florence (Kossoy) S.; m. Ruth Brand, Oct. 19, 1941; children—Karsten, Wendy. B.A., NYU, 1936, M.S., 1938; M.D., N.Y. Med. Coll., 1942, M.S. in Surgery, 1947; grad. Julliard Conservatory of Music, 1933. Diplomate Am. Bd. Abdominal Surgery, Am. Bd. Surgery. Intern Queens Gen. Hosp., Jamaica, N.Y., 1942-43; resident VA Hosp. Newington, Conn., 1947-48, Cumberland Med. Ctr., Bklyn., 1948-51; practice medicine specializing in surgery, Miami, Fla., 1951—; mem. staff Mt. Sinai Med. Ctr., Miami Beach, Fla., Jackson Meml. Hosp., Cedars of Lebanon Health Care Ctr. Variety Children's Hosp., South Shore Hosp., Miami Beach, Victoria Hosp.; former instr. in anatomy L.I. Coll. Medicine, N.Y.; instr. in surgery, instr. in anatomy and surg. anatomy U. Miami; instr. in surg. anatomy and surgery Mt. Sinai Med. Ctr.; med. adviser ARC of Dade County, Fla.; chief med. examiner Miami Beach Boxing Commn.; chief med. adviser World Boxing Assn., U.S. Boxing Assn.; med. adviser World Martial Arts, Judo and Karate; mem. Am. Bd. Quality Assurance and Utilization Rev. Physicians; formerly instr. in diving medicine Underwater Demolition Team Sch., U.S. Navy, Key West, Fla.; lectr., instr. in scuba diving, diving medicine; lectr. on medicine and surgery, cancer, artificial respiration, anatomy, hypnosis, boxing, weight lifting, judo, skin and scuba diving, swimming, water skiing, small craft, wrestling, music. Active ARC, 1936—, now bd. dirs., chmn. safety services ARC of Dade County; instr./trainer in CPR, instr. in advanced cardiac life support Am. Heart Assn.; former mem. N.Y. div. Olympic Wrestling Com. Served to maj. M.C., U.S. Army, World War II; ETO. Contbr. articles to profl. and sports publs. Fellow ACS, Internat. Coll. Surgeons (vice-regent Fla.), Am. Coll. Angiology, Internat. Acad. Proctology; mem. AMA (Physicians Recognition award 1986), So. Med. Assn., Fla. Med. Assn., Dade County Med. Assn., Israeli Med. Assn., Fla. Assn. Gen. Surgeons (charter), Med. Hypnosis Assn. Dade County (past pres.), Am. Coll. Angiology, Pan Am. Med. Assn., Am. Soc. Abdominal Surgeons, Am. Soc. Contemporary Medicine and Surgery, Med. Aspects of Atomic Explosion, Assn. Mil. Surgeons U.S., Am. Coll. Sports Medicine, Commodore Longfellow Soc., Miami Beach Power Squadron (charter), Am. Canoe Assn., Am. White Water Assn., Underwater Med. Soc., Photog. Soc. Am., Contin Hon. Soc. of N.Y. Med. Coll., Phi Delta Epsilon (past pres. chpt.). Democrat. Jewish. Holder black belt in judo; black belt in karate, 2d degree. Home: 44 Star Island Miami Beach FL 33139 Office: 1444 Biscayne Blvd Suite 304 Miami FL 33132

STRUL, GENE M., telecommunications company executive, former TV news dir.; b. Bklyn., Mar. 25, 1927; s. Joseph and Sally (Chartoff) S.; student journalism U. Miami (Fla.), 1945-47; m. Shirley Dolly Silber, Aug. 7, 1949; children—Ricky, Gary, Eileen. News dir. Sta. WIOD AM-FM, Miami, 1947-56; assignment editor, producer Sta. WCKT-TV, Miami, 1956-57, news dir., 1957-79; dir. broadcast news Miami News, 1957; free-lance writer newspapers and mags.; cons. dept. communications U. Miami, 1979, acting dir. public relations, 1979-80; v.p. Hernstadt Broadcasting Corp., 1980-81; dir. corp. communications Burnup & Sims, 1981—. Communications dir. United Way of Dade County, 1981. Served with AUS, 1945. Recipient Peabody award, 1975; Preceptor award Broadcast Industry conf., San Francisco State U.; Peabody award, 1975; Abe Lincoln awards (2) So. Baptist Radio-TV Conf.; Nat. Headliners awards (5); led Sta. WCKT to more than 200 awards for news, including 3 Peabody awards, Emmy award, 2 Nat. Sigma Delta Chi awards; Peabody award, 1975. Mem. Nat. Acad. Television Arts and Scis. (past gov. Miami chpt.), Radio-TV News Dirs. Assn., Fla. AP Broadcasters (past pres.), Greater Miami C. of C., Nat. Broadcast Editorial Assn., Sigma Delta Chi. Home: 145 SW 49th Ave Miami FL 33134

STRUM, LAWRENCE M., medical marketing consultant; b. Ventnor Heights, N.J., Sept. 1, 1935; s. Marcus and Jeanette (Arena) S.; m. Cissy F. Brown, May 26, 1956; children—Michael Gary, Laurie. B.S., Boston U., 1957. Corr. N.Y. Times, Atlantic City, 1948-50; staff announcer Sta. WFPG-AM-FM-TV, Atlantic City, 1951-53, Boston, 1955-70; reporter Boston Herald-Traveler, 1955-67; writer, performer Sta. WGBH-TV, Boston, 1964-70; corr. Christian Sci. Monitor, Boston, 1967-68; press. sec. City of Boston, 1968-70, press aide to gov. State of Boston, 1973-74; communications officer Boston U. Med. Ctr., 1970-74, Comprehensive Cancer Ctr., State of Fla., 1974-77; pres. Health Care Communications, Inc., Miami, Fla., 1979—. Editor: (anthology) Behind Prison Walls 1974; Manual for MDs On New and Unproven Methods of Cancer Therapy, 1979. Pres. South End Innergy Council, Boston, 1973-74, South Fla. Hosp. Assn., Miami, 1978; press officer for Carter and Mondale, Fla., 1976; bd. dirs. Fla. unit Am. Cancer Soc., 1974—; founder, pres. Boston Med. Communications Group, 1972-74; founder 1st health fairs in Dade County; bd. dirs. Nat. Football Found. Hall of Fame, 1964-66. Recipient 1st place for publs. Am. Cancer Soc., 1976. Mem. Am. Med. Writers Assn. (v.p. 1981-83), Fla. Writers Assn. (founder med./health sect.), Kendall Pioneers (founder 1985), Sigma Delta Chi (founder scholarship program New Eng. and Greater Miami chpts.). Democrat. Jewish. Home: 11550 SW 82nd Terr Miami FL 33173 Office: Health Care Communications Inc 11550 SW 82nd Terr Miami FL 33173

STRUM, ORPHIA THEO, university administrator; b. Roxboro, N.C., Dec. 1, 1924; d. Orphia T. and Mattie (Scoggin) S. A.B., Elon Coll., 1945; M.Ed., U. N.C.-Greensboro, 1955; Ph.D., U. N.C.-Chapel Hill, 1965. Tchr., adminstr. Durham County (N.C.) Schs., 1956-63; dean of women Elon Coll., 1964-68, assoc. dean of coll., 1968-69, dean of instrn., 1969-73, dean of coll., 1973-76; chmn. div. profl. programs Campbell U., 1976—. Mem. N.C. Adv. Council on Tchr. Edn., 1979—, N.C. Tchr. Edn. Evaluation Com., 1978—, N.C. Com. on Coll. Transfer, 1982—. Mem. AAUW, Bus. and Profl. Women's Club (past state treas.), Pi Gamma Mu, Phi Theta Kappa, Alpha Chi, Omicron Delta Kappa, Delta Kappa Gamma, Phi Kappa Phi. Democrat. Home: 6 Burkot Rd Buies Creek NC 27606 Office: Taylor Hall Campbell U Buies Creek NC 27506

STRUNK, MARK NEIL, college counselor; b. Kingston, Pa., June 16, 1953; s. Jack Hoyt and Martha Mae (Matheson) S.; m. Rebecca Jane Page, June 24, 1978; 1 child, Kristin Rebecca. B.A., U. Ala.-Tuscaloosa, 1975, M.A., 1977; postgrad. U. Auburn, 1979—. Lic. profl. counselor, Ala. Asst. coordinator career devel. U. Ala., Tuscaloosa, 1976-77; asst. dir. student activities Ga. Coll., Milledgeville, 1977-78; counselor spl. service Columbus Coll., Ga., 1978-79, counselor, coordinator placement, 1979—; cons. Muscogee County Bd. Edn., Columbus, 1982—, Pvt. Industry Council, 1981-82. Mem. Am. Assn. for Counseling and Devel., Am. Coll. Personnel Assn., Am. Soc. Personnel Adminstrs., Ga. Coll. Placement Assn., Columbus Area Personnel Assn. Methodist. Clubs: Fountain City Magic (pres. 1981-82), Internat. Brotherhood of Magicians. Avocations: magic; tennis singing; photography; cooking. Home: Route 5 Box 2211 Phenix City AL 36867 Office: Columbus Coll Counseling and Placement Center Columbus GA 31993

STRUZYNA, GEORGE ARTHUR FELIX, college administrator; b. Breslau, Germany, July 13, 1920; came to U.S., 1958, naturalized, 1964; s. Joseph and Elise (Leppmann) S.; m. Erika Hertha Schomburgk, May 27, 1950; children—Reinhart W., Dieter G., Dorothee E. Diplom-Ingenieur, Hanover Inst. Tech., Germany, 1950; postgrad. U. Bristol, Eng., 1949, Veasey Coll. Engring., South Africa, 1954-56. Registered profl. engr., N.J., S.C. Asst. to plant mgr. German Highgrade Steel Co., Remscheid, 1950; design engr., plant engr. Bayer AG, Leverkusen, Germany, 1951-53; chief engr. No. 1 ammonia plant African Explosives and Chem. Industris, Johannesburg, South Africa, 1954-57, chief engr., v.p. engring. Verona Chem. Corp., Union, N.J., 1958-76; dir. plant engring., maintenance and utilities Mobay Chem. Corp., Pitts., 1976-82; v.p. div. support services Trident Tech. Coll., Charleston, S.C., 1984—; chmn. Internat. Conf. Coal Gasification and Liquefaction, U. Pitts. Contbr. articles to profl. jours. Chmn. bd. dirs. German Lang. Sch., Union, 1964-68. Served with German Army, 1940-45. Decorated Iron Cross 1st and 2d class; Mem. Nat. Soc. Profl. Engrs. (chpt. pres. 1974-75), ASME, Atlantic Council U.S. Republican. Methodist. Lodge: Rotary. Office: Trident Tech Coll PO Box 10367 Charleston SC 29411

STRYKER, STEVEN CHARLES, lawyer; b. Omaha, Oct. 26, 1944; s. James M. and Jean G. (Grannis) S.; B.S., U. Iowa, 1967, J.D. with distinction, 1969; postgrad. Northwestern Grad. Sch. Bus., 1969-70; M.Taxation, DePaul, U., 1971; m. Byrna Dee Litwin, Oct. 20, 1972; children—Ryan, Kevin, Gerrit, Courtney. Bar: Iowa 1969; sr. tax acct. Arthur Young & Co., Chgo., 1969-72; fed. tax mgr. Massey Ferguson, Des Moines, 1972-74; fed./state tax mgr. FMC Corp., Chgo., 1974-78; gen. tax atty. Shell Oil Co., Houston, 1978-81, asst. gen. tax counsel, 1981-83, gen. mgr., 1983-86, v.p., gen. tax counsel, 1986—. C.P.A., Ill., Iowa. Mem. Am. Bar Assn., Am. Inst. C.P.A.s, Tax Execs. Inst., Am. Petroleum Inst., Iowa Bar Assn., Ill. Soc. C.P.A.s, Iowa Soc. C.P.A.s. Republican. Home: 10819 Everwood St Houston TX 77024 Office: 1 Shell Plaza Suite 4570 Houston TX 77001

STUART, BRUCE ROBERT, consultant; b. N.Y.C., Dec. 22, 1943; s. Jack Lord and Mary Joy (Crozier) S.; m. Kathleen Turner, Nov. 6, 1970; children—Ellen Paige, Christopher Lowrie, Keena Dare, m. Jo Ellen Smith, May 28, 1963 (div. Sept. 1970). Student U. Richmond, 1961-65. Co-founder Chesterfield CJ Corp., Richmond, Va., 1965—, chmn. bd., 1983—. Mem. Va. Motorcycle Dealer's Assn. (pres. 1981—). Home: Route 2 Box 1 Amelia VA 23002 Office: Chesterfield CJ Corp 11225 Mid Pike Richmond VA 23235

STUART, WALTER BYNUM, IV, lawyer; b. Grosse Tete, La., Nov. 23, 1946; s. Walter Bynum III and Rita (Kleinpeter) S.; m. Lettice Lee Binnings May 18, 1968; children—Courtney Lyon, Walter Burke. Student Fordham U., 1964-65; B.A., Tulane U., 1968, J.D., 1973. Bar: La. 1973, U.S. Dist. Ct. (ea. and we. dists.) La. 1974, U.S. Tax Ct. 1974, U.S. Supreme Ct. 1981, U.S. Dist Ct. (so. dist.) N.Y. 1983. Ptnr. Stone, Pigman, Walter, Wittman and Hutchinson, New Orleans, 1973-78; ptnr. Singer, Hutner, Levine, Seeman and Stuart, New Orleans, 1978-81; ptnr. Gordon, Arata, McCollam and Stuart, New Orleans, 1981—; instr. Tulane U. Law Sch., 1978-82; dir. First Nat. Bank of Jefferson, Jefferson Parish, La., Inst. Politics, 1975—; mem. adv. bd. City Atty.'s Office, New Orleans, 1978-79. Mem. ABA, La. Bar Assn., New Orleans Bar Assn., La. Bankers Assn. (bank counsel com.). Democrat. Roman Catholic. Office: Gordon Arata McCollam & Stuart Pan Am Life Ctr 601 Poydras St New Orleans LA 70130

STUBBLEFIELD, JAMES BERT, JR., army officer; b. Charleston, Ark., Oct. 9, 1934; s. James Bert and Violet Hettie (Clevenger) S.; m. Patsy Jane Alley, June 24, 1956; children—James Bert III, Kelly Jane. B.S., Ark. Tech. U., 1956; M.H.A., Baylor U., 1969. Commd. 2d lt. U.S. Army, 1956, advanced through grades to col.; chief Supply and Services div. Noble Army Hosp., Ft. McClellan, Ala., 1962-64; med. advisor III Corps Tactical Zone, Vietnam, 1964-65; project officer Combat Devel. Command Inst. Combined Arms and Support, Ft. Leavenworth, Kans., 1966-67; sect. and br. chief Acad. Health Scis., Ft. Sam Houston, Tex., 1970-74; asst. chief health care adminstrn. div., dep. dir. U.S. Army-Baylor U. Grad. Program in Health Care Adminstrn., Acad. Health Scis., Ft. Sam Houston, 1974-75, chief, assoc. prof., 1978-80; exec. officer, chief adminstrv. services Letterman Army Med. Ctr., Presidio of San Francisco, 1980-83, chief of staff Brooke Army Med. Ctr., Ft. Sam Houston, 1983—. Decorated Bronze Star, Air medal. Fellow Am. Coll. Hosp. Adminstrs.; mem. Am. Hosp. Assn., Tex. Hosp. Assn., Am. Mgmt. Assn., Alamo Hosp. Adminstrs. Council, Trinity U. Health Care Adv. Council, Baylor U. Adv. Council. Baptist. Office: Brooke Army Med Ctr Fort Sam Houston TX 78234

STUBBS, SIDNEY ALTON, lawyer; b. Gainesville, Fla., Nov. 29, 1938; s. Sidney Alton and Esther Ann (Witt) S.; m. Annette McIntosh, Feb. 7, 1938; children—Melaine K., Natalie K., Scott M. B.S. in History, Fla. State U., 1960; J.D. with honors, U. Fla., 1965. Bar: Fla. 1966, U.S. Dist. Ct. (so. dist.) Fla. 1967, U.S. Ct. Appeals (5th cir.) 1981, U.S. Ct. Appeals (11th cir.) 1981. Mem. Jones & Foster, P.A., West Palm Beach, Fla., 1972—; spl. counsel to Fla. Gov. Bob Graham, 1983-84; mem. adv. bd. Southwestern Legal Found., 1983. Asst. scoutmaster Boy Scouts Am. Served with USAF, 1960-63. Mem. Fla. Bar Assn. (bd. govs. 1980—), Palm Beach County Bar Assn. (pres. 1978-79). Club: Kiwanis (pres. West Palm Beach Club 1978-79). Office: PO Drawer E West Palm Beach FL 33402

STUCKEY, COATES, mental retardation facility administrator; b. Monroe, La., May 1, 1917; s. E. Coates and Hattie (Kilpatrick) S.; m. Dorothy Iles, Mar. 23, 1940; children—Linnie (Mrs. Kenneth A. Single), Jane (Mrs. Kenny Charbonnet). B.S. in Bus. Adminstrn., La. State U., 1938. Mem. Highway Commn., State of La., Baton Rouge, 1938-41; field auditor La. Div. of Employment Security, Alexandria, 1941-48; mem. Div. of Adminstrn. Office of Gov., Alexandria, 1948-50; bus. adminstr. State Colony and Tng. Sch., Pineville, La., 1950-55, Central La. State Hosp., Pineville, 1955-60; adminstr. Pinecrest State Sch., Pineville, 1960—; organizer La. Dept. Hosp. Credit Union, Baton Rouge, 1956, bd. dirs., 1956—; pres. 1963-67; bd. dirs. Rapides United Givers, Alexandria, 1963-67; mem. adv. com. St. Mary's Residential Tng. Sch., 1983—; mem. Study Com. for Joint Commn. Accreditation of Hosps., Accrediation of Residential Facilities for Mentally Retarded; lectr. in field. Contbr. chpts. in books; author publs. in field. Mem. Gov.'s Commn. on Handicapped. Recipient Pres.' Cup La. Assn. for Retarded Children, 1964; Hon. Mention Charles E. Dunbar Jr. Career Service awards La. Civil Service League, 1964, 70; named Best Supr. in State Service, 1972; recipient Service award Nat. Am. Assn. on Mental Deficiency, 1978. Fellow Am. Assn. on Mental Deficiency (1st ann. Helen Thompson Meml. award Region V, 2d ann. Helen Thompson Meml. award La. Chpt. 1983, regional counsellor 1964-67, mem. legis. and social issues com.); mem. Nat. Assn. Superintendents of Public Residential Facilities for Mentally Retarded (spl. achievement award 1985), La. State U. Alumni Assn. Democrat. Episcopalian. Office: Pinecrest State School PO Box 191 Pineville LA 71360

STUCKEY, JOE WAYLON, lawyer, engineer; b. Atlanta, Tex., Apr. 19, 1943; s. Joseph Norman and Nobie Jane S.; B.S. in Civil Engring., Tex. A&M U., 1965; J.D., U. Houston, 1974; m. Kay Connor, Sept. 3, 1966; children—Harold

Troy, Thomas Nathaniel. Pres., Joe W. Stuckey & Assos., Inc., Cons.-Engrs.-Surveyors-Mgrs., Houston, 1976—; admitted to Tex. bar, 1974. Active Boy Scouts Am. Registered profl. engr., Tex., public surveyor, Tex. Mem. Tex. Soc. Profl. Engrs., Nat. Soc. Profl. Engrs., Nat. Soc. Engring. Heritage, Am. Water Works Assn., Tex. Surveyors Assn., Tex. Utility Dist. Assn., Am. Congress Surveying and Mapping, La. Engring. Soc., Ark. Soc. Profl. Engrs. N.Mex. Soc. Profl. Engrs., Okla. Soc. Profl. Engrs., Am. Bar Assn., Houston Bar Assn., Houston Bd. Realtors, Tex. Assn. Realtors, Nat. Assn. Realtors, Tex. State Archery Assn.; Nat. Archery Assn., Houston C. of C. Methodist. Office: 6100 Corporate Dr Suite 550 Houston TX 77036

STULL, GREGORY JOHN, lawyer; b. Aurora, Ill., Aug. 2, 1952; s. John N. and Edith A. (Tiffany) S.; m. Margaret Aarons, Dec. 17, 1978; 1 child, Tiffany Lee. B.A., Northwestern U., 1973; J.D., John Marshall Law Sch., 1978. Bar: Ill. 1978, U.S. Dist. Ct. (no. dist.) Ill. 1978, Tex. 1980, U.S. Dist. Ct. (we. dist.) Tex. 1983, U.S. Tax Ct. 1984. Editor Commerce Clearing House, Inc., Chgo., 1978-80; regional v.p. Profl. Services, Inc., San Antonio, 1980-82; prin. shareholder Parenti & Stull, P.C., San Antonio, 1982—. Author: VEBA's Explained, 1983; also articles. Mem. ABA, San Antonio Bar Assn. (sec./treas. corp. counsel com. 1983-84, vice chair 1984-85), State Bar Tex. (tax. sect., faculty advanced tax law course 1984), Ill. State Bar Assn. Home: 13743 Hunters Moss San Antonio TX 78230 Office: Parenti & Stull PC 12440 West Ave San Antonio TX 78216

STUMBAUGH, LAWRENCE (BUD), state senator; b. Pensacola, Fla., Aug. 24, 1940; s. James H.R. and Mary (Elkins) S.; B.S., Daivd Lipscomb Coll., 1962; m. Carole Hollingsworth, 1961; children—Stacey Ann, Susan Delight. Mem. DeKalb (Ga.) County Democratic Exec. Com., 1972—, vice chmn., 1972-74; nat. sales trainer EBSCO Industries, Inc., Birmingham, Ala., 1966-68; v.p., regional mgr. Anthony Kane Assos., Inc., N.Y., 1968-72; v.p., gen. mgr. Norrell Security Service, Inc., Atlanta, 1972-76; pres. Stumbaugh Assos., Inc., 1976—, Team Temporaries, Inc., Atlanta, 1980—; mem. Ga. Senate, chmn. indsl. devel. com., 1975—. Bd. dirs. Healthcare, Inc., 1978—; treas., trustee Liberia for God Found., 1973—. Recipient Disting. Service award Kiwanis Internat., 1967; named Legislator of Yr., 1978. Mem. Ch. of Christ. Contbr. articles to Ga. Bus. News. Office: Ga Senate Atlanta GA 30334*

STURDIVANT, SUSAN, psychotherapist; b. Amarillo, Tex., Dec. 12, 1944; d. Wilton Charles and Betty Jane (Shoupe) Sturdivant. postgrad. U. Tex., 1967-71; Ph.D. in Clin. Psychology, Fielding Inst., 1977. Psychol. examiner Region X Ednl. Service Ctr., Richardson, Tex., 1971-72; psychologist Terrell State Hosp. Adolescent Ctr. (Tex.), 1972-79; pvt. practice psychotherapy, Dallas, 1979—; cons. Unit II, East Town Hosp., Dallas. Mem. Dallas Mus. Fine Arts; bd. dirs. Tejas council Girl Scouts U.S. Mem. Am. Acad. Psychotherapists, Am. Assn. Counseling and Devel., Assn. Women in Psychology, Exec. Women Dallas (bd. dirs.). Author: Therapy with Women: A Feminist Philosophy of Treatment, 1980. Home: 5326 Ridgedale St Dallas TX 75206 Office: 5304 E Mockingbird Suite 401 Dallas TX 75206

STURGEON, CHARLES EDWIN, chem. co. exec.; b. Cherryvale; Kans., May 30, 1928; s. William Charles and Lucile Myrtle (Gill) S.; children—Carol Ann, John Randolph, Richard Steven. A.A., Independence Jr. Coll., 1948; B.S., U. Kans., 1951; postgrad., U. Tulsa Grad. Sch., 1953-56; grad., Advanced Mgmt. Program, Harvard Bus. Sch., 1977. Research engr. Standard Oil and Gas, Tulsa, 1953-56; production supr. Vulcan Materials Co., Wichita, Kans., 1956-62, maintenance supt., 1962-64, mgr. tech. services, 1964-69, plant mgr., Newark, N.J., 1970-71, gen. mktg. mgr., v.p. mktg., Wichita, 1971-73, v.p. mfg., Birmingham, Ala., 1974-77, pres. chem. div., 1977—; dir. Jones Hamilton Co., Newark, Calif. Served with U.S. Army, 1951-53. Mem. Am. Inst. Chem. Engrs., Nat. Mgmt. Assn., Chlorine Inst., Chem. Mfg. Assn., Soc. Chem. Industries. Republican. Presbyterian. Clubs: Vestavia Country, Relay House. Office: PO Box 7689 Birmingham AL 35253

STURGILL, VIRGINIA NELL, nurse; b. BetsyLayne, Ky., Mar. 5, 1947; m. Willie G. Sturgill, Sept. 18, 1965; children—Dawn, Gina. A.A., Jefferson Community Coll., 1982. R.N., Ky. Seamstress Cloth World, Louisville, 1971-79; miniature designer Talents Unltd., Louisville, 1975-80; staff nurse Suburban Hosp., Louisville, 1982-83, charge nurse, 1983—; mem. Policy and Procedure Com., City of Louisville, 1982-83. Recipient Jefferson Community Coll. Merit award Jefferson Community Coll., 1981-82; Pollard nursing scholar Carl Pollard of Humana, 1982. Mem. Student Nurse Orgn. Republican. Mem. Ch. of Christ. Club: Blue Grass Bells (Louisville). Home: 9301 Plumwood Pl Crestwood KY 40014

STURGIS, C. M., criminal investigator; b. Memphis, July 8, 1953; m. Demetria Tillery, June 28, 1981; children—Chanté, Johnathan. B.Edn., Memphis State U., 1976. Asst. sales mgr. GT Distbrs., Rossville, Ga., 1977-82; policeman Memphis Police Dept., 1982-85; criminal investigator U.S. Dept. Justice, Louisville, 1985—. Mem. Jaycees. Republican. Avocations: golfing; shooting.

STURGIS, ELLIE TRAYNHAM, psychologist, educator; b. Rock Hill, S.C., Aug. 25, 1952; d. Thomas Johnson and Anna Beth (Lupo) Sturgis. B.A., Furman U., 1974; M.S., U. Ga., 1976, Ph.D., 1979. Lic. psychologist, Miss. Asst. prof. U. N.C., Chapel Hill, 1979-80; asst. prof. U. Miss. Med. Ctr., Jackson, 1981-84, assoc. prof. psychiatry/psychology, 1984—. Contbr. articles to profl. jours., chpts. to books. Mem. Am. Psychol. Assn., Assn. Advancement Behavior Therapy, Assn. for Advancement Psychology, Soc. for Behavioral Medicine, Soc. for Psychophysiol. Research, Chi Beta Phi, Psi Chi. Avocations: backpacking; reading; camping. Home: 127 Cumberland Rd Brandon MS 39042 Office: Dept Psychology/Psychiatry 2500 N State St Jackson MS 39216

STUTT, SHARON DALE GELBAUM, appliance company owner; b. N.Y.C., Apr. 23, 1950; d. Harold and Ruth (Flender) Gelbaum; m. Brian Stutt, Mar. 29, 1976; children—Joshua, Adam. Student Hunter Coll., DePaul U. Pub. sch. tchr., Chgo., 1971-74, N.Y.C., 1974-76; comptroller, owner Warehouse Appliance, Houston, 1978—. Recipient award INC Mag., 1983. Democrat. Jewish. Clubs: Beth Ann Sisterhood, ORT. Office: 11923 Katy Freeway Houston TX 77079

STUTTS, ELBERT HARRISON, b. Royal Armistead and Sallie Ann (Buie) S.; m. Evelyn Ruth Bailey, Jan. 3, 1947; 1 child, Sharon Kay Stutts Carlson. B.S., Flora McDonald Coll., N.C., 1957; M.A., Am. Coll. Fin., Calif., 1982; M.Ed., St. Andrews U., N.C., 1968. Devel. exec. Boy Scouts Am., North Brunswick, N.J., 1973-78, assoc. regional dir., Sunnyvale, Calif., 1978-84, fin. edn. and devel., Las Colinas, Tex., 1984—, fin. mktg. cons., 1979—; pres. Am. Coll. Fin., Sunnyvale, Calif., 1981—, ACF, Inc. of Calif. and Tex., 1981—. Author: Fund Raising Educational Systems, 1979. Mem. Council Advancement and Support of Edn., Am. Soc. Tng. and Devel., Nat. Assn. State Approved Colls. and Univs. Republican. Presbyterian. Avocations: classical music; reading; writing. Home: 122 Surrey Ln Euless TX 76039

SUAREZ, MICHAEL ANTHONY, consulting engineer; b. Havana, Cuba, Dec. 14, 1948; came to U.S., 1961, naturalized, 1973; s. Miguel Angel and Elena Felicia (Sanchez) S.; B.S. in Civil Engring., U. Miami, 1973, postgrad., 1974. Civil engr. Bert Saul, Cons. Engr., Miami, Fla., 1969-72, De-Zarraga & Donnell, Cons. Engrs., Coral Gables, Fla., 1972-76; civil engr., in-house cons. Cadillac Fairview-Southeastern Fla. Properties, Miami, 1976-80; pres. Michael A. Suarez & Assos., Inc., Cons. Engrs., Miami, 1980—, also dir.; pres., dir. Summa Enterprises, Inc., Summa Devel. Corp., Real Devel. Corp., Southeastern Properties Constrn., Inc. Mem. nat. adv. bd. Am. Security Council; chmn.'s adviser U.S. Congl. Adv. Bd.; mem. Republican Presdl. Task Force, Rep. Nat. Com., Fgn. Affairs Council. Registered profl. engr., Fla.; lic. gen. contractor, Fla.; recipient Presdl. Achievement award. Mem. Nat. Soc. Profl. Engrs., ASCE, Fla. Engring. Soc., Constrn. Specifications Inst., Am. Concrete Inst., Pre-Stressed Concrete Inst., Nat. Engring. and Physics Honor Soc. Republican. Roman Catholic. Club: Turnberry Isle Yacht and Country (Miami). Home: 13234 SW 110 Terr #2 Miami FL 33186

SUAREZ, XAVIER, city official. Mayor, City of Miami, Fla. Office: Office of Mayor 3500 Pan American Dr Miami FL 33133*

SUCHLICKI, JAIME, historian, educator; b. Havana, Cuba, Dec. 8, 1939; s. Salomon and Ana (Greenstein) S.; m. Carol Meyer, Jan. 26, 1964; children—Michael, Kevin, Joy. B.A., U. Miami, 1964, M.A., 1965; Ph.D., Tex. Christian U., 1968. Asst. to dir. Ctr. for Advanced Internat. Studies, U. Miami, 1964-65, research assoc., 1967-70, assoc. dir. Inst. Interam. Studies, 1970-71, dir., 1971-73, 82—, asst. prof. history, 1967-71, assoc. prof. history, 1971-75, prof., 1975—, assoc. dir. Ctr. for Advanced Internat. Studies, 1979-80; teaching fellow Tex. Christian U., 1965-66, fellow, 1966-67. Mem. nat. com. B'nai B'rith. Author: The Cuban Revolution: A Documentary Bibliography, 1952-68; University Students and Revolution in Cuba, 1920-1968, 1969; Cuba, Castro and Revolution, 1972; Cuba: From Columbus to Castro, 1975; Latin American Fact Book, 1975. Home: 1135 San Pedro Ave Coral Gables FL 33156 Office: Inst Interam Studies U Miami 1531 Brescia Ave Miami FL 33124

SUD, ISH, mechanical engineer; b. Calcutta, India, Oct. 6, 1949; s. Inder Sain and Santosh Vati (Law) S.; B.Tech., Indian Inst. Tech., Kanpur, 1970; M.S., Duke U., 1971, Ph.D., 1975. Design engr. T.C. Cooke, P.E., Inc., Cons. Engrs., Durham, 1974-77, dir. sect. energy mgmt. and spl. projects, 1978; sr. project engr., systems analyst Duke U., Durham, 1976—; pres. SUD Assocs., Cons. Engrs., Durham, 1979—. Mem. India Assn. (pres. 1973-74), ASHRAE, Nat. Soc. Profl. Engrs., ASME. Hindu. Contbr. articles to profl. jours. Home: 3004 Montgomery St Durham NC 27707 Office: 1805 Chapel Hill Rd Durham NC 27707

SUDDERTH, DIANE JERNIGAN, insurance agent; b. Dunn, N.C., Sept. 2, 1952; d. Josiah W. and Norva (Hawley) Jernigan; m. Clyde Thomas Sudderth, Jr., Feb. 2, 1975; children—Sarah Hawley, Rachel Jennings. B.A., Greensboro Coll., 1973. Sr. underwriter Kemper Group, Richmond, Va., 1974-81; casualty mgr. Md. Casualty Co., Richmond, 1981-84, Chapel Hill Ins. Agy., Inc., 1984—. Auction vol. Sta. WCVE-TV, Richmond, 1977—. Cert. profl. ins. woman Nat. Assn. Ins. Women, 1977. Mem. Durham Assn. Ins. Women, DAR (sec. 1982-83). Republican. Baptist. Home: PO Box 1094 Chapel Hill NC 27514 Office: Chapel Hill Ins Agy Inc PO Box 600 Chapel Hill NC 27514

SUDDETH, STEVEN MARKLEY, insurance agent; b. Tulsa, Feb. 27, 1946; s. Milton Sparks and Ida (Manning) S.; m. Deanne D. Cashman, Jan. 26, 1966; m. 2d Donna L. Vance, May 14, 1977. B.S. in Bus. Adminstrn., Okla. State U., 1970. C.L.U., chartered fin. cons. Agt., Girard Life, Stillwater, Okla., 1964-67; gen. agt. Western Security, Stillwater, 1967-72; asst. gen. agt. Conn. Mut. Ins. Co., Los Angeles, 1973-79, gen. agt., Omaha, 1979-82, Dallas, 1983—. Speaker profl. confs. Recipient awards Conn. Mut., 1975, 77, 80, 81, Omaha C. of C., 1979, 81-82. Mem. Am. Soc. C.L.U.s, Omaha Assn. Life Underwriters (bd. dirs. 1980-82, v.p.), Gen. Agts. and Mgrs. Assn. (bd. dirs. 1983—). Republican. Presbyterian. Clubs: University, Bent Tree Country (Dallas). Home: 5512 Bent Trail Dallas TX 75248 Office: Conn Mut Ins Co 15301 Dallas Pkwy LB 24 Suite 950 Dallas TX 75248

SUDDUTH, WILLIAM MCLEAN, museum director; b. Muskogee, Okla., Nov. 15, 1945; s. Freddy B. and Betty J. (McLean) S.; m. Sharon Kaye Cobb, Sept. 9, 1967. B.S. in Chemistry, U. Okla., 1969, M.A. in History of Sci., 1974, Ph.D. in History of Sci., 1978. Dir. Omniplex Project, Oklahoma City, 1978-79; exec. dir. N.C. Mus. Life and Sci., Durham, N.C., 1979-85; pres. Mus. History and Sci., Louisville, 1985—; mus. cons., 1976—; vis. lectr. Duke U., Durham, 1981-82; vis. prof. U. Okla., 1979; v.p. bd. trustees Assn. Sci. and Tech. Ctrs., Washington, 1980—, trustee, 1978—; trustee Okla. Zool. Soc., 1978-79. Producer, writer videotape presentation; contbr. articles to profl. jours. Cultural planning com. Triangle Council Govts., Durham, 1983; rep. to regional meeting Nat. Sci. Bd., Oklahoma City, 1977; judge Okla. State Sci. Fair, 1978-79; mem. Oklahoma County Democratic Central Com., 1979. Grantee, NEH, 1981, 83, Inst. Mus. Services, 1982, 83. Mem. AAAS, Am. Assn. Museums, Internat. Council Museums, History of Sci. Soc., Southeastern Museums Conf. Office: Museum History and Science 727 W Main St Louisville KY 40202

SUEHS, DERRICK JOURDAIN, health care educator, management consultant; b. Bryan, Tex., Mar. 26, 1954; s. William Anthony and Mavis Lucille (Heine) S.; m. Audrey Elaine Fuller, Jan. 3, 1976; children—Christian Vaughn, Erich Niklas. B.S. in Edn., Tex. A&M U., 1976; M.A. in Bus., Nat. U., 1982. Sr. cons. P.T.I., Houston, 1981-82; orgnl. devel. specialist Nat. Convenience Stores, Houston, 1982-83; tng. coordinator Meth. Hosp., Houston, 1983-86; dir. orgn. devel. St. Paul Med. Ctr., 1986—; hosp. cons. La. and Tex., 1984—. Author: Leading the Way Through Leadership, 1983; Bean Bag, 1985. Speaker Greater Houston Hosp. Mgmt. Systems Soc., 1984, Western Bones, Houston, 1985. Served to lt. USN, 1976-81. Recipient Mil. Excellence award Am. Legion, 1976. Mem. Am. Soc. Tng. and Devel., Am. Soc. Hosp. Edn. and Tng., Tex. Soc. Hosp. Educators, Cutten Green Civic Assn. Republican. Lutheran. Avocations: jogging, writing, water sports, gardening. Home: 11510 Glen Lane Ct Houston TX 77066 Office: St Paul Med Ctr 5909 Harry Hines Blvd Dallas TX 75235

SUESCUN, ELKIN, physician; b. Medellín, Colombia, May 30, 1937; came to U.S., 1965, naturalized, 1974; s. Jorge and Carolina (Gómez) S.; m. Gloria Vargas, Nov. 27, 1967; children—Mauricio Andrés, Ana María. M.D., U. Valley, Cali, Colombia, 1964. Resident in internal medicine Albert Einstein Med. Ctr., Phila., 1965-68, hematology fellowship, 1968-70; mem. staff hematology and oncology Wadley Inst., Dallas, 1971-72; pvt. practice medicine specializing in internal medicine and hematology, San Antonio, Tex., 1973—; chief internal medicine dept. Luth. Gen. Hosp., San Antonio, 1982—, v.p. med. staff, 1982—. Mem. Tex. Internal Medicine Soc., Tex. Diabetic Assn., AMA, Tex. Med. Assn., Bexar County Med. Soc., So. Med. Assn., Colombia Hematology Soc. Democrat. Roman Catholic. Club: Thousand Oaks Country. Office: 700 S Zarzamora St Suite 212 San Antonio TX 78230

SUITER, JOHN WILLIAM, industrial engineering consultant; b. Pasadena, Calif., Feb. 16, 1926; s. John Walter and Ethel May (Acton) S.; B.S. in Aero. Sci., Embry Riddle U., 1964; m. Joyce England, Dec. 3, 1952; children—Steven A., Carol A. Cons. indsl. engr., Boynton Beach, Fla., 1955—. Instr. U. S.C. Tech. Edn. Center, Charleston, 1967-69. Served as pilot USAF, 1944-46. Registered profl. engr., Fla. Mem. Am. Inst. Indsl. Engrs., Soc. Mfg. Engrs. (sr.), Computer and Automated Systems Assn., Methods-Time Measurement Assn. (assoc.), Soc. Quality Control. Home: 190 SE 27th Ave Boynton Beach FL 33435 Office: PO Box 1797 Delray Beach FL 33444

SUITER, JUDITH IRENE, corporation executive, management consultant; b. Sioux Falls, S.D., May 25, 1944; d. Frederick Louis and Lois Irene (Heller) Bohlke; m. Jerry Dean Suiter, Sept. 5, 1964; children—Jerry Brett, Andrew Blake. B.S., Middle Tenn. State U., 1975; postgrad. in managerial scis. Field mgr., staff assoc. Performax Systems Internat.; sales rep. Avon Products, Inc., Smyrna, Tenn., 1970-74, Con-Stan Industries, Smyrna, 1974-75, So. Electric Supply, Russellville, Ark., 1977-78, Apex Supply Co., Atlanta, 1979-80; cons. McIntosh Travel, Atlanta, 1980-81; pres. Competitive Edge, Inc., Peachtree City, Ga., 1981—. Author tng. program: Job Savvy & Options, 1983. Recipient sales awards, Avon, 1973, Con-Stan Industries, 1974; Gold Letter award Clemson U., 1984. Mem. Nat. Assn. Profl. Saleswomen (publicity chmn. 1980-81, Galaxy award 1981), Am. Businesswomen's Assn. (Bus. Assoc. of Yr. 1985), Ga. Assn. Adult Edn., Domestic Policy Assn., Nat. Assn. Female Execs., Fayette County C. of C. (edn. com. 1983-84, forum moderator Fayetteville 1983). Home: 307 Longer Dr Peachtree City GA 30269 Office: Competitive Edge Inc PO Box 2418 Peachtree City GA 30269

SUITER, NORMA JEAN, church official; b. Houston County, Tenn., Oct. 17, 1936; d. Roy Pascal and Emma Pearl (Provo) Mobley; m. Lacy Edward Suiter, Mar. 15, 1958; 1 dau., Melissa Elaine Suiter Gregory. Student U. Tenn., Tenn. State U., 1970-82. Ins. clk. Royal Globe Ins. Co., Nashville, 1955-57; sec. Interbd. Com. on Missionary Edn., The Methodist Ch., Nashville, 1957-66, adminstrv. asst. to gen. sec. Div. of the Local Ch., Bd. Edn., 1966-76, rec. sec. Bd. Discipleship, 1972-73, exec. dir. Gen. Bus. Services, Bd. Discipleship, 1976—, cons. affiliate mem. United Methodist Interagy. Task Force on Telecommunications Gen. Council on Fin. and Adminstrn. subcom. on Use of Personal Computer in Local Ch. Chairperson adminstrv. bd., mem. council on ministries fin. com. Donelson Heights United Meth. Ch. Mem. Am. Mgmt. Assn. Home: 2728 Pennington Bend Rd Nashville TN 37214 Office: United Meth Bd of Discipleship PO Box 840 Nashville TN 37202

SUITT, THOMAS HOWARD, construction company executive; b. Spartanburg, S.C., Aug. 4, 1926; s. Ben Green and Mary (Warwick) S.; m. Hilda Brockman, July 9, 1949; children—Thomas Howard, Nancy Warwick. B.S.C.E., The Citadel, 1948. Registered profl. engr., N.C., S.C. Engr., McKoy Weary, Greenville, S.C., 1949-51, Taylor Colquitt Co., Spartanburg, S.C., 1951-57, S.H. Kress Co., N.Y.C., 1957-60; div. mgr. Daniel Constrn. Co., Greenville and Greensboro, N.C., 1960-67; pres. Suitt Constrn. Co., Inc., Greenville, S.C., 1968—. Bd. dirs. YMCA, Greenville, 1974-81, Carolinas br. Associated Gen. Contractors, Charlotte, N.C., 1984. Mem. Greenville C. of C. (dir. 1980-83, 84). Methodist. Avocations: golf; tennis. Address: Suitt Constrn Co Inc 1400 Cleveland St Greenville SC 29604

SULFARO, JOYCE A., educator, former school principal; b. Bklyn., Oct. 23, 1948; d. John Joseph and Mildred Ann (Credidio) Carvelli; B.A., Molloy Coll., 1970; postgrad. Fla. Atlantic U., 1979-80; M.S. in Adminstrn. and Supervision, Nova U., 1982; m. Guy Sulfaro, Aug. 1, 1971; children—Jacqueline A., Kristin Lynn. Tutor reading Our Lady of Loretto, Rockville Centre, N.Y., 1969-70; tchr. lang. arts and math. Resurrection Sch., Bklyn., 1970-73; tchr. Annunciation Sch., Hollywood, Fla., 1976-80, prin., 1980-84; writer English curriculum for Jr. High for Archdiocese of Miami, 1979. Travel coordinator/sec. Rego Park (N.Y.) Met. Youth Orgn., 1969-70. Mem. Nat. Council Tchrs. Math., Fla. League of Middle Schs., Cath. Educators Guild Archdiocese of Miami, Nat. Cath. Ednl. Assn., Am. Mus. Natural History, Annunciation Athletic Assn. (v.p. 1983-84). Author: (with M. Sue Timmins) The Basket, 1980. Home: 5626 Centennial Dr Durham NC 27712

SULLIVAN, ANGELA MARIA, biologist; b. New Orleans, Nov. 8, 1957; d. Joseph Lee and Doris Mae (Barnes) Sullivan. B.S., St. Mary's Dominion Coll., 1981. Chemistry lab. technician So. U., New Orleans, 1982-83, 85; selling assoc. Goudchase-Maison Blanche, Baton Rouge and New Orleans, 1984-85; research assoc. La. State U. Med. Ctr., New Orleans, 1985—. Mem. Beta Beta Beta. Democrat. Roman Catholic. Avocations: Photography; gourmet cooking; travel. Home: 4708 Odin St New Orleans LA 70126 Office: La State U Med Ctr 1100 Florida Ave New Orleans LA

SULLIVAN, CHARLES ROLAND, real estate broker; b. Balt., Sept. 19, 1931; s. Charles R. and Mabel Lillian S.; B.S. in Bus. Adminstrn., Duquesne U., 1953; m. Helen Louise Bernica, July 31, 1970. Sales and mgmt. ofcl. IBM Corp., Washington and Los Angeles, 1955-68; Computer Scis. Corp. including Internat. div., Sydney, Australia, 1968-73; v.p. Arthur Rubloff & Co., 1973-78; owner, operator Sullivan Properties, Inc., Atlanta, 1978—. Served to 1st lt. USAF, 1953-55. Home: 2572 Circlewood Rd NE Atlanta GA 30345 Office: Sullivan Assocs Freeway Office Park A 125 Atlanta GA 30329

SULLIVAN, FRED MEYRITH, lawyer; b. Grosse Pointe Farms, Mich., Sept. 12, 1930; s. Frederick S. and Wilma (Jensen) S.; B.A., U. Tex., Austin, 1956, J.D., 1959, postgrad. 1970-71; student So. Meth. U., 1951-54; m. Sarah Ann Evans, Feb. 21, 1966; children—Robert, John, Ellen, Janet. Instr. real estate law U. Maine, Lewiston, 1968-70, U. Tex., El Paso, 1981-82; adj. prof. real estate Dallas Bapt. Coll., 1982—; admitted to Tex. bar, 1958; Justice of the Peace, Stratton, 1968-75; pvt. practice law, El Paso, 1980-82, Dallas, 1982—. Served with USMC, 1945-47. Mem. ABA, Fed. Bar Assn., State Bar Tex., El Paso Bar Assn., Plano Bar Assn., Am. Judicature Soc., Tex. Land Title Assn. (judiciary com. 1983), Tex. Mortgage Bankers Assn. (judiciary com. 1984), Tex. Trial Lawyers Assn., AAUP, Tex. Soc. S.A.R. Democrat. Methodist. Clubs: Rotary (pres. 1971), Masons (Shriner). Home: 1492 Larchmont Dr Plano TX 75074 Office: Suite 100 13021 Coit Rd Dallas TX 75240

SULLIVAN, JERRY HAMPTON, electronic engineer; b. Nashville, Jan. 24, 1939; s. Wiley Hampton and Mary (Eubank) S.; m. Mildred Elizabeth Gary, Dec. 31, 1963 (div. 1972); children—Wiley Hampton, James Gary; m. Mildred Joyce Ferguson, Nov. 15, 1975. B.E., Vanderbilt U., 1960, M.S., 1963. Registered profl. engr., Tenn. Instrument engr. ARO, Inc., Tullahoma, Tenn., 1963-65; project engr., electronics engr., sr. electronics engr. So. Ry. System, Alexandria, Va., 1965-78; project mgr. Fed. R.R. Adminstrn., U.S. Dept. Transp., Washington, 1978-80; signal and communications electronic engr. Chessie Systems, Huntington, W.Va., 1980—; instr. Marshall U., 1983-85. Mem. Am. Ry. Engring. Assn., IEEE (sect. pres. 1983—), Nat. Soc. Profl. Engrs. Republican. Baptist. Lodges: Masons (32 deg.), Shriners. Contbr. articles to profl. jours. Home: 2924 Chase St Huntington WV 25704 Office: 801 Madison Ave Huntington WV 25704

SULLIVAN, SISTER MARIE CELESTE, hospital administrator; b. Boston, Mar. 18, 1929; d. Daniel John and Katherine Agnes (Cunniff) S. B.B.A., St. Bonaventure U., Olean, N.Y., 1965. Joined Order Franciscan Sisters. Roman Cath. Ch., 1952; bus. mgr. St. Joseph's Hosp., Providence, 1954-62, asst. adminstr., Tampa, Fla., 1965-70, adminstr., 1970—; bd. dirs. St. Francis Hosp., Miami Beach, Fla.; trustee St. Anthony's Hosp., St. Petersburg, Fla.; mem. Fla. Gulf Health Systems Agy. Adv. Council Hillsborough County, Emergency Med. Planning Council Hillsborough County; adv. com. Hillsborough County Sch. Practical Nursing; coordinator health affairs Diocese of St. Petersburg, 1980—; mem. Fla. Cancer Control and Research Adv. Bd., 1980—; dir. 2d Nat. Bank of Tampa. Recipient Humanitarian award Judeo-Christian Coalition Clinic, Tampa, 1977. Fellow Am. Coll. Hosp. Adminstrs.; mem. Fla. Hosp. Assn. (trustee), Am. Mgmt. Assn., Greater Tampa C. of C., Royal Soc. Health. Office: PO Box 4227 Tampa FL 33677*

SULLIVAN, MICHAEL DAVID, judge; b. Hattiesburg, Miss., Dec. 2, 1938; s. Curran Watts and Mittie (Chambers) S.; m. Nancy Grace Ezell, Dec. 20, 1959; children—David Paul, Rachel Michel. B.S. in History, U. So. Miss., 1960; J.D., Tulane U., 1966. Bar: Miss. 1967. Sole practice, Hattiesburg, Miss., 1967-75; chancellor State of Miss., Hattiesburg, 1975-84; justice Miss. Supreme Ct. Jackson, 1984—; del. Pres.'s Jud. Commn. Victim's Rights, 1984-85. Mem. Civic Arts Council, Hattiesburg, 1974—. Served with USNR, 1961-63. Named Outstanding U. So. Miss. Grad., Forrest County Alumni Assn., 1984; Tulane U. scholar, 1963-66. Fellow Miss. Bar Found. Democrat. Methodist. Lodges: Lions, Elks. Avocations: reading; strategic simulations. Office: Miss Supreme Ct PO Box 117 Jackson MS 39205

SULLIVAN, NEIL MAXWELL, oil and gas company executive; b. McKeesport, Pa., May 25, 1942; s. Thomas James and Jane Mason (Ginn) S.; m. Margaret Pedrick Aug. 10, 1974; children—Margaret Blair, Mason Pedrick. B.S., Dickinson Coll., 1970; postgrad. Tulane U., 1970-74. Exploration geologist Base Enterprises, Midland, Tex., 1976-77; dist. geologist ATAPCO, Midland, Tex., 1977-78, Andarko Prodn. Co., Midland, 1978-79, chief geologist, 1979-80, v.p. exploration, regional mgr., Houston, 1980-82; exploration ops. mgr. Valero Producing Co., San Antonio, 1982-85, v.p. exploration, New Orleans, 1985—. Editor: Guadalupian Delaware Mountain Group of West Texas and Southeast New Mexico, 1979; Ancient Carbonate Reservoirs and Their Modern Analogs, 1977; Petroleum Exploration in Thrust Belts and Their Adjacent Forelands, 1976. Bd. dirs. Permian Basin Grad. Ctr., Midland, 1979; com. chmn. Mus. of S.W., Midland, 1978. Served with USAF, 1964-68. Mem. Geol. Soc. Am., Am. Assn. Petroleum Geologists (cert. petroleum geologist), West Tex. Geol. Soc., Soc. Econ. Paleontologists and Mineralogists (pres. Permian Basin sect. 1979). Republican. Episcopalian. Lodge: Elks. Home: 2814 State St New Orleans LA 70113 Office: Valero Producing Co 1001 Howard Ave Suite 2900 New Orleans LA 70113

SULLIVAN, PATRICK JOSEPH, structural engineer, consultant; b. Austin, Tex., June 14, 1957; s. Thomas James and Mary Jane (Anderson) S.; m. Beth Marie Price, July 28, 1979; children—James, Chris, John. B.S. in Civil Engring., Rice U., 1979, M.C.E., 1984. Registered profl. engr., Tex., La., Fla. Project engr. Linbeck Constrn., Houston, 1979-80; project mgr., corp. sec. Amege, Houston, 1980-81; project engr. Walter P. Moore & Assocs., Houston, 1981-82; br. engr. VSL Inc., Houston, 1982-83; chief engr., v.p. Skyline Structures, Inc., Houston, 1983—. Sec. parish council All Saints Catholic Ch., 1983—; mem. Woodland Heights Civic Club, Houston, 1981—. Mem. ASCE, Am. Concrete Inst. Republican. Office: 10601 Grant St #112 Houston TX 77070

SULLIVAN, RITA PAYNE, oil and marketing company executive; b. Memphis, Feb. 3, 1942; d. Fred G. and Mignon (Shinault) Payne; m. Richard Russell Sullivan, Oct. 18, 1974; stepchildren—Stacy, Russell. B.A., U. Tulsa, 1964. Placement asst. coordinator Skelly Oil Co., Tulsa, 1964-73, assoc. personnel rep., 1973-74, personnel rep., 1974-75; employment and coll. relations rep. Getty Refining & Mktg. Co., Tulsa, 1975-77, wage and salary adminstr., 1977-78, compensation, employment mgr., 1978-84; sr. coordinator Texaco Inc., Tulsa, 1984-85, employee relations mgr., 1985—. Mem. bus. adv. bd. Okla. State Tech. Sch., Okmulgee, 1978—; mem. adv. council Tulsa Pub. Schs., 1978-81. Mem. Am. Compensation Assn., Coll. Placement Council, Southwest Placement Assn. (officer 1973—), Am. Soc. Personnel Adminstrs., U. Tulsa Alumni Assn. (bd. dirs. 1972), Kappa Kappa Gamma. Republican.

Episcopalian. Club: U. Tulsa Hurricane (bd. dirs. 1984). Office: Texaco Inc PO Box 1650 Tulsa OK 74102

SULLIVAN, ROBERT ALLEN, electronics company executive; b. Mpls., Oct. 9, 1940; s. Robert E. and Ida S. B.S., Purdue U., 1966, M.S., 1966, Ph.D., 1968. Tech. dir. Videorama, Caracas, Venezuela, 1972-74; asst. to dept. head U.S. Dept. Energy, Washington, 1974-79, chief instrumentation and control div. Naval Reactors, 1979-81; pres., chmn. TSM, Inc., Reston, Va., 1981—. Served to lt. USN, 1966-71. Mem. IEEE, Tau Beta Pi, Eta Kappa Nu. Patentee in field; contbr. articles to tech. jours. Office: 12343E Sunrise Valley Dr Reston VA 22191

SULLIVAN, ROBERT WOLFE, geologist; b. Harmon, La., Jan. 26, 1926; s. Richard Burl and Grace Jurusha (Wolfe) S.; m. Elizabeth Joan Newton, Dec. 24, 1947; children—Lynda Diane, Robert Wolfe, Jr. B.S., U. Tulsa, 1950. Registered petroleum geologist. Geologist, F. Wm. Carr, Corpus Christi, Tex., 1952-55, Coloma Oil and Gas Co., Corpus Christi, 1955-57; cons. Deadman and Sullivan, Corpus Christi, 1957-60; pvt. practice geologist and engring. cons., Corpus Christi, 1961-80; pres. Sullivan Exploration Co., Corpus Christi, 1980—. Served with USN, 1944-46; PTO; Korea, 1950-52. Mem. Am. Assn. Petroleum Geologists, Soc. Independent Profl. Earth Scientists (chmn. 1983-84, chpt. award 1983), Scouting Coop. of Ind. Geologists (v.p. 1985—), Corpus Christi Geol. Library (pres. 1982-83), Soc. Econ. Paleontologists and Mineralogists, Corpus Christi Geol. Soc., Ind. Petroleum Assn. Am., Tex. Independent Producers and Royalty Owners, AIME, Corpus Christi C. of C. Avocations: hunting; fishing. Home: 59 Townhouse Ln Corpus Christi TX 78412 Office: Sullivan Exploration Co Suite 1170 First City Tower 11 Corpus Christi TX 78478

SULLIVAN, WALTER FRANCIS, bishop; b. Washington, June 10, 1928; s. Walter Francis and Catherine Jeanette (Vanderloo) S. B.A., St. Mary's Sem. U., Balt., 1947, S.T.L., 1953; J.C.L., Catholic U. Am., 1960. Ordained priest Roman Catholic Ch., 1953; asst. pastor St. Andrews Ch., Roanoke St. Mary's, Star of Sea, Ft. Monroe, 1956-58; sec. Diocesan Tribunal, 1960-65; chancellor Diocese of Richmond, Va., from 1965; rector Sacred Heart Cathedral, Richmond, from 1967; ordained aux. bishop of Richmond, 1970, bishop of Richmond, 1974—. Office: 807 Cathedral Pl Richmond VA 23220*

SULLIVAN, WILLIAM JOHN, JR., insurance company sales manager; b. Savannah, Ga., Nov. 27, 1941; s. William John and Ann Josephine (Calhoun) S.; m. Judy Elizabeth Thornburg, June 12, 1971; children—Mary Ann, Diane Elizabeth. Degree in Indsl. Engring., So. Ga. Tech., 1966. Loss prevention rep. Comml. Union, Atlanta, 1971-74; mgr. field service Cotton States Ins. Co., Atlanta, 1974-85, dist. sales mgr., 1985—. Pres. Stephen Hills Civic Club, Duluth, Ga., 1972; active various polit. campaigns. Served with U.S. Army, 1961-65. Recipient Hon. State Trooper award Ga. State Patrol, 1983, Ga. Transp. Dirs. Assn. award, 1981. Mem. Am. Soc. Safety Engrs. Democrat. Roman Catholic. Club: Duluth Wildcat. Home: 2017 Parsons Ridge Circle Duluth GA 30136 Office: Cotton States Ins Co 244 Perimeter Center Park Atlanta GA 30301

SULZBY, JAMES FREDERICK, JR., realty co. exec.; b. Birmingham, Ala., Dec. 24, 1905; s. James Frederick and Annie (Dobbins) S.; student Howard Coll., Birmingham, 1925-26; A.B., Birmingham-So. Coll., 1928; grad. Am. Inst. Banking, 1934; Litt.D., Athens Coll.; m. Martha Belle Hilton, Nov. 9, 1935; children—James Frederick III, Martha Hilton Sulzby Clark. In trust dept. First Nat. Bank of Birmingham, 1929-43; pres. Sulzby Realty Co., 1943—; dir. Ala. Fed. Savs. and Loan Assn. Dir. Birmingham Area Bd. Realtors, 1948-49, sec.-treas., 1948-49, v.p., 1951-52, pres., 1953; past pres. Ala. Bd. Realtors; dir. Nat. Assn. Real Estate Bds., 1952-56. Mem. adv. com. Athens Coll. Chmn., Birmingham Planning Commn., 1948-52; pres. Norwood Gardens, Inc., housing project; mem. Jefferson County Area Planning and Devel. Adv. Bd.; mem. Jefferson County Hist. Commn.; treas. Birmingham Area Ednl. TV, Inc.; mem. Jefferson County Personnel Bd., 1953-56; dir. Ala. Bapt. publ., 1945—; deacon, treas. Southside Bapt. Ch.; historian 75th Anniversary celebration for Birmingham, 1946; pres. Ala. Bapt. Young Peoples Union, 1932-33; trustee Rushton Lectures; bd. govs. Civic Theatre of Birmingham, 1946-48; chmn. Edn. Com., C. of C., 1949-53; mem. humanities advising council Auburn U., Cahawba Commn., Ala. Hall of Fame Com. Recipient Lit. award Ala. Library Assn., 1962. Mem. Newcomen Soc. N.Am., Ala. Hist. Assn. (pres. 1947-49, sec., 1950—), Ala. Bapt. Hist. Soc., Birmingham Sunday Sch. Council (pres. 1960-61, chmn. exec. com. 1962-64), Birmingham Hist. Soc. (sec. 1940-50, trustee 1950—), Birmingham Civic Symphony Assn. (trustee), Ala. Acad. Sci. (past chmn. bd. trustees, pres. 1965-66), Jefferson County Nat. Found. Infantile Paralysis (chmn. 1951-53), Am. Planning and Civic Assn. (dir.), Ala. Writers Conclave (v.p. 1949, pres. 1950-51), Phi Beta Kappa, Phi Alpha Theta, Delta Sigma Phi, Omicron Delta Kappa. Author: Birmingham As It Was in Jackson County, 1944; Birmingham Sketches, 1945; Annals of the Southside Baptist Church, 1947; Historic Alabama Hotels and Resorts, 1960; Arthur W. Smith, A Birmingham Pioneer, 1855-1944. Democrat. Baptist. Home: 3121 Carlisle Rd Birmingham AL 35213 Office: 1019 Massey Bldg Birmingham AL 35203

SUMMER, GEORGE KENDRICK, medical educator, biochemist, researcher; b. Cherryville, N.C., May 8, 1923; s. Thomas Carlisle and Bessie Eunice (Kendrick) S.; m. Elizabeth Ann Koch, Aug. 27, 1952; children—David Elliott, Carol Ann Summer Zachek. B.S. in Chemistry, U. N.C., 1944; M.D., Harvard U., 1951. Diplomate Am. Bd. Pediatrics. Intern Vanderbilt U., Nashville, 1951-52; asst. resident in pediatrics Wake Forest U., Winston-Salem, N.C., 1952-53; sr. resident U. N.C.-Chapel Hill, 1953-54, fellow in pediatric metabolism, 1954-57, instr. in pediatrics, 1957-59, asst. prof., 1959-62, 1963-65, assoc. clin. prof. pediatrics, 1965—, asst. prof. biohemistry and nutrition, 1965, assoc. prof., 1966-72, prof., 1972—, research scientist Biol. Scis. Research Ctr., Child Devel. Inst., 1971—, dir. Automated Biochem. Systems Lab., 1965—; vis. scientist human biol. genetics King's Coll., London and Galton Lab., Univ. Coll., London, 1962-63. Served with USNR, 1944-46. Recipient Research Career Devel. award Nat. Inst. Arthritis, Metabolic and Digestive Diseases, 1965-70. Fellow Am. Acad. Pediatrics; mem. N.C. Pediatric Soc., Am. Chem. Soc., Soc. Exptl. Biology and Medicine, Am. Inst. Nutrition, Am. Soc. Human Genetics. Contbr. numerous articles to profl. jours. Office: 336 Faculty Lab Office Bldg 231H U NC Chapel Hill NC 27514

SUMMER, VIRGIL C., utility company executive; b. Spartanburg, S.C., 1920; grad. Internat. Corr. Schs.; M.S., U. S.C.; married. With S.C. Electric & Gas Co., Columbia, 1937—, v.p. electric ops. and engring., 1966-67, sr. v.p., 1967-77, pres., chief operating officer, 1977-79, pres., chief exec. officer, 1979-82, chmn. bd., 1986—, chief exec. officer, 1982—, also dir. Chmn. Midlands Tech. Edn. Found.; mem. Riverbanks Park Commn., Lexington County Health Edn. Found., Nat. Urban League Commerce and Industry Council, Palmetto Bus. Forum; trustee Lowman Home. Fellow ASME; mem. NAM (bd. dirs.), Nat. Soc. Profl. Engrs. Office: SCANA Corp 1426 Main St Box 764 Columbia SC 29218

SUMMERLIN, LEE ROY, II, chemist, educator, consultant; b. Sumiton, Ala., Apr. 15, 1934; s. Lee Roy and Mildred Caldonna (Ford) S.; m. Catherine Wilson, Dec. 27, 1958; children—Lee Roy, Karin Andrea, Lisa Sloan, Andrew Thomas Ford. A.B., Samford U., Birmingham, Ala., 1955; M.S., Birmingham-So. Coll., 1959; Ph.D., U. Md., 1969. Chemist, U.S. Pipe and Foundry Co., Birmingham, 1952-55, So. Research Inst., Birmingham, 1956-59; asst. prof. Fla. State U., Tallahassee, 1962-70; asst. prof. U. Ga., Athens, 1970-71; prof. chemistry U. Ala.-Birmingham, 1972—, asst. v.p. acad. affairs, 1978-80, interim dean Sch. Sci. and Math., 1980-82; teaching assoc. U. Md., 1968-69; dir. Ga. Sci. Teaching Project NSF, 1970-71; vis. prof. U. Calif., Berkeley, summers 1985, 86. Served to capt. USAR, 1964-70. Recipient Ingalls Teaching award U. Ala., 1974, 76, 83; CMA Catalyst award, 1986; named Exec. of Year, 1982. Mem. Am. Chem. Soc. (James B. Conant award 1969), AAAS, Sigma Xi, Alpha Epsilon Delta, Omicron Delta Kappa. Baptist. Author 8 textbooks including: Chemical Demonstrations: A Source Book for the Teacher, Chemistry, Chemistry of Common Substances, Chemistry For The Life Sciences; contbr. numerous articles to profl. jours.

SUMMERS, HUGH BLOOMER, JR., chem. engr.; b. Lake City, Fla., Aug. 5, 1921; s. Hugh Bloomer and Hazel A. (Flory) S.; B.Chem. Engring., U. Fla., 1943; m. Betty Jane Karstedt, Aug. 17, 1946; children—Hugh Bloomer, III, Carole Anne. Research chem. engr. Dept. Agr., Olustee, Fla., 1947-65; chem. engr. Union Camp Corp., Savannah, Ga., 1965—. Served with USNR, 1943-46. Registered profl. engr., Ga. Mem. Nat. Soc. Profl. Engrs., Am. Inst. Chem. Engrs., Am. Chem. Soc., Am. Inst. Chemists. Democrat. Methodist. Author, patentee in field. Home: 5 Raleigh Dr Savannah GA 31406 Office: PO Box 2668 Savannah GA 31402

SUMMERS, JAMES WILLIAM, chief justice; b. Rusk, Tex., July 8, 1914; s. James Lee and Constance (Rook) S.; B.B.A., J.D., U. Tex., 1937; grad. Inst. for Juvenile Ct. Mgmt., Nat. Coll. for State Judiciary; m. Inez Thompson Steed, Nov. 22, 1969; children—Julia Ann (Mrs. Charles E. Tucker), Raymond C. Steed. Admitted to U.S. Supreme Ct. bar, Tex. bar, 1937, practiced in Rusk, 1937-56; city atty., 1937-41; county atty. Cherokee County, 1941-42, 47-48, county judge, 1949-56; judge 2d Jud. Dist. Tex., Rusk, 1957-78; chief justice Ct. Appeals, 12th Supreme Jud. Dist. Tex., Tyler, 1978—. Dir. Southwestern Title & Guaranty Co. First State Bank, 1937-78; partner Summers and Summers, land, cattle, timber. Faculty, Tex. Coll. for judiciary, 1975-76. Dir. Civil Def., Cherokee County, 1949-56; mem. Cherokee County Heritage Assn., Cherokee Civic Theatre; mem. adv. council Criminal Justice Program, Stephen F. Austin U., vice chmn. Rusk Housing Corp.; chmn. Nacogdoches-Cherokee Counties Probation Bd. Bd. dirs. East Tex. area council Boy Scouts Am., East Tex. Regional Cancer Center, Rusk Indsl. Found., Rusk United Way, Rusk Bicentennial Commn.; bd. dirs., exec. com. Rusk Civic Service, Inc. Served as lt. USNR, 1942-46. Fellow Tex. Bar Found. (life); mem. Am. Judicature Soc., Am. Bar Assn., East Tex. Bar Assn., Cherokee Bar Assn., Smith County Bar Assn., State Bar Tex. (mem. nominating com. jud. sect., vice chmn. juvenile judges continuing legal edn. com.), Nat. Conf. State Trial Judges, Am., Tex., East Tex. Aberdeen-Angus assns., U. Tex. Ex-Students Assn. (exec. council Austin, past pres. Cherokee County alumni club), Rusk C. of C. (chmn. govt. affairs com.), Tex. Farm Bur. Fedn., Tex. State Hist. Found., Cherokee County Hist. Commn. (dir.), Am. Legion, Beta Gamma Sigma, Phi Delta Phi, Phi Eta Sigma, Phi Delta Theta (v.p. East Tex. alumni). Democrat. Methodist (chmn. ofcl. bd. 1955-56, 73-74, trustee, charge lay leader, dist. steward 1975-77, dist. trustee 1979—). Clubs: Masons (Shriners), Kiwanis (past pres.), Willow Brook Country, Willow Brook Country (Tyler). Contbr. to profl. publs. Home: 200 W 5th St PO Box 148 Rusk TX 75785 also 567 Towne Oaks Dr Tyler TX 75701 Office: Ct Appeals 306 Smith County Courthouse Tyler TX 75702

SUMMERS, JOSEPH FRANK, author, publisher; b. Newnan, Ga., June 26, 1914; s. John Dawson and Anne (Blalock) S.; B.A. in Math., U. Houston, 1942; profl. certificate meteorology, U. Calif. at Los Angeles, 1943, U. Chgo., 1943; postgrad., U. P.R., 1943-44; M.A. in Math., U. Tex. at Austin, 1947; postgrad. (fellow math.) Rice U., 1947-49; m. Evie Margaret Mott, July 8, 1939; children—John Randolph, Thomas Franklin, James Mott. With Texaco Inc., Houston, 1933-42, 49-79, mgr. data processing, 1957-67, asst. gen. mgr. computer services dept., 1967-79, automation cons., 1979-83; pres. Word Lab Inc., Houston, 1983—; instr. math. AAC, Ellington Field, Tex., 1941-42, U. Tex. at Austin, 1946-47. Pres. Houston Esperanto Assn., 1934-39. Served to capt. AAC, 1942-46. Mem. Assn. Computing Machinery (pres. 1956-58), Nat. Assn. Accountants (past dir.), Am. Petroleum Inst. (mem. data processing and computing com. 1955-59). Author: Mathematics for Bombadiers and Navigators, 1942; Wholly Holey Holy, An Adult American Spelling Book, 1984. Contbg. author: American Petroleum Institute Drilling and Production Practices. Home: 5517 Tilbury Dr Houston TX 77056 Office: PO Box 53462 Houston TX 77052

SUMMERS, SHARON LORAINE, oncology nurse clinician; b. Yates Ctr., Kans., Apr. 15, 1941; d. Henry Edward and Norma Elaine (Koenig) Horsch; m. Samuel Lloyd Summers, Jan. 21, 1961; children—Stacie Leigh, Stephen Lynn, Sonja Loy. Diploma, Wichita-St. Joseph Sch. Nursing, Wichita, Kans., 1962. Dir. nursing Elk Manor Nursing Home, Moline, Kans., 1962-65; dir. nursing, co-administr. Retirement Manors Am., Topeka, 1965-68; dir. nursing John Lynn Town House, Kansas City, Mo., 1968-69; staff nurse VA Hosp., Kansas City, 1969-70; staff nurse VA Hosp., Oklahoma City, 1970-72, head nurse, 1972-81; oncology nurse clinician VA Med. Ctr., Oklahoma City, 1981—. Mem. nursing edn. com. Am. Cancer Soc. Named Outstanding Young Women Am., Moline Jr. C. of C. (Kans.), 1965. Mem. Am. Nurses Assn. (cert. med.-surg. 1983), Okla. Nurses Assn., Oncology Nursing Soc., Okla. Oncology Nursing Soc. (v.p. 1983-84), Nurses Orgn. VA, LWV. Democrat. Roman Catholic. Club: Westbury (Yukon, Okla.) Home: 1817 Lankestar Pl Yukon OK 73099 Office: VA Med Ctr 921 NE 13th St Oklahoma City OK 73104

SUMMERSELL, CHARLES GRAYSON, history educator; b. Mobile, Ala., Feb. 25, 1908; s. Charles Fishweek and Sallie Rebecca (Grayson) S.; A.B., U. Ala., 1929, A.M., 1930; Ph.D., Vanderbilt U., 1940; m. Frances Sharpley, Nov. 10, 1934. Instr. history U. Ala., University, 1935-40, asst. prof., 1940-46, assoc. prof., 1946-47, prof., 1947—, head dept. history, 1954-71; radio commentator, Tuscaloosa and Selma, Ala., 1941-43. Mem. Ala. Hist. Commn.; chmn. Tannehill Furnace and Foundry Commn., 1980-82; mem. Tuscaloosa County Preservation Authority. Commd. lt. (j.g.), USNR, 1942; active duty, 1943; served with USN, in PTO; lt. comdr., comdr. Res., 1954; officer charge Naval Tng. School, Norfolk, Va., 1951-53; mem. steering com. organizing Tuscaloosa unit Organized Res. of Navy, 1947. Recipient Letter of Commendation USNR, 1945; Outstanding Tchr. award U. Ala. Nat. Alumni, 1978; Ramsey award Ala. Assn. Historians, 1981; Pritchett award Tuscaloosa County Heritage Commn., 1982; Disting. fellow Ctr. for Study of So. History and Culture, U. Ala., 1977; U. Ala. Ind. Study award, 1982. Mem. So., Mississippi Valley, Ala. (pres. 1955-56, emeritus 1982) hist. assns., Orgn. Am. Historians, U.S. Naval Inst., Naval Hist. Found., SAR (pres. Ala. 1957-58), Am. Assn. State and Local History (council 1965-71), Am. Hist. Assn., Hakluyt Soc., Phi Beta Kappa (pres. Ala. chpt. 1953-54), Phi Alpha Theta. Democrat. Clubs: University; Tuscaloosa Country; Army-Navy (Washington). Author: Historical Foundations of Mobile, 1949; Mobile History of a Seaport Town, 1949; Alabama History for Schools, 1957, rev., 1965, 70, 75, 82; (with Howard W. Odum and G.H. Yeuell) Alabama Past and Future, 1941, rev. edit. (with G.H. Yeuell and W.R. Higgs), 1950; (with Frances C. Roberts) Exploring Alabama, 1957, rev., 1961; (with Frances S. Summersell) Alabama History Filmstrips, 1961; (with F.S. Summersell and Rembert W. Patrick) Florida History Filmstrips, 1963; (with others) Texas History Filmstrips, 1965; The Cruise of CSS Sumter, 1965; Ohio History Filmstrips, 1967; (with others) California History Filmstrips, 1968, Illinois History Filmstrips, 1970; (with others) Atlas of Alabama, 1973. Editor: The Journal of George Townley Fullam: Boarding Officer of the Confederate Sea Raider Alabama, 1973; Colonial Mobile (Peter J. Hamilton), 1976. Mem. editorial adv. bd. Am. Neptune, 1946-83; mem. editorial bd. Ala. Rev., 1964—; contbr. articles and revs. to encys. and profl. jours. Home: 1411 Caplewood Dr Tuscaloosa AL 35401 Office: PO Drawer CZ University AL 35486

SUMMERSELL, FRANCES SHARPLEY (MRS. CHARLES GRAYSON SUMMERSELL), club woman; b. Birmingham, Ala.; d. Arthur Croft and Thomas O. (Stone) Sharpley; student U. Montevallo, Peabody Coll., Nashville; m. Charles Grayson Summersell, Nov. 10, 1934. Partner, artist, writer Assn. Educators, 1959—. Mem. Ft. Morgan Hist. Commn., 1959-63. Mem. D.A.R., Magna Charta Dames, U. Women's Club (pres. 1957-58), U.D.C. (state historian 1956-58, pres. Robert Emmet Rodes chpt. Tuscaloosa 1953-55), Daus. Am. Colonists (organizing regent Tuscaloosa 1956-63), English Speaking Union, Marquis Biog. Library Soc. (adv. mem.), Tuscaloosa County Preservation Soc. (trustee 1965-75, Service award 1975), West Ala. Art Assn., Nat. Trust. Clubs: Univ., Country (Tuscaloosa). Co-author: Alabama History Filmstrips, 1961; Viewing Alabama History Filmstrips, 1961; Florida History Filmstrips, 1963; Texas History Filmstrips, 1965-66; Ohio History Filmstrips (Merit award Am. Assn. State and Local History 1968), 1967; California History Filmstrips, 1968; Illinois History Filmstrips, 1970. Home: 1411 Caplewood Tuscaloosa AL 35401

SUMNER, DANIEL ALAN, economics educator; b. Fairfield, Calif., Dec. 5, 1950. B.S. in Agrl. Mgmt., Calif. State Poly. U., 1971; M.A. in Econs., Mich. State U., 1973; M.A. in Econs., U. Chgo., 1977, Ph.D., 1978. Rockefeller Found. post-doctoral fellow, labor and population group, econ. dept. Rand Corp., Santa Monica, Calif., 1977-78; asst. prof. N.C. State U., Raleigh, 1978-83, assoc. prof. econs., 1983—. Author book and monographs; contbr. chpts. to books, articles to profl. jours. Grantee N.C. Agrl. Research Service, 1978-84, N.C. Tobacco Found., 1983—, HHS, 1980-82, U.S. Dept. Labor, 1981-83. Mem. Am. Econ. Assn., Econometric Soc., Am. Agrl. Econs. Assn., Internat. Assn. Agrl. Economists. Home: 327 E Jones St Raleigh NC 27601 Office: Dept Econs and Bus NC State U Box 8110 Raleigh NC 27695

SUMRELL, GENE, research chemist; b. Apache, Ariz., Oct. 7, 1919; s. Joe B. and Dixie (Hughes) S.; B.A., Eastern N.Mex. U.; Ph.D., U. Calif. at Berkeley, 1951. Asst. prof. chemistry Eastern N.Mex. U., 1951-53; sr. research chemist J.T. Baker Chem. Co., Phillipsburg, N.J., 1953-58; sr. organic chemist S.W. Research Inst., San Antonio, 1958-59; project leader Food Machinery & Chem. Corp., Balt., 1959-61; research sect. leader El Paso Natural Gas Products Co. (Tex.), 1961-64; project leader So. utilization research and devel. div. U.S. Dept. Agr., New Orleans, 1964-67, investigations head, 1967-73, research leader Oilseed and Food Lab., So. Regional Research Center, 1973-84, collaborator, 1984—. Served from pvt. to staff sgt. AUS, 1942-46. Mem. Am. Chem. Soc., A.A.A.S., N.Y. Acad. Scis., Am. Inst. Chemists, Am. Oil Chemists Soc., Am. Assn. Textile Chemists and Colorists, Research Soc. Am., AAUP, Sigma Xi, Phi Kappa Phi. Home: PO Box 24037 New Orleans LA 70184 Office: 1100 Robert E Lee Blvd New Orleans LA 70179

SUMWALT, ROBERT LLEWELLYN, JR., construction company executive; b. Columbia, S.C., Dec. 29, 1927; s. Robert Llewellyn and Caroline M. (Causey) S.; B.S. in Civil Engring., U. S.C., 1949; M.S. in Civil Engring., M.I.T., 1950; m. Mary Joyce Mills, Mar. 8, 1952; children—Elizabeth Ladson, Robert Llewellyn III. Area engr. E. I. duPont de Nemours & Co., Camden, S.C., 1950-52; constrn. engr. Columbia City Sch. System, 1952-58; sr. v.p., dir. McCrory-Sumwalt Constrn. Co., Inc., Columbia, 1958-77; chmn. bd., treas., dir. Sumwalt-Mashburn Engring. & Constrn. Co., Inc., Columbia, 1977-79; pres., treas., dir. Sumwalt Constrn. Co., Inc., Columbia, 1979—. Pres., Richland County unit Am. Cancer Soc., 1956; chmn. Carolina Carillon Ball, 1963; sect. chmn. United Community Services, 1957; div. chmn. constrn. div. United Way, 1973; bd. dirs. Am. Cancer Soc., S.C. chpt., 1957, Richland County unit ARC, 1955-56; mem. adv. bd. Salvation Army, 1982—. Served to comdr., C.E.C., USNR. Named Young Man of Yr. Columbia Jr. C. of C., 1958. Registered profl. engr., S.C. Mem. Asso. Gen. Contractors Am., (chmn. bldg. div., dir. Carolinas br. 1977), Am. Inst. Constructers, Columbia Contractors Assn. (pres. 1969), S.C. Soc. Engrs., S.C. Soc. Profl. Engrs., U. S.C. Alumni Assn. (circuit v.p. 1956), Sigma Alpha Epsilon, Phi Beta Kappa, Omicron Delta Kappa, Tau Beta Pi. Presbyn. (chmn. bd. deacons 1968, elder). Kiwanian (pres. 1962). Clubs: Forest Lake Country, Tip Off (pres. 1981-82), Palmetto, Cotillion, Tarantilla, Columbia Ball, Centurion (Columbia); Litchfield Country (Litchfield Beach, S.C.). Home: 1420 Belmont Dr Columbia SC 29205 Office: 4600 Forest Dr Suite 10 Columbia SC 29206

SUNDQUIST, DONALD KENNETH, Congressman, sales corporation executive; b. Moline, Ill., Mar. 15, 1936; s. Kenneth M. and Louise (Rohren) S.; m. Martha Swanson, Oct. 3, 1959; children—Tania, Andrea, Donald Kenneth. B.A., Augustana Coll., Rock Island, Ill., 1957. Div. mgr. Josten's, Inc., 1961-72; exec. v.p. Graphic Sales of Am., Memphis, 1972, pres., 1973-82; mem. 98th Congress from 7th Dist. Tenn.; vice chmn. bd. Bank of Germantown, Tenn. Past mem. White House Commn. Presdl. Scholars; past chmn. Jobs for High Sch. Grads. of Memphis; nat. campaign mgr. Howard Baker for Pres., 1979; dir. com. ops., alt. del. Republican Nat. Conv., 1980; chmn. Shelby County Rep. Party, 1975-77; alt. del. Rep. Nat. Conv., 1976; exec. com. Rep. Nat. Com., 1971-73; nat. chmn. Young Rep. Nat. Fedn., 1971-73; sec. Bedford County Election Commn., 1968-70; chmn. Tenn. Young Rep. Fedn., 1969-70; dir. Mid-South Coliseum, Am. Council Young Polit. Leaders, 1972-74, U.S. Youth Council, 1972-75; bd. govs. Charles Edison Meml. Youth Fund; nat. adv. bd. Distributive Edn. Clubs Am.; mem. U.S. del. study tour, People's Rep. of China, 1978, study tour, Soviet Union, 1975. Served with USN, 1957-59. Lutheran. Lodge: Kiwanis. Home: 3028 Emerald Dr Memphis TN 38115 Office: 515 Cannon House Office Bldg Washington DC 20003

SURBER, DAVID FRANCIS, public relations and advertising consultant, TV producer, journalist; b. Covington, Ky.; s. Elbert and Dorothy Kathryn (Mills) S.; B.A. in Physics, Thomas More Coll., 1960; LL.D. (h.c.), London Inst. Applied Research, 1973. Owner, The P.R. Co., pub. relations and advt. counseling, Covington, 1960—. Spl. corr. Am. newspapers to Vatican II, Rome, Italy, 1965. Mem. Bd. Adjustment (Zoning Appeals), Covington, 1964—, chmn., 1971—; chmn. Covington Environ. Commn., 1971-72, Commn. Strip Mining, 1967-68; mem. pub. interest adv. com. Ohio River Valley Water Sanitation Commn., 1976—; mem. water quality adv. com. Ohio-Ky.-Ind. Regional Council Govts., 1975—; mem. environ. adv. council City of Cin. Mem. rehab. com. Community Chest Greater Cin., 1972—, mem. agy. admissions com., 1972—, mem. priorities com., 1972—. Pres. bd. dirs. Cathedral Found., 1968—; trustee Montessori Learning Center, 1973—, Bklyn. Spanish Youth Choir; mem. Ky. Nature Preserves Commn.; 1976-79. Recipient Community Service award Thomas More Coll., 1975. Mem. AFTRA, Tri-State Air Com. (chmn. 1973-74), Izaak Walton League (pres. Ky. 1973, dir. Ky.; nat. dir.), ACLU, Mousquetaires d'Armagnac. Producer: Make Peace with Nature, WKRC-TV, Cin., Strip Mining Must Be Stopped, 1972; Energy: Where Will It Come From; How Much Will It Cost, 1975; Atomic Power for Ohio, 1976; A Conversation With The Vice President, 1976; The Bad Water, 1977, The Trans-Alaska Pipeline: A Closeup Report, 1977. Home and office: 9 E Southern Ave Covington KY 41015

SURFACE, JAMES RICHARD, management educator; b. Salina, Kans., Feb. 26, 1921; s. Richard Jacob and Lucile (Gary) S.; m. Mary Ellen Shaver, Nov. 28, 1942; children—Mary Lucile, Richard C., Daniel S., John W., Thomas E. A.B., U. Kans., 1942, M.A., 1948; M.B.A., Harvard U., 1950, D.C.S., 1956. Asst. prof. Harvard Bus. Sch., 1953-57; dean sch. bus. U. Kans., 1957-62, vice chancellor and provost, 1962-69; vis. prof. Harvard Bus. Sch., 1967-68, 69—; prof. grad. sch. mgmt. Vanderbilt U., Nashville, 1972-78, exec. vice chancellor, 1978—; dir. Fleming Cos., Inc., 1962—. Bd. dirs. Sr. Citizens Ctr., Nashville, 1971-74, Nashville Symphony Assn., 1979-82. Served to 1st lt. USMCR, 1942-45. Mem. Beta Gamma Sigma. Contbr. articles to profl. jours. Home: 1215 Otter Creek Rd Nashville TN 37215 Office: Office Grad Sch Mgmt Vanderbilt U Nashville TN 37203

SURVINE, CARL FREDERICK, lawyer; b. Shreveport, La., May 4, 1953; s. Murphy and Leona (Survine) Thompson. B.A., So. U., Baton Rouge, La., 1974, M.A., 1976, J.D., 1982; postgrad. NE La. U. Bar: La. 1983, U.S. Dist. Ct. (we. dist.) La. 1984. Aide La. House of Rep. Senate, Baton Rouge, summer 1976, law clk., 1979-82; transp. planner Shreveport Area Council of Govt., 1976-77; city planner Met. Planning Commn., Shreveport, 1977-78; student dir. So. U., Baton Rouge, 1979-82; law clk. atty. 1st Jud. Dist. Ct., Shreveport, 1984—; dir. Gov.'s Office for Minority Bus. Devel.; sr. counselor Employ-Ex, Shreveport, 1978-79. Bd. dirs. La. Task Force on Edn., Shreveport, 1984—, La. Survival Coalition, Shreveport, 1984—; dir. Youth Group, Shreveport, 1983—; exec. dir. Pelican council Girl Scouts U.S., Shreveport, 1983-84. Recipient Am. Legion award, Shreveport, 1971, George Mears Found. award, 1979. Mem. La. Bar Assn., La. Trial Lawyers Assn., La. Juvenile Detention Assn., ABA. Democrat. Baptist. Office: 1st Jud Dist Ct 500 Texas Ave Shreveport LA 71103

SURYAATMADJA, JOHAN, college administrator; b. Bogor, West Java, Indonesia, May 29, 1941; came to U.S., 1974; s. Petrus Jahja and Anna Mariam (Witarsa) S.; m. Janny Damayanti, June 12, 1960; children—Amelia J., David J. B.A., Acad. Fgn. Langs./U. Indonesia, 1974; cert. U. Mich., 1975; M.A., U. Va., 1981. Liaison officer UN, Jakarta, Indonesia, 1960-64; mgr. Grand Ocean Internat. Ltd., Hong Kong, 1965-70, Bangkok I.B. Motors, Thailand, 1970-74; complex mgr. Ratu Sayang Corp., Jakarta, 1980-82; adminstr., instr. English, Houston Community Coll. System, 1982—. Editor, writer Student Fin. Aid Office newsletter, 1984—, Question and Answer bull., 1985—. Mem. Janice Sutton Scholarship Com., Houston, 1984—. Mem. Am. Assn. for Counseling and Devel., Nat. Assn. Student Fin. Aid Adminstrs., Tex. Assn. Student Fin. Aid Adminstrs., Asia Soc., Assn. Coll. Classified Personnel (treas. 1986—). Club: Houston Indonesian (pres. 1986). Home: 13206 Noblecrest Dr Houston TX 77041 Office: Houston Community Coll System 320 Jackson Hill Houston TX 77270

SUSCO, LOYCE JARVIS, college administrator; b. Norfolk, Va., Sept. 18, 1927; d. Leon Hobson and Alice (Pell) Jarvis; m. Roy Ellsworth Hatton, Jan. 31, 1948 (div. July 1967); children—Cary, Richard Dial; m. Milton Leonardo Susco, June 20, 1970 (dec. Mar. 1983). A.A., Centenary Coll., 1946; B.A., Wright State U., 1970; M.S. in Edn., Old Dominion U., 1974, Cert. Advanced Study, 1981. Nat. bd. cert. counselor, Va. Group leader Detention Services, Dayton, Ohio, 1966-68; social worker Children's Services Bd., 1970-72; dir., counselor, trainer Transactional Analysis Assn. Tidewater, Chesapeake, Va., 1973-80; dir. spl. services Coll. of The Albemarle, Elizabeth City, N.C., 1981—; provided workshops for orgns. and cos., 1975-79. Bd. dirs. Council on Status of Women, Currituck, N.C., 1979-82, Albermarle Hopeline, Elizabeth City, 1983-84. Mem. Am. Assn. Counseling and Devel., N.C. Council Ednl. Opportunities Programs (standing com. chair. 1981-85), Southeastern Assn. Ednl. Opportunities Program Personnel, Internat. Transactional Analysis Assn. (clin.), Phi Delta Kappa (treas. 1983-85). Democrat. Avocations:

walking; reading; exploring. Home: Bells Island Star Route Currituck NC 27929 Office: Coll of The Albemarle PO Box 2327 Elizabeth City NC 27909

SUTHERLAND, THOMAS ALLEN, librarian, association executive; b. Owensboro, Ky., Oct. 24, 1940; s. Adron Cohen and Ruth (Christian) S.; m. Gayle Moss, Aug. 28, 1965; children—Ginnia, Todd, Katherine. B.A., Ky. Wesleyan U., 1964; M.L.S., U. Ky., 1965. Page Ky. Wesleyan Coll., Owensboro, 1963-64; regional dir. Ky. Dept. Libraries, Frankfort, 1965-68; dir. Paducah Pub. Library (Ky.), 1968—; exec. dir. Ky. Library Assn., Paducah, 1971—; cons. Washington Court House Pub. Library (Ohio), 1975; mem. Ky. Gov.'s Adv. Council for Libraries, 1973-83, chmn., 1974-75. Served with U.S. Army, 1961-62. Mem. ALA (pres. pub. library systems sect. 1979-80), Southeastern Library Assn., Ky. Library Assn. (Outstanding Pub. Librarian award 1974). Democrat. Methodist. Lodge: Rotary (Paducah). Home: 147 Idlewild Dr Paducah KY 42001 Office: Paducah Pub Library 555 Washington St Paducah KY 42001

SUTHERLAND-HALL, FRANK SHELDON, real estate, oil and gas investment company executive; b. Columbus, Ohio, Oct. 7, 1948; s. Arthur Sheldon and Laura Sue (Teas) Hall; m. Mary Beth Alspaugh, Apr. 1, 1984; 1 child, Laura Elizabeth. Student U. Tex.-Arlington, 1974, U. Tex.-Austin, 1975-76. Pres., Sutherland Cos., Arlington, 1976—, Alspaugh-Sutherland-Hall, Dallas, 1984—. Editor: Bagerly Familys of America, vols 1-4, 1983. Mem. Pi Kappa Alpha. Republican. Methodist. Club: Founders and Patriots (gov. 1985-87). Avocations: antiques; first editions; genealogy. Office: Sutherland Cos PO Box 769 Arlington TX 76010

SUTOWSKI, THOR BRIAN, choreographer; b. Trenton, N.J., Jan. 27, 1945; s. Walter X. and Kathryn (Tang) S.; m. Sonia Arova, Mar. 11, 1965; 1 dau., Ariane. Student San Diego Ballet, 1958-63, San Francisco Ballet, 1963-64, Nat. Ballet, 1964. Cert. solotanzer (solo dancer), Genossenschaft Deutscher Buhnen-Angehorigen, West Germany. Soloist, Norwegian State Opera, Oslo, 1965-70; 1st soloist Hamburgische Staatsoper, Hamburg, Ger., 1970-71; dir. San Diego Ballet, 1971-76, Ballet Ala., Birmingham, 1978-81; dir. State of Ala. Ballet, Birmingham, 1982-83; chmn. Ala. Sch. Fine Arts, Birmingham, 1976—; artistic advisor, choreographer Asami Maki Ballet, Toyko, 1976-79; choreographer Atlanta Ballet, 1980—; dance advisor Ala. State Arts Council, Montgomery, 1977-78. Recipient Pub. TV Emmy award, 1976; Obelisk award for Choreography, 1977, 78, 79, 80; grantee Ford Found., 1964, Nat. Endowment Arts, 1973-74. Mem. Am. Guild Mus. Artists. Republican. Lutheran. Office: Ala Sch Fine Arts 820 N 18th St Birmingham AL 35203

SUTTER, EMILY MAY GEESEMAN, psychologist, educator; b. St. Louis, Nov. 18, 1939; d. George Robert and Cora Hamilton (Glasgow) Geeseman; m. Gordon Frederick Sutter, Aug. 13, 1960; children—John Blaine, Steven George. B.S., U. Pitts., 1960, M. Retailing, 1961; M.Ed., Wayne State U., 1965; Ph.D., U. Tex., 1967. Lic. psychologist, Tex. Chief psychologist Richmond State Sch., Houston, 1967-71; dir. Fairhill Sch., Houston, 1971-72; assoc. dir. Battin Clinic, Houston, 1972-81; asst. prof. U. Houston, 1981—. Contbr. articles to profl. jours. Mem. Am. Psychol. Assn., Southwestern Psychol. Assn. (sec., treas. 1977-79), Tex. Psychol. Assn. (treas. 1978, liaison officer 1985-87, conv. chmn. 1985), Houston Psychol. Assn. (pres. 1976-77). Avocation: gardening. Home: 15719 Heatherdale Dr Houston TX 77059 Office: U Houston 2700 Bay Area Blvd Houston TX 77055

SUTTER, (HOWARD) BRUCE, baseball player; b. Lancaster, Pa., Jan. 8, 1953. Baseball player Chgo. Cubs, 1976-80, St. Louis Cardinals, from 1981, now with Atlanta Braves; mem. Nat. League All-Star Team, 1978-81. Recipient Cy Young award Nat. League, 1979. Office: care Atlanta Braves PO Box 4064 Atlanta GA 30302*

SUTTLE, DORWIN WALLACE, fed. judge; b. Knox County, Ind., July 16, 1906; s. William Sherman and Nancy Cordelia (Hungate) S.; m. Anne Elizabeth Barrett, Feb. 1, 1939 (dec.); children—Stephen Hungate, Nancy Joanna Suttle Walker (dec.); m. Lucile Cram Whitecotton; stepchildren—Fred and Frank Whitecotton. LL.B., U. Tex., 1928. Bar: Tex. bar, also U.S. Supreme Ct. 1960. Practiced law; Uvalde, Tex., 1928-64; U.S. dist. judge Western Dist. Tex., 1964—. Fellow Tex. Bar Found., Am. Judicature Soc.; mem. Am., Tex., San Antonio bar assns., Tex. Law Rev. Assn. Democrat. Methodist. Home: 911 Eventide Dr San Antonio TX 78209 Office: 655 E Durango St San Antonio TX 78206

SUTTLES, DAVID CLYDE, educator; b. Harriman, Tenn., June 14, 1948; s. Clyde and Virginia (Stewart) S.; m. Barbara Chambers, June 3, 1968; children—Julia Kay, Robert David. B.S. in Bus. Adminstrn., U. Tenn., 1972, M.S., 1975. Asst. prof. Cleveland State Coll., Tenn., 1975—. Active Community Devel. Citizens Adv. Com., Cleveland, 1981; bd. dirs. Friends of Library, Cleveland, 1984; active Gov.'s Com. Employment of Handicapped, 1984. Recipient Achiever award Gov. Tenn., 1976; cert. of appreciation Mayor of Cleveland, 1980. Mem. Coll. Media Advisors. Democrat. Episcopalian. Office: Cleveland State Community Coll PO Box 3570 Cleveland TN 37311

SUTTLES, DONALD ROLAND, educator, business consultant; b. Coldsprings, Ky., Nov. 14, 1929; s. Noah Elseworth and Bertha Viola (Seward) S.; m. Phyllis JoAnn McMullen, Dec. 12, 1952; children—Daniel, Ruth, Jonathan, Donna, Joanna, Stephen. Student U. Md., 1949-50, U.S. Naval Acad., 1951-52; B.B.A., U. Cin., 1959; M.B.A., Xavier U., 1966; Ed.D., U. N.C.-Greensboro, 1977. C.P.A., N.C.; cert. mgmt. acct., internal auditor. With Procter & Gamble Co., Cin., 1952-73, supr., 1959-60, indsl. engr., 1960-63, cost engr., 1963-64, mgr. prodn. planning, 1965-68, asst. security coordinator, 1968-70, dept. mgr., 1970-73; dir. bus. affairs Piedmont Bible Coll., Winston-Salem, N.C., 1973-80; assoc. prof. bus. Winston-Salem State U., 1978—; also bus. cons. Deacon, tchr. Bible sch. Salem Bapt. Ch. Served with USAF, 1948-51. Mem. Am. Inst. C.P.A.s, N.C. Assn. C.P.A.s, Nat. Assn. Accts., Inst. Cert. Mgmt. Acctg., Inst. Internal Auditors, Delta Sigma Pi. Republican. Home: 1715 Brewer Rd Winston-Salem NC 27107 Office: Winston-Salem State Univ Winston-Salem NC 27110

SUTTON, EDDIE, college basketball coach; b. Bucklin, Kans.; m. Patsy Sutton; children—Stephen, Sean, Scott. B., Okla. State U., 1958, M., 1959. Asst. basketball coach Okla. State U., Stillwater, 1958-60; basketball coach Tulsa Central High Sch., 1960-66, So. Idaho Jr. Coll., 1967-70, Creighton U., Omaha, 1970-74, U. Ark., Fayetteville, 1974-85, U. Ky., Lexington, 1985—. Office: U Ky Athletic Dept Lexington KY 40506*

SUTTON, FREDERICK ISLER, JR., realtor; b. Greensboro, N.C., Sept. 13, 1916; s. Fred I. and Annie (Fry) S.; m. Helen Sykes Morrison, Mar. 18, 1941; children—Fred I. III, Frank Morrison. Grad. Culver (Ind.) Mil. Acad., 1934; A.B., U. N.C., 1939, student Law Sch., 1939-41; grad. Realtor's Inst., 1956, student Grad. Sch., 1957. Propr., Fred I. Sutton, Jr., realtor, Kinston, N.C., 1946—; comml. airplane pilot, 1949—. Chmn., Kinston Parking Authority; chmn. Kinston Water Resources; pres. Lenoir County United Fund, 1969, 70; trustee, dean U. N.C. Realtors Inst.; trustee Florence Crittenton Services; v.p. N.C. Real Estate Edn. Found.; deacon Presbyn Ch. Served from ensign to lt. comdr. USNR, 1941-46. Named Kinston Realtor of Year, 1963; cert. property mgr. Mem. Kinston Bd. Realtors, (pres.), N.C. Bd. Realtors (v.p., 1957), N.C. Assn. Realtors (regional v.p., chmn. ednl. com., dir. Realtors Ednl. Found.), N.C. Assn. Real Estate Bds. (dir., v.p. 1958-60, 61, 63), Newcomen Soc., Am. Power Boat Assn. (nat. champion 1951, 82, region 4 champion 1976, 78, 79, 80, 82, Eastern Div. Champion 1982), U.S. Power Squadron (navigator; Kinston comdg. officer, sec. Dist. 27), C. of C. (v.p.), S.R. Clubs: Kiwanis (pres., dir. Kinston), Masons (32 deg.), Shriner, Elks. Home: 1101 N Queen St Kinston NC 28501 Office: Sutton Bldg PO Drawer 3309 Kinston NC 28501

SUTTON, GLORIA JEAN, health sciences counselor; b. Salisbury, Md., Oct. 2, 1948; d. Paul Weldon and Doris Mabel (Tribeck) S.; B.S., Towson State U., 1971; M.Ed., Western Md. Coll., 1977. Tchr., counselor Carroll County Bd. Edn., Westminster, Md., 1971-77; vocat. evaluator Goodwill Industries, Austin, Tex., 1977-78; voc. rehab. counselor Tex. Rehab. Commn., Austin, 1978-81; health scis. counselor Austin Community Coll. (Tex.), 1981—, also part-time instr. allied health scis.; pres. Taysa Video. Mem. Nat. Vocat. Guidance Assn., Am. Assn. Counseling and Devel., Jr. Coll. Personnel Assn. of Tex., Tex. Assn. Counseling and Devel., Internat. Arabian Horse Assn., Am. Horse Shows Assn., Central Tex. Arabian Horse Club. Home: 7909 Creekmere Ln Austin TX 78745 Office: Health Sci Ctr Austin Community Coll 707 E 14th St Austin TX 78745

SUTTON, JOHN EWING, lawyer, accountant; b. San Angelo, Tex., Oct. 7, 1950; s. John F. Jr. and Nancy (Ewing) S.; m. Jean Ann Schofield, July 2, 1977; 1 son, Joshue Ewing; 1 stepson, Michael Brandon Ducote. B.B.A., U. Tex., 1973, J.D., 1976. Bar: Tex. 1976, U.S. Tax Ct. 1977, U.S. Ct. Claims, 1977, U.S. Dist. Ct. (no. dist.) Tex. 1977, U.S. Ct. Appeals (5th cir.) 1978, U.S. Dist. Ct. (we. dist.) Tex. 1979, U.S. Supreme Ct. 1980; C.P.A., Tex. Staff acct. Daugherty, Kuperman & Golden, Austin, 1975-76; tax specialist Peat, Marwick, Mitchell & Co., Dallas, 1976-77; tax ptnr. Shannon, Porter, Johnson & Sutton, Attys. at Law, San Angelo, Tex., 1977—. Treas. Good Shepherd Episcopal Ch., San Angelo, 1979-81; co-chmn. profl. div. United Way, San Angelo, 1980-82. Mem. ABA, Tex. Bar Assn., Tom Green County Bar Assn. (sec. treas. young lawyers 1977-78), Am. Inst. C.P.A.s, Tex. Soc. C.P.A.s (dir. 1980—, pres. San Angelo chpt. 1980-81, mem. state exec. com. 1981-82, chmn. profl. ethics com. 1985-86, Young CPA of Yr. 1984-85), Concho Valley Estate Planning Council (v.p. 1979-80, also dir.). Office: 317 W Concho San Angelo TX 76902

SUTTON, PHILIP GARLAND, JR., marketing cons.; b. New Albany, Ind., May 8, 1936; s. Philip Garland and Ona (Tucker) S.; student Western Mich. U., 1954-56; B.S., Purdue U., 1958; postgrad. Northeastern U., 1962-63, Union Coll., 1964-65; m. Marsha Anne McCauley, June 10, 1961; children—Philip Garland III, David Maurice, Elizabeth Tucker. Tech. rep. Am. Cyanamid Co., Boston, 1958-63; market devel. specialist Gen. Electric Co., Waterford, N.Y., 1963-66, mgr. southwestern dist., Dallas, 1966-69, mgr. plastic additive project, Waterford, 1969-71, mgr. fluids sect., 1971-72; pres. Sutton Assos., marketing cons., Houston, 1972—, also Cypress Assos., Inc., Houston. Served with USCGR, 1959-60. mem. Soc. Plastics Industries, Soc. Aerospace Materials and Process Engrs. Delta Chi. Unitarian. Lion. Clubs: Cy-Fair Swim (chmn. bd.), Wimbledon Racquet. Home: 10711 Creektree Dr Houston TX 77070 Office: 12337 Jones Rd Suite 216 Houston TX 77070

SUTTON, WALTER C., clergyman, editor, educator; b. East McKeesport, Pa., Apr. 23, 1927; s. Harold E. and Zora (Harvison) S.; m. Edith McMillan, June 8, 1956; children—Harold M., Stephanie J. B.A., Muskingum Coll., 1950; B.D., Louisville Presbyterian Theol. Sem., 1957, Th.M., 1963. Ordained to ministry Presbyn. Ch. U.S., 1957. Pastor 1st Presbyn. Ch., Elizabethtown, Ky., 1964-76, Eminence, Ky., 1957-63; instr. journalism and communications U. Ky. Elizabethtown Community Coll., 1968-76; dir. pub. relations Louisville Presbyn. Theol. Sem., 1976-79; pastor 1st Presbyn. Ch., Maysville, Ky., 1979-80; pub., editor Presbyn. Survey mag., 1980-83; editorial dir. John Knox Press, Atlanta, 1982—. Mem. Am. Acad. Religion, Soc. for Bibl. Lit. Office: John Knox Press 341 Ponce de Leon Ave NE Atlanta GA 30365

SUVER, JAMES DONALD, health administration educator, accountant; b. Swords Creek, Va., Oct. 21, 1931; s. Van Dula and Marcia Ellen (Davis) S.; m. Margaret Louise Schindler, Mar. 21, 1958 (div. 1977); children—James A., Amanda M.; m. 2d, Jean Claire Cooper, Dec. 31, 1980. B.S.B.A., Calif. State Coll.-Sacramento, 1962; M.B.A., Harvard U., 1965, D.B.A., 1971. Cert. mgmt. acct. Enlisted U.S. Air Force, 1949, advanced through grades to col., 1975; dir. mil. pay Air Force Acctg. and Fin. Ctr., Denver, 1973-75; ret., 1975; prof. acctg. U. Colo.-Colorado Springs, 1975-81, prof. health adminstrn. Health Scis. Ctr., 1978-81; prof. health policy and adminstrn. U. N.C.-Sch. Pub. Health-Chapel Hill, 1981—, dir. masters program, 1982—; cons. in field. Bd. dirs. Peak Health, Ltd., Colorado Springs, Colo., 1981-83; treas. Triangle Hospice, Chapel Hill, 1982-84. Decorated D.F.C., Legion of Merit, Air medal, Bronze Star; recipient Outstanding Teaching award U. Colo., 1977, 78, 81. Mem. Nat. Assn. Acctg. (Cert. of Merit 1977-79), Am. Pub. Health Assn., Health Care Fin. Mgmt. Assn., Assn. Govt. Acctg. (Disting. Research award 1978). Republican. Roman Catholic. Author: Management Accounting for Health Care Organizations, 1981; contbr. articles in field to profl. publs. Office: Univ NC Dept Health Policy and Adminstrn Sch Pub Health Chapel Hill NC 27514

SUZUKI, HOWARD KAZURO, educator; b. Ketchikan, Alaska, Apr. 3, 1927; s. George K. and Tsuya S.; B.S., Marquette U., 1949, M.S., 1951; Ph.D., Tulane U., 1955; m. Tetsuko Fujita, Sept. 12, 1952; children—Georganne, Joan, James, Stanley. Instr. anatomy Yale U. Sch. Medicine, 1955-58; asst. prof. U. Ark. Med. Center, Little Rock, 1958-62, asso. prof., 1962-67, prof. anatomy, 1967-70; prof., asso. dean U. Fla. Coll. Health Related Professions, Gainesville, 1970-71, prof., acting dean, 1971-72, dean, prof., 1972-79, prof. anatomy and health related professions, 1979—; mem. gen. research support program NIH, 1972-77, Health Manpower Program, VA, 1974-77. Bd. dirs. Civitan Regional Blood Bank; div. chmn. United Way; pres. Gulfview Guild, State Adv. Council Vocat. Edn.; regional v.p. Fla. Assn. Retarded Citizens, 1974-76. Fellow AAAS; mem. Soc. Exptl. Biology and Medicine, Am. Soc. Anatomists, Am. Soc. Allied Health Professions, So. Assn. Allied Health Deans at Acad. Health Centers (chmn. 1979—), Sigma Xi. Episcopalian. Home: 4331 NW 20th Pl Gainesville FL 32605 Office: Box J-235 J Hillis Miller Health Center U Fla Gainesville FL 32610

SVETLIK, J(OSEPH) FRANK, lawyer; b. Borger, Tex., June 30, 1945; s. Joseph Frank and Milton Florine (Woodall) S.; m. Barbara Gere Bauman, Nov. 17, 1973; children—David Scott, Stephanie Laura. B.S., Mich. State U., 1967; J.D., U. Houston, 1973. Bar: Tex. 1973; ptnr. law firm Burleson & Svetlik, Houston, 1974-81; ptnr. law firm Webb Flaum & Svetlik, Houston, 1982—. Pres. Larkwood Civic Assn., Houston, 1974. Mem. ABA, Tex. Bar Assn. (grievance com. 1974-78, fee arbitration com. 1980), Houston Bar Assn., Maritime Law Assn. U.S. Clubs: Briar, Houston. Lodges: Masons, Shriners. Home: 3504 Audubon Pl Houston TX 77006

SWAEBE, RICHARD, diamond and precious gem dealer; b. N.Y.C., Dec. 4, 1938; s. Leslie and Rosa (Landau) S.; m. Lily Kalkstein, Sept. 25, 1963; children—Theodore Aaron, Daniela. Pres., chmn. bd. Richard Swaebe Inc., Miami, Fla., 1963—; cons. Diamond and Precious Gem Index, Smithsonian Instn. dept. mineral sci. Treas., mem. exec. bd. Fla. region Anti-Defamation League. Served with U.S. Army, 1956-59. Mem. Diamond Dealers Assn., Diamond Trade Assn., Ocean Power Boat Racing Assn. Republican. Jewish. Clubs: Bankers, Palm Bay, Cricket, Jockey (Miami). Office: Ainsley Bldg Suite 1500 14 NE 1st Ave Miami FL 33132

SWAIM, OSCAR RANDALL, air force officer, pilot; b. Aberdeen, Md., June 28, 1954; s. Thomas Grey and Shirl Temple (Woodard) S.; A.A.S. in Respiration Therapy, Forsyth Tech. Inst., 1974; B.S. in Applied Math., N.C. State U., 1979. Staff therapist Sarasota (Fla.) Meml. Hosp., 1974-75; supr. N.C. Baptist Hosp., Winston-Salem, 1975; enlisted U.S. Air Force, 1979, advanced through grades to capt., 1983; crew mem. Seymour-Johnson AFB, N.C., 1981—; comml. single and multi-engine and comml./instrument pilot. Mem. Air Force Assn., Exptl. Aircraft Assn., Internat. Aerobatics Club. Lutheran. Home: 700C Spence Dr Apt 5 Goldsboro NC 27530 Office: Seymour Johnson AFB NC 27530

SWAIN, ALICE MARIE MCNEELY, reading specialist; b. Oklahoma City, Feb. 3, 1924; d. William Henry and Lucy Bruce (McCuiston) McNeely; B.S., Langston U., 1946; M.E., U. Okla. 1952; m. Robert Alphonso Swain, Aug. 24, 1946 (dec.); children—Robert Alphonso II, Lecia Danee. Tchr. schs., Oklahoma City, 1950—; pres. Together Enterprises, Oklahoma City, 1971—; asst. prof. English and reading Langston (Okla.) U. Recipient S.W. Regional Sigma of Year award, 1962. Outstanding Citizen award local chpt. Omega Psi Phi, 1976; U. Okla. math grantee, 1963, Livingtext book grantee, 1964; named one of 10 outstanding nat. Sigma women, 1965. Mem. Urban League Guild, NAACP, YWCA, Okla. Edn. Assn., NEA, Nat. Pan-Hellenic Council (sec. 1970-72, v.p. 1972—, nat. pres. 1974-75, Excellence in Service award 1974-76), Sigma Gamma Rho (past chmn. bd. dirs., Hall of Fame; chpt. Leadership award, 1st v.p. 1978-80). Mem. Christian Ch. Club: Tes Trams Social (Oklahoma City). Editor: Alice's Short Stories, 1972. Contbr. column The Black Dispatch, 1974; social columnist Black Chronicle, 1978. Home: 3016 Norcrest Dr Oklahoma City OK 73111 Office: 3016 Norcrest Dr Oklahoma City OK 73111

SWAIN, CLAUDIA NELL JONES, educator; b. Fort Worth, Dec. 15, 1937; d. Vidal Leonard and Wynona (Dews) J.; B.S., East Tex. Bapt. Coll., 1962; M.Ed., North Tex. State U., 1980, postgrad., 1980—; m. Richard Edward Swain, Jr., Apr. 28, 1973. Tchr., N.E. Houston Ind. Sch. Dist., 1962-64, Duncanville (Tex.) Ind. Sch. Dist., 1964-65, Dallas Ind. Sch. Dist., 1965-69; asst. dean students East Tex. Bapt. Coll., Marshall, 1969-70, dir. preschool and children's orgns. Woman's Missionary Union Tex., Bapt. Gen. Conv. Tex., Dallas, 1970-77; tchr. B.F. Darrell Community Center, Dallas Ind. Sch. Dist., 1977—. Named Outstanding Tchr. B.F. Darrell Community Center, 1979-80, 80-81. Mem. Assn. Childhood Edn. Internat., Internat. Reading Assn., Assn. Supervision and Curriculum Devel., Delta Kappa Gamma, Phi Delta Kappa. Baptist. Author: God Leads His Children, 1979. Office: 4730 S Lancaster Rd Dallas TX 75216

SWAIN, DONALD CHRISTIE, historian, university president; b. Des Moines, Oct. 14, 1931; s. George C. and Irene L. (Alsop) S.; B.A., U. Dubuque, 1953; M.A. in History, U. Calif.-Berkeley, 1958, Ph.D., 1961; m. Lavinia Kathryn Lesh, Mar. 5, 1955; children—Alan Christie, Cynthia Catherine. Asst. research historian U. Calif.-Berkeley, 1961-63; asst. prof. history U. Calif.-Davis, 1963-67, asso. prof., 1967-70, prof., 1970-81, acad. asst. to chancellor, 1967-68, asst. vice chancellor acad. affairs, 1971, vice chancellor acad. affairs, 1972-75, acad. v.p. U. Calif. System, Berkeley, 1975-81; pres. U. Louisville, 1981—, prof. history, 1981—; dir. Louisville Gas and Electric Co. Mem. Project 2000, Louisville Devel. Com.; bd. govs. J.B. Speed Art Mus.; bd. dirs. Louisville Orch., Ky. Econ. Devel. Council, Louisville C. of C., Boy Scouts Am.; mem. exec. com. urban affairs div. Nat. Assn. State Univs. and Land Grant Colls. Served to lt. (j.g.) USN, 1953-56. Recipient Disting. Teaching award U. Calif.-Davis, 1972. Mem. Am. Hist. Assn., Orgn. Am. Historians, Forest History Soc., Agrl. History Soc. Democrat. Presbyterian. Author: Federal Conservation Policy, 1921-33, 1963; The Politics of American Science 1939 to the Present, 1965; Wilderness Defender: Horace M. Albright and Conservation, 1970. Office: Office of President U Louisville Louisville KY 40292

SWAIN, JAMES JOSEPH, industrial engineering educator; b. Binghamton, N.Y., June 7, 1952; s. Arthur C. and Margaret Louise (Robinson) S.; m. Avi Jamshed Madan, Aug. 27, 1983. B.A., U. Notre Dame, 1974, B.S., 1975, M.S., 1977; Ph.D., Purdue U., 1982. Systems analyst Air Products & Chems., Allentown, Pa., 1977-79; asst. prof. Sch. Indsl. and Systems Engring. Ga. Inst. Tech., Atlanta, 1983—. Author: (with William E. Biles) Optimization and Industrial Experiments, 1980. Named Outstanding Grad. Instr., Purdue U., 1980; NSF New Engring. Faculty Research Incentive grantee, 1982-83. Mem. Am. Statis. Assn., Soc. Computer Simulation, Am. Soc. Engring. Edn., Ops. Research Soc. Am., Inst. Indsl. Engring. Roman Catholic. Office: Sch Indsl and Systems Engring Ga Inst Tech 225 North Ave Atlanta GA 30332

SWAMI, UMESH MANILAL, mathematics educator, consultant; b. Patan, India, Feb. 23, 1942; came to U.S., 1967; s. Manilal N. and Sitaben M. Swami; m. Vasu V. Khatri, May 10, 1966; 1 son, Anil U. M.Sc., Gujarat U., 1964; M.S., U. Iowa, 1968. Lectr. Dhrangadhra (India) Coll., 1964-65, Kadi (India) Sci. Coll., 1965-67; instr. Tex. Coll., Tyler, 1968; asst. prof. S.C. State Coll., Orangeburg, 1968-81, assoc. prof. math., 1981—. Democrat. Hindu. Home: 377 Adden St NW Orangeburg SC 29115 Office: S C State Coll PO Box 1975 Orangeburg SC 29117

SWAN, GEORGE STEVEN, law educator; b. St. Louis, Feb. 9, 1948; s. Raymond A. and Lorene (Kennedy) S. B.A., Ohio State U., 1970; J.D., U. Notre Dame, 1974; LL.M., U. Toronto, 1976, S.J.D., 1983. Bar: Ohio 1974. Asst. atty. gen. state of Ohio, Columbus, 1974-75; jud. clk. Supreme Ct. Ohio, Columbus, 1976-78; asst. prof. Del. Law Sch., Wilmington, 1980-83, assoc. prof., 1983-84; prof. law St. Thomas U. Law Sch., Miami, Fla., 1984—. Contbr. articles to law jours. Mem. ABA, Ohio State Bar Assn., Am. Polit. Sci. Assn. Republican. Roman Catholic. Office: 16400 NW 32d Ave Miami FL 33054

SWANGO, BILLY JOE, curtainwall contracting company executive; b. Dallas, Aug. 7, 1928; s. Erb T. and Lela Shirley (Beard) S.; m. Ada Beth Godwin, July 23, 1955; children—Kimberly, Tracey. B.S. in Archtl. Constrn., Tex. A&M U., 1949. Sales engr. Gene Paige Co., Dallas, 1950-54; mgr. engring. sales Am. Metal Window Co., Dallas, 1954-56; dist. sales mgr. Michael Flynn Mfg. Co., Dallas, 1956-61; pres. Olden & Co., Dallas, 1961—; organizer/dir. Pavillion Nat. Bank, Dallas. Served with U.S. Army, 1949-50; to 1st lt., 1951-53. Decorated Bronze Star. Mem. North Tex. Contractors Assn., Assoc. Gen. Contractors Am., Tex. A&M Former Students Assn. Republican. Baptist. Lodge: Masons. Patentee in field. Home: 10029 Woodgrove Dr Dallas TX 75218 Office: 4141 N St Augustine St Dallas TX 75227

SWANN, JOHN BUCK, credit union executive, personal financial consultant; b. Warren, Ark., Apr. 29, 1937; s. Charles Tillman and Carmen Ercell (May) S.; L.H.D., Linda Vista Baptist Bible Coll. and Sem., 1981; m. Joyce Degele, June 15, 1963; children—Alexandra, Christopher, Francesca, Dominic, Victoria, Benjamin, Israel, Gabrielle, Stefan, Judah. Mgr., Gen. Fin. Corp., El Paso, Tex., 1962-67; sr. loan officer Air Def. Center Fed. Credit Union, El Paso, 1967-68, treas.-mgr., 1968-84, pres., 1984—; cons. nat. credit union adminstrn.; lectr. Tex. Credit Union League; pub. Beautiful Feet newspaper, 1972-74. Served with USAF, 1956-60. Mem. El Paso C. of C., Better Bus. Bur., Credit Union Exec. Soc., Tex. Credit Union League. Republican. Mem. Ch. at Chaparral. Home: Star Route Box 7A Canutillo TX 79835 Office: PO Box 6082 El Paso TX 79906

SWANN, RUSSELL EUGENE, ophthalmologist; b. Jackson, Miss., May 13, 1947; s. Richard Earnest and Edythe (Kengla) S.; m. Renee Presley, Dec. 30, 1977; children—Russell Presley, Forrest Beau. B.S., Tulane U., 1969; M.D., Tulane U., 1975. Diplomate Am. Bd. Ophthalmology. Intern, Baylor U. Med. Ctr., Dallas, 1975-76; resident Oschner Found. Hosp., New Orleans, 1978-81; pvt. practice, medicine specializing in ophthalmology; Waco, Tex., 1981—; clin. instr. McLennan County Med. Soc., Waco., 1983—. Active Greater Waco Beautification Assn., Waco Hist. Found.; sponsor The Art Ctr., Waco, Central Tex. Zoo, Waco Boys Club. Served to capt. U.S. Army, 1976-78. Decorated Army Commendation medal, Washington, 1978. Fellow Am. Acad. Ophthalmology; mem. AMA, Tex. Ophthalmology Assn., Tex. Med. Assn. Republican. Clubs: Ambassador (New Orleans); Ridgewood Country (Waco). Avocation: sailing. Office: Russell E Swann MDPA 3115 Pine Suite 706 Waco TX

SWANN, WILLIAM SHIRLEY, clergyman, theology educator, academic administrator; b. Rome, N.Y., Jan. 7, 1947; s. William S. and Virginia (Norton) S. B.A., St. Joseph Sem., 1970; M.Div., Notre Dame Sem., New Orleans, 1974, S.T.M., 1976; S.T.D., Catholic U., 1981. Ordained priest Roman Catholic Ch., 1974. Tchr. religion St. John Vianney Prep Sch., New Orleans, 1974-75; assoc. pastor St. Matthias Parish, New Orleans, 1975-76; prof. theology Notre Dame Sem., New Orleans, 1979-80, acad. dean., 1980—; prof. Loyola U., New Orleans, 1982-83; adj. prof. Spring Hill Coll., Mobil, Ala., 1981—. Mem. Am. Acad. of Religion, Coll. Theology Soc., Catholic Theology Soc. Am., N.Am. Patristic Soc. Democratic. Avocations: jogging; handball. Home: 2901 S Carrollton Ave New Orleans LA 70118 Office: Notre Dame Sem 2901 S Carrollton Ave New Orleans LA 70118

SWANSON, CHARLES RICHARD, accountant, oil and gas consultant; b. Tulsa, July 19, 1953; s. Donald Charles and Helen Kathryn (Smith) S.; m. Karen Marcelle Pfister, June 10, 1978; children—Kimberly Marcelle, Laura Kathryn. B.A., Tulane U., 1975, M.B.A., 1977. C.P.A., Tex. Staff auditor Ernst & Whinney, Houston, 1977-79; sr. auditor, 1979-81, oil and gas cons., 1981-84, sr. mgr. energy industry services, 1984—; ptnr. Swanson Petroleum Enterprises, Houston, 1979—; dir. Cygnet Group, Inc., Houston. Contbr. articles to profl. jours. Mem. Republican Nat. Com., 1982. Teagle Found. scholar, 1971-75. Mem. Tulane Assn. Bus. Alumni (pres. 1982), Am. Inst. C.P.A.s, Tex. Soc. C.P.A.s, Petroleum Accts. Soc., Ind. Petroleum Assn. Am., Houston Jaycees, Mensa, Delta Tau Delta (pres. 1971-75). Lutheran. Club: Krewe of Bacchus. Home: 13810 Kingsride St Houston TX 77079 Office: Ernst & Whinney 333 Clay St Suite 3100 Houston TX 77002

SWANSON, DONALD CHARLES, geologist; b. Canon City, Colo., Sept. 22, 1926; s. Charles William and Josephine Anne (Kramer) S.; B.S. in Gen. Arts and Sci., Colo. State U., 1950; B.S. in Geology, Tulsa U., 1956; postgrad. U. Okla., 1965-67; m. Helen Kathryn Smith, June 10, 1950; children—Charles Richard, Jeffrey Stuart. Tax engr. and geologist Carter Oil Co., Tulsa, 1951-61; explorationist Humble Oil Co., Tex. and Okla., 1961-67; research geologist Exxon Prodn. Research Co., Houston, 1967-79; cons. geologist Swanson Petroleum Enterprises, Houston, 1979—; partner Swanson & Crow, 1979—. Fellow Geol. Soc. Am.; mem. Am. Assn. Petroleum Geologists (recipient A.I. Levorsen awards 1969, 79), Explorers Club, Sigma Chi. Lutheran. Contbr. articles to profl. jours. Home: 13611 Kingsride St Houston TX 77079 Office: 11999 Katy Freeway Suite 310 Houston TX 77079

SWARTWOUT, JOSEPH RODOLPH, physician; b. Pascagoula, Miss., June 17, 1925; s. Thomas Roswell and Marshall (Coleman) S.; student Miss. Coll., 1943-44; M.D., Tulane U., 1951; m. Risë Deutsch, Nov. 25, 1978. Intern Touro Infirmary, New Orleans, 1951-52; asst. obstetrics and medicine Tulane U., 1952-53, instr., 1955-60; Nat. Found. fellow Harvard, 1953-55; asst. medicine Peter Bent Brigham Hosp., Boston, assoc. obstet. research Boston Lying-in Hosp., 1953-55; asst. prof. U. Pitts., 1960-61; assoc. prof. Emory U., Atlanta, 1961-66; assoc. prof. obstetrics and gynecology U. Chgo., 1967-80; chief ob-gyn at Prime Health, also clin. asso. prof. Kans. U. Sch. Medicine, 1978-80; prof. dept. ob-gyn Mercer U. Sch. Medicine, Macon, Ga., 1980—, assoc. dean for acad. affairs, 1982—. Served with USNR, 1943-46. Fellow Am. Coll. Obstetricians and Gynecologists, Am. Heart Assn., (council clin. cardiology), Am. Acad. Reproductive Medicine; mem. AMA, Bibb County Med. Soc., Population Assn. Am., AAAS, Ga. State Med. Assn., Am. Pub. Health Assn. Home: 319 Alexandria St Macon GA 31210 Office: Mercer U Sch Medicine Macon GA 31207

SWARTZMAN, TERESA ARLENE, bookstore executive; b. Akron, Ohio, May 25, 1936; d. Edward John and Ann (Wacher) Mysock; m. Richard Edwin Swartzman, Nov. 30, 1957; children—Todd Edward, Derek Richard. B.A., U. Akron, 1958. History tchr. Litchfield Jr. High, Akron, 1959-61, Firestone High, Akron, 1961-64; tchr. history, psychology Hempfield Sr. High Sch., Greensburg, Pa., 1964-67; owner Book Swap Inc., Dunedin, Palm Harbor, Tampa, Fla., 1977—. Author booklet Book Swap Franchising, 1980. Pres. PTA, Centerville, Ohio, 1974, Welcome Wagon, Centerville, 1973; Mem. Antiquarian Book Club, Alpha Gamma Delta. Republican. Roman Catholic. Avocations: golf; bridge; reading. Home: 2708 Pinewood Ct Clearwater FL 33519 Office: Book Swap Inc 491 US 19N Palm Harbor FL 33519

SWEARINGEN, CAROL CANFIELD, accountant; b. Wichita, Sept. 1, 1944; d. Charles Calvin and Arlee Jeanne (Featherston) Canfield; children—Gretchen Christine, Jeffrey Blair; m. Robert Goodwin Swearingen, Sept. 13, 1980; 1 dau., Ashley Brooks; stepchildren—Andrew McCraw, Benjamin Patrick. Student U. Ottawa (Ont.), 1961-63, Cambridge (Eng.) U., 1968-70; B.S., 1971; postgrad. Tex. Tech. U., 1978, Rice U., 1984. Lic. pvt. pilot. Analyst, Seiscom-Delta Co., 1974-75; research asst. Alaska Interstate, 1975-76; asst. controller Dan-Tex Internat., 1977-79; controller Levering & Reid, 1980-81; pres. Canfield-Swearingen, 1982—, (all Houston); pres. Canfield Aviation, Inc. Mem. Nat. Women's Conf., Houston, 1977; violinist The Chamber Group, The Houston Symphonetta; mem. Bd. Adjustment, Hedwig Village. Republican. Episcopalian. Home: 11774 Duart St Houston TX 77024 Office: 800 Gessner Suite 170 Houston TX 77024

SWEENEY, ERMENGARDE COLLINS, horse breeder; b. Falfurrias, Tex., Nov. 3, 1922; d. John and Ophelia (Fant) Sweeney; m. William Wallace Walton, Jr., Nov. 8, 1940 (div. 1972); children—William Walton III, Ermengarde Walton, Julia Walton. Student, Tex. Sch. Fine Arts, 1939-40. Horse breeder, exhibitor, Corpus Christi and Helotes, Tex., 1956-70; pres. Paws Gulf Coast Humane Soc., Corpus Christi, 1978-86; lectr. in field. Bd. dirs., dir. region 5 of Tex. Human Info. Network, 1978-81. Mem. Arabian Horse Club of Am. Republican. Club: Corpus Christi Town. Contbr. to Arabian Horse Jour. in Eng. Address: 3461 Floyd St Corpus Christi TX 78411

SWEENEY, EVERETT JOHN, lawyer; b. Thomas, Okla., Mar. 22, 1945; s. John and Lucille (Wright) S. m. Sherryl M. Sweeney, Sept. 27, 1964; children—John Chad, Andrea Rachelle. B.S., Southwestern State Coll., 1967; J.D., U. Okla. 1970. Bar: Okla. 1970, U.S. Dist. Ct. (we. dist.) Okla. 1970, U.S. Ct. Apl.s (10th cir.) 1970, U.S. Supreme Ct. 1982. Instr., Southwestern State Coll., Weatherford, Okla., 1970-72; counsel Am. Fidelity Assurance Co., Oklahoma City, 1972-74; assoc. Robert G. Grove, Oklahoma City, 1974-76; legal asst. Supreme Ct. Okla., Oklahoma City, 1976-77; assoc. Miskovsky & Sullivan, Oklahoma City, 1977-78; ptnr. Sweeney & Lankford, Norman, Okla., 1978—. Mem. Cleveland County Bar Assn., Oklahoma County Bar Assn., Okla. Trial Lawyers Assn., Assn. Trial Lawyers Am. Democrat. Baptist. Home: 1609 Post Oak Rd Norman OK 73069 Office: Sweeney & Lankford 303 S Peters St Norman OK 73069

SWEENEY, GEORGE BERNARD, JR., planning consultant, broadcast executive; b. Cleve., May 9, 1933; s. George Bernard and Ethel E. (Wise) S.; B.S. in Bus. Adminstrn., John Carroll U., 1955; M.B.A., Wharton U. Pa., 1957; m. Molly Jane O'Neill, July 13, 1963; children—Brian, Kelly, Mark, Kevin, Kim. With Exxon Corp., 1956-78, chmn., pres. Esso Pakistan Fertilizer Co., Karachi, 1969-74, v.p. Exxon Corp. and Exxon Chem. U.S.A., Houston, 1974-78; dir., prin. Chagrin Valley Co. Ltd., Cleve., 1977-81; dir. Nevamar Corp., Odenton, Md., Liqui-Lawn Corp., Cleve., Evergreen Capital Corp., Austin, Tex., Mapleleaf Capital Corp., Houston; chmn. bd. A/L Sports, Inc., Denver, 1979-83; pres., prin. Questers, Inc., Houston, 1979-83; pres., prin. KMUV Radio, Conroe, Tex., 1984—, Sweeney Broadcasting Co., 1984—. Bd. dirs. Houston Symphony, 1976—; trustee John Carroll U., Cleve., 1977—, Strake Jesuit Coll. Prep., Houston, 1979—; trustee, chmn. bd. Trinity Coll., Washington, 1974-80; exec. bd. Wharton Grad. Sch., U. Pa., 1980—; trustee U. St. Thomas, Houston, 1982—; bd. dirs. Tex. Hunter-Jumper Assn., 1981—. Served with Transp. Corps, U.S. Army, 1958. Recipient in Pakistan U.S. State Dept. citation of appreciation, 1974. Clubs: Houston, Houstonian, Del Lago. Home: Route 1 Box 12 Macedonia Rd Hockley TX 77447

SWEENEY, ROBERT BOYCE, accounting educator, consultant; b. San Antonio, Aug. 13, 1930; s. Charles Franklin and Ella A. (Lockett) S.; m. Beverly Jane Shivers, Oct. 26, 1957; children—Robert Boyce, Katherine B., William F., John E. B.B.A. with highest honors, U. Tex., 1951, M.B.A., 1953, Ph.D., 1960. C.P.A., Tex. Acct., Gen. Electric Co., 1954; instr. acctg. U. Tex., Austin, 1959-60; prof. acctg. U. Ala., University, 1960-83, dir. Sch. Accountancy, 1970-83, v.p. fin., 1974-75; MSU prof. accountancy Memphis State U., 1983—; mem. Fin. Acctg. Standards Adv. Council. Served to lt. USN, 1954-57; Korea. Recipient Sarah Healy award U. Ala., 1976; Sigma Chi Outstanding Prof. award U. Ala., 1983; Ford Found. fellow U. Chgo., 1965, U. Mich., 1962. Mem. Am. Inst. C.P.A.s, Nat. Assn. Accts., Fin. Execs. Inst., Inst. Mgmt. Acctg. (chmn. bd. regents), Am. Acctg. Assn. (sec.-treas.), Stuart Cameron McLeod Soc. (hon.), Alpha Lambda Delta (hon.). Baptist. Club: North River Yacht (Tuscaloosa, Ala.). Lodges: Masons, Shriners. Author: Use of Computers in Accounting, 1972; Cost Accounting, 1978; other publs. in field. Office: Coll of Business Memphis State Univ Memphis TN 38152

SWEENEY, ROBERT JOSEPH, JR., oil company executive; b. Montpelier, Vt., Oct. 23, 1927; s. Robert Joseph and Glenna Ethyln (Little) S.; B.S. in Engring. Physics, Auburn (Ala.) U., 1948; M.S. in Petroleum Engring., La. Tech. U., 1961; m. Hazel Miller, Mar. 7, 1947; children—Robert Joseph, III, Theodore C., James Bradford. With Murphy Oil Corp., 1952—, v.p. prodn. and exploration, 1966-69, pres., chief operating officer El Dorado, Ark., 1972-84, chief exec. officer, 1984—; pres. Murphy Eastern Oil Co., 1969-72; dir. Ocean Drilling and Exploration Co., Fed. Res. Bank of St. Louis. Bd. dirs., past pres. Boys Club El Dorado, S.Ark. Arts Center; trustee El Dorado YWCA. Served with USNR, 1945-46. Mem. AIME. Roman Catholic. Club: K.C. Home: 1502 N Euclid St El Dorado AR 71730 Office: 200 Jefferson Ave El Dorado AR 71730

SWEENY, DAVID MCCANN, congressman; b. Wharton, Tex., Sept. 15, 1955; s. Daniel Webster and Billy Kathleen (Sandlin) S.; m. Catherine Hellman, 1982. B.A., U. Tex., 1978, postgrad. Sch. Law, 1979-81. Truck driver, ranch worker, staff aide to Senator Tower, 1977-78, to Gov. J. Connally, 1979-80; dir. adminstrv. ops. White House, Washington, 1981-83; mem. 99th U.S. Congress from 14th dist. Tex. Office: US House of Reps Washington DC 20515*

SWEET, JAMES W., building products company executive; b. 1918. Various positions Scotty's Inc., Winter Haven, Fla., 1939—, pres., chief exec. officer, 1968-71, pres., chmn., 1971-73; chmn., chief. exec. officer, 1973—. Office: Scotty's Inc Recker Hwy PO Box 939 Winter Haven FL 33880*

SWEETMAN, LINDA RUTH, university dean; b. Indpls., Nov. 26, 1942; d. Carl Herman and Doretta Henrietta (Heger) Bulthaup; m. Edward Richard Sweetman, Nov. 20, 1965; children—Dennis Patrick, Jennifer Lynn. B.S. in Elem. Edn., Ind. Central U., 1968; M.A. in Humanities, U. Dallas, 1980. Sec. Indpls. Schs., 1960-66, tchr. kindergarten, 1968-70; tchr. Lincoln Schs., Nebr., 1970-72; adminstrv. asst. to pres. U. Dallas, Irving, 1975-77, asst. dean students, 1977-81, dean students, 1981-85. Mem. adv. com. Congl. award, 1984; mem. Task Force Life Enrichment-WellWay Ctrs., Inc., 1984-85; adminstrv. bd. First United Meth. Ch., Dallas, 1985. Recipient Staff award U. Dallas, 1979, 85. Mem. Nat. Assn. Student Personnel Adminstrs., Tex. Assn. Coll. and Univ. Student Personnel Adminstrs., Am. Coll. Personnel Assn. Democrat. Methodist. Avocations: camping; biking; sewing; traveling. Home: Emma Willard Sch Troy NY 12180 Office: U Dallas 1845 E Northgate Irving TX 75061

SWEEZY, SHIRLEY ALICE, manager antiques firm; b. Beaumont, Tex., July 15, 1935; d. Wiley Greenly and Mary Edna (Stevens) S. Student Lamar U. Sec., Golden Triangle Antiques Dealers Assn., 1970-74; co-owner, mgr. Paul Sweezy Antiques, Beaumont; participant antiques shows, Tex., 1955—. Bd. dirs. Beaumont Assn. Mental Health, 1964-65. Mem. DAR (charter mem.-Jane Long, Pasadena, Tex.). Republican. Baptist. Avocations: collecting fine art, cut glass, rare coins, antiques.

SWEGER, JOHN BOULDIN, savings and loan company executive; b. Quincy, Fla., Nov. 7, 1919; s. Roy Louis and Dicie (Bouldin) S.; m. Ruth Van Zyle, 1941 (div. 1946); 1 child, John B.; m. Gloria Patricia Burke, June 13, 1948; 1 child, Robert L. B.A.J., U. Fla., 1941. Pres., Smith-Sweger Constrn. Co., Largo, Fla., 1948-75; chmn. Fortune Fin. Group, Inc., Clearwater, Fla., 1982—. Former pres. Morton F. Plant Hosp. Assn., Clearwater, Fla., 1974-77; former trustee, 1970-83; trustee Human Services, Inc., Clearwater, 1984-85. Served to maj. U.S. Army, 1941-46; ETO. Democrat. Avocation: ranching. Office: Fortune Federal Savs and Loan Assn 14 S Fort Harrison Ave Clearwater FL 33516

SWENSSON, EARL SIMCOX, architect; b. Nashville, July 28, 1930; s. Earl Ebenezer and Viola Lazelle (Simcox) S.; m. Suzanne Dickenson, June 6, 1953; children—Krista Swensson Oglesby, Lin Swensson Walker, Kurt Dickenson. B.S., Va. Poly. Inst. and State U., 1952, M.S. Arch., 1953; M.S. Arch., U. Ill., 1955. Assoc. Glenn G. Frazier, Urbana, Ill., 1954-56, Perkins & Wills, Chgo., 1956-60; Donald Stoll, Nashville, 1960-61; founder, prin. Earl Swensson Assocs., Inc., Nashville 1961—; adj. prof. Va. Poly. Inst., Blacksburg, 1971-72, Auburn U., 1976-83; dir. Am. Retirement Corp., Nashville. Patentee systamodule for pharmacies. Bd. dirs. Metro Arts Commn., 1979—, Middle Tenn. Health Systems Aug. 1973-78, Salvation Army, 1964-69, Leadership Nashville Alumni Groups, 1984—; mem. bd. advisers U. Tenn. Sch. Architecture, 1982. Recipient Jefferson award Am. Inst. Public Service, Nashville chpt., 1985. Fellow AIA (regional rep.). Presbyterian. Clubs: Nashville City, University, Belle Meade Country. Office: Earl Swensson Assocs 2100 West End Ave Nashville TN 37203

SWETMAN, GLENN ROBERT, educator, poet; b. Biloxi, Miss., May 20, 1936; s. Glenn Lyle and June (Read) S.; B.S., U. So. Miss., 1957, M.A., 1959; Ph.D., Tulane U., 1966; m. Margarita Ortiz, Feb. 8, 1964 (div. 1979); children—Margarita June, Glenn Lyle Maximilian, Glenda Louise. Instr., U. So. Miss., 1957-58, asst. prof., 1964-66; instr. Ark. State U., 1958-59, McNeese U., 1959-61; instr. English, Univ. Coll. Tulane U., 1961-64, spl. asst. dept. elec. engring., 1961-64; assoc. prof. La. Inst. Tech., 1966-67; prof., head dept. langs. Nicholls State Coll., Thibodaux, La., 1967-69, head dept. English, 1969-71, prof., 1971—. Partner, Breeland Pl., Biloxi, Miss., 1960—; stringer corr. Shreveport (La.) Times, 1966—; partner Ormuba, Inc., 1975—; cons. tech. writing Union Carbide Corp., Am. Fedn. Tchrs. State v.p. Nat. Com. to Resist Attacks on Tenure, 1974—. Subdiv. coordinator Republican party, Hattiesburg, Miss., 1964. Served with AUS, 1957. Recipient Poetry awards KQUE Haiku contest, 1964, Coll. Arts contest, Los Angeles, 1966, Black Ship Festival, Yoqosuka, Japan, 1967; Green World Brief Forms award Green World Poetry Editors, 1965. Mem. MLA, S. Central MLA, So. Literary Festival Assn. (v.p. 1975-76, 82-83, pres. 1984-85), Coll. Writers Soc. La. (pres. 1971-72, exec. dir. 1983—), IEEE, Am. Assn. Engring. Edn., La. Poetry Soc. (pres. 1971-74, 85-86), Internat. Boswellian Inst., Nat. Fedn. State Poetry Socs. (2d v.p., nat. membership chmn. 1972-74, pres. 1976-77), Nat. Soc. Scholars and Educators (bd. dirs. 1982—), Am. Fedn. Tchrs. (chpt. pres. 1973-78, 85-86), Nat. Fedn. State Poetry Socs. (1st v.p. 1975-76, exec. bd. 1972—), Phi Eta Sigma, Omicron Delta Kappa. Book reviewer Jackson (Miss.) State Times, 1961. Poems pub. in various publs. including Poet, Prairie Schooner, Trace, Ball State U. Forum, Film Quar.; (books of poems) Tunel de Amor, 1973; Deka #1, 1973; Deka #2, 1979; Shards, 1979; Concerning Carpenters, 1980; Son of Igor, 1980; A Range of Sonnets, 1981; Christmas, 1982; cons. editor (poetry) Paon Press, 1974—, Scott-Foresman, 1975; editorial bd. Scholar and Educator, 1980—. Home: 203 Four Point Dr Raceland LA 70394

SWICK, LEO EMMETT, JR., petroleum geologist; b. Lima, Ohio, July 2, 1917; s. Leo E. and Mildred May (Kennedy) S.; m. Margaret Kathryn Nunemaker, Sept. 28, 1938; children—Sue, Nancy, Kathryn, David. B.A., Ohio State U., 1939, M.S., 1941. Geol. engr. Nickel Plate R.R., Cleve., 1941-43, B.&O. R.R., Balt., 1943-44; exploration geologist Magnolia Petroleum Co., Dallas, 1944-48; ind. petroleum geologist and cons., Gainesville, Tex., 1948—; v.p., chief geologist Reliance Petroleum Corp., Dallas, 1980—. Mem. Gainesville City Council, 1951-52; chmn., pres. Gainesville Bd. Edn., 1954-59. Mem. Gainesville C. of C. (pres. 1954), Am. Assn. Petroleum Geologists (life), Am. Inst. Profl. Geologists (cert. geologist), Explorers Club. Methodist. Avocations: travel; photography; sculpture. Office: 411 E California St Gainesville TX 76240

SWIDERSKI, THEODORE JOHN, JR., oil company executive, oil and gas producer, oil and gas consultant; b. Bklyn., May 29, 1950; s. Theodore John and Ernesteen (Barfoot) S.; m. Nancy Carlene McDonald, June 10, 1970 (div. Jan. 1975); m. Elizabeth Ann Barrett, Jan. 6, 1979; children—Jordan Barrett, Christopher Michael. B.S. magna cum laude in Geology, U. Fla., 1972; M.S. in Geology, U. Colo., 1974. Area exploration geologist Phillips Petroleum, Denver, 1974-79; sr. exploration geologist Amerada-Hess Corp., Denver, 1979; v.p. exploration, prodn. MEG Petroleum Corp., San Angelo, Tex., 1979-85, also dir.; dir. West Tex. Operator's, Inc., San Angelo; dir., pres. TLM Energy Corp., San Angelo; oil and gas cons., San Angelo, 1980—. Mem. Am. Assn. Petroleum Geologists, Soc. Econ. Paleontologists and Mineralogists, Geol. Soc. Am., Rocky Mountain Geol. Soc., W. Tex. Geol. Soc., Phi Beta Kappa, Phi Kappa Phi. Republican. Presbyterian. Club: San Angelo Country. Avocations: study of military and world history; sailing; hiking. Home: 511 S Park St San Angelo TX 76901 Office: 40 W Twohig Suite 403 San Angelo TX 76903

SWIETELSKY, ERNST FERDINAND, importer; b. Linz, Austria, July 30, 1946; came to U.S., 1972; s. Hellmuth Ferdinand and Etelka Ida (Gorog) Bielka S.; m. Andrea Euston, Aug. 7, 1972 (div. 1975). Doctoris Rerum Politicarum, U. Vienna, Austria, 1972; B.S. magna cum laude, U. Miami, Fla., 1974. Pres. Pot Co., Miami, 1975—. Mem. Nat. Republican Senatorial Com., Washington, Better Bus. Bur., Miami, Center for Fine Arts, Miami, Lowe Art Mus., Miami, Greater Miami Opera Assn. Mem. Importers Assn. Am., U.S. C. of C., Greater Miami C. of C., Miami Film Soc., Phi Kappa Phi. Republican. Roman Catholic. Clubs: Grove Isle (Miami); U.S. Senatorial. Avocations: arts; tennis; sailing.

SWIGERT, JAMES LYNWOOD, zoological park adminstrator, cousultant; b. Carlisle, Pa., May 18, 1941; s. Clarence Switgert and Evelyn (Shearer) S.; m. Esther Adams, Sept. 14, 1963; 1 son, Earl Trent. B.S., Coll. Agr., W.Va. U., 1966. Zoologist Mesker Park Zoo, Evansville, Ind., 1967-69; dir. Caribbean Gardnes, Naples, Fla., 1969-72, Randolph Park Zoo, Tucson, 1972-75, Jackson Zool. Park, Miss., 1975—. Office: Jackson Zool Park 2918 W Capital St Jackson MS 39209*

SWIGGETT, HAL, writer, photographer; b. Moline, Kans., July 22, 1921; s. Otho Benjamin and Mildred (Spray) S.; ed. high sch.; m. Wilma Caroline Turner, Mar. 1, 1942; children—Gerald, Vernon. Staff photographer San Antonio Express-News, 1946-67, head dept., 1955-67; freelance writer/photographer San Antonio, 1947—, full-time, 1967—; ordained minister So. Baptist Ch. Served with USAAC, World War II. Recipient 10th ann. Outstanding Am. Handgunner award, 1982. Mem. Wildlife Unltd. (pres. chpt. 1955-58), Outdoor writers Assn. Am. (dir. 1969-72), Tex. Outdoor Writers Assn. (pres. 1967-68), Ducks Unltd., Nat. (life), Tex. (life) rifle assns., Internat. Handgun Metallic Silhouette Assn. (life), Game Conservation Internat. Republican. Contbg. author books game hunting, gun-oriented paperbacks; author: Hal Swiggett on North American Deer, 1980; editor spl. projects Harris Publs.; contbg. editor Gun Digest. Home: 539 Roslyn St San Antonio TX 78204

SWINDALL, PATRICK LYNN, lawyer, congressman; b. Anniston, Ala., Oct. 18, 1950; m. Kimberly Nan Schiesser, 1957; 1 child, Kelley Alice. B.A., U. Ga., 1972, J.D., 1975. Bar: Ga. 1975. Assoc., Heyman and Sizemore, Atlanta, 1975-79, ptnr., 1979-84; owner Atlanta Furniture Co., 1978—; mem. U.S. Ho. of Reps. from 4th dist. Ga., 1984—. Active Young Life Northwest Atlanta Com. 1978-81, Dunwoody High Sch., 1982—; mem., Sunday sch. tchr. First Presbyterian Ch., Atlanta, 1979-81; mem. Dunwoody Community Ch., 1982—; flight coordinator Friendship Force Brussels/Atlanta flight, 1978; mem. exec. com. Atlanta Prison Fellowship, 1978-81; U. Ga. Young Alumni Council, 1975-81; div. chmn. met. Atlanta, Joint Ga.-Ta. Tech. Devel. Drive, 1975-76, United Way, 1978; co-chmn. Atlanta Radio Fellowship, 1979—. Named Outstanding Young Man U.S. Jaycees, 1979. Mem. ABA, Atlanta Bar Assn., Am. Trial Lawyers Assn., Blue Key, Biftad Honor Soc., Omicron Delta Kappa, Pi Kappa Phi. Office: 508 Cannon House Office Bldg Washington DC 20003

SWINDLE, GARY PAUL, garment manufacturing executive, equipment leasing executive; b. Ada, Okla., Jan. 5, 1948; s. Jack S. and Juanita (Smallwood) S.; m. Theresa Louise Wilson, Nov. 13, 1976; children—Carla, Diana. B.B.A. in Mktg., Tex. Tech. U., 1970. Acct., auditor Mobil Oil Corp., Dallas, 1973-77; acctg. supr. Mobil Oil Indonesia, Medan, 1978-81; v.p. and gen. mgr. E.G. Wilson Mfg. Inc., Winnsboro, Tex., 1981—; pres. G.P. Swindle, Inc., Columbus, Tex., 1981—, Columbus Clothing Mfg. Inc., Columbus, Tex., 1983; owner Colorado Cleaners, Columbus. Mem. Columbus City Council, 1986-87; trustee 1st United Methodist Ch., Columbus. Republican. Home: 1303 Milam St Columbus TX 78934 Office: PO Box 219 Columbus TX 78934

SWINDLE, LARRY CLIFFORD, filtration company executive; b. Abilene, Tex., Feb. 12, 1945; s. Clifford Oliver and Virginia Su (Boozer) S.; m. Judy Vernell Kendall, June 15, 1985; children—Clifford Cason, Christopher Canon, Creighton Colin. A.A. with honors, Phoenix Coll., 1965; B.S. with high honors, Ariz. State U., 1967. Sr. salesman Kaiser Aluminum & Chem. Co., Charlotte, N.C., 1967-71, br. mgr., 1971-75, regional distbr. mgr., Phila., 1975-78; pres. Treadle Wheel, Protem, Mo., 1978-79; dir. mktg. services Williams Co., Tulsa, 1979-81; v.p. sales, mktg. Titan Rig Co., Tulsa, 1981-82; group dir. mktg., sales Facet Enterprises, Inc., Tulsa, 1982-86; dir. mktg., sales Perry Equipment Co., 1986—. Patentee printing and camping equipment. Pres., Tarheel Cyclist, Charlotte, 1974; chmn. Lower Providence Twp. Parks and Recreation Bd., Phila., 1976; campaign mgr. U.S. Congl. candidacy, Tulsa, 1982. Named Top Salesman, Sales and Mktg. Execs. Ariz., 1967, Salesman of Yr., Kaiser Aluminum Co., Oakland, Calif., 1972. Mem. Am. Mktg. Assn., Nat. Bus. Aircraft Assn., Am. Mgmt. Assn., Ariz. State U. Bus. Coll. Alumni Assn. (charter), Ariz. State Alumni Assn., Holiday Hill C. of C. (Mineral Wells). Republican. Clubs: Petroleum (Ft. Worth); Financial (Tulsa). Home: 511 SW 1st Mineral Wells TX 76067 Office: Perry Equipment Co PO Box 640 One Peco Place Mineral Wells TX 76067

SWITZER, GWENDOLYN JOHAN, nurse; b. Ada, Okla., Oct. 24, 1935; d. Claud B. and May Alice (Bratcher) Smith; student Bethany Peniel Coll., 1953-54; B.S., E. Central State Coll., 1957; R.N., St. Anthony's Hosp. Sch. Nursing, 1962; 1 dau., Janet Dianne. Office nurse Dr. C.B. Dawson, Oklahoma City, 1962-63; pvt. duty nurse St. Anthony Hosp., Oklahoma City, 1963-64; staff nurse Valley View Hosp., Ada, 1964-66, house supr., 1966-68; dir. nursing Holdenville (Okla.) Gen. Hosp., 1968-69, coronary care nurse, 1969-76, unit dir. med. floor, 1976-78, dir. pediatrics, 1978-79, house supr., 1979—; cons. nurse Stonegate Nursing Home, Stonewall, Okla., 1974-77. Leader Camp Fire Girls, 1970-76, counselor, 1971-72; ch. choir dir. Ch. of the Nazarene, 1968, children's dir., 1974-77; first aide instr. ARC, 1966-68, disaster-nurse, 1964—; bd. dirs. Singles' Ministry of Southeast Okla., 1982—. Recipient ARC Nursing Student award, 1962. Mem. Nat. League for Nursing, Am. Assn. Critical Care Nurses, Okla. Nurses Assn., Nat. Assn. Female Execs. Democrat. Ch. of the Nazarene. Home: 2629 E 14th St Ada OK 74820 Office: 1300 E 6th St Ada OK 74820

SWITZER, ROBERT EARL, lawyer, educator, military law consultant; b. Buffalo, Nov. 24, 1929; s. Earl Alexander and Verne (Nowak) S.; m. Suzanne Marion Van Slyke, May 11, 1957; children—Tracey Ann, Beth Ann. B.A. with distinction in History, Bethany (W.Va.) Coll., 1951; J.D., U. Buffalo, 1956; postgrad. Nat. Jud. Coll., Reno, 1978. Bar: N.Y. 1958, U.S. Ct. Mil. Appeals, 1966, U.S. Supreme Ct. 1976. Estate planner M & T Trust Co., Buffalo, 1956-58; sole practice, Buffalo, 1959-65; asst. county atty. Erie County, Buffalo, 1962-65; commd. 2d lt. U.S. Marine Corps, 1951, advanced through grades to col., 1973; inf. officer, 1951-53; trial csl., def. csl., 1965-66, dep. staff judge adv., 1967-69; staff judge adv., 1969-70, 75-77; dir. Law Ctr., 1971-72; cir. mil. judge, 1973-74, 1978-81; ret., 1981; instr. law criminal justice dept. Coastal Carolina Community Coll., Jacksonville, N.C., 1981—; mil. law cons., 1981—; lectr. on criminal law and trial advocacy, 1970—. Dist. committeeman Erie County Republican Com., 1960-65; del. 8th Jud. Dist. Nominating Conv., 1962-64; scoutmaster Boy Scouts Am., Quantico, Va., 1952-53, advisor Explorer scout post, Jacksonville, 1981-82. Decorated Navy Commendation medal; named Eagle Scout with gold palm Boy Scouts Am., 1947. Mem. ABA, Fed. Bar Assn. (pres. Hawaii chpt. 1977-78), Assn. Trial Lawyers Am., Acad. Criminal Justice Scis., Am. Soc. Criminology, N.C. Assn. Criminal Justice Educators, Inst. for Criminal Justice Ethics. Episcopalian. Club: Masons. Home: 1112 Keating Ct Jacksonville NC 28540 Office: Coastal Carolina Community College 444 Western Blvd Jacksonville NC 28540

SWOFFORD, DONALD ANTHONY, architect; b. Houston, Apr. 14, 1947; s. Harry and Henrian (Engbrock) S.; m. Virginia M. Bauler, May 23, 1985. B.Arch., Tex. A&M U., 1969; M.Arch., U. Va., 1976. Registered architect, Nat. Council Archtl. Registration Bds., cert. pilot. Architect, urban designer City of Dallas, 1970-72; architect Milton L. Grigg, FAIA, Architects, 1972-78; prin. Don A. Swofford, Architect, Charlottesville, Va., 1978—; pres. Traditional Am. Concepts Ltd., 1983—. Prin. works include Joseph Jarvis residence, 1978, Shrinemont Conf. Ctr., Episcopal Diocese of Va., Orkney Springs, 1981, United Coal/Martha Washington Inn, Bristol, Va., 1985. Chmn. parich council Holy Catholic Ch., Charlottesville, 1980-84. Recipient Tex.-AIA Design award, 1969-70; Jefferson fellow, 1972-73. Mem. AIA, Albemarle County Hist. Soc., Nat. Trust Historic Preservation, Soc. Archtl. Historians, Assn. Preservation Tech. Office: Don A Swofford Architect 1843 Seminole Trail Charlottesville VA 22901

SWOPE, WILLIAM RICHARDS, hardware and lumber co. exec., lawyer; b. Washington, Oct. 17, 1920; s. King and Mary Margaret (Richards) S.; A.B., U. Ky., 1941; LL.B., Harvard U., 1947; m. Bobbie Wylie Stringfellow, June 17, 1944; children—Cheryl Swope Browne, Robert Cromwell. Admitted to Ky. bar, 1947; v.p., sales mgr. Stringfellow Lumber Co., Birmingham, Ala., 1951-58; pres., owner Swope Co., Inc., Birmingham, Ala., 1958—, Swope Alabaster Supply, Inc., Birmingham, 1970—, Swope Sandestin Builders Supply, Inc., Santa Rosa Beach, Fla., 1973—. Bd. deacons Ind. Presbyn. Ch., Birmingham, 1953-56, 61-64, 71-74. Served to maj. U.S. Army, 1942-45. Mem. Am. Bar Assn., N. Am. Wholesale Lumber Assn., Nat. Fedn. Ind. Bus., Birmingham C. of C., Order of the Crown, Ams. of Royal Descent, First Families of Va., SAR, Lincoln's Inn Soc., Phi Delta Theta. Republican. Presbyterian. Clubs: Birmingham Country, The Club, Relay House, Lions (pres. 1957-58) (Birmingham); Idle Hour Country (Lexington); Santa Rosa Golf and Beach Club (Fla.). Home: 3821 Glencoe Dr Birmingham AL 35213 Office: PO Box 1447 Birmingham AL 35201

SYED, IBRAHIM BIJLI, medical physicist, educator; b. Bellary, India, Mar. 16, 1939; came to U.S., 1969, naturalized, 1975; s. Ahmed Bijli and Mumtaz Begum (Maniyar) S.; m. Sajida Shariff, Nov. 29, 1964; children—Mubin, Zafrin. B.S. (with honors), Mysore U., 1960, M.S. with honors and distinction, 1962; D.Sc., Johns Hopkins U., 1972; Ph.D. (hon.), Marquis Giuseppe Scicluna Intenat. U., 1985. Lectr. in physics Veerasaiva Coll., Bellary, U. Mysore, 1962-63; WHO trainee, 1963-64; med. physicist, radiation safety officer Victoria Hosp., India, 1964-67, Halifax (N.S., Can.) Infirmary, 1967-69; dir. med. physics, radiation safety officer Baystate Med. Center, Springfield, Mass., 1973-79; med. physicist, radiation safety officer VA Med. Center, Louisville, 1979—; prof. medicine and nuclear medicine tech. U. Louisville Sch. Medicine, 1979—; guest examiner Am. Bd. Radiology; mem. panel of examiners Am. Bd. Health Physics; Ph.D. thesis examiner U. Delhi; assoc. prof. Springfield Tech. Community Coll. (Mass.), 1973-79; adj. prof. radiology Holyoke Community Coll. (Mass.), 1973-79; asst. clin. prof. U. Conn. Health Scis. Center, 1975-79; tech. expert in nuclear medicine IAEA, Bangladesh, 1986. Pres., Springfield Islamic Center, 1973-79, India Assn., Louisville, 1980-81; v.p. Islamic Cultural Assn. Louisville, 1979-80, vice chmn. bd. trustees, 1984—; sec. bd. trustees India Community Found. Louisville, chmn., 1984-85; bd. dirs. Child Guidance Clinic, Springfield, 1973-79, Heritage Corp., Louisville, 1981—, others; active Am. Cancer Soc., Heart Fund. Diplomate Am. Bd. Radiology, Am. Bd. Health Physics. Recipient Disting. Community Service award India Community

Found. Louisville, 1982; USPHS fellow Johns Hopkins U., 1969-72; Fellow Inst. of Physics (U.K.), Am. Inst Chemists, Royal Soc. Health, Am. Coll. Radiology; mem. Am. Coll. Nuclear Medicine, Health Physics Soc., Am. Assn. Physicists in Medicine, Soc. Nuclear Medicine (life), Assn. Med. Physicists of India (life), N.Y. Acad. Scis., Jefferson County Med. Soc., Ky. Med. Assn. AAUP, Sigma Xi. Islamic. Author: Radiation Safety for Allied Health Professionals. Mem. editorial bd. Jour. Islamic Med. Assn., 1981—. Contbr. numerous articles to sci. jours. Home: 7102 Shefford Ln Louisville KY 40222 Office: 800 Zorn Ave Louisville KY 40202

SYKES, DELORES ROSELLE, educator; b. Accomack County, Va., May 22, 1932; d. John Sinclair and Bertha Virginia (Dennis) Roselle; m. William Luther Sykes, Nov. 13, 1954; children—Del Fionn, Ethan Doyle. B.S., Va. State Coll., 1954; M.S., Hampton Inst., 1970; Ph.D., U. Md., 1980. Tchr., chmn. home econs. dept. Chesapeake Sch. System (Va.), 1958-70; instr. human ecology Hampton Inst. (Va.), 1970-78, asst. prof., 1978-81, assoc. prof., 1981—. Mem. NEA, Nat. Council Family Relations, Am. Home Econs. Assn., Am. Vocat. Assn., Va. Home Econs. Assn., Va. Edn. Assn., Kappa Delta Pi. Jehovah's Witness. Home: 316 Rudisill Rd Hampton VA 23669 Office: Hampton Inst Hampton VA 23668

SYKES, GEORGE KUNKEL, investment company executive; b. Phila., Mar. 24, 1921; s. George and Ellen (Kunkel) S.; m. Katherine Louise Carpenter, Nov. 18, 1944; 1 child, Stephen C. Student Pa. State U., 1938-39; B.S., U.S. Mil. Acad., 1939-43; M.B.A., U. Pa., 1950; student Air War Coll., 1959-60. Various positions USAF, ret. as Brig. Gen. 1972; securities broker Charter Capital, Inc., San Antonio, 1972-73; spl. asst. to pres. United Services Automobile Assn., 1973, v.p. investments, 1973-76; exec. v.p. United Services Automobile Assn. Mgmt. Co., 1976-83, pres., chief operating officer, 1983—, also dir.; pres., dir. USAA Mut. Fund, Inc., San Antonio, USAA Tax Exempt Fund, Inc., San Antonio, 1982—, USAA Investment Trust, San Antonio, 1984—; dir. USAA Properties Fund, Inc., San Antonio, 1983—. Chmn. fin. com. United Way San Antonio and Bexar County; bd. dirs. Southwest Tex. Methodist Hosp., San Antonio, also mem. fin. com., personnel and retirement com. Decorated Legion of Merit with two oak leaf clusters, Air medal with three oak leaf clusters, Purple Heart, D.F.C., D.S.M. Mem. Fin. Analysts Fedn., San Antonio Soc. Fin. Analysts, Austin-San Antonio Soc. Fin. Analysts, No-Load Mut. Fund Assn. (adv. bd.). Club: San Antonio Golf Assn. Lodge: Kiwanis. Home: 7330 Ashton Pl Ct San Antonio TX 78229 Office: USAA Investment Mgmt Co 9800 Fredericksburg Rd San Antonio TX 78288

SYKES, MAYME JEAN PHARIS, educational administrator; b. Pineville, La., Feb. 21, 1928; d. Henry Garland and Ethel Fern (Mandeville) Pharis; B.A., La. Coll., 1949; M.Ed., U. Houston, 1954; m. Stephen McKenzie Sykes, Dec. 21, 1950; children—Stephen McKenzie, Sandra Jean. Tchr., La and Tex. schs., 1949-73; prin. Jefferson Elem. Sch., Temple, Tex., 1973—; cons. Ednl. Service Center. Former mem. City Commn. on Safety. Mem. NEA, Assn. Supervision and Curriculum Devel., Nat. Assn. Elem. Prins., Prins. Research Assn., Tex. Tchrs. Assn., Tex. Elem. Prins. Assn. (dist. v.p. 1981-82, dist. pres. 1983-84), PEO, Phi Delta Kappa, Delta Kappa Gamma, Alpha Delta Kappa. Methodist. Clubs: Order Eastern Star, Opti-Mrs. (past. pres.). Home: 3305 Buckeye Ln Temple TX 76501 Office: 400 W Walker St Temple TX 76501

SYKES, ROY EUGENE, JR., oil company executive; b. Lebanon, Va., May 20, 1951; s. Roy Eugene and Norma Jean (Kiser) S.; m. Martha Ann Turner, Nov. 23, 1979; children—Martha Roseann, Roy Arthur Jonathan. A.A.S., S.W. Va. Community Coll., 1971; B.S., Va. Poly. Inst. and State U., 1978. With D.S. Buck Inc., St. Paul, Va., 1977—, supr. computer ops., credit mgr., mgr. purchasing, acctg. mgr., 1978—. Mem. IEEE. Home: PO Drawer K Saint Paul VA 24283

SYKORA, DONALD D., utility company executive; b. Stamford, Tex., Aug. 23, 1930; s. John E. and Lillie A. S.; m. Beverly J. Dawson, Feb. 7, 1952; 1 dau., Sandra Lynn. B.B.A., U. Houston, 1957; J.D., South Tex. Coll. Law, 1969. Bar: Tex. 1969. With Houston Lighting & Power Co., 1956—, asst. mgr. comml. sales, 1970-72, mgr. comml. sales, 1972-74, mgr. orgnl. devel., 1974, gen. mktg. mgr., 1974-77, v.p. mktg., 1977-78, v.p. customer relations, 1978-80, v.p. customer and pub. relations, 1980-81, exec. v.p., 1981-82, pres., chief operating officer, 1982—, also dir.; dir. Houston Industries, Primary Fuels, Inc., Utility Fuels, Inc. Chmn. exec. adv. bd. customer service and mktg. com. Edison Electric Inst., Washington, 1974—; mem. exec. bd. Electrification Council, Washington, 1974—, Salvation Army, Houston, 1980—. Mem. Tex. Bar Assn., Houstron C. of C. Club: Houston. Office: Houston Lighting & Power Co 611 Walker St Houston TX 77002*

SYLVESTER, HAZEL ANN, ednl. adminstr.; b. Lubbock, Tex., Mar. 18, 1931; d. John W. and Bula M. (Hatridge) Harrison; B.S. in Edn., Tex. Tech. U., 1953, M.S. in Edn., 1971; m. Charles A. Sylvester, Aug. 23, 1951; children—Mary Ann, Laurie Lynn, Julie Kay. Tchr. lang. arts grades 6-8 Ropesville (Tex.) Public Schs., 1951-52; part-time English instr. South Plains Jr. Coll., Levelland, Tex., 1961-63; tchr. grade 5 Levelland (Tex.) Public Schs., 1965-71, dir. elem. edn., 1971-74; Title I reading tchr. leader Round Rock (Tex.) Public Schs., 1975-76, supr. elem. edn., 1976-79, dir. elem. edn., 1979—; mem. state com. Tex. Assessment of Basic Skills, 1979-81; mem. Tex. Right to Read Com.; trainer New Adventures in Learning, 1980; cons., speaker various ednl. projects. Sunday sch. tchr., supt. pre-sch. 1st Bapt. Ch., Levelland; pres. South Plains Coll. Faculty Wives, 1959-61. Mem. Assn. Supervision and Curriculum Devel., Capital Area Assn. Supervision and Curriculum Devel., Nat. Assn. Edn. Young Children, Tex. Assn. Edn Young Children, Assn. Childhood Edn. Internat., So. Assn. Colls. and Schs. (state area chmn.), Delta Kappa Gamma (various chpt. coms.), Alpha Chi, Phi Kappa Phi, Phi Delta Kappa. Contbr. articles to edn. jours.

SYMMES, EDWIN CLIFFORD, JR., advertising consultant, photographer; b. Winchester, Mass., Dec. 27, 1939; s. Edwin C. and Cleora Symmes; m. Leila Rhena Howard, Apr. 15, 1960; children—Cynthia Lynn, Rene Elizabeth. B. Design, U. Fla., 1962. Comml. artist Filmart, Atlanta, 1962-67; creative dir. Charles Rawson Assocs., Atlanta, 1967-69; owner, operator Symmes Systems, Atlanta, 1970—; dir. Photog. Investments Gallery, Atlanta, 1978—. Author, photographer: Native Treasures, 1973. Editor, pub.: Yoshimura Commemorative Album, 1975. One-man shows include Madison/Morgan Cultural Ctr., Ga., 1984, U.S. Nat. Arboretum, Washington, 1981, Floriade, Amsterdam, 1982; exhibited in group shows, 1960—. Editor: Ga. Conservancy Newsletter, Atlanta, 1975-78. Founder, Greater Atlanta Aquarium Soc. Recipient Gold Medal award Mid-South Art Dirs. Club. Mem. Am. Soc. Mag. Photographers, Garden Writers Assn. Am. (internat. mem.). Republican. Unitarian-Universalist. Office: Symmes Systems 468 Armour Dr Atlanta GA 30324

SYMONDS, ELSA ORNELAS (BONNIE), lawyer; b. Mexico City, Dec. 15, 1939; came to U.S., 1946; d. Jaime Josue and Esther (Barber) Ornelas; m. Michael F. Symonds, Sept. 5, 1964; children—Bonnie Michael, Joshua Michael. A.A., San Antonio Coll., 1960; B.A. in English and Edn., St. Mary's U., San Antonio, 1967, J.D., 1980; postgrad. in edn. U. Tex.-San Antonio, 1972-76. Bar: Tex. 1980. Sec., Mexicana Airlines, San Antonio, 1960-65; troubleshooter, translator Robert F. Barnes Customhouse Brokers, 1969-72; instr. Fort Sam Houston Gen. Tech. Program, San Antonio, 1972-77, San Antonio Coll., 1972-78; sole practice, San Antonio, 1981—. Contbr. articles to TV and radio programs on law. Bd. dirs. San Antonio YWCA, Guardianship Adv. Bd.; mem. council, bd. dirs. Christian doctrine program Holy Spirit Parish, San Antonio, 1970-72; pres. PTA, St. Geo's Episcopal Sch., 1974; active San Antonio Acad. Parents Club, Bexar County Polit. Women's Caucus, Women's Ctr. San Antonio, Hispanic Women's Com. San Antonio, Alternatives to Juvenile Deliquency and Arrest Program, Peer Counseling, Vol. Advocacy Group; bd. dirs. pub. responsibility com. San Antonio Hosp. Recipient cert. of appreciation Guardianship Adv. Bd., 1983. Mem. San Antonio Bar Assn., San Antonio Trial Lawyers Assn., Tex. Trial Lawyers Assn., Assn. Trial Lawyers Am., ABA, Women in Bus. (bd. dirs.), Delta Theta Phi. Roman Catholic. Office: 809 S St Mary's St San Antonio TX 78204

SYNAR, MICHAEL LYNN, Congressman; b. Vinita, Okla., Oct. 17, 1950; s. Edmond and Virginia Anne (Gann) S. B.B.A., U. Okla., 1972, J.D., 1977; M.A. in Econs., Northwestern U., 1973; postgrad., U. Edinburgh, 1973-74. Farmer, rancher, Muskogee, Okla., real estate broker, Muskogee, 1968-78; mem. 96th-99th Congresses from 2d Okla. Dist. Del. White House Conf. on Aging, 1971. Democrat. Episcopalian. Office: 1713 Longworth Bldg Washington DC 20515*

SYPERT, GEORGE WALTER, neurosurgery educator, clinical neurosurgeon, research neurophysiologist; b. Marlin, Tex., Sept. 25, 1941; s. Claude Carl and Ruth Helen (Brown) S.; m. Nancy Susan Rojo, Dec. 10, 1971; children—Kirsten Dianne, Shannon Ruth. B.A., U. Wash., 1963, M.D. with highest honors, 1967. Intern, Barnes Hosp., St. Louis, 1967-68; asst. resident in neurol. surgery U. Wash. Sch. Medicine, Seattle, 1968, 1970-72, chief resident, 1973-74, instr., 1973-74; asst. prof. neurol. surgery and neurosci. grad. faculty U. Fla. Coll. Medicine, Gainesville, 1974-77, assoc. prof., 1977-80, prof., 1980-84; C.M. and K.E. Family prof. and eminent scholar, 1984—; mem. staff Shands Hosp. U. Fla., 1974—; neurobiology reviewer NSF, NIH, USPHS, 1979—; mem. merit rev. bd. neurobiology VA, 1979-82; examiner Am. Bd. Neurol. Surgery, 1984. Served to capt. U.S. Army, 1968-70. Fellow Internat. Coll. Surgeons; mem. Soc. Neurol. Surgeons, Am. Physiol. Soc., AAAS, Congress Neurol. Surgeons (exec. com. 1980-83), Am. Assn. Neurol. Surgeons (mem. exec. com. sect. spinal disorders 1982-85, pres. 1985-87), Soc. Neurosci., Am. Soc. Stereotactic and Functional Neurosurgery (pres. 1983-85; mem. exec. com. 1985—), Internat. Congress Physiol. Sci., Brain Surgery Soc., Neurosurgery Forum, AMA, Alachua Inst. Union Physiol. Sci., Internat. Neurosurgery Forum (pres. 1984-85), Sigma Xi, Alpha Omega Alpha, Phi Sigma. Club: Gainesville Golf and Country. Home: 3729 SW 65th Ln Gainesville FL 32608 Office: Neurosurgery PO Box J-265 U Fla Health Ctr Gainesville FL 32610

TABAK, MORRIS, lawyer, consultant; b. Warsaw, Poland, July 23, 1944; s. Joseph Irving and Zina Tammy (Basista) T.; m. Karen Elaine Tomber, May 28, 1947; children—Adam Jason, Jessica Lee, Joshue Paul. B.S. in Econs. and Mktg., Ind. 1970, J.D. magna cum laude, 1972. Atty., Alameda Corp., Houston, 1982—. Bd. dirs. Beth El, Missouri City, Tex. Served with spl. forces U.S. Army, 1965-67. Decorated Bronze Star. Mem. ABA, Ind. Bar Assn., Indpls. Bar Assn., Beta Gamma Sigma. Jewish. Clubs: Sweetwater Country, Skyline (Indpls.); Houston City. Home: 2746 Raintree St Sugarland TX 77478 Office: 9301 SW Freeway Suite 510 Houston TX 77074

TABER, CHARLES RUSSELL, theology educator; b. Neuilly, France, Nov. 1, 1928; came to U.S., 1936; s. Floyd William and Ada Dolores (Zellner) T.; m. Betty Joyce Hanna, Aug. 24, 1951; children—Christine Anne, Diana Ruth, Kathleen Lois, Charles Stephen, Patricia Doris. B.A. magna cum laude, Bryan Coll., 1951; postgrad. Grace Theol. Sem., 1951-52; M.A., Hartford Sem. Found., 1964, Ph.D., 1966. Missionary educator Fgn. Missionary Soc. Brethren Ch., Central African Republic, 1952-60; pastor Community Grace Brethren Ch., Warsaw, Ind., 1960-62; translation cons. United Bible Socs. Hamden, Conn., also West Africa, 1966-73; assoc. prof. Milligan Coll., Johnson City, Tenn., 1973-79; prof. theology Emmanuel Sch. Religion, Johnson City, 1979—. Author: (with others) Theory and Practice of Translation, 1969, La Traduction: Théorie et Méthode, 1971. Editor: (with others) Christopaganism or Indigenous Christianity?, 1975; The Church in Africa, 1978. Bd. dirs. Pioneer Bible Translators, Duncanville, Tex., 1976-80, 82—. Fellow Am. Anthrop. Assn.; mem. Assn. Profs. Missions (pres. 1982), Am. Soc. Missiology (1st v.p. 1984, pres. 1985), Internat. Assn. for Mission Studies. Democrat. Home: 906 Huffine Rd Johnson City TN 37601 Office: Emmanuel Sch Religion Route 6 Box 500 Johnson City TN 37601

TABEREAUX, TOM L., association executive; b. Sheffield, Ala., Jan. 26, 1951; s. Alton T. and Mary Ruth (Bradley) T.; m. Charlotte Ann Burcham, Aug. 4, 1973; children—C. Jason, Kevin Bradley. B.S. in Bus. Mgmt., U. North Ala., 1973. Mgmt. trainee, foreman H.D. Lee Co., Guntersville and Florence, Ala., 1973-75; multi-line adjuster Gen. Adjustment Bur., Florence, Ala., 1976-78; exec. dir. Jr. Achievement of Quad-Cities, Ala., 1978-80, Jr. Achievement of Shreveport-Bossier City, Inc., Shreveport, La., 1980-84; regional project bus. dir. Jr. Achievement, Englewood, Coll., 1984-85, regional dir. ops., 1985—; moderator Free Enterprise Symposium; chmn. regional Jr. Achievement Conf. Recipient Acad. Leadership award Nat. Jr. Achievement, Inc., 1979-80, Western Region All-Star award, 1980-81, 82-83, Pioneer award, 1980-81, performance award, 1981-82, Five-Point Plan award, 1982-83. Mem. Am. Exec. Dirs. Jr. Achievement, Shreveport C. of C. (edn. and career coms.), Phi Gamma Delta (treas. and charter mem. Phi Upsilon chpt.). Republican. Baptist. Lodge: Rotary. Office: Jr Achievement Inc 7400 E Arapahoe Rd Suite 205 Englewood CO 80112

TADDIE, DANIEL LAWRENCE, college music educator; b. Cleve., Feb. 25, 1949; s. Lawrence John and Ritamarie Coletta (Bernard) T.; m. Ann Killebrew, Oct. 26, 1974; 1 child, Elena Louise DeZavala. B.A. summa cum laude, Marycrest Coll., 1971; M.A., U. Iowa, 1973, M.F.A., 1974, Ph.D., 1984. Adj. instr. mus. Luther Coll., Decorah, Iowa, 1974-77, Upper Iowa U., Fayette, 1975-77; instr. mus. Miss. County Community Coll., Blytheville, Ark., 1979-83; assoc. prof. mus. Bethel Coll., McKenzie, Tenn., 1983—. Choir dir. First Cumberland Presbyn. Ch., McKenzie, 1983-86. Recipient Rita Benton prize in musicology U. Iowa, 1985. Marycrest Coll. scholar, 1970-71, U. Iowa scholar, 1971-73. Mem. Coll. Mus. Soc., Am. Musicol. Soc., Nat. Assn. Tchrs. of Singing, Am. Choral Dirs. Assn., Presbyn. Assn. Musicians. Democrat. Avocations: gardening; swimming; reading; movies. Home: Route 1 Box 389L McKenzie TN 38291 Office: Bethel Coll Cherry St McKenzie TN 38201

TADLOCK, STEVE TITUS, commercial artist; b. Copiah County, Miss., Sept. 13, 1956; s. Woodrow T. and Virginia B. (Brock) T.; m. Tammy Lynn Wade, Aug. 4, 1979; 1 son, Steven Seth. Student Hinds Jr. Coll., 1974-76; B.F.A. in Graphic Communications, U. So. Miss., 1979. Art dir. Maris, West & Baker, Inc., Jackson, Miss., 1979—. Named Graphic Communication Student of Yr., U. So. Miss., 1979, Art Dir. of Yr., 1979. Mem. Jackson Graphic Arts Soc. (gold and silver awards 1979—). Republican. Baptist. Club: Toastmasters. Home: 512 Plainview Circle Richland MS 39218

TAFT, THOMAS FLEMING, lawyer, wholesale building and hardware distribution executive, real estate developer; b. Greenville, N.C., Dec. 29, 1945; s. Edmund Hoover and Helen Irene (Fleming) T.; m. Kathy Arnold, Jan. 30, 1982; children—Jessica, Paige, Thomas, Jonathan. A.B., Duke U., 1968; J.D., U. N.C., 1972; Summer Cert., City of London Coll., 1971. Bar: N.C. Legal counsel to lt. gov. Office of Lt. Gov., Raleigh, 1972-74; ptnr. Taft, Taft & Haigler, Greenville, N.C., 1974—; pres., dir. Eastern Lumber & Supply Co., Winterville, N.C., Hardware Suppliers Am., Inc., Winterville, Mercer Glass Co., Inc., Greenville. Chmn. bd. dirs. N.C. Ports Authority, 1978-85; mem. N.C. Senate from 9th Dist., 1985—. Served with USAR, 1968-74. Mem. ABA, N.C. Bar Assn., Pitt County Bar Assn., N.C. Acad. Trial Lawyers, Am. Trial Lawyers Assn. Democrat. Methodist. Home: 611 Queen Anne's Rd Greenville NC 27834 Office: Taft Taft & Haigler PO Box 588 Greenville NC 27834

TAGLE, TESSA ARROYO-MARTINEZ, education educator; b. San Antonio, July 15, 1947. B.J., U. Tex.-Austin, 1969; M.A., U. Tex.-San Antonio, 1976. Instr., J.F. Kennedy High Sch., Edgewood Ind. Sch. dist., 1969-71; instr. continuing edn. San Antonio Coll., 1970-72, program developer, 1972-76, 1978-82, program developer occupational edn. and tech., 1982-84; dean occupational edn. and tech., 1984—; dir. Act 101 program U. Pa., Phila., 1977-78; community relations liaison High Tech. High Sch.; film cons. Greater San Antonio C. of C., United San Antonio; mktg. cons. Reston Pub. Co., Winthrop Pub. Co.; employee tng. cons. U. Tex.-San Antonio, Datapoint Corp. Vol. coordinator San Antonio Ballet Co.; mem. San Antonio downtown revitalization com. Madison Square Neighborhood Assn. Recipient 1st place award for advt. film U. Tex., 1969. Mem. Mexican Am. Bus. and Profl. Women (Young Career Woman of Yr. nominee 1976), Council for Occupational Edn., Am. Assn. Women in Community and Jr. Colls. (named a Leader of the 80's, 1983). Tex. Jr. Coll. Tchrs. Assn. Office: 1300 San Pedro St San Antonio TX 78215

TAGUE, JEAN RUTH, recreational educator; b. Kirkman, Iowa, Dec. 20, 1927; d. Clifford and Ruth (Morgan) T. B.S., Drake U., 1950; M.A., Columbia U., 1955; Ph.D., U. So. Calif., 1968. Lectr. dept. recreation, UCLA, 1960-64; pres. Creative Leisure Planning, Inc., Los Angeles, 1965-70; prof. Calif. State U., Northridge, 1970-79; prof., chmn. dept. recreation Tex. Woman's U., Denton, 1979—; cons. in field. Editor mag. Programming Trends in Therapeutic Recreation 1980—. Recipient Citation for Dedicated Leadership and Service, Nat. Therapeutic Recreation Soc.; Innovative Recreation Programs grantee U.S. Office Edn., Washington, 1983—; Therapeutic Recreation Training grantee U.S. Office Edn., Washington, 1975—. Mem. Nat. Recreation and Park Assn. (bd. dirs. 1977-80), Gerontological Soc., Nat. Council on Aging, Tex. Therapeutic Recreation Section (pres. 1982-83), Calif. Therapeutic Recreation Section (bd. dirs. 1982-83; outstanding recreator, 1978). Home: 2225 E McKinney Denton TX 76201 Office: Tex Woman's U Dept Recreation Box 23717 Denton TX 76204

TAI, CHONG-SOO STEPHEN, political science educator; b. Seoul, Korea, Oct. 15, 1940; came to U.S., 1969, naturalized, 1983; s. Hyung-Kyoon and Ock-Hee (Park) T.; m. Susan Gillja Kang, Aug. 28, 1965; children—Angie, Elizabeth, Michael. B.A., Yonsei U., Seoul, 1963; M.A., Ill. State U., 1972; M.A., Northwestern U., 1972, Ph.D., 1974. Lectr., Northwestern U., Evanston, Ill., 1974-75; asst. prof. U. Ark., Pine Bluff, 1976-80, assoc. prof. polit. sci., 1980—; great decisions coordinator Fgn. Policy Assn., Pine Bluff, 1977-84; cons. S.E. Ark. Planning Commn., Pine Bluff, 1979-80. Contbr. articles to profl. jours. Served with Korean AF, 1963-67. Grantee KOTN radio sta., 1978, Ark. Endowment for Humanities, 1979, 80, NEH, 1980; Fulbright-Hays scholar, China, 1985. Fellow Internat. Ctr. for Asian Studies; mem. Am. Polit. Sci. Assn., Ark. Polit. Sci. Assn., Assn. for Asian Studies, Assn. Korean Polit. Scientists in N.Am. Roman Catholic. Avocation: golf. Home: 3903 Royal Forest Dr Pine Bluff AR 71603 Office: U Ark Pine Bluff N Cedar St Pine Bluff AR 71601

TALBERT, ROY, JR., college professor; b. Cheraw, S.C., Aug. 1, 1943; s. Roy and Betty Jean (Harper) T.; B.A. (Furman Scholar), Furman U., 1965; M.A. (NDEA fellow), Vanderbilt U., 1967, Ph.D., 1971; grad. Inst. Ednl. Mgmt., Harvard U., 1981; grad. Computer Literacy Inst., Pepperdine U., 1983; m. Linda Diane Thompson, Aug. 1, 1975; children—Matthew, Rebecca Anne. Sr. teaching fellow Vanderbilt U., Nashville, 1967-70; asst. prof. history Ferrum (Va.) Coll., 1974-76, dir. curriculum and programs, 1976-79; vice chancellor for acad. affairs Coastal Carolina Coll. of U. S.C., Conway, 1979-84; assoc. prof. history, 1979—; producer, host The Public Eye, TV show, 1978-79; host Waccamaw Mag., TV show, 1983; project dir. numerous film, TV and pub. programming projects for community and civic groups, 1975-79. Served to capt. U.S. Army, 1970-72. Mem. So. Hist. Assn., Horry County Hist. Soc. Baptist. Author: (with Rex Stephenson) Too Free for Me, 1979; editor: Studies in the Local History of Slavery, 1978. Home: 1022 Buccaneers Cove Conway SC 29526 Office: Coastal Carolina Coll Conway SC 29526

TALBOT, RICHARD BURRITT, veterinarian, educator; b. Waterville, Kans., Jan. 4, 1933; s. Roy B. and Aleta (Stone) T.; m. Mary Jane Hensley, May 24, 1953; children—Richard Lee, Andrea Jean. B.S., Kans. State U., 1954, D.V.M., 1958; Ph.D., Iowa State U., 1963. From instr. to assoc. prof. dept. physiology and pharmacology Coll. Vet. Medicine, Iowa State U., Ames, 1958-65; prof., chmn. dept. physiology and pharmacology U. Ga. Coll. Vet. Medicine, Athens, 1965-68, dean coll., 1968-75; prof., dean vet. medicine Va. Poly. Inst. and State U., Blacksburg, 1975-85, prof. pharmacology and toxicology, 1985—; dir. 1st Va. Bank SW, Hazelton Labs. Corp.; cons. NIH. Editor: Jour. Vet. Medicine Edn. Dist. commr. Boy Scouts Am. Nat. Heart Inst. postdoctoral fellow, 1959. Mem. AVMA (council on edn. 1972-80, edn. com. fgn. vet. grads. 1972—), Am. Physiol. Soc., Conf. Research Workers Animal Diseases, Nat. Bd. Vet. Med. Examiners, Am. Assn. Lab. Animal Sci., Drug Info. Assn., Am. Soc. Vet. Pharmacology, Am. Soc. Vet. Toxicology, Assn. Am. Vet. Med. Colls., Sigma Xi, Phi Zeta, Phi Kappa Phi. Presbyterian (elder). Clubs: Rotary; Ruritan. Home: Route 2 Box 561 Newport VA 24128

TALBOTT, EUNICE TILLMAN, clubwoman; b. Springfield, Mo., Jan. 25, 1911; d. Sidney Ellis and Nancy Elizabeth (Denney) Tillman; B.S. (Ed.), U. Tampa, 1947; postgrad. U. Fla., 1959-61; m. William W. Talbott, June 23, 1933 (dec.); children—Sharon Lynn Webb. Tchr., Hillsborough County, Fla., 1947-68; lectr. table settings; poet. Recipient awards flower shows, 1968—. Mem. NEA, Fla. Edn. Assn., English Council (program chmn. Hillsborough County 1963-65), DAR (regent 1970-72), Colonial Dames (pres. 1977-79), Magna Charta Dames, Tampa and Fla. Fedn. Garden Clubs, Plantagnet Soc., Tri Sigma. Democrat. Methodist. Clubs: Jasmine Garden Sundial (pres. 1970-72), State Jr. Garden (chmn. 1945-47), Tampa Woman's (librarian 1979-80), Order of Crown. Home: 2810 Parkland Blvd Tampa FL 33609

TALBOTT, PENNY, social worker; b. Glenn Cove, N.Y., Jan. 3, 1953; d. Thomas M. and Lucretia Ann (Penuel) T. B.A., U. Ga., 1975; M.S.W., Atlanta U., 1982. Casework sr. Mcduffie County Dept. Family and Children Services, Thomson, Ga., 1975-78, casework prin., 1978-85, casework supr., 1985—; Systematic Tng. for Effective Parenting facilitator; mem. Dist. 6 Title XX Council and dist. rep. to State Council, 1982. Bd. dirs. Parents Anonymous of Ga., 1982, chmn. Vol. Coordination Com., 1983, rep. Ga. Nat. Conv., 1983, v.p. chpts., 1983; active Ga. Council on Child Abuse, 1984—, mem. program com., 1985; vol. pilot Latchkey project Nat. Council for Prevention Child Abuse, 1984—; Meth. Youth Fellowship counselor, 1983. Recipient Outstanding Sr. award U. Ga. Kappa Deltas, 1975; named Outstanding Child Protective Service Worker of McDuffie County, 1983, 84, 85. Mem. Kappa Delta Alumnae. Republican. Methodist. Home: 415 Apollo Dr Thomson GA 30824 Office: PO Box 507 Thomson GA 30824

TALELE, CHAITRAM JIVARAM, economics educator; b. Satod, Maharashtra, India, Jan. 27, 1939; came to U.S., 1964, naturalized, 1974; s. Jivaram E. and Jai Jivaram T.; m. Nalini C. Tekade, July 3, 1971; children—Kunda, Anjali, Amitabh. B.A. (Hons.), U. Poona, India, 1960, M.A., 1962; M.S., U. Wis., 1967; Ph.D., U. Tenn.-Knoxville, 1981. Tutor in econs. Poona U., 1962-64; instr. Peace Corps, Milw., summers 1966, 67; assoc. prof. econs. Columbia State Coll., Tenn., 1967-85, prof., 1985—; faculty adviser Gamma Beta Phi, 1979—. Author: (with Lewis Moore, Sam Martin) Economic Potential of Maury County, Tenn., 1970; (movie) The Federal Reserve and U.S. Economy, 1977. Bd. dirs. Maury County Daycare, Columbia, 1984—. Mem. Am. Econ. Assn., Tenn. Consortium of Asian Studies (mem. exec. com. 1980-81). Hindu. Avocations: music; reading; swimming. Home: 131 Sunnyside Ln Columbia TN 38401 Office: Columbia State Community Coll Columbia TN 38401

TALIAFERRO, NANCY ANN, former history educator; b. Dallas, Dec. 25, 1921; d. Clarence Erskin and Jennie Chris (Coyle) Kennemer; m. Myrl Arlen Taliafeiro (dec. 1966); children—Jennie Lee Land, John Elliott. B.A., Baylor U., 1943; M.A., Tex. U., 1945. Cert. tchr., Tex. Tchr. St. Mathews Sch. (merged with Tex. Country Day Sch. for Boys, name now St. Mark's), Dallas 1940-50; with Home Service, ARC, 1946-47; prof. Am. history, counselor So. Meth. U., Dallas, 1948-49. Active Republican Women of Highland Park; Dallas Hist. Soc. Recipient service award Dallas Baptist Coll., 1967. Episcopalian. Home: 4049 Westside Dr Dallas TX 75208

TALL, LAMBERT, engineering educator, consultant; b. Sydney, Australia, Jan. 25, 1933; came to U.S., 1955; s. Jack and Leontine E. (Eisman) T.; m. Rita Augusta Csallner, Dec. 26, 1959. B.E. in Civil Engring., U. Sydney, 1954; M.S. in Civil Engring., Lehigh U., 1957, Ph.D. in Civil Engring., 1961. Bridge design engr. New South Wales (Australia) Dept. Main Roads, 1954-55; grad. asst., instr. Lehigh U., Bethlehem, Pa., 1955-61, asst. prof., 1961-64, assoc. prof., 1964-69, prof., 1969-79, dir., 1966-78; vis. fellow U. New South Wales (Australia), 1964; liaison scientist U.S. Office Naval Research, London, 1971-72; dir. USA/Egypt Coop. Program on Low-Cost Housing, 1976-79; dean Coll. Tech., Fla. Internat. U., Miami, 1979-83, prof. civil engring., 1983—. Mem. Fla. Task Force on Sci., Engring. and Tech. Service to Industry, 1980-81. Served with Royal Australian Art., 1955. John Simon Guggenheim Found. fellow, 1964. Fellow ASCE, Instn. Engrs. Australia (Chapman medal 1964); mem. Am. Welding Soc. (Davis silver medal 1963, 71), Internat. Inst. Welding, Internat. Assn. Bridge and Structural Engring., AAAS, ASTM, Am. Soc. Engring. Edn., Assn. Profl. Engrs. Australia, Structural Stability Research Council, Soc. for History of Tech., Am. Mgmt. Soc., Sigma Xi. Editor, chief author: Structural Steel Design, 1st edit., 1964, 2d edit., 1974. Mem. editorial adv. bd. Welding Design and Fabrication mag. Contbr. articles to profl. jours. Office: Sch Engring Fla Internat U Miami FL 33199

TALLANT, KENNETH ALLEN, insurance/real estate agent, broker, consultant; b. Montgomery, Ala., Dec. 10, 1935; s. Elmer Allen and Mary (Tindol) T.; m. Florence Annette Smith, June 4, 1960; children—Teri Tallant Randolph, Tami Tallant Grider, K(enneth) Allen. B.S. U. Ala.-Tuscaloosa, 1958; postgrad. Huntingdon Coll., 1955-59; M.S., Ala. Christian Coll., 1979, postgrad. in religion, 1979-80, postgrad. Internat. Bible Inst. and Sem., 1984, Newport U., Jones Law Inst. Vice pres., sec. Elmer Tallant Agy., Inc., Montgomery, 1954—. Served with N.G., 1952-63. Mem. Nat. Assn. Realtors, Ind. Insurors Am., Profl. Ins. Agts. Am., Commerce Execs. Soc. of U. Ala.-Tuscaloosa, Ala. Ins. Soc. of U. Ala., Pi Kappa Phi. Republican. Mem. Ch. of Christ. Club: Montgomery Civitan. Home: 20 Mountainview Dr Montgomery AL 36109 Office: Elmer Tallant Agy Inc 2100 Mount Meigs Rd PO Drawer 7100 Montgomery AL 36107

TALLEY, CAROLYN CORBIN, physician's office official; b. Greenville, S.C., June 14, 1940; d. Macie (Emory) Corbin; m. James C. Odom, Mar. 13, 1958 (div.); children—Alonda C. Rollison, Vicky A. Walton, Richard J.; m. 2d, Frank H. Talley, May 6, 1978. Student Draughons Bus. Coll., 1962-64. Vice pres. Talley Industries, Greenville, 1978-83; v.p., cons. Talley, Corbin, Jones & Assocs., Greenville, 1982-83; office mgr. adminstrn. Orthopedic Assocs., Greenville, 1960—. Mem. Christian Children's Fund, Worldwide, 1979-83; mem. Abused Children Fund, 1980-83; chmn. Am. Cancer Soc., Greenville, 1976—, Am. Heart Fund, Greenville, 1977. Mem. S.C. Assn. Med. Mgrs. (charter), Greenville C. of C. Baptist. Office: Orthopedic Assocs Greenville 901 W Faris Rd Greenville SC 29605

TALLEY, CHARLES RICHMOND, banker; b. Richmond, Va., Dec. 23, 1925; s. Charles Edward and Marie Cox (Throckmorton) T.; m. Anne Marie Smith, June 4, 1948; children—Laurie Anne, Charles Richmond. B.A., U. Richmond, 1949; postgrad. Northwestern U., 1955, Rutgers U., 1961, U. Va., 1974. With First & Merchants Nat. Bank, Richmond, 1949-83, asst. cashier, 1955-56, asst. v.p., 1956-63, v.p., 1963-69, sr. v.p., 1969-74, exec. v.p. in charge corp. adminstrn., 1974-83; corp. exec. officer adminstrv. services Sovran Bank, N.A. (merger First & Mchts. Nat. Bank and Va. Nat. Bank), 1984—; dir. Sovran Properties Inc., Security Atlantic Life Ins. Co. and Agy. Pres., Va. Bapt. Extension Bd., 1973-75, Richmond Clearing House Assn., 1977; bd. dirs. Richmond Symphony Orch., 1959-68, Richmond Better Bus. Bur., 1967-69, Va. Edn. Loan Authority, 1983—; bd. dirs., mem. exec. com. Richmond Eye and Ear Hosp. Served with USN, 1944-46. Mem. Assn. Bank Holding Cos. (govt. relations com. 1984-86), Am. Inst. Banking, Va. Bankers Assn. (fed. legis. com. 1984-86), Richmond Jaycees (pres. 1961). Clubs: Willow Oaks Country (pres. 1971), Bull and Bear (dir. 1974-75) (Richmond); Farmington Country (Charlottesville, Va.). Lodges: Rotary (dir. 1981-83), Masons.

TALLEY, JOSEPH EUGENE, psychologist; b. Springfield, Mass., May 27, 1949; s. Joseph Addison and Miriam Louise (Ayers) T.; m. Vibeke Absalon, Jan. 3, 1981; 1 child, Kirsten. B.A., U. Richmond, 1971; M.A., Radford Coll., 1973; Ph.D., U. Va., 1978. Lic. psychologist, N.C. Psychologist, clin. faculty Duke U., Durham, N.C., 1977—, coordinator research, program evaluation and testing services, 1979—; gen. practice psychotherapy, Durham, 1980—. Author: Study Skills, 1981. Author, editor: Counseling and Psychotherapy Services, 1985; Counseling and Psychotherapy: A Guide to Treatment, 1985. Contbr. articles to profl. jours. Bd. deacons Hillsborough Presbyn. Ch., N.C., 1983—, chmn., 1985—; bd. dirs. Orange County Mental Health Assn., Chapel Hill, N.C., 1982-83, mem. legis. com., 1983. Mem. Am. Psychol. Assn., N.C. Psychol. Assn., Southeastern Psychol. Assn., Nat. Soc. Clin. Hypnosis, Assn. Advancement Psychology, Phi Kappa Phi, Omicron Delta Kappa, Psi Chi, Phi Kappa Sigma. Democrat. Presbyterian. Home: Route 4 Box 1284 Hillsborough NC 27278 Office: Counseling and Psychological Services Old Chemistry Bldg Suite 214 Duke U Durham NC 27706

TALLEY, LAWRENCE H., chemistry educator; b. Cin., Aug. 16, 1927; s. Thomas Boyd and Sylvia L. (Bowers) T. B.S. in Chemistry, Ohio U., 1952, M.S. in Phys. Chemistry, 1956; Ed.D., W.Va. U., 1972, cert. advanced study, 1974. Research chemist Mound Lab., U.S. AEC, Miamisburg, Ohio, 1948-54, sr. research chemist Nat. Lead of Ohio, Cin., 1956-58; dept. dir. Parker Co., Janesville, Wis., 1958-69; mem. faculty West Liberty (W.Va.) State Coll., 1969—, assoc. acad. dean, 1981-84, acad. dean, 1984—, prof. chemistry, 1972—. Named Prof. of Year, West Liberty State Coll., 1970, 72; Chi Beta Phi Prof. of Year, 1974, 83. Mem. N.Y. Acad. Scis., Sigma Xi, Chi Beta Phi, Phi Delta Kappa, Kappa Delta Pi, Theta Xi. Contbr. articles to profl. jours. Home: 40 Heiskell Ave Wheeling WV 26003 Office: Main Hall West Liberty State Coll West Liberty WV 26074

TALLEY, RONDA CAROL, school psychologist; b. Glasgow, Ky., Nov. 21, 1951; d. Jack Howard and Ronda Mae (McCoy) T.; B.S., Western Ky. U., 1973; M.Ed., U. Louisville, 1974, Ed.S., 1976; Ph.D., Ind. U., 1979. Spl. edn. tchr. Jefferson County Pub. Schs., Louisville, 1973-76; research assoc. dept. sociology U. Calif.-Riverside, 1977; research assoc. dept. spl. edn. Ind. U., Bloomington, 1976-78; adminstrv. intern Bur. Edn. for the Handicapped, HEW, Washington, 1978-81; adj. prof. dept. spl. edn. U. Louisville, 1981-83, dept. psychology Spalding U., 1984-86; coordinator, assessment/placement services Exceptional Child Edn., Jefferson County Pub. Schs., Louisville, 1981—; founder, pres. Tri-T Assocs. Inc., Louisville, 1982—. Crusade for Children grantee, 1974; Bur. Edn. for Handicapped grantee, 1978. Mem. Am. Psychol. Assn. (chairperson adminstrs. of sch. psychol. services), Am. Ednl. Research Assn., Nat. Assn. Sch. Psychologists, Council Exceptional Children, Ky. Assn. Psychologists in Schs. (pres., chairperson liaison and pub. relations), AAUP, Women in Sch. Adminstrn., Phi Delta Kappa, Kappa Delta, Delta Kappa Gamma. Republican. Methodist. Editor: Administrator's Handbook on Integrating America's Handicapped Students, 1982; contbr. articles to profl. jours. Home: 9104 Hurstwood Ct Louisville KY 40222 Office: 4409 Preston Hwy Room 243 Louisville KY 40213

TALLEY, WILLIAM GILES, JR., container mfg. co. exec.; b. Adel, Ga., Sept. 25, 1939; s. William Giles and Mary (McGlamry) T.; B.S. in Bus. Adminstrn., U. S.C., 1961; m. Jacqueline Vickery, Apr. 14, 1962; children—William Giles III, John Lindsey, Bronwyn Ashley. Mgmt. trainee Talley Veneer & Crate Co., Inc., Adel, 1961-62, plant mgr., salesman, Waynesboro, Ga., 1965-67; with Talley's Box Co., Leesburg, Fla., 1962-65, plant mgr., 1967-69; partner, gen. mgr. Growers Container Cooperative, Inc., Leesburg, 1969—; gen. ptnr. Talley Box Co., Ltd., 1974—; pres. Talley Acres, Inc., 1979—; pres. Talley-Selman Wood Products, Inc., 1985—; dir. First Nat. Bank Leesburg. Bd. dirs. Leesburg Hosp. Assn. Served with USAAF, 1961. Mem. Fla. Forestry Assn. (dist. v.p. 1980, dir. 1978—), Leesburg C. of C. (dir.), Sigma Alpha Epsilon. Democrat. Methodist. Clubs: Elks, Kiwanis. Home: Lake Griffin Leesburg FL 32748 Office: PO Box 817 Leesburg FL 32748

TALLEY, WILLIAM JAMES, oil company executive, consultant; b. Waco, Tex., Sept. 23, 1922; s. Joseph Titus and Laura Catherine (Taylor) T.; m. Evelyn Bowman, June 21, 1951 (div. 1975); children—Patricia, Jeffrey. LL.B., Pacific Coast U., 1950; postgrad. UCLA, 1950-51. Landman, Shell Oil Co., 1947-51; div. land mgr. Continental Oil Co., 1951-56; ind. producer, 1956-72; land mgr. Signal Oil, 1972-76; ptnr., land mgr. Banner Petroleum, 1976-79; v.p. land OFT Exploration, Inc., San Francisco, 1979-81; pres. OFT-Tex. Corp., Houston, 1981-83; pres. Aztec Exploration, Inc., Houston, 1983—; cons. Banner Petroleum, OFT Exploration, Inc. Served with USAAF, 1941-45. Mem. Am. Assn. Petroleum Landmen, Houston Assn. Petroleum Landmen. Republican. Clubs: University (Houston); Olympic (San Francisco). Office: 908 Town and Country Blvd Suite 130 Houston TX 77024

TALLEY, WILLIAM WOODROW, II, energy consultant, management consultant, resource analyst; b. Hobart, Okla., Aug. 17, 1942; s. William Woodrow and Jacquita Elizabeth (Surber) T.; m. Sandra Jean Smith, Sept. 12, 1964; children—Kimberly Veda Michelle, Britani Suzanne. B.S. in Chem. Engring., U. Okla., 1964, M.S., 1971, M.S. in Nuclear Engring., 1971, Ph.D. in Nuclear and Chem. Engring., 1973. Chem. engr. Continental Oil Co., Ponca City, Okla., 1963-64; with Coll. of Engring., U. Okla., 1970-73; exec. dir. Okla. Energy Adv. Council, Oklahoma City, 1973-74; asst. to dir. Fossil Fuel and Advanced Systems, Electric Power Research Inst., Palo Alto, Calif., 1974; asso. Resource Analysis and Mgmt. Group, 1974-75; chmn. Okla. Gov.'s Adv. Council on Energy, Oklahoma City, 1975-79; pres., chief exec. officer William W. Talley II, Inc., Oklahoma City, 1976—; mng. partner Resource Analysis and Mgmt. Group, 1976-83; chmn., pres. RAM Group, Ltd., 1984—; cons. energy and fuels tech., 1969-74; dir. Vice-chmn. Okla City C. of C. Energy Council, 1975-79; bd. dirs. Allied Arts Found., 1977-79, Frontiers of Sci. Found., 1977—, Okla. Symphony Orch., 1978-83, Oklahomans for Energy and Jobs, 1980—, Higher Edn. Alumni Council, 1984—, Central Okla. Community Council, 1984—. Oklahoma City Food Bank, 1985—; trustee Omniplex, 1981—, pres., 1984—; commr. parks and recreation Norman (Okla.). Served as nuclear submarine officer USN, 1964-69. Registered profl. engr., Okla. Mem. Am. Nuclear Soc. (founding mem. process heat application com.), Am. Inst. Chem. Engrs., Am. Soc. Petroleum Engring. Oklahoma City C. of C. (bd. dirs. 1985—). Clubs: Economic (dir. 1983—), Petroleum, White Hall, Oklahoma City Golf and Country. Lodge: Rotary (dir. 1983-84). Author: Energy in Oklahoma, 1974; Industrial Development in Oklahoma, 1974; Enhanced Recovery Alternatives, 1975; Oklahoma Energy Facts, 1977; numerous others; author U.S. energy model MANERGY, 1973. Office: 6001 N Robinson Oklahoma City OK 73118

TALLON, ROBERT EUGENE, utility executive; b. Golden, Colo., Aug. 4, 1926; s. Eugene Maurice and Lucy Marie (Pierce) T.; m. Audrey Morilla Porter, June 20, 1948; children—Patrick Doyle, Audrey Roberta. A.A., Fullerton (Calif.) Coll., 1948; LL.B., Southwestern U., Los Angeles, 1951; postgrad., Columbia U. Grad. Sch. Bus., 1975. With So. Calif. Edison Co., Los Angeles, 1952-54; div. v.p. Union Oil Co., Calif., Los Angeles, 1954-73; pres. Moreland Investment Co., Los Angeles, 1965-73; exec. v.p. Fla. Power & Light Co., Miami, 1973—; pres., dir. Land Resources Investment Co., Miami, 1973—, W. Flagler Investment Corp., 1981-85, chmn. bd. dirs., 1985—; chmn. Palm Ins. Co., Ltd., 1986—; dir. Palm Beach Bank & Trust Co. Adv. bd. Salvation Army, Dade County and Fla., 1981—; indsl. commnr. City of Brea, Calif., 1972-73; trustee El Dorado Sch., Fullerton, 1965; chmn. Fla. C. of C. Found. Served with USNR, 1944-46. Mem. Fla. C. of C. (dir.), Greater Miami C. of C. (trustee), U.S. C. of C. Republican. Club: Shriners. Office: 9250 W Flagler St Miami FL 33174

TALLON, ROBIN, congressman, clothing retailer, realtor; b. Hemmingway, S.C., Aug. 8, 1946; s. Robert M. and Mary (Williamson) T.; m. Amelia Louise Johns, Dec. 19, 1982; children—Robert M., Sarah Tatum. Student, U. S.C., 1964-65. Pres. Robin's Men's Wear, Inc., Florence, S.C., 1971-80, Tallon Bldg., 1973-75, Tri-State Advt., Florence, 1975-77; bd. chmn. Tallon Sales Co., Florence, 1979—; broker-in-charge Robin Tallon Real Estate Co., Florence, 1980—; mem. S.C. Ho. of Reps., Columbia, 1980-81, 98th Congress from 6th S.C. Dist., mem. agr. com., mcht. marine and fisheries com., 1983—, mem. steering com., tourism caucus, 1983—. Participant White House Conf. on Small Bus. Democrat. Methodist. Home: 2182 W Evans St Florence SC 29501 Office: 128 Cannon House Office Bldg Washington DC 20515*

TALLY, LURA SELF, state senator; b. Iredell County, N.C., Dec. 9, 1921; d. R.O. and Sara (Cowles) Self; children—John Cowles, Robert Taylor. A.B., Duke U., 1942; M.A., N.C. State U., 1970. Democratic coordinator Congl. and gubernatorial campaigns, N.C., 1954-70; mem. N.C. Ho. of Reps., 1972-82; mem. N.C. Senate, 1982—, mem. appropriations, corrections, edn., health, higher edn., mental health and social service coms., N.C. Gen. Assembly, 1972—; tchr. Fayetteville City Schs. (N.C.), 1943-68, guidance counselor, 1968-72. Mem. Mental Health Assn. Fayetteville. Recipient Outstanding Alumna award Peace Coll., 1962. Mem. Bus. and Profl. Women's Assn., LWV, AAUW, Delta Kappa Gamma, Kappa Delta. Methodist. Club: Fayetteville Women's. Office: NC Senate State Capitol Raleigh NC 27611*

TAMBONE, PETER JOHN, marketing firm executive; b. N.Y.C., June 24, 1938; s. Vito A. and Clara (Riccardi) T.; student Cooper Union, 1958; m. Barbara Gail Yadeska, Feb. 1, 1968; children—Adam, Brian. Account exec. Wunderman, Ricotta & Kline, N.Y.C., 1964-66; account supr. firm Rapp & Collins, N.Y.C., 1966-69; v.p. Jamian Advt. Inc., N.Y.C., 1969-70; pres. firm Campbell Advt. Inc., N.Y.C., 1972-75; v.p. Downe Communications Inc., 1973-75; pres. Greenland Studios, Inc., 1974-78, Tambone Direct Mktg., Inc., 1975—, G.L.S. Communications, Inc., 1976—; exec. v.p. Natural Interiors, Inc., 1979-80; pres. Sterling Mgmt. Corp., 1980-83; pres. CASCO/USA, Sports Medicine Industries, Inc., 1980—. Mem. Direct Mail Advt. Assn., Direct Mail Writers Club, Assn. Third Class Mailers, Fla. Direct Mktg. Assn., Am. Coll. Sports Medicine, Parcel Post Assn. Home: 2204 NE 15th Ct Fort Lauderdale FL 33304 Office: 3221 NW 10th Terr Fort Lauderdale FL 33309

TANG, RUEN CHIU, wood science educator, forest products consultant; b. Kiangsu, China, Oct. 31, 1934; s. Ping H. and I-Chen (Shen) T.; m. Anna C. Huang, Dec. 25, 1960; children—Gina, Sophia, Jayne. B.S., Nat. Chung-Hsing U., 1957; Ph.D., N.C. State U., 1968. Profl. forester, Republic of China. Forester, Taiwan Forest Bur., 1959-63; research asst. N.C. State U., Raleigh, 1963-67; research assoc. U. Ky., Lexington, 1968-69, asst. prof., 1970-74, assoc. prof., 1974-78; prof. Auburn U. (Ala.), 1978—; chmn. Forest Products Tech. Commn., State of Ala., 1986—; adviser wood sci. Miss. State U.; referee forest field contests U. Ky.; cons. forest products. Served to 2d lt. Army of Republic of China, 1957-59. Mem. Soc. Wood Sci. and Tech., Soc. Exptl. Stress Analysis, Soc. Am. Foresters, Forest Products Research Soc. (chmn. physics sect., best paper award 1976), Am. Forestry Assn., ASTM, AAAS, Internat. Assn. Math. Modelling, Soc. Computer Simulation, Ala. Acad. Sci., Sigma Xi, Gamma Sigma Delta. Confucianist. Contbr. sci. research papers to profl. publs. and confs. Office: Sch Forestry Auburn U Auburn AL 36849

TANIGUCHI, ALAN YAMATO, architect, educator; b. Stockton, Calif., Sept. 13, 1922; s. Isamu and Sadayo (Miyagi) T.; m. Leslie E. Honnami, Apr. 29, 1949; children—Evan, Keith. B.A. in Architecture, U. Calif.-Berkeley, 1949. Owner archtl. practice, Harlingen, Tex., after 1952; asst. prof. architecture U. Tex.-Austin, 1961-62, assoc. prof., 1963-65, prof., 1966, dean, 1967-72; prof. and dir. Sch. Architecture, Rice U., 1972-75, Smith Prof. Architecture, 1972-78; prin. and pres. Alan Y. Taniguchi and Assocs., Austin, 1978—. Chmn., Downtown Revitalization Task Force, City of Austin, 1981-85; past chmn. Tex. Com. Humanities; panelist Tex. Commn. on Arts; mem. trade mission to Japan; mem. Austin/San Antonio Corridor Council, 1985; mem. Austin Statue of Liberty Com. Recipient award Progressive Architecture, Tex. Assn. Sch. Bds. and Sch. Adminstrs.; Teaching Excellence awards Student Assembly U. Tex., Austin. Fellow AIA (award Austin chpt.); mem. Tex. Soc. Architects (award), Phi Kappa Phi. Democrat. Home: 2818 Wooldridge Dr Austin TX 78703 Office: Alan Y Taniguchi and Assocs 1609 W 6th St Austin TX 78703

TANKS, MARK DERWIN, import-export company executive; b. Cin., Aug. 24, 1957; s. Lillious and Myrtle Helen (Washington) Thomas T. Student Bowling Green State U., 1975-78. Vice-pres. Yao Devel. Corp., N.Y.C., 1978-81; pres., chmn. Tanks Internat. Corp., Atlanta, 1982—; Fgn. rep. Yao Devel. Corp., N.Y.C., 1978-81. Republican. Home: 1328 Oakland Dr SW Atlanta GA 30310

TANNEBAUM, SAMUEL HUGO, accountant; b. Oklahoma City, Aug. 15, 1933; s. Simon L. and Eva (Kapp) T.; B.B.A. with spl. distinction, U. Okla., 1955; m. Nita Mae Levy, June 12, 1955; children—Joel L., Marilyn J. Staff acct. Alford, Meroney & Co., Dallas, 1955-61; pvt. practice acctg., Dallas, 1961-63; partner Tannebaum & Bindler, C.P.A.s, Dallas, 1963-67; mng. partner Tannebaum, Bindler & Lewis, C.P.A.s, Dallas, 1967-80, Tannebaum, Bindler & Co., C.P.A.s, Dallas, 1980-84; pres. Tannebaum Bindler & Co., P.C., 1984—; dir. Nat. Center Banks, Inc. Bd. dirs. Dallas Home and Hosp. for Jewish Aged, 1973-76; trustee Temple Emanu-El, Dallas, 1976-83, treas., 1980-82, v.p., 1982-83. Named C.P.A. of Yr., Dallas chpt. Tex. Soc. C.P.A.s, 1976; C.P.A., Tex., Okla. Mem. Am. Inst. C.P.A.s (council), Tex. Soc. C.P.A.s (dir., past v.p., past chpt. pres.), Nat. Assn. Estate Planning Councils (dir. 1978-82, treas. 1982-83, v.p. 1983-84, pres. 1984-85), Dallas Estate Planning Council (past pres.). Clubs: Lancers, Brookhaven Country, University. Home: 5820 Meletio Ln Dallas TX 75230 Office: 2323 Bryan St Suite 700 Lock Box 107 Dallas TX 75201

TANNEN, DAVID E., real estate executive; b. Miami, Fla., Aug. 9, 1945; s. Melvin A. and Fredrica M. Tannen; m. Carol Dale Herman, Dec. 5, 1982. B.S.B.A., U. Denver, 1969. Pres., chief exec. officer Procorp Realty Inc., Miami, Fla., 1978-82, Tanneco Internat., Inc., Miami, 1982—, C.I.C. Fin., Inc., 1984—; dir. Comptrex, Inc., Miami. Contbr. articles to profl. jours. Mem. Internat. Assn. Fin. Planning. Clubs: Cricket, Ocean Reef. Office: Tanneco Internat Inc 8900 SW 107 Ave Suite 311 Miami FL 33176

TANNENBAUM, HERBERT WALTER, lawyer; b. N.Y.C., May 13, 1935; s. Hyman Jack and Regina (Izan) T.; m. Muriel Golde, June 25, 1961; children—Ross, Eric, Brett. A.B., Amherst Coll., 1957; J.D., Georgetown U., 1967. Bar: Va. 1961, Fla. 1961. Sr. ptnr. Young, Stern & Tannenbaum, P.A., North Miami Beach, Fla., 1962—; chmn. bd. Turnberry Savs. and Loan Assn., North Miami Beach. Served with USAR, 1960, to lt., USCGR, 1961-68. Mem. North Dade Bar Assn. (pres. 1966-68), ABA. Democrat. Jewish. Address: 4800 Cleveland St Hollywood FL 33021

TANNER, BILLY CHARLES, real estate and holding company executive; b. Hartselle, Ala., July 27, 1935; s. Orville Wright and Mabel Nettie (Landers) T.; B.S., U. Ala., 1958; children—Terry Charles, Billy Renea. Developer, builder homes and shopping centers Circle T Devel. Inc., Hartselle, 1959—; builder Han-O-Way Markets, chain convenience stores, 1964—; pres. Tanner Cos., holding co., Hartselle, 1975—, The Gen. Stores, 1979—. Coordinator North Ala. for Gov. George Wallace, 1964-68; mem. Republican Nat. Com., Presdl. Task Force, 1984. Served with AUS, 1957-58. Mem. Commerce Execs. Soc. of U. Ala. Baptist. Clubs: Rotary (pres. 1979), Rolls Royce Owners, U.S. Senatorial. Office: Tanner Heights Plaza PO Box 944 Hartselle AL 35640

TANNER, CHARLES WILLIAM, professional baseball team manager; b. New Castle, Pa., July 4, 1929. Player Milw. Braves, 1955-57, Chgo. Cubs, 1957-58, Cleve. Indians, 1959-60, Calif. Angels, 1961-62; mgr. Chgo. White Sox, 1970-75, Oakland A's, 1976, Pitts. Pirates, from 1977, now mgr. Atlanta Braves. Recipient Major League Mgr. of Year award The sporting News, 1972, Am. League Mgr. of Year award AP, 1972. Address: care Atlanta Braves PO Box 4064 Atlanta GA 30302*

TANNER, RAYMOND LEWIS, school administrator, radiology educator, consultant; b. Memphis, Dec. 11, 1931; s. Arthur Thomas and Josephine (Pearce) Tanner; m. Margaret Foster, Sept. 4, 1958; children—John William, Paul Russell, Rebecca Lee. B.S. in Phys. Sci., Memphis State U., 1953; M.S. in Physics, Vanderbilt U., 1955; Ph.D. in Med. Physics, UCLA, 1967. Radiation protection cons., 1955-62; asst. prof. physics Memphis State U., 1955-62; radiation protection cons., Memphis, 1967—; cons. physicist VA Med. Ctr., Memphis, 1968-77; prof. radiology dept. U. Tenn. Ctr. Health Scis., 1967—, profl. asst. facilities planning, 1976-82, asst. dean. grad. sch. med. scis., 1982-85. Recipient Am. Chem. Soc. award, 1948; radiology award So. Calif. Health Physics Soc., 1966. Fellow Am. Coll. Radiology; mem. Health Physics Soc., Am. Assn. Physicists in Medicine (pres. 1973, exemplary service award 1975), Am. Coll. Radiology (chancellor 1983—), Tenn. Acad. Sci. (pres. 1976), Radiol. Soc. N.Am. (v.p. 1982), Tenn. Radiol. Soc., Sigma Xi. Methodist. Contbr. articles to profl. jours.

TANNER, RICHARD THOMAS, high tech company executive; b. Omaha, Sept. 16, 1940; s. Robert Burke and Mary Elizabeth (O'Toole) T.; m. Diane Rogish, May 1, 1965; children—Kathleen Beth, Paula Patrice. B.S. in Bus. Adminstrn., Creighton U., 1962; M.A. in Human Resources Mgmt., Pepperdine U., 1979. Commd. 2d lt. U.S. Marine Corps, 1962, advanced through grades to lt. col., 1979; served twice in Vietnam; dir. intelligence 1st Marine Air Wing, Okinawa, Japan, 1978-79; dep. dir. Amphibious Warfare Sch., Quantico, Va., 1983-84; ret., 1984; dir. human resources Nat. Telephone Coop. Assn., Washington, 1984-85; dir. adminstrn. Verdix Corp., Chantilly, Va., 1985—. Author: Individual Small Arms tng. manual, 1973. Decorated Def. Meritorious Service medal, Meritorious Service medal, Navy Commendation medal, Navy Achievement medal. Mem. Am. Soc. for Personnel Adminstrn., Marine Exec. Assn. Republican. Roman Catholic. Avocations: golfing, jogging, reading. Home: 6271 Masefield Ct Alexandria VA 22304 Office: Verdix Corp 14130-A Sullyfield Circle Chantilly VA 22021

TANNER, ROBERT DEANE, JR., foundation executive, real estate executive; b. Akron, Ohio, Aug. 6, 1958; s. Robert Deane and Ann Rose (Baili) T. B.S. in Mgmt., U. Akron, 1981. Lic. real estate broker, Tex. Dir. fin. Tex. Policy Inst., Houston, 1981-82; pres. Investigative Research Found., Inc., Houston, 1982—; v.p., co-founder, dir. Creative Capital, Inc., Houston, 1983—; cons. Tex. Policy Inst., Inc., 1982—; pres., dir. Investigative Research Found., Inc., 1982—. Editor: Legal Aspects of Terrorism, 1983. Mem. U.S. Supreme Ct. Hist. Soc., Washington, 1983, 84. Mem. Houston Bd. Realtors, Am. Assn. Ind. Investors, Conservative Polit. Action Com., Houston C. of C. (small bus. com. 1983. Republican. Home: 2416 S Voss #K-217 Houston TX 77057

TANNER, ROBERT EDWARD, safety engineer; b. Norfolk, Va., May 9, 1939; s. Elzie Lee and Betty Lou (Tripp) T.; m. Maude Wright, Mar. 12, 1979; children—John, Joseph. A.A. in Police Adminstrn., Tenn. Tech. U. Police detective Virginia Beach Police Dept., Va., 1964-69; police chief, Allgood, Tenn., 1969-76; sr. security and safety officer DePaul Hosp., Norfolk, Va., 1976-78; chief security and safety Miss. Meth. Rehab. Ctr., Jackson, 1978—; cons. Miss. Bar Assn., 1979—. Mem. Hinds County-Vicksburg Disaster Planning Com., Jackson, 1978—. Served as tech. sgt. USAF, 1956-64. Mem. Nat. Fire Protection Assn., Am. Soc. Safety Engrs., Am. Soc. Indsl. Security, Internat. Assn. Hosp. Security (charter chpt. chmn. 1980-81, state coordinator 1982-83, regional state chmn. 1984-85). Republican. Baptist. Avocations: fishing, reading. Office: Miss Methodist Rehab Ctr 1350 Woodrow Wilson St Jackson MS 39216

TANNOUS, AFIF, social scientist, international development consultant; b. Lebanon, Sept. 25, 1905; came to U.S., 1937, naturalized, 1943; s. Ishak I. and Theodora (Yazbik) T.; m. Josephine S. Milkey, Sept. 16, 1941; children—David, Paul. B.A., Am. U. of Beirut (Lebanon), 1929; M.A., St. Lawrence U., 1938; Ph.D., Cornell U., 1940. Tchr., American High Sch., Tripoli, Lebanon, 1923-25; adminstrv. ofcl. Sudan Govt., 1929-31; leader rural devel. work in Palestine, Lebanon, Syria, 1931-37; tchr. Am. U. Beirut, 1933-37; teaching fellow St. Lawrence U., Canton, N.Y., 1937-38, Cornell U., Ithaca, N.Y., 1938-40; mem. faculty sociology dept. U. Minn., 1940-43; Middle East regional specialist Office Fgn. Agrl. Relations, U.S. Dept. Agr., 1943-51; lectr. agrl. economy and social orgn. of Middle East, Sch. Advanced Internat. Studies, Washington, 1948-51; dep. dir. U.S. Ops. Mission to Lebanon, 1951-54; liaison for U.S. Dept. Agr. with ICA and chief Africa and Middle East Analysis br. Fgn. Agrl. Service, Washington, 1954-61, area officer Africa and Middle East, 1961-71, ret., 1971; lectr. on Middle East affairs to profl. orgns. and civic groups, 1940-71; cons., bd. dirs. Internat. Center for Dynamics of Devel., Arlington, Va., 1971—; dep. dir. U.S. Agr. Exhibit, Cairo, 1960; cons. on food prodn. project in Morocco, Tunisia and Sudan, AID, 1974; mem. U.S. Dept. Agr. team for Egypt, 1975; adv. editor Middle East Jour., 1947-82; mem. FAO Mission to Greece, 1946, U.S. Agrl. Mission to Middle East, 1946, UN Econ. Survey Mission to Middle East, 1949, U.S. Tech. Task Force to Egypt to organize Egyptian-Am. Rural Devel. Service, 1953, U.S. govt. team to survey wheat relief needs in Tunisia, 1956. Contbr. numerous articles on Middle East affairs to profl. publs., also chpts. to books. Mem. Am. Sociol. Assn., Rural Sociol. Soc., Acad. Ind. Scholars, Am. Acad. Polit. and Social Sci., Soc. Applied Anthropology, Middle East Inst., AAAS, Agrl. Econs. Assn., Assn. Humanistic Psychology, Soc. for Internat. Devel., World Future Soc., Assn. Humanistic Sociology, Acad. Ind. Scholars, Soc. for Human Economy, Sigma Xi.

TANOUS, HELENE MARY, physician; b. Zanesville, Ohio, Oct. 22, 1939; d. Joseph Carrington and Rose Marie (Mokarzel) Tanous; B.A., Marymount Coll., 1961; M.D., U. Tex., 1967; divorced. Diplomate Am. Bd. Radiology. Intern, County Hosp., Los Angeles, 1967-68; resident in radiology U. So. Calif. Hosp., Los Angeles, 1969-71; instr. radiology U. So. Calif. Med. Sch., Los Angeles, 1971-72; practice medicine specializing in radiology, Los Angeles, 1972-73; asst. prof. diagnostic radiology Baylor Med. Sch., Houston, 1973-75; dir. med. student elective in diagnostic radiology Ben Taub Hosp., Houston, 1973-75, chief radiologist Clinic, 1975-79; practice radiology, Tampa, Fla., 1979—; asst. prof. U. S.Fla. Med. Sch., 1980—. Founder, pres. Children's Advocates, Inc.; bd. dirs. Fla. Endowment Humanities, 1979-83. Mem. AMA, So. Med. Assn., Am. Med. Women's Assn. (del. to Internat. Med. Women's Assn., Paris), Hillsborough County Med. Assn., West Coast Radiology Soc., Am. Trauma Soc., L'Alliance Francaise of Tampa (dir. 1984) (pres. 1985-86). Office: VA Hosp 13000 N 30th St Tampa FL 33612

TANSIL, JOAN HENDRIX, pharmacist, freelance photographer; b. Norfolk, Va., Dec. 22, 1944; d. Robert Taylor and Glenn (Ivey) Hendrix; m. Donald Wayne Tansil, Nov. 25, 1967; children—Tice, Parish. Student East Tenn. State U., 1962-64; B.S. in Pharmacy, U. Tenn. Coll. Pharmacy, 1967. Staff pharmacist Meml. Hosp., Johnson City, Tenn. 1967; relief pharmacist Stauffer Pharmacy, Altus, Okla., 1968-69, Lucas Pharmacy, Blacksburg, Va., 1969-70; clin. pharmacist, instr. U. Ga. Sch. Pharmacy, Athens, 1971-73; pharmacist-in-charge Upper Cumberland Regional Office Tenn. Dept. Health and Environment, Cookeville, 1974—; freelance photographer, 1980—. Recipient Merck award U. Tenn. Coll. Pharmacy, 1967; Best of Show award in photography Putnam County Fair, 1979; 2d prize animals div. Tenn. Photo Show and Contest, 1980; photog. award WSMV Photography Contest, Nashville, 1983. Mem. Tenn. Pharm. Assn. (mem. com.), Women's Symphony Guild, Embroiderer's Guild Am., Smacking Arts Guild Am. Methodist. Club: Tennessee Tech University Faculty Women's. Contbr. numerous photographs and articles to various newspapers.

TAPP, JOHN CECIL, physician; b. Horse Cave, Ky., Dec. 1, 1940; s. Ernest and Lottie Belle (Gill) T.; student David Lipscomb Coll., 1958-59, Western Ky. U., 1959-61; postgrad. Sch. Pharmacy, U. Ky., 1962; M.D., U. Louisville, 1966; div.; children—John Randolph, Gregory Patrick. Intern, U. Louisville, 1966-67, resident in internal medicine, 1969-70; practice medicine, Bowling Green, Ky., 1971—; mem. staff Greenview Hosp., Bowling Green Warren

County Med. Center; clin. instr. vol. faculty Travecca-Nazarene Coll., Nashville; asst. clin. prof. vol. faculty Coll. Applied Health Professions, U. Ky., Lexington; Med. dir. Prima Care Home Health Agy.; mem. med. adv. bd. Bowling Green Bus. Coll. Served as maj. USPHS, 1967-69. Fellow Am. Acad. Family Physicians; mem. Am. Acad. Bariatric Physicians, Am. Acad. Family Physicians, Ky. Acad. Family Physicians, Bowling Green Med. Soc., Internat. Ctr. Family Medicine, Hon. Order Ky. Cols., Alpha Omega Alpha, Alpha Kappa Kappa, Kappa Psi, Bowling Green-Warren County C. of C. Office: 414 Old Morgantown Rd Bowling Green KY 40201

TAPPAN, WILLIAM BURGESS, entomologist; b. DeFuniak Springs, Fla., May 9, 1928; s. Walter Lebaron and Bessie (White) T.; B.S., U. Fla., 1953, M.S., 1954; m. Barbara Ann Love, June 5, 1960. Plant insp. Fla. State Plant Bd., Gainesville, 1954-55; agrl. nematologist U.S. Dept. Agr., Lake Alfred, Fla., 1955; entomologist U. Fla., Quincy, 1955—. Served with USAAF, 1946-49; PTO. Registered profl. entomologist. Mem. Am. Phytopathol. Soc., Tobacco Workers Conf. (vice-chmn. 1975-76, chmn. 1977-79), Tobacco Sci. Council (chmn. 1977-79), Lepidoptera Found. ASTM, Am., SW, S.C., Fla., Ga. entomol. socs., Am. Inst. Biol. Sci., Soc. Nematologists, Am. Peanut Research and Ednl. Soc. Inc., Nat. Eagle Scout Assn., Alpha Zeta, Gamma Sigma Delta, Phi Sigma. Democrat. Baptist. Contbr. articles to profl. jours. Home: 106 Cheeseborough Ave Quincy FL 32351 Office: North Fla Research and Edn Center Quincy FL 32351

TARAS, ARNOLD ELIOT, management consultant; b. N.Y.C., Oct. 5, 1935; s. David William and Lillian M. (Peckett) T.; student Yale U., 1952-53; B.A., U. Vt., 1956, M.S., 1957; M.B.A., NYU, 1958; m. Madeleine J. Baumgarten, June 24, 1958; children—Jeffrey Mark, Debra Joy, Buffy Ann. Vice pres., gen. mgr. Diamond Tool Inc., N.Y.C., 1958-65; v.p. Law Engring. Testing Co., Atlanta, 1965-68; pres., chief exec. officer Piedmont Devel. Co., Atlanta, 1968-71; pres., chief exec. officer Crow, Pope and Land Enterprises, Atlanta, 1971-76; pres. Diversified Investment Assos., Atlanta, 1976-79; mng. partner Barton Sans Internat., Atlanta, 1979-83; pres. Taras Assocs. Inc., Atlanta, 1983—; dir. Piedmont Devel. Co., Law Engring; instr. Ga. State U. Div. pres. United Way, Atlanta, 1974-75. Recipient Service commendation Nat. Assn. Homebuilders, Dept. Def. Mem. Urban Land Inst., Am. Land Devel. Assn., Internat. Council Shopping Centers, Nat. Assn. Homebuilders, Inst. Real Estate Mgmt., Atlanta Apt. Owners Assn. Republican. Clubs: Atlanta City; Lan Mar Yacht; Chatahoochie Plantation; B'nai B'rith. Home: 4312 Cove Island Dr Marietta GA 30067 Office: 6 Piedmont Center Suite 703 Atlanta GA 30305

TARBOX, GURDON LUCIUS, JR., museum director; b. Plainfield, N.J., Dec. 25, 1927; s. Gurdon Lucius and Lillie (Hodgson) T.; B.S., Mich. State U., 1952; M.S., Purdue U., 1954; m. Milver Ann Johnson, Sept. 25, 1952; children—Janet Ellen Tarbox Lamb, Joyce Elaine Tarbox Gant, Paul Edward, Lucia Ann. Asst. dir. Brookgreen Gardens, Murrells Inlet, S.C., 1954-59, trustee, 1959—, dir., 1963—. Chmn. Georgetown County Mental Health Commn., 1964-66; mem. exec. council Confedn. S.C. Local Hist. Socs., 1976—; trustee S.C. Hall Fame, 1976—. Served with AUS, 1946-48. Mem. Soc. Am. Foresters, Am. Assn. Bot. Gardens and Arboreta (dir. 1971-74, sec.-treas. 1982, v.p. 1983, pres. 1985—), Georgetown County Hist. Soc. (pres. 1970-74), Am., Royal hort. socs., Am. Assn. Mus. (council 1983), Southeastern Mus. Conf. (dir. 1977-80), S.C. Fedn. Museums (pres. 1974-76), Am. Assn. State and Local History, S.C. Confedn. Local Hist. Socs. Episcopalian. Lodge: Rotary (pres. 1979-80). Home: Brookgreen Gardens Murrells Inlet SC 29576 Office: Brookgreen Gardens Murrells Inlet SC 29576

TARICA, ALBERT ISRAEL, accountant; b. Montgomery, Ala., Aug. 25, 1941; s. Israel J. and Esther (Hasson) T.; m. Ramona June Meadows, Jan. 5, 1964; children—Karen E., Ian B., Wendy R. B.S., U. Ala., 1963. C.P.A., Ga. Audit mgr. Wolf & Co., Atlanta, 1965-72; ptnr. Tarica, Moore & Co., 1972-76, Fox & Co., 1976-77; mng. ptnr. Tarica & Co., 1978—. Chmn. festival div., bd. dirs. Peach Bowl; mem. small bus. task force Ga. State Senate; mem. Ga. adv. council SBA. Served to 1st lt. USAFR, 1964-70. Mem. Internat. Assn. Fin. Planners, Am. Inst. C.P.A.s, Ga. Soc. C.P.A.s, Internat. Festival Assn., Ga. Small Bus. Council. Republican. Jewish. Lodge: Lions (Atlanta). Home: 2513 Foster Ridge Ct Atlanta GA 30345 Office: 3340 Peachtree Rd Suite 1560 Atlanta GA 30026

TARKOFF, MICHAEL HARRIS, lawyer; b. Phila., Oct. 3, 1946; s. Oscar Henry and Frances (Goldhagen) T.; m. Karen Joy Tuchman, Aug. 8, 1976; 1 son, Joshua William. A.B., U. Miami, 1968, J.D., 1971. Bar: Fla. 1973, N.Y. 1983, U.S. Supreme Ct. 1976, U.S. Tax Ct. Trial atty. Pub. Defender, Miami, Fla., 1973-77; ptnr. Flynn, Rubio & Tarkoff, Miami, 1977-83; ptnr. Flynn and Tarkoff, Miami, 1983—; atty. Dade County Democratic Com., Miami, 1977-80; guest lectr. U. Miami Law Sch., 1977; mem. legal com. NORML, Washington, 1981—. Pres. Young Democrats of Dade County, Miami, 1971; committeeman Dade County Dem. Exec. Com., Miami, 1971-73; mem. Tiger Bay Polit. Club, Miami, 1976—; sustaining mem. So. Fla. Council Boy Scouts Am. Mem. ABA, Nat. Assn. Criminal Def. Lawyers, Fla. Criminal Def. Lawyers Assn., Fla. Bar (substancial assistance in trafficing cases com. criminal law sect.); Zool. Soc. Fla., Simon Wiesenthal Ctr., U. Miami Alumni Assn. Jewish. Club: Hurricane. Office: Flynn and Tarkoff 1414 Coral Way Miami FL 33145

TARLTON, SHIRLEY MARIE, college dean; b. Raleigh, N.C., Aug. 8, 1937; d. Lloyd E. and Mary O. (Suycott) Tarlton; diploma Peace Coll., Raleigh, N.C., 1957; B.A. in French, Queens Coll., Charlotte, N.C., 1960; M.S.L.S., U. N.C., Chapel Hill, 1966. Head tech. services div. U. N.C., Charlotte, 1961-68, asst. librarian, 1961-63; asso. dir. tech. services Winthrop Coll. Library, 1968-73, acting dir., 1971, 73-74, dean library services, 1974—; mem. bd. Southeastern Library Network; mem. council Online Computer Library Center. Mem. ALA, Southeastern N.C., S.C., Metrolina, Mecklenburg library assns., Am. Soc. Info. Sci., Rock Hill C. of C., Sigma Pi Alpha, Phi Theta Kappa, Beta Phi Mu, Phi Kappa Phi. Home: 7406 Windyrush Rd Matthews NC 28105 Office: Winthrop College Rock Hill SC 29733

TARRILLION, THOMAS LEE, data processing consultant; b. San Antonio, Apr. 9, 1946; s. Paul William and Annie Ruth (Jansky) T.; B.A., St. Mary's U., 1968, M.B.A., 1971; m. Sylvia Olivia Evans, Aug. 26, 1967; children—Stephen Mark, Michelle Lynn, Cynthia Marie. Asst. dir. Computer Center, St. Mary's U., San Antonio, 1964-68, asst. registrar, 1968-69, registrar, 1969-73; data processing cons., San Antonio, 1973—; pres. Thomas L. Tarrillion Enterprises, Inc., San Antonio, 1978—. Cubmaster, Boy Scouts Am., 1977-79, asst. scoutmaster, 1979—; mem. parish council Roman Catholic Ch., 1977, chmn. fin. com., 1976-77. Cert. data processor. Mem. Data Processing Mgmt. Assn. (pres. 1973-74; Individual Performance Gold award 1980). Home: 7034 Weathered Post San Antonio TX 78238 Office: Suite 112 1747 Citadel Plaza San Antonio TX 78209

TARRY, GEORGE DUDLEY, JR., civil engineer, surveyor, moving company executive; b. Jefferson, Tex., July 17, 1924; s. George D. and Lucile Epps (Wynn) T.; m. Jimmie Patricia Radford, Sept. 2, 1950; 1 son, Radford George. B.S.C.E., U. Tex.-Austin, 1948. Registered profl. engr., Tex., La.; registered surveyor Tex. Asst. resident engr. Tex. Hwy. and Transp. Dept., Houston, 1949-57, dist. planning engr., Tyler, Tex., 1962-70, urban planning engr., 1962-70, environ. engr., 1962-70, asst. dist. engr., 1972-79; cons. engr., surveyor, Thompson and Assocs., Tyler, 1979—. Bd. dirs. Tyler United Fund, active East Tex. Council Govts. Served with USAF, 1943-45. Mem. ASCE, Tex. Soc. Profl. Engrs., Nat. Soc. Profl. Engrs., Tex. Surveyors Assn., Tyler Profl. Engrs. Soc. (dir.). Methodist. Clubs: Tyler Plaza, Tyler Tennis and Swim, Hollytree Country (Tyler). Lodges: Masons, Shriners. Author: Tyler Urban Planning Study, vol. I. Home: 1819 Easy St Tyler TX 75703

TARTE, TERRY AUSTIN, engineering administrator, consultant; b. Muskegon, Mich., June 17, 1948; s. Austin Clifford and Eldonna Mae (Morell) T.; m. Christine Lois Morgan, Jan. 3, 1970; children—Michelle Marie, Sean Michael. B.S. in Engring., U. Mich., 1970; M.S. in Systems Mgmt., U. So. Calif., 1979; M.B.A., Fla. Inst. Tech., 1985. Registered profl. engr., Fla., Pa., Ga. Field engr. Bechtel Power Corp., San Francisco, 1972-74; design engr. Ebasco Services Inc., N.Y.C., 1974-83; engring. mgr. Ebasco Plant Services, Inc., Stuart, Fla., 1983—. Served with U.S. Army, 1970-72. Mem. IEEE, ASME, Power Engring. Soc., Engring. Mgmt. Soc. Republican. Avocations: Photography; stereo equipment. Home: 5051 SW Markel St Stuart FL 33497 Office: Ebasco 1111 S Federal Hwy Stuart FL 33494

TATE, ALBERT, JR., federal judge; b. Opelousas, La., Sept. 23, 1920; s. Albert and Adelaide (Therry) T.; m. Claire Jeanmard, Apr. 23, 1949; children—Albert III, Emma Adelaide, George J., Michael F., Charles E. Student, Yale U., 1937-38, La. State U., 1938-39; B.A., George Washington U., 1941; LL.B., Yale U., 1947; certificate La. State U., 1948. Bar: La. 1948. Practice law Ville Platte, La., 1948-54; judge Ct. Appeals, 1st Circuit La., Baton Rouge, 1954-60; presiding judge 3d Circuit, Lakes Charles, La., 1960-70; assoc. justice La. Supreme Ct., 1958, 70-79; judge 5th circuit U.S. Ct. Appeals, 1979—; prof. law La. State U., 1967-68; mem. faculty Inst. Jud. Adminstrn., N.Y. U., 1965-76; appellate judges seminar U. Ala., 1966, 68, 69, U. Nev., 1967; Vice chmn. study adminstrn. appelate Cts. Am. Bar Found., 1970-76; Am. Bar Assn. rep. adv. council Nat. Center for State Cts., Washington, 1971-72; mem. adv. Council for Appellate Justice, 1971-75; mem. com. and council La. State Law Inst., 1954-59; chmn. Jud. Com. La., 1968-70; mem. jud. council Supreme Ct. La., 1960-70; chmn. La. Jud. Planning Council, 1976-79; del. Constl. Conv. La., 1973-74. Author: Louisiana Civil Procedure, 1968, 3d edit., 1977, Treatises for Judges: A Selected Bibliography, 1971, 2d edit., 1972, 3d edit., 1976; Contbr. articles to profl. jours. Chmn. La. Commn. on Aging, 1956-59; pres. La. Cotton Festival, 1955-57; mem. Evangeline Area council Boy Scouts Am., 1948—, dist. chmn., 1949-50; mem. La. Gov.'s Commn. on Rehab. and Corrections, 1970-75; Bd. dirs. La. State U. Found. Served with CIC AUS, 1942-45; PTO. Recipient Nat. Jud. award of merit Am. Trial Lawyers Assn., 1972; inducted La. State U. Hall of Distinction. Mem. ABA (chmn. exec. com. appellate judges conf. 1966-76, chmn. com. appellate advocacy 1974-78, mem. com. tech. in courts 1973-78, chmn. 1974-76), La. Bar Assn., Am. Judicature Soc. (dir. 1969-73), La. Conf. Ct. Appeal Judges (pres. 1967-70), Am. Legion, V.F.W., Woodmen of World, Delta Kappa Epsilon. Lodges: K.C., Rotary. Office: Room 324 600 Camp St New Orleans LA 70130*

TATE, CAROL FAY, social worker; b. Mitchell, Nebr., Apr. 5, 1937; d. Laurence and Vivian Joan (Powell) T.; B.S., Sioux Falls (S.D.) Coll., 1959; postgrad. Kent State U., 1961-64; M.S.W., Fla. State U., 1969. Asst. dir. health, phys. edn. YWCA, Akron, Ohio, 1959-61; home vis. tchr. Summit County Assn. Retarded Children, Akron, 1961-62, Summit County Child Welfare Bd., Akron, 1962-63; instr. Youngstown (Ohio) U., 1964-65; dir. sch. for trainable mentally retarded Scotts Bluff County (Nebr.) Assn. Retarded Children, 1964-65; tchr. Scotts Bluff County Sch. Bd., 1965-66; with Fla. Dept. Health and Rehab. Services, Tampa, 1966-69; pvt. practice social work, Tampa, 1970-75; dir. social work Hope Haven Children's Hosp., Jacksonville, Fla., 1975; dir. Gulf County Activity Center for Retarded Adults, Port St. Joe, Fla., 1976-77; pvt. practice med. social services, St. Petersburg, Fla., 1977-78; staff social worker Bay Area Home Health Services, St. Petersburg; adminstr. Omni Home Health Services, Inc., Cleveland, Tenn., 1983; researcher Am. Health Enterprises, 1984. Mem. Nat. Assn. Social Workers (v.p.), Acad. Cert. Social Workers, Tenn. Assn. Home Health Social Workers (v.p.). Democrat. Home: 2341 Gale Ln Chattanooga TN 37421

TATE, CHESTER NEAL, political science educator, consultant; b. Gastonia, N.C., Oct. 17, 1943; s. Chester Marshall and Pearl (Whitaker) T.; m. Carol Sue MacKenzie, Dec. 20, 1967; 1 child, Erin Elizabeth. B.A., Wake Forest U., 1965; M.A., Tulane U., 1968, Ph.D., 1971. Vis. instr. Tulane U., New Orleans, 1969-70; asst. prof. North Texas State U., Denton, 1970-75, assoc. prof., 1975-83, chmn. polit. sci. dept., 1980—, prof., 1983—; ptnr. Info.-Research Services, Denton, 1982—. Co-author: Supreme Court in America Politics, 1980; Your TI Professional Computer, 1984; Microcomputers in Research. Contbr. articles to profl. jours. Mem. Am. Polit. Sci. Assn., Southwestern Polit. Sci. Assn. (pres. 1978-79), Southwestern Social Sci. Assn. (sec. 1980—), Internat. Polit. Sci. Assn., So. Polit. Sci. Assn. Democrat. Home: 1400 Auburn Dr Denton TX 76201 Office: North Texas State Univ Dept Polit Sci Box 5338 Denton TX 76203

TATE, ERNEST DESHIELDS, ladies wear manufacturing company executive; b. Va., Oct. 3, 1926; s. John Clifford and Ruby Price (Mills) T.; m. Elizabeth May Moore, Feb. 14, 1947 (div. 1960); children—Patricia, Sandra; m. 2d, Nancy Lee Gray, Dec. 23, 1961 (div. 1970); children—Evelyn, Elaine. Student, U. Richmond, T. C. Williams Law Sch. With Kenrose Mfg., Inc., Roanoke, Va., 1950-66; founder, pres., chmn. bd. Lady Bird Apparel, Inc., Roanoke, 1967—. Active Republican Pary of Va., Air Lee Ct. Bapt. Ch., Am. Legion. Served with USN. Clubs: Elks, Moose.

TATE, HAROLD SIMMONS, JR., lawyer; b. Taylors, S.C., Sept. 19, 1930; s. Harold Simmons and Cleone (Clayton) T.; m. Elizabeth Anne Coker, Dec. 22, 1952; children—Mary Elizabeth Anne, Martha Coker, Virginia Clayton. A.B. cum laude, Harvard U., 1951, J.D., 1956, postgrad., 1954. Bar: S.C. 1956. Ptnr. Boyd, Knowlton, Tate & Finlay, Columbis, S.C., 1962—; lectr. Am. Law Inst.-ABA Seminars. Chmn. Richland County Mental Health Ctr., 1965-66; co-chmn. Columbia Hearing and Speech Ctr., 1962-64; mem. admission and scholarship com. Harvard U., 1961—; chmn. subcom. on legislation, legislation and fin. study commn. Gov.'s Adv. Group on Mental Health Planning, 1963-65; chmn. Columbia Bd. Supervisory of Registration, 1961-70; pres. Columbia Philharmonic Orch., 1966-67; pres. Town Theatre, 1967-70; trustee Richland County Pub. Library, 1983-78, Hist. Columbia Found., 1971-75, Caroliniana Soc., 1978—, Bostick Charitable Trust, 1968—. Served to capt. U.S. Army, 1951-53. Mem. ABA, S.C. Bar Assn., Richland County Bar Assn., Am. Law Inst., Am. Judicature Soc., Harvard Law Sch. Assn., S.C. (sec. treas. 1968-70). Episcopalian. Clubs: Tarantella, Forest Lake Country, Columbia Drama (pres. 1963-64), Palmetto (sec. 1963-70, pres. 1973-76), The Forum, Harvard (N.Y.C.); Harvard of S.C. Contbr. articles and book revs. to profl. jours. Home: 15 Gibbes Ct Columbia SC 29201 Office: Boyd Knowlton Tate & Finlay PO Box 11598 Columbia SC 29211

TATE, JAMES MACK, software quality assurance engineer; b. Wichita, Kans., Nov. 7, 1941; s. Mack James and Alice Mae (Tate) T.; m. Caryn Christine Tracy, June 26, 1965; children—Tracie Lyn, Melissa Leigh, Virginia Gayle. B.A. in Math., Tex. Christian U., Ft. Worth, 1974. Sr. electronics engr. McDonnell-Douglas Astronautics, St. Louis, 1974-75, 76-78; aerosystems engr. Gen. Dynamics, Ft. Worth, 1975-76; sr. quality assurance engr. Vought Corp., Dallas, 1978—. Served with U.S. Army, 1962-65. Recipient Letter of Commendation, NASA, 1974. Mem. IEEE, Nat. Security Indsl. Assn. (mem. software quality subcom.). Author tech. papers and reports. Home: 702 Cavendish Arlington TX 76014 Office: PO Box 225907 MC-15 Dallas TX 75265

TATE, SHIRLEY ANN, public welfare administrator; b. Detroit, Mar. 23, 1943; d. Connie Lee and Bessie (Jennings) Maynard; m. Leonard E. Tate, June 1980; 1 child by previous marriage, Kambui. B.S., Eastern Mich. U., 1965. With State of Mich., 1974-84, pub. welfare adminstr., Detroit, 1978, social services mgr., Taylor, 1978-80, dir. Office Children and Youth Services, Lansing, 1980-84; dir. div. family and children services Ga. Dept. Human Resources, 1984—; mem. Mich. Commn. on Youth Employment, Mich. Adv. Com. on Juvenile Justice, Mich. Commn. on Criminal Justice, Mich. Woman's Commn.; bd. dirs. Children's Trust Fund; mem. Ga. Commn. on Child Support, 1984—; del. White House Conf. on Families; chmn. Mich. Conf. on Children and Youth, 1981. Founding mem. Pan-African Congress-U.S.A., 1970. Mem. Am. Mgmt. Assn., Mich. Assn. Childcaring Agys., Child Welfare League Am., Am. Pub. Welfare Assn., Ga. Council Developmental Disabilities, Atlanta Women's Network, Nat. Negro Bus. and Profl. Women's Assn., Nat. Assn. Black Social Workers, NAACP, Alpha Kappa Alpha. Office: 878 Peachtree St NE Atlanta GA 30309

TATHAM, JULIE CAMPBELL, writer; b. N.Y.C., June 1, 1908; d. Archibald and Julia deFres (Sample) Campbell; student pvt. schs., N.Y.C.; m. Charles Tatham, Mar. 30, 1933; children—Charles III, Campbell. Author more than 30 juvenile books including: The Mongrel of Merryway Farm, 1952; The World Book of Dogs, 1953; To Nick from Jan, 1957; author Trixie Belden series, 1946—, Ginny Gordon series, 1946—; co-author Cherry Ames and Vicki Barr series, 1947—; author: The Old Testament Made Easy, 1985; many series books transl. into fgn. langs.; contbr. numerous mag. stories and articles to popular publs., 1935—; free-lance writer, 1935—; contbr. numerous articles to Christian Sci. publs., including Christian Sci. Monitor, 1960—. Address: 1202 S Washington St Apt 814 Alexandria VA 22314

TATHAM, ROBERT HAINES, geophysicist; b. Merced, Calif., Dec. 10, 1943; s. Robert and Dorothy (Fitzgerald) T.; m. Henna E. Solomin, Aug. 29, 1970; children—Sarah, Rachel, Benjamin. B.S. in Physics, Calif. State U.-Northridge, 1967; M.S. in Applied Geophysics, U. Houston, 1970; Ph.D. in Geophysics, Columbia U., 1975. Geophysicist, Texaco, Inc., Houston, 1967-71; spl. projects geophysicist, 1975-81; research geophysicist Geosource, Houston, 1981—; chmn. steering com. Seismic Acoustics Lab., U. Houston, 1982-84. Contbr. articles to tech. jours. and books. Mem. Soc. Exploration Geophysicists, European Assn. Exploration Geophysicists, Am. Assn. Petroleum Geologists, Am. Geophys. Union, Seismol. Soc. Am., IEEE. Democrat. Jewish. Avocation: gardening. Home: 7710 Candlegreen Ln Houston TX 77071 Office: Geosource 2700 Post Oak Suite 2000 Houston TX 77056

TATUM, ALLYN CARR, lawyer, state official; b. Portia, Ark., Jan. 27, 1942; s. Algin Carr and Nina Ruth (Turney) T.; B.S. in Bus. Administrn., U. Ark., 1967, J.D., 1970; m. Lois Ann Galloway, Apr. 30, 1977; children—Lislie Rochelle, Juliet Kee. Admitted to Ark. bar, 1970; asso. Highsmith, Harkey & Walmsley, Batesville, 1970-72; partner Highsmith, Tatum, Highsmith, Gregg & Hart, 1972-77; regional atty. Ark. Dept. Social Services, 1973-77; chmn. Ark. Workers Compensation Commn., 1977—; vis. prof. Ark. Coll., 1971-74; trust dept. adviser Citizens Bank, 1971-75; legal cons. White River Planning and Devel. Dist., 1972-77. Area Wide Comprehensive Health Planning Council, 1974-75; dir. Independence Fed. Bank, Independence Corp.; dir. Profl. Counseling Assocs. Inc., 1982-84, pres., 1985-86, also dir.; dir. Pro-Max, Inc.; mem. Atty. Gen.'s Task Force on Missing Children, 1985—. Pres., East Side PTA, 1974-75; mem. pres. adv. council Ark. Coll., 1974-75; mem. adv. bd. Gateway Vo-Tech Sch., 1977-78; mem. Batesville (Ark.) Planning Commn., 1971-73, Community Sch. Bd., 1972-77; bd. dirs. Ark. Health Systems Found., 1974-75; bd. dirs. Delta-Hills Health Systems Agy., 1976-80, mem. exec. com., 1977; bd. dirs., exec. com. Ark. Health Coordinating Council, 1976-77; bd. dirs. North Central Ark. Mental Health Center, 1972-81, pres., 1974-80; chmn. exec. com. Region VI SW Assn. Mental Health Centers, 1977-80; bd. dirs. Batesville Community Theater, 1972; bd. dirs. Nat. Community Mental Health Inst., 1976-82, exec. com., 1977-78; bd. dirs. Nat. Council Community Mental Health Centers, 1975-82, pres., 1981-82; mem. Ark. Gov.'s Task Force on Ark. Mental Health, 1986—; mem. adminstrv. bd., pastor parish com. First United Meth. Ch., Jacksonville, Ark. Recipient So. Senator award So. Bapt. Coll., 1974. Mem. So. Assn. Workers Compensation Adminstrs. (exec. com. 1971—, v.p. 1977, pres. 1978-79), ABA, Ark. (chmn. com. on mental disability 1985—), Independence County (pres. 1971-72) bar assns., Ark. Trial Lawyers Assn., Nat. Health Lawyers Assn., Internat. Assn. Indsl. Bds. and Commns. (nominating com. 1978-79, exec. com. 1985—), Assn. Rehab., Bus. and Industry (bd. dirs. 1985—), Scot Booster Club, Ark. Mental Health Assn., Batesville C. of C., Pi Kappa Alpha, Delta Theta Phi. Clubs: Kiwanis, Batesville Country (pres. 1974-75, dir. 1975-76). Home: 2708 Northeastern Ave Jacksonville AR 72076 Office: Office of Chmn Ark Workmen's Compensation Commn Justice Bldg State Capital Grounds Little Rock AR 72201

TATUM, WILLIAM FRANK, electrical engineer; b. Denison, Tex., Mar. 24, 1942; s. Luther Irvy and Grady Lou (Slagle) T.; m. Martha Lou Henderson, Sept. 3, 1965; children—Melissa Lyn, Alesha Karen. B.S.E.E., U. Tex.-Arlington, 1965; M. Elec. Engring., U. Fla., 1967. Elec. engr. Radiation, Inc., Melbourne, Fla., 1965-69; servo control systems mgr. Omega-t System, Richardson, Tex., 1969-71; project engr. Tex. Instruments, Inc., Dallas, 1971-81, program mgr., 1981-85, image processing lab. mgr., 1985—. Pres. Williams High Sch. Band Boosters, 1982-83. Recipient Pat on the Back award Sports Illustrated Mag., 1959; NSF fellow, 1966-67. Mem. Airplane Owners and Pilots Assn., Phi Kappa Phi, Epsilon Nu Gamma, Phi Kappa Theta, Phi Theta Kappa. Republican. Baptist. Home: 2400 Rockbrook Ct Plano TX 75074

TAULBEE, JOHN EARL, utility executive; b. Moline, Ill., July 9, 1934; s. Marion A. and Mabel (Fowler) T.; m. Sylvia I. Beer, Aug. 2, 1959; children—Amy L., J. Eric, Joshua J. B.A., St. Ambrose Coll., Davenport, Ia., 1958; J.D. with honors, George Washington U., 1962. Bar: D.C. bar 1962, Md. bar 1966; C.P.A., D.C. Accountant Price Waterhouse & Co., Chgo., 1958-60; atty. div. corp. finance SEC, 1962-65; atty. Balt. Gas & Electric Co., 1965-68, treas., 1968-72, sec., treas., 1972-74, v.p. finance and acctg., sec., 1974-78; exec. v.p., chief fin. officer, dir. Central & South West Corp., Dallas, 1978—. Served with U.S. Army, 1953-55. Mem. ABA, Phi Delta Phi, Delta Epsilon Sigma. Address: 4220 Stanhope Ave Dallas TX 75205*

TAUNTON, RAYMOND FRANKLIN, SR., mechanical engineer; b. Tallahassee, Nov. 18, 1936; s. John Nathan and Viola Naomi (Bullard) T.; m. Kathleen Bell, Jan. 12, 1974; 1 dau., Sandy Ann. Grad., Union 234 Apprenticeship Program, Jacksonville, Fla. Vice pres., gen. mgr. Goodwin Plumbing Co., Jacksonville, 1955-75; owner KT Industries, Jacksonville, 1975-80; owner, gen. mgr. Vogel Plumbing Co., Jacksonville, 1976-77; asst. project mgr. Galadari-Ernst, Dubai, United Arab Emirates, 1978-79; mech. project mgr. Midmac Saudi Ltd. (Saudi Arabia), 1979-80; project mgr. Atlas-Tompkins-Beckwith, Nassau, Bahamas, 1980-82; mech. project mgr. United FMI, Nassau, 1982-83, Poole & Kent Co., Tampa, 1984—. Mem. Seaplane Pilots Assn., Nat. Assn. Plumbing, Heating, Cooling Contractors Am. (cert.). Club: Jacksonville Jetty-Jumpers. Patentee universal plastic flange. Office: 1715 W Lemon St Tampa FL

TAUZIN, WILBERT J., congressman; b. Chackbay, La., June 14, 1943; B.A., Nicholls State U., 1964; J.D., La. State U., 1967; m. Gayle Theresa Clement, 1965; children—Kristie Rene, Wilbert J. III, John Ashton, Thomas Nicholas, Michael James. Former legis. aide La. Senate; admitted to La. bar, 1968; partner firm Marcel, Marcel, Fanguy & Tauzin, Houma, La., 1968-72, Sonnier & Tauzin, 1976; individual practice law, 1972; mem. 96th-99th Congresses from 3d Dist. La., mem. energy and commerce, mcht. marine, fisheries coms. Former mem. La. Ho. of Reps. Democrat. Office: Room 222 Cannon House Office Bldg Washington DC 20515*

TAVS, HENRY WOODROW, marketing executive; b. N.Y.C. Nov. 5, 1922; s. Saul A. and Cilia (Ratner) T.; m Virginia Schultheis, Apr. 12, 1960; children—Robert, Richard, James, John, Cynthia. Sales mgr. Belding Hemingway Co., N.Y.C., 1948-52; sales and mktg. mgr. PLAYTEX Corp. 1952-53; v.p. sales and mktg. Ludman Corp., Miami, Fla., v.p. sales/mktg. Piedmont Industries 1955-58; sr. v.p. sales/mktg. Revlon Corp., N.Y.C. 1958-71; pres. Revlon (P.R.), 1971-74; v.p. sales/mktg. Robino-Ladd Corp., 1974-74; pres. Fomento Mktg. Corp., 1974-77; dir. sales and mktg. Bonaventure 1977; pres. Bond Chem. Mfg., 1977-81; pres. IPMC, 1981-82; pres. Bond Chem. Mfg. 1982-84. Served as capt. AUS; ETO, PTO. Mem. Amateur Golfers Assn. Am. (pres. 1985—). Clubs: Jockey, Cricket, Miami. Home: 11111 Biscayne Blvd Miami FL 33161

TAYLOE, EDWARD DICKINSON, II, bank trust executive; b. Norfolk, Va., May 21, 1942; s. Edward Thornton and Virginia Barron (Baird) T.; B.S., East Carolina U., 1971; cert. N.Y. Inst. Fin., 1972; C.F.P., Coll. Fin. Planning, 1977; m. Louise Miller Fletcher, June 13, 1970; children—Michaux Stuart, Edward Thornton. Account exec. Thomson McKinnon Securities, Charlottesville, Va., 1971-81; investment officer Wheat First Securities, Kilmarnock, Va., 1981; trust officer Va. Nat. Bank (now Sovran Bank N.A.), Charlottesville, 1981-84, v.p., regional investment officer, 1984—; chmn. Indsl. Devel. Authority of City of Charlottesville, 1977-80. Trustee Miller Endowment Fund for U. Va.; bd. dirs. Lee-Jackson Found., Am. Cancer Soc.; team capt. for various fund-raising orgns. Served with Spl. Forces, U.S. Army, 1967-68, as spl. agt., 1969; Vietnam. Decorated Bronze Star with V device, Army Commendation medal. Mem. Internat. Assn. Fin. Planners, Inst. Cert. Fin. Planners, Am. Inst. Banking. Episcopalian. Clubs: Greencroft (dir. 1983—, pres. 1985—), Young Men's Bus. (pres. Charlottesville and Albemarle County club 1976-77); Red Lands (pres. club 1980-81) (Charlottesville). Home: 1603 Concord Dr Charlottesville VA 22901 Office: PO Box 351 Charlottesville VA 22902

TAYLOR, A. STARKE, city official. Mayor City of Dallas. Office: Office of Mayor 1500 Marilla 5EN Dallas TX 75201*

TAYLOR, B. RICHARD, former government official; b. Chickasha, Okla., Sept. 26, 1926; s. Wylie James and Eva Helen (McCauley) T.; m. Lera Wayne Griffith, Nov. 6, 1948; 1 dau., Vicki Lynn. LL.B., Baylor U., 1952, J.D., 1969. Bar: Tex. 1952, Colo. 1971, U.S. Supreme Ct. 1964. Ptnr. firm Arnold and Taylor, Waco, Tex., 1952-54; asst. U.S. atty. Western dist. Tex., Waco, 1954-63, San Antonio, 1963-64; trial atty. Dept. Justice, Washington, 1964-68, atty.-in-charge land and natural resources div., Denver, 1968-82; lectr. Lands Div. Seminars, 1966, 71, 73, 77, 79. Pres. bd. dirs. Heart O'Tex. Fed. Credit Union, 1956-63. Served with AUS, 1944-46. Mem. Tex. Bar Assn., Colo. Bar Assn., Delta Theta Phi (dean emeritus James P. Alexander senate). Lodge: Masons. Editorial staff Baylor Law Rev., 1951-52. Home and office: 517 N 36th St Waco TX 76710

TAYLOR, CYNTHIA AGNES, interior designer, horse breeder; b. Wye, Ark., Aug. 11, 1937; s. Dudley Rufe and Linnea Juno Cynthia (Nelson) Harrell; m. William Raymond Brown, Sept. 4, 1955 (div. May 1968); children—Karen, David, Linnea, Ray; m. 2d, Charles Alvin Taylor, Sept. 19, 1973 (div. Oct. 1980); 1 dau., Crystal. Student Capitol City Bus. Coll., 1956-57, U. Central Ark., 1968. With Lincoln Nat. Bank, Louisville, 1957, Blass, Little Rock, 1968, Dillards of Little Rock, 1969-70, Ark. Furniture, Little Rock, 1970-73; owner Luineas Fashion Shoppe, Inc., Conway, Ark., 1963-73; interior designer, Bigelow, Ark., 1965—; owner, operator First Love Arabian Horse Farm, Bigelow, 1972—; mem. Harrell Family Singers, 19—. Recipient Sweepstakes award Art Show, Morrilton, Ark., 1963. Democrat. Baptist. Home: Route 1 Box 261 Bigelow AR 72016

TAYLOR, DONALD M., advertising agency executive; b. Whiteville, Tenn., July 7, 1944; s. Willie Clifford and Cradie Bernice (Jacobs) T.; m. Carolyn Louise Fain, Aug. 19, 1965; children—Laura Ann, Paul David. Student U. Tex.-Arlington, 1962-63, So. Meth. U., 1969-71, Dallas Bapt. Coll., 1971-72. Regional mgr. advt. and sales promotion Gen. Electric, Dallas, 1969-79; pres. Donald Taylor & Assocs., Dallas, 1979—. Deacon Lakeside Baptist Ch., Dallas. Served to 1st lt. U.S. Army, 1967-69. Decorated Army Commendation medal. Mem. Dallas Advt. League, Dallas C. of C. Republican.

TAYLOR, DONALD MICHAEL, real estate developer; b. Columbia, S.C., Feb. 9, 1959; s. Don E. and Audrey (Headden) T.; m. Kimberly Cosper, Aug. 6, 1983. B.A. in Econs., Wofford Coll., 1982. Lic. real estate, S.C. Vice pres. Don E. Taylor & Assoc., Columbia, 1982—. Athletic scholar Wofford Coll., 1978. Mem. Internat. Council Shopping Ctrs., Columbia C. of C. (Pres.'s Club 1985), Kappa Alpha. Order. Baptist. Avocations: hunting, fishing, biking, softball. Home: 5020 Wofford Ave Columbia SC 29206 Office: Don E Taylor & Assoc PO Box 6788 Columbia SC 29260

TAYLOR, DONALD STUART, retail executive; b. Richmond, Va., July 12, 1949; s. Elbert Gray and Margaret Eleanor (Garthright) T.; m. Teresa Carol Vassey, July 16, 1978. B.A. in English Lit., Coll. of William and Mary, 1975. Receiving supt. Clowe & Cowan, Lubbock, Tex., 1975-76; store mgr. Mister Doyce, Lubbock, Wichita Falls and Amarillo, Tex., 1976-80; ptnr. Norwood, Taylor & Assocs., Amarillo, 1980-82; retail mgr. Hastings Books and Records, Amarillo, 1983—. Served with USAF, 1971-74. Mem. Young Poets of Am., Mensa. Republican. Contbr. poems to nat. publs.

TAYLOR, DOUGLAS JENNINGS, retired process safety and fire protection specialist; b. Worcester, Mass., Mar. 12, 1917; s. Henry and Lavena Alice (Jennings) T.; m. Edith Louise Harding, June 10, 1967. B.S. in Chem. Engring., MIT, 1939. Devel. engr. Linde Air Products Co., Tonawanda, N.Y., 1939-55; safety engr. Union Carbide Corp., Sistersville, W.Va., 1955-67, process safety and fire protection specialist Union Carbide Corp., Sistersville and Marietta, 1967-82; cons., 1983—; gen. chmn. Central Ohio Valley Indsl. Emergency Orgn., 1963. Dir., Pleasants County (W.Va.) Emergency Services, 1961—; chmn. Pleasants County Housing Com., 1975; sec. bd. dirs. Pleasants County Community Action, 1976-79; bd. dirs. Pleasants County Housing Rehab. Program, 1980; mem. Pleasants County Democratic Exec. Com.; bd. dirs. FIRETAC. Named Ky. Col. Mem. Am. Soc. Safety Engrs. (profl.), Nat. Fire Protection Assn. (life), Am. Def. Preparedness Assn. (life), Sigma Xi. Episcopalian. Clubs: Kiwanis (gov. W.Va. dist. 1971-72) (St. Marys, W.Va.); Masons, Elks. Home and Office: 501 Sycamore St Saint Marys WV 26170

TAYLOR, EDWARD EUGENE, school principal; b. Greeneville, Tenn., Dec. 10, 1924; s. Frank Hiram and Cecil Elizabeth (Brown) T.; m. Mattise Wilson, June 30, 1947; children—Inza Ehren Taylor Washington. B.S., Allen U., 1945; Dr.Humanities (hon.), Allen U., 1976; M.S. in Edn., U. Mich., 1952; Ph.D., U. S.C., 1979; postgrad. Harvard U., 1957-58. Instr., Allen U., 1945-48; tchr. math./physics C.A. Johnson High Sch., Columbia, S.C., 1948-61; prin. F.C. Benson Elem. Sch., Columbia, 1961-71; asst. dir. adult edn. Richland Sch. Dist. One, 1971-77; prin. Roosevelt Village Elem. Sch., Columbia, 1977—; summer instr. Tuskegee Inst., 1959, 60, 61, 65, 66, Claflin Coll-Upward Bound, 1967-71. Bd. dirs. S.C. Edn. Assn., 1967-84; chmn. bd. dirs. Opportunities Industrialization Ctr./S.C., 1981—; mem. Vol. Action Council United Way, 1983—; pres. Richland Tchrs. Council Fed. Credit Union, 1965—; bd. dirs., sec. Bethel Bishop Chappelle Meml. Apts., Inc., 1971—; treas. Booker T. Washington High Sch. Found., 1974—. NSF fellow, 1957-58, various summer inst. grants, 1955-64. Mem. NEA (life mem.; past pres. Black Caucus), S.C. Edn. Assn. (mem. Black Caucus), Palmetto Edn. Assn. (past v.p.), Richland County Tchrs. Assn. (past pres.), Richland County Edn. Assn. (past pres.), Columbia Tchrs. Assn., Dist. #1 Elem. Prins. Assn., S.C. Assn. Elem. Sch. Prins. (past v.p.), S.C. Assn. Sch. Adminstrs., Nat. Assn. Elem. Sch. Prins., NAACP, Alpha Phi Alpha, Phi Delta Kappa. Democrat. Mem. African Meth. Episcopalian Ch. Clubs: Columbia Luncheon, Columbia Cosmopolitan. Home: 3817 Ardincaple Dr Columbia SC 29203 Office: Roosevelt Village Elementary Sch McRae St Columbia SC 29203

TAYLOR, EDWARD SCHAEFFER, JR., accountant; b. Norfolk, Va., Sept. 12, 1948; s. Edward Schaeffer and Sara Elizabeth (Rock) T.; m. Susan Martha Resch, Sept. 28, 1973; 1 son, Daniel Patrick. B.S. magna cum laude in Bus. Adminstrn., Old Dominion U., 1974. C.P.A., Va. Supr., Goodman & Co., Norfolk, 1974-83; pvt. practice acctg., Virginia Beach, Va., 1983—; fin. cons. Served with U.S. Army, 1969-72. Mem. Am. Inst. C.P.A.s, Va. Soc. C.P.A.s, Internat. Assn. Fin. Planners (v.p. pub. relations 1983), Virginia Beach C. of C. (chmn. membership 1982, local legis. affairs 1983, recipient Best Membership Recruitment Yr. award 1982), Virginia Beach Jaycees (adminstrv. v.p. 1978-79, state dir. 1979, 80, pres. 1980, 81, Life Membership award 1981, Presdl. awards of honor 1978, 79, 80, 82). Episcopalian. Club: Virginia Beach Forward. Lodge: Corinthians (Norfolk). Home: 6335 Taylor Dr Norfolk VA 23502 Office: 533 Newton Rd Suite 112 Virginia Beach VA 23462

TAYLOR, ELDON DONIVAN, association executive; b. Holdenville, Okla., July 29, 1929; s. Rome B. and Alma Edith (Collins) T.; m. Hypatia Ethyl Roberts, Feb. 7, 1953; 1 dau., Teresa Lynn Taylor McDermott. B.S. cum laude, Am. U., 1959, M.S., 1965. Dir. program rev. and resources mgmt., office of space scis. and applications NASA, 1962-70; dep. asst. adminstr. resources mgmt. EPA, Washington, 1970-73; dep. asst. dir. adminstrn. NSF, Washington, 1973-74, asst. dir. adminstrn., 1974-79; insp. gen. NASA, Washington, 1979-80; mgmt. cons. Office Mgmt. Budget, Annandale, Va., 1981-83; dir. adminstrn. Va. Ctr. for Innovative Tech., 1983-84; v.p. Assn. Univs. for Research in Astronomy, 1984—. Served with USAF, 1951-54. Recipient Superior Accomplishment award Dept. Navy, 1958; William A. Jump Meritorious award, 1964; NASA Exceptional Service award, 1969; EPA Spl. Achievement award, 1972; NSF Disting. Service award, 1977; NASA Outstanding Leadership award, 1981.

TAYLOR, ELLEN BORDEN BROADHURST, civic worker; b. Goldsboro, N.C., Jan. 18, 1913; d. Jack Johnson and Mabel Moran (Borden) Broadhurst; student Converse Coll., 1930-32; m. Marvin Edward Taylor, June 13, 1936; children—Marvin Edward, Jack Borden, William Lambert. Bd. govs. Elizabethan Garden, Manteo, N.C., 1964-74; mem. Gov. Robert Scott's Adv. Com. on Beautification, N.C., 1971-73; mem. ACE nat. action com. for environ. Nat. Council State Garden Clubs, 1973-75; bd. dirs. Keep N.C. Beautiful, 1973-85; mem. steering com., charter mem. bd. dirs. Keep Johnston County (N.C.) Beautiful, 1977-88; life judge roses Am. Rose Soc.; chmn. local com. that published jointly with N.C. Dept. Cultural Resources: An Inventory of Historic Architecture, Smithfield, N.C., 1977; co-chmn. local com. to survey and publish jointly with N.C. Div. Archives and History: Historical Resources of Johnston County, 1980-86. Mem. Nat. Council State Garden Clubs (life; master judge flower shows), Johnston County Hist. Soc. (charter), N.C. Geneal. Soc. (charter), Johnston County Geneal. Soc. (charter), Nat. Soc. Daus. Founders and Patriots Am. (N.C. chpt.), Nat. Soc. New Eng. Women (charter mem. Carolina Capital Colony 1984), Hist. Preserva- Soc. N.C. (life), N.C. Art Soc. (life), N.C. Lit. and Hist. Assn., DAR (organizing vice-regent chpt. 1976), Gen. Soc. Mayflower Descs. (life), Descs. of Richard Warren, Nat. Soc. Colonial Dames Am. (life), Democrat. Episcopalian. Clubs: Smithfield (N.C.) Garden (charter; pres. 1969-71), Smithfield Woman's (v.p. 1976). Magna Charta Dames. Home: 616 Hancock St Smithfield NC 27577

TAYLOR, EMERY FOLGER, chemist; b. Somerville, Mass., June 27, 1910; s. William Emery and Gladys Estelle (Carr) T.; m. Isabel Hamilton Elliott, Feb. 27, 1943 (dec. 1981); children—Emery Folger. B.S. in Indsl. Chemistry, Harvard U., 1932, M.S. in Phys. Chemistry, 1938. Research chemist B.B. Chem. Co., Cambridge, Mass., 1933-36; teaching fellow in chemistry Harvard U., Cambridge, 1936-41; research chemist E.I. duPont de Nemours & Co., Waynesboro, Va., 1941, tech. supr., 1947-49, supr. process control, 1950-51, area supr. acid recovery, 1951-53, textile, 1953-55, orlon polymer, 1955-57, environ. supr., 1959-75. Statewide adv. com. Va. Water Resources Ctr., Va. Poly. Inst. and State U., 1966-75; tech. adv. com. State Air Pollution Control Bd., 1967-75; dir. Shenandoah Valley Council, Navy League U.S., 1982—; dir., assoc. dir. Headwaters Soil and Water Conservation Dist., 1972—; chmn. State Water Plan Adv. Com., 1983—; mem. State Air Pollution Control Bd., 1976-82, chmn., 1979-82. Elder, First Presbyn. Ch., 1983—. Served with U.S. Army, 1941-43, 43-46, USAR to lt. col., 1957-61. Recipient Indsl. Wastes Medal, Water Pollution Control Fedn., 1965; Enslow-Hedgepath award Va. Water Pollution Control Assn., 1970; Service award Va. Water Polution Control Assn., 1968-71; Disting. Service award Va. State Air Pollution Control Bd., 1976-82; Va. Wildlife Fedn. Clean Air Conservationist of Yr., 1982. Mem. Va. Water Pollution Control Assn. (pres. 1966-67), Am. Chem. Soc., Air Pollution Control Assn., AAAS, Sigma Xi, Tau Beta Pi, Alpha Chi Sigma. Presbyterian. Contbr. articles to profl. jours.; patentee in field. Address: 105 Woodland Dr Staunton VA 24401

TAYLOR, FOSTER JAY, university president; b. Gibsland, La., Aug. 9, 1923; s. Lawrence Foster and Marcia Aline (Jay) T.; student La. Poly. Inst., 1940-42; B.A., U. Calif.-Santa Barbara, 1948; M.A., Claremont (Calif.) Grad. Sch., 1949; Ph.D. in History and Govt., Tulane U., 1952; 1 son, Terry Jay. Assoc. prof. history, dean men. La. Coll., Pineville, 1952-56, prof., 1956-62, dean coll., 1960-62; pres. La. Tech U., Ruston, 1962—. past chmn. La. Labor Mediation Bd.; arbitrator Am. Arbitration Assn., Fed. Mediation and Conciliation Service, former mem. Am. La. Adv. Council on Vocat.-Tech Edn.; bd. dirs. River Cities High Tech. Group, Ruston Civic Symphony trustee Falcon Found.; mem. Gov.'s Task Force on High Tech.; former mem. Air Force ROTC Adv. Council. Served to lt. comdr., aviator, USNR, 1942-46. Recipient citation for outstanding achievement U. Calif. Alumni Assn., 1971. Mem. Ruston C. of C. (dir.), Am., Miss. Valley, So. hist. assns., Am. Assn. State Colls. and Univs. (com. on sci. and tech.), So. Assn. Colls. and Schs. (chmn. appeals com. commn. on colls.), Nat. Acad. Arbitrators, Phi Alpha Theta. Lodge: Rotary. Author: The United States and the Spanish Civil War, 1936-39, 1956; Reluctant Rebel, The Secret Diary of Robert Patrick, 1861-1865, 1959. Office: La Tech U Ruston LA 71272

TAYLOR, FRED J., university administrator. Chancellor, U. Ark.-Monticello. Office: U Ark-Monticello Monticello AR 71655*

TAYLOR, GAIL BATTLES, state official; b. Oklahoma City, Oct. 15, 1943; d. Sam O. and Dorothy (Blackwell) Battles; B.A., Oklahoma City U., 1964; M.Ed., Central State U., 1965; 1 dau., Laura Gail. Records officer Oklahoma County Assessor's Office, Oklahoma City, 1968-69; program mgr. ednl. programs Okla. Hwy. Safety Office, Oklahoma City, 1975-81; info. officer Okla. Tax Commn. Motor Vehicle Div., Oklahoma City, 1981—. Program chmn. Women's Dem. Club, 1980-84. Served with USAF, 1970-72. Mem. Women in Communications, Res. Officers Assn., Delta Zeta. Democrat. Roman Catholic. Club: Faculty House. Office: 2501 N Lincoln Blvd Oklahoma City OK 73194

TAYLOR, GEORGE DODSON, real estate developer; b. Chester, Pa., Oct. 10, 1943; s. George Holden and Ernestina Alice (Brumfield) T.; m. Claudia Evelyn O'Hearn, June 11, 1966; children—Todd, Christopher, Leigh Ann. B.S.M.E., Clemson U., 1965; student in exec. mgmt. U. Tenn., 1967. Registered profl. engr., S.C. Design engr. E.I. DuPont, Chattanooga, 1965-69; v.p. resort devel. Sea Pines Co., Hilton Head, S.C., 1970-74, Kiawah Island Co., Charleston, S.C., 1974-78; ptnr. Leonard, Call, Taylor & Assocs., Myrtle Beach, S.C., 1978—; advisor in field. Trustee, bd. dirs. Coastal Acad., Myrtle Beach, 1982—; mem. exec. council Urban Land Inst., Washington, 1984—. Recipient Best Comml. Bldg. award City of Myrtle Beach, 1984, Best Multi Family Bldg. award, 1984. Mem. Am. Land Devel. Assn. Club: Dune. Avocations: tennis; golfing; traveling.

TAYLOR, GRACE ELIZABETH (BETTY) WOODALL, law educator, library administrator; b. Butler, N.J., June 14, 1926; d. Frank E. and Grace (Carlyon) Woodall; m. Edwin S. Taylor, Feb. 4, 1951 (dec.); children—Carol Lynn Taylor Crespo, Nancy Ann. A.B., Fla. State U., 1949, M.A., 1950; J.D., U. Fla., 1961. Instr., asst. librarian Univ. Libraries, U. Fla., 1950-56, asst. law librarian, 1956-62, now dir. Legal Info. Ctr., prof. law, 1976—; cons. law libraries; bd. dirs. Southeastern Library Network; chmn. LAWNET network legal info. Contbr. articles on automation and law to library publs. Fla. legislature Lewis scholar, 1946-50; grantee Nat. Endowment for Humanities, 1981-82. Mem. Am. Assn. Law Libraries (exec. bd.), Am. Assn. Law Schs., ABA, Am. Soc. Info. Scis., Fla. Library Assn. Democrat. Methodist. Office: U Fla Legal Info Ctr Gainesville FL 32611

TAYLOR, HELEN WICKHAM, physician; b. Anking Anwhei, China, Apr. 12, 1919; came to U.S., 1933; d. Harry Baylor and Alma (Booth) T. B.S., Sweet Briar Coll., 1940; M.D., U. Va., 1943. Intern, Montreal Gen. Hosp., 1944-45, Doctor's Hosp., N.Y.C., 1945-46; ob-gyn resident Bellevue Hosp., N.Y.C., 1974-47, Presbyn. Hosp., 1947-48; missionary St. James Hosp., China, 1948-51; ob-gyn resident Bellevue Hosp., N.Y.C., 1951-52; practice medicine specializing in ob-gyn, Norfolk, Va., 1952-71; dir. Family Planning Clinic, Norfolk Health Dept., 1971—; pres. med. staff DePaul Hosp., 1964-65. Fellow Am. Coll. Ob-Gyn; mem. AMA, Med. Soc. Va., Norfolk Acad. Medicine. Club: Soroptimist (pres. 1964) (Norfolk-Virginia Beach, Va.). Episcopalian.

TAYLOR, HENRY EMMANUEL, bookdealer; b. Texarkana, Tex., Aug. 6, 1925; s. Henry Emmanuel and Essie Faye (Walker) T.; Martha Jean Allen, July 15, 1950; children—Michael H., Mary C., Julie A. B.A., Baylor U., 1949. Dir., Baylor U. Student Hosp. and Health System, Waco, Tex., 1947-49; adminstr. Hillsboro Clinic Hosp., Tex., 1949-51; cons. adminstr. Snyder Hosp. & Clinic, Tex., 1951-52; adminsr. Torbett Clinic & Hosp., Marlin Tex., 1952-54, Sweetwter Mcpl. Hosp., Tex., 1955-60, Med. Arts Hosp., Dallas 1955-60; dir. Exchange Park Med. Ctr., Dallas, 1960-63; exec. dir. Locke Med. Ctr., v.p. Locke Enterprises, Dallas, 1963-67; exec. v.p. Bristol Gen. Hosp., Dallas, 1968-69; regional dir. Hosp. div. Extendicare Inc., Dallas, 1970; owner, mgr. Preston Books, Dallas, 1969—; chmn. bd. Taylors, Inc., Dallas, 1973—; dir. Parkway Bank & Trust, Dallas. Contbr. articles on bookselling to profl. jours. Chmn., Dallas County Grand Jury, 1984; chmn. adv. council Sch. Arts and Humanities, U. Tex., Dallas, 1979-83; bd. dirs. Library Congress Ctr. for the Book, 1982—. Served with USN, 1943-46. Mem. Am. Booksellers Assn., Dallas Hosp. Council (pres. 1958), North Dallas C. of C. Republican. Presbyterian. Club: Eisenhower Yacht (Dennison). Avocations: boating; gardening; painting; Home: 6050 Desco Dr Dallas TX 75225 Office: Taylors Inc 5455 Belt Line Rd Dallas TX 75240

TAYLOR, HOWARD EARLE, bank executive; b. Columbus, Ga., Mar. 4, 1952; s. Thomas Earl and Beverly Nita (Smith) T.; m. Karen Harriet Muller, Jan. 12, 1980. B.A., Furman U., 1974; postgrad. Ga. State U., 1976-78. Mktg. rep. First Nat. Bank, Columbus, Ga., 1974-76; asst. cashier Bank of the South, Atlanta, 1976-79; v.p. ops., dir. So. Ambulance Builders, Inc., LaGrange, Ga., 1979-83; cons. health care delivery systems, 1983-84; pres. Thunderwood Corp., Thunderwood Holdings, Inc. Vice pres. Viron Internat., Inc., 1981-83. Methodist. Home and Office: RR 2 Box 1565 Pine Mountain GA 31822

TAYLOR, ISOM RENARD, international educational and training analyst; b. Winnsboro, La., Dec. 5, 1951; s. Leo Nathaniel and Elsie Mae (Wilson) T.; m. Bonnie Marie Baker, Mar. 20, 1981. B.A., U. Calif.-Irvine, 1976; M.S. in Econs.-Mgmt., U. Utah, 1978. Broadcast ops. scheduler CBS-TV, 1968-70; youth service dir. Los Angeles City Schs., 1970-73; Manpower A Program adminstr., Los Angeles and Orange counties, 1973-76; mgmt. analyst Salt Lake County, 1976-79; research program planner analyst Boeing Co., Seattle, 1979-82; adj. prof. Cogswell Coll., Seattle, 1979-82; planning and program analyst ARAMCO Services Co., Houston, 1982—; v.p. CDC Mgmt. Group, Inc., Salt Lake City, 1979. Chmn. planning council Urban League, Salt Lake City, 1977-78. Mem. NAACP, Am. Soc. Pub. Adminstrn., Internat. City Mgmt. Assn., Indsl. Scientist Assn., Am. Soc. Personnel Adminstrs., Urban League. Home: 12403 Vinking Ct Houston TX 77071 Office: ARAMCO Services Co PO Box 53211 Houston TX 77052

TAYLOR, JACKSON, JR., history educator; b. N.Y.C., Feb. 12, 1938; s. Jackson and Gladys (McCracken) T. A.B., Dartmouth Coll., 1960; M.A., NYU, 1963, Ph.D., 1970. Salesman, Stokely-Van Camp Co., Indpls., 1960-62; tchr. Cheshire Acad. (Conn.), 1963-66; asst. prof. history U. Miss., Oxford, 1967-71, assoc. prof., 1971—. Mem. Lafayette County Republican Com., Oxford, 1971—. Recipient NYU Founders Day award, 1971. Mem. Am. Hist. Assn., Am. Assn. Advancement Slavic Studies. Club: Oxford Country. Lodge: Kiwanis. Contbr. articles to profl. jours. Home: Box 659 University MS 38677 Office: 305 Bishop Hall University MS 38677

TAYLOR, JAMES ALTON, educational administrator; b. Shreveport, La., Oct. 2, 1945; s. Olney Alton and Mary Lee (Caskey) T.; B.A., La. Poly. Inst., 1968; M.Ed., Tulane U., 1972; Ph.D., U. New Orleans, 1981; m. Myrna Rae Williams, Sept. 2, 1967; 1 son, James Alton. Music tchr., choral dir. Hahnville High Sch., Boutte, La., 1968-76; prin. Carver Jr. High Sch., Hahnville, La., 1976-77; prin. Hahnville (La.) Jr. High Sch., 1977-79; dir. evaluation, research and devel. St. Charles Parish Schs., Luling, La., 1979-84, supr. curriculum and instrn., 1984—; asso. music dir. Concert Choir New Orleans, 1973—. Mem. Council Basic Edn., Assn. Supervision and Curriculum Devel., Am. Ednl. Research Assn., La. Ednl. Research Assn., Nat. Council Measurement Edn., Music Educators Nat. Conf., La. Assn. Sch. Execs., Phi Delta Kappa, Kappa Delta Pi. Democrat. Methodist. Home: 4925 Elysian Fields New Orleans LA 70122 Office: PO Box 46 Luling LA 70070

TAYLOR, J(AMES) BENNETT, management consultant; b. Sarasota, Fla., June 15, 1943; s. Thurman Ralph and Lucille (Bennett) T. divorced; 1 child, Kelly Christine. B.S. in Advt., U. Fla., 1965. Dist. mgr. The Coca-Cola Co., Shreveport, La., 1966-68; allied product specialist Coca-Cola U.S.A., Dallas, 1968-70, dist. mgr., Cin., Indpls., 1970-75; v.p. Ott Research and Devel., Miami, Fla., 1975-78; pres., chief exec. officer Exec. Group, Inc., Tampa, Fla., 1978—. Mem. Assn. Outplacement Cons. Firms. Home: 855 N Village Dr 101 Saint Petersburg FL 33702

TAYLOR, JAMES DANIEL, beverage and chemical companies executive; b. Rahway, N.J., Nov. 21, 1928; s. James Daniel and Ella Sophie (Sneedse) T.; student Bates Coll., 1948, Sch. Fgn. Service, Georgetown U., 1949-51, U. Mex., summer 1949; M.B.A., Ateneo of Manila, 1964; postgrad. Bus. Sch., Harvard U., 1978; m. Teresa Frances Lavers, Dec. 18, 1965; children—Anita Teresa, Andrea Ella, Alex James. With Standard Vacuum Oil Co., Philippines, 1951-65; mktg. exec. Esso Standard Oil Co., C.Am., 1965-68; dir. mgmt. cons. Price Waterhouse Co., N.Y.C., Tampa, Fla., 1968-74; pres. Jim Taylor Corp., Orlando, Fla., 1974—, Autochlor Suncoast, 1978—, Sarasota Beverage Co., 1980—, St. Petersburg Beverage Co. (Fla.), 1983— dir. So. Data Co., So. Cons. Co.; mem. wholesale adv. bd. Schlitz Brewing Co. Mem. Mountainside (N.J.) Sch. Bd., 1971-72; patron Rollins Coll., U. Central Fla.; mem. panel United Cerebral Palsy Found.; bd. dirs. Union County Sch. Bd., 1972; cons. Fla. Senate, 1974; Jaycee senator, 1969—. Served with U.S. Army, 1946-48. Recipient Inner Circle award Jos. Schlitz Brewing Co., 1978, 80, C.Am. award Govt. of Honduras, 1950. Mem. Am. Mgmt. Assn., Sales Execs. Club, Central Fla. Wholesalers Assn. (pres.), Beer Industry Fla. (dir.), Econs. Club of Orlando (dir.), Georgetown U. Alumni Assn. (bd. govs. interviewing com. chmn. Fla.). Republican. Episcopalian. Clubs: Winter Park Racquet (pres.), University, Tar Boosters; Manila Polo, Interlachen Country. Contbr. articles to profl. publs. Home: 187 Atlantic Dr Maitland FL 32251 Office: 187 Atlantic Dr Maitland FL 32751

TAYLOR, JEREMIAH, youth worker, educator; b. Montgomery, Ala., July 5, 1958; s. Walter and Rebecca (Croskey) T. B.S., Ala. State U., 1981, M.S., 1982. Substitute tchr. Montgomery Pub. Schs., 1982-84; activity program asst. Dept. of Mental Health, Montgomery, 1983-84; childcare worker Dept. of Youth Services, Montgomery, 1984—. Recipient Award of Merit, The Nat. Dean's List, 1980-81. Mem. Am. Assn. for Counseling and Devel., Am. Mental Health Counselor Assn., Assn. for Specialist In Group Work, Am. Criminal Justice Assn. Democrat. Baptist. Avocations: reading; coin collecting; jogging. Office: State Dept of Youth Services Route 5 Box 542 Montgomery AL 36117

TAYLOR, JESSE FREDERICK, community relations counselor, foundation executive; b. Phoenix, Apr. 8; s. Frederick J. and Grace S. Taylor; B.A., Ariz. State U., 1952, M.A., 1957; Ph.D. (hon.), Rochdale Coll., Toronto, Ont., Can. Instr. English, Prairie View (Tex.) Coll., 1957-59; teaching fellow English dept. Ariz. State U., Tempe, 1959-60; asso. prof. English, humanities So. U., New Orleans, 1960-65; lectr., cons., counselor Inst. Afro-Am. and Comparative Cultures, New Orleans, 1965-73; counselor Div. Vocat. Rehab., New Orleans, 1973-75; instl. counselor La. Family Planning Program, New Orleans, 1974-75; med. and social services specialist Mental Health Services, New Orleans, 1975-76; personal and rehab. counselor, New Orleans, 1976-77; acad. adv. legal tng. program, cons. communication, part-time tutor English, Am. Found. Negro Affairs, New Orleans, 1977—; community relations counselor New Orleans City Council, 1977—. Mem. adv. bd. Nat. Black Firefighters Am.; mem. bd. advisors Coll. Edn., Ariz. State U., Tempe; mem. U.S. Congl. Adv. Bd. Served with USAF, 1952-56. Certified rehab., family, marriage and counselor. Mem. Nat., La. rehab. assns., Nat. Rehab. Counselors Assn., Am. Soc. Adlerian Psychology, Am. Personnel and Guidance Assn., Nat. Council Tchrs. English, Assn. Black Psychologists, Nat. Psychol. Assn., Am. Psychotherapy Assn., Am. Acad. Polit. and Social Scis., Assn. Black Anthropologists, Am. Humanist Assn. Home: 3140 New Orleans St New Orleans LA 70122

TAYLOR, JOHN COMER, telecommunications analyst; b. Gadsden, Ala., July 31, 1953; s. Charles Comer and Vesta Ramona (Ledford) T.; m. Jo Lynn Schellack, Sept. 22, 1979; children—John Caleb, Joshua Nathan. B.A., Wofford Coll., 1975; J.D., Woodrow Wilson Coll. Law, Atlanta, 1978; M.B.A., Ga. State U., 1979. Service cons. So. Bell Tel.&Tel., Atlanta, 1979-83; telecommunications analyst Bank South Atlanta, 1983—. State Ga. Gov.'s intern, 1978; Am. Leaders fellow Shavano Inst., Keystone, Colo., 1984 fellow Found. for Econ. Edn., Irvington-on-Hudson, N.Y., 1984; Cato Inst. fellow, Washington, 1985. Coordinator 4th dist. Citizens Choice, U.S. C. of C., 1983. Mem. Ga. Telecommunications Assn. (sec.-treas. 1984, 1st v.p. 1986), Am. Mensa. Libertarian. Presbyterian. Home: 2426 Sherbrooke Ct Atlanta GA 30345 Office: 55 Marietta St Atlanta GA 30303

TAYLOR, JOHN MCKOWEN, lawyer; b. Baton Rouge, Jan. 20, 1924; s. Benjamin Brown and May (McKowen) T.; 1 son, John McKowen. B.A., La. State U., 1948, J.D., 1950. Bar: La. 1950, U.S. Supreme Ct. 1960. Asso., Taylor, Porter, Brooks, Fuller & Phillips, Baton Rouge, 1951-55, Huckaby, Seale, Kelton & Hayes, Baton Rouge, 1955-58; ptnr. Kelton & Taylor, Baton Rouge, 1958-61; sole practice, Baton Rouge, 1961—. Served with AUS, 1943-46; to maj. USAR, 1946—; ATO, ETO, PTO. Mem. ABA, La. State Bar Assn., Baton Rouge Bar Assn., AAAS, Mil. Order of World Wars, Am. Radio Relay League, Baton Rouge C. of C., Sigma Chi. Republican. Presbyterian. Clubs: Baton Rouge Country, City of Baton Rouge, Baton Rouge Amateur Radio. Home and Office: 2150 Kleinert Ave Baton Rouge LA 70806

TAYLOR, KENNETH MICHAEL, social worker, educator; b. Grayson County, Va., June 16, 1949; s. Squire O. and Hope (Bartlett) T.; A.A., Hiwassee Coll., 1969; B.A., Scarritt Coll., 1971, M.C.W., 1973; M.S. in Social Work, U. Tenn., 1975; m. Sharon Regina Clemons, Jan. 19, 1985; 1 child, Mary Joan. Social group worker Magness Center, Nashville, 1971-73; psychiat. social worker Mental Health Clinic, Inc., Wise, Va., 1975-81; lectr. in social welfare Clin. Valley Coll., U. Va., 1976-81; clin. social worker Patrick Henry Mental Health Center, Martinsville, Va., 1981-84; coordinator Franklin County Satellite Clinic, Rocky Mount, Va., 1981-84; Patrick County Satellite Clinic, Stuart, Va., 1981-84; psychiat. social worker St. Mary's Psychiat. Ctr., Norton, Va., 1984—; pvt. practice, 1981—; asst. prof. social gerontology Ferrum Coll. (Va.), 1982; instr. psychology Mountain Empire Community Coll., 1984—. Bd. dirs. planning dist. I, Community Mental Health and Mental Retardation Services Bd., 1979-81; mem. Wise County Health Services Adv. Bd., 1980-81; bd. dirs. Va. Council Social Welfare, 1984—, Wise County Youth Adv. Bd., 1984—. Mem. Nat. Assn. Social Workers, Am. Assn. Marriage and Family Therapists, Acad. Cert. Social Workers. Methodist. Home: 139 11th St NW Norton VA 24273 Office: 910 Virginia Ave Norton VA 24273

TAYLOR, LYNN, public relations executive, writer; b. Queens, N.Y., Apr. 3, 1957; d. Norman and Homa Bahary; m. Douglas Anthony Taylor, Dec. 16, 1979. B.A., NYU, 1978. Account exec. Burson-Marsteller, N.Y.C., 1978-81; account supr. corp. communications and mktg., 1981; dir. pub. relations So. Biotech, Inc., Tampa, Fla., 1981-82; pres. Taylor & Assocs., Inc., Tampa and Miami, 1982—. Mem. Pub. Relations Soc. Am. (accredited). Office: Lincoln Center 5401 W Kennedy Blvd Tampa FL 33609 and Concorde Center 2875 NE 191 St Suite 803 North Miami Beach FL 33180

TAYLOR, MARK WILLIAM, JR., occupational safety and health professional; b. Wilson, N.C., May 21, 1952; s. Mark William and Florence Lee (Hawkins) T.; m. Carolyn Duane Mathews, Aug. 7, 1971; children—Brian, Eric, Mark. Assoc. in Applied Sci., Wilson Tech. Inst., 1978. Supr. James I. Miller Tobacco Co., Wilson, 1970-72, safety dir., 1977-80; safety coordinator City of Durham, N.C., 1980—. Author and illustrator: (training manual) Public Utilities Safety Series, 1983; Affects of Noise and Vibration, 1984; (photographer) Safety for the New Employee, 1981. Designer traffic cone retrieval invention, 1982. Vol. safety cons. numerous local govts., N.C., 1980—, Occoneechee council Boy Scouts Am., 1983—, Durham Arts Council, 1983—, Durham Tech. Inst., 1983; Little League coach Whipporwill Athletic Assn., Durham. Served with USCG, 1972-77. Recipient award of Honor for City of Durham, Reliance Ins. Co., 1981. Mem. Am. Soc. Safety Engrs. (sec. 1985—), N.C. Assn. Local Govtl. Employee Safety Officials (pres. 1983-84), Mid-State Safety Council (bd. dirs. 1982—). Democrat. Avocations: designing and building furniture; golf; oil painting; comedy writing; public speaking. Office: City of Durham 101 City Hall Plaza Durham NC 27701

TAYLOR, MARY ROSE, former television anchor, reporter; b. Denver, May 26, 1945; d. Walter Gorringe and Marylynn (Eusterman) King; m. Charles Peete Rose, Aug. 10, 1968 (div.); m. 2d, Charles McKenzie Taylor, Feb. 26, 1983; stepchildren—Andrew McKenzie, Camille Williams. B.A. in Polit. Sci., U. N.C., 1967. Researcher, CBS-TV News, N.Y.C., 1968-71; assoc. producer BBC-TV Documentaries, N.Y.C., London, 1971-73; assigment editor Sta. WNEW-TV Metromedia, N.Y.C., 1973-74; documentary producer PBS, N.Y.C., Washington, 1974-76; producer, assigment editor Sta. WTOP-TV Post-Newsweek, Washington, 1976-77; anchor, reporter KTUL-TV News, Tulsa, 1978-79; anchor, reporter Gannett Broadcasting Sta. WXIA-TV, Atlanta, 1980-84; cons. producer documentary film Pumping Iron, N.Y.C., 1975-76; cons. producer Marshall McLuhan-the Man and his Message, N.Y.C., Toronto, 1982—. Bd. dirs. Atlanta Chamber Orch., 1981-83; trustee Robert W. Woodruff Arts Ctr. Recipient 1st place State UPI award, Ga., 1982. Mem. Am. Women in Radio TV, Nat. Acad. TV Arts & Scis., Sigma Delta Chi. Roman Catholic. Researcher: File on the Tsar, 1980-81; researcher on cities European Economic Community, German Marshall Fund, 1976.

TAYLOR, MELTON EUGENE, hospital administrator; b. Birmingham, Ala., Jan. 16, 1950; s. Raymond Eugene and Gloria (Stovall) T.; B.S., Samford U., 1971; M.B.A., Western Colo. U., 1982; m. Deborah G. Taylor, Feb. 24, 1984; children—Joshua Eugene, Amy Lynn. Dir. acctg. Jefferson Health Found., Inc., Birmingham, 1974-78; controller/chief fin. officer Bapt. Med. Center, Cherokee, Centre, Ala., 1978-79; dir. acctg. services Brookwood Med. Center, Birmingham, 1979; asst. adminstr. fin. Shelby Med. Center, Alabaster, Ala., 1979-84; assoc. adminstr. fin. Brookwood Med. Ctr., Birmingham, 1984—. Mem. Am. Coll. Hosp. Adminstrs., Am. Fin. Assn., Am. Hosp. Assn., Healthcare Fin. Mgmt. Assn. (advanced mem.), Soc. Hosp. Planning. Republican. Presbyterian. Home: 4720 Quarter Staff Rd Birmingham AL 35223 Office: Brookwood Med Center 2010 Medical Center Dr Birmingham AL 35209

TAYLOR, MILDRED LOIS, nursing home administrator; b. Conroe, Tex., July 23, 1927; d. George Carl and Bertha Elizabeth (Swift) Ferguson; student Hunter Coll., 1944, U.S. Navy Hosp. Corps Sch., Bethesda, Md., 1944, corr course Am. Sch., Chgo., 1971, Central Tex. Coll., 1971, U. Tex., Austin, 1975; m. Thomas Nielsen Taylor, Dec. 1, 1945; children—Linda Sue, Thomas Grant, Charles Nielsen. Nurse aide St. David's Hosp., Austin, Tex., 1965-67; adminstr.-in-tng. North Lamar Nursing Home, Austin, 1971-72, adminstr., 1973-75; adminstr. Austin Nursing & Convalescent Center, 1976—, sec., treas., 1976—. Pres. Episcopal Women of the Ch., Austin, 1966; mem. Tex. Nursing Home Adminstrs. Polit. Action Com., 1976—. Served with WAVE, USNR, 1944-45. Lic. nursing home adminstr., Tex. Mem. Tex. Nursing Home Assn., Am. Health Care Assn., Austin C. of C., U.S. C. of C. Clubs: Lost Creek Country, Order Eastern Star, St. David's Hosp. Women's Aux. (Austin). Home: 1909 Glencliff Dr Austin TX 78704 Office: 110 E Live Oak Austin TX 78704

TAYLOR, NOEL C., clergyman, mayor; b. Bedford County, Va., July 15, 1924; s. Noel and Hettie Lee (Murphy) T.; B.S. with honors, Bluefield State Coll., 1949; B.D., Va. Sem. and Coll., 1955, D.D., 1959; M.A. in Religious Edn., N.Y. U., 1963; m. Barbara Jean Smith, July 16, 1955; children—Sabrina Leochia, Deseree Charletta. Tchr., Bedford County Public Sch., 1949, elem. sch. prin., 1950-52; ordained to ministry Baptist Ch.; pastor 3 chs., 1954, First Bapt. Ch., Clifton Fordge, Va., 1955-58, First Bapt. Ch. (Berkley), Norfolk, Va., 1958-61, now High St. Bapt. Ch., Roanoke, Va.; mem. Roanoke City Council, 1970—, vice-mayor, 1974-75, mayor, 1975—; dir. First Nat. Exchange Bank Va. Bd. dirs. local ARC, Blue Cross and Blue Shield Southwestern Va., Bapt. Children's Home, Blue Ridge Mountains council Boy Scouts Am.; pres. Opportunities Industrialization Center of Roanoke Valley; mem. Roanoke City Library Bd., Adv. Bd. Public Welfare, Jud. Selection Commn. Western Dist. Va.; bd. mgrs. Va. Sem., Hunton YMCA; mem. adv. bd. Central YWCA; mem. Va. Coal Research and Devel. Adv. Com.; mem. exec. com. Va. Mcpl. League, also chmn. transp. policy com., mem. task force on property tax; mem. Local Govt. Adv. Council, 1977—, also mem. com. adminstrn. and fin. Served in U.S. Army, 1943-46. Named Man of Yr. (twice), Omega Phi Psi; recipient cert. of merit Nat. Phi Delta Kappa; cert. of appreciation Roanoke Jaycees; Brotherhood award NCCJ; Tri-Ominis Celebrity award; Man of Yr. award Nat. Masons; Community Service award Delta Sigma Theta. Mem. Va. Bapt. State Conv. (pres.), Roanoke Ministers Conf. (pres.), Valley Bapt. Assn. (moderator), Am. Bapt. Conv., Nat. Bapt. Conv., Lott Carey Bapt. Fgn. Missions Conv., Bapt. Ministers Conf. Roanoke, U.S. Conf. Mayors, NAACP, Nat. Conf. Black Mayors, Nat. League Cities, Alpha Phi Alpha. Clubs: Masons (33 deg.; mem. united supreme council), Kiwanis. Office: 215 Church Ave SE Roanoke VA 24011

TAYLOR, NORMAN EUGENE, public relations firm executive; b. Newark, Nov. 12, 1948; s. Edwin Alfred and Martha Raye (Small) T.; children—Assaf, Amman, Joy; m. 2d, Theresa LaVerne Singleton, Apr. 26, 1980; children—Todd, Autier. B.A., Bethune-Cookman Coll., 1970; M.Pub. Adminstrn., Fla. Altantic U., 1976. Exec. dir. October Center, Inc., Ft. Lauderdale, Fla., 1974-80; host Taylor & Co., Sta. WRBD/WCKO, Ft. Lauderdale, 1975-81, Sta. WMBM, Miami, Fla., 1981-82; v.p. Systems Mgmt. Assocs., Inc., Miami, 1978-81; pres. Norman E. Taylor & Assocs., Inc., Miami, 1979—; editor Enhance Mag., Ft. Lauderdale, 1982—; dir., assoc. pub. Communications Four, Inc., Ft. Lauderdale, 1982—. Mem. Fla. Black Republican Council, 1982—. Served with U.S. Army, 1971-73. Recipient Broward County Human Relations award for broadcasting, 1978; NAACP City award, 1979, County award, 1980. Mem. Am. Soc. Pub. Adminstrn., Pub. Relations Soc. Am., Broward Industry Council, NAACP, Miami-Dade C. of C. (pub. relations com. 1981-82), Omega Psi Phi. Office: 4050 SW 14th Ave Fort Lauderdale FL 33315

TAYLOR, ORVILLE WALTERS, historian, educator; b. El Dorado, Ark., Sept. 20, 1917; s. William Oscar and Minnie Belle (White) T.; A.B., Ouachita Bapt. U., 1947; M.A., U. Ky., 1948; Ph.D., Duke U., 1956; m. Evelyn Adelle Bonham, Dec. 5, 1942; children—Michael, Priscilla Taylor Norvell, Melissa, Penelope Taylor-Pullen. Instr. history Little Rock Jr. Coll., 1950-55; prof. history Bapt. Coll., Iwo, Nigeria, 1955-62, U. N.C., Asheville, 1963-65; prof., chmn. dept. Wesleyan Coll., Macon, Ga., 1965-69; prof., chmn. dept. Ga. Coll., Milledgeville, 1969-84, prof. emeritus, 1984—; vis. or adj. prof. East Tex. State U., U. Ark., Coll. of William and Mary, Duke U., U. Ga., Ind. State U.; exec. sec., state historian Ark. History Commn., 1959; cons. Ministry of Edn., Nigeria, 1956-62; cons. Nat. Endowment for Humanities, 1972-79. Justice of peace, Pulaski County, Ark., 1952-55; chief fed. electoral officer Iwo Dist., Nigeria, 1957; bd. dirs. Ark. Ednl. TV Assn., 1953-55; mem. nat. adv. com. Civil War Centennial Commn., 1959; Am. del. 14th Internat. Congress of Hist. Scis., 1975. Served to capt. U.S. Army, 1941-46; lt. col. USAF (ret.), 1977—. Am. Philos. Soc. grantee, 1968-69; Shell Found. grantee, 1966, 67, 68; NEH grantee, 1969, 72. Mem. AAUP, Royal African Soc. (life), Am., So., Ark. (sec.-treas. 1954-55, Shader Meml. prize 1958) hist. assns., Ga. Assn. Historians (pres. 1973-74), Ga. Polit. Sci. Assn. (pres. 1970-71, Disting. Service award 1978), Assn. for Study Afro-Am. Life and History, Phi Beta Kappa, Phi Kappa Phi. Democrat. Baptist. Author: Negro Slavery in Arkansas, 1958; contbr.: A History of Baptists in Arkansas, 1979; Religion in the Southern States, 1983; Persistance of the Spirit, 1986; contbr. articles and revs. to profl. jours. and encys. Home: 800 Lantana Ave Clearwater Beach FL 33515

TAYLOR, PRISCILLA HUNT, mental health counselor, nurse; b. Greenville, S.C., July 5, 1936; d. Joseph Wilson and Ruth Mozelle (Brown) Hunt; Asso. in Nursing, Bapt. Coll. Charleston, 1973, B.S., 1973; M.S. in Nursing, Med. Coll. Ga., 1976; M.S.Ed., So. Ill. U., Edwardsville, 1976; Ph.D., U. S.C., 1983; m. William Haynie Taylor, Jr., Oct. 7, 1955; children—Billy, Cindy, Mandy. Nursing instr. Bapt. Coll., Charleston, 1973-76, nursing instr., 1973-74; asst. prof. Med. U. S.C., Charleston, 1976-81; career counselor U. S.C., 1981-82; breavement coordinator Hospice of Charleston, 1983—; instr. psychology Trident Tech. Coll., 1977; vol. counseling Dorchester Mental Health Clinic; mental health counselor and cons. to individuals and orgns. Public mem. Palmetto Low Country Health Systems Agy., 1976—. NIH trainee, 1974-76; cert. counselor. Mem. Am., S.C. nurses assns., Am. Assn. Counseling and Devel., S.C. Personnel and Guidance Assn., Sigma Theta Tau. Baptist. Home: 104 Race Club Rd Summerville SC 29483 Office: 171 Ashley Ave Charleston SC 29403

TAYLOR, R. LEE, II, food products company executive; b. Memphis, 1941; married. B.S., Princeton U., 1964. With The Fedral Co., Memphis, 1966—, v.p., 1967-78, exec. v.p., 1978-80, pres. v.p., 1980—, chief exec. officer, 1981—, dir. Office: The Federal Co Inc 1755-D Lynnfield Rd Box 17236 Memphis TN 38117*

TAYLOR, RICK DALE, restaurant owner; b. El Reno, Okla., July 24, 1954; s. Delbert Kirk and Elsie Louise (Caves) T. B.B.A., U. Okla., 1976. Mgmt. trainee McDonalds Corp., Oklahoma City, 1977-78, supr., ops. mgr. restaurant franchise group, 1978-81; franchisee, owner, Burger King-R.J.T. Enterprises, Inc., Jasper, Huntsville and Livingston, Tex., 1982—; food concessionnaire Rayburn Country Club, Lake Sam Rayburn, Tex., 1983—, George Jones Music Park, North Tyler County, Tex., 1984—. Mem. First Christian Ch. Club: Lions. Home: 14 Broadmoor St Sam Rayburn TX 75951 Office: Rayburn Hall PO Box 140 Sam Rayburn TX 75951

TAYLOR, ROBERT BRAY, orthodontist; b. Middletown, Ohio, June 30, 1944; s. Clarence Hufford and Verna Bernice (Bray) T.; m. Judith Ann Klein, July 4, 1970; children—Kristina Ruth, Robert Bray Jr. B.A., Miami U., Oxford, Ohio, 1966; D.D.S., cum laude, Ohio State U., 1970; M.S. in Orthodontics, U. N.C., 1974. Pvt. practice orthodontics, Asheville, N.C., 1974—. Mem. ch. council St. Mark's Lutheran Ch., Asheville, 1976-79, 84—. Served as lt. Dental Corps, USN, 1970-72. Mem. Buncombe County Dental Soc. (pres. 1982-83), N.C. Dental Soc., N.C. Orthodontic Soc., ADA, Am. Assn. Orthodontists. Republican. Avocations: family vacations; trumpet; raquetball; golf; swimming. Home: 65 Brookwood Rd Asheville NC 28804 Office: 131 McDowell St Asheville NC 28801

TAYLOR, ROBERT L., judge; b. Embreeville, Tenn., Dec. 20, 1899; s. Alfred Alexander and Florence Jane (Anderson) T.; Ph.B., Milligan Coll., 1921; student Vanderbilt Law Sch., 1922-23; LL.B., Yale, 1924; m. Florence Fairfax McCain, May 27, 1933; children—Ann, Robert. Admitted to Tenn. bar, 1923; practice law, Johnson City, 1924-49; U.S. judge Eastern Dist. Tenn., 1949—. Trustee Milligan Coll. Mem. ABA, Fed. Bar Assn., Tenn. Bar Assn., Jud. Conf. U.S., Am. Judicature Soc., Sigma Alpha Epsilon, Phi Delta Phi, Corby Court. Mem. Christian Ch. Home: 3567 Talahi Dr Knoxville TN 37919 Office: Federal Bldg PO Box 2068 Knoxville TN 37901

TAYLOR, ROBERT WAYNE, criminal justice educator, consultant; b. Helena, Mont., Nov. 10, 1951; s. Harvey Walter and Rosemary (Muffuletto) T.; m. Sherri Ann Moore, Nov. 25, 1972; children—Matthew Walter, Scott Michael, Laura Marie. B.S. in Adminstrn. Justice, Portland State U., 1973, Ph.D. in Urban Studies, 1981; M.S. in Criminal Justice Adminstrn., Mich. State U., 1974. Grad. teaching asst. Sch. Criminal Justice, Mich. State U., East Lansing, 1973-74; police officer Portland Police Bur. (Oreg.), 1974-78, detective, 1978-80; instr. Adminstrn. of Justice Dept. Portland State U., 1976-77; instr. dept. sociology Ark. State U., Jonesboro, 1981; asst. prof. dept. criminal justice U. South Fla., Tampa, 1981—, research fellow Internat. Ctr. Study of Violence, Human Resources Inst., 1982—; cons. and lectr. in field. Mem. Acad. Criminal Justice Scis., Am. Soc. Pub. Adminstrn., Amnesty Internat., Alpha Phi Sigma. Roman Catholic. Contbr. numerous articles to profl. jours.

TAYLOR, ROGER NORRIS, immunologist; b. Farmington, Utah, Oct. 23, 1941; s. Norris John and Josephine (Hardy) T.; m. Sydney Moulton, Apr. 1, 1965; children—Michael, Stephen, Reuben, Melissa, Marcus, Benjamin, Lettita. Student, Oceanside-Carlsbad Jr. Coll., 1960-62, Brigham Young U., 1964-65, Weber State Coll., 1965-67, Japan, 1962-63, U. Md., Zama, B.S., U. Utah, 1969, M.S., 1971, Ph.D., 1974. Clin., research microbiologist VA Hosp., Salt Lake City, 1969-72; teaching assoc. U. Utah Coll. Medicine, Salt Lake City, 1970-74; microbiologist-lab. improvement Utah State Div. Health, 1972-74; chief diagnostic immunology Ctrs. for Disease Control, Atlanta, 1975—; clin. lab. dir. Am. Bd. Bioanalysis, 1976—; mem. subcom. for standardization of rheumatoid factor tests Nat. Com. for Clin. Lab. Standards, 1977—, subcom. for standardization of tests for carcinoembryonic antigen, 1981—. Substitute sem. tchr. of Jesus Christ of Latter-day Saints, 1975—, elders quorum presidency, 1971-73, 76-78, deacons quorum advisor, 1979-82, stake primary scouting dir., 1980-82, primary sch., Sunday sch. tchr., 1982-83; scouting coordinator Boy Scouts Am., 1978-83, explorer adviser, 1978-79, dist. scout com. mem. 1978—, scoutmaster, 1979-82, dist. scout tng. com., dist. tng. staff, 1981-83, asst. scoutmaster, 1982-83, dist. tng. chmn., 1983—, mem. Atlanta Area Council tng. com., 1983—, recipient Order of Arrow, Scouters Tng. award, woodbadge, On My Honor Religious Scouting award, 1981, Dist. Merit award, 1982. Served with USMC, 1960-63. Mem. Am. Soc. for Microbiology, Am. Acad. Microbiology, Am. Assn. Immunologists, Internat. Soc. Immunology Labs. (nat. adv. com. 1982—), N.Y. Acad. Sci., Sigma Xi. Contbr. numerous articles in field to profl. jours. Home: 308 Westwind Dr Lilburn GA 30247 Office: Dept Diagnostic Immunology Centers for Disease Control 1600 Clifton Rd Atlanta GA 30333

TAYLOR, RUTH ELINOR HOSTETTER, logistics management specialist; b. Portland, Maine, June 12, 1929; d. Paul Eugene Hostetter and Ethel Emily (Butler) Alden; m. David E. Taylor, Apr. 9, 1949 (div. June 1978); children—Anna Christine Slifkin, Laura Jean Myers, Steven Albert. B.S. in Bus. Mgmt., Evans-Carolina Coll., Charlotte, N.C., 1949; postgrad. N.C. State U., 1958; spl. courses U.S. Army. Program analyst U.S. Army, Ft. Bragg, N.C., 1968-78, Ft. Sheridan, Ill., 1979-79, chief mgmt. div., 1979-80, chief supply and services div., 1980-81, asst. chief of logistics, 1981-84, logistics mgmt. specialist, Ft. Lee, Va., 1984—. Author: Symbolism, 1983. Leader Girl Scouts U.S.A., 1963-77; pres. woman's guild Lutheran Ch., Fayetteville, 1970, mem. council, 1972-73. Recipient Teamwork award U.S. Army, 1980, Civilian of Yr. nomination, 1981, Exceptional Performance awards, 1978-83, 85. Mem. Nat. Assn. Female Execs., Art Inst. Chgo., Art Council Waukegan, LWV, Assn. U.S. Army, Luth. Ch. Women. Democrat. Club: Waukegan Newcomers. Lodge: Eastern Star (worthy matron 1977, 83, personal page to grand officer 1983). Home: 16101 Tri-Gate Rd Chester VA 23831 Office: US Army Logistics Ctr Concepts and Doctrine Fort Lee VA 23801

TAYLOR, RUTHFORD T., mechanical engineer; b. Leesburg, Fla., Jan. 14, 1933; s. Berle W. and Martha A. Taylor; A.A., Northeastern Okla. A&M Coll., 1952; B.S., Okla. State U., 1961; m. Frances L. Erion, May 20, 1953; children—Beverly, Brenda, Barbara, Beth, Paul. With Employers Casualty Ins. Co., Amarillo, Tex., 1961-63; with Mason & Hanger-Silas Mason Co., Amarillo, 1963—, various engring. positions, 1963-71, sr. project engr., supervisory head work analysis and control sect., 1971-74, sr. project engr., supervisory head estimating sect. plant design dept., 1974-75, sr. project engr., supr. head maintenance and modification sect. plant design dept., sect. engr., 1975-81, supr. head crafts maintenance sect. mech. dept. sect. engring., 1982-83, dept. supr. property mgmt. and gen. stores, 1983—. Mem. Amarillo Retarded Citizens Bd., 1981-82. Served with U.S. Army, 1951-57. Registered profl. engr., Tex. Mem. Nat. Property Mgmt. Assn., Full Gospel Bus. Men's Fellowship Internat. (v.p. Amarillo chpt. 1978-82). Presbyterian. Home: 3413 Lipscomb St Amarillo TX 79109 Office: PO Box 30020 Amarillo TX 79177

TAYLOR, SAMUEL WAYNE, judge; b. Mobile, Ala., Aug. 8, 1935; s. George Samuel and Oclis (Waldrip) T.; m. Emily Allen Thrasher, June 3, 1960; children—Samuel Wayne, George Samuel II, Emily Allen Thrasher. B.S. in Bus. Adminstrn., U. Ala., 1956, J.D., 1958; LL.M., NYU, 1959. Bar: Ala. 1958. Sole practice, Montgomery, Ala., 1965-75; judge Montgomery County Ct., Montgomery, 1975-77, Dist. Ct., Montgomery, 1977, Cir. Ct., Montgomery, 1977-83, Ct. of Criminal Appeals, State of Ala., Montgomery, 1983—; instr. Jones Law Inst., Montgomery, 1965-73. Mem. Ala. Ho. of Reps., 1971-75. Served to capt. U.S. Army, 1962-64. Mem. ABA (jud. administr. div. and criminal law sect.), Ala. State Bar, Montgomery Bar Assn., Dist. Judges Assn. (pres. Ala. 1977), Pi Kappa Alpha, Phi Alpha Delta. Democrat. Methodist. Club: Lions (dir. 1983-85) (Montgomery). Lodges: Masons, Shriners. Home: 2429 Woodley Rd Montgomery AL 36111 Office: Court of Criminal Appeals State of Ala PO Box 351 Montgomery AL 36101

TAYLOR, SHAHANE RICHARDSON, JR., ophthalmologist; b. Greensboro, N.C., Sept. 5, 1928; s. Shahane Richardson and Mary Hoke (Hooker) T.; A.B., U. N.C., 1955, M.D., 1959; m. Betty Jane Teague, Aug. 2, 1952; children—Shahane R. III, Anne Teague, Mary Hooker. Intern, N.C. Meml. Hosp., Chapel Hill, 1959-60; resident in ophthalmology U. N.C.-McPherson Meml. Hosp., 1960-63; practice medicine specializing in ophthal. surgery, Greensboro, N.C., 1963—; chief ophthalmology Wesley Long Hosp.; attending staff Moses Cone; staff Humana Hosp. (all Greensboro); cons. in ophthalmology N.C. State Employees Health Plan, Prudential Medicare, Title 19 program, Pilot Life Ins. Co.; vis. instr. opthal. surgery U. N.C., Chapel Hill, 1964-73; pres. North Central Peer Rev. Found. Mem. N.C. State Health Care Council, 1981. Served to capt., M.I., U.S. Army, 1951-54. Diplomate Am. Bd. Ophthalmology. Mem. AMA, So. Med. Assn., N.C. Med. Soc. (exec. council 1979—), Med. Assn. U. N.C. (pres. 1981), Guilford County Med. Soc. (pres. 1977), Am. Acad. Ophthalmology and Otolaryngology, N.Y. Acad. Scis., Pan Am. Ophthal. Soc., Soc. Eye Surgeons, Mensa, Quarter Century Wireless Assn., Intertel. Episcopalian. Clubs: Greensboro Whist, Greensboro Country, Greensboro City (dir.). Home: 2207 Carlisle Rd Greensboro NC 27408 Office: 348 N Elm St Greensboro NC 27401

TAYLOR, SHEILA ANNETTE, actress educator; b. Dayton, Ohio, Sept. 2, 1938; d. Earl Julian and Martha Annette (Ruhl) T.; m. Morley Schang, Sept. 15, 1956 (dec. Feb. 1966); 1 son, Kyle Gregory Taylor. Student in voice Theodore Heiman, Munich, W.Ger.; student acting Sorbonne, U. Paris, Royal Acad., London; student in drama Claudia Frank, N.Y.C., Actor's Studio, N.Y.C., Maria Gambrielli Theatre, student in music, speech and drama Bowling Green State U.; B.Edn. in Drama and Speech, U. Miami, 1959, M.Ed. in Drama, 1975; also dance and music lessons. Tchr. vocat. English, Manpower Devel. Programs, 1964-68; tchr. English for fgn.-born, various schs., 1965-67; tchr. drama and English, Parkway Jr. High Sch., Dade County Sch. System (Fla.), 1968-70, Booker T. Washington Jr. High Sch., 1970-74, tchr. drama Miami High Sch., summer 1974, tchr. drama and speech Miami Central Sr. High Sch., 1974-75, Miami Killian Sr. High Sch., 1975-82; drama dir. Performing and Visual Arts Ctr., Miami-Dade Community Coll., South Campus, 1982—; actress Broadway shows: Diary of Anne Frank (understudy); Damn Yankees; Dark of the Moon; Liliom; off-broadway: Arms and the Man; Another Part of the Forest; various dramatic and comml. TV appearances; also road shows, summer stock and repertory theatre appearances; mem. Taylor and Root saagio ballroom team; numerous appearances in U.S. Europe; condr. workshops in field, 1980-81. Developer ednl. programs. Mem. Secondary Sch. Theatre Assn. (Fla. rep.), Southeastern Theatre Conf. (vice-chairperson secondary div. 1982-84, chairperson div., Am. Theatre Assn., Phi Kappa Phi, Epsilon Tau Lambda, Alpha Delta Pi, Theta Alpha Phi. Republican. Episcopalian. Home: 2570 NE 201 St North Miami Beach FL 33100 Office: Miami-Dade Community Coll-South Performing and Visual Arts Ctr 11011 SW 104 St Miami FL 33180

TAYLOR, STEPHEN LOUIS, hospital administrator; b. Evansville, Ind., July 26, 1946; s. Fenton F. and Martha N. (Scherer) T.; m. Ruth Ann Barr, May 7, 1971; children—Stephanie, Melissa, Michelle, Lauren, Christian. B.A., U. Evansville, 1968; M.B.A., Indiana U., 1971. Administr., Suburban Hosp., Satsuma, Ala., 1971, Meml. Hosp., Center, Tex., 1972-74, Bristol Hosp., Dallas, 1974-76, Nautilus Hosp., Waverly, Tenn., 1976-81; exec. dir. Humana Hosp., Morristown, Tenn., 1981—. Bd. dirs. Hamblen County United Way, Morristown, 1982—, Hamblen County Central Services, Morristown, 1985, KC Home, Morristown, 1985. Mem. Am. Coll. Hosp. Administrs. Roman Catholic. Lodges: Rotary, KC. Home: 1845 Seven Oaks Dr Morristown TN 37814

TAYLOR, THOMAS CHARLTON, radio consulting engineer, flight instructor; b. Flint, Mich., Mar. 24, 1952; s. Howard C. and Lois L. (Horton) T.; m. Jo Ann Smith, Sept. 18, 1981; 1 child, Christine Taylor. Student Ohio State U., 1981—, flight instr. refresher AOPA Air Safety Found., Indpls., 1983, 85; B.Div. (hon.) Christian Congregation, LaFollette, Tenn., 1974, D.Div., 1975. Chief engr. Sta. WTTO-AM, Toledo, 1971-73, Sta. WLQR-FM, Toledo, 1973-78; pres. Taylor Broadcast Cons., Toledo, 1978-80; service mgr. Sound Systems, Inc., Tiffin, Ohio, 1980-81; dir. engring. Sta. WIMA/WIMT-FM, Lima, Ohio, 1981-85; prin. Eagle Enterprises, Inc., Old Fort, N.C., 1985—; frequency coordinator N.C. Broadcasting Services; flight instr. Two Wings and a Prop, Inc., Old Fort, 1985—. Ordained minister Christian Congregation, LaFollette, 1975. Author reports in field; cons. 1st solar powered radio sta. WBNO, Bryah, Ohio, 1979. Notary public State of N.C., 1985; trustee Cable Road Alliance Ch., Lima, 1983-84; mem. Greenlee Bapt. Ch., Old Fort, N.C., 1985, dir. outreach and evangelism, 1985. Recipient Disting. Work citation FCC, 1978. Mem. Soc. Broadcast Engrs. (cert., frequency coordinator Old Fort, N.C. 1985), Nat. Assn. Radio & Telecommunications Engr. (1st class 1985), Nat. Assn. Ednl. and Bus. Radio (cert.), Internat. Soc. Cert. Electronics Technician (cert.), Nat. Pilots Assn. (advanced 1978). Republican. Baptist. Club: Lima Pilots, Inc. (sec. 1984-85). Avocations: boating; flying; fishing; photography. Office: Eagle Enterprises Inc PO Box 1527 Old Fort NC 28762

TAYLOR, THOMAS HUDSON, JR., import co. exec.; b. Somerville, Mass., June 8, 1920; s. Thomas Hudson and Virginia Gwendolyn (Wilson) T.; B.S. in Econs., Wharton Sch. Fin. and Commerce, U. Pa., 1947; m. Mary Jane Potter, Dec. 1, 1943; children—Thomas Hudson, III, James R., Jane, John E., Virginia. Acctg. exec. Collins & Aikman Corp., Phila., 1947-55, divisional controller automotive div., Albemarle, N.C., 1956-59, asst. dir. purchases, 1960-64; exec. v.p. Carolina Floral Imports, Inc., Gastonia, N.C., 1965-67, pres., treas., 1968—. County commr. Stanly County, Albemarle, N.C., 1962-66. Served to capt. USAAF, 1941-45. Decorated Air medal. Mem. Beta Theta Pi. Republican. Methodist. Clubs: City of Gastonia; Princeton. Home: 4537 Forest Cove Rd Belmont NC 28012 Office: Box 2201 Gastonia NC 28054

TAYLOR, WILLIAM AL, church administrator; b. Danville, Va., Sept. 26, 1938; s. P.F. and Helen Elizabeth (Doss) T.; m. Brenda F. Owen, June 4, 1961; children—Fawnia Rae, Albert Todd, Athena Dawn. A.A., Lee Coll., 1957; student Ann. and Deferred Gifts Inst., 1977, Inst. Advanced Studies in Personal Fin. Planning, 1980; Br. mgr. Ency. Brit., Greensboro, N.C., 1960-62, div. trainer, Mpls., 1963, dist. mgr., Omaha, 1964-72; adminstrv. asst. Forward in Faith Internat. Broadcast, Cleveland, Tenn., 1972-80; gen. mgr. Sta. WQNE, Cleveland, 1980; dir. stewardship Ch. of God Gen. Offices, Cleveland, 1980—; chmn. NAE Stewardship Com., 1985—. Pres., Clean Water Soc., Gastonia, N.C., 1974-75, Pathway Credit Union, 1983—; exec. dir. Vision Found., 1979-80, pres., 1985—; speaker Citizens Against Legalized Liquor, 1973, cons., 1975; adv. Mothers on March, 1976; mem. Com. for Nat. Conf. on Drug Abuse, 1978; master ceremonies Nat. Religious Leaders Conf. on Alcohol & Drug Abuse, 1979. Recipient named master of sales award Ency. Britannica, 1960, top dist. mgr. award, 1967, Million Dollar Dist. award, 1968; Mass Communications award Forward in Faith, 1980. Mem. Nat. Religious Broadcasters. Contbr. articles to profl. jours. Home: 915 Robin Hood Dr Cleveland TN 37311 Office: Keith at 25th St Cleveland TN 37311

TAYLOR, WILLIAM BARRETT, III, international marketing executive, lawyer; b. Winston-Salem, N.C., July 7, 1919; s. William Barrett, II, and Frances Dinsdale (Swann) T.; A.B., U. Tenn., 1941; J.D., U. Fla., 1950; postgrad. Oxford U., 1943, George Washington U., 1948, U. Denver, 1957, U. Md., 1958; m. Gwendoline Madge Abbott, May 1, 1945; children—Sally Hill (Mrs. Christopher Brunton), William Barrett IV, Richard A., Michael A. Bar: Fla. 1950, U.S. Supreme Ct. 1953. Commd. 2d lt. U.S. Air Force, 1941, advanced through grades to col., 1954; with 8th AF, 1942-45; with Office of Legislative Liaison, Office Sec. of Air Force, 1950-54; asst. chief of staff, chief staff USAF Acad., 1955-58; with Joint U.S. Mil. Group, Spain, 1958-62; with Office of Asst. Sec. of Def., 1962-64; ret., 1964; internat. liaison McDonnell Douglas Corp., Washington, 1964-75; dir. internat. devel. Lykes Youngstown Corp., 1975-77; pres. Wm. B. Taylor Assos., 1978-79, Arthur Andersen & Co., 1979—; commr. South Pacific Commn., Noumea, New Caledonia, 1969, sr. commr., 1970-74, with rank of dep. asst. sec. of state; v.p. Taylor Bros., Inc., Winston-Salem, 1947-50. Mem. Trans Atlantic council Boy Scouts Am., 1960-62; nat. v.p., bd. dirs. Nat. Alliance Sr. Citizens; chmn. srs. div. Reagan-Bush campaign Republican party, 1984. Mem. Am., Inter-Am., Fla. bar assns., Air Force Assn., Navy League, Am. Def. Preparedness Assn., Assn. U.S. Army, Armor Assn., Middle East Inst., Iran Am. Soc. Author: Pictorial History 14th Combat Bomb Wing, 1946. Home: 3209 N Columbus St Arlington VA 22207 also 983 Narcissus Ave Clearwater FL 33515 Office: Suite 404 2201 Wilson Blvd Arlington VA 22201

TAZEWELL, CALVERT WALKE (PSEUDONYM WILLIAM STONE DAWSON), ret. air force officer, author, historian; b. Wilmington, Del., Apr. 13, 1917; s. Calvert W. and Sophie (Goode) T.; student Air Corps Tech. Sch., 1940, Air Tactical Sch., 1948, Sophia U., Tokyo, 1951, Air Command and Staff Sch., USAF Air. U., 1952, Ind. U., 1956; m. Beverly Mae LaCour, Jan. 14, 1943 (div. Apr. 1959); children—Lyn Diane, Patricia Marie, Beverly Ann; m. 2d, Belle Gordon, July 7, 1959 (div.); 1 son, William Bradford; m. 3d, Theresa Hoey, Feb. 20, 1976; adopted children—Valera Marie and Sabrina Lienemann Tazewell; 7 stepchildren. Pvt., Va. NG, 1934-35; radio technician, San Antonio, 1936-37; pvt., USAC, 1937, m/sgt. weather observer and forecaster, 1941; commd. 2d lt. USAAF (by direct appointment while overseas), 1942, advanced through grades to lt. col.; comml. multi-engine pilot; communications specialist on USAF meteorol. flight, flew over North Pole, 1947; during World War II developed and supervised for USAAF pioneer worldwide weather communications system, which principles and techniques accepted by World Meteorol. Orgn. and Internat. Civil Aviation Orgn.; apptd. officer Regular Army, 1947; transferred to USAF, 1948; comdr. 1951st AAGS Squadron, Nagoya, Japan, 1950-51; dep. dir. plans and requirements Hdqrs. 1808th AACS Wing, Tokyo, 1951-52; comdr. 1300th Student Squadron, Great Falls, Mont., 1953-54, 818th AC & W Squadron, Randolph, Tex., 1955-56, Kangnung Air Base, Korea, 1957, Takaoyama Air. Sta., Japan, 1958; dir. communications-electronics 314th Air div. Osan, Korea, 1956-57. Duluth Air Def. Sector, 1958-59; ret., 1959; civil def. coordinator Dade County, Fla., 1961; organizer chmn. Met. Dade County Public Library Adv. Bd., 1963-64; instr. N.Y. U., 1962-63, Old Dominion U., 1964-65, 77; microcomputer mktg. and systems specialist, 1977-82. Trustee, Assn. Preservation Va. Antiquities, 1967-69; bd. dirs. Boush-Tazewell-Waller House, Norfolk, 1982-83. Recipient awards Writers Digest, 1974, 75, Nat. Writers Club, 1976. Decorated Bronze Star. Mem. Norfolk Hist. Soc. (1st pres., founder 1965), Va. History Fedn. (1st pres., founder 1967). Amateur radio sta. operator, 1934—; amateur nutritionist, computerist. Contbr. articles on nutrition, electronics and history to periodicals in U.S., Gt. Britain. Address: 3517 Sandy Point Key Virginia Beach VA 23452

TEAGUE, PAMELA ANN, building consultant, residential designer; b. Birmingham, Ala., Aug. 14, 1952; d. Sam Gerald and Laura Kate (Anderson) Cobb; m. Durall Robert Teague, Mar. 13, 1976; 1 child, Laura Kathryn. A.S., Gadsden State Jr. Coll., 1974; B.A., Upper Iowa U., 1982; postgrad. archtl. design Marshall Tech. Sch., Ala., 1983. Inventory specialist H.D. Lee Co., Guntersville, Ala., 1971; purchasing asst., inventory control specialist Monsanto Textiles, Guntersville, 1972-76; adminstrv. asst. Wright Industries, Nashville, 1976-77; owner, mgr. Sunbrite Cleaners, Albertville, Ala., 1978-84; bldg. cons., residential designer, Albertville, 1984—. Active U.S. Savs. Bond Drive, United Givers Fund Drive, Guntersville, 1972-76; mem. membership drive com. United Way Albertville, 1982. Mem. Albertville C. of C. (membership drive com. 1980-83), Omega Chi Delta (fin. com. 1982-84). Republican. Baptist. Avocations: drafting; boating. Home: 810 Christopher Circle Albertville AL 35950

TEAGUE, PEYTON CLARK, chemist, emeritus educator; b. Montgomery, Ala., June 26, 1915; s. Robert S. and Sara McGehee (Clark) T.; ed. Huntingdon Coll., 1932-34; B.S., Auburn U., 1936; M.S., Pa. State U., 1937; Ph.D., U. Tex., 1942; m. Patricia Cussons Lamb, June 12, 1937; 1 dau., Norah Teague Grimball. Research chemist Am. Agrl. Chem. Co., Newark, 1937-39; instr. dept. chemistry Auburn (Ala.) U., 1941-42, asst. prof., 1943-45; research chemist U.S. Naval Research Lab., Washington, 1942-45; asst. prof. U. Ga., Athens, 1945-48, U. Ky., Lexington, 1948-50; assoc. prof. dept. chemistry U. S.C., Columbia, 1950-56, prof., 1956-82, assoc. dean Grad. Sch., 1966-68, chmn. grad. council, 1980-81, deptl. dir. grad. studies, 1971-82, disting. prof. emeritus, 1982—; vis. prof. U. Coll., Dublin, Ireland, 1963-64, 77; dir. Teague Hardware Co., Montgomery, Ala., 1955-74. Vestryman, Trinity Episcopal Cathedral, 1968-71, lay reader, 1963—; bd. dirs. S.C. chpt. Arthritis Found., 1983—; bd. govs. Columbiatown Theatre, 1985—. Recipient Outstanding Tchr. award U. S.C., 1976. Mem. Am. Chem. Soc. (chmn. S.C. sect. 1958-59), Phytochem. Soc. N. Am. (pres. 1969-70), S.C. Acad. Sci., Sigma Xi (pres. U. S.C. chpt. 1962-63), Phi Kappa Phi, Phi Lambda Upsilon, Blue Key, Phi Delta Theta. Clubs: Kiwanis, Forest Lake Country. Contbr. articles to sci. jours. Home: 1550 Adger Rd Columbia SC 29205 Office: Dept Chemistry U SC Columbia SC 29208

TEAL, GILBERT EARLE, industrial engineer; b. Balt., July 22, 1912; s. Cecil Armstrong and Margaret (Trimble) T.; B.S. in Civil Engring., U. Md., 1937; postgrad. George Washington U., 1946; M.A., N.Y. U., 1947, M. Adminstrv. Engring., 1947, D.Sc. in Engring., 1952, Ph.D., 1956; m. Evangeline Maxine Piper, Apr. 4, 1947; children—Saundra Gail, Sue Anne, Gilbert Earle. Commd. 1st lt. U.S. Army, 1941, advanced through grades to lt. col, 1947; engr. Travelers Ins. Co., Washington and N.Y.C., 1937-39; indsl. relations engr. U.S. Rubber Co., Naugatuck, Conn., 1939-41; commd. lt. col. U.S. Air Force, 1947, advanced through grades to col., 1960, ret., 1960; chief scientist, v.p. Dunlap & Assos., Darien, Conn., 1960-70; ret., 1970; dean coll. Western Conn. State U., Danbury, 1970-75, v.p. acad. affairs, 1975-76, v.p. emeritus, 1976—; pres. Public Service Research Inst., Stamford, Conn., 1961-63, Mil. Personnel Assos., Washington, 1968-71; instr., prof. aerospace sci. Purdue U., Lafayette, Ind., 1958-60; instr. U. Md., Germany and France, 1952-55, vis. lectr., 1974-75; research asso. prof. edn. N.Y. U., 1968-70, instr. Mgmt. Inst., 1966-67; instr. U. Conn., 1974-76, cons. faculty Charter Oak Coll., 1974-76, now emeritus faculty; pres. Gilbert E. Teal & Assos., Newtown, Conn., 1960—; chief exec. officer Randolph-Macon Acad., Front Royal, Va., 1977-78; chmn. mgmt. faculty Shenandoah Coll. and Conservatory Music, 1978-83, prof. emeritus, 1983—. Dir., Community Devel. Action Program, Newtown, 1969-70; mem. Newtown Bd. Edn., 1962-63; 1st v.p. Danbury ARC, 1975-76; bd. mgrs. Conn. State PTA, 1974-76. Served to 2d lt., inf., U.S. Army, 1935-37. Decorated Bronze Star medal; recipient Founders Day award N.Y. U., 1957; registered profl. engr., Calif. Fellow Am. Public Health Assn., Soc. Applied Anthropology; mem. Am. Psychol. Assn., Royal Soc. Health, Am. Assn. Sch. Adminstrs., Soc. Am. Mil. Engrs., Am. Soc. Safety Engrs., Ret. Officers Assn., Air Force Assn., Aircraft Owners and Pilots Assn., Am. Ordnance Assn., Arnold Air Soc., Scabbard and Blade, Sigma Xi, Phi Delta Kappa, Psi Chi, Delta Mu Delta, Greater Danbury C. of C. (dir. 1975-76). Republican. Clubs: Army-Navy, Army-Navy Country, Masons, Shriners, Rotary. Author: (with R. Fabrizio) Your Car and Safe Driving, 1962; editor 8 books; contbr. articles to profl. jours. Home: Route 1 Box 23 Stephens City VA 22655 Office: Shenandoah Coll Winchester VA 22601

TEAM, WILBUR HAYES, physics educator; b. Little Rock, Ark., Oct. 9, 1926; s. Leslie D. and Thyra (Hayes) T.; m. Cora Belle Powell, Nov. 21, 1954; children—Robert C., Patty Team Vincent. B.S., Univ. Okla., 1949; M.S., Tex. A&M Univ., 1962. Dept. chmn. Sunray Ind. Sch. Dist., Tex., 1955-62; instr. phys. sci. dept. Amarillo Coll., Tex., 1962—, chmn. dept., 1975—. Author: (lab manual) Lab Manual for Engineering Physics I, 1978; Lab Manual for Engineering Physics II, 1979; Lab Manual for General Physics, 1976. Served as ACM/1C USN, 1944-46. Recipient Pres. award Innovation Amarillo Coll., 1974. Mem. Tex. State Jr. Coll. Tchrs. Assn., Phi Delta Kappa. Republican. Mem. Ch. of Christ. Avocation: nature study. Home: 6703 Sandie Dr Amarillo TX 79109 Office: Amarillo Coll Box 447 Amarillo TX 79178

TEARE, IWAN DALE, research scientist; b. Moscow, Idaho, July 24, 1931; s. Mylrea Henry and Crystal Ann (Atkinson) T.; m. Claudia Joy Patterson, Jan. 31, 1934; children—Steven, Bradley, Kurtis, Kelly. B.S. in Agronomy, U. Idaho, 1953; M.S. in Agronomy, Wash. State U., 1957; Ph.D., Purdue U., 1963. Instr. agronomy Purdue U., West Lafayette, Ind., 1961-63; asst. prof. agronomy Wash. State U., Pullman, 1963-69; prof. agronomy Kans. State U., Manhattan, 1969-79; dir. Agrl. Research and Edn. Ctr., U. Fla., Quincy, 1979-82; research scientist U. Fla., Quincy, 1982—. Active Boy Scouts Am. Served to 1st lt. U.S. Army, 1954-56. Recipient Disting. Grad. Faculty award Kans. State U., 1974. Mem. Am. Soc. Agronomy, Am. Soc. Crop Sci., Sigma Xi, Phi Kappa Phi, Gamma Sigma Delta. Mem. Ch. Jesus Christ of Latter-Day Saints. Assoc. editor Agronomy Jour., 1979-84, tech. editor, 1986—; co-editor: Crop-Water Relations, 1983; contbr. numerous articles to profl. jours. Home: 104 Greenwood Dr Quincy FL 32351 Office: Box 638 Route 3 Quincy FL 32351

TEAS, JOHN P., JR., accountant, data processing executive; b. Clarendon, Ark., Feb. 26, 1935; s. John P. and Sarah E. (McDaniel) T.; B.S.B.A., U. Tulsa, 1970; m. Nancy G. Parks, May 21, 1961; children—Johnna Renee, David Russell. Controller, Service Petroleum Co., Tulsa, 1959-64; acct., system analyst Amoco Prodn. Co., Tulsa, 1965-71; gen. mgr. Holarud Services Co., Tulsa, 1972-75; dir. mgmt. info. systems Ken's Restaurant Systems, Inc., Tulsa, 1976-84; exec. v.p. William J. Butts, Inc., 1984—; pres. C&S Computer Services, 1984—; v.p. Major Controls, Inc., Tulsa; cons. acctg. systems and data processing systems. Treas., Eagles Athletics, Inc., 1980-81. Served with U.S. Army, 1955-58. C.P.A., Okla. Mem. Okla. Soc. C.P.A.s, Am. Inst. C.P.A.s, Data Processing Mgmt. Assn., Beta Gamma Sigma. Home: 4545 E 38th Pl Tulsa OK 74135 Office: 9920 E 42d Suite 210 Tulsa OK 74145

TEASLEY, EDGAR WILLIAM, association executive, realtor; b. Toccoa, Ga., Oct. 7, 1912. A.B. in Econs., George Washington U., 1936; m. Margaret Pitney, Sept. 15, 1939; children—Stewart P., Russell W. Jr. exec. W.R. Grace & Co., N.Y.C., 1936-41; gen. mgr., owner Sta. WTNT, Augusta, Ga., 1947-49; self-employed land developer, home builder, realtor, Greenville, S.C., 1950-63; exec. v.p. Home Builders Assn., Greenville, 1963-85; exec. dir. Home Builders Ins. Trust, Home Builders Self Insurers Fund, Home Builders Pension Fund; pres. Am. Claims Corp. Trustee, Watson Brown Found., Thomson, Ga. Served with USNR, 1941-46. Recipient 8 awards as exec. v.p. Home Builders Assn. Greenville. Mem. Am. Soc. Assn. Execs. (cert. assn. exec.), Internat. Platform Assn., Nat. Assn. Home Builders (life dir.), Home Builders S.C. Presbyterian (elder). Editor, pub. Home Building Newsletter, 1962-85. Home: 8 Sunset Dr Greenville SC 29605 Office: 702 E McBee Ave Greenville SC 29601

TEATE, JAMES LAMAR, educator, administrator; b. Moultrie, Ga., Mar. 4, 1932; s. Luther Nathaniel and Emmie Lou (Smoot) T.; m. Martha Jacqueline Hall, Dec. 26, 1953; children—Cathy Susan, John Michael, Stephen Gregory. B.S., U. Ga., 1954, M.F., 1956; Ph.D., N.C. State U., 1967. Info. and edn. forester Fla. Forest Service, 1956-58; instr. forestry, research asst. Auburn U., 1958-60; instr., asst. forester Miss. State U., 1960-62; asst. prof. forestry Wis. State U., Stevens Point, 1965-67; assoc prof. forestry Okla. State U., 1967-76; prof., dir. sch. forestry La. Tech. U., Ruston, 1976—. Mem. Soc. Am. Foresters, Am. Forestry Assn., Forest Farmers Assn., La. Forestry Assn. Presbyterian. Lodge: Mason. Home: 1811 Wade Dr Ruston LA 71270 Office: Sch Forestry La Tech U Ruston LA 71272

TEBO, HEYL GREMMER, anatomy educator; b. Atlanta, Oct. 17, 1916; s. Clarence Decker and Olna Maudest (Patterson) T.; m. Ruth Elizabeth Davidson, Feb. 14, 1940. A.B., Oglethorpe U., Atlanta, 1937, M.A., 1939; D.D.S., Emory U., 1947. Prof. gross human anatomy U. Tex. Dental Bd., Houston, 1962-82, prof., 1978-83, adj. prof., 1984—, chmn. dept. anatomy, 1978-84. Contbr. articles to profl. publs. Served to capt. U.S. Army, 1940-43. Fellow AAAS; mem. ADA (life), Assn. Mil. Surgeons (life), Am. Assn. Anatomists, Am. Assn. Dental Research (life). Avocations: Antique gun collecting and restoration. Home: 5822 Queensloch Houston TX 77096

TEDDER, CHLOE JEAN, volunteer service administrator; b. Ft. Smith, Ark., Aug. 7, 1929; d. Eric Norquest and Roberta Luella (McLaughlin) Jordan; student Ft. Smith Jr. Coll., 1947-50, Newspaper Inst. Am., 1954-56; m. Robert F. Tedder, Jr., Apr. 3, 1947; children—Michael Eric, Stephen Mark, Robert David, Daniel Lee. With advt. sales SW Times Record, Ft. Smith, Ark., 1962-70; office div. mgr. Manpower, Ft. Smith, 1970-72; dir. vol. service Sparks Regional Med. Center, Ft. Smith, 1972—. Christmas seal chmn. Ark. Lung Assn.; active Ft. Smith Community Concert, Ft. Smith Art Center, Ft. Smith Hist. Soc., Ft. Smith Symphony Assn., The Bonneville House Assn., Old Fort Mus. Assn., Sparks Aux., Sparks Guild; mem. Sparks Woman's Bd. Mem. Am. Soc. Dirs. of Vol. Service, Ark. Soc. Dirs. of Vol. Service (pres., 1975-76, 83-84). Republican. Baptist. Contbr. to Volunteer Leader. Home: 436 N 39th St Fort Smith AR 72903 Office: 1311 South I St Fort Smith AR 72901

TEDDLIE, KATHY BOWER, medical technologist; b. San Juan, P.R., May 5, 1944; d. David William and Gladys Marie (Tollinche) Bower; m. M. B. Teddlie, May 27, 1970 (div. May 1976); 1 dau., Andrea Lee. B.S. in Med. Tech., U. Tex.-Arlington, 1966. Staff endocrinology Baylor U. Med. Ctr., Dallas, 1966-68; supr. spl. chemistry Presbyn. Hosp., Dallas, 1968-75; mktg. rep. Curtin Mathison Sci., Dallas, 1975-78; coagulation specialist Gen. Diagnostics div. Warner Lambert, Morris Plains, N.J., 1978—. Mem. Assn. Women Execs., AAUW. Republican. Episcopalian. Club: 500, Inc.

TEED, CYNTHIA CASON, author, art educator; b. Dallas, Mar. 9, 1941; d. Jack Charles and Gladys (Swope) Cason; m. Michael Joseph Pizzitola, Aug. 1, 1982; children by previous marriage—Bayard Swope and Bret Cason (twins). B.A., Newcomb Coll., 1962; M.A., Middlebury Coll., 1963; diploma Sorbonne, Paris, 1964, U. Dijon (France), 1967. Lectr. lang. and art U. Houston, 1965-66 79-82; tour guide Mus. Fine Arts, Houston, 1975-81. Author: Guidebook for American Bar Association; Walking Tour of Museum of Fine Arts, Houston, 1981; Conversational Spanish for Medical and Allied Health Personnel, 1983. Vol. translator Ben Taub Hosp., 1968-70. Govt. of Spain travel stipend, 1962. Mem. AAUP, Soc. Profl. Journalists, Kappa Kappa Gamma. Episcopalian.

TEEKELL, BYRUM WEBSTER, insurance sales executive; b. Shreveport, La., Mar. 22, 1929; s. Walker Webster and Elda Mae (Matlock) T.; m. Jan Gray, Aug. 18, 1950; children—Judson Gray, Andrew Walker, Scott Aylmer, Charles Hassell. B.A., La. State U., 1950, J.D., 1951. C.L.U.; chartered fin. cons. Salesman, Lincoln Nat., Shreveport, 1948-61, gen. agt., 1961-73; chmn. bd. Brill/Teekell & Assocs., Inc., Shreveport, 1973—; pres. The Teekell Co., Inc., Shreveport, 1977—; pres. Holiday Inn Dixie, Shreveport, 1965; chmn. bd. Bank of Commerce, Shreveport, 1978-81. Mem. conf. bd. Coll. Bus. Adminstrn., La. State U., Baton Rouge. Mem. the Forum (charter), Million Dollar Round Table, Ark.-La.-Tex. Tax Inst., Am. Soc. C.L.U.s, (past pres. local chpt.), Shreveport Assn. Life Underwriters (past pres. local chpt.), Advanced Assn. Life Underwriting (past mem. bd. dirs.), La. Assn. Life Underwriters (pres. 1972-73, man of yr. 1974), La. State U. Found. Democrat. Methodist. Clubs: Shreveport Country, Petroleum (Shreveport); Preston Trail Golf (Dallas). Lodge: Masons (32 degrees). Avocations: twin-engine aircraft; golf; hunting. Home: 5655 Mirador Circle Shreveport LA 71119 Office: The Teekell Co Inc 400 Texas Suite 1400 Shreveport LA 71101

TEER, NELLO LEGUY, JR., construction executive; b. Durham, N.C., Mar. 8, 1914; s. Nello Leguy and Gertrude (Adcock) T.; m. Dorothy Foster, Nov. 10, 1934 (dec. May 1976); children—Sondra Teer Robertson, Nello Leguy III, Dorothy Teer Liptzin, Michael Page; m. Ethel Vredevoogd Wyngaarden, Nov. 4, 1978. Student, U. N.C., 1932-35; D.Sc., N.C. State U., 1968. Pres., Nello L. Teer Co., Durham, 1954—, Nello L. Teer Internat., Inc., Central Engring. & Contracting Corp.; founding dir. Better Hwys. Info. Found.; pres. N.C. Engring. Found., 1963-65; chmn. world council Internat. Rd. Fedn., 1976. Pres. Occoneechee council Boy Scouts Am., 1964, Friends of Watts Hosp., 1965-68. Recipient Civilian Meritorious Service award U.S. Bur. Yards & Docks, USN; Silver Beaver award, 1963; Silver Antelope award, 1969; Disting. Citizen award, 1980, all Boy Scouts Am.; Ann. Civic award Durham C. of C., 1972; Disting. Achievement award, 1974; Nat. Brotherhood award NCCJ, 1975. Mem. Assoc. Gen. Contractors Am. (pres. 1973), Am. Rd. Builders Assn. (pres. 1959-60, award 1962), Internat. Rd. Fedn. (dir., mem. exec. com., world council), Carolina Rd. Builders Assn. (pres. 1944-45). Episcopalian. Home: 3200 Rugby Rd Durham NC 27707 Office: PO Box 1131 Durham NC 27702

TEGTMEYER, CHARLES JOHN, radiologist, educator; b. Hamilton, N.Y., July 25, 1939; s. Charles Edwin and Eusebia (Petgrave) T.; B.A. (N.Y. Regents scholar) with honors, Colgate U., 1961; M.D. (USPHS Research scholar), George Washington U., 1965; m. Virginia Peters, June 1, 1963. Extern in surgery French Hosp., N.Y.C., 1964; surg. intern George Washington U. Hosp., Washington, 1965-66, surg. resident, 1966-68, resident in radiology, 1968-71; fellow in cardiovascular radiology Peter Bent Brigham Hosp., Boston, 1971-72; practice medicine specializing in radiology, Charlottesville, Va., 1972—; asst. prof. of radiology U. Va. Med. Center, Charlottesville, 1972-75, asst. prof. anatomy, 1973-77, dir. radiology edn. for med. students, 1972-81, assoc. prof. radiology, 1975-78, prof., 1978—, assoc. prof. of anatomy, 1977—, dir. of angiography dept. radiology, 1974—; mem. staff U. Va. Hosp. Served to maj. AUS, 1966-72. Diplomate Am. Bd. Radiology (examiner June 1979, 81, 84, 85), Nat. Bd. Med. Examiners. Fellow Am. Coll. Angiology, Am. Coll. Radiology; mem. Radiol. Soc. N.Am., Med. Soc. Va., Am. Roentgen Ray Soc., Eastern Radiol. Soc., AMA, Albemarle County Med. Soc., Soc. Cardiovascular and Interventional Radiology (sec.-treas. 1983, pres. 1985), Trout Unltd., Salt Water Fly Rodders Am., Sigma Xi, Nu Sigma Nu, Sigma Chi. Editorial bd. Radiographics, 1983—; adv. editorial bd. Radiology, 1985—. Contbr. numerous articles on angiography and interventional radiology to med. jours.; inventor of lymph duct cannulator. Home: Bass Hollow 2040 Earlysville Rd Earlysville VA 22936 Office: Dept Radiology U Va Med Center Charlottesville VA 22908

TEHEL, FRANK DAVID, financial executive; b. Postville, Iowa, Mar. 31, 1946; s. Frank Adrin and Marilyn May (Heims) T.; B.S. in Acctg., Old Dominion U., 1975; ed. U.S. Navy Advanced Electronics and Meteorology Sch. Cert. fin. planner Va. Salesman bus. computer systems, Norfolk, Va., 1975-81; owner, operator Gen. Bus. Services, Norfolk, 1978-81; owner, operator, dir. Tehel & Co. Inc., TW Investment Corp., Atlantic Fin. Corp., Norfolk, 1981—; lectr. Norfolk Adult Ednl. Programs. Served with USN, 1968-75. Mem. Nat. Assn. Accts., Nat. Soc. Pub. Accts., Sales and Mktg. Execs., Inst. Cert. Fin. Planners, Internat. Assn. Fin. Planners, Norfolk C. of C. Lutheran. Club: Sports (Norfolk). Lodge: Lions (Norfolk). Home: 4532 Lauderdale Ave Virginia Beach VA 23455 Office: 15 Koger Exec Ctr Norfolk VA 23502

TEICH, NORMAN PAUL, public relations counselor; b. Waltham, Mass., Dec. 24, 1933; s. Julius Robert and Ruth (Stroum) T.; m. Ruth Halpern, June 14, 1958; children—Paul, David, Michael, Mark. B.S. in Pub. Relations, Boston U., 1958. With Fairchild Publs., Inc., N.Y.C., 1959-60; press relations mgr. Lab. For Electronics, Inc., Waltham, Mass., 1960-63; account rep. Carl Byoir & Assocs., Inc., Wellesley Hills, Mass., 1963-68, assoc. account exec., 1968-69; v.p. and account supr. R.S. Weeks and Assocs., Inc., Chgo., 1969-70; pub. relations mgr. Vought Corp., Dallas, 1970-74; group supr. Bloom/Harshe-Rotman & Druck, Inc., Dallas, 1974; mgr. corp. communications Recognition Equipment, Inc., Dallas, 1975-76; pres. Teich Communications, Co., Dallas, 1974—. Served with USMC, 1951-54. Mem. Pub. Relations Soc. Am. (accredited; chmn. Task Force City Dallas; sec. N. Tex. chpt. 1975, v.p. and sec. 1976, v.p. 1977, pres. 1978, nat. assembly del. 1980-81, 84-86, dir. 1974-86, chmn. investor seminar 1976, 80, 81, 83; nat. dir.-at-large, bd. dirs. 1982-83, nat. treas. 1985), Internat. Assn. Bus. Communicators, Nat. Investor Relations Inst. (sec./treas. Dallas chpt. 1972, 77-78, v.p. 1973, pres. 1974), Data Processing Mgmt. Assn., Tex. Pub. Relations Assn. (bd. dirs. 1985-87), N. Dallas C. of C. (bd. dirs. 1986—), Greater Dallas Planning Council, Aviation and Space Writers Assn. Office: Teich Communications Co 4455 LBJ Freeway Dallas TX 75244

TEMPLE, FRANCES ELIZABETH, business executive; b. Marlin, Tex.; d. W.H. and Louise (Czirr) Meyer; grad. high sch.; ed. Draughon's Bus. Coll.; m. L.O. Temple, 1944 (dec. 1975); children—Lee O., Terri E. Temple Bratton. Bookkeeper, Temple, Inc., San Antonio, 1955-72, pres., 1972-80, chmn., 1980—, dir., 1955—; founding dir., chmn. Met. Nat. Bank; pres. ISIS, Inc.; ptnr. Temple & Temple. Bd. dirs. Tex. Research League; hon. chmn. San Antonio Coalition for Children, 1983, bd. dirs., 1984. Recipient Headliner award San Antonio chpt. Women in Communications, 1983; named to Savvy Mag.'s Savvy Sixty List of women directed business. Mem. San Antonio Council of Pres., Com. of 200 (founding). Club: Altrusa. Office: 4314 Dividend Dr San Antonio TX 78219

TEMPLE, ROBERT WINFIELD, engineering consulting company executive; b. New Albany, Ind., Feb. 25, 1934; s. Edgar Winfield and Kathryn (Rady) T.; m. Katrina Voorhis, Jan. 4, 1954 (div. Oct. 1970); children—James V., Robert K., Jennifer; m. Katharine Ann Stobbs, Apr. 29, 1977; children—Andrew, Philip. B.S. in Chem. Engring., B.S. in Indsl. Mgmt., MIT, 1955; postgrad., Chem. Engring. Sch. MIT, 1955, Sch. Bus. Adminstrn. NYU, 1955-58, Mgmt. Devel. Program, Columbia U., 1966. Dist. sales mgr. ACF Industries, 1955-59; sr. staff cons. Arthur D. Little, Inc., 1959-64; dir. planning and devel. Am. Cryogenics, Inc., Atlanta, 1964-69; v.p. Williams Bros. Co., Atlanta, 1969-70; pres. Lang Engring., Coral Gables, Fla., 1970-74; pres. Western Process Co., Geneva and Houston, 1974—. Sunday sch. tchr. Presbyterian Ch.; bd. dirs., sec. MIT Enterprise Forum of Tex.; bd. dirs. Dads Club Swim Team, YMCA. Fellow Am. Inst. Chemists and Chem. Engrs.; mem. Am. Chem. Soc., Am. Mgmt. Assn., (seminar spkr.), Assn. Cons. Chemists and Chem. Engrs., Chem. Mktg. Research Assn., MIT Alumni Assn. (past regional pres.) Clubs: Cherokee Town and Country (Atlanta); Univ. (Houston). Contbr. articles to profl. jours. Home: 11602 Habersham Ln Houston TX 77024 Office: Western Process Co 6100 Corporate Dr 110 Houston TX 77036

TEMPLES, PAMELA REAMES, interior design and furnishings company executive, consultant; b. Columbia, S.C., Mar. 27, 1949; s. Marvin C. and Margaret (Berry) Reames; m. Samuel E. Temples, Feb. 6, 1971 (div. Dec. 1981); children—Stephanie Dawn, Melissa Gayle. B.F.A., U. S.C., 1971. Teaching assoc. U. S.C., Columbia, 1975-81; designer Stig Sjoberg Interiors, Columbia, 1970-73; designer, salesperson R. L. Bryan Co., Columbia, 1973-75, Archtl. Interiors, Columbia, 1976-78; pres., founder PTI Inc., Columbia, 1979—. Active Women's Symphony Assn., Columbia, 1980-84, Leadership Columbia, 1983-84; bd. dirs. Quail Hollow Community Assn., West Columbia, 1981-83. Named one of Ten Best Dressed Career Women, Columbia Career Council, 1978. Mem. Am. Soc. Interior Designers, Constrn. Specifications Inst., Nat. Fire Protection Assn., Am. Land Devel. Assn. (chmn. design bd. 1984—, sec. bd. dirs. S.C. chpt.; 1st pl. award resort category 1984, 2d pl. award comml. category 1984; 1st pl. award renovation and restoration 1985), Nat. Timeshare Council (sec., bd. dirs. 1984-85), Am. Resort and Residential Devel. Assn. (bd. dirs. 1985-86), Zeta Tau Alpha. Republican. Baptist. Avocations: water skiing; bicycling; racquetball; traveling. Home: 2212 Quail Hollow Ct West Columbia SC 29169 Office: PTI 2009 Lincoln St Columbia SC 29201

TENENBAUM, ZELDA BEHR, human resource development company executive; b. LaGrange, Ga., Dec. 17, 1946; d. Harry Shames and Marie (Hallbauer) Behr; m. Sheldon Usher Tenenbaum, Sept. 15, 1969; 1 child, Jessica Lane. B.A. in Sociology, U. Ga., 1968; M.A. in Psychology, Ga. So. U., 1978. Research asst. La. State U. Med. Sch., New Orleans, 1968-69; caseworker in child services Chatham County Dept. Family and Children's Services, Savannah, Ga., 1969-71; substitute tchr. Chatham Bd. Edn., Savannah, 1971; family care coordinator Tidelands Mental Health Ctr., Savannah, 1971-73; instr. Armstrong State Coll., 1973-80, workshop leading trainer, 1975-85; v.p. Aenchbacher & Tenenbaum, Savannah, 1980-85; family care cons. Ga. Dept. Human Resources, 1973-74; cons. Johnson Sq. Health Club, Savannah, 1984; trustee Ga. Infirmary, Savannah, 1982—. Author manual: A Guide for Family Care Workers, 1973. Mem. Ga. Commn. Internat. Yr. of the Child, Atlanta, 1979; del; White House Conf. on Families, Bethesda, Md., 1980; pres. Vol. Action Ctr., Savannah, 1976; bd. dirs. Jr. League, Savannah, 1979-80, 82-83; mem. nat. task force on children and youth Nat. Council Jewish Women, N.Y., 1980-82; mem. adv. council Parents Anonymous Ga., Atlanta, 1981-83; chmn. child services Chatham County Dept. Human Resources, Savannah, 1980-82; v.p. bd. dirs. chmn. planning allocation and community services United Way of Coastal Empire, Savannah, 1985. Recipient Young Careerist award Oglethorpe Bus. and Profl. Women's Club of Savannah, 1975, Outstanding Community Vol. of Yr., Vol. Action Ctr., 1979, Arch award U. Ga. Alumni Soc., 1985. Mem. Am. Mgmt. Assn., Am. Soc. Tng. and Devel., Oglethorpe Bus. and Profl. Women's Club, Child Advocacy-Coalition of Chatham Savannah, Inc. (bd. dirs.), Women Bus. Owners Savannah, Savannah C. of C. (mem. edn. com., women in mgmt. com., bd. dirs. 1985). Democrat. Jewish. Home: 324 Hewsham St Savannah GA 31401 Office: Aenchbacher & Tenenbaum 601 E 66th St Suite A Savannah GA 31405

TENNANT, JERALD LEE, physician, educator; b. Dodge City, Kans., June 28, 1940; s. Harold and Nellie (Smith) T.; student Tex. Tech. U., 1957-60; M.D., U. Tex. Southwestern Med. Sch., 1964; m. Marilyn Lois Dickerson, Mar. 26, 1982; children—Scott Edward, John Grier, Thomas Bruce, Jared Lane, Tasha Zerriah. Intern, Methodist Hosp., Dallas, 1964-65; resident Parkland Meml. Hosp., 1965-68; postgrad. Basic Sci. Opthalmology, Harvard Med. Sch., 1966; dir. Ophthalmic Plastic Surgery Clinic, Parkland Meml. Hosp., Dallas,

1968-74; pvt. practice medicine, specializing in ophthalmology, Dallas, 1968—; tchr. lens implant surgery U.S. and abroad, 1974—; founder, dir. Dallas Eye Inst., Dallas Eye Surgicenter; mem. staff Meth. Hosp., Oak Cliff Med. and Surg. Hosp., Parkland Meml. Hosp., VA Hosp., Med. City Hosp., all Dallas. Served with AUS, 1964-69. Diplomate Am. Acad. Ophthalmology and Otolaryngology. Mem. Phi Kappa Phi. Designer, Tennant Intraocular Lens; Tennant Anchorflex Lens; Tennant Posterior Chamber Lens. Office: 710 S Cedar Ridge Duncanville TX 75137

TENNIS, GAY HARGIS, business administration educator; b. Atlanta, June 20, 1936; d. James Othnel and Margaret (Whittle) Hargis; m. William K. Price III, Aug. 14, 1955 (div. 1974); children—William Kyle IV, James Kerrick, John Charles; m. Eugene H. Tennis, 1975. B.A., Ga. State U., 1970, M.A., 1974, Ph.D., 1976. Asst. prof. Kennesaw Coll., Atlanta, 1976-78; research coordinator United Presbyn. Ch. U.S.A., N.Y.C., 1979-82; computer cons., Atlanta, 1983-84; asst. prof. bus. adminstrn., North Ga. Coll., Dahlonega, 1984—; cons. Presbyn. of South New Eng., Old Saybrook, Conn., 1984. Contbr. articles to profl. jours. Home: Route 2 Box 7 Country Pl Dawsonville GA 30534 Office: N Ga Coll Dahlonega GA 30597

TEPLITZ, JERRY V., professional speaker, consultant; b. Bklyn., Mar. 19, 1947; s. Herbert and Celia (Ozer) T. B.A., Hunter Coll., 1968; J.D., Northwestern Law Sch., 1972; M.A., Columbia Pacific U., 1981, Ph.D., 1983. Bar: Ill. 1973. Atty., Ill. EPA, Chgo., 1972-73; tng. cons. Lakeview Edn. Assn., Chgo., 1973-74; owner, pres. Jerry Teplitz Enterprises, Virginia Beach, Va., 1974—; assoc. mem. adv. bd. Nat. Assn. for Campus Activities, Columbia, S.C., 1980-84. Author: How to Relax and Enjoy, 1978; Managing Your Stress, 1982. Named Top Rated Speaker, Internat. Platform Assn., Washington, 1984. Mem. Nat. Speakers Assn., Nat. Assn. Campus Activities. Avocations: reading; travel.

TERCILLA, ORLANDO AMANCIO, manufacturing company executive; b. Oriente, Cuba, Nov. 7, 1955; came to U.S., 1962; s. Amancio Orlando and Maria (Carmen) T. Student P.R. Jr. Coll., 1975-78. Service mgr. Quick Service A/C Corp., San Juan, P.R., 1974-78; purchasing mgr. Refricenter of Miami, Inc. (Fla.), 1978-82; v.p. sales Ig-Lo Products Corp., 1982—. Mem. N.Am. Heating and Air Conditioning Wholesalers Assn. Republican. Roman Catholic. Office: Ig-Lo Products Export Corp 8086 NW 74th Ave Miami FL 33166

TEREKHOV, MIGUEL R., educator, choreographer; b. Montevideo, Uruguay, Aug. 22, 1928; came to U.S., 1954, naturalized, 1963; s. Miguel George and Antonia (Rodriguez) T.; grad. Montevideo public schs.; m. Yvonne Chouteau, Aug. 31, 1956; children—Christina, Elizabeth. Soloist, Teatro Sodre, Montevideo, 1941-43; soloist, lead dancer Original Ballet Russe, 1943-49, prin. dancer Teatro Sodre, Montevideo, 1949-51; prin. dancer Boris Kniaseff Ballet Co., Buenos Aires, 1951-52; choreographer weekly TV program Night at the Ballet, Havana, Cuba, 1954; lead dancer Ballet Russe de Monte Carlo, 1954-58, regisseur gen., 1957; prin. dancer Teatro Sodre, Montevideo, 1952-54; staged own choreography ballet Don Quixote, Tex. Christian U. Ballet, Ft. Worth, 1976; staged own choreography Arensky Variations for Allegro Ballet Co., Houston, 1976; artist-in-residence Okla. U., 1961-63, asst. prof. ballet, 1963-67, asso. prof., 1967-70, prof., 1970—, chmn. dept. dance, 1973—; choreographer full length ballets of The Nutcracker, Coppelia, Undine, Romeo and Juliet, Giselle, Okla. City Civic Ballet, also U. Okla. Ballet; choreographer one act ballets; choreographer operas La Traviata and Carmen, Oklahoma City Lyric Opera; Die Fledermaus and The Unicorn, The Gorgon, The Manticore, Okla. U. Sch. Music; guest lectr. Ballet Club, N.Y.C.; instr. master classes Southwest Regional Ballet Festival; dir. Oklahoma City Civic Ballet, 1963-71; co-dir. Okla. Indian Ballerina Festival, 1967. Bd. dirs. Oklahoma Summer Arts Inst. Mem. Nat. Assn. for Regional Ballet, Okla. Arts and Humanities Adv. Bd., Okla. Summer Arts Inst. Roman Catholic. Office: Dept Dance 563 Elm Ave Room 209 U Okla Norman OK 73019

TEREKHOV, YURIY, physician, educator; b. Kazan, Russia, Jan. 21, 1924; came to U.S., 1971, naturalized, 1978; s. Vladimir and Lubov (Rgekhiua) T.; m. Ida Abramicheva (div. 1956); 1 child; m. 2d, Elvira Kogan, 1962; 1 child. Student Saratov State Med. Inst. (Russia), 1947-51; M.D., Kirov Med. Acad., Leningrad, Russia, 1953; Ph.D., Institut of Normal and Pathologic Physiology, Acad. of Med. Scis. (Russia), 1967. Intern, Research Inst. of Phys. Therapy and Rehab., Sverdlovsa, Russia, 1959-62, attending physician and sr. clin. research investigator, 1962-72; cons. U.S. Air Force Sch. Aerospace Medicine, 1972-73; research scientist U. Tex. Health Sci. Ctr., 1973-74, instr., 1974-79; pres. Teretronics Co., San Antonio, 1982—. Served to sr. med. officer Russian Army, 1953-59. Mem. IEEE, Aerospace Med. Assn. Greek Orthodox. Editor, pub. Jour. of Clin. Engring., 1979; contbr. articles to profl. jours.; patentee in field.

TER KEURST, WILLIAM JACK, aviation executive; b. Grand Rapids, Mich., July 17, 1934; s. Herman and Jennie (Karsten) T.; m. Joan Marie Hathaway, Oct. 9, 1954; children—Barbara Joan, Laura Elizabeth, Susan Jean, William Jack. B.A., U. Tex., 1959. Pres., Trade Winds Aviation, Miami, Fla., 1960-64, Casada, Caracas, Venezuela, 1964-69, Aircraft Leasing of Miami, 1969-74, Bahamas/USA Airways, 1969-74, Dade Helicopter Jet Service, 1977—; chmn. bd. Tropical Helicopter Airways. Served with USN, 1952-55. Mem. Nat. Air Transp. Assn., Helicopter Assn. Am., Miami C. of C. Democrat. Presbyterian. Club: Tiger Bay. Office: Dade Helicopter Jet Service 950 MacArthur Causeway Miami FL 33132

TERRASSA, JUAN ANTONIO, insurance company executive; b. San Juan, P.R., Oct. 29, 1946; s. Antonio and Maria (Nolla) T.; m. Viola T. Benitez, Dec. 16, 1969; children—Juan A., Viola M., Carlos M., Margarita I. B.B.A. in Fin. and Ins., U. P.R., 1969. Ins. adjuster West Indies Adjustment Inc., San Juan, 1967-68; claims mgr. Carlos M. Benitez Inc., San Juan, 1969-70, v.p. underwriting, 1970-75, pres., 1975—; pres. Standard Underwriters MGA Inc., Coral Gables, Fla., Ins. Adjusters & Appraisals, Inc.; dir. Nat. Ins. Co., Nat. Life Ins. Co., Manuel Casiano, Inc.; mem. adv. bd. Gen. Gases, Inc. Bd. dirs. P.R. Symphony Orch. Mem. Profl. Ins. Agts., C. of C., Young Pres.'s Orgn. Roman Catholic. Home: 9 Jardines de Vedruna Santa Maria Rio Piedras PR 00927 Office: Box 147 San Juan PR 00902

TERREL, CHARLES LYNN, management science and financial information systems consultant; b. DeGraff, Ohio, Apr. 19, 1904; s. Charles and Rose Belle (Pence) T.; m. Lela Fern Heaston, June 15, 1935 (div. 1952); children—Sondra Lee, Mark Heaston; m. 2d, Mary Emily Masterson, Sept. 3, 1956. B.A., Ohio State U., 1928; M.B.A. cum laude, Harvard Bus. Sch., 1932. Pres., Internat. Cons., Inc., San Diego, Calif., 1953-60; chief indsl. devel. div. Dept. State, Lagos, Nigeria, 1960-63; dir. Devel. Service Inst., Accra, Ghana, 1963-66; fin. adviser Nat. Investment Bank, Accra, 1966-68, Korea Devel. Fin. Corp., Seoul, 1968-73, Korea Investment and Fin. Corp., Seoul, 1971-73, Korea Capital Corp., Seoul, 1973-74, Indsl. Devel. Bank, Saigon, 1973-75, Kuwait Indsl. Devel. Bank, 1974, Banco Unido de Fomento, Santiago, Chile, 1974; mission Chief Internat. Fin. Corp., Washington, World Bank, 1974; fin. adviser Compagnie Financiere et Touristique, Tunis, Tunisia, 1975-78; program evaluator AID, Abidjan, Ivory Coast, 1978; fin. adviser Saudi Indsl. Devel. Fund, Riyadh, Saudi Arabia, 1979, Devel. Indsl. Bank, Cairo, Egypt, 1980-83, Caribbean Fin. Services Corp., Barbados, 1984; pres. Internat. Devel. Cons., Inc., Alexandria, Va., 1966—. Editor Long-term Trends in The Terrel Letter, 1956—; inventor PERT-COST system, 1956. Decorated Order of Bn. of George I, Greece. Mem. Research Soc. Am. Republican. Methodist. Home and Office: 6301 Stevenson Ave Alexandria VA 22304

TERRILL, JAMES E., administrative executive; b. Houston, Aug. 11, 1944; s. Paul M. and Betty (Beene) T.; m. Elizabeth K. Boy, Mar. 25, 1967; children—James III, Jennifer, Stephanie. B.S., La. State U. Statis. acct. Crown-Zellerbach Paper Co., Inc., St. Francisville, La., 1967; personnel asst. U.S. Sugar Corp., Clewiston, Fla., 1971-72, personnel officer, 1972-76, 1st asst. v.p. personnel, 1976-80, v.p. personnel, 1980-84, v.p. adminstrn., 1984—; bd. dirs. Everglades Credit Union. Bd. dirs. Nat. Council Agrl. Employees, 1981-83; mem. Fla. Employment Service Com., 1980—, labor com. Fla. Farm Bur. 1980—, Fla. Job Service Improvement Com., 1982—, labor com. Am. Farm Bur., 1984—. Served to capt. USAF, 1967-71. Mem. Clewiston C. of C. (bd. dirs.), Am. Soc. Personnel Adminstrn. Episcopalian. Club: Clewiston Country (pres. 1979-80). Home: 1045 Palmetto St Clewiston FL 33440 Office: US Sugar Corp PO Drawer 1207 Clewiston FL 33440

TERRY, GEORGE ALVIN, state official; b. Oneida, Tenn., Dec. 19, 1926; s. William Claude and Paralee (Cowan) T.; m. Sarah Ellen Winn, June 9, 1950; children—Stephanie, Saralee, Sereessa, Rachel. B.S., U. Tenn., 1950. Owner, mgr. Ben Franklin Store, Oneida, 1962-72; dir. personal property Tenn. Dept. Gen. Services, Nashville, 1972—. Mem. Tenn. Ho. of Reps., 1957, Tenn. Senate, 1961-67. Served to 2d lt. U.S. Army, 1945-46. Republican. Mem. Ch. Christ. Home: 304 Highland Heights Goodlettsville TN 37072 Office: Tenn Dept Gen Services Fed Property Sect 6500 Centennial Blvd Nashville TN 37209-1199

TERRY, HOWARD ROBERT, agriculture educator; b. Hobart, Okla., June 15, 1937; s. Howard Leon and Daisy Elizabeth (Briggs) T.; m. Barbara Jane Honeycutt, May 15, 1959; children—Rob, Val. B.S. in Agrl. Edn., Okla. State U., 1959, M.S., 1962; Ph.D., Ohio State U., 1969. Instr. vocat. agr. Perry/Summer High Sch., 1959-63, Lone Wolf High Sch., 1963-67; asst. prof. agrl. edn. Okla. State U., 1969-72, assoc. prof., 1972-75, prof., head dept., 1975—; cons. in field. John Deere Found. Research fellow, 1967-69. Mem. Am. Vocat. Assn., Okla. Vocat. Assn., Nat. Vocat. Agr. Tchrs. Assn. (Service award 1973), Okla. Vocat. Agr. Tchrs. Assn., Am. Assn. Tchr. Educators in Agr., Okla. State U. Alumni Assn., Nat. FFA Alumni Assn., Okla. FFA Alumni Assn., Phi Delta Kappa, Alpha Zeta, Phi Kappa Phi, Gamma Sigma Delta, Alpha Tau Alpha. Democrat. Baptist (deacon). Author: Robert R. Price-Leader in Agricultural Education, 1971; (with others) Agricultural Education Student Recruitment: What Means-How Effective?, 1975, The Image of Vocational Education, 1973, The Image of the FFA as Perceived by Active Members and Advisors, 1974. Home: 1605 W Liberty Ave Stillwater OK 74075 Office: 448 Agricultural Hall Oklahoma State U Stillwater OK 74078

TERRY, MARSHALL NORTHWAY, JR., English educator, author; b. Cleve., Feb. 7, 1931; s. Marshall Northway and Margaret Louise (Carpenter) T.; m. Antoinette Barksdale, Sept. 5, 1953; children—Antoinette Ansley Terry Bryant, Mary Marshall. Student, Amherst Coll., 1949-50, Kenyon Coll., 1950-51; B.A., So. Meth. U., 1953, M.A., 1954. Teaching fellow English, So. Meth. U., 1954, dir. pub. relations, lectr. English, 1957-65, instr. English, 1956, 65-67, asst. prof., 1968, assoc. prof., 1969-71, prof., 1972—, chmn. dept., 1971-75, 79-82, also dir. creative writing program; copywriter Bloom Advt., Dallas, 1955; book critic Dallas News, 1970-75. Past trustee Incarnate Word Coll., San Antonio; sec. bd. trustees Fort Burgwin Research Ctr., Ranchos de Taos, N.Mex. Recipient Jesse H. Jones fiction award Tex. Inst. Letters, 1968; Best Short Story award S.W. Rev., 1973; Mem. AAUP (pres. chpt. 1971), Coll. Conf. Tchrs. English, South Central Modern Lang. Assn., Tex. Inst. Letters (pres. 1977-79, councilor 1980—). Democrat. Methodist. Author: Tom Northway, 1968; Old Liberty, 1961; book reviewer Dallas News; contbr. short stories to various jours. and mags. Home: 2717 Lovers Ln Dallas TX 75225 Office: English Dept So Meth U Dallas TX 75275

TERRY, MARY SUE, attorney general; b. Martinsville, Va., Sept. 28, 1947; d. N.C. and Nannie Ruth Terry. B.A., Westhampton Coll., 1969; M.A., U. Va., 1970, J.D., 1973. Asst. Commonwealth's atty. Patrick County, Va., 1973-77; mem. Va. Ho. of Dels., 1977-85; ptnr. B.H. Cooper Farm, Inc., Stuart, Va., 1978—, Terry & Rogers, Stuart, 1978—; atty. gen. elect of Va., Richmond, 1986—; dir. First Nat. Bank Stuart. Mem. Piedmont Planning Dist. Crime Commn., 1974-77; bd. dirs. West Piedmont Health Planning Council, 1975-77, Patrick Henry Mental Health Ctr., 1975-77, Va. YMCA, 1980—; mem. pres.'s bd. advisors Ferrum Coll., Va., 1978-83; bd. trustees U. Richmond, 1980—; chmn. Gov.'s Task Force to Combat Drunk Driving, 1982. Named Outstanding Mem. of Freshman Class, Ho. of Dels., 1979; recipient Disting. Alumna award for disting. service U. Richmond, 1984; Service to Youth award Va. YMCA, 1981. Mem. Va. Trial Lawyers Assn., ABA, Va. State Bar, Patrick County-Stuart C. of C. (charter pres., pres. 1974-76), Omicron Delta Kappa. Democrat. Baptist. Office: Atty Gen Va 101 N Eighth St Richmond VA 23219

TERRY, RONALD ANDERSON, bank holding company executive; b. Memphis, Dec. 5, 1930; s. John Burnett and Vernon (Lucas) T.; m. Beth Howard, Feb. 1, 1953; children—Natalie Carol, Cynthia Leigh. B.S., Memphis State U., 1952; postgrad., So. Meth. U., 1961, Harvard U., 1970. Mgmt. trainee First Tenn. Bank, Memphis, 1957; pres. First Tenn. Nat. Corp., Memphis, 1971, chmn., chief exec. officer, 1973-79, First Tenn. Bank N.A., Memphis, 1979—. Past pres., bd. dirs. Boys Clubs Memphis, Arts Appreciation Found.; past chmn. Memphis Jobs Conf.; bd. dirs., pres. Future Memphis. Served to lt. USN, 1953-57. Mem. Am. Bankers Assn. (treasury adv. com., bd. dirs., past chmn. govt. relations council), Assn. Res. City Bankers (dir., past chmn. govt. relations com. and pub. affairs com.), Assn. Bank Holding Cos. (legis. policy com., past pres. fed. adv. council), Econ. Club of Memphis (past pres.). Office: PO Box 84 Memphis TN 38101*

TERRY, WINFIELD CLINTON, III, educator; b. N.Y.C., Mar. 24, 1943; s. Winfield Clinton and Virginia L. Terry; m. Patricia Anderson, June 27, 1965; children—Jerusha Elizabeth, Winfield Clinton IV. B.A. in History, Fla. State U., TAllahassee, 1965; B.D., Yale Div. Sch., 1968; M.A. in Sociology, U.Calif.-Santa Barbara, 1969, Ph.D. in Sociology, 1978; postgrad. Georg-August Universitaet, Goettingen, W.Ger., 1969-72. Instr. sociology U. Md. Extension, W.Ger., 1970-71; reader in sociology U. Calif.-Santa Barbara, 1973-74, instr. sociology extension program, 1973-76, teaching asst. in sociology, lectr. sociology, 1974-76; instr. sociology Ventura (Calif.) Community Coll., 1973-74; lectr. sociology Calif. State U.-Fresno, 1976-77; asst. prof. sociology and criminal justice U. Fla., Gainesville, 1977-82; asst. prof. Fla. Internat. U., North Miami, 1982-86, assoc. prof., 1986—. Author: Teaching Religion: The Secularization of Religion Instruction in a West German School System, 1981; Policing Society: An Occupational View, 1985. Contbr. articles to profl. jours. Editor: Jour. Justice Issues, 1985—. Behavioral and Social Scis. Inst. grantee; grantee Deutscher Akademischer Austauschdienst, Deutsche Forschungsgemeinschaft. Mem. Am. Soc. Criminology (mem. internat. liaison com. 1982-83, mem. fellows com. 1980-82, mem. student affairs com. 1979-80), Acad. Criminal Justice Scis. (mem. program com. 1982-83, mem. history of field com. 1982—, mem. subcom. on criminal justice edn. and tng. 1979, mem. assn. and standards com. 1980-81, mem. publs. com. 1980-81), Fla. Criminal Justice Educators Assn. (mem. exec. bd. 1981—, sec. treas. 1982—, chmn. research com. 1981-84, mem. membership com. 1980-81, mem. program and devel. com. 1979-80), So. Assn. Criminal Justice Educators (mem. info.-dissemination com. 1980-81), So. Sociol. Soc., Am. Sociol. Assn. Democrat. Mem. United Ch. of Christ. Home: 10410 NW 20th St Pembroke Pines FL 33026 Office: Dept Criminal Justice Fla Internat Univ Bay Vista Campus North Miami FL 33181

TERWILLIGER, ROBERT ELWIN, bishop; b. Corland, N.Y., Aug. 28, 1917; s. Melville and Ella May (Seman) T.; m. Viola Mae Terwilliger, Dec. 27, 1942; 1 dau., Anne Elizabeth. B.A. summa cum laude, Syracuse U., 1939; B.D., Episcopal Theol. Sch., Cambridge, Mass., 1943; Ph.D., Yale U., 1948; S.T.M., Gen. Theol. Sem., N.Y.C., 1949; D.D. hon., Seabury Western Theol. Sem., Evanston, 1970, U. of South, Sewanee, Tenn., 1976; postgrad., Nashotah House, Wis. Ordained deacon, Episcopal Ch., 1942; ordained priest, Episcopal Ch., 1943; consecrated bishop, Episcopal Ch., 1975. Curate All Saints Ch., Worcester, Mass., 1942-44; asst. Christ Ch. Cathedral, Hartford, Conn., 1944-47; fellow, tutor Gen. Theol. Sem., N.Y.C., 1947-49; rector Christ Ch., Poughkeepsie, N.Y., 1949-60, St. James Ch., Los Angeles, 1960-62; assoc. pastor All Saints Ch., N.Y.C., 1963-67; founding dir. Trinity Inst., N.Y.C., 1967-75; suffragan bishop Episcopal Diocese of Dallas, 1976—; chaplain Com. of Holy Spirit, N.Y.C., 1968-75, St. Hilda's and St. Hugh, 1965-67; Episcopal visitor Com. of St. Mary, Peekskill, N.Y., 1967—; adj. prof. theology Gen. Theol. Sem., 1967-75. Author: Receiving the Word of God, 1959, Christian Believing, 1973; editor, contbr.: The Charismatic Christ, 1973; co-editor: To Be A Priest, 1975. Trustee U. of South, 1975—, Gen. Theol. Sem., N.Y.C., 1977-79, Nashotah House, 1980—. Mem. Anglican-Orthodox Internat. Dialogue, Phi Beta Kappa, Phi Kappa Phi. Office: Episcopal Diocese of Dallas 1630 N Garret St Dallas TX 75206*

TESTERMAN, KYLE, mayor. Mayor City of Knoxville, Tenn. Office: City-County Bldg Knoxville TN 37902*

TETI, CATHERINE POWER, lawyer; b. Charleston, W.Va., Nov. 17, 1945; d. Francis Ray and Mary Jo (Crozier) P; m. John Joshua Teti, Jr., Aug. 27, 1966; children—John Joshua III, Sarah Margaret. A.B., W.Va., U., 1967; J.D., U. Richmond, 1979. Bar: Va. 1979, Fla. 1980. Social worker Preston County Dept. Welfare, Kingwood, W.Va., 1967-68; mng. editor King George (Va.) News, 1972-74; sole practice law, Clearwater, Fla., 1980-82; legal counsel Hillsborough County Office of Child Support Enforcement, Tampa, Fla., 1982—. Chmn., King George Bicentennial Commn., 1974-76; mem. Germana Community Coll. Citizen's Adv. Panel, King George, 1974-76, King George Planning Commn., 1978-79, King George Democratic Com., 1978-79; del. Va. Dem. Conv., 1978. Mem. ABA, Va. Bar Assn., Fla. Bar (arts and entertainment com.), Fla. Assn. Women Lawyers, Hillsborough County Assn. Women Lawyers, LWV, Sigma Sigma Sigma. Office: Office of Child Support Enforcement Suite 401 505 Twiggs St Tampa FL 33601

TEW, E. JAMES, JR., electronics company official; b. Dallas, July 7, 1933; s. Elmer James and Bessie Fay (Bennett) T.; student Arlington State Jr. Coll., 1955-57; B.B.A. in Indsl. Mgmt., So. Meth. U., 1969; M.S. in Quality Systems, U. Dallas, 1972, M.B.A. in Mgmt., 1975; m. Barbara Dean Evans, Dec. 12, 1952; children—Teresa Annette, Linda Diane, Brian James. Mgr. quality assurance ops. and corp. reference standards lab. Tex. Instruments Inc., Dallas, 1957—, chmn. corp. metric implementation com., mem. credit com. Texis Credit Union; adj. faculty Richland Coll., Mountain View Coll. Precinct chmn., election judge, 1961-64, del. several county and state convs. Served with U.S. Army, 1953-55. Decorated Army Commendation medal with oak leaf cluster; registered profl. engr., Calif. Fellow Am. Soc. Quality Control (cert. as quality and reliability engr., chmn. Dallas-Ft. Worth sect. 1974-75), U.S. Metric Assn., mem. Optical Soc. Tex. (charter), Am. Nat. Metric Council, Tex. Metric Council (charter; dir. Dallas region), U.S. Metric Assn., Res. Officers Assn., Dallas C. of C. (chmn. world mfg. com. 1974-77, chmn. spl. task force career edn. adv. bd. 1973-74), Nat. Rifle Assn., Mensa. Baptist. Clubs: Texins Rod and Gun (pres. 1969-70), Texins Flying, Masons (32 deg.). Contbr. articles to profl. jours. Home: 10235 Mapleridge Dallas TX 75238 Office: PO Box 225214 MS 368 Dallas TX 75265

TEWS, HANS W., banker; b. Dusseldorf, Germany, Aug. 15, 1934; came to U.S., 1949; s. Curt J. and Elsa (Roesch) T.; m. Martha Wilkerson, Dec. 28, 1963; children—Charles C., Melissa Jacquelyn. B.A., Fla. State U., 1956; cert., Sch. Banking, La. State U.; cert. exec. mgmt., Columbia U., Wharton Sch. Asst. v.p. Nat. bank Sarasota, (Fla.), 1958-62; cashier First Nat. Bank, Lakeland, Fla., 1963, First Nat. Bank at Orlando (Fla.) (now Sun Bank N.A.), 1963-66, v.p., 1966-70, pres., chief adminstrv. officer, 1977—; also dir. First Nat. Bank at Orlando (Fla.) (now Sun Bank N.A.); pres. Sun Bank of St. Ludie County, Ft. Pierce, Fla., 1970-76; exec. v.p. corp. and internat. banking Sun Banks, Inc., 1981—, also dir. Bd. dirs. United Way of Orange County, 1979—; pres. Loch Haven Art Ctr., Inc., Orlando, 1980-82, trustee, Orlando, trustee Fla. State U. Found., 1978—; advisor Coll. of Bus., Fla. State U., 1980—. Served to 1st lt. U.S. Army, 1956-58. Mem. Am. Bankers Assn., Fla. Bankers Assn., Orlando Area C. of C. (pres. 1983). Clubs: Country Club of Orlando, University, Citrus. Office: Sun Bank N A 200 S Orange Ave Orlando FL 32801*

THACKER, ANDREW JACKSON, business educator, photographer; b. Richmond, Va., Nov. 19, 1939; s. Andrew Jackson and Helen Marie (Landers) T.; m. Carol Ann Janak, June 24, 1972. B.S., Va. Mil. Inst., 1961; M.B.A., U. Houston, 1970, Ed.D., 1977. Intermediate scientist Rohm & Haas Co., Phila., 1961-62; assoc. chemist Texaco Experiment, Inc., Richmond, Va., 1963-65; chemist Shell Chem. Co., Deer Park, Tex., 1965-66; technologist Shell Chem. Co., Union, N.J., 1966, tech. and sales rep., Houston, 1966-68; mktg. mgr. Analytical Cons., Inc., Houston, 1968-69; instr. quantitative mgmt. sci. U. Houston, 1969-74; instr. vocat. office edn. Houston Community Coll., 1974; lectr. bus. tech. U. Houston, 1974-77, asst. prof. bus. tech., 1976-80, asst. prof. indsl. tech., 1980-83; assoc. prof. mktg. mgmt. Calif. State Poly. U., Pomona, 1983—; chmn. bd. Photographic Services Unlimited, Inc.; past dir. Chemco Sales Corp., Inc., Lovely Lady Cosmetics, Inc., Lovely Lady Enterprises, Inc.; dir. Am. Condor, Inc. Bd. dirs., treas. Harris County Water Control and Improvement Dist. #94, 1976-78; pres. Bellaire West Civic Improvement Assn., 1979-80, bd. dirs., 1977-80; mem. Horizon 76 Com., Alief Bicentennial Commn., 1975-77. Served with AUS, 1961-63. Recipient U. Houston Teaching Excellence award, 1976, Coll. Tech. Teaching Excellence award, 1979, Dean's Teaching Excellence award, 1978, Coll. Tech. Faculty Devel. award, 1979. Mem. Nat. Bus. Edn. Assn., Tex. Bus. Edn. Assn., Sales and Mktg. Execs. Los Angeles, Am. Mktg. Assn. (bd. advisors bus. and internat. div. So. Calif.), Los Angeles Distbrs. Assn., Profl. Photographers Am., Golden Key (nat. acad. coordinator 1981-83), Alief Jaycees, Pi Sigma Epsilon (div. educator dir. 1981-83, educator v.p. 1983-84, educator dir. 1984—; Nat. Top Faculty Adv. award 1979, 80, 81), Kappa Alpha Order, Pi Omega Pi, Phi Delta Kappa, Mu Kappa Tau. Republican. Roman Catholic. Contbr.: Retail Security; contbr. articles to profl. jours. Home: 11418 Triola Ln Houston TX 77072 Office: Dept Mktg Mgmt Calif State Poly U Pomona CA 91768

THAKORE, VIJAY RAMESHCHANDRE, chemical company executive; b. Ahmedabad, Gujarat, India, Sept. 12, 1941; came to U.S., 1970, naturalized, 1970; s. Rameschandre B. and Sulochna R. Thakore; m. Rajnika Vijay, Apr. 26, 1969; children—Nilima, Trupti. B.Sc., Gujarat U., Ahmedabad, 1964; M.Sc., M.S., U. Baroda, Gujarat, 1967; M.S., Tuskegee Inst., Ala., 1972. Asst. research officer Anand Agrl. U., Gujarat, 1968-70; research assoc. A&M U., Normal, Ala., 1971-76; pres. tech. dir. Biochem. Analysis, Inc., Huntsville, Ala., 1974—. Avocations: photography, music, gardening.

THAMES, BILLY HOWARD, state senator; b. Magee, Miss., Apr. 2, 1944; student Hinds Jr. Coll., U. So. Miss.; m. Lynda Kowatch. Mem. Miss. Senate; businessman. Mem. Farm Bur., U. So. Miss. Alumni Assn. Democrat. Baptist. Club: Mason. Office: Miss State Senate Jackson MS 39205*

THAMES, REDDEN JEFFERSON, business executive; b. Elba, Ala., Oct. 31, 1932; s. Aaron Preston and Ruth (Bass) T.; A.B., Stetson U., 1958; B.D., So. Bapt. Theol. Sem., 1962, M.Div., 1970; m. Joanne Ellen Reeves, Sept. 1, 1952; children—Ruth, Nancy, Joe, Jim. Ordained to ministry So. Bapt. Ch., 1952; pastor chs., Lake View, S.C., 1962-67, Loris, S.C., 1967-70; dir. Horry County Dept. Social Services, Conway, S.C., 1970-73; dist. dir. S.C. Dept. Social Services, Columbia, 1973-85; v.p. WeCare Distbrs., Inc., Charlotte; dir. Catawba Regional Planning Council, 1973-81; v.p. Interval Mktg. Cons., Inc., North Myrtle Beach, S.C., 1981-82; v.p. pub. relations We Care Distbrs., Inc., Charlotte, N.C., 1983—. Bd. dirs. Dillon County Rural Recreation Commn., 1964—, Central Midlands Regional Planning Council, 1973—, Coastal Plains Mental Health Commn., 1971-73, Coastal Plains Regional Home Health Council, 1971-73; chmn. S.C., Nat. Multiple Sclerosis Soc. Named Rural Minister of Yr., Progressive Farmer mag., 1965, Outstanding Alumnus, Stetson U., 1971; Nat. Multiple Sclerosis Hope Chest award, 1982. Mem. Am. Mgmt. Assn., Adminstrv. Mgmt. Soc., Child Welfare League Am., Am. Public Welfare Assn. (human resources adv. com. 1975-79). Lodge: Masons. Author: Dynamic Supervision, 1977. Home: 5500 E Strawberry Hill Dr Charlotte NC 28211 Office: PO Box 222138 Charlotte NC 28222

THARP, JOHN ROBERT, educator, army reserve officer; b. Clifton, Ohio, June 24, 1944; s. Herbert William and Cleo Rebecca (Pond) T.; m. Ann Lewis Scott, Aug. 11, 1968; 1 dau., Natalie. B.S. in Edn., Eastern Ky. U., 1968, M.A. in Edn., 1974; Rank I Certificate Sch. Adminstrn., Western Ky. U., 1979; grad. numerous mil. schs. Tchr. phys. edn. Jeffersontown Elementary Sch., Louisville, 1968-69; commd. 2d lt. U.S. Army, advanced through grades to lt. col., 1983; served in Europe, Vietnam, 1969-72; various assignments, Louisville, 1972—; tchr. driver edn., coach football Durrett High Sch., Louisville, 1972-78; tchr. driver edn. Mill Creek Vocat. Sch., Louisville, 1978-83. Decorated Bronze Star medal, Army Commendation medal, Vietnam Service medal, Vietnam Campaign medal, Nat. Def. Service medal, Armed Forces Reserve medal, Army Reserve Component Achievement medal, Army Service medal, Overseas medal, Parachute Badge, Expert Marksman Badge. Mem. NEA, Ky. Edn. Assn., Phi Delta Kappa. Democrat. Methodist. Club: Lion (Louisville). Home: 5119 Cool Brook Rd Louisville KY 40291 Office: 2 Gast Blvd Louisville KY 40205

THAYER, PAUL, diversified company executive; b. Henryetta, Okla., Nov. 23, 1919; s. Paul Ernest and Opal Marie (Ashenhurst) T.; m. Margery Schwartz, Feb. 14, 1947; 1 child, Brynn. Student U. Wichita, 1937-38, U. Kans., 1939-41. Pilot, Trans World Airlines, 1945-47; chief exptl. test pilot Chance Vought Corp., 1948-50, sales mgr., 1951, sales and service mgr., 1952-54, v.p. sales and service, 1954-58, v.p. Washington ops., 1958-59, v.p., gen. mgr. Vought Aeros div., 1959-63, pres., 1963; chief flight test Northrop Aircraft Co., 1950-51; sr. v.p. Ling-Temco-Vought, Inc., Dallas, 1963, exec. v.p., 1964, chmn. bd., chief exec. officer, 1970—; chmn. bd., chief exec. officer LTV Aerospace Corp., Dallas, 1965-70; chmn. bd. LTV Corp., 1970-83; dep. sec. def., Washington, 1983-84. Served to lt. comdr. USNR, 1941-45. Decorated D.F.C., Air medal with 9 oak leaf clusters; recipient Disting. Service award Sec. Navy, 1962. Mem. Soc. Exptl. Test Pilots, NAM (dir.), Nat. C. of C. (vice chmn.), Bus. Roundtable, Conf. Bd., Phi Gamma Delta. Office: 14840 Landmark Blvd Suite 200 Dallas TX 75240

THAYER, WILLIAM ALFRED, civil engr.; b. Queens, L.I., N.Y., Nov. 17, 1945; s. Richard Francis and Irene Teresa (Cody) T.; m. Linda J. Conklin, Sept. 25, 1982. A.A. in Civil Engring., Miami-Dade Community Coll., 1975; B.S. in Civil Engring., Fla. Internat. U., 1979. Draftsman, City of Coral Gables, Fla., 1964-67; technician Fla. Dept. Transp., Miami, 1968-78, engr., coordinator, 1978-81; engr. Dade County Rapid Transit System, 1981-84; pres. Thayer & Assocs., Inc., engring. cons., Miami, 1984—. adj. prof. dept. civil engring. Fla. Internat. U., Miami, 1981-82. Mem. exec. council, dist. VI liaison com. Fla. Dept. Transp. Served with AUS, 1968-71. Decorated Army Commendation medal, Vietnam Commendation medal; recipient Eagle Scout award, 1962. Mem. Am. Concrete Inst., ASCE (affiliate), Am. Inst. Steel Constrn., Dade County Constrn. Coordination Council, Monroe County Coordination Council, World Future Soc., Dade County Safety Council, Smithsonian Assocs., Fla. Utility Liaison Council, Fla. Internat. U. Alumni Assn. (dir. 1981—, v.p. 1983-84, pres. 1984—), Phi Theta Kappa (hon. Theta of Fla. chpt.). Home and office: 911 NW 202d St Miami FL 33169

THEIL, WILLIAM FRED, JR., manufacturing company executive; b. Cleve., Dec. 21, 1944; s. William Fred and Yolanda Mary (Golop) T.; m. Nadine Joanne Kendra, Dec. 27, 1965; 1 son, Christopher. Student, Carnegie-Mellon U., 1962-63; B.B.A., Cleve. State U., 1973. Sports editor The News-Herald, Conneaut, Ohio, 1963-64; sports writer Decatur Herald and Rev. (Ill.), 1968-69; sports editor News-Herald, Willoughby, Ohio, 1969-70; margin analyst Paine-Weber-Jackson & Curtis, 1970-73; asst. office mgr. Hendershot & Smith, Inc., Wickliffe, Ohio, 1973-75; office mgr. Hendershot & Smith, Inc., 1975-76, controller, 1976-78, corporate sec., gen. mgr., 1978—, also Carolina Comml. Heat Treating, Inc., 1978—, gen. mgr. of same; data processing cons., 1973-78; dir. Auburn Career Center, 1977-78. Served to 1st lt., U.S. Army, 1964-68. Decorated Army Commendation medal. Mem. Am. Mgmt. Assn., Data Processing Mgmt. Assn., Metrolina S/3-34 Users Group. Roman Catholic. Club: Charlotte (N.C.) Tennis. Office: 6313 Old Pineville Rd PO Box 240867 Charlotte NC 28210

THEISS, PHYLLIS BROOKS (SCOTTIE), transactional analysis counselor; b. Ashtabula, Ohio, Aug. 3, 1926; d. Ralph Irwin and Alma Mildred Onel (Peden) Brooks; m. Chester B. Theiss, Jr., June 19, 1949; children—Anne, Ellen, Marsha, John. R.N., Youngstown Hosp. Sch. Nursing, Ohio, 1947; cert. Internat. Transactional Analysis Assn. 1976; student St. Joseph's Coll., Maine, 1985—. Psychiat. nurse, VA Hosp., Louisville, 1947-49; home delivery nurse, Harlan, Ky., 1949-50; transactional analysis mental health counselor, Louisville, 1972—; bloodmobile coordinator ARC, Delaware, Ohio, 1953-55; nurse recruit Chmn. Med. Aux., Delaware, 1953-55; health nurse vol. coordinator local PTA's, Louisville, 1959-63; presenter workshops in field. Author: Parenting for High Self Esteem, 1983. Sec. Louisville, PTA, 1963-65; den leader Boy Scouts Am., 1966-68, 4H, Louisville, 1968-70; dist. cookie chmn. Louisville council Girl Scouts U.S., 1965-69; speaker on scuba diving to local schs., on Ecuador, and Africa to local schs., chs., and civic groups; active local Presbyterian ch. Mem. Internat. Transactional Analysis Assn., Ky. Transactional Analysis Assn., Am. Assn. Counseling and Devel., Am. Nurses' Assn., Ky. Nurses' Assn., DAR, 17th Century Colonial Dames. Democrat. Club: Beckham Bird (Louisville). Avocations: birding; photography; boating; sailing; scuba diving; swimming. Home: 3420 Nandina Dr Louisville KY 40222 Office: Scottie Theiss Counseling 3420 Nandina Dr Louisville KY 40222

THEOFANIS, CHRIS CHARLES, university administrator; b. Phoenix, Mar. 12, 1930; s. Constantinos and Aglaia (Zabaras) T.; m. Katherine Pulos, Apr. 17, 1955; children—Lee Ann, Dean, Florie. B.S., Butler U., 1952. Asst. dir. sch. community relations Indpls. Pub. Schs., 1955-57; dir. pub. relations Butler U., Indpls., 1957—; cons. pub. relations to various orgns., 1957—. Vice pres. Sertoma Charities, 1979-82. Served with U.S. Army, 1953-55. Mem. Indpls. Pub. Relations Soc. (pres. 1973), Indpls. Press Club, Pub. Relations Soc. Am. (assoc.), Council for Advancement and Support Edn., Phi Kappa Phi. Republican. Greek Orthodox. Home: 7843 Buckskin Dr Indianapolis IN 46250 Office: Butler U 4600 Sunset Ave Indianapolis IN 46208

THERRIEN, FRANCOIS XAVIER, JR., bus. and tax cons.; b. Amesbury, Mass. June 6, 1928; s. Francis Xavier and Doris Alma (Cote) T.; B.S., U.S. Mil. Acad., 1950; M.S., U. Ariz., 1962; m. Yoshiko Kashima, July 22, 1969; children—Francois Xavier, Norman, Sakura, Izumi. Commd. 2d lt., U.S. Army, 1950, advanced through grades to lt. col., 1965, ret., 1970; dist. dir. R. J. Carroll Asso., Inc., Atlanta, 1970-71; with Treasure Lake, Atlanta, 1971; pres. Identiseal of Fla., Orlando, 1972-74; owner Yoshiko Enterprises, Winter Park, Fla., 1974—; instr. Seminole Community Coll., 1974-79; sec. Buck Enterprises, Orlando, 1978—, Cosmic Corp., Orlando, 1978—, Abney's Enterprises, Inc., Winter Park, 1982—; dir. E. J. Air Services, Inc., Art Works, Inc., Arabian Express, Inc. Decorated Army Commendation medal, Air medal, Bronze Star medal, Silver Star; Croix DeGuerre with palm. Mem. Nat. Assn. Enrolled Agts. Roman Catholic. Home: 1492 Canterbury Circle Casselberry FL 32707 Office: 2265 Lee Rd Suite 223 Winter Park FL 32789

THEUS, B. J., actor, media and public affairs liaison; b. Abilene, Tex., Oct. 19, 1947; s. C. Ralph Theus and Betty Lou (Wagener) Haddock T. B.S., E. Tex. State U., 1972; postgrad. Trinity U., San Antonio, 1972-74, Army Inst. Profl. Devel., Newport News, Va., 1982—. Bus. mgr., student asst. dept. speech and drama E. Tex. State U., 1970-72; resident co. apprentice Dallas Theater Ctr., 1972-74; freelance entertainer Los Angeles, 1977—; asst. to chief of news Am. Forces Radio and TV Programming Ctr., Hollywood, Calif., 1981-82; pub. affairs and broadcast project officer Office of the Chief of Army Pub. Affairs, 6325th Individual Mgmt. Augmentation, Los Angeles, 1980—; liaison cons. Barrymore Inst., Los Angeles, 1981—; appeared in Am. Coll. Theater Festival Tarot of Otho McCain, 1971, Dallas Theater Ctr. as Lee Harvey Oswald in Jack Ruby...All-American Boy, 1972, Gen. Hosp. ABC-TV, 1983; tech. advisor media, pub. affairs specialist Res. Component Personnel and Adminstrn. Ctr., St. Louis, 1980—; radio prodn. specialist Armed Forces Info. Service, Arlington, Va., 1981-82; pub. service appointee Dept. Def. Office of Asst. Sec., Washington, 1981-82. Vol. counselor United Youth, Van Nuys, Calif., 1980-81; campaign supporter John Glenn Presdl. Campaign Com., Los Angeles, 1983. Served to capt. U.S. Navy, 1967-69. Recipient Award of Excellence Kennedy Ctr. of the Performing Arts, 1971, Am. Coll. Theatre Festival, 1972; Spl. Media award Pub. Interest Radio and TV Ednl. Soc., 1982. Mem. Tex. Assn. Film and Tape Profls., Screen Actors Guild, AFTRA, Actors Equity, Publicity Club of Los Angeles, Greater Los Angeles Press Club, Hollywood Radio and TV Soc. Pentacostal. Clubs: Holiday Health, Am. Legion.

THEUS, WINNIE WANDA, health care administrator, nurse; b. Glenwood, Ark., Nov. 30, 1929; d. Leonard Webster and Ozelle Thomas; m. Robert William Theus, Sept. 27, 1954; children—Nancy, Robert, Jean, Sue Ann, John. R.N., St. Vincent Infirmary, Little Rock, 1954; B.S., Bradley U., 1977; M.A. in Edn., U. Ark., 1982. Staff nurse Acute Care Hosps., Ark., 1954-67, charge nurse, Ill., 1967-78, educator, Peoria, Ill., 1978-79; educator Jefferson Regional Med. Ctr., Pine Bluff, Ark., 1979-80, adminstrv. asst., 1981, assoc. adminstr., 1982—. Mem. Ark. Nurse Execs. (dir., program chmn. 1983-84), Am. Orgn. Nurse Execs., Am. Nurses Assn., Nat. League Nurses, Am. Hosp. Assn., Pine Bluff C. of C., Am. Cancer Soc. Democrat. Baptist. Avocations: reading; music; board games. Home: 517 W 20th Ave Pine Bluff AR 71601 Office: Jefferson Regional Med Ctr 1515 W 42d Ave Pine Bluff AR 71603

THIBODEAUX, CAROLE ANN LE BLANC, nursing home administrator; b. Krotz Springs, La., June 14, 1941; d. Vernon and Mary (Hollinghead) Leblanc; m. Aarol Anthony Thibodeaux, Apr. 20, 1963; children—Aarol Anthony, Veronica Celeste. L.P.N., T.H. Harris Vocat. Sch., 1960; A.S. in Nursing, La. State U.-Eunice, 1978; A.A., La. State U.-Alexandria, 1982. Lic. practical charge nurse Lafayette Charity Hosp. (La.), 1960-64, Opelousas Gen. Hosp. (La.), 1965-68, Sr. Village Nursing Home, Opelousas, 1976-79; dir. nurses Acadia-St. Landry Guest Home, Church Point, La., 1982—, adminstr., 1983—. Parent mem. PTA, 1970—; lectr. Pre-Cana Marriage Courses, Church Point, 1982; chmn. Opelousas Garden Club Ball Masque, 1976. Recipient 1st place in floral design and arrangements Opelousas Garden Club, 1975. Mem. La. Health Care Assn., (region 3 dir.). Democrat. Roman Catholic. Home: Route 3 Box 35 Church Point LA 70525 Office: Acadia St Landry Guest Home 830 S Broadway St Church Point LA 70525

THIEL, JOHN MELVIN, physician, b. Cin., Nov. 10, 1912; s. John Nicholas and Mary Ida (Renschen) T.; m. Dorothy Felicie Taggart, June 6, 1942; children—Beverly, Diane, Camille, John Joseph, Louis Joseph. Student Xavier U., 1930-32; B.S., U. Cin., 1934, M.B., 1936, M.D., 1937; Sc.D., St. Edwards U., 1957. Intern Good Samaritan Hosp., Cin., 1936-37, resident, 1937-40; assoc. Venable Clinic, San Antonio, 1940-41; practice medicine specializing in surgery, Galveston, Tex., 1941—; mem. staff John Sealy Hosp., St. Mary's Hosp.; mem. control group 1st State Bank of Hitchcock, Tex., Bank of W. Galveston, Bank of Santa Fe, Tex., Gulf Nat. Bank, Texas City, Gulf Shore Bank, Crystal Beach, Tex.; owner Circle JT Ranches, Atascosa County, Coryell County and Victoria County, Tex.; real estate executive; involved in oil and gas prodn.; horse breeder and racer. Bd. dirs. Galveston County unit Am. Cancer Soc. Served to surgeon USPHS. Fellow ACS; mem. SW Surg. Congress, Tex. Surg. Soc., Singleton Surg. Soc., Tex. Med. Assn., So. Med. Assn., Galveston County Med. Assn., AMA, Nat. Rifle Assn. Am., AAUP. Clubs: Serra of Galveston, Galveston Country, Pelican, Galveston Skeet and Trapshooting Assn., Galveston Rifle and Pistol, Galveston Artillery, Bob Smith Yacht, Sunday Morning Coffee, Port Bay Hunting and Fishing, Quarterdeck, Tandem. Lodge: Rotary. Home: 2626 Ave 0 1/2 Galveston TX 77550 Office: Sealy and Smith Profl Bldg 200 University Blvd Galveston TX 77550

THIEMAN, EUGENE ALBERT, management consultant for physicians; b. Louisville, Oct. 7, 1927; s. Albert Charles and Otillia Margaret (Miller) T.; m. Mary Jane Doll, Oct. 21, 1950; 7 children. B.S., U. Louisville, 1951. With Service Bur. for Doctors, Louisville, 1951—, owner, gen. mgr., 1964—. Served with U.S. Army, 1946-48. Mem. Soc. Profl. Bus. Cons. (nat. pres. 1982-83), Inst. Cert. Profl. Bus. Cons. (nat. pres. 1976-77), Nat. Soc. Pub. Accts., Ky. Assn. Accts., Louisville Employee Benefit Council. Republican. Roman Catholic. Editorial cons. Physician's Mgmt. Mag., 1962—, Dental Mgmt. Mag., 1962—; contbr. articles to profl. jours. Office: Service Bur for Doctors 2823 Preston Hwy Louisville KY 40217

THIES, AUSTIN COLE, utility company executive; b. Charlotte, N.C., July 18, 1921; s. Oscar Julius and Blanche (Austin) T.; B.S. in Mech. Engring., Ga. Inst. Tech., 1943; m. Marilyn Joy Walker, June 26, 1945; children—Austin Cole, Robert Melvin, Marilyn Leone. With Duke Power Co., Charlotte, 1946—, mgr. steam prodn., 1963-65, asst. v.p., 1965-67, v.p. prodn. and operation, 1967-71, sr. v.p., 1971-82, exec. v.p. power ops., 1982—, also dir.; past chmn. prodn. com., engring. and operating div. Southeastern Electric Exchange; chmn. tech. advisory com. Carolinas Va. Nuclear Power Assos.; chmn. N.C. Air Control Advisory Council. Mem. nat. adv. bd. Ga. Inst. Tech.; pres. Arts and Scis. Council; chmn. bd. dirs. Mercy Hosp.; trustee Alexander Childrens Center; bd. visitors Boy's Town. Served with USNR, 1943-46. Decorated Purple Heart. Mem. Edison Electric Inst., Charlotte C. of C., ASME (past chmn. Piedmont Carolina sect.), Am. Nuclear Soc., Air Pollution Control Assn., N.C. Soc. Engrs. (past pres.), Charlotte Engrs. Club, Nat. Rifle Assn. (life), Kappa Sigma. Presbyterian (elder). Clubs: Rotary (past pres., dir. N. Charlotte), Cowans Ford Country, Quail Hollow Country, Charlotte City, Charlotte Ga. Inst. Tech. (past pres.), Charlotte Rifle and Pistol (past pres.). Home: 2429 Red Fox Trail Charlotte NC 28211 Office: 422 S Church St Charlotte NC 28242

THOEM, ROBERT LEROY, consulting engineering company executive; b. Davenport, Iowa, Aug. 26, 1940; s. LeRoy Henry and Maurine Ethyl (Wymore) T.; m. Jean Ann Osburn, Sept. 2, 1963; children—Robin Jean, Wendy Ann, Kevin Robert. B.S. in Civil Engring., Iowa State U., 1962; M.S. in San. Engring., Rutgers U., 1967. Registered profl. engr., Ala., Ga., Ill., Iowa, S.C., Va. Project engr. Stanley Cons., Inc., Muscatine, Iowa, 1966-73, environ. engring. dept. head, 1973-76, resource mgmt. dept. head, Atlanta, 1976-82, assoc. chief environ. engr., 1980-83, ops. group head, office mgr., 1982-83; sr. project mgr. Engring.-Sci., Inc., Atlanta, 1983-85, mgr. solid and hazardous waste engring. sect., 1985—. . Chmn. bd. deacons Presbyn. Ch. Iowa, Muscatine, 1969-70; chmn. Cub scout pack Boy Scouts Am., Muscatine, 1974-75; pres. Grant Elem. Sch. PTA, Muscatine, 1975-76; mem. recreation expansion com., archtl. controls com. Willow Point Homeowners Assn., Atlanta, 1977-78, chmn. planning/external affairs, 1981-82, pres., 1982-83; bd. adminstrs. Methodist Ch., Atlanta, 1979-82, treas. Sunday Sch. class, 1982-83; treas. Dickerson Middle Sch. PTA, Atlanta, 1981-82. Served to lt. USPHS, 1962-65. USPHS trainee Rutgers U., 1965-66. Mem. Am. Acad. Environ. Engrs., ASCE, Nat. Soc. Profl. Engrs. (pres. Muscatine chpt. 1970-71), Water Pollution Control Fedn., Ga. Profl. Engrs. in Pvt. Practice (vice chmn. 1981-82), Ga. Cons. Engrs. Council (rep. 1982-83). Contbr. articles to profl. jours. Home: 1712 Huntingford Dr Marietta GA 30067 Office: 57 Executive Park S NE Atlanta GA 30329

THOM, CAROL ELAINE, educator, coach; b. Charleston, W.Va., Nov. 25, 1950; d. Charles Ray and Dorma Dell (Gay) T. B.A., Purdue U., 1972; M.S., W.Va. U., 1976, postgrad., 1976-83. Tchr., coach Washington Jr. High Sch., Parkersburg, 1973-78; tchr., coach South Charleston High Sch. (W.Va.), 1978—; coach W.Va. Girls High Sch. All-Star Basketball Team, W.Ger., summer 1978, Eng., summer 1980, Hawaii, summer 1982. Recreational Fitness grantee Union Carbide Corp., 1983. Mem. Kanawha County Edn. Assn., W.Va. Edn. Assn., NEA, W.Va. Assn. Health Phys. Edn. Recreation and Dance (sec. 1983-84, v.p. 1978-79), W.Va. High Sch. Coaches Assn., AAHPERD. Democrat. Baptist. Home: 314 Central Ave South Charleston WV 25303 Office: South Charleston High Sch One Eagle Way South Charleston WV 25309

THOMANN, RICHARD LOUIS, medical sales executive; b. Akron, Ohio, Sept. 6, 1950; s. Richard Andrew and Lucille (Shaheen) T.; m. Linda Kay Jones, June 10, 1972; children—Kaley Lynn, Shawn Nicole, Erin Monica. B.B.A. in Mgmt., Notre Dame U., 1972; postgrad. U. North Fla., 1976-78. Profl. football player World Football League, Jacksonville, Fla., 1974-76; coach Gardner-Webb Coll., Boiling Springs, N.C., 1977-78; sales rep. Princeton Ind. Corp., Ind., 1978-81; terr. mgr. U.S. Surg. Corp., Norwalk, Conn., 1981-82; terr. mgr. Cilco, Inc., Huntington, W.Va., 1982—. Sustaining mem. Republican Nat. Com., Jacksonville, 1984-85. Roman Catholic. Club: Notre Dame (v.p. 1983—). Avocations: golf; tennis; racquetball; bodybuilding; basketball. Home: 1115 Executive Cove Jacksonville FL 32223 Office: Cilco Inc 1616 13th Ave Huntington WV 25701

THOMAS, ALVIN L., oil company executive, lawyer; b. Lubbock, Tex., Dec. 5, 1946; s. Alvin L. and Thelma Joyce (Casey) T.; m. Debra Jean Palmer, Apr. 16, 1983. B.A. in History, U. Okla., 1969, J.D., 1972. Bar: Okla. 1972, Tex. 1980. Assoc. Lytle, Soule and Emery, Oklahoma City, 1975-76; counsel gen. Okla. Securities Commn., 1976-78; ptnr. Kratz Thomas Williams and Patton, Oklahoma City, 1978-79; land mgr. Santa Fe Minerals Inc., Dallas, 1979-81, v.p., 1981-83, v.p. exploration, 1983-85; sr. v.p. Trafalgar House Oil and Gas Inc., 1985—. Served to capt. U.S. Army, 1972-75. Mem. Okla. Bar Assn., State Bar Tex. Office: 8584 Katy Freeway Suite 222 Houston TX 77024

THOMAS, BENNETT ARTHUR, JR., oil company executive; b. Shreveport, La., Jan. 7, 1946; s. Bennett Arthur and Mary Ethel (Rosalee) T.; m. Mary Louise Bizet, Apr. 24, 1965; children—Derek A.R., Adam L., Carey E. B.S. in Petroleum Engring., La. Tech. U., 1967; postgrad. in Bus. Adminstrn., Tulane U., 1970-74. Petroleum engr. Mobil Oil Corp., Tripoli, Libya, 1967-70, sr. reservoir engr., New Orleans, 1970-74, sr. planning analyst, N.Y.C., 1975-76; planning mgr. Superior Oil Co., Houston, 1976-77; pres. Neptune Oil Co., Tel Aviv, Israel, 1977-78; acquisitions mgr. Superior Oil, Houston, 1979; sr. v.p. McIntyre Mines, Calgary, Alta., Can., 1980-81; v.p. Mark Producing, Houston, 1981-82; sr. v.p. Natural Resources Mgmt. Corp., Dallas, 1983-84, pres., 1985—. Mem. Am. Petroleum Inst., Soc. Petroleum Engrs., Natural Gas Men of Houston, Tex. Ind. Producers and Royalty Owners Assn., Phi Epsilon Tau, Sigma Gamma Epsilon. Republican. Presbyterian. Club: Exchange, Royal Oak Country (Dallas). Home: 3816 Stratford Ave Dallas TX 75205 Office: 2600 San Jacinto Tower Dallas TX 75201

THOMAS, BYRON K., geologist; b. Small, Idaho, Apr. 22, 1922; s. Daniel W. and Mary (Evans) T.; B.S., U. Idaho, 1942; Ph.D., Johns Hopkins U., 1952; m. Mary B. Neidig, Aug. 3, 1945; children—Byron Andrew, Barbara Kay Barrett, Mary Patricia Kiser, Judy Lee Walters, Barry Dan. Geologist, U.S. Bur. Reclamation, 1945-49; geologist Olin Mathieson Chem. Corp., 1952-55; cons. geologist, ind. oil operator, Longview, Tex., 1955—; prof. geology Kilgore Coll., 1966-67. Served with USN, 1942-45; ETO, PTO. Mem. Am. Assn. Petroleum Geologists, Geol. Soc. Am., E. Tex. Geol. Soc., Soc. Petroleum Engrs., Sigma Xi, Sigma Gamma Epsilon. Lutheran. Address: 1306 Montclair St Longview TX 75601

THOMAS, CHARLES F., professional basketball team executive. Co-owner, chmn. bd. Houston Rockets, Nat. Basketball Assn., 1982—. Office: care Houston Rockets The Summit Ten Greenway Plaza E Houston TX 77046

THOMAS, DANIEL HOLCOMBE, judge; b. Prattville, Ala., Aug. 25, 1906; s. Columbus Eugene and Augusta (Pratt) T.; LL.B., U. Ala., 1928; m. Dorothy Quina, Sept. 26, 1936 (dec. 1977); children—Daniel H., Jr., Merrill Pratt; m. 2d, Catharine J. Miller, Oct. 25, 1979. Bar: Ala. Practice law, Mobile, Ala., 1929; asst. solicitor Mobile County; mem. firm Lyons, Chamberlain & Courtney, 1937-43, Lyons & Thomas, 1943-46, Lyons, Thomas & Pipes, until 1951; judge U.S. Dist. Ct., Mobile, 1951—. Mem. exec. bd. Mobile Area council Boy Scouts Am., 1963—, v.p., 1967-69, pres., 1973-74, mem. nat. council, 1973-81. Trustee dept. archieves and history State of Ala. Served to lt. USNR, 1943-45. Recipient Silver Beaver award Boy Scouts Am., 1970, Silver Antelope award, 1975. Methodist. Club: Mobile Country. Home: 13 Dogwood Circle Mobile AL 36608 Office: US Fed Bldg Mobile AL 36602

THOMAS, E. C., church association adminstrator; b. Lulu, Fla., Dec. 13, 1920; s. Elver E. and Essie Thomas; m. Alice Douglas, July 19, 1941; children—Charmaine, Cheryl. D.D. (hon.), Lee Coll.; D.Lit., Am. Div. Sch. Publisher Ch. of God, Cleveland, Tenn., 1954-70; state overseer Ch. of God, Va., Ala., N.C., 1970-78; gen. sec.-treas. Ch. of God, Cleveland, Tenn., 1978-82, gen. overseer, 1982—. Nat. Assn. Evangelicals (bd. adminstrn. 1982—). Office: Ch of God Gen Offices Keith at 25th St NW PO Box 2430 Cleveland TN 37320-2430

THOMAS, EDWARD WILFRID, physics educator; b. Croydon, Eng., May 9, 1960; s. Gilbert Wilfrid and Helena Josephina (Geeraerts) T.; m. Rebecca Louise Worsham, Aug. 30, 1971; 1 son, Graham Edward. B.S., Univ. Coll. London, 1961, Ph.D., 1964. Asst. prof., assoc. prof., prof. physics Ga. Inst. Tech., Atlanta, 1964—, dir. Sch. Physics; cons. Union Carbide. Fellow Am. Inst. Physics, Inst. Physics (London); mem. Optical Soc. Am. Contbr. numerous articles on physics to profl. jours.; patentee in field. Office: Physics Dept Ga Tech Inst Atlanta GA 30332

THOMAS, FRANCIS EDWARD (JEFF), agri-business executive; b. Clewiston, Fla., June 3, 1940; s. Charles Edward and Bonita C. (Clemson) T.; m. Georgiana Mills, Aug. 17, 1962; children—Cynthia G., Jeffrey A. B.B.A., U. Miss., 1964. Pres., gen. mgr. Thomas Bros. Inc., Belle Glade, Fla., 1965—. Active Young Republican Club, 1965—; mem. Rep. Nat. Com., U.S. Senatorial Club. Baptist. Clubs: Sailfish of Fla. (Palm Beach); Mayacoo Country (West Palm Beach); Governors; Palm Beach Yacht. Lodges: Masons, Elks. Office: Thomas Bros Inc PO Box 818 Belle Glade FL 33430

THOMAS, GARNETT JETT, accountant; b. Farmington, Ky., July 27, 1920; s. Pinkney Madison and Ethel (Drinkard) T.; B.S., Lambuth Coll., 1947; student U. Notre Dame, 1943-44; M.S., Miss. State U., 1949; m. Nell Penton, May 23, 1981; stepchildren—Vernon Bice, Michael Bice, Gena Bice. Clk./acct. Ill. Central R.R., Paducah, Ky., 1941-42; mgr. Coll. Bookstore, Lambuth Coll., Jackson, Tenn., 1946-47; acct. Miss. Agrl. and Forestry Expt. Sta., Mississippi State, 1948-60, chief acct., 1960-75, adminstrv. officer and chief acct., 1975—; mem. adv. bd. Nat. Bank of Commerce of Miss., 1974—; pres. Starkville PBR Corp. (Miss.), 1977—; fin. adminstr. seed tech. research internat. programs, Brazil, India, Guatemala, Columbia, Thailand, Kenya, 1958—. Bd. dirs. Govt. Employees Credit Union, 1967—, pres., 1969-73. Served with USN, 1942-46. Decorated Bronze Star medal with oak leaf cluster. Mem. Nat. Assn. Accts., Assn. Govt. Accts., Am. Assn. Accts., Acad. Acctg. Historians, So. Assn. Agrl. Scientists. Republican. Methodist. Club: Rotary (pres. 1959-60, dist. gov. dist. 682, 1977-78, adv. com. to pres. 1979-80). Home: 114 Grand Ridge Dr Starkville MS 39759 Office: PO Drawer ES Mississippi State MS 39762

THOMAS, JAMES CARL, hospital administrator; b. Ottawa, Ill., June 10, 1930; s. James Carl and Olive Leona (Knudson) T.; m. Nancy Lou Puckett, Apr. 30, 1983. B.S. in Pharmacy, U. Okla., 1959. Vice pres. Hosp. Corp. Am., Nashville, 1967-73; asst. dir. Lakeland Gen. Hosp., Fla., 1973-75; assoc. dir. Halifax Hosp. Med. Ctr., Daytona Beach, Fla., 1975-81; adminstr. Lake Community Hosps., Leesburg, Fla., 1981-82; adminstr. Jenkins Community Hosp., Ky., 1982—, exec. dir., 1981—. Mem. planning bd. City of Ormond Beach, Fla., 1975-81. Served with USN, 1950-54, Korea. Fellow Am. Acad. Med. Adminstrs.; mem. Am. Coll. Hosp. Adminstrs., Leesburg C. of C. (v.p. 1981). Republican. Episcopalian. Lodges: Rotary, Kiwanis (v.p. 1975-81). Avocations: Bridge; tennis; sailing; home projects; family activities. Home: Lakeside Dr PO Box 670 Jenkins KY 41537 Office: Jenkins Community Hosp Main St PO Box 472 Jenkins KY 41537

THOMAS, JAMES EDWARD, JR., telecommunication company executive; b. Aiken, S.C., Sept. 14, 1952; s. James E. and Ruth N. T. B.S. in Bus. Adminstrn., S.C. State Coll., 1976; M.S. in Govt. and Adminstrn., Ga. State U., 1983. Sales rep. Armour-Dial Co., Chamblee, Ga., 1976-78; assoc. trainer AT&T Techs., Norcross, Ga., 1980—. Mktg. advisor Jr. Achievement, Norcross, 1983-84. Served with U.S. Navy, 1970-72. Regent's Opportunity scholar Ga. Bd. Regents, 1978. Recipient Outstanding Young Man. Am., U.S. Jaycees, 1983. Mem. S.C. State Alumni Assn., Ga. State U. Alumni Assn., Young Folks Union Soc., Am. Mgmt. Assn., Nat. Geographic Soc., Smithsonian Instn., Omega Psi Phi. Methodist. Club: Atlanta Track. Home: 6654 M Peachtree Ind Blvd Doraville GA 30360 Office: AT&T Technologies 2000 NE Expressway Norcross GA 30071

THOMAS, JAMES WELDON, geophysicist; b. Gainesville, Tex., Apr. 2, 1909; s. Charles M. and Gladys Pearl (Moon) T.; B.A., N. Tex. State U., 1929, B.S., 1930; postgrad. U. Tex., Austin, 1930; D.C.L. (hon.), Atlanta Law Sch., 1975; m. Isabel Cunningham Edwards, Aug. 23, 1930 (dec. 1968); children—Ann Tamsin Thomas Boardman, William Lee, Diana Craig Thomas Childress; m. 2d, Bess Fleming. With Geophys. Service Inc. (now subs. Tex. Instruments, Inc.), Dallas, 1930—, v.p., to 1960, mem. pres.'s council, 1960—, past dir. U.S. and fgn. subs.; cons. geophysics, Dallas, 1960—; pres. Diversified Properties Inc., Dallas. Trustee Tex. Presbyn. Found.; bd. dirs. Presbyn. Pan Am. Sch., Kingsville, Tex., Internat. Linguistics Center, Dallas; past mem., chmn. Good Neighbor Commn. Tex.; past chmn. bd. dirs. Salvation Army Adv. Bd., Mexico City; hon. consul Rep. of Korea, Dallas-Fort Worth; dean Dallas-Ft. Worth Consular Corps. Mem. Am. Assn. Petroleum Geologists (emeritus), Soc. Exploration Geophysicists (emeritus), Dallas Geophys. Soc., Dallas Geol. Soc., Dallas-Ft. Worth Consular Corps. Clubs: Dallas Petroleum, Brook Hollow Golf, Cadence, University. Lodges: Masons (past grand master and potentate) Lions (past chpt. pres.).

THOMAS, JOAB LANGSTON, university president, biology educator; b. Holt, Ala., Feb. 14, 1933; s. Ralph Cage and Chamintney Elizabeth (Stovall) T.; m. Marly Dukes, Dec. 22, 1954; children—Catherine, David, Jennifer, Frances. A.B., Harvard U., 1955, M.A., 1957, Ph.D, 1959; D.Sc. (hon.), U. Ala., 1981. Teaching fellow Harvard U., 1955-59; cytotaxonomist Arnold Arboretum, Harvard U., 1959-61; asst. prof. biology U. Ala., University, 1961-62, assoc. prof., 1962-66, prof., 1966, asst. dean, 1964-65, dean of students, 1969-74, v.p., 1974-75, pres., 1981—; chancellor N.C. State U., 1976-81; dir. Am. Defender Life Ins. Co., Blount, Inc.; mem. exec. com. So. Regional Edn. Bd. Trustee Internat. Potato Center, 1977-83, chmn. bd., 1981-83. Named to Ala. Acad. of Honor, 1983. Mem. Bot. Soc. Am., Internat. Assn. Plant Taxonomists, Am. Soc. Plant Taxonomy, So. Assn. Schs. and Colls. (exec. com.), Ala. C. of C. (dir.), Tuscaloosa C. of C. (dir.), Phi Beta Kappa, Sigma Xi, Omicron Delta Kappa, Alpha Lambda Delta. Episcopalian. Club: North River Yacht. Author: (with Blanche Dean and Amy Mason) Wildflowers of Alabama, 1973; (with Donald Noble) The Rising South, 1976. Office: PO Box B University AL 35486

THOMAS, JOHN CHARLES, state supreme court justice; b. Norfolk, Va., Sept. 18, 1950; s. John and Floretta V. (Sears) T.; m. Pearl Walden, Oct. 9, 1982. B.A. with distinction in Am. Govt., U. Va., 1972. Bar: Va. 1975, U.S. Dist. Ct. ea. and we. dists 1976, U.S. Ct. Appeals 4th cir. 1976, U.S. Supreme Ct. 1979, U.S. Ct. Appeals D.C. cir. 1980. Law clk. civil rights div. Dept. Justice, Washington, summer 1973; mem. staff spl. council to pres. and legal advisor to rector and visitors U. Va., Charlottesville, 1973-74, 74-75; assoc. Hunton & Williams Richmond, Va., 1975-82, ptnr. 1982-83; justice Supreme Ct. of Va., Richmond, 1983—. Mem. Gov.'s Commn. of Future of Va.; former mem. bd. dirs. Leadership Met. Richmond; operating bd. Met. Econ. Devel. Council, Richmond. Mem. Va. State Bar (former mem. 3d dist. com.), Va. Bar Assn. (law sch. liaison), Bar Assn. City of Richmond, Old Dominion Bar Assn.

(former mem. exec. com.), U. Va. Alumni Assn. Office: Supreme Ct Va PO Box 1315 Richmond VA 23210

THOMAS, JOHN EDWIN, university chancellor; b. Fort Worth, Tex., Apr. 23, 1931; s. John L. and Dorothy F. T.; B.S.E.E., U. Kans., 1953; J.D., U. Mo., Kansas City, 1961; M.S., Fla. State U., 1965, D.B.A., 1970; m. Janice Paula Winzinek, Jan. 29, 1967; children—John L., Christa T., Scott A., Brandon F. With Wagner Electric Corp., St. Louis, 1955-63, mgr. elec. apparatus div., Atlanta, 1961-63; with NASA, Cape Kennedy, Fla., 1963-70, chief requirements and resources office, dir. tech. support, 1966-70; prof., head gen. bus. dept. East Tex. State U., 1970-72; dean Coll. Scis. and Tech., 1972-74; vice chancellor for acad. affairs Appalachian State U., Boone, N.C., 1974-79, chancellor, 1979—. Served with USN, 1949-50; with USMC, 1953-55. NDEA fellow, 1968. Mem. Fed. Bar Assn., Soc. Advancement Mgmt., So. Mgmt. Assn., Phi Delta Kappa, Delta Gamma Sigma. Methodist. Club: Kiwanis. Home: Appalachian State Univ Chancellor's Home Boone NC 28608 Office: Office of Chancellor Appalachian State U Boone NC 28608

THOMAS, JOHN PERRY, accountant; b. Tallahassee, Fla., May 2, 1944; s. John D. and Sara (Quaile) T.; m. Kay W. Thomas, Aug. 13, 1966; children—Cathryn, Sara. B.S., Fla. State U., 1966, M.Accountancy, 1968. C.P.A., Fla. Acct. Price Waterhouse & Co., Miami, Fla., 1968-72; ptnr. Barineau, Walker, Cherry & Thomas, Tallahassee, 1972-78; ptnr. May Zima & Co., Tallahassee, 1978-82, mng. ptnr., 1983—. Mem. Am. Inst. C.P.A.s, Fla. Soc. C.P.A.s, Assoc. Industries of Fla. (bd. dirs.), Fin. Acctg. Standards Adv. Council. Episcopalian. Club: Governors. Home: Route 13 Box 396 Tallahassee FL 32303 Office: May Zima & Co 215 S Monroe St Tallahassee FL 32301

THOMAS, JULIAN DEWAYNE, lawyer, state legislator; b. Carthage, Miss., Mar. 16, 1954; s. Walter Julian and Bobbie Ruth (Moore) T.; m. Linda Jeanette Dickerson, Oct. 2, 1982; children—David, Ryan. B.A., U. Miss.-Oxford, 1977; J.D., Miss. Coll. Sch. Law, 1980. Bar: Miss. 1980, U.S. Dist. Ct. (so. dist.) Miss. 1981, U.S. Ct. Appeals (5th cir.) 1982. Sole practice law, Jackson, Miss., 1981—. Mem. Miss. Ho. of Reps., Jackson, 1984—. Mem. Hinds County Bar Assn., Miss. Bar Assn., Miss. Trial Lawyers Assn., Am. Trial Lawyers Assn., Jackson Jaycees (dir. 1982). Republican. Baptist. Lodge: Exchange (pres. 1984). Home: 3802 Camilla Dr Jackson MS 39212 Office: PO Box 1695 Jackson MS 39265

THOMAS, LEE BALDWIN, mfg. co. exec.; b. Alma, Nebr., Sept. 17, 1900; s. Rees and Fannie (Baldwin) T.; B.B.A., U. Wash., 1923; m. Margaret Thomas, 1924 (dec.); m. 2d, Elizabeth C. Bromley, 1967; children—Lee Baldwin, Margaret Ellen Thomas Dunbar, Susan Jane Thomas Hamilton. Advt. mgr. Ernst Hardware Co., Seattle, 1923-24, sales mgr., 1926-29; buyer R.H. Macy Co., N.Y.C., 1924-25; dir. home goods merchandising Butler Bros., Chgo., 1929-41; pres. Ekco Products Co., Chgo., 1941-47; with Am. Elevator & Machine Co., Louisville, 1947-48; now chmn. bd. Thomas Industries, Inc., Louisville, Ct. Am. Corp., Louisville; owner Honey Locust Valley Farms, Cloverport, Ky. Episcopalian. Clubs: Owl Creek (Anchorage, Ky.); Harmony Landing Country (Goshen, Ky.); Huntg Creek Country (Prospect, Ky.), Jefferson, Pendennis, Louisville, Union League, Mid-Day, Chgo., Lake Region Yacht and Country, Delray Dunes (Fla.), Mountain Lake (Lake Wales, Fla.). Office: 100 E Liberty Louisville KY 40202

THOMAS, LINDSEY KAY, JR., research biologist, educator, consultant; b. Salt Lake City, Apr. 16, 1931; s. Lindsey Kay and Naomi Lurie (Biesinger) T.; m. Nancy Ruth Van Dyke, Aug. 24, 1956; children—Elizabeth Nan Thomas Cardinale, David Lindsey, Wayne Hal, Dorothy Ann. B.S., Utah State Agrl. Coll., 1953; M.S., Brigham Young U., 1958; Ph.D., Duke U., 1974. Park naturalist Nat. Capital Parks, Nat. Park Service, Washington, 1957-62, research park naturalist Region 6, Washington, 1962-63, research park naturalist Nat. Capital Region, Washington, 1963-66, research biologist S.E. Temperate Forest Park Areas, Washington, 1966, Durham, N.C., 1966-67, Great Falls, Md., 1967-71, research biologist Nat. Capital Parks, Great Falls, 1971-74, research biologist Nat. Capital Region, Triangle, Va., 1974—; instr. Dept. Agr. Grad. Sch., 1964-66; ecol. cons. Fairfax Count (Va.) Fedn. Citizens Assns., 1970-71; guest lectr. U. D.C., 1976. Asst. scoutmaster and scoutmaster, merit badges counselor Boy Scouts Am., 1958—, Scouters Tng. award, 1961. Recipient incentive awards Nat. Park Service, 1962; research grantee Washington Biologists Field Club, 1977, 82. Mem. AAAS, Bot. Soc. Washington, Ecol. Soc. Am., George Wright Soc., Nature Conservancy, Soc. Early Hist. Archaeology, Washington Biologists Field Club, Sigma Xi. Mormon. Contbr. articles profl. jours. Home: 13854 Delaney Rd Woodbridge VA 22193 Office: PO Box 209 Prince William Forest Park Triangle VA 22172 also Nat Capital Region of Nat Park Service 1100 Ohio Dr SW Washington DC 20242

THOMAS, LOWELL, business exec., state senator; b. Fountain City, Tenn., Jan. 14, 1907; student Tenn. Wesleyan Coll., U. Tenn., Knoxville; married. Sheriff, Madison County, Tenn., 1960-66; mem. Tenn. Senate. Mem. VFW. Democrat. Baptist. Clubs: Jackson Lions, Elks, Moose, Masons, Shriners. Office: Room 11 Legislative Plaza Nashville TN 37219*

THOMAS, MARY ANN SELLARO, court reporter; b. Morgantown, W.Va., Dec. 24, 1949; d. Antonio Mark Sr. and Catherine (Chico) Sellaro; m. Robert Stanley Thomas, Sept. 2, 1972; 1 child, Catherine Louise. Cert. W.Va. Career Coll., 1968, Duff's Bus. Inst., Pitts., 1981; B.S. in Bus. Edn., W.Va. U., 1972. Tchr. bus. edn. Clay-Battelle High Sch., Blacksville, W.Va., 1972-74, Lakewood High Sch., Ohio, 1974-76; tchr. remedial math. John A. Holmes High Sch., Edenton, N.C., 1979; tchr. bus. edn. Duff's Bus. Inst., 1980-81; ofcl. ct. reporter N.C. Superior Ct., Raleigh, 1982—; mem. N.C. Ct. Reporter Standards Com., Raleigh, 1985—. Dir. pub. relations Edenton Little Theatre Group, 1978; program chmn. Edenton Women's Club, 1978-79; active spl. events Peanut Festival, Edenton, 1978; del. W.Va. Democratic Conv., Charleston, 1980. Named to Outstanding Young Women Am., U.S. Jaycees, 1984. Mem. Nat. Shorthand Reporter's Assn., N.C. Shorthand Reporter's Assn. (treas. 1985—, bd. dirs. eastern area 1984-85), Alpha Delta Pi (membership adviser 1979-81, Meritorious Service award 1980). Roman Catholic. Avocations: reading; crocheting; swimming.

THOMAS, MARY BARTON, marriage and family counselor; b. Sherman, Tex., Nov. 4, 1954; B.S. in Social Sci. and Elem. Edn., Southeastern Okla. State U., 1976; M.Ed. in Ednl. Diagnosis and Psychology, Abilene Christian U., 1979; m. William M. Thomas, 1978. Lic. profl. counselor, Tex.; basic, intermediate, advance and instrs. certs. Tex. Commn. on Law Enforcement Officer Standards and Edn. Tchr. Durant (Okla.) Middle Sch., 1976; substitute tchr. Sunset Elem. Sch., Healdton, Okla., 1976; asst. ednl. diagnostician spl. edn. dept. Abilene Ind. Sch. Dist., 1978; police officer Dallas Police Dept., 1979—, staff counselor, investigator, 1981—. Recipient Life Saving award Dallas Police Dept., 1983, Safe Driving award, 1985. Delta Kappa Epsilon scholar, 1973; Red River Valley Hist. scholar, 1975-76. Mem. Internat. Law Enforcement Stress Assn., Dallas Psychol. Assn., Am. Assn. Counseling and Devel., Tex. Mcpl. Police Assn., Dallas Police Assn., Kappa Delta Pi, Phi Alpha Theta. Club: Ko Jai Kai. Home: 16208 Fallkirk Dr Dallas TX 75248 Office: 8700 Stemmons Freeway Suite 352 Dallas TX 75247

THOMAS, MAXINE, educational administrator; b. Broken Arrow, Okla., Oct. 21, 1936; d. Grover M. and Ethel Lee (Watts) Norwood; m. Bobby Gene Thomas, June 29, 1957; children—Rinda Lee, Jana Kay, James Dowell. B.S., Northeastern Okla. State U., 1957. Tchr., Owasso High Sch., Okla., 1957-70; tchr., counselor Tulsa Skills Ctrs., 1971-75, asst. dir., 1974-77; instr. Tulsa Vo-Tech Sch., 1977-82, adult edn. supr., 1982—; liaison Jobs Tng. Partnership Authority, Tulsa, 1984-85. Mem. Refugee Relocating Com., Tulsa, 1983-85; leader Owasso 4-H Club, 1979-85; mem. Owasso Band Patrons, 1970-85. Recipient Great Am. Family award Tulsa County Home Extension, 1984; Tchr. of Yr. award Owasso Pub. Schs., 1967; Leader of Yr., Tulsa County 4-H, 1983; Clover award Okla. 4-H Found., 1983-85. Mem. Owasso C. of C., Am. Vocat. Assn., Okla. Vocat. Assn., NEA, Okla. Edn. Assn., Am. Soc. Tng. and Devel., 4-H Leaders Council (sec. 1982). Democrat. Baptist. Avocations: photography; owl collecting. Home: 7841 N 134 E Ave Owasso OK 74055 Office: 3802 N Peoria St Tulsa OK 74055

THOMAS, MICHAEL CONDON, real estate developer; b. Ada, Okla., Mar. 23, 1950; s. Tom Albert and Bette (Condon) T.; B.B.A., U. Okla., 1972; m. Deborah Amanda Feldman, June 30, 1973; children—Michael C., Megan Charls. With Thomas Concrete Products Co., Oklahoma City, 1973-77; pres. Michael C. Thomas Cos., Inc., Oklahoma City, 1977—. Bd. dirs. Okla. Symphony Orch., 1978-83, treas., 1981-83; bd. dirs. Oklahoma Heritage Assn., 1982—. Recipient Award of Excellence, Oklahoma City, 1980; Award of Honor, Oklahoma City Bicentennial Commn., 1976. Mem. Okla. C. of C., Nat. Assn. Indsl. and Office Parks, Bldg. Owners and Mgrs. Assn., Oklahoma County Hist. Soc. Clubs: Confederate Air Force, Oklahoma City Golf and Country. Home: 6803 Grand Blvd Oklahoma City OK 73116 Office: 525 Central Park Dr Suite 100 Oklahoma City OK 73105

THOMAS, MICHAEL RANDALL, financial banking network company executive; b. Evanston, Ill., June 9, 1943; s. Charles Randall and Dorothy (Starkel) T.; m. Beverly Carrol, Sept. 20, 1983; children—Kathryn Ann, Michael Scott. B.S., U. Ill., 1965; postgrad. U. Mich., 1966-67; M.B.A., Ga. State U., 1968. Controller, Ogden Equipment Co., Atlanta, 1967-68; accountant Arthur Andersen & Co., 1968-71; ptnr., chief exec. officer Libby, Thomas & Braxton, 1971-80; ptnr. Arthur Young & Co., 1980-82; mng. ptnr., chief exec. officer Standard Ventures Ltd., 1982-84; chief exec. officer The Thomas Fin. Group Ltd., Atlanta, 1984—; dir. Kasko, Inc. Bd. govs. World Trade Club, 1982-84; founder, mem. Ga. Cert. Devel. Corp. Mem. Nat. Assn. Small Bus. Investment Companies, Am. Inst. C.P.A.s, Ga. Soc. C.P.A.s, Atlanta C. of C., German Am. C. of C. Democrat. Episcopalian. Clubs: Capital City, World Trade. Office: Thomas Fin Group 225 Peachtree St NE Atlanta GA 30303

THOMAS, NORMAN DAY, government official; b. Kingsport, Tenn., Nov. 2, 1933; s. James Earl and Georgia Louise (Day) T.; m. Carole Dolores Williams, Sept. 1, 1962; children—Diane Lee, Mark Alexander. Student U. Tenn., 1952-53, Valdosta State Coll., 1978-79. Joined U.S. Army, 1956, advanced through grades to chief warrant officer, 1967, ret., 1977; attache specialist Def. Attache Office, Warsaw, Poland, 1965-67; acting def. attache, Accra, Ghana, 1968-70; spl. agt. Def. Investigative Service, Washington, 1970-73, Tampa and Valdosta, Ga., 1975-82 resident spl. agt., Daytona Beach, Fla., 1982—; ops. coordinator Vientiane, Laos, 1973-75; Pres. Am. Community Assn., Vientiane, Laos, 1974; treas. North Pointe Homeowners Assn., Tampa, 1977. Republican. Presbyterian. Home: 412 N Oleander Ave Daytona Beach FL 32018 Office: Defense Investigative Service PO Box 270 Daytona Beach FL 32015

THOMAS, PHILIP ROBINSON, operational management consulting company executive; b. Torquay, Devon, Eng., Dec. 9, 1934; s. Leslie Robinson and Margaret (Burridge) T.; came to U.S., 1963, naturalized, 1969; B.Sc., U. London, 1959, M.Sc., 1961, postgrad., 1961-64; m. Wayne Laverne Heirtzler, Apr. 6, 1973; children by previous marriage—Martin N.R., Stephen D. R. With Tex. Instruments Corp., 1961-72, ops. mgr., Dallas, 1963-72, Bedford, Eng., 1961-63; v.p., gen. mgr. MOS/LSI div. Gen. Instruments Co., N.Y.C., 1972-73; gen. mgr. MOS Products div. Fairchild Camera and Instrument Corp., Mountainview, Calif., 1973-75; v.p. Integrated Circuits div. RCA, Somerville, N.J., 1975-78; chmn., chief exec. officer Thomas Group Inc., Irving, Tex. 1978—. Mem. IEEE, Brit. Inst. Radio and Electronics Engrs. Contbr. articles to profl. jours.; patentee semicondrs. Home: 220 Steeple Chase Irving TX 75062 Office: Thomas Group Inc 5215 N O'Connor Rd Suite 2500 Irving TX 75039

THOMAS, RALPH STEPHENS, manufacturing company executive; b. East St. Louis, Ill., July 30, 1923; s. Joe N. and Florence (Stephens) T.; student Washington U., St. Louis, 1942; m. Bertha M. Farenzena, Dec. 14, 1944; children—Judith A. Thomas Ghaffari, Barbara J. Thomas Harris. Works mgr. Walworth Co., Greensburg, Pa., 1941-65; with Robertshaw Controls Co., Richmond, Va., 1965—, pres., chief exec. officer, 1972—; dir. Reynolds Metals Co., Bank of Va. Trust Co., Bank of Va. Co. Trustee Richmond Meml. Hosp. Served with USNR, 1943-46. Mem. Am. Gas Assn., Nat. Elec. Mfrs. Assn., Gas Appliance Mfrs. Assn. (chmn. 1979), Richmond C. of C. (dir.). Clubs: Commonwealth, Country of Va. (Richmond). Office: 1701 Byrd Ave Richmond VA 23261*

THOMAS, ROBERT ALLEN, nature and science center administrator, educator; b. Luling, Tex., Apr. 10, 1946; s. Julian H. and Katie (Schneider) T.; m. Paulette M. Jung, Aug. 17, 1968; children—Jennifer Leigh, Aimee Kathryn, Patrick Julian. B.S., U. So. La., 1970; M.S., Tex. A&M U., 1974, Ph.D., 1976. Lectr. Tex. A&M U., College Station, 1976-77; instr. La. State U. Med. Ctr., New Orleans, 1977-78; exec. dir. La. Nature and Sci. Ctr., New Orleans, 1978—; adj. prof. biol. sci. U. New Orleans, 1979—; cons. for environ. issues, New Orleans. Contbr. articles to profl. jours.; columnist. Recipient Elsie Naumburg award Nat. Sci. for Youth Found., 1983. Mem. Soc. for Study of Amphibians and Reptiles, Herpetologists League, Am. Soc. Ichthyologists and Herpetologists, La. Assn. Mus. (v.p. 1985—), Am. Assn. Mus., Southwestern Assn. Naturalists (bd. govs. 1982-85), East New Orleans C. of C. (exec. com.). Roman Catholic. Lodge: Rotary (pres. 1984-85). Avocations: tennis; writing. Office: La Nature & Sci Ctr 11000 Lake Forest Blvd New Orleans LA 70127

THOMAS, ROBERT LINDSAY, congressman; b. Patterson, Ga., Nov. 20, 1943; m. Melinda Ann Fry, 1966; children—Lindsay, Ransom, Nell. B.A., U. Ga., 1965. Investment banker, 1966-73, farmer, 1973-82; mem. 98th Congress from 1st Dist. Ga., 1982—. Mem. County Agrl. Stblzn. and Conservation Service, Ga. Agrl. Commodity Commn. for Tobacco; active Leadership Ga., Leadership Savannah; bd. stewards Screven United Meth. Ch. Mem. Wayne County Young Farmers, Wayne County Farm Bur., County Bd. Realtors. Democrat. Office: Room 431 Cannon House Office Bldg Washington DC 20515

THOMAS, ROYCE PHELPS, state senator, fruit and vegetable distributor; b. Avon Park, Fla., Jan. 3, 1932; s. J.R. and Eunice M. (Phelps) T.; m. Margaret C. Stonecipher, May 19, 1951; children—James Royce, Mary Cecille Thomas Vieira, Richard Latt. Student Duke U., 1948-51, U.S. Army Advanced Infantry Officers Sch., Ft. Benning, Ga., 1957-58. Mem. N.C. Senate, 1979-80, 81—; chmn. small bus. com., 1981; vice chmn. fin. com., 1981; mem. election laws, ins., judiciary III, local govt. and regional affairs, mfg., labor and commerce, redistricting of Senate coms., 1981. Chmn. 11th Congl. Dist. Dem. Party of N.C., 1980-81; Served to capt. U.S. Army, 1951-60. Mem. Hall of Fame, U.S. Army Infantry Officers Candidate Sch. Democrat. Lodges: Elks, Lions. Office: NC Senate State Capitol Raleigh NC 27611*

THOMAS, RUBLE ANDERSON, utility company executive; b. Birmingham, Ala., July 14, 1921; s. James A. and Grace (Smith) T.; B.S. in Mech. Engring., Ga. Inst. Tech., 1947, B.S. in Elec. Engring., 1948, M.S. in Elec. Engring., 1949; student Oak Ridge Sch. Reactor Tech., 1953-54; m. Mary Jo Bass, Feb. 16, 1941; children—James Lewis, Janice Thomas Jones. Electric design engr. Commonwealth & So. Corp., Birmingham, 1948; with So. Co. Services Inc., Birmingham, Ala., 1949—, mgr. nuclear power, 1959-65, asst. to pres., 1965-66, v.p., 1966—; v.p. Ga. Power Co., 1984—. Mem. So. Interstate Nuclear Bd., 1966-77; dir. Power Reactor Devel. Co., Detroit, 1968-73; trustee High Temperature Reactor Devel. Assos., 1967-73. Served to 1st lt. AUS, 1943-44, USAAF, 1944-46. Registered profl. engr., Ala., Fla., Ga., Mich., Miss. Mem. Am. Nuclear Soc. (dir.), ASME, Atomic Indsl. Forum, Edison Electric Inst., Electric Power Research Inst., IEEE. Clubs: Kiwanis, Downtown, Inverness Country. Home: 5033 Kerry Downs Rd Birmingham AL 35243 Office: PO Box 2625 Birmingham AL 35202

THOMAS, SANDRA PAUL, nurse educator, researcher; b. Moline, Ill., Mar. 9, 1940; d. Raymond Spencer and Oceana Lee (Agee) Paul; m. Eddie King Thomas, Dec. 17, 1960 (div. June 24, 1977); children—Kenneth, Tommy, Shana. B.S. in Edn., U. Tenn., 1974, M.S. in Edn., 1977, Ph.D. in Edn., 1983, M.S. in Nursing, 1984. Staff nurse East Tenn. Baptist Hosp., Knoxville, 1964-74; instr. psychiat. mental health nursing East Tenn. Bapt. Sch. Nursing, Knoxville, 1975-80; project dir. Kellogg grant U. Tenn., Knoxville, 1983—. Contbr. articles to profl. jours. and research presentations to nat. confs. Mem. governing bd. East Tenn. Health Improvement Council, Knoxville, 1976-82; mem. Knoxville Mental Health Assn.; bd. dirs. Greater Knoxville Epilepsy Found., 1980-83. Fellow Nat. Inst. Edn., 1981-82; recipient Jessie Harris award U. Tenn., 1983, Outstanding Dissertation award, 1984; named Outstanding Doctoral Student U. Tenn., 1983. Mem. Am. Nurses Assn., Tenn. Nurses Assn. (dist. pres. 1978-80, vice chmn. nurse educators spl. interest group 1984—; Nurse of Yr. award 1980), Am. Psychol. Assn., Soc. Behavioral Medicine, Sigma Theta Tau, Phi Kappa Phi. Presbyterian. Avocations: Travel, writing, music. Office: U Tenn Coll Nursing 1200 Volunteer Blvd Knoxville TN 37996

THOMAS, WILLIAM CHARLES, publishing executive; b. Chgo., Dec. 25, 1926; s. Charles Murrel and Louise Frances (Hoeppner) T.; m. Jane Thomas, June 7, 1947; children—Valerie, Susan, Kimberly. Advt. salesman, bur. mgr. St. Petersburg Times, Fla., 1946-60; v.p., adv. dir. Worrell Newspapers, Inc., Bristol, Va., 1960-61, pub., Suffolk, Va., 1961-62, asst. to pub., Florence, Ala., 1967-68; asst. gen. mgr. Cox Newspapers, Miami, Fla., 1962-66; advt. dir., pub. Hearst Corp., San Antonio, 1968—; now chief operating exec.; dir. Republic Bank San Antonio. Bd. dirs. Santa Rosa Health Care Corp., San Antonio chpt. ARC, San Antonio Econ. Devel. Found., San Antonio Zool. Soc., San Antonio Performing Arts Assn., San Antonio Symphony; trustee Santa Rosa Med. Ctr., Southwest Research Inst. Served with AC USN, 1944-46. Mem. Greater San Antonio C. of C. (bd. dirs.), World Affairs Council, Univ. Round Table, Am. Newspaper Pubs. Assn., So. Newspaper Pubs. Assn., Tex. Daily Newspaper Assn. (bd. dirs.), Tex. Press Assn. Clubs: San Antonio Golf Assn. (bd. dirs.), One Hundred (bd. dirs.) Lodges: Lions (v.p. 1959-60); Masons, Rotary. Office: San Antonio Light 420 Broadway San Antonio TX 78205

THOMASSON, SYLVIA MCCARDEL, human service educator, administrator; b. Telogia, Fla., July 31, 1938; d. Allison Chesley and C.A. Victoria (Elmore) McCardel; m. Ray Gerald Thomasson, Sept. 20, 1956; children—Victoria Lee, Donna Ray, Cathy Lynn, Charles Jack, II. B.S. in Edn., Fla. So. Coll., 1968; M.A. in Counseling and Guidance, U. So. Fla., 1972, S.Ed. in Counseling and Guidance, 1974; D.Ed., Nova U., 1982. Counselor Pasco-Hernando Community Coll., Brooksville, Fla., 1974-77, coordinator counseling, 1977-78, campus dean North Campus, 1978-82, dir. title III dist. office, Dade City, Fla., 1982-84, dir. human services, New Port Richey, Fla., 1984—; chmn. staff and program devel. com., college wide, 1984-85. Communication chmn. Am. Heart Assn. of Fla., St. Petersburg, 1982—, mem. state and local bd., 1981; sponsor Human Service Club, New Port Richey, 1984—. Mem. Internat. Soc. for Coll. and Univ. Planning, Nat. Assn. Human Services Educators, So. Assn. Human Services Educators, Fla. Assn. of Community Colls., Phi Delta Kappa. Democrat. Baptist. Club: Music (Brooksville) (pres. 1983-84, v.p. 1984-85). Avocations: lecturer; writting; art collecting; music. Home: 4320 White Rd Brooksville FL 33512 Office: Pasco-Hernando Community Coll 7025 State Rd 587 New Port Richey FL 33552

THOMPSON, ANDREW BOYD, JR., publishing company executive; b. West Point, Ga., Mar. 30, 1930; s. Andrew Boyd and Frieda Jaqueline (Smith) T.; student Auburn U., 1948-49; m. Laura June Guy, Mar. 13, 1959; children—Guy Bradly, Eric Kiepp. Materials engr. asst. Ala. Hwy. Dept., Montgomery, 1949-51, 54-55; lab. technician So. Testing Labs., Montgomery, 1955; salesman, mgr. Mel's Photo Shop, Montgomery, 1955-57, 58-66; agt. Prudential Ins. Co. Am., Montgomery, 1957-58; furniture salesman Sears, Roebuck & Co., Montgomery, 1966; v.p., gen. mgr. Nat. Photo Pricing Service, Inc., Montgomery, 1966-81, pres., 1981—; pres. Nat. Pricing Services, Inc., Montgomery, 1981—. Bd. dirs. Friends of Epilepsy, 1977—, pres., 1977-78, sec., 1978—; mem. Ala. Gov.'s Task Force on Epilepsy; active Boy Scouts Am. Served with U.S. Army, 1951-54; lt. col. Res. ret. Recipient numerous awards including Dist. Award Merit, Boy Scouts Am. Mem. Photo Mktg. Assn. Internat., Photog. Mfrs. and Distbrs. Assn., Nat. Audio-Visual Assn., Mil. Order World Wars, Ret. Officers Assn. (life), Res. Officers Assn. (life), Internat. Platform Assn., Ala. C. of C., Montgomery C. of C., Am. Legion, Am. Biog. Inst. Research Assn. (life). Methodist. Office: PO Box 3008 Eastbrook Sta Montgomery AL 36109

THOMPSON, ANNETTE SHIREY, deaf education educator, educational consultant; b. Little Rock, May 1, 1940; d. Alton J. and Freida Elizabeth (Yarbrough) Shirey; m. Charles D. Thompson (dec. Apr. 1977). B.A., Centenary Coll., 1961; M. Communication Disorders, U. Okla., 1965. Council on Edn. of Deaf. Tchr., Pilot Sch. for Deaf, Dallas, 1965-68; supr. and curriculum coordinator Callier Hearing and Speech Center, Dallas, 1968-70; prin. W.Va. Schs. for Deaf and Blind, Romney, W.Va., 1970-80; instr. deaf edn. tchr. tng. program U. Tulsa, 1980—; ednl. cons. to pub. sch. deaf edn. programs; mem. state adv. bd.; mem. Early Identification Task Force Com.; officer Okla. Council on Hearing Impaired. Mem. bd. March of Dimes; vol. worker United Way. Recipient Outstanding Faculty award U. Tulsa, 1981. Mem. Am. Conv. of Instrs. of Deaf, A.G. Bell Assn., Conf. Ednl. Adminstrs. Serving the Deaf (assoc.), Okla. Council on Hearing Impaired, Okla. Tchrs. of Hearing Impaired; Okla. Univ. Personnel Assn., Tulsa Speech and Hearing Assn. (bd. dirs. 1980—). Republican. Presbyterian. Home: 7357 E 58th Pl Tulsa OK 74145 Office: University of Tulsa 600 S College Ave Tulsa OK 74104

THOMPSON, BARRY B., university president. Pres. Tarleton State U., Stephenville, Tex. Office: Office of Pres Tarleton State U Tarleton Sta Stephenville TX 76402

THOMPSON, BILLY WEBSTER, air force officer; b. Pioneer, La., Aug. 18, 1947; s. Webster Able and Tressie Pauline (Buchannan) T.; m. Mary Evelyn Cannon, Oct. 30, 1970; 1 child, Patricia. B.S. in Biology, N.E. La. U., 1969; A.A.S. in Edn., Community Coll. of Air Force, 1977; M.A. in Counseling, La. Tech. U., 1977. Joined U.S. Air Force, 1969, advanced through grades to capt., 1972; tchr., counselor U.S. Dept Interior, Puxico, Mo., 1978-79; air traffic controller FAA, Childress, Tex., 1979-80; guidance counselor U.S. Air Force, Dyess AFB, Abilene Tex., 1980-85; edn. services officer U.S. Air Force, Cannon AFB, Clovis, N.Mex., 1985—; adv. council Eastern N.Mex. U., Clovis, 1985—; aviation mgmt. officer U.S. Army Res., St. Louis, 1985—. Decorated Air medal. Mem. Am. Assn. Counseling and Devel. Democrat. Lodge: Masons. Home: Route 1 Pioneer LA 71266 Office: 27 CSG/DPE Cannon AFB Clovis NM 88103

THOMPSON, CARSON R., specialty retail and leather manufacturing company executive; b. Wilson, Okla., Feb. 10, 1939; s. Silas and Della (Woods) T.; m. Charlotte Arwine, Dec. 26, 1959; children—Shelley Elaine, Susan Denise. B.S., Tex. Wesleyan Coll., 1962. Leather buyer, mdse. mgr. Tandy Leather Co., Ft. Worth, 1970-74, 74-77; pres. Tex Tan Welhausen Co., Yoakum, Tex., 1978; v.p. Tandy Brands Corp., Fort Worth, 1981—, chmn. bd., chief exec. officer, 1982—. Home: 8873 Random Rd Forth Worth TX 76179 Office: 550 Bailey Suite 400 Fort Worth TX 76107

THOMPSON, CHARLES GLOVER, architect; b. Boston, Dec. 10, 1928; s. Richard Cowles and Margaret (Peterson) T.; m. Thelma M. Thoms, Jan. 28, 1956; children—David G., Mark K. A.A., Boston U., 1952; B.S. in Architecture, R.I. Sch. Design, 1959. Architect, N.E. region Howard Johnson Co., Braintree, Mass., 1963-67; architect C. Glover Thompson Architect, AIA, Brockton, Mass., 1967-77, St. John, V.I., 1983—; chief architect V.I. Housing Authority, 1978-83; pres. Thompson Cons., Inc., 1984—. Mem. Commn. for Handicapped, 1982. Served with CIA, 1947-49. Mem. AIA, Nat. Council Archtl. Registration Bd. Republican. Archtl. projects: restoration of Slater Mill Mus., Pawtucket, R.I., 1960; first parish in U.S., W. Bridgewater, Mass., 1964; Emmaus Manse, St. John; author, lectr.: Do It Yourself Architecture. Home: Coral Bay St John VI 00830

THOMPSON, CHRISTINE EPPS, librarian; b. Ft. Worth, Nov. 1, 1940; d. John Robert Epps and Eva May (Taylor) Epps McKee; m. Robert Edgar Thompson, Jr., Sept. 28, 1957; children—Thomas Len, Robert Kearn. B.A., North Tex. State U., 1964, M.A., 1966, M.L.S., 1970. Teaching asst. North Tex. State U., Denton, 1964-65, library clk., 1968-70; librarian Tarleton State U., Stephenville, 1970-83; teaching asst. Tex. Woman's U., Denton, 1983-84; head original cataloging dept. Tex. A&M U. Library, College Station, 1984—. Author bibliographies. Mem. ALA, A Coll. Research Libraries, Tex. Library Assn. (chmn. scholarship com. 1980-81, chmn. intellectual freedom com. 1983-84), Tex. Assn. Coll. Tchrs. (exec. bd. 1980-81, nomination com. 1983-84), Library Adminstrn. and Mgmt. Assn., Am. Mgmt. Assn. Democrat. Baptist.

THOMPSON, DEAN ALLAN, cattleman; b. Peru, Ind., Jan. 29, 1934; s. Paul Franklin and Pauline St. Clair (Thrush) T.; student Purdue U., 1952-54. Mgr. Thompson Farms, breeders registered Hereford cattle, Peru, 1956-69; owner Thompson Farms, Wartrace, Tenn. and Peru, 1970—, Dean Thompson Prodns., Wartrace, Wartrace Records; chmn. bd. Instant Copy and Printing, Inc., Monterey, Calif., Trenton Energy Inc., 1977-83, Bloomfield, Ind.; v.p., dir. 5B Cattle Co., Twin Bridges, Mont.; internat. beef cattle judge; dir. Maine Manna, Gorham. Bd. dirs. H.A. Thrush Found., Peru; trustee Middle Tenn. State U. Found., 1981-83, 85—, chmn. fin. com., 1982-83, 85—, mem. exec. com., 1983; precinct committeeman, chmn. Miami County (Ind.) Young Republican Com., 1962-67; treas. 5th Dist. Young Reps., 1965-66. Served with U.S. Army, 1955-56. Mem. Nat. Western (dir.), Ind. (dir. 1958-68, pres. 1960) polled Hereford assns., Ind. Cattleman's Assn. (founding dir.), Ind. Livestock Breeders Assn., Am. Hereford Assn. (v.p. pres.'s council 1981, pres. 1982),

Tenn. Hereford Assn. (dir. 1977-81, v.p. 1979, pres. 1980-81). Presbyterian. Clubs: Toastmasters (pres., area gov.); Columbia (Indpls.). Home and Office: Box 230 Route 1 Wartrace TN 37183

THOMPSON, DOLA SEARCY, anesthesiologist; b. Benton, Ark., Sept. 15, 1926; d. Ben Veo and Imogene (Anderson) Searcy; m. Bernard W. Thompson, June 20, 1948; children—Elizabeth Ann, Cynthia Thompson Feinberg. Student Little Rock Jr. Coll., 1943-44, Baylor U., 1944-45; M.D., U. Ark., 1949. Diplomate Am. Bd. Anesthesiologists. Intern, Women's and Children's Hosp., San Francisco, 1949-50; resident U. Ark. Coll. Medicine, Little Rock, 1951-53; practice medicine specializing in anesthesiology, Little Rock, 1953-59; chief div. anesthesiology U. Ark. for Med. Scis., Little Rock, 1959-74, prof., chmn. dept. anesthesiology, 1974—; cons. Little Rock VA Hosp., 1974—, Ark. Children's Hosp., 1974—. Mem. CPR adv. com. Ark. Heart Assn., 1974-75. Named to Alumni Elite 500, U. Ark., 1977—. Mem. AMA, Am. Coll. Anesthesiologists, Am. Coll. Chest Physicians, Soc. Acad. Anesthesia Chairmen, AAUW, Sigma Xi. Presbyterian. Office: U Ark for Med Scis 4301 W Markham St Little Rock AR 72205

THOMPSON, DOUGLAS HERSCHEL, JR., business executive, accountant; b. Alexandria, Va., Aug. 8, 1942; s. Douglas H. and Ruth B. Thompson; m. Sara P., Sept. 13, 1970; children—Scott, Ryan. B.S. in Bus. Adminstrn., U. Fla., 1965. C.P.A. Exec. dir. Fla. Bd. Accountancy, 1968-81; adj. prof. acctg. Sch. Acctg. U. Fla., Gainesville, 1975-80; presdl. exec. editor Ind. Profl., Inc., Gainesville, 1981—; exec. dir. Acctg. Firms Assoc., Inc., Gainesville, 1982—. Active Fla. Heart Assn., Children's Home Soc., Salvation Army. Served with USAR, 1965-71. Mem. Am. Inst. C.P.A.s, Fla. Inst. C.P.A.s, Fla. Soc. Assn. Execs., Fla. Press Assn., Fla. Mgmt. Assn., Assn. Area Bus. Publs. Methodist. Office: Acctg Firm Assoc PO Box 14698 Gainesville FL 32604

THOMPSON, ELIZABETH DENHAM, association executive; b. Houston, Nov. 17, 1956; d. William Ernest, Jr. and (Emma) Priscilla (Kelley) Denham; m. Phillip Allen Thompson, May 5, 1979. B.S. in Edn., Baylor U., 1978. Cert. tchr., Tex. Adminstrv. asst. Word, Inc., Waco, Tex., 1978-79; account exec. Charles Wallis, Inc., Waco, 1979-80, program dir., 1980-81; pub. communications specialist, City of Waco, 1981-84; program coordinator Leukemia Soc. Am., 1985—. Active 7th and James Baptist Ch., 1974-85, Manor Bapt. Ch., San Antonio, 1985-86, Bapt. Ch. of Covenant, Birmingham, 1986—; blood drive chmn. ARC, Waco, 1978-84; vol. worker, mem. speakers bur. Waco Rape Crisis Ctr., 1980-84; active Gen. Fedn. Women's Clubs, 1980-84; co-chmn. docent div. Historic Waco Found., 1981-83; mem. publicity com. Caritas of Waco, 1980-82; regional Alcohol Adv. Com., Heart of Tex. Council Govts., 1982-84; mem. Downtown Waco Goals Com., 1983. Mem. Pub. Relations Soc. Am. (chpt. dir.-at-large 1983-84, accredited pub. relations 1984), Am. Advt. Fedn. (Waco seminar chairperson 1983-84), Chi Omega, Theta Kappa. Democrat. Southern Baptist. Home: 4428 8th Ave S Birmingham AL 35222 Office: 1608 13th Ave S Suite 103 Birmingham AL 35205

THOMPSON, FRANK JAMES, real estate broker, radio station official, author; b. Rowan County, N.C., June 4, 1947; s. Richard Hunter and Virginia Catherine (Blair) T.; m. Mitsy Diane Rivers, June 12, 1980; children—Frank James, Susan. B.S., U. Va., 1969. Enforcement officer Rowan County Alcoholic Beverage Commn. Police, Rowan County, 1969-72; agt. dept. alcoholism, tobacco and firearms U.S. Treasury North Wilkesboro, N.C., 1972-75; program dir. Sta. WTIK, Durham, N.C., 1975-80, 82—; real estate broker Lowder Real Estate Co., Durham, 1980—. Pres., Young Republican Club, 1980. Served to lt. USAFR. Mem. N.C. Sheriff's Assn., Radio Broadcasters Am., Nat. Assn. Broadcasters, Nat. Bd. Realtors. Baptist. Club: Exchange. Lodge: Kiwanis (v.p. 1979). Author: The Horses Have It, 1980; The New Wave, 1982. Home: 707 Leon St Durham NC 27707 Office: PO Box 1571 Durham NC 27702

THOMPSON, FRANK MARION, military medical technician; b. Montgomery, Ala., June 28, 1955; s. Frank Marion Savage and Martha Janet (Parsons) Thompson; m. Sarah Jane Dorsey, Apr. 30, 1977; 1 son, Frank Edward. B.S., Troy State Coll., 1984. Lic. practical nurse, emergency med. technician. Mgr., Ranch House, Kissimmee, Orlando and Melborne, Fla., 1974-76; kitchen mgr. House of Plenty, Merit Island, Fla., 1976-77; enlisted U.S. Air Force, 1977; med. service specialist USAF Regional Hosp., Montgomery, Ala., 1977-81; emergency room shift leader, 1981-83, ob-gyn supr., 1983—; instr. basic cardiac life support Am. Heart Assn., Tex., Ala., 1981—. Mem., rep. Montgomery Men's Assn., 1983. Mem. Nat. Rifle Assn. Republican. Presbyterian.

THOMPSON, HENRY EDWARD, real estate consultant; b. Dighton, Mich., Sept. 19, 1918; s. John Mark and Eva Melvina (Cusick) T.; m. Mary Kathleen Frost, June 3, 1965; children—James, Jane, Kristy, Scott. A.B.B.S., U. Western Mich., 1940; postgrad. U. Ga., 1973-74. Real estate cons., Fla. Owner Hank Thompson Realty, Inc., Boynton, Fla., 1958—, pres., 1984—. Trustee Fla. Kiwanis Found., 1975-84, Habilitation Ctr. Physically Handicapped, 1979-84; chmn. Community Redevel. Agy., Boynton Beach, Fla., 1983-84. Served with inf. U.S. Army, 1943-46; PTO. Decorated Bronze Star; recipient Indsl. award Gov. of Fla., 1968; named Fla. Real Estate Assoc. of Yr., 1965, Man of Yr., City of Boynton Beach (Fla.), 1967. Mem. Realtors Nat. Mktg. Inst., Nat. Assn. Realtors, Internat. Assn. Realtors, Fla. Assn. Realtors. Presbyterian. Clubs: Kiwanis (pres.). Lodges: Elks, Masons. Contbr. articles to profl. jours.

THOMPSON, JACK NEAL, economics educator, investor, consultant; b. Millerton, Okla., Oct. 10, 1931; s. Frank James and Connie Cornelia (Logan) T.; m. Ingrid Kringstad, Oct. 7, 1958; children—Erik, Susanne. B.A. in Econs., U. Okla., 1968; M.A. in Econs., Tex. Christian U., 1976. Cons. economist U.S. Govt., 1968—; prof. econs. Tex. Christian U., Ft. Worth, 1981—. Served with USAF, 1948-62. Mem. Omicron Delta Epsilon. Democrat. Club: Headliners (Ft. Worth). Home and Office: 4632 Brandingshire Pl Fort Worth TX 76133

THOMPSON, JAMES HENRY, television broadcasting company executive; b. Taylors, S.C., July 8, 1928; s. Lawrence Edwin and Esther Rozelle (Wood) Thompson; m. Joanne Upton, Apr. 22, 1955; 1 son: Vincent Gene. B.Th., Holmes Theol. Seminary, 1950. D.D., 1976; B.A., Furman U., 1952; D.D. (hon.), United Christian Internat. Bible Inst., 1983. Pres., Carolina Christian Broadcasting Co., Greenville, 1972—; owner, mgr. Faith Printing Co., Taylors, 1958—. Author: First Steps, 1984. Pres., Mountain View Elem. PTA, 1968. Home: RR 2 Taylors SC 29687

THOMPSON, JAMES TIPTON, university dean, animal nutritionist; b. Murray, Ky., Apr. 23, 1941; s. James E. and Larue (Hendon) T.; m. Patricia King, June 8, 1963; children—Lora, Heather. B.S., Murray State U., 1963; M.S., U. Ky., 1964, Ph.D., 1966. Assoc. prof. Ill. State U., Normal, 1966-75; head dept. agr. Murray State U., 1975-79; dean Sch. Agr., West Tex. State U., Canyon, 1979—. Contbr. articles to profl. jours. Active Ky. Bd. Agr., Frankford, 1975-79. Recipient Agri scholarships Houston Livestock Show, 1980-85. Mem. Agr. Consortium Tex. (pres., v.p. 1979-80), Water, Inc., Am. Assn. Schs. and Colls. Agr. and Renewable Resources, Amarillo C. of C., Alpha Gamma Rho. Avocations: camping; hunting; stained glass. Home: 92 Hunsley Hills Blvd Canyon TX 79015 Office: West Tex State U Sch Agr PO Box 998 WT Canyon TX 79016

THOMPSON, JANNAT CROSSAN, computer software company executive; b. Brainard, Minn., June 16, 1954; d. Frank P. and Catherine C. (Crossan) T. Student U. Colo., 1972-73. Soloist, publicist, advance promotion Ice Capades, 1976-79; dir. pub. relations Universal Restaurants, B & M Enterprises, Dallas, 1979-81; cons., mgr. A.S.G.I., Dallas, 1980-82; v.p. fin. and adminstrn., dir., sec.-treas. Image Scis., Inc., Dallas, 1982—. Nat. Merit scholar finalist; gold medalist U.S. Figure Skating Assn., 1969, U.S. Pair Champion, 1972, others. Mem. Mensa. Republican. Clubs: Willow Bend Polo and Hunt, University. Home: 6211 W NW Hwy Apt 2407 Dallas TX 75225 Office: 8350 N Central St Suite 700 Dallas TX 75206

THOMPSON, JEFFREY CRONER, school administrator; b. Pitts., Sept. 20, 1947; s. William Earl and Jane (Croner) T.; m. Madeleine Clark Hillman, June 12, 1970; children—Brett McLeod, Jeremy Hillman, Peter Rhodes. B.A., Kenyon Coll., 1969; M.A., Williams Coll., 1975. Cert. high sch. prin., N.C. Tchr. Hill Sch., Pottstown, Pa., 1969-70, Choate-Rosemary Hall, Wallingford, Conn., 1970-73; instr. Williams Coll., Williamstown, Mass., 1973-75; tchr., dept. chmn. St. Louis Country Day Sch., 1975-78; headmaster Rossman Sch., St. Louis, 1978-83, Greenfield Sch., Wilson, N.C., 1983—, trustee, 1983—. Lay leader St. Timothy's Episc. Ch., Wilson, 1983—. Mem. So. Assn. of Schs. and Colls. (cons. 1985—), Council for Religion in Ind. Schs., St. Louis Elem. Sch. Heads Assn. (pres. 1981-82). Democrat. Club: Wilson Country. Lodge: Rotary Internat. (sec. 1984—). Avocations: scuba diving; golfing; Caribbean travel. Home: 2109 Canal Dr Wilson NC 27893 Office: Greenfield Sch PO Box 3525 Wilson NC 27893

THOMPSON, JOHN B(YRON), corporation operation manager; b. North Tonawanda, N.Y., Mar. 11, 1945; s. John Calvin and Sara Lee (Butterbaugh) T.; m. Delores Ann Armiger, Feb. 20, 1965 (div. 1979); children—Susan Marie, Julie Ann, John Larry; m. 2d, Barbara Kolojay, Dec. 6, 1980. B.S.E.E., SUNY-Buffalo, 1967. Electronic design engr. Bell Aerospace, Buffalo, 1967-69; plant and factory elec. engr. Western Electric, Atlanta, 1969-74, devel. engr., Buffalo, 1974-76; plant elect. engr. Nassau Recycle Corp., Gaston, S.C., 1976-77; sr. staff project engr., Gen. Cable Co., Woodbridge, N.J., 1977-82; ops. mgr. Nokia Inc., Atlanta, 1982—; committeeman Internat. Wire and Cable Symposium, Ft. Monmouth, N.J., 1982—. Republican. Roman Catholic. Office: Nokia Inc 4015 Presidential Pkwy Atlanta GA 30340

THOMPSON, JOHN P., retail food executive; b. Dallas, Nov. 2, 1925; s. Joe E. and Margaret (Philip) T.; m. Mary Carol Thomson, June 5, 1948; children—Mary Margaret, Henry Douglas, John P. B.B.A., U. Tex., 1948. With Southland Corp., 1948—, pres., 1961-69, chmn., chief exec. officer, 1969—. Office: Southland Corp 2828 N Haskell Ave Dallas TX 75221*

THOMPSON, JOHN ROBERT, minister; b. Wabash, Ind., Aug. 12, 1932; s. Raymond C. and Paulene (Paullus) T.; m. Susan Kay Wood, May 3, 1975; children—Eric Allen, Kristen Ann. Cert. Armed Forces Info. Coll., 1952; student Ind. U.-Fort Wayne, 1955-58; D.D., Internat. Bible Coll. and Sem., 1985. Ordained to ministry Assn. Internat. Gospel Assemblies, Inc., 1978. Incentive cons. Top Value Enterprises, Dayton, Ohio, 1971-74; dist. rep. U.S. Congressman E.H. Hillis, Kokomo, Ind., 1974-77; pres. Christian Faith Ministries Internat., Inc., Dallas, 1978-85; bus. mgr. Full Gospel Businessmen's Fellowship Internat., Houston, 1978-80; assoc. pastor Word of Faith World Outreach Ctr., Dallas, 1981—; dir. Christian Faith Ministries Internat., Inc., 1978—, HELPS Internat., Inc., Dallas, 1983—; ptnr. Metroplex TV Broadcasting Ltd., Dallas, 1983-85. Co-author: The Trial of the Messiah, 1985; The Marriage-Go-Round, 1985. Mem. Farmers Branch City Bonding Council, Tex., 1985-86, Farmers Branch Citizens Council, 1984-85; pres. Fort Wayne Young Republicans, 1959-61. Served with USN, 1951-55. Named Outstanding Young Man of Yr., City of Ft. Wayne, 1961. Mem. Am. Legion (adj. 1956-58). Lodge: Toastmasters (area gov. 1963). Avocations: sailing; golf. Home: 1212 Huntington Dr Richardson TX 75080 Office: Word of Faith Outreach Ctr 13675 Stemmons Freeway Farmers Branch TX 75234

THOMPSON, KATHLEEN O'LEARY, investment advisor, stockbroker; b. Washington, Dec. 17, 1946; d. Patrick Christopher and Hilda Elizabeth (Gobrecht) O'Leary; children—Kara Ann, Scott Patrick, Ryan Arthur, Kelly Marie Thompson. Student Montgomery Jr. Coll., 1964-66; Colo. State U., 1974; B.S. in Bus. Adminstrn., U. Md., 1975. Account exec. Sta. WSBT-AM-FM-TV, South Bend, Ind., 1972-74; mgr. advt. and promotion Sta. WGHP-TV, High Point, N.C., 1978-83; account exec. Wheat, First Securities, Greensboro, N.C., 1983-85; investment broker Legg Mason Wood Walker, Greensboro, 1985—; lectr. in field. Exec. producer TV show Classic Memories, 1985. Founder, 1st pres., bd. dirs. Big Bros./Big Sisters of High Point, 1981-85; founder, sec.-treas. Furniture City Classic, Inc., High Point, 1981—; founder, bd. dirs. Henredon Classic LPGA Golf Tournament, High Point, 1981—; com. mem. Challenge: High Point grad. and steering com. mem. High Point C. of C., 1984-85; bd. dirs. met. bd. YMCA of High Point, 1981, 82, Adams Meml. YWCA, High Point, 1985—, Salvation Army Boys Club, 1980-81, Vols. to Ct., Guilford County, 1980-81; Sunday sch. tchr. Immaculate Heart of Mary Ch., High Point, 1980-82. Mem. Ladies Profl. Golf Assn. Sponsors Assn. Democrat. Roman Catholic. Avocations: creative writing; classical piano. Home: 1737 Stoneybrook Dr High Point NC 27260 Office: Legg Mason Wood Walker 100 S Elm St Greensboro NC 27401

THOMPSON, K(ENNETH) REED, electrical engineer; b. Alma, Ga., Feb. 20, 1931; s. Howard and Larue (Head) T.; B.E.E., Ga. Inst. Tech., 1953, M.S. in Elec. Engring., 1954; m. Margaret Louise Drody, Mar. 22, 1952; children—Larry Stephen, Fred Lamar. With Ga. Power Co., Atlanta, 1950-52; with Gen. Electric Co., 1954—, systems engr., 1958-61, sr. systems engr., 1961-66, engring. unit mgr., 1966-71, GE Drive Systems Dept. engring. subsect. mgr., 1971-78, mgr. metal industry engring., Salem, Va., 1978-82, mgr. automation systems engring., 1982-84, mgr. advanced systems engring., 1985—; dir. Southcon, Inc., Trendy Enterprises, Inc.; adj. faculty Ga. Inst. Tech., 1953-54, U. Va. Extension, Roanoke, 1955-58. Recipient Gen. Electric Cordiner award, 1963; registered profl. engr., Va. Mem. Va. Soc. Profl. Engrs. (pres. Roanoke chpt. 1986, bd. dirs. 1985-86), IEEE (sr. mem., region 3 chmn. 1982-83, dir. 1982-83; Centennial award 1984, Outstanding Service award 1986), Nat. Soc. Profl. Engrs., Assn. Iron and Steel Engrs., Tau Beta Pi, Eta Kappa Nu, Phi Kappa Tau. Club: Briaereans. Patentee in field. Office: 1501 Roanoke Blvd Room 250 Salem VA 24153

THOMPSON, LEE BENNETT, lawyer, business executive; b. Miami, Indian Ter., Mar. 2, 1902; s. P.C. and Margerie Constance (Jackson) T.; B.A., U. Okla., 1925, LL.B., 1927; m. Elaine Bizzell, Nov. 27, 1928; children—Lee Bennett, Ralph Gordon, Carolyn Elaine. Admitted to Okla. bar, 1927, since practiced in Oklahoma City; sec., gen. counsel, dir. Mustang Fuel Corp.; spl. justice Okla. Supreme Ct., 1967-68; chmn. Fed. Judiciary Nominating Com., 1981, 84, 86. Former mem. bd. dirs. Oklahoma County Tb Assn., Inc.; former sec. Masonic Charity Found. Okla.; chmn. Oklahoma Co. chpt. ARC, 2 terms, chmn. resolutions com., nat. conv., 1953; past dir. Community Fund, Symphony Orch., Oklahoma City. Served from capt. to col. AUS, 1940-46. Decorated 5 campaign stars, Legion of Merit; recipient Disting. Service citation U. Okla., 1971. Fellow Am. Bar Found. (past state chmn.), Am. Coll. Trial Lawyers (former state chmn.); mem. Oklahoma City (past dir.), Oklahoma City Jr. (past pres.), U.S., Jr. (past dir., v.p.) chambers commerce, Am. (ho. of dels. 1971-72, spl. com. fed. rules procedure, standing com. on law and nat. security), Okla. (past mem. ho. dels., pres. 1972, Pres.'s award 1979), Oklahoma County (past pres.) bar assns., Okla. Bar Found. (trustee 1973-79, 81-84, Thou Good and Faithful Servant award 1980, Journal-Record award 1984), U. Okla. Alumni Assn. (past exec. com.), U. Okla. Meml. Student Union (past pres.), Am. Legion, Beta Theta Pi (past v.p., trustee), Phi Beta Kappa (Phi Beta Kappa of the Yr. 1982). Democrat. Mem. First Christian Ch. (former deacon, former elder, lifetime elder). Clubs: Masons (33 deg.), Shriners, Jesters, Seventy Five, Rotary (past pres.; Paul Harris fellow), Men's Dinner (past exec. com.), Beacon, Oklahoma City Golf and Country; Univ. (Norman, Okla.). Home: 539 NW 38th St Oklahoma City OK 73118 Office: 2120 First Nat Bldg Oklahoma City OK 73102

THOMPSON, LEROY, JR., army reserve officer, radio engineer; b. Tulsa, July 7, 1913; s. LeRoy and Mary (McMurrain) T.; B.S. in Elec. Engring., Ala. Poly Inst., 1936; m. Ola Dell Tedder, Dec. 31, 1941; 1 son, Bartow McMurrain. Commd. 2d lt. U.S. Amy Res., 1935, advanced through grades to col., 1963; signal officer CCC, 1936-40; radio engr. Officer Hdqrs. 4th C A., 1941, signal officer OSS, Burma, 1945, signal officer Hdqrs. OSS, China, 1945, radio engr., tech. liaison officer, Central Intelligence Group, CIA, 1945-50; chief radio br. Hdqrs. FEC, Tokyo, 1950-53, chief radio engring br. Signal C Plant Engring. Agy., 1953-55; radio cons. to asst. dir. def. research and engring. communications, 1960-62; ret., 1973; pvt. research and devel. on communication and related problems, 1963—; owner Thompson Research Exptl. Devel. Lab. Lic. profl. radio engr., Ga. Mem. IEEE (life sr.), Vet. Wireless Operators Assn., Am. Radio Relay League, Nat. Rifle Assn., Mil. Order World Wars, Res. Officers Assn., Am. Motorcycle Assn., Nat. Wildlife Fedn. Baptist. Home: 6450 Overlook Dr Alexandria VA 22312

THOMPSON, MARGUERITE MYRTLE GRAMLING, librarian; b. Orangeburg, S.C., Apr. 23, 1912; d. Thomas Laurie and Rosa Lee (Stroman) Gramling; B.A. cum laude in English, U. S.C., 1932, postgrad., 1937; B.L.S., Emory U., 1943; m. Ralph B. Thompson, Sept. 17, 1949 (dec. Oct. 1960). Tchr. English public high schs., S.C., 1932-43; librarian Rockingham (N.C.) High Sch., 1943-45, Randolph County (N.C.) Library, Asheboro, 1945-48, Colleton County (S.C.) Library, Walterboro, 1948-61; dir. Florence (S.C.) County Library, 1961-78. Sec. com. community facilities, services and instns. Florence County Resources Devel. Com., 1964-67; vice chmn. Florence County council on Aging, 1968-70, 78-79, sec., 1976-77, exec. bd., 1968-82, treas., 1974-75; mem. Florence County Bicentennial Planning Com., 1975-76; mem. agy. relations and allocations com. United Way, 1979-80; chmn. adv. com. Orangeburg Meth. Home, 1984—. Named Boss of Yr., Florence County chpt. Nat. Secs. Assn., 1971; named Career Woman of Yr., Florence Bus. and Profl. Women's Club, 1974. Mem. ALA (council 1964-72), Southeastern Library Assn., S.C. Library Assn. (pres. 1960, chmn. assn. handbook revision com. 1967-69, 80, fed. relations coordinator 1972-73), Delta Kappa Gamma (state scholarship chmn. 1967-73, internat. scholarship com. 1970-74, internat. exec. bd. 1975-77, 78-80, internat. adminstrv. bd. 1978-80, constn. com. 1980-82, dir. SE region 1978-80, coordinator Golden Anniversary Conf. SE region 1979, state pres. 1975-77, chmn. state handbook com. 1977-81, chmn. state adv. com. 1980-83, chmn. state fin. com. 1980-83, cons. state adv. com. 1983—, chmn. state bylaws com. 1983—, exec. bd. 1971—), Greater Florence C. of C. (div. vice chmn. 1968; women's div. chmn. 1969-70, dir. 1975-77), Southeastern Regional Conf. Women in Chambers Commerce (dir. 1970-71), Florence Lit. Club (pres. 1970-72, v.p. 1972-74 sec. 1979-82). Methodist (chmn. ch. library com. 1965-71, chmn. com. ch. history, 1968-69, sec. adminstrv. bd. 1979-82, chmn. ch. circle 1980-81). Home: Route 2 Box 1000 Apt 8B Orangeburg SC 29115

THOMPSON, MORGAN ELWIN, state agency official; b. Wagoner, Okla., June 17, 1932; s. Charles Archie and Irene Ethel (McPherson) T.; m. Wanda J. Ennis, June 19, 1951; children—Deborah Lynn, Bruce Alan, Teresa Ann. B.A., Okla. U., 1958, M.A., 1960; M.A., Central State U., 1983. Staff psychologist Children's Home, 1958-60; questioned document examiner, Oklahoma City, 1958—; adminstrv. hearing officer State Okla., Oklahoma City, 1975—; faculty Rose State Coll., 1978—. Served with USAF, 1950-58. Mem. Nat. Acad. Criminology, Nat. Assn. Adminstrv. Law Judges (pres. 1984), Alpha Phi Sigma. Methodist. Contbr. articles in field to profl. jours. Home: 109 Gill Dr Midwest City OK 73110 Office: 531 W Couch Dr Oklahoma City OK 73102

THOMPSON, NANCY JO, consulting geophysicist; b. San Antonio, Aug. 21, 1950; d. Richard Lewis and Dorothy Lee (Vogt) Terwilliger; children—Kevin Neil, Barbara Joy. A.S., Amarillo Coll., 1970; B.S. in Geology, West Tex. State U., 1972. Geophys. trainee Mesa Petroleum Co., Amarillo, 1972-73; geologist, geophysicist Diamond Shamrock Corp., Amarillo, 1978-81; geophysicist Santa Fe Energy Co., Amarillo, 1981-83, Midland, Tex., 1983-85; cons. geophysicist, Midland, 1985—. Student-tchr. Bethel Bible course Holy Trinity Episcopal Ch., Midland, 1983—; mem. various Episcopal ch. choirs, 1959—. Mem. Soc. Exploration Geophysicists, Am. Assn. Petroleum Geologists (dist. chmn. com. on drilling stats. 1978-81), West Tex. Geol. Soc., Permian Basin Geophys. Soc., Oklahoma City Geol. Soc., Panhandle Geol. Soc. (treas. 1979-80, sec. 1980-81, v.p. 1981-82, 1st female pres. 1982-83), Soc. Econ. Paleontologists and Minerologists (Permian Basin sect.), Alpha Chi. Club: Amarillo Toastmasters 211 (sec. 1980, ednl. v.p. 1981, 1st female pres. Amarillo chpt. 1981). Avocations: choir; swimming; volleyball; arts and crafts.

THOMPSON, R. LEE, advertising agency executive; b. San Antonio, Sept. 12, 1946; s. S.L. and Marie Aleene (Dennis) T.; m. Judyth Lynn Myer, Apr. 30, 1971 (div. 1983); children—Robert Lawrence, Richard Lee. Student, San Antonio Jr. Coll., 1965-68, U. Tex., Austin, 1968-70. Announcer Sta. KITE, San Antonio, 1968; newscaster, program dir. Sta. KHFI-AM/FM/TV, Austin, 1968-70; program dir., announcer Sta. KTAP-AM/KRMH-FM, Austin, 1970-76; ops. mgr., sta. mgr. Sta. KIXL-AM, Austin, 1976-78; creative dir. Young & Assocs., Advt., Austin, 1978-81; sole owner Lee Thompson Advt., 1981-82; sec.-treas., chmn. bd. TCP, Inc., Austin, 1983—; creative dir. Thompson, Curtiss, Parsons & Johnson mktg., Advt. & Pub. Relations, Austin, 1983—. Recipient Addy awards Austin Advt. Club, 1981; Gold Award for Collateral Packaging, 1981, 4 Silver awards for radio advt., 1981, 2 silver awards for splty. advt., 1981. Mem. Austin Alliance Advt. Agy. Prins. (arbitration com.), Austin C. of C. Office: 151 S 1st St Suite 100 Austin TX 78704

THOMPSON, RALPH FRANKLIN, management executive, consultant; b. Goff, Kans., June 12, 1919; s. Frank Hayes and Mabel Lorena (Fowler) T.; m. Mary Lilla Willis, Sept. 25, 1943; children—Mary Lee Thompson Lannoye, Peter Hayes. B.S. in Engring., George Washington U., 1955. Cert. tchr., Kans. Engring. aide Office Chief of Ordnance, U.S. Army, Washington, 1946-49, ordnance, mechanical engr., 1949-62; gen. engr. U.S. Army Material Command, Washington, 1962-80, supr. gen. engr., Alexandria, Va., 1980-84, retired, 1984—; cons. Vitro Corp., Silver Spring, Md., 1985—; mem. Integrated Logistic Support Adv. Com. Dept. Defense, Washington, 1968-70, Life Cycle Cost Planning Group, 1968-70. Contbr. articles to profl. jours. Officer PTA, Alexandria, 1960-61, Methodist Men, Trinity Ch., Alexandria, 1970-80. Served with U.S. Army, 1943-46, NATOUSA, ETO. Mem. Soc. Logistic Engrs., Def. Preparedness Assn., Nat. Rifle Assn. (pres.). Republican. Club: Acorns Jr. Rifle (officer 1959-64). Avocation: gardening. Home: 1504 Oakcrest Dr Alexandria VA 22302

THOMPSON, RALPH GORDON, judge; b. Oklahoma City, Dec. 15, 1934; s. Lee Bennett and Elaine (Bizzell) T.; B.B.A., U. Okla., 1956, J.D., 1961; m. Barbara Irene Hencke, Sept. 5, 1964; children—Lisa, Elaine, Maria. Bar: Okla. 1961. Spl. agt. Office Spl. Investigations, U.S. Air Force, 1957-60; partner Thompson, Thompson, Harbour & Selph, and predecessors, Oklahoma City, 1961-75; judge U.S. Dist. Ct. Western Dist. Okla., 1975—; mem. Okla. Ho. of Reps., 1966-70, asst. minority floor leader, 1969-70; spl. justice Supreme Ct. Okla., 1970-71. Republican nominee for lt. gov. Okla., 1970; chmn. bd. ARC, Oklahoma City, 1970-72, chmn. Midwestern area adv. council, 1973-74; pres. Okla. Young Lawyers Conf., 1965; bd. visitors U. Okla., 1975-78; pres. bd. dirs. St. John's Episcopal Sch., Oklahoma City, 1977-79. Served as lt. USAF, 1957-60, col. USAFR. Named Outstanding Fed. Trial Judge, Okla. Trial Lawyers Assn., 1980; Okla. City's Outstanding Young Man, Jr. Chamber Commn., 1967, Outstanding Young Oklahoman, 1968. Fellow Am. Bar. Found.; Mem. Nat. Conf. Fed. Trial Judges, ABA, Fed. Bar Assn., Okla. Bar Assn. (chmn. sect. internat. law and gen. practice 1974-75), Oklahoma County Bar Assn. (dir.), Jud. Conf. U.S. (com. on ct. adminstrn. 1981—), U. Okla. Dad's Assn. (pres. 1986), Order of Coif, Phi Beta Kappa (pres. chpt.), Beta Theta Pi, Phi Alpha Delta. Episcopalian. Club: Rotary (hon.). Office: US Courthouse Oklahoma OK 73102

THOMPSON, RICHARD EDWARD, consulting civil engineer; b. Seattle, Aug. 22, 1950; s. Robert Cecil and Gloria Elizabeth (Smith) T.; m. Carolyn Lois Pruett, Apr. 18, 1981; stepchildren—Robin, Brian. B.S. in Civil Engring., Va. Poly. Inst. and State U., 1974. Registered profl. engr., Va. Engring. asst. Byrd, Tallamy, MacDonald & Lewis, Falls Church, Va., 1971-74, jr. engr., 1974, engr., 1976, staff engr., 1979, sr. systems design engr., 1982—. Mem. ASCE, Inst. Transp. Engrs. Methodist. Office: 2921 Telestar Ct Falls Church VA 22047

THOMPSON, THEODORA, nurse; b. El Paso, Tex., Apr. 1, 1929; d. Ysabel and Genoveva (Nava) Reyes; m. Arthur Carl Thompson, Dec. 15, 1951; children—Claudine Marie, Olga Louise, Arthur Carl, Jr. R.N., Hotel Dieu Sch. of Nursing, El Paso, 1951. R.N., Tex., La. Staff nurse surgery Hotel Dieu Hosp., El Paso, 1951-53, St. Francis Sanitarium, Monroe, La., 1953-61; nurse, operating room head nurse St. Francis Hosp., Monroe, 1961-77, staff nurse recovery room, 1978-80; nurse, dir. central supply St. Francis Med. Ctr., Monroe, 1980—. Mem. Tex. State Nurses, La. State Nurses, La. Central Supply Mgrs. (bd. dirs.). Democrat. Roman Catholic. Avocations: photography; rock and shell collection; travel. Home: 317 Tennessee Monroe LA 71203 Office: St Francis Med Ctr 209 Jackson St PO Box 1901 Monroe LA 71201

THOMPSON, THOMAS GLOVER, JR., social worker; b. St. Jo, Tex., Mar. 23, 1930; s. Thomas Glover and Gladys Maureen (Rone) T.; B.A., Midwestern U., 1962; M.S.W., Our Lady of the Lake, 1968; m. Shirley Pope, May 25, 1957. Caseworker, Tex. Dept. Pub. Welfare, 1962-66; field cons. various state insts., 1968-69; chief instl. services Tex. Dept. Public Welfare, 1969-77; utilization review officer Tex. Dept. Health, Austin, 1977—. Pres., Midwestern U. Young Dems., 1961-62. Served with USN, 1951-53. Mem. Nat. Assn. Social Workers (chpt. treas. 1973-76), Tex. Public Employees Assn. (chpt. v.p. 1964-65, treas. 1971-72), Tex. Public Health Assn. Democrat. Baptist. Home: 2303 A Mahone St Austin TX 78758 Office: 1100 W 49th St Austin TX 78756

THOMPSON, THOMAS WILLIAM, business educator, financial editor, writer, consultant; b. Chgo., Sept. 6, 1934; s. Thomas Henry and Edna Bernice (Stelzer) T.; m. Ellen Anne Ferraro, May 24, 1958; children—Lisa Caitlin, Thomas Howard, Amy Martha. B.S. in Journalism, Northwestern U., 1957; M.S. in History, NYU, 1962; Ph.D. in Am. Studies, George Washington U., 1976. News editor Am. Banker, N.Y.C., 1959-62; v.p., dir. research Conf. State Bank Suprs., Washington, 1962-69; assoc. Carter H. Golembe Assos.,

Washington, 1969-71; pvt. practice as cons. and fin. writer, 1971-73; v.p., dir. communications Bank of Va. (bank holding co.), Richmond, 1973-77; assoc. prof. mktg. Sch. Bus., Va. Commonwealth U., Richmond, 1977—; fin. cons.; pres. Am. Communications Resources, Inc., Washington; dir. Lafferty Publs., Ltd.; sr. contbg. editor U.S. Banker, Cos Cob Conn., editor, 1977-83; assoc. editor Jour. Retail Banking, 1985—. Officer, Overseas Mission Soc., Protestant Episcopal Ch. U.S.A., 1969-72; bd. dirs. United Way of Richmond, 1976-79, ALIVE, Alexandria, Va., 1970-73; mem. Urban League, 1970-80, Housing Opportunities Made Equal, Richmond, 1975-80. Served with Med. Service Corps, U.S. Army, 1957-59. Mem. Bank Mktg. Assn., Am. Mktg. Assn., Exchequer Club (Washington), Richmond C. of C. (communications council 1983), Sigma Delta Chi, Beta Gamma Sigma. Author: Checks and Balances: A History of the American Banking System, 1962, Issues in Communications, 1978, The Home Mortgage: Tomorrow's Core Service, 1978: columnist: Retail Banker, Internat., London; contbr. articles to profl. jours.; co-editor: The Bank Holding Company Act Amendments of 1970, 1971; editor, research dir. A Profile of State-Chartered Banking, 1965, 67, 69; co-author: Banking Tomorrow, 1978, rev. 1981; The Changing World of Banking, 1982; Marketing Financial Services: A Strategic Vision, 1985. Home: 510 Plantation Dr Richmond VA 23227 Office: Sch Bus Va Commonwealth Univ Richmond VA 23220

THOMPSON, VERNON EARL (JACK), university administrator; b. Jester, Okla., Dec. 8, 1925; s. Vanis Earl and Oma (Wallach) T.; B.B.A., Tex. Tech. U., 1949; postgrad. in mgmt., 1949-51; m. June Stine, Sept. 1, 1948; children—James Earl, Vernon Earl. Asst. comptroller Tex. Tech. U., Lubbock, 1949-59; bus. mgr. Midwestern U., Wichita Falls, Tex., 1959-63; bus. mgr. U. Tex. Southwestern Med. Sch., Dallas, 1963-66; dir. Office Facilities Planning and Constrn., U. Tex. System, Austin, 1966-67; exec. v.p. adminstrn. and bus. affairs U. Tex. Med. Br., Galveston, 1967—. Served with Inf., AUS, 1944-46. Mem. Galveston C. of C. (dir.), Assn. Am. Med. Colls., Nat. Assn. Coll. and Univ. Bus. Officers, Central Assn. Coll. and Univ. Bus. Officers, So. Assn. Coll. and Univ. Bus. Officers, Tex. Assn. State Sr. Coll. and Univ. Bus. Officers. Episcopalian. Office: U Tex Med Branch Suite 621 Adminstrn Bldg Galveston TX 77550

THOMPSON, VIVIAN OPAL, nurse; b. Lebanon, Va., Nov. 30, 1925; d. Luther Smith and Cora Belle (Baugh) Thompson; R.N., Knoxville (Tenn.) Gen. Hosp., 1947. Supr. obstetrical dept. Knoxville Gen. Hosp., 1947-48; gen. duty nurse Clinch Valley Clinic Hosp., Richlands, Va., 1948-52, supr., 1957-61, 68-78; indsl. nurse, Morocco, Africa, 1952-56; charge nurse Bluefield Sanitarium, W.Va., 1961-65, Rochingham Meml. Hosp., Harrisonburg, Va., 1965-68; charge nurse obstet. dept. Clinch Valley Community Hosp., 1978—. Mem. Nat. League Nursing. Democrat. Presbyterian. Home: 205 Pennsylvania Ave Richlands VA 24641

THOMPSON, WILLIAM, public relations executive, consultant; b. Escanaba, Mich., Sept. 16, 1922; s. Waino Alexander and Viola Ellen (Wood) T.; m. Dorothy Elizabeth Zum Buttel, July 11, 1945; children—Stephanie Jo Thompson Graves, Craig Donald, Brian William. Student Wabash Coll., 1944-45; B.S., George Washington U., 1965; grad. Harvard U. Bus. Sch. Advanced Mgmt. Program, 1970. Enlisted U.S. Navy, 1942, commd. ensign, 1945, advanced through grades to rear adm., 1971; spl. asst. for pub. affairs Sec. of Navy, 1964-70; dep. chief of info. Navy Dept., Pentagon, Washington, chief of info., 1971-75, ret., 1975; pres. Admiralty Communication, Inc., McLean, Va., 1978—, U.S. Navy Meml. Found., Washington, 1978—, Nat. Under Water and Marine Agy., Washington, 1978—; chmn. bd., dir. Admiralty Gen. Corp. (Real Estate Fund), McLean, 1983—; pub. relations cons., 1975—. Decorated D.S.M., Legion of Merit. Mem. Pub. Relations Soc. Am. (Silver Anvil award for best press relations 1962), Sigma Chi. Club: Army Navy Country (Arlington, Va.). Home: 6529 Divine St McLean VA 22101 Office: Admiralty Comm Inc PO Box 184 McLean VA 22101

THOMPSON, WILLIAM EDWARD, charitable association executive; b. Oklahoma City, Sept. 16, 1942; s. Thomas Edward and Lorette Bynum T. B.B.A., U. Okla., 1964. Mgmt. understudy Am. Airlines, Los Angeles, 1968-70; adminstr. Transcon Lines, Los Angeles, 1970-82; adminstr. Western Okla./Tex. Panhandle div. ARC, Oklahoma City, 1982—. Chmn. resident com. Marina Area Community Council, 1979-82; mem. Oklahoma City Beautiful, 1982—. Served to capt. USMC, 1965-76. Mem. Oceanic Soc. (dir. Los Angeles chpt. 1981-82), U.S. Naval Inst. (assoc.), Res. Officers Assn., Navy League, USCG Acad. Alumni Assn. (assoc.), USCG Aux. (div. vice capt. 1984), U. Okla. Alumni Assn., Beta Theta Pi. Republican. Episcopalian.

THOMPSON, WILLIAM MOREAU, radiologist, educator; b. Phila., Oct. 20, 1943; s. Charles Moreau and Aileen (Haddon) T.; m. Judy Ann Seel, July 27, 1968; children—Christopher Moreau, Thayer Haddon. B.A., Colgate U., 1965; M.D., U. Pa., 1969. Diplomate Am. Bd. Radiology. Intern, Case Western Res. U., Cleve., 1969-70; resident in radiology Duke U., Durham, N.C., 1972-75, asst. prof. Med. Center, 1976-77, assoc. prof., 1977-82, prof. radiology, 1982—. Served with USPHS, 1970-72. Recipient James Picker Found. Scholar in Acad. Medicine award, 1975-79; research and devel. grantee VA, 1977—. Fellow Am. Coll. Radiology; mem. Radiology Soc. N.Am., AMA, N.C. Med. Soc., Am. Roentgen Ray Soc., Assn. Univ. Radiologists, Soc. Gastrointestinal Radiology, Sigma Xi. Republican. Presbyterian. Contbr. chpts. to books, articles to profl. jours. Home: 1502 Micheax Rd Chapel Hill NC 27514 Office: Duke U Med Ctr PO Box 3808 Durham NC 27710

THOMS, DAVID OGDEN, JR., banker; b. Las Vegas, Sept. 6, 1944; s. David Ogden and Daisy McLaurin (Stevens) T.; m. Judy Marie Ellis, Apr. 17, 1971; children—David Ogden III, Gregory Ellis. B.S., Miss. State U., 1966; cert. U. Wis.-Madison, 1972, La. State U., 1979. Dist. mgr. Richton Tie and Timber Co., Miss., 1967-68; examiner Miss. Banking Dept., Jackson, 1968-69; auditor Comml. Nat. Bank, Laurel, Miss., 1969-71, v.p., auditor, 1972-78, v.p., comptroller, 1979-84, v.p., cashier, 1985—. Mgr. Dixie Youth Baseball Team, Laurel, 1983-85; treas. 1st United Meth. Ch., Laurel, 1985. Recipient Eagle Scout badge Boy Scouts Am., 1960. Mem. Bank Adminstrn. Inst. (chpt. treas.-pres. 1970-73, state bd. dirs. 1973-75, dist. bd. dirs. 1977-79), Miss. Bankers Assn. (bd. dirs. young bankers sect. 1977-78), Laurel C. of C. Club: Laurel Rotary (pres. 1985-86). Avocations: family; tennis; golf. Home: 45 Oak Crest Dr Laurel MS 39440 Office: Comml Nat Bank and Trust Co 415 N Magnolia St Laurel MS 39440

THORBURN, JAMES ALEXANDER, educator; b. Martins Ferry, Ohio, Aug. 24, 1923; s. Charles David and Mary Edna (Ruble) T.; B.A., Ohio State U., 1949, M.A., 1951; postgrad. U. Mo., 1954-55; Ph.D., La. State U., 1977; m. Lois McElroy, July 3, 1954; children—Alexander Maurice, Melissa Rachel; m. 2d, June Yingling O'Leary, Apr. 18, 1981. Head English dept. high sch., Sheridan, Mich., 1951-52; instr. English, U. Mo., Columbia, 1952-55, Monmouth (Ill.) Coll., 1955-56, U. Tex., El Paso, 1956-60, U. Mo., St. Louis, 1960-61, La. State U., Baton Rouge, 1961-70; asso. prof. English, Southeastern La. U., Hammond, 1970—; examiner testing and cert. div. English Lang. Inst., U. Mich., 1969—. Served with F.A., AUS, 1943-46. Mem. MLA, Linguistic Assn. Southwest, Linguistic Soc. Am., Am. Dialect Soc., Nat. Council Tchrs. of English, Conf. Coll. Composition and Communication, Southeastern Conf. Linguistics, Avalon World Arts Acad. (hon. life), Sigma Delta Pi, Phi Mu Alpha Sinfonia, Phi Kappa Phi. Republican. Presbyterian. Contbg. author: Exercises in English, 1955; also poetry; book rev. editor Experiment, 1958—, co-editor Innisfree. Home: 602 Susan Dr Hammond LA 70401 Office: Dept English Southeastern La Univ Hammond LA 70402

THORE, STEN ANDERS, economics educator, finance educator; b. Stockholm, Apr. 22, 1930; came to U.S., 1978, naturalized, 1985; s. Eric and Elsa (Ostberg) T.; m. Margrethe Munck; children—Susanne, Alexander, Clementine. M. Commerce, U. Birmingham, Eng., 1954; Filosofie Doktor, U. Stockholm, 1961. Prof. econs. Norwegian Sch. Econs. and Bus. Adminstrn., Bergen, Norway, 1964-78; Gregory A. Kozmetsky Centennial fellow IC2 Inst., U. Tex., Austin, 1984—; vis. prof. Northwestern U., Carnegie-Mellon U., U. Va. Author: Programming the Network of Financial Intermediation, 1980. Contbr. articles to profl. jours. Named Hon. Citizen, State of Tex., 1981. Mem. Inst. Mgmt. Scis. Econometric Soc. Home: 809 Electra Austin TX 78734 Office: IC2 Inst 2815 San Gabriel Austin TX 78705

THORINGTON, TREVOR ERSKINE, computer software company executive; b. Barbados, W.I., June 28, 1943; came to U.S., 1966; s. Charles Christopher and Enid Undine (Husbands) T.; m. Rosemary Allison Morris, July 11, 1968; children—Terrence Erskine and Sonja Lynn (twins), Diana Allison. B.S. in Acctg. magna cum laude, U. Hartford, 1973, M.S. in Profl. Acctg., 1972. C.P.A., Conn. Sr. staff auditor Peat, Marwick, Mitchell & Co., C.P.A.s, Hartford, Conn., 1973-76; mgr. corp. acctg. Dexter Corp., Windsor Locks, Conn., 1976-78; acctg. cons. Travelers Corp., Hartford, 1978-82; comptroller Travelers/EBS, Inc., 1982—; owner, dir. Sta. WNOU-FM, Thompson Transp. Lines, Teson Corp.; adj. prof. acctg. Orlando Coll.; tchr. Jr. Achievement. Served with USAF, 1967-71. Univ. scholar; First Security Ins. acad. scholar, 1972. Mem. Am. Inst. C.P.A.s, Nat. Assn. Accts., Fla. Soc. C.P.A.s. Address: 696 Canopy Ct Winter Springs FL 32708

THORNAL, CHARLES HILL, educational admistrator; b. Waco, Tex., June 2, 1935; s. James Augustus and Fannie Alberta (Hill) T.; m. Dorothy Lynn Maxwell, Apr. 19, 1957; children—Charles Keith, Kaylyn Ann. B.A., Baylor U., 1957, M.A., 1961; postgrad. Tex. A&M U., 1965-69. Dir. fed. programs Waco Pub. Schs., 1965-80; dir. sch.-community relations Waco (Tex.) Ind. Sch. Dist., 1980—; mem. So. Assn. Secondary Schs. and Colls. team to evaluate Sp. Tex. Sch. Dist., 1970-72. Served with Tex. N.G., 1957-66. Mem. Tex. Sch. Pub. Relations Assn. (v.p. 1982-83). Baptist (minister music). Lodge: Lions. Statewide editor Tex. Assn. Compensatory Educators Newsletter, 1978-80: editor WISD Communicator, 1980-84; contbr. articles in field to profl. jours. Club: Waco Adminstrs. (pres. 1979-80). Home: 5318 Lake Crest Waco TX 76710 Office: Waco Ind Sch Dist Box 27 Waco TX 76703

THORNBURG, CHERYL ANN, public health nurse; b. Lincolnton, N.C., Sept. 10, 1956; d. Joe Nelson and Lena Marie (Carpenter) Thornburg. B.S.N., Lenoir-Rhyne Coll., 1979. Registered nurse, N.C. Staff nurse McLeod Regional Med. Ctr., Florence, S.C., 1979-82; pub. health nurse Lincoln County Health Dept., Lincolnton, 1982—; with young careerist program Lincolnton Bus. and Profl. Women's Club, 1982-83. Chmn. com. to form Hospice of Lincoln County, Lincolnton, 1983—; bd. dirs. Am. Cancer Soc., Lincolnton, 1983—. Mem. Am. Nurses Assn., N.C. Nurses Assn. (v.p. 1984-86), Western N.C. Pub. Health Assn., N.C. Pub. Health Assn. (sec. 1982-85), Bus. Profl. Women's Club. Democrat. Baptist. Office: Lincoln County Health Dept Rural Route 8 PO Box 1527-C Lincolnton NC 28092

THORNBURG, LACY, N.C. state's attorney general; b. Charlotte, N.C., Dec. 20, 1929; m. Dorothy Todd, 1953; A.A., Mars Hill Coll., 1950; B.A., U. N.C., 1950, J.D., 1954. Staff aide to U.S. congressman, 1959-60; mem. N.C. Ho. of Reps., 1961-65; judge Superior Ct. 30th Jud. Dist. N.C., 1967-83; atty. gen. State of N.C., Raleigh, 1985—. Office: NC Justice Dept PO Box 629 Raleigh NC 27602*

THORNDIKE, ALLEN BRIAN, financial management consultant; b. Tyler, Tex., May 26, 1950; s. Allen Kingsland and Nina Sue (Bizzell) T.; B.A., Stephen F. Austin State U., 1972; postgrad. U. Houston, 1980; m. Janet Menotti, Nov. 24, 1973; children—Trisha Dawn, Jarod Michael. Rate analyst Tex. Eastern Corp., Shreveport, La., 1972-75; sr. cons. Zinder Cos., Inc., Houston, 1975-79; energy economist Price Waterhouse & Co., Houston, 1979-80; v.p. regulatory affairs Tatham Corp., Houston, 1980-82; chief operating officer NTEC, Inc., 1982-85; pres. Thorndike Interests, Inc., Longview, Tex., 1985—. Mem. Am. Econ. Assn., Econometric Soc., Western Econ. Assn., Am. Mgmt. Assn., Stephen F. Austin Alumni Assn. Office: PO Box 5562 Longview TX 75608

THORNE, JOHN THOMAS, indsl. instrument control system engr. and designer; b. Port Arthur, Tex., Apr. 17, 1926; s. Ernest Eugene and Mary (Wooldridge) T.; student Tex. Coll. Mines, 1944-45, LeTourneau Tech., 1949-50, Lamar Coll., 1952-53, Lee Coll., 1964-65; U. Houston, 1967-68, 78-79; m. Patricia McBride, Feb. 12, 1949; children—John Thomas, Ernest E., Alida Diane, Jerry Allen. Instrument technician Texas City Refining Inc. (Tex.), 1953-63; instrument and electronics instr. Lee Coll., 1963-66; instrument supr. Tech. Maintenance, Inc., Pasadena, Tex., 1963-67; ind. cons., Houston area, 1967-68; ind. cons. Diamond-Shamrock, Tenneco, U.S. Indsl. Chems., Olin Corp., 1967-68; instrument tech. dept. head San Jacinto Coll., 1966-68; regional systems mgr. Robertshaw Controls Co., Houston and Anaheim, Calif., 1968-70; ind. cons. Olin Corp., Pasadena Ind. Sch. Dist., 1970-72; mgr. tng. sales Tex-A-Mation Engring., La Porte, Tex., 1971-72; ind. cons. Forney Engring., Dallas also J.E. Sirrine Co., Houston, 1972; instrument designer Stubbs, Overbeck & Assos., Houston, assigned to Celanese Chm. Co., Bishop, Tex., 1972; instrument design supr. S.I.P., Inc., Houston, assigned to Shell Chem. Co., Houston, 1972-74; sr. instrument engr., design supr. Tellepsen Petro-Chem. Constrn. Co., Houston, 1974-79; prin. Thorne Cons. Service, Houston, 1979—. Mem. Tex. Senate Com. for Tech. and Vocational Edn., 1971-75; Tex. rep. for instrumentation HEW Conf., Los Alamos, 1967. Served with AUS, 1946, 50-53; with USAAF, 1946-49. Registered profl. engr. Mem. Instrument Soc. Am. (edn. dir. Houston sect. 1972-74), Am. Soc. Engring. Technicians, Internat. Platform Assn., Nat. Soc. Profl. Engrs. Club: Masons. Home: 16922 Blackhawk St Friendswood TX 77546 Office: PO Box 37 Friendswood TX 77546

THORNE, ROBERT EARL, language educator; b. Goldsboro, N.C., June 16, 1943; s. Henry Earl Thorne and Doris Mae (Elks) Fergerson; m. Judy Gardner Guillet, July 27, 1968; children—Ashlee Maria, Anna Barrett. A.B., U. N.C., 1968, M.A.T., 1970; Ph.D., Duke U., 1972. Tchr. English, Githens Jr. High Sch., Durham, N.C., 1968-70; English master tchr. Demonstration Enrichment Sch., Duke U., Durham, N.C., 1970-72; assoc. prof. English Coll. Albemarle, Elizabeth City, N.C., 1972-77; assoc. prof., dir. English edn. Elizabeth City State U., 1977-82, prof. modern langs., 1982—. Mem. Pasquotank Arts Council, 1972—. Served with USAF, 1962-66. Mem. Nat. Council Tchrs. English, Internat. Soc. Gen. Semantics, Kappa Delta Pi. Democrat. Methodist. Clubs: Pine Lakes Country, Duplicate Bridge. Author: A Semanticist and Campus Unrest: A Study of Samuel Ichiye Hayakawa in Thought and Action, 1972; contbr. poetry to anthologies and mags. Home: 402 Pineview Dr Elizabeth City NC 27909 Office: Elizabeth City State U Box 112 Elizabeth City NC 27909

THORNSBERRY, MARY GASWINT, nurse; b. Sioux City, Iowa, May 10, 1943; d. Dale and Louise (Zurn) Gaswint; m. Willis Lee Thornsberry, Jr., June 19, 1965; children—Brian, Michele. R.N., St. Vincent Sch. Nursing, Sioux City, 1964. Staff nurse Meadowcrest Hosp., Gretna, La., 1979-81, area supr., 1981-83, house supr., 1983—. Pres., George Cox Sch. PTA, Gretna, 1978; den mother Cub Scouts, Gretna, 1973-78; troop leader Girl Scouts USA, 1977-81. Democrat. Roman Catholic. Home: 549 Lynnmeade Rd Gretna LA 70053 Office: Meadowcrest Hosp 2500 Belle Chasse Hwy Gretna LA 70053

THORNTHWAITE, WILFRED LEE, actuarial firm executive, software company executive; b. Huntsville, Ala., June 29, 1943; s. William Leslie and Mildred Marion (Bridges) T.; m. Evelyn Carrie Hopkins, June 17, 1973; children—Alanna Eden, Jennifer Dawn, Geoffrey Hopkins. B.S., David Lipscomb Coll., 1963; postgrad. Northeastern U., 1970; M.B.A., U. Tenn., 1979. Enrolled actuary. Asst. actuary Fidelity Mut. Life Ins. Co., Phila., 1973-76, asst. v.p., asst. actuary, 1976-79, 2d v.p., assoc. actuary, 1979-81; v.p. Nat. Life and Accident Ins. Co., Nashville, 1981-84; pres. Thornthwaite & Co., Brentwood, Tenn., 1984—; ptnr. Wildan Microsystems Co.; dir., sec.-treas. Cytophysics, Inc., Nashville. Author publs. in field. Served to 1st lt. USAF, 1966-69. Fellow Soc. of Actuaries; Life Mgmt. Inst.; mem. Am. Acad. Actuaries, Chartered Life Underwriter Am. Coll., Chartered Fin. Cons. Am. Coll. Republican. Mem. Church of Christ. Clubs: Music City Civitan (pres. Nashville 1980-81), Valley Dist. Civitan (lt. gov. 1985-86). Home: 5412 Forest Acres Dr Nashville TN 37220 Office: Thornthwaite & Co One Maryland Farms Suite 200 Brentwood TN 37027

THORNTON, KENNETH MONROE, clergyman, chaplain, financial executive; b. Alden, Iowa, July 7, 1923; s. Guy and Emma Alma (Risse) T.; m. Velma Rose Claude, Sept. 6, 1942; children—Ronald Kent, Donald Karl. Engring. degree Ellsworth Coll., 1942; divisional natural sci. degree Iowa Wesleyan Coll., 1961; B.Div., Hartford Sem., 1966, M. Div., 1966. Asst. dist. mgr. Fuller Brush, Blakesburg, Iowa, 1958-59; ordained to ministry Meth. Ch., as deacon, 1964, as elder, 1966; pastor Blakesburg Circuit, 1959-61, Malden Bridge Circuit, Old Chatham, N.Y., 1961-62, Brownsville Circuit (Vt.), 1962-63; sr. pastor Agawam United Meth. Ch. (Mass.), 1963-69, Maple Street United Meth. Ch., Lynn, Mass., 1969-74, Holyoke United Meth. Ch. (Mass.), 1974-76; comptroller United Meth. Reporter, Dallas, 1976—, Religious News Service, Dallas, 1983—; asst. conf. sec. So. New Eng. Conf., Boston, 1968-74, trustee, 1974-76, conf. sec., 1974-76; chaplain Lynn Fire Dept., 1971-74; mem. supervisory com. North Tex. Conf. Fed. Credit Union, Farmersville, Tex., 1981-84. Second vice comdr. Amvets, State Iowa, 1954-55; pres. Greater Lynn Mental Health Assn., 1973-75. Stowell fellow for travel and study in Holy Land, So. New Eng. Conf. United Meth. Ch., Boston, 1969. Recipient This Is Your Life award Lynn, 1974. Mem. Nat. C. of C. Lodge: Lion (pres. 1982-84, zone chmn. 1983, del. internat. conv. 1985). Home: 1288 N Bagley St #144 Dallas TX 75211 Office: The United Methodist Reporter PO Box 660275 Dallas TX 75266-0275

THORNTON, RAY, university president; b. Conway, Ark., July 16, 1928; s. R.H. and Wilma (Stephens) T.; m. Betty Jo Mann, Jan. 27, 1956; children—Nancy, Mary, Stephanie. B.A., Yale, 1950; J.D., U. Ark., 1956. Bar: Ark. 1956, U.S. Supreme Ct. Pvt. practice in Sheridan and Little Rock, 1956-70; atty. gen. Ark., 1971-73, mem. 93d-95th congresses 4th Ark. Dist.; exec. dir. Joint Ednl. Consortium, Arkadelphia, Ark., 1979-80; pres. Ark. State U., Jonesboro, 1980-84; now pres. U. Ark. Central Office; pres. Ark. State U. System; chmn. Ark. Bd. Law Examiners, 1967-70. Del. 7th Ark. Constl. Conv., 1969-70. Chmn. pres.'s devel. council Harding Coll., Searcy, Ark., 1971-73. Served with USN, 1951-54; Korea. Mem. AAAS (chmn. com. on sci., engring. and public policy 1980—). Office: Univ of Ark Central Office Fayetteville AR 72701*

THORNTON, RICHARD JOSEPH, lawyer; b. Indpls., Dec. 24, 1922; s. Maurice Emerson and Helene Emelia (Biederman) T.; B.S. in Bus., Ind. U., 1943; LL.B., U. Miami (Fla.), 1949; m. Edna Jean Thompson, Dec. 25, 1944; children—Charlotte Anne, Joseph Thompson. Bar: Fla. 1949. Practice law, Miami; ptnr. Walton, Lantaff, Schroeder & Carson, 1954-81; pres. Thornton, David & Murray, P.A., 1981—. Deacon, Presbyterian Ch., 1972-75, 76-79, elder, 1980-82. Served as capt. inf. U.S. Army, World War II. Fellow Am. Acad. Trail Lawyers; mem. ABA, Fla. Bar Assn., Dade County Bar Assn. (dir.), Internat. Assn. Ins. Counsel, Am. Judicature Soc., Beta Theta Pi, Phi Delta Phi. Democrat. Lodge: Elks. Home: 10401 NE 6th Ave Miami Shores FL 33138 Office: 2950 SW 27th Ave Suite 100 Miami FL 33133

THORNTON, RUSSELL JAMES, lawyer; b. Lockney, Tex., Dec. 7, 1955; s. Herman B. and Mildred D. (Deavenport) T. B.B.A., Abilene Christian U., 1977; J.D., Tex. Tech U., 1980. Bar: Tex. 1980, U.S. Dist. Ct. (no. dist.) Tex. 1981. Sole practice, Plainview, Tex., 1981-82; county atty. Hale County, Plainview, 1982—. Revision co-editor: Texas Crimes and Punishment, 1983. Treas., adminstrv. v.p. Plainview Jaycees, 1982-84; bd. dirs. Plainview Symphony, 1982-83; adv. counsel Sr. Vol. Program, Plainview, 1983—. Mem. Hale County Bar Assn., Tex. Dist. and County Atty.'s Assn. (pub. relations com. 1983-84), ABA (criminal justice com. 1982-84), Nat. Dist. Atty.'s Assn., Tex. Trial Lawyers Assn. Democrat. Mem. Ch. of Christ. Home: 410 Mesa Circle Plainview TX 79072 Office: County Attys Office Hale County Courthouse Plainview TX 79072

THORNTON, WILLIAM LEWIS, surgeon; b. San Antonio, Oct. 21, 1923; s. Daniel Raymond and Rhoda (Lewis) T.; B.S., U. Miss., 1945; M.D., U. Pa., 1947; m. Mae Carroll Harrison, June 14, 1945; children—Carroll Hodges, Rhoda Gayle, William Lewis, Lee Kinsey. Intern, Parkland Hosp., Dallas, 1947-48, surg. resident, 1948-52; pvt. practice medicine, specializing in gen. surgery, Meridian, Miss., 1952—; pres. Med. Arts Surg. Group, Meridian, 1972—; chief of staff Anderson Hosp., Meridian, 1976-77. Pres., Lauderdale County Cancer Soc., 1954—; pres. Meridian Mus. Art, 1975—; steward Central United Methodist Ch., Meridian, 1956—; 1st v.p. Meridian C. of C. Jr. Aux. Mardi Gras, 1972. Served with U.S. Army, 1943-46. Diplomate Am. Bd. Surgery. Mem. A.C.S. (pres. Miss. chpt. 1960), Meridian C. of C. (dir. 1970-73), Southeastern Surg. Soc., AMA, So., Miss. med. assns., E. Miss. Med. Soc., Meridian C. of C. (pres. 1980). Methodist. Clubs: Exchange (pres. Meridian 1960), Northwood Country (pres. 1971-72). Home: 4000 Country Club Dr Meridian MS 39301 Office: 2111 14th St Meridian MS 39301

THORNTON, WINFRED LAMOTTE, railroad executive; b. Winston-Salem, N.C., July 9, 1928; s. Winfred Lewis and Mildred (Cain) T.; B.S., Va. Mil. Inst., 1950; m. Mary Ann Hege, Aug. 18, 1951; children—Winfred LaMotte, Mary Ann. With So. Ry. System, 1950-59; chief operating officer Fla. East Coast Ry. Co., St. Augustine, 1960, v.p., chief operating officer 1961-64, pres., 1964—, also chmn., chief exec. officer, dir.; pres., dir. Fla. Sugar Refinery, Inc., Talisman Sugar Corp.; dir. Charter Co., St. Joe Paper Co., Fruit Growers Express Co., Bd. dirs. U.S. Indsl. Council; bd. dirs. Nat. Right to Work Com.; v.p., bd. dirs. Nemours Children's Hosp., Inc.; bd. dirs. Nemours Health Clinic, Inc.; mem. Fla. Council 100; co-trustee Alfred I. duPont Estate. Mem. Am. Ry. Engring. Assn., Am. Assn. R.R. Supts. Baptist (deacon). Office: Fla East Coast Ry Co St Augustine FL 32084

THORNTON-TRUMP, WALTER EDMOND (TED), manufacturer, inventor; b. Edmonton, Alta., Can., Aug. 8, 1918; came to U.S., 1970, naturalized, 1977; s. Walter Edward and Olga Wilhelmena Lyntine (Lund) Thornton-T.; m. Bernice Ruth Boale, Mar. 18, 1942; children—William Hamilton, Alexander Beverly, Belva Lynn, Anne Louise; student U. B.C., Vancouver, Can., 1939-41. Pres., Trump, Ltd., Oliver, B.C., 1944-64, Trump Hydraulics, Ltd., Toronto, Ont., Can., 1964-70, Trump, Inc., Plattsmouth, Nebr., 1970—; pres. Trump Engrs., Inc., Talb, Inc., 1978—, Trump Fabricators, Inc., 1980—; pres. Trump Industries Inc., Elberta, Ala., 1980—, Ted Trump Co., Elberta, 1983—, TRF Inc., Elberta, 1983—. Mem. Soc. Automotive Engrs., Rotary Club (past pres.). Patentee Fire Dept. "Snorkel" aerial device, Cherry Picker, Power Co. Bucket Trucks, Hot Water aircraft ramp deicing, also 12 basic hydraulic machines. Home: 3342 Spanish Cove Lillian AL 36549 Office: PO Drawer 410 Elberta AL 36530

THORPE, ALMA LANE KIRKLAND, broadcaster; b. Sylacauga, Ala., Dec. 20, 1941; d. Pierce and Dolly Odessa (Pardue) Kirkland; student Trevecca Nazarene Coll., 1961, Columbia Sch. Broadcasting, 1974; m. Jim Thorpe, Oct. 8, 1961; 1 dau., Margie. With W.T. Grant, Anniston, Ala., 1957-59; with So. Bell Telephone Co., Atlanta, 1963-65; religious broadcaster, Atlanta, 1974—. Office: PO Box 10634 Station A Atlanta GA 30310

THORPE, DEBORAH LEE MOOREHEAD, nurse; b. Lima, Ohio, Aug. 8, 1948; d. Lee Charles and Betty May (Birmingham) Moorehead; 1 dau., Abigail Lee. B.S.N., Ill. Wesleyan U., 1970; M.S., Boston U., 1972; postgrad. Tex. Woman's U. R.N. Staff nurse Tufts New Eng. Med. Ctr., Boston, 1972-74; instr. Children's Hosp. Sch. Nursing, Boston, 1974-77, Burlington County Meml. Hosp., Mt. Holly, N.J., 1978-80; clin. nurse specialist St. Francis Hosp., Tulsa, 1981-82, U. Tex. System Cancer Ctr., M.D. Anderson Hosp. and Tumor Inst., Houston, 1983—. Active Newton (Mass.) Symphony, 1972-74, Plymouth (Mass.) Philharm., 1974-78. W.K. Kellogg Found. fellow, 1980. Mem. Am. Nurses Assn., Council Clin. Nurse Specialists, Nat. League Nursing, Nat. Assn. Orthopaedic Nurses, Oncology Nursing Soc., Tex. Nurses Assn. (bd. dirs. dist. 9), Am. Pain Soc. Sigma Theta Tau, Sigma Kappa, Alpha Tau Delta. Episcopalian. Editor Dimensions in Oncology Nursing; mem. editorial bd. Orthopaedic Nursing; contbr. Working with Orthopedic Patients; also articles.

THORPE, EDWIN MORRIS, college dean; b. Monroe, N.C., Dec. 2, 1916; s. Charles Herman and Cora Lee (Dunham) T.; m. Annette Pinkston; children—Elaine, Edwin, Jean, Charles. B.S., N.C. A&T State U., 1938; M.S., U. Ill., 1948; Ph.D., Fla. State U., 1975. Instr. math., coach Oaklawn High Sch., Lincolnton, N.C., 1938-44; asst. to dean Johnson C. Smith U., Charlotte, N.C., 1944-47; grad. asst. in edn. adminstrn. U. Ill., Urbana, 1947-48; registrar Fla. A&M U., Tallahassee, 1948-72, asst. to pres., 1972-78, dean student affairs, 1978—; cons. Ala. State U., Montgomery, 1971, Moton Consortium, Washington, 1972, St. Augustine's Coll., Raleigh, N.C., 1972. Contbr. articles to ednl. jours. Chmn. United Way at Fla. A&M U., 1960-84; mem. Dem. Exec. Com., Tallahassee, 1975-84; bd. dirs. Tallahassee Habitat for Humanity, 1980—, Capital Health Plan, 1979—. Recipient numerous awards United Way. Mem. Am. Heart Assn. (chpt. bd. dirs. 1978-82), Nat. Assn. Coll. Deans, Registrars, and Admissions Officers (past pres., editor publs., 1949-73), Fla. Assn. Coll. Registrars and Admissions Officers (v.p. 1972-73), Phi Delta Kappa, Pi Gamma Mu., Alpha Phi Alpha, Sigma Pi Phi. Democrat. Roman Catholic. Lodge: Kiwanis. Avocations: international travel; reading; golf; tennis. Office: Dean Student Affairs Fla A&M U 1700 S Martin Luther King Blvd Tallahassee FL 32307

THRAILKILL, DANIEL B., lawyer; b. Fayetteville, Ark., Sept. 21, 1957. B.S. in Bus. Adminstrn., U. Ark., 1979, J.D., 1981. Bar: Ark. 1982, U.S. Dist. Cts. (ea. and we. dists.) Ark. 1982, U.S. Ct. Appeals (8th cir.) 1983, U.S. Supreme Ct. 1985. Ptnr. Tucker & Thrailkill, Mena, Ark., 1981—. Recipient Appellate Advocacy award U. Ark. Sch. Law, 1981. Mem. Assn. Trial Lawyers Am., ABA, Nat. Dist. Attys. Assn., Ark. Bar Assn., Phi Alpha Delta. Methodist. Lodge: Lions. Home: 1717 W Church St Mena AR 71953 Office: Tucker and Thrailkill 311 De Queen St Mena AR 71953

THRASH, BILL, TV executive; b. Ada, Okla., Sept. 25, 1939; s. Guy and Lucille (Williams) T.; m. Billie Allen, Feb. 16, 1967. B.A., E. Central U., 1961. Program dir. Sta. KTEN-TV, Ada, 1955-62, Sta. KOCO-TV, Oklahoma City, 1962-71; dir. ops. Sta. KTVY, Oklahoma City, 1971—. Producer, dir. TV programs including Stars and Stripes Show, Pop! Goes the Country, Nashville On the Road, Hoyt Axton, Bill Banowsky Visits. Pres. bd. Lyric Theatre Okla., Inc., Oklahoma City, 1985. Served with AUS, 1962-67. Mem. TV Programming Conf., Nat. Assn. TV Program Execs., E. Central Alumni Assn. (past pres.). Republican. Baptist. Club: Quail Creek. Avocation: music.

THRASH, THOMAS WOODROW, lawyer; b. Birmingham, Ala., May 8, 1951; s. Thomas Woodrow and Catherine (Pope) T.; m. Margaret Lines, June 20, 1981; children—Andrew Stiles, Margaret van Buren. B.A., U. Va., 1973; J.D. cum laude, Harvard U., 1976. Bar: Ga. 1976. Assoc. McClain, Mellen, Bowling & Hickman, Atlanta, 1976-77; asst. dist. atty. Atlanta Jud. Dist. 1977-81; ptnr. Finch, McCranie, Brown & Thrash, Atlanta, 1981—; instr. Atlanta Law Sch., 1977, Atlanta Coll. Trial Advocacy, 1984-85. Active High Mus. Art, Atlanta, 1982—, Atlanta Hist. Soc., 1977—; bd. dirs. Current Historians, 1983—, Ga. Conservancy, 1982—. Mem. Ga. Bar Assn., Atlanta Bar Assn., Lawyers Club Atlanta. Democrat. Episcopalian. Contbr. articles to profl. jours. Home: 57 Lakeland Dr NW Atlanta GA 30305 Office: 1510 1st Atlanta Tower Atlanta GA 30383

THREEFOOT, SAM ABRAHAM, internist, educator; b. Meridian, Miss., Apr. 10, 1921; s. Sam Abraham and Ruth Francis (Lilienthal) T.; m. Virginia Rush, Feb. 6, 1954; children—Ginny Ruth, Tracyann Rush, Shelly Ann. B.S., Tulane U., 1943, M.D., 1945. Diplomate Am. Bd. Internal Medicine. Intern, Michael Reese Hosp., Chgo., 1945-47; fellow in internal medicine Tulane U., New Orleans, 1947-49, instr. to prof. medicine, 1948-70, prof., 1976—; dir. research and med. edn. Touro Infirmary, New Orleans, 1953-70; chief of staff VA Med. Center Augusta, Ga., 1970-76, also prof. medicine, asst. dean Med. Coll. Ga., Augusta, 1970-76; assoc. chief of staff for research VA Med. Center, New Orleans, 1976-79, chief of staff, 1979—; cons. physician in medicine Lallie Kemp Charity Hosp., Independence, La., 1951-53; cons. Charity Hosp. of La., New Orleans, 1969-70, 76—; dir. Am. Heart Assn., N.Y.C. and Dallas, 1966-75; regional adv. group La. Regional Med. Program, New Orleans, 1965-70. Served with A.S.T.P., 1943-45. La. Heart assn. grantee, 1953-55; USPHS grantee, 1953-66; honor scholar Tulane U., 1938-41; Am. Heart Assn. grantee, 1959-61; research grantee John A. Hartford Found., 1954-72. Fellow ACP, Am. Coll. Cardiology; mem. So. Soc. Clin. Investigation, Central Soc. Clin. Research, Am. Heart Assn., Internat. Soc. Lymphology, Phi Beta Kappa. Contbr. articles to profl. jours., chpt. in book. Home: 347 Millaudon St New Orleans LA 70118 Office: VA Hosp 1601 Perdido St New Orleans LA 70146

THRESHER, ALISON JEAN DEMAREST, obstetrician-gynecologist, computer analyst; b. Glen Ridge, N.J., Aug. 30, 1946; d. David Franklin and Alison Jean (Clark) Demarest; m. Dean Thresher, Jr., Aug. 26, 1967; children—Caroline Clark, Daniel Demarest, Charles Dean. B.A. in Math. cum laude, U. Colo., 1966; M.D., U. Miami (Fla.), 1975. Diplomate Am. Bd. Ob-Gyn. Computer programmer Airco, Union, N.J., 1966-67, McCormick-Schilling Co., San Francisco, 1967-68; systems analyst Dade County Sch. Bd., Miami, 1968-70; intern Jackson Meml. Hosp., Miami, 1975-76, resident in ob-gyn, 1976-79; practice medicine specializing in ob-gyn, Miami, 1979—; mem. staff Drs. Hosp., Coral Gables, Fla., Bapt. Hosp. Miami; clin. asst. prof. medicine U. Miami. Recipient Alumni award U. Miami Sch. Medicine, 1975; S. Atlantic Assn. Obstetricians and Gynecologists fellow, 1972. Mem. AMA, Fla. Med. Assn., Dade County Med. Assn., So. Med. Assn., Am. Coll. Ob-Gyn, Alpha Omicron Pi. Republican. Mem. United Ch. Christ. Office: 9000 SW 87th Ct Suite 207 Miami FL 33176

THRIFT, ROBERT DAVID, marriage and family therapist; b. San Antonio, Dec. 1, 1948; s. David Benjamin and Bonnie Elizabeth (Reading) T.; m. Susan Louise Ledbetter, May 29, 1971; children—David Bradley, Kristin Brooke. B.A., Tex. Tech. U., 1970; postgrad. Southwestern Sem., 1970-71; M.Ed., Tex. Tech. U., 1973; postgrad. Austin Presbyn. Sem., 1973-74, U. Miami, 1980—. Lic. marriage and family therapist/mental health counselor, Fla. Asst. dir. Bapt. Student Union, Tex. Tech. U., Lubbock, 1971-72; minister to coll. students Univ. Bapt. Ch., Austin, Tex., 1972-75, First Bapt. Ch., Waco, Tex., 1975-79; dir. counseling Univ. Bapt. Ch., Coral Gables, Fla., 1979—. Mem. Am. Personnel and Guidance Assn., Nat. Council on Family Relations, So. Bapt. Assn. Family Ministers, Am. Assn. Marriage and Family Therapy (assoc.), Coral Gables C. of C. Author: The Ball Park, 1976. Home: 930 Malaga Ave Coral Gables FL 33134 Office: 624 Anastasia Ave Coral Gables FL 33134

THRONE, VIRGIL MICHAEL, data processing executive; b. Springfield, Mo., Nov. 19, 1942; s. Virgil and Exah Berline (Thomason) T.; m. Constance Faye Arnall, Dec. 19, 1964; children—Melanie LaKaye, Shelli Leigh. B.S. in Ed., Southwest Mo. State U., 1966; postgrad. Southwestern Baptist Theol. Sem., 1966-68. Minister music and edn. First Bapt. Ch., Lancaster, Tex., 1969-73; programming team leader Southland Corp., Dallas, 1973-75; asst. mgr. devel. and maintenance Dallas County Hosp. Dist., 1975-79; systems engr. mgr. Electronic Data Systems, Dallas, 1979-85; sr. group mgr., 2d v.p. Lomas & Nettleton Info. Systems, Dallas, 1985—. Mem. bd. trustees Grand Prairie Ind. Sch. Dist., Tex., 1983—, pres., 1984-85, sec., 1985-86; minister of music Indian Hills Bapt. Ch., Grand Prairie, 1978—. Republican. Lodge: Rotary. Home: 3650 Racquet Club Grand Prairie TX 75051

THUMANN, ALBERT, association executive, engineer; b. Bronx, N.Y., Mar. 12, 1942; s. Albert and Ella (Josephy) T.; m. Susan Stock, Jan. 23, 1966; 1 son, Brian. B.S., CUNY, 1964; M.S. in Elec. Engring., NYU, 1967, in Indsl. Engring., 1970. Registered profl. engr., N.Y., Ga., Ky. Project engring. mgr. Bechtel Corp., N.Y.C., Louisville, 1964-77; exec. dir. Assn. Energy Engrs., Atlanta, 1977—; adj. prof. environ. engring. U. Louisville, 1974-75. Recipient Young Engr. of Yr. award Ky. Soc. Profl. Engrs., 1974-75, Ky. Col.; Disting. Service award Assn. Energy Engrs., 1980. Mem. IEEE, Nat. Soc. Profl. Engrs., Am. Soc. Assn. Execs., City Coll. Alumni Assn. Author: Electrical Consulting-Engineering and Design, 1973; (with R.K. Miller) Secrets of Noise Control, 1976, Plant Engineers and Managers Guide to Energy Conservation, 1977, 82; Biorhythms and Industrial Safety, 1977, How to Patent Without a Lawyer, 1978, Electrical Design, Safety and Energy Conservation, 1978, Handbook of Energy Audits, 1979, 83; Fundamentals of Energy Engineering, 1984; Energy Audit Sourcebook, 1983; Introduction to Efficient Electrical Systems Design, 1985; editor; Emerging Synthetic Fuel Industry, 1981; contbr. articles to profl. jours; lectr. on energy conservation. Home: 931 Smoketree Dr Tucker GA 30084 Office: 4025 Pleasantdale Rd Suite 340 Atlanta GA 30340

THURMAN, FRANK, sheriff; b. Dewey, Okla., Oct. 23, 1925; s. John Andrew and Dottie Mae (Greer) T.; m. Norma Jean Shuck, July 11, 1959. Officer, Claremore Police Dept., Okla., 1946-49; trooper Okla. Hwy. Patrol, 1950-58; chief criminal dep. Tulsa County Sheriff's Office, 1959-74, under-sheriff, 1974-82, sheriff, 1982—; past pres. FBI Nat. Acad. Grads., 1963, 79, 80; chmn. Regional Organized Crime Information Ctr., 1979-80, 84-85. Named Outstanding Law Enforcement Officer Okla. Dist. Attys. Assn., 1984. Mem. Okla. Sherriff's Assn. (v.p.), Okla Sherrifs Peace Officers Assn. (pres. 1985), Tulsa C. of C. Clubs: Tulsa County Democratic, Sertoma. Lodges: Masons, Shriners. Avocations: hunting; fishing; golf. Office: Tulsa County Sheriff's Office 500 S Denver Tulsa OK 74103

THURMAN, KAREN, state senator; b. Rapid City, S.D., Jan. 12, 1951; d. Lee Searle and Donna (Altfillisch) Loveland, Jr.; m. John Patrick Thurman, 1973; children—McLin Searl, Liberty Lee. B.A., U. Fla., 1973. Mem. Dunnellon City Council (Fla.), 1974-82; mayor, Dunnellon, 1979-81; mem. Fla. Senate, 1982—; mem. Regional Energy Action Com.; mem. Monroe Regional Med. Ctr. Governance Com.; former mem. Comprehensive Plan Tech. Adv. Com. Former del. Fla. State Democratic Conv. and Dem. Nat. Conv., 1980. Recipient Appreciation for Service award Regional Planning Council. Mem. Dunnellon C. of C. (charter, former dir.; Service above Self award 1980), Fla. Horseman's Children's Soc. (charter). Democrat. Episcopalian. Office: Fla State Senate Office Bldg Tallahassee FL 32304*

THURMON, JACK JEWEL, financial services executive; b. Kilgore, Tex., Aug. 14, 1944; s. Merida Eldridge and Agnes (Jones) T.; B.S. in Indsl. Engring., So. Meth. U., 1967; M.B.A., Harvard U., 1969; m. Barbara Fern Henson, July 1, 1966; children—Gregory, J. Clarke, J. Douglas. Pres., Rimcor, Inc., Houston, 1969-72, Houston Mut. Agy., Inc., 1972—, Jojoba Mgmt., Inc., Houston, 1982—; chmn. Hillsboro Press, Inc., 1985—; sr. v.p. Crump Co., Houston, 1985—. Served with USAR, 1969-75. Republican. Home: 426 Rancho Bauer St Houston TX 77079 Office: 900 Gessner Suite 800 Houston TX 77024

THURMOND, STROM, U.S. senator; b. Edgefield, S.C., Dec. 5, 1902; s. John William and Eleanor Gertrude (Strom) T.; B.S., Clemson Coll., 1923; over 20 hon. degrees; m. Jean Crouch, Nov. 7, 1947 (dec. Jan. 1960); m. Nancy Moore, Dec. 22, 1968; children—Nancy Moore, Juliana Gertrude, J. Strom II, Paul Reynolds. Tchr., athletic coach in S.C. schs., 1923-29, supt. edn., 1929-33; admitted to S.C. bar, 1930; city atty., county atty.; state senator, 1933-38; circuit judge, 1938-46; gov. S.C., 1947-51; mem. Thurmond, Lybrand & Simons, 1951-55; U.S. senator, 1954—, chmn. senate judiciary com., 1981, pres. pro tem, 1981; del. Democratic Nat. Conv., 1932, 36, 48, chmn. S.C. del. and nat. committeeman, 52, 56, 60; chmn. S.C. del. Republican Nat. Conv., 1968, 84, del., 1972, 76, 80; States' Rights Dem. candidate for Pres., 1948. Served with U.S. Army, 1st Army, ETO and PTO; attached to 82d Airborne Div. for invasion of Europe, 1942-45; ret. maj. gen. U.S. Army Res. Decorated 18 medals and awards, including Legion of Merit with oak leaf cluster, Bronze Star with V., Purple Heart, Presdl. Disting. Unit citation, 5 battle stars (U.S.), Croix de Guerre (France), Order of Crown (Belgium). Recipient Patriots award Congressional Medal of Honor Soc., 1974. Past trustee Winthrop Coll. Mem. Am. Bar Assn., Res. Officers Assn. (past nat. pres.; Minuteman of Year award 1971), Am. Legion (nat. def. com., Disting. Public Service award 1975), Mil. Govt. Assn. (past nat. pres.), numerous other vets., civic and fraternal orgns. Baptist. Republican. Author: The Faith We Have Not Kept, 1968. Home: Aiken SC 29801 Office: United State Senate Washington DC 20510

TIBBITTS, BRADFORD WHITTIER, college dean; b. Boston, Mar. 22, 1941; s. Walter Grenville, Jr., and Barbara (Whittier) T.; m. D'Linda Sue Shillingburg, Sept. 3, 1966; children—Matthew Whittier, Emily Sue. B.A., So. Meth. U., 1963; M.A., North Tex. State U., 1967. History instr. Blinn Jr. Coll., Brenham, Tex., 1968-73; dir. social scis. Weatherford Coll., Tex., 1973-75, dean of instruction, 1975—. Del. to state conv. Tex. Democratic Party, 1978; fin. chmn. Comanche Trails dist. Longhorn council Boy Scouts Am., 1985; chmn., pres. Weatherford Pub. Library Bd., 1976-77, 83; pres. Friends of Weatherford Pub. Library, 1975-77; mem. Weatherford Indsl. Devel. Bd., 1981—. Mem. Tex. State Hist. Assn., Tex. Jr. Coll. Tchrs. Assn., Tex. Assn. Jr. and Community Coll. Instrl. Adminstrs. (parliamentarian 1983-84). Methodist. Lodge: Optimist (pres. Weatherford 1980-81, Optimist of Yr. 1980). Avocations: travel; fishing; reading; ships; tennis. Home: PO Box 724 Weatherford TX 76086 Office: Weatherford Coll 308 E Park Ave Weatherford TX 76086

TICHENOR, DORIS ANNIS, home economics educator; b. Butler County, Ky., Oct. 18, 1931; d. Wendell and Amy Annis; m. Carroll Tichenor, Feb. 16, 1952; children—Karen Michele, Annis Caylen. B.S. in Home Econs. with high distinction, U. Ky., 1952, M.S. in Home Econs., 1958, Ph.D. in Animal Scis., 1969. Dir. food and nutrition service ARC, 1952-55; faculty U. Ky., Lexington, 1955-84, assoc. dean Coll. Home Econs., 1969-84, asst. dir. Home Econs.-/Community Devel., 1976-84; dir. home econs. U. Fla., Gainesville, 1984—; writer, speaker in field. Mem. Assn. Adminstrs. of Home Econs., Am. Home Econs. Assn., Am. Meat Sci. Assn., Community Devel. Soc., Inst. Food Technologists, Sigma Xi, Epsilon Sigma Phi (Disting. Service award Alpha Kappa chpt.), Gamma Sigma Delta, Phi Upsilon Omicron. Home: 7616 NW 44th Pl Gainesville FL 32606 Office: 3001 McCarty Hall U Fla Gainesville FL 32611

TIDBALL, TAUN OGLE, insurance agency executive; b. Frederick, Md., June 11, 1953; d. William Henry and Florence Josephine (Naill) Ogle; m. Bruce Mack Tidball, May 6, 1977; 1 son, Steven Mack. Student pub. schs., Frederick. Cert. ins. counselor. Agt. trainee State Farm Ins. Co., Frederick, 1974-75; underwriter James S. Kemper Ins. Co., San Antonio, 1975-77; mgr. Donald E. Miller Agy., San Antonio, 1977—. Mem. council Lutheran Ch. of Resurrection, San Antonio, 1982-84. Mem. Soc. Cert. Ins. Counselors. Republican. Home: 2338 Frontier Trail San Antonio TX 78251 Office: Donald E Miller Agy 1920 Nacogdoches Suite 202 San Antonio TX 78209

TIDWELL, GEORGE ERNEST, federal judge; b. Atlanta, Aug. 1, 1931; s. George Brown and Mary (Wooddall) T.; LL.B., Emory U., 1954; m. Carolyn White, July 1, 1961; children—Thomas George, Linda Carol, David Loran. Admitted to Ga. bar, 1954; practiced in Atlanta, 1954-66; exec. asst. atty. gen., Atlanta, 1966-68; judge Civil Ct., Fulton County (Ga.), 1968-71; judge Superior Ct., Atlanta Jud. Circuit, 1971; now judge U.S. Dist. Ct., No. Dist. Ga., Atlanta. Office: 1967 US Courthouse 75 Spring St SW Atlanta GA 30303*

TIEDEMANN, ALBERT WILLIAM, JR., chemist; b. Balt., Nov. 7, 1924; s. Albert William and Catherine (Madigan) T.; B.S., Loyola Coll., Balt., 1947; M.S., N.Y. U., 1949; Ph.D., Georgetown U., 1958; m. Mary Therese Sellmayer, Apr. 6, 1953; children—Marie Therese, Donna Elise, Albert William III, David Lawrence. Teaching fellow N.Y. U., 1947-50; instr. chemistry Mt. St. Agnes Coll., 1950-55; chief chemist Emerson Drug div. Warner Lambert Pharm. Co., Balt., 1955-60; analytical supr. Hercules Powder Co., Allegany Ballistics Lab., Cumberland, Md., 1960-68; tech. service supt. Hercules Inc., Radford, Va., 1968-72; dir. Va. Div. Consol. Labs., Richmond, 1972-78; vice-chmn. Va. Toxic Substances Adv. Council, 1978—; dep. dir. for labs. Va. Dept. Gen. Services, 1978—. Served to lt. (j.g.) USNR, 1943-46; capt. Res., 1946—. Fellow Am. Inst. Chemists; mem. Am. Mgmt. Assn., Soc. Advancement Mgmt. (treas. Richmond sect. 1982-83, exec. v.p. 1983-84, pres. 1984-85), Am. Soc. Quality Control (chmn. Richmond sect. 1975-76, councilor biomed. div. 1978-80), U.S. Naval Inst., Naval Res. Assn. (dist. pres. 1954-57; nat. v.p. 1962-63, 65-69; nat. chmn. Navy Sabbath Program 1969-75; Nat. Meritorious Service award 1971, Twice a Citizen award 1978), Central Atlantic States Assn. Food and Drug Ofcls. (exec. bd. 1977-83, v.p. 1981-82, pres. 1982-83), Nat. Assn. Food and Drug Ofcls. (chmn. sci. and tech. com. 1981-85, sec.-treas. 1985—). Home: 10511 Cherokee Rd Richmond VA 23235 Office: Div Consol Labs 1 N 14th St Richmond VA 23219

TIEGEN, ELAINE MALIN, accounting company executive; b. Elizabeth, N.J., May 22, 1944; d. Bernard Edwin and Estelle (Radin) Malin; m. Robert A. Tiegen, Feb. 2, 1973 (div. Nov. 1975); 1 dau., Heike-Ann M. B.S. in Acctg., Fairleigh Dickinson U., Madison, N.J., 1966. C.P.A., Fla. Staff auditor Peat, Marwick, Mitchell and Co., Miami, 1968-69; sr. staff auditor J.H. Cohn and Co., C.P.A.s, Newark, N.J., 1969-71; with Clarence Rainess and Co., C.P.A.s, N.Y.C., 1971-73; spl. asst. to sr. ptnr. Wiener, Stern and Hantman, C.P.A.s, Miami, 1973-74; sr. specialist Laventhol & Horwath, Coral Gables, Fla., 1974-78, supr. dept. total acctg. services, 1978-79, mgr., 1979, head dept., 1980-83; prin. Elaine Tiegen & Co., C.P.A.s, Miami, 1983—. Pres. South Fla. Interprofl. Council, 1985-86; rep. small bus. Fed. Res. Bank of Atlanta Adv. Council Mem. Nat. Assn. Women Bus. Owners (bd. dirs. Miami chpt. 1985-86), Am. Women's Soc. C.P.A.s, Am. Soc. Women Accts (chpt. pres. 1975-76; Fla. Acct. of Yr. award 1976), Am. Inst. C.P.A.s (small bus. com.), Fla. Inst. C.P.A.s (recipient Disting. Service award Dade County chpt. 1980, 81, 82, gov. 1983-85, pres. chpt. 1984-85), Fla. Inst. C.P.A.s (chmn. Small bus. com. 1985-86) Am. Arbitration Assn., Mensa. Club: Miami Lakes Zonta (fin. chmn. 1984-85).

TIERNEY, MICHAEL EDWARD, bookstore owner, publisher, writer, artist; b. Pittsburg, Kans., July 6, 1955; s. Thomas Edward and Mary Ruth (Hall) T.; m. Joyce Ann Foster, June 21, 1974 (div. 1977). Student U. Ark., 1981-82. Mailroom supr. Morning Sun Paper, Pittsburg, 1971-73; apprentice machinist Forms Mfrs. Inc., Girard, Kans., 1973-75; journeyman machinist Service Bus. Forms, Wichita, Kans., 1975-77; div. mgr., purchaser Internat. Graphics, Little Rock, 1977-83; owner, operator Collector's Edit. Bookstore, North Little Rock, Ark., 1982—; tech. cons. Crazyhorse Lit. Jour., U. Ark., Little Rock, 1981-83, Equinox Mag., 1981-82. Author, illustrator, pub. jour. The Multiversal Scribe, 1977; contbr. short stories, artwork, art and poetry booklet to various profl. jours., 1969-78, comic book, 1984. Mem. Ark. Booksellers Assn. Avocations: writing; art; publishing. Office: Collector's Edition 5310 MacArthur Dr North Little Rock AR 72118

TIERNEY, PHILIP, lawyer; b. Boston, Nov. 29, 1933; s. Albert Gerard and Myrtle Marie (Curtin) T.; m. Bettina Rathbone Hartley, Mar. 25, 1961; children—Christopher Randolph, Philip Andrew, David Hartley. A.B., Harvard U., 1956; LL.B., Boston U., 1961. Bar: Mass. 1961, D.C. 1963, Va., 1964, U.S. Cts. 1964. Atty. advisor U.S. Tax Ct., Washington, 1961-63; ptnr. Boothe Prichard & Dudley, Alexandria, Va., 1963—; founder, dir. Bank of Alexandria, 1980—. Bd. dirs. Alexandria Seaport Found., 1982—. Served to lt. USNR, 1956-58. Fellow Am. Coll. Probate Counsel; mem. Va. State Bar (chmn. sect. taxation 1973-75), ABA, Va. Bar Assn. Republican. Episcopalian. Clubs: Eastern Yacht, Annapolis Yacht. Avocations: sailing; yacht racing; fly fishing; tennis. Home: 1114 Savile Ln McLean VA 22101 Office: Boothe Prichard & Dudley 1199 N Fairfax St Alexandria VA 22313

TIETJENS, JOEL NASH, safety engr.; b. Carrollton, Mo., July 28, 1953; s. Henry Orval and Lucille Candis Tietjens; student U. Mo., Columbia, 1975-76; B.S. in Indsl. Safety, Central Mo. State U., 1978; m. Jacqueline Aprisa Whitenton, Apr. 17, 1982. Loss prevention rep. St. Paul Fire and Marine Ins. Co., Houston, 1978-80; corp. safety engr. Mitchell Energy and Devel. Corp., The Woodlands, Tex., 1980—. Served with USAF, 1971-75. Mem. Am. Soc. Safety Engrs., Am. Legion. Baptist. Home: 4614 Hickorygate Dr Spring TX 77373 Office: PO Box 4000 2002 Timberloch Pl The Woodlands TX 77380

TIETKE, WILHELM, gastroenterologist; b. Niengraben, Germany, Oct. 15, 1938; came to U.S., 1969, naturalized, 1979; s. Wilhelm and Frieda (Schmeding) T.; M.D., U. Goettingen (W.Ger.), 1968; m. Imme Schmidt, Oct. 15, 1965; children—Cornelia, Claudia, Isabel. Intern, Edward W. Sparrow Hosp., Lansing, Mich., 1970; resident in internal medicine Henry Ford Hosp., Detroit, 1971-73; fellow in gastroenterology, 1973-75; practice medicine specializing in gastroenterology, Huntsville, Ala., 1975—; mem. vol. faculty, cons. U. Ala., Huntsville, 1976; clin. asst. prof. internal medicine, 1979—; pres. Gastroenterology Assocs. P.A., Huntsville, 1979—. Diplomate Am. Bd. Internal Medicine, Am. Bd. Gastroenterology. Mem. AMA, Ala. Med. Soc., Am. Soc. Gastrointestinal Endoscopy. Lutheran. Home: 2707 Westminster Way Huntsville AL 35801 Office: 520 Madison St Suite A Huntsville AL 35801

TIETZ, NORBERT WOLFGANG, clinical chemistry administrator; b. Stettin, Germany, Nov. 13, 1926; s. Joseph and Anna (Kozalla) T.; m. Gertrud Kraft, Oct. 17, 1959; children—Margaret, Kurt, Annette, Michael. Student Tuebingen, Germany, 1945-46; D.Sc., Tech. U., Stuttgart, W.Ger., 1950. Chmn. dept. chemistry Reid Meml. Hosp., Richmond, Ind., 1956-59; prof., dir. clin. chemistry Mt. Sinai Med. Ctr. and Chgo. Med. Sch., Chgo., 1959-76; prof., dir. clin. chemistry U. Ky. Med. Ctr., Lexington, 1976—; research fellow and asst. U. Munich, W.Ger., 1951-54; research fellow dept. pathology U. Chgo. and St. Luke's Hosp., Chgo., 1955-56, Rockford Meml. Hosp., Ill., 1954-55; cons. Ill. Dept. Pub. Health, 1967-76, VA Hosp., Hines, Ill., 1974-76; prof. biochemistry and pathology Rush Med. Coll., Chgo., 1975-76; vol. cons. VA Hosp., Lexington, 1976—. Fellow Acad. Clin. Lab. Physicians and Scientists; mem. Am. Assn. Clin. Chemistry (clin. chemist award 1971, award for outstanding efforts in edn. and tng. 1976, disting. alumnus award 1977, Steuben Bowl award 1978), AAAS, Am. Chem. Soc., Am. Soc. Clin. Pathologists, Am. Inst. Chemists, Sigma Xi. Roman Catholic. Author: Fundamentals of Clinical Chemistry, 1970, 3d edit., 1987; Clinical Guide to Laboratory Tests, 1983; Textile of Clinical Chemistry, 1986; assoc. editor: Dictionary and Encyclopedia of Laboratory Medicine and Technology, 1983; contbr. numerous articles to profl. jours. Home: 2075 Bridgeport Dr Lexington KY 40502 Office: Dept Pathology HL408 U Ky Med Ctr Lexington KY 40536

TIFFANY, JAMES ROBERT, JR., physical education educator, physical fitness company executive; b. Winchester, Va., Dec. 17, 1944; s. James Robert and Lois Virginia (Pangle) T.; m. Anne King Tweedy, July 14, 1973; children—Heather Anne, James Bronson. A.A. in Sci., Montreat-Anderson Jr. Coll., 1964; B.A. in Religion, Lynchburg Coll., 1966; B.S. in Phys. Edn., Wake Forest U., 1967, M.A., 1972; Ed.D., Nova U., 1980. Grad. asst., research lab. asst. Wake Forest U., Winston Salem, N.C., 1968; tchr. phys. edn., biology pub. schs., Fairfax County, Va., 1968-74; soccer coach Annandale High Sch. (Va.), 1971-72; cross country coach Lee High Sch., Springfield, Va., 1972-74; dir. phys. edn. and intramurals No. Va. Community Coll. Loudoun Campus, Sterling Va., 1974-83, prof., 1983—; pres. EXER-TRAIL, Inc., 1978—; cons. on physical fitness; tennis profl. Pres. Lincoln Community League, 1982; co-founder, adv. Loudoun Meml. 10 Miler, 1979-83; clinician Pres.'s Council on Phys. Fitness and Sports. Recipient plaques for outstanding contbns. xerox. Loudoun Meml. 10 Miler; Washington Fittest award YMCA and Channel 4, 1984. Mem. AAHPERD, Va. Assn. Health, Phys. Edn. and Recreation, Am. Coll. Sports Medicine, Am. Assn. Fitness Dirs. in Bus. and Industry. Episcopalian. Club: Potomac Peddlers. Author: (with R.A. Moss) The EXER-TRAIL Guide, 1980; The EXER-TRAIL Guide to Total Physical Fitness, 1983. Office: No Va Community Coll 1000 Harry Flood Byrd Hwy Sterling VA 22170

TILLER, MARTHA RUSSELL, public relations executive, consultant; b. Temple, Tex., Jan. 20, 1940; d. John Lafayette and Cleo (Davidson) Russell; m. David Clyde Tiller, Nov. 26, 1966; 1 son, John Russell. B.F.A. cum laude, U. Tex., 1961; student Nat. U. Mex., 1962, Piaget Inst. of Tex. Christian U., 1970. With radio-TV prodns. dept. U. Tex. and Sta. KTBC-TV, Austin, 1959-61; asst. to producer CBS TV, N.Y.C., 1961-64; with Goodson Todman Prodns., N.Y.C., 1964-66; dir. publs. Tex. Fine Arts Commn., Austin, 1967-69; press and social sec. to Mrs. Lyndon B. Johnson, Austin, 1973-76, also spl. asst. to Pres. Lyndon B. Johnson, Office of the Former Pres., Austin, 1972; dir. pub. info. Southwest Ednl. Devel. Lab., Austin, 1976, media specialist, 1969-72, writer, 1967; dir. pub. affairs Glenn, Bozell & Jacobs, Inc., Dallas, 1977-78; pres., pub. relations counselor Martha Tiller & Co., Dallas, 1978—. Mem. cultural activities task force Goals for Dallas; mem. KLRN-TV Channel 9, Austin, Austin Symphony Orch. Soc., Town Lake Beautification Com. of Austin, Laguna Gloria Art Mus. and Guild, Austin; vice chmn. 8 Arts Ball, TACA Assn., 1981-82; vice chmn. James K. Wilson Luncheon, 1982; mem. March of Dimes Women's Aux., Friends of LBJ Library (life), women's com. Dallas Civic Opera. Recipient Golden Key Pub. Relations award Am. Hotel/Motel Assn., 1982; named Nation's Top Broadcasting Coed, Am. Women Radio and TV, 1959. Mem. Pub. Relations Soc. Am., Tex. Pub. Relations Assn. (Best of Tex. award 1981), Women in Communications, Austin Natural Sci. Assn., Mortar Bd., Alpha Epsilon Rho. Clubs: Plaza Athletic, Bent Tree Country. Conceived and produced award-winning video Basic Steps to Fire Safety, 1981. Office: 4529 McKinney St Dallas TX 75205

TILLER, WENDELL HOWARD, orthopedic surgeon; b. Spartanburg, S.C., Oct. 17, 1920; s. Wendell and Ruth Howard (Lanham) T.; B.S., Wake Forest U., 1942, M.D., 1945; m. Martha Ivey, May 28, 1949; children—Linda Tiller McHam, W. Howard, Barbara Tiller Barragan, Frank, Martha I. Intern, N.C. Bapt. Hosp., Winston-Salem, 1945, asst. resident orthopedic surgery, 1948-50; resident orthopedic Children's Hosp., Boston, 1950-51; chief orthopedics U.S. Naval Hosp., Quantico, Va., 1952-54; practice medicine specializing in orthopedics, Spartanburg, 1951—; mem. staff Spartanburg Gen. Hosp., 1947, 51-52, 54—, Mary Black Hosp., Spartanburg, 1956—; asso. clin. prof. orthopedic surgery Med. U. S.C., Charleston, 1971—; dir. Blue Cross and Blue Shield S.C., 1965-74. Mem. Airport Commn. Spartanburg, 1961-63. Bd. dirs. YMCA Family Center, Spartanburg, 1955—, Jr. Archives of Spartanburg; elder 1st Presbyn. Ch., Spartanburg, 1966—. Served to lt. comdr. M.C., USN, 1946, 52-54. Diplomate Am. Bd. Orthopedic Surgery. Fellow A.C.S.; mem. Am., Pan Am., So., S.C. med. assns., Spartanburg County Med. Soc. (pres. 1969), S.C. Orthopedic Assn. (pres. 1970-71), Am. Acad. Orthopedic Surgeons, Southeastern Surg. Congress, Pan Pacific Surg. Assn., N.Y. Acad. Scis. Rotarian. Home: 210 Edgecombe Rd Spartanburg SC 29301 Office: 711 N Church St Spartanburg SC 29303

TILLERY, HERBERT RANDOLPH, JR., army officer; b. Morehead City, N.C., Dec. 28, 1947; s. Herbert R. Tillery and Elaine Ruth (Boney) Tillery Bell; m. Judy Carolyn Harrison, Feb. 8, 1969 (div.); children—Herbie, Damienne, Michale; m. Elnora Yvonne Hill, June 19, 1981. B.S. in Sociology, N.C. A&T State U., 1970; M.P.A., Jacksonville State U., 1978. Commd. officer U.S. Army, 1971, advanced through ranks to maj., 1982; platoon leader, Aberdeen Proving Ground, Md., 1971-72, chief race relations/equal opportunity office, 1972-74; platoon leader, Korea, 1974; asst. logistics officer, Ft. McClellan, Ala., 1975, co. comdr., 1976-77, instr. common mil. subjects com., 1977-78; community provost marshal, Karlsruhe Mil. Community (Ger.), 1978-81; command and gen. staff, Ft. Leavenworth, Kans., 1982-83; assigned 89th Mil. Brigade, Ft. Hood, Tex., 1983—. Decorated Meritorious Service medal with one oak leaf cluster, Army Commendation medal, Army Achievement medal with one oak leaf cluster, Nat. Def. Service medal, Armed Forces Expeditionary medal, Sec. Army's award Equal Opportunity Programs, 1974. Mem. Assn. U.S. Army, Kappa Alpha Psi (vice polemarch 1977-78). Democrat. Methodist. Home: 2501 Hanson Rd Killeen TX 75641 Office: HQ 89th Mil Police Brigade Fort Hood TX 76544

TILLETT, DOLORES BROOKS, advertising agency executive; b. Morristown, Tenn., Feb. 8, 1932; d. Thomas Dexter and Pearl (Smith) Brooks; m. Samuel Martin Tillett, Aug. 8, 1953; children—Steven Martin, Cynthia Brooks. Student in journalism U. Tenn., 1949-52. Asst. advt. mgr. Miller's Inc.,

Knoxville, Tenn., 1952-56, fashion copy dir., 1972-73; radio and TV copy dir. Sta.-WATE, Knoxville, 1962-69, TV promotion dir., 1969-71; copy dir. Bagwell & Assocs., Knoxville, 1973-77, v.p. creative services, 1977—. Recipient First Place award for superior creativity Greater Knoxville Advtg. Club, 1973, 74, 75, 77, 80, 81, 82, Third Best of Show trophy, 1981; First Place trophy 7th Dist. Advt. Assn., 1982, Nat. Addy trophy Am. Fedn. Advt., 1983. Home: 5421 Mockingbird Circle Knoxville TN 37919 Office: 320-D Troy Circle Knoxville TN 37919

TILLETT, GRACE MONTANA, ophthalmologist, real estate developer; b. Malone, N.Y., Dec. 5, 1924; d. Everett Reed and Althea Adela (Manson) Montana; m. Charles W. Tillett, Aug. 9, 1952; children—Charles, James, Avery. B.A., Syracuse U., 1946, M.D., 1949. Diplomate Am. Bd. Radiology, Am. Bd. Ophthalmology. Intern, Balt. City Hosps., 1949-50, resident, 1950-51; resident Johns Hopkins Hosp., Balt., 1951-53; practice medicine specializing in ophthalmology, Charlotte, N.C., 1957—; v.p. Prof. Optical Service, Charlotte, 1959—; pres. 2200 E. Seventh St. Real Estate Corp., Charlotte, 1965—; mem. staff Presbyn., Mercy, Charlotte Meml. hosps. Bd. dirs. Heart Assn. Charlotte, 1971-73, Dance Charlotte, 1978-79. Mem. Bus. and Profl. Women's Assn., Am. Acad. Ophthalmology, Am. Acad. Radiology, AMA, N.C. Med. Soc., Mecklenburg County Med. Soc., Charlotte Ophthalmol. Soc. Republican. Club: Charlotte Country. Office: 2200 E 7th St Charlotte NC 28204

TILLEY, ROBERT MIRES, psychology educator; b. Houston, Mo., Oct. 11, 1921; s. Robert Bruce and Virginia Agnes (Young) T.; m. Betty Eloise Rudy, June 14, 1947 (div. 1971); children—Anne L., Susan E., Robert B., Michael A., Mary C., Margaret E.; m. Dorotha Louise Treulove, Feb. 4, 1978. B.B.A., U. Mo., 1947; M.S. in Psychology, North Tex. State U., 1964; postgrad. Tex. Tech U., 1972-73. Mgmt. engr. Pollock Paper Corp., Dallas, 1948-63; instr. psychology Amarillo Coll., Tex., 1964-68, dir. testing, 1968-71, prof., 1974—, chmn. psychology dept. 1974—; psychologist Killgore Children's Hosp., Amarillo, 1966-72, State Ctr. for Human Devel., Amarillo, 1967-72; tng. cons. Southwestern Pub. Service, Amarillo, 1969. Bd. dirs. St. Andrews Episcopal Day Sch., Amarillo, 1966-69, Panhandle Community Action Corp., Amarillo, 1970-72; bd. dirs., pres. Suicide Prevention Crisis Intervention, Amarillo, 1966-70, Potter-Randall County Child Welfare, Amarillo, 1966-72; bd. dirs. Amarillo Opportunity House, 1981-83. Served to capt. U.S. Army, 1942-46, PTO. Mem. Assn. Improvement Community Coll. Teaching (bd. dirs. 1984—), Tex. Jr. Coll. Tchrs. Assn. (chmn. psychology sect. 1967). Avocations: fishing; tennis; classical music. Home: 7208 W 35th Amarillo TX 79109 Office: Amarillo Coll PO Box 447 Amarillo TX 79178

TILLMAN, MASSIE MONROE, lawyer; b. Corpus Christi, Tex., Aug. 15, 1937; s. Clarence and Artie Lee (Stewart) T.; B.B.A., Baylor U., 1959, LL.B., 1961; m. Jerra Sue Comer, July 27, 1957; children—Jeffrey Monroe, Holly. Admitted to Tex. bar, 1961, since practiced in Ft. Worth; partner firm Herrick & Tillman, 1961-66, Brown, Herman, Scott, Dean & Miles, 1970-78; sole practice law, 1966-70, 78—. Fellow Tex. Bar Found., Am. Bd. Trial Advocates; mem. Ft. Worth-Tarrant County Bar Assn. (dir. 1970-72, chmn. med.-legal liaison com. 1968-75, sec.-treas. 1976-77), Tex. Assn. Def. Counsel (dir. 1976-77), State Bar Tex. (chmn. pilot project Right of Trial by Jury 1969—), Trial Attys. Am., Am. Trial Lawyers Assn., Tex. Bd. Legal Specialization (cert. personal injury trial law), Tex. Trial Lawyers Assn. Democrat. Presbyterian. Author: Tillman's Trial Guide, 1970. Home: 4612 Briarhaven Rd Fort Worth TX 76109 Office: 4100 S Hulen St Suite 245 Fort Worth TX 76109

TIMAEUS, DANA LEE, lawyer; b. Beaumont, Tex., Sept. 19, 1956; s. Lee Jefferson and Vernell (Lovin) T.; m. Kay Williams, Oct. 17, 1981. B.B.A. with highest honors, Lamar U., 1978; J.D., U. Tex., 1981. Bar: Tex. 1981, U.S. Ct. Appeals (5th and 11th cirs.) 1981—, U.S. Dist. Ct. (ea. and so. dists.) Tex. 1982, U.S. Supreme Ct. 1985. Assoc., Benckenstein & Oxford, Beaumont, Tex., 1981—. Editor, Am. Jour. Criminal Law, 1980-81; contbr. article in law jour. Bd. dirs., pres. Neighborhood Housing Services of Beaumont, 1984. Mem. Jefferson County Bar Assn., Tex. Young Lawyers Assn., Jefferson County Young Lawyers Assn. (mem. continuing legal edn. com. 1984—), ABA (mem. rules and procedures com., subcom. local rules), Blue Key, Phi Kappa Phi, Phi Eta Sigma (pres.). Democrat. Lutheran. Office: PO Box 150 Allied Banks Bldg 3535 Calder Beaumont TX 77704

TIMCHAK, LOUIS JOHN, developer, real estate executive; b. Johnstown, Pa., Jan. 13, 1906; s. John and Mary (Karas) T.; m. Edna A. Bonistall, July 23, 1936; children—Janice Connell, Louis John, Glory McKean, Clifford J., Neil E. Ph.B., U. Chgo., 1934. Pres., Louis J. Timchak and Assocs., Real Estate. Mem. Beta Theta Pi, Phi Delta Phi. Republican. Roman Catholic. Home: 6657 Midhill Pl Falls Church VA 22043

TIMCHAK, LOUIS JOHN, JR., lawyer; b. Johnstown, Pa., June 7, 1940; s. Louis John and Edna Ann (Bonistall) T.; A.B., Georgetown U., 1962; J.D. U. Pitts., 1965; m. Susan Truesdale Mueller, June 3, 1972; children—Louis John, Alexander Mueller, Christopher Truesdale. Admitted to Pa. bar, 1965, D.C. bar, 1966, Fla. bar, 1970, N.Y. State bar, 1973, Ga. bar, 1980; individual practice law, Johnstown, 1968-69; real estate atty. Marriott Corp., Washington, 1969-73; asso. firm Finley, Kumble, Wagner, Heine & Underberg, N.Y.C., 1973-74; v.p., corp. counsel Phipps Land Co., Atlanta, 1974-76; regional v.p. IDR Mgmt., Inc., Atlanta, 1976-79; real estate cons. Boothe Fin. Corp., Atlanta, 1980; v.p., gen. counsel, dir. The Bankers Land Co., Palm Beach Gardens, Fla., 1980-83; v.p., mgr. corp. devel. Merrill Lynch Realty Inc., Stamford, Conn., 1983-84; mem. firm Scott, Royce, Harris & Bryan, Palm Beach, Fla., 1984-85; sr. v.p. Turner Devel. Corp., North Palm Beach, 1985—. Founding dir., past pres. Palm Beach County Devel. Bd., bd. dirs., 1984—. Served to lt. JAGC, USNR, 1965-68; Vietnam. Lic. real estate broker, N.Y., Fla. Mem. Am., D.C. bar assns., Palm Beach County Bar Assn., Urban Land Inst., Nat. Assn. Corp. Real Estate Execs., North Palm Beach County C. of C. (dir. 1981-83, 84— treas. 1983), Am. Heart Assn. (bd. dirs. Palm Beach County chpt. 1983—, sec. 1984, 1st v.p. 1985), Leadership Palm Beach County. Clubs: City Tavern (Washington); Gov.'s (Palm Beach); Univ. (Pitts.); Ponte Vedra (Fla.); Ocean Reef. Office: 1201 US Hwy One Suite 225 North Palm Beach FL 33408

TIMM, JEANNE ANDERSON, musician; b. Sioux City, Iowa, Aug. 15, 1918; d. Milton Earnest and Hazel Fern (Cunningham) Anderson; B.Mus., Morningside Coll., Sioux City, 1940; postgrad. Eastman Sch. Music, La. State U.; m. Everett L. Timm, Aug. 5, 1940; children—Gary Everett, Laurance Milo. Prof. woodwind instruments Morningside Coll., 1943-45, 48—; staff flutist Sta. KSCJ, Sioux City, 1941; prin. flutist Sioux City Symphony, 1943-45; vis. flutist New Orleans Philharm., New Orleans Opera Orch; prof. flute and chamber music La. State U., 1968—; cons., clinician flute cos.; editor Armstrong Edu-tainment Co., 1976—; flutist Baton Rouge Little Theater, summers 1965-81. Mem. Nat. Assn. Wind and Percussion Players, Nat. Flute Assn., Music Educators Nat. Conf., Music Tchrs. Nat. Assn., La. Music Educators Assn., Baton Rouge Music Club, Pi Kappa Lambda, Mu Phi Epsilon. Roman Catholic. Home: 465 Magnolia Woods Baton Rouge LA 70808 Office: 269 Music and Dramatic Arts Bldg La State U Baton Rouge LA 70803

TIMMONS, PAT FRANCIS, lawyer; b. Texarkana, Ark., Nov. 26, 1917; s. Pat F. and Janet (Spidel) T.; B.A., Baylor U., 1939; J.D., S. Tex. Coll., 1947; m. Clara Virginia Penick, Aug. 25, 1940; children—Claire Janet, Patrick F., Terence P. Pub. acct. P.F. Timmons, Houston, 1940-45; staff counsel Superior Oil Co., Houston, 1945-49; tax counsel Transcontinental Gas Pipeline Corp., Houston, 1950-57; admitted to Tex. bar, 1947; practice in Houston, 1957-76, 84— sr. counsel Superior Oil Co., 1976-84. Dist. com. mem. Boy Scouts Am., 1965-66. C.P.A., Tex. Mem. Tex. Soc. C.P.A.s, Am. Inst. C.P.A.s, State Bar Tex., Am. Bar Assn. Home: 7706 Woodway St Houston TX 77063 10200 Old Katz Rd Suite 100 Houston TX 77043

TIMMONS, WILLIAM THOMAS, patent and trademark lawyer; b. Ft. Worth, Feb. 28, 1946; s. Wilburn Charles and Olivia Jeane (Thomas) T.; m. Janet Louise Afterman, June 20, 1970. B.S. in E.E. with highest honors, U. Tex.-Arlington, 1969; M.S. in E.E., Northwestern U., 1971; J.D., U. Tex.-Austin, 1975. Bar: Tex. Liaison engr. Bell Helicopter, Ft. Worth, 1967-69; mem. tech. staff Bell Telephone Labs., Naperville, Ill., 1969-72; assoc. firm Hubbard, Thurman, Turner & Tucker, Dallas, 1975-77; sole practice, Dallas, 1977-80; ptnr. firm Kanz, Scherback & Timmons, Dallas, 1980—. Sec. Dallas Homeowners League, 1980-81, 81-82, pres., 1982-83; pres. U. Tex., Arlington, Engring. Alumni Assn., 1981-82; bd. dirs. U. Tex., Arlington, Alumni Assn., 1982—; treas. Dallas Democratic Forum, 1981-83; chmn. Growth and Devel. Task Force, Dallas County Dem. Party, 1981; chmn., treas. Keep Our Good Judges Com., 1982—; bd. dirs. Shakespeare Festival of Dallas, 1982-85, pres., 1986. Ernst Heyer scholar, 1968. Mem. ABA, State Bar Tex., Am. Patent Law Assn., Dallas Bar Assn. (chmn. lawyer referral and probono com. 1982-84, chmn. sole practitioners sect. 1981, chmn. other coms.). Dallas Assn. Young Lawyers (dir. 1980, co-chmn. domestic violence com. 1981), Dallas-Ft. Worth Patent Assn. (pres. 1980), Dallas C. of C., Mensa, Eta Kappa Nu. Home: 10424 Eastlawn Dallas TX 75229 Office: 1030 S Tower Plaza of the Americas Dallas TX 75201

TINDELL, WILLIAM NORMAN, oil company executive, petroleum geologist; b. Calvin, Okla., Apr. 6, 1921; s. John Lawson and Nona Lou (Baldwin) T.; m. Mary Helen Cozart, Dec. 31, 1983. B.S. cum laude, U. Pitts., 1948, M.S., 1950. Dist. mgr. Mayfair Minerals, Inc., Abilene, Tex., 1953-85; chmn. bd., chief exec. officer Westico Energy Co., Abilene, 1985—. Chmn. Citizens for Better Govt., Abilene, 1974; pres. Goodfellows, Abilene, 1966; pres., bd. dirs. West Central Tex. Mcpl. Water Dist., Abilene, 1968-75. Mem. Abilene C. of C. (v.p., mem. exec. com., bd. dirs. 1984-85, Petroleum Industry award 1984), West Central Tex. Oil and Gas Assn. (pres. 1962-63, Oilman of Yr. 1983), Abilene Geol. Soc. (pres. 1958), Am. Assn. Petroleum Geologists (mem. adv. council), Tex. Ind. Producers and Royalty Owners Assn. (v.p. 1963-64), Ind. Petroleum Assn. Am. (v.p. 1967-68). Republican. Episcopalian. Clubs: Petroleum (v.p.), Exchange (pres. 1965) (Abilene). Avocations: jogging; traveling; reading. Home: 10 Shepherds Cove Abilene TX 79605 Office: Westico Energy Co One Energy Sq Suite 2A Abilene TX 79601

TINGLER, LOYD, retail trade company executive; b. Daviess County, Mo., Aug. 27, 1920; s. Lawrence Henry and Leah Mae (Robinson) T.; grad. Chillicothe (Mo.) Bus. Coll., 1941; postgrad. Harvard U., 1947; m. Arlene Marie Preston, Aug. 8, 1948; children—Martha, Elizabeth, Charles, James. Mgr., Webb's Furniture Store, St. Petersburg, Fla., 1949-62; propr., dir. Loyd Tingler Furniture Inc., Pinellas Park, Fla., 1962—; dir. S.E. Bank of Pinellas Park, 1976-79. Chmn. Pinellas Park Water Mgmt. Dist., 1976—; trustee 5th Ave Bapt. Ch., St. Petersburg, 1980—; bd. dirs. Boys' Club of Pinellas Park, 1965-73, Pinellas Park Girls' Club, 1971-72, Child Guidance Clinic of Pinellas Park, 1973-75, Bay Vista Civic Assn., 1957-72. Served with USN, 1942-47. Mem. Fla. Furniture Dealers Assn. (dir. 1972—), Nat. Home Furnishing Assn., Contractors and Builders of Pinellas County (dir. 1980-82), Pinellas Park C. of C. (dir. 1972-75, transp. chmn. 1972-75 named Citizen of Year 1979). Republican. Baptist. Clubs: Optimists (dir. 1967-70, Friend of the Boy award 1971), Kiwanis (Layman's award 1975), Pres.'s Club, Moose. Home: 3611 93d Ave N Pinellas Park FL 33565 Office: 8010 US Hwy 19 Pinellas Park FL 33565

TINSLEY, JACKSON BENNETT, newspaper editor; b. Ewing, Tex., Dec. 14, 1934; s. Henry Bine and Sallie Alberta (Jackson) T.; m. Claudia Anne Miller, Oct. 3, 1965; children—Jackson Bennett, Anna Melissa. B.S., Sam Houston State U., Huntsville, Tex., 1958. With Lufkin (Tex.) News, 1951-52, 56; editor Diboll News-Bull., 1953-54, Corrigan Times, 1954; news editor Port Lavaca Wave, 1955; info. asst. Southwestern Bell Telephone Co., 1960-62; reporter Ft. Worth Star-Telegram, 1959-60, edn. writer, asst. night city editor, 1962-65, Sunday editor, 1965-70, asst. mng. editor, 1970-74, asst. to editor, 1974-75, exec. editor, 1975—, v.p., 1983—; adj. prof. Tex. Christian U., 1971-72; editor-in-residence various univs., 1982-84. Mem. Ft. Worth Badge and Shield; bd. dirs. Freedom of Info. Found. Tex., Inc.; dir. Sec. of State's Election Central Adv. Task Force. Served with inf. U.S. Army, 1959. Recipient 1st place award Nat. Edn. Writers Assn., 1965, Pub. Service citation AAUP, 1965; Disting. Alumnus award Sam Houston State U., 1984. Mem. Am. Soc. Newspaper Editors, Tex. AP Mng. Editors Assn. (pres. 1979-80), Sigma Delta Chi. Clubs: Ft. Worth, Colonial Country, Headliners (Ft. Worth). Lodge: Ft. Worth Rotary (pres. 1983-84). Office: 400 W 7th St Fort Worth TX 76102

TIPPIE, BRYAN THOMAS, army officer; b. Sedalia, Mo., Aug. 26, 1946; s. Kenward Elwaine and Doris Rae (Lacy) T.; m. Teresa Ann Preuitt, May 24, 1969; children—Bryan Christopher, Amy Rebecca. B.S. in Bus. Adminstrn., Central Mo. State U., 1968; M.S. in Human Resource Mgmt., U. Utah, 1975; grad. Army Command and Gen. Staff Coll., 1979, Air Command and Staff Coll., 1984. Joined U.S. Army, 1968, commd. 2d lt., 1969, advanced through grades to lt. col., 1986, commanding officer HHC 229th Assault Helicopter Bn., Vietnam, 1971-72; tng. officer Directorate of Tng., Ft. Bliss, Tex., 1976-77; comdr. B. Battery student Bn., Ft. Bliss, 1977-79; comptroller 501st MIl. Intelligence Group, Seoul, 1979-80; chief tng. div. XVII Airborne Corps, Ft. Bragg, N.C., 1980-81; ops. officer 3d Battalion 68th Air Def. Artillery, Ft. Bragg, 1981-83; dir. resource mgmt. Vint Hill Farms Sta., Warrenton, Va., 1984—, insp. gen., 1984—. Decorated Bronze Star, Air Medal. Mem. Am. Soc. Mil. Comptrollers (pres. 1984—), Assn. of U.S. Army. Baptist. Avocations: philatelist; playing basketball; football and softball. Home: 110 B Vint Hill Farms Sta Warrenton VA 22186 Office: Directore of Resource Mgmt Vint Hill Farms Sta Warrenton VA 22186

TIPTON, BARBARA FIERCE, business executive; b. Washington, Feb. 21, 1947; d. Harry Francis and Jeanne Elizabeth (Edwards) Krams; m. Donald Leon Fierce, Sept. 24, 1971 (div. 1981); children—Matthew Gabriel, Alison Stacy; m. 2d, John Edgar Tipton, May 29, 1982. Student Carson-Newman Coll., 1966-69; B.S. in Econs. cum laude, U. Md., 1971; postgrad. Va. Poly. Inst.-Reston, 1973. Staff, Com. for Re-election of Pres., Washington, 1971-72; adminstrv. asst. office of counsellor White House, Washington, 1973, 74; U.S. mktg. rep. asst. Australian Wine Bd., Washington, 1976; pres., chief exec. officer Greenscape, Inc., Falls Church and Sterling, Va., 1977—. Mem. Fairfax County (Va.) Republican Com., 1977-79, Alexandria (Va.) Rep. City Com., 1972-74; vice chmn. Alexandria Young Reps., 1973-74; precinct chmn. Lee Dist., Fairfax County, 1976-79. Recipient spl. achievement award U.S. Dept. Treasury, 1968-71. Mem. Landscape Contractors Met. Washington, Assn. Landscape Contractors Am., Loudoun County C. of C., Internat. Platform Assn., Am. Assn. Nurserymen, Interior Plantscape Assn., Nat. Landscape Assn., Better Bus. Bur., Omicron Delta Epsilon. Mormon. Home: Route 2 Box 394 Purcellville VA 22132 Office: Greenscape Inc 1101 W Church Rd Sterling VA 22170

TIRAS, HERBERT GERALD, engineering executive; b. Houston, Aug. 11, 1924; s. Samuel Louis and Rose (Seibal) T.; m. Aileen Wilkenfeld, Dec. 14, 1955; children—Sheryle, Leslie. Student, Tex. A. and M. U., 1941-42; attended, Houston U., 1942-65. Registered profl. engr., Calif. Cert. mfg. engr. in gen. mfg.; robotics; mfg. mgmt. Engr., Reed Roller Bit, Houston, 1942-60; pres. Tex. Truss, Houston, 1960-77; chief exec. officer Omnico, Houston, 1977—; Nat. Defense exec. res. resources officer, Region VI Fed. Emergency Mgmt. Agy., 1982—. Served to 1st lt. CAP, 1954-61. Mem. Soc. Mfg. Engrs., Robot Inst. Am., Robotics Internat., Marine Tech. Soc., Coll. and Univ. Mfg. Ednl. Council (nat. dir.). Lodge: Masons, Shriners. Home: 9703 Runnymeade Houston TX 77096 Office: PO Box 2872 Houston TX 77001

TISCH, JOSEPH LESAGE, priest, social work executive; b. Mount Vernon, N.Y., Sept. 3, 1933; s. Joseph Francis and Deborah Theresa (LeSage) T. B.A. in History, Notre Dame U., New Orleans, 1956, M.A. in History, 1958; D.D. (hon.), Addison State U., Can., 1979. Ordained priest Roman Catholic Ch., 1960; asst. pastor, Newman Club chaplain, dir. rural mission, Woodworth, La., 1960-63; prin. St. Joseph High Sch., Plaucheville, La., 1963-67; social worker Fla. State Welfare Bd., 1968-70; asst. exec. dir. Brevard County Community Action Agy., Inc., 1970-73; dir. City of Melbourne (Fla.) Human Services Dept., 1973—; rector St. Pierre Liberal Cath. Ch.; vicar commissary for Fla.; sec./treas. Provincial Clerical Synod, Liberal Cath. Ch. Chmn., City of Cape Canaveral Recreation Bd., 1968-74, Youth Edn. Commn. Named Humanist of Yr., Space Coast chpt. Am. Humanist Assn., 1974. Mem. Nat. Assn. Social Workers (chmn. Central East Coast unit Fla. chpt.), U.S. Conf. City Human Service Ofcls. (nat. trustee), Theosophical Soc., Theosophical Order of Service (dir. social service dept.). Democrat. Club: Kiwanis. Author: French in Louisiana, 1959; The Big Step, 1963; Adam Before Eve, 1984. Editor: The Evolving Universe, 1979—; Catholic Critiques, 1973—; The Voice of the Synod, 1980—. Home: PO Box 1117 Melbourne FL 32902 Office: 900 E Strawbridge Ave Melbourne FL 32901

TITLE, PETER STEPHEN, lawyer; b. New Orleans, Nov. 24, 1950; s. Harold Benjamin and Beulah (Sterbcow) T.; m. Sheryl Gerber, June 14, 1981. B.A., Columbia U., 1972; J.D., Tulane U., 1975. Bar: La. 1975, U.S. Dist. Ct. (ea., we. mid. dists.) La., U.S. Ct. Appeals (5th cir.). Assoc. Sessions, Fishman, Rosenson, Boisfontaine, Nathan & Winn, New Orleans, 1975-81, ptnr., 1982—; instr. on property Tulane U., 1978; asst examiner com. on Admissions to Bar, 1980—; lectr. on real estate Mem. ABA, La. State Bar Assn. (chmn. sect. on trust estates, probate and immovable property law 1983-84), New Orleans Bar Assn., Republican Am. Judicature Soc., Order of Coif, Phi Delta Phi. Jewish. Lodge: B'Nai Brith. Home: 515 Hillary St New Orleans LA 70130 Office: Sessions Fishman Rosenson Boisfontaine Nathan & Winn 601 Poydras St 25th Floor New Orleans LA 70130

TITONE, RUSSELL EMIL, sales exec.; b. New Brunswick, N.J., Mar. 11, 1948; s. Nicholas and Clara (Cassano) T.; A.S. cum laude in Bus. Adminstrn., Tidewater Community Coll., 1979; B.S. in Bus. Adminstrn., Va. Commonwealth U., 1982; m. Maureen Linda Murphy, June 15, 1968; children—Nicole Colette, Elise Marie, Brenna Beth, Summer Renee, Fawn Noelle. Engr. technician licensing and quality control Va. Electric Power Co., Surry, 1976-77, sr. engr. technician in prodn., ops. and maintenance Surry Nuclear Power Sta., 1977-79, engring. supr. in prodn. ops. and maintenance, 1979-80, sr. staff engr. nuclear ops. and maintenance support services, Richmond, 1980-82; mktg. mgr. IDS div. S.E. region The Computer Co., Richmond, 1982-85; regional sales mgr. Markhurd Corp., Midlothian, Va., 1985—. Served with USN, 1968-76. Mem. Am. Soc. Quality Control, Am. Mgmt. Assn., Phi Theta Kappa. Republican. Roman Catholic. Home: 104 Bondurant Pl Richmond VA 23236 Office: Markhurd Corp PO Box 1152 Midlothian VA 23113

TITUS, KIM VERNON, utilities public relations executive; b. Phoenix, Oct. 15, 1951; s. Merton Claire and Hazel Louise (Shandrow) T.; m. Elise Christina Hite, Aug. 10, 1973; children—Sterling Claire, Preston Starr, Courtney Renee. B.F.A. in Broadcast Film Arts, So. Meth. U., 1973, M.F.A. summa cum laude in Mass Communication, 1982. Audiovisual specialist Salt River Project, Phoenix, 1973-75, audiovisual coordinator, 1975-77; communication specialist Tex. Utilities Services, Inc., Dallas, 1977-81, sr. info. coordinator, 1981-83, supr. creative services, 1983—; adj. prof. TV, So. Meth. U., Dallas, 1980. Contbr. articles to profl. jours. Mem. TV arts cluster adv. com. Skyline High Sch., Dallas, 1982—; deacon Northminster United Presbyterian Ch., Dallas, 1979-81, elder, 1983-85; mem. artistic bd. Emporium Prodns., Dallas, 1985—. Recipient Ariz. Credit Union Booster of Yr. award, 1976. Mem. Internat. Assn. Bus. Communicators (Eddy award 1979; bd. dirs. 1980), Internat. TV Assn., Nuclear Industry Film Council, Delta Sigma Phi. Club: Dallas Press. Home: 9910 Tanglevine Dr Dallas TX 75238 Office: 2001 Bryan Tower Suite 1680 Dallas TX 75201

TIXIER, MAURICE PIERRE, petroleum engineer; b. Clermont-Ferrand, France, Feb. 1, 1913; came to U.S., 1935, naturalized, 1941; s. Lambert and Clementine Marie (Bacconet) T.; m. Allene Beulah Kaderli, Apr. 20, 1939; children—Linda Suzanne, Annette Louise (Mrs. George Harper West). Degree of Engr., Arts et Métiers, Belgium, 1932, Ecole Supèrieure d'Electricité, Paris, 1933. Registered profl. engr., Tex. Dist. mgr. Schlumberger Ltd., Midland, Tex., 1935-39, area mgr., Casper Wyo., Denver, 1941-49, dir. interpretation, Houston, 1949-72, tech. advisor to pres., 1972-77; pres. Tixier Tech. Corp., Houston, 1978-83, cons. engr., 1983—. Contbr. articles to profl. jours. Patentee in field. Served with French Army, 1934, 40. Mem. Am. Assn. Petroleum Geologists, Soc. Petroleum Engrs. of AIME (Disting. Lectr. award 1961), Geophys. Union, Soc. Profl. Well Log Analysts (Gold medal 1969), N.Y. Acad. Scis. Club: Petroleum (Houston). Home: 2319 Bolsover Rd Houston TX 77005

TJOFLAT, GERALD BARD, judge; b. Pitts., Dec. 6, 1929; s. Gerald Benjamin and Sarita (Romero-Hermoso) T.; m. Sarah Marie Pfohl, July 27, 1957; children—Gerald Bard, Marie Elizabeth. Student, U. Va., 1947-50, U. Cin., 1950-52; LL.B., Duke U., 1957; D.C.L., Jacksonville U., 1978. Bar: Fla. 1957. Individual practice law, Jacksonville, Fla., 1957-68; judge 4th Jud. Cir. Ct. Fla., 1968-70, U.S. Dist. Ct. for Middle Dist. Fla., Jacksonville, 1970-75, U.S. Ct. Appeals, 5th Cir., 1975-81, U.S. Ct. Appeals, 11th Cir., 1981—; mem. Advisory Corrections Council U.S., 1975—; mem. com. adminstrn. probation system Jud. Conf. U.S., 1972—, chmn., 1978—. Hon. life mem. bd. visitors Duke U. Law Sch.; pres. N. Fla. council Boy Scouts Am., 1977—; trustee Jacksonville Marine Inst., 1977—, Jacksonville Episcopal High Sch. Served with AUS, 1953-55. Mem. Am. Law Inst., Am. Bar Assn., Am. Judicature Soc., Fla. Bar. Episcopalian. Clubs: Masons, Shriners. Home: 2970 Saint Johns Ave Apt 6-D Jacksonville FL 32205 Office: US Ct Appeals 11th Cir PO Box 960 Jacksonville FL 32201

TOAL, JEAN HOEFER, lawyer, state representative; b. Columbia, S.C., Aug. 11, 1943; d. Herbert W. and Lilla (Farrell) Hoefer; m. William Thomas Toal; children—Jean Hoefer, Lilla Patrick. B.A. in Philosophy, Agnes Scott Coll., 1965; J.D., U. S.C., 1968. Bar: S.C. Ptnr. firm Belser, Baker, Barwick, Ravenel, Toal & Bender, Columbia; mem. S.C. Ho. of Reps., 1975—. Editor S.C. Law Rev. Bd. visitors Clemson U., 1978; parliamentarian S.C. Democratic Conv.; bd. trustees Columbia Mus. Art. Mem. Columbia Bus. and Profl. Women (named Career Woman of Yr. 1974). Roman Catholic. *

TOBIN, GERALD J., lawyer; b. Bklyn., Sept. 11, 1935; s. David and Dorothy (Gnatowsky) T.; m. Helene Pomerantz, June 24, 1956; children—Alyson Beth, Stacey Lynn, Adam Scott. B.A., U. Miami, 1959, J.D., 1962. Bar: Fla. 1962, N.Y. 1980, U.S. Supreme Ct. 1965, U.S. Ct. Appeals (5th cir.) 1964, U.S. Ct. Appeals (11th cir.) 1981. Sole practice, Miami, Fla., 1962—; judge Mcpl. Ct., City of Miami, 1965-72; chief judge, 1970-72; pres., chmn. bd. Nat. Corrections Holding Inc. and subs. cos. Bd. dirs. P.R.I.D.E.-Fla Prison Industries, 1982—, Big Bros., Miami, Congregation Bet Breira. Home: 12005 SW 64th St Miami FL 33183 Office: 1414 Coral Way Miami FL 33145

TOBOLOWSKY, JACK LEHMAN, textile co. exec.; b. Dallas, Jan. 16, 1917; s. Reuben and Etta Gertrude (Tobolowsky) T.; B.B.A., U. Tex., 1937; m. Josephine Pergament, Feb. 7, 1943; children—Donna Tobolowsky Stiffel, Ira, George, Myra Tobolowsky Prescott. Sr. engr. Western Electric Co., N.Y., 1944-49; gen. mgr. Tex Style Mfg. Co., Midlothian, 1949-59; pres. Midlo Textile Co., Midlothian and Dallas, 1959-63; pres. Wolf Textile Co., Dallas, 1963—; also engaged in ranching. Served with AUS, 1942-44. Mem. Phi Sigma Delta. Home: 5909 Waggoner Dr Dallas TX 75230 Office: 2214 Pacific Ave Dallas TX 75201

TODD, BOSWORTH MOSS, JR., investment counselor; b. Frankfort, Ky., Mar. 1, 1930; s. Bosworth Moss and Mary Jouett (Rodman) T.; m. Joan Yandell Henning, June 4, 1955; children—Samuel B., David Yandell, James Rodman. B.S., U. Ky., 1952; M.B.A., Harvard U., 1954. Chartered fin. analyst, investment counselor. Vice pres. Ky. Trust Co., Louisville, 1958-67; pres. Todd-Boston Co., Louisville, 1967-79; pres. Todd Investment Advisors, Louisville, 1979—; mem. The Boston Company Investment Policy Com., 1977, 79; dir. Cumberland Savs. & Loan, Louisville, 1983—. Contbg. editor Business First Weekly, 1984—. Treas., Schizophrenia Research Found., Louisville, 1983—, Schizophrenia Found. Ky., Inc., Louisville, 1982—; founding chmn. St. Francis Sch., Goshen, Ky., 1965-73. Served to capt. USAF, 1954-56. Mem. Investment Counsel Assn., N.Y. Soc. Security Analysts, Louisville Soc. Fin. Analysts. Republican. Episcopalian. Clubs: Pendennis, Juniper (Louisville). Home: 452 Swing Lane Louisville KY 40207 Office: Todd Investment Advisors 3160 First National Tower Louisville KY 40202

TODD, CYNTHIA LOIS BALFOUR, school psychologist, psychoeducational diagnostician; b. Highland Park, Mich., July 13, 1941; d. Harry C. and Eleanor Lucille (Rousseau) Balfour; m. James N. Todd, Aug. 8, 1970; children—Jonathon Barrett, David Bradley. B.A., Mich. State U., 1962; M.A., Eastern Mich. U., 1967; M.A., George Mason U., 1978. Cert. psychologist, Va.; cert. tchr., Va., Calif. Spl. edn. tchr. various sch. systems, Beverly Hills, Calif., Farmington, Mich. and Arlington, Va., 1965-70; diagnostician Huntington Beach Intercommunity Hosp., 1974; cons. Fauquier County Schs., Bishop Ireton High Sch., Alexandria, Va., 1979-84; school psychologist Arlington Pub. Schs., Va., 1977—; dir., owner Psycho-Ednl. Services, Internat., Reston, Va., 1982—; edn. chairperson Calif. Assn. for Neurologically Handicapped, Los Angeles, 1967-69; founder Calif. Assn. for Tchrs. of Educationally Handicapped, Los Angeles, 1967. Author: (pamphlet) Consciousness-Raising, 1975. Farmington Pub. Schs. scholar, 1967; Arlington Pub. Schs. research grantee, 1985-86. Mem. Ind. Hist. Soc., Reston Soccer Assn., NOW, Va. Assn. Sch. Psychologists (historian 1983), Nat. Assn. Sch. Psychologists, Am. Psychol. Assn. (assoc.), Arlington Edn. Assn., Kappa Delta. Democrat. Roman Catholic. Avocations: genealogy, soccer, sailing, traveling. Home: 2647 Wild Cherry Pl Reston VA 22091

TODD, EDWARD PAUL JOSEPH, surgeon, educator; b. Chgo., Aug. 12, 1941; s. Edward William and Georgine Marilyn T.; B.A., Baylor U., 1963, M.D., 1968, Ph.D., 1969; m. Marilyn Debner, Dec. 26, 1965; children—Erin, Edward, Rachael, Daphne. Intern, U. Minn. Hosp. and Clinics, 1969-70; resident in surgery, 1970-74; asst. prof. surgery U. Ky. Med. Center Hosp.,

Lexington, 1974-77, asso. prof. surgery, chmn. dept., 1977-80, prof., 1980—, chmn. cardio-thoracic surgery div., 1977—; cons. staff VA Hosp., Lexington, 1977—. Fellow Am. Coll. Chest Physicians, Am. Coll. Cardiology ACS; mem. AMA, Am. Assn. Thoracic Surgeons, Am. Thoracic Soc., Central Surg. Assn., Royal Soc. Medicine, Internat. Cardiovascular Soc., So. Thoracic Surg. Assn., Thoracic Surgery Dirs. Assn., Soc. Thoracic Surgeons, Am. Heart Assn., Ky. Surg. Soc., Ky. Thoracic Soc., Assn. Acad. Surgery, Southeastern Pediatric Cardiology Soc., Ky. Med. Assn., Fayette County Med. Assn., Lexington Surg. Soc. Contbr. articles to med. jours. Home: 3145 Warren Wood Wynd Lexington KY 40502 Office: Cardio Thoracic Surgery Ky Med Center Lexington KY 40536

TODD, GARY PRICE, ophthalmologist; b. Starr, S.C., Jan. 30, 1941; s. Joseph Archer and Mary Louise (Rainey) T.; m. Clara Sue Whitten, June 1, 1963; children—Frank Whitten, George Stuart. B.S. in Chemistry, Carson-Newman Coll., 1963, B.A. in Math., 1963; M.D., Bowman Grey Sch. Medicine, 1967. Diplomate Am. Bd. Ophthalmology. Commd. ensign U.S. Navy, 1966, advanced through grades to comdr.; intern in medicine, Portsmouth, Va., 1967-68; submarine physician, Charleston, S.C., 1968-70; dir. hyperbaric research, Groton, Conn., 1970-71; resident in ophthalmology, Bethesda, Md., 1971-74; chief ophthalmology, Yokosuka, Japan, 1974-77; resigned, 1977; practice medicine specializing in ophthalmology, Waynesville, N.C., 1977—; pres. Bio-Zoe, Inc., Waynesville, 1985—; mem. staff Haywood County Hosp., Clyde, N.C. Author: The Eternal Triangle, 1977; Nutrition, Health, and Disease, 1985. Inventor analog diving computer, thermal regulating cup. Scoutmaster, Daniel Boone council Boy Scouts Am., 1979—. Recipient Eagle Scout award Boy Scouts Am., 1955, Vigil award Order of Arrow, Boy Scouts Am., 1986. Fellow Am. Acad. Ophthalmology; mem. AMA, Western N.C. Ophthal. Soc., Haywood County C. of C. Lodge: Rotary (Boy Scout coordinator local lodge 1978—). Avocations: photography; backpacking; archery. Office: 112 Academy St Waynesville NC 28786

TODD, HARRY W(AYNE), geologist, petroleum exploration; b. Ardmore, Okla., Nov. 8, 1935; s. Joseph Harold and Leola Marie (Williams) T.; m. Marilyn Elizabeth Myers, Jan. 26, 1960 (div. July 1968); children—Eric Joseph, Dana Katherine, Michael David; m. Janet Aileen Rich, Dec. 31, 1970; children—Jason Ratcliffe, Ian Williams, Allison Kelly. B.S. in Geol. Engring., U. Okla., 1958, M. Geol. Engring., 1960. Cert. petroleum geologist. Jr. geologist, Sunray DX Oil Co., Tulsa, Okla., 1960-63, exploration geologist, Midland, Tex., 1963-67; cons. geologist various oil cos., Tulsa, 1967-72; sr. geologist Helmerich & Payne Inc., Tulsa, 1972-75; exploration mgr Transok Pipe Line Co., Tulsa, 1975-77; pres. Todd Exploration Co., Tulsa and N.Y.C., 1977—; instr. geology Tulsa Jr. Coll., 1970-71; pres. Okla. Well Log Library, Tulsa, 1979-80, bd. dirs., 1980-81. Chmn. Christian service bd. 1st Presbyn. Ch., Tulsa, 1972-76, deacon, 1978-80, elder, 1984—. Mem. Am. Assn. Petroleum Geologists, Oklahoma City Geol. Soc., Petroleum Exploration Soc. N.Y., Soc. Econ. Paleontologists and Mineralogists, Tulsa Geol. Soc., Sigma Gamma Epsilon, Tau Beta Pi. Republican. Avocations: handball, photography. Office: Todd Exploration Co 320 S Boston Ave Tulsa OK 74103

TODD, PATRICIA ANN, human resource specialist, planning analyst; b. Charlotte, N.C., Oct. 1, 1955; d. William Anderson and Bennie (Belk) T. B.A. in Bus. Adminstrn., U. N.C.-Charlotte, 1977, postgrad. 1983—. Mgmt. trainee in personnel Lance, Charlotte, N.C., 1978-80; tng. specialist Duke Power Co., Charlotte, 1980—. Co-author tng. program for Duke Power, 1983. Mem. Am. Soc. Tng. and Devel. (v.p. fin., bd. dirs. Charlotte chpt. 1984—). Democrat. Methodist. Avocations: skiing, aerobics, sailing; swimming; snorkeling. Address: Duke Power Co 311 S Church St Charlotte NC 28242

TODD, ROBERT EDWARD, university official; b. Greenville, Ky., Jan. 18, 1926; s. Delmer Linton and Nanny Myrtle (Hayes) T.; B.S. in Commerce, U. Ky., 1950; m. Mary Louise Webb, June 8, 1948; children—Nancy Ann Todd Draper, Robert Edward. Store mgr. Newberry Co., 1950-65; sr. buyer Commonwealth Ky., Frankfort, 1965-67, prin. buyer, 1967-68, asst. dir. purchases, 1968-69; dir. purchasing U. Louisville, 1969-78, asst. v.p. purchasing services, 1979—. Merit badge counselor Boy Scouts Am. Served with USN, 1944-46. Mem. Nat. Assn. Ednl. Buyers (past chmn. Ky. chpt.), Purchasing Mgmt. Assn. Louisville (dir. nat. affairs 1979-80), Nat. Assn. Purchasing Mgmt. (v.p. dist. VII, Profl. Devel. Person of Year 1978-79, pres. 1984—), Council Procurement Advs. Commonwealth Ky. Democrat. Methodist. Office: Belknap Campus U Louisville Louisville KY 40292

TODD, ROBERT FOREMAN, marketing executive; b. Brunswick, Ga., Feb. 28, 1945; s. Benjamin Herbert and Idella (Foreman) T.; m. Lorraine Angela Ferrera, May 20, 1965 (div.); children—Robert Ferrera, Troy Jasen. B.A., Troy State U., 1967; M.B.A. in Mktg., Ga. State U., 1977. Regional sales mgr. Xerox Corp., Atlanta, 1977-77; mktg. mgr. Hughes Helicopter div. Summa Corp., Atlanta, 1977-80; v.p. mktg. Ficus Group, Miami, Fla., 1980-83; pres. Tomarc/TMC, South Miami, Fla., 1980—. Served as commd. officer U.S. Army, 1967-75; Vietnam. Decorated Silver Star, D.F.C. with two oak leaf clusters, Bronze Star for valor, Purple Heart (4), Air medal (67); Vietnamese Cross of Gallantry (2), ARCOM for valor. Mem. Mensa, Helicopter Assn. Internat., Am. Helicopter Assn., Army Aviation Assn., U.S. C. of C., Greater Miami C. of C., DAV. Republican. Office: 5825 Sunset Dr Suite 203 South Miami FL 33143

TODD, SHIRLEY ANN, educational counselor; b. Botetourt County, Va., May 23, 1935; d. William Leonard and Margaret Judy (Simmons) Brown; m. Thomas Byron Todd, July 7, 1962 (dec. July 1977). B.S. in Edn., Madison Coll., 1956; M.Ed., U. Va., 1971. Cert. tchr., Va. Elem. tchr. Fairfax County Sch. Bd., Fairfax, Va., 1956-66, 8th grade history tchr., 1966-71, guidance counselor James F. Cooper Intermediate Sch., McLean, Va., 1971—; chmn. mktg. Lake Anne Joint Venture, Falls Church, Va., 1979-82, mng. ptnr., 1980-82. Del. Fairfax County Republican Conv., 1985. Fellow Fairfax Edn. Assn. (mem. profl. rights and responsibilities commn. 1970-72, bd. dirs. 1968-70), Va. Edn. Assn. (mem. state com. on local assns. and urban affairs 1969-70), NEA, No. Va. Counselors Assn. (hospitality and social chmn. 1982-83), Va. Counselors Assn., Va. Sch. Counselors Assn., Am. Assn. for Counseling and Devel. Baptist. Club: Chantilly Nat. Golf and Country (v.p. social 1981-82) (Centreville, Va.). Avocations: golf, tennis. Home: 6543 Bay Tree Ct Falls Church VA 22041 Office: James F Cooper Intermediate Sch 977 Balls Hill Rd McLean VA 22101

TODD, WALTER NATHAN, corporation executive; b. Marion, Ind., Oct. 20, 1942; s. Arlin David Todd and Pauline Dexter (McFarland) Eppard; m. Sandra Dianne Lais, Aug. 27, 1967; children—Michelle, Trecia, Travis, Cheri. B.A., B.S., La. State U.-New Orleans, 1967. With sales mgmt. Motorola, Chgo., 1968-70; founder, pres., dir. 6 cos., 1970-82; pres. Am. Performance Monitoring Systems, Inc., Pass Christian, Miss., 1982—; Author: Economics of Heavy Fuel, 1981; Running at Best Profit, 1983. Campaign mgr. state rep. race, New Orleans, 1969; bd. dirs. Nat. River Acad., Helena, Ark., 1973-76; trustee Coast Episcopal Sch., Pass Christian, 1976—. Served with USAF, 1960-65. Mem. Soc. Naval Architects and Marine Engrs., Am. Waterways Operators. Republican. Roman Catholic. Office: One Todd Plaza Pass Christian MS 39571

TODSEN, DANA ROGNAR, foundation executive; b. St. Petersburg, Fla., Oct. 8, 1947; s. Birger Rognar and Elsie (Ewin) T.; m. Janis Hellman, June 13, 1970; children—Matthew Kristian, Jennifer Alana. B.A., U. South Fla., 1970, M.A., 1976. Assoc. dir. So. Health Found., Tampa, Fla., 1976-78; dir. U. Tampa, 1978-82; mng. dir. St. Anthony's Devel. Found., St. Petersburg, 1982-85; pres. Todsen & Assocs., Brandon, Fla., 1983—; dir. devel. Moffitt Cancer Ctr., Tampa, 1985—. Contbr. articles to profl. jours. Bd. dirs. Children's Home Soc., 1983—; mem. Leadership Tampa, 1983—. Mem. Nat. Assn. Hosp. Devel., Council for Advancement and Support Edn., Philanthropic Action Council, Tampa Tiger Bay, Alpha Tau Omega. Democrat. Methodist. Club: Tampa. Home: 407 Park Manor Dr Brandon FL 33511 Office: Moffitt Cancer Ctr PO Box 280179 Tampa FL 33682

TOEPLITZ, GIDEON, symphony society executive; b. Tel Aviv, Nov. 18, 1944; s. Erich and Ruth (Loeb) T.; m. Gail Ransom, Sept. 2, 1978. B.A., Hebrew U., Jerusalem, 1969; M.B.A., UCLA, 1973. Flutist, Israel Philharm. Orch., 1969-71; asst. mgr. Rochester Philharm., 1973-75; asst. mgr. Boston Symphony, 1975-79, orch. mgr., 1979-81; exec. dir. Houston Symphony Soc., 1981—. Trustee, Met. Cultural Alliance. Mem. Nat. Acad. Rec. Arts and Scis. Home: 12503 Vindon Dr Houston TX 77024 Office: Jones Hall 615 Louisiana Houston TX 77002

TOLBERT, CONSTANCE LYNN, business executive; b. Boone, Iowa, Aug. 3, 1945; d. Melvin Emory and Dorothy K. Hitsman; m. James W. Tolbert, Jr., Dec. 30, 1964; children—James, Lisa, Randy Mel. Exec. v.p. Classique Creations, Inc., Dallas, 1976—; dir. Success, Inc.; v.p. Classique Internat., Horses, Inc.; exec. v.p. J.W.T., Inc., 1977—; owner Eagle Ranch. Republican. Baptist. Home: 5936 Meadowcreek Dallas TX 75248 Office: 14240 Midway Rd Dallas TX 75234

TOLLEY, AUBREY GRANVILLE, hospital administrator; b. Lynchburg, Va., Nov. 15, 1924; student Duke, 1942-43; M.D., U. Va., Hosp., 1952; married. Intern, St. Elizabeths Hosp., Washington, 1952-53; asst. resident psychiatry U. Va. Hosp., Charlottesville, 1953-54; resident psychiatry VA Hosp., Roanoke, Va., 1954-56; instr. U. N.C. Sch. Medicine, 1956-61, asst. prof., 1961-66, clin. asst. prof. psychiatry, 1966-72, clin. asso. prof., 1972-76, clin. prof., 1976—; dir. psychotherapy Dorothea Dix Hosp., Raleigh, 1962-67, dir. hosp., 1973—; dir. resident tng. John Ulmstead Hosp., Butner, N.C., 1966-67; dir. profl. tng. and edn. N.C. Dept. Mental Health, Raleigh, 1967-72, asst. dir., 1972-73. Prin. investigator USPHS grant, 1957-59; cons. VA Hosp., Fayetteville, N.C., 1957-78; sr. cons., supervising faculty, community psychiatry sect. dept. psychiatry U. N.C. Sch. Medicine, 1971—; exec. sec. Multiversity Group, 1968-73. Served with USNR, 1943-46. Diplomate Am. Bd. Psychiatry and Neurology. Fellow Am. Psychiat. Assn. (rep. N.C. Dist. br.), Am. Coll. Psychiatrists; mem. N.C., Durham-Orange County med. socs., N.C. Neuropsychiat. Assn. (pres.), Am. Assn. Dirs. Psychiat. Residency Tng. Home: 110 Laurel Hill Rd Chapel Hill NC 27514 Office: Dorothea Dix Hosp Sta B Box 7527 Raleigh NC 27611

TOLLEY, GARY MAURICE, radiologist; b. Lesage, W.Va., Aug. 2, 1935; s. Eugene Franklin Tolley and Mary Virginia (Lunsford) Brandt; m. Wanda Gordon Chain, Aug. 23, 1957; children—Stephen Gregory, Mark Kevin, David Brian, Joseph Andrew. B.S., Marshall Coll., 1957, W.Va. U., 1959; M.D., Med. Coll. Va., 1961. Diplomate Am. Bd. Radiology, Am. Bd. Nuclear Medicine. Intern Charleston Meml. Hosp., W.Va., 1961-62; resident Ind. U. Med. Ctr., Indpls., 1965-68; staff radiologist Cabell-Huntington Hosp., St. Mary's Hosp., Huntington Hosp., VA Hosp., 1968—, Marshall U. Sch. Medicine, 1977—; chief radiology Cabell-Huntington Hosp., 1983—. Served with USN, 1962-65. Am. Cancer Soc. fellow, 1966-67; George Benedum Found. scholar, 1958. Del. Am. Coll. Nuclear Physicians; mem. AMA (Physician's Recognition award 1972, 75, 78, 81, 84), Am. Inst. Ultra Sound in Medicine, Pan Am. Med. Assn., W.Va. State Med. Assn., Caber County Med. Assn., Am. Coll. Radiology, W.Va. State Radiologic Soc., Alpha Epsilon Delta. Home: 323 Woodland Dr Huntington WV 25705 Office: Radiology Inc 319 First Huntington Bldg Huntington WV 25701

TOLLEY, WILLIAM RUSSELL, JR., electronics company official; b. Gay, W.Va., Dec. 5, 1933; s. William Russell and Ruth Evelyn (McIntyre) T.; B.S., W.Va. U., 1955; m. Patricia R. Fike, Oct. 2, 1955; children—James, Timothy, Kimberly. Field scout exec. Boy Scouts Am., Parkersburg, W.Va., 1955-56; with Harris Corp., Melbourne, Fla., 1956—, mgr. mfg. planning and control, 1962-64, mgr. govt. acctg. services, 1964-76, dir. govt. contracting practices, 1977-84, dir. legis. affairs, 1984—. Active Boy Scouts Am., 1957—; active Hope United Methodist Ch., Melbourne, 1960—; bd. dirs. Happy Landing Boys Ranch, Melbourne, 1978—. Mem. Assn. Govt. Accts. (William P. Lemby award 1979), Nat. Contract Mgmt. Assn. (Profl. Service award 1980), Nat. Security Indsl. Assn., Nat. Assn. Bus. Polit. Action Coms. (bd. dirs.). Republican. Home: 4250 Pinewood Rd Melbourne FL 32935 Office: 1025 W Nasa Blvd Melbourne FL 32919

TOMAN, FRANK RAY, biochemistry educator; b. Ellsworth, Kans., June 6, 1939; s. Frank and Anna Marie (Shanelec) T.; m. Judy Kay Stephen, Sept. 1, 1962; children—Troy, Tamara. B.S. in Tech. Agronomy, Kans. State U., 1961, M.S. in Agronomy, 1963, Ph.D. in Biochemistry, 1967. Mem. faculty Western Ky. U., Bowling Green, 1966-73, 1975—, prof. biology, 1979—; research assoc. AEC Plant Research Lab., Mich. State U., East Lansing, 1974; prof. dept. biology, Western Ky. U., 1979-82, 83—; vis. prof. agronomy U. Ky., Lexington, 1982-83; vis. prof. biochemistry Kans. State U., 1984. Active Band Boosters. Faculty Research grantee Western Ky. U., 1968, Faculty devel. grantee, 1982-85; Ogden Found. teaching improvement fellow, 1984. Mem. Am. Chem. Soc., Assn. Southeastern Biologists, Ky. Acad. Sci. Methodist. Home: 825 Cabell Dr Bowling Green KY 42101 Office: Dept of Biology Western Ky U Bowling Green KY 42101

TOMKINS, BRUCE ALLEN, chemist; b. Providence, Aug. 2, 1951; s. Chester and Leonora B. Tomkins. B.A., U. Conn., 1973; M.S., U. Ill., 1975, Ph.D., 1978. Staff chemist analytical chemistry div. Oak Ridge Nat. Lab., 1978—. Mem. Am. Chem. Soc., Phi Beta Kappa, Sigma Xi, Phi Kappa Phi. Contbr. articles to profl. jours. Home: 103 E Holston Ln Oak Ridge TN 37830 Office: Oak Ridge Nat Lab Bldg 4500S Room E-160 Oak Ridge TN 37830

TOMLIN, DONALD ROBERT, JR., company executive; b. Columbia, S.C., Dec. 19, 1947; s. Donald Robert and Frances (Patrick) T. B.S. in Bus. Mgmt., U. S.C.-Columbia, 1971. Pres. Columbia Mgmt. Corp., S.C., 1974-83; chmn. bd., chief exec. officer U.S. Capital Corp., Columbia, 1983—. Author: Making Time Sharing Work, 1975. Address: US Capital Corp 1400 Main St Columbia SC 29211

TOMLINS, C. B., art educator, researcher, sculptor; b. Waco, Tex., Mar. 22, 1941; m. Ann Brennan, Jan. 16, 1976; 1 child, Robynn. B.F.A., Okla. State U., 1964; M.F.A., Ohio State U., 1966. Assoc. instr. Ohio State U., Columbus, 1965-66; instr. Tulsa U., 1966-73, asst. prof. art, 1973-80, assoc. prof., 1980—; dir. S.W. film Festival, Tulsa, 1970-72, Festival 77, Tulsa, 1977; judge Young Talent, Oklahoma City, 1983; mem. Art in Pub. Places Com., Tulsa, 1985. Exhibited one-man shows: Moon Gallery, Berry Coll., Mt. Berry, Ga.; group shows include: Mitchell Galleries, Afton, Okla., 1984, Wilde-Meyer Gallery, Scottsdale, Ariz., 1985; represented in permanent collections Diocese of Okla., Okla. U. Mus., State of Okla.; prin. works include CACACT, Minshall Hill, Fairfax. Inventor alt. materials for ceramic shell. Grantee Okla. Arts Council, 1975, U. Tulsa, 1984, 85. Fellow Inst. for Advancement Contemporary Art; mem. Coll. Art Assn., Internat. Sculpture Assn., Interface (pres. 1980-85), Living Arts (pres. 1969-71). Avocations: flying; swimming; golf. Home: 2204 E 25th St Tulsa OK 74114 Office: Tulsa U Dept Art Tulsa OK

TOMLINSON, H. EVANGELINE, obstetrician-gynecologist; b. Celina, Ohio, May 26, 1945; d. Prentiss F. and Arline L. (Quilling) T. B.A., Olivet Coll., 1967; student U. Dayton, 1966; M.D., Ohio State U., 1971. Resident in ob-gyn Riverside Hosp., Columbus, Ohio, later St. Ann's Hosp., Columbus, 1971-75; fellow in surgery Washington Hosp. Ctr., 1975-76; practice medicine specializing in ob-gyn, Alexandria, Va., 1976—; mem. staff Alexandria Hosp., Circle Terr. Hosp., Alexandria, 1976—. Mem. AMA, So. Med. Assn., Am. Assn. Gynecol. Laparoscopists, Med. Soc. Va., Am. Profl. Practice Assn., Christian Med. Soc. Republican. Presbyterian. Avocations: music, gardening, sewing. Home: 3800 S Fort Worth Ave Alexandria VA 22304 Office: 5249 Duke St Suite 11 Alexandria VA 22304

TOMLINSON, HAROLD LEE, energy company executive; b. Dallas, Aug. 28, 1944; s. Ross W. and Neva (West) T.; m. Margie Smith, Aug. 27, 1964; children—Tracy Lenn, Stacy Lee. B.A., North Tex. State U., Denton, 1968. Chmn. bd. Tomlinson Constrn. Co., Dallas, 1968-79, McKamy Devel. Corp., 1978-82, Am. Empire Oil and Gas, Inc., 1982—, Tomlinson Energy, Inc., 1982—; dir. Keystone Fin. Corp.; assoc. dir. Preston North Nat. Bank. Active Nat. Kidney Found., Golden Charity. Recipient House of Yr. award Nat. Home Builders Assn., 1978. Republican. Baptist. Clubs: Bent Tree Country, University (Dallas); Le Club (Fort Lauderdale, Fla.); Willowbend Polo (Plano, Tex.). Office: 6750 LBJ Freeway Suite 1180 Dallas TX 75240

TOMLINSON, MILTON AMBROSE, clergyman; b. Cleveland, Tenn., Oct. 19, 1906; s. Ambrose Jessup and Mary Jane (Taylor) T.; m. Ina Mae Turner, Sept. 18, 1928; children—Wanda Jean (Mrs. Hugh Ralph Edwards), Carolyn Joy (Mrs. Verlin Dean Thronton). Ed., Tenn. pub. schs. Printer, Herald Printing Co., Cleveland, ten years; pastor ch., Henderson, Ky., 1 yr.; gen. overseer Ch. of God of Prophecy, Cleveland, 1943—; editor and pub. The White Wing Messengers; pres. Bible Tng. Inst., chmn. trustees. Author: Basic Bible Beliefs. Pres., Tomlinson Home for Children. Office: Bible Pl Cleveland TN 37311*

TOMLINSON, NORMAN THOMAS, government official, specialist; b. Alexandria, Va., July 21, 1932; s. Thomas Perry and Beulah Opal (Blackmore) T.; B.B.A, Ga. Coll., Milledgeville, 1979, postgrad. in bus. adminstrn.; postgrad. Air Command and Staff Coll., Robins AFB, Ga.; m. Donna Ruth Dodds, July 28, 1961; children—Jcan Marie, Christine Opal. Automotive repair and serviceman, 1955-60; mem. faculty Keesler Air Tng. Ctr., Miss., 1963-64; life ins. agt., 1965-68; trainer U.S. Govt., 1968-74; staff cons. on productivity and quality of worklife Warner Robins AFB, 1974—. Deacon, dir. Sunday sch. Baptist Ch. Served with USAF, 1951-55, 60-64; Korea. Mem. Am. Soc. Tng. and Devel., Soc. Logistics Engrs., Air Force Assn., Fed. Mgrs. Assn., Better Mgmt. Assn. Home: 1200 Tucker Rd Perry GA 31069 Office: WR-ALC MAWFP Robins Air Force Base GA 31098

TOMLINSON, WILLIAM HOLMES, retired soldier, management educator; b. Thornton, Ark., Apr. 12, 1922; s. Hugh Oscar and Lucy Gray (Holmes) T.; B.S., U.S. Mil. Acad., 1943; grad. Air Command Staff Coll., 1958; M.B.A., U. Ala., 1960; M.S. in Internat. Affairs, George Washington U., 1966; grad. U.S. Army War Coll., 1966; grad. Indsl. Coll. Armed Forces; Ph.D. in Bus. Adminstrn., Am. U., 1974; postgrad. 56th Advanced Mgmt. Program, Harvard U., 1968, 69; m. Dorothy Payne, June 10, 1947 (dec.); children—Jane Axtell, Lucy Gray, William Payne; m. 2d, Florence Mood Smith, May 1, 1969 (div.); m. 3d, Suzanne Scollard Gill, Mar. 16, 1977. Commd. 2d lt. U.S. Army, 1943, advanced through grades to col., field arty., 1966; bn. comdr. 246th FA Bn., Americal Div., Philippines, Japan; aide de camp, comdg. gen. 8th Army, 1945-48; mem. Office of Undersec. Army, Pentagon, Washington, 1961-64; comdr. 2d Bn., 8th Arty. and 7th Div. Arty., South Korea, 1964-65; faculty Indsl. Coll. Armed Forces, Ft. McNair, Washington, 1966-72, ret., 1973; faculty U. North Fla., Jacksonville, 1972—, assoc. prof. mgmt., 1976—; mem. Nat. Def. Exec. Res., Fed. Emergency Mgmt. Agy., 1976—. Decorated Bronze Star, Legion of Merit, Philippine Liberation medal, Japanese Occupation medal; recipient Freedom Found. award, 1973; sr. profl. in human resources. Mem. Acad. Mgmt., So. Mgmt. Assn., Am. Soc. Personnel Adminstrn., Indsl. Relations Research Assn., Acad. Internat. Bus., Co. Mil. Historians, Nat. Eagle Scout Assn. (dir., chmn. 1981), West Point Soc. N. Fla. (pres. 1976), Mil. Order Stars and Bars (Fl. state comdr. 1981-84), Beta Gamma Sigma. Presbyterian (elder). Clubs: Army Navy, Army Navy Country, Fla. Yacht, Kappa Alpha Order, Masons (32 deg.), Shriners. Contbr. articles and case studies to profl. jours. and books. Home: 1890 Shadowlawn Jacksonville FL 32205 Office: U North Fla 4567 St Johns Bluff Rd Jacksonville FL 32216

TOMPKINS, A. KATHLEEN KELLY, civic worker; b. St. Johns, Mich., Jan. 15, 1903; d. William Thomas and Harriet A. (Wright) Kelly; grad. U. Cin. Conservatory of Music, 1926; m. Neil Wright (dec.); children—Neil, Ross; m. Raymond McLaughlin, June 1961 (dec.); m. Lawrence E. Tompkins, June 5, 1975 (dec.), Concert pianist, 1932-37; social dir. Lakeside Hotel, Eaglesmere, Pa., 1938-47; publicity dir. Pocono Manor, 1947-49; resident mgr. Gulf Winds Apts., St. Petersburg, Fla., 1949-50; social dir. Marshall House, York Harbor, Maine, 1951. Bd. dirs. Sarasota Music Club, 1964—, pres., 1966-68, parliamentarian, 1976-81; bd. dirs. Fla. Fedn. Music Clubs, 1968—; pres. Golden Gate Point Assn., 1962—, cons., 1978-85. Named Realtor of Yr., Sarasota Realtors Assn., 1960. Mem. Delta Omicron (nat. pres. 1931-37). Episcopalian. Club: Intercity Bridge (pres. 1960), Sarasota Yacht. Home: 350 Golden Gate Point Sarasota FL 33577

TONEY, MELODY-ANN, government education specialist and guidance counselor; b. Richmond, Va., Oct. 24, 1945; d. Virginia (Blair) Kirschner; m. John Edward Toney, Aug. 18, 1968; 1 son, Richard Edward. B.S. in Elem. Edn., Appalachian State U., 1968; M.Ednl. Leadership, Fla. State U., 1985. Notary pub., Fla. Elem. tchr., pub. schs., Goldsboro, N.C., 1978-70, Lenoir, N.C., 1970-71; sec. First Baptist Ch., Omaha, 1972-73; data processing clk. Sun Bank, Orlando, Fla., 1973-74; Civil Service worker U.S. Air Force, Washington, 1974-76, Ramstein, Germany, 1977-79, Panama City, Fla., 1979—, edn. specialist, 1981—, guidance counselor, 1981—; mgr., asst. edn. officer Fed. Women's Program, Tyndall AFB, Fla., 1983—. Active Sandy Creek Women's Club, Panama City, 1979-85, Multi-Ethnic Group, Panama City, 1983—, Panama City Seminole Boosters, 1985; com. mem. Cub and Weblos Scouts Sand Lake Dist. council Boy Scouts Am., 1983-85. Recipient Spl. Achievement award USAF, 1983, Superior Performance award, 1985. Mem. Am. Assn. Counseling and Devel., Mil. Educators/Counselor Assn., Federally Employed Women (Sandollar chpt.), Am. Bus. Women's Assn. Democrat. Baptist. Avocations: reading; sewing; travel; tennis. Home: Wewa Route Box 75-417 Panama City FL 32404 Office: 325 CSG/DPE Tyndall AFB FL 32403

TONKIN, INA LYNN DYER, cardiovascular radiologist, educator; b. Louisville, Apr. 26, 1944; d. Robert S. and Nancy E. (Camp) Dyer; m. Allen K. Tonkin, June 29, 1968; children—Allison Elizabeth-Ann, Keith Allen. B.A., DePauw U., 1966; M.D., U. Louisville, 1970. Diplomate Am. Bd. Radiology. Intern U. Fla., Gainesville, 1970-71, resident in radiology, 1971-73, fellow in cardiovascular radiology, 1974-75; asst. prof. U. Ariz. Health Sci. Ctr., Tucson, 1975-77, U. Ala.-Birmingham, 1977-79; assoc. prof. radiology U. Tenn., Memphis, 1979—; exec. com. LeBonheur Children's Med. Ctr., Memphis, 1981—. Contbr. chpts. to books. Fellow Am. Heart Assn. (exec. com. Council Cardiovascular Radiology 1980-82), Jour. Rev. Club of Memphis (sec. 1984). Methodist. Home: 3415 Chambers Chapel Arlington TN 38002 Office: LeBonheur Children's Med Center 848 Adams St Memphis TN 38103

TONKOVICH, DAN R., state senator; b. Apr. 17, 1946; B.A., W. Liberty State Coll.; M.A., Maxwell Sch., Syracuse (N.Y.) U. Former mem. congressional staff, Washington; mem. W.Va. Ho. of Dels., 1972-76; mem. W.Va. Senate from 2d Dist., 1976—, now majority leader; alt. mem. exec. com. So. Legis. Conf. and alt. mem. governing bd. of Council State Govts.; mem. energy com. Nat. Conf. State Legislatures, 1983-84. Vice chmn. So. States Energy Bd., 1983-84. Served with USAR. Mem. Lambda Chi Alpha. Roman Catholic. Office: State Capitol 1800 Washington St E Charleston WV 25305

TOOKES, JAMES NELSON, real estate investment co. exec.; b. Tallahassee, Sept. 16, 1934; B.S., Fla. A&M U., 1955, M.Ed., 1956; m. Hortense Latricia James, June 22, 1958; 1 son, Gerald Ray. Tchr., Griffin Elem. Sch., Tallahassee, 1957-58, Douglas Elem. Sch., Wabasso, Fla., 1958-59; tchr. Barrow Hill Sch., Tallahassee, 1959-60, prin., 1960-67; summer sch. math. tchr. various sch. centers Leon County Dist., Tallahassee, 1960-65; prin. Pineview Elem. Sch., Tallahassee, 1967-73; pres. Geray Petroleum, Inc., Tallahassee, 1980—, J.N.T. Properties, Inc., Tallahassee, 1973—; broker Tookes Realty, Tallahassee, 1973—; adv. bd. Barnett Bank of Tallahassee, 1973-76. Bd. dirs. Tallahassee Youth Center, 1952-54, Tallahassee Meml. Regional Med. Center, 1977-82; chmn. div. United Fund campaign, 1962; trustee Tallahassee Community Coll., 1974-82, chmn. bd., 1976-77. Recipient Sch. Adminstr. Service award Pineview Elem. Sch. Student Council, 1967-73; commedation award Bert Roger's Sch. Real Estate, 1973; Contbns. to Community award Phi Beta Lambda, 1974; named 1 of 5 Most Outstanding Black Businessmen in State of Fla., Fla. A&M U. Sch. Bus. and Industry, 1974. Mem. Tallahassee Bd. Realtors, Fla. Assn. Realtors, Nat. Assn. Realtors, Tallahassee C. of C., Phi Delta Kappa, Kappa Alpha Psi (Man of Yr. 1973). Home: 3303 Wheatley Rd Tallahassee FL 32304 Office: JNT Properties Inc 540 W Brevard St Tallahassee FL 32301

TOPLIN, ROBERT BRENT, history educator, television producer; b. Phila., Sept. 26, 1940; s. Maurice Cunningham and Janet Rachel (Belsinger) T.; m. Aida Lee Zukowski, Sept. 3, 1961; children—Cassandra, Jennifer. B.S. Pa. State U., 1962; M.A., Rutgers U., 1965, Ph.D., 1968. Asst. prof. Denison U., Granville, Ohio, 1968-74, assoc. prof., 1976-78; assoc. prof. and program dir. U. Houston-Clear Lake City, 1974-76; assoc. prof. U. N.C. at Wilmington, 1978-80, prof. history, 1980—; project dir. A House Divided, TV series, U.S.A.: A Television History; vis. prof. U. N.C.-Chapel Hill, 1983; media advisor NEH; lectr. in field. Pres. Williston Jr. High Sch. PTA; v.p. New Hanover County PTA. Grantee or fellow Ford Found., 1967, NEH, 1970, 77, 78-79-80, 82-83, 83-84, 85-86, Am. Philos. Soc., 1970, 81, Denison U. Research Found., 1972, Annenberg/Corp. for Pub. Broadcasting, 1983-84. Mem. Am. Hist. Assn., Orgn. Am. Historians (mem. com. on radio, TV, film media 1978-80, Eric Barnouw prize 1985), Conf. on Latin Am. History com. on teaching materials 1978), So. Hist. Assn. Democrat. Jewish. Author: The Abolition of Slavery in Brazil, 1972; Unchallenged Violence: An American Ordeal, 1975; Freedom and Prejudice: The Legacy of Slavery in the United States and Brazil, 1982. Editor: Slavery and Race Relations in Latin America, 1974. Editor anthology: American History Through Film, 1983; contbg. editor Jour. Am. History, 1986—; contbr. articles to hist. jours.; book reviewer various jours.; project dir. Denmark Vesey's Rebellion (PBS TV), 1982, Solomon Northup's Odyssey

(PBS TV), 1984; Charlotte Forten's Mission (PBS TV), 1985. Office: Dept History U NC at Wilmington Wilmington NC 28403

TOPOL, SIDNEY, electronics company executive; b. Boston, Dec. 28, 1924; s. Morris and Dora (Kalinsky) T.; B.S., U. Mass., 1947; postgrad. U. Calif., 1948-49; m. Lillian Friedman, Dec. 15, 1951; children—Deborah Jane, Joanne, Martha Grace. Physicist, Naval Research Lab., 1947-48; engr. Raytheon Co., Boston, 1949-57, asst. mgr. engring., comml. equipment div., 1957-59, dir. planning and mktg. Raytheon-Europe, Rome, Italy, 1959-65, gen. mgr. communications ops., 1965-71; pres., dir. Sci.-Atlanta, Inc., 1971—, chief exec. officer, 1975—, chmn. bd., 1978—; dir. 1st Atlanta Corp., 1st Nat. Bank of Atlanta. Mem. adv. council Coll. Indsl. Mgmt., Ga. Inst. Tech.; mem. exec. com. mgmt. conf. bd. Emory U.; bd. advisors Morris Brown Coll.; chmn. Ga. com. CARE. Served with USAAF, 1943-46. Mem. IEEE, Electronic Industries Assn. (bd. govs.). Club: Rotary. Office: Scientific-Atlanta Inc One Technology Pkwy PO Box 105600 Atlanta GA 30348

TORANO-PANTIN, MARIA ELENA, business executive, management consultant; b. Havana, Cuba, Feb. 13, 1938; d. Julio and Sira M. (Vidal) Diaz-Rousselot; m. Arturo E. Torano, Feb. 9, 1957 (div.); children—Arthur J., Eric J.; m. Leslie Peter Pantin, Sept. 28, 1980. B.A. in Langs., U. Havana, 1958. Tchr. home econs. Demonstration Sch., U. Havana, 1958-60; orientation tchr. Dade County Pub. Schs., Miami, Fla., 1962-63; caseworker family and children services Fla. Dept. Pub. Welfare, 1965-68; with Eastern Airlines, 1968-76, program mgr. Latin Am. Affairs, Miami, 1974-76; dir. Latin Am. affairs Jackson Meml. Med. Ctr., Miami, 1976-77; assoc. dir. pub. affairs U.S. Community Services Adminstrn., Washington, 1977-79; pres. and founder Nat. Assn. Spanish Broadcasters, 1978-80; pres. META Inc., Miami, 1980—. Recipient various commendations, certificates appreciation. Democrat. Roman Catholic. Office: 300 Biscayne Blvd Way Miami FL 33131

TORBERT, CLEMENT CLAY, JR., state chief justice; b. Opelika, Ala., Aug. 31, 1929; s. Clement Clay III and Lynda (Meadows) T.; m. Gene Hurt, May 2, 1952; children—Mary Dixon, Gene Shealy, Clement Clay. Student, U.S. Naval Acad., 1948-49; B.S., Auburn U., 1951; postgrad., U. Md., 1952; LL.B., U. Ala., 1954. Bar: Ala. 1954. Practiced in, Opelika, 1954-77, city judge, 1954-58; partner firm Samford, Torbert, Denson & Horsley, 1959-74; chief justice Ala. Supreme Ct., 1977—; chmn. Ala. Jud Study Commn., Ala. Criminal Justice Info. Systems, Conf. Chief Justices, Jud. Coordinating Com.; supervisory bd. Ala. Law Enforcement Planning Agy., 1977-83; Dir. First Nat. Bank Opelika, Opelika-Auburn Broadcasting Co. Mem. Ala. Ho. of Reps., 1958-62, Ala. Senate, 1966-70, 74-77. Served to capt. USAF, 1952-53. Elected to Ala. Acad. of Honor, 1979. Mem. Am. Judicature Soc. Farrah Law Soc., Phi Delta Phi, Phi Kappa Phi, Alpha Tau Omega. Methodist. Club: Kiwanis. Home: 611 Terracewood Dr Opelika AL 36801 Office: Judicial Bldg PO Box 218 Montgomery AL 36101

TORIAN, MERVILLE RUSSELL, SR., constrn. co. exec.; b. Birmingham, Ala., Nov. 28, 1933; s. Ezra Sullivan and Leona (Friend) T.; student U. Ala., 1956; m. Doris Willene Davis, Aug. 28, 1952; children—Merville Russell, William Michael, James Gregory. Supr., Rust Engring. Co., Birmingham, New Orleans, Cleveland, Tenn. and Escanaba, Mich., 1956-70; resident constrn. mgr. Pullman-Swindell Co., Salt Lake City and Ahwaz, Iran, 1970-76; exec. v.p., dir. John Price Assos., Inc., Salt Lake City, 1976-79; mgr. constrn. mktg. Rust Engring. Co., Birmingham, 1979—. Dir., state dir. Cleveland Jaycees, 1962-65. Recipient several public service awards Jaycees. Mem. Soc. Mining Engrs. Presbyterian. Club: Rotary.

TORKELSON, JOHN ANTHONY, computer systems company executive; b. Bucyrus, Ohio, Mar. 27, 1945; s. Quito P. and Rebecca Ann (Hagen) Massare; m. Sharon Chapman, Sept. 1966; children—J. William, John R., Julia A. Student U. Kans., 1963-66; B.S. in Mech. Engring., U. Houston, 1968; Kans., 1963-66; postgrad. So. Meth. U., 1969-70. Registered profl. engr., Tex. Computer programmer Ray Geophys. Co., Houston, 1966-67; systems engr., mgr. Recognition Equipment Co., Dallas, 1967-72; pres. Systems Research Corp., Dallas, 1972—; exec. v.p. Shared Fin. Systems, Dallas, 1982—; v.p., dir. Descriptive Systems Corp., Dallas, 1977-79; dir. Systems Research Corp., Shared Fin. Systems. Patentee in field of digital image compaction systems. Cubmaster Boy Scouts Am.; coach YMCA, 1971-75. Mem. Nat. Soc. Profl. Engrs., Tex. Soc. Profl. Engrs., Sigma Pi Sigma, Tau Beta Pi. Republican. Lutheran. Club: University (Dallas). Home: 3764 Pallos Verdas St Dallas TX 75229 Office: Systems Research Corp 15301 Dallas Pkwy Suite 650 Dallas TX 75248

TORKELSON, LEIF OSCAR, physician; b. Shelby, Mich., Apr. 5, 1926; s. Ingolf and Anne Martine (Bergsmark von Rockmann) T.; student George Washington U., 1943, U. N.Mex., 1946-47; B.A., Ohio State U., 1949; postgrad. U. Va., 1952-53, M.D., 1957; m. Betty Kirsch, Aug. 29, 1954; children—Kirstann Lee, Leif Erik, Kari Ingabert, Kirk Torleif, Kai Oscar, Inger Kristus. Intern, Mary Fletcher Hosp., Med. Coll. Vt., Burlington, 1957-58; resident in medicine DePaul Hosp., Norfolk, Va., 1958-59; resident in psychiatry N.C. Meml. Hosp., U. N.C., 1959-60; resident medicine Duke U. Affiliated Hosps., Durham, N.C., 1960-61; instr. medicine Sch. Medicine, Western Res. U., Cleve., 1961-62; instr. medicine, asst. prof. medicine U. Ky. Coll. Medicine, 1963-67; vis. physician U. Va. Sch. Medicine, 1967—; practice medicine specializing in internal medicine, Madison, Wis., 1962-63; practice medicine specializing in internal medicine and cardiovascular disease, Harrisonburg, Va., 1968—; clin. investigator for L-Dopa, 1970-71; lectr. in field; conduct of cardiac stress testing studies James Madison Coll., Harrisonburg, 1975-77, also adj. prof. health, 1975-77. Regional cons. Nat. Center Chronic Disease Control of USPHS, Charlottesville, Va., 1967-68. Served with USNR, 1944-45, to lt., 1949-52, lt. col. USAR, 1981—. Recipient research grants for studies cardiac rehab. and cardiac stress testing Sch. Medicine, Western Res. U. and Crile VA Hosp., 1961-62, Coll. Medicine, U. Ky., 1965-67. Mem. AMA (Physician Recognition award 1969, 72, 76-79, 82-85), Am. Heart Assn., Acad. Medicine Cleve., State Med. Soc. Va. (Continuing Edn. award 1979-81), Albemarle, Rockingham County med. socs., Am. Soc. Internal Medicine, Assn. Am. Indian Affairs, Conservation and Wildlife Socs., Pi Kappa Alpha. Republican. Lutheran. Contbr. articles to profl. jours. Home and Office: Route 1 Box 240D Mount Crawford VA 22841

TORRENCE, WILLIAM ERNEST, hospital administrator; b. Chattanooga, Sept. 6, 1923; s. James Madison Torrence and Lela Margaret (Varnell) Brockman; m. Dorothy Katherine Phillips, Feb. 12, 1945 (div. Dec. 1977); children—William Ernest, James Madison; m. Audrey Frances Whitmore, May 13, 1978. Student, U. Chattanooga, 1948-49. Dir. purchasing Erlanger Hosp., Chattanooga, 1946-57; adminstr. Bradley Meml. Hosp., Cleveland, Tenn., 1957—. Bd. dirs. ARC, Cleveland, 1969-75. Served with USN, 1943-45. Recipient Cert. of Appreciation, Boys Club Am., 1971. Fellow Am. Coll. Health Care Adminstrs. (regional advisor 1976-79); mem. Tenn. Hosp. Assn. (trustee 1965-71; Cert. of Appreciation 1960-62, Meritorious Service award 1972). Republican. Baptist. Club: Cleveland Country. Lodges: Rotary (pres. 1966-67; Disting. Service award 1970; Paul Harris fellow 1982), Elks. Home: 3810 Woodbine Circle NW Cleveland TN 37311 Office: Bradley Meml Hosp PO Box 3060 Cleveland TN 37320

TORRES, HECTOR, truck and trailer rental executive; b. Havana, Cuba, Sept. 26, 1952; s. Emilio and Ana Maria (Ramirez) T. Assoc. in Gen. Studies, Miami-Dade Community Coll., 1978. Systems programmer Ryder Truck Rental Co., Miami, Fla., 1974-80; mgr. computer ops. Jartran, Inc., Miami, 1980—. Mem. Assn. Computer Ops. Mgrs. Democrat. Roman Catholic. Home: 448 Cadagua St Coral Gables FL 33146 Office: Jartran Inc 9500 S Dadeland Blvd Miami FL 33156

TORRES, ISRAEL, oral and maxillofacial surgeon; b. El Paso, Tex., Sept. 5, 1934; s. Francisco Mendoza and Manuela (Gallardo) T.; m. Karen Marie Hensley, Aug. 22, 1970; children—Michael, George Stanley, Dianna. B.S., Tex. Western Coll., 1958; D.D.S., U. Tex.-Houston, 1963; postgrad. Health Sci. Ctr., Houston, 1963-66; diploma (hon.) XX Reunion de Provincia, Juarez, Chihuahua, Mexico, 1970, Atteneo Odontologica Mexicano, Valle de Bravo, Mexico, 1973, Colegio de Cirujanos Mexicanos, Juarez, 1975, 84. Diplomate Am. Bd. Oral and Maxillofacial Surgery. Resident in oral surgery Methodist Hosp., Houston, 1963-64, Ben Taub Hosp., Houston, 1964-65, Hermann Hosp., Houston, 1965-66; practice dentistry specializing in oral and maxillofacial surgery, El Paso, 1966—; mem. staff Sun Towers Hosp., chief oral and maxillofacial surgery, 1975, 76, 77; instr. pathology El Paso Community Coll., 1975-76; lectr. in field. Contbr. articles to Jour. Oral/Maxillofacial Surgery. Bd. dirs. Am. Cancer Soc., El Paso, 1971-73, El Paso Cancer Treatment Ctr., 1971-74; bd. dirs. West Tex. Health Systems Agy., 1980-82, chmn., 1981-82. Recipient Bowie Exes award, El Paso, 1982. Fellow Am. Coll. Oral and Maxillofacial Surgeons, Am. Assn. Oral and Maxillofacial Surgeons, Internat. Assn. Oral and Maxillofacial Surgeons, Southwest Soc. Oral and Maxillofacial Surgeons, Acad. Internat. Dental Studies, Pan Am. Med. Assn., EPSDT (dental adv. and rev. com. 1985-86), Tex. Soc. Oral and Maxillofacial Surgeons; mem. El Paso Dist. Dental Soc. (pres. 1979), U. Tex. Dental Br. alumni Assn. (life), Nat. Rifle Assn. (life), Tex. Rifle Assn. (life), Safari Club Internat. (Paso Del Norte chpt.), Am. Found. for N.Am. Wild Sheep, Internat. Sheep Hunting Assn., Anthony Rod and Gun Club. Republican. Roman Catholic. Avocations: high mountain sheep hunting; outdoor activities. Home: 416 Lindbergh St El Paso TX 79932 Office: 1201 E Schuster Bldg 4-A El Paso TX 79902

TORRES DE NAVARRA, CARLOS, civil engineering executive; b. Havana, Cuba, June 14, 1942; came to U.S., 1960; s. Carlos Torres and Adela (Mancebo) De N.; m. Anita Porro, Mar. 27, 1965; children—Carlos, Ana Eliza, Felipe. B.C.E., U. Miami, 1964; M.C.E., U. Kans., 1967. Registered profl. engr., Fla., Tex. Civil engr. Rader & Assoc., Miami, Fla., 1965-66, Black & Veatch, Kans. City, Mo., 1964-65; engr. Monsanto Chem., Texas City, Tex., 1966-69; assoc. engr. Hazen & Sawyer, Hollywood, Fla., 1969-73; exec. v.p. Biscayne Internat., Miami, 1973-79; exec. v.p. Terrinvest, Miami, 1979-81; pres. Intercontinental Bank Properties Co., Miami, 1981—. Mem. ASCE. Republican. Roman Catholic.

TOSH, DANNY JAMES, architect; b. Waxahachie, Tex., Aug. 9, 1946; s. James L. and Mildred Elizabeth (Chenault) T.; student U. Tex., Arlington, 1964-67; B.S. in Archtl. Studies, U. Tex., Austin, 1969; m. Georgeann McLean, Sept. 4, 1976. Draftsman Maples-Jones, Architects, Ft. Worth, 1969-71; job capt. A.S. Komatsu, Ft. Worth, 1971; with Burson Hendricks, Architects, Dallas, 1972, Pierce-Lacy, Architects, Dallas, 1973, Page Southernland Page, Architects, Dallas, 1974-75; partner Danny James Tosh, Architect, Dallas, 1975-78; v.p. Wassell/Tosh, Architects & Planners, Inc., Dallas, 1978—; sec. Guimarin Can Co., Inc. Registered architect, Tex., Colo., Calif.; cert. Nat. Council Archtl. Registration Bds. Club: Aircraft Owners and Pilots Assn. Home: 3129 Weather Vane Ln Dallas TX 75228 Office: 515 Mercantile Continental Bldg Dallas TX 75201

TOSH, JUANITA PRILLAMAN, business executive; b. Axton, Va., Jan. 13, 1930; d. Stuart Owen and Ann Halvorsen (Jamison) Prillaman; student public schs. Bassett, Va.; m. James Cleavon Tosh, June 5, 1961; children—Rebecca Ann Tosh Craze, Cheryl Sue Tosh Tuggle, Mark Cleavon. Owner, Russ Auto Service Co., Norfolk, Va., 1954-59; v.p. Russ & Prillaman Auto Service Inc., Collinsville, Va., 1959-68; co-owner John Allen Estates, Collinsville, 1975—; owner Tosh Tire Town, Collinsville, 1969—; sec.-treas. Cash Oil Sales, Inc., 1982—; v.p., treas. Town Gun Shop, Inc., Collinsville, Va., 1984—. Mem. Retail Mchts. Assn., Va. Tire Dealers and Retreaders Assn., Nat. Tire Dealers and Retreaders Assn. Baptist. Home: 208 Ferndale Dr Collinsville VA 24078

TOTA, FRANK PETER, educational administrator; b. Hoboken, N.J., Dec. 28, 1938; s. Frank and Jeanette (Grimaldi) T.; m. Eileen Virginia Dolan, Aug. 3, 1968; children—Frank, Christopher. B.A., N.J. State Coll., 1960; M.A., Columbia U., 1962, also postgrad. Tchr., coordinator pub. schs., Englewood, N.J., 1960-65; head lang. arts dept. pub. schs., Bedford, N.Y., 1965-70; dir. secondary and elem. edn. pub. schs., New Rochelle, N.Y., 1970-73; supr. for instrn., pub. schs., Rochester, N.Y., 1973-81; supt. schs., Roanoke, Va., 1981—; guest lectr. Cambridge U. (Eng.), 1983. Bd. dirs. Achievement Ctr., ARC, Ronaoke Symphony Orch., Jr. Achievement, Transp. Mus., 1981—. Mem. Am. Assn. Sch. Adminstrs., Nat. Sch. Bds. Assn., Assn. for Supervision and Curriculum Devel., Nat. Forensic League, Roanoke C. of C., Phi Delta Kappa, Kappa Delta Pi, Delta Upsilon. Roman Catholic. Lodge: Rotary (chmn. youth com. Roanoke 1983-84). Home: 430 Bramble Ln SW Roanoke VA 24014 Office: Roanoke City Pub Schs 40 Douglass Ave NW Roanoke VA 24012

TOTH, KENNETH STEPHEN, nuclear scientist; b. Shanghai, China, Mar. 17, 1934 (father Am. citizen); s. Stephen and Anfisa Sylvestrovna (Porseva) T.; m. Roberta Joan Kelly, June 5, 1956; children—Deborah Ann, Kenneth Stephen. B.A. in Chemistry, San Diego State U., 1954; Ph.D. in Nuclear Chemistry, U. Calif.-Berkeley, 1958. Teaching asst. U. Calif.-Berkeley, 1954-55; research asst. Lawrence Berkeley Lab., 1955-58; Fulbright fellow Niels Bohr Inst., Copenhagen, 1958-59; nuclear scientist Oak Ridge Nat. Lab., 1959—; translator sci. articles Russian to English, Am. Inst. Physics, N.Y.C., 1979-82. Contbr. numerous articles to sci. jours. and conf. procs. Guggenheim fellow Niels Bohr Inst., 1965-66; Nat. Acad. Scis. scholar, Dubna, USSR, 1975. Mem. Am. Phys. Soc., Am. Chem. Soc. Avocations: walking; music; reading; sports. Home: 103 Canterbury Rd Oak Ridge TN 37831 Office: Oak Ridge Nat Lab Bldg 6000 Oak Ridge TN 37831

TOUBY, KATHLEEN ANITA, lawyer; b. Miami Beach, Fla., Feb. 20, 1943; s. Harry and Kathleen Rebecca (Hamper) T.; children—Mark Andrew Finkel, Judson David Finkel. B.S. in Nursing, U. Fla., 1965, M.R.C. in Rehab. Counseling, 1967; J.D. with honors, Nova U., 1977. Bar: Fla. 1978, D.C. 1978. Counselor, Jewish Vocat. Service, Chgo., 1967-68; rehab. counselor Fla. Dept. Vocat. Rehab., Miami, 1968-70; spl. asst., asst. U.S. atty. U.S. Dept. Justice, Miami, 1978-80; assoc. firm Pyszka & Kessler, P.A., Miami, 1980-83; ptnr. firm Lococo, Klein, Touby & Smith, P.A., North Miami, Fla., 1983—. Bd. dirs. Bay Point Homeowner's Assn. Mem. ABA, Dade County Bar Assn., Fla. Def. Bar Assn., Am. Assn. Nurse Attys., Am. Bus. Women's Assn., Assn. Am. Trial Lawyers, Fed. Bar Assn., North Miami C. of C., Phi Delta Phi (province pres. 1982-85, bd. dirs. 1985—). Democrat. Roman Catholic. Home: 450 Sabal Palm Rd Miami FL 33137 Office: Lococo Klein and Touby PA 901 NE 125th St North Miami FL 33161

TOUPS, KAREN LOVELADY, state official; b. Oxford, Miss., Dec. 3, 1953; d. Morris Carl and Anita (Simpson) Lovelady; widowed; 1 child, Gregory Clayton. Student, U. Miss., 1972. Sec. Fed. Barge Lines, New Orleans, 1972-74; clk. typist Fed. Res. Bank, Jacksonville, Fla., 1974-75; adminstrv. sec. U. Miss., Oxford, 1979-80; licensing bd. adminstr. State Bd. Architecture, Jackson, Miss., 1980—. Methodist. Avocations: sewing; wood crafts; water skiing; softball; golf. Office: State Bd Architecture 440 Bounds St Suite D Jackson MS 39206

TOUS DE TORRES, LUZ M., bank exec.; b. San Juan, P.R., Apr. 23, 1944; d. Rafael Tous Cortes and Iris Fernos; B.B.A., U.P.R., 1965; M.B.A., Interam. U., 1976, also P.R. Sch. Banking, 1976; m. Manuel A. de Torres, Jr., Feb. 17, 1967; children—Rosa Iris, Lara Sofia. With Banco Popular, San Juan, 1965—, v.p., employee relations dir., 1969—. Co-founder P.R. Indsl. Editors Assn., pres., 1970-72; dir. bank's blood program for ARC, 1972—, dir. bank's personnel donors program United Fund, 1981—. Recipient Outstanding Acad. Achievement award Interam. U., 1976. Mem. Am. Soc. Personnel Adminstrs. (accredited personnel mgr.), Am. Mgmt. Assn., Internat. Assn. Bus. Communicators. Office: GPO Box 2708 San Juan PR 00936

TOWERS, THOMAS R., wholesale leaf tobacco and holding company executive. Pres. Universal Leaf Tobacco Co., Inc., Richmond, Va., 1982—, dir. Office: Universal Leaf Tobacco Co Inc Hamilton and Broad Sts Richmond VA 23230

TOWNES, HOWELL MCKEEL, JR., accountant; b. Nashville, Aug. 7, 1946; s. Howell M. and Edna M. (Mahoney) T.; m. Janet Arlene Helms, Oct. 24, 1971; 1 dau., Heather Margaret. B.S. in Bus. Mgmt., David Lipscomb Coll., 1967; M.B.A., U. Tenn., 1969. Mgmt. trainee Cummings & Co., Nashville, 1969-71; adminstrv. mgr. Modern Maid Homes, Nashville and Knoxville, Tenn., 1971; controller, Henrite Products, Morristown, Tenn., 1972; acctg. mgr. Winner Corp., Dickson, Tenn., 1972-73; acctg. cons., mgr. Trane Co., Clarksville, Tenn., 1973-75; asst. dir. Tenn. Found. for Med. Care, Inc., Nashville, 1975-77; controller Shirt Closet, Inc., Nashville, 1977-80; dir. bus. Tenn. Performing Arts Ctr., Nashville, 1980—; instr. bus. David Lipscomb Coll., Nashville, 1969. Deacon Central Ch. of Christ, 1980—. Served with Army N.G., 1969-75. Mem. Assn. M.B.A. Execs., Nat. Assn. Accts. Home: 2731 Westwood Dr Nashville TN 37204 Office: Tenn Performing Arts Ctr 505 Deaderick St Nashville TN 37219

TOWNES, MARY MCLEAN, university dean; b. Southern Pines, N.C., July 12, 1928; d. Mitchell and Nora Jane (McPhatter) McLean; m. Ross Emile Townes, Aug. 28, 1954; children—Emilie M., Tricia L. B.S., N.C. Central U., 1949, M.S.P.H., 1950; M.S., U. Mich., 1953, Ph.D., 1962. Mem. faculty N.C. Central U., Durham, 1950—, prof. biology, 1968—, chmn. dept., 1976-79, dean Grad. Sch. Arts and Scis., 1979—. Bd. advisors N.C. Sch. Sci. and Math. Gen. Edn. Bd. fellow, 1953-54; recipient Danforth Tchr. study award, 1958-59. Mem. Am. Soc. Zoologists, Soc. Gen. Physiologists, N.Y. Acad. Scis., N.C. Acad. Sci., AAAS, Delta Sigma Theta. Democrat. Methodist. Home: 101 W Alton St Durham NC 27707 Office: NC Central U Durham NC 27707

TOWNLEY, CATHERINE JANET, savings and loan association executive; b. Atlanta, Apr. 7, 1950; d. William Milton and Audrey (Warnock) T.; student Dekalb Coll., Inst. Fin. Edn.; grad. Sch. Exec. Devel., U. Conn., 1980. Asst. office mgr. First Fed. Savs. & Loan Assn. of Atlanta, 1968-70; sec., teller Decatur (Ga.) Fed. Savs. & Loan Assn., 1970-71, asst. br. mgr., Stone Mountain, 1972-73, asst. v.p., br. mgr., 1973-78, dist. v.p. So. dist. brs., 1978—, adminstrv. officer INVEST. Vol., ARC, Aidmore Childrens Hosp., Jr. Achievement, DeKalb County Heart Fund, United Way, Am. Cancer Soc., De Kalb C. of C.; membership chmn. DeKalb County Boy Scouts Am. Mem. Stone Mountain Indsl. Park Assn., DeKalb C. of C., DeKalb Gwinnett Young Realtors, Am. Savs. and Loan Inst. Home: 6024 Old Town Pl Norcross GA 30093 Office: 5465 Peachtree Indsl Blvd Chamblee GA 30341

TOWNLEY, JOHN, educational administrator. Supt. of schs. Irving, Tex. Office: PO Box 2637 Irving TX 75061*

TOWNS, JOSEPH ALAN, architect, structural engineer; b. Kansas City, Mo., July 7, 1953; s. Bill and Nadine T.; A.Arch., Longview Community Coll., 1975; B. Environ. Design, U. Kans., 1978, B.S. in Archtl. Engring., 1979; m. Cheryl L. McLemore, Dec. 3, 1971; children—Joseph A., Christopher M. Mem. Kansas City Police Dept., 1971-79; sr. structural engr., architect Corp. Engring. div. Phillips Petroleum Co., Bartlesville, Okla., 1979—; mem. solar design com. Farmland Industries, Inc. Vice-chmn., Bartlesville Traffic Com.; pres. PTO; mem. Supt.'s Communication Council. Registered profl. engr., okla., Mo., Kans., Colo., Cert. pilot. Mem. Nat. Soc. Profl. Engrs., Bartlesville Area C. of C. Republican. Clubs: Masons, Shriners. Home: 408 Fleetwood Dr Bartlesville OK 74006 Office: Phillips Petroleum Co B-41-AB Bartlesville OK 74004

TOWNSEND, DONLEY PAUL, computer company executive; b. Rapid City, S.D., May 14, 1953; s. Donley Paul and Pauline (Heim) T.; m. Christina Godfrey, Apr. 21, 1979; B.A., U. Tex., 1975, M.A., 1977. Assoc. mng. ptnr. Lucas Assocs., Inc., Houston, 1977-80; div. recruiter Hilti Inc., San Francisco, 1980-81, mgr. staffing, Tulsa, 1981-83, mgr. program devel., 1983-84, mgr. orgn. planning and mgmt. devel., 1984-85; dir. orgn. devel. Telex Computer Products, Tulsa, 1985—; dir. adv. bd. Mgmt. Devel. Ctr., U. Tulsa, 1984-85. Contbr. articles to profl. jours. Cons., Leadership Tulsa, 1985, Jr. Achievement, Tulsa, 1985; bd. dirs. Tulsa Urban League, 1982-85. Mem. Am. Soc. Tng. and Devel., Human Resource Planning Soc. Episcopalian. Club: Tulsa Country. Home: 2409 E 18th St Tulsa OK 74104 Office: Telex Computer Products 6422 E 41st St Tulsa OK 74135

TOWNSEND, FRANK MARION, physician, educator; b. Stamford, Tex., Oct. 29, 1914; s. Frank M. and Beatrice (House) T.; m. Gerda Eberlein, 1940 (div. 1944); 1 son, Frank M.; m. Ann Graf, Aug. 25, 1951; 1 son, Robert N. Student San Antonio Coll., 1931-32, U. Tex., 1932-34; M.D., Tulane U., 1938. Diplomate Am. Bd. Pathology. Intern, Polyclinic Hosp., N.Y.C., 1939-40; commd. 1st lt. M.C., U.S. Army, 1940, advanced through grades to lt. col., 1946; resident and instr. pathology Washington U., 1945-47; trans. to USAF, flight surgeon, 1949, advanced through grades to col., 1956; instr. pathology Coll. Medicine, U. Nebr., 1947-48; assoc. pathologist Scott and White Clinic, Temple, Tex., 1948-49; assoc. prof. pathology Med. Br. U. Tex., Galveston, 1949-59; dir. labs. USAF Hosp., Lackland AFB, 1950-54; cons. pathology, chief cons. group Office Surgeon Gen., Hdqrs. SAF, Washington, 1954-55, cons., 1955-63; dep. dir. Armed Forces Inst. Pathology, Washington, 1955-59, dir., 1959-63, vice comdr. aerospace med. div. Air Forces Systems Command, 1963-65; ret., 1965; practice medicine specializing in pathology, San Antonio, 1965—; dir. labs. San Antonio State Chest Hosp.; cons. pathologist Tex. Dept. Health hosps., 1965-72; clin. prof. pathology U. Tex. Med. Sch., San Antonio, 1969-72, prof., chmn. dept. pathology, 1972—; mem. Armed Forces Epidemiol. Bd., 1983—; cons. U. Tex. Cancer Ctr.-M.D. Anderson Hosp., 1966-76, NASA, 1967-75; mem. adv. bd. cancer WHO, 1958-75. Contbr. med. articles to profl. jours. Mem. adv. council Civil War Centennial Commn., 1960-65; bd. dirs. Alamo Area Sci. Fair, 1967-73; bd. govs. Armed Forces Inst. Pathology, 1984—. Decorated D.S.M., Legion of Merit; recipient Founders medal Assn. Mil. Surgeons, 1961. Fellow ACP, Coll. Am. Pathologists (South Central states regional commr. lab. accreditation 1971—), Am. Soc. Clin. Pathologists (Ward Burdick award 1983),Internat. Acad. Pathologists, Acad. Clin. Lab. Physicians and Scientists, Aerospace Med. Assn. (H.G. Moseley award 1962); mem. Tex. Med. Assn. (sci. publ. com. 1980—), AMA, Internat. Acad. Aviation and Space Medicine, Tex. Soc. Pathologists, Am. Assn. Pathologists, Soc. Med. Cons. to Armed Forces, Gonzales (Tex.) Farm Bur., S.W. Cattle Raisers Assn., Nat. Cattleman's Assn. Club: Torch. Home: Box 77 Harwood TX 78632 Office: Dept. Pathology U Tex health Sci Ctr 7703 Floyd Curl Dr San Antonio TX 78284

TOWNSEND, LAWRENCE WILLARD, theoretical physicist, educator; b. Jacksonville, Fla., May 13, 1947; s. Willard Hyram and Marion Patricia (McCann) T.; m. Linda Susan Summerlin, June 5, 1969; children—Laura Suzanne, David Matthew, Jeremy Peter. B.S., U.S. Naval Acad., 1969; M.S., U.S. Naval Postgrad. Sch., 1970; Ph.D., U. Idaho, 1980. Research asst. prof. physics Old Dominion U., Norfolk, Va., 1980-81; research scientist Langley Research Ctr., NASA, Hampton, Va., 1981—, prin. investigator NASA space radiation protection research program, 1982—; mem. adj. faculty Old Dominion U., Norfolk, Va., 1981—. Treas. Va. peninsula chpt. Full Gospel Businessmen's Fellowship Internat., 1983, pres., 1979, 85-86, v.p. Palouse River chpt., 1978. Served to lt. comdr. USN, 1969-77. Recipient NASA Spl. Achievement award, 1984. Whittenberger Found. fellow, 1979-80. Mem. Am. Phys. Soc., Sigma Xi (award 1980-81). Contbr. articles to profl. jours. Office: Mail Stop 160 NASA Langley Research Center Hampton VA 23665

TOWNSON-SWANSON, MARILYN, clothing company executive; b. Fort Oglethorpe, Ga., Jan. 25, 1959; d. Hurshel Milford and Treva Anne (Finch) T.; m. Charles Strickland Swanson, Apr. 20, 1985. A.A., Am. Coll. Art, 1979; B.S. in Textiles and Clothing, U. Tenn., 1983. Sales rep. Lily of France, Atlanta, 1978-79; asst. mgr. Givenchy, Atlanta, 1979; sales clk., security bd. mem. Neiman-Marcus, Atlanta, 1979-80, asst. buyer, Dallas, 1983-85, mail order merchandise assoc. buyer women's apparel, 1985—; mgr. trainee Sakowitz, Houston, 1982-83. Student of hist. costume Atlanta Hist. Soc., 1978-79; pres. Merchandising Students Assn., Knoxville, Tenn., 1981-82; chmn. Prof. Seminars for Success, Knoxville, 1981-82. Republican. Episcopalian. Avocations: reading; needlepoint; tennis; horseback riding. Home: 5539 McCommas Blvd Dallas TX 37206 Office: Neiman-Marcus Main at Ervay Dallas TX 75201

TRACHTENBERG, JOSEPH SIDNEY, political science educator; b. Portland, Oreg., Dec. 26, 1948; s. Isaac N. and Gladys (Goodman) T.; m. Wendy Silver, June 9, 1985. B.A., Willamette U., 1970; M.A., Portland State U., 1973; Ph.D., Emory U., 1978. Assoc. prof. polit. sci. Ga. Clayton Coll., Morrow, Ga., coll. rep. Regents adv. panel in polit. sci., 1979—. Mem. So. Polit. Sci. Assn., Ga. Polit. Sci. Assn., Am. Polit. Sci. Assn. Democrat. Club: Multnomah Athletic (Portland). Office: Clayton Coll Morrow GA 30260

TRAHANT, WILLIAM JAMES, management consultant; b. Malden, Mass., Aug. 5, 1945; s. Robert A. and Evelyn (Trainor) T.; m. Nedra Jean Pipher, June 12, 1976; children—Timothy Pipher, Christopher Earl. B.A., Mt. Carmel Coll. (Ont., Can.), 1967; M.P.A., Am. U., Washington, 1976. Tchr., Mt. Carmel High Sch., Chgo., 1968-69; vice prin. Eberhard Sch., Washington, 1970-75; dir. ops. Leadership Systems, Inc., Silver Spring, Md., 1976-79; assoc. dir. Clary Inst., Washington, 1979-80; pres. William J. Trahant & Assocs., Arlington, Va., 1981-83; v.p. IMR Corp., Energy, Mktg. and Mgmt. div., Falls Church, Va., 1983—. Served with USAR, 1970-76. Mem. Am. Soc. Tng. and Devel., Am. Soc. Pub. Adminstrn., D.C. Jaycees (dir. tng. and devel. 1975). Roman Catholic. Home: 812 N Danville St Arlington VA 22201

TRAMMELL, VIRGINIA ANN, telephone co. ofcl.; b. Grayson County, Tex., May 8, 1930; d. James L. and Emma D. Lankford; grad. Tyler Comml. Coll., 1957; m. B.C. Trammell, June 16, 1980; 1 dau., Sharon Dee Hail. Dental asst., Grapevine, Tex., 1953-56; acctg. clk. Gulf States United Telephone Co.,

Tyler, Tex., 1957-61, asst. to auditor, 1961-66, asst. auditor, 1966-67, asst. sec., asst. controller, 1967-80, internal audit mgr., 1980-82, staff acct., 1982—. Mem. Am. Bus. Women's Assn. (Woman of Yr. 1971), Telephone Pioneer Assn. Presbyterian. Home: 823 Bama Ln Tyler TX 75701 Office: 123 S Broadway Tyler TX 75702

TRANTHAM, WILLIAM EUGENE, music educator, organist, director; b. Elkland, Mo., Aug. 6, 1929; s. Harvey Wilson and Lola Jane (Minor) T.; m. Patsy Ann Starr, June 7, 1959; children—Rachel Ann, Gene. B.S., B.S.E., Southwest Mo. State U., 1951; Mus.M., Northwestern U., 1955, Ph.D., 1966. Instr., Northwestern U., Evanston, Ill., 1954-55; prof. Southwest Baptist U., Bolivar, Mo., 1955-60; prof. Ouachita Bapt. U., Arkadelphia, Ark., 1960—, dean Sch. Music, 1966-82; organist-dir. Westminster Presbyn. Ch., Hot Springs, Ark., 1975—. Contbr. articles to Jour. Research in Mus. Edn., The Church Musician. Served to cpl. U.S. Army, 1951-53. Named Musician of Yr., Ark. Federated Music Clubs, 1981. Mem. Ark. State Mus. Tchrs. Assn. (pres. 1977-79, Outstanding Coll. Tchr. 1982), Music Tchrs. Nat. Assn., Coll. Music Soc., Am. Guild of Organists, Phi Mu Alpha Sinfonia, Pi Kappa Lambda. Avocations: travel; cooking. Home: 688 Carter Rd Arkadelphia AR 71923 Office: Ouachita Baptist U Box 3789 Arkadelphia AR 71923

TRAPNELL, BEATRICE JOAN, nursing administrator; b. Jackson, Mich., June 4, 1933; d. Cassell Lee and Glenadine M. (Priddy) Pursell; m. Richard H. Trapnell, Nov. 29, 1958 (div. Dec. 1983); children—Ann Cassell, Sarah E., James G. B.S., U. Mich., 1955; M.S., U. Calif.-San Francisco, 1980. R.N.; lic. nurse, N.C., Calif. Staff nurse Marin Crisis Unit, San Rafael, Calif., 1974-80; clin. nurse San Mateo Community Mental Health, 1980-81; head nurse McAuley Neuropsychiat. Inst., San Francisco, 1981-82; asst. dir. nursing Sutter Meml. Hosp., Sacramento, 1982-84; dir. nursing Highland Hosp., Asheville, N.C., 1985—; guest lectr. Calif. State U.-Sacramento, 1982-84; cons. U. Calif.-Davis Med. Ctr., 1982-84, Am. River Hosp., Sacramento, 1983. Mem. Am. Orthopsychiatry Assn., Calif. Nurses Assn. Avocations: hiking, cross country skiing, reading.

TRAPOLIN, FRANK WINTER, insurance executive; b. New Orleans, Jan. 29, 1913; s. John Baptiste and Florence Bertha (Winter) T.; B.S. in Econs., Loyola U. of South, New Orleans, 1935; m. Thelma Mae Mouledoux, Oct. 27, 1937; children—Timothy, Patricia, Jane, Anne. Agt., Godchaux & Mayer, New Orleans, 1935-42, 46-51; pres. Trapolin Ins. Agy., Inc., New Orleans, 1953—; mem. faculty Loyola U.; ins. cons. Former pres. Cath. Human Relations Commn. Greater New Orleans, Associated Cath. Charities New Orleans, Maryland Dr. Homeowners Assn.; former chmn. adv. bd. New Orleans Juvenile Cts., Ursuline Nuns New Orleans; former scoutmaster Boy Scouts Am.; former v.p. Community Relations Council Greater New Orleans, La. Interch. Conf.; former trustee United Fund Greater New Orleans Area; former mem. adv. bd. Coll. Bus. Adminstrn., Loyola U., Mother-house of Sisters of Holy Family; former bd. dirs. St. John Berchman Orphanage, New Orleans Interfaith Conf., St. Elizabeth's Home for Girls, Cath. Book Store Found., Manresa Retreat House; pres. Greater New Orleans Execs. Assn. Served in USN, 1942-46, 51-53; to capt. Res. Recipient Merit cert. City of New Orleans, 1972; Order of St. Louis. Mem. La. Assn. Ins. Agts., Nat. Assn. Ins. Agts., New Orleans Ins. Exchange, Navy League, Mil. Order World Wars, New Orleans Photog. Soc., Sierra Club, Loyola U. Alumni Assn. (past pres.), Blue Key. Democrat. Roman Catholic. Clubs: Sertoma (pres. New Orleans 1955-56), Serra (pres. New Orleans 1973-74), Internat. House, New Orleans Track, New Orleans Yacht, KC (4 deg.). Patentee gunnery, tng. and machinery devices for USN. Home: 119 Audubon Blvd New Orleans LA 70118 Office: Trapolin Ins Agy Inc 837 Gravier St Suite 1212 New Orleans LA 70112

TRAPP, CLAYTON LESLIE, JR., civil engineer; b. Wellington, Kans., Mar. 13, 1929; s. Clayton Leslie and Lee Fern (Goff) T.; B.S. in Civil Engring., Kans. State U., 1951; m. Dixie Jeanne Bradshaw, Apr. 15, 1972. Airworthiness dir. Boeing Co., Wichita, Kans., 1970-71; sec.-treas. Tyson Bldg. Corp., Ft. Worth, 1971-80; pres., chief exec. officer Multisound Corp., Ft. Worth, 1975-81; chmn. bd., chief exec. officer Comml. Floorcovering Co., Houston, 1977-80; v.p. Ronco Properties Co., Ft. Worth, 1977-79; pres., chief exec. officer Fin. Services Tex., Dallas and Ft. Worth, 1981—. Recipient various certs. of appreciation. Registered profl. engr., Kans., V.I., Tex. Mem. Nat. Soc. Profl. Engrs., ASCE, Tex. Soc. Profl. Engrs., Internat. Soc. Financiers, Internat. Platform Assn. Address: PO Box 1952 Ft Worth TX 76101

TRAUTWEIN, JAMES WILLIAM, optoelectric component company executive; b. Washington, Mo., Aug. 24, 1935; s. Edwin Herman and Octavia (Raymond) T.; student S.E. Mo. U., 1953-55; B.S.E.E., Mo. U., Rolla, 1957; M.S. in Solid State Physics, Western Ky. U., 1967; 1 dau., Susan. Engring. trainee Gen. Electric Co., Owensboro, Ky., Tyler, Tex. and Syracuse, N.Y., 1957-58, research engr., Owensboro, Ky., 1958-60, design engr., 1960-63, engring. mgr., 1963-67; engring. supr. Monsanto, Decater, Ala., 1967; design engr. Tex. Instrument Inc., Dallas, 1967-69, engring. mgr., 1969-72, project mgr., 1972-74; mktg. mgr. TRW Optron, Carrollton, Tex., 1975-80; v.p. mktg. Optek, McKinney, Tex., 1980—; condr. tech. seminars. Boys' counselor Royal Ambassadors, Owensboro, Ky., 1960-66; counselor Jr. Achievement, Owensboro, 1964-67. Registered profl. engr., Mo., Ky. Mem. IEEE, Profl. Engrs. Soc. (v.p. Green River br. 1966), Mark Twain Soc. Republican. Lutheran. Author: Increasing Speeds of Response in Photocell, 1967; contbr. articles to profl. jours. Office: 345 Industrial Blvd McKinney TX 75069

TRAVIS, JUDITH ANN, nursing administrator; b. Tampa, Fla., Feb. 21, 1934; d. Thomas McIntyre and Niza (Brooker) Morris; m. Marvin Thomas Travis, Mar. 19, 1955; children—Karen Lee, David Thomas. B.S. in Nursing, Emory U., 1955; D.P.A., Nova U., Fort Lauderdale, Fla., 1982. Staff nurse VA Hosp., Shreveport, La., 1955-56, Sinai Hosp., Balt., 1957-58; dir. in-service edn. Manassas Manor Nursing Home, Va., 1967-70; dir. in-service edn. Habana Plaza Nursing Ctr., Tampa, 1970-72, asst. dir. nursing, 1972-73; dir. nursing Delaware Valley Medictr., Tampa, 1973-74; exec. dir. Vis. Nurse Assn. Tampa Bay, Inc., 1974—; clin. dir. dept. comprehensive medicine U. South Fla., 1981—; mem. founding bd. dirs., v.p. Hospice of Hillsborough, Inc., Tampa, 1982-84; mem. founding bd. dirs. Eldermed of Hillsborough, Inc., Tampa, 1983—; presenter coms. on aging, also other issues to U.S. Senate, Ho. of Reps., Fla. Ho. of Reps., 1976-80; del. Fla. Conf. on Aging, Orlando, 1980; observer White House Conf., 1981; mem. Hillsborough adv. council Fla. Gulf Health Systems Agy., pres. 1979-81. Sec. Keystone Park Civic Assn., Odessa, Fla., 1982-83. Named Tampa Bay Area Bus. Woman of Yr., Eastlake Mall and Sta. FM101, 1982. Mem. Vis. Nurse Assns./Services (exec. com. Am. affiliation 1983-85), Am. Soc. Pub. Adminstrn., Fla. Assn. Home Health Agys. (v.p. 1976-77, pres. 1977-80), Nat. League Nursing, Nat. Assn. for Home Care (accrediation and quality assurance com.), Fla. Council Vis. Nurses Assns. (pres. 1982-83), Sigma Theta Tau. Democrat. Home: 546 Blake Rd Odessa FL 33556 Office: Vis Nurse Assn Tampa Bay Inc 4100 W Kennedy Blvd Suite 210 Tampa FL 33609

TRAVIS, MARVIN THOMAS, business educator, retired air force officer, consultant; b. Charlotte, N.C., June 7, 1932; s. Thomas T. and Esther (Sutherland) T.; m. Judith Ann Morris, Mar. 19, 1955; children—Karen Lee, David Thomas. B.A., Emory U., 1954; M.B.A., Ariz. State U., 1967; D. in Pub. Adminstrn., Nova U., 1982. Commd. 2nd lt. U.S. Air Force, 1954; advanced through grades to lt. col., 1971; chief adminstr. Directorate of Civil Engring., Hdqrs. U.S. Air Force, Pentagon, 1966-70; chief of personnel Utapao AFB, 1970-71; sec. joint staff U.S. Readiness Command MacDill A.F.B., 1971-77; ret. 1977; adj. prof. U. Tampa, Fla., 1971-84; coordinator doctoral program, adj. prof. Nova U., Tampa, 1982—; asst. prof. business St. Leo Coll., Fla., 1982-83, prof. mgmt., chmn. div. bus., 1984—; presentor seminars in field. Author publs. in field. Mem. Keystone Civic Assn., Odessa, Fla., 1978-85. Mem. Am. Mgmt. Assn., Am. Soc. for Pub. Adminstrn., Air Force Assn., Beta Gamma Sigma, Sigma Iota Epsilon. Democrat. Mem. Christian Ch. (Disciples of Christ). Home: 546 Blake Rd Odessa FL 33556 Office: Div of Bus Saint Leo College PO Box 2067 Saint Leo FL 33574

TRAYLOR, THOMAS REID, physician, medical educator; b. Montgomery, Ala., Apr. 15, 1949; s. Herschel Reid and Betty (Wilson) T.; m. Brenda Gail Royall, 1966 (div. 1970); 1 son, Thomas Stephen; m. Rikki Roach, June 5, 1971; children—Joshua Reid, Matthew Austin. B.S., Auburn U., 1971; M.D., U. S. Ala., 1977. Intern, Richmond Meml. Hosp., Columbia, S.C.; resident in ob-gyn, 1978-81; practice medicine specializing in ob-gyn, Knoxville, 1981—; instr. U. Tenn. Hosp., Knoxville, 1981—; asst. med. dir. regional perinatal program, Knoxville, 1981—. Assoc. fellow Am. Coll. Ob-Gyn; mem. Knoxville Acad. Medicine, S.C. Med. Assn., U. South Ala. Med. Alumni Assn., Tenn. Med. Assn., AMA, East Tenn. Ob-Gyn Soc. (program chmn.), Am. Inst. Ultrasound and Medicine, Tenn. Perinatal Assn., Internat. Corr. Soc., A.W. Diddle Soc. (charter). Republican. Baptist. Club: LeConte. Contbr. articles to profl. jours. Home: 1809 Northwood Dr Knoxville TN 37923 Office: 1924 Alcoa Hwy Dept Ob-Gyn Knoxville TN 37920

TREACY, JAMES BERNARD, corporate executive; b. Indpls., 1921. B.S., U. Notre Dame, 1943. With Pan Am. World Airways Inc., 1943-50, Bendix Corp., 1950-76; with Facet Enterprises Inc., Tulsa, 1976—, chief exec. officer, until 1984, now chmn. bd., chmn. exec. com., dir. Office: Facet Enterprises Inc 7030 S Yale St Tulsa OK 74136

TREAGY, PAUL EVERETT, retired naval officer, consultant; b. Pembroke, Maine, Oct. 3, 1930; s. Paul Alden and Beatrice Louise (Morang) T.; m. Julia Ann Drenning, Aug. 11, 1962; children—Michael Edward, Carrie Barker Treagy. B.S. in Engring., U.S. Naval Acad., 1954; M.S. in Mgmt., Naval Postgrad. Sch., Monterey, Calif., 1970; grad. Naval War Coll., Newport, R.I., 1965, Nat. War Coll., Washington, 1975. Commd. ensign U.S. Navy, 1954, advanced through grades to capt., 1979; exec. officer to dir. for ops. Joint Staff, Washington, 1972-73; dep. comdt. midshipmen U.S. Naval Acad., Annapolis, Md., 1975-77; comdg. officer of frigate Fanning, San Diego, 1970-72; comdr. Destroyer Squadron Five, San Diego, 1978-79; project engr. TRW, McLean, Va., 1984—; mil. aide White House, Washington, 1960-62. Scouting coordinator Nat. Capital Area council Boy Scouts Am., 1980—; mem. adminstrv. council Epworth United Methodist Ch., Annandale, Va., 1985—. Decorated Legion of Merit. Mem. U.S. Naval Inst., Nat. Geog. Soc. Republican. Clubs: Sleepy Hollow Bath & Racquet. Avocations: preservation, restoration of houses, antiques, landscaping, jogging. Home: 3412 Stoneybrae Dr Lake Barcroft Falls Church VA 22044 Office: TRW Systems Engring and Applications Div 7600 Colshire Dr McLean VA 22102

TREECE, JAMES WILLIAM, JR., sociology educator; b. Parkerton, Wyo., July 12, 1924; s. James William and Myrtle (Chaney) T.; m. Eleanor Mae Walters, Apr. 11, 1954. Degree in Bus. Adminstrn., Barnes Sch. Commerce, 1948; B.R.E., St. Paul Bible Coll., 1962; B.A. in Sociology, Bethel Coll., 1965; M.A. in Sociology, U. Minn., 1967, postgrad., 1967-69. Part-time instr. St. Paul Bible Coll., 1967-68, S.D. State U., St. Paul Extension, 1968-69, Arthur B. Ancker Meml. Sch. Nursing, St. Paul, 1968-69; asst. prof. sociology Bethel Coll., St. Paul, 1969-74; assoc. prof. sociology Liberty Bapt. Coll., (now Liberty U.), Lynchburg, Va., 1978—; condr. workshops in field. Served with U.S. Army, 1943-46. Paul and Priscilla Johnson scholar, 1961. Mem. Am. Sociol. Assn., So. Sociol. Soc., Soc. for Sci. Study of Social Problems, Wyo. Hist. Soc., Va. League for Nursing, Internat. Platform Assn., Smithsonian Assocs., Wycliffe Assocs. Republican. Baptist. Author: (with Eleanor Walters Treece) Elements of Research in Nursing, 3d edit., 1982, 4th edit., 1986. Home: PO Box 234 Forest VA 24551 Office: Liberty U Lynchburg VA 24506-8001

TREIB, SEYMOUR LAZARUS, water equipment company executive; b. Bklyn., Feb. 23, 1918; s. William and Jennie (Lewitzky) T.; m. Ethel Malament, Feb. 10, 1953 (dec. 1971); 1 dau., Elinor Alexander; m. 2d, Suzanne M. Rosenthal, June 2, 1975. A.B., Johns Hopkins U., 1940; postgrad. Columbia U., 1941. Asst. research mgr. Dreyfus & Co., N.Y.C., 1947-49; gen. sales mgr. Crystal Springs Water Co., Miami, Fla., 1956-73; cons. water problems, Miami, 1973-75; pres., chmn. bd. Agua Pure, Inc., Sarasota and Miami, Fla., 1975—. Served to capt. USCG, 1942-46, 49-53. Mem. Armed Forces League, Res. Officers Assn. U.S., Res. Officers Assn. Fla. Democrat. Club: Army-Navy of Coral Gables. Office: Agua Pure Inc PO Box 431096 Miami FL 33243

TREISTER, ALAN WILLIAM, architect; b. Miami, Fla., Aug. 23, 1957; s. Kenneth and Helyne (Bressler) T. B.A., U. Pa., 1979, M.Arch., 1981. Registered architect, Fla. Architect, Alfred Browning Parker, Coconut Grove, Fla., 1978-79, Cossutta & Assocs., N.Y.C., 1981-82, Treister & Cantillo, Coconut Grove, 1982—. Artist watercolor travel sketches, 1980 (Silver medal AIA exhibit 1982); architect interior design Office for Allen W. Greenwald, 1982. Recipient 2d class merit award U. Edinburgh (Scotland) Dept. Architecture, 1978; Dales traveling fellow U. Pa. Grad. Sch. Fine Arts, 1980. Democrat. Jewish. Home: Apt 7-A 3304 Virginia St Coconut Grove FL 33133 Office: Treister & Cantillo Architects 2699 S Bayshore Dr Coconut Grove FL 33133

TRELOAR, ALAN E(DWARD), medical biometrician; b. Melbourne, Australia, Sept. 27, 1902; s. William Tremayne and Annie Oliver (McBean) T.; B.Sc. in Agr., Sydney U. (Australia), 1926; M.S., U. Minn., 1928, Ph.D., 1930; m. Molly Innes, Aug. 1929 (dec.); m. 2d Dorothy Elizabeth Buchanan, Mar., 1948; children—Anne M., Alayne G., Harriette E. Belmore scholar Sydney U., 1922-23; Farrer scholar (Australia), 1926-27; Internat. Edn. Bd. fellow Rockefeller Found., 1927-28; research assoc. U. Minn., 1928-29, prof. pub. health, 1929-56; dir. research Am. Hosp. Assn., 1957-60; chief statistics and analysis br. NIH, 1961-76; research fellow N.C. Population Center, 1977-80; research prof. (voluntary) U. Utah Coll. Nursing, 1984—. Author 4 books on biometry; internat. authority on realities of menstruation. Mem. 5 sci. socs.

TREMBLAY, SHARYN ANN, nurse, educator, consultant, author; b. Fort Lauderdale, Fla., May 30, 1945; d. Angelo Francis and Bada Frances (Kinsey) Ferrara; 1 child, Angela. Diploma Jackson Meml. Sch. Nursing, 1966; B.S. in Nursing, Fla. Internat. U., 1976, M.S. in Edn., 1980; M.S. in Nursing Adminstrn., Barry U., 1986. Staff nurse various hosps., N.Y. and Fla., 1966-75; dir. edn. Broward County Emergency Med. Services, Fort Lauderdale, 1975-81; nursing instr. Broward Community Coll., Fort Lauderdale, 1980-82, dept. head nursing, 1982—; cons. Consultation Edn. Unltd., Coral Springs, Fla., 1978—. Author: Paramedic Review, 1980; First Care, 1981; Critical Care Review for Nurses, 1984; Manual of Emergency Nursing, 1986. Recipient Service award Am. Heart Assn., Fort Lauderdale, 1976. Mem. Deans and Dirs. Assn., Nat. League Nursing, Fla. Nurses Assn. Republican. Roman Catholic. Avocations: tennis; hunting; snow skiing. Home: 1067 NW 87th Ave Coral Springs FL 33065 Office: Broward Community Coll 1000 Coconut Creek Blvd Pompano Beach FL 33066

TRENT, JAMES WILSON, JR., educator, social worker; b. Durham, N.C., Feb. 4, 1948; s. James Wilson and Margaret Leigh (Yarborough) T.; m. Carolyn Sue Norman, Dec. 21, 1974; children—Mary Shelley, Rachel Elizabeth. B.A., Wake Forest U., 1970; M.Div., Duke U., 1973; M.S.W., U. N.C., 1980; Ph.D., Brandeis U., 1982. Social worker Murdoch Ctr., Butner, N.C., 1973-75; devel. disabilities coordinator Durham County Community Mental Health Ctr., 1976-78; asst. prof. Barrington Coll., R.I., 1980-83; asst. prof. social work U. So. Miss., Hattiesburg, 1983—. Contbr. articles to profl. jours., chpt. to book. Nat. Inst. Child Health and Human Devel. grantee, 1978-81; NEH grantee, 1985. Mem. Nat. Assn. Social Workers (sec. chpt. 1984-86); Am. Sociol. Assn. Democrat. Home: 101 N 22d Ave Hattiesburg MS 39401 Office: U So Miss Box 5114 Hattiesburg MS 39406

TRENT, JOYCE MILLER, librarian; b. Dayton, Ohio, Dec. 7, 1946; d. Fielding Leo and Joyce (Henry) Miller; m. Robert Cody Trent, Mar. 17, 1973; children—Michael Frederick Cody, Paul Templeton. B.A., Stephen F. Austin State U., 1969; M.L.S., U. Tex., Austin, 1975. Pub. service librarian Deer Park Pub. Library, Tex., 1969-73; system interlibrary loan librarian San Antonio Pub. Library, 1975-76; dir. system, county librarian Atascosa County Library System, Jourdanton, Tex., 1976-81; library dir. N.W. Community Library, Leon Valley, Tex., 1981—. Biweekly columnist N.W. Leader, 1981—. Pres. parish council St. Brigid's Ch., San Antonio, 1980-81; del. Met. Congl. Alliance, San Antonio, 1982—; mem. civic affairs com. Tex. Sesquicentennial Com., Leon Valley, 1984—. Mem. ALA, Tex. Library Assn. (treas. dist. 10), Leon Valley Bus. and Profl. Assn., San Antonio Geneal. Hist. Soc. (sec. 1977-78). Democrat. Roman Catholic. Home: 5903 Forest Rim San Antonio TX 78240 Office: Leon Valley NW Community Library 6500 Evers Rd San Antonio TX 78238

TRENT, MARY CAROLYN, oilfield equipment sales company executive; b. Independence, Mo., July 15, 1938; d. George Lawrence and Mildred Louise T. Student Columbia Coll., U. Mo., Katherine Gibbs Secretarial Sch. Sec., Phinney, Hallman & Coke, 1960-67, U.S. Industries, Inc., 1967-74, The McDaniel Co., 1977-78, (all Dallas); sec.-treas. Wing Pipe & Supply, Dallas, 1978—. Bd. dirs. DAR, United Daus. Confederacy, Daus. Am. Colonists, Freedoms Found. Valley Forge; active Dallas Opera Women's Bd., Opera Guild, Opera Action, Dallas Symphony Orch. League, The 500, Inc.; state chmn. Tex. Children Am. Revolution Hdqrs. Fund. Club: Engineers (Dallas). Office: 300 University Tower Dallas TX 75206

TRESE, THOMAS JOSEPH, physician; b. Toledo, Ohio, July 10, 1950; s. Ralph Edward and Virginia Marie (Farrell) T.; m. Susan Rose Slomski, May 12, 1972; children—Steven, Megan. B.A., U. Mich., 1972; D.O., Mich. State U., 1975. Diplomate Am. Osteo. Bd. Neurology and Psychiatry. Intern, Botsford Gen. Hosp., Farmington Hills, Mich., 1975-76, resident in neurology, 1976-79; asst. prof. medicine (neurology) Tex. Coll. Osteo. Medicine, Fort Worth, 1980, clin. asst. prof. medicine, 1982—; adj. prof. neurology W.Va. Coll. Osteo. Medicine, Lewisburg, 1984—; chief staff Fort Worth Osteo. Med. Ctr., 1983—. Mem. profl. adv. bd. Tarrant County Epilepsy Assn., Fort Worth, 1983—; mem. med. adv. bd. Tarrant County Multiple Sclerosis Soc., 1983—. Mem. Am. Osteo. Assn., Am. EEG Soc., Am. Coll. Neuropsychiatry (sr.), Am. Soc. Neuroimaging, Am. Assn. Electromyography and Electrodiagnosis, Tex. Osteo. Med. Assn., Am. Acad. Neurology. Roman Catholic. Club: Serra (Fort Worth). Avocations: golf; tennis; skiing. Office: 3607 W 7th St Fort Worth TX 76107

TRESSER, MELVIN, physician; b. N.Y.C., Oct. 31, 1931; s. Max and Hannah (Levy) T.; m. Bella Kerner, Feb. 11, 1956; children—Debra Ilene, Steven Jeffrey, Andrea Michel. A.B., Columbia Coll., 1952; M.D., NYU, 1956. Diplomate Am. Bd. Internal Medicine. Intern, Montefiore Hosp., N.Y.C., 1956-57, resident, 1957-58, 61-62; resident in gastroenterology Mt. Sinai Hosp., N.Y.C., 1960-61; practice medicine specializing in gastroenterology and internal medicine, Orlando, Fla., 1962—; chief gastroenterology Orlando Regional Med. Ctr., 1977-83. Served as capt. USAF, 1958-60. Fellow Am. Coll. Gastroenterology; mem. Am. Soc. Gastrointestinal Endoscopy, ACP, AMA, So. Med. Assn., Fla. Gastroenterologic Soc., Orange County Med. Soc., Am. Heart Assn. Office: W Lake Beauty Dr Orlando FL 33806

TREVEY, JACK, state senator, physician; b. Big Island, Va., May 2, 1933; s. John and Mary H. T.; m. Mary Jo Dove, 1960; children—John Harrison, Mary Elizabeth. B.S., Va. Mil. Inst., 1955; M.D., Med. Coll. Va., 1959. Rotating intern Roanoke Meml. Hosp. (Va.), 1959-60; indsl. medicine staff IBM, Lexington, Ky., 1966—; courtesy staff Central Baptist, Good Samaritan, and St. Joseph hosps., 1967—; assoc. clin. prof. community medicine U. Ky., 1967—; mem. Ky. Ho. of Reps., 1978-79; mem. Ky. Senate, Frankfurt, 1979—, chmn. subcom. health professions, mem. labor and industry, state govt. capitol constrn. oversight and health and welfare coms. Pres. Fayette County Young Republicans, 1969, campaign chmn. Fayette County, 1971, mem. exec. and adv. coms. Fayette County Rep. Party, 1971-78, chmn., 1972-74; bd. dirs. profl. div. United Way of Bluegrass, 1972—, campaign chmn., 1974, mem. campaign cabinet, 1975; mem. fin. com. Ephraim McDowell Community Cancer Network. Served to capt. M.C., USAF, 1960-62; col. M.C., USAR. Mem. Ky. Med. Assn. (del. 1970—, chmn. occupational health and phys. medicine and rehab. coms.), AMA, Fayette County Med. Assn. (chmn. legis. and pub. health com. 1970-77, v.p., 1974, mem. exec. com. 1981), Alpha Sigma Chi. Club: Lexington Country. Lodge: Kiwanis. Office: Ky Senate State Capitol Frankfurt KY 40601*

TREVINO, MANUEL, JR., agricultural and industrial machinery company executive; b. McAllen, Tex., Apr. 25, 1927; s. Manuel Trevino and Jesusa (Jaime) Garza; m. Maria Luisa Gallegos, July 17, 1954; children—Victor, Jaime, Norma, Mario, Marinela, Alfredo, Javier. B.A. in Mktg. and Mgmt., Antioch U., Yellow Springs, Ohio, 1978. Sales mgr. Astro Marble Products Inc., McAllen, Tex., 1972-78; owner, operator M. Trevino & Sons Distbrs., Pharr, Tex., 1978-80; v.p. mktg. and purchasing, dir. Finders Internat. Inc., McAllen, 1980—. Commr., Little League Baseball, 1973-77; scoutmaster Boy Scouts Am., 1978-80; mem. City Council, Pharr, Tex., 1982—; founder, exec. dir., bd. dirs. David Renk Found. Inc., 1983—; bd. dirs. Indsl. Found., City of Pharr, Tex.; bd. dirs. Internat. Good Neighbor Council, 1985-87, pres., 1983-84; treas. Boys Club of Pharr, 1983-84; pres. Internat. Bridge Com., Pharr, 1983-84. Served with U.S. Army, 1944-48; ETO. Mem. Am. Mgmt. Assn., Pharr C. of C. Clubs: Pharr Rotary (dir. 1975-81), Masons. Home: 1006 N Athol St Pharr TX 78577 Office: 4404 S 23d St McAllen TX 78501

TRIBBLE, LAVIECE EDITH, counselor; b. Campbell, Mo., Nov. 7, 1925; d. James Herman and Grace Elizabeth (Grimes) Anders; A.B., George Washington U., 1960; M.S., U. Hawaii, 1965; m. Cecil Wayne Tribble, July 7, 1945; children—Suzanne Beth, Jana Kay. Tchr. pub. schs., Mo., 1954-57, Guantanamo Bay, Cuba, 1955-58, Arlington, Va., 1960-64, Kanmehameha Schs., Honolulu, 1964-67; resource tchr. Custis Elementary Sch., Arlington, Va., 1967-68; dir. guidance Swanson Intermediate Sch., Arlington, Va., 1968—. Ward chmn. Polit. Action Com., 1977. Mem. NEA, Va., Arlington edn. assns., Am., Va. personnel and guidance assns., No. Va. Guidance Assn., Am. Sch. Counselors Assn., Delta Kappa Gamma. Democrat. Methodist. Home: 2924 S Grant St Arlington VA 22202 Office: 5800 Washington Blvd Arlington VA 22205

TRIBLE, PAUL SEWARD, JR., U.S. senator; b. Balt., Dec. 29, 1946; s. Paul Seward and Katherine (Schilpp) T.; B.A., Hampden-Sydney Coll., 1968; J.D., Washington and Lee U., Lexington, Va., 1971; m. Rosemary Dunaway; children—Mary Katherine, Paul Seward III. Admitted to Va. bar, 1971; law clk. to U.S. dist. judge Albert V. Bryan, Jr., 1971-72; asst. U.S. atty. Eastern Dist. Va., 1972-74; commonwealth's atty. Essex County, Va., 1974-76; mem. 95th-97th Congresses from 1st Va. dist.; U.S. senator from Va., 1982—. Bd. govs. St. Margaret's Sch., Tappahannock, Va.; trustee Hampden-Sydney Coll. Named Outstanding Young Man of Va., Jaycees, 1978. Republican. Episcopalian. Mem. Law Rev., Washington and Lee U. Office: 517 Hart Senate Office Bldg Washington DC 20510

TRICKEY, SAMUEL BALDWIN, physics educator, researcher; b. Detroit, Nov. 28, 1940; s. Samuel Miller and Betty Irene (Baldwin) T.; m. Lydia Hernandez Dec. 28, 1962 (div. June 1981); children—Matthew J., Phillip J.; m. 2d, Cynthia Karle, Aug. 13, 1983. B.A. in Physics, Rice U., 1962; M.S., Tex. A&M U., 1966, Ph.D. in Theoretical Physics, 1968. Research scientist Mason & Hanger-Silas Mason Corp., 1962-64; asst. prof. physics U. Fla., Gainesville, 1968-73, assoc. prof., 1973-77, prof. physics and chemistry, 1979—, dir. J.C. Slater Meml. Computing Facility, 1981—; prof. physics, chmn. physics and engring. physics Tex. Tech U., Lubbock, 1977-79; cons. Redstone Arsenal Ala., 1972-76; vis. research scholar Mich. Tech. U., 1982, 83, 84; vis. scientist IBM Research Ctr., San Jose, Calif., 1975-76; assoc. or dep. dir. Sanibel Symposia; cons. T div. Los Alamos Nat. Lab., 1984—. Exec. v.p. U. Fla. chpt. United Faculty of Fla., 1981-83. Named Tchr. of Yr., Coll. Arts and Scis., U. Fla., 1973-74. Fellow Am. Phys. Soc.; mem. Am. Assn. Physics Tchrs., S.W. R.R. Hist. Soc., Phi Kappa Phi, Sigma Xi, Sigma Pi Sigma. Democrat. Presbyterian. Contbr. articles to profl. jours. Home: 723 NW 19 St Gainesville FL 32603 Office: Quantum Theory Project Williamson Hall U Fla Gainesville FL 32611

TRIEN, STEPHEN ROY, telephone communications consultant; b. N.Y.C., Mar. 11, 1944; s. Irving H. and Frances E. (Weiner) T.; m. Gwendolyn O'Kelley, Mar. 26, 1977; 1 dau., Laura Frances. B.B.A., U. Miami, 1965. Owner, Trien & Assocs., North Miami, Fla., 1967—. Mem. Internat. Orgn. Women in Telecommunications, AIA (assoc.). Office: Trien & Assocs 1065 N E 125th St North Miami FL 33161

TRIMBLE, LUTHER GRADY, dentist; b. Formosa, Ark., Mar. 5, 1920; s. Luther Gordon and Delcenia (Gross) T.; m. Marjorie Imogene Lieblong, Dec. 18, 1945; children—Kathy Ann, Grady Ellis. Student U. Ark., 1939-40; D.D.S., Baylor U., 1949. Gen. practice dentistry, Ft. Smith, Ark., 1949-50, Little Rock, 1950-84. Served as 1st lt. U.S. Army, 1941-46, ETO. Decorated Bronze Star, 5 Battle Stars. Mem. ADA, Ark. State Dental Assn., Pulaski County Dental Soc. (pres. 1960), Pierre Fuchard Acad. (hon.). Baptist. Lodges: Shriners, Trinity, Lions Internat. Home: 8 Glenridge Rd Little Rock AR 72207

TRIPLETT, RUFUS MORGAN, banker; b. Nashville, Oct. 12, 1946; s. Marquis Jackson and Betty Jane (Bondurant) T.; m. Wilson Hunt, Oct. 27, 1972; 1 dau., Noel Elizabeth. B.S. cum laude, Tenn. Wesleyan Coll., 1968; postgrad. U. Wis., 1978. Adminstrv. asst. Am. Nat. Bank, Chattanooga, 1968, credit card officer, 1968-71, br. officer, 1971-72, asst. cashier, 1972-77, cashier, 1978-83. v.p., cashier, 1983—; instr. Am. Inst. Banking, Chattanooga, 1978—; mem. faculty Sch. Bank Adminstrn., U. Wis., Madison, 1979-82. Chmn. fin. com., trustee Tenn. Wesleyan Coll., Athens, 1975-83; treas., trustee The Sentor Sch., Chattanooga, 1983—; treas., bd. dirs. The Little Theatre, Inc., Chattanooga, 1975-81; pres. The Riverbend Festival, Chattanooga, 1984-85, past pres., 1986; mem. U. Tenn.-Chattanooga Sports Arena Use Com., 1980-84.

Recipient Miss Annie award The Little Theatre, Inc., Chattanooga, 1973. Methodist. Clubs: Downtown Kiwanis, Golf and Country (Chattanooga). Lodge: Masons. Home: 1614 Hillcrest Rd Chattanooga TN 37405 Office: Am Nat Bank and Trust Co 736 Market St Chattanooga TN 37401

TRIPLETT, WILLIAM GEORGE, insurance agency executive; b. South Charleston, W.Va., Feb. 15, 1921; s. General Francis and Vivian Ethel (Eastep) T.; student public schs., W.Va.; m. Donna Maxine Morgan, Mar. 11, 1944; children—James Francis, Robert Gary, Daniel Morgan, Richard Alan, John Quintin, Mark Fitzwilliam. Sales rep. Nat. Equipment Co. and Anchor Fixture Co., Inc., Charleston, W.Va., 1946-48; owner Tri-Ax-Land Co., Charleston, 1968—, Triplett Shores Agy., Charleston, 1960—, Triplett Enterprises, Charleston, 1977—; ins. agt. State Farm Ins. Cos., Bloomington, Ill., 1949—. Republican ward commr., Charleston, 1951-59; sec. Charleston Football Inc., 1980-82; v.p. Charleston Rockets Football, 1982-83. Served with USMC, 1942-45. Recipient State Farm Ins. Career Achievement Concept award, 1954-81. Mem. Charleston Life Underwriters Assn. Republican. Club: Masons (32 deg.). Home: 877 Sherwood Rd Charleston WV 25314 Office: 804 Kanawha Blvd Charleston WV 25301

TRIPP, PETER ALAN, artist, artistic environmental consultant; b. Miami, Fla., Nov. 2, 1947; s. Percival Arthur and Anne Laura (Dias) T. Cert. Ringling Sch. Art. Cert. interior designer. Furniture designer Mansfield Manor, Ltd., N.Y.C., 1972-74; actor, playwright Children's River Theatre, Vero Beach, Fla., 1977-79; fabric artist, designer Steven Shatz, MGS Designs, N.Y.C., 1979-81; exhibited in group shows at Ann. Ringling Sch. Art Exhibit, 1970-72, Fire Island Pines Art Show, 1970-75, Philip Daniel Showroom, N.Y.C., 1973, Interior Design Mag., 1973, Gindi Fine Jewels, N.Y.C., 1975-81, Bloomingdale's, N.Y.C., 1976, Bonwit-Teller, N.Y.C., 1975, Saks Fifth Ave., N.Y.C., 1976, Glamour Mag., 1977, Les Mouches nightclub, N.Y.C., Aureus Art Jewelry, Coral Gables, Fla., 1982, Gallery Los Olas, Ft. Lauderdale, Fla., 1983, Brenner Gallery, Boca Raton, Fla., 1983, Winthrop Gallery, Vero Beach, 1984-85; numerous painting commns.; artist numerous residences; executed numerous murals. Ringling Sch. Art scholar, 1971-72. Mem. Vero Beach Art Club. Republican. Avocation: reading. Home and Office: 1000 SW 27th Ave Lot 64 Vero Beach FL 32962

TRIPP, TIMOTHY GARLAND, school principal; b. Toledo, Dec. 27, 1948; s. Charles John and Dorothea Rodgers (Smith) T.; m. Priscilla Ann Moody, Feb. 4, 1970; 1 child, William Joseph. A.A., U. Fla., 1969; B.A., U. Central Fla., 1971; M.S., Fla. State U., 1978. Tchr., Taylor County Sch. Dist., Perry, Fla., 1971-78, prin., 1978-82, asst. prin., 1982-85, prin., 1985—; interviewer Taylor County Sch. Bd., Perry, 1984—, trainer, 1984—, negotiator, 1981. Co-chmn. arts and crafts Fla. Forest Festival, Perry, 1975; mem. choir 1st United Methodist Ch., Perry, 1971—. Recipient Golden Sch. award Fla. Dept. Edn., 1982. Mem. Fla. Assn. Sch. Adminstrs., Fla. Assn. Elem. Prins. Democrat. Lodge: Elks. Avocations: Model ship building; fishing; reading. Office: Gladys Morse Elm Sch 800 Ash St Perry FL 32347

TRITICO, FRANK EDWARD, historian, educational administrator; b. Houston, Aug. 1, 1930; s. Leonard Frank and Aletha Agnes (McBride) T.; B.A., U. St. Thomas, 1955; M.Ed., U. Houston, 1963; postgrad. U. Va., 1967, Columbia U., 1968; m. Marilyn Ann Stewart, Sept. 8, 1956 (dec.); Robert Blakey, Mark Douglas, Mary Lindsey, Frank Edward. Chmn. dept. Houston Ind. Sch. Dist., 1960-67; cons. Harris County (Tex.) Dept. Edn., Houston, 1967-71, dir. adult edn., 1968-70; dir. curriculum and instruction Katy (Tex.) Ind. Sch. Dist., 1971-79; guest lectr. Am. Petroleum Inst., U. Houston, 1962-76, Rice U., 1978, 79; adminstr. St. Charles Sch., 1982-84; chmn. Spanish Tex. Microfilm Center, 1975—, LaBahia Research Awards, 1975—. Mem. Tex. Civil War Centennial Commn., 1959-63; chmn. Harris County Hist. Commn., 1968—; commr. Battleship Tex., 1971-77, 84—; mem. Tex. Medal of Honor Grove Com., 1976; chmn. San Jacinto Battleground Hist. Adv. Bd., 1979-84. Bd. dirs. St. Thomas Found., 1975-83; bd. dirs. Morality in Media of Tex., 1976-82, mem. adv. bd., 1983—; mem. Battleship Tex. Hist. Adv. Bd., 1984—. Recipient Tex. Heritage Disting. Service medal, 1963; knight comdr. Knights of San Jacinto, 1963; Freedom Fellowship award, 1970; SAR Gold Good Citizenship medal, 1970; Alcalde de La Villita Hon. Mayor of San Antonio, 1971; Jefferson Davis award, 1973; DAR medal of Honor, 1973; William Paca award, 1975; Marianer Knight of Teutonic Order (Austria); papal knight, knight comdr. Equestrian Order of Holy Sepulchre of Jerusalem (Vatican); knight officer Order of Isabel la Catolica (Spain); George Washington Honor medal Freedoms Found., 1978; cert. of commendation Tex. Hist. Commn., 1965-79. Mem. Tex. State Tchrs. Assn., Nat., Tex. assns. supervision and curriculum devel., Am., Tex. assns. sch. adminstrs., Katy Edn. Assn. (pres.), Tex. State Hist. Assn. (life), Am. Assn. State and Local History, Harris County Heritage Soc., Philos. Soc. Tex., Tex. Hist. Found. (dir. 1979-86), Granaderos de Galvez (gov. gen. nat. soc. 1983-85). Roman Catholic. Author: (with E.M. Carrington) Women in Early Texas, 1975; editorial bd. Heraldry, 1976-79; contbr. articles to profl. jours. Home: 11931 Kimberley Ln Houston TX 77024

TRIVEDI, MANMOHAN MANUBHAI, electrical, computer engineering educator; b. Wardha, India, Oct. 4, 1953; s. Manubhai J. and Tanuben M. (Trivedi) T.; m. Nayana N. Mehta, Aug. 22, 1982. B.Engring. with honors, Birla Inst. Tech. and Sci., 1974; M.Engring., Utah State U., 1976, Ph.D., 1979. Teaching, research asst. Space Dynamics Lab., Utah State U., Logan, 1975-79; assoc. prof. elec., computer engring. La. State U., Baton Rouge, 1979—; co-chmn. Applications Artificial Intelligence, 1985, 86. Assoc. editor; Jour. Approximate Reasoning. Univ. research scholar Utah State U., 1976. Mem. IEEE, Am. Soc. Photogrammetry and Remote Sensing, Am. Assn. Artificial Intelligence, Pattern Recognition Soc., Internat. Soc. Optical Engring., Sigma Xi, Phi Kappa Phi, Tau Beta Pi. Guest editor Optical Engring. Jour. Contbr. articles in remote sensing, image analysis and computer vision to profl. jours. Home: 327 McDonald Ave Baton Rouge LA 70808 Office: Dept Elec and Computer Engring La State Univ Baton Rouge LA 70803

TRIVETTE, WILLIAM LOYD, JR., educational administrator; b. Winston-Salem, N.C., Mar. 8, 1955; s. William Loyd and Gladys Jewel (Pearson) T.; m. Sandra Jane Thomas, Apr. 7, 1979; children—Stephen Albert, David Ross. B.S., East Tenn. State U., 1978, M.A., 1982. Tchr., Elizabethton City Schs., Tenn., 1978-80; dean students Elizabethton High Sch., 1980-81; asst. prin. T.A. Dugger Middle Sch., Elizabethton, 1981-84, prin., 1985—. Composer hist. ballads. Deacon, Meml. Presbyterian Ch. Mem. Prins.' Study Council, Nat. Trust for Historic Preservation, Broadcast Music, Tenn. Assn. for Sch. Supervision and Adminstrn. Presbyterian. Avocation: botany; guitar music.

TROGDON, DEWEY LEONARD, JR., textile company executive; b. Summerfield, N.C., Feb. 17, 1932; s. Dewey Leonard and Ethel (Miller) T.; A.B. in Econs., Guilford Coll., Greensboro, N.C., 1958; postgrad. U. N.C., 1967-68, U. Va., 1970, Advanced Mgmt. Program, Harvard U., 1978; m. Barbara Jean Ayers, Sept. 10, 1955; children—Mark, Leonard. With Cone Mills Corp., Greensboro, 1958—, staff asst. to chief exec. officer, 1970-74, pres. Otto B. May, subs. co., 1974-78, v.p. Cone Mills Mktg. Co., 1977-78, exec. v.p. Cone Mills Corp., 1978, pres., from 1979, chief exec. officer, 1980—, chmn., 1981—; mem. Midtown adv. bd. Chem. Bank. Served with USNR, 1949-53. Mem. Am. Textile Mfrs. Inst. (1st v.p.), N.C. Textile Mfrs. Assn. (dir.). Methodist. Office: Cone Mills Corp 1201 Maple St Greensboro NC 27405

TROOST, BRADLEY TODD, physician, educator; b. Mankato, Minn., July 5, 1937; s. Henry Bradley and Elizabeth (Todd) T.; m. Elizabeth Gail Godet, Apr. 17, 1976; children—Elizabeth Claire, Laurie Anne. B.S. with honors in Biophysics, Yale U., 1959; M.D., Harvard U., 1963. Diplomate Am. Bd. Psychiatry and Neurology. Intern, Colo. Gen. Hosp., Denver, 1963-64; resident in neurology U. Colo., Denver, 1966-69; NIH fellow in neuro-ophthalmology U. Calif.-San Francisco, 1969-70; asst. prof. U. Miami (Fla.), 1970-76; assoc. prof. U. Pitts., 1976-80; prof. Case Western Res. U., Cleve., 1980-83; prof., chmn. dept. neurology Bowman Gray Sch. Medicine, Winston-Salem, N.C., 1983—; chief dept. neurology VA med. ctrs., Pitts., Cleve. Bd. dirs. Greater Miami Epilepsy Found., 1973-76. Served to capt. U.S. Army, 1964-66. Fellow Am. Acad. Neurology; mem. Am. Neurol. Assn., Barany Soc. Republican. Episcopalian. Contbr. numerous articles to profl. publs.

TROPP, HARRY ERNEST, science author, educator; b. St. Louis, Dec. 27, 1912; s. Solomon and Masha (Levin) T.; m. Muriel Liebmann, Nov. 7, 1943; 1 child, Robert Alan. B.S., St. Louis U., 1935; M.S., Vanderbilt U., 1936; postgrad. U. Ill., 1937, U. Fla., 1962, Yale U., 1959-60. Postgrad. cert. in edn. supervision and adminstrn. Prof. physics Buena Vista Coll., Storm Lake, Iowa, 1936-38, dean of men, 1937-38; with dept. hydrology U.S. Engrs. Office, Little Rock, 1939-41; instr. physics Hillsborough County Pub. Schs., Tampa, Fla., 1949-58, supr. sci., 1958-77; sci. textbook author Holt, Rinehart & Winston, N.Y.C., 1958—; dir. Fla. State Sci. Fair and Talent Search, Fla. Found. of Future Scientists, Tampa, 1963. Author: (with George R. Tracy and Alfred Friedl) Modern Physical Science, 7 edits., 1958—. Chmn. radiol. monitoring sect. Hillsborough County Civil Def., 1952-57; v.p. Tampa chpt. Res. Officers Assn., 1956-57. Served to lt. col. Signal Corps U.S. Army 1941-46; Europe. Teaching fellow in physics Vanderbilt U., 1935-36; recipient Most Valuable Sci. Educator award Fla. Assn. Sci. Tchrs., 1977. Mem. Fla. Assn. Sci. Suprs. (pres. 1964), Nat. Sci. Tchrs. Assn., Ret. Officers Assn. Democrat. Jewish. Lodge: Rotary (bd. dirs. Tampa 1968-70). Avocations: world travel. Home and Office: 4141 Bayshore Blvd #603 Tampa FL 33611

TROTTER, SHIRLEY ANN, computer specialist, author; b. Oklahoma City, Nov. 30, 1934; d. Charles George and Bessie Lee (Armstrong) Huber; B.S. in Bus. Edn., Oklahoma City U., 1961, M.A. in Teaching Math., 1973; m. George Monroe Hilton Trotter, Jr., Oct. 11, 1980; children—Darrell Lynn, Darren Lee Smith; stepchildren—David, Paige. Tchr. math. and bus., Putnam City Schs., 1961, 69-79; adminstrv. asst. Nat. Assn. Mature People, Oklahoma City, 1979; instr. FAA, Oklahoma City, 1980-81; co-founder, pres. DocuWrite, Inc., Bethany, Okla., 1981-83; sr. CBT analyst First Data Mgmt. Co., Oklahoma City, 1981-83; mgr. interactive product devel. Advanced Systems, Inc., Arlington Heights, Ill., 1983-84; sr. mem. tech. staff Computer Data Systems, Inc., 1984-85; supervisory programmer/analyst Office of Naval Research, Arlington, Va., 1985; co-founder, pres. Info. Resource Mgmt., Inc., Alexandria, Va., 1985—. Mem. alumni bd. Oklahoma City U., 1963-64. Mem. Assn. Devel. Computer-Based Instructional Systems, Balt.-Washington Info. Systems Edn., Soc. for Applied Learning Tech., Nat. Soc. for Programmed Learning Instrn., Mensa, Beta Gamma. Democrat. Mem. Christian Ch. (Disciples of Christ). Home: 309 Yoakum Pkwy 408 Alexandria VA 22304 US Army Services and Tng Directorate Falls Church VA

TROUBLEFIELD, WILLIAM EDWARD, JR., educational administrator; b. Hickory, N.C., Jan. 28, 1947; s. William Edward and Margaret (Elliott) T.; m. Trudy Benbow, June 11, 1967; children—Kimberly Ann, William Craig. B.S. in Banking, Fin., Ins. and Real Estate, U. S.C., 1969, M.Acctg., 1978. Office mgr. phys. plant div. U. S.C., Columbia, 1969-71, asst. budget dir., 1971-78, dir. budget and systems, 1978-79; v.p. bus. and adminstrn. Lander Coll., Greenwood, S.C., 1979—. Mem. United Way, Greenwood, 1981-83. Mem. Greenwood C. of C. (chmn. econ. devel. com. 1983-84, mem. bus. and indsl. devel. com. 1984—), Nat. Assn. Coll. and Univ. Bus. Officers, So. Assn. Coll. and Univ. Bus. Officers. Methodist. Lodge: Rotary (bd. dirs. 1984—). Avocations: tennis, woodworking. Home: 115 Kennedy Ct Greenwood SC 29646 Office: Lander Coll Stanley Ave Greenwood SC 29646

TROUSE, ALBERT CHARLES, JR., soil scientist, consultant; b. Hanford, Calif., May 19, 1921; s. Alfred Charles and Mary Catherine (Jungers) T.; m. Lois Katherine Hull, June 24, 1947; children—Albert Charles III, James M., Frederic E., David R. B.S., U. Calif.-Berkeley, 1943; M.S., U. Calif.-Davis, 1948; Ph.D., U. Hawaii, Honolulu, 1963. Soil scientist USDA, Nevada, Calif., Hawaii, 1946-51; agronomist Hawaii Sugar Planters, Honolulu, 1951-63; soil scientist USDA, Auburn, Ala., 1964-83; pres. Tilth Internat., Auburn, 1982—; collaborator Nat. Tillage Machinery Lab., Auburn, 1983—; cons. Ford Found., Nigeria, 1973, 1977, Devel. Alternatives U.S. AID, Cairo, Egypt, 1983, Weyerhauser Lumber, Peabody Ind., Ill., Ohio, 1983-85. Contbr. chpts. to books on soil. Producer-dir. movie Bottom of the Wheel, 1972. Served to maj. USMCR, 1943-46. Recipient nat. award Soil Conservation Service, Yerington, Nev., 1949, Western Region award, 1949. Mem. Internat. Soil Tillage Research Orgn. Lodge: Kiwanis (Auburn, Ala.). Avocations: study of history and development of foods of early man. Home: 275 Oak St Auburn AL 36830 Office: Tilth Internat. PO Box 449 Auburn AL 36830

TROUT, MARGIE MARIE MUELLER, civic worker; b. Wellston, Mo., Apr. 27, 1923; d. Albert Sylvester and Pearl Elizabeth (Jose) Mueller; student Webster Coll., 1944-45; cert. genealogist Bd. Cert. Genealogy; m. Maurice Elmore Trout, Aug. 24, 1943; children—Richard Willis, Babette Yvonne. Sec. offices Robertson Aircraft Corp., St. Louis, 1942; speed lathe and drill press operator Busch-Selzer Diesel Engine Co., St. Louis, 1942-43; Cub Scout den mother, Vienna, Austria, 1953-55, Mt. Pleasant, Mich., 1955, London, 1956-57; leader Nat. Capitol council Girl Scouts U.S.A., Bethesda, Md., 1963-65; co-chmn. Am. Booth YWCA and Red Cross Annual Bazaars, Bangkok, Thailand, 1970-72; worker ARC, Vientiane, Laos, 1959-60, Bangkok, 1970-72; activities co-chmn., exec. bd. mem. Women's Club Armed Forces Staff Coll., Norfolk, Va., 1975-77; mem. Am. Women's Clubs, Embassy Clubs, Internat. Women's Clubs Vienna, 1952-55, London, 1956-59, Vientiane, 1959-61, Bangkok, 1969-72, Munich, Germany, 1965-69, Norfolk, 1975-77. Crochet articles exhibited Exhibition of Works of Art by the Corps Diplomatique, London, Eng., 1958. Home: 6203 Hardy Dr McLean VA 22101

TROUT, WILLIAM EDGAR, III, geneticist, historic canal consultant, writer; b. Staunton, Va., Apr. 21, 1937; s. William Edgar and Harriet Creighton (McCurley) T.; B.S., U. Richmond, 1959; A.M., Ind. U., 1964, Ph.D., 1965. Research fellow in radiation genetics biology div. Oak Ridge Nat. Lab., 1965-66; research scientist biology City of Hope Med. Ctr., Duarte, Calif., 1966-82; v.p. Am. Canal Soc., Inc., 1972-85, pres., 1985—; pres. Va. Canals and Navigations Soc., Richmond, 1982-84; editor The Am. Canal Guide. Mem. AAAS, Genetics Soc. Am., Behavior Genetics Assn. Address: 35 Towana Rd Richmond VA 23226

TROUTMAN, GEORGE WILLIAM, consulting firm executive, geological consultant; b. Brandenburg, Ky., Aug. 8, 1949; s. George I. and Ellen G. (Parker) T.; m. Marcia Lyn Roseman, Aug. 14, 1971; children—Nancy, Anthony, Janet, David, Barbara, Jonathan. Student Murray State U., 1967-68; B.S. in Geology, Western Ky. U., 1974. Geophys. engr. Birdwell div. Seismograph Service Corp., Ohio, Pa., W.Va., 1974-77; geologist Consolidated Natural Gas, Clarksburg, W.Va., 1977-79; exploration geologist Mountain Fuel Supply Corp., Denver, 1979-80; regional exploration geologist Al-Aquitaine Exploration, Ltd., Denver, 1980-81; sr. staff geologist Resources Investment Corp., Denver, 1981-82; geol. mgr. Petro-Lewis Corp., MCR, Oklahoma City, 1982-84; pres., geologist Troutman Geol., Inc., Oklahoma City, 1984—; geol. adviser SITCO, Inc., Oklahoma City, 1984—. Served with USN, 1968-70. Mem. Am. Assn. Petroleum Geologists (cert.), Soc. Profl. Well Log Analysts, Oklahoma City Geol. Soc., Kans. Geol. Soc., Rocky Mountain Assn. Geologists (mem. govtl. action com. 1981). Republican. Mem. Ch. of Jesus Christ of Latter-day Saints. Home: 4406 Karen Dr Edmond OK 73034 Office: Troutman Geol Inc 4406 Karen Dr Edmond OK 73034

TROUTMAN, GERALD STEVENSON, bishop; b. Andrews, N.C., Dec. 16, 1933; s. Edwin Flavious and Estelle (Brown) T.; m. Marihope Shirey, Aug. 19, 1959; children—Steven, Lee Frances. A.B., Lenoir Rhyne Coll., 1956; M.Div., Luth. Theol. So. Sem., 1960; D.D., Newberry Coll., 1976. Ordained to ministry Luth. Ch. in Am., 1960. Pastor Reformation Luth. Ch., Greeneville, Tenn., 1960-63, St. John's Luth. Ch., Atlanta, 1963-69; sec. Southeastern Synod. Luth. Ch. in Am., Atlanta, 1969-75, pres. Southeastern Synod., 1975—, Southeastern synodical bishop, 1980—; chaplain Greenville Fire Dept., 1960-63. Bd. dirs. Druid Hills Civic Assn., 1965-68, Lutheridge Assembly, Arden, N.C., 1962-69; trustee Luth. Theol. So. Sem., Newberry Coll., Williams-Henson Luth. Home for Children, Luthridge Assembly, 1975—. Mem. Ga. Interch. Assn. (dir. 1972—), Atlanta Luth. Ministerial Assn. (pres. 1967-68). Club: Druid Hills Golf. Office: Luth Ch in Am 756 W Peachtree St NW Atlanta GA 30308*

TROWBRIDGE, CYRUS PFEIFFER, judge; b. Ottawa, Ill., Aug. 24, 1928; s. Cyrus Pomeroy and Doris (Merner) T.; m. Doris Bittinger, Apr. 4, 1953 (div. Apr. 1974); children—Teri, Leslie, Ashley, Allison, Christian; m. Patricia Winford, Apr. 7, 1974. B.A., Denison U., 1950; J.D., U. Va., 1953. Bar: Va. 1952, Fla. 1956. Sole practice, Stuart, Fla., 1956-60; circuit judge 19 Jud. Circuit of Fla., Stuart, 1960—, chief judge, 1977—. Editor-in-chief, Vol. 38, Va. Law Rev., 1952-53. Contbr. articles to profl. jours. and books. Lt. col. CAP; flotilla comdr. U.S. Coast Guard Aux. Served with U.S. Army, 1953-56. Mem. Va. State Bar Assn., Fla. State Bar, Scribes, Mensa, Order of Coif. Congregationalist. Clubs: Quiet Birdmen, Intertel. Lodge: Rotary of India-Lucie (charter pres.). Office: PO Box 445 Stuart FL 33495

TRUAX, DENNIS DALE, civil engineering educator, consultant; b. Hagerstown, Md., July 25, 1953; s. Bernard James and Dorothy Hilda T.; m. Jeanie Ann Knable, Aug. 20, 1977. B.S. in Civil Engring., Va. Poly. Inst. and State U., 1976; M.S., Miss. State U., 1978, Ph.D., 1985. Registered profl. engr., Miss. Asst. dep. constrn. mgr. Fairfax County, Va., 1972-74; design engr., Washington County, Md., 1976; instr. Miss. State U., Starkville, 1980-81, asst. prof. civil engring., 1981—; cons. and expert witness environ. engring. and constrn. Lay leader Aldersgate United Meth. Ch., Starkville, 1982-85, chmn. pastor/parish relations, 1985-86, chmn. council on ministries, 1986—; adviser Triangle Fraternity, Starkville; bd. dirs. Meth. Student Ctr., Miss. State U., 1983—, chmn. pastor/parish relations, 1984-86, v.p. bd., 1986. Named Outstanding Young Man Am., U.S. Jaycees, 1983. Mem. ASCE, Am. Water Works Assn., Miss. Acad. Sci., Miss. Engring. Soc. (bd. dirs., v.p., pres. Tombigbee chpt.), Nat. Soc. Profl. Engrs., Water Pollution Control Fedn., Sigma Xi, Tau Beta Pi, Chi Epsilon. Democrat. Contbr. engring. articles to profl. jours. Home: 108 Dogwood Dr Starkville MS 39759 Office: Miss State U PO Drawer CE Mississippi State MS 39762

TRUCKS, LOUIS BARCLAY, industrial engineering consultant, educator; b. Birmingham, Ala., June 14, 1916; s. James F. and Janet (Nett) T.; m. Elizabeth Jordan, June 28, 1941; children—Louise, Annette, Mary Jane. B.S. in Indsl. Engring., Auburn U., 1939; M.S. in Indsl. Engring., U. Pitts., 1951; Ph.D. in Indsl. Engring., Okla. State U., 1974. Registered profl. engr., Ala., Pa.; cert. safety profl. Engr., gen. foreman Westinghouse Electric Group, Pitts. and S.C., 1940-64; assoc. prof. Auburn U., Ala., 1964-82, adj. prof., 1982—; cons., Auburn, 1978—. Served to major U.S. Army, 1941-46, ETO. Mem. Inst. Indsl. Engrs. (pres.), Am. Soc. Safety Engrs. (chmn. Auburn-Montgomery chpt. 1983-84; named Safety Profl. of Yr. Ala. chpt. 1983-84), Human Factors Soc., Alpha Pi Mu, Saugatchee C. of C. Republican. Baptist. Lodge: Lions (pres.). Avocations: old cars; building doll houses. Home: 875 Cherokee Rd Auburn AL 36830 Office: Auburn Univ Industrial Engring Dept Auburn AL 36849

TRUDNAK, STEPHEN JOSEPH, landscape architect; b. Nanticoke, Pa., Feb. 25, 1947; s. Stephen Adam and Marcella (Levulis) T.; B.S. in Landscape Arch., Pa. State U., 1970; m. Arden Batchelder Weill, Sept. 6, 1980. Jr. landscape architect Kling Partnership, Phila., 1970-72; landscape architect firm Keith French Assocs., Washington, 1972-73; head dept. landscape architecture Linganore Center Design, Frederick, Md., 1973-74; head dept. landscape architecture Toups and Loiederman, Rockville, Md., 1974-76; project landscape architect Dade County Transit Improvement Program, Kaiser Transit Group, So. Calif. Rapid Transit Dist., Metro Rail Transit Cons.; v.p. Harry Weese & Assocs., Ltd., Miami, Fla., 1976-84; prin Trudnak & Assocs.; v.p. landscape architecture Canin Assocs., Orlando, Fla., 1984—. Mem. Am. Soc. Landscape Architects (pres. Fla. chpt. 1983, chpt. adv. bd. 1984-85), Nat. Speleol. Soc. SCARAB. Home: 224 Clemens Ct Orlando FL 32826 Office: 500 Delaney Ave Suite 404 Orlando FL 32801

TRUE, CHARLES WESLEY, JR., agriculturalist; b. Bishop, Tex., July 26, 1916; s. Charles Wesley and Allye Vera (Hines) T.; B.S. in Agrl. Edn. and Agrl. Sci., Tex. Coll. Arts and Industries, 1941; m. Ruth Oleta Hulen Smith, May 2, 1970; children by previous marriage—Martha Ann True Lehne Strunk, Charles Wesley. Agr./sci. tchr., Lolita, Tex., 1941; farm loan officer U.S. Dept. Agr., Groveton, Tex., 1942, soil and water conservationist, Benavides, Tex., 1944-52; trace element fertilizer promoter Umbaugh Fertilizer Co., Miss. Delta, 1953; range conservationist U.S. Dept. Agr., Alice, Tex., 1954; agrl. scientist S.W. Research Center, San Antonio, 1954-66; chief natural resources U.S. Army Air Def. Center and Ft. Bliss, Tex., 1966-80; self-employed editor, pub. family history and genealogies, El Paso, 1981—; cons. Sec.-treas., Rio Bravo Turf and Golf Course Supts. Assn., 1968—; bd. dirs. Beautify El Paso Assn., 1967-81, pres., 1977; mem. hort. program adv. com. El Paso Community Coll., 1981, instr., 1983; mem. vocat. adv. council, El Paso Ind. Sch. Dist., 1976—. Served with U.S. Army, 1945-46. Recipient U.S. Dept. Def. Natural Resources Conservation citation for meritorious achievement, 1975; spl. award for exceptional service Rio Bravo Turf and Golf Course Supts. Assn., 1975, 85; commendation for sustained superior performance U.S. Dept. Army, 1978; Alumni Silver Spur award Tex. A&I U., 1982. Mem. Am. Soc. Agronomy, Crop Sci. Soc. Am., Council Agrl. Sci. and Tech., Nat. Wildlife Fedn., Soc. Am. Mil. Engrs. (sec. El Paso chpt. 1972-77), SAR (pres. El Paso chpt. 1983), Am. Assn. Ret. Persons, Assn. Old Crows. Methodist. Club: El Paso Knife and Fork. Contbr. articles to profl. jours.; editor, pub.: True Family History, 1981; Family of True Genealogy, 1984. Address: 9324 McFall St El Paso TX 79925

TRUETT, BOB, zoo ofcl.; b. Jacksonville, Tex., July 17, 1932; s. Robert E. and Katherine (Sheets) T.; m. Lisa Vila Wys, July 14, 1956; children—Marietta, Bob. B.S. in Zoology, U. Ark., 1955. Animal keeper Cin. Zoo, 1957; zoologist Lincoln Park Zoo, Chgo., 1957-60; dir. Birmingham (Ala.) Zoo, 1960—. Appeared on TV and radio shows.; Actor in community theaters, Town and Gown, 1962-80, Center Players, 1963-72, Birmingham Festival Theater, 1972-77; Contbr. articles to mags. Served with U.S. Army, 1955-57. Fellow Am. Assn. Zool. Parks and Aquariums (profl. fellow); mem. Phi Beta Kappa. Clubs: Am. Sunbathing Assn., Gymno Vita Park (founder, owner). Home and office: 2630 Cahaba Rd Birmingham AL 35223

TRUETT, CASEY, physician; b. Gatesville, Tex., Sept. 26, 1944; s. Herbert Winters and Gladys (Reed) T.; student U. Ala., 1962-63; B.S. with honors, U. Okla., 1965, M.D., 1969; m. Lisa A. Truett, Jan. 20, 1979; children—Melinda Katherine, Amy Elisabeth. Intern, St. Francis Hosp., Tulsa, 1969-70; practice medicine, Norman, Okla., 1972-79, Tulsa, 1979—; cons. MEDCOM, N.Y.C., 1974-76; asso. clin. prof. dept. family practice and community medicine and dentistry U. Okla. Coll. Medicine, 1975-79; med. examiner Cleveland County (Okla.), 1973; asst. prof. Oral Roberts U. Sch. Medicine, 1979-81; dir. Emergency Room, City of Faith Hosp., 1983-84, dir. employee health service, 1983-84; physician Prucare of Tulsa, 1984-85; pres. Casey Truett, M.D., Inc. Chmn. Okla. Med. Polit. Action Com., 1976-77; bd. dirs. Norman C. of C., 1975-77, Norman Christian Fellowship, 1978, Norman Alcohol Info. Center, 1978-79; mem. health occupations adv. com. Moore/Norman Vocat.-Tech. Sch.; mem. Norman Mayor's Task Force, 1974; mem. Republican State Com., 1973-75; chmn. worship task force Tulsa Christian Fellowship, 1983; bd. dirs. Campfire Girls, Norman, 1974-75. Served with USPHS, 1970-72. Recipient Kiwanis Spl. award, Tahlequah, Okla., 1972; elected as Eagle Scout, 1958, to Student AMA Com. on Med. Edn., 1968; USPHS grantee, 1966-67; diplomate Am. Bd. Family Practice. Fellow Am. Acad. Family Practice; mem. Okla. Med. Assn. (trustee 1974-77), So. Med. Assn., Okla. Acad. Family Practice, Am. Coll. Emergency Physicians, Cleveland McClain County Med. Soc. (pres. 1979), Tulsa County Med. Soc. (alt. del., council on pub. relations 1982-84), Royal Soc. Medicine (London) (affiliate), U. Okla. Alumni Assn. Republican. Club: Kiwanis. Home: 8001 S Quebec Ave Tulsa OK 74136 Office: Med Care Assocs Tulsa 3218 S 79th East Ave Tulsa OK 74145

TRUMBLY, WILLIAM DALE, geologist; b. Osage County, Okla., Sept. 27, 1921; s. Oliver William and Mary Frances (Cornett) T.; m. Earlene Elizabeth Cox, Dec. 31, 1945; children—William D., Mary Adair Trumbly Brown, Toya Trumbly Thomas, James E., Nancy I. B.S. in Mil. Sci. and Tactics, Okla. State U., 1943; B.S. in Geology, U. Okla., 1947. Geologist, Tex. Pacific Coal & Oil Co., Midland, 1947-51, Republic Natural Gas Co., Midland and Oklahoma City, 1952-62; assoc. geologist Mobil Oil Corp., Oklahoma City, 1962-69; regional geologist Royal Resources Corp., Oklahoma City, 1969-70; chief geologist Vanderbilt Resources Corp., Oklahoma City, Dallas, 1970-73; pres., owner Trumbly Petroleum Cons., Inc., Dallas, 1973—. Served to 1st lt. AUS, 1943-45. Decorated Bronze Star, Purple Heart with Cluster. Mem. Soc. Ind. Profl. Earth Scientists, Am. Assn. Petroleum Geologists (ho. of dels. 1970-72, 77-80, ins. com. 1977-78), Oklahoma City Geol. Soc. (exec. com. 1965-69, pres. 1968-69), Dallas Geol. Soc. (pres. 1982-83), W. Tex. Geol. Soc. Roman Catholic. Club: Energy (charter) (Dallas). Contbr. articles to profl. jours.

TRUNDLE, W(INFIELD) SCOTT, newspaper executive; b. Maryville, Tenn., Mar. 24, 1939; s. Winfield Scott and Alice (Smith) T.; m. Diana Shanklin, Apr. 21, 1962; children—Stephen, Allison. B.A., Vanderbilt U., 1961, J.D., 1967. Bar: Tenn. bar 1967. Spl. agt. U.S. Secret Service, 1963-66; asso. to partner firm Hunter, Smith, Davis & Norris, Kingsport, Tenn., 1967-72; pub. Kingsport (Tenn.) Times-News, 1972-78; pres. Greensboro (N.C.) Daily News, 1978-80; exec. v.p. Jefferson Pilot Publs., Inc., Greensboro and Clearwater, Fla., 1980-82; v.p., bus. mgr. Tampa Tribune (Fla.), 1982—; assoc. prof. E. Tenn. State U., 1973-77. Bd. dirs. Tampa United Way, Tampa Prep. Sch., Better Bus. Bur. Mem. Tenn. Bar Assn., N.C. Bar Assn., Am. Newspaper Pubs. Assn., So. Newspaper Pub. Assn., ABA. Methodist. Club: Tampa Downtown Rotary. Office: Box 191 Tampa FL 33601*

TRUSDELL, MARY LOUISE CANTRELL, state educational administrator; b. Chandler, Okla., Oct. 24, 1921; d. George Herbert and Lois Elizabeth

(Bruce) Cantrell; m. Robert William Trusdell, Jan. 7, 1943; children—Timothy Lee, Laurence Michael. B.A., Ga. So. Coll., 1965; M.Ed., U. Va., 1974. Dir. spl. learning disabilities program Savannah Country Day Sch., Ga., 1960-65; learning disabilities tchr. Richmond pub. schs., Va., 1966-73; dir. New Community Sch., Richmond, 1974-75; dir. Fed. Learning Disabilities Project, Dept HEW, Middle Peninsula, Va., 1975-76; supr. programs for learning disabled Va. Dept. Edn., Richmond, 1976—; former bd. dirs. Learning Disabilities Council, Richmond; mem. adv. com. Learning Disabilities Research and Devel. Project, Woodrow Wilson Rehab. Ctr., Fisherville, Va., 1983—. Bd. dirs. Savannah Assn. Retarded Children, 1957-60, Meml. Guidance Clinic, Richmond, 1966-69. Named Tchr. of Yr., Learning Disabilities Ctr., Richmond, 1972. Mem. Assn. for Children and Adults with Learning Disabilities, Orton Dyslexia Soc. (pres. capital area br. 1968-70, nat. bd. dirs. 1970-72). Presbyterian. Avocations: camping; travel; theater; reading. Office: Va Dept Edn PO Box 6-Q Richmond VA 23216

TSCHINKEL, VICTORIA JEAN, state environmental official; b. Mt. Vernon, N.Y., Oct. 30, 1947; d. William Aaron and Edith (Meyerson) Nierenberg; m. Walter Rheinhardt Tschinkel, June 15, 1968. A.B. in Zoology, U. Calif.-Berkeley, 1968; postgrad. in Fortran programming Fla. State U., 1974, program in environ. policy and mgmt. Harvard U. Sch. Pub. Health, 1978. Biologist, librarian Tall Timbers Research Sta., Tallahassee, Fla., 1970-74; field insp. Trustees of the Internal, Improvement Trust Fund, Fla. Dept. Environ. Regulation, Tallahassee, 1974-76; environ. specialist Fla. Dept. Environ. Regulation, Tallahassee, 1976, asst. to sec., 1976-77, asst. sec., 1977-81, sec., 1981—; mem. energy research adv. bd. Dept. Energy, Washington, 1979—; mem. OTA-Adv. Panel Energy in City Bldgs., 1980-81; mem. adminstrs. toxic substances adv. com. EPA, Washington, 1982—; mem. adv. council Gas Research Inst., 1983—; mem. space applications bd. NRC, Washington, 1983—; bd. dirs. Environ. and Energy Inst., Washington, 1984—. Contbr. articles on environ. issues to various publs. Mem. community adv. bd. Ctr. for Profl. Devel., Tallahassee, 1983—. Mem. Am. Soc. Pub. Adminstrn. (North Fla. chpt., Pub. Adminstr. of Yr. 1984), Capital Women's Network. Office: Fla Dept Environ Regulation 2600 Blair Stone Rd Tallahassee FL 32301

TSCHOEPE, THOMAS, bishop; b. Pilot Point, Tex., Dec. 17, 1915; s. Louis and Catherine (Sloan) T.; student St. Thomas Sch. Pilot Point, 1930, Pontifical Coll. Josephinum, Worthington, Ohio, 1943. Ordained priest Roman Cath. Ch., 1943; asst. pastor in Ft. Worth, 1943-46, Sherman, Tex., 1946-48, Dallas, 1948-53; adminstr. St. Patrick Ch., Dallas, 1953-56; pastor St. Augustine Ch., Dallas, 1956-62, Sacred Heart Cathedral, Dallas, 1962-65; bishop of San Angelo, Tex., 1966-69, Dallas, 1969—. Address: PO Box 190507 Dallas TX 75219

TSIANTIS, LEONIDAS ANGELO, film librarian, historian, consultant; b. Columbia, S.C., Mar. 29, 1954; s. Angelo and Violet (Brethes) T. B.A. in Journalism, U. S.C.-Columbia, 1975. Account exec. Films Inc., Atlanta, 1975-76; teaching asst. U. S.C., Columbia, 1976-78; film librarian Films Inc., Atlanta, 1979—; research assoc. PBS Series Cinematic Eye, 1976-78, PBS program Caligari Legacy, 1983; guest lectr. Ga. State U., Atlanta, 1981; cons. Atlanta Jour.-Constitution, 1981—. Contbg. author: Dictionary of Literary Biography, 1984, St. James Press Film Project, 1984, World Film Directors, 1985. Mem. Omicron Delta Kappa. Greek Orthodox. Office: Films Inc 476 Plasamour Dr NE Atlanta GA 30324

TSUI, ANNE S., business educator; b. Shanghai, China, Sept. 4, 1948; came to U.S., 1970; m. Yueh Wang, May 31, 1975. A.A., Northcote Coll. Edn., Hong Kong, 1970; B.A., U. Minn.-Duluth, 1973; M.A., U. Minn.-Mpls., 1975; Ph.D., UCLA, 1981. Personnel specialist U. Minn. Hosps., Mpls., 1974-77; sr. personnel adminstr. Control Data, Mpls., 1977-79, personnel cons., 1979-81; asst. prof. bus. Duke U., Durham, N.C., 1981—. Contbr. articles to profl. jours. Recipient UCLA Grad. Sch. Mgmt. alumni award for acad. distinction, 1981, grad. fellow, 1978-81; Duke U. Research Council grantee, 1983-84; Office Naval Research grantee, 1983-84; Control Data grantee, 1981-84; Hewlett Packard fellow, 1980-81, others. Mem. Acad. Mgmt., Am. Psychol. Assn., Durham Triangle Personnel Assn., Am. Inst. Decision Scis. Democrat. Roman Catholic. Office: Fuqua Sch Bus Duke U Science Dr Durham NC 27706

TSUJI, KOHSUKE, geologist; b. Osaka, Japan, May 9, 1955; came to U.S. 1981; s. Naoki and Kanae Tsuji. B.S., U. Tokyo, 1978, M.S., 1980. Geologist, Idemitsu Oil Devel. Co., Tokyo 1980-81, Niigato, Japan, 1981, staff geologist, Denver, 1981-82, chief geologist, 1982-83, exploration mgr., Houston, 1983—. Mem. Japanese Assn. Petroleum Tech., Am. Assn. Petroleum Geologists. Office: Idemitsu Oil Exploration Corp 5051 Westheimer Suite 500 Houston TX 77056

TU, HO CHUNG, pediatrician-neonatologist; b. Viet-nam, Jan. 1, 1946; came to U.S., 1974; s. Ho Thuc Tu and Vo Thi Cang., m. Tran Hoang Lan; children—Ho Hoang Viet, Ho Viet Dung, Ho Dung Anh. M.D., Vietnam, 1971. Resident, Jamaica-Queen Gen. Hosp. (N.Y.), fellow in neonatology Jackson meml. Hosp./U. Miami (Fla.), 1979-81; dir. neonatology Mt. Sinai Med. Ctr., Miami, 1981—. Inventor exchange-transfusion machine. Vice chmn. Free Vietnamese League, Washington; chief exec. bd. Vietnamese-Am. Republican Heritage Council. Office: Pediatrics Dept Mount Sinai Med Ctr Miami FL 33140

TUCK, LESLIE ERNEST SIDNEY, aerospace company executive; b. Bedford, Eng., Apr. 22, 1928; s. Lester Ernest and Maud Alice (Webb) T.; m. Joan Frances Pinder; children—Roger, Paul, Simon. Student, de Havilland Aero. Tech. Sch., Hatfield, Eng., 1945-49. Sales exec. Bristol Siddeley Engines, Bristol, Eng., 1962-66; sales mgr. Hawker Siddeley Aviation, Hatfield, Eng., 1966-71, regional exec., Lima, Peru, 1971-75, exec. v.p., Washington, 1975-77, Brit. Aerospace, 1977-80, pres., chief exec. officer, 1980—; pres. DIAI, Washington, BJAC, Brit. Aerospace Services. Adv. council Washington Dulles Task Force, Washington. Decorated comdr. Order Brit. Empire. Fellow Royal Aero. Soc., Flight Safety Found. (gov.). Clubs: Wings (N.Y.); Internat., Aero. of Washington, Nat. Aviation.

TUCKER, ANNE WILKES, photographic historian and critic, lecturer; b. Baton Rouge, Oct. 18, 1945. A.A.S. in Photographic Illustration, Rochester Inst. Tech., 1968; B.A. in Art History, Randolph-Macon Woman's Coll.; M.F.A. in Photographic History, SUNY-Buffalo, 1972. Research asst. Internat. Mus. Photography at the George Eastman House, Rochester, N.Y., 1968-70; research assoc. Gernsheim Collection U. Tex., Austin, summers 1969, 79; curatorial intern (N.Y. State Council on the Art grant) dept. photography Mus. Modern Art, N.Y.C., 1970-71; photography cons. Creative Artists Pub. Service program, N.Y.C., 1971-72; vis. lectr. New Sch. for Social Research, Photography spring 1973; dir. photography lecture series Cooper Union Forum, N.Y.C., 1972-75; lectr. Cooper Union for the Advancement of Arts and Sci., N.Y., 1972-75; vis. lectr. Phila. Coll. Art, 1973-75; affiliate artist U. Houston, 1976-80; curator of photography Mus. Fine Arts, Houston, 1976—, also Gus and Lyndall Wortham curator, photographic historian and critic, lectr.; trustee Visual Studies Workshop, 1980—; visual arts panel The Houston Festival, 1981-83; adv. bd. Randolph-Macon Woman's Coll. Art Gallery, 1982-84. Author of books and catalogues: Walker Evans: Photographs, 1971; (with William C. Agee) The Target Collection of American Photography, 1977; Phot Notes and Filmfront, 1977; The Museum of Fine Arts, Houston: A Guide to the Collection, 1981; Unknown Territory: Photography by Ray K Metzker, 1957-83, 1984; Fifth Annual International Fine Art Photograpy Exposition, 1984. Editor: The Woman's Eye, 1973; The Anthony G. Cronin Memorial Collection, 1979; Susanne Bloom and Ed Hill (Manual), 1980; Target II: 5 American Photographers, 1981; Target III: In Sequence, 1982; (with Philip Bicohman) Robert Srank: New York to Nova Scotia, 1986; also articles to profl. jours. and mags. Director of numerous exhbns. and workshops; lecturer; mem. numerous juries and panels. Nat. Endowment Arts grantee, 1976; John Simon Guggenheim Meml. Found fellow, 1984. Mem. Soc. Photographic Edn. (nat. bd. dirs. 1976-80), sec., 1977-79), Coll. Art Assn., Art Table, Inc.

TUCKER, BOYCE LYNN, architect; b. Houston, Jan. 12, 1939; s. Gilliam Boyce and Steryl Valentine (George) T.; student Westmont Coll., 1957-58; B.S. in Arch., U. Houston, 1963; m. Penelope Flos Meier, June 9, 1961; children—Katherine Ann, Tamara Lynn. With Caudill Rowlett Scott, Houston, 1965-66, Lundgren & Maurer, Austin, Tex., 1966-67; partner Musemeche Tucker Davis, Houston, 1967-70; prin. Boyce Tucker, Inc., Houston and Marble Falls, Tex., 1970—; dir. Tech Design, Inc., GFG, Inc. Chmn. citizens com. Marble Falls Ind. Sch. Dist.; bd. dirs. Christ's Mission, Austin, 1968—, Lindale Assembly of God Ch., Houston, 1970-72; elder Central Christian Ch., Marble Falls, 1979-82; bd. dirs., v.p. Marble Falls Community Devel. Corp., 1979-81; mem. adv. bd. Am. Christian Trust, Washington, 1982—. Mem. AIA, Tex. Soc. Architects, Nat. Heritage Soc., Tex. Ind. Producers and Royalty Owners Assn., Katy Royalty Owners Assn. (pres.). Republican.

TUCKER, CHARLES RAY, metalworking company executive, sales and service engineer; b. Somerset, Ky., Jan. 18, 1950; s. Arthur William and Mildred Gladys (Taylor) T.; m. Charlotte Ann Wood, July 26, 1969; children—Shawn Dell, Ryan Scott. Student, U. Cin., 1968-70; grad. engring. program Cin. Milacron, 1970. Registered mech. engr., Ky., Miss. Asst. engring. lab mgr. Tecumseh Products Co., Somerset, Ky., 1971-76, engring. lab mgr., Tupelo, Miss., 1977-82; tech. sales mgr. Cin. Milacron, Grand Prairie, Tex., 1982-84; sales rep. E.F. Houghton & Co., Valley Forge, Pa., 1984—; lectr. in field. Named So. Div. Performer of Year E.F. Houghton & Co., 1985. Mem. Somerset-Pulaski County Jaycees (bd. dirs. 1976). Democrat. Baptist. Avocations: golf; fishing; hunting; travel.

TUCKER, DONALD HUGH, physician, educator; b. Greenville, N.C., June 2, 1934; s. Arden L. and Susan Corrine Tucker; m. Barbara Lane, June 25, 1955; children—Donald Hugh, Barbara Lynn, Susan Leigh, Michael Arden. M.D., Duke U., 1958, B.S. in Medicine, 1959. Diplomate Am. Bd. Internal Medicine, Am. Bd. Cardiovascular Disease. Intern dept. medicine Duke U., 1958-59; asst. resident in medicine N.Y. Hosp., 1959-60; fellow in cardiopulmonary disease dept. medicine Duke U., 1960-61, sr. resident, 1961-62; mem. staff Pitt County Meml. Hosp., Greenville, N.C., 1964—; practice medicine specializing in internal medicine and cardiology Quadrangle Internal Medicine, Greenville, N.C., 1964—; clin. assoc. prof. medicine East Carolina U. Med. Sch., 1978—; mem. regional adv. bd. Duke Hosp., 1982-87; Greenville dir. N.C. Nat. Bank. Past trustee Pitt County Meml. Hosp.; past bd. dirs. Shepard Meml. Library, Enstern Carolina Heart Assn.; pres. PTA. Served to lt. comdr. USN, 1962-64. Fellow Am. Coll. Cardiology, ACP; mem. Am. Soc. Internal Medicine, N.C. Soc. Internal Medicine (past bd. dirs.), N.C. Med. Soc., Pitt County Med. Soc. (past pres. 1977), Pitt County Duke U. Alumni Assn. (pres.), Sigma Xi. Republican. Methodist. Club: Noon Rotary. Contbr. articles to profl. jours.

TUCKER, FRANCIS MICHAEL, financial company executive; b. Washington, Nov. 22, 1947; s. Clyde Davis and Doris Eleanor (Mullen) T.; m. Mary Jessica McLoud, Dec. 30, 1966 (div. Dec. 1974); children—Joan Frances, Abigail Frances; m. Eleanor Irene Chiampa, Apr. 20, 1978. C.P.A. Corporate budget asst. Fed. Nat. Mortgage Assn., Washington, 1970-72, corp. acctg. mgr., 1972-78, sr. acctg. systems analyst, 1978-80, sr. fin. analyst, 1980-82, mgr. fin. analysis, 1982-83; v.p. fin. Criterion Fin. Corp., Dallas, 1983—. Mem. Am. Inst. C.P.A.s, Acctg. Research Found. Democrat. Roman Catholic. Office: Criterion Financial Corp 5055 Keller Springs Rd Suite 401 Dallas TX 75248

TUCKER, GARLAND SCOTT, III, investment banker; b. Raleigh, N.C., June 17, 1947; s. Garland Scott Jr. and Jean Smith (Barnes) T.; m. Greyson Conrad Shuff, Jan. 15, 1972; children—Greyson Carrington, Elizabeth Bradford. B.S. magna cum laude, Washington and Lee U., 1969; M.B.A., Harvard U., 1972. Vice-pres. Tucker Furniture Co., Wilson, N.C., 1972-76; corp. fin. assoc. Investment Corp. of Va., Norfolk, 1976-78; v.p., to pres., chief exec. officer Carolina Securities Corp., Raleigh, N.C., 1978—; mem. regional firms com. N.Y. Stock Exchange. Dir. Raleigh Rescue Mission, 1980-83; vestry Christ Episcopal Ch., Raleigh, 1981—. Mem. Carolina Securities Corp. (bd. dirs. 1979—), Securities Industry Assn. (bd. dirs. Mid-Atlantic region 1981-82, 84—, regional firms com. 1983—), Raleigh C. of C. (bd. dirs. 1984—), Newcomen Soc., Phi Beta Kappa. Republican. Clubs: Capital City (dir.), Carolina Country (Raleigh); Harvard of N.Y.C. Home: 2327 Lake Dr Raleigh NC 27609 Office: Carolina Securities Corp 127 W Hargett St Raleigh NC 27602

TUCKER, GEORGE GREGORY, government official; b. Gadsden, Ala., Sept. 30, 1952; s. James Russell and Ruby Estelle (Bellew) T.; m. Amelia Diane McCord, July 2, 1983. Asst. mgr. Transameric Fin., Gadsden, 1972-74; supr. mails U.S. Postal Service, Gadsden, 1977-79; postmaster, Steele, Ala., 1979-83, Fyffe, Ala., 1983-85, supt. postal ops., Albertville, Ala., 1984—. Editor The Alabamian, 1982. Coordinator Chocolloco council Boy Scouts Am., 1981. Mem. Nat. League Postmasters (exec. v.p. 1980), Nat. Assn. Postal Suprs. (pres. 1979), Fyffe Jaycees (external v.p. 1983). Baptist. Lodge: Masons. Avocation: work with youth athletic organizations. Home: Route 1 Box 71 Fyffe AL 35971 Office: US Postal Service 210 S Hambrick St Albertville AL 35950

TUCKER, JAMES FRANCIS, architect; b. Washington, Jan. 19, 1946; s. Eugene and Margaret (Garner) T.; divorced; 1 son, Matthew James. B.Arch., Va. Poly. Inst., 1969. Registered architect, Va., D.C., N.C. Architect, Albert P. Hinckley, Jr., AIA, Architect, Warrenton, Va., 1971-75; prin. James F. Tucker, AIA, Architect, Warrenton, 1975—. Served with U.S. Army, 1969-71. Mem. AIA (dir. No. Va. chpt. 1982, Design award 1980), Va. Soc. AIA (chmn. design awards 1983, 84). Home and Office: 28 Main St Warrenton VA 22186

TUCKER, KENNETH IRBY, JR., real estate executive, security and life safety consultant; b. Greenwood, Miss., Jan. 21, 1944; s. Kenneth I. and Gladys (York) T.; m. Patsy Carolyn Baker, Dec. 28, 1983. B.A., U. Miss., 1965; postgrad. in corp. security Cornell U., 1977, in polygraph Tex. A&M U., 1974. Cert. protection profl.; lic. real estate agt. Tex. Probation officer Dallas County, Tex., 1971-76; polygraph examiner Winn Dixie, Inc., Ft. Worth, 1974-76; chief investigator Tandy Corp., Ft. Worth, 1976-79; dir. security Wynne/Jackson, Dallas, 1979-82, v.p. ops., 1982—; guest lectr. U. Tex., Arlington, Tex. A&M U., Tarrant County Jr. Coll., Bldg. Owners and Mgrs. Assn., Inst. Real Estate Mgmt., 1979-83; bd. dirs. Internat. Council Shopping Ctr. Security, Dallas, 1982; advisor Office Emergency Preparedness, Dallas, 1980-81. Civilian mem. Chiefs High Rise Com. Dallas Fire Dept., 1980-81; telephone canvasser Dallas Fine Arts, 1982; pres. Am. Diabetes Assn., Dallas County, 1981-82; mem. Dallas Crime Com., Dallas County, 1983. Mem. Am. Soc. Indsl. Security (treas. North Tex. chpt. 1981), Am. Polygraph Assn., Dallas Assn. Dirs. of Security (pres. 1981), Dallas Crime Commn. Clubs: Rotary, Lions.

TUCKER, LARRY A., state senator; b. Fayette County, W.Va., Nov. 11, 1935; s. Thomas E. and Frances (Monday) T.; m. Jean Copeland, May 19, 1978; children—Gregory A., Pamela J., Larry A., Mark D., Gary W., Kelly; 1 stepson, Steven Copeland. Grad. W.Va. Inst. Tech. Mem. W.Va. Ho. of Dels., 1970-82, W.Va. Senate, 1982—, vice chmn. banking and ins. com. Trustee Summersville Meml. Hosp. (W.Va.); mem. adv. council, fund chmn. Buckskin council Boy Scouts Am.; bd. dirs. Summersville Little League. Served with U.S. Army. Mem. C. of C., Am. Legion, DAV. Democrat. Methodist. Lodges: Rotary, Masons, Shriners. Office: West Virginia Senate Charleston WV 25305*

TUCKER, PAUL WILLIAM, retired petroleum company executive; b. Liberty, Mo., Dec. 21, 1921; s. Nova William and Georgia May (Cuthbertson) T.; m. Beverly Caryl Livingston, June 2, 1943; children—Ann Caryl Tucker Worland, Linda Louise Tucker Smith. B.S., William Jewell Coll., 1942, LL.D. (hon.), 1968; M.S. in Chemistry, La. State U., 1944; Ph.D. (George Breon fellow 1946-48), U. Mo., 1948. Registered profl. engr., Okla. Chemist, spectroscopist Tenn. Eastman Corp., Oak Ridge, 1944-46; with Phillips Petroleum Co., 1948-85, mgr. internat. gas and gas liquids, Bartlesville, Okla., 1974-78, v.p. gas and gas liquids, 1979-80, v.p. gas and gas liquids group, 1980-85, ret., 1985. Recipient Disting. Service award N. Mex. Petroleum Industries Com., 1956. Fellow Inst. Petroleum (U.K.), Instn. Gas Engrs. (U.K.); mem. Nat. Soc. Profl. Engrs., Am. Chem. Soc., AAAS, Okla. Soc. Profl. Engrs., Sigma Xi, Phi Lambda Upsilon, Alpha Chi Sigma. Republican. Baptist. Clubs: American (London); Hillcrest Country (Bartlesville). Author articles in field. Home: 1533 Pecan Pl Bartlesville OK 74003 Office: 17 Phillips Bldg Bartlesville OK 74004

TUCKER, RICHARD DAVID, psychology educator; b. Richmond, Va., Feb. 7, 1927; s. Joseph and Alease (Hill) T.; B.A., Va. Union U., 1949; M.S., Va. State Coll., 1951; Ed.D., UCLA, 1964. Grad. asst. Va. State Coll., Petersvurg, Va., 1950-51; tchr. Randolph (Richmond, Va.) Sch., 1951-54, Luther Jackson High Sch., Merrifield, Va., 1954-59; faculty Summer Session, Hampton (Va.) Inst., 1962; asst. prof. Tuskegee (Ala.) Inst., 1964-65; prof. history Miss. Valley State Coll., Itta Bena, 1965-70; instr. psychology, econ., sociology Mary Holmes Coll., W. Point, Miss., 1970—, faculty senate pres., 1974-75, chmn. scholarship com., 1982-84; cons. Nat. Endowment for the Humanities, 1974-77; dir. acad. honors program Mary Holmes Coll., 1978—, advisor student newspaper, 1978—, dir. edn. and social sci. div., 1979—; adviser Sigma Phi Sigma Frat. Minority Student fellowship scholar, 1972-73. Mem. Mary Holmes Coll. Edn. Assn. (pres. 1975-76), Miss. Edn. Assn., NEA, Am. Hist. Soc., AAUP, Assn. for Supervision and Curriculum Devel., Phi Theta Kappa, Phi Delta Kappa, Alpha Phi Alpha, NAACP. Roman Catholic. Contbr. articles to profl. jours.; author booklets: The Psychology of Personality, 1977; Social Forces in Education, 1984. Home: Mary Holmes Coll West Point MS 39773 Office: PO Box 1257 Mary Holmes Coll West Point MS 39773

TUCKER, ROBERT EDWIN, JR., oil and gas exploration executive; b. San Antonio, June 24, 1938; s. Robert Edwin and Josephine Vance (Spencer) T.; m. Lucijane Strozier, Apr. 30, 1966; (div. 1977); children—Maria Vance, Lucy Lea; m. Anne Criswell Gregory, Nov. 16, 1979. Student U. Tex.-Austin, 1956-61. Landman Hunt Oil Co., Williston, N.D. and Midland, Tex.; ptnr. Tucker & Collins Oil Exploration, Midland, 1965-68, Tucker & Heath Oil Exploration, Midland, 1968-77, Tucker & Snyder Oil Exploration, Denver, 1977-79; pres., chmn. bd. West Bay Exploration Co., Midland and Traverse City, Mich. Republican. Episcopalian. Clubs: San Antonio Country, Argyle (San Antonio); Midland Country, Racquet (Midland); Traverse City Country. Office: 3000 N Garfield #165 Midland TX 79705

TUCKER, SALLY (SARAH ANN), art appraiser; b. Austin, Tex., Dec. 24, 1934; d. Jim and Lorena Leah (Kinsey) Tucker; m. Peter S. Solito, Aug. 31, 1978; 1 son, Keny Jim. B.A., U. St. Thomas, 1975; postgrad. S.W. Tex. State U., Ind. U. Ins. agt., Houston, 1952—; legal sec., 1960-70; real estate broker, owner Sally Tucker Investments, 1970—; fine arts appraiser, owner Tucker Appraisal Assocs., 1975—. Docent, Houston Mus. Fine Arts. Mem. Internat. Soc. Fine Arts Appraisers (charter), Internat. Soc. Appraisers (ethics com., chmn. dist. fine arts rev. com., pres. Houston chpt.), Mensa, Am. Soc. Appraisers (cert.), Phi Alpha Theta. Democrat. Methodist. Clubs: Houston, Riv-O-Lon Garden (pres. 1981). Home: 3219 Ella Lee Lane Houston TX 77019 Office: Tucker Appraisal Assocs Houston TX 77019

TUCKER, SAMUEL MAYBERRY, consulting electrical engineer; b. Merchantville, N.J., Apr. 7, 1925; s. Joseph R. and Anna (Stierlan) T.; m. Mary Jean Marshall Tucker, May 12, 1925; children—Joseph, Cherl Ann, Richard. B.A., Rutgers U., 1957; M.A., U. Pa., 1959, M.S. in Elec. Engring., 1965. Engr., engring. leader Communications Systems div. RCA, Camden, N.J., 1958-65; engring. mgr. Computer div., Palm Beach Gardens, Fla., 1965-67; cons. corp. systems Data Systems Analysts, Pensauken, N.J., 1967-69; engring. mgr. Computer div. RCA, Palm Beach Gardens, 1969-71, mem. corp. staff, N.Y.C., 1971-72; v.p. tech. Transystems Internat. div. Northwest Industries, Winchester, Mass., 1972-74, corp. staff parent co., Chgo., 1974-75; project mgr. N.Am. Philips, Brazil, 1975-78; pres. Comucomp Internat., Gulf Breeze, Fla., 1978—. Served with U.S. Maritime Service, 1942-45. Mem. Assn. Computing Machinery, IEEE. Home: 96 Bayridge Gulf Breeze FL 32561 Office: 115 Baybridge Gulf Breeze FL 32561

TUCKER, STANLEY COLE, cardiologist; b. Richmond, Va., Dec. 2, 1942; s. Harry Ellsworth and Marjorie Louise (McGhee) T.; m. Sandra Levy Townsend, June 25, 1966; children—Cole, Kendall, Townsend. B.S. in Chemistry, U. Richmond, 1965; M.D., U. Va., 1969. Diplomate Am. Bd. Internal Medicine. Intern, Med. Coll. Va., Richmond, 1970, resident in medicine, 1970-72, fellow in cardiology, 1972-74, instr. medicine, 1974—; cardiologist McGuire Clinic, Richmond, 1974—; pres. med. staff St. Luke's Hosp., 1984. Served to maj. USAR, 1971-82. Fellow Am. Coll. Cardiology, ACP; mem. Am. Heart Assn. (pres. Richmond Area chpt. 1983—). Club: Ruritan. Contbr. articles to med. jours.

TUCKER, STEPHEN GUYNN, data processing consultant; b. Atlanta, Aug. 14, 1946; s. Benton Aubry and Marion Lee (Haymore) T.; B.S. with honors in Bus. Edn., U. Ga., 1977; children—Adam, Amber, Carrie. Programmer, analyst Service Bur. Corp., Dallas, 1968-70; devel. programmer, analyst IBM, White Plains, N.Y., 1970-74, systems engr., Atlanta, 1974-77, systems engr., Jacksonville, Fla., 1977-80; mgr. systems programming Advanced Micro Devices Co., Sunnyvale, Calif., 1980-81; dir. data processing services Fla. Associated Services div. Am. Heritage Life Ins. Co., Jacksonville, 1981-82; owner Tucker Enterprises, data processing consulting firm, Jacksonville, 1982—. Served with USAF, 1969-70. Cert. in data processing Inst. Cert. Computer Profls., also cert. in computer programming (systems). Mem. Data Processing Mgmt. Assn., EDP Auditors Assn., Assn. Systems Mgmt. Home: 1600 Long Creek Dr Columbia SC 29210

TUCKER, THOMAS JAMES, banker; b. Atlanta, Sept. 5, 1929; s. Thomas Tudor and Carol (Govan) T.; m. Mary Ann Garland, Nov. 23, 1953. B.A. in Econs., U. of the South, 1952. Asst. sec. CIT Corp., 1957-72; pres., chief exec. officer Am. South Fin. Corp., Birmingham, Ala., 1972-82, chmn. of bd., 1982; exec. v.p. Am. South Bancorp., Birmingham, 1982—, AmSouth Bank N.A., Birmingham, 1983—; dir. AmSouth Fin. Corp., AmSouth Mortgage Corp., Alabanc Properties Inc., Birmingham. Contbr. articles to profl. jours. Served to 1st lt. USAF, 1952-56. Mem. Planning Forum, Strategic Planning Exchange (chmn. 1984). Episcopalian. Clubs: The Club, Relay House, Jefferson, Birmingham Canoe (chmn. 1981), Vulcan Trail; Ala. Trail Riders Assn. (chmn. 1982). Office: AmSouth Bancorp PO Box 11007 Birmingham AL 35288

TUCKER, VIKI LEWIS, travel agency executive; b. Big Springs, Tex., Sept. 2, 1957; d. William Nathan and Maxine Minnie (Woodard) Lewis; m. Donald Wayne Tucker, Sept. 9, 1982. B.S. in Sociology, Okla. State U., 1979. Travel agt. Trailblazers, Oklahoma City, 1981-83; travel agt. mgr. Bartlett Tours, Oklahoma City, 1983; pres., owner Country Travel and Tours Inc., Oklahoma City, 1983—. Mem. Young Republicans, Oklahoma City, 1984, Ballet Okla., 1984, Okla. Symphony, 1984. Mem. Am. Retail Travel Agts (pres. 1985-86), Am. Soc. Travel Agts. (cert. travel counselor), Christians Womens Orgn. (project chmn. 1983-85), Jr. Hospitality. Baptist. Club: Oklahoma City Tips. Lodge: Eastern Star. Home: 2756 N Grand Blvd Oklahoma City OK 73116

TUCKER, WILLIAM EDWARD, university administrator, clergyman; b. Charlotte, N.C., June 22, 1932; s. Cecil Edward and Ethel Elizabeth (Godley) T.; m. Ruby Jean Jones, Apr. 8, 1955; children—Jan Tucker Scully, Will, Vance. Student, East Carolina U., 1949-51; B.A., Atlantic Christian Coll., 1953; B.D., Tex. Christian U., 1956; M.A., Yale U., 1958, Ph.D., 1960; LL.D., Atlantic Christian Coll., 1978; D.H.L., Chapman Coll., 1981; D.H., Bethany Coll., 1982; D.D., Austin Coll., 1985. Ordained to ministry Christian Ch. (Disciples of Christ), 1956. Mem. faculty Atlantic Christian Coll., Wilson, 1959-66, prof. religion and philosophy, 1962-66, chmn. dept., 1961-66; assoc. prof. church history, asst. dean Brite Divinity Sch., Tex. Christian U., Fort Worth, 1966-69, prof. church history, 1969-76, assoc. dean, 1969-71, dean, 1971-76, chancellor, 1979—; pres. Bethany Coll. (W.Va.); 1976-79; moderator Christian Ch., 1983-85; dir. Justin Industries, Tandy Corp. Bd. dirs. Fort Worth Symohony Orch. Assn., W. Tex. Region Conf. Christians and Jews; bd. dirs., exec. com. Van Cliburn Internat. Piano Competition. Author: J.H. Garrison and Disciples of Christ, St. Louis, 1964; (with Lester G. McAllister) Journey in Faith: A History of the Christian Church, 1975; contbr. encys. Mem. Am. Soc. Ch. History, Am. Acad. Religion, Newcomen Soc. N.Am. Home: 2900 Simondale Dr Fort Worth TX 76109 Office: Tex Christian U Box 32909 Fort Worth TX 76129

TUCKER, WILLIAM THOMAS, manufacturing company official; b. Monticello, Ark., Aug. 7, 1928; s. Pinkey Eugene and Lura Mae (O'Bryant) T.; m. Margery Josephine Noble, Aug. 3, 1952 (div. Sept. 1973); children—Bill Thomas, Sheryl, Melanie, Alicia; m. 2d, Patricia Ann Cook, Apr. 21, 1979. B.S., Miss. State U., 1955. Prodn. engr. Union Carbide Corp., Charlotte, N.C., 1955-57; indsl. engr. McQuay Inc., Grenada, Miss., 1958-59; prodn. mgr. Tex. Instruments, Dallas, 1959-73; materials mgr. Franklin Electric Co., Jacksonville, Ark., 1973-74; materials mgr. Taylor Instruments, Asheville, N.C., 1975-77; prodn. mgr. Emerson Electric Co., Mena, Ark., 1978—. Mem. Sherman (Tex.) Sch. Bd., 1972-73; sec. Polk County Republican Com., 1983-84. Served with USN, 1947-52; Korea. Mem. Am. Prodn. and Inventory Control Soc., Ark. Pvt. Industry Council. Baptist. Lodge: Lions. Home: Star Route 9 Box 6D Mena AR 71953 Office: 311 DeQueen St Mena AR 71953

TUERFF, JAMES RODRICK, insurance company executive; b. Gary, Ind., Jan. 17, 1941; m. Julie K. Luttinen; children—Brian J., Kevin A., Jeffrey J., Gregory S. B.A. in Econs., St. Joseph's Coll., 1963. C.L.U. Asst. v.p. Life and Casualty Ins. Co., Nashville, 1967-75; v.p. Commonwealth Life Ins. Co., Louisville, 1975-77; v.p. Am. Gen. Life Ins. Co., Houston, 1977-78, sr. v.p., exec. v.p., 1979-83; v.p. Am. Gen. Corp., Houston, 1978-79, exec. v.p., 1983—; dir. Am. Gen. Fire & Casualty Co., Houston. Pres. Norchester Maintenance

Fund, Inc., Houston, 1985—. Fellow Life Mgmt. Inst. Soc. Greater Houston; mem. C.L.U. Republican. Roman Catholic. Club: Raveneaux Country (Houston). Home: 10810 Creektree St Houston TX 77070 Office: Am Gen Corp 2929 Allen Pkwy Houston TX 77019

TUGGLE, DAVID CLEM, forest products company executive, lawyer; b. Kansas City, Mo., Apr. 14, 1943; s. Charles Clem and Ruth (Jenkins) T.; m. Joyce Elliott, Dec. 30, 1973; children—Amy, Mark. B.S., Kansas State U., 1965; J.D., Southern Meth. U., 1971. Bar: Tex. 1971, Kans. 1982. Mktg. mgr. L. R. McCoy, Inc., Worcester, Mass., 1975-81; pres., chief exec. officer Roanoke Forest Products Co., Inc., Va., 1981—. Mem. ABA. Republican. Lodge: Masons.

TUGGLE, EMMIT RAY, architect; b. Lindsay, Okla., Apr. 16, 1922; s. Emmett C. and Emelie Lois (Ray) T.; m. Mae Benzaquin Waldman, Mar. 24, 1953; 1 son, Thomas Matthew; 1 stepdau., Dana Lee Waldman. Student, Edinburg Jr. Coll. (Tex.), 1939-40, U. Tex., 1948. Registered architect, Tex., Nat. Council Archtl. Registration Bds. Draftsman, Ford & Rogers, San Antonio, 1948-50; ptnr. Peery & Tuggle, San Antonio, 1952-56; prin. Emmit R. Tuggle, San Antonio, 1956-73; ptnr. Tuggle & Graves, Architects, San Antonio, 1973-82, 86—; pres. Tuggle & Graves, Inc., San Antonio, 1982-86. Sch. dist. architect San Antonio, and South San Antonio , Crystal City. Served as 1st lt. USAAF, 1942-46. Recipient cert. of citation Tex. Ho. of Reps., 1970. Mem. ACLU, Amnesty Internat., AIA. , Clubs: Friends of the McNay, Giraud (San Antonio). Home: 204 Terrell Rd San Antonio TX 78209 Office: 215 Broadway San Antonio TX 78205

TULL, DAVID ADOLPHUS, physician, hospital administrator; b. Phila., Oct. 15, 1933; s. Dewey H. and Beulah Mae (Lewis) T.; B.A., Lincoln U., Oxford, Pa., 1954; M.D., Howard U., 1961; m. Maxine F. Webb, Sept. 6, 1959 (div. 1974); children—Heidi M., David Adolphus, II, Leilani M. Intern, St. Rita Hosp., Lima, Ohio, 1962; resident in phys. medicine and rehab. VA Hosp., Phila., 1963-66, mem. phys. medicine and rehab. staff, 1966-69, asst. chief phys. medicine and rehab., 1967-69, chief phys. medicine and rehab., 1969-71; chief of staff VA Hosp., Ft. Howard, Md., 1972-73, VA Hosp., Pitts., 1973-76; dir. VA Hosp., Tuskegee, Ala., 1976—; asst. phys. medicine and rehab. dept. U. Pa., 1966-69, asso., 1969-71; prof. clin. medicine dept. phys. therapy Tuskegee Inst., 1977—; adj. asst. prof. hosp. and health adminstrn., public and allied health U. Ala., Birmingham, 1977—, mem. V.A. Deans Com., 1976—; Ala. VA rep. governing Body of S.E. Ala. Health Systems; mem. mgmt. bd. John A. Andrew Hosp., Tuskegee Inst.; lectr., speaker in field. Chmn. Combined Fed. Campaign, Tuskegee, Ala. area, 1976-78; hon. chmn. United Negro Coll. Fund, 1977. Served with U.S. Army, 1954-56; Korea. Named Hon. Adm., Ala. Navy, 1976, Hon. Lt. Col. Aide-de-Camp, Ala. Militia, 1976, hon. mem. Lt. Gov.'s Staff, State Ala., 1978, Hon. Citizen of New Orleans, 1978; recipient award for loyal and devoted services to disabled vets. DAV of Ga., 1977, cert. appreciation Optimist Club Tuskegee, 1977, proclamation Martin Luther King, Jr. Community Players, New Brunswick, N.J., 1978, cert. appreciation Carver dist. Boy Scouts Am., 1978, Tuskegee Lions Club, 1978. Mem. AMA, Nat. Med. Assn., Am. Acad. Phys. Medicine and Rehab., Am. Congress Rehab. Medicine, Pa. Soc. Phys. Medicine and Rehab., Omega Psi Phi. Republican. Methodist. Home: Cottage 63 VA Med Center Tuskegee AL 36083 Office: VA Med Center Tuskegee AL 36083

TULLIS, EDWARD LEWIS, bishop; b. Cin., Mar. 9, 1917; s. Ashar Spence and Priscilla (Daugherty) T.; A.B., Ky. Wesleyan Coll., 1939, L.H.D., 1975; B.D., Louisville Presbyn. Theol. Sem., 1947; D.D., Union Coll., Barbourville, Ky., 1954, Wofford Coll., 1976; D.Hum., Claflin Coll., 1976, Lambuth Coll., 1984; m. Mary Jane Talley, Sept. 25, 1937; children—Frank Loyd, Jane Allen (Mrs. William Nelson Offutt IV). Ordained to ministry Methodist Ch., 1941; service in chs., Frenchburg, Ky., 1937-39, Lawrenceburg, Ky., 1939-44; asso. pastor 4th Ave. Meth. Ch., Louisville, 1944-47, Irvine, Ky., 1947-49; asso. sec. ch. extension sect. Bd. Missions, Meth. Ch., Louisville, 1949-52; pastor First Meth. Ch., Frankfort, Ky., 1952-61, First Meth. Ch., Ashland, Ky., 1961-72; resident bishop United Meth. Ch., Columbia, S.C., 1972-80, resident bishop Nashville area, 1980-84; instr. Bible, Ky. Wesleyan Coll., 1947-48; instr. Louisville Presbyn. Theol. Sem., 1949-52. Mem. Meth. Gen. Conf., 1956, 60, 64, 66, 68, 70, 72, Southeastern Jurisdictional Conf., 1952, 56, 60, 64, 68, 72; bd. mgrs. Bd. Missions, 1962-72; mem. bd. discipleship, 1972-80. Chaplain, Ky. Gen. Assembly, 1952-61; chmn. Frankfort Com. Human Rights, 1956-61; chmn. Mayor's Advisory Com. Human Relations, Ashland, 1968-72. Pres. bd. dirs. Magee Christian Edn. Found.; trustee Meth. Assembly, Lake Junaluska, N.C., 1966—, Emory U., 1973-80, Alaska Meth. U., 1965-70, Ky. Wesleyan Coll., Martin Coll., Lambuth Coll., McKendree Manor, Meth. Hosps., Memphis. Recipient Outstanding Citizen award Frankfort VFW, 1961, Mayor's award for outstanding service. Ashland, 1971. Club: Kiwanis. Author: Shaping the Church From the Mind of Christ, 1984; contbr. articles to religious jours. Home and Office: 2 S Lakeshore Dr PO Box 754 Lake Junaluska NC 28745

TULLY, CHRISTOPHER CARL, physician, hospital administrator; b. Charleston, W.Va., June 22, 1913; s. Christopher Columbus and Eva Lena (Lanham) T.; B.S. magna cum laude, Morris Harvey Coll., 1937; B.S., W.Va. U., 1945; M.D., Med. Coll. Va., 1947; m. Virginia Belle Tully, Apr. 9, 1937 (dec. 1963); children—Christopher Carl II, Richard R.; m. 2d, Margaret A. Plumley, Oct. 29, 1966. With Charleston Fire Dept., 1935-39, U.S. P.O., Charleston, 1939-43; intern U.S. Marine Hosp., 1947-48; gen. practice medicine, South Charleston, W.Va., 1948-79; mem. staff H. J. Thomas Meml. Hosp., South Charleston, 1948—, pres., 1966, med. coordinator, 1979-81; med. coordinator St. Francis Hosp., Charleston, W.Va., 1981— prof. family practice Kanawha Valley Family Practice Center, 1973-79. Dir., mem. exec. com. First Nat. Bank of South Charleston. Mem. South Charleston Recreation Com.; chmn. South Charleston Park Bd.; mem. Kanawha County Bd. Edn., 1959-70, pres., 1963-64; mem. Charter Bd. South Charleston, W.Va.; pres. W.Va. div. Am. Cancer Soc., 1981-83. Served with U.S. Army, 1944-46, 47-48, 51-53, 71. Diplomate Am. Bd. Family Practice. Fellow Am. Acad. Family Physicians; mem. Am. Acad. Family Practice (pres. Kanawha chpt. 1962-63; pres. W.Va. chpt. 1969-70, chmn. bd.), W.Va. Acad. Family Practice (dir. 1960-64), AMA, W.Va., Kanawha med. socs., So. Med. Assn., Am. Soc. Contemporary Medicine and Surgery, Phi Beta Pi. Lodges: Masons, Shriners, Lions (pres. Spring Hill 1957-58, Citizen of Yr. South Charleston 1956-57). Home: 4530 Spring Hill Ave South Charleston WV 25309 Office: 519 Donnally St Charleston WV 25322

TUMA, JUNE MILDRED, clinical child psychologist, educator; b. Rapides Parish, La., June 22, 1934; s. Harry and Mary (Pospisil) T.; B.A., La. State U., 1958, M.A., 1962, Ph.D., 1965. Lic. psychologist, Calif., La., Tex. Postdoctoral fellow Reiss Davis Child Study Center, Los Angeles, 1965-67; staff psychologist Mental Health Devel. Center, Los Angeles, 1967-69; asst. prof. U. Tex.-Galveston, 1969-74, assoc. prof., 1974-79; assoc. prof. La. State U., Baton Rouge, 1979-83, prof., 1983—. Fellow Am. Psychol. Assn., Am. Orthopsychiat. Assn.; mem. Soc. Personality Assessment, Soc. Pediatric Psychology, Editor: Handbook for the Practice of Pediatric Psychology, 1982; Jour. Clin. Child Psychology; contbr. chpts. to books, articles to profl. jours. Office: Dept Psychology La State U Baton Rouge LA 70803

TUMAY, MEHMET TANER, geotechnical consultant, educator; b. Ankara, Turkey, Feb. 2, 1937; came to U.S., 1959; s. Bedrettin and Muhterem (Uybadin) T.; m. Karen Nuttycombe, June 15, 1962; children—Peri, Suna. B.S. in Civil Engring., Robert Coll. Sch. Engring. (Turkey), 1959; M.C.E., U. Va., 1961; postgrad. UCLA, 1963-64; Ph.D., Tech. U. Istanbul (Turkey), 1971; Fugro-Cesco postdoctoral research fellow U. Fla., Gainesville, 1975-76. Instr. civil engring. U. Va., Charlottesville, 1961-62; asst. prof. civil engring. U. Louisville, 1962-63; teaching fellow UCLA, 1963-64; asst. prof. civil engring. Robert Coll. Sch. Engring., Istanbul, 1966-71; asso. prof. dept. civil engring. Bogazici U., Istanbul, 1971-75; asso. prof. then prof. civil engring., coordinator geotech. engring. La. State U., Baton Rouge, 1976—; maitre de conferences Ecole Nationale des Ponts et Chaussees, Paris, 1980—; geotech. cons. Sauti, Spa, Cons. Engrs., Italy, 1969-72, SOFRETU-RATP, Paris, 1972-73, D.E.A., Cons. Engrs., Istanbul, 1974-75, BOTEK, Ltd., Istanbul, 1975—, Senler-Campbell Assos., Louisville, 1979—, Fugro Gulf-Geogulf, Houston, 1980—; cons. UN Devel. Program, 1982-84; cons. in field. Contbr. articles to profl. jours. AID scholar, 1975-76; qualified fallout shelter analyst and instr. Dept. Def.; lic. civil engr., La., Turkish Chamber of Civil Engring; NSF grantee, 1982—; French Ministry External Relations scholar, 1982. Mem. ASCE, Am. Soc. Engring. Edn., ASTM, La. Engring. Soc., Turkish Soil Mechanics Group (charter), Turkish Chamber Civil Engrs., Internat. Soc. Soil Mechanics and Found. Engring., Sigma Xi, Chi Epsilon, Tau Beta Pi. Home: 1915 W Magna Carta Pl Baton Rouge LA 70815 Office: Dept Civil Engring La State Univ Baton Rouge LA 70803

TUNNER, WILLIAM SAMS, urological surgeon; b. San Antonio, Nov. 14, 1933; s. William Henry and Sarah Margaret (Sams) T.; student Washington and Lee U., 1952-55; M.D., U. Va., 1960; m. Sallie Berry Woodul, Dec. 4, 1965; children—William Woodul, Jonathan Sams. Intern in surgery, then asst. surg. resident Duke Hosp., 1960-62; fellow cancer surgery Cancer Inst. NIH, Bethesda, Md., 1962-64; resident in urol. surgery Cornell-N.Y. Hosp., 1964-68, fellow transplantation, dialysis and biochemistry, instr. surgery, 1968-70; asst. prof. urol. surgery U. Tex. Med. Sch., San Antonio, 1970-72; practice medicine specializing in pediatric and adult urology, Richmond, Va., 1972—; chief urology St. Mary's Hosp., also bd. dirs., sec. to bd., trustee; mem. staff Henrico County, Chippenham, Johnston-Willis hosps.; asst. clin. prof. urology Med. Coll. Va., 1972—. Valentine research fellow, 1970-72; grantee Hearst Research Found., 1970-72. Diplomate Am. Bd. Urology. Fellow ACS, (pres. Va. chpt.), Am. Acad. Pediatrics (affiliate); mem. AMA, Societé Internationalde Urologié, Transplantation Soc., Soc. Pediatric Urology, Am. Urol. Assn., Am. Nephrology Assn., SR, Alpha Epsilon Delta, Beta Theta Pi. Episcopalian. Club: Country of Va. Contbr. articles to med. jours., films. Home: Braedon Box 158 Manakin-Sabat VA 23103 Office: St Mary's Hosp Profl Bldg 5855 Bremo Rd Richmond VA 23226

TURBYFILL, JOHN RAY, railway executive; b. Newland, N.C., Sept. 28, 1931; s. Thomas Manuel and Della Isabell (Braswell) T.; m. Joyce Lorraine Wainwright Bolton, Aug. 14, 1954; children—Karen Denise, John Ray. B.A., Roanoke Coll., 1953; LL.B., U. Va., 1956. Bar: Va. 1956, N.Y. 1956. Assoc. mem. firm Cravath, Swaine & Moore, N.Y.C., 1956-60; mem. law dept. Norfolk & Western Ry. Co., Roanoke, Va., 1960-70; sr. v.p. Erie Lackawanna Ry. Co. and Delaware & Hudson Ry. Co., Cleve., 1970-72; v.p. Dereco, Inc., Cleve., 1970-72, 73—; v.p. adminstrn. Norfolk & Western Ry. Co., Roanoke, 1972-74, v.p. fin., 1974-80, exec. v.p., 1980—; now with Norfolk So. Corp.; v.p. Va. Holding Corp., Roanoke, 1973—. Mem. ABA, Roanoke Valley C. of C. (v.p. 1974-76, pres. 1976), Phi Delta Phi. Democrat. Office: PO Box 3609 Norfolk So Corp Norfolk VA 23514*

TURCHI, PETER JOHN, research laboratory director, scientist; b. N.Y.C., Dec. 30, 1946; s. Charles Orlando and Fay Florence (Breglia) T.; m. Judith Ann Radogna, June 13, 1967; children—Janita Nicole, Rebecca Lenore. B.S.E. in Aerospace and Mech. Sci./Physics, Princeton U., 1967, M.A., 1969, Ph.D., 1970. Research assoc. Plasma Propulsion Lab., Princeton U. (N.J.), 1963-70; plasma physicist Air Force Weapons Lab., Kirtland AFB, N.Mex., 1970-72; research physicist Naval Research Lab., Washington, 1972-77, chief Plasma Tech. br., 1977-80; scientist R&D Assocs., Arlington, Va., 1980-81; dir. RDA Washington Research Lab., Alexandria, Va., 1981—; chmn. Megagauss Inst., Inc., Alexandria; lectr. Air Force Pulsed Power Lecture Program; cons. on pulsed power tech.; chmn. 2d Internat. Conf. on Megagauss Fields, Arlington, 1979; chmn. Spl. Conf. on Prime-Power for High Energy Space Systems, Norfolk, Va., 1982; mem. organizing com. Megagauss Magnetic Field Confs. Pres., Collingwood Civic Assn. (Va.), 1980-81; rep. Mt. Vernon Council, Mt. Vernon Dist., Fairfax County, Va. Served to 1st lt. USAF, 1970-72. Recipient Invention award U.S. Air Force, 1972; Research Publ. award Naval Research Lab., 1976, U.S. Navy and Air Force invention awards, 1978-83; NSF fellow, 1967-70. Mem. Am. Phys. Soc., IEEE (chmn. tech. 5th pulsed power conf.), (tech. com. on plasmadynamics and lasers, internat. chmn. 18th internat. electric propulsion conf. 1985), Planetary Soc., Sigma Xi, Tau Beta Pi. Clubs: Princeton Campus, Va. Ki Soc. Editor: Megagauss Physics and Tech., 1980; contbr. numerous articles in field to profl. jours.; patentee in field. Office: Washington Research Lab 301A S West St Alexandria VA 22314

TURCHIN, ROBERT LOUIS, construction company executive; b. N.Y.C., Feb. 22, 1922; s. Benjamin B. and Gertrude (Grogin) T.; m. Lillian Grace Athey, Nov. 11, 1944; children—Barbara, Robert L., Melanie, Thomas, John. B.B.A., Tulane U., 1943. Registered gen. contractor, Fla. Pres., chief exec. officer Robert L. Turchin, Inc., Miami Beach, Fla., 1946—; pres. GAC Realty, Inc., 1969-72; dir. Gulfstream Land and Devel. Corp.; pres., dir. Gulfstream Constrn. Services Corp.; dir. Chase Fed. Savs. and Loan, Keller Industries, Atico Fin. Corp.; constrn. mgmt. cons. Pres. Miami Better Bus. Bur.; active Pres.' Council Tulane U., Soc. Founders U. Miami; chmn. Dade County Contractors Examining Bd., Dade County Fire Prevention Safety Appeals Bd., Dade County Contractors Mediation Bd., Met. Dade County Bd. Rules and Appeals; bd. dirs., v.p. Dade League Municipalities; councilman, vice mayor City of Miami Beach, 1963-67; adv. bd. Miami Dade Community Coll.; curriculum com. Fla. Internat. U.; panel arbitrators Am. Assn. Arbitrators; bd. dirs. Cedars Med. Ctr. Served to lt. USN, 1941-46. Recipient Nat. Industry Leader award B'nai Brith, 1972; named Man of Yr., Miami Beach Democratic Club, 1965; Outstanding Alumnus, Tulane U., 1983. Mem. Assoc. Gen. Contractors, Miami Builder's Exchange, Marine Council, Internat. Game Fish Assn., Internat. Oceanographic Assn., Am. Legion. Lodge: Elks. Home: 4499 N Meridian Ave Miami Beach FL 33140 Office: Robert L Turchin Inc 1835 Purdy Ave Miami Beach FL 33139

TURK, JAMES CLINTON, judge; b. Roanoke, Va., May 3, 1923; s. James Alexander and Geneva (Richardson) T.; A.B., Roanoke Coll., 1949; LL.B., Washington and Lee U., 1952, J.D., 1972; m. Barbara Duncan, Aug. 21, 1954; children—Ramona Leah, James Clinton, Robert Malcolm Duncan, Mary Elizabeth, David Michael. Admitted to Va. bar, 1952; mem. firm Poff & Turk, Radford, Va., 1952-72; mem. Va. Senate, 1959-72, minority leader; chief U.S. dist. judge Western Dist. Va., Roanoke, 1972—. Trustee Radford Community Hosp., 1959-74. Served with AUS, 1943-46. Mem. Order of Coif, Phi Beta Kappa, Omicron Delta Kappa. Baptist (deacon). Office: US Dist Ct Fed Bldg 210 Franklin Rd Roanoke VA 24001

TURK, MARTIN ERWIN, real estate developer; b. Balt., Sept. 5, 1945; s. Jerome and Shirley (Amorky) T.; m. Mary Agnes Lovinski, Nov. 24, 1980. B.A., U. Md., 1970. Sales mgr. Cavalier Formals, Alexandria, Va., 1971-77; salesman Lewis & Silverman Realty, Burke, Va., 1977-78; comml. mgr. White House Real Estate, Annandale, Va., 1978-84; pres. New Homes Realty, Inc., Falls Church, Va., 1984—, Nat. Greetings Corp., Falls Church, 1985—; cons. Woodward & Lothrop, Washington 1985—. Mem. No. Va. Bd. Realtors (Top Producer award 1981, 83), No. Va. Builders Assn. Lodge: Optimist (pres. 1981). Avocation: tennis. Home: 4500 Park Rd Alexandria VA 22312 Office: 6526 Arlington Blvd Falls Church VA 22042

TURKHEIMER, ARNOLD IVAN, communications specialist; b. Mt. Vernon, N.Y., June 20, 1939; s. Milton S. and Lillian G. (Goldberg) T.; B.A., U. Iowa, 1961, M.A., 1962; m. Andrea J. Widelitz, June 13, 1965; children—Mitchell, Roberta. Dist. mgr. United World Films, div. Universal Pictures, N.Y.C., 1962-67; public relations mgr. spl. projects British Airways, N.Y.C., 1967-76; v.p., div. mgr. Booke & Co., Vicom Communications div., Winston-Salem, N.C., 1976-78; mgr. Southeastern U.S. employee benefit communications William M. Mercer Inc., Atlanta, 1979—, asst. v.p., 1982—, assoc., 1983—. Recipient gold medals, N.Y. Film Festival, 1969, 72, 73; 1st pl. Bus. Ins. award, 1981; Silver medal Chgo. Internat. Film Festival, 1982. Mem. Internat. Communications Council, Soc. Motion Picture TV Engrs., Nat. Audio-Visual Assn. (cert. media specialist). Club: Masons. Home: 4752 Big Oak Bend Marietta GA 30062 Office: 133 Peachtree Suite 3500 Georgia Pacific Center Atlanta GA 30326

TURLEY, JOHN PAUL, computer programmer, analyst; b. Shreveport, La., Nov. 25, 1955; s. John Robert and Wanda Jean (Rancier) T.; m. Julia Ann Leisk, May 27, 1978; children—Stephen Glen, Laura Elizabeth. B.S., La. Tech. U., 1977. With South Central Bell Tel. Co., Birmingham, Ala., 1977-85, analyst info. systems, 1979-80, staff analyst info. systems, 1980-85; staff analyst fin. systems Bell South Services Co., Birmingham, 1986—. Mem. Assn. Computing Machinery, Phi Kappa Phi, Upsilon Pi Epsilon. Republican. Methodist. Office: 1876 Data Dr PO Box 2394 Birmingham AL 35201

TURLEY, STEWART, retail drug chain executive; b. Mt. Sterling, Ky., July 20, 1934; s. R. Joe and Mavis (Sternberg) T.; student Rollins Coll., 1952-53, U. Ky., 1953-55; m. Judith Anne Hall, July 10, 1953; children—Carol Anne, Turley Cohen, Karen Elaine. With Crown Cork & Seal Co., Phila., and Orlando, Fla., 1955-66, plant mgr., Phila., 1964-66; with Jack Eckerd Corp., Clearwater, Fla., 1966—, sr. v.p., 1971-74, pres., 1974-75, pres., chmn. bd., 1975—, also dir.; dir. Barnett Banks of Fla., Jacksonville, United Telecommunications Inc., Springs Industries, Inc. Mem. Fla. Council of 100; mem. World Bus. Council; trustee Eckerd Coll., St. Petersburg, Fla.; vice chmn. Fla. Council on Econ. Edn. Mem. Am. Retail Fedn. (dir.), Nat. Assn. Chain Drug Stores (chmn. 1978-79, dir.), Young Pres.'s Orgn., Chief Execs. Orgn., Bus. Roundtable, Kappa Alpha. Clubs: Carlouel Yacht, Belleview Biltmore Country. Office: PO Box 4689 Clearwater FL 33518

TURLINGTON, RALPH DONALD, state official; b. Gainesville, Fla., Oct. 5, 1920; s. John Edwin and May (Baldwin) T.; m. Ann Gellerstedt, Oct. 2, 1946; children—Ralph Donald, Katherine Wright. B.S., U. Fla., 1942; M.B.A., Harvard U., 1943; LL.D. (hon.), U. Miami, 1977, Stetson U., 1975. Asst. prof. U. Fla., Gainesville, 1947-49; agt. State Farm Ins., 1949-74; commr. edn. State of Fla., 1974—. Mem., Fla. Ho. of Reps., 1950-74, speaker, 1967-68, chmn. appropriations com., fin. and taxation com.; pres. So. Scholarship Found Inc. Served with U.S. Army, 1943-46, 51-52; Korea. Mem. Am. Assn. Sch. Adminstrs., Nat. Assn. State Bds. Edn., Nat. Sch. Bd. Assn., Nat. Econ. Edn. Council, Edn. Council States, Joint Council Econ. Edn., Am. Legion, VFW, Phi Delta Kappa, Sigma Phi Epsilon. Democrat. Baptist. Club: Elks. Home: 2612 Lucerne Dr Tallahassee FL 32303 Office: PL 08 The Capitol Tallahassee FL 32301

TURNER, CHARLES ARTHUR, artist, educator; b. Houston, Tex., Nov. 17, 1940; s. Lloyd T. and Modest A. (Wainwright) T.; B.A., N. Tex. State U., 1962; M.F.A., Cranbrook Acad. Art, 1966. Instr., Birmingham (Mich.) Art Assn., 1965-66; asst. prof. Madison Coll., Harrisonburg, Va., 1966-68; guest instr. U. Houston, Tex., 1973, Glassell Sch. Art, Mus. Fine Arts, Houston, 1968—, Anderson Ranch Arts Ctr., Aspen, Colo., 1985; one-man shows include: Columbia Mus. Art, Columbia, S.C., 1968, Circle Gallery, New Orleans, 1969, Beyond Baroque Gallery, Venice, Calif., 1969, Art Gallery, Sam Houston State U., Huntsville, Tex., 1971, Beaumont (Tex.) Art Mus., 1972, Art Mus. of S. Tex., Corpus Christi, 1973, Art Gallery, Madison Coll., Harrisonburg, Va., 1967, 74, Sol Del Rio Gallery, San Antonio, Tex., 1975, 78, Moody Gallery, Houston, 1976, 77, 78, 80, 82, Patricia Moore Gallery, Aspen, 1983, 85, numerous group shows, latest being: U. Minn., Mpls., 1975, Moody Gallery, Houston, 1975, The Art Center, Waco, Tex., 1977, Mus. Fine Arts, Houston, 1978, U. Houston, 1979, Jurgen Schweinbraden, Berlin, Germany, 1980, Stavanger Mus. (Norway), 1982, McAllen Internat. Mus. (Tex.), Chgo. Navy Pier Art Fair, 1984, Morgan Gallery, Kansas City, Kans.; represented in permanent collections: Mus. of Fine Arts, Houston, First City Nat. Bank, Bellaire, Tex., Alcoa Corp., Detroit, Cranbrook Acad. Art, Bloomfield Hills, Mich., Del Mar Coll., Corpus Christi, Tex., AT&T, N.Y.C., East Tenn. State U., Johnson City, Dresser Industries Inc., Houston. Mem. Coll. Art Assn. Am., Tex. Fine Arts Soc., Tex. Watercolor Soc. Office: 5101 Montrose St Houston TX 77005

TURNER, DONALD, JR., book store executive; b. Dallas, Dec. 4, 1932; s. Donald and Etta Mae (Sutton) T.; m. Mary Evelyn Jefferson, Nov. 3, 1956; children—Donald III, Mary Elizabeth, James Alan, Rachel Lynne. B.A., Baylor U., 1954; M. Div., New Orleans Bapt. Theol Sem., 1959. Mgr. Bapt. Book Store, Bapt. Sunday Sch. Bd., Roanoke, Va., 1959-64, San Antonio, 1964-69, Oklahoma City, 1969—; area rep. Christian Book Sellers Assn., Colorado Springs, Colo., 1977—. Home: 820 Ramblewood Terr Edmond OK 73034 Office: Bapt Book Store 3023 NW 23 Oklahoma City OK 73034

TURNER, EDDIE, bookstore executive; b. Sweetwater, Tex., Apr. 13, 1950; s. Cecil Edwin and Kathleen Louise (Freeman) T.; m. Anita Sue Hammit, Feb. 25, 1978; children—Erin Michelle, Andrea Danee. B.A., Wayland Bapt U.; M.S.M., Houston Bapt. U. Missionary, So. Bapt. Conv., Okinawa, Japan, 1972-74; purchasing officer, bookstore mgr., Wayland Bapt. U., Plainview, Tex., 1975—. Mem. Nat. Assn. Coll. Stores, Nat. Assn. Bus. Officers, Christian Booksellers Assn. Baptist. Avocations: snow skiing, music. Home: Rt 2 Hale Center TX 79041 Office: Wayland Bapt U 1900 W 7th St Plainview TX 79072

TURNER, ELBERT DAYMOND, JR., educator; b. Gainesville, Fla., Nov. 15, 1915; s. Elbert D. and Lena (Baird) T.; B.A. with honors, Davidson Coll., 1937; M.A., U. N.C., 1939, Ph.D., 1949; m. Irma Aboy, Aug. 2, 1945; children—Carmen Irma (Mrs. Joseph Lipe), Ana Maria (Mrs. Timothy Lomperis), Victoria (Mrs. Todd Powers), Elbert D. III, Rosa. Teaching fellow U. N.C., 1937-38, part-time instr. 1938-39; instr. Ga. Tchrs. Coll., 1939-41; instr. Spanish, U. N.C., 1946-49; asst. prof. U. Del., 1949-58, dir. lang. lab., 1955-66, assoc. prof. modern langs., 1958-61, prof. modern languages, 1961-66; prof. Spanish, chmn. dept. fgn. langs. U. N.C., Charlotte, 1966-71, dir. grad. studies, 1970-80, prof. Spanish, emeritus, 1981—; vis. prof. NDEA Inst., Utah State U., 1963-64, Utah State U., Oaxaca, (Mex.), summer 1966; cons. public schs. Del., 1951-52, 56, Del. Dept. Public Instrn., 1959-66, Memphis State U., 1967-70, Profl. Child Care Centers, Inc., 1969-73, Nat. Endowment Humanities, 1980. Chmn. test devel. Nat. Spanish Exams., 1965-74. Served from 1st lt. to lt. col. AUS, 1941-46; col. Res. ret. Research grantee Nat. Endowment Humanities, 1979-82, Comité Conjunto Hispan. Norteamericano Para Asuntos Educativos y Culturales, 1980-81. Fellow Southeastern Inst. Medieval and Renaissance Studies, 1968; fellow Huntington Library, 1982. Mem. Am. Assn. Tchrs. Spanish and Portuguese (life), Assn. for Latin-Am. Studies, Am. Council on Teaching Fgn. Langs., Charlotte Area Ednl. Consortium (sec. 1971-72), S. Atlantic LA, Renaissance Soc. Am., Phi Beta Kappa, Delta Sigma Pi, Eta Sigma Phi, Sigma Phi Epsilon. Republican. Presbyterian (elder). Clubs: U. N.C. Faculty. Author: Gonzalo Fernández de Ovideo y Valdés: An Annotated Bibliography, 1967; The Conquest and Settlement of Puerto Rico, 1975. Contbr. to numerous profl. publs. Mem. adv. bd. N.C. Fgn. Lang. Tchr., 1970-74. Home: 233 Fenton Pl Charlotte NC 28207

TURNER, JAMES ELDRIDGE, anatomy educator, researcher; b. Richmond, Va., Oct. 1, 1942; s. Shelly Ivy and Aylease (Moore) T.; m. Virginia Clark, May 27, 1967; children—Catherine Aylease, Annamarie Frances, James Eldridge. B.S. in Biology, Va. Mil. Inst., 1965; M.S., U. Richmond, 1967; Ph.D. in Zoology, U. Tenn., 1970. NIH postdoctoral trainee dept. anatomy Case Western Res. Sch. Medicine, Cleve., 1970, NIH postdoctoral fellow, 1972-74; asst. prof. biology Va. Mil. Inst., Lexington, 1971-72; asst. prof., assoc. prof. dept. anatomy Bowman Gray Sch. Medicine, Winston-Salem, N.C., 1974-83, prof., 1983—, vis. prof. dept. neurochemistry Max-Planck Inst., Munich, W.Ger., 1980-81. Pres. ch. council Augsburg Luth. Ch., 1983. NIH fellow, 1968-70, 72-74; Basil O'Connor research fellow, 1975-78; NIH research career devel. awardee, 1978-83. Mem. AAAS, Am. Inst. Biol. Sci., Am. Soc. Zoologists, Am. Assn. Anatomists, Soc. for Neurosci. Contbr. articles to profl. jours. Home: 450 Lynn Ave Winston-Salem NC 27104 Office: Dept Anatomy Bowman Gray Sch Medicine 300 Hawthorne Rd Winston-Salem NC 27103

TURNER, JAMES MORTON, JR., business executive; b. San Diego, Oct. 21, 1944; s. James Morton and Dorothy (Jenkins) T.; m. Suzette Stafford; children—James Morton, J. Stafford, Margaret Hunter, Catherine Phipps. B.S., Washington and Lee U., 1967, J.D., 1971. Clk. to justice Supreme Ct. Va., 1971-72; assoc. Woods Rogers Muse Walker & Thornton, Roanoke, Va., 1972-78; v.p. J.M. Turner & Co., Inc., Salem, Va., 1978—. Chmn. Roanoke Valley Civic Ctr. Commn., 1985, trustee Roanoke Meml. Hosp., 1985; mem. Roanoke City Sch. Bd.; bd. dirs. United Way Roanoke Valley, Inc., Roanoke Valley Sci. Mus. Served with USMCR, 1967-73. Named Disting. Citizen, Roanoke Valley Jaycees, 1985. Mem. C. of C. of Roanoke Valley (pres. 1985). Episcopalian. Avocations: skiing; canoeing; golf.

TURNER, JAMES RICKEY, exploration geologist; b. Timpson, Tex., Jan. 31, 1950; s. James R. and Jarrett H. (Birdwell) T.; m. Lenda J. Godwin, June 24, 1979; children—Trent, Summer. B.S. in Geology, Stephen E. Austin U., 1973; M.S. in Geology, Tex. A&M U., 1977. Exploration geologist Gulf Oil, Houston, 1977-80, Braddock exploration, Shreveport, La., 1980-81, Pruet Oil, Shreveport, 1981-85; cons. geologist, Shreveport, 1985—. Contbr. articles to profl. jours. Served to 1st lt. U.S. Army, 1973-76. Named Outstanding Student, Stephen F. Austin U., 1973. Mem. Am. Assn. Petroleum Geologists (cert.), Soc. Econ. Paleontologists and Mineralogists, Gulf Coast Assn. Geol. Socs., Soc. Profl. Well Log Analysts. Baptist. Avocation: private pilot. Office: 206 Beck Bldg Shreveport LA 71101

TURNER, JOE STEWART, electrical engineer; b. Sherman, Tex., 1909; s. Ethelbert and Annie Lee (Stewart) T.; grad. Chgo. Radio and T.V. Inst., 1932; B.A. with honors, U. Tex., 1934; m. Vivian Dybwad, Jan. 7, 1932; children—Jo Ann (Mrs. Lawrence Albert Westhaver), Robert Roger. Elec. engr. Cooney Mining Co., Glenwood, N.M., 1934-35, Internat. Milling Co., Greenville, Tex., engr., sect. supr. CAA, Ft. Worth, and Washington, 1936-47, supt. Pacific area communications, Honolulu, 1948-52; chief radar div. FAA, Washington, 1953-59; project dir. systems div. dir. Collins Radio Co., Dallas, 1960-65; supr.

cost control and new tech. reporting Bendix Launch Support, Kennedy Space Center, Fla., 1966-73; research and devel. on alt. energy sources, Titusville, Fla., 1974—. Coach, Annandale (Va.) Swim Team, 1956; bd. dirs. Annandale Recreation Center, 1956; charter mem. Republican Presdl. Task Force. Served with AUS, 1943-44. Named Bendix/NASA launch honoree, Nov. 1973, Man of Month, Dec. 1973; honored by astronauts for work on Apollo program; Dept. Energy research grantee, 1981. Mem. IEEE (sr.; chmn. Pacific sect. 1951), Bendix Mgmt. Club. Author: DOD/Commerce Joint Use of Radar Agreement, 1958; Airport Surface Detection Equipment, 1959; Performance Standards for Communications Systems, 1960; patentee in field. Home: 2825-614 S Washington Ave Titusville FL 32780

TURNER, JOE VERNON, JR., apparel manufacturing executive; b. Lubbock, Tex., Oct. 22, 1944; s. Joe Vernon and Estelle (Arp) T.; student Tex. Technol. U., 1963-66; m. Elizabeth Ann Haynes, Aug. 23, 1966; 1 dau., Mary Elizabeth. Asst. store mgr. Howard Bros. Discount Stores, Ft. Walton Beach, Fla., Ft. Lauderdale, Fla., Smyrna, Ga., 1966-69; regional softlines supr. Arlans Dept. Stores, Atlanta, 1969-70; buyer, v.p. softlines Howard Bros. Discount Stores, Monroe, La., 1970-83; pres. Braxton Jeans, Carrollton, Tex., 1983—. Republican. Covenant Presbyn. Home: 1940 Garden Grove Ct Plano TX 75075 Office: 1702 Metro Dr Carrollton TX 75006

TURNER, JUSTIN LEROY, consultant; b. Madrid, Iowa, May 26, 1915; s. John and Mabel (Smith) T.; student Northwestern U., 1934-41, N.Y.U., 1949-52; m. Roberta Gertrude Beaty, Aug. 13, 1937 (dec. Feb. 1979); m. Dorothy Y. Weaver, Feb. 14, 1985. Plant controller, div. controller, mgr. adminstrv. standards Am. Can. Co., N.Y.C., 1933-56; dir. adminstrn. Remington-Rand Univac div. Sperry Rand Co., Stamford, Conn., 1956-61; pres. chief exec. officer, dir. Foregger Co., Roslyn, N.Y., 1961; pres., chief exec. officer, chmn. exec. com. Soundscriber Corp., North Haven, Conn., 1961-64; chmn. bd. Soundscriber Sales Corp., 1961-64 indsl. mgmt. cons., 1964-66; pres., chief exec. officer, dir. Ednl. Service Programs, Inc., New Haven, 1966-73; dir. Soundscriber Corp. Japan, Ltd.; cons., gen. investor, 1973—. Chmn. troop com., scout master Boy Scouts Am., Oak Park, Ill.; chmn. publicity com. Conn. Regional Export Expansion Council. Trustee Conn. Distributive Edn. Com. Mem. Nat. Mfg. Assn., AIM, (pres.'s council), Am. Assn. Mus., Am. Assn. Zool. Parks and Aquariums, Smithsonian Mus. Assos., Yale Peabody Assos., Newcomen Soc. N.Am. Baptist (deacon). Clubs: Bayside Yacht, Lake County Executive, Douglaston, Sedgwood, Quinnipac, Darien Country, Darbonne Country, Kiwanis, Elks. Patentee in field. Home: Route 1 Box 46 Clermont FL 32711

TURNER, L.S., JR., retired utilities company executive; b. Dallas, Nov. 5, 1926; s. James A. and Fay Sims; B.S. in Civil Engring., Tex. A&M U., 1948; J.D., So. Meth. U., 1957; m. Donetta Mae Johnson, Jan. 17, 1947. Engr. Dallas Power & Light Co., 1948, various exec. positions, pres. chief exec., 1967-76; exec. v.p. Tex. Utilities Co., Dallas, 1976-84; cons. Trustee Com. for Econ. Devel., Southwestern Med. Found.; past pres., bd. dirs. Dallas Citizens Council, Children's Med. Center; past chmn., bd. dirs. YMCA Met. Dallas, United Way of Met. Dallas; sr. mem. Conf. Bd. Served with U.S. Army, 1945-46. Mem. Salesmanship Club. Presbyterian. Office: 13101 Preston Rd Dallas TX 75240

TURNER, LOYD LEONARD, business executive; b. Claude, Tex., Nov. 5, 1917; s. James Richard and Maude (Brown) T.; B.A., Baylor U., 1939, M.A., 1940; postgrad. U. Pa., 1940-42; m. Lee Madeleine Barr, Apr. 13, 1944; children—Terry Lee, Loyd Lee. Instr., U. Pa., 1940-42; public relations coordinator Consol. Vultee Aircraft Corp., San Diego, 1946-48, dir. public relations, Ft. Worth, 1948-53; asst. to pres. Ft. Worth div. Gen. Dynamics Corp., 1953-71, dir. public affairs Convair Aerospace div., Ft. Worth, 1971-72; exec. asst. to chmn. bd. and pres. Tandy Corp., Ft. Worth, 1972-76, v.p., 1976-85; sr. v.p. Witherspoon & Assos., Ft. Worth, 1986—, also dir. Pres., Ft. Worth Public Library Bd., 1958-63, Casa Mañana Musicals, Inc., 1978-80; v.p. Ft. Worth Bd. Edn., 1962-65, pres., 1965-71; mem. exec. com. Tex. Assn. Sch. Bds., 1966-71, v.p., 1970-71; mem. steering com. Council Big City Bds., Nat. Sch. Bds. Assn., 1967-69, mem. Gov's Com. on Public Sch. Edn., 1966-69; pres. Tex. Council Maj. Sch. Dists., 1968-69. Bd. dirs. Tarrant County chpt. ARC, 1956-59, Tex. Com. Public Edn., 1961-69; trustee Baylor U., 1980—; bd. dirs. Public Communication Found. N.Tex., 1970-76, One Broadway Plaza, 1978—, Tex. Research League, 1979—, Longhorn council Boy Scouts Am., 1976—; bd. dirs. Child Study Center, 1974-82, 85—, v.p., 1986—; bd. dirs. Parenting Guidance Center, 1976-78, Planning and Research Council of United Way Met. Tarrant County, 1976-80, Ft. Worth Safety Council, 1980-83, Christian Edn. Coordinating Bd. Bapt. Gen. Conv. Tex., 1976-80; v.p. Ft. Worth Citizens Organized Against Crime, 1977—; bd. dirs. Jr. Achievement of Tarrant County, 1982—, North Central Tex. chpt. March of Dimes, 1983-84. Served with USAAF, 1942-46. Named Library Trustee of Yr., Tex. Library Assn., 1961, Pres. of Best Bd. of Large Sch. Systems in U.S., NEA, 1968; recipient citation Air Force Assn., 1962; Leadership award West Tex. C. of C., 1966, 69; Man of Merit award Baylor U., 1980; Silver medal Am. Advt. Fedn., 1981. Mem. Pub. Relations Soc. Am. (pres. N.Tex. chpt. 1977, Paul Lund public service award 1980), Tex. Assn. Bus. (bd. dirs. 1977-82, 83—, exec. com. 1979-82), Assn. for Higher Edn. of N.Tex. (dir. 1978-82), Air Force Assn., Nat. Mgmt. Assn., Advt. Club Ft. Worth (pres. 1977-78), Friends Ft. Worth Library (v.p. 1971), Ft. Worth C. of C. (dir. 1974-76, 78-81 83—, vice chmn. 1985—), West Tex. C. of C. (dir. 1982, v.p. 1985—), Arts Council Ft. Worth and Tarrant County (dir. 1973-75, 80—), Baylor U. Devel. Council (pres. 1975-77), Baylor U. Alumni Assn. (dir. 1958-61), Sigma Delta Chi (pres. Ft. Worth 1961-62). Baptist. Clubs: Rotary (pres. Fort Worth 1974-75, dir. 1972-76, Paul Harris fellow 1983), Knife and Fork (dir. 1963-66, pres. 1965-66), Colonial Country, Century II. Author: The ABC of Clear Writing, 1954. Home: 3717 Echo Trail Fort Worth TX 76109 Office: 1000 W Weatherford Fort Worth TX 76102

TURNER, LUTHER SOHMERFIELD, JR., retired government official, search consultant; b. Atlanta, Oct. 6, 1929; s. Luther S. and Dorothy (Norris) T.; m. Ann Dellinger, Sept. 1, 1956; children—Helen Lynn, Doris Leigh, Luther S. III. B.S. in Bus. Adminstrn., U. Ala., 1956. Asst. mgr. Luther Turner Advt. Co., Guntersville, Ala., 1956-60; civilian personnel specialist Dept. Army, Huntsville, Ala., 1960-61; dir. coll. recruitment NASA Johnson Space Ctr., Houston, 1961-67; dir. exec. search Dept. HEW, Washington, 1967-81; dir. exec. devel. HHS, Washington, 1981-84, ret.; search cons. Odyssey Co., Fairfax, Va., 1984—; cons. U.S. Army, Washington, 1981-82. Awards chmn. Cub Scouts, Fairfax, 1974; jr. warden Ch. of Epiphany, Guntersville, 1960; jr. warden, lay reader St. John's Episcopal Ch., Centreville, Va., 1985; dir. field maintenance Chantilly Youth Assn., Fairfax, 1976-77. Served with USN, 1950-54. Mem. Fed. Exec. Inst. Alumni Assn., Jr. C. of C. (program chmn. 1958), Sigma Nu. Republican. Club: Val Monte Country. Lodge: Lions. Avocations: camping; hiking; jogging.

TURNER, MARGUERITE ROSE COWLES, library administrator; b. Port Sulphur, La., June 21, 1941; d. John Clinton and Marguerite Eileen (Slaybaugh) Cowles; B.A., U. New Orleans, 1963; M.L.S., La. State U., 1966; M.A. in History, U. So. Miss., 1970; divorced; 1 son, Jeffrey Jason. Reference librarian edn. div. U. So. Miss., 1966-70; librarian Pascagoula (Miss.) Jr. High Sch., 1970-71, Irwin County High Sch., Ocilla, Ga., 1971-72; dir. Fitzgerald (Ga.) Carnegie Library, 1974-80; adminstrv. librarian Assumption Parish Library, Napoleonville, La., 1980-83; dir. Jacob S. Mauney Meml. Library, Kings Mountain, N.C., 1983—. Sunday sch. tchr. First Baptist Ch., Fitzgerald, 1978-80, Napoleonville, 1980-83. Mem. ALA, N.C. Library Assn. Democrat. Author poems, short stories, contbr. articles profl. jours. Home: 202 S Gaston St Kings Mountain NC Office: 100 S Piedmont St Kings Mountain NC

TURNER, MATTHEW SCOTT, geologist, geomorphologist; b. Bayshore, N.Y., Aug. 28, 1951; s. Eugene Everett and Margaret Louise (McNulty) T.; m. Paula Phoebe Shrout, June 23, 1979. B.S., No. Ariz. U., 1973; M.S., Fort Hays State U., 1983. Cert. profl. geologist, Ind., Va.; lic. profl. geologist Alaska. Geologist, Ertec, Inc., Redwood City, Calif., 1973-75; geologist Holosonics, Inc., Fairbanks, Alaska, 1975-76; geologist Western Techs., Las Vegas, 1977-80; geologist Technos Inc., Miami, Fla., 1983—. Mem. Assn. Engring. Geologists. Republican. Methodist. Office: Technos Inc 3333 NW 21st St Miami FL 33142

TURNER, RALPH (CHIP) WILSON, JR., clergyman, religious organization and religious television network administrator; b. Shreveport, La., Jan. 18, 1948; s. Ralph W. and Gladys Pearl (Ma Gouirk) T.; B.A. cum laude in Speech Edn., La. Coll., 1970; M.R.E., New Orleans Bapt. Theol. Sem., 1973; m. Sandra Elaine Aymond, May 23, 1970; children—Christopher Layne, Cory Wilson. Ordained to ministry Bapt. Ch., 1972; assoc. pastor and minister edn. 1st Bapt. Ch., Farmerville, La., 1968-71, 1st Bapt. Ch., Summit, Miss., 1971-73, 1st Bapt. Ch., Slidell, La., 1973-75, 1st Bapt. Ch., Port Arthur, Tex., 1975-76; minister edn., bus. adminstr. 1st Bapt. Ch., Beaumont, Tex., 1976-79; assoc. dir. missions, teaching and tng. Greater New Orleans Bapt. Assn., 1979-81; dir. media services dept. La. Bapt. Conv., 1981—, also state dir. The Acts Satellite Network, 1983—; guest faculty religious edn./communications courses New Orleans Bapt. Theol. Sem., 1979-80, 84, 86; Sunday sch. dir. St. Tammany Bapt. Assn., Slidell, 1973-75; ch. tng. dir. Concord Bapt. Assn., Farmerville, 1970-71; mem. nat. bd., nat. exec. com. Ch. Commn. on Civic and Youth Serving Agys. Merit badge counselor, exec. bds. New Orleans Area, Three Rivers and Attakapas councils Boy Scouts Am., 1973—, relationships v.p., 1983—; mem. nat. Protestant Com., Boy Scouts Am., 1980—; dist. rep. Nat. Eagle Scout Assn., 1975-79; protestant chaplain gen. Nat. Boy Scouts Jamboree, 1985; nat. chmn.-elect. Commn. for Ch. and Youth Agy. Relationships, 1986-88; faculty mem. Bapt. Week at Philmont Scout Ranch, 1978, 80; state coordinator Bapt. Telecommunications Network, 1983—. Recipient Alexandria (La.) Civitan Citizenship award, 1969, 70; Silver Beaver award Boy Scouts Am., 1982; Good Shepherd award Nat. Assn. Baptists for Scouting. Mem. Nat. Assn. of Ch. Bus. Adminstrs., La. Bapt. Religious Edn. Assn., Bapt. Public Relations Assn., Met. Assn. of Religious Edn. Dirs., So. Bapt. Religious Edn. Assn., Golden Triangle Religious Edn. Assn., Nat. Audio-Visual Assn., Tex. Bapt. Public Relations Assn., Southwestern Bapt. Religious Edn. Assn., Nat. Assn. Local Ch. Communicators (charter), Assn. Bapt. for Scouting (nat. bd. 1978—), Internat. TV Assn., Assn. for Ednl. Communications and Tech., La. Assn. for Ednl. Communications and Tech., Internat. Platform Assn., Nat. Assn. Local Cable Programmers, La. Cable TV Assn. (assoc.), Young Men's Bus. League of Beaumont, Alpha Phi Omega (life mem.; chpt. founder). Republican. Clubs: Lions, Rotary (newsletter editor 1976, chorister 1976), Masons. Author: Training Sunday School Workers, 1982; How To Use Audiovisuals; The Church Video Answerbook; A Nontechnical Guide for Ministers and Laypersons, 1986 contbr. articles to religious, adminstrv. and scouting publs. Office: PO Box 311 Alexandria LA 71309

TURNER, RANDALL MEAD, real estate development executive, banker; b. Maracaibo, Venezuela, May 2, 1949; came to U.S., 1952; s. Jo Thomas and Jane Ann (Allerton) T.; m. Joan Denise Howell, Aug. 11, 1979; children—Jennifer Howell, Mead. B.A., U. Tex., 1971, M.B.A., 1985; postgrad. U. Madrid, 1969-70. Vice-pres., chief operating officer, dir. Sutherland Properties, Inc., Houston, 1972-78; pres. Landtana Corp., Houston, 1978—; adv. dir. Bank of Harris County, 1978-81; organizer, dir. Westhollow Nat. Bank, Houston, 1981—. Mem. Urban Land Inst., Inst. Real Estate Mgmt., Bldg. Owners and Mgrs. Assn., Nat. Realtors Assn., Houston Bd. Realtors, C. of C. Methodist. Clubs: University, The Forest (Houston); Giraud, Argyle (San Antonio). Office: 150 E Main St Fredericksburg TX 78624

TURNER, ROBERT EDWARD (TED TURNER), III, broadcasting and sports executive, yachtsman; b. 1938; m. Jane Turner. Ed., Brown U. Chmn. bd., pres. Turner Broadcasting System, Inc.; pres. Atlanta Braves, 1976—; chmn. bd. Atlanta Hawks, 1977—. Won America's Cup in his yacht Courageous, 1977. *

TURNER, ROBERT GERALD, university administrator; b. Atlanta, Tex., Nov. 25, 1945; s. Robert B. and Oreta Lois (Porter) T.; m. Gail Oliver, Dec. 21, 1968; children—Angela Jan, Jessica Diane. A.A., Lubbock Christian Coll., 1966; B.S., Abilene Christian U., 1968; M.A., U. Tex., 1970, Ph.D., 1975. Tchr. Weatherford High Sch., Tex., 1968-69, Lanier High Sch., Austin, Tex., 1969-70; instr. dept. psychology San Antonio Coll., Tex., 1970-72; instr. extension div. Prairie View A&M U., Tex., 1973-75; asst. prof. psychology Pepperdine U., Malibu, Calif., 1975-78, assoc. prof., 1978-79, dir. testing, 1975-76, chmn. social sci. div., 1976-78, assoc. v.p. univ. affairs, 1979; assoc. prof. psychology U. Okla., Norman, 1979-84, exec. asst. to pres., 1979-81, acting provost, 1982, v.p. exec. affairs, 1981-84; chancellor U. Miss., Oxford, 1984—. Co-author: Readings About Individual and Group Differences, 1979. Contbr. articles to profl. jours. NIMH trainee, 1972. Mem. Am. Assn. Univ. Adminstrs., Am. Psychol. Assn., Western Psychol. Assn., Southwestern Psychol. Assn., Miss. Psychol. Assn., Phi Theta Kappa, Alpha Chi. Mem. Ch. of Christ. Avocations: golf; tennis; reading; traveling. Office: U Miss 109 Lyceum St University MS 38677

TURNER, STEPHEN PARK, sociology and philosophy educator; b. Chgo., Mar. 1, 1951; s. Lawrence Lynn and Natalie (Stephens) T.; m. K. Summer Hebb, Jan. 14, 1978. A.B., U. Mo., 1971, A.M. in Sociology, 1971, A.M. in Philosophy, 1972, Ph.D. in Sociology, 1975. Prof., U. South Fla., St. Petersburg, 1984—, dir. Ctr. for Interdisciplinary Studies in Culture and Society, 1984-85; vis. prof. Ctr. for Study Sci. in Soc., Va. Poly. Inst., Blacksburg, 1982; vis. prof. Sociology U. Notre Dame, 1985. NDEA fellow, 1970-73. Mem. Inst. Internat. Sociologie, Internat. Sociol. Assn., Am. Sociol. Assn., So. Sociol. Soc., Soc. for Social Studies Sci. Club: Prairie. Author: Sociological Explanation as Translation, 1980; (with F. Weed) Conflict in Organizations, 1983; (with R. Factor) Max Weber and the Dispute Over Reason and Values, 1984; co-editor (with M. Wardell): Sociological Theory in Transition, 1986; The Search for a methodology of Social Science: Durkheim, Weber, and the 19th Century Problem of Cause, Probability, and Action, 1986; mem. editorial bd. Am. Sociologist, 1979-82, Human Studies, 1983—, History of Sociology, 1984—. Home: 1803 Sunrise Blvd Clearwater FL 33520 Office: U South Fla 140 7th Ave S Saint Petersburg FL 33701

TURNIPSEED, BARNWELL RHETT, III, journalist, public relations consultant, government official; b. Gainesville, Ga., Apr. 6, 1929; s. Barnwell Rhett and Leone (Rogers) T.; m. Jane Whitley, June 12, 1982. B.A. in Journalism, U. Ga., 1950, M.A. in Journalism, 1960. Program dir., ops. cons. Ga. broadcasting stas., 1953-60; sr. corr., sci. editor Voice of Am. Worldwide English, 1960-72; coordinator rado-TV pub. affairs HEW, 1972-73; mem. staff Ga. congressman Phil Landrum, 1974-75; dir. tech. info. dissemination Solar Energy Program, ERDA and Dept. Energy, 1975-77; spl. asst. Office of Asst. Sec. for Conservation and Solar Energy, Dept. Energy, Washington, 1977-81; cons. energy devel., pub. relations, Atlanta, 1981—; promoter aviation and aerospace devel.; comml. pilot. Symphony Guild rep. for Louisville and Columbus, Ga. Jaycees; active community symphony and arts devel. Served to sgt., U.S. Army, 1950-52; Korea. Recipient 2 meritorious service awards USIA. Mem. Nat. Assn. Sci. Writers, Aircraft Owners and Pilots Assn., Sigma Delta Chi. Democrat. Methodist. Author: History of Georgia Broadcasting, 1972; prin. corr. Voice of Am. Peabody award-winning space exploration broadcasts, 1969. Home: 4297 Doublegate Dr Douglasville GA 30135

TURPEN, MICHAEL, state attorney general; b. Tulsa; B.S., U. Tulsa, 1972, J.D., 1974. Legal advisor Muskogee Police Dept., 1975-76; asst. dist. atty., Muskogee County, 1976-78, dist. atty., 1978-82; atty. gen. State of Okla., Oklahoma City, 1983—; vice chmn. Okla. Crime Commn., 1980—; mem. Okla. State Bur. Investigation Commn., 1980—; adj. prof. Northeastern State U., 1977, also Connors State Coll. Mem. County Girls Softball Assn., Boy's League Baseball Assn. Recipient Donald Santarelli award Nat. Orgn. Victim for Assistance, 1981, One of 10 Outstanding Nat. Leaders in field victim rights, 1985; named One of 40 Men and Women under 40 Changing the Nation, Esquire mag., 1985. Mem. Okla. Dist. Attys. Assn. (pres. 1980—), ABA, Okla. Bar Assn. (Outstanding Young Lawyer award 1975, Golden Quill award 1980), Muskogee County Bar Assn., Jaycees. Democrat. Presbyterian. Lodge: Rotary. Office: State Capitol Bldg Suite 112 Oklahoma City OK 73105

TURRENTINE, ROBERT CLEVELAND, boot manufacturing company executive; b. Steubenville, Ohio, Aug. 15, 1925; s. Chesley Dean and Grace Lillian (Evans) T.; student Austin Peay State U., Clarksville, Tenn., 1946-47; m. Imogene Morgan, May 31, 1951; children—Carol, Richard, Ross, Grace. With Acme Boot Co., Inc., Clarksville, Tenn., 1947—, gen. mgr., then v.p. ops., 1950-62, pres., 1962—, chief exec. officer, 1970—; dir. First Nat. Bank, Clarksville. Trustee Meml. Hosp., Clarksville. Served with USAAF, 1943-46. Mem. Am. Footwear Industries Assn., Tenn. Mfrs. Assn., Tenn. Taxpayers Assn. Methodist. Office: 1002 Stafford St Clarksville TN 37040

TUTTLE, ELBERT PARR, federal judge; b. Pasadena, Calif., July 17, 1897; s. Guy Harmon and Margie Etta (Parr) T.; m. Sara Sutherland, Oct. 22, 1919; children—Elbert Parr, Jane T. (Mrs. John J. Harmon). Student, Punahou Acad., Honolulu, 1909-14; A.B., (Cornell U., 1918, LL.B., 1923; LL.D., Emory U., 1958, Harvard U., 1965, Georgetown U., 1978, Atlanta U., 1984. Bar: Ga. 1923. News and editorial writer N.Y. Evening Sun, N.Y.C.; also Army and Navy Jour. and Am. Legion Weekly, Washington, 1919; practiced in, Atlanta and Washington, 1923-53; mem. firm Sutherland, Tuttle & Brennan; gen. counsel, head legal div. Treasury Dept., 1953-54; judge 5th circuit U.S. Ct. Appeals, 1954-81, judge 11th circuit, 1981—, chief judge, 1961-67; Chmn. adv. com. on civil rules Jud. Conf. U.S., 1972-78, chmn. adv. com. on jud. activities, 1969-77. Trustee Atlanta Community Chest, 1947-49; v.p. Atlanta Community Planning Council, 1951; Past trustee Interdonominational Theol. Center, Cornell U., Atlanta U., Spelman Coll., Morehouse Coll., Piedmont Hosp. Served to col. F.A., 77th Inf. Div. U.S. Army, 1941-46; comdg. gen. 108th Airborne Div. (res.), 1947-50; brig. gen. U.S. Army Res. Decorated Legion of Merit, Bronze Star, Purple Heart with oak leaf cluster; recipient Presdl. medal of freedom, 1981. Mem. ABA, Atlanta Bar Assn. (pres. 1948), Atlanta C. of C. (pres. 1949), Phi Kappa Phi, Pi Kappa Alpha (nat. pres. 1930-36), Order of Coif. Episcopalian.

TUTTLE, RON LUTHER, academic administrator; b. Winston-Salem, N.C., May 22, 1941; s. Roland Luther and Alta May (Fulton) T.; m. Shirley Louise Clowney, May 31, 1969; children—Alise, Susanne. B.A., U. N.C., 1963, Ed.D., 1972; M.A., Columbia U., 1967. Dean Grad. Sch., Appalachian State U., Boone, N.C., 1979-80; research asst. to v.p. U. N.C., Chapel Hill, 1981; prof. ednl. stats. Appalachian State U., 1981-83; dean of univ., chief exec. officer U. S.C. at Beaufort, 1983—, mem. presdl. commn. on undergrad. missions U. S.C., 1984-85, mem. alumni council, 1985—. Contbr. articles to profl. jours. Chmn. Beaufort Tourism Com., 1984-85; bd. dirs. Beaufort Salvation Army, 1983-85; mem. dist. com. Low Country council Boy Scouts Am., 1983-85. Mem. Am. Ednl. Research Assn., Assn. Regional Campus Adminstrs., Navy League, Phi Delta Kappa. Democrat. Baptist. Club: Sea Island Rotary. Avocations: running, skiing. Home: 111 Fort Marion Rd Beaufort SC 29902 Office: U SC at Beaufort 800 Carteret St Beaufort SC 29902

TWELL, CHARLES FOSTER, geologist, consultant; b. Hays, Kans., Nov. 14, 1935; s. George Norman and Flavel (Kelley) T.; m. Virginia Ann Horner, Jan. 3, 1960; children—Charles Archer, Catherine Ann. B.S., Kans. State U., 1958, M.S., U. Kans., 1964. Geologist, Empire Drilling Co., Wichita, Kans., 1958-62; mgr. geology Sun Oil Co., Dallas, 1964-81; sr. geologist Evergreen Oil Co., 1981-82; cons. geologist Twell, Inc., Dallas, 1982—; geol. cons. Baker & Taylor Drilling Co., Amarillo, Tex., 1982—, Maguire Oil Co., Dallas, 1983—, Transam. Energy, Ltd., 1984—. Mem. Collin County Republican Com., Plano, Tex., 1978. Mem. Am. Assn. Petroleum Geologists, Dallas Geol. Soc., Sigma Xi. Episcopalian. Avocation: antique autos. Home: 1424 Debon Dr Plano TX 75075 Office: Twell Incorp 2007 N Collins Blvd 207 Richardson TX 75080

TWIFORD, H. HUNTER, III, lawyer; b. Memphis, Sept. 19, 1949; s. Horace Hunter and Elizabeth (Andrews) T.; m. Frances Dill, June 27, 1970; children—Elizabeth Smith, Horace Hunter IV. B.A., U. Miss., 1971, J.D., 1972. Bar: Miss. 1972, U.S. Dist. Ct. Miss. 1972, U.S. Ct. Appeals (5th cir.) 1977, U.S. Supreme Ct. 1977. Assoc., Holcomb, Dunbar, Connell, Merkel & Tollison, Clarksdale, Miss., 1972-75, H. Hunter Twiford III, Clarksdale, 1975-77; ptnr. Garmon, Wood & Twiford, Clarksdale, 1977-78, Wood & Twiford, P.A., Clarksdale, 1978-85; Twiford & Webster, P.A., 1985—; adj. prof. Coahoma Jr. Coll., Clarksdale, 1976—; firm city atty. City of Clarksdale, 1977—, Town of Friars Point, Miss., 1981—; mcpl. judge pro tempore City of Clarksdale, 1974-76. Mem. vestry St. George's Episc. Ch., Clarksdale, 1974-76, 82-83, sr. warden, 1984-86; mem. Coahoma County C. of C., Clarksdale, 1975—; mem. Gov.'s Commn. on Drug Abuse, Jackson, Miss., 1976-80; sec. Clarksdale-Coahoma County Joint Airport Bd., Clarksdale, 1981—. Mem. Assn. Trial Lawyers Am., Miss. Trial Lawyers Assn., Nat. Assn. Criminal Def. Lawyers, Miss. Bar Assn., Miss. Prosecutors Assn., Am. Judicature Assn., Coahoma County Bar Assn. Lodge: Rotary (pres. 1984-85). Home: 1420 Rose Circle Clarksdale MS 38614 Office: Twiford & Webster PA 148 Sunflower Ave Clarksdale MS 38614

TWIGG, CHRISTOPHER JOHN RAYMOND, blood center executive; b. Sheffield, Eng., Sept. 23, 1945; came to U.S., 1976; s. Raymond Albert and Betty (Gascoigne) T.; m. Judith Mary Long, Jan. 10, 1970; 1 son, Robin James Christian. Diploma in bus. Sheffield Coll. Tech., 1967; Diploma in Mktg., Sheffield Poly. Inst., 1970; D.B.A., Calif. Coast U., 1983. Dir. ARC Blood Program, St. Louis, 1978-80; pres. Blood Ctr. for Southeast La., New Orleans, 1980—; pres. Force Five, Inc., 1980—; ptnr. African Artifacts, 1982—. Bd. dirs. New Orleans chpt. ARC, 1982—; chmn. Health Systems Agy., 1980-82; bd. dirs. Council Community Blood Ctrs., Washington, 1981—. Mem. Am. Assn. Blood Banks, Am. Assn. Donor Recruitment Profls. Lodge: Rotary. Contbr. articles to profl. jours. Home: 9205 Hermitage Pl River Ridge LA 70123 Office: Blood Ctr for SE La 312 S Galvez St New Orleans LA 70119

TWINAM, JOSEPH WRIGHT, international relations educator, former foreign service officer; b. Chattanooga, July 11, 1934; s. John Courtenay and Daisy (Murphy) T.; m. Janet Carolyn Ashby, May 30, 1959; children—Courtenay Jane, Marshall Ashby. B.A. with honors, U. Va., 1956; postgrad. Georgetown U., 1960-61. Commd. fgn. service officer Dept. State, 1959; various assignments within the fgn. service in Netherlands, Kuwait, Saudi Arabia, Dept. State; ambassador to Bahrain, 1974-76; dir. Arabian Peninsula affairs Dept. State, Washington, 1976-79; dep. asst. Sec. of State, Washington, 1979-82, dean of sr. seminar and profl. studies Fgn. Service Inst., 1983-85; vis. prof. U. Va., 1982-83; John C. West disting. vis. prof. internat. relations The Citadel, Charleston, S.C., 1985—. Served to lt. (j.g.) USN, 1956-59. Democrat. Episcopalian.

TWYMAN, JOSEPH PASCHAL, university president; b. Prainie Hill, Mo., Nov. 21, 1933; s. William L. and Hazel (Dry) T.; B.A., U. Mo. at Kansas City, 1955, M.A., 1959, Ph.D., 1962; m. Patricia Joanne Harper, July 26, 1953; children—Mark Kevin, Patricia Lynn. Asst. prof., then asso. prof. Okla. State U., 1960-66, asso. dir. Research Found., 1965-66; dir. research U. Mo. at St. Louis, 1966-67; v.p. U. Tulsa, 1967-68, pres., 1968—; cons. in field, 1960—; dir. Sooner Fed. Savs. & Loan Assn., Atlas Life Ins. Co.; mem. Commn. on Instns. Higher Edn., North Central Assn. Colls. and Schs., 1975—. Mem. adv. panel Southwestern Coop. Ednl. Lab., 1967-68; adv. bd. Tulsa Opera, 1968-77, St. John's Hosp., Tulsa, 1969-76. Bd. dirs. Okla Council Econ. Edn., 1968—, Tulsa Area United Way, 1968-77, Tulsa Civic Ballet, 1968-78, Arts Council Tulsa, 1970-77, Thomas Gilcrease Mus. Assn., 1970—, Goodwill Industries of Tulsa, Inc., 1975-82; bd. dirs., acting chmn. Tulsa Area Health Edn. Center, 1977-79; trustee Undercroft Montessori Sch., Tulsa, 1967-72, Children's Med. Center, Tulsa, 1968-73, Tech. Edn. Research Center Inc., Cambridge, Mass., 1977—; Hillcrest Med. Center, Tulsa, 1969-80, 81—; mem. exec. com. Okla.'s Future Inc., 1981—; bd. dirs. Tulsa Mental Health Assn., 1967-74, 75—, Mid-Continent Research and Devel. Council, 1967-68. Ford Found. grantee, 1963-66, U.S. Office Edn. grantee, 1958-60, 61-62, 62-63, 64-65, 64-66. Mem. AAAS, Am. Acad. Polit. and Social Sci., Okla. Cattlemen's Assn., Belted Galloway Soc., Phi Delta Kappa, Omicron Delta Kappa. Presbyterian. Clubs: Southern Hills, University and Summit (Tulsa). Author: (with others) The Concept of Role Conflict, 1964; also articles.

TYLER, DONALD STEPHEN, electrostatic equipment company executive; b. Aurora, Ill., Aug. 2, 1946; s. Claude Trull and Erba Waneeta (Ames) T.; m. Janet K. Murchie, Aug. 13, 1967 (div. 1970); children—Sandra Marie; m. Leah Elizabeth Cromer, July 1, 1978; children—Jennifer Ann, Julia Elizabeth, Jessica Lynn. With Armstrong Products Co., Warsaw, Ind., 1968-75; v.p. Advance Poly. Assocs., Orlando, Fla., 1975-76; with Tyler Machinery Co., Warsaw, 1976-79; product mgr. Armstrong Products Co., 1979-80; gen. sales mgr. Volstatic Inc., Florence, Ky., 1980—, gen. mgr., 1981—; dir. The Powder Coating Inst., Greenwich, Conn.; dir., v.p. Chem. Coaters Assn., Cin. Served with U.S. Army, 1966-68. Mem. Powder Coating Inst., Chem. Coatings Assn. (dir.), Am. Chem. Soc., ASTM, Am. Mgmt. Assn., Am. Electroplaters Soc., Assn. Finishing Process, Soc. Mfg. Engrs. Address: 7960 Kentucky Dr Florence KY 41042

TYLKOWSKI, CHESTER MITCHELL, orthopedic surgeon; b. Chgo., Dec. 24, 1946; s. Mitchell Francis and Marie (Helinski) T.; m. Maureen Hennaghan, Sept. 9, 1972; 1 child, Daniel. Student, St. Procopius Coll., Lisle, Ill., 1969-70; B.S., U. Ill.-Chgo., 1969, M.S., M.D., 1973. Diplomate Am. Bd. Orthopedic Surgery. Intern, U. Ill. Hosps., 1973-74, resident dept. orthopedic surgery, 1974-78, Children's Hosp. Med. Ctr., Harvard U. Med. Sch., 1978-79; assoc. prof. orthopedic surgery U. Fla., 1979—, dir. Cerebral Palsy Clinic and Gait Analysis Lab., 1979—; mem. sch. health adv. bd. Alachua County, 1974—. Mem. Am. Acad. Orthopedic Surgeons, Pediatric Orthopedic Soc., Am. Acad. Cerebral Palsy and Devel. Medicine, Scoliosis Research Soc. Roman Catholic. Contbr. articles to profl. jours. Office: Coll Medicine U Fla Box J 246 Health Ctr Gainesville FL 32610

TYNER, MAX RAYMOND, clergyman; b. Kokomo, Ind., Nov. 21, 1925; s. Paul Raymond and Dora May (Schroeder) T.; m. Marjorie Jane Tobias, Dec. 30, 1949; children—Renita (Mrs. Thomas Odom), Shawnee Marthel (Mrs. James Overstreet). Student Ind. U. extension, 1946; B. Liberal Studies, U. Okla.; postgrad. Calif. State U.; Gen. mgr. Becraft Motor Express, Inc., Kokomo, 1946-58; owner Tyner Realty & Ins., McAllen, Tex., 1959-72; buyer Summer Inst. Linguistics, Mexico City, 1972-73; ordained to ministry Methodist Ch., 1968; pastor 1st United Meth. Ch., George West, Tex., 1973-77, First United Meth. Hosp., Port Isabel, Tex.; Author: The Tyner Family and Some Other Relatives. Bd. dirs., sec. Rio Grand Children's Home, Mission, Tex., 1968-72; bd. dirs. Alliance Village Nursing Home, McAllen, 1970-72, Salvation Army, 1965-69. Served with USNR, 1944-45. Named hon. citizen, Guadalajara, Mexico, 1964, Xalapa, 1963; named outstanding mem. Kokomo Jr. C. of C., 1956. Mem. Am. Assn. Christian Counselors, Internat. Platform Assn., Am. Legion, Wycliffe Assocs., Christian Writers Guild, Christian Motorcyclists Assn., Circuit Riders. Republican. Clubs: Masons, Shriners. Home: PO Box 1072 Port Isabel TX 78578 Office: PO Box 1074 Port Isabel TX 78578 Office: PO Box 1074 Port Isabel TX 78578

TYRE, JOSEPH BYRON, JR., pharmacist; b. Albany, Ga., Sept. 3, 1957; s. Joseph Byron and Mary Jacqueline (Harris) T. A.A., Albany Jr. Coll., 1977; B.S. in Pharmacy, U. Ga., 1980. Registered pharmacist, Ga. Pharmacist, Revco Drugs, Dunwoody, Ga., 1980—. Mem. Ga. Pharm. Assn., Phi Lambda Sigma, Phi Delta Chi (pres. 1978-79). Republican. Baptist. Home: 204 Treecorners Pkwy Norcross GA 30092 Office: Revco Drugs Inc 1420 Dunwoody Village Pkwy Dunwoody GA 30338

TYREE, TERRY LYNN, educator; b. Benham, Ky., Sept. 21, 1955; s. Franklin and Wilma Doris (Gilliam) Fields. A.S., S.E. Community Coll., Cumberland, Ky., 1975; B.A., U. Ky., 1977. Tchr., Lexington (Ky.) Sch., 1978-79; tchr., coach Bishop Kenny High Sch., Jacksonville, Fla., 1979—; camp counselor Falling Creek Camp for Boys, Tuxedo, N.C., 1977—; basketball coach Jacksonville AAU, 1982—. Named Coach of Yr., North Fla. Conf., 1980, 82, 83, Mr. Inspiration, Falling Creek Camp, 1978. Mem. Fla. Athletic Coaches Assn., Nat. Catholic Edn. Assn. (tchr. assoc.), Nat. Audubon Soc., Wilderness Soc., Nat. Wildlife Fedn. Democrat. Baptist. Club: Sierra. Home: 8276 San Jose Manor Ct Apt 3 Jacksonville FL 32217 Office: Bishop Kenny High Sch 1055 Kingman Ave Jacksonville FL 32207

TYSON, HELEN FLYNN, civic leader, retired budget analyst; b. Wilmington, N.C.; d. Walter Thomas and Fannie Elizabeth (Smith) Flynn; A.A., Pineland Jr. Coll., 1931; student Guilford Coll., 1932-33, Am. U., Washington, 1961-62; m. James Franklin Tyson, Dec. 25, 1940 (dec.). Auditor, Disbursing Office, U.S. Civil Service, AUS, Ft. Bragg, N.C., 1935-46, chief clerical asst. Disbursing Office, Pope AFB, N.C., 1946-49, asst. budget and acctg. officer, 1949-55, supervisory budget officer hdqrs. Mil. Transport Command, USAF, 1955-57, budget analyst Hdqrs. USAF, Washington, 1957-74. Active, Arlington Com. 100, Arlington Hosp. Found., Salvation Army Women's Aux., Inter-Service Club Council of Arlington; pres. Operation Check-Mate Council of Arlington, 1981-82; charter asso. Alexandria City Hosp. Found. Recipient awards U.S. Treasury, 1945, 46, U.S. State Dept., 1970; Good Neighbor award Ft. Belvoir Civilian-Mil. Adv. Council, 1978; awards U.S. First Army, 1973, ARC, 1977; named Arlington County Woman of Yr., 1975; Vol. Activist of Yr. of Washington Met. Area, 1981. Mem. Nat. Fedn. Bus. and Profl. Women's Clubs, Nat. Assn. Ret. Fed. Employees, Am. Soc. Mil. Comptrollers, Am. Inst. Parliamentarians, Am. Assn. Ret. Personnel, Guilford Coll. Alumni Assn., N.C. Soc. Washington. Clubs: Mil. Dist. of Washington Officers, Altrusa Internat. Home: 4900 N Old Dominion Dr Arlington VA 22207

TYSON, KAREN WINDAU, economist, industry consultant; b. Sandusky, Ohio, Nov. 25, 1951; d. Robert G. and Lola (Light) Windau; m. Herbert L. Tyson III, June 14, 1974. B.A. in Econs. and Govt., Georgetown U., 1973; M.A. in Econs., Mich. State U., 1975, Ph.D., 1980. Economist Abt Assoc., Cambridge, Mass., 1977-78; sr. economist Chase Econometrics, Bala Cynwyd, Pa., 1978-81; sr. fellow Ctr. Health Policy Studies, Georgetown U., Washington, 1982-85; cost. analyst Inst for Def. Analyses, Alexandria, Va., 1986—; cons. in field. Mem. Fedn. Orgn. Profl. Women, Washington Women Economists, Nat. Econs. Club (sec. 1984—), Nat. Assn. Bus. Econs., Am. Econ. Assn., Mt. Vernon Amateur Radio Club. Office: Inst for Def Analyses 1801 N Beauregard St Alexandria VA 22311

TYSON, PHOEBE WHATLEY, painter; b. Wichita Falls, Tex., May 5, 1926; d. Mertic Boyd and Susie Phoebe (Creath) Whatley; student Abilene Christian U., 1943-45; B.A., N. Tex. State U., 1946, M.A., 1951; m. Josiah William Tyson, Jr., Dec. 20, 1946; children—Josiah William III, Phoebe Creath Tyson McDavid. Elem. art tchr. Ft. Worth Ind. Sch. Dist., 1946-47; pvt. tchr. art, Haskell, Tex., 1948-50; painter watercolors, acrylics, Seabrook, Tex., 1971-79, Austin, Tex., 1979—; exhibitor Biennial Exhbn., Nat. League Am. Pen Women, Kennedy Center, Washington (award of distinction), 1976, Rocky Mountain Nat. Watermedia Exhbn., Golden, Colo., McNay Art Inst., San Antonio, Tex. Watercolor Ann. Exhbn. (purchase award); pres. McLean (Va.) Art Club, 1971. Mem. Tex. Fine Arts Assn., Nat. League Am. Pen. Women (nat. art bd. 1972-74, Tex. v.p. 1972-74, Meml. br. pres. 1976-78), Art League Houston, AAUW (v.p. Austin 1955-56), Clear Creek Art League, Watercolor Art Soc. Houston, Tex. Watercolor Soc., Waterloo Watercolor Group, Nat. Watercolor Soc. (assoc.), San Antonio Water Color Group, Waterloo Watercolor Group. Mem. Ch. of Christ. Home and Office: 8600 Appalachian Austin TX 78759

TZAMTZIS, ANTHONY EUGENE, architect; b. Thessaloniki, Macedonia, Greece, May 23, 1949; came to U.S. 1973, naturalized 1978; s. Euthimios Constantine and Helen (Karras) T.; m. Christine McBriarty, Nov. 11, 1972 (div. 1977). B.A. in Architecture, Inst. Architecture of Venice, Italy, 1972; M.A. in Architecture, U. Pa. Louis I Kahn Studio, 1974. Registered architect, 1982. Sr. planner Del. County Planning Dept., Media, Pa., 1974-76, Dade County Planning Dept., Miami, 1976-79; architect Greenleaf-Telesca, Inc., Miami, 1979-82; pres., prin. architect In-Architecture, Inc., Miami, 1982—; tchr., special cons. Miami Dade Community Coll., 1982—. Author: Passive Design Principles for Hot and Humid Climates, 1983. Guest, lectr. ednl. video tape: Passive Design - part of the Solstice TV services, 1984. Fgn. student scholar Ministry of Edn., Venice, Italy, 1969; U. Pa. scholar, 1973. Mem. AIA. Roman Catholic. Avocations: carpentry, painting, yoga, chess. Home: 2421 Tigertail Ave Miami FL 33133 Office: In-Architecture Inc 4055 Ponce De Leon Coral Gables FL 33146

UEKERMANN, MANFRED NORBERT, bank holding company executive; b. Sontra, W.Ger., Oct. 6, 1950; s. Hans and Gisela (Kalus) Sonnenschein; m. Nancy Jones, Aug. 19, 1971; 1 child. B.S. in Bus. and Econs., Okla. State U., 1973, M.S. in Econs., 1976. Dir. mgmt. info. systems and research, planning and devel. Tri-County Employment and Tng. Authority, Inc., Tulsa, 1977-79; coordinator planning and product devel. Blue Cross & Blue Shield of Okla., Tulsa, 1979-80; dir. corp. planning Hinderliter Industries, Inc., Tulsa, 1981-83; mgr. corp. devel. Midland Fin. Co., Tulsa and Oklahoma City, 1983—; prof. econs. Tulsa Jr. Coll., part-time, 1977—; instr. econs. Okla. State U. Mem. budget com. local United Way; active Sand Springs (Okla.) Soccer Club. Mem. Strategic Planning Inst., Planning Execs. Inst., Am. Econs. Assn., Tulsa Bus. Econs. Club, Am. Mgmt. Assn., Sand Springs C. of C. Office: 7010 S Yale St Suite 215 Tulsa OK 74177

UENG, CHARLES EN-SHIUH, engineering educator, consultant; b. Kiangtu, Kiangsu, China, Sept. 8, 1930; s. San Yu and Shu Chi (Hsu) U.; m. Shirley Wen-Hwa Chen, Oct. 20, 1962; children—Vivian, Grace. B.S., Nat. Cheng-Kung U., Tainan, Taiwan, 1953; M.S., Kans. State U., 1960, Ph.D., 1963. Registered profl. engr., China. Asst. structural engr. Taiwan Power Co., 1954-58; asst. prof. engring. Kans. State U., 1963-64; asst. prof. engring., Ga. Inst. Tech., Atlanta, 1964-67, assoc. prof., 1967-77, prof., 1977—; cons. to industry. NSF grantee, 1964, 74; NASA grantee, 1967, 68; Soc. Mfg. Engring. grantee, 1981. Mem. Soc. Engring. Sci., ASCE (award 1983), Am. Soc. Engring. Edn., Am. Acad. Mechanics. Republican. Baptist. Contbr. articles profl. jours. Home: 2037 Chesterfield Dr NE Atlanta GA 30345 Office: School of Engineering Science and Mechanics Georgia Institute of Technology Atlanta GA 30332

UGELOW, ALBERT JAY, mechanical engineer; b. Bklyn., Mar. 16, 1950; s. Seymour Joseph and Leah (Payenson) U.; m. Paula Statsky, Apr. 29, 1973; children—Sharon Heather, Brianne Melissa. B.S., Columbia U., 1971; M.Engring., Stevens Inst. Tech., Hoboken, N.J., 1976. Registered profl. engr., N.Y., Fla. Asst. engr. Ebasco Services, N.Y.C., 1971-73, assoc. engr., 1973-74, engr., 1974-77, lead nuclear steam supply system engr., 1977-80, prin. engr., 1980-81, prin. engr., Stuart, Fla., 1981-84, supervising engr., 1984—. Mem. ASME, Nat. Soc. Profl. Engrs., Am. Nuclear Soc., N.Y. State Soc. Profl. Engrs. (Young Engr. of Yr. 1982, dir. Queens County chpt.). Democrat. Jewish. Lodge: K.P. Office: Ebasco Services 1111 S Federal Hwy Stuart FL 33497

UHDE, GEORGE IRVIN, physician; b. Richmond, Ind., Mar. 20, 1912; s. Walter Richard and Anna Margaret (Hoopes) U.; M.D., Duke, U., 1936; m. Maurine Elizabeth Whitley, July 27, 1935; children—Saundra Uhde Seelig, Thomas Whitley, Michael, Janice. Intern, Reading (Pa.) Hosp., 1936-37, resident in medicine, 1937-38; resident in otolaryngology Balt. Eye, Ear Nose and Throat Hosp., 1938-40, U. Oreg. Med. Sch., Portland, 1945-47; practice medicine specializing in otolaryngology, Louisville, 1948—; asst. prof. otolaryngology U. Louisville Med. Sch., 1945-62, prof. surgery (otolaryngology), 1963—, head dept., 1963-81, dir. otolaryngology services, 1963—; mem. staff Meth., Norton's-Children's, Jewish, St. Joseph's, St. Anthony's, St. Mary and Elizabeth's hosps.; cons. Ky. Surg. Tb Hosp., Hazelwood, VA Hosp., Louisville; cons. U. Louisville Speech and Hearing Center. Bd. dirs. Easter Seal Speech and Hearing Center. Served to lt. col. M.C., AUS, 1940-45; ETO; chief gas casualty and biol. warfare ETOUSA; Research Officer under Sir Lovatt Evans. Recipient Distinguished Service award U. Louisville, 1972; Sower's award Founders Soc.; endowed George I. Uhde, M.D. Endowment Fund, Duke U., Uhde Otolaryngology Fund, George I. Uhde, M.D. Award for Excellence in otolaryngology, U. Louisville. Fellow A.C.S., Am. Acad. Ophthalmology and Otolaryngology, So. Med. Soc.; mem. N.Y. Acad. Scis., Am. Coll. Allergists, Am. Acad. Facial Plastic and Reconstructive Surgery, AAAS, Assn. U. Otolaryngologists, AAUP, Assn. Mil. Surgeons U.S., Am. Laryngol., Rhinol. and Otol. Soc., Am. Audiology Soc., Soc. Clin. Ecology, Am. Soc. Otolaryngology Allergy, Centurian Otol. Research Soc. (Ky. rep.), Am. Council Otolaryngology (Ky. rep. 1968—), Hoopes Quaker Found., Centurion Found., SAR (life), Alpha Kappa Kappa. Democrat. Methodist. Clubs: Filson, Big Spring Country, Jefferson. Author 4 books; contbr. articles to profl. jours. Home: 708 Circle Hill Rd Louisville KY 40207 Office: Med Towers South Louisville KY 40202

UHLIR, GLADYS ANN, university dean; b. Kokomo, Ind., Aug. 13, 1934; d. George C. and Gladys (Young) U. B.S., Ball State U., 1955; M.A., Tchrs. Coll., Columbia U., 1956, Ed.D., 1962. Assoc. prof. phys. edn. SUNY-Brockport, 1956-65; prof., chmn. dept. phys. edn., project dir. women's ednl. equity Eastern Ky. U., 1965-79; exec. dir. Assn. Intercollegiate Athletics for Women, Washington, 1979-82; edn. and sport cons., 1982-83; dean Coll. Health, Phys. Edn., Recreation and Dance, Tex. Woman's U., Denton, 1983—; speaker. Mem. Ky. Nat. Women's Yr. Com., 1977, Phys. Educators for Ednl. Equity, 1978-79; mem. ho. of dels. U.S. Olympic Com., 1980-82. Recipient Outstanding Service award and Founders award Ky. Women's Intercollegiate Conf., 1981; Columbia Alumni fellow, 1959-60. Mem. AAHPER and Dance, Nat. Assn. Girls and Women in Sport (pres. 1973; Disting. Service award 1974), Women's Equity Action League, Coll. and Univ. Adminstrs. Council, Ky. Assn. Health, Phys. Edn. and Recreation, Nat. Assn. Women Deans, Adminstrs., Counselors. Congregationalist.

UHRIG, ROBERT EUGENE, engineering educator; b. Raymond, Ill., Aug. 6, 1928; s. John Matthew and Anna LaDonna (Fireman) U.; m. Paula Margaret Schnepf, Nov. 27, 1954; children—Robert J., Joseph C., Mary C., Charles W., Jean M., Thomas P., Fredrick J. B.S. with honors, U. Ill., 1948; M.S. Iowa State U., 1950, Ph.D., 1954; grad. Advanced Mgmt. Program, Harvard U., 1976. Registered profl. engr., Iowa, Fla. Instr., Iowa State U., Ames, 1948-51, research engr., 1951-52, grad. asst., 1952-54, assoc. prof. nuclear engring., 1956-60; chmn. dept. nuclear engring. U. Fla., Gainesville, 1960-68, dean Coll. Engring. 1968-73; v.p. advanced systems and tech. Fla. Power & Light Co., Miami, Juno Beach, 1982-86; Disting. prof. engring., dept. nuclear engring. U. Tenn., Knoxville, 1986—. Served with USAF, 1954-56. Recipient Meritorious Civil Service award U.S. Dept. Def., 1968; Disting. Service in Engring. award U. Ill. Alumni, 1970; Disting. Achievement citation Iowa State U. Alumni, 1980. Fellow ASME (Richards meml. award 1969), Am. Nuclear Soc., AAAS; mem. Nat. Soc. Profl. Engrs., Fla. Engring. Soc. Roman Catholic. Author: Random Noise Techniques in Nuclear Reactor Systems, 1970 (transl. into Russian 1974); editor: Neutron Noise, Wave, and Pulse Propagation, 1966; Noise Analysis In Nuclear Systems, 1963; contbr. articles to profl. jours. Office: Dept Nuclear Engring U Tenn Knoxville TN 37996

ULLBERG, KENT JEAN, sculptor; b. Gothenburg, Sweden, July 15, 1945; came to U.S., 1974; s. Jean Wilgot and Kerstin A. (Axelsson) U.; m. Veerle Rufina Vermeir, May 5, 1978; children—Robert, Gerald. Grad., Swedish State Sch. Art, Stockholm, 1966. Cert. German Assn. Museologists, 1966. Tech. dir. Botswana Game Industries, 1968-70; curator Botswana Nat. Mus. and Art Gallery, 1971-74; curator Denver Mus. Natural History, 1974-75; sculptor, Corpus Christi, Tex., 1976—; works include PUMA, Gothenburg Mus., 1980; Lincoln Ctr. Eagle monument, Dallas, 1981; Watermusic, Corpus Christi, 1981; Wind in the Sails, Corpus Christi, 1983; Genesee Eagle, Genesee Mus., Rochester, N.Y., 1983; Mem. NAD (Barnett prize, 1975), Nat. Sculpture Soc. (Dietsch award, 1979, Meisner award, 1981, Gold medal, 1983), Nat. Acad. Western Art, (Gold medals for sculpture, 1981-82), Soc. Animal Artists, Am. Soc. Marine Artists. Home and Studio: 14337 Aquarius St Corpus Christi TX 78418

ULLMANN, STEVEN GEORGE, economics educator; b. San Francisco, May 29, 1953; s. Gunter and Ilse (Chaska) U.; m. Rhonwyn Alice Edwards, June 29, 1980; children—Jeffery, Bryan. B.A., U. Calif.-Berkeley, 1974; M.A., U. Mich., 1976, Ph.D., 1980. Research asst. U. Mich., Ann Arbor, 1975-78, fellow, instr., 1975-78, research assoc., 1977-79; research assoc. Policy Analysis, Inc., Ann Arbor, 1978; instr. Ferris State Coll., Big Rapids, Mich., 1978-79; asst. prof. dept. econs. U. Miami, Coral Gables, Fla., 1980—, assoc. dir. health adminstrn. programs, 1985; cons. econs. Mgr. hurricane shelter ARC, Coral Gables, 1983-85. U. Miami Sch. Bus. grantee, 1980, 81, 82, 84; Am. Assn. Ret. Persons-Andrus Found. grantee, 1982-83; recipient excellence in teaching award U. Miami Sch. Bus., 1980, 84, U. Miami Student Body, 1981, 84. Mem. Am. Econ. Assn., Health Econs. Research Orgn., Phi Kappa Phi. Democrat. Jewish. Avocations: playing piano; bicycle riding; model building. Office: Dept Econs U Miami 517 Jenkins Bldg Standard Dr Coral Gables FL 33124

ULLRICH, GUSTAVE, educator; b. Bklyn., June 12, 1915; s. Rudolph Maximilian and Alma Ida (Blendow) U.; A.A.S., Bklyn. Coll., 1962; B.A., Trinity U., 1968; M.A., S.W. Tex. State U., 1975; m. Ada Laura Dilworth, Sept. 26, 1948; 1 dau., Lisa Lynne. Lt. Tng. Inst., unit asst. mgr. N.Y.C. Police Acad., 1941-66; tchr. English and math. San Antonio Comml. Coll., 1968-69; faculty traffic adminstrn. S.W. Tex. State U., San Marcos, summer 1976; tchr. English, New Braunfels (Tex.) Ind. Sch. Dist., 1968—, chmn. dept. English, 1978-80. Served with USAF, 1941-46; ETO, PTO; to lt. col. USAF, 1950-52; Korea. Cert. profl. tchr., Tex. Mem. MLA, Assn. of Tex. Profl. Educators, Assn. for Supervision and Curriculum Devel., New Braunfels C. of C., Soc. Profl. Investigators, Central Tex. Council Tchrs. of English, Nat. Rifle Assn., Alpha Sigma Lambda, Alpha Chi, Sigma Tau Delta, Pi Gamma Mu. Republican. Baptist. Club: Masons. Asst. editor Bull. Soc. Profl. Investigators, 1962-68; editorial bd. Valor Mag., 1963-65. Home: 3 Ridge Dr New Braunfels TX 78130 Office: 2551 Loop 337 N New Braunfels TX 78130

ULMER, DEBORAH LUXTON, medical training administrator, nurse, consultant; b. Phila., Apr. 1, 1953; d. Elvin Lamar and Charlotte Mabel (Herring) Luxton; m. David Dewitt Ulmer, Jan. 10, 1976. B.S. in Nursing, W.Va. Wesleyan U., 1975; M.Edn., Va. Commonwealth U., 1980. R.N., Va. Staff nurse St. Francis Hosp., Pitts., 1976; pub. health nurse Va. Health Dept., Richmond, 1977; head nurse Corrections Commn. of Va., Richmond, 1978, dir. edn. and tng. Chippenham Hosp., Richmond, 1978—; mem. faculty mgmt. tng. Ctr. for Health Studies, Nashville, 1980—; cons., 1982—. Author: (tng. programs) Communication by Caring, 1979, Why Bother?, 1984. Mem. adv. com. Va. Commonwealth U. Sch. Health Occupations, Richmond, 1983—, John Tyler Community Coll., Richmond, 1983. Mem. Am. Soc. Tng. and Devel., Am. Soc. for Health, Edn. and Tng. Democrat. Methodist. Home: 503 Kennesaw Ct Richmond VA 23236 Office: Chippenham Hosp 7101 Jahnke Rd Richmond VA 23225

ULMER, MELVIN ULRIS, JR., insurance company executive; b. Meridian, Miss., June 15, 1921; s. Melvin Ulris and Maud Belle (Eason) U.; student Tulane U., 1939-41; m. Ollie Mae cInnis, Sept. 21, 1941 (dec.); children—Beverly Carol Ulmer Robertson, Melvin Ulris III; m. 2d, Mary Beth Hawkins, Mar. 7, 1981. Accessory salesman Philco Corp., Phila., 1948-49; parts mgr. McWhorter Weaver Co., Nashville, 1949-53; with N.Y. Life Ins. Co., 1953—, ins. cons., New Orleans 1960—. Ordained deacon Baptist Ch.; v.p. Ulmer Family Reunion. Served with USN, 1942-45. Mem. Nat. Assn. Life Underwriters, SAR, SCV. Democrat. Clubs: Masons, Shriner, High Twelve. Home: 832 Legion Dr Gretna LA 70053 Office: New York Life Ins Co 1 Shell Sq Suite 636 New Orleans LA 70139

ULMER, SHIRLEY SIDNEY, political science educator; b. North, S.C., Apr. 15, 1923; s. Shirley Shakespeare and Anna Rebecca (Reed) U.; m. Margaret Anel Lipscomb, Mar. 18, 1946; children—Margaret, William, Susan, John, Mary. B.A. cum laude, Furman U., 1952, LL.D. with honors, 1981; M.A. (Rockefeller fellow) Duke U., 1954, Ph.D. (Otis Greene fellow), 1956. Instr. polit. sci. Duke U., Durham, N.C., 1954-55; instr. U. Houston, 1956; mem. faculty Mich. State U., East Lansing, 1956-63, assoc. prof., 1960-63, chmn. dept. polit. sci., 1961-62; chmn. dept. polit. sci. U. Ky., Lexington, 1963-69, prof., 1963-78, Alumni prof., 1978—; vis. prof. SUNY-Buffalo, 1969, U. Wis.-Milw., 1974, Ariz. State U., 1980; mem. polit. sci. panel NSF, 1968-70, chmn. bd. overseers Data Base Project, U.S. Supreme Ct., 1984—. Served with USAAF, 1942-45. Decorated Air medal with 4 oak leaf clusters; named Disting. Prof. Arts and Scis., U. Ky., 1975-76, recipient Sang award, 1973, 74; Phi Sigma Alpha award, 1983. NSF grantee, 1969-71, 79-82; Social Sci. Research Council fellow, 1958, 1967. Mem. Am. Polit. Sci. Assn., So. Polit. Sci. Assn. (exec. council, pres. 1971-72), Midwest Polit. Sci. Assn., Ky. Polit. Sci. Assn. (v.p. 1966-67), Inter-Univ. Consortium Polit. Research (exec. council 1966-67, council chmn. 1967-68), Phi Beta Kappa. Author: Military Justice and the Right to Counsel, 1971; Courts as Small and Not So Small Groups, 1971; Supreme Court Policy Making and Constitutional Law, 1985; editor: Introductory Readings in Political Behavior, 1961; Political Decision Making, 1969; Courts, Law, and Judicial Processes, 1981; contbr. chpts. to books, articles to profl. jours. Home: 1701 Williamsburg Rd Lexington KY 40504 Office: Patterson Office Tower Univ KY Lexington KY 40506

ULRICH, DALE VERNON, educational administrator; b. Wenactchee, Wash., Mar. 11, 1932; s. Herbert Elmer and Esther DeEtta (Webb) U.; m. Claire Marie Gilbert, June 6, 1953; children—Vernon Wayne, Daniel Warren, Sharon Elaine. B.A., U. LaVerne, Calif., 1954; M.S., U. Oreg., 1956; Ph.D., U. Va., 1964. Instr. physics Bridgewater Coll., Va., 1958-61, from asst. prof. to prof. physics, 1964-85, dean of coll., 1967-82, provost, 1985—; asst. prof. James Madison U., Harrisonburg, Va., summer, 1961; Sec., Brethren Ency., Inc., Ambler, Pa., 1977—; pres. On Earth Peace Assembly, New Windsor, Md., 1981—. NIH fellow, 1963-64. Fellow Va. Acad. Scis. (pres. 1978-79); mem. Am. Assn. Physics Tchrs., Am. Phys. Soc. Mem. Brethren Ch. Lodge: Rotary Internat. (pres.). Home: Route 1 Box 4 Bridgewater VA 22812 Office: Bridgewater Coll Bridgewater VA 22812

ULRICH, RUSSELL DEAN, osteopathic physician; b. LaPorte, Ind., Apr. 15, 1947; s. Russell Denzel and Betty Faye (Higgins) U.; m. Evelyn Kay Gove, July 14, 1967; children—Tonya Kay, Nolan Dean, Bryce Alan. B.A. in Religion, Wesleyan Holiness Coll., Phoenix, 1970; B.A. in Psychology, U. Ariz., 1974; D.O., Coll. Osteo. Medicine and Surgery, Des Moines, 1978. Tchr., Montezuma Schs., Cottonwood, Ariz., 1970-72; intern William Beaumont Army Med. Ctr., 1978-79; gen. practice medicine Piedmont Med. Clinic, Ala., 1982-85, Piedmont Family Practice Ctr., 1985—; asst. chief of staff Piedmont Hosp., 1983-84, chief of staff, 1984—. Med. adviser Piedmont Rescue Squad, 1982—; mem. Calhoun County Disaster Preparedness Com., Anniston, Ala., 1984—. Served to capt. U.S. Army, 1978-82. Mem. AMA (Physician's Recognition award 1982, 85), Am. Osteo. Assn. Republican. Methodist. Home: Route 4 Box 335 Jacksonville AL 36265 Office: Piedmont Family Practice Ctr 800 W Smith St PO Box 450 Piedmont AL 36272

ULRING, RICHARD HENRY, material handling equipment corporation executive; b. St. Paul, Apr. 18, 1939; s. Marvin B. and Bessie A. (Laverenz) U.; m. Catherine Elaine Edwards, July 25, 1964 (div. 1972); children—David R., Michael E.; m. 2d, Brenda Louise Bender, Oct. 18, 1978. B.S.M.E., U. Minn., 1962. Various positions mfg. group Gen. Electric Co., 1962-71; regional sales and ops. mgr. Litton Unit Handling Systems, Cin., 1971-80; v.p. sales Conveyor Corp. Am., Crowley, Tex., 1980-81, v.p., gen. mgr., 1981—; v.p., gen. mgr. Stearns Mfg. Co. Mem. Am. Inst. Indsl. Engring., Internat. Material Mgmt. Soc. Republican. Lutheran. Contbr. developments various automated systems in field. Office: 2300 W Risinger Rd Crowley TX 76036

UMANA, UFOT FRANK, counselor educator; b. Ikot Akpan Afaha Cross River, Annang, Nigeria, June 14, 1952; came to U.S., 1977. s. Frank and Mary (Frank) U.; m. Mfon William udom Ufot, Sept. 5, 1970; children—Unyime, Mfonobong, Ufot Jr. B.Sc., East Tex. State U., 1980, M.Sc., 1980; M.Ed., Tex. So. U., 1983. Headmaster, Govt. Sch., Cross River State, 1970-76; counselor Mental Health and Retardation, Terrell, Tex., 1979-81, Richmond State Sch., Tex., 1982-83; instr. asst. Tex. So. U., Houston, 1983—. Mem. nat. council Nigeria and Caemroon Party, Cross River State, 1969; sec. Village Council Ikot Akpan Afaha, 1976. Cross River State scholar, 1977; Govt. Nigeria scholar, 1983-85. Mem. Am. Assn. Counseling and Devel., Am. Coll. Personnel Assn., Phi Delta Kappa. Roman Catholic. Avocations: Photography; jogging. Home: Ikot Akpan Afaha Ukanafun Cross River State Nigeria Office: Tex So Univ PO Box 14277 Houston TX 77221

UMBACH, CLAYTON AUGUST, JR., publisher; b. New Orleans, Aug. 30, 1930; s. Clayton August and Gladys (Meyer) U.; B.J., U. Mo., 1952; m. Patricia J. Young, Oct. 16, 1954; children—Clayton August, III, Ellen Kay, Alice Claire. With Gulf Pub. Co., Houston, 1956—, dir. book pub. div., 1962—, corp. v.p., 1979—; chief exec. officer, dir. Gulf Pub. Video subs. Gulf Pub. Co., Houston, 1982—; lectr. S.W. Writers Conf., Rice U., publishing program Tex. A&M U., U. Houston. Disaster info. dir. Harris County chpt. ARC, 1965-70. Served with inf. AUS, 1952-54, Korea. Mem. Harris County C. of C. (info. com. 1964-66), Am. Soc. Tng. and Devel., Internat. Assn. Bus. Communicators, Tex. Pubs. Assn. (dir. 1979—, pres. 1981-86), Houston Area Booksellers Assn. (dir. 1973-85), Phi Theta Kappa. Lutheran. Club: Houston Press. Author: How to Prepare for Management Responsibilities, 1964. Home: 8006 Neff St Houston TX 77036 Office: PO Box 2608 Houston TX 77001

UMHOLTZ, CLYDE ALLAN, fin. analyst; b. Du Quoin, Ill., Dec. 20, 1947; s. Frederick Louis and Opal Kathleen (Beard) U. B.S., U. Ill., 1969; postgrad. U. Ark., 1969-70; M.S., U. Miss., 1972; M.B.A., Memphis State U., 1983. Chartered fin. analyst; registered profl. engr.; cert. in data processing. Supr. quality control Champion Internat. Corp., Oxford, Miss., 1971-72; mgr. div. quality control Cook Industries, Memphis, 1973; engring. planner Northwest Industries and subsidiaries, Memphis, 1974-75; long range planning and analysis, W.R. Grace & Co. and subsidiaries, Memphis, 1975-78, mgr. planning and analysis Center Nuclear Studies, Memphis State U., 1979-83; data processing mgr. Shelby County Govt., 1983—; cons. in field. Contbr. articles to profl. publs. Active presdl. election campaigns, 1968, 72, 80, mayoral campaign Memphis, 1975, 83, Mid-South Billy Graham Crusade, 1978. Recipient Oratorical award Optimist Club, 1963, Leadership and Human Relations award Dale Carnegie Inst., 1977; NSF fellow, 1970-72. Mem. Memphis Jaycees, AAAS, U. Ill. Alumni Assn., U. Miss. Alumni Assn., Memphis State U. Alumni Assn., Am. Mgmt. Assn., Am. Rose Soc., Am. Inst. Chem. Engrs., Am. Chem. Soc., Assn. M.B.A. Execs., Data Processing Mgmt. Assn., Planning Execs. Inst. Baptist. Clubs: Admirals, Order of De Molay. Inventor angle trisector, 1966; researcher energy considerations of Haber cycle, 1969, comprehensive bus. and fin. studies of sulfur, sulfuric acid, and phosphate industries, 1975-78, cost and materials sci. studies for nuclear industry, 1979, 80, studies of distillation with vapor recompression, 1983. Home: 3580 Hanna Dr Memphis TN 38128

UMLAND, JEAN BLANCHARD, educator; b. Elizabeth, N.J., Sept. 26, 1924; d. Donald and Evelyn (Haring) Blanchard; m. Carl William Umland II, June 18, 1955; children—Anne Whiting, Susan Schallert. B.A., Swarthmore Coll., 1945; Ph.D., U. Wis., 1953. Research chemist Am. Cyanamid Co., Stamford, Conn., 1945-50; instr. Mt. Holyoke Coll., South Hadley, Mass., 1953-55, asst. prof. 1955-56; research chemist Esso Research & Engring., Linden, N.J., 1956-58; lectr. Union Coll., Cranford, N.J., 1967-73, instr., 1958-61; lectr. U. Houston, 1975-81, asst. prof. chemistry, 1981-85, assoc. prof., 1985—. Pres., PTA, Cranford, 1969-71; mem. Union County Council, 1969-73; mem. Cranford Recycling Program Bd., 1971-73, county committeewoman, 1972-73. Mem. AAAS, Am. Chem. Soc., Phi Beta Kappa, Sigma Xi, Phi Kappa, Iota Sigma Pi. Republican. Congregationalist. Contbr. articles to profl. jours. Office: 1 Main St Suite N813 Houston TX 77002

UMLAUF, KARL ALLEN, artist; b. Chgo., May 16, 1939; s. Charles Julius and Angeline McMoran (Allen) U.; m. Shirley Ann Franks, Jan. 25, 1961; children—Stuart, Kurt. B.F.A., U. Tex., 1961; M.F.A., Cornell U., 1963. Teaching asst. Cornell U., Ithaca, N.Y., 1961-63; instr. U. Pa., Phila., 1963-66; asst. prof. U. No. Iowa, Cedar Falls, 1966-67, East Tex. State U., Commerce, 1967—; vis. prof. art Ind. U., Bloomington, 1974-75, 1980; vis. artist Baylor U., Waco, Tex., 1978, 80, Austin Coll., Sherman, Tex., 1974, So. Colo. State U., Pueblo, 1973; vis. lectr. Longview Mus., 1983, Joslyn Mus., Omaha, 1975. Represented in permanent collections Everson Mus., Okla. Art Ctr., Silvermine Guild, Masur Mus., Dallas Mus., Joslyn Mus., Ark Arts Ctr., Cornell U., New Orleans Mus. Art, IBM Corp., N.Y.C. Recipient purchase award Joslyn Mus. 1974, New Orleans Mus. Art 1973, Evansville Mus. Art 1975, Ark. Art Ctr. 1981; East Tex. State U. grantee 1969, 72, 73, 78, 82. Mem. Coll. Art Assn., Tex. Assn. Coll. Tchrs., Tex. Assn. Schs. Art, Tex. Fine Arts Assn. Home: 109 Royal Ln Commerce TX 75428

UMPIERRE, LUIS FRANCISCO, clinical psychologist, neuropsychologist; b. Santurce, P.R., Aug. 14, 1953; s. Francisco and Doris (Vela) U.; m. Maggie Ferrer, Nov. 17, 1984. B.A. in Psychology, Inter-Am. U., San Juan, P.R., 1976; M.S., Caribean Ctr. Advanced Studies, San Juan, 1981, Psy.D. in Clin. Psychology, 1983. Lic. clin. psychologist, P.R. Clin. psychologist Psychol.-Psychiat. Ctr., Hato Rey, P.R., 1979-85; dir. community mental health service Carribean Ctr. Advanced Studies, Santurce, P.R., 1983—, neuropsychol. coordinator, 1983—, tng. cons., 1983—; mem. sch. health program Dept. Health, Caguas, P.R., 1982—; instr. psychology Cayey Sch. Medicine, P.R., 1983—. Vice pres. Brenas Assn., Dorado, 1983-84. Recipient Head Start Recognition award, 1980, Outstanding Clin. Practice award Carribean Ctr. Advanced Studies, 1981, Outstanding Intern award Carribean Ctr. Advanced Studies, 1983. Mem. Intenat. Neuropsychol. Soc., Am. Psychol. Assn., Biofeedback Soc. Am., P.R. Psychol. Soc., Behavioral Neuropsychol. Assn. Roman Catholic. Club: Villa Marina (Fajardo). Avocations: sport fishing; scuba diving; windsurfing; skiing. Home: Camino de las Rosas B-9 Bayamon Enramada PR 00936 Office: Condominium Midtown Office 510-511 Ave Ponce de Leon 420 Hato Rey PR 00918

UMSTOTT, MARTHA LOUISE, training and development educator; b. Cumberland, Md., May 21, 1951; d. Haven Dawson and Marian Louise (Ours) U. B.A., Coll. of William and Mary, 1973; Ed.M., U. Va., 1974, Ednl. Specialist, 1975; Ph.D., Am. U., Washington, 1985. Career devel. counselor U. Md., Balt., 1975-78; prof. tchr. edn. Am. U., Washington, 1978-81, withdrawals coordinator, 1982-84; prof. Montgomery Coll., NIH, Bethesda, 1985—; cons. in field; lectr. in field. dir., asst. sec.-treas. HADA, Inc., McLean, Va.; ptnr. Umstott and Umstott, McLean, 1972—; dir., sec. Am. Splty. Fibers, Inc., Springfield, Va., 1984—. Am. U. scholar, 1984, grantee, 1984—; recipient Service award Am. U., 1981. Mem. Nat. Assn. Women Deans, Adminstrs. and Counselors (exec. bd. 1985—), Am. Assn. Counseling and Devel., Am. Coll. Personnel Assn., Am. Soc. Tng. and Devel., Phi Delta Kappa. Avocations: swimming; reading.

UNDERWOOD, ARTHUR LOUIS, JR., chemistry educator, researcher; b. Rochester, N.Y., May 18, 1924; s. Arthur Louis and Grace Ellen (Porter) U.; m. Elizabeth Knapp Emery, June 30, 1948; children—Paul William, Robert Emery, Susan Elizabeth. B.S. in Chemistry, U. Rochester, 1944, Ph.D., in Biochemistry, 1951. Research assoc. Atomic Energy Project, U. Rochester, 1946-51; research assoc. in chemistry MIT, Cambridge, 1951-52; asst. prof. chemistry Emory U., Atlanta, 1952-57, assoc. prof., 1957-62, prof., 1962—; research assoc. chemistry Cornell U., 1959-60; vis. prof. chemistry Mont. State U., summers 1979—. Served with USN, 1944-46. Fellow AAAS; mem. Am. Chem. Soc., Phi Beta Kappa, Sigma Xi. Republican. Methodist. Co-author: Quantitative Analysis, 5th edit., 1986; contbr. articles to profl. jours. Home: 1354 Springdale Rd NE Atlanta GA 30306 Office: Dept Chemistry Emory U Atlanta GA 30322

UNGER, JOHN WILLIAM, lawyer; b. Danville, Ill., June 11, 1954; s. John William and Lena Rivers (Roach) U.; m. Melinda Lark White, May 18, 1974 (div. Aug. 1982); m. Carolyn Ruth Welch, Sept. 17, 1982; children—Ashley Suzanne, Adriana Michelle, John William. B.A., U. Ark., 1977, J.D., 1978. Bar: Ark. 1978, U.S. Dist. Ct. Ark. 1978, U.S. Ct. Appeals (8th cir.) 1978, U.S. Tax Ct. 1979. Assoc., Jones & Segers, Fayetteville, Ark., 1978-80; assoc. Crumpler, O'Connor and Wynne, El Dorado, Ark., 1980-83, ptnr., 1983-85; sole practice, 1985—. Mem. ABA, Ark. Bar Assn. (committeeman environ. law sect. 1982-83, natural resources sect. 1982—), Union County Bar Assn., Assn. Trial Lawyers Am. Republican. Presbyterian. Home: 1300 Briarwood El Dorado AR 71730 Office: 204 Petroleum Bldg El Dorado AR 71730

UNGLESBY, LEWIS O., lawyer; b. New Orleans, July 6, 1949; s. Lewis Huber and Mary Jane (Holloway) U.; m. Gail Hoy, Aug. 15, 1970; children—Lewis, Lance, Blake. B.S., U. Miss., 1971; J.D., La. State U., 1974. Diplomate Am. Trial Lawyers Assn. Bar: La. 1974, U.S. Dist. Ct. (ea., mid. and we. dists.) La. 1974, U.S. Ct. Appeals (5th cir.) 1974, U.S. Supreme Ct. 1980. Ptnr. Ungles By & Brown, Baton Rouge, 1974—; mem. Gov. La. Pardon Parole and Rehab. Commn., 1978; mem. judge's benchbook com. La. Supreme Ct., 1982—. Fellow Am. Bd. Criminal Lawyers. Mem. Nat. Assn. Criminal Defense Lawyers, Am. Trial Lawyers Assn., ABA, La. Trial Lawyers Assn. (chmn. criminal law sect. 1983-85, bd. govs. 1983-86), La. Bar Assn. (ho. of dels. 1979-87). Home: 14415 Highland Rd Baton Rouge LA 70810 Office: 246 Napoleon St Baton Rouge LA 70802

UNGS, THOMAS DALE, political science educator; b. Dyersville, Iowa, Oct. 3, 1928; s. Charles and Leona (Holscher) U.; m. Theresa M. Lamm, Aug. 13, 1955; children—Susan, Elizabeth, Andrea, Lisa, Matthew. B.A., U. Iowa, 1951, M.A., 1952, Ph.D., 1957. Asst. prof. U. N.D., Grand Forks, 1957-60; assoc. prof. Wichita State U., Kans., 1960-68; prof., chmn. Kent State U., Ohio, 1968-71; prof., head dept. polit. sci. U. Tenn., Knoxville, 1971—, dir. Bur. Pub. Adminstrn., 1971—. Co-author: American Political Patterns, 1973. Contbr. articles to profl. jours. Served to cpl. U.S. Army, 1952-54. Mem. Am. Polit. Sci. Assn., So. Polit. Sci. Assn., Tenn. Polit. Sci. Assn. (pres. 1974-76), Law and Soc. Assn., Am. Soc. Pub. Adminstrn. Home: 3525 Bluff Pt Dr Knoxville TN 37920 Office: Univ Tenn Knoxville Dept Polit Sci Knoxville TN 37916

UNTERKOEFLER, ERNEST LEO, bishop; b. Phila., Aug. 17, 1917; s. Ernest L. and Anna Rose (Chambers) U.; A.B., Cath. U. Am., 1940, S.T.L., 1944, J.C.D., 1950. Ordained priest Roman Cath. Ch., 1944; asst. pastor Richmond, Va., 1944-47, 50-60, Arlington, Va., 1947-50, sec. Richmond Diocesan Tribunal, 1954-60; moderator Council Cath. Women, 1956-61; chancellor Richmond Diocese, 1960-62, vicar gen., 1962-64, papal chamberlain, 1961; aux. bishop Richmond, titular bishop Latopolis, 1962-64; Father, Second Vatican Council, 1962-65; bishop of Charleston (S.C.), 1965—. Sec., U.S. Cath. Bishops Meeting, 1963; asst. sec. adminstrv. bd. Nat. Cath. Welfare Conf. (now U.S. Cath. Conf.), 1963-66, sec., mem. com. on budget and fin., adminstrv. bd., 1966-69; sec. Nat. Conf. Cath. Bishops, 1966-69, mem. com. for Dept. Internat. Affairs (now Social Devel. and World Peace), from 1971, ad hoc com. on women in church and society, from 1971, chmn. region IV, 1972-74, mem. adminstrv. com., 1975-77; chmn. Bishop's Com. Permanent Diaconate, 1975-77. Mem. Nat. Conf. Cath. Bishops' Commn. for Ecumenical and Interreligious Affairs, 1965-69, cons., 1969—, chmn. sub-commn. for dialogue with Presbyn. and Reform Roman Cath.-Anglican Joint Sub-Commn. on Theology of Marriage, from 1967, mem. adv. com., from 1975; mem. Com. on Social Devel. and World Peace, from 1971; chmn. Bishops' Com. on Permanent Diaconate, 1968-71, 75-77; dir. Center for Applied Research in the Apostolate, from 1969, pres., from 1972; co-chmn. Charleston Religious Com. for Bicentennial, 1976. Mem. alumni bd. govs. Cath. U. Am.; adv. com. Ams. for Energy Independence. Decorated Grand Cross Panama; recipient Pax Christi award St. John's U., 1970; Pro-Life Citizen of Yr. award S.C. Citizens for Life, 1978; Nat. Dirs. of Permanent Diaconate award, 1978; award Cath. Youth, 1979; award for applied research in the Apostolate, 1983; James Fitzgerald award Nat. Assn. Diocesan Ecumenical Officers, 1983. Editor: The Unity We Seek; The American Catholic Church and the Negro Problem in the XVIII-XIX Centuries; also articles. Home: 114 Broad St Charleston SC 29401 Office: 119 Broad St Charleston SC 29401*

UNTHANK, G. WIX, U.S. district judge; b. Tway, Ky., June 14, 1923; s. Green Ward and Estell (Howard) U.; J.D., U. Miami (Fla.), 1950; m. Marilyn Elizabeth Ward, Feb. 28, 1953. Admitted to Ky. bar, 1950; judge Harlan County, 1950-57; asst. U.S. atty., Lexington, Ky., 1966-69; commonwealth atty., Harlan, 1970-80; judge U.S. Dist. Ct., Eastern Dist. Ky., Pikeville, 1980—. Served with AUS, 1940-45; ETO. Decorated Purple Heart, Bronze Star, Combat Inf. badge. Mem. Am. Bar Assn., Am. Judicature Soc., Ky. Bar Assn., Fla. Bar Assn. Democrat. Presbyterian. Office: US Courthouse PO Box 278 Pikeville KY 41501

UPADHIAYA, UMESH CHANDRA, sugar engineer; b. Dabha, India, July 11, 1927; came to U.S. 1977; s. Bhagwati Prashad and Shri (Devi) U.; m. Susila Devi, Nov. 7, 1954; children—Anita, Amit. Diploma in Elec. and Mech. Engring., Tech. Coll., Dayalbagh, India. Registered profl. engr., Fla. Asst. engr. Hindusthan Sugar, Gola, India, 1954-60; mech. engr. Bagpat Sugar, (India), 1060-61; erection engr. Dhampur Sugar (India), 1961-62; cons. Mehta Group Uganda, 1962-73; project mgr. KCP Ltd., Madras, India, 1973-74; design engr. joint sugar project unit, Surabaya, Indonesia, 1974-77; cons. engr. Tate & Lyle Enterprises Inc., Miami, Fla., 1977—. Contbr. articles to profl. publs. Home: 2350 SW 26th St Miami FL 33133

UPCHURCH, AVERY C., city official. Mayor, City of Raleigh, N.C. Office: PO Box 590 Raleigh NC 27602*

UPCHURCH, SAM BAYLISS, geology educator; b. Murfreesboro, Tenn., June 30, 1941; s. Sam Clemmons and Martha Miriam (Anderson) U.; m. Mary Ann Comer, Aug. 25, 1964; children—Samantha Ann, Samuel William Joseph. A.B., Vanderbilt U., 1963; M.A., Northwestern U., 1966, Ph.D., 1970. Cert. profl. geol. scientist. Geologist, Tenn. Div. Geology, Nashville, 1959-64; resident in research Northwestern U., Evanston, Ill., 1967-68; research phys. scientist Great Lake Research Ctr., NOAA, Detroit, 1970; asst. prof. Mich. State U., East Lansing, 1971-74; assoc. prof. geology U. South Fla., Tampa, 1974-82, prof., chmn. dept., 1982—. Served to capt. C.E., U.S. Army, 1968-70. Grantee in field. Mem. Am. Assn. Petroleum Geologists, Soc. Econ. Mineralogists and Paleontologists, Geol. Soc. Am., Am. Inst. Profl. Geologists, Nat. Water Well Assn., Am. Water Research Assn., Internat. Assn. Math. Geologists, Southeastern Geol. Soc. (pres. 1981), Sigma Xi. Lodge: Elks. Contbr. articles to profl. jours.; co-editor; Miocene of the Southeastern U.S., 1982. Office: Dept Geology U South Fla Tampa FL 33620

UPCHURCH, THURMAN HOWELL, pipe products company executive; b. Raleigh, N.C., Nov. 6, 1926; s. Auba Merriman and Mertie Mae (Howell) U.; m. Elizabeth Short Daniels, Aug. 7, 1949; children—William Howell, Thurman, Daniel, Mary Elizabeth. B.S. in Metall. Engring., N.C. State U., 1961; grad. Inst. Mgmt., Lynchburg (Va.) Coll., 1970; grad. Mng. Corp. Resources Program, U. Va., 1970, grad. Indsl. Mgmt. Basic Comuter Systems Program, 1968. Asst. mgr. Sungas of the Carolinas, Inc., Raleigh, 1947-49; mgr. Blue Flame Gas Co., Durham, N.C., 1949-55; research asst. dept. engring. research N.C. State U., 1955-61; dir. engring. and prodn. Hardy & Newsome, Inc., LaGrange, N.C., 1961-65; dir. maintenance Glamorgan Pipe and Foundry Co. (name now Griffin Pipe Products Co.), Lynchburg, 1965-66, plant engr., 1966-67, prodn. mgr., 1967, works mgr., 1967-71, dir. mfg., 1971-73, dir. ops., 1971-73, dir. ops. and central iron research and devel., 1973-78, dir. research, 1978—. Chmn. Old Dominion Com. for Fair Utility Rates; past bd. dirs. Lynchburg Central YWCA; City of Lynchburg rep., chmn. Central Va. Air Pollution Control Com. Served with USN, 1944-46. Mem. Am. Soc. for Metals (past chmn. Central Va. chpt.), Lynchburg Soc. Engring. and Sci. (past chmn.), Am. Foundrymen's Soc. (past dir. Piedmont chpt.), Aircraft Owners and Pilots Assn. Republican. Southern Baptist. Clubs: Boonsboro Country, Peakland Swimming (Lynchburg). Patentee control of centrifugal pipe casting operation. Home: 2427 Castle Pl Lynchburg VA 24503 Office: PO Box 740 Lynchburg VA 24505

UPDEGROVE, PAT FORD, library coordinator; b. Jacksonville, Fla., Dec. 12, 1925; d. George and Esther Jane (Wicker) Ford; m. Robert Chester Updegrove, Sept. 12, 1949; 1 son, Glen Ray. B.A., Coll. of William and Mary, 1940; M.A., U. Houston, 1955. Tchr., librarian, Lawrenceville High Sch. (Va.), 1940-41; librarian Blair Jr. High Sch., Norfolk, Va., 1941-47, Armed Forces Staff Coll., Norfolk, 1947-49, U. Tex.-Austin, 1949-51; tchr., Texas City Jr. High Sch. (Tex.), 1951-58; librarian, Texas City, 1959-67; library coordinator Tex. City Ind. Sch. Dist., 1967—. Mem. Tex. Congress Parents and Tchrs. (hon. life), Tex. Assn. Sch. Librarians (chmn. 1976-77), Tex. State Tchrs. Assn., Tex. Library Assn., Tex. Classroom Tchrs. Assn., ALA, Tex. Hist. Found., AAUW (pres. Texas City br. 1981-83), Delta Kappa Gamma. Presbyterian (elder; librarian). Home: 111 Seaside Ln Texas City TX 77590 Office: Texas City Ind Sch Dist 1800 9th Ave North Texas City TX 77590

UPHAM, CHESTER ROBERT, JR., oil and gas company executive, skiing corporation executive; b. Mineral Wells, Tex., May 19, 1925; s. Chester Robert and Ida Irene (Schafer) U.; m. Virginia Frances Lee, Dec. 16, 1946; children—Barbara, Kathy, Robert, Richard (dec.). B.S. in Mech. Engring., U. Tex., 1945. Vice pres. Upham Gas Co., Mineral Wells, Tex., 1947-56, managing co-owner, 1956—; vipe, dir. Loveland Skiing Corp., Georgetown, Colo., 1956-72; chmn. bd. dirs., pres. Clear Creek Skiing Corp., Denver, 1972—; dir. City Nat. Bank, Mineral Wells, 1966—. Pres., Palo Pinto Area Found., Mineral Wells, 1961-80; state fin. chmn. Tex. Republican Party, 1970-71, mem. state exec. com., 1964-70, state chmn., 1979-83. Served with USNR, 1943-46. Mem. Tex. Ind. Producers and Royalty Assn. Am. (pres. 1977-79), Ind. Petroleum Assn. Am. (exec. com. 1982—), North Tex. Oil and Gas Assn., West Central Oil and Gas Assn., Phi Gamma Delta, Tau Beta Pi, Pi Tau Sigma. Republican. Office: 999 Energy Ave PO Box 940 Mineral Wells TX 76067

UPP, JERRY ELI, geologist, exploration researcher, consultant; b. Fairbury, Nebr., Oct. 23, 1904; s. Jehu David and Eva Dell (Rucker) U.; m. Elsie Martha Thomas, Sept. 15, 1928 (dec. Sept. 1983); 1 child, Jerry Everett. B.Sc., Nebr. U., 1929, M.Sc., 1932. Geologist, Nebr. Geol. Survey, Lincoln, 1927-29, 1932-34; micropaleontologist The Pure Oil Co., Tulsa, 1929-32; selemium cons., field geologist U.S. Bur. Chem. and Soils, Tulsa, Lincoln, Montana, Mexico, 1933-34; regional geologist Amerada Petroleum, Tulsa, Can., 1934-50; adminstr. geologist central div. Sinclair Oil & Gas Corp., Tulsa, 1950-60, exploration geologist, 1957-60; research geologist, asst. to v.p. petroleum, coal, sulfur and phosphate, Skelly Oil Co., Tulsa, 1960-70, oil exploration geologist, Venezuela, sulfur exploration, Mex., phosphate exploration, Can., 1965-70; cons. in geology, Tulsa, 1970—. Author, contbr. papers to Nebr. Geol. Survey, other publs. Deacon, First Christian Ch., Tulsa; mem. exec. bd. Indian Nations Council, Boy Scouts Am., Tulsa, 1951—, life mem.; dist. chmn., mem. fund drive Tulsa United Fund, 1946—; precinct chmn. Republican Party, Tulsa, 1946-76, del. to county, state Rep. convs., 1955-85. Recipient Nat. Silver Beaver award Boy Scouts Am., 1952. Fellow Geol. Soc. Am.; mem. Am. Assn. Petroleum Geologists (mem. Disting. Lectr. com. 1951, ballot com. 1975-85); Am. Inst. Profl. Geologists (mem. nat. exec. bd. 1972-73, adv. bd. 1971, chmn. eastern Okla. sect. 1977, cert.), Tulsa Geol. Soc. (pres. 1948-49, hon. life mem. 1979), Tulsa Geol. Study Group (hon. membership award 1977). Avocations: Boy Scouts; youth activities; bowling; reading; music. Home and Office: 1548 S College St Tulsa OK 74104

UPSHAW, SHERWIN DOUGLAS, corporate safety executive; b. Denver City, Tex., Mar. 5, 1952; s. Glenn and Violet Jim (Hargrove) U.; m. Sheila Ruth Justiss, Aug. 10, 1974; children—Brandon, Ross, Justin, Meagan. B.S., McMurry Coll., 1974; postgrad. Tex. A&M U., 1974-77. Cert. tchr., Tex. Safety specialist Brown & Root, Houston, 1976-79, E.I. Dupont de Nemours, Wilmington, Del., 1979-82; corp. safety supr. Tesoro Petroleum Corp., San Antonio, Tex., 1982—. Bd. dirs. Northeast sect. YMCA, 1985—. McMurry Coll. scholar, 1974. Mem. Am. Soc. Safety Engrs. (chmn. scholar com. 1984—), Am. Petroleum Inst. (com. mem. 1982—), Nat. Petroleum Refiner's Assn. (exec. com. 1982—), Internat. Assn. Drilling Contractors (accident com. 1982—), IHR Fraternal Orgn. (pres. 1974—). Avocation: family outdoor activities. Home: 16503 Cypress Park San Antonio TX 78247 Office: Tesoro Petroleum Corp 8700 Tesoro Dr San Antonio TX 78286

UPTON, CHRISTOPHER STANLEY, architect; b. Oceanside, N.Y., Sept. 9, 1953; s. Gerard Stephen and Grace (Hawkins) U. B.Arch., La. State U., 1977. Intern architect Smith, Hinchman & Grylls, Detroit, 1977-78; project architect KTC Architects, Houston, 1978-80, Falick/Klein, Houston, 1980-82; ptnr. Williams/Upton, Architects, Houston, 1982—. Mem. U.S. C. of C., Nat. Soc. for Historic Preservation. Roman Catholic. Avocations: art, photography. Home: 8383 Sandspoint Dr Houston TX 77036 Office: Williams/Upton Architects 5177 Richmond Blvd Suite 1000 Houston TX 77056

UPTON, GERALD WILLIAM, oral and maxillofacial surgeon, infectious diseases researcher; b. Washington, Mar. 5, 1949; s. William Bruce, Jr. and Addie Morine (Williams) U.; m. Nancy Gail Henshaw, Dec. 11, 1976. B.S. in Biology, Va. Mil. Inst., 1971; M.S. in Microbiology, Med. Coll. Va., 1975, D.D.S., 1975; Ph.D. in Exptl. Pathology, U. N.C., 1981. Diplomate Am. Bd. Oral and Maxillofacial Surgery. Resident oral and maxillofacial surgery U. N.C., Chapel Hill, N.C., 1977-80, AAOMS post doctoral research fellow, 1980-81; practice of oral and maxillofacial surgery, Raleigh, N.C., 1981—; adj. prof. U. N.C. Sch. Dentistry, Chapel Hill, 1984—; prin. investigator Clin. Research Study, Burroughs-Wellcome Co., Raleigh, N.C., 1984—; bd. dirs. Blue Ridge Ambulatory Surgery Ctr., Raleigh, N.C., 1983-84. Mem. Va. Mil. Inst. Alumni Assn. (new cadet recruiting chmn. Central Carolina chpt. 1983-84, v.p. Central Carolina chpt. 1985), ADA, N.C. Dental Soc., Raleigh-Wake County Dental Soc., Am. Assn. Oral and Maxillofacial Surgeons (recipient research fellow 1979), Omicron Kappa Upsilon, Sigma Zeta, Mu Beta Psi. Avocations: snow skiing; jogging Office: 2310 Myron Dr Raleigh NC 27607

UPTON, WILLIAM WINGATE, investment company executive; b. Norfolk, Va., Feb. 26, 1918; s. George Thomas and Vivian Elizabeth (Boushall) U.; 1 child, William Wingate, Jr. B.S. in Commerce, U. of N.C., 1939; M.B.A., Harvard U., 1947. With investment mgmt. dept. Dominick & Dominick, N.Y.C., 1952-56; dir. research Phila. Nat. Bank, 1957-67; investment mgr. E.W. Axe & Co., Tarrytown, N.Y., 1967-70; dir. investments Flagship Banks, Miami, Fla., 1970-76; owner, mgr. William W. Upton, Inc., Palm Beach, Fla., 1980—. Bd. dirs. Palm Beach Republican Club, 1981-82; mem. gen. Fund Council Harvard Bus. Sch., Boston, 1966-69. Served to lt col. USMCR, 1940-46, PTO. Mem. Fin. Analysts Fedn. (pres. Miami chpt. 1974), Inst. Chartered Fin. Analysts, Harvard Bus. Sch. Assn. South Fla. (1st v.p., bd. dirs. 1975-78), Mensa, Mil. Order Stars and Bars, Beta Gamma Sigma. Republican. Club: Harvard (Palm Beach). Lodge: Rotary (pres. 1982-83). Office: William W Upton Inc Box 428 Palm Beach FL 33480

URALIL, FRANCIS STEPHEN, physicist; b. Monippally, India, June 3, 1950; s. Stephen Chacko and Chechamma (Joseph) U.; m. Annie Kuruvilla, Dec. 15, 1980; 1 child, Sherene Elizabeth. B.S., U. Kerala, 1969; M.S., Marquette U., 1972; Ph.D., U. Del., 1976. Scientist Case Inst. Tech., 1976-78; scientist Schlumberger, Ridgefield, Conn., 1978-79, scientist Battelle, Columbus, Ohio, 1979—. Mem. Am. Phys. Soc. Home: 4503 Mobile Dr Columbus OH 43220

URBAN, JOHN CARL, JR., devel. co. exec.; b. Woodbury, N.J., Aug. 28, 1942; s. John Carl and Anne Elizabeth (Marville) U., Sr.; student Am. U., 1960-61, U. of Va., 1961-64. Sr. cert. valuer Internat. Inst. Valuers. Acctg. clk. IBM, Washington D.C., 1961-63; real estate salesman Herring Realty, Falls Ch., Va., 1964-66, Regent Realty, 1969-70; real estate broker Rosslyn Asso., Arlington, Va., 1970—; builder, developer, Sarasota, Fla., 1971—; owner, pres. Wexford Inc., Sarasota, 1975—; v.p. Burgundy-Wexford Corp., Dallas; pres. Property Tax Service Corp., Sarasota. Pres. Shadybrook Village, Fla., 1972-82. Mem. Builders Nat. Adv. Council, 1978, Nat. Assn. Rev. Appraisers and Mortgage Underwriters (registered mortgage underwriter) Served to 1st. lt. with U.S. Army, 1966-69. Named hon. Tex. ranger, adm. Tex. Navy. Mem. Nat. Assn. of Home Builders. Home: 707 S Gulfstream Ave Sarasota FL 33577 Office: 1900 Main St Sarasota FL 33577

URBAN, MICHAEL EDWARD, political science educator; b. Los Angeles, May 28, 1947; s. Edward L. and Rose Kiska Urban; m. Veronica McGill, Apr. 28, 1971; children—Emily, George Michael. B.A., Seattle U., 1969; M.A., U. Alta., Edmonton, Can., 1972; postgrad. U. Glasgow, Scotland, 1974-75; Ph.D., U. Kans., 1976. Asst. prof. U. Mont., Missoula, 1976-78, SUNY-Oswego, 1978-82; assoc. prof. polit. sci. Auburn U., Ala., 1982—; postdoctoral research fellow Moscow State U., USSR, 1979-80, 82. Author: The Ideology of Administration, 1982. Contbr. articles to profl. jours. Internat. Research and Exchange Bd. fellow 1979-80; SUNY-Albany grantee, 1982. Mem. Am. Polit. Sci. Assn., Am. Assn. Advancement Slavic Studies, So. Polit. Sci. Assn. Avocations: blues guitar; basketball. Office: Auburn U Dept Polit Sci Auburn AL 36849

URBINA, SUSANA PATRICIA, psychology educator, psychological assessment consultant; b. Lima, Peru, Jan. 20, 1946; came to U.S., 1962; d. Fernando Alfredo and Patricia (Galofre) U. B.A. magna cum laude, Mary Manse, Toledo, 1966; M.A., Fordham U., 1968, Ph.D., 1972. Lic. psychologist, Fla. Asst. prof. psychology Marywood Coll., Scranton, Pa., 1972-73, Mary Manse Coll., Toledo, 1973-75; dir. YMCA Women's Ctr., Toledo, 1975; lectr. in psychology U. Md. European Div., Germany, 1975-76; adviser, asst. prof. psychology U. North Fla., Jacksonville, 1976-80, assoc. prof. psychology, 1980—; field supr. Psychol. Corp., N.Y.C., 1979; pvt. practice psychol. assessment, 1978—. Author reports and jour. articles in field. Bd. dirs. Hubbard House, Jacksonville, 1983—; mem. Mental Health Assn., Jacksonville, 1977—. Mem. Am. Psychol. Assn. (vol. abstractor 1977-81), Southeastern Psychol. Assn., Soc. for Personality Assessment, Sigma Xi, Kappa Gamma Pi. Democrat. Avocations: bicycling; swimming; reading; movies. Office: Dept Psychology U North Fla 4567 St Johns Bluff Rd S Jacksonville FL 32216

URBINE, KEVIN MICHAEL, aviator, insurance agent; b. Ft. Wayne, Ind., Dec. 22, 1956; s. Robert William and Kay Francis (Archibald) U.; m. Charlotte Mae Davis, Dec. 22, 1979; 1 dau., Jade Sorrell. Diploma, N.C. State U., 1979, student Guilford Tech., 1981-82. Lic. gen. contractor, N.C.; lic. ins. agt., N.C.; lic. pilot. Owner, operator Urbine Constrn. Co., Greensboro, N.C., 1976—; salesman Aviation Underwriting Agy., Greensboro, 1977—, also v.p. Reno br. (Nev.); rep. Lloyds of London, 1982, 83; speaker aviation safety seminars. Mem. Exptl. Aircraft Assn. Roman Catholic. Club: Toastmasters. Office: PO Box 19267 Greensboro NC 27419

URIBE, HECTOR, state senator, lawyer; b. Jan. 17, 1946; B.A., J.D., U. Miami (Fla.). Mem. Tex. Ho. of Reps., 1978-81; mem. Tex. Senate, 1981—, mem. fin., health and human resources, and natural resources coms. Democrat. Office: Tex Senate PO Box 12068 Austin TX 78711*

URIEGAS-TORRES, CARLOS, business executive, consultant; b. Mexico City, Sept. 20, 1921; s. Gustavo and Esther (Torres) Uriegas; m. Laura Avendano, Jan. 24, 1948; children—Carlos, Laura, Juan Jose, Teresa, Maria. B.S.C.E., U. Tex.-Austin, 1943; Degree in Civil Engring., U. Nacional Autonoma de Mex., 1944. Project engr. Sec. of Pub. Works, Mexico City, 1954, supt. constrn. North zone Petroleos Mexicanos, Tampico, Mex., 1954-63, asst. mgr. constrn., 1963-64, asst. mgr. inspection, Mexico City, 1965-76, mgr. informatics, 1977-80; dir. Uriegas Torres & Assocs., Mexico City, 1981—; mem. Tech. Commn. Pub. Works, Mexico City, 1968-76; cons. bd. Postgrad. div. LaSalle U., Mexico City, 1978-81; exec. dir. Ctr. Profl. Devel., Mexico, 1981—. Author: Economic Analysis of Engineering Projects, 1975; also articles. E.D. Farmer Internat. scholar U. Tex., 1941. Fellow ASCE; mem. Am. Assn. Cost Engrs., Colegio de Ingenieros Civiles de Mex. (service award 1981), Soc. Mex. de Ingenieria de Costoas (founder 1979), Am. Soc. Engring. Edn. Home: Chichen-Itza 301 Mexico DF Delegacion Benito Juarez 03600 Mexico Office: Uriegas Torres y Assocs Av Cuauhtémoc 1202-P2 Mexico DF Delegacion Benito Juarez Mexico 03650

URSCHLER, FRIEDRICH KARL, physician; b. Fuerstenfeld, Austria, Aug. 26, 1927; s. Karl and Helene (Mann) U.; came to U.S., 1953, naturalized, 1961; M.D., Karl Franzens U., Graz, Austria, 1952; m. Judith Ann Sheets, July 10, 1972; 1 son, Mark Brian. Intern, Swedish Hosp., Seattle, 1954-56; resident Grant Hosp., Columbus, Ohio, LK Hosp., Fuerstenfeld, 1955, Miami Hosp., Dayton, Ohio, 1964, Ohio State U., 1965-66; practice medicine specializing in family practice Columbus, Ohio, 1957-69; mem. staff Grant Hosp., Ohio State U. Hosp., Mercy Hosp., Childrens Hosp., St. Anns Hosp., Community Hosp. of New Port Richey, Tampa Gen. Hosp., U. Community Hosp. Tampa, Tarpon Springs Gen. Hosp., West Pasco Hosp. Diplomate Am. Bd. of Family Practice, apptd. consulate physician by consulate Gen. of Fed. Republic of Germany in Atlanta, 1977, Austria, 1979; lic. physician Ohio, Fla., Wash., Wyo., Nev. Mem. Am. Acad. of Family Physicians, Am. Health Care Med. Dirs. Assn. (Fla. pres.), AMA, Ohio Acad. of Family Practice FMA, Pasco County med. assns., FAFP Am. Med. Soc. of Vienna, Am. Geriatrics Soc. Clubs: Elks, German Cultural Soc. Home: 143 Colonial Dr New Port Richey FL 33552 Office: 515 Forest Ave New Port Richey FL 33552

URSICH, DONALD WEAVER, marriage and family counselor, clergyman, drug and alcohol counselor; b. Morgantown, W.Va., Mar. 24, 1939; s. Charles and Freda Marie (Weaver) U.; m. Barbara Christina Neeser, Sept. 22, 1962; children—Christine, Sarena. B.A., Southeastern Coll., 1968; M.Div., Interdenominational Theol. Ctr., 1971; M.Ed., Boston U., 1979; M.A. in Edn., East Carolina U., 1980. Cert. alcoholism counselor, N.C.; cert. marriage and family therapist, N.C.; registered practicing counselor, N.C. Ordained to ministry United Ch. of Christ, 1981; officer Salvation Army, 1958-81; pvt. practice marriage and family counselor, Fayetteville, N.C., 1979—; drug and alcohol counselor U.S. Army, Ft. Bragg, N.C., 1981—; lectr. and cons. in field. Bd. dirs. Mental Health Assn. Cumberland County (N.C.); asst. dist. commr. Occoneechee council Boy Scouts Am. Served as chaplain U.S. Army, 1971-79. Decorated Commendation medal. Mem. Nat. Alliance for Family Life, Am. Assn. Marriage and Family Therapy, Am. Assn. Counseling and Devel., Nat. Acad. Counselors and Therapists, Am. Group Psychotherapy Assn. Republican. Lodges: Masons, Shriners.

USSERY, BENJAMIN BASCOM, JR., tobacco company executive; b. Wilmington, N.C., Jan. 16, 1948; s. Ben B. and Sarah Elizabeth (Howell) U.; m. Carol Birkhead, Nov. 7, 1969. A.A., Chowan Coll., 1968; B.S., U. Richmond, 1970; M.B.A., Ind. U., 1972. Mktg. trainee Philip Morris, Richmond, Va., 1972-75, sr. logistician, 1975-78, mgr. domestic leaf logistics, 1978-81, asst. dir. logistics and warehousing, 1981—. Trustee Central Va. chpt. Multiple Sclerosis. Alfred E. Lyon scholar Philip Morris, Inc., 1969-70. Mem. Beta Gamma Sigma, Omicron Delta Kappa, Alpha Kappa Psi. Republican. Baptist. Clubs: Spider U. Richmond, Richmond Traffic (bd. dirs.). Author: The Role of the Brand Manager, 1972. Home: 9303 Venetian Way Richmond VA 23229 Office: PO Box 26603 Richmond VA 23261

UTBERG-HOOD, DONALD LEROY, health service company executive, biomedical engineer; b. Pitts., Feb. 9, 1940; s. William John and Ruth Helen (Marks) Hood; m. Carolyn Ann Utberg, Mar. 6, 1982. A.A., Allan Hancock Coll., 1974; A.A.S., Community Coll. of Air Force, 1978; B.S., Wayland U., 1981. Joined U.S. Air Force, 1959, advanced through grades to master sgt., ret., 1981; asst. dir. dept. biomed. engring. Harris Meth. Health Services, Fort Worth, 1982-84, dir. dept. biomed. engring., 1984—; mem. tech. equipment rev. group Am. Health Care Systems, 1984—. Mem. Assn. Advancement Med. Instrumentation, Soc. Radiol. Engring., Am. Soc. Hosp. Engring. Office: Harris Meth Health Services 1423 W Pruitt St Fort Worth TX 76104

UTLEY, EDWIN EMERY, utility company executive; b. Wadesboro, N.C., Apr. 10, 1924; s. Edwin Emery and Stella (Ray) U.; m. Hellon Norma Lawrence, Mar. 1, 1947; children—Nancy Utley Hutchins, Sharon Utley Weigle, James, Douglas. Student, N.C. State U., 1941-42, Louisburg Coll., 1946-47. With Carolina Power & Light Co., Raleigh, 1951—, v.p., sr. v.p., until 1980, exec. v.p.-power supply and engring and constrn., 1980—, dir., Leslie Coal Mining Co., Cleve., McInnes Coal Mining Co. Served with USN, 1943-46; PTO. Mem. ASME (chmn. eastern sect. 1962), N.C. Soc. Engrs. (dir. 1981-82), Am. Nuclear Soc., Nat. Soc. Profl. Engrs. (sr. assoc. mem.), Profl. Engrs. N.C. (sr. assoc.). Democrat. Methodist. Office: Carolina Power & Light Co 411 Fayetteville St Raleigh NC 27602*

UTLEY, JON BASIL, real estate developer, journalist, lecturer; b. Moscow, Mar. 10, 1934; came to U.S., 1939, naturalized, 1952; s. Arcadi and Freda (Utley) Berdichevsky; B.S., Georgetown U., 1956; student U. Munich, 1952, Alliance Française (Paris), 1956; m. Ana Maria Hijar, 1978. Mgr., Am. Internat. Underwriters, Cali, Colombia, 1959-60; editor, pub. Bogotá Bull., 1960-61; v.p. Universal Investors Services, Nassau, 1962-67; real estate developer, Washington, 1968—; fgn. corr. Jour. of Commerce, Internat. Reports, S.Am., 1969-74; assoc. editor, columnist Times of the Ams., 1974-82; columnist Washington Inquirer, 1981—, N.Y.C. Tribune, 1982, Washington Times, 1982-83; mng. gen. ptnr. Kimwill Oil Assocs., Warren, Pa., 1978—; lectr. Freedoms Found. at Valley Forge, 1978—. Bd. dirs. Accuracy in Media, Washington, 1985—; bd. govs. Council on Nat. Policy, 1985—. Mem. Nat. Press Club, Army Navy Club of Washington, Apt. and Office Bldg. Assn., Army Navy, Appalachian Petroleum Club of Washington (dir.). Republican. Editorial adv. bd. Internat. Reports, Internat. Bus. Intelligence, Fgn. Letter; contbg. editor Conservative Digest, 1984—; weekly commentator Voice of Am., 1985—; contbr. articles to Washington Post, Harvard Bus. Rev., Nat. Rev., Human Events, Jour. of Commerce, Miami Herald, others. Office: 6031 Crimson Ct McLean VA 22101

UWAYDAH, IBRAHIM MUSA, medicinal chemist, pharmacologist; b. Qalqiliya, Jordan, Sept. 18, 1943; s. Musa Mahmud and Sa'adiya Yusif (Ismail Hassan) U.; came to U.S., 1969, naturalized, 1976; B.S. in Pharmacy with distinction, Am. U. Beirut, 1967; Ph.D., U. Kans., 1974; m. Afifeh Muhamed Kasem, Sept. 18, 1968; children—Nema, Basem, Hani, Nabeel. Profl. sales rep. Bristol-Myers Middle East Inc., Beirut, 1967-69; teaching asst. U. Kans., 1969-70, research asst., 1970-72, NIH research trainee, 1972-74; postdoctoral research assoc. Med. Coll. Va., Richmond, 1974-77; sr. research chemist, research assoc. A.H. Robins Co., Richmond, 1977—; adj. asst. prof. pharmacology Med. Coll. Va., 1978—. Pres., Islamic Center Va., 1975-76, chmn. bd. trustees, 1981-82, 84-85. Mem. Am. Chem. Soc., Chem. Soc. (London), Internat. Soc. Heterocycl. Chemistry, New York Acad. of Scis., Va. Acad. Sci., Va. Jr. Acad. Sci. (com. 1985-88), Sigma Xi. Contbr. articles to profl. jours. Home: 7100 Able Rd Chesterfield VA 23832 Office: AH Robins Research Labs 1211 Sherwood Ave Richmond VA 23220

VACCA, ANNA MARIA, principal; b. Birmingham, Ala., Jan. 17, 1947; d. Joseph John and Maggie Jo (Petruzella) V.; B.S., Birmingham So. Coll., 1968; M.A., U. Ala., 1972, A.A., 1975, M.A., 1978, Ph.D., 1984. Tchr. gen. and advanced biology Minor High Sch., Birmingham; now prin. Hewitt Trussville Jr. High Sch., Trussville, Ala.; speaker on role of microcomputers in future. Named Outstanding Tchr. of Yr., Ala. Congress Parents and Tchrs., 1980. Mem. NEA, Nat. Activities Advisers Assn., Internat. Soc. Ednl. Planners, Ala. Council Computer Edn. (pres. elect), Mid South Assn. Ednl. Data Systems, Apple Corps Internat. (editor Apple Peel, pres. Apple Blossom), Nat. Assn. Sci. Tchrs., Ala. Edn. Assn., Jefferson County Edn. Assn., Birmingham Bus. and Profl. Womens Club, Delta Zeta. Roman Catholic. Home: 2301 Winterberry Way Birmingham AL 35216 Office: Hewitt Trussville Jr High Sch 601 Parkway Trussville AL

VACHE, CLAUDE CHARLES, bishop; b. New Bern, N.C., Aug. 4, 1926; s. Jean Andre and Edith Virginia (Fitzwilson) V. B.A., U. N.C., 1949; M.Div., Seabury Western Theol. Sem., 1952, D.D., 1976. Ordained priest Episcopal Ch., 1953. Rector St. Michael's Ch., Bon Air, Va., 1952-57, Trinity Ch., Portsmouth, Va., 1957-76, bishop coadjutor Diocese of So. Va., Petersburg, 1976-78; pres. standing com. Diocese of So. Va., Episcopal Ch., 1975. Pres. Tidewater Regional Health Planning Council, 1974-75; chmn. Portsmouth Sr. Citizens Com., 1973-76, Ch. Deployment Bd., 1985-887; mem. Standing Comm. on Ecumenical Relations, 1983-86, Standing Comm. on Constitution and Canons, 1985-91, Com. on Pastoral Develop., 1976—; mem., bd. trustees Episcopal High Sch., Alexandria, Va., Chatham (Va.) Hall, Trinity High Sch., Bon Air Va., St Paul's Coll., Lawrenceville, Va., Va. Theol. Sem., Alexandria, Seabury-Western Theol. Sem., Evanston, Ill., Westminster-Canterbury, Virginia Beach. Address: 600 Talbott Hall Rd Norfolk VA 23505*

VACHER, CAROLE DOUGHTON, psychologist; b. Rocky Mount, Va.; d. John Harold and Mamie Katherine (Frith) Doughton; B.A., W.Va. Wesleyan U., 1960; M.A., Ohio U., 1962; Ph.D., N.C. State U., 1973; m. A. Ray Mayberry, Sept. 2, 1978; 1 child, Elizabeth Michele Vacher. Birth defects coordinator W.Va. U. Med. Sch., Morgantown, 1962-63; research assoc. U. N.C. Med. Sch., Chapel Hill, 1965-70, psychology research cons. N.C. Dept. Mental Health, Raleigh, 1971-73, research psychologist, 1973-75; asst. prof. psychology family practice residency program E. Tenn. U. Med. Sch., Johnson City, 1975-77; dir. community services Overlook Mental Health Center, Knoxville, 1977—; pvt. practice clin. psychology Maryville (Tenn.) Psychiat. Service, 1980-84; research fellow Emory U., Atlanta, 1985—; cons. Knox County Child Abuse Rev. Team, Knoxville, 1977—; asst. prof. psychology U. Tenn., Knoxville, 1978—. Organizer, Community Psychology Task Force, Knoxville, 1977, Mental Health Assns. in Sevier and Monroe Counties, Tenn., 1979, various workshops. vol. Knoxville Med. Assn. Aux., 1979—; vol. mission to Haiti, Methodist Ch., 1979; bd. dirs. Orange County Mental Assn., Chapel Hill, N.C., 1967-68, Contact Ministries, 1980—; exec. bd. Knoxville Med. Assn. Aux., 1980-81; mem. exec. bd. Tenn. Med. Assn. Aux., 1981-82; bd. dirs. Contact Teleministries of Knox County, 1980-83, Bloundt County Bd., 1984—; health and welfare chmn. Maryville Dist., United Methodist Ch., 1983—. Recipient Wesleyan Key award, 1960; Outstanding Vol. Service award Tenn. Dept. Human Services, 1978; N.C. Dept. Mental Health scholar, 1970-71; lic. clin. psychologist, Tenn. Mem. Am. Psychol. Assn., Tenn. Psychol. Assn., Knoxville Area Psychol. Assn., Phi Kappa Phi, Psi Chi, Alpha Psi Omega. Methodist. Co-author: Health and Mental Health Mutual Aid/Self Help Groups in East Tennessee, 1985; author: Consultation Education: Development and Evaluation, 1976; contbr. articles to profl. jours. Home: Route 23 Topside Rd Knoxville TN 37920 Office: 822 Tuckaleechee Pike Maryville TN 37801

VACHON, REGINALD IRENEE, technical company executive; b. Norfolk, Va., Jan. 29, 1937; s. Rene Albert Vachon and Regina (Galvin) Radcliffe; student U.S. Naval Acad., 1954-55; B.M.E., Auburn U., 1958, M.S., 1960; Ph.D., Okla. State U., 1963; LL.B., Jones Law Sch., 1969; m. Mary Eleanor Grigg, Jan. 16, 1960; children—Reginald Irenee, Jr., Eleanor Marie. Engr., Hayes Internat., 1958; instr., research asst. Auburn U., 1958-60, research asso., 1961, asso., prof., 1963-78; research and devel. engr. E.I. DuPont, 1960; aerospace engr., technologist NASA Marshall Space Flight Center, summers 1964, 65; pres. Vachon Nix & Assocs., 1977—; chmn. bd. Optimal Systems Internat., Inc., 1969—; chief operating officer Thacker Constrn. Co., Thacker Orgn. Inc., 1981—; admitted to Ala. bar, 1971. Served with U.S. Army, 1960-61. Registered profl. engr., Ala., Ga., Miss., La., Wis. Mem. ASME, Am. Inst. Aeros. and Astronautics, Nat. Soc. Profl. Engrs., Ala. Bar Assn., Am. Bar Assn. Roman Catholic. Club: Cosmos (Washington). Contbr. articles to profl. jours.; patentee in field. Home: 1414 Epping Forest Atlanta GA 30319 Office: PO Box 467069 Atlanta GA 30346

VACLAVEK, CARIDAD LOZADA, physician; b. Cebu, Philippines, Feb. 20, 1938; came to U.S., 1963, naturalized, 1971; d. Naun Lozada and Juanita L. Alpuerto; m. Alan John Vaclavek, Apr. 14, 1967; 1 son, Mark Lance. A.A., U. San Carlos, Cebu, 1957; M.D., Inst. Coll. Medicine, Cebu, 1962. Instr. physiology and pharmacology Cebu Inst. Coll. Medicine, 1962-63; intern St. Mary's Hosp., Huntington, W.Va., 1963-64; resident Jewish Hosp. Cin., 1964-66, U. Miami Hosp. (Fla.), 1966-69; emergency room physician Baptist Hosp., Miami, 1969-70; fellow in infectious diseases Jackson Meml. Hosp./U. Miami, 1970-71; pvt. practice, Miami, 1971—. Mem. Dade County Med. Assn., Fla. Med. Assn. Republican.

VAIL, MATTHEW ALLISON, physician; b. Halifax, N.S., Can., Nov. 22, 1949; came to U.S., 1981; naturalized, 19; s. Gilbert Frank and Pauline Mary (Tully) V.; m. Barbara Marion Nowlan, June 22, 1973; children—Peter Stuart, Lisa Maureen. B.Sc., Dalhousie U., Can., 1971, M.D., 1976. Intern Royal Alexandra Hosp., Edmonton, Alta., Can., 1976-77; practice medicine specializing in family practice, N.S., 1977-81, Austin, Tex., 1981—; dir., co-founder Medictr. Inc., Austin; cons. Tex. Instruments, Austin, 1985—, Tex. State Sch. for Blind, 1985—; chief family practice St. Davids Hosp., Austin, 1983-84, employee health physician, 1982-84. Dalhousie U. scholar, 1967. Mem. Tex. Med. Assn., AMA, Am. Med. Soccer Assn., N.S. Arthritis Soc. (past pres.), Sigma Chi, Phi Chi. Roman Catholic. Avocations: soccer; running; baseball coaching. Home: 4214 Endcliffe Dr Austin TX 78731 Office: 6343 Cameron Rd Medictr Inc Austin TX 78723

VAISMAN, DANIEL, reinsurance executive; b. Lima, Peru, Apr. 23, 1951; s. William and Harriet (Kurlan) V.; m. Tetje Miedema, June 25, 1976. B.S., Boston U., 1973; Diploma Internat. Program, Netherlands Sch. Bus., 1972. Staff acct. Price, Waterhouse & Co., Miami, Fla., 1973-74; jr. acct. I.I. Blitt, C.P.A., Miami, 1974-75; internat. acct. Am. Life Ins. Co., Wilmington, Del. and Lagos, Nigeria, 1975-78; fin. dir. Spain, Am. Internat. Underwriters, Madrid, 1978-80; regional mgr. for Latin Am., Hudig-Langeveldt, Rotterdam, Amsterdam, 1980-82; v.p. product Armco Reins., Boca Raton, Fla., 1983—; reins. cons., 1983—; pres. Ins. Workshop, Inc., Coral Gables, Fla., 1984—. Mem. Jaycees (past v.p.), U.S. Rowing Assn. (life). Club: U.S. Propeller.

VAJDA, STEVEN ALAN, data processing official; b. Milw., Nov. 18, 1943; s. George F. and Lois B. (Feldman) V.; B.S. in Elec. Engring. (Alumni Scholar), Purdue U., 1965; M.B.A., Northwestern U., 1971; div.; 1 son, Jeffrey Matthew. Systems mgr. RCA Info. Systems, Chgo., 1965-71; mgr. MIS planning and control Ryder System, Inc., Miami, Fla., 1972-81; dir. MIS planning and internat. devel. Burger King Corp., Miami, 1982-83; mgr. MIS, DWG Corp., Miami, 1984—; pres. Continental Cons.; lectr. NCC, 1979; internat. lectr., seminar leader DPMA Internat. Conf., 1980, Communicaiones Expo, 1981, Internat. Conf., Brazil, 1981, U.S. Trade Center, Mexico City, 1981. Vocat. data processing com. Dade County Sch. Bd. and Miami-Dade Community Coll., 1975—; counselor in data processing Boy Scouts Am.; active Kendale Homeowners Assn., 1972—. Mem. Data Processing Mgmt. Assn. (pres. Miami chpt. 1975, internat. dir. 1976—, govt. and industry relations com. 1977—; nat. award 1975), Software Commn. for the Eighties (charter), Northwestern U., Purdue U. alumni assns. Home: 9157 SW 72d Ave S-6 Miami FL 33156 Office: 6917 Collins Ave Miami Beach FL

VALADEZ, STEPHEN KENT, dentist; b. Chattanooga, July 28, 1950; s. Henry Madrid and Frances Virginia (Eakes) V.; m. Dabney James, June 16, 1973; children—Stephen James, William Dabney. B.A. in Econs., U. Tenn.-Chattanooga, 1972; D.D.S., U. Tenn.-Memphis, 1976. Instr., U. Tenn. Coll. Dentistry, Memphis, 1976-79; pvt. practice gen. dentistry, Chattanooga, 1979—; pres., chief exec. officer Brainerd Dental Ctr. Group Dental Practice, Chattanooga, 1983—. Team dentist Chattanooga Lookouts Baseball Team, 1980—; patron Chattanooga chpt. Am. Lung Assn. Tenn., 1983—. Recipient Philanthrophy award Council Corp. Responsibility, 1985. Mem. Am. Acad. Cosmetic Dentistry, Acad. Gen. Dentistry, ADA, Am. Soc. Clin. Hypnosis, Internat. Soc. Clin. Hypnosis, Brainerd C. of C. (bd. dirs. 1985-86). Republican. Presbyterian. Lodge: Masons. Home: 4 Watson Dr Lookout Mountain TN 37350 Office: Brainerd Dental Ctr 5742 Brainerd Rd Chattanooga TN 37411

VALDES, GABRIEL MANUEL, foreign language program specialist; b. Havana, Cuba, Jan. 1, 1937; came to U.S., 1969, naturalized, 1974; s. Gabriel and Hortensia (Fonseca) V.; m. Margarita C. Clarens, Jan. 6, 1961; children—Ana Maria, Gabriel Jesus. B.S. in French, Fla. Internat. U., 1973; M.S., Biscayne Coll., 1976. Cert. tchr., Fla. Adult edn. instr. Dade County Schs., Miami, Fla., 1973-74; instr., asst. coordinator summer programs tchrs. of migrant children Fla. Dept. Edn., Tampa and Boca Raton, 1975-77; freelance tech. translator Miami, 1977-78; adj. prof., coordinator fgn. lang. courses Fla. Internat. U., Miami, 1973-78; bilingual, fgn. lang. edn. cons. Fla. Dept. Edn., Tallahassee, 1978-82, fgn. lang. program specialist, 1982—. Author: (curriculum devel.) Conversational French, 1973. Author and co-producer: (videotapes) Cuban Literature, 1977. U.S. Dept. Edn. fellow, 1975-76. Mem. Fla. Fgn. Lang. Assn. (bd. dirs. 1978—), Am. Assn. Tchrs. French, Am. Assn. Tchrs. Spanish and Portuguese, Am. Council Teaching Fgn. Langs., Nat. Council State Suprs. Fgn. Langs. Democrat. Roman Catholic. Avocations: music; films; reading. Home: 5600 Old Hickory Ln Tallahassee FL 32303 Office: Fla Dept Edn Knott Bldg Tallahassee FL 32301

VALDÉS-CHAO, JOSÉ ANTONIO, advertising agency executive; b. Havana, Cuba, Feb. 19, 1930; s. Pedro Sergio and María Josefa (Chao) V.; Advt. Agt., Profl. Sch. Commerce, Havana, Cuba, 1954; Profl. in Advt., U. Havana, 1956; m. Nee Hilda R. Villavol, Dec. 15, 1957; 1 dau., Viviana. Co-owner, gen. dir. Aguila Publicitaria, Havana, Cuba, 1954-61; office mgr. Internat. Rescue Com., Miami, 1961-63; copywriter, ad divisional supr. Milw. Boston Store, 1963-64; copywriter, creative coordinator, account rep., account supr. J. Walter Thompson Co., San Juan, P.R., 1965-68; v.p., gen. mgr. Ross Roy N.Y., Inc., San Juan, 1968-70; pres. J. A. Valdes-Chao, Inc., San Juan, 1971—; prof. sales and advt. Profl. Sch. Commerce, Havana, Cuba, 1954-61. Recipient Silver Medal, Internat. Film and TV Festival, 1971, Bronze Medal, 1975; Cuspide award, 1983. Mem. Am. Mgmt. Assn., Advt. Agy. Assn. P.R. (dir. 1982-84, v.p. 1973-74), C. C. P.R. Democrat. Roman Catholic. Club: Caribe Hilton Swimming and Tennis (San Juan, P.R.). Contbr. articles in field to profl. jours. Home: 902 Ponce de León Ave Apt 1001 Miramar Santurce PR 00907 Office: 804 Ponce de León Ave Suite 202 Santurce PR 00907

VALENTIN, ROBERTO HERMAN, mfg. co. exec.; b. Mayaguez, P.R., July 31, 1940; s. Martiniamo and Isabel (Serrano) V.; Indsl. Engr., U. P.R., 1964; m. Diana Arabia, Dec. 9, 1960; children—Roberto Luis, Dianissa. Pres., El Morro Corrugated Box Corp., Vega Alta, P.R., 1968-78; v.p. Inland Container Corp., Indpls., 1972-78; pres. Cartonera Antillana, Inc., P.R., 1969-81; pres., chmn. bd. P.R. Container, Inc., Bayamon, 1981—; pres. ABC Cargo Container Corp., 1981—; pres. Erics Swiss Products; dir. Pan Am. Savings, Inc., Girod Velar Cia. Trustee, U. Sacred Heart, San Juan, P.R., 1981, Ashford Meml. Hosp., 1981; bd. dirs. Am. Heart Assn., 1974. Paul Harris fellow Rotary Internat., 1976; named Mfr. of Yr., P.R. Mfrs. Assn., 1974. Mem. Fed. Savs. and Loan League, P.R. Mfrs. Assn. (bd. dirs.), Nu Sigma Beta. Clubs: Caparra Country, Rio Mar Country, Villa Caparra Rotary, Rotary Internat. (past dist. gov., Rio Mar Country. Home: GA 21 Paseo Del Parque Garden Hills Guaynabo PR 00657 Office: Carr No 2 KM 15.2 Hato Tejas Bayamon PR 00619

VALENTINE, ROBERT JOHN, professional baseball manager; b. Stamford, Conn., May 13, 1950; m. Mary Branca, Jan. 8, 1976. Major league baseball player Los Angeles Dodgers, 1969-72, Calif. Angels, 1973-75, San Diego Padres, 1975-77, N.Y. Mets, 1977-78, Seattle Mariners, 1979; infield instr. San Diego Padres, 1980-81; minor league infield instr. N.Y. Mets, 1982, first base coach, 1983-85; mgr. Tex. Rangers, Arlington, 1985—. Address: Tex Rangers Arlington Stadium PO Box 1111 Arlington TX 76010*

VALENTINE, TIM, U.S. Congressman; b. Nashville, Mar. 15, 1926. A.B., The Citadel, 1948; LL.B., U. N.C., 1952. Atty., 1952—; mem. N.C. House of Reps., 1955-60; legal advisor to Gov. N.C., 1965, legis counsel, 1967; mem. 98th-99th congresses from 2d Dist., N.C. Served with USAF, 1944-46. Address: Room 1107 Longworth House Office Bldg Washington DC 20515

VALENZUELA, RAUL ENCINA, ophthalmologist; b. Linarea, Chile, Oct. 2, 1923; came to U.S., 1971; s. Humberto V. and Marina (Sommers) V.; m. Carmen Luisa Barrenechea, Mar. 25, 1952; children—Raul Santiago, Carmen Luz, Maria Soledad, Alvaro Rodrigo. B. Medicine and Surgery, Cath. U., Santiago, Chile, 1949; M.D., U. Chile, Santiago, 1950. Diplomate Am. Bd. Ophthalmology. Intern Cath. U. Clin. Hosp., Santiago, 1947-49, resident, 1951; resident San Francisco de Borja Hosp., Santiago, 1952-53; Rockefeller Found. fellow in disease and surgery of the retina Wilmer Inst., Johns Hopkins Hosp. and U., Balt., 1958-60; asst. prof. surgery Baylor Coll. Medicine, Houston, 1971-74; assoc. prof. surgery U. Miss., Jackson, 1974-76, prof. surgery, 1976-81; practice medicine specializing in diseases and surgery of the retina, Jackson, 1981—. Fellow ACS; mem. AMA, Am. Acad. Ophthalmology, Macula Soc., Wilmer Residents Assn., Miss. State Med. Assn., Johns Hopkins Med. Assn.; hon. mem. Soc. Colombiana Oftalmologia, Soc. Ecuatoriana Oftalmologia, Fundacion Oftalmologica Argentina, Inst. Oftalmologico Nacional de España. Avocation: orchid growing. Home: 3920 Restbrook Pl Jackson MS 39211 Office: 2969 University Dr Suite 100 Jackson MS 39216

VALINES, A. IRENE, university staff; b. Washington, Oct. 28, 1958; d. David Lynn and Velma Irene (Bailey) Clodfelter; m. Francisco Alberto Valines, July 30, 1983. B.A. in Psychology, U. N.C.-Charlotte, 1981; M.Ed., U. Fla., 1983. Grad. hall dir. Div. Housing, U. Fla., Gainesville, 1981-83; intern Syracuse U., 1982; summer conf. unit mgr. dept. housing and food service Tex. Tech U., Lubbock, 1984, residence hall dir., 1983—, instr. resident asst. tng., 1984—. Mem. Am. Coll. Personnel Assn., Tex. Women's Network (bd. dirs. region III), Assn. Coll. and Univ. Housing Officers, Am. Personnel and Guidance Assn., Nat. Assn. Student Personnel Adminstrs., Nat. Assn. for Campus Activities, Scottish Heritage Soc., Sigma Kappa, Phi Lambda Theta, Kappa Delta Pi. Democrat. Avocations: cross stitch, traveling, photography, stamp collector. Home: PO Box 4543 Tex Tech U Lubbock TX 79409 Office: Horn Hall Office Apt 111 Lubbock TX 79409

VALKOVICH, JOYCE ELAINE, dentist, researcher; b. Sept. 19, 1950; d. George and Ruth (Koonce) V. B.S. in Fashion Merchandising, Tex. Woman's U., 1972; D.D.S., U. Tex., 1983. Diplomate Am. Bd. Dentistry. Asst. mgr. women's accessories Sears, San Antonio, Tex., 1972-75; research asst. Med. Sch., U. Tex.-San Antonio, 1975-79, Faculty Dental Sch., 1985—; sr. dentist, Sherwood Dental Ctr., Inc., Waco, Tex., 1984—, bd. dirs., 1985—. Contbr. articles to profl. jours., chpts. to books. Vol. Med. Ctr. Hosp., San Antonio, 1977-79, observer, 1978-79; bd. dirs. Am. Diabetes Assn., Waco, 1984—; voting judge LWV, San Antonio, 1977; mem. San Antonio Ballet Sch., 1978, Bandera River Ranch Assn., Tex., 1977—; election worker San Antonio, 1984. Mem. ADA, Tex. Dental Assn., San Angelo Dist. Dental Soc., San Antonio Dist. Dental Soc., Am. Diabetes Assn. (bd. dirs.), Sherwood Dental Ctrs., Inc. (bd. dirs.), Soc. Exptl. Biology and Medicine, Waco C. of C. Baptist. Clubs. U. Tex. Health Sci. Ctr. Fencing (San Antonio) (pres. 1978-79), Houston (pres. 1982-83), U. Tex. Health Sci. Ctr. Garden (San Antonio) (pres. 1978-79). Avocations: fencing; gardening; writing; jewelry making; golf.

VALLANDIGHAM, PATRICIA LOUISE, physical education educator; b. Salinas, Calif., Feb. 24, 1944; d. Chester Nicholas and Ann Mae (Chernetsky) Maslac; m. Vance Vernon Vallandigham, Jr., May 17, 1964; children—Sydne Joy, Jill Westberg. B.S., Wash. State U., 1967; M.Edn., Whitworth Coll., 1974. Cert. tchr., Fla. Tchr. Rogers High Sch., Spokane, Wash., 1968-69; tchr., dept. chmn. Salk Jr. High Sch., Spokane, 1969-74; dept. chmn. Boca Raton High Sch., Fla., 1974—; owner, sec./treas. Vallandigham/Reed, Inc. Home Interiors, 1985—; cons. summer Connection, Deerfield Beach, Fla., 1983—. Recipient Community Service award Boca Raton C. of C., 1982, Silver Sch. award State of Fla., 1982-83.; named Mother of Year Wash. State U., 1985. Mem. NEA, Fla. Tchrs. Assn., Fla. Assn. Health, Phys. Edn., Recreation and Dance (Profl. Recognition award), Nat. Assn. for Sports and Physical Edn., Fla. Atlantic Builders Assn., AAHPERD, Palm Beach County Classroom Tchrs. Assn., U.S. Tennis Assn., Nat. Assn. for Girls and Women in Sport, Alpha Delta Kappa. Republican. Roman Catholic. Club: Deerfield Jr. Woman's. Home: 1545 SW 13th Dr Boca Raton FL 33432 Office: 7050 W Palmetto Park Rd Suite 21 Boca Raton FL 33433

VALLONE, RALPH, JR., lawyer, consultant; b. Phila., Apr. 15, 1947; s. Ralph and Carmen Maria (Perez) V. B.A., Yale U., 1966, M. Phil. (Carnegie fellow), 1966; LL.D. Harvard U., 1972. Bar: P.R., 1972, U.S. dist. ct. P.R., 1972, U.S. Sup. Ct., 1972. Ptnr., Ralph Vallone Law Firm, San Juan, P.R., 1972—; prof. comml. law Interam. U. Law Sch., P.R., 1972—; chief hearing examiner for Environ. Quality Bd. of P.R. Trustee Bronx Mus. Arts. Mem. P.R. Inst. Registry Law, Jud. Conf. of P.R. Roman Catholic. Clubs: N.Y. Athletic, Atrium of N.Y. Author: à Tiene Usted un Caso de Malapráctica Médica?Office: 165 Ponce de Leon Ave Penthouse Hato Rey PR 00917

VALLOTTON, WILLIAM WISE, surgeon, educator; b. Valdosta, Ga., Nov. 26, 1927; s. Joseph Edward and Mattie (Rouse) V.; A.B., Duke, 1947; M.D., Med. Coll. Ga., 1952; postgrad. Harvard, 1956; m. Hulda Roberta Jones, Sept. 3, 1950; children—Stephen Ralph, Amie Izaguirre, Mark Hugh, William Wise. Intern, U. Wis., 1952-53; resident ophthalmology Duke U., 1953-55, instr., 1953-55, asso., 1955-56; asso. prof. ophthalmology Med. U. S.C., Charleston, 1958-65, prof., 1965-—, dir. residency program ophthalmology, 1960-70, chmn. dept. ophthalmology, 1967—, dir. Storm Eye Inst., 1976—; v.p. Vallorbe Inc., Valdosta, 1955—. Cons., USN Hosp., Charleston, 1962—, State Hosp. S.C., Columbia, 1963—, U.S. Vets. Hosp., Charleston, 1966—; faculty home study Am. Acad. Ophthalmology and Otolaryngology. Bd. dirs. S.C. Commn. for Blind, 1975-76. Served to lt. M.C., USNR, 1956-58. Diplomate Am. Bd. Ophthalmology. Fellow A.C.S.; mem. S.C. Ophthal. and Otolaryn. Soc. (pres. 1965), Charleston Duke Alumni Assn. (past pres.), Assn. Research in Ophthalmology (chmn. S.E. sect. 1966-67), Am. Acad. Ophthalmology and Otolaryngology (Honors award 1968), Pan Am. Ophthal. Assn., So. Med. Assn. (asso. councilor 1972-75, councilor 1975-80), N.Y. Acad. Scis., Pi Kappa Phi, Alpha Kappa Kappa, Alpha Omega Alpha. Republican. Methodist. Clubs: Charleston Country, Elks. Research and publs. in ophthalmology. Home: 15 Br ıghton Rd Charleston SC 29407 Office: Eye Inst Med U of SC Charleston SC 29425

VALVANO, JAMES THOMAS, university basketball coach; b. Queens, N.Y., Mar. 10, 1946; s. Rosco and Marie Angela (Vitale) V.; m. Pamela Susan Levine, Aug. 6, 1967; children—Nicole, Jamie, Lee Ann. B.A. in English, Rutgers U., 1967, postgrad., 1968-69. Freshman basketball coach Rutgers U., New Brunswick, N.J., 1967-69; head basketball coach Johns Hopkins U., Balt., 1969-70; asst. basketball coach U. Conn., Storrs, 1970-72; head coach Bucknell U., Lewisburg, Pa., 1972-75; head basketball coach Lona Coll., New Rochelle, N.Y., 1975-80, N.C. State U., Raleigh, 1980—; mem. Washington Speaker Bur., Medalist Sports Edn., Sports Illus. Speakers Bur. Author: Too Soon to Quit, 1983; coach: NCAA championship team, 1983. Named Outstanding Sr. Athlete Seaford High Sch., 1963, Sr. Athlete of Yr. Rutgers U., 1967, Coach of Yr. Hawkeye Rebounders Club Cedar Rapids, (Iowa), Medalist Sports Industries St. Louis, Spalding Sporting Goods Co., Eastern Basketball Mag. Roman Catholic. Only athlete in history of Seaford High Sch. to earn all-league honors in three different sports in same yr. Office: NC State U Raleigh NC 27650*

VAMMEN, ADOLPH NATHANIEL, obstetrician-gynecologist; b. Osakis, Minn., July 17, 1919; s. Christian Adolph and Tomina Marie (Neve) V.; m. Hazel Lee Becker, Apr. 9, 1949; children—Vahla Lee Vammen Todd, Susan Rozemarie, Elizabeth Ann. Student Dana Coll., Nebr., 1936-38; B.S., Northeastern State Coll., Okla., 1940; M.D, U. Okla., 1944. Diplomate Am. Bd. Ob-Gyn. Intern, Univ. Hosp., Oklahoma City, 1945-46; resident in ob-gyn, 1950-52; postgrad. ob-gyn U. Vienna (Austria), 1948; staff physician USPHS Hosp., Lawton, Okla., 1948-50; practice medicine, specializing in ob-gyn, Tulsa, 1952—; clin. prof. ob-gyn U. Okla. Coll. Medicine, Tulsa, 1978—; chief of staff Hillcrest Med. Ctr., Tulsa, 1969-72; pres. Tulsa Obstet. and Gynecol. Edn. Found., 1976; chmn. Okla. State Rural Med. Edn. Com., 1973-75; vice-chmn. Gov's com. to Combat Cancer, 1973-75. Contbr. articles to profl. jours. Bd. dirs. Okla. div. Am. Cancer Soc., 1961—, Oaks Mission Children's Home (Okla.), 1971—; chmn. Okla. Maternal Mortality Com., 1979—; past pres. ch. council First Lutheran Ch., Tulsa, also past chmn. stewardship, Christian edn. and ch. planning coms.; past bd. dirs. Bethany Coll., Lindsborg, Kans. Served to capt. M.C., U.S. Army, 1942-44, 46-48; ETO. Recipient Disting. Service citation U. Okla., 1980; Honored Med. Alumnus, Coll. Medicine, 1980. Mem. AMA, Okla. Med. Assn., Tulsa County Med. Soc., Am. Coll. Obstetricians and Gynecologists (treas.), Tulsa Obstet. and Gynecol. Soc. (past pres.), Oklahoma City Obstet. and Gynecol. Soc. Home: 3830 S Florence Pl Tulsa OK 74105 Office: 321 Utica Square Med Ctr Tulsa OK 74114

VAN AALTEN, JACQUES, painter, sculptor, educator; b. Antwerp, Belgium, Apr. 12, 1907; came to U.S., 1917; s. Jacob and Marianna (DeWind) Van A.; m. Miriam Truebell, Apr. 29, 1939. Student Nat. Acad. Design, 1926-30, Art Students League, 1932-34, Acad. Grande Chaumiers, Paris, 1955, Tulane U., 1970-71. Instr. art Nassau Conservatory Art, Long Island, N.Y., 1940, van Aalten Studio Sch., Detroit, 1944-47. Exhibited in group shows at Nat. Acad. Design, N.Y.C., 1930, Whitney Mus., 1940, Beaux Arts, N.Y.C., 1940, Archtl. League, N.Y.C., 1940, Soc. Ind. Artists, N.Y.C., 1940, Munic Artists, N.Y.C., 1941, Detroit Inst. Art Mus., 1946, Isaac Delgado Mus. Art, New Orleans, 1958-59, Rockport Art Assn., Mass., 1962-85, Mus. Norton Gallery, Palm Beach, Fla., 1963, La. Artists Group, La. Art Commn. Gallery, Baton Rouge, others; represented in permanent collections Portrait of Pope Pius XII, Vatican Mus. Permanent Collection, Rome, Relig Ministry Bldg., Jerusalem, Truman Library, Independence, Mo., La. State Art Collections, Baton Rouge, Rockport Art Assn., Mass.; also pvt. collections. Recipient Suydam medal, 1930, Silver Pontificial medal Pope Pius XII, Vatican, Rome, 1956; Tiffany scholar, 1930. Mem. Rockport Art Assn. (life), Art Students League (life), Nat. Soc. Mural Painters, Isaac Delgado Mus. Art Assn. Home: Lyndhurst K-1043 Deerfield Beach FL 33442

VAN AKEN, JOHN HENRY, marine surveyor, engineer, consultant; b. Haarlem, Netherlands, Sept. 26, 1922; came to U.S., 1952; s. Antony and Maria Petronella (Renzen) van A.; m. Hendrika A. Bonneur, Sept. 25, 1947 (div. Feb. 1960); 1 son, Antony Laurens; m. 2d, Helen Jemison, July 17, 1962 (dec. Feb. 1978); m. 3d, Marilyn McDaniel, July 13, 1980. Marine Engr., Acad. Tech. Sci. and Arts of Design, Rotterdam, Holland, 1940. Asst. mgr. repair dept. Wilton-Feyenoord Dockyards, Schiedam, Netherlands, 1945-52; supt. machinery Ala. Dry Dock & Shipbldg. Co., Mobile, 1958-60; project mgr. Kerr-McGee Oil Industries, Oklahoma City, 1954-58, 60-63; insp. George Sharp Co., naval architects, Newport News, Va., 1960; pres. John H. van Aken Co., Inc., marine surveyors and cons., Mobile, 1963—; non-exclusive surveyor Panama Bur. Shipping, Internat. Cargo Gear Bur., Registr. Italiano Navale. Named hon. consul gen. Republic of South Africa; decorated comdr. Order Good Hope (South Africa). Mem. Soc. Naval Architects and Marine Engrs., Nat. Assn. Marine Surveyors, Netherlands Soc. Marine Technologists, Am. Boat and Yacht Council, Northeast Coast Instn. Engrs. and Shipbuilders. Republican. Clubs: Athelstan, Fairhope Yacht. Lodge: Mobile Rotary. Home: 188 Rolling Hill Dr Daphne AL 36526 Office: John H van Aken Co Inc PO Box 1738 Daphne AL 36526

VANATTA, NANCY NORICEA, medical assistant; b. Williamson County, Tenn., Jan. 9, 1942; d. Joe Thomas and Alma W. (Deal) Spicer; student Draughons Bus. Coll., 1970; student cardiopulmonary courses Sch. Medicine, U. Calif., San Diego, 1980-82; m. James Vanatta, Feb. 2, 1957 (dec.); m. 2d, Joseph Tanksley; children—Tony, Janice, Margie, Jeff (dec.). Asst. to physicians, Nashville, Tenn., 1970-82; cardiographics supr., Holter monitor technician Goodlark Hosp., Dickson, Tenn., 1982—. Vol. inservice trainer for EKG by telephone, Lewisburg Community Hosp. and Warren County Hosp., McMinnville, Tenn.; den mother Girl Scouts U.S., Boy Scouts Am., 1969-76; softball coach Fairview Recreation Center, 1969-76; hon. sheriff's dep. Sumner County, Tenn. Cert. med. sec., med. asst., treadmill technician, Ga. Mem. Nat. Assn. Female Execs., Am. Assn. Cardiology Technologists, Nat. Assn. Physicians Nurses, Jaycettes, Moose, Am. Legion, VFW. Democrat. Roman Catholic. Home: Box 92 205 Cox Pike SW Fairview TN 37062 Office: 1325 Carters Creek Pike Franklin TN 37064

VAN AUKEN, ROBERT DANFORTH, educator; b. Chgo., Oct. 31, 1915; s. Howard Robert and Mable (Hanlon) Van A.; student Guilford Coll., 1933-35, Gen. Motors Inst. Tech., 1936-38, U. Pitts., 1953-54; B.S., U. Dayton, 1958; M.A., U. Okla., 1967; m. Ruth Bowen Cutler, Nov. 24, 1939; children—Robert Hanlon, Joseph Marshall, David Danforth, Howard Evans, Jonathan Lewis. Commd. aviation cadet U.S. Air Force, 1938; advanced through grades to lt. col., 1961; fighter pilot, squadron comdr., ops. officer, 1939-45; asst. air attaché, Paris, 1946-49; staff officer, Pentagon 1950-53; procurement-prodn. staff officer Wright-Patterson AFB, 1954-58, Tinker AFB, 1958-60, Holloman AFB, 1960-61, ret., 1961; personnel officer U. Okla., Norman, 1962-65, mem. faculty, 1965—, asst. prof. mgmt., 1979-83, prof. emeritus bus. adminstrn., 1983—, dir. student programs and career devel. Coll. Bus. Adminstrn., 1975-79; mgmt. cons., 1963—. Decorated Silver Star, Purple Heart. Mem. Am. Soc. Personnel Adminstrn., Acad. Mgmt., Internat. Platform Assn., Ret. Officers Assn., Mil. Order of World Wars, Beta Gamma Sigma, Delta Sigma Pi. Republican. Clubs: Lions, Masons. Contbr. in field. Home: 420 Highland Rd Midwest City OK 73110 Office: 307 W Brooks St Norman OK 73019

VAN BRACKLE, LEWIS NAPOLEON, III, mathematics educator; b. Savannah, Ga., Apr. 23, 1948; s. Lewis Napoleon and Helen Ethel (Banks) Van B.; m. Anita Yvonne Short, June 24, 1978; 1 child, Robert Michael. B.S. in Physics, Ga. Inst. Tech., 1970, M.S. in Physics, 1972; M.S. in Stats., Va. Poly. Inst. and State U., 1977. Field engr. Schlumberger Surenco, S.A., Catu, Bahia, Brazil, 1974-76; mem. tech. staff Bell Telephone Labs., Murray Hill, N.J., 1977-79; asst. staff mgr. So. Bell, Atlanta, 1979-81, assoc. staff mgr., 1981-84; instr. dept. math. and computer sci. Kennesaw Coll., Ga., 1984—. Elder Northwoods Presbyn. Ch., Doraville, Ga. Mem. Am. Statis. Assn. (sec. local chpt. 1983-85), Math. Assn. Am. Avocation: running. Home: 2001 Village North Rd Dunwoody GA 30338 Office: Kennesaw Coll Dept Math and Computer Sci Marietta GA 30061

VAN BREDA, MICHAEL FILMER, business educator; b. Vereeniging, South Africa, Feb. 20, 1942; s. Donald Gilbert and Irene Mildred (Filmer) van B.; m. Nancy Webster, Aug. 17, 1978; 1 child, Adrian. B.Sc. cum laude, Stellenbosch U., 1961; M.B.A., Cape Town U., 1969, P.T.D., 1964; Ph.D., Stanford U., 1979. Investment mgr., secondary sch. educator, 1962-68; br. mgr. M.H. Goldschmidt Pty. Ltd., Johannesburg, 1971; lectr. U. Witwatersrand, 1972-73; asst. prof. mgmt. sci. MIT, Cambridge, Mass., 1977-81; vis. sr. lectr. U. Witwatersrand, summer 1982; assoc. prof. business So. Meth. U., Dallas, 1981—; mgmt. cons.; lectr. in field. Fin. chmn. Trinity House Camp, Inc., 1979-81; chmn. vol. opportunities com. Trinity Ch., Copley Sq., Boston, 1978-81, mem. parish life council, 1978-81. Recipient Lybrand Silver medal Nat. Assn. Accts., 1981; Ernst & Ernst doctoral fellow, 1975; Haskins & Sells award, 1974; Old Mutual scholar and gold medal, 1969. Mem. Am. Acctg. Assn., Am. Fin. Assn., Nat. Assn. Accts., Fin. Mgmt. Assn., Acad. Internat. Bus. Lodge: Rotary (pres. club 1985-86), Author: The Prediction of Corporate Earnings, 1981; contbr. articles to profl. jours. Office: E L Cox Sch Bus So Meth Univ Dallas TX 75275

VAN BROEKHOVEN, ROLLIN ADRIAN, administrative judge; b. Dallas, June 3, 1940; s. Harold and Loraine (Chafer) Van B.; m. Diana Gullett, Oct. 6, 1962; children—Gretchen, Heidi. B.S., Wheaton Coll., 1962; J.D. cum laude, Baylor U., 1968; LL.M., George Washington U., 1975. Bar: Tex. 1968, U.S. Ct. Mil. Appeals 1970, U.S. Ct. Claims 1970, U.S. Supreme Ct. 1975. Commd. 2d lt. U.S. Army, 1962, advanced through grades to maj., 1969; trial atty., Ft. Hood, Tex., 1968-70, Heidelberg, W.Ger., 1970-71; gen. counsel U.S. Army Procurement Agy., Frankfurt, W.Ger., 1971-74; asst. gen. counsel Dept. Army, Washington, 1975-77; resigned, 1977; dep. counsel NAVSUP, Dept. Navy, Washington, 1977-80; judge Armed Services Bd. Contract Appeals, Washington, 1980—. Editor-in-chief Baylor Law Rev., 1968. Contbr. articles to legal jours. Contbg. author textbooks. Pres., PTA, Frankfurt, 1972-74; mem. Frankfurt Community Adv. Council, 1972-74; mem. Child Abuse Council, Killeen, Tex., 1968-69; elder, chmn. Evangelical Free Ch., Manassas, Va., 1980-84; bd. dirs. Trinity Sem., Deerfield, Ill., 1982—; trustee Outreach, Inc., Grand Rapids, Mich., 1977—; mem. gen. bd. Evang. Free Ch. of Am., 1982—, mem. standards com. Evans Council for Fin. Accountability, 1982—. Recipient Spl. Recognition award Mariano Galvez U., Guatemala, 1984; decorated in service. Mem. ABA, Tex. Bar Assn., Fed. Bar Assn., Nat. Conf. Bd. Contract Appeals Mems. Republican. Home: 8026 Whitting Dr Manassas VA 22111 Office: 200 Stovall St Alexandria VA 22332

VANBUREN, ARNIE LEE, physicist; b. Reynoldsburg, Ohio, Nov. 28, 1939; s. Arnie Alford and Martha Virginia (Turner) VanB.; m. Marjorie Jacqueline Webb, June 21, 1969 (div. Mar. 1985); children—David Webb, Rebecca Lee. B.S., Birmingham So. Coll., 1961; Ph.D., U. Tenn., 1967. Research assoc. U. Tenn.-Knoxville, 1967-68; research physicist Naval Research Lab., Washington, 1968-76, Orlando, Fla., 1976-78, head methods sect., 1979-80, head measurements br., 1981—; chmn. working group of tech. com. Internat. Electrotech. Commn., 1981-83. Contbr. articles to profl. jours. Patentee in field. Fellow Acoustical Soc. Am.; mem. Phi Beta Kappa, Sigma Xi, Phi Kappa Phi, Alpha Tau Omega. Avocations: bridge; bowling; chess; racquetball; reading. Home: 3508 Emerywood Ln Orlando FL 32806 Office: Naval Research Lab 755 Gatlin Ave Orlando FL 32806

VANCE, DONALD, communication educator, advertising and public relations consultant; b. Kansas City, Mo., Nov. 29, 1923; s. Ralph T. and Helene (von Zartwitz) V.; m. Sarah Jane Hudelson, Jan. 2, 1982. B.A., U. Ariz., 1953; M.A., UCLA, 1968; Ph.D., Syracuse U., 1977. Reporter Los Angeles Examiner, 1946-47, Tucson Daily Citizen, 1951-53, Detroit Free Press, 1953-54; advt. and pub. relations exec. Batten, Barton, Durstine & Osborn Advt., San Francisco and N.Y.C., 1954-67; asst. prof. journalism, advt. and pub. relations Syracuse U., 1968-72; asst. prof. advt. U. Tex., Austin, 1972-78; asst. prof. mktg. and advt. Ariz. State U., Tempe, 1978-80; assoc. prof. communication and bus. mgmt. U. Miami, Coral Gables, Fla., 1980—; cons. advt. and pub. relations Bruce Rubin Assocs. Pub. Relations, Miami, Fla., Gables Acads., Miami, others. Served to lt. col. USAFR. Decorated Air medal with 2 oak leaf clusters, 10 combat stars. Recipient Teaching Excellence award U. Tex., Austin Sch. of Communication, 1974; Nat. Addy 1st place award, 1959. Mem. Am. Advt. Fedn. (Outstanding educator award 1979), Pub. Relations Soc. Am., Am. Acad. Advt., Assn. Edn. Journalism, Pi Delta Epsilon, Kappa Tau Alpha, Phi Kappa Phi. Contbr. articles to profl. jours. Home: 1411 Cadiz Ave Coral Gables FL 33134 Office: U Miami PO Box 248127 Coral Gables FL 33124

VANCE, JON HARLEY, hospital administrator; b. Dothan, Ala., July 1, 1935; s. George N. and Adelaide (Jones) V.; m. Ellene Grant; children—Susan Emily, Jon Clayton. B.A. in Econs., U. Ala.-Tuscaloosa, 1958; M.S. in Hosp. Adminstrn., U. Ala.-Birmingham, 1969, grad. Advanced Health Services Adminstrs. Devel. Program, 1981. Adminstrv. asst. U. Ala. Hosps., Birmingham, 1969-72; asst. adminstr. and acting exec. dir. Cooper Green Hosp., Birmingham, 1972-76, exec. dir., 1976-84; adminstr. Children's Hosp. of Ala., Birmingham, 1984-85, exec. dir., 1985—. Named Boss of Yr., Vulcan chpt. Am. Bus. Women's Assn., Birmingham, 1985. Mem. Am. Coll. Hosp. Adminstrs., Ala. Hosp. Assn., Ala. Assn. Hosp. Execs., Birmingham Regional Hosp. Council (bd. dirs.). Roman Catholic. Avocation: fishing. Office: Children's Hosp of Ala 1600 7th Ave S Birmingham AL 35233

VANCE, ROBERT BELL, SR., marketing executive; b. Owings, S.C., Oct. 3, 1912; s. Zeb and Nettie (Babb) V.; m. Marilyn Herndon, Dec. 11, 1954; 1 son, Samuel H.; children by previous marriage—Robert B., Harriett VanHooser. Cost acct. Gen. Shoe Corp., Nashville, 1936—; sales mgr. GENESCO, Inc., Nashville, 1946-47; gen. mgr. Gen. Wax Ind., Nashville, 1947-49; founder, pres., The Mar-Gold Corp., Atlanta, 1949-59, Robert B. Vance & Assocs., Atlanta, 1960-79, Vance Mktg., Atlanta, 1979—. Served with U.S. Army, 1941-46. Decorated Silver Star, Bronze Star with cluster, Purple Heart; recipient Patriot medal S.A.R., 1983; Patriotism Award, Patriotic Edn. Inc., 1982. Mem. Democrat. Mil. Order World Wars (comdr. 1980, 82), S.A.R., Old Guard (sec. 1983-84). Presbyterian. Clubs: Kiwanis (pres.), Capital City. Home: 5136 Powers Ferry Rd Atlanta GA 30327 Office: Robert B Vance Co Atlanta GA 30327

VANCE, ROBERT MERCER, banker, textile mill executive; b. Clinton, S.C., July 9, 1916; s. Robert Berly and Mary Ellen (Bailey) V.; m. Virginia Sexton Gray, Dec. 27, 1949; children—May Bailey Switt, Robert Mercer, Russell Gray. B.S., Davidson Coll., 1937; H.H.D., Presbyn. Coll., 1968. Paymaster, Lydia Cotton Mills, Clinton, 1937-41; with M.S. Bailey & Son, Bankers, Clinton, 1946—, pres., 1948-75, chmn., 1975—; dir., asst. treas. Clinton Cotton Mills, 1948-58, v.p., 1956-58, pres., treas., 1958-64; dir., asst. treas. Lydia Cotton Mills, Clinton, 1948-58, v.p., 1953-58, pres., treas., 1958-64; pres. Clinton Mills, Inc., 1964-79, chmn. bd., 1979—, treas., 1964-70; dir. Clinton Cottons, Inc., N.Y.C., 1948—, v.p., asst. treas., 1953-58, treas., 1958—; dir. Textile Hall Corp., Greenville, S.C. Pres. Community Chest Greater Clinton, 1958; mem. nominating com. United Community Services S.C., 1959; trustee exec. com. Ednl. Resources Found., 1965; mem. State Adv. Commn. on Higher Edn., 1965-67; mem. State Commn. on Higher Edn., 1967-71, chmn., 1968-71; bd. visitors Davidson Coll. (N.C.), 1959—; trustee, chmn. bd. Presbyn. Coll., Clinton, 1953—; trustee, sec. bd. Thornwell Orphanage, Clinton, 1959-67; trustee Inst. Textile Tech., Charlottesville, Va., S.C. Found. Ind. Colls. Served as p.f.c. Signal Corps, AUS, 1941; served to lt. comdr. USNR, 1941-46. Named Man of Yr., Clinton Lions Club, 1955; named Textile Man of Yr., N.Y. Bd. Trade, 1978. Mem. Am. Textile Mfrs. Inst. (dir. 1965—), Am. Bankers Assn. (v.p. 1953-55), S.C. Bankers Assn. (pres. 1963-64), S.C. Textile Mfrs. Assn. (dir. 1965—), S.C. Textile Assn. (pres. 1967-68), Am. Legion, S.C. State C. of C. (dir. 1959-60), Clinton C. of C. (dir. 1951-54), Kappa Alpha. Presbyterian (elder 1958—). Clubs: Lakeside Country (Clinton); Poinsett (Greenville, S.C.); Piedmont (Spartanburg, S.C.). Lodges: Masons, Shriners, Moose, Kiwanis. Home: 311 S Broad St Clinton SC 29325 Office: Clinton Mills Inc 600 Academy St Clinton SC 29325

VANCE, ROBERT SMITH, federal judge; b. Talladega, Ala., May 10, 1931; s. Harrell Taylor and Mae (Smith) V.; B.S., U. Ala., 1950, J.D., 1952; LL.M., George Washington U., 1955; m. Helen Rainey, Oct. 4, 1953; children—Robert Smith, Charles R. Partner firm Vance, Thompson & Brown, Birmingham, Ala., 1956-77; U.S. circuit judge U.S. Ct. Appeals for 11th Circuit (formerly 5th Circuit), Birmingham, 1978—; lectr. Cumberland Sch. Law, Samford U., 1967-69. Chmn., Ala. Democratic Com., 1966-77; pres. Nat. Assn. Dem. State Chairmen, 1973-75. Served to 1st lt. AUS, 1952-54. Fellow Internat. Soc. Barristers; mem. Am., Ala., Birmingham bar assns., Am. Judicature Soc., Newcomen Soc. N.Am., Omicron Delta Kappa, Beta Gamma Sigma, Delta Chi. Episcopalian. Clubs: Birmingham Kennel, Heart of Ala. Great Dane, Am. Saluki Assn. Home: 2824 Shook Hill Rd Birmingham AL 35223 Office: US Courthouse Room 234 Birmingham AL 35203

VANCE, ROY NEWTON, JR., state supreme court justice; b. Paducah, Ky., Nov. 14, 1921; s. Roy Newton and Mary (Bryan) V.; m. Euleen Hamilton, Oct. 20, 1949; children—Linda, Teresa, Roy. LL.B., U. Ky., 1942. Bar: Ky. 1942. Sole practice, Paducah, 1942-70; county atty. McCrocken County (Ky.), 1949-53; commonwealth atty. State of Ky., 1953-57; 70-76; judge Ky. Ct. Appeals, 1976-83; justice Ky. Supreme Ct., Frankfort, 1983—. Served to 1st lt. U.S. Army, 1942-46. Mem. Order of Coif. Home: 7 Justice Ln Frankfort KY 40601 Office: Ky Supreme Ct Capitol Bldg Frankfort KY 40601

VAN CLEAVE, KIRSTIN (KIT) DEAN, writer, educator, publishing executive; b. Ft. Worth, Jan. 9, 1940; d. Henry Shibley and Lola Kathryn (Wimberly) van C. B.A., N. Tex. State U., 1961; M.A., U. Houston, 1972; D.L. in English, London Inst., 1973. Reporter, Associated Gen. Contractors News Service, Houston, 1961-62; dir. pub. relations Diboll Advt. Agy. (Tex.), 1963-64; writer Goodwin, Dannenbaum, Littman and Wingfield advt. agy., Houston, 1964-65; reporter Houston Tribune, 1965-68; copywriter sales promotion dept. Gulf Publishing Co., 1968-70; Houston editor, then mng. editor Metrobeat, Dallas, 1970; editor publs., dir. pub. relations, press rep. Baroid div. NL Industries, Inc., Houston, 1973-74; chief exec. officer Inner-View Publishing Co., Houston, 1980—; mem. faculty St. Agnes Acad., Houston; past mem. faculty U. Houston and Coll. of Mainland, Texas City, Tex. Author: They Still Do, 1973, Folklore of Texas Cultures, 1975; (poetry) Day of Love (set into a song cycle which was nominated for Pulitzer prize in Mus. Composition), 1978, Amourette, 1979, Laurels, 1980; editor Inner-View Mag., Houston; columnist: Houston Home & Garden, Houston Guide, Scene mag., In Houston, Billboard; contbr. articles to mags. Mem. S.W. C. of C., Houston C. of C., AAUP, Music Critics Assn., Internat. Assn. Bus. Communicators, Am. Soc. Authors and Journalists, World Tae Kwon Do Fedn., Tex. Press Assn., Houston Press Club. Home: PO Box 66156 Houston TX 77266

VAN CURA, BARRY JACK, ballet dancer, choreographer; b. Berwyn, Ill., Nov. 13, 1948; s. John J. and Eleanor (Knize) Van C.; m. Anna Baker Miller, Aug. 18, 1979; children—Anamarie, Anthony, Victoria. B.F.A., N.C. Sch. Arts, Winston-Salem. Trainee, Rebeccah Harkness Found., 1972; dancer, soloist Chgo. Ballet and Lyric Opera, 1970-74, Milw. Ballet, 1974-75; dir., choreographer Ballet Midwest, Chgo., 1977-84; dir. Nat. Acad. Dance, Champaign, Ill., 1979-81; dir., choreographer Chattanooga Ballet, 1984—; mem. part-time faculty U. Ill., Champaign, 1980-82; resident choreographer theatre dept. Youngstown U., Ohio, 1984-85; choreographer Allegheny Coll., Meadville, Pa., 1984-85, Rockford Coll., Ill., 1982-83; cons. on dance Warren Dance Ctr., Ohio, 1983-84. Founder Friends of Ballet Midwest, Youngstown, 1982, Chattanooga Ballet Guild, 1984. Ill. Arts Council grantee, 1979; Ohio Arts Council grantee, 1983, 84; Tenn. Arts Commn. grantee, 1985. Mem. Assn. Ohio Dance Co. (trustee 1983-85), Nat. Assn. Regional Ballet, Southeastern Regional Ballet Ann. Buddhist. Home: 4126 Mountain Creek Rd Apt 5 Chattanooga TN 37415

VANCURA, STEPHEN JOSEPH, radiologist; b. Norton, Kans., June 26, 1951; s. Cyril William J. and Clara Mae (Ruthstrom) V.; B.A. magna cum laude, Kans. State U., 1972; M.D., Kans. U., 1976; m. Lydia Acker, Dec. 10, 1976. Intern in medicine Letterman Army Med. Center, San Francisco, 1976-77, resident in radiology, 1977-80; practice medicine specializing in radiology, 1980—; chief dept. radiology Darnall Army Hosp., Ft. Hood, Tex., 1980-82; pvt. practice diagnostic radiology, 1982—. Served to maj. M.C., U.S. Army, 1976-82 Recipient Ollie O. Mustala award in clin. pharmacology Kans. U. Med. Center, 1974; A. Morris Ginsberg award in phys. diagnosis Kans. U. Med. Center, 1975; Resident Tchr. of Yr. award Letterman Army Med. Center, 1979; Staff Tchr. of Yr. award Darnall Army Hosp., 1982. Trembly Meml. scholar, 1972. Diplomate Am. Bd. Radiology. Mem. Am. Coll. Radiology, Inter-Am. Coll. Radiology, Radiologic Soc. N. Am., AMA, Tex. Med. Assn., Am. Inst. Ultrasound in Medicine, Tex. Radiol. Soc., Central Tex. Physicians Assn., Sigma Xi, Alpha Chi Sigma, Alpha Omega Alpha. Club: Killeen Exchange. Home: 913 Nola Ruth St Harker Heights TX 76543 Office: Dept Radiology Metroplex Hosp 2201 S Clear Creek Rd Killeen TX 76541

VAN DE CASTLE, ROBERT LEON, psychologist; b. Rochester, N.Y., Nov. 16, 1927; s. Omar G. and Linnie (Lampkin) Van de C.; m. Myra S. Swann, May 22, 1981; children—Lance, Keith, Craig, Drake. B.A., Syracuse U., 1951; M.A., U. Mo., 1953; Ph.D., U. N.C., 1959. Lic. psychologist, Va. Instr. Idaho State Coll., Pocatello, 1958-59; asst. prof. U. Denver, 1959-63; assoc. dir. Inst. Dream Research, Miami, 1963-65; assoc. prof. U. N.C., Chapel Hill, 1965-67; prof. U. Va. Med. Sch., Charlottesville, 1967—. Author: The Psychology of Dreaming, 1971; (with others) Content Analysis of Dreams, 1966. Mem. Parapsychol. Assn. (pres. 1970), Assn. Study of Dreams (pres. 1985). Home: 670 E Rio Rd Charlottesville VA 22901 Office: Blue Ridge Hosp 6th Floor E Charlottesville VA 22901

VANDEGRIFT, VAUGHN, chemistry educator, administrator; b. Jersey City, Dec. 7, 1946; s. Frederick M. and Marjorie A. (Frelond) V.; m. Suzanne Margaret Bouchoux, July 26, 1969; children—Beth Ann, David Vaughn, Mark Frederick. B.A., Montclair State Coll., 1968, M.A., 1970; Ph.D., Ohio U., 1974. Asst. prof. chemistry Ill. State U., Normal, 1974-76; asst. prof. Murray State U., Ky., 1976-79, assoc. prof., 1979-84, chmn. dept. chemistry, prof., 1982—; vis. assoc. prof. So. Ill. U., Carbondale, 1980-81. Reviewer for pubs. Contbr. articles to profl. jours. NDEA fellow, 1970-74; grantee Fats and Proteins Research Found., 1977-81, NSF, 1980. Mem. Am. Chem. Soc. (Ky. Lake sect.) (chmn. 1983-84; reviewer Jour. Chem. Edn., Jour. Agr. and Food Chemistry 1980—), Sigma Xi (pres. Murray State U. chpt. 1980-81, southeast regional lectr. 1984—), Phi Kappa Phi, Omicron Delta Kappa (Outstanding Murray State U. Faculty mem. 1984). Home: 1700 Magnolia Murray KY 40071 Office: Dept Chemistry Murray State U Murray KY 42071

VAN DER MEER, DENNIS DOUGLAS, administrator tennis school, tennis instructor; b. Windhock, Namibia, Mar. 2, 1933; came to U.S., 1961, naturalized, 1972; s. Isaac Jacobus and Maria Dorothea (Haagen) Van der M.; m. Patricia Joyce Skinner, Feb. 12, 1981. Student U. Cape Town, South Africa, 1950-52. Head, Berkeley Tennis Club, Calif., 1961-73; pres. Van der Meer Tennis U., Hilton Head Island, S.C., 1973—; pres. U.S. Profl. Tennis Registry, Hilton Head Island, 1975—. Author: Van der Meer's Complete Book of Tennis, 1982. Hon. chmn. Shoestrings for Handicapped, Houston, 1984. Mem. U.S. Tennis Assn. Office: Van der Meer Tennis Ctr Box 4739 De Allyon Rd Hilton Head Island SC 29938

VANDER MEER, ROBERT KENNETH, research chemist; b. Chgo., Nov. 29, 1942; s. Robert Valentine and Marion Kelso (MacBratney) Van; children—Jeffrey Scott, Elizabeth Vanessa. B.A., Blackburn Coll., 1964; M.S., John Carroll U., 1966; Ph.D., Pa. State U., 1972. Lectr. chemistry U. of South Pacific, Suva, Fiji Islands, 1972-76; postdoctoral fellow Cornell U., Ithaca, N.Y., 1976-77; research chemist USDA, Gainesville, Fla., 1977—. Editor: Fire Ants and Leaf-Cutting Ants: Biology and Management, 1986. Inventor in field. Contbr. articles to profl. jours. Mem. Am. Chem. Soc., Royal Chem. Soc., Entomol. Soc. Am., Fla. Acad. Sci., Fla. Entomol. Soc., Sigma Xi. Avocations: racquetball; horseback riding; running; photography. Office: US Dept Agr PO Box 14565 Gainesville FL 32604

VANDER MYDE, PHILIP LOUIS, architect; b. Whiteside County, Ill., Apr. 4, 1931; s. Louis John and Ann Marie (Pals) Vander M.; student Central Coll., 1949-50; B.A. in Arch., U. Minn., 1958; m. Martha T. Grier, Mar. 15, 1969; children—John Philip, Martha Maslin. Registered architect, Va., Md., D.C., N.C., Tenn., Pa., Mich., N.J., Ill. Architect, Vosbeck-Ward & Assocs., Alexandria, Va., 1962-64; assoc. partner Vosbeck Vosbeck & Assocs., Alexandria, 1966; partner VVKR Partnership, Alexandria, 1967-70, mng. partner University Park, Md., 1970-80; prin. archtl. ops. VVKR Inc., Alexandria, Va., 1980-82, mng. ptnr. Dewberry & Davis. Architecture, Fairfax, Va., 1983—. Exec. com. Seminary Hill Citizens Assn., 1979-81; pres. Vauxcleuse Citizens Assn., 1972-80; mem. Alexandria Hosp. Corp., 1981—. Served with USAF, 1951-54; capt. USNR. Recipient Honor award Bicentennial Design awards, 1976. Mem. Nat. Council Archtl. Registration Bds., AIA (pres. Potomac Valley chpt. 1977-78), Sigma Alpha Epsilon (chpt. pres. 1954). Republican. Presbyterian. Clubs: Belle Haven Country, Greater Washington Bd. Trade. Archtl. works include Prince Georges Gen. Hosp., 1977, U. Md. Law Library, 1978, Frederick County Courthouse, 1978, Md. Dept. Agr. Headquarters, 1979, Inglewood Office Complex, 1981, Wolf Trap Ctr. for Performing Arts, 1984, First Am. Bank of Va. Hdqrs., 1984, Fairfax Govt. Ctr., 1984, Times/Jour. Hdqrs., 1984, Smithsonian Air and Space Mus., 1986, Courthouse Place, 1986, Huntwood Plaza, 1986, others. Home: 1100 N Howard St Alexandria VA 22304 Office: 8401 Arlington Blvd Fairfax VA 22031

VANDERPOOL, BOBBY, educator; b. Knott County, Ky., Jan. 22, 1931; s. Andrew J. and Maude (Dyer) V.; m. Marian Coleman, June 8, 1957; children—April Suellen Vanderpool Schneider, Andy Jack. B.S., Morehead State U., 1957. With Newport (Ky.) City Schs., 1957—, football coach Newport High Sch., 1958-67, coach basketball, 1958-77, head coach, 1970-77, instr. phys. edn., 1957—. Served with USMC, 1948-52. Decorated Purple Heart (2). Mem. Ky. High Sch. Athletic Assn. (life). Home: 54 Holly Woods Dr Fort Thomas KY 41075 Office: Newport High Sch 900 E 6th St Newport KY 41071

VANDERSLICE-BELLER, SUELLYN, clinical psychologist, air force officer; b. Baytown, Tex., Oct. 10, 1948; d. Thomas J. Vanderslice Jr. and Teodosia E. (Bevers) Loerwald; student Brevard Community Coll., 1966-67; B.A. in Sociology, La. State U., 1970; M.S. in Recreation Therapy, Calif. State U., 1975; Ph.D. in Psychology, U. Hawaii, 1986; m. John Walter Patrick Jr., May 30, 1970 (div. 1975); m. 2d, James Edward Beller, Dec. 18, 1983. Community social worker City of Pensacola (Fla.), 1970-71; therapeutic recreation supr. Salvation Army, Honolulu, 1973-74; community social worker Girl Scout Council of the Pacific, Honolulu, 1974-75; psychiat. social worker Mental Health Div., State of Hawaii, summer 1977; lectr. dept. psychology U. Hawaii, Honolulu, 1978-82; state mental health program dir. for women Dept. Health, State of Hawaii, 1979; pvt. practice marriage and family counseling, Honolulu, 1977-82; resident in clin. psychology USAF, Wilford Hall, Lackland AFB, Tex., 1982-83; chief psychol. services USAF Hosp., Tyndall AFB, Fla., 1983—; adj. faculty in psychology Gulf Coast Community Coll., Panama City, Fla.,

Fla. State U., Panama City. Mem. Lt. Gov.'s Com. on Women and Family, State of Hawaii, 1979-82; bd. dirs. Panhandle Alcohol Council, 1985—; founder Panama City chpt. Compassionate Friends, 1985-86; mem. Gov.'s Constituency on Women, 1985—. Mem. Am. Psychol. Assn., Hawaii Assn. for Humanistic Psychology (v.p. 1976-77, sec.-treas. 1977-78), Nat. Assn. Parks and Recreation, Am. Personnel and Guidance Assn., Democrat. Baptist. Contbr. articles to jours. in psychology. Home: 601 S Berth Ave Panama City FL 32404 Office: SGHMA/USAF Hosp Tyndall AFB FL 32403

VANDEVEER, JAMES WELLINGTON, oil/gas production, real estate development executive; b. Cleve., May 24, 1925; s. Welzie Wellington and Wilda (Ruth) V.; m. Betty Lou Ober, June 22, 1946; children—Vicki, Cindi. B.S., UCLA, 1949. Sales engr. Allied Oil Co., Inc., Cleve. and Chgo., 1949-52; ind. oil operator, Dallas, 1952—; pres., chmn. bd. Vantex Enterprises, Inc., Dallas, 1983—; dir. Ashland Oil Inc. Served with U.S. Army, 1943-46; ETO; PTO; ATO. Mem. Am. Petroleum Inst., Mid-Continent Oil and Gas Assn., Ind. Petroleum Assn. Am., Am. Assn. Petroleum Geologists, Wine and Spirits Guild, Am. Fighter Pilots Assn. Republican. Clubs: Northwood Country, Tower, Petroleum, Bent Tree Country.

VANDEVENDER, LEONARD GRESHAM, air force officer; b. West Point, Miss., Jan. 22, 1942; s. Leonard Green and Elma Pauline (Gresham) V.; m. Dolores Boaz, July 13, 1969; children—Leonard Gresham Jr., Shawn Derek. B.S. in Acctg., Miss. State U., 1965; M.B.A. in Mgmt., Golden Gate U., 1975. Commd. 2d lt. U.S. Air Force, 1966; advanced through grades to lt. col., 1980; instr. pilot Craig AFB, Selma, Ala., 1966-70, aircraft comdr. Udorn AFB, Thailand, 1971-72; instr. pilot Shaw AFB, Sumter, S.C., 1973-76; chief ops. Hdqrs. 1 Group, Bawtry, Eng., 1976-78, student Air Command and Staff Coll., Maxwell AFB, Montgomery, Ala., 1979-80, advisor Ala. Air N.G. 187 Tng. Unit, 1981-83; wing chief Air Command and Staff Coll., 1983—. Mgr. Dixie Youth Baseball, YMCA Football Program, Montgomery. Decorated D.F.C. (4), Air medal (10), Commendation medal, Meritorious medal (2). Republican. Methodist. Address: 2201 Semmes Dr Montgomery AL 36106

VANDEVENTER, VERNON EARL, college administrator; b. Sturgis, S.D., Oct. 16, 1943; s. Fred E. and Roszella M. (Westberg) VanD.; m. Jane Marilyn Scheurer, Sept. 2, 1966; children—Janelle Rae, Brian Lee, Jon Earl. B.S., Black Hills State U., 1967, M.S., 1975. Cert. tchr. S.D. Tchr. Fort Yates High Sch., N.D., 1966-69, Bur. of Indian Affairs, Manderson, S.D., 1969-75; prin. Bur. of Indian Affairs, Kyle, Oglala, S.D., 1975-77; Christian edn. dir., pastor Ch. of God of Prophecy of Can., Vancouver, B.C., 1977-82, auditor, mem. nat. bd. dirs., bishop, 1979-82; dean of bus. services Tomlinson Coll., Cleveland, Tenn., 1982—, bookstore mgr., 1982—. Mem. Assn. of Bus. Officers, Nat. Assn. Coll. and U. Bus. Officers, Coll. and U. Personnel Assn., Nat. Assn. of Ednl. Buyers. Republican. Avocations: reading; walking. Home: 1252 Crown St NW Cleveland TN 37311

VANDIVER, FRANK EVERSON, university president, author, educator; b. Austin, Tex., Dec. 9, 1925; s. Harry Shultz and Maude Folmsbee (Everson) V.; Rockefeller fellow in humanities U. Tex., 1946-47, Rockefeller fellow in Am. Studies, 1947-48, M.A., 1949; Ph.D., Tulane U., 1951; M.A., Oxford (Eng.) U., 1963; H.H.D. (hon.), Austin Coll., 1977; m. Carol Sue Smith, Apr. 19, 1952 (dec.); children—Nita, Nancy, Frank Alexander; m. Renee A. Carmody. Apptd. historian Army Service Forces Depot, Civil Service, San Antonio, 1945, Air U., 1951; prof. history La. State U., summers 1954-57; asst. prof. history Washington U., St. Louis, 1952-55; asst. prof. history Rice U., Houston, 1955-56, assoc. prof., 1956-58, prof., 1958-65, Harris Masterson Jr. prof. history, 1965-79, chmn. dept. history and polit. sci., 1962-63, chmn. dept. history, 1968-69, acting pres., 1969-70, provost, 1970-79, v.p., 1975-79; pres. North Tex. State U., Denton and Tex. Coll. Osteo. Medicine, 1979-81, Tex. A&M U., College Station, 1981—; Harmsworth prof. Am. history Oxford U., 1963-64; prof. history U. Ariz., summer 1961; master Margarett Root Brown Coll., Rice U., 1964-66. Harman lectr. Air Force Acad., 1963; Keese lectr. U. Chattanooga, 1967; Fortenbaugh lectr. Gettysburg Coll., 1974; Phi Beta Kappa asso. lectr., 1975—; vis. prof. mil. history U.S. Mil. Acad., 1973-74; hon. pres. Occidental U., St. Louis, 1975—; Confederate Inaugural Centennial speaker Va. Civil War Centennial, 1962; mem. adv. council Civil War Centennial Commn.; cons. Nat. Endowment Humanities, 1966—; mem. adv. council, office chief mil. history Dept. Army, 1969-74; exec. dir. Am. Revolution Bicentennial Commn. Tex., 1970-73; mem. selection com. Ft. Leavenworth Hall of Fame Assn. U.S. Army, 1971-72, 74-76; bd. dirs. Inst. Civil War Studies, 1975—; chmn. adv. council U.S. Mil. Hist. Research Collection, Carlisle Barracks, Pa., 1972—; mem. Nat. Council for Humanities, 1972-78, vice-chmn., 1976-78; mem. Commn. Internat. Edn. Am. Council Edn., 1982—; mem. Sec. of Navy's Adv. Bd. Edn. and Tng., 1983—. Bd. visitors Air U. Recipient research grants Am. Philos. Soc., 1953, 54, 60; Guggenheim fellow, 1955-56; Carr P. Collins prize Tex. Inst. Letters, 1957; Huntington Library research grant, 1961; Harry S. Truman award Kansas City Civil War Round Table; Jefferson Davis award Confederate Meml. Lit. Soc., 1970; Fletcher Pratt award N.Y. Civil War Round Table, 1970; laureate Lincoln Acad., Ill., 1973; First Outstanding Alumnus award Tulane U. Grad. Sch., 1974; Nevins-Freeman award Chgo. Civil War Round Table, 1982; Outstanding Civilian Service medal Dept. Army, 1974. Fellow Tex. Hist. Assn.; mem. Am., So. (assoc. editor jour. 1959-62, pres. 1975-76) hist. assns., Assn. Am. Colls. (bd. dirs. 1982—), Tex. Inst. Letters (past pres.), Jefferson Davis Assn. (pres., chmn. adv. bd. editors of papers), Soc. Am. Historians (councillor), Tex. Philos. Soc. (pres. 1978), Civil War Round Table (Houston), Phi Beta Kappa. Club: Cosmos (Washington). Editor: The Civil War Diary of General Josiah Gogas, 1947; Confederate Blockade Running Through Bermuda, 1861-65, Letters and Cargo Manifests, 1947; Proceedings of First Confederate Congress, 4th Session, 1954; Proceedings of Second Confederate Congress, 1959; A Collection of Louisiana Confederate Letters; new edit. J.E. Johnston's Narrative of Military Operations; new edit. J.A. Early's Civil War Memoirs; The Idea of the South, 1964. Author: Ploughshares Into Swords: Josiah Gorgas and Confederate Ordnance, 1952; Rebel Brass: The Confederate Command System, 1956; Mighty Stonewall, 1957: Fields of Glory (with W. H. Nelson), 1960; Jubal's Raid, 1960; Basic History of the Confederacy, 1962; Jefferson Davis and the Confederate State, 1964; Their Tattered Flags: The Epic of the Confederacy, 1970; The Southwest: South of West?, 1975; Black Jack: The Life and Times of John J. Pershing (Nat. Book Award finalist 1978), 1977; also hist. articles. Mem. bd. editors U.S. Grant Papers, 1973—. Office: Texas A&M Univ College Station TX 77843

VANDIVER, PATSY DIANNE, nursing administrator; b. Lexington, Ala., Dec. 17, 1948; d. Albert Newton and Thetus Marie (Balch) McCain; m. William E. Vandiver, III, Sept. 14, 1968; children—Michael W., Jason L. B.S.N., U. Ala.-Birmingham, 1970, now postgrad. in nursing. R.N., Ala. Staff nurse Univ. Hosp., Birmingham, 1970-71, South Highlands Hosp., Birmingham, 1971-72; staff nurse, team leader Cooper Green Hosp., Birmingham, 1972-73, head nurse nurseries, 1973-75, nursing supr., 1975-78, asst. dir. maternal-infant nursing, 1978-83, asst. dir. nursing, 1983-85, interim dir. nursing, 1985-86, asst. adminstr. nursing, 1986—. Sec. Epic Sch. PTA, 1982, Five Points South Neighborhood Assn., Birmingham, 1985, bd. dirs. Southside Neighborhood Devel. Corp., 1985; Mem. Am. Orgn. Nursing Execs., Am. Hosp. Assn., Am. Nurses Assn., Nursing Assn. of Am. Coll. Ob- Gyn. Democrat. Presbyterian. Home: 1610 12th St S Birmingham AL 35205 Office: Cooper Green Hosp 1515 6th Ave S Birmingham AL 35233

VANDIVER, RAYMOND FRANKLIN, III, state official; b. Huntsville, Ala., Jan. 1, 1955; s. Raymond Franklin Jr. and Martha Jane (McCown) V.; m. Terrie Lynn Brooks, Mar. 20, 1982; 1 child, Raymond Franklin IV. B.S., Auburn U., 1977. Estimator W. Chester Williams Co. Inc., Montgomery, Ala., 1977-78, Caldwell Constrn. Co. Inc., Huntsville, 1978; v.p. J.T. Schrimsher Co. Inc., Huntsville, 1978-83; dir. State Bldg. Commn., Montgomery, 1983—. Mem. Ala. Hist. Commn., Montgomery, 1983—; mem. Gov.'s Mansion Adv. Bd., Montgomery, 1983—; mem. Dexter Ave. Historic Devel. Com., Montgomery, 1985; bd. dirs. YMCA, Huntsville, 1982-83. Mem. So. Bldg. Code Congress Internat., Nat. Fire Protection Assn., Jaycees. Presbyterian. Club: Acme (Huntsville). Home: 6013 Forest Grove Ct Montgomery AL 36117 Office: State Bldg Commn 800 S McDonough St Montgomery AL 36130

VAN DYKE, GENE, energy company executive; b. Normal, Ill., Nov. 5, 1926; s. Harold and Ruby (Gibson) Van D.; B.S. in Geol. Engring., U. Okla., 1950; m. Kerstin Rohr, Feb. 27, 1981; children—Karen, Scott, Janice, Mary Katherine. Geologist, Kerr-McGee, Oklahoma City, 1950; chief geologist S.D. Johnson Co., Wichita Falls, Tex., 1950-51; ind. geologist and oil operator, 1951-58; partner Van Dyke and Mejlaender, Houston, 1958-62; owner, pres. Van Dyke Oil Co. (name now Van Dyke Energy Co.), Houston, 1962—; also dir.; dir. Van Dyke Netherlands, Inc. Served with AC, U.S. Army, 1945. Mem. Am. Petroleum Inst., Ind. Petroleum Assn. Am., Am. Assn. Petroleum Geologists, Tex. Mid-Continent Oil and Gas Assn. Republican. Methodist. Clubs: Houston, Houston Petroleum, Houston City. Compiler index of geol. articles in South La. Home: 3815 Olympia St Houston TX 77019 Office: One Greenway Plaza Houston TX 77046

VAN EKRIS, ANTHONIE CORNELIS, trading corporation executive; b. Rotterdam Netherlands, June 3, 1934; came to U.S., 1963; s. Cornelis and Evertje (Mulder) van E.; m. Heather Frances Button, Sept. 7, 1960; children—Anthonie Cornelis, Marijke Karin. Trainee Van Rees, Ltd., Rotterdam, 1952-57; mgr. African Coffee Trading Ops., Mombasa, E. Africa, 1957-63, Ralli Trading Co., N.Y.C., 1963-67; pres. Van Ekris & Stoett, Ltd., N.Y.C., 1967-70; pres., dir. Ralli-Am. Ltd., N.Y.C., 1970-72; pres., chief exec. officer Kay Corp., N.Y.C., 1972—, also dir.; chmn. Kay Jewelers, Inc., Balfour, Maclaine Internat. Ltd., Van Ekris & Stoett, Inc., Marcus & Co., Inc. Served with Royal Dutch Navy, 1951-53.

VAN ETTEN, MARGUERITE RUBY, dietitian; b. Sayre, Okla., July 2, 1921; d. Monroe Clarence and Susie Estella (Larkey) Baggett; B.S. in Home Econs. and Dietetics, U. Okla., 1945; M S. in Behavioral Sci. and Human Services, Nova U., 1981; m. George Douglas Van Etten, June 9, 1945; children—Karen Lynette, Janel Anne, Vicki Tina. Dietitian Montgomery County (Md.) Jewish Day Camp, Bethesda, 1949; clin. dietitian and relief dietitian Chestnut Lodge Mental Health Facility, Rockville, Mo., 1949-50; relief clin. and adminstrv. dietician, dir. dietary service Suburban Hosp., Bethesda, 1954-64; dir. dietary services; cons. dietitian Althea Nursing Home, Silver Spring, Md., 1964-65; adminstrv. and clin. dietitian Holy Cross Hosp., Silver Spring, 1964-72; clin. dietitian St. Michael's Hosp., nr. Stevens Point, Wis., 1972-73; dietitian, preceptor dietetic assts., preceptor coordinated undergrad. dietetic program U. Wis., Stevens Point, 1972-73; cons. dietitian St. Jude's Nursing Home, Wis., 1972; clin. and adminstrv. dir. dietary services South Fla. Bapt. Hosp., Plant City, 1973-74; pub. health nutrition cons. Fla. State Health and Rehab. Services Office of Licensure and Cert., Miami, 1974-84. Mem. Am. Dietetic Assn., Broward County Dietetic Assn. (pres.-elect, acting pres. 1983, pres.'s plaque 1985), Fla. Council on Aging, Cons. Dietitians of Health Care Facilities of Fla., Broward County Geneal. Soc. (life mem.; v.p. 1982, pres. 1983, life mem. 1984—), DAR (1st vice regent Cypress Chpt. 1982, regent 1984, life mem. 1985—), Cherokee Hist. Soc., Madison County Geneal. Soc. (life), U. Okla. Alumni Assn. (life), Plantation (Fla.) Hist. Soc., AAUW, LWV, New Eng. Hist. and Geneal. Soc. Congregationalist. Lodge: Order Eastern Star (past matron Rockville, Md. 1964, dep. grand lectr. 1965, 66, 67). Author: Masters Practicum-Cons. Dietitians Handbook, 1980. . Home: PO Box 16326 Plantation FL 33318

VANGILDER, GLORIA EUDORA, health care company executive; b. Sikeston, Mo., Mar. 4, 1938; s. A.L. and J. Lucille (Ragsdale) Goatcher; m. John R. Van Gilder, Aug. 11, 1979; children—Jack Terry, III, Richard, Susie. B.S., U. Houston, 1958, M.B.A., 1959; postgrad. U. Tex., 1959-61. Teaching fellow U. Tex.-Austin, 1959-61; instr. Coll. Bus. Adminstrn., U. Houston, 1961-64; mgmt. devel. coordinator San Jacinto Coll., Pasadena, Tex., 1964-73; dir. human resources devel. Meml. Care Systems, Houston, 1973—; cons. in field; v.p. Records Etc., Inc., Houston, 1984—; speaker, affiliated socs. Tex. Hosp. Assn., Dallas, Austin, San Antonio and Houston, 1974—; Author: Behavior Insights, 1973, 82, also tng. manuals. Contbr. articles to profl. publs. Mem. adv. com. U. Houston, 1984—, Houston Community Coll., 1984—. Mem. Am. Soc. Tng. and Devel. (Torch award 1976, v.p., chmn., Outstanding Mem. award 1975-77), Tex. Soc. Hosp. Edn. (bd. dirs. 1976, 82, 85), Am. Soc. Hosp. Edn. and Tng., Alpha Chi Omega. Republican. Baptist. Avocations: writing, gardening. Office: Meml Care Systems 7600 Beechnut St Houston TX 77074

VAN GORDER, DAVID ROBERT, marketing executive; b. Gary, Ind., Apr. 14, 1955; s. Lawrence Allen and Nancy Louise (Travis) Van G.; married. B.A., Temple U./LaRoche Coll., 1978. Cons., 1978-80; asst. to v.p. Christian Broadcasting Network, Virginia Beach, Va., 1980-82; dir. mktg. Jimmy Swaggart Ministries, Baton Rouge, 1982—. Author Pa. Student Bill of Rights, 1973. Recipient Hearst Journalism award, 1974; Nat. Merit scholar, 1973. Mem. Am. Mgmt. Assn., Direct Mktg. Assn. Republican. Presbyterian.

VAN HOOSE, HELEN HALL, visual information specialist; b. Allen, Ky., Oct. 13, 1945; d. Troy and Stella (Branham) Hall; m. Ernest W. VanHoose, Feb. 4, 1967. B.A., U. Ky., 1968; postgrad. U. Gent, 1974; M.A., Eastern Ky. U., 1975; postgrad. U. Louisville, 1976. Art tchr. Fayette County Sch. System, Lexington, Ky., 1968-69, Jefferson County Sch. System, Louisville, 1969-75; illustrator U.S. Army Darcom Materiel Readiness Support Activity, Lexington-Bluegrass Depot Activity, 1976-78; med. illustrator, free-lance artist, Lexington and Louisville, 1974-82; visual info. specialist U.S. Army, Lexington, 1978—; evaluator PS Mag., Art Contract, U.S. Army, 1982. Fulbright-Hays scholar Commn. Ednl. Exchange, 1974; recipient Exceptional Performance awards U.S. Army Materiel Readiness Support Activity, 1981, 82, 83, Sustained Superior Performance award, 1982. Mem. Bus. and Profl. Women's Orgn. Clubs: Ky. Watercolor Soc. (Louisville); Lexington Art League. Home: 3804 Forsythe Ct Lexington KY 40503

VAN HOOSE, WILLIAM HENRY, educational psychology educator; b. Louisa, Ky., Sept. 20, 1929; s. Millard and Elizabeth (Moore) Van H.; children—Frederick, Pamela. A.B., Morehead State U., 1951; M.S., Ind. U., 1957; Ph.D., Ohio State U., 1965. Psychologist, Akron pub. schs., Ohio, 1960-62; asst. prof. ednl. psychology U. Mich., Ann Arbor, 1962-65; prof. Wayne State U., Detroit, 1965-72; prof. counselor edn. U. Va., Charlottesville, 1972—, dir. Ctr. for Research and Career Devel., 1979—. Author: Midlife: Myths and Realities, 1985; Tecumseh: An Indian Moses, 1984. Contbr. articles to profl. jours. Mem. citizens adv. com. on developmental counseling Va. Gen. Assembly, 1980-84. Served with U.S. Army, 1951-53. Named Outstanding Ph.D. Grad., Ohio State U., 1983. Mem. Am. Psychol. Assn. Democrat. Presbyterian. Avocations: fishing; golf. Address: U Va 405 Emmet St Charlottesville VA 22903

VAN HORN, JAMES EDWARD, college administrator; b. San Francisco, Oct. 28, 1937; s. James Harmon and Margaret (Henderson) Van H.; m. Martha Jane Long, Nov. 21, 1959; children—Sonya Denise Van Horn Hood, Barbara Leigh. B.S., U. Ala., 1960, M.A., 1965, Ed.D., 1971. Div. chmn. Jefferson State Jr. Coll., Birmingham, Ala., 1965-76; dean instrn. Wallace State Community Coll., Hanceville, Ala., 1976—. Commr. Ala. Jr. Coll. Conf., 1972—; regional bd. dirs. Nat. Jr. Coll. Athletic Assn., Colorado Springs, Colo., 1976—; fundraiser Cullman County Heart Assn., 1978—; ops. officer Fed. Emergency Mgmt. Agy, Cullman, 1984—. Served to capt. U.S. Army, 1960-64. Mem. Ala. Acad. Dean's Assn. (treas. 1977-78, pres. 1978-79). Methodist. Avocations: fishing. Home: 1829 Glover St NW Cullman AL 35055 Office: Wallace State Community Coll PO Box 250 Hanceville AL 35077

VAN HOWE-NEZELEK, ANNETTE EVELYN, real estate agent; b. Chgo., Feb. 16, 1921; d. Frank and Susan (Linstra) Van Howe; B.A. in History magna cum laude, Hofstra U., 1952; M.A. in Am. History, SUNY-Binghamton, 1966; m. Edward L. Nezelek, Apr. 3, 1961. Editorial asst. Salute Mag., N.Y.C., 1946-48; asso. editor Med. Econs., Oradell, N.J., 1952-56; nat. mag. publicist Nat. Mental Health Assn., N.Y.C., 1956-60; exec. dir. Diabetes Assn. So. Calif., Los Angeles, 1960-61; corporate sec., v.p., editor, public relations dir. Edward L. Nezelek, Inc., Johnson City, N.Y., 1961-82; mgr. condominium, Fort Lauderdale, Fla., 1982-83; dir. Sky Harbour East Condo, 1983-85; substitute tchr. high schs., Binghamton, N.Y., 1961-63. Bd. dirs. Broome County Mental Health Assn., 1961-65, Fine Arts Soc., Roberson Center for Arts and Scis., 1968-70, Found. Wilson Meml. Hosp., Johnson City, 1972-81, Found. SUNY, Binghamton; trustee Broome Community Coll., 1973-78; v.p. Broward County Commn. on Status of Women, 1982—, Broward Art Guild, 1985—; trustee Unitarian-Universalist Ch. of Ft. Lauderdale, 1982—. Mem. AAUW (v.p. 1983-84), Am. Med. Writers Assn., LWV (dir. Broome County 1969-70), Alumni Assn. SUNY Binghamton (dir. 1970-73), Am. Acad. Polit. and Social Sci., Nat. Assn. Female Execs., Am. Heritage Soc., Nature Conservancy, Nat. Hist. Soc., Alpha Theta Beta, Phi Alpha Theta, Phi Gamma Mu. Clubs: Binghamton Garden, Binghamton Monday Afternoon, Acacia Garden (pres.). Editor newsletter Mental Health Assn., 1965-68, newsletter Unitarian-Universalist Ch., weekly 1967-71, History of Broome County Meml. Arena, 1972. Home: 2100 S Ocean Dr Apt 16K Fort Lauderdale FL 33316 Office: 1439 SE 17th St Fort Lauderdale FL 33361

VAN KEUREN, ROBERT EUGENE, JR., public relations executive; b. Washington, Aug. 2, 1947; s. Robert Eugene and Mary Elizabeth (Mattox) Van K. B.A. in History, U. S.C., 1968, M.A. in Journalism, 1979. Communication dir. Roddey for Congress com., Lancaster, S.C., 1973-74; archtl. reporter F.W. Dodge div. McGraw-Hill Info. Systems Co., Inc., Charlotte, N.C., 1974-77; grad. asst. in pub. relations Computer Services div. U. S.C., 1977-79; pub. relations officer Atlanta Area Tech. Sch., 1980—; mem. publicity com. U.S. Skill Olympics and Internat. Skill Olympics, Atlanta, 1981. Mem. arrangements com. Ga. Occupational Awards of Leadership, Atlanta, 1981—; rep. Atlanta Area Tech. Sch. at Stewart Ave. Area Bus. Assn., 1981—, St. Peter's Episcopal Ch. on Charlotte Uptown Coop. Ministries, 1975-77; mem. Richland County (S.C.) Dem. Exec. com., 1978-79. Served with USN, 1969-73. Recipient Clara Hammond award for outstanding extracurricular leadership U. S.C., 1966, others. Mem. Pub. Relations Soc. Am., Nat. Assn. Vocat. Tech. Edn. Communicators (bd. dirs. 1985—), Kappa Tau Alpha. Episcopalian. Home: 3572 Buford Hwy Apt 1 Atlanta GA 30329 Office: 1560 Stewart Ave SW Atlanta GA 30310

VAN LANDINGHAM, LEANDER SHELTON, JR., patent lawyer; b. Memphis, July 15, 1925; s. Leander Shelton Van L.; B.S. in Chemistry, U. N.C., 1948, M.A. in Organic Chemistry, 1949; J.D., Georgetown U., 1955; m. Henrietta Adena Stapf, July 5, 1959; children—Ann Henrietta, Leander Shelton III. Bar: D.C. 1955, Md. 1963, Va. 1976. Patent adviser Dept. Navy, Washington, 1953-55; practiced in Washington; 1955—; cons. patent, trademark and copyright law, chem. patent matters, 1955—. Served to lt. USNR, 1943-46, 1951-53. Mem. Am. Chem. Soc., Sci. Assn., ABA, Fed., D.C., Va., Md. bar assns., Am. Patent Law Assn., Am. Judicature Soc., Sigma Xi, Phi Alpha Delta. Methodist. Home: 10726 Stanmore Dr Potomac Falls Potomac MD 20854 Office: 2001 Jefferson Davis Hwy Arlington VA 22202

VAN LANDINGHAM, WILLIAM JENNINGS, banker; b. Louisville, Sept. 10, 1937; s. Zack Jennings and Corinne (Brown) VanL.; m. Barbara McMillan, Feb. 16, 1985; children by previous marriage—William Jennings II, Teri Leigh, Joseph Templeton. B.S., Ga. Inst. Tech., 1959; postgrad. Emory Law Sch., 1964-67; P.M.D., Harvard U., 1972. Prodn. mgr. Procter & Gamble, Columbus, Ohio and Dallas, 1959-64; asst. to v.p. Rich's Inc., Atlanta, 1964-66; exec. v.p. No. Ga. banking Citizens and So. Ga. Corp., Atlanta, 1966—. Mem. Atlanta Bd. Edn., 1971-74; bd. dirs. Spl. Audiences, Inc., Research Atlanta, Inc., Volunteer Atlanta, Ga. Safety Council, Met. Atlanta Found.; mem. Mayor's Task Force on Ethics in City Govt.; pst gen. chmn. Tech-Ga. Devel. Fund; trustee Pace Acad., Alexander Tharpe Scholarship Fund, Inc.; mem. exec. com. Ga. Council on Econ. Edn.; founding chmn. Leadership Ga.; Inc. Served to lt. (j.g.) USNR. Mem. Ga. Inst. Tech. Nat. Alumni Assn. (past pres.), ANAK Hon. Soc. (Ga. Inst. Tech.). United Methodist. Office: Citizens and So Georgia Corp 35 Broad St NW Atlanta GA 30303

VANMEER, MARY ANN, publisher, writer, researcher; b. Mt. Clemens, Mich., Nov. 22; d. Leo Harold and Rose Emma (Gulden) VanM.; stepdau. of Ruth (Meek) VanM. Student Mich. State U., 1965-66, 67-68, Sorbonne U., Paris, 1968; B.A. in Edn., U. Fla., 1970. Pres. VanMeer Tutoring and Translating, N.Y.C., 1970-72; freelance writer, 1973-79; pres. VanMeer Publs., Inc., Clearwater, Fla., 1980—, VanMeer Media Advt., Inc., Clearwater, 1980—; exec. dir., founder Nat. Ctrs. for Health and Med. Info., Inc., Clearwater, 1982—; pres. Physicians Research Ctr., Inc., 1985—. Author: Traveling with Your Dog, U.S.A., 1976; How to Set Up A Home Typing Business, 1978; Freelance Photographer's Handbook, 1979; See America Free, 1981; Free Campgrounds, U.S.A., 1982; Free Attractions, U.S.A., 1982; VanMeer's Guide to Free Attractions, U.S.A., 1984; VanMeer's Guide to Free Campgrounds, 1984. Pub. info. chairperson, bd. dirs. Pinellas County chpt. Am. Cancer Soc., Clearwater, 1983-84. Mem. Am. Booksellers Assn., Author's Guild. Republican. Club: RAND Real Estate Investment (Tampa, Fla.). Office: VanMeer Publs Inc PO Box 1289 Clearwater FL 33517

VAN METRE, MARGARET CHERYL, artistic director, dance educator; b. Maryville, Tenn., Nov. 24, 1938; d. Robert Fillers and Margaret Elizabeth (Goddard) Raulston; m. Mitchell Robert Van Metre II, Aug. 25, 1956; 1 child, Mitchell Robert. Elem., intermediate and advanced teaching certs. Dir. Van Metre Sch. of Dance, Maryville, 1958—; artistic dir. Appalachian Ballet Co., Maryville Coll., 1972—; chmn. dance panel Tenn. Arts Commn.; 1973-74; chmn. Bicentennial Ballet Project, Tenn., 1975-76. Choreographer ballets: DeLusion, 1965; Hill Heritage Suite, 1972; Dancing Princesses, 1983. Mem. Tenn. Assn. of Dance (pres. 1972). Democrat. Episcopalian. Home: 609 Kendrick Pl Knoxville TN 37902 Office: Van Metre Sch of Dance Maryville College Maryville TN 37801

VAN MOURIK, RONALD, petroleum geologist; b. Willemsted, Curacao, Netherlands Antillies, Feb. 27, 1956; came to U.S., 1958, naturalized, 1979; s. Hans and Ine (Westhoven) van M.; m. Nancy Eugenia Miles, Sept. 21, 1979; children—Maureen, Lindsey. B.S. in Geology, La. State U., 1979. Sr. petroleum geologist Exxon Co., U.S.A., New Orleans, 1979—. Mem. Am. Assn. Petroleum Geologists. Avocations: snow skiing; golf; raising 2 children; music. Home: 134 Woodside Dr Mandeville LA 70448 Office: Exxon Co USA 1555 Poydras St New Orleans LA 70161

VAN NAME, MARK LAWRENCE, computer software company executive; b. Haverhill, Mass., Mar. 14, 1955; s. Donald Louis and Nancy Ann (Bergeron) Van N.; m. Mary Anne Frazier, Aug. 18, 1976. B.S., Fla. State U., 1976; M.S., Pa. State U., 1977. Computer programmer II, Fla. State U., Tallahassee, 1975-76; teaching asst. Pa. State U., State College, 1976-77; computer scientist HRB-Singer, Inc., State College, 1977-78; mem. tech. staff Data Gen. Corp., Research Triangle Park, N.C., 1978-81; co-founder, pres. Blue Ridge Info. Systems, Inc., Raleigh, N.C., 1981-82; co-founder, v.p. research and devel. Foundation Computer Systems, Inc., Cary, N.C., 1982—. Mem. Assn. for Computing Machinery, IEEE, Sci. Fiction Writers Am. Democrat. Contbr. short stories to mags. Home: 10024 Sycamore Rd Durham NC 27703 Office: Foundation Computer Systems Inc 8000 Regency Pkwy Cary NC 27511

VAN NESS, JAMES SAMUEL, academic administrator, historian; b. Houston, Feb. 26, 1932; s. John Bishop and Ruth (Ryan) Van N.; m. Nedra Tracy, June 18, 1955; children—Lynn, Paul. B.A., U. Md., 1954, M.A., 1962, Ph.D., 1968. Asst. prof. history U. Md., Coll. Park, 1967-74, supt. history and govt. European div., Heidelberg, Fed. Republic Germany, 1969-71, dir. summer sch., Coll. Park, 1972-74; asst. dean St. Lawrence U., Canton, N.Y., 1974-78; dean instrn. Central Wyo. Coll., Riverton, 1978-82; dean arts and scis. Temple Jr. Coll., Tex., 1982—. Editor: (with J. Raths and J. Pancella) Studying Teaching, 1971. Contbr. chpt. to book, articles to profl. jours. Mem. bd. advisors Inst. for Humanities at Salado, Tex., 1983-85; vice chmn. Wyo. Council for Humanities, Laramie, 1981-82; mem. exec. com. Assn. for Innovation in Higher Edn., 1977-79; bd. dirs. Central Tex. Orchestral Soc., Temple, 1984-85; chmn. Canton Village Rep. Club, 1975-78. Named Rotarian of Yr., Canton, 1978, Outstanding Tchr., U. Md. History Honorary, 1969; faculty devel. fellow U. Md., 1961-63. Mem. Orgn. Am. Historians, Nat. Assn. Instructional Adminstrs. Methodist. Club: Rotary. Home: 4502 Cactus Trail Temple TX 76502 Office: Temple Jr Coll 2600 S 1st St Temple TX 76501

VAN PATTEN, JAMES JEFFERS, educator; b. North Rose, N.Y., Sept. 8, 1925; s. Earl F. and Dorothy (Jeffers) Van P.; B.A., Syracuse U., 1949; M.E., Tex. Western Coll., 1959; Ph.D., U. Tex., Austin, 1962; m. Sept. 10, 1961. Asst. prof. philosophy and edn. Central Mo. State U., Warensburg, 1962-64, asso. prof., 1964-69; asso. prof. vis. overseas U. Okla., Norman, 1969-71; prof. edn. U. Ark., Fayetteville, 1971—. Served with inf., U.S. Army, 1944-45. Decorated Purple Heart. Mem. Philosophy of Edn. Soc., So. Futures Soc., World Future Soc., Am. Philosophy Assn., Southwestern Philosophy of Edn. Soc. (pres. 1970), Ark. Edn. Assn. (pres. chpt. U. Ark.), Phi Delta Kappa (pres. chpt. U. Ark. 1976-77). Club: Kiwanis. Editor: Conflict, Permanency and Change in Education, 1976; contbr. articles to books, profl. jours.; founder Jour. of Thought. Home: 434 Hawthorn St Fayetteville AR 72701

VANPELT, ARNOLD FRANCIS, JR., biology educator, biologist, researcher; b. Orange, N.J., Sept. 24, 1924; s. Arnold Francis and Fredericka Emma (Kleiber) VanP.; m. Gladys Mae Smith, June 24, 1947; children—Stephen Arnold, Susan Frances. B.A., Swarthmore Coll., 1945; M.S., U. Fla., 1947, Ph.D., 1950. Assoc. prof. biology Appalachian State U., Boone, N.C., 1950-54; prof. Tusculum Coll., Greeneville, Tenn., 1954-63, prof. Greensboro Coll. (N.C.), 1963—, chmn. dept. sci. and math., 1964-71, 82-83, dir. Allied Health programs, 1975—, chmn. div. sci. math., 1983—; adj. faculty mem. U.

N.C., Greensboro, 1974, Moses H. Cone Meml. Hosp., Greensboro, 1975, 77, Forsyth Meml. Hosp., Winston-Salem, 1972—. Grantee: NSF, Research Corp., N.Y., Big Bend (Tex.) Hist. Soc., Piedmont U. Ctr., Winston-Salem, Oak Ridge Nat. Lab., Savannah River Ecology Lab., S.C., Greensboro Coll. Mem. AAAS, Entomol. Soc. Am., N.C. Acad. Sci., Sigma Xi. (Greensboro chpt. treas. 1978-79, sec. 1980-81, pres. 1983). Quaker. Contbr. articles to profl. jours. Home: 203 Howell Pl Greensboro NC 27408 Office: 815 W Market St Greensboro NC 27401

VANREKEN, MARY K., clinical psychologist; b. East Grand Rapids, Mich., Dec. 13, 1947; d. Donald L. and Elsa M. (DeWind) vanR. Cert. Trinity Christian Coll., 1967; B.A. magna cum laude, Hope Coll., 1969; M.A., Appalachian State U., 1970; Ph.D., Purdue U., 1977. Lic. psychologist, Tenn., Ga. Vis. asst. prof. psychology Ind. U., Bloomington, 1977-78; asst. prof. Ind. State U.-Terre Haute, 1978-80; psychologist Valley Psychiat. Hosp., Chattanooga, 1980-82, adolescent program dir., 1983, chief psychologist, 1982-84; pvt. practice, Chattanooga, 1982—; adv. council Family and Children's Services, Chattanooga, 1981-85. Named Outstanding Young Woman, Ind. State U., 1979. Mem. Am. Psychology Assn., Assn. for Women in Psychology, Southeastern Psychol. Assn., Tenn. Psychol. Assn., Ga. Psychol. Assn., Chattanooga Area Psychol. Assn. (treas. 1983, ethics com. 1984—), NOW (treas. Tenn., 1983-85, sec. Tenn. 1985—), Women's Network of Chattanooga, Chattanooga Bus. and Profl. Women, LWV, Psi Chi. Democrat. Methodist. Avocation: photography. Office: Northgate Psychology Group Suite 301 1 Northgate Park Chattanooga TN 37415

VAN RIPER, PAUL PRITCHARD, political science educator; b. Laporte, Ind., July 29, 1916; s. Paul and Margaret (Pritchard) Van R.; m. Dorothy Ann Dodd Samuelson, May 11, 1964; 1 child, Michael Scott Samuelson. A.B., DePauw U., 1938; Ph.D., U. Chgo., 1947. Instr., Northwestern U., Evanston, Ill., 1947-49, asst. prof. polit. sci., 1949-51; mgmt. analyst Office Comptroller Dept. Army, 1951-52; mem. faculty Cornell U., 1952-70, prof., 1957-70; chmn. governing bd., exec. com. Social Sci. Research Ctr., Cornell U., 1956-58; prof., head dept. polit. sci. Tex. A&M U., College Station, 1970-77, prof., 1977-81, prof. emeritus, 1981—, coordinator M.P.A., program, 1979-81; vis. prof. U. Chgo., 1958, Ind. U., 1961, U. Strathclyde, Scotland, 1964, U. Mich., 1965, U. Okla., 1969, 84, U. Utah, 1979. Author: History of the United States Civil Service, 1958; Some Educational and Social Aspects of Fraternity Life, 1961; (with others) The American Federal Executive, 1963; Handbook of Practical Politics, 3d edit., 1967. Served to maj. AUS, 1942-46. Decorated Croix de Guerre, France. Mem. Am. Polit. Sci. Assn., So. Polit. Sci. Assn., Southwest Polit. Sci. Assn. (exec. com. 1975-77), Am. Soc. Pub. Adminstrn. (Dimock award 1984), Internat. Personnel Mgmt. Assn., Phi Beta Kappa, Beta Theta Pi (v.p. 1962, gen. sec. 1963-65), Pi Sigma Alpha, Phi Kappa Phi, Sigma Delta Chi. Republican. Baptist. Home: 611 Montclair College Station TX 77840 Office: Tex A&M U Dept Polit Sci College Station TX 77843

VAN SANT, GEORGE MONTGOMERY, philosophy educator; b. State College, Pa., Nov. 20, 1927; s. Edward R. and Beatrice (Snow) Van S.; m. Peggy Ann Hutchinson, Sept. 12, 1953 (dec.); children—Edward Dunbar, Mary Montgomery; m 2d, Susan Jane Hanna, Oct. 1, 1975. A.B., St. John's Coll., 1948, M.A., 1955; Ph.D., U. Va., 1958. Ednl. researcher Nat. Council Episc. Ch., N.Y.C., 1948-49; dir. printing, bookstore mgr. St. John's Coll., Annapolis, Md., 1949-50; editor, head report sect., Va. Hwy. Research Council, Charlottesville, 1953-58; from asst. prof. to prof., chmn. dept. philosophy Mary Washington Coll., 1958—. Bd. dirs. United Way, 1968—; mem. Dem. Com. Fredericksburg, 1964—, chmn., 1975-80; mem. Fredericksburg City Council, 1980. Served to col. USMCR, 1945-77. Decorated Bronze Star, Purple Heart, Meritorious Service medal. Mem. Am. Philos. Assn., Conf. Philosophy Dept. Chairmen (chmn. 1982-84), Va. Philos. Assn. (past pres.), Washington Philosophy Club (past pres.), Marine Corps Assn., Va. Mcpl. League; Omicron Delta Kappa, Episcopalian. Club: Cotillion of Fredericksburg. Contbr. articles to profl. jours. Home: 1407 Washington Ave Fredericksburg VA 22401 Office: Dept Classics Philosophy and Religion Mary Washington College Fredericksburg VA 22401

VAN SETERS, JOHN, religion educator; b. Hamilton, Ont., Can., May 2, 1935; s. Hugo and Anna (Hubert) Van S.; m. Elizabeth Marie Malmberg, June 11, 1960; children—Peter, Deborah. B.A., U. Toronto, 1958; M.A., Yale U., 1959, Ph.D., 1965; B.D., Princeton Theol. Sem., 1962. Asst. prof. Near Eastern studies Waterloo Luth. U., 1965-67; assoc. prof. Andover Newton Theol. Sch., 1967-70; assoc. prof. Near Eastern studies U. Toronto, 1970-76, prof., 1976-77; James A. Gray prof. Bibl. lit. dept. religion U. N.C., Chapel Hill, 1977—, chmn., 1980—. Woodrow Wilson fellow, 1958-59; J.J. Oberman fellow Yale U., 1962-64; Agusta Hasard fellow, 1964-65; Can. Council research grantee, 1973; John Simon Guggenheim meml. fellow, 1979-80; Nat. Endowment Humanities research fellow, 1985-86. Mem. Soc. Bibl. Lit., Am. Oriental Soc., AAUP, Soc. Study Egyptian Antiquities, Am. Schs. Oriental Research. Mem. Ch. of Christ. Author: The Hyksos, A New Investigation, 1966; Abraham in History and Tradition, 1975; In Search of History, 1983. Home: 303 Hoot Owl Ln Chapel Hill NC 27514 Office: Dept Religion 101 Saunders Hall U NC Chapel Hill NC 27514

VANSICKLE, JOHN JAY, agricultural economist, economic educator, researcher; b. Jefferson, Iowa, Sept. 22, 1952; s. Carl and Lois May (Godwin) VanS.; m. Kristen Ann Little, Sept. 4, 1978; children—Carl David, Laura Kathleen. B.S., Iowa State U., 1974, Ph.D., 1980. Research assoc. Iowa State U., Ames, 1976-80; asst. prof. U. Fla., Gainesville, 1980-85, assoc. prof., 1985—; hon. dir. Fla. Council of Farmer Coops., Gainesville, 1983—; chmn. Nat. Adv. Com. for Computerized Mktg. of Fresh Produce, 1984—. Contbr. articles to profl. jours. Recipient Am. Inst. Coop. award for Best Ph.D., Thesis, 1980. Mem. Am. Agrl. Econs. Assn., Am. Econs. Assn., So. Agrl. Econs. Assn. Democratic. Presbyterian. Lodge: Masons. Home: 4216 NW 77th Terr Gainesville FL 32606

VAN SICLEN, DEWITT CLINTON, geologist, consultant, lecturer; b. Carlisle, Pa., Oct. 25, 1918; s. Clinton DeWitt and Mary (Coyle) Van S.; m. Beverly Gayle King, Apr. 10, 1949; children—Mary, Clinton, Sally, Henry. B.A., Princeton U., 1940; M.S., U. Ill., 1941; Ph.D., Princeton U., 1951. Geologist Drilling & Exploration Co., Abilene, Tex., 1947-51; staff geologist Amoco Prodn. Co. and predecessors, Houston, 1952-59; prof. U. Houston, 1959-82; geol. cons., Houston, 1974—. Served to capt. USAF, 1942-46, 51-52. Recipient Disting. Service award Gulf Coast Assn. Geol. Socs., 1984. Mem. Am. Assn. Petroleum Geologists (del.), Am. Inst. Profl. Geologists (cert., editor Tex. sect. 1975-79), Soc. Petroleum Engrs., Nat. Assn. Geology Tchrs. (pres. Tex. sect. 1965-66), Houston Geol. Soc. (chmn. numerous coms., Disting. Service award, 1981). Republican. Episcopalian. Avocations: travel; gardening; reading. Home and Office: 4909 Bellaire Blvd Bellaire TX 77401

VAN TASSELL, G. LANE, political science educator; b. Murray, Utah, Apr. 14, 1942; s. Glen and Erma Harriet (Marchant) VanT.; m. Christine J. Smith, June 5, 1965; children—Darin, Dwight Huong, Danielle, Dana Dru, Maria Dawn, Dyana Nu, David L. B.A., Brigham Young U., 1966; Ph.D., Claremont Grad. Sch., 1971. Instr., vis. prof. Brigham Young U., 1959-60, 77; prof. Ga. So. Coll., Statesboro, 1970—, head. dept. polit. sci. Active NAACP. Served with USAR, 1960-68. NEH grantee 1974, 76-77, 80. Mem. Am. Polit. Sci. Assn. Democrat. Contbr. articles to profl. jours. Home: 507 Peg-won Blvd Statesboro GA 30458 Office: Ga So U PO Box 8101 Statesboro GA 30460

VAN VALKENBURG, DAVID RAYNOR, cable company executive; b. Tecumseh, Mich., May 19, 1942; s. Raynor Waldron and Mary Pauline (Powell) Van V.; m. Doris Colleen Bowers, June 6, 1964; children—Enid Suzanne, Chadwick Bowers. B.A., Malone Coll., 1964; M.S., U. Kans.-Lawrence, 1966; postgrad. in radiation biophysics U. Pitts., 1966-67; M.B.A., Harvard U., 1969. Investment security analyst Investors Diversified Services, Mpls., 1969-73; v.p. Am. TV and Communications Corp., Denver, 1973-80; exec. v.p. United Cable TV Corp., Denver, 1980-82; exec. v.p. Cox Cable Communications, Inc., Atlanta, 1982-83, pres., 1983-85; pres. ATC/HI Cable TV Corp., Denver, 1986—; dir. Calif. Cable TV Assn., 1974-76, Cable TV Advt. Bur., 1981-82, C-Span, 1982-84; mem. exec. com. Council for Cable Info., 1983—. Bd. trustees Malone Coll., 1969-74, 1982—; bd. deacons Wellshire Presbyn. Ch., Denver, 1978-80; bd. dirs. Alliance Theatre, Atlanta, 1985—; bd. dirs. Walter Kaitz Found., 1984—. Included in Outstanding Young Men Am., 1970; recipient Outstanding Jaycee Mpls. Jaycees, 1971; named Alumnus of Yr. Malone Coll., 1985. Mem. Nat. Cable TV Assn. (bd. dirs. 1983—). Republican. Presbyterian. Club: Cherokee Town and Country (Atlanta). Avocations: tennis; reading. Office: Cox Cable Communications Inc 1400 Lake Hearn Dr Atlanta GA 30319

VAN VALKENBURGH, MARY ELIZABETH, public relations consultant; b. Kingston, N.Y., May 25, 1921; d. Raymond H. and Ruth (Terwilliger) Van V. B.A., St. Lawrence U., 1943. Library researcher Netherlands Info. Bur., N.Y.C., 1943-45; exec. dir. YWCA, Kingston, N.Y., 1947-49; various positions in local councils Girl Scouts U.S.A., 1945-47, 50-56, 57-60, 80-83, pub. relations cons. on nat. staff Dallas, Atlanta, N.Y.C., 1960-80; free-lance pub. relations cons., 1983—. Mem. Pub. Relations Soc. Am., Women in Communications, NOW, LWV, Atlanta Women's Network, Am. Cut Glass Assn., Nat. Assn. Van Valkenburgh Family. Democrat. Episcopalian. Home and Office: 615 Kenilworth Circle Stone Mountain GA 30083

VAN VRANKEN, ROSE, sculptor; b. Passaic, N.J., May 15, 1919; d. Gilbert and Rose Ann (Camwell) Van V.; m. Robert Cornelius Hickey, June 11, 1942; children—Kathryn, Robert, Stephen, Dennis, Sarah. B.A. cum laude, Pomona Coll., 1935-39; student of William Zorach and Robert Laurent, Art Students League, N.Y.C., 1939-42; postgrad. NYU Grad. Inst. Fine Arts, 1941-42; M.A. in Art, U. Iowa, 1943; D.F.A. (hon.), Ricker Coll., 1976. Represented in permanent collections Coventry Cathedral, Eng., Saint Cyril of Alexandria Ch., Houston, Mitchell Energy Corp., Houston, Tex. Commerce Bank, Houston, Des Moines Art Ctr. Mus., Mus. Fine Arts, U. Iowa, Smith Coll., Pomona Coll., Laguna Gloria Mus., Austin, Tex., Brand Art Gallery, Glendale, Calif., Crowne Plaza Hotels, Houston, Tex. Investment Bank, Houston, Finial Investment Corp., Houston Pub. Library, U. Houston Law Sch., numerous other pvt. and corp. collections. Recipient awards for sculpture Los Angeles County Mus., 1944, nat. ann. Oakland Mus., 1945, 46, Iowa ann. Des Moines Art Ctr., 1953, midwest biennal Walker Art Ctr., 1951, Midwest ann. Joslyn Mus., 1950, award for graphics Pasadena Mus., 1951, Madison Art Ctr. Mus., Wis., 1965, 66, 67, Catharine Lorillard Wolfe Art Exhbn., Nat. Arts Club, N.Y.C., 1969, So. Assn. Sculptors, 1973, art in embassies program U.S. Dept. State, Washington, 1977-80. Mem. Nat. Assn. Women Artists (graphic chosen for European Touring Exhbn. 1956), Salmagundi Club (numerous awards 1980—), Internat. Platform Assn. (awards 1981, 1984), Artists Equity, Tex. Soc. Sculptors (past pres. Houston chpt.), Acad. Artists Assn. (nat. ann. Council award 1979, assn. award 1980, Medal of Honor 1985). Gallery: Hobe Sound Galleries 11870 SE Dixie Hwy Hobe Sound FL 33455 also Sol del Rio Galleries San Antonio TX

VANWALLEGHEM, ANDRE JACQUES, safety engineer, fire protection executive, consultant; b. Lima, Peru, Aug. 9, 1937; came to U.S., permanent resident, 1960; s. Andre Omer and Enriqueta (Malaga) VanW.; m. Joyce Evelyn Cary-Barnard, May 26, 1960; children—Lorraine, Janine, Joyce, Paul. C.E., NTL Engring. U., Peru, 1959; postgrad. Pace U., 1963. Sr. market analyst Standard Oil Co. (now Exxon), N.Y.C., 1960-69; dir. Latin Am. ops. Elgin Leach Internat., Chgo., 1969-72; mng. dir. Protecsa, Lima, 1972-76, Ibamatic S.A., Caracas, Venezuela, 1976-83; dir. Latin Am. ops. Nat. Foam System Inc., Houston, 1983—; v.p., dir. NAFOMEX, Mex., 1984—; v.p., dir. Nafobras, Sao Paulo, 1985—; lectr. Tex. A&M U., College Station, 1984—. Author: (with others) Volume Forecasting, 1963. Mem. U.S. Pan Am. Hockey team 1967, Olympic Team 1968; mayor San Borja, Lima, Peru, 1975-76; poll watcher Republican Party, Houston, 1984. Mem. Am. Soc. Safety Engrs., Nat. Fire Protection Assn. Avocations: Woodworking, tennis. Home: 11818 Fawnview Dr Houston TX 77070 Office: Nat Foam System Inc 523 North Belt Suite 450 Houston TX 77060

VAN WAY, MARILYN MATHEWS, school counselor, consultant; b. Columbus, Ga., Sept. 1, 1936; d. Clifford Laurence and Mary Emily (Johnson) Mathews; m. James William Van Way, June 27, 1956 (div. 1969); children—Laura Emily Metyko, Cheryl West Ownby. Student So. Methodist U., 1954-55, U. Houston, 1955-57; B.A., Houston Baptist U., 1970, M.Ed., 1981. Elem. tchr. Houston Sch. Dist., 1970-72, 75-80, counselor gifted students, 1980—; seminar presenter. Author: Windy, 1970. Bible sch. tchr. 1st Meth. Ch., Houston, 1963-68; Sunday sch. tchr. Westminster Meth. Ch., Houston, 1974-76; vol. Republican Com., Houston, 1972-80; vol. Cancer Soc., Leukemia, Cystic Fibrosis, March of Dimes, Houston, 1970-78. Mem. Nat. Assn. Counseling and Devel., Tex. Assn. Counseling and Devel., Tex. Assn. Gifted and Talented, Houston Assn. Counseling and Devel., Kappa Delta Pi, Psi Chi, Delta Kappa Gamma. Avocations: gardening; writing; genealogy. Office: Lanier Middle Sch 2600 Woodhead Houston TX 77098

VAN WINKLE, PETER KEMBLE, banker; b. Providence, Dec. 30, 1941; s. E. Kingsland and Kate Louise (Vondermuhll) Van W.; B.A., Denison U., 1964; M.B.A., Columbia U., 1968; C.F.A., U. Va., 1979; m. Prudence Anderson Bridges, Aug. 16, 1969; children—Trintje Anderson, Prudence Elizabeth. Trust investment officer State St. Bank, Boston, 1969-73; v.p. Lemire & Van Winkle Investment Counselors, Boston, 1973-74; chief investment officer Choate Hall & Stewart, Boston, 1974-75; v.p. First Nat. Bank in Palm Beach (Fla.), 1975-80; exec. v.p., head trust dept. Sun 1st Nat. Bank of Palm Beach County, 1981—; pres. Palm Beach Water Sports Inc., 1975—; prof. Palm Beach Atlantic Coll. Treas., Parents and Teachers of Montessori Children; mem. gifts com. Boca Raton Hosp.; bd. dirs., pres. Community Chest Delray Beach; trustee Boca Raton Acad.; bd. dirs. Visiting Nurse Assn.; treas. Bethesda-by-the-Sea Gift Shop. Served with Army N.G., 1964-70. Chartered fin. analyst. Mem. Fin. Analysts Fedn., Boston Soc. Security Analysts, Fin. Analysts Soc. S. Fla., Delray Beach C. of C. (dir.), Internat. Water Hockey Assn. (v.p.). Republican. Episcopalian. Club: Holland Soc. (N.Y.). Home: 110 Seaspray Ave Palm Beach FL 33480 Office: 255 S County Rd Palm Beach FL 33480

VARGA, DORLINDA APRIL, pediatrician, anesthesiologist; b. Trenton, N.J., Aug. 13, 1952; d. Joseph and Doris Pauline (Hoffman) V. B.A., Goucher Coll., Md., 1974; M.D., U. Fla., 1980. Pediatric intern Shands Teaching Hosp., Gainesville, Fla., 1980-81, resident, 1982-83, resident dept. anesthesiology, 1984—; emergency physician Sunland Tng. Ctr., Gainesville, part-time 1981-83; team physician Eastside High Sch. Football Team, Gainesville, 1983. Area admissions rep. Goucher Coll., 1982—, class agt., 1974—. Recipient Luther W. Holloway award U. Fla. Dept. Pediatrics, 1980; March of Dimes award U. Ala. Sch. Medicine, 1976. Jr. fellow Am. Acad. Pediatrics (Bronze medal 1981); mem. Phi Beta Kappa. Office: Dept Anesthesiology J 296 Shands Hosp Gainesville FL 32611

VARGO, ROBERT FRANK, lawyer; b. St. Louis, Oct. 21, 1948; s. Frank John and Hazel Emma (Brisch) V.; m. Alice Anne McClelland, Sept. 23, 1977. B.A. in Econs. U. South Fla., 1970; J.D. with distinction, St. Mary's U., 1975; postgrad. in law U. Miami, 1983—. Bar: Ala. 1975, Tex. 1984. Assoc. atty. Judge Hugh Rozelle, Atmore, Ala., 1975-76; sole practice law, Atmore, 1976-81, Bay Minette, Ala., 1976-81, 82-84; assoc. atty. Holbrook, Kaufman & Becker, San Antonio, 1984—; ptnr. firm Wills & Vargo, Bay Minette, 1981-82; instr. Jefferson Davis Jr. Coll., Brewton, Ala., 1976—. Contbr. articles to profl. jours. Campaign chmn. North Baldwin United Fund, 1980, bd. dirs., 1980—, pres., 1981-82; bd. dirs. Atmore Fine Arts Council, 1976-77. Mem. ABA, Ala. Bar Assn., John M. Harlan Soc. Presbyterian. Lodge: Kiwanis (dir. 1979-80). Home: 13414 Vista Del Mar San Antonio TX 78216 Office: 2300 Interfirst Plaza 300 convent San Antonio TX 78205

VARMA, JAYDEV R., physician; b. Bulsar, India, Jan. 1, 1936; came to U.S., 1975; s. Ranchodji G. and Amba R. Varma; m. Lila J. Chauhan, July 25, 1965; children—Darshana, Pratim. M.B.B.S., U. Bombay, India, 1964; D.P.H., London Sch. Pub. Health, 1975. Intern, Med. Coll. Ga., Augusta, 1964-65; med. officer Zambia Ministry Health, 1965-69; pvt. practice medicine, Chingiola, Zambia, 1970-73; with Nat. Health Service, London, 1973-75, Med. Coll. Ga., 1976—. Mem. So. Med. Assn., Am. Acad. Family Physicians, AMA, Soc. Tchrs. Family Medicine, Richmond County Med. Soc. Republican. Hindu. Office: Med Coll Ga Laney Blvd Augusta GA 30912

VARNELL, EMILY DIMILLA, medical researcher; b. Boston, Apr. 15, 1936; d. Thomas and Elsa Deitz (Lehniger) DiM.; m. Ray Varnell, Oct. 6, 1971; 1 son, Brian Thomas. B.S. in Chem. Engring., Northeastern U., 1958. Chemist, U.S. Army Biol. Labs., Fort Detrick, Md., 1958-59; head research asst. Uveitis Lab., Mass. Eye and Ear Infirmary, Boston, 1959-62; asst. research prof. dept. ophthalmology U. Fla., Gainesville, 1962-77; asst. prof. dept. ophthalmology La. State U. Med. Center, New Orleans, 1977—. Mem. Assn. Research in Vision and Ophthalmology, Am. Soc. Microbiology, Am. Fedn. Clin. Research, N.Y. Acad. Sci., Sigma Xi. Contbr. articles to profl. jours. Office: La State U Eye Center 136 S Roman St New Orleans LA 70112

VARNER, ROBERT EDWARD, judge; b. Montgomery, Ala., June 11, 1921; s. William and Georgia (Thomas) V.; m. Carolyn Hood Self, Sept. 2, 1947; children—Robert Edward, Carolyn Stuart; m. Jane Dennis Hannah, Feb. 20, 1982. B.S., Auburn U., 1946; J.D., U. Ala., 1949. Bar: Ala. 1949. Atty. City of Tuskegee, 1951; asst. U.S. atty. Middle Dist. Ala., 1954-58; practice in, Montgomery, 1958-71; partner firm Jones, Murray, Stewart & Varner, 1958-71; U.S. dist. judge, Montgomery, 1971—; guest lectr. bus. law Huntingdon Coll. Pres. Montgomery Rotary Charity Found.; v.p., fin. chmn. Tukabatchee Area council Boy Scouts Am.; Mem. Macon County Bd. Edn., 1950-54. Served with USNR, 1942-46. Recipient Silver Beaver award Boy Scouts Am. Mem. ABA, Fed. Bar Assn., Montgomery Bar Assn. (pres. 1971), Macon County Bar Assn., Am. Trial Lawyers Assn., Jud. Conf. of U.S. (com. on operation of jury system), Phi Alpha Delta, Phi Delta Theta. Republican. Methodist. Club: Rotarian (pres. 1961). Office: PO Box 2046 Montgomery AL 36103*

VARNES, PAUL RAY, recreation educator; b. Gainesville, Fla., June 12, 1934; s. Harley Ozieth and Julia (Anderson) V.; m. Martha Vlacos, Dec. 25, 1954 (div. 1975); children—Paula, Patricia; m. Nancy Jull Tutton, Nov. 24, 1977; 1 child, Julia Rae. B.S., U. Fla., 1960, M.S., 1961, Ed.D., 1967. Tchr., coach Pensacola High Sch., Fla., 1961-64; program dir. U. Fla., Gainesville, 1964-67, dept. chmn., 1968-86; project dir. for five Fla. counties, Ocala, 1967-68; cons. in field. Author: Contemporary Views on Drug Education, 1974; Drug Abuse: Intramurals-A Viable Alternative, 1974. Contbr. articles to profl. jours. Mem. Selective Service Bd. Alachua County, 1982-85; mem. building codes com. City of Gainesville, 1982-85. Served as sgt. U.S. Army, 1952-56, Korea. Recipient honor award Fla. Assn. Health, Phys. Edn., Recreation and Dance, 1979, Outstanding Service award Gov.s Council, 1981. Mem. Nat. Recreation and Parks Assn. (cert.), AAHPERD, So. Dist. Assn. Health, Phys. Edn., Recreation and Dance (pres. 1985-86, honor award 1985), Internat. Council Health, Phys. Edn., Recreation and Dance, Fla. Recreation and Parks Assn. Lodge: Elks. Avocations: hunting; fishing. Office: U Fla Room 227 Gainesville FL 32611

VASILAKOS, NICHOLAS PETROU, chemical engineer; b. Athens, Greece, Jan. 1, 1954; s. Petros and Theodora (Sotiropoulou) V.; B.S., Nat. Tech. U., Athens, 1976; M.S., Calif. Inst. Tech., 1978, Ph.D., Calif. Inst. Tech., 1980. Asst. prof. chem. engring. U. Tex., Austin, 1981—; founding mem. Separations Research Council, Ctr. for Energy Studies, Austin; cons. Exxon Enterprizes, Inc., 1980, Arco Petroleum Products Co., 1982—, Norton Co., 1983—, U.S. Dept. Energy Coal Liquefaction Reviewers Bd., 1982. Recipient cert. recognition NASA, 1982; Disting. Faculty Advisor award U. Tex. Student Engring. Council, 1982, 83. Mem. Am. Inst. Chem. Engrs., Am. Chem. Soc., Sigma Xi.

VASS, LACHLAN MAURY, JR., geologist, consultant; b. New Orleans, June 11, 1925; s. Lachlan M. Vass and Louise (Voorhies) Bushnell; m. Bette John, Sept. 7, 1947; children—Katherine, William, Julie. B.S. in Geology, Tulane U. Cert. profl. petroleum geologist. Vice pres. Amerada Hess, Tulsa, 1970-74, v.p. offshore joint ventures, Houston, 1974-81, dir., sr. v.p. exploration Mitchell Energy, Houston, 1981-84, Transco Energy, Houston, 1981-84; pres. Exploration Mgmt. Cons., Houston, 1984—. Served to lt. (j.g.), USNR, 1944-46. Mem. Am. Assn. of Petroleum Geologists, Soc. Exploration Geophysicists, Houston Geol. Soc., Am. Petroleum Inst. Avocations: golf; tennis. Home and Office: 17911 Fall River Circle Houston TX 77090

VASSER, RICHARD EDWARD, state agency official; b. Spokane, Wash., Sept. 29, 1942; s. Roy and Mary Elizabeth (Johnson) V.; student Emory U., Atlanta, 1960-61, Schreiner Inst., Kerrville, Tex., 1961-62; B.S., S.W. Tex. State U., 1965, M.P.A., 1977; m. Sue Dodgen, June 16, 1973; children—Elizabeth, Sharon. Dir. evaluation San Antonio Dept. Parks and Recreation, 1971, grant adminstr. youth services project, 1971-72; project mgr. planning div. Tex. Dept. Human Resources, Austin, 1972-74, acting dir. analysis sect. planning div., 1974-75, project mgr. planning bur., 1975-79, adminstr. research and demonstration div., med. programs, 1979, project and grant mgr. policy planning div., 1979-80, dir. research and demonstration, policy and planning div., med. programs, 1980, project mgr. nursing home programs and hospice program office research, demonstrations and evaluation Tex. Dept. Human Resources, 1981—. Served with USAF, 1965-71, Res., 1978—. Decorated D.F.C., Air medals. Mem. Lambda Chi Alpha (pres. 1976-81). Republican. Episcopalian. Club: Austin Skiers (v.p. programs 1977-78, asst. v.p. trips 1978-79, v.p. trips 1979-80). Home: 5107 Saddle Circle Austin TX 78727 Office: PO Box 2960 Dept Human Resources Austin TX 78769

VASSILIOU, MARIOS SIMOU, geophysicist, educator; b. Nicosia, Cyprus, June 7, 1957; came to U.S., 1961; s. Simos Georghiou and Avra (Papadopoullou) V. A.B., Harvard U., 1978; M.S., Calif. Inst. Tech., 1979, Ph.D., 1983. Cons., Rockwell Internat. Sci. Ctr., Thousand Oaks, Calif., 1981-82, TRW, Inc., Los Angeles, 1982-83; sr. research geophysicist ARCO Resources Tech., Plano, Tex., 1983—; vis. lectr. U. Tex.-Dallas, 1984—. Contbr. articles to profl. jours. Mem. Seismol. Soc. Am., IEEE, Soc. Exploration Geophysicists, Sigma Xi. Office: ARCO Resources Tech 2300 W Plano Pkwy/Pat Plano TX 75075

VASSY, LAWRENCE KENNETH, electronic engineering technology educator, consultant; b. Laurens, S.C., Aug. 27, 1930; s. William Lawrence and Vivian Elizabeth (Pinson) V.; m. Joann Smiley, May 24, 1951; children—Cynthia Dianne, Teresa Lynn, Lisa Carol. B.S. in Vocat. Edn., Western Carolina U., 1984. Repair bus. owner, Gaffney, S.C., 1951; chief engr., ops. mgr. radio WADA Radio, Slielby, N.C., 1958-78, contact engr., 1978-82; instr. Cleveland Tech. Coll., Shelby N.C., 1978—. Contbr. articles to profl. jours. Served as staff sgt. USAF, 1951-55. Republican. Baptist. Avocations: electronics; fishing; woodworking. Home: 1320 King's Circle Shelby NC 28150

VASTBINDER, EARL EDWARD, pediatrician, educator; b. Dayton, Ohio, July 26, 1935; s. Ernest Clayton and Lucy (Smith) V.; m. Joyce Elaine Mangum, June 30, 1962; children—Jennifer Elizabeth, Heidi Ruth. Student Olivet Nazarene Coll., 1953-55; B.S., U. Dayton, 1957; M.D., Ohio State U., 1961, M.S., 1967. Diplomate Am. Bd. Pediatrics. Intern Miami Valley Hosp., Dayton, 1961-62; resident Columbus Children's Hosp., Ohio, 1964-66; assoc. prof. pediatrics U. Ky. Coll. Medicine, Lexington, 1967-72, assoc. prof. allied health Coll. Allied Health, 1972-76, dir. clin. assoc. program, 1972-76; prof., chmn. dept. allied health Trevecca Nazarene Coll., Nashville, 1976-85, dir. physicians asst. program, 1976-83, dir. student health services, 1977-85; chief clin. services Student Health Service, Vanderbilt U., 1985—. Served to capt. USAF, 1962-64. Recipient Faculty Mem. of Yr. award Trevecca Nazarene Coll., 1978. Fellow Am. Acad. Pediatrics; mem. Soc. for Adolescent Medicine (charter), Am. Med. Dirs. Assn., Tenn. Assn. Long Term Care Physicians. Avocations: gardening; music. Home: 889 Lakemont Dr Nashville TN 37220 Office: Zerfoss Student Health Ctr Sta 17 Vanderbilt U Nashville TN 37232

VATH, JOSEPH G., bishop; b. New Orleans, Mar. 12, 1918. Ed., Notre Dame Sem., New Orleans, 1935-41; J.C.L., Catholic U. Am., 1948. Ordained priest Roman Catholic Ch., 1941; asst. pastor Ascension Ch., Donaldsonville, La., 1941-46, Incarnate Word Ch., New Orleans, 1948, St. Michael's Ch., 1948-49; vice-chancellor Archdiocese of New Orleans, 1948-66, sec. to bishop, 1949-62, sec. diocesan tribunal, 1955; adminstr. Our Lady of Perpetual Help Ch., Kenner, La., 1952; pastor Little Flower Ch., 1966-69; consecrated bishop, 1966, vicar gen., aux. bishop, Mobile-Birmingham (Ala.) and titular bishop of Novaliciana, 1966-69, bishop of Birmingham, 1969—. Office: PO Box 2086 Birmingham AL 35201*

VAUGHAN, DALE ETTER, landscape contractor; b. St. Louis, Mar. 4, 1947; s. Ervin Heartwell and Charlotte (Etter) V.; m. Gail Bernice Vaughan, Oct. 19, 1969; children—Michael Dale, Paul Nicholas, Rebecca Susan. B.S. in Christian Ministry, Southwest Assembly of God Coll., Waxahachie, Tex., 1977. Regional mgr. Big Chief Stone, Ft. Worth, 1976-79; owner Shirt Tales, Inc., St. Louis, 1979-82; v.p. mktg. Bot. Concepts, Ft. Worth, 1982—; owner, operator wholesale nursery, Wilmer, Ala. Served with U.S. Army, 1964-68. Decorated Purple Heart. Mem. Assn. Gen. Contractors, Tex. Assn. Landscape Contractors, Tex. Assn. Nurserymen, Am. Assn. Nurserymen. Democrat. Assemblies of God. Home: 7617 Bermejo Rd Fort Worth TX 76112 Office: Bot Concepts Inc 4800 Wichita St Fort Worth TX 76119

VAUGHAN, DONALD SHORES, political science educator; b. Cape Girardeau, Mo., Oct. 17, 1921; s. Arthur Winn and Harriett (Shores) V.; m. Sarah Janes Auten, Nov. 3, 1945; children—Beverly Winn, Kenneth Auten. Student, Southeast Mo. State U., 1939-41; B.A., Vanderbilt U., 1943; M.A., U. Ala., 1947; Ph.D., Columbia U., 1967. With U. Ala., 1949-55; instr. to prof. polit. sci. U. Miss., University, 1955—, chmn. dept., 1968-82, successively asst.

dir., assoc. dir., dir. Bur. Govtl. Research, 1957-77. Contbr. articles to profl. jours. Pres. Oxford Community Band, 1984-85. Served to lt. USNR, 1943-1946. Fellow Vanderbilt U. 1942-43; U. Ala. scholar 1947; Columbia U. fellow, 1947-49, NSF fellow, 1973. Mem. Am. Soc. Pub. Adminstrn., So. Polit. Sci. Assn. (v.p.-elect 1983-84, v.p. 1984-85), Miss. Polit. Sci. Assn. (pres. 1972), Pi Alpha Alpha (exec. council 1977-78), Omicron Delta Kappa (assoc.), Kappa Alpha. Democrat. United Methodist. Club: Oxford Tennis. Home: 109 Philip Rd Oxford MS 38655 Office: U Miss University MS 38677

VAUGHAN, JACK CHAPLINE, retired physicist, author; b. Sarasota, Fla., Dec. 17, 1912; s. Alfred Jefferson and Blossom Creighton (Chapline) V.; B.A. in Physics and Math., Tex. Christian U., 1967; postgrad. U. Tex., Arlington, 1967-68, Ark. Law Sch., 1934-35; m. Anne Gwin, Sept. 4, 1942 (div. Mar. 1955); children—Jack Chapline, Gwin Barnum Vaughan (dec.), Thomas A.J., Anne; m. Lanette Worthington, Mar. 12, 1965. Propr. cattle ranch, Chicot County (Ark.), 1950, Adams County (Miss.), 1945-52; specifications writer Navy carrier-based aircraft programs Douglas Aircraft Corp. Los Angeles, 1952-55; head specifications group TITAN intercontinental ballistic missile nosecone Research and Adv. Devel. Div., AVCO, Boston, 1956; analyst, writer research and devel. proposals LTV Aerospace Corp., Dallas, 1956-59, sr. analyst progress reporting and contractually required data submissions LTV-NASA-SCOUT launch vehicle program, 1959-74. Served to maj. inf. AUS, 1940-45. Mem. Am. Phys. Soc., AAAS, Honourable Soc. of Cymmrodorion (Wales). Author: (all Vaughan's American Histories) Frontier Ambassador, 1957; Vaughan's Brigade Army of Tennessee, vols. 1-10, 1960-75; The British History of Geoffrey of Monmouth, 1975; Blossom Chapline and Alfred Vaughan 3d, 1975; The Chronicles of Wales, 1976; Martha Jane, 1977; William Vaughan. . .Renaissance Scholar; American Colonist, 1978; Gyges, Ancient Lydians, 1978; Conquest of the South (1861-1865), Part I, 1979; Welsh Colony of Virginia, 1980; Genesis, 1981; World War II, 2 vols., 1982; Florence Plantation, 1983; translator: (from Russian, Latin and Welsh) in Vaughan's Eurasian Histories, vol. 1, Caucasians, 1984, vol. 2, Cimmerians and Cymry, 1985, vol. 3, Cumbrian Romano-Britons, 1986. Address: PO Box 7632 Little Rock AR 72217

VAUGHAN, JOHN WILLIS, utility company executive; b. Blackstone, Va., 1925; married. B.S.E.E., Duke U., 1947; S.M. in Indsl. Mgmt., MIT, 1962. With Appalachian Power Co., Roanoke, Va., 1947—, comml. mgr. Roanoke div., 1947-71, asst. v.p., 1971-72, exec. v.p., 1972-80, pres., chief operating officer, dir., 1980—; dir. Am. Electric Power Service Corp., Dominion Bankshares Corp.; v.p., dir. various subs. Am. Electric Power Co. Served with USN, World War II. Office: Appalachian Power Co 40 Franklin Rd Roanoke VA 24009*

VAUGHAN, JOHN WILLIS, JR., lawyer; b. Martinsville, Va., June 13, 1951; s. John Willis and Audrey Virginia (Hatcher) V., m. Brenda Louise Foley, June 19, 1976. B.S. in Commerce, U. Va., 1973; J.D., U. Richmond, 1976. Bar: Va. 1976. Assoc. firm Hirschler, Fleischer, Weinberg, Cox & Allen, Richmond, Va., 1980—. Mem. Va. State Bar, Va. Bar Assn., Richmond Bar Assn., Richmond Trial Lawyers Assn., Richmond Jaycees. Office: Main St Centre 629 E Main St Richmond VA 23202

VAUGHAN, MICHAEL RAY, research wildlife biologist, educator; b. Hampton, Va., Aug. 11, 1944; s. Ray and Elizabeth (Bradshaw) V.; m. Lillian Marie Wolfe, Sept. 5, 1971; children—Benjamin Ray, Jodi Lynn, Lindsay Elizabeth. B.S., N.C. State U., Raleigh, 1971; M.S., Oreg. State U., 1974; Ph.D., U. Wis., 1979. Research assoc. Wis. Coop Wildlife Research Unit, Madison, 1979-80; asst. leader Va. Coop Wildlife Research Unit, Blacksburg, Va., 1980—. Organizer, 1st pres. Support Group for Gifted/Talented Edn., Montgomery County, Va., 1984-85. Served with USAF, 1962-66. Mem. Wildlife Soc. (organizer Va. chpt., pres. 1982-83, Pub. award 1982). Baptist. Home: 130 Thelma Ln Christiansburg VA 24073

VAUGHAN, RICHARD ALLEN, life insurance underwriter; b. Sherman, Tex., July 18, 1946; s. John W. and Margaret Ann (Fires) V.; student U. Tex., Austin, 1964-68; B.B.A., N. Tex. State U., 1969; m. Terence Hall Thompson, Jan. 12, 1968; children—Shannon, Elizabeth, Todd. Mgr., Vaughan Dept. Stores, Sherman, 1968-73; asso. Fallon Co., Sherman, 1973-76; with Fallon & Vaughan, C.L.U.s, Sherman, 1976—; founder, dir. Consol. Printing, Inc.; dir. Wexford Fin. and Leasing Corp.; instr. Life Underwriter Tng. Council, Washington. Bd. dirs. Grayson County (Tex.) chpt. Am. Cancer Soc., 1973-77, pres., 1976-77; bd. dirs. Salvation Army, 1975-77; mem. Sherman City Council, 1977-79. Qualifying and life mem. Million Dollar Round Table; named Agt. of Yr., Indpls. Life Ins. Co., 1975; C.L.U. Mem. Am. Soc. C.L.U.s, Nat. Assn. Life Underwriters, Life Underwriters Assn. (dir.), Assn. for Advanced Life Underwriting, Tex. Assn. Life Underwriters, Mensa Internat., Greater Sherman Tex. Area C. of C. (bd. dirs. 1986—), Sigma Alpha Epsilon. Baptist. Office: 111A N Travis Sherman TX 75090

VAUGHAN, WILLIAM WALTON, atmospheric scientist; b. Clearwater, Fla., Sept. 7, 1930; s. William Walton and Ella Vermelle (Warr) V.; m. Wilma Geraldine Stapleton, Dec. 23, 1951; children—Stephen W., David A., William D., Robert T. B.S. with honors, U. Fla., 1951; grad. cert. Fla. State U., 1952; Ph.D., U. Tenn., 1976. Sci. asst. Air Force Armament Ctr., 1955-58, Army Ballistic Missile Agy., 1958-60; chief aerophysics and astrophysics br. NASA-Marshall Space Flight Ctr., Ala., 1960-64, chief aero-astrophysics office, 1964-67, chief aerospace environ. div., 1967-76, chief atmospheric scis. div., 1976—. Bd. dirs. Huntsville Youth Orch., chmn. troup com. Boy Scouts Am. Served to capt. USAF, 1951-55. Recipient Exceptional Service medal NASA, 1970; various govt. performance awards USAF, U.S. Army, NASA. Mem. Am. Meteorologist Soc. (mem. nat. com. meteorol. aspects of aerospace systems), Am. Geophys. Union, AIAA (mem. nat. com. atmospheric environ., Losey atmospheric sci. award 1980), AAAS, Sigma Xi. Baptist. Contbr. articles to profl. jours. Office: Mail Code ED41 NASA Marshall Space Flight Ctr Marshall Space Flight Center AL 35812

VAUGHEN, VICTOR CORNELIUS ADOLPH, chemical engineer; b. Wilmington, Del., Oct. 8, 1933; s. John Victor and Charlotte (Leicht) V.; m. Judith Shaver, Apr. 5, 1959 (div. Jan. 1975); children—Leonard Karl, Bruce Kevin, Eric John; m. Salli Lou Kimberly, June 4, 1977 (div. Oct. 1984); 1 child, Rebecca Susan Kimberly-Vaughen. B.S. in Chemistry, Stetson U., 1957; B.S. in Chem. Engring., MIT, 1956, M.S. in Chem. Engring., 1957, Ph.D. in Chem. Engring., 1961. Registered profl. engr., Tenn. With Oak Ridge Nat. Lab., 1960—, mgr. hot cell ops., 1975-80, program mgr., 1980-81, sect. head, 1981—; exchange scientist Kernforschungsanlage, Julich, Fed. Republic Germany, 1972-74; leader on energy, various workshops, seminars, 1970—; speaker on ethics of tech., 1980—. Author numerous tech. reports; also articles, chpt. Mem., past pres. Oak Ridge Symphony Orch.; active, past treas. Oak Ridge Civic Music Assn.; treas. Southern Appalachian yearly meeting, 1975-79; sec. Sportsman's Assn., Oak Ridge, 1977-79. Served to capt. U.S. Army, 1961. Scholar Stetson U., DeLand, Fla., 1952-54, MIT, 1956. Mem. Am. Inst. Chem. Engrs. (chmn. edn. com. 1981-82), Am. Nuclear Soc. (ethics com. local sect. 1981—), Nat. Soc. Profl. Engrs. (chmn. arrangements 1984-85, ethics com. 1985-86), AAAS, Sigma Xi, Tau Beta Pi. Republican. Mem Society of Friends. Avocations: music performance; woodworking; hiking; canoeing. Home: 106 Gordon Rd Oak Ridge TN 37830 Office: Oak Ridge Nat Lab PO Box X Oak Ridge TN 37831

VAUGHN, EDWARD MCDONALD, JR., behavioral consultant; b. Hamlet, N.C., Aug. 7, 1935; s. Edward McDonald and Ruth (Dickson) Martin; m. Anne Wilkerson, Dec. 6, 1958 (div. Jan. 1971); children—Edward, Elizabeth, Katherine; m. Mary Humphrey, Aug. 16, 1975; 1 child, David; 1 stepchild, Gregory. B. Gen. Edn., U. Nebr., 1964; M.A. in Psychology, Catholic U. Am., 1982; postgrad. Va. Poly Inst., 1985—. Commd. pvt., 1955, advanced through grades to col. U.S. Army Dept. Def., D.C., 1955-68, 77-81; asst. v.p. Bache & Co., Inc., N.Y.C., 1968-70; pres. Martin & Vaughn, Inc., Woodcliff Lake, N.J., 1970-77; dir. Creative Focus, Springfield, Va., 1981-85; behavioral cons. Darnoc Enterprises, Arlington, Va., 1984—. Finance chmn. County Rep. Party, Raleigh, 1970; vol. therapist Mt. Vernon Mental Health, Springfield, 1981-84. Decorated Silver Star, Legion of Merit, 3 Bronze Stars, Air medal, Purple Heart. Mem. Am. Psychol. Assn., Eastern Psychol. Assn. Episcopal. Lodges: Masons, Lions (pres. 1976). Avocations: painting; sports. Home and Office: 7902 Colorado Springs Dr Springfield VA 22153

VAUGHN, GAROLD FORREST, construction company executive; b. Elkton, Mo., Apr. 12, 1919; s. Welford and Monta Willetta (Crank) V.; student So. Mo. U., 1937-40; m. Jacqueline Kirtland, July 9, 1941; children—Carol Ann, Sarah Smith. Fin. and ops. systems mgr., program mgmt., contract claims mgr. Litton Systems, Pascagoula, Miss., 1969-78; project configuration control bd. mgr. Parsons-Gilbane, New Orleans, 1978; mgr. configuration mgmt. Orbital Astron. Obs., 1978-79; configuration mgmt. mgr., engring. mgr. Dravo Utility Constructors, Inc., New Orleans, 1979-81, exec. mgmt. cons., 1981, configuration mgmt. officer, petroleum ops. support services, 1982-84; pres. Applied Science Inc., New Orleans, 1983—; cons. configuration and data mgmt., integrated logistics support, 1984—. Recipient Mgmt. Assn. Service award, 1963. Club: St. Andrews Golf and Country. Home: 3730 River Pine Dr Moss Point MS 39563

VAUGHN, GLENN, JR., newspaper executive; b. Newton County, Ga., May 19, 1929; s. Glenn and Sallie (Thomason) V.; student U. Ga., 1949-52; m. Nancy Jean Weeks, Aug. 30, 1952; children—Valorie Vaughn Riley, Penny Vaughn Byrd, Robert W., William. Reporter, Albany (Ga.) Herald, 1952-55; copy editor Columbus (Ga.) Ledger, 1955-56, news editor, city editor, mng. editor, 1959-65, v.p., gen. mgr. Ledger-Enquirer Newspapers, 1973-77, pres., 1977—, pub., 1980—; pub. Phenix City (Ala.) Citizen, 1956-57; reporter Atlanta Jour., 1957-59; editor, pub. Athens (Ga.) Daily News, 1965-69; editor Columbus Enquirer, 1969-73. Bd. dirs. Columbus United Way, 1977—, pres.-elect, 1981. Served with USMC, 1946-48. Mem. So. Newspaper Pubs. Assn., Am. Newspaper Pubs. Assn., Columbus C. of C. (dir. 1978-83). Methodist. Office: Columbus Ledger-Enquirer 17W 12th St Columbus GA 31901

VAUGHN, JEANNETTE WRIGHT, business educator; b. Bonham, Tex., June 20, 1927; d. Joseph Franklin and Lois Catherine (Coleman) Wright; m. Oris Durelle Vaughn, June 21, 1958; children—Steven Vaughn, Kathryn Vaughn. B.A., Tex. Woman's U., 1948; M.B.A., U. Tex., 1954. Cert. tchr., Tex. Instr. Lamar U., Beaumont, Tex., 1954-57, asst. prof. dept. adminstrv. services, 1957—. Assoc. editor: Business Education's Response to the Changing Technologies, 1984. Wesley Found. bd. dirs. Lamar U., Beaumont, 1984-85. Recipient Regents' Merit award Lamar U., 1972, 84; Lamar Research Council grantee, 1981, 82. Mem. Nat. Bus. Edn. Assn., Nat. Collegiate Assn. for Secs., Am. Bus. Communication Assn., Mountain Plains Bus. Edn. Assn., S.W. Adminstrv. Services Assn., Tex. Bus. Tchrs. Edn. Council, Tex. Bus. Edn. Assn. (Collegiate Tchr. of Yr. 1985, pres. dist. 5, 1983-84), Delta Sigma Pi, Beta Gamma Sigma (sec.-treas. Lamar chpt. 1981-83). Office: Lamar U Box 10033 Beaumont TX 77710

VAUGHN, KAREN, economics educator; b. N.Y.C., July 21, 1944; d. Willy and Cecelia (Douglas) Iversen; m. Garrett Alan Vaughn, Sept. 7, 1968; 1 child, Jessica Susan. B.A., Queens Coll. CUNY, 1966; M.A., Duke U., 1969, Ph.D., 1971. Asst. prof. U. Tenn., Knoxville, 1969-75; assoc. prof. George Mason U., Fairfax, Va., 1978-84, chmn. dept. econs., 1982—, prof. econs., 1984—; adj. scholar CATO Inst., Washington, 1982—. Author: John Locke: Economist and Social Scientist, 1980. Mem. editorial bd. History of Polit. Economy Jour., 1984—. Editor: HES Bull., 1978-84. Contbr. articles to profl. jours. NDEA fellow, 1966-69. Mem. So. Econs. Assn. (exec. com. 1978-80), Am. Econs. Assn., History of Econs. Soc., Mont Pelerin Soc. Office: George Mason U Fairfax VA 22030

VAUGHN, PEARL HENDERSON, retired educator, recreation administrator; b. Chattanooga; d. Cicero C. and Fannie (Strickland) Henderson; B.S., Tenn. A&I State U., 1956, M.S., 1957; m. Roy O. Vaughn, Sept. 10, 1930, (div. May 1942); 1 son, Roy Orlando II. Tchr. public schs., summer playground dir. City of Chattanooga, 1940-42; recreation dir. and organizer, first aid and water safety instr., ARC, Chattanooga, 1942-54; water safety instr. SE Nat. Aquatic Sch., ARC, Nashville, 1954; asst. prof. phys. edn. and recreation, profl. counselor, asst. dean women Tenn. A&I State U., Nashville, 1957-60; asso. prof. phys. edn. Lemoyne Coll., Memphis, 1960-62; head tennis counselor Camp Kokosin, Bedford, Vt., summer 1961; asso. prof. health, phys. edn. and recreation Grambling Coll., 1962-77, recreation curriculum coordinator, 1970-77, ret., 1977, coordinator recreation Major's Soc., 1963-76, sec. library com., 1964-66, mem. student union bd., 1964—, mem. coll. curriculum com., 1967-68, mem. edn. com., 1965-68, dir. adult edn. project Continuing Edn. Program, 1979-80, also dir. Therapeautic Recreation Consortium, 1970s; cons. high sch. phys. edn. and recreation career days. Leader, Pelican council Girl Scouts U.S.A., 1966—, dir. day camp, 1966-69; coordinator recreation com. Town of Grambling (La.), 1964-66; pres. North La. br. Mental Health Program, 1967-72; exec. dir. Grambling Community Recreation and Playground Summer Program, 1977-80; dir. Recreation Leadership Tng. Workshop, 1968-69, 69-70, 70-71; recreation cons., specialist Lincoln Parish Emergency Sch. Assistance Program, summers 1972, 73; cons. Sr. Citizens Camping Program, Williams Bay (Wis.) Coll.; mem. La. Ednl. Books Com., 1980—; formerly recreation coordinator, v.p. sr. choir, dir. bd. Christian edn., other offices Lewis Temple Christian Meth. Ch.; arts and crafts dir. Ann. Leadership Tng. Sch., La. Conf. of Christian Meth. Epis. Ch.; recreation dir., coordinator bd. Christian edn. Bethel African Meth. Ch., 1982—; mem. Citizen's Adv. Bd. for Recreation in Hamilton County (Tenn.), 1982—, also chmn. contact com.; adv. bd. East 5th St. Day Care Ctr., 1982—; mem. Task Force for Renovation Booker T. Washington State Park, 1983—; spl. adviser to supt. recreation, adv. bd. recreation dept. City of Chattanooga, 1984—. Pearl H. Vaughn night named in her honor, sponsored by Met. Recreation Athletic Assn. Mem. Nat. Recreation and Park Assn. (nat. council membership services task force 1971-72), La. Recreation and Parks Assn. (adminstr., chmn. 6th dist. 1970-71), Am. Park and Recreation Soc. (chmn. minority groups relation com. 1971-73), AAHPER, Am. Forestry Assn., Am. Camping Assn., AAUP (pres. Grambling 1976), Soc. Parks and Recreation Educators (dir. 1973-76), Grambling Ret. Tchrs. Assn. (sec. cultural com. 1979-81), Delta Psi Kappa (nat., charter), Delta Sigma Theta (pres. 1972-73), LWV. Designer nature sanctuary for outdoor edn. and camp counseling classes. Home: 6102 Emery Dr Chattanooga TN 37421

VAUGHN, WILLIAM PRESTON, historian, educator; b. East Chicago, Ind., May 28, 1933; s. James Carl and Georgiana (Preston) V.; A.B., U. Mo., Columbia, 1955; M.A., Ohio State U., 1956, Ph.D., 1961; m. Virginia Lee Meyer, June 10, 1961; 1 dau., Rhonda Louise. Instr. in history U. So. Calif., 1961-62; asst. prof. history N. Tex. State U., 1962-65, assoc. prof., 1965-69, prof., 1969—. Served with arty. U.S. Army, 1956-57. Mem. So. Hist. Assn. (life), Orgn. Am. Historians, Tex. United Faculty, Phi Beta Kappa, Phi Alpha Theta (Manuscript Competition winner 1972). Republican. Episcopalian. Clubs: Lions, Masons, Shriners. Author: Schools for All: The Blacks and Public Education in the South, 1865-77, 1974; The Antimasonic Party in the United States, 1826-43, 1983; contbr. numerous articles on black edn. and polit. antimasonry to profl. jours. Home: 908 Hilton Pl Denton TX 76201 Office: History Dept North Tex State U Denton TX 76203

VAUX, VICTOR VAN, quality engineer; b. Tucumcari, N.Mex., July 11, 1954; s. George McClay and Sara Byrl (Abercrombie) V. Student in petroleum engring. Tex. A&M U., 1972-73; B.S. in Mech. Engring., U. Tex.-Arlington, 1979. Insp. apprentice Otis Engring. Co., Dallas, 1974, class B insp., 1974-75, class A insp., 1975-77, precision insp. supr., 1977-78, quality engr., 1979—; tchr. Mt. View Coll., Dallas, 1982; mng. ptnr. Southwest Investment Group, 1985—. Mem. Am. Soc. Quality Control (cert.), ASME, Phi Eta Sigma, Pi Tau Sigma, Alpha Chi. Baptist. Home: 1000 Noble St Carrollton TX 75006 Office: Otis Engring Co 2601 Beltline Rd PO Box 34380 Dallas TX 75234

VAZIRI, MANOUCHEHR, civil engineering educator, researcher, consultant; b. Tehran, Iran, June 3, 1951; came to U.S., 1975; s. Gholamhossian and Fakhrieh (Mahabadi) V. B.S. in Civil Engring., Pahlavi U., Shiraz, Iran, 1975; M.S. in Civil Engring., U. Calif.-Davis, 1976, Ph.D. in Civil Engring., 1980; M.B.A., Armstrong Coll., 1979; M. in Pub. Adminstrn., Golden Gate U., 1980. Registered profl. engr., Ky. Asst. prof. civil engring., U. Ky., Lexington, 1980—; researcher, cons. in field. Recipient Monbusho award Japanese Govt., 1982; Urban Mass Transp. Adminstrn., Dept. Transp. grantee. Mem. ASCE, Transp. Research Bd., Inst. Transp. Engrs., Soc. Automotive Engrs. (Ralph Teetor award 1981), Acad. Mgmt., N.Y. Acad. Sci., Assn. M.B.A. Exec., Nat. Soc. Profl. Engrs., Chi Epsilon, Sigma Xi. Club: Spindle Top. Contbr. studies and reports in transp. field. Office: Dept Civil Engring 212 Anderson Hall U Ky Lexington KY 40506

VAZQUEZ, ANDREW, county official, financial analyst; b. Havana, Cuba, Sept. 18, 1928; s. Andres and Carmen (Dieguez) V.; came to U.S., 1956; m. Delia Villavicencio, Nov. 14, 1951; 1 dau., Julia Vazquez Pulles. Procurator, U. Habana Law Sch., 1952; A.A., Wright Jr. Coll., 1961, B.S., U. So. Calif., 1971; postgrad. U. Miami Sch. Continuing Studies, Fla. Inst. Tech., Inst. Internal Auditors. Cert. price analyst. Controller, Sonia Investments, 1949-52; procurator Vasquez & Diaz Law Partnership, 1952-55; controller Am. Aluminum Venezuela, 1955-57; with trade, maintenance and constrn. Western Electric, 1957-62; operator So. Calif. Rapid Transit Dist., 1962-70; asst. fin. sec. Inst. of Aerospace Safety and Mgmt., U. So. Calif., 1970-71; auditor Bancshares of Fla., 1971-72; sr. auditor Defense Contract Audit Agy., 1972-75; team leader Fla. Dept. Energy, Miami, 1975-78; dir. of audit Transp. Adminstrn., Miami, 1978-79; internal auditor, dir. internal audit dept. Met.-Dade County, Miami, 1979—; lectr. in field. Robert Hall fellow, 1970-71; recipient award FEA, 1977; commendations Metro Dade County Mgr. and Office of Transp. Adminstrn., 1978-83; Achievement award to Transp. Dept. Audit Div., Nat. Assn. Counties, 1981. Mem. So. Fla. Regional Audit Dirs. Council (chmn., outstanding contbn. award 1983), Assn. Govt. Accts. Miami Chpt. (past pres., outstanding contbn. to nat. symposium award 1981, outstanding contbn. chpt. pres. award 1983), Am. Pub. Transp. Assn. (audit subcom.), Inst. of Cost Analysis, Inst. Internal Auditors, Inc., Mcpl. Fin. Officers Assn. Republican. Lutheran. Author tng. manuals and other publs; contbr. articles to profl. jours. Home: 13 SW 113 Ave #102 Sweetwater FL 33174 Office: Internal Auditing Dept Met Dade County 140 W Flagler St Miami FL 33130

VAZQUEZ, ELOY, accountant; b. Spain, Mar. 9, 1935; s. Jesus and Carmen V.; grad. Accts. Sch. Bus., LaCoruna, Spain, 1952; grad. U. Havana, 1960; postgrad. Fla. Internat. U., 1972; m. Lydia Alvarez, June 15, 1958; children—Jorge E., Carlos, Lydia M. Controller, Chacon Alvarez & Co., Havana, 1956-61; practice acctg., Havana, 1961-67; adminstrv. dir. Nuovo Pignone, Madrid, Spain, 1968-69; sr. acct. W. Charles Becker, C.P.A., 1969-74; pres. Eloy Vazquez & Assos., Inc., Miami, Fla., 1974—; exec. dir. Hispanic Heritage Festival Com., Inc., 1981—. Pres., Spanish Soc. of Fla., Inc., 1974; chmn. Hispanic Heritage Week Com., 1976; 1st v.p. Latin Orange Festival Council, Inc., 1979; mem. task force Hispanic affairs Met. Dade County, 1980. Mem. Nat. Assn. Public Accts., Fla. Accts. Assn. Roman Catholic. Club: Ponce de Leon (charter pres. 1976). Home: 3430 E 1st Ave Hialeah FL 33013 Office: 4011 W Flagler St Miami FL 33134

VAZQUEZ, ROLANDO, school administrator; b. Santiago, Cuba, July 25, 1949; s. Pedro M. and Graciela Luisa (Cruz) V.; m. Maria del Carmen Boucugnani, Aug. 16, 1969; children—Alejandro Javier, Juan Carlos. A.A., Miami Dade Jr. Coll., 1969; B.A., U. Miami, 1971; M.S., Fla. Internat. U., 1973. Tchr. social studies Booker T. Washington Jr. High Sch., Miami, 1971-74; asst. to prin. Miami Beach Sr. High Sch., 1974-75; asst. prin. West Miami Jr. High Sch., Miami, 1975-78; prin. Guri Internat. Sch. (Venezuela), 1978-79, 80-82; asst. prin. Jackson Sr. High Sch., Miami, 1979-80; asst. prin. Rockway Jr. High Sch., Miami, 1982—; instr. Miami Dade Community Coll., part time 1975-78. Merit scholar, 1969. Mem. Phi Kappa Phi, Phi Alpha Theta, Phi Theta Kappa. Republican. Roman Catholic. Clubs: Country of Coral Gables, Ciudamar Yacht (Miami). Home: 1742 SW 102d Pl Miami FL 33165 Office: Rockway Jr High Sch 9393 SW 29th Terr Miami FL 33165

VAZQUEZ-SANTONI, CARLOS AUGUSTO, civil engineer; b. Cayey, P.R., Feb. 19, 1930; s. Francisco M. and Belen M. (Santoni) Vazquez; m. Maria I. Camunas, May 1, 1955; children—Maria B., Carlos J. B.S. in Civil Engring., Davis and Elkins Coll., 1952; cert. Weaver Sch. Real Estate, 1958. Supt. engr. Jorge I. Rosso Constrn. Corp., 1952-53, 55-57; v.p. Triangle Engring. Corp., 1958-82; mem. fin. com. Coop. Devel. Adminstrn. Commonwealth P.R., 1969-72; pres. evaluating com. Planning Bd. Commonwealth P.R., 1974; bd. dirs. Free Enterprise Assn., 1975, Banco Popular de P.R., 1978—; pres. Shop Centre Devel. Corp., 1978—; bd. dirs. P.R. Cement Corp., 1980—. Bd. dirs. P.R. chpt. ARC, 1976-81, Pro-Arte Musical de P.R., 1976-79. Served with U.S. Army, 1952-55. Mem. Nat. Soc. Profl. Engrs. (award for outstanding service 1968), Associated Gen. Contractors Am. (pres. 1973-74, cert. of merit 1974), Am. Concrete Inst., Coll. Engrs. P.R., Soc. Civil Engrs. P.R., Alpha Sigma Phi. Roman Catholic.

VEACH, ALLEN MARSHALL, research physicist; b. Lancaster, S.C., Sept. 21, 1933; s. Alvis Lindell and Ruth Delia (Frith) V.; m. Lynn Marie Hawkins, Sept. 15, 1973; children—Allen Marshall, Olivia Anne, Alvis Leonard, Sarah Ruth. Student Auburn U., 1951-52; B.S. in Physics and Math., U. Ala., 1956; M.S. in Physics and Math., U. Akron, 1959. Physicist, B.F. Goodrich Co., Akron, Ohio, 1956-57; microscopist-chemist, Oak Ridge Nat. Lab., 1957-59, devel. specialist, 1959-60, isotope separation plasma physicist, 1960-70, research physicist in ion sources, 1970—. Patentee plasma physics, ion sources, isotope separation, vacuum tech. Mem. Am. Phys. Soc. Avocation: inventing. Home: PO Box 323 Oak Ridge TN 37831 Office: Oak Ridge Nat Lab Bldg 9204-3 PO Box Y Oak Ridge TN 37831

VEATCH, JESSE WILLIAM, JR., surgeon; b. Dalton, Ga., Dec. 2, 1914; s. Jesse William V.; m. Mildred Jarrett, Oct. 24, 1943; children—Jesse William III, Robert Jarrett, Michael. A.B., Emory U., 1936, M.D., 1940. Diplomate Am. Bd. Surgery. Intern Grady Meml. Hosp., Atlanta, 1940-41, resident in surgery, 1941-44; practice medicine specializing in surgery, Atlanta, 1946—; chief surgery Crawford W. Long Hosp. of Emory U.; mem. staff Piedmont., Ga. Bapt. Hosps.; clin. assoc. prof. surgery Emory U. Med. Sch.; mem. research rev. bd. Ga. Inst. Tech. Served to lt. USNR, 1944-46. Mem. ACS, AMA, Ga. Surg. Soc. (pres. 1983-84), Med. Assn. Ga., Med. Assn. Atlanta, Atlanta Clin. Soc. (pres. 1953), Emory Med. Alumni Assn. (pres. 1985—). Methodist. Club: Capital City (Atlanta). Home: 373 Pinetree Dr NE Atlanta GA 30305 Office: 25 Prescott St NE Suite 3441 Atlanta GA 30308

VEAUDRY, WALLACE FRANCIS, hospital administrator, retired army officer; b. Attleboro, Mass., Dec. 9, 1924; s. Edward Leon and Viola Dean (Nickerson) V.; m. Pauline Riley, Apr. 2, 1948; children—Paula Dean, Patricia May Veaudry Wells. B.S., U.S. Mil. Acad., 1947; postgrad. Command and Gen. Staff Coll., 1959-60; M.S., Tulane U., 1962; postgrad. Spl. Warfare Officers and Insurgency Sch., 1962-63, Army War Coll., 1964-67, Naval Postgrad. Sch., 1968, Dept. State Fgn. Service Inst., 1971; M.Ed., Ga. State U., 1975. Commd. 2d lt. U.S. Army, 1947, advanced through grades to col., 1968; faculty U.S. Mil. Acad., West Point, N.Y., 1951, 53, 54, U.S. Naval Acad., 1952-53, U.S. Army War Coll., 1969-71; asst. comdr. Inf. Ctr., Fort Benning, Ga., 1974-77, ret., 1977; dir. outpatient dept. Med. Ctr., Columbus, Ga., 1977-79, dir. gen. services, 1979-82, dir. ambulatory services, 1982-84, mgr. family practice program, 1984—. Contbr. articles to profl. jours. Bd. dirs., chmn. combined fed. campaign fund drive United Way, 1974-77; bd. dirs. Columbus Urban League, 1980; mem. Civilian-Mil. Council, 1973-77. Decorated Legion of Merit with 2 oak leaf clusters, Bronze Star medal, Meritorious Service medal with oak leaf cluster, Air medal, Army Commendation medal with oak leaf cluster, Vietnamese Cross of Gallantry with bronze star, Honor medal 1st class, Chinese Army badge, U.S. Combat Infantry badge, Airborne Wings. Mem. Ret. Officers Assn., Assn. U.S. Army (bd. dirs. Columbus-Phenix City chpt. 1975-85, chpt. pres. 1982-83), Am. Hosp. Assn., U.S. Mil. Acad. Alumni Assn., Tulane U., Alumni Assn., Ga. State U. Alumni Assn., West Point Soc. Columbus. Club: Columbus Rotary (bd. dirs., treas. 1981-85). Home: 3341 Shirehill Ln Columbus GA 31904 Office: Med Ctr Dept Family Practice PO Box 951 Columbus GA 31994

VEAZEY, JOHN HOBSON, physician; b. Van Alstyne, Tex., June 27, 1901; s. James and Malta Augusta (Blassingame) V.; student Austin Coll., 1918-20; M.D., U. Tex., 1926; m. Elizabeth May Chandler, Mar. 14, 1935; children—Samuel James. Intern, Sherman (Tex.) Hosp., 1926-28; pvt. practice medicine, Madill, Okla., 1929-35, Ardmore, Okla., 1935—; co-founder Med. Arts Clinic, Ardmore, Okla., 1952—; pvt. practice internal medicine, Ardmore, 1957—; chief staff Meml. Hosp., So. Okla., 1958—, chmn. dept. Internal Medicine, 1973; mem. staff Ardmore (Okla.) Hosp.; pres. Med. Arts Bldg. Co. Ardmore, Med. Arts Clinic of Ardmore; chmn. pattern gift com. Meml. Hosp. of So. Okla. Hosp. Expansion Program, 1983—. Co-chmn. profl. div. United Fund, 1969. Recipient 50-Year Cert. of Appreciation, bd. trustees Alumni Assn. U. Tex. Med. Br., 1976. Mem. AMA (Physician's Recognition award 1976, 79, 82, 85), Okla. State (council 1944-56, life) Med. Assn., Carter-Love-Marshall Med. Soc. (pres. 1955, life), Ardmore C. of C. (dir., v.p.), Am. Soc. Internal Medicine. Presbyn. (elder). Mason. Home: 2 Overland Route Ardmore OK 73401 Office: 921 14th St NW Ardmore OK 73401

VEERISETTY, VENKATESWARLU, research microbiologist, educator; b. Obulakkapalle, India, June 1, 1949; s. Subbaiah and Ankamma V.; m. Indira, Nov. 6, 1978. B.Sc., Andhra Pradesh Agrl. U., Bapatla, India, 1970; M.Sc., Indian Agrl. Research Inst., New Delhi, 1972, Ph.D., U. Nebr., 1976. Postdoctoral fellow U. Mo.-Columbia, 1976-79; NIH postdoctoral trainee U.

Ala.-Birmingham, 1979-80; postdoctoral fellow U. Miss. Med. Ctr., Jackson, 1980-82, instr. microbiology, 1982—; mem. exec. com., plant virus subcom. Internat. Com. on Taxonomy of Viruses, 1978-81. Contbr. articles and abstracts to profl. jours.; proposed theoretical relationships between protein subunits and nucleic acid chain of helical viruses, 1978, new classification of helical plant viruses, 1979, drug resistance in herpes simplex virus, 1981-84. Sec., India Student Assn., U. Nebr., Lincoln, 1974-75, pres., 1975-76; v.p.-elect India Assn. Miss., 1983-84, v.p., 1984—. Co-investigator Am. Heart Assn., 1983—, Nat. Inst. Dental Research, 1983—. Mem. Am. Soc. Microbiology, Am. Soc. Virology, Sigma Xi. Office: U Miss Med Ctr 2500 N State St Jackson MS 39216

VEERKAMP, PATRICK BURKE, art educator, administrator; b. Joplin, Mo., Nov. 22, 1943; s. William E. and Loretta Cathrine (Burke) V.; m. Mary Lynne Moore, Feb. 8, 1964; children—Christine, Anne. B.A., Adams State Coll. Colo., 1965; M.A., U. Denver, 1976; M.F.A., Colo. State U., 1981. Instr. art Mesa Coll., Grand Junction, Colo., 1973-78; asst. dir. spl. visual arts program Colo. State U., Fort Collins, 1981-82; instr. art N. Idaho Coll., Coeur d'Alene, 1982-83; chmn. dept. art, assoc. prof. Southwestern U., Georgetown, Tex., 1983—. Exhibited throughout U.S. Bd. dirs. Western Colo. Ctr. for Arts, Grand Junction, 1977-78. Colo. State U. grantee, 1978-79. Mem. Coll. Art Assn., Nat. Council Art Adminstrs. Democrat. Roman Catholic. Office: Southwestern U Dept Art Georgetown TX 78626

VEINOTT, CYRIL GEORGE, electrical engineer, consultant; b. Somerville, Mass., Feb. 15, 1905; s. Jason A. and I. Laura (Fales) V.; m. Dorothy Helen Bassett, Nov. 28, 1936; 1 child, Richard A. B.S.E.E. cum laude, U. Vt., 1926; E.E., 1939; D.Engring. (hon.), 1951. Mgr. indsl. motor sect. Westinghouse, Lima, Ohio, 1926-52; chief engring. analyst Reliance Elec. Co., Cleve., 1953-70; invited prof. Laval U., Quebec City, Can., 1970-72; vol. exec. Internat. Exec. Service Corps, N.Y.C., 1972-79; pvt. practice as consultant in computer-aided design of electric motors, Sarasota, Fla., 1970—. Author: Fractional HP Electric Motors, 1939, 4th edit. in press; Theory and Design Small Motors, 1959; Computer-Aided Design Electric Machines, 1972. Patentee in field. Recipient Merit award Research Inst. Rotating Machines, CSSR, 1968; IEEE Tesla medal, 1977; named to Hall of Fame Small Motors Mfg. Assn., 1985. Fellow IEEE (chmn. standards com. 1961-63), AIEE (v.p. 1949-51, chmn. rotating machines com. 1951-53, chmn. standards com. 1961-63); mem. Navy League U.S., Phi Beta Kappa, Eta Kappa Nu, Tau Beta Pi. Republican. Presbyterian. Club: High Twelve. Lodges: Masons, Shriners. Avocations: photography; prepare and present travelogues. Home: 4197 Oakhurst Circle W Sarasota FL 33583

VEIT, EDWIN THEODORE, finance educator, investment advisor, consultant; b. West Chester, Pa., Oct. 13, 1945; s. Edwin Warren and Sarah (Twaddell) V.; m. Marcia Raley, July 6, 1968; children—Shawn K., Erica L. B.S., Marietta Coll., 1967; M.S., U. Ark., 1972, Ph.D., 1977. Registered rep. Merrill Lynch, West Chester, 1972-73; instr. U. Ark., Fayetteville, 1974-76; asst. prof. fin. W. Va. U., Morgantown, 1976-78; assoc. prof. fin. U. Central Fla., Orlando, 1978—; investment advisor Fla. Fin. Advisors, Inc., Winter Springs, 1979—; cons. Sun Banks Fla., Orlando, 1980-84; adj. prof. Coll. Fin. Planning, Denver, 1984—. Contbr. articles to profl. jours. Served to capt. USAF, 1967-71. Mem. Inst. Chartered Fin. Analysts, Internat. Assn. Fin. Planners, Fin. Analysts Assn. Central Fla., Fin. Mgmt. Assn., Fin. Analysts Fedn., Sigma Iota Epsilon, Beta Gamma Sigma. Presbyterian. Avocations: travel; golf; reading. Office: U Central Fla Alafaya Trail Orlando FL 32816

VELA, FILEMON B., federal judge; b. Harlingen, Tex., May 1, 1935; s. Roberto and Maria Luisa Cardenas V.; student Tex. Southmost Coll., 1954-56, U. Tex., 1956-57; J.D., St. Mary's U., San Antonio, 1962; m. Blanca Sanchez, Jan. 28, 1962; children—Filemon, Rafael Eduardo, Sylvia Adriana. Admitted to Tex. bar, 1962; judge dist. 107, Tex. Dist. Ct., 1975-78; judge U.S. Dist. Ct., So. Dist. Tex., Brownsville, 1980—; instr. Law Enforcement Coll. Past city commr., Brownsville. Served with U.S. Army, 1957-59. Mem. State Bar Tex. Democrat. Office: PO Box 1072 Brownsville TX 78520*

VELA-CREIXELL, MARY ISABEL, law librarian, consultant; b. Brownsville, Tex., Nov. 15, 1938; d. Alfredo Nicolás and Maria Isabel (Creixell) V.; m. Apr. 11, 1959 (div. 1983); children—Deborah A., Joan Rachelle, Donald R. II (dec. 1983). B.A. cum laude, St. Thomas U., Houston, 1971; M.A., U. Denver, 1980. Children's librarian Houston Pub. Library, 1978-79, librarian NEH project dir., 1980-82, law librarian, 1982—, chmn. Hispanic resource librarians, 1982-83; law librarian legal dept. City of Houston, 1982—; cons. law libraries, Hispanic women, women's studies, Hispanic affairs, 1980—. Spanish book reviewer Lector, Berkeley, Calif., 1983. Mem. adv. com. Action's RSVP Program, Houston, 1981—, chmn., 1983-84. Mem. ALA, Am. Assn. Law Libraries (com. on legal info. to pub., spl. com. to attract minorities to the profession), Am. Assn. Sch. Libraries (early childhood edn. com. 1981—), Am. Assn. Law Libraries. Home: 9530 Winsome St Houston TX 77063 Office: Legal Dept City of Houston PO Box 1562 Houston TX 77251

VELARDE, ROBERT M., nursing, hospital administrator; b. Tampa, Fla., Oct. 28, 1950; s. Jesus Manuel and Angela (Velasco) V. A.S. in Nursing, Hillsborough Community Coll., Tampa, 1972; B.S. in Nursing, Samford U., 1975; M.Pub.Adminstrn., Golden Gate U., 1980. R.N., Fla., Ala.; cert. in nursing adminstrn. advanced Am. Nurses Assn.; cert. surg. technologist Assn. Surg. Technologists. Surg. technologist attendant Centro Espanol Hosp., Tampa, 1965-72, nursing supr., 1972-74, asst. adminstr. patient services, 1975-85, adminstr., chief exec. officer, 1985—; charge nurse emergency room Brookwood Med. Ctr., Birmingham, Ala., 1974-75; mem. blue ribbon task force to Fla. Bd. Nursing, 1982-83; mem. adv. bd. Fla. Nursing News. Recipient award from bd. dirs. Centro Espanol Hosp., 1977; Contbns. to Nursing award Minority Nurses Assn., 1979. Mem. Am. Orgn. Nurse Execs., Fla. Soc. Nursing Service Adminstrs., ARC, Sigma Theta Tau (chpt. v.p. 1983-84). Democrat. Methodist. Home: 2618 W Saint John St Tampa FL 33607 Office: Centro Espanol Meml Hosp 4801 N Howard Ave Tampa FL 33603

VELASQUEZ, OSCAR, painter; b. Pharr, Tex., Apr. 5, 1945; s. Cresencio and Vicenta (Castillo) V.; m. Pamela Ann Margaret Szymkowski, Dec. 22, 1972. A.A., Cooper Sch. of Art, 1965. One man shows: Cannon Bldg. Gallery, Washington, 1983, Defience Coll. Art Ctr., Ohio, 1973. Mem. Am Water Color Soc. (recipient Mary S. Litt medal 1973, 74, High Winds medal 1976, nat. juror 1978, Dolphin fellow 1981). Home: Route 1 Box 160 Abbeville SC 29620

VELEBER, DAVID MATTHEWS, clinical psychologist, educator; b. N.Y.C., Feb. 16, 1954; s. Edwin Reeves and Doris (Matthews) V.; m. Velyn Morris, Apr. 13, 1980; 1 child, Matthew Morris. B.A. in Psychology, Muhlenberg Coll., 1976; M.A. in Clin. Psychology, Fairleigh Dickinson U., 1978; Ph.D. in Clin. Psychology, Calif. Sch. Profl. Psychology, 1981. Lic. clin. psychologist., Va. Psychology intern Fresno Community Hosp., Calif., 1979-80, Merced County Mental Health Services, Merced, Calif., 1981; psychol. asst. William Edgar Boblitt, Ph.D., Modesto, Calif., 1981; clin. psychologist Western State Hosp., Staunton, Va., 1981—; teaching asst. Fairleigh Dickinson U., Madison, N.J., 1977-78; clin. faculty Inst. Clin. Psychology, U. Va., Charlottesville, 1984, asst. prof. behavioral medicine and psychiatry, 1985—; clin. psychologist, Waynesboro, Va., 1985—. Contbr. articles to profl. jours. Mem. Am. Psychol. Assn., Va. Psychol. Assn. Avocations: golf; tennis.

VELIZ, RUBEN DE JESUS, physician; b. Manzanillo, Oriente, Cuba, Apr. 23, 1941; s. Ruben Nueva and Ismenia Petronila (Oliva) V.; m. Maria Nieves, Nov. 11, 1969; children—Nieves Maria, Ruben Miguel. Student U. Havana (Cuba), 1959-62, U. Miami, 1962-64, UCLA, 1965-66, U. So. Calif., 1965-66; M.D., U. Madrid, Spain, 1970. Intern, U. Madrid Hosps. and Clinics, 1973-74; pvt. practice family medicine Los Angeles, 1970-73, Miami, Fla., 1973-75; resident surgery Coll. Medicine and Dentistry N.J.-Morristown 1975-76; commd. lt. USPHS, 1976, advanced through grades to comdr., 1978; med. resident Columbia U. Coll. Physicians Surgeons/Morristown Meml. Hosp., 1978-81; pvt. practice medicine specializing in internal medicine-critical care medicine Miami, 1981—; mem. staffs Jackson Meml. Hosp./U. Miami Med. Center, Cedar's Med. Center, Miami, Mercy Hosp., Miami, South Miami Hosp., Coral Gables Hosp. (Fla.), Am. Hosp., Miami, Palmetto Gen. Hosp., Hialeah, Hialeah Hosp. (Fla.). Mem. Republican Nat. Com., Washington, 1983, Cuban Am. Nat. Found., Miami and Washington, 1983. Mem. AMA, ACP, Am. Soc. Internal Medicine, Assn. Mil. Surgeons U.S., Soc. Critical Care Medicine, So. Med. Assn., Am. Acad. Family Physicians. Republican. Roman Catholic. Office: Ruben de J Veliz MD 475 Biltmore Way Suite 206 Coral Gables FL 33134

VELLER, MARGARET PAXTON, physician; b. Beaver Dam, Ky., Dec. 14, 1925; d. Darrell K. and Gladys (Myers) Veller; B.A., Vanderbilt U., 1947, M.D., 1950. Intern, resident Vanderbilt U. Hosp., Nashville, 1950-54; pvt. practice, 1954—. Mem. Am., Miss. (com. maternal and child welfare 1956-73) med. assns., Homochitto Valley Med. Soc., Natchez Assn. of Commerce, Miss. Obstet. and Gynecol. Soc., Phi Beta Kappa, Alpha Omega Alpha. Baptist. Club: Pilgrimage Garden. Home: 28 S Circle Dr Natchez MS 39120 Office: Natchez Med Clinic 49 Sgt S Prentiss Dr Natchez MS 39120

VENDITTO, JAMES JOSEPH, chemical engineer; b. Dobbs Ferry, N.Y., Nov. 13, 1951; s. Vincenzio Rocco and Maria Nichola (Cassetti) V.; B.S.Ch.E., U. Okla., 1973; m. Annabelle Ruth Carson, Dec. 26, 1972; children—Vincent James, Joseph Ryan. Engr.-in-tng., Victoria, Tex., 1973-74; field engr. Halliburton Services, Alice, Tex., 1974-75, dist. engr., Mission, Tex., 1975-77, regional service sales engr., New Orleans, 1977-80, asst. div. engr., Corpus Christi, Tex., 1980-83, supt. stimulation dept., 1983, div. engr., 1983—; cons. in field. Active United Way. Registered profl. engr., Tex. Mem. Am. Inst. Chem. Engrs., Soc. Petroleum Engrs., AIME, Am. Petroleum Inst., Internat. Platform Assn., Nat. Soc. Profl. Engrs., Tex. Soc. Profl. Engrs. Republican. Roman Catholic. Contbr. article to jour. Researcher chem. stimulation S. Tex. sandstones, devel. new API cementing temperatures for oil and gas industry; developed refracturing technology. Home: 2211 Live Oak St Portland TX 78374 Office: 1220 First City Bank Tower FCB119 Corpus Christi TX 78477

VENERO, RAMON JOSE, property management executive; b. Escalante, Santander, Spain; Sept. 21, 1955 (parents Am. Citizens); s. Jose Antonio Venero Fonfrias and Lucia (Matanzas) De Venero; m. Catherine Rosalyn Pannullo, Aug. 22, 1981 (div. Dec. 1984). B.A., Rutgers U., 1976. Acct., Mayor's Office, Newark, N.J., 1977-79; loan officer NHDRC, Newark, 1979-80; rehab. coordinator, State of N.J., Trenton, 1980-81; sr. dist. mgr. Nat. Corp. for Housing Partnerships, Washington, 1981—; cons. R.J. Venero & Assoc., McLean, Urban Alternative, Inc. Newark. Campaigner, Essex County Democratic County com., Newark, 1977-81; bd. dir. Newark Ctr. of Arts, 1977-80, Ironbound Edn. and Cultural Ctr., Newark, 1976-77, Assn. Pro Zarzuela en Am., N.Y.C., 1978-80. Mem. Inst. Real Estate Mgmt., Apartment Office Bldg. Assn. of Greater Washington, Nat. Assn. Home Builders, Internat. Inst. Valuers, Nat. Assn. Realtors. Club: Espana (bd. dirs. 1975-78, 1st v.p., 2nd v.p.). Avocations: golf; tennis; travel. Office: Nat Corp for Housing Partnerships Property Mgmt Inc 1350 Beverly Rd Suite 216 McLean VA 22101

VENINGA, JAMES FRANK, humanities educator, editor, writer; b. Milw., Aug. 26, 1944; s. Frank and Otila Ann (Mauch) V.; m. Catherine M. Williams, Apr. 5, 1969; 1 child, Jennifer Elisa. B.A., Baylor U., 1966; M. Theol. Studies, Harvard U., 1968; M.A., Rice U., 1973, Ph.D., 1974. Instr. U. St. Thomas, Houston, 1971-73, asst. prof. humanities, 1974; asst. dir. Tex. Com. for Humanities, Austin, 1975, exec. dir., 1976—; dir. Nat. Fedn. State Humanities Councils, Mpls., 1980-83; trustee Inst. for Humanities at Salado, Tex., 1982—; vis. prof. Am. studies Univ. Tex., Austin, 1984. Editor: The Biographer's Gift, 1983; Vietnam in Remission, 1985. Editor in chief Tex. Humanist mag., 1982—. Recipient Baylor Man of Merit award Baylor Univ., 1985. Democrat. Home: 607 Burleson St Smithville TX 78957 Office: Tex Com for Humanities 1604 Nueces St Austin TX 78701

VENTULETT, THOMAS WALKER, III, architect; b. Albany, Ga., Oct. 29, 1935; s. Thomas Walker, Jr. and Edith Mae (Poole) V.; B.S., Ga. Inst. Tech., 1957, B.Arch., 1958; M.Arch., U. Pa., 1961; m. Elizabeth Paulick, Dec. 29, 1956; children—Suzanne, Thomas, Jonathan. With archtl. firms in Ga. and Fla., 1959-67; v.p., prin. charge design Thompson, Ventulett & Stainback, Inc., Atlanta, 1968-76; v.p., dir. design Thompson, Ventulett, Stainback & Assocs., Inc., Atlanta, 1977—; mem. regional public adv. panel archtl. and engring. service GSA, 1975; mem. So. G.F. Design Awards Jury, 1974-76. Div. chmn. Atlanta United Way, 1974; exec. bd. Atlanta Area council Boy Scouts Am., 1977. Served as capt. AUS, 1958. Recipient Kawneer prize Student Design competition, 1957; Leadership and Merit medal Alpha Rho Chi, 1958; Wade meml. scholar, 1961; Archtl. award excellence Am. Inst. Steel Constrn., 1973, 77. Fellow AIA (pres. Atlanta 1976, mem. nat. coms. design and urban planning, various design awards juries; Honor award Ga. chpt. 1973, 76, 78, Nat. Bronze medal 1975, South Atlantic Region Conf. Honor award 1976, 78); mem. Tau Sigma Delta (hon.). Democrat. Presbyterian. Prin. works include Omni Arena, Atlanta, 1972, Omni Internat., 1975, NCNB Plaza, Charlotte, 1974-77, Commerce Pl., Nashville, 1977, Ga. World Congress Center, Atlanta, 1976, IBM-NMD Hdqrs. Bldg., Atlanta, 1977, Merc. Bank Tower, St. Louis, 1974, IBM-SCD, Charlotte, 1980, AT&T Regional Hdqrs., Atlanta, Buckhead Plaza, Atlanta. Home: 4234 Conway Valley U Atlanta GA 30327 Office: 1200 N Omni Internat Atlanta GA 30335

VEREEN, HENRY STACY, physician; b. Montgomery, Ala., Jan. 10, 1942; s. Catherine Louise Stansel; m. June Marie Petryszn, Jan. 10, 1974; children—Jason Andrew, Matthew Stefan; m. Dana Lous Akin, June 13, 1985. B.S., Auburn U., 1968; M.D., U. Graz (Austria), 1975. Cert. aviation med. examiner and accident investigator FAA. Intern Univ. Hosp., Graz, 1973-75, resident in surgery, 1975; resident in surgery Piedmont Hosp., Atlanta, 1975-77; practice medicine specializing in surgery, Blue Ridge, Ga., 1977—; chief emergency service Fannin Regional Hosp., Blue Ridge, 1977-79, chief surgery, 1978-79; mem. staff Copper Basin Med. Ctr., Copperhill, Tenn., 1980—, chief staff, 1980—; med. examiner Fannin County (Ga.), 1982—, Polk County (Tenn.), 1983; chmn. bd. J.T. Industries, Chgo., 1979-81; pres. Transaire, Inc., Moultrie, Ga., 1980-82; med. chmn. Polk County chpt. Am. Heart Assn. Mem. So. Med. Assn., Aircraft Owners and Pilots Assn. Episcopalian. Club: Atlanta City. Translator several books.

VEREEN, WILLIAM JEROME, uniform manufacturing company executive; b. Moultrie, Ga., Sept. 7, 1940; s. William Coachman and Mary Elizabeth (Bunn) V.; student Episcopal High Sch.-Va., 1954-57; grad. Culver Mil. Acad., 1959; B.S. in Indsl. Mgmt., Ga. Inst. Tech., 1963; m. Lula Evelyn King, June 9, 1963; children—Elizabeth King, William Coachman. Engr. Riverside Mfg. Co., Moultrie, Ga., 1967-70, v.p., 1970-73, exec. v.p., 1973-77, pres., 1977—, pres., treas., chief exec. officer, 1984—, also dir.; v.p., dir. Moultrie Cotton Mills, 1969—; v.p., dir. Riverside Industries, Inc., Moultrie, 1973-77, pres., 1977—, pres., treas., chief exec. officer, 1984—; pres., treas., chief exec. officer, dir. Riverside Uniform Rentals, Inc., Moultrie, Riverside Mfg. Co. (Ireland) Ltd., G.A. Rivers Corp., Right Image Inc.; pres. Riverside Mfg. Co. (W.Ger.) GmbH. advisor apparel tariffs U.S. State Dept. Bd. dirs. Moultrie-Colquitt County (Ga.) Devel. Authority, 1973—, Moultrie-Colquitt County United Givers, Moultrie YMCA, Colquitt County Cancer Soc.; trustee Community Welfare Assn., Moultrie, Pineland Sch., Moultrie, Leadership Ga. Served to capt. USMC, 1963-67. Decorated Bronze Star, Purple Heart. Mem. Am. Apparel Mfrs. Assn. (bd. dirs.), Young Pres.'s Orgn. (Rebel chpt.), Nat. Assn. Uniform Mfrs., Sigma Alpha Epsilon. Presbyterian (chmn. bd. deacons). Lodges: Elks, Kiwanis. Home: 21 Dogwood Circle Moultrie GA 31768 Office: PO Box 460 Moultrie GA 31768

VERGHESE, KUMARI DANIEL, psychiatrist; b. Edanad, India, Nov. 25, 1947; came to U.S., 1973; d. John and Kunjamma (Varghese) Daniel; m. Chacko Perakathu Verghese, Sept. 21, 1972; children—Tikku Jacob, Tisha Sarah. M.B., B.S. Kasturba Med. Coll., 1972. Resident in gen. psychiatry Henry Ford Hosp., Detroit, 1975-77; fellow in child psychiatry Fairlawn Ctr., Pontiac, Mich., 1977-80; staff psychiatrist adult admissions John Umstead Hosp., Butner, N.C., 1980-81, staff psychiatrist geropsychiatry unit, 1981—, staff, 1983—; sec. med. cons. resident pediatric dept. Pontiac Gen. Hosp., 1977-80, Oakland County Schs., Pontiac, 1977-80, Juvenile Ct. Oakland County, 1977-80; resident rep. Task Force on Resident Recruitment Dept. Mental Health, Lansing, Mich., 1979. Mem. Butner Presbyn. Kindergarten Sch. Bd., 1983. Mem. Am. Psychiat. Assn., N.C. Neuropsychiat. Assn., Am. Assn. Psychiatrists for India, Assn. Kevala Med. Grads.

VERIGAN, TERRENCE, computer and telecommunications corporation executive; b. Seattle, May 18, 1948; s. Donald Calvin and Mary (Voigt) V.; m. Kathy Jeannette Higgins, Aug. 28, 1970. B.A., U. New Orleans, 1971, postgrad., 1972-74; postgrad. Law Sch. Loyola U., New Orleans, 1980-82. Tchr., Jefferson Parish Schs., Metairie, La., 1971-75; sr. sales rep. Xerox Corp., Metairie, 1975-79; owner Terry Verigan, Cons., Metairie, 1979-83; market analyst AT&T, Metairie, 1983-84, sales mgr., 1984—; spl. lectr. Inst. Politics Loyola U., New Orleans, 1979, La. Close Up Found., 1983. Rep. Dist. 8 Jefferson Parish Pub. Sch. Bd., Metairie, 1977-82, chmn. exec. com., 1979, chmn. ins. com., 1980, v.p., 1981; mem. Jefferson Parish exec. com. Republican Party of La., 1977-83. Recipient Community Leader of the Yr. award U. New Orleans, 1981; award of Excellence for Br. Leadership AT&T, 1983; Mgmt. Excellence award AT&T, 1984; Inst. Politics Loyola U., fellow, 1975. Mem. New Orleans C. of C., Omicron Delta Kappa, Kappa Delta Pi (pres. 1969-70), Phi Delta Kappa. Roman Catholic. Club: Press of New Orleans. Home: 4009 W Esplanade Ave Metairie LA 70002 Office: AT&T 3500 N Causeway Blvd 10th Floor Metairie LA 70002

VERMEER, RICHARD DOUGLAS, oil drilling contractor; b. Bronxville, N.Y., July 2, 1938; s. Albert Casey and Helen Valentine (Casey) V.; m. Grace Dorothy Ferguson, May 22, 1960; children—Carin Dawn, Catherine Jeanne, Robert Brooke. B.S., Fairleigh Dickinson U., 1960; M.B.A., Lehigh U., 1967. Mgmt. trainee Gen. Electric Co., Phila., 1961-63; auditor Campbell Soup Co., Camden, N.J., 1963-64; auditor, sr. systems analyst Air Products & Chems., Inc., Allentown, Pa., 1964-67; mgr. fin. systems Trans World Airlines, N.Y.C., 1967-71; dir. mgmt. services Kaufman & Broad, Inc., Los Angeles, 1971-73, group controller, 1974-76; asst. to pres. Global Marine, Inc., Los Angeles, 1976-77, v.p. corp. planning, controller, 1977-81, v.p. control and adminstrn., Houston, 1982, sr. v.p., 1982—; dir. Republic Bank, Eldridge. Adviser Jr. Achievement Phila., 1962-63. Served with AUS, 1960. Recipient awards Am. Legion, 1956, Am. Mktg. Assn., 1960. Fin. Execs. Inst., Am. Mgmt. Assn., Mensa. Republican. Clubs: Falcon Point (dir.), Westlake (dir.). Home: 19807 Summerset Way Houston TX 77094 Office: 777 N Eldridge St Houston TX 77076

VERMEY, GERARD JOSEPH, architect, artist; b. Port-de-Bouc, France, Apr. 28, 1935; s. Antony Nicolas and Helen Rose (Landolfi) V.; m. Barbara Ryan Cantor, June 12, 1959 (div. June 1969); 1 dau., Michelle; m. 2d, Deby Ann Chalcraft, Sept. 23, 1978; children—Ryan, Aaron. B.Arch., U. Fla., 1963. Pvt. practice architect, Neptune Beach, Fla., 1970-79, 80—; prof. U. S.W. La. State U., 1980. Served with U.S. Army, 1954-57. Wood Products Am. scholar, 1962. Mem. Gargoyle Honor Soc. Democrat. Unitarian. Club: Beaches Soccer Assn. (bd. dirs.) (Jacksonville Beach, Fla.).

VERMILLION, WILLIAM JOSEPH, audio recording engineer, computer consultant, writer; b. Wallace, Idaho, July 23, 1936; s. William Joseph and Irene Horton Vermillion; m. Bonnie Jean Bishop, Dec. 15, 1985; 1 child, William Fred. B.A. in Redio-TV, U. Idaho, 1958. Announcer/engr. Sta. KTFI, Twin Falls, Idaho, 1958-61; announcer/disc jockey Sta. KXLY, Spokane, Wash., 1961-62; disc jockey/program dir. Sta. WLOF, Orlando, Fla., 1962-73; columnist Orlando (Fla.) Sentinel, 1968-71; chief engr. Bee Jay Studios, Orlando, 1973-83; ind. radio engr., computer cons., 1983—; audio instr. Recipient RIAA Cert. Gold Record award, 1981. Mem. Audio Engring. Soc., Central Fla. Computer Soc., Exptl. Aircraft Assn. (pres. 1977-80).

VERNER, JOHN VICTOR, JR., physician; b. Greenville, S.C., Apr. 26, 1927; s. John Victor and Ruth Adele (Groce) V.; A.B., Duke U., 1950, M.D., 1954; m. Sally Prosser, Aug. 5, 1950; children—Sally Verner German, Victor (dec.), James, Edward. Intern, Duke U., Durham, N.C., 1954-55, resident in medicine, 1956-57; resident in medicine U. Mich., Ann Arbor, 1955-56; instr., resident Duke U. Med. Sch., 1957-58, A.C.P. fellow in endocrinology, 1958-59, asso. in medicine, staff mem. Pvt. Diagnostic Clinic, 1959-62; practice internal medicine Watson Clinic, Lakeland, Fla., 1972—; mem. staff Lakeland Gen. Hosp.; dir. 1st Nat. Bank Lakeland. Served with AUS, 1944-47. Diplomate Am. Bd. Internal Medicine (gov. 1974-81); Mosby scholar, 1954. Fellow A.C.P.; mem. Am. Soc. Internal Medicine (trustee 1974-76), Fla. Soc. Internal Medicine (pres. 1972-73), AMA, Fla. Med. Assn., Polk County Med. Assn., AAAS, West Coast Acad. Medicine (pres. 1973), Endocrine Soc., Am. Fedn. Clin. Research, Alpha Omega Alpha. Contbr. articles to profl. jours. Office: PO Box 1429 Lakeland FL 33802

VERNON, MARY EMMA LOUISE, pediatrician; b. Spartanburg, S.C., June 17, 1950; d. James Arthur and Violet (Copeland) Vernon; m. James Smiley, June 8, 1974; children—Derek Lamont, Miranda Victoria. B.S. in Biology, S.C. State Coll., Orangeburg, 1972; M.D., Columbia U., 1976. Diplomate Nat. Bd. Med. Examiners. Intern, Duke U. Med. Ctr., Durham, N.C., 1976-77, pediatric resident, 1977-79, Robert Wood Johnson gen. acad. fellow, 1979-81, assoc. in pediatrics, 1981-83, asst. prof. pediatrics, 1983—; coordinator adolescent services Lincoln Community Health Ctr., Durham, 1981—, Contbr. articles to profl. jours. Mem. Durham County Task Force on Teenage Pregnancy, 1980, Durham County Community Based Alternative, 1981; bd. dirs. Mental Health Assn. Durham, 1984. Recipient Dr. Harry S. Altman Ambulatory Pediatrics award Columbia U., 1976. Mem. Soc. Adolescent Medicine, N.C. Pediatric Soc., Nat. Beta Honor Soc., Alpha Kappa Mu. Democrat. Baptist. Office: PO Box 3176 Duke U Med Center Durham NC 27710

VERNON, SHELDON IRA, management educator, consultant; b. N.Y.C., Aug. 1, 1922; s. Aaron K. and Anna R. (Schwartz) V.; m. Kathryn Marie McRae, Sept. 4, 1948; children—Dixi Lynn Vernon Chandler, Gregory E. B.S. in Elec. Engring., Okla. STate U., 1955; M.B.A., U. Tex.-Arlington, 1976; Ph.D., U. Houston, 1985. Commd. 2d lt. U.S. Army Air Force, 1943, advanced through grades to col. U.S. Air Force, 1968; dir. mgmt. analysis, pilot, navigator, various locations, 1943-72; ret., 1972; property mgr. Vought Systems div. LTV, Dallas, 1972-76; chmn. dept. mgmt., mktg. and computer info. systems, Houston Baptist U., 1980—, asst. prof. mgmt., 1980-85; instr. mgmt. devel. ctr. U. Houston, 1978-80, div. profl. devel. Houston Bapt. U., 1980—. Charter mem. Republican Presdl. Task Force, Washington, 1982—. Decorated Legion of Merit, D.F.C. Mem. Acad. Mgmt., Planning Execs. Inst., Air Force Assn. (pres. Dallas chpt. 1974-75). Baptist. Avocations: electronics; aviation; gardening. Home: 1007 Glacier Hill Dr Houston TX 77077 Office: Houston Bapt U 7502 Fondren Houston TX 77074

VERNON, WALTER NEWTON, JR., minister, historian; b. Verden, Okla., Mar. 24, 1907; s. Walter Newton and Fannie Hawling (Dodd) V.; m. Ruth Mason, Dec. 27, 1931; children—Walter Newton III, Kathleen Frances Vernon Clark. B.A., So. Meth. U., 1928, B.D., 1931, M.A., 1934; Litt.D., W.Va. Wesleyan U., 1963. Ordained to ministry United Methodist Ch., 1929. Pastor, Lakewood Meth. Ch., Dallas, 1931-38; assoc. editor Ch. Sch. Publs., 1938-72. Author: Methodism Moves Across North Texas, 1967; Methodism in Arkansas, 1976. Mem. N. Tex. conf. United Meth. Ch., 1929—, conf. historian, 1967—; mem. div. Christian edn. Nat. Council Chs., 1944-72; del. World Sunday Sch. Assn., Tokyo, 1958; Fair lectr. Southwestern U., Georgetown, Tex., 1962. Editor The Ch. Sch., 1944-72, Daily Christian Adv.,1 940-72, Contact, 1945-46; assoc. editor Ency. World Methodism, 1974. Editor, co-author: The Methodist Excitement in Texas, 1984. Contbr. articles to ch. jours. Weekly columnist Christian Adv., 1948-53. Spl. corr. Dallas News, Dallas Times Herald, others. Named to United Meth. Communicators Hall of Fame, 1983. Mem. Sigma Delta Chi, Tau Kappa Alpha. Home: 4835 W Lawther Dr Apt 802 Dallas TX 75214

VERON, EARL ERNEST, federal judge; b. Smoke Bend, La., Jan. 2, 1922; s. Dyer M. and Edna (Rodriguez) V.; B.A., McNeese State U., 1958; J.D., La. State U., 1959; m. Alverdy Heyd, Oct. 10, 1948; children—J. Michael, Douglas E. Admitted to La. bar, 1959; pvt. practice law, Lake Charles, La., 1959-67; judge 14th Jud. Dist., Lake Charles, La., 1967-77, U.S. Western Dist. of La., Lake Charles, 1977—; mem. Orleans Parish Criminal Ct., 1972; Circuit Ct. Appeal, 1974. Office: US Dist Ct PO Box 1404 Lake Charles LA 70602*

VERON, REX BROWN, construction designer; b. Lafayette, La., Dec. 3, 1943; s. Wesley Anthony and Hazel Nure (Guidry) V.; m. Sharon K. Williamson, Aug. 17, 1964 (div. Feb. 1981); children—Lauri Lynn, Rex Brown; m. Priscilla Ann Babineaux, Sept. 12, 1982. Student La. State U., 1962-63, Southwestern U., 1963-65; B.F.A., Central State U., 1968. Registered profl. bldg. designer, Okla. Design tchr. Okla. Sch. System, Oklahoma City, 1968-71; designer Frankfurt/Short, 1971-72; assoc. Wood/Wilkins/Walker, 1972-73; ptnr. Wilkins/Walker, 1973-74; owner, pres. Rex Veron Design, Inc., Oklahoma City, Okla. and Lafayette, La., 1974—; owner, ptnr. Andrus & Veron, Lafayette, 1984—. One man shows include Guaranty Bank, Lafayette, Hub City Bank, Central State U. Recipient Copper Rivet award for design of custom residences Times of Acadiana, 1979, 80, 81. Vice-pres. Full Gospel Bus. Fellowship Internat., Lafayette, 1974-84, pres. 1985—. Mem. Lafayette C. of C., Better Bus. Bur., Am. Inst. Bldg. Design (nat. bd. dirs. 1984—). Republican. Mem. Assembly of God Ch. Avocations: golfing; swimming; canoeing; camping. Home: 117 Candda Dr Lafayette LA 70506 Office: Andrus & Veron 101 Southwood Dr Lafayette LA 70503

VERRASTO, RALPH EDWARD, music educator, administrator; b. Scranton, Pa., Mar. 12, 1933; s. Anthony Gregory and Stella (Mahosky) V.; m.

Judith Ann Barlett, July 31, 1963; children—Jennifer, Philip. B.S., Mansfield State Coll., 1958; M.S., Ithaca Coll., 1962; Ed.D. in Music Edn., Pa. State U., 1970. Cert. secondary tchr. Music tchr. Montgomery Area High Sch., Pa., 1958-64; asst. to assoc. prof. E. Carolina U., Greenville, N.C., 1964-72; prof. U. Okla., Norman, 1972-77; prof., dir. Blossom Sch. Festival, Kent State U. Ohio, 1977-79; prof., dir. music U. Ga., Athens, 1979—; cons. Manhattanville Music Project, Purchase, N.Y., 1967-72, Contemporary Music Project, Washington, 1968-72, various colls. and univs., 1970—. Contbr. articles to profl. jours. Recipient Dean's Excellence award U. Okla., 1976. Mem. Music Educators Nat. Conf., Coll. Music Soc., Phi Kappa Phi, Phi Kappa Lambda, Phi Mu Alpha Sinfonia. Lutheran. Home: 209 Dunwoody Dr Athens GA 30605 Office: Sch Music U Ga Athens GA 30602

VERRILL, CHARLES OWEN, JR., lawyer, educator; b. Biddeford, Maine, Sept. 30, 1937; s. Charles Owen and Elizabeth (Handy) V.; m. Mary Ann Blanchard, May 22, 1937; children—Martha Anne, Edward Blanchard, Elizabeth Handy, Matthew Lawton, Peter Goldthwait. A.B., Tufts U., 1959; J.D., Duke U., 1962. Bar: D.C. 1962. Ptnr., Wiley & Rein, Washington, 1984—; adj. prof. internat. trade law and regulation Georgetown U. Law Ctr. Chmn. bd. trustees Internat. Law Inst. Recipient Service citation Tufts U., 1959. Mem. ABA. Clubs: Met. (Washington), Chevy Chase (Md.); Tarratine (Dark Harbor, Maine). Home: 8205 Dunsinane Ct McLean VA 22101

VESPERI, MARIA DAVOREN, anthropologist, educator, journalist, gerontology specialist; b. Worcester, Mass., June 24, 1951; d. Arthur Ernest and Mary Elizabeth (Davoren) V.; 1 dau., Corinna Aline Calagione. B.A., U. Mass.-Amherst, 1973; M.A., Princeton U., 1975, Ph.D., 1978. Vis. asst. prof. anthropology, U. South Fla., Tampa, 1978-81, adj. asst. prof. anthropology, 1981—, mem. Grad. Coll., 1981—; cons., writer St. Petersburg Times (Fla.), 1980, staff writer, 1981—; vis. asst. prof. anthropology New Coll., Sarasota, Fla., 1985-86; project dir. folk arts documentary supported by Nat. Endowment for Arts; cons. hist. photo exhibit Mus. Fla. History. Active Gray Panthers. Commonwealth scholar, U. Mass., 1969-73; Princeton U. fellow, 1973-75; NIH Pub. Health Service research fellow, 1976-78; doctoral dissertation grantee NSF, 1975-76; grantee Adminstrn. on Aging, 1975-76, Nat. Endowment for Arts, 1983. Mem. AAAS, Am. Anthropol. Assn., Gerontol. Soc. Am., N.Y. Acad. Scis., Assn. for Anthropology and Gerontology (newsletter editor), Nat. Council on Aging, Fla. Press Club, Phi Beta Kappa, Alpha Lambda Delta. Author: City of Green Benches: Growing Old in a New Downtown, 1985. Contbr. articles to publs. in field. Home: 1209 Alcazar Way S Saint Petersburg FL 33705 Office: PO Box 1121 Saint Petersburg FL 33731

VESS, GEORGE DAVID, JR., tax accounting firm executive; b. Chattanooga, May 22, 1925; s. George David and Chrystol (De Friese) V.; m. Jean Thomas, Sept. 14, 1947; children—Mary Susan Vess Adams, Barbara Jo Vess Gibbs, Robert David. B.B.A., U. Chattanooga, 1949. C.P.A. Acctg. instr. Nat. Sch. Bus., Cleveland, Tenn., 1949-50; shipping/receiving clk. E.I. DuPont de Nemours Nylon Co., Chattanooga, 1950; tax acct. So. Ry. Co., Chattanooga, 1950-72; owner George Vess Co., Chattanooga, 1972—; tax cons. Lester Bowden C.P.A., Chattanooga, 1967. Mem. Nat. Soc. Pub. Accts. Served with AUS, 1944-46. Democrat. Baptist. Club: Kiwanis. Address: 1007 Altamont Rd Chattanooga TN 37415

VESSELS, ALLEN RAYMOND, hospital administrator; b. Louisville, Oct. 12, 1949; s. Raymond Carl and Patricia (Rohmann) V.; m. Karen Dale Curtsinger, June 12, 1971; children—Jennifer Karen, Christian Allen, Nanci Gretchen. B.A., U. Louisville, 1971; postgrad. U. Cin., 1981—. Adminstr. Nat. Health Enterprises, Jackson, Tenn., 1973-74, Elizabethtown, Ky., 1974-78; exec. dir. United Med. Corp., Louisville, 1978-80, adminstr., chief exec. officer, Shelbyville, Ky., 1980-82; adminstr. Red Bank Community Hosp., Chattanooga, 1982—. Mem. state adv. council ARC, Louisville, 1979-80; bd. dirs. Red Bank Area Council, 1983—. Mem. Am. Acad. Med. Adminstrs., Am. Coll. Hosp. Adminstrs., Shelby County C. of C. (bd. dirs. 1980-82), Alpha Phi Omega. Democrat. Roman Catholic. Avocations: golf; fishing, racquetball; antique collecting, jogging. Lodge: Kiwanis. Home: 911 Glamis Circle Signal Mountain TN 37377 Office: Red Bank Community Hosp 632 Morrison Springs Rd Chattanooga TN 37415

VEST, DEED LAWRENCE, university medical facility administrator; b. San Antonio, Mar. 21, 1944; s. Deed Lafayette and Martha (Lee) V.; B.A. cum laude, U. Tex., 1968, M.B.A., 1970; m. Carol Ann Hanna, Aug. 28, 1964; children—Kelly Rene, John David; m. 2d, Diane H. Davies; 1 stepson, John C. Stelzer. Assoc. auditor Trans World Airlines, Kansas City, Mo., 1970-71, auditor, 1971-72, sr. fin. analyst, 1972, div. controller, sales and services Tex. Internat. Airlines, Houston, 1972-73, dir. inflight services, 1973-74; assoc. mgr. M.D. Anderson Hosp., U. Tex., Cancer Center, Houston, 1974-75, sr. assoc., adminstrv. officer physicians referral service med. practice, 1976-77, managerial adv. to exec. council, exec. retirement bd., univ. cancer found., 1976-77; mng. dir. central food service facility U. Tex. Med. Ctr., Houston, 1977—, asst. v.p. adminstrn., 1980-81, assoc. v.p. facilities, 1981-84, bus. dir. Cancer Bull. med. publ., sec., treas. to bd. dirs. Med. Arts Publs. Found.; chmn. waste handling com. Tex. Med. Center, 1981, mem. com. disaster and security. Mem. Sigma Iota Epsilon. Home: 18223 Barbuda Ln Houston TX 77058 Office: University of Texas 6723 Bertner Houston TX 77054

VEST, HERBIE DARWIN, investment firm executive, investment advisor; b. Battle Creek, Mich., Aug. 12, 1944; s. Horace Wilson and Ruth (Blakely) Powers; m. Barbara Jean Howard, Sept. 18, 1965; children—Matthew, Daniel. M.S. in Taxation, Tex. Tech U., 1973. C.P.A., Tex.; Col. U.; cert. fin. planner lic. real estate broker, Tex.; chartered fin. cons., fin. analyst. Acct. various pub. acctg. firms, Amarillo, Tex. and Fort Worth, 1973-75; propr. Herb Vest, Irving, Tex., 1975—; pres. H.D. Vest Investment Securities, Inc., Irving, 1983—; speaker in field. Contbr. articles to profl. jours. Served to capt. U.S. Army, 1966-71. Decorated Bronze Star, Purple Heart, Air medal. Fellow Fin. Analyst Fedn.; mem. Dallas Estate Planning Council, Soc. Security Analysts, Real Estate Securities and Syndication Inst., Nat. Assn. Bus. Economists, Inst. Cert. Fin. Planners, Mensa. Lodges: Rotary, Mason, Shriners. Avocations: computers; jogging; option writing; canoeing; hiking. Home: 3309 Hadalgo St Irving TX 75062 Office: HD Vest Investment Securities Inc 433 E Las Colinas Blvd Suite 1230 Irving TX 79039

VEST, HYRUM GRANT, JR., horticulture educator; b. Salt Lake City, Sept. 23, 1935; s. Hyrum Grant and Gwendolyn (Lund) V.; m. Gayle Pixton, Sept. 18, 1958; children—Kelly Grant, Lani Kae, Kari Lyn, Kamille, Kyle. B.S., Utah State U., 1960, M.S., 1964; Ph.D., U. Minn., 1967. Agronomist U.S. Dept. Agr., Beltsville, Md., 1967-70; assoc. prof. Mich. State U., East Lansing, 1970-76; prof. horticulture, dept. head Okla. State U., Stillwater, 1976-83, Tex. A&M U., College Station, 1983—. Contbr. articles to profl. jours. Served to 1st lt. U.S. Army, 1960-63. Fellow Am. Soc. Hort. Scis. (bd. dirs. 1984-85); mem. Am. Soc. Agronomy, Council Agrl. Sci. and Tech. Home: Route 2 Box 200 College Station TX 77840 Office: Dept Hort Scis Tex A&M U College Station TX 77840

VIAR, JOSEPH FRANKLIN, JR., computer consulting company executive; b. Phila., June 15, 1941; s. Joseph Franklin and Alice Lee (Williams) V.; B.S., Hampden-Sydney (Va.) Coll., 1963; m. Penelope Lusby; children—Elizabeth Anne, Amy Laura, Mgr., IBM Corp., Research Triangle Park, N.C., 1967-69; v.p. Systems Engring. Corp., Richmond, Va., 1969-71; dir. environ. programs Chase, Rosen & Wallace, Inc., Alexandria, Va., 1971-76; pres. Viar and Co., Inc., Alexandria, 1976—. Mem. Hampden-Sydney Alumni Council; trustee Hampden-Sydney Coll., 1985—; bd. dirs. Alexandria Hosp. Found., 1986—. Episcopalian. Clubs: Hampden-Sydney Alumni (pres. 1984-85). (Washington area); Commonwealth (Richmond, Va.); Trans-Potomac. 8710 Highgate Rd Alexandria VA 22308 Office: 300 N Lee St Alexandria VA 22314

VICKERS, MOZELLE CARVER, English educator, writer, poet; b. Durham County, N.C., Mar. 5, 1927; d. Isaiah Thomas and Sadie Blanche (Ball) Carver; m. Victor Graham Vickers, Feb. 1, 1946 (div. 1963); children—Sandra C. Vickers Haas, Mark G. B.A. in Religion and English, Tex. Christian U., 1965; M.A. in Religion and Edn., U. Tex.-Austin, 1969, Ph.D. in Edml. Adminstrn. and English, 1979; postgrad. So. Ill. U., Edwardsville, 1970-75. Life cert. English and core curriculum, Mo.; life cert. English, Tex. Part time dir. Christian edn. Christian Chs. Ft. Worth, 1962-69; English instr. State Community Coll., East St. Louis, Ill., 1970-76; part time and temporary instr. English, U. Tex.-Austin, 1976-79; high sch. tchr., also cons. Tex. state comptroller, Eagle Pass, 1980; prof. English, Brevard Coll. (N.C.), 1981—. Vice pres. Am. Penwomen, Cahokia, Ill., 1975. Grantee, Piper Found. of San Antonio, 1978. Mem. Am. Coll. Tchrs. of English, AAUW, Am. Bus. Women's Assn., Delta Kappa Gamma, Phi Theta Phi. Methodist. Contbr. poetry to various periodicals. Office: English Dept Brevard Coll Brevard NC 28712

VICKERS, STEPHEN ALLEN, lawyer; b. Bristol, Tenn., July 17, 1955; s. Charles Allen and Mary E. (Payne) V.; m. Valerie Agatha Fleenor, Aug. 9, 1980; 1 child, Whitney Elizabeth. B.A. magna cum laude, Emory and Henry Coll., 1977; J.D., U. Richmond, 1981. Bar: Va. 1981, U.S. Dist. Ct. Va. 1981, U.S. Ct. Appeals (4th cir.) 1982, U.S. Bankruptcy Ct. 1983. Cost acct. Sperry Inc., Bristol, 1977-78; ptnr. Copeland, Molinary & Vickers, Abingdon, Va., 1981-82, Vickers & Via, Bristol, 1983-84; corp. legal staff Nuclear Power div. Babcock and Wilcox Co., Lynchburg, Va., 1985—; arbitrator United Steelworkers Am. and Reynolds Metals, Bristol, 1983-84; legal intern supr. Emory and Henry Coll., Va., 1982-84. Democratic candidate for commonwealth's atty. Washington County, Abingdon, 1983; Dem. conv. del., Bristol, 1977, 78; spokesman, lobbyist Citizens for Responsive Govt., Washington County, Va., 1982. Mem. ABA, Va. Trial Lawyers Assn., Am. Judicature Soc., Assn. Trial Lawyers Am., Jaycees, Phi Delta Phi. Home: 1016 Mary Ann Dr Lynchburg VA Office: Nuclear Power Div Babcock and Wilcox Co 3315 Old Forest Rd Lynchburg VA 24504

VICKERS, TOMMY EUGENE, pharmaceutical company sales representative, pharmacist; b. Gainesville, Ga., Sept. 8, 1945; s. John Tilmon and Grace Marie (Crane) V.; m. Ethel Jean Ellis, Dec. 20, 1969; children—Timothy Scott, John Allen. A.A., Truett-McConnell Jr. Coll., 1965; B.S. in Pharmacy, U. Ga., 1972. Registered pharmacist, Ga. Laborer J.D. Jewell, Inc., Gainesville, 1963-64, Ralston Purina, Gainesville, 1965-66; structural assembler Lockheed Aircraft Corp., Marietta, Ga., 1966-68; warehouse mgr. West Bldg. Materials, Clarksdale, Miss., 1968-70; staff pharmacist Palmyra Park Hosp., Albany, Ga., 1972-74; sales rep. Dista Products Co., Indpls., 1974—. Treas. Church St. PTO, Tupelo, Miss., 1984-85. Republican. Baptist. Avocations: woodworking; hunting; fishing; golf. Home: 4 Brandywine Dr Belden MS 38826

VICKERY, EUGENE BENTON, JR., lawyer; b. New Orleans, Nov. 23, 1936; s. Eugene Benton and Esther (Cleveland) V.; m. Anne Saunders Porteous, Aug. 25, 1961; children—Eugene Benton III, Saunders P., Ninette C., William A. A.B., Williams Coll., 1962; J.D., Loyola U., New Orleans, 1967. Bar: La. 1967, U.S. Dist. Ct. (ea. dist.) La. 1967, U.S. Ct. Appeals (5th cir.), 1967. Supr. computer systems, sr. tech. programmer New Orleans Data Ctr., Shell Oil Co., 1962-67; jr. ptnr. Porteous, Toledano, Hainkel & Johnson, New Orleans, 1968-73; ptnr. Sutterfield & Vickery, New Orleans, 1974-82; sole practice, New Orleans, 1983—. Procurator adviser Met. Tribunal for Archdiocese of New Orleans; trustee, St. George's Episcopal Sch., 1976-83, chmn. bd. trustees, 1978-79; mem. Met. Crime Commn., Uptown Neighborhood Improvement Assn. Served with U.S. Army, 1956-59. Mem. ABA, La. Bar Assn., New Orleans Bar Assn., La. Assn. Def. Counsel, New Orleans Assn. Def. Counsel, Def. Research Inst., Am. Judicature Soc., Am. Arbitration Assn. (panel arbitrators 1968—), Notaries Assn. New Orleans, La. Landmarks Soc., Delta Phi. Republican. Roman Catholic. Clubs: Boston, Louisiana, Pickwick, Lake Shore (New Orleans); Williams (N.Y.C.). Home: 5526 Chestnut St New Orleans LA 70115 Office: 600 Maritime Bldg New Orleans LA 70130

VIDA, ROSA MARÍA RAMIREZ, education educator, consultant; b. Laredo, Tex., Oct. 7, 1947; d. Eloy and Anna Maria (Velasquez) Ramirez; m. Frank Alex Vida, July 26, 1974; children—Frank Alex, Roberto Antonio. B.S. in Secondary Edn., Tex. A & I U., 1970, M.S. in Elem. Edn., 1974; Ph.D., U. Tex., 1980. Cert. elem., secondary tchr., Tex. Tchr., Laredo Ind. Sch. Dist., 1970-74; tchr. and bilingual supr. Austin (Tex.) Ind. Sch. Dist., 1975-79; program devel. specialist Laredo State U., 1979-82, asst. prof. edn., 1982—; cons. Santillana Pub. Co., Austin Ind. Sch. Dist., Laredo Ind. Sch. Dist., United Ind. Sch. Dist. Research grantee Laredo State U., 1982. Mem. Tex. State Tchrs. Assn., NEA, Tex. Assn. Coll. Tchrs., Tex. Assn. Bilingual Edn., Tex. Assn. Gifted and Talented, Laredo Philharm. Assn., Civic Music Assn., Las Damas de la Repblica del Rio Grande.

VIELE, GEROGE BROOKINS, library executive; b. Flint, Mich., Apr. 20, 1932; s. Roy Millard and Mable Anna (Brookins) V.; m. Shirley Louise Larzelere, Aug. 27, 1955; 1 child, Sara (dec.). B.S., Central Mich. U., 1960, M.A., 1965; M.S.L.S., U. N.C., 1969. Cert. pub. librarian; cert. adminstrv. mgr. Asst. dir. Wake County Pub. Library, Raleigh, N.C., 1968-71; dir. Greensboro Pub. Library, N.C., 1971—; instr. library sch. U. N.C.-Greensboro, 1977-79. Contbr. articles to profl. jours. Bd. dirs. Lawndale Community Club, Greensboro, 1976-78; councilman Twining Town Council, Mich., 1963-65; mem. fin. com. Fellowship Presbyn. Ch., Greensboro, 1978-80. Served to cpl. U.S. Army, 1953-55. Mem. N.C. Library Assn. (stats. com. Pub. Library sect., chmn. 1977-79, devel. com. 1977-79). Republican. Lodges: Torch, Lions, Rotary. Avocations: bridge, photography, gardening. Office: Greensboro Public Library 201 N Greene St Greensboro NC 27402

VIERA, CRISTOBAL EUGENIO, general and vascular surgeon; b. Camguey, Cuba, Sept. 6, 1941; s. Cristobal J. and Luz Marina (Garcia) V.; came to U.S., 1959, naturalized, 1966; children from a previous marriage—Estelle Marie, Christopher; m. 2d, Ady Pino, Sept. 15, 1982; children—Adymari, Anibal. Student Candler Coll., Havana, Cuba, 1960; B.S., U. Miami, Fla., 1966, M.D., 1970. Straight surg. intern Sch. Medicine, U. Miami, 1970-71, asst. resident in surgery, 1971-72, resident, 1972-73, sr. resident, 1973-74, chief resident, 1974-75, clin. instr., 1976-81, clin. asst. prof. dept. surgery, 1981—; individual practice medicine specializing in gen. and vascular surgery, Miami, 1975—; staff Am. Mercy, Hialeah hosps. Co-chmn. Philharm. chpt. Interam. Found. for Endowment of Fine Arts, 1978—; bd. dir. League Against Cancer; mem. Greater Miami Opera Assn. Served to capt. M.C., USAR, 1971. Diplomate Am. Bd. Surgery. Fellow A.C.S.; mem. Dade County Med. Soc., Fla. Med. Assn., So. Med. Assn., Am. Cancer Soc., Phi Chi. Republican. Roman Catholic. Clubs: Racquet of Royal Biscayne, Big Five, Key Biscayne Yacht.

VIETH, RICK, lawyer, law educator; b. Spartanburg, S.C., Aug. 27, 1947; s. Walter Richard and Evelyn (Lenz) V.; m. Mary Fagan, Nov. 15, 1981 (div. Aug. 1985). B.A., Methodist Coll., 1969; postgrad. Am. U., 1971-74; J.D., U. S.C., 1975. Bar: U.S. Dist. Ct. 1975, U.S. Ct. Appeals (4th cir.) 1976. Assoc., Vieth & Wilson, Spartanburg, 1975-76; tchr. Rutledge Coll., Spartanburg, part-time 1975-78; dep. solicitor, prosecutor Solicitor Office, Spartanburg, 1977-84; ptnr. Henderson, Brandt & Vieth, Spartanburg, 1984—; faculty Spartanburg Meth. Coll., 1984—. Served to E5 USN, 1971-74. Mem. S.C. Trial Lawyers Assn., Am. Trial Lawyers Assn., S.C. Bar Assn., Greenville Fedn. Musicians, ABA. Democrat. Methodist. Club: Pebble Creek Country (chmn. bd. dirs. 1978-80). Avocations: golf, tennis, swim, ski. Home: 6A Terrell St Spartanburg SC 29302 Office: Henderson Brandt & Vieth 360 E Henry St Spartanburg SC 29302

VIGANDER, SVEIN, mechanical engineer, research specialist, fluid mechanics consultant; b. Oslo, Mar. 3, 1934; came to U.S., 1956, naturalized, 1970; s. Haakon Sverreson and Signy (Horn) V.; m. Marianne Ullery, Dec. 27, 1957; children—Nancy Marie, Dagny, Lisen, Hakon. B.S.M.E., Purdue U., 1958, M.S.M.E., 1959; Ph.D. in Engring. Mechanics, U. Kans., 1965. Research engr. Kimberly-Clark Corp., Neenah, Wis., 1959-61, TVA, Norris, 1965—; test engr., cons. Bechtel Inc., San Francisco, 1976, U.S. Army Corps of Engrs., Savannah, Ga., 1976, Chgo., 1981. Contbr. articles to profl. jours. Explorer skipper local council Boy Scouts Am., 1965-70; coach, referee Am. Youth Soccer orgn., Norris, 1975-85. Mem. ASCE, ASME, Internat. Assn. Hydraulic Research. Republican. Lutheran. Club: Optimist Internat. Avocations: viticulture; oenology; camping; fishing. Home: 32 Laurel Pl Box 303 Norris TN 37828 Office: TVA Engring Lab Pine Rd PO Drawer E Norris TN 37828

VIGTEL, GUDMUND, mus. dir.; b. Jerusalem, Palestine, July 9, 1925; came to U.S., 1948, naturalized, 1966; s. Arne Jonsen and Elisabeth (Petri) V.; m. Solveig Lund, 1951 (div. 1964); 1 dau., Elisabeth; m. Carolyn Gates Smith, July 18, 1964; 1 dau., Catherine Higdon. B.F.A., U. Ga., 1952, M.F.A., 1953. Adminstrv. asst., asst. to dir. Corcoran Gallery Art, Washington, 1954-61, asst. dir., 1961-63; dir. High Mus. Art, Atlanta, Ga., 1963—. Author essays and articles in field. Served with Royal Norwegian Air Force, 1944-45. Mem. Am. Assn. Mus., Assn. Art Mus. Dirs. Home: 2082 Golf View Dr NW Atlanta GA 30309 Office: 1280 Peachtree St NE Atlanta GA 30309

VILA, CARLOS RAMÓN, accountant; b. San Juan, P.R., Feb. 26, 1950; s. Carlos A. and Nilda E. (Ruiz) V.; m. Lucía María Navarro, May 18, 1973; children—Lucía Isabel, Carlos Amado. B.S. in Acctg. cum laude, Boston Coll., 1972. C.P.A., P.R. Acct., Arthur Andersen & Co., San Juan, 1972-78, audit mgr., 1977-78; audit ptnr. Vila Del Corral & Torres De Jess, San Juan, 1978-79; mng. ptnr. Sánchez Muñoz & Vila Ruíz, San Juan, 1979-84; owner, pres. Vila-Ruiz, C.P.A., San Juan, 1984—; dir: Anglo Puerto Rican Ins. Co., Amado Salon, Inc.; cons., dir. Luis E. Mainardi & Assocs., 1984. Bd. govs. United Fund P.R., 1977-80, treas., mem. exec. com., 1977, mem. admissions com., 1978-80. Mem. Am. Inst. C.P.A.s, Assn. C.P.A.s P.R. (v.p. San Juan chpt.). Office: GPO Box 1857 San Juan PR 00936

VILCHES-O'BOURKE, OCTAVIO AUGUSTO, acctg. co. exec.; b. Havana, Cuba, Aug. 15, 1923; came to U.S., 1962, naturalized, 1967; s. Bartolome and Isabel Susana (O'Bourke) Vilches; C.P.A., U. Havana, 1949, J.D., 1951, Ph.D. in Econ. Scis., 1953; m. Alba Del Valle Junco, July 24, 1954; 1 son, Octavio Roberto. Owner, Octavio Vilches & Assos., Havana, 1949-61; comptroller United R.R. of Cuba, 1950-53; cons. econ. affairs Cuban Dept. Labor, Havana, 1953; auditor Cuban Dept. Treasury, 1952-59; pres. Roble Furniture, Inc., San Juan, P.R., 1963-65, owner, Hato Rey, P.R., 1963—; pres. Mero Constrn. Corp., San Juan, 1973; prin. Octavio Vilches & Assocs., C.P.A., Hato Rey, 1983—. Mem. Circulo Cubano P.R., Colegio Contadores Publicos en el Exilio, Colegio Abogados en el Exilio, Cuban Nat. Bar Assn. Republican. Roman Catholic. Home: 146 Turquesa St Guaynabo PR 00920 Office: Centro II Suite 1402 Hato Rey PR 00920

VILE, JOHN RALPH, political science educator; b. Wilmington, Del., Apr. 29, 1951; s. Ralph and Joanna Virginia (Griffith) V.; m. Linda Kay Christensen, June 27, 1976; children—Virginia, Rebekah. B.A. in Govt., Coll. William and Mary, 1973; Ph.D. in Govt., U. Va., 1977. Asst. prof. McNeese State U., Lake Charles, La., 1977-81, assoc. prof. polit. sci., head dept. soc. sci., 1981—. Contbr. articles to profl. jours. NEH fellow, summers 1979, 82, 85. Mem. Am. Polit. Sci. Assn., So. Polit. Sci. Assn., Southwestern Polit. Sci. Assn., La. Polit. Sci. Assn. (editor newsletter 1981-83, 85-86), Phi Beta Kappa, Omicron Kappa, Lychns Hon. Soc. Democrat. Baptist. Office: McNeese State Univ Dept Soc Scis Lake Charles LA 70609

VILES, HENRY, pathologist; b. Cali, Colombia, Dec. 24, 1938; s. Pedro and Tulia V.; M.D., U. del Valle (Colombia), 1968; m. Mary Jo Oliver, Oct. 10, 1980; children—Maurice, Andrés, Tabatha, Joshua. Rotating intern Hosp. U. del Valle, Cali, 1967-68; resident in pathology Stamford (Conn.) Hosp., 1971-75, chief pathology resident, 1975-76; dir. labs. Mayfield (Ky.) Community Hosp., 1976—. Diplomate Am. Bd. Pathology. Fellow Coll. Am. Pathologists; mem. AMA, Am. Soc. Clin. Pathologists, Am. Soc. Microbiology, AAAS. Home: Lakeview Dr Mayfield KY 42066 Office: 206 W South St Mayfield KY 42066

VILLA, JOAN, management consultant, writer, educator; b. San Mateo, Calif., June 14, 1949; d. Leonard Charles and Angeline Josephine (Arena) Calabrese; m. Anthony Q. Villa, Jan. 20, 1973. B.S. in Exceptional Child Edn., State U. Coll. Buffalo, 1973; M.S. in Edn., Nova U., 1978. Cert. tchr. nursery sch., kindergarten, grades 1-6, N.Y.; cert. tchr. handicapped children, the emotionally handicapped, jr. coll., adminstrn., supervision, Fla. Tchr. emotionallly disturbed Broward County Schs., Ft. Lauderdale, Fla., 1974-79; sr. coordinator Personal Dynamics Inst., Mpls., 1978-85, resident mgr., 1985—; pres., owner Personal and Profl. Devel. Ctr., Coral Springs, Fla., 1979—; adj. prof. edn. U. La Verne, Calif., 1979, 80; adj. prof. bus. edn. Nova U., Davie, Fla., 1981—; sponsor continuing profl. edn. program Fla. State Bd. Accountancy, Gainesville, Fla., 1982—. Writer, Profit mag., 1985—. Contbr. articles and poems to profl. jours., mags. Coordinator exceptional child week Council Exceptional Children, Broward County Chpt., 1979, communications chmn., 1977-78, sec. 1976-77. Recipient Outstanding Young Woman Am. award, 1984. Mem. Am. Soc. for Tng. Devel. (chmn. strategic planning Broward/Palm Beach chpt. 1985, chmn. nat. issues 1985, Appreciation award 1983, chmn. strategic planning Region IX Conf. 1984, bd. dirs. 1984, pres. 1983, v.p. 1982, chmn. membership 1981, Dedicated Service award 1983, Chpt. of Yr. award 1983, Regional Chpt. Excellence award 1983, Nat. Profl. Contbn. award 1983, Outstanding Leadership award 1982, Outstanding Service award 1981), Classroom Tchrs. Assn. (chmn. 1976-79), Fla. Teaching Profession of NEA (women's leadership tng. cadre 1980—), Network Connection, Women in Sales Assn. (writer SE Fla. chpt. 1984, 85), Coral Springs Exec. Club, Women's Exec. Club, Ft. Lauderdale-Broward County C. of C. (edn. task force 1984-85), Coral Springs C. of C., Fla. Freelance Writers Assn. Democrat. Mem. Christian Ch. Avocations: bicycling; reading; rug hooking; leather craft; dancing. Home: 8811 NW 21st Ct Coral Springs FL 33065 Office: Personal Profl Devel Ctr PO Box 9003 Coral Springs FL 33075

VILLA, MARIE, nurse practitioner; b. El Paso, Tex., June 5, 1943; d. Leo R. and Josephine (Sanchez) Perez; m. Joe Villa, Dec. 26, 1964; children—Virginia, Frances, Diana, Joseph. Grad. Hotel Dieu Sch. Nursing, El Paso, 1964. Cert. Ob-Gyn nurse practitioner, nursing adminstrn. Charge nurse Hotel Dieu Hosp., El Paso, 1965-66, Providence Meml. Hosp., El Paso, 1966-73; asst. dir. Tigua Gen. Hosp., El Paso, 1973-82; infection control practitioner, quality assurance coordinator Sun Towers Hosp., El Paso, 1982—; mem. faculty Am. Heart Assn., El Paso, 1980—; dir. Med. Personnel Pool, 1985. Co-editor: Suggested Resources for Infection Control Practitioners, 1982. Mem. Hispanic task force Am. Cancer Soc., 1983-85; mem. sch. bd. Our Lady of Valley Sch., El Paso. Mem. Tex. Soc. Infection Control Practitioners (outstanding service award 1982), Am. Practitioners of Infection Control, Nurses Assn. Am. Coll. Ob-Gyn, City Assn. Practitioners Infection Control (program chmn. 1983). Roman Catholic. Avocation: reading. Office: Sun Towers Hosp 1801 N Oregon St El Paso TX 79902

VILLALON, AUGUSTO, marine design company executive, consultant; b. Havana, Cuba, Jan. 19, 1931; s. Jose Ramon and Elodia (Sorzano) V.; m. Maria Eugenia Capmany, Sept. 20, 1953 (div. Aug. 1972); children—Maria E. Ferguson, Jose R., Augusto; m. 2d, Barbara Ann Young, Dec. 8, 1978. M.S., U. Havana, 1953; B.S. in Bus. Adminstrn., U. Ark., 1962. With Gulf Atlantic Sugar Co., 1955-60, sugar mill mgr., 1959-60; asst. mgr. Winrock Farms, Carlisle, Ark., 1961-62; asst. chief engr. Traveler Boat Co., Little Rock, 1962-64; chem. engr. Reynolds Metals, Bryant, Ark., 1964-69; chief engr. Caravelle Boat Co., Jacksonville, Ark., 1969-72; exec. v.p. Ouachita Marine, Little Rock, 1972-75; pres., founder Marine Concepts, Inc., Cape Coral, Fla., 1975—; prof. engring. U. Ark., Little Rock, 1963-64; pres. Ancon, Inc., Cape Coral, Fla., 1983—; dir. Twistee-Freez Corp. Scoutmaster Boy Scouts Am., Little Rock, 1970-73; mem. Parochial Sch. Bd., 1970-73; mem. campaign com. Connie Mack for Congress, 1982. Mem. Soc. Naval Architects and Marine Engrs., Nat. Marine Mfrs. Assn., Am. Boat and Yacht Council, Assn. Sugar Engrs. in Exile. Republican. Roman Catholic. Club: Useppa Island (Pineland, Fla.). Co-inventor disappearing fittings. Home: 1804 SE 13th Terr Cape Coral FL 33904 Office: 1009 SE 12th Pl Cape Coral FL 33904

VILLAMAR, HECTOR E., federal flight examiner, pilot, aviation consultant; b. Havana, Cuba, Oct. 20, 1937; came to U.S., 1960; s. Reynerio and Maria Luisa Villamar; m. Sara Catalina Estevez, May 15, 1958; 1 son, Hector E. Grad. in bus. adminstrn. Havana Bus. U., 1957. Lic. airline transport pilot FAA. Flight engr., 1st officer Airlift Internat., Miami, Fla., 1966-68; capt., dir. flight tng. Fla. Atlantic Airlines, Miami, 1968-70; capt., aviation cons. Kamarakas Airline, Cambodia, 1970-74; flight examiner FAA, Miami, 1974—; aviation and aviation accident cons. Bd. dirs. Spanish Am. League Against Discrimination. Mem. Quiet Birdmen. Republican. Roman Catholic. Home and Office: 4144 Alton Rd Miami Beach FL 33140

VILLEGAS, HUGO ARMANDO, international financial consultant; b. La Paz, Bolivia, Oct. 31, 1950; came to U.S., 1979; s. Hugo Rene and Maria Julia (Vargas) V.; m. Maria Elvira Gomez, June 25, 1971 (div. 1973); 1 dau., Monica Patricia; m. 2d, Deborah Louise Tarvin, June 15, 1975; 1 son, Hugo Nicholas. B.B.M., Northwood Inst., 1974; M.A. in Econs., U. Cin., 1975. Assoc. prof. econs. U. Mayor J.M.S., Bolivia, 1976; pres. Hugo A. Villegas, La Paz, Bolivia, 1975-79; account exec. D.L.J. Securities, Miami, Fla., 1980-81; v.p. First Fla. Leasing, Miami, 1981-83; Latin Am. and Caribbean rep. Gold Hill Services S.A., Lausanne, Switzerland, 1984—; dir. COTRANS, La Paz, Grace & Co., La Paz, Sertrans, La Paz. Mem. Soc. Boliviana de Cemento (dir.), Internat. Sci. Honor Soc., Internat. Honor Soc. Econs. Home: 22204 SW 103d Ave Miami FL 33190 Office: Gold Hill and Kesperry Futures Ltd 125 Pall Mall London SW1 England

VILLELLA, EDWARD JOSEPH, ballet dancer, choreographer; b. L.I., N.Y., Oct. 1, 1936; s. Joseph and Mildred (DeGiovanni) V.; m. Janet (div. Nov. 1970); m. Linda; 1 dau., Christa F. B.S. in Marine Transp., N.Y. State Maritime

Coll., 1959. Lectr. in field. Dancer, N.Y. City Ballet, from 1957; guest appearance, London, 1962, Royal Danish Ballett Co., 1963, Boston Ballet, 1968, 69, Miami Ballet, 1968-69, N.Y.C. Opera, 1969, White House, London, 1971; appearances on TV shows, summer theatres, festivals, U.S. and abroad, 1957—; artistic coordinator, Eglevsky Ballet Co. (now André Eglevsky State Ballet of N.Y.), N.Y.C., 1979-84; choreographer, Eglevsky Ballet Co., N.Y.C., 1980-84, N.J. Ballet, 1980—; artistic dir., Ballet Okla., Oklahoma City, 1984—. Mem. Nat. Council on Arts, 1968-74; chmn. Commn. for Cultural Affairs City N.Y., 1978. Recipient Emmy award for program Harlequin on CBS Festival of Lively Arts, 1975. Address: Prodigal Prodns 129 W 69th St New York NY 10023*

VILLERE, ANDRE LOUIS, JR., architect; b. New Orleans, July 25, 1949; s. Andre Louis and Marie Elise (Jaubert) V.; m. Mary Catherine Greco, July 29, 1978; 1 child, Paul Louis. B.Arch., Tulane U., 1973. Registered architect, Tex., La. Staff architect Sizeler & Muller, Architects, New Orleans, 1973-74, E. Eean McNaughton & Assocs., 1974-79; project architect Barron/Toups, Architects, 1979-83; owner, pres. Andre L. Villere Jr. Architect, AIA, New Orleans, 1983—. Commr., Vieux Carre Commn., New Orleans, 1983-85; bd. advisors Habitat for Humanity, Inc., 1985—; bd. dirs. Bouligny Found., 1985—, St. Joseph Sem. Alumni Assn., 1978-80. Mem. Nat. Trust for Hist. Preservation, Preservation Resource Ctr., Friends of Cabildo, New Orleans Mus. Art, AIA, Constrn. Specifications Inst., Assn. Preservation Tech., Tulane Alumni Assn. Roman Catholic. Club: Serra Internat. Avocations: calligraphy; running; history. Home: 4600 S Johnson St New Orleans LA 70125 Office: 619 Chartres St Suite C New Orleans LA 70130

VILLOLDO, PEDRO ANTONIO, lawyer, developer, builder; b. Havana, Cuba, Mar. 9, 1918, naturalized, 1964; s. Pedro Jose and Maria Luisa (Campos) V.; m. Elena Ramirez de Arellano, July 30, 1948; children—Pedro, Alberto, Elena Villoldo Carpenter. J.D., U. Havana, 1940. Bar: P.R. 1960. Practice law, Havana, 1942-58; land developer in charge Gables-by-the-Sea, Coral Gables, Fla. Author: The Capital Structure of Corporations, 1956; Latin-American Resentment, 1959. Recipient Order of Cespedes (Cuba); cert. of Merit, Home Builders Assn., 1970. Mem. P.R. Bar Assn., Nat. Home Builders Assn. (dir. 1970), Home Builders Assn. P.R. (pres. 1969). Republican. Roman Catholic. Office: 30 SW 27th Ave Miami FL 33135

VINAMATA PASCHKES, CARLOS, lawyer; b. Barcelona, Spain, Sept. 19, 1944; s. Carlos Vinamata Castaner and Martha Paschkes Sibibin; gen. law degree U. Nacional Autónoma de Mex., 1968; m. Carolina Chávez Moran, Jan. 16, 1964; children—Caroline, Claudia Alejandra, Ingrid, Carlos. Admitted to Mexican bar, 1968; mem. firm Basham, Ringe & Correa, Mexico City, 1968-74; partner firm Vinamata, Melesio and Fernandez, Mexico City, 1974—; prof. U. Acatlán, 1979-80; owner Bufete Juridico Intercontinental, 1981-83; ptnr. Vinamata y Asociados, S.C., 1983—; gen. commr. Indian Community Rights, 1978-80; under dir. Land Tenancy, 1980-81; counsellor adminstrv. council Instituto Nacional Indigenista, 1978-81; mem. Tech. Commn. Nat. Countrymen Census, 1979-81. Dir. internat. studies Confederacion de Profesionistas y Tecnicos Revolucionarios, del Partido Revolucionario Institucional, Mexico City, 1969, 70, 71. Mem. Mexican Assn. Indsl. Property, Instituto Mexicano de Derecho Procesal. Director of Agrarian Rights of Confederación Nacional de la Pequeña Propiedad, 1984. General Commr. of Juridical Matters of Confederación Nacional de la Pequeña Propiedad, 1985. President of the commision of economic fiscalization of Colegio de Abogadosforo de México, A.C. 1985. Office: Bajio 335 Desp 303 Col Roma-Sur Delegacion Cuauhtemoc 06760 Mexico City Mexico Home: ixtacihuatl 6-502 Colonia Hipodromo Condesa Delegación Cuauhtémoc 06170 México DF

VINCENT, CHARLES JAMES, engineer; b. Ocean City, N.J., Sept. 14, 1930; s. Leslie H. and Catherine V. Geisinger; B.S. in Elec. Engring., Drexel U., 1957; B.S. in Civil Engring., U. Mo., Rolla, 1965; M.S. in Civil Engring., George Washington U., 1975; m. Judith Suzanne Deojay, Jan. 31, 1959; children—Anne Marie, Robert Michael, Sondra Jean, Jacqueline Danielle. Engr. coop. student Westinghouse Electric Corp., Balt., 1954-57; commd. 2d lt. U.S. Army, 1957; advanced through grades to lt. col., 1973, served with C.E.; ret., 1974; dep. dir. public works Prince William County, Va., 1974-77, dir. constrn. services, 1977-80, dir. project mgmt., 1980-83; assoc. Kidde Cons., Inc., Manassas, Va., 1983—; part-time instr. No. Va. Community Coll., 1975-77; mem. water resources planning bd. Met. Washington Council of Govts., 1975-83, chmn. water supply adv. com., 1979-83; mem. environ. quality com. Va. Mcpl. League, 1982-83. Mem. Prince William-Manassas Jail Bd. Served with USMC, 1950-53. Decorated Bronze Star with 3 oak leaf clusters, Air Medal with oak leaf cluster, Vietnamese Cross of Gallantry (2). Mem. ASCE (chpt. pres., 1977), Va. Soc. Profl. Engrs. (state dir., 1980-81, state v.p. Profl. Engrs. in Govt., 1978-79, chpt. pres., 1978), Am. Public Works Assn., Am. Water Works Assn., Bldg. Ofcls.-Code Adminstrs. Internat., Aircraft Owners and Pilots Assn. Baptist. Home: 12077 Winona Dr Woodbridge VA 22192 Office: 8315 Wellington Rd Manassas VA 22110

VINCENT, LLOYD DREXELL, university president; b. DeQuincy, La., Jan. 7, 1924; s. Samuel and Lila (Dickerson) V.; m. Johnell Stuart, Aug. 30, 1947; children—Drexel Stuart, Sandra. Student Rice U., 1946-47, 49-50; B.S., U. Tex., Austin, 1952, M.A., 1953, Ph.D., 1960; Asst. prof. U. Southwestern La., 1953-55, assoc. prof., 1956-58; instr. Tex. A&M U., 1955-56; Danforth Found. tchr. study grantee, NSF Sci. faculty fellow. U. Tex., 1958-59; research scientist Tex. Nuclear Corp., Austin, 1959-60; prof., dir. physics dept. Sam Houston State U., 1960-65, asst. to pres., 1965-67; pres. Angelo State U., San Angelo, Tex., 1967—; co-owner, mgr. ACME Glass Corp., Baytown, Tex., 1947-49; physics cons. Columbia U. Tchrs. Coll., U.S. AID, India, summer 1966; dir. W.Tex. Utilities Co., 1978—; vice chmn. Council Pres. of Public Sr. Colls. and Univs. Tex., 1980-81; chmn. Council Presidents of Lone Star Athletic Conf., 1981-83, 86-87; bd. dirs. Assn. Tex. Colls. and Univs., 1981—. Bd. dirs. West Tex. Rehab. Center, 1977-85; bd. visitors Air U., Maxwell AFB, Ala., 1981—. Served to 2d lt. USAAF, 1942-45. Named Citizen of Year San Angelo C. of C., 1975. Fellow Tex. Acad. Sci.; mem. Am. Phys. Soc., Am. Assn. State Colls. and Univs. (state rep. 1972-74), Am. Assn. Physics Tchrs. (sect. chmn. 1965-67, mem. del. to USSR and China 1983), Am. Assn. State Colls. and Univs. (mission of presidents and chancellors to Malaysia 1986), West Tex. C. of C. (bd. dirs., chmn. cultural affairs com. 1985—), Sigma Xi, Sigma Pi Sigma. Democrat. Baptist. Rotarian. Home: 2602 Live Oak St San Angelo TX 76901 Office: President's Office Angelo State U San Angelo TX 76909

VINCENT, NICHOLAS MARIO, psychologist, educator; b. Phila., Sept. 8, 1921; s. Paul P. and Grace Georgia V.; B.S. in Bus. Adminstrn., U. Fla., 1948; M.S., Fla. State U., 1949, Ph.D., 1955; m. Jean Lois Grider, Feb. 1, 1952; children—Nicholas Gregory, Paul Christopher. Asst. prof. U. Tenn., Martin, 1954-55; assoc. prof. Richmond (Va.) Profl. Inst., 1955-56; assoc. prof. East Tenn. State U., 1956-57; assoc. prof. Jacksonville U., 1957-64; prof. psychology U. South Ala., Mobile, 1968—, chmn. dept., 1965-76, dir. Univ. Counseling Service, 1966-69, dir. Psychol. Services Inst., 1967-73 dir. career planning and devel., 1977—; dir. Intergroup Relations for Law Enforcement Officers, Mobile, 1972-73; bd. dirs. Mobile Assn. Mental Health, 1971-77. Served with A.C., USN, 1942-45. Mem. Am. Psychol. Assn., Southeastern Psychol. Assn., Ala. Psychol. Assn., Psi Chi, Alpha Kappa Psi, Beta Gamma Sigma, Phi Kappa Phi. Author: (with David Hale) The Multilevel Vocabulary Test, 1966; editor The Ala. Psychologist, 1967-69, Jour. Sports Behavior, 1982—. Home: 1062 Woodside Dr W Mobile AL 36608 Office: Dept Psychology U South Ala Mobile AL 36688

VINCES, OSCAR H., banker; b. Trujillo, Peru, Nov. 18, 1946; came to U.S., 1976; s. Oscar H. and Maria Julia (De Bracamonte) V.; m. Elena Vinces, June 25, 1971; children—Oscar H., Maria. M.B.A. in Fin., St. Louis U., 1972. With Banco de la Nacion, Lima, Peru, 1964-67; gen. mgr. Parquet Sta. Ines S.A., Lima, 1967-68; with PetroPeru, Lima, 1968-71; treas. Estudios 501, S.A., Lima, 1974-76; internat. loan officer Mercantile Trust Co., St. Louis, 1976-78; sr. auditor Monsanto Co., St. Louis, 1978; internat. loan officer Southeast Bank, Miami, Fla., 1979-80, No. Trust, Miami, 1980-82; asst. v.p., head internat. corp. banking Bank of Boston Internat. South, Miami, 1982—. Hon. dep. Consul of Peru, 1976. PetroPeru grantee, 1970-71; Fulbright fellow, 1971-72. Mem. Washington Export Council, Fla. Internat. Bankers Assn., Internat. Ctr. of Fla. Clubs: Bankers, Kendall Lakes Golf and Country, King's Bay Yacht and Country. Office: Bank of Boston Internat South 800 Brickell Ave Suite 1500 Miami FL 33131

VINES, DARRELL LEE, electrical engineering and computer science educator, consultant; b. Crane, Tex., Mar. 7, 1936; s. Perry O. Vines. m. Mary P. Marcom, Sept. 6, 1957. Ph.D., Tex. A&M U., College Station, 1967. Registered profl. engr. Instr. Tex. A&M, 1963-66; prof. elec. engring. and computer sci. Tex. Tech U., Lubbock, 1966—, dir. undergrad. engring. programs, assoc. dean Coll. of Engring., 1984—; disting. vis. prof. U.S. Air Force Acad., Colo., 1981-82. Author: Inst. for Oilfield, 1972. Mem. bd. elec. examiners City of Lubbock, 1970-76, bldg. code bd., 1974-80. Recipient Abell Teaching award Tex. Tech U., 1985, Amoco Teaching award, 1976. Mem. IEEE (sect. chmn. 1969-71, bd. dirs. 1978-80, Centennial Medal 1984), Am. Soc. Engring. Educators (Recipient Western Electric award 1977). Home: Box 6015 Lubbock TX 79493 Office: Tex Tech U Box 4200 Lubbock TX 70409

VINES, DWIGHT DELBERT, university president; b. Jonesboro, La., Sept. 27, 1931; s. Dwight N. and Bessie (Barlow) V.; student Fla. State U., 1950-51; B.S., Northwestern State Coll., 1957; M.B.A., La. State U., 1958; D.B.A., U. Colo., 1966; m. Frances Imogene Varnado, June 4, 1956; children—Michael Allan, Timothy Wayne, David Ray. Sales rep. Burroughs Corp., Shreveport, La., 1956-57; instr., asst. prof. NE La. State Coll. (now N.E. La. U.), Monroe, 1958-63, assoc. prof. mgmt., 1964-69, dean Sch. Bus., 1964-69, prof., dean Sch. Bus. Adminstrn., 1969-75, pres. univ., 1975—, cons., 1960—. Chmn. bus. adminstrn. div. Conf. La. Colls. and Univs.; chmn., bd. dirs. Monroe Indsl. Mgmt. Council; mem. adv. bd. Fed. Property Assistance Agy.; bd. dirs. Northeast La. Edn. Found. Served with USAF, 1950-55. Mem. Southwest Acad. Mgmt., Southwest Mgmt. Assn. (officer); Sr. Mgmt. Assn., Monroe C. of C. (pres., dir.), Omicron Delta Kappa, Delta Sigma Pi, Pi Sigma Epsilon, Phi Kappa Phi, Sigma Iota Epsilon, Beta Gamma Sigma, Pi Omega Pi, Pi Kappa Delta. Office: 700 University Ave NE La U Monroe LA 71209*

VINING, MARK RICHARD, geologist; b. Seattle, Dec. 14, 1951; s. Merwin W. and Phyllis L. (Baber) V.; m. Donna G. Fisher, July 7, 1984. B.S., U. Wash., Seattle, 1974; M.S., U. B.C., Vancouver, Can., 1977. Engring. geologist Roger Lowe Assocs., Inc., Seattle, 1977-79; geologist Exxon Co. U.S.A., Midland, Tex., 1980—. Mem. Am. Assn. Petroleum Geologists, Nat. Speleological Soc., W. Tex. Geol. Soc., Phi Beta Kappa. Avocations: photography; hiking; outdoor exploring; geological fieldwork; computer applications. Home: 4601 Erie St Midland TX 79703 Office: Exxon Co PO Box 1600 Midland TX 79702

VINING, ROBERT L., JR., U.S. district judge; b. 1931. B.A., U. Ga., 1959, J.D., 1959. Atty. Mitchell & Mitchell, 1958-60, McCamy, Minor & Vining, 1960-69; solicitor gen. Conasauga Jud. Circuit, 1963-68; Superior Ct. judge Consauga Jud. Ctr., 1969-79; judge U.S. Dist. Ct. for No. Ga., Atlanta, 1979—. Office: 2167 US Courthouse 75 Spring St SW Atlanta GA 30303*

VINING, WILLIAM MACON, JR., industrial hygienist; b. Rusk, Tex., Dec. 19, 1947; s. William Macon and Eddie B. (Roark) V.; m. Tonya Jo Kallsen, July 27, 1985. B.A., Tex. Christian U., 1970; M.S., U. Tex., 1978. Cert. indsl. hygienist; diplomate Am. Acad. Indsl. Hygiene. Safety health coordinator Johnson Controls, Garland, Tex., 1973-77; sr. indsl. hygienist Tex. Industries, Inc., Dallas, 1977-81, Dresser Industries, Inc., Dallas, 1981-85; pres. Occupational-Environ. Control, Inc., 1985—. speaker to orgns. on environ. health. Author: Ventilation Design Guide, 1980. Mem. Am. Indsl. Hygiene Assn. (pres., bd. dirs. N. Tex. sect. 1981-83, engring. com. 1981-84), Am. Soc. Safety Engrs. (v.p. communications SW chpt. 1976-77), Dallas C. of C. (hazardous materials com.). Republican. Methodist. Avocations: sailing; snow skiing; tennis. Home: 7001 Fair Oaks St 233 Dallas TX 75231 Office: Occupation-Environ Control Inc 7001 Fair Oaks St 233 Dallas TX 75231

VINSON, C. ROGER, U.S. district judge; b. Cadiz, Ky., Feb. 19, 1940; m. Ellen Vinson; children—Matt, Todd, Kate, Patrick, Joey. B.S., U.S. Naval Acad., 1962; J.D., Vanderbilt U., 1971. Atty., Beggs & Lane, Pensacola, Fla., 1971-83; judge U.S. Dist. Ct. for No. Fla., Pensacola, 1983—. Office: 105 US Courthouse 100 N Palafax St Pensacola FL 32501*

VINSON, CYDONNA YOUNG, nurse; b. Madisonville, Ky., Jan. 10, 1956; d. June Elbert Young and Wanna Jo (Brown) Penick; m. James Michael Cherry, Aug. 21, 1973 (div. June 1978); 1 son, John Marcus; m. Henry Richard Vinson, Jr., Nov. 26, 1983; 1 son, Justin Kyle; 1 stepson, Henry Richard Vinson. A.Sci. Nursing, Hopkinsville Community Coll., 1980. R.N. Nursing asst. Jennie Stuart Med. Ctr., Hopkinsville, Ky., summer 1979, charge nurse CCU, 1980-81, 82—; dir. nursing Medco Ctr., Penbroke, Ky., 1981-82. Democrat. Methodist. Home: 2626 Kenwood Dr Hopkinsville KY 42240 Office: Jennie Stuart Med Ctr Hospital Ln Hopkinsville KY 42240

VINSON, JUDY ANN, university administrator; b. Pine Bluff, Ark., Sept. 1, 1946; d. Edward Boyd and Myra June (Burris) V.; m. William Carl Shockley, Jr., Apr. 10, 1982. B.A., Henderson State U., 1968; M.S., Okla. State U., 1976. Field exec. Circle T council Girl Scouts U.S., Fort Worth, 1972-73; student services officer Pan Am. U., Edinburg, Tex., 1977-78, asst. dean students, 1978-81, asst. dean student life, 1981-82, dean students, 1982—. Charter pres. Women Together, Inc., 1978-80; bd. dirs. Hidalgo County United Way, 1980-84; bd. dirs. Tip of Tex. council Girl Scouts U.S., 1982-84, sec., 1984—. Mem. Tex. Assn. Women Deans, Adminstrs., and Counselors (1st v.p. 1983—), Nat. Assn. Fgn. Student Affairs, Nat. Assn. Student Personnel Adminstrs., Tex. Assn. Coll. and Univ. Student Personnel Adminstrs., So. Assn. Coll. Student Affairs. Avocations: sailing; reading; tatting; aerobic exercise. Home: 1102 S 8th St Edinburg TX 78539 Office: Pan Am U 1201 W University Dr Edinburg TX 78539

VINSON, MICHAEL COOPER, pharmacist, administrator; b. Jackson, Miss., May 11, 1945; s. J.W. and Martha Jean (Varner) V.; m. Doris Marie Thibodeaux, Sept. 4, 1965; children—Sharron Marie, Troy Michael, Tara Lynn. B.S. in Pharmacy, U. Ms., 1969, M.S. in Hosp. Pharmacy, 1973; Pharm.D., Phila. Coll. Pharmacy, 1973. Staff pharmacist Univ. Hosp., Jackson, 1969-70; asst. prof. Sch. Pharmacy, U. Miss., Jackson, 1973-79, instr. 1980—; dir. pharmacy Miss. Methodist Rehab. Ctr., Jackson, 1979—; instr. clin. pharmacology Hinds Jr. Coll., Jackson, 1984—; chmn. pharmacy purchasing group Miss. Hosp. Assn., Jackson, 1981—; team pharmacist Honduras Med. Mission Trips, Central Am., 1982, 84, 85. Contbr. articles to profl. jours., chpt. to book. Chilton Meml. scholar, 1968. Mem. Am. Soc. Hosp. Pharmacists, Miss. Pharmacists Assn. (drug utilization com. 1984—), Miss. Soc. Hosp. Pharmacists (pres. 1980-81, named Hosp. Pharmacist of Yr. 1980). Episcopalian. Avocations: calligraphy; stained glass. Home: 1564 Wingfield Dr Jackson MS 39204 Office: Miss Methodist Rehab Ctr 1350 E Woodrow Wilson Dr Jackson MS 39216

VIOLETTE, JOHN-PAUL J., lawyer, educator; b. Ipswich, Eng., Mar. 31, 1953; s. Norman J. and Eileen A. (Cody) V. A.S. in Engring., U.S. Air Force Acad., 1973; B.A. in Math, Fla. Atlantic U., 1977; S.M. in Engring., MIT, 1979; J.D., U. Miami, Fla., 1983. Bar: Fla. 1983, U.S. Dist. Ct. (so. dist.) Fla. 1984, U.S. Ct. Appeals (11th cir.) 1984. Intern, jud. clk. U.S. Dist. Ct. (so. dist.) Fla., Miami, 1982; spl. asst. pub. defender State of Fla., Miami, 1983-84; sole practice, Miami, 1983—; adj. prof. bus. law U. Miami, Coral Gables, Fla., 1983—; dir. Violette Corp., Palm Beach, Fla., 1979—. Sponsor, Palm Beach Round Table, 1981-83, Boston Ballet, 1977-79, Met. Opera, Boston, 1977-79, Copley Art Gallery, Boston, 1977-79. Served with USAF, 1971-73. Mem. ABA, Fla. Bar Assn., Fed. Bar Assn., Assn. Trial Lawyers Am., IEEE, Phi Alpha Delta. Republican. Clubs: MIT of Palm Beach, Tower (Fort Lauderdale, Fla.). Office: Consol Bank Bldg 168 SE 1st St Miami FL 33480

VIOT, PETER ARNOLD, engineer, manufacturing company executive; b. Aarberg, Switzerland, July 18, 1945; s. Oscar Arnold and Dora Lina (Baur) V.; m. Penny A. Bell, Nov. 18, 1984; children—Erich Gene, Marcus Gerard. Grad., Technicum Biel, Switzerland, 1965. With dept. research and devel. ITT of Can., 1967-69; tool designer I.D. Watch Co., 1969-71; mfg. engr. Meltronics Inc., Leeds, Ala., from 1971, now chief engr., v.p.; pres. Swiss Precision Machine, 1979; cons., lectr. in field. Served with Swiss Air Force, 1966. Mem. Soc. Mfg. Engrs. Episcopalian. Club: Civitan. Lodge: Masons. Office: PO Box 569 Leeds AL 35094

VIRE, THOMAS NORMAN, industrial hygienist; b. Terre Haute, Ind., Dec. 10, 1948; s. George Talt and Minnie Laverne (Green) V.; m. Edna Wilhelmina Pendleton, Aug. 25, 1973; children—James Thomas, Joshua Todd, Jarrett Talt. B.S. in Environ. Scis., Ind. State U., 1976. Cert. indsl. hygienist. Indsl. hygienist OSHA sect. Va. State Health Dept., Richmond, 1976-78; indsl. hygienist enforcement div. N.C. Dept. Human Resources, Raleigh, 1978-80; corp. indsl. hygienist Sandoz Chems. Corp., Charlotte, N.C., 1980—. Vol. ARC, Charlotte, Gastonia, N.C., 1982, Am. Heart Assn., Charlotte, 1982; scoutmaster Boy Scouts Am., Gastonia, 1983. Served with USMC, 1968-72, Vietnam. Mem. Am. Indsl. Hygiene Assn., Eta Sigma Gamma. Republican. Morman. Lodge: Kiwanis. Avocations: camping; backpacking. Home: 302 Greenwood Pl Belmont NC 28012 Office: Sandoz Chems Corp PO Box 669246 Charlotte NC 28266

VISH, DONALD H., lawyer, educator; b. Ft. Benning, Ga., Jan. 18, 1945; s. D.H. Jr. and Dorris (Parrish) V.; m. Catherine Pence Hamilton, Aug. 20, 1966; children—Donald Hamilton, Daphne Mershon. B.A. in English, Bellarmine Coll., 1968; J.D. cum laude, U. Louisville, 1971. Bar: Ky. 1971, Fla. 1972, U.S. Ct. Appeals (6th cir.) 1974. Sec., gen. counsel Gen. Energy Corp., Lexington, Ky., 1978-83; ptnr. firm Wyatt, Tarrant & Combs, Lexington, 1980—; assoc. prof. Coll. of Law, U. Ky., Lexington, part-time 1977-80, adj. assoc. prof. mineral law, 1979-85. Contbr. to legal ency. American Law of Mining, 2d edit., 1984; co-editor, contbr. Coal Law and Regulation, 1983. Trustee Sayre Sch., Lexington, 1980—, chmn. bd., 1985—. Mem. Am. Law Inst., Eastern Mineral Law Found. (trustee 1979—, exec. com. 1979-82, chmn. coal subcom. 1984-85), Am. Judicature Soc., ABA, Fla. Bar Assn., Ky. Bar Assn. (ethics com. 1983—), Am. Soc. Corp. Secs., English Speaking Union: Republican. Episcopalian. Clubs: Pendennis (Louisville); Keeneland (Lexington). Home: 1107 Richmond Rd Lexington KY 40502 Office: Wyatt Tarrant & Combs 1100 Kincaid Towers Lexington KY 40507

VISOT-SAUZA, LUIS RAUL, educational adminstrator; b. Ponce, P.R., Jan. 25, 1957; s. Luis Raul and Lolita (Sauza) Visot. B.A. in Spanish, Marquette U., 1978; M.Ed. in Higher Edn., U. Ga., 1980. Resident advisor dept. housing Marquette U., Milw., 1976-77, asst. hall dir., 1977-78; grad. resident dept. housing U. Ga., Athens, 1978-80; resident instr. dept. housing U. S. Fla., Tampa, 1981-82, area coordinator, 1982—. Mem. Am. Coll. Personnel Assn. (commn. III bd. dirs. 1984-87), Nat. Assn. Coll. and Univ. Residence Halls, Am. Soc. Tng. and Devel., Assn. Coll. and Univ. Housing Officers. Roman Catholic. Avocations: jogging; reading; listening; sports. Home: U S Fla 618 Tampa FL 33620

VITZ, THOMAS WILLARD, dentist, dental services administrator; b. San Diego, June 16, 1947; s. Robert Herman and Ruth Mabel (Dreibelbis) V.; m. Velda Rose Atokuku, Dec. 10, 1977; children—Tory Don, Kelly Anne. B.A. in Biolo. Scis., San Jose State U., 1970; D.D.S., Georgetown U., 1974. Chief dental services USPHS, Keams Canyon, Ariz., 1975-77; dir. dental services Meml. Med. Ctr., Corpus Christi, Tex., 1978—. Served to major USPHS, 1974-77; served in U.S. Coast Guard, 1968-69. Mem. ADA, Am. Assn. Functional Orthodontists, Clin. Found. Orthopedics and Orthodontics, Nueces Valley Dist. Dental Soc. Republican. Baptist. Lodge: Lions (Corpus Christi). Avocations: hunting; fishing; tennis. Home: 5206 Crestwick Corpus Christi TX 78413

VIVIANI, PHILIP RICHARD, government official; b. Bklyn., Jan. 11, 1930; s. Vincent Brennan and Alessandria (Stellato) V.; m. Margaret Eloise Kelly, Aug. 7, 1952 (div. 1976); children—Elizabeth, Margaret, Philip, Michael. A.B. in Econs./Psychology, Mercer U., 1963, M.Ed., 1971; Ed.S., Ga. Coll., 1975. Lic. tchr., Ga.; lic. pvt. pilot FAA. With B. Lloyds Products, Barnesville, Ga., 1953-55, Binswanger Glass Co./Willingham Sash & Door Co., Macon, Ga., 1955-58; with U.S. Civil Service, 1958—, contracting officer, 1966-74, procurement analyst, 1969-71, supervisory contract negotiator, 1969-78, supervisory procurement analyst, 1978—, chmn. contracts com., directorate of contracting and mfg. Robins AFB, Ga., 1978—. Mem. Ga. Commn. to Study Economy and Efficiency in Macon and Bibb County, Ga., 1972, 75; pres. Crawford County Citizens for Tax Reduction, 1983—. Served with USAF, 1950-53. Named Supr. of Month, Robins AFB, 1972; recipient Disting. Toastmaster award, 1976. Mem. Smithsonian Assocs., Ga. Sheriffs Assn. (hon. mem.), Nat. Assn. Sports Ofcls., Air Force Assn., Aircraft Owners and Pilots Assn., Middle Ga. Baseball Umpires Assn. Republican. Roman Catholic. Clubs: Toastmasters (internat. dir. 1969-71), Robins AFB Aero, Robins AFB Officers.

VLADIMIR, MAREK, ballet director, teacher; b. Uzhorod, Czechoslovakia, Sept. 26, 1928; s. Jaroslav and Julia (Valkova) Sourek. Grad. Gymnasium, Prague, Czechoslovakia, 1938-40, Bus. Acad., Prague, 1940-46; student various ballet schs., Prague, 1945-47. Soloist, Czechoslovakia Nat. Theater Ballet, Prague, 1947-50, prin. dancer, Bratislava, 1950-69, ballet master, 1958-68; founder, artistic dir. San Antonio Ballet, 1970—; owner V. Marek Ballet Acad., San Antonio, 1970—; instr. ballet Our Lady of the Lake U., San Antonio, 1970-78. Home: 800 Babcock T-4 San Antonio TX 78201 Office: San Antonio Ballet 212 E Mulberry San Antonio TX 78212

VLATTAS, NICHOLAS E., architect; b. Newport News, Va., Oct. 26, 1952; s. Emmanuel N. and Anne (Vainas) V.; m. Barbara Burgin, June 18, 1977; 1 child, Kristen Nicole. B.Arch., Va. Poly. Inst. and State U., 1976. Sports writer Daily Press, Newport News, 1967-73; intern architect Design Collaborative, Newport News, 1976-78, S. Michael Evans, Architect, Poquoson, Va., 1978-79; prin., architect Hanbury Evans Newill Vlattas & Co., Norfolk, Va., 1979—. Mem. AIA (1st v.p. Tidewater chpt. 1985, pres. 1986), Soc. Am. Mil. Engrs., Va. Soc. Architects (bd. dirs. 1985). Greek Orthodox. Lodge: Rotary (pres. 1987). Avocations: photography; running; sailing. Home: 407 Woodroof Rd Newport News VA 23606 Office: Hanbury Evans & Co., Vlattas & Co 120 Atlantic St Norfolk VA 23510

VOCELLE, CHARLES, lawyer; b. St. Marys, Ga., Sept. 4, 1923; s. James Thomas and Mary Della (Schmitt) V.; m. Betty Paige Todd, Feb. 4, 1948; children—Charlene Paige, Douglas Scot. A.A., U. Fla., 1947; J.D., U. Miami, 1950. Bar: Fla. 1950. Spl. asst. atty. gen. Fla., 1955-60; mem. Fla. Bd. Bar Examiners, 1970-74; mem. Fla. Gov.'s Task Force Workers' Compensation, 1973-74; mem. Workers' Compensation Adv. Council, Fla., 1974—; chmn. Workers' Compensation com., 1970-74; mem. Workers' Compensation Rules com. Served with USMCR, 1942-45. Republican. Presbyterian. Office: PO Box 1029 Lake City FL 32055

VOCKROTH, GEORGE BYROM, petroleum geologist; b. Atlanta, May 16, 1928; s. Ewald George and Katherine Eoline (Byrom) V.; m. Dora Danelle Knight, June 5, 1953 (div. July 1967); children—George Laird, Amanda Katherine, Graham Byrom; m. Marilyn Reynolds, Oct. 9, 1976. B.S., Va. Poly. Inst., 1949; A.M., Harvard U., 1951. Sub-surface geologist, geophysicist Calif. Co., Jackson, Miss., 1951-55, 66, 69, devel. geologist, New Orleans, 1955, 57-59, dist. devel. geologist, Jackson, 1959-66; sr. geologist Chevron Oil Co., New Orleans, 1969-75, staff geologist, 1975-77; owner, pres. Vantage Oil Co., Jackson, 1977—; lectr. in field; mem. People to People Petroleum Tech., Del. to China, 1985. Chief, YMCA Indian Guides, Jackson, 1964; pres., dist. v.p. Unitarian-Universalist Assn., 1963-67; advisor Jr. Achievement, New Orleans, 1970-73; scoutmaster, dist. chmn. New Orleans Area Council Boy Scouts Am., 1973-77. Served to capt. USAFR, 1955-57. Decorated Nat. medal, SAR, 1949; recipient Holden award, Sigma Gamma Epsilon, 1949. Mem. Soc. Ind. Profl. Earth Scientist, Am. Assn. Petroleum Geologists, Am. Inst. Profl. Geologists, Soc. Profl. Well Log Analysts, Soc. Petroleum Engrs. of AIME, Miss. Assn. Petroleum Landman (bd. dirs. 1985—), Tau Beta Pi, Omicron Delta Kappa, Phi Kappa Phi. Republican. Unitarian. Clubs: Toastmasters Internat. (Tokyo); Diamonhead Country. Avocations: gardening; forestry; photography; camping. Home: 6221 Ferncreek Dr Jackson MS 39211 Office: Vantage Oil Co 125 S Congress St L-154 Jackson MS 39201

VOERMAN, DAVID PETER, lawyer; b. Poughkeepsie, N.Y., Sept. 27, 1947; s. Louis and Eunice Amelia (Lane) V.; m. Mary Elizabeth Janson (div.); children—Kristina Ann, Lara Louise; m. Barbara Anne Ethridge, Aug. 11, 1980; 1 son, David Louis; 1 stepchild, Ashley Paige Wood. A.B. in History, Coll. Holy Cross, 1969; J.D., Duke U., 1972. Bar: Ohio 1972, N.C. 1972, U.S. Dist. Ct. (ea. dist.) N.C. 1972, U.S. Ct. Mil. Appeals 1972, U.S. Ct. Appeals (4th cir.) 1977, U.S. Ct. Appeals (fed. cir.) 1984. Law clk. U.S. Dist. Ct. (ea. dist.) N.C., Trenton, N.C., 1971-72; spl. asst. Office of U.S. Atty., Honolulu, 1973-74; assoc. Beaman, Kellum, Mills, Kafer, New Bern, N.C., 1977-80; ptnr. Perdue, Voerman & Alford, New Bern, 1980-83; ptnr. Voerman & Ward, P.A., New Bern, 1983—. Served to lt. comdr. JAGC, USN, 1972-77. NROTC scholar Coll. Holy Cross, 1965. Mem. Assn. Trial Lawyers Am. (patron 1977—), N.C. Acad. Trial Lawyers (patron 1977—), N.C. Bar Assn. Democrat. Episcopalian. Home: 306 W Wilson Creek Dr New Bern NC 28560 Office: Voerman & Ward PA 605 Broad St PO Box 1534 New Bern NC 28560

VOGAN, CHARLES EDWARD, educator, choral conductor; b. Sandy Lake, Pa., Sept. 26, 1910; s. Cassius Edward and Myra Sysanna (Weber) V.; m. Frieda Alice Op't Holt, Sept. 14, 1942; children—Charles Edward Jr., Judith Anne,

David Nicholas. Mus. B., Oberlin Coll., 1932; M. Mus., U. Mich., 1946; Ph.D., U. Mich., 1949. Dir. mus. Central Reformed Ch., Grand Rapids, Mich., 1932-41; instr. U. Mich., Ann Arbor, 1946-48; asst. prof. U. Mo., Columbia, 1948-50; prof. Old Dominion U., Norfolk, Va., 1950-76; adj. prof. Va. Wesleyan Coll., Norfolk, 1978—; program notes dir. Va. Symphony, Norfolk, 1954-81; condr. Vogan Chorale, Norfolk, 1975—. Author: French Organ Music in the 17th and 18th Century, 1948; composer: In Memorium, 1939; Christmas Tryptich, 1946. Bd. dirs. Community Music Sch., Norfolk, 1955—. Served with U.S. Army, 1941-46. Recipient Selby Houston award Oberlin Coll., 1932. Mem. Am. Musicol. Soc., Va. Music Educators Assn. (coll. chmn. 1966-68), Pi Kappa Lambda, Phi Kappa Phi; assoc. mem. Am. Guild Organists (dean 1954-56). Republican. Presbyterian. Lodge: Rotary. Home: 1305 Harmott Ave Norfolk VA 23509 Office: Va Wesleyan Coll Wesleyan Dr Norfolk VA 23502

VOGEL, DONALD STANLEY, gallery executive, artist; b. Milw., Oct. 20, 1917; s. Walter Frederick and Francis Osborne (Talmadge) V.; m. Margaret Katherine Mayer, Oct. 14, 1947 (dec. June 1974); children—Eric Stefan, Kevin Eliot, Katherine Barley; m. Erika Kjar Farkac, Oct. 4, 1980. Student Chgo. Art Inst., 1936. With WPA Easel Project, Chgo., 1940; tech. dir. Dallas Little Theatre, 1942-43; dir. Betty McLean Gallery, Dallas, 1951-54; dir., owner Valley House Gallery, Dallas, 1954—; dir., ptnr. Main Place Gallery, Dallas, 1968-70. Author: (with Margaret Mayer) Aunt Clara: The Paintings of Clara McDonald Williamson, 1966. Author essays and catalogues. Mem. Art Dealers Assn. Am. Inc. Avocations: travel; swimming. Office: Valley House Gallery 6616 Spring Valley Rd Dallas TX 75240

VOGEL, GEOFFREY KENT, geophysicist; b. Austin, Tex., July 13, 1957; s. Ralph F. and Cecelia H. (Rohrs) V.; B.A. in Geology, Rice U., 1979. Geophysicist, Houston dist. Gulf Oil Corp., 1979-80, internat. exploration support, 1981-83, R.V. Hollis Hedberg seismic acquisition, 1984—. Mem. Am. Assn. Petroleum Geologists, Soc. Exploration Geophysicists. Home: 4327 Pease St Houston TX 77023

VOGEL, JOHNNA B., music educator, symphony musician; b. El Reno, Okla., Sept. 2, 1941; d. John Jacob and Bessie Juanita (Townsend) V. B. Music Edn., Oklahoma City U., 1964, Mus.B. in Violin Performance, 1964, M.A. in Teaching Music Edn., 1968. Tchr. string orch. Oklahoma City Pub. Schs., 1964—; musician playing sect. violin and viola Okla. Symphony Orchestra, 1965-84, Lawton Philharm. Orchestra, 1965—; musician playing prin. and sect. viola Wichita Falls Symphony Orchestra, Tex., 1984-85. Mem. Am. String Tchr. Assn., Music Educators Nat. Assn., Am. Fedn. Musicians (v.p. local 375) 1983-84. Methodist. Avocations: reading; needlepoint; cats; plants.

VOGEL, MARION LACK, college dean, librarian; b. Jersey City; d. Philip and Rose (Fondiller) Lack; m. Harry S. Vogel, Nov. 2, 1947; children—Nancy Roslyn Lack Feldman, Joan Elinor, Stephen Howard, Richard Joseph. B.A., Rutgers U., 1942; M.A., Columbia U., 1946. Reference, research librarian Am. Geog. Soc., N.Y.C., 1943-46; librarian, files analyst Elec. Bond Share Co., Inc., N.Y.C., 1946-49; head librarian Palmer Coll., Charleston, S.C., 1969-73; dir. learning resources Palmer campus Trident Tech. Coll., Charleston, 1973-78, dean learning resources, from 1978; cons. St. Francis Hosp., Charleston, 1st Fed. S.C., 1968. Pres. Nat. Council Jewish Women, Charleston, 1969-71; v.p. Mental Health Assn., Charleston, 1973-75, sisterhood Synagogue Emanu-El, Charleston, 1966-70; chmn. Family Life Forum Mental Health Assn., 1970-77. Recipient Citizenship award Synagogue Emanu-El, 1961. Mem. S.C. Library Assn., Columbia U. Grad. Assn., Soc. Am. Archivists, Soc. Ga. Archivists. Club: Charleston Bridge. Home: 624 Rebellion Rd Charleston SC 29407 Office: Trident Tech Coll 1 LR/M Box 29411 Charleston SC 29411

VOGEL, ROGER CRAIG, music educator, composer; b. Cleve., July 6, 1947; s. Joseph Casper and Nora Elsa (Farmer) V.; m. Kimberly Beth Horne, Aug. 26, 1978; 1 child, Craig Harrison. B.Mus., Ohio State U., 1971, M.A., 1972, Ph.D., 1975. Asst. prof. U. Ga., Athens, 1976-82, assoc. prof. music, 1982—. Composer: Concerto for Horn and Strings, 1981, other mus. compositions. Recipient Voice Category prize Delius Composition Competition, 1981. Mem. Am. Musicol. Soc., Coll. Music Soc., Broadcast Music Inc., Southeastern Composers' League, Pi Kappa Lambda. Avocation: photography. Home: 315 Camelot Dr Athens GA 30606 Office: U Ga Sch Music Athens GA 30602

VOGEL, WERNER PAUL, retired machine company executive; b. Louisville, June 15, 1923; s. Werner George and Emma (Bartman) V.; B. Mech. Engring., U. Louisville, 1950; m. Helen Louise Knapp, Oct. 2, 1954. With Henry Vogt Machine Co., Louisville, 1942—, asst. plant supt., 1957-60, plant supt., 1961-73, v.p., 1974-85, ret., 1986. Trustee, City of Strathmoor Village, Ky., 1959-61; clk. City of Glenview Manor, Ky., 1967-73, trustee, 1974-75; bd. dirs. Louisville Protestant Altenheim, 1979—, pres., 1984-86. Served with USAAF, 1944-46. Mem. ASME, Am. Welding Soc., Am. Def. Preparedness Assn., Tau Beta Pi, Sigma Tau. Republican. Methodist. Home: 29 Glenwood Rd Louisville KY 40222

VOGL, ERIC GEOFFREY, petroleum geologist; b. Wilmington, Del., Oct. 10, 1957; s. Otto and Jane (Cunningham) V.; m. Lisa Gail Smith, Aug. 1981. B.S., U. N.H., 1978; M.S., Kans. U., 1980. Petroleum geologist Exxon Co. U.S.A., Lafayette, La., 1980—. Mem. Am. Assn. Petroleum Geologists. Republican. Avocations: fishing; gardening; training labrador retrievers. Home: 131 Sandest Dr Lafayette LA 70508 Office: Exxon Co USA PO Box 50000 Lafayette LA 70505

VOGLER, HERBERT ALEXANDER, III, geologist; b. Winston-Salem, N.C., Dec. 11, 1955; s. Herbert A. and Frances Miller (Sowers) V.; m. Teracia Lane Gardner, July 30, 1983. B.S. with honors, U. N.C., 1978; M.S., U. N.Mex., 1983. Geologist Energy Reserves Group, Albuquerque, 1979; research asst. Lawrence Berkeley Labs., Calif., 1980; research asst. dept. geology U. N.Mex., Albuquerque, 1980-83; geologist Shell Offshore Inc., New Orleans, 1983—. Author: Major and Trace Element Geochemistry of the Laguna Del Perro Playa-Bolson Complex, 1983. Contbr. articles to profl. jours. Mem. Am. Assn. Petroleum Geologists, Soc. Econ. Geologists. Democrat. Mem. Moravian Ch. Avocations: photography; cross-country skiing. Home: 372 Blossom Ct Waggaman LA 70094 Office: Shell Offshore Inc One Shell Sq PO Box 61933 New Orleans LA 70161

VOGT, FRANCIS ELWOOD, consultant remote computing services and ADP systems and procurements; b. Steubenville, Ohio, Oct. 16, 1944; s. Francis Sebastian and Daisy (Darsic) V.; B.A. (scholar), Coll. of Steubenville, 1966; postgrad. Denver U., 1970-71; m. Donna Lee Philyaw, Oct. 28, 1978. Data systems mgr. State of Ohio, 1973-74; mathematician U.S. Navy, 1974-75; ops. research analyst U.S. Army, 1975-76; tech. adviser, negotiator teleprocessing services program GSA, 1976-77; gen. partner TSP Tng. Assos.; cons. automated data processing. Served as capt. USAF, 1966-70. Mem. Mensa. Research, implementation and deployment of guided bombs. Home: Route 621 Leesburg VA 22075 Office: PO Box 878 Leesburg VA 22075

VOGTLE, JESSE, electric utility company executive; b. 1934; married. A.B., U. Va., 1955, LL.B., 1958. Bar: Ala. 1958. Atty. firm Martin, Balch, Bingham, Hawthorne & Williams, until 1969; with Ala. Power Co., Birmingham, 1969—, sr. v.p., 1975-79, exec. v.p., 1978—. Office: Alabama Power Co Inc 600 N 18th St Box 2641 Birmingham AL 35291*

VOIGT, LYDIA, sociology educator; b. Bad Aibling, Fed. Republic Germany, Sept. 15, 1946; came to U.S. 1957, naturalized, 1969; d. Karl Gustav and Maria (Podhayni) V.; m. Thomas C. Cerullo, July 27, 1968 (div. 1982); children—Karl, Tanya; m. William E. Thornton, Jr., Sept. 15, 1984. B.A., Boston U., 1969; M.A., Boston Coll., 1971, Ph.D., 1977. Research assoc. Boston Coll., Chestnut Hill, Mass., 1969-73; research assoc., sociology lectr. Tulane U., New Orleans, 1974-76; asst. prof. Loyola U., New Orleans, 1977-83, assoc. prof., chmn. sociology dept., 1984—; cons., mem. New Orleans Social Welfare Adv. Bd., 1985—. Author: Limits of Justice, 1984; Delinquency and Justice, 1986. Contbr. articles to profl. jours. Cons. Youth study Ctr., New Orleans, 1980—. Mem. Am. Sociol. Assn., So. Sociol. Soc., Am. Assn. for Advancement of Slavic Studies, AAUW, Am. Criminological Soc., Acad. Criminal Justice Scis., Soc. for Study of Social Problems. Avocations: painting; piano; opera.

VOISINET, JAMES RAYMOND, building materials manufacturing company executive; b. Buffalo, June 18, 1931; s. Walter E. and Hildegarde M. (Optiz) V.; m. Virginia M. Waud, Sept. 14, 1957; children—James Raymond, Sarah, Anne. B.M.E., Cornell U., 1951; B.A. in Econs. cum laude, St. Lawrence U., 1954. Partner Weber, Loes, Weber Assos., Buffalo, 1956-62; dir. mktg. Gold Bond div. Nat. Gypsum Co., Charlotte, N.C., 1962-72, v.p. merchandising Gold Bond div., 1973-74, corp. group v.p., Dallas, 1974-80, v.p. internat. ops., 1980-81, v.p. corp. devel., 1982-83, corp. pres., chief operating officer, 1984—; dir. Compagnie du Platre, Isle sur Sorque, France, U.S. C. of C., Concorde Bank, Dallas. council U. Tex., Dallas. Served to 1st lt. U.S. Army, 1954-56. Republican. Roman Catholic. Clubs: Dallas (bd. dirs.), Northwood. Home: 6938 Meadowcreek Dr Dallas TX 75240 Office: 4500 Lincoln Plaza Dallas TX 75201

VOITH, CHARLES PATRICK, computer company sales executive; b. San Antonio, Nov. 7, 1950; s. Charles Kenneth, Jr. and Margaret Mary (Fogarty) V.; m. Nancy Lee Sharp, Jan. 5, 1955; children—Patrick Sharp, Austin Ousely. B.S. in Ops. Analysis, U.S. Naval Acad., 1973; M.B.A., Webster Coll., St. Louis, 1976. Instr., U.S. Naval Acad., Annapolis, Md., 1973-74; systems programming br. mgr. U.S. Marine Corps Automated Services Ctr., Kansas City, Mo., 1975-78; product mgr., bus. systems div. EDS Corp., Dallas, 1979-80; br. sales mgr., computer systems div. Tex. Instruments Corp., Dallas, 1981-82; Southwest ter. mgr. HBO and Co., Dallas, 1983—. Active Big Brothers Program, Dallas; Sunday sch. instr. Ch. of Resurrection Episcopal; treas. Copperridge Homeowners Assn., 1982—. Served to capt. USMC, 1973-78. Recipient Tex. Instruments Corp. Computer Sales Achievement award, 1981. Mem. Healthcare Fin. Mgmt. Assn., Tex. Hosp. Assn., Data Processing Mgmt. Assn., Tex. Hosp. Info. System Soc. Republican. Home: 13210 Roaring Springs Ln Dallas TX 75240 Office: 12700 Park Central Pl Suite 1406 Dallas TX 75251

VOLKER, JOSEPH FRANCIS, educator; b. Elizabeth, N.J., Mar. 9, 1913; s. Francis Joseph and Rose G. (Hennessey) V.; D.D.S., Ind. U., 1936; A.B., U. Rochester, 1938, M.S., 1939, Ph.D., 1941; D.Sc. (hon.), U. Med. Sci., Thailand, 1967; Dr. honoris causa, Lund U., Sweden, 1968, U. Louis Pasteur de Strasbourg, 1972; D.Sc. (hon.), Ind. U., 1970, U. Ala., 1970, Coll. Medicine and Dentistry, N.J., 1973, U. Rochester, 1975, Georgetown U., 1978, Fairleigh Dickinson U., 1978, U. Ariz., 1978; Professor (honoris causa), Federal do Rio de Janeiro, 1977; LL.D., Troy State U., 1980; m. Juanita Berry, Feb. 6, 1937; children—Joseph Francis, Juanita Anne, John Berry. Dental intern Mountainside Hosp., Montclair, N.J., 1936-37; Carnegie fellow in dentistry U. Rochester, 1937-41, asst. prof. biochemistry, 1941-42; prof. clin. dentistry Dental Sch., Tufts Coll., 1942-47, dean, 1947-49; dean U. Ala. Sch. Dentistry, 1948-62, dir. research and grad. studies U. Ala. Med. Center, 1955-65, v.p. health affairs, 1962-66, v.p. Birmingham Affairs, 1966-68, dir. Med. Center, Birmingham, 1966-68, exec. v.p. U. Ala. Birmingham, 1968-69, pres., 1969-76, disting. prof., 1982—; chancellor U. Ala. System, University, 1976-82; dir. Ariz. Med. Sch. Study, 1960-61, Dept. State teaching specialist, Thailand, 1951; mem. Unitarian Service committee's med. teaching mission to Czechoslovakia, 1946, Germany, 1948. Bd. regents Nat. Library Medicine, 1973-77. Decorated Order White Lion (Czechoslovakia), Most Noble Order Crown (Thailand); comdr. Order Falcon, Republic Iceland; fellow in dental surgery Royal Coll. Surgeons Eng., 1961; fellow faculty dentistry Royal Coll. Surgeons Ireland, 1973. Diplomate Am. Bd. Oral Medicine. Mem. Inst. Medicine of Nat. Acad. Scis., Soc. Exptl. Biology and Medicine, ADA, Am. Chem. Soc., Internat. Assn. Dental Research, Sigma Xi, Omicron Kappa Upsilon, Alpha Omega Alpha. Club: Cosmos. Home: 2725 11th Ave S Birmingham AL 35205 Office: University of Ala Box 85 SDB University Station Birmingham AL 35294

VOLKER, JUANITA ANNE, counselor, educator, administrator; b. Boston, July 5, 1944; d. Joseph Francis and Juanita Anne (Berry) V.; 1 child, Jennifer Elizabeth. B.A. in Speech, U. Montevallo, 1966; M.A. in Spl. Edn., U. Ala.-Tuscaloosa, 1969, Ph.D. in Adminstrn. Higher Edn., 1986; Ed.S. in Counseling, Vanderbilt U., 1977; postgrad. Rutgers U., 1982, U. Ga., 1982. Lic. profl. counselor; cert. alcoholism counselor; grad. cert. gerontology. Intake counselor Diagnostic Clinic for Mentally Retarded Children, Birmingham, Ala., 1966-68; tchr. edn. mentally retarded Nashville Davidson County, Nashville, 1969-70; welfare worker State Tenn., Nashville, 1970-71; spl. edn./social work liaison Ctr. Devel. and Learning Disabilities, Birmingham, 1971-73; coordinator Employee Assistance Service Alcoholism Council, Birmingham, 1981-82, dir., 1982—. Bd. dirs. Birmingham Urban League, 1971-73, ARC Youth Com., Birmingham, 1972-73, Nashville, 1973-74; del. Nat. Red Cross Conv. New Orleans, 1973, Ala. Jud. System, Birmingham, 1973. Fellow U. Ala., 1968-69, Brookwood Lodge Found., 1982. Mem. Am. Assn. Counseling and Devel., Assn. Labor-Mgmt. (sec. treas. state chpt. 1982-83), Adminstrs. and Cons. on Alcoholism (v.p. state chpt. 1985—), Nat. Assn. for Alcoholism and Drug Abuse Counselors, State Cert. Bd., North Am. Congress on Employee Assistance Programs (charter mem.), Zeta Phi Eta, Kappa Delta Phi. Episcopalian. Avocations: reading, drawing, cooking, writing. Home: 1600 Barry Ave Birmingham AL 35209

VOLKMAN, ALVIN, pathologist, educator; b. Bklyn., June 10, 1926; s. Henry Phillip and Sarah Lucille (Silverstein) V.; m. Winifred Joan Grinnell, June 12, 1947 (div. Aug. 1967); children—Karl Frederick, Nicholas James, Rebecca Jane Evans, Margaret Rose Werrell, Deborah Ann Falls; m. 2d, Carol Ann Fishel, Jan. 26, 1973; 1 dau., Natalie Fishel. B.S., Union Coll., 1947; M.D., U. Buffalo, 1951; D.Philosophy, U. Oxford (Eng.), 1963. Diplomate Nat. Bd. Med. Examiners, Am. Bd. Pathology. Intern, Mt. Sinai Hosp., Cleve., 1951-52; research fellow dept. anatomy Western Res. U. Sch. Medicine, 1952-54; resident, then sr. resident, then asst. in pathology Peter Bent Brigham Hosp., Boston, 1956-60; asst. prof. pathology Columbia U. Coll. Physicians and Surgeons, 1960-66; asst. mem., then assoc. mem. Trudeau Inst., Saranac Lake, N.Y., 1966-67; prof. dept. pathology East Carolina U. Sch. Medicine, Greenville, N.C., 1977—; mem. NIH study sect. immunological scis., 1975-79, chmn., 1977-79. Served to lt. USNR, 1952-54. Am. Cancer Soc. scholar, 1961-63. Mem. Am. Assn. Immunologists, Am. Soc. Hematology, Reticuloendothelial Soc., Am. Soc. Microbiologists, AAAS, N.Y. Acad. Scis. Contbr. articles to sci. jours. Office: Dept Pathology Brody Bldg East Carolina U School Medicine Greenville NC 27834

VOLLBEER, FRED H., financial executive; b. Davenport, Iowa, Jan. 3, 1944; s. Walter H. and Fern J. (Holst) V.; B.B.A., U. Iowa, 1966; 1 son, Robert Scott. With Berlage Bernstein Builders, Alexandria, Va., 1971-72; v.p. fin. L.A. Clarke & Son, Inc., Washington, 1972-76, also dir.; controller Micro Systems, Inc., Vienna, Va., 1976-77; chief fin. officer Williams Lumber Co. Inc., Rocky Mount, N.C., 1977-78; personal bus. mgr. to Roy J. Carver, founder, chmn. bd. Bandag, 1978-82; gen. mgr. Carver Enterprises, Miami, Fla., 1978-82; personal bus. mgr. to J.B. Fuqua, founder, chmn. bd. Fuqua Industries, 1982-83; pres. Fuqua Nat., Inc., Atlanta; v.p. investments Acorn Fin. Services, Inc., Atlanta, also dir.; owner Fred H. Vollbeer Fin. Services. Served with USAF, 1968-71. Mem. Alpha Kappa Psi. Club: Benvenue Country (Rocky Mount). Home: 2740 Habersham Rd Atlanta GA 30305 Office: 8 Piedmont Center Suite 608 Atlanta GA 30305

VOLLERTSEN, RUSSELL ARMIN, computer company executive, antiques retailer; b. Berger, Mo., Jan. 11, 1924; s. Harry George and Verona Emelia (Schaeffer) V.; m. Loys Marie Howell, Sept. 14, 1943; children—Conrad, Vernon, Bruce, Jon. B.S., U.S. Naval Acad., 1947; B.S. in Elec. Engring., U.S. Naval Postgrad. Sch., 1957, M.S. Computer Sci., 1972; grad. Command and Staff Coll., 1961, Naval War Coll., 1966. Commd. ensign U.S. Navy, 1947, advanced through grades to capt., 1968; ret. 1975; asst. br. mgr. System Devel. Corp., Slidell, La., 1975-76, br. mgr., 1976—. Mem. NASA Productivity Council, Marshall Space Flight Ctr., Ala., 1983-84. Originator Operation Sea-Dragon, 1967, recipient Vietnam Cross Gallantry, 1968. U.S. rep. NATO Armaments group, Paris, 1961-63, chmn. electronic data transmission com., Brussels, 1970-71, chmn. communications navigation com., Brussels, 1974-75. Decorated Bronze Star with Combat V; Disting. service Order (Vietnam). Mem. Naval Inst., Naval Acad. Alumni Assn., New Orleans Automatic Data Processing Council. Republican. Club: Nat. Space. Avocations: Outdoor activities; hunting; fishing. Home: 130 Middle Pearl Dr Slidell LA 70458 Office: System Devel Corp 1010 Cause Blvd Slidell LA 70458

VOLPE, ANGELO ANTHONY, university administrator, chemistry educator; b. N.Y.C., Nov. 8, 1938; s. Bernard Charles and Serafina (Martorana) V.; m. Jennette Murray, May 15, 1965. B.S., Bklyn. Coll., 1959; M.S., U. Md., 1962, Ph.D., 1966; M.Engring. (hons.), Stevens Inst. Tech., 1975. Research chemist U.S. Naval Ordnance Lab., Silver Spring, Md., 1961-66; asst. prof. to prof. of chemistry Stevens Inst. Tech., Hoboken, N.J., 1966-77; chmn. dept. chemistry East Carolina U., Greenville, N.C., 1977-80, dean. coll. arts and scis., 1980-83, vice chancelor for acad. affairs, 1983—; adj. prof. textile chem. N.C. State U., Raleigh, 1978-82; guest lect. Plastics Inst. Am., Hoboken, 1967—. Contbr. articles to profl. jours. Recipient Ednl. Service award Plastics Inst. Am., 1973; named Freygang Outstanding Tchr., Stevens Inst. Tech., 1975. Mem. Am. Chem. Soc., N.C. Acad. of Scis., Sigma Xi, Phi Kappa Phi. Democrat. Roman Catholic. Avocations: golf; reading. Home: 109 Queen Anne's Rd Greenville NC 27834 Office: East Carolina U Greenville NC 27834

VON DER LIPPE, EDWARD JOSEPH, museum director; b. Newark, Jan. 24, 1934; s. John C. and Josefine (Sixt) von der L.; m. Hannelore A. Eckhardt, July 30, 1964; children—Kevin, Douglas and Bruce (twins). A.A., Fairleigh Dickinson U., 1960, B.A., 1963. Mus. asst. Newark Mus., 1958; mus. docent (part-time) Am. Mus. Natural History, N.Y.C., 1959-61; supr. jr. mus. Newark Mus., 1964-66; dir. Natural Sci. Ctr., Greensboro, N.C., 1966—; zoo cons. Turtle Back Zoo, West Orange, N.J., 1964-65; mus. cons. Dan Nicholas Nature Ctr., Salisbury, N.C., 1974-75. Asst. scoutmaster Gen. Greene council Boy Scouts Am. Louis S. Thompson scholar, 1960; Fairleigh Dickinson U. archaeol. scholar, 1963; recipient Elsie M.B. Naumburg award Nat. Sci. for Youth Found., 1973; named Man of Yr., Greensboro Beautiful, 1984. Fellow Am. Assn. Zool. Parks and Aquariums; mem. Am. Assn. Museums, Nat. Sci. for Youth Found., Assn. Sci. Mus. Dirs., N.C. Mus. Council. Republican. Lutheran. Lodge: Optimists (sec. Greensboro 1970-73). Avocations: stamp, coin collecting. Office: Natural Sci Ctr of Greensboro 4301 Lawndale Dr Greensboro NC 27408

VON NIMITZ, WALTER WILHELM, research institute executive, consultant; b. Ukraine, Apr. 18, 1926; came to U.S., 1951, naturalized, 1957; s. Wilhelm A. and Anna (Ruban) von N.; m. Martha D. Duke, Dec. 3, 1983. Dipl. Eng., Tech. U. Munich, Fed. Republic Germany, 1950; Ph.D., Internat. Coll., Los Angeles, 1980. Sr. research physicist SW Research Inst., San Antonio, 1957-66, sect. mgr., 1966-69, asst. dir., 1969-74, dir., 1974—, cons., 1966—; guest lectr. Tex. A&M U., College Station, 1979—. Contbr. numerous articles to profl. publs.; author, contbr. research reports, tng. seminar vols. Bd. dirs. Contact Crisis Line, San Antonio, 1983—. Recipient Disting. Service award So. Gas Assn., 1979. Mem. ASME (v.p. 1983—. vice chmn. council on engring. 1984—). Home: 6616 Countess Adria Ln San Antonio TX 78238 Office: SW Research Inst 6220 Culebra Rd San Antonio TX 78284

VON RAFFLER-ENGEL, WALBURGA, linguist, educator; b. Munich, Germany, Sept. 25, 1920; came to U.S., 1949, naturalized, 1955; d. Friedrich J. and Gertrud E. (Kiefer) von Raffler; m. A. Ferdinand Engel, June 2, 1957; children—Lea Maxine, Eric Robert von Raffler. D.Litt., U. Turin, Italy, 1947; M.S., Columbia U., 1951; Ph.D., Ind. U., 1953. Freelance journalist, 1949-58; mem. faculty Bennett Coll., Greensboro, N.C., 1953-55, Morris Harvey Coll., Charleston, W.Va., 1955-57, Adelphi U., CUNY, 1957-58, NYU, 1957-59, U. Florence, Italy, 1959-60, Istituto Post Universitario Organizzazione Aziendale, Italy, 1960-61, Bologna Center of Johns Hopkins U., 1964; mem. faculty Vanderbilt U., Nashville, 1965—, asso. prof. linguistics, 1966-77, prof., 1977—, dir. linguistics program, 1978—; chmn. com. on linguistics Nashville Univ. Center, 1974-79; vis. prof. U. Ottawa, 1971-72, Inst. for Lang. Scis., Tokyo, 1976, faculty devel. course Shanxi U., People's Republic of China; sr. research assoc. Inst. for Pub. Policy Studies, 1986—; grant evaluator NSF, NEH, Can. Council; manuscript reader Ind. U. Press, U. Ill. Press, Prentice-Hall; cons. Trinity U., Simon Frazer U. Author: Il prelinguaggio infantile, 1964; The Perception of Nonverbal Behavior in the Career Interview, 1983; co-author: Language Intervention Programs 1960-74, 1975. Editor, co-editor 10 books. Author film and videotape. Contbr. over 250 articles to profl. and popular publs. Grantee Am Council Learned Socs., NSF, Can. Council, Ford Found., Kenan Venture Fund, Japanese Ministry Edn., NATO, Finnish Acad., Meharry Med. Coll., Internat. Sociol. Assn., Internat. Council Linguists, Tex. A&M U., Vanderbilt U., also others. Mem. AAUP, Internat. Linguistics Assn., Linguistic Soc. Am. (chmn. golden anniversary film com. 1974, session chmn. profl. conf. 1983), Internat. Assn. Applied Linguistics (com. on discourse analyses, sessions chmn. 1978), Internat. Sociol. Assn. (research com. on sociolinguistics, session co-chmn. profl. conf. 1983), Inst. Nonverbal Communication Research (workshop leader 1980, 81), Lang. Origins Soc. (exec. bd. 1984—), Tenn. Conf. on Linguistics (pres. 1976), Semiotic Soc. Am. (organizing com. Internat. Semiotics Inst. 1981), Internat. Assn. for Study of Child Lang. (chmn. internat. conf. 1972, v.p. 1975-78). Office: Vanderbilt U Nashville TN 37235

VON ROSS, HANS-WILHELM, architect, consultant; b. Velbert, Germany; came to U.S., 1957, naturalized, 1961. B. Arch., U. Houston, 1976. Pres., owner von Ross & Co., Dallas, 1974—; cons. Oasis Oil Co., Lybia, Tripoli, 1975-77, Aramco, Dhahran, Saudi Arabia, 1979-81, Arabian Rukan, Dammam, Saudi Arabia, 1981-83, Wright-Rich Architects, Dallas, 1985—. Mem. Constrn. Specification Inst., AIA, Profl. Engring. Inst. Republican. Avocations: sailing; snow skiing; travel; chess.

VON SELDENECK, JUDITH CROWELL, educator, interior designer; b. New Rochelle, N.Y., Feb. 12, 1945; d. Robert Kenyon and Susan Ann (Mitchell) Crowell; B.A., U. Richmond (Va.), 1967; cert. N.Y. Sch. Interior Design, 1971; m. Roger Dean von Seldeneck, June 24, 1967; 1 son, Jeffrey Dean. Tchr. English, Augusta County (Va.), 1967-69; asst. to designers Young Assos., Staunton, Va., 1969-70; self-employed interior designer, Lynchburg, Va., 1971-74; tchr. design Balt. County Adult Edn., 1976-78; tchr. bus. English and interior design Patricia Stevens Career Coll., Balt., 1979; substitute tchr. Harrisonburg City and Rockingham County (Va.), 1981-83. Instr., Harrisonburg Recreation Dept., 1980-83; interior designer, sales/showroom mgr. Va. Craftsmen, Inc., 1983-85; owner von S Interiors, 1985—. Mem. DAR (chpt. 2d vice regent 1981-83, chpt. regent 1983—, asst. to state treas. 1983—, nat. vice chmn. pages) U. Richmond Westhampton Coll. Alumnae Assn. (nat. v.p. 1975-77). Republican. Clubs: Lynchburg Jr. Woman's (rec. sec. 1973-74); Valley Intermediate Pacesetters (sec. 1980-82) (Harrisonburg); Harrisonburg Jr. Woman's Club (co-chmn. hospitality com. 1982-83). Address: 88 Maplehurst Ave Harrisonburg VA 22801

VON TRESCKOW-NAPP, RALPH, psychotherapist, consultant, educator; b. Bridgeport, Conn., Sept. 5, 1921; s. Emil A. Napp and Helene (von Tresckow) N.; m. Hannelore Rath; children—Ralph Jr., Winifred-Alice. B.A., U. Ala., 1947; postgrad. U. Munich, 1951-57; M.Ed. in Edn., Duke U., 1960, Ed.D., 1964. Cert. marital and family therapist, N.C. Lectr., U.S. Dept. State, W.Ger., 1951-57, 68; grad. asst. sociology and anthropology Duke U., Durham, N.C., 1958-59; from asst. prof. to assoc. prof. sociology East Carolina U., 1957-69; assoc. prof. sociology James Madison U., 1969-71; prof., coordinator sociology, rep. univ. council internat. programs Winston-Salem U., 1971-82; Intern group psychotherapy Western Va. State Hosp., Staunton, summer 1971; intern group marital psychotherapy with Dr. Ali Jarrahi, Winston-Salem, N.C., 1974-76; tng. marriage and family counseling and therapy dept. psychiatry Bowman Gray Sch. Medicine, Winston-Salem, 1978-79; marital psychotherapist, Winston-Salem, N.C., 1974—. Mem. Interracial Council, Greenville, N.C., 1966-69; pres. Jr. High Sch. PTA, 1966-67; state and precinct del. Democratic Party, 1972; cons. Upward Bound, 1972. Served with USAR, 1943-50 ETO; officer, parachutist, Korea. Named 1 of 10 outstanding profs. East Carolina U., 1965; recipient cert. of honor Winston-Salem Pub. Safety Dept., 1977. Mem. N.C. Sociol. Assn., So. Sociol. Soc., AAUP (treas. 1966, pres. 1972-74), Am. Sociol. Assn., Internat. Council Edn. for Teaching, Nat. Council Family Relations, Popular Culture in South (pres. 1979-80), Am. Assn. Marriage and Family Therapists (clin. mem.), Nat. Psychiat. Assn. (life), Kappa Delta Pi, Pi Gamma Mu. Co-author: Breaking Down the Barrier, 1961; author book revs. and poems; contbr. articles to profl. jours. Home: 2605 Club Park Rd Winston-Salem NC 27104 Office: Psychol Evaluation and Therapy Clinic 322 N Spring St Winston-Salem NC 27101

VOORHEES, LARRY DONALD, environmental science researcher; b. Benson, Minn., Dec. 23, 1946; s. Donald Henry and Eunice Judell (Fragodt) V.; m. Carol Jean Groneberg, Sept. 6, 1970; children—Luke, Kimberly. B.A., U. Minn., 1970; M.S., N.D. State U., 1972, Ph.D., 1976. Cert. wildlife biologist. Instr. N.D. State U., Fargo, 1974-75, research assoc., 1975-76; mem. research staff Oak Ridge Nat. Lab., 1976—. Mem. Transp. Research Bd., Nat. Research Council, 1978-84, mem. Task Force Wildlife and Fisheries Issues, 1981. Served with U.S. Army N.G., 1965-71. Mem. Wildlife Soc., Ecol. Soc. Am., AAAS, N.D. Natural Sci. Soc., Sigma Xi. Lutheran. Contbr. articles to profl. publs. Home: 213 Newport Rd Knoxville TN 37922 Office: PO Box X Oak Ridge Nat Lab Oak Ridge TN 37831

VOORHEES, LOUIS EUGENE, horticulturist, former naval officer, publisher; b. Merced, Calif., Dec. 12, 1918; s. Louis Carlyle and Hazel Ellen

(Chandler) V.; m. Jeanette Cox, Nov. 14, 1946; children—James Cox, Steven Chandler. A.B. in Edn., Fresno State U., 1942. Served with U.S. Navy, 1942-63, comdr., 1958; Mich. rep. Oakite Products, Inc., 1963-78; owner Garden Cons., Atlanta, 1978—; pub. Yardman's Atlanta Almanac, 1978—; writer, editor, lectr. Supplier, St. Luke's Community Kitchen, Atlanta, 1982—; lectr. Emory Sr. U., Atlanta, 1981—. Recipient David S. Ball award Oakite Products, Inc., 1972. Mem. Am. Hort. Soc., Ga. Hort. Soc., Am. Camellia Soc. Methodist. Lodges: Masons, Elks.

VOORHIES, RICHARD JOSEPH, civil engineer; b. Wellsville, N.Y., July 23, 1948; s. James Francis and Levinia (Cronin) V.; m. Linda Byron, Nov. 15, 1969; children—Ryan Joseph, Duane Spencer. Assoc. Applied Sci., Monroe Community Coll., Rochester, N.Y., 1973; B.Engring., Rochester Inst. Tech., 1976. Civil technician Robert E. Smith, Rochester, 1967-68, Lozier Engrs., Inc., Rochester, 1969-71; civil technologist Pipeline Services, Inc., New Harford, N.Y., 1972, Erdman, Anthony Assocs., Rochester, 1973-76; asst. project mgr. Edminster, Hinshaw, Russ, Houston, 1976-78; v.p., civil engr. Century Engring., Inc., Houston, 1978—. Mem. Houston Livestock Show and Rodeo, 1983—. Served with U.S. Army, 1968-69, Vietnam. Mem. Water Pollution Control Fedn., Am. Congress Surveying and Mapping, Constrn. Specification Inst., Tex. Surveyors Assn. (assoc.). Roman Catholic. Club: Sports Car of Am. (Houston). Avocations: sports car racing. Home: 619 Sancroft Ct Katy TX 77450 Office: Century Engring Inc 9950 Westpark St Suite 200 Houston TX 77063

VOROUS, MARGARET ESTELLE, educator; b. Charles Town, W.Va., Feb. 14, 1947; d. Benjamin Welton and Helen Virginia (Owens) Vorous; A.A. in Pre-Edn. (Laureate scholar), Potomac State Coll., W.Va. U., 1967; B.S. in Elem. Edn., James Madison U., 1970, M.S. in Edn., 1975, postgrad., spring 1978, fall 1979, summer 1979, 81; postgrad. U. Va., summers 1977, 78, fall 1978. Tchr. 3d-4th grade Highview Sch., Frederick County, Va., 1968-69, 3d grade Kernstown Elem. Sch., Frederick County, 1970-71, E. Wilson Morrison Elem. Sch., Front Royal, Va., 1971-72, Stonewall Elem. Sch., Frederick County, 1972-78; tchr. 4th grade South Jefferson Elem. Sch., Jefferson County (W.Va.) Schs., 1978-79, Emergency Sch. Aid Act reading tchr./reading specialist, 1980-82, reading tchr./specialist Page Jackson Solar Elem. Sch., 1983—; adult basic edn. tchr. Dowell J. Howard Vocat. Ctr., Winchester, Va., 1984-86, G.E.D. tchr., 1985-86; tchr. 4th grade Ranson (W.Va.) Elem. Sch., 1979; reading tutor; art rep. Creative Arts Festival at Kernstown, 1971, Stonewall elem. schs., 1973-77; mem. cultural task force Frederick County Sch., 1974-75, music task force, 1973-74, textbook adoption com. for reading, writing, 1976-77. Active Pilot Club of Winchester (Va.), Inc., 1976-81, rec. sec., 1979-80, chaplain, 1980-81, edn. area leader, 1981-82; vol. fundraiser Am. Cancer Soc., Frederick County, Va., 1981. Mem. Frederick County Polit. Action Com., Jefferson County Polit. Action Com.; del. 103-109th Ann. Diocesan Convs., Episcopal Ch., registrar of vestry Grace Episcopal Ch., Middleway, W.Va., 1980—, lic. lay reader, 1980—, lic. chalice bearer, 1983—. Recipient various awards, including being named Miss Alpine Princess, Sigma Phi Omega, 1967. Mem. Internat. Reading Assn., Va. Reading Assn., Shenandoah Valley Reading Council, Assn. Supervision and Curriculum Devel., W.Va. Edn. Assn., NEA. Jefferson County Edn. Assn. (faculty rep.), South Jefferson PTA, Potomac State Coll. Alumni Assn., James Madison U. Alumni Assn., Frederick County Democratic Women, Kappa Delta Pi. Founder, editor The Reading Gazette, The Reading Tribune, Emergency Sch. Aid Act Reading Program, South Jefferson Elem. Sch., 1980-81, Shepherdstown Elem. Sch., 1981-82; creator numerous reading games, activities. Office: Page-Jackson Solar Elem Sch Route 1 Box 322M Charles Town WV 25414

VORWERK, E. CHARLSIE, artist; b. Tennga, Ga., Jan. 28, 1934; d. James A. and Hester L. (Davis) Pritchett; A.B., Ga. State Coll. for Women, 1955; m. Norman T. Vorwerk, Feb. 9, 1956; children—Karl, Lauren, Michael. Billboard design artist Vanesco Poster, Chattanooga, 1955; cartographic draftsman TVA, Chattanooga, 1955; fashion illustrator Loveman's, Chattanooga, 1956; free lance comml. artist, 1957—; pvt. art instr. children and adults, all media, 1966—; art instr. continuing edn. Bapt. Coll. Charleston, S.C., 1979-82; coordinator Washington Park Picolo Spoleto Art Exhibit, 1983. Mem. Bd. Archtl. Rev., Summerville, 1976—; YMCA Flowertown Festival Art Exhibit chmn., 1972-84; mem. women's bd. St. Paul's Episcopal Ch. 1968-83; active Boy Scouts Am., Girl Scouts U.S.A.; vol. Mental Health Clinic, 1972-74, others. Recipient Centaur award Italian Art Acad., 1982. Mem. Charleston Artists Guild, League of Charleston Artists, Miniature Art Soc. Fla., Beaufort Art Assn., Am. Art Soc., Italian Art Acad. Illustrator: Tales and Taradidales; St. Paul's Epitahs; Captain Tom, others. Address: 315 W Carolina Ave Summerville SC 29483

VOTAW, ROBERT HENRY, wholesale and retail hardware company executive, business management educator; b. Walters, Okla., May 7, 1936; s. Hershel Edward and Hazel (Turnage) V.; m. Emily Joan Harden, July 25, 1958; children—Robert Glenn, Wesley Scott, Kelly Christine, Laura Sue. B.B.A., U. Okla., 1962; diploma LaSalle Extension U., Chgo., 1969; M.B.A., Pepperdine U., 1980. Sales mgr. Hallmark Cards Inc., Kansas City, Mo., 1964-80; pres., gen. mgr. Votaw Properties, Inc., Garland, 1980—; prof. bus. mgmt. Amber U., Garland, Tex., 1981—; cons. in field Author: Profit Management, 1985; How to Start a Business, 1985; Financing a Business, 1985; Acquisition Analysis, 1985. Chmn. Tex. Assn. Bus., Garland, 1985, Warehouse Edn. Research Council, Dallas, 1985; active Nat. Fedn. Ind. Bus., Dallas, 1985. Served with USMC, 1954-57. Republican. Mem. Ch. of Christ. Avocation: tennis. Home: Route 2 Box 45AA Royse City TX 75089 Office: Votaw Properties Inc 2609 Forest Ln Garland TX 75042

VOYLES, JAMES HOMER, III, architect, developer, architectural consultant; b. Munich, Germany, Feb. 5, 1950; s. James Homer and Doris (Patterson) V.; m. Susan Foster, Aug. 21, 1976; children—Mary Elizabeth, Kathryn Foster. A.A., Los Angeles Valley Coll., 1970; B.Arch., U. Ariz., 1974; M.Arch., U. So. Calif., 1977. Lic. architect, Calif. Designer Archisystems Internat., Van Nuys, Calif., 1974-78; asst. project architect Thompson, Ventulett, Stainback Assocs., Inc., Atlanta, 1978-81; project architect Toombs, Amisano, Wells, Inc., Atlanta, 1981-82; project dir., architect W.B. Johnson Properties, Inc., Atlanta, 1982-84; mgr.-architect Equitable Life Assurance Soc. Am., 1984—; v.p. architecture HAPVAS, Inc. Cons. Services, Atlanta, 1981—. Chmn. adv. council 2d Ponce de Leon Baptist Ch., Atlanta, 1982-83, coach recreation sport team, 1970-72. Gerontology fellow, 1976-77. Mem. AIA (Assoc. award 1979), Atlanta Hist. Soc. Republican. Home: 275 Apt 34 Collier Rd Atlanta GA 30309 Office: 3414 Peachtree Rd Suite 252 Atlanta GA 30326

VYAS, DILEEPKUMAR RAMANLAL, physician; b. Kadod, Gujarat, India, May 22, 1941; s. Ramlal Manishanker and Nirmalaben V.; M.B., B.S., M.P.Shah Med. Coll., Jamnagar, Gujarat, 1970; m. Kokila Patel, Mar. 13, 1967; 1 son, 1 dau. Intern, New Civil Hosp. and B.J. Med. Coll., Ahmedabad, India, 1970-71; resident in pediatrics Harlem Hosp. Center, N.Y.C., 1971-74; fellow in pediatric hematology oncology Babies Hosp., Columbia U., N.Y.C., 1974-75, Montefiore Hosp., Bronx, 1975-76; practice medicine specializing in pediatrics and pediatric hematology, Tigard, Oreg., 1978-79, El Dorado, Ark., 1979—; clin. instr. U. Oreg. Health Sci. Center, Portland, 1978-79; asst. clin. prof. pediatrics and community medicine Area Health Edn. Center U. Ark. for Med. Scis., El Dorado, 1982—. Diplomate Am. Bd. Pediatrics. Mem. Ark. Med. Assn., Union County Med. Soc., Am. Soc. Pediatric Hematology-Oncology, Am. Profl. Practice Assn. Office: 317 Thompson St El Dorado AR 71730

VYAS, PREMILA HARIPRASAD, education educator, researcher, consultant; b. Dholka, India, Aug. 19, 1928; came to U.S., Apr. 11, 1964, naturalized, 1975; d. Bhimshanker and Pramoda (Desai) Oza; m. Harjprasad Vyas, May 2, 1957 (dec. May 9, 1964). B.A. with honors, Gujarat U., India, 1947; B.Ed., M.S. U., India, 1954; diploma in edn. London U., 1962; M.A., U. Houston, 1964, D.Ed., 1967. Instr. M.S. U., Baroda, India, 1962-63; research fellow Gulf Sch., Houston, 1967-68; asst. prof. Tex. So. U., Houston, 1967-77, assoc. prof. edn., 1977—; presentor numerous papers to profl. assns. Contbr. articles to profl. jours., to Houston Post. Editor Joyti Hindu Workshop Soc., 1976-77. Author: (booklet) Indian Cookbook, 1964. Recipient Fulbright-Hays award, 1981, cert. achievement Tex. So. U., 1976, scholarship Tex. State Tchrs. Assn., 1967, Alpha Tchrs. Sorority, 1966-67, Altrusa Internat. Orgn. 1965-66. Mem. Am. Coll. Personnel Assn. (chmn. conv. session 1979, dir. Commn. X, 1983, 84, 85), AAUP (v.p. Tex. So. U. chpt. 1975). Avocations: swimming; dancing. Home: 4038 O'Meara Houston TX 77025 Office: Texas So U 3201 Wheeler Ave Houston TX 77004

WACHS, ROBERT FAULL, cemetery company executive; b. Covington, Ky., Mar. 24, 1932; s. Carl Bernard and Elizabeth (Faull) W.; m. Mildred Desmond, June 7, 1952; children—Cheryl Elizabeth, Teresa Lynn, Helen Lorraine, Robert Douglas. B.S. in Agr., U. Ky., 1954. Mem. staff Lexington Cemetery, Ky., 1956-58, asst. mgr., 1958-73, gen. mgr., 1973—. Mem. adv. bd. Salvation Army, Lexington, Served with U.S. Army, 1952-54. Mem. Am. Cemetery Assn., So. Cemetery Assn., Cremation Assn. N.A., Am. Assn. Bot. Gardens and Arborets, Inc. Mormon. Avocations: nature; hiking; camping; boating; photography. Home: 1027 W Main St Lexington KY 40508 Office: Lexington Cemetery Co 833 W Main St Lexington KY 40508

WACHTER, ROBERT GORDON, commercial land development company executive; b. Waynesboro, Pa., Apr. 3, 1952; s. Lester Pryor and Thelma (Gordon) W.; m. Susan Rebecca Short, Aug. 18, 1973; 1 dau., Kourtney Christine. B.Arch. Engring., Pa. State U., 1976; student U. Pa., 1970-72, U. Dayton, 1980-81. Constrn. project mgr. B.G. Danis Co., Dayton, Ohio, 1976-81; design project mgr. U.S. Lend Lease, Inc., Dallas, 1981-82; v.p. comml. land devel. Dimension Devel. Co., Inc., Dallas, 1982—. Address 3700 Cross Bend Plano TX 75023

WACKENHUT, GEORGE RUSSELL, security services executive; b. Phila., Sept. 3, 1919; s. William Henry and Frances (Hogan) W.; student U. Pa. 1937-38, State Tchrs. Coll., West Chester, Pa., 1938-41; B.S., U. Hawaii, 1943; postgrad. Temple U., 1946; M.Ed., Johns Hopkins U., 1949; m. Ruth Johann Bell, Apr. 8, 1944; children—Janis Lynn Wackenhut Ward, Richard Russell. Dir. phys. edn. profl. program tchr. tng., head coach soccer wrestling and track Johns Hopkins, 1946-50; civilian cons. recreational sports br. Office Spl. Services, U.S. Army, Washington, 1950-51; spl. agt. FBI, 1950-54; dir. personnel, security and safety Giffin Industries, Inc., Miami, Fla., 1954; pres., chmn. bd. Spl. Agt. Investigators, Inc., Spl. Agts. Security Guards, Inc., Security Services Corp. (all Miami), 1954-58; pres., chmn. bd., dir. Wackenhut Corp., Coral Gables, Fla., 1958—; chmn. Wackenhut Systems Corp., Titania Advt., Inc., Wackenhut of Alaska, Inc.; chmn., pres. Wackenhut Services, Inc.; chmn. bd., dir. NUSAC, Inc., Stellar Systems, Inc., Am. Guard and Alert, Inc., Wackenhut Internat., Inc., Wackenhut of North Africa, Inc.; pres. Titania Ins. Co., Ltd.; dir. chmn. bd. Wackenhut del Ecuador SA, Wackenhut N. Africa Inc., Titania Advt., NUSAC, Steelar Systems, Wackenhut of Alaska, Inc., Am. Guard an Alert Inc. Wackenhut of Can., Ltd., Wackenhut S.A., Wackenhut U.K. Ltd., Wackenhut Dominicana, S.A., Wackenhut del Ecuador, S.A., dir. S.A., Wackenhut Research Corp., Wackenhut Keibi, K.K.-Japan Servicos Profesionales de Proteccion y Seguridad, S.A., Wackenhut Korea corp., Venezolana de Sequridad y Vigilancia C.A., PROSEC, Inc. Mem. law enforcement council Nat. Council Crime and Delinquency, 1971—. Bd. dirs. Heart Assn. of Greater Miami, 1965-66, Gov.'s War on Crime, Fla., 1967-70; bd. visitors U.S. Army M.P. Sch., 1972-74. Served with AUS, 1941-45. Mem. Soc. Former Spl. Agts. FBI, Inc., Am. Soc. for Indsl. Security, AIM (pres.'s council 1964-66). Christian Scientist. Clubs: Ocean Reef (Key Largo, Fla.); Palm Bay, Grove Isle (Miami). Home: 20 Casuarina Concourse Gables Estates Coral Gables FL 33143 Office: 3280 Ponce de Leon Blvd Coral Gables FL 33134

WACKER, JOHN AUGUST, construction company executive; b. Temple, Tex., Oct. 24, 1920; s. John August and Charlotte (Dickson) W.; m. Lee Pinkston, Oct. 20, 1950; children—Lisa, Lauren. B.S. in Archtl. Engring., U. Tex., Austin, 1943. With J.W. Bateson Co., Dallas, 1946-66, chmn., 1966—; exec. v.p. Centex Corp., Dallas, 1983—, dir., 1966—; chmn. Rooney Enterprises, Ft. Lauderdale, Fla., 1979—, M.H. Golden Co., San Diego, 1982; dir. Eugene Simpson & Brother, Alexandria, Va., Sherry Ln. Nat. Bank. Chmn. U. Tex. System Bd. Regents Adv. Com. for Capital Improvement; chmn. nat. sci. studies com. Assn. Children with Learning Disabilities; pres. Wacker Found. Served to 1st lt. USAF, 1943-45. Methodist. Author: The Dyslogic Syndrome, 1975. Home: 10848 Strait Ln Dallas TX 75229 Office: 4600 Republic Bank Tower Dallas TX 75201

WADDELL, CHARLES LINDY, state senator; b. Braselton, Ga., May 13, 1932; m. Marie V. Dawson. Mem. Va. Senate, 1972—. Mem. Democratic State Central Com., Loudoun County Bd. Suprs., 1968-71, Vets. Affairs Commn.; state dir. Va. Wildlife Fedn.; founding mem. Potomac Baptist Ch.; active Lower Loudoun Little League. Named Man of Yr., Loudoun Times Mirror, 1971; Handicapped Unlimited Legislator of Yr., 1981; VWF Conservationist of Yr., 1978. Mem. Sterling Park Jaycees (charter), Va. Jaycees (life). Lodge: Masons. Office: Va Senate Gen Assembly Bldg 9th and Broad Sts Richmond VA 23219*

WADDELL, GUILFORD THOMAS, III, financial adviser; b. Charlotte, N.C., Sept. 10, 1949; s. Guilford Thomas and Ella Frances (Cochrane) W.; B.A., U. N.C., 1971, M.B.A., 1974; m. Mary Gwendolyn Hightower, Aug. 20, 1972; children—Jennifer Mary, Guilford Thomas, IV. Asso., Chris C. Crenshaw & Assos., ins. brokers, Durham, N.C., 1974-75; mng. partner Easton & Waddell, Chapel Hill, N.C., 1975-79; pres. Waddell Benefit Plans, Inc., Chapel Hill, 1979—; pres. JenMar Securities, Inc., 1983—; vis. lectr. U. N.C., Chapel Hill, 1978-81. Ruling elder Univ. Presbyn. Ch., 1980-85, co-chmn. bldg. fund campaign, 1979; dist. chmn. Carolina Ann. Giving, 1979—, United Way, 1978, 83; mem. U. N.C. Ednl. Found., 1976—. Recipient Disting. Service award Nat. Assn. Life Underwriters, 1979; C.L.U. Mem. N.C. Assn. Life Underwriters (ethics com. 1979, legis. com. 1981), Durham Assn. Life Underwriters (pres. 1981), Am. Soc. C.L.U.s, Chapel Hill-Carrboro C. of C., Durham C. of C., Am. Mgmt. Assn., U. N.C. Gen. Alumni Assn. (treas.), Million Dollar Round Table, Order Golden Fleece, Chartered Fin. Cons. Democrat. Clubs: Chapel Hill Country (golf com. 1978, tennis com. 1979), Chancellor's (U. N.C.). Contbr. articles to profl. publs. Home: 2110 N Lake Shore Dr Chapel Hill NC 27514 Office: 890 Airport Rd PO Drawer 3616 Chapel Hill NC 27515

WADDELL, MATHIS THERON, JR., political science educator; b. Goose Creek, Tex., Dec. 10, 1941; s. Mathis Theron and Alva Olive (Eason) W.; m. Judith E. Smith, Aug. 25, 1962 (div. June 1979); 1 dau., Wendy Lee; m. Jeri Lynette Jaquis, July 13, 1985. B.A., U. Tex., 1962, M.A., 1963, postgrad. Adminstrv. aide to state senator, 1963-65, 67; instr. Sam Houston State U., 1963-64, Houston Bapt. U., 1964, San Antonio Coll., 1965-66, San Jacinto (Tex.) Coll., 1967-69; prof. polit. sci. Galveston Coll. (Tex.), 1969—, also asst. to pres. Chmn. Democratic Party, Galveston County, Tex., 1980—. Mem. Nidwest Polit. Sci. Assn., S.W. Polit. Sci. Assn., So. Polit. Sci. Assn., Tex. Jr. Coll. Tchrs. Assn. Democrat. Presbyterian (ruling elder). Contbr. articles to In Between Mag. Office: M-330 Galveston Coll 4015 Ave Q Galveston TX 77550

WADDILL, MARCELLUS EMRON, mathematics educator; b. North Garden, Va., Apr. 28, 1930; s. Charles Wilson and Sallie Ann (King) W.; m. Shirley Ann Funk, Aug. 10, 1957; children—David Howard, Dan Wilson. B.A., Hampden-Sydney Coll., 1952; M.A., U. Pitts., 1953, Ph.D., 1962. Instr. Hampden-Sydney Coll. (Va.), 1956-58; grad. asst. U. Pitts., 1958-61, instr., 1962; asst. prof. Wake Forest U., Winston-Salem, N.C., 1962-67, assoc. prof., 1967-77, prof., chmn. dept. math., 1980—; cons. Western Electric Co., Princeton, N.J., 1965—. Served to 1t. USNR, 1953-61. Mellon fellow, 1961. Mem. Math. Assn. Am., Am. Math. Soc., Fibonacci Assn., AAUP, N.C. Acad. Sci., Phi Beta Kappa, Sigma Chi. Democrat. Baptist. Contbr. articles to profl. jours. Home: 3385 Sledd Ct Winston-Salem NC 27106 Office: Box 7311 Winston-Salem NC 27104

WADDLE, GERALD LEE, marketing educator; b. Conneaut, Ohio, Aug. 16, 1943; s. Thomas Edward and Elizabeth (Glisson) W.; m. Pamela Stowers, Nov. 3, 1973; children—Laura Elizabeth, Erin Leigh. B.A., Baldwin Wallace Coll., 1965; M.B.A., Kent State U., 1968; Ph.D. in Bus. Adminstrn., U. S.C., 1973. Asst. dir. admission Baldwin Wallace Coll., Berea, Ohio, 1967-68; instr. mktg. Ind. State U., Terre Haute, 1968-70, U. S.C., Columbia, 1971-73; prof. Clemson U., S.C., 1973—, chmn. mktg. dept., 1982—, dir. Small Bus. Inst.; cons. Palmetto Bank, Laurens, S.C., 1977-78; advisor Greenville Tech. Coll., 1984—. Contbr. articles to profl. jours. NDEA fellow U. S.C., 1970-73. Mem. So. Mktg. Assn., Mid-Atlantic Mktg. Assn., Am. Mktg. Assn., Sierra Club (mem. exec. com.), Omicron Delta Epsilon, Beta Gamma Sigma. Republican. Presbyterian. Home: 103 Shady Ln Clemson SC 29631 Office: Dept Mktg Clemson U Clemson SC 29631

WADE, ARNOLD, college administrator; b. Huntingburg, Ind., Jan. 24, 1943; s. Clarence Wesley and Marjorie Mae (Leathco) W.; m. RuthAnn Helena Popp, June 5, 1965; 1 child, James Kevin. B.M.E., Evansville Coll., 1964; M.S. in Edn., Purdue U., 1966, Ph.D., 1972. Counselor U. Evansville, Ind., 1966-69; counselor, asst. dir. Purdue U., West Lafayette, Ind., 1969-72; asst. prof. edn. U. Wis.-Superior, 1972-80; assoc. prof. edn. Hardin-Simmons U., Abilene, Tex., 1980-81; dir. counseling services Ga. Coll., Milledgeville, 1981—. Contbr. articles to profl. jours. Musical dir. SPEBSQSA, Duluth, 1975-80, Macon, Ga., 1984—; actor, singer Ga. Coll. Theater, Milledgeville, 1984. Recipient Spl. Merit Teaching award U. Wis.-Superior, 1977. Mem. Am. Assn. Counseling and Devel., Am. Coll. Personnel Assn., Assn. Measurement and Evaluation in Counseling and Devel., Assn. Counselor Edn. and Supervision, So. Assn. Coll. Student Affairs, Ga. Coll. Personnel Assn. Methodist. Avocations: singing; golf; photography. Home: 1844 Holly Hill Rd Milledgeville GA 31061 Office: Ga Coll CPO 61 Milledgeville GA 31061

WADE, HENRY MENASCO, district attorney; b. Rockwall, Tex., Nov. 11, 1914; s. Judge Henry M. and Lula Ellen (Michie) W.; m. Gladys Yvonne Hillman, Jan. 10, 1948; children—Michelle Wade Branderburger, Kim, Henry M. Jr., Wendy Wade Ballew, Bari Wade Tiffin. LL.B. with highest honors, U. Tex., 1938. Bar: Tex. 1938. Pres. U. Tex. Law Sch., 1937-38, chancellors, 1938; county atty. Rockwall County, Tex.; spl. agt. FBI, 1939; asst. dist. atty. Dallas County, Dallas, 1947-49, dist. atty., 1951—. Served to lt. j.g. USN, 1943-46. Order of Coif, 1938; named Citizens of Yr. Kiwanis Club Dallas, 1973; recipient Orchids & Onions award Free Enterprise of So. Meth. U., 1976; named Father of Yr.; recipient Press Club All-Time Headliner award, Dallas, 1980. Mem. Dallas Alliance of Business, Dallas County Juvenile Services Adv. Com., FOCAS (Foster Care Child Placement Program), Youth Services Network, Soc. Former Spl. Agts. FBI, Open, Inc., Delta Theta Phi., YMCA. Democrat. Mem. First Community Ch. Lodges: Lions (Oak Cliff); Masons. Office: District Attorney's Office 600 Commerce St 7th Floor Dallas TX 75202

WADE, KATHLEEN ANN, nurse, administrator; b. Waterloo, Iowa, June 23, 1945; d. George Dewy and LaVon Fay (Short) Zimmer; m. Eugene Robert Wade, Aug. 20, 1963; children—Kelly Suzanne, Dianne Kay, Janelle Lynn, Brenda Jean. B.A. in Social Sci., U. South Fla., 1972; B.A. in Nursing, U. Central Fla., 1982. Cert. critical care nurse; cert. emergency nurse. Staff nurse Bay Front Med. Ctr., St. Petersburg, Fla., 1976-77, Sebastian River Med. Ctr., Fla., 1978-82; nurse mgr. Humana Hosp., Sebastian, 1982-83, assoc. exec. dir. nursing, 1983—; adv. Fla. Inst. Tech. Coll. Health, Jensen Beach, Mem. Fla. Soc. Hosp. Nursing Service Adminstrs., U. Central Fla. Nursing Honor Soc., Phi Kappa Phi. Republican. Lutheran. Home: 3160 Ellis Dr Melbourne FL 32901 Office: Humana Hosp 13695 US 1 Sebastian FL 32958

WADE, NEILL GILLESPIE, lawyer; b. Jacksonville, Fla., Jan. 16, 1951; s. Neill G. and Virginia (Sikes) W.; m. Debborrah Ponder, June 23, 1973. B.S. in Criminology, Fla. State U., 1974, J.D., 1977. Bar: Fla. 1977, U.S. Dist. Ct. (mid. dist.) Fla. 1978, U.S. Dist. Ct. (no. dist.) Fla. 1980. Asst. state atty. 20th Jud. Cir. Fla., Fort Myers, 1977-80, 2d Jud. Cir. Fla., Quincy, 1980—; mem. exec. council criminal law sect. Fla. Bar, 1980-83; lectr. in field. Contbr. chpt. to Florida Criminal Rules and Practice, 1983. Mem. Gadsden County Bar Assn. (pres. 1983-84), Nat. Dist. Attys. Assn., Fla. Peace Officers Assn. Lodge: Kiwanis (Quincy) (pres. 1983-84). Office: Office of State Atty Gadsden County Courthouse Quincy FL 32351

WADSWORTH, HARRISON MORTON, JR., industrial engineering educator, consultant; b. Duluth, Minn., Aug. 20, 1924; s. Harrison Morton and Alice English (Densmore) W.; m. Irene Hawkins, Nov. 16, 1950; children—Harrison M. III, Alice E. Wadsworth Lunsford. B.S. in Indsl. Engring., Ga. Inst. Tech., 1950, M.S. in Indsl. Engring., 1955; Ph.D., Case Western Res. U., 1960. Registered profl. engr., Ohio. Quality control engr. Union Carbide Corp., Cleve., 1954-56; asst. prof. indsl. engring. Mich. State U., East Lansing, 1956-57; research assoc. Case Western Res. U., Cleve., 1957-60; vis. prof. Middle East Tech. U., Ankara, Turkey, 1967-68; assoc. prof. Ga. Inst. Tech., Atlanta, 1960-64, prof., 1964—; pvt. practice cons., Atlanta, 1960—. Author: (with others) Modern Methods for Quality Control and Improvement, 1986. Editor: Jour. Quality Tech. (Appreciation award 1982), 1979-82; Handbook of Statistics, 1985. Contbr. articles to profl. jours. Served with U.S. Army, 1943-46, PTO. Fellow Am. Soc. Quality Control (Brumbaugh award 1970, Austin Bonis award 1985); mem. Inst. Indsl. Engrs. (sr.), Am. Statis. Assn., Am. Soc. Engring. Edn., Sigma Xi. Home: 660 Valley Green Dr NE Atlanta GA 30342 Office: Ga Inst Tech Atlanta GA 30332

WAESCHE, R(ICHARD) H(ENLEY) WOODWARD, combustion research scientist; b. Balt., Dec. 20, 1930; s. J(oseph) Edward and Margaret Steuart (Woodward) W.; m. Lucy Spotswood White, June 29, 1957; children—Charles Russell, Ann Spotswood. B.A., Williams Coll., 1952; postgrad. U. Ala., 1956-58; M.A., Princeton U., 1962, Ph.D., 1965. Research scientist Rohm & Haas Redstone div., Huntsville, Ala., 1954-59; research asst. Princeton U., 1961-64; sr. research scientist Rohm & Haas, Huntsville, 1964-66; sr. research engr. United Tech. Research Ctr., East Hartford, Conn., 1966-81; prin. scientist Atlantic Research Corp., Gainesville, Va., 1981—; cons. Goodyear Corp., 1959-60, Princeton U., 1965. Assoc. editor Jour. Spacecraft and Rockets, 1975-80, editor-in-chief, 1980—; contbr. numerous articles to profl. jours. Chmn. Fine Arts Commn., Glastonbury, Conn., 1975-77. Served to cpl. U.S. Army, 1952-54. Guggenheim fellow, 1959-61. Mem. Am. Phys. Soc., Combustion Inst., AIAA (chmn. propellants and combustion tech. com. 1975-77, propulsion tech. group coordinator 1979-81, tech. activities com. 1979—, publs. com. 1980—), Sigma Xi. Episcopalian. Club: Evergreen Country (Haymarket, Va.). Home: 4319 Banbury Dr Gainesville VA 22065 Office: Atlantic Research Corp 7511 Wellington Rd Gainesville VA 22065

WAGENBLATT, FREDERICK JOSEPH, chef; b. New Haven, May 15, 1955; s. Francis Lewis and Ola Janet (Everett) W.; m. Kay Marie Schaar, Oct. 15, 1982. Assoc. Occup. Studies in Culinary Arts, Culinary Inst. Am., 1979. Sous chef Jackson Lake Lodge, Moran, Wyo., 1980, 81, 82; chef Park Plaza Hotel, Helena, Mont., 1982-83; cons. Grand Union Hotel, Fort Benton, Mont., 1983-84; exec. chef Clydes of Tyson's Vienna, Va., 1984—. Mem. Am. Culinary Fedn. Roman Catholic. Avocations: gardening; hiking; winemaking; reading; canoeing. Home: 1434 1-B Northgate Sq Reston VA 22090 Office: Clydes of Tysons Corner 8332 Leesburg Pike Vienna VA 22020

WAGENER, JAMES WILBUR, university president; b. Edgewood, Tex., Mar. 18, 1930; s. James W. and Ima (Crump) W.; m. Ruth Elaine Hoffman, May 31, 1952; children—LuAnn Wagener Powers, Laurie Kay Wagener Hill. B.A., So. Methodist U., 1951; M.A., U. Tex., Austin, 1967, Ph.D. (Ellis fellow 1967-68), 1968. Instr. edn. U. Tex., Austin, 1967-68, asst. prof., 1970-74, U. Tenn., Knoxville, 1968-70; asst. to chancellor acad. affairs U. Tex. System, 1974; assoc. prof. U. Tex., San Antonio, 1974-78, acting pres., 1978, pres., 1978—, prof. div. edn. Coll. Multidisciplinary Studies, 1978—; asst. to pres., then exec. asst. to pres. U. Tex. Health Sci. Center, San Antonio, 1974-78, acting dean Dental Sch., 1976-78. Author articles, book revs. in field. Bd. govs. Southwest Found. Research and Edn., San Antonio, 1978—; bd. dirs., trustee Southwest Research Inst., San Antonio, 1978—. Mem. Am. Ednl. Studies Assn., Assn. Instl. Research, Soc. Profs. Edn., Soc. Coll. and Univ. Planning, Greater San Antonio C. of C., Phi Delta Kappa, Phi Theta Kappa. Club: Torch. Lodge: Rotary. Office: Univ Tex San Antonio TX 78285*

WAGENER, LEE EDSON, airport management executive; b. Chgo., June 21, 1920; s. William F. and Charlotte (Williams) W.; B.B.A., Northwestern U., 1941; m. Anne E.; children—Carol J., David L. With Western Electric Co., 1941-48; dir. airports Broward County, Ft. Lauderdale, Fla., 1948-83; pres. Airport Mgmt. Services, 1983—; dir. Barrett, Inc., Joliet, Ill., Barrett Hardware Co., Joliet; dir. Airport Ops. Council Internat. Served to lt. comdr. USNR, 1942-46; PTO. Recipient Top Mgmt. award Sales and Mktg. Execs. Club, Ft. Lauderdale, 1962. Mem. Southeastern Airport Mgrs. Assn. (pres. 1957), Am. Assn. Airport Execs. (pres., 1968-69), Ft. Lauderdale C. of C., Am. Legion, Quiet Birdmen, Assn. Naval Aviation. Mason. Club: Congressional Flying (Washington). Home: 1668 S Ocean Ln Fort Lauderdale FL 33316 Office: 1668 S Ocean Ln Fort Lauderdale FL 33316

WAGENHEIM, CHARLES, builder/developer executive; b. N.Y.C., May 10, 1946; s. Walter and Beatrice (Maniloff) W.; m. Mary Ellen Matthews, June 8, 1969; children—David Walter, Daniel Abraham, Michael Jeffery. A.S., Miami Dade Community Coll., 1969; B.S., Fla. Internat. U., 1978; M.B.A., U. Miami, 1982. Pres., Wagenheim Constrn. Corp., Miami, 1970-73; dir. constrn. Centex Homes of Fla., Miami, 1973-81; pres. Lexington Homes of Fla., Inc., Boca Raton, 1981—. Arbitrator, Am. Arbitration Assn., Miami, 1978-86; mem. 11th jud. cir. grievance com. Fla. Bar, Miami, 1983-86; mem. Palm Beach County Citizens Task Force. Served with USMCR, 1967-73. Mem. Am. Inst. Constructors, Constrn. Specifications Inst., Nat. Assn. Homebuilders, Fla. Home Builders Assn. (dir. 1985-86), Homebuilders and Contractors Assn. of

Palm Beach County (dir. 1984-865), Builders Assn. S. Fla. (dir. 1981-83), Sigma Lambda Chi (pres. 1977-78). Republican. Jewish. Home: 8441 SW 180th St Miami FL 33157 Office: Lexington Homes Fla Inc 5521A Coach House Circle Boca Raton FL 33432

WAGGONNER, JOSEPH DAVID, III, architect; b. Shreveport, La., Feb. 27, 1949; s. Joseph David Jr. and Mary Ruth (Carter) W. B.A., Duke U., 1971; M. Arch., Yale U., 1975. Draftsman, Architect of the Capitol, Washington, 1974; archtl. designer Bechtel Corp., San Francisco, 1976-78; staff architect DMJM Curtis & Davis, New Orleans, 1978-80; assoc. Labouisse, Graeber Ltd., New Orleans, 1980-82; prin. Labouisse & Waggonner, New Orleans, 1982—; vis. critic Tulane U., New Orleans, 1980—, design prof., 1983-84; vis. Critic Williams Coll., 1985. Architect: 400 Lafayette St. (Gambit Best Comml. Renovation award 1984), 1981-84, 430 Notre Dame St (LAA Honor award 1984), 1982-84. NEA grantee, 1983, 85. Mem. AIA, La. Architects Assn. (Design Festival Presentation 1984), Nat. Trust Hist. Preservation, Preservation Resource Ctr., Am. Film Soc. Democrat. Methodist. Office: Labouisse & Waggonner Architects 2200 Prytania St New Orleans LA 70130

WAGNER, ALAN B., manufacturing and financial executive; b. Balt., June 8, 1938; s. Robert Ellsworth and Anna Margaret (Schnitzlein) W.; B.Engring. Sci. (scholastic leadership award) John Hopkins, 1960; M.M.E., Case-Western Res. U., 1962, Ph.D. in Bus. Mgmt., 1965; m. Lynn Felton Wynant, June 26, 1964; children—Brian Alan, David Scott, Elizabeth Lynn. Mgr. orgn. planning and devel. Internat. Minerals & Chem. Corp., Libertyville, Ill., 1964-67, dir. indsl. relations, 1967-70, v.p. div. orgn. and indsl. relations, 1970-73, corporate v.p. adminstrn., 1973-79; pres. Taylor Tot Products, Inc., 1979-80, Fed. Mining Co., Inc., Lexington, Ky., 1980-82; pres. Wagner Mgmt. Corp., Lexington, 1982—; dir. Sobin Chems., Inc., Hilliard-Lyons, Wagner Assocs., Ky. Metals, Inc.; lectr. in field. Trustee Union Coll. Fellow Alfred P. Sloan Nat. Found. Mem. Chgo. Assn. Commerce and Industry, Chem. Industries Council of Midwest, ASME, Am. Mgmt. Assn., ASHRAE (Homer Addams award), AAAS, Ky. Coal Assn. (dir. 1977—), Lexington C. of C., Sigma Xi, Omicron Delta Kappa. Clubs: Knollwood (Lake Forest, Ill); Greenbriar Golf and Country, Lafayette (Lexington, Ky.). Home: 1523 Lakewood Ct Lexington KY 40502 Office: 110 W Vine St Lexington KY 40507

WAGNER, BERNARD RAYMOND, public residential facility administrator; b. Chgo., June 17, 1940; s. Bernard Anthony and Anne (Leemputtee) W.; m. Joyce Stumpf; children—Christine, Amy, Gary. B.A., U. Denver, 1962; M.A., U. Ill., 1965, Ph.D., 1967. Dir. PACE, Decatur, Ill., 1968-73; acting area dir. Devel. Disabilities Area Central Ind., 1978-81; supt. New Castle Hosp., Ind., 1973-82, Ga. Retardation Ctr., Atlanta, 1982—; mem. adj. faculty Ga. State U., Atlanta, 1985, U. Ill., Urbana, 1969-73; cons. in field. Contbr. articles to profl. jours. Chmn. bd. dirs. Henry County Community Action Program, Ind., 1980, Fontainebleau Community Ctr., Atlanta, 1985. Named Outstanding State Employee Ill., 1971. Fellow Am. Assn. on Mental Deficiency (v.p. 1985—); Nat. Assn. Supts. Pub. Residential Facilities for Mentally Retarded (pres. 1983-84), Nat. Assn. of Devel. Disabilities Mgrs. (pres. 1985—). Club: New Castle Country (Ind.) (bd. dirs. 1981-82). Home: 7158 Chalet Ct Doraville GA 30360 Office: Ga Retardation Ctr 4770 N Peachtree Rd Atlanta GA 30338

WAGNER, FRED JOHN, JR., petroleum geologist; b. Phila., Feb. 7, 1929; s. Fred John and Dorothy V. (Burrows) W.; m. Carolyn Lipe, June 4, 1955; children—Fred John III, Kristin L. B.S. in Geology, Franklin and Marshall Coll., 1951; M.A. in Geology, Washington U., St. Louis, 1954; postgrad. Tulsa U., 1969-71. Research geologist Standard Oil Co. of N.J. including Carter Oil Co., Tulsa, Jersey Prodn. Research Co., Tulsa, Esso Standard Libya, Tripoli, 1953-68; petroleum systems engr. IBM, Tulsa, 1968-69; staff geologist, profl. specialist, planning geologist Skelly Oil Co. (merged with Getty Oil Co.), Tulsa, 1969-79, ops. research coordinator Getty Oil Co., Tulsa, supr. geologic research, Houston, 1979-81; mgr. exploration/exploitation, Williams Exploration Co., Tulsa, 1981-82; lead geologist offshore ops., mgr. exploration computing systems, Getty Oil Co., Houston, 1982-84, regional exploration geologist, 1984-85; exploration systems adviser; mem. com. on U.S. drilling stats., com. on drilling and producing expenditures Am. Petroleum Inst.; mem. Adv. Council Petroleum Data System; instr. continuing edn. Tulsa U., 1981-82. Editor Geobyte, Am. Assn. Petroleum Geologists, Tulsa, 1985—. Served with U.S. Army, 1955-57. Mem. Am. Assn. Petroleum Geologists (AAPG-Am. Petroleum Inst. joint com. for statis. integrity of discovery data 1981—, cert. petroleum geologist, chmn. com. on stats. of drilling 1973-75, cert. of merit 1975), Am. Inst. Profl. Geologists (cert. geologist), Soc. Petroleum Engrs. of AIME, Tulsa Geol. Soc., Houston Geol. Soc. Home: 5206 S Harvard Unit 232 Tulsa OK 74135 Office: PO Box 979 Tulsa OK 74101

WAGNER, FREDERIC EMIL, oil and gas company executive; b. Waco, Tex., Aug. 14, 1920; s. Frederic Emil and Ernestine (Clements) W.; student U. Tex., Arlington, 1940-42, So. Meth. U., 1942-43; B.S., U. Tex., Austin, 1946; m. Ellen Marie Seay, Dec. 15, 1964; children—Jory, Hilda. Founder, Williams & Wagner Constrn. Co., Inc., Dallas, 1946, founder oil div. Eldorado Oil and Gas, Inc., 1950, pres. Williams & Wagner Constrn., Co., Inc. and Eldorado Oil and Gas, Inc., 1946—; U.S. rep. Lifefield N.V. Mem. oil and gas com. Tex. Gov.'s Energy Commn., 1976-77; mem. oil and gas com. Tex. Energy Adv. Council, 1978-79. Recipient Disting. Service award Nat. Exchange Club, 1950. Mem. Council Sci. Socs., Am. Soc. Photogrammetry, Photogrammetry Soc. London, Calif. Racing Hall of Fame, Soc. Petroleum Engrs., Tex. Thoroughbred Breeders Assn., Tex. Thoroughbred Racing Assn., Calif. Thoroughbred Breeders Assn., Horsemen's Benevolent Protective Assn., U.S. Power Squadron, USCG Aux., Dallas Opera Guild, others. Clubs: Brookhaven Country, Cipango, Petroleum, Commerce, Dallas Gun, Pala Mesa Golf, Brook Hollow Golf. Author: Aircraft Lofting Practice, 1943. Home: 8801 Jourdan Way Dallas TX 75225 Office: Eldorado Oil & Gas Inc 8150 N Central Expwy Suite 225 Dallas TX 75206

WAGNER, HENRY CARRH, III, hospital executive; b. Charleston, W.Va., Oct. 30, 1942; s. Henry C. and Margurite (Halstead) W.; m. Elisabeth Anne Tibbott, Sept. 12, 1964; children—Stephanie, Jeffrey, Alex. B.S., W.Va. U., 1964; M.H.A., Duke U., 1966. Assoc. dir. Univ. Hosp., Cleve., 1966-73; exec. v.p. Jewish Hosp., Louisville, Ky., 1973-82, pres., 1982—; pres. Hosp. Council Met. Louisville, 1979, Ohio Valley Hosp. Dist., Louisville, 1980. Bd. dirs. Louisville Orch., 1983-85, Met. United Way, Louisville, 1984—, Spalding U., Louisville, 1985—; alumnus Leadership Louisville, 1983—, Louisville C. of C., 1986—. Served to 1st lt. U.S. Army, 1966-68. Mem. Am. Coll. Healthcare Execs., Ky. Hosp. Assn. (bd. dirs. 1979-84), Premier Hosps. Alliance (treas. 1984—). Republican. Methodist. Club: Hunting Creek (Louisville). Lodge: Masons. Office: Jewish Hosp 217 E Chestnut St Louisville KY 40202

WAGNER, JOHN EDWARD, former army officer, civil engineer; b. Springfield, Mo., Oct. 11, 1927; s. Nicholas Edward and Esther Caroline (Anderson) W.; m. Louise Wagner, July 29, 1950; children—John Edward, Mary Louise. Student Drury Coll., 1945-46; B.S., U.S. Mil. Acad., 1950; M.S., U. Ill., Urbana, 1959, Ph.D., 1961; M.B.A., George Washington U., 1980. Registered profl. engr., N.Y., Ill. Commd. 2d lt. U.S. Army, 1950, advanced through grades to col., 1970; engr. 1st field Force, Vietnam, 1970-71; dir. U.S. Army Engr. Topographic Lab., Ft. Belvoir, 1971-74; dep. dir. Army research Dept. Army, Washington, 1974-77; asst. for energy conservation Office Sec. Def., Washington, 1977-79; dep. div. engr. Corps Engrs., N.Y.C., 1979-81; sr. staff officer NRC, 1981-84; sr. civil engr. ANSER, 1984—. Decorated Legion of Merit, Meritorious Service Medal, Air medal. Fellow ASCE; mem. Soc. Am. Mil. Engrs., Nat. Soc. Profl. Engrs., Am. Soc. Photogrammetry, Assn. U.S. Army, Sigma Xi, Phi Kappa Phi. Antarctic geol. feature Wagner Spur named in his honor, 1971. Home: 3229 First Pl N Arlington VA 22201 Office: 1215 Jefferson Davis Hwy Arlington VA 22202

WAGNER, JON REED, dentist; b. Orange, Calif., Nov. 8, 1935; s. John S. and Elizabeth E. (Allen) W.; m. Sharon M. Nall, Aug. 27, 1960; children—Suzanne, Jonathan, Jason. A.A., Fullerton Jr. Coll., 1961; student U. Oreg.; D.D.S., Marquette U., 1966. Dentist in pvt. practice, Pensacola, Fla., 1970—; v.p. Wagner Investments Corp., Pensacola. Contbr. articles to profl. jours. Fellow Internat. Congress Oral Implantology; mem. ADA, Am. Endodontic Soc., Am. Soc. Preventive Dentistry, Am. Acad. Implant Dentistry, Am. Coll. Implantology. Avocations: saltwater fishing; investing; painting; music. Office: 7100 Plantation Rd Suite 9 Pensacola FL 32504

WAGNER, RENÉE MICHELLE, chemist; b. Pa.; d. Elmer L. Wagner; B.S., Wake Forest U., 1978; Ph.D., Pa. State U.-State College, 1982. Research chemist U.S. Dept. Agr., College Station, 1982—. Contbr. articles to profl. jours. Mem. N.Y. Acad. Sci., Internat. Union Pure and Applied Chemistry, Am. Inst. Chemists, Am. Chem. Soc. Republican. Roman Catholic. Office: US Dept Agr College Station TX 77841

WAGNER, SARA BAILEY, consulting company executive; b. Connellsville, Pa., May 20, 1921; d. William Orel and Bertha (Hooper) Bailey; m. William Vernon Wagner, Jr., Mar. 24, 1945; children—Mary Louise, William Vernon, III. B.A., Pa. State U., 1942; M.A., Mich. State U., 1967; Ed.D., Wayne State U., 1972. Dir. research Nat. Council on Aging, Washington, 1972-75; sr. assoc. JWK Internat. Corp., Annandale, Va., 1975-78, v.p., 1978—; adj. prof. Wayne State U., Detroit, 1967-72, Marygrove Coll., Detroit, 1971-72, George Mason U., Fairfax, Va., 1972-74. Contbr. reports to profl. publs. Mem. Am. Psychol. Assn., Nat. Council Measurement in Edn., Am. Soc. Tng. and Devel. Republican. Presbyterian. Avocations: photography; travel; flowers. Office: JWK Internat Corp 7617 Little River Turnpike Annandale VA 22003

WAGNER, STANLEY PAUL, university president; b. Ambridge, Pa., Mar. 22, 1923; s. Stephan and Anna (Wojtkowski) W.; B.A., U. Pitts., 1947, M.A., 1949, Ph.D., 1953; m. Diana Mills, Oct. 20, 1945; 1 dau., Kathleen Anne (Mrs. James E. Lawler). Instr. social scis. Muskingum Coll., 1950-54; asst. prof. Allegheny Coll., 1954-62; prof. history and polit. sci., chmn. dept., asso. dean arts and scis. Oklahoma City U., 1962-68; vice-chancellor acad. affairs Minn. State Colls., 1968-69, pres. East Central Okla. State U., Ada, 1969—; cons. Allegheny Coll. Guidance Clinic, summers 1955-69. Mem. Commn. Orgn. Govt. for Conduct Fgn. Policy, 1972-75. Chmn. Ada Community Chest drive, 1970. Pres. East Central Okla. State U. Found. Served with AUS, 1942-45. Episcopalian. Rotarian. Author: The End of Revolution, 1970. Office: Office of Pres East Central Okla State U Ada OK 74820

WAGNON, DAVID JONES, oil and gas investment executive; b. Oklahoma City, Apr. 30, 1937; s. Joseph Preston and Mable Rozelle (Jones) W.; m. Mary Jane Aikman, Mar. 4, 1972; children—Jay David, Jeffrey Dane, David Jordan. B.A. in Mktg., Okla. State U., 1960; M.B.A. in Fin., So. Meth. U., 1976. Dist. mktg. dir. Phillips Petroleum Co., 1960-63; regional mktg. mgr. hosp. div. Johnson & Johnson, 1963-67; project mgr. Americare Corp., 1967-72; exec. v.p. Metal Market, 1972-76; v.p. corp. devel. Hunt Internat. Resources, 1976-78; exec. v.p., chief operating officer, dir., chmn. fin. com. Sunshine Mining Co., 1977-81; pres. Mission Energy Corp., Dallas, 1981—; chmn. bd., chief exec. officer Texona Petroleum Co. Mem. Gov.'s Bus. Task Force, Tex. and Idaho. Mem. Am. Mgmt. Assn., Am. Mining Congress, Nat. Assn. Corp. Dirs., Silver Inst. (bd. dirs.), Northwest Mining Assn., Alaska Mining Assn. Republican. Methodist. Clubs: Royal Oaks Country; City, Chaparral (Dallas). Office: 9400 N Central Expressway Suite 414 709 Dallas TX 75231

WAGONER, JENNINGS LEE, JR., history of education educator; b. Winston-Salem, N.C., July 26, 1938; s. Jennings Lee and Carolyn Nelme (Phifer) W.; m. Shirley Canady, Aug. 12, 1962; children—David Carroll, Brian Jennings. B.A., Wake Forest U., 1960; M.A.Teaching, Duke U., 1961; Ph.D., Ohio State U., 1968. Tchr. High Point Pub. Schs., N.C., 1960-62; instr. Wake Forest U., 1962-65; teaching assoc. Ohio State U., 1965-68; from asst. prof. to prof. history of edn. U. Va., Charlottesville, 1968—, chmn. leadership and policy studies, 1985—; vis. research scholar Harvard U., 1972, U. Calif., Berkeley, 1984. Author: Thomas Jefferson and the Education of the New Nation, 1976; also articles in profl. jours. Co-editor: Changing Politics of Education, 1978; editorial bd. History of Edn. Quar., Ednl. Studies jour. Active Outward Bound, CAP. Sesquicentennial fellow U. Va., 1972, 84. Mem. History of Edn. Soc. (pres. 1983-85, bd. dirs. 1979-81), Am. Ednl. Research Assn. (v.p. div. F 1981-83), Orgn. Am. Historians, Am. Ednl. Studies Assn. (bd. dirs.), Assn. Study Higher Edn., Raven Soc., Kappa Delta Pi, Phi Delta Kappa. Democrat. Baptist. Avocations: hiking, fishing, canoeing, rock climbing. Home: 100 Juniper Ln Charlottesville VA 22901 Office: Univ of Va 405 Emmet St Charlottesville VA 22903

WAGONER, WILLIAM HAMPTON, university chancellor; b. Washington, N.C., May 12, 1927; s. William Gotha and Lossie Bell (Barrington) W.; B.S. cum laude, Wake Forest U., 1949, LL.D., 1981; M.A., East Carolina U., 1953; Ph.D. in Ednl. Adminstrn. and Polit. Sci., U. N.C., Chapel Hill, 1958; m. June 3, 1952; children—William Michael, David Robin, Mark Hampton. Tchr., Washington (N.C.) High Sch., 1950-53; asst. prin. Elizabeth City (N.C.) High Sch., 1953-55; prin. Hattie Harney Elementary Sch., Elizabeth City, 1956; instr. U. N.C., 1957; asso. exec. sec. N.C. State Sch. Bds. Assn., 1958-59; supt. Elizabeth City Schs., 1959-61; supt. Wilmington-New Hanover County Schs., 1961-68; pres. Wilmington Coll., 1968; chancellor U. N.C., Wilmington, 1969—. Speaker before various profl. groups at confs., convs. Pres., N.C. Div. Supts., 1967-68; chmn. bd. govs. N.C. Advancement Sch., 1967, mem. Gov.'s Tech. Coordinating Com. for Marine Sci. Council; pres. N.C. Assn. Colls. and Univs., 1981. Served with USNR, 1945-46. Recipient East Carolina Alumni award as Univ.'s Outstanding Alumni Award Winner, 1968. Mem. N.E.A. (life). Democrat. Episcopalian. Office: U NC at Wilmington South College Rd PO Box 3725 Wilmington NC 28406

WAGUESPACK, CHARLOTTE LANGLINAIS, guidance counselor, educator; b. Erath, La., Sept. 19, 1956; d. Wilfred and Anna Jeanne (Broussard) Langlinais; m. Glynn Joseph Waguespack, Aug. 4, 1979; children—Nicole Andree, Christopher Ryan. B.S., U. Southwestern La., 1976, M.A., 1980. Cert. tchr., La. Tchr. Northside High-Lafayette Parish, La., 1977, Kaplan High-Vermilion Parish, La., 1977-80; acad. counselor, instr. U. Southwestern La., 1980-85; guidance counselor N. Vermilion High-Vermilion Parish, Maurice, La., 1985—; presenter various workshops on teaching. Mem. Am. Assn. Counseling and Devel., Am. Coll. Personnel Assn., La. Coll. Personnel Assn., La. Personnel Guidance Assn., Nat. Vocat. Guidance Assn., Phi Kappa Phi, Kappa Delta Pi. Democrat. Roman Catholic. Home: Route 2 Box 720 Erath LA 70533 Office: N Vermilion High Sch Route 1 Box 55 Maurice LA 70555

WAHBA, ALBERT J., biochemistry educator, researcher; b. Alexandria, Egypt, Feb. 27, 1928; s. Jacques A. and Camille (deMaloul) W.; m. Judith Weinberg, May 1, 1965; children—Jeffrey, Danielle, Michael. A.B., U. Calif., 1951; M.A., U. Tex., 1954; Ph.D., Tufts U., 1961. Instr. dept. biochemistry NYU Sch. Medicine, 1963, asst. prof., 1963-65, assoc. prof., 1966-69; prof., dir. Lab. Molecular Biology, U. Sherbrooke Sch. Medicine, Quebec, Can., 1970-77; prof., chmn. dept. biochemistry U. Miss. Med. Ctr., Jackson, 1977—; vis. scientist Salk Inst. Biol. Studies, 1966. NIH fellow, 1956-58; Jane Coffin Childs Fund for Med. Research fellow, 1962. Mem. Am. Soc. Biol. Chemists, Am. Chem. Soc., AAAS, Am. Soc. Microbiology, Sigma Xi. Contbr. articles to sci. jours. Office: Dept Biochemistry U Miss Med Ctr 2500 N State St Jackson MS 39216

WAHBEH, CAMILLE JAMIL, physician; b. Tripoli, Lebanon, Oct. 14, 1952; d. Jamil Saleh and Ellen Kamel (Wehbe) W.; m. Rima Elie Zaroubi, May 4, 1980. B.S., Am. U. Beirut, 1972, M.D., 1977. Diplomate Am. Bd. Ob-Gyn. Resident in Ob-Gyn, Am. U. Med. Ctr., Beirut, 1977-80, U. Chgo., 1980-81; fellow in maternal-fetal medicine Duke U. Med. Ctr., 1981-83, assoc. in ob-gyn, 1981-83, asst. prof., 1983—, assoc. dir. Ob-Gyn Program, Fayetteville, N.C., 1983—, dir. maternal-fetal medicine, 1985—. Contbr. articles to med. jours. Mem. Am. Coll. Ob-Gyn, Bayard Carter Soc. Ob-Gyn, Soc. Perinatal Obstetricians. Greek Orthodox. Home: 2001 Dockside Dr Fayetteville NC 28304 Office: Fayetteville Area Health Edn Found 1601 Bowen Dr Fayetteville NC 28306

WAHLBERG, PHILIP LAWRENCE, clergyman; b. Houston, Jan. 18, 1924; s. Philip Lawrence and Ella Alida (Swenson) W.; m. Rachel Mary Conrad, June 1, 1946; children—David, Christopher, Pauli, Sharon. A.A., Tex. Lutheran Coll., 1942, D.D. (hon.), 1963 A.B., Lenoir Rhyne Coll., 1944; M.Div., Luth. Theol. Sem., 1946. Ordained to ministry Lutheran Ch., 1946. Pastor St. Luke Luth. Ch., Thunderbolt, Ga., 1946-50; organizing pastor Redeemer Luth. Ch., Wilmington Island, Ga., 1946-50; pastor St. Mark. Luth. Ch., Corpus Christi, Tex., 1950-59; pres. Tex.-La. Synod, United Luth. Ch. Am., Austin, Tex., 1959-62; pres., bishop Tex.-La. Synod, Luth. Ch. Am., Austin, 1963—; bd. dirs. Tex. Conf. Chs., Austin, 1959—. Contbr. articles to profl. jours. Bd. dirs. Luth. Sch. Theology, Chgo., 1967—, Luth. Social Service Tex., Austin, 1959—; bd. regents Tex. Luth. Coll., Seguin, 1959—; bd. dirs. Tex. Impact, Austin, 1983-85; mem. CUANES (Christian Urgent Action Network for El Salvador), Chgo., 1985, Interfaith Task Force on Central Am. Refugees, Austin, 1985. Named Man of Yr., Thunderbolt C. of C., Ga., 1950, Disting. Alumnus, Lenoir Rhyne Coll., Hickory, N.C., 1961, Tex. Luth. Coll., Seguin, 1972, Disting. Churchman, Tex. Luth. Coll., Seguin, 1978. Democrat. Avocations: photography; winemaking; hunting; fishing; golf; reading. Home: 5804 Cary Dr Austin TX 78757 Office: Tex-La Synod Luth Ch Am Box 4367 Austin TX 78765

WAID, ERIC TEAL, natural gas company executive; b. Vandergrift, Pa., Oct. 17, 1944; s. Frederick T. Waid and Shirley Cole (Painter) McCray; m. Virginia Kathleen, Feb. 2, 1964 (div. June 1972); children—Bryan Teal, Travis Cole; m. 2d, Claudia Kay, Jan. 3, 1973; children—Shelly, Leslie. Student public schools, Corpus Christi, Tex. Cert. quality analyst. Mail boy computer ops. Coastal State Gas Co., Corpus Christi, Tex., 1964-65, computer operator, 1965-70, ops. supr., 1970-74, sr. systems analyst, Houston, 1974-77; systems engr. E.D.S., Houston, 1977; mgr. prodn. systems Valero Energy Corp., San Antonio, 1977-83, mgr. quality assurance, 1983—. Campaigner United Way, San Antonio, 1983, 84. Named Employee of Month, Valero Energy Corp., 1978. Mem. Quality Assurance Inst. (charter). Republican. Methodist. Office: Valero Energy Corp PO Box 500 San Antonio TX 78292

WAITE, SCOTIA BALLARD KNOUFF, criminal justice specialist; b. Willis Wharf, Va., Apr. 8, 1909; d. Warren Alan and Lotta Mondera (Chard) Ballard; B.L.I., Emerson Coll., 1931; M.Ed., Boston U., 1933; diploma Sch. Social Work, Columbia U., 1939; m. William Francis Knouff, Oct. 9, 1943 (dec. Jan. 1968); children—Mary Francis Knouff Linn, Warren Irving Knouff; m. Frederick Waite, Jan. 3, 1976. Dir., Mathews County (Va.) Relief Office, 1932-35, Rappahanock County Relief Office, 1935-36, dir. relief offices Norfolk County and City of S. Norfolk (Va.), 1936-37, case worker Henry Watson Children's Aid Soc., Balt., 1937, with New Orleans Council Social Agys., 1940-43, dir. Social Service exchange and family and child welfare div., 1940-44, asst. dir. Detroit Council Social Agys., 1944-45, tech. dir. juvenile delinquency Dept. Justice, Washington, 1948-50, instr., dir. Sociology Research Lab. CCNY, 1950-55, faculty dept. Sociology Adelphi U., 1955-63; dir. research and staff devel. Nassau County (N.Y.) Probation Dept., 1963-78; co-dir. Improving Victim Services Through Probation project Am. Probation and Parole Assn. of Aberdeen (N.C.) and Blackstone Inst. of Washington, 1978-80; cons. criminal justice, Pinehurst, N.C., 1980—; examiner Nat. Commn. on Accreditation for Corrections, 1979—; mem. Adminstrn. of Justice Task Force, 1980; adj. assoc. prof. Sch. Criminal Justice, C.W. Post Coll., L.I.U., 1967—; mem. Child Placement Rev. Com. Moore County, N.C.; chmn. Youth Services Commn., Moore County. Mem. Nat. Republican Com. Recipient Outstanding Achievement award C.W. Post Coll. Sch. Criminal Justice, 1977, Spl. award Nassau County Probation Dept., 1978. Mem. Am. Probation and Parole Assn. (Walter Dunbar award 1977), Am. Correctional Assn., Northeastern Assn. Correctional Educators, Tex. Correctional Assn., AAUW, LWV. Episcopalian. Clubs: Pinehurst Country. Author numerous reports in corrections, victim services. Home: PO Box 456 McDonald Rd Pinehurst NC 28374

WAITKUS, ALAN JOSEPH, army officer, topographic engineer, cartoonist; b. Detroit, Aug. 26, 1949; s. Joseph Charles Waitkus and Luella Isabella (Gignac) Waitkus Olmstead; m. Ann Elizabeth Roggenbach, Jan. 25, 1974; children—Eric Alan, Tracey Lynne, Addam Lee. Grad. Army M.P. Sch., 1968, Air Force Sch., 1969; A.A., Henry Ford Coll., 1974; B.S., Ea. Mich. U., 1976; basic engr. grad. Army Engr. Sch., 1976, advance engr. grad., 1980; postgrad. Def. Mapping Sch., 1983. Joined U.S. Army, 1968, advanced through grades to capt., 1980; service in Ky., Ga., Tex., Mich., Alaska, Australia and Vietnam, 1969-75; platoon leader 8th Engring. Bn., Fort Hood, Tex., 1976-79; ops. officer 3d Bn., 4th Tng. Brigade, Fort Leonard Wood, Mo., 1980-81; sr. instr. Army Engr. Sch., Fort Belvoir, Va., 1981-83; Co. comdr. 3d Engring. Bn., Fort Stewart, Ga., 1983-84; instr. chief constrn. drafting Def. Mapping Sch., Fort Belvoir, 1985—, also mem. acad. rev. bd., 1985—. Author course design in tng. mgmt., 1983 (Army Commendation medal 1983); author cartoon strips: Turnin' Green, Army's Engr. mag. Def. Mapping Sch. newspaper, 1985—, Gowf Corse, 1985—, Dynasaurus Wrecks, 1985—, Crackshot, 1986—. Editor course design in army constrn. drafting, 1985 (SAC award 1985). Mem. Adult Concert Band, Garden City, Mich., 1971; active Spl. Olympics, Rolla, Mo., 1980, Springfield, Va., 1982. Decorated Army Achievement medal; recipient Humanitarian award U.S. Army, Joint Service Commendation medal. Fellow So. Assn. Colls. (accredited 1985), Assn. U.S. Army VFW (life). Roman Catholic. Club: Officers (Fort Stewart). Avocations: cartooning; model wood ship building; sports. Home: PO Box 1362 Fort Belvoir VA 22060 Office: Def Mapping Sch Attention TSD-Mapping/Charting Div Bldg 220 Fort Belvoir VA 22060

WAITS, THOMAS POPE, dentist; b. Vardaman, Miss., July 13, 1935; s. Tommy Alford and Thelma (Hawkins) W.; m. Sarah Maloy Hodges, May 19, 1985. B.S. in Zoology, Miss. Coll., 1956; D.M.D., U. Louisville, 1960. Gen. practice dentistry, Bruce, Miss., 1963—; oral surgeon Community Hosp. Calhoun County, Pittsboro, Miss., 1975—; past tri-county health adviser Miss. Action for Progress, Inc., Bruce. Alderman, Town of Bruce, 1973-77; mem. Miss. Welfare Bd., Jackson. Mem. ADA, Miss. Dental Assn., N.E. Miss. Dental Soc. Baptist. Lodge: Rotary (past pres. local club). Avocations: raising Tennessee walking horses; fishing; hunting; gardening. Home and Office: PO Box 280 Bruce MS 39815

WAKEFIELD, JOHN FREDERICK, teacher educator, psychological researcher; b. Evanston, Ill., Jan. 28, 1952; s. Ernest Henry and Hilda Gertrude (Overholt) W.; m. Janelle McMurtrey, June 1, 1985. A.B., U. Ill., 1974, Ph.D., 1981. Asst. prof. psychology Eastern Ill. U., Charleston, 1981-82; asst. prof. edn. U. North Ala., Florence, 1982—. U. North Ala. grantee, 1982—. Mem. Am. Psychol. Assn., Am. Ednl. Research Assn., Southeastern Psychol. Assn., Mid-South Ednl. Research Assn. Avocations: reading; gardening. Home: 1805 Hermitage Dr Florence AL 35630 Office: Box 5208 U Station Florence AL 35632

WAKIN, MICHAEL BRUCE, toy and hobby company executive; b. Texarkana, Ark., July 21, 1948; s. Edward Wakin and Charlene (Cowgill) Sebulsky; m. Sandra Kay Paulk, Dec. 4, 1970 (div. 1985); children—Michael Bruce Jr., Jason Anthony. B.B.A. in Mktg., No. Tex. State, 1972. With sales mgmt. dept. Lachman-Rose (W.R. Grace), San Antonio, 1972-76; sales v.p. Elmex (W.R. Grace), Cin., 1976-79; exec. Southeast Toys, Atlanta, 1980-84, Distrib-U-Toys, Grand Prairie, Tex., 1985—; cons., Atlanta, 1983-85. Republican. Baptist. Avocations: racquetball; golf; camping. Office: Distrib-U-Toys Inc 901 Ave S Grand Prairie TX 75050

WALDECK, JACQUELINE ASHTON, author; b. Chgo.; d. John and Maria Teresa (Arneri) Ashton; m. William George Waldeck, Sept. 20, 1947 (div. June 1964). B.A., U. Colo., 1948; postgrad. Tex. A&M U., 1969. Staff and vol. writer Montrose Daily Press, Colo., 1949-66; feature editor Fiesta Mag., Boca Raton, Fla., 1971-76; free-lance writer, historian, pub., lectr., Boca Raton area, 1977—. Author: Boca Raton from Pioneer Days, 1980, Boca Raton, a Romance, 1981, Boca Raton Pioneers and Addison Mizner, 1984; also numerous mag. articles. Sec., Tri-County Mental Health Assn., Montrose, 1964-65; pub. relations chmn. Montrose County chpt. ARC, 1950-63; bd. dirs. Friends Boca Raton Mus. Art, 1983-84; mem. Friends Boca Raton Library; active Friends Caldwell Play House, Boca Raton, 1983—. Mem. Nat. League Am. Pen Women (br. v.p. 1984-86, Nat. Biennial award for non-fiction article 1984), Nat. Soc. Arts and Letters (chpt. bd. dirs. 1983-86, pub. relations chmn. drama and dance contests 1984-86), Boca Raton Hist. Soc., Greater Boca Raton C. of C. Avocations: dancing, psychology, anthropology, international relations. Home: 398 W Camino Real Apt 1 Boca Raton FL 33432

WALDEN, JENELLE BROWN, bank executive; b. El Doredo, Kans., Jan. 1, 1955; d. A.K. and Virginia (Frogge) Brown; m. Blake Kuhlman, July 23, 1977 (div. July 1979); m. Peter J. Walden, Aug. 31, 1985. B.S. in English and Communication, U. Tex., 1977. Data processing tng. coordinator First City Services, Houston, 1979-81; tng. dir. Gibraltar Savs., Houston, 1980-81; v.p. tng. and devel. Interfirst Bank Austin, 1981—. Contbr. articles to profl. jours. Bd. dirs. Parks and Recreation Bd., Austin, 1984—, Live Oak Theatre, Austin, 1984—. Mem. Tex. Bankers Assn. (bd. dirs. edn. com. 1983—), Am. Soc. Tng. and Devel. (v.p. communication 1981-82), Nat. Soc. Performance Instruction. Republican. Avocations: photography; music; exercise. Home: 848 Banister Austin TX 78704 Office: Interfirst Bank Austin PO Box 908 Austin TX 78781

WALDEN, PHILIP MICHAEL, recording and publishing company executive; b. Greenville, S.C., Jan. 11, 1940; s. Clemiel Barto and Carolyn (McLendon) W.; A.B. in Econs., Mercer U., 1962; m. Peggy Hackett, Sept. 13, 1969; children—Philip Michael, Amantha Starr. Pres., Phil Walden Artists & Promotions, 1961, Walden Artists & Promotions, 1963-69, Phil Walden & Assos., 1965—, Capricorn Records, Inc., 1969—, Rear Exit Pub. Co., 1969—, No Exit Music Pub. Co., 1969— (all Macon, Ga.). Campaign chmn.

Muscular Dystrophy Assn., 1975; past mem. Macon-Bibb County Planning and Zoning Commn.; mem. com. for Preservation of White House; chmn. Macon Heritage Found., Inc.; mem. In-Town Macon Neighborhood Assn.; mem. nat. fin. com. Jimmy Carter Presdl. Campaign. Served to 1st lt. AUS. Recipient 14 Gold Record awards, 3 Platinum Record awards, 11 pub. awards; Rolling Stone Red Suspenders award, 1977; named a Top Exec. of Tomorrow, Billboard Mag., 1976; Martin Luther King Jr. Humanitarian award, 1977; Big Bear award Mercer U., 1975; Shriners plaque, 1976, 77; Human Relations award Am. Jewish Com., 1978. Mem. Rec. Industry Assn. Am. (dir.), Nat. Assn. Rec. Merchandisers, Nat. Assn. Rec. Arts and Scis. (past v.p., trustee), Nat. Trust Historic Preservation, Middle Ga. Hist. Soc., Brandywine Conservancy, Common Cause Ga. (dir.), Phi Delta Theta Alumni Assn., Phi Mu Alpha Sinfonia (hon.). Clubs: Elks; River North Golf and Country; Gov.'s of Ga.; Pres.'s (Mercer U.); Sea Pines. Founder Otis Redding Scholarship fund and Phil Walden Scholarship, Mercer U. Home: 401 Bowling Ave 93 Nashville TN 37205 Office: 561 Cotton Ave Macon GA 31201

WALDRON, ROBERT LEROY, II, physician; b. Carbondale, Ill., Feb. 6, 1936; s. Robert Leroy and Violet Mae (Thompson) W.; A.B., Princeton U., 1958; M.D., Harvard U., 1962; m. Carol Ann Fairman, June 17, 1972; children—Richard, Robert Leroy III, Ryan. Intern, Mass. Gen. Hosp., Boston, 1962-63; resident in radiology Columbia-Presbyn. Med. Center, N.Y.C., 1965-68; instr. radiology Coll. Physicians and Surgeons, Columbia U. and spl. fellow in neuroradiology Neurol. Inst., N.Y.C., 1968-69; clin. asst. in radiology Harvard Med. Sch., asst. radiologist Mt. Auburn Hosp. and M.I.T., Cambridge, 1969-71; asso. prof. clin. radiology Coll. Physicians and Surgeons, 1971-73; dir. radiology French Hosp. and French Med. Clinic, San Luis Obispo, 1973-80, v.p., dir., 1976-77; asso. clin. prof. radiology Loma Linda U. Sch. Medicine, 1977-80; dir. radiology Richland Meml. Hosp., Columbia, S.C., 1980—; dir. First South Savs. Bank, Columbia. Bd. dirs. Am. Cancer Soc., San Luis Obispo. Served with USPHS, 1963-65. Recipient grants James Picker Found., Am. Cancer Soc., NRC, Nat. Acad. Scis., Nat. Cancer Inst.; diplomate Am. Bd. Radiology. Fellow Am. Coll. Radiology; mem. Am. Roentgen Ray Soc., Radiol. Soc. N.Am., Am. Soc. Neuroradiology, Western Neuroradiol. Soc., Southeastern Neuroradiol. Soc., AMA, S.C. Med. Assn., San Luis Obispo County Med. Soc. (pres. 1979), Columbia Med. Soc., Sierra-Cascade Trauma Soc. (pres. 1983-84), S.C. Radiol. Soc. Republican. Methodist. Clubs: Ivy of Princeton; Wildewood, Summit (Columbia). Contbr. articles to profl. jours. Home: 1420 Adger Rd Columbia SC 29205 Office: 1814 Bull St PO Box 11620 Columbia SC 29211

WALDROP, FRITZ CARL, JR., safety engineer; b. Brevard, N.C., July 7, 1951; s. Fritz Carl Waldrop, Sr. and Eunice Lovell (Hitt) Justus; m. Margaret Elizabeth Moseley, Aug. 1, 1981. B.S. in Indsl. Engring., Ga. Inst. Tech., 1974. Employment supr. Union Carbide Corp., Greenville, S.C., 1974-76, prodn. control supr., Matamoros, Mex., 1976-78, indsl. engr. planning, Greenville, 1978-79, prodn. supr., 1979-80, safety engr., 1980—. Nat. Merit scholar, 1969. Mem. Inst. Indsl. Engrs., Am. Soc. Safety Engrs. (treas. local chpt. 1984-86). Club: Co-op (sec. 1971-72, pres. 1972-73). Avocations: golf; tennis. Office: Union Carbide Corp Electronics Div PO Box 5928 Greenville SC 29606

WALDROP, GERRY LUTHER, army officer, data processing analyst; b. Kilgore, Tex., May 13, 1943; s. Curtis Luther and Gladys Miriam (Cox) W.; B.A., Austin Coll., 1965; M.B.A., Tex. Tech. U., 1974; m. Joyce Janelle Buchanan, Nov. 6, 1965; children—Elbridge Gerry, Sara Kathleen, Amy Allison. Dept. mgr. J. C. Penney Co., Dallas, 1965-66; enlisted in U.S. Army, 1966, advanced through grades to lt. comdr., 1983; platoon leader, Vietnam, 1967-68; co. comdr., Ft. Bragg, N.C., 1968-70, div. chief project corps automation requirements, 1975-77; co. comdr., Ft. Huachuca, Ariz., 1970-72; div. chief project combat service support test hdqrs., Ft. Hood, Tex., 1974-75; requirements analyst Supreme Hdqrs. Allied Powers Europe, Mons, Belgium, 1977-80; bn. exec. officer 142d Signal Bn., Ft. Hood, Tex., 1981-83; J-6 Exercise Ocean Venture, 1984; grad. asst. Tex. Tech. U., 1972-74, instr. in ADP, 1972-74. Cubmaster Occoneechee council Boy Scouts Am., 1975-77. Decorated Bronze Star, Meritorious Service medal; Vivian Thyng scholar, 1961-65; Bruce McMillan Jr. scholar, 1961-65; Austin Coll. scholar, 1961-65. Mem. Assn. U.S. Army, Sigma Iota Epsilon. Presbyterian. Author: Corps Information Requirements Analysis Methodology, 1975 Command and Control Requirements Analysis Methodology. Home: PO Box 28 Kilgore TX 75662 Office: 3d Signal Brigade Fort Hood TX 76544

WALDROP, MARY FRANCES, English language educator; b. Denison, Tex., July 30, 1926; d. Clark Alexander and Estelle (Ivie) Johnson; m. Robert Owen Waldrop, July 15, 1947; children—Robert Rush, Laura Louise. B.A., Austin Coll., 1946, M.A., 1950; postgrad., U. Tex., 1957, North Tex. State U., 1958-64. Cert. secondary tchr. Tchr., dir. English, Sherman Ind. Sch. Dist., Tex., 1946-62; instr., dean div. humanities and social scis. Tyler Jr. Coll., Tyler, Tex., 1962—. Recipient Meritorious Service award Austin Coll., 1973. Mem. Tex. Jr. Coll. Tchrs. Assn., Community Coll. Humanities Assn., Alpha Chi. Democrat. Mem. Disciples of Christ. Avocations: sewing; traveling. Office: Tyler Jr Coll PO Box 9020 Tyler TX 75711

WALDROP, WILLIAM ALLEN, JR., federal services personnel director; b. Atlanta, May 31, 1951; s. William Allen and Susan Hixie (Brewer) W.; B.B.A., W. Ga. Coll., 1974; m. Debra Ann Waldrop, 1981; children—Patrick Alan, Jason Craig. With IRS, 1974, U.S. Postal Service, 1974; with EPA, 1974—, chief of classification S.E. regional office, Atlanta, 1979-82, regional personnel dir., 1982— Recipient Sustained Superior Performance award EPA, 1976, 80, 82, 83; cert. of appreciation Atlanta Clean City Commn., 1977; Bronze Medal commendable service, 1984; lt. col. a.d.c. Gov.'s staff. Mem. Internat. Personnel Mgmt. Assn., Classification and Compensation Soc., Fed. Classification Assn. Atlanta, Atlanta Assn. Fed. Execs. (pres. Atlanta fed. personnel council 1985). Baptist. Club: Toastmasters (club pres. 1976, 81, dist. gov. 1979—, lt. gov. adminstrn. 1978, 82, Able Toastmaster award 1978, 81, Outstanding Toastmaster, Peachtree Center club 1976, Area Gov. of Yr. award 1977, Disting. Toastmaster award, 1980). Home: 127 Jonathan Rd Riverdale GA 30274 Office: EPA 345 Courtland St Atlanta GA 30365

WALIGORSKI, BETH ELLEN, college administrator; b. Cleve., May 2, 1954; d. Leo Francis Waligorski and Carol Maurine (Finefrock) Meyer. B.A. in Music Edn., Heidelberg Coll., 1976; M.A., Bowling Green State U., 1977. Grad. asst. Bowling Green State U., Ohio, 1976-77; residence hall dir. SUNY-Cortland, 1977-79, assoc. dir. residence life, 1979-83, U. Tampa, Fla., 1984—. Organist, Sacred Heart Ch., Tampa, 1986—. Mem. North East Assn. of Coll. and Univ. Housing Officers (at large 1981-82), Nat. Assn. Student Personnel Adminstrs., Assn. Coll. Personnel Adminstrs. Democrat. Presbyterian. Home: 4003 S Westshore Blvd 3113 Tampa FL 33611 Office: Univ Tampa 401 W Kennedy Blvd Box 109F Tampa FL 33606

WALK, FRANK HUMPHREY, consulting engineer; b. Decatur, Ala., Aug. 30, 1920; s. Francis Albert and Laura Adeline (Humphrey) W.; m. Consuelo Faust, Sept. 6, 1947; children—Wendelyn, Karen, Frank, Wade, Wesley. B.S. in Mech. Engring., La. State U., 1942. Registered profl. engr., La. Vice pres. Dunham Wilson Co., Baton Rouge, 1946-54; mgr. Am. Metal Works, Baton Rouge, 1954-55; v.p. Truman B. Wayne Assocs., New Orleans, 1955-59; chmn. bd. Walk, Haydel & Assocs., New Orleans, 1959—. Contbr. articles to engring. jours. Pres., New Orleans C. of C., 1980, bd. dirs., 1979—; chmn. Econ. Devel. Council, New Orleans and River Region, 1975-77, bd. dirs., 1975—, mem. com. of "50", 1968—; co-chmn. Met. Forum for Econ. Devel. Action, 1977-78; mem. Mayor's Bus. Devel. Council, 1980—, Council on Internat. Trade, 1979-80; bd. dirs. Internat. Trade Mart, 1979—, mem. internat. bus. com., 1980—; mem. Mississippi Valley Coal Exporters Council, 1982—, La. Bd. Commerce and Industry, State of La., 1980-84, Industry Sect. Adv. Com. on Service for Trade Policy Matters, 1980, Central Bus. Dist. Hist. Landmarks Commn., 1979-85; mem. Hist. Dist. Archtl. Rev. Com., 1979-85, chmn., 1983; chmn. New Orleans Image Devel. Com., 1980—; v.p. Met. Area Council, 1978-80; bd. dirs. La. State U. Found.; chmn. U. New Orleans Engring. Devel. Adv. Council, 1982—, sec. engring. devel. fund, 1982—, mem. Met. Coll. of Higher Edn., 1979—. Served to col. AUS, 1942-46. Decorated Bronze Star. Recipient Frank Evans award Energy-sources Tech. Conf. and Exhbn., 1984. Fellow ASME (past chmn. nat. exec. com. petroleum div., hydrocarbon processing com.; past chmn. New Orleans sect.; past chmn. Energy Sources Tech. Conf. and Exhbn., Edgar Pavia award 1984), Am. Cons. Engrs. Council, Cons. Engrs. Council of La. (past pres., past chmn. indsl. and utilities relations com., Am. Cons. Engrs. Polit. Action Council, past project mgmt. program com., constrn. mgmt. com., past nat. dir. La.); mem. Soc. Am. Mil. Engrs. (past pres. La. post; bd. dirs.; past regional v.p. Lower Miss. region, John W. Morris award 1983), Nat. Soc. Profl. Engrs., Profl. Engrs. in Pvt. Practice, ASCE, Am. Petroleum Inst., Miss. Soc. Profl. Engrs., Instrument Soc. Am., La. Engring. Soc. (Andrew M. Lockett award, 1977, A.B. Patterson award for engrs. in mgmt.), Engrs. Club of New Orleans. Republican. Roman Catholic. Clubs: Plimsoll of New Orleans, Boston of New Orleans, Pendennis of New Orleans, Lakeshore of New Orleans, City of New Orleans, Petroleum of New Orleans, Internat. House, Avoca Duc, Baton Rouge City, Camelot (Baton Rouge). Home: 1543 Henry Clay Ave New Orleans LA 70118 Office: Walk Haydel & Assocs Inc 600 Carondelet St New Orleans LA 70130

WALKER, ALAN EDWARD, aircraft company executive; b. Pitts., Mar. 13, 1938; s. Edward Eberli and Mildred Florence (Roth) W.; m. Barbara Ann Fisher, Apr. 12, 1960 (div. 1974); children—Dawn Michelle, Craig Alan; m. 2d Gail L. Toolan, Apr. 14, 1977; children—Cristine, Cynthia. B.A., Va. Mil. Inst., 1960; M.S., Troy State U., 1972. Commd. 2d lt. U.S. Air Force, 1960, advanced through grades to col., 1979, ret., 1983; mgr. aerospace advanced systems mktg. Beech Aircraft Corp., Arlington, Va., 1983—. Decorated D.F.C., Air medal, Legion of Merit. Mem. Air Force Assn., Am. Def. Preparedness Assn., Nat. Aviation Club. Lutheran. Club: Harrington Harbour Yacht (vice commodore 1983-84) (Rose Haven, Md.). Office: Beech Aircraft Corp 1777 N Kent St Arlington VA 22209

WALKER, BEASOR BARROW, county sheriff; b. Tuscaloosa, Ala., Dec. 16, 1921; m. Kathlynn Simkins, Mar. 13, 1942; children—Beasor Barrow, Jr., William Arthur. B.S., U. Ala., 1950. Owner, Walker Bros. Oil Co., Tuscaloosa, 1952-71; sheriff Tuscaloosa County, 1971—. Served with inf. U.S. Army, 1940-45, 50-52; col. USNG. Decorated D.S.C., Silver Star with oak leaf cluster, Bronze Star with 2 oak leaf clusters, Purple Heart with oak leaf cluster. Mem. Ala. Sheriffs Assn. (pres. 1977), Democrat. Baptist. Clubs: Exchange (past pres.), Shrine (past pres.). Home: 2425 Prince Ave Tuscaloosa AL 35401 Office: Sheriffs Dept 714 1/2 Greensboro Ave Tuscaloosa AL 35401

WALKER, BENTON LEROY, electrical engineer, aerospace technician; b. Atlanta, Jan. 4, 1939; s. Charlie Frank and Laura Frances (Baber) W.; m. Mary Agnes Maher, May 3, 1968; children—Steven M., Douglas S. Diploma elect engring. tech., Capitol Radio Engring. Inst. and N.Y. Inst. Tech., 1973; B.S. in Polit. Sci. and History, SUNY-Albany, 1984. Enlisted U.S. Navy, 1956, resigned, 1966; civilian elec. specialist U.S. Navy, Jacksonville, Fla., 1966-69; tech. analyst Delta Air Lines, Atlanta, 1969—. Decorated Air medal. Mem. IEEE, AIAA. Home: 2043 Campfire Dr Riverdale GA 30296 Office: Delta Air Lines Atlanta Airport Atlanta GA 30320

WALKER, CAROLYN EVA, lawyer; b. Kansas City, Kans., Jan. 3, 1951; d. Carl Jerome and Emerald Stewart (Pena) W.; m. Federico Guillermo Rodriquez, Dec. 16, 1978; 1 child, Sabrina Lisel. B.A., U. Tex., 1972; J.D., St. Marys U., 1978. Bar: Tex. 1981. Tax examiner/auditor IRS, Austin, Tex., 1972-75; legal intern Bexar County Dist. Atty's. Office, San Antonio, 1977-79; assoc. Driscoll & Walker, San Antonio, 1981-82; land title atty. Alamo Title Co., San Antonio, 1982—. Campaign worker, Bill White for dist. atty. Bexar County, Tex., 1978, Mark White for gov., 1982; vol. atty. Mayor's Com. Progress, San Antonio, 1982, Com. to Set Child Support Formula, San Antonio, 1984. Named Outstanding Young Woman of Am. 1983. Mem. San Antonio Bar Assn., Bexar County Women's Bar Assn. (adv. to bd. dirs. 1983-84, mem. bd. 1985). Democrat. Roman Catholic. Home: 13906 Bluff Oak San Antonio TX 78216 Office: Alamo Title Co 613 NW Loop 410 San Antonio TX 78216

WALKER, DANIEL JOSHUA, JR., lawyer; b. Gibson, N.C., Nov. 27, 1915; s. Daniel Joshua and Annie (Hurdle) W.; A.B., U. N.C., 1936, J.D., 1948; m. Sarah Elizabeth Nicholson, June 14, 1941. Claim dept. Barnwell Bros. Trucking Co., Burlington, N.C., 1936-42; admitted to N.C. bar, 1948; clk. Superior Ct., Alamance County, Graham, N.C., 1948-53; partner Long, Ridge, Harris & Walker, Graham, 1953-67; county atty. Alamance County, Graham, 1964-77, county mgr., 1971-76; sr. mem. firm Walker Harris & Pierce, Graham, 1967-71; partner firm Allen & Walker, and predecessor, Burlington, N.C., 1977—. Mem. Human Relations Council, Alamance County, 1963-71, chmn., 1970; mem. N.C. Environ. Mgmt. Commn., 1972-77. Pres., Alamance County Young Democratic Club, 1950; chmn. Alamance County Dem. Exec. Com., 1956-58; mem. N.C. Dem. Exec. Com., 1958-66. Trustee Tech. Inst. of Alamance, 1964-71; bd. dirs. Alamance County United Fund, Cherokee council Boy Scouts Am., Community YMCA, Burlington; trustee Presbyn. Found., Presbyn. Ch. U.S., 1969-73, mem. exec. com., 1971-73, moderator Orange Presbytery, 1980. mem. council Orange Presbytery, 1972-74. Served with AUS, 1942-46. Decorated Bronze Star. Mem. Am. Judicature Soc., Alamance County C. of C. (pres.-elect 1980, pres. 1981), Am., N.C., Alamance County (pres. 1977) bar assns., N.C. Assn. County Attys. (v.p. 1971, pres. 1972, named county atty. of yr. 1971), Phi Alpha Delta. Democrat. Presbyn. (elder; trustee ch.). Lodge: Kiwanis. Home: PO Drawer 29 Burlington NC 27216 Office: 500 S Main St Burlington NC 27215

WALKER, DAVID FRANK, accountant; b. Indpls., Nov. 16, 1953; s. Thomas C. and Dorothy L. (Henson) W.; m. Gwendolyn Locke Butler, Sept. 6, 1980. B.A., DePauw U., 1975; M.B.A., U. Chgo., 1980. C.P.A., Ill., Fla. Staff acct. Arthur Andersen & Co., Chgo., 1975-80, acctg. and audit mgr., Tampa, Fla., 1980—. Bd. dirs. Boys Clubs Pinellas County, 1980-84. Mem. Am. Inst. C.P.A.s, Fla. Inst. C.P.A.s. Clubs: Tower (Tampa); Feather Sound Country (Clearwater, Fla.). Home: 3035 Mockingbird Ct Clearwater FL 33520 Office: 111 Madison St Suite 2400 Tampa FL 33602

WALKER, DEBORAH KLUTZ, pharmacist; b. Boone, N.C., Nov. 3, 1952; d. Mitchell Harris and Mary (Klutz) W. B.S. in Biology, Agnes Scott Coll., Decatur, Ga., 1974; B.S. in Pharmacy, Mercer U., Atlanta, 1977, Pharm.D., 1978. Asst. prof. clin. pharmacy Mercer U., 1978-80; asst. dir. pharmacy services Doctors Meml. Hosp., Atlanta, 1979-80, dir. clin. pharmacy, 1980-82, dir. pharm. services, 1982-85; corp. mktg. mgr. pharmacy systems HBO & Co., Atlanta, 1985—; mem. preceptor faculty Mercer U., 1978—, mem. admissions com. Sch. Pharmacy, 1985-86. Organist Rowland United Methodist Ch. (N.C.), 1967-70; recruiting alumnus vol. Agnes Scott Coll., 1974—. Mem. Am. Soc. Hosp. Pharmacist (cert. pharmakokinetic dosing services), Am. Pharm. Assn., Ga. Pharm. Assn., Atlanta Acad. Instl. Pharmacists, AAUW, Kappa Epsilon, Rho Chi. Home: Post Pl 3036-B Clairmont Rd NE Atlanta GA 30329 Office: HBO & Co 301 Perimeter Center N Atlanta GA 30346

WALKER, DEE BROWN, retired judge, lawyer; b. Royse City, Tex., Dec. 3, 1912; s. Dee Alexander and Lela Blanche (Jones) W.; LL.B., So. Meth. U., 1935; m. Ruthe Elizabeth Edwards, Mar. 28, 1942; children—Susan Hays, Stephen Craig; m. 2d, Anna Lee Gandy, Sept. 13, 1952. Admitted to Tex. bar, 1935; atty. Tex. Fire & Casualty Underwriters, 1935-36, Standard Accident Ins. Co., 1936-41, Glens Falls Indemnity Co., 1941-42; gen. practice law, Dallas, 1946-59; atty. Southland Life Ins. Co., 1959-63; judge 162d Jud. Dist. Ct. Dallas County, 1963-85. Mem. Dallas County Democratic Com., 1952-63. Trustee Dallas Pub. Library; v.p., dir., trustee Royse City Cemetery Found., Chisholm Cemetery Found., Cottonwood Cemetery Found. Served from pvt. to 1st lt. AUS, 1942-46. Mem. Am., Dallas bar assns., State Bar Tex., Dallas County Bar Assn., Dallas County Criminal Bar Assn., Am. Judicature Soc., Southwestern Legal Found., So. Meth. U. Alumni and Law Sch. Alumni Assn., Res. Officers Assn., Dallas Geneal. Soc. Dallas (pres. dir. 1963-65), S.A.R. (past pres. Dallas), Am. Legion, Mil. Order World Wars, D.A.V., V.F.W., Soc. Colonial Wars, Sons Confederate Vets., Phi Alpha Delta. Mem. Christian Ch. Mason (K.T., 33 deg., Shriner), Lion. Home: 5918 Vanderbilt Dallas TX 75206 Office: Renaissance Pl 714 Jackson St Dallas TX 75202

WALKER, DONALD IRVINE, petroleum product consultant; b. Winnipeg, Man., Can., July 21, 1911; s. John Irvine and Alberta Louise (Wahn) W.; student Park Coll., 1928-31; A.B., Grinnell Coll., 1933; postgrad. State U. Iowa, 1934, Iowa State Coll., 1935, Princeton U., 1944; m. Marie Hubbard, July 9, 1931; 1 dau., Donna Marie Walker West. Tchr. chemistry high sch. Newton, Iowa, 1933-37; chief chemist Maytag Co., Newton, 1937-39; with AMOCO Oil Co. (formerly Standard Oil Co., Ind.), Chgo., 1939-74, product mgr., 1961-74; petroleum product cons., Ormond Beach, Fla., 1974—. Mem. fund raising com. Child Care Center, Evanston, Ill., 1966-67; trustee Park Coll., Parkville, Mo., 1975—; juvenile justice arbitrator Volusia County (Fla.), 1981—; bd. dirs. Daytona Beach Civic Music Inc., 1983—, v.p., 1986—. Served to lt. USNR, 1943-45. Mem. ASTM (sec. 1959-68, Outstanding Service award 1976), TAPPI (sec. 1959-68, Outstanding Service award 1967), Am. Chem. Soc., Am. Petroleum Inst. Congregationalist (Ill. state bd. 1955-57, local ch. trustee 1975-77). Patentee in field; contbr. articles to profl. jours. Home: 910 Old Mill Run Ormond Beach FL 32074

WALKER, DONALD ROY, counselor, history educator; b. Beaumont, Tex., Oct. 2, 1941; s. Gaus Wilburn, Jr., and Juanita (Sellars) W.; B.A. in Zoology, U. Tex., Austin, 1969; M.A. in History, Lamar U., Beaumont, 1974; Ph.D., Tex. Tech U., Lubbock, 1983; m. Jonette McElroy, Mar. 21, 1977; children—Jennifer Debs, Jolie Marguerite. Counselor, Tex. Sch. for Deaf, Austin, 1964-65; Peace Corps vol., Mekambo, Gabon, 1965-68; with Dept. of State, AID, Hue, South Vietnam, 1969-72; teaching asst. Lamar U., 1972-74; instr. Tex. Tech. U., 1975—, internat. student counselor Internat. Programs Office, 1978—; instr. history Western Tex. Coll., Snyder, 1978—. Bd. govs. Lubbock County ACLU, 1978-79; pres. Llano Estacado Audubon Soc., 1978—. Recipient Grad. Student Teaching award Tex. Tech. U., 1976-77. Mem. Am. Hist. Assn., Orgn. Am. Historians, So. Hist. Assn., Nat. Assn. Fgn. Student Affairs, Delta Phi Epsilon, Phi Alpha Theta, Phi Kappa Phi, Omicron Delta Kappa. Editor: (with others) Studies in History, 1978-79; contbg. editor Stirpes, 1979. Office: PO Box 4248 Texas Tech University Lubbock TX 79409

WALKER, DOYLE RAY, educational administrator; b. Temple, Tex. Sept. 2, 1949; s. Malcolm Young and Vera Dell (Owen) W.; m. Catherine Ann Schutz, June 7, 1969; 1 son, Christopher Scott. A.A., Temple Jr. Coll., 1969; B.S. in History and Bus., U. Mary Hardin Baylor, 1972; M.Ed., North Tex. State U., 1978, mid-mgmt. cert., 1980. Tchr. social studies Plano High Sch., Tex., 1972-75; asst. prin. Plano Sr. High Sch., 1975-76; asst. prin. Vines High Sch., Plano, 1976-80, prin., 1980—; asst. supr. coll. night courses, summer sessions Grayson County Coll.-Plano, 1981—. Bd. dirs., v.p. Child Welfare, Tex. Dept. Human Resources, McKinney, 1980-82; bd. dirs. Plano Child Guidance Clinic, 1977-78, Plano Info. and Referred Ctr., 1986—. Recipient cert. of merit K.C., Dallas, 1979. Mem. Tex. Assn. Secondary Sch. Prins., Nat. Assn. Secondary Sch. Prins., Plano Prins. Assn. Avocation: fishing. Home: 4421 Birdsong Ln Plano TX 75075 Office: Vines High Sch 1401 Highedge Plano TX 75075

WALKER, EDGAR WARREN, pharmacist; b. El Dorado, Ark., July 12, 1946; s. Edgar Doyle and Mattie Pauline (Murphy) W.; m. Frances J. Mcbride, July 8, 1972 (separated). B.S. in Pharmacy, Northeast La. U., 1970. Registered pharmacist, La. Pharmacist, Aron's Pharmacy, Monroe, La., 1971-80; pharmacist, v.p. Lee's Super Drug, Bastrop, La., 1980-82; pharmacist Medic Pharmacy of Bastrop, Inc., 1980—; mem. Nat. Assn. Bd. Acals. testing com. Nat. Assn. Bds. Pharmacy, 1976-81; cons. in field. Avocations: deer hunting; fishing; writing articles on medicine and outdoors. Home: Route 2 Box 509 Bastrop LA 71220 Office: Medic Pharmacy of Bastrop Inc 103 Tully Dr Bastrop LA 71220

WALKER, ESPER LAFAYETTE, JR., civil engineer; b. Decatur, Tex., Sept. 22, 1930; s. Esper Lafayette and Ruth (Mauldin) W.; B.S., Tex. A&M U., 1953; B.H.T., Yale U., 1958; m. Sara Lynn Dunlap, Oct. 2, 1955; children—William David, Annette Ruth. Design engr. Tex. Hwy. Dept., Austin, 1956-57; dir. Dept. Traffic Engring., High Point, N.C., 1958-63; v.p. Wilbur Smith & Assos., Houston, 1963—. Pres. Meadowbrook PTA, 1976-77; chmn. pack 902 com. Sam Houston council Boy Scouts Am., 1973-74, treas. troop 904 com., 1976-80; treas. Stratford High Band, 1981-82, bd. dirs., 1980-82; baseball team mgr. Spring Br. Sports Assn., 1975-77; mem. adminstrv. bd. Meml. Drive Meth. Ch., 1971-77, 83-86, bldg. com., 1974-82, fin. com., 1975-77, 83-85, trustee, 1983-86. Served to 1st lt. C.E., AUS, 1953-56. Recipient Key Man award High Point Jaycees, 1962. Registered profl. engr., Tex., S.C., Colo., Ark., Wis., La., Okla., Wyo. Mem. Nat., Tex. socs. profl. engrs., High Point Jaycees (dir.), Houston C. of C. (chmn. transit com. 1975-79), Inst. Transp. Engrs. (pres. So. sect. 1963). Clubs: Warwick, Summit, Beaumont, Plaza. Home: 14216 Kellywood Ln Houston TX 77079 Office: 908 Town and Country Blvd Suite 400 Houston TX 77024

WALKER, ETHEL, pediatrician; b. Nashville, May 21, 1909; d. Bradley and Ethel (Mathews) Walker. A.B., Vassar Coll., 1931; A.M., Vanderbilt U., 1933, M.D., 1936. Diplomate Am. Bd. Pediatrics. Intern in pediatrics John Hopkins Hosp., Balt., 1936-37, resident in pediatrics, dispensary chief, 1938-43; asst. resident in pediatrics Yale U.-New Haven, Conn., 1937-38; individual practice medicine specializing in pediatrics, Nashville, 1943—. Recipient Founder's medal Vanderbilt Univ. Med. Sch., 1936, Woman of Yr. award Nashville Bus. and Profl. Women, 1975, Disting. Alumna award Univ. Sch. Nashville, 1980. Mem. AMA, Am. Acad. Pediatrics, Tenn. Med. Assn., Davidson County Med. Soc., Davidson County Pediatric Soc., Phi Beta Kappa, Alpha Omega Alpha. Democrat. Methodist. Clubs: Belle Meade Country, Jr. League (both Nashville). Home: 3016 West End Ave Nashville TN 37203 Office: 3017 Hedrick St Nashville TN 37203

WALKER, EUNICE MIRIAM ARNAUD, writer; b. Monett, Mo.; d. Emile and Pauline (Barriquand) Arnaud; student S.W. Mo. State U.; B.A., U. Ark.; postgrad. George Washington U., 1956; m. Joseph Edward Walker (div.); children—Diane Leigh Walker Smith, Carole Cecile Walker Baker; m. 2d, William Roy Little. Reporter, feature writer Monett Times, Kansas City (Mo.) Star; publs. writer Woodrow Wilson Centennial Celebration Commn., Washington, 1957; pub. relations writer Senator Joseph S. Clark, Washington, 1958-59; asst. pub. relations Ho. of Reps. Com. on Sci. and Astronautics, 1959-61; officer U.S. ACDA, Washington, 1961-65, policy reports officer, Washington, 1965-70, officer; pub. info. officer U.S. Dept. Agr., Washington, 1970-76; free lance writer, 1956—. Mem. LWV, Nat. League Am. Penwomen, Nat. Fedn. Press Women, Nat. Press Club, Assn. Agr. Coll. Editors, Nat. Hist. Soc., Am. Hist. Soc., Nat. Archives, Smithsonian Assos., Nat. Trust Historic Preservation, Am. Hort. Soc., Nat. Cathedral Assn., Huguenot Soc., Aaron Burr Assn., Kappa Delta Pi, Lambda Tau. Episcopalian. Club: City Tavern (Washington). Author: Woodrow Wilson, 1958; contbr. articles to various publs. Home: 205 James Thurber Ct Falls Church VA 22046

WALKER, EVELYN, retired public radio-tv broadcasting executive; b. Birmingham, Ala.; d. Preston Lucas and Mattie (Williams) Walker; A.B., Huntingdon Coll., 1927, L.H.D. (hon.), 1974; postgrad. Cornell U., 1927-29; M.A., U. Ala., 1963, postgrad., 1965-75; spl. TV course U. Ill., summer 1953. Tchr. speech Phillips High Sch., Birmingham, Ala., 1930-34; head speech dept. Ramsay High Sch., Birmingham, 1934-52; chmn. schs. radio, TV, 1944-75, producer, coordinator TV-radio Birmingham Public Schs., 1952-69; head instrnl. TV programming services, 1969-75; radio broadcaster daily children's program, Birmingham, 1946-57; staff producer Birmingham Ednl. TV Studio for Ala. Public TV Network, 1954-75; cons. Gov.'s Ednl. TV Legis. Study Com., 1953. Mem. Def. Adv. Com. on Women in the Services, 1958-60; chmn. TV and radio competition Festival of Arts, 1962-65; bd. dirs. Women's Com. of 100 for Birmingham, 1968—; TV radio co-chmn. Gov's Adv. Bd. to State Safety Com., 1965-68; nat. del. Asian-Am. Women Broadcaster's Conf. 1966; media chmn. Gov.'s Commn. Ala. Yr. of Child; mem. Salvation Army Aux.; audio visual chmn. Birmingham Council PTA, 1966-75. Bd. dirs. Women's Army Corps Found.; trustee Arlington Hist. Assn. Recipient Educator's Medal award Freedoms Found. at Valley Forge, 1963; Spl. award for the Arts Birmingham Festival of Arts. 1962; Red Cross TV award, 1964; Nat. Headliner award Women in Communications, 1965; Key to City of Birmingham, 1966; Ala. service award Nat. Exchange Club, 1969; named Ala. Woman of Achievement, 1964, Birmingham Woman of Yr., 1965; Ala. Woman of Yr., Progressive Farmer mag., 1966; named hon. col. Ala. militia, hon. lt. a.d.c.; 20-Year Service award Ala. Ednl. TV Commn.; Obelisk award Children's Theatre, 1976; Cert. of Appreciation, USMC, 1959, Air Force Recruiting Service, 1961, 3d Army Corps, 1961, N.Am. Air Def. Command, 1962. Mem. Nat. League Am. Pen Women, Nat. Assn. Ednl. Broadcasters, Ala. Hist. Assn., Colonial Dames XVII Century, Daus. Am. Colonists (state TV chmn. 1966-76), Noble Order of Crown, Colonial Order of Crown, Am. United Daus. 1812, Huntingdon Coll. Alumnae Bd. (achievement award, 1958, 1st nat. v.p. 1959-60, internat. pres. 1961-63, 2d v.p. 1973-76), Ams. Royal Descent, Royal Order Garter, Magna Charta Dames (former sec.-treas.), DAR (state program chmn. 1979-85), Plantagenet Soc., Humane Soc., Birmingham-Jefferson Hist. Assn. (trustee), Women's Golf Assn., Women of Yr. Ltd. of Birmingham, Ala. Congress PTA (audio visual chmn. 1966-75), Arlington Hist. Assn. (pres. 1981-83), Ala. Dist. Exchange Clubs (hon. life, bronze plaque award 1969), Art Assn., Art Mus., Symphony Women, Nat. Trust Historic Preservation, English-Speaking Union, Greater Birmingham Arts Alliance, Nat. Eagle Forum, Delta Delta Delta Alumnae (Golden Circle). Methodist. Clubs: Press, The Club, Downtown, Birmingham Country. Home: 744 Euclid Ave Birmingham AL 35213

WALKER, FRANCIS CHARLES, consulting industrial psychologist; b. Knox County, Ill., Feb. 1, 1926; s. Ivan Banks and Hazel Anna (Weiler) W.;

m. Donna Jean Bender, Sept. 1, 1946; children—Gregory C., Taffy Leigh. B.A. in Humanities with honors, Bradley U., 1949, M.A. in Psychology, 1950. Lic. psychologist, Fla., Ill.; cert. rehab. counselor, cert. tchr., Fla.; diplomate Am. Bd. Vocat. Experts. Personnel counselor Caterpillar Tractor Co., Inc., Peoria, Ill., 1950-55; indsl. psychologist Byron Harless and Assocs., Inc., Tampa, 1955; indsl. relations cons. Sangamo Elec. Co., Inc., Springfield, Ill., 1955-60; sec., dir. adminstrv. services Byron Harless, Schaffer, Reid Assocs., Inc., Tampa, 1960-69; v.p. Rutenberg Homes, Inc., Belleair Bluffs, Fla., 1969-70, cons., 1970-71; pres. Frank Walker Assocs., Inc., Tampa, 1970—. Contbr. articles to profl. jours. Served with USAF, 1944-46. Mem. exec. com. Boys' and Girls' Clubs. of Tampa, 1982—; past clk. of session Bayshore Presbyn. Ch., Tampa. Mem. Internat. Assn. Applied Psychology, Am. Psychol. Assn., Southeastern Psychol. Assn., Fla. Psychol. Assn. (past pres., chapter rep.), Nat. Mgmt. Assn., Tampa Bay Psychol. Assn. (past pres.), Nat. Rehab. Assn., Nat. Rehab. Counseling Assn., Greater Tampa C. of C. (past chmn. law enforcement com.). Republican. Clubs: Exchange, University (Tampa). Avocations: photography; bicycling; reading. Home: 215 S Hesperides Tampa FL 33609 Office: Frank Walker Assocs Inc 1300 N Westshore Blvd Suite 140 Tampa FL 33607-4618

WALKER, GAIL LORNA, aerospace and defense technology company executive; b. Yonkers, N.Y., Mar. 10, 1946; d. John Michael and Lillian Christine (Lohrfink) Toolan; m. Stephen Chupak, Aug. 5, 1967 (div. July 12, 1975); children—Christine, Cynthia; m. Alan E. Walker, Apr. 14, 1977 (div. Oct. 22, 1984). B.A., Salve Regina Coll., 1977, M.A., 1978; Ph.D., Catholic U., 1983. Research assoc. Systems Research Corp., Alexandria, Va., 1978-79; researcher Montgomery County Pub. Schs., Rockville, Md., 1979; sr. program analyst Applied Mgmt. Scis., Silver Spring, Md., 1979-80, AMCOR, Alexandria, Va., 1980; dir. adv. mgmt. systems Dynamic Sci. Inc., Fairfax, Va., 1980-82; market devel. mgr. very high speed integrated circuits Honeywell, Inc., McLean, Va., 1982-85; advanced tech. mktg. mgr. Honeywell, Inc., Clearwater, Fla., 1985—. Author: (with others) The Annual Test Report 1978-79-Montgomery County Public Schools, 1978; The Relation Among Cognitive Ability, Taking an Assigned Perspective, and Type of Story Ideas Remembered, 1983. Mem. Am. Astronautical Soc. (Washington bd. dirs. 1984-85, Appreciation award 1984), Air Force Assn., Inst. of Navigation, Am. Def. Preparedness Assn., Nat. Space Club, Nat. Security Indsl. Assn. (mem. LOMAC com. 1983-84), Electronic Industries Assn. (contracts com. 1983-85). Republican. Baptist. Home: 4170 Harbor Hills Dr Clearwater FL 33540 Office: Honeywell Inc 13350 US Highway 19 S Clearwater FL 33546

WALKER, GEORGE KONTZ, educator; b. Tuscaloosa, Ala., July 8, 1938; s. Joseph Henry and Catherine Louise (Indorf) W.; B.A., U. Ala., 1959; LL.B., Vanderbilt U., 1966; M.A., Duke U., 1968; LL.M., U. Va., 1972; postgrad. (Sterling fellow), Yale U., 1975-76; m. Phyllis Ann Sherman, July 30, 1966; children—Charles Edward, Mary Neel. Admitted to Va. bar, 1967, N.C. bar, 1976; law clk. Judge John D. Butzner, Jr., U.S. Dist. Ct., Richmond, Va., 1966-67; asso. firm Hunton, Williams, Gay, Powell & Gibson, Richmond, 1967-70; practiced in Charlottesville, Va., 1970-71; asst. prof. Wake Forest U. Law Sch., Winston-Salem, N.C., 1972-73, asso. prof. law, 1974-77, prof., 1978—; vis. prof. law Marshall-Wythe Sch. Law, Coll. William and Mary, Williamsburg, Va., 1979-80, U. Ala., 1985; cons. Naval War Coll., 1976—, JAG, USN, 1981—. Served from ensign to lt. (j.g.) USNR, 1959-62; capt. Res. Woodrow Wilson fellow Duke U., 1962-63. Mem. Am., N.C., Va. bar assns., Am. Soc. Internat. Law, Am. Judicature Soc., Maritime Law Assn., Order of Barristers, Phi Beta Kappa, Sigma Alpha Epsilon, Phi Delta Phi. Democrat. Episcopalian. Author: International Law for the Naval Commander. Contbr. articles to profl. jours. Home: 3321 Pennington Ln Winston Salem NC 27106 Office: PO Box 7206 Winston-Salem NC 27109

WALKER, GEORGE PINCKNEY, III, consulting geologist; b. El Paso, Tex., June 28, 1934; s. George Pinckney and Helen (Griffith) W.; m. Estella Jeanne Livingston, Sept. 4, 1955; children—George Pickney, Charlisa Ann, Betsy Kim. Profl. Degree in Petroleum Engring., Colo. Sch. Mines, 1956; M.A. in Geology, U. Tex., 1967. Cert. profl. petroleum engr., La.; cert. petroleum geologist. From jr. petroleum engr. to dist. petroleum engr. Tenneco Oil Co., Wichita Falls, Tex., Great Bend, Kans., Lafayette, La., 1956-64; from geologist to div. geologist AMOCO Prodn. Co., Midland, Tex., Fort Worth, Houston, 1966-80; cons. geologist, owner Walker Exploration Co., Sattler, Tex., 1980—; cons. Amarex, Inc., Oklahoma City, 1980-83, Texland Petroleum, Inc., Fort Worth, 1983-84, BWAB, Inc., Denver, 1984—, McNallen Oil Co., Inc., Breckenridge, Tex., 1984—. Author: Subsurface Geologic Reconnaissance of Kerr Basin and Adjacent Areas, South-Central Texas, 1966. First vice chmn. Lafayette Republican Club, La., 1963; mem. Republican Parish Exec. Com., Lafayette, 1963-64. Mem. Am. Assn. Petroleum Geologists, Soc. Ind. Petroleum Earth Scientist, Am. Inst. Profl. geologists, Geol. Soc. Am., West Tex. Geol. Soc., Soc. Econ. Palenotologists and Mineralogists, Soc. Petroleum Engrs. of AIME, Soc. Econ. Geophysicists, Soc. Profl. Wireline Log Analysts. Episcopalian. Avocations: fishing; hunting; hiking; travel. Home: Route 5 Box 637A Canyon Lake TX 78130 Office: Walker Exploration Co PO Box 2022 Sattler TX 78130

WALKER, HAROLD DAVID, vocational administrator; b. Oak Hill, W.Va., Apr. 10, 1939; s. John A. and Mollie D. (Shepherd) W.; m. Betty Lee Bradshaw, Sept. 7, 1962; children—Carmella, Shelley, Harold. B.A. in Social Studies, Marshall U., 1961, M.A. in Bus. Edn., 1966. Cert. vocat. adminstrn., W.Va. Tchr., Wyoming County Bd. Edn., Pineville, W.Va., 1961-66; tchr. Kanawha County Bd. Edn., Charleston, W.Va., 1966-71, coordinator adult edn., 1971-72, asst. dir., 1972, mem. adv. com., 1975—; dir. Garnet Career Ctr., Charleston, 1972—. Coach, Piedmont Elem. Soccer Team, Charleston, 1977-80; asst. cub scout master First Presbyn. Ch., Charleston, 1978-80. Named Boss of Yr. Am. Bus. Women's Assn., Charleston, 1980. Mem. Am. Vocat. Assn. (sec. 1981-83), W.Va. Local Adminstrs. (treas. 1971-75), W.Va. Adult Edn. Assn., W.Va. Vocat. Assn., W.Va. L.P.N. Assn. Democrat. Lodge: Greenbrier Lions. Home: 709 Mayflower Dr Charleston WV 25311 Office: Garnet Career Ctr 422 Dickinson St Charleston WV 25301

WALKER, HAROLD EMMETT, accountant; b. Columbus, Ga., Nov. 27, 1932; s. Emmett Boyd and Grace Truman (Wadsworth) W.; m. Janice Carter, June 9, 1956; children—Mark Jackson, Margaret Anne. B.S. in Bus. Adminstrn., U. Tenn., 1954. With audit staff Ernst & Whinney, Knoxville, Tenn., 1954-66, ptnr., Miami, Fla., 1966-71, mng. ptnr., Ft. Lauderdale, Fla., 1971-76, Miami, 1976—. Pres., Broward County United Way, Ft. Lauderdale, 1975; pres. citizens bd. U. Miami, 1979-80, trustee, 1980-81; mem. exec. com. Miami Citizens Against Crime, 1982-84, trustee Greater Miami United, 1981-84. Mem. Am. Inst. C.P.A.s (nat. council 1977-82), Fla. Inst. C.P.A.s (pres. 1977-78), Nat. Assn. Accts. (pres. Knoxville chpt. 1962), Greater Miami C. of C. (vice chmn. 1981-84). Republican. Congregationalist. Clubs: Miami (pres. 1981-82), Bankers, Bath, Riviera Country, Grove Isle, 200 Greater Miami (pres. 1983). Home: 10800 Old Cutler Rd Miami FL 33156 Office: Ernst & Whinney 2700 One Biscayne Tower Miami FL 33131

WALKER, HARRY GREY, presiding justice state supreme court; b. Ovett, Miss., Sept. 30, 1924; s. Chester A. and Ina (Mangum) W.; LL.B., U. Miss., 1952; m. Carrie Thorne Lang, Apr. 4, 1953; children—Harry Grey, Fred Wallace. Admitted to Miss. bar, 1952; practiced in Gulfport, Miss., 1952-64; judge Harrison County (Miss.) Ct., 1964-68; judge Circuit Ct., 2d Dist. Miss., 1968-72; assoc., then presiding justice Miss. Supreme Ct., 1972—. Mem. Miss. Ho. of Reps., 1964. Served with USCG, 1942-44. Mem. Am. Judicature Soc., Miss. State Bar, DAV, Paralyzed Vets. Am., Phi Alpha Delta, Kappa Alpha. Democrat. Methodist. Clubs: Am. Legion, Elks, Gulfport Yacht, Magnolia Hunting. Home: 2107 Plantation Blvd Jackson MS 39211 Office: Miss Supreme Ct Bldg Jackson MS 39205

WALKER, HARVEY DALE, oil and gas exploration company executive, petroleum engineer; b. Harrison, Ark., Apr. 8, 1946; s. Albert Monroe and Ruby Clementine (Klepper) W.; m. Judith Ann Kimes, Apr. 18, 1965 (div. Mar. 1969); 1 child, Stacie Ann; m. Sylvia Ann Verde, Feb. 2, 1973. B.S. in Petroleum Engring., U. Tex., 1979. Prodn. engr. Andover Oil Co., Tulsa, 1979-81, Davis Oil Co., Tulsa, 1981-83; prodn. mgr. Essex/CNG Producing Co., Tulsa, 1983—; counselor U. Tex., Austin, 1976-79; asst. to pres. Garrett Computing Systems, Dallas, 1973-76. Social dir. Young Republicans Club, Houston, 1968; supporting mem. Palmer Drug Abuse Ctr., Tulsa, 1985. Served with USN, 1965-67. Mem. Soc. Petroleum Ergrs., Soc. Profl. Well Log Analysts, Am. Assn. Petroleum Geologists (assoc.). Democrat. Methodist. Avocations: geology; classic car restoration; reading; classical music. Home: 3632 E 142d St S Bixby OK 74008 Office: Essex/CNG Prodn Co 810 S Cincinnati St Tulsa OK 74119

WALKER, HELEN ROSALIE, county official; b. Victoria, Tex., Feb. 14, 1937; d. Frank Henry and Beatrice (Vanek) Dusek; A.A., Victoria Coll., 1956; student U. Houston-Victoria, Tex. A&M U.; m. Walter C. Walker, Mar. 20, 1956; children—Randy, Vicki. Proofreader, Victoria Advocate, 1956; dep. treas. Victoria (Tex.) County, 1956-73, treas., 1973—. Adult leader O'Connor 4-H Club, 1971-75; bd. dirs., treas. Victoria County Democratic Women's Club; bd. dirs. Victoria County United Way; past treas., sponsor Victoria Girls' Fastpitch Assn.; mem. Gov.'s County Ofcls. Adv. Commn., 1982-83. Mem. County Treasurers Assn. Tex. (pres. 1981-82, Outstanding County Treas. Tex. 1983), Nat. Assn. County Treasurers and Fin. Officers (dir.), Tex. Assn. Elected Women, Victoria Profl. Women's group, Nat. Assn. for Female Execs. Clubs: Pilot (past pres., dir.), Toastmistress (past pres.). Recipient New Counties U.S.A. Achievement award Nat. Assn. Counties, 1975, 81. Home: 3601 Bobolink Ln Victoria TX 77901 Office: 115 N Bridge St Room 116 Victoria TX 77901

WALKER, JAMES GORDON, educator; b. Jones County, Miss., Aug. 27, 1947; s. James Alton and Janie Mae (Tullos) W.; A.A., East Central Jr. Coll., 1968; B.S. in Edn. (Sperry scholar 1968), Miss. Coll., 1970, M.Ed., 1971; Ed.D. (univ. fellow 1974), U. So. Miss., 1975; m. Senita Ann Arthur, Nov. 5, 1967; children—James Gordon, Arthur Merkel Kelly. Tchr., then prin. elem. schs. in Miss., 1970-72; prin. Harrison Central Elem. Sch., Harrison County (Miss.) Schs., Gulfport, 1972-76, county dir. instrn., 1976-80; supt. schs. Grenada (Miss.) Separate Sch. Dist., 1980—; mem. adj. faculty William Carey Coll., Hattiesburg, Miss., U. So. Miss.; v.p. Miss. Acad. Sch. Execs., 1982-83, pres., 1983-84; bd. dirs. Grenada Higher Edn. Council, 1980-84, Miss. Sch. Study Council, 1980-84; cons. in field. Treas. Harrison County PTA, 1972-75; bd. dirs. Miss. PTA, 1978-84, v.p., 1981-84; bd. dirs. Grenada County ARC, 1981-84. Mem. Am. Assn. Sch. Adminstrs., Miss. Assn. Sch. Adminstrs., Miss. Assn. Asst. Supts., Miss. Assn. Educators, Assn. Supervision and Curriculum Devel., Miss. Edn. Assn. (del. 1973-76), U. So. Miss. Alumni Assn. (dir. Grenada County chpt.), Kappa Delta Pi, Phi Delta Kappa (v.p. 1980—). Baptist. Clubs: Orange Grove Civitan (sec. 1978-80), Rotary, Masons.

WALKER, JAMES PRENTICE, oil company executive; b. Tahoka, Tex., Sept. 29, 1936; s. John Prentice and Helen Marr (Applewhite) W.; children—Sheryl, James, Mike, Jeff. B.S. in Geology, Tex. Tech U., 1958. Exploration mgr. Humphrey Oil Corp., Dallas, 1959-66; pvt. practice as geologist, Oklahoma City, 1966-68; pres. Gold Crest Corp., Oklahoma City, 1968-73, The Walker Corp., Oklahoma City, 1973—. Bd. dirs., mem. exec. bd. Okla. Symphony Orch., 1982—; mem. exec. bd. Red Raider Club, 1981—. Mem. Am. Assn. Petroleum Geologists, Oklahoma City Geol. Soc., Am. Assn. Petroleum Landmen, Okla. Ind. Petroleum Assn. Am. (bd. dirs.). Clubs: Dallas, Quail Creek Country, Petroleum, Twin Hills Country (Oklahoma City). Office: Walker Corp 210 W Park Ave Oklahoma City OK 73102

WALKER, JERALD CARTER, college president; clergyman; b. Bixby, Okla., May 22, 1938; s. Joseph Carter and Trula Tosh (Jackson) W.; m. Virginia Canfield, Apr. 14, 1963; children—Elisabeth Katherine, Anne Carter. B.A. in Sociology, Oklahoma City U., 1960; B.Div., U. Chgo., 1964; D.Religion, Sch. Theology at Claremont, 1966. Ordained to ministry Methodist Ch.; dir., campus minister Campus Christian Assn., Chgo., 1961-64; minister of outreach Temple Meth. Ch., San Francisco, 1965-66; chaplain, asst. prof. religion Nebr. Wesleyan U., 1966-69; pres. John J. Pershing Coll., 1969-70; v.p. univ. relations, asso. prof. Southwestern U., Georgetown, Tex., 1970-74; pres. Baker U., Baldwin, Kans., 1974-79; pres. Oklahoma City U., 1979—; cons. Rice U., 1973. Author: (with Daisy Decazes) The State of Sequoyah. Contbr. articles to profl. jours. Recipient Pres.'s Creative Young Prof. award Nebr. Wesleyan U., 1968; Alumni Recognition award Nebr. 4H Club, 1970, Okla. 4H Club, 1970; Disting. Alumnus award Oklahoma City, U., 1974; Student Commn. Outstanding Person of Yr. award Baker U., 1977. Mem. Am. Soc. Christian Ethics, Okla. Ann. Conf. United Methodist Ch., Nat. Assn. Schs. and Colls. United Meth. Ch. (past pres.), Okla. Ind. Coll. Found., Oklahoma City C. of C. (exec. com.). Club: Rotary. Home: 2501 N Blackwelder Oklahoma City OK 73106 Office: Oklahoma City U Oklahoma City OK 73106

WALKER, JERRY DON, chiropractor; b. Ft. Worth, Nov. 25, 1952; s. Weldon Maurice and Annie Arlee (Fuller) W.; m. Katherine Lynn Guyse, May 21, 1977; children—Jonathan Lynn, Jason Alan. Student U. Tex.-Arlington, 1971-73; D.Chiropractic, Tex. Chiropractic Coll., 1977. Diplomate Nat. Bd. Chiropractic Examiners. Pvt. practice chiropractic, Ft. Worth, 1978—. Mem. Am. Chiropractic Assn., Tex. Chiropractic Assn. (Dr. of Yr. award dist. IV, 1981, pres. dist. IV, 1982-83; mem. radiology com., ins. relations com.), Am. Chiropractic Assn. Council on Roentgenology, Omega Psi. Republican. Baptist.

WALKER, JERRY TYLER, plant pathologist, educator, researcher; b. Cin., Sept. 7, 1930; m. Mary Elizabeth Bridges, June 6, 1953; children—Robert W., Ann Elizabeth. A.B., Miami U., Oxford, Ohio, 1952; M.S., Ohio State U., 1957, Ph.D., 1960. Grad. asst. Ohio State U., Columbus, 1955-59; research assoc. Ohio Agrl. Research and Devel. Ctr., Wooster, 1959-61; plant pathologist Bklyn. Bot. Garden, 1961-69; acting chmn. Kitchawan Research Lab., 1967-69; prof., head dept. plant pathology U. Ga., 1969—. Mem. United Fund com. Griffin-Spalding County Facilities Plan. Served with Chem. Corps, U.S. Army, 1953-55. NSF grantee 1963-66; Am. Rhododendron Soc. grantee, 1982. Mem. Am. Phytopathol. Soc., Soc. Nematologists, Ga. Hort. Soc., Ga. Assn. Plant Pathologists, Internat. Soc. Arboriculture, Council for Agrl. Sci. and Tech., Sigma Xi, Gamma Sigma Delta, Phi Kappa Alpha. Episcopalian. Lodge: Rotary. Contbr. articles to profl. jours., popular mags. and encys. Office: Dept Plant Pathology U Ga Georgia Station Experiment GA 30212

WALKER, JEWETT LYNIUS, clergyman, church official; b. Beaumont, Tex., Apr. 7, 1930; s. Elijah Harvey and Ella Jane (Wilson) W.; B.A., Calif. Western U., 1957; M.A., Kingdom Bible Inst., 1960; B.R.E., St. Stephens Coll., 1966, D.D., 1968; LL.D., Union Bapt. Sem., 1971; grad. Nat. Planned Giving Inst., 1981; m. Dorothy Mae Croom, Apr. 11, 1965; children—Cassandra Lynn, Jewett L., Kevin, Michael, Ella, Betty Renne, Kent, Elijah H. Ordained to ministry A.M.E. Zion Ch., 1957; pastor Shiloh A.M.E. Zion Ch., Monrovia, Calif., 1961-64, Martin Temple A.M.E. Zion Ch., Los Angeles, 1964-65, 1st A.M.E. Zion Ch., Compton, Calif., 1965-66, Met. A.M.E. Zion Ch., Los Angeles, 1966-73, Logan Temple A.M.E. Zion Ch., San Diego, 1973-74, Rock Hill A.M.E. Zion Ch., Indian Trail, N.C., 1974-79, Bennettsville A.M.E. Zion Ch., Norwood, N.C., 1979—; sec.-treas. depts. home missions, brotherhood pensions and relief A.M.E. Zion Ch., Charlotte, N.C., 1974; mem. exec. bd. ch. and soc. Nat. Council Chs.; mem. World Meth. Council, del. 14th World Conf.; pres. Jewett L. Walker and Assocs., Inc. Trustee, Clinton Coll., Rock Hill, Lomax-Hannon Coll., Greenville, Ala., Union Bapt. Theol. Sem., Birmingham, Ala.; bd. mgrs. McCrorey br. YMCA; pres. Am. Ch. Fin. Service Corp., Carolina Home Health Service Inc., Methodist Life Ins. Soc. Inc. Mem. Nat. Assn. Ch. Bus. Adminstrs. (fellow in ch. bus. adminstrn.), Presbyn Ch. Bus. Adminstrs. Assn., NAACP (life). Clubs: Shriners, Masons (33 deg.). Author articles. Home: 910 Bridle Path Ln Charlotte NC 27211 Office: PO Box 30846 401 2d St Charlotte NC 28202

WALKER, JOHN CARL, school principal; b. New Orleans, July 6, 1945; s. J.D. Walker and Mable (Folse) W.; m. Linda Lowry, Aug. 1, 1968; 1 child, Johnny. B.S., La. State U., 1969, M.Ed., 1976; postgrad. Tulane, Loyola, Nicholas U., New Orleans, 1979-84. Tchr. St. Charles Parish Sch., Luling, La., 1969-76, asst. prin. Jr. High, 1976-77, prin. R.J. Vial Middle, 1978-80, prin. Lakewood Jr. High, 1980—; dir. St. Charles Parish Recreation Dist., Luling, 1977-79. Recipient Lakewood Jr. High-Secondary Sch. Recognition Program Dept. Edn., 1982-83; grantee State Dept. Edn., 1982-83. Mem. Am. Assn. Curriculum Devel., La. Assn. Prins. (parish pres.), Nat. Assn. Secondary Sch. Prins., La. Assn. Sch. Execs., Phi Delta Kappa. Avocations: tennis, horses, fishing. Home: 217 Dunleith St Destrehan LA 70047

WALKER, JULIUS, educational administrator; b. N.Y.C., Feb. 9, 1945; s. Julius Edward and Ruth Odessa (Grimes) W.; B.S., Elizabeth City (N.C.) State U., 1967; M.S., N.C. Central U., 1974; Ed.S., East Carolina U., Greenville, N.C., 1980; D.Hum. (hon.), Urban Bible Inst., 1984; m. Katie Louise Johnson, Aug. 24, 1968; children—Shawn Edward, Kendra Lynette. Elem. sch. tchr. Washington County Union Sch., Roper, N.C., 1967-74, prin., 1977-83; prin. Creswell (N.C.) Elem. Sch., 1974-77; mem. Prins. Info. and Research Center. Democratic judge Lees Mill Precinct, 1971-74; del. Washington County Precinct Conv., 1981; bd. dirs. Spl. Olympics Washington County, 1979-81, Washington County Heart Fund, 1979-80, Roanoke Devel. Center, 1980-81, Washington County Salvation Army. vice chmn. Washington County Recreation Commn., 1979-81, chmn., 1981—; commr. Men's Softball League Washington County, 1976; del. dist. conf. A.M.E. Zion Ch., 1980-81; steward to pastor, primary Sunday sch. tchr.; vice-chmn. Selective Service Bd., 1983. Recipient various tchr. of yr. awards, service awards. Mem. NEA, Nat. Polit. Action Community Edn., Am. Sch. Bd. Jour. Assn., Assn. Elem. Prins., Assn. Supervision and Curriculum Devel., N.C. Assn. Educators, N.C. Athletic Ofcls. Assn., Kappa Alpha Psi. Club: Masons. Home: PO Box 358 Roper NC 27970 Office: PO Box 308 Roper NC 27970

WALKER, LARRY DON, hospital administrator; b. Jonesboro, Ark., Mar. 8, 1949; s. Cornelia (McMasters) Walker; m. Linda Carol, June 20, 1971; children—Paul Adrian, Allison Leight. B.S., U. Ark., 1976; M.P.A., Memphis State U., 1981; M.S., Trinity U., San Antonio, 1984. Dept. dir. Bapt. Meml. Hosp., Memphis, 1971-80, adminstr., 1980-82; adminstr. Bapt. Meml. Hosp., Forrest City, Ark., 1982—. Bd. dirs. St. Francis County Hosp. Authority, Forrest City, 1984—. Mem. Ark. Hosp. Assn. (bd. dirs. non-profit hosp. council), Am. Hosp. Assn., Healthcare Fin. Mgmt. Assn., Corning C. of C. (bd. dirs. 1980-82). Mem. Assembly of God Ch. Lodges: Kiwanis, Rotary. Avocations: fishing; hunting. Office: PO Box 667 Forrest City AR 72335

WALKER, LAURENCE COLTON, forestry educator, clergyman, forestry consultant; b. Washington, Sept. 8, 1924; s. Hobart Theodore and Laura Pearl (Johnson) W.; m. Anne Sinclair, June 17, 1948; children—Janet Anne, Stephen Laurence, Wendy Elizabeth, Jean Marie. B.S., Pa. State U., 1948; M. of Forestry, Yale U., 1949; Ph.D., SUNY-Syracuse, 1953; cert. Oak Ridge Inst. Nuclear Studies, 1956; cert. U. Paris, 1946. Ordained to ministry Cumberland Presbyn. Ch., 1981. With U.S. Forest Service, Tex. and Ala., 1948-54; assoc. prof. U. Ga., 1954-63; dean Sch. Forestry Stephen F. Austin State U., 1963-76, Lacy Hunt prof., 1976—; chief forester Nat. Plant Food Inst., 1958-70. Vice pres. E. Tex. Area council Boy Scouts Am., 1974—; pres. Deep E. Tex. Devel. Assn., 1974-75; pres. United Way County of Nacogdoches, 1979. Recipient Disting. Eagle Scout award Boy Scouts Am. 1975, Silver Beaver award 1974, Silver Antelope award, 1984. Fellow Soc. Am. Foresters (Disting. Service to Forestry award 1968), AAAS (councilman 1974), Am. Sci. Affiliation. Lodge: Rotary (Nacogdoches, Tex.). Author: Ecology and Our Forests, 1972; Axes, Oxen & Men, 1975; Reporting Technical Information, 2d edit., 1975; Trees, 1984. Home: 514 Millard Dr Nacogdoches TX 75961 Office: PO Box 6109 Stephen F Austin State U Nacogdoches TX 75962

WALKER, LEROY TASHREAU, educator, university administrator, coach; b. Atlanta, June 14, 1918; s. Willie and Mary Elizabeth (Thomas) W.; B.S., Benedict Coll., 1940; M.A., Columbia U., 1941; Ph.D., NYU, 1957; H.H.D., Benedict Coll., Defiance Coll.; LL.D., Eastern Ky. U.; D.Sports Sci., U.S. Sports Acad.; m. Katherine McDowell, Dec. 31, 1938 (dec.); children—LeRoy, Carolyn. Chmn. dept. phys. edn., coach basketball, football, track and field Benedict Coll., Columbia, S.C., 1941-42, Bishop Coll., Marshall, Tex., 1942-43, Prairie View State U., 1943-45; chmn. dept. phys. edn. and recreation, coach basketball, football, track and field N.C. Central U., Durham, 1945-73, vice-chancellor for univ. relations, 1974-76, chancellor, 1983-86; ednl. specialist Cultural Exchange Program, Dept. State, 1959, 60, 62; dir. program, planning and tng. Peace Corps, Africa, 1966-68; coach Ethiopian and Israeli Olympic teams, Rome, 1960; adv. Jamaican Nat. Team in track and field Carreras Games, 1962, Trinidadian Olympic Team, Mexico City, 1968; track and field coach Western Hemisphere Team, Germany, England, 1969; head coach U.S. Nat. Track and Field Team, France, Germany and Russia, 1970; organizer, coordinator Pan-Africa vs. U.S.A. Internat. Track and Field Meet, Durham, 1971, U.S.A. Nat. Track and Field Team, Germany, Italy, Russia and West Africa, 1973, U.S.A. vs. USSR Internat. Track and Field Meet and Arts Festival, Durham, 1974, U.S.A.-Pan-Africa-Germany Internat. Track and Field Meet, Durham, 1975; tech. cons. Kenyan Olympic Team, Munich, 1972; commr. Mid-Eastern Athletic Conf., 1971-74; mem. U.S. Collegiate Sports Council, 1971; chmn. Coll. Commrs. Assn., 1971-74; chmn. Athletic Union of U.S.A. Track and Field Com., 1973-75; head coach U.S.A. Olympic Track and Field Team, Montreal, 1976; bd. dirs. U.S. Olympic Com., U.S.A.-China Relations Com. Recipient Hamilton Watch Co. award for James E. Shepard Outstanding Tchr. at N.C. Central U., 1964; Achievement award Central Intercollegiate Athletic Assn., 1967; Disting. Alumni Service award Benedict Coll., 1968; Disting. Service awards Kiwanis Internat., 1971, City of Durham, 1971, Durham C. of C., 1973; Gov.'s Ambassador of Goodwill award, 1974; O. Max Gardner award, 1976; N.C. Disting. Citizen award, 1977; Achievement in Life award Ency. Brit., 1977; elected to N.C. Hall of Fame, 1975; S.C. Hall of Fame, 1977; Nat. Assn. Sport and Phys. Edn. Hall of Fame, 1977; Central Intercollegiate Athletic Assn. Hall of Fame, 1980; Mid Eastern Athletic Conf. Hall of Fame, 1981; Benedict Coll. Hall of Fame, 1982. Mem. AAHPERD (nat. pres., Honor award 1972, Luther Halsey Gulick award), NEA, U.S. Track Coaches Assn. (Nat. Track Coach of Yr. award 1972), Nat. Assn. Intercollegiate Athletics, Nat. Collegiate Athletic Assn. (Nat. Coach of Yr. award 1972), N.C. Assn. Health, Phys. Edn. and Recreation (Honor award 1971, v.p. phys. edn. div., dir.), Internat. Assn. Athletic Fedns. (U.S. rep. 1976—), Sigma Delta Psi, Alpha Phi Omega, Omega Psi Phi. Episcopalian. Author: Manual of Adapted Physical Education, 1960; Physical Education for the Exceptional Students, 1965; Championship Techniques in Track and Field, 1969; Track and Field for Boys and Girls, 1983; contbr. articles to profl. jours. Office: NC Central U Chancellor's Office Durham NC 27707

WALKER, MARY ANN, oil company geologist, benefits consultant; b. Denton, Tex., Mar. 5, 1952; d. Billy Earl and Laura Bell (Nobles) Snow; m. William Carl Collins, Aug. 4, 1973 (div. May 1981); m. Gregory Smith Walker, Oct. 15, 1983. B.S.Edn., Tex. Christian U., 1973; M.S. in Edn., Tex. Tech. U., 1978; B.A. in Geology, U. Houston-Clear Lake, 1983; M.S., U. Houston-Clear Lake, 1986. Tchr., various sch. dists., Tex., 1973-81; geol. technician Williams Exploration Co., Houston, 1981—; co-owner, v.p. Associated Benefits Cons., 1984—. Mem. Am. Assn. Petroleum Geologists (jr.), Houston Geol. Soc. (student mem.), mem. (assoc.) Soc. Profl. Well Log Analysts. Methodist. Avocation: sailing. Home: 2038 Willow Wisp Seabrook TX 77586 Office: Williams Exploration Co PO Box 4664 111 Fannin Suite 1100 Houston TX 77586

WALKER, MARY ELIZABETH, state consultant for gifted; b. Austin, Tex., Aug. 30, 1948; d. William Stewart and Mary Elizabeth (Abel) W. B.Mus. Ed., N.E. La. U., 1970; M.A., Gifted Child Edn., U. South Fla., 1977. Tchr. chorus Calcasieu Parish Sch., Lake Charles, La., 1970-76; resource cons. for gifted Edn. Service Unit 2, Fremont, Nebr., 1977-78; state cons. for gifted Miss. Dept. Edn., Jackson, 1978—; state dir. Miss. Future Problem Solving Program, 1981—; gifted edn. cons., public schs., Nebr., Va., Ark., 1977-84. Sec., v.p. bd. dirs. Unity of Jackson, 1983-84; ptnr. Oral Roberts Assn., 1977—. Office of Gifted, Dept. Edn. grantee, 1978-81. Mem. Council State Dirs. Programs for Gifted (pres. 1984—), Miss. Assn. Talented and Gifted (exec. bd. 1978—), Music Educators Nat. Conf., La. Tchrs. Assn., Council Exceptional Children, Assn. for Gifted (com. chmn. 1984—), Miss. Assn. Women in Ednl. Leadership, Delta Omicron, Alpha Delta Kappa. Avocations: reading; jogging; music; dance. Home: PO Box 593 Clinton MS 39056 Office: Miss Dept Edn PO Box 771 Jackson MS 39205

WALKER, MARY ELLA, nurse; b. St. Louis, Aug. 23, 1945; d. Earl Earnest and Mrytle Emma (Agnew) W.; B.S. in Nursing, Tex. Christian U., 1967; M.S. in Nursing, U. Tex., 1972, Ph.D., 1976. Staff nurse, asst. head nurse, head nurse Barnes Hosp., St. Louis, 1967-71; staff nurse Brackenridge Hosp., Austin, Tex., 1972; research asso. U. Tex. System, 1973-74; research asso. Center Study of Human Resources, Austin, 1975-76, So. Regional Council, Inc., Atlanta, 1975-76; nurse cons. Tex. Med. Found., Austin, 1976-77; vis. lectr. U. Wis., Oshkosh, 1977-78; program dir. Southwest Rural Health Field Services Program Nat. Rural Center, Austin, 1977-78; program dir. Tex. Rural Health Field Services Program, 1979-85; lectr. U. Tex., 1979-85. Mary Gibbs Jones scholar, 1976; Meadows fellow, 1983-85. Fellow Am. Acad. Nursing; mem. Am. Nurses Assn., Am. Rural Health Assn., Sigma Theta Tau, Phi Kappa Phi. Contbr. in field. Office: U Texas Sch Social Work Texas Rural Health Field Services Program 2609 University Ave Austin TX 78712

WALKER, MITCHELL HARRIS, pharmacist; b. Hillsbrough, N.C., Mar. 29, 1930; s. Marion Robert and Madeline Cornelius (Harris) W.; m. Mary Francis Kluttz, May 20, 1951; children—Deborah Kluttz, Michelle Harris Walker Smith. Degree in Pharmacy, Mercer U. Sch. Pharmacy, 1957. Registered pharmacist, N.C. Pharmacist, Walkers Drug, Rowland, N.C. Commr., Town of Rowland, 1967—, mayor-pro-tem, 1973-85, mayor, 1985—; Sunday sch. tchr. Rowland Meth. Ch., 1961-71, 84—; Vice-chmn. Council of Govt., Lumberton, N.C., 1984-85, chmn., 1985—. Served with U.S. Army,

1951-53. Mem. N.C. Pharm. Assn., Am. Legion (comdr. 1965-83), Phi Delta Chi. Democrat. Lodges: Lions (pres. 1982-84), Masons, Shriners. Avocations: golfing; rose gradening. Home: B-207 Rowland NC 28383 Office: Walkers Drug 301 Hwy Rowland NC 28383

WALKER, OSCAR JAMES, III, tobacco sales representative, consultant; b. Winston-Salem, N.C., Oct. 27, 1947; s. Frank and Willie Mae (Longshore) Gunn; m. Sarah Jane Fleming, Dec. 23, 1973; 1 son, Oscar Jermaine. B.S. in Bus. Adminstrn., Johnson C. Smith U., Charlotte, N.C., 1974. Pub. asst. technician, then auditor S.C. Dept. Social Services, Columbia, 1973-77; state mgr. United Motor Club, Columbia, 1976-77; project dir. Columbia Urban League, 1977-79; salesman Philip Morris USA, N.Y.C., 1979—; cons. Jermaine Enterprises, 1981—. Charter pres. Concerned Citizens, Inc., Newberry, S.C., 1976; adv. bd. Beckman's Mental Health Ctr., Greenwood, S.C., 1975; chmn. bd. Miss Fashion Pageant, Newberry, 1982. Served with U.S. Army, 1968-70; Vietnam. Named Citizen of Week, Standard Savs. & Loan, Newberry, 1975; recipient citation of appreciation Concerned Citizens, Inc., 1976, meritorious service award Columbia Urban League, 1979; decorated Bronze Star medal, Army Commendation medal with oak leaf cluster; notary pub. S.C. Mem. Tobacco Action Program. Democrat. Baptist. Club: Arrows Bridge of Newberry (pres. elect 1984). Home: 112 Tillbury Dr Columbia SC 29203

WALKER, R. DIXON, urologist; b. Rochester, N.Y., July 22, 1936; s. Robert Dixon and Lucy Virginia (Wier) W.; m. Joyce Ann Copeland, July 23, 1961; children—Sherri, Lisa, Jeff. B.A. in Psychology, Carson-Newman Coll., 1959, B.S. in Biology, 1959; M.D., U. Miami, Fla., 1963. Diplomate Am. Bd. Urology. Intern, Bowman Gray Sch. Medicine, Winston-Salem, N.C., 1963-64; resident, U. Fla. Coll. Medicine, Gainesville, 1964-68; clin. instr. Coll. Medicine U. Tenn., Memphis, 1968-70; asst. prof. surgery and pediatrics, Coll. Medicine U. Fla., Gainesville, 1970-74, assoc. prof. surgery and pediatrics, 1974-76, prof. surgery and pediatrics, 1976—, dir. of admissions, 1976-79; chief of staff Shands Hosp., Gainesville, 1975-76, med. dir. children's med. service, 1982—, med. dir. operating room, 1985—. Contbr. chpts. to books, articles to publs. Served with USNR, 1968-70, served to comdr. USNR, 1954-80. Fellow Am. Acad. Pediatrics (sec. urology sect. 1976-79, chmn. 1981), ACS (Fla. State Adv. Com. 1983—); mem. Am. Urologic Assn., Soc. Pediatric Urology (sec. 1983—). Avocation: gardening. Office: Div Urology Univ Fla Sch Medicine Box J247 Gainesville FL 32610

WALKER, ROBERT COLEMAN, social sciences administrator, counseling psychologist; b. Mobile, Ala., Feb. 26, 1937; s. Edward George and Venita Grace (Davidson) W.; m. Gerri Kay Howell, Aug. 10, 1963; 1 child, Adam Coleman. B.A., Stetson U., 1959; Ed.M., U. Ga., 1964; Ed.D., Auburn U., 1970; postgrad., U. Ala., La. State U. Tchr., Foley pub. schs., Ala., 1959-61, Atlanta pub. schs., 1961-63; guidance counselor Ala. pub. schs., 1964-68; dir. pupil personnel Rockdale County Schs., Conyers, Ga., 1970-72; prof. psychology DeKalb Coll., Dunwoody, Ga., 1972-74, head psychology dept., 1974-81, head social scis. div., 1982—; counselor Gov.'s Honor Program, Macon, Ga., summer 1964; cons. in field. Contbr. articles to profl. jours. Bd. dirs., sec. Ansley Park Civic Assn., Atlanta, 1974-81; coordinator task force on pub. housing, Atlanta, 1976-79; founder Ansley Park House Garden Tour, 1978—; mem. com. Peidmont Park Beautification; mem. Rockdale County Community Resources Council, Conyers, Ga., 1970-72. Fellow NDEA, 1963-64, 1961, Wall St. Jour., 1960; recipient Wall St. Jour. award, 1961. Mem. Am. Psychol. Assn., Counseling Psychology Assn. Div. 17, Theta Alpha Phi, Sigma Delta Phi, Sigma Tau Delta, Phi Delta Dappa, Sigma Phi Epsilon. Republican. Episcopalian. Avocations: collector-dealer: Am. cutglass, artglass, pottery 1860-1920. Home: 7105 Brandon Mill Rd NW Atlanta GA 30328

WALKER, ROBERT GERALD, corporate executive; b. Austin, Tex., Feb. 25, 1925; s. Robert Gerald and Bess Woodrin (Patterson) W.; m. Pauline Burleson, Feb. 11, 1949; children—Keith, Mark, Susan, Wayne, Sally. B.B.A., U. Tex., 1950. Mfg. mgr. R.H. Folmar Bldg. Products, Austin, Tex., 1950-55; mfg. adminstr. Waste King Corp., Los Angeles, 1955-58, mfg. mgr., 1958-60; mfg. mgr. Digital Computer div. Litton Industries, Beverly Hills, Calif., 1960-63, gen. mgr. Tex. plant, 1963-65, Microwave Oven div., Minn., 1965-67; v.p. corp. adminstrn. Allis-Chalmers, Milw., 1967-68, v.p., gen. mgr., 1968-69, group v.p., 1969-72; chmn. bd., chief exec. officer Kinark Corp., Tulsa, 1972—, also dir.; dir. Boyles Galvanizing Co., Ft. Worth, Lake River Corp., Countryside, Ill., Kinpak Inc., Montgomery, Ala. City councilman and mayor, LaMirada, Calif., 1959-60. Served with USAF, 1943-46; material command contract officer, 1950-51. Home: 3855 S Birmingham Pl Tulsa OK 74105 Office: 7060 S Yale Ave Tulsa OK 74136

WALKER, ROBERT MICHAEL, communication systems engineering manager; b. Los Angeles, May 27, 1940; s. George Frank and Roberta Ruth (Potts) W.; B.S. in Mech. Engring., N.Mex. State U., 1963, M.S. in Mech. Engring., 1964, D.Sc. (fellow), 1967; m. Dickie Tighe, May 20, 1967; children—Katherine Marie, Robert Tighe, Ann Michelle. Grad. asst. mech. engring. dept. N.Mex. State U., 1963-64, instr., 1964-67, instr. extension sch., White Sands Missile Range, 1968-70; prin. scientist BDM Corp., McLean, Va., 1971-79, sr. scientist, El Paso, Tex., 1967-71, project mgr., Tucson, 1971-75, prin. investigator nuclear survivability communication systems, McLean, 1975-77, nat. expert NATO integrated communication system design, SHAPE Tech. Center, The Hague, Netherlands, 1977-78, prin. scientist, McLean, 1978-79; sr. tech. staff engr. TRW Def. Systems Group, Falls Church, Va., 1979-83, mgr. advanced communication systems engring., 1983—. Cub scout webelos den master Boy Scouts Am., Tucson, 1972-73, asst. scoutmaster, Annandale, Va., 1975-77; mem. archtl. com. Canterbury Woods Civic Assn., 1979—. Served to capt. Ordnance Corps, U.S. Army, 1968-70. Decorated Commendation medal; registered profl. engr., N.Mex. Mem. Armed Forces Communications and Electronics Assn., Air Force Assn., SAR (charter mem., pres. Fairfax Resolves chpt. 1982-84; sec.-treas. Tucson chpt. 1971-74), Soc. Pershing Rifles, Sigma Xi, Tau Beta Pi, Pi Tau Sigma. Home: 4928 Althea Dr Annandale VA 22003 Office: 5113 Leesburg Pike Suite 400 Falls Church VA 22041

WALKER, ROBERT YULE, geologist; b. Fort Worth, Sept. 11, 1917; s. Robert Yule and Christine (Taylor) W.; m. Beverly Jensen, Jan. 31, 1942; children—Robert Y., Christopher W., Tina Marie. Ph.B., U. Wis., 1939. Cert. petroleum geologist. Geophysicist, Texaco, So. La., Rocky Mountains, 1939-43; dist. geologist Gt. Lakes Carbon, Abilene, Tex., 1946-53; geologist W. Tex., Abilene, 1953—. Served to lt. USNR, 1943-46; PTO. Mem. Am. Assn. Petroleum Geologists, Am. Ind. Geologists, Abilene Geol. Soc. Republican. Episcopalian. Clubs: Petroleum, Fairway Oaks Country. Avocations: golf; fishing. Home: 49 Pinehrust St Abilene TX 79606 Office: 11-LA One Energy Sq Abilene TX 79601

WALKER, RONALD LAVERN, urban planning economist, consultant; b. Brookhaven, Miss., Nov. 23, 1953; s. Albert J. Walker and Annie P. (Tillman) Walker Kelly; m. Minnie P. Peabody, Aug. 25, 1979. B.S. in Resource Econs., U. Mass., 1975; M. Urban Planning, U. Ill., 1977. Asst. dir. Neighborhood Housing Services of Chgo., 1977-79; asst. tng. dir. Neighborhood Reinvestment Corp., Washington, 1979-80; support officer, 1980-81, regional program rev. mgr., 1981-85, dist. dir., 1986—. Univ. scholar, 1973-74; Ascension Farm scholar, 1974-75; recipient Community Service award Village of Oak Park (Ill.), 1980. Mem. Nat. Econs. Assn., Am. Mgmt. Assn., Am. Planning Assn., Atlanta C. of C., High Mus. Art, Atlanta Urban League, Atlanta NAACP. Alpha Zeta. Home: 3833 Seton Hall Dr Decatur GA 30034

WALKER, RONALD NOBLE, pharmacist; b. Waco, Tex., Feb. 26, 1956; s. Ronald Olan and Janice Claire (Jewell) W. B.S. in Pharmacy with honors, U. Tex., 1978. Registered pharmacist, Tex. Staff pharmacist in charge of unit-dose decentralized drug distbn. Presbyterian Hosp.-Margot Perot Women's and Children's Hosp. Bldg., Dallas, 1981-84; pharmacist in charge Eckerd Drugs, Bedford, Tex., 1984—; nursing in-service lectr., 1982, 83. Jr. asst. scoutmaster Longhorn council Boy Scouts Am.; mem. Nat. Republican Congl. Com., Washington, 1983. Recipient Eagle Scout award Boy Scouts Am., 1969, God and Country award, 1972. Mem. Am. Soc. Hosp. Pharmacists, Tex. Soc. Hosp. Pharmacists, Kappa Psi (sgt.-at-arms chpt. 1977-78), Rho Chi. Baptist. Avocations: photography; video photogaphy; coin collecting; spectator sports; tennis. Home: 6348 Dorchester Tr North Richland Hills TX 76180

WALKER, RONALD R., writer, newsletter editor; b. Newport News, Va., Sept. 2, 1934; s. William R. and Jean Marie (King) W.; m. O. Diane Mawson, Apr. 16, 1961; children—Mark Jonathan, Steven Christopher. B.S., Pa. State U., 1956; postgrad. (Nieman fellow) Harvard U., 1970-71. Reporter, news editor, sr. editor, editorial page editor, mng. editor San Juan Star (P.R.), 1962-73, Washington columnist, 1982-84, city editor, 1984—; instr. journalism Pa. State U., State College, 1973-74; asst. prof. Columbia U. Grad. Sch. Journalism, N.Y.C., 1974-76; editor The Daily News, V.I., 1976-77; press sec. Gov. V.I., 1978-79; adminstrv. asst. Rep. James H. Scheuer, U.S. Congress, 1980-82. Served with U.S. Army, 1957-59. Mem. Soc. Nieman Fellows. Contbr. articles to nat. mags. and jours. Address: 1 Taft St Apt 8-D San Juan PR 00911

WALKER, SCOTT GARY, sales executive; b. Dublin, Ga., Feb. 24, 1958; s. Holland Gary and Ouida Sue (Dixon) W.;. m. Karen S. Walker; 1 child, Aaron P. B.B.A., Augusta Coll., 1982. Turf technician Pride Fertilizer Co., Augusta, Ga., 1979-80; asst. mgr. Westside Tool Rental, Augusta, 1980-82; sales rep. Indsl. Rubber & Safety, Augusta, 1982-83; dist. sales mgr. Willson Safety Products, Reading, Pa., 1984—. Mem. Nat. Asbestos Council, Am. Soc. Safety Engrs. (v.p. 1983). Baptist. Avocations: baseball; golf; music. Home: 1074 Bailing Rd Lawrenceville GA 30245 Office: Willson Safety Products 2d and Washington Sts Reading PA 19603

WALKER, STEPHEN DADE, geologist; b. Durango, Colo., June 25, 1958; s. John Vaughan and Sarah Louise (Grimes) W.; m. Kimberly Robin Lockwood, May 23, 1981; 1 child, Kelly Elaine. B.S. in Geology, Va. Poly. Inst., 1980; postgrad. U. Tex.-Odessa. Project coordinator devel. geology Chevron, USA , Midland, Tex., 1980—. Mem. Am. Assn. Petroleum Geologists, West Tex. Geol. Soc. Mem. Pentecostal Ch. Club: Va. Tech. Geology (pres. 1979-80) (Blacksburg). Home: 1912 Hollywood Odessa TX 79763

WALKER, TOM MORROW, ophthalmologist; b. Mobile, Ala., June 4, 1942; s. Thomas Marshall and Eoliene (Morris) W.; m. Bette Lee Benjamin, June 15, 1968; children—Juliana Anita, Gretchen Elaine. B.S., Auburn U., 1964; M.D., U. Ala., 1968. Diplomate Am. Bd. Ophthalmology. Intern, U. South Ala., Mobile, 1964; resident Gorgas Hosp., Canal Zone, 1970; attending ophthalmologist Gorgas Hosp., Panama Canal Zone, 1976-77; ophthalmologist Mobile Eye, Ear, Nose and Throat Ctr., 1977—; bd. dirs. Ala. Acad. Ophthalmologists, 1978-79. Served to maj. U.S. Army, 1970-74. William Boyd Pathology Med. grantee, U. Ala. Med. Sch., 1968. Fellow Am. Acad. Ophthalmologists, Ala. Acad. Ophthalmologists (bd. dirs. 1978-79); mem. AMA, Phi Delta Kappa, Phi Kappa Phi, Alpha Omega Alpha. Republican. Methodist. Club: Mobile Yacht (rear commodore). Office: Mobile Eye Ear Nose and Throat Ctr 1359 Springhill Ave Mobile AL 36604

WALKER, WILLIAM DELANY, physics educator; b. Dallas, Nov. 23, 1923; s. William and Mildred (Ramsey) W.; m. Suzanne J. Porter, Dec. 23, 1946 (div. Sept. 1975); children—Nancy, Elizabeth, Samuel; m. 2d Constance Kalbach, Oct 10, 1975. B.A., Rice U., 1944; Ph.D., Cornell U., 1949. Physicist, Naval Research Lab., Washington, 1944-45; asst. prof. physics Rice U., Houston, 1949-52; lectr. physics U. Calif.-Berkeley, 1951-52; asst. prof. physics U. Rochester (N.Y.), 1952-54; asst. prof. physics U. Wis., Madison, 1954-57, assoc. prof., prof., 1957-71, Disting. prof., 1969-71, chmn. dept., 1964-66; prof. physics Duke U., Durham, N.C., 1971—, chmn. dept., 1975-81. Served to ensign USNR, 1944-45. Grantee Research Corp., 1949-51, NSF, 1960-61, also AEC, ERDA, Dept. Energy, 1955—, fellow Cornell U., 1945-48. Fellow Am. Phys. Soc.; mem. Phi Beta Kappa, ,Sigma Xi. Episcopalian. Club: Tennis. Contbr. articles to profl. jours. Discoverer/co-discoverer two elem. particles. Home: 907 Green St Durham NC Office: Physics Dept Duke U Durham NC 27706

WALKER, WILLIAM HOMER, III, savings and loan executive; b. Miami, Fla., June 24, 1940; s. William Homer, Jr., and Zoella (Babcock) W.; B.B.A., Westminster Coll., New Wilmington, Pa., 1963; m. Carol Sue Harriman, June 4, 1963; children—William Homer, David Harriman. With AmeriFirst Fed. Savs. & Loan Assn. (formerly First Fed. Savs. & Loan Assn.), Miami, Fla., 1964—, audit clk., 1964-65, programmer-analyst, 1965-69, loan officer, 1969-71, v.p., mgr. loan servicing, 1971-74, v.p., asst. sec., 1974-75, v.p., sec., 1975-79, dir., 1976—, sr. v.p., corp. sec., 1979—. Trustee, United Protestant Appeal, 1979—; trustee Met. Bd. YMCA of Greater Miami, asst. sec., 1975-76, pres., 1979-81; mem. U. Miami Citizens' Adv. Council. Corp. rep. S. Fla. Coordinating Council, Fla. C. of C. Democrat. Presbyterian. Clubs: Rod and Reel of Miami Beach, Univ., Bath, Kiwanis of Miami (dir., 1979-83). Office: 1 SE 3d Ave 17th Floor Miami FL 33131

WALKER, WILLIAM OLIVER, JR., religion educator; b. Sweetwater, Tex., Dec. 6, 1930; s. William Oliver and Frances Baker (White) W.; m. Mary Scott Daugherty, Dec. 22, 1955 (div. Dec. 1978); children—William Scott, Mary Evan, Michael Neal. B.A., Austin Coll., 1953; M.Div., Austin Presbyterian Sem., 1957; M.A., U. Tex., 1958; Ph.D., Duke U., 1962. Instr. religion Austin Coll., Sherman, Tex., 1954-55, Duke U., 1960-62; from asst. to prof. religion Trinity U., San Antonio, 1962—, chmn. dept., 1980—. Contbr. articles and book reviews to profl. jours. Editor: The Relationships, 1978; assoc. editor Harper's Bible Dictionary, 1985. Mem. Studiorum Novi Testamenti Soc., Soc. Bibl. Lit. (regional sec.-treas. 1980—), Am. Acad. Religion (regional pres. 1966-67), Soc. Sci. Study Religion, Catholic Bibl. Assn. Am. Democrat. Presbyterian. Avocations: tennis; traveling. Home: 315 Cloverleaf Ave San Antonio TX 78209 Office: Dept Religion Trinity U 715 Stadium Dr San Antonio TX 78284

WALKUP, HOMER ALLEN, lawyer, historian, writer; b. Dunloup, W.Va., Jan. 28, 1917; s. Homer Allen and Lillie Belle (Harris) W.; m. Edna Mae Tucker, Nov. 19, 1941 (dec. 1966); m. Charlotte M. Tuttle Lloyd, Feb. 4, 1967; children—Homer Allen, Randolph Michael, Pamela Susan. A.B., W.Va. U., 1935, LL.B., 1938; LL.M., Georgetown U., 1947. Bar: W.Va. 1938, U.S. Supreme Ct. 1946, U.S. Ct. Claims 1978, U.S. Ct. Appeals (fed. cir.) 1982, U.S. Claims Ct. 1982. Sole practice, W.Va., 1938-42; complaint atty. W.Va. Office OPA, Charleston, 1942; commd. ensign USNR, 1942, advanced through grades to capt., 1963; appellate judge Navy Ct. Mil. Rev., 1966-68; dep. asst., JAG of Navy, 1968-73; ret., 1973; sole practice, Summersville, W.Va., 1974—. Vice chmn. governing bd. Alexandria (Va.) Community Mental Health Ctr., 1981-82; mem. exec. bd. and social planning com. Alexandria United Way; mem. exec. bd. No. Va. Family Service, 1978-82. Mem. ABA, Fed. Bar Assn., W.Va. State Bar, W.Va. Bar Assn., Bar Assn. D.C. Fed. Circuit Bar Assn., Judge Advs. Assn. (bd. dirs.), Assn. Trial Lawyers Am., Am. Judicature Soc., Mil. Order World Wars, Res. Officers Assn., Ret. Officers Assn., Order of Coif, Phi Alpha Delta. Democrat. Presbyterian. Club: Mil. Dist. Washington Officers.

WALL, BENNETT HARRISON, history educator; b. Raleigh, N.C., Dec. 7, 1914; s. Bennett Louis and Evie David (Harrison) W.; A.B., Wake Forest Coll., 1933; M.A., U. N.C., 1941, Ph.D., 1947; m. Neva Olive White, Sept. 7, 1968; children by previous marriage—Mae (Mrs. John E. Clark) (dec.), Diana (Mrs. John Freckman), Ann Bennett. Instr., N.C. State U., 1942-43; instr. U. N.C., 1943-44; instr. U. Ky., 1944-46, asst. prof., 1946-52, assoc. prof., 1952-64; prof. history dept. Tulane U., New Orleans, 1968-80, head dept., 1968-73, dir. Tulane Center Bus. History Studies, 1974-80; lectr. Am. history U. Ga., Athens, 1980-85. Mem. Orgn. Am. Historians, Agrl. History Soc., Bus. History Soc., Econ. History Assn., Newcomen Soc., La. (pres. 1974-75), So. (sec.-treas. 1953—) hist. assns., Omicron Delta Kappa, Phi Alpha Theta. Co-author: Teagle of Jersey Standard, 1974; Louisiana, A History. Contbr. numerous articles to profl. jours. Home: 150 Ashton Dr Athens GA 30606 Office: U Ga Dept History Athens GA 30602

WALL, CHARLES DONALD, pharmacist, realty company owner; b. Greenville, S.C., Sept. 2, 1943; s. Charles Heyward and Mary (Hightower) W.; m. Sylvia Ellen Turmo, June 25, 1966; children—Charles D., Jr., James Edward. B.S. in Pharmacy, U.S.C., 1967. Registered pharmacist. Pharmacist, pres. Profl. Pharmacy of Greer, S.C., 1967—; owner DW Leasing Co., Greer, 1984—, Kempson Rexall Drugs, Inman, S.C., 1984—, Kash & Karry Pharmacy, Greenville, S.C., 1984—; co-owner DW Realty Co., Greer, 1984—; dir. First Fed. S.C., Greer, Greenville TEC-Pharmacy Program, Greenville, 1983—. Cubmaster, Blue Ridge council Cub Scouts Am., Greer, 1976-82; mem. Greer Planning and Zoning Bd., Greer, 1984—, Mayor's Adv. Com., Greer, 1984—. Served with S.C. Air N.G., 1968-74. Mem. Am. Pharm. Assn., S.C. Pharm. Assn., 13th Dist. Pharm. Assn., Nat. Assn. Retail Druggists. Episcopalian. Clubs: Ducks Unlimited (Long Grove, Ill.); Commerce (Greenville). Avocations: hunting, fishing, racquetball, Rosarian. Home: 115 Peachtree Dr Greer SC 29651 Office: Profl Pharmacy Greer Inc 320 Memorial Dr Greer SC 29651

WALL, EVERN RANDOLPH, utility executive; b. Borger, Tex., Nov. 20, 1932; s. Evern T. and Janie (Hyman) W.; m. Phyllis M. Parker, June 8, 1952; children—Debbie, Randy. B.S., N.Mex. State U., 1957. Registered profl. engr., Tex. With El Paso Electric Co., 1957—, v.p. engring. and ops., 1968-74, pres., 1975—, chmn. bd., chief exec. officer, 1980—, also dir.; dir. State Nat. Bank El Paso, Franklin Land & Resources Inc. Bd. dirs. El Paso Indsl. Devel. Corp.; bd. dirs. utility mgmt. program N.Mex. State U., Presidents Assos. U. Tex., El Paso, Presidents Assos. N.Mex. State U., El Paso Boys Club, Yucca council Boy Scouts Am., El Paso Sci. Center. Recipient Disting. Alumnus award N.Mex. State U., 1976. Mem. Rocky Mountain Elec. League (past pres.), Tex. Atomic Energy Research Found. (past pres.), El Paso C. of C. (past pres.). Episcopalian. Club: El Paso Rotary. Office: Box 982 El Paso TX 79960*

WALL, JEFFRIE LYN PERKINS, ballet teacher, choreographer; b. Lake Charles, La., Mar. 19, 1953; d. W. L. (Buddy) and JoAnne (Deax) Perkins; m. H. Kent Wall, Feb. 7, 1976; children—Maurea Laine, Logan Hatch. Grad. Nat. Ballet Acad. Sch., Washington; cert. of study Grades 1-6 USSR State Ballet Sch. Minister of Culture, Tbilisi, Georgia, 1982, 83. Apprentice dancer Nat. Ballet, Washington, 1969-72; mem. corps Md. Ballet, Balt., 1972-73; tchr., dir. Lafayette Ballet, La., 1979—; tchr., owner Jeffrie Perkins Wall Ballet Studio, Lafayette, 1975—; dance panelist La. State Arts Council Grants Rev. Bd., Baton Rouge, 1985; guest faculty mem. Nat. Acad. Arts, Champaign, Ill., 1985. Dancer, Larry Logan in Concert, Lafayette, 1985. Mem. Southwest Regional Ballet Assn. Republican. Avocations: camping; outdoors; horseback riding. Office: Lafayette Ballet 215 Devalcourt St Lafayette LA 70506

WALL, WALTER VIRGIL, logging company executive; b. Abbeville, S.C., Dec. 27, 1925; s. William Lenzie and Alice Mable (Strother) W.; m. Patsy Blandena Timmerman, Nov. 15, 1947; children—Walter Virgil, William Timmerman, Sharon Elaine, Richard Dennis. Student Newberry Coll., 1946-47. Farmer, nr. Edgefield, S.C., 1950-60; owner, mgr. W.V. Wall Logging Co., Edgefield; dir. First Citizens Bank & Trust Co. Mem. fin. com. McKendree United Meth. Ch., chmn. adminstrv. bd., 1980—; mem. Edgefield County Bd. Trustees, 1970—. Served with USN, 1943-46. Mem. S.C. Forestry Assn. (chmn. Timber Suppliers Task Force; dir. 1982—), Am. Legion (comdr. 1983-84). Lodges: Masons, Shriners. Office: WV Wall Co Box 174 RR2 Edgefield SC 29824

WALL, WILLIAM CARTER, JR., engineering and business management consultant, educator, author; b. Huntsville, Ala., June 30, 1930; s. William Carter and Marion Elizabeth (Terry) W.; m. Shirley Lenore Matzet, June 18, 1955; children—William August, Kathleen Mary, Linda Lee, Christie Lynn, Terri Elizabeth, Julie Catherine. B.S. in Mech. Engring., Lafayette Coll., 1953; M.A. in Pub. Adminstrn., U. Okla., 1971, M.B.A., 1975, Ph.D., 1978. Cert. profl. estimator. Engr. Allis-Chalmers, Milw., 1953-55; with Dept. Army, Redstone Arsenal, Ala., 1957-81, chief mgmt. data systems office, Ballistic Missile Def. Systems Command, 1968-76, chief program mgmt. office HAWK Project Office, Missile Materiel Readiness Command, 1976-78, dep. project mgr. ground laser designators project office, Missile Research and Devel. Command, 1978-79, chief def. advanced research projects agy. projects office, Missile Command, 1979-80, dep. project mgr. Tow Project Office, 1980-81; pres. WCW Assocs., Inc., Huntsville, Ala., 1981—; adj. prof. mgmt. Fla. Inst. Tech., Melbourne, 1978—; part time faculty U. Ala., Huntsville, 1979—; prof. mgmt., nat. grad. faculty, dir. Huntsville Ctr., Ctr. for Study of Adminstrn., Nova U., Ft. Lauderdale, Fla., 1981—. Contbr. articles to profl. publs. Active Better Bus. Bur. N.Ala., Nat. Eagle Scout Assn. Served with U.S. Army, 1955-57. Recipient cert. of merit Dept. Army, 1971. Mem. Am. Mgmt. Assn., Assn. U.S. Army, So. Mgmt. Assn., Project Mgmt. Inst., Acad. of Mgmt., Nat. Estimating Soc., Huntsville-Madison County C. of C., Beta Gamma Sigma, Omicron Delta Epsilon. Roman Catholic. Clubs: Redstone Arsenal Officers, K.C. Home: 2200 Woodmore Dr Huntsville AL 35803 Office: 3609 Memorial Pkwy SW Huntsville AL 35801

WALLACE, ANDERSON, JR., lawyer; b. Cleve., Sept. 24, 1939; s. Anderson and Agatha Lee (Culpepper) W.; 1 son, Anderson III. Student Ga. Inst. Tech., 1957-58; B.A., George Washington U., 1962, J.D., 1964, LL.M., 1966. Bar: Tex. 1968, U.S. Dist. Ct. (no. dist.) Tex. 1968, U.S. Ct. Claims 1968, U.S. Tax Ct. 1968, U.S. Ct. Appeals (5th cir.) 1968, U.S. Supreme Ct. 1971, U.S. Ct. Appeals (11th cir.) 1981. Program mgmt. asst. NASA, Washington, 1962-64; atty. U.S. Dept. Treasury, Washington, 1964-66; tax atty. Price Waterhouse & Co., Atlanta, 1966-67; tax ptnr. Jackson, Walker, Winstead, Cantwell & Miller, Dallas, 1967-84; head tax dept., dir. Baker, Smith & Mills, Dallas, 1984—; instr. Sch. Law So. Meth. U. Trustee S.W. Mus. Sci. and Tech., Dallas, 1974—; N. Tex. Rehab. Assn., Dallas Girls Found. Chmn. Inst. on Employee Benefits, Southwestern Legal Found., 1976. Mem. ABA. Home: 10633 Park Preston Dallas TX 75230 Office: 500 LTV Ctr 2001 Ross Dallas TX 75201

WALLACE, DAVID HAROLD, automotive corporations executive; b. Mobile, Ala., Feb. 10, 1936; s. Roshier Lee and DeAlva (Shannon) W.; m. Sondra Scott; children—John Gray, Julie Scott, Susan Scott; adopted children—Karen Jane, Kelley June, David Harold. B.S. in Commerce and Bus. Adminstrn., U. Ala., 1958, postgrad., 1958-59. Founder, chmn., chief exec. officer U & W Industries, Inc., Selma, Ala., Laura Industries, Inc., Selma Rentals, Inc., U & W Truck Co., Ins., Bibb Corp., Brent, Ala., 1960-70; founder, chmn. bd., chief exec. officer Nat. Automotive Superstores, Inc., Pensacola, Fla., 1972, Wallace Automotive Distbrs., 1974—, 6 retail stores, Mobile, Ala., 4 retail stores, warehouse, service corp., Pensacola, 4 retail stores, New Orleans, also Nat. Automotive Distbrs., Inc., trucking co.; organizer, dir. First Nat. Bank of Escambia County, Pensacola. Jr. warden, sr. warden St. Christopher's Episcopal Ch., Pensacola, 1977-79; vestryman, 1982-84, mem. choir, Diocesan Venture in Mission Com., chmn. Venture in Mission Com. of Parish; mem. Pensacola Jr. Coll. Booster Club, Pensacola YMCA, Panhandle Tiger Bay Club; bd. dirs. Azalea Trace; v.p., pres.-elect bd. regents U. West Fla. Served to 1st lt. USAR, 1959-65. Named Man of Year sta. WCOA-WJLQ, 1983; named Knight Ct. of DeLuna, Fiesta of Five Flags, Pensacola, 1981. Mem. Automotive Parts and Accessories Assn. U.S., U.S. C. of C., New Orleans C. of C., Greater Mobile C. of C., Fla. C. of C., Pensacola Area C. of C., U. Ala. Alumni Assn., Sigma Chi Nat. Alumni Assn. Republican. Clubs: Pensacola Ski, Top Twenty, Pensacola Country (bd. dirs.), Pensacola Open Tournament Com. (vice chmn. 1985, chmn. 1986 tournament), Pensacola Sports Assn. Found. (sec., bd. dirs.), Pensacola Sports Assn., Rotary. Home: 3640 Menendez Dr Pensacola FL 32503 Office: 4317 N Palafox Hwy Pensacola FL 32505

WALLACE, GEORGE CORLEY, governor of Alabama; b. Clio, Ala., Aug. 25, 1919; s. George C. and Mozell (Smith) W.; LL.B., U. Ala., 1942; m. Lurleen Burns, May 23, 1943 (dec.); children—Bobbie Jo, Peggy Sue, George Corley, Janie Lee; m. 2d, Cornelia Ellis Snively, Jan. 1971 (div. Jan. 1978); m. 3d, Lisa Taylor, Sept. 1981. Admitted to Ala. bar, 1942; asst. atty. gen. Ala., 1946-47; mem. Ala. Legislature from Barbour County, 1947-53; judge 3d Jud. Dist. Ala., 1953-58; pvt. practice, Clayton, Ala., 1958-62; gov. Ala., 1963-66, 71-79, 83—; dir. rehab. resources U. Ala., 1979-83; counselor to Gov. of Ala., from 1979; pres. Ala. Bd. Edn. Sponsor, Wallace Act for state trade schs., 1947; candidate for pres. Am. Ind. party, 1968, Democratic primary, 1972, 76; bd. dirs. Ala. Tb Assn. Served with USAAF, 1942-45; PTO. Mem. Am. Legion, VFW, DAV. Democrat. Methodist (past Sunday sch. tchr. and supt.). Clubs: Masons, Shriners, Moose, Elks, Modern Woodman of World, Order Eastern Star, Civitan Internat. Office: Office of Governor Room 100 State Capitol Bldg Box 17222 Montgomery AL 36130*

WALLACE, GLADYS BALDWIN, librarian; b. Macon, Ga., June 5, 1923; d. Carter Shepherd and Dorothy (Richard) Baldwin; B.S. in Edn., Oglethorpe U., 1961; M.Librarianship, Emory U., 1966; Edn. Specialist, Ga. State U., 1980, doctoral candidate; m. Hugh Loring Wallace, Jr., Oct. 14, 1941; (div. Sept. 1968); children—Dorothy, Hugh Loring III. Librarian public elem. schs., Atlanta, 1956-66; librarian Northside High Sch., Atlanta, 1966—. Ga. Dept. Edn. grantee, 1950; NDEA grantee, 1963, 65. Mem. NEA, Ga., Atlanta assns. educators, Atlanta Symphony Orch. League Madison-Morgan Cultural Center; Oglethorpe U. Nat. Alumni Assn., Emory U. Alumni Assn., Ga. State U. Alumni Assn., Atlanta Hist. Soc., Ga. Trust for Historic Preservation. Home: 136 Peachtree Memorial Dr NW North Carolina 6 Atlanta GA 30309 Office: 2875 Northside Dr NW Atlanta GA 30305

WALLACE, HAROLD LEW, historian; b. Montgomery, Ind., Nov. 9, 1932; s. Lewis Alfred and Winifred Maria (Summers) W.; A.B., Ind. U., 1961, M.A. (univ. grantee 1964, Eli Lilly fellow 1962), 1964, Ph.D., 1970; m. Janice J. Inman, June 6, 1957; children—Stefanie Ann, Stacy Elizabeth, Jason Lew.

Tchr. history and English, Mooresville (Ind.) High Sch., 1961-63; teaching asst. Ind. U., 1963, univ. fellow, 1964-65; asst. prof., then asso. prof. Murray (Ky.) U., 1965-71; prof. history, chmn. dept. No. Ky. U., Highland Heights, 1971-81, prof. history, dir. oral history, 1981—; adv. com. Ky. Public Documents Com., 1973—; cons. in field. Mem. No. Ky. Bd. Regents, 1985—. Served with USNR, 1952-56. Harry S. Truman research scholar, 1965, 71; Mott fellow, 1973-75; grantee Murray State U., 1967, 71, No. Ky. U., 1973, 76, 78, 81, 85—, Oral History Commn., 1980-82, Gen. Electric, 1982, Ky. Humanities Council, 1982; Smithsonian fellow, 1983. Mem. Am. Hist. Assn., Nat. Hist. Soc., Center Study Democratic Instns., So. Hist. Assn., Ind. U. Alumni Assn., Mended Hearts Orgn., Mensa (coordinator, proctor Greater Cin. area 1978—), Intertel, Phi Alpha Theta, Alpha Epsilon Delta, Phi Delta Kappa. Democrat. Author articles in field. Home: 22 Orchard Terr Cold Spring KY 41076 Office: 4th Floor Landrum Hall Highland Heights KY 41076

WALLACE, JAMES P., justice Supreme Ct. Tex.; b. Sidon, Ark., Apr. 8, 1928; s. Harvey J. and Belma G. Wallace; B.S. in Bus. Adminstrn., U. Ark., 1952; J.D., U. Houston, 1957; m. Martha J., Sept. 18, 1954; children—James, Jill. Admitted to Tex. bar; partner law firms, 1958-75; mem. Tex. Senate, 1970-75; judge 215th Dist. Ct., Harris County, Tex., 1975-78; assoc. justice Ct. Civil Appeals, 1st Supreme Jud. Dist. Tex., 1978-81; justice Supreme Ct. Tex., 1981—. Served with USNR, 1946-49. Mem. Am. Bar Assn., Tex. Bar Assn., Houston Bar Assn. Democrat. Baptist. Office: Box 12248 Supreme Ct Tex Capitol Station Austin TX 78711

WALLACE, JAMES RANDALL, international economist; b. Jamestown, N.Y., Oct. 27, 1955; s. Maynard Blaine and Viola Jean (Tewinkle) W.; m. Carolyn Jean Vaughn, June 16, 1978. B.A. cum laude, U. Tex.-Arlington, 1978, M.A., 1982. Economist, Council on Wage and Price Stability, Exec. Office of Pres., Washington, 1980-81; staff economist Overseas Devel. Council, Washington, 1981-83; internat. economist U.S. Treasury Dept., Washington, 1984—; cons. Overseas Devel. Council, 1983. Author: Statistical Annexes in U.S. Foreign Policy and the Third World: Agenda 1983, 1983, Agenda 1982, 1982. Mem. Am. Econ. Assn., Omicron Delta Epsilon (outstanding sr. award). Avocations: softball; basketball; running; rowing; reading. Home: 4317-B1 S 36th St Arlington VA 22206 Office: Office Internat Investment US Treasury Main Bldg Pennsylvania Ave Washington DC

WALLACE, JOHN DOUGLAS, roofing contractor, consultant; b. Chattanooga, June 3, 1947; s. James Raymond and Mary S. W.; m. Rose Marie Crume, Jan. 31, 1969; children—Thaddeus Edward, Cameron Matthew, Cameron Rayne. B.A., U. N.C., 1969; M.A., U. Okla., 1976. Asst. prof. U. Okla., 1974-77; dir. personnel and tng. Ivey's Dept. Stores Fla., 1977; v.p. Tiptop Roofing Co., Inc., Orlando, Fla., 1978—; v.p. Roof Repair Specialists, Orlando, 1979—; pres. William John Assocs., Orlando, 1979—. Served as aviator USN, 1969-77; comdr. Res. Mem. Nat. Roofing Contractors Assn., Naval Res. Officers Assn., Central Fla. Roofing and Sheet Metal Assn., Winter Park C. of C. (v.p. community affairs div. 1983, div. 1982—, exec. com. 1982, 83). Lodge: Orange County East Rotary. Compiling editor: To Get the Job Done, 1976; Readings in Leadership and Management, 1976; Instructors Guide-Leadership and Management, 1976. Home: 825 Palmer Ave Winter Park FL 32789 Office: 6400 University Blvd Winter Park FL 32793

WALLACE, JOYCE GRODEMAN, information services executive; b. Knoxville, Tenn., May 3, 1934; s. Louis T. and Bonnie W. (Waggoner) Grodeman; m. James A. Wallace, Sept. 25, 1952 (div. May 1974); children—James Gregory, Jamie Yvonne. Student, U. Tenn.-Knoxville, 1974—. Cert. profl. sec. Sr. sec. chemistry dept. U. Tenn., 1964-74; sec. applications lab. ORTEC, Inc., Oak Ridge, 1974; office mgr., prin. sec. geol. scis. U. Tenn., 1974-76; freelance editor/cons. Gen. Coll. Chemistry textbook, 1966-80; adminstrv. asst. Energy, Environ. and Resources Ctr., U. Tenn., 1976-78, asst. to dir., 1978-80; mgr. info. services dept. Tech. for Energy Corp., Knoxville, Tenn., 1980—. East Tenn. regional dir. Tenn. Congress of P.T.A.s, 1977-78, dist. pres., bd. mgrs., 1976-77; pres., legislation chmn. Knox County Council P.T.A., 1972-80; mem. adv. bd. for office automation Roane State Community Coll. Mem. Adminstrv. Mgmt. Soc. (v.p. 1983-84), Internat. Info. and Word Processing Assn., Nat. Assn. Female Execs., Gamma Beta Phi. Republican. Baptist. Home: 3208 Bellevue St Knoxville TN 37917 Office: Tech for Energy Corp 1 Energy Center Pellissippi Pkwy Knoxville TN 37922

WALLACE, KATHLEEN MARIE, personnel executive; b. Chgo., May 2, 1955; d. Raymond William and Barbara Elaine (Justeson) Richardson; m. Michael Lee Wallace, Mar. 18, 1978. B.S. in Psychology, MacMurray Coll., 1977; M.A. candidate U. Tulsa, 1983. Word processor Arthur Andersen & Co., Chgo., 1977-78; sales asst., new account supr. Dean Witter Reynolds, Inc., Tulsa, 1978-79; personnel recruiter Bus. Resources and Exec. Search, Tulsa, 1979; dir. personnel State Fed. Savings and Loan, Tulsa, 1979-85; human resource rep. Agrico Chem. Co., Tulsa, 1985—. Leader spl. assignment Girl Scouts U.S.A., Tulsa, 1962-84. Recipient award of appreciation Girl Scouts U.S.A., Jacksonville, Ill., 1975. Mem. Inst. Fin. Edn. (v.p. 1981-83, pres. 1983-85), Tulsa Personnel Assn., Am. Soc. Personnel Adminstrn. Democrat. Roman Catholic. Lodge: Kiwanitas (bd. dirs. Tulsa 1982). Home: 6407 S 109th E Ave Tulsa OK 74133 Office: Agrico Chem Co PO Box 3166 Tulsa OK 74101

WALLACE, LENETA JEAN, career counselor, consultant, lecturer; b. Athens, Tex., Aug. 17, 1941; d. Preston Wells and Pearlie Francis (Jordan) Gideon; m. Don Thomas Wallace, June 12, 1965; children—Gregory Bryan, Scott Trevor. B.A., East Tex. State U., 1963; M.A., Austin Coll., 1969. Lic. profl. counselor. Tchr. Dallas Ind. Sch. Dist., 1963, 65; tchr. Sherman Ind. Sch. Dist., Tex., 1965, 71, counselor, 1971, 73; counselor Austin Coll., Sherman, 1977—; with C. & P.C., South and Southeast U.S., 1977—. Mem. adminstrv. bd. First United Methodist Ch., Sherman; mem. library bd. Sherman City Library, 1978-84; v.p., pres. Perrin Elem. Sch. PTA, Sherman, 1983-85; v.p. Dillingham Middle Sch. PTA, Sherman, 1985—. Mem. Am. Assn. Counseling and Devel., Nat. Vocat. Guidance Assn., Texoma Counseling and Devel. Assn., Sigma Tau Delta. Avocations: Tennis; skiing; aerobics; reading; travel. Office: Austin Coll Box 1629 Sherman TX 75090

WALLACE, MINOR GORDON, JR., architect, landscape architect, mayor; b. Texarkana, Tex., Oct. 30, 1936; s. Minor Gordon and Dessie (Bledsoe) W.; B.A., U. Ark., 1961, B. Arch., 1961; children—Rayma, Minor Gordon III. Project architect Bruce R. Anderson, Architect, Little Rock, 1964-67; univ. architect U. Ark., Fayetteville, 1968—; prin. Minor G. Wallace, Jr., Architect, 1969—, Wallace & Estes, Architects, Fayetteville, 1978-80; dir. facilities planning and constrn. U. Ark. System, Fayetteville, 1968-81, dir. facilities planning, 1981-84, asst. v.p. facilities planning, 1984—; cons. ednl. planning, architecture. Alderman, City of Prairie Grove, (Ark.), 1981-83, mayor, 1983—; chmn. bd. dirs. Northwest Ark. Arts and Crafts Guild, 1977-79; bd. dirs. Northwest Ark. Cultural Center, 1978—, acting pres., 1981-84, pres., 1984—; pres. D & W Devel. Co., Inc., 1985—; ptnr. Country Inn Restaurants and Antiques, 1985—. Mem. AIA, Am. Soc. Landscape Architects, Council Ednl. Planners, Soc. Coll. and Univ. Planning, Nat. Trust Hist. Preservation, Assn. Univ. Architects, Am. Planning Assn. Democrat. Unitarian. Campus landscaping Pine Bluff and Fayetteville campuses U. Ark., 1977-78, indoor tennis center, Fayetteville campus, 1979-80, also botany greenhouse and sports arena. Home: PO Box 586 Prairie Grove AR 72753 Office: PO Box 1384 Fayetteville AR 72702

WALLACE, PETER RUDY, lawyer, state legislator; b. St. Petersburg, Fla., Apr. 13, 1954; s. John Powell and Martha (Rudy) W.; m. Helen Pruitt, Mar. 3, 1984; 1 child, Daniel McSwain. A.B., Harvard U., 1976, J.D., 1979. Bar: Fla., U.S. Dist. Ct. (mid. dist.) Fla. 1981. Law clk. to justice U.S. Ct. Appeals (5th cir.), St. Petersburg, 1979-80; assoc. atty. Greene & Mastry, P.A., St. Petersburg, 1980—; mem. Fla. Ho. of Reps., 1982. Bd. dirs. Big Bros./Big Sisters of Pinellas County, 1981—, Leadership St. Pete Alumni Assn., 1982—. Presdl. scholar U.S. Dept. Edn., 1972; Harvard nat. scholar, 1972-79. Mem. Fla. Bar, St. Petersburg Bar Assn. Democrat. Episcopalian. Club: Suncoast Tiger Bay. Lodge: Kiwanis. Office: PO Box 3022 Saint Petersburg FL 33731

WALLACE, ROBERT EDWARD, dentist; b. Charleston, W.Va., Nov. 2, 1939; s. Rodney Boyd and Margaret Kathlyn (Maddy) W.; m. Mary Elizabeth Chappell, Aug. 31, 1964; 1 child, Terry Glenn. B.S., Hampden-Sydney Coll., 1961; D.D.S., W.Va. U., 1965. Dentist, Salem, Va., 1968—; instr. Va. Western Community Coll., Roanoke, 1971-72. Served to capt. U.S. Army, 1965-68. Mem. Roanoke Valley Dental Soc., Piedmont Dental Soc., Va. Dental Assn., ADA. Presbyterian. Avocations: back packing; photography.

WALLACE, ROBERT GLENN, petroleum company executive; b. Webb City, Okla., Oct. 8, 1926; s. Glenn McKinsey and Sarah Elizabeth W.; m. Kelmor Wallace, Oct. 9, 1954; 1 son, John. B.S.Ch.E., Tex. A&M U., 1950; grad., Advanced Mgmt. Program, Harvard U.-U. Hawaii, 1972. Registered profl. engr., Okla. Mgr. internat. sales and devel. Phillips Petroleum Co., 1970-71; pres. Sealright Co., Inc., Kansas City, Mo., 1972-73; v.p. plastics Phillips Petroleum Co., Bartlesville, Okla., 1974-78, sr. v.p., 1978-80, exec. v.p., 1980—; dir. Phillips Chem. Co., Valmont Industries Inc. Mem. devel. council Tex. A.&M. Coll. Bus. Adminstrn., Tex. A&M Coll. Engring. Served with USNR, 1944-46. Republican. Office: Phillips Petroleum Co 18 Phillips Bldg Bartlesville OK 74004*

WALLACE, WILLIAM HARWELL, JR., state planner, community and economic developer; b. Eastaboga, Ala., Dec. 11, 1939; s. William Harvell and Bettye Lou (Wingo) W. B.S. in Bus. Adminstrn., Auburn U., 1965. Cartographer, Aero. Chart and Information Center, St. Louis, 1965-69; planning dir. East Ala. Regional Planning & Devel. Commn., Anniston, 1970-72; state planner Ala. Devel. Office, Montgomery, 1973-82; sect. chief econ. devel. Dept. Econ. and Community Affairs, Montgomery, 1982—; mem. adv. com. Ala. Rail Services, Montgomery, 1974—, Gov.'s Pvt. Industry Council, 1982—, So. Appalachian Regional Coal Team, 1976—, adv. bd. Fed.-State Coal Team, 1976—, Ala. Occupational Information Coordinating Com., 1985—. Served with USAF, 1960-63. Mem. Am. Soc. Pub. Adminstrs. Baptist. Home: 170 Canyon Rd Wetumpka AL 36092 Office: Ala Dept Econ and Community Affairs 3465 Norman Bridge Rd Montgomery AL 36105-0939

WALLACE, WILLIAM RAY, fabricated steel manufacturing company executive; b. Shreveport, La., Mar. 25, 1923; s. Jason Mohoney and Mattie Evelyn (Adair) W.; m. Minyone Milligan Rose, Oct. 5, 1966; children—Jayne Cecile Rose McDearman, Susan Rose, H. Robert Rose; children by previous marriage—Patrick Scott, Michael B., Timothy, Shelly. B.S. in Engring, La. Tech., 1944. Field engr. Austin Bridge Co., Dallas, 1944-45; core analyst Core Labs., Bakersfield, Calif., 1945-46; chief engr., then sec.-treas., exec. v.p. Trinity Industries, Inc., Dallas, 1946-58, pres., 1958—, also dir.; dir. Redman Industries, Inc., Lomas & Nettleton Financial Corp., Republic Bank Dallas, Tex. Employers Ins. Assn., ENSERCH Corp. Methodist. Home: Dallas TX Office: 2525 Stemmons Freeway Dallas TX 75207*

WALLER, BURTON WOODROW, JR., health care executive; b. Jackson, Tenn., Nov. 30, 1949; s. Burton Woodrow and Jeanne Elizabeth (Russell) W.; m. Sandra Desbien, Mar. 22, 1970; children—Craig, Catherine. B.S. cum laude, U. Tenn., 1971; M.H.A., Washington U., St. Louis, 1974. Asst. adminstr. Methodist Hosp. Dallas, 1975-78, v.p., 1978-82, sr. v.p., adminstr., 1982-85; v.p., gen. mgr. Cigna Healthplan of Tex., 1985—; dir. Dallas-Ft. Worth Hosp. Council. Mem. Am. Coll. Hosp. Adminstrs. (chmn. Dallas chpt. 1984—), Tex. Hosp. Assn. Democrat. Baptist. Office: City Center Tower II 301 Commerce St Fort Worth TX 76102

WALLING, JOHN BELL, manufacturing company executive; b. Knox County, Tex., Oct. 5, 1928; s. Wade Hampton and Ida (Partridge) W.; B.S., Midwestern U., Wichita Falls, Tex., 1949; m. Bobbie Marie Boggs, Apr. 13, 1947; children—Danny Michael, John Scott, Candace Suzanne Walling Davis. Program dir. Boys Club Wichita Falls, 1948-49; ednl. dir. Floral Heights Meth. Ch., Wichita Falls, 1949-50; pres. World Oil & Gas Corp., 1958-62; chmn. bd. Appalachian Coal & Timber Co., 1966-69; pres. Everman Success, Inc., 1968-72; cons., 1976-78; pres. Fluid Lift Internat., Inc., Ft. Worth, 1978-80, chmn. bd., 1980—. Mem. Tex. Ho. of Reps. from 111th Dist., 1951-59, chmn. common carriers com., 1955-59; del. So. Govs. Conf., 1958; mem. U.S. Com. for UN, 1981—, vice chmn., 1982, 83, assoc. chmn., 1984—; mem. support council U.S. Com. for UNICEF, 1984, bd. dirs. U.S. Com. for UNICEF; 1984—. Mem. UN Assn. U.S. (nat. bd. dirs. 1983—), Dallas UN Assn. (bd. dirs. 1984). Democrat. Methodist. Home: 5613 Trail Lake Dr Fort Worth TX 76133 Office: Fluid Lift Internat Inc 4100 Equitable Dr Tower 1 Suite 150 Fort Worth TX 76109

WALLIS, BEN A., JR., lawyer; b. Llano County, Tex., Apr. 27, 1936; s. Ben A. and Jessie Ella (Longbotham) W.; B.B.A., U. Tex., 1961, J.D., 1966; postgrad. So. Meth. U., 1971; children—Ben A. III, Jessica. Bar: Tex. 1966, D.C. 1975, U.S. Supreme Ct., 1974, U.S. Ct. Appeals (5th, 8th, 11th and D.C. cirs.), U.S. Dist. Ct. (we., no. and so. dists.) Tex., U.S. Dist. Ct. (no. dist.) Calif., U.S. Dist. Ct. (ea. dist.) Wis., U.S. Dist. Ct. (D.C.). Individual practice law, Llano, Tex., 1966-68, Dallas, 1971-72, San Antonio, 1974—; atty., investigator Tex. Securities Bd., Austin and Dallas, 1968-71; v.p. devel. Club Corp. Am., Dallas, 1973; asso. counsel Com. on the Judiciary Impeachment and Inquiry, U.S. Ho. of Reps., Washington, 1974; chmn. Nat. Land Use Conf., 1979-81; pres. Inst. for Human Rights Research; guest lectr. in field. Mem. Am. Bar Assn., State Bar Tex., D.C. Bar Assn., Fed. Bar Assn., San Antonio Bar Assn., Dallas Bar Assn., Nat. Cattlemen's Assn., Delta Theta Phi. Office: 2400 Tower Life Bldg San Antonio TX 78205

WALLIS, JOHN MERCER, III, architect; b. Atlanta, Oct. 26, 1943; s. John Mercer and Martha Jean (Kirkland) W.; m. Johnnie Faye McKnight, July, 1966 (div. 1973); 1 child, Mary Wendalyn; m. Jacqueline Ann Cabala, May 6, 1977. A.A., Norman Coll., 1964; Nat. Council Archtl. Registration Bds. Coll. Equivalency Exam, 1980. Registered architect, Ga. Designer, Wellman Power Gas, Lakeland, Fla., 1964-72; Setliff & Regnvall Architects, Lakeland, 1972-80; ptnr., v.p. Kendrick Regnvall & Assoc., Inc., Lakeland, 1980—; guest lectr. Fla. So. Coll., Lakeland, 1983. Bd. dirs. Polk County Assn. Handicapped Citizens, Lakeland, 1984-85, Am. Cancer Soc., Lakeland, 1984-85. Mem. AIA (sect. v.p. 1983-84), Lakeland Area C. of C. Democrat. Baptist. Lodges: Elks, Sertoma (pres. 1985-86). Avocations: boating; golf; reading; travel. Office: Kendrick Regnvall & Assoc Inc 211 S Tennessee Ave Lakeland FL 33801

WALLS, CARL EDWARD, JR., communications company official; b. Magnolia, Ark., Sept. 9, 1948; s. Carl E. and Melba Rene (Garrard) W.; student San Antonio Coll., 1966-68; m. Doris Duhart, Aug. 1, 1970; children—Carl Edward, Forrest Allen. Div. mgr. Sears Roebuck & Co., San Antonio, 1967-73, area sales mgr., 1973-78; service cons. Southwestern Bell, 1978-79, account exec., 1979-82; account exec., industry cons. AT&T Info. Systems, 1983—. Mem. citizens advisory com. Tex. Senate, 1975-81; legis. aide Tex. Ho. of Reps., 1981—; commr. Alamo Area council Boy Scouts Am., 1970-79, Capitol Area council, 1980—, nat. jamboree staff, 1973, 77, 81, 85; mem. Republican Nat. Com., 1980—, Rep. Senatorial Club, 1981—. Recipient Patriotic Service award U.S. Treasury Dept., 1975, 76; Scouters Key and Commrs. award also Dist. Merit award, 1978, Boy Scouts Am. Mem. Scouting Collectors Assn. (pres. South Central region 1979-80, v.p. region 1980-81, sec. 1983-86), Nat. Eagle Scout Assn., Assoc. Photographers Internat., Am. Legion. Baptist. Lodge: Kiwanis. Home: 11712 D-K Ranch Rd Austin TX 78759 Office: 3700 Executive Center Dr 200 Austin TX 78731

WALLS, JULIE, social worker; b. Hershey, Pa., Oct. 4, 1954; d. Edward Joseph Walls and Nancy (Schule) Walls Kapp. B.S.W., Pa. State U., 1976; M.S.W., Norfolk State U., 1984. Lic. social worker, Va. Sr. social worker York Poquoson Social Service Bur., Grafton, Va., 1977-83; trainer, cons. Family Resources, Inc., Williamsburg, Va., 1982-85; admissions social worker Charter Colonial Inst., Newport News, Va., 1985—. Bd. dirs. Planned Parenthood Southeastern Va., Peninsula Sexual Abuse Prevention Team. Mem. Nat. Assn. Social Workers, Family Forum, Inc. Office: 17579 Warwick Blvd Newport News VA 23607

WALLS, MARGARET SUSAN, make-up artist; b. Tampa, Fla., Mar. 13, 1951; student Fla. Coll., 1969-70, U. S. Fla., 1979—. Free lance public relations cons., Tampa; adv. editor, columnist DanceScene mag.; coordinator Artswatch, Greater Tampa C. of C., 1979; now dir. cosmetics Star Styled, Inc.; mem. nightclub vocal duo Two of Us; v.p. Stage I Theatrical Enterprises; asso. dir. community theater prodns.; guest lectr.; mem. faculty Theatre Confs. of the S.E., NILO Toledo Dance Camps; tchr. stage makeup Dance Masters Am.; judge beauty pageants; fashion show coordinator. Vocalist Tampa's 91st Birthday Celebration. Mem. Fla. Vocat. Assn., Fla. Public Relations Assn., Publicity Club N.Y., Fla. Personnel and Guidance Assn., Nat. Assn. Cosmetic Boutique Owners, Tampa C. of C. Republican. Author slide presentation: You and the World of Work, 1975. Office: 4235 Henderson Blvd Tampa FL 33609

WALSH, DAVID ALASTAIR, biostatistician; b. Springfield, Mass., Feb. 14, 1955; s. Thomas Francis and Mary (Cumming) W.; m. Marjorie Anne Martin, July 12, 1980; children—Sara Jane, Zachary David. B.S. magna cum laude, Providence Coll., 1976; Ph.D., U. Wash., 1981. Asst. prof. div. biostatistics U. Miss. Med. Ctr., Jackson, 1981—; cons. Community Control of Hypertension, Goodman, Miss., 1981—, dept. math. scis. San Diego State U., 1983, Doctors Hosp., Jackson, 1982-83, VA Med. Ctr., Jackson, 1985—. Author: Clinical Research Design, 1983; also articles in profl. jours. Recipient award Citizens for Treatment High Blood Pressure, Inc., 1984. Mem. Am. Statis. Assn., Alpha Epsilon Delta. Roman Catholic. Home: 128 Bent Creek Dr Brandon MS 39042 Office: Dept of Preventive Medicine U of Miss Med Ctr 2500 N State St Jackson MS 39216

WALSH, GWENDOLYN ELROY, professional studies educator; b. Cambridge, Mass., Mar. 19, 1925; d. Chesley and Elizabeth (Furey) Elroy; m. Douglas Francis Walsh (div. 1962); children—Kevin Douglas, Robyn Elizabeth. Diploma Bouve Boston, 1945; B.S., Tufts U., 1946; postgrad. San Jose State U., 1961, Stanford U., 1962; M.Ed., U. Va., 1967; diploma theatre Ecole Mouvement et Pensee, Paris, 1976. Tchr. Abbot Acad., Andover, Mass., 1946-50, Katherine Delmar Burke Sch., San Francisco, 1951-58, San Carlos High Sch., Calif., 1961-62; asst. prof. dept. profl. studies Mary Baldwin Coll., Staunton, Va., 1962—; tchr. Gov. Sch. to Gifted, Staunton, 1974-76, Gov. Sch. for Arts, Staunton, 1984; dir. Staunton Puppets, 1970-85. Editor: Fencing Guide, 1982. Mem. AAUP, AAUW, AAHPER and Dance, Puppeteers of Am., Nat. Capitol Puppet Guild, Va. Assn. Health, Phys. Edn. and Dance. Republican. Episcopalian. Club: Summer Tennis (Staunton) (dir. 1968-76). Avocation: painting. Home: 340 E Beverley St Staunton VA 24401 Office: Mary Baldwin Coll Frederick and New Sts Staunton VA 24401

WALSH, JAMES HAMILTON, lawyer; b. Astoria, N.Y., May 20, 1947; s. Edward James and Helen Smith (Hamilton) W.; m. Janice Ausherman, Aug. 3, 1968; children—Tracy, Courtney, Eric. B.A. in Psychology, Bridgewater Coll., 1968; J.D., U. Va., 1975. Bar: Va. 1975, U.S. Dist. Ct. (ea. and we. dists.) Va. 1975, U.S. Ct. Appeals (4th cir.) 1976, U.S. Supreme Ct. 1982. Assoc. McGuire, Woods & Battle, Richmond, Va., 1975-82, ptnr., 1982—; spl. prosecutor U.S. Dist. Ct. (ea. dist.) Va., 1979, 84. Mem. staff Va. Law Rev. Served with U.S. Army, 1969-72. Mem. ABA (mem. antitrust sect. health care com. and task force on health planning), Am. Trial Lawyers Assn., Va. State Bar (vice chmn., bd. govs. antitrust sect. 1984—), Va. Bar Assn., Richmond Bar Assn., Order Coif, Phi Delta Phi. Episcopalian. Clubs: Willow Oaks, Bull and Bear (Richmond, Va.). Contbr. articles to profl. jours. Home: 3035 Stratford Rd Richmond VA 23225 Office: McGuire Woods & Battle One James Ctr Richmond VA 23219

WALSH, LAWRENCE ADRIAN, lawyer; b. New Orleans, Mar. 7, 1955; s. Joseph Wayne and Lorraine Beverly (Mason) W.; m. Virginia Obriotti, Aug. 16, 1980; 1 child, Katherine Nicole. Student Tulane U., 1974-75; B.A., St. Mary's U., 1976, J.D., 1978. Bar: Tex. 1978, U.S. Dist. Ct. (so. dist.) Tex. 1979, U.S. Ct. Appeals (5th cir.) 1981, U.S. Supreme Ct. 1984. Ptnr. Walsh & Assocs., Brownsville, Tex.; cons., atty. Johnson Internat. Materials, Inc., Brownsville, Mexican Consulate, Brownsville, 1983—, Hoteles El Presidente, Mexico City, 1983—. Active ACLU. Mem. ABA, Tex. Bar Assn., Cameron County Bar Assn., Assn. Trial Lawyers Am., Tex. Trial Lawyers Assn., Valley Trial Lawyers Assn., Tex. Criminal Def. Assn., Tex. Assn. Bank Counsel. Democrat. Roman Catholic. Home: 444 Calle Retama Brownsville TX 78520 Office: Walsh and Assocs 950 E Van Buren Brownsville TX 78520

WALSH, MARY D., civic worker; b. Whitewright, Tex., Oct. 29, 1913; d. William Fleming and Anna Maud (Lewis) Fleming; B.A., So. Meth. U., 1934; LL.D. (hon.), Tex. Christian U., 1979; m. F. Howard Walsh, Mar. 13, 1937; children—Richard, Howard, D'Ann (Mrs. Wm. F. Bonnell), Maudi (Mrs. H.B. Roe, Jr.), William Lloyd. Pres. Fleming Found.; v.p. Walsh Found.; partner Walsh Co. Guarantor, Ft. Worth Arts Council, Ft. Worth Ballet, Tex. Boys Choir, Ft. Worth Theatre, Ft. Worth Opera, Schola Cantorum; hon. mem. Opera Bd., 1960-84, hon. v.p., 1967—; hon. mem. Ballet Bd.; co-founder Am. Field Service in Ft. Worth; mem. Tex. Commn. for Arts and Humanities, 1968-72, mem. adv. council, 1972-84; hon. bd. dirs. Van Cliburn Internat. Piano Competition; mem. Colorado Springs Day Nursery, Colorado Springs Symphony; bd. dirs. Wm. Edrington Scott Theatre; hon. chmn. Opera Ball, 1975, Opera Guild Internat. Conf., 1976; mem. Lloyd Shaw Found., Colorado Springs, Colo.; ann. sponsor Christmas presentation of The Littlest Wiseman, Ft. Worth. Recipient numerous awards, including Altrusa Civic award as 1st Lady of Ft. Worth, 1968; (with husband) Disting. Service award So. Bapt. Radio and TV Commn., 1972; Opera award Girl Scouts U.S.A., 1977, 78, 79; award Streams and Valleys, 1976-80; (with husband) Brotherhood citation Tarrant County chpt. NCCJ, 1978, Royal Purple award Tex. Christian U., 1979, Friends of Tex. Boys Choir award, 1981; (with husband) Appreciation award Southwestern Bapt. Theol. Sem., 1981, citation for contbns. to Christianity and the arts, 1981, B.H. Carroll founders award, 1982; spl. recognition award Ft. Worth Ballet Assn., 1978; named (with husband) Patron of Arts in Ft. Worth, 1970, Edna Gladney Internat. Grandparents of 1972; library at Tarrant County Jr. Coll. N.W. campus dedicated to Mary D. and F. Howard Walsh, 1978; 1978-79 season of Fort Worth Ballet dedicated to Mary D. and F. Howard Walsh; med. bldg. at Southwestern Bapt. Theol. Sem. named for them; recipient Sr. Citizen award, 1985. Mem. Ft. Worth Boys Club, Ft. Worth Children's Hosp., Jewel Charity Ball, Ft. Worth Pan Hellenic (pres. 1940), Opera Guild, Fine Arts Found. Guild of Tex. Christian U., Girl's Service League, AAUW, Goodwill Industries Aux., Child Study Center, Tarrant County Aux. of Edna Gladney Home, YWCA (life), Ft. Worth Art Assn., Ft. Worth Ballet Assn., Tex. Boys Choir Aux., Round Table, Colorado Springs Fine Art Center, Am. Automobile Assn., Nat. Assn. Cowbelles, Ft. Worth Arts Council (dir.), Rae Reimers Bible Study Class (pres. 1968), Tex. League Composers (hon. life), Chi Omega (pres. 1935-36), others. Baptist. Clubs: Chi Omega Mothers, The Woman's (Club Fidelite). Home: 2425 Stadium Dr Fort Worth TX 76109 also 1801 Culebra Ave Colorado Springs CO 80907

WALSH, MAURICE DAVID, JR., business executive; b. N.Y.C., Dec. 24, 1924; s. Maurice David and Helen Merlyn (Flynn) W.; m. Alice Louise Flynn, Oct. 18, 1952; children—Maud Maureen Byerly, Michael Sean, James Liam, Douglas Padraic. B.J., U. Mo., 1949; M.S. in L.S., La. State U., 1963; grad. U.S. Army Command and Gen. Staff Coll., 1967. With Jefferson Parish Library, Metairie, La., 1959-80, head librarian, 1963-80; area dir. Housing Authority New Orleans, 1980-85; exec. v.p. GTF, Inc., 1985—. Author: (motion picture) (with Charles A. Wagner) The Jefferson Parish Story, 1961; contbr. articles to mil. and library publs. Pres., Pontchartrain Shores Civic Assn., 1981-82. Served with AUS, 1943-45, 50-52. Decorated Bronze Star with V device and oak leaf cluster, Purple Heart with oak leaf cluster. Mem. Jefferson Performing Arts Soc., 1st Cav. Div. Assn., 11th Armored Div. Assn., Urban League New Orleans, Lafreniere Park Found., Alpha Delta Sigma. Republican. Roman Catholic. Lodges: Rotary, Elks. Home and Office: 4536 Folse Dr Metairie LA 70006

WALSH, ROBERT E., investment analyst, market strategist; b. Madison, Wis., July 31, 1934; s. Martin Patrick and Mildred (Harmon) W.; m. Ellen Pophal, July 6, 1957; children—Linda, Patrick, Timothy. B.B.A. in Fin., Mgmt., U. Wis., 1957. Vice pres. A.G. Beckery & Co., Chgo., 1965-80; Blunt, Ellis & Leuwi, Milw., 1980-82; sr. v.p. Rotan Mosle Inc., Houston, 1982—, also dir. Author monthly mktg. report, 1980—. Mem. Houston Analysts Soc. Republican. Lutheran. Home: 1503 Briar Park Dr Houston TX 77042 Office: Rotan Mosle Inc 4000 Republic Ctr Houston TX 77002

WALSH, THOMAS ARTHUR, psychologist, management consultant; b. Rockville Ctr., N.Y., Apr. 22, 1950; s. Thomas John and Mable (Canfield) W.; m. Gretchen Richards, May 27, 1978. B.A., Marist Coll., Poughkeepsie, N.Y., 1972; M.S., SUNY-Albany, 1973, Ed.D., 1974; Ph.D., U. Pacific, 1978. Lic. psychologist, Calif.; cert. community coll. counselor, Calif. Adminstr., SUNY-Albany, 1972-73; pres. Fla. Import, Miami, 1973-76; pvt. practice psychology, N.Y.C., 1976-77; chief ednl. psychologist Calif. Youth Authority, 1978-80; mgmt. cons. Fran Tarkenton, Atlanta, 1980-82; pres., chief exec. officer Creative Consultation Corp.: The Productivity Mgrs., Orlando, 1982—; mgmt. cons. Consol. Foods, Continental Canned Corp., Crown Zellerbach, Pan Am. Airlines, Greenwood Textiles. SUNY fellow, 1972. Fellow Council Internat. Ednl. Exchange; mem. Am. Psychol. Assn. Republican. Author: The Response-Ability Series, 1981; Productivity Management System, 1982; (tape series) Excellence, 1983. Office: Creative Consultation Corp.: The Productivity Mgrs 200 Maitland Ave Altamonte Springs FL 32701

WALSH, WILLIAM JOHN, educational administrator; b. Natrona Heights, Pa., Mar. 29, 1941; s. William Henry and Helen Constance W.; B.A. in Sociology, Duquesne U., 1969; M.Ed. in Ednl. Adminstrn., Pa. State U., 1971; m. Carol Jean Miller, Sept. 3, 1966; children—Keirsten, Shannon. Classification analyst Pa. State U., University Park, 1969-73; asst. personnel dir. W.Va. U., Morgantown, 1973-78; dir. personnel adminstrn., dir. purchasing audit W.Va. Bd. of Regents, Charleston, 1978—; cons. in field. Served with USMC, 1962-66; Vietnam. Mem. Am. Compensation Assn., Inst. Internal Auditors, Coll. and Univ. Personnel Assn. Democrat. Roman Catholic. Home: 102 Shan Ln Hurricane WV 25526 Office: 950 Kanawha Blvd East Charleston WV 25301

WALTER, CHARLES LINDBERGH, psychologist; b. Colwyn, Pa., Mar. 23, 1930; s. Charles Wesley and Irene Martha (Pohlsen) W.; m. Janet Ann Peterson, Sept. 14, 1957; children—Bernadette Ruth, Charles Wesley. B.A., U. Pa., 1952; Ph.D., U. Tenn., 1962. Lic. psychologist, Tenn. Psychologist, VA Med. Ctr., Johnson City, Tenn., 1967—; mem. faculty Quillen-Dishner Coll. Medicine, 1980—. Mem. Am. Psychol. Assn., Tenn. Psychol. Assn. (pres. 1978, Psychologist of Yr. award 1982), Intermountain Psychol. Assn. (pres. 1984-85). Lutheran. Club: Toastmasters. Lodge: Elks. Home: 201 Dogwood Ln Johnson City TN 37601 Office: VA Med Ctr Johnson City TN 37684

WALTER, JAMES NORTHCUTT, company executive; b. Montgomery, Ala., Nov. 15, 1928; m. Adele Voltz; children—James N., Robert L. B.S., U.S. Mil. Acad. Pres. Algernon Blair, Inc., Montgomery, 1959—. Office: Algernon Blair Inc One Algernon Blair Pl Montgomery AL 36116

WALTER, JOHN PAUL, economist; b. Gainesville, Tex., Oct. 7, 1939; s. Joseph Bernard and Anna Marie (Walterschied) W.; B.S.Econs., Benedictine Coll., 1961; M.B.A. in Mgmt., North Tex. State U., 1962, M.A. in Econs., 1965; Ph.D. in Econs. (Univ. fellow), U. Notre Dame, 1970; m. Carol Diane Atkins, Aug. 17, 1974. Vis. Fulbright-Hayes prof. econs. Universidad Nacional de Trujill (Peru), 1970; indsl. research economist Fed. Res. Bank, Dallas, 1971-72; dir. econ. research Turner, Collie & Braden. Houston 1972-73; corp. economist Shell Oil Co., Houston, 1973-81; group planning mgr. Dresser Magcobar, 1981—; adj. prof. U. Houston, U. St. Thomas. Mem. Mayorial Com. to Study Airspace Rights in Houston, 1972-73; adviser on econ. impacts of changing weather patterns in Houston Mayor of Houston, 1972-76; mem. advisory com. NSF Chambers County (Tex.) Environ. Controls System Study, 1973-75. Served with USN, 1963-65. UNICEF grantee, 1969. Mem. Western Econs. Assn., Assn. Social Econs., Nat. Assn. Bus. Economists (pres. Houston chpt. 1976, dir. chpt. 1977-78), Notre Dame Alumni Assn. of Houston (v.p. 1976—), Nat. Notre Dame Alumni Assn., Omicron Delta Epsilon, Delta Tau Kappa. Author: Deprived Urban Youth, 1975; contbr. numerous articles to econ., sociol. jours., 1969-83; pioneer in econs. of nutrition. Office: PO Box 6504 Houston TX

WALTER, MICHAEL JOSEPH, lawyer; b. N.Y.C., Mar. 2, 1943; s. Samuel Lewis and Hilda (Finn) W.; m. Carla James, Mar. 2, 1973; children—Kristen, Lindsay. B.A., U. Bridgeport, Conn., 1964; J.D., Bklyn. Law Sch., 1967. Bar: N.Y. 1968, Tex. 1976. County atty. Broome County, Binghamton, N.Y., 1971-72; assoc. Drazen, Carmien & Young, Binghamton, 1972-74; pvt. practice, Binghamton, 1974-76, Houston, 1976-80; v.p., gen. counsel Meineke Discount Mufflers, Houston, 1980-82; sr. v.p. law Computerland Corp., Oakland, Calif., 1983-84; gen. counsel Entre Computer Ctrs., Inc., Vienna, Va., 1984—; assoc. editor Litigation Mag., Chgo., 1981—. Contbr. articles to various publs. Served with U.S. Army, 1968-70. Republican. Office: Entre Computer Ctrs Inc 1951 Kidwell Dr Vienna VA 22180

WALTER, RAY ALLISON, school counselor; b. Groesbeck, Tex., July 24, 1927; s. Frank William and Tina Onita (Priddy) W. B.A., Baylor U., 1949, M.A., 1952. Lic. profl. counselor. Counselor, supr. McLennan County Schs., Waco, Tex., 1963-80; coop. counselor Edn. Service Ctr. XII, Waco, Tex., 1980-81, Mt. Calm Ind. Sch. Dist., Tex., 1981-85; counselor, curriculum dir. Mart Ind. Sch. Dist., Tex., 1985—. Author: History of Limestone County, Texas, 1960, Checklist of Known Publications, Limestone County, 1964, History of Negroes of Limestone County, Texas, 1966. Editor: The McKinley Clan, 1963. Life mem. Friends Waco-McLennan Library, Friends Maffett Meml. Library, Groesbeck, Tex., Limestone County Mus., Groesbeck; past pres. Limestone County Hist. Survey Coms., Groesbeck. Recipient Service award Limestone County Commrs., Groesbeck, 1969. Mem. Am. Assn. Counseling and Devel., Am. Sch. Counseling Assn., Nat. Vocat. Guidance Assn., Tex. Assn. Counseling and Devel., Tex. Sch. Counseling Assn. Democrat. Methodist. Home: 3025 Homan Ave Waco TX 76707-0032 Office: Mart Ind Sch Dist 800 Navarro St Mart TX 76664

WALTER, TOMMY JOE, telecommunications corporations executive; b. San Angelo, Tex., Aug. 21, 1945; s. Joseph Weldon Bailey and Lula Agnes (Spencer) W.; m. LaJan Kiker, June 22, 1968; 1 child, Kerry Joe. B.S., Angelo State U., 1967, M.A.T., 1974; postgrad. U. Wash., 1975-76; Ed.D., Nova U., 1986. Coach, tchr. Bronte High Sch., Tex., 1967-68, Ranger High Sch., Tex., 1968-71; tng. instr. Gen Telephone Co. of S.W., Garland, Tex., 1971-73, tng. analyst, supervising analyst, San Angelo, Tex., 1973-74; tng. adminstr. Gen. Telephone Co. NW, Everett, Wash., 1974-76; tech. tng. adminstr. GTE World Hdqrs., Stamford, Conn., 1976-77; ops. tng. mgr. Gen. Telephone Co. Calif., Santa Monica, 1977-79; tng. dir. Gen. Telephone Co. Ind., Ft. Wayne, 1979-80; tng., communication dir. GTE Data Services, Tampa, Fla.; dir. network tng., mktg./sales tng., curriculum devel. GTE Telephone Ops. Hdqrs., Irving, Tex., 1982—. Coach YMCA, Tex., 1982-85; vol. ARC, Washington, 1974-75; active various chs., 1968—. Mem. Am. Soc. Tng. and Devel., IEEE, Republican. Methodist, Baptist. Avocations: reading; swimming; golf; gardening.

WALTERICK, RONALD EUGENE, aerospace engineer; b. Alexandria, Va., Mar. 22, 1951; s. Eugene Woodrow and Virginia Rhea (Richardson) W.; m. Candice Elaine Walker, June 23, 1973; 1 dau., Jennifer Rebecca. B.Aerospace Engring., Ga. Inst. Tech., 1974; M.Aero. Engring., Air Force Inst. Tech., 1980. Aerospace engr. Wright Patterson AFB, Ohio, 1974-81; research engr. Ga. Inst. Tech., Atlanta, 1981—. Cubmaster Boy Scouts Am., 1976-77. Mem. Sigma Xi. Baptist. Contbr. articles to profl. jours. Home: 4591 N Landing Dr Marietta GA 30066 Office: School of Aerospace Engineering Georgia Institute of Technology Atlanta GA 30332

WALTER-RYAN, WILLIAM GEORGE, psychiatrist; b. Berkeley, Calif., Jan. 7, 1951; s. William George and Natalie Elizabeth (Harris) Ryan; m. Kimerly Ann Walter, July 26, 1980. Student, Princeton U., 1969-71; A.B., Ind. U., 1974, M.D., 1978. Diplomate Am. Bd. Psychiatry and Neurology. Resident in psychiatry N.C. Meml. Hosp., Chapel Hill, 1978-82; asst. prof. psychiatry U. Ala., Birmingham, 1982—; attending physician Univ. Hosp., Birmingham, 1982—. NSF grantee, 1972. Mem. Am. Psychiat. Assn., Ala. Conservacy, Phi Beta Kappa, Alpha Omega Alpha. Episcopalian. Office: 390 N University Hosp Birmingham AL 35294

WALTERS, ARTHUR M., social service organization administrator; b. Magnolia, Ky.; m. Noralee Bryant; children—Reginald G., Artye M., Michele Walters Barnett. Grad. Colo. Coll.; postgrad. U. Louisville; assoc. advance engring. tng. Engr. Sch., Ft. Belvoir, Va. Commd. U.S. Army, advanced through grades to lt. col.; ret., 1962; mem. staff Louisville Urban League, to 1970, exec. dir., 1970—. Chmn., West Louisville Appreciation Celebration Com., 1983-84; bd. dirs. Spirit of Louisville, Leadership Louisville; mem. Pvt. Industry Council, Louisville/Jefferson County, State Job Tng. Coordinating Council, Louisville Labor Mgmt. Com., Louisville Police Adminstrn. Adv. Com., Louisville/Jefferson County Hypertension Task Force, Chickasaw Block Club Fedn., Ky. Coalition of Conscience; mem. adv. com. Ky. Ednl. TV; mem. coms. Metro United Way, Louisville. Recipient Service award Greater Louisville AFL-CIO, 1970, citation Louisville Bd. Edn., 1971, Meritorious Community Service award Louisville/Jefferson County Human Relations Commn., 1972, Whitney M. Young, Jr., award Lincoln Found., 1976, Disting. Service citation United Negro Coll. Fund, 1976, Cato Watts award for Black Progress in Louisville, 1977, Louisville Community award Urban League Guild, 1980, Fellowship award West Chestnut St. Baptist Ch., 1981, resolution Ky. Ednl. TV, 1982, cert. of merit Louisville Bd. Aldermen, 1983, Disting. Citizen award City of Louisville, 1983, Haycraft Civil Rights Leadership award Ky. Conf. NAACP, 1984, numerous others. Mem. Sigma Pi Phi, Alpha Phi Alpha, NAACP, Ret. Officers Assn. Office: Louisville Urban League 1202 S 3d St Louisville KY 40203

WALTERS, BILL PETER, state senator, lawyer; b. Paris, Ark., Apr. 17, 1943; s. Peter Louis and Elizabeth Cecelia (Wilhelm) W.; children—Jamie Elizabeth, Sherry Ann; m. Shirley Ann Dixon, Aug. 20, 1971. B.S., U. Ark., 1966, J.D., 1971. Bar: Ark. 1971. Asst. pros. atty. 12th Jud. Dist. Ark., Ft. Smith, 1971-74; ptnr. firm Walters Law Firm, P.A., Greenwood, Ark., 1975—; mem. Ark. Senate, Little Rock, 1982—; dir. First Ark. Title Ins. Co., Pine Bluff; dir., sec.-treas. Mineral Owners Collective Assn., Inc., Greenwood, 1973—; v.p., dir. Sebastian County Abstract and Title Ins. Co., Greenwood, 1981—; abstractor Ark. Abstract & Title Ins. Com., 1980—. Regional committeeman Ark. Republican Com., Ft. Smith, 1980; search pilot CAP, Ft. Smith; Recipient Silver medal of Valor CAP, 1983; cert. of honor Justice for Crimes Victims, 1983. Mem. ABA, Sebastian County Bar Assn., Profl. Landmen's Assn. (speaker 1983), Roman Catholic. Home: PO Box 700 Greenwood AR 72936 Office: Walters Law Firm PO Box 280 Greenwood AR 72936

WALTERS, CHESTER HUEL, bakery executive, aerospace engineering consultant; b. Bklyn., Miss., June 28, 1936; s. James Porter and Maudie Allie (Tingle) W.; children—Mark, Pamela, Marsha. Owner, mgr. Knead-um Donuts & Bakery, Pensacola, Fla., 1978—; owner Caretaker Services, Pensacola, 1979—; owner So. Handling of Pensacola, 1980—; mgr. so. div. Rail Co., Pensacola, 1981—. Served to lt. comdr. USNR. Club: Pensacola Yacht. Lodge: Shriners. Home: 4677 Saufley Field Rd Pensacola FL 32506 Office: 3190 Navy Blvd Pensacola FL 32505

WALTERS, JAMES KURT, exploration geologist; b. Dallas, Feb. 27, 1959; s. James G. and Mary Jo (Anderson) W. B.S. in Geology, Baylor U., 1982; M.S., Tex. A&M U., 1984. Field asst. Calumet Corp., Dallas, 1980, geotech. aide, 1981-82, geologist, 1982—. Mem. Am. Assn. Petroleum Geologists (jr. mem.), Sigma Chi. Republican. Presbyterian. Avocations: swimming; fishing; hunting. Office: Calumet Corp PO Box 31763 Dallas TX 75231

WALTERS, KAY LYNN, software company executive; b. Big Spring, Tex., Nov. 27, 1942; d. Lesley Albert and La Verne (Holden) Clawson; B.A. in English, U. Tex., Arlington, 1974; M.B.A., So. Meth. U., 1978; children—David Ryan, Stephen Paul. Programmer, Bank of A. Levy, Oxnard Calif., 1966-68; project leader 1st Data Processing, Big Spring, 1968-70, Results, Inc., Dallas, 1970-72; dir. application systems ENSERCH Corp., Dallas, 1973-80; mgr. devel. Performance Assos., Inc., Plano, Tex., 1980-81; v.p. Directions, Inc., Dallas, 1981—. Mem. So. Meth. U. M.B.A. Assn. Baptist. Office: 15301 Dallas Pkwy Suite 400 LB 23 Dallas TX 75248

WALTERS, NORMAN VALENTINE, JR., training executive; b. Jacksonville, Fla., Dec. 21, 1936; s. Norman Valentine and Mary Elizabeth (Rankin) W.; children—Deborah Lynn, David Glenn, Robert Michael, Pamela Jo. B.S.E.E., U. Beverly Hills, 1977, M.B.A., 1979, Ph.D., 1981; B.S. in Math. cum laude, Coll. Notre Dame-Belmont, 1978, B.S. in Bus. cum laude, 1978. Software engr. Dalmo Victor Co., Belmont, Calif., 1974-77; gen. mgr. Jade Co., Lawndale, Calif., 1977; pres. Wameco, Inc., San Jose, Calif.; software engr. research and devel. dept. Fairfield Industries, Houston, 1978, mgr. quality control mfg., 1978-79, prodn. mgr., 1980; asst. tng. mgr. Petty Ray Geophys., Houston, 1980; tng. mgr. tech. div. Geosource Inc., Houston, 1981—; guest lectr. U. Houston, 1985—; lectr. in field. Mem. Nat. Republican Congl. Com., 1982-83; charter mem. Rep. Presdl. Task Force, 1981—. Served with USN, 1959-74. Decorated Air medal; recipient Presdl. Achievement award, 1982, Am. Spirit Honor medal Citizens Com. for Army, Navy and Air Force, 1959, Medal of Merit, Pres. Reagan, 1982. Mem. Am. Soc. Tng. and Devel. (sec.-treas. petroleum spl. interest group 1983-84, nat. conf. chmn. 1984-85, bd. dirs. 1985-86), Soc. Exploration Geophysicists, Nat. Rifle Assn., Nat. Def. Preparedness Assn., Am. Film Inst., Mensa, Am. Mus. Natural History, Naval Inst., Delta Epsilon. Episcopalian. Lodges: Masons, Shriners. Author: Basic Instructional Principles and Techniques; The New First Line Supervisor or Manager. Home: 6930 Falling Waters Spring TX 77379 Office: 6909 Southwest Freeway Houston TX 77036

WALTERS, REBA NELLE, nursing educator, administrator; b. Lenox, Ga., Apr. 20, 1933; d. John Roy and Essie (Barton) Rowan; m. Charles Ray Walters, Sept. 3, 1955; children—Charles Ray, Jr., Nancy Walters Harman, J. Douglas. B.S. in Nursing, U. N.C., 1969; Ed.M., N.C. State U., 1973; M.S. in Nursing, East Carolina U., 1982. R.N., N.C. Staff nurse Monongalia Gen. Hosp., Morgantown, W.Va., 1955-56, Vincent Pallotti, Morgantown, 1957; Kingston Hosp., N.Y., 1960-65; nursing instr. Rex Hosp., Raleigh, N.C., 1969-75, Wake Tech. Coll., Raleigh, 1975-82; chmn. health edn., dir. nursing edn. Vance Granville Community Coll., Henderson, N.C., 1982—. Recipient Best Ob Nurse award Crawford Long, 1955. Mem. Am. Nurses Assn. (pres. dist. 13 1979-80, bd. dirs. 1980-82), Am. Vocat. Assn. (v.p. community coll. and tech. edn. div. 1977-79), So. Sociol. Assn., Assoc. Degree Nursing Dirs., Alpha Kappa Delta, Sigma Theta Tau. Democrat. Baptist. Avocation: gardening. Home: 719 Williamsboro St Oxford NC 27565 Office: Vance Granville Community Coll PO Box 917 Henderson NC 27536

WALTERS, SHARON RUTH, psychologist; b. Dallas, Mar. 15, 1949; d. Edward Earl and Dorothy Marie (Kelley) W. B.A., So. Meth. U., 1971; M.A. Tex. Women's U., 1975, Ph.D., 1983. Lic. psychologist, Tex. Instr., Mountain View Coll., Dallas, 1974-84; cons. psychologist in pvt. practice, Dallas, 1985—. Author: (with George R. Mount) The Art of Child Management, 1982. Contbr. articles to profl. jours. Mem. Am. Psychol. Assn., Tex. Psychol. Assn., Dallas Psychol. Assn. Avocations: ballroom dancing; ice skating; horseback riding; art. Office: 1450 Preston Forest Sq 267 Dallas TX 75230

WALTERS, SUE FOX, business woman, corporate executive; b. Louisville, June 9, 1941; d. Thomas Burke and Reva (Crick) Fox; m. Hugh Alexander Walters; children—Thomas Wade, Susan Alexandra. Student N.C. State U., Ky. Wesleyan Coll. Acct., legal sec. to various fin. instns. and firms; free-lance designer; ct. adminstr. 45th Jud. Cir. Ct. Ky.; v.p., treas. Alexander and Assocs., CATV cons. firm, Greenville, Ky.; corp. adminstr. Pres., Jr. Woman's Club Greenville, 1964-65; pres. Woman's Club Greenville, 1976-78, art chmn. beautification com., mem. fund-raising com.; vice gov. 2d dist. Ky. Fedn. Women's Clubs, 1980. Mem. Epsilon Sigma Omicron. Democrat. Club: Woman's of Greenville. Home and Office: Route 2 Amde Lo Greenville KY 42345 also Seattle WA

WALTNER, BEVERLY RULAND, artist; b. Kansas City, Mo.; d. Harry George and Ruth Anna (Laitner) Waltern, Jr. Student Columbia U., 1950-51, Yale U., 1951-53; B.A., U. Miami, Fla., 1955; M.F.A., No. Ill. U., 1968; postgrad. Kent State U., summer 1968. Tchr. art pub. schs. N.Y., Fla., Mo., Ill., 1960-65; instr. art Barry Coll., Miami Shores, Fla., 1969-70; artist-designer, Coral Gables, Fla., 1972—; One-woman shows: Art Gallery, No. Ill. U., DeKalb, 1968, Lyons Meml. Library, Point Lookout, Mo., 1968, Jewish Community Ctr. Gallery, Kansas City, Mo., 1969; juried exhbns. include: New Horizons in Painting, North Shore Art League, 1966, 68, Chautauqua Exhbn. Am. Art, 1968-73, 78, 10th Midwestern Bienniel, Joslyn Mus., 1968, Mid-Am. I, Nelson Gallery and St. Louis Mus., 1968, Nat. Soc. Painters in Casein and Acrylic, 1969, 70, 72, 73, Ark. Nat., Ark. State U., 1970, 35th Ann. Mid-Yr. Show, Butler Inst. Am. Art, 1970, Ann. Exhbn. Am. Painting, Soc. Four Arts, 1971, 74, IV and V Ann. Pan. Am. Exhbns., 1972, 73; represented in permanent collections: No. Ill. U., Arlen Realty Mgmt., Inc., Alexander Muss and Sons, Equitable Life Assurance Soc. U.S., Gen. Devel. Corp., Zuckerman-Vernon Corp., also numerous pvt. collections. Recipient 1st place award Ann. Chautauqua Exhbn. of Am. Art, 1968, Louis E. Selden award, 1972; top award New Horizons in Painting Show, 1966, honorable mention, 1968. Mem. Artists Equity Assn., Cultural Execs. Council Profl. Artists Guild (treas. 1977-78, v.p. 1978-79, editorial staff newsletter 1977—), Chautauqua Art Assn., Coral Gables C. of C. (cultural affairs com. 1979—).

WALTON, CHESTER LEE, JR., management consultant; b. Annapolis, Md., Oct. 10, 1926; s. Chester Lee and Mildred Dolores (Farnen) W.; m. Doris Beloian Lange, Nov. 3, 1981; children by previous marriage—Bret Lee, Candace Susan, Gregory Tod. Maintenance engr. Pam Am. Petroleum and Transport Co., Texas City, Tex., 1948-51; research engr. Babcock & Wilcox Co., Alliance, Ohio, 1953-54; sales engr. Bunting Brass & Bronze Co., Indpls., 1954-55; cons. McKinsey & Co., Inc., Chgo., London, 1955-60; prin. McKinsey & Co., Inc., London, N.Y.C., 1960-63, dir., mgr., Chgo., 1963-67, mng. dir., 1967-73, dir. Dallas, mgr. Tex. offices, 1973-84. Mem. adv. bd. Dallas Symphony Assn., 1979—; dir. Dallas Symphony Found., 1982—; chmn. adv. council U. Tex., Dallas, 1976—; mem. vis. com. Calif. Inst. Tech., 1973—; mem. adv. council Carnegie-Mellon U., 1973—; mem. centennial commn. U. Tex., Austin, 1982—; mem. chancellors council U. Tex. System, 1978—. Served with USNR, 1944-46; to 1st lt. USAF, 1951-53. Recipient Nelle C. Johnston award U. Tex., Dallas, 1979. Republican. Lutheran. Clubs: Links (N.Y.C.); Chicago; Dallas. Office: 5944 Luther Ln Suite 600 Dallas TX 75225

WALTON, CONRAD GORDON, SR., architect; b. Houston, June 18, 1928; s. John Edward and Evelyn Lucille (Gordon) W.; B.S. (Walsh scholar), Rice U., 1951; postgrad. U. Houston, 1955; m. Rilda Ellen Akin, Dec. 10, 1954; children—Conrad Gordon, Evelyn Coleman, Roberta Agnes. Registered architect Nat. Coll. Archtl. Registration Bds. Chief supt. Welton Becket & Assos., Houston, 1961-63; partner Alexander, Walton & Hatteberg, Houston, 1963-68; owner Conrad G. Walton, Houston, 1968—, D.C.W. Architects, 1974—; Realtor, 1982—; co-owner subdiv. Holiday Oaks, Lake Somerville, Tex., 1964—; registered fallout shelter analyst Def. Dept., 1966—. Pres. Woodrow Wilson Elem. PTO, Houston, 1969-70, Houston Great Books Council, 1976-77; chmn. Troop 345, Roberts Sch., Boy Scouts Am., 1960-71; Republican precinct chmn., 1964-71; trustee Fair Haven United Meth. Ch., 1976-77. Served with AUS, 1952-54; Korea. Mem. AIA (treas. 1968), Tex. Soc. Architects, Houston C. of C. (mem. small bus. com.). Methodist. Optimist. Architect U. Houston Sci. Bldg. renovation, 1979. Home: 9014 Springview Houston TX 77080 Office: 7011 Southwest Freeway Suite 206 Houston TX 77074

WALTON, CONRAD GORDON, JR., microcomputer retailing company executive; b. Houston, Mar. 2, 1956; s. Conrad Gordon and Rilda (Akin) W. B.S. in Computer Sci., Tex. A&M U., 1981. Programmer, Omnus Computer Corp., Houston, 1971-79; programmer analyst SynerCom Tech., Houston, 1981-82; service mgr. ComputerCraft, Inc., Houston, 1982-83; pres. YES Computers, Inc., Bryan, Tex., 1983—. Served with U.S. Army, 1974-77. Mem. Tex. A&M U. Microcomputer Club (pres. 1980-81). Republican. Home: 3302 Coastal St College Station TX 77840

WALTON, JOHN WAYNE, air pollution engineer; b. St. Louis, July 11, 1937; s. John Van Allen and Clara (Huskey) W.; m. Elizabeth Ann Ellis, Sept. 29, 1962; children—Richard John, Eric Van Allen, Robyn Carole. B.S. in Civil Engring., U. Mo.-Rolla, 1961; M.S. in Engring., U. Cin., 1969. Registered profl. engr., Ky., Mo., Tenn. Engr., Ky. Dept. Pub. Health, Frankfort, 1965-68; devel. engr. Ga. Kraft Co., Rome, 1969-71; dep. dir. Tenn. Div. Air Pollution, Nashville, 1971—. Served to 1st lt. U.S. Army, 1962-64. Mem. Air Pollution Control Assn. (dir. 1973-75, chmn. so. sect. 1970-71), Nat. Soc. Profl. Engrs., Tenn. Soc. Profl. Engrs. Club: Civitan (dir. 1979-80) (Brentwood, Tenn.). Home: 8116 Millview Dr Brentwood TN 37027 Office: Tenn Div Air Pollution Control 150 9th Ave N Nashville TN 37219-5404

WALTON, MILDRED LEE, educational administrator; b. Atlanta, Dec. 8, 1926; d. James Forest and Pauline (Dickerson) Collier; m. Borah Wayne Walton, June 26, 1971; children—Berle Burse, Denise Burse Mickelbury, Charna Michelle Burse Turner. A.B., Spelman Coll., 1947; M.A., Atlanta U., 1962; Ed.D., Nova U., 1976; postgrad. fellow Harvard U., Summer 1984. Tchr. Dekalb County Bd. Edn., Atlanta, 1947-56; tchr. Atlanta Pub. Schs., 1956—, prin. Harwell Elem. Sch., 1969-73, Miles Elem. Sch., 1973—; asst. prof. Atlanta U., summer 1970. Mem. adv. bd. Rockefeller Bros. Found. for Art Edn., 1980-84; vestrywoman St. Paul's Episc. Ch., 1984—. Mem. Nat. Assn. Elem. Sch. Prins. (dir. 1980-83, pres. elect 1984-85, pres. 1985-86, past pres. 1986-87), Ga. Assn. Elem. Prins., Spelman Coll. Alumnae Assn. (chpt. pres. 1982-86), Southeastern Council Elem. Sch. Prins. (dir. 1980-83), AAUW (Ednl. Resources Info. Service bd.), Phi Delta Kappa (bd. dirs. chpt. 1984-86). Zeta Phi Beta. Democrat. Office: Miles Elem Sch 4215 Bakers Ferry Rd Atlanta GA 30331

WALTON, RONALD C., geophysicist, consultant; b. Rexburg, Idaho, July 28, 1929; s. Charles Lewis and Mable Irene (Merrill) W.; m. Patsy Rae Nesbitt, July 28, 1953; children—Debra K., Karen R. B.A. in Geology, Idaho State U., 1952. Civil engr., party chief City of Idaho Falls, Idaho, 1952-53; field helper, geophysicist Western Geophys. Co., 1953-62, ops. mgr., 1962-67, mgr. interpretation, 1967-69, seismologist, 1969-74; geophys. explorationist major oil companies, Houston, 1974—; geophys. cons. Geosci. Cons., Houston, 1974—. Contbr. articles to profl. jours. Mem. Republican Presdl. Task Force, 1982-84. Mem. Am. Assn. Petroleum Geologists, Soc. Exploration Geophysicists, Houston Geol. Soc., Geophys. Soc. Houston, Assn. Petroleum Cons. (treas. 1981-83, 2d v.p. 1983—). Mem. Ch. of Jesus Christ of Latter-day Saints. Home: 9222 Beechnut Houston TX 77036

WALTON, SAM M., retail discount chain company executive. Founder, chmn. Wal-Mart Stores, Bentonville, Ark. Office: Wal-Mart Stores 702 SW Eighth Bentonville AR 72712*

WALTON, TERENCE MICHAEL, librarian; b. Norwalk, Conn., May 28, 1938; s. Charles Cameron and Mildred V. (Welch) W.; m. Geraldine Ryan Quinn, Jan. 3, 1964 (dec.); B.A., Ariz. State U., 1967; M.L.S., U. Hawaii, 1968. Asst. dir. adult edn. Ariz. Dept. Pub. Instrn., Phoenix, 1964-67; adult edn. coordinator Phoenix Coll., 1968-69; sr. reference librarian N.Y. Pub. Library, N.Y.C., 1969-70; head acquisitions Hunter Coll., CUNY, N.Y.C., 1970-75, U. Petroleum and Minerals, Dhahran, Saudi Arabia, 1975-77; assoc. dean Old Dominion U., Norfolk, Va., 1978-82; dir. Captiva Meml. Library, Captiva Island, Fla., 1983—; adj. instr. Cath. U. Am., 1979-82; automation cons. U. Petroleum and Minerals, 1975-77, various libraries; adult edn. cons. Contbr. articles to profl. jours. NDEA fellow, 1964-67. Mem. Va. Council Higher Edn. (com. chmn. 1978-82), Va. Library Assn. (com. chmn. 1978-80), Tidewater Library Consortium (cons.), Southeastern Library Network (cons.), ALA, Library Info. Tech. Assn., Fla. Library Assn. Democrat. Roman Catholic. Home: PO Box 672 Captiva Island FL 33924 Office: Captiva Meml Library PO Drawer 99 Captiva Island FL 33924

WALTON, WALTER GREGORY, clinical psychologist; b. Jacksonville, N.C., Dec. 8, 1947; s. Walter Parrott and Ethleen Louise (Rochelle) W.; m. Linda Kay Crouch, June 21, 1975; 1 child, Noah Matthew. B.S., Pembroke State U., 1974; M.A., Appalachian State U., 1980; Ph.D., U. Ga., 1983. Lic. psychologist, N.C.; cert. S.C., Ga. Clin. psychologist Meckenburg Mental Health, Charlotte, N.C., 1976-80, Alexander Children's Ctr., Charlotte, 1980-81; asst. prof. psychology Presbyn. Coll., Clinton, S.C., 1983-84; dir. psychol. services Brynn Marr Hosp., Jacksonville, N.C.; pvt. practice clin. psychology, Jacksonville, 1984—. Served with U.S. Army, 1969-72. Mem. Am. Psychol. Assn., S.E. Psychol. Assn. Avocations: distance running; writing children's stories. Home: 13E Jupiter Trail Jacksonville NC 28540 Office: Brynn Marr Office Park Suite 14 Jacksonville NC 28540

WALTZ, ALAN KENT, clergyman, denominational executive; b. Normal, Ill., Oct. 10, 1931; s. James Edwin Sr. and Ethel Leona (Hawkins) W.; m. Mary Joyce Horton, June 5, 1966; children—Sharon Kay, Reid Alan. B.A., Ill. Wesleyan U., 1953; M.Div., Garrett Theol. Sem., Evanston, Ill., 1957; M.A., Northwestern U., 1958, Ph.D., 1961. Ordained to ministry United Methodist Ch., 1957. Pastor Braceville Meth. Ch., Ill., 1954-56; denominational exec. United Meth. Ch., 1960—, asst. dir. bd. Missions, Phila., 1960-64, asst. gen. sec. Council on Fin., Evanston, 1964-68, assoc. gen. sec. Gen. Council on Ministries, Dayton, Ohio, 1969-84; assoc. gen. sec. Gen. Bd. Discipleship, Nashville, 1984—. Author: Images of the Future, 1980; To Proclaim the Faith, 1983. Editor book series Into Our Third Century, 1981-84. Trustee Ill. Wesleyan U., Bloomington, 1984—. Mem. Am. Sociol. Soc., Soc. Sci. Study Religion, Religious Research Assn., World Future Soc. Office: Gen Bd Discipleship United Meth Ch PO Box 840 Nashville TN 37202

WALZ, ROBERT BRADSHAW, historian; b. Ashdown, Ark., Sept. 27, 1918; s. Joe and Lolla (Bradshaw) W.; A.A., Magnolia A. and M. Coll., 1939; B.A., Henderson State Tchrs. Coll., 1941; M.A., U. Tex., Austin, 1952, Ph.D., 1958; m. Curtistine Parsons, Apr. 28, 1951. Instr., Texarkana Coll., 1946-51; teaching fellow U. Tex., Austin, 1952-55; instr., asst. prof. history E. Tex. State U., Commerce, 1955-58; mem. faculty dept. history So. Ark. U., Magnolia, 1958—, prof., 1968—. Bd. dirs. Southwest Ark. Regional Archives, 1978—. Served with USAAF, 1943-45. Named Ark. Humanist of Yr., Ark. Endowment for Humanities, 1979. Mem. Orgn. Am. Historians, So. Hist. Assn., Ark. Hist. Assn. (mem. bd. 1963-80, pres. 1968-69, 69-70), Ark. Archaeol. Soc. Democrat. Methodist. Home: 1502 N Jackson St Magnolia AR 71753 Office: PO Box 1292 So Ark Univ Magnolia AR 71753

WANAMAKER, TAMMY LYNNE, counselor; b. Canadian, Tex., June 28, 1956; d. Burl and Vona (Brooks) Benge; m. George Sturdevant Wanamaker. B.S. in Edn., West Tex. State U., 1977, M.A. in Psychology, 1980. Lic. profl. counselor, Tex. Tchr. Hereford Independent Sch. Dist., Tex., 1977-78; ednl. cons., Amarillo, Tex., 1979-80; instr. St. Edwards U., Austin, Tex., 1981, Mary Hardin Baylor U., Belton, Tex., 1981; counselor Family Service Ctr., Georgetown, Tex., 1982—. Regional leader March of Dimes, Georgetown, 1984; youth dir. First Presby. Ch., Georgetown, 1981-82; mem. Am. Heart Assn. Psi Chi scholar, 1979. Mem. Am. Psychol. Assn., Stepfamily Assn. Am.,

Tex. Assn. Children and Adults with Learning Disabilities. Democrat. Home: 501 Esparada Dr Georgetown TX 78628 Office: Family Service Ctr PO Box 997 Georgetown TX 78627

WANDER, MARTIN JOSEPH, architect; b. Albany, N.Y., July 7, 1949; s. Jerome and Ellen Judith (Loeb) W. B.Arch., Cornell U., 1972; M.Arch., U. Calif.-Berkeley, 1976. Registered architect. Designer, Perry Dean Ptnrs., Boston, 1973-75, Gensler Assocs., San Francisco, 1976-77; sr. designer Perry, Dean, Stahl & Rogers, Cambridge, Mass., 1979-82; v.p. Arquitectonica, Miami, Fla., 1982—; instr. Boston Archtl. Ctr., 1973-79; adj. prof. Fla. Internat. U., 1985—. Author cover article Abitare Mag., 1979. Mem. Beacon Hill Civic Assn., Boston, 1980-82. Recipient Merit award Boston Bd. Realtors, 1982. Mem. AIA, Archtl. Club Miami. Office: Arquitectonica Internat Corp 4215 Ponce de Leon Blvd Coral Gables FL 33146

WANDERMAN, RICHARD GORDON, pediatrician; b. N.Y.C., Apr. 17, 1943; s. Herman L. and Helen L. (Cohn) W.; m. Judy Rosenberg, Nov. 2, 1980; children—Richard Gordon, Gregory Lloyd, Adam Joseph; 1 stepdau., Shana Abraham. B.A., Western Res. U., Cleve., 1965; M.D., SUNY-Bklyn., 1969. Diplomate Am. Bd. Pediatrics. Intern, Kings County Hosp. Ctr., Bklyn., 1969-70, resident in pediatrics, 1970-71; resident in pediatrics L.I. Jewish-Hillside Med. Ctr., New Hyde Park, N.Y., 1971-72; practice medicine specializing in pediatrics, adolescent clin. ecology and allergy, Merrick, N.Y., 1972-74, Charleston, W.Va., 1974-78, Memphis, 1978—; pres. DCT and Assocs., 1982—; mem. staff L.I. Jewish-Hillside Med. Ctr., 1972-74, Nassau County Med. Ctr., 1972-74, Hempstead Gen. Hosp., 1972-74, Charleston Area Med. Ctr., 1974-78, LeBonheur Children's Hosp., 1978—, St. Joseph Hosp., 1978—, St. Francis Hosp., 1978—, Bapt. Meml. Hosps., 1978—, Meth. Hosps., 1978—; asst. instr. pediatrics Downstate Med. Ctr., SUNY-Bklyn., 1970-71; clin. asst. prof. W.Va. U. Med. Sch., 1974-78, clin. assoc. prof., 1978; clin. assoc. prof. U. Tenn. Sch. for Health Scis., 1979—. Chmn. parent adv. com. Headstart Program, Kanawha, Boone and Clay counties, W.Va., 1977-78; Sunday Sch. tchr. Temple Israel Memphis, 1978-80; coach swim team Memphis Jewish Community Ctr., 1979-80, chmn. adolescent problems task force, 1980; mem. council Memphis chpt. Jewish Nat. Fund, 1981—; bd. dirs. Midsouth Area Jewish Nat. Fund, 1983—. Mem. Am. Physician Fellowship, Inc., Tenn. Med. Assn., Memphis-Shelby County Med. Soc. (mem. grievance com.), Soc. for Adolescent Medicine (mem. sch. and coll. health com. 1978), Am. Acad. Pediatrics (fellow adolescent medicine sect.), Tenn. Pediatric Soc., Soc. Clin. Ecology, Mensa, Les Amis du Vin, Zeta Beta Tau. Democrat. Office: 6584 Poplar Ave Suite 420 Memphis TN 38138

WANDERS, HANS WALTER, banker; b. Aachen, Germany, Apr. 3, 1925; s. Herbert and Anna Maria (Kusters) W.; came to U.S., 1929, naturalized, 1943; B.S., Yale U., 1947; postgrad. Rutgers U. Grad. Sch. Banking, 1961-64; m. Elizabeth Knox Kimball, Apr. 2, 1949; children—Crayton Kimball, David Gillette. With Gen. Electric Co., 1947-48, Libbey-Owens-Ford Glass Co., 1948-53, Allied Chem. Co., 1953-55, McKinsey & Co., Inc., 1955-57; asst. cashier, then 2d v.p., v.p. No. Trust Co., Chgo., 1957-65; v.p. Nat. Blvd. Bank, Chgo., 1965-66, pres., 1966-70, also dir.; exec. v.p. Wachovia Bank & Trust Co., N.A., Winston-Salem, N.C., 1970-74, chmn., dir., 1977—; pres., dir. Wachovia Corp., 1974-76, chmn., dir., 1977—; v.p., dir. Winton Mineral Co., dir. Hanes Cos., Inc. Mem. com. on bank relationships Council on Founds., Inc., 1973-74; chmn. Winston-Salem Found. Com., 1981-82; trustee, mem. exec. com. Tax Found., Inc.; mem. exec. com. President's Pvt. Sector Survey on Cost Control, 1982-84; bd. visitors Fuqua Sch. Bus., Duke U.; bd. dirs. N.C. Engring. Found., Inc., N.C. Textile Found., Inc. Served to lt. USNR, 1943-46, 51-53. Mem. Am. Bankers Assn. (chmn. mktg. div. 1979-80, dir. 1971-73), Assn. Bank Holding Cos. (dir., mem. exec. com. 1981-83), Assn. Res. City Bankers, Internat. C. of C. (trustee U.S. council 1974-80), Conf. Bd. (So. regional adv. council), Newcomen Soc. N.Am. Clubs: Commonwealth, Chgo. (Chgo.); Yale (N.Y.C.); Old Town (Winston-Salem); Roaring Gap (N.C.). Home: 2760 Old Town Club Rd Winston-Salem NC 27106 Office: 301 N Main St Winston-Salem NC 27101

WANG, TSEN CHEN, chemical engineer; b. Taiwan, Apr. 26, 1943; came to U.S., 1967, naturalized, 1969; s. Ken Sun and Lain (Chou) W.; m. Huei Li Lee, Aug. 29, 1970; children—Clifford, Sean. B.S. in Chem. Engring., Chun Yuan U., Taiwan, 1966; M.S., U. Iowa, 169, Ph.D., 1972. Registered profl. engr., Fla. Research chemist Dunn Edward Corp., Los Angeles, 1969; presdl. intern Smithsonian Inst., Ft. Pierce, Fla., 1972-73; chem. engr. Harbor Br. Found., Ft. Pierce, 1973-79, chief chem. engr., 1979—; cons. City of Vero Beach, Fla., 1982—, Piper Aircraft, Corp., Vero Beach, 1981—. Contbr. articles to profl. publs. Grantee Piper Aircraft, 1981—, City of Vero Beach, 1982—. Mem. Am. Inst. Chem. Engring., Am. Chem. Soc., Am. Water Works Assn., AAAS. Office: Harbor Br Found Inc RR 1 Box 196 Fort Pierce FL 33450

WANNAN, BRIAN DOUGLAS, computer company executive; b. Toronto, Ont., Can., Aug. 18, 1942; came to U.S., 1980; s. Lloyd Rieve and Emma Lilla (Lowe) W.; m. Carol J. Ritchie, Sept. 10, 1965 (div. June 1980). Cert., Fich Inst. Data Processing, 1962. Sales rep. Mai Can. Ltd., Toronto, 1967-69; sales mgr. Sperry Univac Ltd., 1969-75; owner, operator Curly's, 1977-78; sales mgr. ICL Computers Ltd., 1978-80, ME29 launch mgr. N.Am., London, 1980, Toronto, 1980, advanced systems mgr., Irving, Tex., 1981, western regional mgr., 1982; pres., owner, chief exec. officer MicroSolve, Inc., Dallas, 1982—. Mem. Republican Presdl. Task Force, Washington, 1983. Mem. Dallas C. of C. Club: Inwood Racquet. Office: MicroSolve Inc One Lincoln Ctr Suite 200 Dallas TX 75240

WARBERG, CARLA MARIE, bank executive; b. Denver, Dec. 14, 1943; d. Carl William and Myrtle Marie (Corsberg) W.; m. Gerard Joseph Kelly, Aug. 12, 1973; 1 child, Sean Warberg. B.A., U. Colo., 1965; M.A., U. Wis., 1968, Ph.D., 1970. Fin. economist Fed. Res. Bank Dallas, 1969-73, research officer, 1974-77, asst. v.p., asst. controller, 1977-81, v.p. personnel, 1982—. Harold Stonier fellow, 1965, 66, 67. Mem. Am. Econ. Assn., Am. Fin. Assn., Am. Inst. Banking, Phi Beta Kappa., Methodist. Lodge: Zonta (sec.-treas. 1972-76). Home: 6811 Kenwhite Dallas TX 75231 Office: Fed Res Bank Dallas Sta K Dallas TX 75222

WARBURTON, RALPH JOSEPH, architect, engineer, urban planner; b. Kansas City, Mo., Sept. 5, 1935; s. Ralph Gray and Emma Frieda (Niemann) W.; B.Arch., M.I.T., 1958; M.Arch., Yale U., 1959, M.C.P., 1960; m. Carol Ruth Hychka, June 14, 1958; children—John Geoffrey, Joy Frances. With various archtl., planning and engring. firms, Kansas City, Mo., Boston, N.Y.C., Chgo., 1952-64; asso., chief of planning Skidmore, Owings & Merrill, Chgo., 1964-66; spl. asst. for urban design HUD, Washington, 1966-72, cons., 1972-77; adv. to govts. Iran, 1970, France, 1973, Ecuador, 1974, Saudi Arabia, 1984-85; prof. architecture, archtl. engring. and planning U. Miami, Coral Gables, Fla., 1972—, chmn. dept., 1972-75, asso. dean engring. and environ. design, 1973-74; cons., 1972—; lectr., critic, design juror, 1965—; mem., chmn. Coral Gables Bd. Architects, 1980-82. Mem. Met. Housing and Planning Council of Chgo., 1965-67; mem. exec. com. Yale Arts Assn., 1965-70; chmn. Yale U. Planning Alumni Assn., 1983—; mem. ednl. adv. com. Fla. State Bd. Architecture, 1975. Skidmore, Owings & Merrill Traveling fellow M.I.T., 1958; vis. fellow Inst. Architecture and Urban Studies, N.Y.C., 1972-74; NSF grantee, 1980-82; recipient W. E. Parsons medal Yale U., 1960; Spl. Achievement award HUD, 1972; commendation Fla. State Bd. Architecture, 1974; group achievement award NASA, 1976; Honor award Fla. Trust Hist. Preservation, 1983; registered architect, Colo., Fla., N.J., Md., Ill., N.Y., Va., D.C.; registered profl. engr., Fla., N.J.; registered community planner, Mich., N.J. Fellow ASCE, Fla. Engring. Soc. (dir. 1984-85); mem. AIA (nat. housing com. 1968-72, nat. regional devel. and natural resources com. 1974-75, nat. systems devel. com. 1972-73, nat. urban design com. 1968-73; dir. Fla. S. chpt. 1974-75), Am. Inst. Cert. Planners (mem. exec. com. dept. environ. planning 1973-74), Am. Soc. Engring. Edn. (chmn. archtl. engring. div. 1975-76), Nat. Soc. Profl. Engrs., Fla. Engrs. in Edn. (chmn. 1984-85), Nat. Sculpture Soc. (allied profl. mem.), Nat. Trust for Hist. Preservation (mem. principles and guidelines com. 1967), Am. Soc. Landscape Architects (hon. mem., chmn. nat. design awards jury 1970-72), Am. Planning Assn. (award of excellence Fla. chpt. 1983), Internat. Fedn. Housing and Planning, Am. Soc. Interior Designers (hon. mem.), Greater Miami C. of C. (chmn. new neighborhoods action com. 1973-74), Sigma Xi (pres. U. Miami chpt. 1983-84), Tau Beta Pi. Club: Cosmos (Washington). Assoc. author: Man-Made America: Chaos or Control, 1963; editor: New Concepts in Urban Transportation, 1968; Housing Systems Proposals for Operation Breakthrough, 1970; Focus on Furniture, 1971; National Community Art Competition, 1971; Defining Critical Environmental Areas, 1974; contbg. editor, corr. Progressive Architecture, 1979-84; contbr. numerous articles to profl. jours.; mem. adv. panel Industrialization Forum Quar., 1969-79; mem. editorial adv. bd. Jour. of Am. Planning Assn. Home: 6910 Veronese St Coral Gables FL 33146 Office: 420 S Dixie Hwy Coral Gables FL 33146 also Sch Architecture U Miami Coral Gables FL 33124

WARCHOL, CHARLES MICHAEL, charcoal manufacturing company marketing executive; b. Lawrence, Mass., Dec. 17, 1941; s. Michael Frank and Julia Alicia (Malek) W.; m. Tula Rosa Ugarteche, Sept. 4, 1969; children—Michelle Elizabeth, Alexander Frank. B.A., Harvard U., 1963; M.A., Institut d'Études Politiques, Paris, 1965; M.B.A., Stanford U., 1967. Product mgr. The Pillsbury Co., 1969-74; product mgr. Chesebrough Ponds, Greenwich Conn., 1974-79; mktg. dir. William Wrigley Jr. Co., Chgo., 1979-81; v.p. mktg. and sales Husky Industries, Inc., Atlanta, 1981—. Served with U.S. Peace Corps, 1967-69. Mem. Am. Mktg. Assn., Barbecue Industry Assn. (chmn. research com. 1981—). Clubs: Harvard of Atlanta, Fox. Home: 1620 Lazy River Ln Atlanta GA 30338 Office: 35 Glenlake Pkwy Atlanta GA 30328

WARD, ALVAH HAFF, JR., state official; b. Wanchese, N.C., Oct. 25, 1929; s. Alvah Haff and Tracy (Cahoon) W.; m. Dolores Zittrouer, Mar. 21, 1954 (div. Sept. 1965); m. 2d, Rachel Teague, June 3, 1972. B.S., The Citadel, 1951; M.B.A., U. N.C., 1955. Owner, mgr. Dare County Ice & Storage Co., Manteo, N.C., 1954-69; marine industries and seafood cons. N.C. Dept. Commerce, Raleigh, 1969-77, indsl. devel. rep., 1977-80, dir. indsl. devel., 1980—; dir. Marine Industries and Seafood Mktg., Raleigh, 1972-74. Pres. Dare County Tourist Bur., Manteo, 1957-58; chmn. Oregon Inlet Project, Manteo, 1956-69; chmn. Wanchese Harbor Task Force, 1975-77. Mem. N.C. Fisheries Assn. (v.p. 1960-61), Am. Indsl. Devel. Council, So. Indsl. Devel. Council, N.C. Indsl. Developers Assn. Served to capt., inf. U.S. Army, 1951-54. Democrat. Baptist. Lodges: Masons (past master), Shriners (pres. Dare County 1961-62), Manteo Lions (pres. 1960-61). Home: 105 Thomas Pl Knightdale NC 27545 Office: Div Indsl Devel NC Dept Commerce 430 N Salisbury St Raleigh NC 27611

WARD, BEN LEONARD, mining technology educator, civil engineering consultant; b. Offutt, Ky., Jan. 23, 1936; s. Felix and Samantha (Arrowood) W.; m. Geneva Amburgey, June 10, 1959; children—Martha Ellen, Eliot Felix. B.S. in Civil Engring., U. Ky., 1960; M.S. in Environ. Engring., U. Tenn., 1971; postgrad. in profl. devel. U. Wis., 1980. Registered profl. engr., Ky., Tenn., Va., W.Va. Civil engr. TVA, Knoxville, Tenn., 1965-77, Appalachian Regional Commn., Pikeville, Ky., 1977-80; instr. and chmn. dept. mining tech. Pikeville Coll., 1980—. Served to 1st lt. USAF, 1960-64. Mem. ASCE, Nat. Soc. Profl. Engrs., Ky. Soc. Profl. Engrs. Avocations: photography; geology; guitar. Home: 212 Bank St Apt 5 Pikeville KY 41501 Office: Pikeville Coll Dept Mining Tech Pikeville KY 41501

WARD, BENJAMIN PORTER, retired naval officer, educator; b. LaFayette, Ind., July 2, 1897; s. Harry Van Devanter and Nellie Clara (Armbruster) W. ; B.S., U.S. Naval Acad., 1919; M.S., Columbia U., 1927; m. Mary Ellen Estes Moore, May 6, 1928; 1 son, Benjamin Porter. Commd. ensign U.S. Navy, 1919, advanced through grades to capt., 1942, ret., 1950; assoc. prof. mech. engring. Auburn U., Auburn, Ala., 1950-68, emeritus, 1968—. Decorated Victory medal, World War I, World War II, Korean War. Registered profl. engr., N.Y., D.C. Mem. Am. Soc. Naval Engrs., Soc. Naval Architects and Marine Engrs., U.S. Naval Acad. Alumni Assn., Columbia Engring. Sch. Alumni Assn.; Pi Tau Sigma. Clubs: N.Y. Yacht (N.Y.C.); Saugahatchee Country (Auburn), Masons. Home: 815 S College St Auburn AL 36830

WARD, CHESTER DOUGLAS, naval officer; b. Council Bluffs, Iowa, Aug. 30, 1944; s. Chester Bennett and Caroline Elizabeth (Chapman) W.; m. Pamela Sue, Oct. 7, 1967 (div. 1972); children—Elisabeth Courtney, Serene Rosalee; m. Nancy Jane, Aug. 28, 1977; 1 son, Joseph Chester. B.S., Iowa State U.; M.S., U. So. Calif. Asst. instr. Iowa State U., Ames, 1967; commd. U.S. Navy, 1967; div. officer engr. ops. U.S.S. Henry Clay, Pearl Harbor, 1969-73; head, tactics dept. Naval Sub Ctr., Pearl Harbor, 1976-78; head engring. dept. U.S.S. Ethan Allen, Pearl Harbor, 1973-76; exec. officer U.S.S. Puffer, 1978-81; comdg. officer U.S.S. James Madison, Miami, Fla., 1982—. Decorated Navy Commendation medal. Mem. Am. Mgmt. Assn. Republican. Lutheran. Home: 100 White Heron Ln Summerville SC 29483 Office: USS James Madison (SSBN627) B FPO Miami FL 34092

WARD, CONNIE MICHELE, psychologist, educator; b. Hampton, Va., June 11, 1954; d. Wallace W. and Elsie Saline (Polk) W. B.A., U. Calif.-Santa Cruz, 1976; M.A., Ohio State U., 1978, Ph.D., 1980. Asst. prof. Ga. State U., Atlanta, 1980—, counseling psychologist Counseling Ctr., 1980—, dir. Career Reference Library, 1980—. Contbr. articles to profl. jours. Recipient Outstanding Adminstr. award Intersorority Council Ga. State U., 1984. Mem. Am. Psychol. Assn. Baptist. Avocations: reading, chinese cooking, music. Home: 309 Camelot Dr Colldge Park GA 30349 Office: Ga State Univ Counseling Ctr University Plaza Atlanta GA 30303

WARD, DAVID HENRY, television news reporter, anchorman; b. Dallas, May 6, 1939; s. H. M. and Mary W.; m. Glenda Lois Odom, Nov. 10, 1959 (div.); children—Linda Ann, David H.; m. 2d, Debra Rene Holland, Apr. 25, 1976. Student Tyler Jr. Coll., Tex., 1957-59. Announcer Sta. KGKB, Tyler, 1958-60; program director Sta. WACO (Tex.), 1960-62; news dir. Sta. KNUZ, Houston, 1962-66; news reporter, photographer, writer, producer Sta. KTRK-TV, 1966—; free lance writer, producer, cons.; chmn. pub. affairs adv. bd. Houston Bus. Council; pub. info. com. Am. Cancer Soc.; pres. bd. dirs. Easter Seal Soc., Harris, Fort Bend counties. Recipient Best TV Newscast award Tex. UPI, 1968, 72, 73-80; TV Service award Houston Jaycees, 1982; named Man of Yr., Houston Sertoma Club, 1973; TV Personality of Yr. Am. Women in Radio and TV, 1983. Mem. Sigma Delta Chi. Baptist. Club: Press (Houston). Office: 3310 Bissonnet Houston TX 77005

WARD, EVAN, JR., pharmacist; b. Selma, Ala., Sept. 13, 1942; s. Evan and Hattie Mae (Hunter) W.; children from previous marriage—Donna Janine, Jennifer Lynn, Christopher Evan; m. Rita M. Lacey, Sept. 3, 1983; children—Nicholas Cameron, Dustin Roman. B.S., Fla. A&M U., 1965. Pharmacist, Triangle Prescription, Atlanta, 1966-70; pharmacist, asst. mgr. Walgreen Drugs, Atlanta, 1968-70; pharmacist, pres. Medics Drug Marts, Inc., Atlanta, 1970—; exec. v.p., founder W&W Pharms., Atlanta, 1982-84; cons. Sadie Mays Nursing Home, Atlanta, 1973-77; staff pharmacist McClendon Hosp., Atlanta, 1976-79; mem. adv. com. State Ga., 1984—. Mem. United Negro Coll. Fund, 1985, Nat. Urban League, 1985. Recipient Bus. Man of Year award Atlanta Bus. League, 1970, Cert. Appreciation award CETA, 1980. Mem. Ga. Pharm. Assn., Nat. Assn. Retail Druggists, Fla. A&M Sch. Pharmacists Alumni Assn. (pres. 1973, Pharmacist of Year 1973), Fla. A&M Alumni Assn. (Disting. Service award 1984), C. of C., Kappa Alpha Psi. Baptist. Office: Medics Drug Marts Inc 75 Peidmont Ave NE Atlanta GA 30303

WARD, GEORGE TRUMAN, architect; b. Washington, July 24, 1927; s. Truman and Gladys Anna (Nutt) W.; B.S., Va. Poly. Inst., 1951, M.S., 1952; postgrad. George Washington U., 1966; m. Margaret Ann Hall, Sept. 10, 1949; children—Carol Ann Ward Dickson, Donna Lynne Ward Hale, George Truman, Robert Stephen. Archtl. draftsman Charles A. Pearson, Radford, Va., 1950; head archtl. sect. Hayes, Seay, Mattern & Mattern, Radford and Roanoke, 1951-52; with Joseph Saunders & Assos., Alexandria, Va., 1952-57, asso. architect, 1955-57; partner Vosbeck-Ward & Assos., Alexandria, 1957-64, Ward/Hall Assocs., Fairfax, Va., 1964—; dir. United Va. Bank/Greater Washington Region. Pres. PTA Burke (Va.) Sch., 1970-71; mem. bd. mgrs. Fairfax (Va.) County YMCA, 1964-76; mem. adv. com. Coll. Architecture, Va. Poly. Inst.; bd. dirs. Va. Tech. Found., Inc.; pres. Springfield Rotary Found., 1978-79; vice chmn. county adv. bd. Salvation Army; mem. Gen. Bd. Va. Bapts.; bd. visitors Va. Poly. Inst. Served with AUS, 1946-47. Registered profl. architect, Va., Md., D.C., W.Va., Ohio, N.J., Del., Pa., Tenn., Ga., N.C., N.Y., Tex. Paul Harris fellow. Mem. AIA (corp.), Interfaith Forum on Religion, Art and Architecture, Va. Assn. Professions, Va. C. of C., Tau Sigma Delta, Omicron Delta Kappa, Phi Kappa Phi, Pi Delta Epsilon. Baptist (deacon, moderator). Mason (Shriner, K.T.), Rotarian (charter mem., pres. Springfield 1973-74). Home: Route 1 Box 30 Marshall VA 22115 Office: 12011 Lee Jackson Meml Hwy Fairfax VA 22033

WARD, HARRY PFEFFER, university administrator, physician; b. Pueblo, Colo., June 6, 1933; s. Lester L. and Alysmai (Pfeffer) W.; m. Betty Jo Stewart, Aug. 20, 1955; children—Perry Stewart, Leslie, Elizabeth, Mary Alice, Amy. A.B., Princeton U., 1955; M.D., U. Colo., 1959; M.S., U. Minn., 1963. Diplomate Am. Bd. Internal Medicine. Intern in internal medicine Bellevue Hosp., N.Y.C., 1959-60; resident internal medicine Mayo Clinic, Rochester, Minn., 1960-63; chief hematology Denver VA Hosp., 1964-69, chief med. service, 1967-72; dean Coll. Medicine, U. Colo., Denver, 1972-78; chancellor U. Ark. Sch. Med. Sci., Little Rock, 1979—; trustee Am. Bur. Med. Advisers China, N.Y.C., 1981—. Bd. dirs. Little Rock chpt. ARC, 1979—, Ark. Child Hosp., Little Rock, 1980—. Fellow ACP; mem. Am. Fedn. Clin. Research, AMA, Central Soc. Clin. Research, Western Soc. Clin. Research, Alpha Omega Alpha. Office: U Ark Sch Med Sci 4301 W Markham St Little Rock AR 72205

WARD, HIRAM HAMILTON, federal judge; b. Thomasville, N.C., Apr. 29, 1923; s. O.L. and Margaret A. Ward; student Wake Forest Coll., 1945-47; J.D., Wake Forest U., 1950; m. Evelyn M. McDaniel, June 1, 1947; children—William McDaniel, James Randolph. Bar: N.C. 1950. Practiced law, Denton, N.C., 1950-51; staff atty. Nat. Prodn. Authority, Washington, 1951-52; partner firm DeLapp, Ward & Hedrick, Lexington, N.C., 1952-72; U.S. dist. judge Middle Dist. N.C., 1972—, chief judge, 1982—; mem. Jud. Council of 4th Cir., 1984—; bd. visitors Wake Forest U. Sch. Law, 1973—. Mem. N.C. Bd. Elections, 1964-72; trustee Wingate Coll., 1969-72. Served with USAAF, 1940-45. Decorated Air medal, Purple Heart. Mem. ABA, N.C. Bar Assn., Am. Judicature Soc., N.C. State Bar, Jud. Conf. Fourth Circuit, Phi Alpha Delta (hon. life). Republican. Baptist. Clubs: Lions, Masons (Denton). Contbr. legal opinions to Fed. Reporter System, 1972—. Office: 246 Fed Bldg and US Courthouse Winston-Salem NC 27101

WARD, HORACE TALIAFERRO, federal judge; b. LaGrange, Ga., July 29, 1927; A.B., Morehouse Coll., 1949; M.A., Atlanta U., 1950; J.D., Northwestern U., 1959; m. Ruth LeFlore (dec.); 1 son. Instr. polit. sci. Ark. A.M. and N. Coll., 1950-51. Ala. State Coll., 1951-53, 55-56; claims authorizer U.S. Social Security Adminstrn., 1959-60; admitted to Ga. bar, 1960; asso. firm Hollowell Ward Moore & Alexander and successors, Atlanta, 1960-71; individual practice law, Atlanta, 1971-74; judge Civil Ct. of Fulton County, 1974-77, Fulton Superior Ct., 1977-79; now U.S. Dist. Ct. judge No. Dist. Ga., Atlanta; lectr. bus. and sch. law Atlanta U., 1965-70; dep. city atty., Atlanta, 1969-70; asst. county atty. Fulton County, 1971-74. Trustee, Friendship Baptist Ch., Atlanta; mem. Ga. adv. com. U.S. Civil Rights Commn., 1963-65; assisting lawyer NAACP Legal Def. and Edn. Fund, Inc., 1960-70; mem. Jud. Selection Commn., Atlanta, 1972-74; mem. Charter Commn., Atlanta, 1971-72; mem. Ga. Senate, 1964-74, jud. com., rules com., county and urban affairs com.; mem. State Democratic Exec. com., 1966-74; bd. dirs. Atlanta Legal Aid Soc., Atlanta Urban League, Fed. Defender Program, No. Dist. Ga.; trustee Met. Atlanta Commn. on Crime and Delinquency, Atlanta U., Fledgling Found. Mem. Am. Bar Assn., Nat. Bar Assn. (chmn. jud. council 1978-79), State Bar Ga., Atlanta Bar Assn., Gate City Bar Assn. (pres. 1972-74), Atlanta Lawyers Club, Phi Beta Kappa, Alpha Phi Alpha, Phi Alpha Delta, Sigma Pi Phi. Office: 2388 US Courthouse 75 Spring St SW Atlanta GA 30303*

WARD, JAMES HUBERT, social work educator, university dean, researcher, consultant; b. Lawndale, N.C., Apr. 8, 1937; s. Frank A. and Helen (Wray) W.; m. Jacqueline Ferman Ward, Dec. 29, 1966; children—Dawn Alese, Audran Maria, James H., Christopher F. B.S., N.C. A&T State U., 1960; M.S.W., U. Md., 1968; Ph.D., Ohio State U., 1974. Tchr., counselor Ohio Youth Commn., Columbus, 1962-66, dep. dir., 1971-73; adj. instr. social work dept. sociology and anthropology, U. Dayton (Ohio), 1968-69; exec. dir. Montgomery County Community Action Agy., Dayton, 1969-71; asst. prof. sociology and anthropology, Central State U., Wilberforce, Ohio, 1973; asst. prof., sr. research assoc. Sch. Applied Social Scis., Case Western Res. U., Cleve., 1975-76, asst. prof., assoc. dean, 1976-79, assoc. prof., assoc. dean, 1979-81; prof. Sch. Social Work, U. Ala., Tuscaloosa, 1981—, dean, 1983—; cons. in field; mem. Ala. Juvenile Justice Adv. Com., 1983—; mem. adv. council on social work edn. Ala. Commn. on Higher Edn., 1982—; mem. ho. of dels. Council on Social Work Edn., 1981—; mem. annual program planning com. Council on Social Work Edn., 1984-85; mem. task force on licensing for social work practice, Ala. State Bd. Social Work Examiners, 1985; mem.local human resources bd. Tuscaloosa County Dept. Pensions and Security, 1982—, mem. external central adminstrv. rev. panel, 1985. Bd. dirs. Greater Tuscaloosa chpt. ARC, 1982—; pres. Eastwood Middle Sch. PTA, Tuscaloosa Bd. Edn., 1983-84; hon. mem. bd. Parents Anonymous of Ala. State Bd., 1982; mem. W. Ala. Nat. Issues Forum, 1984—; bd. dirs., chmn. fin. com. Tuscaloosa County Mental Health Assn., 1984—. Served to capt. U.S. Army, 1960-68. Recipient Pace Setters award for disting. achievement Coll. Adminstrv. Sci., Ohio State U., 1974; named Outstanding Profl. in Human Services, Acad. Human Services, 1974. Mem. Acad. Cert. Social Workers (cert), Council on Social Work Edn., Internat. Assn. Schs. Social Work, Internat. Council on Social Welfare, Nat. Assn. Social Workers (mem.-at-large, bd. dirs. Ala. Chpt. 1985), Am. Assn. Deans and Dirs. of Grad. Schs. of Social Work (chair deans group S.E. region 1985—), Ala. Conf. of Social Work (chmn. program com.), Greater Tuscaloosa C. of C. Contbr. numerous articles to various profl. jours., also chpts. to books. Home: 2526 Woodland Hills Dr Tuscaloosa AL 35405 Office: Sch Social Work U Ala PO Box 1935 University AL 35486

WARD, JAMES KIRK, manufacturing company executive; b. Winston Salem, N.C., Aug. 23, 1932; s. James Leonard and Evelyn (Edwards Kirk) W.; m. Joe Anne Frier, July 1, 1956; children—Sidney Kirk, Julie Anne. A.A., Mars Hill Coll., 1952; B.F.A., Coll. William and Mary, 1955. Dir. advt. Erwin Lambeth Inc., Thomasville, N.C., 1958-60; v.p. design Heirloom Furniture Inc., High Point, N.C., 1960-78, pres., 1978—, also dir. Rep., Triad Council Govts., Greensboro, 1978; mem. adv. bd. Mars Hill Coll. (N.C.), 1973; pres. Sch. Bd. Thomasville, N.C., 1976; pres. N.C. Bapt. Homes for Aging, Winston Salem, 1983. Named Lion of Yr., 1974. Mem. Am. Soc. Interior Design Industry Found. Democrat. Baptist. Club: Furniture. Lodge: Lions (pres. 1975-76 Thomasville). Home: 416 E HollyHill Rd Thomasville NC 27360 Office: Heirloom Furniture Inc 500 Old Thomasville Rd High Point NC 27261

WARD, JOE HENRY, JR., lawyer; b. Childress, Tex., Apr. 18, 1930; s. Joe Henry and Helen Ida (Chastain) W.; m. Carlotta Agnes Abreu, Feb. 7, 1959; children—James, Robert, William, John. B.S. in Acctg., Tex. Christian U., 1952; J.D., So. Meth. U., 1964. Bar: Tex. 1964, Va. 1972, D.C. 1972; C.P.A., Tex. Mgr. Alexander Grant & Co., C.P.A.s., Dallas, 1956-64; atty. U.S. Treasury, 1965-68; tax counsel U.S. Senate Fin. Com., 1968-72; sole practice, Washington, 1972-83; asst. gen. counsel, tax mgr. Epic Holdings, Ltd., 1983, Crysoft Corp., Alexandria, Va., 1983—. Served to lt. USNR, 1952-56. Mem. ABA, Am. Inst. C.P.A.s, Am. Assn. Atty.-C.P.A.s. Club: Univ. (Washington). Home: 2639 Mann Ct Falls Church VA 22046 Office: Crysoft Corp 3101 Park Center Dr Suite 1450 Alexandria VA 22302

WARD, JOHN EVERETT, JR., microbiology educator; b. Mocksville, N.C., Feb. 23, 1941; s. John Everett and Maurine Ruby (Todd) W., m. Louella May Richards, Feb. 1, 1964; children—Emily, Everett. B.S., High Point Coll., 1963; M.A., Wake Forest U., 1965; Ph.D., U. S.C., 1970. Asst. prof. biology Gaston Coll., 1965-67; prof. biology High Point Coll., 1970—; vis. Lilly scholar Duke U., 1977. Mem. N.C. Acad. Sci., Assn. Southeastern Biologists, Mycol. Soc. Am., Sigma Xi. Methodist. Contbr. articles to profl. jours. Office: Dept Biology High Point Coll High Point NC 27262

WARD, JOHN PUGH, JR., state official, writer, editor; b. Kinston, N.C., Feb. 22, 1926; s. John Pugh and Edith Earl (Harper) W.; m. Katie Louise Willingham, Aug. 25, 1951. B.A., Mercer U., 1950; cert. in profl. devel. U. Ga., 1954; postgrad. in ednl. and counseling psychology U. S.C., 1985. Profl. intern, writer Macon Telegraph Newspaper Publishing Co., Macon, 1949-53; assoc. editor Bowen Press, Inc.-Dixie Contractor Publishing Group, Atlanta, 1953-64, contbg. editor, 1965-74; editor, proprietor Indsl. News Bur., Columbia, S.C., 1964-74; vocational, ednl. counselor and coordinator Occupational Div. State of S.C., Columbia, 1974—; S. Atlantic regional media del. Internat. Bldg. Industry Exposition, Chgo., 1957, 63; academic practicum rep. Richland County Sch. Dist. I, Columbia, 1985; grad. sch. studies rep. to Nat. Inst. in Rational-Emotive Psychology, 1986. Contbr. articles to profl. jours. Publicity chmn. Jr. C. of C., Macon, 1953; vol. United Way, Atlanta, Columbia, 1958—; mem. edn. com. and sch. rep. Animal Protection League Columbia, 1984-85. Recipient McDonald award Mercer U., 1950. Mem. Am. Assn. Counseling and Devel., Assn. Humanistic Edn. and Devel. (mem. U. S.C. seminar com. 1982), Nat. Vocat. Guidance Assn., S.C. Press Assn., Lambda Chi Alpha (life; chmn. chpt. publications). Club: Griff's (Columbia). Avocations: reading; creative writing; personal and family library; farming; preservation of wildlife. Office: State Govt SC Employment Services Div 700 Taylor St Columbia SC 29202

WARD, JOHN WESLEY, pharmacologist; b. Martin, Tenn., Apr. 8, 1925; s. Charles Wesley and Sara Elizabeth (Little) W.; A.A., George Washington U., 1948, B.S., 1950, M.S., 1955; Ph.D., Georgetown U., 1959; m. Martha Isabelle

Hendley, Dec. 7, 1947; children—Henry Russell, Judith Carol, Charles Wesley, Richard Little. Pharmacologist, Hazleton Labs., Falls Church, Va., 1950-59; prin. pharmacologist, dir. pharmacology A. H. Robins Co., Richmond, Va., 1959-71, dir. research, 1980-82, v.p. Office of Research, 1982—; adj. research assoc. prof. pharmacology Med. Coll. Va., 1982—, mem. research adv. council, 1984—; expert pharmacologue toxicologue Republique Francaise, 1986—. Served with USMC, 1943, USN, 1944-46, U.S. Army, 1943-44. Mem. Am. Assn. Accreditation Lab. Animal Sci. (trustee 1970—, chmn. 1976-80, vice-chmn. 1981, 85—), Pharm. Mfrs. Assn. (mem. drug safety steering com. 1974—, chmn. color additive com., 1978—, chmn. animal care and use 1970—). Assn. Biomed. Research (dir. 1983-84), AAAS, Am. Chem. Soc., Soc. Toxicology, Am. Soc. Pharmacology and Exptl. Therapeutics, Assn. Food and Drug Ofcls. U.S., N.Y. Acad. Sci., Va. Acad. Sci., Internat. Soc. Reg. Toxicology and Pharmacology, Sigma Xi. Clubs: Cosmos; Willow Oaks Country (Richmond, Va.). Patentee in field. Home: 10275 Cherokee Rd Richmond VA 23235 Office: 1211 Sherwood Ave PO Box 26609 Richmond VA 23261-6609

WARD, LEW O., oil producer; b. Oklahoma City, July 24, 1930; s. Llewellyn Orcutt and Addie (Reisdorph) W. II; student Okla. Mil. Acad. Jr. Coll., 1948-50; B.S., Okla. U., 1953; m. Myra Beth Gungoll, Oct. 29, 1955; children—Casidy Ann, William Carlton. Dist. engr. Delhi-Taylor Oil Corp., Tulsa, 1955-56; partner Ward-Gungoll Oil Investments, Enid, Okla., 1956—; owner L.O. Ward Oil Operations, Enid, 1963—; v.p. 1420 Lahoma Rd. Inc., Enid, 1967—, also dir.; pres., chmn. Ward Petroleum Corp., Ward Drilling Co. Inc.; dir. Community Bank & Trust Co., Mag. of Okla. Bus. Vice chmn. Indsl. Devel. Commn., Enid, 1968—; mem. Okla. Gov.'s Adv. Council on Energy. Active YMCA. Chmn., Garfield County Republican Com., 1967-69; bd. dirs. Okla. Polit. Action Com., now chmn. mem. bus. adv. council Phillips U.; bd. dirs. Bass Meml. Hosp.; bd. visitors Coll. Engring., U. Okla. Served as 1st lt. C.E., AUS, 1953-55. Registered profl. engr., Okla. Mem. AIME, Okla. Ind. Petroleum Assn. (dir., pres.), Ind. Petroleum Assn. Am. (dir., v.p.), C. of C. (dir., chmn. indsl. devel. com. 1970-72, pres.-elect 1981, pres. 1982-83), Enid C. of C. (pres.), Nat. Petroleum Council, Am. Bus. Club (pres. 1964), Order Ky. Cols., Alpha Tau Omega. Methodist. Mason (Shriner), Rotarian. Clubs: Metropolitan Dinner (dir. Enid), Falcon, Toastmasters (pres. Enid 1966). Home: 900 Brookside Dr Enid OK 73701 Office: 502 S Fillmore Enid OK 73701

WARD, MARK EDISON, pharmacist; b. Canton, Ill., Apr. 10, 1950; s. Howard Elmer and Mable May (Neear) W.; m. Della Ann Pochel, Apr. 15, 1978; children—Nicholas Anthony, Brenda Diane, Rebecca Dawn. B.S., U. Iowa, 1974. Registered pharmacist. Staff pharmacist Brokaw Hosp., Normal, Ill., 1974-79; dir. drug info. poison control, dir. pharmacy Shelby Meml. Hosp., Shelbyville, Ill., 1979-83; dir. pharmacy Hardtner Med. Ctr., Olla, La., 1983—. Asst. editor Drug Dex, 1979—. Bd. dirs. LaSalle Parish Mus. Assn., Jena, La., 1985—; founder Tea Leaf Club Internat., 1979. EMS Pub. Service grantee Ill. Dept. Pub. Health, 1977. Mem. Am. Assn. Hosp. Pharmacists, Central La. Soc. Hosp. Pharmacists. Methodist. Avocation: antiques. Home: PO Box 690 Olla LA 71465

WARD, ROBERT ERNEST, English literature educator; b. Utica, N.Y., Apr. 17, 1927; m. Catherine Coogan, Apr. 7, 1969. A.B., Syracuse U., 1953; M.A., SUNY-Albany, 1954; Ph.D. in English, U. Iowa, 1969. Tchr., English, Bainbridge Central Sch. (N.Y.), 1954-55, Utica Free Acad., 1955-65; asst. prof. English, Western Ky. U., Bowling Green, 1969-73, assoc. prof., 1973-77, prof., 1977—; researcher 18th century Anglo-Irish culture and lit. Mem. Am. Soc. 18th Century Studies, Can. Assn. Irish Studies, Am. Com. on Irish Studies, Popular Culture Assn., Internat. Assn. Study Anglo-Irish Lit., MLA. Author: Prince of Dublin Printers, The Letters of George Faulkner, 1972; (with Catherine Ward) A Checklist and Census of 400 Imprints of the Irish Printer and Book Seller, George Faulkner 1725-1775, 1973; The Correspondence of Charles O'Conor of Belanagare, Vol. 1, 1731-1771, Vol. 2, 1772-1790, 1980. Contbr. to Studies, an Irish Quar., Eire-Ireland. Office: Dept of English Western Kentucky U Bowling Green KY 42101

WARD, ROBINSON JESTER, JR., newspaper editor; b. Birmingham, Ala., July 29, 1934; s. Robinson Jester and Laura Margaret (Leland) W.; m. Barbara Ann Byrne, Aug. 17, 1957; children—Michael Dennis, Nancy Laura, Robert Hanly, student Auburn U., 1952-54; B.A. in Journalism, U. Ala., 1956. Pub. relations asst. The Ingalls Cos., Birmingham, Ala., 1956-57; staff writer Huntsville (Ala.) Times, 1957-66, Sunday editor, 1966-70, assoc. editor, 1970-74, mng. editor, 1974—. Bd. dirs. Huntsville/Madison County Indsl. Devel. Assn., 1976-80; mem. City Research Park Bd., 1982—. Recipient ann. state newswriting awards AP Assn. Ala., 1957-72; U.S. Dept. State Journalist Exchange Travel grantee to People's Republic of China, 1980. Mem. AP Assn. Ala. (pres. 1977-78), AP Mng. Editors Assn., Huntsville Press Club (pres. 1967-68), Huntsville C. of C. (chmn. 1985), Sigma Delta Chi. Clubs: Rotary; Heritage (bd. govs 1983—) (Huntsville). Home: 1012 San Ramon Ave Huntsville AL 35802

WARD, THOMAS MONROE, lawyer, educator; b. Raleigh, N.C., Mar. 6, 1952; s. Melvin Francis and Margaret Alice (Fulcher) W.; m. Ann Frances Sharky, July 28, 1980. B.S.B.A., U. N.C., 1974, J.D., 1978. Bar: N.C. 1978, U.S. Dist. Ct. (ea. dist.) N.C. 1978. Ptnr. Ward, Ward, Willey & Ward, New Bern, N.C., 1978—; instr. bus. law Craven Community Coll., New Bern, 1982—. Bd. dirs. Footlight Theatre/Lollipop Playhouse Inc., New Bern, 1980—; vol. Craven County Recreation Dept., New Bern, 1982—; chmn. Richard Dobbs Spaight Constl. Commemorative Com., 1985—. Mem. Craven County Bar Assn., N.D. Bar Assn., N.C. Acad. Trial Lawyers, Assn. Trial Lawyers Am., Phi Beta Kappa, Beta Gamma Sigma. Democrat. Methodist. Lodge: Rotary. Office: Ward Ward Willey & Ward 409 Pollock St New Bern NC 28560

WARD, WILLIAM TERRY, city administrator; b. Lebanon, Ky., Sept. 3, 1944; s. William Richard and Elizabeth Gertrude (Downs) W.; A.B., U. Notre Dame, 1968; M.A., Eastern Ky. U., 1969; postgrad. St. Mary's Sem. and Univ., Balt., 1970-73. Tchr., Lebanon (Ky.) High Sch., 1966-68; instr. St. Mary's Coll., St. Mary, Ky., 1969-70; exec. dir. Central Ky. Community Action Agy., Lebanon, 1973-82; adminstr. City of Lebanon, 1982—. Bd. dirs. North Central Comprehensive Care, Nat. Center for Appropriate Tech. Mem. Lebanon City Council, 1978-81, chmn. budget com., 1978-81. Mem. Nat. Assn. Community Action Agy. Exec. Dirs. (v.p. 1980-82), Ky. Assn. Community Action Agys. (pres. 1977-78), S.E. Assn. Community Action Agys. (dir. 1977-82, sec. 1979), Jr. C. of C. Democrat. Roman Catholic. Club: Kiwanis. Home: 226 E Mulberry St Lebanon KY 40033 Office: PO Box 840 113 S Proctor Knott Ave Lebanon KY 40033

WARDELL, ARLENE BATEMAN HANCOCK, educational administrator; b. L.I., N.Y., Sept. 29, 1934; d. Olan Wright and Hilda (Yerkes) Hancock; student Fla. State U., 1953; A.A., Miami-Dade Jr. Coll., 1967; B.A., Barry Coll., 1969, M.S., 1975; M.B.A., Barry U., 1983 m. Robert Lynn Wardell, July 6, 1957; children—Robert Lynn II, Thomas Stephen. Tchr., Thomas Jefferson Jr. High Sch., Dade County public schs., Miami, Fla., 1969-76, resource tchr., N.E. Area-Dade County, 1976-77, dept. chmn. Highland Oaks Jr. High Sch., 1977-79, evaluation specialist I, 1979—. Vice chmn. Dade County Republican Exec. Com., 1969; bicentennial chmn. Thomas Jefferson Jr. High Sch., 1975-76, pres. P.T.A., 1974-75. Mem. Internat. Reading Assn., Nat. Council Tchrs. English, Fla. Ednl. Research Assn., Am. Ednl. Research Assn., Fla. Reading Assn., Fla. Council Tchrs. English, Dade Reading Council (past pres.), Dade County Sch. Adminstrs. Assn., Alpha Delta Kappa, Delta Kappa Gamma, Phi Delta Kappa. Republican. Presbyterian. Home: 555 NE 15th St Apt 30J Miami FL 33132 Office: 1450 NE 2d Ave Room 500 Miami FL 33132

WARDEN, WALDIA ANN, former college president, dietitian; b. New Orleans, Jan. 15, 1933; d. Walter Emmer and Lydia Eugenie (LeBlanc) W.; B.S., St. Mary's Dominican Coll., 1961; M.S. in Dietetics, St. Louis U., 1964; postgrad. Cath. U. Am., 1986—. Joined Dominican Sisters, Congregation of St. Mary, Roman Catholic Ch., 1953, gen. councillor Congregation of St. Mary, 1976-84; tchr. elem. schs., 1954-62; instr. foods and nutrition Dominican Coll., New Orleans, 1964-66, chmn. home econs. dept., 1966-69, asst. dean students, 1969-75, chmn. dept. home econs., 1975-78, chmn. Coll. Planning Council, 1972-76; dir. Rosaryville Center, Ponchatoula, La., 1979-81; pres. St. Mary's Dominican Coll., New Orleans, 1983-86; cons. Pike Meml. Hosp. Trustee, St. Mary's Dominican Coll., 1973-79, 83-86. Mem. La. Dietetic Assn. (editor jour. 1966-68), La. Leadership Conf. Women Religious, Am. Dietetic Assn., AAUW. Address: 580 Broadway New Orleans LA 70118

WARD-GARY, JACQUELINE ANN, nurse, nursing administrator; b. Somerset, Pa., Oct. 23, 1945; d. Donald C. and Thelma R. (Wable) Beas; married; children—Charles L. Jr., Shawn M. B.S. in Nursing, U. Pitts., 1966; M.A. in Counseling and Guidance, W.Va. Coll. Grad. Studies, 1976; M.B.A., Columbus Coll., 1983. Staff nurse W.Va. U. Hosp., Morgantown, 1966-67; staff nurse, head nurse Meml. Hosp. Charleston, W.Va., 1967-69; staff nurse Santa Rosa Hosp., San Antonio, 1969; staff nurse, supr. Bexar County Hosp., San Antonio, 1970; charge, staff nurse Rocky Mountain Osteo. Hosp., Denver, 1971; staff nurse Charleston Area Med. Ctr., 1971-74, asst. dir. nursing, 1974-82; dir. nursing H.D. Cobb Meml. Hosp., Phenix City, Ala.; clin. instr. Chattahoochie Valley Community Coll., Phenix City, 1982-84; v.p. nursing Venice Hosp., Fla., 1984—; pres.-elect region III-South Fla. Am. Orgn. Nurses Execs., 1985—. Mem. Fla. Hosp. Assn., Nat. League Nursing, Articulation Council of Sarasota and Manatee Counties. Office: Venice Hosp 540 The Rialto Venice FL 33595-3298

WARD-MCLEMORE, ETHEL, research geophysicist, mathematician; b. Sylvarena, Miss., Jan. 22, 1908; d. William Robert and Frances Virginia (Douglas) Ward; B.A., Miss. Woman's Coll., 1928; M.A., U. N.C., 1929; postgrad. U. Chgo., 1931, Colo. Sch. Mines, 1941-42, So. Meth. U., 1962-64; m. Robert Henry McLemore, June 30, 1935; 1 dau., Mary Frances. Head math. dept. Miss. Jr. Coll., 1929-30; instr. chemistry, math. Miss. State Coll. for Women, 1930-32; research mathematician Humble Oil & Refining Co., Houston, 1933-36; ind. geophys. research, Tex. and Colo., 1936-42, Ft. Worth, 1946—; geophysicist United Geophys. Co., Pasadena, Calif., 1942-46; tchr. chemistry, physics, Hockaday Sch., Dallas, 1958-59, tchr. math., 1959-60; tchr. chemistry Ursuline Acad., Dallas, 1964-67, Hockaday Sch., 1968-69. Bd. dirs. Geol. Info. Library Dallas. Mem. Am. Math. Soc., Math. Assn. Am., Am. Geophys. Union, Seismol. Soc. Am., Soc. Exploration Geophysicists, AAAS, Soc. Indsl. and Applied Math., Tex Acad. Sci. (dir.), Sigma Xi. Author annotated bibliographies of 4 U.S. Sedimentary Basins, selected bibliography of ground water in U.S. Contbr. articles to profl. jours. Home: 11625 Wander Ln Dallas TX 75230

WARDREP, BRUCE, finance and real estate educator, management consultant; b. Oxnard, Calif., Sept. 20, 1945; s. Royce Edgar and Helen Elizabeth (Niece) W.; m. Barbara Ann Ridenhour, June 12, 1969 (dec. 1976); m. 2d Mary Anne Segrave, Dec. 28, 1978; children—Christopher, Andrew, Katherine. B.B.A. in Fin., Ga. State U., 1971, Ph.D. in Bus. Adminstrn., 1974. Parts and service mgr. R.G.A. Motors, Inc., Atlanta, 1969-71; sr. analyst Land Devel. Analysts, Atlanta, 1971-73; prof. fin. and real estate, chmn. fin. dept. East Carolina U., Greenville, N.C., 1973—; mgmt. cons., Greenville, 1974—. Contbr. articles on fin. and industry to profl. jours. Editor: Future Face of Banking, 1983. Chmn; Bd. Adjustments, Greenville, 1982—. Mem. Fin. Mgmt. Assn., Am. Real Estate and Urban Econs. Assn., So. Fin. Assn., Fin. Execs. Inst., Beta Gamma Sigma. Lodge: Rotary. Office: East Carolina U Dept Fin Greenville NC 27834

WARE, ALYCE MARTIN, educator; b. Birmingham, Ala., June 19, 1930; d. Nethadius Mentor and Alice (Bell) M.; m. J. Lowell Ware, Aug. 15, 1952; children—Rhonda Ware, Janis Ware. B.S., A&M Coll., Huntsville, 1951; M.A., Tuskegee Inst., 1965. Tchr. Marengo County Demopolis, Ala., 1951-53, DeKalb County, Decatur, Ga., 1957-65; tchr. Atlanta Pub. Schs., 1965-79, teleclass instr., 1979—. Author: Handbook for Homebound Teachers, 1968; columnist Atlanta Scene, 1975. Vice pres. orgn. for homebound exceptional children, 1983. Recipient Leadership award Profl. Women of Atlanta, 1981, Mem. Nat. Assn. Media Women (pres. 1983, Media Woman of Yr. 1980), Ga. Tchrs. Assn., Alpha Kappa Alpha (service to handicapped award 1983). Club: Bus./Profl. Women's, Juts and Etucs Bridge. Address: 2720 Laurens Circle SW Atlanta GA 30311

WARE, THOMAS CLAYTON, English educator; b. Louisville, Apr. 7, 1929; s. Charles Lindsay and Marie Josephine (Branham) W.; m. Judith Pauline Klosterman, Dec. 12, 1953; children—Susan Elizabeth, Linda Kathleen, Thomas Clayton, Jr., Matthew O'Hara, Christopher Branham. B.A., U. Louisville, 1957; M.A., U. N.C., 1960, Ph.D., 1969. Instr. English, U. Cin., 1962-66, asst. prof., 1966-67; asst. prof. English, U. Chattanooga, 1967-69; assoc. prof. English, U. Tenn.-Chattanooga, 1969-74, prof., 1974—. Contbr. articles to profl. jours. Served with USN, 1949-53. So. fellow, 1957-60. Mem. So. Atlantic Assn. Depts. of English (trustee), South Atlantic MLA. Home: 620 E Brow Rd Lookout Mountain TN 37350 Office: U Tenn-Chattanooga English Dept Hooper Hall 259 615 Oak St Chattanooga TN 37403

WARE, WILLIAM THOMAS, JR., college administrator; b. Longview, Tex., Feb. 10, 1936; s. William Thomas and Nina Yvonne (Matthews) W.; m. Margaret Ann Ogletree, Aug. 7, 1960; children—William Thomas III, Julia Michelle. B.S., Miss. State U., 1959. Sales service mgr. So. Bag Corp., Yazoo City, Miss., 1961-64; mgr. market research and devel. Miss. Chem. Corp., Yazoo City, 1964-69; bus. mgr. Mid-South Bible Coll., Memphis, 1970—; cons. U.S. Dept. Edn. Student Fin. Aid, summer 1974, 75. Active Rotary Club, Yazoo City, 1962-69; chmn. exec. com. Yazoo County Republican Party, 1966. Served with U.S. Army, 1959. Mem. Nat. Assn. Coll. and Univ. Bus. Officers, Assn. Bus. Adminstrs. Christian Colls. (bd. dirs. 1985—). Republican. Baptist. Avocations: tennis; hunting; flying. Home: 6245 Malloch Dr Memphis TN 38119 Office: Mid-South Bible Coll 2485 Union Ave Memphis TN 38112

WARFFORD, TONY WAYNE, accountant; b. Lexington, N.C., Dec. 9, 1943; s. Herbert Ree and Virginia (Hunt) W.; m. Linda Crook, Aug. 12, 1962; children—Michelle J., Michael Justin, Jarrett P. Student Mars Hill Coll., 1962-64; B.S. in Acctg., U. N.C., 1966. C.P.A., N.C. Staff acct. A.M. Pullen & Co., Greensboro, N.C., 1966-69; from staff acct. to mgr. Craven & Co., Greensboro, 1969-73; owner T.W. Warfford, C.P.A., Greensboro, 1973-78; pres. Warfford, Comstock & Co., Greensboro, 1979-83; resident mng. ptnr. Cherry, Bekaert & Holland, Greensboro, 1983—. Fellow N.C. Assn. C.P.A.s; mem. Am. Inst. C.P.A.s. Baptist. Lodges: Kiwanis, Elk. Home: 600 Blanton Pl Greensboro NC 27408 Office: Cherry Bekaert & Holland CPAs Forum VI Suite 654 Greensboro NC 27408

WARING, JOHN ALFRED, research writer, lectr., cons.; b. San Francisco, Dec. 30, 1913; s. John A. and Mary (Wheeler) W.; student pub. schs. Yachting, marine editor Chgo. Tribune, 1934-47; editor Kellogg Messenger, Kellogg Switchboard & Supply Co., Chgo., 1945-49; research cons. Baxter Internat. Econ. Research Bur., Inc., investment counselling, N.Y.C., 1951-52; research asst. mktg. research dept. Fuller, Smith & Ross, Inc., advt., N.Y.C., 1953; research writer, cons. Twentieth Century Fund, N.Y.C., 1953-54; research cons. Ford Motor Co., Dearborn, Mich., 1955; chief researcher Internat. Fact Finding Inst., Lawrence Orgn., public relations cons., N.Y.C., Washington, 1957-58; lectr. on energy, tech. and history World Power Conf., Montreal, 1958, First Energy Inst., Am. U., Washington, 1960, Nat. Archives, Washington, 1962, Smithsonian Mus. History and Tech., Washington, 1968; guest lectr. social responsibility in sci. U. Md., 1972, guest lectr. sci. and environment, 1974; lectr. Internat. Conf. on Energy and Humanity, Queen Mary Coll., U. London, 1972, World Energy Conf., Detroit, 1974, History of Sci. Soc., Norwalk, Conn., 1974, 83; research cons. PARM Project, Nat. Planning Assn., Washington, 1961-62; cons. Sci., Tech. and Fgn. Affairs Seminar, Fgn. Service Inst., Dept. State, 1965; vis. lectr. social implications of sci. for N.Am., U. Alta. (Can.), Edmonton, 1981; cons. U.S. energy statistics Smithsonian Instn., U.S. Bur. Census, 1960—; research cons. Program of Policy Studies in Sci. and Tech., George Washington U., 1967-68; del. U.S. commn. UNESCO Conf., San Francisco, 1969; inaugural lectr. Future of Sci. and Soc. in Am. Seminar U.S. Civil Service Commn., Washington, 1970; editorial cons. Nat. Acad. Engring., Washington, 1971; research cons., analyst Seminar Sch., Indsl. Coll. Armed Forces, Ft. Lesley J. McNair, Washington, 1959-74; researcher Office Plans and Programs, U.S. Army Med. Dept., Washington, 1975-76; asst. editor Def. Systems Mgmt. Rev. mag. Def. Systems Mgmt. Coll., Ft. Belvoir, Va., 1977-78; ret., 1979. Mem. Soc. History of Tech. (charter), History Sci. Soc., Technocracy, AAAS, Washington Acad. Scis., Washington Soc. Engrs. (sec. 1977), Phi Beta Kappa Assn. in D.C., Internat. Soc. Gen. Semantics, N.Y. Acad. Sci. Technol. trends editor The Futurist Mag., 1968—. Contbr. chpts. to books; compiler statis. tabulations. Home: 1320 S George Mason Dr Arlington VA 22204

WARNER, ALLEN RUSSELL, curriculum and instruction educator, consultant; b. Chgo., Aug. 26, 1943; s. Henry Carl and Ann Marie (Kiefer) Woldhausen W.; m. Hildegard Ann Herbst, Aug. 26, 1967; children—David Eric, Robin Leigh. B.S.Edn., No. Ill. U., 1968, M.S.Edn., 1969, Ed.D., 1973. Grad. asst. student teaching office No. Ill. U., 1968-69; tchr. social studies, team leader Downers Grove South High Sch., Ill., 1969-72; instr. dept. secondary profl. edn. No. Ill. U., 1972-73; asst. prof. curriculum and instrn., dir. clin. experiences U. Houston Victoria Campus, 1973-74; assoc. dir. Improving the competence of sch. based tchr. educators through CBTE tng. and credentialing systems Fund for the Improvement of Postsecondary Edn., 1975-77; assoc. prof. curriculum and instrn., dir. clin. experiences Coll. Edn., U. Houston, 1979-80, asst. prof., 1974-79; assoc. prof., chair dept. curriculum and instrn. U. Houston, University Park, 1980—: nat. bd. state reps. Am. Nat. Bus. Hall of Fame, 1980—; chair faculty standards redesign subcom. Nat. Council for Accreditation Tchr. Edn., 1983—, mem. standards com., 1983—. Cons. editor: (with Kenneth W. Brown) Economics of Our Free Enterprise System, 1982. Mem. editorial bd. Action in Tchr. Edn., 1985—, Capstone Jour. Edn., 1983—, So. Social Studies Quar., 1983—; manuscript reviewer Jour. Classroom Interaction, 1981—. Contbr. articles to profl. jours., chpts. to books. Lay minister St. Martin's Lutheran Ch., Houston, 1976—, mem. ch. council, 1983—; bd. dirs. Brays Forest Improvement Corp., 1982-83; v.p. Belle Park Community Assn., 1977-78. Served with U.S. Army, 1961-64. Recipient Finalist award U. Houston Coll. Edn., 1978, First Annual Disting. Service award U. Houston Coll. Edn. Found. Fund, 1980. Mem. World Futures Soc., NEA, Assn. Tchr. Educators (life, disting. mem., Pres.'s award for disting. service 1984, 85, bd. dirs. 1978-81), Nat. Council Social Studies (editorial bd. Social Edn. 1981-83, ethics com. 1983—), Assn. Supervision and Curriculum Devel., S.W. Ednl. Research Assn., Tex. Assn. Tchr. Educators (Ben E. Coody disting. service award 1984, 2d v.p. 1984—), Tex. Council Social Studies (research com. 1985—), Tex. State Tchrs. Assn. (chair dist. IV instrn. and profl. devel. com. 1984—, outstanding service award 1985), Tex. Soc. Coll. Tchrs. Edn., Tex. Assn. Coll. Tchrs. Democrat. Lutheran. Home: 4322 Braysworth Dr Houston TX 77072 Office: 4800 Calhoun Blvd Houston TX 77004

WARNER, CECIL RANDOLPH, JR., lawyer; b. Fort Smith, Ark., Jan. 13, 1929; s. Cecil Randolph and Reba (Cheeves) W.; m. Susan Curry, Dec. 10, 1955; children—Susan Rutledge, Rebecca Jane, Cecil Randolph III, Matthew Holmes Preston, Katherine Mary. B.A. magna cum laude, U. Ark. 1950, LL.B., Harvard U., 1953, Sheldon fellow, 1953-54. Bar: Ark. bar 1953. Practiced in, Fort Smith, 1954—; partner firm Warner & Smith (and predecessor), 1954—; pres., dir. Fairfield Communities, Inc.; dir. Mid-Am. Industries, Inc., 214, Inc., Wortz Co.; Instr. U. Ark. Sch. Law, 1954, 56; vice chmn. Ark. Constl. Revision Study Commn., 1967; v.p. 7th Ark. Constl. Conv., 1969-70. Scoutmaster troop 23 Boy Scouts Am., Fort Smith, 1955-58; commn. Ark. State Police Commn., 1970; mem. alumni bd. U. Ark.; Bd. dirs. United Fund, ARC, Ark. Community Found.; trustee Sparks Regional Med. Center. Fellow Am., Ark. bar founds.; mem. Fort Smith C. of C. (dir.), Am. Law Inst., ABA, Ark. Bar Assn. (past chmn. exec. com., past chmn. young lawyers sect.), Sebastian County Bar Assn., Am. Trial Lawyers Assn., Phi Beta Kappa, Phi Eta Sigma, Omicron Delta Kappa, Sigma Alpha Epsilon. Presbyterian. (elder). Office: 214 N 6th St Fort Smith AR 72901 also 1207 Rebsamen Park Rd Little Rock AR 72203*

WARNER, CHARLES HENRY, JR., architect; b. Tucson, May 2, 1952; s. Charles Henry and Joan Ruth (Boone) W.; B.S. in Environ. Design, U. Okla., 1974; B.S. in Architecture, 1975, M.S. in Architecture, 1975; m. Mary L. Briggs, Mar. 22, 1974; 1 dau., Rebecca Gayle. Elec. designer/project mgr. Binnicker Assos., Oklahoma City, 1975-77; project mgr. Jones Hester Bates Reik, Oklahoma City, 1977; project architect Howard & Porch Inc., Oklahoma City, 1977-79; prin.-in-charge prodn. Quentin Remy Assocs., Norman, Okla., 1979-82; sole propr. CHW Assocs., 1982—; cons. in field. Youth soccer referee. Recipient Reynolds Aluminum Co. award, 1973. Registered architect, Okla., Tex. Mem. AIA, Nat. Council Archtl. Registration Bds., South Can. Amateur Radio Soc., Norman Softball League, Norman Adult Soccer Assn. Democrat. Methodist. Clubs: Demolay, Masons (32 deg.). Author instructional publs. for U. Okla. archtl. courses. Home: 3915 Waverly Dr Norman OK 73072 Office: 3915 Waverly Dr Suite 133 Norman OK 73072

WARNER, CLINTON ELLSWORTH, surgeon; b. Atlanta, July 11, 1924; m. Sally E. Johnson, Aug. 28, 1976; 1 son, Clinton Ellsworth III. B.S., Morehouse Coll., 1948; M.D., Meharry Med. Sch., 1951. Diplomate Am. Bd. Surgery, also recert. Intern, Michael Reese Hosp., Chgo., 1951-52; resident in surgery St. Louis City Hosp., 1952-56; practice medicine specializing in surgery, Atlanta, 1956—; mem. staffs S.W. Community (chmn. bd. trustees 1978-83), Grady Meml., St. Joseph, Hughes Spalding, Crawford W. Long Meml., Northside, Physician Surgeon Community hosps.; instr. preventive medicine Emory U., 1971-73; chmn. exec. com. Mut. Fed. Savs. & Loan Assn.; dir. Blue Cross Blue Shield Inc., Atlanta Inquirer, 1958—; mem. exec. com., chmn. Hughes Spalding com. Fulton DeKalb Hosp. Authority, 1975-83; dir. health service Spelman Coll., 1958—; treas. Enterprise Investment, Inc., 1958—; pres. Flamingo Estates Inc., 1960—; pres. Lew-Arner Profl. Bldg., 1960—. Treas. Sickle Cell Found. of Ga., 1971—; chmn. bd. trustees Morehouse Sch. Medicine, 1979—. Fellow ACS; mem. Nat. Med. Assn., Ga. Med. Assn., Atlanta Surg. Profl. Assn. (pres. 1969—), Atlanta Med. Assn., Atlanta Health Care Found., Med. Assn. Atlanta, Omega Psi Phi. Home: 1253 Clearbrook Dr SW Atlanta GA 30311 Office: 319 W Lake Ave NW Atlanta GA 30318

WARNER, DAVID COOK, public affairs educator; b. Boston, Apr. 22, 1940; s. Roger Lewis and Dorothy Flora (Cook) W.; m. Phyllis Gail Erman, July 9, 1967; children—Ann Fitch, Michael Beers. B.A., Princeton U., 1963; M.P.A., Syracuse U., 1965, Ph.D. in Econs, 1969. Research assoc. Ctr. Urban Studies, Wayne State U., Detroit, 1969, asst. prof. econs., 1969-71; dep. dir. program analysis and budget N.Y.C. Health and Hosp. Corp., 1971-72; lectr. Yale U., New Haven, 1973-75; assoc. prof. L.B.J. Sch. Pub. Affairs, U. Tex., Austin, 1975-81, prof. pub. affairs, 1981—. Bd. dirs. Brackenridge Hosp., Austin, 1976-83; mem. Tex. Diabetes Council, 1983—, chmn., 1985—. Mem. U.S.-Mex. Border Health Assn. (chmn. research, edn., tng. com. 1982-84), Am. Pub. Health Assn. Democrat. Congregationalist. Author: Health of Mexican Americans in South Texas, 1979; Developing Programs to Prevent and Control Diabetes, 1982. Editor: Toward New Human Rights, 1977, Public Affairs Comment, 1978—; mem. editorial bd. Jour. Health, Politics, Policy and Law, 1975—; Contbr. numerous articles to profl. publs. Home: 5701 Trailridge Dr Austin TX 78731 Office: U Tex LBJ Sch Pub Affairs Austin TX 78712

WARNER, JOHN WILLIAM, U.S. Senator; b. Washington, Feb. 18, 1927; s. John William and Martha Stuart (Budd) W.; B.S., Washington and Lee U., 1949; LL.B., U. Va., 1953; children—Mary Conover, Virginia Stuart, John William IV. Law clk. to U.S. judge, 1953-54; spl. asst. to U.S. atty., 1956-57; asst. U.S. atty. Dept. Justice, 1957-60; partner Hogan & Hartson, 1960-68; undersec. of Navy, 1969-72, sec. of Navy, 1972-74; adminstr. Am. Revolution Bicentennial Adminstrn., 1974-76; mem. U.S. Senate from Va., 1979—. Served with USNR, 1944-46; to capt. USMCR, 1949-52. Mem. Bar Assn. D.C., Beta Theta Pi, Phi Alpha Delta. Republican. Episcopalian. Clubs: Metropolitan, Burning Tree, Alfafa, Alibi. Office: 421 Russell Senate Office Bldg Washington DC 20510

WARNER, LEE HOWLAND, museum director; b. Parkersburg, W.Va., Jan. 21, 1943; s. Edwin Brooks and Rebecca (Dailey) W.; m. Wenefred Gail Harter, Apr. 3, 1983; children by previous marriage—Jill, Gregory Lee. B.A. Juniata Coll., 1964; M.A., U. Wis., 1965, Ph.D., 1971. Asst. prof. Fla. State U., Tallahassee, 1968-75; assoc. curator Hist. Tallahassee Pres. Bd., 1975-79; hist. preservation bd. coordinator Fla. Dept. State, Tallahassee, 1979-81; asst. dir. Div. Archives History and Record Mgmt., Tallahassee, 1981-82; dir. Mus. Fla. History, Tallahassee, 1982—; trustee Tallahassee Jr. Mus., 1983—; dir., sec. Fla. History Assocs., Tallahassee, 1983—. Editor: Photos of Alvin S. Harper, 1984. Contbr. articles to profl. jours. NSF fellow, 1968; Council for Faculty Research grantee, 1974; Am. Philos. Soc. grantee, 1976. Mem. Am. Hist. Assn., Orgn. Am. Historians, Am. Assn. State and Local History, Fla. Hist. Records Com. Home: 2701 Everett Ln Tallahassee FL 32312 Office: Museum of Florida History 500 S Bronough St Tallahassee FL 32301

WARNER, MICHAEL KENDALL, architect; b. Oakland, Calif., Oct. 4, 1941; s. Hollis Moore and Hannah Jane (Kendall) W. B.Arch., N.C. State U., 1966. Registered architect, N.C. Assoc., Odell Assocs. Inc., Charlotte, N.C., 1966—. Bd. dirs. Charlotte Opera Assn., 1979-80. Mem. AIA (sec. Charlotte sect. 1984, treas., 1985.) Republican. Episcopalian. Home: 203 The Poplar 301 W 10th St Charlotte NC 28202 Office: Odell Assocs Inc 129 W Trade St Charlotte NC 28202

WARNER, WAYNE GILBERT, librarian; b. Duquesne, Pa., Sept. 25, 1939; s. William M. and Verna Grace (Radcliffe) W. B.A., Duke U., 1962; M.Div., Boston U., 1965; M.Ed., U. Pitts., 1968; M.L.S., SUNY-Geneseo, 1975; Ph.D., Vanderbilt U., 1981; Ed.S., Middle Tenn. State U., 1982; postdoctoral studies

East Tex. State U., 1983—. Cert. library media specialist, prin., supr. of instrn., supt. Ordained to ministry Methodist Ch., 1963; assoc. pastor Grace Meth. Ch., Waterloo, Iowa, 1965-67; head religious studies Fay Sch., Southborough, Mass., 1968-71; minister edn. Asbury 1st United Meth. Ch., Rochester, N.Y., 1971-75; library media specialist Sam Houston Elem. Sch., Lebanon, Tenn., 1977—. Vice pres. Wilson County Assn. for Gifted (Tenn.), 1982-83. Mem. ALA, Assn. Supervision and Curriculum Devel., Assn. Ednl. Communications and Tech., Nat. Assn. Gifted Children, Religious Edn. Assn. Republican. Home: PO Box 855 Lebanon TN 37088 Office: Sam Houston Elem Sch Oakdale Dr Lebanon TN 37087

WARNS, MARIAN KINCAID, labor relations arbitrator; b. Louisville, Oct. 3, 1923; d. Horace L. and Laura (Law) Kincaid; B.A., U. Louisville, 1944, M.Ed., 1972, Ph.D., 1976; m. Carl Arthur Warns, Jr., Sept. 14, 1946. Asst. tng. dir. Richard Store Co., Miami, Fla., 1947-48; personnel and tng. dir. Kaufman Straus Co., Louisville, 1948-52; tchr., asst. coordinator Ahrens Trade High Sch., 1952-56; personnel, tng. dir. H.P. Selman Co., 1956-57; research asso. in arbitration Carl A. Warns Jr., 1957-64; indsl. psychology cons. Raymond Kemper & Assos., 1970-72; instr. psychology U. Louisville, 1972-76; pvt. practice labor relations arbitrator, 1971—; adj. prof. indsl. psychology, 1984—; mem. numerous permanent arbitration panels in pub. and pvt. sector. Mem. Nat. Acad. Arbitrators, Am. Psychol. Assn., Am. Soc. Tng. Dirs., Indsl. Relations Research Assn., N.Y. Acad. Scis., Mortar Bd., Phi Kappa Phi, Psi Chi. Episcopalian. Contbr. articles in field to profl. jours. Home: 312 Brunswick Rd Louisville KY 40207 Office: 312 Brunswick Rd Louisville KY 40207

WARREN, CYNTHIA ANN, hospital administrator; b. Flint, Mich., Feb. 21, 1956; d. James Anderson and Norma Jean (Thatcher) Weaver; m. Michael Ray Warren, June 11, 1977; children—Jennifer Rene, Anna Michelle. Student Ark. State U., 1974-76; B.S. in Pharmacy, U. Ark., 1979. Asst. mgr. Revco Discount Drugs, Newport, Ark., 1979-82, mgr., 1982-83; dir. pharmacy Newport Hosp., 1983—. Active Newport Service League, 1980-82. Mem. Am. Pharm. Assn., Ark. Pharm. Assn. Baptist. Home: 1201 Cherokee Newport AR 72112 Office: Newport Hosp Pharmacy 2000 McClain Newport AR 72112

WARREN, DARLENE HOWELL, college administrator; b. Fayetteville, N.C., July 14, 1944; d. Marvis Eugene and Kathryn (Wooten) Howell; m. Herman Denning Warren, June 24, 1970. B.S. in Business Administration, Campbell U., 1965; M.Ed. in Community Coll. Edn., N.C. State U., 1973, Ph.D., 1980. Acctg. instr. James Sprunt Tech. Coll., 1966-68, Sampson Tech. Coll., Clinton, N.C., 1968-74; dean fiscal affairs Martin Community Coll., Williamston, N.C., 1976—; dir. Mid-East Commn., Washington, 1984—. Contbr. articles to profl. jours. Mem. ACCBO (exec. com. 1981-82), Coll. and Univ. Personnel Assn., Nat. Assn. Coll. and Univ. Bus. Officers, So. Assn. Coll. and Univ. Bus. Officers. Democrat. Baptist. Avocations: reading; swimming; skiing; needlework; traveling. Home: PO Box 1212 Williamston NC 27892 Office: Martin Community Coll Kehukee Park Rd Williamston NC 27892

WARREN, DAVID BOARDMAN, art curator; b. Balt., Mar. 11, 1937; s. Robert Otey Yancey Warren and Florence Elizabeth Prickett Hershey; m. Gabrielle Lavielle Fraser, Apr. 24, 1971 (div. July 1978); 1 son, Robert Wilson Fraser; m. 2d, Janie Currie Lee, Jan. 2, 1980. A.B. cum laude, Princeton U., 1959; M.A., U. Del., 1965. Curator Bayou Bend Collection, Mus. Fine Arts, Houston, 1965—, assoc. dir., 1974—; cons. Friends of Gov.'s Mansion, Austin; mem. bd. Winterthur Mus.; dir. Winterthur Corp.; mem. adv. com. Tex. Area Project, Archives Am. Art. Author: Bayou Bend: American Furniture Paintings and Silver in the Bayou Bend Collection, 1975; (with others) Texas Furniture: The Cabinetmakers and Their Work 1940-1880, 1975; author, co-author exhbn. catalogs. Served to lt. USNR, 1960-63. Mem. Philos. Soc. Tex. Republican. Episcopalian. Office: Museum of Fine Arts 1001 Bissonnet Houston TX 77005

WARREN, DONALD WAYNE, dentist; b. Tulsa, Okla., Mar. 16, 1948; s. Harold Eugene and Loyce Elaine (Morgan) W.; m. JoNell Tumlison, Sept. 13, 1969; children—David, Darryl, Dennis. B.A., Hendrix Coll., 1970; D.D.S., U. Tenn., 1973. Gen. practice dentistry, Clinton, Ark., 1975—. Dep. coroner Van Buren County, Clinton, Ark., 1984—; airport commnr. Clinton Municipal Airport, 1981—. Mem. ADA, Ark. Dental Assn., Northwest Dist. Dental Soc. Home: SIM-Lock Acres Clinton AR 72031 Office: Donald W Warren DDS SIM-Lock Acres Clinton AR 72031

WARREN, FRANK RAYMOND, general contractor; b. Ft. Towsen, Okla., Mar. 7, 1915; s. Frank Homer and Ethel Estell (Mann) W.; student Lamar Jr. Coll., Beaumont, 1935, U. Tex., Austin, 1937; m. Sept. 17, 1938; m. Edith Van Riper; children—Carol Temple, Frank R., Elaine Sutherland. Research dir. Foley's of Houston, 1946-47; asst. v.p. Tenn. Gas Transmission Co., Houston, 1960-66; pres., chmn. bd. Mid-South Constrn. Co., Pinehurst, Tex., 1967-85, Greenville, S.C., 1985—, Central Testing Co. Inc., Lake Charles, La., 1969—; dir. Tex. Commerce Nat. Bank, Conroe; pres., chmn. bd. Mid-South Devel. Corp. Active Big Bros. Houston, Nat. Right to Work Com.; trustee Montreat-Anderson Coll., Montreat, N.C., vice chmn. Found. Fund; bd. dirs. Covenant Fellowship of Presbyns, St. Louis; bd. dirs. Presbyn. Layman, 1984—; trustee King Coll., 1985—. Named Outstanding Citizen of Houston, Big Bros. Am., 1972. Presbyterian. Clubs: Panorama Country (pres. bd. dirs.), Rotary (Conroe). Home: 4 Winged Foot Dr Conroe TX 77304 Office: PO Box 1266 Conroe TX 77301

WARREN, FREDERICK MARSHALL, ret. army officer, former judge; b. Newport, Ky., Aug. 23, 1903; s. William Ulysses and Katherine (Lampe) W.; A.B., LL.B., LL.M., LL.D., U. Cin.; m. Peggy Beaton, Feb. 20, 1926; 1 son, Frederick Marshall. Various positions with lumber and millwork cos., 1926-32; police judge, Southgate, Ky., 1932-35; admitted to Ky. bar, 1935; city atty., Southgate, 1935-40, 46-49; city solicitor, Newport, 1950-52; county judge, Campbell County, 1954-58; cons. to under sec. army, 1958; spl. asst. to asst. sec. army for manpower personnel and res. forces, 1959; recalled to active duty as maj. gen. U.S. Army, 1959; chief U.S. Army Res. and ROTC Affairs, 1959-63; circuit judge 17th Jud. Dist. Ky., Newport, 1964-76. Field rep. Alcoholic Beverage Control Bd. Ky., 1949; mem. U.S. Army Gen. Staff com. N.G. and army res. policy, 1953-56; mem. res. forces policy bd. Dept. Def., 1958-59. Served to col. AUS, 1941-46. Decorated D.S.M., Silver Star, Bronze Star, Army Commendation medal (U.S.); Croix de Guerre (France, Belgium). Mem. Am., Ky., Campbell County (past pres.) bar assns., Am. Legion, VFW, DAV, Assn. U.S. Army, Res. Officers Assn. (past nat. v.p.), Mil. Order World Wars. Mason, Elk. Home: 20 Crow Hill Fort Thomas KY 41075

WARREN, GRETCHEN WARD, dance educator, costume designer, choreographer; b. Princeton, N.J., Apr. 7, 1945; d. Herman Matthew and Margery (Brearley) Ward; m. Alan Warren, Dec. 1967 (div. 1972). Student Royal Ballet Sch., London, 1963-64, Acad. Nat. Ballet of Washington, 1964-65, Polakov Studio and Forum of Stage Design, N.Y.C., 1977-79. Soloist, Pa. Ballet, Phila., 1965-76; ballet mistress Am. Ballet Theatre II, N.Y.C., 1978-83; costume designer numerous nat. and internat. dance prodns., 1976—; assoc. prof. dance U. South Fla., Tampa, 1983—; guest faculty Banff Centre for Arts, Canada, 1982, Interlochen Arts Acad., Mich., 1979-84, Walnut Hill Acad., Mass., 1980; faculty Fla. State Dance Assn. Workshop, 1984, 85. Choreographer (ballets) Songsteps, 1979, Journeys, 1984, Duo, 1984, Ghosts, 1985. Faculty adviser Univ. Peace Alliance, Tampa, 1984—; mem. Tampa Coalition for Survival, 1984—, Common Cause, 1985. Recipient Dean's Spl. award U. South Fla. Coll. Fine Arts, 1984, Creative Research award U. South Fla. Sponsored Research Div., 1985; Research award U. South Fla. Press, 1985; Div. Cultural Affairs award Fla. Dept. State, 1985. Mem. United Faculty of Fla., Sierra Club. Democrat. Avocations: environmental causes; horticulture; sailing; cultural activities. Office: U South Fla Dance Dept Tampa FL 33620

WARREN, HERBERT ALBERT, lawyer; b. Birmingham, Ala., Dec. 18, 1922; s. Herbert Allen and Ethel Virginia (Price) W.; student Auburn U., 1940-43; B.S., U. Chgo., 1947; LL.B. magna cum laude, U. Miami, 1951; m. Marjorie Mathis, June 6, 1953; children—Richard Alan, Pamela Jayne. Bar: Fla. 1951, U.S. Supreme Ct. 1960; law clk., U.S. Dist. Judge J. Holland, 1950-51; mem. firm Carr & Warren, 1951-74; prin. Herbert A. Warren, P.A., 1974—; lectr. U. Miami Law Sch., 1951-54. Served with USAF, 1943-46. Mem. Fla., Am. bar assns., Fla. Acad. Trial Lawyers, Am. Trial Lawyers Assn., Com. of 100, Phi Delta Phi. Presbyn. (deacon). Clubs: Bath, Viscayans, La Gorce Country. Miami Shores Country, La Gorce Country. Lodges. Lions, Kiwanis. Home: 398 NE 100th St Miami Shores FL 33131 Office: 1401 Brickell Ave Suite 801 Miami FL 33131

WARREN, JAMES WALTER, JR., pharmaceutical company executive; b. Lincolnton, N.C., Aug. 17, 1944; s. James Walter and Edith (Abernethy) W.; m. Nancy Wallace Warlick, Jan. 19, 1964; children—James Walter, Beverly Joy. B.S. in Pharmacy, U. S.C., 1967; M.S. in Pharmaceutics, Butler U., Indpls., 1973; Ph.D. in Pharmaceutics, U. Ga., 1976. Pharmacy supr. Greenville Hosp., S.C., 1967-69; research pharmacist Eli Lilly & Co., Indpls., 1969-73; instr. U. Ga., Athens, 1973-76; prof., dir. dept. Med. U. S.C., 1976-81; v.p. research and devel. R.P. Scherer Co., Clearwater, Fla., 1981-84; v.p. sci. div. Reid-Rowell, Inc., Atlanta, 1984—. Author numerous research papers. Mem. Am. Pharm. Assn., Acad. Pharm. Scis., Sigma Xi, Rho Chi. Episcopalian. Club: Gamecock. Avocations: golf, writing. Home: 4752 Township Chase Marietta GA 30066 Office: Reid-Rowell Inc 25 5th St Atlanta GA 30308

WARREN, JERRY LEE, college administrator, conductor; b. Montgomery, Ala., Jan. 12, 1935; s. H.L. and Lula B. (Dowdy) W.; m. Dorothy Glen Floyd, Aug. 17, 1955; children—Dorothy Lee, Laura Ellen, John Floyd. B.M., Samford U., 1955; M.C.M., Sch. Ch. Music, So. Bapt. Theol. Sem., 1959, D.M.A., 1967. Minister music First Bapt. Ch., Cartersville, Ga., 1956-57, Auburn, Ala., 1959-63; asst. prof. music Shorter Coll., Rome, Ga., 1966-69; chmn. dept. music Belmont Coll., Nashville, 1969-83, dean Sch. Music, 1983—; choral performer Broadman Singers Recording Group, Nashville, 1972-80; clinician sch. and ch. choral groups. Tenor soloist First Presbyn. Ch., Nashville, 1970-75, 77-79. Mem. Am. Choral Dirs. Assn. (state pres. 1979-81), Music Educators Nat. Conf., Tenn. Music Educators Assn. (state bd. 1976—), Middle Tenn. Vocal Assn. (coll. rep. 1976—), Coll. Music Soc., Nat. Assn. Tchrs. Singing (local pres. 1974-76), Pi Kappa Lambda. Republican. Baptist. Avocations: golf; reading. Home: 5325 Overton Rd Nashville TN 37220 Office: Belmont Coll Sch of Music Nashville TN 37203

WARREN, LINDA RUTH, psychology educator; b. Richmond, Va., June 22, 1945; d. Ramon Eldridge and Ruth Elizabeth (Braudrick) W.; m. Robert Lee Duke, Jr. Apr. 29, 1978; children—Elizabeth Ruth, Kathryn Bernice. B.A., Duke U., 1967; Ph.D., U. Calif.-Berkeley, 1972. Asst. prof. Williams Coll., Williamstown, Mass., 1972-76; asst., then assoc. prof. psychology U. Ala., Birmingham, 1976—. NIH postdoctoral fellow, 1975-76. Mem. Am. Psychol. Assn., Gerontol. Soc., Soc. for Psychophysiol. Research, Psychonomic Soc. Contbr. articles to profl. jours. Home: 2417 Sceptor Ln Birmingham AL 35226 Office: 238 Campbell Hall U Ala Birmingham AL 35294

WARREN, MARK EDWARD, political scientist, theorist, educator; b. Berkeley, Calif., Mar. 26, 1952; s. Charles Edward and Margaret Louise (Smith) W.; m. Janet Elizabeth Joy, Apr. 15, 1980. B.A., Lewis and Clark Coll., 1974; M.A., U. Toronto, 1976, Ph.D., 1982. Mellon postdoctoral fellow Rice U., Houston, 1982-84; vis. asst. prof. U. Tex.-San Antonio, 1984—. Contbr. writings to publs. in field. Doctoral fellow U. Toronto, 1976-80. Mem. Am. Polit. Sci. Assn., Founds. of Polit. Theory Group. Democrat. Home: 908 Jewell St Austin TX 78704 Office: Div Social and Policy Scis U Tex-San Antonio San Antonio TX 78285

WARREN, MCWILSON, parasitologist, international health officer, educator, consultant; b. Goldsboro, N.C., Aug. 29, 1929; s. Lorenzo Blake and Ethel (Bass) W.; m. Mary Isaobel Keany, Aug. 2, 1975; 1 son, James Russell. A.B., U. N.C., 1951, M.S.P.H., 1952; Ph.D., Rice U., 1957. Assoc. prof. preventive medicine Sch. Medicine, U. Okla., 1957-61; commd. officer USPHS, 1961—, advanced through grades to scientist dir., 1979, with Far East Research Unit, Kuala Lumpur, Malaysia, 1961-65, NIH, Bethesda, Md., 1965-67, U. London, 1967-68, NIH, 1968-69, C.Am. Research Sta. (Ctrs. for Disease Control), El Salvador, 1970-74, Center for Disease Control, Atlanta, 1975-81, team leader WHO Malaria Tng. Sec. for Asia and Pacific, Kuala Lumpur, 1981-84; dir. Div. Sci. Services CID, Ctrs. for Disease Control, Atlanta, 1985—; adj. prof. Tulane U., 1981—; cons. on malaria WHO, Walter Reed Army Inst. of Research, USN Med. Research Unit. Mem. Am. Soc. Tropical Medicine and Hygiene (sci. program chmn. 1976-80), Am. Soc. Parasitology, Royal Soc. Tropical Medicine and Hygiene, Malaysian Soc. Parasitology and Tropical Medicine (sec. treas. 1962-63, v.p. 1982-83, pres. 1983-84), AAAS, Am. Mosquito Control Assn., Sigma Xi. Contbr. articles in profl. jours. Home: 2153 Kodiak Dr Atlanta GA 30345 Office: Centers for Disease Control Atlanta GA 30333

WARREN, RANDALL FULTON, clergyman; b. Longview, Tex., July 4, 1949; s. Ollie Woodrow and Vera Belle (Richardson) W.; m. Carol Sue Oefinger, Aug. 7, 1976; children—Mark, David, Laura Kristin. B.S., Stephen F. Austin State U., 1971; postgrad. Emory U., 1971-72; Th.M., So. Meth. U., 1975. Ordained elder United Meth. Ch., 1976. Pastor, Walter Fair United Meth. Ch., Tyler, Tex., 1975-77, First Meth. Ch., Malakoff, Tex., 1977-81; campus minister Wesley Found., coordinator dept. Bible Stephen F. Austin State U., Nacogdoches, Tex., 1981-85; pastor, First Meth. Ch., Trinity, Tex., 1985—; mem. com. on protection of human subjects, 1983-85; dir. edn. Nacogdoches Dist. United Meth. Ch., 1981-85; dir. ch. summer camp, Pal.-Nacogdoches Dist., Tex. Ann. Conf., United Meth. Ch., 1977—. City fire marshall City of Malakoff, Tex., 1977-81; mem. Child Welfare Bd., Henderson, Tex., 1978-79. Recipient Copeland award Tex. Conf. United Meth. Ch., 1979. Mem. Nat. Com. on Adoption, Nat. Com. Campus Ministry. Democrat. Lodge: Toastmasters (Nacogdoches, Tex.). Avocations: reading; snow skiing; fishing; travel; historical studies. Home: Tomne St Trinity TX 75862 Office: Trinity United Meth Ch Drawer 31 Trinity TX 75862

WARREN, ROBERT DAVIS, state senator; b. Sampson County, July 22, 1928; s. Opheus and Neta (Jackson) W.; m. Ann Sparks, Jan. 20, 1951; children—Robert Davis, Gary Burrell. B.S., N.C. State U., 1950, M.Ed., 1968; postgrad. East Carolina U. Mem. Miss. Senate; vice chmn. econ. com., edn. com.; mem. agr. appropriations com., appropriations com. edn., banking com., judiciary I com., redistricting Senate com., state govt. com., transp. com., 1981; mem. Gov.'s Adv. Com. Vocat. Edn., 1969-73, Benson Recreation Commn. Deacon, Benson Bapt. Ch., 1950-80, chmn., Sunday Sch. supt., Sunday sch. tchr., 1966-80. Recipient Young Man of Yr. award Benson Jaycees, 1960; Boss of Yr. award Johnston County; Benson Citizen of Yr. award, 1980; Hon. Chpt. Farmer Degree and Hon. State Farmer Degree, Future Farmers Am. Mem. N.C. Assn. Educators, NEA, N.C. Prins. and Asst. Prins. Assn., N.C. Farm Bur., Johnston County Arts Soc., N.C. Wildlife Fedn., Mental Health Assn. of Johnston County, Benson C. of C. Democrat. Clubs: Coats Hunting and Fishing, Sampson County Dem. Men's Lodges: Masons, Shriners. Office: N C Senate State Capitol Raleigh NC 27611*

WARREN, ROBERT LEE, dentist, educator; b. Boone, N.C., July 20, 1943; s. John Floyd and Maude Elizabeth (Roark) W.; m. Dorthea Irene Carroll, Aug. 31, 1983. B.S. in Biology, Appalachian State U., 1965; postgrad. Duke U., summer 1967; D.D.S., U. N.C., 1972. Instr. biology and chemistry West High Sch., North Wilkesboro, N.C., 1965-68; instr. chemistry Lee's McRae Coll., Banner Elk, N.C., summer 1966; gen. practice dentistry, Boone, 1972—; part-time clin. instr. dept. operative dentistry U. N.C. Sch. Dentistry, Chapel Hill, 1972-79, vis. clin. asst. prof. dept. fixed prosthodontics, 1982-84. Fellow Acad. Gen. Dentistry (bd. dirs.); mem. ADA, N.C. Dental Soc., First Dist. Dental Soc., Dental Alumni Assn. (bd. dirs.), Tar Heel Dental Study Club (pres.), Boone C. of C., Delta Sigma Delta (grand master). Republican. Baptist. Avocations: tar heel sports; water skiing; sports cars. Home: Teaberry Hills Boone NC 28607 Office: R Lee Warren 40 Doctors Park Boone NC 28607

WARREN, THOMAS EDMOND, university administrator; b. Turkey, N.C., Feb. 9, 1947; s. Ollen Edward and Martha Laurine (Carr) W.; m. Mary Ethel Pollock, Mar. 31, 1966; children—Cameron Mitchell, Angelia Renea. B.B.A., Campbell Coll.-Buies Creek, N.C., 1974. Mgr., Family Dollar Stores, Inc., Fayetteville, N.C., 1969-70; acct. Ed Renfrow and Assocs., Smithfield, N.C., 1974-75; bus. mgr. N.C. Dept. Justice, Raleigh, dir. adminstrv. services U. Houston, 1979—; cons. in field. Served with USAF, 1966-69. Decorated Bronze Star, Air Medal, Purple Heart, Vietnam Service ribbon. Campbell scholar, 1973-74. Mem. N.C. Soc. Accts., Nat. Assn. Coll. and Univ. Bus. Officers, So. Assn. Coll. and Univ. Bus. Officers, Tex. Assn. State Sr. Coll. and Univ. Bus. Officers, Nat. Assn. Coll. Aux. Services, Soc. Property Adminstrs., Adminstrv. Mgmt. Soc., Houston Apt. Mgmt. Assn. Democrat. Baptist. Home: 606 Briar Creek Dr La Porte TX 77571 Office: Univ Houston 4800 Calhoun St Houston TX 77004

WARREN, WILLIAM DAVID, data processor; b. Austin, Tex., Sept. 3, 1931; s. William Frederick and Eleanor Faver (Hill) W.; B.A., U. Tex., 1957; certificate data processing Inst. for Certification Computer Profls, 1963. Tabulating equipment operator data processing div. U. Tex., Austin, 1958-61, computer programmer, systems analyst, 1961—; with Lumbermen's Investment Corp., Austin, 1980—. Served with AUS, 1952-53. Mem. Data Processing Mgmt. Assn. (sec. Austin chpt. 1969-70), Am. Philatelic Soc. (life), U. Tex. Ex-Students Assn. (life), Nat. Geog. Soc. (life), Order DeMolay (sr.). Episcopalian. Club: Stamp (pres. 1951-52) (Austin). Lodges: Masons, Shriners. Home: 1502 Hardouin Ave Austin TX 78703

WARREN, WILLIAM MICHAEL, association executive; b. Bancroft, Mich., July 5, 1917; s. Perrin Charles and Gladys May (Hill) W.; m. Rebecca Carolyn Glass, Dec. 20, 1945; children—William Michael, Jr., Charles, John, James, Joseph, Andrew. B.S., Mich. State U.-East Lansing, 1940; M.S., Tex. A&M U., 1948; Ph.D., U. Mo., 1952. Instr. Tex. A&M U., Coll. Sta., 1940-42, asst. prof., 1946-50, assoc. prof., 1952-55; prof. Auburn U., Ala., 1955-57, prof., dept. head, 1957-80, prof. emeritus, 1980—; exec. dir. Santa Gertrudis Breeders Internat., Kingsville, Tex., 1980—. Contbr. articles to scientific jours. Gen. Edn. Bd. scholar, 1950-52. Mem. Am. Soc. of Animal Sci., Southern Sect., Am. Soc. of Animal Sci. Lodge: Kiwanis. Methodist. Home: 1405 Christy St Kingsville TX 78363 Office: Santa Gertrudis Breeders Internat PO Box 1257 Kingsville TX 78363

WARRICK, CLIFTON EUAL, association executive, rancher; b. Wellington, Tex., Sept. 11, 1935; s. John W. and Margille (Sigler) Stroud; m. Ethel M. Curry, Oct. 3, 1957; children—John Russell, Craig Randall. B.S., Tex. A&M U., 1957, M.Ed., 1965. Freshman football coach Tex. A&M U., College Station, 1964-65; phys. edn. coach Gary Job Corps Ctr., San Marcos, Tex., 1965-68; athletic and aquatic dir. Park and Recreation Dept., Austin, Tex., 1968-79; dep. exec. dir. Amateur Softball Assn., Oklahoma City, 1979—; head insp. Tex. Relays, Austin, 1969—, NCAA Outdoor Track and Field Championships, 1980, 85, NCAA Indoor Track and Field Championships, 1986; state commr. Tex. Amateur Athletic Fedn., Austin, 1970-79. Author: Coaching Junior Olympic Softball, 1982. Coordinator softball U.S. Olympic Com. Nat. Sports Festival, Indpls., 1982, Colorado Springs, 1983, Baton Rouge, 1985, U.S. Olympic Festival Houston, 1986; bd. dirs. Youth Athletic Council, Austin, 1972-79. Mem. Tex. Parks and Recreation Soc. (exec. com. 1974-79), Tex. Amateur Athletic Fedn. (Koger Stokes award 1980; exec. bd. 1975-79), Nat. Park and Recreation Assn. (S.W. Council 1977-79), So. Tex. Amateur Athletic Union (v.p. 1975-79), Amateur Softball Assn. (regional v.p.), Nat. Council Youth Sports Dirs. (exec. bd. 1979—, pres. 1983-85. Republican. Methodist. Home: PO Box 18366 Oklahoma City OK 73154 Office: Amateur Softball Assn 2801 NE 50th St Oklahoma City OK 73111

WARRINER, DAVID DORTCH, federal judge; b. Brunswick County, Va., Feb. 25, 1929; s. Thomas Emmett and Maria Clarke (Dortch) W.; B.A. in Polit. Sci., U. N.C., 1951; LL.B., U. Va., 1957; m. Barbara Ann Jenkins, Jan. 31, 1959; children—Susan Wells, David Thomas Dortch, Julia Cotman. Va. 1957, U.S. Supreme Ct. 1970. Ptnr. Warriner & Outten, Emporia, Va., 1957-74; judge U.S. Dist. Ct. Eastern Dist. Va., Richmond, 1974—. Mem. Va. Republican Central Com., 1963-74, gen. counsel, 1972-74. Served as lt. USNR, 1951-54. Mem. Am., Va. bar assns. Home: Route 2 Box 280 Brodnax VA 23920 Office: US Courthouse 10th and Main Sts Richmond VA 23219

WARRINGTON, ROBERT O'NEIL, JR., mechanical engineering educator, researcher; b. Sparta, Wis., Mar. 13, 1945; s. Robert O'Neil and Virginia (Johnson) W.; m. Anne Cabell, Aug. 14, 1968; children—Robert O'Neil III, Daniel Scott, Kristy Cabell. B.S. in Aerospace Engring., Va. Poly. Inst., 1967; M.S. in Mech. Engring., U. Tex.-El Paso, 1971; Ph.D. in Mech. Engring., Mont. State U., 1975. Instr. U. Tex.-El Paso, 1971; instr. Mont. State U., Bozeman, 1975-76, asst. prof., 1976-80, assoc. prof., 1980-83; prof. mech. engring., dept. head La. Tech. U., Ruston, 1983—, track and field ofcl., 1983—; cons. Atlas Processing Co., Shreveport, La., 1984—. Author: Montana Energy Primer, 1978. Contbr. articles to profl. jours. Coach Little League, Bozeman, 1978-83, Soccer League, Bozeman, 1981-83. Served with U.S. Army, 1968-70. Grantee NSF, Exxon Found., Hewlett-Packard Corp., C.E., Dept. Energy, 1975—. Mem. ASME (K-8 com. 1983—), Am. Soc. for Engring Edn., Mont. Engring. Assocs. (sec.-treas. 1979—), Nat. Ski Patrol, Sigma Chi. Republican. Roman Catholic. Office: Mech Engring Dept La Tech U Ruston LA 71272

WARSHAUER, STEVEN MICHAEL, exploration geologist; b. N.Y.C., May 20, 1945; s. Milton J. and Murial (Porter) W.; m. Yvette L. Perez, Sept. 2, 1967; children—Michelle, Eric. B.A. in Geology, Queens Coll., 1967; M.S. in Geology, U. Cin., 1969, Ph.D., 1973. Asst. prof. geology W.Va. U., 1972-77, assoc. prof., 1977-81; exploration geologist Tenneco Oil Co., Houston, 1981-83, sr. exploration geologist, 1983—. Contbr. numerous articles to profl. jours. Mem. Am. Assn. Petroleum Geologists, Houston Geol. Soc., Sigma Xi. Office: Tenneco Oil Co Frontier Exploration PO Box 2511 Houston TX 77001

WARSHAWSKY, HOWARD, political science educator; b. N.Y.C., Feb. 19, 1947; s. Norman and Frances (Wolgang) W. B.A., Queens Coll., CUNY, 1967; M.A., U. Va., 1969, Ph.D., 1974. Instr. U. Va., Charlottesville, 1973-74; prof. polit. sci. Roanoke Coll., Salem, Va., 1974—. Served to 1st lt. U.S. Army, 1969-72. N.Y. State Regents scholar, 1963-67; NDEA fellow, 1967-73; Du Pont scholar, 1973-74; NEH summer fellow, 1977. Mem. Am. Polit. Sci. Assn., Internat. Polit. Sci. Assn., So. Polit. Sci. Assn., Internat. Studies Assn. Office: Dept Polit Sci Roanoke Coll Salem VA 24153

WARTHAN, HELEN PATRICIA, educator; b. Alexandria, Va., June 14, 1941; d. Anthony John and Elizabeth Radcliff (Etchison) Trovato; B.S., Fairmont State Coll., 1964; M.Ed., Tex. A&M U., 1969; postgrad. Fla. State U., 1966-70; U. Ga., 1975-79. Tchr., counselor Carrabelle (Fla.) High Sch., 1964-70; tchr., chmn. dept. sci. Towers High Sch., Decatur, Ga., 1970—. Pres., Decatur Civic Chorus, 1975-76, treas., 1979-80. Benedum acad. scholar, 1959-64; named Tchr. of Yr., Ga. Tchrs. Assn. 4th Dist., 1976, Towers High Sch., 1980-85, Dekalb County Tchr. of Yr., 1985. Mem. Sci. Tchrs. Assn. Rockdale and DeKalb (pres. 1980, Sci. Tchr. of Yr. 1984-85), Nat. Earth Sci. Tchrs. Assn., Ga. Sci. Tchrs. Assn., AAAS, Nat. Assn. Biology Tchrs., Nat. Sci. Tchrs. Assn., Assn. Supervision and Curriculum Devel., Nat. Oceanographic Soc., Internat. Oceanographic Found. Episcopalian. Home: 1910-D Bodwin Pl Decatur GA 30035 Office: 3919 Brookcrest Circle Decatur GA 30032

WASCHKA, RONALD WILLIAM, independent oil and gas producer; b. Memphis, Sept. 2, 1932; s. Frederick William and Hazel Celeste (Guidroz) W.; B.A., U. Miss., 1960; M.A., Memphis State U., 1970, Ph.D., 1977; m. Patricia Janet Sinclair Hanney, July 27, 1963; children—Michael, John, Anne Marie, Helen Marissa. Service asst. Memphis State U., 1970, teaching asst., 1972-75; with Legis. Reference Service, Library of Congress, Washington, 1955; founder, owner Ronald Co., Inc., Memphis, 1963-81; ind. oil and gas producer, Ft. Worth, 1972—. Com. mem. Boy Scouts Am., Germantown, 1975-81. Served with USAF, 1955-59, Tenn. Air N.G., 1963-69. Mem. Res. Officers Assn., Ind. Producers Assn. Am., Tex. Ind. Producers and Royalty Owners, Am. Petroleum Inst., Am. Econ. History Assn., Am. Hist. Assn., Orgn. Am. Historians. Republican. Roman Catholic. Clubs: Sturgeon Bay (Wis.) Yacht; Memphis Equestrian Assn. (past pres.); Petroleum (Ft. Worth); Padre Isles Country (Corpus Christi, Tex.); Summit (Memphis); Rotary. Home: 2108 Oak Knoll Dr Colleyville TX 76034 Office: 210 W 6th St Suite 1202 Fort Worth TX 76102

WASH, ALLEN GARDNER, accounting educator; b. Augusta, Ga., Apr. 21, 1946; s. William Holman and Emmie Mae (Gardner) W.; children—Bradley, Jason. B.B.A., Augusta Coll., 1968; M.B.A., U. S.C., 1972, M.Acctg., 1973. C.P.A., N.C. loan adminstr. S.C. Nat. Bank, North Augusta, S.C., 1969-71; instr. Gaston Coll., Dallas, N.C., 1973-76, chmn. acctg. dept., 1978—; asst. prof. Gardner-Webb Coll., Boiling Springs, N.C., 1977; prin. Allen G. Wash, C.P.A., Gastonia, N.C., 1974—. Recipient Econs. award Wall St. Jour., 1968. Fellow N.C. Assn. C.P.A.s. Democrat. Baptist. Office: Gaston Coll Dallas NC 28034

WASHBURN, JOHN ROSSER, medical-surgical supply company executive, financial/investment consultant; b. Hopewell, Va., July 24, 1943; s. Winthrop Doane and Mary Virginia (Overstreet) W.; m. Judith Ann Rosen, May 16, 1971 (div. Feb. 1982); m. Tana Jean Demro, July 9, 1982; children—Eric Joseph Harrison, Amanda Ashley. Student Louisburg Jr. Coll., 1963, Va. Commonwealth U., 1963-64, U. Richmond Extension, 1967-69, Williams Coll., 1985, Stanford U., 1986. Asst. mgr. Liberty Loan Corp., Richmond, Va., 1965-67; loan interviewer Central Fidelity Bank, Richmond, 1967-69; regional credit/sales supr. Moores Bldg. Supplies, Inc., Roanoke, Va., 1969-74; corp. credit mgr. Owens & Minor, Inc., Richmond, 1974—; fin., investment cons. JA-GO Enterprises, Richmond, 1982—, Washburn Enterprises, 1984—; instr., lectr.

investment, fin., credit mgmt., 1970—. Active Nat. Republican Congl. Com., 1980—, YMCA, 1979—, Am. Mus. Nat. History, 1982—, U.S. Def. Com., 1981—; mem. Credit Research Found. Mem. Internat. Platform Assn., Nat. Assn. Credit Mgmt. (Appreciation cert for outstanding service 1980-81, pres. Central Va. sect. 1979-80, chmn. legis. com. 1977-79, dir. 1983—), Am. Mgmt. Assn., Nat. Wildlife Fedn. Episcopalian. Clubs: Congressional (Washington); Hopewell (Va.) Yacht. Lodge: Moose. Office: Owens & Minor Inc 2727 Enterprise Pkwy Richmond VA 23229

WASHINGTON, CRAIG A., state senator, lawyer; b. Oct. 12, 1941. B.S., Prairie View A&M U.; J.D., Tex. So. U. Mem. Tex. Ho. of Reps., 1973-83; mem. Tex. Senate, 1984—, mem. health and human resources, jurisprudence, and state affairs coms. Democrat. Office: Tex Senate PO Box 12068 Austin TX 78711*

WASHINGTON, EARLIE M., social worker; b. Madison County, Miss. Sept. 28, 1956; d. Early B. and Mary (Burnett) W. B.A., Tougaloo Coll., 1976; M.S.W., Ohio State U., 1978. Drug counselor, then drug program coordinator Jackson Mental Health Ctr. (Miss.), 1978-82; instr. Tougaloo Coll., 1979-82, dir. mental health tng. program, 1982—; pvt. cons., Jackson, 1982—. Bd. dirs. Cath. Charities Youth Program, Contact of Jackson. Recipient Maggie Drake Humanitarian award Tougaloo Coll., 1976, outstanding instr. psychology/-mental health award, 1984; scholastic award NIMH, 1977. Mem. Nat. Assn. Social Workers, Nat. Assn. Black Social Workers. Baptist. Home: 4112 Oak Hill Dr Jackson MS 39206 Office: Dept Psychology Tougaloo Coll Tougaloo MS 39174

WASHINGTON, MICHAEL HARLAN, historian, educator, consultant, writer; b. Cin., Sept. 25, 1950; s. Herbert William and Willa Alice (Battle) W.; m. Sandra LaVonne Walker, Sept. 23, 1972; children—Michael Jr., Milo Robeson. A.A., Raymond Walters Coll., 1971; B.S., U. Cin., 1973, M.Ed., 1974, Ed.D., 1984. Social edn. dir. Fleischmanns Boy's Clubs of Greater Cin., 1972-74; instr. reading Vets. Upward Bound Program, U. Cin., 1974, asst. dir. Employees Developmental Edn. Program, 1974-76, instructional specialist Ctr. Devel. Edn., 1974-79; assoc. prof. history No. Ky. U., Highland Heights, 1980—; cons. various orgns. Asst. football coach Finneytown Parent Boosters, 1980-83, head coach, 1985; active Williams YMCA, Cin., 1979—; founder Minority Student Leadership award No. Ky. U. Recipient award of appreciation Fishermen's Concerned Citizens of Plaqucmens Parish, La.; Ky. Council Higher Edn. devel. grantee, 1979, 80. Mem. AAUP, U.S. Tang-soo-do Fedn., Ky. Assn. Tchrs. History, Coll. Reading Assn., Youth Against Militarism (founder), Phi Alpha Theta. Baptist. Author tech. papers; contbr. articles to profl. jours. Creator Voices of Youth radio program.

WASHINGTON, VALORA, educator; b. Columbus, Ohio, Dec. 16, 1953; d. Timothy Lee and Elizabeth (Jackson) W. B.A. with honors, Mich. State U., 1974; Ph.D., Ind. U., 1978. Work study participant Mich. State U., East Lansing, 1971-73, resident asst., 1973-74; grad. research asst. Ind. U., Bloomington, 1974, dir. black studies St. Rita's Summer Youth Program, Indpls., 1975; assoc. instr. Sch. Edn., Ind. U., 1975-77; spl. asst. to dir./program cons. for research and evaluations, Human Relations Consortium, Indpls., 1977-78; substitute tchr. Indpls., 1978; dir. Sex Desegregation Tng. Inst. U. N.C., Chapel Hill, 1980-82, asst. prof., 1978-82, assoc. prof. Sch. Edn., 1982-83; assoc. prof. Howard U., Washington, 1981-82, asst. dean, assoc. prof., 1983—. Congl. Sci. fellow, Soc. for Research in Child Devel., AAAS, 1981-82; lectr. in field; cons. in field; condr. workshops in field; mem. various panels, confs. So. Fellowships Fund fellow, 1977-78; U. N.C. Research Council grantee, 1978-80; Spencer Found. grantee, 1979-80; Ednl. Research Mgmt./Nat. Acad. Edn. fellow, 1979; Carolina Challenge Awards for Jr. Faculty Devel., U. N.C., 1980-81; Soc. for Research in Child Devel. Congr. Sci. fellow, 1981-82; recipient award of distinction Ohio Bd. Edn., 1971; Wright-Effie scholar, 1971; LaVerne Noys scholar, 1972-74, others. Mem. Assn. Women Faculty, LWV (dir. 1981-82), Nat. Black Child Devel. Inst., Nat. Council Negro Women, N.C. Assn. Black Educators, N.C. Assn. Black Psychologists, Soc. Research in Child Devel., Phi Delta Kappa. Contbr. articles to profl. jours.

WASHINGTON, WALTER, college president; b. Hazlehurst, Miss., July 13, 1923; s. Kemp and Mable (Comous) W.; B.A., Tougaloo Coll., 1948; M.S., Ind. U., 1952; Edn. Specialist, Peabody Coll., 1958; postgrad. Yale U., 1953; Doctorate, U. So. Miss., 1969; LL.D., Tougaloo Coll., 1972, Ind. U., 1983; m. Carolyn Carter, July 31, 1949. Tchr., Holtzclaw High Sch., Crystal Springs, Miss., 1948-49; asst. prin., tchr. Parrish High Sch., Hazlehurst, 1949-52; prin. Utica Jr. Coll. High Sch., Miss., 1952-54; dean Utica Jr. Coll., 1954-55, pres., 1957-69; pres. Alcorn (Miss.) State U., 1969—; prin. Sumner Hill High Sch., Clinton, Miss., 1955-57; dir. Miss. Power & Light Co., Middle South Utilities, Blue Cross Blue Shield of Miss., Klingler Industries, Ltd. Pres., Nat. Pan-Hellenic Council, 1964-67, Nat. Alumni Council of United Negro Coll. Fund, 1959-60; past mem. adv. council Miss. Vocational Edn. Program; past mem. adv. council Miss. Regional Med. Programs; mem. Miss. Econ. Council; mem. S.E. regional exec. com. Boy Scouts Am., mem. exec. com. Andrew Jackson council; mem. adv. council Miss. 4-H Clubs. Bd. dirs. Miss. Heart Assn., Miss. Mental Health Assn., Miss. Easter Seal Soc. Mem. So. Assn. Colls. Secondary Schs. (past dir., past chmn. secondary commn., past trustee), Am. Assn. Sch. Adminstrs., Nat. Assn. State Univs. and Land Grant Colls., NEA, Miss. Educators Assn. (pres. 1964-65), Miss. Tchrs. Assn., Tougaloo Nat. Alumni Assn. (pres. 1960), Nat. Soc. Study Higher Edn., John Dewey Soc., Assn. Supervision and Curriculum Devel., Alumni Assn. George Peobody Coll. (past v.p. exec. com.), Delta Kappa Pi, Phi Delta Kappa, Alpha Kappa Mu, Alpha Phi Alpha (gen. pres. 1974-76). Address: Alcorn State U Office of President Lorman MS 39096

WASINGER, VIRGINIA LEE, quality assurance engineer; b. Paris, Tex., Sept. 21, 1932; d. Theo L. and Elizabeth V. (Carter) White; children—Janet M. Wasinger Dickson, James L., Richard J., Lee Anne, Cynthia S. B.B.A., Tarleton State U., 1978. Cons., Nat. Bus. Cons., Dallas, 1969; owner Granbury Picture Framing (Tex.), 1973-76; mgr. Sky-Harbour Lake Property, Granbury, 1974-75; indsl. relations mgr. Voltaic Internat. Corp., Dallas, 1969-71; quality assurance engr. H.J. Kaiser, Moscow, Ohio, 1983, Brown & Root Contrn., Glen Rose, Tex., 1979-83, Nat. Inspection and Cons., Inc., Pullman Power Co., Perry, Ohio, 1983—. Mem. AAUW, Am. Soc. Quality Control, Nat. Carvers Mus. Address: PO Box 129 Bluff Dale TX 76433

WASON, KELLY DON, business executive; b. San Antonio, July 12, 1958; s. Don Ralph and June Juanell (Spray) W.; m. Susan Ann Livesay, Apr. 27, 1981. B.S., Wayland Bapt. U., 1981; M.B.A., U. Tex., 1983. Gen. mgr. Wason Installation, Plainview, Tex., 1979-81; sr. research technician El Paso Products Co., Odessa, Tex., 1981-83; key accounts mgr. Interphase Corp., Dallas, 1983—. Mem. Mgmt. and Mktg. Assn., Tex. Acad. Sci. Coll. Acad. Republican. Methodist. Lodges: Toastmasters. Office: 2925 Merrell Rd Dallas TX 75229

WASSERMAN, ALBERT JULIAN, educational administrator; b. Richmond, Va., Jan. 25, 1928; s. Stanley Lewis and Ann (Greenberg) W.; m. Martele Sporn, June 27, 1948; children—Gail Hart, Rae Rosenthal, Beth Wasserman. B.A., U. Va., 1947; M.D., Med. Coll. Va., 1951. Diplomate Am. Bd. Internal Medicine. Chief resident Med. Coll. Va., 1956-57, sr. asst. resident in medicine, 1955-56; teaching fellow Harvard U., Boston, 1952-53; instr. medicine Med. Coll. Va., Richmond, 1956-57, assoc. in medicine, 1957-60, asst. prof. medicine, 1960-63, assoc. prof., 1963-67, prof. medicine and pharmacology, 1967—, assoc. dean curriculum, 1978—, exec. assoc. dean Sch. Medicine, 1979—; chief med. service VA Hosp., Richmond, 1960-63; editorial activities and reviewer AMA Drug Evaluations, 1970—, Am. Jour. Digestive Diseases, New Eng. Jour. Medicine, Annals of Internal Medicine; prin. investigator FDA Contract, Intensive Drug Surveillance in Selected Hosp. Units, 1973-75; mem. cardiovascular panel U.S. Pharmacopeia, 1974-80; cons. VA Drug Info. and Consultative Service, VA Hosp.; attending physician Med. Coll. Va. Hosp. Pres. Temple Beth El, 1981-82; attending physician Beth Shalom Home of Va. Served with USAF, 1953-55. Named Tchr. of Yr., Med. Coll. Va., 1977, 78, 79; NIH, USPHS grantee, 1957-60. Fellow ACP, Am. Coll. Chest Physicians, Am. Coll. Clin. Pharmacology; mem. So. Soc. Clin. Investigation, Am. Soc. Clin. Pharmacology and Therapeutics, Am. Heart Assn., Am. Fedn. Clin. Research, Assn. Am. Med. Colls., Am. Physicians Fellowship for Israel Med. Soc., Richmond Area Heart Assn., Richmond Acad. Medicine, Med. Soc. Va. Contbr. articles to profl. jours. Address: 1305 Lake Ave Richmond VA 23226

WASSERMAN, ELVIRA, psychiatrist; b. N.Y.C.; d. Charles W. and Zena (Berlin) W.; A.B., Hunter Coll., 1933; M.D., Women's Med. Coll. Pa., 1938; cert. N.Y. Sch. Psychiatry, 1962, Postgrad. Center for Mental Health, 1965; children—James G. Wallach, Lewis R. Wallach. Intern, Wilkes Barre (Pa.) Gen. Hosp., 1938-39; resident Creedmoor State Hosp., N.Y.C., 1959-62, supervising psychiatrist, 1962-65; practice medicine specializing in psychiatry, psychoanalysis and hypnoanalysis, N.Y.C., 1959-76, specializing in metaphysical psychotherapy, West Palm Beach, Fla., 1976—; asst. prof. guidance and counseling L.I.U., 1972-76; med. dir. Long Beach Mental Health Clinic, 1965-70, West Nassau Mental Health Clinic, 1970-76. Mem. Am. Psychiat. Assn., Internat. Soc. Clin. and Exptl. Hyponosis, Soc. Med. Analysts, N.Y. Council Child Psychiatry, Nat. League Am. Pen Women. Mem. Artist Guild of Norton Mus.

WASSERMAN, FRED, physician, medical educator; b. Norfolk, Va., Oct. 18, 1924; s. Fred and Frances (Sommers) W.; m. Lillian Mehalic, Nov. 19, 1953; children—Fred III, Frances S., John D., Janet C. B.A., U. Va., 1948, M.D., 1952. Diplomate Am. Bd. Internal Medicine. Intern, Norfolk Gen. Hosp. (Va.), 1952-53; resident in medicine U. Pa. Hosps., Phila., 1953-54, 55-56, resident in cardiology, 1954-55; resident in cardiology Phila. Gen. Hosp., 1956-57; chief med. service VA Hosp., Miami, 1959-64, cons. cardiology, 1964-79; prof. medicine U. Miami Sch. Medicine, 1963-64, clin. prof., 1964—; chief dept. medicine Cedars Med. Ctr., Miami, 1980-82; practice medicine specializing in internal medicine and cardiology, Coral Gables, Fla., 1964-83; regional med. dir. AV-Med Health Plan, Tampa, Fla. 1984-85; chief gen. internal medicine sect. Bay Pines Med. Ctr. (VA hosp.), Fla., 1985; dir. VA Outpatient Clinic, Ft. Myers, Fla., 1985—; mem. med. adv. com. Hosp. Crippled Children and Adults, 1971-82; bd. dirs. Cedars Med. Ctr., 1965-82; mem. Task Force on Heart Disease Fla. Regional Med. Program, 1971-72; bd. dirs. Health Systems Agy. South Fla., Inc., 1978-79, Charron Williams Coll., 1983—. Served with U.S. Army, 1943-46; ETO. Fellow ACP, Am. Coll. Cardiology, Am. Coll. Chest Physicians; mem. Am. Heart Assn., Fla. Heart Assn. (bd. dirs.), AMA, Fla. Med. Assn., Pinellas County Med. Assn., Phi Beta Kappa, Sigma Xi. Contbr. articles to med. jours.

WASSOM, JOHN CLARK, economics educator; b. Davenport, Iowa, Nov. 13, 1939; s. Samuel Jesse and Jane Deloras (Becknell) W.; m. Sharon Mae Ferneau, Sept. 2, 1961; 1 son, Gregory Scott. B.A. in Econs., Grinnell Coll., 1961; M.A., Ind. U., 1963, Ph.D., 1970. Asst. prof. fin. U. Fla., Gainesville, 1966-71; assoc. prof. econs. Western Ky. U., Bowling Green, 1971-77, prof., 1977—, head dept. econs., 1978—, developer, coordinator 2 yr. banking program, 1974-78. Mem. Am. Econ. Assn. (transp. and pub. utilities sub-group), So. Econ. Assn. Researcher, contbr. articles to profl. publs. Office: Econs Dept Western Ky Univ Bowling Green KY 42101

WASSON, THERON VIVION, retail store executive; b. Decatur, Ga., July 11, 1931; s. Word Ray and Lula Blanche (House) W.; student Smith Hughes Vocat. Sch., 1954-56; B.A., Ga. State Coll., 1958; m. Grace Ann Atkins, Oct. 21, 1954; children—Vivian, Gail, Patricia. With Decatur Police Dept., 1954-60, with detective div., 1965-70; adult probation asst. chief DeKalb County, Ga., 1960-65; with Richway Stores, Atlanta, 1970-82; dir. loss prevention The Home Depot Inc., Atlanta, 1982—. Lt. col., aide de camp Gov.'s Staff, State of Ga., 1971. Served with U.S. Army, 1951-54. Decorated Bronze Star medal (3). Cert. protection profl. Mem. Ga. Assn. Security Personnel (v.p. 1975—), Nat. Mass Retail Inst., Ga. Assn. Chiefs of Police, Ga. Retail Mchts. Assn., Home Ctr. Inst. Loss Prevention Council. Home: 3365 Colony Dr SE Conyers GA 30208 Office: 45 Broad St PO Box 50359 Atlanta GA 30302

WATABE, NORIMITSU, biology and marine science educator; b. Kure, Hiroshima, Japan, Nov. 29, 1922; came to U.S., 1957; s. Isamu and Matsuko (Takamatsu) W.; m. Sakuko Kobayashi, Dec. 12, 1952; children—Shoichi, Sachiko. B.S., 1st Nat. High Sch., Tokyo, 1945; M.S., Tohoku U., Sendai, Japan, 1948, D.Sc., 1960. Research investigator Fuji Pearl Co., Mie-ken, Japan, 1948-52; instr. Prefect U. Mie, Tsu, Mie-ken, Japan, 1952-55, asst. prof., 1955-59; research assoc. Duke U., Durham, N.C., 1957-70; assoc. prof. U. S.C., Columbia, 1970-72, prof. biology, marine sci., 1972—, dir. Electron Microscopy Ctr., 1970—; cons. in field. Author: Studies on Pearls, 1959. Editor: Mechanisms of Mineralization, 1976; Mechanisms of Biomineralization, 1980. Contbr. numerous sci. articles to profl. jours. Recipient Pearl Research award Elmer W. Ellsworth, 1952, Alexander Von Humboldt award Fed. Republic Germany, 1976, Russel award U. S.C., 1981; grantee NIH, 1971-76, NSF, 1973—. Fellow AAAS, Royal Micros. Soc. Gt. Britain; mem. Am. Micros. Soc. (rev. bd.), Am. Malacological Union (rev. bd.), Am. Soc. Zoologists, Electron Micros. Soc. Am. Avocations: music; piano playing. Home: 3510 Greenway Dr Columbia SC 29206 Office: Electron Microscopy Ctr U SC Columbia SC 29208

WATANABE, DANIEL HIROSHI, microbiologist; b. Los Angeles, Aug. 6, 1929; s. Takeo and Tai (Iwasaki) W.; m. Akiko Ito, May 16, 1963; children—Fujio M., Midori A. B.S., Pa. State U., 1957; M.A., U. Calif.-Berkeley, 1959; Ph.D., SUNY Upstate Med. Center 1973. Asst. prof. Coll. Osteo. Medicine and Surgery, Des Moines, 1972-74; research asst. prof. N.Y. Med. Coll., Valhalla, 1974-78; research asst. prof. Baylor Coll. Medicine, Houston, 1978-84; dir. research Interface-Internat. Conf. Developers, 1983—; instr. Houston Community Coll. System, 1981—. Pres., Japanese Am. Citizens League, Houston, 1982—; bd. dirs. Houston Ctr. for the Humanities, 1983—; 1st pres. Japan Am. Cultural Exchange Soc., Syracuse, 1972-73; 1st chmn. Asian Am. Festival Com. Houston, 1980. Served with AUS, 1949-52; Japan. Recipient Merit cert. City Houston, 1981. Mem. Am. Soc. Microbiology, AAAS, Assn. Advancement Med. Instrumentation, Japan-Am. Soc. Houston (dir. 1982—), Meeting Planners Internat. Office: 1212 Cedar Post Ln Suite D Houston TX 77055

WATERHOUSE, RUSSELL RUTLEDGE, artist, painter; b. El Paso, Aug. 11, 1928; s. Charles Ewing and Lucille (Rutledge) W.; children—Robert M., Quentin. B.S., Tex. A&M U., 1950; postgrad. Art Ctr., Coll. Design, Pasadena, Calif., 1953-56. Art dir. El Paso Nat. Gas Co., 1956-71; adv. dir. Tony Lama Co., El Paso, 1971-72; free-lance painter, El Paso, 1972—. One man shows include El Paso Mus. of Art, Wichita Falls Mus. Art, Americana Mus., Tex. A&M U; represented in permanent collections El Paso Mus. Art, Tex. Tech U., Tex. A&M U. Mem. Tex. Commn. Arts and Humanities, 1970-75. Served to 1st lt. U.S. Army, 1951-53. Home and Studio: 5500 Westside Dr El Paso TX 79932

WATERMAN, DANIEL, comptroller; b. Havana, Cuba, Sept. 17, 1953; came to U.S., 1961; s. Samuel S. and Gladys (Madina) Perez. A.A., Miami-Dade Community Coll., 1973; B.A., Fla. Internat. U., 1975. Gen. mgr. Toughlite Lens, Miami, Fla., 1970-73; comptroller Key Enterprises, Miami, 1973-78, Tour-Op Inc., Miami, 1978-80, Aircraft Metals, 1980—; dir. W & W Bus. Cons., Miami, 1978—; cons. Parodi Printers, Miami, 1981—. Contbr. articles to profl. jours.; author: Reflections, 1978. Recipient Literary award Diario Las Americas, 1971. Democrat.

WATERS, BETTY JUNE, medical records specialist; b. Chattanooga, Aug. 13, 1934; d. William Jennings Caldwell and Lois Irene (Hale) Irwin; m. Charles Richard Waters, Sr., Oct. 17, 1954; children—Cynthia R. Milliron, Elaine K. Machiela, Elizabeth L. Pemberton, Charles R., Jr. Student Tenn. State U. With personnel records dept. Bethesda Naval Hosp., Md., 1976-80; med. records specialist Vets. Hosp., Nashville, 1983—. Mem. Nat. Trust for Hist. Preservation. Republican. Mem. Ch. of the Nazarene. Avocations: history, reading, jogging. Home: 131 General Jackson Ln Hermitage TN 37076

WATERS, H. FRANKLIN, U.S. district judge; b. Hackett, Ark., July 20, 1932; s. William A. and Wilma H. Waters; m. Janie Waters, May 31, 1958; children—Carolyn Denise, Melanie Jane, Melissa Ann. Engr., atty. Ralston Purina Co., St. Louis, 1958-66; atty. Crouch, Blair, Cypert & Waters, 1967-81; judge U.S. Dist. Ct. for Western Ark., Fort Smith, 1981—. Mem. ABA, Ark. Bar Assn., Springdale C. of C. (bd. dirs.). Address: PO Box 1908 Fayetteville AR 72702

WATERS, JOHN WILLIAM, insurance company executive; b. Alexandria, La., Aug. 22, 1910; s. Charles Milton and Elizabeth (Texada) W.; m. Rosemary Bennet, Sept. 25, 1940; 1 child, John Bennet. Student Mercer U., Macon, Ga., 1927, La. Coll., Pineville, 1928. Chmn. bd., sec. Fireside Comml. Life Ins. Co., Shreveport, La., 1932—. Active Episcopal Ch., Shreveport, 1960—; pres. Rapides United Givers, 1960; mem. adv. com. Profl. Golfers Assn., 1964-75; dir. Life Begins at 40 Golf Tournament, 1964—. Served to lt. comdr. USN, 1942-46. Recipient Disting. Service award Alexandria Jaycees, 1942. Mem. La. State Golfers Assn. (pres. 1948-49), Alexandria-Pineville C. of C. (pres. 1962-63), So. Golf Assn. (pres. 1966-67, dir. emeritus). Home: 8614 Glenhaven Dr Shreveport LA 71106 Office: Fireside Comml Life Ins Co 6001 Financial Plaza Shreveport LA 71130

WATERS, LENORA DELORES, teacher educator; b. Crescent, Okla., May 11, 1935; d. Robert Lee and I.V. (Kendrick) Jones; m. Cleon Marvin Waters, Dec. 15, 1957. B.S. in Edn. cum laude, Langston U., 1955; M.S. in Edn., Okla. State U., 1960; Ed.D., Baylor U., 1972. Public sch. tchr., Ponca City, Okla., 1955-66; reading instr. Phillips U. Speech and Hearing Ctr., Enid, Okla., summers 1962-63; instr. Paul Quinn Coll., Waco, Tex., 1966-69, 71-72, cons., 1972-74; dir. basic studies program Huston-Tillotson Coll., Austin, 1972-82, chairperson div. edn., 1982-85, v.p. acad. affairs, 1985—; exchange edn. instr. SW Tex. State U., San Marcos, spring 1976; cons. Langston U., Okla., 1981-84. Contbr. articles to profl. jours. Mem., sec.-treas. Austin-Travis County Mental Health-Mental Retardation, 1981-83; mem. bd. Austin Ind. Sch. Dist. Evaluation Adv. Com., Austin, 1983-85; mem. Travis County Adult Literacy Bd., Austin, 1984-85. Ford Found. fellow, 1969-71; fgn. study fellow Tex. So. U., Houston, summer 1977; Nat. Ednl. Policy fellow Inst. Ednl. Leadership, Washington, 1982-83; recipient Outstanding Alumni award Baylor U., 1977, award Bd. Higher Edn., United Methodist Ch., summer 1977, Excellence in Edn. award Austin Ind. Sch. Dist., 1984. Mem. Austin Coop. Tchr. Edn. Ctr. (sec. 1982—), Tex. Assn. Colls. for Tchr. Edn., Assn. Tchr. Educators, Tex. Assn. Tchr. Educators, Delta Sigma Theta (chmn. scholarship com. 1980—), Phi Delta Kappa (1st v.p. 1983—). Democrat. Baptist. Avocations: reading, walking, singing. Home: 6509 Greensboro Dr Austin TX 78723 Office: Huston-Tillotson Coll 1820 E 8th St Austin TX 78702

WATERS, MICHAEL COOPER, medical center and development corporation executive; b. Cisco, Tex., Oct. 29, 1942; m. Kathy Street, Apr. 17, 1976; children—Tiffany, Allison. Student, Baylor U., 1961-63; B.S., Lamar U., 1965; M.S., U. Pitts., 1967. Adminstrv. resident U. Tex. Med. Branch Hosp., Galveston, 1966-67; v.p. Meml. Hosp. System, Houston, 1969-78; exec. dir. Bapt. Meml. Hosp., Kansas City, Mo., 1978-80; pres. Hendrick Med. Ctr., Hendrick Med. Devel. Corp., Abilene, Tex., 1980—; dir. First Nat. Bank of Abilene. Bd. dirs. United Healthcare Systems, Kansas City, Hospice of Abilene, 1981—, Hosp. Receivables, Carrollton, Tex., 1983—, Untied Way, Abilene, Abilene Pastoral Care and Counseling Ctr., Abilene, 1981—. Served to lt. USPHS, 1967-69. Recipient W.F. Yates medallion William Jewell Coll., Liberty Mo., 1980. Mem. Am. Hosp. Assn., Am. Protestant Hosp. Assn. (bd. dirs. 1983—), Tex. Hosp. Assn. (chmn. Forts and Pecos div. 1983-84), Tex. Asn. Hosp. Auxs. (chmn. 1982-83), Abilene C. of C. Republican. Am. Baptist. Lodge: Abilene Kiwanis. Office: Hendrick Med Ctr N 19th and Hickory Sts Abilene TX 79601*

WATERS, ROLLIE ODELL, consulting firm executive; b. Charleston, S.C., Oct. 14, 1942; s. Rollie Robert and Mary Olivia (Brown) W.; A.A., Spartanburg Coll., 1968; B.S., U. S.C., 1969; M.B.A., Pepperdine U., 1980; m. Nancy Yvonne Chapman, May 3, 1975; children—Wendie Kay, Lauren Olivia. Supr. communications and spl. activities Owens-Corning Fiberglas, Aiken, S.C., 1970-71, asst. personnel dir., Fairburn, Ga., 1971-72; personnel dir. Meisel Photochrome Corp., Atlanta, 1972-73, dir. corp. personnel, Dallas, 1973-76, asst. v.p., dir. human resources, after 1976; sr. ptnr., chief exec. officer cons. firm Waters, Trego & Davis, 1979—1979-85, pres., chief exec. officer, 1985—; dir., program dir. 35th and 36th North Tex. Personnel Confs.; guest lectr. Lorch Found., London, Calif. Inst. Tech., Dallas C. of C., U. Md., Am. Mgmt. Assn., Pa. State U. Served with USAF, 1962-66. Mem. Am. Soc. Personnel Adminstrn. (nat. compensation and benefits com.), Am. Compensation Assn., Dallas Personnel Assn. (v.p. membership 1977-78), Am. Mgmt. Assn., Am. Soc. Tng. and Devel., Mensa, Psi Chi, Phi Theta Kappa, Omicron Delta Kappa, Beta Phi Gamma. Contbr. articles to profl. jours. Home: 278 Creekwood Lancaster TX 75146

WATERS, WILLIAM CARTER, III, internist, educator; b. Atlanta, Dec. 12, 1929; s. William Carter and Nannie Ellen (Starr) W.; m. Sarah Ann Bankston; children—William Carter IV, Sarah Walker Waters McEntire. A.B., Emory U., 1950, M.D., 1958. Diplomate Am. Bd. Internal Medicine, Am. Bd. Nephrology. Resident in internal medicine Grady Meml. Hosp., Emory U., Atlanta, 1958-60, 61-62; fellow in nephrology New Eng. Med. Ctr., 1960-61; practice medicine specializing in internal medicine and nephrology, Atlanta, 1962—; from instr. to assoc. prof. Emory U. Sch. Medicine, 1962-70, clin. assoc. prof., 1970—; chief staff internal medicine Piedmont Hosp., Atlanta. Served with USAF, 1951-52. Fellow ACP (gov. for Ga.); mem. Med. Assn. Met. Atlanta, Med. Assn. Ga., AMA, Am. Soc. Nephrology, Southeast Clin. Club. Methodist. Clubs: Atlanta Country, Big Canoe. Contbr. articles to med. jours. Office: 35 Collier Rd Suite 350 Atlanta GA 30309

WATKINS, A.J., lawyer; b. Austin, Tex., July 27, 1924; s. Beda D. and Winnie Juel (Roper) W.; m. Jean Voss, May 11, 1946; children—Gregory Lee, Rebecca Lynn Watkins Oliver. B.A., U. Tex., 1948; J.D., Harvard U., 1951. Bar: Tex. 1951, U.S. Dist. Ct. (ea. dist.) Tex., U.S. Dist. Ct. (we. dist.) Tex., U.S. Dist. Ct. (so. dist.) Tex., U.S. Ct. Appeals (5th cir.), U.S. Ct. Appeals (11th cir.), U.S. Supreme Ct. Briefing atty. Tex. Supreme Ct., Austin, 1951-52; assoc. Baker, Botts, Shepherd & Coates, Houston, 1952-63; ptnr. Baker, Heard, Elledge & Watkins, Houston, 1963-66; ptnr. Watkins, Ryan & Hamilton, Houston, 1966-70; ptnr. Watkins & Marshall, Housotn, 1970-73; mem. Law Offices of A.J. Watkins, Houston, 1973-82; ptnr. Watkins & Kempner, 1982—. Lectr. trial tactics Bates Coll. Law, U. Houston, 1967-68; juvenile adv. counsel Spring Branch Meml., 1966-71. Served with USMCR, 1943-45. Decorated Bronze Star. Fellow Tex. Bar Found. (life); mem. State Bar Tex. (advocacy com., dir.), Houston Bar Assn. (Pres.'s award 1978), Am. Bd. Trial Advs., Internat. Assn. Ins. Counsel (v.p. casualty ins. com. 1965-66), Houston C. of C. Home: 9673 Doliver St Houston TX 77056 Office: 3000 Smith St Houston TX 77006

WATKINS, CLIFTON EDWARD, JR., psychology educator; b. Westminster, S.C., Sept. 9, 1954; s. Clifton Edward and Betty (Land) W.; m. Wallene Grantland, Aug. 14, 1976. A.A., Anderson Coll., 1974; B.A., Carson-Newman Coll., 1976; M.A. in Edn., Western Carolina U., 1977; Ph.D., U. Tenn., 1984. Psychol. technician Knoxville Counseling Ctr., Tenn., 1977-78; psychotherapist Cherokee Mental Health Ctr., Morristown, Tenn., 1978-79; counselor Coll. Counseling Ctr., Jefferson City, Tenn., 1980-82; psychology intern VA Med. Ctr., Durham, N.C., 1983-84; asst. prof. psychology North Tex. State U., Denton, 1984—. Contbr. chpts. to books, articles to profl. jours. Mem. editorial bd. Individual Psychology Jour., 1984-87, Am. Mental Health Counselors Assn. Jour., 1984-87. Mem. exec. bd. Denton County Mental Health Ctrs., 1984—. Mem. Am. Assn. for Counseling Devel., Am. Psychol. Assn. Home: 1908 Parkside Denton TX 76201 Office: Dept Psychology N Tex State U Denton TX 76203

WATKINS, FELIX SCOTT, printing co. exec.; b. Sutton, W.Va., Nov. 27, 1946; s. Felix Sutton and Helena Sara (Cogar) W.; student W.Va. Inst. Tech.; m. Vivian L. Watkins, June 20, 1970; children—Jeffrey Scott, Jamie Leigh. Salesman, Kingsport Press (Tenn.), 1971-73; sales mgr. George Banta Co., N.Y.C., 1973-74; production mgr. Fuller Typesetting, Phila., 1974-75; account exec. Rocappi, Pennsauken, N.J., 1975-78; pres. Photo Data, Inc., Washington, 1978—. Mem. Washington Club Printing House Craftsman (1st v.p.), Washington Printing Guild, Printing Industries of Met. Washington (dir. master printers). Home: 9521 Orion Ct Burke VA 22015 Office: 419 7th St NW Washington DC 20004

WATKINS, HALCYON OLIVETTE, veterinarian, educator; b. Bryan, Tex., June 14, 1939; d. Oliver W. and Sylvia V. (Sealey) Sadberry; B.Sc., Tex. So. U., 1961; D.V.M., Tuskegee Inst., 1968; m. Aubrey B. Watkins, June 1, 1968; children—Russell S., Shane O. Vet. officer Republic of Guyana; asst. prof. biology Prairie View A&M U. (Tex.); veterinarian Stirling (N.J.) Animal Hosp.; now asst. prof. biology Tex. So. U., Houston; cardiovascular research, dept. pharmcology U. Houston; fellow virology dept. Baylor U., Houston, summer 1965. Pres.'s asso. Tuskegee Inst., 1982; recipient Tchr.'s Appreciation award Prairie View A&M U., 1969-70; postdoctoral fellow U. Houston. Mem. Coll. Tchrs. Adv. Assn., Nat. Inst. Sci., E.B.O.N.Y. Orgn. (pres. 1982-83), Beta Kappa Chi. Democrat. Roman Catholic. Office: 3200 Cleburn Ave Houston TX 77004

WATKINS, HAYS THOMAS, transportation executive; b. Fern Creek, Ky., Jan. 26, 1926; s. Hays Thomas and Minnie Catherine (Whiteley) W.; B.S. in Accounting, Western Ky. U., 1947; M.B.A., Northwestern U., 1948; m. Betty Jean Wright, 1950; 1 son, Hays Thomas III. With C.&O. Ry. Cleve., 1949-80, v.p. finance, 1964-67, v.p. adminstrv. group, 1967-71; pres., chief exec. officer, 1971-73, chmn. bd., chief exec. officer, 1973-80; with B.&O. R.R., 1964-80, v.p. finance, 1964-71, pres., chief exec. officer, 1971-73, vice chmn. bd., chief exec. officer, 1973-80; chmn., chief exec. officer Chessie System, Inc., 1973-80; pres. and co-chief exec. officer CSX Corp. (merger of Chessie System, Inc. and Seaboard Coast Line Industries, Inc.), Richmond, Va., 1980-82; chmn., chief exec. officer CSX Corp., 1982—; dir. Black & Decker Mfg. Co., Westinghouse Electric Corp., Bank of Va. Co. Chmn. Va. Ctr. Innovative Tech.; trustee, vice rector Coll. William and Mary; trustee Johns Hopkins U. Mus. Arts Assn. (Cleve. Orch.). Served with AUS, 1945-47. C.P.A. Mem. Nat. Assn. Accts., Am. Inst. C.P.A.s, Ohio Soc. C.P.A.s. Clubs: Center (Balt.); Commonwealth (Richmond, Va.); Sky (C.); Union (Cleve.) Country of Va. (Richmond). Home: 8912 Gingerway Dr Richmond VA 23229 Office: One James Ctr Richmond VA 23219

WATKINS, JERRY WEST, lawyer, oil company executive; b. Vernon, Tex., Dec. 10, 1931; s. Terrell Clark and Daisy Dean (West) W.; m. Elizabeth Jill Cole, Sept. 3, 1955. Student Hendrix Coll., 1949-50; La. Poly. Inst., 1950-51; LL.B., U. Ark., 1954. Bar: Ark. 1954. Law clk. Supreme Ct. Ark., 1954-55; landman Murphy Oil Corp., El Dorado, Ark., 1955-57, atty., 1957-66, sec., 1966—, gen. atty., 1966-71, gen. counsel, 1971—, v.p., dir., 1975—. Mem. Ark. Bd. Law Examiners, 1969-74; trustee Barton Library, El Dorado, 1966—, Ark. State U., 1982—, Warner Brown Hosp., El Dorado, bd. dirs. South Ark. Arts Ctr., 1979-82, 85—. Mem. Ark. Bar Assn., ABA, Am. Soc. Corp. Secs., Am. Petroleum Inst. Home: 111 Watkins Dr El Dorado AR 71730 Office: Murphy Oil Corp 200 Jefferson Ave El Dorado AR 71730

WATKINS, JOEL SMITH, JR., geophysicist, former oil company executive; b. Poteau, Okla., May 27, 1932; s. Joel Smith, Sr. and Eva (Byers) W.; m. Carolyn DeHaven Shoup, May 12, 1956 (div. 1971); m. Billie K. Dore, Mar. 27, 1971; children—Catherine D., Victoria B. A.B. in Geology, U. N.C., 1953; postgrad., U. Wis., 1956-58; Ph.D. in Geology, U. Tex., 1961. Prof., U. N.C., Chapel Hill, 1967-72, Mgmt. Sci. Inst., U. Tex., Galveston, 1973-77; exploration researcher Gulf Research and Devel. Co., Hamarille, Pa., 1977-81; exploration mgr. Gulf Oil, Houston, 1981-83, v.p. exploration research, 1983-85; co-investigator NASA, Houston, 1965-73; cons. U.S. Dept. Interior, Washington, 1983-84. Contbr. articles to profl. jours. Served to 1st lt. USMC, 1953-56. Recipient Exceptional Sci. Achievement medal NASA, 1973. Fellow Geol. Soc. Am. (v.p., pres. geophysics div. 1981-83, recipient spl. commendation 1972), Royal Astron. Soc.; mem. Am. Assn. Petroleum Geologists (assoc. editor 1984—), Soc. Exploration Geophysicists, Am. Geophys. Union. Club: Cosmos (Washington). Home: 6724 Vanderbilt Houston TX 77005

WATKINS, JOHN CLETIS, lawyer; b. Black Oak, Ark., Mar. 26, 1917; s. Joseph Cleveland and Sylvia Ann (Hamilton) W.; m. Arna Lana Shields, Sept. 11, 1924; 1 child, Mary lana Watkins Schult. Student Ark. State U., 1939-40, 46-48; J.D., U. Ark., 1952. Practice law, West Memphis, Ark., 1951-54, Paragould, Ark., 1954-73; of counsel Joe Hollifield, Paragould; mcpl. judge City of Paragould, 1959-63. Author: (novel) With Another Mans Gold, 1986. Served to sgt. AUS, 1940-45. Mem. Greene Clay Bar Assn. (pres. 1965), Ark. Bar Assn., VFW, Am. Legion, DAV. Lodge: Masons. Home: 28 Hillcrest Dr Paragould AR 72450

WATKINS, LEWIS BOONE, artist; b. Beckely, W.Va., July 24, 1945; s. Fred Boone and Margaret Theodoris (Laurie) W.; m. Marinda Ann Hogan, Aug. 18, 1979; children—Mary Sheridan, Marinda Laurie. B.S., W.Va. State Coll., 1978; postgrad. U. South Fla., 1979-82. Artist in residence Boxwood Gallery, Brooksville, Fla., 1978-79; instr. of gifted, Hernando County, Fla., 1979-81; artist in residence Casa Serena Gallery, Brooksville, 1981—; vis. artist W. Va. State Coll., Samford U., St. Leo Coll., U. Tampa (Fla.); works include numerous lithograph print edits., sculpture represented in permanent collections Fla. State Mus., U. Fla., Gainesville, Vatican Mus., Vatican City, Italy, W.Va. Fine Arts and Cultural Ctr., Charleston, also numerous pvt. collections; sculptures include Hernando Heritage Sculpture, 1981, Crosses of Life, 1982, Youth of Today, 1983; Am. Farmer Meml. Sculpture, Bonner, Kans., 1986. Bd. advisors Hernando County YMCA (Fla.); pres. Boxwood Art Guild, 1978; treas. Hernando County Young Republicans, 1981. Recipient various awards including Ambassador Artistic Achievement award State of W.Va., 1981; Outstanding Achievement award State of Fla., 1982; proclamation declaring Lewis Watkins Day, Hernando County, Fla., 1981; cert. of Recognition in Art, State of Ga., 1983, award for sculpture, Tampa, Fla., 1984, Pub. Service award City of Atlanta, 1984. Mem. Hernando Heritage Mus. Assn. (bd. dirs.), Hernando County C. of C.

WATKINS, PAUL JUNNES, III, psychological counselor, alcohol counselor; b. Bklyn., Oct. 13, 1947; s. Paul Junnes and Elizabeth Mae (Taylor) W.; m. Doris Junnetta Green, Aug. 31, 1969 (div. Apr. 1980); 1 child, David Lamarcus; m. Wanda Joyce Thomas, July 18, 1981; 1 child, Candice Nichole. B.A. in Polit. Sci., Fla. A. and M. U., 1971, postgrad., 1974-77. Disability examiner Health and Rehab. Services, Tallahassee, Fla., 1973-78; program cons. Dept. Community Affairs, Tallahassee, 1978-82; employment interviewer Div. Employment & Tng., Tampa, 1983; alcohol counselor II, Pinellas County Alcohol Services, Clearwater, Fla., 1984—; psychol. counselor Operation PAR, St. Petersburg, Fla., 1984—. Mem. policy adv. com. Tampa Urban League, 1982—; bd. dirs. Hillsborough Sickle Cell Assn., Tampa, 1983—, Split Feather Indian Council, Safety Harbour, Fla., 1983—. Named Little League Coach of Yr., Kiwanis Little League Team, Tallahassee, 1982. Mem. Ams. for Substance Abuse Prevention, Fla. Assn. Alcohol and Drug Abuse, Fla. A&M U. Alumni Assn., Omega Psi Phi. Democrat. Episcopalian. Avocation: sports. Home: 12615 Logan Pl Tampa FL 33625 Office: Operation PAR 1900 9th St S Saint Petersburg FL 33705

WATKINS, SAMUEL RAYBURN, association executive; b. Benton, Ky., Apr. 21, 1923; s. Gipp and Keron (Wyatt) W.; student Tufts U., 1942-43; B.S. in History, Econs. and Journalism, Murray State U., 1944; M.S. in Mass Communications, History and Econs., U. Ill., 1951; m. Evelyn W. Ellis, Mar. 6, 1954; children—Julia Ellis, Samuel R. Night editor S.I. (N.Y.) Advance, 1946-48; instr. journalism U. Ill., 1948-49; editor, pub. Tribune-Democrat, Benton, 1948-54; adminstrv. sec. Louisville Area C. of C., 1950-55; pres. Assoc. Industries of Ky., Louisville, 1955-85; exec. v.p. Ky. Safety Council, 1980—. Pres. Nat. Labor-Mgmt. Found., 1970—; mem. Pres.' Com. on Employment of Physically Handicapped, 1968-72; mem. Ky. Labor Mgmt. Adv. Council, 1979—; vice chmn. Ky. Employer Com. Support Guard and Res., 1979-84, chmn., 1985—. Served to lt. USNR, 1942-46. Recipient Disting. Alumnus award Murray State U., 1979. Mem. Am. Soc. Assn. Execs. (past pres., chartered assn. exec.), Govt. Research Assn., Kappa Delta Pi, Tau Kappa Alpha, Sigma Delta Chi. Clubs: Louisville Pendennis, Louisville Boat. Author: Management Success Patterns, 1965; How to Be A Good Supervisor, 1969; Management Strategy in Labor Relations, 1970. Home: 2704 Poplar Hill Ct Louisville KY 40207 Office: 200 W Chestnut St Louisville KY 40202

WATKINS, VINCENT GATES, supermarket executive, real estate broker; b. Wichita, Kans., Nov. 27, 1945; s. Joseph Wade and Martha Geneve (Gates) W.; m. Josephine Anna Prickett, July 6, 1968 (div. 1985); children—Paul Clayton, Jason Wade, Vernon Curtis. B.S. in Real Estate and Urban Devel., Am. U., 1973; M.B.A., Wake Forest U., 1976. Mortgage loan officer Better Homes Realty, Arlington, Va., 1969-72, Carey Winston Co., McLean, Va., 1972-73; real estate officer, property mgr. NCNB Nat. Bank, Charlotte, N.C., 1973-77; v.p. spl. projects and devel. Food Lion, Inc., Salisbury, N.C., 1977—; pres. In Good Spirits, Ltd., Little River, S.C. mem. bus. adv. council East Carolina U., Greenville, N.C., 1984—; dive control specialist Scuba Schs. Internat., Fort Collins, Colo., 1984. Mem. Civitan, Am. Soc. Tng. and Devel., Am. Mgmt. Assn., Les Amies du Vin. Lutheran. Clubs: Tower (Charlotte), High Rock Ski (Salisbury). Avocations: scuba diving; racketball; snow and water skiing; cooking; carpentry. Home: 10 Waters Edge Salisbury NC 28144 Office: Food Lion Inc PO Box 1330 Salisbury NC 28144

WATKINS, WESLEY LEE, accountant; b. Norfolk, Va., Dec. 4, 1953; s. Morrell and Mary Elizabeth (Washington) W. B.S., Norfolk State U., 1977. Inventory acct. specialist Norfolk State U. Bookstore (Va.), 1977-79; acct-./auditor DMTS, HEW, 1979-80; acct. McClure Lundberry Assocs., 1980-81; contractual acct. Acad. Contemporary Problems, Washington, 1982; fin. cons. Watkins & Watkins, Washington, 1982—, Watkins Auto Shop, Norfolk, 1983-84. Bd. dirs. Jerusalem Baptist Ch. Credit Union, 1976—. Mem. NAACP, Nat. Assn. Accts., Nat. Assn. Black Accts., Phi Beta Lambda. Democrat. Home: 5019 Fillmore Ave #100 Alexandria VA 22311

WATKINS, WESLEY WADE, congressman; b. DeQueen, Ark., Dec. 15, 1938; B.S. in Agr. Edn., Okla. State U., 1960; M.S. in Ednl. Adminstrn., 1961; m. Elizabeth Lou Rogers, June 9, 1963; children—Sally, Martha, Wade. Mem. staff Dept. Agr., Washington, 1963; asst. dir. admissions Okla. State U., 1963-66; exec. dir. Kiamichi Econ. Devel. Dist., Okla., 1966-68; owner, operator constrn. bus., 1968-76; mem. Okla. Senate, 1974-76; mem. 95th-98th Congresses from 3d Okla. Dist., chmn. Congressional Rural Caucus, mem. ho. appropriations com.; mem. Democratic Steering Com. Past Okla. chmn. Nat. Future Farmers Am. Found. Served with Air N.G., 1961-67. Recipient award Nat. Fedn. Ind. Bus., 1977-78; Guardian of Small Bus. award; Recognition award Okla. 4-H; Disting. Alumnus award Okla. State U. Presbyterian. Clubs: Masons, Lions. Office: 2440 Rayburn House Office Bldg Washington DC 20515

WATKINS, WILLIAM LAW, lawyer; b. Anderson, S.C., Dec. 26, 1910; s. Thomas Franklin and Agnes (Law) W.; A.B., Wofford Coll., 1932; LL.B., U. Va., 1933; m. Frances Sitton, Oct. 23, 1937; children—Sarah (Mrs. Allen S. Marshall), Anna (Mrs. Alexander C. Hattaway III), Elizabeth (Mrs. Anderson Mills Kinghorn, Jr.), Jane (Mrs. Roger W. Mudd). Admitted to S.C. bar, 1933; since practiced in Anderson; mem. firm Watkins & Prince, 1936-46, Watkins & Watkins, 1946-54, Watkins, Vandiver & Freeman, 1954-64, Watkins, Vandiver, Kirven & Long, 1964-67, Watkins, Vandiver, Kirven, Long & Gable, 1968-77; mem. firm Watkins, Vandiver, Kirven, Gable & Gray, 1977-84, of counsel, 1984—; dir. emeritus Duke Power Co., Perpetual Fed. Savs. & Loan Assn. Mem. S.C. Ho. of Reps., 1935-36; mem. S.C. Probation, Parole and Pardon Bd., 1954-69. Trustee Presbyn. Coll., Clinton, S.C., 1966-75, Anderson County Hosp. Assn., 1964-74. Served with AUS, 1942-46. Decorated Bronze Star with oak leaf cluster. Fellow Am. Coll. Trial Lawyers, Am. Bar Found.; mem. Am., S.C., Anderson bar assns., Phi Beta Kappa, Sigma Alpha Epsilon. Presbyn. Club: Rotary. Home: 317 North St Anderson SC 29621 Office: 500 S McDuffie St Anderson SC 29624

WATSON, BETTY JEAN SMITH, medical technologist; b. Fairfield, Ala., Nov. 15, 1929; d. Gilbert Fram and Lela Mae (Wood) Smith; m. Richard Morey Watson, Aug. 30, 1952; children—Gilbert Morey, Richard Alan, Nancy Jean. B.S. in Med. Tech., Auburn U., 1951. Trainee Lloyd Noland Hosp., Fairfield, 1951-52; med. technologist, research dept. Strong Meml. Hosp., Rochester, N.Y., 1953, Holston Valley Community Hosp., Kingsport, Tenn., 1968-74; gen. technologist Pathology Assos. (Now Medex Labs. of Pathology Assos.), Kingsport, 1974-76, lab. supr., 1976—. Treas. Diversified Study Club, 1954-55. Mem. Am. Soc. Clin. Pathologists, Clin. Ligand Assay Soc. Presbyterian (elder). Club: Auburn Alumni (Kingsport). Home: 4325 Stagecoach Rd Kingsport TN 37664 Office: 102 E Ravine St Kingsport TN 37660

WATSON, BURL STEVENS, management consultant; b. N.Y.C., June 15, 1927; s. Burl Stevens and Emitom (Burns) W.; m. Nita Jean Burnett, Oct. 4, 1956; children—Burl Douglas, Emily Jean, Byron Stevens. B.S. in Elec. Engring., Worcester Poly. Inst., 1950; cert. exec. program Columbia U., 1969. Registered profl. engr., Okla. Sales engr. Ethyl Corp., Los Angeles, 1954-57; with Cities Service Co., Tulsa, 1957-83, dir. internat. treasury, 1970-79, dir. corp. fin., 1979-83; cons. in field. Mem. Tulsa County Exec. Com.; trustee Coll. of Ozarks; active Republican Party, 1950—. Served to lt. USAF, 1950-54. Mem. Am. Petroleum Inst., Fin. Execs. Inst. Presbyterian. Club: Summit (Tulsa). Home: 3442 E 61st Pl Tulsa OK 74136

WATSON, DARLIENE KEENEY, painter; b. Amarillo, Tex., Mar. 16, 1929; d. James L. and Anna G. (Reimers) Keeney; m. David Alton Watson, Aug. 14, 1953; children—Gregory, Kendra, Kathryn, Steven. Student Amarillo Coll., 1947-49, Art Inst. Chgo., 1949; B.F.A., Colo. U., 1953. Illustrator, Amarillo AFB, Tex., 1953-56; pvt. art tchr., Oklahoma City, 1963-66, Linwood, N.J., 1966-68; art tchr. Fairfax County Schs., Va., 1976-78, No. Va. Community Coll., Manassas, 1980-82; judge 13th ann. exhbn. Sumi-e Soc. Am., 1978; dir. Herndon Old Town Gallery, Va., 1985—. Exhbns. include: Potomac Valley Watercolorists, Va., D.C., Md., 1973-85, Sumi-e Soc. Am., Washington, N.Y.C., 1983-85, Va. Watercolor Soc., Charlottesville, 1984 S. Watercolor Soc. represented in permanent collection St. John's U., Jamaica, N.Y. Mem. Sumi-e Soc. Am. (chpt. chair 1976-78), Va. Watercolor Soc., Potomac Valley Watercolor Soc., So. Watercolor Soc., Ga. Watercolor Soc. Presbyterian.

WATSON, DAVID BRUCE, psychologist, researcher; b. Monterey Park, Calif., Aug. 20, 1953; s. Richard Haley and Lois Audrey (Bercaw) W.; m. Lee Anna Clark, June 23, 1979; children—Bartholomew Clark, Erica Watson Clark. B.S., U. Santa Clara, 1975; Ph.D., U. Minn., 1982. NIMH postdoctoral research fellow dept. psychiatry Washington U. Sch. Medicine, St. Louis, 1982-84; adj. asst. prof. dept. psychology So. Methodist U., Dallas, 1984-85, vis. asst. prof., 1985—. Contbr. articles to sci. jours. Bush Found. fellow, St. Paul, 1975-78; research grantee U. Minn. Found., Mpls., 1980. Mem. Am. Psychol. Assn. Democrat. Avocations: medieval and early modern European history; art; classical music; films; sports. Home: 7220 Lehigh Dr Dallas TX 75214 Office: Dept Psychology So Meth U Dallas TX 75275

WATSON, DONALD CHARLES, cardiothoracic surgeon, educator; b. Fairfield, Ohio, Mar. 15, 1945; s. Donald Charles and Pricilla W.; m. Susan Robertson Prince, June 23, 1973; children—Kea Huntington, Katherine Anne, Kirsten Prince. B.A. in Applied Sci. Lehigh U., 1968, B.S., in Mech. Engring., 1968; M.S. in Mech. Engring., Stanford U., 1969; M.D., Duke U., 1972. Diplomate Am. Bd. Thoracic Surgery, Am. Bd. Surgery. Intern in surgery Stanford U. Med. Ctr., Calif., 1972-73, resident in cardiovascular surgery, 1973-74, resident in surgery, 1976-78, chief resident in heart transplant, 1978-79, chief resident in cardiovascular and gen. surgery, 1978-80; clin. assoc. surgery br. Nat. Heart and Lung Inst., 1974-76, acting sr. surgeon, 1976; assoc. cardiovascular surgeon dept. child health and devel. George Washington U., Washington, 1980-83, asst. prof. surgery, asst. prof. child health and devel., 1980-84, attending cardiovascular surgeon dept. child health and devel., 1983-84; assoc. prof. surgery, assoc. prof. pediatrics U. Tenn.-Memphis, 1984—, chmn. cardiothoracic surgery, 1984—; mem. staff Le Bonheur children's Med. Ctr., Memphis, chmn. cardiothoracic surgery, 1984—; mem. staff William F. Bowld Med. Ctr., Memphis, Regional Med. ctr. at Memphis, Baptist Meml. Med. Ctr., Memphis; cons. in field; instr. advanced trauma life support; profl. cons., program reviewer HHS. Contbr. chpts., numerous articles, revs. to profl. pubs. Served to lt. comdr. USPHS, 1974-76. Smith Kline & French fellow Lehigh U., 1967; NSF fellow Lehigh U., 1968; univ. interdepartmental scholar and univ. scholar Lehigh U., 1968. Fellow Am. Coll. Cardiology, Am. Coll. Chest Physicians (forum cardiovascular surgery, council critical care), Southeastern Surg. Congress, Am. Acad. Pediatrics (surgery sect.); mem. Assn. Surg. Edn., Am. Assn. Thoracic Surgery, Soc. Thoracic Surgeons, So. Thoracic Surg. Assn., Am. Thoracic Soc., Assn. Acad. Surgery, Internat. Soc. Heart Transplantation, Am. Fedn. Clin. Research, Found. Advanced Edn. in Scis., Andrew G. Morrow Soc., Council on Cardiovascular Surgery of Am. Heart Assn., AAAS, N.Y. Acad. Sci., AMA, NIH Alumni Assn., Stanford U. Med. Alumni Assn., Duke U. Med. Alumni Assn., Duke U. Alumni Assn., Stanford U. Alumni Assn., Lehigh U. Alumni Assn., Smithsonian Assocs., Sierra Club, U. Tenn. Pres.'s Club, LeBonheur Pres.'s Club, U.S. Yacht Racing Assn., Pilots Internat. Assn., Nat. Assn. Flight Instrs., Aircraft Owners and Pilots Assn., Order Ky. Cols., Phi Beta Kappa, Tau Beta Pi, Pi Tau Sigma, Phi Gamma Delta. Republican. Presbyterian. Club: Memphis Racquet. Avocations: sailing; racquet sports; flying. Office: U Tenn 956 Court Ave Room E 230 Memphis TN 38163

WATSON, EDWARD EUGENE, fire protection engineer; b. Terre Haute, Ind., Aug. 2, 1946; s. Edward E. and Dorothy Evelyn (Conklin) W.; m. Mary Catherine Edrington, June 21, 1980. B.S., So. Ill. U., 1969. Resident engr. Factory Mutual Engring., St. Louis, 1969-77; sales rep. Fendall, Memphis, 1978-79; cons. Royal Ins., Charlotte, N.C., 1979—. Mem. Nat. Fire Protection Assn., Soc. Fire Protection Engrs., Am. Soc. Safety Engrs. Democrat. Baptist. Avocations: racquetball; golf. Home: 723 Conestoga Dr Matthews NC 28105 Office: Royal Ins 9300 Arrowpoint Charlotte NC 28210

WATSON, GREGORY HARRISS, defense systems analyst, consulting company executive; b. Englewood, N.J., July 16, 1948; s. Robert John and Anne Faye (Bellotte) W.; B.A. cum laude, Taylor U., 1970; M.S., U. So. Calif., 1975; diploma, Nat. Def. U., 1981; m. Cynthia Sue Sandberg, June 6, 1971 (div. 1983); 1 son, Andrew Daniel. Grad. fellow in philosophy Am. U., Washington, 1970-71; commd. ensign U.S. Navy, 1971, advanced through grades to lt., 1976, resigned, 1977; regional mgr., sr. analyst San Jose (Calif.) Office for Atlantic Analysis Corp., 1977-78; profl. staff Center for Naval Analyses (affiliate U. Rochester), Alexandria, Va., 1978-80; recalled to active duty, promoted to lt. comdr., 1980; weapon system acquisition mgr., 1981-83; pres. So. Cons. Services, Inc., 1983—; adj. prof. systems acquisition Def. Systems Mgmt. Coll., 1981; instr. continuing edn. Naval Postgrad. Sch., 1977. Mem. Mil. Ops. Research Soc., Ops. Research Soc. Am., Naval Inst. Republican. Home: 6120 Edsall Rd Apt 201 Alexandria VA 22304

WATSON, JACK BORDEN, JR., sociology educator; b. Tyler, Tex., Jan. 15, 1954; s. Jack Borden and Billie Marie (Anderson) W.; m. Rita Dale Nelson, Dec. 30, 1978; children—Jack Borden, Mary Etta. B.A., N.E. La. U., 1976; M.A., Tex. Christian U., 1978; postgrad. N.Tex. State U., 1977-82, 83—. Grad. asst. sociology dept. Tex. Christian U., Fort Worth, 1976-78; teaching fellow N. Tex. State U. sociology dept., Denton, 1977-81, research asst. Ctr. on Aging, 1978-82; asst. prof. sociology Miss. Coll., Clinton, 1982—. Co-author jour. articles. Dir. nursing home ministry First Baptist Ch., Clinton, 1984—, Sunday Sch. tchr., 1984—; mem. YMCA, Jackson, Miss., Childbirth Edn. Assn., Jackson. Mem. Gerontol. Soc. Am., Am. Sociol. Assn., Assn. for Sci. Study of Religion Southwest, Mid-South Sociol. Assn., Miss. Council on Family Relations, N.E. La. U. Alumni Assn. (bd. dirs. 1983—), N.E. La. U. Sociology Alumni Assn. (pres. Monroe, 1983—), Alpha Kappa Delta, Pi Gamma Mu. Avocations: Running; camping; racquetball. Office: Dept Sociology Miss Coll PO Box 4166 Clinton MS 39058

WATSON, JACK CROZIER, state court justice; b. Jonesville, La., Sept. 17, 1928; s. Jesse Crozier and Gladys (Talbot) W.; B.A., U. Southwestern La., 1949; LL.B., La. State U., 1956; m. Sue Carter, Dec. 28, 1958; children—Carter (dec.), Wells. Bar: La. 1956. Practiced in Lake Charles, La., 1956-64; mem. firm Watson & Watson, 1960-64; prosecutor City of Lake Charles, 1960; asst. dist. atty. 14th Jud. Dist. La., 1961-64; dist. judge 14th Jud. Dist. La., Lake Charles, 1964-72; judge ad hoc 1st Circuit Ct. Appeal, 1972-73, 3d Circuit Ct. Appeal, 1974-79; justice La. Supreme Ct., 1979—. Faculty, adv. Nat. Coll. State Judiciary, 1970, 73; mem. La. Jud. Council, 1972-74; del. Internat. Conf. Appellate Magistrates, Manila, 1977. Served to 1st lt. USAF, 1950-54. Mem. Am. Bar Assn., La. Bar Assn., S.W. La. Bar Assn. (pres. 1973), Nat. Council Juvenile Ct. Judges (pres. La. council 1969-70), Am. Legion, S.W. La. Camellia Soc. (pres. 1973—), Blue Key, Sigma Alpha Epsilon, Phi Delta Phi, Pi Kappa Delta. Club: Lake Charles Yacht (commodore 1970). Home: 5018 DeSoto St Lake Charles LA 70605 Office: 301 Loyola Ave New Orleans LA 70112 also 368 Audubon St New Orleans LA 70118 also 5018-C DeSoto St Lake Charles LA 70605

WATSON, JERRY ALLAN, geologist, consultant; b. Lubbock, Tex., Aug. 14, 1935; s. Clarence Emmett and Lena (Porter) W.; m. Cozette Terrell, July 17, 1955; children—Steven Allan, Mark Porter, Dana Cozette, Lee Ann. B.S. in Geology, Tex. Western Coll., 1961; M.S. in Oceanography, Tex. A&M U., 1968. Cert. petroleum geologist; cert. profl. geologist. Geologist, Standard Oil, Midland, Tex., 1961-66; oceanographer Tex. Instruments, Dallas, 1966-72; pres. Geo-Marine, Inc., Richardson, Tex., 1972-78; geologist Gruy Cos., Houston, 1978-79; v.p. W.L. Tidwell & Assocs., Houston, 1979-81; cons. geology, Houston, 1981—. Contbr. articles to profl. jours. Served with USAF, 1955-57. Mem. Am. Assn. Petroleum Geologists, Am. Inst. Profl. Geologists (editor Tex. sect. 1985), Soc. Ind. Profl. Earth Scis., Houston Geol. Soc. (editor bull. 1983-84), Dallas Geol. Soc. Home: 12843 Ashford Chase Houston TX 77082 Office: 11490 Westheimer 5410 Houston TX 77077

WATSON, JERRY FRANKLIN, gen. surgeon; b. Martin, Tenn., Aug. 30, 1936; s. Paul Leon and Alta Mae (Stringer) W.; student David Lipscomb Coll., Nashville, 1954-55; A.A., U. Tenn., Martin, 1957, M.D., Memphis, 1960; m. Doris Maurine Harris, June 15, 1957; children—Edith Maurine, Susan Kay, Anne Marie. Intern John Gaston Hosp., Memphis, 1960-61; commd. capt. AUS, 1961, advanced through grades to lt. col., 1972; resident surgery Brooke Gen. Hosp., San Antonio, 1964-68; comdg. officer 44th Surg. Hosp., Korea, 1969-70; chief dept. surgery DeWitt Army Hosp., Ft. Belvoir, Va., 1970-72; pvt. practice gen. surgery, North Wilkesboro, N.C., 1972—; mem. staff Wilkes Gen. Hosp., North Wilkesboro, 1972—, chief dept. surgery, 1982—. Diplomate Am. Bd. Surgery. Fellow ACS, Internat. Coll. Surgeons, Southeastern Surg. Congress; mem. AMA, Assn. Mil. Surgeons, Alpha Omega Alpha. Baptist (deacon 1974—). Club: Kiwanis. Home: 605 Magnolia Rd North Wilkesboro NC 28659 Office: Corner C and 8th Sts North Wilkesboro NC 28659

WATSON, KITTIE WELLS, speech communication educator; b. Newburgh, N.Y., July 31, 1953; d. Cody Usry and Bettie Richards (Todd) Watson. A.A., Gainesville Jr. Coll., 1973; B.S., U. Ga., 1975; M.A., Auburn U., 1977; Ph.D., La. State U., 1981. Cert. tchr., Ga. Grad. teaching asst. Auburn U. (Ala.), 1975-77, instr., 1977-79; instr. Tulane U., New Orleans, 1979-81, asst. prof. speech communication, 1981-85, assoc. prof., 1985—, also acting head dept. speech communication, 1981-82, chmn. dept., 1982-84; assoc. dir. Inst. Study of Intrapersonal Processes; staff writer and reviewer Prentice-Hall, Wm. C. Brown, Addison Wesley pub. cos.; co-owner, v.p. SPECTRA Communication Assocs.; co-owner SPECTRA Creations. Mem. editorial bd. several jours. Author: Instructional Objectives and Evaluation, 1980; Effective Listening, 1983; contbr. numerous articles to scholarly jours.; creator audio tapes: Watson-Barker Listening Test; Willing Yourself to Listen. Mem. Am. Council for Career Women. Recipient Mortar Bd. Teaching Excellence award Tulane U., 1982. Mem. Speech Communication Assn., Internat. Communication Assn., So. Speech Communication Assn., Eastern Speech Assn., Am. Soc. Tng. and Devel., Internat. Listening Assn. (member-at-large, chmn. research com.), Delta Delta Delta. Home: 119 Avenue E Metairie LA 70005 Office: Dept Communication Newcomb Hall Tulane U New Orleans LA 70118

WATSON, LAUREN HILDITCH, quality assurance specialist; b. Chester, Pa., Aug. 13, 1949; d. Albert Edwin and Louise (Price) Hilditch; m. Aubrey Pliny Watson, Dec. 19, 1981. A.A., Harcum Coll., Bryn Mawr, Pa., 1969; B.S., West Chester U., 1974, M.A., 1976; postgrad. U. North Ala., 1984—. Research asst. U. Pa., Phila., 1969-71; instr. Harcum Coll., 1971; indsl. microbiologist supt. Wyeth Pharm. Co., West Chester, Pa., 1973-75; quality assurance specialist Reynolds Metals Co., Sheffield, Ala., 1978—; grad. asst. West Chester U., 1976; research asst. U. Ala., Birmingham, 1977. Patron Tennessee Valley Arts Assn., 1983, Muscle Shoals Concert Assn., 1977. Mem. Am. Soc. Quality Control (membership chmn. 1983, edn. chmn., 1984, program chmn. 1985), Internat. Assn. Quality Circles. Office: Reynolds Metal Co PO Box 910 Sheffield AL 35660

WATSON, PAUL FRANCIS, company executive; b. Wilmington, Del., Nov. 20, 1932; s. Elmer and Sara Louise (Woodburn) W.; m. Josephine Smith, May 5, 1958; children—Leroy, Nicola. B.S.E.E., Bridgeport Engring. Inst., 1964. Ordained permanent deacon Roman Catholic Ch., 1983. Electronic technician Stelma Inc., Stamford, Conn., 1958-60; mgr., configuration mgmt. Barnes Engring Co., Stamford, 1960-74; asst. to v.p. engring. Homelite Div. of Textron, Byram, Conn., 1974-76, mgr. product integrity, Charlotte, N.C., 1976-82, mgr. product safety, 1982—. Adviser Woman's Aglow Evening Chpt., Charlotte, 1983-85; v.p. non-denominational Evangelist Ministry, Charlotte, 1980—. Served with U.S.A.F., U.S. Army, 1950-57. Home: 1516 Plumstead Rd Charlotte NC 28216 Office: Homelite-Div of Textron 14401 Carowinds Blvd Charlotte NC 28217

WATSON, PHIL, state senator; b. Aug. 31, 1933; B.A. Harding Coll., 1959; M.A., U. Mo., 1960. Ordained to ministry Ch. of Christ, 1956; minister Ch. of Christ, Columbia Mo., 1959-61; v.p. for devel., Okla. Christian Coll., 1961-67; minister Ch. of Christ, Edmond Okla. 1967-72; in real estate ins., commercial properties 1964—; mem. Okla. Senate, 1973—. Chmn. bd. dirs. Zambia Christian Schs., 1984—. Home: Edmond OK 73034

WATSON, ROBERT ALLAN, lawyer; b. San Diego, Calif., Dec. 30, 1933; s. Albert Orville and Nadia Florence (Herman) W.; m. Elizabeth Ellen Payne, Apr. 7, 1956; children—Terri Elizabeth, Robert Allan, Leslie Margaret, Richard Payne. B.S.C., Tex. Christian U., 1955; J.D., So. Meth. U., 1958. Bar: Tex. 1958, D.C. 1981; cert. estate planning and probate law, tax law Tex. Bd. Legal Specializations, 1977. With Office of Regional Counsel, IRS, Atlanta, 1958-59; atty. advisor Tax Ct. U.S., 1960; with Cantey, Hanger, Johnson, Scarborough & Gooch, and successor firms, 1961-79, Watson, Ice & McGee, Ft. Worth, 1979-84, Watson, Ice, McGee, Morgan, Hughes & Liles, 1984—; dir. Merc. Nat. Bank Arlington. Trustee, Tex. Christian U. Fellow Am. Coll.

Probate Counsel; mem. Tex. Bar Assn., D.C. Bar Assn., Ft. Worth/Tarrant County Bar Assn., ABA, Fed. Bar Assn., Tex. Bar Found. Republican. Mem. Christian Ch. Clubs: Ft. Worth, Colonial Country, Masons. Home: 4444 Overton Crest Fort Worth TX 76109 Office: 1212 Texas American Bank Bldg Fort Worth TX 76102

WATSON, ROBERT WINTHROP, author, educator; b. Passaic, N.J., Dec. 26, 1925; s. Winthrop and Laura Berdan (Trimble) W.; m. Elizabeth Rean, Jan. 12, 1952; children—Winthrop, Caroline. B.A., Williams Coll., 1946; Swiss Am. exchange fellow U. Zurich, 1946-47; M.A., Johns Hopkins U., 1950, Ph.D., 1955. Instr. English, Williams Coll., 1946, 1947-48, 1952-53, Johns Hopkins U., 1950-52; instr. U. N.C.-Greensboro, 1953-55, asst. prof., 1955-59, assoc. prof., 1959-63, prof., 1963—, dir. assoc. writing programs, 1957-72; vis. prof. Calif. State U.-Northridge, 1968-69. Served with USN, 1943-45. Recipient Am. Scholar Poetry prize, 1959; Lit. award Am. Acad. and Inst. Arts and Letters, 1977; fellow Nat. Endowment Arts, 1976. Author: A Paper Horse, 1962, Advantages of Dark, 1966, Christmas in Las Vegas, 1971, Selected Poems, 1974, Night Blooming Cactus, 1980, Three Sides of the Mirror, 1966, Lily Lang, 1979. Address: Dept English University of NC Greensboro NC 27412

WATSON, TERRY R., osteopathic physician; b. Fort Worth, Nov. 10, 1950; s. Orlette and Frances (Terry) W. B.S. with honors, U. Tex., 1974; D.O., North Tex. State U., 1978. Resident physician, Parkland Hosp., Dallas, 1978-79, Presbyn. Hosp., Dallas, 1979; gen. practice medicine, Dallas, 1980—; chief gen. practice dept. Mesquite Community Hosp., Dallas, 1983; active med. staff Med. City Dallas Hosp., Meth. Hosps. Dallas; also real estate investor. Instr. Heart O'Tex. council Boy Scouts Am.; big bro. Big Bros. Am., 1970-74; vol. dr. Buckner Bapt. Children's Home, Dallas, 1982-84. Recipient Eagle Scout award Boy Scouts Am. 1968. Mem. Tex. Med. Assn., Am. Osteo. Assn., Sigma Phi Epsilon. Club: Atlas. Avocations: coin collecting; antique automobiles; snow skiing. Office: Family Med Ctr 9709 Bruton Rd Dallas TX 75217

WATSON, WELDON WARD, JR., automotive company executive; b. Cairo, Ill., May 25, 1947; s. Weldon Ward and Alfreda Ree (Shortz) W.; m. Nancy Ann Hauber, Mar. 19, 1974; 1 dau., Stephanie Hauber. B.S. in Engring. Mgmt., U. Mo. Schedule planner Deere & Co., Dubuque, Iowa, 1973, prodn. supr., 1973-77, gen. supr., 1977-81; dir. prodn. Zimmer Motorcars Corp., Pompano Beach, Fla., 1981-82, v.p. mfg., 1982—. Bd. dirs. Dubuque Area chpt. Am. Nat. ARC, 1976-81. Mem. Am. Soc. Engring. Mgmt., Am. Mgmt. Assn. Democrat. Baptist. Home: 1076 NW 84th Dr Coral Springs FL 33065 Office: 777 SW 12th Ave Pompano Beach FL 33060

WATSON, WILLIAM DOWNING, JR., economist, educator; b. Durango, Colo., Aug. 9, 1938; s. William Downing and Carrie Elizabeth (Bailey) Blanchard; m. Dolores Marie Boisclair, Sept. 7, 1968; children—Kelli, Adam, Seth. B.A. in Math., No. Colo. U., 1964; M.A. in Econs., Syracuse U., 1965; Ph.D. in Econs., U. Minn., 1970. Asst. prof. Wash. State U., Pullman, 1971-72; economist EPA-Washington, 1972-73; sr. fellow Resources for the Future, Washington, 1973-78; adj. prof. Va. Poly. Inst. and State U., Falls Ch., 1981—; economist U.S. Geol. Survey, Reston, Va., 1978—; staff economist dirs. office U.S. Geol. Survey, Reston, 1984—. Author: To Choose a Future, 1980; contbr. articles to profl. jours. Served with U.S. Army, 1956-59. Earhart fellow, U. Minn., 1967; Resources for the Future Dissertation fellow, Washington, 1969. Mem. Am. Econs. Assn., Internat. Assn. Energy Economists, Assn. Environ. and Resource Economists. Avocations: tennis; hiking; skiing. Home: 1927 Upper Lake Dr Reston VA 22091

WATTERS, RAYMOND WENDELL, family medicine physician; b. Cin., Apr. 14, 1948; s. Lawrence Lauder and Lelia Wanda (Odell) W.; m. Vicki Jean Caccia, July 20, 1985. Student Union Coll., 1966-67; B.S., Purdue U., 1970; M.D., U. La Laguna, Spain, 1981. Diplomate Am. Bd. Family Practice. Intern, St. Elizabeth Med. Ctr., Covington, Ky., 1981-82; resident U. Louisville Affiliated Hosp., 1982-85; physician emergency medicine Ireland Army Hosp., Fort Knox, Ky., 1983-85; physician Prewett and Watters Family Physicians, Corbin, Ky., 1985—. Participant Appalachian Project AMA, Va., summers 1972-73; vol. missions Bd. Global Missions United Methodist Ch., Ganta Liberia, 1984. Served to capt. M.C. USAR, 1985—. Recipient Research award Year U. Louisville, 1985; Union Coll. scholar, 1966. Mem. Am. Acad. Family Physicians, Ky. Acad. Family Practice, AMA, Ky. Med. Assn., Christian Med. Fellowship (London), Am. Heart Assn. (instr. advanced cardiac life support), Am. Coll. Surgeons (instr. advanc trauma life support). Republican. Avocations: Racketball; reading; running; hiking; music. Home: 1401 Sherwood Dr Corbin KY 40701 Office: Prewett & Watters Family Physicians Drs Pk Corbin KY 40701

WATTERSON, WILLIAM BURROUGHS, English educator, author, musician, stained glass company executive; b. Shelby, N.C., Aug. 23, 1943; s. William Monroe and Myra Maryl (Burroughs) W.; m. Carol Juanita Sisk, June 3, 1962; children—Eric, Kelly. A.A., Gardner-Webb Coll., 1963; B.S., Appalachian State U., 1965, M.A., 1970. Tchr. English, Winston-Salem Schs., N.C., 1965-70; prof. English Lees-McRae Coll., Banner Elk, N.C., 1970-71, prof. English, Brevard Coll., N.C., 1971-73; dir. admissions, 1973-79, prof. chmn. dept. English, 1979—, acting dean, dept. chmn., 1984—; owner stained glass craft Co. Editor: Carolina Voices, 1983; asst. editor: Hemlocks and Balsams, 1980-85. Contbr. articles to profl. jours. R.J. Reynolds Industries scholar Harvard U., 1968. Mem. Nat. Council Tchrs. English. Democrat. Baptist. Avocations: acting; playing guitar and Appalachian dulcimer; building stained glass windows and lamps. Home: PO Box 163 Banner Elk NC 28604 Office: Lees-McRae Coll PO Box 128 Banner Elk NC 28604

WATTIER, DEBBIE STEWART, journalism educator, public relations practitioner; b. Lubbock, Tex., June 25, 1951; d. William Benton Stewart and Thelma J. (Thompson) S.; m. Mark J. Wattier, Dec. 15, 1979; 1 dau., Rachel Lynn. B.A., Baylor U., 1973; M.S., Northwestern U., 1974. Editorial asst. Baptist World Alliance, Washington, 1974-76; info. cons. Bapt. Gen. Conv. Tex., Dallas, 1977-79; instr. journalism Murray (Ky.) State U., 1980—. Recipient Intern of Yr. award Tex. Daily Newspaper Assn., 1973; 1st place prize for news Bapt. Pub. Relations Assn., 1978. Mem. Pub. Relations Soc. Am. (accredited), Women in Communications, Soc. Profl. Journalists, Kappa Kappa Gamma. Democrat. Office: Murray State U Dept Journalism Murray KY 42071

WATTS, ANTHONY LEE, savings and loan executive; b. Griffin, Ga., Jan. 24, 1947; s. Edgar Lee and Eula Mae (Benton) W.; A.A., Gordon Mil. Coll., 1967; A.B.J., U. Ga., 1969; m. Barbara Malinda Harp, Oct. 11, 1969; children—Natalie Paige, Barbara Leigh, Melanie Marie. Conventional loan rep. Fed. Nat. Mortgage Assn., Atlanta, from 1971, asst. regional appraiser, quality control and property mgr., until 1976; v.p., dir. ins. services Ticor Mortgage Ins. Co., Atlanta, 1976-82, v.p., regional sales and exec. v.p. Ticor Indemnity Co., 1982-85; sr. v.p., regional mgr. Ticor Mortgage Ins. Co., Atlanta, 1984, sr. v.p. Eastern div. mgr., 1984-85; pres. Mt. Vernon Fed. Savs. and Loan, Dunwoody, Ga., 1985—; lectr. trade assns. Served with U.S. Army, 1969-71. Decorated Bronze Star, Army Commendation medal. Mem. Nat. Assn. Rev. Appraisers (sr.), Ga. Mortgage Bankers Assn. Office: 2408 Mt Vernon Rd Dunwoody GA 30338

WATTS, CECIL EUGENE, optometrist; b. Little Rock, Sept. 20, 1953; s. James Kalep and Geneva Bessie (Dewey) W.; m. Vicky Ann Hamaker, Aug. 12, 1978; children—Brian Eric, Nicole Elise. D. Optometry, U. Houston, 1978. Gen. practice optometry, North Little Rock, Ark., 1978-81, Searcy, Ark., 1981—. Mem. Tex. Assn. Optometrists. Mem. Assembly of God. Home: 507 Country Club St Searcy AR 72143 Office: 2810 E Race St Searcy AR 72143

WATTS, JACK NORTHINGTON, JR., building products company executive; b. Shreveport, La., Feb. 11, 1943; s. Jack Northington and Norma (Franklin) W.; m. Julie Ann Ronson, Apr. 7, 1966 (div. 1975); m. 2d, Merry Lynn Jones, July 3, 1977; children—Jeffrey Lee, Jack Northington III. B.S., La. Poly. Inst., 1967. Mgr. indsl. engring. Sperry Rand, Shreveport, 1961-73; dir. indsl. engring. Redman Industries, Dallas, 1973-76; ops. mgr. Alenco, Bryan, Tex., 1976-81, dir. mfg., gen. mgr. archtl. div., 1981—. Served with USAF, 1968-73. Mem. Bryan-College Station C. of C., Am. Legion. Republican. Episcopalian. Home: 2361 Briargate Bryan TX 77801 Office: Alenco 615 Carson St Bryan TX 77801

WATTS, JIMMY CARL, banker; b. Little Rock, June 27, 1943; s. Carl Thomas and Mary Lois (Ramsey) W. B.A., U. Ark.-Little Rock, 1968; postgrad. Sch. Bank Mktg., U. Colo., 1980. With Union Nat. Bank of Little Rock, 1967—, v.p. mktg., 1976—, Adv. bd. dirs. Quapaw Council area Boy Scouts Am., 1982; dir. Ark. Arts, Crafts and Design Fair, 1977-78, Ballet Co. of Ark., 1979-80, Ark. State Festival of Arts, 1974-76. Recipient Disting. Salesman award Sales and Mktg. Execs. Assn., 1973. Mem. Pub. Relations Soc. Am. (accredited, pres. Ark. chpt. 1982, dir. 1978-83), Ark. Advt. Fedn., Bank Mktg. Assn., Ark. Pub. Relations Edn. Found. (dir. 1982-85), Nat. Assn. Freight Payment Banks (pres. 1978-79). Democrat. Episcopalian. Home: 2717 Old Forge Dr Little Rock AR 72207 Office: PO Box 1541 Little Rock AR 72203

WATTS, LARRY LEE, residence hall director, personel and career counselor; b. Luling, Tex., June 18, 1950; s. Alton Lee and Jo Nelle (Ussery) W.; m. Catherine M. Loosbrock, Nov. 18, 1983; children—Michelle Lynne, Jessica Anne. B.A., Chadron State Coll., 1983, M.A., 1984. Box officer mgr. Post Playhouse, Ft. Robinson, Nebr., summer 1983; grad. asst. Chadron State Coll., Nebr., 1982-83, vocat. asst., 1983-84; residence hall dir. Southwest Tex. State U., San Marcos, 1984—, counselor, 1984—. Mem. Am. Assn. Counseling and Devel., Southwest Assn. Coll. and Univ. Housing (profl. devel. and publication rev. 1984—, community service com. 1985—), Phi Kappa Tau. Republican. Avocations: self-defence; weight-lifting; chess; volleyball; tae kwon do. Home: Arnold Hall Dir Apt San Marcos TX 78666 Office: Southwest Tex State U Housing Office Southwest Tex State U San Marcos TX 78666

WATTS, LEE DENSON, public relations executive, editor; b. Bklyn., May 2, 1942; d. Irving and Judith (Goldman) Colby; m. James Edward Watts, May 18, 1981; 1 dau., Audrey Julia Denson. Student, Miami Dade Community Coll., 1972-74, NYU, 1961, China Inst., N.Y.C., 1958. Communication specialist, mng. editor United Tchrs. Dade County, 1971-74; mng. editor Am. Fedn. State, County and Mcpl. Employees Local 1363, 1974-75; dir. corp. relations Ryerson & Haynes, Miami, 1975-76, nat. media dir., v.p. communications group, 1976-79; pres. Lee Denson Pub. Relations, Inc., North Miami, Fla., 1979-82; pub. relations dir. Dade County Police Benevolent Assn., Miami, 1982—, editor H.E.A.T., 1983—. Mem. Gov. Graham Pub. Relations Council; co-chmn. Asaault on Police Officers Com., Dade County Crime Watch; dir. Dade County Crime Watch; sec. citizens adv. com. Metro-Dade Police, Sta. 6; dir. Retired Officers' Council. Recipient cert. of appreciation Dade County Pub. Safety Dept., 1979, North Dade C. of C., 1979, 80, 81, 82, 83; Meritorious Service award Dade County Assn. Chiefs of Police, 1983; Cert. of Appreciation, Ret. Officers Council, Dade County Police Benevolent Assn., 1982, Blue Knights Law Enforcement Motorcycle Club, 1983. Mem. Women in Communication, Women's Inst. for Freedom of Press, Nat. Women's Polit. Caucus, NOW, North Dade C. of C. (dir.). Democrat. Jewish. Contbr. articles in field to profl. jours.

WATTS, MARY PORCHE, accountant; b. Houma, La., Mar. 9, 1936; d. Albert Narcisse and Nettie Mary (Bergeron) Porche; m. Allen John LeBoeuf, Apr. 10, 1954 (div. 1974); children—John Blair, JoAnne Marie; m. Harry Feather Watts, Mar. 12, 1976; stepchildren—Richard H., Wesley R., Carol F. Ed. Tulane U. Bookkeeper, Seither Sales, New Orleans, 1958-60; cordex operator White Sales, 1965-68; legal sec. Joseph Clay, 1968-70; acct., Metairie, La., 1969-74, South Boston, Va., 1975—; sec. Southwestern Mech., 1982—. Mem. Nat. Soc. Pub. Accts., Am. Bus. Women's Assn., La. Acctg. Assn. Democrat. Roman Catholic.

WATTS, RUFUS C., high school principal; b. Columbia, S.C., Feb. 16, 1939; s. Horace and Louise (Walker) W.; m. Ruby Carolyn Waiters, May 28, 1966; children—Brian, Kerwin, Sharon. B.S. in Math., Benedict Coll., 1961; M.S. in Math., Atlanta U., 1966; postgrad. U. S.C., 1964, 77-78. Cert. elem., secondary sch. prin., supr. Math. tchr. B.T. Washington High, Columbia, 1961-66, Columbia High Sch., 1967-70; asst. prin. Eau Claire High Sch., Columbia, 1970-77, prin., 1982—; asst. prin. Crayton Middle Sch., Columbia, 1977-78; prin. Gibbes Middle Sch., Columbia, 1978-82; mem. adv. com. Dept. Edn. Math., Columbia, Prin.'s Resolutions Com., Prin.'s Adv. Com. to Supt.; chmn. Richland One Classification Com., Columbia. Bd. dirs. Palmetto Place, Columbia, 1983-85; commr. Greenview Baseball League, Columbia, 1977-84. Recipient Cert. of Worthwhile Contbns. Nat. Council of Negro Women, 1982. Mem. Nat. Assn. Secondary Sch. Prins., S.C. Assn. Sch. Adminstrs., Assn. for Supervision and Curriculum Devel., S.C. Middle Sch. Assn., Phi Delta Kappa, Alpha Psi (sec. 1979-84), Alpha Phi Alpha. Democrat. Baptist. Avocations: checkers, deep sea fishing. Home: 607 Easter St Columbia SC 29203 Office: Eau Claire High Sch 4800 Monticello Rd Columbia SC 29203

WATTS, TED GLEN, vocational-technical educator, electro-mechanical engineer; b. Des Moines, May 5, 1932; s. Theodore Glen and Gertrude Maud (Collins) W.; divorced; children—Linda Louise, Steven Eugene, Hope Annette; m. Dena Marie Foster, Feb. 17, 1979. B.S. in Mech. Engring., Iowa State U., 1957; M.S. in Electro-Mech. Engring., Okla. State U., 1971, U. So. Fla., 1985. Engr. Loudin Machinery Co., Fairfield, Iowa, 1958-60, Gen. Dynamics, San Diego, 1960-63; engr., mgr. Stroco Inc., Cheyenne, Wyo., 1963-65; engr. Tampa Bay Engring. Co., St. Petersburg, Fla., 1965-67; engr., mgr. Radiation Concepts, St. Petersburg, 1975-77; instr., curriculum coordinator Pinellas Vocat. Tech. Inst., Clearwater, Fla., 1967-75, 1977—; cons. U.S. Postal Service, Norman, Okla., 1971-72, Foods div. Coca Cola Co., Houston, 1975-78, Klopp Internat., St. Petersburg, 1981-83, U. South Fla., Tampa, 1982-84, Fla. Steel Corp., Tampa, 1973-74, Fla. Mus. Holography, St. Petersburg, 1984—. Author: Mechanisms Linkages, 1971; (with others) Electro-Mechanical Series, 1971. Patentee in field. Team mem. leader So. Assn. Colls. and Schs., Atlanta, 1972-74; com. mem. Fla. Common Course Numbering System, Tallahassee, 1984—. Served as sgt. USMC, 1949-52, Korea. Okla. State U. scholar 1969; Okla. State U. fellow 1969. Mem. NEA, Fla. Teaching Profession, Am. Vocat. Assn., Fla. Vocat. Assn., Pinellas Adult and Vocat. Educators, Pinellas Classroom Tchrs. Assn. Avocations: scuba diving; boating. Home: 6665 27th Way N Saint Petersburg FL 33702 Office: Pinellas Vocat Tech Inst 6100 154th Ave N Clearwater FL 33520

WATTS, WILLIAM CAREL, educator, educational administrator; b. Prentiss, Miss., Mar. 28, 1939; s. Rufus Garfield and Velmae (Buckley) W.; m. Anne Wimbush, Mar. 25, 1967; children—Michael Kevin, Christopher Nolan. B.S., Alcorn State U., 1961; M.S., Atlanta U., 1968, adminstrn. and supervision cert., 1972; career devel. cert., postgrad. U. Ga., 1974-75. Tchr. Simpson County Pub. Schs., Magee, Miss., 1961-65; instr. Utica Jr. Coll., 1966-67; tchr. coordinator career devel., adminstr. Atlanta Pub. Schs., 1968—; mem. Middle Sch. Adv. Task Force, 1980-84, Council Vocat. Educators, 1982-84; supr. Career Devel. Club, Atlanta. Sch.'s chmn. United Negro Coll. Fund, Atlanta, 1979—; asst. supr. Sandtown League Assn., Atlanta, 1980-83; youth advisor NAACP, Atlanta, 1982-84. Served with U.S. Army, 1957-58. Named Tchr. of Yr., Atlanta Pub. Sch. System, 1972, 74, Star Tchr., 1972, recipient acad. incentive award, 1983; NSF grantee, 1965-66. Mem. Ga. Vocat. Assn. (life mem.; chmn. program improvement council 1977-82, bylaws and parliamentary procedure 1982-83, v.p., sec. dir. 1979—; pres. guidance div. 1982—), Atlanta Assn. Career Devel. (pres., treas. 1975-81), Am. Vocat. Assn. (life), Nat. Assn. Educators, Ga. Assn. Educators, Kappa Alpha Psi. Baptist. Lodge: Masons. Home: 5245 Orange Dr SW Atlanta GA 30331 Office: Atlanta Pub Schs 320 Irwin St NE Atlanta GA 30312

WATTS, WILLIAM PARK, naval officer, university administrator, consultant; b. Huntsville, Ala., Mar. 25, 1916; s. Clarence Lee and Inez Elizabeth (Looney) W.; m. Eleanor Ruth Roth, July 2, 1949; children—Deborah Clark Watts Holley, Lauren McCrary Watts Buchner. B.S., U.S. Naval Acad., 1938; grad. Naval War Coll., 1949; M.B.A., NYU, 1961; Ph.D. in Bus. Adminstrn., U. Ala., 1977. Commd. ensign U.S. Navy, 1938, advanced through grades to capt., 1962, duty assignments include commdg. officer of naval supply depot, various Navy, joint, NATO staffs and in combatant ships; adminstrv. mgr. Research Inst., U. Ala., Huntsville, 1963-70, mem. faculty, 1970-77, asst. prof. 1970-74, acting chmn. dept. bus. adminstrn., 1974-75; mgr. high tech. program Guest Assocs., Inc., 1979-80; owner, Mgmt. Sci. Applications Assocs., Huntsville, 1978-82. Pres., 1st v.p., mem. exec. com. Huntsville-Madison County Council for Internat. Visitors, 1978—; com. chmn. Huntsville Symphony Orch. Assn., 1983—; officer, vestryman Episcopal Ch. of the Nativity, Huntsville, 1982-84; founding pres. Randolph Sch. Athletics and Activities Assn., Huntsville, 1966-67; mem. budget com. Huntsville-Madison County United Way, 1968-70; mem. Huntsville-Madison County Library Devel. Council, 1985; mem. Huntsville Community Chorus, 1980—, bd. dirs., 1981-82. Awarded with Bronze Star, Asiatic-Pacific Campaign Medal with three stars, WWII Victory medal, Occupation service medal, Am. Campaign Joint service Commendation medal, Comdr. Joint Task Force One, 1946, Nat. Defense Service medal, 1954; recipient plaque San Pedro C. of C., 1955. Mem. U.S. Naval Inst., Am. Assn. Individual Investors, Redstone Arsenal Officers Club. Republican. Episcopalian. Club: Heritage (Huntsville) (chmn. various coms.). Lodge: Rotary. Avocations: singing in choir, community chorus concerts, musical comedies, operas, jogging, walking, gardening, reading. Home: 2300 Big Cove Rd Huntsville AL 35801

WAUFLE, ALAN DUANE, museum director, consultant; b. Hornell, N.Y., Feb. 11, 1951; s. Robert Karl and Heather (Gunn) W.; m. Catherine Lynn Chandler, Aug. 11, 1973; children—Erik Alan, Mark Chandler. A.B., Coll. William and Mary, 1973; M.A., Duke U., 1976. Dir., Gaston County Mus., Dallas, N.C., 1976—; cons. Gaston Hist. Properties Commn., Gastonia, N.C., 1983—. Author: Guide to North Carolina Galleries, 1982. Bd. dirs. Gastonia Little Theater, 1977-79; v.p. Gaston County Art Guild, Gastonia, 1980-82. Mem. N.C. Mus. Council (bd. dirs. 1978-83), Am. Assn. of Mus., Nat. Trust, Am. Assn. of State and Local History. Democrat. Methodist. Lodge: Rotary (Gastonia). Avocations: collecting cut glass; cooking; gardening. Home: 3308 Sherwood Circle Gastonia NC 28054 Office: Gaston County Mus 131 Main St PO Box 429 Dallas NC 28034-0429

WAUGH, JOHN DAVID, university administrator, engineering educator, consultant; b. Charleston, W.Va., Sept. 20, 1932; s. Oran Waugh and Audrey Jewel (DeWees) Lively; div.; children—Debra, Donna, David; m. Sylvia Hill, Mar. 18, 1983. B.S. in Engring., U. S.C., 1954, U. Notre Dame, 1958; M.S. in Engring., Yale U., 1964. Registered profl. engr., S.C. Design engr. Bendix, South Bend, Ind., 1953-58; from instr. to prof U. S.C., Columbia, 1959-68, assoc. dean engring., 1968-76, dean engring., 1977—; pvt. cons., 1960—. Editor: Development in Mechanics, 1968. Pres. PTA, Columbia; mem. Gov.'s Commn. for Econ. Devel., S.C., 1983—; founder, pres. U. S.C. Credit Union, Columbia; mem. Com. of 100, Columbia, 1980—. Named Litman Outstanding Prof., U. S.C., 1979; recipient Order of Palmetto, Gov. S.C. Fellow ASCE; mem. Nat. Soc. Profl. Engrs. (Engr. of Yr. 1984), Am. Soc. Engring. Edn., Assn. Media-Based Continuing Engring. Edn. (bd. dirs. 1976—), Council Engring. Deans (bd. dirs. 1983—). Methodist. Club: Summit (Columbia). Avocations: bridge; boating; travel; restaurants. Office: Coll Engring U SC Columbia SC 29208

WAUGH, MARK HOWARD, clinical psychologist; b. Augusta, Ga., Oct. 25, 1954; s. William Howard and Eileen (Garrigan) W.; m. Marcia Snowden, Nov. 29, 1975; 1 child, Robert Mark. A.B., U. N.C., 1976; M.S., U. Fla., 1979, Ph.D., 1982; postgrad. Yale U. Med. Sch., 1984. Asst. prof. Roosevelt U., Chgo., 1982-83; staff psychologist Ridgeview Hosp., Oak Ridge, 1984—, dir. psychol. testing, 1984—, dir. Harriman Clinic, 1984—. Cons. editor Jour. Personality Assessment, 1982—. Contbr. articles to profl. jours. Mem. Am. Psychol. Assn., Soc. for Personality Assessment, Tenn. Psychol. Assn. Democrat. Avocations: brewing beer; basketball; running. Home: 718 Morgan St Harriman TN 37748 Office: Ridgeview Psychiat Hosp 240 W Tyrone Rd Oak Ridge TN 37830

WAWRYKOW, GEORGE MICHAEL, psychologist; b. Winnipeg, Man., Can., Jan. 31, 1945; s. Michael George and Frances Warykow; m. Lea Anna Bond, June 3, 1966; children—Taras Michael George, Tania Lea Ann, Teresa Lara Francine, Tamera Virginia Jean. B.Sc., U. Man., 1966; M.A.Sc., U. Waterloo, 1970; Ph.D., North Tex. State U., 1975. Diplomate Am. Bd. Family Psychologists, Am. Bd. Profl. Psychotherapists, Internat. Acad. Profl. Counseling and Psychotherapy; lic. psychologist, Tex. Sr. psychologist Brandon (Man.) Mental Health Ctr., 1969-72; cons. psychologist Edn. Service Ctr., Richardson, Tex., 1972-73, Nat. Consortium for Humanizing Edn., Dallas, 1972-75, Mini Skools Ltd., Houston Day Care, 1975-76, Gulf Coast Community Services Assn., Houston Head Start, 1976-78; dir. spl. services Houston Head Start, 1976-78; research specialist Tex. Research Inst. Mental Scis., 1976-77; counseling psychologist Spring (Tex.) Ind. Sch. Dist., 1978-81; pvt. practice psychology, Spring, 1980—. Bd. dirs. Mental Health Assn., Community Unified for Responsible Family Life Edn. Govt. Man. fellow, 1966; Can. Council fellow; State of Tex. grantee. Mem. Am. Psychol. Assn., Can. Psychol. Assn., Tex. Psychol. Assn., Psychol. Assn. Man., Houston Psychol. Assn., Am. Personnel and Guidance Assn., Am. Research Assn., Can. Guidance and Counseling Assn., Mental Health Assn. Byzatine Catholic. Contbr. articles to profl. jours. Home: 21802 Greengate Dr Spring TX 77379 Office: 21802 Greengate Dr Spring TX 77379 also 2400 Augusta Suite 274 Houston TX 77057

WAX, GEORGE LOUIS, lawyer; b. New Orleans, Dec. 6, 1928; s. John Edward and Theresa (Schaff) W.; LL.B., Loyola U. of South, 1952, B.C.S., 1960; m. Patricia Ann Delaney, Feb. 20, 1965; children—Louis Jude, Joann Olga, Therese Marie. Admitted to La. bar, 1952; practice in New Orleans, 1954—. Served with USNR, 1952-54. Mem. Am., La., New Orleans bar assns., Am. Legion. Roman Catholic. Kiwanian. Clubs: New Orleans Athletic, Suburban Gun and Rod, Pendennis. Home: 6001 Charlotte Dr New Orleans LA 70122 Office: First Nat Bank Commerce Bldg New Orleans LA 70112

WAXMAN, HERSHOLT CHARLES, curriculum educator; b. Chgo., Mar. 10, 1951; s. Max and Helen (Sokolsky) W. B.A., U. Ill.-Chgo., 1972, M.Ed., 1978, Ph.D., 1982. Asst. prof. dept. curriculum and instrn. U. Houston, dir. Ednl. Research Ctr., 1983—. Contbr. articles to profl. jours. Mem. Am. Ednl. Research Assn., S.W. Ednl. Research Assn. Office: Ednl Research Ctr Coll of Edn U Houston Houston TX 77004

WAY, WILSON SPENCER, osteopathic physician and surgeon; b. Guatemala City, Guatemala; Feb. 24, 1910; s. Wilson Spencer and Lydia Caroline (Walker) W.; m. Louise Edrington, May 20, 1938 (div. May 1953); children—Flora Ann Way Arnold, Wilson Edrington; m. Olga Cheves, May 25, 1953. D.O., Kirksville Coll. Osteo. Medicine, 1941; Ph.D., Donsbach U., 1979; D. Christian Lit. (hon.), Freedom U., 1984. Gen. practice osteo. medicine, Orlando, Fla., 1941; staff Orlando Gen. Hosp., 1941-72; cert. instr. Dale Carnegie, Orlando, 1957-63. Author: Total Life, 1978; Miracle of Enzymes, 1979. Bd. dirs. Sta. WTGL-TV, Cocoa-Orlando, 1980—; deacon Assembly of God Ch. Fellow Internat. Coll. of Applied Nutrition; mem. Am. Osteo. Assn., Fla. Osteo. Med. Assn., Fla. Acad. Osteopathy, Nat. Acad. Osteopathy, Internat. Acad. of Preventive Medicine. Democrat. Lodge: Toastmasters Internat. (pres. Orlando, Fla. 1966—). Avocation: fishing. Home: 827 Nancy Winter Springs FL Office: Way Clinic 500 N Mills Orlando FL 32803

WAYBURN, GATES JORDAN, JR., ophthalmologist; b. Macon, Ga., Mar. 3, 1944; s. Gates J. and Frances J. (Thames) W.; m. Martha E. Haxthausen, June 13, 1970; children—Christopher Gates, Leigh Elizabeth. A.B., Princeton U., 1966; M.D., Baylor Coll. Medicine, 1970; Diplomate Am. Bd. Ophthalmology. Intern U. Ala., Birmingham, 1971, resident Eye Found. Hosp., 1973-76; practice medicine specializing in ophthalmology, Nashville, 1976—; clin. instr. ophthalmology Vanderbilt Sch. Medicine, Nashville, 1979—. Served to capt. USAF, 1971-73. Mem. Nashville Acad. Ophthalmology (pres. 1979-80, v.p. 1978-79), Princeton Alumni Assn. (pres. Nashville chpt. 1983-85). Republican. Baptist. Avocations: scuba diving; golf; backpacking; fishing. Home: 1981 Sunnyside Dr Brentwood TN 37027 Office: 4301 Hillsboro Rd Nashville TN 37215

WAYNE, ALAN, educator; b. N.Y.C., June 18, 1909; s. Adolph Otto Johann and Martha (Horvath) Wiesenburg; B.S., Coll. City N.Y., 1931, M.S. in Edn., 1937; postgrad. Columbia, 1945-49, (A.A.A.S. Secondary Sch. fellow) N.Y. U., 1961-68; m. Muriel Rothstein, Aug. 25, 1934; children—Linda Wayne Weiss, Susan Wayne McKee. Tchr. math. and sci. Rhodes Sch., N.Y.C., 1930-45; tchr. math. James Fenimore Cooper Jr. High Sch., N.Y.C., 1940-45, Williamsburgh Vocational High Sch., N.Y.C., 1945-51; asst. prin., supr. math. and sci. Eli Whitney Vocational High Sch., N.Y.C., 1951-72; adj. instr. math. Cooper Union, N.Y.C., 1949-67, adj. prof., 1967-72; instr. math. edn. N.Y. U., 1950-51, Yeshiva U. Grad. Sch., 1959-61; adj. asst. prof. math. Queensborough Community Coll., N.Y.C., 1965-72; instr. math. and physics Pasco-Hernando Community Coll., Fla., 1975-86; editorial cons. vocat.-indsl. edn. SUNY, 1949-57; mem. curriculum devel. coms. N.Y.C. Bd. Edn., 1950-70. Vice chmn. finance com. Beacon Sq. Pool Assn.; sec. Richey Symphony Soc., 1973-77. Committeeman, N.Y. County Democratic Com., 1940. Mem. Sch. Sci. and Math. Assn., Council Supervisory Assns., AAUP, Am. Math. Soc., Soc. for Indsl. and Applied Math., Math. Assn. Am., Nat. Council Tchrs. Math., Assn. Tchrs. Math. N.Y.C. (pres. 1948-50); exec. bd., historian 1951-71), Assn. Tchrs. Math. N.Y. State (charter, county chmn. 1951-72), Math. Chmns. Assn. N.Y.C. (v.p. 1971-72), Nat. Puzzlers League, Epsilon Pi Tau. Club: N.Y. Riddlers (pres. 1952). Author: Basic Mathematics I, 1951; Basic Mathematics

II, 1954; (with Olivo) Basic Applied Science, 1957; (with Bold) Number Systems, 1971; (with Peters, Schor, Meng) Exploring Mathematics, 1974. Editor: Metals Technology, 1955. Home: 6614 Springfield Dr Holiday FL 33590

WEAKLEY, CLARE GEORGE, JR., insurance executive; b. Dallas, Apr. 14, 1928; s. Clare George and Louise (Cunningham) W.; m. Eddy J. Smallfeldt, Feb. 13, 1948 (div. 1960); children—Clare George III, Carol J., Charles E.; m. Jean C. Weakley, July 20, 1962. B.B.A., So. Meth. U., 1948, Th.M., 1967. Ordained minister Christian Community, 1967. With Employers Ins., Dallas, 1948-52; owner Weakley & Co., Dallas, 1952—. Author/editor: Holy Spirit and Power, 1977; Happiness Unlimited, 1979. Bd. dirs. Dallas Cerebral Palsy, 1962; mem. Dallas County Grand Jury, 1959; hon. chaplain Casa Blanca Hosp., Dallas, 1960-74. Mem. Dallas Assn. Mut. Agts. (pres. 1953), Tex. Assn. Mut. Agts. (dir. 1954-59). Republican. Home: 7106 Gateridge Dallas TX 75240 Office: Am Service Found Inc Box 7347 Dallas TX 75209

WEAKS, CHESTER ARTHUR, JR., mining company manager; b. Blair, S.C., Nov. 27, 1930; s. Chester Arthur and Marjorie Calhoun (Ragsdale) W.; student Newberry Coll., 1949-50; m. Connie Sue Ratledge, Dec. 23, 1956; children—James Arthur, Blake Hunter. Equipment operator Superior Stone Co., Greensboro and Hickory, N.C., 1950-59, foreman, Woodleaf, N.C., 1959-66; plant mgr. Martin Marietta Aggregates, Fountain, N.C., Augusta and Macon, Ga., 1966-78, S.C. prodn. mgr., Columbia, 1978-82, prodn. mgr. Eastern dist., Raleigh, N.C., 1982—; dir. Fountain Apparel Corp. Served with U.S. Army, 1952-54. Recipient Jefferson Cup Martin Marietta Aggregates, 1975, 50 Year Service award, 1985. Mem. Nat. Crushed Stone Assn. Republican. Presbyterian. Home: 1502 Bloomingdale Dr Cary NC 27511 Office: Martin Marietta Aggregates PO Box 30013 Raleigh NC 27622

WEARN, WILSON CANNON, media company executive; b. Newberry, S.C., Oct. 7, 1919; s. George F. and Mary (Cannon) W.; B.E.E., Clemson U., 1941; m. Mildred Colson, Feb. 21, 1948; children—Jean Wearn Held, Joan Wearn Gilbert, Wilson Cannon. Engr. Westinghouse Electric Corp., Pitts., 1941; engr. FCC, Washington, 1946-48; assoc. cons. electronic engr. firm Weldon & Carr, Washington, 1948-50; partner firm Vandivere, Cohen & Wearn, cons. engrs., Washington, 1950-53; with Multimedia Broadcasting Co., Greenville, S.C., 1953—, organizer of corp., 1953, became corp. officer, 1960, pres., 1966-77; pres., Multimedia, Inc., Greenville, 1977-81, chief exec. officer, 1978—, chmn. bd., 1981—; instr. electronic engring. Clemson U., 1946; dir. Bankers Trust of S.C., Broadcast Music, Inc., Liberty Life Ins. Co. Mem. S.C. Hosp. Adv. Council, 1969-71. Bd. dirs. Family and Children Service of Greenville County, 1967-69, pres., 1969; bd. dirs. Newspaper Advt. Bur.; trustee Greenville Symphony Assn., 1960-62, 71-77, pres., 1977; trustee Greenville Hosp. System, 1964-70, chmn., 1968-70; trustee Broadcast Rating Council, 1969-73, chmn., 1971-73; trustee Clemson U. Found., 1973-79, pres., 1979; trustee Presbyn. Coll. Served to capt. Signal Corps, AUS, 1941-45; PTO. Decorated Bronze Star; recipient Outstanding Alumni award Clemson U., 1972. Mem. Nat. Assn. Broadcasters (chmn. bd. 1975-77), S.C. Broadcasters Assn. (pres. 1967), Nat. Communications Club, Greater Greenville C. of C. (pres. 1972). Presbyn. (elder). Kiwanian. Clubs: Poinsett, Green Valley Country (Greenville); University (N.Y.C.). Office: PO Box 1688 Greenville SC 29602

WEATHER, LEONARD, JR., gynecologist, laser surgeon; b. Albany, Ga., July 6, 1944; s. Leonard and Lucille (Reese) W.; m. Bettye Jean Roberts, Apr. 13, 1970; children—Marcus Brandon, Kirstin Anita. B.S. in Pharmacy, Howard U., 1967; M.D., Rush Med. Coll., 1974. Internship Johns Hopkins U., 1974-75, residency, 1975-78; dir. Chef Women's Clinic, New Orleans, 1979—; instr. Tulane Med. Sch., New Orleans, 1979—; asst. prof. Xavier U. Coll. Pharmacy, New Orleans, 1983—; chief dept. ob-gyn New Orleans Gen. Hosp., 1982-83; med. staff, sec., treas. Humana Women's Hosp., New Orleans, 1985; host. program Sta. WYLD, New Orleans, 1984—. Author: Why Can't We Have A Baby, 1985. Contbr. articles to profl. jours. Bd. dirs., v.p. Bayou Fed. Savs. and Loan, New Orleans, 1983—; bd. dirs. Dryade St. YMCA, New Orleans, 1983—; med. conv. dir. Push New Orleans Nat. Conv., 1982, NAACP Nat Conv., New Orleans, 1983. Mem. Am. Fertility Soc., AMA, Nat. Med. Assn., Chi Delta Mu (pres. 1983—, nat. pres. 1986—). Democrat. Baptist. Clubs: Original Ill., Idle Wilds Pine. Avocations: writing; fishing; car collector; art. Home: 6831 Lake Willow Dr New Orleans LA 70126 Office: Chef Womens Clinic 7820 Chef Menteur New Orleans LA 70126

WEATHERLY, JAY, hospital administrator; b. Birmingham, Ala., Aug. 19, 1956; s. Jesse Orel and Emma Sue (Montgomery) W.; m. Sharon Michelle Bowen, Ja. 15, 1983; 1 child, Hunter. B.S. in Health Care Mgmt., U. Ala.-Tuscalousa, 1978; M.S. in Hosp. Adminstrn., U. Ala.-Birmingham, 1980. Adminstrv. resident Regional Med. Ctr., Anniston, Ala., 1979-80, dir. of personnel, 1980-82; adminstr. Bowdon Area Hosp., Ga., 1982-86; v.p. Bapt. Med. Ctr. Montclair, Birmingham, Ala., 1986—; mem. council of smaller hosps. Ga. Hosp. Assn., Atlanta, 1983—, mem. council of assoc. devel. and clin. lab. adv. council, 1984—. Brotherhood dir. Bowdon Bapt. Ch., Ga., 1985; mem. Bowdon Beautification Com., 1985. Mem. Am. Coll. Hosp. Adminstrs., Anniston C. of C. (pres.'s com. 1982). Republican. Lodge: Lions. (sec., treas. Bowdon chpt. 1985). Avocations: golf, camping, outdoor activities. Office: Bowdon Area Hosp 501 Mitchell Ave Bowdon GA 30108

WEATHERLY, MARK GIVENS, educator, marital and family therapist; b. Alco, La., Mar. 7, 1923; s. Obie Lee and Lilla (Givens) W.; m. Katherine Burge, Aug. 18, 1951; children—Mark Givens, Jr., Susan Weatherly Book, Robert O'Connor. B.S., Stetson U., 1949; M.Ed., U. Va., 1967, Ed.D., 1970; postgrad. Fla. State U., 1961. Pres., corp. owner Camp Tenn. and Sch., Winchester, 1950-68; instr. Lynchburg Coll., Va., 1965-66; instr., football coach Fork Union Mil. Acad., Va., 1949-53; instr. U. Va. Sch. Gen. Studies, Charlottesville, 1970-71; assoc. prof. edn. Longwood State Coll., Farmville, Va., 1970—; pvt. practice marital and family therapy, Farmville and Lynchburg, 1965-81; cons. pub. and pvt. schs. in Central Va., juvenile and domestic cts. Central Va. Author: Readings in Adolescence, 1986. Chmn. for Democratic campaign Senator Harry F. Byrd, Jr., Appomattox County. Served to 2d lt. U.S. Army, 1942-45, PTO. Recipient Mayor's Gold Key, Memphis, 1968; recipient Disting. Service medal Liberty U., Lynchburg, 1985. Mem. Am. Psychol. Assn., Am. Assn. Marital and Family Therapy, Am. Assn. Counseling and Devel., Am. Mental Health Counselors Assn., Phi Delta Kappa, Sigma Chi Iota. Avocations: gardening; fishing; writing. Office: Longwood Coll Sch Edn Farmville VA 23901

WEATHERLY, ROBERT STONE, JR., aluminum company executive; b. Birmingham, Ala., May 12, 1929; s. Robert Stone and Gladys (Manning) W.; m. Mary Anne Burr, May 1, 1955; children—Robert Stone, III, Henry, William. A.B., Princeton U., 1950; LL.B., Harvard U., 1953, grad. advanced mgmt. program, 1972. Bar: Ala. 1953. Assoc. firm Burr, McKamy Moore & Thomas, Birmingham, 1955-62; asst. gen. atty. Vulcan Materials Co., Birmingham, 1962-69; v.p. chems. div., Wichita, Kans., 1969-71, treas., 1971-74, v.p. and controller, 1974-77, pres. metals div., Birmingham, Ala., 1977—, pres. Middle East div., 1982—; disting. lectr.-practitioner U. Ga. Served with U.S. Army, 1953-55. Mem. Am. Bar Assn., Fin. Exec. Inst., Nat. Assn. Accts. (cert. mgmt. acct.). Presbyterian. Club: Country of Birmingham. Home: 4608 Old Leeds Rd Birmingham AL 35213 Office: 1 Metroplex Dr Birmingham AL 35223

WEATHERLY, SAMUEL FRANCIS, professional investigator, consultant; b. Savannah, Ga., Sept. 19, 1945; s. Isaac Walter and Nell Mae (Grant) W.; m. Susan Lee Owens, Aug. 12, 1966; children—Samuel Francis Jr., John Edward, Jennifer Ashby. B.S. in Criminal Justice, Armstrong State Coll., 1976; J.D., John Marshall Law Sch., Atlanta, 1979. Detective sgt. criminal investigations Chatham County Police Dept., 1966-74; capt., asst. chief criminal investigations, Tybee Island Police Dept., Ga., 1974-76; owner, pres., sr. investigator Weatherly & Assocs., Inc., Savannah, Ga., 1976—; cons. Criminal Def. Lawyers Assn.; cons. various utility cos., law firms, police depts. Served as cpl. USMC, 1963-67. Named Chatham County Police Officer of Yr., 1972; recipient Cert. Commendation, Am. Legion, 1970; Cert. of Commendation Jaycees, 1975-76; Cert. of Commendation Grumman Aircraft, 1972. Mem. Savannah C. of C., Tybee Island C. of C., Internat. Assn. Arson Investigators, Inst. Criminal Justice Ethics. Methodist. Lodge: Masons. Office: 124 E Oglethorpe Ave Savannah GA 31401

WEATHERSBY, A(UGUSTUS) BURNS, entomologist, educator; b. Pinola, Miss., May 19, 1913; s. Augustus Benton and Louie Jane (Burns) W.; m. Olive Pearl Hammons, Apr. 8, 1945; children—Richard Michael, Robert Benton. B.S., La. State U., 1938, M.S., 1940; Ph.D., 1954; postgrad. George Washington U., 1953. Asst. entomologist-at-large La. Dept. Agr., 1940-42; commd. ensign U.S. Navy, 1942, advanced through grades to comdr., 1957; served with 3d Marines, Pacific, 1943-45; entomologist Office Naval Med. Research, Cairo, and Teheran, 1946-47, Bethesda, Md., 1947-55; comdr. Naval Forces Far East, Japan, 1955-57; entomologist-parasitologist Naval Med. Research Inst., Bethesda, 1957-62; ret., 1962; research assoc. dept. entomology U. Ga.-Athens, 1962—; spl. advisor to Iranian Minister of Health, 1946. Author: (with others) Manual Medical Entomology, 1958. Contbr. chpts. to books. 50 articles to profl. jours. Organizer, pres. Fedn. Community Assns., 1967-69; pres. Little League Baseball, 1969-74; chmn. bd. deacons Bapt. Chs. Md. and Ga., 1949-75. Decorated Navy Commendation medal (2); NIH grantee, 1962-75; recipient Outstanding Tchr. award U. Ga., 1981; Disting Achievement award for teaching Southeast br. Entomol. Soc. Am., 1982, Entomol. Soc. Am., 1983. Fellow Royal Soc. Tropical Medicine and Hygiene; mem. AAAS, Am. Soc. Tropical Medicine and Hygiene, Am. Soc. Parasitology, S.E. Soc. Parasitologists (pres. 1974-75), Am. Mosquito Control Assn., Entomol. Soc. Am. (Disting. Teaching award 1983), Ga. Entomol. Soc., Loyal Order of Boar, Internat. Wood Collectors Soc., Sigma Xi. Phi Kappa Phi (pres. 1976-77, emeritus 1985), Phi Sigma. Home: 210 Bishop Dr Athens GA 30606 Office: Dept Entomology Univ Ga Athens GA 30602

WEAVER, BOBBY STEVE, sheriff; b. Athens, Tex., Jan. 31, 1947; s. Ralph Jack and Weaver and Elizabeth Marie (Davis) McClenden; m. Nancy LaVern Davis, Aug. 21, 1965; children—Tonya Michelle, Paul Justiss. A.A., Kilgore Coll., 1971; B.S., Baylor U., 1975; M.S., U. Tex.-Tyler, 1979. Patrolman, Tex. State Police, 1967-71; instr. Kilgore Coll., Tex., 1971-80; sheriff Gregg County, Longview, Tex., 1980—; guest instr. East Tex. Police Acad. Pres., White Oak Sch. Bd. Edn., Tex., 1978-80; bd. dirs. Gregg County Mental Health Assn., 1983—. Recipient cert. of commendation Am. Legion, 1984; Disting. Service award Res. Law Officers Assn., 1984. Mem. East Tex. Police Officers Assn. (v.p. 1984-85), Nat. Sheriffs Assn., Tex. Sheriffs Assn., Longview C. of C. Republican. Mem. Ch. of Christ. Lodges: Masons, Lions (pres. 1977-78) (White Oak). Avocations: fishing, hunting. Home: 2 Leona Circle White Oak TX 75693 Office: PO Box 506 Longview TX 75606

WEAVER, CARMON JOYCE, educational administrator; b. Indpls., Sept. 19, 1956; d. Clenard and Sara Ailene (Campbell) W. Student Butler U., 1976; B.A., U. Cin., 1978; M.A., Atlanta U., 1980. Counselor Etes, Inc., Bluffton, Ind., 1980; resident hall dir. Ball State U., Muncie, Ind., 1980-81; resident counselor U. Cin., 1981-83, resident coordinator, coordinator minority and internat. students Hollins Coll., Roanoke, Va., 1983-85, asst. dean students, 1985—. Mem. NAACP, Am. Coll. Personnel Assn. (editor com. for multicultural affairs newsletter 1984—), Am. Assn. Counseling and Devel., Assn. Black Women in Higher Edn., Black Career Women, Va. Assn. Student Personnel Adminstrs. Home: PO Box 9713 Hollins Coll Roanoke VA 24020

WEAVER, CHARLES EDWARD, geology educator; b. Lock Haven, Pa., Jan. 27, 1925; s. Clair William and Kathryn Harriet (Best) W.; m. Janice Beatrice Hartland, Nov. 29, 1946; children—Alaine Robin, Patrice Kathryn, Allison Hartland. B.S., Pa. State U., 1948, M.S., 1950, Ph.D., 1952. Research geologist Shell Oil Co., Houston, 1952-59; research group leader Continental Oil Co., Ponca City, Okla., 1959-63; prof. Ga. Inst. Tech., Atlanta, 1963-70, dir. Sch. Geophys. Scis., 1970-81, prof., 1981—. Served to lt. (j.g.) USNR, 1943-46. Recipient Battelle Exceptional Performance award, 1979, grantee in field. Mem. Geol. Soc. Am., Am. Mineral. Soc. (research award 1958), Clay Mineral Soc. (Disting. mem. 1985), Ga. Geol. Soc., Soc. Econ. Paleontology and Mineralogy, Geochem. Soc. Am., Trout Unltd., Sigma Xi (research award 1972). Author: The Chemistry of Clay Minerals, 1972; Miocene of the Southeastern United States, 1977; Shale-Slate Metamorphism Southern Appalachians, 1983; editor: Changing Identity of Graduate Earth Science Education, 1966. Contbr. numerous articles on geology to profl. jours. Home: 3276 Craggy Point Atlanta GA 30339 Office: Geophys Scis Ga Tech Inst Atlanta GA 30332

WEAVER, GERALD CECIL, wood products manufacturing manager; b. Laurel, Miss., Nov. 13, 1939; s. Robert Franklin, Sr., and Annie Margaret (Herring) W.; m. Laura Faye Grantham, July 10, 1959; children—Junicha D. Weaver Gordon, Cossondra Lea Weaver George. Student in Forestry and Bus. Mgmt., La. Tech. U., Miss. State U., 1957-73. Supr., Masonite Corp., Laurel, Miss., 1960-66, Elizabeth, N.J., 1966-67; supr. Ga. Pacific Corp., Crossett, Ark., 1967-68; supr., gen. foreman, Louisville, Miss., 1968-78, supt., plant mgr., 1978—. Instr. hunter safety tng. Nat. Rifle Assn.-Miss. Game and Fish Commn. Methodist. Office: Ga Pacific Corp PO Box 309 Louisville MS 39339

WEAVER, JACK WAYNE, English language educator; b. Damascus, Va., Apr. 7, 193[illegible]; s. Elihu Joshua and Bina Mathilda (Elliott) W.; m. Betty Jane Nester, Dec. 27, 1957; children—Laura, Rebecca, Stephen. B.A. in English, Berea Coll., 1954; M.A., U. N.C., 1959, Ph.D., 1966. Instr. English, Oak Ridge Mil. Inst., 1957-58; asst. prof. English, Greensboro (N.C.) Coll., 1959-61, assoc. prof., 1963-66; assoc. prof. English, Winthrop Coll., Rock Hill, S.C., 1967-72, prof., 1972—, dir. Internat. Yeats Symposium, 1983, dir. Scotch-Irish Heritage Festivals, 1980, 83, 85; cons. reader for various jours. Precinct vice chmn. Rock Hill Democratic Com.; mem. local exec. com. Boy Scouts Am., Rock Hill. Served with U.S. Army, 1954-56. NEH summer stipend, 1973; S.C. Com. for Humanities grantee, 1978, 80, 83; S.C. Arts Council grantee, 1985. NEH grantee, 1983. Mem. MLA, South-Atlantic Modern Lang. Assn., Am. Com. for Irish Studies, Philol. Assn. of Carolinas, Scotch-Irish Soc. U.S.A. (mem. corp.). Presbyterian. Author: (with E.J. Wilcox) Annotated Bibliography of Writings about Arthur Wing Pinero, 1980; Selected Proc. of the Scotch-Irish Heritage Festival, 1981, 84; (with Dee Gee Lester) Immigrants form Great Britain and Ireland; contbr. articles and poems to various publs. Home: 144 Brookwood Ln Rock Hill SC 29730 Office: 325 Kinard Winthrop College Rock Hill SC 29733

WEAVER, JACQUELYN ALEXANDER, ednl. adminstr.; b. Seattle, Sept. 28, 1947; d. Banard Llewellyn and Ann Joye (Winborne) Alexander; B.S., Hampton Inst., 1971, M.A., 1974; C.A.S., Old Dominion U., 1981; m. Herman Adolphus Weaver, Sept. 2, 1978; children—Alicia Denise, Dameron Alane. English tchr. Chesapeake (Va.) Sch. System, 1971-74, dir. Emergency Sch. Aid Act Human Relations Program, 1974-81, asst. prin., 1981—; instr. English Tidewater Community Coll.; cons. human relations; mem. adv. bd. Old Dominion U. Recipient service award City of Chesapeake, 1974-75. Mem. NEA, Va. Edn. Assn., Chesapeake Edn. Assn., Assn. for Supervision and Curriculum Devel., Delta Kappa Gamma, Alpha Kappa Alpha. Contbr. articles to profl. jours. Home: 1393 Watson St Portsmouth VA 23707 Office: 1100 Holly St Chesapeake VA 23324

WEAVER, JAMES D., art museum director; b. Houston, Oct. 13, 1949; s. James D. and Mary (Hancock) W.; m. Sharyn Cecil Aydam. B.A., U. Houston, 1975; M.F.A., Syracuse U., 1978. Asst. curator Lowe Art Gallery, Syracuse, N.Y., 1976-78; curator edn. Springfield Art Mus., Mo., 1978-81; dir. Tyler Mus. Art, Tex., 1981—; guest lectr. Southwest Mo. State Univ., Springfield, 1981; guest prof. U. Tex., Tyler, 1983—. Author and editor numerous catalogues, 1982-85. Mem. Am. Assn. Museums (Merit award 1984), Am. Fedn. Arts, Tex. Assn. Museums (Mitch Wilder award 1983), Coll. Arts Assn., Art Mus. Assn. Am. (Excellence award 1984). Office: Tyler Mus Art 1300 S Mahon Tyler TX 75701

WEAVER, JOHN W., oil company executive; b. York, Pa., Sept. 7, 1924; s. Norman H. and Grace A. (Schaefer) W.; B.S. in Chem. Engring., Drexel U.; m. Patricia Grove, July 21, 1974; children—LeeAnn, Lorri, Robert, Michael. Successively refinery analyst, tech. asst., sales rep., supply mgr., v.p. supply and distbn. Standard Oil Calif., 1953-75; exec. v.p. adminstrn., ops., supply and distrbn. Standard Oil Co. (Ky.), 1975-82; exec. v.p. Coral Petroleum; pres. United Refining Co.; pres. Ind. Refining Corp., 1983—; cons. U.S. Bankruptcy Ct. dir. Asphalt Inst. Trustee Drexel U. Mem. Nat. Petroleum Refiners Assn. (dir.), Am. Petroleum Inst. Clubs: Shriner, Scottish Rite, Masons; Indian Wells (Calif.) Country; Desert Island Country (Calif.); Champions Country; Pendennis (Ky.). Audubon Country. Home: 11601 Katy Freeway 609 Houston TX 77079 Office: 908 Town and Country Blvd #600 Houston TX 77024

WEAVER, MARGUERITE (PEGGY) MCKINNIE, plantation owner, investor; b. Jackson, Tenn., June 7, 1925; d. Franklin Allen and Mary Alice (Caradine) McKinnie; children—Lynn Weaver Hermann, Thomas Jackson Weaver III, Franklin A. McKinnie Weaver. Student U. Colo., 1943-44, 44-45, Am. Acad. Dramatic Arts, 1945-46, S. Meisner's Profl. Classes, 1949. Actress theatrical cos., Can., New Eng., N.Y.C., 1946-52; mem. staff Mus. Modern Art, N.Y.C., 1949-50; radio/TV editor Sta. WTJS-AM FM Jackson Sun Newspaper, 1952-55; plantation owner, Hickory Valley, Tenn. Founder, hon. bd. dirs. Paris-Henry County Arts Council, Tenn., 1965—; charter mem. adv. bd. Tenn. Arts Commn., Nashville, 1967-74, Tenn. Performing Arts Ctr., Nashville, 1972—; chmn. Tenn. Library Assn., Nashville, 1973-74; regional chmn. Opera Memphis, 1979-85; active mem. Met. Opera Nat. Council, N.Y.C., 1980—. Mem. Am. Women in Radio and TV. Republican. Methodist. Clubs: Paris Country (pres. ladies assn. 1964-65, 70-71, 80-81), Delphian (pres. 1959-60, 83-84). Avocations: horseback riding; horse shows; field trials; travel; theatre; art museum galleries; golf; dancing. Home: Heritage Hall Heritage Farms Hickory Valley TN 38042

WEAVER, NATALIE DEWITT, religious educator, legal assistant; b. Detroit, Oct. 4, 1928; d. Edward Manning and Nathalie Galpine (LaFerte) DeWitt; m. Edward Leroy Weaver, Oct. 30, 1976 (dec. 1982). Ph.B., Siena Heights Coll., 1956, M.A. in Edn., 1967. Cert. elem. tchr., prin., Mich., Ohio, Fla., N.Y. Notary pub., Va. Research librarian Inst. Internat. Edn., Washington, 1975-78; religious educator, dir. Ecumenical Chs., Alexandria, Va., 1978-85; dir. United Coll. Ministries, Alexandria, 1984-85; legal asst. Cremins, Snead & Annunziata, Fairfax, Va., 1985-86; instr. Flagler Coll.; beauty-color cons., Arlington, Va., 1983-85; edn. cons. Weaver Assocs., Arlington, 1982-85. Contbr. articles to profl. jours. Vice chmn. United Coll. Ministries No. Va., 1985-86. Mem. Nat. Assn. Legal Secs., Capitol Color Cons. (pres. 1984-85), Nat. Cath. Edn. Assn., Religious Edn. Assn., Network, Cath. Social Justice Lobby, D.A.R. Home: 1068 Rio del Mar St Augustine FL 32084

WEAVER, RONALD L., lawyer; b. Winston-Salem, N.C., June 8, 1949; s. Robert Lee and Laura (Reich) W.; m. Jacquelyn Kay Witt, June 12, 1971; children—Lara Alison, Ronald Lee. A.B., U. N.C.-Chapel Hill, 1971; J.D. cum laude, Harvard U., 1974. Bar: Fla. Mem. Carlton, Fields, Ward, Emmanuel, Smith & Cutler, Tampa, Fla., 1974-79; ptnr. Stearns, Weaver Miller, Weissler, Alhadeff & Sitterson, Tampa, 1979—; dir. Founders Life Ins. Co., Majestic Towers, Pasadena, Fla. Chmn. Am. Heart Assn., Tampa, 1983. Served to 1st lst. USAF, 1971-81. Mem. ABA (chmn. real estate fin. subcom. comml. and fin. services com.), Hillsborough County Bar Assn. (program chmn. 1980), Tampa C. of C. (chmn. cultural affairs, bd. govs. 1983). Clubs: University, Palma Ceia Country (Tampa). Author: Florida and Federal Banking, 1981; Commercial Real Estate Acquisition, 1983. Home: 4304 W Azeele Tampa FL 33609 Office: Steans Weaver Miller Alhadeff & Sitterson 3300 One Tampa City Ctr Tampa FL 33602

WEAVER, SAMUEL EUGENE, JR., pharmacist; b. Gorman, Tex., Mar. 3, 1949; s. Sam Eugene and Alzira Eugenia (Robertson) W.; m. Glenda Faye Hardin, Mar. 9, 1969; children—Denise D'anne, Sam Eugene III, Trey Wesley, Jonathan Wesley. B.S. in Pharmacy, U. Tex., 1974. Lic. pharmacist, Tex. Student pharmacist Ace Drug Mart, Austin, Tex., 1972-74; pharmacist Eastland Drug-U-Save, Tex., 1974-79, Gorman Pharmacy, Tex., 1974-79; pharmacist Weaver Drug, DeLeon, Tex., 1974—; v.p. T.P. Weaver & Sons, Inc., DeLeon, 1980—. Pres. Peach and Melon Festival, DeLeon, 1981, DeLeon Baseball Assn., 1984; cubmaster Comanche Trail council Boy Scouts Am., 1984. Mem. DeLeon C. of C. (pres. 1980, Citizen of Yr. 1982). Methodist. Club: Par Country (bd. dirs. 1980-82) (Proctor, Tex.). Avocations: horses; golf; baseball; snow skiing. Home: 1104 Holland St DeLeon TX 76444 Office: TP Weaver & Sons Inc 104 N Texas St DeLeon TX 76444

WEAVER, VIRGINIA DOVE, museum executive; b. Westerly, R.I.; d. Ronald Cross and Elva Gertrude (Burdick) Dove; m. Water Albert Weaver, Jr. (div. Apr. 1982); children—Marshall Gueringer, Claudia Cross, Leila Jane. B.A., Tulane U., 1973; M.A., 1977. Dir. volunteers Hermann Grima Historic House, New Orleans, 1976-77; adminstrv. analyst City Chief Adminstrv. Office, New Orleans, 1977-83; dir. public relations New Orleans Mus. Art, 1983—. Coeditor: Letters From Young Audiences, 1971. Chmn. bd. New Orleans chpt. Young Audiences, Inc., 1969-71; co chmn. New Orleans Symphony Book Fair, 1973-74; mem. city council investigative panel SPCA, New Orleans, 1981-82; nat. public relations chmn. Nat. Soc. Daughters of Founders and Patriots Am., 1985—. nat. Council Jewish Women grantee, 1977. Mem. Pub. Relations Soc. Am. (anvil award 1985), La. Press Assn. (assoc.), La. Travel and Promotion Assn., Deep South Hotel/Motel Assn., La. Restaurant Assn. Episcopalian. Bd. dirs. Symphony Womens Com., 1982—, New Orleans Young Audiences, 1975—; mem. steering com. Mayors Arts Task Force, New Orleans, 1978-79. Clubs: Orleans (fine arts com.); Le Petit Salon. Avocation: Piano. Home: 7478 Hurst St New Orleans LA 70118 Office: New Orleans Mus Art PO Box 19123 New Orleans LA 70179

WEBB, DAVID ALAN, lawyer; b. Washington, May 11, 1954; s. Edwin Hull and Dorothy Augusta (Dryden) W.; m. Karen Leigh McDonald, June 24, 1978; children—Mariah Christine, Rachael Lyric. B.A., U. Ky., 1975; J.D., U. Okla., 1979. Bar: Okla. 1980. Asst. dist. atty. 20th Dist., Ardmore, Okla., 1980-82, Madill, Okla., 1982—. Research editor Am. Indian Law Rev., 1979. Mem. adv. bd. Mental Health of So. Okla., Madill, 1983—. Mem. Okla. Bar Assn., Marshall County Bar Assn. Baptist. Lodge: Rotary. Home: 407 W Tishomingo St Madill OK 73446 Office: Marshall County Courthouse Plaza Madill OK 73446

WEBB, DONALD W., lawyer, developer; b. Letcher County, Ky.; m. Julie Howser; 1 child, Woodford. B.A. in Commerce and Econs., Georgetown Coll., 1960; J.D., U. Ky., 1967. Bar: Ky. With Ky. Dept. Econ. Devel., Lexington; spl. asst. to commr. Ky. Dept. Commerce; legal adv. Nat. Adv. Com. on Civil Disorders, Washington, 1967-68; dir. Katherine Peden for U.S. Senate Campaign, Ky.; assoc. Handmaker, Weber & Meyer, Louisville, to 1971; ptnr. Webb & Webb, Lexington, from 1971, Webb, Dickey, Sullivan & LeMaster, Lexington, to present, Webb Properties, Lexington, to present. Office: Webb Dickey et al 17th Floor Vine Ctr Office Tower Lexington KY 40507

WEBB, EDGAR LELAND, dental educator; b. Reidsville, N.C., Aug. 18, 1950; s. Charlie Elton and Claudia (Harrison) W.; m. Tamsen Banks, May 12, 1973; children—Bethany Claire, Peter Harrison. B.S. in Biology, U. N.C., 1972, D.D.S., 1975, M.S. in Dentistry, 1978. Instr. U. N.C. Sch. Dentistry, Chapel Hill, 1976, asst. prof., 1978-85, assoc. prof., 1985—. Contbr. articles to profl. jours. Bd. dirs. Chapel Hill PTA, 1984—. HEW grantee, 1976-78; recipient Dentsply Internat. award, 1976. Mem. ADA, Internat. Assn. Dental Research, N.C. Dental Soc., Third Dist. Dental Soc., Durham-Orange Dental Soc., Delta Sigma Delta (dep. 1982-85). Democrat. Home: 814 Churchill Dr Chapel Hill NC 27514 Office: U NC Sch Dentistry Manning Dr Chapel Hill NC 27514

WEBB, ELEANOR ELAINE, educational administrator; b. Greensburg, La., Aug. 18, 1936; d. Robert Maurice and Bertha (Raborn) W. B.A., Southeastern La. U., 1958; M.Ed., La. State U., 1965, Ed.D., 1978. Tchr. Woodlawn High Sch., Braithewaite, La., 1958-60, Lutcher High Sch., La., 1960-65, Nicholls State U., Thibodaux, La., 1965-77; teaching asst. La. State U., Baton Rouge, 1977-78; dir. vocat. bus. edn. Nicholls State U., Thibodaux, 1978-84; asst. supt. vocat. edn. State Dept. Edn., Baton Rouge, 1984—; cons. Chromalloy Natural Resources, Houma, La., 1974-79. Editor procs. Conf. La. Colls. and Univs., Coll. Bus. Adminstrn. Contbr. articles to profl. jours. Mem. library com. First Bapt. Ch., Thibodaux; judge sci. fairs Thibodaux High Sch. Recipient Disting. Service award La. Assn. Higher Edn., 1974-75. Mem. Nat. Assn. State Dirs. Vocat. Edn., Conf. La. Colls. and Univs. (sec.), La. Assn. Higher Edn. (pres.), Coll. Bus. Adminstrn. (senator), La. Assn. Tchr. Educators (sec.), Office Systems Research (treas.), Delta Kappa Gamma (sec.). Democrat.

WEBB, ELMER JAMES, geology educator, consultant; b. Springfield, Mo., Dec. 28, 1925; s. Earl Lee and Mildred Geraldine (Watson) W.; m. Catherine Amy Sutton, Dec. 27, 1949; (div. Sept. 28, 1983); children—Catherine Susan, James Sutton, Drayton Clark. B.S. in Econs., B.S. in Geology, Drury Coll., 1950; Ph.D. in Geology, U. Cin., 1980. Exploration mgr. Texaco, Inc., various locations, 1950-68; consulting geologist, Lexington, Ky., 1968-75; exploration mgr. Anadarko Product Co., Houston, 1975-78; pres. Winchester Oil & Gas, Vancouver, B.C., 1980-82; v.p. exploration ConVest Energy, Houston, 1982-83; assoc. prof. U. Southwest La., Lafayette, 1983—; adv. bd. Womprop Resources, Oklahoma City, 1980—; pres. E.J. Webb & Assocs., Houston, Lafayette, 1983—. Contbr. geologic articles to profl. jours. Mem. Citizens of Dist. A, Lafayette, 1984. Served to lt. USNR, 1944-64, PTO. Mem. Am. Assn. Petroleum Geologists, Soc. Econ. Paleontologists and Mineralogists, Internat. Assn. Sedimentologists, Houston Geol. Soc., Lafayette Geol. Soc. Republican. Episcopalian. Club: Houston. Lodge: Sertoma Internat. Avocations: sailing; camping; rock collecting; gardening. Home: 107 Manassa Circle Carencro LA

70520 Office: U Southwestern La Dept Geology USL BOX 44530 Lafayette LA 70504

WEBB, ERNEST PACKARD, publisher; b. Junta, W.Va., Aug. 30, 1907; s. Robert Moses and Josephine (Harvey) W.; student Fed. Schs. Comml. Designing, Mpls., 1926-29; student advt. Internat. Corr. Schs., 1946-48, Alexander Hamilton Bus. Sch., 1948-52. Artist, Mountain State Engraving Co., 1929, Huntington Engraving Co. (W.Va.), 1930, Charleston Engraving Co. (W.Va.), 1931; owner, mgr. Profl. Art Studio, Roanoke, Va., 1931-40; v.p., treas. Roanoke Engraving Co., 1940-48; pres. Va. Engraving Co., Richmond, 1947—; v.p. Dixie Engraving Co., Roanoke, 1961—; pres. W.&H. Corp., Richmond, 1968—. Served with USAAF, 1942-45. Mem. Va., Richmond chambers commerce, Internat. Craftsman's Club. Republican. Baptist. Clubs: Richmond Industrial, Willow Oaks Country, Westwood (Richmond). Home: 2000 Riverside Dr Richmond VA 23225 Office: 2003 Roane St Richmond VA 23222

WEBB, GLENDA JEFFERSON, nurse; b. Elberton, Ga., Jan. 6, 1954; d. James Ray and Regenia (Blackmon) Jefferson; m. Michael Ayers Webb, Dec. 15, 1974; children—Bridget Dawn, Derrick Michael. B.S. in Nursing cum laude, Med. Coll. Ga., 1975. R.N., Ga. Staff nurse Self Meml. Hosp., Greenwood, S.C., 1975-78; pub. health nurse Elbert County Health Dept., Elberton, Ga., 1978-80, div. dir. med./surg. area, 1978—, emergency med. care first respondent, 1980—. CPR instr., 1979-83; mem. Emergency Med. Service Region 10 Council, Athens, Ga., 1980-82. Mem. Sigma Theta Tau. Home: Route 6 Box 149-A Elberton GA 30635

WEBB, HARRY CHARLES, cons.; b. Felsenthal, Ark., Sept. 30, 1905; s. Victor Leach and Lillian Zenobia (Stinnett) W.; student U. Tex.; m. Ruth Alene Brown, July 5, 1959; children—Harry Charles, Richard C. With Tex. Gulf Sulpher Co., Houston, 1929-53, exec. asst., asst. to v.p., dir. pub. relations; pres. Pan Am. Sulphur Co., Houston, 1954-70, dir., 1953-70, ret.; now cons. Mem. AIME. Clubs: Houston Country, Petroleum, Coronado River Oaks Country. Office: 1919 Bank of Southwest Bldg Houston TX 77002

WEBB, HENRY EMILE, church history educator, minister; b. Detroit, June 11, 1922; s. Hubert and Mabel Lavina (Postiff) W.; m. Emerald Mae Stevenson, Aug. 24, 1943; children—Karen, Mark, Wendy. A.B., Cin. Bible Sem., 1943; Ph.B., Xavier U., 1944; B.D., So. Bapt. Theol. Sem., 1947, Ph.D., 1954. Ordained to ministry Christian Ch. (Disciples of Christ), 1943. Minister Clifton Christian Ch., Louisville, Ky., 1944-49, First Christian Ch., Erwin, Tenn., 1950-63; prof. ch. history Milligan Coll., Tenn., 1950—. Contbr. articles to religious publs. Mem. Am. Soc. Ch. History, Disciples of Christ Hist. Soc., Theta Phi. Democrat. Lodge: Civitan (pres. 1979-80). Home: 1601 Idlewild Dr Johnson City TN 37601 Office: Milligan Coll Milligan College TN 37682

WEBB, IVA BRIDWELL, physician; b. Deland, Fla., July 24, 1954; d. John Wesley and Patricia Lavell (Tomlinson) Bridwell; m. Raoul Avington Webb, Dec. 21, 1975; children—Cooper Avington, Wesley Alden. B.S., U. Central Fla., 1975; M.D., U. South Fla., 1977. Diplomate Nat. Bd. Med. Examiners, Am. Bd. Pediatrics. Resident, Tampa (Fla.) Gen. Hosp., 1977-79; fellow Shands Teaching Hosp., Gainesville, Fla., 1979-81; asst. prof. pediatrics U. Tenn. Coll. Medicine, Knoxville, 1981-83; dir. neonatology Humana Hosp. Brandon (Fla.), 1983—. Jr. fellow Am. Acad. Pediatrics; mem. AMA, So. Soc. Pediatric Research, Fla. Med. Assn., Hillsborough County Pediatric Soc., Hillsborough County Med. Assn. Republican. Office: Humana Hosp Brandon 119 Oakfield Dr Brandon FL 33511

WEBB, JAMES PETER, dentist; b. Norristown, Pa., Jan. 23, 1949; s. James Carlin and Esther Marie (Reiner) W. B.S., Pa. State U., 1971; D.D.S., Temple U., 1976. Dentist U.S. Navy, 1977-80; gen. practice dentistry, Hopewell, Va., 1980—. Bd. dirs. United Way, Hopewell, 1984-85. U.S. Navy scholar, 1972-76. Mem. Southside Dental Soc., ADA, Hopewell C. of C. (bd. dirs. 1985), Hopewell Cancer Soc. (bd. dirs. 1983-85). Lodges: Moose, Lions. Avocations: snow skiing; racquetball; sailing; swimming; jogging. Home: 700 Quarterpath Ln Colonial Heights VA 23834 Office: 100 N 2d Ave PO Box 501 Hopewell VA 23860

WEBB, JANIS LEE, banker; b. Dumas, Tex., July 27, 1941; d. William Lee and Frances Inez (Tidwell) W.; student Draughons Bus. Coll., Amarillo, Tex., 1960-61. Sch. Banking, Tex. Tech U., 1983. Divorced. Various clerical and bookkeeping positions, 1961-62, with First Nat. Bank, Dumas, 1962—, v.p. installment loan dept., 1962—; seminar leader, 1980—. Co-chmn. bd. dirs. Moore County Art Assn.; mem. Dumas Sr. High Sch. Bd. Spl. Adult Edn. Mem. Nat. Assn. Bank Women, Bus. and Profl. Women's Club, Dumas C. of C. (pres. 1984). Republican. Lutheran. Office: PO Box 1117 500 Main St Dumas TX 79029

WEBB, JOHN ROBERT, personnel service company executive; b. Leland, Miss., July 22, 1940; s. Robert Melvin and Hazel Louise (McDaniel) W. Process engr. Uniroyal, Inc., Baton Rouge, 1963-64; pilot plant engr. Copolymer Rubber & Chem. Co., Baton Rouge, 1964-67; asst. prodn. supt. Baxter Labs., Kingstree, S.C., 1967-68; research engr. Celanese Chem., Corpus Christi, Tex., 1968-70; pres., chmn. bd. W-J Enterprises, Inc., San Antonio, 1970—; pres., dir. Dunhill Temporary of San Antonio, Inc., 1983—; dir. Dunhill Personnel Service, San Antonio, 1973—. Registered profl. engr., Tex. Mem. Nat. Employment Assn., Am. Inst. Chem. Engrs., Tex. Pvt. Employment Assn., San Antonio Pvt. Employment Assn. Republican. Baptist. Home: 2434 Rockaway St San Antonio TX 78232 Office: 9601 McAllister Freeway San Antonio TX 78216

WEBB, JOSEPH BERNARD, educational administrator; b. Galax, Va., Mar. 27, 1936; s. Bernard and Opal Naomi (Collier) W.; m. Marianne Baker, Aug. 14, 1960; 1 child, Mary Camille. B.A. cum laude, Wake Forest U., 1958; M.A., George Peabody Coll., 1959; postgrad, UCLA, 1962, East Carolina U., 1965-67, U. N.C., 1969, N.C. State U., 1972-73. Cert. secondary tchr., prin. Tchr., Winston-Salem/Forsyth Schs., Winston-Salem, N.C., 1959-65; prin. Kinston City Schs., N.C., 1965-69, dir. staff devel. and instrn., 1969-70; fed. program dir. N.C. Dept. Edn., Raleigh, 1970-82, asst. state supt., support services, 1983-84, asst. state supt. instructional services, 1984—. Deacon, St. Paul's Christian Ch., Raleigh, 1970—. Reynolds fellow Reynolds Industries, 1962. Mem. Assn. Supervision and Curriculum Devel., N.C. Assn. for Supervision and Curriculum Devel., N.C. State Employees Assn. Avocations: music; tennis. Home: 7205 Bolero Circle Raleigh NC 27609 Office: NC Dept Edn Edn Bldg Raleigh NC 27611

WEBB, LEE HAMPTON, architectural products group sales manager; b. Cordele, Ga., Mar. 31, 1928; s. Robert Leon and Ruth (Warters) W.; m. Beverly Butcher, Apr. 4, 1959; children—William West, Lee Hampton. B.S. in Archtl. Engring., Ga. Inst. Tech., 1951. Sales mgr. J.W. O'Donnell Constrn. Co., Atlanta, 1960-65; with H.B. Fuller Co., Atlanta, 1965—, salesman southeastern region, 1965-74, southeastern region sales mgr., 1974-78, so. region sales mgr., 1978-80, industry sales mgr., Walls, 1980-83, nat. sales mgr., archtl. products, Atlanta and Palatine, Ill., 1983—; bds. dirs. Giles Sales Co., Atlanta, 1976—, B & L Distbrs., Atlanta, 1976—, E.I.M.A., Washington, 1983—. Republican. Baptist. Home: 534 Collier Rd NW Atlanta GA 30318 Office: H B Fuller Co 315 S Hicks Rd Palatine IL 60067

WEBB, MARGARET ANNE, optometrist; b. Akron, Ohio, Apr. 4, 1953; d. James Henry and Anna Ross (Collins) Konneker; m. John A. Webb, Jr., Apr. 5, 1980; 1 child, Steve Ross. Student Lamar U., 1972-74; B.S., U. Houston, 1976, O.D., 1977. Optometrist with Dr. Crawford, Orange, Tex., 1978-80, Dr. Kever, Sherman, Tex., 1980-82; pvt. practice optometry, McKinney, Tex., 1980—. Recipient Gold Key Internat. U. Houston, 1976; Rookie of Yr. award Altrusa Club Sherman, 1983. Mem. Tex. Assn. Optometrists (sec. Golden Triangle chpt. 1979-80), Alpha Chi Omega (pres. 1979), Pi Delta Phi, Alpha Lambda Delta. Club: Altrusa (pres. 1984-85). Avocations: sewing; water sports; needlework; camping; cooking. Home: 1502 Andy Sherman TX 75090 Office: Tex State Optical 312 A Hwy 75 N McKinney TX 75069

WEBB, PAUL LAFAYETTE, II, educator, historian; b. Huntington, W.Va., Oct. 20, 1935; s. Paul Lafayette and Amanda Elizabeth (Cunningham) W.; m. Evangeline Marcella Humann, Aug. 8, 1964; children—Kathryn Elizabeth, Victoria Lea. B.A., U. Redlands, 1958; M.Div., Eastern Bapt. Theol. Sem., 1961; M.A., Ohio State U., 1968, Ph.D., 1977. Minister youth and music 1st Baptist Ch., Wellington, Kans., 1961-63; minister Christian edn. and music Trinity Bapt. Ch., Marion, Ohio, 1964-66; assoc. prof. history, chmn. div. social scis. Bacone Coll., Muskogee, Okla., 1970—, long range planner, 1983-84. Author, editor: Strategies for College Success, 1979, 80. Bd. dirs. Muskogee Coop. Ministries, 1981-85; co-chmn. Muskogee CROP Walk, 1982; Democratic precinct chmn., Muskogee, 1974. Mem. Orgn. Am. Historians, Am. Hist. Assn., AAUP. Baptist. Lodge: Lions. Avocations: music; travel; drama. Office: Bacone Coll East Shawnee Muskogee OK 74403

WEBB, PERRY FLYNT, JR., clergyman; b. Malvern, Ark., Feb. 9, 1925; s. Perry Flynt and Thelma Fern (Stall) W.; m. Virginia Louise Powell, Oct. 3, 1949; children—Deborah Webb Smith, Perry F. III. B.A., Baylor U., 1946; M.Div., So. Bapt. Theol. Sem., 1949. Ordained to ministry Baptist Ch., 1946. Pastor, Bapt. chs., Poteet, Tex., 1949-52, Natchitoches, La., 1952-64; Albany, Ga., 1964-75; First Bapt. Ch., Baton Rouge, 1975—; past pres. and former pres. exec. bd. Dist. Eight Bapt. Conv.; past mem. and officer La. Bapt. Exec. Bd.; past state pastor advisor Bapt. Student Union; past mem. exec. com. Ga. Bapt. Conv.; past mem. radio and television commn. So. Bapt. Conv.; mem. program coordination com. La. Bapt. Conv. Woman's Missionary Union; guest speaker Bapt. Sem. of East Africa, Kenya, 1983; pres. La. Bapt. Conv., 1981-83, also mem. and pres. exec. bd. Contbr. articles to religious publs. Past mem. adv. bd. Sowega Youth Home; past mem. hosp. commn. Ga. Bapt. Hosp.; mem. adv. bd. Baton Rouge Gen. Hosp.; mem. Dist. Atty.'s Crime Commn.; past mem. bd. dirs. ARC; past trustee La. Bapt. Coll., Tift Coll.; trustee So. Bapt. Theol. Sem., La. Moral and Civic Found. Republican. Avocations: woodworking, golf. Home: 8022 Oakbrook Dr Baton Rouge LA 70810 Office: First Bapt Ch PO Box 1309 Baton Rouge LA 70821

WEBB, ROBERT CARROLL, SR., physics educator, researcher; b. Petersburg, Va., Mar. 6, 1947; s. Robert O. Sr. and Anna Mae (Blankenship) W.; m. Patricia Ann Wiley; children—Robert Carroll Jr., Suzanne W., Nicole M. B.A., U. Pa., 1968; M.A., Princeton U., 1970, Ph.D. in Physics, 1972. Adj. asst. prof. UCLA, 1972-75; research assoc. Princeton U., 1975-76, asst. prof., 1976-80; assoc. prof. physics Tex. A&M U., College Station, 1980—. Contbr. articles to profl. jours. Mem. exec. com. Raintree Homeowners Assn., College Station, 1981-82, pres., 1982-83. U.S. Dept. Energy grantee, 1981—; Robert A. Welch Found. grantee, 1982-85. Mem. Am. Phys. Soc. Avocations: travel; gardening; photography. Home: 2508 Antietam Dr College Station TX 77840 Office: Physics Dept Tex A&M U College Station TX 77843

WEBB, ROBERT COLEMAN, optometrist; b. Lucasville, Ohio, Aug. 15, 1922; s. James G. Webb and Lorene (Gilbert) Boggs; m. Linda Faye Mobley, Dec. 28, 1959; children—Robin Lynn, Robert Charles. Student Ohio State U., 1941; O.D., No. Ill. U., 1949. Lic. optometrist, Ky. Practice optometry, Grayson, Ky., 1954—. Patentee optometric screwdriver. Served as aviation cadet pilot USAF, 1942-45. Named Hon. City Fireman, Grayson Fire Dept., 1979; recipient U.S. Pratt award Grayson C. of C., 1983. Mem. Ky. Optometric Assn. (legis. com. 1975—), Am. Optometric Assn., League Ky. Sportsmen (Ky. sportsman of Yr. 1965), Fish and Wildlife Ky. (chmn. 8th dist. 1975, 84, 85). Republican. Methodist. Lodges: Masons, Shriners, Lions (v.p. 1976). Avocations: farming; hunting; golfing; fishing. Home: Route 1 Box 115 Grayson KY 41143 Office: 107 E Main St Grayson KY 41143

WEBB, STEPHANIE TILSON, educator; b. Indpls., Sept. 26, 1946; d. Stephen William and Bertie Ruth Tilson; m. Milam Ross Weeb, Sept. 9, 1967; children—Elizabeth Ellen, Bret Maxwell. B.Ed., U. Miami, 1968, M.Ed. with honors, 1979. Tchr., Villas Elem. Sch., Ft. Myers, Fla., 1968-70, 72-74, 75-77; music tchr. Canterbury Sch., Ft. Myers, 1970-71; tchr. resource tchr. Lee County Bilingual Edn. Programs, Ft. Myers, 1977—; workshop leader for bilingual paraprofls., 1977-80; guest lectr. Fla. Internat. U., Winter Haven, 1981. Bd. dirs. Edison Players, 1968-70, Lee County Children's Theater, 1968-70; sec., registrar S.W. Fla. Summer Music Festival, 1973-75; pianist Jr. Welfare League Follies; leader, troop services dir. Gulfcoast council Girls Scouts U.S.A.; mem. Lee County Mental Health Assn., Nature Ctr. of Lee County. Project Trial grantee, 1976. Mem. Fla. Pharmacy Assn. Ladies Aux., Tchrs. of English to Speakers of Other Langs., Nat. Assn. Bilingual Educators. Republican. Lutheran. Home: 3955 McGregor Blvd Fort Myers FL 33901 Office: Lee County Schools Bilingual Dept 2055 Central Ave Fort Myers FL 33901

WEBB, STEVEN E(UGENE), insurance agent, real estate broker; b. Mineral Wells, Tex., May 26, 1955; s. William Steven Webb and Dorothy Nan (Sturdivant) Barnes; m. Jann Cawthon, May 26, 1980; children—Heather Elizabeth, Stephanie Janene, Boone Arza. Student Weatherford Jr. Coll., 1973-75, Tarleton State U., 1977-79. Lic. real estate broker, ins. agt. Clay pipe mill operator, Can-Tex Industries, Mineral Wells, 1973-76; owner Webb Roofing Co., Mineral Wells, 1976-77; owner, agt. Webb Ins. and Real Estate, Mineral Wells, 1977—. Commr., Optimist Pee Wee Football, Mineral Wells, 1979—, Babe Ruth League Baseball, 1980. Mem. Mineral Wells Bd. Realtors (sec.-treas. 1983-84, v.p. 1985-86, pres. 1986-87), Mineral Wells Ind. Ins. Agts. (sec. treas. 1981—), Nat. Assn. Self Employed, Am. Assn. Entrepreneurs, Internat. Mktg. Assos. (Eagle award 1982). Club: Optimist (pres. Mineral Wells 1980-81, Optimist of Yr. 1980). Home: 4 Preston Pl Mineral Wells TX 76067 Office: Webb Ins and Real Estate PO Box 220 Mineral Wells TX 76067

WEBB, THOMAS FREDERICK, periodontist, real estate developer, grain merchant; b. Elizabeth City, N.C., Dec. 26, 1947; s. James Fred and Nellie Mae (Webb) W.; m. Karen Elaine Farless, June 30, 1973; children—Karen Elizabeth, Blair Lawrence, Laura Thomas. Student U. N.C., 1966-69, D.D.S., 1973; cert. in periodontics U. Ky., 1976. Grain dealer Fred Webb Grain Inc., Greenville, N.C., 1962-66, 85—; gen. practice dentistry, 1973-74; practice dentistry specializing in periodontics, New Bern, N.C., 1976—; pres. Kari Blue Properties, New Bern, 1983—; pres. TFW, Inc.; sec. Timberlands Unltd., Windsor, N.C., 1982-85. Mem. ADA, Am. Acad. Periodontics, N.C. Dental Soc., N.C. 5th Dist. Dental Soc. (pres. 1983-84), Loblolly Study Club (pres. 1982-83), Craven County Dental Soc. (pres. 1978-79), N.C. Soc. Periodontics, N.C. Dental Implant Study Club, Carteret County Dental Study Club, N.C. Hist. Soc., N.C. Art Soc., Democrat. Methodist. Avocations: tennis; golf; skiing; hunting; fishing; basketball; volleyball; raquetball. New Bern Golf and Country Club (singles and doubles champion, 1981). Home: 4701 Trentwoods Dr New Bern NC 28560 Office: PO Box 2681 New Bern NC 28560

WEBB, THOMAS YANCEY, realtor, interior designer; b. Portsmouth, Ohio, Dec. 17, 1948; s. George Kenneth and Frances (Scarborough) W. B.S., Bapt. Coll., 1971; A.B., Atlanta Sch. Design, 1976; grad. Nat. Ctr. Paralegal Tng., 1981; postgrad. Atlanta Law Sch., 1983—. Real estate broker Doris Meddin Real Estate, Charleston, S.C., 1977—; pres. Thomas Webb & Co. Ltd., Charleston, 1977-80; owner Sophisticated Interiors, Charleston, 1980-83. Recipient John Myers English award Ky. Mil. Inst., 1967. Mem. Am. Soc. Interior Designers (assoc.), Trident Bd. Realtors, Pi Gamma Mu, Delta Theta Phi. Republican. Episcopalian. Address: 64 Murray Blvd Charleston SC 29401

WEBB, W. ROGER, university president; b. Bristow, Okla., Apr. 28, 1941; s. E.A. and Grace ; W.; B.A., Okla. State U., 1963; J.D., U. Okla., 1967; m. Gwen Moulton, Sept. 7, 1963; children—Roger Brett, Brandon R. Bar: Okla. Asst. to sec. U.S. Senate, 1965; adminstrv. asst. to commr. pub. safety Oklahoma City, 1967-68; gen. counsel Okla. Dept. Public Safety, 1968-71, asst. commr. pub. safety, then commr., 1971-78; pres. Northeastern Okla. State U., Tahlequah, 1978—; instr. Central State U., Edmond, Okla., 1970-71; chmn. Okla. Employees Suggestion Com., 1972; chmn. Council Univ. Pres., 1984-85; chmn. Okla. Coll. and Univ. AASCU Pres., 1983-85. Bd. dirs. Oklahoma City Council Alcoholism. Ford Found. legis. intern. 1963. Mem. Internat. Assn. Chiefs Police, Am. Assn. Motor Vehicle Adminstrs., Okla. Bar Assn., Lambda Chi Alpha. Baptist. Address: Office Pres Northeastern Okla State U Tahlequah OK 74464

WEBBER, CLYDE RAY, JR., court official; b. Jonesville, La., Nov. 1, 1936; s. Clyde R. and Violet (Kirby) W.; m. Gwen Huff, June 20, 1957; children—Trey, Sue Ann, Phillip. B.A., La. Coll., 1959. Reporter, F.W. Dodge Corp. div. McGraw Hill Pub. Co., 1960-62; tchr. Ferriday High Sch., 1962-63; instr. pub. speaking U. So. Miss., Natchez, 1962-78, Copiah-Lincoln Jr. Coll., Natchez, 1975-78, Alcorn State U., Natchez, 1978; clk. of ct. 7th Jud. Dist., Parish Concordia, Vidalia, La., 1966—; profl. after-dinner speaker; guest lectr. Ala. Jud. Coll., 1981, Miss. Jud. Coll., 1985; fellow Inst. for Ct. Mgmt., Denver, 1972-78; mem. Jud. Council La., 1975-76, La. Commn. on Law Enforcement and Adminstrn. Criminal Justice, 1972-79; mem., sec. New Courthouse Bldg. Com., Concordia Parish, 1972—; mem. task force com. on cts. Red River Delta Law Enforcement Planning Council, 1978; mem. jud. planning commn. La. Supreme Ct., 1977—. Editor: Concise History and Statistical Look at Concordia Parish (Dabney Calhoun), 1967. Pres. Bd. Suprs. of Elections, Concordia Parish, 1972—; mem. Concordia Parish Sch. Bd., 1964-66; mem. Gov.-Elect Edward's Transition Com. on Criminal Justice, 1984; bd. dirs. Concordia Parish Council on Aging, 1972—, project co-ordinator Kitchen Keepsakes cookbook, 1978—; trustee La. Clks. of Ct. Retirement and Relief Fund, 1969-79; bd. dirs. Red River Delta Law Enforcement Planning Council, 1977—. Served with U.S. Army, 1961, USAR, 1961-67. Recipient Disting. Service award Ferriday Jaycees, 1971; named Ky. col., Hon. Tar Heel (N.C.). Mem. La. Clks. of Ct. Assn. (bd. dirs. 1969-78, legis. chmn. 1975-79, pres. 1975-76, exec. com. 1974-78, editor newsletter 1970—), Internat. Assn. Clks., Recorders, Election Ofcls. and Treasurers (pres. 1980, membership chmn. 1981—, editor newsletter 1977—), Nat. Assn. Trial Ct. Adminstrs., Nat. Assn. Ct. Adminstrs., Nat. Assn. County Ofcls., Nat. Speakers Assn., Ala. Jud. Coll. Faculty Assn. (hon.). Home: Box 871 Vidalia LA 71373 Office: New Parish Courthouse 1 Advocate Row Vidalia LA 71373

WEBBER, DAVID BENJAMIN, petroleum geophysicist, real estate broker; b. Elkton, Md., Sept. 9, 1958; s. Irving Wade and Wanda (Holtsclaw) W.; m. Susan Gamage, Oct. 1, 1983. B.S. in Chemistry, East Tenn. State U., 1980; M.S. in Oceanography, Old Dominion U., 1982. Research chemist Research Found., Norfolk, Va., 1980-82; geophysicist Amoco Prodn. Co., New Orleans, 1982-85; broker, pres. Webber Properties, New Orleans, 1984—. Contbr. articles to profl. jours. Vice pres. local civic assn., New Orleans, 1985—. Mem. Soc. of Exploration Geophysicists, Am. Assn. of Petroleum Geologists, Southeastern Geophys. Soc. (editor 1985—), Nat. Assn. of Realtors. Republican. Methodist. Home: 4705 Sonfield St Metairie LA 70006 Office: Amoco Prodn Co PO Box 50879 New Orleans LA 70150

WEBBER, JOE MARTIN, pathologist, medical examiner, educator; b. Indpls., Jan. 15, 1924; s. Martin Inman and Ercel Pleuma (Crawford) W.; m. Marion Stevenson, July 16, 1949 (div. 1968); children—Deborah Lynn, Martin Inman, Paul Joseph, Christine Sue, Johanna Stephanie, Nathan Timothy; m. 2d, Mary Margaret Bayer, Nov. 9, 1968; children—Holly Mary Margaret, Mary Kim. B.S., Middlebury Coll., 1944; M.D., Albany Med. Coll., 1948. Diplomate Am. Bd. Pathology. Intern Rochester (N.Y.) Gen. Hosp., 1948-49; resident in surgery Good Samaritan Hosp., Cin., 1949-50; practice medicine, Orangeburg N.Y., 1950-51; med. dir. Banmethuot Leprosarium, Vietnam, 1951-53; resident in pathology Miami Valley Hosp., Dayton, Ohio, 1953-57; practice medicine specializing in pathology, Columbus, Ga., 1957—; chief pathology Cobb Hosp., Phenix City, Ala., 1960-73, VA Med. Ctr., Tuskegee, Ala., 1973—; med. examiner State of Ga., 1957—; prof. allied health Tuskegee Inst., 1974—; pres. Interstate Labs., Inc., 1960—, Joe M. Webber, M.D., P.C. Lab.; med. dir. Am. Family Life Ins. Co., 1961-77, Columbus Intermediate Care Home, 1975—; cons. in pathology, 1960—. Organist Sherwood United Meth. Ch., Columbus. Mem. AMA, Acad. Forensic Scis., Nat. Assn. Med. Examiners, Soc. Nuclear Medicine, Nat. Assn. VA Physicians, Assn. VA Chiefs of Lab. Service, So. Med. Assn., Med. Assn. Ala., N.Y. Acad. Scis., Coll. Am. Pathologists, Am. Soc. Clin. Pathologists, Aircraft Owners and Pilots Assn., Am. Guild Organists. Mem. Assemblies of God Ch. Office: 1300 Wynnton Rd Suite 108 Columbus GA 31906

WEBBER, LINDSAY CAMPBELL, nurse, health agency administrator; b. St. Petersburg, Fla., Feb. 9, 1952; d. Robert Mathers and Mary Adele (Clark) Campbell; m. Stephen Perry Shaw, May 5, 1975 (div. May 1980); m. 2d Frank Arthur Webber, Apr. 3, 1982. B.S. in Nursing, U.Fla., 1974; postgrad. in nursing U. South Fla. R.N., Fla. Neuro/burn staff nurse Shands Teaching Hosp., Gainesville, Fla., 1974-75; staff nurse ICU/CCU, North Fla. Regional Hosp., Gainesville, 1975-76, Univ. Community Hosp., Tampa, Fla., 1977-78; staff nurse radiation therapy St. Joseph's Hosp., Tampa, 1978-82; field nurse Forest Terr. Home Health Agy., Tampa, 1982-83; supr. Univ. Home Health Agy., Tampa, 1983—; vol./mem. Hospice of Hillsborough, Tampa, 1983—. Mem. Gerontol. Assn. Am., Internat. Soc. Nurses in Cancer Care, Sigma Theta Tau, Phi Kappa Phi. Democrat. Home: Route 3 Box 169 Lithia FL 33547

WEBBER, PAMELA CLARK, construction scheduling executive; b. Ft. Hood, Tex., Apr. 20, 1947; d. John Lanham and Alice Paula (Collier) Clark; ed. Radford Coll., 1965-68; m. David L. Webber, Sept. 24, 1976; 1 dau., Stacey Michele. Civil enging. technician with various cons. engrs., 1969-75; critical path method cons. Winn & Assos., Richardson, Tex., 1974-75; co-owner, exec. v.p. DLW Infosystems, Inc., Richardson, 1975—; pres. ON SCHEDULE, Inc. div. W.B.E., 1983—. Mem. Beta Sigma Phi (sec. 1973). Republican. Episcopalian. Office: 1216 Executive Dr W Richardson TX 75081

WEBER, ANTHONY JOHN, geophysicist, geologist; b. Urbana, Ill., Aug. 1, 1953; s. Ralph Harold and Evelyn C. (Babcock) W.; m. Dierdre Elice Duggan, Apr. 21, 1979; 1 son, John Anthony. B.S. in Geophys. Engring., Colo. Sch. of Mines, 1975; M.S. in Geology, U. S.W. La., 1979. Cert. geol. scientist. Area geophysicist South La. dist. Atlantic Richfield Co., Lafayette, 1975-81; sr. explorationist Gulf Coast div. Delta Drilling Co., Lafayette, 1981-85; cons., Lafayette, 1983—; sr. explorationist Gt. So. Oil and Gas Co., Lafayette, 1985—; ptnr. LAFDEL Partnership, Penta Ptnrs., Comanche Flyers Inc.; prin. Phoenix Exploration Co. Recipient Cecil Green Gold medal Colo. Sch. Mines, 1975, Waltman award, 1975. Mem. S.W. La. Geophys. Soc. (past pres.), Lafayette Geol. Soc., Soc. Exploration Geophysicists, Am. Assn. Petroleum Geologists, Am. Inst. Profl. Geologists, Aircraft Owners and Pilots Assn. Baptist. Club: City of Lafayette. Contbr. articles to profl. jours. Home and office: 114 Normandy Rd Lafayette LA 70503

WEBER, FREDERICK ALVIS, communications company executive; b. St. Louis, Feb. 17, 1944; s. Frederick Daniel and Zelma Grace (Alvis) W.; m. Janice Jensen, May 10, 1970; 1 child, Lynn. B.A., Dana Coll., 1966; M.A., U. Guam, 1970; postgrad. in mgmt. Ga. State U., 1984—. Tchr. Govt. of Guam, Agana, 1966-70, media specialist, 1971-74, asst. dir. learning resource ctr., 1975-80; tng. coordinator Cox Communications, Inc., New Orleans, 1981-83, tng. mgr., 1984—, condr. nat. tech. needs assessments, 1981—, tech. tng. mgr., 1984—. Contbr., researcher for Constitution of Guam, 1972, Constitution No. Marianas, 1972. Nat. social sci. rep. Nat. Social Sci. Conf., Omaha, 1970; mem. Destrehan Plantation Restoration Soc., La., 1983, Old Kenner Railway Assn., Kanner, La., 1985. Mem. Am. Soc. Tng. and Devel., Phi Delta Kappa. Lutheran. Home: 507 Dell Dr Saint Rose LA 46368 Office: Boeing Petroleum Services 850 S Clearview Pkwy Metairie LA 70123

WEBER, LOUIS CARL, JR., home building firm executive; b. Lorain, Ohio, Aug. 8, 1947; s. Louis Carl and Lucille Mae (Richards) W.; m. Linda Radcliffe Bucher, June 10, 1967 (div. 1975); children—Kristen Marie, Gretchen Lou; m. 2d Elizabeth Betts Weber, Nov. 21, 1981; 1 dau., Stephanie Elizabeth. B.B.A., Ohio U., 1969. Lic. gen. contractor, N.C., S.C., Fla. Estimator, Dickerson Inc., Monroe, N.C., 1973, Ervin Co., Charlotte, N.C., 1973-74; v.p. Century Home Builders, Inc., Pineville, N.C., 1974-78; pres. Horizon Home Builders, Inc., Mathews, N.C., 1979-82, Nola Properties, Inc., Charlotte, N.C., 1982—. Bd. dirs. Ind. Living Ctr., Charlotte, 1981—. Served to 2d lt. U.S. Army, 1969-75. Recipient Commendation, Gov. N.C., 1982. Mem. N.C. Solar Energy Assn. (pres. Charlotte chpt. 1981), N.C. Home Builders Assn., Charlotte Home Builders Assn., N.C. Bd. Realtors, Charlotte Bd. Realtors. Republican. Episcopalian. Address: 6313 Gay Wind Dr Charlotte NC 28211

WEBER, PAUL JOSEPH, political science educator; b. Dubuque, Iowa; Nov. 1, 1937; s. Les R. and Iven E. (Willenborg) W.; m. Madeline C. Reno, Aug. 30, 1977; 1 child, Benjamin J. Reno-Weber. B.A., St. Louis U., 1964, Philosophy & Letters, 1965, M.A., 1971; Ph.D., U. Chgo., 1977. Asst. prof. Marquette U., Milw., 1973-75; prof. polit. sci. U. Louisville, 1984—; chairperson social sci. div. U. Louisville, 1980—. Author: Private Churches and Public Money, 1981. Contbr. articles to profl. jours. Expert witness Conn. Legislature, Hartford, 1985, Mich. legislature, Lansing, 1985 Ky. Senate, Frankfort, 1978. Recipient ACE Teaching Incentive award East Central States, 1985, Grawmeyer award Kentuckiana Metroversity, 1984, Dist. Teaching award U. Louisville, 1984, Affirmative Action award U. Louisville, 1984. Mem. Am. Polit. Sci. Assn., Southern Polit. Sci. Assn., Southeastern Pre Law Advisor Assn., Am. Judicature Soc., Golden Key. Democrat. Roman Catholic. Avocations: tennis; basketball; jogging. Office: U Louisville Dept Polit Sci Louisville KY 40292

WEBER, ROBERT DONALD, minister, psychotherapist; b. Apache, Okla., June 12, 1935; s. Henry G. and Tressa Arlyn (Windsor) W.; m. Patricia Anne Brashear, Apr. 9, 1957; children—Patricia Gayle, James Robert, Paul Kevin. B.S., Howard Payne U., 1966; TH.M., New Orleans Bapt. Theol. Sem., 1969.

Ordained to ministry So. Baptist Ch., 1961; pastor Trinity Bapt. Ch., Oakdale, La., 1969-71, First Bapt. Ch., LeCompte, La., 1971-74, Southside Bapt. Ch., Carthage, Tex., 1974-75; chaplain Lufkin State Sch. (Tex.), 1975-77; pastor First Bapt. Ch., Anthony, N.M., 1977-78; pastoral psychotherapist, adminstrv. asst. Pastoral Care and Counseling Ctr., Abilene, Tex., 1981—; pastor Rochele Bapt. Ch., 1982—; assoc. pastor of counseling Harris Ave. Bapt. Ch., San Angelo, Tex., 1982—. Bd. dirs. Mothers Against Drunk Drivers, 1982—. Served with USAF, 1953-60. Mem. Am. Assn. for Marriage and Family Therapy (clin.), Am. Assn. Pastoral Counselors, Tex. Bapt. Family Minister Assn. Lodges: Rotary. Home: 2102 Westview Abilene TX 79603 Office: 702 Hickory St Abilene TX 79601

WEBER, ROBERT EUGENE, pharmacist; b. Altoona, Pa., July 19, 1935; s. Kenneth Jay and Sara (Snyder) W.; m. Anne Virginia Heafner, Sept. 5, 1959. B.S. in Sci., Coll. William and Mary, 1959; B.S. in Pharmacy, Med. Coll. of Va., 1964. Lic. pharmacist, Va. Tchr. sci. Cradock High Sch., Portsmouth, Va., 1960-61; pharmacist Irwin's Pharmacy, Portsmouth, 1964-66, Portsmouth Gen. Hosp., 1966—, dir. pharmacy services, 1969—; clin. instr. Sch. Pharmacy, Med. Coll. of Va., Richmond, 1978—. Contbr. articles to profl. jour. Served with U.S. Army, 1958-60. Mem. Va. Soc. Hosp. Pharmacists, Am. Soc. Hosp. Pharmacists, Alpha Sigma Chi, Sigma Zeta. Methodist. Avocation: photography. Office: Portsmouth Gen Hosp 850 Crawford Pkwy Portsmouth VA 23704

WEBRE, PRESTON JOSEPH, JR., dentist; b. Thibodaux, La., Aug. 17, 1949; s. Preston J. and Gladys (Roux) W.; m. Sydney Blanchard, June 2, 1970; 1 child, Douglas. B.S., Nicholls State U., 1971; D.D.S., La. State U., 1975. Dentist U.S. Army, Augusta, Ga., 1975-77; gen. practice dentistry, Lafayette, La., 1977—. Bd. dirs. Fatima Parents Club, Fatima Boosters Club, mem. Fatima Found. Served to capt. U.S. Army, 1975-77. Democrat. Roman Catholic. Clubs: K'rewe of Bonaparte, Cricket (bd. dirs.). Lodge: Rotary. Avocations: golf; gardening.

WEBSTER, BURNICE HOYLE, physician; b. Leeville, Tenn., Mar. 3, 1910; s. Thomas Jefferson and Martha Anne (Melton) W.; B.A. magna cum laude, Vanderbilt U., 1936, M.D., 1940; D.Sc., Holy Trinity Coll., 1971; Ph.D., Fla. Research Inst., 1973; m. Georgia Kathryn Foglemann, May 6, 1939; children—Brenda Kathryn, Phillip Hoyle, Adrienne Elise. Intern St. Thomas Hosp., Nashville, 1940-42, resident, 1942-43; practice medicine, specializing in chest disease, Nashville, 1943—; mem. staff St. Thomas, Bapt., Nashville Gen., Westside hosps.; clin. prof. allied health Trevecca Coll.; cons. VA Hosp.; assoc. in medicine Vanderbilt Med. Sch., 1943—; med. dir. Nashville Health Care Corp., Univ. Health Care Corp.; prof. anatomy Gupton-Jones Sch. Mortuary Sci., 1941-43. Pres., Middle-East Tenn. chpt. Arthritis Found. Served to med. dir. USPHS. Decorated baliff grand cross Hospitaller Order St. John of Jerusalem; chevalier Sovereign Mil. Order Temple of Jerusalem recipient Disting. Service award Arthritis Found. Fellow Am. Coll. Chest Physicians, Am., Internat. colls. angiology, Royal Soc. Health, Internat. Biog. Assn. (life); mem. Am. Cancer Soc. (dir., past pres. Nashville), AMA, Am. Thoracic Soc., So. Med. Soc. (life), Tenn. Med. Assn., Nashville Acad. Medicine, SCV (surgeon-in-chief), Order St. John of Jerusalem, Royal Soc. Medicine, Tenn. Assn. Long Term Physicians (past pres.), Phi Beta Kappa, Alpha Omega Alpha, Delta Phi Alpha. Research in mycotic and parasitic diseases. Home: 2315 Valley Brook Rd Nashville TN 37215 Office: 2015 Patterson St Nashville TN 37203

WEBSTER, DEBORAH ANN STEWART, marketing executive; b. Charleston, W.Va., Jan. 25, 1953; d. John Carlton and Sarah Ann (Knapp) Stewart; m. David Robert Webster, Sept. 8, 1973; 1 son, Jared Scott. B.S. in Communications with honors, U. Tenn.-Knoxville, 1979. APC technologist State of Tenn., 1973-76, student supr. U. Tenn., 1976-79; pub. relations intern Nuclear div. Union Carbide, Oak Ridge Nat. Lab., 1978; staff writer Gallatin (Tenn.) News Examiner, Multi Media, Inc., 1980; bus. devel. asst. Gresham, Smith & Ptnrs., Nashville, 1980-81, communication specialist, 1981, communications coordinator, 1982-83; sr. mktg. exec. Barge, Waggoner, Sumner & Cannon, Nashville, 1983—. Mem. Hist. Nashville, Inc. Mem. Pub. Relations Soc. Am., CABLE, Exec. Women Internat., Internat. Assn. Bus. Communicators. Republican. Mem. Ch. of Christ. Contbr. articles to newspapers. Office: 404 James Robertson Pkwy Nashville TN 37219

WEBSTER, EDWIN HENRY, steel company executive; b. Hulmeville, Pa., Feb. 7, 1918; s. Jesse Gilbert and May Flowers (Hibbs) W.; m. Mildred Theresa Matthews, Feb. 16, 1948; children—Marian Webster Olson, Jes Gilbert. B.S.C.E., U. Pa., 1939. Registered profl. engr., Pa. Engr., draftsman Am. Bridge-Dravo, Trenton, N.J., Pitts., 1939-43; v.p. Luria Engring. Corp., Behelehm, Pa., 1947-56; exec. v.p. Whitehead & Kales Co. (river Rouge), Mich., 1956-74; chmn., chief exec. officer Carolina Steel Corp., Greensboro, N.C., 1974—; pres. W & K Erectors, River Rouge, 1964-74, W & K Engrs., 1964-74; dir. Greenville Machinery Corp., S.C., 1978-73. Served to lt. USN, 1943-47. Fellow ASCE; mem. Am. Inst. Steel Constrn. (pres. 1970-71), NAM (regional v.p. 1979-82). Republican. Presbyterian. Clubs: City, Country (Greenboro, N.C.). Lodge: Masons. Office: Carolina Steel Corp 1451 S Elm Eugene St Greenboro NC 27420*

WEBSTER, GORDON DOUGLAS, automotive accessory distribution company executive; b. Nashville, Oct. 3, 1939; s. Isham Gordon and Catherine Leland (Todd) W.; m. Carol Mooneyhan, Aug. 29, 1969 (div. Jan. 1976); 1 dau., Casey Lee. B.A., Tenn. Tech. U., 1965; postgrad. U. Tenn., 1965-66. Mgmt. trainee Genesco, Nashville, 1966-67, asst. to pres., 1967-69; equipment order entry mgr. Xerox Co., Birmingham, Ala., 1969, br. adminstrn. mgr., Memphis, 1969-71, br. controller, Dallas, 1971-74, adminstrn. ops. mgr., 1974-75, regional dist. mgr., Atlanta, 1975-82; chmn. bd. Gordon Enterprises, Inc., Smyrna, Ga., 1983—; pres., gen. mgr. C.J.R. Distbg., Smyrna, 1983—; v.p. Charlton Jones Racing, Inc., Smyrna, 1983—; pres. J-W Properties, Marietta, Ga., 1983—; owner Daniell Aero. Co., Marietta, 1983—; v.p., dir. S.E. Continental Warranty; dir. Charlton Jones Racing, Inc., Gordon Enterprises, Inc. Served with USAF, 1957-62. U. Tenn. scholar, 1965; named Br. Adminstrv. Mgr. of Yr., Xerox Co., 1970, 71, Br. Controller of Yr., 1972, Pres.'s Outstanding Coop. Achievement award, 1982. Republican. Sportscar racing reporter Road Racers Mag., 1980. Home: 2741 Georgian Terr Marietta GA 30067 Office: 4292 Camp Highland Rd Smyrna GA 30080

WEBSTER, MURRAY ALEXANDER, JR., sociologist; b. Manila, Philippines, Dec. 10, 1941; s. M.A. and Patricia (Morse) W.; A.B., Stanford U., 1963, M.A., 1966, Ph.D., 1968. Asst. prof. social relations Johns Hopkins U., Balt., 1968-74, assoc. prof., 1974-76; prof. sociology, adj. prof. psychology U. S.C., Columbia, 1976—; vis. prof. sociology Stanford U., 1981-82, 85; v.p. W&D Assocs., Inc., research and cons. co. NIH fellow, 1966-68; grantee NSF, Nat. Inst. Edn. Mem. Am. Sociol. Assn., So. Sociol. Soc. Republican. Presbyterian. Author: (with Barbara Sobieszek) Sources of Self-Evaluation, 1974; Actions and Actors, 1975; mem. editorial bd. Am. Jour. Sociology, 1976-79, Social Psychology Quar., 1977-80, 84-87, Social Sci. Research, 1975—. Home: 1829 Senate St Apt 10A Columbia SC 29201 Office: Dept Sociology U SC Columbia SC 29208

WEBSTER, REX, advertising agency executive; b. Gatesville, Tex., May 29, 1918; s. Roscoe and Fannie (Hooser) W.; B.A., Tex. Tech. U., 1938, M.A., 1939; m. Madge Malone, June 1, 1941; children—Len Rex, Robin Bass. Program dir., commercial mgr. Radio Sta. KFYO, Lubbock, Tex., 1935-47; partner, Buckner, Craig & Webster Advt. Agy., 1947-52; partner, Craig & Webster Advt. Agy., Lubbock, 1952-59; partner, Webster, Harris, Welborn Advt. Agy., Lubbock, 1959-72; partner, Webster & Harris Advt. Agy., Lubbock, Tex., 1972-85, Rex Webster Assocs., Lubbock, 1985—; v.p., pub. relations dir. Great Plains Life Ins. Co., Lubbock, Tex., 1955-57. Advt. and pub. relations cons., instr. Tex. Tech. U., 1953-71. Pres. Lubbock council Camp Fire Girls, 1960; v.p. South Plains Council Boy Scouts Am., 1958-59; pres., Lubbock (Tex.) Better Bus. Bur., 1965. Chmn. bd. dirs. Lubbock Symphony Orch., 1949-50, charter mem., 1947, vocal soloist, dir. Pops Nite Chorus, 1963-71; chmn. bd. dirs. Lubbock (Tex.) Cerebral Palsy Treatment Center, 1962-63, 72-74, sec.-treas., 1974—; bd. dirs. Goodwill Industries, Lubbock; pres. Lubbock Area Extended Rehab. Services, 1983; trustee Wayland Bapt. U., Plainview, Tex., 1983—. Served as lt. USNR, 1943-45. Recipient Distinguished Service award Lubbock Jr. C. of C., 1955, Silver Medal award for distinguished service to advt. Lubbock Tex. Advt. Club, 1967. Mem. Am. (chmn. S.W. council 1957-58), Southwestern (pres. 1955) assns. advt. agys., Am. Automobile Assn., Panhandle Plains Auto Club (v.p. 1971-78), Lubbock Advt. Club (pres. 1954-55), Tex. Pub. Relations Assn. (dir. 1958-64), Baptist (mem. exec. com. gen. conv. Tex. 1968-74, chmn. bd. deacons 1972-73). Clubs: Mason (32 deg.), Rotary Internat. (pres. Lubbock 1947-48, dist. gov. 1956-57, dir. 1967-69, v.p. 1968-69, trustee Found. 1981-84). Home: 3305 44th St Lubbock TX 79413 Office: 1313 Broadway Suite 2 Lubbock TX 79401

WEBSTER, STOKELY, artist; b. Evanston, Ill., Aug. 23, 1912; s. Henry Kitchell and Mary Ward (Orth) W.; m. Iva Kitchell, Aug. 23, 1933; 1 dau., Stephanie. Student Yale U., 1931-32, NAD, 1934, Art Students League, 195; student of Wayman Adams, 1937. One-man shows include James St. L. O'Tolle Gallery, N.Y.C., 1940, Albert Roullier Gallery, Chgo., 1940, Vallombreuse Gallery, Biarritz, France, 1971, Vallombreuse Gallery, Palm Beach, Fla., 1973, Hobe Sound (Fla.) Gallery, 1974, Eric Galleries, N.Y.C., 1975, Ormond Beach Meml. Gallery, 1983, Polk Pub. Mus., Lakeland, Fla., 1984, Brevard Mus., Melbourne, Fla., 1984, Fla. Gulf Coast Art Ctr., Belleair, 1984, Cornell Fine Arts Ctr., Winter Park, Fla., 1984, Scarfone Gallery, U. Tampa (Fla.), 1985, Mus. Arts and Scis., Daytona Beach, Fla., 1985; exhibited in group shows including Corcoran Bienniel, Washington, Allied Artists and Nat. Acad., N.Y.C., Art Inst. Chgo., Salon des Independants, Paris, Salon des Artistes Francais, Paris, Heckscher Mus., Huntington, N.Y., State Mus. Albany (N.Y.), Parrish Mus., Southampton, N.Y.; represented in permanent collections Nat. Collection Fine Art, Smithsonian Instn., Mus. N.Y.X., Philips Collection, Washington, Indpls. Mus. Art, Ill. State Mus., Springfield, Fitchburg (Mass.) Mus. Art, Northwestern U. Library, Evanston, Newark Mus., Parrish Mus., Heckscher Mus., Mus. Arts and Scis., Cornell Mus., Rollins Coll., Winter Park. Recipient 1st Halgarten prize NAD, 1941. Address: 255 Ocean Palm Dr Flagler Beach FL 32036

WECHSLER, EDWARD CHARLES, school administrator; b. N.Y.C., Nov. 4, 1946; s. Morris and Rose (Barbers) W. B.A., Fla. So. Coll., 1968; M.A., U. Fla., 1972. Tchr. Duval Dist. Schs., Jacksonville, Fla., 1968-73, asst. prin., 1973-80, vice prin., 1980-81, prin., 1981—. Contbr. articles to profl. jours. Recipient Asst. Adminstr. of Yr. award Duval County Assn. Secondary Sch. Adminstrs., 1981. Mem. Duval County Assn. Secondary Sch. Adminstrs. (bd. dirs. 1973-74, 84-85), Fla. Assn. Sch. Adminstrs., Nat. Assn. Secondary Sch. Adminstrs., Duval County Jr. High Athletic Assn. (sec. 1981-82, v.p. 1982-83, pres. 1984-85). Home: 3565 Northride Dr Jacksonville FL 32217 Office: Duval County School Bd 1701 Prudential Dr Jacksonville FL 32207

WECHSLER, SHELDON, optometrist, educator; b. N.Y.C., July 16, 1926; s. Harry H. and Rose A. (Goldberg) W.; m. Dorothy Weddle, Apr. 24, 1953; children—Keith O., Gail M. Student Hunter Coll., 1946-47, San Diego State Coll., 1947-48; B.S., U. Calif.-Berkeley, 1951, M. Optometry, 1952; O.D., Pa. Coll. Optometry, 1980. Practice optometry Oakland, Calif., San Francisco, Palo Alto, Calif., 1958-73; assoc. prof. optometry U. Ala.-Birmingham, 1973-76; assoc. prof. optometry U. Houston, 1977-80, prof., 1980-81; dir. new product devel. Vistakon, Inc. subs. Johnson & Johnson Inc., Jacksonville, Fla., 1982—; cons. to various optical mfg. cos., 1970—; guest lectr. various profl. groups and symposia, 1960—. Mem. Santa Clara County Planning Commn., Calif., 1964-68. Served with USN, 1944-46, PTO. Fellow Am. Acad. Optometry; mem. Assn. Research in Vision and Ophthalmology, Am. Optometric Assn., AAAS, Internat. Assn. Contact Lens Research, Contact Lens Educators Assn., U. Calif. Optometry Alumni Assn. Home: 961 Mapleton Terr Jacksonville FL 32207 Office: PO Box 10157 Jacksonville FL 32247

WEDDING, CHARLES RANDOLPH, architect; b. St. Petersburg, Fla., Nov. 16, 1934; s. Charles Reid and L. Marion (Whitaker) W.; m. Audrey Whitsel, Aug. 18, 1956 (div. Apr. 1979); children—Daryl L., Douglas R., Dorian B.; m. Vonnie Sue Hayes, June 22, 1984; stepchildren—Stephanie M., Brian E. B.Arch., U. Fla., 1957. Registered architect, Fla., Ga., N.C., S.C., Del., Va., Tex. Architect in tng. Harvard & Jolly AIA, St. Petersburg, 1957-60; architect, prin., pres. Wedding & Assocs., St. Petersburg, 1960—. Mayor City of St. Petersburg, 1973-75; past chmn. Pinellas County Com. of 100, Bldg. Dept. Survey Team, City of St. Petersburg; trustee All Children's Hosp., 1968-70; sect. leader St. Petersburg United Fund, 1965-70; mem. city council Action Team for Pier Redevel., 1967-68; mem. exec. com. Goals for City of St. Petersburg, 1970-72; den. leader Weblos, Boy Scouts Am., 1971-72; chmn., trustee Canterbury Sch. YMCA, 1968-72; mem. adv. com. Tomlinson Vocat. Sch., 1969-79; past trustee Mus. Fine Arts; past bd. dirs. Neighborly Ctr., Jr. Achievement Pinellas County. Served to 1st lt. U.S. Army, 1958-60. Mem. AIA (5 Silver Spike awards, Merit of Honor, Medal of Honor), Am. Soc. Landscape Architects, St. Petersburg Assn. Architects (past. pres.), Fla. Assn. Architects (8 Merit Design awards). Republican. Episcopalian. Clubs: Suncoasters; St. Petersburg Yacht. Avocations: sailing; hunting; golfing; tennis. Home: 3000 58th Ave N Saint Petersburg FL 33714 Office: Wedding & Assocs Inc 360 Central Ave Saint Petersburg FL 33701

WEDEMEYER, RICHARD CHARLES, petroleum geologist; b. Bklyn., Dec. 31, 1953; s. Henry and Elizabeth (Koch) W.; m. Candy Jan Strobel, Aug. 14, 1976 (div. 1979); m. Danie Pauline Jones, Nov. 21, 1982. B.S., Furman U., 1975; M.S., E. Carolina U., 1978. Ops. mgr. Eagle Printing Co., Greenville, S.C., 1975-76; teaching fellow E. Carolina U., Greenville, 1976-78; research technician U. Ga., Athens, 1979-82; geologist Sun Exploration and Prodn. Co., Oklahoma City, Okla., 1982—. Author: (with others) Stress Management: A Guide to Better Living, 1985. Crisis counselor, counselor trainer CONTACT of Met. Oklahoma City, 1983—, bd. dirs., 1985—, profl. concerns com., 1985—, case rev. com., 1985—; adv. S.C. Pub. Interest Research Group, Greenville, 1973-76. Mem. Am. Assn. Petroleum Geologists, Oklahoma City Geol. Soc., Union Concerned Scientists (charter 1981—), Chi Beta Phi. Avocations: volleyball; tennis; golf; photography; counseling psychology. Home: 5917 NW 49th St Oklahoma City OK 73122 Office: Sun Exploration Prodn Co 525 Central Park Dr Oklahoma City OK 73105

WEDICK, FRANK MICHAEL, civil engineer; b. Laconia, N.H., Feb. 6, 1940; s. John Lawrence and Florence Nettie (Clifford) W.; m. Deborah Lynn Webb, Dec. 26, 1970; children—Nicole Marie, Victoria Devon. B.S., New Eng. Coll., 1969. Registered profl. engr., Ga., S.C. With Howard Needles Tammen & Bergendoff, various locations, 1969—, resident engr., Atlanta Internat. Airport, 1970-81, Charleston (S.C.) Internat. Airport, 1981—. Served with USMC, 1959-63, Res. ret. Mem. ASCE, Soc. Am. Mil. Engrs. (bd. dirs. Charleston), Civil Engrs. Club of Charleston. Home: 44 Hunters Forest Dr Charleston SC 29407 Office: PO Box 10948 Charleston SC 29411

WEED, ALBERT CHARLES, II, vintager, winery executive; b. Bklyn., May 23, 1942; s. Lowrey Albert Weed and Solace Adelaide (Smith) Radspinner; m. Emily Louise Chan, Nov. 4, 1966; children—Albert Charles III, Julia Meredith. A.B. cum laude, Yale U., 1968; M.Pub.Affairs, Princeton U., 1970. Asst. to U.S. dir. World Bank, Washington, 1970-72; dir. Washington office Arthur Lipper Corp., 1972-73; pres., winegrower La Abra Farm and Winery, Lovingston, Va., 1973-80, 81—; pres., chief exec. officer Gen. Wood Processors, Inc., Easley, S.C., 1980-81; former dir. Nelson County Mut. Ins. Co., Arrington, Va. Contbr. articles to profl. publs. Democratic candidate for Nelson Supr., Lovingston, 1975; treas. Amherst Country Day Sch., Va., 1979; pres. Jefferson-Madison Regional Library Bd., Charlottesville, Va., 1980. Served with U.S. Army, 1962-66, Vietnam; to command sgt. maj. Res. Decorated Bronze Star. Mem. Va. Wineries Assn. (pres. 1983-85), Spl. Forces Assn. Democrat. Episcopalian. Home and Office: Route 1 Box 139 Lovingston VA 22949

WEEKS, ARTHUR FULTON, artist; b. Birmingham, Ala., June 1, 1930; s. Fulton and Viola Lillian (Wright) W. Student Howard Coll., Birmingham, 1953-54. One-man shows include Birmingham Mus. Art, Birmingham, 1971, Littlehouse Art Ctr., 1971-85, Jemison Carnaige Found., Talladega, Ala., James Hunt Barker, Palm Beach, Fla.; group shows include Hunter Mus., Chattanooga, 1st So. Contemporary, Art in Embassies program, New Delhi, 1966; represented in permanent collections Southtrust Bank, Birmingham, Am. South Banks Inc., Birmingham, 1st Ala. Bank, Birmingham. Recipient 1st Place and Best of Show awards 1st So. Contemporary Art Show, 1965; numerous juried awards in SE region. Avocation: gardening. Home and Studio: 1906 15th Ct S Birmingham AL 35205

WEEKS, BOBBY CHARLES, electronic company executive; b. Whitney, Tex., Oct. 19, 1932; s. Charles Leo and Tracy (Ivy) W.; m. Billie Gayle Stephens, Sept. 1, 1956; children—Charles, Vickie Weeks Frost. Student pub. schs., Whitney, Tex. Machine parts insp. Tex. Instruments, Dallas, 1956-62, supr., 1962-74, fabrication quality control mgr., 1974—. Mem. adv. com. Dallas County Community Coll.; deacon, chmn. Valwood Park Bapt. Ch., 1983; mem. credit com. Texans Credit Union. Served with U.S. Army, 1954-56. Mem. Am. Soc. for Quality Control. Home: 1601 Milam Way Carrollton TX 75006 Office: Tex Instruments 5900 Lemmon Ave Dallas TX 75266

WEEKS, CHARLES, JR., real estate executive, retired publishing company executive; b. Palo Alto, Calif., Apr. 25, 1919; m. Patricia Anne Blair, Apr. 7, 1949; children—Patricia Alice, Charles Blair, Clayton Brian, Phyllis Anne. s. Charles and Mary Alice (Johnson) W.; Student U. Fla., 1936-38. Prin., Fla. Airmotive, Inc., Lantana, Fla., 1946-50; v.p., dir. Perry Publs., Inc., West Palm Beach, Fla., 1950-69; dir. Perry Oceanographics, Inc., Riveria Beach, Fla., 1969, dir. mgmt. bd. Flagler Nat Bank, West Palm Beach. Mem. Planning and Zoning Bd., Lantana, 1962-65; assoc. trustee John. F. Kennedy Hosp., Atlantis, Fla. Served to 1st lt., pilot, USAF, 1943-46: ETO. Decorated Air medal. Recipient Pilot Safety award Nat. Bus. Aircraft Assn., 1970, 74, 78. Mem. Quiet Birdman. Episcopalian. Democrat. Clubs: Handersonville (N.C.) Country; Sailfish of Fla. (Palm Beach), Governors of The Palm Beaches (West Palm Beach) (charter). Home: PO Box 3411 Lantana FL 33462 Office: Boalt Properties 400 Royal Palm Way Palm Beach FL 33480

WEEKS, PATSY ANN LANDRY, librarian, teacher; b. Luling, Tex., Mar. 3, 1930; d. Lee and Mattie Wood (Callihan) Landry; m. Arnett S. Weeks, Dec. 2, 1950; children—Patsy Kate, Nancy Ann, Janie Marie. B.S., Southwest Tex. State U., San Marcos, 1951; M.L.S., Tex. Woman's U., Denton, 1979. Tchr. art, reading, math. Grandview Ind. Sch. Dist., Tex., 1950-52; tchr. phys. edn. Beaumont Ind. Sch. Dist., Tex., 1953; tchr. art, coll. algebra Cisco Jr. Coll., Tex., 1957-58; tchr. remedial reading Taylor County Schs., Tuscola, Tex., 1965-66; tchr. remedial reading Anson Ind. Sch. Dist. Tex., 1971-73; librarian Bangs Ind. Sch. Dist., Tex., 1973-79, learning resources coordinator, 1979—; adv. com. Edn. Service Ctr., 1978-84; coordinator Reading is Fundmental Program, 1978-83. Bd. dirs. Anson Pub. Library, Tex., 1971-72. Exhibitor oil paintings, pastels at Tex. fairs (1st prize 1952, 60). Mem. ALA, Assn. Library Service to children (Caldecott award com. 1986), Am. Assn. Sch. Librarians, Intellectual Freedom Round Table, Assn. Supervision and Curriculum Devel., Tex. Library Assn. (mem. intellectual freedom and profl. responsibility com. 1979-81; mem. Tex. Bluebonnet award com. 1982-85), Tex. Assn. Sch. Librarians (media prodns. award com. 1985-86), Tex. Assn. Improvement Reading, Teenage Library Assn. Tex. (chmn. audio-visual award com. 1984), Tex. Assn. Sch. Library Adminstrs., Tex. State Tchr. Assn. (life), Kappa Pi, Alpha Chi, Beta Phi Mu, Delta Kappa Gamma. Baptist. Clubs: Bangs Progressive Women's (treas. 1974-76). Home: 110 Poco St Bangs TX 76823 Office: Bangs Ind Sch Dist PO Box 969 Bangs TX 76823

WEEKS, ROSS LEONARD, JR., foundation/museum executive; b. Jamestown, N.Y., Sept. 11, 1936; s. Ross Leonard and Cecile Forbes (Carrie) W.; A.B., Colgate U., 1958; M.S., George Washington U., 1971; m. Patricia Ann Earley, June 10, 1951; children—Susan Woodall, Ross Leonard, III, William Andrew, David James. Reporter, Jamestown Post-Jour., 1958-60, Richmond (Va.) News Leader, 1960-65; dir. public info., then asst. to exec. v.p. Coll. William and Mary, Williamsburg, Va., 1965-74, asst. to pres., dir. univ. communications, 1974-81; exec. dir. Jamestown (Va.)-Yorktown Found., 1981—; mem. adj. faculty Christopher Newport Coll., Golden Gate U. Chmn. Williamsburg-James City Bicentennial, 1975-77; bd. dirs. Williamsburg Pre-Sch. Spl. Children, 1970-75; pres. Williamsburg Sch. PTA, 1974-77; bd. dirs. Williamsburg C. of C., 1982—; exec. dir. Va. Independence Bicentennial Commn., 1981-83; trustee council, Thirteen Original States, 1982—. Recipient award excellence for programs Council Advancement and Support Edn., 1978, 79. Mem. Public Relations Soc. Am., Am. Assn. Mus., Am. Assn. State and Local History, St. Andrews Soc., Sigma Delta Chi. Episcopalian. Clubs: Nat. Press (Washington); Masons. Home: 308 Indian Springs Rd Williamsburg VA 23185 Office: Jamestown-Yorktown Found Drawer JF Williamsburg VA 23187

WEEMS, JOHN EDWARD, writer; b. Grand Prairie, Tex., Nov. 2, 1924; s. J. Eddie and Anna Lee (Scott) W.; B.J., U. Tex., 1948, M.Journalism, 1949; M.A. in L.S., Fla. State U., 1954; m. Jane Ellen Homeyer, Sept. 11, 1946; children—Donald, Carol, Mary, Barbara, Janet. Telegraph editor Temple (Tex.) Daily Telegram, 1950; instr. Calif. State Poly. Coll., San Dimas, 1950-51; night news editor San Angelo (Tex.) Standard-Times, 1951; copy editor Dallas Morning News, 1952-53; asst. prof., head cataloger main library Baylor U., 1954-57; asst. prof. U. Ala., also asst. mgr. Ala. Press Assn., 1957-58; asst. to dir. U. Tex. Press, 1958-68; prof. English, Baylor U., 1968-71, lectr. creative writing, fall 1979; reference librarian McLennan Community Coll., Waco, Tex., 1969-70; freelance writer, 1971—. Served with USNR, 1943-46, 51-52; lt. Res. (ret.). Am. Philos. Soc. grantee, 1964. Mem. Nat. Book Critics Circle, Authors Guild, Tex. Inst. Letters, AAUP, Sigma Delta Chi, Beta Phi Mu. Author: A Weekend in September, 1957; The Fate of the Maine, 1958; Race for the Pole, 1960; Peary: The Explorer and the Man, 1967; Men Without Countries, 1969; Dream of Empire (Amon G. Carter award), 1971; To Conquer a Peace: The War Between the United States and Mexico (Richard Fleming award), 1974; Death Song, 1976; The Tornado, 1977; (with John Biggers and Carroll Simms) Black Art in Houston, 1978; —If You Don't Like the Weather,— 1986; editor: A Texas Christmas: A Miscellany of Art, Poetry, Fiction, Vol. I, 1983, Vol. II, 1986. Address: 2012 Collins Dr Waco TX 76710

WEEMS, WILLIAM ARTHUR, physiologist; b. Carlsbad, N.Mex., July 3, 1944; s. John Warren and Ida (Brooke) W.; B.S., Baylor U., 1967, M.S., 1969; Ph.D., U. Ill., 1973; m. Betty Susan Stanhouse, Aug. 21, 1965; children—John Mark, Jennifer Rene. Research fellow Mayo Clinic, Rochester, Minn., 1973-76; asst. prof. physiology U. Tex. Med. Sch., Houston, 1976-82, assoc. prof., 1982—. Minn. Heart Assn. fellow, 1974-76; recipient Research Career Devel. award, 1980; NIH grantee. Mem. Neurosci. Soc., Am. Physiol. Soc., Sigma Xi. Baptist. Assoc. editor Physiol. Revs., 1982—; contbr. articles to profl. jours. Home: 12219 Alston St Stafford TX 77477 Office: PO Box 20708 Houston TX 77025

WEGMAN, EDWARD JOSEPH, statistician, educator, researcher; b. Terre Haute, Ind., July 4, 1943; s. Andrew Joseph and Adelaide Mary Wegman; m. Barbara Jean Bordeaux, Sept. 2, 1967; children—Lisa Anne, Katherine Dawn. B.S. St. Louis U., 1965; M.S., U. Iowa, 1967, Ph.D., 1968. Prof. stats. U. N.C., Chapel Hill, 1968-78; vis. prof. math. Manchester (Eng.) U., 1976-77; head math. scis. div. Office Naval Research, Arlington, Va., 1978-86; dir. Ctr. Computational Stats. and Probability, George Mason U., 1986—. NSF Sr. Faculty fellow, 1976; recipient Meritorious Civilian Service medal U.S. Navy, 1981. Fellow Am. Statis. Assn., royal Statis. Soc., AAAS, Inst. Math. Stats.; sr. mem. IEEE; mem. Internat. Statis. Inst., Math. Assn. Am., Soc. Indsl. and Applied Math. Roman Catholic. Author: (with dePriest) Statistical Design of Weather Modification Experiments, 1980; (with Smith) Statistical Signal Processing, 1984; (with De Priest) Statistical Image Processing and Graphics, 1985. Office: Ctr Computational Stats and Probability 217 Thompson Hall George Mason U 4400 University Dr Fairfax VA 22030

WEHMEYER, JANET ADELINE, recreation administrator; b. St. Louis, Dec. 26, 1934; d. Celestine August and Adeline Helen (Bucher) Wehmeyer. A.A., Orlando Jr. Coll., 1960; B.S. in Recreation, U. Fla., 1962. Switchboard operator, bookkeeper George Stuart, Inc., Orlando, Fla., 1952-57; office mgr., bookeeper F & R Office Supply, Orlando, Fla., 1957-60; arts and crafts dir. McCoy AFB, Fla., 1962-63; program dir. U.S. Army, Ft. Benjamin, Ind., 1963-64; recreation adminstr. USAF MacDill AFB, Fla., 1963—. Pres. bd. dirs. Sr. Scouters, Girl Scouts Am., St. Louis; bd. dirs. MacDill Fed. Credit Union, vice chmn., 1983; bd. dirs. United Services Orgn. Recipient Dept. AF Superior Performance award, 1967; Fed. Employee Recognition award Tampa Bay Area Assn. Fed. Adminstrs., 1974; Service award USO, 1980. Mem. Fla. Parks and Recreation Assn., Nat. Parks and Recreation Assn., Phi Mu. Democrat. Roman Catholic.

WEHOVZ, JOACHIM, artificial intelligence developer; b. Koeflach, Austria, July 18, 1947; s. Sepp and Gaby Wehovz; m. Teofila Echevarria, Nov. 15, 1975; children—Josef, Oscar. B.A., Bundes Gymnasium, Graz, Austria, 1967, postgrad, 1975. Advertiser, Sepp Wehovz sculptor, Austria, 1973-74; adj. prof. math. U. P.R., Rio Piedras, 1976-82, statis. researcher, 1979-84; artificial intelligence developer, Rio Piedras, 1984—; high sch. tchr. Lincoln Mil. Acad., Guaynabo, P.R., 1978-79. Mem. Am. Statis. Assn. Avocation: multilingual command of communication; creation of graphic symbols. Home: Calle 207 4-I-11 Fairview Rio Piedras PR 00926

WEHR, ALLAN GORDON, chemical engineering educator, consultant; b. Bklyn., July 31, 1931; s. Martin Henry and Hazel Gordon (Hilson) W.; m. Margaret Rita Wylie, Oct. 20, 1951; children—Kathryn, Robert. B.S. in

Metall. Engring., Mo. Sch. Mines, 1958; Ph.D. in Metall. Engring., U. Mo., 1962. Registered profl. engr., Miss. Research engr. P.R. Mallory, Indpls., 1960-61; head dept. materials engring. Mississippi State (Miss.) U., 1963-73, prof. chem. engring., 1973—; materials cons. Served with USN, 1951-55. Mem. Am. Inst. Chem. Engrs., Am. Soc. Metals, Am. Soc. Engring. Edn., Miss. Acad. Scis., Sigma Xi. Club: Rotary (Starkville, Miss.).

WEHRLE, HOWARD FRANKLIN, III, army officer, management educator, consultant; b. Kansas City, Mo., Oct. 30, 1919; s. Howard Franklin and Anna Masten (Estill) W.; m. Verlie Louise Wilbert, Nov. 22, 1957 (div. July 1961); m. Mary Elizabeth Ashley, Dec. 14, 1974. A.S., Jr. Coll. Kansas City, Mo., 1938; B.S., U.S. Mil. Acad., 1943; M.E.E., U. Pa., 1952; M.Ed., Coll. William and Mary, 1972, M.B.A., 1974, cert. advanced grad. study in edn., 1977, postgrad., 1978-81; grad. U.S. Army Command and Gen. Staff Coll., 1956. Commd. 2d lt. infantry, U.S. Army, 1943; advanced through grades to lt. col., 1959; comdr. 1st Reconnaissance Squadron, 11th Armored Cavalry, Straubing, Fed. Republic Germany, 1961-62; dir. mil. characteristics Joint U.S.-Fed. Republic Germany Main Battle Tank Program, Augsburg, 1964-65; chief plans br. Logistics Div. Hdqrs. U.S. Army Europe, Heidelberg, Fed. Republic Germany, 1965-66; chief maneuvers br. Office DC/S Ops., Ft. Monroe, Va., 1966-69; dep. dir. Security Plans and Ops., U.S. Army Support, Thailand, 1969-70; mobilization designee in nat. emergency Transp. Ctr., Ft. Eustis, Va., 1983-84; v.p., gen. mgr. western ops. Sawadee Ltd., Gen. Cons., Hampton, Va., 1974—; asst. prof. bus. dept. mgmt. Hampton Inst., 1977-84. Author: (with Ruth Swan) Financial Aid for Minority Students in Business, 1980. Mem. Hampton Bd. Bank Voluntary Action Ctr., 1983. Decorated Legion of Merit with one oak leaf cluster, Meritorious Service medal, Army Commendation medal. Mem. Am. Mgmt. Assn., Assn. Computing Machinery, Am. Philatelic Soc., Am. Youth Hostels, Nat. Rifle Assn., Soc. Logistic Engrs., World Future Soc., Order Daedalians, U.S. Armor Assn., Assn. U.S. Army, Assn. Grads. U.S. Mil. Acad., Blackhorse Assn., VFW, Phi Kappa Phi. Episcopalian. Clubs: Army and Navy (Washington); Army and Navy Country (Arlington, Va.). Lodge: Mil. Order World Wars.

WEHRLE, RUSSELL SCHILLING, industrial executive; b. Charleston, W.Va., Oct. 26, 1926; s. Henry Bernard and Elizabeth (Herscher) W.; B.A. summa cum laude, Princeton U., 1947; m. Martha Gaines, Oct. 16, 1954; children—Michael H., Ebersole Gaines, Katherine Schilling, Philip Noyes, Martha Chilton. With McJunkin Corp., Charleston, 1947—, asst. to pres., 1951-64, exec. v.p., 1964-80, pres., 1980—, dir., 1964—; pres. dir. McJay Internat. Corp., Charleston, 1977—, dir. Heck's, Inc., K.R.M. Petroleum. Mem. W.Va. Labor-Mgmt. Adv. Council, 1977-81; mem. W.Va. Gov.'s Econ. Adv. Council, 1978—; mem. Charleston Bldg. Council, 1980—; mem. Kanawha County Bd. Edn., 1966-72; trustee United Fund Kanawha Valley, Inc., 1963-75, pres., 1965-66; trustee Sunrise Found., Inc., 1961-77; trustee U. Charleston, 1967—, vice chmn. bd., 1976-79, chmn. bd., 1979-82; past trustee Charleston Area Med Center, YMCA, YWCA; bd. dirs. W.Va. Edn. Fund, 1982—, Bus.-Industry Polit. Action Com., 1983—; chmn. Nat. Inst. Chem. Studies, 1985—. Served with USNR, 1944-46. Mem. Am. Supply Assn. (dir.), Petroleum Equipment Suppliers Assn., NAM (dir.), Phi Beta Kappa. Home: 1440 Louden Heights Rd Charleston WV 25314 Office: PO Box 513 Charleston WV 25322

WEHUNT, J. DONALD, dentist; b. Louisville, Feb. 19, 1935; s. Luther E. and Mildred S. (Self) W.; m. Jo Ann Schafner, Apr. 1954 (div. 1963); 1 child, Donna Beth; m. Barbara I. Peterman, Feb. 12, 1965; children—Nicole S., January N. Student U. Tenn., 1966-68; D.M.D., U. Ky., 1972. Sole practice gen. dentistry, El Paso, Tex., 1980—. Fellow Acad. Gen. Dentistry; mem. ADA, Tex. Dental Assn., Am. Endodontic Soc., Am. Orthodontic Soc., Am. Acad. Implant Dentists, Internat. Coll. Oral Implantologists, Internat. Assn. Orthodontists, Acad. Sports Dentistry, Am. Straight Wire Assn., El Paso C. of C. Baptist. Avocation: building and flying model airplanes. Office: 5320 Will Ruth El Paso TX 79924

WEIBEL, DENNIS EARL, dentist; b. Enid, Okla., May 12, 1947; s. Earl Leroy and Doreen Frances (Suppes) W.; m. Anita Bearden, July 31, 1971; children—Adam, Beth, Collin. B.A. in Biology, Trinity U., 1969; D.D.S., Baylor U., 1973. Dentist Dallas County Health Dept., 1973, Muskogee County Health Dept., Okla., 1974-75; gen. practice dentistry, Muskogee, 1975—. Elder, deacon 1st Presbyn. Ch., Muskogee, 1980—; bd. dirs. Eastern Okla. Hospice, Muskogee, 1984—. Served to capt. U.S. Army, 1973-75. Fellow Acad. Gen. Dentistry; mem. ADA, Okla. Dental Assn., Am. Soc. Dentistry for Children, Blue Key. Lodge: Rotary. Office: 204 N 37th St Muskogee OK 74401

WEIDEMEYER, CARLETON LLOYD, lawyer, musician; b. Hebbville, Md., June 12, 1933; m. Diane Draper, 1962; children—Karen, Kurt, Katherine, Kristen. B.A. in Polit. Sci., U. Md., 1958; J.D., Stetson U., 1961. Bar: Fla. 1961, D.C. 1971, U.S. Dist. Ct. (mid. dist.) Fla. 1963, U.S. Ct. Appeals (5th cir.) 1967, U.S. Ct. Appeals (D.C. cir.) 1976, U.S. Supreme Ct. 1966, U.S. Ct. Appeals, (11th cir.) 1982. Research asst. Fla. 2d Dist. Ct. Appeals, 1961-65; ptnr. Kalle and Weidemeyer, St. Petersburg, Fla., 1965-68; asst. pub. defender 6th Jud. Cir., Fla., 1966-69, 81—; ptnr. Wightman, Weidemeyer, Jones, Turnbull and Cobb, Clearwater, Fla., 1968-82; dir. Fla. Bank Commerce, Clearwater, 1973-77; dir. First Nat. Bank and Trust Co., Belleair Bluffs, Fla., 1974-78. Bd. advisors Musicians Ins. Trust. Mem. Musicians Assn. Clearwater (pres. 1976-81), Fla. Conf. Musicians (sec., treas. 1974-76), AFM, So. Conf. Musicians (pres. 1979-80), Assn. Trial Lawyers Am., Fla. Acad. Trial Lawyers, Fla. State Hist. Soc., Am. Fedn. Musicians (internat. law com.), Am. Legion, DAV, Phi Delta Phi, Sigma Pi, Kappa Kappa Psi. Club: Sertoma (v.p. 1984—).Lodges: Masons, Moose, Shriners. Home: 2261 Belleair Rd Clearwater FL 33546 Office: 501 S Fort Harrison Suite One Clearwater FL 33516

WEIDLER, JAMES HOWELL, sports association executive; b. New Kensington, Pa., June 15, 1944; s. Wellington Earl Jr. and Lois Ann (Howell) W.; m. Mary Lillian Duncan, Dec. 27, 1977; stepchildren—Alison, Lesie, Melissa. B.A., Southwestern U., 1966; M.A., Old Dominion U., 1976. Account exec. Calvin Jones & Assocs., advt. and pub. relations, Houston, 1976; regional mgr. for promotions and advt. Astroworld div. Six Flags Corp., Houston, 1977-79; dir. govtl. affairs and spl. projects Houston Sports Assn., Inc., 1979—; polit. cons.; expert witness Tex. Legislature. Producer TV and radio commls., print advertisements, 1975—, Astros baseball highlights film, 1979; contbr. to mil. and civilian publs. Campaign mgr. Houston Conv. Ctr. Election, 1983; mem. Met. Tech. Adv. Com. for Subregional Transit Devel. Plan; chmn. Harris County Young Profls. for Reagan-Bush, 1984. Served from 2d lt. to capt., USAF, 1967-75. Decorated Air Force Commendation medal (2); Vietnam Cross of Gallantry with palm unit citation. Mem. Pub. Relations Soc. Am., Houston Com. Fgn. Relations, South Main Ctr. Assn., Air Force Assn., U.S. Naval Inst., Houston C. of C. (govt. affairs com. 1981—, chmn. subcom. 1984—), Assn. for Tex. Entertainment (v.p. 1984—). Home: 20623 Chestnut Hills Dr Katy TX 77450 Office: PO Box 288 Houston TX 77001

WEIDMAN, DALE EMIL, interior designer; b. Wichita, Kans., Nov. 8, 1929; s. Fred Dewey and Freda Emma (Volckmann) W. Student, Kans. State U., 1947-49, Colo. Sch. Floral Design, 1949. Floral designer, Calif., Fla., 1947-50; asst. Jack Cameron Designs, Miami, Fla., 1951-56; dir. interior design Mackle Co./Gen. Devel. Corp., Miami, 1956-62; owner, interior designer Interiors by Dale E. Weidman, Miami, 1962—; owner Marco Interiors, Inc., Marco Island, Fla., 1968-75; interior design cons. Mem. Am. Soc. Interior Design (Fla. bd. 1975-76, area chmn. 1976-77, treas. 1971). Republican. Lutheran. Home: 1965 Ixora Rd North Miami FL 33181 Office: Interiors by Dale E Weidman 1965 Ixora Rd North Miami FL 33181

WEIDNER, CAROL LYNN, corporate marketing director; b. Cleve., Dec. 1, 1946; d. Bernard Julius Pasterniak and Lillian Helen (Brazek) Wysocki; m. John W. McDowell, Feb. 4, 1967 (div. 1975); 1 child, John Christopher; m. Richard Joseph Weidner, July 3, 1976; 1 child, Kenneth Richard. Student U. Fla., 1964, North Miami Dade Jr. Coll., 1964-65. Clk., buyer Sears Roebuck Co., Miami, Fla., 1965-66; asst. to comptroller Fla. Cycle Supply, Jacksonville, Fla., 1973-75; acct. Pinebreeze Eggs, Jacksonville, 1975-76; bus. mgr. Crisp County Animal Hosp., Cordele, Ga., 1976-85; mktg. dir., adminstrv. asst. Perlis Corp., Cordele, 1985—. Contbr. articles and poetry to local newspaper. Recipient Silver Knight award Knight Publs., 1964. Mem. Cordele Jr. Women's Club (v.p. 1982), Cath. Women's Council (pres. 1982, 83). Republican. Roman Catholic. Avocations: Water sports; flower arranging; reading and writing poetry. Office: Perlis Corp I-75 & Exit 31 Cordele GA 31015

WEIGAND, DENNIS ALLEN, physician, educator; b. Alva, Okla., Mar. 17, 1939; s. Carl and Helen J. (Wesner) W.; m. Janet DeAnn White, July 7, 1961; children—Christopher, Rebecca. B.S., Northwestern Okla. State Coll., 1960; M.D., U. Okla., 1963. Diplomate Am. Bd. Dermatology, Am. Bd. Dermatopathology. Intern, St. Francis Hosp., Wichita, Kans., 1963-64; resident in dermatology U. Okla. Health Sci. Ctr., Oklahoma City, 1964-67; asst. prof. dermatology U. Okla., Oklahoma City, 1970-74, assoc. prof. dermatology, 1974-78, adj. prof. pathology, 1977—, prof. dermatology, 1978—, vice-head dept. dermatology; chief dermatology service VA Med. Ctr., Oklahoma City, 1978—. Served to maj. U.S. Army, 1968-70. Decorated Army Commendation medal. Fellow Am. Acad. Dermatology, Am. Soc. Dermatopathology; mem. Am. Dermatological Assn., AMA, Sigma Xi, Alpha Omega Alpha. Episcopalian. Contbr. articles to books and profl. jours. Home: 141 Barbara Dr Edmond OK 73034 Office: 619 NE 13th St Oklahoma City OK 73104

WEILAND, ALAN LAWSON, dentist, biologist; b. N.Y.C., Mar. 24, 1950; s. Harry and Violet (Lawson) W.; m. Linda Elise Farmer, Apr. 12, 1980. B.S. in Biology, SUNY-Stony Brook, 1972; M.A. in Biology, William and Mary U., 1974; D.D.S., Med. Coll. Va., 1978. Lic. dentist, Fla., Va., Md., D.C. Gen. practice dentistry Clewiston, Fla., 1981—; mem. staff Hendry Gen. Hosp., Clewiston. Contbr. articles to sci. jours. Med. adviser Am. Cancer Soc., Clewiston, 1984—. Served to lt. comdr. USPHS, 1978-81. A.D. Williams Research fellow, 1977. Fellow Acad. Gen. Dentistry; mem. ADA, Mensa. Lodges: Lions (bd. dirs. 1983—), Elks. Avocations: boating; fishing; S.C.U.B.A., beekeeping. Home: 316 E Trinidad St Clewiston FL 33440 Office: Box 2132 Clewiston FL 33440

WEILER, HAROLD HAUSER, ophthalmologist, educator, naval officer; b. Washington, July 13, 1942; s. Harold Frederick and Carmen (Mejia) W.; m. Sharon Lee Kesling, June 28, 1981; children—Amy, Susan, Tamara, Heather. A.B., Dartmouth Coll., 1964; M.D., Med. Coll. Va., 1969. Diplomate Am. Bd. Ophthalmology. Commd. lt. U.S. Navy, 1971, advanced through grades to capt., 1981; chief ophthalmology, Portsmouth, Va., 1981-83, med. hosp. quality assurance adminstr., 1983-84; vice-chmn. Lions Eye Bank, Norfolk, Va., 1983-85, chmn., 1985—; asst. clin. prof. Eastern Va. Med. Sch., 1981—. Contbr. articles to profl. jours. Fellow Am. Acad Ophthalmology; mem. Tidewater Ophthalmology and Otolaryngology Soc., Assn. Mil. Ophthalmologists. Episcopalian. Clubs: Austin Healey Tidewater (pres.), Austin Healey of Am. Avocation: sailing. Home: 994 Kelso Ct Virginia Beach VA 23464 Office: US Naval Hosp Portsmouth VA 23708

WEIMER, PETER DWIGHT, mediator, lawyer; b. Grand Rapids, Mich., Oct. 14, 1938; s. Glen E. and Clarabel (Kauffman) W.; children—Melanie, Kim. B.A., Bridgewater Coll., 1962; J.D., Howard U., 1969. Assoc. counsel Loporto & Weimer Ltd., Manassas, Va., 1970-75; chief counsel Weimer & Cheatle Ltd., Manassas, 1975-79, Peter D. Weimer, P.C., Manassas, 1979-82; pres., mediator Mediation Ltd., Manassas, 1981—; pres. Citation Properties, Inc., Manassas, 1971—; pres. Preferred Research of No. Va. Inc., Fairfax, 1985—. Address: PO Box 1616 Manassas VA 22110

WEINBAUM, ELEANOR PERLSTEIN, estate manager; writer; b. Beaumont, Tex., Sept. 3; d. Hyman Asher and Mamie (Gordon) Perlstein; student Ward-Belmont Coll., 1920, Benjamins' Coll., N.Y.C., 1922, writers conf. Boulder U., 1931; L.H.D., U. Libre, 1972; m. Charles Weinbaum, Aug. 25, 1923 (div.); 1 son, Charles H. Partner estates mgmt. 23d St. Shopping Center, Beaumont, 1956—; founder Eleanor Poetry Room at Lamar U., 1960, Pulse, lit. mag., 1962. Donor Poetry Room So. Meth. U., Dallas, 1965, sponsor ann. lecture by internat. poet, 1960—; donor award to sr. grad. in English, Lamar U. Recipient D. Modern Humanities, Internat. Acad., 1969; named one of internat. women of yr. with laureate honors Poet Laureate Internat., 1975; recipient Disting. Service citation World Poetry Soc., 1970. Mem. Beaumont C. of C., Heritage Soc., Tex., Nat. Press Women, Internat. Acad. Poets, Acad. Am. Poets, Tex. Council Promotion Poetry, World and Nat. Poetry Day Com. (hon. life), Sigma Tau Delta. Jewish. Club: Beaumont. Author: From Croup to Nuts, 1941; The World Laughs With You, 1950; Jest for You, 1954; Shalom, America, 1970; Conrad's Scrabble Babble, 1977; God's Eternal Word, 1978; contbr. to Adventures in Poetry mag. Home: Hotel Beaumont Apt 415 Beaumont TX 77701 Office: 1215 Beaumont Savs Bldg Beaumont TX 77701

WEINBERG, FREDRICK LEWIS, optometrist; b. Bklyn., Feb. 25, 1944; s. Ira and Vivian (Greenberg) W.; children—Cindy, Suzanne. B.S., U. Tampa, 1965; O.D., Mass. Coll. Optometry, 1971. Gen. practice optometry, Spring Hill, Fla., 1971—. Mem. Am. Optometric Assn., Fla. Optometric Assn., Hillsborough County Optometric Assn. (v.p. 1974). Avocations: golf, tennis, skiing. Office: 11025 Spring Hill Dr Spring Hill FL 33526

WEINBERG, RICHARD BRUCE, psychologist, author, consultant; b. Chgo., Nov. 11, 1951; s. Jack D. and Dorothy L. Weinberg; m. Rebecca Liddell, Aug. 26, 1979; children—Joanna Rose, Charles Evan. B.A. cum laude, U. Mich., 1975; M.A., Xavier U., 1977; Ph.D., U. South Fla., 1983. Psychology intern Mass. Gen. Hosp., Boston, 1980-81; clin. fellow Harvard Med. Sch., Boston, 1980-82; faculty U. South Fla.-Fla. Mental Health Inst., Tampa, 1981—, dir. psychology tng., 1984—; cons.; pvt. therapy practice, Tampa, 1983—. Co-author: Competence Development, 1985. Bd. dirs. Tampa Bay Family Times, 1984—, Victim Assistance Program, Tampa, 1985—. NIMH grantee, 1983; U. South Fla. Grad. Council grantee, 1984. Mem. Am. Psychol. Assn., Fla. Psychol. Assn., Sigma Xi, Psi Chi. Jewish. Avocations: canoeing; swimming; triathalon. Office: Fla Mental Health Inst 13301 N 30th St Tampa FL 33612

WEINBERG, RICHARD JAMES, ophthalmologist; b. Cleve., Dec. 29, 1941; s. Phillip and Malvina Ruth (Abramson) W.; m. Mary Kathleen Kohler, June 15, 1974 (div. May 1985); children—Brian, Kevin. B.A., Washington and Jefferson Coll., 1963; M.D., Ohio State U., 1967. Diplomate Am. Bd. Ophthalmology. Intern Los Angeles County-U. So. Calif. Gen. Hosp., Los Angeles, 1967-68; resident dept. ophthalmology Georgetown U., Washington, clin. asst. prof. 1978—; cornea research fellow F.I. Proctor Found., San Francisco, 1974-75; asst. prof. U. Pitts. Med. Sch., 1975-78; mem. med. adv. com. Lions Eye Bank, Washington, 1978-85, med. dir., 1982-84; bd dirs. Old Dominion Eye Bank, Richmond, Va., 1985—. Contbr. articles to profl. jours. Trustee Va. Lions Eye Inst., Falls Church, 1982—. Served to capt. USAF, 1968-70, Vietnam. Research grantee Nat. Eye Inst., 1974. Fellow ACS, Am. Acad. Ophthalmology; mem. Assn. for Research in Vision and Ophthalmology, Castroviejo Soc. (assoc.). Home: 9609 Clarks Crossing Rd Vienna VA 22180 Office: Tysons Corner Ophthalmic Assocs Ltd 8150 Leesburg Pike Vienna VA 22180

WEINBERG, ROBERT STEPHEN, physical education educator; b. N.Y.C., June 15, 1948; s. Harold and Jeanette (Stone) W.; m. Kathleen Susan Kolodny, Apr. 21, 1985; children—Josh, Kira. B.S. in Phys. Edn., Bklyn. Coll., 1969; M.S. in Psychology, UCLA, 1972, M.A., 1975, Ph.D., 1978. Postdoctoral fellow UCLA, 1978; tchr. N.Y.C. Pub. Schs., Bklyn., 1970; lectr. Bklyn. Coll., 1972-74, UCLA, 1977-78; assoc. prof. phys. edn. North Tex. State U., Denton, 1978—; cons. U.S. Olympic Com., Colorado Springs, Colo., 1981; vis. prof. Wingate Inst., Netanye, Israel, 1983. Author: Psychological Foundations in Sport, 1984. Contbr. articles to profl. jours. Fellow Research Consortium; mem. Am. Psychol. Ann., N.Am. Soc. Sport Psychology, AAHPERD. Avocations: tennis; basketball; running. Home: Rt 3 Box 513 Roanoke TX 76262 Office: North Tex State U Dept Phys Edn Denton TX 76203

WEINBERG, ROBERT STEPHEN, ophthalmologist; b. Washington, Aug. 10, 1945; s. Benjamin Abra and Jean (Matlin) W.; m. Shifri Alper, Mar. 22, 1970; children—F. Naomi, Ari I., Ethan M. B.A., Johns Hopkins U., 1966, M.D., 1969. Diplomate Am. Bd. Ophthalmology. Intern in medicine Johns Hopkins U., Balt., 1969-70, resident in medicine, 1970-71; resident in ophthalmology U. Ill., Chgo., 1973-76, chief resident in ophthalmology, 1977-78; fellow in ophthalmology Francis Proctor Found., U. Calif.-San Francisco, 1976-77; assoc. prof. ophthalmology Med. Coll. Va., Richmond, 1978—. Served to lt. comdr. USN, 1971-73. Fellow Am. Acad. Ophthalmology. Office: Med Coll Va Box 262 MCV Sta Richmond VA 23298

WEINBERG, STEVEN, physics educator; b. N.Y.C., May 3, 1933; s. Fred and Eva (Israel) W.; m. Louise Goldwasser, July 6, 1954; 1 dau. B.A., Cornell U., 1954; postgrad. Copenhagen Inst. for Theoretical Physics, 1954-55; Ph.D., Princeton U., 1957; A.M. (hon.), Harvard U., 1973; Sc.D. (hon.), Knox Coll., 1978, U. Chgo., 1978, U. Rochester, 1979, Yale U., 1979, CUNY, 1980, Clark U., 1982, Dartmouth Coll., 1984; Ph.D. (hon.), Weizmann Inst., 1985; D.Litt. (hon.), Washington Coll., 1985. Research assoc., instr. Columbia U., 1957-59; research physicist Lawrence Radiation Lab., Berkeley, Calif., 1959-60; mem. faculty U. Calif.-Berkeley, 1960-69, prof. physics, 1965-69; vis. prof. MIT, 1967-69, prof. physics, 1969-73; Higgins prof. physics Harvard U., 1973-83, Morris Loeb vis. prof. physics, 1983—; sr. scientist Smithsonian Astrophys. Lab., 1973-83; Josey Regental prof. U. Tex., Austin, 1982—; cons. Inst. for Def. Analyses, Washington, 1960-73, ACDA, 1970-73; sr. cons. Smithsonian Astrophys. Obs., 1983—; mem. Pres.'s Com. on Nat. Medal of Sci., 1979-80; Richtmeyer Meml. lectr., 1974; Scott lectr. Cavendish Lab., 1975; Silliman lectr. Yale U., 1977; Lauritsen Meml. lectr. Calif. Inst. Tech., 1979; Bethe lectr. Cornell U., 1979; de Shalit lectr. Weitzman Inst., 1979; Henry lectr. Princeton U., 1981; Cherwell-Simon lectr., Oxford, 1983; Bampton lectr. Columbia U., 1983; Loeb lectr. in physics Harvard U., 1966-67; dir. Jerusalem Winter Sch. Theoretical Physics, 1983—; mem. council of scholars Library of Congress, 1983-85; bd. overseers SSC Accelerator, 1984—; bd. advisors Santa Barbara Inst. Theoretical Physics, 1983—; bd. govs. Tel Aviv U., 1984—. Author: Gravitation and Cosmology: Principles and Applications of the General Theory of Relativity, 1972; The First Three Minutes: A Modern View of the Origin of the Universe, 1977; The Discovery of Subatomic Particles, 1982; mem. editorial bd. Progress in Sci. Culture, Monographs on Mathematical Physics, Nuclear Physics; Issues in Science and Technology; research and publs. on elem. particles, quantum field theory, cosmology. Recipient J. Robert Oppenheimer Meml. prize, 1973; chair in physics, College de France, 1971; Dannie Heineman prize in math. physics, 1977; Am. Inst. Physics-U.S. Steel Found. sci. writing award, 1977; Nobel prize in physics, 1979; Elliott Cresson medal Franklin Inst., 1979; Sloan fellow, 1961-65. Mem. Am. Acad. Arts and Scis. (past councilor), Am. Phys. Soc. (past councilor at large), Nat. Acad. Sci., Internat. Astron. Union, Council on Fgn. Relations, Am. Mediaeval Acad., Am. Philos. Soc., Royal Soc. London. Office: Dept Physics U Tex Austin TX 78712

WEINBRENNER, GEORGE RYAN, aerospace engineer; b. Detroit, June 10, 1917; s. George Penbrook and Helen Mercedes (Ryan) W.; B.S., MIT, 1940, M.S., 1941; grad. Advanced Mgmt. Program, Harvard U., 1966; m. Billie Marjorie Elwood, May 2, 1955. Commd. 2d lt. USAAF, 1939, advanced through grades to col., 1949; def. attaché Am. embassy, Prague, Czechoslavakia, 1958-61; dep. chief staff intelligence Air Force Systems Command, Washington, 1962-68; comdr. fgn. tech. div. U.S. Air Force, Wright-Patterson AFB, Ohio, 1968-74; comdr. Brooks AFB, Tex., 1974-75; ret., 1975; exec. v.p. B.C. Wills & Co., Inc., Reno, Nev., 1975—; lectr. Sch. Aerospace Medicine Brooks AFB, Tex., 1976; chmn. bd. Hispaño-Technica S.A. Inc., San Antonio, 1977—; cons. Def. Dept., 1981, Dept. Air Force, 1975-84. Decorated D.S.M., Legion of Merit, Bronze Star, Air medal, Purple Heart; Ordre National du Merite, Medaille de la Resistance, Croix de Guerre (France). Fellow AIAA (asso.); mem. San Antonio C. of C., Air Force Assn. (exec. sec. Tex. 1976-82; Presdl. citation 1983), Assn. Former Intelligence Officers (nat. dir.), Air Force Hist. Found. (dir.), Am. Def. Preparedness Assn., U.S. Strategic Inst., World Affairs Council San Antonio, Am. Astronautical Soc., Aerospace Ednl. Found. (dir.), Mil. Order World Wars, Am. Legion, Assn. Old Crows, Kappa Sigma. Roman Catholic. Clubs: Army-Navy, University (Washington); Army-Navy Country (Arlington, Va.); Josef, St. Anthonys, Josef (San Antonio); Spl. Forces (London). Home: 1236 Wiltshire Ave San Antonio TX 78209 Office: PO Box 18484 San Antonio TX 78218

WEINER, BERNARD KARL, physician; b. Gary, Ind., Jan. 2, 1929; s. Isidore and Anna (Alterman) W.; B.S., Ind. U., 1950, M.D., 1953; m. Marcia Myra Spitzer, Sept. 15, 1952; children—Audrey Cheryl Scheinberg, Jodi Lynn Groff, Karen Elizabeth Miller. Intern, Meth. Hosp., Gary, 1953-54; gen. practice medicine, San Antonio, 1958—; active staff Meth. Hosp., chief dept. family practice, 1969, sec. staff, 1974, vice chief staff, 1975, chief staff, 1977; courtesy staff Bapt. Meml. Hosp., St. Luke's Luth. Hosp., Humana Hosp., Santa Rosa Hosp.; clin. asst. prof. family practice U. Tex. Med. Sch., San Antonio, 1978-82, clin. assoc. prof., 1982—; clin. asst. prof. Tex. Tech Med. Sch., Lubbock, 1979—. Trustee Jewish Community Center, 1970-73. Served to capt. USAF, 1954-58. Recipient Nat. Membership award Zionist Orgn. Am., 1969, Citation of Honor, 1972; Physician's Recognition award AMA, 1972, 75, 78, 79, 81, 83; Nat. Retention award B'nai B'rith, 1974; Maimonides award State of Israel, 1977. Diplomate Am. Bd. Family Practice. Fellow Am. Acad. Family Physicians, Royal Soc. Health, Am. Geriatrics Soc.; mem. Tex., So., Pan Am. med. assns., Tex., Alamo (pres. 1985) acads. family physicians, Am. Soc. Contemporary Medicine and Surgery, Soc. Tchrs. Family Medicine, Internat. Med. Assembly (trustee 1963-65), Bexar County Med. Soc. (exec. com. 1976-79, mem. peer rev. com. 1973-76), Zionist Orgn. Am. (dist. pres. 1968-72), Assn. Am. Physicians and Surgeons, Am. Physicians Fellowship, Phi Chi. Jewish (pres. synagogue 1975-78). Mem. B'nai B'rith (pres. lodge 1973-74). Home: 6603 Moss Oak St San Antonio TX 78229 Office: 929 Manor Dr San Antonio TX 78229

WEINER, BRIAN LANDAU, magazine and book distributing company executive, real estate investment company executive, rancher; b. Galveston, Tex., Jan. 7, 1943; s. Stanford and Selma (Landau) W.; m. Katina Anthony, Apr. 13, 1962; children—Danny, Ellyce. B.S. in Agr. and Econs., Tex. A&M U., College Station, 1965. Mktg. specialist Tex. Dept. Agr., Austin, 1965-66; mgr. Weiner News Co., San Antonio, 1975-77; chief exec. officer Periodical Mgmt. Group, San Antonio, 1975—; gen. ptnr. S&B Properties, San Antonio, 1974—; dir. Fidelity Bank, San Antonio. Contbr. articles to profl. jours. Mem. U.S. Senatorial Bus. Adv. Bd.; bd. dirs. Anti-Defamation League, San Antonio, 1982-83; rep. Republican Jewish Coalition, Bala Cynwyd, Pa., 1983; mem. Tex. fin. com. Reagan/Bush 84 Campaign, San Antonio, 1983-84. Mem. Council for Periodical Distbrs. Assn., Ind. Mag. Wholesalers Assn. Southwest, Mid-Am. Periodical Distbrs. Assn. (dir., sec. 1975-80), San Antonio C. of C., Mexican C. of C. of San Antonio, San Antonio Homebuilders Assn., Tex. Cattle Raisers Assn., Southwestern Cattle Raisers Assn., Assn. Former Students Tex. A&M U. Jewish. Club: Aggie (College Station). Home: 2 Lazy Hollow San Antonio TX 78230 Office: Periodical Mgmt Group Inc 1011 N Frio St San Antonio TX 78207

WEINER, EDWARD TERRY, architect; b. N.Y.C., Feb. 22, 1945; s. Irving Louis and Harriett Francis (Davison) W.; m. Nancy Blossom Miller, Dec. 22, 1973; children—Chad Eric, Jorian Beth. Student, Dean Jr. Coll., 1962-63; B.A., U. Nebr., 1969; postgrad. NYU, 1970-71. Registered profl. architect, Fla. Draftsman/designer F.R. Harris, Inc., Stamford, Conn., 1970-72; project architect Haack-Crawford & Assocs., Wilton Manors, Fla., 1972-76; project mgr. Peabody & Childs, Pompano, Fla., 1976-77; assoc. Steven Cohen, architect, Plantation, Fla., 1977-78, Ronald Kall, Architect, Plantation, 1978-82; pres. etw & Assocs., Inc., architect/planner, inc., Plantation, 1982—. Pres., Miss Broward County Pageant, 1978—; sec. Cultural Arts Ctr., Plantation, 1983, 84; candidate Plantation City Council, 1983; mem. Plantation Code Enforcement Bd., 1984. Recipient various awards Ft. Lauderdale Jaycees, 1973, 74, 1st pl. Project award U.S. Jaycees, 1973-74, Speak Up award Fla. Jaycees, 1973-74. Mem. AIA, Soc. Am. Registered Architects (sec. Fla. council 1983-84), Am. Inst. City Planners, Am. Planning Assn., Am. Soc. Planning Ofcls., Constrn. Specifiers Inst., Broward Builder's Exchange, Plantation C. of C., Broward County YMCA, Sigma Alpha Mu. Democrat. Club: Toastmasters Early Bird (pres. 1974). Lodges: Rotary, B'nai B'rith (exec. v.p. 1980). Home: 5960 S W 16th St Plantation FL 33317 Office: etw & Assocs 4080 W Broward Blvd Plantation FL 33317

WEINFURTER, ROBERT WAYNE, consultant; b. Appleton, Wis., May 17, 1928; s. George John and Esther Rose (Kumbier) W.; B.S., Lawrence U., 1953, postgrad., 1956; m. Cathryn Janice Masterson, June 20, 1953; children—Erich, Kurt, Karl, Hans. With Bechtel Corp., San Francisco, 1956-59; engr.-in-charge for O'Hare Field Project Soil Testing Services, Inc., Chgo., 1959-62; pres. Soil Testing Services Wis., Green Bay, 1962-70; adminstrv. v.p. Soil Testing Services Inc., Chgo., 1970-74; exec. v.p. Soil Testing Services Iowa, Cedar Rapids, 1974-79, also dir.; pres. Soil Testing Services Kans., Kansas City, 1975-80, dir., 1980-83; prin., dir. Terracon Consultants Inc., Kansas City; pres. Western Technols., Inc., Tulsa, 1983-85; with Raba-Kistner Consultants, Inc., Austin, Tex., 1985—. Mem. chancellor's bldg. adv. bd. U. Wis., Green Bay, 1968-70. Served with USAF, 1946-49. Registered profl. geologist, Ga., profl. engr., Nev., Wis. Mem. Soc. Mining Engrs. Assn. Soil and Found. Engrs. (past pres.), Assn. Engring. Geologists, Am. Inst. Profl. Geologists, Tex. Soc. Profl. Engrs., ASCE, Profl. Engrs. in Pvt. Practice. Phi Delta Theta. Republican. Presbyn. (ch. trustee 1967-70, deacon 1973-74). Home: 1601 E Anderson Ln 507 Austin TX 78752 Office: 8100 Cameron Rd Austin TX 78753

WEINHAUER, WILLIAM GILLETTE, bishop; b. N.Y.C., Dec. 3, 1924; s. Nicholas Alfred and Florence Anastacia (Davis) W.; B.S., Trinity Coll.,

Hartford, Conn., 1948; M.Div., Gen. Theol. Sem., 1951, S.T.M., 1956, Th.D., 1970; m. Jean Roberta Shanks, Mar. 20, 1948; children—Roberta Lynn, Cynthia Anne, Doris Jean. Ordained to ministry Episcopal Ch. U.S.A., 1951; pastor Episcopal parishes Diocese N.Y., 1951-56; prof. N.T., St. Andrews Theol. Sem., Manila, Philippines, 1956-60; asst. prof. N.T., Gen. Theol. Sem., 1961-71; rector Christ Ch., Poughkeepsie, N.Y., 1971-73; bishop Episcopal Diocese of Western N.C., 1973—; chaplain to mil. bases, colls. hosps. Served with USN, 1943-46. Mem. Soc. Bibl. Lit. Office: PO Box 368 Black Mountain NC 28711*

WEINHOLD, DONALD LEROY, JR., lawyer, engineer; b. Salisbury, N.C., Mar. 27, 1946; s. Donald Leroy and Merrea L. (Smith) W.; m. Patricia Lynn Heffner, May 15, 1966; children—Melena Lynn, Donald Brandt. B.S. in Engring., N.C. State U., 1969; J.D., Cath. U. Am., 1973. Bar: N.C., D.C.; cert. N.C. Bd. Engrs. and Land Surveyors. Patent examiner U.S. Dept. Commerce, Washington, 1970-74; mem. firm Davis Ford & Weinhold, Salisbury, 1974-76, Ford & Weinhold, Salisbury, 1976-80; pres. firm Donald L. Weinhold, P.A., Salisbury, 1980—; commr. N.C. Gen. Statutes Commn., 1977-81, N.C. Criminal Justice and Tng. Standards Council, 1979-81. Mayor, mayor pro tem City of Salisbury, 1977-81; pres. Nat. Sportscasters and Sportswriters Found., Ind., 1982—; chmn. Rowan County Democratic Party; dir. community orgns. including Salisbury Community Found., Citizens for Older Adults, Salisbury Community Service Council. Served with USAF, 1966. Recipient Superior Performance awards U.S. Dept. Commerce, 1971, 72, 73, Disting. Service awards Salisbury Jaycees, 1980. Mem. Am. Soc. Indsl. Engrs., ABA, N.C. Bar. D.C. Bar, Rowan County Bar Assn., N.C. Acad. Trial Lawyers, Assn. Trial Lawyers Am., Am. Legion, Salisbury Rowan C. of C. Lutheran. Clubs: Rotary, Sales Exec. Mktg. Club of Salisbury, KC. Author: Brief History of Politics, 1981. Home: 228 W Bank St Salisbury NC 28144 Office: 318 N Main St Salisbury NC 28144

WEINKRANTZ, ALAN LANDAU (FORMERLY ALAN SAMUEL FADER), advertising and public relations executive, marketing consultant; b. Dallas, Mar. 29, 1953; s. Philip Henry Weinkrantz and Rosette (Landau) Fader; m. Barbara P. Roth, Mar. 1, 1985. B.A. in Bus., Antioch Coll., 1976. Mgr. mktg. services Contemporary Mktg., Inc., Bensenville, Ill., 1976-77; regional rep. Chgo. and N.Y.C., Mailers Services, Inc., St. Cloud, Minn., 1977-78; dir. mktg. Columbia Galleries, Inc., Dallas, 1978-79; account exec. Mitchell & Co., Inc. Advt., Dallas, 1979-80; pres. Alan Weinkrantz & Co. (formerly Alan S. Fader Advt./Dir. Mktg./Pub. Relations), Dallas, 1980—, 21st Century Space Commerce/Space Industrialization Consulting, Dallas, 1980—. Mem. Nat. Space Inst., Dallas C. of C. Home: 115 S Willomet Dallas TX 75208 Office: 4255 LBJ Pkwy Suite 265 Dallas TX 75244

WEINSTEIN, ALLEN ISAAC, anthropological linguist, consultant; b. Bklyn., Feb. 7, 1933; s. Louis H. and Harriette (Siegel) W.; m. Claire Frant, June 9, 1954; children—Lynette H. Weinstein Maton, Howard L. B.A., Columbia U., 1955, M.A., 1956; Ph.D., SUNY-Buffalo, 1966. Instr. German, SUNY-Buffalo, 1959-65, asst. prof. German, 1965-66; sci. linguist Sch. Lang. Studies, Fgn. Service Inst., Dept. State, Washington, 1966-81, chmn. resource support, 1981-84, asst. dean ops., 1984-85; systems devel. mgr. CACI, Inc., Arlington, 1985—. Co-author: Deutsche Stunden, 1964; FSI Dutch Reader, 1976; editor: FSI Swedish Basic Course, 1983; also articles. Served with U.S. Army, 1956-58. Recipient Meritorious Honor award U.S. Dept. State, 1976, 82, 85. Fellow Am. Anthrop. Assn.; mem. AAAS, Linguistic Soc. Am., AAUP. Jewish. Home: 6236 23d St N Arlington VA 22205 Office: CACI Inc Lang Ctr 1815 N Fort Myer Dr Arlington VA 22209

WEINSTEIN, BRUCE HOWARD, insurance and investment counselor; b. Birmingham, Ala., May 17, 1946; s. Hyman David and Mayme (Wilson) W.; m. Germaine Zalta, Dec. 25, 1977; children—Harris, Brooke, Michael. B.A., U. Ala., 1970. C.L.U. Nat. dir. chpt. relations Zeta Beta Tau, N.Y.C., 1970-72; salesman Equitable Life Assurance Soc., Atlanta, 1972-75, dist. mgr., 1975-79; owner Profl. Planning Services, Atlanta, 1979—; speaker ins. industry. Bd. dirs. Atlanta Jewish Community Ctr., Atlanta Jewish Fedn. Served with USCGR, 1967-73. Recipient Leadership award B'nai B'rith Youth Orgn., 1978, Atlanta Jewish Welfare Fedn., 1980, also various ins. industry awards and recognitions. Mem. Nat. Assn. Life Underwriters, C.L.U. Assn., Internat. Assn. Fin. Planners, Atlanta Jaycees, Atlanta C. of C., U. Ala. Alumni Assn. (bd. dirs.). Jewish. Lodge: B'nai B'rith (pres. 1982, Leadership award 1982, bd. dirs. Atlanta). Home: 4867 Vermack Rd Atlanta GA 30338 Office: 2635 Century Pkwy Suite 600 Atlanta GA 30345

WEINSTEIN, CLAIRE ELLEN, psychology educator; b. Bklyn., Nov. 8, 1946; d. Sidney and Fannie Weinstein. B.S., Bklyn. Coll., 1967; Ph.D., U. Tex., 1975. Dir. Research Learning Concepts, Inc., Austin, Tex., 1975-79; asst. prof. U. Tex., Austin, 1975-83, assoc. prof. psychology, 1983—; also dir.; cons. Dept. of Army, Washington, Community Colls. Author: (booklet) How to Help Your Child Achieve Better in School, 1982; also articles and chpts. in books. Policy asst. Dept. of Edn., Dept. of Def. Recipient Teaching Excellence award U. Tex., 1982; Spencer fellow, 1978-83; grantee Nat. Inst. Edn., Hogg Found., 1976—. Mem. Am. Ednl. Research Assn. (asst. program chair 1983), S.W. Ednl. Research Assn. (pres. 1985), Am. Psychol. Assn. (co-program chair 1984), AAUP, AAAS. Democrat. Jewish. Home: 6108A Shadow Valley Dr Austin TX 78731 Office: Dept Ednl Psychology U Texas EDB 504 Austin TX 78757

WEINSTEIN, JAY A., social science educator, researcher; b. Chgo., Feb. 23, 1942; s. Lawrence E. and Jacqueline L. (Caplan) W.; m. Diana S. Staffin, Sept. 16, 1961; m. 2d, Marilyn L. Schwartz, Nov. 30, 1971; children—Liza, Bennett. A.B., U. Ill., 1963; Ph.D., 1973; M.A., Washington U., St. Louis, 1965. Teaching fellow U. Ill., Urbana, 1963-64; teaching asst. McGill U., Montreal, Que., Can., 1966-68; instr. Sir George Williams U., Montreal, 1967-68; lectr. Simon Fraser U., Vancouver, 1968; asst. prof. North Central Coll., Naperville, Ill., 1970-71; asst. prof. U. Iowa, 1973-77; prof. social scis. Ga. Inst. Tech., Atlanta, 1977—; researcher; cons. pub. and pvt. agys. Fulbright prof., Ahmedabad, India, 1975-76, Hyderabad, India, 1981-82; Faculty Devel. grantee Ga. Tech. Found., 1981-82; World Order Studies Course Devel. grantee, 1974-75; Steinberg fellow, 1967. Mem. Nat. Sci. Hon. Soc., Am. Sociol. Assn., Soc. S. Indian Studies, Population Assn. Am., So. Sociol. Soc., Sigma Xi. Jewish. Author: Madras: An Analysis of Urban Ecological Structure in India, 1974; Demographic Transition and Social Change, 1976; Sociology/-Technology: Foundations of Postacademic Social Science, 1982; The Grammar of Social Relations: The Major Essays of Louis Schneider, 1984; editor: Studies in Comparative International Development, 1978—; editorial bd. Social Development Issues, 1977—; specialized contbr. Calcutta Municipal Gazette, 1979—; editor: Social and Cultural Change, 1974-75; editorial reviewer: Jour. of Asian Studies, Social Devel. Issues, Tech. and Culture, The Am. Sociologist, Technological Forecasting and Social Change; Contbr. chpts. to books, articles to profl. jours. Office: Ga Inst Tech 300 DM Smith Bldg Atlanta GA 30332

WEINSTEIN, JON LEONARD, stockbroker; b. New Orleans, Feb. 19, 1946; s. Benjamin Bernard and Clarice (Groner) W. B.A., La. State U., 1970. Agt. MetroLife Ins. Co., New Orleans, 1970-72; account exec. Merrill Lynch, Pierce, Fenner & Smith, Shreveport, La., 1972-76; registered rep. Kidder, Peabody, Dallas, 1976—. Active The 500, Inc., Dallas; mem. Am. Jewish Com., U.S. Equestrian Team; treas. Stults Road Homeowners Assn. Mem. Dallas Security Dealers Assn., Dallas Mus. Art, U.S. Combined Tng. Assn. Clubs: Chimeras, Assemblage, North Tex. Combined Tng. Assn., Jewish Community Ctr. Office: Kidder Peabody 3939 InterFirst Bldg Two Dallas TX 75270

WEINSTEIN, LEWIS, lawyer; b. New Orleans, Apr. 30, 1932; s. Israel and Norma Rebecca (Levy) W.; m. Mary Cox, Oct. 22, 1964; children—Terri. Steven, Linda, Marilyn. B.S., La. State U., 1951, J.D., 1955. Bar: La. 1955. Assoc. with asst. atty. gen. State of La., 1955-62; atty. State of La. Tax Dept., 1958-62; sole practice, Shreveport, La., 1962—; instr. law So. U., Shreveport. Mem. Republican Club, Downtown Shreveport Unlimited. Mem. ABA, La. Bar Assn., Assn. Trial Lawyers Am., Am. Judicature Soc., Fed. Bar Assn., Zionist Orgn. of Am. (past pres.). Club: Jewish Men's (v.p.). Home: 305 Wayne Dr Shreveport LA 71105 Office: 609 Texas St Shreveport LA 71101

WEINSTEIN, MARTIN, aerospace manufacturing executive, materials scientist; b. Bklyn., Mar. 3, 1936; s. Benjamin and Dora (Lemo) W.; m. Sandra Rebecca Yaffie, June 5, 1961; children—Hilary Ann, Sarah Elizabeth, Joshua Aaron. B.S. in Metals Engring., Rensselaer Poly. Inst., 1957; M.S., MIT, 1960, Ph.D., 1961. Mgr. materials sci. Tycolabs, Waltham, Mass., 1961-68; tech. dir. turbine support div. Chromalloy Am. Corp., San Antonio, 1968-71, v.p., asst. gen. mgr., 1971-74, pres. 1975-79; pres. Chromalloy Compressor Techs., San Antonio, 1979—; group pres. Chromalloy Gas Turbine, San Antonio, 1982—; supervisory mng. dir. Turbine Support Europe, Tilburg, Netherlands, 1975—; dir. Internat. Coating Co., Tokyo, Japan. Bd. dirs. Jewish Fedn., 1981—, Chamber Players of San Antonio, 1979—, NCCJ, 1982—. Recipient Turner Meml. award Electrochem. Soc., 1963; Achievement award NASA, 1965; Am. Iron and Steel Inst. fellow, 1960. Mem. Am. Soc. Metals, Am. Inst. Metall. Engrs., N.Y. Acad. Sci., Sigma Xi. Patentee diffusion coating of jet engine materials. Contbr. articles to profl. jours. Home: 111 Sheffield Pl San Antonio TX 78213 Office: 4430 Director Dr San Antonio TX 78220

WEINSTEIN, PETER M., lawyer, state senator; b. N.Y.C., Feb. 3, 1947; s. Moses and Muriel W.; m. Barbara Ann Forman; children—Andrew, Michael. B.S., NYU; J.D., Bklyn. Law Sch. Bar: N.Y., Fla. Asst. dist. atty. Queens County, N.Y.; asst. state's atty., Broward County, Fla.; now ptnr. Weinstein & Zimmerman, Ft. Lauderdale, Fla.; mem. Fla. State Senate, Tallahassee, 1982—, chmn. Broward County legis. del., 1985-86. Mem. Broward County Charter Rev. Commn.; mem. Coral Springs Planning and Zoning Bd. Served to capt. U.S. Army. Recipient Allen Morris award Fla. Senate; named Most Effective Freshman, Fla. Senate. Clubs: Jewish War Vets.; Coral Springs Democratic (pres. 1980-82). Avocation: photography. Office: 6191 W Atlantic Blvd Suite 4 Margate FL 33063

WEINSTEIN, ROY, physicist, university administrator, researcher; b. N.Y.C., Apr. 21, 1927; s. Harry and Lillian (Ehrenberg) W.; m. Janet E. Spiller, Mar. 26, 1954; children—Lee Davis, Sara Lynn. B.S., MIT, 1951, Ph.D., 1954; Sc.D. (hon.), Lycoming Coll., 1981. Research asst. MIT, 1951-54, asst. prof., 1956-59; asst. prof. Brandeis U., Waltham, Mass., 1954-56; assoc. prof. Northeastern U., Boston, 1960-63, prof. physics, 1963-82, exec. officer, chmn. grad. div. physics dept., 1967-69, chmn. physics dept., 1974-81; dean Coll. Natural Scis., Math., prof. physics U. Houston, 1982—, dir. Inst. for Beam Particle Dynamics, 1985—; vis. scholar and physicist Stanford, 1966-67, 81-82; dir. Perception Tech., Inc., Winchester, Mass., Omniwave Inc., Gloucester, Mass.; cons. Visidyne Inc., Burlington, Mass., Stanford U., Calif., Cambridge Electron Accerlerator, Harvard U., Cambridge, Mass., also mem. adv. com., 1967-69; mem. program mgmt. group Tex. Accelerator Ctr., Woodlands, 1983—, chmn., 1985—; dir., mem. exec. com. Houston Area Research Corp., 1984—; 3d ann. faculty lectr. Northeastern U., 1966; chmn. organizing com. 4th ann. Internat. Conf. on Meson Spectroscopy, 1974, chmn. program com. 5th ann., 1977, mem. organizing com., 1980, 83. Author: Atomic Physics, 1964; Nuclear Physics, 1964; Interactions of Radiation and Matter, 1964. Editor: Nuclear Reactor Theory, 1964; Nuclear Materials, 1964. Editor procs 5th Internat. Conf. on Mesons, 1977. Contbr. articles to profl. jours. Vice chmn. Lexington Council on Aging, Mass., 1977-84; mem. Lexington Town Meeting, 1973-76, 77-84. Served with USNR, 1945-46. NSF fellow Bohr Inst., Copenhagen, 1959-60, Stanford U., 1969-70; Guggenheim fellow Harvard U., 1970-71; recipient numerous research awards NSF. Fellow Am. Phys. Soc.; mem. Am. Assn. Physics Tchrs., N.Y. Acad. Scis., Sigma Xi, Phi Kappa Phi (pres. chpt. 1977-78, nat. Triennial disting. scholar prize 1980-83), Pi Lambda Phi. Democrat. Unitarian. Lodge: Masons. Home: 4368 Fiesta Ln Houston TX 77004 Office: Coll Natural Sci Math U Houston Houston TX 77004

WEINTRAUB, E(LIOT) ROY, economics educator; b. Bklyn., Mar. 22, 1943; s. Sidney and Sheila E. (Tarlow) W.; m. Margaret Edwards, Aug. 24, 1968; children—Matthew, Garth. A.B., Swarthmore Coll., 1964; M.S., U. Pa., 1967, Ph.D., 1969. Asst. prof. Rutgers U., New Brunswick, N.J., 1968-70; assoc. prof. Duke U., Durham, N.C., 1970-75, prof. econs., 1975—, chmn. econs. dept., 1982—; cons. editor Cambridge U. Press, N.Y.C., 1980—. Author: Conflict and Cooperation, 1974; Microfoundations, 1979; Mathematics for Economists, 1983; General Equilibrium Analysis, 1985. Advisor, Kudzu Alliance, Durham, 1979-82; trustee Carolina Friends Sch., Durham, 1975-78. Mem. Am. Econ. Assn., History of Econs. Soc. Home: 411 Lakeshore Ln Chapel Hill NC 27514 Office: Econs Dept Duke U Durham NC 27706

WEINTRAUB, LAWRENCE HOWARD, ins. co. ofcl.; b. Oklahoma City, July 11, 1941; s. Sig and Pearl W.; B.S., U. Okla., 1963; postgrad. Ga. Inst. Tech., 1966-68; C.L.U., Am. Coll. Life Underwriters, 1979, C.H.F.C., 1982; m. Carol Blufston, Dec. 26, 1960; children—Douglas Lee, Nancy Ann, James Hardy. Engr., Rockwell Internat., Tulsa, 1963-66; sr. engr. Lockheed Aircraft Co., Marietta, Ga., 1966-69; agt. Nat. Life of Vt., Atlanta, 1969-73; gen. agt. Am. United Life Ins. Co., Atlanta, 1973—, mem. Pres. Club. Mem. Nat. Assn. Life Underwriters, Am. Soc. C.L.U.s, Million Dollar Round Table. Republican. Jewish. Home: 6340 Blackwater Trail Atlanta GA 30328 Office: Suite 112 6400 Powers Ferry Rd Atlanta GA 30339

WEINTRAUB, MICHAEL, banker, lawyer; b. Miami, Fla., June 5, 1938; s. Joseph and Hortense W.; B.A. in Econs., U. Va., 1960, J.D., 1963; m. Barbara Anderson, Sept. 5, 1968; 1 dau., Lori Ellen Southern. Bar: Fla. Assoc., Smathers & Thompson, Miami, 1963-69, partner, 1969—; v.p. Pan Am. Bancshares Inc., Miami, 1969-73, chief exec. officer, pres., 1973-81, vice chmn. bd., 1981—; dir. Continental Corp., City Gas Co. of Fla., Key Pharms., Inc. Trustee Miami Heart Inst., U. Miami. Recipient award for patriotic service U.S. Treasury, 1979. Mem. Am. Bankers Assn., Fla. Bankers Assn. (Disting. Service award 1978-79, pres. 1978-79), ABA, Fla. Bar Assn., Dade County Bar Assn. Clubs: Westview Country, Bankers, Miami, Standard. Office: 150 SE 3d Ave Miami FL 33131

WEINZETTLE, FRANCES REGINA, nurse; b. Phila., Aug. 22, 1952; d. Joseph Cornelius and Mary (Redner) Eichman; m. John Paul Weinzettle, Nov. 24, 1978; 1 dau., Marcella M. B.S.N., Gwynedd Mercy Coll., 1975. Cert. emergency room nurse. Capt. U.S. Army, 1976—; staff nurse trauma unit William Beaumont Army Med. Ctr., El Paso, Tex., 1976-77; staff nurse med. 121st Evacuation Hosp., Seoul, 1977-78; pediatrics head nurse U.S. Army Hosp., Wuerzburg, W.Ger., 1978-79, med./pediatrics head nurse 1979-83; head nurse emergency room 67th Evacuation Hosp., 1983; head nurse emergency room Dewitt Army Hosp., Ft. Belvoir, Va., 1983—. Active ARC. Recipient cert. of achievement ARC, Wuerzburg, 1983. Mem. Emergency Dept. Nurses Assn., DAR. Republican. Roman Catholic. Home: 3432 Beverly Dr Annandale VA 22003 Office: Dewitt Army Hosp Fort Belvoir VA 22060

WEIR, EUGENE ARNOLD, architect, industrial real estate official; b. Baton Rouge, Sept. 15, 1926; s. Claude Arnold and Myrtis (Downing) W.; student La. State U., 1944-46, 47; B.S. in Archtl. Engring., Kans. State U., 1950, B.S. in Architecture, 1951; m. Nancy Jean Fitzgerald, Apr. 3, 1954; children—Eugene Marcus, Jefferson Arnold, Nancy Kathryn. Constrn. aide Fed. Housing Adminstrn., Birmingham, Ala., 1950; with Ethyl Corp., Baton Rouge, 1951—, dir. corp. real estate, 1974-83, dir. corp. real estate and services dept., 1983—. Mem. Va. Mus.; bd. dirs. Central Richmond Assn. Served with USNR, 1944-46. Mem. AIA, Va. Soc. Architects, Indsl. Devel. Research Council, Internat. Assn. Corp. Real Estate Execs. (dir. 1977-81), Am. Inst. Corp. Asset Mgmt. (bd. govs.), Kans. State U. Alumni Assn., Clubs: Brandermill Country; Downtown, Engineers (Richmond). Internat. Platform Assn., Sigma Tau, Tau Sigma Delta, Kappa Alpha. Episcopalian. Clubs: Brandermill Country, Downtown of Richmond. Home: 3303 Fortune's Ridge Rd Midlothian VA 23113 Office: 330 S 4th St Richmond VA 23119

WEIR, GLORIA JANE, physician; b. Baton Rouge, Jan. 18, 1921; d. Claude Arnold and Peggy (Downing) Weir; student Sullins Coll., 1936-37; B.S., La. State U., 1940, M.D., 1943; m. N. Lyle Evans, July 26, 1952; children—Peggy Jane, David Lyle. Intern, Charity Hosp. La., New Orleans, 1944, resident, then chief resident in pediatrics, 1949-51; practice medicine specializing in pediatrics, Baton Rouge, 1952-81; staff mem. Baton Rouge Gen. Hosp., vice-chief staff, 1965, vice-chief pediatrics, 1969, chief pediatrics, 1970-71; mem. staff Our Lady of Lake Hosp., Baton Rouge, vice chief pediatrics, 1959-60; mem. staff Women's Hosp., chief pediatrics, 1969-70; mem. cons. staff Mary Bird Perkins Treatment Center of Cancer, Radiation and Research Found.; vis. staff Earl K. Long Meml. Hosp.; mem. instnl. rev. bd. Our Lady of Lake Regional Med. Ctr., 1983—; clin. instr. pediatrics La. State U. Med. Sch.; pediatric cons. Baton Rouge Med. Ctr. Child Day Care Ctr.; chief med. cons. Disability Determination Services State of La.; bd. dirs. Baton Rouge Assn. Retarded Citizens, 1974-77; adv. bd. East Baton Rouge Parish Med. Aux.; patron Baton Rouge Symphony. Diplomate Am. Bd. Pediatrics. Fellow Am. Acad. Pediatrics (alt. state chmn. 1975-78); mem. AMA, La. 6th Dist., East Baton Rouge Parish med. socs., La. Heart Assn., La. Pediatric Soc. Baton Rouge Pediatric Soc. (v.p. 1968-69, pres. 1969-70), Am. Med. Women's Assn., Baton Rouge Women in Medicine, Children's Hosp. Found., Cancer Soc. Baton Rouge (dir. 1963-67, 76-81), Sullins Alumnae Assn., Baton Rouge Alumnae Assn., Baton Rouge Symphony Aux., La. State U. Alumni Fedn. Episcopalian. Clubs: Harlequins (v.p. 1979-80, 83-84). Home: 5885 Eastwood Dr Baton Rouge LA 70806 Office: 2730 Wooddale Blvd PO Box 96074 Baton Rouge LA 70896

WEIRICK, WILLIAM NEWTON, economics educator; b. Long Beach, Calif., June 16, 1952; s. Richard Carver and Jane Margaret (Rumble) W.; m. Ellen Ann Johnson, Oct. 29, 1975; children—Lauren, Carlin. B.A., Pomona Coll., 1974; Ph.D., U. Wyo., 1984. Fin. mgr. So. Calif. Coop. Community, Los Angeles, 1975-79; research asst. U. Wyo., Laramie, 1980-84; asst. prof. econs. NE La. Univ., Monroe, 1983—; research aide EPA, 1981-84. Contbr. articles to profl. jours. Interim period research grantee NE La. Univ., 1984-85, La. Real Estate Bd. grantee NE La. Univ., 1985; Bugas fellow U. Wyo., 1982-84. Mem. Am. Econ. Assn., Regional Sci. Assn., Assn. Environ. and Resource Economists, Acad. La. Economists (parliamentarian 1985, program chmn. 1986). Avocations: auto restoration; gardening; back packing. Home: 2313 Jasmine St Monroe LA 71201 Office: NE La Univ Dept Econs and Fin Monroe LA 71209-0130

WEISE, BONNIE RENEE, petroleum geologist; b. Taylor, Tex., Dec. 1, 1952; d. Obie Eddie and Alice Charlotte (Tiemann) W. B.S. in Geology, U. Tex., 1974, M.A. in Geology, 1979. Research geologist Bur. Econ. Geology, Austin, Tex., 1974-81; exploration geologist Placid Oil Co., San Antonio, 1982-83; geol. cons., San Antonio, 1983-84; sr. geologist Valero Producing Co., San Antonio, 1984-85; geol. cons., San Antonio, 1986—; lectr. various seminars. Author: Wave-Dominated Delta Systems of the Upper Cretaceous San Miguel Formation, Maverick Basin, South Texas, 1980; (with others) Padre Island National Seashore-A Guide to the Geology, Natural Environments, and History of a Texas Barrier Island, 1980, Wilcox Sandstone Reservoirs in the Deep Subsurface Along the Texas Gulf Coast, 1982. Mem. editorial com.: Contributions to South Texas Geology, 1985. Contbr. geol. articles to profl. publs. Mem. Am. Assn. Petroleum Geologists (chmn. poster session 1984, book reviewer 1985), Soc. Econ. Paleontol. and Mineralogists, Soc. Econ. Paleontol. and Mineralogists (bus. rep. Gulf Coast sect. 1984—, awards com. 1984—), Gulf Coast Assn. Geol. Socs. (registration com. 1977, editorial com. ann. meeting 1977, judge best paper award 1979, 82), S. Tex. Geol. Soc. (v.p. 1982-83, pres. 1983-84, co-chmn. continuing edn. com. 1984-85, nominating com. 1985), W. Tex. Geol. Soc., San Antonio Geophys. Soc., San Antonio Logging Soc. Club: Petroleum. Republican. Lutheran. Avocations: tennis; hiking; dancing; reading. Home and office: 19902 Encino Cove San Antonio TX 78259

WEISE, FRANK EARL, JR., steel executive; b. Allegheny County, Pa., June 25, 1919; s. Frank E. and Caroline S. (Stork) W.; m. Marian M. Hagerman, Jan. 17, 1942; children—Frank Earl, III, Pamela D., Kathryn A. B.S. in Metall. Engring., Lehigh U., 1941. With Bethlehem Steel Co., 1941-49; with Detroit Steel Corp., 1949-64, v.p. ops., 1961-64; with Koppers Co. Inc., Pitts., 1964-69, v.p. engring. and constrn. div., 1966-69; with Fla. Steel Corp., Tampa, since 1969, v.p. mills, 1971, exec. v.p., 1974-80, pres., chief operating officer, 1980—, also dir.; dir. Atlanta Constrn. Products Inc., Bricmont and Assocs., Applied Process Controls, Ameritrust Southeast Nat. Assn. Mem. Am. Iron and Steel Inst., Am. Iron and Steel Engrs., Am. Inst. Steel Constrn., Wire Assn., Asso. Gen. Contractors. Presbyterian. Clubs: Belleview Biltmore Country, Innisbrook Country, Ponte Vedra Country, Tower, Rotary, Masons. Office: PO Box 23328 Tampa FL 33630

WEISER, ERNEST LEOPOLD, language and linguistics educator; b. Buffalo, Oct. 17, 1930; s. James A. and Elsie (Hechter) W.; m. Marsha A. McCullen, June 16, 1967; children—Robert E., Edward J. B.A., U. Buffalo, 1952; A.M., Syracuse U., 1954; Ph.D., UCLA, 1966. Instr. to asst. prof. German and humanities Reed Coll., Portland, Oreg., 1958-63; asst. prof. German, U. Miami, Coral Gables, Fla., 1963-66; asst. prof. to prof. langs. and linguistics Fla. Atlantic U., Boca Raton, 1966—, chmn. dept., 1968—. Contbr. articles to profl. jours. Acad. freedom chmn. Fla. ACLU, Miami, 1965-66; bd. dirs. Palm Beach Council Humanistic Values, Palm Beach County, 1980-81; asst. dir. Democrats of Boca Raton, 1982-83. Grantee Goethe Inst. and Fed. Rep. Germany, 1961,79, NEH, 1976,79. Mem. Am. Assn. Tchrs. German (pres. Fla. chpt. 1970-72), MLA, Fla. Fgn. Lang. Assn., Assn. Depts. Fgn. Langs., Am. Council Teaching Fgn. Langs., Am. Assn. Coll. Profs. (sec., treas. Reed Coll. chpt. 1960-61). Unitarian. Avocations: computer languages; bridge; tropical gardening. Home: 121 St Cloud Ln Boca Raton FL 33431 Office: Fla Atlantic U 500 NW 20th St Boca Raton FL 33431

WEISHEIT, RICHARD LANE, accountant; b. Houston, Jan. 27, 1951; s. Oscar George and Shirley Ann (Spickerman) W.; B.B.A. in Acctg., Tex. Tech U., 1973; m. Margaret Lynette Willis, May 12, 1973. Staff acct. Frank B. Egan, C.P.A., Dallas, 1973-77; sr. acct. Isham P. Nelson, P.C., C.P.A.s, Dallas, 1977-78; owner Richard L. Weisheit, P.C., C.P.A.s, Dallas, 1979—; assoc. dir. Grand Bank/Stemmons, Dallas; adv. dir. Founders Nat. Bank, 1985—; dir. Spaghetti Importing and Warehouse Co. Mem. editorial bd. C.P.A. Mktg. Report, Atlanta. Treas. Dallas Hist. Preservation League, 1984-86. C.P.A., Tex. Mem. Am. Inst. C.P.A.s, Am. Mgmt. Assn., Tex. Soc. C.P.A.s, Sigma Chi. Republican. Methodist. Home: 6327 Riverview Ln Dallas TX 75248 Office: 9221 LBJ Freeway Suite 207 Dallas TX 75243

WEISIGER, EDWARD INNES, tractor and equipment company executive; b. Rowan County, N.C. Oct. 29, 1931; s. Leslie Marshall and Katharine (Van Benthuysen) W.; m. Ellen Harrington Jan. 17, 1959; (div.) children—Edward Innes, Leslie Marshall; m. Agnes Watkins Binder, Jan. 8, 1983. B.S. in Mech. Engring., N.C. State U., 1954. Mgr. Charlotte br. Carolina Tractor & Equipment Co., 1956-58, v.p., gen. mgr., 1958-65, pres. 1965—; pres. EIW Equipment, Inc., Charlotte and Raleigh, N.C., 1984—; dir. Washovia Bank & Trust Co., Charlotte. Active Mecklenburg County chpt. ARC, Charlotte; trustee St. Andrews Coll.; vice chmn. bd. trustees N.C. State U.; mem. bus. adv. council U. N.C.-Charlotte; bd. dirs. YMCA of Charlotte and Mecklenburg, Charlotte Jr. Achievement, Crossmore Sch., N.C. bd. visitors Davidson Coll. Served to 1st lt. U.S. Army, 1954-56. Mem. Assoc. Equipment Distbrs. (govt. relations com., tax reform adv. com.), Better Transp. N.C., Newcomen Soc., Assoc. Gen. Contractors, Engring. Found., Southeastern Caterpillar Dealer Assn. (pres.), Southeastern Caterpillar Lift Truck Assn. (pres.), Charlotte C. of C., Pi Kappa Alpha. Democrat. Presbyterian. Clubs: Quail Hollow Country (Charlotte); Grandfather Golf, Country (Linville, N.C.); Shoal Creek Country (Birmingham, Ala.); MacGregor Downs (Raleigh); Sportsman's, Ducks Unltd., Charlotte Country, Mecklenburg Wolfpack (Charlotte); Core Banks (N.C.). Lodge: Rotary. Home: 1634 Queens Rd W Charlotte NC 28207 Office: US 21 N Charlotte NC 28221

WEISINGER, RONALD JAY, mortgage banker; b. Youngstown, Ohio, Feb. 13, 1946; s. David S. and Sterna (Woolf) W.; m. Wendy Doris Cowen, Dec. 19, 1976. B.S., Carroll Coll., 1968. Notary public. Dir. cash dept. United Jewish Appeal, N.Y.C., 1975-78; exec. dir. Jewish Fedn. Pinellas County, Inc., Clearwater, Fla., 1978-80; pres. Capital Investment Co. Am., Inc., West Palm Beach, Fla., 1980-82; v.p. Worldwide Merc. Trading Co., Inc., West Palm Beach, 1982-83; v.p. W.J. Miller Mortgage Co., Inc., West Palm Beach, 1983, V.I.P. Mortgage Trust Co., West Palm Beach, 1984—; chmn. bd. Israeli Deli World Inc.; fin. cons. residential and comml. mortgages; bd. dirs. USA Homeowners Fed. Credit Union. Mem. Nat. Republican Congl. Com., 1980—, Boca Raton Rep. Club. Mem. Lake Worth Jaycees. Jewish. Club: Sertoma (Clearwater and Palm Beach, Fla.).

WEISS, ARMAND BERL, economist; b. Richmond, Va., Apr. 2, 1931; s. Maurice Herbert and Henrietta (Shapiro) W.; B.S. in Econs., Wharton Sch. Fin., U. Pa., 1953, M.B.A., 1954; D.B.A., George Washington U., 1971; m. Judith Bernstein, May 18, 1957; children—Jo Ann Michele, Rhett Louis. Officer, U.S. Navy, 1954-65; spl. asst. to auditor gen. Dept. Navy, 1964-65; sr. economist Center for Naval Analyses, Arlington, Va., 1965-68; project dir. Logistics Mgmt. Inst., Washington, 1968-74; dir. systems integration Fed. Energy Adminstrn., Washington, 1974-76; sr. economist Nat. Commn. Supplies and Shortages, 1976-77; tech. asst. to v.p. System Planning Corp., 1977-78; pres. Assns. Internat., Inc., 1978—; v.p., treas. Tech. Frontiers, Inc., 1978-80; sr. v.p. Weiss Pub. Co., Inc., Richmond, Va., 1960—; v.p. Condo News Internat., Inc., 1981; adj. prof. Am. U., 1979-80; vis. lectr. George Washington U., 1971; assoc. prof. decision scis. George Mason U., 1984; chmn. U.S. del., session chmn. NATO Symposium on Cost-Benefit Analysis, The Hague, Netherlands, 1969, NATO Conf. on Operational Research in Indsl. Systems, St. Louis, France, 1970; pres. Nat. Council Assns. Policy Scis., 1971-77; chmn. adv. group Def. Econ. Adv. Council, 1970-74; resident asso. Smithsonian Instn., 1973—; expert cons. Dept. State, GAO. Del. Pres.'s Mid-Century White House Conf. on Children and Youth, 1950; scoutmaster Japan, U.S., leader World Jamborees, France, Can., U.S., 1945-61; U.S. del.

Internat. Conf. on Ops. Research, Dublin, Ireland, 1972; organizing com. Internat. Cost-Effectiveness Symposium, Washington, 1970; speaker Internat. Conf. Inst. Mgmt. Scis., Tel Aviv, 1973, del., Mexico City, 1967. Mem. bus. com. Washington Nat. Symphony Orch., 1968-70, Washington Performing Arts Soc., 1974—; bus. mgr. Nat. Lyric Opera Co., 1983—; exec. com. Mid Atlantic council Union Am. Hebrew Congregations, 1970-79, treas., 1974-79, mem. nat. MUM com., 1974-79; mem. dist. com. Boy Scouts Am., 1972-75; bd. dirs. Nat. Council Career Women, 1975-79, Fairfax Cable Assn., 1982-85. Recipient Service award FBI. Fellow AAAS, Washington Acad. Scis. (gov. 1981-82, chmn. membership com. 1984—); mem. Ops. Research Soc. Am. (chmn. meetings com. 1969-71; chmn. cost-effectiveness sect. 1969-70), Washington Ops. Research Council 9editor newsletter 1969-78; sec. 1971-72, pres. 1973-74, trustee 1975-77, bus. mgr. 1976-85), Internat. Inst. Strategic Studies (London), Am. Soc. Assn. Execs. (membership com. 1981-83), Inst. for Mgmt. Sci., Am. Econ. Assn., Wharton Grad. Sch. Alumni Assn. (exec. com. 1970-73), Am. Acad. Polit. and Social Sci., Alumni Assn. George Washington U. (governing bd. 1974-82, chmn. univ. publs. com. 1976-78, Alumni Service award 1980), Alumni Assn. George Washington U. Sch. Govt. and Bus. Adminstrn. (exec. v.p. 1977-78, pres. 1978-79), George Washington U. Doctoral Assn. (sr. v.p. 1968-69). Jewish (pres. temple 1970-72). Club: Wharton Grad. Sch. Washington (sec. 1967-69, pres. 1969-70). Co-editor: Systems Analysis for Social Problems, 1970; The Relevance of Economic Analysis to Decision Making in the Department of Defense, 1972; Toward More Effective Public Programs: The Role of Analysis and Evaluation, 1975. Editor: Cost-Effectiveness Newsletter, 1966-70, Operations Research/Systems Analysis Today, 1971-73, Operation Research/Mgmt. Sci. Today, 1974—; Feedback, 1979—, Condo World, 1981; assoc. editor Ops. Research, 1971-75; editor newsletter Internat. Soc. Parametric Analysts, 1983-85. Served as FBI undercover agt. for 3 years and uncovered Soviet espionage agent, 1983. Home: 6516 Truman Ln Falls Church VA 22043

WEISS, CHARLES MANUEL, environmental biologist, educator; b. Scranton, Pa., Dec. 7, 1918; s. Morris and Fannie (Levy) W.; B.S., Rutgers U., 1939, postgrad., 1939-40; postgrad. Harvard U., 1940; Ph.D., Johns Hopkins U., 1950; m. Shirley Friedlander, June 7, 1942. Fellow in marine microbiology, research assoc. marine biology Woods Hole (Mass.) Oceanographic Instn., 1939-47; chemist, biologist Balt. Harbor Project, Johns Hopkins U. Dept. San. Engring., 1947-50; basin biologist div. water pollution control USPHS, N.Y.C., 1950-52; biologist med. labs. Army Chem. Center, Edgewood, Md., 1952-56; prof. dept. environ. scis. and engring. U. N.C.-Chapel Hill, 1956—; Bigelow fellow Woods Hole Oceanographic Instn., 1970; cons. limnology Duke Power Co.; mem. standards com. for triennial rev. state water quality standards, div. environ. mgmt. N.C. Dept. Natural Resources and Community Devel., 1981-82. Mem. Chapel Hill Planning Bd., 1969-76, chmn., 1970-72, 75-76; trustee Chapel Hill Preservation Soc., 1972. Fellow AAAS, Am. Public Health Assn., N.Y. Acad. Scis.; mem. Am. Chem. Soc., Am. Geophys. Union, Am. Fisheries Soc., Am. Soc. Limnology and Oceanography, Ecol. Soc. Am., Water Pollution Control Fedn. (chmn. research com. 1966-71), Am. Water Works Assn. (com. on quality control in reservoirs), Am. Soc. Microbiology, AAUP (chpt. pres. 1980-81, N.C. conf. pres. 1982-83), N.C. Acad. Sci., Sigma Xi, Delta Omega. Author: Water Quality Investigations, Guatemala: Lake Atitlan 1968-70, 1971; Water Quality Investigations, Guatemala: Lake Amatitlan 1969-70, 1971; The Trophic State of North Carolina Lakes, 1976; The Water Quality of the Upper Yadkin Drainage Basin, 1981; Water Quality Study, B. Everett Jordan Lake, N.C., Year 1, 1981-82, 1984, Year II, 1982-83, 1985. Home: 155 Hamilton Rd Chapel Hill NC 27514 Office: 104 Rosenau 201H U NC Chapel Hill NC 27514

WEISS, HERBERT SAUL, pharmacist; b. Bklyn., Sept. 6, 1932; s. Morris Adolf and Lillian (Rogg) W.; m. Gloria Rita Silverman, Sept. 4, 1954 (div. May 1980); children—Ilyce Sharri, Holly-Jill; m. Kathleen Johnson, May 12, 1982. B.S. in Pharmacy, L.I.U., 1956. Lic. pharmacist, Fla., N.Y. Pres., Shiller/Weiss Pharmacy, Inc., Liberty, N.Y., 1968-78; dir. pharm. service Ellenville Community Hosp., N.Y., 1978-80, Highlands Regional Med. Ctr., Sebring, Fla., 1980—; pres. Herb Weiss, Inc., Sebring, 1984—. Author: Hyperalimentation/TPN, 1982; Pharmpro/XT, 1984. Mem. Am. Soc. Hosp. Pharmacists, Fla. Soc. Hosp. Pharmacists, Am. Soc. Nutrition. Lodges: Rotary (pres. 1984, sec. 1985), Elks. Avocations: golfing; sailing. Home: 2402 Valerie Blvd Sebring FL 33870 Office: Highlands Regional Med Ctr S Highlands Ave Sebring FL 33870

WEISS, HERMAN ROBERT, psychologist; b. Bklyn., Oct. 3, 1913; s. Julius and Fanny (Backman) W.; m. Sylvia Weiss, Jan. 30, 1938; children—Jeffrey, Daniel. B.A., L.I. U., 1934; M.A., Columbia U., 1936; Ph.D., NYU, 1951. Lic. psychologist, N.Y.; diplomate Am. Bd. Profl. Psychology. Psychologist, Bellevue Hosp., N.Y.C., 1940-44; chief psychologist VA Hosp., Bklyn., 1946-74; spl. examiner N.Y.C. Civil Service, N.Y. State Civil Service, N.Y.C. Bd. Examiners, 1946-74. Contbr. articles to profl. jours. Assoc. editor Ednl. Abstracts, 1935-38. Chmn. Bd. Social Services, Tamarac, Fla., 1976-80; mem. County Bd. Gerontology (now Services for Elderly), Broward County-Fort Lauderdale, 1980-85; bd. dirs. Sr. Ednl. Experience, Broward Community Coll. (North), 1976-85. Served as lt. (j.g.) USMC, 1944-46; to capt. USAF, 1951-53. Named Vol. of Yr., Broward County Council on Aging, 1983. Fellow Am. Psychol. Assn. (emeritus). Jewish. Avocations: music; photography. Home: 9411 NW 74th Pl Tamarac FL 33321

WEISS, JEFFREY J., business exec.; b. Bklyn., July 13, 1943; s. Louis M. and Miriam (Solow) W.; student Miami Dade Jr. Coll., 1961-63, U. Miami, 1974—; children—Lara J., Gina J. Pres., chmn. bd., founder Atlantic Industries, Inc., Miami, Fla., 1965-74, spl. cons., 1974-76; chmn. bd., v.p. Exposition Corp. of Am., Miami, 1968—; v.p., dir. Scarlet O'Hara, 1970-79, Glenda Products Inc., 1972—, Gazebo Food Corp., 1973-74; founder, prin., dir. First Bank of North Kendall Assos., 1974-76; prin., dir. Allstate Realty & Investment Co., 1974—; pres., founder Advance Devel. Corp., 1975—, Custom Land, Inc., 1975—, Advance Investment Properties, Inc., 1977—, Advance Fin. Corp., 1978—, 1st Advance Realty Corp.; gen. partner Flagler St. Ltd., 1979—; founder, dir. Miami Dinnerkey Boat Show, 1970—, So. Marine, 1965-68; v.p., founder Kitchencraft Inc., 1976-77; founder, chmn. bd. Advance Fin. Corp., 1977—; founder, prin. So. Marine Corp., 1966-70, So. Fla. Savs. & Loan Assn., 1982—; dir. Underwriters Fin. of Fla., Inc., Creative Ideas; cons. Walter E Heller & Co. S.E.; fin. cons. to numerous corps. and lending instns. Exec. com. Ednl. Community TV, 1973—. Recipient ann. corp. award March of Dimes Walkathon. Mem. Direct Selling Assn. (dir.), Smithsonian Instn. Office: 1320 S Dixie Hwy Penthouse Suite Coral Gables FL 33146

WEISS, JEROME IRWIN, psychologist; b. Chgo., Aug. 22, 1934; s. Harry and Helen Weiss; B.A., Ariz. State Coll., 1955; M.A., CUNY, 1962; M.S. (teaching asst.), U. N.D., 1971, Ph.D., 1974. Tchr., Jr. High Sch. 142, Bronx, N.Y., 1961-65; instr. Phoenix Coll., 1965-67; therapist U. N.D., Grand Forks, 1969-73; intern clin. psychology Health Sci. Center, U. Tex., Dallas, 1973-74; sr. clinician Dallas County Cocare Outpatient Unit, 1974-76; pvt. practice clin. psychology, 1976—; psychologist Beverly Hills Hosp., Dallas, 1973, Meth. Hosp., Dallas, 1977; cons. North Dallas Pain Clinic, 1980-81; clin. asso. prof. health care scis. U. Tex. Health Sci. Center, Dallas, 1980-82. Mem. Am. Soc. Behavioral Medicine, Am. Psychol. Assn., Tex. Psychol. Assn., Dallas Psychol. Assn., Am. Assn. Marriage and Family Therapists, Tex. Assn. Marriage and Family Therapists, Dallas Assn. Marriage and Family Therapists, Am. Acad. Behavioral Medicine, Am. Soc. Clin. Hypnosis, Internat. Soc. Hypnosis, Dallas Soc. Clin. Hypnosis. Author: Crisis Intervention with Children, 1980; editor Jour. Am. Acad. Behavioral Medicine, 1980—. Office: The Registry 6350 LBJ Freeway #283 Dallas TX 75240

WEISS, LEONARD, international economics consultant; b. Chgo., June 5, 1918; s. Ben and Esther (Tepper) W.; m. Mary L. Barker, Sept. 21, 1946; children—Susan R., David A. B.A., U. Chgo., 1939; M.A., Fletcher Sch. Law and Diplomacy, 1940. Research asst. Ill. Tax Commn., 1938, Carnegie Endowment for Internat. Peace, 1940; fellow Brookings Instn., 1941-42; economist Office Inter-Am. Affairs, 1942-43, 46; ofcl. Dept. State, 1946-56, fgn. service officer, 1956-74; asst. chief trade agreements div., alt. chmn. interdeptl. trade agreements com., until 1957; dep. dir. and acting dir. USOM, Belgrade, Yugoslavia, 1957-60, also 1st sec., 1957-58; then counselor econ. affairs Am. embassy, Belgrade, 1959-60; with Dept. of State, Washington, 1960-63, dep. dir., then dir. Office Internat. Trade and Fin., 1960-63; counselor econ. affairs, 1963-65; also minister-counselor polit. and econ. affairs Am. embassy, New Delhi, 1965-67; minister econ. and comml. affairs Am. embassy, Bonn, 1968-70; dep. dir. Bur. Intelligence and Research, Dept. State, Washington, 1970-74; chief World Bank Mission, Bangladesh, 1974-78; internat. econs. cons., mem. trade policy group U.S. Atlantic Council, 1978—; mem. Research and Study Panel, Am. Soc. Internat. Law, 1982—; U.S. del. ECOSOC, 1951, GATT, 1950, 53-54, 55, 61, 62, 63, OEEC Council of Ministers meeting, 1954; vice chmn. U.S. del. to ECAFE, 1965, 66, 67, alt. U.S. rep., 1966-67; spl. rep. for Offset Talks, 1968; mem. U.S. del. to Offset Talks, 1969, Sr. Seminar Fgn. Policy, State Dept., 1967-68, World Bank del. to Bangladesh Aid Group meeting, 1974, 75, 76, 77. Contbr. articles to profl. publs. Served to lt. j.g. USNR, 1943-46. Recipient Superior Service award Dept. of State, 1963. Mem. Am. Econ. Assn., Am. Soc. Internat. Law (research and study panel on internat. trade issues 1982—), Am. Fgn. Service Assn., Diplomatic and Consular Officers Assn., Alumni Assn. Fletcher Sch. Law and Diplomacy, Chgo. Alumni Assn., 1818 Soc. (World Bank), Phi Beta Kappa. Home: 4126 N 34th St Arlington VA 22207

WEISS, MARVIN ARNOLD, manufacturing company executive; b. Chgo., Oct. 10, 1924; s. Nathan and Sarah (Kushner) W.; B.S., Sch. Bus., Northwestern U., 1948; m. Martha Hirsh, Feb. 1, 1948; children—Michael Joel, Robert Steven. Sales rep. Nikoh Tube Co. div. Internat. Rolling Mills, Chgo., 1948-53; pres. Marvin Weiss & Assocs., mfrs. rep., Chgo., 1953-63; v.p. mktg. Unarco Industries, Oklahoma City, 1964-81, sr. v.p., gen. mgr., 1981-84, pres., 1984—. Pres. Oklahoma City Jewish Community Council, 1979-80, Emanual Synagogue, 1982. Served as sgt. U.S. Army, 1942-46. Mem. Mgmt. Group. Clubs: Petroleum, Oak Tree Golf, B'nai B'rith. Office: 1316 W Main St Oklahoma City OK 73106

WEISS, SHIRLEY F., urban and regional planner, economist; b. N.Y.C.; d. Max and Vera (Hendel) Friedlander; B.A., Douglass Coll., Rutgers U., 1942; postgrad. Johns Hopkins U., 1948-50; M.Regional Planning, U. N.C., 1958; Ph.D., Duke U., 1973; m. Charles M. Weiss, June 7, 1942. Asso. research dir. Center for Urban and Regional Studies U. N.C., Chapel Hill, 1957—, lectr. planning, 1958-62, assoc. prof., 1962-73, prof., 1973—, research assoc. Inst. for Research in Social Sci., 1957-73, research prof., 1973—, mem. chancellor's adv. com., 1977-80, chmn., 1979-80, mem. tech. com. Water Resources Research Inst., 1976-79; mem. adv. com. on housing for 1980 census Dept. Commerce, 1976-81; cons. Urban Inst., Washington, 1977-80; mem. rev. panel Exptl. Housing Allowance Program, HUD, 1977-80, mem. Adv. Bd. on Built Environment, Nat. Acad. Scis./NRC, 1981-83. Fellow Urban Land Inst. (exec. group community devel. council 1978—); mem. Am. Inst. Cert. Planners, Am. Planning Assn., Am. Econ. Assn., So. Regional Sci. Assn. (v.p., program chair 1976-77, exec. council 1971-74, 79—, pres. 1977-78), Regional Sci. Assn. (councillor 1971-74, v.p. 1976-77), Interamerican Planning Soc., Internat. Fedn. Housing and Planning, Town and Country Planning Assn. (Eng.), Econometric Soc., Econ. History Assn., Internat. New Towns Assn., History Econs. Soc., Am. Statis. Assn., Am. Real Estate and Urban Econs. Assn. (dir. 1977-81, regional membership chair 1976-82, 84-85), Royal Econ. Soc. (Eng.), AAUP (chpt. pres. 1976-77, N.C. Conf. pres. 1978-79, nat. council 1983-86), Douglas Soc., Order of Valkyries, Phi Beta Kappa. Author: The Central Business District in Transition, 1957; New Town Development in the United States; Experiment in Private Entrepreneurship, 1973; co-author: A Probabilistic Model for Residential Growth, 1964; Residential Developer Decisions: A Focused View of the Urban Growth Process, 1966; New Communities U.S.A., 1976; co-author, co-editor: Urban Growth Dynamics in a Regional Cluster of Cities, 1962; co-editor: New Community Development: Planning Process, Implementation and Emerging Social Concerns, vols. 1, 2, 1971; City Centers in Transition, 1976; New Communities Research Series, 1976-77; mem. editorial bd. Jour. Am. Inst. Planners, 1963-68, Rev. of Regional Studies, 1969-74, 82—, Internat. Regional Sci. Rev., 1975-81. Office: Dept City and Regional Planning 207 New East Bldg 033A Univ NC Chapel Hill NC 27514

WEISSENBURGER, JAN ELIZABETH, research psychologist and consultant; b. Sterling, Ill., Mar. 16, 1953; d. Harold E. and Marian E. (McNinch) Stone; m. David Allen Weissenburger, Aug. 20, 1977; 1 child, Jon Eric. B.S., Western Ill. U., 1975; M.A., U. Tex.-Arlington, 1977. Research technician U. Tex. Health Sci. Ctr., Dallas, 1978-80, psychol. asst., 1980-82, psychol. assoc., 1982-84, sr. research assoc., 1984-85, research scientist, 1985—; co-owner, cons. Statpak Research Cons., Dallas, 1982—. Contbr. chpt. to books, articles to profl. jours. Mem. Am. Psychol. Assn. (assoc.), Smithsonian Instn. Avocations: swimming; bicycling; gardening; travel; reading. Home: 1104 Berkshire Ct Trophy Club TX 76262 Office: Dept Psychiatry U Tex Health Sci Ctr 5323 Harry Hines Blvd Dallas TX 75235

WEITZEL, MARLENE HELEN, nurse educator, administrator; b. Hastings, Nebr., Nov. 12, 1937; d. Lester C. and Helen (Trautman) Weitzel. Diploma in nursing St. Francis Hosp. Sch. Nursing, 1957; B.S. in Nursing, Duchesne Coll., 1958; M.S. in Nursing, Cath. U. Am., 1963; Ph.D., U. Tex., 1977. R.N., Nebr., S.D., N.Y., Ariz., Tex. Staff nurse, instr. St. Francis Hosp., Grand Island, Nebr., 1958-61; instr. Mt. Marty Coll., Yankton, S.D., 1963-65; asst. prof., curriculum coordinator Niagara U., Niagara Falls, N.Y., 1965-70; asst. prof. Ariz. State U., Tempe, 1970-74; asst. dean, assoc. prof. Coll. of Nursing and Allied Health, U. Tex.-El Paso, 1981-84; asst. prof. Sch. Nursing U. Tex., Austin, 1984—; cons. in field. Recipient acad. award U.Tex. at El Paso, 1981; Am. Cancer Soc. scholar, 1958; Faculty Devel. grantee, 1980. Mem. Am. Nurses Assn., Nat. League for Nursing, Am. Ednl. Research Assn., AAUP, Am. Heart Assn., AAUW, Pi Lambda Theta, Sigma Theta Tau, Pi Lambda Theta. Democrat. Roman Catholic. Contbr. articles on nursing to profl. jours. Office: 1700 Red River TX 78701

WEITZEL, WILLIAM DAVID, psychiatrist; b. Detroit, Sept. 16, 1942; s. William Howard and Mary Ann (Buscanics) W.; B.S. cum laude, Xavier U., 1964; M.D., St. Louis U., 1968; m. Joan Carol Heiser, June 8, 1968; children—Erica Marie, Jennifer Joan, Sarah Elizabeth. Intern, William Beaumont Gen. Hosp., El Paso, Tex., 1968-69; psychiat. resident Walter Reed Gen. Hosp., 1969-72; postgrad. tng. family therapy The Washington Sch. Psychiatry, 1971-72; chief dept. psychiatry and neurology Moncrief Army Hosp., Columbia, S.C., 1972-74; asst. prof. psychiatry and dir. Hosp. Inpatient Psychiatry Service, Coll. Medicine, U. Ky., Lexington, 1974-78, asso. prof. psychiatry, 1979, asso. clin. prof. psychiatry, 1980—, lectr. Coll. Law, 1977-82; supervising and cons. psychiatrist William S. Hall Psychiat. Inst., Columbia, S.C., 1973-74; psychiat. cons. Commn. on Ministry Episcopal Diocese of Lexington, 1975-85; psychiat. cons. Clin. Research Center Project, Ky. Bur. Health Services, Homestead Nursing Center, Lexington, Ky., 1978—; mem. adv. com. U. Ky. Grant on Rural Aging and Mental Health, 1978-81; mem. profl. adv. bd. Mental Health Assn. Central Ky., 1979-80. Mem. Ky. Gov.'s Task Force on Welfare Reform, 1978-79; mem. Ky. Mental Health Task Force, 1977-79. Served to maj. MC AUS, 1968-74. Diplomate Am. Bd. Psychiatry and Neurology, Am. Bd. Forensic Psychiatry. Mem. Group for Advancement of Psychiatry, AAAS, Am. Psychiat. Assn. (pres. Ky. dist. br. 1979-80), Am. Acad. Psychiatry and the Law, Am. Coll. Psychiatrists. Contbr. numerous articles to profl. jours. Home: 330 Chinoe Rd Lexington KY 40502 Office: Suite A580 1401 Harrodsburg Rd Lexington KY 40504

WEITZMAN, DONALD OSCAR, psychologist, educator; b. N.Y.C., Nov. 27, 1933; s. Max and Rose (Bienenfeld) W.; m. Edna Marcia Freeman, Apr. 19, 1970; children—Erica S., Michael S. B.A., U. Conn., 1955; M.S., Lehigh U., 1960; Ph.D., U. Md., 1966. Research psychologist Naval Med. Research Ctr., Groton, Conn., 1965-68; head human performance lab. Riverside Research Inst., N.Y.C., 1969-75; sr. research psychologist Army Research Inst., Alexandria, Va., 1975-80; mem. tech. staff Bell Telephone Labs., Whippany, N.J., 1980-82, Mitre Corp., McLean, Va., 1982—; adj. lectr. U. R.I., Kingston, 1966-68; adj. assoc. prof. Hunter Coll., N.Y.C., 1969-75; cons. Mt. Carmel Guild Hosp., Newark, 1975; vis. prof. U. Md., College Park, 1976-79. Contbr. articles to profl. jours. Served to lt. col. USAF, 1957—. Fellow Centre Nat. de la Recherche Scientifique, 1968; NIH grantee, 1970. Mem. Human Factors Soc., Psychonomic Soc., N.Y. Acad. Scis., Am. Psychol. Assn., AAAS. Avocations: theatre; music. Home: 10240 Dunfries Rd Vienna VA 22180 Office: Mitre Corp 1820 Dolley Madison Blvd McLean VA 22102

WEITZNER DE SHWEDEL, ESTHER JUDITH, psychologist, researcher; b. Veracruz, Mex., b. Aug. 8, 1946; d. Kive and Eva (Jonas) W.; m. Stuart Kenneth Shwedel, Dec. 18, 1971; children—Yosef B., Daniel J. B.A., U. Tex., 1968; M.A., Mich. State U., 1973; Ph.D., 1980. Asst. researcher Mich. State U., East Lansing, 1973-74; assoc. prof. Nat. U. Costa Rica, 1974-75; assoc. prof. U. Iberoam., Mexico City, 1978; head researcher Ctr. for Ednl Studies, Mexico City, 1978-81, Research on Edn., Mexico City, 1981-83; dept. head CONAFE - Dept. Diseno Sistemas Edn., Mexico City, 1983—; head researcher Nat. Edn. Council, Mexico City, 1980-81; advisor to rector Nat. Aut. Met. U., 1981; guest lectr. Ctr. for Univ. Studies, Veracruz, 1979. Contbr. articles to profl. jours. Mem. Am. Edn. Research Assn., Am. Psychol. Assn., Interam. Psychol. Assn. Jewish. Avocations: writing; reading. Home: Cda de Moctezuma 43 La Herradura Mexico 10 DF Mexico

WEKKIN, GARY DON, political science educator, researcher; b. Durand, Wis., June 6, 1949; s. Donald and Nellie Almeda (Newell) W.; m. Julia Maurene Pierson, June 26, 1971; children—Clifford Donald, Erik Lloyd. B.A., U. Wis.-Madison, 1971; M.A., U. B.C., Vancouver, 1972, Ph.D., 1980. Grad. asst. Inst. Internat. Relations, Vancouver, 1973-74; del. selection coordinator Wis. Democratic Party, Madison, 1975-76; lectr. U. Wis. Ctr., Janesville, Wis., 1978-81; vis. asst. prof. U. Mo., Kansas City, 1981-82; asst. prof. polit. sci. U. Central Ark., Conway, 1982—; referee Ark. Polit. Sci. Jour., Conway, 1983—. Author: Democrat vs Democrat, 1984. Contbr. articles to profl. jours. Campaign mgr. Ada Deer for Sec. State, Madison, 1978; mem. exec. com. Dane County Democrats (Wis.), 1976-77; del. Ark. State Conv., Hot Springs, 1984; advisor U. Central Ark. Young Dems., Conway, 1982—. Recipient Dr. MacKenzie Am. Alumni award U. B.C., 1971-72; grantee U. Central Ark. Research Council, 1985, U. Wis. Ctr. System, 1980. Mem. Am. Polit. Sci. Assn., Midwestern Polit. Sci. Assn., Acad. Polit. Sci., So. Polit. Sci. Assn., Com. for Party Renewal. Presbyterian. Avocation: mil. strategy games. Home: 145 Oaklawn St Conway AR 72032 Office: U Central Ark Dept Polit Sci Conway AR 72032

WELBORN, MYLES BRANTLEY, JR., dentist; b. McKinney, Tex., Sept. 1, 1928; s. Myles Brantley and Edna Loraine (Renfro) W.; m. Pansy Dale Turpen, Nov. 24, 1950; children—Todd Lee, Tracy Brant, Tandy Vee. A.A., Wayland Coll., 1945-47; B.S., Hardin Simmons U., 1949; postgrad. Tex. Tech. U., 1955-56; D.D.S., Baylor Coll., 1960. Lic. dentist, Tex. Gen. practice dentistry, Richardson, Tex., 1960—. Served to cpl. U.S. Army, 1953-55. Fellow Tex. Dental Assn.; mem. Dallas County Dental Assn. (sec.-treas. 1970-71), ADA, Tex. Dental Assn., Omicron Kappa Upsilon. Lodges: Masons, Order Eastern Star, Shriners. Avocations: flying; skiing; boating. Home: 419 Fall Creek Dr Richardson TX 75080 Office: 670 W Arapaho St Suite 1 Richardson TX 75080

WELBORN, W. WAYNE, safety engineer, consultant; b. Memphis, Aug. 20, 1947; s. Harold Wayne and Iris (Hooper) W.; m. Donna Ann Porter, June 9, 1967 (div. 1976); children—Michael Clark, Jarred Christopher. B.S., Tenn. Tech. U., 1969; postgrad. Clemson U., 1973, U. Ala., 1974, 76, Memphis State U., 1975. Registered cert. safety exec. World Safety Orgn. Sr. safety engr. TVA, 1970-73; Sr. program mgr. OSHA, 1973-78; dir. corp. environ./safety affairs Alcon Labs worldwide ops., Ft. Worth, 1978—; expert witness congl. subcom. on ethylene oxide exposure; citizen ambassador environ./safety/health issues Govt. South Africa. Mem. Am. Soc. Safety Engrs., Am. Congress Govt. Indsl. Hygienists, Internat. Soc. Pharm. Engrs. Home: 485 Spruce Dr Lewisville TX 75067 Office: Alcon Labs 6201 S Freeway Fort Worth TX 76134

WELCH, ARTHUR STELLHORN, association executive, consultant; b. Sewanee, Tenn., Aug. 15, 1930; s. James Tracy and Rachel Catherine (Stellhorn) W.; m. Ingrid Beeken, Nov. 20, 1954; children—Suzanne Tracy Welch Monroe, Christine Anne. Student George Washington U., 1948-50; B.C.S., Benjamin Franklin U., 1952, M.C.S., 1953. Acct. Lamon and Henderson, Washington, 1952-54; treas. Assn. U.S. Army, Arlington, Va., 1954—. Founding pres. Adminstrv. Mgmt. Soc. Found., 1980-81, trustee 1980—, treas., 1984—; planning cons. Prospect Mgmt., Inc., 1982—; active Arlington Com. 100, Arlington C. of C. Served to capt. U.S. Army, 1961-62. Decorated Armed Forces Res. medal. Mem. Adminstrv. Mgmt. Soc. (Diamond award 1978, Ambassador award 1983; internat. pres. 1980-81; internat. dir. 1978-82), Am. Soc. Assn. Execs., Greater Washington Soc. Assn. Execs., Acad. Cert. Adminstrv. Mgrs. (cert. adminstrv. mgr.; dir. 1974-76). Republican. Episcopalian (sr. warden). Home: 3437 N Randolph St Arlington VA 22207 Office: 2425 Wilson Blvd Arlington VA 22201

WELCH, DANIEL WAYNE, physics educator, administrator, consultant; b. Baton Rouge, Sept. 7, 1949; s. Johnnie Lyman and Hilda Meredith (Hundley) W.; m. Shannon Marie Cashin, Dec. 18, 1971; children—Sean Michael, Heather Kathleen, Erin Colleen. B.S., U. SW La., 1971; M.S. in Physics, Clemson U., 1974, Ph.D., 1977. Planetarium lectr. Lafayette Nat. Hist. Mus. and Planetarium, La., 1969-71, Clemson U., S.C., 1971-77; dir. Planetarium, Wofford Coll., Spartanburg, S.C., 1978—, chmn. physics dept., 1984—; cons. Upstate Machine & Tool, Landrum, S.C., 1983—, Butler et al (attys.), Spartanburg, 1984. Contbr. articles to profl. jours. Mem. Am. Assn. of Physics Tchrs., Math. Assn. of Am., Sigma Xi, Pi Mu Epsilon, Sigma Pi Sigma. Baptist. Clubs: Spartanburg Amatuer Radio. Avocation: ham radio. Office: Physics Dept Wofford Coll Spartanburg SC 29301

WELCH, DAVID ULYSSES, psychologist, army officer; b. Vinton, Iowa, May 8, 1941; s. Lloyd LaVerne and Alice Loraine (Butler) W.; m. Suzanne April Regnier, Jan. 23, 1965; children—Kathleen, Mark, Mary, Christie, Michael. B.A., Iowa No. U., 1965; postgrad., South Tex. Coll. Law, 1966-70; M.Ed., North Tex. State U., 1974, Ed.D., 1977. Lic. psychologist, Ariz. Lic. marriage and family therapist, N.C. Cert. coll. tchr., Ariz. Cert. secondary sch. tchr., Iowa, Tex. Clin. dir. Psycho-Phys. Research and Treatment Ctr., Dallas, 1977-78; asst. chief psychologist, Ariz. State Prison, Florence, 1978-79; dir. Family Off-Post Ministry, Fort Bragg, N.C., 1979-83; army officer Ft. Hood, Tex., 1979—. Served to airman 1st class U.S. Air Force, 1961-63, capt. U.S. Army, 1979—. Diplomate Am. Bd. Christian Psychology, Am. Bd. Family Psychology; mem. Am. Psychol. Assn., Am. Assn. Marriage and Family Therapists, Assn. Mormon Psychotherapists, Kappa Delta Pi. Mormon. Avocation: swimming. Home: 112 Hardman St Copperas Cove TX 76522

WELCH, DOTTY JANE, university administrator, counselor; b. Steubenville, Ohio, Oct. 11, 1949; d. Edward R. and Sarah J. Welch. B.S., Akron U., 1972; M.A., Austin Peay State U., 1978; doctoral candidate Ohio U., 1983—. Cert. counselor. Elem. sch. tchr., Cambridge, Ohio, 1972-73, Spring Lake, N.C., 1973-74, Enterprise, Ala., 1974-75, Clarksville, Tenn., 1975-78; vocat. guidance counselor, Rio Grande, Ohio, 1978-80; dir. admissions Shawnee State Community Coll., Portsmouth, Ohio, 1980—. Bd. dirs. Portsmouth LWV, 1982-84; mem. adv. council Scioto County Joint Vocat. Sch., 1984—. Mem. Am. Assn. Counseling and Devel., Ohio 2-Yr. Admissions Officers (v.p. 1984-85, pres. 1985-86), Phi Delta Kappa, Women, Inc. Republican. Mem. Christian Ch. Avocations: water skiing; reading. Home: Route 10 Box 325 South Portsmouth KY 41174 Office: Shawnee State Community College 940 2d St Portsmouth OH 45662

WELCH, FRANCES CLAYTON, education educator, psychologist; b. Orangeburg, S.C., Oct. 10, 1947; d. Samuel William and Dorothy (Shuler) Clayton; m. Robert Wayne Welch, July 26, 1969; children—Lee Ann, William. B.A., Columbia Coll., 1969; M.A. U. S.C., 1971, Ph.D., 1978. Tchr. mentally retarded Summerville Sch. Dist., S.C., 1970-71; sch. psychologist Charleston County Sch. Dist., 1971-76, human relations specialist, 1977-78, spl. edn. cons., 1978-79, evaluator, researcher, 1979-80; prof. edn. Coll. Charleston, S.C., 1980—; mem. Children's Case Resolution Commn., Columbia, 1983—; pvt. practice psychology, Summerville, 1983—. Author: Teaching in the Elementary School, 1984. Contbr. articles to profl. jours. Bd. dirs. Pinewood Summerville Prep. Sch., 1982—, Assn. for Retarded Citizens, 1984—. Mem. Am. Psychol. Assn., S.C. Assn. Sch. Psychologists (pres. 1977-78), Council for Exceptional Children, Am. Edn. and Research Assn. Methodist. Home: Route 2 Box 191 Ridgeville SC 29472 Office: Coll Charleston Edn Dept Charleston SC 29424

WELCH, JAMES MONROE, personnel consultant firm executive; b. Chattanooga, June 4, 1916; s. Benjamin H. and Laura (Gill) W.; m. Elizabeth DeMars, Dec. 24, 1936; children—Suzanne, James M. Grad. McKenzie Coll., 1934; student U. Chattanooga, 1936-39. Tech. sec., drafting instr., elec. engr. TVA, Chattanooga, 1936-43, recruiter sci. personnel-indsl. relations counselor, 1943-45; asst. to v.p., dir. research Tenn. Eastman Co., Oak Ridge and Kingsport, 1945-64, mgr. adminstrv. services and research, 1964-81; owner, pres. Appalachian Mgmt Assistance, Kingsport, 1981—. Pres. Kingsport Symphony Orch. Assn., 1949-51, Kingsport Coll. Found., 1959—, East Tenn. State U. Found., 1980-81; chmn. Tenn. March of Dimes, 1956; bd. dirs. Kingsport Community Chest, 1947-61. Named Hon. Alumnus, East Tenn. State U., 1979. Mem. Adminstrv. Mgmt. Soc. (area dir. 1964-66, Ambassador award 1985), Am. Mgmt. Assn. (planning council, gen. services div. 1970-81), Internat. Platform Assn., Jaycees (Outstanding Young Man 1948; life mem.), Am. Legion (Disting. Service award 1971) Methodist. Club: Ridgefields Country (Kingsport). Lodge: Kiwanis. Contbr. articles to publs. Office: Applachian Mgmt Assistance 4022 Fort Henry Dr Kingsport TN 37663

WELCH, JUNE RAYFIELD, historian, educator, lawyer; b. Brownwood, Tex., Nov. 24, 1927; s. Frank Albert and Elizina Jane (Prigmore) W.; m. June Curtis (div. 1966); children—Ransom Frank, Susan Curtis; m. Lynda Marie Chalk, Jan. 16, 1981. Bar: Tex. 1951. Sec. to Senator Lyndon Johnson, Washington, 1950; asst. city atty. City of Fort Worth, 1953-55; city atty. City of Grand Prairie, Tex., 1955-57; ptnr. Ashley and Welch, Dallas, 1960-67; acad. dean U. Dallas, Irving, 1967-69, chmn. history dept., 1969—; commentator daily program Sta. KRLD, 1983—. Author: Dave's Tune, 1975; The Colleges of Texas, 1982; Riding Fence, 1984; The Texas Courthouse Revisited, 1985. Columnist Las Colinas Jour., 1983—. Served to sgt. U.S. Army, 1947-48, lt. col. USAFR, 1959-82. Named Outstanding Faculty mem. U. Dallas, 1976; recipient Katy award Dallas Press Club, 1983. Mem. Tex. Bar Assn., Tex. Hist. Assn. Home: 5535 Willow Ln Dallas TX 75230 Office: U Dallas Dept History Box 466 Irving TX 75061

WELCH, LOUIE, former association executive, former mayor; b. Lockney, Tex., Dec. 9, 1918; s. Gilford E. and Nora (Shackelford) W.; m. Iola Faye Cure, Dec. 17, 1940; children—Guy Lynn, Gary Dale, Louie Gilford, Shannon Austin, Tina La Joy. B.A. magna cum laude, Abilene Christian U., 1940, LL.D. (hon.), 1981, H.H.D., Okla. Christian U., 1982. Councilman at large, Houston, 1950-52, 56-62, mayor of Houston, 1964-73, mayor emeritus, 1974—; past pres. Houston C. of C. Pres. Tex. Municipal League, 1959-60; pres. U.S. Conf. of Mayors, 1972-73; trustee Abilene Christian U.; mem. Tex. Water Devel. Bd. Mem. Tex. Mayors and Councilmens Assn. (past pres.), Nat. League Cities (past v.p.), Am. C. of C. Execs. (dir.). Office: 1100 Milam 25th Floor Houston TX 77002*

WELCH, NELDA KAY, nursing administrator; b. Gilmer, Tex., July 9, 1946; d. Woodie Melvin and Frankie Louise (Copeland) Cooper; m. Terry Dale Welch, May 21, 1965; children—Terry Brent, Kerry Brennan, Tara Suzanne, Kara Leanne. Diploma Tex. Eastern Sch. Nursing, 1967. Registered nurse, Tex. Staff nurse operating room Med. Ctr. Hosp., Tyler, Tex., 1967—, instr. and head nurse operating room, 1973-75; supr. operating room Med. Ctr. Hosp., Nacogdoches, Tex., 1975-77; staff nurse, supr. operating room Anderson County Meml. Hosp., Palestine, Tex., 1977—; cons. operating room technician program Henderson County Jr. Coll., Athens, Tex., 1984—; cons. program, 1983—. Vaughn Found. scholar, 1964. Mem. Assn. Operating Room Nurses, E. Tex. Assn. Operating Room Nurses, Tex. Assn. Operating Room Nurses. Democrat. Baptist. Avocations: oil painting; sewing. Home: Route 2 PO Box 102A Frankston TX 75763 Office: Anderson County Meml Hosp PO Box 740 Palestine TX 75801

WELCH, PAUL CLAUDE, business exec.; b. Horton, Kans., Sept. 24, 1900; s. Frank and Grace (Walker) W.; m. Lucile Irene Sherman, May 1, 1920 (dec.); children—Robert Paul, Byron Eugene, William Frank. Asst. to pres. Bankers Mortgage Co., Kansas City, Mo., 1926-28; C.P.A., Mo Pac Lines, Kansas City, Mo., 1928-44; sales mgr. William B. Ward Co., Kansas City, 1944-45; dist. traffic mgr. Mid-Continent Airlines Co., Houston, 1946-48; gen. traffic mgr. Trans-Tex. Airways, Houston, 1949-51; dist. salesman Ada Oil Co., Houston, 1951-54; partner Tex. Gulf Coast Distributors, Houston, 1949-69; pres. Tex. Sales Reps. Co., Houston, 1954-69; exec. v.p., treas. Welch Assos., Inc., Houston, 1965—. Mem. Am. Soc. Safety Engrs., Nat. Soc. Fund Raising Execs., Houston Soc. Fund Raising Execs. Republican. Home: 2220 Westcreek Ln 36E Houston TX 77027 Office: 3701 Kirby Center Suite 1010 Houston TX 77098

WELCH, RIZPAH L., educator; b. Wilmington, N.C., Sept. 13, 1920; d. H.M. and A. Louise (Sampson) Jones; m. W. Bruce Welch; B.S. in Elem. Edn., Elizabeth City (N.C.) State Coll., 1944; M.S. in Elem. Edn. and Remedial Reading, Ind. U., Bloomington, 1952, Ed.D. in Elem. Edn. and Spl. Edn., 1966. Certified in reading, mental retardation, elem. edn., Va.; specialist in lang. devel., reading and lang. disabilities. Tchr. elem. grades Richmond (Va.) Pub. Schs., 1956-60, spl. edn. tchr., 1960-66, spl. edn. cons., 1966-67; asso. prof. edn. Va. Commonwealth U., Richmond, 1967-75, prof. edn., 1975—, chmn. dept. spl. edn., 1970-79, dir. Ednl. Devel. Centers Complex, 1979—; cons. early childhood edn. programs, P.R., 1968. Contr. articles to profl. jours., chpts. to books. Chmn., Commonwealth of Va. Devel. Disabilities Planning and Adv. Council, 75-77; mem. (Va.) Gov.'s Com. on Edn. of Handicapped, 1976-77; adv. bd. New Community Sch., Richmond, 1975—; mem. vestry St. Philip's Episc. Ch., Richmond, 1978—; 1st v.p., sec. Friend's Assn. for Children, 1969-75. Mem. AAUP, Council for Exceptional Children, Am. Assn. on Mental Deficiency, Va. Edn. Assn., Orton Soc., AAUW, Internat. Reading Assn., Nat. Council Tchrs. of English, Richmond Assn. for Retarded Citizens. Developed a model for tng. spl. edn. resource tchrs. Home: 1728 Forest Glen Rd Richmond VA 23228 Office: 2095 Oliver Hall Va Commonwealth U Richmond VA 23284

WELDON, FRANK EDWIN, III, college administrator; b. Westfield, N.J., Apr. 29, 1931; s. Frank Edwin and Mildred Isabel (Hand) W.; m. Janice Aiken, July 28, 1956 (dec. Sept. 1980); children—Tamara, Frank; m. Erlene White, Dec. 24, 1983; children—Jerry, James, Joseph, Donna, Jon. B.S., The Citadel, 1953; M.S., Columbia U., 1955; M.R.E.-B.C.M., SW Baptist Sem., 1959; Ph.D., Fla. State U., 1977. Minister of edn. and music Bklyn. Ave. Bapt. Ch., Seattle, 1959-65; prof. econs., bus., music Allegany Community Coll., Cumberland, Md., 1965-82; dean Sch. Bus., William Carey Coll., Hattiesburg, Miss., 1982—; cons., Wel-don Fin., Hattiesburg, 1983—; counselor, v.p. M.A.R.C.H., Hattiesburg, 1984—. Author: Junior College Student Understanding in Economics, 1977. Contbr. articles to profl. jours. Bd. dirs. Western Md. Symphony Soc., Cumberland, 1970-77; pres., v.p., bd. dirs. Community Concert Assn., Cumberland, 1974-82. Served to 1st lt. U.S. Army, 1953-55. NSF fellow, 1966. Mem. Lebanon Bapt. Assn. (bd. dirs.), Phi Delta Kappa. Democrat. Avocations: organist; gardening; soloist; choral dir. Home: 111 Briarcliff Dr Hattiesburg MS 39401 Office: Sch Bus William Carey Coll Tuscan Ave Hattiesburg MS 29401

WELDON, JOHN WESLEY, lawyer; b. St. Charles, S.C., Mar. 12, 1920; s. Ariel Koga and Wilhelmina (Scott) W.; A.B., Presbyterian Coll., Clinton, S.C., 1941; LL.B., U. Va., 1950; m. Louis Christy, May 3, 1947; children—John Wesley, Christy Scott, William Heathley. Admitted to N.C. bar, 1952; corp. atty. Atlantic Coast Line R.R., Wilmington, N.C., 1950-57, asst. gen. atty., 1957-60, gen. atty., 1960-62, gen. solicitor, Jacksonville, Fla., 1962-73; v.p. law Seaboard Coast Line R.R. Co., Jacksonville, 1973-81, v.p., gen. counsel, 1981—; gen. counsel Duval Connecting R.R. Co., Jacksonville, 1967—; dir. Central Fla. Pipeline Co., Tampa, 1963—; v.p., gen. counsel Seaboard Tampa Investment Corp. (Fla.), 1980—, Cybernetics & Systems, Inc., Jacksonville, 1981—, Seacoast Transp. Co., Jacksonville, 1981—. Commr. City of Atlantic Beach (Fla.), 1964-70, mayor pro tem, 1969-70; mem. bd. dirs. Southeastern Region Boy Scouts Am., Atlanta, 1980—, Silver Beaver award, 1976, chmn. area 1 Explorers, Jacksonville, 1979—; mem. bd. dirs. Fla. chpt. Arthritis Found., Jacksonville, 1979-84. Served to maj. U.S. Army, 1941-47; to lt. col. USAR, 1947-68. Mem. Am. Bar Assn., N.C. Bar Assn., Va. C. of C., Fla. C. of C., Jacksonville Area C. of C. Democrat. Presbyterian. Clubs: Rotary (Jacksonville Beaches chpt. pres. 1977-78, dir. 1976-78), Nat. Lawyers Club, River, (Jacksonville); Ponte Vedra. Office: 500 Water St Jacksonville FL 32202

WELDON, NORMAN ROSS, manufacturing company executive; b. Greencastle, Ind., July 21, 1934; s. David M. and Lenora F. (Evens) W.; B.S., Purdue U., 1956, M.S. in Indsl. Mgmt., 1962, Ph.D., 1964; m. Carol J. Warne, Oct. 2, 1954; children—Thomas D., Cynthia M. With CTS Corp., Elkhart, Ind., 1964-79; exec. v.p., 1970-76, pres., 1976-79, chief exec. officer, 1977-79, also dir.; pres. Cordis Corp., Miami, Fla., 1979—; adv. bd. Investment Co. Am., Inc. Served to capt. USAF, 1956-60. Recipient Disting. Alumnus award Krannert Grad. Sch. Mgmt., Purdue U., 1979; NSF fellow, 1962-63; Ford Found. fellow, 1963-64. Mem. Tau Kappa Epsilon, Phi Eta Sigma, Alpha Zeta. Presbyterian. Club: Royal Palm Tennis. Office: Cordis Corp PO Box 025700 Miami FL 33152 33102-5700*

WELLER, JOHN ALBERT, JR., architect, landscape architect; b. Havana, Cuba, Dec. 4, 1944; s. John Albert and Idalia Victoria (Gou) W.; B.A. in Architecture; B.A. in Landscape Architecture; grad. Nat. Landscape Inst.; m. Beatrice Cox, June 20, 1963; children—Donald Shawn, Kimberly Dawn. Pvt. practice architecture and landscape architecture, 1973—. Contbr. numerous articles to mags., newspapers, and books. Trustee, Palmer Sch. Registered architect, Grand Canyon, B.W.I., Bahamas Fla., N.C., S.C., Ga., Tenn., Calif., Colo., Vt., U.K., N.Y. State, Va., W.Va., Tex., Mass., Maine, Ky., La., Hawaii, Nat. Council Archtl. Registration Bds., Archtl. Registration Council of U.K. Fellow Faculty Architects and Surveyors U.K.; mem. AIA, Coral Gables C. of C., South Fla. Orchid Soc., South Fla. Palm Soc., Am. Hist. Soc. Episcopalian. Clubs: Coral Reef, Cat Cay Yacht (dir.), Coral Oaks Tennis. Home and Office: 5200 N Kendall Dr Miami FL 33156

WELLER, MARIAN ELIZABETH, nurse educator; b. Monterrey, Calif., Dec. 3, 1946; d. Robert Vance and Marian Georgiana (Fleck) Weller. B.S. in Nursing, U. Pitts., 1967; M.S. in Nursing, U. Tex.-San Antonio, 1982. Registered nurse, Tex. Intensive care nurse clinical Brooke Army Med. Ctr., 1976; staff nurse Magee Women's Hosp., Pitts., 1968, Walter Reed Army Med. Ctr., Washington, 1968, head nurse neurosurg. and surg. spltys. unit, 95th EVAC DaNang, Vietnam, 1969-70, head nurse emergency room Ft. Lee, Va., 1970, charge nurse U.S. Army Med. Research Inst. Infectious Diseases, Frederick, Md., 1970-71, intensive care nurse Tripler Army Hosp., Hawaii, 1970-73, head nurse med. and intensive coronary care, Ft. Gordon, Ga., 1973-75, coordinator coronary rehab. program, 1973-75, evening supr. Ft. Deven's, Mass., 1976-78, intensive care nurse Audie Murphy VA Hosp., San Antonio, 1978-83; instr. nursing Bapt. Meml. Hosp. System, San Antonio, 1983—. Ednl. chmn. nurses' adv. bd. San Antonio chpt. Myasthenia Gravis Found. Served with Nurse Corps, U.S. Army, 1966-78, to maj., USAR, 1978-83. Decorated Army Commendation medal with 2 oak leaf clusters, Vietnam Service medal; named Imagemaker, Sigma Theta Tau. Mem. Am. Assn. Critical Care Nurses (cert.), U. Tex. Sch. Nursing Alumni Assn., Am. Heart Assn., Mil. Order World Wars, VFW, Alpha Delta Pi. Methodist. Office: 111 Dallas St San Antonio TX 78233

WELLFORD, HARRY WALKER, judge; b. Memphis, Aug. 6, 1924; s. Harry Alexander and Roberta Thompson (Prothro) W.; B.A., Washington and Lee U., 1947; student U. N.C., 1943-44; postgrad. U. Mich. Law Sch., 1947-48; LL.D., Vanderbilt U., 1950; m. Katherine E. Potts, Dec. 8, 1951; children—Harry Walker, James B. Buckner P., Katherine T., Allison R. Admitted to Tenn. bar, 1950; atty. McCloy, Myar & Wellford, Memphis, 1950-60, McCloy, Wellford & Clark, Memphis, 1960-70; judge U.S. Dist. Ct., Memphis, 1970—. Campaign chmn. Sen. Howard Baker campaigns, 1964, 66, Gov. Winfield Dunn, 1970; mem. Charter Drafting Com. City of Memphis, 1967; chmn. Tenn. Hist. Commn.; mem. Tenn. Am. Revolution Bicentennial Commn., 1976; mem. Com. on Adminstrn. of Fed. Magistrates System. Served as ensign USNR, 1944-45; PTO. Recipient Sam A. Myar award for service to profession and community Memphis State Law U., 1963; Tenn. Sr. Tennis Champion, 1974. Mem. Sixth Circuit Dist. Judges Assn. (sec. 1981), Phi Beta Kappa, Omega Delta Kappa. Presbyterian (clk. of session, commr. Gen. Assembly, elder). Office: US Ct Appeals 1176 Federal Bldg 167 N Main St Memphis TN 38103

WELLINGTON, JAMES ELLIS, educator; b. Arlington, Mass., July 9, 1921; s. William Edward and Jessie (Dennett) W.; A.B., Dartmouth Coll., 1948; M.A., Boston U., 1950; Ph.D., Fla. State U., 1956; m. Mary Canfield Grier, July 22, 1952 (div. 1982); children—Georgia Grier, Anne Ross; m. 2d, Patricia Collier Kuett, Apr. 11, 1984. Instr. dept. English, U. Nebr., 1950-53; teaching asst., instr. English, Fla. State U., 1953-56; instr., asst. prof. English, U. Miami, Coral Gables, Fla., 1956-63, asso. prof., 1963-70, prof., 1970—, acting chmn. dept. English, 1981-82; lang. cons., 1958—. Served with USNR, 1941-46. Mem. Modern Lang. Assn., AAUP, South Atlantic Modern Lang. Assn., Southeastern Renaissance Conf., Augustan Reprint Soc., Delta Upsilon. Democrat. Anglo-Catholic. Author: Alexander Pope's Epistles to Several Persons, 1963; Pope's Eloisa to Abelard, with the Hughes Letters, 1965. Home: 1200 Mariposa Ave Apt D-104 Coral Gables FL 33146 Office: Dept English U Miami Coral Gables FL 33124

WELLMAN, JAMES DALE, safety engineer; b. Carrolton, Mo., June 24, 1957; s. Kenneth D. and Myra Sue (Lybarger) W.; m. Angela Lee Jones, Oct. 27, 1979; 1 child, James Ryan. B.S., Central Mo. State U., 1979, postgrad., 1982-83. Safety and property protection engr. Monsanto Co., St. Peters, Mo., 1980-83; safety specialist Gen. Electric Co., Largo, Fla., 1983—; mem. robotics safety com. U.S. Dept. Energy, Albuquerque, 1984—. Mem. Am. Soc. Safety Engrs., Sigma Phi Epsilon. Methodist. Lodge: Elks. Avocations: reading; swimming; racquetball; sports. Home: 12820 126 Terr N Largo FL 33544 Office: Gen Electric Co 7887 Bryan Dairy Rd Largo FL 34294

WELLMAN, ORA MAX, business educator, consultant; b. Terre Haute, Ind., Feb. 5, 1922; s. Henry Davis Wellman and Mabel Madoline Pemberton; m. Betty Lee Lawrence, Jan. 2, 1944; children—Ruth Janine, Myra Gale, Amy Ann. B.S., Purdue U., 1947; M.A., Ind. State U., 1961; Ph.D., Okla. U., 1975. Asst. prof. John Brown U., Siloam Spring, Ark., 1957-65; assoc. prof., dept. chmn. Le Tourneau Coll., Longview, Tex., 1965-77; prof. bus., div. chmn. Liberty U., Lynchburg, Va., 1977—; edn. accreditation evaluator So. Assn. Colls. and Schs., Atlanta, 1977-78; bd. dirs. FOMCO Inc., Longview, 1977; cons. U.S. Small Bus. Adminstrn., Longview, Lynchburg, 1972—. Contbr. articles to profl. jours. Staff dir. Siloam Spring Republican Com., 1962. Served to staff sgt. U.S. Army, 1943-46, PTO. Grantee U. S.C., 1967. Mem. Am. Bus. Law Assn., Va. Bus. Edn. Assn., Acad. Mgmt., Delta Phi Epsilon. Baptist. Avocations: tennis; fishing; hiking; music. Home: Route 3 Box 478-7 Rustburg VA 24588 Office: Liberty U Div Bus Lynchburg VA 24506

WELLS, BETTE EVANS, psychotherapist; b. Hot Springs, Ark., Oct. 31, 1944; d. Basil Brent and Betty (Gandy) Evans; m. John W. Wells, July 25, 1969. B.A., Bob Jones U., 1967; cert. edn. Fla. Atlantic U., 1976; M.S., Nova U., 1979. Tchr. pvt. and public schs., Fla., 1967-76; psychotherapist Christian Counseling Services, Inc., Ft. Lauderdale, Fla., 1979-81; dir. therapy Residential Alcholism Treatment Ctr., Ft. Lauderdale, 1982-83; pvt. practice psychotherapy, Ft. Lauderdale, 1981—. Contbr. articles to profl. jours. Mem. Task Force Commn. on Status of Women, 1981-82. Mem. Nat. Council on Family Relations, Am. Mental Health Counselor Assn., Am. Assn. Counseling and Devel. Republican. Mem. Reformed Ch. Am. Avocations: Solo and choral work; pottery; painting; shelling. Office: North Broward Profl Ctr Suite 230 100 E Sample Rd Pompano Beach FL 33064

WELLS, CECIL MONROE, chemist; b. Madison, Wis., Feb. 22, 1934; s. Cecil Gale and Ethel Florence (Cook) W.; B.S., U. New Orleans, 1966, M.S., 1970; m. Karen Marie Cucullu, Jan. 21, 1961; children—Michael Scott, John Patrick. Chef, Hoffman House, Madison, Wis., 1950-54; chemist U. New Orleans, 1962—, sci. materials mgr., 1974—; cons. USDA Research Lab., New Orleans, 1974. Bd. dirs. Brother Martin Parents Club, 1976-78. Recipient St. Louis medallion, 1977. Mem. U. New Orleans Alumni Assn. (rep. at large 1975-76), Nat. Assn. Sci. Materials Mgrs. (organizer, 1975, pres. 1977, treas. 1979—). Democrat. Roman Catholic. Home: 2526 Barracks St New Orleans LA 70119 Office: Dept Chemistry U New Orleans LA 70148

WELLS, CLARA ELIZABETH, electronics company executive; b. Kokomo, Miss., July 16, 1923; d. Benjamen Alexander and Harriette Morgan (McLean) Lee; student Massey Bus. Coll., Atlanta, 1957; m. Robert Leonard Wells, Aug. 31, 1942; children—Harriette Ann, John Robert, Richard Leonard. Bookkeeper, Printing Industry Atlanta, 1957-59; v.p. TV-Electronics Co., Atlanta, 1959-64, pres., 1964—. Trustee, The Prosperos; treas. Atlanta Dogwood Festival, 1982. Mem. Nat. Assn. Bus. and Ednl. Radio, Nat. Fedn. Ind. Bus., U.S. C. of C., Women's C. of C. Atlanta (treas. 81, 84-85), Southeastern Motorola Service Stas. Assn. (co-founder), Bus. and Profl. Womens Club, Women Bus. Owners, Assn. Women Entrepreneurs. Clubs: Pilot, Women's Commerce Home: 707 Sherwood Rd NE Atlanta GA 30324 Office: 1254 Techwood Dr NW Atlanta GA 30318

WELLS, DAMON, JR., investment company executive; b. Houston, May 20, 1937; s. Damon and Margaret Corinne (Howze) W.; B.A. magna cum laude, Yale U., 1958; B.A., Oxford U., 1964, M.A., 1968; Ph.D., Rice U., 1968. Owner, chief exec. officer Damon Wells Interests, Houston, 1958—; Mem. sr. common room Pembroke Coll., Oxford U., 1972—, hon. fellow, 1984—; asso. fellow Jonathan Edwards Coll., Yale U., 1982—; mem. pres.'s council Tex. A&M U., 1983—; bd. Bd. dirs. Child Guidance Center of Houston, 1970-73; trustee Christ Ch. Cathedral Endowment Fund, 1970-73, 84—, Kinkaid Prep. Sch., Houston, 1972—, Jefferson Davis Assn., 1973-81, Episcopal Diocese of Tex. Retreat at Camp Allen (Tex.), 1976-79; mem. Houston Com. on Fgn. Relations. Recipient prize for biography Tex. Writers Roundup, 1971. Mem. English-Speaking Union (nat. dir. 1970-72, v.p. Houston br. 1966-72), Brit. Inst. U.S. (founding dir. 1978-81), Council on Fgn. Relations, Phi Beta Kappa, Pi Sigma Alpha. Episcopalian. Clubs: Coronado, Houston Country, Houston; Yale (N.Y.C.); United Oxford and Cambridge Univs. (London); Cosmos (Washington). Author: Stephen Douglas: The Last Years, 1857-1861, 1971. Home: 3435 Westheimer Rd Houston TX 77027 Office: River Oaks Bank Bldg 2001 Kirby Dr Houston TX 77019

WELLS, LARRY WAYNE, insurance broker, consultant; b. Burlington Junction, Mo., Jan. 25, 1938; s. Elvin Lee and Lucille Wells; m. Martha Lynn Pollock, Sept. 12, 1967; children—Shannon Scott, Jon Lee. B.S. Central Mo. State Coll., 1960; B.C., U. Ariz., 1970; student U. Mo., 1958, Little Rock U., 1965. Factory rep. Fram Corp., Providence, 1960-66; computer sales engr. Singer Corp., San Leandro, Calif., Tucson and Little Rock, 1966-70; bank cons. Northwest Ark., 1970-80; ins. broker-cons., Fort Smith, Ark., 1970—. Active Fort Smith Optimist Club, pres. PTA, Fort Smith Foster Parents; troop leader Westark council Boy Scouts Am. Mem. Data Processing Mgmt. Assn., Confederate Air Force. Republican. Methodist. Lodges: Masons, Shriners. Avocation: World War II aircraft and history. Address: 2408 Queensbury Way Fianna Hills Fort Smith AR 72903

WELLS, PAM, television executive; b. Tyler, Tex., June 22, 1949; d. Cecil H. and Polly (Willis) Payne; m. James Robert Wells, Dec. 31, 1969; children—Aimee P., Robert Cecil. Student pub. schs., tex. Adminstrv. asst. to sr. v.p. Inter First Bank, Tyler, 1979-84; adminstrv. asst. to gen. mgr. Sta.-KLTV, Tyler, and personnel dir. Buford TV, Tyler, 1984-85; program dir., community relations coordinator Rose Channel, Tyler, and Sta.-KTET-TV, Tyler, 1985—. Bd. dirs. East Tex. Crisis Ctr., Tyler, 1983—. Mem. East Tex. Symphony League, Tyler Bus. and Profl. Women, Beta Sigma Phi (chpt. sec. 1983). Republican. Methodist. Avocations: painting; ceramics; swimming.

WELLS, ROBERT DALE, biochemistry educator; b. Uniontown, Pa., Oct. 2, 1938; s. Charles O. and Margaret Elizabeth (Sturm) W.; m. Dorothy Jackson Smart, June 25, 1960; children—Robert Kevin, Cynthia Gail. B.A., Ohio Wesleyan U., 1960; Ph.D., U. Pitts., 1964. Fellow Inst. for Enzyme Research, U. Wis., Madison, 1964-66, mem. faculty, 1966-81, prof. biochemistry, until 1981; prof. biochemistry U. Ala., Birmingham, 1982—, chmn. dept., 1982—. John Simon Guggenheim Found. fellow, 1976-77. Mem. Am. Soc. Biol. Chemists, AAAS, Am. Assn. for Microbiology, Biophys. Soc., Sigma Xi, Phi Lambda Upsilon, Alpha Sigma Phi. Methodist. Assoc. editor Jour. Biol. Chemistry, 1978—; contbr. articles to profl. jours. Office: 201 Volker Hall U Ala Birmingham AL 35294

WELLS, ROBERT LYNN, pharmacist, air force officer; b. Mathiston, Miss., Aug. 18, 1942; s. William Herman and Flossie Dell (Sewell) W.; m. Hannie Marie Sistrunk, June 13, 1965; children—William David, Marianne Elizabeth. B.S. in Pharmacy, U. Miss., 1965; postgrad. Air Command and Staff Coll., 1978, Air War Coll., 1982. Cert. pharmacist Commd. 2d lt., U.S. Air Force, 1966, advanced through grades to lt. col., 1983; chief pharmacy services U.S. Air Force Hosp., Blytheville AFB, Ark., 1967-70, Incirlik, Turkey, 1970-72, Vandenberg AFB, Calif., 1972-75; chmn. dept. pharmacy, Keesler AFB, Miss., 1975-79; chief pharmacy services RAF Lakenheath, Eng., 1979-82; chmn. dept. pharmacy; Carswell AFB, Tex., 1982—; preceptor U. Miss., Oxford, 1977-79. Chmn. troop support com. Transatlantic council Boy Scouts of Am., RAF Lakenheath, 1981-82; mem. adminstrv. bd., pres. Open Line Class Overton Park United Methodist Ch., Fort Worth, 1984, 85. Mem. Am. Soc. Hosp. Pharmacists. Republican. Avocations: camping; hiking; canoeing; computers. Home: 5021 Whistler Dr Fort Worth TX 76133 Office: USAF Regional Hosp Carswell AFB Fort Worth TX 76127

WELLS, WAVEL LOU, pediatric dentist; b. Neodesha, Kans., Oct. 30, 1946; s. Orval R. and Fredia Marie W.; m. Laura Lynne Williams, June 12, 1971; children—Gia, Shannon, Jason. B.A., Kans. State Tchrs. Coll., 1967; D.D.S., U. Mo.-Kansas City, 1971. Intern, St. Anthony's Hosp., Oklahoma City, 1971-72; resident U. Ind./Ind. Med. Ctr., Indpls., 1974-76; practice dentistry specializing in pediatric dentistry, Oklahoma City, 1976-77, Lawton, Okla., 1977—; part-time instr., lectr. Children's Meml. Hosp., Oklahoma City, 1976-77; cons. U.S. Army Dental Activity, Ft. Sill, Okla., Okla. Nursing Assn. Mem. Okla. Health Systems Agy., Lawton, 1982—; lectr. Pre-Natal Classes Meml. Hosp., Lawton, 1979—; coach elem. soccer, Lawton, 1984—. Served to capt. U.S. Army, 1972-74. Recipient Cert. of Merit Am. Acad. Oral Medicine, 1971; Army Commendation medal, Ft. Campbell, 1974. Mem. Comanche County Dental Soc. (past pres. 1979- 80), Okla. Dental Assn. (past pres. So. Central Dental Dist. 1981-82, dental health care com. 1984—), Am. Acad. Pediatric Dentistry, ADA, Omicron Kappa Upsilon. Republican. Presbyterian. Club: Amateur Radio (Lawton/Ft. Sill, Okla.). Avocations: family; travel; fishing; physical fitness; amateur radio. Home: 723 Heinzwood Circle Lawton OK 73505 Office: 4417 W Gore Suite 11 Lawton OK 73505

WELSH, JUDITH SCHENCK, communications educator; b. Patchogue, N.Y., Feb. 5, 1939; d. Frank W. and Muriel (Whitman) Schenck; B.Ed., U. Miami (Fla.), 1961, M.A. in English, 1968; m. Robert C. Welsh, Sept. 16, 1961; children—Derek Francis, Christopher Lord. Co-organizer Cataract Surg. Congress med. meetings, 1963-76; grad. asst. instr. Dale Carnegie Courses Internat., 1967; adminstr. Office Admissions, Bauder Fashion Coll., Miami, 1976-77, instr. communications, 1977—, also publisher coll. monthly paper; freelance writer; guest speaker Optifair Internat., N.Y.C., 1980; guest speaker, mem. seminar faculty Optifair West, Anaheim, Calif., 1980, Optifair Midwest, St. Louis, 1980. Mem. Nat. Assn. Female Execs., Fla. Freelance Writers Assn., Nat. Writers Club (award), Delta Gamma. Congregationalist. Clubs: Coral Reef Yacht, Riviera Country, Royal Palm Tennis. Co-editor: The New Report on Cataract Surgery, 1969, Second Report on Cataract Surgery, 1974; editor: Cataract Surgery, National Ophthalmology Writers, 1984. Home: 1600 Onaway Dr Miami FL 33133 Office: 160 Onaway Dr Miami FL 33133

WELSH, WARREN JOHN, clinical psychologist, magician; b. Schenectady, N.Y., Jan. 18, 1935; s. John S. and Regina G. (Miller) W.; m. Kathleen Anne Campbell, Aug. 2, 1969; children—John Lee, Leanne Marie. M.A. in Edn., U. Notre Dame, 1964; Ph.D. in Psychology, Bowling Green State U., 1973. Lic. clin. psychologist, Ky. Dean of studies O.L.C. Sem., Carey, Ohio, 1963-65; staff psychologist Ypsilanti, Mich., 1969-72, Marquette Prison, Mich., 1972-74, Fedn. Correctional Instn., Lexington, Ky., 1974—; cons. to local industry. Mem. Am. Psychol. Assn., Am. Soc. Clin. Hypnosis, Internat. Bro. Magicians (pres. Lexington chpt. 1984-85), Am. Taekwondo Assn. (Lexington chpt.). Roman Catholic. Avocations: magic; music; karate; jogging. Home: 1598 White Oak Rd Stamping Ground KY 40379 Office: Federal Correctional Instn Box 2000 Leestown Pike Lexington KY

WELSH, WILMER HAYDEN, music educator, composer, organist; b. Cin., July 17, 1932; s. Wilmer Wesley Welsh and Dorothy Mary (Exon) Hamilton; m. Constance Teri DeBear, June 30, 1957 (div. 1982); children—Benjamin Hayden, Stephen Andrew. B.S., Johns Hopkins U., 1953; artist diploma Peabody Conservatory Music, 1953, B.Music, 1954, M.Music, 1955. Asst. prof. music Winthrop Coll., Rock Hill, S.C., 1959-63; assoc. prof. music Davidson Coll., N.C., 1963-72, prof. music, 1972—, chmn. dept. music 1981—; organ recitalist specializing in Am. music from Colonial period to present; subject doctoral dissertation, 1985. Composer symphonies, concertos, operas; also music for ch. festivals. Contbr. articles to profl. jours. Grantee Ford Found., 1959, Nat. Endowment Arts, 1969; recipient Thomas Jefferson award McConnell Found., 1976. Mem. Am. Guild Organists, AAUP, Music Educators Nat. Conf., Coll. Music Soc., Am. Music Ctr., The Sonneck Soc. Republican. Episcopalian. Avocations: writing; antiques; gardening; swimming. Home: 510 South St Davidson NC 28036 Office: Davidson Coll PO Box 358 Davidson NC 28036

WELT, GLENN MARTIN, entrepreneur; b. N.Y.C., Aug. 28, 1948; s. David Irwin and Rhoda Lila (Shapiro) W. A.A., Miami-Dade Jr. Coll., 1968. Founder, pres. Design Shack, Inc., Miami, Fla., 1968-73; v.p. Welt/Safe-Lock, Inc., Hialeah, Fla., 1973-74; pres. ARSCO Internat., Inc., Hialeah, 1974—; founder, pres. Video Warehouse, Inc., Atlanta, 1980-81, American Phone Ctrs., Inc., Atlanta, 1982-83, Welt Industries, Inc., Atlanta, 1984—; cons. Comdial Corp., Charlottesville, Va., 1984-85. Inventor video caddy for Welt/Safe-Lock, Inc., 1973; snapper paint roller system for Arsco Internat., Inc., 1974; lipstick phone, 1982; Valentino telephone for Am. Phone Ctrs., 1983, portable suntan system, 1984. Mem. Atlanta C. of C., TeleCommunications Dealers Assn. (founder, pres., 1983-84), Suntanning Assn. for Edn. (founder 1985, pres. 1986—). Jewish. Office: 1117 Perimeter Center W Suite N-122 Atlanta GA 30338

WELTNER, CHARLES LONGSTREET, state supreme court justice; b. Atlanta, Dec. 17, 1927; s. Philip and Sally (Cobb) Hull; m. Betty Jean Center, Sept. 16, 1950 (div. 1972); children—Elizabeth Shirley, Philip II, Susan Martin, Charles Longstreet; m. Anne Fitten Glenn, Mar. 22, 1978; children—June Spalding, Anne Glenn. A.B., Oglethorpe U., 1948; J.D., Columbia U., 1950; M.A., Columbia Theol. Sem., Decatur, Ga., 1983; LL.D., Tufts U., 1967. Bar:

Ga. 1949. Sole practice, Atlanta, 1950—; mem. 88th and 89th Congresses from Ga., 1963-67; judge Superior Ct. Atlanta Jud. Cir., 1976-81; assoc. justice Supreme Ct. Ga., 1981—; chmn. Jud. Council Ga., 1980-81. Author: Southerner (NEA award) 1966; John Willie Reed, 1970; Heavens of Babylon, 1980; Process and Service, 1962. Dep. chmn. Dem. Nat. Com., Washington, 1967. Served to 1st lt. U.S. Army, 1955-57. Mem. State Bar Ga., Am. Law Inst. Presbyterian. Office: Supreme Court of Georgia State Judicial Bldg Atlanta GA 30334

WELTY, ELMER ELIAS, lawyer, retired army officer; b. Pandora, Am. Legion, Res Sept. 3, 1906; s. Elias and Elizabeth (Amstutz) W.; m. Dorothy Tolford, June, 1929; 1 dau., Nancy Lee; m. 2d, Gertrude Kintzer, June, 1936 (div. 1946); children—Linda Ann, Rebecca Lou, Richard Edward; m. 3d, Lyla Rogers, Feb. 23, 1946. Student, Ohio No. U., 1924-26, LL.D. (hon.), 1982; grad. Fgn. Affairs Study Course, Yale U., 1945. Bar: Ohio 1928, Japan 1949. Served with Ohio Nat. Guard, 1926-33; commd. 2d lt. U.S. Army, 1933, advanced through grades to col. 1949, ret. 1978; served in CBI, 1943-45, with Gen. Hdqrs. staff, Tokyo, 1946-49; solicitor City of Lima (Ohio), 1929-33; pros. atty., Logan County, Ohio, 1940; ptnr. Welty, Shimeall and Kasari Internat., Tokyo, 1949-78, of counsel, Pompano Beach, Fla., 1978—. Decorated Bronze Star, China medal. Mem. ABA, Ohio Bar Assn., Dai Ichi Bar Assn., Am. Soc. Internat. Law, Interamerican Bar Assn., World Peace Through Law (charter mem.), Am. Legion, Res Officers Assn., Ret. Officers Assn., Mil Order of World Wars, Am. C. of C. in Japan (pres. 1952-53, dir. 1950-60) Am. Club of Tokyo (past pres., bd. of govs. 1948-64). Republican. Clubs: Bohemian (San Francisco); Explorers (N.Y.C.); Outriggers (Honolulu). Lodge: Elks (past exalted ruler). Address: 43 Avista Circle Saint Augustine FL 32084

WENDEL, JOHN FREDRIC, lawyer, consultant; b. Newark, N.J., Nov. 8, 1936; s. John J. and Margaret D. (Mortimer) W.; m. Barbara Vaughn Smith, Dec. 17, 1960 (dec. July, 1978); children—David I., Stephen F.; m. 2d, Carlene M. Arnoldini, May 30, 1981; 1 dau., Carlene Margaret. B.A., U. Fla., 1958; J.D., Stetson U., 1963. Bar: Fla. 1963, U.S. Dist. Ct. (mid., and so. dists.) Fla., U.S. Ct. Appeals (5th cir.) 1964, U.S. Supreme Ct. 1968, U.S. Tax Ct. 1976, U.S. Ct. Appeals (11th cir.) 1982. Assoc. Troiano & Roberts, Attys., Lakeland, Fla., 1963; assoc. Law Offices George C. Dayton, Dade City, Fla., 1965; sole practice, Lakeland, 1965, 70-73; ptnr. Wendel & Schott, Attys., Lakeland, 1965-70; ptnr. Wendel & McArthur, P.A., Lakeland, 1973-75; ptnr. Wendel & Chritton, Chartered, and predecessor firms Wendel, McArthur, Broderick & Chritton, Wendel, Broderick & Chritton, Wendel, Broderick, Chritton & Klepetko, Wendel, Broderick & Chritton, Lakeland, 1975—, pres., 1983—; town atty., St. Leo, 1964-78; town judge, 1968; asst. mcpl. judge, Lakeland, 1966; atty. Citrus County, Fla., 1976-81; mem. adj. faculty Fla. So. Coll., Lakeland, 1963-65, St. Leo Coll., 1963-73. Del. 2d internat. conf. Ptnrs. of Alliance of Progress; Mem. Fla.-Columbia Alliance coms. and sub-coms. Served to 1st lt. USMC, 1958-59; Mem. Fla. Bar, ABA, Fla. Assn. County Attys. (pres. 1981), Lakeland Bar Assn., Acad. Fla. Trial Lawyers, Canon Law Soc. Am., Sports Lawyers Assn. (bd. dirs., v.p.), Pi Kappa Alpha, Phi Delta Phi. Democrat. Roman Catholic. Clubs: Lakeland Yacht & Country, Univ. of Tampa, St. Petersburg Yacht & Country. Lodges: Elks, K.C. Office: Wendel & Chritton 5300 S Fla Ave PO Box 5378 Lakeland FL 33803

WENDLANDT, RUTH BECKER, accounting executive; b. Plauen, Germany, June 16, 1927; d. Rudolf Arthur and Elsa Anna (Dressel) Becker; came to U.S., 1952, naturalized, 1959; m. Ernest Walter Wendlandt; 1 child, Claudette Emily. Grad. Wirtschafts Ober Schule, Plauen, 1945. Agy. mgr. United Ins. Co. Am., Atlanta, 1955-79; acctg. mgr. WBRC-TV, Birmingham, Ala., 1979—. Campaigner for Democratic candidates, Atlanta, 1960-75; active LWV, College Park, Ga., 1965-75; pres. College Park Jaycettes, 1966-67; treas.-sec. Service League, College Park, 1970-73. Lutheran. Home: 2857 K Regal Circle Birmingham AL 35216 Office: WBRC-TV Atop Red Mountain Birmingham AL 35201

WENGLER, ANTOINETTE TARTOUE, interior designer; b. McAllen, Tex., Jan. 15, 1947; d. Pierre and Virginia (Nelson) Tartoue; m. Kenneth John Wengler, Aug. 30, 1968; children—Steven Bradley, Amber Lee. B.A. in Applied Arts and Scis., El Centro Coll., 1976. Studio asst. Payne Assoc. Inc., Dallas, 1971-73; asst. designer, office asst. Travers & Johnston AIA, Dallas, 1973-75; owner, designer TW Interiors, Plano, Tex., 1970—. Contbr. articles to profl. jours. Vice pres., initiator Plano Lead Exchange, 1984. Mem. Women in Constrn., Metrocrest C. of C., Plano C. of C. (ambassador 1981). Republican. Mem. Christian Sci. Ch. Avocations: weaving; raquetball; travel; architecture; tennis. Office: 2008 Lakeside Plano TX 75023

WENGROW, ARNOLD, theatre director, educator; b. Columbia, S.C., June 27, 1944; s. Sam and Sura (Wolff) W. A.B., U. N.C., 1964; M.A., Tufts U., 1967. Asst. curator Harvard Theatre Collection, Cambridge, Mass., 1966-68; drama dir. Mount Airy Fine Arts Project, N.C., 1968-70; dir. theatre U. N.C.-Asheville, 1970—, prof. drama, 1983—. Author theatre adaptations, scripts for children, also articles. Active publicity and pub. relations com. Community Arts Council Western N.C., 1979-80; bd. dirs. Asheville Contemporary Dance Theatre, 1981-84, N.C. Arts Council, 1984—; mem. exec. com. N.C. Dance Alliance, 1983-84. Mem. Carolina Dramatic Assn. (exec. com. 1970-72, v.p. 1972-74, pres. 1974-76, John W. Parker award for service to theatre in N.C.). Office: U NC-Asheville Dept Drama Asheville NC 28804

WENNER, LINDA SUE, educator; b. Phila., May 8, 1936; d. Dan Bradley and Sylvia W. (Segal) Cooper; student Huntingdon Coll., 1954-57; B.A., Chapman Coll., 1968, M.A., 1970; m. Warren Wenner, Dec. 15, 1956; children—Warren M., Charlotte Louise. Tchr., Lompoc, Calif., 1968-71, Sedalia, Mo., 1971-72; substitute tchr. Knob Noster, Mo., 1972-77; tchr., La Monte, Mo., 1978-80, Apopka, Fla., 1980-83, Orlando, Fla., 1983—; adj. instr. Ga. Mil. Coll., Whiteman AFB, Mo., 1974, Central Mo. State U., 1975-76; needlepoint instr. Officers' Wives Club, Whiteman AFB, 1974-78; tchr. 5th grade La Monte (Mo.) Elem. Sch., 1978—. Active Boy Scouts Am., Red Cross; craft chmn. Officer's Wives Club, 1974-78; chmn. volunteers Whiteman AFB, 1976-78. Recipient many needlepoint awards: named Woman of Yr., Vandenburg AFB, 1968, Woman of Yr., Bus. and Profl. Women's Club, Knob Noster, Mo., 1976. Republican. Lutheran. Clubs: Officers' Wives, Bus. and Profl. Women's Club. Author: Knob Noster: A Little History of a Little Town, 1976. Home: 832 Haulover Dr River Run S Altamonte Springs FL 32714

WENTZ, DENNIS KEITH, physician, educator; b. Napoleon, N.D., Sept. 1, 1935; s. Edwin J. and Bertha Louise (Kaz) W.; B.A., North Central Coll., Naperville, Ill., 1957; M.D., U. Chgo., 1961; grad. exec. program health systems mgmt., Harvard U., 1975; m. Anne Colston, Sept. 28, 1968. Intern, U. Md. Hosp., 1961-62, resident, 1962-64, 66-67; fellow in gastroenterology Scott and White Clinic, Temple, Tex., 1964-66; asst. dean U. Md. Med. Sch., 1971-77; assoc. dir. clin. affairs U. Md. Hosp., 1974-77; asst. vice chancellor acad. affairs U. Tenn. Center Health Scis., Memphis, 1977-80; dir. med. services, asso. dean clin. affairs Vanderbilt U. Sch. Medicine and Hosp., 1980-84, assoc. dean for grad. and continuing med. edn., 1984—, asst. prof. medicine, 1971—, assoc. prof. med. adminstrn., 1980—. Bd. dirs., treas. Memphis Orch. Soc.; bd. dirs. Salvation Army, Nashville, Nashville Opera Assn. Served to lt. comdr. M.C., USNR, 1977-79. Mem. AMA, Am. Coll. Physician Execs., Am. Acad. Med. Dirs., Am. Assn. Med. Systems and Informatics, Am. Soc. Cytology, Am. Soc. Internal Medicine, Meeting Planners, Internat. Profl. Conv. Mgmt. Assn., Soc. Med. Coll. Dirs. of Continuing Edn., So. Med. Assn., Tenn. Med. Assn., Nashville Acad. Medicine. Episcopalian. Clubs: Maryland (Balt.); Gibson Island (Md.). Author articles in field. Home: 4390 Chickering Ln Nashville TN 37215 Office: Vanderbilt U Med Center Nashville TN 37232

WERFEL, SANDRA DIANE, clinical social worker; b. Kew Gardens, N.Y., Feb. 23, 1947; d. Israel Harry and Charlotte (Lustryn) Leibowitz; m. Mark Werfel, Oct. 25, 1970; children—Justin Keith, Erica Elizabeth. B.A., Queens Coll., 1968; M.S.W., Simmons Coll., 1970. Lic. social worker, Va., Md. Staff social worker Child Guidance Ctr. Greater Lynn, Mass., 1970-73; supervising social worker Union Hosp. Community Mental Health Ctr., Lynn, 1973-77; cons. Paragon Assocs., McLean, Va., 1980-82, Enterprise Sch., McLean, 1982-83, Marriage and Family Clinic, Annandale, Va., 1982-85, Silver Hill Services to Families and Children, Temple Hills, Md., 1984—; founder, pres. Met. Stress Cons., Burke, Va., 1985—. Bd. dirs. No. Va. Jewish Community Ctr. Family Day Care Program, Fairfax, 1984—; mem. sch. com. Congregation Beth-El, Alexandria, Va., 1983-85. Recipient Maida H. Solomon honorable mention citation Simmons Coll. Sch. Social Work, 1979; NIMH scholar, 1968, 69. Mem. Nat. Assn. Social Workers, Acad. Cert. Social Workers, Am. Orthopsychiat. Assn., Greater Washington Soc. Clin. Social Work. Avocations: reading, music, needlework, bike riding. Office: Burke Profl Ctr 5206-B Rolling Rd Burke VA 22015

WERKHOVEN, KATHRYN REGINA, nursing adminstrator; b. Memphis, Apr. 11, 1936; d. Stephen Grier and Mary (McKenize) Edmundson; m. William Edward Werkhoven, July 8, 1961; children—Thomas, Jerome, Michael, Mary Anne, John. Diploma nursing Nazareth Coll., 1957; B.Profl. Studies, Memphis State U., 1979. Cert. nursing adminstr. Scrub nurse Dr. McCarthy Demere, Memphis, 1960-62; instr. St. Joseph Hosp., Memphis, 1962-71, dir. surgery, 1971-74; dir. surgery St. Francis Hosp., Memphis, 1974-79, dir. nursing, 1979—. Wharton's fellow in nursing mgmt. Wharton's and Johnson & Johnson, 1984. Mem. Am. Soc. Nursing Adminstrs., Tenn. Hosp. Assn. (chmn. council on nursing 1984-85), Tenn. Soc. Nurse Adminstrs. (bd. dirs. 1982-84). Democrat. Roman Catholic. Avocations: swimming; reading. Office: St Francis Hosp 5959 Park St Memphis TN 38187

WERMAN, DAVID SANFORD, psychiatrist, psychoanalyst, educator; b. N.Y.C., Jan 1, 1922; s. Morris and Blanche (Heftel) W.; m. Marjolijn R. DeJager, Oct. 25, 1958 (div. 1975); children—Marco W., Claudia J. B.A., Queens Coll., 1942; postgrad. Columbia U., 1946-47; M.D., Cert. d'Etudes Medicales, U. Lausanne (Switzerland), 1952. Diplomate Am. Bd. Ob/Gyn., Am. Bd. Psychiatry and Neurology. Intern, Beth Israel Hosp., N.Y.C., 1953-54, resident, 1954-57; resident Montefiore Hosp., Bronx, N.Y., 1964-67; practice medicine specializing in Ob/Gyn, N.Y.C., 1957-64; faculty acad. psychiatry, U. N.C.-Chapel Hill, 1967-76, assoc. prof., instr. psychoanalytic tng. program, 1974—; prof. psychiatry Duke U. Med. Center, Durham, N.C., 1976—, supervising and tng. analyst Psychoanalytic Tng. Program, 1981—; cons. Durham VA Hosp. Served with AUS, 1943-45. Named Outstanding Tchr., psychiatry U. N.C., 1975, honored tchr. psychiatry, Duke U., 1978. Fellow ACS, Am. Psychiat. Assn., Am. Coll. Psychoanalysts, others. Author: The Practice of Supportive Psychotherapy, 1984. Contbr. chpts. to books, articles to profl. jours. Home: Bartram Dr Chapel Hill NC 27514 Office: Dept Psychiatry Box 3812 Duke Univ Med Center Durham NC 27710

WERNER, ARTHUR STEPHEN, environmental consulting company executive; b. N.Y.C., Dec. 19, 1945; s. William and Thelma (Bernstein) W.; m. Mary Beatrice Hughes, Sept. 5, 1977; children—Jacob Thomas, Rebecca Elizabeth. B.S. in Chem. Engring., Poly. Inst. Bklyn., 1966; M.S. in Chem. Engring., 1967; Ph.D. in Phys. Chemistry, U. Calif.-Berkeley, 1971. Teaching and research fellow Brandeis U., Waltham, Mass., 1971-72; research assoc. U. N.C., Chapel Hill, 1972-75; mgr. Analytical Lab., GCA/Tech. Div., Bedford, Mass., 1976-78, br. mgr., Chapel Hill, 1979—; mem peer rev. panel Environ. Engring. and Pollution Control Process, EPA, Washington, 1980—. Contbr. articles to profl. publs. Pres. Chaple Hill Alliance of Neighborhoods; councilman Town of Chapel Hill, 1985—. N.Y. State Regents scholar, 1962; N.Y. State fellow, 1966. Mem. Air Pollution Control Assn., Am. Chem. Soc., Sigma Xi. Democrat. Jewish. Home: 2510 Millwood Ct Chapel Hill NC 27514 Office: GCA/Tech Div 500 Eastowne Dr Chapel Hill NC 27514

WERNER, JEANNE ELDER, management consultant; b. Clarion County, Pa.; d. John O. and Grace Elder; m. Wayne E. Werner, 1965; 1 child, Elon. B.S. in Edn., Clarion State Coll., 1958; M.Ed., SUNY-Buffalo, 1965, Ed.D., 1969; postgrad. Oreg. State U., 1966-67. Asst. prof. counseling and psychology Tuskegee Inst. Ala., 1972; coordinator community services and women's programs, Auburn U., Ala., 1973-74; dir. student devel. services E. Tex. State U., Texarkana, 1975-79; pres. Werner Assocs, Texarkana, 1979—. Mem. allocations com. United Way, 1976-77; bd. dirs. Conifer council Girl Scouts U.S., 1981—, Greater Texarkana United Way, 1979-84, Texarkana Community Concerts Assn. NDEA fellow, 1964-65, 66-67. Mem. Am. Assn. Counseling and Devel., Am. Soc. Tng. and Devel., Nat. Vocat. Guidance Assn. (nat. sec. 1979-80), Am. Assn. for Counseling and Devel. (com. for women 1973-74, 76-77), Tex. Personnel and Guidance Assn. (chair human relations com.), Texarkana C. of C. (women's involvement), Pi Gamma Mu. Office: Werner Assocs PO Box 3380 4066 Sommerhill Sq Texarkana TX 75504

WERNER, PAUL HOWARD, pediatric dentist; b. N.Y.C., Oct. 5, 1949; s. Robert Alexander and Alice (Burger) W.; m. Anita Ellen Grossberg, Aug. 10, 1980; children—Lisa Ilona, Karolina Maxine. B.S., SUNY, Albany, 1971; D.D.S., Georgetown U., 1975; pedodontic cert. Eastman Dental Ctr., 1979; postgrad. Doyle Orthodontic Seminars, 1986. Practice pediatric dentistry, Boca Raton, Fla., 1980—; co-chmn. pediatric dentistry, Atlantic Coast Research Clinic, Lake Worth, Fla., 1985. Chmn. architecture rev. bd. Home Owners Assn., Thorn Hill Green, Boca Raton, 1982-83. Mem. ADA, Fla. Dental Assn., Am. Soc. Dentistry for Children, Am. Acad. Pediatric Dentists, S.E. Soc. Pediatric Dentists, Fla. Soc. Pediatric Dentists, Fla. Soc. Dentistry for Children, Atlantic Coast Dist. Dental Assn., South Palm Beach County Dental Soc.; Alpha Omega. Democrat. Jewish. Lodge: B'nai B'rith (pres. 1984-85). Office: 2200 W Glades Rd 706 Boca Raton FL 33431

WERNER, SANDRA LEE, county ofcl.; b. Lake City, Fla., Oct. 10, 1938; d. George Washington and Frances Fair (Clark) Blankenship; A.A., Pasco-Hernando Community Coll.; m. Eugene Vernon Werner, Jan. 31, 1970; children—Clark, Addine, Reed Nessler, Paul Nessler, Jeffrey Nessler, Frances. Legal Asst. Delzer, Edwards & Martin, Port Richey, Fla., 1964-71, Roy M. Speer, Holiday, Fla., 1971-72; congressional aide, 1975; county commr. Pasco County, Fla., New Port Richey, 1980—. Sec., chmn. Pasco County Republican Exec. Com., 1974-80; precinct committeewoman; del. Rep. Nat. Conv., 1976; chmn. Pasco County Ford Campaign, 1976. Mem. Pasco County Legal Secs. (charter pres. 1968), Fla. Assn. Legal Secs., Nat. Assn. Legal Secs. (charter), Nat. Assn. Legal Assts. Presbyterian. Home: 19 Marlin Dr New Port Richey FL 33552 Office: 4025 Moon Lake Rd New Port Richey FL 33552

WERNLUND, RUSSELL JOHN, petroleum geologist; b. Baldwin, Wis., July 12, 1948; s. John Henry and Arlene Jane (TeBeest) W.; m. Monica Jo Mantey, Sept. 13, 1969 (div. July 1975); 1 child, Alyssa Ann. B.S., U. Wis.-Madison, 1971; M.S., Tex. Tech U., 1977. Cert. petroleum geologist. Exploration geologist, Getty Oil Co., Midland, Tex., 1975-84, Texaco, Coral Gables, Fla., 1985—. Mem. Am. Assn. Petroleum Geologists, Am. Inst. Profl. Geologists, Soc. Econ. Paleontologists and Mineralogists (Permian Basin sect.), Paleontology Soc., West Tex. Geol. Soc., Miami Geol. Soc., N.Mex. Geol. Soc., Soc. Econ. Paleontologists and Mineralogists. Lutheran. Avocations: reading; snow skiing. Home: 17620 SW 84th Ct Miami FL 33157 Office: Texaco Latin Am/West Africa 150 Alhambra Circle Coral Gables FL 33134

WERRIES, E. DEAN, wholesale food distribution executive; b. Tescott, Kans., May 8, 1929; s. John William and Sophie E. Werries; B.S. in Bus., U. Kans., 1952; m. Marjean Sparling, May 18, 1962. With Fleming Co., Inc., 1955—, exec. v.p. Eastern ops., then pres. Fleming Foods, 1976-81, pres., chief operating officer parent co., Oklahoma City, 1981—, dir., 1979—; dir. First Nat. Bank Oklahoma City. Served with AUS, 1952-54. Mem. Food Mktg. Inst. (dir.), Nat. Am. Wholesale Grocers Assn. (dir.), Ind. Grocers Assn., Okla. C. of C. (dir.), Omicron Delta Kappa. Republican. Office: 6301 Waterford Blvd Oklahoma City OK 73126

WESBERRY, JAMES PICKETT, clergyman; b. Bishopville, S.C., Apr. 16, 1906; s. William McLeod and Lillian Ione (Galloway) W.; m. Ruby Lee Perry, Sept. 5, 1929 (dec. Dec. 1941); 1 son, James Pickett; m. Mary Sue Latimer, June 1, 1943 (dec. 1982); m. Alice Margaret Spratlin, Oct., 1983. A.B., Mercer U., 1929, M.A., 1930, D.D., 1957; B.D., Newton Theol. Inst., 1931; M. Sacred Theology, Andover Newton Theol. Inst., 1934; postgrad., Harvard U., 1931, Union Theol. Sem., N.Y.C., summers 1934, 65, Yale U., 1946, So. Bapt. Theol. Sem., 1957, Mansfield Coll., Oxford U., 1979; LL.D., Atlanta Law Sch., 1946; L.H.D., LaGrange Coll., 1962; Litt. D., Bolen-Draughan Coll., 1967. Ordained to ministry Bapt. Ch., 1926; pastor, Soperton, Ga., 1928-30, Medford, Mass., 1930-31, Kingstree, S.C., 1931-33, Bamberg, S.C., 1933-44, Morningside Bapt. Ch., Atlanta, 1944-75, pastor emeritus, 1975—; engaged in evangelism, counseling, editing, publishing and chaplaincies, 1975—; mem. exec. com. So. Bapt. Conv., 1959-65, 74—, mem. chaplains commn., 1973-79, mem. adminstrv. com., 1974—; pres. Ga. Bapt. Conv., 1956-57, 57-58, rec. sec., 1970—; pres. So. Bapt. Ministers Conf., 1967; prof. Mercer U. extension, Atlanta, 1944-53; pres. Highview Nursing Home, Atlanta, 1947-60, chaplain, 1975—; pres. Nat. Youth Courtesy Found., 1971—; staff corr. Christian Century, 1951-58; editor column The People's Pulpit; columnist Atlanta Times, 1964-65; chaplain Yaarab Temple, 20 yrs. Author: Prayers in Congress, 1949, Every Citizen Has A Right to Know, 1954, Baptists in South Carolina Before the War Between the States, 1966, Rainbow Over Russia, 1962, Meditations for Happy Christians, 1973, Evangelistic Sermons, 1974, When Hell Trembles, 1974, The Morningside Man (Wesberry's biography by James C. Bryant), 1975, Bread in a Barren Land, 1982; The Lord's Day, 1986; editor: Sunday Mag., 1975—; editor: Basharet, 1976-77; asst. editor, 1977—. Chmn. Ga. Lit. Commn., 1953-74; acting chaplain U.S. Ho. Reps., July-Aug., 1949; mem. Gov.'s Citizens Penal Reform Commn., 1968, Fulton County Draft Bd., 1968-71; Bd. dirs. Atlanta Fund Rev. Bd., 1964-70, Grady Met. Girls Club, 1969-72, hon. bd. dirs., Atlanta Union Mission, 1972—, Dogwood Assn. Festival, 1970-71; trustee Mercer U., 1944-49, 54-57, 72-74, mem. pres.'s council, 1974-81; also mem. adv. com. Sch. Pharmacy; trustee Atlanta Bapt. Coll., 1964-72, Truett McConnell Coll., Cleveland, Ga., 1960-65; mem. president's council Tift Coll., Forsyth, Ga., 1976—; bd. mgrs. Lord's Day Alliance U.S., 1971—, exec. dir., 1975—. Elected Man of the South Dixie Bus. mag., 1972; named to South's Hall of Fame, 1972. Mem. Atlanta Area Mil. Chaplains Assn. (hon.), SAR (chaplain 1981). Clubs: Mason (Shriner), Lion., Atlanta Harvard, Atlanta Athletic, Atlanta Amateur Movie. Home: 1715 Merton Rd NE Atlanta GA 30306 Office: Suite 107 Baptist Center 2930 Flowers Rd S Atlanta GA 30341

WESLER, KIT WAYNE, archaeologist, consultant; b. Washington, Feb. 27, 1955; s. John E. and Ann (Nichols) W. B.A., Washington U., St. Louis, 1975; M.A., U. N.C., 1977, Ph.D., 1982. Project archaeologist Md. Hist. Trust, Annapolis, 1980-81; staff archaeologist Murray (Ky.) State U., 1981-83, dir. archaeol. services program, 1981-83, coordinator grants, 1981-83, dir. Wickliffe Mounds Research Ctr., 1983—; Fulbright prof. U. Ibadan, Nigeria, 1985-86. Ky. Heritage Council research grantee, 1982; Ky. Humanities Council grantee, 1982; NSF grantee, 1985. Mem. Am. Soc. Ethnohistory, Archaeol. Inst. Am., Internat. Platform Assn., Soc. Am. Archaeology, Soc. Hist. Archaeology, Soc. History of Discoveries, Australian Soc. Hist. Archaeology, Southeastern Archaeol. Conf., Sigma Xi. Office: Wickliffe Mounds Research Ctr PO Box 155 Wickliffe KY 42087

WESLEY, CHARLES PARMER, JR., public health dentist; b. Portsmouth, Va., Aug. 3, 1950; s. Charles Parmer, Sr. and Ravada Olive (Bowser) W.; m. Katie Broadbent, Sept. 10, 1983. B.A., Va. Wesleyan Coll., 1972; D.D.S., Va. Commonwealth U., 1976. Dental assoc. Dr. Jerome Schonfeld Ltd., Portsmouth, Va., 1976-78; practice dentistry, Virginia Beach, Va., 1978-82; pub. health dentist Va. Dept. Pub. Health, Norfolk, 1982—; clin. prof. community dentistry Va. Commonwealth U. Dental Sch., Richmond, 1982—; dental supr. students Va. Inst. Tech., Norfolk, 1982—. Mem. Va. Wesleyan Coll. Alumni Fund Com., Norfolk, 1981, V.W.C. Jobs Fair, Norfolk, 1980, 81, 82, 83. Mem. ADA, Va. Dental Assn., Tidewater Dental Assn. (Nat. Children's Health Month com. 1984), Va. Pub. Health Dental Assn. (pres.-elect). Methodist. Avocations: photography; tennis; basketball; softball. Home: 129 Osage St Virginia Beach VA 23462 Office: Norfolk Dept Pub Health 7665 Sewells Point Rd Norfolk VA 23513

WESNER, SUSAN KENYON, geologist; b. Columbus, Ohio, July 14, 1955; d. George Paul and Rose (Pujazon) Kenyon; m. Mark Lee Wesner, May 14, 1983. A.B., Middlebury Coll., 1977. Petroleum geologist Gulf Oil Co., New Orleans, 1981-85; geologist Chevron U.S.A. Inc., 1985—. Served to capt. U.S. Army, 1977-81. Mem. Am. Assn. Petroleum Geologists, Soc. Profl. Well Log Analysts. Democrat. Avocations: architectural restoration; running. Home: 2334 Marengo St New Orleans LA 70115 Office: Chevron USA Inc PO Box 61590 New Orleans LA 70161

WESSON, ROBERT MICHAEL, sales executive, consultant; b. Lynn, Mass., Jan. 13, 1935; s. Charles Henry and Helen (Hogan) W.; m. Michelle Long, Feb. 20, 1982; children—Robert Michael, Kerry Ann. B.A., Merrimack Coll., 1956, LL.D., 1980; M.A., Villanova U., 1961; M.A., Augustinian Coll., 1962. Asst. prof. Merrimack Coll., North Andover, Mass., 1962-68, Villanova U., Pa., 1968-79; v.p., pres. The Augustinians, Villanova, 1971-81; v.p. Pandick SE, Inc., Arlington, Va., 1981—. Trustee Biscayne Coll., 1975-81, Villanova U., 1977-81, Merrimack Coll., 1975-81. Democrat. Roman Catholic. Lodge: KC (Lynn). Avocations: American history; politics; sports; reading. Home: 1631 Montmorency Dr Vienna VA 22180 Office: Pandick SE 1801 N Oak Arlington VA 22209

WEST, BENJAMIN HARRISON, regional planner; b. Calhoun, Ga., Sept. 26, 1941; s. Eulas Spurgin and Amer (Bramblett) W.; B.B.A., U. Ga., 1962, M.P.A., 1969; m. Jane Munday, June 8, 1962; children—Jeff, Susan. Asst. personnel dir. DeKalb County (Ga.), 1962-64; adminstrv. asst. to county mgr., Fulton County, Ga., 1964-67, asst. county mgr., 1968-69, acting county mgr., 1969-70, county mgr., 1970-72; dir. dept. govtl. services Atlanta Regional Commn., 1972-73, exec. dir., 1973—. Recipient awards Leadership Atlanta, Leadership Ga., Atlanta Jaycees. Mem. Nat. Assn. Regional Councils, Govt. Fin. Officers Assn., Am. Soc. Pub. Adminstrn., Ga. City and County Mgrs., Internat. City Mgmt. Assn., U. Ga. Alumni Soc. (past v.p.), Gridiron Secret Soc. Presbyterian. Office: 100 Edgewood Ave NW Suite 1801 Atlanta GA 30335

WEST, BETTY AARON, banker; b. Chatham, Va.; d. Lester George and Ellen (Crocker) Aaron; grad. Teller Tng. Seminar, Am. Inst. Banking; m. Henry Marvin West, Apr. 21, 1946; children—Mary Elizabeth West Branch, Robert Marvin, Stephen Dale. Successively bookkeeper, teller, head teller, First Nat. Bank of Martinsville (Va.) (now United Va. Bank), 1955-77, bank officer, asst. cashier, 1977-82, br. ops. officer, 1982—. Active Nat. Arthritis Soc., United Fund Campaign. Recipient Boss of Yr. award local chpt. Am. Bus. Women's Assn., 1980. Baptist. Home: Route 6 PO Box 148 Martinsville VA 24112 Office: PO Box 4911 Martinsville VA 24112

WEST, BILL GRAYUM, mgmt. and tng. cons.; b. Paducah, Tex., May 24, 1930; s. Kade and Ruth (Grayum) W.; B.A., Baylor U., 1951; Th.D., Southwestern Sem., 1957; postgrad. U. Houston, 1970; m. Ann Radnor, June 12, 1976; 1 son, Jason. Ordained to ministry Bapt. Ch., 1951; minister First Bapt. Ch., Okmulgee, Okla., 1957-65, River Oaks Bapt. Ch., Houston, 1965-72; asso. prof. Houston Bapt. U., 1972-75; profl. speaker and mgmt. cons., 1975—; pres. West and Assos., Houston, 1975—; owner, pres. Seroyal South Central Inc., 1982—. Bd. dirs. Baptist Conv. Okla., 1958-65; trustee Houston Bapt. U., 1966-72, mem. exec. com., 1970-71. Mem. Am. Soc. Tng. and Devel., Nat. Speakers Assn., Tex. Soc. Assn. Execs., Houston Speakers Assn. (dir.). Republican. Author: Free To Be Me, 1971; How To Survive Stress, 1980; The Platform to Success, 1982; contbg. editor Indsl. Distbn. mag., 1979—; contbr. articles to various publs. Office: PO Box 218551 Houston TX 77218

WEST, BRYAN CLINTON, JR., manuscript dealer, physician; b. Kinston, N.C., June 19, 1928; s. Bryan Clinton and Margaret Dilts (Hunt) W.; m. Margaret Elizabeth Hammet, Nov. 12, 1955; children—Laura, Bryan III, Walter, Richard. B.S., Wake Forest U., 1945-51; M.D., Duke U., 1955. Diplomate Am. Bd. Obstetrics and Gynecology. Obstetrician and gynecologist, Elizabeth City, N.C., 1960-72; manuscript dealer, Elizabeth City, 1974—. Exec. bd. Tidewater council Boy Scouts Am., 1976-84; bd. dirs. N.C. Cancer Soc., 1983; deacon Cann Presbyn. Ch. Served to lt. USN, 1956-58. Fellow ACS, Am. Coll. Ob-Gyn, Manuscript Soc. (trustee); mem. Coastal Plain Ob-Gyn Soc., N.C. Ob-Gyn Soc., Bayard Carter Soc. Obstetricians and Gynecologists. Republican. Lodge: Rotary (dist. gov. 1980-81). Home and Office: 105 Pine Lake Dr Elizabeth City NC 27909

WEST, DORENE BUDNICK, geologist; b. Indpls., June 26, 1952; d. Joseph Budnick and Beverly Bee (Izsak) Budnick Goldstein; m. Stephen R. West, June 17, 1978 (div. Jan. 1985). Cert. in Bus. Mgmt. and Adminstrn., Ind. U., 1973; B.A. in Geology, Ind. U., 1975, M.A. in Geology, 1978. From geologist to sr. project geologist Gulf Oil Exploration & Prodn. Co., 1978-84; sr. geologist Sohio Petroleum Co., Houston, 1984—. Mem. Am. Assn. Petroleum Geologists, Gulf Coast Sect. Soc. Exploration Paleontologists and Mineralogists. Republican. Jewish. Avocations: water skiing; snow skiing; fishing; walking. Home: 14635 Stanbridge Dr Houston TX 77083 Office: Sohio Petroleum Co 9401 SW Freeway Suite 1200 Houston TX 77074

WEST, GARY WAYNE, educator, administrator, computer educator, consultant; b. So. Pines, N.C., Jan. 21, 1947; s. Daniel Burdette and Anna Elizabeth (Chisholm) W.; m. Kathryn Marie Dietz, Jan. 1, 1983; children—Brian Edwin Rood, Kelly Ann West. A.B. in Math., E. Carolina U., 1969; M.Ed., U.S.C., 1983. Cert. math. tchr., counselor. Educator Eden City Schs., N.C., 1969-72, Andrews Acad., S.C., 1973-75; educator Allendale County Schs., S.C., 1975—, administrator, 1979—; instr. U.S.C., Columbia, 1982—; dir. CETA-YETP Programs, Allendale, 1978-79; cons. Allendale County govt., 1985; cons., programmer S.C. Dept. Edn., Columbia, 1985; computer cons. to various sch. dists., small bus., local govts., 1982—. Author: (computer program) Chapter

1 Evaluation S.C. State Dept. Edn., 1985. Mem. Assn. for Supr. and Curriculum Devel., Am. Assn. for Counseling and Devel. Democrat. Avocations: anthropology, astronomy, archaeology, tennis, computers. Home: 414 Jackson St Allendale SC 29810 Office: Allendale County Schs 919 Railroad Ave Allendale SC 29810

WEST, GENE A., dentist; b. Gadsden, Ala., Nov. 10, 1947; s. Hershel Charles and Kathryn (Wood) W.; m. Shirley Jean Whisenant, Sept. 6, 1969; children—Kathryn Dale, Elizabeth Jane. B.S., Auburn U., 1969; D.M.D. (hon.), U. Ala., 1973. Gen. practice dentistry, Atmore, Ala., 1975—. Bd. dirs. State Heart Assn., County Cancer Assn.; missionary Baptist Fgn. Missionary Bd. Served to capt. USAF, 1973-75. Mem. 4th Dist. Dental Assn., ADA, Ala. Dental Assn., Atmore C. of C., Jaycees. Republican. Lodge: Lions. Office: 109 7th Ave Atmore AL 16504

WEST, GLENN EDWARD, association executive; b. Kansas City, Mo., Nov. 19, 1944; s. Ernest and Helen (Cecil) Johnson W.; m. Vicki Lynn Knox, May 22, 1970; children—Kelle Kaye, Kallen Chandler, Ashley Knox. B.S. in Acctg. and Mktg., N.W. Mo. State U., 1966; postgrad. Inst. Orgn. Mgmt., U. Colo., 1976, Acad. Orgn. Mgmt., U. Notre Dame, 1979. Staff auditor Arthur Young & Co., Kansas City, Mo., 1966-67; salesman Procter & Gamble, St. Joseph, Mo., 1967-68, dist. head salesman, Kansas City, Mo., 1968-69; mgr. membership and pub. relations St. Joseph Area C. of C., Mo., 1961-71, mgr. econ. devel., 1971-74; exec. v.p. Lawrence C. of C., Kans., 1974-81, Greater Macon C. of C., Ga., 1981—. Author: Career Planning and Position Search, 1981. Pres. Macon chpt. ARC, 1984. Served with Air Nat. Guard, 1968-74. Recipient Leadership award Kiwanis Club, St. Joseph, 1974. Mem. Am. C. of C. Execs. (dir. 1981—), Ga. C. of C. Execs. (dir. 1982—). Republican. Methodist. Club: Idle Hour Golf and Country (Macon). Lodge: Rotary (pres. 1979). Avocations: sports, photography; yard work. Home: 500 Yorkshire Dr Macon GA 31210 Office: Greater C of C PO Box 169 Macon GA 31298

WEST, HAROLD, lawyer; b. Bklyn., June 26, 1929; m. Donna West. B.A., U. Colo., 1951; LL.B., St. John's U., 1958. Bar: N.Y. 1958, Fla. 1960. Ptnr. West & Lindley, Miami, 1963—. Mem. ABA, Dade County Bar Assn., Fla. Bar, Assn. Trial Lawyers Am., Acad. Fla. Trial Lawyers. Home: 5424 Jackson St Hollywood FL 33021 Office: 2320 NE 171st St North Miami Beach FL 33160

WEST, HARVEY GORDON, JR., information systems company executive; b. Phila., June 11, 1945; s. Harvey Gordon and Helen Elaine (Eustace) W.; B.A., Trinity U., San Antonio, 1972; M.L.S., U. Tex., Austin, 1973; m. Jaton Louise Holder, Dec. 21, 1967; 1 son, Stephen MacPherian. Staff Library of Congress, 1973-80; cons. CWS Office Systems, Springfield, Va., 1980-81; sales rep. Xerox, 1982; project mgr. Info. Systems & Networks Corp., 1982-85; mem. tech. staff Contel, Fairfax, Va., 1985—. Served with U.S. Army, 1968-69; Vietnam. Mem. Spl. Libraries Assn., Aircraft Owners and Pilots Assn. Mem. Ch. of Jesus Christ of Latter Day Saints. Home: 11313 Nancyann Way Fairfax VA 22032 Office: 12015 Lee Jackson Hwy Fairfax VA 22033

WEST, LEE ROY, lawyer; b. Clayton, Okla., Nov. 26, 1929; s. Calvin and Nicie (Hill) W.; B.A., U. Okla., 1952, J.D., 1956; LL.M. (Ford Found. fellow), Harvard U., 1963; m. Mary Ann Ellis, Aug. 29, 1952; children—Kimberly Ellis, Jennifer Lee. Bar: Okla. 1956. Sole practice law, Ada, Okla., 1956-61, 63-65; faculty U. Okla. Coll. Law, 1961-62; judge 22d Jud. Dist. Okla., Ada, 1965-73; mem. CAB, Washington, 1973-78, acting chmn., 1977; individual practice law, Tulsa, 1978—; spl. justice Okla. Supreme Ct., 1965; U.S. dist. judge Western Dist. Okla., 1979—. Served to capt. USMC, 1952-54. Mem. U. Okla. Alumni Assn. (dir.), Phi Delta Phi (pres. 1956), Phi Eta Sigma, Order of Coif. Editor Okla. Law Rev. Home: 2705 Old Farm Ln Edmond OK 73034 Office: 3001 Federal Courthouse Oklahoma City OK 73102

WEST, RHEA HORACE, JR., educator; b. Loudon, Tenn., Oct. 5, 1920; s. Rhea Horace and Verna (Quillen) W.; B.S. in Accounting, U. Tenn., 1947; postgrad. (Sloan fellow, M.I.T. fellow), M.I.T., 1959-60, 63, Case Inst. Tech., summer 1960; Ph.D., U. Ala., 1964. Asso. prof. mgmt. Wake Forest Coll., 1950-51; budget and reports analyst AEC, Oak Ridge, 1951-55; teaching fellow U. Ala., Tuscaloosa, 1956-57; asst. prof. mgmt. U. Ark., Fayetteville, 1957-59; Sloan teaching intern M.I.T., Cambridge, 1959-60; asso. prof. econs. Carson-Newman Coll., Jefferson City, Tenn., 1960-65; prof. mgmt. Ga. State Coll., 1965-70; prof. mgmt., dir. grad. studies Auburn (Ala.) U., 1970-75; acad. dean Cooper Inst., Knoxville, Tenn., 1976-82; chmn. dept. bus. Winston-Salem (N.C.) State U., 1982—; mgmt. cons.; cons. Cape Kennedy and Huntsville (NASA), Lockheed Aircraft Co., U.S. CSC, others; exec. v.p. Enviro South. Active Center for Study Democratic Instns., Atlanta High Mus. Art; mem. men's com. Internat. Debutantes Ball, N.Y.C., 1976—; supr. registration U. Tenn., 1946-50. Served with AUS, 1943-46. Mem. Am. Accounting Assn., Am. Mgmt. Assn., Am. Soc. Personnel Adminstrn. (nat. dir. industry edn. com. 1958-60), Inst. Mgmt. Scis., Soc. Advancement Mgmt., Acad. Mgmt., Soc. Sloan Fellows, Opelika Arts Assn., Acad. Polit. Sci., Am. Acad. Polit. and Social Scis., AAUP, Am. Legion, Opelika C. of C., Am. Ordnance Assn., Smithsonian Assos., Am. Acad. Arts and Scis., AAAS, AIAA, Am. Inst. Decision Scis., Am. Judicature Soc., N.Y. Acad. Scis., Internat. Platform Assn., UN Assn. U.S., Newcomen Soc. N.Am., East Tenn. Personnel and Guidance Assn., Sigma Iota Epsilon, Alpha Kappa Psi (dist. dir. 1965—), Alpha Phi Omega, Kappa Phi Kappa (pres. 1969-70), Alpha Iota Delta, Phi Beta Lambda. Baptist. Clubs: Mass. Inst. Tech., Harvard Faculty, Kiwanis (pres. 1965). Book rev. editor Personnel Adminstr., 1960—. Contbr. numerous articles and book revs. to profl. publs. Home: 3411 Old Vineyard Rd Apt E-3 Winston-Salem NC 27103 Office: Winston-Salem State U Winston-Salem NC 27101

WEST, ROBERT HUNTER, English literature educator; b. Nashville, May 20, 1907; s. Olin and Susie (Hunter) W.; m. Conn Harris, June 23, 1934; 1 dau., Susan McConnell. A.B., Vanderbilt U., 1929, M.A., 1930, Ph.D., 1939. Mem. faculty Vanderbilt U., Nashville, 1933-36; asst. prof. U. Ga., Athens, 1936-47, assoc. prof., 1947-54, prof., 1954-64, Alumni Found. prof., 1964-74; vis. prof. of U. Va., 1959-60; mem. Fulbright com., 1969-70. Served to capt. USAAF, 1942-46. Recipient publ. prize U. Ky. Press, 1967. Mem. MLA, Milton Soc. Am. (pres. 1974), Shakespeare Assn., South Atlantic Modern Lang. Assn., Phi Delta Theta. Episcopalian. Author: The Invisible World, 1939; Milton and the Angels, 1955; Shakespeare and the Outer Mystery, 1968; Reginald Scot and Witchcraft, 1984; contbr. numerous articles on English lit. to profl. jours.; columnist Athens Observer. Home: 133 West View Dr Athens GA 30606

WEST, ROBERT VAN OSDELL, JR., petroleum company executive; b. Kansas City, Mo., Apr. 29, 1921; s. Robert Van Osdell and Alma Josephine (Quistgard) W.; B.S., U. Tex., 1942, M.S., 1943, Ph.D., 1949; children—Robert Van Osdell, III, Kathryn Anne, Suzanne Small, Patricia Lynn. Pres., Slick Secondary Recovery Corp., San Antonio, 1956-59, Texstar Petroleum Co., San Antonio, 1959-64; pres. Tesoro Petroleum Corp., San Antonio, 1964-71, chmn. bd., 1971—, also chief exec. officer; dir. Frost Nat. Bank of San Antonio, Charter Co., Jacksonville, Fla., Continental Telecom, Inc., Atlanta, Trinidad-Tesoro Petroleum Co. Ltd., Port-of-Spain, Trinidad. Chmn. exec. com. Caribbean/Central Am. Action, Washington; past sr. warden St. Luke's Episcopal Ch., San Antonio; chmn. bd. Tiwanaku Archeol. Found., La Paz, Bolivia; past trustee City Pub. Service Bd., San Antonio; mem. Engring. Found. Adv. Council, U. Tex., Austin, bd. visitors McDonald Obs. and dept. astronomy; mem. adv. council Sch. Bus. Adminstrn., St. Mary's U., San Antonio; trustee SW Research Inst., San Antonio, San Antonio Symphony Soc.; past chmn. San Antonio Econ. Devel. Found.; bd. dirs. Cascia Hall Prep. Sch., Tulsa; bd. dirs. World Affairs Council, San Antonio; bd. govs. Fords Theatre, Washington Named Disting. Grad. Coll. Engring. U. Tex., Austin, 1973; Significant Sig award, 1979; People of Vision award Soc. to Prevent Blindness, 1982. Mem. Am. Petroleum Inst. (nat. dir.), Ind. Petroleum Assn. Am., Tex. Mid-Continent Oil and Gas Assn., All-Am. Wildcatters, 25 Year Club of Petroleum Industry, Americas Soc. (dir.). Home: 2602 Country Hollow San Antonio TX 78209 Office: 8700 Tesoro Dr San Antonio TX 78286*

WEST, TERRELL RANDALL, physical education educator, tennis professional; b. Altavista, Va., June 1, 1942; s. George Rosser and Ruth Leigh (Shelton) W.; m. Nora Clarice West, Aug. 7, 1966; children—Gray Antony, Ryan Terrell. B.S., Appalachian State Coll., 1964, M.A., 1965; Ed.D., U. N.C.-Greensboro, 1979. Tchr., Milford High Sch., Del., 1965-68; head dept. phys. edn. Sandhills Community Coll., Southern Pines, N.C., 1968—; teaching fellow Univ. N.C.-Greensboro, 1971-72, Appalachian State Coll., Boone, N.C., 1964-65; tennis profl. Country Club of N.C., Pinehurst, 1970-71, Seven Lakes Tennis Club, West End, N.C., 1984—. Contbr. author: Right to Participate, 1982. Republican. Baptist. Avocations: golf; tennis; canoeing; angling. Home: 510 W New Jersey Southern Pines NC 28387 Office: Sandhills Community Coll Route 3 Box 182-C Carthage NC 28327

WEST, WARWICK REED, JR., biology educator; b. Evington, Va., Feb. 9, 1922; s. Warwick Reed and Otelia (Woodford) W.; m. Alyce Liggon Johnson, May 29, 1946; children—Warwick Reed III, Leila, Jane. B.S., Lynchburg Coll., 1943; Ph.D., U. Va., 1952. Instr. biology Lynchburg Coll., 1946-49; asst. prof. biology U. Richmond (Va.), 1952-56, assoc. prof., 1956-66, prof., 1966—, chmn. dept. biology, 1965—. Served with USMCR, 1943-46. Mem. AAAS, AAUP, Va. Acad. Sci., Assn. Southeastern Biologists, Sigma Xi. Methodist. Home: 6806 Lakewood Dr Richmond VA 23229 Office: Dept Biology U Richmond Richmond VA 23173

WESTAFER, ANITA SLOAN, physician; b. Salisbury, N.C., Aug. 2, 1953; d. Ben Eugene and Vivian Olene (Stirewalt) Sloan; m. John Michael Westafer, July 17, 1978; children—Ryan Sloan, Lauren Michelle. B.S., U.N.C., 1975, M.D., 1978. Intern, N.C. Meml. Hosp., Chapel Hill, 1978-79; resident in family practice Pensacola Ednl. Program (Fla.), 1978-81; practice family medicine, Pensacola, Fla.; mem. staffs Bapt. Hosp., Sacred Heart Hosp., Pensacola. Mem. AMA, Am. Acad. Family Physicians, Fla. Med. Assn., Escanbia County Med. Soc. Office: Cordova Sq Suite 37 4400 Bayou Blvd Pensacola FL 32503

WESTBERRY, WILLIE DONALD, educational administrator; b. Jesup, Ga., Mar. 10, 1942; s. Willie and Othel (Johnson) W.; m. Sandra Elizabeth Roberson, Aug. 18, 1963; children—Timothy Donald, David Elbert. B.S. in Edn., Ga. So. Coll., 1964; M.Ed., U. Ga., 1967; Ed.S., Ga. So. Coll., 1970, cert., 1975. Tchr. Wayne County Bd. Edn., Odum, Ga., 1964-66; counselor Pierce County Bd. Edn., Blackshear, Ga., 1967-73, prin., 1973-83; prin. Wayne County Bd. Edn., Jesup, 1983—. Mem. Ga. Assn. Ednl. Leaders. Baptist. Club: Pine Forest Country (Jesup). Avocations: golf; fishing. Home: Route 4 Box 158B Jesup GA 31545 Office: Wayne County Jr High Sch 1425 W Orange St Jesup GA 31545

WESTBROOK, ROBERT JOSEPH, lawyer; b. Balt., Jan. 16, 1952; s. Andrew Joseph and Adriana Bianca (Buttarelli) W. B.A., Dickinson Coll., 1974; J.D. with honors, U. Tulsa, 1981. Bar: Okla. 1981, U.S. Dist. Ct. (no. dist.) Okla. 1981, U.S. Ct. Appeals (10th cir.) 1982, U.S. Dist. Ct. (we. dist.) Okla. 1983, U.S. Dist. Ct. (ea. dist.) Okla. 1984. Assoc. Crawford, Crowe & Bainbridge, P.A., Tulsa, 1981-83, Marsh & Armstrong, Tulsa, 1983-84; gen. atty. Fed. Deposit Ins. Corp., Oklahoma City, 1984—. Served to 1st lt. U.S. Army, 1974-78. Mem. ABA, Okla. Bar Assn., Assn. Trial Lawyers Am., Am. Judicature Soc., Phi Alpha Delta, Sigma Chi. Republican. Roman Catholic. Home: 2734 NW 62d St Oklahoma City OK 73112 Office: Fed Deposit Ins Corp PO Box 26208 Oklahoma City OK 73126

WESTBURY, JOHN BURNET, educator; b. Dorchester County, S.C., May 7, 1933; s. John Andrew and Malvina Ruth (Avinger) W.; student Wofford Coll., 1951-53; B.S., U. S.C., 1955; M.Ed., U. Ga., 1966; postgrad. U.S.C., 1956, 60, 62, 63, Birmingham So. Coll., summer 1961, Cornell U., 1967, St. Cloud State Coll., 1968, U. San Francisco, 1970, 75, The Citadel, 1970-71, 73, 79, Mich. State U., 1971, Clemson U., 1972. Tchr. math. Andrews (S.C.) Pub. Schs., 1955-57, North Charleston (S.C.) High Sch., 1959-60; tchr. math., head dept. Walterboro (S.C.) Jr. High Sch., 1960-64, 65-69; tchr. math., supr. St. George (S.C.) High Sch., 1969—; part-time instr. Trident Tech. Coll., 1978—, Fla. Jr. Coll. at Jacksonville Navy Campus High Sch. Studies Program, 1981; program participant Charleston (S.C.) Nat. Council Tchrs. Math. meeting, 1973, Orlando (Fla.) meeting; mem. cons. com. NASTEC, 1985. 1976. Mem. regional adv. com. S.C. Instructional TV, 1973-76, mem. com. to develop TV geometry series, 1972-74; mem. com. to develop. math. learning activities packages Dorchester Vocat. Sch., 1977. Served with AUS, 1957-59. Shell Merit fellow, summer 1967; NSF grantee, summers 1961-63, 66, 68, 70, 71, 75, also 1964-65; S.C. Commn. on Higher Edn. grantee, summers 1972-73. Mem. Nat. Council Tchrs. Math., Math. Assn. Am., Assn. Tchrs. Math (U.K.), Sch. Sci. and Math. Assn., NEA, S.C. Edn. Assn., Dorchester County Edn. Assn. (sec. 1975-76), Assn. S.C. Math Tchrs. (v.p. 1973-74, treas. 1974-75, 77-78), S.C. Math Council (v.p. 1973-74), S.C. Council Tchrs. Math. (sec. 1978-79), Phi Delta Kappa. Methodist. Home: 423 N Parler Ave St George SC 29477 Office: 600 Minus St St George SC 29477

WESTCOTT, RUTH OSTMAN, nurse; b. Orlando, Fla., Sept. 19, 1955; d. Wilbur James and Virginia E. (Derhammer) Ostman; m. Gerald David Westcott, June 29, 1980. A.S. cum laude in Office Adminstrn., So. Coll., 1977, A.S. cum laude in Nursing, 1978, postgrad., 1978—. R.N., Tenn. Med. records technician Madison Hosp., Tenn., 1977; nurse technician East Ridge Hosp., Chattanooga, Tenn., 1978; charge nurse orthopedics Parkridge Hosp., Chattanooga, 1979, charge nurse ICU, 1982-83, head nurse ICU, 1983—, critical care clin. instr., 1983. Mem. Chattanooga Venture, 1985. Mem. Assn. Seventh-day Adventist Nurses, Am. Critical Care Nurses. Home: PO Box 1513 Collegedale TN 37315 Office: Parkridge Hosp 2333 McCallie Ave Chattanooga TN 37404

WESTHEIMER, JEROME MAX, SR., independent oil operator, petroleum geologist; b. Marietta, Okla., Feb. 14, 1910; s. Simon and Rose (Munzesheimer) W.; m. Ellen Louise Woods, Feb. 22, 1936; children—Beverly, Jerome M., Jr., Valerie. B.A., Stanford U., 1933. Chief geologist Simpson-Fell Oil Co., Ardmore, Okla., 1936-40, Samedan Oil Corp., Ardmore, 1940-51; cons. geologist, Ardmore, 1951—. Primary trustee C.B. Goddard Ctr. for the Visual and Performing Arts, Ardmore, 1974-85; trustee Mid-Am. Arts Alliance, Kansas City, Mo., 1978-85, Okla. Art. Ctr., Oklahoma City, 1967-85; dir. Okla. Summer Arts Inst., Okla. City, 1977-85, pres. 1983. Mem. Am. Assn. of Petroleum Geologists, Am. Inst. of Profl. Geologists, Soc. of Econ. Paleontologists, Soc. of Ind. Exploration Scientists, Sigma Xi. Avocation: art collectors.

WESTMAN, CARL EDWARD, lawyer; b. Youngstown, Ohio, Dec. 12, 1943; s. Carl H. and Mary Lillis (Powell) W.; m. Carolyn J., July 17, 1965; children—C. Forrest, Stephanie A. B.B.A., Sam Houston State U., 1966; J.D., U. Miami, 1969, LL.M. in Taxation, 1972. Bar: Fla. 1969. mng. ptnr. Frost & Jacobs, Naples and Marco Island, Fla., 1978—; v.p. Comunity Found. of Collier County, N.C. Exec. bd. S.W. Fla. council Boy Scouts Am., 1980—; trustee Found. for Mental Health, Inc., 1976—, chmn. 1985-86; past pres. bd. trustees, elder Moorings Presbyterian Ch. Mem. ABA, Fla. Bar, Collier County Bar Assn., Estate Planning Council. Club: Coral Reef Yacht, Useppa Island. Lodge: Rotary. Home: 1952 Crayton Rd Naples FL 33940 Office: Frost & Jacobs Suite 303 1300 3d St S Naples FL 33940

WESTMORELAND, THOMAS DELBERT, JR., chemist; b. near Vivian, La., June 2, 1940; s. Thomas Delbert and Marguerite Beatrice (Moore) W.; B.S., N. Tex. State U., 1963, M.S., 1965; Ph.D., La. State U., 1971, postdoctoral fellow, 1971-72; m. Martha Verne Beard, Jan. 1, 1966; children—Anne Laura, Kyle Thomas. Chemistry tchr., research dir. Lewisville (Tex.) High Sch., 1964; summer devel. program student Tex. Instruments, Inc., Dallas, 1966; sr. exptl./analytical engr. Power Systems div. United Technologies, South Windsor, Conn., 1972-76; sr. research chemist Pennzoil Co., Shreveport, La., from 1976, now research assoc., Houston; chem. cons. Active Parent Tchrs. Orgn. Recipient E.I. du Pont tching. award La. State U., 1968-69. Mem. Am. Chem. Soc. (treas. 1978-79, chmn. 1979-80), Assn. Research and Enlightenment, Sigma Xi (sec.), Phi Eta Sigma (pres. 1959-60), Alpha Chi Sigma, Kappa Mu Epsilon. Clubs: Jaycees (state dir. Conn. 1976, gov.'s civic leadership award Conn. 1975-76, C. William Brownfield Meml. award 1976), Masons. Contbr. sci. articles to profl. jours. Home: 143 Melmont Ln Conroe TX 77302 Office: PO Box 7569 The Woodlands TX 77387

WESTON, JAMES CHARLES, airline official; b. St. Louis, July 17, 1951; s. Charles Newton and Georgia Marie (Schutzel) W.; m. Deborah Ann Owensby, June 2, 1972; children—Jered Charles, Christopher M. B.Aerospace Engring., U. Mo.-Rolla., 1972. Flight simulator technician, programmer Delta Airlines, Atlanta, 1976-85, supr. communications data analysts, 1985—, mem. simulator design team and instr. on maintenance of simulators operated by color graphics system; owner, operator Weston Computing, Jonesboro, Ga., 1982—. Contbr. articles to profl. jours. Served with USAF, 1972-76. Mem. Christian Ch. Home: 2293 Camden Ct Jonesboro GA 30236 Office: Dept 184 Hartsfield Internat Airport Atlanta GA 30320

WESTON, LOIS JEANETTE, nurse; b. Shreveport, La., Dec. 15, 1943; d. Harry Slater and Olga Amee (Ballard) W. A.A. Nursing, El Centro Coll., 1983. L.P.N., Tex. Student asst phys. and social sci. div. El Centro Coll., Dallas, 1981-83; nurse extern Presbyn. Hosp., Dallas, 1982-83; nurse Baylor U. Med. Ctr., Dallas, 1983—. Active Dallas County Mental Health Assn., Dallas County chpt. ARC, 1983—. Dye Found. scholar Presbyn. Hosp., 1981-83, Baylor U. Med. Ctr. scholar, 1982-83; Am. Med. Internat. Assn.-Nat. Student Nurses Assn. grantee, 1983. Mem. Am. Nurses Assn., Tex. Nurses Assn., Tex. Nursing Students Assn., Brookhaven Student Nurses Assn. Democrat. Presbyterian. Lodge: Order Eastern Star. Office: Telemetry Unit Jonsson Med and Surg Hosp Baylor Univ Med Ctr 3500 Gaston Ave Dallas TX 75246

WESTPHELING, ROBERT PAUL, JR., newspaper publisher; b. St. Joseph, Mo., Jan. 2, 1914; s. Robert Paul and Martha Theresa (Amelunxen) W.; B.J., U. Mo., 1936; m. Johanna Serio, Feb. 4, 1940; children—Robert Paul III, Mary Johanna. With St. Joseph News-Press, 1936-37, Effingham (Ill.) Daily Record, 1937, Gallatin (Tenn.) Examiner, 1937-38, Racine (Wis.) Day, 1938-39, Clarksdale (Miss.) Daily Register, 1939-41, Clarksdale (Miss.) Daily Press, 1941-42; mgr. advt. Washington Post, 1946-47; pub. Fulton (Ky.) News, 1947-72; pub. Hickman (Ky.) Courier, 1972—; pres. Ken-Tenn Broadcasting Corp., Fulton, 1962-67. Mem. Ky. Econ. Devel. Commn., 1963-70; activity chmn. Internat. Banana Festival, Fulton, 1964-68; chmn. Hickman-Fulton County River Port Authority, 1976-80, bd. dirs., 1983—. Served to maj. AUS, 1942-46; ETO, PTO. Decorated AF Commendation Medal; hon. Rotarian; Ky. col.; recipient 57 excellence awards in newspaper publishing Ky. Press Assn., 1948-76. Mem. Ky. Press Assn. (pres. 1960), Am. Fedn. Musicians, Fulton C. of C., Delta Tau Delta. Democrat. Roman Catholic. Clubs: Rotary (pres. Fulton 1960), K.C. Home: The Highlands PO Box 821 Fulton KY 42041 Office: PO Box 70 Hickman KY 42050

WETHINGTON, JOHN ABNER, JR., nuclear engineering and science educator; b. Tallahassee, Apr. 18, 1921; s. John Abner and Mary McQueen (Hale) W.; m. Kathryn Kemp Green, Aug. 28, 1943; 1 son, John Abner, III. B.A., Emory U., 1942, M.A., 1943; postgrad. Princeton U., 1943-44; Ph.D., Northwestern U., 1950. Vis. research asst. Princeton U. (N.J.), 1943-44; chemist Ferclave Corp., Oak Ridge, 1944-45; assoc. chemist Oak Ridge Nat. Lab., 1945-46, chemist, 1946-47, sr. chemist, 1949-53, vis scientist, 1979-80; mem. faculty U. Fla., Gainesville, 1953—, prof. nuclear engring. sci., 1958-85, prof. emeritus, 1985—, acting chmn., 1982-85; faculty participant Oak Ridge Sch. Reactor Tech., 1957-58; del. 2d Internat. Conf. on Peaceful Uses of Atomic Energy, Geneva, Switzerland, 1958, Radiation Congress, Harogate, Eng., 1963; vis. scientist P.R. Nuclear Ctr., 1962-63; vis. fellow Lawrence Livermore Nat. Lab. (Calif.), 1971-72; del. 2d Symposium on Nat. Radiation Environment, Bombay, India, 1981. Recipient award for outstanding contbn. in research Southeastern sect. Am. Soc. Engring. Edn., 1960. Fellow AAAS; mem. Am. Chem. Soc., Am. Nuclear Soc., Fla. Aero. Club (v.p. 1978-79), Phi Beta Kappa, Sigma Xi, Tau Beta Pi, Alpha Chi Sigma. Democrat. Methodist. Contbr. articles to profl. jours. Home: 109 NW 22d Dr Gainesville FL 32605 Office: 202 Nuclear Sci Ctr U Fla Gainesville FL 32611

WETHINGTON, WILLIAM ORVILLE, agriculturist, investor; b. Goltry, Okla., Feb. 5, 1906; s. Urban Green and Rosa Mae (Stoke) W.; m. Louise Etta Glaser, July 27, 1933 (dec. Feb. 1985). B.S. in Geology, U. Okla., 1931; M.S. in Geology, 1932. Tenant farmer Grant County, Okla., 1927-45; tenant farmer, ptnr., operator Grant County, Okla., 1945-66; owner, operator Grant & Alfalfa Co., 1966-71, pres., owner, 1971—. Mem. County Equalization Bd., Grant County, 1950-71, Okla. Pub. Expenditures council, 1965-80; judge Republican Party Precinct, Grant County, 1941-55; state committeeman Rep. Party, 1948-62; mem. Grant County Soil Conservation Service, 1985. Mem. Farm Bur. (chmn. county 1960-61), Grange (exec. com. 1940-50), Am. Assn. Petroleum Geologists, Enid C. of C., Sigma Gamma Epsilon. Lodge: Lions (Enid). Avocations: traveling; fishing. Home and Office: 1809 Indian Dr Enid OK 73703

WETZEL, ALBERT JOHN, former air force officer, university official, systems analyst, consultant; b. New Orleans, Dec. 29, 1917; s. Albert John and Emelie (Willoz) W.; B.Engring., Tulane U., 1939; M.S., Johns Hopkins U., 1950; postgrad. UCLA, 1956; grad. Command and Gen. Staff Coll., U.S. Armed Forces Staff Coll.; m. Helen Elizabeth Zurad, Sept. 7, 1946; children—Albert John, Elizabeth Ann, Joan Clark, Edward Russell. Commd. 2d lt. C.E., U.S. Army, 1941, advanced through grades to col. USAF, 1956; service in Europe, Asia, Middle East; exptl. test pilot, 1943-45; fighter pilot, 1945-47; tech. staff officer Armed Forces Spl. Weapons Project, Washington, 1950-52; exec. asst. to dir. guided missiles Office Sec. Def., Washington, 1952-55; wing comdr. SAC, 1955-57; dir. Titan ICBM and Gemini Space Program, 1957-62; exec. dir. U.S. Air Force Council, 1962-63; dir. strategic programs, def., research and engring., Office Sec. Def., 1963-65; ret., 1965; dir. research and sponsored programs, then dir. univ. devel. Tulane U., 1965-76, v.p. alumni and univ. affairs, 1976-80, asst. to pres., from 1980, now v.p., adj. prof. mgmt. and engring. mgmt., 1965—; mem. rocket and space panel President's Sci. Adv. Com., 1965-71; bd. dirs. Gulf South Research Inst., Inst. Def. Analysis, Washington; del. Nat. Conf. Advancement Research. Bd. dirs. Walter Clark Teagle Found., N.Y.C., Oak Ridge Assn. Univs., Air Force Assn., Navy League U.S., Crippled Children's Hosp., New Orleans, La. Council Music and Performing Arts, Council Devel. French in La.; trustee Delgado Jr. Coll., Girl Scouts U.S.A.; exec. com. local Boy Scouts Am.; commr. La. Ednl. TV Authority; pres. New Orleans Cath. Found. Decorated Legion of Merit, Armed Forces and Air Force Commendation medal; papal knight Order Holy Sepulchre of Jerusalem; Order of St. Louis; registered profl. engr., Ohio. Fellow AIAA; mem. AAAS, Greater New Orleans Area C. of C. (v.p.), Sigma Xi, Kappa Sigma, Tau Beta Pi, Omicron Delta Kappa. Clubs: Internat. House, Bienville, Plimsoll (New Orleans); University (N.Y.C.); Army-Navy (Washington); Rotary. Home: 7 Richmond Pl New Orleans LA 70115 Office: Tulane Univ University Station New Orleans LA 70118

WETZEL, EDWARD THOMAS, II, hospital official; b. Parkersburg, W.Va., June 5, 1937; s. Ralph Hugh and Beulah May (King) W.; m. Carolyn Tyson Rice, June 25, 1982; 1 son, Edward Thomas III. B.S., W. Va. U., 1959, M.A., 1961; M.A., Niagara U., 1963. Congl. asst. 40th dist. State NY., 1963-65; tchr., Niagara Falls, N.Y., 1965-68; Dir. Speakers Bur., Ohio Edison Co., Akron, 1968-75; dir. pub. relations and devel. Salvation Army, Cleve., 1975-78; pres. Program Cons., Inc., Beachwood, Ohio, 1978-80; dir. pub. relations Calhoun Gen. Hosp., Grantsville, W.Va., 1980-81; adminstrv. asst. Huntington (W.Va.) Hosp., Inc., 1981—; instr. Cleve. State U., 1969-73. Mem. Hudson (Ohio) Bd. Edn., 1971-80; pres. Young Republican Club W.Va., 1958-60; county committeeman, Niagara County, N.Y., 1965-68. Mem. Pub. Relations Soc. Am., Internat. Assn. Bus. Communicators, Internat. Platform Assn., Am. Soc. Hosp. Pub. Relations. Republican. Methodist. Lodges: Kiwanis, Masons. Home: 9 Bayberry Dr Huntington WV 25705 Office: 1230 6th Ave Huntington WV 25701

WETZEL, (HUGH) DONALD, supermarket executive; b. Owensboro, Ky., Oct. 24, 1945; s. Hugh Thomas and Lovie (McGehee) Wetzel Mitchell; B.A., Ky. Wesleyan Coll., 1968; m. Sara Ann Ireland, June 17, 1967; children—Shannon, Melanie, Ross. Sch. tchr. Daviess County Pub. Sch. System, 1968-70; part-owner, pres. Wetzel's Super Markets, Inc., Owensboro; dir. Great Fin. Fed. Assn. Trustee Christian Ch. Named Ky. Col. Mem. Super Market Inst. Clubs: Campbell (pres., dir.), Owensboro Country. Office: PO Box 2200 Owensboro KY 42302

WEXLER, JEFFREY, journalist; b. N.Y.C., May 25, 1947; B.A. in Econs. and Contemporary Civilization, Washington and Lee U., 1969; postgrad. Columbia U. Sch. Law, 1969-71, Equine Inst., Old Westbury Coll., 1974. Mgr., Atlantic Beach Bridge, Nassau County, N.Y.; journalist in Va. and N.Y., 1965—; commentator Sta. WLUR, Lexington; editor Lynbrook (N.Y.) News, Meadowbrook (N.Y.) Times; columnist Nassau Herald; pub. affairs counsel to Congressman J.W. Wydler of N.Y.; mng. editor South Shore Record, Hewlett, N.Y., 1971-79; editor, pub. Oceanside (N.Y.) Beacon, 1976-79, Shenandoah Valley Mag., Shenandoah Valley Almanac, Staunton, Va., 1979-81, Shenandoah (Va.) Town & Country mag., 1982—, Virginian Mag., 1984—; pres. Shenandoah Valley Mag. Corp., 1978—; commr. pub. affairs Village of Cedarhurst (N.Y.), 1974-79. Trustee Iron Mountain Inst.; historian Village of Cedarhurst; counsel Nassau County Village Ofcls. Assn.; commr. Nassau council Boy Scouts Am.; bd. dirs. Five Towns Community Council, Happy Birthday U.S.A., 1979-82; mem. N.Y.C. Aux. Police, 1970-73; pres. South Shore Bicentennial Soc., 1975-77; bd. dirs. Cedarhurst Bus. Assn., Oceanside Bd. Trade, Five Towns Community Center, 1979—; active Waynesboro YMCA. Robert E. Lee research scholar, 1968-69; recipient award Va. chpt. Soc. Cincinnati, 1968; named an Outstanding Young Man of Am., Jaycees, 1976. Mem. English Speaking Union, Am. Numis. Assn. (life), Am. Numis.

Soc., Nat. Rifle Assn. (life), South Shore Numis. Assn., Va. Numis. Assn. Washington and Lee U. Alumni (pres. L.I. chpt.), Token and Medal Soc., Soc. Paper Money Collectors, Council Strategic Policies, Security and Intelligence Fund of Washington, U.S. Naval Inst. (life), Smithsonian Instn. (resident assoc.), Sigma Delta Chi, Pi Sigma Alpha, Phi Epsilon Pi, Zeta Beta Tau. Author: Our Towns, A Bicentennial History, 1976; Stone Ground Poems, 1970; (novel) Wet Goods, 1973; also short stories. Clubs: Internat. House, Overseas Press, Deadline (N.Y.C.); Colonnade (Lexington, Va.); Peninsula Rifle and Pistol (exec. officer); Staunton Athletic, Cavalry of Va. (Staunton); Ruritan (Mint Spring, Va.). Address: Box 1212 Waynesboro VA 22980

WHALEN, DENNIS JOEL, communications consultant; b. Detroit, Oct. 19, 1948; s. Dennis W. and Mary Ellen (Patterson) W.; B.S., U. Fla., 1972; M.S., Fla. State U., 1982, Ph.D., 1984. News editor Sta. WSRF/WSHE-FM, Ft. Lauderdale/Miami, 1973-76; producer News Blimps, Ft. Lauderdale/Miami, San Francisco, 1974-76; pres. Joel Whalen and Assocs., Tallahassee, 1976—; v.p. Interactive Design Systems; mktg. cons. Fla. Pub. Broadcasting, 1983, Burger King, North Fla., 1980; cons. Charles McArthur Ctr. for Am. Theatre, 1976-79. Vol. TV personality Pub. TV, Tallahassee, 1976—; media cons. Springtime Tallahassee Festival, 1983; campaign media strategist Hon. Bill Grant, Fla. senator, 1982; bd. dirs. Still Moving Dance Co., Gainesville, Fla., 1980; bd. dirs. Tallahassee Fine Arts Council, 1977-78; pres. Southeastern United States Presbyn. Youth, 1965. Fla. Energy Office Communication Research grantee, 1979; U.S. Dept. Agr. fellow, 1979; Nat. Endowment Arts/Fla. Endowment Humanities grantee, 1979; Fla. Inst. Food and Agrl. Scis. TV Research grantee, 1977-78; recipient Excellence in Radio Journalism award Ft. Lauderdale News, 1968. Mem. Nat. Advt. Fedn. (5 Addie awards 1977-80), Internat. Communication Assn., Speech Communication Assn., Fla. Speech Communication Assn., Fla. Capitol Press Corps, Sigma Delta Chi, Alpha Epsilon Rho. Democrat. Presbyterian. Club: Kiwanis. Home: 1474-B Willow Bend Way Tallahassee FL 32301

WHALEY, CHARLOTTE TOTEBUSCH, publisher, editor, writer; b. Pitts., June 21, 1925; d. Charles R. and Elizabeth G. (Dunn) Totebusch; m. Gould Whaley, Jr., Aug. 24, 1951; children—John Gould, Robert Dunn. B.A., So. Meth. U., 1970, M.A., 1976. Editorial asst., Southwest Rev., S.M.U. Press, So. Meth. U., Dallas, 1971-72, asst. editor, 1972-74, assoc. editor, 1974-75, asst. to dir. S.M.U. Press, mng. editor Southwest Rev., 1975-81, editor Southwest Rev., 1981-83, asst. dir., editor SMU Press, 1981-82, editor, 1982-83; editor/pub. Still Point Press, 1984—. Mem. Tex. Pubs. Assn., S.W. Booksellers Assn., So. Meth. U. Colophon Assn. (bd. dirs.), Phi Beta Kappa asst. sec. So. Meth. U. chpt. 1979-82, pres. North Tex. chpt. 1982-84). Home and Office: 4222 Willow Grove Rd Dallas TX 75220

WHALEY, JAMES LEE, advertising agency executive; b. Traverse City, Mich., Aug. 6, 1940; s. Robert Roy and Mary Elizabeth (North) W.; m. Lynda Mary Doenges, Sept. 20, 1963; children—Coryee Ann, Andrew Doenges. Student in advt. design Soc. Arts and Crafts, Detroit, 1958-62. Art dir. Kenyon & Eckhardt, Detroit, 1962-65; art dir. Sales Communications Inc. div. McCann-Erickson, Detroit, 1965-70, sr. art dir., creative group head parent co., Houston, 1970-79; exec. art dir. Allen & Dorward, Inc., Houston, 1979-82, v.p., creative dir., 1982—. Baseball coach, football coach Alief Youth Assn. (Tex.); active Christ the Lord Ch., Alief. Recipient numerous awards Am. Fedn. Advt., Nat. Agrl. Mktg. Assn., Houston Advt. Fedn. Mem. Houston Art Dirs. Club, Houston Advt. Fedn. Republican. Lutheran. Club: Alief Hawghunters (co-founder, past pres.). Home: 13326 Trompilla Ln Houston TX 77083 Office: 4747 Bellaire Blvd Suite 200 Bellaire TX 77401

WHANG, ROBERT, physician, educator, researcher; b. Honolulu, Mar. 7, 1928; s. Won Tai and Grace Maria (Lee) W.; m. May Taeko Yamaoka, June 3, 1956; children—Robin, David, Cynthia, Lisa. B.S., St. Louis U., 1952, M.D., 1956. Diplomate Am. Bd. Internal Medicine, Am. Bd. Nutrition. Intern in medicine Johns Hopkins Hosp., 1956-57; resident in medicine Balt. City Hosp., 1957-60; fellow in metabolism U. N.C., 1960-63; from instr. to assoc. prof. medicine U. N.Mex., 1963-71; prof. medicine U. Conn., chief of staff VA Hosp., Newington, Conn., 1971-73; prof. medicine Ind. U., chief of staff VA Hosp., Indpls., 1973-78; prof., vice-head dept. medicine U. Okla., 1978—; chief of medicine VA Med. Center, Oklahoma City, 1978—. Served with U.S. Army, 1946-48; col. USAR. Life. Ins. Med. Research Fund fellow, 1960-62; Willard O. Thompson Travelling Scholar, ACP, 1967. Fellow ACP, Am. Coll. Nutrition (bd. dirs. 1978-79, pres., 1981-83); mem. Am. Fedn. Clin. Research, Western Soc. Clin. Research, Am. Soc. Nephrology, Internat. Soc. Nephrology, Central Soc. Clin. Research, Mem. editorial bd. Jour. of Lab. and Clin. Medicine, 1976-81; assoc. editor Jour. Am. Coll. Nutrition, 1976—; contbr. articles to profl. publs. Home: 3708 Surrey Rd Edmond OK 73034 Office: VA Med Center 921 NE 13th Oklahoma City OK 73104

WHARTON, JAMES HENRY, university chancellor; b. Mangum, Okla., July 23, 1937; s. John Henry and Emma Faye (Walling) W.; B.S., N.E. La. Coll., 1959; Ph.D., La. State U., 1962; m. Joan Monette McPherson, Nov. 21, 1956; children—Sherri Shannon, John Scott. Instr. chemistry La. State U., Baton Rouge, 1962, asst. prof., 1965-69, asso. dean chemistry and physics, then dean jr. div., 1969-75, dean Gen. Coll., 1975-81, acting chancellor, Alexandria, 1978, chancellor, Baton Rouge, 1981—; scientist Marshall Space Flight Center-NASA, 1963-64. Served with U.S. Army, 1962-65. Mem. Am. Chem. Soc., Phi Kappa Phi, Omicron Delta Kappa. Democrat. Methodist. Address: Office of Chancellor 156 Thomas Boyd Hall La State Univ Baton Rouge LA 70803

WHARTON, WALTER JOHN, insurance company executive; b. Athens, Ohio, Dec. 30, 1945; s. Walter and Ruth (Cabeen) W.; B.A., Ohio Dominican Coll., 1974; M.A., Central Mich. U., 1975; M.B.A., Ohio U., 1981; m. Beverly Gail Arnoff, Jan. 17, 1971. Mgr., Wharton's Super Market, The Plains, Ohio, 1964-69; trainee Continental Ins. Co., Columbus, Ohio, 1969, underwriter, 1970, sr. underwriter, 1972, supervising underwriter, 1974, multi-line adminstrv. mgr., 1975, sr. methods and procedures analyst, 1976, supt. methods and procedures, 1977-79, supt. regional systems and procedures, 1979-80, asst. sec., 1979—, zone mgr. field ops. Midwest and So. U.S., 1983-85, dir. regional ops., 1985—; asst. sec. Buckeye Union Ins. Co., 1979—; real estate cons.; speaker in field. Recipient Alumni Service award Ohio Dominican Coll., 1977. Mem. Am. Mgmt. Assn., Air Safety Found., Aircraft Owners and Pilots Assn., Jr. C. of C. Republican. Clubs: Masons (32 deg.), Shriners, Order of Demolay. Home: 904 Elmwood Ct Euless TX 76039 Office: Plaza of Ams 600 N Pearl St PO Box 960 Dallas TX 75221

WHATLEY, JACQUELINE BELTRAM, lawyer; b. West Orange, N.J., Sept. 26, 1944; d. Quirino R. and Eliane (Gruet) Beltram; B.A., U. Tampa, 1966; J.D., Stetson U., 1969; m. John W. Whatley, June 25, 1966. Admitted to Fla. bar, 1969, Alaska bar, 1971; practiced in Anchorage, 1971-73; mem. firms Gibbons, Tucker, McEwen, Miller & Whatley & Stein, Tampa, Fla., 1969-71, 1973—, pres., 1983—; dir. Fla. Investment and Devel. Corp. Arbitrator Am. Can Co., Continental Can Co., United Steelworkers Am., Tampa, 1974—. Bd. dirs. Traveler's Aid Soc. Tampa. Mem. Am., Alaska, Fla., Tampa-Hillsborough County, Anchorage bar assns., Tenn. Walking Horse Breeders' and Exhibitors' Assn. (bd. dirs. 1981—, v.p. enforcement 1985), Fla. Walking Horse Assn. (pres. 1979-81), Athena Soc., Nu Beta Epsilon, Delta Phi Epsilon, Phi Alpha Theta. Home: PO Box 17595 Tampa FL 33682 Office: 606 Madison St Tampa FL 33602

WHATLEY, JAMES ROYCE, oil and gas production company executive; b. Pittsburg, Tex., Oct. 29, 1926; s. Mason and Florence (Jackson) W.; m. Elizabeth Hoggatt, Sept. 2, 1947; 1 child, James M. B.S. in Acctg., Tex. A&M U., 1949, M.S. in Acctg., 1951. C.P.A., Tex. Acct. Exxon, Houston, 1951-52; sr. acct. Peat Marwick Mitchell, Houston, 1952-55; v.p. fin. Kaneb Services Inc., Houston, 1955-60, sr. v.p., 1960-68, pres., chief exec. officer, 1968-83, chmn., 1983—; dir. United Fin. Group Inc., Houston, Daniel Industries Inc., Houston; chmn. bd. Pittsburg Nat. Bank, Tex., 1973—. Chmn. bd. Northeast Tex. Community Coll., Chapel Hill, 1984-90; mem. adv. council Coll. Bus. Adminstrn. Tex. A&M U., 1979—, Coll. Geosci., 1978—; chmn. bd. Pittsburg Hosp., 1984—. Served with USN, 1943-45, PTO. Mem. Am. Inst. C.P.A.s, Am. Petroleum Inst. Episcopalian. Clubs: River Oaks (Houston); Sugar Creek (Sugarland, Tex.). Office: Kaneb Services Inc 14141 SW Freeway Sugarland TX 77478

WHEAT, THOMAS EDWARD MOSS, architect, structural engineer; b. Detroit, July 28, 1925; s. Thomas Edward Moss and Lucille Hayden (Daniels) W.; m. Audrey Marie Louise Castiglione, June 30, 1948; 1 child, Thomas Edward Moss III. Sc.B., Mich. State U., 1951; student U. Mich. 1946-47, 1952. Registered profl. engr., Mich., N.Y., Tex. Registered architect, Mich., Tex. Ptnr. O'Dell Hewlett-Luckenbach, Birmingham, Mich., 1961-66; v.p., dir. Eberle M. Smith Assocs., Detroit, 1966-75; asst. to sr. v.p. Giffels Assocs., Southfield, Mich., 1975-78; sr. mgr. Smith, Hinchman & Grylls, Detroit, 1978-82; pres. Robert Arburn & Assoc., San Antonio, 1982-86; mgr. structural div. The Dabney Group, San Antonio, 1986—. Del. Republican party, Birmingham, 1964; pres. Mensa, Detroit, 1967; mem. adv. bd. Bus. Coms. for Arts, San Antonio, 1985—; mem. Fine Arts Commn., San Antonio. Recipient Award of Merit Am. Inst. Steel Construction, 1966, Cert. Merit Mich. Soc. Architects, 1981. Mem. AIA, Tex. Soc. Architects (bd. dirs. San Antonio chpt., govt. affairs com. 1986—, chmn. pub. relations com. San Antonio chpt. 1986—). Republican. Episcopalian. Club: Sonterra Country (San Antonio). Avocations: flying; golf; reading. Home: 305 Cloverleaf Ave San Antonio TX 78209 Office: The Dabney Group 2391 NE Loop 410 Suite 404 San Antonio TX 78217

WHEATLEY, DAVID COE, architect; b. St. Louis, Feb. 21, 1929; s. Thomas and Nora (Allen) W.; student Washington U., St. Louis, 1950-53, Frank Lloyd Wright Sch. Architecture, 1953-59; m. Susan Jacobs, Mar. 30, 1957. Staff architect Frank Lloyd Wright Found., Spring Green, Wis. and Phoenix, 1959-69; participated in constrn. Guggenheim Mus., N.Y.C., 1958-60, Marin County Govt. Center, San Raphael, Calif., 1960-63; architect Wheatley-Merritt Assos., Dallas, 1969-73; v.p. planning and design Centex Homes Corp., Dallas, 1973—. Mem. City of Dallas Task Force, Historic Preservation Commn. Served with USMC, 1946-49. Registered architect, Ariz., Calif., Colo., Fla., Ga., Ind., Ill., Iowa, Kans., La., Md., Minn., N.J., N.Y. State, Nev., S.C., Tex., Va., Wash., Wis., D.C. Mem. AIA, Soc. Archtl. Historians, Tex. Soc. Architects, Historic Preservation League, Nat. Council Archtl. Registration Bds., Nat. Trust for Historic Preservation, Internat. Conf. Bldg. Ofcls., Bldg. Ofcls. Code Adminstrs., Am. Planning Assn., Constrn. Specifications Inst., Urban Land Inst. (exec. council). Prin. works include Aitken residence, Woodside, Calif., 1961, Warren residence, St. Joseph, Mich., 1962, Kittleson residence, Scottsdale, Ariz., 1972, Royse residence, LaGrange, Tex., 1973, Holmdel Garden Center, N.J., 1973, Menard residence, Hillsboro, Tex., 1973, Harborside, Foster City, Calif., 1974, La Laderas, Hercules, Calif., 1975, Pitcairn, Foster City, 1976, Langley Oaks, McLean, Va., 1976, Woodbury Village, Miami, 1978, Burke Village, Va., 1979, Mountain Vista Village, Westminster, Colo., 1980, Walter Lee Culp residence, Dallas, Paul R. Seegers residence, William Pasztor residence, Folsom, Calif., 1981, Harry P. Leonhardt residence, James E. Lewis residence, Breckenridge, Colo., 1982, Stockbridge Village, Elk Grove, Ill., 1983. Home: 3632 McFarlin Blvd Dallas TX 75205 Office: 4258 Spring Valley Rd Dallas TX 75234

WHEATLEY, EDWARD WARREN, marketing educator, consultant; b. Woodbury, N.J., June 30, 1936; s. William Wheatley and Sara Agnes (Buckley) Bozarth; m. Elizabeth Ann Burkitt, Oct. 25, 1980; children—Lisa Hill, Richard, Sarah. B.C.S., Fairleigh Dickinson U., 1958; M.B.A., Wharton Grad. Sch. Fin. and Commerce, U. Pa., 1959; Ph.D., Fla. State U., 1969. Vice-pres., dir. of advt. R.A. Bozarth, Inc., Vineland, N.J., 1953-62; mgmt cons. Ernst & Whinney, San Antonio, 1962-65; instr. mktg. Fla. State U., Tallahassee, 1965-68; prof., chmn. dept. mktg. U. Miami, Fla., 1968-82, East Carolina U., Greenville, N.C., 1982—; cons. in field. Author: Marketing Professional Services, 1983; Values in Conflict, 1976; (with others) Modern Marketing, 1978; also articles. Served to capt. U.S. Army, 1959-62. Recipient Outstanding Scholar award, Sales Exec. Club, N.J., 1958. Mem. Am. Mktg. Assn. (award, 1982; nominated Fla. Marketer of Yr. 1982.), So. Mktg. Assn., Acad. Mktg. Sci. (editorial bd. 1978—), Delta Sigma Pi, Beta Gamma Sigma, Alpha Mu Alpha, Phi Kappa Phi. Republican. Avocations: sailing; fishing; music. Office: E Carolina U Dept Mktg Greenville NC 27834

WHEATLEY, EUGENE AUSTIN, JR., physicist; b. Cin., Aug. 12, 1928; s. Eugene Austin and Grace (Appleton) W.; M.E., U. Cin., 1951, M.S. in Physics, 1954; m. Dolores Gerhardt, June 9, 1956 (div. Dec. 1965); m. 2d, Carol Betty Houck, Nov. 8, 1969. Controls systems engr. Gen. Electric Co., Evendale, Ohio, 1955-58; staff mem. nuclear rocket div. Los Alamos Sci. Lab., 1958-61; asst. sr. engr. NERVA nuclear rocket div. Aerojet Gen., Azusa, Calif., 1961-63; staff mem. AC spark plug div. Gen. Motors, El Segundo, Calif., 1963-64; prin. engr. Saturn V flight evaluation working group Boeing Co., Huntsville, Ala., 1964-69; cons. Code Research Corp., Huntsville, 1970; sr. engr. Skylab, Space Shuttle Martin Marietta Corp., Huntsville, New Orleans, 1971—. Mem. Am. Phys. Soc., Am. Nuclear Soc., ASME, AIAA, Pi Tau Sigma. Contbr. articles to profl. jours. Home: 1619 Drake Ave SE Huntsville AL 35802 Office: Martin Marietta Corp PO Box 29304 New Orleans LA 70189

WHEATLEY, RICHARD DUNCAN, SR., clinical psychologist; b. McAlester, Okla., July 30, 1938; s. Joseph Richard and Mildred Kyle (Coffield) W.; B.A., U. Louisville, 1962, M.A. (NSF scholar), 1973, Ph.D., 1976; children—Thomas Warren, Richard Duncan. Commd. officer U.S. Air Force, 1962-68, 76-81, Res., 1981—; chief clin. psychologist Sch. Aerospace Medicine, Brooks AFB, San Antonio, 1976-81; clin. psychology cons., dir. alcohol-drug treatment program VA Med. Center, Kerrville, Tex., 1981—. Cert. and lic. in clin. psychology, Tex. Mem. Am. Psychol. Assn., Internat. Neuropsychol. Soc., Tex. Psychol. Assn., Assn. Advancement Psychology, Assn. VA Chiefs Psychology. Office: VA Med Center Kerrville TX 78028

WHEATON, DAVID JOE, aerospace mfg. co. exec.; b. Las Vegas, N.Mex., June 5, 1940; s. Joseph Charles and Estella Marie (Grubbs) W.; B.S., U. Colo., 1962; m. Gail Ellen Moody, July 17, 1965; children—Deanna Lynn, Kimberly Gail, Joseph Charles II. Predesign engr., mktg. mgr. Convair div. Gen. Dynamics, San Diego, 1967-75, F-16 mktg. mgr. Fort Worth div., 1975-77, engring. program mgr., 1977-79, dir. F-16 domestic mktg., 1979-80, v.p. mktg., 1980—. Served with USN, 1962-67. Decorated Air medal (6). Mem. Air Force Assn., Am. Def. Preparedness Assn., Navy Tailhook Assn., Red River Fighter Pilots Assn., Nat. Mgmt. Assn., Sigma Tau, Scabbard and Blade, Tau Beta Phi. Republican. Home: 7801 Regatta Ct Fort Worth TX 76179 Office: PO Box 748 Fort Worth TX 76101

WHEELER, ANGELA LOUISE, college administrator, counselor, consultant; b. Charlotte, N.C., Dec. 11, 1950; s. Howard Augustine and Kathleen Louise (Dobbins) W. B.A., Sacred Heart Coll., 1972; M.Ed., Winthrop Coll., 1978. Cert. counselor. Asst. dean students Sacred Heart Coll., Belmont, N.C., 1972-77; counselor, psychometrist Mary Dore Ctr., Charlotte, 1977-78; tchr. Central Piedmont Community Coll., Charlotte, 1978-79; dir. counseling Belmont Abbey Coll., N.C., 1979—; counselor, cons., Belmont, 1978—. Mem. Am. Assn. Counseling and Devel., Am. Coll. Personnel Assn., N.C. Sch. Counselors Assn. Democrat. Roman Catholic. Avocations: bicycling; sailing; camping. Home: 125 Country Ln Belmont NC 28012 Office: Counseling Ctr Belmont Abbey Coll Belmont NC 28012

WHEELER, CHARLES VAWTER, lawyer; b. Fay, Okla., Nov. 12, 1920; s. Claude A. and Bertha (Cooke) W.; m. Maryjo Meacham, Jan. 23, 1943; children—Allison Ann, Meacham. Student Harding Coll., 1938-39; student U. Okla., 1939-43, LL.B., 1948; student U. Tex., 1947; LL.M., NYU, 1973. Bar. Okla., 1943. Atty., Southwestern Bell Telephone Co., Oklahoma City, 1948-53; mem. firm Cantrell, Carey & McCloud, Oklahoma City, 1953-58; with Cities Service Co., Tulsa, 1958-83, gen. counsel, 1969-83; counsel Gable & Gotwalls, Tulsa, 1983—; asst. adj. gen. State of Okla., 1966-68. Served with AUS, 1943-47, 50-52. Decorated Legion of Merit. Mem. ABA, Okla. Bar Assn., N.Y. State Bar Assn., N.G. Assn., Delta Tau Delta. Democrat. Presbyterian. Clubs: Metropolitan (N.Y.C.); Tulsa, So. Hills Country. Home: 2300 Riverside Dr Apt 18-1 Tulsa OK 74114 Office: 2000 4th Nat Bldg Tulsa OK 74119

WHEELER, DAVID WOODRING, construction and development executive; b. Bethlehem, Pa., Aug. 23, 1955; s. Donald Bingham, Jr. and Mary Louise (Woodring) W.; m. Trudy Kay Scamehorn, Apr. 18, 1981. B.Arch., Cornell U., 1978. Project coordinator Internat. Systems, Mobile, Ala., 1978-80; project mgr. Hardin Assocs., Inc., Atlanta, 1980—. Democrat. Club: Cornell of Atlanta. Avocations: sailing; swimming; cycling. Home: 4674 Andalusia Trail Dunwoody GA 30360 Office: Hardin Assocs Inc 1380 W Paces Ferry Rd Atlanta GA 30327

WHEELER, DONALD JEFFERSON, statistician, consultant; b. Oklahoma City, Sept. 30, 1944; s. Henry Raymond and Cleo E. (Manly) W.; m. Frances Louise Vaughan, May 28, 1966; children—David J., Elaine F. B.A., U. Tex., 1966; M.S., So. Methodist U., 1968, Ph.D., 1970. Asst. prof. U. Tenn., Knoxville, 1970-74, assoc. prof. stats., 1974-82; cons. stastician Statis. Process Controls, Inc., Knoxville, 1982—; cons. various corps., U.S., Portugal and Brazil. Author: Understanding Statistical Process Control, 1984. Contbr. articles to profl. publs. Mem. Am. Statis. Assn., Am. Soc. Quality Control, Math. Assn. Am., Inst. Mgmt. Sci., Alpha Chi, Kappa Mu Epsilon. Office: Statis Process Controls Inc 7026 Shadyland Dr Knoxville TN 37919

WHEELER, GENEVIEVE STUTES, library administrator, educator; b. Duson, La., Dec. 13, 1937; d. Noah and Natalie (Falcon) Stutes; m. Richard Anthony Musemeche, Feb. 3, 1956 (div. 1975); children—Sabrina Marie Musemeche Beckham, Susan Ann; m. 2d, Berle Steele Wheeler, July 1, 1978. B.A., U. Southwest La., Lafayette, 1959; M.S. in Library Sci., La. State U., Baton Rouge, 1970. Cert. tchr. Tchr. Iberia Schs., New Iberia, La., 1959-60; sch. librarian Lafayette Parish Sch., 1960-69; tchr., librarian La. State Sch. Deaf, Baton Rouge, 1970-71; librarian East Baton Rouge System, 1971-78; library adminstr. St. Bernard Community Coll., Chalmette, La., 1978—, cons., 1978—; cons. library La. State Dept. Edn., Baton Rouge, 1975-76. Author tchr. guides, 1975, 77. Co-organizer, co-sponsor Project LesEfants, 1975. Mem. La. Assn. Sch. Librarians (pres. 1982-83), ALA, La. Assn. Sch. Execs., La. Library Assn., Gov.'s Conf. Libraries, Delta Kappa Gamma (v.p. Baton Rouge 1975-76), Phi Kappa Phi. Club: Republican Women's (New Orleans). Home: 12987 N Lake Carmel Dr New Orleans LA 70128 Office: St Bernard Parish Community Coll Library 1100 E Judge Perez Chalmette LA 70043

WHEELER, HAROLD AUSTIN, SR., lawyer, former educational administrator; b. Montverde, Fla., Oct. 5, 1925; s. Bureon Kylus and Susan Ella (Bible) W.; m. Myrtle Edna Suggs, Sept. 30, 1949; children—Brenda Lynn, Harold Austin, Stephen Wayne, Donna Kay. B.S.B.A., U. Fla., 1950; M.Ed., Fla. Atlantic U., 1970; J.D., U. Miami (Fla.), 1973, LL.M., 1977. C.P.A., Fla.; bar: Fla. 1973. Auditor to supr. auditor Fla. State Auditing Dept., 1950-62; asst. supt. fin. and acctg. Palm Beach County, Fla. Pub. Schs., 1962-65; dir. fin., treas. Fla. Pub. Schs., Dade County, 1966-81; sole practice, Miami, 1982—. Mem. Fla. Inst. C.P.A.s, Am. Inst. C.P.A.s, Fla. Bar Assn., Dade County Bar Assn., ABA, Assn. Sch. Bus. Ofcls. of U.S. and Can. Democrat. Baptist. Lodge: Kiwanis. Home: 6695 SW 112th St Miami FL 33156 Office: 7210 SW 57th Ave Suite 215 South Miami FL 33143

WHEELER, HOWARD AUGUSTINE, JR. (HUMPY), speedway exec.; b. Gastonia, N.C., Oct. 23, 1938; s. Howard A. and Kathleen (Dobbins) W.; A.B. in Journalism, U. S.C., 1961; m. Patricia Adele Williams, May 12, 1962; children—Mary Patricia, Tracy, Howard Augustine, III. Dir. spl. events Firestone Tire & Rubber Co., Akron, 1964-70; promotor racing, spl. events, Charlotte, N.C., 1970-72; dir. corp. affairs Real Estate div. Am. Cyanamid, Charlotte, 1972-75; pres. Charlotte Motor Speedway, 1975—. Bd. dirs. Boy Scouts Am., Belmont Abbey Coll., Charlotte Drug Edn., Boys Town, Richard Petty Safety Found.; mem. N.C. Gov.'s Travel Adv. Bd., 1980—. Named Nat. Racing Promoter of Yr., Motorsports Weekly, 1977, 81; recipient N.C. Travel Attraction award N.C. Travel Council, 1980; Affinity award Charlotte Public Relations Soc., 1976. Mem. Nat. Assn. Stock Car Racing, Public Relations Soc. Am., N.C. Travel Council. Democrat. Roman Catholic. Club: Rotary. Author: Mechalete Conditioning. Office: PO Box 600 Harrisburg NC 28075

WHEELER, MARK THOMAS, geologist; b. Sept. 14, 1955; s. R. Phillip and Dorothy A. (Beddoe) W. Student U. Calif.-Berkeley, 1975-76; B.S. in Geology, St. Lawrence U., Canton, N.Y., 1978; M.S. in Geology, Wash. State U., 1980. Geologist, Conoco Inc., Houston, 1980-84, project supr., Lafayette, La., 1984, project dir. exploration, 1984-85, ops. dir., New Orleans, 1985—. Mem. fund raiser com. YMCA, Lafayette, 1985. Mem. Am. Assn. Petroleum Geologists, Houston Geol. Assn., Lafayette Geol. Assn. Republican. Club: University (Houston). Avocations: tennis, skiing. Office: Conoco Inc 3500 Gen DeGaulle New Orleans LA 770114

WHEELER, MARY ELLEN QUIRK, architect; b. Springfield, Mass., Apr. 30, 1946; d. John Thomas and Mary Elizabeth (Hurley) Q.; m. Robert Clews Wheeler, II, Mar. 4, 1972; children—Mary Elizabeth, Sarah Brockenbrough. B.Arch., Syracuse U., 1969. Registered architect, Mass., Va. City planner City of Springfield, 1967; designer, architect Samuel Glazer & Ptnrs., Boston, 1969-72; architect VVKR Ptnrs., Alexandria, Va., 1972-73; architect, Fredericksburg, Va., 1973—. Contbr. chpt. to book. Mem. Downtown Devel. and Design Coms., Fredericksburg, 1975-79; mem. Archtl. Rev. Bd., 1983—; bd. dirs. YMCA, 1985—. Avocations: reading; traveling; sewing; gardening. Home and Office: 1201 Princess Anne St Fredericksburg VA 22401

WHEELER, ROGER MILTON, JR., energy company executive; b. Tulsa, July 3, 1948; s. Roger Milton and Patricia (Wilson) W.; m. Patricia Diane Foor, Mar. 4, 1978; children—Roger Milton III, Clark Wilson. B.S. in Petroleum Engring., U. Tulsa, 1977. Pres. Wheeler Energy Co., Tulsa, 1977—; gen. ptnr. W.J.A. Realty, Tulsa, 1978—. Served with USN, 1968-72. Mem. Soc. Profl. Engrs. (cert.), Soc. Petroleum Engrs. (cert.), Am. Assn. Petroleum Geologists, Young Pres. Orgn. Republican. Presbyterian. Office: 810 S Cincinnati Suite 200 Tulsa OK 74119

WHEELER, WILLIAM BLAINE, college administrator; b. King, Ark., Apr. 14, 1942; s. Marion Morris and Estella (Wylie) W.; m. Nadia Wheeler, Nov. 22, 1978; 1 dau., Yasmin Alexandra. B.A. with honors, U. Ark.-Fayetteville, 1964, M.A., 1965, Ph.D., 1971. Faculty, prof. lang. Oral Roberts U., Tulsa, 1968-72; dean acad. affairs Am. Christian Coll., Tulsa, 1972-75; dir. English program U. Benghazi, Libya, 1975-79; vis. prof. Glasgow U. (Scotland), 1979-81; ednl. cons. Eagle & Assocs., Tulsa, 1981—; dean acad. affairs Okla. Coll., Tulsa, 1983—; pres. Internat. Mktg. Services, 1984—; dir. classical music KBJH-FM, Tulsa, 1972-75. Author: English as 2nd Language, 2 vols., 1976; contbr. articles to profl. jours. Mem. City Commn., City of Jenks (Okla.), 1974. NDEA Title IV fellow, 1964-67; Hamburg Exchange fellow, 1966; named Outstanding Faculty Mem., Am. Christian Coll., 1975, Benghazi U., 1977. Mem. Phi Beta Kappa. Republican. Episcopalian. Office: 6931 S 66th East Ave Suite 310 Tulsa OK 74133

WHEELER, WILLIAM BRYAN, III, systems company executive; b. Kissimmee, Fla., June 21, 1940; s. William Bryan and Olive Mae (Criner) W.; m. Mary Sue Lewis, Dec. 29, 1961; children—Alicia Nanette, Bryan. Student U. Fla., 1958-59, U. Md., 1967-68; B.L.A., U. Ga., 1975; Ph.D., Bangor Inst. Meteorol. supr. Pan Am. World Airways, 1962-63; asst. engr. Fla. Road Dept., Orlando, 1963-64; tech. supr. Xerox Corp., 1964-65; sr. field engr. Fed. Electric Corp., Rome, 1965-66; systems engr. Bendix Corp., 1966-70; devel. dir. East Coast Stainless Steel, Lanham, Md., 1970-71; regional planner Middle Flint Planning and Devel. Commn., Ellaville, Ga., 1975-78; planning dir. Northeast Ga. Area Planning and Devel. Commn., Athens, 1978-81; dist. mgr. CASA Data Systems, Athens, 1981-82; v.p. Select Systems, Inc., Atlanta, 1982—. Vice pres. Sumter County Bicentennial Beautification Com., 1976-77. Author: (Pseudonym Rhuddlwm Gawr) The Quest - The Discovery of the Cauldron of Immortality. Served with USMC, 1958-61. Mem. Am. Soc. Landscape Architects, Am. Soc. Med. Computing and Electronics, Am. Planning Assocs. Democrat. Office: 2000 Clearview Ave Atlanta GA 30340

WHEELESS, JAMES NORMAN, construction executive; b. Thomaston, Ga., May 27, 1952; s. Huell Otto and Nell (Beeland) W.; m. Deborah Elaine Hoyal; children—Tim, Jeff, Lori. Student, Tift Coll. Owner, Wheeless Constrn. Co., Thomaston, 1971-75; asst. dir. Upson County EMS, Thomaston, 1975-79; inspector Ga. Power Co., Juliette, Ga., 1975-81, constrn. safety supr., 1981—, chmn. labor-mgmt. safety com. Plane Scherer, Juliette, 1983—. Mem. exec. bd. Atwater PTA, Thomaston, 1984-85, v.p., 1985-86, pres., 1986-87. Recipient Disting. Safety award Ga. Dept. Labor, 1983, Cert. of Appreciation, Southeastern Electric Exchange, 1984. Mem. Am. Soc. Safety Engrs. Baptist. Avocations: camping; fishing; playing guitar. Home: 169 Maple Ridge Thomaston GA 30286 Office: Ga Power Co PO Box 56 Juliette GA 31046

WHEELESS, KAREN JEAN, government official; b. Dallas, June 2, 1954; d. E.E. And Aileen Witten W. B.A., Baylor U., 1976, M.B.A., 1979. Asst. mgr. direct mail clubs Word DMS, Inc., Waco, Tex., 1976-77; account exec. Charles Wallis, Inc., Waco, 1977-79; mktg. mgr. Smithsonian Sci. Info. Exchange, Washington, 1979-80; pub. affairs officer U.S. Forest Service, Gainesville, Ga., 1980—. Mem. Pub. Relations Soc. Am., Orgn. Profl. Employees in Dept. of Agr., LWV, Ga. Environ. Edn. Council (treas.), Soil Cons. Soc. Am. Baptist. Contbr. book revs. to newspapers and mags. Office: 601 Broad St Gainesville GA 30501

WHELAN, DENNIS EDWARD, antique book dealer; b. Morristown, N.J., Feb. 14, 1949; s. George Joseph Whelan and Jessie (McPartlin) DeFelice. Student, George Washington U., 1967-69. Self-employed antique dealer, Newberry, Fla., 1970—. Promoter antique and nostalgia festivals. Mem. North Fla. Nostalgia Assn. (founder). Avocations: Canoeing; snorkeling; astrology; poetry; history. Home and Office: PO Box 729 Newberry FL 32669

WHELAN, PATRICK JOSEPH, geologist, geophysicist; b. Washington, Apr. 12, 1950; s. Thomas Malcolm and Catherine Winnifred (Carnazza) W.; m. Louise Ann Schneider May 22, 1971; children—Shawn Catherine, Conor, B.S., Trinity U.; M.S., E. Tex. State U. Mudlogger, Splty. Logging, Gonzales, Tex., 1977-78, Exploration Services, Midland, Tex., 1978-79; grad. asst. E. Tex. State U., Commerce, 1979-80; geophysicist, geologist Superior Oil Co., Midland, 1980-85; regional geologist Mobil Oil Co., Midland, 1985—. Served with U.S. Army, 1971-74. Mem. Am. Assn. Petroleum Geologists, Soc. Exploration Geophysicists, Permian Basin Geophys. Club, Permian Basis Geol. Club. Avocations: running; biking; camping; hiking; rugby. Home: 1606 Harvard St Midland TX 79701

WHELAN, WILLIAM JOSEPH, biochemistry educator; b. Salford, Lancashire, U.K., Nov. 14, 1924; s. William Joseph and Jane Antoinette (Bertram) W.; m. Margaret Miller Birnie, Dec. 22, 1951. B.S., U. Birmingham (U.K.), 1945, Ph.D., 1948, D.Sc., 1955. Asst. lectr. U. Birmingham, 1947-48; sr. lectr. U. Wales, Bangor, Wales, U.K., 1948-55; sr. mem. Lister Inst., U. London, 1956-64; prof. and chmn. Royal Free Hosp. Sch. Medicine, U. London, 1964-67; prof. and chmn. dept. biochemistry U. Miami (Fla.), 1967—. Recipient Alsberg award Am. Assn. Cereal Chemists, 1967; award of Merit Japan Soc. Starch Sci., 1975; Sare medal Assn. Cereal Chemists (W.Ger.), 1979. Mem. Fedn. European Biochem. Socs. (sec. gen. 1965-67, diplome-d'honneur 1974), Am. Soc. Biol. Chemists, Brit. Biochem. Soc. (sec. 1959-67, Ciba medal 1969), Pan-Am. Assn. Biochem. Socs. (sec. gen. 1970-71), Royal Coll. Physicians London (hon.), Internat. Union Biochemistry (gen. sec. 1973-83, Wood-Whelan travel fellow 1985—; chmn. ICSU Press 1983—). Club: Athenaeum (London). Editor: Carbohydrate Metabolism, 1964-82; editor-in-chief Trends in Biochem. Scis., 1975-78, BioEssays, 1984—, Fedn. Procs., 1986—. Office: Biochemistry-UMED PO Box 016129 Miami FL 33101

WHERRY, JEFFREY NEIL, psychologist, guidance center director; b. Huntsville, Tex., Mar. 14, 1954; s. Douglas Holcomb Wherry and Sue (Ferguson) Davies; m. Diane Elaine Morgan, Aug. 6, 1977; 1 child, Ashley Nicole. B.S., Abilene Christian U., 1977, B.S. in Edn., 1977; M.S., U. Tex.-Tyler, 1979; Ph.D., U. Southern Miss., 1982. Lic. psychologist, Tex. Tchr. Chapel Hill High Sch., Tyler, 1977-79; psychology extern Hattiesburg Schs., Miss., 1979-80; research asst., instr. U. Southern Miss., Hattiesburg, 1979-81; clin. psychology intern Childrens Village, Dobbs Ferry, N.Y., 1981-82; postdoctoral fellow U. Tex. Med. Br., Galveston, Tex., 1982-83; dir. psychol. services Children's Guidance Ctr., Waco, Tex., 1983—. Co-author: (with others) Group Therapies for Children and Youth, 1982. Contbr. articles to profl. jours. Counselor Crestview Ch. of Christ, Waco, 1984-85. Mem. McLennan County Psychol. Assn. (pres. 1985), Am. Psychol. Assn., Tex. Psychol. Assn., Nat. Assn. Sch. Psychologists, Soc. Pediatric Psychology (limited), Sigma Xi, Psi Chi, Pi Kappa Alpha. Avocations: photography; bicycling; jogging; racquetball. Home: 324 Spring Valley Rd Hewitt TX 76643 Office: Children's Guidance Ctr 1111 Herring Ave Waco TX 76708

WHETSELL, GEORGE IRVAN, JR., educational administrator; b. Orangeburg, S.C., Nov. 1, 1941; s. George Irvan and Alice (Hoy) W.; m. Brenda Wiggins, June 15, 1963; children—George Irvan, III, Mary Catherine. B.S., Wofford Coll., Spartanburg, S.C. 1963; M.Ed., S.C. State Coll., 1975. Sec.-treas. Mut. Wholesale Co., Orangeburg, 1963-69; dean student affairs Orangeburg Calhoun Tech. Coll., 1969—; cons. Limestone Coll., Gaffney, S.C., 1981—. Bd. dirs. Boy's Club, Orangeburg, 1981. Served to vice comdr. USCG, 1980—. Mem. Phi Theta Kappa. Lodge: Rotary. Methodist. Avocations: hunting; fishing; gun collecting. Home: 996 Boulevard Orangeburg SC 29115 Office: Orangeburg Calhoun Tech Coll 3250 St Matthews Rd Orangeburg SC 29115

WHETSTONE, JAMES RANDOLPH, accountant, educator; b. Calhoun County, Ala., July 3, 1940; s. John Harvey and Mishie (Lawler) W.; m. Ruth Ann Beaird, Nov. 27, 1959; children—Janet Arlene, Mary Elizabeth. B.S., Jacksonville State U., 1970; student Gadsden State Jr. Coll., 1966-67. C.P.A., Ala. Billing clk. Ala. Pipe Co., Anniston, 1961-66; civilian Anniston Army Depot, Bynum, Ala., 1966-68; acct. Gene E. Evans, C.P.A., Gadsden, Ala., 1968-69; acct. Kirkland, Smith, Taylor & Payne, C.P.A.s, Anniston, 1969-74; comptroller Rainbow Home Improvement Co., Gadsden, 1974-75; ptnr. McBrayer & Whetstone, C.P.A.s, Anniston, 1975-77; pres. Kemp, Whetstone & Ray, PC, C.P.A.s, Oxford, Ala., 1978-79 Davis, Kemp, Goodgame, Whetstone, Mosley & Ray, PC, C.P.A.s, Oxford, 1979-80; owner Profl. Typing Service, Oxford, 1981—; individual practice acctg. James R. Whetstone, C.P.A., Oxford, 1980—; instr. Gadsden State Jr. Coll., Anniston, 1971-78, 81—. Served with USN, 1958-61. Mem. Ala. Soc. C.P.A.s, Am. Inst. C.P.A.s. Mem. Full Gospel Ch. Club: Kiwanis. Home: Route 1 Box 118 Wellington AL 36279 Office: 909 Snow St Oxford AL 36203

WHIDDEN, SANDRA KAY, insurance underwriter; b. Tampa, Jan. 11, 1946; d. Claude Clifford and Gloria (Lackey) W. Student pub. schs., Tampa. Cert. profl. ins. woman. Examiner, Fla. Insp. and Rating Bur., Tampa, 1964-66; rater Md. Casualty Co., Tampa, 1966-71, underwriter, 1971-82, sr. underwriter, 1982—. Mem. Ins. Women Tampa Assn. (corr. sec. 1975-76), Tampa Assn. Ins. Women (pres. 1977-78), Beta Sigma Phi. Democrat. Baptist. Home: 7415 El Encanto Ct Apt 213 Tampa FL 33617 Office: Md Casualty Co 1408 N Westshore Blvd Suite 400 Tampa FL 33607

WHIDDON, FREDERICK PALMER, university president; b. Newville, Ala., Mar. 2, 1930; s. Samuel Wilson and Mary (Palmer) W.; A.B., Birmingham So. Coll., 1952; B.D. cum laude, Emory U., 1955, Ph.D. in Philosophy, 1963; m. June Marie Ledyard, June 14, 1952; children—Charles Wilson, John Tracy, Karen Marie and Keith Frederick (twins). Grad. asst. Inst. Liberal Arts, Emory U., 1955-56; asst. prof. philosophy, dean students Athens (Ala.) Coll., 1957-59; dir. Mobile Center U. Ala., 1960-63; pres. Univ. S. Ala., Mobile, 1963—; presdl. adv. com. Fed. Home Loan Bank, Atlanta. Bd. dirs. Mobile Mus. Named Outstanding Young Man in Ala., 1964, in Am., 1965, Outstanding Administr. in Ala., Am. Assn. Univ. Adminstrs., 1981. Mem. Mobile C. of C. (dir.). Methodist (steward). Club: Kiwanis (Mobile). Home: 2157 Venetia Rd Mobile AL 36605 Office: Univ So Ala Mobile AL 36688

WHILLOCK, CARL SIMPSON, electric cooperative executive, lawyer; b. Scotland, Ark., May 7, 1926; m. Margaret Moore Carter; 2 sons, 2 daus., 3 stepdaus., 3 stepsons. B.S. in Social Welfare, U. Ark., 1948, M.A., 1951; J.D., George Washington U., 1960. Exec. asst. to U.S. congressman, 1955-63; practice law, 1963-66; pros. atty. 14th Jud. Dist. Ark., 1965-66; asst. to pres. U. Ark., 1966-71, dir. univ. relations, 1971-74; v.p. govtl. relations and pub. affairs, 1978-80; campaign mgr. David Pryor for Gov. Ark., 1974-75; exec. sec. to Gov. Ark., 1975; pres. Ark. State U., Jonesboro, 1978-80; pres. Ark. Electric Coops., Inc., and Ark. Electric Coop. Corp., Little Rock, 1980—; dir. Comml. Nat. Bank, Little Rock. Mem. Ark. Ho. of Reps., 1953-56; bd. dirs. Van Buren County Hosp., 1953-55; chmn. Clinton Water and Sewer Commn., Ark., 1964-66; pres. bd. dirs. Clinton Sch. Dist., 1965-66; chair Fayetteville Housing Authority, 1975-81; mem. exec. com. So. Growth Policies Bd., 1975-81; mem. ofcl. bd. First United Methodist Ch., Little Rock, 1982—; bd. dirs. St. Vincent Infirmary Found., Little Rock, 1980—. Mem. Little Rock C. of C. (exec. com. of bd. dirs. 1980—), Nat. Rural Electric Coop. Assn. (long-range study com. 1982-83). Office: Ark Electric Coop Corp 8000 Scott Hamilton Dr Little Rock AR 72209

WHISENANT, ALLEN DALE, pharmacist, army officer; b. Gadsden, Ala., May 17, 1947; s. Ray Elvester and Angelou (Felton) W.; m. Janis Carol Garrett, June 7, 1969; children—Christopher, Allen, Michael Ryan. B.S. in Pharmacy, Auburn U., 1970; M.S. in Edn., U. So. Calif., 1980. Enlisted U.S. Army, 1971, advanced through grades to maj., 1984; with Med. Services Corps, from 1972; stationed at 41st Combat Support Hosp., Comayagua, Honduras, 1983-84; pharmacy resident Brooke Army Med. Ctr., Fort Sam Houston, Tex., 1984—. Contbr. articles to profl. jours. Asst. coach NE Youth Soccer Orgn., San Antonio, 1983; asst. den leader San Antonio council Boy Scouts Am., 1984—. Decorated Joint Service Commendation medal, Meritorious Service medal, U.S. Army Commendation medal, Army Achievement medal. Mem. Am. Soc. Hosp. Pharmacists, Am. Pharm. Assn., Acad. Pharmacy Practice, Assn. Mil. Surgeons of Uniformed Services, Tex. Soc. Hosp. Pharmacists. Home: 5410 El Tejano St San Antonio TX 78233 Office: Brooke Army Med Ctr Pharmacy Service Fort Sam Houston TX 78234

WHISENHUNT, MARGARET JEAN, nuclear power facility administrator, psychologist; b. Hamlet, N.C., Oct. 22, 1944; d. Robert Eugene and Edith Iola (Leonard) W. A.B., E. Carolina U., 1965, M.A., 1969; J.D., N.C. Central U., 1976. Psychol. assoc., N.C. Clin. psychologist So. W.Va. Regional Health, Beckley, 1968-71, Southeastern Mental Health, Wilmington, N.C., 1971-76; law clk., Southport, N.C., 1979-80; radiation control trainee Carolina Power and Light Co., Southport, 1983—; cons. Neighborhood Youth Corps., Beckley, 1970, Brunswick County Sch., Southport, 1974-76, Juvenile Ct., Southport, 1974-76. Mem. Yaupon Beach Planning Bd., N.C., 1985—. Mem. Am. Psychol. Assn. (assoc.), Am. Bus. Women (treas. 1984-85). Democrat. Methodist. Avocations: reading; gardening; needlework; cooking. Home: 106 Sellers St Yaupon Beach NC 28461

WHISONANT, ROBERT CLYDE, geology educator, scientist; b. Columbia, S.C., Apr. 20, 1941; s. Clyde Webb and Mary Perrylee (Lanford) W.; m. Brenda Dale Lark, June 7, 1963; children—Dell Raye, Robert Dowling. B.S. in Geology, Clemson U., 1963; M.S., Fla. State U., 1965, Ph.D. in Geology, 1967. Petroleum geologist Humble Oil & Refining Co., Houston/Kingsville, Tex., 1967-71, cons., 1972; mem. faculty Radford (Va.) U., 1971—, prof. geology, 1981—, chmn. geology dept., 1981—; cons. Nat. Geographics, 1981. Commr., Va. Oil and Gas Conservation Commn., 1982—. NASA grantee, 1963-66, Petroleum Research Fund grantee, 1983-85, Jeffress Meml. Trust grantee, 1983-85. Fellow Geol. Soc. Am. (Penrose Research grantee 1972); mem. Am. Assn. Petroleum Geologists, Soc. Econ. Paleontologists and Mineralogists, Va. Acad. Sci. Methodist. Lodge: Lions. Contbr. articles to jours. in field. Home: 29 Round Hill Dr Radford VA 24141 Office: Radford Univ Geology Dept Radford VA 24142

WHITACRE, VERNON C., state senator; b. Capon Bridge; s. Boyd U. and Bessie O. Whitacre; m. Madeline Anderson, Sept. 3, 1935; 1 dau., Shelva J. Whitacre Switzer. Tchr., 1931-41; with W.Va. Tax Dept., 1941-57; former fed. land commr.; apptd. W.Va. Senate, 1982—, vice chmn. transp. com. Chmn. Hampshire County Democratic Exec. Com. (W.Va.). Office: W Va Senate Charleston WV 25305*

WHITACRE, WALTER EMMETT, aeronautical engineer; b. Detroit, Sept. 28, 1931; s. Arthur James and Reba Adeline (England) W.; B.S. in Aero. Engring., Purdue U., 1959, M.S. in Indsl. Mgmt., 1968; D.Sc. in Mgmt., Southeastern Inst. Tech., 1983; m. Donna Lee Longstreet, Nov. 26, 1950; children—Donn Arthur, Kirk Alexander, Chris Martin. Project engr. Lockheed Missiles & Space Co., 1959-64; aerospace engr. Marshall Space Flight Center, NASA, Huntsville, Ala., 1964—. Active Tenn. Valley council Boy Scouts Am., chmn. sea exploring com. Southeast Region; mem. nat. exploring com. Boy Scouts Am.; mem. adminstrv. bd. Latham United Methodist Ch. Recipient Valley Scouter award Boy Scouts Am., 1971, Silver Beaver award, 1974, Silver Antelope award, 1986, Spurgeon award, 1977, 85 Youth Group Conservation award Ala. Environ. Quality Assn., 1981; Service to Mankind award Huntsville Sertoma Club; 1981, Group Achievement award NASA, 1981, 85; Liberty Bell award Madison County Bar Assn., 1979; Scoutmaster award Nat. Eagle Scout Assn., Ala. chpt., 1983; God and Service award United Meth. Ch., 1985. Club: Elks. Home: 301 Belvidere Dr Huntsville AL 35803 Office: Marshall Space Flight Center Huntsville AL 35812

WHITAKER, GORDON PREVO, public administration educator; b. Terre Haute, Ind., July 18, 1943; s. Prevo Loren and Mary Gordon (Boling) W. A.B., Cornell Coll., 1965; M.A., Ind. U., 1970, Ph.D., 1972. Asst. prof. Bklyn. Coll., 1971-73; asst. prof. U. N.C., Chapel Hill, 1973-80, assoc. prof., dir. master of pub. adminstrn. program, 1980—. Author: Patterns of Metropolitan Policing, 1978; Basic Issues in Police Performance, 1982. Contbr. articles to profl. jours. Grantee NSF, 1974, 76, Nat. Inst. Justice, 1978, 80, 82. Mem. Am. Soc. Pub. Adminstrn. (chpt. pres. 1982-83), Am. Polit. Sci. Assn., Policy Studies Orgn., Assn. for Pub. Policy Analysis Mgmt., Law Soc. Assn. Office: U NC Dept Polit Sci Hamilton Hall Chapel Hill NC 27514

WHITAKER, JACK HARRY, microbiologist; b. Fairbanks, Alaska, Feb. 10, 1953; m. Connie Ervin. B.S. in Biology, East Tenn. State U., 1975, M.S. in Microbiology, 1982. Grad. asst. dept. microbiology East Tenn. State U. Coll. Health, 1977, student researcher dept. surgery, 1977-79, advanced research technician, 1979-82; clin. research assoc. Beecham Labs. div. Beecham, Inc., Bristol, Tenn., 1982—. Mem. Sigma Xi. Contbr. articles to profl. publs. Home: Route 3 Box 112 Jonesboro TN 37659

WHITAKER, JOHN KING, economist, educator; b. Burnley, Eng., Jan. 30, 1933; came to U.S., 1967; s. Ben and Mary (King) W.; m. Sally Bell Cross, Aug. 26, 1957; children—Ann Elizabeth, Jane Claire, David John. B.A. in Econs., U. Manchester, Eng., 1956; M.A., Johns Hopkins U., 1957; Ph.D., U. Cambridge, Eng., 1962. Lectr. U. Bristol, Eng., 1960-66, prof., 1966-69; vis. prof. U. Va., Charlottesville, 1967-68, prof. econs., 1969—, chmn. dept. econs., 1979-82. Author and editor: The Early Economic Writings of Alfred Marshall, 1867-1890, 2 vols., 1975. Mem. History Econs. Soc. (v.p. 1982-83, pres. 1983-84), Am. Econ. Assn., Royal Econ. Soc. Home: 1615 Yorktown Dr Charlottesville VA 22901 Office: Dept Econs U Va Rouss Hall Charlottesville VA 22901

WHITAKER, R. SCOTT, architect; b. Frankfort, Ky., Dec. 1, 1945; s. Martin Vanbruen and Cecilia Bell (Florian) W.; B.Arch., U. Ky., 1971; m. Wendy Lou Plath, Apr. 29, 1977; 00040, 1983—; dau., Holly Paige. With Brighton Engring., 1964-68, Hugg, Blakeman & Carter, 1968-69, Burris & Thompson, 1969-72, Luckett & Farley, 1972-74; architect, chief plan reviewer, div. bldgs. and grounds Ky. Dept. Edn., 1974; architect L. Wayne Tune, 1974-76, William Johnson & Assos., 1976-77; sr. architect, project mgr., adminstrv. asst. to pres. Luckett & Farley, Louisville, 1977-83; ptnr. Whitaker, 1983—; designer Ky. Democratic Hdqrs., Samuel V. Noe Middle Sch., Strickler Hall of U. Louisville, U.H.T. Milk Plant. Mem. scholarship rev. com. U. Ky. Sch. Architecture, 1975; leader Girl Scouts U.S.A.; youth counselor United Methodist Christ Ch. Recipient C.A. Coleman, Jr., honor award, 1971. Mem. So. Sch. Plant Mgrs. Assn., U. Ky. Sch. Architecture Alumni Assn. (past pres. Class 1971). Democrat. Office: Whitaker Architects Engrs and Interior Designers 4500 Upper River Rd Louisville KY 40222

WHITBECK, DOLORES IRENE, nurse; b. Nassawadox, Va., Aug. 11, 1944; d. Harry Cleveland, Jr. and Dolores June (Huether) Tatum; m. David Lamar Whitbeck, Aug. 10, 1963; children—Lisa Renee, Stacey Michelle, David Lamar. Diploma, Norfolk Gen. Hosp., 1965. Registered nurse, Va. Staff nurse recovery room Norfolk Gen. Hosp., Va., 1965-66, nursery, 1966-68; head nurse central supply Children's Hosp. of King's Daus., Norfolk, 1968—. Mem. Internat. Assn. Hosp. Central Service Mgmt., Va. Nurses Assn. Baptist. Avocations: bowling; dancing; church activities. Home: 2113 Sparrow Rd Chesapeake VA 23325 Office: Children's Hosp of King's Daus 800 W Olney Rd Norfolk VA 23507

WHITBECK, ELAINE ESTHER, lawyer; b. Fayetteville, N.C., Sept. 13, 1954; d. Robert Earl and Joanne Lee (Barber) W.; m. Lonnie Eugene Lindsey, Jan. 15, 1982. B.A. with highest honors, U. Va., 1976, J.D., 1979. Bar: Tex. 1979, U.S. Ct. Appeals (5th cir.) 1979, U.S. Dist. Ct. (no. dist.) Tex. 1979. Protocol asst. to def. secs. Dept. Def., Washington, 1975-76; assoc. Vial, Hamilton, Koch, Tubb, Knox & Stradley, Dallas, 1979-82; dir. legal ops., asst. sec. Mary Kay Cosmetics, Inc., Dallas, 1982—. Author: Securities Regulation, 1982; also articles. Counselor Dallas Rape Crisis Ctr.; participant Leadership Tex.; active Dallas Women's Polit. Caucus. Echols scholar U. Va., 1973—; recipient Outstanding Women of Dallas award, 1985, Leadership Tex. award, 1984. Mem. Assn. Trial Lawyers Am., Dallas Bar Assn., Tex. Bar Assn., ABA, Dallas Assn. Trial Attys., Dallas Assn. Young Lawyers, Nat. Orgn. Female Execs., Direct Selling Assn. (lawyers council), Am. Soc. Corp. Secs., Inter-Am. Bar Assn., Union Internationale des Avocats, Am. Corp. Counsel Assn., U. Va. Alumni Club. Club: Las Colinas Sports. Home: 2416 Peachtree Plano TX 75074 Office: Mary Kay Cosmetics Inc 8787 Stemmons Freeway Dallas TX 75247

WHITE, ARLYNN QUINTON, JR., marine science educator, consultant; b. Norfolk, Va., Jan. 17, 1946; s. Arlynn Quinton and Mazie Alice (Herrington) W.; m. Susan Hite, June 16, 1958. B.S., N.C. Wesleyan Coll., 1968; M.S., U. Va., 1972; Ph.D., U. S.C., 1976. Research asst. U. S.C., 1972-74; asst. prof. biology Jacksonville U. (Fla.), 1976-83, assoc. prof. biology and marine sci., 1983—; assoc. dir. Environ. Ctr., 1980—, Charter Marine Sci. Ctr., 1982—. Mem. adminstrv. bd. Arlington United Meth. Ch., 1978—, chmn. council on ministries, 1981-83; pres. Shadowood Community Assn., 1981-82; mem. citizen adv. bd. Coastal Zone Mgmt. Planning Bd., City of Jacksonville, 1977-80, mem. indsl. site rev. com., 1978; mem. artificial reef adv. panel Fla. Sea Grant, 1981—, adv. bd. marine adv. program, 1982—; mem. marine edn. inst. adv. bd. Fla. 4-H, 1982-83. Served with U.S. Army, 1968-70. Recipient Nat. Conservation award DAR, 1980; Disting. Alumnus award N.C. Wesleyan Coll., 1982; named Outstanding Young Man of Jacksonville, Jacksonville Jaycees, 1981; grantee NSF, 1971, 79-82, Explorers Club, 1974-75, Sigma Xi, 1976, Port of Jacksonville, 1982-83. Mem. Am. Soc. Zoologists, Am. Inst. Biol. Scis., Estuarine Research Fedn. (newsletter editor 1980-82), AAAS, N.Am. Benthological Soc., Nat. Marine Edn. Assn., Crustacean Soc., Southeastern Estuarine Research Soc. (sec.-treas. 1979-81), Fla. Marine Edn. Assn., Jacksonville Shell Club (pres. 1980-81), Sigma Xi (pres. 1984-85). Democrat. Methodist. Contbr. articles to profl. jours. Office: Dept Biology Jacksonville U Jacksonville FL 32211

WHITE, BARBARA ANN, advertising agency account executive; b. Indpls., Dec. 2, 1957; d. Raymond H., Jr., and Patricia R. (Chamberlain) White. A.B. in Telecommunications, Ind. U., 1980. Account exec., sta. WLPR-FM, Mobile, Ala., 1980-81, sta. WKRG-AM, Mobile, 1981, sta. WKSJ-FM, Mobile, 1981-82, J.H. Lewis Advt. Agy., Mobile, 1982—. Dir. publicity Friends of WHIL Pub. Radio, 1983; dir. promotion Dauphin Way Lodge Rehab. Center, 1983; maj. United Way campaign, 1982. State of Ind. acad. scholar, 1976; recipient Award of Excellence, Dixon Hild Coalition Advt. Agy., 1979. Mem. Am. Mktg. Assn. (pres. Gulf Coast Chpt. 1983-84), Advt. Fedn. Greater Mobile, Exec. Women's Forum, Nat. Hon. Broadcasting Soc. (pres. Ind. U. chpt. 1979-80, Mem. of Year). Lodge: Job's Daus. (hon. queen 1974). Home: 124 Golf Terr Daphne AL 36526 Office: 105 N Jackson Mobile AL 36601

WHITE, BRUCE N., safety engineer; b. Columbus, Ga., Mar. 26, 1952; s. Clarence H. and Eleanor (Lindsey) W. A.A., U. Louisville, 1974, B.S. in Police Adminstrn., 1976, M.S. in Community Devel., 1978. Patrolman, Jefferson County Police Dept., Louisville, 1973-76, burglary detective, 1977-80; security shift supr. Ford Ky. Truck Plant, Louisville, 1980-81, fire protection engr., 1981-83, safety engr., 1983—. Sunday Sch. tchr. Green Castle Baptist Ch., Louisville, 1983. Mem. Am. Soc. Safety Engrs., Nat. Assn. Chiefs Police, E. End Democrat Club, NAACP, Louisville Urban League, Kappa Alpha Psi. Avocations: tennis; racquetball; softball. Office: Ford Ky Truck Plant PO Box 32310 Louisville KY 40232

WHITE, CARL MULLINS, consultant; b. Salem, Ark., Sept. 29, 1907; s. Robert Lee and Mary Elizabeth (Mullins) W.; m. Helen Margaret Mylrea, Mar. 30, 1929; 1 dau., Margaret Elizabeth Cordray. B.S., Northwestern U., 1931; M.A., U. Tulsa, 1955; postgrad. Okla. State U., 1930-31, 32, Corpus Christi Coll., Oxford (Eng.) U., 1945, U. Tulsa, 1948-55. Traffic clk. Stanolind Pipe Line Co. (later Service Pipe Line Co.), 1935-42, aviation coordinator, 1947-57, supr. tng. specialist, 1957-65; staff devel. cons., tchr. human relations and supervision Okla. State Tech., Okmulgee, 1965-66; mgmt. and tng. cons. Pub. Service Co. Okla., Tulsa, 1966-72; owner Orgn. and Mgmt. Devel. Services, Tulsa, 1972-84; instr. evening divs. U. Tulsa, Okla. State U., Tulsa Jr. Coll., 1962-83. Mem. adminstrv. bd. First United Methodist Ch.; past bd. mem. Girl Scouts U.S. Served to lt. col. USAF, 1942-47; ETO. Mem. Am. Soc. Tng. and Devel. (life; past pres. Tulsa chpt.), Am. Soc. Personnel Adminstrs., Tulsa Personnel Assn. (hon. life), Res. Officers Assn. (life), Ret. Officers Assn. (life), Nat. Mgmt. Assn., Am. Assn. Ret. Persons, Tulsa C. of C., Amoco Alumni Assn. (co-founder), Northwestern U. Alumni Assn., U. Tulsa Alumni Assn. Democrat. Author: People, Productivity and Growth, 1966; contbr. articles to profl. jours. Home and Office: 4940 S Columbia Ave Tulsa OK 74105

WHITE, CHARLES AUGUSTINE, JR., government official; b. Richmond, Va., Feb. 19, 1949; s. Charles Augustine and Shirley Bernice (Jones) W.; m. Brenda Ruth Wells, June 4, 1971 (div. 1975); m. Ruth Ann Wyche, Sept. 5, 1976; children—Tamara Nicole, Charles Augustine III. B.A., Shaw U., 1971. Lic. pvt. pilot. Employee relations specialist Dept. of Army, Ft. Belvoir, Va., 1971-78, D.C. Govt., 1978-79; personnel mgmt. specialist Def. Communications Agy., Washington, 1979—. Served with Army N.G., 1971—. Mem. Seaplane Pilots Assn., Aircraft Owners and Pilots Assn., D.C. N.G. Officers Assn., Kappa Alpha Psi.

WHITE, CHRISTOPHER J., educator; b. Worcester, Mass., Aug. 14, 1945; s. James Joseph and Marion (Logan) W.; m. Mary Margaret Macklin; children—Megan, Maura, Mathew. B.S. in Social Studies, Mass. State Coll., 1968; M.Ed., U. Va., 1972. Guidance counsellor Fairfax County pub. schs., Va., 1968—; pres. Potomac Valley Homes, Alexandria, Va., 1978—. Pres. bd. dirs. Mt. Vernon on the Potomac Citizens Assn., Alexandria, 1985-86. Mem. NEA, Va. Edn. Assn., Fairfax Edn. Assn. Republican. Roman Catholic. Avocations: Running; triathletics. Home: 9414 Mt Vernon Cir Alexandria VA 22309 Office: Potomac Valley Homes Inc 108 S Columbus St Suite 201 Alexandria VA 22314

WHITE, DANIEL BOWMAN, lawyer; b. Charlotte, N.C., Apr. 12, 1948; s. William Garner and Elizabeth (Bowman) W.; m. Sarah deSaussure Peterson, May 29, 1976; 1 child, Bentley Parker. A.B., Davidson Coll., 1970; J.D., U. S.C., 1976. Bar: S.C. 1976, U.S. Dist. Ct. S.C. 1976, U.S. Ct. Appeals (4th cir.) 1978. Ptnr. Rainey, Britton, Gibbes & Clarkson, P.A., Greenville, S.C., 1976—. Comments editor U. S.C. Law Rev., 1975-76. Commr. Greenville Zoning Commn., 1980—. Served to 1st lt. U.S. Army, 1971-73. Decorated Bronze Star; Dana scholar Davidson Coll., N.C., 1966-70. Mem. Def. Research Inst., Nat. Assn. R.R. Trial Counsel, Greenville Young Lawyers Club (pres. 1981). Episcopalian. Home: 104 Garden Trail Greenville SC 29605 Office: Rainey Britton Gibbes & Clarkson PA 330 E Coffee St Greenville SC 29603

WHITE, EDWARD ALFRED, lawyer; b. Elizabeth, N.J., Nov. 23, 1934. B.S. in Indsl. Engring., U. Mich., 1957, J.D., 1963. Bar: Fla. 1963, U.S. Supreme Ct. 1976; cert. civil trial lawyer Fla Bar, Assoc. Jennings, Watts, Clarke & Hamilton, Jacksonville, Fla., 1963-66, ptnr., 1966-69; ptnr. Wayman & White, Jacksonville, 1969-72; sole practice, Jacksonville, 1972—; mem. clients security fund com. Fla. Bar, 1975-79, mem. aviation law com. Fla. Bar, 1976—, chmn., 1979-81, bd. govs., 1984—. Mem. Jacksonville Bar Assn. (chmn. legal ethics com. 1975-76, bd. govs. 1976-78, pres. 1979-80), ABA, Fla. Bar Assn., Assn. Trial Lawyers Am., Acad. Fla. Trial Lawyers (diplomate), Lawyer-Pilots Bar Assn., Nat. Bd. Trial Advocacy (cert. trial lawyer), Am. Judicature Soc., Southeastern Admiralty Law Inst. (dir. 1982—). Home: 1959 Largo Rd Jacksonville FL 32207 Office: 902 Barnett Bank Bldg Jacksonville FL 32202

WHITE, ETHYLE HERMAN (MRS. S. ROY WHITE), artist; b. San Antonio, Apr. 10, 1904; d. Ferdinand and Minnie (Simmang) Herman; ed. pvt. schs., instrs.; m. S. Roy White, Mar. 3, 1924 (dec.); children—De Lois Eileen (Mrs. William Marion Mohrle), Patsyruth (Mrs. Henry Wheeler). Exhibited numerous one-man, group shows, Tex.; represented pub. collections in U.S., pvt. collections in Switzerland, Germany, Sweden. Del. Internat. Com. Centro Studi E. Scambi Internationali. Mem. Anahuac Fine Arts Group, San Antonio, Beaumont, Galveston, Houston art leagues, Daus. Republic Tex., UDC, Pastel Soc. Tex., Watercolor Soc., Nat. League Am. Pen Women. Episcopalian. Mem. Order Eastern Star. Clubs: Fine Arts (Anahuac); Artist and Craftsmen (Dallas). Author, illustrator: Arabella. Author: Poet's Hour. Home: PO Box 176 Anahuac TX 77514

WHITE, FAYE ANN, social worker, counselor; b. Birmingham, Ala., Feb. 1, 1952; d. S.L. and Ophelia W. B.A., Miles Coll., 1974; M.A., U. Ala., 1982. Claims clk. Ala. Dept. Indsl. Relations, Ensley, 1975-76; lab. asst. U. Ala.-Birmingham, 1976-77; research interviewer, 1977-79; social worker, counselor Housing Authority of Birmingham, 1980—. Mem. Prejudice Reduction Task Force, Birmingham, 1985. Mem. Am. Assn. Counseling and Devel., Ala. Conf. Social Work, Ala. Gerontol. Soc., Alpha Kappa Alpha. Democrat. Baptist. Avocations: Reading. Home: 1114 Coosa St Birmingham AL 35234 Office: Housing Authority Birmingham Dist 1826 3d Ave S Birmingham AL 35233

WHITE, GERALD RAYMOND, human factors consultant; b. Spencer, Okla., Oct. 16, 1920; s. Willis F. and Reeda M. (Bone) W.; m. Ruth L. McCoy, 1939 (dec. Nov. 1977); children—Gerald Leland, George Lavon, Laura Lou; m. Ethel Lee Uselton, 1979. Grad. Lighthouse Bible Coll., Ill., 1943; B.S. in Journalism, East Tex. State U., 1963, M.S., 1967, M.S. in Psychology, 1971.

Ordained to ministry Gen. Council Assemblies of God, 1942. Nat. Sunday sch. rep. Assemblies of God, Springfield, Mo., 1949-53; sr. pastor 1st Assembly of God, Billings, Mont., 1953-56; supr. tech. writers E-Systems Inc., Greenville, Tex., 1956-64, human factors/systems safety engr., 1965-75, engrng. specialist E-Systems, 1981-85; ret., 1985; human factors cons., 1985—; pastor, minister human relations Assembly of God, Garland, Tex., 1975-84; psychol. cons. Teen Challenge, Dallas, 1977-81; engring. cons. def. industry, 1975-82. Chmn. sch. bd. North Buckingham Christian Sch., Garland, 1981-85. Mem. Human Factors Soc., Am. Soc. Safety Engrs., System Safety Soc., Christian Assn. Psychol. Studies, Soc. Profl. Journalists. Avocations: golf; music; art. Home: 7309 Lakeshore Rowlett TX 75088

WHITE, GERALD ROBERT, industrial applications consultant; b. Stillwater, Okla., May 28, 1947; s. Perry Leonard and Roberta (Treadway) W.; m. Vicki Ann White, July 15, 1973 (dec. 1980); 1 child, Gerald Arthur; m. Sandra R. White, Sept. 30, 1983. B.S. in Chem. Engring., N.Mex. State U., 1971, M.S., 1976; postgrad. in chem. engring. Tulane U. Polyolefin research engr., Dow Chem. Co., Freeport, Tex., 1971-74; mgmt. trainee Mobil Chem. Co., Temple, Tex., 1974-75; process control engr. Setpoint, Houston, 1977-78; sr. process control engr. Biles & Assocs., Houston, 1978-80; pres. GRTW Inc., Beaumont, Tex., 1980-82; sr. indsl. applied cons. Foxboro Co., Houston, 1982—; mng. ptnr. BSW Trust, Houston, 1979—; dir., chief exec. officer GRTW Inc., Beaumont, 1980—; cons., lectr. in field. Author: (poem) A Dogs Life, 1962 (1st Place N.Mex. Poets Assn. 1963), (short story) The Dating Complex (1st Place N.Mex. Writers Guild 1964); artist stained glass works; photographer mag. covers; patentee in chemistry. Charter mem. Com. to Re-elect Reagan, 1983—; dir. Chelford Mcpl. Water Dist., Houston, 1985—. EPA research grantee, 1975, NSF grantee, 1977. Mem. Instrument Soc. Am. (keynote speaker 1980—, session chmn. 1985, program developer 1986), Am. Inst. Chem. Engrs. (lectr. 1977—), Soc. Mfg. Engrs., IEEE, Nat. Speakers Assn., Statue of Liberty Found. (charter), Houston Mus. Natural Sci., Contemporary Arts Mus. Houston, Mensa. Republican. Methodist. Home: 5155 Cripple Creek Houston TX 77017 Office: Foxboro Co 6440 SW Freeway Houston TX 77074

WHITE, GERALDINE POTTS, nurse; b. Bradenton, Fla., Jan. 20, 1941; d. Will and Burnell (Potts) Williams; A.A. in Nursing, Manatee Jr. Coll., Bradenton, 1970; B.S. in Psychology, Barry Coll., Miami, Fla., 1975; B.S. in Nursing, Fla. Internat. U., 1978, M.S., 1980; postgrad. Nova U., 1981—; m. Gladstone Joseph White, July 15, 1973. Dental asst., 1959-63; practical nurse Sarasota (Fla.) Meml. Hosp., 1964-69, registered nurse, 1970-72; asst. head nurse surg. ICU, North Shore Hosp., Miami, 1973-75; psychiat. supr. Highland Park Gen. Hosp., Miami, 1975-77; dept. head health occupations, dir. Miami Lakes practical nursing program Dade County Public Schs., Miami, 1977—; adj. prof. nursing Miami Dade Community Coll. Hartman scholar, 1975. Mem. Am. Nurses Assn., Fla. Nurses Assn., Nat. League Nursing, Am. Heart Assn., Nat. Assn. Female Execs., Fla. Notary Public Soc., Fla. Vocat. Assn., Health Occupations Educators Assn. Fla., South Fla. Consortium Nursing Edn., NAACP, Fla. Bus. and Profl. Women's Assn., United Tchrs. Dade County, Am. Soc. Notaries, Barry U. Alumni Assn., Fla. Internat. U. Alumni Assn., Kappa Delta Pi, Epsilon Pi Tau. Methodist. Club: Ebony (Sarasota). Home: 15120 SW 105th Ave Miami FL 33176 Office: 5780 NW 158th St Miami FL 33014

WHITE, JAMES CHRISTOPHER (CHRIS), accountant, management firm executive; b. Tulsa, Sept. 28, 1946; s. Loftin Ellette and Ruby Stuart (Blackmore) W.; m. Ann Merdese Morton, June 15, 1968; children—Theresa Ann, Bradford Peter, B.S.B.A., in Acctg., Tulsa U., 1968; M.B.A. in Mgmt., Ind. U., 1970. C.P.A. With Arthur Young & Co., 1970—, mgr., Tulsa, 1975-79, prin., 1979-82, ptnr. mgmt. services dept., 1982—, nat. practice dir. for petroleum industry cons. Bd. dirs. Youth Services of Tulsa County, treas., 1980-82, 83-85, chmn., 1982-83. Served to 1st lt. USAF, 1970-71. Mem. Am. Inst. C.P.A.s, Okla. Soc. C.P.A.s, Planning Forum. Republican. Presbyterian. Clubs: Tulsa, Tulsa Country, Golf of Okla. Office: Arthur Young 4300 One Williams Ctr Tulsa OK 74101

WHITE, JAMES EDMUND, architect, educator; b. Anson, Tex., Feb. 21, 1933; s. Victor Philemon and Lucy Alice (Baker) W.; m. Wanda Sue Sandlin, Aug. 6, 1970. B.Arch., U. Tex., 1957; M.S., Tex. Tech U., 1973. Registered architect, Tex. Draftsman, F.C. Olds., Abilene, Tex., 1957; draftsman, ptnr. Peters and Fields, Odessa, Tex., 1962-71; mem. faculty Tex. Tech U., Lubbock, 1971—; pres. White Assocs., Lubbock, 1971—; mem. intern devel. com. Nat. Council Archtl. Registrations Bd., Washington, 1984—, regional dir. Intern Devel. Program; Served with USAF, 1957-61. Mem. AIA (sec. Lubbock chpt. 1974, 1977, treas. chpt. 1979), Tex. Soc. Architects (state coordinator intern devel. 1982-84, bd. dirs. 1986—), Tau Kappa Epsilon (chpt. advisor 1981—). Democrat. Methodist. Avocations: painting; golf. Office: White Assocs AIA Architects 1220 Broadway Suite 1308 Lubbock TX 79401

WHITE, JAMES FILE, physician; b. Columbia, S.C., May 26, 1934; B.S., U. S.C., 1955; M.D., Duke U., 1959; M.S., State U. Iowa, 1965. Intern State U. Iowa, Iowa City, 1959-60; resident in otolaryngology, 1961-63, chief resident in otolaryngology, 1963-64; resident in gen. surgery VA Hosp., Denver, 1960-61; chief otolaryngology and ophthalmology U.S. Naval Hosp., Beaufort, S.C., 1964-66; practice medicine specializing in ear, nose and throat, Columbia, 1966—; vice chief of staff Providence Hosp., Columbia, 1981, chief of staff, 1982; cons. Lost Chord Club, Columbia, 1966—, S.C. Dept. Vocat. Rehab., 1970—, S.C. Dept. Health and Environ. Control, 1975—; mem. exec. council dept. communicative disorders and Projece Scooter, U. S.C., 1977-82, mem. adv. bd., 1982—. Bd. dirs. Babcock Ctr. for Mentally Retarded, 1970-72. HEW grantee, 1982-83; NIH grantee, 1982-85. Mem. S.C. Speech and Hearing Assn. (honors 1983), S.C. Soc. Otolaryngology (pres. 1983-84), S.C. Oncology Soc., Am. Assn. Cosmetic Surgeons, Am. Acad. Facial Plastic and Reconstructive Surgery, Triological Soc., Am. Soc. Head and Neck Surgery, ACS, Columbia Med. Soc., AMA, S.C. Med. Soc., S.C.-N.C. Soc. Otolaryngology and Maxillo Facial Surgery, S.C. Soc. Otolaryngology-Head and Neck Surgery (pres. 1984-85), Am. Acad. Otolaryngology. Contbr. papers and articles to profl. lit. Office: 1639 Brabham St Columbia SC 29204

WHITE, JAMES RICHARD, real estate broker, consultant; b. Denison, Tex., Apr. 8, 1941; s. Basil Lowell and Neoma Rossi (Saunders) W.; m. Mitty Kay Smith, Dec. 15, 1962; children—James R., Gregory B. B.S. in Bible, Abilene Christian Coll., 1965. Lic. Realtor, Tex. Successively student salesman, field mgr., dist. sales mgr. Southwestern Pub. Co., Nashville, Tenn., 1959-67; tchr. San Antonio Pub. Schs., 1963-66; exec. dir. YMCA, San Antonio, 1971-73; real estate broker, cons., exec. mgr. James R. White Assocs., Austin, Dallas, Midland and San Antonio Tex., 73—; owner, pres. Computer Search, Inc., Austin, Art Buyer's Alliance. Austin; cons. and tchr. various bus. groups and individuals in real estate and computer related activities throughout Tex. Bd. dirs. San Antonio YMCA, 1975-76; com. mem. Young Life, Midland, Tex., 1980-81; mem. Leadership Midland, 1980-81; fund-raising leader Abilene Christian U. Alumni Assn., 1976-78; coordinator various youth related activities, 1962-81. Recipient numerous sales and mgmt. awards Southwestern Pub. Co., 1959-67; sales and mgmt. awards in real estate, 1973-82. Mem. Austin Bd. Realtors, Tex. Assn. Realtors, Nat. Assn. Realtors, Realtors Nat. Mktg. Inst. Democrat. Office: PO Box 162017 Austin TX 78716

WHITE, JAMES WILSON, political science educator; b. Cleve., Aug. 22, 1941; s. Wilbur Wallace and Edwarda Jane Curran (Williams) W.; m. Marion Lewis Sullivan, Jan. 7, 1967; children—James V.B., Erin S., Christopher D. A.B. with highest honors, Princeton U., 1964; M.A., Stanford U., 1965, Ph.D., 1969. Prof. polit. sci. U. N.C., Chapel Hill, 1969—; Am. adv. com. Japan Found.; dir. N.C. Japan Ctr., Assn. Asian Studies. Woodrow Wilson fellow, 1964; NDEA fellow, 1964-67; grantee NSF, Ford Found., Social Sci. Research Council, Japan Found., Fulbright Commn. Mem. Am. Polit. Sci. Assn., Assn. Asian Studies, Internat. House Japan. Presbyterian. Club: Orange County Fish and Wildlife (Hillsborough, N.C.). Author: The Sokagakkai and Mass Society, 1970; Social Change and Community Politics in Urban Japan, 1976; The Urban Impact of Internal Migration, 1979; Migration in Metropolitan Japan, 1982. Home: 105 Ridge Ln Chapel Hill NC 27514 Office: Polit Sci Dept U NC Chapel Hill NC 27514

WHITE, JOHN CHARLES, history educator; b. Washington, Apr. 14, 1939; s. Bennett Sexton, Jr. and Mary Elizabeth (Wildman) W.; B.A. magna cum laude, Washington and Lee U., Lexington, Va., 1960; M.A., Duke U., 1962, Ph.D., 1964; m. Carolyn Ruth West, July 6, 1963. Mem. faculty U. Ala., Huntsville, 1967—, prof. history, 1976—, chmn. dept., 1970—; dir., sec.-treas. Consortium on Revolutionary Europe, 1979-86. Vice chmn. Constn. Hall Park Bd., 1980-82, chmn., 1982-84; bd. dirs. Ala. Humanities Found., 1985—. Served to capt. USAR, 1964-67. Recipient award of merit Ala. Historic Commn., 1978; Robert E. Lee scholar, 1956-60; So. fellow, 1960-63. Mem. Nat. Trust Historic Preservation, Ala. Hist. Soc., Ala. Assn. Historians (pres. 1978-80), Huntsville Lit. Assn., L'Alliance Française Huntsville (pres. 1970), Phi Kappa Phi, Phi Alpha Theta, Phi Sigma Iota, Omicron Delta Kappa. Club: Huntsville Rotary. Author articles, revs. in field; editor Proc. on Revolutionary Europe, 1977, 81. Home: 220 Longwood Dr Huntsville AL 35801 Office: UAH Huntsville AL 35899

WHITE, JOHN POSTON, architect, educator; b. Anson, Tex., Feb. 21, 1933; s. Victor Philemon and Lucy Alice (Baker) W. B.Arch., U. Tex., 1957; M.Arch., U. Nebr., 1973. Registered architect, Tex., Ariz., N.Mex. Architect Peters & Fields, AIA, Odessa, Tex., 1962-72; draftsman Bahr Vermeer Haecker, Lincoln, Nebr., 1972-73; asst. prof. Tex. Tech U., Lubbock, 1973-77, assoc. prof. architecture, 1977—; prin. White Assocs., AIA Architects, Lubbock, 1975—; project supr. Hist. Am. Bldgs. Survey, summers 1974-85. Served with USAF, 1957-61. Mem. AIA, Tex. Soc. Architects (chmn. hist. resources com. 1984), AIA (treas. Lubbock chpt. 1985), Lubbock Heritage Soc., Tau Sigma Delta, Delta Chi (chpt. adviser 1982—). Democrat. Methodist. Home: 2430 24th St Lubbock TX 79411 Office: White Assocs AIA Architects 1220 Broadway Suite 1308 Lubbock TX 79401

WHITE, JOHN W., mathematical statistician; b. Reading, Pa., July 24, 1941; s. Jason Whitney and Margaret Josephine (Smith) W.; m. Sally Ann Collins, Mar. 31, 1965; children—John W., Richard, Rebecca, Elizabeth. B.S., Ga. State U., 1963; M.S., U. Notre Dame, 1967; Ph.D., So. Methodist U., 1976. Instr., U. Notre Dame, South Bend, Ind., 1967-68, Murray State U., Ky., 1968-72, So. Meth. U., Dallas, 1972-76; asst. prof. Va. Tech. Inst., Blacksburg, 1976-79; math. statistician Ctrs. for Disease Control, Atlanta, Ga., 1980—. Contbr. articles to profl. jours. Vol., Heart Fund, Atlanta, 1984. Recipient Cert. of Teaching Excellence, Va. Tech. Inst., 1977. Cert. of Superior Work Performance, USPHS, 1980, unit award USPHS, 1985. Mem. Am. Statis. Assn. Democrat. Methodist. Club: Drayton Woods Recreation (Tucker, Va.) (v.p. 1984—). Avocations: tennis; bridge; reading. Home: 1537 Idlehour Way Tucker GA 30084 Office: Ctrs for Disease Control 1600 Clifton Rd Atlanta GA 30333

WHITE, JOYCE FIELDER, educator; b. Cochran, Ga., Mar. 24, 1933; d. Harley Leslie and Christine (Scott) Fielder; B.S., Ga. State U., 1963, postgrad., 1980—; M.A.T., Emory U., 1970; Ed.S., U. Ga., 1977; Ph.D., Ga. State U., 1984; m. Aubrey Hoyt White, Apr., 1951; children—Phillip, Timothy, Elizabeth, Susan. Bench electronics mechanic Lockheed Aircraft, Marietta, Ga., 1951-56; buyer and supr. non-prescription drugs E. Marietta Drug Co., 1956-63; tchr. math. Marietta High Sch., 1963-65; tchr. math. East Cobb Middle Sch., 1965-70; math. supr. k-12 Cobb County Bd. Edn., 1970-81, Title I project writer, coordinator, 1974-75; pvt. practice ednl. cons., 1982—; part-time math. instr. So. Tech. Coll., 1980-82, instr., 1982—. Mem. St. Joseph Sch. Bd. Edn., 1977-79. NSF grantee, 1967-70. Mem. Assn. Supervision and Curriculum Devel., Nat. Council Tchrs. Math, Ga. Council Tchrs. Math, Metro Math Club, Cobb County Adminstrv. Assn., Ga. Council Suprs. Math., U. Ga. Alumni Assn., Ga. State Alumni Assn., Emory U. Alumni Assn., Delta Kappa Gamma, Mu Rho Sigma. Club: Eastern Star. Home: 2825 Okawana Dr NE Marietta GA 30067 Office: 121 Clay St Marietta GA 30060

WHITE, KATHY RUTH, hospital pharmacist; b. Russellville, Ala., May 5, 1954; d. Bobby J. and Terrell J. (Hargett) Grissom; m. Edward C. White Jr., Aug. 12, 1979. Student NW Ala. State Jr. Coll., 1972-74; B.S. in Pharmacy, Auburn U., 1978. Pharmacy intern Lanier Hosp., Langdale, Ala., 1975-78, staff pharmacist, 1978, asst. dir. pharmacy, 1978-79; pharmacy supr. Flowers Hosp., Dothan, Ala., 1979-81, dir. pharmacy, 1981—; cons. Immediate Care Ctr., Dothan, 1982—. Mem. Ala. Pharmacy Assn., Am. Soc. Hosp. Pharmacists, Wiregrass Pharm. Assn. Democrat. Home: 10 Camelot Apt Dothan AL 36303 Office: Flowers Hosp 3228 W Main St Dothan AL 36301

WHITE, KENNETH JULIUS, pharmacist; b. Ozark, Ala., July 26, 1945; s. Eli David and Irene (Silverman) W.; m. Glenda Carol Sizemore, Oct. 15, 1977; children—Janice, Michael. B.S.A., U. Ga., 1967, B.S.Ph., 1969. Registered pharmacist, Ga., Fla. Pharmacist Reed Drugs, Atlanta, 1969-72, Springhill Pharmacy, Marietta, Ga., 1972-73, Rexall Drugs, Naples, Fla., 1973-75; pharmacist, mgr. K-Mart Corp., Marietta, Ga., 1975—. Recipient Conchologists of Am. award, 1981. Mem. Ga. Shell Club (pres. 1979-81, corr. sec. 1984-85, Outstanding Exhibit award 1983), Kappa Psi (pres. U. Ga. chpt. 1969). Avocations: collecting seashells; speaking to clubs and sch. children. Home: 2587 Ballew Ct Marietta GA 30062 Office: K-Mart 7184 4269 Roswell Rd Marietta GA 30062

WHITE, K(ING) PRESTON, JR., systems engineering educator, researcher, consultant; b. Port Chester, N.Y., Dec. 31, 1948; s. K. Preston and Rosamond (Conley) W.; m. Charlotte Rebekah O'Cain, Apr. 9, 1977; 1 son, William Preston. B.S.E., Duke U., 1970, M.S., 1972, Ph.D., 1976. Grad. teaching and research asst. Duke U., Durham, N.C., 1970-75; asst. prof. dept. operations research and systems analysis Poly. Inst. N.Y., Bklyn., 1975-77; asst. prof. dept. mech. engring., dept. engring. and pub. policy Carnegie-Mellon U., Pitts., 1977-79; asst. prof. systems engring. U. Va., Charlottesville, 1979-85, assoc. prof., 1985—; researcher, cons. in field; jour. referee. Mem. Ops. Research Soc. Am., Am. Soc. for Engring. Edn., IEEE, Systems, Man, and Cybernetics Soc., Control Systems Soc., Soc. Automotive Engrs., Tau Beta Pi, Omega Rho (charter), Sigma Xi, Pi Tau Sigma. Contbr. articles to profl. jours., chpts. to books; U.S. editor Internat. Abstracts in Ops. Research; contbr. to Ency. of Systems and Control. Home: Route 1 Box 132 Shipman VA 22971 Office: Dept Systems Engring Thornton Hall U Va Charlottesville VA 22901

WHITE, LEON SAMUEL, college administrator; b. West Palm Beach, Fla., Mar. 31, 1946; s. Edward Julius and Carmeta Francis (Ferguson) W.; m. Anne Fryer, Sept. 29, 1969; children—Nigel, Kanika Pele. B.S., Tuskegee Inst., 1969, M.Ed., 1973; Ph.D., Ohio State U., 1976; cert. in journalism Columbia U., 1970. Research assoc. Ohio State U., Columbus, 1974-76; coordinator counseling St. Augustine's Coll., Raleigh, N.C., 1976-77, dean of students, 1977-81; dean of students Savannah State Coll., Ga., 1981-84; vice chancellor, student affairs Elizabeth City State U., N.C., 1984—. Psychol. cons. Franklin County Drug Treatment Program, Columbus, Ohio, 1975-76; mentor Boys Club of Raleigh, 1978-81; vol. counselor Tidelands Community Mental Health, Savannah, 1982-84. Contbr. articles to profl. jours. Tuskegee Inst. scholar, 1963, grad. internship, 1971. Mem. So. Assn. Coll. Student Personnel, Nat. Assn. Personnel Workers, Am. Assn. Counseling and Devel., Phi Delta Kappa. Democrat. Methodist. Avocations: writing; gardening; swimming; tennis; running. Home: 1511 College St Elizabeth City NC 27909 Office: Elizabeth City State U PO Box 773 Elizabeth City NC 27909

WHITE, LEONARD RAYMOND, optometrist; b. Cin., May 14, 1920; s. Raymond Harris and Sarah (Schear) W.; m. Hadassah Ruth Frankel, Apr. 26, 1944 (dec. Aug. 1983); children—Bernard Henry, Harris Herman, Raymond Magnus, Sidney Gordon. O.D., Ill. Coll. Optometry, 1948. Practice optometry, Fort Worth, 1948—; guest lectr. Tarleton State U., Stephenville, Tex., 1974—. Served as pharmacists's mate 1st class USN, 1942-45. Fellow Coll. Optometrists in Vision Devel. Jewish. Lodges: Lions (pres. local clubs 1957, 72), Masons (worshipful master 1977-78, dist. dep. grand master 1983). Home: 5233 Cockrell St Fort Worth TX 76133 Office: 2606 Hemphill St Fort Worth TX 76110

WHITE, LOUISE HUMPHRIES, publisher, psychological counselor; b. Grayson, La., Mar. 30, 1926; d. Ernest Christopher and Mary Vina (Elder) Humphries; B.A., Centenary Coll. of La., 1962; M.S. in Counseling, Ga. State U., 1971; m. Verlin Ralph White, Mar. 11, 1944 (div. 1986); children—Carol Louise White Kelly, Verlin Ralph, Jr. Employment counselor La. State Employment Service, Shreveport, 1966-68; master counselor Ga. Dept. of Labor, Profl. Office, Job Service Center, Atlanta, 1968-81; owner Counseling Assocs., Atlanta, 1981—; pub., owner Archive Enterprises. Mem. Cathedral of St. Philip, Atlanta, 1968—, Sunday sch. tchr., 1975-78, Daughter of the King, 1973—, Episcopal ch. women, 1973—, Internat. Christian Community Network, 1973-79; Foyer group leader for reconciliation, 1974-84; bd. dirs. Resource Center at Cathedral St. Philip, 1983-84. Recipient Jongleurs award for service to Marjorie Lyons Playhouse, Centenary Coll., 1963; Nat. award for service in resettlement of Indochinese refugees U.S. Catholic Conf. Mem. Am. Personnel and Guidance Assn., Nat. Employment Counselors Assn., Internat. Assn. Personnel in Employment Service, Atlanta C. of C., Cobb County C. of C. AAUW, LWV, Atlanta Hist. Soc., Ga. Hist. Soc., Kennesaw Hist. Soc. (treas.; editor soc. book on local families 1980—). Episcopalian. Club: Northside Woman's (dir., chmn. arts dept. 1979-80). Home: 3286 Wetherbyrne Rd Kennesaw GA 30144 Office: 1800 Water Pl Atlanta GA 30339

WHITE, MARK WELLS, JR., governor of Texas; b. Henderson, Tex., Mar. 17, 1940; s. Mark Wells and Sarah Elizabeth White; B.B.A., Baylor U., 1962, J.D., 1965; m. Linda Gale Thompson, Oct. 1, 1966; children—Mark Wells III, Andrew, Elizabeth Marie. Admitted to Tex. bar, 1965; asst. atty. gen. ins., banking and securities div. State of Tex., Austin, 1966-69; asso. firm Reynolds, White, Allen & Cook, Houston, 1969-71, partner, 1971-73; sec. of state State of Tex., Austin, 1973-79, atty. gen., 1979-83; gov. of Tex., 1983—. Bd. dirs. St. David's Hosp., Austin; mem. adv. panel on voter registration Fed. Election Commn.; mem. adv. council Southwestern Baptist Theol. Sem.; mem. Christian Edn. Coordinating Bd. Served with Tex. N.G., 1966-69. Named Lawyer of Year, Baylor U. chpt. Phi Alpha Delta, 1975. Mem. Nat. Assn. Secs. State (pres. 1977—). Democrat. Baptist. Office: Office of Governor PO Box 12428 Capitol Station Austin TX 78711*

WHITE, MICHAEL DARWIN, dentist; b. Hamlet, N.C., Oct. 20, 1947; s. David Franklin and Ruby Maye (Russell) W. A.B. in Psychology, U. N.C., 1970, D.D.S., 1974. Pub. health dentist Anson and Richmond counties, N.C., 1976-83, Hoke County, N.C., 1983—. Chmn. dental sect. N.C. Pub. Health Assn.; bd. dirs. Richmond County and Anson County Cancer Soc. Served with Dental Corps, USN, 1974-76. Recipient Appreciation award Am. Lung Assn. Fellow Acad. Gen. Dentistry; mem. ADA, N.C. Dental Assn., Greater Fayetteville Dental Soc., Sand Hills Dental Study Club, Am. Soc. Dentistry for Children, Am. Pub. Health Assn., So. Health Assn., U. N.C. Ednl. Found., Chancellor's Club U. N.C., U. N.C. Dental Found., U. N.C. Gen. Alumni Assn., U. N.C. Dental Alumni Assn. (life), Xi Psi Phi Methodist. Clubs: Bachelors (Raleigh) (Greensboro); Civitan. Home: 216 River Rd Rockingham NC 28379

WHITE, PHILIP HAYDEN, ophthalmologist; b. Natick, Mass., Apr. 4, 1945; s. Harlow Hayden and Rachel Harriet (Wheat) W.; m. Zella Marie Hubbard, Nov. 23, 1974. B.A., Dartmouth Coll., 1967; M.D., Tufts U., 1971. Diplomate Am. Bd. Ophthalmology. Intern, Madigan Army Med. Ctr., Tacoma, 1971-72; resident in ophthalmology Brooke Army Med. Ctr., San Antonio, 1976-79; practice medicine specializing in ophthalmology, Sulphur Springs, Tex., 1980—; mem. staff Hopkins County Meml. Hosp., Sulphur Springs, Tex.; treas. Misczellaneous, Inc., Sulphur Springs, 1983—; clin. instr. U. Tex. Med. Sch., Dallas, 1983—. Served to lt. col. U.S. Army, 1971-80. Fellow Am. Acad. Ophthalmology; mem. Am. Intraocular Implant Soc., AMA, Tex. Med. Assn., Hopkins Franklin County Med. Soc. (sec. 1985), Classic Car Club Am. Lodge: Shriners, Masons. Avocations: collecting, driving, and exhibiting antique and classic autos. Home: Rt 3 Sulphur Springs TX 75482 Office: 109 Medical Circle Sulphur Springs TX 75482

WHITE, RALPH ERNEST, artist, educator; b. Mpls., Jan. 3, 1921; s. Ralph Ernest and Ann (Billings) W.; m. Dorthy Ann Nance, June 28, 1947 (div. Oct. 1949); Ruby Irene Bergherr, Jan. 12, 1951; children—Ralph III, Brett, Katherine. Cert., Mpls. Sch. Art, 1942. Painter, 1942—; cons. art dir. Austin, San Antonio, Tex., 1947-70; prof. art U. Tex., Austin, 1946-82, acting chmn. dept., 1965-82. dir. Tex. Fine Arts Assn., Austin, 1956-60. Illustrator numerous books, 1955-65. Exhibited in numerous one-man and group shows, US., Europe and Mex. Served to 1st lt. USAAF, 1942-46. Recipient numerous awards and purchase prizes for fine arts paintings; research grantee U. Tex., 1970; Ford Found. grantee U. Tex., 1975; Vander Lip fellow Mpls. Sch. Art, 1942. Home: 4701 Agarita Cove Austin TX 78734

WHITE, RANDALL PHILLIP, sociologist, management researcher, educator; b. Sacramento, June 5, 1952; s. George William and Mildred Ruth (Johnson) W.; m. Betty Ann Bailey, June 11, 1978; children—Jessica Ann, Logan Kathleen. A.B. in Sociology, Georgetown U., 1974; M.S. in Sociology, Va. Poly. Inst. and State U., 1976; Ph.D. in Devel. Sociology, Cornell U., 1982. Grad. asst. Va. Poly. Inst. and State U., 1974-77, Cornell U., 1978-80; vis. asst. prof. N.C. A.&T. State U., Greensboro, 1980-82; research assoc. Ctr. for Creative Leadership, Greensboro, 1982-85, program assoc., 1985—; cons. Westinghouse Electric, Pitts., Goodyear Tire & Rubber, Akron, Ohio, Merrill Lynch & Co., N.Y.C., 1983—. Co-author: Career Experience of Successful Women Executives, 1986. Contbr. articles to sociol. jours. Pres. St. Paul's Parish Council, Greensboro, N.C., 1984-85, v.p., 1983; mem. tng. com. United Way, Greensboro, 1985 . Summer fellow U. Mich., 1977; grad. scholar Va. Poly. Inst. and State U., 1977. Mem. Am. Psychol. Assn. (div. program com.), Am. Sociol. Assn., Acad. Mgmt. (program com. 1983—), Alpha Kappa Delta, Phi Kappa Phi. Avocations: racquetball; tennis; playing the stock market. Home: 3509 Kirby Dr Greensboro NC 27403 Office: Ctr for Creative Leadership 5000 Laurinda Dr PO Box P-1 Greensboro NC 27402

WHITE, RANDY, football player; b. Wilmington, Del., Jan. 15, 1953; s. Guy and Laverne White; m. Vicci Hanes, 1978; 1 child, Jordan. Student U. Md. Defensive tackle Dallas Cowboys, 1975—; participant NFL All Star Game, 1977, 79-84. Recipient Outland Trophy winner, best coll. lineman, 1974. Address: Dallas Cowboys 6116 N Central Expressway Dallas TX 75206*

WHITE, RAY, hospital administrator; b. Macon, Ga., Apr. 5, 1949; s. Jackson and Izella (Williams) W.; m. Bertha Lee Davis, Nov. 25, 1967 (div. 1972); children—Regina, Valerie; m. 2d, Bertha Lee Brooks, Apr. 7, 1979; children—Derrick, Sherrie, Ray. A.S. in Environ. Health Tech., Community Coll. of Air Force, 1979; B.S., SUNY-Albany, 1980; M.S. in Allied Health Services, U. North Fla., 1980. Lic. hosp. adminstr., mortgage broker. Warehouseman, Winn/Dixie and Atlantic & Pacific Tea Co., Jacksonville, Fla., 1970-74; salesman Met. Life Ins. Co., Jacksonville, 1977-78; environ. health technician Jacksonville Naval Regional Med. Ctr., 1978-80; asst. v.p. Meth. Hosp., Jacksonville, 1980—; v.p. Boardwalk Mortgage Cons., 1985—; adj. prof. U. North Fla., 1982-84. Mem. Jacksonville Democratic Exec. Com.; active Duval unit Am. Cancer Soc. Served with USAF, 1974-76, Ga. Air N.G., 1976-80. Mem. Am. Coll. Hosp. Adminstrs., Nat. Assn. Quality Assurance Profls., Fla. Assn. Quality Assurance Profls., Am. Lung Assn., Eta Sigma Gamma, Alpha Phi Alpha. Democrat. Episcopalian. Clubs: Sertoma, Royal Ambassadors. Lodge: Masons. Home: 8676 Old Plank Rd Jacksonville FL 32220 Office: Meth Hosp 580 W 8th St Jacksonville FL 32209

WHITE, RAYMOND PETRIE, JR., health sciences educator; b. N.Y.C., Feb. 13, 1937; s. Raymond Petrie and Mabel (Shutz) W.; m. Betty Pritchett, Dec. 27, 1961; children—Karen Elizabeth, Michael Wood. Student Washington and Lee U., 1955-58; D.D.S., Med. Coll. Va., 1962, Ph.D. in Anatomy, 1967. Diplomate Am. Bd. Oral and Maxillofacial Surgery, 1969. Resident in oral and Maxillofacial surgery Med. Coll. Va., 1964-67; asst. prof. U. Ky., 1967-70, assoc. prof., 1970-71, chmn. dept. oral and maxillofacial surgery, 1969-71; asst. dean adminstrn., prof. oral and maxillofacial surgery Med. Coll. Va., 1971-74; prof. oral and maxillofacial surgery U. N.C., Chapel Hill, 1974—, dean Sch. Dentistry, 1974-81, assoc. dean medicine, 1981—; dir. Robert Wood Johnson Dental Services Research Program; assoc. chief of staff, chmn. dentistry N.C. Meml. Hosp. Fellow Internat. Coll. Dentists, Am. Coll. Dentists; mem. Inst. Medicine, Am. Dental Assn., Am. Assn. Oral and Maxillofacial Surgeons, Am. Assn. Dental Schs. Roman Catholic. Home: 1506 Velma Rd Chapel Hill NC 27514 Office: Dept of Oral and Maxillofacial Surgery University of North Carolina School of Dentistry Chapel Hill NC 27514

WHITE, REX NAMOND, principal; b. Gilmer, Tex., Jan. 27, 1930; s. Robert Nathaniel and Dollie Mae (Dunagan) W.; student Kilgore Jr. Coll., 1947-49; B.S., East Tex. State U., 1950, M.Ed., 1955; m. Gloria Green, June 4, 1955; children—Kevin Clyde, Brent Nathaniel, Shelly. Elem. tchr., Campus Ward Sch., Longview, Tex., 1950-51, Foster Elem. Sch., Longview, 1953; tchr., coach New London (Tex.) Jr. High Sch. and Sr. High Sch., 1953-55, tchr. advanced math. and physics, coach, 1955-65; prin. West Rusk County Jr. High Sch., New London, 1965-67; supt. Tatum Ind. Sch. Dist., Tatum, Tex., 1967-73; tchr. advanced math. Robert E. Lee High Sch., Tyler, Tex., 1973-77; prin. James S. Hogg Middle Sch., Tyler, 1977—. Mem. NEA, Nat. Middle Sch. Assn., Tex. Middle Sch. Assn., Tex. Tchrs. Assn., Tex. Assn. Secondary Sch. Prins., East Tex. Middle Sch. League, Tex. Middle Sch. Assn. (pres.-elect). Baptist. Club: Optimists. Lodge: Kiwanis. Office: James S Hogg Middle School 920 S Broadway Tyler TX 75701

WHITE, RICHARD EUGENE, finance educator; b. Hutchinson, Kans., July 16, 1942; s. Blaine White and Eunice Elizabeth (Shunk) White Richardson. Ph.D., U. Mo., 1973. Assoc. prof. fin. U. North Fla., Jacksonville, 1973—. Mem. Fin. Analysts Soc. (bd. dirs.), Fin. Mgmt. Assn., Eastern Fin. Assn., So. Fin. Assn. Republican. Roman Catholic. Home: 6162 Briarforest Rd N Jacksonville FL 32211 Office: U North Fla 4567 St Johns Bluff Rd Jacksonville FL 32216

WHITE, RICHARD STANTON, JR., banker; b. Cedar Rapids, Iowa, Mar. 14, 1934; s. Richard Stanton and Geraldine Frances (O'Leary) W.; B.M.E., Ga. Inst. Tech., 1956; Advanced Mgmt. Program, Emory U., 1974; Nat. Grad. Trust Sch., Northwestern U., 1969-71; m. Vivian Therese Cantrall, Sept. 22, 1956; children—Cynthia Lynn, Richard Stanton, Robert Lamar, Kathleen Marie. Trust investment officer Hamilton Nat. Bank, Chattanooga, 1958-70; trust investment officer Citizens & So. Nat. Bank, Atlanta, 1970-71, sr. v.p., 1972-79; v.p. Citizens & So. Investment Counseling, Inc., Atlanta, 1971-72, exec. v.p. RepublicBank Houston (formerly Houston Nat. Bank), 1979—; vice chmn. bd. Republic Bank Trust Co., 1981, chmn. bd., pres., 1982—; mng. dir. Republic Bank Corp., 1985—; dir. Depository Trust Co. tchr. Southeastern Trust Sch., Pacific Coast Banking Sch., U. Wash., 1984, 85. Bd. regents Southeastern Trust Sch., Campbell Coll., N.C., Tex. Woman's U., 1985—. Served with U.S. Army, 1956-58. Mem. Am. Bankers Assn., Tex. Bankers Assn. (1st vice chmn. trust fin. services div. 1985), So. Pension Conf., S.W. Pension Conf., Inst. Chartered Fin. Analysts (chartered fin. analyst), Houston Soc. Fin. Analysts, Houston Estate and Fin. Forum, Houston C. of C., Dallas Estate Planning Council. Roman Catholic. Clubs: Houston, Raveneaux Country, Rotary, Kiwanis (Kiwanian of Yr. 1967; pres. club 1965-66, dist. lt. gov. 1966-67, dist. chmn. 1967-68). Office: RepublicBank Houston PO Box 299001 Houston TX 77299

WHITE, ROBERT ALTON, JR., biochemical entomologist; b. Atlanta, Jan. 7, 1947; s. Robert Alton and Lorraine Catherine (Davis) W.; m. Carol Ruth Lord, June 9, 1973; 1 son, John Robert. B.S., Fla. State U., 1968; M.S. in Entomology U. Ga., Athens, 1973, Ph.D. in Entomology, 1980. Postdoctoral fellow zoology dept. U. Ga., 1980, 84, biochemistry dept., 1981, pharmacology dept., 1982-83; cons., research assoc. RTD Corp., Lexington, Ga., 1984-85. Served with U.S. Army, 1969-70. Decorated Bronze Star, Air medal, Army Commendation medal with cluster. Mem. Am. Chem. Soc., Am. Entomol. Soc., Ga. Entomol. Soc., Am. Philatelic Soc., Sigma Xi. Democrat. Methodist. Contbr. articles to profl. jours.

WHITE, ROBERT BRUCE, aviation company executive; b. St. Louis, May 30, 1942; s. Bruce and Alice (Probst) W.; m. Margaret M. Hargreave, Sept. 12, 1964; children—Robert B. Jr., Christopher B. B. Acctg., Nat. Coll. Arts and Scis., 1979; student in Animal Husbandry, Calif. State Poly. Coll., 1963. Horseshoer, St. Louis, 1963-66; mechanic Royal Crown Cola, Columbus, Ga., 1966-68; prodn. supr. W.C. Bradley Co., Columbus, 1968-72; controller Wireways, Inc., Panama City, Fla., 1972-80; v.p., gen. mgr. Sowell Aviation Co., Inc., Panama City, 1980—; dir., treas. Delwood Estates Homeowners Assn., Panama City, 1976—; dir., pres. Gulf Coast Goodwill, Inc., Panama City, 1983—. Pres. Panama City Civitan Club, 1980; bd. dirs. Ala., West Fla. Civitan Dist., 1985—, lt. gov., 1984; allocations com. mem. Bay County United Way, Inc., Panama City, 1985; notary State of Fla., 1972—. Recipient Leadership Bay award Bay County C. of C., 1984-85, 500 Plus award Claxton Fruit Cake, 1982-83; named Outstanding lt. gov. Ala. West Fla. Civitan Dist., 1984. Mem. Nat. Air Transportation Assn. (mgmt. inst. 1980), Am. Mgmt. Assn. Democrat. Presbyterian. Home: 1025 W 19th St Unit 12A Panama City FL 32405 Office: Sowell Aviation Co Inc PO Box 1490 Panama City FL 32402

WHITE, ROBERT CLARENCE, retired company executive; b. St. Louis, June 2, 1918; s. Robert Rinier and Eleanor Violet (Moody) W.; m. Dorothy Mae Weidle, May 11, 1946; children—Pamela Jean White Riebesell, Carolyn Irene White Hack, Robert Raymond. B.S. in Chem. Engring., Washington U., 1939. Vice pres. Warner-Chilcott Div., Morris Plains, N.J., 1964-70, Warner-Lambert Co., Morris Plains, 1970-79, ret., 1979—. Trustee Beaufort County Library, S.C., 1984—; dir. Environ. and Hist. Mus., Hilton Head Island, S.C., 1985—; pres. Hilton Head Island Audobon Soc., 1985—. Served to comdr. USN, 1942-46, 50-52. Mem. Am. Chem. Soc. Republican. Presbyterian. Clubs: Bear Creek Golf, Dolphin Head Golf, Morris County Golf. Home: 33 Bent Tree Ln Hilton Head Island SC 29928

WHITE, ROBERT DEAN, oral and maxillofacial surgeon; b. San Angelo, Tex., July 30, 1946; s. Edwin Cole and Mary Eva (Underwood) W.; m. Vickie Lynn Shoffner, June 20, 1970; children—Jennifer Leigh, Lindsay Ellen, Shannon Cole. Student Amarillo Jr. Coll., 1964-66; D.D.S., U. Tex.-Houston, 1970, M.S. in Biomed. Scis., 1974. Diplomate Am. Bd. Oral and Maxillofacial Surgery. Practice dentistry specializing in oral and maxillofacial surgery, Bedford, Tex., 1974—; mem. staff North Hills Med. Ctr., Ft. Worth, 1974—, Harris Hurst-Euless-Bedford Hosp., Bedford, chief dental dept., 1984—. Contbr. articles to Jour. Oral Surgery, Tex. Dental Jour., Oral Surgery, Oral Medicine, Oral Pathology jour. Pres. N.E. Tarrant County sect. Am. Cancer Soc., 1976. Fellow Am. Dental Soc. Anesthesiology; mem. N. Tex. Soc. Oral Surgeons (past pres. 1980), Tex. Soc. Oral and Maxillofacial Surgeons (pres.-elect 1984), Am. Soc. Oral and Maxillofacial Surgeons, ADA, Tex. Dental Assn. Republican. Avocations: tennis; golf; snow skiing; jogging. Office: 2121 Central Dr Bedford TX 76021

WHITE, ROBERT MILES FORD, life insurance company executive; b. Lufkin, Tex., June 9, 1928; s. Sullivan Miles and Faye Clark (Scurlock) F.; B.A., Stephen F. Austin State U., 1948; B.B.A., St. Mary's U., San Antonio, 1955; M.S. in Fin. Services, Am. Coll., 1981; C.L.U.; m. Mary Ruth Wathen, Nov. 10, 1946; children—Martha, Robert, Benedict, Mary, Jesse, Margaret, Maureen, Thomas. Chartered fin. cons. Tchr., Douglas (Tex.) Public Schs., 1946-47, Houston Public Schs., 1948-51; office mgr. Heat Control Insulation Co., San Antonio, 1951-53; acct. S.W. Acceptance Co., San Antonio, 1953-55; sec.-treas. Howell Corp., San Antonio, 1955-64; agt. New Eng. Mut. Life Ins. Co., San Antonio, 1964-71; br. mgr. Occidental Life Ins. Co. of Calif., San Antonio, 1971-84, gen. agt., 1984—. Mem. EEO Council, 1974—. Mem. San Antonio C. of C., San Antonio Estate Planners Council, S.W. Pension Conf., Nat., Tex., San Antonio assns. life underwriters, Am. Soc. CLUs, Am. Risk Mgmt. Assn., Gen. Agts. and Mgrs. Assn., Internat. Assn. Fin. Planners, Internat. Platform Assn., Tex. Leaders Round Table (life), San Antonio, S.E. Tex. geneal. and hist. socs., Sons of Republic of Tex., SAR, Children Am. Revolution, Kappa Pi Sigma. Republican. Roman Catholic. Home: 701 Sunshine Dr E San Antonio TX 78228 Office: 4805 Fredericksburg Rd San Antonio TX 78229

WHITE, ROGER KREIS, lawyer; b. Nashville, Mar. 16, 1957; s. Roger Kreis White and Mary Anne (Hall) Scroggs; m. Jennifer Lynn Junker, Aug. 1, 1975; children—Matthew William, Joshua Thomas. B.A., U. Tenn., 1978; J.D., Vanderbilt U., 1981. Bar: Tenn. 1981, U.S. Dist. Ct. (mid. dist.) Tenn. 1981, U.S. Dist. Ct. (ea. dist.) Tenn. 1986, U.S. Ct. Appeals (6th cir.) 1983, U.S. Supreme Ct. 1984. Ptnr., Guenther, White & Jordan, Nashville, 1981-85; assoc. Brown & Brown, 1985—. Mem. editorial bd. Law and Social Problems, 1981. Deacon, Bellevue Bapt. Ch., Nashville, 1984—, also ch. tng. dir., 1984—. Mem. ABA, Tenn. Bar Assn., Nashville Bar Assn. Democrat. Home: Route 4 Green Valley Dr Ashland City TN 37015 Office: Brown & Brown 633 Thompson Ln Nashville TN 37204

WHITE, RONALD LEON, soft drink company executive; b. West York, Pa., July 14, 1930; s. Clarence William and Grace Elizabeth (Gingerich) W.; m. Estheranne Wieder, July 31, 1931; children—Bradford William, Clifford Allen, Erick David. B.S. in Econs., U. Pa., 1952, M.B.A., 1957. Cost analysis supr. Air Products & Chem. Corp., Allentown, Pa., 1957-60; cost control mgr. Mack Trucks, Inc., Allentown, 1960-64; mgmt. cons. Peat, Marwick, Mitchell & Co., Phila., 1964-66; mgr. profit planning Monroe, The Calculator Co. div. Litton Industries, Orange, N.J., 1966-67, controller, 1967-68, group v.p. fin., Beverly Hills, Calif., 1968-70; pres. Royal Typewriter Co. div., Hartford, Conn., 1970-73; exec. v.p., chief operating officer, treas., dir. Tenna Corp., Cleve., 1973-75, pres., dir., 1975-77; v.p. fin. Arby's, Inc., Youngstown, Ohio, 1978-79; exec. v.p., dir. Roxbury Am., Inc., 1979-81; v.p. fin., treas. Royal Crown Cos., Inc., Miami Beach, Fla., 1981—; instr. acctg. Wharton Sch., U. Pa., 1952-53, instr. industry, 1953-54. Div. chmn. United Way campaign. Served to lt. USNR, 1954-57. Mem. Am. Mgmt. Assn., Nat. Assn. Accts., Fin. Execs. Inst., Acacia, Nat. Assn. Corp. Dirs. Republican. Mem. United Ch. of Christ. Lodge: Masons.

WHITE, SAMUEL AUGUSTUS, JR., security company executive, former air force officer; b. Savannah, Ga., Nov. 16, 1918; s. Samuel Augustus and Henrietta Lynah (Glover) W.; m. Sara Crigler, Sept. 14, 1946 (dec. Nov. 1973); children—Samuel Augustus III, W. Kingman, Catherine R., Sara E. Student Va. Mil. Inst., 1939-41; B.S., Air U., 1956. Commd. 2d lt. U.S. Air Force, 1941, advanced through grades to lt. col., 1955; chief combat ops. div. Air Def. Command, Colorado Springs, Colo., 1951-54; chief air def. div. Hdqrs. U.S. Air Forces in Europe, Wiesbaden, W.Ger., 1954-58; with War Plans Directorate, Hdqrs. U.S. Air Force, Washington; research dir. Aerospace Studies Inst., Maxwell AFB, Ala., 1962-66; dir. ops. JUSMAG, Bangkok, 1966-68; ret., 1969; pres. So. Security Inc., Savannah, 1971-73, Preventor Security Ctr., Inc., Savannah, 1973—; Author analytical studies on mil. pacts. Campaigner Republican Nat. Com., 1980—. Recipient numerous mil. awards and decorations. Mem. Nat. Burglar and Fire Alarm Assn., Air Force Assn., Ret. Officers Assn., Mil. Order World Wars, Soc. of Cincinnati of S.C., Soc. Colonial Wars of Ga., Savannah C. of C. (crime prevention com. 1974-75). Episcopalian. Club: Oglethorpe (Savannah). Lodge: Rotary. Home: 818 Wilmington Island Rd Savannah GA 31410 Office: Preventor Security Center Inc 118 E 34th St Savannah GA 31401

WHITE, SANDRA LYNN, educator; b. Toledo, Apr. 25, 1939; d. Charles Glenn and Jennie Ruth (Smith) Mull; B.S., U. Tenn., 1961; M.S. in Edn., Fla. State U., 1975; postgrad. U. So. Fla., 1982—; children—Liesl Lynn, Jennifer Leigh. Flight attendant Delta Air Lines, 1961-65; tchr. Charlotte County Schs., Fla., 1975—; Served to capt., USAF, 1966-70. Mem. AAUW, Internat. Reading Assn., Am. Ednl. Research Assn., Assn. Supervision and Curriculum Devel., Fla. State Reading Council, Phi Kappa Phi, Phi Delta Kappa, Delta Gamma Alumni. Republican. Methodist. Club: Jr. Women's. Home: 447 Blossom Ave NW Port Charlotte FL 33952 Office: FAO 247 Coll of Edn U S Fla Tampa FL 33620

WHITE, STEVEN LEIGH, geologist; b. Enid, Okla., Dec. 13, 1955; s. Harold Ray and Elaine Hope (Myers) W. B.S. in Geology, U. Tex.-Austin, 1978. Mudlogger, The Analysts-Schlumberger, Houston, 1979-80; staff geologist Intercontinental Petroleum Co., Houston, 1980-81; sr. geologist Tex. Oil & Gas Corp., Tyler, Tex., 1981—. Author: (with others) The Jurassic of East Texas, 1984. Mem. Am. Assn. Petroleum Geologists, Soc. Profl. Well Log Analysts, Houston Geol. Soc., East Tex. Geol. Soc., Soc. Econ. Paleontologists and Mineralogists. Republican. Methodist. Office: Tex Oil & Gas Corp One American Ctr Suite 500 Tyler TX 75703

WHITE, SUSANNE TROPEZ, pediatrician, educator; b. New Orleans, Apr. 13, 1949; d. Maxwell Sterling and Ethel (Ross) Tropez; m. James Carnell White, Apr. 10, 1971; children—Lisa, Janifer, James Carnell. B.S., Bennett Coll., 1971; M.D., U. N.C., 1975, M.P.H., 1982. Diplomate Am. Bd. Pediatrics. Resident in pediatrics N.C. Meml. Hosp., Chapel Hill, 1975-76, 77-79; pediatrician Darnell Army Hosp., Ft. Hood, Tex., 1976-77; acting dir. pediatric day clinic Wake County Med. Ctr., Raleigh, N.C., 1979-82, dir. pediatric day clinic, 1982—, dir. teens with tots clinic, 1980—; asst. prof. pediatrics U. N.C. Chapel Hill, 1982—, mem. coordinating com. for curriculum rev., 1981-83; pediatrician Shelly Child Devel. Ctr., Raleigh, 1981—, child med. examiner program, Raleigh, 1979—. Contbr. articles to profl. jours. Mem. Walnut Terr. Child Devel. Ctr., Raleigh, 1981-83, chmn., 1982-83; chmn. pastor of parish com. Longview Ch., Raleigh, 1982-84. Fellow Am. Acad. Pediatrics; mem. Ambulatory Pediatric Assn., Adolescent Pregnancy Coalition United Way, Bennett Coll. Alumnae Assn., United Methodist Women. Democrat.

WHITE, THOMAS HARRY, photographer; b. Spartanburg, S.C., Sept. 5, 1930; s. Jimmie A. and Clara (Cothran) W.; student N.Y. Inst. Photography, 1947; student journalism U. N.C., 1950; m. Lillian Ruth Hughes, Mar. 15, 1949; children—Diane Elizabeth, Karen Patryce, Thomas Harry. With editorial staff Spartanburg Herald Jour., 1947-50; organized B. & B. Studios, Inc., Spartanburg, 1950, pres., gen. mgr., 1962—; exec. v.p. Graphico, Inc., 1971—, King Photo. Recipient awards including Nat. Art League award, 1948, S.C. Press Assn. award, 1949. Mem. Photog. Soc. Am., Nat. Press Photographers Assn., Royal Order of Scotland. Mem. United Methodist Ch. (lay leader). Clubs: Masons (33 deg.; grand master), Shriners, Sertoma. Photog. works in traveling photog. exhbns. Home: 230 Cart Dr Spartanburg SC 29302 Office: 268 E Main St Spartanburg SC 29302

WHITE, TIMOTHY JOSEPH, physicist, industrial company executive; b. Nashville, Apr. 3, 1942; s. Francis Peter and Frances Rita (Marcisovsky) W.; B.A., Vanderbilt U., 1964; M.S., U. Ala. in Huntsville, 1974, M.A.S., 1976; M.P.A., Nova U., 1978, D.P.A., 1978; m. Christine Helen Spond, Sept. 5, 1964; children—Marcia Ann, Angela Marie, Charlene Kay. Jr. engr. Air Reduction Co., Jersey City, 1964-66; physicist Sperry Rand Corp., Huntsville, 1966-67, sr. physicist, 1967-74, sr. staff physicist, group leader, 1974-77; sr. staff analyst, asst. security supr. Consol. Industries, Inc., Huntsville, 1977-78; sr. staff engr. SCI Systems, Inc., 1978-79; sr. staff scientist Sci. Applications, Inc., 1979-80; pres. Dynamic Enterprises, Inc., 1979—; cons. NASA, 1966-67, 1976-77, adj. asst. prof. U. Ala., Fla. Inst. Tech. Pres., Holy Spirit Sch. PTA, 1974-76; mem. Radio Amateur Civil Emergency Service, 1974—; mem. crafts com. J.F. Drake State Tech. Coll., 1976—; instr. Christian Formation Program, 1973-75; vol. donor ARC, 1973—. Recipient Apollo Achievement award NASA, 1959, Skylab Achievement award NASA, 1974; Outstanding Service award J.F. Drake Coll., 1979. Mem. Am. Mgmt. Assns., Am. Phys. Soc., Ala. Acad. Sci., Am. Def. Preparedness Assn., Am. Soc. for Pub. Adminstrn. (v.p. 1980-81, sec.-treas. 1984—), Policy Studies Orgn., Soc. Logistics Engrs. (vice chmn. ops. 1983-84), Am. Radio Relay League, Vanderbilt U. Alumni Assn., U. Ala. in Huntsville Alumni Assn., Nova U. Alumni Assn., Sigma Pi Sigma, Mu Alpha Theta. Roman Catholic. Contbr. articles to profl. jours. Home: 11230 Hillwood Dr Huntsville AL 35803 Office: Dynamic Enterprises Inc 8200 S Memorial Pkwy Suite B Huntsville AL 35802 also PO Box 4389 Huntsville AL 35815

WHITE, TOMMY BURFORD, health officer; b. Alexandria, La., Feb. 3, 1943; s. Samuel J. and Doris J. (Parker) W.; m. Sharon L. Brown, June 4, 1966; children—Marco Lamar, Marcia Rene. B.S. in Biology, Central State U., 1965; M. Environ. Scis., U. Okla., 1973, Th.D., 1979. Chief consumer protection Oklahoma City-County Health Dept., 1976-81, dir. environ. health services, 1976-81, adminstrv. health dir., 1982—; dir. commns., coms. relating to mental and pub. health. Coordinator Northeast Coalition for Better Health; mem. Okla. State Judiciary Reform Commn.; mem. Gov.'s State Mental Health Planning Bd. Recipient numerous awards Nat. Assn. Restaurants, EPA, profl. socs. Mem. Nat. Pub. Health Assn., U.S. Conf. City Health Officers, Alpha Phi Alpha. Mem. Pentecostal Ch. Clubs: Kiwanis Internat., Toastmasters Internat. Home: 4700 Thompson Ave Oklahoma City OK 73105 Office: County Health Dept 921 NE 23d St Oklahoma City OK 73105

WHITE, TRENTWELL MASON, retired naval officer, professional services researcher, educator; b. Boston, Dec. 28, 1931; s. Trentwell Mason and Helen Thompson (Hawley) Studley W.; children—Trentwell M. III, Dana B., Stephen H., Markell H., Meredith C.; m. Harriet Camden, Apr. 10, 1976. B.A., Tufts U., 1954, M.A. in Edn., 1955; M.A. in Personnel Mgmt., George Washington U., 1963. Commd. ensign U.S. Navy 1955, advanced through grades to commdr., 1969; mgr. naval programs BDM Corp., McLean, Va., 1977—; instr. U.S. Naval Acad., 1960-62. adj. prof. Northern Va. Community Coll., Alexandria, 1977—, George Mason U., Fairfax, Va., 1980-81. Pres., Homeowners Assn., Alexandria, 1977-78, Vienna, 1982-83. Mem. Nat. Mil. Intelligence Assn. (v.p. Potomac chpt. 1984—), Naval Intelligence Profls., Inc. (sec., founder 1985—). Republican. Avocations: tennis; carpentry; gardening. Home: 10200 Wandering Creek Rd Vienna VA 22180 Office: BDM Corp 7915 Jones Br Dr McLean VA 22102

WHITE, VIRGINIA LUCILLE, diversified holding company executive; b. Yoakum, Tex., May 9, 1924; d. Deo Valentine and Eddie Lucille (Williams) W. B.B.A., U. Tex., 1947. Cert. prof. sec. Legal sec., then exec. sec. various cos., San Antonio and Houston, 1947-63; exec. sec. Joe L. Allbritton and Perpetual Corp., Houston, 1963-70, adminstrv. asst., 1970, adminstrv. officer, 1970—; sec.-treas. Perpetual Corp., University Bancshares, Inc., Jobaro Corp., Perfin Corp., Houston, Allbritton Communications Co., Allbritton News Bur., Inc., Washington, WJLA, Inc., Washington, KATV-TV Inc., Little Rock, KTUL-TV, Inc., Tulsa, First Charleston Corp. (S.C.), WSET, Inc., Lynchburg, Va., Hudson Dispatch, Union City, N.J., News Printing Co., Paterson, N.J., Trenton Times Corp., Westfield News Advertiser, Inc., Westmoreland Jours., Inc., Irwin, Pa.; asst. sec. Pierce Nat. Life Ins. Co., Los Angeles; asst. sec. First Internat. Bancshares, Inc., Dallas, 1972-74; sec. Evening Star Newspaper Co., Washington, 1976-78, Star Press, Inc., Washington, 1977-78, Star Syndicate, N.Y.C., 1976-78, Wallace Pennysaver, Westfield, Mass., 1977-79. Sec.-treas. The Allbritton Found. Mem. Profl. Secs. Internat., DAR. Episcopalian. Office: 5615 Kirby Dr Suite 310 Houston TX 77005

WHITE, WILLIAM CLINTON, physician; b. Scottsville, Va., Nov. 22, 1911; s. Llewellyn Gordon and Caroline Rebecca (Rawlings) W.; m. Frances Evelyn Daniel, July 2, 1938; children—William Clinton, Elizabeth White Martin. B.S., Va. Mil. Inst., 1933; M.D., U. Va., 1937. Diplomate Am. Bd. Pathology. Intern, Walter Reed Gen. Hosp., Washington, 1937-39; resident in pathology U. Colo. Med. Ctr., Denver, 1949-53, assoc. prof., 1949-65; med. dir. Los Alamos Hosp., 1946-49; cons. U. Calif. Sci. Labs, Los Alamos, 1949-59; chmn. dept. pathology Denver Gen. Hosp., 1953-65; dir. med. edn. and research Pensacola Found. for Med. Edn. and Research (Fla.), 1965-78; bd. dirs., 1976—; cons. med. edn., emeritus dir. med. edn. Pensacola Edn. Program (Fla.), 1978—; co-founder, dir. Rocky Mountain Natural Gas Co.; dir. Midwest Nat. Gas Co. Bd. govs. Fellowship Concerned Churchmen, 1982-85, pres., 1983-85. Mem. Selective Service Bd., N.Mex., 1946-49; mem. adv. bd. on cancer to Gov. of Colo., 1960-65; mem. Community Hosp. Council, Fla. Bd. Regents, 1971-74; mem. vestry, chmn. fin. com., sr. warden Christ Ch.; active Salvation Army, Boy Scouts Am. Served to col., M.C., U.S. Army, 1938-46. Recipient Cert. of Appreciation, Selective Service, 1951; Citation of Merit, Bd. Health and Hosps., Denver, 1963. Mem. AMA, Am. Soc. Clin. Pathologists (counselor), Colo. Soc. Pathology (pres.), Internat. Acad. Pathology, Colo. State Med. Soc., Denver Med. Soc., Escambia County Med. Soc. (hon. life), Los Alamos County Med. Soc. (pres.). Clubs: Andalusia Country (Ala.); Pensacola Country. Lodges: Rotary Internat., St. Andrew's Soc. (trustee 1981—), Masons, Shriners. Contbr. articles in field to profl. jours. Home: 615 Bayshore Dr Apt 101 Warrington FL 32507 Office: Route 6 Box 251A Andalusia AL 36420

WHITE, WILLIAM EARLE, lawyer; b. Dinwiddie County, Va., Aug. 19, 1898; s. William Richard and Annie Eliza (Hone) W.; m. Marian Louise Molloy, Apr. 24, 1924; children—Marion White DiStanislao, William Earle Jr., Stephen Graham. B.A., Richmond Coll., 1917; student Law Sch. Am. Expeditionary Forces, Beaune, France, 1919, Harvard Law Sch., 1920. Bar: Va. 1920, U.S. Ct. Appeals (4th cir.) 1940, U.S. Supreme Ct. 1941. Ptnr. Lassiter & White, 1922-24, White Hamilton Wyche & Shell, Petersburg, Va., 1927—; ret. dir. 1st & Mechants Nat. Bank (now part of Sovran Bank N.A.), Commonwealth Natural Gas (now part of Columbia Gas). Chmn. Hosp. Authority City of Petersburg. Served to cpl. USMC, 1917-1919. Fellow Am. Coll. Trial Lawyers, Am. Bar Found., Am Coll. Probate Counsel; mem. Am. Judicature Soc., Petersburg C. of C. (past pres.), Petersburg Bar Assn., Va. State Bar (pres. 1963-64). Democrat. Baptist. Home: Walnut Hill Apts Petersburg VA 23803 Office: White Hamilton Wyche & Shell 20 E Tabb St Petersburg VA 23803

WHITE-CROSS, TINA RENÉE, science educator, research entomologist, consultant; b. Augusta, Ga., Apr. 12, 1953; d. Edward Wilson and Helen (Jeffrey) White; m. Victor W. Cross, Jan. 15, 1982. B.S. in Biology, Augusta Coll., 1975; M.S. in Zoology, Clemson U., 1977, Ph.D. in Entomology, 1980. Guest lectr., research asst. Clemson U. (S.C.), 1975-80; chmn. sci. dept. Curtis Bapt. Sch., Augusta, 1980-83; research assoc. Fla. State Collection of Anthropods, 1980—; sci. educator Appling County Schs., 1983—; instr. Brewton Parker Coll., 1983—; taxonomic cons. Greenville County Bd. Health, Water Resources Research Inst., Savannah River Ecology Labs., EPA, Burlington Industries. Recipient Max Planck Inst. award, 1980; Star Tchr. award Curtis Bapt. Sch., 1981-82; Exchange Club award in sci. and tech. photography, 1982; Outstanding Tchr. award CSRA Sci. Fair, 1983. Mem. Societas Internationalis Odonatologica, N.Am. Benthological Soc., Entomol. Soc. Washington, Entomol. Soc. Am., S.C. Entomol. Soc. (Outstanding Student Presentation award 1980), S.C. Acad. Sci., Ga. Entomol. Soc., Sigma Xi. Methodist. Clubs: Augusta Country, Vidalia Country. Contbr. articles to profl. jours. Home: PO Box 1792 Vidalia GA 30474 Office: Route 7 PO Box 36 Baxley GA 31513

WHITEFIELD, BEN TAYLOR, energy company executive; b. Houston, Apr. 6, 1937; s. Franklin Wolcot and Louise (Gilliam) W.; m. Claudette Dee Peters, Aug. 23, 1964; children—Christopher, Dulci. B.S. in Geology, U. Tex., 1960, B.A., 1961. Landman Anadarko Prodn. Co., Liberal, Kans., 1961-65, div. landman, Denver and Calgary, Can., 1965-72, exploration mgr., Denver, 1972-76, v.p., Houston, 1976-81; pres. dir. Egret Energy Corp., Houston, 1981—; owner, pres. Whitefield Oil Co., Houston, 1983—. Mem. Am. Assn. Petroleum Landmen, Am. Assn. Petroleum Geologists. Republican. Avocations: fishing; ranching. Home: 13138 Boheme Houston TX 77079 Office: 3223 Smith St Suite 303 Houston TX 77006

WHITEHORNE, ROBERT ALVIN, business educator; b. Portsmouth, Va., June 20, 1925; s. Stanford Laferty and Ruth (Speight) W.; B.E.E., Va. Poly. Inst., 1948, M.E.E., 1951; m. Margaret Kirby, Sept. 6, 1946; children—Lynn Whitehorne Sacco, Robert Alvin, Cynthia Leigh Moore. Engr., IBM Corp., Poughkeepsie, N.Y., 1950-54, lab. adminstr., Kingston, N.Y., 1954-56, dir. employee relations, Armonk, N.Y., 1956-72, resident mgr. Mid-Hudson Valley, Poughkeepsie, 1972-74; v.p.-personnel and orgn. planning Sperry & Hutchinson Co., N.Y.C., 1976-79; exec. v.p. Michelin Tire Corp., Grenville, S.C., 1974-76; dir. CODESCO, Inc., SPAN-America, Inc.; mem. faculty Coll. Bus. Adminstrn., U. S.C., Columbia, 1979—. Former trustee U. S.C. Bus. Partnership Found.; mem. plans for progress com. Pres.'s Commn. on Equal Employment Activity, 1963-68. Served with USMCR, 1944-46. Methodist. Clubs: Quail Hollow. Home: 2400 Owl Circle West Columbia SC 29169 Office: U SC Coll Bus Columbia SC 29208

WHITEHURST, BROOKS MORRIS, chemical engineer; b. Reading, Pa., Apr. 9, 1930; s. David Brooks and Bessie Ann (Lowry) W.; B.S., Va. Poly. Inst. and State U., 1951; m. Carolyn Sue Boyer, July 4, 1951; children—Garnett, Anita, Robert. Sr. process asst. Am. Enka Corp., Lowland, Tenn., 1951-56; sr. process devel. engr. Va.-Carolina Chem. Corp., Richmond, Va., 1956-63; project engr. Texaco Inc., Richmond, 1963-66; mgr. engring. services Texasgulf, Inc., Aurora, N.C., 1967-80, mgr. spl. projects and long range planning, 1980-81; pres. Whitehurst Assos., Inc., New Bern, N.C., 1982—; instr., lectr., cons. alternative sources of energy community colls. and univs. Co-chmn. N.C. state supt. task force on secondary edn., 1974—; mem. N.C. Personnel Commn. for Public Sch. Employees; mem. N.C. state adv. com. on trade and indsl. edn., 1971-77; chmn. Gov.'s Task Force Vols. in the Workplace, 1981; chmn. State Adv. Council Career Edn., 1977—; gov.'s liaison for edn. and bus., 1978-79. Registered profl. engr., N.C. Recipient commendation Pres. U.S., 1981. Mem. Am. Inst. Chem. Engrs., Am. Inst. Chemists (dir. 1980-84; cert.), N.C. Inst. Chemists (pres. 1975-77), Nat. Soc. Profl. Engrs., N.C. Soc. Profl. Engrs., Internat. Solar Energy Soc., Royal Soc. Chemistry. Patentee in field. Home: 1983 Hoods Creek Dr New Bern NC 28560 Office: PO Box 3335 New Bern NC

WHITEHURST, GEORGE WILLIAM, congressman; b. Norfolk, Va., Mar. 12, 1925; s. Calvert Stanhope and Laura (Tomlinson) W.; m. Jennette Seymour Franks, Aug. 24, 1946; children—Frances Seymour, Calvert Stanhope. B.A., Washington and Lee U., 1950; M.A., U. Va., 1951; student W.Va. U., 1956-57, Ph.D., 1962. Mem. faculty Old Dominion U., 1950-68, dean students, prof. history, 1963-68; news analyst Sta. WTAR-TV, 1962-68; mem. 91st-99th congresses from 2d dist. Va., 1969—; del. N. Atlantic Assembly. Mem. Norfolk Council Alcoholism; past chmn. Norfolk crusade Am. Cancer Soc. Served with USNR, 1943-46. Decorated Air medal with oak leaf cluster. Mem. Am. Hellenic Ednl. and Progressive Assn., V.F.W., Am. Legion, Deutsche Marine-Akademie (asso.), Delta Upsilon. Methodist (past chmn. bd.). Lion, Rotarian. Office: Rayburn House Office Bldg Washington DC 20515*

WHITELEY, MARILYNN MAXWELL, educator; b. Columbus, Ohio, Apr. 17, 1929; d. Marion Wilbur and Thelma (McGrady) Maxwell; B.S., East Carolina U., 1949; M.Ed., U. Tenn., Chattanooga, 1975; Ed.D., U. Tenn., Knoxville, 1981; children—Kay, Janet, Kenneth. Tchr. Edgecombe County (N.C.) schs., 1949-51; Hamilton County (Tenn.) schs., 1966-69, Chattanooga public schs., 1969—; adj. prof. edn. U. Tenn., Chattanooga, 1980—. Delta Kappa Gamma scholar, 1974. Mem. Assn. Supervision and Curriculum Devel., Internat. Reading Assn., Nat. Council Tchrs. English, AAUW, United Teaching Profession, Phi Delta Kappa, Delta Kappa Gamma. Methodist. Home: 6433 Brookmeade Circle Hixson TN 37343

WHITELOCK, ALFRED THEODORE, librarian, clergyman; b. Dorchester, Dorset, Eng., June 5, 1933; s. Frederick Alfred and Kathleen Ann (Whitelock)

Woodward. Diploma in pianoforte, Royal Acad. Music, London, 1950; B.A. in Theology, U. Bristol, Eng., 1958; diploma (Fulbright scholar), Va. Theol. Sem., 1960; M.L.S., U. Ind., 1970. Ordained priest Ch. of Eng., 1960; curate, priest St. Bartholomew with St. Andrew, Bristol, 1960-62; welfare officer St. Anne's Bd. Mill Co., Bristol, 1962-65; asst. librarian Indpls. Pub. Library, 1965-68; librarian Cath. Sem. Found. Library, Indpls., 1968-71; county librarian Laramie County (Wyo.) Library System, Cheyenne, 1971-77, Park County (Wyo.) Library System, 1977-78; city librarian Roanoke (Va.) City Public Library System, 1978—. Served with RAF, 1952-54. Mem. Wyo. Library Assn. (pres. 1975-76). Office: 706 S Jefferson Roanoke VA 24016

WHITELY, PATRICIA ANN, college administrator, campus minister; b. N.Y.C., Oct. 16, 1958; d. William L. and Margaret (Dickinson) W. B.S. in Mgmt., St. John's U. Coll. Bus., 1980; M.Edn., U. S.C., 1982. Coordinator residence edn. U. Miami, Coral Gables, Fla., 1982—, campus minister, 1983—. Mem. Am. Coll. Personnel Assn. (mem. directorate body commn. XV 1983-86). Republican. Roman Catholic. Avocation: running. Home: PO Box 248567 Coral Gables FL 33146 Office: U Miami 1211 Dickinson Dr Coral Gables FL 33146

WHITEMAN, EDWARD RUSSELL, artist, painter; b. Buffalo, Dec. 16, 1938; s. Edward Russell and Hildagarde Mikelite W.; m. Rosalie Martha Shambra. A.A. in Applied Sci., U. Buffalo, 1959. Exhibited in group shows at U. Mich., 1965, New Orleans Mus. Art, 1975, Whitney Mus. Art, N.Y.C., 1975, Carnegie Inst., 1982, La. World Expn., 1984, Southeastern Ctr. for Contemporary, Winston, N.C., 1984; represented in permanent collections Nat. Collection of Fine Arts, Washington, Albright-Knox Art Gallery, Buffalo, New Orleans Mus. Art, Montgomery Mus. Fine Arts, Ala., Nat. Endowment for the Arts/Southeastern Ctr. for Contemporary Art Artist fellowship, 1979; grantee Ford Found.; recipient award citation New Orleans Mus. Art, 1975. Home and Office: 601 Constantinople St New Orleans LA 70115

WHITENER, ROBERT WILFONG, psychiatrist; b. Thomasville, N.C., Nov. 21, 1927; s. Sterling Wilfong and Marie Anna (Hegnauer) W.; m. Marion Talley Lefler, Feb. 9, 1952; children—Donald, Louise. B.A., Catawba Coll., 1950; M.D., Northwestern U., 1954. Intern, Charity Hosp., New Orleans, 1954-55; resident in psychiatry U. N.C., Chapel Hill, 1955-58; mem. staff U. Ill. Student Health Service, 1958-61, assoc. prof. hygiene, 1961; pvt. practice medicine, specializing in psychiatry, Greensboro, N.C., 1961—; clin. assoc. prof. psychiatry U. N.C., Chapel Hill, 1975—; med. dir. Greensboro Drug Action Council, 1972-81. Served with USAF, 1946-47. Named Physician of Yr., Greensboro. Mem. Am. Psychiat. Assn., N.C. Psychiat. Assn., N.C. Med. Soc., Guilford County Med. Soc., Am. Group Psychotherapy Assn., Carolinas Group Psychotherapy Soc. Democrat. Mem. United Ch. Christ. Home: 1102 Hobbs Rd Greensboro NC 27410 Office: 1024 Professional Village Greensboro NC 27401

WHITESIDE, MARIAN DAVIS, nursing educator; b. Rutherfordton, N.C., Feb. 27, 1932; d. Julius R. and Corrine (Miller) Davis; m. Herbert Ray Whiteside, July 22, 1962; children—Patricia Ann, Anthony Edward, Susan Rae. B.S.N., A&T State U., Greensboro, N.C., 1962; M.P.H., U. N.C., 1971. R.N., N.C. Staff nurse N.Y.U. Hosp., N.Y.C., 1962-63, North Hudson Vis. Nurse Service, WeeHawken, N.J., 1963-64; staff nurse Guilford County Health Dept. (N.C.), 1966-68, supr. pub. health nursing, 1971-74; dir. pub. health nursing Cabarrus County Health Dept. (N.C.), 1974-75; asst. prof. nursing U. N.C.-Greensboro, 1975—. Author: (with others) A Model for Inservice Education, 1968. Mem. ARC Nursing Service Program, Greensboro, 1976-82; mem. N.C. Health Manpower Adv. Council, Chapel Hill, 1978; chmn. Ret. Sr. Vol. Program, Greensboro, 1978-79; mem. N.C. Family Planning Council, Raleigh, 1980-82. Recipient Nurse of Yr. citation Chi Eta Phi, Greensboro, Outstanding Alumni citation N.C. State A&T U. Sch. Nursing, 1978, cert. Ret. Sr. Vol. Program U.S.A., Greensboro, 1976, 77, 78, cert. recognition Forsyth County Bd. edn.; Nat. Endowment for Humanities grantee Mich. State U., 1981. Mem. Am. Nurses Assn. (chmn. Commn. on Human Rights 1978-82, vice chmn. Commn. on Human Rights 1982-84), N.C. Nurses Assn. (dir. Raleigh chpt. 1978-80) pres. Dist. 8 1976-77, N.C. Pub. Health Assn., Nat. Council Negro Women, Sigma Theta Tau, Delta Omega. Club: Sr. (Greensboro).

WHITESIDE, OSCAR REX, educational administrator; b. Grapevine, Tex., Oct. 23, 1928; s. Leander Brandon and Nellie Lee (Harrison) W.; m. Freda Boyer, Dec. 13, 1952; children—Cindy E., Douglas W., Sherri. B.S., Tex. A&M U., 1955; M.S., Tex. Christian U., 1961; Ed. D., Baylor U., 1974. Tchr. Arlington Heights Sch., Ft. Worth, 1955-56; asst. prof. Arlington State Coll., Tex., 1956-62; registrar Hill Jr. Coll., Hillsboro, Tex., 1962-64, dean, 1964-75; dean Victoria Coll., Tex., 1975—. Served with USN, 1947-48, U.S. Army, 1950-52. Mem. Tex. Assn. Jr.-Community Coll. Instrnl. Adminstrs. (bd. dirs. 1981-83), Math. Assn. Am. Victoria C. of C. (chmn. free enterprise com. 1983-85). Lodge: Kiwanis. Avocations: golf; physical fitness) Home: 203 Tanglewood Victoria TX 77901 Office: Victoria Coll 2200 Red River Victoria TX 77901

WHITESIDES, VIRGIL STEWART, JR., geologist; b. Tupelo, Miss., Sept. 19, 1929; s. Virgil Stewart and Lucille (Evans) W.; m. Eleanor Joyce McLeroy, July 15, 1961 (dec. Dec. 1982); children—Audrey, Rachel; m. Sandra Lois Whitaker Gantenbein, May 11, 1984; children—Sam Gantenbein, Peter Gantenbein, Becca Gantenbein, Jennie Gantenbein. B.A., Vanderbilt U., 1951; M.S., U. Okla., 1957. Geologist, Exxon, Tyler, Tex., 1957-67, Robbins Petroleum Corp., Longview, Tex., 1967-68; area staff geologist Enserch Exploration, Dallas, 1968—; lectr. in geoscis. U. Tex.-Dallas, 1980—. Deacon, Scofield Meml. Ch., Dallas, 1978-82, elder, 1983-84. Served with USAF, 1951-54. Mem. Am. Assn. Petroleum Geologists, Dallas Geol. Soc. (Outstanding Service award 1983, chmn. continuing edn. com. 1982—), East Tex. Geol. Soc., Shreveport Geol. Soc., Miss. Geol. Soc. Republican. Avocations: photography; nature study; cycling. Home: 9524 Whitehurst Dallas TX 75243 Office: Enserch Exploration Inc Two Energy Sq Suite 1200 Dallas TX 75206

WHITESITT, LINDA MARIE, musicologist, violinist, radio producer; b. Great Falls, Mont., Jan. 13, 1951; d. Donald Lee and Judith Elaine (Johnson) W.; m. Bennett Lentczner, Jan. 16, 1982. B.Mus., Peabody Conservatory, 1973, M.Mus., 1975; Ph.D., U. Md., 1981. Teaching asst. Peabody Conservatory, Balt., 1973-75; instr. Gettysburg Coll., Pa., 1975; asst. prof. Radford U., Va., 1978-84; freelance writer and radio producer, Christiansburg, Va.; violinist Artemis Chamber Players, Blacksburg, Va., 1981—, New River Valley Symphony Orch., Blacksburg, 1980—, Charleston Symphony Orch., W.Va., 1984—. Author: The Life and Music of George Antheil, 1983. Producer: (radio program) WomanSpace, 1984—. Contbr. articles to profl. jours. Co-founder, My Sister's Place, A Women's Library, Blacksburg, 1985—. Nat. Endowment for Arts grantee, 1982; Va. Commn. for the Arts grantee, 1983; NEH fellow, 1984. Mem. Coll. Music Soc., Sonneck Soc., Am. Musicol. Soc. Avocations: hiking; drawing. Home: 1285 Chestnut Dr Christiansburg VA 24073

WHITFIELD, GRAHAM FRANK, orthopedic surgeon; b. Cheam, Surrey, Eng., Feb. 8, 1942; came to U.S., 1969, naturalized, 1975; s. Reginald Frank and Marjorie Joyce (Bennett) W.; m. Doreen Koester, May 17, 1980. B.Sc. magna cum laude, King's Coll., U. London, 1963, Ph.D., Queen Mary Coll., U. London, 1969; M.D., N.Y. Med. Coll., 1976. Research scientist Unilever Research Lab., Welwyn, Hertfordshire, Eng., 1963-66; postdoctoral fellow Temple U.-Phila., 1969-71, instr., 1971-72, asst. prof. chemistry, 1972-73; intern, Met. Hosp. Ctr., N.Y.C., 1976-77; resident in surgery N.Y. Med. Coll. Affiliated Hosp.-N.Y.C., 1977-78, resident in orthopedics, 1978-79, sr. resident in orthopaedic surgery, 1979-80, chief resident orthopedic surgeon, 1980-81; attending orthopedic surgeon Good Samaritan Hosp., West Palm Beach, Fla., 1981—, John F. Kennedy Meml. Hosp., Lake Worth, Fla., 1981—. Cons. practice panel in orthopedic surgery, Infections in Surgery, 1982—. Recipient N.Y. Med. Coll. Surg. Soc. award, 1976; Indsl. Studentship awardee Sci. Research Council, London, 1966-69. Mem. AMA, Fla. Med. Assn., Palm Beach County Med. Soc., Royal Inst. Chemistry (Eng.), So. Orthopaedic Assn., Sigma Xi. Republican. Clubs: Poinciana, Governor's of the Palm Beaches, The Beach, Rotary, Colette (Palm Beach); Brit. Schs. and Univs., Soc. of Sons of St. George (both N.Y.C.). Co-author: Critical Care Readings, 1981; contbg. editor, mem. editorial bd.: Hospital Physician, 1978-82; orthopedic cons.: Convention Reporter, 1980-82; assoc. editor in chief: Critical Care Monitor, 1980-82; cons. editor: Physician Assistant and Health Practitioner, 1979-82; editorial bd. Complications in Orthopaedics, 1986—. Home: 235 Queens Ln Palm Beach FL 33480 Office: 1870 Forest Hill Blvd West Palm Beach FL 33406

WHITINGTON, GENE LUTHER, pediatric gastroenterologist; b. Memphis, May 7, 1929; s. Frank Everett and Mary Lena (Hollingsworth) W.; m. Mary Francis Snider, Apr. 15, 1947 (div. Oct. 1947); m. Martha Gene Gaines, Feb. 2, 1950; children—Jeanie Whitington Mercer, Peggy Reynolds, Gene Luther, Deborah, Frank. Student Miss. State U., 1947-50; M.D., U. Tenn., 1953. Intern, Brooke Army Hosp., San Antonio, 1953-54; resident in pediatrics U. Tenn., 1955-58, fellow in gastroenterology, 1978-80; practice medicine specializing in pediatrics, Memphis, 1958-78; assoc. prof. pediatric gastroenterology U. Tenn., Memphis, 1980—, chief dir. pediatric gastro enterology, 1984—; teaching staff LeBonheur Childrens Hosp., 1980—; cons. Bapt. Hosp., 1980—, St. Jude Children's Hosp., Memphis; owner M&W Farms, Parkin, Ark., Faronia Townhouses, Memphis; pres. Cross Country Farms, Inc., Parkin. Served to capt. AUS, 1953-55. Mem. AMA, Am. Gastroenterol. Assn. Republican. Club: University. Contbr. articles to profl. jours. Home: 981 Palmer St Memphis TN 38116 Office: 848 Adams St Rm 311 Memphis TN 38103

WHITLEY, CHARLES ORVILLE, Congressman; b. Siler City, N.C., Jan. 3, 1927; s. J.B. and Mamie G. (Goodwin) W.; m. Audrey Kornegay, June 11, 1949; children—Charles Orville, Martha, Sara. B.A., Wake Forest U., 1948, LL.B., 1950. Bar: N.C. 1950. Sole practice law, Mt. Olive, 1950-60, town atty., 1951-56; adminstrv. asst. to Congressman David Henderson, 1961-76; mem. 95th-98th Congresses from 3d N.C. Dist., mem. Agr. and Armed Services coms. Served with AUS, 1944-46. Democrat. Baptist. Lodges: Masons, Woodmen of World. Office: 404 Cannon House Office Bldg Washington DC 20515*

WHITLEY, DONALD LEE, petroleum geologist; b. Pueblo, Colo., Aug. 21, 1956; s. Charles N. and Dolly J. (Boyns) W.; m. Katharine D. Fulker, Aug. 4, 1984. B.S. in Geology, U. So. Colo., 1978; M.S. in Geology, U. Iowa, 1980. Petroleum geologist Amoco Prodn. Co., Houston, 1980—. Mem. Am. Assn. Petroleum Geologists, Houston Geol. Soc. Republican. Methodist. Avocations: camping; photography; backpacking; mineral collecting. Home: 17310 Thorhill St Spring TX 77379 Office: Amoco Prodn Co PO Box 3097 Houston TX 77253

WHITLOCK, PAUL AUSTIN, JR., surgeon; b. Carrollton, Ga., Aug. 5, 1942; s. Paul Austin and Martha Louise (Ford) W.; m. Barbara Jean Mohr, Mar. 22, 1969; children—Clarice, Bessie Elizabeth, Paul Austin, Nolan Arthur. B.S., U. Ga., 1964; M.D., Emory U., 1968. Diplomate Am. Bd. Surgery. Intern Camp Pendleton (Calif.) Naval Hosp., 1968-69; resident in surgery San Diego Naval Hosp., 1969-73; practice medicine specializing in surgery, Statesboro, Ga., 1975—; mem. staff Bulloch Meml. Hosp. 1975—, pres. staff, 1979. Served to lt. comdr. M.C., USN, 1968-75. Fellow ACS; mem. Ogeechee River Med. Soc. (pres. 1976, 77), Bulloch County C. of C. (pres. 1982), 1st Dist. Med. Soc. (pres. 1981), Phi Beta Kappa, Phi Kappa Phi, Alpha Tau Omega. Lodge: Republican. Statesboro Rotary.

WHITLOCK, RUTH HENDRICKS SUMMERS, music educator; b. McAllen, Tex., May 10, 1934; d. Harold Glen and Lucile (McKee) Hendricks; m. B. McIntosh Summers, Jan. 26, 1955 (div. July 1970); 1 son, Harold McIntosh; m. Robert E. Whitlock, June 2, 1972; stepchildren—Karen Whitlock Williams, Bob. B.A., Tulane U., 1955; M.A., Occidental Coll., 1970; Ph.D., North Tex. State U., 1981; postgrad. U. Tex., Mich. State U. Cert. tchr., Tex. Music tchr. Georgetown (Tex.) Ind. Sch. Dist., 1955-58, Austin (Tex.) Ind. Sch. Dist., 1958-59, Edinburgh (Tex.) Sch. Dist., 1959-67, McAllan Ind. Sch. Dist., 1970-72, Carrollton-Farmer's Branch (Tex.) Ind. Sch. Dist., 1972-73; assoc. prof. music Tex. Christian U., Ft. Worth, 1975—; condr., cons. Recipient Outstanding Faculty award Mu Phi Epsilon 1980; Theodore Presser scholar, 1954; Mu Phi Epsilon grantee, 1980. Mem. Music Educators Nat. Conf., Tex. Music Educators Conf., Tex. Music Educators Assn., Am. Choral Dirs. Assn., Tex. Choral Dirs. Assn., Tex. Congress Parents and Tchrs. (hon. life mem.), Mu Phi Epsilon, Pi Kappa Lambda. Republican. Episcopalian. Author: Choral Insights—General Edition, 1982; Choral Insights—Renaissance Edition, 1982; Choral Insights-Baroque Edition, 1985. Home: 2712 6th Ave Fort Worth TX 76110 Office: Department of Music Texas Christian University Fort Worth TX 76129

WHITMAN, RONALD LOUIE, owner health club, chef; b. Pitts., Mar. 16, 1948; s. Louie Alford and Estelle Grace (Walker) W.; m. Linda Lee Milberger, Dec. 17, 1969 (div. Mar. 1977); 1 son, Richard Nance; m. Kaye Ellen Garner, Dec. 19, 1977; 1 dau., Tiffany Diane. B.A. in Acctg., Tex. A&M U., 1970. Mgr. Wyatts Cafeteria, 1970-72; chef Hyatt Corp., Houston, 1972-76; mktg. mgr. Trammell Temple and Staff, Houston, 1976-83; pres. N.W. Athletic Ctr., Inc., Houston, 1982—; mgr. The Sports House, Houston, 1982—; vis. lectr. U. Houston, San Jacinto Jr. Coll.; cons. lectr. Am. Dietetic Assn. Instr. safety programs, mem. safety com., bd. dirs. ARC. Recipient Humanitarian award ARC, 1981. Mem. Am. Culinary Fedn. (cert. working chef), Tex. Chefs Assn. (bd. dirs.). Republican. Home: 5021 Libbey Ln Houston TX 77092 Office: 11460 West FM 1960 Houston TX 77065

WHITMIRE, JOHN, state senator, lawyer; b. Aug. 13, 1949. B.S., U. Houston. Mem. Tex. Ho. of Reps., 1973-83; mem. Tex. Senate, 1983—; mem. health and human resources com., vice chmn. subcom. pub. health; mem. intergovtl. relations. Democrat. Office: Tex Senate PO Box 12068 Austin TX 78711*

WHITMIRE, KATHRYN JEAN, mayor of Houston; b. Houston, Aug. 15, 1946; d. Karl Niederhofer and Ida Reeves; m. James M. Whitmire (dec.). B.B.A., U. Houston, 1968, M.S. in Acctg., 1970. Audit mgr. Coopers and Lybrand, Houston, 1971-76; mem. faculty U. Houston, 1976-77; controller City of Houston, 1977-79, 79-82, mayor, 1982—; chairperson standing com. on arts, culture and recreation U.S. Conf. of Mayors, 1982—. Mem. adv. bd. dirs. Houston YWCA, 1979-81; bd. dirs., treas. Juvenile Diabetes Found., Houston, 1977. Recipient Disting. Alumnus award U. Houston Alumni Assn., 1982; Disting. Pub. Service award Houston chpt. Tex. Soc. C.P.A.s, 1982. Methodist. Office: Office of Mayor City Hall PO Box 1562 Houston TX 77251

WHITMORE, JACOB LESLIE, III, forester, researcher, consultant; b. Pontiac, Mich., Jan. 21, 1939; s. Jacob Leslie and Grace Mae (Wall) W.; m. Menandra Sabina Mosquera Moreno, Jan. 7, 1965; children—Jacqueline Grace, Michelle Jacinta. B.S., U. Mich., 1961, M.F., 1968; postgrad. U. Wash., 1968-69. Forester, Am. Friends Service Com., San Martin, Puebla, Mex., 1962-64; instr., researcher silviculture and tree improvement Tropical Agrl. Research and Tng. Ctr., Turrialba, Costa Rica, 1974-76; research forester Inst. Tropical Forestry, U.S. Dept. Agr. Forest Service, Rio Piedras, P.R., 1969-74, 76-80; internat. forester U.S. Dept. Agr. Forest Service, Washington, 1980—; U.S. del. Latin Am. Forestry Commn., Mex., 1980, Com. Forest Devel. in Tropics, Rome, 1983; USDA-Forest Service liaison to Peace Corps, 1982-85, Asia coordinator, 1981-82; program coordinator Man and Biosphere, 1980-81, research coordinator, 1985—; cons. AID, FAO, Peace Corps, others, 1969—; sec. U.S. nat. com. 9th World Forestry Congress, Mexico City, 1985. Contbr. articles to profl. jours.; editor/author other publs.; mem. editorial bd. Jour. Forestry, 1985—. U. P.R. grantee, 1979; Block Drug Co. grantee, 1967; Orgn. Tropical Studies grantee, 1967. Mem. Soc. Am. Foresters, Ecol. Soc. Am., Internat. Soc. Tropical Foresters (membership chmn. 1983-85), Internat. Union Forestry Research Orgn. (working party chmn. 1978—), Orgn. Profl. Employees of Dept. Agr. (v.p. chpt. 1984-86). Roman Catholic. Clubs: Soc. Les Voyageurs (chief 1966), Trigon. Home: 3807 Ridge Rd Annandale VA 22003 Office: USDA Forest Service-Internat Forestry 1621 N Kent St Rosslyn VA 22209

WHITNER, LILLIAN (LILLIE) MADDOX, interior designer, consultant; b. Birmingham, Ala.; d. Milton udoxious and Harriette (Newell Coleman) Maddox; m. James Harrison Whitner II, Feb. 27, 1923 (div. 1942); children—Harriette, James Harrison III, Lillian II. Sweet Briar Coll., Owner, operator Mary Lewis Dress Shop, Charlotte, N.C., 1939-42; researcher Fortune mag., Charlotte, 1942-45, Nat. Research Ctr., Denver, 1942-45; artist's rep., Charlotte, 1946-48; prin. Lillian Whitner's Interiors, Charlotte, 1948—. Exhibited at Mint Mus. Art, Charlotte, 1955; decorator Queen's Sorority House, Charlotte, 1958; Davidson Coll. frat. (N.C.), 1958; asst. decorator Gov's home, Charlotte, 1958. Pres. Alumnae Orgn. Sweet Briar Coll., Charlotte, 1932; asst. Handicraft Div. Regional Art, Mint Mus. Art, 1938-39; radio worker Community Chest, Charlotte, 1939-40. Mem. Am. Soc. Interior Designers (cert.), Mint Mus. Art. Presbyterian. Clubs: Charlotte Country, Jr. League Charlotte (soc. editor 1929-30, corr. sec. 1931-32, chmn. ways and means com. 1933-34, editor-in-chief 1935-36, chmn. local advt. 1940-41), Jr. League U.S.

WHITNEY, CAROLYN JOYCE, psychiatric nurse; b. Boston, Oct. 4, 1933; d. William Joseph and Rachel Elsie (Kimball) Armstrong; children—Richard Armstrong, Jennifer Rachael; m. 2d, Whitney Harold Thornton, Sept. 27, 1967 (dec. Aug. 1979). Grad. Lowell Gen. Sch. Nursing, 1957; B.A., Framingham State Coll., 1980; M.A. with distinction, Webster U., 1983. From asst. to supr. Boston Dispensary, 1961-64; nurse Framingham (Mass.) Union Hosp., 1964-75; charge nurse Alcohol Detoxication Ctr., Framingham, 1975-78; program coordinator Medfield (Mass.) State Hosp., 1978-80; intensive care nurse No. Trident Hosp., Charleston, S.C., 1981-82; charge nurse crisis unit So. Pines Hosp., Charleston, 1982—; associated with Dr. Roger Adler, 1985—; mem. Palmetto-Low Country Health Systems Agy, Inc., Summerville, S.C., 1982—. Chmn. Ashland (Mass.) Planning Bd., 1969-76; guardian ad litum Family Cts. and D.S.S., Summerville, 1984. Mem. Am. Pub. Health Assn. Republican. Baptist. Home: 417 Red Fox Run Summerville SC 29483 Office: So Pines Hosp Speissiger Dr Charleston SC 29405

WHITNEY, CARROLL SHAW, training and consultant executive; b. Fairmont, W.Va., Oct. 8, 1948; d. Ralph Edward and Rhoda Lee (Carroll) Shaw; m. Frederick Joseph Whitney, Sept. 2, 1972; children—Sarah, Timothy. B.A., W.Va. U., 1970; Ed. D., N.C. State U., 1984. Manpower devel. specialist Dept Manpower, Washington, 1970-74; research assoc. Conserva, Inc., Raleigh, N.C., 1979; pres., owner Occupational Tng. and Devel., Inc., Raleigh, 1979—. Author series of tng. books: Supervisory Skills Program, 1985. Mem. Am. Soc. Tng. and Devel. (v.p. Research Triangle Area chpt. 1983, bd. dirs. 1984). Democrat. Avocations: reading; beach trips. Office: Occupational Tng and Devel Inc 612 W Peace St Raleigh NC 27605

WHITNEY, HAROLD TICHENOR, JR., engineering company executive; b. Evansville, Ind., Oct. 1, 1938; s. Harold Tichenor and Ruth (Schomburg) W.; B.S., U. Cin., 1961; M.S., Northwestern U., 1962, Ph.D., 1969; m. Doris Guinevere Phillips, Apr. 16, 1961; children—Gregory Alan, Jennifer Lynn. Soil testing technician U.S. Army C.E., Cin., 1956-61, found. engr., Louisville, 1961-63; found. engr. E. D'Appolonia Assos., Pitts., 1965-69; dept. mgr. Law Engrng. Testing Co., Birmingham, Ala., 1969-72, found. cons., Atlanta, 1972-73, project mgr., found. cons. Met. Atlanta Rapid Transit Project, 1973-85, project dir. Dade County Transp. Improvement Program, Miami, Fla., 1977-82, asst. v.p. Law Engr. Testing Co., 1977—, dir., 1979-81; pres., dir. Law/Geoconsult Internat., 1982-85, NIKE/DERP hazardous waste program, 1985—; guest lectr. numerous univs. Bd. dirs. Murphey Candler Youth Sports, 1975-82, Atlanta Ballet Co., 1982—. Mem. ASCE (com. on earth retaining structures 1971-82), ASTM, Internat. Soc. Soil Mechanics and Found. Engrs., Am. Public Transit Assn., Sigma Xi, Chi Epsilon, Tau Beta Pi, Delta Tau Delta. Club: Atlanta Sports Collectors (dir.). Contbr. articles to profl. jours. Office: 1140 Hammond Dr NE Suite 5150 Bldg E Atlanta GA 30356

WHITT, GREGORY SHAWN, architectural illustrator; b. Maryville, Tenn., Jan. 27, 1955; s. Walter Rufus and Joan Maxine (Hawkins) W.; m. Julia Leigh Watson, Dec. 31, 1981; 1 child, Brandon Shawn. Student Walters State Community Coll., 1973-75, U. Tenn., 1975-78. Illustrator, Oak Ridge Nat. Lab., Tenn., 1978-80, 81-82; automobile designer Porsche Automobiles, Stuttgart, W. Ger., 1980; illustrator Martin Marietta Corp., Orlando, Fla., 1982-83; archtl. illustrator Evans Group Architecture, Orlando, 1983—; pvt. practice, Orlando, 1984—; illustrator Litton Corp., Orlando, 1984—; archtl. illustrator Greater Constrn., Orlando, 1984—; free lance illustration Road & Track Mag., Newport Beach, Calif., 1980—. Recipient Excellance award Internat. Graphics, Inc., 1981, 82; 5th place award Nat. Competition Model Products Corp., 1972. Democrat. Southern Baptist. Avocations: Automobile collector; tennis; art. Home and Office: 1008 Pine Shadow Dr #2 Apopka FL 32712

WHITT, MARCUS BURNS, II, counseling agency administrator; b. Oklahoma City, Mar. 12, 1948; s. Marcus Burns and Peggy Jane (Gassaway) W.; m. Barbara Ann Gallagher, July 10, 1971 (div. 1982); 1 son, Marcus Burns; m. 2d, Pamela Sue Chapin, Nov. 26, 1982. A.S., No. Okla. Coll., 1972; B.S. in Edn., East Central State U., 1974; M.S. in Sociology, Okla. State U., 1976. Registered social worker; cert. parent effectiveness trainer. Juvenile officer, family counselor Kay Juvenile Services, Inc., Perry, Okla., 1974-76; exec. dir. Kay County Youth Services Ctr. and Shelter, Ponca City, Okla., 1976—; instr. No. Okla. Coll., 1978, 79, 80. Served with AUS, 1967-70. Recipient Ponca City Outstanding Young Man award, 1981; Eagle Scout award, 1961. Mem. Am. Correctional Assn., Am. Personnel and Guidance Assn., Nat. Criminal Justice Assn., Okla. Assn. Youth Services, Nat. Assn. Prevention Profls., Am. Soc. Criminology, Am. Pub. Welfare Assn., Ponca City Arts Assn., VFW, Am. Legion. Democrat. Presbyterian. Club: Ambucs. Lodge: Rotary. Home: 2301 Glenmore Pl Ponca City OK 74601 Office: 415 W Grand St Ponca City OK 74601

WHITT, WILLIAM O'NEAL, electric utility company executive; b. Blanch, Tenn., 1923; married. B.S., Auburn U., 1947. With Alabama Power Co. Inc., Birmingham, 1948—, sr. engr., 1949-58, Birmingham dist. supt., 1958-61, dist. mgr., 1961-65, asst. to v.p., 1964-65, div. v.p., 1965-75, corp. sr. v.p., 1975-78, exec. v.p., 1978—. Office: Alabama Power Co Inc 600 N 18th St Box 2641 Birmingham AL 35291*

WHITTEMORE, DOROTHY JANE, librarian; b. San Jose, Calif., Nov. 9, 1920; d. Glen James and Jane Dorothy (Katz) Gordon; A.B., San Jose State Coll., 1941, cert. of librarianship, 1942, postgrad., 1952-53; m. Robert Clifton Whittemore, June 15, 1959; children by previous marriage—Stanley Allen Lawton, Shirley Anne (Mrs. Anthony Kopcych). Sch. library supr. Piedmont (Calif.) Sch. Dist., 1942-43; asst. post librarian Presidio of San Francisco, 1943-49; jr. librarian San Jose (Calif.) State Coll., 1951-53; reference librarian Tulane U. Library, New Orleans, 1953-76, acting dir., 1976-78, asst. librarian for public services, 1978-80, dir. Norman Mayer Bus. Library, 1980—. Bd. dirs. New Orleans chpt. LWV, 1964-66, dir. La. chpt., 1967-69, 73-78; mem. citizens adv. com. City Planning Commn. of New Orleans, 1965-67; sec. New Orleans chpt. La. Consumers League, 1972-74; adv. council La. State Bd. Nursing, 1977—; active Pub. Affairs Research Council. Council on Library Resources research grantee, 1972. Mem. Spl. Libraries Assn. (pres. La. chpt. 1975-76), La. Library Assn. (chmn. coll. and reference sect. 1968-69, exec. bd. 1973-74), New Orleans Library Club (past pres.), Am. Soc. Info. Sci., Nat. Microfilm Assn. Author: (with others) Citizen's Guide to Louisiana Government, 1969. Home: 7521 Dominican St New Orleans LA 70118 Office: Tulane U Library New Orleans LA 70118

WHITTEN, DAVID OWEN, economics educator, b. Beaver Falls, Pa., Nov. 30, 1940; s. Paul Harry and Bula (Owens) Ehrenbergh. B.S., Coll. Charleston, 1962; M.A., U. S.C., 1963; Ph.D., Tulane U., 1970. Instr. econs. and fin. U. New Orleans, 1965-68; asst. prof. econs. Auburn U., Ala., 1968-74, assoc. prof., 1974-82, prof., 1982—; cons. U.S. Army C.E., New Orleans, summers 1964, 65. Author: Andrew Durnford: A Black Sugar Planter, 1981 (La. honor award 1982); Emergence of Giant Enterprise, 1983. Editor, Wall St. Rev. of Books, 1981—, contbr., 1976-80. Served with USMCR, 1957-63. Tulane Edn. Found. fellow, 1964, 65. Mem. Am. Econ. Assn. Agrl. History Soc., Soc. for History Early Am. Rep., Econ. History Assn., So. Econs. Assn. Home: 515 Foxrun Pkwy 5M Opelika AL 36801 Office: Dept Econs Auburn U Auburn AL 36849

WHITTEN, JAMIE LLOYD, congressman; b. Cascilla, Miss., Apr. 18, 1910; s. Alymer Guy and Nettie (Early) W.; m. Rebecca Thompson, June 20, 1940; children—James Lloyd, Beverly Rebecca. Student lit. and law depts. U. Miss., 1926-31. Prin. Cowart Pub. Sch., 1931; elected Miss. State Legislature, 1931; dist. atty. 17th Dist. of Miss., 1933, reelected, 1935 and 1939; mem. 77th-99th congresses from 1st Miss. Dist., 1941—, chmn. house appropriations com. Mem. Beta Theta Pi, Phi Alpha Delta, Omicron Delta Kappa. Democrat. Mason. Home: Charleston MS 38921 also 5804 Nebraska Ave Washington DC 20015 Office: House of Representatives Washington DC 20515

WHITTIER, CHARLES TAYLOR, JR., investment company executive; b. Cedar Falls, Iowa, Nov. 29, 1941; s. Charles Taylor and Sara Jane (Leckrone) W.; student Montgomery Jr. Coll., 1959-62; B.S., Morehead U., 1964; M.B.A., Temple U., 1968; postgrad. U. Okla., 1971-77; m. Wendi Lynn Walker, June 18, 1978; children—Megan Rose, Courtney Lynn. Cost analyst Philco-Ford Corp., Ft. Washington, Pa., 1967, programs adminstr., 1967-69, sr. salary adminstr., 1969-70, mgr. indsl. relations for U.S. and Third Country nats., Saigon, Vietnam, 1970, Southeast Asia liason, Phila., 1971; pres. Internat. Enterprises, Norman, Okla., 1971-76, Transnational Corp., Norman, Okla., 1977—, v.p., treas. mining co., 1977-81; pres. CTEC Inc., 1979—, TACSAW Inc., 1982—, Transnat. Energy Corp., 1983—, Whittier Fin. Corp., 1979—, WTS Inc., 1981—, Whittier Exploration and Devel. Co., 1983—; oil and gas cons., 1975—; ins. cons., 1983—; past cons. to Okla. Aeronautical Commn.; past cons. and acting pres. Aviation FBO Co. Mem. AAUP, Aircraft Owners and Pilots Assn., Oklahoma City Internat. Trade Club, Licensing Execs. Soc., World Mariculture Soc., Colo. Mining Assn. Mem. Christian Ch. (Disciples of Christ). Co-editor: The Conduct of Bus. Overseas: An Okla. Perspective, 1974. Home: 2226 Lindenwood Ln Norman OK 73071 Office: PO Box 5969 Norman OK 73070

WHITTINGTON, JEFFERY LEE, optometrist; b. Montgomery, W.Va., Oct. 11, 1957; s. Bobby Lee and Jacqueline Carol (McCoy) W.; m. Sandra Mae Hess, Sept. 10, 1983; 1 child, Jennifer Logan. Student W. Va. U., 1975-78; D.O., So. Coll. Optometry, 1982. Pvt. practice optometry, Charleston, W. Va., 1982—. Pres. Shawnee Lions Club, Charleston, 1983—. Mem. Kanawha Valley Optometric Assn. (pres. 1982—). Democrat. Baptist. Avocations: tennis; racquetball. Home: 25 Seneca Hills Dr 1 Elkview WV 25071 Office: 3840 Pennsylvania Ave Charleston WV 25302

WHITWORTH, CHARLES DARWIN, veterinarian; b. Huntsville, Ala., May 7, 1955; s. Thomas Jerome and Sara (Landman) W.; m. Kimberly Leigh Allen, Mar. 15, 1980; children—Allison Lynn, Chase Allen, Mark Thomas. D.V.M., Auburn U., 1980. Pvt. practice vet. medicine, Waverly Animal Clinic (Tenn.), 1980-81; owner Whitworth Animal Clinic, Madison, Ala., Whitworth Farm. Mem. North Ala. Vet. Med. Assn., Madison County Vet. Med. Assn., Ala. Cattleman's Assn., Alpha Psi. Club: Acme. Home: 1044 Mill Rd Madison AL 35758 Office: 106 Rainbow Dr Madison AL 35758

WHITWORTH, RANDOLPH HOWARD, educator, psychologist; b. Robstown, Tex., May 18, 1929; s. Howard J. and Pearl (Randolph) W.; B.S., U. Tex., Austin, 1951, Ph.D., 1960; m. Selina Morgan, Mar. 17, 1966; children—Kirsten, Randolph T., Caroline S. Asst. prof. psychology Tex. Western Coll., 1960-63; asso. prof. psychology U. Tex., El Paso, 1963—, dir. counseling service, 1962-67, asst. dean Coll. Liberal Arts, 1977-83, chmn. dept. psychology, 1983—; pvt. practice psychology, El Paso, Tex., 1960—; adj. prof. Tex. Tech. Med. Sch., 1977—. Served with USAF, 1951-55. Mem. Am. Psychol. Assn., Southwestern Psychol. Assn., Rocky Mountain Psychol. Assn., Tex. Psychol. Assn., El Paso Psychol. Assn., Sigma Xi. Contbr. articles to profl. jours. Home: 6600 Camino Fuente El Paso TX 79912 Office: 6006 N Mesa Suite 301 El Paso TX 79912

WHOLEBEN, BRENT EDWARD, teacher educator, educational administrator; b. Olean, N.Y., July 7, 1946; s. Bernard Edward and Mildred Florence (Camp) W.; m. Judith Ann Braun, June 22, 1968; children—Melissa Anne, Kevin Patrick. B.S. in Math., St. Bonaventure U., 1968; M.Ed. in Psychology, U. Hawaii, 1972, M.Ed. in Adminstrn., 1974; Ph.D. in Ednl. Adminstrn., U. Wis., 1979. Cert. emergency med. technician, Wash., Tex. Tchr. math., coordinator student activities, dir. guidance services Hawaii Dept. Edn., 1970-75; family psychotherapist, vocat. guidance specialist interim dept. supr. Family Tng. Ctr., Glasgow, Mont., 1975-77; project asst., research cons. U. Wis.-Madison, 1977-79, teaching asst. computer applications in edn., 1978-79; systems evaluation cons. to sch. dists., 1978-79; asst. prof. ednl. adminstrn., assoc. dir. Research Bur., U. Wash., 1979-82; assoc. prof. ednl. adminstrn. U. Tex.-El Paso, 1982-84, dir. instructional computer labs., 1984—; internat. cons. on applications of data and info. processing to roles of instrn. and decision-making; internat. cons. UN Ednl., Sci. and Cultural Orgn., 1985—. Author books, articles, and research reports in field; manuscript and publs. reviewer N.W. Regional Ednl. Labs., Assn. Ednl. Data Systems, Univ. Press Am., Jour. Ednl. Computing Research, Univ. Press Am., Jour. Tchr. Edn. Served with arty. U.S. Army, 1968-70, Vietnam. Mem. Am. Ednl. Research Assn., Wash. Inst. Mgmt. Scis., Wash. Ednl. Research Assn., Wash. Assn. Supervision and Curriculum Devel., Assn. Ednl. Data Systems, Phi Delta Kappa. Democrat. Roman Catholic. Lodge: KC. Home: 6700 Southwind Dr El Paso TX 79912 Office: Edn Bldg Room 712 El Paso TX 79963

WHORTON, JUDSON SEABORN, life insurance executive; b. Gadsden, Ala., Dec. 26, 1929; s. George Seaborn and Jennie (Griffin) W.; m. Carolyn Buckner, Aug. 23, 1953; children—Jane, Elaine, Alan, Bruce. B.S. in Bus., Jacksonville State U., 1953. Acct., Winston, Brooke C.P.A.s, Anniston, Ala., 1953-55; chief acct. Atlantic Nat. Life Ins. Co., Anniston, 1955-57; chief acct., treas., v.p. and treas., sr. v.p. and treas. Am. Heritage Life Ins. Co., Jacksonville, Fla., 1957—; mem. adv. bd. Atlantic Bancorp., Jacksonville, 1973—. Bd. dirs. Bapt. Med. Ctr., Jacksonville. Served with USN, 1948-49. Mem. Fin. Analysts Soc. Jacksonville, Jacksonville C. of C. Democrat. Clubs: River (Jacksonville), Univ. Country (Jacksonville), Ponte Vedra (Fla.). Home: 5443 John Reynolds Dr Jacksonville FL 32211 Office: 11 E Forsyth St Jacksonville FL 32202

WHYBARK, DALE LEE, geologist; b. Oklahoma City, Apr. 28, 1957; s. Dale Beeson nd Mildred Lee (Clark) W. B.A., Okla State U., 1979. Prospect geologist PSEC Inc., Oklahoma City, 1979—. Deacon, Britton Christian Ch., Oklahoma City, 1983—. Mem. Am. Assn. Petroleum Geologists (jr.), Oklahoma City Geol. Soc. Republican. Mem. Christian Ch. (Disciples of Christ). Club: Petroleum. Home: 2116 NW 115th St Oklahoma City OK 73120 Office: PSEC Inc 100 Park Ave Bldg Suite 200 Oklahoma City OK 73102

WIANT, HARRY VERNON, JR., forestry educator, consultant; b. Burnsville, W.Va., Nov. 4, 1932; s. Harry Vernon and Allegra (McNemar) W.; m. Jeanne Dean, Nov. 6, 1954; children—Kurt Vernon, Teresa Jeanne. B.S., W.Va. U., 1954; M.F., U. Ga., 1959; Ph.D., Yale U., 1963. Registered forester, W.Va. Forester Forest Service, U.S. Dept. Agr., Blairsville, Ga., 1957; asst. prof. forestry Humbolt State U., Arcata, Calif., 1961-65; asst. to dean, assoc. prof. forestry Stephen F. Austin State U., Nacogdoches, Tex., 1965-72; asst. dir. research, prof. forestry W. Va. U., Morgantown, 1972—. Served with U.S. Army, 1954-56. Mem. Soc. Am. Foresters, Sigma Xi, Xi Sigma Pi, Gamma Sigma Delta. Baptist. Author: Elementary Timber Measurements, 1979; editor No. Jour. Applied Forestry, 1984—; contbr. numerous articles to profl. jours. Home: 113 Scenery Dr Morgantown WV 26505 Office: WVa U Morgantown WV 26506

WIBLE, JUDITH LAINE, psychiatrist; b. Portland, Ind., Oct. 7, 1940; d. John F. and June V. (Young) W.; children—Pamela, Frederick. Student U. Houston, 1959-61; M.D., U. Tex., 1965. Intern, Jewish Hosp. and Med. Ctr., N.Y.C., 1965-66; resident Phila. Psychiat. Ctr., Ancora Psychiat. Hosp., Phila. State Hosp., 1972-74; research psychiatrist Phila. Gen. Hosp., 1973-75; clin. dir., staff psychiatrist Phila. State Hosp., 1974-76; clin. asst. psychiatrist Pa. Hosp., Phila., 1976-78; inpatient unit dir. Dallas County Mental Health Ctr., 1977-78; pvt. practice psychiatry, Dallas, 1978—; chmn. dept. psychiatry Richardson Med. Ctr. (Tex.), 1984—. Diplomate Am. Bd. Psychiatry and Neurology. Mem. Am. Med. Women's Assn., Am. Psychiat. Assn., Pres. Assocs. Women's Med. Coll. Pa., NOW, Nat. Women Polit. Caucus, Alpha Epsilon Delta, Dallas C. of C. Office: 13601 Preston Rd Dallas TX 75240

WICH, DONALD ANTHONY, JR., lawyer; b. Detroit, Apr. 13, 1947; s. Donald Anthony and Margaret Louise (Blatz) W. B.A., Notre Dame U., Ind., 1969, J.D., 1972. Bar: Fla. 1972, U.S. Dist. Ct. (so. dist.) Fla. 1972; U.S. Ct. Appeals (5th and 11th cirs.) 1982, U.S. Supreme Ct. 1976. Assoc. VISTA, Miami, Fla., 1972-74; atty. Legal Services, Miami, 1973-75; adj. prof. law U. Miami, Fla., 1974-75; ptnr. Sullivan, Bailey, Wich & Stockman, P.A., Pompano, and Ft. Lauderdale, Fla., 1976—; pres., dir. Legal Aid of Broward, Ft. Lauderdale, 1976-82. Mem. ABA, Lawyers Title Guaranty Fund, Am. Arbitration Assn., North Broward Bar Assn. (pres. 1983-84), Acad. Fla. Trial Lawyers Assn., Broward County Trial Lawyers Assn. (v.p. 1985-86), Broward Bar Assn. (chmn. legis. com. 1984-85), Assn. Tex. Trial Lawyers, Assn. Trial Lawyers Am., Pompano Beach C. of C. (dir. 1984-87, Govtl. Affairs Chmn. 1983-84, Art Show chmn. 1984-85, Seafood Festival chmn. 1985-86). Office: Sullivan Bailey Wich & Stockman PA 2335 E Atlantic Blvd Suite 301 Pompano Beach FL 33062

WICKENS, NANCY BEVAN, health care administrator, nurse; b. New Haven, July 7, 1936; d. James Stuart and Edith (Newcomb) W.; m. Roger Elliot Thies, Sept. 7, 1957 (div. Dec. 1970); children—J. Eric, David N.; m. Alfred Charles Taylor, Nov. 29, 1977. Student Bates Coll., 1954-56; B.S. in Nursing, Cornell U., 1959. R.N., N.Y., Fla. Sr. Staff nurse N.Y. Hosp., N.Y.C., 1959-60; instr. N.Y. Hosp.-Cornell U., N.Y.C., 1960-61; supr. nursing Coyne Campbell Hosp., Oklahoma City, 1969-75; tng. mgr. Upjohn HealthCare Services, Tampa, Fla., 1976—. Mem. Am. Nurses Assn., Am. Soc. Tng. and Devel., Nat. League Nursing, Nurse Educators Assn. Tampa, Sigma Theta Tau (corr. sec.). Democrat. Episcopalian. Avocations: reading; needlepoint. Home: 8205 Crenshaw Circle Tampa FL 33615 Office: Upjohn HealthCare Services 14802 N Dale Mabry Suite 306 Tampa FL 33624

WICKER, JAMES EUGENE, psychologist; b. Whittenburg, Tex., Jan. 26, 1935; s. Elbert Shelton and Mrytle Blanche (Brown) W.; children—Tamra Michelle, David Andrew. A.A., Del Mar Coll., 1955; B.A. in Psychology, U. Tex., 1960, M.A., 1962; Psy. D., Tex. Sch. Profl. Psychology, 1987. Lic. psychologist, Tex. Electronics technician various cos., Austin, 1953-57; tech. staff asst. II, research scientist asst. Radiobiol. Lab., U. Tex. and U.S. Air Force, 1957-64; cons. psychologist, Austin, Ft. Worth, 1962-70; pvt. practice psychology, Ft. Worth, 1970—; spl. instr. psychology U. Tex., 1964; human factors engr. Gen. Dynamics, Ft. Worth, 1964-65, sr. human factors psychologist, 1966—; condr. seminars, lectr., cons. in field. Contbr. articles to profl. jours. Mem. Am. Psychol. Assn., Midwestern Psychol. Assn., Tex. Psychol. Assn., Tarrant County Psychol. Assn. (chmn. referral com.), Mensa. Republican. Episcopalian. Avocations: hiking; camping; tennis; chess. Address: 3436 Clayton Rd E Fort Worth TX 76116

WICKER, THOMAS CAREY, JR., judge; b. New Orleans, Aug. 1, 1923; s. Thomas Carey and Mary (Taylor) W.; B.B.A., Tulane U., 1944, LL.B., 1949; m. Veronica Jean Di Carlo; children—Thomas Carey III, Catherine Anne. Admitted to La. bar, 1949; law clk. La. Supreme Ct., New Orleans, 1949-50; asst. U.S. Atty., 1950-53; practiced in New Orleans, 1953-72; mem. firm Simon, Wicker & Wiedemann, 1953-67; partner firm Wicker, Wiedemann & Fransen, 1967-72; dist. judge Jefferson Parish (La.), 1972—, mem. faculty Nat. Jud. Coll., Tulane U. Sch. Law. Past bd. visitors Tulane U; bd. dirs. La. Jud. Coll.; treas. Sugar Bowl. Served from ensign to lt. (j.g.), USNR, 1944-46. Mem. ABA (jud. div. council), La. (chmn. jr. bar sect. 1958-59, gov. 1958, mem. ho. of dels. 1960-72), Jefferson Parish, bar assns., Tulane U. Alumni Assn. (past pres.), Am. Judicature Soc., La. Dist. Judges Assn. (past pres.), Nat. Conf. State Trial Judges (exec. com.), Order of Coif, Beta Gamma Sigma (former chmn. nat. alumni adv. council), Pi Kappa Alpha. Democrat. Episcopalian. Clubs: Rotary (pres. 1971-72), Metairie (La.) Country. Home: 3700 Cleveland Pl Metairie LA 70003 Office: New Courthouse Bldg Gretna LA 70053

WICKER, VERONICA DICARLO, judge; b. Monessen, Pa., Nov. 26, 1930; s. Vincent James and Rose Margaret DiCarlo; B.F.A., Syracuse U., 1952; J.D., Loyola U. of South 1966; m. Thomas Carey Wicker, Jr.; children—Cathy, Carey. Bar: La. 1966. U.S. magistrate, New Orleans, 1977-79; judge U.S. Dist. Ct. Eastern Dist. La., New Orleans, 1979—. Mem. vis. com. Loyola U. Sch. Law, 1981—. Mem. Fed. Bar Assn., ABA, La. Bar Assn., New Orleans Bar Assn., Assn. Women Judges, Fed. Judges Assn., Assn. Women Attys., Women's Caucus for Art, Justinian Soc. Jurists, Alpha Xi, Phi Mu. Office: US Courthouse 500 Camp St Rm C-406 New Orleans LA 70130

WICKEY, EDWARD LEWIS, proprietary school executive; b. N.Y.C., Oct. 20, 1942; s. Edward Lewis and Martha Elizabeth (Franke) W.; m. Faye Donna Delucia, Dec. 29, 1963 (div. 1970); 1 son, Keith Christopher; m. Karen Ann Swanner, Feb. 27, 1971 (div. 1976); children—Gina Michelle, Robert William (dec.); m. Nancy Ann Evans, Feb. 26, 1977. A.S. with honors, Grossmont Coll. Chief operating officer Bill Wade Sch., San Diego, 1969-75; admissions dir. San Diego Coll. Bus., 1975-79; chief exec. officer Bryman Schs., Dallas, 1979-80, Airco Tech. Inst., Houston, 1980-81, Gen. Industries, Houston, 1981—; chmn., chief exec. officer NTDS, Inc., Houston, 1983—; cons. San Diego County Orgn. Pvt. Edn., 1977-79, Hargest Coll., Houston, 1982—. Served with AUS, 1959-62. Mem. Tex. Assn. Pvt. Schs., Houston Assn. Pvt. Schs., Calif. Assn. Pvt. Edn., Nat. Assn. Accts., Nat. Rehab. Assn. Republican. Home: 10611 Village Trail Houston TX 77065

WICKHAM, DAVID WHEELER, communications educator, administrator; b. Abilene, Tex., Nov. 27, 1946; s. Robert Elde and Johnnie (Wheeler) W.; m. Sharifeh Sokhansanj, May 20, 1976; 1 child, Athena. B.A., So. Methodist U., 1969, M.A., 1974. English instr. Peace Corps., West Africa, 1969-72, Rasht, Iran, 1975-77, Esfahan, Iran, 1978-79; part-time instr. Mountain View Coll., Dallas, 1980-84, chmn. dommunications div., 1984—; instr. So. Meth. U., Dallas, summer 1984. Mem. Dallas Mus. Fine Arts, Tex. Jr. Coll. Tchrs. Assn. Democrat. Home: 2956 Binkley St #5 Dallas TX 75205 Office: Mountain View college 4849 W Illinois St Dallas TX 75211

WICKMAN, JOAN PIERCE, educator; b. Susquehanna, Pa., May 17, 1933; d. Fred Ray and Hazel Marion (Hupman) Pierce. B.A. magna cum laude in Sociology, SUNY-Potsdam, 1977; M.B.A., Clarkson U., Potsdam, 1978; postgrad. Queen's Coll., Kingston, Ont., Can., 1979, U. Tex. Office trainee IBM, Endicott, N.Y. and N.Y.C., 1952-57; exec. sec. Gulf Oil Co., Binghamton, N.Y., 1957-59; adminstrv. asst. bus. and indsl. devel. Marine Midland Corp., Buffalo, 1959-68; dir., treas. So. Tier Shares, Inc., Binghamton, 1965-68; stockbroker trainee First Albany Corp. (N.Y.), 1965-68; owner Circuit, Houston, 1969-74; asst. dir. spl. programs SUNY, 1977, assoc. dir. sponsored research, 1979; fin. mgmt. cons., Houston, 1980, Potsdam, 1981-83; prof. Clarkson Coll. Sch. Mgmt., 1983, Dallas Bapt. Univ. Sch. Mgmt., 1984—. Bd. dirs. Music Theatre North, Potsdam, 1980—; active numerous civic and charitable orgns. Recipient various nat. and state awards for work with rural children Patrons of Husbandry. Mem. Adminstrv. Mgmt. Soc., Data Processing Mgmt. Assn., Assn. Computing Machinery, Sales and Mktg. Execs., DAR, Alpha Kappa Delta. Republican. Baptist. Club: Altrusa. Home: 611 Oriole Blvd Duncanville TX 75116

WIDENER, HIRAM EMORY, JR., judge; b. Abingdon, Va., Apr. 30, 1923; s. Hiram Emory and Nita Douglas (Peck) W.; m. Jo Smith O'Donnell; children—Molly Berentd, Hiram Emory III. Student Va. Poly. Inst., 1940-41; B.S. U.S. Naval Acad., 1944; LL.B, Washington and Lee U., 1953, LL.D., 1977. Bar: Va. 1951. Pvt. practice law, Bristol, Va., 1953-69; judge U.S. Dist. Ct., Western Dist. Va., Abingdon, 1969-71, chief judge, 1971-72; judge U.S. Ct. Appeals, 4th Circuit, Abingdon, 1972—. U.S. commr. Western Dist. Va., 1963-66; mem. Va. Election Laws Study Commn., 1968-69, Chmn. Republican party 9th Dist. Va., 1966-69; mem. Va. Republican State Central Com., 1966-69, state exec. com., 1966-69. Served to lt. (j.g.) USN, 1944-49, to lt., USNR, 1951-52. Decorated Bronze Star with combat V. Trustee Va. Intermont Coll.; mem. Am. Law Inst.; mem. Va. Bar Assn., Va. State bar, Am. Legion, Phi Alpha Delta. Republican. Presbyterian. Home: RFD 1 Box 485AA Abingdon VA 24210 Office: PO Box 868 Abingdon VA 24210

WIDMAN, RUDOLPH PAUL, college administrator; b. Abington, Pa., Sept. 19, 1940; s. Rudolph Paul and Sara (Brinker) W.; m. Alberta Elanora Sabino, May 20, 1963; children—Rudi Paul, Karl Albert. A.B., Eastern Nazarene Coll., Wollaston, Mass., 1963; M.S., Northeastern U., 1965, Ph.D., 1971; M.B.A., Fla. Inst. Tech., Jensen Beach, 1982. Tchr., Plymouth-Carver High Sch. (Mass.), 1964-66; prof. chemistry Curry Coll., Milton, Mass., 1966-68; research fellow U. Va., Charlottesville, 1971-73; adminstrv. asst. Piedmont Va. Community Coll., Charlottesville, 1974; dir. ednl. services Indian River Community Coll., Ft. Pierce, Fla., 1974—. Pres. bd. dirs. Sun Grove Montessori Sch., Ft. Pierce, 1975—; bd. dirs. St. Michael's Sch., Stuart, Fla., 1977—, Fla. Found. Future Scientists, Gainesville, 1977—, Community Action Orgn., Ft. Pierce, 1975-78. Recipient 4th Annual award Soc. Applied Spectroscopy, 1970. Mem. Fla. Assn. Community Colls., Sigma Xi, Phi Kappa Phi, Phi Delta Kappa. Contbr. articles to profl. publs. Office: 3209 Virginia Ave Fort Pierce FL 33450

WIDMER, DIANE ELIZABETH, language educator; b. Coral Gables, Fla., Nov. 1, 1951; d. Frederick Shannon and Dorothy Anne (Lorber) Smith; m. James A. Widmer, Dec. 26, 1981. Student U. Munich, 1972-73; B.S., U. Pitts., 1975; postgrad. U. Hamburg, 1975-76; M.S., Fla. Internat. U., 1979. Lic. tchr., Pa., Fla. Adj. prof. Fla. Internat. U., 1978-79; asst. prof. German and English as 2d lang. Miami (Fla.)-Dade Community Coll., 1977—; owner German Translating Service, Miami, 1980—. Fulbright-Hays scholar to W.Ger., 1975-76; Goethe Inst. tchr.'s scholar, 1979. Mem. DAR. Republican. Methodist. Home: 7701 SW 57th Ave Apt 3 South Miami FL 33143 Office: Miami Dade Community Coll 300 NE 2nd Ave Miami FL 33132

WIEBE, MICHAEL JOHN, special education educator, psychologist; b. Wichita, Kans., Sept. 20, 1945; s. Carl Edward and Ella Marie (Warkentin) W.; m. Norma Jean Buller, Aug. 12, 1967; children—Michael John, II, Matthew Carl, Mark Edward. B.S., Bethel Coll., 1967; M.S., Kans. Tchrs. Coll., 1971, Ed.S., 1971; Ph.D., George Peabody U., 1973. Lic. psychologist, Tex. Educator Menniger Found., Topeka, 1967-71, prof. spl. edn. Tex. Woman's U., Denton, 1973—. Mem. Am. Psychol. Assn., Council for Exceptional Children. Presbyterian. Avocation: woodworking. Home: 905 Hilton Pl Denton TX 76201 Office: Tex Woman's U Box 23029 Denton TX 76204

WIEDEMANN, FREDERIC FRANKLIN, insurance company executive; b. N.Y.C., Apr. 1, 1923; s. Rudolph Franklin Edward and Margaret Elizabeth (Lord) W.; m. Florence Leachman, Mar. 25, 1927; children—Frederic Franklin, Harden H., Jonathan L. B.S. in Elec. Engring., U.S. Naval Acad., 1945. C.L.U.; chartered fin. cons. Agt., Minn. Mut. Co., Dallas, 1947-50; regional sales dir. Franklin Life Ins. Co., Dallas, 1950-53; v.p. Continental Life, Ft. Worth, 1953-55; ptnr. Jones & Wiedemann, Dallas, 1955-65; chmn. bd. Wiedemann & Johnson Cos., Dallas, 1966—. Bd. dirs. St. Marks Sch. Tex., 1960-76, Dallas Art Mus., 1970-74, Theatre Three, 1968-76, Dallas Civic Opera, 1957—, Colo. Outward Bound Sch., 1980—; bd. dirs. S.W. Outward Bound Sch., 1969-80, chmn., 1971-78. Served with USN, 1941-47. Episcopalian. Club: Dallas Petroluem, Idlewild. Office: 3626 N Hall St Dallas TX 75219

WIEDEMANN, JEFFERSON ALLEN, coal company executive; b. Lexington, Ky., Nov. 24, 1921; s. George Stanhope and Mary McIlwaine (Purcell) W.; m. Dorcas Noel Hollingsworth, June 20, 1950; children—Jefferson Mark, Randal Armistead, Holly Boal, Britton Boal, Hope Hall B.A., Yale U., 1943; M.Litt., U. Pitts., 1947. Gen. mdse. mgr., treas. Purcell Co., Lexington, 1947-68; underwriting agt. Mass. Mutual Life Ins. Co., Lexington, 1968-78; pres. Wiedemann & Assocs., Lexington, 1978-85, Wiedemann Coal, Lexington, 1980—; pres., editor Holly Pub. Co. Pres. Montessori Sch. Bd., Georgetown, Ky.; bd. dirs. Lexington Credit Bur.; pres., bd. dirs. Ky. Retail Fedn., Lexington; mem. Republican Predsl. Task Force, Washington, 1983—. Served to lt. (j.g.) USN, 1943-46, PTO. Mem. Lexington C. of C. (mem. exec. com.), Nat. Retail Merchants Assn. Episcopalian. Clubs: Spindletop, Thoroughbred of Am., Iroquois Hunt (bd. dirs.) (Lexington). Lodge: Rotary. Avocations: Polo; hunting. Home: the Hollys 1589 Newtown Pike Georgetown KY 40324 Office: Wiedemann Coal Co 100 W Vine St Lexington KY 40507

WIEDENMANN, BARBARA NAOMI, retail executive; b. LaPorte, Ind., Dec. 24, 1938; d. Lloyd Noble and NaomiRuth (Cook) Overton; m. Mark Joseph Wiedermann, May 27, 1961 (div. Nov. 1976); children—Ferrin Ruth, Andrea Marie, Megan Suzanne. Student U. Mo.-Columbia, 1959-60. Sec., Ditto, Inc., Tulsa, 1958; office asst. Okla. Natural Gas, Tulsa, 1960-61; owner The Fair, Tulsa, 1963-76; owner, pres. Dish Bar, Inc., Tulsa, 1974—. Officer, Childrens Day Nursery, Tulsa, 1973-76. Mem. Tulsa C. of C., Better Bus. Bur., Tulsa Philharm. Soc. Republican. Presbyterian. Office: Dish Barn Inc 6528 E 51st St Tulsa OK 74145

WIEDERANDERS, DAVID GENE, engineering executive; b. Vernon, Tex., Apr. 25, 1943; d. Edward John and Virginia Mae (Freeling) W.; B.S. in Engring. Sci., U. Tex., Austin, 1968. Mktg. rep. IBM, San Antonio, 1968-70; sr. research engr. SW Research Inst., San Antonio, 1970-72; mgr. sales engring. Datapoint Corp., San Antonio, 1972-75; v.p. Trinity Chem. Corp., San Antonio, 1975-78; v.p. mfg. and ops., dir. Refrigeration Engring. Corp., San Antonio, 1978-81; pres. Infotech Systems, Inc., San Antonio, 1981—; dir. Trinity Chem. Corp., Cynetics Inc., The Alpha Group, Inc., AutoMasters, Inc., Fusion BioTech, Inc. Pres., Checkpointers, 1973, Coast, 1974, Data Processing Mgmt. Assn., 1972-73. Served with U.S. Army, 1961-64. Recipient certs. of appreciation Data Processing Mgmt. Assn., World War I Pilots Assn. Mem. Tex. Assn. Bus., North San Antonio C. of C. Republican. Lutheran. Author: Quality Assurance in Nuclear Power Plant Construction, 1971. Office: 130 W Rhapsody San Antonio TX 78216

WIEGAND, FREDERICK WILLIAM, JR., petroleum engineer; b. Austin, Tex., Dec. 22, 1945; s. Frederick William and Navene R. (Lee) W.; m. Patricia Ann Yesenik Jan. 24, 1970 (div. 1979); children—Gretchen Eileen, Carl Jonathan; m. Charlotte Harriet Watson, Oct. 15, 1983; children—Sandra, Bryan Frederick. B.S. in Geology, U. Tex., 1969, B.S. in Petroleum Engring., 1969, M.S. in Petroleum Engring., 1970. Registered profl. engr., Tex. Reservoir engr. Gulf Oil Co., Houston, 1970; reserve engr. State Tex., Austin, 1973-74; drilling engr. Esso Exploration Co., Houston, 1977-78; internat. cons., S. Am. and Middle East, 1978—; owner, pres. Wiegand Drilling and Producing Co., Lockhart, Tex. and Houston, 1978—. Pres. Young Adult Republicans, San Antonio, 1978. Served to 1st lt. U.S. Army, 1971-72; Vietnam; maj. C.E. (Res.), 1983—. Mem. Am. Assn. Petroleum Geologists, Soc. Petroleum Engrs. Roman Catholic. Avocations: radio amateur, pilot, marksmanship. Office: Ranch-house Office and Equipment Yard Route 1 Box 101 Lockhart TX 78644

WIEGAND, ROBERT C., television executive; b. Springfield, Mass., Feb. 6, 1927; s. Kurt Eric and Helen (Carroll) W.; children—Kurt, Kenneth, Kimberly, Keith, Kristin. Student Boston U., Worcester Poly. Inst. (Mass.), Union Coll., Emerson Coll. Vice pres., gen. mgr. WTVN-TV, Columbus, Ohio, 1960-67, WGR-TV, Buffalo, 1967-70, WTAF-TV, Phila., 1970-75, WKRC-TV, Cin., 1975-80; exec. v.p., gen. mgr. WPEC-TV, West Palm Beach, Fla., 1980—. Treas., mem. exec. com. Better Bus. Bur., West Palm Beach; chmn. edl. adv. com. West Palm Beach Sch. Bd.; mem. Arbitron Adv. Council. Served with USN, World War II. Mem. West Palm Beach C. of C. (bd. dirs., treas.), Soc. Profl. Journalists. Clubs: Governors (West Palm Beach); Jonathan's Landing (Jupiter, Fla.). Home: 12916 Barrow Rd Juno Isles North Palm Beach FL 33408 Office: WPEC-TV Fairfield Dr West Palm Beach FL 33407

WIELENGA, JAMES LEE, pharmacist; b. Paterson, N.J., Apr. 18, 1948; s. Claude Louis and Nellie (Letsch) W.; m. Lesliee Ann Sparks, June 26, 1971; children—Brian, Stacey, Erin. B.S. in Pharmacy, U. S.C., 1971; Dr. Pharmacy, U. Tenn., 1973. Pharmacy intern Richmond Meml. Hosp., Columbia, S.C., 1971-72; staff pharmacist West Tenn. Chest Hosp., Memphis, 1973; dir. pharmacy Lonesome Pine Hosp., Big Stone Gap, Va., 1973-78, HPI Health Care, Cleveland, Tenn., 1978-84, dir. health care, 1984-85, regional coordinator ops., 1985—; cons. Bradley County Nursing Home, Cleveland, 1983—; clin. asst. U. Tenn., Memphis, 1983—; instr. Med. Coll. Va., Richmond, 1977. Contbr. articles to profl. jours. Fellow Am. Soc. Cons. Pharmacists; mem. Am. Soc. Hosp. Pharmacists, Tenn. Soc. Hosp. Pharmacists (Innovative Hosp. Pharmacy Practice award 1983), Chattanooga Soc. Hosp. Pharmacists (pres. 1980-81). Avocations: running; golf. Home: 2365 Interlackin Circle Cleveland TN 37311 Office: HPI Health Care Services Inc PO Box 3775 Cleveland TN 37320-3775

WIEMANN, JOAN ANN, chemist, educator; b. New Orleans, Oct. 3, 1948; d. Joseph Leonard and Ethel Rose Mary (Raftery) Kirschenheuter; m. Cyril Joseph Wiemann, Feb. 22, 1969; 1 dau., Gretchen Ann. B.S. in Physics, U. New Orleans, 1975, M.S. in Applied Physics Chemistry, 1977. Environ. quality specialist Jefferson (La.) Parish Civic Service, 1978-79; chemist New Orleans Pub. Service, Electric Power Dept., 1979—; instr. physics U. New Orleans, part-time, 1978—. Mem. Com. for Responsible Govt., New Orleans Pub. Service, River Ridge Community Assn., 1983. Recipient award for scholarship, leadership and service, faculty of U. New Orleans physics dept., 1975. Mem. Am. Phys. Soc., AAAS, La. Fern Soc. Republican. Home: 37 Hennessey Ct River Ridge LA 70123 Office: 3601 Paris Rd New Orleans LA 70128

WIENANDT, ELWYN ARTHUR, music educator, author, composer; b. Aniwa, Wis., July 23, 1917; s. Charles Herman and Ida O. (Loehrl) W.; m. Lois Patricia Trachsel, July 7, 1950; children—Alan Christopher, Linda Beth Wienandt Gandy, Thomas David. B.Mus. cum laude, Lawrence Coll., 1939; M.Mus., U. Denver, 1948; Ph.D., U. Iowa, 1951. Asst. prof. music N.Mex. Highlands U., Las Vegas, 1951-56; assoc. prof. music Baylor U., Waco, Tex., 1956-58, prof. musicology, 1959-85, prof. emeritus, 1985—, assoc. dean music, 1973—, acting dean music, 1981-83; choir dir. First Presbyterian Ch., Waco, 1957-72. Author: Choral Music of the Church, 1965, reprint, 1980; Opinions on Church Music, 1974. Co-author: Anthem in England and America, 1970; Thematic Catalogue, Instrumental Works of Johann Pezel, 1983. Contbr. Acad. Am. Ency., 1980. Editor music, ch. and chamber works. Served with USNR, 1943-46, Europe. Recipient Disting. Service award Lawrence U. Alumni Assn., 1974. Mem. Music Library Assn., Am. Musicol. Soc. (pres. Tex. chpt. 1961-63), Pi Kappa Lambda, Phi Mu Alpha Sinfonia. Democrat. Episcopalian. Avocations: Gardening; travel. Home: 1216 Cliffview Rd Waco TX 76710

WIENANDT, LOIS PATRICIA, editor, violist; b. Iowa City, Sept. 14, 1922; d. Charles Schlatter and Elizabeth Marguerite (Hilles) Trachsel; m. Elwyn Arthur Wienandt, July 7, 1950; children—Alan Christopher, Linda Beth, Thomas David. B.Mus., U. Iowa, 1944, M.A., 1940; postgrad. Curtis Inst. Music, Phila., 1944-46, 47-48. Instr. music U. Iowa, Iowa City, 1948-50; instr. music Baylor U., 1964-69; mem. Waco Symphony Orch., 1963—, prin. violist, 1971-84; freelance copy editor, Waco, Tex., 1966-69; asst. editor Word Books, Pub., Waco, 1970-72, assoc. editor, 1972-74, editor, 1974-80, sr. editor, 1980-85, sr. acad. editor, 1985—. Mem. Am. Musicol. Soc., Am. Viola Soc. Episcopalian. Club: PEO (pres. 1961-62, Waco). Avocations: travel; golf; gardening. Office: Word Books Pub PO Box 1790 Waco TX 76796

WIENER, WILLIAM BENJAMIN, JR., architect; b. Shreveport, La., Nov. 15, 1936; s. William B. and Babette (Levy) W. B.Arch., Cornell U., 1961. Registered architect, La. Prin. Bill Wiener, Architect, Shreveport, 1973—; pres. I.B. Magazette Inc., Shreveport, 1982—; dir. selection La. Architects, 1975-76. Pres. Hist. Preservation Shreveport, 1976-77, 82; chmn. adv. bd. Nat. Parks, Dept. Interior; trustee Nat. Parks and Conservation Assn., 1983—; mem. nat. adv. council Sierra Club Found. Recipient Preservationist of Yr. award La. Preservation Alliance, 1981. Mem. La. Architects Assn. (bd. dirs. 1971-74), AIA (pres. sect. 1973-74). Office: 1307 Petroleum Tower Shreveport LA 71101

WIER, LEIGHTON ARTHUR, dentist; b. Pine Bluff, Ark., Dec. 15, 1943; s. Max Harris and Grace Adele (Hargis) W.; m. Linda Leighton Childress, Sept. 14, 1968; children—Matthew Morgan, Brad Michael, Mary Beth. A.A., San Antonio Coll., 1963; student U. Tex.-Austin, 1963-64; D.D.S., U. Tex.-Houston, 1968. Pvt. practice dentistry, San Antonio, 1971—. Served to capt. U.S. Army, 1968-71. Recipient Past Pres. award Am. Dental Interfraternity Council, 1983. Fellow Acad. Gen. Dentistry, Am. Coll. Dentists, Internat. Coll. Dentists; mem. ADA (del. 1986-87), Tex. Dental Assn. (chmn. council on ann. session 1985-86, del. 1986-87), Tex. Acad. Gen. Dentistry (pres.-elect 1986-87, editor jour. 1982-84, spl. citation 1983), San Antonio Dist. Dental Soc. (dir. 1985-87, v.p. 1986-87, del. 1987-89, editor newsletter 1979-82, Dentist of Yr. 1982), San Antonio C. of C., Xi Psi Phi (internat. pres. 1980-82). Republican. Methodist. Clubs: Congressman's, San Antonio Country, DDD Golf Assn. (San Antonio) (pres. 1979-80). Home: 126 Cave Ln San Antonio TX 78209 Office: 104 W Magnolia Ave San Antonio TX 78212

WIER, THOMAS PERCY, JR., engineering consultant; b. Houston, June 10, 1919; s. Thomas Percy and Elinor (Jones) W.; m. Marjorie Parsons, Dec. 23, 1942 (dec. 1966); children—Thomas Percy, Donna, Janet; m. Margery McDonald, May 13, 1967. B.S. in Chem. Engring., Rice U., 1940, M.A., 1942, Ph.D., 1943. Registered profl. engr., Tex. Sr. research chemist Shell Devel., Emeryville, Calif., 1943-44, Shell Oil Co., Houston, 1944-51; pres. Wood-Protection Co., Houston, 1951-71; pres. Wier & Assocs., Houston, 1971—; pres. Vacuum Wood Preservatives Inst., Houston, 1953-58. Author: Self-Discipline, 1984; contbr. tech articles to publs.; patentee. Vice pres. bd. trustees Space Ctr. Meml. Hosp., Houston, 1970-72. Mem. Rice Engring. Alumni (pres. 1970-72), Sigma Xi, Phi Beta Kappa, Tau Beta Pi, Tau Beta Pi Alumni (pres. 1969), Phi Lambda Upsilon. Club: Rotary (editor 1985). Avocations: boating; photography; bird watching; travel; sculpture; woodworking. Home: 207 Bluepoint Clear Lake Shores TX 77565 Office: Wier and Assocs PO Box 58403 Houston TX 77258

WIER, VERNON SAINT CLAIR, JR., small business owner; b. San Antonio, Nov. 17, 1952; s. Vernon Saint Clair and Lucy Morninglory (Schultz) W.; m. Cassandra Joyce Hancock, June 16, 1974; children—David Edward, Keith Allen. B.S. in Indsl. Arts/Edn., Southwestern Union Coll., Keene, Tex., 1976; M.S. in Indsl. Arts/Edn., North Tex. State U., 1978. Tchr. indsl. arts Ft. Worth Ind. Sch. Dist., 1975-79; co-owner, mgr. W-R Industries San Antonio, 1979-80; mech. engr. So. Tech., Inc., San Antonio, 1980-81; owner, operator The Repair Shop, San Antonio, 1982—. Adventist. Home and Office: 201 Golden Crown San Antonio TX 78223

WIERCIOCH, MARIANNE, lawyer; b. Chgo., June 29, 1958; d. Richard Stanley and Virginia Valentine (Lisiecki) Wiercioch. B.A. in Polit. Sci. and Journalism, Fla. Atlantic U., 1978; J.D., Pepperdine U., 1982; postgrad. in taxation U. Miami (Fla.). Bar: Fla. 1983. Sole practice, Boca Raton, Fla., 1985—; cons. So. Terr. Builders and Interiors, Boca Raton; mem. Attys.' Title Ins. Fund. Mem. Gold Coast Republican Club, Boca Raton. Mem. ABA, Fla. Assn. Women Lawyers, Fla. Bar Assn. Young Lawyers, Profl. Women's Assn., Boca Raton Hosp. Aux., Boca Raton Hist. Soc.,Boca Raton C. of C., Women's Forum, Delta Theta Phi, Pi Sigma Alpha. Republican. Office: PO Box 4215 Boca Raton FL 33429

WIERENGO, CYRIL JOHN, JR., chemistry educator; b. Nicholson, Miss., Mar. 7, 1940; s. Cyril John and Mary Helen (Thigpen) W.; m. Mary Elaine Spence, Jan. 21, 1962; children—Cyril John III, Marcy Elaine. B.A., U. So. Miss., 1962, M.S., 1964; Ph.D., Miss. State U., 1974. Research chemist La. div. Dow Chem. Co., 1964-67; prof. chemistry Miss. U. for Women, Columbus, 1967—. Active Boy Scouts Am. Named Faculty Mem. of Yr., Miss. U. for Women, 1981; Miss. U. for Women summer research grantee, 1969, 75. Mem. Am. Chem. Soc. (Outstanding Chemist, Miss. sect. 1985), SCV, Sigma Xi, Phi Kappa Phi. Baptist. Home: 840 Cannon Trace Columbus MS 39702 Office: Box W119 Miss U for Women Columbus MS 39701

WIESER, JOAN ELIZABETH, university administrator, employee development programs consultant; b. Fall River, Mass., Mar. 14, 1948; d. James Edward and Theresa (O'Gara) Lenaghan; m. Paul B. Wieser, Sept. 7, 1968. Student Triton Coll., River Grove, Ill., 1969-71, Brown U., 1973; M.B.A., U. Miami-Coral Gables, 1982. Cost acct. Sylvaniz Electric, Fall River, Mass., 1967-68; support staff mem. Alberto-Culver, Melrose Park, Ill., 1968-70; exec. sec. Profl. Marketers, Inc., Broadview, Ill., 1970-71; asst. mgr. East Providence Credit Union, R.I., 1972-75; asst. personnel dir. U. Miami, Coral Gables, 1975-84, personnel dir. Med. Campus, Miami, 1984—; mem. credit com. U. Miami Credit Union, 1979—; cons. devel. employment skills John S. Koubek Ctr., Miami, 1981—; condr. workshops and seminars in field. Named Outstanding Young Women in Am., Sales & Mktg. Execs. of Ft. Lauderdale, Inc., 1983, Woman of Year Am. Bus. Women's Assn., 1984. Mem. U. Miami Women's Commn., Am. Bus. Women's Assn., Am. Mgmt. Assn., Am. Soc. Personnel Adminstrn., Am. Soc. Tng. and Devel. Club: Toastmasters Internat. (Coral Gables). Office: Univ of Miami Med Campus 1800 NW 10th Ave Miami FL 33101

WIESNER, SHARON MARIE, investment banker; b. Omaha, July 16, 1938; d. Ralph Remmington and Evelyn Adeline (Morris) Bremers; m. Virgil James Wiesner, Apr. 4, 1959 (div. 1982); children—Scott James, Lydia Marie, Michelle Elizabeth. B.A., Creighton U., 1959; M.A., U. Nebr.-Omaha, 1964, postgrad., 1979-82. Owner, v.p. Wiesner Distbg. Co. Inc., Lincoln, Nebr., 1966-72, Wiesner Tire Co. Inc., Omaha, 1972-75; v.p. Fin. Inc., Omaha, 1975-82; with fin., sales oil Am. Internat. Sales Corp., Dallas, 1982-83; pres. Joint Capital Resources, Dallas, 1983—. Editor: Born Rich: A Historical Book of Omaha, 1978. Author: Slanting News, 1959; Critical Study of Iago's Motivation, 1964. Vice pres. Assistance League Omaha, 1973-78; fund raiser Opera Omaha; v.p. women's bd. Omaha Community Playhouse; v.p. Lincoln Symphony Guild, 1966-71; bd. dirs. Omaha Jr. Theatre, 1975-79. Named Outstanding Young Woman Jr. C. of C., Norfolk, Nebr., 1964; recipient Valuable Service awards Lincoln Gen. Hosp., Omaha Community Playhouse. Mem. Omaha Writers Group, The Quill, Landmarks Inc., Nat. Beer Wholesalers, AAUW, Omaha Symphony Guild (v.p. 1973-78), Omaha C. of C., Lincoln C. of C., Brownville Hist. Soc., Brownville Fine Arts Assn., Nebr. Kennel Club, Dalmatian Club Am., Minn.-St. Paul Dalmatian Club, Blue Ribbon Dog Breeders, Beta Sigma Phi, Omicron Delta Kappa, Phi Delta Gamma, Theta Phi Alpha (pres. 1958-59). Club: Womens (v.p. 1966-70). Avocations: painting; music; art; knitting; writing. Home: PO Box 20841 Dallas TX 75220 Office: Joint Capital Resources PO Box 20841 Dallas TX 75220

WIGDERSON, MAURICE BRAYTON, labor arbitrator, consultant; b. Antigo, Wis., May 17, 1918; s. David L. and Myrth Elizabeth (Smith) W.; m. Caroline Elizabeth Ashline, July 24, 1972; children—William D., Patricia K., Michael B. Ph.B., U. Wis.-Madison, 1942, LL.B., 1950, J.S.D., 1964. Bar: Wis. 1950, Ill. 1960, U.S. Supreme Ct. 1962. Mem. firm Wigderson, Lindholm & Brueger, Madison, 1950-57; chief counsel, legal dir. Air Line Pilots Assn., Chgo., 1957-65; sr. staff v.p. Air Line Employees Assn., 1965-85; labor arbitrator, cons., Hollywood, Fla., 1985—. Served to capt. USAAF, 1942-46. Decorated Bronze Star, Silver Star, Purple Heart. Republican. Roman Catholic. Lodge: Elks. Avocations: tennis, biking, swimming, hiking. Home and Office: 204 St Andrews Rd Hollywood FL 33021

WIGGINS, CHARLES WILLIAM, political science educator, researcher; b. Clarion, Iowa, Feb. 26, 1937; s. Arthur Lyle and Mary (Gross) W.; m. Mary Jane Burkett, Oct. 30, 1958; children—Angila Sue, Scott William, Theodore Arthur, Mary Beth. B.A., State U. Iowa, 1959; M.A., Washington U., 1963, Ph.D., 1964. Prof., Iowa State U., Ames, 1964-81; prof. polit. sci. Tex. A&M U., College Station, 1981—; mem., vice chmn. Iowa Campaign Fin. Commn., Des Moines, 1973-77; specialist intergovtl. relations EPA, Kansas City, Mo., 1979-81. Author: The Legislative Process in Iowa, 1972, The Arizona Legislature, 1975. Contbr. articles to profl. jours. Mem. College Station Capital Improvements Com., 1983-84; pres. Greater Ames Ice Assn., 1976-81; chmn. precinct Democratic Party, Ames, 1965-79, chmn. county conv. Mem. Am. Polit. Sci. Assn., So. Polit. Sci. Assn., Midwest Polit. Sci. Assn., Southwestern Polit. Assn., Tex. Assn. Schs. of Pub. Affairs, Administrn., (pres. 1983-85), Pi Sigma Alpha, Pi Alpha Alpha. Avocations: art collector; fishing; travel. Home: 1302 Deacon Dr College Station TX 77840 Office: Dept Polit Sci Tex A&M Univ College Station TX 77843

WIGGINS, DAVID L., JR., systems analyst; b. Durham, N.C., Oct. 19, 1940; s. David Lee and Nixola (Burnette) W.; m. Barbara A. Williams, Jan. 10, 1961 (div. 1967); 1 child, Raphael; m. Dorothy A. Cobb, June 10, 1967; 1 child: David L. III. A.B. in History, N.C. Central U., 1962, postgrad., 1973-75; postgrad N.C. A&T U., 1964. Cert. tchr. N.C. Tchr. secondary sch. West Charlotte High Sch., Charlotte, S.C., 1962-66; prodn. analyser IBM Corp., Research Triangle Park, N.C., 1966-67, system programmer, 1974-78, systems analyst, 1978—. Scoutmaster, Troop & Cub Pack 129, Durham, 1968—; mem. Sch. Systemwide Adv. Bd., Durham, 1983—; pres. Durham City PTA Council, 1983—; v.p. Precinct #11, Durham, 1984—. Recipient Award of Merit, Durham Dist., Boy Scouts Am., 1983. Democrat. Am. Baptist. Mem. Omega Psi Phi. Clubs: Modern Men (treas. 1983-85), Hillside Class of '58 (pres. 1978—), Sertoma (Durham). Avocations: Model airplanes; softball. Home: 318 Wayne Cir Durham NC 27707 Office: IBM Corp PO Box 12195 Research Triangle Park NC 27709

WIGGINS, GENE BERGLUND, III, consulting petroleum engineer, educator; b. El Paso, Tex., Sept. 12, 1951; s. Gene Berglund and Bettye (Northcutt) W.; m. Deborah Susan Head, Feb. 29, 1976 (div. 1983). B.S. in Mech. Engring., U. Houston, 1978; M.B.A., Tulane U., 1985. Registered profl. engr., La., Tex., Miss., Ala. Asst. structural analyst Zapata Tech. Services, Houston, 1976; asst. engr. Hughes Tool Co., Houston, 1976-77; petroleum engr. Getty Oil Co., Mobile, Ala., 1978-80; cons. petroleum engr. Atwater Cons., Ltd., New Orleans, 1980-85, v.p., 1985—; adj. asst. prof. petroleum engring. Tulane U., New Orleans, 1985—. Mem. Soc. Petroleum Engrs. of AIME, Am. Assn. Petroleum Geologists, New Orleans Geol. Soc. Club: Petroleum (New Orleans). Avocations: sports; music. Home: 801 Rue Dauphine Apt 103 Metaire LA 70005 Office: Atwater Cons Ltd 318 Camp St New Orleans LA 70130

WIGGS, SHIRLEY JOANN, educator; b. Johnston County, N.C., Nov. 6, 1940; d. William H. and Sallie P. (Barden) W.; B.A., Atlantic Christian Coll., 1963; postgrad. Duke U., 1966, East Carolina U., 1979-80; grad. Newspaper Inst. Am. Tchr. public schs. South Hill, Va., 1963-64; tchr. lang. arts and social studies Glendale Chapel High Sch., Kenly, N.C., 1964-65, Benson (N.C.) High Sch., 1965—; tchr. advanced placement English, lang. arts, journalism and dramatics South Johnston High Sch., Four Oaks, N.C., 1969—, chairperson lang. arts dept., 1971—, coordinating adminstr. curriculum, 1974—, student adv., 1978—; evaluator profl. books Allyn and Bacon, Inc., 1974, 79. Sunday sch. tchr. 1st Bapt. Ch., Smithfield, N.C., 1964-66, asso. supt. young people's dept., 1964-67; co-chmn. Keep Johnston County Beautiful, 1979—. Named Woman of Yr., Atlantic Christian Coll., 1962; recipient Keep Johnston County Beautiful Appreciation award, 1980, Internat. Cheerleading Found. award, 1972. Mem. NEA, Nat. Council Tchrs. English, Assn. Supervision and Curriculum Devel., N.C. English Tchrs. Assn. (dir. dist. 12, 1980-84), Johnston County Assn. of Educators, N.C. Assn. Educators. Home: 102 E Sanders St Smithfield NC 27577 Office: South Johnston High School Route 3 Four Oaks NC 27524

WIGHT, DONALD LEO, dentist; b. Beloit, Wis., Aug. 23, 1924; s. Charles Leo and Mary Lucille (Bittner) W.; m. Barbara Lee Cole, June 12, 1946; children—Barbara Ann, Charles Foster. A.B., Transylvania U., 1946; D.D.S., Northwestern U., 1950. Gen. practice dentistry, Marion, Ky., 1950—. Chmn. Crittenden County Bd. Edn., Marion; elder Disciples of Christ Ch., Marion. Mem. West Central Dental Soc., Ky. Dental Assn., ADA, Kappa Alpha, Psi Omega. Republican. Lodges: Masons, Shriners. Avocations: hunting; fishing; raising bird dogs; reading. Home: PO Box 249 Marion KY 42064 Office: 123 E Belleville St Marion KY 42064

WIGINTON, JAY SPENCER, chemical company executive; b. Lubbock, Tex., Sept. 21, 1941; s. Clarence Elbert and Faye (George) W.; B.S., Tex. Tech. U., 1963, M.S., 1968; m. Billye Kay Freitag, Nov. 28, 1968; children—Lauren, Lindsay. Sales rep. West Tex. ter. Syntex Labs., Lubbock, 1968-70, regional sales rep., 1970-72, Far East regional mgr., Des Moines, 1972-73, dir. mktg., 1973-74; regional sales mgr. Zoecon Corp., Dallas, 1974-76, nat. accounts mgr. Custom div., 1976-78; gen. mgr. V.A. Snell & Co. div. Gt. Plains Chem. Co., San Antonio, 1978-83, Southwest regional mgr., 1983-84, dir. field devel., 1984-85; dist. mgr. Agri-Sales Assocs., Inc., 1985—. Served with AUS, 1964-66; Vietnam. Mem. Tex. Grain and Feed Assn., Tex. Cattle Feeders Assn., Tex. Chem. Assn., Kappa Sigma. Mem. Christian Ch. (Disciples of Christ). Office: 12915 N Hunters Circle San Antonio TX 78230

WIGLEY, DAVID ALAN, educational adminstr.; b. McClellan County, Tex., July 12, 1945; s. Albert Gar and Bonibel (Burt) W.; B.S., Howard Payne Coll., 1967, M.Ed., 1970; postgrad. Tex. Tech. U., 1970-73; Tchr., coach Lubbock (Tex.) Ind. Sch. Dist., 1967-76; prin. Crosbyton (Tex.) Consol. Ind. Sch. Dist., 1976—; jr. partner The Fashion Outlook, Brownwood, 1974—. Mem. Crosbyton C. of C. (dir. 1979-81), Tex. Elem. Prins. and Suprs. Assn., Tex. State Tchrs. Assn., Nat. Rifle Assn. Phi Delta Kappa, Delta Zeta. Republican. Methodist. Lodges: Lions, Masons, Shriners. Contbr. in field. Home: Rural Route 2 Crosbyton TX 79322 Office: 204 S Harrison St Crosbyton TX 79322

WIIK, CAROL ANNE, correspondent; b. Norwood, Mass., Apr. 21, 1951; d. Uuno and Virginia Hope (Hinchliffe) W. B.A., U. Mass., 1973; M.A., Am. U., 1980. Security clk. select com. on Presdl. campaign activities U.S. Senate, Washington, 1973-74, select com. on intelligence, 1975-76; chief security clk. permanent select com. on intelligence U.S. Ho. of Reps., Washington, 1977-79; corr. Cable News Network, Washington, 1980—. Mem. Radio and TV Corrs. Assn., Mortarboard.

WIJNHOLDS, HEIKO DE BEAUFORT, marketing educator, consultant; b. Amsterdam, Netherlands, Dec. 9, 1940; came to U.S., 1974, naturalized, 1983; s. Heiko W. and Benudina Maria (de Beaufort) W.; m. Carolyn Marie-Therese Williams, May 22, 1980; children—Annamarie Elizabeth, Monique Constance, Heiko Aernout. B.Commerce cum laude, U. Pretoria, South Africa, 1962, B.Commerce (Honours) cum laude, 1964; M.Commerce, U. South Africa, 1967, D.Commerce, 1970. From asst. prof. to prof. bus. adminstrn. U. South Africa, Pretoria, 1964-74, acting chmn. bus. adminstrn., 1974; chmn. mktg. dept. U. N.D., Grand Forks, 1975-78, assoc. prof., then prof. mktg., 1975-79; assoc. prof. mktg. Va. Commonwealth U., Richmond, 1979—, chmn. mktg. dept., 1982—. Author: (with others) Marketing Management: A South African Approach, 1974. Contbr. research reports and articles to profl. jours. Scholar Inst. for Internat. Edn. (award not accepted), 1964, U. Pretoria, 1962, Nat. Cash Register, 1960-61; U. N.D. grantee, 1977. Home: 1410 Cedarbluff Dr Richmond VA 23233 Office: VA Commonwealth U Richmond VA 23284

WIKSTROM, NELSON, political science educator; b. Upper Darby, Pa., June 19, 1940; s. Gunnar and Anna Carolina (Nelson) W.; m. Mary Bardon Kimmes, June 7, 1969; children—Amy, Sarah, Jessica. B.A., Northeastern U., 1963; M.A., U. Conn., 1965, Ph.D., 1969. Instr. U. Wis.-Superior, 1967-68; asst. prof. U. Maine, Orono, 1968-71; asst. prof. Va. Commonwealth U., Richmond, 1971-75, assoc. prof., 1975—; sr. intern Joint Legis. Audit and Rev. Com., Commonwealth Va., Richmond, summer 1984. Author: Councils of Governments, 1977; co-editor: Municipal Government, Politics and Public Policy, 1982; contbr. articles to profl. jours. Mem. Va. Social Sci. Assn. (v.p. 1980-81, pres. 1981-82). Democrat. Episcopalian. Home: 300 Sunset Dr Richmond VA Office: Va Commonwealth U Polit Sci Dept Richmond VA 23284

WILBANKS, DARREL JAY, human resources development executive; b. Dover, N.J., May 12, 1944; s. Carey J. and Laura (Hill) W.; divorced; children—Denise, Cale. Student Newark Coll. Engring., 1962-65. Mech. engr. Haggar Slacks, Dallas, 1966-78, prodn. mgr., 1979-81, tng. dept. mgr., 1982-83; human resource devel. mgr. Fox Photo, San Antonio, 1983—; tng. cons. Phlash Prodns., San Antonio, 1984—; photog. cons. La Quinta Motels, San Antonio, 1984—. Patenteee mech. devices. Mem. Internat. TV Assn. (v.p. San Antonio chpt.), Am. Soc. Tng. and Devel. Avocations: bowling; raquetball; travel. Office: Fox Photo 1734 Broadway San Antonio TX 78215

WILBERT, MARTHA TOMLIN, nursing home and home health agency administrator, hospice nurse; b. Atlanta, Oct. 13, 1941; d. Samuel Stokes and Elizabeth (Barge) Tomlin; m. David Allen Wilbert, May 20, 1962; children—John Spencer, Lawrence Allen. Diploma in Nursing, Crawford W. Long, Emory U., Atlanta, 1964; Assoc. in Social Services, Kennesaw Coll., 1985; student U. Ga., 1968, Med. Coll. Ga., 1980. Instr. practical nursing Marietta-Cobb Area Vocat. Tech. Sch., Marietta, Ga., 1966-67; staff nurse coronary care unit Kennestone Hosp., Marietta, 1967-68; dir., instr. Cartersville (Ga.) Manpower-Devel. Act Practical Nurse Tng. Ctr., 1968-69; dir. nursing services Springdale Convalescent Ctr., Cartersville, 1969-70; adminstr. Hideaway Hills Convalescent Ctr., Austell, Ga., 1971-73; nursing home adminstrv. cons. Marcy Corp., Atlanta, 1972-74; instr. Coosa Valley Vocat. Sch., Rome, Ga., 1974-75; owner, operator Camelite Book and Info. Ctr., Cartersville, Ga., 1975-81; precertification nurse Ga. Med. Care Found., Atlanta, 1981; psychiat. clinic nurse Anneewakee Treatment Ctr., Douglasville, Ga., 1981-82; pvt. duty nurse homes and hosps. Upjohn Healthcare Services Med. Personnel Pool, Atlanta, 1981-82; owner Pvt. Hospice Service, Cartersville, Ga., 1984—; hospice nurse Kennestone Regional Hospice, Marietta, 1985—; pvt. psychol. cons., 1978—; vol. counselor Crisis Pregnancy Service, Atlanta, 1980-81; sec. community action group Interagency Council, Cartersville, Ga., 1975. 1975. Mem. profl. edn. com. Am. Cancer Soc., Atlanta, 1983. Home: 13 Attaway Dr Cartersville GA 30120

WILCOX, LINDA PATTERSON, college career planning and placement director, counselor; b. Asbury, W.Va., Sept. 10, 1950; d. Akie and Janice (Cole) P.; m. James Galen Wilcox, Nov. 26, 1977; children—Benjamin, Joshua. B.S. in Edn., Trevecca Nazarene Coll., 1973; M.A. in Guidance and Counseling, U. Mo.-Kansas City, 1979. Tchr. Met. Schs., Nashville, 1973-76; program asst. Kansas City Regional Council for Higher Edn., Mo., 1976-77; social worker, counselor Jackson County Juvenile Ct., Kansas City, Mo., 1977-79; dir. career planning and placement Bethany Nazarene Coll., Okla., 1979—, also counselor; mem. Oklahoma City Job Pursuit Consortium, 1984-85. Presenter profl. confs. in field. Sunday Sch. tchr. Bethany First Ch. of the Nazarene, Okla., 1985—; mem. Evang. Women's Caucus, 1984-85, Nat. Impact Polit. Assn., 1985. Mem. Am. Soc. Tng. and Devel., Am. Assn. Counseling and Devel., Okla. Coll. and Univ. Personnel Assn. (sec. 1985—), Okla. Coll. Personnel Assn. Democrat. Avocations: aerobics; reading; travel. Office: Bethany Nazarene Coll Bethany OK 73008

WILCOX, OLUYOMI TUAMOKUMO, pharmacist; b. Bonny, Rivers-State, Nigeria, Dec. 22, 1954; came to U.S., 1976, naturalized, 1985; d. Lazarus and Mercy (Jumbo) W.; m. Francois Olayo Tuamokumo, Jan. 9, 1978; children—Nimi, Fini, Timin Tomini. B.S. in Pharmacy, Creighton U., 1980; M.S. in Pub. Health, Tulane U., 1983; D.Pharmacy (hon.), La. Pharmacist Assn., 1983. Registered pharmacist, La. Pharmacy intern Drug Info. Ctr., Omaha, Nebr., 1978-79, St. Joseph Hosp., 1979-80, Taylor's Pharmacy, Lafayette, La., 1980-81; pharmacist B&R Pharmacy, New Orleans, 1982-83, Univ. Med. Ctr., Lafayette, 1983—. Contbr. articles to profl. jours. Mem. La. Pharmacists Assn., New Orleans Progressive Pharmacist Assn., South Central La. Hosp Pharm. Assn., Am. Soc. Hosp. Pharmacists. Methodist. Home: 1512 Louisiana Ave Lafayette LA 70501 Office: Univ Med Ctr 2390 W Congress St Lafayette LA 70506

WILCOXON, SEARCY ALLEN, III, counselor educator, marriage and family therapist; b. Crossett, Ark., Sept. 12, 1953; s. Searcy Allen Jr. and Helen Jean (Beavers) W.; m. Cynthia Wilson, July 4, 1981; children—Searcy Allen, IV, Andrew Dudley. B.A., Ouachita Baptist U., 1975; M.A., Stephen F. Austin State U., 1978; Ed.D., E. Tex. State U., 1982. Staff psychologist Mental Health and Mental Retardation Services of S.E. Tex., Beaumont, 1978-80; grad. teaching asst. E. Tex. State U., Commerce, 1980-82; counseling intern Tex. A&M U., College Station, 1982-83; asst. prof. counselor edn. U. Ala., Tuscaloosa, 1983—. Contbr. articles to profl. jours. Family minister, Sunday sch. tchr. First Bapt. Ch., Tuscaloosa, 1983—. U. Ala. grantee, 1984-85. Mem. Am. Assn. for Marriage Family Therapy, Am. Assn. for Counseling Devel., Nat. Council on Family Relations, Southeastern Psychol. Assn., Assn. for Counselor Edn. Supervision. Republican. Avocations: golf; woodworking; photography. Home: 200 Manora Estates Tuscaloosa AL 35405 Office: Program Counselor Edn U Ala University AL 35486

WILDER, ANNETTE BEDFORD (MRS. EUGENE WILDER), librarian; b. Natchez, Miss.; d. George Madison and Ella (Ford) Bedford; B.A., Miss. Woman's Coll., 1929; postgrad. Tulane U., 1932, U. So. Miss., 1940; M.A., Vanderbilt U., 1948; m. Eugene Wilder, July 10, 1919; 1 son, Eugene. Instr. French and Spanish, U. So. Miss., 1928-33, librarian Demonstration Sch., 1940-55, acquisitions librarian, asst. prof. library sci., 1955-60, reference librarian, 1960-64, reference librarian, assoc. prof., 1964-70. Pres., Hattiesburg Music Club, 1927-28; chmn. bd. dirs. Hattiesburg Civic Music Assn., 1927-29; v.p. Original Home and Garden Club, 1938-39; pres. Hattiesburg High Sch. PTA, 1938-39; bd. dirs. Garden Clubs of Miss., 1938-42; sec. bd. dirs. Hattiesburg Community Chest, 1942-43; chmn. bd. dirs. Hattiesburg council Girl Scouts Am., 1942; with Canteen Corps, ARC, 1942-45; pres. Womans Club, 1954-55; trustee Hattiesburg Pub. Library, 1955-75, chmn., 1958-61; bd. dirs. Miss. dist. YWCA, 1956-60; bd. dirs. Hattiesburg br. AAUW Scholarship Fund, 1953. Mem. Am., Southeastern, Miss. library assns., D.A.R. (regent John Rolfe chpt. 1955-57, registrar Norvell Robertson chpt. 1961-80), Daus. Am. Colonists (state regent 1964-67, So. regional chmn. 1967-70), Daus. Founders and Patriots Am. (state sec. 1952-60, state registrar 1970-74), Magna Charta Dames, Order Americans of Armorial Ancestry, Colonial Dames Am., Order First Families of Miss. 1699-1817, Miss. Geneal. Soc., Delta Kappa Gamma, Sigma Delta Pi, Pi Delta Phi, Kappa Delta Pi. Baptist. Address: 902 W Pine PO Box 785 Hattiesburg MS 39401

WILDER, JOHN SHELTON, lieutenant governor of Tennessee; b. Fayette City, Tenn., June 3, 1921; s. John Chamblee and Martha (Shelton) W; m. Marcelle Morton, Dec. 31, 1941; children—John Shelton, David Morton. Student, U. Tenn.; LL.B., Memphis Law U., 1957. Bar: Tenn. 1957. Engaged in farming, Longtown, Tenn., 1943—; supr. mgmt. Longtown Supply Co.; judge Fayette County Ct.; mem. Tenn. Senate, 1959—; lt. gov. Tenn., 1971—; past pres. Nat. Assn. Soil Conservation Dists., Tenn. Soil Conservation Assn., Tenn. Agrl. Council; exec. com. So. Legis. Conf., Conf. Lt. Govs.; dir. Oakland Deposit Bank, Tenn., Somerville Bank and Trust Co. Served with U.S. Army, 1942-43. Mem. Tenn. Cotton Ginners Assn. (past pres.), Delta Theta Phi. Democrat. Methodist. Lodge: Shriners. Office: Suite 1 Legislative Plaza Nashville TN 37219*

WILDER, LAWRENCE DOUGLAS, lieutenant governor of Virginia; b. Richmond, Va., Jan. 31, 1931; children—Lynn, Larry, Loren. B.S., Va. Union U., 1951; J.D., Howard U., 1959. Bar: Va. Mem. Va. Senate, 1969-85; lt. gov. Va., 1985—; del. Democratic Nat. Conv., 1980; agt. NAACP legal def. fund. Served with U.S. Army, 1952-53. Decorated Bronze Star. Bd. dirs. United Givers Fund; chmn. bd. Red Shield Boys' Club. Mem. ABA, Va. Bar Assn., Nat. Bar Assn., Am. Judicature Soc., C. of C., Urban League (dir. Richmond), Omega Psi Phi. Clubs: Masons, Shriners. Office: Office of Lieutenant Governor State Capitol Richmond VA 23219*

WILDER, MILTON RUSSELL, JR., university administrator; b. Jackson, Miss., Oct. 7, 1943; s. Milton Russell and Essie Lee (Tubbs) W.; m. Kathryn Hardwick, Sept. 20, 1970; children—Kelly Marie, James Byron. B.S. in Edn., Samford U., 1967; M.Ed., U. Ala.-Birmingham, 1972; Ed.D., U. Ala., Tuscaloosa, 1975. Tchr. elem. phys. edn. Mt. Brook City Schs., Ala., 1967, 67-68; jr. phys. edn. tchr., coach Jefferson County Schs., Ala., 1968-69, 70-71; asst. prof. health and phys. edn. U. Ala.-Birmingham, 1974-78, U. New Orleans, 1978-82; chmn. div. health, phys. edn. and recreation Delta State U., Cleveland, Miss., 1982—. Recipient Heart Fund Citation, Ala. Heart Assn.,

1977, Presdl. Sports award Pres. Council for Sports and Fitness, 1977, Cert. of Merit, Ala. Heart Assn., 1978, La. Heart Assn., 1979, 80, Phys. Edn. Pub. Info. award La. Assn. Health, Phys. Edn. and Recreation, 1981. Mem. AAHPER and Dance, Miss. Assn. Health, Phys. Edn. and Recreation (newsletter editor 1982—, v.p. health 1985—, bd. dirs. 1982—), Phi Delta Kappa, Kappa Delta Phi. Democrat. Baptist. Lodge: Rotary (chmn. projects com. 1984-85). Avocations: racquetball; swimming. Home: 509 Robinson Dr Cleveland MS 38732 Office: Delta State U Box B-2 Cleveland MS 38733

WILDER, ROBERT ALLEN, finance and leasing company executive, leasing broker, consultant; b. Memphis, Feb. 13, 1944; s. Donald Byrd and Marion S. (Brown) W.; m. Betty Michael, Apr. 23, 1977; 1 dau., Elizabeth Michael. B.S., Memphis State U. Sch. Engring., 1967, M.S., 1973. Regional sales mgr. Hertz Corp. Truck div., Atlanta, 1974-77; regional dir. Itel Corp., Atlanta, 1978-79; pres. Interstate Systems, Inc., Atlanta, 1979-81; dir. corp. lease programs No. Telecom Fin. Corp., Atlanta and Nashville, 1981—; also cons. Served with U.S. Army, 1967-72. Mem. Am. Assn. Equipment Lessors, Memphis State U. Alumni. Methodist. Home: 4791 Fairville Ct Marietta GA 30062 Office: No Telecom Fin Corp 4170 Ashford Dunwoody Rd NE Suite 450 Atlanta GA 30319

WILDER, WARREN JOSEPH, council executive; b. Baton Rouge, May 12, 1943; s. Alton Emmett, Jr., and Adele Effie (Mary) W.; m. Sarah Elizabeth DePriest, Aug. 31, 1966; children—Patrick Michael, Bradley Alton, Christopher Dewey. B.A. in Geography, Southeastern La. Coll., 1966; postgrad. La. State U., 1966-67. Buyer, mgr. Goudchaux's Dept. Store, Baton Rouge, 1967-73; br. mgr. Steinberg's Sports Ctr., Baton Rouge, 1973-75; exec. dir. Cons. Engrs. Council of La., Inc., Baton Rouge, 1975—, pres. Nat. Assn. of Cons. Engrs. Council Execs., 1981-82. Bd. dirs. Oak Hills III Civic Assn., 1981—, rec. sec., 1984—; mem. choir Nat. Sports Festival, 1985, St. George Catholic Ch. Mem. La. Engring. Soc. (affiliate), Nat. Rifle Assn., Tau Kappa Epsilon. Democrat. Clubs: Cath. High Men's, St. George Sch. Men's. Office: Cons Engrs Council La Inc PO Box 1549 Baton Rouge LA 70821

WILDEY, ROY ALLEN, physician; b. Moscow, Ohio, Dec. 1, 1930; s. Tom and Texie Lee (Kirk) W.; m. Carol Ann Walter, June 9, 1956; children—David Allen, Steven Walter, Susan Elizabeth. B.S., U. Cin., 1952; M.D., 1956. Intern, Cin. Gen. Hosp., 1956-57, resident in radiology Emory U., 1967-70; physician United Mine Workers Hosp., Man, W.Va., 1957-58; gen. practice medicine, Bucyrus, Ohio, 1960-67; clin. instr. radiology Emory U., Atlanta, 1970-71; staff radiologist Athens Gen. Hosp., Ga., 1971-72, Middle Ga. Hosp., Macon, 1972-73, Candler Gen. Hosp., Savannah, Ga., 1973—. Served to capt. USAF, 1958-60. Mem. Am. Coll. Radiology, Radiol. Soc. N.Am., Soc. Nuclear Medicine, Am. Coll. Nuclear Physicians, AMA. Lodge: Masons. Avocation: squaredancing. Home: 111 N Millward Rd Savannah GA 31410 Office: Chatham Radiologists PA 9 Medical Arts Ctr Savannah GA 31405

WILDFEUER, DAVID, consulting company executive; b. Prague, Czechoslovakia, Oct. 3, 1920; s. Adolph and Rose W.; m. Frieda Baum, Oct. 24, 1943; children—Sharon, Roger. B.E.E., CCNY, 1942. Intermediate engr. Am. Transformer Co., Newark, 1944-49; sr. staff engr. Arma div. United Tech. Corp., Roosevelt Field, N.Y., 1949-69; head dept. REL, Inc., L.I., N.Y., 1969-75; pres. ElectroMagnetic Cons., Inc., Tamarac, Fla., 1975—; prof. electronics and elec. machinery Hudson Tech. Inst., Union City, N.J., part-time, 1950-56. Served with AUS, 1943. Mem. IEEE (electromagnetic measurements com., computer rules transformer com., electronic transfer com., standards com.). Contbr. articles to tech. jours. Address: 9520 NW 65th St Tamarac FL 33321

WILDHACK, WILLIAM AUGUST, JR., lawyer; b. Takoma Park, Md., Nov. 28, 1935; s. William August and Martha Elizabeth (Parks) W.; m. Martha Moore Allston, Aug. 1, 1959; children—William August III, Elizabeth Louise. B.S., Miami U., Oxford, Ohio, 1957; J.D., George Washington U., 1963. Bar: Va. 1963, D.C. 1965, Md. 1983. Agt., IRS, No. Va., 1957-65; assoc. firm Morris, Pearce, Gardner & Beitel, Washington, 1965-69; sole practice, Washington, 1969; corp. counsel, v.p. B.F. Saul Co. and affiliates, Chevy Chase, Md., 1969—; sec. B.F. Saul Real Estate Investment Trust, Chevy Chase. Mem. Arlington Tenant Landlord Commn., 1976—, former vice chmn.; pres. Arlington unit Am. Cancer Soc., 1970-71; elder Little Falls Presbyn. Ch. Mem. Am. Soc. Corp. Secs., ABA, D.C. Bar Assn., Md. Bar Assn., Va. Bar Assn., Arlington County Bar Assn., Washington Bd. Realtors, Phi Alpha Delta. Home: 6104 N 28th St Arlington VA 22207 Office: 8401 Connecticut Ave Chevy Chase MD 20815

WILDING, ALBERT LEONARD, manufacturing company executive; b. Louisville, Feb. 23, 1929; s. Andrew John and Lorene Augusta (Vollmer) W.; B.S.M.E., Speed Sci. Sch., U. Louisville, 1953; M.M.E., Purdue U., 1955; m. Judie A. Richards, Feb. 14, 1976; children—David Wayne, Jonathan Wayne. Materials and mfg. mgr. Gen. Electric Co., Pittsfield, Mass. and Kuhlman Electric, Versailles, Ky., 1960-72; pres., gen. mgr. Guilbert div. Am. Sterilizer Co., Phila., 1973-75, gen. mgr. Montgomery div., 1976-79, pres. Lombard Lense div., Norfolk, Va., 1979-80; v.p., gen. mgr. Hager Hinge Co., Montgomery, Ala., 1980-84; pres. Mid-South Industries, Gadsden, Ala., 1981-85; pres. B.F. Shaw Co., Laurens, S.C., 1985—; prof. engring. Purdue U., 1953-55; prof. engring. U.S. Coast Guard Acad., 1955-59. Chmn., Mass. United Fund, 1965, Erie (Pa.) Big Bros., 1973; bd. dirs. St. Margaret's Hosp., United Fund, 1980-81; bd. dirs. ARC, blood drive chmn., 1979; mem. Etowah Expansion Authority. Served to lt. comdr. USCGR, 1955-60. Mem. Am. Soc. Profl. Engrs., ASME, Am. Mgmt. Assn., Tau Beta Pi, Sigma Tau. Methodist. Clubs: Men of Montgomery, Arrowhead Country (pres.), Rotary. Home: 144 Arrowhead Dr Montgomery AL 36117 Office: BF Shaw Co PO Box 169 Laurens SC 29360

WILENSKY, ALVIN, business executive; b. Scranton, Pa., Nov. 3, 1921; s. Isaac and Sarah (Barnett) W.; m. Ruth L. Gross, June 3, 1945; children—David, Robert B. A.A., Keystone Jr. Coll., La Plume, Pa., 1939-41; B.A., Pa. State U., 1943. C.P.A., Pa. Sr. acct. Alberts, Kahn, Levess, N.Y.C., 1945-48; prin. Alvin Wilensky, C.P.A., Scranton, 1948-72; pres. Century Village, Inc., West Palm Beach, Fla., 1973-81; chmn., pres. Cenvill Investors, Inc., mem. N.Y. Stock Exchange, West Palm Beach, 1981—; mem. mgmt. bd. 1st Am. Bank and Trust, West Palm Beach. Vice pres. Jewish Fedn. Palm Beach County, 1984—. Served to 1st lt. USAAF, 1943-45. Decorated Air medal with 4 oak leaf clusters; recipient Humanitarian award Mid-County Med. Ctr., West Palm Beach, Fla., 1981. Mem. Am. Inst. C.P.A.s, Fla. Inst. C.P.A.s, Pa. Inst. C.P.A.s, Am. Mgmt. Assn., Nat. Assn. Real Estate Investment Trusts (bd. govs. 1983—). Republican. Clubs: Forum of the Palm Beaches, President Country. Home: 2480 Presidential Way West Palm Beach FL 33401 Office: Cenvill Investors Inc East Dr Century Village West Palm Beach FL 33409

WILEY, JEROLD WAYNE, air force officer; b. Urbana, Ill., Jan. 7, 1944; s. Jesse Scott and Eula Eileen (Deffenbaugh) W.; B.S., So. Ill. U., 1967; M.S., U. N.D., 1973; m. Gloria J. Uselton, May 6, 1982; children—Jackson Scott, Justin Wayne. Commd. 2d lt. U.S. Air Force, 1968, advanced through grades to maj., 1982; Minuteman II launch officer 321 Strategic Missile Wing, 1969-73; Minuteman II initial qualification instr. 4315 Combat Crew Tng. Squadron, 1973-76; asst. prof. aerospace studies Coll. St. Thomas, St. Paul, 1976-79; dir. tng. and devel. 325 Fighter Weapons Wing, Ops. Tng. Devel. Team, Tyndall AFB, Fla., 1979—. Mem. Am. Soc. Tng. and Devel., Am. Mgmt. Assn., Am. Assn. Community and Jr. Colls., Soc. Am. Foresters, Air Force Assn. Republican. Contbr. articles to Tng. mag. Home: PO Box 15008 Panama City FL 32406 Office: 325 FWW/DOTI Stop 56 Tyndall AFB FL 32403

WILEY, KATHY ROSE, biology educator; b. Canton, Ohio, Aug. 29, 1948; d. Edwin Lee and June Kathryn (Laiblin) W. B.A., Miami U.-Oxford, Ohio, 1970; M.A., U. Tex., 1974, Ph.D., 1980. Asst. prof. Huston-Tillotson Coll., Austin, Tex., 1981-85, assoc. prof., 1985—, acting head dept. biology, 1982-84, head dept., 1984—. Contbr. articles to Biochemistry, Biochem. Genetics. NIH genetics grantee, 1972-75; Welch fellow, 1975-79. Mem. AAAS, Tex. Native Plant Soc., Sierra Club, Nat. Audubon Soc. Democrat. Office: Huston-Tillotson Coll 1820 E 8th St Austin TX 78702

WILEY, MILLICENT YODER, educator, realtor; b. Mercedes, Tex., June 7, 1923; d. Frank and Grace Mae (Setter) Yoder; B.S., Tex. State Coll. Women, 1949; postgrad. U. Houston, 1950-53; m. William Gregory Wiley, Mar. 25, 1946; children—Sandra Kay, Patti Gayle Wiley Diamond. Choral dir., music tchr. schs. in Tex. and La., 1945-60; tchr. Kingsville (Tex.) Ind. Sch. Dist., 1960-80, now also trustee; choral dir. H.M. King High Sch., 1964-80, ret., 1980; area admissions adv., adminstr. Pacific Am. Inst., 1976-80; state dir. South Tex. for Am. Internat. Edn. and Tng., 1980-83; Tex. rep. Internat. Travel Study, Inc., 1983—; pianist Kingsville Rotary Club, 1966—. Bd. dirs. Kingsville chpt. Am. Heart Assn., Community Concerts Assn. Recipient various certs. appreciation. Mem. Am. Choral Dirs. Assn., Music Educators Nat. Conf., NEA, Tex. Music Educators Assn. (dir. 1973-74), Tex. Choral Dirs. Assn. (state clinic condr. 1977), Tex. Tchrs. Assn., Kingsville Bd. Realtors, Tex. Assn. Realtors, Multiple Listing Service Kingsville, Nat. Bd. Realtors, Fgn. Study League (adv., adminstr. 1971-76), Music Club of Kingsville (pres. 1982-84), Nat. Ret. Tchrs. Assn., Kingsville Ret. Tchrs. Assn., Tri-City Ret. Tchrs., Kingsville C. of C., Tex. Assn. Sch. Bds., Nat. Sch. Bd. Assn. Republican. Methodist. Clubs: Kingsville Music, Exxon Bridge, Monday Night Bridge. Home: 229 Helen Marie Ln Kingsville TX 78363

WILHELM, SHERRY ANN, statistician; b. Stamford, Tex., Dec. 4, 1944; d. Duard Worth Counts and Sophia Ann (Walker) Counts Hix; m. Charles Dale Wilhelm, Aug. 24, 1963; children—Lavena Ann, Dale Worth. B.Applied Arts and Scis., S.W. Tex. State U., 1979. Fuels stock fund specialist Directorate of Energy Mgmt., Kelly AFB, Tex., 1978-79; refuge clk. Arctic Nat. Wildlife Refuge, Fairbanks, Alaska, 1980-81; statistician U.S. Army Patient Adminstrn. Systems and Biostatistics Activity, Ft. Sam Houston, Tex., 1982-85; computer programmer U.S. Army Health Care Systems Support Activity, Ft. Sam Houston, 1985—. Recipient Spl. Achievement award U.S. Fish and Wildlife Service, Fairbanks, 1980; Exceptional Performance award U.S. Army, Ft. Sam Houston, 1984, 85. Mem. Am. Statis. Assn., San Antonio Statis. Assn., UDC, San Antonio Bulldog Club (sec. 1985). Home: 5810 Mission Bend San Antonio TX 78233 Office: US Army Health Care Systems Mgmt Div Systems Maintenance Br Fort Sam Houston TX 78234

WILHELM, STEPHANIE ANNE, mobile catering company executive; b. Inglewood, Calif., Sept. 6, 1950; d. Robert Franklin and Eva Earl (Alexander) Wilhelm. A.A. in Phys. Therapy, Fullerton Coll., 1978; student San Antonio Coll., 1973, 80-84, U. Md., 1974-75, City Coll. Chgo., 1974. U. Tex., 1982-83. Commd. airman USAF, 1968, advanced through grades to staff sgt., 1975; document control clk., Offult AFB, Nebr., 1969-70; personnel adminstr., Japan, 1970-72; telecommunications mgr., Kelly AFB, Tex., 1972-74; acctg. and fin. adminstr., Crete, 1974-75; instr. arts and crafts Anaheim Parks, Recreation and Arts Dept. (Calif.), 1976, instr. sports, spl. olympics coach 1976; exec. sec. Holovision Internat. Corp., Anaheim, 1976; exec. sec. Link Realtors, Fullerton, Calif., 1976; admissions clk. Fullerton Coll., 1976-77; dir. membership San Antonio Bd. Realtors, 1979-80; mfg. dir. Comp-Data Service, Inc., San Antonio, 1980-84; owner Charter Point Enterprises, San Antonio, 1983. Decorated Air Force Commendation medal. Mem. North San Antonio C. of C., Nat. Assn. Female Execs., Am. Entrepreneurs Assn. Democrat. Roman Catholic. Office: PO Box 380555 San Antonio TX 78280

WILHELMUS, KIRK ROBERT, ophthalmologist, researcher, educator; b. Evansville, Ind., Oct. 26, 1949; s. Gilbert M. and Helen (Hauselmire) W. A.B., Ind. U., 1971; M.D., Vanderbilt U., 1975. Diplomate Am. Bd. Ophthalmology. Intern Baylor Coll. Medicine, Houston, 1975-76, resident, 1976-79; clin. fellow Moorfields Eye Hosp., London, 1979-81; asst. prof. ophthalmology Baylor Coll. Medicine, Houston, 1981—. Contbr. numerous articles, chpts. to profl. publs. Mem. Am. Acad. Ophthalmology, Tex. Ophthalmol. Assn., AMA, Brit. Med. Assn. Home: 1404 Michigan St Houston TX 77006 Office: Cullen Eye Inst 6501 Fannin St Houston TX 77030

WILHIDE, JAMES ALFRED, language arts consultant, educator; b. Youngstown, Ohio, Apr. 27, 1939; s. Harry and Ruth Kathryn (Bates) W.; m. Joan Margaret Weaver, Aug. 20, 1960; children—Scott, Karen, Kevin. B.S., Youngstown State U., 1960; M.Ed., U. Ariz., 1968; Ed.D., U. S.C., 1985. Tchr., Canfield Local Schs., 1960-69; lang. arts and reading cons. Curriculum Improvement Ctr., 1969-71; reading cons. S.C. Dept. Edn., Columbia, 1971-72, lang. arts cons., 1976—; prin. Richland Dist. #1, 1972-76; instr. W.Va. U., 1969-71, U. S.C., 1971—, Columbia Coll., 1972—. Co-author: Teaching Language Arts, 1984; cons. author: Spelling Textbook series, 1983. Com. chmn. Columbia council Boy Scouts Am., 1972—. Fellow U. Ariz., 1967-68. Mem. Internat. Reading Assn., Nat. Council Tchrs. of English, Assn. Supervision and Curriculum Devel., S.C. State Council Internat. Reading Assn. (pres. 1983-84). Presbyterian (elder). Avocations: hiking; camping. Home: 56 Beacon Hill Ct Columbia SC 29210 Office: SC State Dept Edn 801 Rutledge Bldg Columbia SC 29201

WILHITE, JAMES PATRICK, communications company executive; b. Shawnee, Okla., July 12, 1943; s. James Edgar and Aline (Patrick) W.; m. Tommye Ann Lilley, July 29, 1977; children—Tressa Rae Bischoff, Walter Scott Bischoff. B.S., Okla. State U., 1967. Account exec. Storz Broadcasting Co., Oklahoma City, 1968, Sammons-Ruff Broadcasting Co., Amarillo, Tex., 1969-73, Motorola C & E Inc., Amarillo, 1973-79; owner, pres. Mobilcomm of Hereford (Tex.), 1979-84; service mgr. Motorola C&E, Dallas Service Center. dir. electronics dept. Tex. State Tech. Inst., 1978-82; VHF communications advisor West Tex. area, 1980-83. Bd. dirs., pub. relations advisor Panhandle Emergency Med. Services, 1979-80. Grantee NSF, 1964. Mem. Telecator Network Am., Am. Radio Relay League, Aircraft Owners and Pilots Assn. Home: 1808 Mojave Pl Irving TX 75061 Office: Motorola Service Center 2120 Regency Irving TX 75062

WILHITE, JIM O., gas company executive; b. Greenwood, Ark., Mar. 31, 1938; s. Raymond I. and Margaret E. (Oliver) W.; m. Shirley Parker, June 23, 1963; children—Kimberly Kay, Jeffrey Scott. B.S., Okla. State U., 1960. With Ark. La. Gas Co. (now Arcla, Inc.), Shreveport, La., 1963—, v.p. in charge of employee and indsl. relations, 1972-73, exec. v.p., 1973—. Bd. dirs. Central YMCA, Shreveport, Shreveport Norwella council Boy Scouts Am., Sports Found., Shreveport; campaign chmn. United Way, Shreveport, 1978. Mem. So. Gas Assn., Sales and Mktg. Execs., Mid Continent Oil and Gas Assn., Shreveport C. of C. (dir.), La. Assn. Bus. and Industry (dir.). Methodist. Clubs: Pierremont Oaks Tennis, Shreveport. Office: PO Box 21734 Arkla Bldg Shreveport LA 71151*

WILHOIT, HENRY RUPERT, JR., U.S. district judge; s. Henry Rupert and Kathryn (Reynolds) W.; m. Jane Horton, Apr. 7, 1956; children—Mary Jane, M. Rupert, William. LL.B., U. Ky., 1960. City atty. City of Grayson, Ky., 1962-66; county atty., Carter County, Ky., 1966-70; assoc. Wilhoit and Wilhoit, 1960-81; judge U.S. Dist. Ct. for Eastern Ky., Catlettsburg, 1981—. Recipient Disting. Service award U. Ky. Alumni Assn., 1980. Mem. ABA, Ky. Bar Assn. Address: PO Box 695 25th and Broadway Catlettsburg KY 41129*

WILKEN, DOROTHY HARRIS, graphic designer, county official; b. Annville, Pa., Jan. 2, 1936; d. William Henry and Mary Magdalen (Kreider) Harris; A.B., George Washington U., 1957; M.P.A., Fla. Atlantic U., Boca Raton, 1979; divorced; children—Melany Ruth, Stephany Mary, Marjory Frances, Lorilee Elizabeth; m. 2d Thomas Martin Burckes III, Jan. 14, 1984. Art dir. Jour. AIA, 1957-59; art editor Qualified Contractor, Nat. Elec. Contractors Assn., 1959-60; studio mgr. graphics dept. Fla. Atlantic U., Boca Raton, 1965-82; county commr. Palm Beach County (Fla.), 1982—; cons., lectr. in field. Mem. Boca Raton City Council, 1974-78, mayor, 1976-77; mem. Palm Beach County Commn., 1982—; chmn. Boca Raton Com. on Annexation, 1974-75; mem. Treasure Coast Regional Planning Council, 1982—, Ethical Conduct Bd. Boca Raton, 1980-82; charter bd. dirs. Citizens Crime Watch Boca Raton, 1980—, pres., 1982. Recipient various civic awards; grantee Fla. Bd. Regents, 1978. Mem. Acad. Polit. Sci., Am. Planning Assn., Am. Soc. Pub. Adminstrs., AAUW, LWV, Women's Polit. Caucus, Fla. Atlantic U. Alumnae Assn., Audubon Soc., Sierra Club, Fla. Assn. County Commrs., Nature Conservancy, Common Cause. Democrat. Clubs: Wells Coll. Alumnae, George Washington U. Alumnae. Home: 490 NW 20th St Boca Raton FL 33431 Office: 345 S Congress Ave Delray Beach FL 33944

WILKERSON, PHILIP LAYTON, social science educator, college official; b. Paragould, Ark., June 30, 1945; s. Cecil E. and Mildred A. (Songer) W.; m. Shelia Sue Reynolds, Sept. 26, 1969; children—Philip Wesley, Daniel Wade. A.A., York Coll., 1965; B.A., Harding U., 1967; M.A., U. Ark., 1969. Instr. Crowley's Ridge Coll., Paragould, 1968-75, registrar, 1975-82, acad. dean, 1976-82, asst. prof. social sci., 1973—, v.p., chief ops. officer, 1982—. Mem. Am. Hist. Assn., Ark. Coll. Tchrs. Assn., Ark. Deans Assn., Chief Acad. Officers Ark. Ind. Colls. and Univs. Democrat. Mem. Ch. Christ. Avocations: fishing; camping; hunting; softball; reading. Home: Route 4 Box 175 Paragould AR 72450 Office: Crowleys Ridge Coll Route 4 Box 192 Paragould AR 72450

WILKERSON, RICHARD PAUL, exploration geologist; b. Chester, S.C., June 8, 1955; s. William Eugene and Joyce Maxine (Faile) W. B.S., Coll. Charleston, 1977; M.S., U. Ala., 1981. Research asst. State Oil & Gas Bd., Tuscaloosa, Ala., 1977-78; teaching asst. U. Ala., 1978-79; geol. trainee Cities Service Co., Tulsa, Okla., 1979-80, geologist, Houston, 1980-83; sr. geologist Cities Service Oil & Gas Corp., Houton, 1983—. Contbr. articles to profl. jours. Mem. Am. Assn. Petroleum Geologists, Houston Geol. Soc. Baptist. Avocations: yacht racing; tennis. Home: 6121 Winsome #38 Houston TX 77057 Office: Cities Service Oil & Gas Corp 1980 S Post Oak Houston TX 77227

WILKERSON, WILLIAM HOLTON, banker; b. Greenville, N.C., Feb. 16, 1947; s. Edwin Cisco and Agnes Holton (Gaskins) W.; m. Ellen Logan Tomskey, Oct. 27, 1973; 1 child, William Holton Jr. A.B. in Econs., U. N.C., 1970. Asst. v.p. First Union Nat. Bank, Greensboro, N.C., 1972-77; v.p. Peoples Bank & Trust Co., Rocky Mount, N.C., 1977-79; sr. v.p. Hibernia Nat. Bank, New Orleans, 1979—. Bd. advisor Jr. League, New Orleans, 1985. Mem. Robert Morris Assoc., New Orleans C. of C., Omicron Delta Epsilon, Chi Beta Phi, Phi Sigma Phi. Republican. Episcopalian. Clubs: Boston, Pickwick, New Orleans Country (New Orleans). Avocations: golf; tennis.

WILKERSON, WILLIAM ROBERT, university official, history educator; b. Richmond, Va., May 23, 1947; s. Willard Roland and Winnifred Jane (Bowen) W.; m. Elizabeth Duke Pearce, June 15, 1971; children—Elizabeth, Mary Lindsay. B.A. with honors, Washington and Lee U., 1969; M.A., U. Va., 1973, Ph.D., 1975. Editor, Ctr. for Advanced Studies, U. Va., Charlottesville, 1975, spl. asst., lectr. bus. history, 1975-81, asst. treas., 1981-84, assoc. prof., 1984—, assoc. provost for research, 1975—; cons. Va. Dept. Mental Health, 1979. Bd. dirs. Camp Holiday Trails, Charlottesville, 1979—. Mem. Am. Hist. Assn., Soc. Research Adminstrs., Nat. Council Univ. Research Adminstrs., Conf. Brit. Studies, AAAS. Episcopalian. Club: Greencroft (Charlottesville). Home: 1864 Winston Rd Charlottesville VA 22903 Office: Box 533 Newcomb Hall Stadium Charlottesville VA 22904

WILKES, JOSEPH WRAY, educator; b. Ft. Worth, May 10, 1922; s. Luther Lawson and Hattie (Wray) W.; B.S. in Mech. Engring., So. Meth. U., 1944; M.S. in Indsl. Engring., Washington U., St. Louis, 1951, D.Sc. in Indsl. Engring., 1954; m. Mary Lillian Allen, Sept. 26, 1947; children—Dorothy Ann, Mary Susan, Robert Wray. Lectr. mech. engring. So. Meth. U., 1946-48, instr., 1948-49; lectr. indsl. engring. Washington U., St. Louis, 1949-50, instr., 1950-54; asst. prof., asso. prof., prof. indsl. engring., U. Ark., Fayetteville, 1954-85, prof. computer sci. engring., 1985—; asso. supr. Computing Center, 1960-62, supr., 1962-72, asso. dir. instrn. and research, computing services, 1972-81, chmn. computer sci., 1966-85, asst. to v.p./provost, 1958-59, prin. investigator NSF computer expansion grant, 1965-68, NSF inst. engr. systems optimization, 1967; sec. data processing com. Conf. on Edn., 1963-66. Vestryman, Episcopal Ch., 1967-70, lay reader, 1968—, mem. Third Order Soc. St. Francis, 1975—. Served to lt. USNR, 1943-46. NSF grantee, 1959, 61, 63. Registered profl. engr., Ark., Tex. Mem. Am. Inst. Indsl. Engrs., IEEE Computer Soc., Am. Soc. Engring. Edn., Assn. Computing Machinery, Sigma Tau, Alpha Pi Mu, Sigma Xi (v.p. Ark. chpt., 1965-66, pres., 1966-67). Democrat. Panel chmn., session chmn., speaker nat. profl. confs. in field; editor, author U. Ark. Computing Center Technical Memorandum Series, 1966-73; author Users Manual U. of Ark. Computing Center, 1973; contbr. articles to profl. publs. Home: 1923 E Joyce Fayetteville AR 72703 Office: Computer Science Engring Dept Engr Bldg 314 U Ark Fayetteville AR 72701

WILKINS, HENRY, III, state legislator; b. Pine Bluff, Ark., Jan. 4, 1930; s. Henry, Jr. and Minnie Bell (Jones) W.; B.A. in Polit. Sci., Ark. M. and N. Coll., 1957; M.A., Atlanta U., 1961; postgrad U. Pitts., 1966-67; m. Josetta Edwards, 1954; children—Henry, IV, Cassandra Felecia, Mark R., Angela J. Teletype technician Pine Bluff Comml., 1954-59; instr. history and govt. Ark. M. and N. Coll., 1959-60; asst. prof. urban affairs U. Pitts., 1966-67; project dir. coop. coll. devel. program Phelps-Stokes Fund, N.Y.C., 1967-68; asso. prof. polit. sci. U. Ark., Pine Bluff, 1968—; mem. Ark. Ho. of Reps. from 82d Dist., 1973—. Sec. Ark. NAACP, 1964; mem. Jefferson County Democratic Com., 1964; mem. Ark. Dem. Com., 1972—, Ark. Dem. Exec. Com., 1976—; pres. Ark. Dem. Black Caucus, 1982; del. Ark. Constl. Conv., 1970, 80. Served with AUS, 1952-54. Merrill Lynch fellow, 1960; Ford Found. intern, 1966; recipient Disting. Service in Politics and Govt. award 12th Episcopal dist. A.M.E. Ch., 1973; Babe Ruth Little League award, 1975; award Morris Booker Meml. Coll., 1975, Friend of Edn. award Pine Bluff Edn. Assn., 1977, Legis. Service to Aging award Southeast Ark. Econ. Devel. Office on Aging, 1977, Outstanding Leadership for Sr. Citizens award, 1981, Disting. Service award Jaycees, 1978; Disting. Community Service award, 1985; 75th Gen. Assembly Leadership award, 1985. Mem. Am. Assn. Coll. and Univ. Profs., Am. Polit. Sci. Assn., Ark. Polit. Sci. Assn., Ark. Wildlife Assn., Jefferson County Forum, Omega Psi Phi. Methodist. Club: Elks. Author: Some Aspects of the Cold War, 1945-1950, 1963. Home: 303 N Maple St Pine Bluff AR 71601 Office: U Ark Pine Bluff AR 71601

WILKINS, RICHARD SANDEFUR, architect, planning consultant; b. Madison, Wis., Sept. 27, 1933; s. Robert A. and Alice (Metcalf) W.; m. Beatrice Bernshausen, Feb. 14, 1964; 1 child, Karl. B.S., B.Arch., U. Houston, 1957. With Suniland Furnishings, Houston, 1952, David D. Red, AIA, 1953-55, Robert W. Maurice, AIA, 1955-60, Raymond Brogniez, AIA, 1960-61; gen. ptnr. Maurice and Wilkins, Architects, Planning Consultants, Landscape Architects, Houston, 1961—. Bd. dirs. Kiwanis Found., 1983—; chmn. Zoning Bd. Adjustment City of West University Place, Tex., 1972-73. Served to capt. U.S. Army, 1957-58. Mem. AIA, Tex. Soc. Architects (merit award). Republican. Presbyterian. Author: (with Robert W. Maurice) Juveniles of Harris County, 1965; contbr. articles to profl. jours. Office: 3221 Marquart St Houston TX 77027

WILKINS, WAYNE ALLEN, freight company executive; b. Atlanta, Oct. 30, 1940; s. Waymon V. and Grace M. (Mosley) W.; children—Allen, Lisa, Mandy. Grad. Valdosta (Ga.) State U., 1'60. Agt., So. Airways, Valdosta, 1959-61; regional mgr. Airborne Freight Corp., Atlanta, 1967-68; v.p. Inter-Jet Cargo Systems, Atlanta, 1968-70; gen. mgr. Tri-City Delivery, Atlanta, 1970-72; pres., owner Omni Express, College Park, Ga., 1972—. Mem. Transp. Club Atlanta, Ga. Motor Trucking Assn. Methodist. Home: 1150 Longview Dr Fayetteville GA 30214 Office: 640 Terrell Mill Rd College Park GA 30349

WILKINS, WILLIAM WALTER, JR., judge; b. Anderson, S.C., Mar. 29, 1942; s. William Walter and Evelyn Louise (Horton) W.; m. Carolyn Louise Adams, Aug. 15, 1964; children—Lauren, Lyn, Walt. B.A., Davidson Coll., 1964; J.D., U. S.C., 1967. Bar: S.C. 1967, U.S. Dist. Ct. S.C. 1967, U.S. Ct. Appeals (4th cir.) 1969. Law clk. to judge U.S. Ct. Appeals 4th Cir., 1969; legal asst. to U.S. Senator Strom Thurmond, 1970; ptnr. Wilkins & Wilkins, Greenville, S.C., 1971-75; solicitor 13th Jud. Cir., 1976-81; judge U.S. Dist. Ct., Greenville, 1981—; chmn. U.S. Sentencing Commn., Washington, 1985—; lectr. Greenville Tech. Coll. Editor-in-chief: S.C. Law Rev., 1967; contbr. articles to legal jours. Served with U.S. Army, 1967-69; served to capt. USAR, 1969—. Named Outstanding Grad. of Yr. U. S.C. Sch. Law, 1967. Mem. ABA, S.C. Bar Assn., Wig and Robe. Republican. Baptist. Office: US Dist CT PO Box 10857 Greenville SC 29603 also US Sentencing Commn National Pl Suite 1400-A 1331 Pennsylvania Ave NW Washington DC 20004

WILKINSON, BRUCE HERBERT, religious publisher, educator; b. Kearny, N.J., Sept. 4, 1947; s. James S. and Joan M. (Heddy) W.; B.A., Northeastern Bible Coll., N.J., 1969, Th.B., 1970; Th.M., Dallas Theol. Sem., 1974; m. Darlene Marie Gahres, Aug. 23, 1969; children—David Bruce, Jennifer Sue. Lic. to ministry Baptist Ch., 1969; editorial asst. Dallas Theol. Sem., mem. faculty, public relations dir. Dallas Theol. Sem. Lay Inst., 1972-74; prof. Bible, Multnomah Sch. Bible, Portland, Oreg., 1974-77; pres., founder Walk Thru the

Bible Ministries, Atlanta, 1972—, pres. Christian Growth Center, 1979—; pres. Nat. Inst. Bibl. Studies, 1980-84, chmn. bd. dirs., 1981; mem. adj. faculty Columbia Bible Coll., 1980—; seminar leader, 1972—; pres., club mgr. Christian Growth Club, 1980-82; bd. dirs. Fellowship of Cos. for Christ, 1979—; mem. Internat. Council Bibl. Inerrancy, 1978—, Com. on Bible Expn., 1982—; chmn. Bible reading and study emphasis Yr. of Bible, 1983—. Named Alumnus of Year, Northeastern Bible Coll., 1976. Mem. Am. Mgmt. Assn., Pres. Assn. Author: Walk Thru the Old Testament, 1974; Walk Thru the New Testament, 1975; Walk Thru Personal Bible Study Methods, 1978; pub., exec. editor monthly mag. Daily Walk, 1978—, Timeless Insights, 1980—, Family Walk, 1983—, Year of the Bible Devotional Guide, 1983—. Home 4851 Adams Rd Dunnwoody GA 30338 Office: 61 Perimeter Park Atlanta GA 30341

WILKINSON, CHARLES DAVIS, investment company executive; b. Morton, Miss., Jan. 12, 1944; s. Charles Elton and Mary Margaret (Sigrest) W.; m. Noma Sue Midkiff, May 27, 1967; children—Lon Davis, Shea Seban. B.S., U.S. Air Force Acad., 1966; M.B.A., Emory U., 1973. Chartered fin. analyst. Trust portfolio mgr. First Nat. Bank, Mobile, Ala., 1973; investment mgr. Pub. Employee's Retirement System Miss., Jackson, 1976-86; pres. Langford Investment Co., Jackson. Served to capt. USAF, 1966-71. Mem. Nat. Assn. State Investment Officers (exec. com. 1979-82), Miss. Chpt. Fin. Analysts, Miss. Bridge Assn. (pres. 1982-83). Avocation: duplicate bridge. Office: Langford Investment Co 2 Bastille St Brandon MS 39042

WILKINSON, CLYDE WINFIELD, business educator; b. Coleman, Tex., July 4, 1910; s. John Lee and Mabel (Herring) W.; m. Lota Rea Spell, July 3, 1935 (div. 1973); m. Dorothy Ellen Colby, Dec. 14, 1974. A.A., Weatherford Coll., 1930; B.S., U. Tex., 1932, M.A., 1934; Ph.D., U. Ill., 1947. Prin. High Sch., Rockwood, Tex., 1932-33; instr., then asst. prof. Tex. A&M U., College Station, 1935-40; asst. prof., then assoc. prof. U. Ill., Urbana, 1940-50; prof. Mich. State U., E. Lansing, 1950-59; prof. English, U. Fla., Gainesville, 1959-75; prof. bus. U. Ala., Tuscaloosa, 1975—; cons. Mich. Bell, 1954-59, Fla. Farm Ins. Bur., 1962-70. Author various textbooks in field. Served with M.C., U.S. Army, 1942-46. Fellow Assn. Bus. Communication (editor publs. 1948-50, pres. 1954), Phi Theta Kappa, Delta Alpha Epsilon, Beta Gamma Sigma. Democrat. Methodist. Avocations: fishing; gardening; travel. Home: 46 Guilds Woods Tuscaloosa AL 35401

WILKINSON, DON GREENE, architect; b. Chelsea, Mass., Apr. 17, 1929; s. Charles Henry and Helen Thompson (Holt) W.; div.; 1 son, Rafe Wesley. B.A., Dartmouth Coll., 1952; M.Arch., Harvard U., 1959. Registered architect, Fla., Calif. practice architecture, San Jose, Calif., 1966-68, Sarasota, Fla., 1968—; lectr. U. South Fla. Served with AUS, 1946-47, 50-51. Patentee plywood crystal; research three dimensional projection of simple whole numbers, discovering codes of natural objects and processes. Home: 5509 Calle del Invierno Sarasota FL 33581 Office: 32 S Palm Ave Sarasota FL 33577

WILKINSON, DOROTHY COLBY, business educator; b. Chgo., June 10, 1920; d. Merrill Whitney and Harriet Ellen (Shade) Colby; m. Jack Harwood Menning, Mar. 6, 1943 (dec. 1973); children—Whitney Harwood, Colby Harwood; m. Clyde Winfield Wilkinson, Dec. 14, 1974. B.S., U. Ill., 1942, M.A., U. Ala., 1966. Instr. U. Ala., Tuscaloosa, 1948-62, asst. prof., 1976—; instr. City Bd. Edn., Tuscaloosa, 1964-76; cons. in field. Co-author: Communicating Through Writing and Speaking in Business, 1986. Author textbooks in field. Contbr. articles to profl. jours. Pres. Tuscaloosa City Tchrs., 1968; mem. Beautification Com. Womens C. of C. Mem. Assn. Bus. Communicators (com. 1984-86), Commerce Exec. Soc. Episcopalian. Clubs: U. Womens, Masquers, Cook Guild, Avant Garde. Avocations: travel; cooking; gardening; photography; swimming. Home: 46 Guilds Woods Tuscaloosa AL 35401

WILKINSON, JOHN PAUL, JR., accountant; b. Bay City, Tex., Nov. 6, 1939; s. John Paul and Lydia (Rasmussen) W.; m. Pamela Fannin, Nov. 14, 1964; children—John Paul III, Damon Everett. Student U. Tex., 1957-60; B.B.A., Southwestern U., 1966; grad. with honors Sch. Bank Adminstrn., U. Wis., 1974. C.P.A., Tex. With Montgomery Ward & Co., Austin, Tex., 1966-68, controller trainee, 1966, mem. field audit staff, 1967, store controller, Colorado Springs, Colo., 1967-68; with Nat. Bank of Commerce, San Antonio, 1969—, asst. comptroller, 1970-71, auditor, 1971-82, v.p., 1975-82; gen. auditor Nat. Bancshares Corp. Tex., 1978-82, v.p., 1981-82; ptnr. Eidson & Wilkinson, C.P.A.s, San Antonio, 1982—. Served with AUS, 1960-63. Mem. Am. Inst. C.P.A.s, Tex. Soc. C.P.A.s, Inst. Internal Auditors, Bank Adminstrn. Inst., San Antonio Golf Assn. (pres. 1983, gen. chmn. Tex. Open 1983). Methodist. Club: Fair Oaks Country. Office: 10202 Heritage Suite 206 San Antonio TX 78216

WILKINSON, LARRY DALE, minister; b. Charlotte, N.C., Sept. 27, 1936; s. Paul B. and Edna (Todd) W.; m. Blevin Ann Gillis, July 20, 1957; children—Eric Eugene, Cynthia Sue, Dale Ann. A.B., High Point Coll., 1958; M.Div., Duke U. Div. Sch., 1961; M.A. in Edn., Wake Forest U., 1972; Ed.D., U. N.C.-Greensboro, 1976; attended numerous religious seminars. Ordained to ministry United Meth. Ch., 1959. Pastor Woodmont United Meth. Ch., Reidsville, N.C., 1961-66, First United Meth. Ch., Valdese, N.C., 1966-69, Maple Springs United Meth. Ch., Winston-Salem, N.C., 1969-72, Christ United Meth. Ch., High Point, N.C., 1972-76, First United Meth. Ch., Waynesville, N.C., 1976-79, Providence United Meth. Ch., Charlotte, N.C., 1984—; dist. supt. The North Wilkesboro Dist., N.C., 1979-80, The Marion Dist., N.C., 1980-84; vis. prof. psychology dept. High Point Coll., 1974-76; bd. mgrs. The Pastors' Sch. Duke Div. Sch., 1977-80; mem. exec. com. The Regional Commn. on Campus Ministry, 1979-80, Bd. Higher Edn. and Campus Ministry, The Western N.C. Ann. Conf., 1979-84, The State Commn. on Campus Ministry, 1980-84; mem. Bd. Ordained Ministry Western N.C. Ann. Conf., 1975-79; chmn. psychol. guidance com. Western N.C. Ann. Conf., 1976-79; charter mem., bd. mgrs. The Western N.C. Conf. Learning Ctr., Winston-Salem, 1980-84, chairperson, 1980-81; del. to Jurisdictional Conf. of United Meth. Ch., 1980, Gen. and Jurisdictional Confs. of United Meth. Ch., 1984. Contbr. articles to profl. jours. Mem. exec. com., bd. dirs. Greater Winston-Salem Wesley Found., 1969-72, Appalachian State U. Wesley Found., 1979-80; mem. exec. com. High Point Coll. Alumni Assn., 1974-76; bd. mgrs., exec. com. Givens Estates Meth. Retirement Community, 1980-84; trustee High Point Coll., 1983—; bd. dirs. High Point Youth Service Bur., High Point chpt. Am. Cancer Soc., High Point Urban Ministries; pres. Reidsville Ministerial Assn., The Valdese Ministerial Assn. Named Boss of Yr., Furniture Capital chpt. Am. Bus. Women's Assn., 1976. Mem. Am. Psychol. Assn., The Am. Assn. Pastoral Counselors, Pfafftown Jaycees (named top Jaycee Club in U.S. 1971). Lodges: Lions, Rotary, Kiwanis. Avocations: aquatic sports; golf; walking; gardening. Home: 216 N Wendover Rd Charlotte NC 28211 Office: Providence United Meth Ch 2810 Providence Rd Charlotte NC 28211

WILKINSON, ROBERT WARREN, lawyer; b. Oak Ridge, Tenn., Dec. 7, 1950; s. Michael Kennerly and Virginia (Sleap) W.; B.A. cum laude, Emory U., 1972; J.D., U. Tenn., 1975; LL.M., Georgetown U., 1978; m. Patsy Ann McFall, Jan. 3, 1980; 1 son, Michael McFall. Bar: Tenn. 1975. Asst. staff judge adv. U.S. Army, U.S. Army Materiel Devel. and Readiness Command, Alexandria, Va., 1976-79; assoc. partner firm Buxton, Lain & Buxton, Oak Ridge, 1979-83; ptnr. Buxton, Layton, Webster & Wilkinsen, 1983—. Bd. dirs. HOPE of Oak Ridge, Arts Council of Oak Ridge. Served to capt. U.S. Army, 1976-79. Decorated Army Commendation medal. Mem. Am. Bar Assn., Tenn. Bar Assn., Anderson County Bar Assn. Episcopalian. Club: Rotary. Home: 211 Connors Circle Oak Ridge TN 37830 Office: 31 E Tennessee Ave Oak Ridge TN 37830

WILKINSON, STANLEY RALPH, soil scientist; b. West Amboy, N.Y., Mar. 28, 1931; s. Ralph Ward and Eva Goldie (Perkins) W.; m. Jean Saye; children—Rachael, Stanley R. Jr., Augusta J. B.S., Cornell U., 1954; M.S., Purdue U., 1956, Ph.D., 1961. Soil scientist U.S. Regional Pasture Research Lab., University Park, Pa., 1960-64, So. Piedmont Conservation Research Ctr., Watkinsville, Ga., 1964—. Past advance chmn. Boy Scouts Am. Served to capt. USAF, 1955-57. Recipient 3d prize Freedoms Found., 1956. Mem. Am. Soc. Agronomy, Soil Sci. Soc. Am., Soil Conservation Soc. Am., Sigma Xi. Methodist. Contbr. articles to profl. jours.

WILKINSON, STEPHEN THOMAS, college administrator; b. Dallas, Feb. 23, 1943; s. Lionel S. and Irma (Redmon) W.; m. Sharon Elizabeth Roberson Wilkinson, June 4, 1966; 1 dau., Shara Deeann. A.A., Tyler Jr. Coll., 1963; B.S., East Tex. State U., 1965, M.Ed., 1972. Tchr., Edgewood Ind. Sch. Dist. (Tex.), 1965-67, Terrell Ind. Sch. Dist. (Tex.), 1967-74; counselor Canton Ind. Sch. Dist. (Tex.), 1974-77, Henderson County Jr. Coll., Athens, Tex., 1977-78; dean students Frank Phillips Coll., Borger, Tex., 1978—. Mem. Tex. Student Personnel and Guidance Assn., Tex. Assn. Student Fin. Aid Adminstrs., Nat. Assn. Student Fin. Aid Adminstrs., Tex. Assn. Coll. and U. Personnel Adminstrs., C. of C., Beta Beta Beta. Lodges: Lions (pres. 1972-73), Elks. Home: PO Box 1225 Borger TX 79007 Office: Frank Phillips Coll PO Box 5118 Borger TX 79008

WILKINSON, VANCE K., systems analyst; b. Freewater, Oreg., Apr. 4, 1935; s. Clarance Edgar and Velma Fay (Stahly) W.; m. Annette Davis, Sept. 18, 1960; children—Angela Fay, Todd Davis. B.S. in Aero. Engring. (disting. grad.), Air Force Inst. Tech., 1969, M.S. in Systems Engring., 1975; M. Indsl. Engring., U. Tenn., 1980. Registered profl. engr. Tenn., Tex., Ohio. Commd. airman U.S. Air Force, 1957, advanced through grades to maj., 1974; combat officer, 1958-67, weapons systems devel. officer, 1968-77; ret., 1977; systems analyst Oak Ridge Nat. Lab., 1977—; cons., tchr. econ. analysis, quality control, ops. research. Decorated D.F.C., Meritorious Service medal, Air medal (6), Air Force Commendation medal, Vietnamese Cross of Gallantry with palm. Mem. Inst. Indsl. Engrs. (nat. bd. dirs., past chpt. pres., Engr. of Yr. award 1983, 85) ASME, Am. Statis. Soc., Air Force Assn. Contbr. articles to tech. jours. Office: Oak Ridge Nat Lab 9108 MSI PO Box Y Oak Ridge TN 37831

WILKINSON, WILLIAM DURFEE, museum director; b. Utica, N.Y., Sept. 2, 1924; s. Winfred Durfee and Edith (Lockwood) W.; m. Dorothy May Spencer, Apr. 2, 1966. B.S., Harvard U., 1949; postgrad., Munson Inst. Am. Maritime History, Mystic, Conn., 1961-62. Group ins. underwriter Home Life Ins. Co., N.Y.C., 1949-59; adminstr., marine curator Mus. City of New York, 1960-63; registrar Met. Mus. Art, N.Y.C., 1963-71; asso. dir. Mariners Mus., Newport News, Va., 1971-73, dir., 1973—. Bd. dirs. Council Am. Maritime Museums, 1975-79, pres., 1978-79; bd. dirs. Mus. Computer Network, Inc., 1972-83, Coast Guard Acad. Found., Inc., Future of Hampton Roads, Inc.; trustee War Meml. Mus. of Va. Served with C.E. AUS, 1943-45. Mem. Am. Assn. Museums, Soc. for Nautical Research (Gt. Britain), Nat. Trust Hist. Preservation (maritime preservation com. 1978-80), Steamship Hist. Soc. Am., Propeller Club of U.S., Explorers Club of N.Y.C., Propeller Club of Port of Newport News (bd. govs.). Clubs: Hampton Yacht, Town Point. Home: 101 Museum Pkwy Newport News VA 23606 Office: Museum Dr Newport News VA 23606

WILKS, JACQUELIN HOLSOMBACK, educator; b. Oakdale, La., Jan. 18, 1950; d. Jack and Ida Mae (Bass) Holsomback; B.S., La. Coll., 1972; M.A.T., Okla. City U., 1982; postgrad. So. Bapt. Theol. Sem., Louisville, 1974, S.E. Mo. State U., 1977; m. Thomas M. Wilks, Jan. 28, 1972; children—Thomas David, Bryan Emerson. Sec. to adminstr. Allen Parish Hosp., Kinder, La., 1968-69; tchr. horseback riding, swimming Triple D Guest Ranche, Warren, Tex., 1969; singer, speaker Found. Singers, including TV and radio appearances, record albums, 1970-71; tchr. English, reading Pine Bluff (Ark.) High Sch., 1972-74; tchr. kindergarten Doyle Elem. Sch., East Prairie (Mo.) R-2 Sch. Dist., 1974-75; tchr. 1st grad. Bertrand (Mo.) Elem. Sch., 1975-76; tchr. 6th grade sci. A.D. Simpson Sch., Charleston, Mo., 1976-78; dir. admissions and fin. aid Mo. Bapt. Coll., St. Louis, 1978-80; fin. adminstr. Control Data Inst., Control Data Corp., St. Louis, 1980-81; dir. tutorial services, instr. tutorial methods Okla. Bapt. U., 1981—; instr. horsemanship St. Gregory's Jr. Coll., Shawnee, Okla., 1981, dir. Resource Ctr., 1985—; counselor Gordon Cooper Area Vocat. Tech. Sch., 1982-83, Shawnee Jr. High Sch., 1983-85; tutor for children under jurisdiction Juvenile Ct., Jefferson County, Ark., 1972-73, leader group counseling/therapy sessions, 1972. Choreographer, First Bapt. Ch. Youth Choir, Pine Bluff; v.p. St. Gregory's Coll. Therapeutic Horsemanship Program; Republican election judge. Recipient Kathryn Carpenter award La. Bapt. Conv., 1971; Real Scope award Realty World, St. Louis, 1980; lic. Realtor, Mo. Mem. Nat. Hist. Soc., Univ. Alliance Okla. Bapt. U., Nat. Assn. Fin. Aid Adminstrs., Nat. Assn. Admissions Counselors, Athenian Lit. Soc., Nat. Geog. Soc., Gamma Beta Phi, Kappa Delta, Phi Kappa Phi. Republican. Baptist. Clubs: Kathryn Boone Music, Civinette Booster. Home: Route 3 Box 143 Shawnee OK 74801 Office: Shawnee Jr High Sch Highland and Union Sts Shawnee OK 74801

WILL, W. MARVIN, political science educator; b. Peace Valley, Mo., Mar. 25, 1937; m. Doreen Huebner, 1962. B.A., McPherson Coll., 1960; M.A. in Polit. Sci., U. Mo., 1963, Ph.D., 1972. Asst. to dir. Brethren Service Commn., Elgin, Ill., 1958-59; instr. Gasconade R-11 Schs., Owensville, Mo., 1960-62; asst. instr. to instr. U. Mo.-Columbia, 1962-64, 67-69; instr. St. Louis Community Coll., 1964-69; adj. prof. Washington U., St. Louis, 1976-78; dir. Civic Edn. Ctr., St. Louis, 1976-78; asst. prof. to assoc. prof. U. Tulsa, 1969-76, 79—; lectr., cons. in field. Author: Revolution or Order?, 1985. Editor/author: (with R. Millett) Crescents of Conflict, 1986; The Restless Caribbean, 1979. Contbr. articles to profl. jours. Mem. Greater Tulsa Council and Planning Team, 1975-76. Mellon-ILAS fellow, 1984; U. Tulsa fellow, 1982, 84; Hazen Found. grantee, 1977-78, 80, many others. Mem. Midwest Assn. Latin Am. Studies (exec. council, pres. 1985-86), Caribbean Studies Assn. (exec. council), Congress of Americanists, Am. Polit. Sci. Assn. Internat. Studies Assn., Southwestern Social Sci. Assn., So. Polit. Sci. Assn., Pi Sigma Alpha. Ch. of Brethren. Address: Dept Polit Sci U Tulsa 600 S College Ave Tulsa OK 74104

WILLEFORD, CATHERINE PROCTOR, civic worker; b. Greenwood, S.C., Sept. 9, 1935; d. Benjamen Moye and Catherine Proctor; B.S., Winthrop Coll., 1957; M.S., La. State U., 1959; m. Brice J. Willeford, Jr., July 22, 1961; children—Brice J. III, Catherine Elizabeth. Instr., La. State U., 1957-58, Duke U., 1958-61; tchr. Cannon Jr. High Sch., Kannapolis, N.C., 1961-62; bd. dirs. Cabarrus County United Way, 1974-79, ARC, 1976—, N.C. United Way, 1977-79; bd. dirs. Cabarrus County chpt. Am. Cancer Soc., 1981—, Cabarrus-Kannapolis Library, 1983—; chmn. Womens Democratic County Com., 1973; chmn. Gov.'s Involvement Council, 1978-79; vice chmn. Democratic Precinct Com., Kannapolis, N.C., 1970-77; mem. planning bd. So. Piedmont Health Assn., 1978-79; chmn. Tchr. Parent Council, 1978-79; leader Girl Scouts U.S.A., 1970-78, Cub Scouts, 1969; sec. bd. Library Arts Council, 1977-79; bd. dirs. Old Courthouse Theatre, 1977—, Cabarrus-Concona Friends of Library; chmn. Episc. Churchwomen, 1982; chmn. Kannapolis II Book Club, 1981-82; co-chmn. Holt Art Gallery, 1980—, Arts Council Ball, 1983; pres. Parnasis Book Club, 1983; sec. Cabarrus chpt. ARC. Co-editor: The Churchmouse Cookbook. Recipient Gov.'s Spl. Vol. cert., 1979; La. State U. fellow, 1957-58. Mem. DAR, N.C. Hist. Assn., Internat. Platform Assn. Episcopalian. Clubs: Friends of Library, Garden. Home: 1646 Eastwood St Kannapolis NC 28081

WILLEY, BENJAMIN TUCKER, JR., lawyer; b. Richmond, Va., Feb. 23, 1946; s. Benjamin Tucker and Virginia (Bradshaw) W.; m. Beverly Jane Buscanics, Jan. 21, 1984; children by previous marriage—Benjamin Tucker III, Theresa. B.A., U. Tex.-Arlington, 1973; J.D., Oklahoma City U., 1976. Bar: Okla. 1976, Tex. 1985, U.S. Dist. Ct. (we. dist.) Okla. 1976. Ptnr. Evans & Willey, Oklahoma City, 1976-80; sr. ptnr. Willey & Kilpatrick, Oklahoma City, 1980—; chmn. continuing legal edn. program-title exam. basics and oil and gas title exam. U. Tulsa, 1984. Coach, N. Oklahoma City Soccer Club, 1980-83. Served to capt. U.S. Army, 1966-72, Vietnam. Decorated Bronze Star medal, Combat Infantryman's Badge. Mem. Okla. Bar Assn. (chmn. continuing legal edn. program-Indian land titles 1983, mem. faculty oil and gas continuing legal edn. program 1983), State Bar Tex., Phi Delta Phi. Episcopalian. Home: 6640 Avondale Dr Oklahoma City OK 73116 Office: Willey & Kilpatrick 501 Northwest Expressway Suite 525 Oklahoma City OK 73118 also 601 Pacific at Market Suite 220 Dallas TX 75202

WILLEY, MARYANN PICH, home economist, artist; b. Stuttgart, Ark., Jan. 28, 1932; d. George and Kathryn (Bilyk) Pich; m. Donald Joe Willey, Feb. 15, 1958; children—Donald Steven, Barry Conrad. B.S.H.E., U. Ark., 1954; postgrad. U. Houston, 1972-74. Exec. trainee Foley's, Houston, 1954-56; draftsperson Gulf Oil Co., Houston, 1956-57; with home service dept. Houston Light and Power, 1957-58; group shows include Mablevalle Gallery, 1966, Ark. Art Ctr. Rental Gallery, 1967-71; represented in pvt. collections; dir. Pich Farms Inc. Treas. Quilt Guild; bd. dirs. Spring Shadows Civic Assn., Houston, 1978-82, chmn. publs., 1983—. Recipient Monsanto Art award Little Rock Arts Festival, 1977, award of Excellence Fiber Artists Tex., 1981. Mem. Home Economists in Bus., Fiber Artists Houston, Houston Area Home Economists. Methodist. Club: Houston Yacht (LaPorte, Tex.); Plaza (Houston). Address: 2602 Bandelier Houston TX 77080

WILLIAMS, ADELE FULLER, geophysicist; b. Scottsbluff, Nebr., May 22, 1937; d. George Bert and Lois (Kent) Fuller; m. Robert Lawson Lovett, Aug. 17, 1958 (div. Feb. 1976); children—Shana, Steven, Wren, John, Paul; m. Jerry Alan Williams, Dec. 28, 1976; 1 child, Benjamin. B.A., U. Iowa, 1958; B.S., Southwestern Mo. State U., 1976; M.S., U. Houston, 1983. Geophysicist, Texaco, Inc., Bellaire, Tex., 1977-80; sr. geophysicist Sohio Petroleum Co., Houston, 1981—. Mem. Am. Assn. Petroleum Geologists (com. mem. 1984—), Soc. Exploration Geophysicists, Am. Geophys. Union, Assn. Woman Geoscientists. Democrat. Home: 8511 Cookwind St Houston TX 77072

WILLIAMS, ALBERT SIMPSON, horticulture and landscape architecture educator and administrator; b. York County, S.C., Jan. 23, 1924; s. Herman Pearson and Della (Thompson) W.; m. Stella Senn, Aug. 29, 1946; 1 child, Alice Maria. B.S. in Biology, Emory U., 1948; M.S. in Botany, U. Tenn., 1949; Ph.D. in Plant Pathology, N.C. State U., 1954. Asst. prof. Athens Coll., Ala., 1950-51; assoc. prof. Va. Poly. Inst., Blacksburg, Va., 1954-68; prof. plant pathology U. Ky., Lexington, 1968-75, prof., chmn. horticulture and landscape architecture, 1975—. Served to 1st lt. USAF, 1943-46. Mem. Am. Hort. Soc., Am. Phytopath. Soc., Nematology Soc., European Soc. Nematologists. Methodist. Avocations: travel; photography. Home: 790 Cindy Blair Way Lexington KY 40503 Office: Dept Horticulture and Landscape Architecture U Ky Lexington KY 40546

WILLIAMS, ALFRED BLYTHE, business communication educator; b. Oakland City, Ind., Sept. 17, 1940; s. Ross Merl and Jesse Adell (Helsley) W. B.S. cum laude, Oakland City Coll., 1963; M.S., Ind. U., 1964; Ph.D., Ga. State U., 1974. Cert. tchr. bus. edn. and English, Ind. Tchr. Arlington High Sch., Indpls., 1964-65, Oakland City Coll., 1965-69; editor Southwestern Pub. Co., Cin., 1969-72, cons., 1981; adj. prof. Ga. State U., Atlanta, 1972-74; assoc. prof. bus. communications U. Southwestern La., Lafayette, 1975—; cons. John Wiley Pub. Co., N.Y., 1981-82. Author study guides. Editor Information Systems Bus. Communication Jour., 1983. Patron Lafayette Community Concerts, 1984; contbr. La. and Nat. Republican parties, Baton Rouge, Washington, 1983, 84. Mem. Assn. Bus. Communicators (Francis W. Weeks Merit award 1984), AAUP, La. Assn. Higher Edn., Sierra Club, Phi Delta Kappa, Delta Pi Epsilon. Methodist. Lodge: Kiwanis.

WILLIAMS, ALICE TRUMP, mathematics educator; b. Martinsburg, W.Va., Feb. 1, 1940; d. Fred Trump and Florence May (Foshnocht) Sperow; m. Henry Gordon Williams, Mar. 27, 1959; children—Barbara J., Henry G., Nancy J. B.A., W.Va. U., 1968; M.S., James Madison U., 1973. Tchr., Lexington High Sch. (Va.), 1968-72; chair dept. math. So. Sem. Jr. Coll., Buena Vista, Va., 1973-85; faculty mem. James Madison U., 1985—; lectr. Active Am. Field Service, Rockbridge Arts Guild, Lexington Flute Quintet. Danforth assoc. So. Sem., 1975; NSF fellow, 1983. Mem. Math. Assn. Am. Republican. Presbyterian. Club: Ladies Lunch (Lexington, Va.). Home: Route 2 Box 88 Lexington VA 24450 Office: So Seminary Buena Vista VA 24416

WILLIAMS, ANNETTA MARIE, nursing executive; b. Burlington, N.C., Nov. 30, 1952; d. Arthur and Constance (Cummings) Dilworth; children—Annetta, Sydney, Gustav, William; m. Ronald Kevin Williams, Nov. 14, 1981. L.P.N., Guilford Tech. Community Coll., 1977, student Gen. Edn. 1981, student emergency med. tech., 1981. Lic. practical nurse, N.C. Staff nurse L. Richardson Hosp., Greensboro, N.C., 1979-80; charge nurse Carolina Nursing, Greensboro, 1978-80; health care supr. Beverly Enterprises, Virginia Beach, Va., 1980-83; exec. dir. Unique Nursing Care, Inc., Greensboro, 1981—. Mem. L.P.N. Assn. N.C., Nat. Assn. Female Execs., Am. Entrepreneurs Assn. Democrat. Baptist.

WILLIAMS, ANNIE JOHN, volunteer educator; b. Reidsville, N.C., Aug. 26, 1913; d. John Wesley and Martha Anne (Walker) W.; A.B., Greensboro Coll., 1933; M.A., U. N.C., Chapel Hill, 1939; postgrad. Appalachian State U., summer 1944, Duke U., summer 1936, (Shell Merit fellow) Cornell U., summer 1961. Tchr. math. Blackstone (Va.) Coll., 1934-35; tchr. public schs., Hoke High Sch., Raeford, N.C., 1935-37, Massey Hill High Sch., Fayetteville, N.C., 1937-42, Alexander Graham Jr. High Sch., Fayetteville, 1942-43, Carr Jr. High Sch., Durham, N.C., 1943-53; supr. math. N.C. Dept. Public Instrn., Raleigh, 1959-62; tchr. math. Durham High Sch., 1953-59, 62-78, ret., 1978; vol. in math. N.C. Sch. Sci. and Math., Durham, 1980—; adj. asst. prof. math. and sci. edn. N.C. State U., Raleigh, 1966-73. Recipient cert. of recognition dept. math. and sci. edn. N.C. State U., 1979; named Community Key Vol., N.C. Sch. Sci. and Math., 1982. Mem. Nat. Council Tchrs. Math. (life), (dir., 1957-60), Math. Assn. Am. (life), N.C. Council Tchrs. Math. (W. W. Rankin Meml. award 1975), Internat. Platform Assn., Delta Kappa Gamma, Mu Alpha Theta (hon.). Methodist. Clubs: Pierian Lit. (sec. 1979-80, pres. 1980-81), Durham Woman's (co-chmn. internat. affairs dept. 1985-87), DAR (chmn. chpt. Am. History Month 1980-82, chpt. corr. sec. 1982-84, chpt. chaplain 1984-86). Author: (with Brown and Montgomery) Algebra, First Course, 1963, Algebra, Second Course, 1963. Home: 2021 Sprunt Ave Durham NC 27705

WILLIAMS, ARTEE, state personnel administrator; b. North Little Rock, Ark., Sept. 20, 1947; s. Robert L. and Lethel W.; m. Charlotte Marie Hutchinson, Nov. 16, 1968; children—Simone Eunice, Erica Celeste. B.A. in Psychology, Philander Smith Coll., 1970; postgrad. Ark. State U., 1978. Cert. completion of pub. personnel mgmt. fellowship program Nat. Civil Service League. Asst. personnel officer Ark. Hwy. Dept., Little Rock, 1971-74; personnel officer Dept. Higher Edn., Little Rock, 1974-76; personnel dir. Ark. State U., Jonesboro, 1976-79; personnel mgr. State Fin. Dept., Little Rock, 1979-80; state personnel adminstr., State Office Personnel Mgmt., Little Rock, 1980—. Active Am. Heart Assn., Little Rock, 1982-83. Recipient certs. of appreciation Nat. Commn. Jobs for Vets., 1973, Nat. Alliance of Bus., 1981-82, Am. Heart Assn., 1983. Mem. Nat. Assn. State Personnel Execs. (pres. 1984-85), Am. Soc. Personnel Adminstrn., Internat. Personnel Mgmt. Assn., Am. Compensation Assn., Am. Soc. Pub. Adminstrs. Baptist. Avocations: Fishing; travel; reading. Office: State Office of Personnel Mgmt 7th and High PO Box 3278 Little Rock AR 72203

WILLIAMS, ARTHUR MIDDLETON, JR., lawyer, electric utility executive; educator; b. Charleston, S.C., Sept. 16, 1914; s. Arthur Middleton and Katherine (Ward) W.; B.S. in Textile Chemistry, Clemson U., 1936, LL.D. (hon.), 1985; J.D., magna cum laude, U.S.C., 1942, LL.D. (hon.), 1981; m. Katherine Murphy, Nov. 4, 1943; children—Katherine Elizabeth (Mrs. Mahon), Patricia LaBruce (Mrs. Boykin), Elizabeth Middleton. Bar: S.C. 42, U.S. Supreme Ct. 1954. Joined U.S. Army, 1936, served in cav. until 1938; transferred to inactive duty, 1938-42; active duty with armored forces, 1942-43; ret., 1943, practice law Columbia, S.C., 1943-44; with S.C. Electric & Gas Co., Columbia, 1944-82, sr. v.p., 1961-66, pres., 1966-77, chief exec. officer, 1967-79, chmn. bd., 1977-82, chmn. emeritus, 1982—, also dir.; tchr. law U. S.C. Law Sch., 1947-50, 81—; dir. emeritus Liberty Corp., S.C. Nat. Bank. Columbia; dir. S.C. Nat. Corp. Chmn. S.C. Employment Security Commn. Merit System Council, 1950-56, mem. Gov. S.C. Fiscal Survey Commn., 1955, S.C. Commn. Human Affairs, 1971-75; mem. So. Govs.' Conf. Peacetime Uses Nuclear Energy, 1955-59; mem. exec. com. So. Interstate Nuclear Bd., 1959-63; sec. S.C. Nuclear Energy and Space Commn., 1962-63. Mem. bd. sch. commrs. Dist. 1, Richland County, S.C., 1958-71; mem. U. S.C. Bus. Partnership Found., pres., 1969-71; mem. U. S.C. Law Partnership Bd., pres., 1981—; mem. Carolina Research and Devel. Found., U. S.C., pres., 1980—; mem. Ednl. Found., U. S.C.; mem. pres.'s nat. adv. council U. S.C.; mem. Gov.'s Mansion Found. Bd. dirs. United Fund Community Services, Columbia and Richland County, 1955-58, pres., 1956, bd. dirs. Richland County chpt. ARC, 1945-48, Family Welfare Assn. Richland County, 1950-55. Columbia U.S.O., 1948-51; bd. dirs. Carolinas United, 1959-62, exec. com., 1959-62; trustee Porter Gaud Sch., Charleston, 1966-68, Converse Coll., 1971-75, Benedict Coll., 1979—, Voorhees Coll., 1985—, S.C. Episcopal Retirement Community at Still Hopes, 1985—. Recipient Freedoms Found. award, 1950. Algernon Sydney Sullivan award U. S.C., 1972. Disting. Alumni award, 1975. Mem. S.C. (v.p. 5th jud. circuit 1954). Am., Richland County bar assns.; Columbia C. of C. (dir. 1951-57, 61-64, pres. 1955, nat. counselor 1956). S.C. C. of C. (dir. 1963-66, pres. 1968, chmn. bd. 1969). Edison Electric Inst. (dir. 1973-76, 78-81). Southeastern Electric Exchange (pres. 1970-71, bd. dirs. 1966-79). NAM (dir. 1970-73). Phi Beta Kappa Scabbard and Blade, Blue Key, Phi Psi, Beta Gamma Sigma, Sigma Nu (Centennial award 1969). Episcopalian (vestryman) Clubs: Palmetto (pres. 1967-71, bd. govs. 1959—), Cotillion, Quadrille, Pine Tree Hunt, Centurian, Forest Lake, Summit, Columbia Sailing (Columbia); Winyah Indigo Soc. (Georgetown); Carolina Yacht (Charleston). Office: Lady and Marion Sts Columbia SC 29201 also PO Box 764 Columbia SC 29218

WILLIAMS, AVON NYANZA, JR., lawyer, state senator; b. Knoxville, Tenn., Dec. 22, 1921; s. Avon Nyanza and Carrie Belle Williams; A.B., Johnson

C. Smith U., Charlotte, N.C., 1940; LL.B., Boston U., 1947, LL.M., 1948; m. Joan Marie Bontemps, 1956; children—Avon Nyanza, Wendy Janette. Bar: Mass. 1948, Tenn. 1949, U.S. Supreme Ct. 1963. Practice law, Knoxville, 1949-53; partner firm, Nashville, 1953-69; individual practice law, Nashville, 1969—; mem. Tenn. State Senate, 1968—; prof. dental jurisprudence Meharry Med. Coll., 1970-84. Founding mem. Tenn. Voters Council, 1966—, chmn., 1966-85; founding mem. Davidson County Ind. Polit. Council, 1962—, pres., 1962-66; mem. State Dem. Steering Com., 1964; del. Nat. Dem. Conv., 1972; mem. exec. com. Nashville br. NAACP, 1953—; elder, trustee St. Andrews Presbyn. Ch., Nashville, 1966—; mem. appeals and rev. com. Meharry Med. Coll., 1970-76; bd. dirs. So. Regional Council, 1968—, Family and Children's Service, 1956-60. Served to lt. col., JAGC, U.S. Army Res. Recipient certs. of achievement for civil rights legal work. Mem. ABA, Am. Judicature Soc., Omega Psi Phi, Sigma Pi Phi. Home: 1818 Morena St Nashville TN 37208 Office: 203 2d Ave N Nashville TN 37201

WILLIAMS, BARRON, corporate executive, microcomputer consultant; b. St. Louis, Aug. 23, 1951; s. Anderson, Sr. and Mary B. (Gilkey) W. B.A. in Polit. Sci., Washington U.-St. Louis, 1973. Mktg. rep. IBM, St. Louis, 1974-77, Four Phase Systems, St. Louis, 1977-80; AT&T Corp., Atlanta, 1980-83; corp. account exec. Micro Mart, Inc., Atlanta, 1983—; cons. in field. Campaign worker Andrew Young for Mayor, Atlanta, 1981, John Lewis for City Council, Atlanta, 1985; vol. Christmas Hungry Club, Atlanta, 1983-85; fund raiser Atlanta Jaycees, 1985. Acad. scholar Washington U., 1969. Mem. AAUP, Assn. Black Law Students, Atlanta Regional Minority Purchasing Council, Kappa Alpha Psi (v.p., del. nat. conv., pres. 1971-80). Democrat. Baptist. Avocations: racquetball; basketball; tennis; jogging; weight lifting; karate. Home: 2607 Pineview Dr Decatur GA 30030 Office: Micro Mart Inc 3159 Campus Dr Norcross GA 30071

WILLIAMS, BARRY THOMAS, junior high school principal; b. Salisbury, N.C., Apr. 25, 1952; s. Booker Thomas and Lillian Victoria (Gaither) W.; m. Sandra Wannatta Jackson, June 8, 1974; 1 child, Barry Lamont. B.A., Livingstone Coll., 1974; M.Ed., SUNY-Buffalo, 1975; M. Sci. Edn., N.C. Agrl. Tech. State U., 1981; postgrad. U. N.C., 1984, Appalachian State U., 1984—. Sr. counselor Buffalo Gen. Hosp., N.Y., 1975; counselor Greensboro Optional Sch., N.C., 1975-76, coordinator program, 1976-78; asst. prin. Philip J. Weaver Edn. Ctr., Greensboro, 1978-79; prin. William M. Hampton Sch., Greensboro, 1979-82, Claude Kiser Jr. High Sch., Greensboro, 1982—; cons. Greensboro Pub. Schs., 1981-82, mem. task force, 1980-84; rep. jr. high prins., 1983-86. Mem. steering com. United Way, Greensboro, 1984-85; bd. dirs. Greensboro Youth Services Bur., 1976-78, United Arts Council, 1982-85, Gen. Greene Council Boy Scouts Am. Mem. Assn. Sch. Curriculum Devel., Nat. Assn. Secondary Sch. Prins., N.C. Assn. Educators (div. prins.), Greensboro Prins. Assn., Phi Delta Kappa, Alpha Phi Alpha (v.p. Greensboro chpt. Livingstone Coll. alumni assn. 1982-85). Democrat. Methodist. Lodges: Masons, Davie Education Union. Avocations: basketball; travel; reading; music. Home: 2704 New Garden Rd Greensboro NC 27408 Office: Kiser Jr High Sch 716 Benjamin Pkwy Greensboro NC 27408

WILLIAMS, CALVIT HERNDON, JR., chemist, consultant, financial planner; b. Houston, Dec. 28, 1936; s. Calvit Herndon and Julia Eloise (Tybor) W.; B.A., U. St. Thomas, 1958; Ph.D., Brown U., 1964; m. Margaret Florence Jeter, Dec. 27, 1959; children—Sabina Anne, Terence Jeter, Russel Herndon, Damon Andrew. AEC postdoctoral fellow Rice U., Houston, 1964-66; research assoc. Sandia Labs., Albuquerque, 1966-70; tchr. St. Pius High Sch., Albuquerque, 1970-71; prof. chemistry U. Campinas, São Paulo, Brazil, 1971-76; lab. dir., cons. Aer-Aqua Labs., Inc., Houston, 1976-77; sr. staff scientist, group leader Radian Corp., Austin, Tex., 1977-84, 85—; registered rep. IDS/Am. Express, 1984-85. Cert. in indsl. hygiene Am. Bd. Indsl. Hygiene. Fellow Am. Inst. Chemistry; mem. Am. Chem. Soc. (chmn. Central Tex. 1981-82), Am. Soc. Mass Spectrometry, Am. Indsl. Hygiene Assn., Sigma Xi, Delta Epsilon Sigma. Contbr. articles to profl. jours. Home: 1200 Barton Hills Dr Apt 339 Austin TX 78704 Office: 8501 MoPac Blvd Austin TX 78753

WILLIAMS, CECILIA LEE PURSEL, optometrist; b. Lewisburg, Pa., Nov. 15, 1948; d. Lee LaVerne and Geraldine May (Steininger) Pursel; student Lycoming Coll., 1966-68; B.S. (Women's Aux. of Pa. Optometrists scholar 1968-70, Pa. State grantee 1968-70), Pa. Coll. Optometry, 1970, O.D. (Women's Aux. of Pa. Optometrists scholar 1970-72, Pa. State grantee 1970-72), 1972; m. Richard Lee Williams, May 17, 1975; 1 son, Kent Lee. Research optometrist in soft lens materials Gumpelmayer Optik, Vienna, Austria, 1973; optometrist Sterling Optical Co. Contact Lens Center, Washington, 1974-79; pvt. practice optometry, Springfield, Va., 1980—. Recipient Clin. Efficiency award Pa. Coll. Optometry, 1972; lic. and/or cert. optometrist, D.C., Pa., N.Y., N.J., Va. Mem. Optometric Center of Nation's Capital (dir. 1977-80), Am. Optometric Assn., Va. Optometric Assn., No. Va. Optometric Soc., Nat. Honor Soc. for Optometry, Omega Delta. Home: 3600 Wilton Hall Ct Alexandria VA 22310 Office: 6795A Springfield Mall Springfield VA 22150

WILLIAMS, CHARLES C., agricultural products company executive; b. 1923; married. B.S., Presbyn. Coll., 1943. With Gold Kist Inc., Atlanta, 1962. sr. v.p., 1973-78, chmn. bd., 1978—, dir. Served to 1st lt. AUS, 1943-45. Office: Gold Kist Inc 244 Perimeter Center Pkwy NW Box 2210 Atlanta GA 30301*

WILLIAMS, CHARLES HANSEL, public accountant; b. Tifton, Ga., Sept. 2, 1938; s. Amos McKendall and Hattie Idella (Allen) W.; student Ga. Inst. Tech., 1956, Ga. State Coll., 1965, B.B.A., 1965; M.Profl. Accountancy, Ga. State U., 1970; m. Celia Carolyn Trammell, June 27, 1970; children—Trammell Allen, Delia Jane. With So. Bell Tel. and Tel. Co., Atlanta, 1957-60; staff acct. William A. Freeman, C.P.A., Atlanta, 1960-63; cons. Chuck Shields Advt. Agy., Atlanta, 1963, U.S. Plastics Co., Inc., Atlanta, 1963; student summer missionary So. Bapt. Home Mission Bd., Ill., 1963, Ariz., 1964; student staffer Glorieta (N.Mex.) Bapt. Assembly, 1964; state auditor Ga. Dept. Audits, Atlanta, 1965-69; sr. staff acct. Touche, Ross, Bailey & Smart, Atlanta, 1970; pvt. practice pub. acctg., Atlanta, 1970; acctg. instr. Abraham Baldwin Agrl. Coll., Tifton, Ga., 1970-71; mng. partner Allen & Williams, C.P.A.s, Tifton, 1971-78; pvt. practice public acctg., Newnan, 1978—; auditor Powers Crossroads County Fair and Arts Festival, 1981-83. Pres., Ga. State Coll. Bapt. Student Union, 1962-64; enlistment chmn. Ga. Bapt. Student Union, 1963-64; bd. dirs. Hansel & Gretel Nursery Sch., Inc., Atlanta, 1963-83, Abraham Baldwin Agrl. Coll. Found., 1972-78, Flint River council Girl Scouts U.S.A., 1973-76, Tifton Concert Assn., 1974-78, United Givers Fund, 1975-83; chmn. Wiregrass Arts and Crafts Show, Tifton, 1976; councilman Ga. State U. Student Govt. Council, 1964-65; deacon, brotherhood dir., co-dir. ch. tng. 1st Bapt. Ch. of Newnan, 1980—. Served with U.S. Army, 1956-57. C.P.A., Ga. Mem. Am. Inst. C.P.A.s, Ga. Soc. C.P.A.s, Tiftarea Ducks Unltd., Newnan-Coweta County C. of C. Baptist. Clubs: Exchange (dir. 1974-76), Tifton; Newnan Kiwanis; Springhill Country. Home: 13 Hawthorn Dr Newnan GA 30263 Office: 44 Jefferson St PO Box 2323 Newnan GA 30264

WILLIAMS, CHARLES OLIVER, JR., dentist; b. Greensboro, N.C., Sept. 1, 1939; s. Charles Oliver and Amy (Groves) W.; m. Nancy Jane McIntosh, July 31, 1965; children—Cristin McIntosh, Charles Oliver III. Student U. N.C., 1957-61; D.M.D., U. Louisville, 1966. Practice dentistry, Winnsboro, S.C., 1966—; assoc. mem. staff Fairfield Meml. Hosp., Winnsboro. Editor-in-chief S.C. Dental Jur., 1970-83. State publs. chmn. Nat. Children's Dental Health Week, Fairfield County, 1967; vice chmn. bd. dirs. Richard Winn Acad.; bd. visitors Med. U. S.C., Charleston; chmn. profl. div. United Fund, Fairfield County, 1967-68; mem. Fairfield County Mental Health Assn., 1970—; bd. dirs. Fairfield County council Boy Scouts Am. Recipient Dental Editors award Ohio State U., ADA, 1970. Mem. S.C. Central Dist. Dental Assn. (pres.; past pres. peer rev. bd.), S.C. Dental Assn. (past bd. govs.), Mid Carolina Dental Study Acad. (pres.), AAAS, ADA, Nat. Rehab. Assn., Fairfield Jr. C. of C. (past v.p.), Am. Soc. Dentistry for Children, Southeastern Acad. Prosthodontics, Am. Assn. Dental Editors, Mid Carolina Dental Study Acad., Fedn. Dentaire Internat., Royal Soc. Health (Gt. Britain), Order Ky. Cols., Delta Sigma Delta (Nat. Lit. Excellence award 1966). Past sr. warden Episcopal Ch. Office: 204 E Washington St Winnsboro SC 29180

WILLIAMS, CLIFFORD GLYN, economics educator; b. Pembrokeshire, Wales, Feb. 23, 1928; came to U.S., 1958, naturalized, 1967; s. Arthur J. and Annie M. Williams; m. Nancy K. Hammons, Mar. 24, 1977; children—Karen Jean, John Andrew. B.A., U.Wales, Aberystwyth, 1956; M.A., Victoria U., Manchester, Eng., 1958; Ph.D., U. Va., 1962. Asst. prof. econs. U. Alta., Edmonton, Can., 196-163, Ind. U.-Bloomington, 1963-66, Boston Coll., Chestnut Hill, Mass., 1966-69; assoc. prof. U. S.C., Columbia, 1969-73, prof., 1973—. Author: Labor Economics, 1970. Contbg. editor Wall St. Review of Books. Book rev. editor The Economics of Education Review. Contbr. articles to profl. publs. Mem. Am. Econ. Assn., Indsl. Relation Research Assn. Baptist. Home: 201 Tyborne Circle Columbia SC 29210 Office: U SC Dept Econs Columbia SC 29208

WILLIAMS, CLYDE, retail food store executive, consultant; b. Floydada, Tex., Mar. 21, 1926; s. Owen Lester and Bettie Willie (Walker) W.; m. Nona Helen Kingery, May 27, 1944; children—Sandra, Karen, Clyde, Kerry, James, Jerry. Student Tex. Tech U., 1943-44, Southwestern La. Inst., 1944-45. Mgr. Williams Food Store, Levelland, Tex., 1946, butcher, Clovis, N.Mex., 1949-50, owner, Roaring Springs, Tex., 1950-65; owner, operator Thrift Mart Food Store, Comanche, Tex., 1965-78, owner of 8 chain stores, Granbury, Tex., 1978-85; pres. Circle 8 Enterprise, Inc., Granbury, 1975—; dir. 1st Comanche Bank, Tex., Grocery Industry Service Corps.-Affiliated Ins. Bd., Keller, Tex. Bd. dirs. Roaring Springs Ind. Sch. Dist., Tex., 1953-65, Comanche Ind. Sch. Dist., 1966-68; mem. council City of Roaring Springs, 1958-63; Democratic chmn. Motley County, Tex., 1960. Served with USN, 1944-46. Mem. Ch. of Christ. Lodges: Lions, Masons. Avocations: golf; raising quarter horses.

WILLIAMS, CLYDE ELTON, petroleum geologist, consultant; b. Belcher, La., Sept. 17, 1929; s. Bryant Houston and Odie C. (Brumley) W.; m. Patricia Anne Casey, Aug. 29, 1953; children—Karen A. Grider, Mark, Cynthia L. Fowler, Linda. B.S., U. Tex., 1956. Geologist Exxon Co. U.S.A., Tyler, Tex., Houston, 1956-79; dist. geol. mgr. Alamo Petroleum, Houston, 1979-80; cons. Carlson Petroleum Co., Houston, 1980-82, Fagin Exploration Co., Houston, 1983, Houston, 1984—. Served with U.S. Army, 1951-53. Mem. Houston Geol. Soc., Am. Assn. Petroleum Geologists (cert. petroleum geologist). Republican. Avocations: naturalist; fishing. Home: 12510 Vindon Houston TX 77024 Office: 10405 Town & Country Way/100 Houston TX 77024

WILLIAMS, DALE ARDEN, chemistry educator, administrator; b. Greenfield, Mass., Oct. 30, 1938; s. Ronald Walter and Vesta Vera (York) W.; m. Edythe Louise Brown, Aug. 26, 1961; children—Eileen Marie, Ryan Bradford, Leanna Laurel, Priscilla Jean. B.A., Taylor U., 1961; postgrad. Iowa State U., 1961-62; M.S., Wayne State U., 1972, Ph.D., 1973. Asst. prof. chemistry Thiel Coll., Greenville, Pa., 1966-74; asst. prof. chemistry Oral Roberts U., Tulsa, 1974-77, assoc. prof., 1977-86, prof., 1986—, chmn. natural sci. dept., 1977—; cons. in field. Mem. choir Boston Ave. United Methodist Ch., Tulsa, 1974—, leader prayer breakfast. NSF fellow, 1966-68. Fellow Am. Inst. Chemists; mem. Okla. Acad. Sci., Am. Chem. Soc., AAAS, Soc. Applied Spectroscopy, Sigma Xi, Phi Lamba Upsilon, Alpha Epsilon Delta. Office: Oral Roberts U 7777 S Lewis St Tulsa OK 74171

WILLIAMS, DAN C., ins. co. exec.; b. Brenham, Tex., Feb. 22, 1913; s. Dan C. and Harriet (Wilkin) W.; m. Ellen Carolyn Carpenter, June 18, 1936; children—Carolyn Williams Marks, Harriet Williams Peavy, Suzanne Williams Nash. B.S. in Petroleum Engring, U. Tex., Austin, 1935. Petroleum engr. Magnolia Petroleum Co., Dallas, 1935-49; pres., dir. Southland Life Ins. Co., Dallas, 1952-69; chmn. bd., dir. Southland Fin. Corp., Dallas, 1969—. Bd. dirs. Dallas chpt. ARC, Dallas County United Way, State Fair Tex.; bd. regents U. Tex. System, 1968-81, chmn., 1979-81; mem. coordinating bd. Tex. Colls. and Univs., 1965-71; elder Highland Park Presbyn. Ch., Dallas. Recipient Linz award, 1961; Disting. Alumnus award U. Tex. Sch. Engring., 1962. Clubs: Dallas Country, Las Colinas Country, Dallas Petroleum, City, Dallas, Chapparral. Home: 3711 Lexington Ave Dallas TX 75205 Office: PO Box 619208 Dallas TX 75261-9208

WILLIAMS, DANIEL, architect; b. Portage, Wis., Feb. 23, 1944; s. Roger and Ruth Williams. B.Arch., U. Fla., 1968, postgrad. in urban and regional planning; postgrad. U. Tex.-Austin, 1969-70, U. Calif.-Berkeley, 1970, U. Wash., 1970-71. Registered architect, Fla. With Vista Housing, Tex., 1968; architect/planner, San Francisco, 1969-71; housing planner Small Tribes of Western Wash. State, 1971-72; research assoc. NIMH grant, 1972-75; asst. prof. design U. Fla., Gainesville, 1972-74; grad. research assoc. land use planning and ecology U. Fla., 1974-76; architect/energy planner Connell/Metcalf/Eddy, 1976-78; lectr. energy and land use planning Sch. Architecture, U. Miami (Fla.), 1977-79; architect/owner Daniel Williams Architects & Planners, Coconut Grove, Fla., 1978—; solar energy lectr. Active Jr. Achievement, 1977. Recipient honors Dade County Design Co.; Rockefeller Conservation Found. sect. author, 1975. Mem. AIA, Fla. Acad. Sci., Internat. Solar Energy Soc., C. of C., Nat. Council Archtl. Registration Bds., Am. Planning Assn. Club: Architecture (Miami). Contbr. articles to profl. jours.

WILLIAMS, DAVID KENDALL, architect; b. Shreveport, La., Jan. 1, 1949; s. Carl Smith and Wanda Jean (Cole) W. B.Arch., Tex. A&M U., 1971. Registered architect. Draftsman E. Trant Assocs., Bryan, Tex., 1968-71; architect in tng. Richard Colley Architect, Corpus Christi, Tex., 1971-72; architect Ralph Kelman Assocs., Dallas, 1972-74; architect, prin. Burson Hendricks Walls, Dallas, 1974-81; architect, owner Bethel & Williams Architects, Inc., Dallas, 1982—. Editor: Dallasights, 1979. Mem. AIA (sec., v.p. Dallas chpt. 1978, Young Architect of Yr. 1976). Club: A&M (Dallas). Home: 3203 Hudnall St Apt 3101 Dallas TX 75235 Office: Bethel & Williams Architects Inc 4300 MacArthur St Suite 214 Dallas TX 75209

WILLIAMS, DAVID LEE, financial executive, marine transportation company executive; b. Logansport, Ind., Oct. 16, 1947; s. L. Paul and Eva Marie (Richards) W. B.A., Manchester Coll., Ind., 1968; M.B.A., Vanderbilt U., 1982. Staff acct. Ernst & Whinney, Indpls., 1968-69; dir. operational acctg. Genesco, Inc., Nashville, 1969-78; pres. Ingram Book Co., Nashville, 1978-83; sr. v.p. fin. and adminstrn. Ingram Barge Co., Nashville, 1983—; instr. Belmont Coll., Nashville, 1970-71, U. Tenn.-Nashville, 1971-74, Tenn. Soc. C.P.A.s, 1983-84; adj. lectr. Vanderbilt U., Nashville, 1983-85. Treas., Nashville City Ballet, 1985, Rochelle Tng. and Habilitation Ctr., Nashville, 1985. Served to sgt. 1st class U.S. Army, 1969-74. Mem. Fin. Execs. Inst. (bd. dirs.), Am. Inst. C.P.A.s, Inst. Mgmt. Acctg. (cert.). Republican. Roman Catholic. Office: Ingram Barge Co 4304 Harding Rd Nashville TN 37205

WILLIAMS, DAVID ROGERSON, JR., civil engineer; b. Tulsa, Oct. 20, 1921; s. David Rogerson and Martha Reynolds (Hill) W.; B.S. in Civil Engring., Yale U., 1943; m. Pauline Bolton, May 28, 1944; children—Pauline Bolton Williams d'Aquin, David Rogerson III, Rachel Katharine. Constrn. engr., foreman, supt. Williams Bros. Corp., Tulsa, 1939-49; co-founder Williams Companies, 1949, v.p., 1949-56, exec. v.p., 1956-66, chmn. exec. com., 1966-70; chmn. Williams Bros. Can. Ltd., Calgary, Alta., 1957—, The Resource Scis. Corp., Tulsa, 1970-83, Williams Technologies, Inc.; dir. Williams Cos., Burlington No. Inc., St. Paul, Williams Bros. Engring. Ltd., London. Trustee, Nat. Symphony Orch., Washington, Hudson Inst., Croton-on-Hudson, N.Y. Served to capt. USAF, World War II. Fellow ASCE; mem. Am. Petroleum Inst., Am. Gas Assn., Ind. Natural Gas Assn., Royal Arts Soc. (London), Yale Engring. Assn., Alta. Assn. Profl. Engrs. Episcopalian. Clubs: Ranchmen's (Calgary); Toronto; Chagrin Valley Hunt (Gates Mill, Ohio); Petroleum, Southern Hills Country, Summit (Tulsa); Racquet and Tennis, Sky, Yale (N.Y.C.); Rolling Rock (Ligonier, Pa.); Springdale Hall (Camden, S.C.); Union (Cleve.). Office: 320 S Boston Suite 831 Tulsa OK 74103

WILLIAMS, DAVID RUSSELL, music educator; b. Indpls., Oct. 21, 1932. s. H. Russell and Mary Dean (Whitmer) W.; m. Elsa Bühlmann, Jan. 30, 1960. A.B., Columbia U., 1954, M.A., 1956; Ph.D., U. Rochester, 1965. Chief band instr. U.S. Army, Ft. Chaffee, Ark., 1957-59; dir. music Windham Coll., Putney, Vt., 1959-62; opera coach Eastman Sch. Music, Rochester, N.Y., 1962-65, assoc. prof. theory, 1965-80; prof. dept. music Memphis State U., 1980—, chmn. dept., 1980—; mem. exec. bd. Opera Memphis, 1980—; mem. bd. sponsors Mid-South regional auditions Met. Opera Nat. Council, 1983—. Active Friends of Memphis and Shelby County Libraries, 1981—, Ballet Guild, Symphony League, Opera Guild, also others. Served with U.S. Army, 1957-59. Recipient Edward Benjamin Contest for Tranquil Music award, 1963; publ. award Eastman Sch. Music 1970. Mem. Coll. Music Soc. (sec. 1973-83), Tenn. Assn. Music Execs. of Colls. and Univs. (sec. 1981-83; pres. elect 1985—), Am. Music Ctr., Nat. Assn. Schs. Music (sec. region 1983—), Music Tchrs. Nat. Assn., Nat. Acad. Rec. Arts and Scis. (treas. Memphis chpt. 1984—), Southeastern Composers League, Phi Beta Kappa (pres. Memphis Area alumni chpt. 1983-85), Phi Mu Alpha, Pi Kappa Lambda. Republican. Episcopalian. Club: Summit (Memphis). Author: Bibliography of the History of Music Theory, Accura Music, 1971; editor: Opera vol. of New Scribner Music Library, 1972; contbr. articles to profl. jours.; producer Highwater Records album 8201, John Stover, Guitar, 1983. Home: 295 Central Park W Apt 2 Memphis TN 38111 Office: Music Dept Memphis State U Memphis TN 38152

WILLIAMS, DELLA CHRISTINE, neurologist; b. Bassett, Va., Nov. 8, 1943; d. Claude and Christine (Craig) Williams; m. Jon Dudley Dorman. B.S., Columbia U., 1969; M.D., U. Va., 1973. Intern in pathology Cornell Med. Center, N.Y.C., 1973-74; intern in medicine Harlem Hosp., N.Y.C., 1974-75; fellow in medicine Columbia U., N.Y.C., 1975-76, resident neurology, 1976-79; pvt. practice medicine specializing in neurology, Lynchburg, Va., 1979-81, Danville, Va., 1981—; mem. staffs Meml. Hosp., Danville. Office: 115 S Main St Danville VA 24541

WILLIAMS, DON DUANE, insurance company manager, underwriter, consultant; b. Beaver County, Okla., Oct. 7, 1925; s. Arthur Clyde and Mayme (Kilpatrick) W.; m. Yvonne McLeod, Aug. 29, 1947; children—Michael Duane, Gail Williams Jones, Jean Yvonne Williams Ragland, Timothy Don, Dona Owen. B.S., Abilene Christian U., 1949; M.Music Edn., Tex. Tech. U., 1955. C.L.U., chartered fin. cons., Tex. Band dir. pub. schs., Sudan, Tex. and Olton, Tex., 1949-55; with Am. Founders Life Ins. Co., 1955—; mgr. Amarillo agy. (Tex.), 1961-65, Lubbock-Amarillo agy., 1965—. Elder, Bible tchr. Monterey Ch. of Christ, Lubbock. Recipient Nat. Quality awards, Nat. Sales Achievement awards, Ins. Salesman Honor awards, New Agy. of Yr. award, 1981, Profl. Growth award, 1974; inducted to Million Dollar Round Table (life), Top Ten Club, Pres.'s Council. Mem. Lubbock Assn. Life Underwriters (past pres.), Lubbock Chpt. C.L.U.s (past pres.), Gen. Agts. and Mgrs. Assn. Lubbock (past pres.). Home: 5511 26th St Lubbock TX 79407 Office: Am Founders Life Ins Co 3702 Ave Q Lubbock TX 79412

WILLIAMS, DONALD RAY, geologist; b. Harrison, Nebr., May 16, 1929; s. Charles Sidney and Laverne Lillious (Sturdivant) W.; m. Elaine Ruth Witt, Aug. 31, 1950; children—Charles Sidney, III, Steven Ray, Judy Ann Williams Hoos, Jeffrey Lee, Donald Darwin. B.A., Fresno State U., 1961; M.S., U. Ill., 1962. Geologist, regional geologist Monsanto Co., Midland, Tex. and Calgary, Can., 1962-74; western region exploration supr. Kerr-McGee Corp., Oklahoma City, 1974-76; div. mgr. L.R. Feanch, Jr., Oklahoma City, 1976-78; div. geologist Hamilton Bros. Oil Co., Oklahoma City, 1978-83; sr. geologist Citation Oil and Gas Corp., Oklahoma City, 1983—. Contbr. articles to newspapers. Congregation sec. Lutheran Ch., Oklahoma City, 1979-83. Mem. Am. Assn. Petroleum Geologists, Oklahoma City Geol. Soc., Petroleum Club, Farm Club. Republican. Avocations: archaeology; ranching cattle breeding; history. Home: 4620 NW 31 Oklahoma City OK 73122

WILLIAMS, DONALD RAY, operations research educator; b. Ponca City, Okla., June 17, 1937; s. James Lester and Opal Angeline (Taylor) W.; m. Mary Frances Reeg, Mar. 6, 1976; m. Dixie Lee Carroll, Sept. 6, 1957 (div. Dec. 1975); children—Donna, Dee Ann, Donald Ray, Deborah, Doris. A.S., Eastern Okla. A&M Coll., 1957; B.S., Okla. State U., 1959, M.S., 1960, Ph.D., 1963. Sr. computing specialist Aerojet Gen. Corp., Sacramento, 1963-64; sr. research specialist Tex. Instruments Inc., Dallas, 1964-67; asst. prof. mgmt. sci. U. Tex., Arlington, 1967-70; assoc. prof. mgmt. sci. Okla. State U., Stillwater, 1970-74, prof. N. Tex. State U., Denton, 1974—. Cons., 1974—; dir. Citizens Nat. Bank, Denton; pres. Mgmt. Resource Assocs., Denton, 1977—. Co-author: Statistical Analysis for Business, 1970; Mathematical Analysis for Business, 1979, Modern Mathematics with Applications, 1975, Finite Mathematics with Applications, 1975, Applied Calculus with Applications, 1976; contbr articles to profl. jours.; pub. Stockmarket Newsletter The Cycle Technician, 1982-84. Pres., PTA, Stillwater, 1973; coach City League Basketball, 1971-74; bd. dirs. Denton Assn. Retarded Citizens, 1983—. Mem. Am. Inst. Decision Scis. (v.p. student liaison 1973-74, council 1974-79), Southwest Fedn. Adminstrv. Disciplines (v.p. 1974-75, pres. 1975-76), Inst. Mgmt. Sci., Am. Statis. Assn. Mem. Ch. Jesus Christ Latter-day Saints. Avocations: flying; basketball; jogging; stockmarket analysis, skiing. Home: 2515 Jamestown St Denton TX 76201 Office: Mgmt Resource Assocs 2515 Jamestown St Denton TX 76201

WILLIAMS, EARLE CARTER, professional services executive; b. Selma, Ala., Oct. 15, 1929; s. Henry Earle and Nora Elizabeth (Carter) W.; B.E.E., Auburn U., 1951; postgrad. U. N.Mex., 1959-62; m. June Esther Anson, Sept. 7, 1951; children—Gayle Marie, Carol Patrice, Sharon Elaine. Utilities design engr. Standard Oil Co. Ind., Whiting, 1954-56; mem. tech. staff Sandia Corp., Albuquerque, 1956-62; sr. engr. BDM Internat., Inc., El Paso, Tex., 1962-64; spl. projects dir., 1964-66, dir. ops., 1966-68; v.p., gen. mgr., Vienna, Va., 1968-72, pres., chief exec. officer, Vienna and McLean, Va., 1972—, also dir.; mem. adv. bd. 1st Am. Bank Va., 1978—; exec. com., steering com. El Paso Community Coll., 1968-69, trustee, 1969-76; commr. Fairfax County Econ. Devel. Authority, 1976-80, chmn., 1978-80; mem. Va. State Bd. for Community Colls., 1980—; mem. Naval Research Adv. Com., 1984—, vice chmn. bd. dirs., 1985; treas. Wolf Trap Found., 1984; trustee Va. Found. Ind. Colls., 1984; mem. Am. Bus. Conf. bd. dirs. Central Va. Ednl. TV Corp., 1978—; bd. dirs. No. Va. Community Coll. Ednl. Found., 1980-84, pres. 1980-81; chmn. indsl. policy bd. George Mason (U.) Inst., 1982—. Served with AUS, 1951-53. Registered profl. engr., N.Mex. Mem. Profl. Services Council (dir. 1974—, pres. 1976-79), Am. Mgmt. Assn., Armed Forces Communications and Electronics Assn. (dir. 1978, internat. v.p. 1979—), Nat. Soc. Profl. Engrs., Pres. Assn., Fairfax County C. of C. (dir. 1976—), Eta Kappa Nu. Presbyterian. Clubs: International, Metropolitan (Washington). Office: BDM Internat Inc 7915 Jones Br Dr McLean VA 22102

WILLIAMS, EDWARD KENT, architect; b. Lynchburg, Va., July 2, 1934; s. Edward and Lucy Fenton (Kent) W.; m. Emily Louise McMullen, Mar. 15, 1955; children—Jane, Kent, Elizabeth. B.Arch., U. Va., 1962. Registered architect, Va., D.C., Md. Assoc., Strang & Childers, Annandale, Va., 1962-67; project mgr. Allen J. Dickey, Arlington, Va., 1967-70; assoc. Beery, Rio & Assocs., Annandale, 1970-74; ptnr. Peck, Peck & Williams, Woodbridge, Va., 1974-81; owner, prin. Archtl. Evaluation & Analysis Services, Clifton, Va., 1981—. Mem. Fairfax (Va.) Planning Commn., 1967-71, chmn., 1969; mem. No. Va. Regional Planning Commn., 1967-69; mem. Faifax Policy Adv. Com., 1969-70. Served with USAF, 1953-57. Mem. Am. Arbitration Assn., Community Assns. Inst. Mem. Ch. Disciples of Christ. Home: 12216 Quinque Ln Clifton VA 22024 Office: Box 128 Clifton VA 22024

WILLIAMS, ELLIS, law enforcement officer, clergyman; b. Raymond, Miss., Oct. 27, 1931; s. Currie and Elise (Morrison) W.; student Union Baptist Theolk. Sem., New Orleans, 1963-64; B.A. in Criminology, Loyola U. South, New Orleans, 1972, M.Ed., 1974, M.Criminal Justice, 1981; m. Priscilla Norman, Jan. 9, 1954; children—Debra, Rita, Claude, Lathan, Glenn, Zelia. Patrolman, dept. police City of New Orleans, 1964-77, police sergeant, asst. platoon comdr., 1977-79, police lt., platoon comdr., 1979—; past v.p. La. Polygraph Bd.; asso. minister Historic 2d Baptist Ch., New Orleans. Cert. fingerprint identification technician. Mem. Fraternal Order Police, Am. Fedn. Police, Police Mut. Benevolent Assn., Internat. Assn. Identifications, La. Assn. Identification, Am. Polygraph Assn., (cert.), La. Polygraph Assn. (cert.), Cross Keys, Kappa Delta Pi. Democrat. Club: Mason. Home: 3108 Metropolitan St New Orleans LA 70126 Office: 715 S Broad St New Orleans LA 70119

WILLIAMS, ELYNOR ALBERTA, director corporate affairs; b. Baton Rouge, La., Oct. 27, 1946; d. Albert Berry and Naomi Theresa (Douglas) W.; B.S., Spelman Coll., 1966; M.S., Cornell U., 1973. Home econs. tchr. Eugene Butler Jr.-Sr. High Sch., Jacksonville, Fla., 1966-68; publicist, pkg. editor, copy editor Gen. Foods Corp., White Plains, N.Y., 1968-71; writer, researcher Expanded Nutrition Edn. program Cornell U., summer 1972, tutor, com. on spl. edn. projects, 1972-73; communication specialist N.C. Agrl. Ext. Service, N.C. A & T State U., Greensboro and N.C. State U., Raleigh, 1973-77; sr. public relations specialist Western Electric, Greensboro, 1977-83; dir. corp. affairs Hanes Group, Winston-Salem, N.C., 1983—. Bd. dirs. Greensboro Drug Action Council, 1977-83, v.p., 1983; mem. Carolina Theatre Commn., 1977-81; mem. steering com. Guilford County Women's Coalition, 1978; agy. bd. mem. solicitor United Way Campaign, 1977-82; issues chmn. Triad council Girls Scouts Am., 1979-82; mem. Mayor's Energy Conservation Commn., 1977-78; vice-chmn. adv. com. dept. communication arts Cornell U., 1978-79; bd. dirs. Leadership Greensboro Alumni Assn., 1980-81, Women's Aid, 1980, Guilford Tech. Coll., 1981-84; pres. Guilford County Women's Polit. Caucus, 1980-81, Friends of Greensboro Coll. Adv. Com., 1980-82, Greensboro Symphony's Audience Devel. Adv. Com., 1980-82; candidate N.C. Ho. of Reps., 1980; mem. adv. bd. Greensboro Daily News Summer Journalism Inst., 1981; vice chmn. 6th Congressional Black Leadership Caucus, 1980-81, mem. pub. relations adv. bd. YWCA, 1980-81; trustee U. N.C., Greensboro, 1981—; mem. steering com. N.C. 2000, 1982; mem. policy council N.C. Women's Polit.

Caucus, 1982; chmn. Employment Task Force, Gov.'s Assembly on Women and the Economy, 1981; bd. dirs. Hayes-Taylor YMCA, 1983-84, YWCA, Winston-Salem/Forsyth County, 1984—; mem. adv. council Office of Women in Econ. Devel., N.C. Dept. Commerce, 1985; mem. exec. com. Nat. Women's Econ. Alliance, 1985; mem. nat. tech. adv. com. OICs of Am., Inc., 1985; mem. Greensboro Dialogue Task Force, 1983. Recipient United Negro Coll. Fund scholarship, 1962-66; Cornell U. Grad. Sch. fellowship, 1972-73; regional finalist White House fellowship program, 1981-82. Mem. Internat. Assn. Bus. Communicators, NAACP, Greensboro C. of C. (chmn. subcom. fed. legislation 1982-83), Pub. Relations Soc. Am., Women's Forum N.C., LWV, Alpha Kappa Alpha. Democrat. Methodist. Home: PO Box 7328 Winston Salem NC 27109 Office: PO Box 2760 Winston-Salem NC 27102

WILLIAMS, ERIC CURTIS, architect; b. Louisville, Nov. 21, 1950; s. Benjamin Virgil and Aline (Franklin) W.; m. Deborah Evon Edison, June 25, 1977; children—Nyeesha Renelle, Domini Aneska. B.Arch., U. Ky., 1975. Lic. architect, lic. real estate agt.,Ky. Draftsperson J. Ward, Architect, Louisville, 1970; design cons. Louisville Community Design Ctr., 1973-74; apprentice architect Schulhafer, Architect, Louisville, 1976; architect, group leader Bechtel Corp., Louisville, 1977-83, co. rep., 1979-83; corp. architect Ky. Fried chicken, Louisville, 1983—; prin. Eric Curtis Williams, Architect, Louisville, 1983—; realtor-assoc. Century 21. Chmn. community-parents com. Income/N.A.C.M.E., Louisville, 1980-82; adult adviser J.E.T.S./Explores, Louisville, 1981-83. Recipient Disting. Citizen award City of Louisville, 1977. Mem. AIA, Project Mgmt. Inst., Nat. Trust Hist. Preservation, NAACP. Democrat. Baptist. Avocations: karate (black belt); photography. Home: 1805 Allston Ave Louisville KY 40210 Office: Ky Fried Chicken Corp 1930 Bishop Ln Louisville KY 40210

WILLIAMS, ERIC JOSEPH, transportation executive; b. Havana, Cuba, Nov. 15, 1945; came to U.S., 1961; s. Eric and Frances (Waterhouse) W.; m. Maria Julia Williams, Mar. 30, 1984. B.S. in Fgn. Service, Georgetown U., 1968. With Emery Worldwide, 1970—, sales rep., Miami, Fla., 1970-74, sales mgr., 1975-76, country mgr., Caracas, Venezuela, 1976-77, regional mgr. S.Am., Miami, 1977-81, dist. mgr. Latin Am.-Caribbean, Miami, 1981-84, div. gen. mgr. Latin Am.-Caribbean, 1984—; adult edn. tchr., Miami, 1973-75. Served to 1st lt. U.S. Army, 1968-70. Mem. Forwarders and Brokers Assn., Georgetown U. Alumni Assn. (com.). Episcopalian. Clubs: Coconut Grove Sailing (com. 1975-76), Biltmore Tennis. Home: 501 Raven Ave Miami Springs FL 33166 Office: Emergy Worldwide Suite 530 1150 NW 72d Ave Miami FL 33126

WILLIAMS, ERNEST GOING, paper company executive; b. Macon, Miss., Sept. 24, 1915; s. Augustus Gaines and Mary (Sanford) W.; m. Cecil Louise Butler, Aug. 18, 1951; children—Ernest Sanford, Turner Butler, Elizabeth Cecil. B.S. in Comml. and Bus. Adminstrn., U. Ala., 1938. Asst. to treas. U. Ala., 1938-42, 45-48, treas., 1948-56; dir. First Nat. Bank Tuscaloosa, Ala., 1956-83; v.p., dir. Gulf States Paper Corp., Tuscaloosa, 1958-77; chmn. bd., dir. Affiliated Paper Cos. Inc., Tuscaloosa, 1977—; mem. local bd. First So. Fed. Savs. and Loan Assn.; dir. New Southland Nat. Ins. Co. Trustee U. Ala., David Warner Found.; past pres. Jaycees Tuscaloosa County, YMCA, United Way Tuscaloosa County; past chmn. Tuscaloosa County ARC; elder First Presbyterian Ch. Tuscaloosa. Served with USNR, 1942-45. Mem. Greater Tuscaloosa C. of C. (past pres.), Associated Industries of Ala. (past pres., trustee group trust), Newcomen Soc. N.Am., DCH Found., Omicron Delta Kappa, Kappa Alpha, Beta Gamma Sigma. Clubs: Exchange, Civitan (Citizen of Yr. 1974), NorthRiver Yacht (dir.), Univ. (past pres.), Indian Hills Country; River (Jacksonville, Fla.). Home: 156 The Highlands Tuscaloosa AL 35404 Office: PO Drawer 31 Tuscaloosa AL 35402

WILLIAMS, FRED ALTON (AL), JR., business educator, college administrator; b. Paris, Tex., June 13, 1923; s. Fred Alton and Mary Catherine (Gilliland) W.; B.B.A., U. Tex., Austin, 1950; m. Patsy Ruth Williams, Dec. 17, 1954; children—Marilyn Williams Dixon, Carol Williams Huska. Partner, Williams Air Activities, Civilian Flight Sch., Sales & Service Tyler, Tex., 1946-52; partner, v.p. Williams Marine Co., Tyler, Holiday Marina-Resort, Inc., Lake Tawakoni, Tex., 1952-65; recruiter Dallas Fashion Merchandising Coll., 1965-70; exec. dir. Tyler Comml. Coll., 1970-76; dir. fin. aid and secretarial studies Northwood Inst. Tex., Cedar Hill, 1976-79, dir. ops. and fin. aid, instr., 1979—; cons. in field; coordinator workshops. Served with USAF, World War II; capt. Res. ret. Mem. Nat., Tex. assns. student fin. aid adminstrs., Kappa Sigma. Baptist (Sunday Sch. tchr.). Home: 127 Rowland Pl Tyler TX 75701 Office: PO Box 58 Cedar Hill TX 75104

WILLIAMS, GEORGE HENRY, political science educator, researcher; b. Wellsburg, W.Va., Sept. 28, 1950; s. Russell Luther Williams and Ursula Gertrude (Wilson) Williams Durbin; m. Judy Ann Utt, Mar. 10, 1973; 1 child, Stephanie Ann. B.S. in Social Work, W.Va. U., 1972, M.A., 1974, M.P.A., 1975, Ph.D., 1986. Community devel. extension agt., W.Va. U., New Cumberland, 1976-79; prof. polit. sci. U. S. Ala., Mobile, 1985—; research asst. W.Va. U., Morgantown, 1979-82, 82-83. Planning commr. Hancock County, W.Va., 1977-79, exec. dir. Bi-Centennial Commn., 1976, Fair Bd., 1978-79; bd. dirs. W.Va. Health Systems Agy., 1976-79. Swiger fellow, 1985. Mem. Am. Polit. Sci. Assn., Am. Soc. Pub. Adminstrn., Policy Studies Orgn., Am. Pub. Health Assn., Evaluation Research Soc., Phi Kappa Phi. Democrat. Roman Catholic. Avocations: running; reading. Home: 3854 Michael Blvd Mobile AL 36609 Office: Univ S Ala Polit Sci Dept Mobile AL

WILLIAMS, GERALD LEE, insurance executive, consultant; b. Toledo, Jan. 21, 1932; s. John Hawley and Dorothy Hausman (Moore) W.; m. Patricia Irene Mack, Feb. 17, 1956; children—Vikki Lee Williams Grodner, Lori Sue, Sheri Lynn Williams Moire, Student Ohio State U., 1957-62. Diplomate Internat. Claim Assn. Claim supr. Nationwide Life Ins. Co., Columbus, Ohio, 1960-63, regional claim mgr., Portland, Oreg., 1963-70, Atlanta, 1970-78; asst. v.p. Investors Fidelity Life Ins., Birmingham, Ala., 1978-81; pres., chief operating officer Med-Fund Services, Birmingham, 1981—; chmn., chief exec. officer Sunbelt Benefits, Inc., Birmingham, 1986—; dir. Pash & Co., Birmingham; state chmn. Oreg. Health Ins. Council, 1969-70. Contbr. articles to publs. Served with USAF, 1951-55. Recipient spl. commendation Health Ins. Assn. Am., 1976, recognition award, Health Ins. Council, 1970. Fellow Life Mgmt. Inst.; mem. Ala. Life and Health Claim Assn., Ala. Soc. Profl. Benefit Adminstrs., Ala. FLMI Soc., So. Claims Assn. Republican. Presbyterian. Clubs: Birmingham Track, Georgetown Swim and Tennis (pres. Atlanta 1975-76). Office: Sunbelt Benefits Inc PO Box 7672 Birmingham AL 35253

WILLIAMS, GLEN MORGAN, U.S. district Judge; b. Jonesville, Va., Feb. 17, 1920; s. Hughy May and Hattie Mae W.; m. Jane Slemp, Nov. 17, 1962; children—Susan, Judy, Rebecca, Melinda. A.B. magna cum laude, Milligan Coll., 1940; J.D., U. Va., 1948. Bar: Va. 1947. Practiced law, Jonesville, 1948-76; judge U.S. Dist. Ct. for Western Va., 1976—; commonwealth's atty., Lee County, Va., 1948-51; Mem. Va. Senate, 1953-55. Editorial bd.: Va. Law Rev, 1946-47. Mem. Lee County Sch. Bd., 1972-76; trustee, elder First Christian Ch., Pennington Gap, Va. Served to lt. USN, 1942-46; MTO. Mem. Va. State Bar, Va., Am., Fed. bar assns., Am. Legion, 40 and 8. Republican. Club: Lee Players. Lodges: Lions, Masons, Shriners. Home: Jonesville VA 24263 Office: Fed Bldg Abingdon VA 24210*

WILLIAMS, GRIER MOFFATT, music educator, symphony conductor; b. Tampa, Fla., June 18, 1931; s. Jonathan Beatty and Mary Agnes (Moffatt) W.; m. Louise Stephanas Harvin, July 9, 1954; children—Stephen Harvin, Grier Moffatt, Jr. B.S., Davidson Coll., 1953; M. in Music, U. Mich., 1956; Ph.D., Fla. State U., 1961. Asst. prof. music U. S.E. LA., Hammond, La., 1958-61; assoc. prof. music Davidson Coll., N.C., 1961-68; prof. music U. W. Fla., Pensacola, 1968—, chmn. dept. music, 1968—; music dir. Fla. State Music Tchrs. Assn., 1977-79; dir. Pensacola Symphony, 1979—. Chmn., Cultural Affairs Bd., Pensacola, 1979-81. Served with U.S. Army, 1953-55. Research grantee U. W. Fla., 1980, 82. Mem. Music Educators Nat. Conf., Music Tchrs. Nat. Assn., (state v.p. 1977, mag. editor 1976-79). Home: 3407 Connell Dr Pensacola FL 32503 Office: Dept Music U W Fla Pensacola FL 32514

WILLIAMS, H. RUDOLPH, railroad executive; b. Wilmington, N.C., Oct. 23, 1919; s. Henry R. and Virginia L. (Heweltt) W.; B.C.S., Benjamin Franlin U., 1949; M.B.A., George Washington U., 1952; m. Elsie Virginia Gray, Apr. 25, 1942; children—Cheryl A., Deborh L. With Hamilton Nat. Bank, Washington, 1937-42, IRS, 1945-52, ICC, Washington, 1952-67, Office of Sec., U.S. Dept. Transp., Washington, 1967-69, U.S. Fed. R.R. Adminstrn., Washington, 1969-74; sr. fin. analyst U.S. Ry. Assn., Washington, 1974-75; asst. to v.p.-fin. Mo.-Kans.-Tex. R.R. Co., Denison, Tex., 1975, successively asst. v.p.-fin., asst. v.p. and comptroller; dir. Okla.-Kans.-Tex. R.R. Co. Served in U.S. Army, 1942-45, 61-62. Recipient Meritorious Achievement award U.S. Dept. Transp. Mem. R.R. Ins. Mgmt. Assn., Assn. Am. R.R.s, Denison C. of C. Republican. Baptist. Club: Denison Rod and Gun Country. Home: 2600 Brookhaven Circle Denison TX 75020 Office: 104 E Main St Denison TX 75020

WILLIAMS, HARRY JOHN, JR., accountant; b. Marion, Ill., Mar. 10, 1924; s. Harry John and Helita (Durham) W.; B.B.A., Tulane U., 1948; m. Joanne Elizabeth Schwartz, Nov. 1, 1947 (dec. Jan. 1985); m. Mary Elizabeth Spencer, July 3, 1985; children—Kathleen Anne Trenchard, Marianne Elizabeth (Mrs. Eugene A. Antoine, Jr.), Barbara Helen (Mrs. Richard L. Moose), Harry John III. With Peat, Marwick, Mitchell & Co., St. Louis, 1948-53; pvt. practice acctg., New Orleans, 1953-76; pres. Harry Williams Co., P.C., 1976—; lectr. Tulane U., 1953-56; co-founder Asso. Regional Accounting Firms, chmn., 1969-71. Served with USNR, 1943-46. Mem. Am. Inst. C.P.A.s, Soc. La. C.P.A.s (pres. New Orleans chpt. 1964-65, parliamentarian 1971-72, dir. 1964-65, 71-72, mem. trial bd., 1972-75, chmn. 1972-73, chmn. numerous coms.), Accounting Research Assn., New Orleans Estate Planning Council (treas. 1970-71), New Orleans Bd. Trade (bd. dirs. 1984—), Internat. Trade Mart (bd. dirs. 1984—), Greater New Orleans C. of C., Econ. Devel. Council, Com. of 50, Pi Kappa Alpha. Clubs: Pickwick, Southern Yacht, Internat. House (dir. 1975—, pres. 1984), World Trade Ctr. (bd. dirs. 1975—, pres. 1984) (New Orleans). Roman Catholic. Democrat. Editor: La. C.P.A., 1961-62. Contbr. articles to profl. jours. Home: 6824 Vicksburg St New Orleans LA 70124 Office: 940 First Nat Bank of Commerce Bldg New Orleans LA 70112

WILLIAMS, HENRIETTA VER MEER, psychologist, educator; b. Pella, Iowa, Apr. 2, 1924; d. Otto Henry and Dena Catherine (Stadt) Ver M.; m. Richard Hays Williams, Feb. 19, 1971; children—Marylie Catherine Karlovac, Robert Harold, Frank Rendler. Student Central Coll., Pella, Iowa, 1941-43; B.A. in Philosophy, U. Iowa, 1944; M.A. in Psychology, U. Ill., 1946, Ph.D. in Exptl. Psychology, 1949; postgrad. U. Md., 1966-67. Psychologist NIMH, Washington, 1965-67; postdoctoral intern in clin. psychology St. Elizabeths Hosp., Washington, 1967-68, staff psychologist, psychologist-in-charge of div., 1969-72, clin. adminstrn., 1972-74; dir. psychol. services Pitt County Mental Health Ctr., Greenville, N.C., 1974-78; pvt. practice psychology, Greenville, 1978—; assoc. The Nelson Clinic, Greenville, 1978—; clin. asst. prof. psychology Sch. Medicine, Eastern Carolina U., Greenville, 1977—. Contbr. articles to profl. jours. Mem. vestry St. Luke's Episcopal Ch., Rockville, Md., 1968-71; mem. incorporating body, chmn. personnel com. St. Luke's Half-Way Houses, Rockville; pres. Univ. Condominium Assn., Greenville, 1980-82, 84—. Mem. Am. Psychol. Assn., N.C. Assn. for Advancement of Psychology, PEO, Phi Beta Kappa. Republican. Home: 111 Cardinal Dr Greenville NC 27834 Office: The Nelson Clinic Med Pavilion Suite 9 1800 W 5th St Greenville NC 27834

WILLIAMS, HIRAM DRAPER, painter, educator; b. Indpls., Feb. 11, 1917; s. Earl Boring and Inez Mary (Draper) W.; m. Avonell Agnes Baumunk, July 5, 1941; children—Curtis Earl, Kim Avonell. B.S., Pa. State U., M. Ed. Art tchr. Harrington High Sch., Del., 1951-53; mem. faculty art dept. U. So. Calif., Los Angeles, 1953-54, U. Tex., Austin, 1954-60; prof. dept. art U. Fla., Gainesville, 1960-82, Disting. Service prof., 1982—. Author: Notes For A Young Painter, 1963, rev., 1983. Served to capt. U.S. Army, 1941-45, ETO. U. Tex. grantee, 1958; Guggenheim fellow 1963. Home: 2804 NW 30th Terr Gainesville FL 32605

WILLIAMS, JAMES B., banker; b. Sewanee, Tenn., Mar. 21, 1933; s. Eugene G. and Ellen (Bryan) W.; A.B., Emory U., 1955; m. Betty G. Williams, July 11, 1980; children—Ellen, Elizabeth, Bryan. Pres., Peachtree Bank & Trust Co., Chamblee, Ga., 1962-64, chmn. bd. 1st Nat. Bank & Trust Co., Augusta, Ga., 1971-73; vice chmn. Trust Co. of Ga., Atlanta, 1977-81, pres., 1981—; dir. Coca-Cola Co., Atlanta, Genuine Parts Co., Atlanta. Rollins, Inc., Ga. Internat. Life Ins. Co., Merry Cos., Inc., Augusta. Trustee, Emory U., Westminster Schs., Henrietta Egleston Hosp. for Children. Woodruff Med. Center; bd. visitors Berry Coll. Served to lt. USAF, 1955-57. Mem. Am. Bankers Assn., Res. City Bankers Assn. Presbyterian. Clubs: Piedmont Driving, Capital City. Commerce (Atlanta). Office: Trust Co Ga One Park Pl Atlanta GA 30303*

WILLIAMS, JAMES HOWARD, research exec.; b. Wheat, Tenn., Dec. 19, 1920; s. William Wess and Sallie (Shelton) W.; A.B., Carson-Newman Coll., 1942; M.A., George Peabody Coll., 1947; Ph.D., Vanderbilt U., 1956; m. Mary Helen Mewshaw, Aug. 31, 1946; children—James Howard, Edward Robert, Nancy Jean. Instr. dept. sociology U. S.C., 1950-55; asst. dir. Nat. Inst. Mental Health Project, Vanderbilt U., 1956-58; asst. prof. social welfare and sociology Fla. State U., 1958-61; research dir. Fla. Bur. Alcoholic Rehab., Avon Park, 1961-75; research asso. Fla. Aging and Adult Services, 1975-76; planner, evaluator Fla. Alcoholic Rehab. Program, Tallahassee, 1976—. Social sci. cons. City of Columbia (S.C.) Planning Comm., 1950-55. Served to lt. USNR, 1942-46. Mem. N.Am. Assn. Alcohol Programs, So. Sociol. Soc., Soc. Study Social Problems, Am. Sociol. Assn., Nat. Rehab. Assn., Population Assn. Am., Fla. Acad. Sci. Kiwanian (pres. Avon Park club 1970-71, 74-75). Contbr. articles to profl. jours. Home: 1537 Woodgate Way Tallahassee FL 32312 Office: 1323 Winewood Blvd Tallahassee FL 32301

WILLIAMS, JAMES PAUL, human resources director, minister, consultant; b. Wetumka, Okla., Nov. 4, 1940; s. Hubert Avery Williams and Lou Cele (Moon) Fox; m. Sally Rae Whiteley, Apr. 8, 1977; children—James Paul, Lisa Rae, Beth Ann. B.A. in Communications, Okla. Bapt. U., 1963; M.Div., Southwestern Bapt. Theol. Sem., 1967. Ordained to ministry Baptist Ch., 1963. Pastor various So. Bapt. Chs., Okla., Tex., Ohio, 1963-77; service mgr. H-E-B Foods & Drugs, San Antonio, 1977-78, store dir., Waco, Tex., 1978-79, tng. mgr., Corpus Christi, Tex., 1979-83, dir. human resources, McAllen, Tex., 1983-85, dir. human resources, Corpus Christi, 1985—. Adv. bd. chmn. Cornell U., 1979-82; mem. adv. bd. McAllen Blood Bank, Tex., 1985. Mem. Orgn. Devel. Soc., San Antonio Soc. Tng. Devel., Columbus Ohio Jaycees (chaplain 1972-74). Lodge: Rotary. Home: 223 Sandpiper Portland TX 78374 Office: H-E-B Foods & Drugs 4326 Kostoryz Corpus Christi TX 78415

WILLIAMS, JAMES VERNON, gas company executive; b. Winnsboro, La., Sept. 16, 1946; s. James Vernon and Gracie Mae (Foster) W. B.S.E.E., Tex. A&I U., 1972; B.S. in Geology, U. Tex.-Permian Basin, 1981. Registered profl. engr., Tex. Engr. Tex.-N.Mex. Pipeline, Midland, Tex., 1972-74; engr., mgr. No. Natural Gas Co., Midland, 1974-82, gas buyer Delhi Gas Pipeline, Midland, 1982-84; v.p. gas supply Colony Natural Gas Corp., Midland, 1984—. Mem. Tex. Soc. Profl. Engrs., Am. Assn. Petroleum Geologists. Presbyterian. Avocations: tennis; golf. Home: 3602 W Storey St Midland TX 79703 Office: Colony Natural Gas Corp PO Box 50550 Midland TX 79710

WILLIAMS, JEAN TAYLOR, artist; b. Town Creek, Ala., Mar. 27, 1912; d. Woodie Richard and Ella Ross (Harrison) Taylor; B.S., U. Montevallo, 1933; student Chgo. Art Inst., 1936; student of Robert Brackman, Noank, Conn., 1958-60; m. James Hayes Williams, June 18, 1935; children—James Richard, Hayes Taylor, Jean Williams Johnson. Art tchr. high sch., Ala., 1933-35; tchr. pvt. classes own studio, Birmingham, Ala., 1976—; art chmn. Mountain Brook Jr. High Sch., Birmingham, 1966; one-woman shows: Samford U., Nat. Soc. Arts and Letters; exhibited work in Jerome Hines Exhbn., 1977; represented in numerous pvt. collections; organizer Ala. state art competition, 1981, Ala. state piano competition, 1982. Recipient grand award in oil painting State of Ala., 1961; Crusade citation Am. Cancer Soc., 1979. Mem. Am. Artists Profl. League (life), Nat. League Am. Pen Women (1st v.p. 1983-84), Nat. Soc. Arts and Letters (art chmn. Birmingham chpt., pres. 1983-84), Ala. Art League, Birmingham Art Assn. Presbyterian. Clubs: Vestavia Country, Turtle Point Yacht and Country, The Club. Address: 2801 Mountain Brook Pkwy Birmingham AL 35223

WILLIAMS, JERRE STOCKTON, judge; b. Denver, Aug. 21, 1916; s. Wayne Cullen and Lena (Day) W.; A.B., U. Denver, 1938; J.D., Columbia, 1941; m. Mary Pearl Hall, May 28, 1950; children—Jerre Stockton, Shelley Hall, Stephanie Kethley. Bar: Colo. 1941, Tex. 1950, U.S. Supreme Ct. 1944. Instr., U. Iowa Law Sch., 1941-42; asst. prof. U. Denver Law Sch., 1946; mem. faculty U. Tex. Law Sch., Austin, 1946-80, John B. Connally prof. civil jurisprudence, 1970-80; judge U.S. Ct. Appeals Fifth Circuit, 1980—; mem. faculty Inst. Internat. and Comparative Law San Diego U.; mem. faculty Merton Coll. Oxford (Eng.) U., 1977, Magdalen Coll., 1979; chmn. Adminstrv. Conf. U.S., 1967-70, pub. mem., 1972-78. Labor arbitrator, bd. govs. Nat. Acad. Arbitrators, 1964-67, v.p., 1974-75; chmn. Southwestern Regional Manpower Adv. Com., 1964-66; cons. Bur. Budget, 1966-67. Served to capt. USAF, 1942-46. Mem. Internat. Soc. Labor Law and Social Legis., Am. (winner Ross Essay contest 1963, chmn. sect. adminstrv. law 1975-76), Fed., Tex. bar assns., Assn. Am. Law Schs. (pres. 1980). Methodist. Author: Cases and Materials on Employees Rights, 1952; The Supreme Court Speaks, 1956. Editor-in-chief: Labor Relations and the Law, 3d edit., 1965; Constitutional Analysis, 1979. Home: 3503 Mount Barker Dr Austin TX 78731 Office: 1620 American Bank Tower 221 W 6th St Austin TX 78701

WILLIAMS, JIMMIE SHERWOOD, sociology educator; b. Los Angeles, May 22, 1938; s. Sherwood and June E. (Woods) Meek; m. Carolyn Ann Hayes, Jan. 10, 1958; children—Robert S., Jon S., Merrily T. A.A., Compton Coll., 1962; B.A., Calif. State U.-Long Beach, 1964, M.A., Calif. State U.-Los Angeles, 1968; Ph.D., Wash. State U., 1972. Probation officer Los Angeles County, 1964-68; lectr. Calif. State U., Los Angeles, 1967-68; asst. prof. sociology Va. Commonwealth U., Richmond, 1971-75, assoc. prof., 1975—, dir. survey research lab., 1982—; asst. prof. George Washington U., D.C., 1975; referee various revs. Contbr. articles to profl. jours. Mem. Am. Sociol. Assn., Internat. Sociology Honor Soc. (pres. 1968-72), Am. Soc. Criminology, Soc. Study Social Problems, So. Sociol. Soc. Office: Dept Sociology Va Commonwealth U 312 N Shafer St Richmond VA 23284

WILLIAMS, JOHN BARRY, dentist; b. Austin, Tex., May 19, 1928; s. J.B. and Ethyl (Clark) W.; m. Beth Lynn, May 28, 1983; children—John, Marilee. B.A., U. Tex., 1948; D.D.S., Baylor Coll., 1951. Gen. practice dentistry, Austin, 1954—. Treas., Child & Family Service, Austin, 1959-61. Served as capt. USAF, 1952-54. Mem. Tex. Dental Assn. (mem. council on ann. sessions), ADA, Acad. Dentistry, Acad. Operative Dentistry (v.p. 10th dist. 1965). Club: Headliners. Avocations: traveling; reading. Home: 6618 E Hill Dr Austin TX 78756 Office: 4213 Burnet Rd Austin TX 78756

WILLIAMS, JOHN BRAXTON, JR., real estate development executive; b. Indpls., Aug. 10, 1933; s. John Braxton and Jeanette Jane (Webb) W.; B.S. in Civil Engring., So. Meth. U., 1957; 1 son, John Kevin. Pres., co-owner Isles Constrn. Co., Dallas, 1955-58; chief civil engr. Wyatt C. Hedrick Architect-/Engr., Dallas, 1958-60; asso., Don Fleming & Assos. Architects/Engrs., Dallas, 1961-62; constrn. engr., overseas projects, M.W. Kellogg Co., N.Y.C., 1963-65; constrn. mgr. J.C. Penney Co., Atlanta, 1966-79; chmn. bd. Arco Properties Inc., Atlanta, 1971-80, Atlanta Intown Loan & Mfg. Co., Inc., Atlanta, 1981—; dir. Creative Properties, Atlanta/Dallas, Righetti Designs, Atlanta. Bd. dirs. Ga. Gifted Children's Scholarship Fund, Atlanta, 1984—. Republican. Unitarian. Contbr. articles to engring. jours. Home: 926 G Waverly Way NE Inman Park Atlanta GA 30307 Office: Box 54032 Atlanta GA 30308

WILLIAMS, JOHN CARL, educator, researcher; b. Sedalia, Mo., Feb. 19, 1952; s. Frank and Kathleen W. B.A., Columbia Coll., Mo., 1979; M.Ed., U. Mo.-Columbia, 1981, Ed.S., 1984; postgrad. Northeast Mo. State U., Central Mo. State U., U. Ariz., U. Mo.-Columbia, U. Mo.-St. Louis. Elem. Tchr. Jamestown Pub. Schs., Mo., 1979-80; tchr. California Pub. Schs., Mo., 1980-85; elem. curriculum coordinator, 1982-85; officer, instr. English, Camden Mil. Acad., S.C., 1985; com. Statewide Testing and Evaluation Service, 1984; instr. math. Adm. Farragut Acad., St. Petersburg Fla., 1986—. Contbr. articles to profl. jours. Mem. Assn. Supervision and Curriculum Devel., Mo. State Tchrs. Assn., NEA, Mo. NEA, Pi Lambda Theta, Phi Delta Kappa. Club: Optimists. Lodges: Masons, Order Eastern Star. Office: Dept Math Adm Farragut Acad 501 Park St N Saint Petersburg FL 33743

WILLIAMS, JOHN MAYNOR, public relations executive, editor, consultant; b. Long Beach, Calif., Jan. 16, 1957; s. John D. and Bobbie (Maynor) W.; m. Kim Nichols, Aug. 8, 1981. B.S. in Communications, U. Tenn.-Knoxville, 1979. Service engr. Middle Tenn. Electric Membership Corp., Murfreesboro, 1980; pub. relations rep., publs. editor Opryland USA (includes Opryland, Grand Ole Opry, Opryland Revue, Inside Opryland USA, The Opryland Sound, The Opryland News, Opryland Hotel, Nashville Network), Nashville, 1980-84; account exec. Holder Kennedy & Co. Inc., Pub. Relations, Nashville, 1984, sr. account exec., 1984—; speaker journalism and pub. relations. Mem. Pub. Relations Soc. Am., Internat. Assn. Bus. Communicators (v.p.). Republican. Methodist. Office: 2020 21st Ave S Nashville TN 37212

WILLIAMS, JOHN TOLLIVER, newspaper executive; b. San Angelo, Tex., Nov. 4, 1944; s. Tom L. and Virginia W. (Potter) W.; B.B.A., Baylor U., 1967; M.B.A., U. Pa., 1969; m. Carol Anne Tennison, June 1, 1968; children—Christine, Tolliver. Supr. Ernst & Whinney, San Antonio, Tex., 1971-75; treas. Harte-Hanks Communication, Inc., San Antonio, 1975-79; gen. mgr. San Angelo Standard-Times, 1979-80; pres., pub. Bryan-College Station (Tex.) Eagle, 1980—; v.p. Harte-Hanks Communications, Inc., also pres. So. region Harte-Hanks Newspaper Group; pub. Tex. Poll. Served with U.S. Army, 1969-71. C.P.A., Tex. Mem. Am. Newspaper Pubs. Assn., Inst. Newspaper Controllers and Fin. Officers., Am. Inst. C.P.A.s. Baptist. Clubs: Rotary, Briarcrest Country. Home: 2809 Barwick Circle Bryan TX 77802 Office: PO Box 3000 Bryan TX 77805

WILLIAMS, JOHNNY PRESTON, JR., pharmacist; b. Milledgeville, Ga., May 24, 1956; s. Johnny Preston and Vera Estelle (Johnson) W., Sr.; m. Vickey Nell Wood, June 24, 1977 (div. 1980); m. Lynda Gene Bauer, Feb. 18, 1984. B.S. in Pharmacy, U. Ga., 1979. Staff intern Parker Pharmacy, McIntyre, Ga., 1976-79; staff pharmacist Evans' Pharmacy, Milledgeville, 1979-80; staff pharmacist Baldwin County Hosp., Milledgeville, 1980-84, assoc. dir. pharmacy, 1984—. Recipient Merck award Merck, Sharp & Dohme, 1979. Mem. Ga. Pharm. Assn., Ga. Soc. Hosp. Pharmacists. Baptist. Avocations: piano; reading; fishing. Home: 1679 Valley Rd Milledgeville GA 31061

WILLIAMS, JOSEPH HILL, diversified industry exec.; b. Tulsa, June 2, 1933; s. David Rogerson and Martha Reynolds (Hill) W.; B.A., Yale U., 1956, M.A. (hon.), 1977; postgrad. Sch. Pipeline Tech. U. Tex., 1960; m. Terese T. Ross, May 7, 1977; stepchildren—Margot Ross, Jennifer Ross; children—Joseph Hill Jr., Peter B., James C. Field employee domestic constrn. div. Williams Cos., Tulsa, 1958-60, project coordinator engring. div., 1960-61, project supt., Iran, 1961-62, asst. resident mgr., Iran, 1962-64, project mgr., 1964-65, resident mgr., 1965-67, exec. v.p., 1968-71, pres., chief operating officer, 1971-78, chmn., chief exec. officer, 1979—, also dir.; former chmn. Fed. Res. Bank of Kansas City; dir. Parker Drilling Co. Bank of Okla., Am. Express Co.; bd. dirs. Industries for Tulsa, Tulsa Area United Way, Okla. C. of C.; mem. adv. com. Jr. Achievement; trustee and fellow Yale Corp., trustee U. Tulsa. Served with AUS, 1956-58. Mem. Am. Petroleum Inst. (dir.), Young Pres.'s Orgn., Nat. Petroleum Council, Conf. Bd., Council on Fgn. Relations, Met. Tulsa C. of C. (past chmn.). Episcopalian. Clubs: Southern Hills Country, Summit, Tulsa, Springdale Hall (Camden, S.C.), Augusta (Ga.) Nat. Golf, Castle Pines Golf (Denver) Grandfather Golf and Country (Linville, N.C.). Office: One Williams Center Tulsa OK 74172

WILLIAMS, JOYCE ELAYNE, sociology educator, researcher; b. Rockdale, Tex., Feb. 4, 1937; d. Harry Lee and Essie Marie (Fergeson) W. B.A., Mary Hardin-Baylor Coll., Belton, Tex., 1958; M.A., So. Meth. U., 1962; Ph.D., Washington U., St. Louis, 1971. Social caseworker Social Service Dept. Buckner Childrens Home, Dallas, 1958-62; from instr. to asst. prof. sociology Mary Hardin-Baylor Coll., Belton, 1962-65; instr. sociology Arlington State Coll., Tex., 1965-67; teaching asst., lectr. dept. sociology-anthropology Washington U., St. Louis, 1967-69; from asst. prof. to assoc. prof. Sociology U. Tex., Arlington, 1969-74, Trinity U., San Antonio, 1974-80; vis. faculty dept. Sociology U. Tex. Austin, summer 1977; assoc. prof. dept. sociology and social work Tex. Woman's U., Denton, 1980—, acting chairperson, fall 1984; cons. in field. Author: (with others) Black Community Control: A Study of Transition in a Texas Ghetto, 1973, American Ethnic Revival, 1977, Sociology: A Pragmatic Approach, 1981, 2d rev. edit., 1984; The Second Assault: Rape and Public Attitudes, 1981. Contbr. articles to profl. jours. Adviser, Como Community Betterment Council, 1969-74; bd. dirs. Tarrant County Legal Aid, 1972-74; Alamo area vol. advocate program, 1974-80; mem. Am. Issues Forum, 1975, Citizens United for the Rehab. of Errants, Denton County NAACP, Denton County Friends of the Family; proposal evaluator NSF, NIMH, 1983. Recipient Organized Research award Tex. Woman's U., 1981-82; recipient numerous grants, 1971—. Mem. NOW, Am. Sociol. Assn., Soc. for Study of Social Problems, Southwestern Social Sci. Assn. (mem. nominations com. 1980-82), Southwestern Sociol. Assn. (pub. info. com., various other coms.),

Soc. Women in Sociology, Southwestern Assn. Criminal Justice Educators, Nat. Acad. Criminal Justice Scis., Am. Soc. Criminology, Alpha Sigma Phi (nat. advisor 1983-84). Office: Dept Sociology and Social Work Tex Womans U PO Box 23928 Denton TX 76204

WILLIAMS, KEITH WILBUR, educator, clergyman; b. Los Angeles, Aug. 31, 1928; s. Walter Oliver and Helen (Jarvis) W.; m. Carmella Nacci, July 22, 1950; children—Timothy Keith, David Walter. B.A., Wayne State U., 1950; M.Div., Fuller Theol. Sem., 1953; M.A., La. State U., 1964; postgrad. Fla. State U., U. Miami, San Jose State U., Stetson U., Northwestern U., Loyola U., Chgo. Ordained to ministry, Baptist Ch., 1953. Home missionary CBHMS, Penobscot Indians, Maine, 1954; minister West Cannon Bapt. Ch., Grand Rapids, Mich., 1955-57, Berean Bapt. Ch., South Holland, Ill., 1957-58; asst. pastor Marquette Manor Bapt. Ch., Chgo., 1958-60; tchr. math. North Miami Sr. High Sch. (Fla.), 1960-64; prof. math Miami Dade Community Coll. North Campus, 1964—. Mem. Nat. Council Tchrs. Math., Fla. Tchrs. Math., Math. Assn. Am., United Faculty of Fla. (pres.), Two Year Coll. Council of Tchrs. Math in Fla. (past pres.), Nat. Model R.R. Assn., South Fla. Soc. Model Engrs., Rwy. and Locomotive Hist. Soc., Humane Soc. Broward County, Gold Coast R.R. and Mus. Mem. Fla. Bible Ch. Lodge: Gideons Internat. Author: Arithmetic—A Semi Programmed Text, 1970; (with others) Introduction to College Mathematics, 1972. Home: 611 SW 68th Ave Pembroke Pines FL 33023 Office: 11380 NW 27th Ave Miami FL 33167

WILLIAMS, KELL C(OLEMAN), culvert manufacturing company executive; b. Daytona, Fla., Apr. 6, 1919; s. Coleman and Ethel (Kell) W.; m. Mary Frizzelle, Feb. 5, 1939; children—Kell C., Rebecca Williams Schulze. Student Brewton Parker Coll., 1937-38. Salesman, 1939-59; exec. v.p. Fla. Culvert, 1959-60; chmn. bd., pres. Culvert Mfg. Co., Nat. Pipe Co., Kelwil and Epip, Inc., 1961-72; gen. mgr. Culvert ops. St. Regis Corp. Pinellas Park, Fla., 1972—; chmn. bd. Marine Nat. Bank, 1971-74; dir. N.E. Bank of St. Petersburg, 1965-67; mem. adv. bd. Liberty Nat. Bank, 1966-73. Chmn. exec. com., dir. Flagship Bank St. Petersburg, 1974—. Mem. adv. bd. St. Petersburg Jr. Coll. Served with U.S. Army, 1944-46. Decorated Bronze Star. Mem. Nat. Corrugated Steel Pipe Assn. (dir., pres. 1980-81), Com. of 100. Clubs: Feather Sound Country, St. Petersburg Yacht, Safari, Ducks Unltd. Lodges: Masons, K.T., Scottish Rite, Shriners. Home: 8415 Tallahassee Dr NE Saint Petersburg FL 33702 Office: 8250 62nd St N Pinellas Park FL 33565

WILLIAMS, LAURENCE PAUL, government agency administrator; b. Cohasset, Mass., Aug. 16, 1932; s. Laurence Paul and Hilda (Johnson) W.; m. Margie Marie Franklin, Mar. 19, 1955; children—Christy, Laurence, Lila, Ricky, Michael, Matthew. B.S. in Vocat./Tech. Edn., U. So. Miss., 1982. Electronics instr. U.S. Civil Service, Keesler AFB, Miss., 1955-57, 58-81, logistics mgr., 1981—, logistics mgmt. supr., 1985—; prodn. operator City Services Corp., Hackberry, La., 1957-58. Served with USAF, 1951-55. Recipient Meritorious Air Force Civilian award Air Tng. Command, 1979. Mem. Soc. Logistics Engrs. Republican. Roman Catholic. Avocations: amateur radio; computers. Home: 111 Bradford Circle Ocean Springs MS 39564 Office: KTTC/LGXS Keesler AFB MS 39534

WILLIAMS, LAURENCE PHILIP, college administrator; b. Wheeling, W. Va., Dec. 8, 1940; s. Paul Ralston and Katherine (Volinger) W.; m. Jane Lou Delbrugge, June 3, 1967; children—Paul David, Eric Philip, Cristin Lynn. B.A., West Liberty State Coll., 1968; M.A., W. Va., U., 1975. Mktg. rep. 3M Co., Wheeling, 1967-71; coll. adminstr. West Liberty State Coll., W. Va., 1971—. Active pub. relations com. Democratic Exec. Com., W. Va., 1967-69; higher edn. instrnl. TV com. State of W. Va., Charleston, 1975—; pres. Parish Council Corpus Christi Ch., Wheeling, 1977-79, Sch. Bd. Corpus Christi Sch., 1979-81, Men's Club Corpus Christi Ch., 1982-83; sec. bd. dirs. Warwood Redbirds Little League, 1983-84. Served with U.S. Army, 1961-65. Roman Catholic. Club: Warwood Vets. Avocations: jogging; handball; reading; video taping business. Home: 900 Warwood Ave Wheeling WV 26003 Office: West Liberty State Coll West Liberty WV 26074

WILLIAMS, LEAH ANN, biologist, researcher, educator; b. Clarksburg, W.Va., July 20, 1932; d. George Woodbridge and Marguerite (Shanabarger) W. B.A., W.Va. U., 1954, M.S., 1958, Ph.D., 1970. Inst. zoology Pa. State U., 1958-59; instr. W.Va. U., Morgantown, 1959-68, asst. prof. biology, 1968-74, assoc. prof., 1974—. USPHS predoctoral fellow, 1967-68; NSF sci. faculty devel. grantee, 1977-78; Nat. Eye Inst. grantee, 1983-85. Mem. Soc. Developmental Biology, Am. Assn. Zoologists, AAAS, Assn. for Research in Vision and Ophthalmology, Sigma Xi, Kappa Delta. Presbyterian. Lodge: Order Eastern Star. Contbr. articles to profl. jours. Office: W Va U Dept Biology 206 Brooks Hall Morgantown WV 26506

WILLIAMS, LEE ALLEN, industrial salesman; b. Pineville, La., Oct. 19, 1919; s. John W. and Allie L. (Williams) W.; m. Catherine Helen Bruins, Sept. 7, 1945; children—John Lee, Philip James. B.S. in Phys. Edn., La. Coll., 1941. Salesman Alexandria Seed and Feed, La., 1946, Marchant Calculator Co., Baton Rouge, Gasden, Ala., Beaumont, Tex., Little Rock, 1947-62; with indsl. sales Automatic Pump and Equipment Co., Beaumont, 1962—. Served to lt. U.S. Naval Air Corps, 1941-45. Recipient Crime Prevention award Beaumont C. of C., 1982-83. Republican. Baptist. Lodge: Lions (pres. Forest Park 1984-85). Home: 5925 Pinkstaff Ln Beaumont TX 77706 Office: Automatic Pump and Equipment Co PO Box 1281 Beaumont TX 77704

WILLIAMS, LEONARD JACKSON, dentist, educator; b. Roanoke, Ala., May 14, 1933; s. Leonard Clarence and Emily Adeline (Wilder) W.; m. Kathleen McKnight, Oct. 8, 1955 (div. 1974); m. May Belle Laechlein, May 16, 1974. A.A., So. Union Jr. Coll., 1953; student Tex. A&I U., 1958-60; D.D.S., U. Tex., 1964. Gen. practice dentistry, Houston, 1964—; instr. U. Tex. Dental Br., Houston, 1964—. Served to lt. USN, 1954-59. Mem. ADA, Tex. Dental Assn., Houston Dist. Dental Soc. (mem. various coms.), Bellaire-Southwest Houston C. of C. (past dir.). Republican. Methodist. Lodges: Elks, Optimists. Avocations: hunting; fishing; gardening; flying. Home: 5423 Cheena St Houston TX 77096 Office: 6601 Tarnef St Suite 207 Houston TX 77074

WILLIAMS, LOUIS BOOTH, former junior college president; b. Paris, Tex., Oct. 15, 1916; s. William Louis and Maggie Jo (Booth) W.; A.A., Paris (Tex.) Jr. Coll., 1935; B.B.A., U. Tex., 1937; M.B.A., E. Tex. State U., 1961; LL.D. (hon.), Tex. Wesleyan U., 1976; m. Mary Lou Newman, Oct. 15, 1939; children—Joanne Williams Click, Louis Booth. Profl. local C. of C. exec., Austin, Navasota and Paris, Tex., 1938-44; mgr. Bireley's Beverages, Denison, Tex., 1946-49; asst. to pres. Paris Jr. Coll., 1949-52, pres., 1967-83; pres. emeritus 1983—; personnel mgr. Paris Works, Babcock & Wilcox Co., 1952-67; dir. Liberty Nat. Bank, Paris, 1980. Recipient Silver Beaver award Boy Scouts Am., 1957; Paul Harris fellow Rotary Internat., 1974. Mem. Am. Assn. Community Jr. Colls., Assn. Tex. Jr. Colls. (past pres.), Tex. Public Jr. Coll. Assn., Assn. Tex. Colls. and Univs. (pres. 1981-82), Tex. Eastern Athletic Conf. (pres. 1982-83). Democrat. Methodist. Club: Rotary. Author: The Organization, Functions, and Administration of a Local Chamber of Commerce, 1937. Home: 3170 Laurel Ln Paris TX 75460

WILLIAMS, LUTHER FRANCIS, educator, minister; b. Etowah, Tenn., May 14, 1932; s. Frelon Charles and Mattie Lee (Gentry) W.; Asso. Sci., Freed Hardeman Coll., 1957; B.S., Tenn. Wesleyan Coll., 1964; M.M. Math., U. S.C., 1967; Ed.D., U. Tenn., 1977; m. Barbara Ann Gibson, July 20, 1950; children—Carol Ann, Patricia Lynn, Barbara Kay. Ordained to ministry Church of Christ, 1951; minister Dublin (Ga.) Ch. of Christ, 1957-61; tchr. math. Meigs High Sch., Decatur, Tenn., 1961-66; instr. math. Cleveland (Tenn.) State Community Coll., 1966-74, 75-77, dir. instl. research, 1977-84, asst. dean health and life scis., 1984—; minister Central Ch. of Christ, Athens, Tenn., 1969-72, Calhoun, Tenn., 1973-75, Etowah, Tenn., 1976—. Chmn. bd. dirs. Cleveland State Christian Student Center, 1978-82; bd. dirs. Richmond-Tatum Christian Sch., 1979; elder Etowah Ch. of Christ, 1981—. Recipient Disting. Service to Edn. award Freed Hardeman Coll., 1984. Mem. East Tenn. Edn. Assn. (research com. 1985-86), Southeastern Assn. Coll. Researchers, Phi Delta Kappa. Republican. Home: Box 41 Route 5 Athens TN 37303 Office: PO Box 1283 Cleveland TN 37311

WILLIAMS, LYLE RUSSELL, JR., pharmacist, electronics educator; b. Marked Tree, Ark., Apr. 18, 1940; s. Lyle Russell and Delsa Dee (Waskom) W.; m. Nathalie Cecile Baum, May 21, 1971; children—Jennifer, Scott, Rebecca. B.S.E.E., U. Ark., 1963; B.S.P.H. cum laude, Xavier U., New Orleans, 1974. Lic. pharmacist, La. Test engr. McDonnell Aircraft, St. Louis, 1964-67, 69-71; design engr. Emerson Electric, St. Louis, 1968; pharmacist Mercy Hosp., New Orleans, 1974—; instr. computer programming KUGNO, Inc., New Orleans, 1985; instr. electronics, owner, operator Williams Schs., New Orleans, 1985—. Active River Ridge Community Assn., La., 1985. Mem. La. Pharmacist Assn. Democrat. Unitarian. Clubs: KUGNO (New Orleans); Paradise Manor Community (River Ridge). Avocations: electronic design; photography; computers; history; natural history. Home: 705 Wendy Ln River Ridge LA 70123 Office: Mercy Hosp 301 N Jefferson Davis Pkwy New Orleans LA 70119

WILLIAMS, MALVIN AUSBORN, dean, statistical consultant; b. Mayersville, Miss., Apr. 20, 1942; s. Oscar O. and Catherine (Pickett) W.; m. Delores Garner, June 5, 1966; children—Angela, Katrina, Tiffany, Malvin Ausborn. B.S., Alcorn State U., 1962; M.S., Ariz. State U., 1966; postgrad. U. Wis., summer 1967; Ph.D., Southwestern La. U., 1975. Math. tchr. Greenville Pub. Schs., Miss., 1962-65; instr. math. Alcorn State U., Lorman, Miss., 1966-71, registrar, 1975-76, acad. dean, 1976—; grad. asst. Southwestern La. U., Lafayette, 1972-75. Author statis. cons. reports. Steering com. Mgmt. Info. System, Jackson, Miss., 1979—; trustee Watson Chapel A.M.E. Ch., Port Gibson, Miss., 1975—; mem. EEOC com. Waterways Expt. Sta., Vicksburg, Miss., 1978-82. NSF sci. faculty fellow, 1971. Mem. Am. Statis. Assn., Am. Assn. Higher Edn., Am. Assn. Acad. Vice Pres., Miss. Acad. Scis., Claiborne County C. of C. (bd. dirs. 1982-84), Phi Delta Kappa, Omega Psi Phi (basileus 1982-85). Democrat. Avocation: fishing. Home: PO Box 869 Alcorn State U Lorman MS 39096 Office: Alcorn State U PO Box 569 Lorman MS 39096

WILLIAMS, MARGARET BUTLER, psychotherapist, dance/movement therapist; b. Shreveport, La., Sept. 12, 1949; m. Richard W. Williams, Sept. 8, 1979; 1 child, Nicole. B.A. in Psychology with high honors, Sweet Briar Coll., Va., 1968-72; M.S., Northwestern La. U., 1975; postgrad. Fielding Inst., Santa Barbara, Calif., 1978—. Psychotherapist, Phychiat. Services, Inc., Shreveport, 1979—; instr. psychology La. State U., Shreveport, 1975-80. Bd. dirs. Resolve, Inc., Shreveport, 1983—, La. Dance Found., Shreveport, 1984—. Mem. Am. Psychol. Assn., Am. Group Psychotherapy Assn., Am. Dance Therapy Assn., Jr. League Shreveport, Psi Chi. Democrat. Episcopalian. Avocations: modern dance, jazz, ballet, tennis, snow skiing, scuba, saling. Home: 2437 Fairfield Ave Shreveport LA 71104 Office: Psychiatric Services Inc 1541 Irving Pl Shreveport LA 71101

WILLIAMS, MARGARET CLICK, art educator, artist, art historian; b. Surry County, N.C., Feb. 15, 1930; d. James Harold and Esther (Eads) C.; m. Benjamin Forrest Williams, July 2, 1955. B.F.A., U. N.C.-Greensboro, 1952, M.F.A., 1954; D.Edn., N.C. State U., 1979. Dir. fine arts crafts program N.C. State U., Raleigh, N.C., 1954-56; prof. art, chmn. art dept. St. Mary's Coll., Raleigh, N.C., 1956—; participant Rijksbureau, The Hague, Holland, 1964; com. chmn. Cooperating Raleigh Coll., Raleigh, 1969-75; participant Attingham Sch., Eng., 1979, Brit. Odyssey, St. Benet's Hall, Oxford, Eng. 1980, 81, 83, 84, 85. One man shows include: Elliot Hall Gallery, Greenboro, N.C., Little Art Gallery, Asheville, N.C. Mem. bd. Raleigh Civic Music, 1856-60, Raleigh Chamber Music Guild, 1960-72, also officer, Raleigh Fine Arts Soc., 1967—; mem. Sierra Club, N.C., 1968—. Mem. Southeastern Coll. Art Assn., Epsilon Pi Tau. Avocations: music; conservation; nature study; gardening; hiking. Home: 2813 Mayvies Rd Raleigh NC 27607 Office: St Mary's Coll 900 Hillsborough St Raleigh NC 27603

WILLIAMS, MARILYNN CLARKE, educational administrator; b. Lavonia, Ga., Feb. 29, 1924; d. Addison Bowman and Maude (McCarter) Clarke; B.A., Lander Coll., Greenwood, S.C., 1943; M.A., Tchrs. Coll., Columbia U., 1949; m. Hoke Gassaway Williams, Jan. 23, 1953. Tchr. elem. schs., Carnesville, Ga., 1943-45, Greenville, S.C., 1945-67, Kaiserslautern, W. Ger., 1967-69; prin. Grove Elem. Sch., Greenville, 1969-81, Plain Elem. Sch., Greenville, 1982—; dir. summer seminar on Brit. infant schs., Oxford, Eng., 1974; mem. vis. teams So. Assn. Schs. and Colls., 1975—; mem. edn. com. Appalachian Council Govts., 1977—; mem. Gov.'s Task Force on Citizen Participation in Edn., 1979—. Recipient sustained superior performance award Dept. Army, 1968; named PTA Prin. of Yr., 1984; Nat. Disting. Prin., U.S. Dept. Edn., 1985; R.L. Bryan award as outstanding adminstr., 1986. Mem. Assn. for Childhood Edn., Assn. Elem. Sch. Prins., Assn. Supervision and Curriculum Devel. (Outstanding Project of Yr. award, 1979), Internat. Reading Assn., S.C. Council Tchrs. Math., PTA (life), Delta Kappa Gamma, Phi Delta Kappa. Methodist. Club: Altrusa (Greenville). Home: 219 Edgewood Dr Mauldin SC 29662

WILLIAMS, MARK CHARLES, data communications specialist, consultant; b. Montgomery, W.Va., Mar. 14, 1952; s. Charles Henry and Olive Eirvin (Thompson) W.; m. Ann Marie Tucker, Feb. 15, 1975; 1 child, Jason Mark. Network mgr. Computer Network Corp., Washington, 1977-79; network account coordinator GTE Telenet Communications Corp., Reston, Va., 1979-81, mgr. maintenance mgmt. and reporting, 1981-83, sr. tech. specialist, 1983-84, mgr. spl. programs and tng., 1984—; cons. Bob Wainwright & Assoc., San Diego, 1977-79. Pet therapy leader Arlington Animal Welfare League, Va., 1981-85, bd. dirs., 1983-85. Served as staff sgt. USAF, 1970-77. Mem. Telenet Employee Assn. (treas., chmn. bd.). Republican. Mem. Ch. of Christ. Avocations: woodworking; camping. Home: 205 Trail Ct Sterling VA 22170 Office: GTE Telenet Communications Corp 12490 Sunrise Valley Dr Reston VA 22096

WILLIAMS, MARSHA RHEA, computer scientist, educator, researcher, consultant; b. Memphis, Aug. 4, 1948; d. James Edward and Velma Lee (Jenkins) W.; B.S., Beloit Coll., 1969; M.S. in Physics, U. Mich., 1971; M.S. in Systems and Info. Sci., Vanderbilt U., 1976, cert. data processing (CDP), 1981, Ph.D. in Computer Sci., 1982. Engring. coop. student Lockheed Missiles & Space Co., Sunnyvale, Calif., 1967-68; asst. transmission engr. Ind. Bell Telephone Co., Indpls., 1971-72; systems analyst, instr. physics Memphis State U., 1972-74; computer-assisted instrn. project programmer Fisk U., 1974-76; mem. tech. staff Hughes Research Labs., Malibu, Calif., 1976-78; assoc. systems engr. IBM, Nashville, 1978-80; research and teaching asst. Vanderbilt U., Nashville, 1980-82, spl. asst. to dean Grad. Sch., spring 1981; cons. computer-assisted instrn. project Meharry Med. Coll., Nashville, summer 1982; assoc. prof. computer sci. Tenn. State U., Nashville, 1982-83, 84—, U. Miss., Oxford, 1983-84; presenter papers profl. meetings. Editor-in-chief newspaper Pilgrim Emanuel Bapt. Ch., 1975-76; adv. Chi Rho Youth Fellowship, Temple Bapt. Ch., 1975-81, adv. com. 60-Plus Sr. Citizens Fellowship, 1979-80, 86—, Women's Day speaker, 1979, 81; adviser Soc. Black Engring. Students, 1983-84. Mem. Assn. Computing Machinery, IEEE Computer Soc., Am. Soc. Engring. Mgmt., Profl. Data Processing Assn. of Nashville, NAACP. Office: Tenn State U Dept Math and Computer Sci Nashville TN 37203

WILLIAMS, MARTIN, editor, writer, educator; b. Richmond, Va., Aug. 9, 1941 s. John Bell and Rebecca (Yancey) W.; children from former marriage—Charles, Frederick, Frank. B.A., U. Va., 1948; M.A., U. Pa., 1950. Lectr., instr. Columbia U., N.Y.C., 1952-56; editor Macmillan Co., N.Y.C., 1955; free-lance writer, N.Y.C., 1956-71; editor Ency. Americana, N.Y.C., 1959-60; editor Smithsonian Instn., 1971—, now editor Smithsonian Press; lectr. numerous ednl. instns. Author numerous books. Address: 2101 Shenandoah Rd Alexandria VA 22308

WILLIAMS, MARY LOU NEWMAN, former museum and archives coordinator; b. Harleton, Tex., Dec. 21, 1918; d. Ray Maxie and Corine (Baker) Newman; A.A., Coll. of Marshall, 1935; B.A., Mary Hardin-Baylor U., 1937; postgrad. U. Tex., Austin, 1937-38; M.A., E. Tex. State U., 1961; m. Louis Booth Williams, Oct. 15, 1938; children—Joanne Williams Click, Louis Booth. English instr. Paris (Tex.) Jr. Coll., 1953-68, chmn. communications div., 1965-68, coordinator for devel. A.M. and Welma Aikin Regional Archives, 1977—; English instr. E. Tex. State U., Commerce, 1970-74; coordinator for devel. R.F. Voyer Regional Mus., Honey Grove, Tex., 1977-83. Pres., McQuistion Regional Med. Center Aux., 1975-77; dist. bd. Nat. Multiple Sclerosis Soc.; mem. YWCA, Lamar County Hist. Commn. Winedale Mus. seminar scholar, 1977. Mem. AAUW, Am. Assn. State and Local History, Soc. Am. Archivists, Am. Assn. Museums, Tex. Assn. Museums, Tex. State Hist. Assn., NE Tex. Geneal. Soc., LWV, Phi Theta Kappa (hon.). Methodist. Clubs: Cosmos (pres. 1977), Paris Garden (pres. 1944), Garden Study (pres. 1955), Mary Emma Bible (pres. 1975, 80). Home: 3170 Laurel Ln Paris TX 75460

WILLIAMS, MILLER, poet, translator, publisher; b. Hoxie, Ark., Apr. 8, 1930; s. Ernest Burdette and Ann Jeanette (Miller) W.; B.S., Ark. State Coll., 1951; M.S., U. Ark., 1952; postgrad. La. State U., 1951, U. Miss., 1957; m. Lucille Day, Dec. 29, 1951 (div.); m. Rebecca Jordan Hall, Apr. 11, 1969; children—Lucinda, Robert, Karyn. Instr. in English, La. State U., 1962-63, asst. prof., 1964-66; vis. prof. U. Chile, Santiago, 1963-64; assoc. prof. Loyola U., New Orleans, 1966-70; Fulbright prof. Nat. U. Mexico, Mexico City, 1970; co-dir. grad. program in creative writing U. Ark., 1970—, assoc. prof., 1971-73, prof. English and fgn. langs., dir. program in transl., 1973—, dir. poetry-in-the prisons programs div. continuing edn., 1973-83, chmn. program in comparative lit., 1978-80; dir. U. Ark. Press, 1980—; fellow Am. Acad. in Rome, 1976—, mem. adv. council Sch. Classical Studies, 1985—; first U.S. del. Pan Am. Conf. Univ. Artists and Writers, Concepcion, Chile, 1964; mem. poetry staff Bread Loaf Writers Conf., 1967-72; founder, exec. dir. Ark. Poetry Circuit, 1975. Recipient Henry Bellaman Poetry award, 1957, award in Poetry, Arts Fund, 1973; Prix de Rome Am. Acad. Arts and Letters, 1976; Bread Loaf fellow in poetry, 1961; Amy Lowell Travelling scholar in poetry, 1963. Mem. South Central MLA, MLA, Am. Lit. Translators Assn. (v.p. 1978-79, pres. 1979-81), ACLU, AAUP. Author: (poems) A Circle of Stone, 1964; (poems) Recital, 1965; (poems) So Long At the Fair, 1968; The Achievement of John Ciardi, 1968; Ozark, Ozark: A Hillside Reader, 1981; Distractions, 1981; (poems) The Only World There Is, 1971; The Poetry of John Crowe Ransom, 1971; Contemporary Poetry in America, 1972; Halfway From Hoxie: New & Selected Poems, 1973; The Boys on Their Bony Mules, 1983; (with John Ciardi) How Does a Poem Mean?, 1974; Why God Permits Evil (poems), 1977; Imperfect Love (poems), 1986; Patterns of Poetry: An Encyclopedia of Forms, 1986; translator: Poems & Antipoems, 1967, Emergency Poems, 1972 (Nicanor Parra); Sonnets of Giuseppe Belli, 1981; editor: 19 Poetas de Hoy en Los Estados Unidos, 1966; (with John William Corrington) Southern Writing in the Sixties: Poetry, 1967, Southern Writing in the Sixties: Fiction, 1966; Chile: An Anthology of New Writing, 1968; (with James A. McPherson) Railroad: Trains and Train People in American Culture, 1976; A Roman Collection: An Anthology of Writing about Rome and Italy, 1980; poetry editor La. State U. Press, 1966-68; founding editor New Orleans Rev., 1968-69; contbg. editor Translation Rev., 1978—; contbr. articles to profl. pubs. Home: 1111 Valley View Dr Fayetteville AR 72701 Office: Press U Ark Fayetteville AR 72701

WILLIAMS, NANCY JEANEANE, educational administrator; b. Alamance County, N.C., Dec. 11, 1940; d. Wilburn Harley and Mary Linda (Flynn) W.; m. Barney Bradford Stahl, May 12, 1973 (div. 1981). B.A., U. N.C., 1963. Promotion supr. McGraw Hill Book Co., N.Y.C., 1965-68; dir. promotion and advt. Garrett Press Inc., N.Y.C., 1968-71; tech. editor U. Colo., Boulder, 1973-74; spl. asst. to vice chancellor U. N.C., Chapel Hill, 1975-77; assoc. editor U. N.C. Gen. Alumni Assn., Chapel Hill, 1977-81; dir. pub. relations and publs. Guilford Coll., Greensboro, N.C., 1981—. Author mag. series Carolina in Fiction, 1980; contbg. author: Successful Sports Management, 1985. Mem. Eastern Music Festival Mktg. Com., Greensboro, 1981—, long range planning com., 1984—; mem. Council on Bus. Communications, Greensboro, 1983—; publicity chmn. O. Henry Festival, Greensboro, 1983-84. Recipient cert. Leadership Greensboro, 1981. Mem. Pub. Relations Soc. Am. (bd. dirs. 1985—), Council for Advancement and Support of Edn., Carolinas News Assn. Club: P.E.O. (sec. 1978-80, v.p. 1980-82). Avocations: music; theatre; African violets. Home: 3223B Regents Park Ln Greensboro NC 27405 Office: Guilford Coll 5800 W Friendly Ave Greensboro NC 27410

WILLIAMS, NEAL ROTH, interior designer; b. Alice, Tex., Aug. 31, 1950; s. Joseph Harold and Thurston Nyleen (Daniels) W. Student Tulane U., 1968-69; B.S., La. State U., 1972; B. Interior Design, 1980. Curator collections La. State Mus., New Orleans, 1975-77; interior designer Design for Living, Baton Rouge, La., 1981—. Pres. Hist. Spanish Town Civic Assn., Baton Rouge, 1984-85; commn. mem. Mayor's Hist. Dist. Study Commn., Baton Rouge, 1984-85. Served with U.S. Army, 1973-75. Mem. Am. Soc. Interior Designers (assoc.). Republican. Methodist. Avocations: snorkeling; swimming; tennis; antiques; historic building renovations. Home: 635 N 9th St Baton Rouge LA 70802 Office: Design for Living Inc 8146 One Calais Pl #101 Baton Rouge LA 70809

WILLIAMS, PATRICE VONZELL, nurse; b. Miami, Fla., Nov. 21, 1959; d. Homer and Audrey Delane (Scott) W. A.A., Miami Dade North Community Coll., 1980; A.S. in Nursing, Miami Dade Med. Ctr., 1981. R.N.; lic. practical nurse. Nursing asst. Jackson Meml. Hosp., Miami, Fla., 1980-82; lic. practical nurse Hialeah Hosp. (Fla.), 1982—, R.N., 1982—Recipient cert. outstanding acad. achievement Miami Dade North Campus, 1980-81. Democrat. Home: 9815 NW 30th Ct Miami FL 33147

WILLIAMS, PATRICIA CAROLYN, telecommunications company official; b. Jacksonville, Fla., Feb. 28, 1954; d. Robert Lee Charles Williams and Mary Ella (Bigham) Stallings; B.A., Spelman Coll., 1975; M.A., Northwestern U., 1976. Bus. office supr. So. Bell Tel. & Tel. Co., Columbus, Ga., 1976-78, asst. mgr. tng., Decatur, Ga., 1978-79, assoc. mgr. tng., 1979, mgr. work relationships, Atlanta, 1980-84, mgr. legis. affairs, 1984—; mgmt. skills cons., 1978—. Bd. dirs. Urban League, Columbus, 1976-78; adv. Jr. Achievement, 1976-83; active Future Pioneers Am., 1976-78, Ga. Soc. for Prevention Blindness, 1976-78; chmn. Spelman Coll. Interest Group, 1976-78; Explorer Scouts adv. Boy Scouts Am., 1978-80; solicitor United Negro Coll. Fund, 1978-79, team capt., 1980; fund raiser Am. Cancer Soc., 1978. Nat. Fellowship Found. fellow, 1975-76. Mem. Spelman Coll. Alumni Assn. (Centennial program com. co-chmn. 1981, mem. Alumni Glee Club 1976—), Atlanta U. Cluster Nat. Alliance Businessmen, Am. Bus. Women's Assn. (pres., Woman of Yr. 1984), Nat. Black M.B.A. Assn. (Outstanding Service award 1984), Atlanta Women's Network (mid-career seminar co-chmn. 1981), Am. Soc. Tng. and Devel., World Future Soc., Alpha Kappa Alpha. Democrat. Methodist. Office: So Bell Tel & Tel Co 32S Southern Bell Center Atlanta GA 30075

WILLIAMS, PATTI MCBRIDE, diet center executive; b. Shreveport, La., July 31, 1950; d. William Andrew and Lucy Opal (Fussell) McBride; m. Richard Warren Williams, Aug. 25, 1973 (div.); 1 dau., Jennifer Nicole. B.S., La. State U., 1972; M.S., Northwestern State U. La., 1980. Bookkeeper, co-therapist W.A. McBride, M.D., Shreveport, La., 1972-77; dir. profl. and community relations Brentwood Hosp./Humana, Inc., Shreveport, 1979-85; owner, dir. Diet Ctr. Shreveport, Inc., 1985—. Mem. communications com. United Way, 1983, mem. budget com., 1985; publicity chmn. Shreveport Opera, 1981, 82, 83; bd. dirs. Mothers Against Drugs, 1982—; bd. dirs. Little Theater Guild, publicity chmn., 1985-86; past pres. St. Mary's Women Guild, St. Paul's Episcopal Ch.; bd. dirs. Explore 1981—, exec. dir., 1985-86. Recipient 1st place Newsletter award Nat. Hosp. Assn., 1980. Mem. Am. Women in Radio and TV (v.p. local chpt.), Pub. Relations Soc. Am. (pres. local chpt. 1984-86), Nat. Assn. Mental Health Info. Officers (communications awards 1980, 81), Jr. League Shreveport, Leadership Bossier. Democrat. Office: Diet Center Shreveport 2001 E 70th 506 Shreveport LA 71105

WILLIAMS, PEGGY FOWLER, management consultant; b. nr. Seymour, Tex., May 8, 1933; d. Leon Dockrey Fowler and Annie Bell (Williams) Dodd; B.S., North Tex. U., 1954; M.B.A., Rollins Coll., 1963; cert. of advanced study Am. Grad. Sch. Internat. Mgmt., Phoenix, 1980; m. George S. Moranz, June 5, 1953 (div. Aug., 1979); children—Leigh Ann, Walter Lochran. With Tex. Instruments, Dallas, 1957-58; with Temco Aircraft, Dallas, 1951-53, 55-57; owner Williams Cons. (formerly Moranz Cons.), Dallas, 1963—. Mem. UDC, Dallas Hist. Soc., Nat. Assn. Female Execs., Am. Mgmt. Assn. Episcopalian. Club: Listener's. Address: PO Box 7173 Dallas TX 75209

WILLIAMS, PHILLIP WAYNE, securities and diversified company executive, former army officer, consultant; b. Birmingham, Ala., Nov. 1, 1939; s. Louie Alfred and A. Banks (Osborn) W.; m. Jinnett McBride, Apr. 4, 1964 (div.); children—Phillip Wayne, Christopher N.; m. Jennie L. Wallace, Mar. 21, 1984; stepchildren—Michelle, John. B.S. in Math. and Physics, Florence State Coll., Ala., 1961; M.Adminstrv. Sci., U. Ala.-Huntsville, 1977; D.Pub. Adminstrn., Nova U., 1978. Dep. sheriff, Lauderdale County, Florence, 1960-61; commd. 2d lt. U.S. Army, 1961, advanced through grades to lt. col., 1977; served as comdr., staff officer, platoon, co., bn., project mgr. laser designators Redstone Arsenal, Ala., 1973-74, ret., 1982; chmn., pres. COMTEL-South, Inc., Huntsville, Ala., 1982-85, Joint Capital Securities, WIC, Inc., 1985—; cons. Huntsville, 19843—; cons. def. industries, 1983—. Bd. dirs. Better Bus. Bur. No. Ala., 1985. Decorated Legion of Merit, Bronze Star with V and 5 oak leaf clusters, Air Medal with V and no. 7, Army Commendation medal with V and 3 oak leaf clusters; Vietnam Gallantry Cross with Silver Star, Vietnam Gallantry Cross with Palm, Vietnam Tech. Service Medal 1st Class, Vietnam Honor Medal 1st Class, Vietnam Civic Action Medal, Mem. U.S. Armor Assn., Assn. U.S. Army, Blackhorse Assn., Am. Def. Preparedness Assn. (dir. 1982-84, regional v.p. 1985—), Am. Soc. Pub. Adminstrn. (pres.

1982-84), Huntsville/Birmingham C. of C. Office: Joint Capital Securities 225 A Holmes Ave Huntsville AL 35801

WILLIAMS, RALPH MAYNARD, oral surgeon; b. Johnson City, Tenn., Sept. 11, 1927; s. Dewey Maynard and Mary Alice (Crumley) W.; m. Ann Marie Ryan, Dec. 29, 1955; children—William Joe, Dewey Maynard, Dana Beth. B.S., Lincoln Meml. U., 1949; D.D.S., U. Tenn. Coll. Dentistry, 1953. Resident in oral surgery U. Okla. Hosps., 1953-54, Scott and White Hosp., Temple, Tex., 1954-55; pvt. practice oral surgery, Bartlesville, Okla., 1956—. Deacon First Bapt. Ch., Bartlesville, 1970—; bd. reps. Fellowship Christian Athletes for Okla., March Dimes, 1984-85; chmn. Washington County Republican Party, 1969-73. Mem. ADA, Okla. Dental Assn., Internat. Soc. Oral and Maxillofacial Surgeons, Am. Soc. Oral and Maxillofacial Surgeons, Southwest Soc. Oral and Maxillofacial Surgeons (pres. 1977), Midwest Soc. Oral and Maxillofacial Surgeons, Okla. Soc. Oral and Maxillofacial Surgeons (pres. 1961-63), Am. Coll. Oral and Maxillofacial Surgeons, Internat. Acad. Dentistry, No. Dist. Dental Assn. (pres. 1965-67), Bartlesville C. of C., Delta Sigma Delta. Club: Sunset Country (Bartlesville). Lodges: Rotary: (bd. dirs.), Elks. Home: 3432 Hawthorn Ct Bartlesville OK 74006 Office: 3500 SE State St Bartlesville OK 74006

WILLIAMS, RALPH WATSON, JR., investment executive; b. Atlanta, July 2, 1933; s. Ralph Watson and Minnie Covington (Hicks) W.; m. Nancy Jo Morgan, Mar. 19, 1955; children—Ralph Watson III, Nancy Jane, John. B.B.A., U. Ga., 1955. Account exec. Courts Co., 1955-57; municipal bond specialist First Southeastern Co., 1957-60; account exec., br. mgr., gen. ptnr., mem. exec. com., exec. v.p., dir. Francis I. duPont & Co., DuPont-Glore Forgan Dupont Waiston, 1960-74; exec. v.p., dir. E.F. Hutton & Co., Inc., Atlanta, 1974—. Mem. Nat. Assn. Security Dealers (chem. dist. com.); Pres. Club U. Ga. Alumni Assn., Phi Delta Theta. Republican. Methodist. Clubs: Commerce; Capital City; Piedmont Driving.

WILLIAMS, RANDALL ALAN, orthopedic surgeon; b. Chattanooga, Apr. 7, 1936; s. Fred Madison and Ethelyn (Smtih) W.; student U. Chattanooga, 1954-56; M.D., Tulane U., 1960; m. Adelle Crowell, Dec. 28, 1957; children—Laura W. Bergeron, E. Kelley. Intern, Charity Hosp., New Orleans, 1960-61, resident in orthopedic surgery, 1961, 63-67; instr. orthopaedic surgery Tulane U. Sch. Medicine, New Orleans, 1967-69, clin. asst. prof. orthopaedic surgery, 1978—; emergency med. advisor Jefferson Parish Sheriff's Office, 1974—, Jefferson Levee Dist. Police, 1976-80; bd. dirs. Emergency Med. Services of S.E. La., 1978-80; active staff E. Jefferson Gen. Hosp., Metairie, Lakeside Hosp., Metairie; examiner Am. Bd. Cert. in Orthotics and Prosthetics, 1967, 68, 69; NIH co-clinic chief Juvenile Amputee Clinic for U.S. and Can., New Orleans, 1967-73; chief scoliosis clinic Crippled Children's Program, State of La., New Orleans, 1967-73; cons. orthopaedic surgery VA Hosp., Pineville, La., 1967-70, Huey P. Long Charity Hosp., Pineville, 1967-70, Lallie Kemp Charity Hosp., Independence, La., 1967-69; emergency med. advisor Kenner (La.) Police Dept., 1974—, Jefferson Levee Dist. Police, 1976-80; instr. cardiopulmonary resuscitation Am. Heart Assn. of La., 1977—. Served with USAF, 1961-63. Diplomate Am. Bd. Orthopaedic Surgery. Fellow A.C.S., Am. Acad. Orthopaedic Surgeons, Internat. Coll. Surgeons; mem. La. Med. Soc., So. Med. Assn., Mid-Am. Orthopedic Assn. (charter), La. Orthopaedic Assn., Jefferson Parish Med. Soc. La., Greater New Orleans Orthopaedic Soc. Episcopalian. Contbr. articles to profl. jours. Address: 3939 Houma Blvd Suite 16 Metairie LA 70002

WILLIAMS, RANDALL HAROLD, agriculture educator; b. Shamrock, Tex., June 14, 1949; s. Harold Hart and JoAnne (Draper) W.; m. Susan Denise Dollar, May 30, 1981; children—Matthew Wyre, Derek Randall, Braden Daniel. B.S., Tex. Tech. U., 1975, M.Ed., 1976; Ph.D., Okla. State U., 1981. Instr. vocat. agr. Pampa High Sch., Tex., 1975-77, Caprock High Sch., Amarillo, Tex., 1977-79; grad. teaching instr. Okla. State U., Stillwater, 1979-81; prof., dept. chmn. Vernon Regional Jr. Coll., Tex., 1982—; sub-com. chmn. coordinating bd. Tex. Coll. and Univ. System, Austin, 1985—. Bd. dirs. Wheeler County Jr. Livestock Show, Tex., 1981-82, South Wheeler County Hosp. Dist., Shamrock, Tex., 1982, First United Meth. Ch., Shamrock, 1981-82, Vernon, 1982-85. Served with USN, 1970-72. Recipient Eagle Scout award Boy Scouts Am., 1964. Mem. Tex. Jr. Coll. Tchrs. Assn. (agr. vice-chmn. 1985-86), Tex. Jr. Coll. Agrl. Assn. (pres. 1985-86), VFW, Greenbelt Agrl.-Bus. (v.p. 1985-86), Alpha Zeta, Alpha Tau Alpha, Phi Delta Kappa. Club: Santa Rosa Palomino (Vernon). Lodge: Lions. Avocations: snow skiing; sky diving. Home: 4801 Country Dr Vernon TX 76384 Office: Vernon Regional Jr Coll 4400 College Dr Vernon TX 76384

WILLIAMS, RANDALL MARVIN, environmental engineer; b. Baton Rouge, Mar. 1, 1950; s. Sam Sharp and Angie (Germany) W.; m. Brenda Diane McCorkle, June 17, 1972 (div. 1982); m. Elizabeth Jane Holden, Mar. 10, 1984. B.S., La. State U., 1973. Wireline engr. Welex-Halliburton Co., Lafayette, La., 1973-75; prodn. engr. Kerr McGee Corp., Oklahoma City, Okla., 1975-77; insp. U.S. Geol. Survey, Oklahoma City, 1977-79; sr. environ. safety engr. Tenneco Oil Co., Lafayette, La., 1979—. Mem. Tenneco Polit. Action Com., Lafayette. Recipient Disting. Service citation Okla. Corp. Commn., 1982. Mem. Am. Soc. Safety Engrs., Gulf Coast Environ. Affairs Group, Gulf Coast Safety and Tng. Group, Mid Continent Oil and Gas Assn., Soc. Petroleum Engrs. Democrat. Methodist. Clubs: Lake Arthur Yacht, Lafayette Amateur Radio. Avocations: amateur radio; computers; racing sailboats. Home: 936 Rosedown Ln Lafayette LA 70503 Office: Tenneco Oil Co 4023 Ambassador Caffery Pkwy Lafayette LA 70503

WILLIAMS, RICHARD DONALD, wholesale food company executive; b. Audubon, Iowa, Feb. 19, 1926; s. Walter Edward and Olga M. (Christensen) W.; B.A., Ohio Wesleyan U., 1948; M.B.A., Northwestern U., 1949; m. Carol Francis, June 17, 1950; children—Gayle, Todd, Scott. Dir. indsl. and public relations Gardner div. Diamond Nat. Corp., Middletown, Ohio, 1949-61; with Fleming Cos., Inc., 1961—, v.p. personnel, Oklahoma City, 1972-76, sr. v.p. human resources, 1976-82, exec. v.p., 1982—. Pres. Jr. Achievement, Topeka, Kans., 1972; v.p. Last Frontier council Boy Scouts Am., Oklahoma City, 1980; campaign chmn. United Way Greater Oklahoma City, 1980, v.p., 1981, now pres.; bd. dirs. Better Bus. Bur., Oklahoma City Beautiful, Community Council Central Okla. Served with USN, 1944-46. Mem. Am. Soc. Personnel Adminstrn., Food Mktg. Inst. (human resources com.), Am. Mgmt. Assn., Phi Gamma Delta. Clubs: Quail Creek Country, Whitehall (Oklahoma City); La Chaine des Rotisseurs.

WILLIAMS, RICHARD LEROY, U.S. district judge; b. Morrisville, Va., Apr. 6, 1923; s. Wilcie Edward and Minnie Mae (Brinkly) W.; m. Eugenia Kellog, Sept. 11, 1948; children—Nancy Williams Davies, Richard Gregory, Walter Lawrence, Gwendolyn de Grove. LL.B., U. Va., 1951. Bar: Va. 1951. Ptnr. McGuire, Woods & Battle, and predecessor firms, Richmond, Va., 1951-72, 76-80; judge circuit ct. City of Richmond, 1972-76; judge U.S. Dist. Ct. for Eastern Dist. Va., Alexandria, 1980—. Served as 2d lt. USAAF, 1940-45. Fellow Am. Coll. Trial Lawyers. Office: US Dist Ct PO Box 2-AD Richmond VA 23205*

WILLIAMS, ROBERT C., paper company executive; b. 1930. B.S. in Mech. Engring., U. Cin.; M.B.A., Xavier U.; postgrad., Inst. Paper Chemistry. Various tech. and supervisory positions Gardner div. Diamond Internat. Corp., 1947-59; v.p. research, Albermarle Paper Co., 1963-68; founder James River Corp. of Va., Richmond, 1969—, now pres., chief operating officer. Office: James River Corp Va Tredegar St Box 2218 Richmond VA 23217

WILLIAMS, ROBERT CARSON, gastroenterologist; b. Tuscaloosa, Ala., Oct. 28, 1944; s. Robert E. and Clara Gladys (Carson) W.; m. Eunice Padilla, Dec. 27, 1969; children—Robert Bradley, Amy Elizabeth. B.A., David Lipscomb Coll., Nashville, 1965; M.D., U. Tenn., 1968. Diplomate Am. Bd. Internal Medicine, Am. Bd. Gastroenterology. Intern, U. Tex. Teaching Hosp., San Antonio, 1969-70; resident in internal medicine U. Tenn. Hosp., Memphis, 1970-72; fellow in gastroenterology U. Colo. Hosp., Denver, 1972-74; practice medicine, specializing in gastroenterology, Birmingham, Ala., 1976—; v.p. med. staff Med. Ctr. East, 1985-86. Served to lt. comdr. USNR, 1974-76. Mem. AMA, ACP, Ala. Soc. Gastrointestinal Endoscopy (v.p. 1985—), Med. Assn. State of Ala., Jefferson County Med. Soc. Contbr. articles to profl. jours. Office: 52 Med Park E Suite 311 Birmingham AL 35235

WILLIAMS, ROBERT PATE, lawyer; b. Asheboro, N.C., Aug. 30, 1947; s. John Richard and Sarah Elizabeth (Pate) W.; m. Pamela Jean DeWeese, Feb. 24, 1974 (div. May 7, 1985); children—John Matthew DeWeese. A.B., High Point Coll., 1970; J.D., U. N.C., 1973. Bar: N.C., 1973, U.S. Dist. Ct., 1976. Legal adviser to property office U. N.C., Chapel Hill, 1973-76; mem. firm Moser & Moser, Asheboro, N.C., 1976-78; sole practice, Asheboro, 1978—. Bd. dirs. United Way of Randolph County, 1978-84, Randolph County Mental Health, 1978-80; missions chmn. First United Meth. Ch., Asheboro, 1981-85; mem. local bd. SSS, 1983—. Mem. ABA, N.C. Bar Assn., N.C. Acad. Trial Lawyers, N.C. Coll. Advocacy, Randolph County Bar Assn., Asheboro-Randolph C. of C. (dir. 1982-84, 86—), Phi Delta Phi. Democrat. Methodist. Office: 125 Worth St Asheboro NC 27203

WILLIAMS, RONALD JOHN, electrical engineer, educator; b. Blue Ash, Ohio, Dec. 14, 1927; s. John Wolfe and Ethel Virginia (Scheve) W.; B.S., Okla. A. and M. Coll., 1949; M.S., Okla. State U., 1963; Ph.D., Tex. A. and M. U., 1969; m. Patricia Whelan, Aug. 10, 1946; children—Carolyn Virginia (Mrs. Dan Roy Byrne), Eamonn Timothy. Asst. dean applied scis. Del Mar Coll., Corpus Christi, Tex., 1969-71, chmn. engring. tech., 1967-70, prof. engring. tech., 1968—, Piper prof., 1984—; dir. engring. tech. programs U. Ala., 1985-86; vis. prof. engring. tech. Tex. A&M U., 1971-72; cons. in field. NSF-Sci. Faculty fellow, 1964-65; named tchr. of year Tex. Jr. Coll., 1969; AEC trainee, 1965. Mem. IEEE (centennial medal 1984), Nat. Soc. Profl. Engrs., Tex. Soc. Profl. Engrs., (pres. chpt. 1983-84, state ethics com. 1984-85), Am. Nuclear Soc., ASME, Soc. Mfg. Engrs., AIME, ASCE, Am. Soc. Engring. Edn. (sec.-treas. sect. 1983—), N.Y. Acad. Scis., Sigma Xi, Eta Kappa Nu, Tau Beta Pi, Tau Alpha Pi. Democrat. Roman Catholic. Home: PO Box 6027 Corpus Christi TX 78411

WILLIAMS, ROSLIN ETHEL, librarian, b. Arkadelphia, Ark., Dec. 23, 1948; d. Thomas Isaac and Suedonia (Wingfield) Heyward; m. Arthur R. Williams, Nov. 6, 1966 (div. 1982); 1 son, Phillip Jerome. B.S.Ed., Ouachita U., Arkadelphia, 1972, M.S.Ed., 1975; M.L.S., U. Miss., 1983; postgrad. in ednl. adminstrn. Miss. State U., 1984—. Head librarian Central Jr. High Sch., Hot Springs, Ark., 1972-81, Hot Springs High Sch., 1981-82; grad. asst. Farley Library, U. Miss., University, 1982-83; librarian Water Valley (Miss.) Elem. Sch., 1983—; mem. north central evaluating com. State of Ark., 1981-82. Sec. Arkadelphia Women's Devel. Council, 1981; sec. bd. dirs. Ione Bynum Child Care Ctr., Arkadelphia, 1981. Mem. Ark. Library Assn., Miss. Library Assn. Phi Delta Kappa, Kappa Delta Pi. Home: PO Box 736 Mississippi State MS 39762

WILLIAMS, SERELLA HARRIS, health educator; b. Southampton County, Va., Sept. 25, 1928; d. Newit and Annie Beck (Brown) Harris; m. Earl LeGrant Williams, Jr., Feb. 27, 1957; children—N. Wynta, LeGrant Harris. Student Norfolk State Coll., 1947-49; B.S., Morgan State Coll., 1952; M.Edn., Boston U., 1955; postgrad. U. Calif.-Berkeley, U. San Francisco, San Francisco State U. Asst. tumbling coach Norfolk (Va.) State Coll., 1952, women's basketball coach, 1953-60, fencing instr., 1954-60; mem. faculty Hampton (Va.) Inst., now asst. prof. health edn., asst. coordinator health, 1968-70. Vol. ARC; mem. deaconess bd., asst. Sunday sch. tchr. Baptist Ch. Mem. AAHPER and Dance, Morgan Alumni Assn., Boston Alumni Assn., Delta Sigma Theta. Democrat. Home: 6331 Avon Rd Norfolk VA 23513 Office: Holland Physical Education Center Room 130 Hampton Institute Hampton VA 23668

WILLIAMS, SHERRY PHYLLIS, nurse; b. Louisville, Nov. 28, 1949; d. Marvin Gibbs and Ruby Imogene (Adams) W. Assoc. in Nursing, Jefferson Comunity Coll., 1980. Lic. practical nurse St. Anthony Hosp., Louisville, 1967-80, emergency room nurse, 1980—; advanced cardiac life support Heart Assn., Louisville, 1983—. Choir soloist Trinity Coll. and Career Ensemble, Louisville, 1982. Republican. Baptist. Home: 2261 Beargrass Ave Louisville KY 40218

WILLIAMS, STEVEN CLIFFORD, specialty food manufacturer; b. Rochelle, Ill., Jan. 3, 1957; s. Robert C. and June A. (Schmidt) W. Ed. No. Ill. U. Lic. employment counselor, Ill., 1974. Founder Help Employment Agy., Inc., Rochelle, 1974-77; co-founder Claimcheck, Inc., 1977-79; founder, pres., chief exec. officer Cattlebaron Foods, Inc. (formerly Williams Mfg. Co., Inc.), Dallas, 1979-85; founder, pres., chief exec. officer Poor Stephen's, Inc., 1985—. Sponsor Barre Assn. of Dallas Ballet; mem. exec. com. Miss Dallas Pageant; mem. North Dallas Christian Businessman's Assn., Austin Big Bros. Recipient 1st place Addy award in sales promotion and package design, 1982. Mem. Am. Mktg. Assn. (pres. Dallas chpt. 1982-85). Republican. Baptist. Lodge: Masons. Office: PO Drawer 800267 Dallas TX 75380

WILLIAMS, TEMPLE WEATHERLY, JR., medicine, microbiology and immunology educator, physician; b. Wichita Falls, Tex., Apr. 19, 1934; s. Temple W. and Dorothy (Coleman) W.; m. Diane Clare, Aug. 2, 1958; children—Holly, Temple III. B.S., So. Meth. U., 1955; M.D., Baylor U., 1959. Intern, Duke U. Hosp., Durham, N.C., 1959-60, resident in medicine, 1962-63; NIH fellow in infectious diseases Baylor U. Coll. Medicine, Houston, 1960-62, prof. medicine, microbiology and immunology, 1965—. Served with USPHS, 1963-65. Mem. ACP, Infectious Disease Soc. Am. Republican. Methodist. Home: 3766 Nottingham Houston TX 77005 Office: 6565 Fannin Houston TX 77030

WILLIAMS, TERRY LEE, optometrist; b. Wheeling, W.Va., May 17, 1952; s. Charles Ronald and Estella Rosina (Venskoske) W.; m. Linda Pelley, Aug. 18, 1973; children—Anne, Matthew, Melissa, Kathryn, Steven. Student West Liberty State Coll., 1970-72; O.D., So. Coll. Optometry, 1972-76. Gen. practice optometry, Moundsville, W.Va., 1976—, pres. Terry L. Williams O.D., Inc., Moundsville, 1982—; cons. Mound View Health Care Ctr., 1983—. Mem. W.Va. Optometric Assn. (zone chmn. 1980-85, sec.-treas. 1985—), Moundsville Area Jaycees (bd. dirs. 1985), Fraternal Order Police (assoc.), Beta Sigma Kappa, Sigma Alpha Sigma. Democrat. Roman Catholic. Lodge: K.C. Avocations: golf; jogging; basketball. Home: 1102 4th St Moundsville WV 26041 Office: 511 5th St Moundsville WV 26041

WILLIAMS, THOMAS EDGAR, engineer, former army officer; b. Fulton, Ky., Nov. 2, 1928; s. Joshua Faulkner Williams and Vernita (Tribble) Penland; m. Martha Joan Foster, June 11, 1955; children—Kelli, Todd, Martha Lane. B.S. in Mil. Sci., U.S. Mil. Acad., 1953; M.S. in Mech. Engring., Ga. Inst. Tech., 1961. Registered profl. engr. Enlisted man U.S. Army, 1946-53, commd. 2d lt., 1953, advanced through grades to col., 1974; chief test design div. Hdqrs. Ops. Test and Evaluation Agy., Falls Church, Va., 1973-75, comdr. 1st brigade Armor Ctr., Ft. Knox, Ky., 1975-77; dir. instrumentation and automatic data processing, Ft. Hood, Tex., 1977-79; exec. for interoperability SHAPE, Mons, Belgium, 1979-81, sr. army advisor to Tex. N.G., Austin, 1981-83; sr. U.S. rep. NATO Panel No. 2, Brussels, 1971-74; mem. NATO Standardization Group, Brussels, 1979-81, NATO Armaments Group, 1979-81, ret., 1983; state engr. Tex. Adj. Gen.'s Dept., Austin, 1983—; test dir. Laser Guided Weapons in Close Air Support, 1972-73; Pentagon project officer XM-1 Tank Program, 1970-73. Decorated Legion of Merit with oak leaf cluster, Bronze Star with oak leaf cluster, various U.S. and fgn. decorations. Mem. Nat. Soc. Profl. Engrs., Am. Soc. Indsl. Security, Nat. Assn. Chiefs of Police, Am. Def. Preparedness Assn., Assn. U.S. Army, Mil. Order World Wars (dep. comdr. 1983-84). Republican. Baptist. Lodges: Rotary, Masons, Shrine. Office: Adj Gen Dept PO Box 5218 Austin TX 78763

WILLIAMS, THOMAS EUGENE, pediatric hematologist-oncologist; b. Texarkana, Ark., May 13, 1936; s. Thomas Earle and Frankie Jo (Garner) W.; B.A., Yale, 1958; M.D., U. Tex. Southwestern Med. Sch., 1962; m. Peggy Jane O'Neill, May 31, 1958; children—Thomas Eugene, Elizabeth Anne, James David. Rotating intern Hermann Hosp., Houston, 1962-63; pediatric resident Children's Med. Center, Dallas, 1963-65; fellow pediatric hematology U. Va. Sch. Medicine, Charlottesville, 1967-68; research asso. Cancer Research Lab., U. Va., Charlottesville, 1968-69; asst. prof. pediatrics and pathology U. Tex. Health Sci. Center at San Antonio, 1969-72, asso. prof. pediatrics and asst. prof. pathology, 1972-73, assoc. prof. pediatrics and assoc. prof. pathology, 1973-79; med. dir. Santa Rosa Children's Hosp. Cancer Research and Treatment Center, 1974-79, 85—; med. dir. South Tex. Comprehensive Hemophilia Center, 1977-79; sr. clin. research scientist Burroughs Wellcome Co., 1979-85; clin. assoc. prof. pediatrics U. N.C. Sch. Medicine, 1979-85; clin. fellow bone marrow transplantation program Johns Hopkins U. Sch. Medicine, Balt., 1985; assoc. prof. pediatrics U. Tex. Health Sci. Ctr., San Antonio, 1985—. Served to lt. comdr. USN, 1965-67. Named Intern of the Year, Hermann Hosp., 1962-63; Am. Cancer Soc. Advanced Clin. fellow, 1968-69, 70-72; Am. Soc. Pharmacology and Exptl. Therapeutics travel awardee, 1968; diplomate Am. Bd. Pediatrics, Am. Bd. Pediatric Hematology-Oncology. Mem. World Fedn. Hemophilia, Am. Soc. Clin. Oncology, Am. Assn. for Cancer Research, Am. Soc. Hematology, Am. Assn. for Cancer Edn., Am. Fedn. Clin. Research, Am. Acad. Pediatrics, Children's Cancer Study Group. Episcopalian. Contbr. articles to med. jours. Office: 7703 Floyd Curl Dr San Antonio TX 78284

WILLIAMS, THOMAS RICE, banker; b. Atlanta, Sept. 14, 1928; s. George K. and Isabel (Rice) W.; B.S. in Indsl. Engring., Ga. Inst. Tech., 1950; M.S. in Indsl. Mgmt., MIT, 1954; m. Loraine Plant, Mar. 18, 1950; children—Janet, Susan, Thomas Rice. Indsl. engr. Dan River Mills, Danville, Va., 1950-53; dir. indsl. engring. Riegel Textile Corp., Ware Shoals, S.C., 1954-59; v.p. Bruce Payne & Assos., Inc., N.Y.C., 1959-64; asst. to pres. Patchogue-Plymouth Co., N.Y.C., 1964-65; from v.p. to exec. v.p. Nat. City Bank, Cleve., 1965-72; pres. First Nat. Bank Atlanta, 1972-76, chief exec. officer, 1976—, chmn. bd., 1977—; pres. First Nat. Holding Corp. (now First Atlanta Corp.), 1974—, chmn. bd., 1977—; chmn. First Wachovia Corp., 1985—; dir. Nat. Service Industries, Inc.; dir. Nat. Life Ins. Co., Equifax, Inc., ConAgra, Inc., BellSouth Corp., Eastern Air Lines, Ga. Power Co.; dir.-at-large VISA Inc. Trustee Atlanta U. Center, 1977—, Ga. Tech. Found., 1975—, Agnes Scott Coll., 1975—, Atlanta Arts Alliance, 1976—; bd. dirs. Fulton County unit Am. Cancer Soc., 1973—; bd. dirs. Atlanta Area council Boy Scouts Am., 1973-75, adv. bd. mem., 1975—; bd. dirs. Central Atlanta Progress; adv. bd. Christian Council Met. Atlanta, 1977—. Mem. Conf. Bd., Assn. Res. City Bankers (dir.), Am. Inst. Banking, Assn. Bank Holding Cos., Internat. Monetary Conf., Atlanta C. of C. (immediate past pres.), Gridiron Soc., Sigma Alpha Epsilon. Episcopalian. Clubs: Rotary (dir. 1976-79), Capital City (gov. 1977-80), Piedmont Driving, Commerce (dir. 1976—), Peachtree Golf (Atlanta); Union (Cleve.); Farmington Country (Charlottesville, Va.). Office: 1st Nat Bank of Atlanta 2 Peachtree St NW Atlanta GA 30383

WILLIAMS, THOMAS THACKERY, educator; b. N.C., Mar. 13, 1925; s. George and Eliza Williams; B.S., Agrl. & Tech. U. N.C., 1948; M.S., U. Ill., 1949; Ph.D. (sr. research asst. 1952-54), Ohio State U., 1955; postgrad. Case Inst. Tech., 1957; 2 children. Instr. agrl. econs. Tuskegee (Ala.) Inst., 1949-50, asst. to dean agr., 1950-52; asst. prof., chmn. agrl. econs. So. U., Baton Rouge, 1955-66, prof., chmn. agrl. econs. and dir. research and devel., 1959-66, adminstrv. asst. and prof. agrl. econs., 1969-80, dir. Inst. for Internat. Econ. Devel., 1972-80, prof. and adminstrv. asst. for fed. programs, 1972-80; dir. Human Resources and Devel. Center, Tuskegee Institute, Ala., 1980—; OEO Title III program coordinator, 1969-76; cons. in field. Vice pres. Baton Rouge Sister City Internat., 1978, chmn., 1977; mem. Baton Rouge Bd. Christian Giving to Disadvantaged Children, 1976; mem. Scotlandville Devel. Adv. Council, 1976; pres. So. Heights Property Owners Assn., 1970, Baton Rouge Human Relations Com., 1970; mem. Fulbright Selection Com. for Manpower, 1966; La. Manpower Adv. Com., 1969; nat. Fulbright adv. bd. Inst. Internat. Edn., 1970, others. Farm Found. grantee, Russia, 1970, Brazil, 1973; Fulbright Travel grantee, 1967; Ford Found. grantee, 1967-68; AID grantee, 1968; CIES Fulbright Lecture grantee, Tel Aviv, 1967; USOE Fulbright Teaching grantee, Serdang, Malaysia, 1966-67; Fulbright Travel grantee, 1966; Equitable Life Assurance Soc. grantee, 1961; others. Mem. Am. Assn. Agrl. Econs., Nat. Council Social Studies, Acad. Polit. Sci., So. Assn. Profl. Workers, Southwestern Social Sci. Assn., Internat. Devel. Assn. Institutors, Nat. Assn. Land Grant Colls. and State Univs., Assn. Black Economists, Assn. U.S. Univ. Dirs. of Internat. Agrl. Programs, Am. Agrl. Econs. Assn., Western Econs. Assn., Am. Assn. Univ. Adminstrs., SE Consortium for Internat. Devel., Omega Psi Phi named Man of Yr., Omega Psi Phi, 1964, Regional Man of Yr., 1969; Sigma Pi Phi. Club: Kiwanis. Contbr. articles to profl. jours. Address: PO Box 681 Tuskegee Institute AL 36088

WILLIAMS, TIMOTHY JAMES, sanctuary administrator, naturalist; b. Covington, Ky., Sept. 22, 1950; s. Carl Henry and Marcella Virginia (Neff) W.; m. Deborah Louise LeForce, Feb. 15, 1975. B.S. in Biology, No. Ky. State U., 1974. Waiter various restaurants in No. Ky.; park aide Mammoth Cave Nat. Park, 1971; sanctuary mgr. Nat. Audubon Soc.'s Clyde E. Buckley Wildlife Sanctuary, Frankfort, Ky., 1975—. Mem. Nat. Audubon Soc., Assn. of Interpretive Naturalists, Ky. Assn. Environ. Edn. (bd. dirs.).

WILLIAMS, WAYNE KARLTON, petroleum geologist, petroleum engineer; b. Chattanooga, Feb. 5, 1957; s. Frank Williams and Margaret Ruth (Stroud) W.; m. Janice Lynn Marshall, July 9, 1977; 1 child, Steven Marshall. B.A. in Geology, U. Tenn., 1978; M.S. in Geology, Memphis State U., 1980. Prodn. geologist The Dow Chem. Corp., Bay City, Tex., 1980-82, Apache Corp., Houston, 1982-83; prodn. mgr. S. Ranch Oil Co., St. Louis, 1983-84; logging geologist IDL, Inc., Houston, 1985—. Mem. Am. Assn. of Petroleum Geologists, Houston Geol. Soc., Soc. Petroleum Engrs. Republican. Baptist. Avocations: mineral and fossil collecting; outdoor activities. Home: 7829 Windward Passage Houston TX 77072

WILLIAMS, WESLEY KEITH, educator; b. DuQuoin, Ill., Aug. 7, 1953; s. Benjamin Wesley and Jessica Lovedith (Newman) W.; m. Carol Lynn Wise, June 13, 1975; 1 child, Allison Suzanne. B.S., Union U., Jackson, Tenn., 1975; M.R.E., Southwestern Bapt. Theol. Sem., 1977. Minister of edn. First Bapt. Ch., Wills Point, Tex., 1978-80, Englewood Bapt. Ch., Jackson, Tenn., 1980-83; adult cons. Miss. Bapt. Conv., Jackson, 1984—. Mem. Am. Soc. Tng. and Devel., Southwestern Bapt. Religious Edn. Assn., Miss. Bapt. Religious Edn. Assn. Avocation: running. Home: 124 Spanish Moss Dr Clinton MS 39056 Office: Miss Bapt Conv PO Box 530 515 Mississippi St Jackson MS 39205

WILLIAMSON, DAVID GLENN, JR., health service company executive; b. Rock Hill, S.C., Feb. 20, 1929; s. David Glenn and Ola Mae (McMillan) W.; m. Betty Owen, Oct. 18, 1952; children—Beth Ann, Mary Glynn, David Glenn, III. A.B., Wofford Coll., Spartanburg, S.C., 1950; M.H.A., Med. Coll. Va., Richmond, 1957. Adminstrv. resident Riverside Hosp., Newport News, Va., 1951-52, Norfolk (Va.) Gen. Hosp., 1952; adminstrv. asst. Med. Coll. Va. Hosp., 1955; adminstr. Bedford (Va.) County Community Hosp., 1955-61; adminstr., exec. v.p. Lewis Gale Hosp., Salem, Va.; also exec. v.p. Lewis Gale Clinic, 1961-74; v.p. Hosp. Corp. Am., Nashville, 1974-75, sr. v.p., 1975-79, exec. v.p., from 1979, now vice chmn.; chmn. study com. nursing Nat. Commn. Productivity, 1974; alt. health industry adv. com. Cost of Living Council, 1974. Chmn. Roanoke Valley chpt. ARC, 1966-68; exec. commnr. Appalachian Regional Blood Program.; Pres. Roanoke Boosters Club, 1970-71; campaign chmn. United Fund Roanoke Valley, 1967, pres., 1968. Served to 1st lt. USAF, 1952-55. Named Young Man of Year Bedford, Va. Jr. C. of C., 1956. Mem. Am. Coll. Hosp. Adminstrs., Fedn. Am. Hosps. (pres. 1975), Am. Hosp. Assn. (trustee 1980—), Va. Hosp. Assn. (pres. 1971), Tenn. Hosp. Assn., Med. Coll. Va. Alumni Assn. Clubs: Belle Meade Country; Hillwood Country (Nashville); Capitol Hill (Washington). Office: PO Box 550 Nashville TN 37202*

WILLIAMSON, ERNEST LAVONE, petroleum company executive; b. Perryton, Tex., Sept. 10, 1924; s. Ernest and Mabel Robert (Donnell) W.; B.S. in E.E., U. Okla., 1950; student Hill's Bus. Coll., 1943; m. Gertrude Florence Watkins, Dec. 2, 1950; children—Richard Dean, Judith Watkins, Mary Nan, David Ernest. Sales and service rep. Hughes Tool Co., 1950-52; with land dept. Phillips Petroleum Co., 1952-54; with La. Land & Exploration Co., New Orleans, 1954—, exec. v.p., 1967-74, pres., 1974-83, chief exec. officer, 1984—, now chmn. bd.; dir. Hibernia Nat. Bank, New Orleans, Halliburton Co. Mem. adv. bd. Salvation Army, 1971—; bd. dirs. World Trade Ctr., New Orleans, Jr. Achievement. Served with U.S. Army, 1943-46; PTO. Mem. Am. Assn. Petroleum Landmen, Ind. Petroleum Assn. Am., Mid-Continent Oil and Gas Assn. (chmn.), Am. Petroleum Inst. Presbyn. Clubs: Plimsol, Petroleum, Internat. House, New Orleans Country (New Orleans); Tchefuncta Country; Denver. Office: La Land & Exploration Co PO Box 60350 New Orleans LA 70160

WILLIAMSON, HENRY GASTON, JR., banker; b. Whiteville, N.C., Aug. 18, 1947; s. Henry Gaston and Elizabeth Lee (Brittain) W.; m. Nancy Thomas Williamson, Aug. 30, 1969; children—Leigh, Clay. B.S. in Bus. Adminstrn., East Carolina U., 1969, M.B.A., 1972; grad. Young Execs. Inst., Grad. Sch. Bus., U. N.C., 1979. Vice pres., regional loan adminstr. Branch Banking & Trust Co., Wilson, N.C., 1977-80, v.p., city exec., Tarboro, N.C., 1980-81, sr. v.p., mgr. bank ops. div., Wilson, 1981, exec. v.p. ops./human resources div. mgr., 1981-83, sr. exec. v.p., adminstrv. group mgr., 1983—, dir. BB&T Ctr. Mgmt. Devel., East Carolina U., 1983—; dir. Branch Corp. Author: American Antiques: A Case Study (1st place Robert Morris Assocs. 1973). Bd. dirs. Wilson Heart Fund Assn., 1983, pres., 1985-86; bd. dirs. East Carolina U. Found., Inc. 1983—; bd. dirs. Wilson County chpt. ARC, 1984—; mem. exec. com. East Carolina council Boy Scouts Am., 1984—; past pres. Wilson Kiwanis. Mem. Wilson C. of C. (chmn. health care cost containment com. 1983—, v.p. 1986), Beta Gamma Sigma, Omicron Delta Epsilon, Delta Sigma

Pi (scholarship key). Republican. Baptist. Club: Wilson Country. Office: 223 W Nash St Wilson NC 27893

WILLIAMSON, HORACE HAMPTON, architect; b. Butts County, Ga., May 4, 1924; s. Hampton Daughtry and Pearl (Griffin) W.; B.S., Ga. Inst. Tech., 1951, B.Arch., 1952; M.S., M.Arch., Rensselaer Poly. Inst., 1969; Ph.D. in Psychology, U. Utah, 1975; m. Doris Stewart, Nov. 27, 1947; children—Tom S., Larry M., J. Douglas. Draftsman, Aeck Assos., Atlanta, 1948-49; chief designer Woodward and Robert, Spartanburg, S.C., 1952-58; pvt. archtl. practice, Highlands, N.C., 1958-71; from instr. to asso. prof. Clemson (S.C.) U., part-time 1959-71; asso. prof. architecture Tex. Tech. U., Lubbock, 1973—; pvt. archtl. practice, Lubbock, 1978—; campus planning officer Clemson U., 1960-71; design and planning cons. TVA, 1963-65; design cons. psychology dept. Fisk U., Nashville, 1974—; prin. works include Spartanburg Sr. High Sch., Catholic Mission Chapel competition, Park Hills Elem. Sch., Spartanburg. Served with USMC, 1943-46. Recipient 1st prize Louisville Home Show nat. residence competition, 1960, citation Nat. High Sch. design competition, 1958, elem. sch. design competition, 1953; Commn. prize Internat. Cath. Mission Chapel design competition, 1960; NIMH fellow, 1971-73. Mem. Tex. Soc. Architects. Methodist. Club: Lake Ridge Country (Lubbock). Co-author: Creativity in the Home, 1973; contbr. articles to profl. publs. Home: 2122 53d St Lubbock TX 79412 Office: 3403 73d St Lubbock TX 79423

WILLIAMSON, HUGH JACKSON, statistician; b. Dallas, Jan. 12, 1943; s. Hugh and Edna (Mays) W.; m. Sheri Lynn Wooten, Jan. 19, 1980; 1 child, Laura Elizabeth. B.A. in Math., U. Tex., 1965, M.A. in Math., 1967, Ph.D. in Mech. Engring., 1975. Engr., scientist Tracor, Inc. and subs. Austin, Tex., 1967-73; research engr., scientist assoc. U. Tex.-Austin, 1973-77; sr. scientist Radian Corp., Austin, 1977—. Contbr. articles, reports to profl. publs. Mem. Am. Statis. Assn., Sigma Xi, Phi Kappa Phi. Baptist. Avocations: reading; gourmet cooking; music appreciation; golf. Home 2401 Indian Trail Austin TX 78703 Office: Radian Corp PO Box 9948 Austin TX 78766

WILLIAMSON, JAMES THOMAS, JR., automobile agy. exec.; b. Mobile, Ala., Aug. 4, 1935; s. James Thomas and Sadie Louise (Yerkes) W.; student U. Ala., 1953-54, Spring Hill Coll., 1954; m. Lavonne Harris; children—Sandra, Tom III, Renee. Office mgr. Rowe Engring. Co., Mobile, 1956-58; chief estimator Folmar & Flinn Inc., Montgomery, Ala., 1958-59; v.p., gen. mgr. Jack Hamel Volkswagen, Montgomery, 1960-72; owner, pres. Roebuck Mazda Inc., Birmingham, Ala., 1973—; mem. Volkswagen Nat. Dealer Council, 1975, 76. Mem. Automobile Dealers Assn., Ala. Automobile Dealers Assn., Birmingham Automobile Dealers Assn. (pres. 1981-83), Mazda Motors of Am. East (chmn. nat. dealer council 1979, 1982-83). Republican. Roman Catholic. Home: 3512 Kingshill Rd Mountain Brook AL 35223 Office: Roebuck Mazda Inc 9008 Parkway E Birmingham AL 35206

WILLIAMSON, JOHN NICHOLS, oil company official; b. Texarkana, Ark., Feb. 18, 1947; s. Jacob Evans and Mary Gene W.; m. Kay Longino, Oct. 4, 1969; 1 son, Chad. B.B.A., S.E. Ark. U., 1970; M.S. in Interdisciplinary Studies, East Tex. State U., 1981. Secondary mktg. dir. and br. coordinator Tyler Savs. and Loan (Tex.), 1976-79; area personnel adminstr. Gen. Telephone Co. of Southwest, Texarkana, Tex., 1979-80; tng. mgr. Santa Fe Minerals, Dallas, 1980—. Instr. supervisory skills CPR and first aid, ARC; adv. council Longhorn dist. Boy Scouts Am.; Sunday sch. tchr., mem. adv. bd. nursery dept. First Baptist Ch.; mem. Timberline Homeowners Assn. Mem. Am. Soc. Tng. and Devel., Assn. Record Mgrs. and Adminstrs., Dallas Personnel Assn. Clubs: Sen-I Judo, Mid-cities Running.

WILLIAMSON, JUANITA V., English educator; b. Shelby, Miss.; d. John M. and Alice E. (McAllister) W. B.A., LeMoyne-Owen Coll., 1938; M.A., Atlanta U., 1940; Ph.D., U. Mich., 1961. Asst. prof. English, LeMoyne-Owen Coll., Memphis, 1947-56, prof., 1956—, Disting. Service prof. English, 1977—; adj. prof. Memphis State U., 1975—; vis. prof. Ball State U., Muncie, Ind., 1963-64, U. Wis.-Milw., summer 1973, U. Tenn., Knoxville, summer 1975; linguist French Inst. Atlanta U., summer 1963, Hampton Inst., Va., summer 1964, U. Wis., Milw., summer 1966, 67, Memphis State U., summer 1969, 73, 75, U. Ark.-Pine Bluff, summer 1981. Editor: A Various Language, 1971. Contbr. articles to profl. jours. Mem. exec. com. United Way, Memphis, 1953-56; cons. Girl Scouts U.S., Memphis, 1956; bd. dirs. Integration Service, Memphis, 1952-58; mem. exec. com. hist. council United Ch. Christ, 1976. Recipient Citation Excellence in Edn., Memphis City Council, 1973; Rockefeller Found. fellow, 1949-51; Ford Found. fellow, 1954; HEW grantee, 1964-68. Mem. MLA (program com., minority affairs com.), Nat. Council Tchrs. English (coll. sect. exec. com. 1976-79), Am. Dialect Soc. (exec. com. 1979-82), Conf. on Coll. Composition and Communication (exec. com. 1969-71), Delta Sigma Theta. Home: 1217 Cannon St Memphis TN 38106 Office: LeMoyne-Owen Coll 807 Walker Ave Memphis TN 38126

WILLIAMSON, LOWELL ALLEN, educational administrator; b. Savannah, Ga., May 21, 1948; s. Lowell Franklin and Imogene (Allen) W.; m. Marie Aleen Rahn, Mar. 25, 1972; children—Lori Aleen, Amy Marie. B.S. in Indsl. Mgmt., Ga. Inst. Tech., 1970; M.Ed. in Pub. Sch. Adminstrn. and Supervision, Ga. So. Coll., 1976, Ed.S. in Adminstrn. and Supervision, 1979. Tchr., chmn. math. dept. Tompkins High Sch., Savannah, Ga., 1970-71, tchr., coach, 1971-74, STAR tchr., 1974; asst. prin., instructional dir. Appling County High Sch., Baxley, Ga., 1974-82; asst. prin. Ware County Sr. High Sch., Waycross, Ga., 1982—; instr. math. Brewton-Parker Coll., Mt. Vernon, Ga., 1980-82, Waycross Jr. Coll. (Ga.), 1983—. Mem. Ga. Tech. Nat. Alumni Assn., 8th Dist. Principals Assn. (pres. 1983-84), Phi Kappa Phi, Kappa Delta Pi, Pi Mu Epsilon. Methodist. Lodge: Baxley Kiwanis (sec., treas. 1975-77). Home: 2604 Winchester Rd Waycross GA 31501 Office: 2553 Cherokee Ave Waycross GA 31501

WILLIAMSON, MICHAEL LEE, oil company executive; b. Urbana, Ill., Nov. 8, 1955; s. Lee Foster and Joyce Ann (Vergason) W.; m. Carol Collins Standridge, June 5, 1976; children—Bridget Anne, Jamie Michelle. B.S. in Geology U. So. La., 1978. Geol. asst. Great So. Oil & Gas, Lafayette, La., 1977-78; retail mgr. Gayle Oil Co., New Iberia, La., 1978-79; tech.-service rep. Milchem Inc., Lafayette, 1979-82; staff engr. Milchem Internat. Ltd., Athens, Greece, 1982-83, dist. tech. supr., Cairo, Egypt, 1983-84, area tech. mgr., 1984—. Mem. Am. Assn. Petroleum Geologists. Republican. Episcopalian. Office: Care Milchem Internat Ltd PO Box 22111 Houston TX 77027

WILLIAMSON, MIRIAM BEDINGER, medical librarian; b. Asheville, N.C., Nov. 18, 1919; d. Robert Dabney and Mary Julia (Smith) Bedinger; m. Robert Lewis Williamson, June 9, 1944 (div. June 1969); children—Robert Lewis, John Bedinger, Ellen Richmond, Thomas Reid. B.A., Agnes Scott Coll., 1941; M. Christian Edn., Presbyn. Sch. Christian Edn., 1943; postgrad. U. Tenn., 1969. Ch. social worker, kindergarten tchr. N.E. Community Ctr., Italian Presbyn. Mission, Kansas City, Mo., 1943-44; med. librarian Blount Meml. Hosp., Maryville, Tenn., 1972—; tchr. vocat. edn. programs, adult reading program Alcoa, Blount County, Maryville sch. systems. Mem. Blount County unit Bread for the World; vol. worker Contact Teleministries of Blount County. Grantee Library Medicine, HEW, 1973, HHS, 1981, Blount County unit Am. Cancer Soc., 1982; recipient Outstanding Service award Vocat. Edn. Dept., 1983, 85. Mem. Med. Library Assn., Tenn. Hosp. Assn., Tenn. Health Sci. Library Assn., Knoxville Area Health Sci. Library Consortium. Democrat. Presbyterian. Home: 103 Hopi Dr Maryville TN 37801 Office: 907 Smoky Mountain Hwy Maryville TN 37801

WILLIAMSON, RALPH EDWARD, plant physiologist, researcher, educator; b. Wilson, N.C., Feb. 28, 1923; s. John Thomas and Libby W. (Lamm) W.; m. Doris Lamm, Dec. 21, 1946; children—Ralph Edward, Barbara Jean. B.S., N.C. State U., 1948; M.S., U. Wis., 1950, Ph.D., 1958. Botanist Chem. Corps, Dept. Army, Frederick, Md., 1948-49, plant physiologist, 1950-51, 53-57; Wis. Alumni research asst. U. Wis., Madison, 1952; plant physiologist, soil and water conservation research div. Dept. Agr., Raleigh, N.C., 1957-74, Tobacco Research Lab., Dept. Agr., Oxford, N.C., 1974—; assoc. prof. botany N.C. State U., Raleigh, 1967—. Served with USAAF, 1943-46. Decorated Air medal; Rockefeller fellow, 1953. Mem. Am. Soc. Plant Physiologists, Am. Soc. Agronomy, Soil Sci. Soc. Am., Tobacco Research Chemists, Tobacco Workers, Sigma Xi, Phi Kappa Phi, Sigma Pi Alpha, Phi Sigma. Presbyterian. Contbr. articles to profl. jours.; asst. editor Jour. Agrl. Water Mgmt., 1976—. Home: 716 Currituck Dr Raleigh NC 27609 Office: Route 2 Box 16G Oxford NC 27565

WILLIAMSON, THOMAS GARNETT, nuclear engineering and engineering physics educator; b. Quincy, Mass., Jan. 27, 1934; s. Robert Burwell and Elizabeth B. (McNeer) W.; m. Kaye Darlan Love, Aug. 16, 1961; children—Allen, Sarah, David. B.S., Va. Mil. Inst., 1955; M.S., Rensselaer Poly. Inst., 1957; Ph.D., U. Va., 1960. Asst. prof. nuclear engring. and engring. physics dept. U. Va., Charlottesville, 1960-62, assoc. prof., 1962-69, prof., 1969—, chmn. dept., 1977—; with Gen. Atomic (Calif.), 1965, Combustion Engring., Windsor, Conn., 1970-71, Los Alamos Sci. Lab., 1969, Nat. Bur. Standards, Gaithersburg, Md., 1984-85; cons. Philippine Atomic Energy Commn., 1963, Va. Electric & Power Co., 1975—, Babcock & Wilcox, Lynchburg, Va., 1975—. Vestryman Ch. of Our Savior, Charlottesville, Va. Fellow Am. Nuclear Soc.; mem. AAAS, Am. Soc. Engring. Edn., Sigma Xi, Tau Beta Pi. Episcopalian. Home: 2234 Brandywine Dr Charlottesville VA 22901 Office: Univ of Va Reactor Facility Charlottesville VA 22901

WILLIAMSON, WILLIAM PAUL, JR., journalist; b. Des Moines, Mar. 30, 1929; s. William Paul and Florence Alice (Dawson) W.; m. Vania Torres Nogueira, Nov. 27, 1959; children—MaryLiz, Jon Thadeus, Margaret Ann. Student, Mexico City Coll., 1952, U. Havanna, 1955; B.A., U. No. Iowa, 1953; M.A., U. Iowa, 1954. Editor, Brazilian Bus., Rio de Janeiro, 1958-60; mng. ptnr. Editora Mory Ltda., Rio de Janeiro, 1960-79; editor Brazil Herald, Rio de Janeiro, 1960-80; exec. dir. Inter Am. Press Assn., Miami, Fla., 1981—, dir., 1966-80, chmn. awards com., 1975-80. Editor for Brazil, Fodor's South America, 1970-79; contbr. articles to various newspapers and mags. Pres., Am. Soc. Rio de Janeiro, 1968; bd. dirs. Instituto Brasil-Estados Unidos, Rio de Janeiro, 1977-80; bd. dirs. Am. C. of C. for Brazil, Rio de Janeiro, 1964-68. Served with USMC, 1946-48. Decorated Order of Rio Branco (Brazil); recipient Citizen of Rio de Janeiro award State Legislature, 1975; Hon. Carioca award O Globo Newspaper, Rio de Janeiro, 1972; Ralph Greenberg award Am. Soc. of Rio de Janeiro, 1977. Mem. Am. Soc. Assn. Execs., South Fla. Soc. Assn. Execs. (v.p.), Sigma Delta Chi, Kappa Tau Alpha. Clubs: American, Yacht, Gavea Golf and Country (Rio de Janeiro). Home: 2600 Castilla Isle Fort Lauderdale FL 33301 Office: Inter Am Press Assn 2911 NW 39th St Miami FL 33142

WILLIFORD, LAWRENCE BRUMBY, banker; b. Atlanta, Apr. 19, 1953; s. William Bailey and Amelia Cadwallader (Brumby) W.; m. Helen Baskin Hatcher, Oct. 1, 1983; 1 child, L. Grier. B.B.A., U. Ga., 1975. With Robinson-Humphrey Co., Inc., Atlanta, 1978-85, v.p. pub. fin., 1982-85; Southeastern regional mgr. for pub. fin. Mfr.'s Hanover Trust Co. N.Y., 1985—. Mem. Phi Delta Theta. Episcopalian. Clubs: Benedicts, Capital City. Home: 4000 E Brookhaven Dr NE Atlanta GA 30319 Office: Suite 1850 Peachtree Ctr 230 Peachtree St NW Atlanta GA 30303

WILLIFORD, WILLIAM BAILEY, corporation executive; b. Sanford, Fla., July 12, 1921; s. William Francis and Frances Elizabeth (Williford) Bailey; student U. Florence (Italy), 1945, U. Tenn., 1946, 46-47, U. Ga., 1947-48, U. Wis., 1960; m. Julia (Benton) Swann Miller, June 23, 1969; 1 son by previous marriage, Lawrence Brumby Williford. Pub. relations exec. with various corps. and govt. agys., 1949-68; pres. Cherokee Pub. Co., 1968-83; chmn. bd. Larlin Corp., 1983—; lectr. creative writing Emory U., Atlanta, 1964. Mem. bd. counselors Oxford Coll., 1972-78. Served with USAAF, 1942-46, USAF, 1950-52; maj. USAF Res. ret. Recipient spl. award Dixie Council Authors and Journalists, 1976. Named Ky. Col., 1968. Mem. Ga., Atlanta (trustee 1960-66), Newton County (trustee 1971-75, chmn. bd. 1971-73) hist. socs., SAR, Ga. Trust for Historic Preservation, Sumter Historic Preservation Soc., Inquiry Club, Phi Delta Theta. Episcopalian (Lay reader 1954-62, vestryman 1972-75). Clubs: Commerce, Capital City (Atlanta). Author: Americus Through the Years, 1960, rev. edit. 1975; Williford and Allied Families, 1961; Peachtree Street, Atlanta, 1962; The Glory of Covington, 1973. Compiler: A Source Book on the Early History of Cuthbert and Randolph County, Georgia, 1982. Home: 1164 Floyd St Covington GA 30209 Office: 1151 Monticello St Covington GA 30209

WILLIG, BILLY WINSTON, machine shop and foundry executive; b. Temple, Tex., Mar. 11, 1929; s. Bruno William and Mary (Barth) W.; student San Angelo Jr. Coll., 1946-47; B.S. in Mech. Engring., U. Tex., 1951; m. Lanelle Brooks, Sept. 11, 1951; children—Bruce Wayne, Jana Lynn. With Western Iron Works, Inc., San Angelo, Tex., 1951—, gen. mgr., pres., chmn. bd., 1971—. Skipper, Sea Scout Ship 22, Boy Scouts Am., 1965—; chmn. Lake Nasworthy Adv. Bd., 1968-70, Area Environ. Council, 1973-74. Trustee, San Angelo Ind. Sch. Dist., 1966—, v.p., 1969, 72, sec., treas., 1968, 71, 73, pres., 1975, 76. Bd. dirs. San Angelo Govtl. Computer Ctr., Tex. Sch. Service Found.; chmn. Unemployment Compensation Trust, 1983; chmn. Pvt. Industry Council, 1983—; bd. dirs. YMCA San Angelo, 1977, v.p., 1979, pres., 1980, chmn. bldg. com., 1979; v.p. San Angelo Industries, 1975-76, pres., 1976-79, dir., 1970—; pres. West Tex. Indsl. Devel. Corp., 1980—; mem. bd., exec. com. bd. Concho Valley council Boy Scouts Am., v.p. exploring, 1974-78, council commr., 1978-80, pres. council, 1981-83, recipient Silver Beaver award, 1975. Served with C.E., AUS, 1952-54. Recipient Vol. Indsl. Developer of Yr. award Tex. Indsl. Devel. Council, 1983. Mem. Tex. Mfrs. Assn., Tex. Assn. Bus., Tex. Assn. Pvt. Industry Councils (trustee 1985—), Tex. Assn. Sch. Bds. (exec. com. 1975-80, sec.-treas. 1983), Nat. Rifle Assn., C. of C. (dir. 1976-77, chmn. mfrs. com. 1976—, exec. bd. 1976—, pres. 1978; Citizen of Year 1979, chmn. hwy. com. 1986), Am. Foundry Soc., San Angelo Mfg. Assn. (pres. 1982—), Tex. PTA (hon. life). Presbyn. (deacon, elder, clk. session 1968-71, 76-77, 79-80). Mason (Shriner), Rotarian (sec. San Angelo 1973-74, v.p. 1978, pres. 1979-80, Rotarian of Yr. 1981). Club: Concho Yacht (past commodore San Angelo). Home: 1618 Shafter St San Angelo TX 76901 Office: 21 E 6th St San Angelo TX 76901

WILLINGHAM, JEANNE M., dance educator; b. Fresno, Calif., May 8, 1923; d. Harold F. and Gladys (Ellis) Maggart. Student Tex. Woman's U. Owner/tchr., Beaux Arts Dance Studio, Pampa, Tex.; artistic dir. Pampa Civic Ballet. Office: 315 N Nelson Pampa TX 79065

WILLINGHAM, ROBERT MARION, JR., university library curator, appraiser; b. Washington, Ga., Aug. 31, 1946; s. Robert Marion and Helen Pittard (Armour) W. Student Davidson Coll., 1964-66; A.B., West Ga. Coll., 1968; M.A., U. Ga., 1972; postgrad. Duke U., 1972-74; M.Librarianship, Emory U., 1978. Tchr. English, coach Wilkes Acad., Washington, 1970-72, 74-76; instr. English, Duke U., Durham, N.C., 1973-74; rare books specialist U. Ga. Libraries, Athens, 1976-79, curator rare books and manuscripts, 1979—; trustee Mary Willis Library, Washington, 1976—. Author: We Have This Heritage, 1969; No Jubilee, 1976; Georgiana, 1980; Touchdown, 1983; contbr. numerous articles to profl. jours. Councilman, City of Washington, 1975-83; bd. dirs. Washington-Wilkes Recreation Commn., 1976-79; pres. Washington-Wilkes Hist. Found., 1978-82, Young Preservationists of Ga., Atlanta, 1980—. Named Citizen of Yr. Rotary Club, Washington, 1977; Ford Found. fellow for grad. study, 1969. Mem. ALA, Assn. Coll. and Research Libraries (rare books and manuscripts sect.), Ga. Library Assn., So. Hist. Assn., Ga. Hist. Soc., Ga. Trust for Historic Preservation (dir. 1980—), Southeastern Bibliophiles (dir. 1983—). Methodist. Home: 405 S Alexander Ave Washington GA 30673 Office: Univ Ga Libraries Jackson St Athens GA 30602

WILLIS, BERNICE HOLLEY, educational administrator; b. New Haven, Mar. 2, 1938; d. William A. and Vermelle (Campbell) Holley; m. Carroll Tinsley Willis, Jr., July 3, 1965; 1 dau., Holley Vermelle. B.A., Oberlin Coll., 1959; M.A., Vanderbilt U., 1963; Ed.D., Duke U., 1976. Supr. curriculum and tng. Wright Sch., Durham, N.C., 1966-69; adj. prof. N.C. Central U., Durham, 1970-71; assoc. dir. programs Learning Inst. N.C., Durham, 1972-78; asst. prof. N.C. A&T State U., Greensboro, 1978-80; coordinator policy analysis S.E. Regional Council for Ednl. Improvement, Research Triangle Park, N.C., 1980-81, dep. dir., 1981-85; mgr. dissemination and tech. program Southeastern Ednl. Improvement Lab., Research Triangle Park, 1985—; cons. in field; field reader U.S. Dept. Edn., 1980, 81, 83, 84, 86; mem. Nat. Task Force on Paraprofl. Cert., Washington, 1979-80. Author: (report) Schooling and Technology, 5 2 vols., 1983-85; editor: Visions, Issues and Reality, 1981; author tng. modules. Pres., Durham Mental Health Assn., 1976. Mem. Council Exceptional Children, World Future Soc., Assn. for Edn. Young Children, N.C. Council Children with Behavior Disorders, Links Inc., Delta Sigma Theta. Democrat. Home: 33 Stoneridge Pl Durham NC 27705 Office: Southeastern Ednl ImprovementLab PO Box 12746 200 Park Plaza Research Triangle Park NC 27709

WILLIS, DENNIS DARYL, cons. mining engr.; b. Norton, Va., Apr. 29, 1948; s. Virgil Hyman and Reva May (Hubbard) W.; B.S. in Civil Engring., Va. Poly. Inst. and State U., 1970; m. Elizabeth J. Short, July 15, 1967; children—Kristi René, Kimberly Denise. Project engr. Island Creek Coal Co., Keen Mountain, Va., 1970-73; design engr. Wiley & Wilson, Inc., consultants, Lynchburg, Va., 1973-74; v.p., dir., head mining div. Thompson & Litton, Inc., consultants, Wise, Va., 1974-80, pres., 1980-85; pres. Highland Land & Mineral Co., Inc., Willis Enterprises, Corpotal, Inc.; founder, pres. Sheen & Assocs., P.C., Cons., Norton, Va. Recipient Cons. Engrs. Council/Va. engring. design excellence award for Sediment Structure, 1979. Registered profl. engr., Va., Ky., Tenn., W.Va.; recipient Aviation award State of Va., 1985. Mem. ASCE, Cons. Engrs. Council (v.p. Western div. Va., mem. energy com., chmn. mining com.), Soc. Mining Engrs., Profl. Engrs. in Pvt. Practice, Nat. Soc. Profl. Engrs., Va. Surface Mine and Reclamation Assn. (dir., vice-chmn.), Wise Jaycees (sec. 1974-75), Va. Soc. Profl. Engrs. Baptist. Club: Lions. Contbr. articles to profl. publs. Home: 513 Chestnut St Norton VA 24273 Office: PO Box 1307 Wise VA 24293

WILLIS, ISAAC, dermatologist; b. Albany, Ga., July 13, 1940; s. R. L. and Susie (Miller) W.; B.S., Morehouse Coll., 1961; M.D., Howard U., 1965; m. Alliene Horne, June 12, 1965; children—Isaac Willis, Alliric Willis. Intern, Phila. Gen. Hosp., 1965-66; resident in dermatology Howard U., 1966-67, U. Pa., 1967-69; asso. in dermatology U. Pa. Sch. Medicine, 1969-70; asst. attending physician Phila. Gen. Hosp., 1969-70; research assoc., clin. instr. U. Calif. Sch. Medicine, San Francisco, 1970-72; asst. prof. dermatolgoy Johns Hopkins U. Sch. Medicine, 1972-73; asst. prof. dermatology Howard U. Coll. Medicine, 1972-75; asst. prof. dermatology Emory U. Sch. Medicine, 1973-75; chief dermatology VA Hosp., Atlanta, 1973-82; assoc. prof. dermatology Emory U. Sch. Medicine, 1975-82; prof. dermatology Morehouse Sch. Medicine, Atlanta, 1982—; bd. dirs. gen. med. study sect. NIH, 1985-89; panel mem. grants rev. panel U.S. Environ. Health Agy. Bd. med. dirs. Atlanta Lupus Erythematosus Found.; bd. dirs. Skin Cancer Found. Mem. Soc. Investigative Dermatology, Am. Soc. Photobiology, Am. Acad. Dermatology, Nat. Med. Assn., AMA, Am. Fedn. Clin. Research, Internat. Soc. Tropical Dermatology, So. Med. Assn., Pan Am. Med. Assn., Atlanta Dermatol. Assn., Am. Dermatol. Assn., Phi Beta Kappa. Contbr. articles to med. jours.; contbr. chpts. to textbooks. Home: 1141 Regency Rd NW Atlanta GA 30327 Office: 3280 Howell Mill Rd NW Suite 342 Atlanta GA 30327

WILLIS, JANE MARLOW, writer; b. Brandenburg, Ky., Mar. 8, 1942; d. James Mercer and Thelma (Marlow) Willis; B.A., So. Meth. U., 1964; postgrad. (Mark Ethridge fellow), U. N.C., 1966; B.S. in Fire Prevention, Eastern Ky. U., 1979; M.S. in Criminal Justice, Eastern Ky. U., 1985. Mem. staff Meade County Messenger, Brandenburg, 1964—, editor, 1966—, pub., 1978-83; freelance writer; firefighter. Former den mother local Cub Scouts; mem. drive com. Patton Mus. Fund, 1965; mem. local com. Ky. Bicentennial, 1973; patron Pioneer Playhouse, Danville, Ky., 1972; mem. Brandenburg Vol. Fire Dept., 1975; com. chmn. Brandenburg Unity Festival, 1975-76; patron Actors Theatre Louisville Les Boutiques de Noel, 1976; chmn. Fireman's Ball, 1977. Named Ky. col. Mem. Ky., Western Ky. (pres. 1971) press assns., Nat. Newspaper Assn., Internat. Soc. Fire Service Instrs., Women of Moose, Mensa, Sigma Delta Chi. Democrat. Methodist. Editor: Since April Third, 1974; Happy Holidays Cookbook, 1975; Summertime and the Cookin' is Easy, 1977; contbr. articles to profl. publs.

WILLIS, JERRY WELDON, educator; b. Tuscumbia, Ala., Jan. 27, 1943; s. Elbert Carter and Lavice Mae (McAlpin) W.; m. Deborrah Lynn Smithy, Dec. 31, 1977; 1 dau., Amy Elizabeth. B.A., Union U., 1966; Ph.D., U. Ala., 1970. Asst. prof. U. Guelph (Ont., Can.), 1972-74; asst. prof. U. Western Ont., London, 1974-76; asst. prof. U. B.C. (Can.), Vancouver, 1976-78; prof. edn. Tex. Tech U., Lubbock, 1978—. Mem. Am. Psychol. Assn., Assn. Ednl. Data Systems, Assn. Devel. of Computer Based Instructional Systems. Author: Peanut Butter and Jelly Guide to Computers, 1978 (Outstanding Computer Book, Am. Library Jour.); Nailing Jelly to a Tree, 1981; Computers for Everybody, 1981 (Outstanding Computer Book, Am. Library Jour.); Computers for People, 1982; Computers, Teaching and Learning, 1983; Educational Computing: An Introduction, 1986; Computer Simulations: A Guide to Educational Applications, 1986; 28 other books; translations in 8 langs.; edn. series editor Dilithium Press. Home: Box 2010 Lubbock TX 79408 Office: Coll Edn Tex Tech U Lubbock TX 79409

WILLIS, LEONARD W., III, automobile dealership executive; b. Bainbridge, Ga., Dec. 18, 1952; s. Leonard W. and Frankie Olivia (Reynolds) W.; m. Donna Grady White, Feb. 6, 1982; 1 dau., Ellen Larkin. B.A., Presbyn. Coll., 1976; M.B.A., Georgia Coll., 1979. Pres. Bo Willis Pontiac-Porsche Audi, Inc., Macon, Ga., 1982—. Named Pontiac Achiever Dealer, 1982, Pontiac Master Dealer, 1983. Mem. Macon-Bibb County C. of C., Ga. Automobile Dealers Assn., Nat. Automobile Dealers Assn. Presbyterian. Clubs: Elks, Kiwanis, Shield (Macon). Home: 1268 Twin Pines Dr Macon GA 31211 Office: 1090 Riverside Dr Macon GA 31213

WILLIS, MCDONALD, educational administrator; b. Atlanta, Dec. 18, 1937; s. William Paul and Essilee (McDonald) W.; m. Pamela Noel Williams, Sept. 9, 1961; children—Pamela Candace, Rachael Anne. B.A., Oglethrope U., 1959; postgrad Ga. State U., 1963-66, West Ga. Coll., 1968-71. Cert. fund raising exec. Nat. Soc. Fund Raising Execs. Mgmt. officer trainee Trust Co. Ga., Atlanta, 1963-66; dir. alumni affairs West Ga. Coll., Carrollton, 1966-70; headmaster Rutledge Acad., Ga., 1970-71, Oak Mountain Acad., Carrollton, 1971-73; mortgage loan officer Days Inns Am., Atlanta, 1973-74; v.p. devel. Reinhardt Coll., Waleska, Ga., 1974—. Served to lt. (j.g.) USNR, 1959-63. Mem. Council Advancement and Suport Edn., Nat. Soc. Fund Raising Execs. Democrat. Baptist. Avocations: Racquetball; tennis; golf; reading; music. Office: Reinhardt Coll PO Box 98 Waleska GA 30183

WILLIS, ROBERT ERWIN, financial executive; b. Atlanta, Jan. 2, 1942; s. William Leslie and Margaret Louise (Nail) W.; B.S., So. Ill. U., Edwardsville, 1968; m. Sherrin Newsome, Oct. 26, 1973; children—Robert Erwin II, William Eugene, Valerie Lorene. Supr. mail service So. Ill. U., 1962-66; accountant Prince Gardner Co., St. Louis, 1966-68; controller Northwestern Constrn. Co., Chamblee, Ga., 1968-69; sr. accountant Touche Ross & Co., Charlotte, N.C., 1969-72; controller Savannah Foods & Industries (Ga.), 1972-78; corporate controller, asst. treas. Rollins, Inc., Atlanta, 1978-84; chief fin. officer Ellmans, Inc., Atlanta, 1984-85; v.p. fin. RTM Inc., Atlanta, 1985—. C.P.A., Ga., N.C. Mem. Fin. Execs. Inst., Nat. Assn. Accountants (pres. chpt. 1975—), Am. Inst. C.P.A.s, Am. Acctg. Assn., Am. Assn. Bus. Economists. Home: 2761 Breckenridge Ct Atlanta GA 30345 Office: 2130 LaVista Exec Park Tucker GA 30084

WILLIS, ROY EDWARD, corporate program manager, consultant; b. Waukesha, Wis., Aug. 28, 1930; s. Orea Willis and Blanche Josephine (Boyle) Wanchura; m. Dorothy Mae Gest, Apr. 28, 1951 (div. 1977); children—Anne, Kathy Boehm, Mary, Pam Drimilla; m. Alice Jane Fairlee, June 23, 1979. B.S., U. Wis.-Platteville, 1952; M.S., U. Wis.-Madison, 1955. Tchr., coach Clifton Jr. High Sch., Ill., 1955-57, Crystal Lake Jr. High Sch., Ill., 1957-64, McHenry High Sch., Ill., 1964-65; prin. McHenry Jr. High Sch., 1965-66; with IBM, Chgo., 1966-74 Rochester, Minn., 1974-76, Austin, Tex., 1976—, program mgr., Austin, 1982—; cons. ARC, Tex. Legal Services. Recreation dir. Crystal Lake Park Bd., 1959-64. Served to cpl. U.S. Army, 1952-54. Mem. Am. Soc. Tng. and Devel. Republican. Presbyterian. Lodge: Elks. Avocations: Reading; golf; travel; bridge. Office: IBM 2525 Brockton Dr Austin TX 78731

WILLIS, WILLIAM DAVID, JR., educational psychologist, educational administrator; b. Southport, N.C., Dec. 22, 1945; s. William David and Martha Gray (Brown) Willis; m. Denise White, Aug. 10, 1985. B.A., Furman U., 1968, M.A., 1969; Ph.D., U. S.C., 1981. Tchr., Greenville County Schs., S.C., 1968-69; dir. social service Winchester Meml. Hosp., Va., 1969-73; residential supr. Grafton Sch., Inc., Berryville, Va., 1975-77; unit adminstr. O Berry Ctr., Goldsboro, N.C., 1978; dir. phys. and mental health Hannah Moore Ctr., Reisterstown, Md., 1979-80; dir. diagnostic and evaluation services. S.C. Dept. Mental Retardation, Clinton, 1981-83; ednl. psychologist Ednl. Indsl. Systems, Spartanburg, S.C., 1983—; acad. dean mgmt. program Limestone Coll., Spartanburg, 1983—. Psychol. cons., Charles Lea Ctr., Spartanburg, 1983-85; dir. social services Warren Meml. Hosp., Front Royal, Va., 1975-78. Baptist. Home: 718 Gatewood Dr Roebuck SC 29376 Office: 180 Library St Spartanburg SC 29301

WILLNER, EUGENE BURTON, food and liquors executive; b. Chgo., July 27, 1934; s. Fred and Mae (Goodhartz) W.; B.A., Northwestern U., 1956; m. Karen Nell Kaye, Feb. 22, 1962; children—Tracy Fran, Kelly Kaye. Pres., World Wide Fisheries Inc., Chgo., 1956-60; merchandiser Edison Bros. Stores Inc., St. Louis, 1960-66; v.p. Mo. Supreme Life Ins. Co., St. Louis, 1966-67; exec. v.p. Exec. Agys., Inc., St. Louis, 1966-67; pres. Bluff Creek Industries, Inc., Ocean Springs, Miss., 1967-69, Purse String Stores, Inc., Miami, Fla., 1968-69, World Wide Fisheries, Inc., Miami, Fla., 1969-73, Universal Fisheries, Inc., Miami, 1974-76, Renwill Seafoods, Inc., 1979—; chmn. bd. Astral Liquors, Inc., Foxy Laidy Lounges, Prime Universal Seafood Corp., Miami, also Key West, Fla., Caracas, Venezuela, San Juan del Sur, Nicaragua, Quito, Ecuador; pres., chmn. bd. Common Markets, Inc., Miami, London and Moscow, 1980—; dir. Mo. Supreme Life Ins. Co., Lite Am. Corp. Clubs: Kingsbay Country, Turnberry, Jockey, Crickett, Grove Isle. Home: 8400 SW 146th St Miami FL 33158 Office: 6507 SW 40th St Miami FL 33155 also PO Box 570326 Miami FL 33157 also Beverly Hills CA

WILLOUGHBY, CHERYL ANN, association executive, consultant; b. Cocoa Beach, Fla., Jan. 13, 1955; d. Thomas and Margaret (Murray) Watterson. B.A., U. Ala., 1978. Pub. relations dir. Autographics Inc., Birmingham, Ala., 1977-78; tchr. Snead Jr. Coll., Boaz, Ala., 1978-79; mgr. Killian Quarter Horses, Boise, Idaho, 1980-81; pub. Southeastern Rodeo Sports Report, Rainsville, Ala., 1981-83; nat. media dir. Intenat. Pro Rodeo Assn., Pauls Valley, Okla., 1983—; media cons. Southeastern Rodeo Sports Report, Rainsville, Ala., 1983—. Contbr. articles to rodeo mags. Mem. Am. Mktg. Assn., Rodeo Media Assn., Internat. Pro Rodeo Assn. (com. mem. 1983), Am. Rodeo Assn. (dir. 1978), Nat. High Sch. Rodeo Assn. (dir. 1981). Democrat. Roman Catholic. Office: Internat Pro Rodeo Assn PO Box 615 Am Fidelity Bldg Pauls Valley OK 73075

WILLS, JAMES ALLEN, holding company executive; b. Wilkes-Barre, Pa., Mar. 13, 1947; s. William John and Arlene E. (Wolfskeil) W.; m. Linda Marie Diamanti, Nov. 21, 1972. B.S., Wilkes Coll., 1969; M.S., George Washington U., 1978. Contract specialist USAECOM, Fort Monmouth, N.J., 1970-72; dir. contract adminstrn. Telcom Inc., Vienna, Va., 1972-77; dir. fin. and adminstrn. Adaptronics, Inc., McLean, Va., 1977-78; v.p. Corvus Systems, Inc., Vienna, 1978-80; exec. v.p. Corvus Corp., Vienna, 1980—; also dir.; dir. Microwave Systems, Inc.; adviser to bd. JWM Inc., 1985—; cons., Reston, Va., 1978—. Mem. Reston Homeowners Assn., 1983—. Mem. Assn. M.B.A. Execs., George Washington U. Alumni Assn. Republican. Avocations: snorkeling; track; marine fish; gardening. Home: 10718 Cross School Rd Reston VA 22091 Office: Corvus Corp 8150 Leesbur Pike Vienna VA 22180

WILLS, LYNN RUTHAFORD, JR., air force officer; b. Montgomery, Ala., May 29, 1952; s. Lynn Rutherford and Marie Elizabeth (Davies) W.; m. Gail D'Anne, May 21, 1977; children—Brant Davies, Jordan Taylor. B.S. with distinction, U. Ala., 1974; M.A., Ball State U., 1979; grad. Def. Lang. Inst., 1980. Commd. 2d lt. U.S. Air Force, 1974 advanced through grades to maj., 1985; air weapons controller Pope AB, N.C., 1974-75; chief standardization and evaluation br., Mangil-San, Korea, 1975-76; chief weapons tng. br. Borfink, Germany, 1976-79; dir. ops. Joint Air Control and Coordination Ctr., Torrejon AB, Spain, 1980-83; chief tactical air control system tng. br. Hdqrs. Tactical Air Command, Langley AFB, Va., 1983—. Recipient Meritorious Service medal, Air Force Commendation medal with oak leaf cluster. Mem. Air Force Assn. Baptist. Avocations: tennis; classical guitar. Home: 1220 Powderhouse Dr Newport News VA 23602 Office: Hdqrs TAC DOY Langley AFB VA 23365

WILLS, RICHARD BURDEN, charter bus company executive; b. Macon, Ga., May 13, 1913; s. Edgar Crawford and Hallie Lillian (Daugherty) W.; m. Willie Ruth Wilburn, July 22, 1937; children—Dorothy Ann, Wilma Ruth, Margaret Louise. Student pub. schs., Orlando, Fla. Sales mgr. Datson Dairies, Inc., Orlando, 1937-51; sales mgr. Boutwell Dairies, Inc., Lake Worth, Fla., 1951-57, Sealtest, Lakeland, Fla., 1961-63; v.p., sec., treas. Cities Transit, Inc., Lakeland and Tallahassee, Fla., 1963-76; pres., comptroller Cities Transit, Inc., Lakeland, Tallahassee and Sarasota, Fla., 1976—; v.p., dir. Cities Transit of Ga., Inc., 1963-75; dir. Coleman Sales, Inc., Tallahassee, CTI, Lakeland. Decorated Ky. Col. Mem. Nat. Ind. Dairy Salesmgr. Assn. (pres. 1949-57), Ford Philpot Evangelistic Assn. (dir.). Democrat. Methodist. Home: 330 W Wellington St Lakeland FL 33803 Office: 415 S Ingraham Ave Lakeland FL 33801

WILLS, STANLEY EWING, education educator; b. Monte Vista, Colo., Nov. 7, 1922; s. Silas Ezra and Anna Eliza (Dolan) W.; m. Ruth Marie Osborne, May 30, 1947; children—Karen Wills Kelton, Martha Wills Pedersen, Kyle Stanley, Sean Eric, Kristi Ann. A.B., Adams State Coll., 1948, Ed.M., 1954; postgrad. Colo. Coll., 1949-50; Ed.D., U. No. Colo., 1966. Tchr., adminstr. Colo. pub. schs., 1948-54; supt. schs. Marsing, Idaho, 1955-59; asst. to dir. Inst. Edn. and Research, U. Dacca, Pakistan, 1961-63; asst. prof. edn. and registrar Wayne State Coll. (Nebr.), 1963-67, prof. edn., asst. dean faculties, 1967-73, provost, 1973-75; prof. edn. U. Houston, Victoria, Tex., 1975—, chmn. div. edn., 1977-80; accreditation cons. Tex. Edn. Agy. and Nat. Accrediting Commn. of Cosmetology Arts and Scis. Served with U.S. Army, 1943-46. Doctoral fellow U. No. Colo., 1960-61; Title III grantee, 1967-71, 73-75; State of Tex. grantee, 1978, 79, 83. Mem. Am. Assn. Sch. Adminstrs., Idaho Assn. Sch. Adminstrs., Tex. Assn. Sch. Adminstrs., Tex. Assn. Tchr. Educators, Tex. Soc. Coll. Tchrs. of Edn., Tex. Dirs. of Field Experiences, Tex. Assn. Aerospace Tchrs., Civil Air Patrol, Kappa Delta Pi, Phi Delta Kappa. Editor: Teachers' World, Dacca, 1961-63; co-author: Master Plan for Nebraska State Colleges, 1974. Home: 207 Simpson Rd Victoria TX 77904 Office: 2302-C Red River St Victoria TX 77901

WILLS, WILLIAM RIDLEY, II, former insurance company executive, historian; b. Nashville, June 19, 1934; s. Jesse Ely and Ellen (Buckner) W.; m. Irene Weaver Jackson, July 21, 1962; children—William Ridley III, Morgan Jackson, Thomas Weaver. B.A., Vanderbilt U., 1956. Agt., staff mgr. Nat. Life & Accident, Nashville, 1958-62, supr., 1962-64, asst. sec., 1964-67, asst. v.p., 1967-70, 2d v.p., 1970-75, v.p., 1975-81, sr. v.p., 1981-83; sr. v.p. Am. Gen. Services Co., Nashville, 1982-83; dir. Nat. Life & Accident, Nashville, 1976-83. Pres. Tenn. Hist. Soc., 1985, YMCA Met. Nashville, 1984; gen. chmn. United Way Campaign, Nashville, 1978; pres. Cumberland Mus. and Sci. Ctr., Nashville, 1977; nat. chmn. Vanderbilt U. Living Endowment Drive, Nashville, 1974; mem. Tenn. Hist. Commn., 1985—; trustee Ladies Hermitage Assn. Served to lt. USN, 1956-58. Recipient awards YMCA, 1977, 83. Fellow Life Office Mgmt. Assn. Presbyterian. Clubs: Belle Meade Country, YMCA Athletic (Nashville), Coffee House. Office: 4428 Warner Pl Nashville TN 37205

WILLSHIRE, KELLI FRANCISCO, human factors engineer; b. Springfield, Ohio, July 13, 1953; d. Earl Bertram and Ruth Isabell (Matthews) Francisco; m. Michael Rabon Key, Jan. 18, 1975 (div. 1978); m. 2d William Lyle Willshire, Jr., Aug. 14, 1981. B.S., Ga. State U., 1974; M.S., Ga. Inst. Tech., 1979; Ph.D., N.C. State U., 1984. Research asst. Ga. State U., 1972-74; research asst. for dean grad. studies Ga. Inst. Tech., 1977-79; life scientist NASA-Langley Research Ctr., Hampton, Va., 1979—; also cons. Mem. Human Factors Soc., Tidewater Human Factors Soc. (pres. 1986), Inst. Indsl. Engrs., Peninsula Women's Network, Sigma Xi, Delta Gamma. Contbr. articles to tech. jours. Home: 3 Westmont Dr Hampton VA 23666 Office: Mail Stop 288 NASA Langley Research Ctr Hampton VA 23665

WILLY, DONALD JOSEPH, oil company executive; b. Kansas City, Kans., Dec. 29, 1951; s. Donald G. and Marie A. (Ford) W. B.S., U. Mo., 1972; J.D., U. Kans., 1974. Bars: Kans. 1976, Pa. 1977, Tex. 1981, D.C. 1981. Corp. counsel, sec. Neville Chem. Co., Pitts., 1976-79; div. counsel CPC Internat., Englewood Cliffs, N.J., 1979-80; sr. counsel Coastal Corp., Houston, 1980-85; pres., dir. QWIXM Corp., Houston, 1985—; dir. Resources Conservation. Mem. Allegheny County Hazardous Waste Study Group, 1980—; active Boy Scouts Am., United Way. Served to lt. col. USAR, 1971—. Mem. Am. Chem. Soc., ABA, Fed. Bar Assn., Internat. Bar Assn., Am. Def. Preparedness Assn., Am. Indsl. Health Council (dir. 1979-81). Clubs: Union League (Chgo.); Kansas City; Houston; Univ. (Pitts.) Office: Suite 2100 United Bank Plaza Houston TX 77002

WILMER, HARRY ARON, psychiatrist; b. New Orleans, Mar. 5, 1917; s. Harry Aron and Leona (Schlenker) W.; B.S., U. Minn., 1938, M.B., 1940, M.S., 1940, M.D., 1941, Ph.D., 1944; m. Jane Harris, Oct. 31, 1944; children—Harry, John, Thomas, James, Mary. Intern, Gorgas Hosp., Ancon, C.Z., 1940-41; resident in neurology and psychiatry Mayo Clinic, Rochester, Minn., 1945-49, cons. in psychiatry, 1957-58; physician Palo Alto (Calif.) Clinic, 1949-51; pvt. practice medicine, Palo Alto, 1951-55, 1958-64; prof. psychiatry U. Calif. Med. Sch., San Francisco, 1964-69; sr. psychiatrist Scott & White Clinic, Temple, Tex., 1969-74; prof. psychiatry U. Tex. Health Sci. Center, San Antonio, 1972—; founder, dir. Internat. Film Festivals on Culture and Psychiatry, U. Tex. Health Sci. Center, 1972-80; founder, pres., dir. Inst. Humanities, Salado, Tex., 1980—; practice medicine, specializing in psychiatry, Salado, Tex., 1982—. Served to capt. M.C., USNR, 1955-57. Guggenheim fellow, Zurich, 1969-70; NRC fellow, Johns Hopkins Hosp., 1944-45. Fellow Am. Psychiat. Assn., Am. Coll. Psychiatrists, Am. Acad. Psychoanalysis; mem. AAAS, Internat. Assn. Analytical Psychology. Author: Huber the Tuber, 1942; Corky the Killer, 1945; This is Your World, 1952; Social Psychiatry in Action, 1958; First Book for the Mind, 1963; (film) People Need People, 1961;Vietnam in Remission, 1985. Home: PO Box 215 Salado TX 76571

WILMER, MARY CHARLES, artist; b. Atlanta, Aug. 25, 1930; d. William Knox and Harriott Creighton (Thomas) Fitzpatrick; student Wellesley Coll., 1948-50; A.B., Agnes-Scott Coll., 1970; B.F.A., Coll. of Art, 1974; m. John Grant Wilmer, Dec. 28, 1950; children—John Grant, Knox Randolph, Charles Inman, Mary Catherine; m. 2d, Olin G. Shivers, 1982. One-woman shows: Image South Gallery, 1974, Aronson Gallery, 1977, 79, Heath Gallery, 1982, Coach House, 1983; exhibited in group show: Colony Sq., 1975; portrait painter, 1974—. Bd. dirs. Hillside Cottages, 1963-65, Atlanta Child Services, 1965-68, Atlanta Coll. Art, 1965—. Episcopalian. Club: Piedmont Driving.

WILMOTH, PATRICIA BARANOWSKI, counseling psychologist; b. Burlington, Ont., Can., Mar. 15, 1950; d. Leslie B. and Margaret (Spence) Baranowski. Student Lynchburg Coll., 1968-69; B.A. in English, Tenn. Tech. U., 1973; M.Ed., U. Mo.-Columbia, 1975, Ph.D., 1979. Nat. register Health Service Providers in Psychology; lic. psychologist Fla. Intern, student health services, women's ctr. U. Mo., Columbia, 1976-78; mental health worker Cole County Mental Health Services, Jefferson City, Mo., 1978; pvt. practice Adult and Child Psychology Clinic, Clearwater, Fla., 1979-83, Suncoast Psychol. Services, 1983—; instr. St. Petersburg (Fla.) Jr. Coll., 1980—; cons. Su Casa, Spouse Abuse Program, St. Petersburg; mem. adv. bd. Bridgeway Counseling Services, Alternative Human Services; lectr. Pinellas County Mental Health Assn.; dir. Suncoast Women's Network. Mem. Am. Psychol. Assn., Nat. Acad. Neuropsychologists, Am. Soc. Clin. Hypnosis, Mental Health Assn. Pinellas County, Phi Delta Kappa. Editor: Suncoast Women's Newsletter. Office: Suncoast Psychological Services 2085 US 19N Suite 302 Clearwater FL 33575

WILMOTH, WILLIE HAROLD, financial executive, minister; b. Grayson County, Va., Aug. 3, 1934; s. William Tise and Ila Fay (Baugus) W.; m. Shelba Jean Johnson, June 14, 1966; children—Krystal Dawn, April Denise. A.A., Surry Community Coll., 1969; B.S., East Tenn. State U., 1971. Auditor, Def. Contract Audit Agy., Winston-Salem, N.C., 1971-72 operating acct. Nat. Park Service, Atlanta, 1972-75; systems acct. Dept. Army, Atlanta, 1975-78; fin. mgr. Soil Conservation Service, Raleigh, 1978-83, Richmond, Va., 1984—. Served with USAF, 1961-65. Mem. Orgn. Profl. Employees Dept. Agr. (chpt. pres.). Democrat. Baptist. Clubs: Toastmasters, Woodmen of the World. Home: 127 N Franklin Rd Mount Airy NC 27030 Office: 126 E Pine St Mount Airy NC 27030

WILSON, ADDISON (JOE) GRAVES, lawyer, state senator; b. Charleston, S.C., July 31, 1947; s. Hugh deVeaux and Wray Smart (Graves) W.; m. Roxanne Dusenbury McCrory, Dec. 30, 1977; children—Michael Alan, Addison Graves, Julian Dusenbury. B.A., Washington and Lee U., 1969; J.D., U. S.C.-Columbia, 1972. Bar: S.C. 1972. Staff mem. Sen. Strom Thurmond, Washington, 1967, Congressman Floyd Spence, Columbia, S.C., 1970-72; atty./ptnr. Kirkland, Taylor, Wilson, Moore, Allen & Deneen, West Columbia, S.C., 1972—; dep. gen. counsel U.S. Energy Sec. Jim Edwards, Washington, 1981-82; dir. Citizens and So. Nat. Bank, Lexington, S.C.; senator State of S.C., Columbia, 1984—. Campaign mgr. Congressman Floyd Spence, Columbia, 1974, 78, 80, 82; vice chmn. S.C. Republican Party, 1972-74; bd. dirs. S.C. Lung Assn., Columbia, 1980—, S.C. Kidney Found., 1982—. Served to maj. S.C. Army N.G., 1975—. Mem. ABA, Am. Judicature Soc. Presbyterian. Lodges: Rotary, Masons, Shriners. Home: 2825 Wilton Rd West Columbia SC Office: Kirkland Taylor Wilson Moore Allen & Deneen 1700 Sunset Blvd West Columbia SC 29169

WILSON, ALBERT JOHN ENDSLEY, III, social gerontologist, administrator, consultant; b. Pitts., Oct. 9, 1934; s. Robert Endsley and Dorothy Mae (Parry) W.; m. Nancy Jean Hooton, Sept. 29, 1955 (div. Mar. 1963); children—Linda Jean, Albert John Endsley IV, Patrick Lee; m. Nera Bernice Kennedy, Nov. 24, 1965. A.A. in Liberal Arts, St. Petersburg Jr. Coll., 1954; B.S. in Mgmt., Fla. State U., 1956; M.R.C., U. Fla., Gainesville, 1958, Ph.D. in Sociology, 1966. Research sociologist Fla. Dept. Health, St. Petersburg, 1961-66; dir. Inst. on Aging, U. S. Fla., Tampa, 1967-74; dep. dir. geriatric ctr. VA, Bay Pines, Fla., 1974-76, cons., Bay Pines and Waco, Tex., 1972-74, 76-77, 79-82; dir. grad. study gerontology Baylor U., Waco, 1978-81; dir. Boone Gerontology Ctr., Lynchburg Coll., Va., 1983—; vis. prof. Calif. State U.-Chico, 1976-77; adj. prof. rural sociology Pa. State U., 1978-79; cons. in field; del. White House Conf. on Aging, Washington, 1971; expert witness U.S. Senate Com. on Aging, Washington, 1973; bd. dirs. Adult Care of Central Va., Lynchburg, 1984—, Alzheimers Disease Support, Lynchburg, 1984—. Author: Social Services for Older Persons, 1984; also chpt., articles. Editor: Ethical Considerations in Long Term Care, 1977. Vice pres. bd. Presbyterian Social Ministries, St. Petersburg, 1972-76, Interfaith Coalition on Aging, Pinellas County, Fla., 1974-76; mem. adv. com. Va. Baptist Hosp. Day Ctr., Lynchburg, 1984—. Grantee Adminstrn. on Aging, HEW, 1969-72, 71-74, Health Services and Mental Health Adminstrn., USPHS, 1972-73, Calif. Dept. on Aging, 1976-77. Mem. Gerontol. Soc. Am., Nat. Council on Aging, Am. Pub. Health Assn., So. Sociol. Soc., Va. Assn. on Aging (pres. 1985-86), So. Gerontol. Soc. Democrat. Methodist. Avocations: antique and special interest autos; hiking; exploring; travel. Home: 222 Nottingham Circle Lynchburg VA 24502 Office: Belle Boone Beard Gerontology Ctr Lynchburg Coll Lynchburg VA 24501

WILSON, ALEXANDER FREDERICK, geneticist; b. Balt., Jan. 23, 1953; s. Alexander Charles Robinson and Margaret Anne (Eierman) W.; B.A. magna cum laude, Western Md. Coll., 1975; Ph.D., Ind. U., 1980; m. Joan Ellen Bailey, June 24, 1978. Instr. dept. math. Ind. U.-Purdue U., Indpls., 1978-79; postdoctoral tng. dept. biometry La. State U. Med. Center, New Orleans, 1980-82, asst. prof. dept. biometry and genetics, 1982—. Editor software sect. Thrombosis Research, 1984—. Recipient H. P. Sturdivant award Western Md. Coll., 1975; Prize for Poetry, Ind. U.-Purdue U., 1975; USPHS predoctoral fellow, 1975-78; NIH-Nat. Heart, Lung and Blood Inst. research grantee, 1982—. Mem. Am. Soc. Human Genetics, AAAS, Assn. Computing Machinery, Am. Running and Fitness Assn., Sigma Xi, Beta Beta Beta. Lutheran. Office: Dept Biometry and Genetics 1901 Perdido St New Orleans LA 70112

WILSON, ALLEN SHERWOOD, air force noncommissioned officer; b. Mountain, Wis., Sept. 21, 1937; s. Melvin Woodrow and Delilia Beryl (Richardson) W.; A.A.S., Community Coll. Air Force, 1979; m. Sharon Patricia Collins, June 25, 1960; children—Cheri Ann, Renee Lynn, Mark Allen, Stephanie Marie; m. 2d, Jill Marie Combes, July 27, 1974 (div. 1980). Served as enlisted man U.S. Navy, 1956-60; joined U.S. Air Force, 1961, advanced through grades to chief master sgt., med. service specialist, Selfridge AFB, Mich., 1961-65, Mil. Provencial Hosp. AuGumentee program, Viet Nam, 1965-66; supr. on the job tng. Scott Hosp., Belleville, Ill., 1966-70; noncommd. officer in charge hosp. surg. ward, Wiesbaden, Germany, 1970-72; supr. nursing service F.E. Warren AFB, Wyo., 1972-79, U.S. Air Force Clinic, Ramstein AFB, W. Ger., 1979-80; mgr. dept. nursing USAF Regional Hosp., Carswell AFB, Tex., 1980—. Decorated Bronze Star, Meritorious Service medal; Air Force commendation medal; decoration Vietnam Armed Forces. Mem. Noncommd. Officers Grad. Assn. (v.p. 1974-75), Air Force Assn., VFW. Republican. Lutheran. Home: 2705 Cedar Park Blvd Richland Hills TX 76118 Office: USAF Regional Hosp Carswell AFB TX 76127

WILSON, ANN STALLINGS, state official; b. York, Ala., May 11, 1941; d. Raymond S. and L. Sigrid (McGowen) Stallings. B.S., Livingston U., 1962; M. Combined Sci., U. Miss., 1969; Ph.D., U. Ala.-Tuscaloosa, 1973. Tchr. Baldwin County Bd. Edn., Bay Minette, Ala., 1962-64, Mobile County Bd. Edn., Ala., 1964-68, Tuscaloosa, Bd. Edn., 1968-70; research assoc. State Dept. Edn., Montgomery, Ala., 1972-74, fiscal officer div. vocat. edn., 1974-79, asst. dir., 1979—; adj. faculty Ala. State U., Montgomery, 1973-74, Troy State U., 1973-76. Baptist. Home: 1255 Huie St Prattville AL 36067 Office: State Dept Edn 501 Dexter Ave Room 844 State Office Bldg Montgomery AL 36130

WILSON, ANNIE MAE, nursing educator; b. Marlin, Tex., Oct. 31, 1942; d. Richard and Lillie (Williams) W. B.S. cum laude, Prairie View A&M U., 1964; M.S. in Med.-Surg. Nursing, Ind. U., 1970; D.Pub.Health, U. Tex.-Houston, 1982. Family nurse practitioner, Tex. Staff nurse VA Hosp., Marlin, Tex., 1964-68; instr., chairperson lower div., assoc. dean nursing Prairie View A&M U., Tex., 1970-74, asst. prof., 1978-81; nurse practitioner VA Hosp., Houston, 1975-78; dir. assoc. degree nursing program Coll. of Mainland, Texas City, Tex., 1982—; instr. U.S. Army Res., Houston, 1975—; mem. profl. adv. bd. Superior Care, temporary nursing agy., Houston, 1981-82. Contbr. to profl. newsletters. Alt. del. Precinct Democratic Caucus, Houston, 1984; mem. Crown Colony I Homeowners Assn., Houston, 1976. Tuition scholar Prairie View A&M U., 1960-64; USPHS trainee Ind. U., Indpls., 1968, U. Tex., Houston, 1978. Mem. Am. Nurses Assn., Nat. League for Nursing, Tex. Jr. Coll. Tchrs. Assn., Council Deans and Dirs., Sigma Theta Tau. Baptist. Avocations: bowling; aerobics; sewing. Home: 7010 Jetty Ln Houston TX 77072 Office: Coll of Mainland 8001 Palmer Hwy Texas City TX 77591

WILSON, ARTHUR JESS, clinical and forensic psychologist, consultant; b. Yonkers, N.Y., Oct. 25, 1910; s. Samuel Louis and Anna Lee (Gilbert) W.; m. Lillian Moss, Sept. 16, 1941; children—Warren David, Anton Francis. B.S., NYU, 1935, M.A., 1949, Ph.D., 1961; LL.B., St. Lawrence U., 1940; J.D., Bklyn. Law Sch., 1967. Lic. clin. psychologist, N.Y. Dir. adult edn. Yonkers Pub. Sch., 1935-40; supr. rehab. State Edn. Dept., N.Y., 1940-42; personnel exec. for pvt. industry, N.Y.C., 1942-44; dir. rehab. Westchester County Med. Ctr., Valhalla, N.Y., 1948-67; dir. Manhatten Drug Abuse Rehab. Ctr., State Drug Abuse Control Commn., N.Y., 1967-68; clin. psychologist Va Hosp., Montrose, N.Y., 1968-73; pvt. practice clin. psychology, Coral Springs, Fla., 1974—; instr. in psychology Westchester Community Coll., Valhalla; spl. lectr. rehab. Sch. Pub. Health Adminstrn. Med. Columbia U., NYU; cons. in field. Author: The Emotional Life of the Ill and Injured, 1950; A Guide to the Genius of Cardozo, 1939. Contbr. ednl. guide, 1941; also articles. Served with USN, 1944-46. Recipient Founders Day award NYU, 1961, Westchester Author honor Westchester County Hist. Soc., 1957. Mem. Am. Psychol. Assn., N.Y. State Psychol. Assn., Internat. Mark Twain Soc. (hon.), N.Y. Acad. Scis., Internat. Platform Assn., Kappa Delta Pi, Phi Delta Kappa, Epsilon Pi Tau. Avocations: photography; acrylic painting; tennis; bowling; writing. Home: 4121 NW 88th Ave Coral Springs FL 33065

WILSON, BETTY ANN, health and physical education educator, consultant; b. Orange, Tex., May 21, 1945; d. Jack William Gunstream and Elvada Hortence (Casey) Gatlin; m. Samuel Paschal Wilson, Aug. 28, 1965; children—S. Philip, William Derek, A. Janelle. B.S., Baylor U., 1966; M.A., S.W. Tex. State U., 1971; Ph.D., N. Tex. State U., 1974. Cert. tchr., Tex. Instr. McMurry Coll., Abilene, Tex., 1972-74; researcher Concho Valley Council of Govt., San Angelo, Tex., 1975-77; assoc. prof. Angelo State U., San Angelo, 1977-78; dept. head health and phys. edn. Hillsdale Coll., Mich., 1978-81; prof., dept. head health and phys. edn. Howard Payne U., Brownwood, Tex., 1981—; camp dir. Sportsworld, San Diego, summers 1982, 83. Author: (with others) Olympic Annals, 1983. Contbr. articles to profl. jours. Bd. dirs. Kimball YMCA Ctr., Hillsdale, 1980-81; coordinator Spl. Olympics, Hillsdale, 1980. Fellow N. Tex. State U., 1971-72. Mem. Tex. Assn. Health, Phys. Edn. and Dance (editorial bd. 1982—), Delta Psi Kappa, Sigma Alpha Sigma. Republican. Baptist. Avocations: accordian playing; sports; camping. Office: Howard Payne U Dept Health and Phys Edn Brownwood TX 76801

WILSON, BILLY JOE, accountant; b. Cleveland, Tenn., Nov. 25, 1933; s. William L. and Nell D. (Davis) W.; A.A. in Bus., Tenn. Wesleyan Coll., 1954; B.B.A. in Accounting, Ga. State U., 1968; LL.B., John Marshall U., 1972. With tax dept. Touche, Ross, Bailey & Smart, C.P.A.'s, Atlanta, 1967-68; accounting supr. Lockheed-Ga. Co., Marietta, 1968-80; pvt. practice accounting, Tucker, Ga., 1972—. Treas., pres. Laurel Ridge PTA. Served in USMCR, 1955-58. Mem. Nat. Assn. Enrolled Agts. (nat. pres. 1977, 78, dir.), Nat. Soc. Pub. Accountants, Ga. Assn. Pub. Accountants, Sigma Delta Kappa (life), Sigma Phi Epsilon (life), Sigma Delta (pres.). Clubs: Masons, Lions (fin. sec.). Home: PO Box 33458 Decatur GA 30033 Office: 2284 Brockett Rd Tucker GA 30084

WILSON, CARLOS EUGENE, symphony director; b. Kansas City, Kans., Dec. 17, 1935; s. Alva Curtis and Jessie Arline (Grace) W.; m. Mary Jane Anderson, Nov. 1, 1963. Grad. U. Denver. Gen. mgr. Kalamazoo Symphony, 1968-71, Fresno Philharm., Calif., 1971-73; gen. mgr., asst. gen. mgr. Houston Symphony, 1973-77; exec. dir. Denver Symphony, 1977-82; mng. dir. San Antonio Symphony, 1982—. Served with U.S. Army, 1953-57. Office: San Antonio Symphony 109 Lexington St Suite 207 San Antonio TX 78209

WILSON, CHARLES, congressman; b. Trinity, Tex., June 1, 1933; student Sam Houston State U., Huntsville, Tex., 1951-52; B.S., U.S. Naval Acad., 1956. Commd. ensign U.S. Navy, 1956, advanced through grades to lt.; ret., 1960; mem. Tex. Ho. of Reps., 1960-66; mem. Tex. Senate, 1966-72; mem. 93d-99th Congresses from 2d Dist. Tex. Mgr. lumber yard. Democrat. Office: 2265 Rayburn House Office Bldg Washington DC 20515

WILSON, CHARLES GLEN, zoo administrator; b. Clinton, Okla., Aug. 24, 1948; s. Claude Lee and Alva Dean (Gaskins) W.; B.S., Okla. State U., 1972, M.S., 1981; m. Susan Elizabeth Mosher, Nov. 21, 1975; children—Erica Dean, Grant Mosher. Research asst. Oklahoma City Zool. Gardens, 1972-73, zool. curator, 1973-75; dir. Little Rock Zool. Gardens, 1975-76; dir. Memphis Zool. Gardens, 1976—. Served with AUS, 1968-70. Recipient Ark. Traveler award, 1977. Profl. fellow Am. Assn. Zool. Parks and Aquariums; mem. Am. Soc. Mammalogists. Contbr. articles to profl. jours. Office: 2000 Galloway St Memphis TN 39112

WILSON, DANIEL CLYDE, construction company executive; b. Jasper, Ala., Sept. 14, 1947; s. Clyde and Martha (Rogers) W.; m. Virginia Teresa Tuggle, Feb. 24, 1973; children—Amanda Teresa, Matthew Daniel, Meredith Leigh. B.Indsl. Engring., Auburn U., 1972, postgrad., 1980. Registered profl. engr., Calif. Project civil quality control engr. Daniel Internat. Corp., Farley Nuclear Plant, Dothan, Ala., Callaway Plant, Fulton, Mo., 1972-78; mgr. quality assurance Blount Bros. Corp., Montgomery, Ala., 1978—. Mem. Am. Soc. Quality Control, Am. Soc. Nondestructive Testing (level III examiner), Am. Concrete Inst. (level III engr.), ASME, Am. Welding Soc., Auburn Alumni Assn. Republican. Methodist. Club: Methodist Men (Montgomery). Home: 172 Fox Hollow Rd Montgomery AL 36109 Office: PO Box 949 Montgomery AL 36192

WILSON, DANIEL EARL, security and safety company executive; b. Nashville, June 9, 1944; s. Jesse David and Mary Marine (Daniel) W.; m. Wanda Jane Masters, May 30, 1966; children—Mark Daniel, Scott David. B.A., Eastern Ky. State Coll., 1966; M.A., Eastern Ky. U., 1971. Commd. 2d lt. M.I., U.S. Army, 1966, advanced through grades to capt., 1968, resigned, 1975, now lt. col. res.; v.p. Lunday Thagard Oil Co., South Gate, Calif., 1975-78; regional mgr. Security Forces Inc., Charlotte, N.C., 1978-79; pres., sr. cons. Asset Protection Assocs., Inc., Charlotte, 1979—. Mem. editorial adv. bd. Hotel/Motel Security & Safety Mgmt., 1983—. Contbr. security related articles to profl. jours. Mem. Am. Soc. for Indsl. Security (cert. protection profl.; vice chmn. N.C. chpt. 1985-86), Am. Soc. Safety Engrs., Internat. Assn. Chiefs of Police. Republican. Baptist. Lodge: Masons. Avocation: skiing. Office: Asset Protection Assocs 4115 Crossgate Rd Charlotte NC 28226

WILSON, DAVID JAMES, chemistry educator; b. Ames, Iowa, June 25, 1930; s. James Calmar and Alice Winona (Olmsted) W.; m. Martha Carolyn Mayers, Sept. 6, 1952; children—John Wesley, Charles Steven, William David, Andrew Lyman, Joyce Ballin. B.S., Stanford U., 1952; Ph.D., Calif. Inst. Tech., 1958. Mem. faculty U. Rochester, 1957-68, assoc. prof., 1963-67, prof. phys. chemistry, 1967-69; vis. sr. lectr. U. Ife (Nigeria), 1964-65; prof. phys. chemistry Vanderbilt U., Nashville, 1969—, prof. environ. engring., 1977—; mem. Tenn. Environ. Council, 1972—, v.p., 1982-83, pres., 1985-86; mem. Rochester Com. for Sci. Info., 1960-69, v.p., 1966-68; chmn. Nashville Com. for Sci. Info., 1971-74. Served with AUS, 1953-55. Recipient awards Monroe County Conservation Council, 1967, Tenn. Conservation League, 1971; Alfred P. Sloan Found. fellow, 1964-66; Alexander Heard Disting. service prof., 1983-84. Mem. Am. Chem. Soc., Am. Phys. Soc., AAAS, Tenn. Acad. Scis., Phi Beta Kappa, Sigma Xi. Author: Foam Flotation Theory and Applications, 1983. Home: 3600 Wilbur Pl Nashville TN 37204 Office: Dept Chemistry Vanderbilt U Nashville TN 37235

WILSON, DAVID JOHN, fluid power design and sales engineer, pilot; b. San Bernardino, Calif., Dec. 10, 1943; s. Harold Lowell and Marjorie Genevieve

(Loop) W.; m. Carolyn Elaine Woods, Jan. 21, 1978. Student, Northwestern State, 1962-64, Okla. State U., 1964-66. Test engr. Cessna Aircraft Co., Wichita, Kans., 1969; pilot Southwest Sportsman, Dallas, 1970; design engr. Forrest & Cotton Cons. Engrs., Dallas, 1971-72; dept. mgr. Barker & Bratton Steel Works, Dallas, 1972-76; sales engr. Otis Engring. Corp., Carrollton, Tex., 1976-78; sales engr. Wilson Co., Addison, Tex., 1978—. Precinct clk., 1982; mem. adminstrv. bd. Carrollton Meth. Ch. Served with U.S. Army, 1966-68. Mem. ASME, Nat. Fluid Power Assn., Exptl. Aircraft Assn., Christian Action Alliance, Triangle. Club: Tae Kwon Do (Black belt) (Seoul, Korea). Home: 109 Oak Tree Lewisville TX 75067 Office: Wilson Co PO Box 217 Addison TX 75001

WILSON, DAVID WINSLOW, advertising firm executive; b. Kansas City, Mo., May 22, 1939; s. Edward Graham and Anne Elizabeth (Saunders) W.; m. Sandra Louise Slough, Aug. 26, 1961; children—Glen Mackie, Heather Louise. M.A., cum laude, U. South, 1961; M.S. in Journalism, Northwestern U., 1962. Acct. exec. Marsteller, Inc., Chgo., 1962-68, Shattuck Roether, Orlando, Fla., 1968-72, ptnr. Shattuck, Roether, Frailey and Wilson, Orlando, 1972-77; ptnr., pres. Frailey and Wilson, Inc., Orlando, 1977—; dir. Orlando Bus. Jour., Central Fla. Safety Council, Better Bus. Bur., Orlando. Bd. dirs. Loch Haven Art Ctr., Orlando, Maitland Art Ctr., Fla. Symphony, 1973, John Young Mus., Orlando, 1979-81, Lukemia Soc., Orlando, 1978, Orlando Sports Organizing Com. Mem. U. Fla. Advt. Council (chmn. 1985), U. Central Fla. Mktg. Council, Orlando Advt. Fedn. (pres. 1971), Fla. Pub. Relations Assn. (bd. dirs. 1981). Republican. Episcopalian. Clubs: Interlachen Country (Winter Park); University, Citrus, Downtown Athletic (Orlando). Lodge: Rotary (pres. 1986).

WILSON, DONALD LOY, professional football team executive; b. Tulsa, Aug. 16, 1929; s. Ira Loy and Jennie Louise (Moore) W.; m. Joyce Elaine Todd, June 25, 1955 (div. Aug. 1979); children—Michael Loy, David Todd; m. 2d, Gloria Jean Dameron, Sept. 29, 1979. B.S.B.A., U. Tulsa, 1955. C.P.A., Kans. Acct., Arthur Andersen & Co., Kansas City, Mo., 1955-57, Oklahoma City, 1957-65; controller Bath Iron Works Corp. (Maine), 1965-69; v.p., treas. Parkwood Laminates, Inc., Lowell, Mass., 1969-71, Dallas Cowboys Football Club, 1971—. Mem. Am. Inst. C.P.A.s. Office: Dallas Cowboys Ctr One Cowboys Pkwy Irving TX 75063-4727

WILSON, DOUGLAS DOWNES, lawyer; b. Astoria, N.Y., Jan. 20, 1947; s. Douglas and Mildred P. (Payne) W.; m. Joan Bottorf, Feb. 1, 1969; children—Douglas S., Debra J. A.B., Grove City Coll., 1968; J.D., Am. U., 1970; LL.M., George Washington U., 1974. Bar: Md. 1971, D.C. 1971, U.S. Ct. Appeals (D.C. cir.) 1972, U.S. Ct. Mil. Appeals 1972, U.S. Supreme Ct. 1975, Va. 1978, U.S. Tax Ct., U.S. Ct. Claims, U.S. Ct. Appeals (4th cir.), U.S. Dist. Ct. (we. dist.) Va. 1978, U.S. Dist. Ct. (ea. dist.) Va. 1979, U.S. Dist. Ct. (ea. dist.) Ky. 1981. Staff judge advocate Air Force Office Sci. Research, Arlington, Va., 1971-74; trial atty. Office Chief Trial Atty., Dept. Air Force, Wright Patterson AFB, Ohio, 1974-77; assoc. Martin, Hopkins & Lemon, P.C., Roanoke, Va., 1977-78; ptnr. Gardner, Moss & Brown, Washington and Roanoke, 1978-83; ptnr. Parvin & Wilson, 1984—; guest lectr. Old Dominion U., Norfolk, U. Wis., Madison, Alaska Pacific U., Anchorage. Deacon, chmn. fin. com. First Presbyn. Ch., Roanoke, 1979-82; mem. Roanoke Valley Estate Planning Council, 1979-82; dir. Legal Aid Soc., Roanoke Valley, 1982-84. Served to capt. USAF, 1971-77. Decorated Air Force Commendation medal with oak leaf cluster. Mem. ABA (pub. contract law sect.), Md. Bar Assn., D.C. Bar Assn., Fed. Bar Assn., Am. Trial Lawyers Assn., Va. Trial Lawyers Assn., Va. Bar Assn., Nat. Assn. Bond Lawyers. Presbyterian. Clubs: Elks (exalted ruler 1973-74), Forest Ridge Civic Assn. (dir. 1974-77). Home: 3030 Bancroft Dr SW Roanoke VA 24014 Office: Dominion Bank Bldg 213 S Jefferson St Suite 700 Roanoke VA 24011

WILSON, EDMUND EDWARD, marketing specialist; b. Boston, Dec. 14, 1943; s. Clinton Boyd and Florence Louise (Forsythe) W.; m. Cora Ann Partee, Dec. 7, 1975; 1 dau., Elnora Marie. Student, Ind. Inst. Tech., 1963-64, U. Mass., 1966-68. With Wilson Systems, Boston, 1973-79, Mail Systems, Boston, 1978-79, Home Party Plans, Boston, 1977-79, Commls. of Boston, 1975-80; with Security Installation Services, Inc., Alexandria, Va., 1982—, G & C Mktg., Alexandria, 1981—, NTC, Alexandria, 1983—, NA-RU Enterprises, Washington, 1984—, Greater Way Bible Sales & Ministry, Arlington, Va., 1984—; lectr. and cons. in field. Served with U.S. Army, 1964-66. Named Outstanding Bus. Leader in Alexandria, Distributive Edn. Clubs of Am., 1983. Mem. Nat. Small Bus. Assn., Internat. Entrepreneurs Assn. Contbr. articles to profl. jours.; inventor shower attachement. Home: 421 N Thomas St Suite 3 Arlington VA 22203 Office: 6911 Richmond Hwy Suite 410 Alexandria VA 22206 also 2021 K St NW Suite 305 Washington DC 20007

WILSON, EDWARD JOHN, clergyman, spiritual and mental health counselor; b. Memphis, Mar. 16, 1946; s. Richard Clark Wilson and Helen Jane (Jordan) Burcl; m. Marilyn E. May, May 6, 1978 (div. 1983); 1 child, Elizabeth Claire. B.S. in Psychology, U. Houston, 1983, M.Ed. in Counseling Psychology, 1985; postgrad. Houston Grad. Sch. Theology; D.D. (hon.), Universal Life Ch., Modesto, Calif., 1981. Ordained to ministry Universal Life Ch., 1980. Prin. Wilson Vending Co., Houston, 1968-74; salesman Century 21 Westway Realty, Houston, 1974-75; sales mgr. Century 21 James L. Berry Realty, Houston, 1975-77; v.p. broker services Century 21 of Tex., Inc., Houston, 1977-80; pastor Universal Life Ch., Houston, 1980—; instr. Houston Bapt. U., 1983-85; exec. dir. Motivational Counseling and Hypnosis Ctr., Houston. Editor, pub. ULC News newsletter, 1984—. Mem. Am. Assn. Counseling and Devel., Am. Mental Health Counselors Assn., Assn. for Religious and Values Issues in Counseling, Am. Assn. Profl. Hypnotherapists, Nat. Assn. Clergy Hypnotists, Assn. for Specialists in Group Work, Nat. Soc. Hypnotherapists, Nat. Assn. Religious Counselors, Mensa. Republican. Club: Toastmasters (pres. Houston club 1982). Avocations: camping; photography. Home: 9700 Court Glen 2007 Houston TX 77099 Office: Universal Life Church 2715 Bissonnet 409 Houston TX 77005

WILSON, FRANCES CHAPPELL, ophthalmologist; b. St. Louis, Jan. 2, 1919; d. Jesse Irving and Frances (Bigger) C.; m. Byron Gibbs Wilson, Jan. 24, 1948; children—Ann Lynn, Byron Gibbs, Frances Leigh. A.B., Washington U., St. Louis, 1940, M.D., 1943. Diplomate Am. Bd. Ophthalmology. Intern, Barnes Hosp., St. Louis, 1945; resident ophthalmology Barnes McMillan Hosp., St. Louis; practice medicine specializing in ophthalmology, St. Louis, 1946-47, Tampa, Fla., 1948—. Mem. Tampa Ophthalmology Soc. Methodist. Club: Palma Ceia Golf and Country (Tampa). Home and office: 1700 S MacDill Ave Tampa FL 33629

WILSON, FRANK LYNDALL, surgeon; b. Oct. 29, 1926; children—Frank L. III, Patricia L.; m. Kristina F. Wilson, June 29, 1984. B.S., Emory U., 1948, M.D., 1952. Diplomate Am. Bd. Surgery, 1960. Surg. intern Univ. Hosps. Cleve., 1952-53; asst. surg. resident Grady Meml. Hosp., Atlanta, 1953, 55-58, chief surg. resident, 1958-59, now mem. surg. staff; pvt. practice surgery, Atlanta, 1959—; chmn. dept. surgery Piedmont Hosp., Atlanta, 1984—, also trustee, mem. surg. staff; clin. assoc. prof. surgery Emory U. Sch. Medicine; mem. staff Crawford W. Long Meml. Hosp.; courtesy staff mem. St. Joseph's West Pace's Ferry, Drs. Meml., Northside hosps. Trustee Lovett Sch., 1971-79; chmn. med. div. United Way Atlanta, 1978. Served with USN, 1944-46, 53-55. Fellow ACS (pres. Ga. chpt. 1976-77); mem. Med. Assn. Atlanta (dir. 1977-82, pres. 1980, chmn. med. adv. com. selective service, peer rev. com.), Atlanta Med. Heritage Inc. (pres. 1980-83), Med. Assn. Ga. (vice councilor 1966-68, del.), Ga. Surg. Soc., So. Med. Assn., AMA, Atlanta Clin. Soc. Rocky Mountain Traumatological Soc. Presbyterian. Club: Piedmont Driving. Office: 35 Collier Rd NW Suite 670 Atlanta GA 30309

WILSON, FRED TALBOTT, architect; b. Houston, Oct. 2, 1912; s. Fred Taylor and Irene (Davis) W.; m. Irene Lee, Nov. 27, 1945 (div. 1979); children—Elizabeth Valentine (dec.), Michael Talbott. Student Vanderbilt U., 1930-31; B.A., Rice U., 1934, B.S., 1935. Registered architect. Jr. ptnr. Claud Hooton, Houston, 1934-35, 36-37; designer, draftsman Johnson & Porter, N.Y.C., 1935-36; founder, pres. Talbott Wilson Assocs. Inc., and predecessor firms, Houston, 1938—. Bd. dirs. Nat. Com. on U.S. China Relations, Inc., 1968-72; chmn. Houston Com. on Fgn. Relations, 1962-63. Served to lt. col. AUS, 1941-45. Decorated Bronze Star; Order Cloud and Banner (China); recipient design excellence awards. Fellow AIA (pres. Houston 1950, bd. dirs. 1952-54, chmn. AIA guide to Houston Architecture 1970-72), Tex. Soc. Architects, Rice U. Assocs., Breakfast Assn., Houston Philos. Soc. Ruling elder Presbyterian Ch. Clubs: Breakfast, Forest, Houston C. of C. (com. chmn. 1960-61). Office: 4295 San Felipe 220 Houston TX 77027

WILSON, GAIL ALVIN, furniture manufacturing company executive; b. Harrison, Ark., Feb. 21, 1945; s. Rupert (Dick) and Oneta Cordelia (McFerrin) W.; m. Judith Marie Cooper, Feb. 4, 1966 (div. 1976); 1 son, James Alvin. A.A., So. Baptist Jr. Coll., 1965; B.S. in Bus. Mgmt., Ark. State U., 1972. Machinist, Cloud Oak Flooring, Harrison, 1965-66; machine inspector/operator Flexsteel Industries, Harrison, 1969; mgr. mktg. and pub. relations Am. Pioneer and Life Ins. Co., Trumann, Ark., 1970-71; assembly operator Gen. Electric, Inc., Jonesboro, Ark., 1971-75; indsl. engr. Charisma Chairs, Inc. subs. Flexsteel Industries, Sweetwater, Tenn., 1975—. Mem. Mayor's Citizens Affairs Com., Sweetwater Indsl. Bd., 1983—; election judge Sweetwater Democratic com. Served with U.S. Army, 1967-69, Vietnam. Decorated Purple Heart, Bronze Star with oak leaf cluster. Mem. Sweetwater Jaycees (Outstanding Jaycee 1976-77, fin. v.p. 1976, 80), VFW (sr. vice comdr. Sweetwater Gold Star post 1983, outstanding achievement plaque 1982-83). Baptist. Lodge: Odd Fellows.

WILSON, GARY WAINE, ophthalmologist, surgeon; b. Oklahoma City, Oct. 22, 1942; s. Harold W. and Dorothy A. Wilson; m. Nancy Coffman, Dec. 27, 1964; children—Dan, Teri. M.D., U. Okla., 1968. Diplomate Am. Bd. Ophthalmology. Intern, Henry Ford Hosp., Detroit, 1968-69, resident in ophthalmology 1971-75; ophthalmologist, Lawton, Okla., 1975—; chief of surgery Southwestern Hosp., Lawton, 1977, 81, chief of staff, 1978, 82, governing bd., 1978, 82. Pres., Lawton Christian Sch. Bd., 1980—. Served to capt. U.S. Army, 1969-71. Fellow Am. Acad. Ophthalmology; mem. Am. Intraocular Implant Soc., Outpatient Ophthalmic Surg. Soc. Democrat. Avocations: landscape architecture; pecan farmer. Office: 2720 Gore Blvd Lawton OK 73505

WILSON, GAYNELLE, employment counselor; b. Knoxville, Tenn., Aug. 23, 1942; d. Henry Wade and Bernice Janet (Johnson) W. B.A., Carson-Newman Coll., 1964; M.S., U. Tenn., 1970. Cert. profl. counselor, Tenn. Counselor I, Tenn. Dept. Employment Security, Knoxville, 1964-65, counselor II, 1965-75, technician, Nashville, 1975-76, counselor III, 1976-78, employment counseling specialist supr., 1978—; counseling cons. U.S. Dept. of Labor, Jerusalem, 1981. Recipient Award of Merit, Internat. Assn. Personnel in Employment Security, 1981. Mem. Nat. Employment Counselors Assn. (pres. 1985-86), Tenn. Assn. Counseling and Devel. (pres. 1984-85), Middle Tenn. Assn. Counseling and Devel. (pres. 1982-83), AAUW. Baptist. Avocations: traveling; reading; music. Home: 1725 Gen George Patton Dr 707 Franklin TN 37064 Office: Tenn Dept Employment Security C1-114 Cordell Hull Bldg Nashville TN 37219

WILSON, HAROLD WOODROW, chemist; b. Colorado Springs, Colo., July 10, 1917; s. Edwin and Paula (Wolter) W.; student Colo. Sch. Mines, 1935-36, Ind. U., 1938-39; B.Chemistry, U. Mo., 1945. Teaching asst. U. Oreg., 1946-47; lead analytical chemist Sheffield Steel Corp., Kansas City, Mo., 1940-44; sr. organic research chemist Cook Paint & Varnish Co., Kansas City, 1944-45; chief analytical chemist Am. Marietta Corp., Chgo., 1947-53; pres., lab. dir. Wilson Labs., El Paso, Tex., 1953-74, Harmax Labs., Inc., El Paso, 1974—. Served with USNR, World War II; PTO. Fellow Am. Inst. Chemists; mem. Profl. Chemists Assn. (life accreditation), ASTM, Am. Inst. Chemists. Patentee in field. Office: PO Box 9851 El Paso TX 79989

WILSON, HARRISON B., college president; b. Amstead, N.Y., Apr. 21, 1928; m. Lucy Wilson; children—Benjamin, Harrison, John, Richard, Jennifer, Marquarite. B.S., Ky. State U.; M.S., D.H.S., Ind. U. Head basketball coach Jackson State Coll., 1951-60, chmn. dept. health and phys. edn., 1960-67; dir. coop. edn. Tenn. State U.; exec. asst., pres. Fisk U.; pres. Norfolk State Coll. (Va.), 1975—; dir. Va. Nat. Bank. Mem. Va. State Adv. Council on Vocat. Edn.; bd. dirs. Health, Welfare, Recreation Planning Council; mem. lay adv. bd. DePaul Hosp. Mem. Alpha Kappa Mu. Office: Norfolk State U 2401 Corprew Ave Norfolk VA 23504*

WILSON, HARTWELL THOMAS, psychologist, psychology educator; b. Corpus Christi, Tex., July 20, 1947; s. Hartwell Thomas and Jess Harkness (Curl) W. A.B., Washington U., St. Louis, 1969, M.S.W., 1971; Ph.D., Fla. Inst. Tech., 1986. Cert. social worker, 1978; lic. marriage and family therapist, 1984. Asst. prof. U. Ark., Fayetteville, 1978-81; dir. of treatment Youth Estate, Brunswick, Ga., 1982-84; adj. faculty U. N. Fla., Jacksonville, 1984—; pvt. practice, Jacksonville, 1984—; cons. in field. Author: (with others) Out of the Mainstream, 1978. Mem. Am. Psychol. Assn., Fla. Psychol. Assn., Am. Orthopsychiat. Assn., Nat. Assn. Social Workers. Democrat. Presbyterian. Club: Exchange. Avocations: camping; boating; video; photography; travel. Home: Harmony Hall Doctors Inlet FL 32030 Office: Baymeadows Ctr for Psychotherapy Suite 303 9471 Baymeadows Rd Jacksonville FL 32216

WILSON, HOMER MARVIN, elec. engr., electronic instruments mfg. co. exec.; b. St. Louis, Oct. 3, 1934; s. Homer Marvin and Ogarita (Bailey) W.; student Loughborough Coll. (Eng.), 1955-56; B.A., Rice U., 1959; B.S. in Elec. Engring., 1960; m. Rita Jeanne Evans, Mar. 11, 1979. Electronic design engr. Hamner Electronics Co., Princeton, N.J., 1960; tech. mgr. Palmer Physics Labs., Princeton, 1961; v.p. Tech. Enterprises Corp., Houston, 1963-64; pres. H.M. Wilson Co., Houston, 1965—. Served with U.S. Army, 1955-56. Registered profl. engr., Tex. Mem. Nat. Soc. Profl. Engrs., IEEE, Nat. Assn. Corrosion Engrs., Instrument Soc. Am., ASTM., Aircraft Owners and Pilots Assn., Exptl. Aircraft Assn. Republican. Episcopalian. Patentee in field. Home: 353 N Post Oak Ln Apt 725 Houston TX 77024 Office: 11501 Chimney Rock St Houston TX 77035

WILSON, J. TYLEE, business executive; b. Teaneck, N.J., June 18, 1931; s. Eric J. and Florence Q. Wilson; A.B., Lafayette Coll., 1953; m. Patricia F. Harrington, July 17, 1970; children—Jeffrey J., Debra L., Christopher F. Group v.p., dir. Chesebrough-Pond's Inc., 1960-74; pres., chief exec. officer, dir. RJR Foods, Inc., 1974-76; chmn. chief exec. officer, dir. R.J. Reynolds Tobacco Internat., Inc., Winston-Salem, N.C., from 1976, exec. v.p., dir. R.J. Reynolds Industries Co. Inc., Winston-Salem, from 1976; now chmn., chief exec. officer, dir. R.J. Reynolds Industries, Inc., Winston-Salem. Bd. visitors Bowman Gray Sch. Medicine; trustee Randolph-Macon Coll. Served with U.S. Army, 1954-56. Clubs: Old Town, The Links; Ocean Reef (Key Largo, Fla.); Ponte Vedra (Fla.). Office: RJ Reynolds Industries Inc 1100 Reynolds Blvd Winston-Salem NC 27102

WILSON, JAMES HAMLETT, investment broker, adviser; b. Richmond, Va., July 14, 1954; s. George Price and Louise (Smith) W.; m. Ginger Garrison, Mar. 26, 1982. B.A. in Econs., Hampden-Sydney Coll., 1976. Corporate banking officer nat. accounts Bank of Va., Richmond, 1976-79; investment broker Cecil, Waller & Sterling, Richmond, 1980-83; v.p. E.F. Hutton & Co., Richmond, 1983—; mgr. various investment clubs. Mem. Henrico County Republican Com., 1985; del. Va. Republican conv., 1985; bd. dirs. Am. Heart Assn., Richmond, 1982—. Named to Pres.' Club, E.F. Hutton, 1983, Blue Chip Club, 1984, 85. Clubs: Country of Va., Issac Walton (Richmond). Presbyterian. Avocations: car collector; tennis; hunting; martial arts. Home: 9302 Erlwood Rd Richmond VA 23229 Office: E F Hutton & Co Inc 629 E Main St Richmond VA 23219

WILSON, JAMES JOHN, constrn. and real estate exec.; b. N.Y.C., Apr. 18, 1933; s. Daniel J. and Mary (O'Donnell) W.; B.C.E., Manhattan Coll., 1955; m. Barbara A. Wilson, July 27, 1957; children—Kevin John, Elizabeth Ann, Thomas Brian, Mary Patricia, James Michael, Brian Joseph. Pres., chmn. Interstate Gen. Corp., Hato Rey, P.R., 1965—; pres., chmn. Wilson Securities Corp.; chmn. Interstate Land Devel. Corp., Inc., Interstate St. Charles, Inc.; dir. Va. Stallion Sta. Inc.; adv. council Banco Popular de P.R., 1968-70. Pres., Buck Hill Falls Community Assn.; bd. dirs. Hill Sch., Middleburg, Va. Recipient Alumni award for outstanding businessman Manhattan Coll., 1969. Mem. New Communities Council, Urban Land Inst., Am. Arbitration Assn., Va. Thoroughbred Assn., No. Va. Angus Assn., Soc. Am. Mil. Engrs. (pres. 1958), Nat. Assn. Home Builders (pres. P.R. chpt. 1963, dir. 1962-65), Young Pres. Orgn. (pres. Caribbean chpt. 1968-69), Manhattan Coll. Alumni Assn., World Bus. Council, Chief Execs. Orgn. Clubs: Caparra Country; N.Y. Athletic (N.Y.C.); University (Washington). Middleburg (Va.) Tennis; Banker's of P.R. Home: Dresden Farm Box 392 Middleburg VA 22117 also Buck Hill Falls PA Office: 222 Smallwood Village Center St Charles MD 20601 also Box 3908 San Juan PR 00936

WILSON, JAMES LAURENCE, real estate development executive, financial services consultant; b. Jamaica, N.Y., Mar. 20, 1945; s. William Henry and Beulah (Baylis) W.; m. Marilyn Murray, June 13, 1981; children—Leigh William, Robin Steele. B.S., Union Coll., 1968. Dir. World Assocs., Inc., Ft. Lauderdale, Fla., 1975-81; div. head Royal Trust Bank, Miami, Fla., 1981-83; sr. lending officer S.E. Bank, Tampa, 1983; sr. v.p. Southcoast, Inc., shopping ctr. devel. co., Tampa, 1984—; pres., dir. Gulfcoast Capital Resource Corp., Tampa, 1984—. Mem. Mortgage Bankers Assn., Am. Bankers Assn., Econ. Soc. South Fla., Am. Inst. Banking, Internat. Council Shopping Ctrs. Republican. Clubs: Avila Golf and Country, Centre. Home: 5002 Barrowe Pl Tampa FL 33624 Office: Southcoast Inc 2502 Rocky Point Rd Suite 760 Tampa FL 33607

WILSON, JAMES MILTON, JR., bank executive; b. Newport News, Va., Feb. 17, 1934; s. James Milton and Pearle (Forrest) W.; m. Jacqueline Rose Willingham, Aug. 19, 1962 (div. 1969); 1 child, James Milton, IV. B.A., U. Richmond, 1955, M.S., 1963. Sales rep. Met. Life Ins. Co., Newport News, 1956-58; personnel officer United Va. Bank, Richmond, 1959-70, sr. v.p., human resources dir., 1970-85, exec. v.p., dir. human resources, 1985—; tchr. U. Richmond, 1969—. Bd. dirs. Family and Children's Service, Richmond, 1975-82, St. John's Hosp. Inc., Richmond, 1983—. Williams fellow U. Richmond, 1958. Mem. Met. C. of C. (chmn. edn. com. 1984-85), Internat. Transactional Analysis Assn., Am. Soc. Personnel Adminstrs. (bd. dirs. 1983, chmn. region IV conf. 1983), Personnel Accreditation Inst. (sr. profl. in human resources), Nat. Speakers Assn. Republican. Clubs: Bull and Bear (Richmond), Rector's. Office: United Va Bank 919 E Main St Richmond VA 23229

WILSON, JAMES ROBERT, nitrogenous fertilizer manufacturing manager; b. Tremont, Miss., Aug. 26, 1932; s. James Gordy and Eva D. (Ledbetter) W.; m. Floyce B. Barnett, Mar. 1, 1952; children—Deborah Susan, James Larry, Michael Stuart. Trainee operator Am. Cyanamid Co., New Orleans, 1954-56, prodn. supr., 1956-59, start-up supr., engring. constrn. div., Ont., Can., 1959-60, prodn. supr., New Orleans, 1960-66; prodn. supr., safety dir. First Nitrogen Corp., Donaldsonville, La., 1966-69; ops. supt., safety dir., CF Industries, Inc., Donaldsonville, 1969-74, prodn. mgr. complex I, 1974-83, supt. safety security and med., 1983—; owner, pres. Wilson Fabric Ctr., Donaldsonville, 1967—. Chmn. St. Charles Parish Republican Orgn., La., 1965, Mem. La. Loss Prevention Assn., Nat. Safety Council, Greater Baton Rouge Indsl. Mgrs. Assn., Am. Soc. Safety Engrs. Baptist. Club: Indsl. Mgrs. Conf. (Baton Rouge). Lodges: Rotary (pres. 1982-83), Masons, Shriners. Avocations: golf; fishing; hunting. Home: 10336 Oliphant Rd Baton Rouge LA 70809 Office: C F Industries Inc PO Box 468 Donaldsonville LA 70346

WILSON, JANICE ELIZABETH, librarian; b. Boone, N.C., Apr. 24, 1951; d. Chapell and Myrtle (Brandon) W. B.S., Appalachian State U., 1973; M.L.S., George Peabody Coll., 1977. Media specialist Gaston County Schs., Gastonia, N.C., 1973-76; librarian Truett-McConnell Coll., Cleveland, Ga., 1977—. Mem. Ga. Library Assn. ALA, S.E. Library Assn., Beta Phi Mu (membership award 1978). Baptist. Home: PO Box 721 Cleveland GA 30528 Office: Cofer Library Truett-McConnell Coll Cleveland GA 30528

WILSON, JOHN DELANE, university president; b. Lapeer, Mich., Aug. 17, 1931; s. Myron John and Helen (O'Conner) W.; m. Anne Veronica Yeomans, Sept. 21, 1957; children—Stephen, Anthony, Patrick, Sara. B.A., Mich. State U., 1953; Ph.D., 1965; B.A. (hon.), Oxford (Eng.) U., 1955. Asst. to v.p. acad. affairs Mich. State U., East Lansing, 1958-59, assoc. dir., dir. honors coll. and dir. undergrad. edn., 1963-66; asst. to pres. SUNY-Albany, 1959-63; pres. Wells Coll., Aurora, N.Y., 1968-75; exec. v.p., provost Va. Poly. Inst., Blacksburg, 1975-82; pres. Washington and Lee U., Lexington, Va., 1982—. Bd. dirs. Va. Found. for Humanities and Pub. Policy, 1978-84; mem. Gov.'s Commn. on Future of Va., 1982-84. Served to 1st lt. USAF, 1955-57. Rhodes scholar, 1953-55. Mem. Assn. Am. Rhodes Scholars, Phi Beta Kappa, Phi Alpha Theta, Phi Kappa Phi, Omicron Delta Kappa. Clubs: University, Princeton (N.Y.C.). Home: 2 University Pl Lexington VA 24450 Office: Washington and Lee U Lexington VA 24450

WILSON, JOHN ERIC, biochemist; b. Champaign, Ill., Dec. 13, 1919; s. William Courtney and Marie Winette (Lytle) W.; m. Marion Ruth Heaton, June 7, 1947; children—Kenneth Heaton, Douglas Courtney, Richard Mosher. B.S., U. Chgo., 1941; M.S., U. Ill., Urbana, 1944; Ph.D., Cornell U., 1948. Research asst. Pyroxylin Products, Inc., Chgo., summers 1941-42, Gen. Foods Corp., Hoboken, N.J., summer, 1943; asst. in chemistry U. Ill., 1941-44; asst. biochemistry Cornell U. Med. Coll., N.Y.C., 1944-48, research assoc., 1948-50; asst. prof. biochemistry U. N.C., Chapel Hill, 1950-60, assoc. prof., 1960-65, prof., 1970—, dir. grad. studies, dept. biochemistry, 1965-71, acting dir. neurobiology program, 1968-69, assoc. dir., 1969-72, dir., 1972-73; Kenan prof. U. Utrecht (Netherlands), 1978. Scoutmaster Occoneechee council Boy Scouts Am., 1959-66; adv. council Chapel Hill Twp., 1978-85; mem. Orange County (N.C.) Planning Bd., 1979-85. Fellow AAAS; mem. Am. Chem. Soc., Am. Soc. Biol. Chemists, Am. Soc. Neurochemistry, Soc. Neurosci. (council 1969-70, chmn. fin. com. 1973-78, organizer, mem. exec. com. N.C. chpt. 1974-75), Harvey Soc., N.Y. Acad. Sci., N.C. Acad. Sci., Sigma Xi, Phi Lambda Upsilon, Alpha Chi Sigma, Beta Theta Pi. Contbr. numerous articles on biochemistry and neurochemistry to profl. jours. Home: 214 Spring Ln Chapel Hill NC 27514 Office: U NC Sch Medicine Dept Biochemistry and Nutrition Chapel Hill NC 27514

WILSON, JOHN TRUESDELL, retired banker; b. Faubush, Ky., July 23, 1898; s. William Floyd and Doretta (Combest) W.; student Jefferson Sch. Law, 1929-31, Stonier Grad. Sch. Banking, Rutgers U., 1956-68; m. Evangeline Cooper, Apr. 28, 1917 (dec.); children—John Dave (dec.), James Truesdell (dec.), Eva Elizabeth (Mrs. Ollie Caplin, Jr.); m. Mary C. Pierce, Mar. 1938. Partner Truesdell Wilson Sales & Service, Somerset, Ky., 1945-52; farmer, Ky., 1921-49; salesman Swift & Co., Somerset, 1923-24; plant mgr., engr. Wood-Mosiac Co., Monticello, Ky. and Louisville, 1931-35; with First Farmers Nat. Bank, Somerset, 1933-85, pres., 1961-73, chmn., 1973-84, also dir.; dealer Chevrolet Co., Somerset, 1937-39, Chrysler Co., Somerset, 1945-52; owner, pres., operator Ky. Oil Co., Somerset, 1935-52. Dir., pres. Farmers Tobacco Warehousing Corp., 1948—, Peoples State Bank, Monticello, Ky., 1934-35. Mgr. various Democratic campaigns, 1935-58. Bd. dirs. Somerset-Pulaski County Airport, 1948-85, chmn., 1952-85. Mem. Am., Ky. bankers assns., Ky. (dir. 1950-69), Somerset-Pulaski County (pres. 1957) chambers of commerce. Clubs: Masons, Kiwanis (pres. 1955, lt. gov. 1958). Author: History of Banking in Pulaski County, 1970. Home: Dutton Hill Somerset KY 42501 Office: One Fountain Sq Somerset KY 42501

WILSON, KAREN SUE, educator; b. Columbia, Ky., Nov. 23, 1940; d. Clyde Nelson and Irene (Burton) Pendleton; m. Dan Coleman Wilson, June 19, 1965; 1 step-dau., Valerie Ann Geary. A.A., Lindsey Wilson Jr. Coll., 1960; B.S., Campbellsville Coll., 1963; M.S., Western Ky. U., 1970; Ed.S., Nova U., 1982. Tchr. English, coach drama Dayton High Sch. (Ky.), 1963-65, Western High Sch., Louisville, 1965-67; tchr. speech, English, debate coach Southwest Miami High Sch., Fla., 1967-77; head lang. arts dept. Sunset Sr. High Sch., Miami, Fla., 1977-82; tchr. gifted program Southwest High Sch., Miami, Fla., 1982—; chmn. Nat. Forensic League, Miami, Fla., 1972-73, 75-76; pres. Ambu, Inc.; v.p. DCWI Construction Co. Author manual Step-By-Step Procedure for Writing A Research Paper, 1982. Named Southwest Miami Jr. C. of C. Outstanding Young Educator, 1975; Dade County speech Tchr. of Year, Dade County Speech Tchrs. Assn., 1975; Tchr. of Year, Southwest High Sch., Miami, Fla., 1977. Mem. Nat. Council Tchrs. English, Delta Kappa Gamma (pres. Alpha Zeta Chpt. 1984—). Republican. Methodist. Home: 11731 SW 97th Ave Miami FL 33176 Office: Southwest Miami Sr High Sch 8855 SW 50 Terr Miami FL 33165

WILSON, LARRY JOSEPH, editor; b. St. Charles, Mo., Mar. 21, 1948; s. Clyde Marvin and Maxine Mary (Schwendeman) W.; 1 child, Heather Renee. B.A. in English, U. Mo.-St. Louis, 1969; postgrad. U. Mo., 1969-70, Am. U., 1977. Tech. writer, U.S. Army Missile Command, Huntsville, Ala., 1970-71, U.S. Army Munitions Command, Dover, N.J., 1971-72; chief writer, editor Atmospheric Scis. Lab., White Sands, N.Mex., 1972-75; assoc. editor Def. Mgmt. Jour., Alexandria, Va., 1975-78, editor, 1978-82, 82—; chief pub. affairs officer U.S. Army Depot Systems Command, Chambersburg, Pa., 1982; lectr. in field. Contbr. articles to profl. jours. Bd. dirs. Boys' Club Am., Las Cruces, N.Mex., 1974. Fellow Inter-Univ. Seminar on Armed Forces and Soc.; mem. Brookings Instn. Inter-agy. Seminar Group. Avocations: bicycling; gardening; musician. Home: 5415 Montgomery St Springfield VA 22151 Office: Def Mgmt Jour OASD (A&L) 716-R Church St Alexandria VA 22314

WILSON, LAVERNE, nursing administrator; b. Fontaine, Ark., July 27, 1931; d. James Gordon and Sophronia (Scott) Nutt; m. John Bruce Wilson, June 30, 1950 (div. 1971); children—Deborah French, Emily Wilson, Valerie Keating, John B. Wilson Jr., B.G. Scott Wilson. A.A., Ark. State U., 1974.

Charge nurse Ark. Methodist Hosp., Paragould, 1975-78; instr. Delta Vo-Tech, Marked Tree, Ark., 1978-81; clin. nurse educator VA Hosp., North Little Rock, 1981-83; adminstr. coordinator Ark. Methodist Hosp., Paragould, 1983—, in-service coordinator, 1983—; pres. J.G.N., Inc. Mem. Ark. Assn. Critical Care Nurses, Alpha Gamma Delta. Democrat. Baptist. Avocations: Travel; boating. Home: 4 Ridgeway Paragould AR 72450

WILSON, LAWRENCE A., construction company executive; b. Nashville, 1935. Grad., Vanderbilt U., 1957. Pres., chief exec. officer HCB Contractors, Dallas. Office: HCB Contractors 4600 First Nat Bank Bldg Dallas TX 75202*

WILSON, LEONARD RICHARD, geology educator, museum curator, consultant; b. Superior, Wis., July 23, 1906; s. Ernest and Sarah Jane (Cooke) W.; m. Marian DeWilde, Sept. 1, 1930; children—Richard Graham, Marcia Wilson Roe. Ph.B., U. Wis., Madison, 1930, Ph.M., 1932, Ph.D., 1935. From instr. to prof. Coe Coll., Cedar Rapids, Iowa, 1934-46; prof., head dept. geology and mineralogy U. Mass., Amherst, 1946-56; prof. geology NYU, 1956-57; prof. geology U. Okla., Norman, 1957-61, research prof., 1961-77, George Lynn Cross Research prof. of geology and geophysics, 1968-77, prof. emeritus, 1977—; geologist IV Okla. Geol. Survey, Norman, 1957-77; curator of paleobotany Stovall Mus. Sci. and History, Norman, 1970—; leader Greenland ice cap expdn. Am. Geog. Soc., 1953; cons. in palynology, 1945—; mem. editorial bd. Elsevier Sci. Pubs., Netherlands, 1967—. Contbr. articles and papers to tech. jours. Mem. Cedar Rapids City Planning Commn., 1945-47. Melhaup fellow Ohio State U., 1939-40. Fellow Geol. Soc. Am., AAAS, Palynological Soc. India (Gunnard Ertman Internat. Medal 1974); mem. Am. Assn. Petroleum Geologists, Iowa Acad. Sci. (life fellow, editor 1935-45), Sigma Xi, Explorers Club, Audubon Soc. (pres. local chpt. 1983-84), Am. Assn. Stratigraphic Palynologists (hon. mem.), Phi Beta Kappa. Avocations: gardening; photography; British history. Home: 933 Wilson St Norman OK 73072 Office: Stovall Mus Sci and History 1335 Asp Ave Norman OK 73019

WILSON, LILLIAN GRACE, English educator; b. Glasgow, W.Va., July 30, 1925; d. Augustus Alexander and Grace Virginia (Buckland) Love; m. Blair Larue Wilson, 1943 (dec. 1954); 1 child, Paul Richard. B.S., Alderson-Broaddus Coll., 1953; M.A., W.Va. U., 1960; Ph.D., Ohio U., 1968. Cert. secondary tchr., W.Va. Tchr. pub. schs., W.Va., 1953-62; instr. Morris Harvey Coll., Charleston, W.Va., 1962-63, Ohio U., Athens, 1963-68; prof. U. Charleston, 1968—. Mem. Delta Kappa Gamma (1st v.p. 1984—). Baptist. Avocations: reading; music; hiking; gardening. Home: 4110 Virginia Ave SE Charleston WV 25304

WILSON, LINDA GAIL, international relations specialist; b. Bryan, Tex., Dec. 26, 1957; d. Edmon Doak and May Beth (Herron) W. B.A., SW Tex. State U., 1979; M.A., U. Tex., 1982, Ph.D., 1983. Copy editor Univ. Star, San Marcos, Tex., 1979; research asst. U. Tex., Austin, 1979-81; research assoc. Human Interaction Research, Austin, 1981-84; market analyst U. Tex., San Antonio, 1984-85; internat. relations specialist City of San Antonio, 1985—. Co-author: A Study of Adult University Students, 1980. Mem. Am. Statis. Assn., Am. Psychol. Assn., San Antonio Alliance of Bus. (com. mem. 1984—), Future San Antonio, Alpha Lambda Delta, Alpha Chi. Democrat. Methodist. Home: 4822 Gus Eckert Apt 1214 San Antonio TX 78240 Office: Office of Internat Relations City of San Antonio PO Box 9066 San Antonio TX 78285

WILSON, LOIS SCHILLER, instructional executive, consultant; b. Yonkers, N.Y.; d. Harry Joseph and Helen Claudia (Schiller) Friedman; m. Peter Mason Wilson, July 13, 1957; children—Katherine Rose, Kenneth Mason, II. B.S., Fla. State U., 1957, M.A., 1965, Ph.D., 1974. Cert. tchr., Ga. Sr. faculty mem. U.S. Dept. State, Ibadan, Nigeria, 1965-66; mem. teaching faculty Fla. A&M U., Tallahassee, 1969-70; teaching asst. Fla. State U., Tallahassee, 1966-69, editor Intermediate Sci. Curriculum Study, 1970-74, research faculty Individual Sci. Instructional System, 1974-79; courseware mgr. Hazeltine Corp., Reston, Va., 1979—; mem. task force Fla. Ednl. Assessment Programs, Tallahassee, 1979; cons. Marymount Coll., Alexandria, Va., 1985. Author: Sending the Message, 1975. Assoc. editor Tng. Tech. Jour., 1984—. Contbr. numerous books and articles to profl. jours. Sch. supt. Holy Comforter Episcopal Ch., Vienna, Va., 1983—; v.p. Fla. State U. United Faculty of Fla. chpt., Tallahassee, 1978-79; bd. dirs. Fla. State U. Alumni Assn., Atlanta, 1963-65. Mem. Am. Ednl. Research Assn. (chmn. div. C-5 1984-85), Interservice Industry Tng. Equipment Conf. Nat. Security Indsl. Assn. (program chmn. 1984—), Mil. Edn. Tng. Assn. (program chmn.), Am. Ednl. Research Assn., Am. Soc. for Tng. Devel. (bd. dirs. 1985-86), Alpha Xi Delta. Republican. Club: Quill and Scroll (faculty adv. 1958-65). Office: Hazeltine Corp 10800 Parkridge Blvd Reston VA 22091

WILSON, MACK ALEXANDER, agricultural sciences educator; b. Quitman, Ga., Apr. 13, 1948; s. Eddie Alexander and Fannie Frances (Robinson) W.; m. Dollie Culver, Feb. 12, 1971; 1 dau., Dawn K.M. B.S., Ft. Valley State Coll., 1970; M.S., Tuskegee Inst., 1975; Ph.D., U. Ill., 1979. Soil conservationist trainee U.S. Dept. Agr., Willmar, Minn., 1970; grad. asst. Tuskegee (Ala.) Inst., 1971, asst. prof. agrl. scis., 1981—; grad. asst. U. Ill., Urbana, 1976-79; asst. prof. Fla. A&M U., Tallahassee, 1979-81. Served with U.S. Army, 1971-73. Mem. Am. Soc. for Hort. Sci., So. Region Am. Soc. Hort. Sci., Ala. Fruit Growers Assn., Ala. Sweet Potato Assn., Ala. Higher Edn. Assn., Ala. Acad. Scis. Mem. Ch. of Christ. Contbr. articles to profl. jours. Home: Route 1 Box 52-C Tuskegee AL 36083 Office: Dept Agrl Scis Tuskegee Inst Tuskegee Institute AL 36088

WILSON, MARJORIE HARHI, museum store manager; b. Patuxent River, Md., Dec. 2, 1949; d. Theodore Francis and Ruth (Gale) Harhi; m. Robert James Wilson, May 14, 1983. Student St. Petersburg Jr. Coll., Fla., 1981-83. Mus. store mgr. Salvador Dali Mus., St. Petersburg, 1981—. Mem. The Arts Ctr., St. Petersburg, 1982, 83. Mem. Fla. Retail Fedn., Mus. Store Assn., Art League of Burke County, Burke County Arts Council. Democrat. Office: Morning Star Gallery Rt 1 Box 198-A Banner Elk NC 28604

WILSON, MILLARD FILLMORE, educator, management consultant; b. Sanderson, Fla., Oct. 16, 1911; s. George Washington and Martha Christopher (Houston) W.; B.E., U. Fla., 1939, M.Ed., 1940; postgrad. Duke U., 1941; D.B.A. (hon.), Catawba Coll., 1981; m. Helen P. Brown, Sept. 20. Instr. Andrew Jackson Sch., Jacksonville, Fla., 1940-44, dean of men, 1944-48; asso. prof. commerce Catawba Coll., Salisbury, N.C., 1948-79, prof. emeritus, 1979—, dir. placement office, 1948-78, chmn. dept. commerce, 1950-79, chmn. emeritus, 1979—; pres., dir. Dr. Millard Wilson and Assocs., mgmt. cons., 1979—. Pres., Rowan County Inter-Civic Council, Rowan County Friends of Library; bd. dirs. N.C. Assn. Friends of N.C. Libraries; mem. nat. speakers bur. Boy Scouts Am., vice chmn. Rowan County council; mem. Rowan County Blind Council. Named Rowan County Man of Year, 1967. Mem. Am. Acad. Polit. and Social Sci., So. Econ. Assn., Adminstrv. Mgmt. Soc. (exec. v.p., treas.), Sales-Mktg. Execs. Club (exec. Salisbury), Am. Accounting Assn., Soc. Advt. Mgmt., Acad. Mgmt., Am. Mktg. Assn., N.C. Bus. Edn. Council, N.C. Assn. for Blind, Internat. Platform Assn., Acad. Certified Adminstrv. Mgrs., Kappa Delta Pi. Mason (K.T., Shriner), Lion (pres. Salisbury, zone chmn., dist. gov., internat. counselor). Club: Salisbury Country (dir.). Address: Catawba Coll Salisbury NC 28144

WILSON, NANCY VINES, statistician; b. Jasper, Ala., July 19, 1936; d. Carl Donald and Virginia (Morris) Vines; m. Joseph Edwards Wilson, Jr., Oct. 10, 1959; children—Joseph Edwards III, Carl Vines, Lisa Caroline. B.A., U. Tenn., 1957; M. Liberal Arts, So. Meth. U., 1972; M.S., U. Tex.-Dallas, 1976. Engr. Ling-Temco, Garland, Tex., 1957-60; statistician Inst. for Aerobics Research, Dallas, 1977-80, Am. Heart Assn., Dallas, 1980, U. Tex. Health Sci. Ctr., Dallas, 1980-84, Future Computing, Inc., Dallas, 1984—. Contbr. articles to profl. jours. Officer, bd. dirs. Richardson Environ. Action League, 1972—. Mem. Am. Statis. Assn., Am. Heart Assn. Council on Epidemiology, LWV Richardson (bd. dirs. 1961—), Mensa. Office: Future Computing Inc 8111 LBJ Freeway Dallas TX 75251

WILSON, OLEN EDWARD, petroleum geologist; b. Perryton, Tex., May 17, 1959; s. Floyd Clifton and Sarah (Norton) W. B.S., West Tex. State U.,1980. Geologist, Falcon Petroleum, San Antonio, 1981-83; exploration mgr. MRR Oil Inc., Perryton, Tex., 1983-84; ind. geologist, Perryton, 1984—; cons. in field of prospect generation. Mem. Am. Assn. Petroleum Geologists, Panhandle Geol. Soc., Tulsa Geol. Soc., Oklahoma City Geol. Soc., Sigma Gamma Epsilon. Avocations: Outdoor sports. Home: 906 Loyola Perryton TX 79070 Office: PO Box 1233 Perryton TX 79070

WILSON, OLIVE FULLER, librarian; b. Martinsville, Tex., Feb. 18, 1922; d. Fulton and Lillian B. (Brewer) F.; m. William T. Lander, Jr., Mar. 31, 1943 (dec. 1968); children—Susan Lander Pierce, Margaret Lander Shaw, Mary Laura Lander; m. 2d Jack Crymes Wilson, Feb. 25, 1973. B.Mus., Mary Hardin Coll., 1943; M.L.L., U. S.C., 1979. Tchr. English, Williamston pub. schs. (S.C.), 1948-50; tchr. Spartanburg, S.C., 1952-53, Pelzer Elem. Sch. (S.C.), 1953-56; dean women, hostess S.C. Opportunity Sch., West Columbia, 1961-68, dir. music, 1965-68, tchr., 1967-68, trustee, 1976—; tchr. Palmetto High Sch., Williamston, 1968-70, librarian, 1970—; pvt. piano tchr., 1945-60. Sec. Williamston Democratic Com., 1969-70, 73-74; legis. appointee Anderson County Animal Shelter, 1976—. Mem. S.C. Edn. Assn., NEA, Alpha Delta Kappa (chpt. pres. 1974-76, chaplain 1982—). Methodist. Club: Williamston Garden (pres. 1958-60, 68-70, 74-76, 80-82). Author: History of Williamston, S.C., 1970. Home: 106 Hardy St Williamston SC 29697 Office: PO Box 428 Hamilton St Extension Williamston SC 29697

WILSON, ORME, JR., former foreign service officer; b. N.Y.C., July 3, 1920; s. Orme and Alice (Borland) W.; S.B. cum laude, Harvard U., 1942; M.A., George Washington U., 1951; diploma USAF War Coll., 1965; m. Mildred Eddy Dunn, Feb. 16, 1950; children—Marshall, Elsie Dunn, Orme III. jr. pilot Pan Am. World Airways, 1946-47, U.S. Army Map Service, 1950; joined Fgn. Service, 1950; vice consul Frankfurt/am/Main, W.Ger., 1951-53; vice consul, Southampton, Eng., 1953-54; 2d sec., Belgrade, Yugoslavia, 1958-61; 2d, then 1st sec., Athens, Greece, 1961-64; assigned, Washington, 1965-70; consul gen., Zagreb, Yugoslavia, 1970-74; adviser U.S. Mission to UN, 1974-77; polit. counselor U.S. Mission to NATO, 1977-80; ret., 1980; dir. Laurel Race Course, Md., 1968-84. trustee Bishop Rhineland Found. for Episcopal Chaplaincy, Harvard U. and Radcliffe Coll., 1967-71, 76-83; adv. bd. visitors Mary Baldwin Coll., 1982—; bd. mgrs. Seamen's Ch. Inst. of N.Y. and N.J., 1984—; pres. Friends of Blandy Farm, U. Va., Boyce, 1984—. Served to lt. USNR, 1942-46. Fellow Am. Geog. Soc.; mem. Explorers Club, U.S. Tennis Assn. (Prentice Cup Com.), Thoroughbred Club Am., Va. Thoroughbred Assn. (dir. 1981—, treas. 1983-84, v.p. 1984—), Am. Horse Council. Episcopalian. Mason. Clubs: Internat. Lawn Tennis of U.S.A., Harvard, Racquet and Tennis, Brook (N.Y.C.); Metropolitan, Chevy Chase (Washington). Contbr. to Eastern Europe: Essays in Geographical Problems, 1970. Home: White Post VA 22663

WILSON, PATRICIA JANE, educator, librarian, educational consultant; b. Jennings, La., May 3, 1946; d. Ralph Harold and Wilda Ruth (Smith) Potter; m. Wendell Merlin Wilson, Aug. 24, 1968. B.S., La. State U., 1967; M.S. U. Houston-Clear Lake, 1979; Ed.D., U. Houston, 1985. Cert. tchr., learning resources specialist (librarian), Tex. Tchr., England AFB (La.) Elem. Sch., 1967-68, Edward White Elem. Sch., Clear Creek Ind. Schs., Seabrook, Tex., 1972-77; librarian C.D. Landolt Elem. Sch., Friendswood, Tex., 1979-81; instr./lectr. children's lit. U. Houston/Central, 1983—; with editor Rev. Sampler, U. Houston-Clear Lake, 1984—. Trustee, Freeman Meml. Library, Houston, 1982—, v.p., 1985-86; mem. Armand Bayou Nature Ctr., Houston, 1980—; bd. dirs. Sta. KUHT-TV, 1984—. Mem. ALA, Am. Assn. Sch. Librarians, Internat. Reading Assn., Tex. Assn. Improvement of Reading, Tex. Council Tchrs. of English, Nat. Council Tchrs. English, Kappa Delta Pi, Alpha Delta Kappa, Phi Delta Kappa. Methodist. Club: Lakewood Yacht (Seabrook). Home: 1118 Appleford Dr Seabrook TX 77586

WILSON, PAUL LOWELL, lawyer; b. Rockingham County, Va., May 12, 1951; s. James Joseph and Edna Vivian (Halterman) W.; m. Thea Elaine Hermit, June 21, 1975; children—Meredith Elaine, Taylor Halterman. A.B., W.Va. U., 1973; J.D., Coll. of William and Mary, 1976. Bar: W.Va. 1976, U.S. Dist. Ct. (so. dist.) W.Va. 1976, Va. 1979. Assoc. Brown & Peyton, Charleston, W.Va., 1976-78; title atty. Lawyers Title Ins. Corp., Williamsburg, Va., 1978-80; assoc. S.J. Baker, Williamsburg, 1981-83; counsel edn. com. W.Va. Legislature, Charleston, 1977-78; gen. counsel A.J.&L. Corp., Williamsburg, 1983—, v.p., 1985—; dir. Lafayette Ednl. Fund, Inc., Williamsburg, First Va. Bank-Commonwealth, Grafton, 503 Cert. Devel. Co., Richmond. Mem. ABA, Va. Bar Assn., Va. State Bar, W.Va. State Bar, Williamsburg Bar Assn., Sigma Phi Epsilon (dist. gov. Richmond, Va. 1982—), trustee Nat. Housing Corp. 1985—). Methodist. Lodge: Kiwanis (Williamsburg). Home: 102 Cambridge Ln Williamsburg VA 23185 Office: A J & L Corp 1408 Richmond Rd Williamsburg VA 23185

WILSON, PERKINS, lawyer, linguist; b. Cin., Aug. 17, 1929; s. Russell and Elizabeth Baldwin (Smith) W.; A.B., Princeton U., 1951; J.D., U. Va., 1956; m. Mary Earle Mackall, June 8, 1957; children—Russell Perkins, William Mackall, Elizabeth Drake. Admitted to Ohio bar, 1956, N.Y. State bar, 1958, Va. bar, 1959; asso. firm Shearman & Sterling, N.Y.C., 1956-58, Hunton & Williams, Richmond, Va., 1958-62; atty. Reynolds Metals Co., Richmond, 1962-77; asst. atty. gen. State of Va., Richmond, 1979-82; of counsel Thompson & McMullan, Richmond, 1983—. Served with U.S. Army, 1951-53. Mem. Linguistic Soc. Am., Am. Bar Assn., Assn. Computational Linguistics, Soc. History Tech., Va. Bar Assn., Richmond Bar Assn. (past chmn. corp. counsel sect.), Am. Assn. Tchrs. of German, Am. Assn. Tchrs. of French, Am. Assn. Tchrs. Spanish and Portuguese. Episcopalian. Clubs: Commonwealth, Country of Va. Author: Guide to French Noun Gender, 1978; Beginner's French Gender, 1983; Beginner's German Nouns, 1983; Basic Spanish Gender, 1984; Basic French Gender, 1985; Basic German Nouns, Part I, 1985; Basic Italian Gender, 1985; Basic Portuguese Gender, 1986. Home: 204 Tuckahoe Blvd Richmond VA 23226 Office: Thompson & McMullan 100 Shockoe Slip Richmond VA 23219

WILSON, RALPH SLOAN, retinal surgeon; b. El Dorado, Ark., Nov. 12, 1937; s. George Evander and Lauree Eta (Doss) W.; A.B., Davidson Coll., 1959; B.S., U. Ark., 1963, M.D. (Research fellow), 1963; m. Sarah Mignon Ross, Dec. 27, 1958; children—Ralph Sloan, William Gregory, Steven Robert. Intern, U. Ark. Hosps., Little Rock, 1963-64; postgrad. ophthalmology Harvard Med. Sch., Boston, 1964-65; resident ophthalmology U. Ark. Hosps., 1965, U. Tex. Med. Br., Galveston, 1965-67; Heed fellow retinal pathology and surgery Mass. Eye and Ear Infirmary, Harvard Med. Sch., Boston, 1969; asst. prof. and dir. retina services dept. ophthalmology U. Ark. Med. Center, Little Rock, 1970-75, asso. prof., 1975-81, prof., 1981—, acting chmn. ophthalmology dept., 1974-75; practice medicine specializing in retinal surgery Retinal Group, LTD., Little Rock, 1975—; mem. Ark. State Bd. Dispensing Opticians; dir. Retina Service, U.S. VA Hosp., Little Rock; chief staff, exec. com. Doctors Hosp.; dir. Ritchie Grocer Co., S.W. Trading Corp. Chmn. admissions com. U. Ark. Coll. Medicine; trustee Ark. Coll.; pres., bd. dirs. Retinal Research Fund; bd. dirs. Ark. Eye & Kidney Bank, Ark. Soc. for Prevention of Blindness, 1971-73. Served to lt. comdr. USNR, 1967-69. Diplomate Am. Bd. Ophthalmology (asso. examiner); Hoffmann La Roche grantee, 1966-67; recipient AMA Physicians Recognition awards, 1969, 75, 78, 81. Mem. Am. Acad. Ophthalmology (speakers bur.), Assn. Research and Vision in Ophthalmology, AMA, Ark., Pulaski County med. socs., Am., Ark. assns. ophthalmology, Am. Ophthal. Soc., AAUP, Research to Prevent Blindness, So. Med. Assn., Pan Am. Soc. Ophthalmology, Société Française d'Ophthalmologie, Sociedad Boliviana de Oftalmologia, New Orleans Acad. Ophthalmology, Soc. Eye Surgeons, Internat. Eye Found., U. Tex. Med. Br. Ophthalmology Alumni Assn. (pres. 1970-72), Univ. Med. Group, Soc. of Heed Fellows, Little Rock Acad. of Surgery, Retina Soc., Ark. Acad. of Ophthalmology (pres. 1975-76), Ark. Found. for Med. Care, Assn. of VA Ophthalmologists, Ark. Ophthalmology sect. of Ark. Med. Soc. (pres. 1977-78), Assn. Mil. Surgeons, Alpha Omega Alpha, Sigma Xi. Contbr. articles to profl. jours., holder patents in field. Home: 120 N Woodrow St Little Rock AR 72205 Office: Doctors Bldg Suite 519 500 S University St Little Rock AR 72205

WILSON, RICHARD LEE, political science educator; b. Worthington, Minn., Dec. 20, 1944; s. G. Roy and Dorothy Eileen (Johnson) W.; m. Carolyn Ann Dirks, Aug. 24, 1968 (div.); 1 son, Kevin Richard; m. Nora Ann McCarthy, May 15, 1982 (div.). B.A., U. Chgo., 1966, postgrad., 1966-67; Ph.D., Johns Hopkins U., 1971. Congl. aide 4th Congl. Dist. Md., 1971; asst. prof. polit. sci. U. Tenn., Chattanooga, 1971-76, assoc. prof. polit. sci., 1976—; registrar at-large Hamilton County Election Commn, 1977-84; lectr. Robert A. Taft Inst. Govt., U. Tenn., Nashville, 1978, 79, 81; supr. state legis. and met. internship program U. Tenn., Chattanooga, 1980—. Chmn. Hamilton County Health Planning Adv. Council, 1975-79; bd. dirs. Ga.-Tenn. Regional Health Commn., 1978-82; active Tenn. State Health Coordinating Council, 1977-81; exec. com. State Health Coordinating Council, 1979-81; candidate Democratic Nomination Hamilton County Council, 1974; del. Tenn. State Democratic Conv., 1972; co-chmn. Hamilton County Dem. Adv. Com., 1973-74. Recipient Outstanding Educator of Yr. Signal Mountain, Tenn. Jaycees, 1973; Polit. Edn. award NAACP, 1980. Mem. So. Polit. Sci. Assn., Midwest Polit. Sci. Assn., Tenn. Polit. Sci. Assn., Nat. Soc. Internships and Exptl. Edn., SAR. Methodist. Author: Tennessee Politics, 1976; contbr. chpts. to books.

WILSON, RICHARD OSBORN, JR., educational administrator, adult education educator; b. Sylva, N.C., Mar. 14, 1936; s. Richard, Sr. and Virginia (Campbell) W.; m. Myrtha Ann Reagan, Mar. 17, 1957; children—Richard Eric, Haynes Christopher. B.S. in Edn., Western Carolina Coll., 1961, M.A. in Edn., 1967. Cert. secondary tchr., N.C. Advt. agent Cherokee Hist. Assn., Cherokee, N.C., 1958-61; tchr. Scott Creek Sch., Sylva, N.C., 1961-63; prin. Qualla Sch., Sylva, 1963-66; dir. adult edn. Southwestern Tech. Coll., Sylva, 1966-67, dir. student services, 1967-82, dean student services, 1982—. Contbr. articles to newspapers, newsletters. Treas., Southwestern Econ. Devel. Planning Commn., Jackson County, N.C., 1967-70; sec., treas. Sylva Vol. Fire Dept. Mem. dean's div. N.C. Community Coll. Student Services Personnel Assn. (state chmn. 1982-83), Phi Delta Kappa, Phi Theta Kappa. Democrat. Methodist. Home: 27 Fisher Creek Rd Sylva NC 28779 Office: Southwestern Tech Coll 275 Webster Rd Sylva NC 28779

WILSON, ROBERT GARNER, hospital administrator; b. Princeton, Ky., Nov. 1, 1930. B.S. with distinction, Murray State U., 1959; M.S., U. Mich., 1961. Adminstrv. dir. Clin. Labs. Nashville, Inc., 1970-71; adminstr. Colbert County Hosp., Sheffield, Ala., 1970; asst. dir., adminstrv. research coordinator Vanderbilt U. Hosp., Nashville, 1968-70; adminstr. Murray-Calloway County Hosp., Murray, Ky., 1965-68; asst. dir. Parkview Hosp., Nashville, 1964-65; adminstr. Hinds Gen. Hosp., Jackson, Miss., 1974—; adj. faculty U. Ala., Birmingham. Bd. dirs. Sun Health, Inc., Miss. Blood Services. Mem. Am. Hosp. Assn., Am. Coll. Hosp. Adminstrs. (sec.-treas. Miss. affiliates), Jackson-Vicksburg Hosp. Council (pres.), Miss. Hosp. Assn. (govt. relations com., bd. dirs.), Jackson C. of C. (chmn. com. med. and dental affairs). Mem. non-physician health care practitioners adv. com. Miss. Found. for Med. Care, Inc.; bd. dirs. Miss. United Givers Way; mem. Gov.'s Vol. Services for Jackson; mem. Mayor's Water/Sewer Authority; mem. exec. bd. Boy Scouts Am., Jackson. Avocations: woodworking; golf. Office: Hinds Gen Hosp 1850 Chadwick Dr Jackson MS 39204

WILSON, ROBERT GODFREY, radiologist; b. Montgomery, Ala., Mar. 18, 1937; s. Robert Woodridge and Lucille (Godfrey) W.; B.A., Huntingdon Coll., 1957; M.D., Med. Coll. Ala., 1961; m. Dorothy June Waters, Aug. 31, 1957; children—Amy Lucille, Robert Darwin, Robert Woodridge II, Lucy Elizabeth. Intern, Letterman Gen. Hosp., San Francisco, 1961-62; resident in radiology U. Okla. Med. Center, Oklahoma City, 1965-68, clin. instr. in radiology, 1968—; practice medicine specializing in diagnostic and therapeutic radiology, nuclear medicine, Shawnee, Okla., 1968—; mem. med. staff Shawnee Med. Center, Mission Hill Meml. Hosp., Shawnee, 1968—. Served to capt. M.C., USAF, 1960-65. Diplomate Nat. Bd. Med. Examiners, Am. Bd. Radiology, Am. Bd. Nuclear Medicine. Mem. AMA, Okla., Pottawatomie County med. socs., Okla., Greater Oklahoma City radiol. socs., Am. Coll. Radiology, Soc. Nuclear Medicine, Radiol. Soc. N.Am. Methodist. Home: 26 Sequoyah Blvd Shawnee OK 74801 Office: 1110 N Harrison St Shawnee OK 74801

WILSON, ROBERT KEITH, medical educator, consultant; b. Abilene, Tex., Aug. 5, 1945; s. Raymond and Madge Lucille (Campbell) W.; m. Marilyn Lange Huffman, June 30, 1982. B.S. cum laude in Chemistry, N. Tex. State U., 1967; M.S. in Pharmacology, Baylor U., 1972, M.D. cum laude, 1972. Diplomate Am. Bd. Internal Medicine; lic. physician, Tex. Intern Baylor Affiliated Hosps., Houston, 1972-73, resident in internal medicine 1973-75; asst. prof. medicine Baylor U., Houston, 1977—; asst. dir. pulmonary lab. Meth. Hosp., Houston, 1977—, dir. respiratory therapy, 1981—, acting chief pulmonary sect., 1983—; lectr.; cons. Chlorine Inst., 1980-83, Johnson & Johnson, Windsor, N.H., 1979-83; cons. Houston-Galveston Area council Am. Lung Assn., 1979. Fellow A.C.P., Am. Coll. Chest Physicians; mem. Harris County Med. Soc., Tex. Med. Assn., AMA, Am. Soc. Internal Medicine, Am. Occupational Med. Assn., Blue Key, Alpha Omega Alpha, Alpha Chi, Phi Eta Sigma. Contbr. articles to profl. jours. Address: 3610 Aberdeen Way Houston TX 77025

WILSON, RON J., computer co. co. exec.; b. East Chicago, Ind., Oct. 5, 1944; s. Foy and Donna (Morris) W.; B.S., Purdue U., 1976; m. Clarice Roberta Banks, June 8, 1968; children—Ronnie Mark Wilson, Jill Lynette. Schedule clk. Jones & Laughlin Steel Co., East Chicago, 1963-65, supervisory trainee, 1965-68, computer programmer, 1968-72, supr. programming, 1972-77, mgr. process control div., 1977-79; program mgr. Computer Scis. Corp., Falls Church, Va., 1979-80, mgr. systems engring., Atlanta, 1980-83; dir. ops. Comml. Systems div. Systems & Applied Scis. Corp., Atlanta, 1983-84; MIS coordinator Lockheed Ga. Co., Marietta, 1984—; lectr. in field. Pres. Eastside Elem. Sch. PTA, Douglasville, Ga., 1982-84; pres. Burnett Sch. PTA, Douglasville, 1984-85. Cert. mgr. Inst. Cert. Profl. Mgrs. Mem. Nat. Mgmt. Assn. (dir. 1977, sec. chpt. 1979, dir. Chicagoland council 1979, chmn. profl. cert. com. 1985-86), Am. Iron and Steel Engrs. Mem. Ch. of Nazarene. Contbr. articles to trade publs.; columnist Douglas County Sentinel Newspaper. Home: 8981 Par Dr Douglasville GA 30134 Office: 86 S Cobb Dr Marietta GA 30063

WILSON, SAMUEL, JR., architect; b. New Orleans, Aug. 6, 1911; s. Samuel and Stella (Poupeney) W.; m. Ellen Elizabeth Latrobe, Oct. 20, 1951. B.Arch., Tulane U., 1931. Architect office Moise H. Goldstein, 1930-33, Historic Am. Bldgs. Survey in La., 1934-35; architect office Richard Koch, 1935-42, asso., 1945-55; partner Richard Koch & Samuel Wilson Jr., New Orleans, 1955-72, Koch and Wilson, Architects, 1972—; lectr. La. architecture Tulane U. Author: other publs. in field. A Guide to Architecture of New Orleans, 1699-1959; Editor: Impressions Respecting New Orleans (by B. H. B. Latrobe), 1951; Contbr. articles profl. publs. Mem. exec. bd. area council Boy Scouts Am.; bd. dirs. Maison Hospitaliere, Friends of Cabildo (pres. bd. 1979-81). Served with USCGR, 1942-45. Recipient Edward Langley scholarship AIA, 1938; citation Nat. Trust for Historic Preservation, 1968; Merit award Am. Assn. State and Local History, 1977; Elizabeth T. Werlein award Vieux Carre Commn., 1985; Honor award U. New Orleans Sch. Urban and Regional Studies, 1985; decorated officer companion Mil. and Hospitaliere Order St. Lazarus of Jerusalem, Chevalier de l'Ordre des Arts et des Lettres (France). Fellow AIA; mem. Soc. Archtl. Historians, La. Landmarks Soc. (pres. 1950-56; bd.), La. Hist. Assn. (pres. 1985). Roman Catholic. Club: Boston (New Orleans). Home: 1121 Washington Ave New Orleans LA 70130 Office: 1100 Jackson Ave New Orleans LA 70130

WILSON, SANDRA JEAN, psychologist, mental health center administrator; b. Kansas City, Kans., Aug. 31, 1946; d. George W. and Jean Lucy (Danforth) Hurst; m. Jimmy Charles Jones, June 11, 1970 (div. Feb. 1980); 1 child, Jason Clifton; m. Virgil Ray Wilson, June 4, 1982; 1 child, Leah Michell. B.S., U. Central Ark., 1968; M.A., U. Ark., 1970. Psychologist asst. Ark. Children's Colony, Conway, 1968-72, dir. evaluation, 1972-74; coordinator cons. and edn. Human Services Ctr. West Central Ark., Conway, 1974-76; ctr. coordinator Delta Counseling and Guidance Ctr., Dermott, Ark., 1976-79; dir. Southwestern Ark. Counseling and Mental Health Ctr., De Queen, 1979—; treas. Ark. Bd. Examiners in Psychology, 1976-80. Fellow Ark. Psychol. Assn.; mem. Ark. Sch. Psychology Assn., Ark. Behavior Therapy Assn., Am. Psychol. Assn., Am. Assn. Children with Learning Disabilities (pres. chpt.). Democrat. Baptist. Avocations: sewing; gardening; crafts. Home Rt 1 Box 332-OA De Queen AR 71832-9704 Office: Southwest Ark Counseling Ctr PO Box 459 De Queen AR 71832-0459

WILSON, THOMAS J., lawyer; b. Jacksonville, Fla., July 17, 1951; s. William H. and Christina (Dulan) W.; m. Diane Ellen Darden, Nov. 7, 1974 (div. Feb. 1981); 1 child, Thomas Shane. B.A., Augusta Coll., 1973, J.D., 1977, LL.M., 1978. Bar: Ga. 1980. Br. mgr. Gen. Electric, Columbia, S.C., 1976-79; sole practice, Augusta, Ga., 1980—; pres. L'Ectra Skate Corp., 1984. Inventor of electric skates, shown on various TV shows including That's Incredible, CBS Morning News. Vice chmn. Tax Assessor's Bd., Augusta, Ga. 1983. Mem. ABA, Assn. Trial Lawyers Am., Ga. Trial Lawyers Assn. Republican. Baptist. Club: Augusta Flying. Home: 1688 Goshen Rd Augusta GA 30906 Office: 512 Telfair St Augusta GA 30901

WILSON, THOMAS LAMONT, dielectric heating consultant; b. Salt Lake City, June 4, 1914; s. Nathan Lamont and Christina V. (McAllister) W.; m. Carolyn Rosaline Woodmansee, June 4, 1937; children—Carolyn Sylvia Wilson Willie, John Lamont. B.S.E.E., U. Utah, 1940; M.S. in Physics, U. Louisville, 1963. Transmitter operator sta. KSL, Salt Lake City, 1933-40; student engr. RCA, Camden, N.J., 1940-41; chief engr. indsl. electronics div. Fed. Telephone & Radio, ITT, Newark, 1941-46; mgr. electronics research and devel. Votator

Div. Chemetron Corp., Louisville, 1946-77; cons. Dielectric Heating, Louisville, 1977—. Author papers; patentee. Former mem. stake presidency of Louisville, Ky. Stake Mormon Ch. U.S. del. Comite Internacional Spl. Perturbations Radio, 1981—; mem. U.S. del. to Consultative Comité Internacional Radio, 1982—. Fellow IEEE (chmn. Louisville sect. 1970-71, chmn. high frequency heating com., Outstanding Engr. Region III 1977, Achievement award IE Soc. 1979, Centennial medalist 1984), Tau Beta Pi (Eminent Engr. 1977), Sigma Pi Sigma, Theta Tau (regent 1939). Office: 1407 Ormsby Ln Louisville KY 40222

WILSON, WILBURN MARTIN (WILLIE), radio executive; b. Cerulean, Ky., Mar. 13, 1930; s. Robert Estill and Verdya Marie (Shanks) W.; grad. high sch.; m. JoAnn Campbell, May 23, 1954; children—Donna Jo and Deborah Gay (twins). With Princeton Broadcasting Co., Princeton, Ky., 1951-66, news and sports dir., 1955-65; founder WKDZ Am, Cadiz, Ky., 1966, WKDZ FM, 1972, gen. mgr., 1966—. Chmn. deacons Cerulean Bapt. Ch., 1980—. Served with USN, 1951-55. Recipient Communications award Ky. State Farm Bur., 1975. Mem. Trigg County C. of C. (Man of Yr. 1982, past dir.), Ky. AP Broadcasters (past pres.), Broadcasters Assn. Ky. (bd. dirs. 1985-86). Club: Civitan (past pres.). Home: Route 6 Sunset Circle Cadiz KY 42211 Office: Will Jackson Rd Cadiz KY 42211

WILSON, WILLIAM B, oil and gas executive; b. Sonora, Tex., June 21, 1914; s. John William and Nancy Belle (Word) W.; m. Mary Glover, Aug. 31, 1940 (div.); children—John W., Duke G., Word B.; m. 2d, Monetta Bradshaw, Oct. 31, 1962; 1 son, Byron B.; 1 stepson, Michael H. J.D., U. Tex., 1937. Lic. pilot. Owner, chmn. bd. Wm. B. Wilson and Sons, Inc., Midland, Tex., 1980—, W. Wilson Corp., 1973—, Wilson Systems, Inc., 1967—, Wm. B. Wilson Ranches, 1930—, Wm. B. Wilson Mfg., 1969—; Micronet, Inc., Kappa Systems, Inc., Washington, 1981—; Wilson & Sons Energy, Inc., 1981—; Wilson Computer Systems, Montreal and Toronto, Can., 1982—. Past mem. nominating com. ARC, San Angelo, Tex. Served to 2d lt. USAF, 1942-45. Recipient Chmn.'s Cup U.S. Polo Tournament, 1971, finalist U.S. Open, 1977, Gold Cup, 1978, Silver Cup, 1976, 78; winner Inter-Circuit Cup, 1973, Sherman Meml. Championship, 1964, Pacific Coast Open, 1976, 82. Mem. Tex. Bar Assn., U.S. Polo Assn. (gov. 1969-72), Am. Angus Assn. Republican. Episcopalian. Clubs: Midland Country, Midland Polo, Retama Polo (San Antonio), Santa Barbara Polo and Racquet, Midlander Health (Midland, Tex.); Ox 5. Author, pub. Fun Learn Vocabulary Tapes. Patentee automatic irrigation system. Home: 2700 N Garfield Suite 500 Midland TX 79701

WILSON, WILLIAM FEATHERGAIL, petroleum geologist; b. San Antonio, Dec. 25, 1934; s. Glenn Caldwell and Marion (Hord) W.; B.A., U. Tex., Austin, 1957, B.S. with honors, 1960, M.S., 1962; m. Elizabeth Gail Harmison, Mar. 17, 1979; children—Douglas Hord, Clayton Hill, Wendy Elanore. With dept. geology U. Tex., 1958-61, Texaco, Inc., 1961-65, El Paso Natural Gas Co., 1965-66; ind. petroleum geologist, rancher, real estate exec., 1966-70; environ. geologist Alamo Area Council Govts., 1970; account exec. Merrill Lynch Fenner & Smith, 1970-74; sr. exploration geologist Tesoro Petroleum Corp., San Antonio, 1974, exploration mgr. Tex. dist., 1974-76, Eastern hemisphere, 1976-78; chief geologist Placid Oil Co., Dallas, 1978—, also v.p. exploration geology and geophysics. Adj. instr. geology U. Tex., San Antonio, 1976—. Mem. Am. Assn. Petroleum Geologists (cert.), Geol. Soc. Am., Assn. Profl. Geol. Scientists (cert.), S. Tex. Geol. Soc. (pres., editor bull. 1976—), AAAS, Sigma Gamma Epsilon. Contbr. stories to San Antonio mag., articles to profl. jours. Home: 7918 Briaridge Dallas TX 75248 Office: 3900 Thanksgiving Tower Dallas TX 75201

WILSON, WILLIAM HALL, JR., telecommunications company executive; b. Clarksburg, W.Va., Jan. 25, 1942; s. William Hall and Mary Elizabeth (Wamsley) W.; m. Jeri Sue Ishida, Oct. 15, 1976; 1 child, Kauialohaokalani Rae. B.S.E.E., U. Tenn.-Knoxville, 1964; M.S. in Systems Mgmt., U. So. Calif., 1972. Field engr. IBM, Atlanta, 1964-65; engr. Hawaiian Telephone Co., Honolulu, 1969-72, personnel adminstr., 1972-73; mgr. regulatory relations Hawaiian Telephone Co/GTESC, Honolulu and Washington, 1973-78; dir. regulatory relations Hawaiian Telephone Co., 1978-79; dir. systems and procedures GTE Service Corp., Lexington, Ky., 1979-84; mgr. govt. communications GTE Telecom, Inc., Washington, 1984—. Pres. Waikiki Jaycees, 1974. Served to capt. USAF, 1965-69. Named Jaycee of Yr., Waikiki Jaycees, 1975. Mem. Armed Forces Communications and Electronics Assn., Ind. Telephone Pioneer Assn. IEEE Engring. Mgmt. Soc., Inst. Mgmt. Scis., Nat. Contract Mgmt. Assn., Mensa. Republican. Home: 9363 Robnel Pl Vienna VA 22180 Office: GTE Telecom Inc Suite 900 1120 Connecticut Ave NW Washington DC 20036

WILSON, WILLIAM JOE, statistics educator; b. McAllen, Tex., June 30, 1940; s. Jack I. and Ruth (Urban) W.; m. Patricia Ann Susil, June 22, 1965; children—Chad, Bryan, Kerry. B.S., Pan Am. U., 1966; M.S., Tex. A&I U., 1970; Ph.D., 1974, Tex. A&M U. Assoc. prof. stats. U. North Fla., Jacksonville, 1975—; vis. prof. U. Southwest La., Lafayette, 1982-83; cons. in statistics, Jacksonville, 1975—. Mem. Am. Statis. Assn., Biometric Soc., Fla. Assn. Sci. Office: Dept Math Sci U N Fla Jacksonville FL 32216

WILSON, WOODROW, clinical psychologist, association executive; b. Atlanta, Dec. 28, 1948; s. Bennie and Velma Louise (Ford) Blalock; m. Sharon Yvonne Watson, Nov. 14, 1976; children—Shawn Amber, Shane Woody. B.A., Morehouse Coll., Atlanta, 1970; Ph.D. in Clin. Psychology, SUNY-Stony Brook, 1974. Lic. psychologist, Fla.; cert. Nat. Register Health Service Providers in Psychology. Clin. psychologist Community Mental Health Ctr., West Palm Beach, Fla., 1974-76; asst. prof. Morehouse Coll., 1976-77; clin. psychologist Children's Psychiat. Ctr., Miami, Fla., 1977-78; unit dir. Community Mental Health Ctr., Miami, 1977-78; dir. Child Day Treatment Ctr., Miami, 1978—, also pres. Assn. Minority Mental Health, Miami, 1982—; adj. instr. U. Miami, 1978—, Fla. Sch. Profl. Psychology, 1979-81; host weekly radio program Getting Your Act Together, 1982. Author: (poem) Courtesy, 1979 (recipient award); columnist Getting Your Act Together, 1982. Cons. NAACP, 1978, So. Christian Leadership Conf., 1982; active in voter registration. Mem. Am. Psychol. Assn., Assn. Black Psychologist (So. regional dir. 1975-78), Nat. Assn. Black Social Workers (chmn. West Palm Beach 1975), Dade-Monroe Dist. Mental Health Bd., Mental Health Assn. Dade County, Delta Tau Kappa. Democrat. Baptist. Home: 9361 SW 62d St Miami FL 33173 Office: Associates for Minority Mental Health Inc 1400 NW 36th St Suite 207 Miami FL 33142

WILSON-WILKE, NEDA EULANE, computers service and consultation companies executive; b. Beaumont, Tex., Apr. 21, 1942; d. O. Woodrow and Ardelle Ann (Wheeler) Wilson; m. Michael Dettmer Wilke, Sept. 25, 1982. B.A., Lamar U., 1963; M.S.W., U. Houston, 1971; postgrad. U. Ark., 1963-64. Cert. social worker, lic. nursing home adminstr., Tex. With Tex. Dept. Human Resources, 1965-76, regional dir. for planning and devel., Beaumont, to 1976; prof. social work Lamar U., Beaumont, 1976-81; pres., chmn. bd. NEW Interests, Inc., Beaumont, 1981—, Am. Interactive Mgmt. Systems, Inc., Beaumont, 1981—. Chmn. com. S.E. Tex. Regional Planning Commn., 1971-76; mem. Title 1 adv. bd. South Park Ind. Sch. Dist., Beaumont; bd. dirs. Tex. Inst. on Children and Youth, Austin. Named Outstanding Social Worker of Yr., S.E. Tex. Social Welfare, 1974, Vol. of Yr., Mental Health Assn., 1977, Hon. Beaumont Police Officer, 1979; recipient cert. appreciation Gov. Tex. Office, 1978, five-yr. cert. Tex. Dept. Human Resources, 1981. Mem. Tex. Assn. Home Health Agys. (state chmn. volunteerism), Am. Health Care Assn., Tex. Nursing Home Assn., Electronic Computer Health Oriented, Nat. Home Care Assn., Beaumont Coalition on Child Advocacy. Democrat. Primitive Baptist. Home: 4385 Dalton Vidor TX 77662 Office: 3010 Harrison Beaumont TX 77706

WILTZ, ALLEN JOSEPH, safety engineer; b. Krotz Springs, La., Jan. 1, 1938; s. Alfred and Lovina (Guidry) W.; m. Bobbie Jean Lowery, Aug. 10, 1957; children—Connie, Donna, Allen Jr. B.S. in Safety and Health, Our Lady of Holy Cross Coll., 1977. Cert. safety profl.; lic. pvt. pilot. Office mgr. Williams-McWilliams Industries, Inc., Morgan City, La., 1959-67, safety supr., New Orleans, 1967-72; safety engr. T.L. James & Co., Inc., Kenner, La., 1972—. Mem. Am. Soc. Safety Engrs., Bd. Cert. Safety Profls. of Ams. Roman Catholic. Avocations: fishing, flying. Home: 4633 Hastings St Metairie LA 70006 Office: T L James & Co Inc PO Box 10 Kenner LA 70063

WILTZ, CARROLL JOSEPH, sociologist, educator; b. Parks, La., Mar. 10, 1948; s. Joseph Dupre and Anna Mae (Lewis) W.; m. Velda Leona Smith, Aug. 14, 1982; 1 child, Lindsey. B.S., So. U., Baton Rouge, 1970; M.A., Kans. State U., 1973; Ph.D., U. Iowa, 1978. Asst. prof. sociology Dillard U., New Orleans, 1978-80, assoc. prof., 1980—, chmn. div. social scis., 1979—. Mem. adv. bd. Bus. in Action-Urban League, New Orleans, 1983. Dept. Transp. grantee, 1983—. Mem. Am. Sociol. Assn., Am. Soc. Criminology, Nat. Council on Crime and Delinquency, So. Sociol. Soc., Acad. Criminal Justice Sci., NAACP. Roman Catholic. Avocations: reading; listening to music; jogging. Office: Dillard U 2601 Gentilly Blvd New Orleans LA 70122

WIMBERLEY, RONALD C., sociology educator; b. Mobile, Ala., Nov. 7, 1942. B.A., La. Coll., 1963; M.S., Fla. State U., 1967; Ph.D., U. Tenn., 1972. Instr. to prof. N.C. State U., Raleigh, 1971-81, prof., head dept. sociology and anthropology, 1981—; chmn. census adv. com. for agrl. stats. U.S. Dept. Commerce, 1984. Mem. Am. Sociol. Assn., So. Sociol. Soc., Rural Sociol. Soc., Assn. for Sociology of Religion, So. Assn. Agrl. Scientists, Religious Research Assn., Soc. Sci. Study of Religion. Contbr. articles to profl. jours. Address: Dept Sociology and Anthropology NC State Univ Raleigh NC 27695-8107

WIMBERLY, ANNE ELIZABETH STREATY, music educator; b. Anderson, Ind., June 10, 1936; d. Robert Harold and Valeska Bea (Cunningham) Streaty; B.Sc., Ohio State U., 1957; M.Mus., Boston U., 1965, postgrad., 1965-72; grad. cert. gerontology Ga. State U., 1979, Ph.D., 1981; m. Edward Powell Wimberly, June 4, 1966; 1 foster son, Michael A. Haynie. Dir. music Harwood Girls' Sch., Albuquerque, 1957-58; music specialist Detroit Public Schs., 1958-64; teaching fellow Boston U., 1964-66; music cons. Newton Public Schs., jr. high vocal music tchr., Newton, Mass., 1966-68; music cons. Worcester (Mass.) Public Schs., 1968-73; asst. prof. music Worcester State Coll., 1973-75; asso. prof. music, instr. gerontology Atlanta Jr. Coll., 1975-83, faculty coordinator faculty campus ministry outreach, 1981-83, faculty coordinator performing arts series, 1977-83; assoc. prof. Oral Roberts U., Tulsa, 1983—. Vol., Pineview Convalescent Center, 1975-78; mem. adv. com. Bethlehem Sr. Center, 1977—; mem. bd. discipleship family life com. United Meth. Ch., 1980-84; mem. World Meth. Family Life Com., 1981-86; bd. dirs. Dekalb Community Council on Aging, Dekalb County, Ga., 1981-84; mem. planning com. N.Am. Family Life Convocation, United Meth. Ch., 1982. Sch. of Theology at Claremont scholar in residence, 1982, Adminstrn. on Aging grantee, Ga. State U., 1979; Nat. Endowment Humanities grantee Atlanta Jr. Coll., 1977-81. Mem. Music Educators Nat. Conf., Internat. Soc. Music Edn., AAUW, Ga. Music Educators Assn. (chmn. state coll. div. 1979-81), Ga. Gerontol. Soc., Kappa Delta Pi, Pi Kappa Lambda. Democrat. Methodist. Club: Knollview Civic (Dekalb County, Ga.). Home: 6414 E 94th Pl Tulsa OK 74136 Office: 7777 Lewis Tulsa OK

WIMBERLY, BEADIE RENEAU, financial services executive; b. Fouke, Ark., Apr. 18, 1937; d. Woodrow Wilson and Grace B. (Winkley) Reneau; m. Benjamin Leon Price, 1954 (div. 1955); m. Elbert William Wimberly, Dec. 16, 1956; children—Stephanie Elaine Wimberly Davis, Jeffrey Scott, Lael Ruoyn Wimberly Carter. Student William & Mary Coll., 1964-65, U. Md.-Ludwigsburg/Stuttgart, 1966-68, Northwestern State U. La., 1973-75, Cornell U., 1979, Leonard Sch., 1983. Cert. ins. agt.; registered gen. securities rep. SEC.; registered investment adviser; notary public. Internat. trainer of trainers North Atlantic council Girl Scouts, W.Ger., 1965-69, 76-78; inventory master The Myers Co., Inc., El Paso, Tex., 1970; abstract asst. Vernon Abstract Co., Inc., Leesville, La., 1970-71; sec. to chief utilities and pollution control Dept. Army, U.S. Civil Service, Ft. Polk, La., 1971-72, asst. to post safety officer, 1972-73, adminstr. tech. Adj. Gen.'s Office, 1973-75, sr. library technician post libraries, 1975, personnel staffing specialist, Stuttgart, Germany, 1976-79, voucher examiner Fin. and Acctg. Office, Ft. Polk, 1980-81; ins. agt., mgr. Fin. Strategies, Inc., Leesville, La., 1981—, stockbroker, corp. exec., 1983—, mktg. exec., 1983—; labor cons. AFL/CIO, Ft. Polk, 1981-86; sr. resident mgr. Anchor Nat. Fin. Services Inc.; dir., treas. Wimberly Enterprises, Inc.; guest columnist Leesville Daily Leader, Ft. Polk Guardian. Bd. dirs. Calcasieu Parish council Boy Scouts Am., 1982-83; treas. LWV of La., Leesville, 1982-86; pres., bd. dirs. Vernon Parish Helpline/Lifeline, 1985—; network dir. Nat. Assn. Female Execs.; charter mem. Nat. Mus. of Women in the Arts. Mem. Pilot Internat., Am. Soc. Mil. Comptrollers, Internat. Assn. Fin. Planners, Nat. Assn. Govt. Employees (v.p. Ft. Polk chpt. 1980-81), Vernon Parish Hist. Soc., Soc., Internat. Platform Assn., C. of C. (chmn. improvement com.), Assn. U.S. Army, Am. Assn. Fin. Profls., Nat. Women's Polit. Caucus, LWV (state bd. dirs.), NOW. Republican. Club: Toastmasters Internat. (named Competent Toastmaster, 1979). Office: Fin Strategies Inc 302 N 5th St Leesville LA 71446

WIMMER, DONALD NEIL, retail stores executive; b. Roanoke, Va., Jan. 8, 1936; s. Howard Roger and Toyia (Quesenberry) W.; m. Lorraine Agnes Garman, Sept. 2, 1961; children—Sandra Gayle, Randall Neil. Student, U. Va. Extension, Roanoke, 1963-65. Inventory, prodn. control specialist Gen. Electric Corp., Schenectady, N.Y., Salem, Va., 1956-76; owner, operator 5 franchises World Bazaar, Inc. div. Munford Corp., Roanoke, 1974—. Served with USNG 1953-61. Mem. Tanglewood Mchts. Assn., Roanoke C. of C. Baptist. Club: Hidden Valley Country (Salem). Home: 5010 Falcon Ridge Rd SW Roanoke VA 24014 Office: World Bazaar of Roanoke Ltd 4502 Starkey Rd Suite 105 Profl Park Bldg 1 Roanoke VA 24014

WIMPRESS, GORDON DUNCAN, JR., educator, foundation executive; b. Riverside, Cal., Apr. 10, 1922; s. Gordon Duncan and Maude A. (Waldo) W.; B.A., U. Ore., 1946, M.A., 1951; Ph.D., U. Denver, 1958; LL.D., Monmouth Coll., 1970; L.H.D., Tusculum Coll., 1971; m. Jean Margaret Skerry, Nov. 30, 1946; children—Wendy Jo, Victoria Jean, Gordon Duncan III. Dir. pub. relations, instr. journalism Whittier (Cal.) Coll., 1946-51; asst. to pres. Colo. Sch. Mines, Golden, 1951-59; pres. Monticello Coll., Alton, Ill., 1959-64, Monmouth (Ill.) Coll., 1964-70, Trinity U., San Antonio, 1970-77; vice chmn. bd. govs. S.W. Found. Research and Edn., San Antonio, 1977-82; pres., S.W. Found. for Biomed. Research, 1982—; bd. govs. The Dominion; dir. InterFirst Bank, San Antonio; exec. cons. Donald W. Reynold Founds., Inc. Bd. dirs. Am. Inst. Character Edn.; mem. Burlington No. Scholarship Selection Com., Valero Energy Scholarship Com.; trustee Mind Sci. Found., San Antonio Med. Found.; bd. dirs. ARC, Southwest Research Inst., KPAC, Mil. Affairs Council, Mission Road Devel. Ctr., Am. Heart Assn., trustee Sigma Phi Epsilon Found., World Bus. Council, San Antonio Medication Found.; chmn. San Antonio Area Employer Support of Guard and Res. Served to 1st lt. AUS, 1942-45. Decorated Bronze Star. Mem. Am. Acad. Polit. and Social Sci., Am. Assn. Higher Edn., Am. Inst. for Character Edn., Aircraft Owners and Pilots Assn., Council Advancement and Support Edn., Greater San Antonio C. of C., Pilots Internat. Assn., San Antonio Pilots Assn., Assn. Am. Colls., San Antonio C. of C. (bd. dirs.), San Antonio Golf Assn. (treas.), Am. Council on Edn., Nat. Pilots Assn., World Bus. Council, Mensa, Sigma Delta Chi, Sigma Delta Pi, Sigma Upsilon, Pi Gamma Mu, Sigma Phi Epsilon. Presbyn. Clubs: Rotary (dist. gov. 1983-84), Argyle, Newcomen, St. Anthony, San Antonio Country. Author: American Journalism Comes of Age, 1950. Office: PO Box 28147 San Antonio TX 78284

WINBURN, JACK LEE, bank executive, real estate advisor; b. Ft. Worth, Jan. 28, 1943; s. Jack Burton and Zella Loretta (Webb) W. Student, U. Md., 1967-68; B.A., So. Meth. U., 1974; A.A., Odessa Coll., 1979; B.B.A. summa cum laude, U. Tex.-Odessa, 1981; grad. Weaver Sch. Real Estate, 1970, Graham Sch. Comml. Real Estate, 1970, Leonard Sch. Real Estate, 1979. Cert. comml. investment. Fin. cons. Dr. J.D. Cone Estate, Odessa, 1976-81; owner/broker Comml. Investors, Odessa, 1981-83; head comml. real estate div. Home Savs. Assn., Odessa, 1983-84; v.p., loan officer Comml. Real Estate Div. Murray Savs. Assn., 1984—; chmn. Multiple Listing Service, Comml. Real Estate Commn., Odessa, 1983; adj. prof. Odessa Coll., 1981-84. Pres., Allied Youth Club, McKinney, Tex., 1960. Served with USAF, 1964-71. Named Top Comml. Salesperson, Odessa Bd. Realtors, 1982, 83, Million Dollar Sales Club, 1982, 83. Mem. Internat. Assn. Fin. Planners, Am. Morgage Brokers Assn., Real Estate Securities and Syndication Inst., Realtors Nat. Mktg. Inst., Cert. Comml. Investment Mems. (regional v.p. West Tex. High Plains chpt. 1983-84), Am. Property Investment and Mgmt. Assn., Am. Soc. Profl. Cons., Phi Theta Kappa. Republican. Home: 14100 Montfort #3140 Dallas TX 75240 Office: Murray Savs Association 5550 LBJ Freeway LB55 Suite 950106 Dallas TX 75240

WINDER, LARRY NEIL, hospital administrator; b. Galion, Ohio, July 10, 1935; s. Neil George and Kathryn Marie (Weaver) W.; m. Diane Elenor Holden, May 1, 1965; children—Beth Ann, Larry Neil. A.A. in Bus., Brevard Jr. Coll., 1971; B.A. in Fin., Central Fla. U., 1973; M.B.A. in Hosp. Adminstrn., U. Fla., 1973. Adminstr. Cedar Crest Hosp., Humboldt, Tenn., 1974-80; exec. dir. King Kahlid Mil. City Hosp., Hafar Al Batin, Saudi Arabia, 1980-82; adminstr. J. Archer Smith Hosp., Homestead, Fla., 1982-84, Meml. Hosp., Siloam Springs, Fla., 1984—. Dir. Sager Creek Arts Assn., Siloam Springs, 1985-87. Served with USAF, 1957-60. Mem. Am. Coll. Hosp. Adminstrs. Club: Rotary. Avocation: theatre directing. Home: Route 5 Box 144A Siloam Springs AR 72761 Office: Hosp Corp of Am Siloam Springs AR 72761

WINDHAM, ELDORA BROACH, geriatics nurse; b. Roxboro, N.C., May 24, 1917; d. William Edward and Carrie Oliver (Rice) Broach; m. Milton Eugene Windham, June 17, 1942 (div. 1978); children—Bobbie Almira, Youel Travis, Wray Earle, Twila Janel. R.N., N.C. Pvt. nurse So. Baptist Hosp., New Orleans, 1941-45, 47; supr. Columbia Hosp. (Mo.), 1948-49; ward supr. Community Hosp., Placerville, Calif., 1950-51; missionary nurse, mother Am. Baptist Mission, Assam, India, 1952-61; night supr. obstetrics Person County Meml. Hosp., Roxboro, N.C., 1965-79; charge nurse geriatrics, 1979—. Named Dr. Frist humanitarian Person County Meml. Hosp., 1982. Democrat. Baptist. Home: Route 4 Box 213AA Roxboro NC 27573 Office: Person County Meml Hosp Ridge Rd Roxboro NC 27573

WINDSOR, CARL DOUGLAS, university administrator, program producer; b. Peoria, Ill., Oct. 2, 1942; s. George Albert and Madelyn Gail (Leak) Guindon; m. Beverly June Margetts, June 15, 1969; children—Trent Matthew, Todd Michael, Heather Jean. A.A., N. Central Mich. Coll., 1966; B.A. in TV-Radio, Mich. State U., 1969, M.A. in TV-Radio, 1970; Ph.D. in Communications, Ohio State U., 1981; diploma Liberty Home Bible Inst., 1985. News anchor/reporter Sta. WJIM-TV, Lansing, Mich., 1970-71; teaching asst. Mich. State U., East Lansing, 1969-70; asst. prof. John Brown U., Siloam Springs, Ark., 1971-78; teaching assoc. Ohio State U., Columbus, 1978-79; assoc. prof. telecommunications Liberty U., Lynchburg, Va., 1979-80, prof., chmn. telecommunications, 1980—; news dir. Sta. WJML, Petoskey, Mich., 1965-66, Sta. WTOM-TV, Cheboygan, Mich., 1966-67; asst. news dir. Sta. WKAR, East Lansing, 1967-68; radio program host Sta. WFMK, East Lansing, 1968-70; producer, host A Quiet Place, 1981—. Conv. del. Va. Republican Conv., Virginia Beach, 1982. Served to lt. comdr. USNR, 1961—. Recipient Outstanding Young Educator award Jaycees, 1973; Founders award Nat. Religious Broadcasters, 1984. Mem. Nat. Religious Broadcasters (bd. dirs. 1985), Broadcast Edn. Assn., Broadcast Promotion Assn. Baptist. Office: Liberty U 3765 Candlers Mountain Rd Lynchburg VA 24506

WINDSOR, OLIVER DUANE, business administration educator; b. Compton, Calif., Mar. 27, 1947; s. Samuel Tilden and Florence Anne (Sallee) W.; m. Sandra Max, Apr. 20, 1981. B.A. summa cum laude, Rice U., 1969; A.M., Harvard U., 1975, Ph.D., 1978. Research assoc. Rutgers U., New Brunswick, N.J., 1972-74; instr. U. Iowa, Iowa City, 1974-77; instr., then asst. prof. Rice U., Houston, 1977-82, assoc. prof., 1983—; dir. First Houston Bank, Support Ctr. Houston, Gemcraft, Support Ctr. Network. Author: (with others) Housing Development and Municipal Costs, 1973; Fiscal Zoning in Suburban Communities, 1979; The Foreign Corrupt Practices Act, 1982. Editor: (with others) The Changing Boardroom, 1982. Contbr. articles to profl. jours. Fellow Woodrow Wilson Found., 1969, NDEA, 1969-72. Mem. Phi Beta Kappa, Pi Delta Phi. Office: Jesse Jones Sch Rice U PO Box 1892 Houston TX 77251

WINDUS, J. PRESTON, JR., communications company executive; b. Bayshore, N.Y., Feb. 6, 1943; s. Joseph Preston and Margaret (Toomey) W.; B.B.A., St. Francis Coll., 1964; m. Eileen B. O'Rourke, June 12, 1965; 4 children. With budget dept. Avis Rent-a-Car, 1964-65; mgr. Price Waterhouse & Co., L.I., N.Y., 1965-72; asst. treas. Comtech Labs., Inc., Smithtown, N.Y., 1972-76; sec.-treas. Comtech Telecommunications Corp., Smithtown, 1976-80; v.p. Comtech Antenna Corp., Orlando, Fla., 1980-82, pres., 1982—, dir., 1980—; dir. Comtech Data Corp. Pres., Bishop Moore Band Parents Assn., 1981—. C.P.A., N.Y. State. Mem. Am. Inst. C.P.A.s, N.Y. Soc. C.P.A.s. Democrat. Roman Catholic. Office: 3100 Communications Rd Saint Cloud FL 32769

WINFREY, DORMAN HAYWARD, state librarian; b. Henderson, Tex., Sept. 4, 1924; s. Luke Abel and Linnie (Fears) W.; B.A., U. Tex., 1950, M.A., 1951, Ph.D., 1962; m. Ruth Carolyn Byrd, June 12, 1954; children—Laura, Jennifer. Social sci. research asso. Research in Tex. History, Tex. Hist. Assn. at U. Tex., 1946-58; state archivist, 1958-60; archivist U. Tex., 1960-61; dir., librarian Tex. State Library, 1962—. Chmn. State Bd. Library Examiners, 1962-81; chmn. State Records Preservation Adv. Com., 1965-83; vice chmn. Tex. 1986 Sesquicentennial Commn.; bd. dirs. Internat. Festival Inst. at Round Top; adv. bd. Tex. Hist. Records. Served with AUS, 1943-46, ETO. Clara Driscoll scholar for research in Tex. history, 1952-54. Fellow Tex. Hist. Assn. (exec. council, pres. 1971-72), Soc. Am. Archivists (council), Am. Assn. for State and Local History (council), mem. Tex. Inst. Letters, Philos. Soc. Tex. (sec., editor procs. 1976—), ALA, Tex. Library Assn., Am. Hist. Assn., Tex. Hist. Assn., Tex. Travel Trails Com., Bicentennial Assn. Tex., Phi Alpha Theta, Pi Sigma Alpha. Mem. Disciples of Christ Ch. Author, editor: Texas Indian Papers, 1825-1843, 1959; Texas Indian Papers, 1844-1845, 1960; Texas Indian Papers, 1846-1859, 1961; A History of Rusk County, Texas, 1961; Julien Sidney Devereux and His Monte Verdi Plantation, 1964; Indian Papers of Texas and the Southwest, 1825-1916 (5 vols.), 1966; Arturo Toscanini in Texas: The 1950 NBC Symphony Orchestra Tour, 1967; spl. editor Tex. Ency. for Young People, 1964; asso. editor Jr. Historian mag., 1951-58; Seventy-Five Years of Texas History: The Texas State Historical Association, 1897-1972, 1975. Home: 6503 Willamette Dr Austin TX 78723 Office: Tex State Library Box 12927 Capitol Sta Austin TX 78711

WINICK, PAULINE, communications executive, city official; b. N.Y.C., Sept. 19, 1946; d. Morris and Frances (Fox) Leiderman; m. Bruce Jeffrey Winick, June 19, 1966 (div. 1977); children—Margot Scott, Graham Douglas. B.A., Bklyn. Coll., 1966; M.A., NYU, 1971; A.S., Miami-Dade Community Coll., 1977. Tchr. N.Y.C. Pub. Schs., 1966-66, 69-74, Bloomington (Ind.) Pub. Schs., 1968-69; producer Sta. WPLG-TV, Miami, Fla., 1975-79; dir. Office of Communications, Metro-Dade County, Miami, Fla., 1979-86; exec. asst. city mgr. City of Miami, 1986—. Bd. dirs. Fla. Close-Up, Miami, 1979—; mem. exec. com. Leadership Miami Conf., 1980—; bd. dirs. LWV, Miami, 1980; mem. planning com. United Way, Miami, 1980—; bd. dirs. Anti-Defamation League, 1983. Home: 11420 SW 72nd Ave Miami FL 33156 Office: City of Miami Pan American Dr Miami FL 33133

WINKEL, ERWIN CHARLES, urologist; b. Houston, July 7, 1934; s. Erwin Charles and Annie (Walther) W.; B.A., Baylor U., 1956, M.D., 1959; m. Jacquelyn Yvonne Watson, Sept. 3, 1960; children—Erwin Charles III, Carolyn, Todd. Intern, Hermann Hosp., Houston, 1959-60, resident in urology, 1960-62, 64-66, now mem. staff; practice medicine specializing in urology, Houston, 1966—; a founder North Central Gen. Hosp., Houston, 1974, chief of staff, 1974-75; a founder Houston Northwest Med. Center Hosp., 1973, chief of staff, 1977-78; mem. staff Meml. Hosp. System, clin. assoc. in urology U. Tex. Med. Sch., Houston, 1967—. Committeeman Troop 9, Boy Scouts Am., 1952-82, instl. rep., 1960-66, merit badge counsellor, 1967-71; mem. adv. bd. Volunteers of Am., 1968-76. Served with U.S. Army, 1962-64. Diplomate Am. Bd. Urology. Fellow Internat. Coll. Surgeons, ACS; mem. AMA (Physicians Recognition award 1969, 72, 75, 77, 80, 83), Am. Urol. Assn., Am. Assn. Clin. Urologists, Tex. Med. Assn., Am. Fertility Soc., Am. Geriatrics Soc., Am. Assn. Physicians and Surgeons, World, So. med. assns., Nat. Kidney Found., Harris County Med. Soc., Houston Urol. Socs., Houston Acad. Medicine. Republican. Methodist. Home: 5523 Foresthaven St Houston TX 77066 Office: 829 Peakwood St Suite 101 Houston TX 77090

WINKELMAN, BENJAMIN EARL, geophysicist; b. Milw., June 26, 1958; s. Earl Leroy and Elaine (McAllister) W.; m. Jean Marie Leffler, May 31, 1980. B.S., U. Wis., 1979, M.S., 1981; postgrad. Houston Bapt. U. Geophysicist Arco Exploration Co., Dallas, 1981-82, Houston, 1982-85, Dallas, 1985—. Mem. Am. Assn. Petroleum Geologists, Soc. Exploration Geophysicists, Houston Geol. Soc., Geophys. Soc. Houston. Roman Catholic. Avocations: running; autocross. Home: 1308 Chickasaw Richardson TX 75080 Office: Arco Exploration and Tech Co 2300 W Plano Pkwy PAL1423 Plano TX 75075

WINKLE, CHARLES WAYNE, psychologist, consultant; b. Sheridan, Ark., Apr. 8, 1948; s. James Charles and Nannie Lovell (Hopson) W.; m. Vicki Lynn Bratton, Apr. 10, 1971; children—Amanda, Megan. B.A., Ouachita U., 1970; M.S., U. Central Ark., 1973; Ed.D., East Tex. State U., 1980. Lic. psychologist, Ark., Mo.; diplomate in profl. counseling Internat. Acad. Profl. Counseling and Psychotherapy; cert. law enforcement instr., Ark. Psychol. examiner Western Ark. Counseling and Guidance Ctr., Fort Smith, 1973-78; adminstrv. coordinator Marriage and Family Counseling Ctr., Commerce, Tex., 1979-80; assoc.

Smock and Assocs., family therapist, Liberty, Mo., 1981-82; dir. counseling and testing ctr., instr. William Jewell Coll., Liberty, 1980-82; instr. psychology Northwestern Ark. Community Coll., Rogers, 1983—; psychologist Performance and Diagnostic Clinic, Bentonville, Ark., 1982—; psychol. cons.; bd. dirs. Northwestern Ark. Crisis Intervention Ctr.; mem. health services adv. com. Northwestern Ark. Head Start. Contbr. articles to profl. mags., weekly column to local newspaper. Chmn. profl. div. United Fund, Bentonville, 1983; deacon Bella Vista Bapt. Ch., Ark., 1983—; pres.-elect PTA, Bentonville, 1984—. East Tex. State U. grantee, 1979-80; NIMH grantee, 1980; recipient research award Am. Assn. for Marriage and Family Counseling, 1980. Served to lt. U.S. Army, 1972-73. Mem. Am. Psychol. Assn., Am. Assn. for Marriage and Family Therapy (clin.), Am. Assn. for Counseling and Devel., Am. Mental Health Counselors Assn. Avocations: writing fiction; fishing; camping; racketball; tennis. Home: 1812 Crouch St Bentonville AR 72712 Office: Performance and Diagnostic Clinic 906 NW 8th St Bentonville AR 72712

WINKLER, HUGH DONALD, college administrator, public relations consultant; b. Cobden, Ill., Nov. 25, 1932; s. Hugh Stelle and Vesta Marguerite (Schimpf) W.; m. Azile Thomson, Dec. 21, 1956; children—Donald Thomson, James Randolph. Student So. Ill. U., 1952-53; A.B. magna cum laude, McKendree Coll., 1954; M.S., Ohio U., 1956. Grad. asst. Ohio U., Athens, 1954-55; projects sec., editor-in-chief Nat. Conf. Methodist Youth, Nashville, 1955-57; acting dir. communications, instr. N.D. State U., Fargo, 1957-59; dir. info. services Randolph-Macon Woman's Coll., Lynchburg, Va., 1959-66; dir. pub. relations George Washington U., Washington, 1966-72; dir. pub. affairs Calif. State U., Fresno, 1972-78, East-West Ctr., Honolulu, 1978-82; assoc. v.p., exec. dir. pub. affairs and publs. Longwood Coll., Farmville, Va., 1982—; cons. Publs. Authority, San Diego State U., 1978, Valley Regional Tng. Ctr., Fresno, 1975-78; lectr. Nat. Sch. for Ednl. Adminstrs., Council for Advancement and Support Edn., 1973, mem. bd. advs. Nat. Cert. Program, 1977-80, judge Nat. Direct Mail Competition, 1968, Nat. Publs. Competition, 1972; dir. Mason-Dixon Dist. Pub. Relations Workshop, 1971; lectr. nat. ednl. confs. Chmn., East-West Ctr. Aloha United Way Campaign, Honolulu, 1980. Recipient 3 awards for excellence McGraw-Hill Instl. Publs., 1975, 76; cert. excellence Am. Inst. Graphic Arts, 1967. Mem. Nat. Press Club, Soc. Profl. Journalists, Pub. Relations Soc. Am., Ednl. Press Assn. Am. (dir. workshop on urban edn. 1969, Golden Lamp award for Mag. of Yr. 1981, 22 Disting. Achievement awards 1969-85), Council for Advancement and Support of Edn. (Instl. Booklet of Yr. award 1963, Top 5 Alumni Newspapers award 1970, Spl. Merit cert. for info. program 1971, 1st runner-up for Best Total Publs. Program in U.S. 1972, Time-Life Periodical Achievement award 1973, Exceptional Achievement award for newsletter pub. 1977, 78, Spl. Merit award 1980, Top 10 Ednl. Mags. award 1980), Va. Broadcasters Assn., Va. Press Assn. Editor, founder East-West Perspectives Mag., 1979, 80; editor Concern mag., 1955-57, R-MWC Today mag., 1959-66, GW News mag., 1970, Discovery mag., 1975, Contact mag., 1972-78; contbg. editor The Omnibus of Fun, 1957; contbr. numerous articles to profl. jours., newspapers, univ. publs. and religious jours. Home: Route 4 Box 418 Farmville VA 23901 Office: Pub Affairs Office Longwood Coll Farmville VA 23901

WINKLER, L. C., pharmacist; b. Fayetteville, Tenn., May 14, 1955; s. Herman Lee and Ruby Irene (Williams) W. A.A., Martin Coll., 1975; B.S. in Pharmacy, U. Tenn., 1978. Registered pharmacist, Tenn., Ala., W.Va. Pharmacy mgr. Giant K Pharmacy, Fayetteville, 1978-79; staff pharmacist Carter's Drug Store, Fayetteville, 1979-80; pharmacy mgr., pharmacy tng. mgr. Rite Aid Pharmacy, Fayetteville, 1980—; mem. adv. bd. Mt. Sinai Home Health Service, Fayetteville, 1983—. Tchr. CPR, Am. Heart Assn., Fayetteville, 1983; adv. Lincoln County Humane Soc., 1985. Mem. Am. Pharm. Assn., Tenn. Pharm. Assn. U. Tenn. Alumni Assn., Ala. Pharm. Assn., W.Va. Pharm. Assn. Republican. Mem. Church of Christ Ch. Avocations: sports; reading; real estate; stocks. Home: Route 8 Box 487-A Fayetteville TN 37334 Office: Rite Aid Pharmacy 1414 Huntsville Hwy Fayetteville TN 37334

WINN, DEAN, telecommunications company executive; b. Nashville, Sept. 30, 1941; s. Sam and Evelyn (Sadler) W.; m. Carole Overby, June 8, 1968; children—Barry, Mark, Adam. B.S., Tenn. Technol. U. Lic. single engine pilot. Sales rep. Executone of Nashville, Inc. (Tenn.), 1965-70, pres., 1970—; v.p. Ind. Telephone Equipment Suppliers of Tenn., 1974-78; land communications cons. Deacon 1st Baptist Ch., Hendersonville, Tenn., 1982—. Served as 1st lt. U.S. Army, 1963-65. Republican. Clubs: Cages Bend Swim and Tennis. Office: Executone of Nashville Inc 809 Meridian St Nashville TN 37207

WINN, EDWARD LOWRY, JR., finance educator; b. Jacksonville, Fla., Apr. 27, 1925; s. Edward Lowry and Clemmie (Welch) W.; m. Azile Whittemore, Nov. 29, 1946; children—Edward III, Sherry, Nita. B.S., U. Fla., 1948; M.A., Vanderbilt U., 1959; D.B.A., Ind. U., 1965. Asst. prof. U. S.C., Columbia, 1960-65; prof. So. Ill. U., Carbondale, 1965-73, U. Miss., Oxford, 1973-77; dean, prof. fin. Belmont Coll., Nashville, 1977—. Home: 8 Rosebud Dr Nashville TN 37215 Office: Belmont Coll Nashville TN 37202

WINN, LARRY MARSHALL, sales executive, systems specialist; b. Memphis, Oct. 19, 1945; s. Homer Powell and Mary Algood (Pryor) W.; m. Jane Keith, June 20, 1970 (div. 1976); m. Jane Powell, June 1, 1979; 1 child, Conley Powell. B.S. in Mktg., U. Tenn., 1970, M.B.A., 1975. Office mgr. Culbert Constrn. Co., Nashville, 1970-71; purchasing mgr. Opryland U.S.A., Nashville, 1971-72; acct. exec. Liggett & Myers, Nashville, 1972-75; terr. mgr. How Co., Nashville, 1975-83, selected account mgr., Atlanta, 1983—. Served to 1st lt. U.S. Army, 1966-69. Mem. Atlanta Office Products Assn., Ga. Office Products Assn., Ga. Travelors Assn., So. Travelers Assn., Nat. Products Assn. Methodist. Lodge: Elks. Avocations: golf; bass fishing; raquetball. Home and Office: 755 Upper Hembree Rd Roswell GA 30076

WINNINGHAM, CLARENCE GLENN, traffic safety training services executive; b. Myrtle Point, Oreg., Jan. 8, 1940; s. Joseph R. and Helen E. W.; m. Antoinette Vendetti, June 28, 1969; children—Tonya Lynn, Glenn Philip. Student S.A. Coll. Mortuary Sci., 1961; B.A., Ariz. State U., 1966; M.Ed., Central State U., 1973; postgrad. Tex. A&M U., 1975. Instr. Ariz. State U., Tempe, 1966-67; regional edn. rep. Aetna Life & Casualty Co., Houston, 1967-80; traffic safety cons. Aetna Tech. Services, Houston, 1980-82; pres. Driver Tng. Assocs. Inc., Houston, 1983—; cons. State Offices Traffic Safety, 1969-83; mem. adv. com. Fed.-State Edn., Bus. and Industry, 1969-83; curriculum advisor Tex. Edn. Agy., 1969-81. Scriptwriter/cons. Traffic Safety Tng. Films, 1967-82. Goodwill ambassador U.S. State Dept., East Africa, 1962; testifier Legis. Com. Meetings, Austin, Tex., 1981-85. Served with U.S. Army, 1959-63. Recipient Honor award Tex. Driver and Traffic Safety Assn., 1979. Mem. Am. Driver and Traffic Safety Edn. Assn. (chmn. adult div. 1980), Nat. Assn. Fleet Adminstrs. (chmn. safety 1983-85), Tex. Driver and Traffic Edn. Assn. (pres. 1985-86), Tex. Alcohol Traffic Safety Edn. Assn. (bd. dirs. 1982-84), Kappa Delta Pi. Democrat. Presbyterian. Home: 8339 Langdon Ln Houston TX 77036 Office: Driver Tng Assocs Inc PO Box 37225 Houston TX 77237

WINSLETT, LINDA STONER, ballet company artistic director; b. Jacksonville, Fla., Aug. 17, 1958; d. Usher Thomasson and Linda (Stoner) W.; m. Todd Ivan Pankoff, July 30, 1983. A.B. summa cum laude, Smith Coll., 1980. Dir., The Richmond Ballet, Va., 1980—. Choreographer: (ballets) Windows, 1980, Orchestra, 1985, The Nutcracker, 1984. Recipient Alumnae of Yr. award Hammond Acad., 1984. Talent scholar N.C. Sch. of Arts, 1979. Mem. Phi Beta Kappa. Presbyterian. Club: Smith (v.p. 1981-83). Office: The Richmond Ballet 614 N Lombardy St Richmond VA 23220

WINSTEAD, RICHARD MCLEOD, accountant; b. Madisonville, Ky., Dec. 9, 1946; s. William Strauther and Margaret Marie (McLeod) W.; m. Beverly Easterly, July 24, 1976; children—Rachel Elizabeth, Richard Andrew. B.S. magna cum laude, Georgetown Coll., 1969; M.B.A., Ind. U., 1973. C.P.A., Tenn. Staff accountant Arthur Andersen & Co., Chattanooga, Tenn., 1969, 73-77, ptnr., Nashville, 1985—; v.p. fin., comptroller Chesson Oil Co., Inc., Lake Charles, La., 1977-79; mem. Dean's Assocs. for Sch. Bus., Ind. U., Bloomington, 1974—, Estate Planning Council, Nashville, 1981—. Bd. dirs. Adv. Bd. Georgetown Coll., Ky., 1981-83, Fannie Battle Social Workers, Nashville, 1981-83; ambassador Tenn. Ind. Colls. Fund, Nashville, 1980—; active mem. Assocs. of Georgetown Coll., 1983—. Recipient Student Achievement award Wall Street Jour., 1969. Mem. Am. Inst. CPAs, Nat. Assn. Accts., Tenn. Soc. CPAs, Alpha Beta Pi. Baptist. Lodges: Lions, Gideon Internat. Home: 6221 Bridlewood Ln Brentwood TN 37027 Office: Arthur Andersen & Co 315 Deaderick St Nashville TN 37238

WINSTEAD, THOMAS ARNOLD, loss control representative; b. Rocky Mount, N.C., Mar. 20, 1954; s. John Thomas and Odell Mavis (Joyner) W.; m. Peggy Jean Whitehurst; children—Brandy Melissa, John Thomas II. B.S. in Health and Phys. Edn., Atlantic Christian Coll., 1976; postgrad., Pa. State U., 1979-81, Wilson Tech. Coll., 1980, Nash Tech. Coll., 1983. Farmer, Nash County, N.C., 1970-77; tchr., coach, summer recreation dir. Nash County Pub. Schs., Nashville, N.C., 1977-79; engr. aide N.C. Dept. Transp., Nashville, 1979-80, fleet safety supr., Wilson, N.C., 1980-81; loss control rep. Utica Mut. Ins., Richmond, Va., 1981—; mem. Nat. Com. Motor Fleet Safety, Pa. State U., 1980—. Chief Coopers Vol. Fire Dept. and Rescue Squad, Elm City, N.C., 1973—; coach, asst. Tri-Community Little League Baseball, Elm City, 1980—; hon. mem., instr. N.C. 4-H, Nashville, 1980, 84. Recipient various prodn. crop awards Future Farmers Am., 1968-72. Mem. Am. Soc. Safety Engrs., Sandy Cross Jaycees (sec. 1980-81). Democrat. Methodist. Avocations: hunting; class A softball. Home: Rt 1 Box 282-E Rocky Mount NC 27801

WINSTON, DONALD SKEER, trauma surgeon; b. Chgo., Apr. 2, 1945; s. Bernard Harry and Roberta (Skeer) W.; M.D., U. Mo., Kansas City, 1975. Intern, Baylor Coll. Medicine, Houston, 1975-76, resident in gen. surgery, 1976-77; resident in gen. surgery St. Joseph Hosp., Houston, 1978-81, chief resident, 1980-81; clin. research fellow Cardiovascular Surg. Research Labs., Tex. Heart Inst. of St. Luke's Episcopal and Tex. Children's hosps., Houston, 1977-78; pvt. practice medicine specializing in indsl. medicine and trauma, vascular, and gen. surgery, Houston, 1981—; lectr. in field; asst. dir. Clin. Circulatory Support Service, Tex. Heart Inst., 1977-78. Diplomate Nat. Bd. Med. Examiners. Mem. AMA (chmn. cost effectiveness work group, editor Cost Effective Med. Care 1978-79, del. 1980-81), Tex. Med. Assn. (chmn. reference com. on health care facilities), Harris County Med. Soc., Am. Coll. Emergency Physicians, IEEE, IEEE Computer Soc., Assn. Advancement Med. Instrumentation, Am. Soc. Artificial Internal Organs, AAAS, Soc. Advanced Med. Systems, Soc. Computers in Medicine, Ops. Research Soc. Am. Contbr. articles to profl. jours.; editorial asso. and med. cons. Cardiovascular Diseases bull. Tex. Heart Inst., 1977-78. Home: 2346 University Blvd Houston TX 77005 Office: 5085 Westheimer Suite 4700 Galleria II Houston TX 77056

WINSTON, STEPHEN EDWARD, editor; b. N.Y.C., Nov. 1, 1949; s. Ralph and Irene (Sochrin) W. B.A. in Polit. Sci., C.W. Post Coll., 1972. Freelance writer newspapers and mags. U.S. and abroad, 1972-75; features editor Tarter Communications, Manhassett, N.Y., 1975-77; writer Hartford (Conn.) Inst. Criminal and Social Justice, 1977-78; reporter Palm Beach Times, West Palm Beach, Fla., 1978-79; editor-in-chief Halsey Pub. Co., North Miami, Fla., 1979—; cons. Metropolis mag. Editor: Management, 1984; contbr. articles to mags., UPI. Named one of 84 for '84, Miami Mag., 1984. Mem. Soc. Am. Travel Writers, Assn. Am. Travel Editors, Fla. Mag. Assn. Office: Halsey Publishing Co 12955 Biscayne Blvd North Miami FL 33181

WINSTON, THOMAS COLEMAN, hospital administrator; b. Raleigh, N.C., Nov. 18, 1943; s. Thomas D. and Gladys (Coleman) W.; m. Sue McNeill, Apr. 14, 1965; children—Elizabeth Leigh, Thomas M., Courtney Lynn. B.A. in History, Memphis State U., 1965; M. Hosp. Adminstrn., Washington, U., 1967. Vice-pres. Barnes Hosp., St. Louis, 1967-79; assoc. dean U. Calif.-Davis, 1979-84, dir. hosp. and clinics, 1979-84; pres., chief exec. officer Chattanooga-Hamilton County Hosp. Authority, 1984—; bd. dirs. Chattanooga Psychiat. Clinic, 1984—. Contbr. articles to profl. jours. Bd. dirs. Chattanooga United Way, 1984—, Hospice Chattanooga, 1984—. Mem. Am. Coll. Hosp. Adminstrs., Assn. Am. Med. Colls. (del.), Chattanooga C. of C. (bd. dirs. 1985—). Presbyterian. Lodge: Rotary (Chattanooga). Avocations: family travel; golf; photography. Home: 17 Rock Crest Signal Mountain TN 37377 Office: Erlanger Med Ctr 975 E 3d St Chattanooga TN 37403

WINTER, JOAN ELIZABETH, psychotherapist; b. Aiken, S.C., Feb. 24, 1947; d. John S. and Mary Elizabeth (Caldwell) Winter. B.S., Ariz. State U., 1970; M.S.W., Va. Commonwealth U., 1978. Lic. clin. social worker, Va. Counselor Child Psychiatry Hosp., Phoenix, 1969-70, Ariz. Job Coll., Casa Grande, 1970-71; dir. Halfway House, Richmond, Va., 1971-73; state supr. resdl. treatment, Richmond, 1973-75; psycotherapist Med. Coll. Va., Richmond, 1975-76, Va. Commonwealth U., 1976-77; exec. dir. Family Research Project, Richmond, Va., 1979-81; dir. Family Inst. Va., Richmond, 1980—; examiner Bd. Behavioral Scis., Commonwealth of Va., 1982-86; mem. Avanta Network, Exec. Council and Faculty, Nat. Inst. of Drug Abuse, Research Adv. Com. Author: The Phenomenon of Incest, 1977; contbr. articles to profl. jours. Mem. Nat. Assn. Social Workers, Am. Soc. Cert. Social Workers, Am. Assn. Marriage and Family Therapy, Avanta Network Faculty. Address: 2910 Monument Ave Richmond VA 23221

WINTER, MARTIN, lawyer, builder; b. N.Y.C., Dec. 29, 1907; s. Louis and Rose W.; B.A., Columbia U., 1928; LL.B, Fordham U., 1930; m. Adele Godfrey, Feb. 2, 1941; children—Carolyn Bybee, Marjorie Krieger. Admitted to N.Y. State bar, 1933; trust dept. exec. Central Hanover Bank, N.Y.C., 1932-33; assoc. firm Seligsberg & Lewis, N.Y.C., 1933-35; founder, partner firm Chorosh & Winter, N.Y.C., 1935-77; builder housing projects, L.I., N.Y., 1947—; mem. faculty Columbia U.; lectr. Practicing Law Inst. Ofcl. adviser Mayor Lindsay's Office of S.I. Devel., 1966-72; chmn. bldg. com. Village Russell Gardens, Nassau County, N.Y. Mem. Regional Plan Assn., Nassau County Bar Assn. Club: North Shore Country (Glen Head, N.Y.). Author: Inside Staten Island, 1964. Home: Palm Beach County FL

WINTERS, LEO, state official, lawyer; b. Hooker, Okla., Nov. 7, 1922; s. David and Gertrude (Strochin) W.; A.B., Panhandle A&M Coll., Goodwell, Okla., 1950; LL.B., U. Okla., 1957. Bar: Okla. 1957. Since practiced in Oklahoma City; lt. gov. Okla., 1963-67, treas., 1967—. Served as pilot USAAF, World War II. Mem. Am. Quarter Horse Assn. Democrat. Lodge: Masons. (32 deg.). Office: PO Box 53411 Oklahoma City OK 73152

WINTERSHEIMER, DONALD CARL, state supreme court justice; b. Covington, Ky., Apr. 21, 1932; s. Carl E. and Marie A. (Kohl) W.; m. Alice T. Rabe, June 24, 1960; children—Mark, Lisa Ann, Craig, Amy, Blaise. B.A., Thomas More Coll., 1953; M.A., Xavier U., 1956; J.D., U. Cin., 1959; Bar: Ky. 1960, Ohio 1960; sole practice law, Covington, Ky., 1960-76, Cin., 1960-76; city solicitor City of Covington, 1962-76; judge Ky. Ct. of Appeals, Frankfort, 1976-82; justice Ky. Supreme Ct., Frankfort, 1982—; disting. jurist in residence Chase Coll. Law, No. Ky. U. Mem. ABA, Ky. Bar Assn., Ohio State Bar Assn., Am. Judicature Soc., Inst. Jud. Adminstrn. Democrat. Roman Catholic. Home: 224 Adams Ave Covington KY 41014 Office: Supreme Ct of Ky 201 State Capitol Frankfort KY 40601

WINTON, JAMES FREDERICK, construction company executive; b. Flint, Mich., May 20, 1944; s. Orlum Hardin and Jane Louise (Gidley) W.; m. Bertha M. Taylor, May 7, 1966; 1 child, Robert James. B.Arch., U. Mich., 1967. Registered architect, Ill., Mich., Ohio, Tenn., Ky. Draftsman, Albert Kahn & Assocs., Detroit, 1967-68; engrng. coordinator Lombard Co., Alsip, Ill., 1970-73; asst. mgr. design-bldg. Lathrop Co., Toledo, Ohio, 1973-82; v.p. Lacona, Inc., Nashville, 1982—. Commr., Brentwood Planning Commn., Tenn., 1985. Served with U.S. Army, 1968-70. Methodist. Avocations: sailing; golf; camping. Home: 1209 Hood Dr Brentwood TN 37027 Office: Lacona Inc PO Box 23857 Nashville TN 37202

WINZELER, TED J., oil company executive; b. Columbus, Ohio, Dec. 24, 1948; s. Edwin Clarence and Charlotte Mae (Whiteley) W.; m. Linda Meyer, Sept. 30, 1972; 1 child, Alissa Meyer. B.S. in Geology, Wittenburg U., 1970; M.S. in Geology, Bowling Green State U., 1974. Geologist Amoco Prodn. Co., Houston, 1974-80, div. geologist, 1980-84, regional geologist, 1984—. Vol. worker Women's Christian Home Aux., Houston, 1984. Mem. Am. Assn. Petroleum Geologists (cert.), Soc. Exploration Paleontologists and Mineralogists, Houston Geol. Soc., Sigma Gamma Epsilon. Methodist. Clubs: Meyerland, Westlake (Houston). Avocations: golf, tennis. Office: Amoco Prodn Co 501 Westlake Park Blvd PO Box 3092 Houston TX 77253

WIORKOWSKI, JOHN JAMES, mathematics educator; b. Chgo., Sept. 30, 1943; s. John Stanley and Harriet Elizabeth (Bedra) W.; B.S., U. Chgo., 1965, M.S., 1966, Ph.D., 1972; m. Gabrielle K. Hollis, June 4, 1966; children—Fleurette Anne. Research asso. U. Chgo., 1972; asst. prof. Pa. State U., University Park, 1973-74; assoc. prof. U. Tex. at Dallas, Richardson, 1975, assoc. prof. and program head Math Scis. Program, 1979-81, prof., 1981—, asst. to v.p. acad. affairs, 1980-85, asst. v.p. acad. affairs, 1985—; cons. to Fed. Energy Adminstrn., 1975, Tex. Instruments, 1977, Frito-Lay Inc., 1977-78, Republic Nat. Bank, 1979; mem. panel studying 55 mile per hour speed limit Nat. Acad. Sci. Served to capt. U.S. Army, 1968-71. Decorated Army Commendation medal. NSF grantee, 1975—. Am. Council Edn. fellow, 1981-82. Mem. Am. Statis. Assn. (chpt. pres. 1974, v.p. 1977, chpt. pres. 1978), AAAS, Inst. Math. Stats., Biometric Soc., Sigma Xi. Presbyterian. Contbr. articles to profl. jours. Home: 428 Bedford St Richardson TX 75080 Office: U Tex at Dallas Box 688 Richardson TX 75080

WIPPEL, STEPHEN ALEX, geophysicist, educator; b. Huntington, W.Va., May 30, 1949; s. Richard Edward and Rosalie (Smith) W.; m. Bess Marie Bailey, July 21, 1974; children—Stacey, Ryan, Pamela. A.A. in Math., Palm Beach Jr. Coll., 1967; B.A. in Physics, Fla. Atlantic U., 1971, B.S. in Geology, 1974. Petroleum geologist Amoco Oil Exploration and Prodn. Co., New Orleans, 1975-76; geophysicist Superior Oil Co., New Orleans, 1976-77; sr. geologist Amerada Hess Corp., Lafayette, La., 1977-80; dist. explorationist Williams Exploration Co., Houston, 1980-84; sr. geophysicist Lear Petroleum Corp., Houston, 1984—; adj. instr. geology N. Harris Community Coll., Houston, 1981—. Served with U.S. Army, 1970. Mem. Am. Assn. Petroleum Geologists, Soc. Exploration Geophysicists, Am. Geophys. Union, Houston Geophys. Soc. Republican. Roman Catholic. Avocations: computer programming, stamp collecting, rock collecting, racquetball, basketball. Office: Lear Petroleum Corp 515 W Greens Rd Suite 1200 Houston TX 77067

WIRGES, MANFORD FRANK, engineering design company executive; b. Beatrice, Nebr., Jan. 18, 1925; s. Frank J. and Leta (Coon) W.; m. Joan Kelly; 1 child, Kelly Marie. B.S. in Chem. Engring., U. Okla., 1944, M.S., 1945. With Cities Service, N.Y.C., 1946-79, Tulsa, 1979-82, v.p. research, 1979-82; exec. v.p. Flexivol, Inc., Houston, 1982—. Mem. engring. adv. bd. U. Okla., Norman, 1981-85, U Tulsa, 1979-82. Mem. Am. Inst. Chem. Engrs., Am. Petroleum Inst., Founders Club Petrochemical, 25-Yr. Petroleum Club. Republican. Club: Metropolitan (Houston). Home: 3208 E 69th St Tulsa OK 74136 Office: Flexivol Inc PO Box 702588 Tulsa OK 74170

WIRT, MICHAEL ALLEN, safety specialist; b. Roanoke, Va., Sept. 12, 1947; s. Robert C. Wirt and Charlotte (Taylor) Krayer; m. Jean Carol Chambers, Aug. 16, 1969; children—Roger A., Rachel K., Pamela R. A.S. cum laude, St. Clair County Community Coll., Mich., 1975; B.S., Madonna Coll., Mich., 1977; A.S. in Bus. Adminstrn., Maple Woods Community Coll., Mo., 1979. Fire protection specialist U.S. Air Force, Mount Clemens, Mich., 1966-70, U.S. Govt., Mount Clemens, 1970-77, Ford Motor Co., Kansas City, Mo., 1977-79; engrng. rep. Travelers Ins. Co., San Antonio, 1979-81; safety specialist S.W. Research Inst., San Antonio, 1981—; mem. adv. com. safety technician program San Antonio Coll., 1983— part-time lectr. San Antonio Coll. Served with USAF, 1966-70. Mem. Am. Soc. Safety Engrs. (profl., pres. chpt. 1985-86), Greater San Antonio Safety Council (3d vp. 1984-86), Vets. of Safety (chpt. sec.-treas. 1984-85), Fed. Safety and Health Council, Nat. Safety Council (assoc. research and devel. sect.). Republican. Baptist. Clubs: Toastmasters (pres. 1985-86). Avocations: bowling; sports. Office: Southwest Research Inst PO Drawer 28510 San Antonio TX 78284

WISDOM, JERRY LEE, computer systems analyst, business researcher, former army officer; b. Wichita Falls, Tex., July 6, 1941; s. Glenn Roy and Lola Mae (Whisenant) W.; m. Klara Gruner, Sept. 1, 1962; children—Robert J., Hans Michael, Barbara, Carolyn. B.S. in Bus. Adminstrn., Cameron U., 1972; M.A. in Econs., U. Okla., 1978; cert. Command and Gen. Staff Coll., 1981. Cert. quality and reliability engr. Enlisted U.S. Army, 1959, advanced through grades to maj., 1976, chief operating officer 36th Field Artillery Detachment, 4th German Infantry Div., Hemau, W.Ger., 1973-75, chief Ops. Ctr. 59th Ordnance Group, Pirmasens, W.Ger., 1976-77, ops. research analyst TRADOC Combined Arms Test, Fort Hood, Tex., 1977-82, ret., 1982; mng. ptnr. Floors Unique, Copperas Cove, Tex., 1982; bus. systems analyst Tex. Dept. Human Resources, Austin, 1983—; pvt. practice investment and tax cons., Killeen, Tex., 1978-81. Author test design, test report Eight Titles, 1977-82; author article. Zoning com. Austin North Oaks Neighborhood Assn., 1985. Decorated D.F.C., Vietnam, Ehren Nadel, 4th German Div., 1975. Mem. Am. Soc. Quality Control (membership chmn. 1985), Ops. Research Soc. Am., Am. Statis. Assn., Retired Officers Assn. (bd. mem., army rep. 1985—), First Cavaley Div. Assn. (life). Republican. Baptist. Clubs: Golden Life Fit, Bridge, Forget Me Not. Avocations: writing; water sports; running; reading. Home: 8007 Scotland Yard Austin TX 78759-4312 Office: Tex Dept Human Resources PO Box 2960 MC 413-W 701 W 51st St Austin TX 78769

WISDOM, JOHN MINOR, judge; b. New Orleans, May 17, 1905; s. Mortimer Norton and Adelaide (Labatt) W.; m. Bonnie Stewart Mathews, Oct. 24, 1931; children—John Minor, Kathleen Mathews, Penelope Stewart Wisdom Tose. A.B., Washington and Lee U., 1925; LL.B., Tulane U., 1929, LL.D., 1976; LL.D., Oberlin U., 1963, San Diego U., 1979, Haverford Coll., 1982. Bar: La. 1929. Mem. firm Wisdom, Stone, Pigman & Benjamin, New Orleans, 1929-57; judge U.S. Ct. Appeals 5th Circuit, 1957—; mem. Multi-Dist. Litigation Panel, 1968-79, chmn., 1975-79; mem. Spl. Ct. Regional Reorgn. of R.R.s, 1975—; adj. prof. law Tulane U., 1938-57. Mem. Pres.'s Com. on Govt. Contracts, 1953-57; past pres. New Orleans Council Social Agys.; Republican nat. committeeman for, La., 1952-57; trustee Washington and Lee U., 1953—. Served from capt. to lt. col. USAAF, 1942-46. Decorated Legion of Merit; Army Commendation medal. Mem. Am. Acad. Arts and Scis., ABA (chmn. appellate judges conf.), La. Bar Assn., New Orleans Bar Assn., Am. Law Inst. (mem. council), La. Law Inst., Order of Coif, Delta Kappa Epsilon, Phi Alpha Delta (Tom C. Clark Equal Justice under Law award), Omicron Delta Kappa. Episcopalian. Clubs: Boston, Louisiana (New Orleans); Metropolitan (Washington). Office: 600 Camp St New Orleans LA 70130*

WISE, GARY LAMAR, electrical engineering and mathematics educator, researcher; b. Texas City, Tex., July 29, 1945; s. Calder Lamar and Ruby Lavon (Strom) W.; m. Mary Estella Warren, Dec. 28, 1974; 1 child, Tanna Estella. B.A. summa cum laude, Rice U., 1971; M.S.E., Princeton U., 1973, M.A. 1973, Ph.D., 1974. Postdoctoral research assoc. Princeton U., N.J., 1974; asst. prof. Tex. Tech U., Lubbock, 1975-76; asst. prof. U. Tex., Austin, 1976-80, assoc. prof., 1980-84, prof. elec. engring. and math., 1984—; tech. reviewer Army Research Office, Durham, N.C., 1976, Air Force Office Sci. Research, Washington, 1980, 83-85, Harper and Row Pubs., N.Y.C., 1982-83, NSF, 1984; cons. Baylor Coll. Medicine, Houston, 1972; speaker at numerous tech. confs. Contbr. chpts., numerous articles to profl. publs. Recipient award for outstanding contbns. to Coll. Engring., U. Tex. Engring. Found., 1979, 81; Air Force Office Sci. research grantee, 1976—; Carroll D. Simmons Centennial teaching fellow U. Tex., Austin, 1982-84. Mem. IEEE, Soc. Indsl. and Applied Math., Am. Math. Soc., Inst. Math. Stats., Phi Beta Kappa, Tau Beta Pi. Methodist. Home: 8705 Collingwood Dr Austin TX 78748 Office: U Tex Dept Elec and Computer Engring Austin TX 78712

WISE, GEORGE WILKINSON, financial executive; b. Crichton, Red River Parish, La., Dec. 2, 1915; s. Jacob Zeigler and Mattie (Wilkinson) W.; m. Maitland Allums, Sept. 11, 1938; children—George Wilkinson, Mary Ann, Nathan Howard, Marjorie Louise, Edwin Paul, Jacob Zeigler, Mark Maitland. Student Northwestern State U., 1932-34, 35-37, La. State U., 1934-35. Social worker, 1938-46; mcht. Wise Appliance & Hardware Co., Coushatta, La., 1946-69; columnist Coushatta Citizen, 1946—; owner, mgr. Credit Bur. of Coushatta, 1969—. Bd. dirs. Red River Parish and Coushatta CD, 1953—; scoutmaster Boy Scouts Am., 1938-46; firefighter, Coushatta Vol. Fire Dept., 1946-71, hon. mem., 1971—. Episcopalian. Lodge: Masons. Mailing Address: PO Box 98 Coushatta LA 71019 Home: Alligatorville Coushatta LA 71019 Office: PO Box 98 Coushatta LA 71019

WISE, JERRY LEE, investment manager, portfolio manager; b. Tulsa, May 30, 1953; s. Gerald A. and Loeta M. (Whitesell) W.; m. Cathy M.T. Carey, Sept. 22, 1979; children—Kelley, Scott. B.B.A. in Acctg., Okla. U., 1978, M.B.A. in Fin., 1984. C.P.A.; chartered fin. analyst. Auditor, Peat, Marwick, Mitchell, Tulsa, 1979-80; security analyst, portfolio mgr. First Nat. Bank & Trust Co., Oklahoma City, 1981—. Served with U.S. Army, 1972-75. Mem. Beta Gamma Sigma. Republican. Avocations: tennis; water-skiing; reading. Office: First Nat Bank & Trust Co PO Box 25189 Oklahoma City OK 73125

WISE, KATHLEEN ROSE VERONICA, psychotherapist, researcher; b. Forest Hills, N.Y., July 10, 1947; d. Irwin Thomas and Rosemary (Bacchini) Doty; children—Bruce Kenwood, Marc; m. Helbert Wise, Mar. 1, 1983. B.A., Hofstra U., 1967; M.A., SUNY, 1969; Ph.D., Met. Coll. London, 1985; Ph.D. (hon.), Southwestern U., 1985. Staff counselor U.S. Systems, Dallas, 1976-80; psychotherapist Garland Ctr. for Behavioral Sci., Garland, 1982-84; psychotherapist pvt. practice, Irving, Tex., 1984—; cons. Dallas Med. Ladies Clinic,

1983-84. Active Dallas Alliance for Mental Recovery, 1985. Mem. Am. Assn. Profl. Hypnotherapists, AAUW, Menninger Found., Am. Assn. Counseling and Devel. Roman Catholic. Avocation: oil painting.

WISE, ROBERT CHAPPELL, architect; b. Jacksonville, Fla., June 29, 1931; s. Leland E. and Marie E. (Ellis) W.; m. Patricia Ann Wilson, Jan. 25, 1958; children—Jeffrey, Lynn. B.Arch., U. Fla., 1954. Registered architect, Fla. Draftsman, Reynolds, Smith, Hills, Jacksonville, 1958-63, Hardwick & Lee, Jacksonville, 1963-64, Gordon, Drake & Patillo, 1964-67; project architect Kemp/Alford, Jacksonville, 1967-68; prin. Robert Wise Architect, Jacksonville, 1968—. Mem. Gator Bowl Assn., 1975—. Served with USAF, 1954-58. Corp. mem. AIA (chpt. treas. 1972-73, chpt. sec. 1975-76, chpt. alt. state dir. 1979-80); mem. Execs. Assn. Jacksonville (pres. 1978, treas. 1983). Democrat. Baptist. Club: German/American. Avocations: photography; travel; arts and crafts; collectables. Home: 2757 Arapahoe Ave Jacksonville FL 32210 Office: 2523 Herschel St Jacksonville FL 32204

WISE, ROBERT E., JR., congressman; b. Washington, Jan. 6, 1948; m. Sandra Casber, 1984. A.B., Duke U., 1970; J.D., Tulane U., 1975. Atty., legis. counsel judiciary com. W.Va. Ho. of Dels., 1977-78; dir. W.Va. for Fair and Equitable Assessment of Taxes, Inc., 1977-80; mem. W.Va. Senate, 1980-82; mem. 98th-99th congresses from 3rd Dist. W.Va. Mem. ABA, W.Va. State Bar Assn. Address: Ho of Reps Washington DC 20515*

WISE, SHERWOOD WILLING, JR., geology educator; b. Jackson, Miss., May 31, 1941; s. Sherwood Willing and Elizabeth (Powell) W.; m. Cynthia Curtiss, Aug. 21, 1965; children—Sarah Bliss, Sherwood Willing III. B.S., Washington and Lee U., 1963; M.S., U. Ill., 1965, Ph.D., 1970. NSF postdoctoral fellow Swiss Fed. Inst. Tech., Zurich, 1970-71; asst. prof. Fla. State U., Tallahassee, 1971-75, assoc. prof., 1975-80, prof. geology, 1980—; co-chief scientist Deep Sea Drilling Project, Glomar Challenger, 1983. Vice-pres. Sealey Elem. Sch. PTO, 1981-82. Served to capt. U.S. Army, 1965-67. Grantee NSF, 1972—, Petroleum Research Fund Am. Chem. Soc., 1974-81. Fellow AAAS; mem. Soc. Econ. Paleontologists and Mineralogists (outstanding paper award Gulf Coast sect. 1971), Am. Assn. Petroleum Geologists, Geol. Soc. Am., Paleontol. Soc., Societe Geologique Suisse. Episcopalian. Editor, Initial Reports of the Deep Sea Drilling Project, 1977, 83. Home: 3318 Northshore Circle Tallahassee FL 32312 Office: Dept Geology Fla State U Tallahassee FL 32306

WISEHART, MARY RUTH, educator; b. Myrtle, Mo., Nov. 2, 1932; d. William Henry and Ora (Harbison) W. B.A., Free Will Baptist Bible Coll., 1955; B.A., George Peabody Coll. Tchrs., 1959, M.A., 1960, Ph.D., 1976. Tchr. Free Will Bapt. Bible Coll., Nashville, 1956-60, chmn. English dept., 1961-85; exec. sec.-treas. Free Will Bapt. Women's Nat. Aux. Conv., 1985—. Author: Sparks Into Flame, 1985; contbr. poetry to jours. Mem. Nat. Council Tchrs. English, Conf. Christianity and Lit., Scribbler's Club. Avocations: photography; music; drama. Office: Woman's Nat Aux Conv Box 1088 Nashville TN 37202

WISEMAN, THOMAS ANDERTON, JR., U.S. district judge; b. Tullahoma, Tenn., Nov. 3, 1930; s. Thomas Anderton and Vera Seleta (Poe) W.; m. Emily Barbara Matlack, Mar. 30, 1957; children—Thomas Anderton III, Mary Alice, Sarah Emily. B.A., Vanderbilt U., 1952, LL.B., 1954. Bar: Tenn. Practice law, Tullahoma, 1956-71; partner firm Haynes, Wiseman & Hull, Tullahoma and Winchester, Tenn., 1963-71; treas., State of Tenn., 1971-74; partner firm Chambers & Wiseman, 1974-78; judge U.S. Dist. Ct. Middle Dist. Tenn., Nashville, 1978—; mem. Tenn. Ho. of Reps., 1964-68. Assoc. editor: Vanderbilt Law Rev, 1953-54. Democratic candidate for gov., Tenn., 1974; Chmn. Tenn. Heart Fund, 1973, Middle Tenn. Heart Fund, 1972. Served with U.S. Army, 1954-56. Mem. ABA, Tenn. Bar Assn. Presbyterian. Club: Amateur Chefs Am. Lodges: Masons; Shriners. Office: 824 US Courthouse Nashville TN 37203*

WISHARD, LINDA GAY, telephone company executive; b. Denver, Sept. 15, 1950; d. Robert A. and Dorothy Bernice (White) Chidsey; 1 dau., Crystalyn Janette. B.S. in Phys. Edn., U. Tex., 1972; M.A., U. So. Calif., 1976. Tchr., Paul Revere Jr. High Sch., Brentwood, Calif., 1972-73; office mgr. Scott, Marshall, Sands & Latta, Inc., Los Angeles, 1973-75; staff Carnation Internat., Los Angeles, 1975-77, coordinator internat. personnel relations, 1979-81; exec. asst. Teton Nat. Ins. Co., Cheyenne, Wyo., 1978-79; adminstr. govt. bids and contracts Carnation Co., Los Angeles, 1981-82; staff asst. U.S. Telephone, Inc., Dallas, 1982-83; benefits adminstr. InteCom., Inc., Allen, Tex., 1983—. Mem. Am. Soc. Personnel Adminstrn., Soc. Advancement Mgmt., Delta Zeta. Republican. Presbyterian. Home: 3400 Custer Rd Apt 1053 Plano TX 75023 Office: 601 InterCom Dr Allen TX 75002

WISMAN, DOUGLAS PEER, optometrist; b. Saumsville, Va., Feb. 19, 1927; s. Ernest and Erva Lorraine (Peer) W.; m. Betty B. Bowman, Nov. 20, 1954; children—Douglas Scott, Ellen, David, Laura. B.S., Randolph-Macon Coll., 1948; postgrad. U. Richmond, 1948; O.D., So. Coll. Optometry, 1950. Practice optometry, Woodstock, Va., 1950—; bd. dirs. Roanoke Eye Bank, Va., 1960-64; lectr. on children's vision, 1974. Cubmaster Boy Scouts Am., 1951-53; chmn. Woodstock Park Commn., 1959-62. Named Ky. col. Gov. Ky., 1963, Young Man of Yr., Woodstock Jaycees, 1960, Optometrist of Yr., Va. Optometric Assn., 1970. Fellow Va. Acad. Optometry. Lodge: Lions (life mem., dist. gov. 1962-63, internat. counselor 1963). Avocations: band and orchestra; photography. Home and office: 124 S Main St Woodstock VA 22664

WISNER, CYNTHIA ANN, oil company geologist; b. Carthage, Mo., July 7, 1957; d. James William and Billie Ann (Glaze) Schooler; m. David Lee Wisner, Feb. 12, 1983. B.S. in Geology, Baylor U., 1980. Geologist, McClelland Engrs., Houston, 1980, Getty Oil (Texaco), Houston, 1981-85, Minatome Corp., Houston, 1985—. Mem. Houston Geol. Soc., Am. Assn. Petroleum Geologists, Delta Gamma Sorority. Home: 9507 Wellsworth Houston TX 77083 Office: Minatome Corp Petroleum Div 1 Allen Ctr Suite 400 Houston TX 77002

WIST, ABUND OTTOKAR, radiation physicist, computer scientist; b. Vienna, Austria, May 23, 1926; s. Engelbert Johannes and Augusta Barbara (Ungewitter) W.; B.S. in Engring., Tech U. Graz, 1947; M.Ed., U. Vienna, 1950, Ph.D. in Physics, 1951; m. Suzanne Gregson Smiley, Nov. 30, 1963; children—John Joseph, Abund Charles. Research and devel. engr. Hornyphon AG, Vienna, 1952-54, Siemens & Halske AG, Munich, Germany, 1954-58; dir. research and devel. Brinkman Instruments Co., Westbury, N.Y., 1958-64; sr. scientist Fisher Sci. Inc., Pitts., 1964-69; mem. faculty U. Pitts., 1970-73; asst. prof. computer sci. Va. Commonwealth U., Richmond, 1973-80, asst. prof. physiology and biophysics, 1977-83, asst. prof. radiology, 1983—. Adj. prof. chemistry, 1977—; founder, gen. chmn. Symposium Computer Applications in Med. Care, Washington, 1977, 78, 79. NASA/Am. Soc. Engring. Edn. faculty fellow, summer 1975. Mem. IEEE (sr.), ASTM, Am. Chem. Soc., N.Y. Acad. Scis., Biomed. Engring. Soc., Am. Assn. Physicists in Medicine, AAAS, Richmond Computer Club (pres. 1977, 78, 79). Roman Catholic. Author: Microcomputer Based Instrumentation and Control Systems. Patentee in electronic and lab. instrumentation. Contbr. numerous articles and chpts. to profl. jours. and books. Home: 9304 Farmington Dr Richmond VA 23229 Office: 1101 E Marshall St Richmond VA 23298

WITHERELL, PETER CHARLES, entomologist; b. Athol, Mass., Sept. 23, 1943; s. Charles Emerson and Ruth Eva (Dodge) W.; m. Beatriz Alicia Plaza Gonzales, Nov. 9, 1981; children—Tina Kang, Philamer Gonzales. B.S., U. Mass., 1965; M.S., U. Calif.-Davis, 1970, Ph.D., 1973. Registered profl. entomologist. Asst. area supr. Aedes aegypti eradication program USPHS, Fla., 1965-68; grad. research asst. entomology U. Calif.-Davis, 1969-72, postdoctoral research entomologist (NSF grantee), 1973-74; asst. dir. research Dadant & Sons, Inc., Hamilton, Ill., 1975-76; grain insp. U.S. Dept. Agr., Balt., 1977-78, plant protection and quarantine officer, 1978-81, sta. supr. Miami Methods Devel. Sta., 1981—. Mem. Entomol. Soc. Am., Fla. Entomol. Soc., Fla. State Hort. Soc., Orgn. Profl. Employees Dept. Agr., Sigma Xi, Alpha Zeta, Phi Kappa Phi. Democrat. Home: 13900 SW 152d St Lot G-724 Miami FL 33177 Office: Methods Devel Sta US Dept Agr 13601 Old Cutler Rd Miami FL 33158

WITHERSPOON, DON MEADE, veterinarian, consultant, researcher, b. Lamar, S.C., Mar. 6, 1930; s. Harris Wister and Lila (Reynolds) W.; m. Frances Edwards, June 20, 1953; children—Donna, Don Meade. B.S., Clemson U., 1953; D.V.M., U. Ga., 1959, Ph.D., 1970. Diplomate Am. Coll. Theriogenology. Gen. practice vet. medicine, Sandersville, Ga., 1959-63; assoc. prof. large animal surgery and medicine Auburn U., 1964-67; research assoc. in physiology U. Ga., 1967-69, prof. large animal medicine and surgery, 1969-76; dir. vet. services, mgr. Spendthrift Farm, Lexington, Ky., 1976—; cons. in equine reproductive problems. Served to sgt. U.S. Army, 1947-48; to capt. 1950-54. Decorated Silver Star; named Alumnus of Yr., Coll. Vet. Medicine, U. Ga., 1982. Mem. Am. Assn. Equine Practitioners, Ky. Assn. Equine Practitioners, AVMA, Ky. Vet. Med. Assn., Coll. Theriogenology, Am. Soc. Theriogenology. Methodist. Contbr. numerous sci. articles to vet. jours. Office: Spendthrift Farm Box 996 Lexington KY 40588

WITHERSPOON, JAMES WINFRED, lawyer; b. Indianola, Okla., Sept. 20, 1906; s. Ernest and Mary Etta (Stafford) W.; m. Margaret Gilliland, July 25, 1930 (dec.); children—Eleanor Irene Witherspoon Couch, Gerald Winfrey (dec.); m. 2d, Elizabeth Spradley Womble, Feb. 14, 1959; 1 dau., Janie Smith. B.A., Montezuma Coll. (N.Mex.), 1926; postgrad. U. Tex., 1926-27; LL.B., U. Okla., 1929. Bar: Tex. 1929, Okla. 1929, U.S. Ct. Claims 1957, U.S. Ct. Appeals (5th cir.) 1949, U.S. Supreme Ct. 1958. Practiced Hereford, Tex., 1929—; sr. ptnr. Witherspoon, Aikin, Langley, 1950—; dist. atty. 69th Jud. Dist. of Tex., 1933-40, dist. judge, 1940-44; chmn. bd. dirs. First Nat. Bank Hereford; founder First Nat. Bank Dumas (Tex.). Bd. regents Tex. A&M U., 1951-57; del. Tex. State Dem. Conv., 1948, 52, 56, 60. Named Deaf Smith County Citizen of Yr., 1961, Hereford Citizen of Yr., 1961. Mem. 69th Jud. Dist. Bar Assn., Tex. Bar Assn., ABA, Am. Judicature Soc., Tex. Assn. Plaintiffs Attys., Nat. Plaintiffs Attys. Assn., Am. Coll. Probate Counsel, Am. Trial Lawyers Assn., Tex. Criminal Def. Lawyers Assn., Deaf Smith County C. of C., West Tex. C. of C., SCV, SAR. Clubs: Hereford Country, Amarillo County, Sugar of N.Y., Hereford Riders, Amarillo Knife and Fork, Amarillo Businessmen's. Lodges: Elks, Masons, Shriners, Rotary, Lions.

WITHERSPOON, WALTER PENNINGTON, JR., orthodontist, philanthropist; b. Columbia, S.C., Sept. 3, 1938; s. Walter P. and Florence Evelyn (Jones) W.; m. Joyce Ann Smith, Sept. 6, 1970; 1 child, Annie Melissa. B.S., U. S.C., 1960; D.D.S., U. N.C., 1964, M.S.O., 1969. Bd. qualified Am. Bd. Orthodontics. Pvt. practice in orthodontia, Columbia, 1969—; med. staff Bapt. Med. Ctr., Columbia, 1970—, Lexington County Hosp., West Columbia, 1974—. Host Nite Line, Dove Broadcasting Co. Adv. bd. 1st Palmetto Bank and Trust, West Columbia, 1982; del. S.C. Rep. Com., 1983; bd. dirs. Southeastern Coll. Assemblies of God, Lakeland, Fla., 1984. Served to lt. USN, 1964-66. Recipient Century Mem. award Boy Scouts Am., 1984. Mem. Greater Columbia Dental Assn. (pres. 1975-76), S.C. Dental Assn. (ho. of dels. 1971-73), ADA, S.C. Orthodontic Assn., Am. Assn. Orthodontists. Club: Sertoma (pres. 1975-76). Lodge: Am. Legion. Home: 250 Lancer Dr Columbia SC 29210 Office: 205 Medical Circle West Columbia SC 29169

WITHROW, JON RICHARD, geologist; b. Seminole, Okla., Jan. 8, 1933; s. Richard Dean and LoLeta (Carroll) W.; student Seminole Jr. Coll., 1950-51; B.S. in Petroleum Engring., U. Okla., 1954, M.Geol. Engring., 1963; postgrad. U. Tex., 1955; m. Carol Ann Ferguson, Nov. 21, 1960 (div. Nov. 1968); 1 stepdau., Ann Todd. Mem. engr. tng. program Humble Oil & Refining Co., Odessa, Tex., 1954, petroleum engr., asst. to dist. engr., Andrews, Tex., 1954-55, Wink, Tex., 1955-56, petroleum engr., Midland, Tex., 1956-57, Houston, 1957, Midland, 1957-58; petroleum engr., geologist Montgomery Oil Co., El Dorado, Ark., 1959-60; self-employed petroleum engr., geologist, Oklahoma City, 1960-62; mgr. geol. and engring. dept. Sarkeys Enterprises, Oklahoma City, 1962-65; mgr. geol. and engring. dept. Sarkeys, Inc., Oklahoma City, 1965-72, v.p., 1966-72; ind. petroleum geol. engr., 1972—; pres. Sundance Oil Co., Oklahoma City, 1977—, Esson Inc., Oklahoma City, 1980—. Registered profl. engr., Okla. Mem. AIME, Soc. Ind. Profl. Earth Scientists, Am. Assn. Petroleum Geologists, Nat., Okla. socs. profl. engrs., Oklahoma City Geol. Soc., Oklahoma City Assn. Petroleum Landmen, SAR, Sigma Nu, Tau Beta Pi, Pi Epsilon Tau. Republican. Methodist. Clubs: Oklahoma City Ski, Woodlake Racquet, Oklahoma City Running. Home: 6412 Galaxie Terr Oklahoma City OK 73132 Mailing Address: PO Box 1239 Oklahoma City OK 73101

WITKOWSKI, PAUL LEWIS, hospital pharmacist; b. Schenectady, N.Y., Jan. 2, 1955; s. Walter J. and Marie (Cornell) W.; m. Mary K. Novak, Sept. 2, 1978; 1 child, Joseph Paul. B.Sc. in Pharmacy, Mass. Coll. Pharmacy, 1978; M.Sc. in Pharmacy, Ohio State U., 1980. Pharmacy resident Ohio State U. Hosps., Columbus, 1978-80; pharmacy supr. Univ. Hosp., Louisville, Ky., 1980-82; asst. dir. pharmacy Humana Hosp. U., Louisville, 1982—; lectr. C.E. Co., Louisville, 1984; instr. basic cardiac life support Am. Heart Assn., Louisville, 1984—, lectr. advanced cardiac life support, 1984—. Mem. human studies com. Instnl. Rev. Bd. for Human Research, U. Louisville, 1982—. Mem. Am. Pharm. Assn., Am. Soc. Hosp. Pharmacists, Ky. Soc. Hosp. Pharmacists, Ohio State U. Alumni Assn., Mass. Coll. Pharmacy Alumni Assn., Rho Chi. Avocations: woodworking; photography. Home: 4942 Winding Spring Circle Louisville KY 40223 Office: Humana Hosp U 530 S Jackson St Louisville KY 40202

WITSCHI, SUSAN MARTHA, student personnel administrator; b. Hialeah, Fla., Aug. 19, 1954; d. Hans Walter and Lieselotte (Schneegass) W. B.S., N.Mex. State U., 1976; M.Ed., U. No. Colo., 1978, North Tex. State U., 1986. Tchr. learning disabilities Central Kans. Coop. in Edn., Salina, 1979-80; program mgr. Country View Care Ctr., Longmont, Colo., 1980-81; coordinator services for off-campus student North Tex. State U., Denton, 1982—. Contbr.: Decision Making: Case Studies in Business and Industry, Education and Community Relations, 1983. Mem. Tex. Assn. Coll. and Univ. Student Personnel Adminstrs., Southwest Assn. Student Personnel Adminstrs. Am. Assn. Counseling and Devel., Am. Coll. Personnel Assn., Nat. Assn. Campus Activities, North Tex. State Univ League for Profl. Women (sec.-treas. 1984-85), Kappa Delta Pi. Home: NT Box 5354 Denton TX 76203-5354 Office: Dean of Students Office North Tex State Univ NT Box 5356 Denton TX 76203-5356

WITT, JAMES WILLIAM, political science educator, consultant; b. Wheeling, W.Va., Oct. 30, 1929; s. John Bernard and Helen Loretta (Dieters) Leithe W.; m. Penny Carol Finn, June 29, 1966; children—Courtney, Jamie, Tierney. B.A., Loyola U., Los Angeles, 1961; M.A., U. Southern Calif., 1966, Ph.D., 1970; postgrad. U. Va. Law Sch., 1961-62. Teaching asst. U. So. Calif., Los Angeles, 1965-67, instr., 1968-69; asst. prof. Clemson U., S.C., 1969-70; assoc. prof., chair Armstrong State Coll., Savannah, Ga., 1970-73; exec. dir. ctr. criminal justice Marquette U. Law Sch., Milw., 1974-76; prof., chmn. Fla. Internat. U. Miami, Fla., 1976-77; prof., chmn. polit. sci. U. West Fla., Pensacola, 1977—, dir. Rayburn-Dirksen inst. Pensacola, 1983—; cons. Pub. Mgmt. Services, Washington, Southern Assn. Colls. and Schs., Atlanta, 1970—. Contbr. articles to profl. jours. Grantee Law Enforcement Assistance Adminstrn., Savannah, Ga., 1972; Nat. Security Edn. Inst. fellow, Colorado Springs, Colo., 1979; named Instr. of Yr., Students U. West Fla., Pensacola, 1983-84. Mem. Am. Polit. Sci. Assn., Am. Soc. Pub. Adminstrn., Acad. of Criminal Justice Scis., Southern Polit. Sci. Assn., Fla. Polit. Sci. Assn. Republican. Avocation: reading.

WITT, NANCY, artist; b. Richmond, Va., 1930; d. Roland Parker and Catherine (Haydon) Riddick; m. Robert Roy Camden (div.); children—John Bradley, Matthew David; m. John Temple Witt, Apr. 12, 1966; 1 son, Jeremy. B.A. in Fine Art, Old Dominion U., 1965; M.F.A., Va. Commonwealth U., 1967. Founder art dept., acting head fine art dept. Richard Bland Coll. div. Coll. William & Mary; comml. artist, 1952-62; work in collections at Chase-Manhattan Bank, N.Y.C., CSX, Richmond, Randolph-Macon Coll., Ashland, Va., others. Recipient Purchase prize (sculpture) Va. Commn. of Arts and Humanities, 1975, Purchase prize Mint Mus., 1971, Purchase prize Valentine Mus. Biennial, 1962. Avocation: gardening. Office: Pratt-Holt Agy 216 Paxton Rd Richmond VA 23226

WITT, ROBERT CHARLES, risk management and insurance educator; b. Tyndall, S.D., Aug. 24, 1941; s. Emmanuel and Hilda (Link) W.; m. Laura Gutierrez-Witt; 1 child, Kristina Monique. B.A., B.S., U. S.D., 1964; M.S., U. Wis.-Madison, 1966; M.A., U. Pa., 1968, Ph.D., 1972. C.L.U. Instr. econs. Augustana Coll., Sioux Falls, S.D., 1965-66; instr. stats. Temple U., Phila., 1969-70; prof. fin. U. Tex., Austin, 1970—; chmn. dept. fin., 1984—; vis. prof. fin. U. B.C., Vancouver, Can., 1979; adviser U.S. Senate Subcom. on Antitrust and Monopoly, Ill. Ins. Laws Study Commn., Office Tex. Atty. Gen., Tex. Ins. Commn.; bd. govs. Internat. Ins. Seminar, 1981—; mem. research com. Huebner Found., 1976—. Assoc. editor Jour. Risk and Ins., 1983—. Contbg. editor Ins. Abstract and Revs., 1970—. Mem. Am. Risk and Ins. Assn. (bd. dirs. 1980—, pres. 1985), Phi Beta Kappa, Pi Mu Epsilon, Beta Gamma Sigma. Avocations: basketball; soccer. Home: 2602 Forest Bend Austin TX 78704 Office: Dept Finance U Tex Austin TX 78712

WITTE, ARLENE MARIE GILL, music educator; b. Mt. Clemens, Mich., June 23, 1948; d. Richard Sullivan and Evelyn (Sherrill) Gill; m. Thomas Alfred Witte, May 22, 1967; 1 son, Peter Thomas. B.Mus.Edn. (Nat. Merit scholar 1966-70; Band Scholar 1967), U. Mich. Sch. Music, 1970; M.Ed. in Adminstrn., Ga. State U., 1977, postgrad., 1980. Orch. dir. Harlandale Ind. Sch. Dist., San Antonio, 1970-73, DeKalb County Schs., Lithonia, Ga., 1973-75; orch. dir., ensemble dir., instr. clarinet Ga. Acad. Music, Atlanta, 1974-76; mem. adj. faculty Emory U., Atlanta, 1975-76, Woodward Acad., College Park, Ga., 1975-76, Holy Innocent's Episcopal Sch., Atlanta, 1975-76; dir. orchs., East Cobb Middle Sch., Wheeler High Sch., Marietta, Ga., 1976-85; dir. bands Northside Sch. Arts, Marietta, 1985; clarinet, strings, 1970—; music resource tchr. Atlanta Pub. Schs., 1985—; founder Atlanta Regional Concert of Orchs., 1983. Mem. Ga. Music Educators Assn. (div. chmn. 1971-81), Am. String Tchrs. Assn. (chpt. pres. 1977-79), Music Educators Nat. Conf., Nat. Sch. Orch. Assn. (v.p. pub. relations), Ga. Educators Assn., Tex. Music Educators Assn.

WITTEN, THOMAS DAVID, health care executive; b. Washington, Dec. 6, 1943; s. Schurl George and Ruth Rollins W.; m. Brenda Jane Pope, Feb. 4, 1967. Salesman, J.M. Mathis Co., Durham, N.C., 1966-67; asst. mgr. Marriott Corp., Washington, 1967-68, food service dir., Easton, Md., 1968-75, food service dir., Kingsport, Tenn., 1975-76, dist. mgr. health care, southeast region, Atlanta, from 1976; now nat. and internat. dir. health care Canteen Corp., Chgo.; v.p., owner Nat. Tape Video, Atlanta. Talbot County chmn. Nat. Cancer Com., 1974; coach, exec. com., pres. Talbot Little League Football, 1971-75; bd. dirs. Chesapeake Rehab. Center; bd. advisers Chowan Coll., Murfreesboro, N.C. Served with N.C. NG, 1965-71. Mem. Am. Hosp. Assn. of Hosp. Food Service Dirs., Exec. Chefs Assn., Nat. Pilot Assn. Democrat. Roman Catholic. Clubs: Elks, Kiwanis (pres. Easton, lt. gov.-elect dist. 15, 1975). Home: 1910 Ardsley Dr Marietta GA 30062 Office: 1430 Merchandise Mart Chicago IL 60654

WITTENBACH, DON LEO, musician, educator, recitalist; b. Electra, Tex., Dec. 3, 1936; s. Adolphe W. and Mattie Elizabeth (Smith) W.; m. Linda Murl Stracener, May 20, 1960 (div. 1963); m. Luellen McLean, June 18, 1966; children—James Christian, Corey McLean. Student So. Meth. U., 1955-56; B.M., Midwestern State U., 1965, B.M.E., 1966, M.M.E., 1966. Organist, dir. Highland Heights Christian Ch., Wichita Falls, Tex., 1963-70; choral music instr. Wichita Falls Pub. Sch., 1966-70; organist, choirmaster Epworth United Methodist Ch., Chickasha, Okla., 1970-73, First Christian Ch., Duncan, Okla., 1974—, pvt. keyboard instr., organist dir. Active Republican Party. Mem. Am. Guild Organists (dean 1959-62, 67-70, founder, dean West Tex. chpt., 1959-62), Piano Guild, Nat. Music Tchrs. Assn., Nat. Fedn. Music Clubs (jr. counselor), Phi Mu Alpha Sinfonia. Lodge: Rotary. Avocations: spectator sports; geneology. Home: 905 S 8th St Chickasha OK 73018 Office: First Christian Ch 10th at Walnut Duncan TX 73533

WITTERHOLT, EDWARD JOHN, geophysicist; b. Osceola Mills, Pa., Nov. 12, 1935; s. Edward A. and Blanche A. (Muchinski) W.; m. Anne V. Jarosz, Aug. 27, 1957; children—Madalene, Suzanne, Catherine, Marianne, Edward C. B.S., Manhattan Coll., 1957; M.Sc., Brown U., 1959, Ph.D., 1964. Sr. research mathematician Schlumberger Research, Ridgefield, Conn., 1963-75; supr. calibration and analysis Seismograph Service Co., Tulsa, 1975-78; research geophysicist Cities Service Oil & Gas, Tulsa, 1978-80, borehole geophysics research mgr., 1980-83, mgr. petrophysics, 1983-84; mgr. borehole geophysics Sohio Petroleum Co., Dallas, 1984—; lectr. Am. Assn. Petroleum Geologists, 1981—. Editor: (with others) Production Logging, 1985; patentee measurement multi phase flow. Fellow Brown U., 1958, Texaco, 1962. Mem. Soc. Exploration Geophysicists (vice chmn. tech. program 1984), Soc. Profl. Well Log Analysts (pres. Tulsa chpt. 1979), Soc. Petroleum Engrs., Am. Assn. Petroleum Geologists. Avocations: Charles Dickens; landscape gardening; sound reproduction. Home: 2712 Gainesborough Dr Dallas TX 75252 Office: Sohio Petroleum Co 5400 LBJ Freeway Dallas TX 75240

WITTMER, LAVELLE JUNE, superintendent schools; b. Eldorado, Kans., June 30, 1914; d. Frederick Julius and Leota Louise (Money) Meyer; m. George Bolton Wittmer, Apr. 15, 1934 (dec. 1980); children—Judyth Lee, George Bolton Jr. B.S., Okla. State U., 1959, M.A., 1970. Tchr. English Ponca City High Sch., Okla., 1959-70, chmn., 1970-78; supt. schs. Kay County, Newkirk, Okla., 1980—. Contbr. articles to profl. jours. Mem. DAR, LWV, Friends of Ponca City Library. Mem. AAUW, Phi Kappa Phi, Sigma Tau Delta, Kappa Delta Pi. Republican. Mem. First Christian Ch. Avocations: reading; bridge; world travel. Home: 820 Spring Rd Ponca City OK 74604 Office: Kay County Supt Schs Courthouse Newkirk OK 74647

WITTY, FRANK, public relations executive, journalist; b. N.Y.C., Apr. 30, 1937; s. Michael John and Adeline Jeanne (Felice) W.; m. Francine Ann Carusiello, July 29, 1964; children—Cassandra Ann, Jason Michael. B.B.A., Fla. Atlantic U., 1968. Reporter, Palm Beach Post-Times, West Palm Beach, Fla., 1961-66; bus. and real estate editor Broward edit. Miami Herald, Ft. Lauderdale, Fla., 1968-69; advt., pub. relations dir. Osias Orgn. Inc. and Osias Resort Hotels, Ft. Lauderdale, 1969-70; weekend mag. editor Ft. Lauderdale News & Sun-Sentinel, 1970-72; sr. v.p. The Communications Group, Ft. Lauderdale, 1972-76; v.p. communications Century Village East Inc., Deerfield Beach, Fla., 1978-79; self-employed, 1979-81; v.p., regional mgr. The Communications Group, Orlando, Fla., 1981—. Served with USN, 1954-58. Mem. Fla. Pub. Relations Assn., Sigma Delta Chi. Office: The Communications Group 812 N Thornton Ave Orlando FL 32803

WNUK, WADE JOSEPH, manufacturing company executive; b. St. Louis, Sept. 2, 1944; s. Edward Joseph and Helen Evelyn (Millick) W.; B.S. magna cum laude in Math., St. Louis U., 1966; M.S. in Engring. Sci. (NSF trainee), Calif. Inst. Tech., 1966-67; M.B.A., Harvard U., 1974; m. Judith Kay Yohe, May 3, 1969; children—Russell Nicholas, Wade Gregory. Govt. research analyst, Washington, 1967-69; planner FMC Corp., Chgo., 1974-75, mgr. bus. devel. petroleum equipment div., Houston, 1975-77, group planning mgr., petroleum equipment group, 1977-78, ops. mgr. FMC Petroleum Equipment S.E. Asia, 1978-80, subsea mgr. FMC Wellhead Equipment div., Houston, 1980-81; pres., dir. corp. devel. Marathon Mfg. Corp., Houston, 1981-82, v.p. corp. devel., 1982-84; exec. v.p. Marathon Power Tech., Houston, 1984—. Served with U.S. Army, 1969-72. Mem. Internat. Bus. Club (past v.p.), Am. Mgmt. Assn., AAAS, Nat. Geog. Soc., Smithsonian Assns., St. Louis U., Calif. Inst. Tech., Harvard alumni assns. Club: Harvard (Houston). Home: 5510 Kingswick Ct Houston TX 77069 Office: Marathon Mfg Corp PO Box 61589 Houston TX 77208

WODARSKI, JOHN STANLEY, research center director; b. Feb. 27, 1943; s. Estelle Wodarski; m. Lois Ann Moon; 1 child, Ann Christine. B.S. in Social Work, Fla. State U., 1965; M.S.S.W., U. Tenn., 1967; Ph.D. in Social Work, Washington U., 1970. Assoc. prof. U. Md., 1975-78; grant counselor Johns Hopkins U., 1975-77; assoc. prof., research assoc. Washington U., 1970-74; instr. Sam Houston State U., 1967-68; dir. research ctr. U. Ga., 1978—; cons. Child & Family Service, Knoxville, 1974-75; project cons. Ga. Alliance for Children, Atlanta, 1982-84, Study of Social Policy, Washington, 1982-84; adj. fellow Program for Family Research, Athens, Ga., 1984—. Author: Teams-Games-Tournaments, 1984. NIMH grantee, 1983. Avocation: racquetball. Home: 150 Greenhills Rd Athens GA 30605 Office: U Ga Sch of Social Work Tucker Hall Athens GA 30602

WODNICKI, JEAN MARIE, nurse; b. Hoboken, N.J., Oct. 5, 1959; d. Raymond Edward and Dorothy Anne (Cannon) Pennie; m. Henry Wodnicki, Apr. 24, 1983. B.S. in Nursing, Coll. Misericordia-Dallas, 1981. R.N. Staff nurse ICU, St. Barnabas Med. Ctr., Livingston, N.J., 1981-83; staff nurse CCU, Mt. Sinai Med. Ctr., Miami Beach, Fla., 1983—. Mem. Am. Nurses Assn., Am. Assn. Critical Care Nurses. Democrat. Roman Catholic. Home: 9369 Fontainebleu Blvd #J203 Miami FL 33172 Office: Mt Sinai Med Ctr 4300 Alton Rd Miami Beach FL

WOERSCHING, JOHN CHARLES, III, oil company executive; b. Queens, N.Y., May 1, 1946; s. John Charles and Ruth (Jensen) W.; m. Magali Trindade, May 18, 1980; children—Jefferson, James, Jason. B.A., Monmouth Coll., 1970; M.B.A., Fairleigh Dickenson U., 1975. Divisional mdse. mgr. Citgo Petroleum Corp., Tulsa, 1977-79, mgr. budgets and internal controls, 1979-80, mgr.

internal controls, 1980-82, petroleum sales mgr., 1982-83, mgr. petroleum logistics, 1983-84, mgr. wholesale pricing and fuel blending, 1984—, mgr. supply and distbn. ops.; dir. Cities Service Co.; instr. fin. Tulsa Jr. Coll. Active Peninsula Fire Dept., Central Soccer League. Named Man of Yr., Cities Service Bd. Dirs., 1972. Republican. Inventor and patentee Math./econometric pricing model.

WOHLFORD, THOMAS CROCKETT, medical company executive; b. Radford, Va., June 25, 1953; s. Thomas and Lucille Ora (Hale) W.; m. Deborah Ann Warren, May 10, 1980; 1 dau., Tracey Ann. B.A., Emory and Henry Coll., 1976; M.H.A., Ga. State U., 1979. Asst. adminstr. Community Hosp. Roanoake Valley, Roanoke, Va., 1979-83; dir. mktg. for So. Region, Health Group, Inc., Atlanta, 1983; mgr. product devel. Am. Med. Internat., Atlanta, 1983-84, dir. product devel., 1984-85, dir. network devel. AMI Group Health Services, Inc., 1985—. Advisor for devel. Roanoke Rescue Service, 1981-83; bd. dirs. consortium Oncology Program of S.W.Va. 1981-83; pub. relations adviser Southwest Va. chpt. Am. Lung Assn., 1983. Mem. Am. Hosp. Assn., Alliance for Continuing Med. Edn., Aircraft Owners and Pilots Assn. Episcopalian. Home: 4074 Wembly Forest Way Doraville GA 30340 Office: Am Med Internat 4170 Ashford Dunwoody Rd NE Suite 500 Atlanta GA 30319

WOHLSTETTER, CHARLES, telephone company executive; b. 1910. With Charles R. Hammerslough & Co., N.Y.C., 1929-32, Theodore Prince Co., 1932-33; partner Rubinger, Wohlstetter & Co., 1933-38; investment dept. Allen & Co., 1938-40; pres. Cyclohm Motor Corp., 1940-48; partner Seskis & Wohlstetter, 1950-71; chmn. bd. Continental Telephone Corp., 1960-71, chmn. bd., chief exec. officer, 1971—, also dir.; partner J.F. Nick & Co.; dir. Tesoro Petroleum Corp., Am. Satellite Corp. Chmn. Billy Rose Round.; trustee Nat. Symphony, Kennedy Center; bd. dirs. Inst. for Ednl. Affairs, Bus. Com. for the Arts; mem. adv. council Rockefeller U.; nat. ambassador Salk Inst. Office: Continental Telecom Inc 405 Park Ave New York NY 10004*

WOHLTMANN, HULDA JUSTINE, pediatric endocrinologist; b. Charleston, S.C., Apr. 10, 1923; s. John Diedrich and Emma Lucia (Mohrmann) W. B.S., Coll. Charleston, 1944; M.D., Med. U. S.C., 1949. Diplomate Am. Bd. Pediatrics. Postdoctoral fellow biochemistry Washington U., St. Louis, 1961-63; intern Louisville Gen. Hosp., 1949-50; resident in pediatrics St. Louis Children's Hosp., 1950-53; mem. faculty Washington U. Sch. Medicine, 1953-65; prof. pediatrics, head pediatric endocrinology Med. U. S.C., Charleston, 1965—. Bd. dirs. Franke Home, Charleston; pres. S.C. Diabetes Assn., 1970-73, 84-85, v.p., 1982-83, pres.-elect, 1983-84, bd. dirs., 1970-81, 82—. Recipient Profl. Service award S.C. Diabetes Assn., 1977. Mem. Am. Pediatric Soc., Ambulatory Pediatric Assn., Endocrine Soc., Am. Diabetes Assn., Am. Acad. Pediatrics, Am. Fedn. Clin. Research, Midwest Soc. Pediatric Research, So. Soc. Pediatric Research, Lawson Wilkins Endocrine Soc., Sugar Club. Lutheran. Contbr. articles to sci. jours. Home: 280 N Hobcaw Dr Mount Pleasant SC 29464 Office: 171 Ashley Ave Charleston SC 29425

WOLBERG, GERALD, immunologist; b. N.Y.C., Aug. 18, 1937; s. Sam and Fannie (Lipshitz) W.; m. Marilynn H. Goldstein, July 1, 1967; children—Alisa, Lori. B.A., NYU, 1958; M.S., U. Ky., 1963; Ph.D., Tulane U., 1967. Postdoctoral fellow Pub. Health Research Inst. N.Y.C., 1967-70; research scientist Burroughs Wellcome Co., Research Triangle Park, N.C., 1970—. Mem. Am. Assn. Immunologists, Am. Soc. Microbiology, Sigma Xi. Home: 1109 Troon Ct Cary NC 27511 Office: 3030 Cornwallis Rd Research Triangle Park NC 27709

WOLBRECHT, JOHN EARL, educator; b. San Antonio, Aug. 6, 1949; s. William Moore and Rosemary Hester (Lott) W.; B.S., SW Tex. State U., 1972; postgrad. U. Tex., San Antonio, 1973-74; A.A. in Bus. Adminstrn., Houston Community Coll., 1977. Tchr., Mathis (Tex.) Ind. Sch. Dist., 1971-72, Edgewood Ind. Sch. Dist., San Antonio, 1973-74; personnel clk. Brown & Root, Inc., Houston, 1975, sect. supr., 1975, sect. mgr., 1980-81; corp. records adminstr. Raymond Internat. Builders, Inc., Houston, 1981-83; instr., coordinator dept. info. and records mgmt. bus. div. North Harris County Coll., 1983-85; office mgr. Dana Monosoff Assocs., Inc., 1986—. Mem. Assn. of Records Mgrs. and Adminstrs. (Chpt. Mem. of Yr. 1980, dir. 1980-82, treas. 1983), Assn. Info. and Image Mgmt., Bus. Forms Mgmt. Assn. Harris County Geneal. Soc. (dir. 1977-80). Roman Catholic. Contbr. articles to profl. jours.; student photography work pub. SW Tex. State U. Yearbook, 1971, summer edits. of newspaper Univ. Star, 1971. Home: 119 Corwin Dr #1 San Francisco CA 94114 Office: 33 Ford St San Francisco CA 94114

WOLD, DONALD CLARENCE, physicist; b. Fargo, N.D., Sept. 24, 1933; s. Clarence Leonard and Emma Mae (Saunders) W.; m. Shelley Anne Thurman, June 11, 1956; children—Sara, Steven, Sheila. B.A. in Physics, U. Wis., 1955, M.A. in Physics, 1957; Ph.D. in Physics, Ind. U., 1968. Lectr. physics and head physics dept. Forman Christian Coll., Lahore, Pakistan, 1958-63; asst. research physicist UCLA, 1968-69; prof., chmn. dept. physics and astronomy U. Ark., Little Rock, 1969—; project dir. for preparation of energy conservation plan State of Ark., 1976-77. Recipient Donaghey Urban Mission award, 1979; Ark. Research Award Am. Assn. Mental Deficiency, 1980; Region V research award, 1980; HEW research fellow, 1978. Mem. Acoustical Soc. Am., Acoustics, Speech and Signal Processing Soc. (IEEE), Am. Assn. Physics Tchrs., Am. Phys. Soc., Assn. for Computing Machinery, Internat. Soc. Phonetic Scis., Am. Speech, Lang. and Hearing Assn., Phi Kappa Phi, Sigma Xi, Sigma Pi Sigma. Home: 38 Pine Manor Little Rock AR 72207 Office: U Ark 33d and University Ave Little Rock AR 72204

WOLDT, JOHN WILLIAM, music educator, horn player; b. Oshkosh, Wis., May 11, 1920; s. August John and Metha (Hasley) W.; m. Harriet Risk, June 10, 1950; children—Richard Andrew, William August, Robert Oland, Constance Louise. Mus.B., U. Wis., 1941; Mus.M., Yale U., 1943; Ph.D., Eastman Sch. Music, U. Rochester, 1947; Reifeprufung in Horn, Acad. Music, Vienna, Austria, 1953-54, Reifeprufung Kapellmeister, 1953-54. Asst. prof. Tex. Christian U., Ft. Worth, 1943-45; instr. U. Houston, 1946-47; assoc. prof. Baylor U., Waco, Tex., 1947-56; prof. music Tex. Christian U., 1956—; tchr. horn Nat. Music Camp, Interlochen, Mich., summers 1945-56; horn player New Haven Symphony, New Haven, 1941-43, Houston Symphony, 1946-47; prin. horn player Ft. Worth Opera, 1956-69, Ft. Worth Symphony, 1957-66. Author: Spanish Madrigals, 1950. Choirmaster Trinity Episcopal Ch., Ft. Worth, 1956-69; chmn. Democratic precinct, election judge City Ft. Worth, Tarrant County, 1979—. Mem. AAUP (pres. Tex. Christian U. chpt. 1982), Am. Musicol. Soc., Am. Soc. for Music Theory, Am. Guild Organists, Ft. Worth Music Tchrs. Avocation: stamp collecting. Home: 4324 Norwich Dr Fort Worth TX 76109 Office: Tex Christian U University Dr Fort Worth TX 76129

WOLENS, MICKEY EARL, constrn. co. purchasing ofcl.; b. Hutchinson, Kans., Jan. 6, 1937; s. Cyril and Elaine (Gore) W.; student Tex. A&M Coll., 1956-58, Arlington State Coll., 1961; M.B.A., B.B.A., Pacific Western U., 1982; m. Mary Bobbie Carter, Mar. 23, 1962; children—Heather Lynne, Jason Zachary. Sr. buyer Trinity Industries, Inc., Dallas, 1962-67, Baifield Industries, Inc., Carrollton, Tex., 1967; asst. purchasing agt. M.W. Kellogg Co., Dallas, 1967-69, supr. field insps. and expediters, Houston, 1969-70, purchasing agt., Houston, 1970-73; sr. buyer Hess Oil V.I. Corp., St. Croix, 1973; project buyer Davy Powergas, Inc., Lakeland, Fla., 1973-74, mgt. inspection, expediting and traffic, 1974, mgr. purchasing, 1974-76; mgr. procurement Litwin Engrs. and Constrs., Inc., Houston, 1976-79, 80; mgr. purchasing BE&K, Birmingham, Ala., 1979, 82—, asst. mgr. purchasing, 1980-82; student profl. seminars. Served with U.S. Army, 1958-61. Cert. purchasing mgr. (CPM). Mem. Purchasing Mgmt. Assn. Ala. Republican. Baptist. Home: 3500 William & Mary Rd Birmingham AL 35216 Office: Bldg 104 Inverness Center Pl Birmingham AL 35243

WOLF, BONNIE STEPHENS, retail company executive, human resources professional; b. Atlanta, Sept. 17, 1950; d. George Roscoe and Mary Dell (Redwine) Stephens; m. Gary Paul Wolf, Sept. 28, 1974; children—Weston Edwards, Whitney Stephens, Warner Hamilton. B.S. in Edn., West Ga. Coll., 1971; Ed.M. in Curriculum and Instrn., Ga. State U., 1973. Tng. rep. Rich's, Atlanta, 1971-73; tng. asst. Richway Co., Atlanta, 1973-75, tng. dir., 1975-78, dir. tng. and devel., 1978-80, div. v.p. human resources and orgn. devel., 1980—; dir. Rich's Credit Union, 1979—. Bd. dirs. So. Christian Home for Children, Atlanta, 1979-83; mem. steering com. Poncey-Highland Neighborhood Assn., Atlanta, 1979-81; campaign vol. Sidney Marcus for Mayor, Atlanta, 1981. Named in Salute to Women of Achievement YWCA, Atlanta, 1981. Mem. Human Resource Planning Soc., Am. Soc. Tng. and Devel. (v.p. Ga. chpt. 1976-77, nat. chmn. insts. com. 1980-82, nat. nominating com. 1984-86). Avocations: travel; jogging; sailing; collecting seashells. Office: Richway 45 Broad St Atlanta GA 30302

WOLF, CHARLOTTE ELIZABETH, sociologist, sociology educator; b. Boulder, Colo., Sept. 14, 1926; s. Marion Guy and Ethel Eugenia (Thomas) Rosetta; m. Rene Arthur, Sept. 3, 1952; children—Christopher Robin, Michele Renee. B.A., U. Colo., 1949, M.A., 1959; Ph.D., U. Minn., 1968. Teaching asst. U. Minn., Mpls., 1963-65; lectr. U. Md., Ankara, Turkey, 1965-67; asst. prof. Colo. State U., Fort Collins, 1968-69, Colo. Women's Coll., Denver, 1969-74; assoc. to full prof., chmn. Ohio Wesleyan U., Delaware, 1974-83; prof., chmn. Memphis State U., Tenn., 1983—; cons. HUD, HEW, EEOC, Office of Civil Rights, Washington, 1970-74; research assoc. Scientific Analysis Corp., San Francisco, 1971—; review panel, outside reviewer NIMH, Washington, 1979-83. Author: Garrison Community: A Study of an Overseas Military Colony, 1969, Ankara: A Social-Historical Study, 1968. Contbr. articles to profl. jours. Pres., Denver Nat. Orgn. for Women, 1970-71; mem. nat. bd. NOW, 1971-73, nat. coordinator, researcher, 1971-74; 2d v.p. NAACP, Delaware, Ohio, 1981-83; bd. dirs. United Way, Delaware, 1981-83. Ohio Wesleyan Research grantee, 1981, 82; Ohio Wesleyan Scholarly Prodn. award, 1982. Mem. Am. Sociol. Assn. (mem. nominations com. 1982-84, chmn. com. on status of women 1973-76), North Central Sociol. Assn. (v.p. 1983-84), Soc. Study Social Problems (treas. 1979-81), AAUP (pres. chpt. 1981-83), Delta Tau Delta. Democrat. Avocations: hiking; swimming; poetry. Home: 287 Stonewall Place Memphis TN 38112 Office: Dept Sociology Memphis State U Memphis TN 38152

WOLF, CLARENCE, JR., stockbroker; b. Phila., May 11, 1908; s. Clarence and Nan (Hogan) W.; student Pa. Mil. Prep. Sch., 1921; grad. Swarthmore (Pa.) Prep. Sch., 1923; m. Alma C. Backhus, Sept. 11, 1942. Founder French-Wolf Paint Products Corp., Phila., 1926, pres. until 1943; admitted to Phila.-Balt. Stock Exchange, 1937; asso. Reynolds Securities Inc. (name now Dean Witter Reynolds Inc.), 1944—, rep., Miami Beach, Fla., 1946-63, spl. rep., 1963-77, v.p. sales, 1977, v.p. investments, 1977—; former dir., vice chmn. bd., mem. exec. com. Amcord, Inc.; dir. Rand Broadcasting Co., owners radio and TV stas., also hotels, 1946-68; past dir. Superior Zinc Co., Hercules Cement Co. Pres. Normandy Isles Improvement Assn., Miami Beach, 1952-53; mem. Presidents Council Miami Beach, 1952—. Mem. Alumnus Assn. Pa. Mil. Coll. (Fla. dir. 1961—), Com. of 100. Clubs: Jockey, Cricket (Miami, Fla.). Author: $even Letter$, The Securities Market and You, 1980. Home: Jockey Club Apt 858 Biscaya Point 11111 Biscayne Blvd Miami FL 33161 Office: care Dean Witter Reynolds Inc 700 Brickell Ave 6th Floor Miami FL 33131

WOLF, EDWARD CHRISTOPHER, music educator; b. Circleville, Ohio, July 21, 1932; s. Edward Christopher and Helen Marie (Groce) W.; m. Marjorie Ann Swanson, June 24, 1961; 1 child, Edward Christopher, III. Mus.B., Capital U., 1953; Mus.M., Northwestern U., 1955; Ph.D., U. Ill., 1960. Dir. Sch. Fine Arts, West Liberty State Coll., W.Va., 1963-75, 78-79, from instr. to prof. music, 1960—. Editor music edn. mag., 1976—. Contbr. articles to profl. jours. Mem. Am. Musicol. Soc., AAUP, W.Va. Music Educators Assn. (pres. 1965-67), Music Educators Nat. Conf. (state editor 1976—), Pa. German Soc., Luth. Hist. Soc., Sonneck Soc., Coll. Music Soc. Republican. Avocations: photography, travel. Office: Hall Fine Arts West Liberty State Coll West Liberty WV 26074

WOLF, FRANK R., Congressman, lawyer; b. Phila., Jan. 30, 1939; B.A., Pa. State U., 1961; LL.B., Georgetown U., 1965; m. Carolyn Stover; children—Frank, Virginia, Anne, Brenda, Rebecca. Admitted to Va. bar; legis. asst. former Congressman Edward G. Biester, Jr., 1968-71; asst. to Sec. of Interior Rogers B. Morton, 1971-74; dep. asst. sec. for Congl. and Legis. Affairs, Dept. Interior, 1974-75; mem. 97th-98th Congress from 10th Dist. Va. Served with U.S. Army. Republican. Presbyterian. Office: 130 Cannon House Office Bldg Washington DC 20515

WOLF, HAROLD ARTHUR, finance educator, consultant; b. Lind, Wash., Feb. 10, 1923; s. Edward Erwin and Olga Natalie (Limert) W.; m. Jeanette Elizabeth Dunn, Mar. 24, 1961; children—Mark, Suellen. B.A., U. Oreg., 1951; M.A., U. Mich., 1952, Ph.D., 1958. Instr. Lehigh U., Bethlehem, Pa., 1955-57; economist Prudential Ins. Co., Newark, 1957-59; prof. U. Colo., Boulder, 1959-67, U. Tex., Austin, 1967—; cons. numerous fin. insts., Colo., Tex., 1960—. Contbr. articles to profl. jours. Served with USN, 1941-47, PTO. Mem. Am. Econ. Assn., Am. Fin. Assn., So. Fin. Assn., Internat. Assn. Fin. Planners. Home: 7004 Edgefield Dr Austin TX 78731 Office: U Tex Dept Finance Austin TX 78712

WOLF, JACK STANLEY, financial executive; b. Kansas City, Mo., Nov. 9, 1934; s. Joseph and Mary (Coppaken) W.; m. R. Marlene Kirkpatrick, July 29, 1969. B.A., U. Mo., 1956. C.L.U., 1972. Mgr. gen. agt. Jack Wolf, C.L.U. Ins., 1967—; pres. Fin. Planning & Pension Cons., Houston, 1979—; gen. agy. mgr. Am. Gen. Life Ins. Co., 1980—. Served with U.S. Army, 1958-63. Recipient numerous awards various ins. cos., 1968—. Mem. East Ft. Bend C. of C., Million Dollar Round Table (life mem.; charter mem. Ct. of Table), Tex. Leaders Round Table, Houston Assn. Life Underwriters, Gen. Agts. and Mgrs. Assn., Am. Soc. C.L.U.s, Am. Contract Bridge League (life mem.), U. Mo. Alumni Assn. (life). Jewish. Lodge: East Ft. Bend Kiwanis (v.p. 1983-84, pres.-elect 1985-86). Home: 2927 Robinson Rd Missouri City TX 77459 Office: 9207 Country Creek Dr Suite 210 Houston TX 77036

WOLF, JEFFREY STEPHEN, physician; b. Hartford, Conn., July 30, 1946; s. Abraham and Norma Wolf; m. Nina Loving Lockridge; children—Sarah Loving, Lawren Hiley. B.S., McGill U., 1968; M.D., Med. Coll. Va., 1972, M.S., 1973. Diplomate Am. Bd. Colon and Rectal Surgery, Am. Bd. Surgery. Intern, in surgery Mt. Sinai Hosp., N.Y.C., 1972-73, resident, 1973-75; resident N.Y. Med. Coll.-Met. Hosp., N.Y.C., 1975-77; chief resident surgery Met. Hosp., 1977-78; fellow colon-rectal surgery Greater Balt. Med. Center, 1978-79; colon-rectal surgeon, Portsmouth, Va., 1979—. Fellow ACS, Am. Soc. Colon and Rectal Surgery; mem. Portsmouth Acad. Medicine, Med. Soc. Va., Am. Soc. Colon and Rectal Surgeons. Office: 620 London Blvd Portsmouth VA 23704

WOLF, JOCELYNE NOEL, hospital pharmacist; b. Haddonfield, N.J., July 3, 1954; d. Roland Yves and Yolande (Dorion) Noel; m. Benjamin Harrison, Jan. 26, 1980; 1 child, Natalie Noel. Student St. Mary's Dominican Coll., 1972-74; B.S. in Pharmacy, U. Fla., 1977. Lic. pharmacist, Fla., Ga. Pharmacist VA Hosp., Gainesville, Fla., 1977-79, St. Vincent's Med. Ctr., Jacksonville, Fla., 1979-83, North Shore Med. Ctr., Miami, Fla., 1983—. Mem. Am. Soc. Hosp. Pharmacists, Fla. Soc. Hosp. Pharmacists, East Central Soc. Hosp. Pharmacists, South Fla. Soc. Hosp. Pharmacists. Republican. Roman Catholic. Avocations: reading; exercise; tennis; snow skiing. Home: 4400 NW 67th Terrace Lauderhill FL 33319 Office: North Shore Med Ctr 1100 NW 95th St Miami FL 33150

WOLF, JOHN CHARLES, psychologist; b. St. Louis, Sept. 29, 1943; s. Howard August and Wilda Lucille (French) W.; m. Carole Sue Bruce, Oct. 21, 1967; children—Allan Bruce, Anne Elizabeth. B.S., Stephen F. Austin State U., 1964, M.A., 1967, M.Ed., 1969; Ph.D., N. Tex. State U., 1976. Staff psychologist Lufkin State Sch. for Mentally Retarded, 1966-67; instr. psychology Stephen F. Austin State U., 1967-68; dir. rehab. services Goodwill Industries, Fort Worth, 1969-70; counselor VA Guidance Ctr., Tex. Christian U., Fort Worth, 1970-73; counseling psychologist U.S. VA, Lubbock, Tex., 1973—; pres. W & R Real Estate Co.; adj. instr. psychology South Plains Coll., Lubbock, 1973—. Mem. Lubbock County Com. on Employment of Handicapped. Contbr. articles to profl. jours. Bd. dirs. Lubbock Civic Chorale, 1983-85; mem. adv. bd., human services South Plains Coll., 1975—; vestryman St. Christopher Episcopal Ch., 1982-85. Served with USNR, 1979-83. Recipient Outstanding Performance award VA, 1978, 82, 84, 85. Mem. Am. Psychol. Assn., Am. Assn. Counseling and Devel., N.W. Tex. VA Psychol. Assn. (past pres.), Am. Rehab. Counseling Assn., Psi Chi, Kappa Delta Pi. Avocations: Choral singing; golf; hunting. Home: 3312 40th St Lubbock TX 79413 Office: VA Office Room 122 1205 Texas Ave Lubbock TX 79401

WOLF, KARL LEE, college administrator; b. Hagerstown, Md., Jan. 16, 1948; s. Frank R. and Mildred (Barr) W. B.S. in Bus. Adminstrn., Shepherd Coll., 1970; M.B.A. in Internat. Bus., George Washington U., 1973; postgrad. W.Va. U., 1973-77. Mem. faculty Shepherd Coll., Shepherdstown, W.Va., 1970—, dir. admissions, 1970—, asst. prof. bus. adminstrn., 1973—; cons. in field. Mem. Nat. Assn. Coll. Admissions Counselors, Potomac and Chesapeake Assn. Coll. Admissions Counselors, Am. Assn. Collegiate Registrars and Admissions Officers, W.V. Assn. Collegiate Registrars and Admissions Officers, Lambda Chi Alpha, Delta Sigma Pi. Club: Kiwanis (Shepherdstown). Office: Shepherd Coll Shepherdstown WV 25444

WOLF, MORRIS PHILIP, educator; b. Bklyn., Apr. 28, 1929; s. Leo and Jeanne (Applebaum) W.; B.A., N.Y. U., 1949, M.A., 1951; Ph.D., U. Ga., 1959. Asst. prof. U. Ga. Centers, Columbus and Ft. Benning, 1953-54, dir. U. Ga. Center, Gainesville, 1954-56, Augusta Center, 1956-58; asso. prof., asst. dean and dir. extended services Augusta Coll., 1959-60, prof., chmn. dept. English and speech, 1960-62; assoc. prof. bus. communication U. Houston, 1962-67, prof., 1970-74, chmn. dept. gen. bus. adminstrn., 1968-70, coordinator, 1970-74; ind. researcher, writer, 1974-82; asso. prof. bus. communication, dept. office adminstrn. and bus. communication Coll. Adminstrn. and Bus., La. Tech. U., Ruston, 1982—; cons. in field; profl. actor with programs broadcast from N.Y.C. on ABC, CBS, NBC including Adventures of Frank Merriwell, Aunt Jenny's Real Life Stories, The Eternal Light, Famous Jury Trials, The Goldbergs, The Greatest Story Ever Told, Hollywood Screen Test, Philco Playhouse, others; performer with Equity A touring stage prodns. The Heiress, Springboard to Nowhere, Little Women, Mr. and Mrs. North, On Borrowed Time, others; producer, performer on public service TV-radio programs, Augusta, 1956-61; narrator Augusta Choral Soc. Bicentennial Program, Song of Affirmation, 1975-77, others; lectr. in field. Served to capt. AUS and U.S. Army Res., 1951-64. Recipient Disting. Faculty award U. Houston Coll. Bus. Alumni Assn., 1967; Teaching Excellence award U. Houston, 1971. Fellow Am. Bus. Communication Assn. (past pres.); mem. Beta Gamma Sigma, Sigma Delta Omicron, Phi Kappa Phi. Author: (with Robert R. Aurner) Effective Communication in Business, 5th edit., 1967, sr. co-author, 6th edit., 1974, 7th edit., 1979, 8th edit. (with S. Kuiper), 1984; sr. co-author: (with Bette A. Stead) Easy Grammar: A Programmed Review, 1970; contbr. articles to profl. jours.; poems incl. Hypocrite, Scent of Lavender, 1951, Of Curricular Concern, 1951, Reconnaissance Patrol, 1957, others; plays incl.: Hatred, 1951; Continuum, 1952; I Want to Report A Suicide, 1956; Mirrors (radio drama), 1974. Home: 410 James St Ruston LA 71270 Office: Dept Office Adminstrn and Bus Communication Coll Adminstrn and Bus Louisiana Tech Univ Ruston LA 71272

WOLF, RICHARD ALAN, investment executive; b. Lake Odessa, Mich., June 20, 1935; s. Harry and Gladys (Gross) W.; m. Judith Ann Schreiner, Oct. 13, 1962; 1 child, Erik Alan. B.B.A., U. Mich., 1957, M.B.A., 1958. Chartered fin. analyst. Security analyst Colo. Nat. Bank, Denver, 1958-60; v.p., portfolio mgr. Commerce Bank, Kans. City, Mo., 1960-66; v.p., trust investment dept. head Omaha Nat. Bank, 1967-77; treas., dir., sr. v.p. fixed income research and trading Citizens & So. Investment Advisors, Inc., Atlanta, 1977—. Mem. Inst. Chartered fin. analyst, Atlanta Soc. Fin. Analysts; fellow Fin. Analysts Fedn. Republican. Episcopalian. Club: Commerce (Atlanta). Avocations: philately; running. Home: 5390 Forest Brook Pkwy Marietta GA 30067 Office: Citizens So Investment Advisors Inc PO Box 4114 Atlanta GA 30302

WOLF, THOMAS ALBERT, insurance company executive; b. Kirksville, Mo., Dec. 23, 1942; s. Donald Edward and Virginia (Wyatt) W.; B.S., Mo. State U., 1965; divorced; children—Jennifer Lynn, Melissa Ann, Thomas Albert II. Personal property underwriter MFA Ins., Columbia, Mo., 1965-73; supervisory systems analyst Gt. Am. Ins. Co., Cin., 1974-76; mgr. systems devel. ARMCO Ins. Group, Dallas, 1976-80; v.p. Millers Ins. Co., Ft. Worth, 1980—. Mem. Data Processing Mgmt. Assn., Alpha Kappa Lambda. Republican. Lutheran. Home: 1807 Eastfield Dr Richardson TX 75081

WOLFE, BARDIE CLINTON, JR., law librarian, educator; b. Kingsport, Tenn., Oct. 21, 1942; s. Bardie Clinton and Joy (Gillenwater) W.; J.D., U. Ky., 1967, M.S.L.S., 1972. Bar: Ky. 1967. Circulation librarian, dir. reader services U. Tex., 1968-71; acquisition librarian, asst. prof. U. Va., 1971-73; law librarian, asst. prof. Cleve. State U., 1973-76., librarian, assoc. prof., 1976-77; librarian, assoc. prof. law U. Tenn., Knoxville, 1977-80; librarian, prof. law Pace U., White Plains, N.Y., 1980-84; librarian, prof. law St. Thomas U., Miami, Fla., 1984—. accreditation insp. ABA, Assn. Am. Law Schs.; cons. Queens Coll. Sch. Law, 1981-82. Mem. ABA, Ky. Bar Assn., Am. Judicature Soc., Am. Assn. Law Libraries, Assn. Am. Law Schs., Nat. Micrographics Assn. Office: St Thomas U Law Library 16400 NW 32d Ave Miami FL 33054

WOLFE, HENRY DAVEGA, diversified company executive; b. Florence, S.C., Sept. 2, 1953; s. Joseph Lester and Caroline (DaVega) W.; B.S. with honors in Zoology, Clemson U., 1976. Plant supr. City Ice & Fuel Co. (subs. DaVega & Wolfe Industries, Inc.), Florence, 1977, v.p., 1977-79, exec. v.p., 1979; chmn. chief exec. officer DaVega & Wolfe Industries, Inc. (formerly The Wolfe Corp.), Florence, 1979—; cons. in field. Team capt. United Way of Florence, 1981, div. chmn., 1982, vice chmn., mem. campaign cabinet, 1983, chmn. pace-setter div., 1984; crusade vol. Am. Cancer Soc., 1980; bd. dirs., chmn. phys. com. Florence Family YMCA, 1981, 82, v.p., 1982-83, pres., 1983-84; chmn. Florence County Dist. Boy Scouts Am., 1982, bd. dirs. Pee Dee Area Council, 1982, Florence Ballet Co., 1982, Florence County Crime Stoppers, 1983-84; pres. Cypress Point Homeowners Assn., Inc., 1979, treas., 1980, chmn. bd., 1981, 82; chmn. adv. council dist. III of S.C. Future Bus. Leaders of Am., 1981-82. Mem. Am. Entrepreneurs Assn., Greater Florence C. of C. (chmn. exec. dialogue group II). Recipient Community Service award Phillips Petroleum Co., 1980; named Outstanding Young Man of Year in Florence, 1980, in S.C., 1980; Outstanding Young Men of Am., 1982. Republican. Episcopalian. Clubs: Florence Country, Florence Rotary (dir., chmn. program com. 1981-82, dir. 1982-83), Toastmasters Internat. (pres. Club 1916 Florence 1981, area gov. area 2 of S.C. Dist. 58 1981). Office: 152 McQueen St PO Box 889 Florence SC 29503

WOLFE, JAMES FRANKLIN, chemistry educator; b. York, Pa., Oct. 5, 1936; s. Joseph Ewell and Mary Esther (Parlett) W.; m. Nancy Lou Gohn; children—John, Carolyn. B.S. in Chemistry, Lebanon Valley Coll., 1958; Ph.D. in Chemistry, Ind. U., 1963. Research assoc. Duke U., Durham, N.C., 1963-64; asst. prof., Va. Poly. Inst. and State U., Blacksburg, 1964-68, assoc. prof., 1968-74, prof., 1974—, head dept. chemistry, 1981—. Mem. Am. Chem. Soc., AAAS, Va. Acad. Sci., Sigma Xi, Omicron Delta Kappa, Phi Lambda Upsilon. Lutheran. Home: 1200 Westover Dr Blacksburg VA 24060 Office: Va Poly Inst and State U Dept Chemistry Blacksburg VA 24061

WOLFE, JAMES HASTINGS, political science educator; b. Newport News, Va., Oct. 3, 1934; s. Walter John and Grace (Hastings) W.; B.A., Harvard U., 1955; M.A., U. Conn., 1958; Ph.D., U. Md., 1962; m. Irmgard Pfender, June 10, 1965; children—Christine, Karin. Asst. prof. polit. sci. U. S.C., 1962-65; asso. prof. U. Md., 1965-75; prof. polit. sci. U. So. Miss., 1975—; cons. State Dept., summers 1967, 79, 83, 85. Served with AUS, 1955-57. Research fellow Alexander von Humboldt Found., 1964-65, 72-73. Mem. Internat. Studies Assn., Am. Soc. Internat. Law, Am. Assn. for Internat. Com. Jurists. Author: Indivisible Germany: Illusion or Reality?, 1963; co-author: Introduction to International Relations: Power and Justice, 1978, 3d edit., 1986; internat. affairs editor USA Today; contbr. articles to profl. jours. Home: 2600 Sunset Dr Hattiesburg MS 39401 Office: Box 8261 U So Miss Hattiesburg MS 39406

WOLFE, JOHN H., sales trainer, association executive; b. Honolulu, June 12, 1924; s. Fred R. and Dorothy W.; m. Alice McCoy; 1 child, Jann. B.A., Dartmouth Coll., 1945. Pres. John Wolfe Inst., Houston, 1964—; pres., exec. dir. Sales/Mktg. Execs., Houston, 1985—. Author: Sell Like an Ace, Live Like a King, 1961; Miracle Platform Power, 1978; The Wrong Target, 1981; Drilling for Death, 1982. Recipient Hall of Fame award Nat. Speakers Assn., 1977. Republican. Mem. Disciples of Christ Ch. Avocation: Flying. Home: 12335 Boheme Houston TX 77024 Office: Sales and Mktg Execs Soc 10405 Town and Country Way Houston TX 77024

WOLFE, TRACEY DIANNE, distbg. co. exec.; b. Dallas, June 13, 1951; d. George F. and Helen Ruth Cline (Lemons) W.; 1 son, Bronson Alan. B.S. in Edn. and Social Sci., E. Tex. State U., Commerce, 1973, M.S. in Elem. Edn., 1976. Asst. to dir. student devel. E. Tex. State U., 1973-74; corp. sec., v.p. Wolfe Distbg. Co., beer distbrs., Terrell, Tex., 1974—. Mem. Kappa Delta (alumnae v.p. 1978-79, alumnae treas. 1979-81, province pres. 1980-82). Republican. Methodist. Home: 3316 Lakeside Dr Rockwall TX 75087 Office: 100 Metro Dr Terrell TX 75160

WOLFE, WILLIAM GREGORY, dentist; b. Iowa City, Jan. 16, 1947; s. William Gerald and Mayrel (Stalnaker) W.; m. Penny Davis, Nov. 27, 1968; 1 son, Travis L. B.S. in Speech Pathology, U. Tex., 1968; D.D.S., Baylor U.,

1972. Lic. dentist, Tex., N.Mex. Practice dentistry, Austin, Tex., 1972-78, Albuquerque, 1978—; Indian Health Service dentist Indian reservations in N.Mex., 1978-81; pres. Aloe-Dent, Inc., Albuquerque, 1982—; lectr. Bd. dirs. Sr. Citizen Aid Found., Albuquerque, 1980—; trustee First Ch. of Religious Sci., Albuquerque, 1983. Recipient first place Auto Club Mex., Monterrey, 1980. Mem. ADA, Holistic Dental Soc., N.Mex. Dental Assn., Tex. Dental Assn., Toxic Element Research Found. Club: Sports Car of Am. (Denver). Author: A Moment in Dental Operatory History, 1983; patentee in field. Office: 8401 Osuna NE Albuquerque NM 87111

WOLFENDEN, RICHARD VANCE, biochemistry educator; b. Oxford, Eng., May 17, 1935; s. John Hulton and Josephine (Vance) W.; m. Anita Gaunitz, May 25, 1965; children—Peter, John. B.A., Princeton U., 1956; B.A. Exeter Coll., Oxford U., 1958, M.A., 1958; Ph.D., Rockefeller Inst., 1964. Asst. prof. chemistry Princeton U., 1964-70; vis. fellow Exeter Coll., Oxford, 1969; assoc. prof. biochemistry U. N.C., Chapel Hill, 1970-73, prof. biochemistry, 1973-83, Alumni disting. prof., 1983—; vis. prof. U. Montpellier (France), 1976; mem. molecular biology panel NSF, Washington, 1973-76; mem. bio-organic and natural products study sect. NIH, Washington, 1981—; cons. Merck & Co., Rahway, N.J., 1973-75, Burroughs-Wellcome Co., Research Triangle Park, N.C., 1981—; chmn. Gordon Research Conf. on Enzymes, Meriden, N.H., 1977. Fellow AAAS; mem. Am. Chem. Soc., Am. Soc. Biol. Chemists, AAAS. Democrat. Mem. editorial bd. Bioorganic Chemistry, 1983—. Home: 1307 Mason Farm Rd Chapel Hill NC 27514 Office: Dept of Biochemistry Univ of NC Chapel Hill NC 27514

WOLFF, ERIC CHARLES, geologist; b. Burlington, Vt., May 12, 1951; s. Richard Charles and Sybil Helen (Burnham) W.; m. Margaret Nell Ross, Dec. 16, 1973; children—Eric Dane, Alexanda Elizabeth. B.S. in Geology, Tex. A&M U., 1973. Cert. profl. geol. scientist. Geologist, Conoco, Kenedy, Tex., 1974-78; dist. geologist Elf Aquitaine, Corpus Christi, 1978-80; geologist Concord Oil Co., San Antonio, 1980—; mem. fellowship com. Tex. Mining and Mineral Resources Research Inst., Austin, 1985. Author: Energy Mining in Southern Texas, 1982; South Texas Energy Minerals, 1984. Mem. Am. Assn. Petroleum Geologists, AIME (sect. chmn. 1984), Am. Inst. Profl. Geologists, Tex. Mineral Land Assn., South Tex. Geol. Soc. Republican. Roman Catholic. Avocations: swimming, water polo. Office: Concord Oil Co 1500 Alamo Bldg San Antonio TX 78205

WOLFF, RONALD GILBERT, zoology educator; b. Lewiston, Idaho, Jan. 17, 1942; s. Robert Raymond and June Olive (Staffelbach) W.; m. Lilia Cristina Koo, Nov. 1, 1979. A.B., Whitman Coll., 1964; M.A., U. Oreg., 1966; Ph.D. in Paleontology, U. Calif.-Berkeley, 1971. USPHS-NSF postdoctoral fellow in anatomy U. Chgo., 1971-72, research assoc., 1972-73; asst. prof. dept. zoology U. Fla., Gainesville, 1973-78, assoc. prof., 1978—. NSF grantee, 1978—. Mem. Soc. Vertebrate Paleontology, Paleontological Soc., Ecol. Soc. Am., Am. Soc. Mammalogists, Sigma Xi. Contbr. articles to profl. jours. Office: Department of Zoology University of Florida Gainesville FL 32611

WOLFHARD, HANS GEORG, research scientist; b. Basel, Switzerland, Apr. 2, 1912; s. Albert Georg and Helene (Bueck) W.; came to U.S., 1956, naturalized, 1961; m. Adelheid Rohde, Jan. 18, 1940; children—George, John, Bernie. Student, U. Berlin, 1934-35; Dr.Rer.Nat., U. Goettingen, 1938. Scientist, Aeronautical Research Sta., Brunswick, Germany, 1939-46; research scientist Imperial Coll., London, Royal Aircraft Establishment, Eng., 1946-56; research scientist Bur. Mines, Pitts., 1956-59; head physics dept. reaction motors div. Thiokol Chem. Corp., Denville, N.J., 1959-63; sr. research staff Inst. Def. Analyses, Alexandria, Va., 1963—. Fellow Am. Optical Soc.; mem. AIAA, Combustion Inst. Presbyterian. Author: Flames, 4th edit., 1979. Home: 3818 N Wakefield St Arlington VA 22207 Office: Inst Defense Analyses 1801 N Beauregard St Alexandria VA 22311

WOLFLE, LEE MORRILL, educational research educator; b. Chgo., June 24, 1941; s. Dael Lee and Helen (Morrill) W.; m. Jane Elizabeth Allen, Aug. 31, 1963; children—James Dael, David Lee, Susan Jane. B.A., U. Colo., 1965; M.S., San Jose State Coll., 1967; Ph.D., U. Mich., 1976. Asst. prof. Radford Coll., Va., 1967-69; instr. U. N.Mex., Albuquerque, 1974-76; from asst. prof. to prof. ednl. research Va. Poly. Inst. and State U., Blacksburg, 1976—; vis. fellow Ednl. Testing Service, Princeton, N.J., 1984-85. Contbr. articles to profl. jours., chpts. to books. Recipient Outstanding Research in Edn. award Va. Edn. Research Assn., 1979-81. Mem. Am. Ednl. Research Assn. (research tng. com. 1984—), Am. Sociol. Assn., AAAS (life). Home: 506 Stonegate Dr Blacksburg VA 24060 Office: Va Poly Inst and State U Coll Edn Blacksburg VA 24061

WOLFORD, DENNIS ARTHUR, hospital administrator; b. Fort Wayne, Ind., Aug. 8, 1946; s. Donald Arthur and Madelyn Marie (Howell) W.; m. Carol Louise Bullen, Oct. 3, 1964; 1 child, Jack Douglas. B.S. in Bus. Adminstrn., Tusculum Coll., 1968. Auditor, U.S. GAO, Washington, 1968-70; exec. mgr. Irene Byron Hosp., Fort Wayne, 1970-73; asst. adminstr. McCray Meml. Hosp., Kendallville, Ind., 1973-78, adminstr., 1978-84, Macon County Gen. Hosp., Lafayette, Tenn., 1984—. Pres. Cole Ctr. Family YMCA, Kendallville, 1982-84. Mem. Am. Coll. Hosp. Adminstrs., Kendallville C. of C. (bd. dirs. 1981-83). Republican. Lutheran. Lodge: Rotary. Avocations: swimming; racquetball; volleyball; skiing; traveling. Home: 1307 Sonoma Dr Lafayette TN 37083 Office: Macon County Gen Hosp 204 Medical Dr Lafayette TN 37083

WOLFSON, MILTON WILLARD, saddlery and veterinary supply owner; b. Phila., Oct. 22, 1932; s. Abraham Lincoln and Beatrice (Flink) W.; m. Gail Pompian, Jan. 27, 1957; children—Bari, Ellen, Rona. B.S. in Animal Sci., U. Ill., 1959; M.Ed., Temple U., 1972. Sci. tchr. Log Coll., Warminster, Pa., 1972-74; farm mgr. Locust Lawn Farm, Ill., 1960-65; race horse trainer Pub. Stable, Ill., Fla., Pa., 1962-80; owner, mgr. Neshaming Turf/Miamar Dist., Pa. and Fla., West Hollywood, Fla., 1969—. Bd. dirs. Horsemen's Benevolent and Protective Assn. Pa., 1974-78. Served with USAF, 1953-57. Republican. Jewish. Home: 5920 SW 33d Ln Fort Lauderdale FL 33312 Office: Miamar Dist 2408 SW 58th Ave West Hollywood FL 33023

WOLFSON, RICHARD FREDERICK, lawyer; b. N.Y.C., Jan. 7, 1923; s. William Leon and Gertrude (Quitman) W.; B.S., Harvard U., 1942; LL.B., Yale U., 1944; m. Elaine Cecile Reinherz, June 6, 1954; children—Lisa Reinherz, Paul Reinherz Quitman. Bar: N.Y. 1945, Fla. 1956. Law clk. to judge U.S. Ct. of Appeals, 2d Circuit, 1944-45, Justice Wiley Rutledge, U.S. Supreme Ct., 1945-47; mem. firm Kurland & Wolfson, N.Y.C., 1947-52; asst. to pres. Wometco Enterprises, Inc., Miami, Fla., 1952-59, v.p., 1959-62, sr. v.p., 1962-72, exec. v.p., gen. counsel, 1973-81, chmn. exec. com., 1976-81; partner Stroock & Stroock & Lavan, Miami, 1981-83; of counsel Kreeger & Kreeger, Miami, 1983—; dir. Wometco Enterprises, Inc., 1959-84; mem. Fla. Bar Commn. on Merit Retention of Judges, 1981. Past pres. Ransom-Everglades Sch.; bd. dirs. Met. Mus. Miami, Miami Philharmonic Soc. (past pres.), Opera Guild Greater Miami, Greater Miami chpt. Am. Jewish Com., Miami chpt. Am. Jewish Congress; chmn. Fla. region NCCJ; trustee Fla. Internat. U. Found. Guggenheim fellow, 1949-50. Mem. Fla., N.Y. State bar assns., Nat. Assn. Theater Owners, Subscription TV Assn. Am. (vice chmn. 1979-81). Clubs: Standard, Palm Bay, Grove Isle, Harvard, Miami (Miami); Harvard (N.Y.C.). Author: (with Kurland) Jurisdiction of the Supreme Court of the United States, 1951; also articles in profl. jours., poetry. Home: 630 University Dr Coral Gables FL 33134 Office: 169 E Flagler St Miami FL 33131

WOLK, ROBERT GEORGE, educator, biologist; b. N.Y.C., Mar. 10, 1931; s. Sol and Mary (Baker) W.; m. Wilhelmina Joan Klein, Mar. 4, 1956; children—Stephanie Elizabeth, David Paul, Jennifer Sally, Nancy Baker, Jonathan Gardner. B.S., CCNY, 1952; M.S., Cornell U., 1954, Ph.D., 1959. Asst. prof. biology St. Lawrence U., Canton, N.Y., 1957-63; assoc. prof. vertebrate morphology and behavior Adelphi U., Garden City, N.Y., 1963-67; curator life sci. Tackapausha Mus. and Preserve, Nassau County Mus., Seaford, N.Y., 1967-78; exec. dir. Nature Sci. Ctr., Winston-Salem, N.C., 1978-82; lectr. in biology Greensboro Coll. (N.C.), 1982-83; dir. edn. N.C. State Mus. Natural History, Raleigh, 1983—. Biology dept. scholar CCNY, 1952; NSF grantee, 1956; Mae P. Smith Fund grantee, Am. Mus. Natural History, 1954, 55. Mem. Am. Assn. Mus., Am. Ornithologists' Union, Linnaean Soc. N.Y. (editor 1970-75), Brit. Ornithologists' Union, Wilson Ornithol. Soc. (Fuertes grantee 1955), Sigma Xi (pres. Adelphi U. 1966-67). Contbr. articles to profl. jours. Office: PO Box 27647 Raleigh NC 27611

WOLKING, JOSEPH ANTHONY, publishing company executive; b. Morris, Minn., May 7, 1934; s. Lawrence William and Tecla Catherine (Loegering) e7W.; m. Kathleen Marie Poehling, Apr. 18, 1959; children—Christopher, Lisbeth, Gergory, Rebecca, Eric. Student, Fordham U., 1952-54; B.A., U. Minn., 1957. With Ojibway Press Inc., Duluth, Minn., 1958-69; asst. to pres. Petroleum Pub. Co. (name changed to PennWell Pub. Co. 1980), Tulsa, 1969; pub. Dental Econs., 1972-75, group v.p., 1975-82, sr. v.p., chief operating officer, 1982—, dir., 1977—, exec. v.p., 1984—. Home: 3775 S Canton St Tulsa OK 74135 Office: 1421 S Sheridan St Tulsa OK 74112

WOLPERT, EDWARD MARTIN, educational administrator; b. Bklyn., June 16, 1935; children—James, Carolyn. B.Mus., U. Rochester, 1959, M.A., 1960; Ed.D., U. Kans., 1970. Prof. edn. Ball State U., Muncie, Ind., 1970-80, chmn. dept. edn., 1980-83; dean edn. Ga. Coll., Milledgeville, 1983—. Author: Understanding Research, 1981. Served with U.S. Army, 1954-56. Mem. Am. Ednl. Research Assn., Nat. Council on Measurement in Edn., Internat. Reading. Assn., Phi Delta Kappa. Avocation: long distance running. Home: 121 Pinecrest Dr Milledgeville GA 31061 Office: Ga Coll Milledgeville GA 31061

WOLZ, LARRY ROBERT, music educator; b. Odessa, Tex., Sept. 1, 1951; s. Johnny Frank and Lucille Evelyn (Brown) W. B.Mus., Hardin-Simmons U., 1973, Mus.M., 1974; Mus.M., Tex. Christian U., 1976; Ph.D., U. Cin., 1983. Assoc. prof. music Hardin-Simmons U., Abilene, Tex., 1978—. Contbr. articles to profl. jours. Composer organ compositions. Vice pres. Abilene Opera Assn., 1981-84. Mem. Nat. Assn. Tchrs. Singing, Am. Musicol. Soc. Am. Guild Organists, Sonneck Soc., Coll. Music Soc., Abilene C. of C. (Mem. com. Paramount Series 1980—). Baptist. Avocation: stamp collecting. Home: 2834 Hickory St Abilene TX 79601 Office: Hardin-Simmons U Sch Music Abilene TX 79698

WOMACK, JOHN CALVIN, architect; b. Fayetteville, Ark., Aug. 31, 1950; s. Leonard Lee and Betty Jane (Slusher) W.; m. Rebecca Elaine Johnston, Aug. 5, 1972; children—Stuart, Bryan, Mary Elizabeth. B.Arch., U. Ark., 1973, B.A., 1973. Intern architect E. Fay Jones Architect, Fayetteville, 1973-76, assoc. architect Fay Jones & Assocs., Fayetteville, 1976-83; pvt. practice architecture, Fayetteville, 1983—. Mem. adminstrv. bd. Central United Methodist Ch., Fayetteville, 1981-84. Mem. AIA (chmn.-elect N.W. Ark. sect. 1986; Citation of Merit 1983). Methodist. Lodge: Rotary. Avocations: drawing; reading; music; book collecting. Home: 27 Wilson Ave Fayetteville AR 72701 Office: 240 N Block Ave Fayetteville AR 72701

WOMACK, SOLOMON ARTHUR, JR., geologist, oil company executive; b. Mt. Selman, Tex., Aug. 29, 1920; s. Solomon Arthur Sr., and Leona (Boone) W.; m. Virginia Helms, Nov. 1, 1975. B.S., La. State U., 1949. Geologist Union Producing Co., Shreveport, La., 1949-55; chief geologist, asst. to pres. Trans-Tex Drilling Co., Shreveport, 1955-57; mgr. ops. Am. Gas Prodn. Co., Lafayette, La., 1957-59; ind. geologist, oil operator Lafayette, La., 1959-71; mgr. exploration Sklar & Phillips Oil Co., Shreveport, 1971—. Mem. Am. Assn. Petroleum Geologists, Assn. Profl. Geol. Scientists, Ind. Petroleum Assn. Am., Shreveport Geol. Soc., East Tex. Geol. Soc. Republican. Clubs: Petroleum (pres. Lafayette 1965) Petroleum (Shreveport). Avocations: golf, photography. Home: Route 1 Box 64 J Benton LA 71006 Office: Sklar & Phillips Oil Co PO Box 3735 Shreveport LA 71133

WOMBLE, GEORGE MORGAN, life insurance company executive; b. Raleigh, N.C., Oct. 9, 1926; s. George Morgan and Dorothy Hempstead (Price) W.; m. Mary Phyllis Cowdery, Aug. 8, 1946; children—George M. III, Robert Byron, Elizabeth Vaughn. J.D., Wake Forest U., 1950; grad., Advanced Mgmt. Program, Harvard U., 1975. Bar: N.C. 1950. Individual practice law, Elizabeth City, N.C., 1950; with Durham Life Ins. Co., Raleigh, 1950—, gen. counsel, 1965-67, exec. v.p. adminstrn., 1967-75, sr. exec. v.p. ops., 1976-78, pres., chief exec. officer, 1978-83, also dir., chmn. bd., 1983—; sr. exec. v.p. ops. Durham Corp., 1983—; chmn. bd. Durham Life Broadcasting Co., State Capital Ins. Co. Chmn. admission and planning United Way Wake County, 1976-79, v.p., 1979, pres., 1980; bd. visitors Wake Forest U. Sch. Law, 1974—; elder, trustee West Raleigh Presbyterian Ch., 1977—; trustee Penn Coll., 1983—. Served with USAAF, 1945-46. Mem. N.C., Wake County bar assns., Raleigh C. of C. (dir. 1978—, pres. 1983—). Club: MacGregor Downs Country. Office: 2610 Wycliff Rd Raleigh NC 27607*

WONG, BETTY JEAN, state official; b. Leland, Miss., Mar. 15, 1949; d. Suey Henry and Pon Chu (Lam) Wong; B.S., Miss. State U., 1971; M.Ed., Delta State U., 1973. Asst. gen. mgr. Sta. WJPR, Greenville, Miss., 1973-74; career devel. specialist Greenville Municipal Sch. Dist., 1974-76; career edn. curriculum specialist Miss. State U., Jackson, 1976-77, research/curriculum specialist, 1977-79; coordinator vocat. research, curricula and tchr. edn. Miss. State Dept. Edn., 1979-80, asst. state dir., 1980-85, Supportive Services Vocat. Bur., div. dir., 1985—; cons. field career edn. Mem. Am., Miss. (exec. bd., chmn. profl. devel. task force, chmn. conv. 1980) personnel and guidance assns., Am. Vocat. Assn. (named one of 16 Outstanding Women in Vocat. Adminstrn. 1983, mem. policy bd. guidance sect.), Miss. Vocat. Assn., AAUW (handbook chairperson 1975-77). Baptist. Contbr. articles to profl. publs.; also handbook. Home: 1137 Woodfield Dr Jackson MS 39211 Office: PO Box 771 Vocat Div Jackson MS 39205

WONG, ELAINE DANG, television executive; b. Canton, China, June 3, 1936 (parents Am. citizens); d. Robert G. and Fung Heong (Woo) Dang; A.A. (Rotary scholar), Coalinga Coll., 1956; B.S. (AAUW scholar, Grad. Resident scholar), U. Calif., Berkeley, 1958, teaching credential, 1959; m. Philip Wong, Nov. 8, 1959; children—Elizabeth, Russell, Roger, Edith, Valerie. Tchr. acctg. San Mateo (Calif.) High Sch., 1959-60; acct., 1960-75; substitute tchr. Richmond County Schs., Augusta, Ga., 1975-77; comptroller Central Savannah River Area, United Way, Augusta, 1977-82; asst. controller Hammermill Hardwoods div. Hammermill Paper Co., Augusta, 1982-84; controller SFN Communications of Augusta, Inc. (WJBF-TV), 1984—; cons. small bus.; pvt. tutor acctg. Panel judge Jr. Achievement Tres. award, 1980, 81; treas. Chinese Lang. Sch., 1973-75, Merry Neighborhood Sch., 1974-75. Recipient Achievement award Bank of Am., 1954. Mem. Nat. Assn. Accts. (dir. 1978—, treas. 1982—), Chinese Assn. Republican. Presbyterian.

WONG, YOUNG-TSU, history educator; b. Shanghai, China, Jan. 29, 1940; s. Te-pei and Hsia-yun Chen Wong; m. Shan-yi (Sylvia) Lu Wong, Apr. 28, 1940; children—Walter Chih-hua, Virgil Chih-wei. B.A., Nat. Taiwan U., 1961; M.A., U. Oreg., 1964; Ph.D., U. Wash., 1971. Research asst. Far Eastern and Russian Inst., U. Wash., Seattle, 1966-70; asst. prof. history Va. Poly. Inst. and State U., Blacksburg, 1971-77, assoc. prof., 1977—; vis. prof. Nat. Taiwan Normal U., 1978-78, Fudan U., Shanghai, China, 1981-82. Recipient C. Ronald Johnson Meml. Scholarship prize; U.S. Research scholar, 1981-82; Nat. Acad. Scis. grantee. Author or editor 3 books on modern China; contbr. numerous articles on history to profl. jours. Home: 615 Owens Blacksburg VA 24060 Office: 516 McBryde Hall Va Poly Inst and State Univ Blacksburg VA 24061

WONNACOTT, JAMES BRIAN, physician; b. Charlottetown, P.E.I., Can., Feb. 24, 1945; came to U.S., 1978, naturalized, 1984; s. Earl Lepage and Eunice Deborah (Eaton) W.; honors diploma, Prince of Wales Coll., 1964; B.Sc. with honors in Biology, Dalhousie U., 1966, M.D., 1972. Intern, Victoria Gen. Hosp., Halifax, N.S., Can., 1971-72; gen. practice medicine, Summerside, P.E.I., 1975-78; practice medicine specializing in family practice, Houston; med. dir. alcoholism treatment unit Raleigh Hills Hosp., 1981-83; preceptor teaching staff U. Tex. Med. Sch., Houston, 1984—; mem. med. adv. bd. Med. World News, 1983—. Served as flight surgeon RCAF, 1967-75. Diplomate Am. Bd. Family Practice, Coll. Family Physicians Can. Fellow Am. Acad. Family Physicians; mem. Tex. Med. Assn., Can. Med. Assn., AMA, Am. Coll. Emergency Physicians, Royal Coll. Medicine, Am. Pub. Health Assn., Tex. Med. Found., Tex. Research Soc. Alcoholism, Soc. USAF Flight Surgeons, Am. Geriatrics Soc. Methodist. Clubs: Rotary of Houston; Univ. Lodge of Halifax. Office: Northwest Med Pavillion 1740 W 27th St Suite 221 Houston TX 77008

WOOD, ALFRED MCCREARY, retired sales executive; b. Wildie, Ky., Nov. 1, 1896; s. Henry Hugh and Eliza (Stewart) W.; student U. Ky., 1916-17; B.A., Harvard U., 1921; m. Mary Swain, Mar. 11, 1958. With Procter & Gamble Co., 1921-61, salesman, gen. salesman, Kansas City, asst. to gen. sales mgr., Cin., sales supr., Phila., gen. sales supr., N.Y. dist. mgr., Boston, spl. assignment, Dallas, 1921-48, div. mgr., Cin., 1949-61, ret., 1961. Served to ensign USN, 1918-19; from maj. to lt. col., USAAF, 1942-45. Decorated Bronze Star, Croix de Guerre with palm. Mem. Am. Acad. Polit. and Social Sci., Newcomen Soc. N.Am., Dallas Council World Affairs (dir.), Sigma Alpha Epsilon. Republican. Presbyterian. Harvard (Dallas), Dallas Country, Dallas. Home: 3525 Turtle Creek Blvd Dallas TX 75219 also Woodlands Box 774 Millerton OK 74750

WOOD, BERT CLARENCE, III, fire operations bureau administrator; b. Washington, Aug. 9, 1943; s. Bert Clarence and Ora Pearl (Allen) W.; m. Carol Elaine Deal, Aug. 14, 1971; children—Christina A., Gail Marie. A.A.S. in Fire Sci. Mgmt. with honors, No. Va. Community Coll., 1979; B.S. in Fire Sci. Mgmt. with honors, U. Md., 1983. Vice pres. systems devel. Nat. Data Ctrs., Silver Springs, Md., 1965-69; sta. comdr. Alexandria Fire Ops. Bur., Va., 1971—. Contbr. articles to profl. jours. Recipient Top Tech. Paper award Inst. Fire Engrs., Eng., 1984, Fireman of Yr. award Ins. Women, 1983. Mem. Internat. Fire Service Instrs. Club: Clans of Scotland (chief exec. officer 1984). Avocations: gardening; sailing. Office: Alexandria Fire Ops Bur 900 2d St Alexandria VA 22314-1395

WOOD, CHARLES ALFRED, JR., educator; b. Woodsville, N.H., May 17, 1950; s. Charles Alfred and America (Caravatti) W. B.S., Plymouth State Coll., 1972, M.Ed., 1973; postgrad. Va. Poly. Inst. and State U., 1978-80. Asst. dir. housing Plymouth State Coll., Radford, Va., 1972-73, admissions recruiter, 1971-72, exec. asst. to pres., 1974—. Mem. Am. Assn. Higher Edn., Council for Advancement and Support of Edn., C. of C. (dir.). Roman Catholic. Home: PO Box 2881 Radford VA 24143 Office: Radford Univ Radford VA 24142

WOOD, CONSTANCE DORIS, psychologist; b. Boston, June 3, 1929; d. Henry and Annie Lena (Miller) Rosen; m. Edwin C. Wood, Dec. 17, 1977; children—Marsha Lasker, Shelley Lasker, Jeffrey Lasker. B.A. in Psychology, Boston U., 1950; M.Ed. Psychol. Examiner, U. Hartford, 1960; Ph.D. in Psychology, Fordham U., 1975; cert. in Psychoanalytic Psychotherapy, Inst. for Study of Psychotherapy, 1977. Lic. psychologist, Tex., N.Y. Grad. asst. in psychology, Boston U., 1950-51; clin. psychologist Mass. Gen. Hosp., Boston, 1951-52, Hartford Health Dept., Conn., 1963; research psychologist Inst. of Living, Hartford, 1963-66; sch. psychologist Conn. Inst. for the Blind, Hartford, 1965-68; clin. psychologist New Rochelle Ctr. for Psychol. Services and Edn., N.Y., 1970-77; sch. psychologist Mt. Vernon Bd. Edn., N.Y., 1968-77; pvt. practice psychology, New Rochelle, 1977; dir. Ima Hogg Therapeutic Sch., Children's Mental Health Services, Houston, 1978-79; pvt. practice psychology, Houston, 1978—; psychol. cons. St. Luke's Hosp., Houston, 1983—, Methodist Hosp., Houston, 1984—, Tex. Children's Hosp., Houston, 1982—, Belle Park Hosp., Houston, 1983—, Houston Internat. Hosp., 1982—, Houston, 1984—, West Oaks Hosp., 1985—, Jefferson Davis Hosp., Houston, 1982-83, Mental Health/Mental Retardation Authority, Houston, 1982—; expert witness, 1980—. Contbr. articles to profl. publs. Mem. Am. Psychol. Assn., Tex. Psychol. Assn., Houston Psychol. Assn., Phi Delta Kappa, Kappa Delta Pi. Home: 2704 Glen Haven Blvd Houston TX 77025 Office: 5300 San Jacinto Suite 150 Houston TX 77004

WOOD, CONSTANCE LOUISE, statistics educator, consultant; b. Lexington, Ky., Dec. 7, 1948; d. Clinton D. and Colona (Kenney) W.; m. Foster B. Cady, Dec. 27, 1980; 1 child, Clinton Foster. B.A., Hollins Coll., 1969; M.S., Fla. State U., 1971, Ph.D., 1975. Asst. prof. Cornell U., Ithaca, N.Y., 1973-77; asst. prof. U. Ky., Lexington, 1977-82, assoc. prof. dept. stats., 1982—, dir. statis. cons., 1981-83, dir. grad. studies, 1984—. Mem. Am. Statis. Assn., Biometrics Soc. Home: 3513 Cheddington Ln Lexington KY 40502 Office: Dept Statistics 801 POT U Ky Lexington KY 40506

WOOD, DANIEL HARRIS, geophysicist; b. Frankfurt, W.Ger., June 19, 1950; (parents Am. citizens); s. Leonard E. and Kathryn N. (Sims) W.; m. Terry Brandt, Oct. 5, 1983. B.A., U. Tex., 1972. Intelligence specialist Central Intelligence Agy., Washington, 1973-76; assoc. scientist Lockheed Electronics Co., Houston, 1976-77; seismologist Geosource, Inc., Houston, 1977-78; geophysicist Amoco Prodn. Co., Houston, 1978—. Mem. Soc. Exploration Geophysicists, Am. Assn. Petroleum Geologists. Avocations: photography; birds; literature. Office: Amoco Prodn Co 501 Westlake Park Blvd Houston TX 77253

WOOD, DAVID SCOTT, personnel agency executive; b. Cleve., July 11, 1936; s. Lewis John and Nelle Matilda (Brewer) W.; m. Nancy Davis (div. 1979); 1 dau., Kimberly. B.S., Ind. U., 1959, M.B.A., 1960; postgrad. Ind. U. Law Sch., 1962. Sr. market research analyst, personnel rep. Eli Lilly & Co., Indpls., 1960-67; founder, pres. David Wood Personnel Agys., West Palm Beach, Fla., also brs. throughout Fla., 1967—; lectr. Butler U. Sch. Bus., 1961-62. Bd. dirs. Palm Beach chpt. Am. Diabetes Assn., 1982—, v.p., 1983-84, mem. state bd. dirs., 1983—, chmn. bd.-elect, 1985-86; co-founder, bd. dirs. Better Bus. Bur. Palm Beach County, 1970—, chmn. bd., 1973; mem. adv. com. Palm Beach Jr. Coll., 1983-84; mem. Palm Beach Democratic Exec. Com., 1983—; candidate for state Senator, 1984; mem. Fla. Bd. Nursing, 1985-87. Served to capt. USAR, 1960-67. Mem. Nat. Assn. Personnel Cons., Home Builders Assn., SAR, Sigma Chi. Democrat. Episcopalian. Home: 12085 Banyan Rd Juno Beach FL 33408 Office: David Wood Personnel Agencies Inc 1897 Palm Beach Lakes Blvd West Palm Beach FL 33409

WOOD, DEBORAH WEAVER, social worker; b. Troy, Ohio, Sept. 20, 1950; d. Frank and Barbara Anne (Sauer) Weaver; m. William Joseph Wood, Jr., June 22, 1974; 1 dau., Elizabeth Ann. B.A., Winthrop Coll., 1971; M.S.W., U. S.C., 1973; postgrad. U. Ala., 1979-80. Social worker Moseley Clinic, Charleston, S.C., 1973-74; social worker, supr. Dallas County Dept. Pensions and Security, 1975-78; supr. Tuscaloosa County Dept. Pensions and Security, Birmingham, Ala., 1978-80; staff devel. trainer Ala. Dept. Pensions and Security, Birmingham, 1980—; chmn. Spouse Abuse Network, Tuscaloosa, Ala., 1979-80; tchr. G. Wallace Jr. Coll., Selma, Ala., 1976-78; project dir. CETA, 1979, Child Sexual Abuse Tng. Project, HHS, 1982-83. Mem. Head Start Policy Council, 1979-81; mem. pub. relations com. Spouse Abuse Network, 1980; mem. adv. com. Ala. Bd. S.W. Examiners, 1981. Grantee NIMH, 1971-73, CETA grantee, 1979. Mem. Nat. Assn. Social Workers (sec. Ala. chpt. 1981-83, chmn. membership com. 1983—), Acad. Cert. Social Workers, Ala. Zool. Soc. Club: Madd (Jefferson County, Ala.). Home: 133 E Glenwood Dr Homewood AL 35209

WOOD, DOROTHY LUNDY, advertising agency executive; b. Macon, Ga., Oct. 3, 1930; d. Walter Aubrey and Ruth (Holden) Lundy; m. Donald Eugene Wood, Dec. 30, 1955 (div. 1959); 1 son, William Thomas. A.B., U. Ga., 1952. Formerly newspaper reporter, advt. copywriter, creative dir.; v.p. Gordon & Wood Advt., Atlanta, 1971-76; pres. Wood-Bowes Advt., Atlanta, 1976-82; pres. Wood & Assocs. Advt., Inc., Atlanta, 1982—. Dir. advt. Sam Nunn, mem. U.S. Senate, 1972, George Busbee, Gov. Ga., 1974, 78. Mem. Phi Beta Kappa, Alpha Omicron Pi. Methodist. Home: 2946 Rockingham Dr NW Atlanta GA 30327 Office: 455 E Paces Ferry Suite 304 Atlanta GA 30305

WOOD, FORREST HESTER, computer science educator, computer consultant; b. Houston, Feb. 19, 1933; s. Forrest Hubert and Grace (Hester) W.; m. Glenda Elnora Winslett, June 30, 1962; children—Grace Elaine, James Evan. B.S., Naval Postgrad. Sch., 1970, M.S., 1971; postgrad., Nova U., 1983—. Cert. data processer, Ala. Enlisted U.S. Navy, 1951, advanced through grades to comdr., 1971; control tower operator U.S. Navy, 1951-55, naval aviator, 1955-76; instr. Troy State U., Dothan, Ala., 1976-81, asst. prof. computer sci., 1981—, dept. chmn., 1983—; cons. Design Assocs., Dothan, 1980-83, Hayes Internat., Dothan, 1982-83, Vision Eye Clinic, Dothan, 1983-84, City of Dothan, 1983-85. Named Flight Instr. of Yr., City of Milton, Fla. 1962; Kiwanis Editor of Yr., Ala. Kiwanis Dist. 1981, 82. Mem. Data Processing Mgmt. Assn. (faculty advisor), Edn. Spl. Interest Group, Mensa, Ala. Council Computer Edn., Officers Christian Fellowship. Republican. So. Baptist. Club: Dothan Landmarks Found. Avocations: microcomputers; flying; reading. Home: 510 Randwick Rd Dothan AL 36301 Office: Troy State U 227 N Foster St Dothan AL 36303

WOOD, HAROLD BLAIR, SR., engineering executive, engineering technician; b. Lauderdale, Miss., Aug. 29, 1932; s. Cofield Blair and Vivian (Miller) W.; m. Barbara Sue Johnson, Jan. 23, 1960; 1 child, Harold Blair, Jr. A.A., East Miss. Jr. Coll., 1952. Cert. sr. engring. technician. Engring. technician Palmer & Baker Engrs., Mobile, Ala., 1956-68, Dixie Labs. Inc., Mobile, 1968-71; supt. L.R. Johnston Co., Mobile, 1971-74; quality control engr. Structual Prestress Inc., Mobile, 1974-76; prodn. mgr. Smith-Kelly Supply Co., Mobile, 1976—. Served as E-4 U.S. Army, 1953-55. Mem. Nat. Inst for Certification of Engring. Technicians (life), Phi Theta Kappa (hon.). Mem. Church of Nazarene. Avocation: hunting. Home: 1411 E Riviera Dr Mobile AL 36605

WOOD, JACK AUBURN, law enforcement trainer, criminal justice instructor; b. Marion, N.C., Jan. 10, 1951; s. William H. and Mozelle (Hilton) W.; m. Donna B. Birchfield, Aug. 2, 1975; 1 child, David Andrew. A.A., Western Piedmont Coll., 1971; B.S., U. N.C.-Charlotte, 1973; M.A., Appalachian State U., 1986. Law enforcement officer McDowell County Sheriff's Dept., N.C., 1973-76; chmn. criminal justice dept. Mayland Tech. Coll., Spruce Pine, N.C., 1976-78, sch. dir. law enforcement tng., 1978—; police instr. Nat. Rifle Assn., 1984—; ind. protective service instr., Spruce Pine, 1983—. Mem. N.C. Criminal Justice Educators Assn., N.C. Sch. Dirs. Assn., Nat. Rifle Assn., N.C. Law Enforcement Officers Assn., N.C. Law Enforcement Tng. Officers Assn. Democrat. Baptist. Lodges: Masons, Mystic Tie. Avocations: pistol competition; auto racing; golf. Home: PO Box 1452 Marion NC 28752 Office: Mayland Tech Coll PO Box 547 Spruce Pine NC 28777

WOOD, JAMES B., hospital administrator; b. Bangkok, Thailand, July 18, 1957; came to U.S., 1963; s. Bruce Tufts and Barbara Jean (Fleming) W.; m. Vicky Darlene Shelton, Mar. 9, 1985. B.S. in Banking and Fin., U. Fla., 1978; M.H.A., Ga. State U., 1980. Mgmt. engr., Southeastern Gen. Hosp., Lumberton, N.C., 1980-81, asst. adminstr., 1981-82; adminstr. Edgefield County Hosp., S.C., 1982—. Bd. dirs. Piedmont Multi-County Mental Retardation Bd., Greenwood, S.C., 1982-84, Three Rivers Health Systems Agy., Columbia, S.C., 1984—; chmn. Red Cross of Edgefield County, 1982—; sec. Augusta Area Hosp. Council, Ga., 1982—; v.p. Upper Savannah Area Health Edn. Consortium, 1982—; campaign chmn. United Way, Edgefield, 1984. Mem. S.C. Hosp. Assn. Republican. Methodist. Lodges: Lions, Kiwanis (sec. 1981-82). Avocations: flying, scuba diving, photography. Office: Edgefield County Hosp Bausket St Edgefield SC 29824

WOOD, JAYNEE SMITH, real estate developer; b. Beaumont, Tex., July 26, 1954; d. John Sterling and Mildred (Sumerow) Smith; m. Samuel Eugene Wood, Apr. 5, 1980; children—Samantha, Stephanie, Amanda. B.S.B.A., Okla. State U., 1976. Lic. engr. N.C. Territory rep. Armstrong World Industries, Raleigh, N.C., 1976-80; owner, developer J.S. Wood Broker Assoc., Raleigh, 1980-85; v.p. Sam Wood Assocs., Inc., Raleigh, 1981-85, dir., sec., 1981—; ptnr. SAJA Assocs., Raleigh, 1982—; owner, cons. Splty. Products, Raleigh, 1983-85. Contbr. articles and designs to profl. jours. Vice pres. Breakfast Club Constrn., Raleigh, 1983-85; mem. various coms. United Methodist Ch., Raleigh, 1984-85, spl. com. United Way, Raleigh, 1985. Recipient sales awards and Outstanding Achievement award Integrated Ceiling Systems, 1985. Mem. Illumination Engrs. Soc. Republican. Presbyterian. Avocations: golf; boating; tennis; skiing. Home: PO Box 31506 Raleigh NC 27622 Office: Sam Wood Assocs Inc 8909 Midway Rd W PO Box 31506 Raleigh NC 27612

WOOD, JEFFREY GILCHRIST, police chief; b. Providence, Dec. 21, 1940; s. Harold L. and Phyllis (Gilchrist) W.; m. Donna Francis Moody, Mar. 22, 1969; children—Pamela Kay, David Allen, Phillip Gilchrist. Student Armstrong State Coll., 1970-74, Northwestern U. Traffic Inst., 1977, FBI Nat. Acad., 1975. Police officer Savannah Police Dept., Ga., 1965-74, dir. tng. and personnel, 1978-79; comdt. Savannah Regional Police Acad., 1975-77; chief of police Garden City Police Dept., Ga., 1979—; bd. dirs. Silent Witness Program, Savannah, 1983—, Chatham County EMS Council, 1983-85. Served with USAF, 1960-64. Recipient Civic Achievement award City of Savannah, 1973. Mem. Chatham Chiefs of Police Assn. (pres. 1980-81), Ga. Chiefs of Police Assn., Internat. Assn. Chiefs of Police, Northwestern U. Traffic Inst. Alumni Assn., FBI Nat. Acad. Assocs. Democrat. Baptist. Lodge: Lions (Garden City). Avocation: woodworking. Home: 69 Lynn Dr Garden City GA 31418 Office: PO Box 7548 Garden City GA 31418

WOOD, JOHN ELBRIDGE, political science educator; b. N.Y.C., Mar. 8, 1945; s. James Elbridge and Virginia (Keefe) W. B.A., Salem Coll., 1967; M.A., Ohio U., 1968; Ph.D., W.Va. U., 1976. Instr., W.Va. U., Morgantown, part-time 1972-75; instr. Alderson-Broaddus Coll., Philippi, W.Va., part-time 1975-76, asst. prof., 1977-81; asst. prof. Quincy Coll., Ill., 1976-77; asst. prof. polit. sci. Salem Coll., W.Va., 1981-82, assoc. prof., 1982—, chmn. dept. polit. sci./criminal justice, 1984—. Served with U.S. Army, 1969-70, Vietnam. Decorated Bronze Star. Mem. Am. Polit. Sci. Assn., W.Va. Polit. Sci. Assn., SAR, Pi Sigma Alpha. Republican. Episcopal. Lodge: Lions. Avocations: travel; family history; antiques. Home: 311-B Johnson Ave Bridgeport WV 26330 also PO Box 745 Sag Harbor NY 11963 Office: Salem Coll Dept Polit Sci Salem WV 26330

WOOD, LEONARD ALTON, hydrogeologist, consultant; b. Gratiot County, Mich., Aug. 22, 1922; s. Clyde Frederick and Arlin (Barnes) W.; m. Yvonne Bumford, Oct. 20, 1942 (dec. 1975); children—Judy Wood Robbins, Beth Wood Plank, Penny Wood Gittings; m. Annie Ott Grimsley, Feb. 5, 1977. B.S. in Geology, Mich. State U., 1946. Registered geologist, Va. Geologist, U.S. Geol. Survey, Lansing, Mich., 1947-52, Houston, Austin, 1952-63, dist. geology, Denver, 1963-67, staff geologist, Washington, Reston, Va., 1967-80; sr. hydrogeologist S.S. Papadopulos & Assocs., Rockville, Md., 1980—. Contbr. articles to profl. jours. Served to maj. USAF, 1943-45, 51-52. Fellow Geol. Soc. Am. (chmn. hydrogeology div. 1982); mem. Internat. Assn. Hydrologists (chmn. U.S. com. 1977-80), Am. Inst. Profl. Geologists, Am. Geophys. Union, Assn. of Engrng. Geologists, Am. Assn. Petroleum Geologists, Nat. Water Well Assn. Republican. Avocation: photography. Home: 10406 Hunter Ridge Dr Oakton VA 22124 Office: SS Papadopulos & Assocs 12250 Rockville Pike Rockville MD 20852

WOOD, MARCIA TODD, medical laboratory technology educator; b. Newberry, S.C., July 13, 1943; d. Marcus W. and Jean (Copeland) Todd; m. Malcolm Onnie Wood, July 24, 1965; children—Kim Michelle, Todd Michael. A.B., Winthrop Coll., 1964; M.Ed., U. S.C., 1984. Tchr. life sci. Camden (S.C.) Jr. High Sch., 1965-66; tchr. phys. sci. Northside Jr. High Sch., Greenwood, S.C., 1966; microbiology supr. Orangeburg Regional Hosp., 1968-71; instr. med. lab. tech. Orangeburg (S.C.)-Calhoun Tech. Coll., 1971—. Active Orangeburg Civic Chorale, 1979-81. Mem. S.C. Tech. Edn. Assn., Am. Soc. Med. Tech., S.C. Soc. Med. Tech., S.C. Employees Assn. Presbyterian. Office: 3250 St Matthews Rd Orangeburg SC 29115

WOOD, MICHAEL LEE, petroleum geologist, petroleum consultant; b. Milw., May 21, 1937; s. Noel Glenn and Elisabeth (Temple) W.; m. Clare Miller, Aug. 12, 1961 (div. Aug. 1982); children—Timothy Charles, Melinda Lee; m. Carolyn Phillips, Dec. 31, 1982. Student U. Wyo., 1962; B.S., U. Tulsa, 1963; M.S., Tex. Christian U., 1965. Certified petroleum geologist; certified profl. geologist. Geologist Union Oil Co. Calif., Houston, 1965-72, Bass Enterprises Prodn. Co., Fort Worth, 1972-76; sr. exploration geologist Damson Oil Corp., Houston, 1976-77; ptnr., geologist Mauldin and Wood, Houston, 1978-81; pres. Leaf River Group, Inc., Houston, 1982; cons. geologist Clements Energy Inc., Laurel, Miss., 1982—. Served to cpl. USMC, 1956-59. Tex. Christian U. fellow, 1963-65. Mem. Am. Assn. Petroleum Geologists, Am. Assn. Profl. Geologists, Miss. Geol. Soc., Fort Worth Geol. Soc. (pres. 1975-76), Sigma Gamma Epsilon, Kappa Alpha. Republican. Methodist. Avocations: cattle and dog breeding; hunting; fishing; collector mil. artifacts. Home: Route 1 Box 846 Moselle MS 39459 Office: PO Box 364 Laurel MS 39441-0364

WOOD, MICHAEL LEWIS, entertainer, songwriter; b. Oakland, Calif., July 7, 1951; s. Lewis Irvan and Dona Jean (Connell) W.; m. Kathleen Dianne Gordon, Apr. 16, 1977. B.S. in Sci. Edn. and Biology summa cum laude, Kennesaw Coll., 1984. Entertainer, songwriter, Jacksonville, Fla., 1975-80, Atlanta, 1985—; cons. Riverside Songwriter's Guild, Jacksonville, 1976; founder Journeyman Songwriter's Guild, Atlanta, 1985. Republican. Congregationalist. Club: Kennesaw Bicycle (co-founder 1980-82). Avocations: bicycling; hiking; camping; reading. Home: 4952 Bartow St Acworth GA 30101

WOOD, OLIVER GILLAN, JR., banking and finance educator; b. Greer, S.C., Apr. 27, 1937; s. Oliver Gillan and Grace (McBrayer) W.; m. Patricia Myers, Apr. 27, 1978; children—Brian Jay, Mary Ross, Merrill Ross, Michael Ross. B.S., U. S.C., 1958, M.A. in Econs., 1963; Ph.D. in Econs., U. Fla., 1965. Asst. prof. U. S.C., Columbia, 1965-68, assoc. prof., 1968-73, prof. banking and finance, 1973—; dir., founder Republic Nat. Bank, Columbia, 1975—; dir., corp. sec. Columbia Bancorporation, 1985—; chmn. U.S.C. Press Com., Columbia, 1981—. Author: Commercial Banking, 1978; Introduction to Money and Banking, 1980; (with others) Analysis of Bank Financial Statements, 1979; How to Borrow Money, 1981. Served to capt. USNR, 1959—. Mem. Am. Econ. Assn., Am. Finance Assn., Fin. Mgmt. Assn., So. Fin. Assn., Eastern Fin. Assn., Beta Gamma Sigma (pres. 1972). Avocations: farming; golf. Home: 3601 Boundbrook Ln Columbia SC 29206 Office: Coll Bus Adminstrn U S C Columbia SC 29208

WOOD, RICHARD ALLEN, construction company executive; b. Lynn, Mass., Sept. 23, 1946; s. Roland Irving and Ruth Athlene (Coggin) W.; m. Sandra Wood, Mar. 14, 1968 (div. 1979); m. Peggy Jeane Mann, Jan. 26, 1981; children—Corrie, Richard, Phillip. B.A., U. Mass., 1968. Sales rep. Pfizer Labs., Knoxville, Tenn., 1971-75; regional sales mgr. Adria Labs., Atlanta, 1975-76; Eastern sales dir. Technicare Corp., Atlanta, 1976-79; v.p. HPI Healthcare Services, Atlanta, 1979-83, Arthur Shuster, Inc., Atlanta, 1983—; assoc. dir. Nat. Assn. Sr. Living Industries. Pres., Hembree Farms Civic Assn., Roswell, Ga., 1985. Served to capt. USMC, 1968-71, Vietnam. Democrat. Avocations: boating, tennis. Home: 215 E Creek Circle Roswell GA 30075 Office: Arthur Shuster Inc 345 Market Pl Ste 110 Roswell GA 30075

WOOD, RICHARD HARVEY, JR., economics educator; b. Phila., Dec. 12, 1938; s. Richard Harvey and Frances (Manning) W.; m. Maria Graciela Jave, Aug. 17, 1968; 1 child, Maria Frances. B.A. in Geography, Antioch Coll., 1963; M.A. in Agrl. Econs., U. Wis., 1965, Ph.D. in Econs., 1972. Asst. prof. econs. U. Portland, Oreg., 1968-70; from asst. prof. to assoc. prof. econs. Stetson U., DeLand, Fla., 1970—; Fulbright lectr., Monterrey, Mex., 1978-79. Pres. bd. dirs. Sugar 'N Spice Day Care Ctr., DeLand, 1984-85, Wesley House, DeLand, 1984-85 . Land Tenure Ctr. fellow U. Wis., Madison, 1963-65. Mem. Am. Econ. Assn., Latin Am. Studies Assn. Democrat. Avocations: tennis; canoeing; hiking; running; camping. Home: 495 Oak Ridge Ave DeLand FL 32724 Office: Stetson U PO Box 8322 DeLand FL 32720

WOOD, ROBERT EDWARD, JR., bank personnel executive, management consultant; b. Bryn Mawr, Pa., Sept. 15, 1945; s. Robert Edward and Virginia (Nolan) W.; m. Elizabeth Murphy, Nov. 17, 1979. A.A., Valley Forge Mil. Acad. Jr. Coll.-Wayne, Pa., 1966; B.S. in Bus. Adminstrn., U. N.H.-Durham, 1969; M.B.A., Fla. State U.-Tallahassee, 1976. Mgr. mgmt. placement Genesco, Inc., Nashville, 1972-73; personnel mgr. Milliken & Co., Spartanburg, S.C., 1973-75; personnel dir. Fairchild, Inc., Beckley, W.Va., 1975-76; mgmt. cons. Sesco Mgmt. Cons., Chattanooga, 1976-82; v.p. human resources Am. Nat. Bank, Chattanooga, 1982—; cons. personnel adminstrn. and orgn. devel., Chattanooga. Bd. dirs. Met. Council Chattanooga, 1982—. Served to lt. U.S. Army, 1969-71. Decorated Bronze Star, Vietnam Service medal. Mem. Am. Soc. Personnel Adminstrn., Am. Soc. Tng. and Devel. (treas. Chattanooga chpt. 1982-83). Republican. Roman Catholic. Author: Management Development Series, 1980; contbr. articles in field to profl. publs. Home: 3412 Alta Vista Dr Chattanooga TN 37411 Office: 736 Market St Chattanooga TN 37401

WOOD, ROBERT LEE, transportation executive; b. Fort Worth, Jan. 26, 1940; s. James A. and Frances (Gilliam) W.; m. Naomi H. Poore, Mar. 5, 1960; children—Robert Lee, Stephen W., Helen Reena. Student, Draughns Jr. Coll., 1960; B.A., Somerset U., 1965; Traffic mgr. H.G. Hill Co., Nashville, 1959-69; terminal mgr. Sears Roebuck Co., Nashville, 1969-74; pres. Rent-A-Driver, Inc., Nashville, 1974—; dir. Maywood Constrn. Co., Nashville. Chmn. recreation com. Nashville Baptist Assn., 1984—; trustee Belmont Coll., Nashville, 1985—. Served with U.S. Army, 1957. Mem. Driver Leasing Council Am. (bd. dirs. 1981-86), Nashville C. of C., Donelson-Hermitage C. of C. Republican. Baptist. Clubs: Andrew Jackson Sertoma (pres. 1982-83); Beech Mountain (N.C.); Nat. Commodore. Lodge: Masons. Avocations: softball; basketball; water and snow skiing; hunting; fishing. Home: 223 Kennett Rd Old Hickory TN 37138 Office: Rent-A-Driver Inc 206 Shady Grove Rd Nashville TN 37214

WOOD, ROBERT WILLIAM, JR., plastic surgeon; b. Virden, Ill., Jan. 10, 1931; s. Robert W. and Mary J. (Peters) W.; M.D., U. Ill., 1955; m. Sarah Norman, Oct. 12, 1957; children—Robert William III, James Norman, John Willard Guy. Intern Baylor U. Hosp., Dallas, 1955-56; resident Christ Hosp., Cin., 1963-65; practice medicine specializing in aesthetic and plastic surgery; mem. active staff Meth. Hosp., Herman Hosp., Park Plaza Hosp., Diagnostic Hosp., St. Luke's Texas Childrens Hosp.; clin. asst. prof. Baylor U. Med. Sch., Houston, clin. asso. U. Tex. Med. Sch., Houston. Basso Profundo in Dallas Civic Opera Co., 1960-63, Houston Grand Opera Co., 1966-71. Served to capt., M.C., USAF, 1956-58. Diplomate Am. Bd. of Plastic Surgery. Mem. Internat. Soc. of Aesthetic Plastic Surgery (sec.-gen. 1981-83), Internat. Soc. of Clin. Plastic Surgery pres. 1977—), Am. Cleft Palate Assn., Am. Burn Assn., Am. Assn. Cosmetic Surgeons (pres. 1979), Houston Soc. of Plastic Surgeons (v.p. 1977—), Tex. Med. Assn., Harris County Med. Soc., Houston Surg. Soc., Am. Soc. of Plastic and Reconstructive Surgeons, Tex. Soc. of Plastic Surgery (v.p. 1977-78, pres. 1978—). Methodist. Clubs: University, Briar (Houston); Tarry House (Austin). Contbr. numerous articles on plastic and reconstructive surgery to profl. jours.; producer (films) on plastic surgery. Home: 15 Pinehill Houston TX 77019 Office: 1213 Hermann Dr Suite 885 Houston TX 77004

WOOD, SANDRA ELAINE, systems analyst programmer; b. Lynchburg, Va., June 27, 1944; d. William Lewis and Mattie Lou Wood; diploma exec. sec. course Phillips Bus. Coll., Lynchburg, 1970; B.A. in Bus. Adminstrn./Mgmt. cum laude, Lynchburg Coll., 1982, postgrad., 1983—. Cert. profl. sec. Various clerical and secretarial positions, 1962-66; with Owens-Ill., Inc., Big Island, Va., 1966—, data processing supr./programmer, Big Island, Va., 1974-76, data processing systems-analyst/programmer, 1977— participant seminars. Sec. Bedford County Transp. Safety Commn., 1974—; active Jerry Lewis Telethon. Mem. Profl. Secs. Internat. (Sec. of Yr. award Lynchburg chpt. 1971, chpt. participation award 1973, chpt. pres. 1974, coordinator S.E. Dist. Conf. 1981-82), Data Processing Mgmt. Assn. (chpt. pres. 1980), CPS Assos. Democrat. Methodist. Home: PO Box 303 Big Island VA 24526 Office: PO Box 40 Big Island VA 24526

WOOD, SARAH YOUNGBLOOD, librarian, administrator; b. Dallas, Jan. 19, 1920; d. George Quincy and Lela Pearl (Brownlee) Youngblood; m. John Ralph Wood, June 29, 1948; (dec. 1975). B.A., Tex. Woman's U., 1968, M.L.S., 1972. Library clk. Greenhill Sch., Dallas, 1963-68, asst. librarian, 1968-70; head librarian Hockaday Sch., Dallas, 1970—. Mem. Dallas County Library Assn. (sec. 1981-82), Tex. Library Assn. (publs. com. 1973-74), ALA (program com. nat. conv. 1983-84), Nat. Assn. Ind. Schs. (staff-summer workshop secondary sch. librarians Dallas 1979), Ind. Schs. Assn. Southwest (evaluation com. 1971, 82), Beta Phi Mu. Republican. Methodist. Home: 7015 Fisher Rd Dallas TX 75214 Office: Hockaday Sch Inc 11600 Welch Rd Dallas TX 75229

WOOD, SHELTON EUGENE, educator; b. Douglas, Ga., May 20, 1938; s. Shelton and Mae Lillie (Pheil) W.; m. Edna Louise Tanner, Aug. 25, 1958; children—Shelton John, Deirdre Louise. A.A., St. John's U., 1958; B.A., U. Nebr., 1969; M.Ed., Coll. William and Mary, 1971; Ph.D., Nova U., 1975; M.A., Central Mich. U., 1977. Area mgr. Marshall Fields Corp., Fla., 1957-58; transp. supr. Greyhound Corp., Jacksonville, Fla., 1959-62; commd. lt. U.S. Army, 1962, advanced through grades to col., 1984; with Army Research Inst., 1975-78; prof. St. Johns River Community Coll., Palatka, Fla., 1984—; pres. S. G. Wood & Assocs., San Mateo, Fla., 1984—. Active Boy Scouts Am., 1977—; lay leader United Meth. Ch., Palatka, 1977—; mem. State of Fla. Long Term Care Council, Northeast Fla. Pvt. Industry Council. Decorated Bronze Star with two oak leaf clusters, Air medal with three oak leaf clusters, Purple Heart. Fellow Sussex Coll., 1969-70. Mem. Am. Soc. Trainers and Developers (pres. Southeastern chpt. 1974-75), Am. Defense Preparedness Assn., Am. Mgmt. Assn., NEA, Phi Kappa Delta, Phi Delta Kappa. Lodges: Masons, Shriners. Address: PO Box 820 San Mateo FL 32088

WOOD, THEO NOEL, JR., rancher; b. San Saba, Tex., Feb. 1, 1946; s. Theo Noel and Ida Byrd (Mayfield) W.; m. Cynthia Sue Mutz, Dec. 19, 1975; children—Theo Noel III, Tamara Crystal. B.S., Howard Payne U., 1969. Tchr. bus. Southside Ind. Sch. Dist., San Antonio, Tex., 1969-71, adminstrv. asst. to supt., 1971-76; rancher, ptnr. Wood Bros., Richland Springs, Tex., 1976—. Pres., bd. dirs. McCulloch Electric Coop., Brady, Tex., 1979—; trustee Richland Springs Ind. Sch. Dist., 1979—. Mem. San Saba County Peanut Growers Assn. (pres., dir. 1978—). Republican. Baptist. Club: Richland Springs Rodeo (dir. 1977-84). Avocations: racoon hunting; riding; trail biking. Home: PO Box I Richland Springs TX 76871

WOOD, THOMAS COALE, rehabilitation consultant; b. Flora, Ill., July 11, 1951; s. Cordell Howard and Connie Euphemia (Coale) W.; m. Linda Louise Hefner, Nov. 2, 1974; children—Julia Merritt, Robert Coale. B.S. in Journalism, U. Colo., 1977; M.Ed. in Counseling and Human Devel. Services, U. Ga., 1982. Reporter, Macon Telegraph & News (Ga.), 1978; asst. dir. phys. plant Mercer U., Macon, 1978-81; rehab. coordinator Underwriters Adjusting Co., 1982-84; rehab. cons. Conservco, Macon, 1984—. Mem. Nat. Rehab. Assn., Nat. Assn. Rehab. Profls. in the Pvt. Sector, Vocat. Evaluation and Work Adjustment Assn., Nat. Rehab. Counseling Assn., Ga. Rehab. Assn., Pvt. Rehab. Suppliers Ga. Home: 714 Valley Trail Macon GA 31204 Office: 2014 Riverside Dr Macon GA 31204

WOOD, WALTER WYVILL, mechanical engineer; b. Louisville, Feb. 5, 1928; s. George Twyman and Louise Fairfax (Robertson) W.; B.M.E., U. Louisville, 1954, M.Engring., 1972; m. Caroline Shelburne Crone, Dec. 29, 1956 (div.); children—Victoria Armistead, Walter Wyville. Product devel. engr. Gamble Bros. Inc., Louisville, 1954-56; sales engr. Air Reduction Sales Co., Louisville, 1956-61; with Naval Ordnance Sta., Louisville, 1962—, dir. engrng. dept., 1973-74, dir. gun systems engrng. center, 1974-78, dir. gun systems engrng. dept., 1978—. Served with AUS, 1950-52; lt. col. Res. Decorated Meritorious Service medal; recipient Outstanding Citizens award City of Louisville, 1977; named Ky. col., 1969; registered profl. engr., Ky. Mem. Am. Welding Soc. (past chmn. Louisville sect.), Am. Soc. Naval Engrs., Louisville Engr. and Sci. Councils Soc., Louisville Habor Assn. (pres. 1979-80), Theta Tau. Democrat. Episcopalian. Club: River Rd. Country (Louisville). Home: 209 Kennedy Ct Louisville KY 40206 Office: Naval Ordnance Station Southside Dr Louisville KY 40214

WOOD, WILLIAM DOUGLAS, safety engineer; b. Nevada, Mo., Apr. 14, 1946; s. William H. and Mary P. (Cook) W.; m. Carolyn Davis; children—William Douglas, Jonahan I. B.A., Adams State Coll., Colo., 1971. Cert. hazard control mgr. Document analyst U.S. Army DCSOPS, Washington, 1969-71; personnel adminstr. City of Norfolk, Va., 1972-73, sr. personnel adminstr., 1973-74, safety officer, 1974—. Author: Fire Department Fitness Guide, 1982. Mem. Norfolk Hwy. Safety Commn., 1980—, sec., 1980-85; bd. dirs. Safety City, Norfolk, 1985. Served with U.S. Army, 1969-71. Adams State Coll. scholar, 1965. Mem. Am. Soc. Safety Engrs. (chpt. sec. 1976), Am. Indsl. Hygiene Assn., Va. Safety Assn. (chmn. pub. sector 1985). Avocations: running; biking; swimming; golf; fishing. Office: 811 E City Hall Ave Safety Section Norfolk VA 23510

WOOD, WILLIAM MCBRAYER, lawyer; b. Greenville, S.C., Jan. 27, 1942; s. Oliver Gillan and Grace (McBrayer) W.; B.S. in Acctg., U. S.C., 1964, J.D. cum laude, 1972; LL.M. in Estate Planning (scholar), U. Miami, 1980; m. Nancy Cooper, Feb. 17, 1973; children—Margaret, Walter, Lewis. Bar: S.C. 1972, D.C. 1973, U.S. Tax Ct. 1972, U.S. Ct. Claims 1972, U.S. Supreme Ct. 1977, Fla. 1979. Intern, Ct. of Claims sect., tax div. U.S. Dept. Justice, 1971; law clk. to chief judge U.S. Ct. Claims, Washington, 1972-74; ptnr. Edwards Wood, Duggan & Reese, Greer and Greenville, 1974-78; asst. prof. law Cumberland Law Sch., Samford U., Birmingham, Ala., 1978-79; faculty Nat. Inst. Trial Advocacy, N.E. Regional Inst., Hofstra U., 1979, 83, teaching team 5th intensive trial techniques course, 1982; teaching team intensive trial techniques course Emory U., 1982; assoc. Shutts & Bowen, Miami, Fla., 1980-83, ptnr., 1984—. Pres. Piedmont Heritage Fund, Inc., 1975—. Served in USAF, 1965-69; Vietnam. Decorated Air Force Commendation medal; recipient Am. Jurisprudence award in real property and tax I, 1971; winner Grand prize So. Living Mag. travel photo contest, 1969. Mem. ABA, S.C. Bar Assn., Fla. Bar Assn., Greer C. of C. (pres. 1977, Outstanding Leadership award 1976), Greater Greenville C. of C. (dir. 1977), Order Wig and Robe, Estate Planning Council South Fla., Omicron Delta Kappa. Episcopalian. Clubs: Masons, Shriners. Office: Shutts & Bowen Attys 1500 Edward Ball Bldg Miami FL 33131

WOODALL, CHARLES DANIEL, elec. engr.; b. Jersey City, Dec. 9, 1940; s. Charles William and Mary Ellen (Laverty) W.; Asso. Sci., Newark Coll. Engring., 1961. Engring. asso. Western Electric Co., Newark, 1961-66, Columbus, Ohio, 1966, Newark, 1966-72; staff asst. New Eng. Telephone Co., Boston, 1972-74; engr. So. Bell Telephone Co., Ft. Lauderdale, Fla., 1974—. Democrat. Roman Catholic. Clubs: PPC Users (Santa Ana, Calif.); Whale and Porpoise (Ft. Lauderdale). Home: 777 S Federal Hwy Pompano Beach FL 33062 Office: 6451 N Federal Hwy Fort Lauderdale FL 33308

WOODALL, LOWERY A., hospital administrator; b. Lincoln County, Miss., June 10, 1929; s. Clem and Ruth (Smith) W.; children—Linda Woodall Sullivan, Lowery A., Margaret Michelle. B.S., U. So. Miss., 1951; postgrad. Baylor U., 1956, U. Chgo., 1959. Bus. mgr. Miss. Bapt. Hosp., Jackson, 1953-56, adminstrv. asst., 1956-58, asst. adminstr., 1958-62; exec. dir. Forrest Gen. Hosp., Hattiesburg, Miss., 1962—; dir. Blue Cross/Blue Shield, Jackson, 1975—, Hattiesburg Community Blood Ctr.; pres., dir. AAA Ambulance Service, Inc., 1967—; past chmn. Southeastern Hosp. Conf. 11-state, 1981-82, Miss. Hosp. Assn., Jackson, 1970-71. Bd. dirs. Indsl. Park Commn., Hattiesburg, 1981—; mem. Forrest County Indsl. Bd., Hattiesburg, 1972—, pres. 1972-73. Named Exec. of Yr., Sales and Mktg. Assn., 1977, Profl. Secs. Internat., 1981; Hub award Community Leaders, 1981; Liberty award South Central Miss. Bar Assn., 1982. Fellow Am. Coll. Hosp. Adminstrs. Baptist. Lodge: Rotary (pres. 1978-79). Home: One Bristol Ln Hattiesburg MS 39401 Office: Forrest Gen Hosp South 28th Ave Hattiesburg MS 39401

WOODALL, ROGER WAYNE, lawyer; b. Gulfport, Miss., May 16, 1956; s. Robert Ellzey and Vanga Elizabeth (Lassabe) W.; m. Shirley Dianne Jackson, Nov. 22, 1979. B.B.A. in Accountancy, U. Miss., 1978, J.D., 1981. Bar: Miss. 1981, U.S. Dist. Ct. (no. dist.) Miss. 1981. Contract adminstr. Pan Am. World Airways, Inc., Miss., 1981—; dir. Moonlit Knights Corp., Gulfport, 1981—, McCleave & Woodall, P.A., Gulfport, 1981—. Active U.S. Jaycees, Gulfport, 1981. Recipient Silver Snoopy award NASA, 1984. Mem. Am. Assn. Trial Lawyers, Harrison County Bar Assn., Phi Alpha Delta. Republican. Baptist. Clubs: Gulfport Yacht; Broadwater Country (Biloxi, Miss.). Home: 2426 Collins Blvd Gulfport MS 39501 Office: Pan Am World Airways Inc Contracts and Legal Dept NSTL MS 39529

WOODALL, RONALD STEVEN, office supply executive; b. Gadsden, Ala., Sept. 19, 1953; s. Ronald Grady and Mary Ellen (Hartzog) W.; B.A. in Bus. Mgmt. and History, Houston Baptist U., 1975, M.B.A., 1982; m. Rebecca Kay Waldrep, Nov. 18, 1972 (div.); children—Jennifer Noel, Ronald Steven, Amy Michelle, Robert Brandon, Angela Kay. Sales clk. Foley's Dept. Store, Houston, 1970-72; with Ron's Krispy Fried Chicken, Houston, 1972-83, exec. v.p., 1977-83, also dir.; pres. Reliant Bus. Products, Inc., 1984—. Pres. Thunderbird West Homeowners Assn., 1978; mem. mktg. and distbrv. edn. adv. bd. Houston Ind. Sch. Dist., 1978-80; trustee Houston Bapt. U., 1986—; mem. adv. com. PACE, 1977, Missouri City, Tex. Mem. Confederate Air Force (life, fin. officer Gulf Coast wing 1985—), SCV. Baptist. Home: 9607 Stroud Houston TX 77036

WOODARD, FRANCIS MERLEY, sociology educator, research and training consultant; b. Richfield, Utah, Mar. 20, 1942; s. Clyde and Harriet (Yates) W.; m. Sheila Ragozzine, Dec. 26, 1969; children—Corby Jo, Joseph, Jared. B.S., Brigham Young U., 1967, M.S., 1970, Ph.D., 1981. Adminstr. juvenile ct. Utah Juvenile Ct., Salt Lake City and Provo, 1967-76; dir. criminal justice Mountland Assn. Govts., Provo, 1978-79; area dir. aging Mountainland Assn. Govts., Provo, 1979-81; prof. U. Wis., Menomonie, 1981-82; prof. dept. sociology Cameron U., Lawton, Okla., 1982—, chmn., 1985—; research cons. State of Utah, 1978; youth research specialist Mountainland Assn. Govts., 1977; research cons. Dept. Aging, Menomonie, 1981-82; tng. cons. Job Corps, Indiahoma, Okla., 1985—. Contbr. articles to profl. jours. Mem. Nat. Council on Family Relations (chmn. family law focus group), Western Social Sci. Assn. (chmn. sociology sect.), Am. Sociol. Assn., Acad. Criminal Justice Scis. Mem. Ch. of Jesus Christ of Latter-day Saints. Avocations: golfing; cross country skiing; travel. Home: 7619 NW Taylor Ave Lawton OK 73505 Office: Cameron U Dept Sociology Lawton OK 73505

WOODARD, JOSEPH ANDERSON, dentist; b. Nashville, Oct. 23, 1949; s. James Edward and Dorothy Louise (Carter) W.; m. Kathleen Noelle Gunn, Aug. 28, 1975 (div. 1985); children—Aaron Benjamin, Andrea Kathleen. B.A., Lambuth Coll., 1971; D.D.S., U. Tenn., 1974. Resident in gen. dentistry VA Hosp., Palo Alto, Calif., 1975, staff dentist, 1976; pvt. practice gen. dentistry, Columbia, Tenn., 1977—. Mem. adminstrn. bd. 1st United Meth. Ch., 1984-85; bd. dirs. United Givers Fund, Columbia, 1981-84. Mem. ADA, Tenn. Dental Assn., 6th Dist. Dental Soc. (pres. 1981-82), Columbia C. of C. Democrat. Lodge: Kiwanis. Avocations: hunting; fishing; gardening. Home: Country Club Ln Columbia TN 38401 Office: 502 N Garden Columbia TN 38401

WOODARD, ROBERT E., bishop. Bishop, Ch. of God in Christ, S.E. Tex., Houston. Office: Church of God in Christ 7722 Mapletree St Houston TX 77088*

WOODBERRY, PAUL FRANCIS, corp. exec.; b. Boston, Dec. 23, 1927; s. Ronald S. and Elsie E. (Carney) W.; m. Margery Ann Brennan, May 7, 1955; children—Laura, Seth, Lesley, Sarah, Strugis. B.A., Dartmouth Coll., 1949, M.B.A., 1950. Group exec. W.R. Grace & Co., N.Y.C., 1955-69; pres. Winston Industries, Birmingham, Ala., 1969-70; v.p. Alleghany Corp., N.Y.C., 1970-76, now dir.; exec. v.p. Centex Corp., Dallas, 1976—; dir. Boothe Fin. Corp. Served to 1st lt. USAF, 1951-55. Decorated Air medal, Commendation medal. Republican. Roman Catholic. Clubs: Bent Tree Country (Dallas); University (N.Y.C.). Office: 4600 Republic Nat Bank Tower Dallas TX 75201

WOODBERRY, SETH MICHAEL, exploration geologist; b. N.Y.C., Aug. 24, 1958; s. Paul Francis and Margaret Ann (Brennan) W. B.A., Dartmouth Coll., 1981. Geol. asst. K.M. McClain, ind. operator, Ft. Worth, 1981-82; exploration geologist Bettis, Boyle and Stovall, Graham, Tex., 1982—. Mem. N. Tex. Oil and Gas Assn., Graham Geol. Soc. (treas. 1983-84, sec. 1984-85), Am. Assn. Petroleum Geologists, N. Tex. Geol. Soc. Republican. Roman Catholic. Clubs: Dartmouth of Dallas, Dallas Boardwalk Lacrosse. Home: 1405 Green St Graham TX 76096

WOODBURN, STEPHEN KENT, broadcasting company executive; b. Monterey Park, Calif., Mar. 2, 1955; s. Edmund Morrison and Marion Ethel (Hefton) W.; m. Stasia Kelly, Mar. 17, 1984. A.A., West Valley Jr. Coll., Saratoga, Calif., 1975. Disc jockey, newscaster KONG AM/FM, Visalia, Calif., 1975-76; talk show host, programmer KBOS-FM, Tulare, Calif., 1976-77; disc jockey KYNO-FM, Fresno, 1977; news dir. KMED-AM, Medford, Oreg., 1979-80; regional mgr. Metro Traffic Control Networks, Atlanta, 1981—; voice tchr. Seitz Agy., Atlanta, 1983-84; actor Theatre in Square, Centerstage North. Named Best Actor in Musical, Theatre in Square, Marietta, Ga., 1983. Mem. Ga. Assn. Broadcasters. Democrat. Office: Met Traffic Control/Met Networks 1100 Spring St Suite 780 Atlanta GA 30309

WOODBURY, MAX ATKIN, mathematician, educator; b. St. George, Utah, Apr. 30, 1917; s. Angus Munn and Grace (Atkin) W.; m. Lida Gottsch, May 30, 1947; children—Carol, Max, Christopher, Gregory. B.A., U. Utah, 1939; M.S., U. Mich., 1940, Ph.D., 1948; M.P.H., U. N.C., 1977. Instr. math. U. Mich., Ann Arbor, 1947-49, Princeton U., 1949-52; research assoc. econs. and math. U. Pa., assoc. prof., 1952-54; prin. investigator logistics research project George Washington U., Washington, 1954-56; prof. NYU, N.Y.C., 1956-65; prof. biomath. Duke U., Durham, N.C., 1966—; cons. govt. agys., corps.; pres. Inst. Biomed. Computing Research, N.Y.C.; ptnr. Brown, Woodbury, Nemerever & Henry, N.Y.C. Served with USAAF, 1941-46. Fellow Inst. Math. Stats., Am. Statis. Assn., AAAS. Mormon. Contbg. author profl. jours. Home: 4008 Bristol Rd Durham NC 27707 Office: Duke Medical Ctr PO Box 3200 Durham NC 27710

WOODBY, PAUL TURNER, health care executive, pharmaceutical consultant; b. Bristol, Tenn., Apr. 1, 1945; s. Claude William and Julia Anne (Eller) W.; m. Rebecca Ann Myers, Jan. 10, 1965 (div. Oct. 1972); children—Sara Deanna, Richard Lee, Zandria Lynn; m. 2d, Cheryl Lynn Duty, July 15, 1974; children—Paul Turner II, Brian Turner. B.A. in Chemistry, King Coll., Bristol, 1967; M.Organic Chemistry, East Tenn. State U., 1971; Ph.D. in Biochemistry, U. Tenn., 1973. Tech. adviser process improvement Tenn. Eastman Co., Kingsport, 1967-69; cardiovascular researcher, clin. assoc. E.R. Squibb & Sons, New Brunswick, N.J., 1969-72; spl. med. adviser Ives Labs., Atlanta, 1972-78; spl. rep. Astra Pharm. Products, Inc., Greensboro, N.C., 1974-78; clin. assoc. Am. Critical Care, Virginia Beach, Va., 1978—; chmn. Woodby & Spradlin Enterprises, Inc., Virginia Beach; pharm. cons. med. schs. Mem. Republican Presdl. Task Force, Rep. Senatorial Com. Roman Catholic. Lodge: Lions.

WOODDELL, MICHAEL STEWART, orthodontist, temporomandibular disease specialist; b. Grafton, W.Va., Jan. 16, 1948; s. Lyle Stewart and JoAnn (Welsh) W.; m. Patricia Anne Lynch, Aug. 13, 1977. B.A., Ohio State U., 1968, D.D.S., 1972; M.S. in Orthodontics, Washington U., St. Louis, 1976; also continuing edn. Lic. dentist, Fla. Practice dentistry and dental research specializing in orthodontics, dentofacial orthopedics and temporomandibular joint disease, St. Petersburg, Clearwater, and Tampa, Fla., 1976—; pres. Hornblower Enterprises, Inc.; bd. dirs. Arthritis Found., St. Petersburg, 1985—; lectr. for local socs., study groups. Served to capt. Dental Corps, USAF, 1972-74. Health Professions scholar Ohio State U. Sch. Dental Medicine, 1968-72. Mem. ADA, Am. Assn. Orthodontists, Upper Pinellas Dental Assn., F.A.C.E. Found., Royal Soc. Medicine, Am. Assn. Functional Orthodontists, Fla. Gulf Coast Art Soc., Fla. Soc. Marine Artists, U.S. C. of C., Mystic Seaport Soc., Friends of English Harbour, Alpha Epsilon Delta, Phi Alpha Theta. Lodge: Rotary. Avocations: sailing; painting (marine subjects); tennis. Office: 4338 1st St N Saint Petersburg FL 33703

WOODDY, L. D., JR., petroleum company executive; married. B.S. in Mech. Engring., Rice U., 1948. Formerly with Humble Oil and Refining Co.; pres., chief exec. officer Exxon Pipeline Co. Inc., dir. Office: Exxon Pipeline Co Inc 800 Bell Box 2220 Houston TX 77001*

WOODEN, PHYLLIS REYNOLDS, public health nutritionist, county program administrator; b. Johnson City, Tenn., Jan. 25, 1927; d. Paul DeLeon and Elizabeth (Lewis) Reynolds; m. Martin E. Wooden, Apr. 4, 1964; 1 child, Andrea Eleanor. B.S. Instl. Mgmt., James Madison U., 1949; dietitic intern Duke U., 1950; M.S. in Nutrition and Biochemistry, Ohio State U., 1964. Clin. dietitian George Washington U. Hosp., 1950-52; clin. dietitian Med. Coll. Va., Richmond, 1952-56, adminstrv. asst. to chief dietitian, 1961-63; dietitian Woman's Coll. U. N.C., Greensboro, 1956-57; asst. chief dietitian Yale-New Haven Med. Ctr., 1957-61; dietary cons., Boston, 1970-73; instr. foods and nutrition Tech. Coll. Alamance, Burlington, N.C., 1975-77; coordinator Older Ams. project Bd. Edn., Caswell County, N.C., 1976-78; nutritionist Dist. Health Dept., Caswell and Person Counties, N.C., 1978-79; dir. Women, Infant Children Services, Caswell-Person-Lee Health Dist., 1979— dir. nutrition, 1984—. Mem. Am. Dietetic Assn., Soc. Nutrition Edn., N.C. Dietetic Assn., N.C. Pub. Health Assn. Baptist. Avocation: collecting antiques.

WOODERSON, JAMES MICHAEL, lawyer, educator; b. Jasper, Tex., Oct. 10, 1944; s. Robert Clyde and Mary Virginia (Ashley) W.; m. Charlotte Loving, Nov. 23, 1968; children—Robert Clyde, Jennifer Kate. B.A., U. Southwestern La., 1967, M.A., 1985; A.A., Ins. Inst. Am., 1972; J.D., La. State U., 1975. Bar: La. 1975, U.S. Dist. Ct. (we. dist.) La. 1977, U.S. Dist. Ct. (ea. dist.) La. 1979. Claims rep. Aetna Life & Casualty Co., New Orleans, 1968-72; claims adjuster Pat Brown Claims Service, Baton Rouge, La., also spl. dep. East Baton Rouge (La) Parish Sheriff's Office, part-time 1972-75; sole practice, Lafayette, La., 1975—; asst. city atty. Lafayette, 1979-81; atty. Lafayette Parish Sch. Bd., 1981—. Scoutmaster Evangeline Area council Boy Scouts Am., 1979-82; candidate Lafayette Parish Police Jury, 1979, Lafayette Parish Sch. Bd., 1980. Served with USMCR, 1962-77. Mem. ABA, La. Bar Assn., Lafayette Parish Bar Assn., Nat. Sch. Bd. Assn. Legal Advisers. Republican. Episcopalian. Office: PO Box 53516 Lafayette LA 70505

WOODHOUSE, JOHN FREDERICK, food distribution executive; b. Wilmington, Del., Nov. 30, 1930; s. John Crawford and Anna (Houth) W.; B.A., Wesleyan U., 1953; M.B.A., Harvard U., 1955; m. Marilyn Ruth Morrow, June 18, 1955; children—John Crawford II, Marjorie Ann. Bus. devel. officer Canadian Imperial Bank of Commerce, Toronto, Ont., 1955-59; various fin. positions Ford Motor Co., Dearborn, Mich., 1959-64; various fin. positions Copper Industries, Inc., Mount Vernon, Ohio, 1964-67, treas., Houston, 1967-69; treas. Crescent-Niagara Corp., Buffalo, 1968-69; fin. v.p. Sysco Corp., Houston, 1969-72, pres., 1972—, chief exec., 1983—, also dir., mem. exec. com.; dir., mem. exec. com. Republic Bank Houston; dir. Barclays Am. Corp. Chmn., Mich. 16th dist. Republican Club, 1962-64. Treas., Cooper Industries Found., 1967-69; trustee Wesleyan U. Mem. Houston Soc. Fin. Analysts, Fin. Execs. Inst., Sigma Chi. Presbyn. (ruling elder). Clubs: Houston, West Side Tennis, Houstonian. Home: 650 Ramblewood Rd Houston TX 77079 Office: 1177 West Loops Houston TX 77027

WOODHULL, DELIGHT, corporate safety official; b. Bellefonte, Pa., Feb. 9, 1952; d. James Edward and Janice (Shively) W.; m. Thomas E. Maxson, July 31, 1978 (div. 1984). B.S., Coll. William and Mary, 1974; M.P.H., U. Mass., 1976. Cert. indsl. hygienist and safety profl. Indsl. hygienist Tenn. Dept. Labor, Nashville, 1977-78, N.C. Dept. Human Resources, Raleigh, 1978-80; indsl. hygienist Scientific-Atlanta, 1980-83, corp. safety mgr., 1983—. Chmn. Fellowship Council, Unitarian Universalist Congregation of Atlanta, 1985. Mem. Am. Indsl. Hygiene Assn. (pres. Ga. sect. 1984-85), Am. Soc. Safety Engrs., Nat. Safety Mgmt. Soc. Democrat. Avocations: music; textile arts; cat breeding; hiking; tennis. Home: 635 Serramonte Dr Marietta GA 30067 Office: Scientific-Atlanta PO Box 105600 Atlanta GA 30348

WOODHURST, ROBERT STANFORD, JR., architect; b. Abbeville, S.C., July 12, 1921; s. Robert Stanford and Eva (Ferguson) W.; m. Dorothy Ann Carwile, Aug. 4, 1945; 1 son, Robert Stanford III. B.S. in Architecture, Clemson U., 1942. Registered architect, S.C., Ga. Designer Harold Woodward, Architect, Spartanburg, S.C., 1946-47; assoc. architect F. Arthur Hazard, Architect, Augusta, Ga., 1947-54; ptnr. Woodhurst & O'Brien, Architects, Augusta, 1954-83; ptnr. Woodhurst Partnership, 1983—; v.p. Southeastern Architects and Engrs., Inc., Augusta, 1964—; lectr. history architecture N. Augusta Community Coll.; mem. nat. exam. com. Nat. Council Archtl. Regis. Bds.; pres. Ga. State Bd. Architects. Chmn. Augusta-Richmond County Planning Commn., 1966-68; trustee Hist. Augusta, Inc.; active Mayor's Adv. Com., 1965-68; mem. Augusta Bldg. Code Bd. Appeals, 1955-58. Served to capt. U.S. Army, 1942-45. Decorated Air medal with 7 oak leaf clusters; Croix de Guerre avec palms (France). Mem. AIA (Bronze medal 1942), Ga. Assn. AIA (Bronze medal 1977), Soc. Archtl. Historians, Nat. Council Archtl. Registration Bds. Democrat. Baptist. Clubs: Augusta Country, Pinnacle, So. Men's. Lodge: Elks. Designed and built: 1st Baptist Ch., Augusta, Univ. Hosp. Med. Ctr., Augusta, Peabody Apts. and Irvin Towers, Augusta, W. Lake Country Club, Augusta, Med. Library, Med. Coll. Ga., Library Voorhees Coll., Denmark, S.C., Ambulatory Care Ctr., Univ. Hosp., Augusta, Married Students Apartments, Med. Coll. Ga., Covenant Presbyn. Ch., Augusta, Student Ctr. Voorhees Coll., Pres.' Home Voorhees Coll., others. Home: 810 Dogwood Ln Augusta GA 30909 Office: Woodhurst Partnership 607 15th St PO Box 1435 Augusta GA 30903

WOODIN, MARTIN DWIGHT, retired university president; b. Sicily Island, La., July 7, 1915; s. Dwight E. and Gladys Ann (Martin) W.; B.S., La. State U., 1936; M.S., Cornell U., 1939, Ph.D., 1941; D.H.L. (hon.), U. New Orleans, 1985; m. Virginia Johnson, Sept. 7, 1939 (dec.); children—Rebecca Woodin Johnson, Pamela Woodin Fry, Linda Woodin Middleton; m. Elisabeth Wachalik, Oct. 5, 1968. Mem. faculty La. State U., 1941-85, prof. agrl. econs., head dept., 1956-59, dir. resident instruction Coll. Agr., 1959-60, dean at Alexandria, La., 1960-62, exec. v.p. at Baton Rouge, 1962-72, pres. univ. system, 1972-85; mem. pres.'s council Am. Assn. State Univs., 1972-85; pres. Council So. Univs., 1975-76. Dep. dir. La. CD Agy., 1961-72; v.p., exec. com. United Givers Baton Rouge, 1962-63; mem. Arts and Humanities Council Greater Baton Rouge, 1974-85; mem. La. Constn. Rev. Commn.; sec. La. State U. Found., 1962-72; mem. council trustees Gulf South Research Inst., 1972—. Served with USNR, 1942-46; PTO. Mem. Am. Agr. Econ. Assn., So. Assn. Land Grant Colls. and State Univs. (pres. 1977-78, 83-84), Am. Mktg. Assn., Am. Legion (post comdr.), Internat. House New Orleans, Sigma Xi, Omicron Delta Kappa, Phi Kappa Phi, Beta Gamma Sigma, Phi Eta Sigma, Gamma Sigma Delta, Alpha Zeta, Pi Gamma Mu. Presbyterian. Clubs: Elks, Rotary. Author articles in field. Home: 234 Court Dr Baton Rouge LA 70810

WOODLEY, JOHN PAUL, lawyer; b. Shreveport, La., July 27, 1926; s. John Earnest and Katherine (Kelly) W.; m. Hazel Eugenia Iles, May 5, 1951; children—John Paul, Anita, Joseph, Thomas, David, Cecilia, Keith. J.D., La. State U., 1948. Bar: La. 1948. Sole practice law, Shreveport, 1948—. Mem. La. Bar Assn., Shreveport Bar Assn., Assn. Trial Lawyers Am., Phi Delta Phi, Kappa Sigma. Republican. Roman Catholic. Club: Petroleum. Lodge: Kiwanis. Office: 1019 Slattery Bldg Shreveport LA 71101

WOODROE, STEPHEN CLARK, lawyer; b. Charleston, W.Va., Oct. 28, 1940; s. William May and Isabel Tomasa (Clark); m. Marla Kathleen Reid, Oct. 2, 1976. B.A. magna cum laude, Harvard Coll., 1963; J.D., U. Va., 1969. Bar: W.Va. 1969. Assoc. Campbell, Love, Woodroe & Kizer, Charleston, 1969-74, ptnr., 1974-76; ptnr. Love, Wise, Robinson & Woodroe, Charleston, 1976-80; asst. atty. gen. State of W.Va., Charleston, 1980—. Mem. W.Va. State Bar, W.Va. Bar Assn., Kanawha County Bar Assn., ABA, Am. Arbitration Assn., Am. Judicature Soc., Phi Delta Phi. Democrat. Episcopalian. Club: Famrington Country (Charlottesville). Lodge: Elks. Home: 513 Linden Rd Charleston WV 25314 Office: E-26 State Capitol Bldg Charleston WV 25305

WOODRUFF, EDWIN CUSHING, geophysicist; b. N.Y.C., July 22, 1926; s. George Percy and Margaret (Neville) W.; student Princeton U., 1947-50; B.S. in Geology, Marietta Coll., 1953; M.A. (grad. asst.), U. Mo., 1954; 1 child, Anne Elizabeth. With Geophys. Service, Inc., Merced, Calif., 1953; seismologist Shell Oil Co., Hobbs, N.Mex. and Midland, Tex., 1954-59, geophysicist, party chief. 1959-65, sr. geophysicist, Midland, 1969-71; sr. geophysicist Basin Geophys. Inc., Midland, 1971-73; chief geophysicist Am. Quasar Petroleum Co., Midland, 1973-82, cons. geophysicist, 1982—; instr. Permian Basin Grad. Center, Midland, 1972—; pres. Lee chpt. Am. Field Service, Midland, 1966-68, liaison v.p., 1969-70. Served with USN, 1944-46. Mem. Am. Assn. Petroleum Geologists, West Tex. Geol. Soc. (chmn. geothermal survey 1969-72), Soc. Exploration Geophysicists, Oklahoma City Geophys. Soc., Houston, Denver, Southeastern, Permian Basin (membership chmn. 1968-70, pres. 1981-82) geophys. socs., Gamma Alpha, Delta Upsilon. Republican. Unitarian. Club: Denver Petroleum. Home: PO Box 4443 Midland TX 79704 Office: 1404 Wilco Bldg Midland TX 79701

WOODRUFF, GEORGE ALFRED, dentist; b. Orlando, Fla., Dec. 2, 1941; s. George Benjamin and Doris Nell (Green) W.; m. Thera Lynn Brackney, Aug. 1, 1964; children—Richard, Randall. Student, Fla. State U., 1959-62; D.D.S., Emory U., 1966. Lic. dentist, Fla. Gen. practice dentistry, Titusville, Fla., 1967—. Bd. dirs. Am. Cancer Soc., 1973—. Mem. Brevard County Dental Assn. (bd. dirs. 1968—), Acad. Gen. Dentistry (bd. dirs. 1974—), ADA (bd. dirs. 1967—). Republican. Baptist. Avocations: Golf; waterskiing; bicycling. Home: 1980 Londontown Ln Titusville FL 32796 Office: 1625 S Washington Titusville FL 32780

WOODRUFF, JUDSON SAGE, lawyer; b. Birmingham, Ala., May 18, 1925; s. Ernest Wrigley and Margaret (Martin) W.; B.S. in Physics, U. Okla., 1948, LL.B., 1950; m. Ruth Eleanor Dick, June 16, 1949 (div.) 1 dau., Jennifer; m. 2d, Millicent Imel Coats, Oct. 25, 1974. Admitted to Okla. bar, 1950, Ohio Bar 1960; with CIA, Washington, 1951-52; asst. econ. attache Fgn. Service, Dept. State, Washington, 1951-52, Tokyo, Japan, 1952-54, Seoul, Korea, 1955; law clk. U.S. Dist. Ct. for Eastern Dist. Okla., Muskogee, 1955-56; atty. Marathon Oil Co., Tulsa, 1956-60, Findlay, Ohio, 1960-62, Geneva, Switzerland, 1962-63, London, Eng., 1962-63, Tripoli, Libya, 1962-63; ptnr. firm McAfee & Taft, Oklahoma City, 1964—; instr. Tulsa U. Law Sch., 1958-60; assoc. bar examiner State of Okla., 1967-69; chmn. Gov.'s Com. Ad Valorem Taxation, 1967-68; mem. Okla. Alcoholic Beverage Control Bd., 1968-69, Okla. Hwy. Commn., 1969-71. Served to lt. (j.g.) USNR, 1942-46. Sterling fellow, Yale U., 1950-51. Mem. Order of Coif, Sigma Pi Sigma, Phi Delta Phi. Republican. Episcopalian. (sr. warden 1968-70). Okla. editor Oil & Gas Reporter, Southwestern Legal Found., 1964—; contbr. articles on law to profl. jours. Home: 3110 Harvey Pkwy Oklahoma City OK 73118 Office: 100 Park Ave Oklahoma City OK 73102

WOODRUFF, MARTHA JOYCE, temporary nursing service executive; b. Unadilla, Ga., Jan. 3, 1941; d. Metz Loy and Helen (McCorvey) Woodruff. B.A., Shorter Coll., 1963; M.A., U. Tenn.-Knoxville, 1972. Tchr., Albany High Sch. (Ga.), 1963-69; instr. U. Tenn.-Knoxville, 1970-72; asst. prof. Valdosta State Coll. (Ga.), 1972-76; coordinator Staff Builders, Atlanta, 1976-78; pres., owner Med. Personnel Pool, Knoxville, 1978—; owner Personnel Pool of Knoxville, 1985—; mem., adviser Owners Adv. Council, Personnel Pool of Am., Ft. Lauderdale, Fla., 1980-82. Mem. Nat. League for Nursing, Franchise Owners Assn., Knoxville C. of C. (com. for cost containment 1982—), Blount County C. of C. (retirement com. 1983, mem. indsl. relations com. 1983). Republican. Methodist.

WOODRUFF, ROBERT FISHER, safety engineer, consultant motorcycle safety, retired army officer; b. Hamilton, Ohio, May 2, 1941; s. R. Fred and Helen (Fisher) W.; m. Marie Moody, Dec. 28, 1971; 1 child, Jonathan Hart. B.S., Ohio State U., 1973. Commd. 2d lt. U.S. Army, 1964, advanced through grades to maj., 1984; chief edn. U.S. Army Safety Ctr., Ft. Rucker, Ala., 1980-82, chief evaluation div., 1982-83, chief tng. mgmt., 1983-84, ret., 1984; safety cons. Wausau Ins. Co., Orlando, Fla., 1984-85; safety engr. Lockheed-Ga. Co., Marietta, Ga., 1985—; instr. Motorcycle Safety Found., Costa Mesa, Calif., 1980-81, chief instr., 1981—. Contbr. articles on motorcycle safety to various Army publs. Decorated Bronze Star medal (3); recipient John Ruether Meml. award Sports Car Club Am., 1980; John Harley Meml. award Motorcycle Safety Found., 1983; gold medal U.S. Army Aviation Ctr., 1984. Mem. Am. Soc. Safety Engrs. Democrat. Episcopalian. Avocation: motorcycling. Home: 31 Gant Quarter Terr Marietta GA 30067 Office: Lockheed-Ga 86 S Cobb Dr Marietta GA 30063

WOODRUFF, WILLIAM RUSSELL, engineer, professional public speaker; b. N.Y.C., Nov. 10, 1920; s. Alfred Louis and Dora Mary (Glenn) W.; m. Robbie Lee Baker, Sept. 9, 1945; children—Holly, Russell. B.S., Lehigh U., 1942; postgrad. U. Va., 1968-69. Engr., mgr. E.I. duPont de Nemours & Co., Ind., Okla., Kans., Del. and Va., 1942-78. Co-author: Professionals At Their Best, 1978. Mem. Am. Soc. Tng. and Devel. (bd. dirs. Piedmont chpt. 1977-82), Nat. Speakers Assn. (bd. dirs. 1980—). Methodist. Clubs: Impresarios (Martinsville, Va.); Martinsville Toastmasters (pres. 1968-69). Avocation: philately. Home: 1126 Cherokee Trail Martinsville VA 24112

WOODRUM, PATRICIA ANN, library administrator; b. Hutchinson, Kans., Oct. 11, 1941; d. Donald S. and Ruby Pauline (Shuman) Hoffman; m. Clayton Eugene Woodrum, Mar. 31, 1962; 1 son, Clayton Eugene. B.A., Kans. State U., 1963; M.L.S., U. Okla., 1966. Br. librarian Tulsa City County Library, 1964-65, asst. to chief of brs., 1965, head brs., 1965-66, head reference, 1966-67, chief extension, 1967-70, chief pub. services, 1970-73, asst. dir., 1973-76, dir., 1976—. Trustee Univ. Center at Tulsa; mem. adv. council Health Systems; bd. dirs. Tulsa Area Council on Aging. Mem. ALA, Okla. Library Assn. (Disting. Librarian award 1982), Tulsa C. of C. Republican. Episcopalian. Contbr. articles to Library Jour. and Jour. Ednl. Media Sci.

WOODS, BARRY ALAN, lawyer; b. N.Y.C., Nov. 21, 1942; s. Harry E. and Lillian (Breath) W.; B.S., N.Y. U., 1965, LL.M. in Taxation, 1969; J.D., Bklyn. Law Sch., 1968; m. Elsie Payne, Dec. 1980; children—Meredith Rose, Pamela Brett, B. Morgan. Bar: N.Y. 1968, U.S. Tax Ct. 1969, P.R. 1970, U.S. Dist. Ct. P.R. 1971; Partner firm Baker & Woods, Santurce, P.R., 1970-76; mng. partner Woods & Woods, Hato Rey, P.R., 1976-81, Woods Rosenbaum Luckeroth & Perez-Gonzalez, 1981—; spl. cons. Tax Mgmt., Inc.; mem. Bur. Nat. Affairs, Adv. Bd. Internat. Taxation. Mem. Am. Soc. Internat. Law, Am. Bar Assn., Colegio de Abogados de P.R. Clubs: Caribe Hilton Swimming and Tennis, Pan Am. Gun, Bankers of P.R., N.Y. U. Author: United States Business Operations in Puerto Rico; Repatriation of Puerto Rico Source Earnings-Implication of Proposed Section 936; other publs. in field. Home: RFD 3 Box 43AA Rio Piedras PR 00928 Office: PO Box 1292 Hato Rey PR 00919

WOODS, HENRY, judge; b. Abbeville, Miss., Mar. 17, 1918; s. Joseph Neal and Mary Jett (Wooldridge) W.; m. Kathleen Mary McCaffrey, Jan. 1, 1943; children—Mary Sue, Thomas Henry, Eileen Anne, James Michael. B.A., U. Ark., 1938, J.D. cum laude, 1940. Bar: Ark. bar 1940. Spl. agt. FBI, 1941-46; mem. firm Alston & Woods, Texarkana, Ark., 1946-48; exec. sec. to Gov. Ark., 1949-53; mem. firm McMath, Leatherman & Woods, Little Rock, 1953-80; U.S. dist. judge Eastern Dist. Ark., 1980—; referee in bankruptcy U.S. Dist. Ct., Texarkana, 1947-48; spl. assoc. justice Ark. Supreme Ct., 1967-74, chmn. com. model jury instrns., 1973-80; chmn. bd. Center Trial and Appellate Advocacy, Hastings Coll. Law, San Francisco, 1975-76; mem. joint cof. com. Am. Bar Assn.-AMA, 1973-78, Ark. Constl. Revision Study Commn., 1967-68. Author treatise comparative fault; Contbr. articles to legal jours. Pres. Young Democrats Ark., 1946-48; mem. Gubernatorial Com. Study Death Penalty, 1971-73. Mem. ABA, Ark. Bar Assn. (pres. 1972-73, Outstanding Lawyer award 1975), Pulaski County Bar Assn., Assn. Trial Lawyers Am. (gov. 1965-67), Ark. Trial Lawyers Assn. (pres. 1965-67), Internat. Acad. Trial Lawyers, Internat. Soc. Barristers, Am. Coll. Trial Lawyers, Am. Bd. Trial Advocates, Phi Alpha Delta. Methodist. Home: 42 Wingate Dr Little Rock AR 72205 Office: PO Box 3683 Little Rock AR 72203

WOODS, JOHN WITHERSPOON, banker; b. Evanston, Ill., Aug. 18, 1931; s. J. Albert and Cornelia (Witherspoon) W.; B.A., U. of South, 1954; m. Loti Moultrie Chisolm, Sept. 5, 1953; children—Loti, Cindy, Corrie. With Chem. Bank, N.Y.C., 1954-69, v.p., head So. div., 1965-69; pres. AmSouth Bank N.A., 1969-72, vice-chmn., 1972-83, chmn., chief exec. officer, 1983—; chmn., pres., chief exec. officer AmSouth Bancorp., 1972-83, chmn. bd., chief exec. officer, 1983—; dir. Avondale Mills, Inc., Sylacauga, Ala., Protective Life Ins. Co., Birmingham, Engel Mortgage Co., Birmingham, Ala. Power Co. Birmingham. Bd. dirs., mem. exec. com. Community Chest-United Way Jefferson County; trustee, So. Research Inst., Birmingham, past pres. Met. Devel. Bd. Birmingham; trustee Tuskegee Inst. Served to 1st lt. USAF, 1955-57. Mem. Modern Banking Assn. (dir.), Assn. Bank Holding Cos. (past chmn.), Birmingham Area C. of C. (past chmn. bd.; pres. 1978), Assn. Res. City Bankers, Ala. Acad. Honor. Office: 1900 5th Ave N PO Box 11007 Birmingham AL 35288

WOODS, PENDLETON, educational administrator, author; b. Ft. Smith, Ark., Dec. 18, 1923; s. John Powell and Mabel (Hon) W.; B.A. in Journalism, U. Ark., 1948; m. Lois Robin Freeman, Apr. 3, 1948; children—Margaret, Paul Pendleton, Nancy. Editor, asst. pub. mgr. Okla. Gas & Electric Co., Oklahoma City, 1948-69; dir. Living Legends of Okla., Okla. Christian Coll., Oklahoma City, 1969-81; projects and promotion dir. Enterprise Square, U.S.A., 1981—. Bd. dirs. Campfire Girls Council, Okla. Jr. Symphony (past pres.), Boy Scout Council, Okla. Found. Epilepsy, Central Park Neighborhood Assn., Zoo Amphitheater of Oklahoma City, Will Rogers Centennial Commn.; past pres. Keep Okla. Beautiful; past pres. Oklahoma City Mental Health Clin.; pub. relations chmn. Oklahoma County chpt. ARC; past chmn. Western Heritage award Nat. Cowboy Hall of Fame; past pres. Variety Health Center; dir. Am. Freedom Council; exec. dir. Oklahoma City Bicentennial Commn.; mem. Okla. Disabilities Council; pres. Lincoln Park Country; chmn. Mus. Unassigned Lands; mem. publicity com. Am. Cancer Soc. Oklahoma County. Served with AUS, World War II and Korean; col., state historian Okla. N.G. Named Outstanding Young Man of Year, Oklahoma City Jr. C. of C., 1953; Silver Beaver award Boy Scouts Am., 1963; also 3 honor medals Freedoms Found. Mem. Soc. Asso. Indsl. Editors (past v.p.), Advt. Fedn. Am. (past dist. dir.), Central Okla. Indsl. Communicators (past pres., hon. life mem.), Okla. Jr. C. of C. (hon. life; past internat. dir.), Okla. Distributive Edn. Clubs (hon. life), Oklahoma City Advt. Club (past pres.), Okla. Zool. Soc., Okla. Geneal. Soc. (past pres.), Okla. Hist. Soc. (publ. editor), Okla. Heritage Assn. (publ. editor), Oklahoma City Beautiful (publ. editor), Oklahoma County Hist. Soc. (dir., pres.), 45th Inf. Div. Assn. (pres., dir.), Mil. Order World Wars (comdr.), Okla. City Hist. Preservation Commn., Sigma Delta Chi, Kappa Sigma (nat. commr. publs., editor). Author: You and Your Company Magazine, 1950; Church of Tomorrow, 1964; Myriad of Sports, 1971; This Was Oklahoma, 1979. Recorded Sounds of Scouting, 1969; Born Grown, 1974 (Western Heritage award Nat. Cowboy Hall Fame); editor: Oklahoma Diamond Jubilee. Home: 541 NW 31st St Oklahoma City OK 73118

WOODS, POWELL, lawyer; b. Ft. Smith, Ark., Jan. 19, 1922; s. John Powell and Mabel Fairfax (Hon) W.; B.A., U. Ark., 1948; LL.B., U. Ark., Little Rock, 1950; m. Lola Lavoy Keener, June 18, 1954; children—Lola Lavoy (Mrs. Steve Walthour), John Powell. Admitted to Ark. bar, 1950; practiced in Ft. Smith, 1950-58; individual practice law, Siloam Springs, 1958—. City atty., Siloam Springs, 1960-62; mcpl. judge, Siloam Springs, 1963-64. Sec.-treas. Siloam Springs Salvation Army, 1962—. Served with AUS, 1943-45. Mem. Am., Ark., Benton County bar assns., Comml. Law League, Nat. Rifle Assn., C. of C., NW Ark. Geol. Soc., Isaac Walton League. Club: Rotary. Home: 411 S Britt St Siloam Springs AR 72761 Office: 207 S Broadway Siloam Springs AR 72761

WOODS, THOMAS JEFFERSON, ophthalmologist; b. Jackson, Miss., June 11, 1948; s. Emmette Abner and Elizabeth (Crofford) W.; m. Laura Lee Jordan, June 15, 1974 (div. 1977); 1 child, Thomas J., II; m. Joyce Minton, Oct. 31, 1979; 1 child, John Andrew. B.A., U. Miss., 1970, M.D., 1974. Diplomate Am. Bd. Ophthalmology. Intern, Bapt. Meml. Hosp., Memphis, 1974-75; resident in ophthalmology U. Tenn. Ctr. Health Scis., Memphis, 1977-80; house physician, emergency dept. coordinator Doctors Hosp. Memphis, 1975-76; practice family medicine with James E. McAfee, M.D., Memphis, 1976; med. examiner Equitable Life Assurance Soc., 1979-80; physician cons. Midsouth Comprehensive Home Health Services Agy., Memphis, 1977-78, Weight Loss Med. Ctr., Memphis, 1977-79; staff physician Orange Mound Community Action Clinic, Memphis, 1979-81; practice ophthalmology Clinch Valley Physicians, Inc., Richlands, Va., 1980-81; pvt. practice ophthalmology, Clinton, N.C., 1981—; research asst. dept. psychology U. Miss., 1968-70, Sch.

Medicine, 1970-73, dept. biochemistry, physiology, biophysics, artificial kidney unit, 1973-74. Contbr. articles to profl. jours. Fellow Am. Acad. Opthalmology, AMA, Contact Lens Assn. Ophthalmologists, Sampson County Med. Soc., N.C. Med. Assn., N.C. Soc. Ophthalmology, Sigma Xi, Alpha Epsilon Delta. Republican. Episcopalian. Lodge: Lions. Avocations: tennis; sports cars. Home: 409 Walking Stick Clinton NC 28338 Office: Thomas JC Woods MD Woodside Profl Bldg Clinton NC 28328

WOODS, WALTER ABNER, marketing executive, educator; b. Lingle, Wyo., Jan. 16, 1915; s. James Abner and Mazeppa (Israel) W.; A.B., U. Wyo., 1937; M.A., Syracuse U., 1942; Ph.D., Columbia U., 1952; student Arts Students League N.Y., 1946, 47; m. Margaret Edmiston, June 16, 1955 (div.); 1 dau., Dana Jeanne. Staff Art Sch., Pratt Inst., 1946-52; asst. dir. Sch. Clin. and Applied Psychology, assoc. prof. Richmond Profl. Inst., 1952-55; v.p., dir. research Nowland & Co., Greenwich, Conn., 1955-61; pres. Cons. in Consumer Research, Inc., Sparta, N.J., 1961-66; pres. Products and Concepts Research, Inc., Sparta, 1967—; pres. Island Matrix, Inc., St. Thomas, V.I., 1967-74; dir. Prognosis S.A., Brussels. County chmn. Ford campaign, Republican party, 1976; county coordinator ind. candidate John Anderson campaign, 1980. Served with USN, 1942-46. Recipient Dist. Mktg. Service award, 1968; Faculty research grantee, 1978, 80, 82. Mem. Am. Psychol. Assn., Acad. Mktg. Sci., Am. Mktg. Assn., Nat. Geneal. Soc., Am. Rifle Assn., AAAS. Author: Consumer Behavior, 1980; editor: Nowland Symposium on Perception Theory, 1959. Home: 389 Smyrna Church Rd Carrollton GA 30117 Office: West Ga Coll Carrollton GA 30118

WOODS, WALTER THOMAS, JR., biologist, educator; b. Nashville, Mar. 13, 1947; s. Walter Thomas and Evelyn Eugenia (Cooper) W.; m. Kathleen Gage Frye, Aug. 23, 1969; children—Thomas Cooper, Kathleen Gage, Helen Frye. B.A., U. of South, 1969; M.A., Appalachian State U., 1971; Ph.D., Bowman Gray Sch. Medicine, Wake Forest U., 1975. NSF trainee Wake Forest U., Winston-Salem, N.C., 1973; Faculty dept. physiology and biophysics Sch. Medicine, U. Ala., Birmingham, 1974—, asst. prof., 1977-83, assoc. prof., 1984—, instr. dept. medicine div. cardiovascular disease, 1976-83, assoc. prof., 1984—, research assoc. Cardiovascular Research and Tng. Ctr., 1974—; cons. in field. U.S. Army Med. Research and Devel. Command grantee, 1983; NIH grantee, 1983. Fellow Am. Heart Assn. Council on Circulation; mem. AAAS, Am. Physiol. Soc. (fellow sect. on heart and circulation), Biophys. Soc., Sigma Xi. Episcopalian. Club: Mountain Brook (Birmingham, Ala.). Contbr. articles in field to sci. publs. Home: PO Box 7662A Birmingham AL 35253 Office: U Ala Univ Sta Birmingham AL 35294

WOODSON, DORIS WALKER, artist, photographer, art educator; b. Richmond, Va., Jan. 13, 1929; children—Bernard R. III, Wayne E., Gerald A., Gregory B. B.A., Xavier U., 1952; M.F.A., Va. Commonwealth U., 1969. Instr. Richard Bland Coll., Petersburg, Va., 1968-69, Va. State U., Petersburg, 1969—; adj. instr. Va. Commonwealth U., 1979-82; vis. artist Va. Mus. Humanities Ctr., Richmond; judge art shows. Recipient numerous awards for painting and photography. Mem. Petersburg Area Art League, Richmond Artists Assn. Roman Catholic. Club: Links (Petersburg). Home: 20007 Roosevelt Ave Colonial Heights VA 23834 Office: 216 C Harris Hall Suite 216 Petersburg VA 23803

WOODWARD, BETTY SHAW, music educator; b. Russellville, Ky., Jan. 15, 1932; d. John Daniel and Martha Margaret (Hutcheson) Shaw; m. James D. Woodward, Aug. 13, 1955; children—Julia Woodward Broyles, James David, Jr. A.A., Va. Intermont Coll., Bristol, 1952; B.Mus., U. Ky., 1954, M.A., 1955. Tchr. elem. music Jefferson County, Louisville, 1955-56; children's choir dir. Vineville Bapt. Ch., Macon, Ga., 1956-59; children's choir dir., supr. First Bapt. Ch., Tulsa, 1959-66; children's choir dir. First Bapt. Ch., Shawnee, Okla., 1966—; mem. music faculty Okla. Bapt. U., Shawnee, 1966—, assoc. prof. music, 1983—; children's choir clinician, 1966—; children's choir cons. Crystal Cathedral, Garden Grove, Calif., 1981-83; curriculum writer Young Musicians, Music Leader mags. Ch. Music Dept., Nashville, 1968—. Author: The Singing Book, 1975, Exploring Music, 1980, Go Out With Joy, 1981, Teaching Harmony and Part Singing, 1982, Leading Younger Children's Choirs, 1985. Mem. Music Educators Nat. Conf., Am. Choral Dirs. Assn., Am. Orff Schulwerk Assn., Okla. Kodaly Educatoro, Hymn Soc. Am., So. Bapt. Ch. Music Conf. Avocations: needlework; gardening; reading. Home: 22 Sequoyah Shawnee OK 74801 Office: Okla Bapt U 500 W University St Shawnee OK 74801

WOODWARD, DAVID LUTHER, lawyer; b. Alexandria, La., Mar. 18, 1942; s. Luther Washburn and Ruby Ellen (Robertson) W.; m. Adeline Myree Peterson, July 12, 1965 (div. 1971); m. 2d, Louisette Marie Forget, Nov. 12, 1973. Student William Carey Coll., 1960-61; B.A., Fla. State U., 1965, J.D., 1969; postgrad. Emory U. Lamar Sch. Law, 1966-67; postgrad. London Sch. Econs. and Polit. Sci., 1981-82; LL.M., U. London, 1982. Bar: Fla. 1969, Okla. 1981, U.S. Supreme Ct. 1973, U.S. Ct. Appeals (5th, 9th, 10th, 11th and Fed. cirs.), U.S. Dist. Ct. (mid. and so. dists.) Fla., U.S. Dist. Ct. (no. and ea. dists.) Okla., U.S. Dist. Ct. (no. dist.) Tex., U.S. Ct. Claims, U.S. Ct. Customs and Patent Appeals, U.S. Ct. Mil. Appeals, U.S. Tax Ct., U.S. Ct. Internat. Trade. Trial atty. gen. regulatory div. Dept. Agr., Washington, 1970; asst. atty. gen. State of Fla., 1971-73; pvt. practice, Tampa, Fla., 1973-80; appellate pub. defender State of Okla., Norman, 1980-81; instr. Coll. Law, U. Okla., Norman, 1980-81; sole practice, Enid, Okla., 1982-84, Brice & Mankoff, Dallas, 1985—; vis. magistrate Crown Ct. of Gloucestershire, Eng., 1972. Contbr. articles to profl. jours. Mem. ABA, Fla. Bar, Okla. Bar Assn., Inter-Am. Bar Assn., Brit. Inst. Internat. and Comparative Law, Assn. Trial Lawyers Am., Phi Mu Alpha Sinfonia, Phi Alpha Delta. Republican. Episcopalian. Home: 4030 Gilbert Ave Dallas TX 75219 Office: Brice & Mankoff 300 Crescent Ct Blvd 7th Floor Dallas TX 75202

WOODWARD, HALBERT OWEN, federal judge; b. Coleman, Tex., Apr. 8, 1918; s. Garland A. and Helen (Halbert) W.; B.B.A., U. Tex., LL.B., 1940; m. Dawn Blair, Sept. 28, 1940; children—Halbert Owen, Garland Benton. Admitted to Tex. bar, 1941; practice in Coleman, 1949-68; chmn. Tex. Hwy. Commn., 1959-68; U.S. dist. judge No. Dist. Tex., 1968—, now chief judge; dir. S.W. State Bank, Brownwood, Tex. Bd. dirs. Overall Meml. Hosp., Coleman. Served with USNR, 1942-45. Mem. Am., Tex. bar assns., Am. Judicature Soc., Beta Theta Pi. Office: C-210 US Courthouse 1205 Texas Ave Lubbock TX 79401*

WOODWARD, HENRY ERNEST, cons. engr.; b. Atlanta, June 27, 1926; s. Henry Thomas and Icie (Green) W.; B.C.E., Ga. Inst. Tech., 1949; student U. Va., 1944; m. Frances Evelyn Puckett, June 13, 1949; children—Scott, Jane, Katherine. Dist. mgr. Worthington Corp., Cin., 1948-56; engring. liaison Trane Co., N.Y.C., 1956-59; mech. contractor Kerby Saunders, Inc. and Alvord & Swift, N.Y.C., 1959-64; prin., chief mech. engr. Tampa Bay Engring., St. Petersburg, Fla., 1964-68; pres. Woodward Air Balance, St. Petersburg, 1968—. Mem. St. Petersburg Planning and Zoning Commn., 1973-75. Named Engr. of Yr., Fla. Engring. Soc., 1972-73, Disting. Service award, 1975. Fellow Fla. Engring. Soc. (pres. 1980-81); mem. Asso. Air Balance Council, Fla. Inst. Cons. Engrs., ASHRAE, Am. Cons. Engrs. Council, Nat. Soc. Profl. Engrs., Fla. Council Engring. Socs. (chmn. 1983-84). Democrat. Mem. United Ch. of Christ. Home: 5165 Dover St NE Saint Petersburg FL 33703 Office: 8720 49th St N Pinellas Park FL 33565

WOODWARD, MARY HARDIN MORRIS, librarian; b. Louisville, Ky., Mar. 18, 1925; d. Benjamin Franklin and Mary Blackiston (Hume) Morris; m. Ernest Woodward II, Mar. 23, 1946; children—Kirk, Frances Woodward Clark, Mary Alan. B.A., U. Louisville, 1967: M.A.L.S., Spalding Coll., 1972. Librarian Ky. Home Sch. for Girls, Louisville, 1969-72; upper sch. librarian Ky. Country Day Sch., Louisville, 1972-75, upper sch. librarian, dept. chmn., 1975-85; ret., 1985. Mem. Fillies Derby Festival Commn., Louisville, 1963-73, Hist. Homes Found., Louisville, 1975—, Speed Mus., Louisville, 1970—; Mem. DAR (John Marshall chpt.), Ky. Hist. Soc., Pi Beta Phi. Republican. Presbyterian. Clubs: Woman's of Louisville.

WOODWARD, RAYMOND LESLIE, exploration geologist, petroleum property evaluator; b. Freeport, Tex., Dec. 19, 1955; s. George Edward and Sammye Gray (Patton) W.; m. Debra Kay Carrico, June 23, 1984. B.S. in Geology cum laude, Baylor U., 1979. Petroleum geologist supr. Marshall Exploration, Inc., Tex., 1979-82; exploration geologist Legacy Petroleum, Inc., Shreveport, La., 1982-83, McMurray Petroleum, Inc., Kilgore, Tex., 1983-84, Clemco, Inc., Tyler, Tex., 1984-85; ind. exploration geologist, Tyler, 1985—, retainer with Worth Petroleum, Inc., Tyler, 1985—; job recruiter, thesis coordinator Marsh Exploration, Inc., 1980-82; cons. in field. Discovering geologist wildcat exploration Carlile & Howell Petroleum & Gas Field, 1982. Mem. East Tex. Geol. Soc., Dallas Geol. Soc., Shreveport Geol. Soc., Am. Assn. Petroleum Geologists, Assn. Engring. Geologists (pres. chpt. 1978-79), U.S. C. of C. Republican. Methodist. Clubs: Tyler Athletic, Shreveport Yacht. Avocations: competitive sailing, wood working on furniture. Home: PO Box 7202 Tyler TX 75711 Office: 623 Fair Found Bldg 121 S Broadway Tyler TX 75702

WOODWORTH, HAROLD CYRIL, physician; b. Wells, Minn., Sept. 23, 1920; s. Harry Clark and Martha Meta (Wiecking) W.; A.B., Dartmouth Coll., 1942; M.D., Harvard U., 1944; Ph.D., Yale U., 1958; m. Evelyn Eileen Mahon, Aug. 17, 1944; children—Richard, Karl. Intern, Mary Hitchcock Hosp., Hanover, N.H., 1944-45; resident internal medicine, White River Junction, Vt., 1947-48; practice family medicine, Bristol, Vt., 1948-52; chief Microbiology Lab., Center Disease Control, USPHS, Atlanta, 1958-68; county health officer Colbert and Lauderdale Counties, Ala., 1968-75; regional health officer N.W. Ala. Regional Health Dept., Tuscumbia, 1975-81; ret., 1981. Served with USN, 1945-46, 52-54. Recipient Physician's Recognition award AMA, 1979-82; Boss of Yr. award Muscle Shoals Bus. and Profl. Women's Assn., 1980; USPHS postdoctoral fellow, 1955-57, Howard Hughes Med. Inst. fellow, 1957-58. Mem. Am. Pub. Health Assn., Ala. Pub. Health Assn., AAAS, Med. Assn. Ala., Lauderdale County Med. Soc. Episcopalian. Club: Civitan (Florence, Ala.). Home: 3808 Chisholm Rd Florence AL 35630

WOODY, JOHN CHARLES, utility manager; b. Miami, Okla., Apr. 16, 1935; s. George W. and Beulah R. (Dent) W.; m. Charlotte Merlene Masters, May 18, 1957; children—Kaime Pettay, Jaime Jon. Assoc. Degree, Northeastern Okla. AYM &., 1955; B.S., Pittsburg State U., 1963, postgrad. Asst. to supt. Miami Utility Dept., Okla., 1963-65, gen. mgr., 1979—; gen. supt. Carthage Water & Electric, Mo., 1965-74; area engr. B.F. Goodrich Co., Miami, 1974-79. Bd. dirs. Municipal Electric Systems of Okla. Served with U.S. Army, to 1961. Recipient Cert. for Heroism, Boy Scouts Am., 1951. Mem. IEEE, Jr. C. of C. Internat. (senator, life mem.). Episcopalian. Home: 1520 Washington Dr Miami OK 74354 Office: 129 5th Ave NW Miami OK 74354

WOODY, WILLIAM PAUL, business and tax cons.; b. San Angelo, Tex., June 8, 1943; s. William M. and Helen (Dickson) W.; B.B.A., U. Okla., Norman, 1966; m. Cynthia S. Gerhardt, Aug. 28, 1965; children—Grant, Lee, Allison. Contract adminstr./negotiator Gen. Electric Co., Schenectady, 1968-72; propr. Gen. Bus. Service, Oklahoma City, 1972—; mem. field faculty SBA, also local ocat.-tech. centers. Served to capt. USAR, 1966-68. Recipient numerous sales awards, also Franny award Internat. Franchise Assn., 1979; Bus. Counselor of Yr. award GBS, Inc., 1980. Mem. Oklahoma City C. of C., Oklahoma City Better Bus. Bur., Exec. Success Club. Republican. Methodist. Home: 4004 NW 57th St Oklahoma City OK 73112 Office: 3205 NW 63d St Oklahoma City OK 73116

WOOLERY, WILLIAM ALAN, osteopathic physician, clinical researcher; b. Ponca City, Okla., July 8, 1952; s. William and Evelyn (Stipp) W. B.S., Central State U., 1974; M.S. (Scholar), U. Okla., 1978; D.O., Okla. Coll. Osteo. Medicine and Surgery, 1982. Registered microbiologist. Grad. Research teaching asst. dept. microbiology U. Okla.-Norman, 1975-78; sr. research assoc. dept. biomembrane research Okla. Med. Research Found., Oklahoma City, 1978-79; mem. faculty div. biol. scis. Oscar Rose Jr. Coll., Midwest City, Okla., part-time 1978-79; mem. faculty div. basic scis. dept. microbiology Okla. Coll. Osteo. Medicine and Surgery, Tulsa, 1980-82; intern Botsford Gen. Hosp., Farmington Hills, Mich., 1982-83; med. dir. Page Clinic, St. Petersburg, Fla., 1983—; cons./collaborator immunology and microbiology Nat. Osteo. Found., 1983—. Okla. Coll. Osteo. Medicine and Surgery Research grantee, 1982; Botsford Gen. Hosp. Research grantee, 1982. Mem. Am. Osteo. Assn., Am. Osteo. Acad. Sports Medicine, Am. Soc. Microbiology, Nat. Osteo. Found. Contbr. articles to profl. jours. Office: 8000 4th St N Saint Petersburg FL 33702

WOOLEY, GARY RICHARD, engineering firm executive; b. New Orleans, Oct. 21, 1946; s. Harold Aloysius and Althea (Herman) W.; B.S., La. State U., 1969, M.S., 1970, Ph.D. (Dissertation fellow 1972), 1972; m. Diana Lynn Picklesimer, Oct. 28, 1967; children—Tanya Jill, Tamara Lynn, Todd Richard. Mechanic, Shell Oil Co., summer 1966; prodn. engr. Chevron Oil Co., summer 1967, constrn. engr., summer 1968; field engr. surface equipment group Humble Oil & Refining Co., La. Offshore Dist., New Orleans. 1969; grad. teaching asst. engring. sci. dept. La. State U., Baton Rouge, 1969-72; sr. research engr. Arctic spl. projects, group leader Prodn. Research Center, Atlantic Richfield Co., Plano, Tex., 1972-78; v.p., dir. Enertech Engring. & Research Co., Houston, 1978—; sec.-treas., dir. Enertech Computing Corp., 1981—. Registered profl. engr., Tex.; NSF trainee, 1969-71. Mem. Soc. Petroleum Engrs.-AIME, ASME (vice chmn. drilling and prodn. com. 1975, chmn. rock mechanics com. 1976, tech. reviewer Applied Mechanics Rev. 1975-80), Sigma Xi, Phi Kappa Phi, Tau Beta Pi, Pi Tau Sigma. Republican. Methodist (ch. adminstrv. bd.). Clubs: Gymnastics Boosters of Houston, Aerobats Boosters (v.p. 1977), Westside Tennis, Lakeside Civic (Houston); Canyon Creek Country (Richardson, Tex.); Lakeside Swim and Tennis (dir. 1983). Contbr. articles to profl. lit. Home: 10911 Tupperlake Dr Houston TX 77042 Office: Enertech Engring & Research Co Suite 1000 5847 San Felipe Houston TX 77057

WOOLF, KENNETH HOWARD, architect; b. N.Y.C., Aug. 19, 1938; s. Howard Walter and Elizabeth Ann (Levy) W.; B.Arch., Cornell U., 1961; m. Elizabeth Adair Rainwater, July 3, 1965; children—Robert Gregg, Susan Adair, Jennifer Adair. Staff architect Look & Morrison, Architects, Pensacola, Fla., 1965-72; pvt. practice architecture, Pensacola, 1972—; instr. architecture Pensacola Jr. Coll., part-time 1967-76. Chmn., Pensacola Archtl. Rev. Bd., 1970-81; mem. Gulf Breeze Planning Bd., 1976-78. Served with USN, 1961-65. Named Jaycee of Yr., 1970. Mem. AIA (sec. N.W. Fla. chpt. 1976-77, 1977-78, pres. N.W. Fla. 1979-81; Comml. Design Honor award 1975). Unitarian. Club: Rotary. Prin. works include: Coca-Cola Bottling Co. Plant, Pensacola, 1974, Beaumont, Tex., 1983, Twin Towers Profl. Office Bldg., Pensacola, 1976, addition Baptist Hosp., 1977, new facilities Rehab. Inst., 1977; The Village, Housing for Elderly, 1978, Azalea Trace Retirement Community Complex, 1980, Northview Community, 1981, Coca-Cola Bottling Plant, Beaumont, Tex., 1983. Home: 15 N Sunset Blvd Gulf Breeze FL 32561 Office: 100 W Gadsden St Pensacola FL 32501

WOOLFENDEN, RAYMOND (COUSIN RAY), broadcasting executive; b. Kopp, Va., Sept. 15, 1916; s. Raymond Marsden and Hattie Mae (Abel) W.; student public schs.; m. Doris Mae Lynch, Feb. 15, 1953; children—Mabel Irene, Raymond Wilson, Reginald Dale, Raynee Casmo, Casmere Sharlene, Ranier Dorine. Band musician on radio in Va., Ohio, N.C. and Miss., 1925—; route supr. for bakeries and dairies, 1933-40; owner grocery store, restaurant and service station, Groveton, Va., 1940-46; pres., owner Sta. WPWC, Dumfries, Va., 1974—. Bd. dirs., treas. Salvation Army of Prince William County. Served with AUS, 1945-46. Recipient various service awards, including Citizens award Cumberland County, N.C. and Yalobusha County, Miss. Mem. Assn. Country Entertainers, Nat. Assn. Broadcasters, Va. Broadcasters Assn., Reunionairs (Country music pioneers) (pres.), Fedn. Internat. Country Air Personalities (dir.), Assn. U.S. Army (dir.), Country Music Assn., Mt. Vernon Lee C. of C., Prince William County C. of C., Greater Manassas C. of C., Country Music Entertainers and Musicians Benevolent Assn., VFW (former post comdr.), Am. Legion, Assn. (former post chmn., Man of Yr. award Post 28, Dumfries 1982), U.S. Army. Lodges: Moose, Odd Fellows, K.C. (Man of Yr. award 1983). Office: 214 S Main St PO Box 189 Dumfries VA 22026

WOOLFLEY, FRANCIS AUGUSTUS, army officer; b. New Orleans, Apr. 30, 1893; s. Franklin Flanders and Mary Florence (Kessler) W.; grad. Inf. Sch., Ft. Benning, Ga., 1926. Command and Gen. Staff Coll., Ft. Leavenworth, Kan., 1935, Army War Coll., Washington, 1938, Chem. Warfare Sch., Edgewood Arsenal, Md., 1938; m. Rosalie Elizabeth Dufour, June 16, 1920; children—Francis Augustus, Rosalie Elizabeth (Mrs. Allen Henry Johness), Horace Louis Dufour. Commd. 2d lt. U.S. Army, 1917, advanced through grades to brig. gen., 1943, inf. advisor to Turkish Army and chief of staff U.S. Army Group, Joint Am. Mil. Mission for Aid to Turkey, Ankara, 1949-52, ret., 1953; dir. La. Civil Def. Agy., 1953-56; asst. adj. gen., dir. La. Civil Def. and dir. Office Emergency Planning for La., 1960-64. Decorated Silver Star with oak leaf cluster, Bronze Star with oak leaf cluster, Legion of Merit, Air medal; Croix de Guerre with palm, chevalier Legion of Honor (France); Croix de Guerre with palm (Belgium); Croix de Guerre (Luxemburg). Mem. SAR (past pres. La. Soc.), Soc. Colonial Wars, Soc. War 1812 (dep. pres. gen.), Mil. Order World Wars (past comdr.), Am. Legion, Civil War Round Table New Orleans (past pres.), Thackery Soc., Mil. Order Fgn. Wars, Royal Soc. St. George. Club: Pendennis (New Orleans). Home: 932 Solomon Pl New Orleans LA 70119

WOOLFOLK, GEORGE RUBLE, historian, author, educator; b. Feb. 22, 1915; s. Lucien Ben and Theodoshia Berry (Jackson) W.; m. Douglass Geraldyne Perry, Aug. 15, 1947; 1 child, George Ruble. A.B. in History, U. Louisville, 1937; M.A., Ohio State U., 1938; Ph.D., U. Wis., 1947. Cert. profl. historian. From asst. prof. to assoc. prof. history Prairie View A&M U., Tex., 1943-60, prof., chmn. dept. history, 1960-80, prof., chmn. dept., div. social and polit. sci., 1980—; mem. various univ. coms.; mem. local, regional, state panel NEH; vice chmn. Am. Revolution Bicentennial Commn. Tex., 1973-78; mem. Tex. State Hist. Document Adv. Bd.; tech. advisor Waller County Hist. Commn.; mem. Tex. Com. on Humanities; cons. TV series Black Frontier, U. Nebr. and Ford Found.; lectr. in field. Author: The Cotton Regency: The Northern Merchants and Reconstruction, 1865-1880, 1958; Prairie View: A Study in Public Conscience, 1878-1946, 1962 (honorable mention Pageant Press Best Book award 1963); The Free Negro in Texas, 1836-1860, 1976. Contbr. articles, book revs. Jour. Negro History, Tex. Standard, Jour. Sol History, others. Mem. editorial bd. Jour. Negro History, Houston Rev. Served with A.S.T.P., 1943-45. Am. Assn. for State and Local History grantee; Piper Found. Prof., 1973. Mem. Assn. for Study of Afro-Am. Life and History, Am. History Assn., Orgn. Am. Historians, So. Hist. Assn., Southwestern Hist. Assn., Alpha Phi Alpha. Democrat. Baptist. Office: Dept of History Prairie View A&M U Prairie View TX 77446

WOOLLEY, CLIFTON WARD, pediatrician; b. Tuscaloosa, Ala., Jan. 15, 1910; s. David Zacchaeus and Mary Benthall (Davis) W.; student Memphis State U., 1930-33; B.S., Union U., 1935; M.D., U. Tenn., 1939; m. Mary Selden Prescott, Sept. 5, 1940; children—Elizabeth Woolley Self, Martha, John, James. Intern, John Gaston Hosp., Memphis, 1939-40, resident, 1941-42, chief resident, 1946; resident Children's Meml. Hosp., Chgo., 1941-42; pub. health officer Maringo County (Ala.), Linden, 1940-41; practice medicine specializing in pediatrics, Memphis, 1947—; mem. staffs Baptist Meml., Meth., St. Joseph, John Gaston, LeBonheur, St. Francis hosps. (all Memphis); instr. U. Tenn. Coll. Medicine, 1951—; v.p., dir. Die Supplies, Inc., 1963—; physician athletic dept. Memphis State U., 1954—; bd. dirs. Greater Memphis State, Inc., 1970-76; physician athletic dept. Shelby State Community Coll., 1972-83; physician Tenn. Baptist Children's Home, Memphis, 1960—; Bd. advisers Hannibal-LaGrange Coll., 1973—, World Evangelism Found., Dallas, 1970-82; mem. fgn. mission bd. So. Bapt. Conv., 1966-72; trustee Luther Rice Sem., Jacksonville, Fla., Woolley Ednl. Found.; chmn. bd. Tenn. Bapt. Children's Homes, 1982. Served to maj. AUS, 1942-45. Decorated Bronze Star medal with oak leaf cluster; Silver Star (Luzon); named to Memphis State U. Football Hall of Fame, 1978, Nat. Football Found. and Hall of Fame, 1981; recipient Golden Tiger award, 1978, Disting. Service award Greater Memphis State, Inc., 1981. Diplomate Am. Bd. Pediatrics, Am. Acad. Sports Medicine. Fellow Am. Acad. Pediatrics; mem. Am., Tenn., Memphis and Shelby County med. socs., Memphis Pediatrics Soc. (pres. 1952), Shelby Bapt. Assn. (missions com. 1966-70, fin. com. 1970-72), Gideons Internat. Contbr. articles to profl. publs. Completed N.Y.C. Marathon, 1980-83. Home: 3604 Midland Ave Memphis TN 38111 Office: 3181 Poplar Ave Memphis TN 38111

WOOTEN, ALVIN JOE, psychologist; b. Douglas, Ga., Apr. 26, 1938; s. Alton W. and Josephine Wooten; m. Sandra Sikes, Nov. 11, 1961; children—Jason M., Leigh E., Jill A. B.A., Jacksonville U., 1962; M.S., Purdue U., 1967; Ph.D., U. Cin., 1973. Lic. psychologist, Fla. Commd. 2d lt. U.S. Air Force, 1963, advanced through grades to lt. col., 1984; dir. clin. psychology residency program Wright-Patterson USAF Med. Ctr., Ohio, 1976-81; chief psychology service Wilford-Hall Med. Ctr., Lackland AFB, Tex., 1981-83; practice clin. psychology Melbourne, Fla., 1984—; cons. Surgeon Gen., USAF, Washington, 1976-84. Contbr. articles to profl. publs. Named Outstanding Clin. Faculty mem. Wright State U., Sch. Profl. Psychology, 1980-81. Mem. Am. Psychol. Assn., Assn. for Advancement Clin. Psychology, Soc. Air Force Clin. Psychologists (pres. 1980-81). Avocations: guitar; boating. Office: Brevard Psychol Ctr 1305 S Valentine St Melbourne FL 32901

WOOTEN, BOBBY GENE, dentist, real estate developer; b. Winston-Salem, N.C., June 3, 1938; s. Willard Eugene and Hazel Mary Bell (Hobson) W.; m. Juanna Lyvonne Carlton, June 2, 1962; children—Anne Denise, Robert Steven, Jennifer Lynn. D.D.S., U. N.C., 1964. Dentist in pvt. practice, Winston-Salem, 1966—; dir. First Citizens Bank, Winston-Salem; vice pres. Yadkin Valley Developers, Winston-Salem, 1967-69, M&W Developers, Winston-Salem, 1979—; dep. examiner N.C. State Bd. Dental Examiners, Raleigh, 1982-85. Served to capt. USAF, 1964-66. Mem. ADA, Acad. Gen. Dentistry, Am. Pedodontic Soc., Nat. Self Storage Assn., Forsyth County Dental Soc. (pres. 1984—), Winston-Salem C. of C. Republican. Quaker. Club: Forsyth Country. Lodge: Masons. Avocations: golf, classic automobile collecting. Home: 570 Knobview Pl Winston-Salem NC 27104 Office: 116 Jonestown Rd Winston-Salem NC 27104

WOOTEN, FELTON BERNARD, nursing home administrator; b. Greensboro, N.C., Mar. 30, 1954; s. Ernest Lee and Della (Pitt) W.; m. Eileen Adger, Sept. 10, 1983; 1 child, Shannan Renee. B.A. in Pub. Adminstrn., N.C. Central U., Durham, 1976. Lic. nursing home adminstr. Personnel asst. The Evergreens, Inc., Greensboro, 1976-77, personnel dir., 1977-79, dir. support services, 1979-81, asst. adminstr., 1981-84, adminstr., High Point, N.C., 1984—. Bd. dirs. R.L. Wynn Meml. Scholarship, Greensboro, 1982—, treas. R.L. Wynn Golf Tournament, 1983—. Mem. High Point Personnel Assn., N.C. Health Care Facilities Assn., N.C. Non-Profit Assn. for Homes for Aged. Democrat. Baptist. Avocation: acrylic art. Home: 2401 Lamroc Rd Greensboro NC 27407

WOOTEN, WILLIAM, psychology educator, management consultant; b. Memphis, July 12, 1951; s. Joseph and Pauline (Bowie) W.; m. Sandra Faye Perkins, Aug. 18, 1979; children—Whitney, Kimberly. B.S., Memphis State U., 1973, M.S., 1976, Ph.D., 1980. Human resources planning analyst Miller Brewing Co., Milw., 1979-81; asst. prof. psychology U. Central Fla., Orlando, 1981—; mgmt. cons., Winter Park, Fla., 1981—. Mem. exec. bd. Christian Ex-offender Employment Devel. Service. Recipient Achievement award Omega Psi Phi, 1979-81. Mem. Am. Psychol. Assn. (exec. liaison), Assn. Black Psychologists, Am. Personnel Mgmt. Assn., Omega Psi Phi. Democrat. Lutheran. Office: Psychology Dept U Central Fla Orlando FL 32816

WOOTTEN, JOHN ROBERT, investor; b. Chickasha, Okla., Feb. 5, 1929; s. Henry Hughes and Ella Gayle (Ditzler) W.; B.S., Colo. A. and M. U., 1953; m. Mary Lou Schmausser, Mar. 15, 1952 (div.); children—Pamela Jean, Robert Hughes; m. Geraldine Ann Theisen, Aug. 14, 1982. Sec., S.W. Radio and Equipment Co., Oklahoma City, 1953-55; pres. Belcaro Homes, Inc., 1955-60; pres. Bob Wootten Ford, Yukon, Okla., 1960-68; pres. Bus. Data Systems, 1968-72; chmn., chief exec. officer 1st Nat. Bank, Moore, Okla., 1970-72; pres. Communications Enterprises, Inc., Liberal, Kans., 1967-80; pres. Trebor Leasing Co., 1965—; pres. Okla. Sch. Book Depository, Inc., Oklahoma City, 1976-80; pres. S.W. Sch. Book Depository Inc., Dallas, 1976—. Pres. Okla. chpt. Am. Cancer Soc., 1966-67; pres. Okla. chpt. Arthritis Found., 1973-76; pres. Lyric Theater Okla., 1976-77; chmn. bd. trustees Bone and Joint Hosp., 1976-81; bd. dirs. Okla. Theater Center, Dallas Theater Center; trustee Oklahoma City U.; pres. Last Frontier council Boy Scouts Am., 1968-70. Recipient Silver Beaver award Boy Scouts Am., 1971. Mem. Ind. Bankers Assn., Am. Bankers Assn., Tex. Bookmans Assn., Navy League. Republican. Episcopalian. Club: Econ. of Okla. Lodges: Masons, NW Oklahoma City Rotary (pres. 1963-64). Home: 6918 Tokalon Dr Dallas TX 75214 Office: 9259 King Arthur Dr Dallas TX 75247

WORD, AMOS JARMAN, III, architect; b. Greenwood, Miss., Mar. 10, 1949; s. Amos Jarman and Mary Frances (Davis) W.; B.Arch., Auburn U., 1973. Grad. architect Brewer, Godbold & Assocs., Clarksdale, Miss., 1973-78; architect, Blondheim, Williams & Golson, Birmingham, Ala., 1978-79; asso. architect The Ritchie Orgn., Birmingham, 1979—. Mem. AIA. Episcopalian. Project architect for expansion of Miami Valley Hosp., 1980-83. Home: 2831 Highland Ave S Apt 719 Birmingham AL 35205 Office: Dept Architecture and Engring U Ala 1825 University Blvd Birmingham AL 35294

WORD, JAMES ALFRED, car dealership executive; b. Scottsboro, Ala., Apr. 2, 1945; s. Fred William and Bertha Jewell (Smith) W.; m. Melissa Leigh Echols, Oct. 8, 1983. A.A., Calhoun U., 1974. Pres. Exxon Service Ctr.,

Huntsville, Ala., 1970-75, Black Angus Corp., Huntsville, 1975-80, Ledbetter Word Auto, Huntsville, 1981-83, Fayetteville Ford Mercury, Tenn., 1985—. Served with USN, 1962-70. Republican. Lodges: Elks, Masons, Moose. Home: Route 8 Box 322 A Fayetteville TN 37334 Office: Fayetteville Ford Mercury Huntsville Hwy Fayetteville TN 37334

WORELL, JUDITH P., educator; b. N.Y.C.; d. Moses and Dorothy Goldfarb; B.A., Queens Coll., 1950; M.A., Ohio State U., 1952, Ph.D., 1954; m. Leonard Worell, Aug. 11, 1947 (div. Jan., 1974); children—Amy, Beth, Wendy; m. H.A. Smith, Mar. 23, 1985. Psychologist, Columbus Mental Health Center, 1953-54; instr. Portland State U., 1954-56; research asso. Iowa Psychopathic Hosp., Iowa City, 1956-59; asst. prof., research assoc. Okla. State U., 1960-66; asst. prof. U. Ky., 1968-70, assoc. prof. ednl. and counseling psychology, 1970-76, prof., 1976—, dir. counseling psychology doctoral program, 1980; cons. Ky. Dept. Human Resources, Lexington Women's Center, Ky. Humanities Council. NIMH research grantee, 1959-67; USPHS fellow, 1953; NIH biomed. grantee, 1984-85. Fellow Am. Psychol. Assn. (pres. clin. psychology of women 1986-88); mem. Ky. Psychol. Assn. (pres. 1981-82), Southeastern Psychol. Assn., Soc. for Research in Child Devel., Am. Ednl. Research Assn., AAUP, Am. Women in Psychology, Midwest Soc. Lifespan Devel., Midwest Soc. Research on Adolescence. Author: (with C. M. Nelson) Managing Instructional Problems, 1974; (with W. E. Stilwell): Psychology for Teachers and Students, 1981; Psychological Development in the Elementary Years, 1982 (with F. Danner) Adolescent Development: Issues for Education, 1986 editorial bd.: Jour. Cons. and Clin. Psychology, Sex Roles; assoc. editor, Psychology of Women Quar.; contbr. articles to profl. jours., chpts. to books. Home: 3892 Gloucester Dr W Lexington KY 40510 Office: 235 Dickey Hall Univ Ky Lexington KY 40506

WORKIE, ABAINEH, psychology educator, researcher; b. Gursum, Harar, Ethiopia, Apr. 15, 1937; came to U.S., 1977; s. Workie and Manyahlishal (Kewie) Gelemmie; m. Roman Mengistu, Jan. 25, 1970; children—Derset, Blane, Fegegta, Haimera, Essey. B.A., Hailie Selassie I U., Addis Ababa, Ethiopia, 1959; B.D., Bethel Theol. Sem., St. Paul, 1962; M.S. in Psychology, Howard U., 1964; Ph.D., Columbia U., 1967. Lectr. psychology Haile Selassie I U., 1967-68, asst. prof., 1968-74, assoc. prof., 1974-77, asst. dean, 1968-69, dean, 1969-71; vis. prof. psychology Mich. State U., 1977-78, Howard U., 1978-82; prof. Norfolk State U., 1982—; nat. dir. tchr. tng. program UNESCO, 1969-71; psychology program evaluator Makerere U., Uganda, 1970-72; cons. Inst. Internat. Edn., Addis Ababa, 1970-73; Sch. Edn. program evaluator Dar es Salaam U., Tanzania, 1971. Contbr. articles to profl. jours. Pres. Ethiopian Youth for Christ, Addis Ababa, 1956-59; pres. African Christian Assn. N.Am., 1960-62; chmn. Ethiopian Relief Assn. in Va., Inc., 1984—. Grantee Midwestern U. Consortium, 1977-78, Ford Found., 1972-73, Swedish Internat. Devel. Agy., 1971-72. Mem. Am. Psychol. Assn., Am. Assn. Advancement Sci., Internat. Assn. Applied Psychologists, Phi Delta Kappa. Ethiopian Orthodox Ch. Office: Norfolk State Univ 2401 Corprew Ave Norfolk VA 23504

WORKMAN, CHARLES CLEVELAND, JR., management consultant; b. Lineville, Ala., Apr. 14, 1913; s. Charles Cleveland and Emma Franklin (Jones) W.; B.S., Auburn U., 1934; m. Jane Pinaire, 1944 (dec. 1966); 1 child, Janet Susan Workman Baltzer; m. Bessie Kate Bradford, Mar. 23, 1968 (dec. Mar. 1984); m. Shelby J. Freeman. Trainee, Consol. Millinery Co. of Chgo., 1934-35, br. mgr., Miami, Fla. also Allentown, Pa., 1935-36; asst. dept. mgr. Stewart Dry Goods Co., Louisville, 1937; with IBM Corp., 1937-70, sales rep., Louisville, 1937-40, br mgr., Shreveport, La., 1946-49, Houston, 1950-54, gen. mgr. Southeast region, Altanta, 1955-62, dir. mktg. Fed. Systems div., Washington, 1963, mgr. aerospace and dist. br., Atlanta, 1964-70; pres. Mgmt. Services, Inc., Atlanta, 1971-74; So. regional mgr. TLW Corp., Atlanta, 1974-76; mgmt. cons., Atlanta, 1977—. Bd. dirs. Goodwill Industries, 1960-73, pres., 1972-73; various offices ARC, 1937-71, United Way, 1937-71; mem. U.S. Congressional Adv. Bd., Am. Security Council, 1980—. Served with AUS, 1940-45. Mem. SAR, Nat. Assn. Accts., Nat. Sales Execs. Club, Pi Kappa Phi, Delta Sigma Pi, Omicron Delta Kappa. Republican. Presbyterian (deacon). Clubs: Kiwanis Internat., Cherokee Town and Country. Address: 9790 Huntcliff Trace Atlanta GA 30338

WORKMAN, WILLIAM DOUGLAS, III, industrial relations executive, mayor; b. Charleston S.C., July 3, 1940; s. William Douglas, Jr. and Rhea (Thomas) W.; B.A., The Citadel, 1961; postgrad. U. S.C., 1962; m. Marcia Mae Moorhead, Apr. 23, 1966; children—William Douglas IV, Frank Moorhead. Reporter, Charleston News & Courier, 1965-66, Greenville (S.C.) News, 1966-70; tchr., adminstr., dean allied health scis. Greenville Tech. Coll., 1967-75; exec. asst. to Gov. of S.C., Columbia, 1975-78; indsl. relations and mktg. exec. Daniel Internat. Corp., Greenville, 1978—; mayor City of Greenville, 1983—. Chmn. Greenville County Republican Conv., 1980-84, S.C. 4th Congressional Dist. Rep. Conv., 1980, 82, 84; chmn. S.C. Rep. Conv., 1984; trustee Sch. Dist. Greenville County, 1969-75, also vice chmn.; bd. dirs. YMCA Camp Greenville, 1973-83, chmn., 1975; chmn. S.C. Health Coordinating Council, 1976-78; founder S.C. Literacy Assn., treas., 1969-73; mem. Greenville City Council, 1981-83; vice chmn. Greenville Central Area Partnership; bd. dirs. Greenville Conv. and Visitors Bur. Served with AUS, 1962-64; lt. col. Res. Decorated Army Commendation medal with 2 oak leaf clusters; named Outstanding State Chmn., S.C. Jaycees, 1969. Mem. Res. Officers Assn., Assn. U.S. Army, U.S. Conf. Mayors, Short Snout Soc., Assoc. Builders and Contractors (nat. legis. com.). Clubs: Greenville Country, Commerce, Rotary, Beaux Arts of Greenville (past pres.), Greenville-Piedmont Citadel (past pres.). Home: 30 Craigwood Rd Greenville SC 29607 Office: Daniel Bldg Greenville SC 29602

WORLEY, CYNTHIA ANNE, nurse; b. Houston, Feb. 21, 1957; d. James Ellis and Valerie Claire (Schaff) W. B.S. in Nursing, U. St. Thomas, Houston, 1981. Registered nurse, Tex. Staff nurse Meth. Hosp., Houston, 1980—. Instr. CPR, Am. Heart Assn., Houston, 1975—; dialogue facilitator Am. Cancer Soc., 1982, vol. coordinator Can Surmount program, 1985. Recipient Vol. Recognition award Am. Cancer Soc., 1982. Mem. Oncology Nursing Soc., United Ostomy Assn. Roman Catholic. Avocations: calligraphy; tennis; sailing; gourmet cooking. Home: 7827 Rue St Cyr Houston TX 77074 Office: Meth Hosp 6565 Fannin Houston TX 77030

WORLEY, OWEN RUSSELL, consultant; b. Goshen Springs, Miss., June 28, 1920; s. Thomas Eugene and Hattie (Davis) W.; m. Carolyn Nicholson, Oct. 15, 1945; children—Owen Russell Jr., Charles Harman, Robert Sparkman. B.S., Miss. State U., 1942. With Coca-Cola Co., 1945—, field liaison mgr., 1980—, cons., Atlanta, 1985—; cons. Screen Art, Knoxville, Tenn., 1985—; pres. ORW Inc. Mem. Presdl. Task Force, 1984-85. Served to 1st lt. USAF, 1943-45, ETO. Mem. Huntcliff Homes Assn. (pres., bd. dirs.). Republican. Presbyterian. Club: Cherokee Town and Country. Home: 960 Buckhorn E Atlanta GA 30338

WORRELL, ANNE EVERETTE ROWELL, newspaper executive; b. Surry, Va., Mar. 7, 1920; d. Charles Gray and Ethel (Roache) Rowell; student Va. Intermont Coll., 1939, U. Richmond, 1965; m. Thomas Eugene Worrell, Sept. 12, 1941; 1 son, Thomas Eugene. Founding stockholder Worrell Newspapers Inc., 1949, v.p., dir., 1969-73; pres. Bristol Newspapers, Inc., Va., pubs. Bristol Herald-Courier, Bristol Va.__Tennessean, 1979—; v.p., sec. Worrell Investment Co., Charlottesville, Va. Pres., Bristol Jr. League, 1959; mem. Va. Mus., Bayly Mus.; mem. Va. Hist. Landmarks Commn. and Rev. Bd. 1921—, Colonial Williamsburg Found., Planning Bd. for Restoration of Poplar Forest; bd. dirs. Preservation Alliance of Va.; trustee Va. Intermont Coll., 1973—, chmn. Centennial Campaign, 1982—, named Outstanding Alumna, 1981; patron Charlottesville-Albemarle Found. for Encouragement Arts. Mem. DAR (Shadwell chpt.), Assn. Preservation Va. Antiquities, Nat. Trust for Hist. Preservation. Clubs: Bristol Country, Farmington Country. Episcopalian. Home: 7 Sunset Circle Farmington Charlottesville VA 22901 Office: Pantops PO Box 5386 Charlottesville VA 22905

WORSHAM, EARL S., real estate investor, developer; b. Knoxville, Tenn., Nov. 15, 1932; s. Earl S. and Melba (Reagan) W.; m. Nancy Davidson, July 10, 1952 (div.); children—Lee, Elizabeth, Lyn; m. 2d, Anita Moiger, 1974. Diploma Culver Mil. Acad., 1950; B.S. in Fin., U. Tenn., 1955; M.B.A., Am. U., 1957. Pres., chmn. Worsham Bros. Co., Inc., Tenn., Ga., Fla., 1952—, chmn. Westley Swift Found., Atlanta, 1983—, Venturi Internat., Atlanta, 1973—; developer, owner Hyatt Regency, Miami, Knoxville, Excelsior Hotel, Little Rock, also others. Active United Fund, Miami, Fla., Served with U.S. Army, 1955-57. Recipient Developer of Yr. award City of Miami, 1979, Dade County, 1979, City of Miami Reach, 1979. Mem. Urban Land Inst. Clubs: Miami; Cherokee Country (Knoxville); Anglers (N.Y.C.). Home: 1 Cherokee Rd Atlanta GA 30305 Office: Worsham Bros Co Inc 1401 W Paces Ferry Rd Atlanta GA 30327

WORSHAM-KELLEY, JANET JEAN, crime prevention executive; b. Coral Gables, Fla., Nov. 23, 1955; d. Robert Joe and Christine Edith (Skipper) Worsham; m. Mitchell Patrick Kelley, Sept. 27, 1981. Grad. high sch. Prodn. staff Criminalistics Inc., Miami, 1971-73, asst. office mgr., 1973-78, v.p. adminstrn., 1978-84, pres., 1984—. Research and developer patent fingerprint powder, 1980. Mem. Opa Locka C. of C. (Miss Directory 1974), Internat. Assn. Indentification (assoc.). Republican. Baptist. Office: Criminalistics Inc 7560 NW 82 St Miami FL 33166

WORTHAM, ALBERT WILLIAM, consultant, engineer, rancher; b. Athens, Tex., Jan. 18, 1927; s. William Albert and Maggie W.; m. Conrad Edwina Peters, Dec. 18, 1965; children—Gary, Ann, Conrad, Kimberly. B.A., East Tex. State U., 1946; M.S., Okla. State U., 1951, Ph.D., 1954. Registered profl. engr., Tex.; lic. real estate broker, N.C. Sr. engr., supr. Chance Vought Aircraft, Dallas, 1951-57; mgr. quality assurance, chief indsl. engr., other mgmt. positions Tex. Instruments, Dallas, 1957-63; prof., chmn. indsl. engring. dept. Tex. A&M U., College Station, 1963-74, prof., 1974-75; cons. FEA, Washington, 1974-75, Internat. Cons., Bryan, Tex., 1975-81; prof., chmn. indsl. engring. dept. N.C. A&T State U., Greensboro, 1981-83; assoc. real estate broker Tice Realty, Greensboro, 1983-84. Served with USN, 1943-44. Charter mem. bd. govs. Okla. State U. Fellow Am. Soc. Quality Control; mem. Nat. Soc. Profl. Engrs., Am. Soc. Engring. Edn., IEEE, Ops. Research Soc. Am., Am. Inst. Indsl. Engrs. (award of excellence in quality and reliability 1983), Profl. Engrs. N.C. Contbr. articles to profl. jours. Home and Office: 3908 Old College Rd Bryan TX 77801

WORTHAM, LINDA ROACH, counseling educator; b. Dayton, Ohio, Nov. 23, 1948; d. John Marvin and Peggy Marie (Palmer) Roach; m. Howard Leroy Wortham, Sept. 4, 1971; children—James Barrett, Peggy Lee. B.S. cum laude, Tenn. Tech. U., 1970, M.A. summa cum laude, 1971; postgrad. North Tex. State U., 1983-85. Lic. profl. counselor, Tex. Juvenile probation officer Fulton County Juvenile Ct., Atlanta, 1973; rehab. counselor Atlanta Employment, Evaluation and Services Ctr., 1973-74; instr. psychology Mississippi County Community Coll., Blytheville, Ark., 1975-80; dir. counseling Navarro Coll., Corsicana, Tex., 1980-81; counselor, human devel. instr. Cedar Valley Coll., Lancaster, Tex., 1981—; cons. Mississippi County Econ. Opportunity Commn., Blytheville, 1978-80, Corsicana C. of C., 1980-81. Editor: Human Services Directory for Miss. County, 1979. Chmn. edn. com. First United Methodist Ch., Ennis, Tex., 1985. Recipient Outstanding Services to Students award Cedar Valley Coll., Lancaster, 1982. Mem. Am. Assn. Counseling Devel., Tex. Coll. Personnel Assn. (charter), Tex. Jr. Coll. Tchrs. Assn., Dallas County Community Coll. Faculty Assn., Am. Coll. Personnel Assn., Phi Mu. Avocations: water skiing; reading; family outings. Home: 214 Hacienda Waxahachie TX 75165 Office: Cedar Valley Coll 3030 N Dallas Ave Lancaster TX 75134

WORTHAM, RICHARD WALTER, III, real estate developer, investment company executive; b. N.Y.C., Sept. 12, 1938; s. Richard Walter and Marjorie (Hodgson) W.; m. Elena Cusi, Nov. 10, 1964; children—Elena, Pia, Erica, Andrea. B.A. in Econs., Yale U., 19. Gen. ptnr. Wortham & Van Liew, Houston, 1978—. Trustee, Mus. Fine Arts, Houston, 1974, Wortham Found., Houston, 1978, St. John's Sch., Houston, 1983. Served with U.S. Army, 1962-63. Home: 4614 Bryn Mawr St Houston TX 77027 Office: Wortham & Van Liew 1010 Lamar St Suite 1350 Houston TX 77002

WORTHEN, DEUARD VON, physicist; b. Oklahoma City, Aug. 15, 1952; s. Deuard Von and Louise Josephine (Spellings) W.; m. Marylou Fair, July 23, 1975; children—Alexander, Meredith. B.A., Oklahoma City U., 1974; M.S., Okla. State U., 1980. Instr., No. Okla. Coll., Tonkawa, 1975-76, Okla. State U., Stillwater, 1976-80; thin film design engr. Tex. Instruments, Inc., Dallas, 1980—. Mem. IEEE, Am. Phys. Soc., Am. Assn. Physics Tchrs. Unitarian. Avocations: running, fencing, computers, science fiction, hypnosis. Home: 2314 Village N Dr Richardson TX 75081 Office: Texas Instruments MS 3189 PO Box 225012 Dallas TX 75265

WORTHINGTON, DAVID WINSLOW, oil contractor executive, geophysical consulting company executive; b. Worcester, Mass., Aug. 27, 1941; s. Everett Aretus and Ruth Eleanor (Griffin) W.; m. Evelyn White Lindamood, June 15, 1968; children—Jennifer, Paige. B.S. in Geology, Marietta Coll., 1966; postgrad., U. Utah, 1967; M.S. in Geophysics, Va. Tech., 1968. Geophysicist, Shell Oil Co., Houston, 1968-75, mgr. geophysics, New Orleans, 1976-80, exploration mgr., New Orleans, 1980; pres. Tomlinson Offshore, New Orleans, 1981-82, TGS Geophys. Co., Houston, 1983—, Calibre Cons., Houston, 1984—. Served with U.S. Army, 1961-64. Mem. Soc. Exploration Geophysicists, Am. Assn. Petroleum Geologists. Republican. Home: 2214 Long Valley Dr Kingwood TX 77345 Office: TGS Geophys Co 1200 Travis Houston TX 77002

WORTHINGTON, RALPH EUGENE, geologist; b. Flagler, Colo., Jan. 20, 1953; s. Robert Riley Worthington and Shirley Margaret (Cronkhite) Morris; m. Tina Marie Wray, June 23, 1973; children—Geoffrey Allan, Karen Ann, Bradley David. A.A.S., Morgan County Community Coll., Ft. Morgan, Colo., 1973; A.S., Pikes Peak Community Coll., 1978; B.S., U. So. Colo., 1980; M.S., U. Iowa, 1982. Geologist, Arco Exploration Co., Denver, 1982-84, Arco Oil and Gas Co., Midland, Tex., 1984—. Contbr. articles to profl. publs. Youth sports coach YMCA, Midland, 1984, 85. Served with USN, 1973-77. Mem. Am. Assn. Petroleum Geologists, Soc. Econ. Paleontologists and Mineralogists, West Tex. Geol. Soc., N.Mex. Geol. Soc., Rocky Mountain Assn. Geologists. Republican. Baptist. Avocations: pilot, jogging, youth sports coaching, traveling, woodworking. Office: Arco Oil and Gas Co 300 N Pecos Midland TX 79702

WORTHINGTON, WARD CURTIS, JR., university dean, anatomy educator; b. Savannah, Ga., Aug. 8, 1925; s. Ward Curtis and Pearl Mabel (Farris) W.; m. Floride Calhoun McDermid, June 21, 1947; children—Ward Curtis III, Amy Lynne Worthington Hauslohner. B.S., The Citadel, 1952; M.D., Med. U. S.C., 1952. Intern, Boston City Hosp., 1952-53; prof. anatomy Med. U. S.C., Charleston, 1966—, asst. dean curriculum, 1966-69, chmn. dept. anatomy, 1969-77, acting v.p. acad. affairs, 1975-77, v.p. acad. affairs, 1977-82, assoc. dean acad. affairs, 1982—, dir. Waring Hist. Library, 1982—. Bd. dirs. Charleston Symphony Orch. Assn., 1980—, 2d v.p., 1982—. Served with USNR, 1944-46. Research grantee The Commonwealth Fund, 1957-61, NIH, 1962-66, 66-73; NIH spl. fellow, 1964-65. Mem. Assn. Anatomy Chmn., Nat. Microcirculatory Conf., Waring Library Soc., S.C. Acad. Sci., S.C. Med. Assn., Charleston County Med. Soc., Endocrine Soc., Am. Physiol. Soc., Am. Assn. Anatomists, Sigma Xi, Alpha Omega Alpha. Episcopalian. Lodge: Rotary (dir. 1982—). Contbr. articles to profl. jours. Home: 17 Morton Ave Charleston SC 29407 Office: 171 Ashley Ave Charleston SC 29425

WORTHY, LANDIS CLEVELAND, architect; b. Painter, Ala., July 23, 1917; s. William Cleveland and Ida Keturah (Upton) W.; m. Kathleen Elizabeth Rushing, June 28, 1947 (dec. Dec. 1974); children—Landis C. Jr. (dec.), Kathleen Marie; m. Rita Binkley, Sept. 26, 1975. B.Arch., Auburn U., 1945. Registered architect, Ala., Ark., Fla., Ga., Ky., La., N.Y., S.C., Tenn., Va. Designer, draftsman Paul Hofferburt, Gadsden, Ala., 1945-47; archtl. designer Bail, Horton, Inc., Ft. Myers, Fla., 1947-49; project mgr. Robert & Co., Atlanta, 1949-78; v.p. architecture B.G. Sanders & Assocs., Atlanta, 1979—. Author: 6 Ideas for Atlanta, 1971. Prin. works include extension of west central front U.S. Capitol, Washington. Chmn. A&E div. United Appeal Fund Drive, Atlanta Metro, 1967. Mem. AIA (Student medal 1945, sec. Atlanta chpt. 1958). Democrat. Episcopalian. Avocation: gardening. Home: 365 Lake Forrest Ln Atlanta GA 30342 Office: BG Sanders & Assocs 6405 Barfield Rd Atlanta GA 30328

WORTMAN, WILLIAM JEROME, JR., obstetrician, gynecologist; b. Morganton, N.C., Aug. 2, 1934; s. William Jerome and Roberta May (Royster) W.; m. Carolyn Mabel Cane, Mar. 28, 1957 (div. 1974); children—Laura Wortman Solitario, Richard Ashley; m. 2d, Mary Ellen Moore, Jan. 18, 1975. A.B., Duke U., 1956; M.D., Wake Forest Coll., 1964. Diplomate Am. Bd. Ob-Gyn. Intern, U.S. Naval Hosp., Charleston, S.C., 1964-65; resident Virginia Mason Med. Center, Seattle, 1965-66, Kings County Hosp., Bklyn., 1966-69; practice medicine specializing in ob-gyn, Charlotte, N.C., 1969—; mem. staff Presbyn. Hosp., Mercy Hosp., Orthopedic Hosp.; instr. ob-gyn SUNY-Downstate Med. Center, 1968-69; cons. in field. Bd. advisors Charlotte Opera, Charlotte Symphony Orch. Served to lt. USN, 1957-64; to lt. comdr. M.C., USN, 1964-67. Mem. So. Med. Assn., Am. Coll. Obstetricians and Gynecologists, Am. Fertility Soc., Am. Assn. for Colposcopy and Colpomicroscopy, Am. Assn. Gynecol. Laparoscopists, Am. Assn. Sex Educators, Counsellors and Therapists, Royal Soc. Medicine Great Britain, Les Chevaliers du Tastevin, Brotherhood of Knights of Vine. Clubs: Tower, Charlotte Athletic, Carmel. Contbr. numerous articles to profl. jours. Home: 2727 Sharon Ln Charlotte NC 28211 Office: 2711 Randolph Rd Suite 309 Charlotte NC 28207

WORTZ, CARL HAGLIN, III, business consultant; b. Ft. Smith, Ark., May 9, 1921; s. Carl H. Wortz and Ed Dell (Haglin) W.; grad. N.Mex. Mil. Inst., 1940, Sparton Sch. Aeronautics, 1943; B.S. in Bus., U. Ark., 1947; m. Charlotte Wacker, June 29, 1943; 1 dau., Carolyn Jane. Former pres. Wortz Co.; pres. Wortz Assocs.; dir. Tex. Group. Served with AUS, 1943-46; CBI. Mem. Internat. House, Assocs. for Corp. Growth, Sigma Alpha Epsilon. Methodist. Office: PO Box 45565 Dallas TX 75245 also 260 Ledgerwood Rd Hot Springs AR 71901

WRATHER, DANIEL MACRAE, psychologist, consultant, educator; b. Kennett, Mo., May 10, 1949; s. James K. and Belva Lee (Forbes) W.; m. Jean Ann Moe, Apr. 30, 1983; children by previous marriage—Matthew, Marcus, Ryan. B.A., U. Okla., 1971, M.S., 1972, Ph.D., 1975. Asst. prof. psychology Northwest Coll., Orange City, Iowa, 1977-82, Earlham Coll., 1975-77; instr. psychology U. Okla., Norman, 1974-75; dir. Columbus Counseling & Cons. (Miss.), 1982-84; exec. dir. Valcom Learning Ctr., Columbus, 1984—; computer edn. cons. Contbr. articles to profl. jours. Named Outstanding Young Man, U.S. Jaycees, 1977; Eagle award, Boy Scouts Am., 1966; Lilly Found. fellow, 1979-82. Mem. Am. Psychol. Assn., Southwestern Psychol. Assn., Okla. U. Assn. Grad. Assts. (pres. 1974), GT Computer Club (sec.-treas.), GT Advt. Fedn. Methodist. Lodge: Rotary. Office: Valcom Learning Ctr 123 Gardner Blvd Columbus MS 39702

WRAY, FRANK, JR., historian, educator; b. Camden, Ind., Apr. 29, 1921; s. Benjamin Franklin and Bessie Leanore (Ayres) W.; m. Betty Marie Binkley, Dec. 28, 1946; children—William Franklin, James Edward, Thomas Frederick, Ellen Elizabeth. A.B. with high honors, Ind. U., 1946, M.A., 1947; Ph.D., 1954. Instr. history U. S.D., Vermillion, 1947-49, U. Conn., Storrs, 1952, U. Vt., Burlington, 1953; from asst. prof. to prof. Berea Coll., Ky., 1953-76, Hutchins Alumni prof., 1976—, dept. chmn. history and polit. sci., 1983—. Contbr. chpt. to book, articles to profl. jours. Served with U.S. Army, 1942-46. Am. Council Learned Socs. grantee, 1964; S.E. Inst. Medieval and Renaissance Studies fellow, 1968. Mem. Am. Hist. Assn., Am. Soc. Ch. History, Medieval Acad. Am., Renaissance Soc. Am., Am. Soc. Reformation Research. Republican. Baptist. Home: 116 Van Winkle Grove Berea KY 40403 Office: Berea Coll CPO 2271 Berea KY 40404

WRAY, MORRIS GARLAND, college administrator, clergyman; b. Emporia, Va., June 7, 1942; s. William Swanson and Helen (Faris) W. B.A., Mars Hill Coll., 1964; M. Div., Southeastern Sem., 1967; M.A., Vanderbilt U., 1969, Ph.D., 1974. Ordained to ministry Baptist Ch., 1965. Minister, Claremont Bapt. Ch., Va., 1964-67; admissions officer Vanderbilt U., Nashville, 1970-73, chmn. grad. colloquim, 1967-69, freshman counselor, 1968-69; assoc. dean student affairs, William and Mary Coll., Williamsburg, Va., 1973-74; dean admissions Andrew Coll., Cuthbert, Ga., 1974-77, pres., 1985—; dean Brevard Coll., N.C., 1977-85; chmn. Private Coll. Tour. Assn. of Pvt. Colls. and Univs. in Ga., 1977. Author: Montaigne and Protestantism, 1975. Mem. adminstrn. bd. First United Methodist Ch., Brevard, 1983, 85. Mem. Smokey Mountain Consortium, So. Assn. of Colls. and Schs. Democrat. Home: Andrew Coll Cuthbert GA 31740 Office: Office of Pres Andrew Coll Cuthbert GA

WRAY, WILLIAM ALAN, psychologist, consultant; b. Somerset, Ky., Jan. 26, 1951; s. Fred Hamilton and Mary Gladys (Hines) W.; m. Mary Susan Jarnagin, Mar. 22, 1975; children—Alan Barton, Thomas Alexander. B.A., U. Tenn., 1973, M.S., 1978, Ed.D., 1979. Lic. clin. psychologist, Tenn.; cert. sch. psychologist, Tenn. Group leader, mental health worker II, psychiat. service St. Mary's Med. Ctr., Knoxville, Tenn., 1973-77; grad. teaching asst. U. Tenn., Knoxville, 1977-79; psychologist, dir. adminstrv. services Team Evaluation Ctr. Inc., Chattanooga, 1977-84; pvt. practice, Chattanooga, 1983—; co-founder, ptnr. Advancement Resources Group, Chattanooga, 1984—. Author: The Personal Construct System of The Learning Disabled Child, 1979. Contbr. articles to profl. jours. Mem. counseling com. First Centenary United Meth. Ch.; mem. speakers bur. Hamilton County United Way; mem. adv. bd. N.W. Ga. Headstart; active Hamilton County Mental Health Assn., Chattanooga Head Injury Support Group, Chattanooga Eating Disorders Support Group, Chattanooga Alzheimers Disease Support Group. Mem. Am. Psychol. Assn., Tenn. Psychol. Assn., Tenn. Assn. Sch. Psychologists, Chattanooga Area Psychol. Assn. (v.p. 1983), Phi Kappa Phi. Club: Chattanooga Track. Avocations: running; snow and water skiing; sailing. Office: 1001 Med Ctr Plaza 979 E 3d St Chattanooga TN 37403

WREN, LAWRENCE BLAISE, lawyer; b. Chgo., May 19, 1952; s. Lawrence Blaise and Rita Francis (Walsh) W. A.B., U. Miami, Fla., 1974, J.D., 1978. Bar: Fla., U.S. Dist. Ct. (so. dist.) Fla., U.S. Ct. Appeals (11th cir.). Assoc. William S. Frates, West Palm Beach, Fla., 1980, Hastings & Goldman, Miami Beach, Fla., 1980-81; ptnr. Vernis, Bowling & Wren, Cocomut Grove, Fla., 1981-82, Sams, Ward, Newman & Beckham, Miami, Fla., 1982-83, Fazio, Dawson & DiSalvo, Ft. Lauderdale, Fla., 1983—. Speaker Floridians against Constl. Tampering, 1984; harvest staff South Fla. Hist. Soc., 1983. Mem. Acad. Fla. Trial Lawyers, Assn. Trial Lawyers Am., ABA, Dade County Bar Assn., Order Ky. Cols. Republican. Clubs: Bath, Surf (Miami Beach). Home: 20918 Estada Ln Boca Raton FL Office: Fazio Dawson and DiSalvo 633 S Andrews Ave 5th Floor Litigation Bldg Fort Lauderdale FL 33302

WREN, OSCAR PUTNAM, JR., aggregate company executive; b. New Orleans, May 26, 1936; s. Oscar P. and Elma R. (Reynolds) W.; m. Linda Rhea Brookreson, Mar. 27, 1959; children—Jason Severy, Heather Lea, Shannon Margaret. B.S. in Polit. Sci., U. So. Miss., 1958. Successively reporter, salesman, nat. dir. sales tng., regional sales mgr. Dun & Bradstreet Inc., Dallas, 1960-65, Baton Rouge, 1965-67, Shreveport, La., 1967-68, N.Y.C., 1968-69, Dallas, 1969-73; pres. Tomaro Oaks Inc., Poplar Bluff, Mo., 1973-82; gen. sales mgr. La. Limestone Aggregates, Baton Rouge, 1982—. Served with U.S. Army, 1959-60, 61-62. Mem. Sales and Mktg. Execs. Assn. Republican. Club: Dallas Athletic, Rotary, Kiwanis. Office: PO Box 2751 Baton Rouge LA 70821

WRIDE, LARRY NELDON, flotation manufacturing company executive; b. Provo, Utah, July 10, 1947; s. Neldon Francis and Rhea (Hatch) W.; m. Kathleen L. Wride, May 16, 1985; children—Jessica J., L. Tyson, Jeremie Kay, Kimberlee Ann. B.A. in Polit. Sci., Brigham Young U., 1972; M.B.A., Century U., 1983; Fgn. lang. specialist in French. Div. sales mgr. Sears Roebuck & Co., Provo, Utah, 1972-76; gen. mgr. Davis Interiors, Spanish Fork, Utah, 1976-77; v.p. Morning Star Corp., Salt Lake City, 1977-78; v.p. mktg. Simmons Advanced Sleep, Atlanta, 1978-82; v.p. Classic Corp., Jessup, Md., 1982—; dir. Watercoil, Inc., Billings, Mont. Inventor in field. Republican campaign worker Reagan for Pres., Oreg., 1980. Mem. Nat. Assn. Bedding Mfrs., Waterbed Mfrs. Assn., Am. Mgmt. Assn. Republican. Mormon. Clubs: Kiwanis, Jaycees. Address: 4691 Bryson Cove Lilburn GA 30247

WRIGHT, ALFRED DAVID, architect; b. Bristol, Va., Dec. 7, 1951; s. Alfred Daxtrell and Margaret Elizabeth (Haney) W.; m. Freida Diane Wagner, Aug. 5, 1978. B.Arch., U. Tenn., 1976. Jr. architect Boyd & Arthor, Architects, Greeneville, Tenn., 1976-78; J. Fred Honeycutt, Architect, Greeneville, 1978-79; architect Boyd & Arthor, Architects, Greeneville, 1979-82; ptnr., architect The Design Group, Architects, Greeneville, 1982—; design cons. Main Street, Greeneville, 1984—. Mem. So. Bldg. Code Congress Internat. Democrat. Methodist. Club: Breakfast Exchange. Avocation: golf. Home: Route 3 Greeneville TN 37743 Office: The Design Group Architects PO Box 1177 Greeneville TN 37744

WRIGHT, ALMA MCINTYRE, publishing company executive; b. Knoxville, Tenn., July 31, 1909; d. William Mobry and Theresa (Biagiotti) McIntyre; B.S. in Edn., U. Tenn., 1932; m. Robert Oliver Wright, Feb. 17, 1931; 1 son, Robert Oliver. Writer stories, articles on African violets, house plants, 1947—; editor African Violet mag., 1947-63; exec. dir. African Violet Soc. Am., Inc., 1960-63; pres. Indoor Gardener Pub. Co., Inc., Knoxville, 1963—; editor Gesneriad-Saintpaulia News, 1963-86. Mem. Auth. Soc. (hon. v.p. 1954), African Violet Soc. Am. (hon. life, rec. sec. 1946-48, nat. pres. 1948-49, membership sec. 1953-63), Saintpaulia Internat. (editor publs., rec. sec. 1963-81, pres. 1983-86). Editor: Master List of African Violets, 1962; editor for Am., Gesneria Soc. Home: 7914 Gleason Rd Apt 1075 Knoxville TN 37919 Office: 1800 Grand Ave Knoxville TN 37901

WRIGHT, BLANDIN JAMES, lawyer; b. Detroit, Nov. 29, 1947; s. Robert Thomas and Jane Ellen (Blandin) W.; m. Kay Emons Heideman, Aug. 28, 1969; children—Steven Blandin, Martha Kay. B.A., U. Mich., 1969; J.D., Dickinson Law Sch., 1972; LL.M. in Taxation, NYU., 1973. Bar: Pa. 1973, Fla. 1976, U.S. TAx Ct. 1977, U.S. Supreme Ct. 1977, D.C. 1979, Va. 1984. C.P.A., Tex., Va. Atty. IRS, Washington, 1973-76; tax dir. Intairdril Ltd., London, 1976-78; tax atty. Allied Chem. Corp., Houston, 1978-79; v.p., gen. counsel Assoc. Oiltools, Inc., London, 1979-82, J. Lauritzen (USA), Inc., Charlottesville, Va., 1982—; sole practice, Charlottesville, 1986—; officer JL Offshore Drilling, Inc., Houston, 1985—; dir. JL Heavyweight Transport, Inc., Houston; arbitrator Am. ARB Assn., N.Y.C., 1985—. Contbr. articles to profl. jours. Coach Charlottesville Youth Soccer and Baseball, 1984—; coach London Youth Baseball, 1982. Mem. ABA, Am. Inst. C.P.A.s, Tex. and Va. Soc. C.P.A.s, Charlottesville C. of C. Roman Catholic. Clubs: Charlottesville, Farmington Country (Charlottesville). Lodge: Rotary. Home: 6 Farmington Dr Charlottesville VA 22901 Office: 2568-B Ivy Rd Charlottesville VA 22901

WRIGHT, BURTON, sociologist; b. Detroit, Jan. 31, 1917; s. Burton and Hazel Marie (Thomas) W.; A.A., C.Z. Coll., 1944; B.A., U. Wash., Seattle, 1947, M.A., 1949; Ph.D., Fla. State U., 1972; m. Marie Fidelis Gallivan, Jan. 22, 1942; children—Burton III, Catherine Margaret (dec.). Enlisted U.S. Navy, 1937, commd. and advanced through grades to comdr., 1957; dir. Naval Res. Recruiting, 1960-64; ret., 1964; mem. faculty U. Wash., 1947-49, Northwestern U., summers 1956-59, George Washington U., Washington, 1954-60, Rollins Coll., Winter Park, Fla., 1966-69; cons. Ford Found., 1951, Dept. Air Force, 1955, U.S. Army Chem. Corps, 1956; prof. dept. sociology U. Central Fla., Orlando, 1972-82, prof. emeritus, 1982—; dir. Am. Sociol. Assn. Nat. Honors Program, 1981—. Decorated Navy Commendation medal. Fellow Am. Anthrop. Assn.; mem. Am. Sociol. Assn. (dir. honors program 1980-86, membership com. 1983-86), Soc. Psychol. Study Social Problems, AAUP, Am. Acad. Arts and Scis., Soc. Study Social Problems, So. Sociol. Soc., North Central Sociol. Soc. Roman Catholic. Club: Univ. (Winter Park). Author: (with John P. Weiss and Charles M. Unkovic) Perspective: An Introduction to Sociology, 1975; (with Vernon Fox) Criminal Justice and the Social Sciences, 1978; (with John P. Weiss) Social Problems, 1980. Home: 640 London Rd Winter Park FL 32792 Office: Dept Sociology U Central Fla Box 25000 Orlando FL 32816

WRIGHT, CALVIN PERSINGER, businessman; b. Rochester, Pa., Dec. 17, 1928; s. Jesse A. and Clara R. (Persinger) W. m. 2d, Anne Graham Lacy, Nov. 14, 1970; children—Calvin Jr., Jacob; children by previous marriage—Cynthia Wright Kern, Sally Wright Hawkins, Lauren Wright Haynes. Pres., Wright Edsel Sales, Covington, 1957-59, Allegheny Motor Corp., 1959-81, Downtown Autowash, 1972—, Riverside Spraywash, 1975—, Sta. WXCF, 1972-79, The Stable Wash, 1983—; animal breeder, antique auto dealer; dir. State Bank Alleghenies. Pres. High Acres Village, Va., 1965—. Active, Alleghany Hist. Soc.; dir. Persinger Meml. Cemetery. Presbyterian. Home and Office: Merry Go Round Farm Covington VA 24420

WRIGHT, CLOYD, clergyman; b. Glenwood, Ark., July 14, 1922; s. Joel S. and Retter (Grant) W.; m. Mildred Marie Short, Dec. 1941; 1 child, Patsy Ann Podbevsek. Ordained to ministry American Baptist Association, 1949. Pastor chs., Ark., N.Mex., 1955-58; evangelistic work Ark., N.Mex., Okla., Tex., 1956-58; missionary, Carlsbad, N.Mex., 1955-58; founder 1st Missionary Bapt. Ch., Carlsbad, 1956; pastor Mt. Moriah Missionary Bapt. Ch., Bonnerdale, Ark., 1980—; chmn. local assn. of 20 Missionary Bapt. chs. in west central Ark. Sec.-treas. Mt. Tabor Cemetery Assn., Montgomery County, 1970—. Office: Rt 1 Bonnerdale AR 71933

WRIGHT, DONALD KENNETH, educator; b. Vancouver, B.C., Can., Feb. 11, 1945; came to U.S., 1970; s. Kenneth William Thomas and Rosemary Humphries (Edmonds) W.; B.A., Wash. State U., 1967; M.A., Calif. State U., 1971; Ph.D., U. Minn., 1974. Editor, Fresno (Calif.) Advertiser, 1970; adminstrv. asst. U. Minn., Mpls., 1971-73; mem. faculty U. Wyo., Laramie, 1973-74, U. Tex., Austin, 1974-77; prof. journalism U. Ga., Athens, 1977-82; prof., chmn. communication U. South Ala., Mobile, 1982—. Mem. Internat. Public Relations Assn., Public Relations Soc. Am., Assn. Edn. Journalism. Episcopalian. Club: Lions. Contbr. articles to profl. jours. Office: Chmn Communication PO Box U-1462 University South Ala Mobile AL 36688

WRIGHT, DONALD KENNETH, clergyman; b. Woodruff, S.C., June 29, 1951; s. James Melvin and Margaret Rebecca (Goodwin) W.; m. Shirley Mae Biggerstaff, Aug. 13, 1972; children—Jonathan Matthew, David Benjamin, Melanie Elizabeth. B.A., Limestone Coll., 1974; M.R.E., So. Bapt. Theol. Sem., 1976. Ordained to ministry So. Baptist Ch., 1979. Minister mus. Cherokee Ave. Bapt. Mission, Gaffney, S.C., 1971-74; children's dir. Deer Park Bapt. Ch., Louisville, 1975-76; minister edn., youth Florence Bapt. Ch., Forest City, N.C., 1976-79; minister edn. First Baptist Ch., Rockingham, N.C., 1979-81; minister edn. to youth and coll. Wieuca Rd. Bapt. Ch., Atlanta, 1981-86; Christian edn. cons. Atlanta Bapt. Assn., Atlanta, 1986—. Mem. student com. Atlanta Bapt. Assn., 1984—; chmn. So. Bapt. Conv. student Adv. Group, 1985—. Mem. Met. Youth Ministers Assn., Met. Atlanta Youth Ministers Assn., Met. Atlanta Bapt. Religious Edn. Assn., Christian Council Met. Atlanta, So. Bapt. Religious Edn. Assn. Avocations: reading; painting; coin collecting; music; weight training. Home: 1912 Innwood Rd NE Atlanta GA 30329 Office: Atlanta Bapt Assn 1340 Spring St NW Suite 100 Atlanta GA 30309

WRIGHT, DORIS JEAN, counselor, educator; b. Independence, Kans., June 7, 1952; d. Lawrence Glendall and Betty Evelyn (Pruitt) W.; B.S. in Psychology, Kans. State U., 1974, M.S. in Edn., 1976; Ph.D. in Counseling Psychology, U. Nebr., 1982. Instr. U. Nebr., Lincoln, 1978-79, 1980-81; psychology intern San Francisco State U., 1979-80; psychologist U. Tex., Austin, 1981—; cons. Nebr. Dept. Edn., Lincoln, 1980-81; cons., trainer Gen. Land Office, State of Tex., 1985, Omaha Pub. Schs., 1985. Contbr. chpt. to book; reviewer of book. Bd. dirs., v.p. Austin Resource Ctr. for Independent Living, 1983—; bd. dirs. Univ. YWCA, Austin, 1984—, pres., 1985. Am. Psychol. Assn. fellow, 1975-78; Congl. intern, 1977. Mem. Am. Psychol. Assn., Div. Counseling Psychology, Am. Assn. Counseling Devel., Am. Coll. Personnel Assn., Assn. Black Psychologist, Phi Delta Kappa. Avocations: photography; collecting antiques; weight training; aerobic dance. Home: 7744 Northcross Dr N230 Austin TX 78757 Office: Counseling & Mental Health Ctr PO Box 8119 Univ Tex Austin TX 78713-8119

WRIGHT, E(LAM) W(INDOM) (BILL), financial printing company executive; b. Thrall, Tex., Mar. 30, 1944; m. Kathleen Kellogg, Sept. 12, 1969; children—Karen, Lisa. B.A. in Polit. Sci., Bus. and Sociology with honors, S.W. Tex. State U., 1970; M.P.A., U. Tex., 1972. Spl. asst. to Pres. Lyndon B. Johnson, 1970-73; exec. asst. to U.S. Senator Lloyd Bentsen, 1973-77; dir. state and fed. relations U. Houston, 1977; exec. Warren-King Cos., Houston, 1978-82; chmn. bd., chief exec. officer August Fin. Printing Co., Houston, 1983—; dir. Parkway Nat. Bank, 1979-80; mem. devel. bd. Western Bank. Founder, chmn. Tex. Alliance; mem. U.S. Fund for Improvement Post Secondary Edn., 1981; mem. bus. and profl. involvement com. Tex. Commn. on Arts; chmn. Tex. Metric System Adv. Council, 1978; bd. regents Tex. State U. System, 1979-85; bd. dirs. Houston Met. Ministries, Tex. Bus. Hall of Fame Found., Guadalupe Local Devel. Corp. Served with USMC, 1963-67. Named Tex. State fellow, 1972; Tex. Rising Star, Tex. Bus., 1980. Mem. Tex. C. of C. (dir.), East Tex. C. of C. (dir., chmn. pub. affairs com.), Houston C. of C., Tex. Lyceum Assn. (dir. 1981-82). Home: 10710 Paulwood St Houston TX 77071 Office: 806 Main St Suite 2000 Houston TX 77002

WRIGHT, HARRY HERCULES, physician; b. Charleston, S.C., Jan. 4, 1948; s. Harry Vernon and Agnes Lucile (Simmons) W.; B.S., U. S.C., 1970; M.D., U. Pa., 1976, M.B.A., 1976. Resident in psychiatry Wm. S. Hall Psychiat. Inst., Columbia, S.C., 1977-79; adminstrv. fellow in psychiatry NIMH, Rockville, Md., 1979; fellow in child psychiatry William S. Hall Psychiat. Inst., 1979-81, teaching child psychiatrist, 1981—; instr. dept. neuropsychiatry and behavioral sci. U. S.C. Sch. Medicine, 1981-82, asst. prof., 1982—. Bd. dirs. Columbia Area Sickle Cell Anemia Found., 1977. Falk fellow, 1977-79; laughlin fellow, 1979; recipient Freed award Hall Psychiat. Inst., 1978. Mem. Am. Acad. Child Psychiatry, Am. Soc. Adolescent Psychiatry, AAAS, Am. Public Health Assn., Am. Hosp. Assn., Am. Chem. Soc., Am. Psychiat. Assn., So. Med. Assn., Com. to Combat Huntington's Disease, Riverbank Zool. Soc., Nat. Soc. for Autistic Children, Sigma Xi. Methodist. Contbr. articles to profl. jours. Home: PO Box 12474 Columbia SC 29211 Office: PO Box 202 Columbia SC 29202

WRIGHT, JAMES C., JR., congressman; b. Ft. Worth, Dec. 22, 1922; s. James C. and Marie (Lyster) W.; student Weatherford Coll., U. Tex.; m. Betty Hay, Nov. 12, 1972; children by previous marriage—Jimmy, Virginia Sue, Patricia Kay, Alicia Marie. Mem. Tex. Ho. of Reps., 1947-49; mayor City of Weatherford (Tex.), 1950-54; mem. 84th-99th Congresses from 12th Tex. Dist., majority leader, 1976—, mem. public works and transp. com., 1955-76, mem. budget com. Mem. Ho. of Reps. del. to U.S.-Mex. Interparliamentary Conf., 1963-84. Served with USAAF, World War II. Decorated D.F.C., Legion of Merit; named Outstanding Young Man, Tex. Jaycees, 1953; named Most Respected Mem. of Ho. of Reps. in survey taken by U.S. News & World Report, 1980, 82. Mem. League Tex. Municipalities (pres. 1953). Presbyterian. Author: You and Your Congressman, 1965; The Coming Water Famine, 1966; Of Swords and Plowshares, 1968; Reflections of a Public Man, 1984; co-author Congress and Conscience, 1970. Address: 1236 House Office Bldg Washington DC 20515

WRIGHT, JAMES CAMPBELL, speech and theatre educator; b. Goldthwaite, Tex., Apr. 3, 1939; s. Ealum Porter and Esther Elector (Spinks) W.; m. Barbara Anne Whitley, June 7, 1969; children—Emily Lorraine, John Campbell, Katheryn Denise. B.A., Hardin-Simmons U., 1962; M.A., Bowling Green State U., 1963; Ph.D., Ohio State U., 1974. Grad. asst. Bowling Green State U., Ohio, 1962-63, Ohio State U., Columbus, 1968-69; from instr. to prof. speech and theatre Stetson U., DeLand, Fla., 1965—, chmn. dept., 1977—. Dir., designer numerous theatrical prodns. Chmn. Starke Elem. Sch. Adv. Bd., DeLand, 1981-82; pres. George Marks Elem. Sch. P-TC, DeLand, 1983-84. Served with U.S. Army, 1963-65. Recipient Voice of Democracy award VFW, 1979, Prin.'s award Starke Elem. Sch., 1982. Mem. Assn. for Communication Adminstrn., Am. Theatre Assn., S.E. Theatre Assn., Fla. Theatre Conf. (bd. dirs. 1979-81). Democrat. Baptist. Home: 60 Melodie Ln DeLand FL 32724 Office: Stetson U Box 8377 DeLand FL 32720

WRIGHT, JAMES RONALD, English and education educator, college administrator; b. Shelby, N.C., Feb. 19, 1948; s. James Hoke and Catherine Elizabeth (Stockton) W.; m. Sandra Kay Wright, Nov. 27, 1971. A.A., Gardner-Webb Coll., 1969, B.A., 1971; M.A. in Edn., Western Carolina U., 1973; Ph.D., U. S.C., 1983. Tchr. secondary English, Rutherford County Schs., Spindale, N.C., 1971-72; pub. relations officer, instr. Cleveland Tech. Coll., Shelby, N.C., 1973-75, instr. English, gen. edn., 1975-84, dept. head gen. edn., communication tech., 1984—; adj. prof. Gardner-Webb Coll., Boiling Springs, N.C., 1977, Western Carolina U., Cullowhee, N.C., 1984, 85. Chmn. publicity United Way Cleveland County, Shelby, 1984. Recipient Hon. awards cert. Student Govt. Assn. Cleveland Tech. Coll., 1984; Edn. Professions Devel. Act fellow U.S. Govt., 1972. Mem. Greater Cleveland County Internat. Reading Assn. (editor newsletter 1982), Nat. Council Tchrs. English, Cleveland Tech. Coll. Faculty Assn., Phi Beta Kappa. Baptist. Home: 800 Kirby St Shelby NC 28150 Office: Cleveland Tech Coll 137 S Post Rd Shelby NC 28150

WRIGHT, JOHN CHARLES, oil company executive; b. Mercer, Pa., May 18, 1925; s. Paul H. and Helen (Munnell) W.; m. Becky Bell Lewis, June 9, 1951; children—John C., William L., Mary Carolyn. B.A., Denison U., 1947; B.S. in Mining Engring., Ohio State U., 1949, M.S. in Petroleum Engring., 1950. Asst. to pres. Wiser Oil Co. and assoc. cos., Sistersville, W.Va., 1950-53, v.p., 1953-61, pres., 1961—, treas., 1961-81, chief exec. officer, 1982—, also dir.; dir. 1st Tyler Bank & Trust Co. Named Outstanding Alumnus, Ohio State U., 1957, W.Va. Oil and Gas Man of Yr., 1976. Mem. Ind. Petroleum Assn. Am. (bd. dirs., v.p. W.Va.), AIME, Engrs. Com. of 100 of Ohio State U., W.Va. C. of C. (v.p. No. region), Am. Legion, Ohio State U. Assn. Club: Sistersville Country. Lodges: Masons, Shriners.

WRIGHT, JOHN COLLINS, university president; b. Oak Hill, W.Va., Aug. 5, 1927; s. John C. and Irene (Collins) W.; B.S., W.Va. Wesleyan Coll., 1948, LL.D. (hon.), 1974; Ph.D., U. Ill., 1951; D.Sc. (hon.), U. Ala., 1979, W.Va. Inst. Tech., 1979; m. Margaret Ann Cyphers, Sept. 11, 1949; children—Jeffrey Cyphers, John Timothy, Curtis Scott, Keith Alexander. Research chemist Hercules, Inc., 1951-57; mem. faculty W.Va. Wesleyan Coll., 1957-64; asst. program dir. NSF, 1964-65; dean Coll. Arts and Scis., No. Ariz. U., 1966-70, W.Va. U., Morgantown, 1970-74; vice chancellor W.Va. Bd. Regents, Charleston, 1974-78; pres. U. Ala., Huntsville, 1978—; interim pres. W.Va. Coll. Grad. Studies, Institute, 1975-76; hon. research asso. Univ. Coll., London, 1962-63; cons. NSF, 1965—, Army Sci. Bd., U.S. Army, 1979. Served with USNR, 1945-46. Mich. fellow Center Study Higher Edn., U. Mich., 1965-66. Mem. Am. Chem. Soc., AAAS, Assn. Higher Edn. Office: U Ala in Huntsville Office of Pres Huntsville AL 35899

WRIGHT, JULIO ARIAS, architect; b. Panama, May 25, 1936; s. Andrew Mark and Clarita (Smith) W.; m. Maria Del Carmen Fernandez, Sept. 9, 1961; children—Carmen Myra, Julio A., Carlos Alberto. Student Ecole Des Beaux Arts, Paris, 1954-56; A.A., C.Z. Jr. Coll., 1958; B.Arch., U. Fla., 1963. Lic. architect, P.R., Fla., Panama. Practice architecture, San Juan, P.R.; prof. Inter-Am. U., 1968; cons. Mem. AIA, Colegio de Arquitectos de P.R., Junta Tecnica de Ingenieria y Arquitectura. Roman Catholic. Club: Fort Buchanan Golf. Home: J-193 Turquesa Guaynabo PR 00922 Office: GPO Box 328 San Juan PR 00936

WRIGHT, LARRY L., political scientist, consultant; b. Fla., June 20, 1954; s. Dennis and Gertrude (Robinson) W. A.A., Chipola Jr. Coll., 1974; B.S., Fla. State U., 1976, M.S., 1978, Ph.D., 1980. Research asst. House Com. on Edn., Tallahassee, 1976; research asst. Fla. State U., Tallahassee, 1977-78, teaching asst., 1978-80; cons. Ctr. for Pub. Affairs and Govt. Services, Tallahassee, 1982-83; asst. prof. Florida A&M U., Tallahassee, 1980—; cons. Gadsden Demonstration Models Program, Quincy, Fla., 1980; mem. faculty Senate Fla. A&M U., 1984—. Contbr. articles to profl. jours. Commentator Facts and Faces, Sta. WAMF-TV/radio, 1984, radio sta. 91.5 FM, 1984. Mem. Fla. Polit. Sci. Assn., Am. Soc. Pub. Adminstrn., Assn. Soc. and Behavioral Scientists, So. Polit. Sci. Assn., Ga. Polit. Sci. Assn., Tallahassee Urban League, NAACP, Pi Sigma Alpha, Pi Gamma Mu. Democrat. Baptist. Home: PO Box 6856 Tallahassee FL 32314 Office: Florida A&M U Dept Polit Sci/Pub Adminstrn PO Box 984 Tallahassee FL 32314

WRIGHT, LINDA ANN, librarian; b. Columbia, Miss., Jan. 20, 1948; d. Howard Wilbur and Dorothy Elaine (Lott) Wright. B.A., U. So. Miss., 1971, M.S., 1972, M.L.S., 1982. Cert. tchr. English, media specialist, Miss. Tchr., English, Columbia Pub. Sch., 1972-73, librarian, 1980—; sec. Van Parkman Constrn. Co., Columbia, 1974-78; teller Foxworth Bank, Columbia, 1978-79; grad. asst. U. So. Miss., Hattiesburg, 1980. Bd. dirs. Columbia-Marion County Library Bd., 1984—. Mem. ALA, Miss. Library Assn., Beta Phi Mu, Alpha Lambda Delta, Lambda Iota Tau, Pi Gamma Mu. Baptist. Home: 910 Porter St Columbia MS 39429

WRIGHT, LINDA JEAN, banker; b. Chgo., Dec. 14, 1949; d. Eugene F. and Rosemary Margaret (Kiely) Kemph; student Loretto Heights Coll., 1967-69, U. Ill.-Urbana, 1970-71; m. Kelly W. Wright, Jr., Feb. 1979. Asst. to v.p. Busey 1st Nat. Bank, Urbana, 1969-72; spa mgr., supr. sales tng. Venus and Apollo Health Club, San Antonio, 1973-76; owner Plant Shop, San Antonio, 1976-77; with Enterprise Bank, Falls Church, Va., 1977-84, comml. lending officer, 1978-84, sr. v.p., 1979-84, corp. sec. of bd. dirs., 1980-84; pres., chief exec. officer Fairfax Savs. Bank, 1984—. Chmn. exec. com. Fairfax-Falls Church United Way; pres. No. Va. Local Devel. Corp. Mem. Fairfax County C. of C. (dir., v.p.), Nat. Assn. Bank Women (chmn. No. Va. group 1980-81). Roman Catholic. Club: Fairfax Hunt.

WRIGHT, LINUS, school administrator; b. Savoy, Tex., Mar. 1, 1927; m. Joyce Vanston, Aug. 11, 1927. B.A., Austin Coll., 1949, M.A., 1951; LL.D. hon., Abilene Christian U., 1979. Coach and tchr., Denison, Tex., 1949-52, asst. prin., 1953-54, prin., Sherman, Tex., 1954-57, asst. supt. adminstrn., 1957-60, bus. adminstr., San Angelo, Tex., 1960-63; bus. mgr. Lubbock Ind. Sch. Dist., Tex., 1963-71; chief fin. officer Houston Ind. Sch. Dist., 1971-74, supt. adminstrn. and support services, 1974-78; gen. supt. Dallas Ind. Sch. Dist., 1978—; vis. instr. edn., ednl. adminstrn., bus., fin. Austin Coll.; vis. instr. edn., ednl. adminstrn., bus., fin. Tex. Tech. U.; vis. instr. edn., adminstrn., bus., fin. U. Houston; vis. instr. edn., ednl. adminstrn., bus., fin. Tex. So. U.; vis. instr. edn., ednl. adminstrn., bus., fin. Tex. A&M U. Active Skillman Ave. Ch. Christ Dallas, Dallas Area C. of C.; trustee Dallas Alliance; vice chmn. pub. service employees unit United Way Campaign, 1983; trustee Goals For Dallas; exec. bd. Circle 10 Council Boy Scouts Am.; bd. dirs. Tex. Council Econ. Edn., Close Up Found., Clean Dallas, Inc., Dallas Alliance Bus.; adv. council Communities Found. Tex., Mexican Am. Legal Def. and Ednl. Fund Leadership Devel. Mem. Am. Assn. Sch. Adminstrs., Tex. Assn. Sch. Adminstrs., Nat. Assn. Sch. Bus. Ofcls., Tex. Assn. Sch. Bus. Ofcls., Sch. Facilities Council, Tex. Assn. Sch. Curriculum Devel., Phi Delta Kappa. Office: Office of Supt/Dallas Ind Sch Dist 3700 Ross Ave Dallas TX 75204*

WRIGHT, LUKE WILLIAMS, lawyer; b. Pasquotank County, N.C., June 3, 1914; s. Silas G. and Ina (Williams) W.; m. Sue Polson, Feb. 4, 1941; children—John G., Sarah N., Susan F. B.A., U. Ala., 1937, LL.B., 1939. Bar: N.C. 1939. With Jefferson Standard Life Ins. Co., Greensboro, N.C., 1939-43; assoc. Smith, Wharton, Sapp & Moore and predecessor, 1943-49, Welch Jordan, 1949-52; ptnr. Jordan, Wright, Nichols, Caffrey & Hill and predecessor, 1952-78; sole practice, Greensboro, 1978—. Mem. ABA, N.C. State Bar, Greensboro Bar Assn. (pres. 1975-76), N.C. Bar Assn., Am. Judicature Soc., Assn. Trial Lawyers Am. Democrat. Methodist. Club: Greensboro City. Home: 2515 Lakeshore Dr Greensboro NC 27407 Office: 430 W Friendly Ave Suite 207 Greensboro NC 27401

WRIGHT, MARY RUTH, psychologist; b. St. Louis, Apr. 2, 1922; d. Leon Carl and Gwendolyn (Travis) Brown; R.N., Washington U., St. Louis, 1944; B.S., U. Houston, 1966, M.A., 1967; Ph.D., Union Grad Sch., 1978; m. William Kemp Wright, Feb. 10, 1945; children—Gwendolyn, Veronica, Victoria, Jennifer. Instr., U.S. Cadet Nurse Corps, USPHS, 1944; instr. surgery Washington U. Sch. Nursing, 1944-45; instr. pediatrics Children's Meml. Hosp., Chgo., 1945-46; instr. S. Tex. Jr. Coll., Houston, 1967-70; mental health cons. St. Joseph Mental Hosp., Houston, 1966-67; staff psychol. services Almeda Clinic, Houston, 1966-70; pvt. practice marriage and family counseling, Houston, 1970—; med.-psychol. researcher and writer, 1970—; psychologist Houston Health Dept., 1971—; clin. asst. prof. psychology dept. otorhinolaryngology and communicative scis. Baylor Coll. Medicine. Recipient Spl. award Security Agy. Mem. Am. Psychol. Assn., Am. Assn. Marriage and Family Counselors, Am. Assn. Sex Educators and Counselors, Internat. Council Psychologists, Nat. Council Family Relations, Nat. Assn. Social Workers, Mental Health Assn. Houston and Harris County (dir.). Contbr. articles to profl. jours.; speaker U.S. and abroad on psychol. implications of elective surgery. Home: 3671 Del Monte St Houston TX 77019 Office: 633 Hermann Profl Bldg Houston TX 77030

WRIGHT, MURRAY BLAIR, JR., architect, consultant, planner; b. Boston, July 22, 1925; s. Murray Blair and Marcella (Buckel) W.; m. Carolyn Harrington, June 30, 1948; children—David, Marcella, Therese, Mary, John, Elizabeth, Michael, Paul. B.S., Ga. Inst. Tech., 1945, B.Arch., 1947. Registered architect, Ga., Fla. Designer, draftsman Snyder & Nims Architects, Miami, Fla., 1947-48, Alfred B. Parker Architects, Miami, 1948-49; designer, architect Edwin T. Reeder Assocs. A/E, Miami, 1950-57; pvt. practice architecture, Miami, 1958-78, Pensacola, Fla., 1984—; architect, dir. planning and bldg. Diocese Pensacola-Tallahassee, Fla., 1978-84; bd. dirs. 3 non-profit projects for elderly under HUD Sect. 202 program. Prin. works include Barry Coll. Sci. Ctr., Book and Film Ctr. (City of Miami Bldg. of Month 1962), Ch. of St. Hugh, Coconut Grove (City of Miami Bldg. of Month 1963), Primary Centerette Sch. Sch., Liberty City, Miami (U.S. Congress citation for best use of fed. Title 2 funds in U.S. 1968). Scoutmaster South Fla. council Boy Scouts Am., 1963-64; coach Khoury League, Miami, 1970-73. Served to lt. comdr. USNR, World War II. Recipient medal of honor Diocese Pensacola-Tallahassee, 1983. Mem. AIA (various offices 1949-74, including chmn. task force for profl. responsibility to community 1969, coordinator Community Edn.-Environ. Ctr. 1966-67), Constrn. Specifications Inst. (profl.), Soc. Am. Mil. Engrs. Roman Catholic. Club: Serra. Lodges: K.C., Rotary. Office: 1419 N Palafox St Pensacola FL 32501

WRIGHT, MYRON ARNOLD, oil field equipment executive; b. Blair, Okla., Apr. 9, 1911; s. Charles Edgar and Hattie Susan (Dillingham) W.; m. Izetta Chattin, June 4, 1935 (dec.); 1 dau., Mary Judith (Mrs. Sidney Reid, Jr.); m. Josephine Primm, June 14, 1969. Student, Northwestern State Tchrs. Coll., 1928-30; B.S., Okla. State U., 1933; D.Sc. (hon.), U. Tulsa, LL.D., Okla. Christian Coll., D. Eng., Worcester Poly. Inst. Various engring. positions Carter Oil Co., Tulsa, 1933-43, chief petroleum engr., 1943-44, asst. mgr. prodn., 1944-46; exec. asst. producing dept. Standard Oil Co. of N.J., N.Y.C., 1946-49, dep. coordinator, 1949-51; exec. v.p. Internat. Petroleum Co., Ltd., Coral Gables, Fla., 1951-52; exec. v.p., dir. Carter Oil Co., Tulsa, 1952-54; producing coordinator Standard Oil Co., N.J., 1954-58, dir., 1958-60, exec. v.p., mem. exec. com., 1960-66; chmn., chief exec. officer Exxon Co. USA, 1966-76; exec. v.p., dir. Exxon Corp., 1973-76; chmn., pres. Cameron Iron Works, Inc., 1977-81, chmn., chief exec. officer, 1981—, chmn., pres., 1981-85, chmn., 1986—; dir., mem. exec com. 1st City Bancorp. Tex., Inc. 1971-85; dir., mem. exec. com., audit com. Am. Gen. Ins. Co., 1976-83; former dir. Evans Products Co.; Bd. govs. U.S. Postal Service, 1971-80, chmn., 1974-80. Mem. council overseers Jesse H. Jones Grad. Sch. Adminstrn., Rice U.; mem. adv. council U. Tex. at Austin Engring. Found. Mem. Am. Inst. Mining, Metall. and Petroleum Engrs., Am. Petroleum Inst. (dir.), U.S. C. of C. (pres. 1966-67, chmn. 1967-68), Houston C. of C. (dir. 1978-84), Nat. Wildlife Fedn. (mem. bd. 1969-75), Tau Beta Pi, Sigma Tau Gamma, Phi Kappa Phi, Lambda Chi Alpha. Clubs: Balboa Bay (Newport Beach, Calif.); River Oaks Country, Houston, Petroleum, Ramada, Met. Racquet (Houston); Garden of Gods (Colorado Springs, Colo.). Office: PO Box 1212 Houston TX 77251

WRIGHT, R(ALEIGH) LEWIS, neurosurgeon; b. Roanoke, Va., Apr. 16, 1931; s. Raleigh Lewis and Mary Lillian (Major) W.; m. Sarah Bird Grant, Sept. 7, 1963; 1 son, Alexander Grant. B.A., U. Richmond, 1951; M.D., Med. Coll. Va., 1955. Intern, Duke U. Hosp., 1955-56, surg. resident, 1956-57; neurosurg. resident Mass. Gen. Hosp., Boston, 1959-63; practice medicine specializing in neurosurgery, Boston, 1964-70, Richmond, Va., 1970—; mem. staff St. Mary's, Retreat, Richmond Met., Stuart Circle hosps., Med. Coll. Va.; faculty Harvard Med. Sch., Boston, 1962-70; faculty neurosurgery Med. Coll. Va., 1970—. Author: Postoperative Craniotomy Infections, 1966; Septic Complications of Neurosurgical Spinal Procedures, 1970; Artists in Virginia Before 1900, 1983. Contbr. articles to profl. jours., also author articles on early so. artists. Served with M.C., USNR, 1957-59. King Trust Fund fellow, 1963-64. Diplomate Am. Bd. Neurol. Surgery, Nat. Bd. Med. Examiners. Fellow ACS; mem. AMA, Am. Assn. Neurol. Surgeons, Congress Neurol. Surgeons, Southern Neurosurg. Soc., Am. Acad. Neurology, Med. Soc. Va., Assn. for Research in Nervous and Mental Diseases, Richmond Acad. Medicine. Episcopalian. Club: Commonwealth. Home: 3505 Old Gun Rd Midlothian VA 23113 Office: 4908 Monument Ave Richmond VA 23230

WRIGHT, REX ALTON, psychologist, psychology educator; b. Sinton, Tex., Sept. 8, 1954; s. Vernon Alton and Dorotha Sue (Miller) W. A.A., Del Mar Jr. Coll., Corpus Christi, 1974; B.A., U. Tex., 1977; M.A., U. Kans., 1979, Ph.D., 1982. NIMH postdoctoral fellow Lab. of Biobehavior, SUNY-Stony Brook, 1982-84; vis. asst. prof. dept. psychology U. Tex., Austin, 1984—. Contbr. author chpts. in books and various publs. Research asst. U. Kans. Gen. Research Fund, 1978; Fed. Tng. grantee NIMH, 1979-81. Mem. Am. Psychol. Assn., Soc. Personality and Social Psychology. Home: 4205 Speedway 304 Austin TX 78751 Office: Dept Psychology U Tex-Austin Austin TX 78712

WRIGHT, ROBERT LAZENBY, biology educator, consultant; b. Goose Creek, Tex., Oct. 3, 1932; s. William Perkins and Ethel Corine (Lazenby) W.; m. Julia Ann Farned, May 8, 1954 (div.); children—Robert Lazenby, Gordon Kenneth, Lydia Colynn; m. Glenda Morgan Elkins, Mar. 3, 1978. B.S., Stephen F. Austin State Coll., 1954; postgrad. U. Houston, 1956-58, Tex. A&M U., 1958-60, 64-67. Jr. engr. Humble Oil Refining Co., Baytown, Tex., 1957; tchr. sci. Goose Creek Pub. Sch., Baytown, 1960-61; instr. biology Lee Coll., Baytown, 1962-64, prof. biology, 1967—; sr. engr. Esso (Humble Oil), Baytown, 1967, cons. water quality, 1967-68. Dist. commr. San Houston Area council Boy Scouts Am., 1968-70; bd. dirs. Bay Area Heritage Soc., Baytown, 1978-82, pres., 1980-81, 81-82; 1st v.p. Lee Coll. Faculty Assembly, 1984-86. Served with U.S. Army, 1954-56. Fish and Wildlife Service, Dept. Interior grantee, 1958; U.S. Forest Service grantee, 1964. Mem. Am. Forestry Assn., Soc. Range Mgmt., Alpha Chi. Republican. Methodist. Avocations: sailing; woodworking; gardening. Home: 606 Scenic Dr Baytown TX 77521 Office: Lee Coll PO Box 818 Baytown TX 77522-0818

WRIGHT, ROBERT MARLOW, retail sales executive; b. Gadsden, Ala., Aug. 25, 1956; s. James Toliver and Bertha Laverne (Haas) W. B.A.,

Jacksonville State U., 1980. Salesman Dawsey Cherry Shoe Corp., Wakefields Dept. Store, Anniston, Ala., 1977-80; head of sales Rich's Dept. Store, Birmingham, Ala., 1980-81, sales mgr., 1981—. Mem. Phi Mu Alpha Sinfonia. Methodist. Avocations: reading; needlepoint. Home: 108 Moss Rock Ln Birmingham AL 35210 Office: Rich's 2600 Riverchase Galleria Birmingham AL 35236

WRIGHT, ROBERT ROSS, III, lawyer, law educator, consultant; b. Ft. Worth, Nov. 20, 1931; s. Robert Ross and Alma Stewart W.; m. Susan Webber, May 21, 1983; children by previous marriage—Robert R., John Forrest, David Stewart. B.A., U. Ark., 1953; M.A., Duke U., 1954; J.D., U. Ark., 1956; S.J.D., U. Wis., 1967. Bar: Ark. 1956, Okla. 1970, U.S. Supreme Ct. Grad. asst. Duke U., 1953-54; atty. Norton, Norton & Wright, Forrest City, Ark., 1956-59; asst. counsel, asst. sec. The Crossett Co. (Ark.), 1960-63; atty. Ga.-Pacific Corp., Crossett, Ark., 1960-63; asst. prof. law U. Ark., prof., 1963-70, Donaghey Disting. prof., 1976—, asst. dean, 1965-66, dir. Continuing Legal Edn.; vis. prof., asst. to pres. U. Iowa, 1969-70; dean Coll. Law, dir. Law Ctr., prof. U. Okla., 1970-76. Mem. Little Rock Planning Commn., 1978-82, chmn., 1982. Fellow Am. Law Inst., Am. Soc. Probate Counsel; mem. ABA (mem. council sect. of gen. practice 1978-81, mem. standing com. on profl. utilization and career devel. 1977-80), Ark. Bar Assn. (ho. of dels. 1978-81, 82-85, exec. council 1985—), Okla. Bar Assn., Pulaski County Bar Assn., Ark. Bar Found., Order Coif, Phi Beta Kappa, Omicron Delta Kappa, Phi Alpha Delta. Episcopalian. Club: Capital (Little Rock). Author: The Law of Airspace, 1968; Cases and Materials on Land Use, 1969, 3d edit., 1982; Land Use in a Nutshell, 1978, 2d edit., 1985; contbr. chpts. to books. Home: 1409 N Hughes Little Rock AR 72207 Office: U Ark Law Sch 400 W Markham St Little Rock AR 72201

WRIGHT, SARAH BIRD, educator, writer; b. Wilmington, N.C., Nov. 25, 1933; d. Richard Oscar and Elise (Martin) Grant; A.B., Bryn Mawr (Pa.) Coll., 1955; M.A., Duke U., Durham, N.C., 1958; m. R.L. Wright, Sept. 7, 1963; 1 son, Alexander Grant. Tchr. English composition and lit. Boston U., 1959-60; research asst. linguistics Harvard Computation Lab., 1960-62; copy editor Beacon Press and Allyn & Bacon, Boston, 1963-70; tchr. English U. Richmond (Va.), 1981—; contbr. to newspapers and mags. including Christian Sci. Monitor, Accent on Living, Newsday, Toronto Globe & Mail, N.Y. Times, Americana, Travel/Holiday, Chgo. Tribune, N.Z. Herald, Jour. Modern Lit. Dist. councillor Bryn Mawr Coll. Alumnae Assn., 1975-78; vol. Va. Mus., 1980-81. Mem. Authors Guild N.Y., MLA. Episcopalian. Club: Richmond Woman's. Home: 3505 Old Gun Rd Midlothian VA 23113 Office: English Dept Room 405 Ryland Hall U Richmond Richmond VA 23227

WRIGHT, STEPHEN CALDWELL, English language educator; b. Sanford, Fla., Nov. 11, 1946; s. Joseph and Bernice Ida (Wright) Caldwell. A.A., St. Petersburg Jr. Coll., 1967; B.A., Fla. Atlantic U., 1969; M.A., Atlanta U., 1972; Ph.D., Ind. U. Pa., 1983. Instr., head dept. English, Crooms High Sch., Sanford, Fla., 1969-70; student tchr. Clark Coll., Atlanta, 1971-72; prof. English, black Am. history Seminole Community Coll., Sanford, 1972—; reviewer NEH, 1981. Mem. Human Rights Com., Seminole County, 1973-76. Three Univs. fellow Inst. for Services to Edn., 1971—; named First Superior Poet, Fla. Poetry Festival, 1969; Gwendolyn Brooks poetry award, 1984. Mem. Nat. Council Tchrs. English, Langston Hughes Soc., Coll. Lang. Assn., Middle Atlantic Writers Assn., NAACP. Baptist. Author: First Statement: A Collection of Poems, 1983; Poems in Movement, 1984; How A Tulip Blooms: Women As Revolution, 1985; contbr. poems to lit. jours. Home: 127 Langston Dr Sanford FL 32771 Office: Seminole Community Coll Sanford FL 32771

WRIGHT, STUART THURMAN, teacher educator, publisher; b. Roxboro, N.C., Mar. 30, 1948; s. Wallace Lyndon and Frances Anne (Critcher) W. B.A., Wake Forest U., 1970, M.A.Ed., 1973, M.A., 1980. Lectr. edn. Wake Forest U., 1977—; publisher Palaemon Press, Winston-Salem, N.C., 1976—. Mem. Am. Coll. Sports Medicine, Brit. Chiropody Assn., Brit. Assn. Sport and Medicine. Republican. Episcopalian. Clubs: Old Town, Torch, Wednesday (Winston Salem); Grolier (N.Y.C.). Author books including: Historical Sketch of Person County, 1975; Forsyth: The History of a County on the March, 1976; editor: The Confederate Letters of Benjamin H. Freeman, 1974; (with Mary Jarrell) Selected Letters of Randall Jarrell, 1983, Randall Jarrell: A Bibliography, 1983, James Dickey: A Bibliography, 1982; Dancer's Guide to Injuries of the Lower Extremity, 1985; others; contbr. articles to profl. jours.

WRIGHT, TIMOTHY UNDERWOOD, pharmacist; b. Athens, Ala., May 29, 1951; s. Grady Underwood and Ora (Howard) W.; m. Jacqueline Gail Breland, May 21, 1982. B.S. in Pharmacy, Samford U., 1973. Registered pharmacist, Ala. Intern pharmacist Univ. Hosp., Birmingham, Ala., 1974; staff pharmacist K Mart Pharmacy, Florence, Ala., 1975-76, mgr. pharmacist Muscle Shoals, Ala., 1976-77, Tuscaloosa, Ala., 1977-83; owner, pharmacist Medicine Shoppe, Tuscaloosa, 1984—. Recipient Outstanding Young Man Am. Award, 1974, 80. Mem. Ala. Pharm. Assn., Tuscaloosa C. of C., Circle K Clubs (gov. 1972-73, v.p. Circle K Internat. 1973-74), Multiple Sclerosis Soc. (mem. Nat. Youth Leadership Council 1973-74), Phi Delta Chi, Omicron Delta Kappa. Republican. Mem. Ch. of Christ. Club. Hasbeens Internat. (bd. dirs. 1977—). Avocations: sports; gardening. Office: Medicine Shoppe 715 15 St E Tuscaloosa AL 35401

WRIGHTER, FRANKLIN JAMES, retail company executive, investment consultant, realtor; b. Sayre, Pa., Sept. 30, 1940; s. Alton Willis and Emily Mae (Tewksbury) W.; m. Patricia Rae Stanelle, Feb. 17, 1959 (div. 1983); children—Laura, Lisa, Linda. Student, Ga. Inst. Tech., 1959-61, U. Ga., 1961-62. Store mgr. Western Auto, Atlanta, 1963-65; div. mgr. Sears Roebuck & Co., Jackson, Tenn., 1965-67, merchanding mgr., 1967-68, field rep., Memphis, 1969-70, operating mgr., Mobile, Ala., 1970—. Cons., Jr. Achievement of Mobile, 1970—. Republican. Mormon. Club: PJI Flying. Home: 285 Larkspur Mobile AL 36609 Office: Sears Roebuck & Co Bel Air Mall Mobile AL 36616

WRIGHTMAN, CAROLINE ANNE MCGHEE, nursing administrator; b. Portland, Oreg., Mar. 14, 1942; d. William Hanen and Lola Jeanette (Oberg) McGhee; m. Larry Keith Wrightman, Mar. 24, 1974. B.S. in Nursing, Loma Linda U., 1965; M.Nursing in Psychiatry, UCLA, 1975. Lic. advanced registered nurse practitioner, Fla. Clin. instr. pediatrics Pacific Union Coll., Glendale, Calif., 1970-72; clin. instr. psychiat. nursing Los Angeles County Sch. Nursing, 1972-73; crisis unit dir., mental health counselor Los Angeles County Mental Health, Arcadia, 1976-79; adminstrv. dir. psychiatry Fla. Hosp., Orlando, 1979—. HEW grantee, 1964, 73-75. Mem. Am. Assn. Suicidology. Adventist. Home: 7748 Waunatta Ct Winter Park FL 32792 Office: 601 E Rollins St Orlando FL 32803

WRISBERG, CRAIG ALAN, physical education educator; b. St. Louis, Oct. 14, 1945; s. Arthur Paul and Madelyn Gertrude (Wilson) W.; m. Ann Morris, Dec. 16, 1967; children—Amy Dawn, Kristin Gay. A.B. in Edn., Greenville, Coll., 1967; M.A. in Edn., Ind. State U., 1969; A.M. in Psychology, U. Mich., 1973, Ph.D. in Edn., 1974. Asst. prof. Va. Tech. Inst. and State U., Blacksburg, 1974-77; asst. prof. U. Tenn., Knoxville, 1977-78, assoc. prof., 1979-85, prof., 1985—. Contbr. articles to ednl. and psychological jours. Mem. N.Am. Soc. for Psychology of Sport and Phys. Activity (sec., treas., 1982-84), AAHPERD (sec. so. dist. research council 1981-83), Sport Psychology Acad., Nat. Assn. for Sport and Phys. Edn., Internat. Soc. Sport Psychology. Presbyterian. Home: 6716 Government Farm Rd Knoxville TN 37920 Office: Sch of Health Dept Phys Edn and Dance U Tenn 1914 Andy Holt Ave Knoxville TN 37996-2700

WROBLE, ARTHUR G., lawyer; b. Taylor, Pa., Jan. 21, 1948; s. Arthur S. and Sophia P. Wroble; m. Mary Ellen Sheehan, Nov. 19, 1977; 2 daus., Sophia Ann, Sarah Jean. B.S. in Bus. Adminstrn. with honors, U. Fla., 1970, M.B.A., 1971, J.D., 1973. Bar: Fla. 1973, U.S. Ct. Appeals (5th cir.) 1974, U.S. Supreme Ct. 1976, U.S. Ct. Appeals (11th cir.) 1981, U.S. Dist. Ct. (so. dist.) Fla., 1974, U.S. Dist. Ct. (mid. dist.) Fla. 1982. Ptnr., Burns, Middleton, Farrell & Faust (now Steel Hector, Davis, Burns & Middleton), Palm Beach, Fla., 1973-82; ptnr. Wolf, Block, Schorr & Solis-Cohen, Phila. and West Palm Beach, Fla., 1982—; mem. 15th Jud. Cir. Ct. Nominating Commn., 1979-83; mem. U. Fla. Law Center Council, 1981-84; mem. adv. bd. alternative sentencing program Palm Beach County. Served to maj. JAG, U.S. Army Res., 1984. Mem. ABA, Fla. Bar (bd. govs. young lawyers sect. 1979-83, bd. govs. 1985—), Palm Beach County Bar Assn. (pres. young lawyers sect. 1978-79, dir. 1979-81, sec.-treas. 1981-83, pres.-elect 1983-84, pres. 1984-85), Guild Cath. Lawyers Palm Beach County, Inc. (pres. 1980-81, dir. 1981—), Legal Aid Soc. Palm Beach County, Inc. (dir. 1981—). Roman Catholic. Clubs: Kiwanis (pres. 1980-81), Palm Beach County Gator (pres. 1982-83), KC (grand knight 1978-79). Contbr. articles to profl. jours. Home: 7645 Clarke Rd West Palm Beach FL 33406 Office: 777 S Flagler Dr Suite 900 PO Box 027515 West Palm Beach FL 33402

WRUCK, ERICH-OSKAR, German language educator, administrator; b. Gr. Kroessin/Pomerania, Germany, Oct. 29, 1928; came to U.S., 1952, naturalized, 1954; s. Erich Albert and Erna (Kroening) W.; m. Esther Emmy Schmidt, Oct. 3, 1953; children—Eric Gordon, Karin Esther, Krista Elisabeth. B.A. magna cum laude, Rutgers U., 1959, M.A., 1961, Ph.D., 1969. Asst. instr. Rurgers U., New Brunswick, N.J., 1959-62; asst. prof. Davidson Coll., N.C., 1962-69, assoc. prof., 1969-73, prof., chmn. dept. German, 1983—, dir. Davidson Abroad Program, Marburg, Fed. Republic German, 1966-67, 71-72. Served to 1st lt. U.S. Army, 1953-57, to col. USAR, 19—. Recipient Meritorious Service medal Dept. Army, 1983. Mem. Goethe Gesellschaft, Freies Deutsches Hochstift, Schiller Gesellschaft, Goethe Soc. of N. Am., Soc. for German Am. Studies. Republican. Lutheran. Avocations: painting; photography; soaring; skiing; running. Office: Dept German Davidson Coll Davidson NC 28036

WU, JAIN-MING (JAMES), aerospace engineering educator, consultant; b. Nanking, China, Aug. 13, 1933; s. Yong-Yu and Sun-See W. Wu; m. Ying-Chu Lin, June 13, 1959; children—Ernest H., Albert H., Karen H. B.S.M.E., Nat. Taiwan U., 1955; M.S., Calif. Inst. Tech., 1959, Ph.D., 1965. Teaching asst. Calif. Inst. Tech., Pasadena, 1958-65; mem. tech. staff Nat. Engr. Sci. Co., Pasadena, 1960-63; successively asst. prof., assoc. prof., prof. aerospace engring. U. Tenn. Space Inst., Tullahoma, 1965—, dir. gas dynamics div., 1975—, now Bernhard H. Goethert prof.; vis. prof. Von Karman Inst. Fluid Dynamics, Rhode-St.-Genese, Belgium, 1970; hon. prof. Beijing Inst. Aeros. and Astronautics, China, 1985; cons. Jet Propulsion Lab., 1965, U.S. Army Research Office, 1968-73, Messerschmitt-Bölkow-Blohm, W. Ger., 1977-79, Beoing Aerospace, 1977-80; pres. Engring. & Cons., Inc., 1977—; cons. Nielsen Engring. and Research, Inc., 1983—; adviser Orbital Scis. Corp., 1983—; hon. prof. Northwestern Poly. U., Xian, China, 1986. Vice pres. Tullahoma Unitarian Fellowship, 1969; adv. Motlow State Community Coll., Tullahoma, 1977-79. Anthony scholar Calif. Inst. Tech., 1965. Assoc. fellow AIAA (chmn. Tenn. sect. 1973, Gen. H.H. Arnold award Tenn. sect. 1970); mem. Am. Rocket Soc., Southeastern Conf. Theoretical and Applied Mechanics, Sigma Xi. Club: Tullahoma Country. Contbr. articles to tech. jours. Home: 111 Lakewood Dr Tullahoma TN 37388 Office: University of Tennessee Space Institute Tullahoma TN 37388

WUENSCH, KARL LOUIS, behavioral research statistician, psychobiologist, educator; b. Parkersburg, W.Va., Nov. 27, 1947; s. Karl R. and Elizabeth A. (Reese) W.; m. Silvia G. Muller, Oct. 18, 1969; children—Athena Iris, Lotus Siva, Sol Xenos. B.A. summa cum laude, Elmira Coll., 1973; M.A., East Carolina U., 1975; Ph.D., Miami U., Oxford, Ohio, 1982. Vis. asst. prof. SUNY-Oswego, 1981-82; lectr. East Carolina U., Greenville, 1982-85, asst. prof., 1985—. Contbr. articles to profl. jours. Recipient Outstanding Young Men Am. award, 1984. Mem. Am. Psychol. Assn., Am. Soc. Mammalogists, Animal Behavior Soc., Phi Beta Kappa, Sigma Xi, Phi Kappa Phi. Avocation: horticulture. Home: Route 1 Box 327 Ayden NC 28513 Office: East Carolina U Dept Psychology Greenville NC 27834

WUKASCH, DORIS LUCILLE STORK, educator, counselor; b. Somerville, Tex., Dec. 30, 1924; d. Edwin William and Clara Rofine (Fuchs) Stork; B.A. with high honors, U. Tex., 1944, M.Ed., 1969; m. Joe Eugene Wukasch, July 7, 1945 (div. 1971); children—Linda Thiering, Susan Wukasch Richter, Jean Wukasch Mihalik, Jonathan. Chemist Tex. Dept. Health, Austin, 1944-45; microbiologist Terrell Labs., Ft. Worth, 1946-47; exec. sec. Wukasch Architects and Engrs., Austin, 1954-66; editorial asst. Steck-Vaughn Pubs., Austin, 1966; rehab. caseworker, job counselor Mary Lee Sch., Austin, 1969-70; spl. tchr. career edn. Austin Ind. Sch. Dist. 1970-85. . Instr. ARC, 1972—; vol. tchr. Austin State Sch., 1958-68. Area chmn. Am. Cancer Soc., 1970; mem. Women's Archtl. Guild, 1954-71, pres., 1964; mem. Tex. Fine Arts Assn., 1960—, Smithsonian Assos., 1972—, Wycliffe Assos., 1973—. HEW grantee, 1968-69. Certified rehab. counselor. Mem. Austin Mental Health Assn., Nat. Rehab. Counselors Assn., Nat., Tex. State tchrs. assn., Nat. Trust Historic Preservation, Christian Bus. and Profl. Women's Council, NOW, Assn. Supervision and Curriculum Devel., Phi Beta Kappa. Lutheran. Contbr. poems and articles to mags. and newspapers. Home: 2500 Inwood Pl Austin TX 78703

WULF, GEORGE RICHARD, petroleum consultant; b. Clinton, Iowa, May 6, 1930; s. Richard Lyle and Bernice Margaret (Thomsen) W.; m. Janis Marie Burrows, June 5, 1955; 1 dau., Jennifer Marie. B.S. in Geol. Engring. with honors, S.D. Sch. Mines, 1951, M.S. in Geology, 1955; Ph.D. in Geology, U. Mich., 1959; LL.B., LaSalle U., 1964. Cert. profl. geologist. Seismologist, Ind. Exploration Co., Gillette, Wyo., 1951-52; dist. geophysicist Mobil Oil, Tripoli, Libya, 1954-62; sr. ops. geologist Pan Am., Casper, Wyo., 1962-63; pvt. oil operator, Casper, 1963-73; chmn., chief exec. officer Wulf Oil, Casper, 1973-82; cons. in seismic stratigraphy Superior Oil Co., The Woodlands, Tex., 1982—. Author tech. papers in field. Pres. Immanuel Lutheran Ch., Chadron, Nebr., 1978; trustee Chadron State Coll. Found., 1981; bd. dirs. Chadron Community Hosp., 1981. Served with U.S. Army, 1952-54. Recipient Bausch & Lomb sci. award, 1943, best paper award Wyo. Geol. Assn., 1964; Mobil Oil scholar, 1954; U. Mich. scholar, 1957. Fellow Geol. Soc. Am.; mem. Am. Assn. Petroleum Geologists, AAAS, Am. Legion, Sigma Tau, Sigma Xi. Republican. Club: Denver Petroleum. Lodge: Elks. Home: PO Box 8187 The Woodlands TX 77387

WUNDER, CHARLES ALAN, engring. co. exec.; b. Greenock, Pa., Nov. 27, 1933; s. James George and Loretta Mary (Murtha) W.; B.S., U. Pitts., 1959, postgrad., 1962; student bus. mgmt. Alexander Hamilton, 1967; m. Melvine Ann Svitlak, Jan. 6, 1953; children—Charles, Elizabeth, Patrick. Chief engr. Power Piping Co., Pitts., 1963-73; pres. Raemel, Inc., 1973-80, C.A. Wunder Engring., Inc. and Wunder Enterprises, Inc., Cape Coral, Fla., 1980—. Chmn. Cape Coral Code Enforcement Bd., Contractors Examing Bd., Bd. Adjustments and Appeals; mem. Cape Coral Archtl. Bd. Served with AUS, 1953-55. Registered profl. engr., Fla., Pa., Ohio, Ind., Ill. Mem. ASME, Nat. Soc. Profl. Engrs., Cape Coral Contractors Assn., Five County Contractors Assn. Democrat. Roman Catholic. Contbr. articles profl. jours. Research in non-destructive testing and welding. Home: 2201 SE 32d Terr Cape Coral FL 33904 Office: 950 Country Club Blvd Cape Coral FL 33904

WURSTER, STEPHEN HARRY, educator, college president; b. Williamsport, Pa., Feb. 19, 1941; s. Clyde Herbert and Grace Anna (Stevens) W.; A.B., Ursinus Coll., 1963; M.Div., Drew U., 1967; M.A., U. Iowa, 1970, Ph.D., 1972; postdoctoral study Inst. Ednl. Mgmt., Harvard U., 1980; m. Jean Elizabeth Miller, June 18, 1966; children—Gregory Stephen, Mark Andrew, Elizabeth Ann. Ordained to ministry, United Methodist Ch., 1967; assoc. minister Armonk (N.Y.) United Meth. Ch., 1964-65, 67; asst. chaplain Topeka State Hosp., 1965; assoc. dir. Wesley Found., U. Oreg., 1965-66; teaching assoc. U. Iowa, 1969-70; asst. to v.p. for instructional affairs, dean of faculties, asst. prof. history Ball State U., Muncie, Ind., 1971-75, assoc. prof. history, 1975-80, prof. history, 1980-81, dean for acad. planning and faculty devel., 1975-81; pres. Catawba Coll., Salisbury, N.C., 1981—; dir. N.C. Nat. Bank. Pres. bd. dirs. Delaware County Assn. for Retarded Citizens, 1979; trustee N.C. Ind. Coll. Fund, 1981—; bd. dirs. Rowan County Assn. Retarded Citizens, 1981-83; bd. deacons 1st Presbyterian Ch., 1977-79, Salisbury Symphony Soc., 1981—. Woodrow Wilson disseration fellow, 1970-71; Danforth asso., 1973—; Paul Harris fellow, 1982. Mem. Am. Assn. Higher Assn., Am. Hist. Assn., Assn. Study Higher Edn., Am. Soc. Ch. History, Orgn. Am. Historians, Soc. Coll. and Univ. Planning, N.C. Assn. Ind. Colls. and Univs. (dir. 1983—). Democrat. Mem. United Ch. of Christ. Lodge: Rotary (dir.). Home: 104 N Park Dr Salisbury NC 28144 Office: Office of Pres Catawba Coll Salisbury NC 28144

WURTH, MARK STEPHEN, pharmacist, consultant; b. Paducah, Ky., Aug. 20, 1953; s. James Bernard and Glenna (Brandt) W.; m. Karen Shea Littleton, Sept. 17, 1974; children—James B., Paul S. Student U. Ky., 1971-74; B.S. in Pharmacy, Samford U., 1976. Registered pharmacist. Pharmacist Eckerd Drug, Birmingham, Ala., 1974-78, Pay Less Drug, Paducah, 1978-79; pharmacist, owner Wurths Pharmacy, Paducah, 1979—; pharmacy cons. Superior Care Home, Paducah, 1982, Medco Ctr., Paducah, 1985—; dir. pharmacy rev. and therapeutics com. Cardinal Health Care, Possum Trot, Ky., 1981—; cons., pharmacy dir. Parkview Convalescent Ctr., Paducah, 1985—. Mem. Am. Pharm. Assn., Nat. Assn. Retail Druggists, Nat. Fedn. Ind. Bus., 1st Dist. Pharm. Assn. Roman Catholic. Avocation: tennis. Home: 3307 Buckner Ln Paducah KY 42001 Office: Wurths Pharmacy/Sickroom Service PO Box 3244 Paducah KY 42002-3244

WURTZEL, ALAN LEON, retail executive; b. Mount Vernon, N.Y., Sept. 23, 1933; s. Samuel S. and Ruth (Mann) W.; A.B., Oberlin Coll., 1955; postgrad. London Sch. Econ., 1955-56; LL.B. cum laude, Yale, 1959; m. Barbara Goldstein, June 16, 1955; children—Judith Halle, Daniel Henry, Sharon Lee. Bar: Conn. 1959, D.C. 1960, Va. 1968. Law clk. Chief Judge David L. Bazelon, U.S. Ct. Appeals, D.C., 1959-60; assoc. firm Fried, Frank, Harris, Shriver & Kampelman, Washington, 1960-65; legis. asst. to Senator Joseph Tydings, 1965-66; with Circuit City Stores, Inc. (formerly Wards Co., Inc.), Richmond, 1966—, exec. v.p., 1968-70, pres., 1970—, chmn. bd., chief exec. officer, 1984—; dir. Craddock-Terry Shoe Corp. Pres., Jewish Community Fedn. Richmond; mem. adv. com. Va. Commonwealth U. Sch. Social Work and Sch. Bus. Adminstrn.; mem. Va. Juvenile Justice and Delinquency Adv. Council. Mem. Yale Law Sch. Assn. (exec. com.), Phi Beta Kappa. Home: 107 N Plum St Richmond VA 23220 Office: 2040 Thalbro St Richmond VA 23230

WURZ, JOHN ARNOLD, architect; b. Clarksdale, Miss., Feb. 11, 1936; s. Arnold George and Mildred (Whittle) W.; B.S., Ga. Inst. Tech., 1958, B.Arch., 1959; m. Janice Beauchamp, Dec. 22, 1973; children—Valli Elizabeth, Susan Priscilla, John Arnold, Corbett Ann, Charles W. Project mgr. Rich's, Inc., Atlanta, 1962-63; project mgr. Heery & Heery Architects & Engrs., Atlanta, 1963-65, asso. architect, 1965-67, partner, 1967-77; v.p. Cadre Corp., 1977-80; founder, pres. Wurz Wisecarver & Pruett, Inc., Architects, 1980—. Adv. bd. Nat. Acad. Sci., 1979-82. Served as capt. USAF, 1959-62, Res., 1962-72. Registered architect, 20 states and U.K. Mem. Atlanta Art Assn., Bldg. Research Adv. Bd., Ga. Indsl. Devel. Assn., Ga. Tech. Alumni Assn., AIA, Sigma Nu Alumni Assn. Club: Cherokee Town and Country (bd. dirs. 1984—). Home: 401 Arbor Trail Marietta GA 30067 Office: 1900 Emery St NW Suite 212 Atlanta GA 30318

WYATT, CHARLES HERBERT, JR., lawyer; b. Birmingham, Ala., Aug. 18 1937; s. Charles Herbert and Elizabeth Florida (Farrell) W.; m. Lane Laverne Bradley, Mar. 18, 1966. B.S. in Bus., Jacksonville State U., 1960; J.D., Cumberland U., 1964. Bar: Ala. 1964, U.S. Dist. Ct. (no. dist.) Ala. 1964, U.S. Ct. Appeals (5th cir.) 1975, U.S. Ct. Appeals (11th cir.) 1981, U.S. Supreme Ct. 1984. Ptnr. Cole, Wyatt & Bradshaw, Birmingham, 1964-73; prin. atty. City of Birmingham, 1973—. Chaplin Vulcan Power Squad, U.S. Power Squad, Birmingham, 1983, asst. sec., 1984, adminstrv. officer, 1985. Mem. Nat. Inst. Mcpl. Law Officers, Sigma Delta Kappa. Home: 1300 Beacon Pkwy E Birmingham AL 35209 Office: City of Birmingham Law Dept 600 City Hall-710 N 20th St Birmingham AL 35203

WYATT, EDWARD AVERY, V, city manager; b. Petersburg, Va., Nov. 1, 1941; s. Edward Avery and Martha Vaughan (Seabury) W.; B.S., Va. Poly. Inst., 1964; M.Commerce, U. Richmond, 1969; M.A. in Polit. Sci., Appalachian State U., 1977; m. Regina Helen Stec, Aug. 23, 1969; children—Edward Avery, Stephen Alexander, Kent Seabury. Asst. to city mgr., Petersburg, Va., 1967-70; city mgr., Washington, N.C., 1970-73, Morganton, N.C., 1973-78, Greenville, N.C., 1978-82, Fairfax, Va., 1982—; part-time lectr. E. Carolina U. Bus. Sch., 1980-82, Gerrge E. Mason U. Bus. Sch., 1985-86. Mem. adv. bd. Fairfax Salvation Army, 1982—, mem. exec. bd. Fairfax United Fund. Served with USAR, 1964-70. Mem. N.C. Code Ofcls. Qualification Bd. (chmn. 1980-82), Internat. City Mgmt. Assn., N.C. City and County Mgmt. Assn. (past dir.), Am. Soc. Public Adminstrn., Soc. Cincinnati in Va. Episcopalian. Clubs: Rotary (sec.). Contbr. numerous articles to profl. jours. Home: 4041 Autumn Ct Fairfax VA 22030 Office: 10455 Armstrong St Fairfax VA 22030

WYATT, FOREST KENT, university executive; b. Berea, Ky., May 27, 1934; s. Forest Earl and Almeda (Hymer) W.; m. Janice Collins, Mar. 4, 1956; children—Tara Wyatt Mounger, Elizabeth Pharr. B.S. in Edn., Delta State Coll., 1956; M.E., U. So. Miss., 1960; Ed.D., U. Miss., 1970; postdoctoral Harvard U., 1975. Instr., coach Univ. Mil. Sch., Mobile, Ala., 1956-60, Bolivar County Dist. IV Schs., Cleveland, Miss., 1960-64; alumni sec. Delta State U., Cleveland, 1964-69, adminstrv. asst. to pres., 1969-75, pres., 1975—. Editor: Needs of Higher Education, State of Mississippi for 1968. Trustee, mem. exec. com. So. Baptist Theol. Sem., Louisville; past pres. Indsl. Devel. Found. Bolivar County, Crosstie Arts Council, PTA; bd. dirs. Grenada Banking System, Miss. Econ. Council; chmn. adv. com. Leadership Miss. Served with U.S. Army, 1957-58. Mem. Miss. Assn. Educators, Gulf South Conf. (past pres.), Miss. Com. for the Humanities (v.p.), Am. Council on Edn., Am. Assn. Sch. Adminstrs., So. Assn. Colls. and Schs., Am. Assn. State Colls. and Univs. (chmn. athletic com.), Miss. Assn. Colls. (past pres.), C. of C. (past pres.), Red Red Rose, Kappa Delta Pi, Phi Delta Kappa (past pres.), Omicron Delta Kappa, Kappa Alpha. Baptist. Clubs: Met. Dinner (past pres., bd. govs.), Cleveland Country (bd. dirs.), Cleveland Lions (past pres.). Home and Office: Box A-1 Delta State Univ Cleveland MS 38733

WYATT, JACK MILLER, utilities company executive; b. Dubach, La., July 29, 1918; s. George Sylinger and Rae D. (Miller) W.; m. Willie C. Stroud, June 14, 1940; 1 son, Jack Miller II. B.S. in Elec. Engring. U. Ark., 1938; M.B.A., Stanford U., 1966. With La. Power & Light Co., 1938-75, exec. asst., New Orleans, 1965-67, v.p., 1967-70, sr. v.p., 1970-75, pres., chief exec. officer, 1976-82, chmn. bd., chief exec. officer, now dir.; pres., chief exec. officer, dir. System Fuels Inc., 1975-76; dir. Middle South Services, Inc., Middle South Energy, Inc., New Orleans Pub. Service Inc., Middle South Utilities, Inc. Bd. dirs. Internat. House, Met. Area Com., Arthritis Found., Econ. Devel. Council, 1978—; trustee United Way, 1978—; mem. council trustees Gulf South Research Inst.; bd. regents Our Lady of Holy Cross Coll., La. Expo, Inc. Served to lt. USNR, 1942-46. Mem. C. of C. Greater New Orleans Area (dir. 1976—), West Bank Council of C. of C. (dir. 1964-69), Elec. Assn. New Orleans, New Orleans Bd. Trade, Internat. Trade Mart, Theta Tau. Clubs: Timberlane Country (Gretna, La.); Propeller U.S., Bacchus and Janus Carnival, Plimsoll (New Orleans); West Bank Petroleum. Lodge: Lions. Office: 142 Delaronde St New Orleans LA 70174*

WYATT, JOE BILLY, university chancellor; b. Tyler, Tex., July 21, 1935; s. Joe and Fay (Pinkerton) W.; m. Faye Hocutt, July 21, 1956; children—Joseph Robert, Sandra Faye. B.A., U. Tex., 1956; M.A., Tex. Christian U., 1960. Systems engr. Gen. Dynamics Corp., 1956-61; mgr. Digital Computer Lab., 1961-65; dir. computer ctr., assoc. prof. computer sci. U. Houston, 1965-72; dir. Office Info. Tech. Harvard U., 1972-76, sr. lectr. computer sci., 1972-82, v.p. adminstrn., 1976-82; chancellor Vanderbilt U., Nashville, 1982—; mem. faculty Kennedy Sch. of Harvard U., 1972-82. Author (with others) Financial Planning Models for Colleges and Universities, 1979; editor-in chief: Jour. Applied Mgmt. Systems, 1982; contbr. articles to profl. jours.; patentee in field of data processing. Trustee Harvard U. Press, 1976-83, pres., 1975-76, chmn. bd., 1976-79; trustee EDUCOM, Princeton, N.J., 1972-81; bd. dirs. Nashville Inst. Arts, 1982—; chmn. adv. com. IST, NSF, 1978-85; vice chmn. bd. Mass. Tech. Devel. Corp., Boston, 1977-83; mem. policy bd. Nat. Assn. Ind. Colls. and Univs., 1980-83; fellow Gallaudet Coll., 1981-83. Recipient award for exemplary leadership CAUSE, Hilton Head, S.C., 1982; mem. alumni bd. dirs. Harvard Bus. Sch., 1982—. Fellow AAAS; mem. Assn. Computing Machinery (pres. Dallas, Ft. Worth chpt. 1963-65), IEEE, Aircraft Owners and Pilots Assn., Sigma Xi, Beta Gamma Sigma. Methodist. Clubs: Harvard (N.Y.C.); Belle Meade Country (Nashville). Office: Vanderbilt University 207 Kirkland Hall Nashville TN 37240

WYATT, KATHRYN ELIZABETH BENTON, psychologist, educator; b. Danville, Va., May 11, 1928; d. Joseph Nelson and Margaret (Davis) Benton; B.A., Randolph Macon Woman's Coll., Lynchburg, Va., 1949; M.Ed., U. Va., 1952; M.A., U. N.C., Greensboro, 1974, Ph.D., 1977; m. Landon Russell Wyatt, Aug. 30, 1952; children—Margaret Wyatt Scott, Landon Russell, III, Elizabeth Benton. Instr., then asst. prof. psychology Stratford Coll., Danville, 1949-74, chmn. dept., 1963-74; asso. prof. psychology Danville Community Coll., 1977—. Mem. Danville Sch. Bd.; deacon, tchr. 1st Bapt. Ch., Danville; pres. so. dist. Va. Sch. Bds. Assn. Mem. Am. Psychol. Assn., Soc. Research Child Devel., Southeastern Psychol. Assn., Va. Psychol. Assn., Va. Acad. Sci. Clubs: Jr. Wednesday (pres.), Gabriella, Wayside Garden, Shakespeare. Author articles in field. Home: 301 Magnolia St Danville VA 25441 Office: Danville Community Coll Danville VA 25441

WYATT, LLOYD DOW, clinical psychologist; b. Kokomo, Ind., Mar. 1, 1927; s. Lloyd Astor and Nellie Kathern (Galloway) W.; m. Jacqueline Jyl Bazzle, Nov. 7, 1964; children—Debra P. Atrostic, Stephen A., Randall S. B.A., Asbury Coll., 1951; B.D., Butler U., 1955, M.S., 1960; Ph.D., Purdue U., 1964. Clin. psychologist intern VA Hosp., Marion, Ind., 1961-64, staff psychologist, 1964-65; chief psychologist Guidance Ctr., Howard County, Ind., 1965-67; pvt. practice psychology, Wichita, Kans., 1967-70; dir. Mahoning County Diagnostic Clinic, Youngstown, Ohio, 1970-76; psychologist, dir. Peninsula Child Devel. Clinic, Newport News, Va., 1976—; mem. policy planning council Youngstown Area Headstart, 1973-76; mem. spl. edn. adv. com. Newport News Schs., 1983—. Bd. dirs. New Beginnings for Boys, Newport News, Va., 1978. Served to cpl. U.S. Army, 1945-47. Recipient Cert. of Appreciation, Service Systems Forum, Youth Services, Newport News, 1981. Mem. Am. Psychol. Assn., Sigma Xi. Roman Catholic. Avocations: sailing; flying; painting; reading. Home: 2248 Criston Dr Newport News VA 23602 Office: Peninsula Child Devel Clinic 416 J Clyde Morris Blvd Newport News VA 23601

WYATT, MARKEL RAY, geologist, consultant; b. Andalusia Ala., Dec. 12, 1953; s. John Ralph and Ruby Mae (Stewart) W. B.S. in Geology, U. Ala., 1976; student in trust banking, Birmingham So. U., 1981-83. Exploration geologist Dresser Industries, Eufaula, Ala., 1976-77; petroleum geologist Oil & Gas Bd., Tuscaloosa, Ala., 1978-79, regional supr., Mobile, Ala., 1979-80; geologist 1st Nat. Bank, Mobile, 1980-85, AmSouth Bank N.A., 1985—. Author: Exploration Techniques for Bauxite, 1976. Mem. Mobile County Wildlife and Conservation, Mobile, 1980—, Gulf Coast Conservation Assn., Mobile, 1983—. Mem. Am. Assn. Petroleum Geologists, Am. Inst. Profl. Geologists, Soc. Petroleum Engrs. of AIME, Mid-Continent Oil and Gas Assn., ABA (trust div., natural resources), Am. Assn. Petroleum Landmen, Sigma Chi. Republican. Baptist. Club: Alba Yacht (Mobile), Athelstan. Avocations: sailing; salt water fishing; hunting. Home: 213 C East Portier Ct Mobile AL 36607 Office: AmSouth Bank NA of Mobile 31 N Royal St Mobile AL 36621

WYATT, OSCAR S., JR., gas company executive; b. Beaumont, Tex., July 11, 1924; s. O.S. and Eva (Coday) W.; B.S. in Mech. Engring., Tex. A. and M. Coll., 1949; m. Lynn Wyatt; children—Carl, Steven, Douglas, O.S. III, Brad. With Kerr-McGee Co., 1949; with Reed Roller Bit Co., 1949-51; partner ind. oil co. Wymore Oil Co., 1951-55; founder Coastal Corp., Corpus Christi, Tex., 1955, now chmn., chief exec. officer. Served as pilot USAAF, World War II; PTO. Office: Nine Greenway Plaza Houston TX 77046

WYATT, ROBERT EDWARD, biology educator; b. Charleston, S.C., July 15, 1950; s. Lloyd Edward and Helen Jean (Holder) W.; m. Ann Hudson Stoneburner, Mar. 8, 1978. A.B. in Botany, U. N.C., 1972; Ph.D. in Botany, Duke U., 1977. Asst. prof. biology Tex. A&M U., Coll. Sta., 1977-79; asst. prof. botany U. Ga., Athens, 1979-83, assoc. prof., 1983—. Grantee NSF, 1975-77, 80-84, 85—, Whitehall Found., 1983-86. Mem. Soc. for Study Evolution, Bot. Soc. Am., Am. Soc. Plant Taxonomists. Home: 1241 Trailwood Dr Watkinsville GA 30677 Office: Dept of Botany Univ of Ga Athens GA 30602

WYCHERLEY, ROBERT ALLEN, college administrator; b. Wheeling, W.Va., June 16, 1949; s. Kenneth Neuman and Clara Virginia (Wolf) W. A.A., W.Va. No. Community Coll., 1975; B.A., W.Liberty State Coll., 1980; postgrad W.Va. U., 1985—; student U. Hawaii, 1970-71. Asst. dept. gmr. Jefferson's Dept. Store, North Maimi Beach, Fla., 1967-68; prodn. employee Wheeling Pitts. Steel Co., W.Va., 1972-80; coordiantor handicap services W.Va. No. Community Coll., Wheeling, 1983—; career planning specialist W.Va. No. Community Coll./W.Va. Penitentiary, Wheeling, 1980—. Editor, No. Star coll. newspaper, 1973-75; regional exhbns. paitnings, prints, sculptures, 1979-81. Served with AUS, 1969-71. Mem. Am. Assn. Counseling & Devel., Correctional Edn. Assn., Am. Correcitonal Assn., W.Va. Assn. Student Personnel Adminstrs., W.Va. Vocat. Guidance Assn., W.Va. No. Community Coll. Alumni Assn. (bd. dirs. 1978—, prs. 1978-83). Avocations: Whitewater kayaking; skydiving; racketball; reading; bicycling. Home: 34 Virginia St Wheeling WV 26003 Office: W Va No Community Coll College Sq Wheeling WV 26003

WYCOFF, JERRY RANDALL, sociologist, researcher; b. West Palm Beach, Fla., Oct. 4, 1946; s. Fredrick Eugene and Frances Louise (Erwin) W.; m. Sarah Ella Walden, Oct. 23, 1972 (div. 1976). B.S. in Bus. Mgmt., Jacksonville State U.; M.A. in Sociology, Ind. State U.; Ph.D. in Sociology, U. Fla. Instr., Jacksonville State U., Ala., 1973-76; student instr. U. Fla., Gainesville, 1976-80; asst. prof. Stetson U., Deland, Fla., 1980-81, U. Richmond, Va., 1981-83; dir. research Ala. Inst. for Deaf and Blind, Talladega, Ala., 1984—. Mem. Talladega County Mental Health Assn., 1984—. Served to 1st lt. USAR, 1972. Mem. Am. Sociol. Assn., So. Sociol. Assn., Assn. for Edn. of Blind, Ala. Gerontol. Soc., Alpha Kappa Delta (pres.). Episcopalian. Avocations: community theatre; hiking; sailing. Home: 4225 Myrtle Ave Anniston AL 36206 Office: Ala Inst for Deaf and Blind PO Box 698 Talladega AL 35160

WYER, JEAN CONOVER, educator, accountant; b. Louisville, Sept. 12, 1950; d. Ramon and Becky (Hutchinson) Wyer; A.B., Vassar Coll., 1970; M.B.A., U. No. Fla., 1973; C.Phil., Northwestern U., 1975; Ed.D., Coll. of William and Mary, 1980. C.P.A. Field staff ARC, Mayport, Fla., 1971-72; research asst. U. North Fla., 1972-73; research asst., lectr. Northwestern U., 1975-76; asst. prof. Coll. of William and Mary, Williamsburg, Va., 1977-82, assoc. prof. bus. adminstrn., 1982—; cons. to various orgns. Mem. bd. Williamsburg-James City County ARC, 1982, chmn. bd., 1983. Recipient Owl and Torch award 1968-70; Am. Acctg. Assn. fellow, 1975-76; Alumni fellow, 1980; Thomas Jefferson Teaching award, 1982. Fellow Am. Acctg. Assn. Doctoral Consortium; mem. Am. Acctg. Assn., Am. Inst. C.P.A.s, Am. Assn. Higher Edn. Author: (with C. Conrad) Liberal Education in Transition, 1980. Office: Coll of William and Mary Williamsburg VA 23185

WYETH, JOHN CHURCHILL, II, geologist; b. Chgo., Aug. 13, 1923; s. John Churchill and Frances (Huster) W.; m. Betty Swain, Aug. 8, 1953; children—Terry Richard, Robert Dru, Gregg, Jeannette Turjilo, Margaret Reed. B.S. in Geology, U. Utah, 1950. Geologist, soil sampler Bur. Reclamation, Salt Lake City, 1950-51; petroleum geologist Conoco, Rocky Mts., Gulf Coast, 1951-68; uranium geologist, Corpus Christi, Tex., 1969-78; uranium geologist, cons. Conoco, Corpus Christi, 1978-81, petroleum geologist, cons., Corpus Christi, 1981—; dist. geologist Conoco, Corpus Christi, 1969-76, frontier explorer, 1976-78; cons. in field. Precinct chmn. Republican Party, Roswell, N.Mex., 1964. Mem. Am. Assn. Petroleum Geologists, AIME, Corpus Christi Geol. Soc. Mormon. Home: 761 Bradshaw Corpus Christi TX 78412

WYLAND, BEN F., clergyman; b. Harlan, Iowa, Mar. 16, 1882; s. Frank and Mary (Griffith) W.; Ph.B., U. Iowa, 1905; B.D., Yale, 1908, M.Div., 1971; Litt.D., Edward Waters Coll., 1954; m. Ada D. Beach, Jan. 14, 1909; children—Gordon B., Hugh C., Robert B., Molly G.; m. 2d, Mildred E. Oeschger, May 5, 1955. Ordained to ministry Congl. Ch., 1908; pastor, Worcester, Mass., 1918-26, Lincoln, Nebr., 1926-36, Bklyn., 1936-39; radio pastor Sta. KFAB, 1926-36; exchange pastor to Eng., 1933; in charge ch. relations for Herbert Hoover's Campaign, Food for Small Democracies, 1940-41; exec. sec. United Chs. Greater St. Petersburg (Fla.), 1948-56, Fla. Council Racial Cooperation, St. Petersburg, 1956—. Chmn. Com. To Preserve Negro Rights; founder Negro Girls Welfare Home, St. Petersburg, St. Petersburg Helping Hand for Sr. Citizens; chmn. United Negro Coll. Fund. Recipient citation from Maj. Gen. Philip Hayes, 3d Service Command; B'nai B'rith Brotherhood award, St. Petersburg, 1954; recipient Oscar, Community Chest dr., 1955; citation Met. Council, Inc., 1958; Bethune Cookman Coll., Edward Waters Coll.; hon. citation Yale Div. Sch., 1982; Key to City of St. Petersburg, 1983. Mem. Am. Relief Assn. (dir.), Am. Com. Christian Refugees in Bklyn. (exec. sec.), Bklyn. Fedn. Chs. (dir.), Crime Prevention Soc. (dir.), N.Y.C. Assn. Chs. (pres. bd. dirs.), Congl. Ministers (pres.), Profl. Sr. Citizens of Eckerd Coll., Americanization Com. (chmn.), Food Commn. (chmn.), Delta Sigma Phi, Alpha Chi Rho. Mason (32 deg., K.T.), Kiwanian. Home: Apt 107 1898 Shore Dr S Saint Petersburg FL 33707

WYLDER, DELBERT E(EUGENE), English language educator; b. Jerseyville, Ill., Oct. 5, 1923; s. Robert Maines and (Alice) Blanche (Coulthard) W.; m. Jean Williams, June 5, 1950 (div. July 1965); children—Stephen John, William Creighton; m. Edith Beverly Perry, July 15, 1965; stepchildren—Paul Greenwood Stamm, Philip Baldridge Stamm (dec.). B.A., U. Iowa, 1948, M.F.A., 1950, Ph.D., 1968; student Universidad Nacional de Mexico, others. Asst. prof. English, Utah State U., Logan, 1965-66, Colo. State U., Fort Collins, 1966-68; assoc. prof. Bemidji State U., Minn., 1968-69; prof. English, S.W. State U., Marshall, Minn., 1969-77, Murray State U., Ky., 1977—; tech. writer Sandia Corp., Albuquerque, 1958-61. Co-author: Toward Better Writing, 1958; author: Hemingway's Heroes, 1968; Emerson Hough, 1981; also articles. Exec. editor Western Am. Lit., 1966-69; mng. editor Crazy Horse, 1978-82; editor Ky. Philol. Assn. Bull., 1984. Served to 2d lt. USAAC, 1942-45; ETO. NEH grantee, 1976; grantee Colo. State U., S.W. State U., Murray State U. Mem. Western Lit. Assn. (pres. 1966-67), Minn.-Dakotas Am. Studies Assn. (pres. 1974-75), Ky. Assn. Depts. of English (pres. 1979-81), Hemingway Soc. (book rev. editor 1983—), AAUP (chpt. pres. 1978-81). Democrat. Avocations: tennis; writing. Home: Route 7 Box 583 Murray KY 42071 Office: Murray State U Murray KY 42071

WYLIE, BETTY RUTH, city official; b. El Dorado, Ark., Nov. 27, 1941; d. Robert Leigh and Mamie Ruth (Rowland) Pye; m. James H. Wylie, Dec. 19, 1964; 1 son, Ross. B.S.E., Ouachita U., 1963. Tchr., Carthage Sch., Ark., 1963-69; now exec. dir. Carthage Housing Authority; clk., treas. City of Carthage, 1984—. Chmn. Dallas County Library, Fordyce, Ark.; pres. Carthage Sch. Bd., 1984—. Mem. Dallas County Cancer Soc., Dallas County Hosp. Aux. Democrat. Presbyterian. Avocations: water skiing; swimming. Home: PO Box 37 Carthage AR 71725 Office: Carthage Housing Authority PO Box 3 Carthage AR 71725

WYLIE, GEORGE, JR., university administrator; b. Gastonia, N.C., Jan. 24, 1941; s. George and Mary Alice (Walker) W.; m. Gloria Agnes Ward, Dec. 22, 1962 (div. Feb. 1983); m. Edna Hall, Feb. 28, 1983; 1 child, Ricky. B.S., Winston-Salem State U., 1961; M.A., A&T U., Greensboro, N.C., 1969; grad. cert. U. N.C.-Greensboro, 1976; D. Edn. Adminstrn., Va. Poly. Inst. and State U., 1979. Asst. prin. Martinsville Middle Sch., Va., 1968-69, prin., 1969-71; asst. recreation dir.City of Martinsville, 1971-73; dir. student teaching, assoc. prof. edn. Shaw U., Raleigh, N.C., 1979-80, div. chmn. edn., 1980—; mem. exec. bd. So. Consortium, 1979-82. Active Wake County Parks and Recreation, Raleigh, 1982-84; v.p. Community Action Com., East Raleigh, N.C., 1983-84. Recipient Disting. Service award Shaw U. Faculty Senate, 1982, Disting. Srevice award CITE, Greensboro, 1984; grantee So. Consortium, 1979, Title II, 1982. Mem. AAUP, N.C. Assn. Tchr. Edn., NEA, Nat. Assn. Black Sch. Educators, So. Council Tchr. Edn., N.C. Council Edn. Assns., Am. Coll. Tchrs., Assn. Tchr. Edn., Nat. Alliance black Sch. Educators (bd. dirs. so. region 1979-81). Democrat. Baptist. Avocations: reading; research; tennis; jogging; music. Home: 620 Peartree Ln Raleigh NC 27610 Office: Shaw U Div Edn Raleigh NC 27611

WYLIE, JANET CHRISTINE, computer services company executive; b. Wilmington, N.C., June 24, 1956; d. John Knox and Geraldine (Talley) W. B.Civil Engring., Ga. Inst. Tech., 1977. Project engr. Exxon Co., U.S.A., New Orleans, 1977-79; regional engring. cons. McDonnell Douglas Automation Co., Atlanta, 1979-80; tech. rep. Boeing Computer Services, Atlanta, 1980-82, mktg. rep., 1982-83, nat. product sales mgr., 1983—; speaker infield. Named Outstanding Sr. Civil Engring. Student, Chi Epsilon, 1976-77, Boeing Computer Services Employee of Year, 1981. Mem. ASCE (Outstanding Service award 1982, com. chmn. ann. conv. 1984). Republican. Office: Boeing Computer Services 7980-90 Gallows Ct Vienna VA 22180

WYLLYS, RONALD EUGENE, information science educator, dean; b. Phoenix, May 14, 1930; s. Rufus Kay and Eugenia (Dunsmore) W.; m. Jean Mary Graham, Nov. 2, 1957; children—A. Erika, R.K. Graham, Athala Lucy, Kaila B. B.A., Ariz. State U., 1950; postgrad. U. Calif.-Berkeley, 1950-52, Am. U., 1953-57, Georgetown U., 1957-59, UCLA, 1959-64; Ph.D., U. Wis.-Madison, 1974. Mathematician, Dept. Def., Washington, 1954-59; assoc. in math. George Washington U., Washington, 1954-59; assoc. info. retrieval Planning Research Corp., Los Angeles, 1959-61; computer systems specialist System Devel. Corp., Santa Monica, Calif., 1961-66; chief systems analyst Univ. Libraries, U. Wis.-Madison, 1966-69, lectr. computer scis. dept., 1966-72; from asst. prof. to prof. Grad. Sch. Library and Info. Sci., U. Tex., Austin, 1972—, acting dean, then dean, 1982—; cons. in field. Co-author: National Document Handling Systems for Science and Technology, 1967. Contbr. articles to profl. jours., chpts. to books. Served to lt. (j.g.) USN, 1948-49, 52-54. Mem. AAAS, ALA, Am. Soc. Info. Sci., Am. Statis. Assn., Assn. Library and Info. Sci. Edn., Tex. Library Assn. Unitarian. Avocations: opera; bird-watching. Home: 2603 Rogge Ln Austin TX 78723 Office: Grad Sch Library and Info Sci U Tex Austin TX 78712

WYNER, GORDON ALAN, marketing research company executive; b. Cleve., Apr. 10, 1949; s. Edward D. and Alice (Garber) W.; m. DiAnne Walters, Nov. 2, 1980. B.A., Northwestern U., 1971; M.A., U. Pa., 1973, Ph.D., 1976. Lectr., U. Pa., Phila., 1975-77; researcher, Mathematica, Inc., Princeton, N.J., 1974-76; research group mgr. Nat. Analysts, Phila., 1976-83; exec. v.p. M/A/R/C Inc., Dallas, 1983—; mem. editorial bd. Jour. Mktg. Research, 1982—. Mem. Am. Mktg. Assn., Am. Statis. Assn. Home: 2233 Delmar Dr Plano TX 75075 Office: M/A/R/C Inc 4230 LBJ Freeway Dallas TX 75234

WYNNE, CAREY HOWARD (JEAN-PIERRE-SOLÒMON), JR., history and religion educator; b. Pine Bluff, Ark., Mar. 16, 1950; s. Carey Howard and Gertie (Lamb) W. A.B., Morehouse Coll., 1970; A.M., U. Chgo., 1972; postgrad., 1972-73; D.D. (hon.), Universal Ch. Faculty assoc. U. Chgo. Div. Sch., 1972-74; assoc. religion dept. history Morehouse Coll., Atlanta, 1973—; cons. U.S. News and World Report, others; advisor Morehouse Coll.; cons. Msgr. A. Lanzoni, dept. head Secretariat of State, The Vatican, also to Pope John Paul II; Episcopal convenor Synod of Bishops, The Vatican, 1984. Exec. sec. Democratic party Fulton County; active Butler St. YMCA, Atlanta U. Ctr. Community Chorus; tenor soloist. Recipient J.J. Starks Best Man of Affairs award Morehouse Coll., 1970; Rockefeller Protestant fellow, 1970; Lyndon Baines award U. Tex.-Austin, 1970; Ford Found. fellow, 1971-75. Mem. Am. Soc. Ch. History, Internat. Patristics Council, Am. Acad. Religion, Songwriters, Resources and Services (Music Union), Internat. Religious Assn., Inc., Phi Alpha Theta. Democrat. Roman Catholic (mem. Faith Community of St. Charles Lwanga). Contbr. to books, profl. jours.; author: The Tradition: Sacerdotium and Regnum and the Two Beckets, 1972; The Spiritual Significance of Pope John Paul II, San Vittorino, Italia, 1978; On the Rhythm of Soul Truth, 1982; What Are Visions and Values without God?, 1983; On Rhythms of Liberation Notes, 1984; Arius and the Castle of Misty Blue, 1985; composer musical score, For Thine is the Kingdom, The Power, and the Glory, Forever, Amen, 1982; composer Obiedence, 1983; God: The Almighty Power, 1984; The Love of God, 1985.

WYNNE, MARTHA VIRGINIA, financial executive; b. Dallas, Nov. 18, 1951; d. Robert Edwards and Rubye Floyd (Davis) W. B.J., U. Tex., 1972; M.B.A. in Fin. and Acctg., U. Houston, 1981. Chartered fin. analyst. Speechwriter Lt. Gov. William P. Hobby, Jr., Austin, Tex., 1973; with prodn. and account services dept. Tracy-Locke/BBDO, Dallas, 1973-77; analyst Fayez Sarofim & Co., Houston, 1977-81; v.p. corp. fin. Rotan Mosle Inc., Houston, 1981—; mem. editorial rev. bd. John Wiley & Sons, N.Y.C., 1985—. Pres. Encorps, Houston, 1979; bd. dirs. Houston Symphony League, 1980, 83. Mem. Houston Soc. Fin. Analysts (bd. dirs. 1983-84), Houston Bus. Forum (treas. 1985), U. Tex. Alumni Assn. Republican. Presbyterian. Avocations: investments; reading. Home: 1100 Augusta St #26 Houston TX 77057

WYNNE, RICHARD THOMAS, agricultural meteorologist; b. Joliet, Ill., July 31, 1951; s. Walter David and Ethel Elizabeth (Lauffer) W.; B.S. in Geography, No. Ill. U., 1973; M.S. in Agronomy, Iowa State U., 1976. With Nat. Weather Service, Dept. Commerce, NOAA, Tex. A&M U., College Station, 1976—, agrl. meteorologist, 1976—; researcher in field. Recipient SAR award, 1969. Mem. Nat. Weather Assn., Am. Meteorol. Soc., Am. Soc. Agronomy, Soil Sci. Soc. Am. Clubs: Tex. A&M Sailing, Toastmasters (club pres. 1982, area gov. 1983-85). Office: Room 341 Soil and Crop Sci Bldg Tex A&M U College Station TX 77843

WYNNE, ROLAND BROOKS, retired lawyer; b. Greenville, S.C., Sept. 8, 1916; s. Roland E. and May (Brooks) W.; A.B., Wabash Coll., 1937; J.D., Ind. U., 1940; m. Helen R. Johnson, Sept. 1, 1939; children—William Thomas, Judith Brooks. Admitted to Ind. bar, 1940, Ill. bar, 1941; atty. Montgomery Ward, Chgo., 1940-51; atty. General Box Co., 1951, asst. sec., atty., 1952-58, sec., gen. counsel, 1958-78; asst. sec., asso. corp. counsel Southwest Forest Industries, Inc., Phoenix, 1973-78, asso. gen. counsel, asst. sec., 1978-81, ret., 1981; labor relations cons. Mem. Am., Chgo. bar assns., Order of Coif, Phi Beta Kappa, Beta Theta Pi. Republican. Presbyn. Elk. Home: 2413 Homewood Dr Orlando FL 32809

WYRICK, CHARLES LLOYD, JR., museum director, author, editor; b. Greensboro, N.C., May 5, 1939; s. Charles Lloyd and Edythe Ellen (Ellis) W.; m. Constance Michelle Hooper, Aug. 22, 1964; children—Charles Lloyd III, Christopher Conrad Hooper. B.A., Davidson Coll., 1961; M.F.A., U. N.C., 1967. Instr. Stephens Coll., Columbia, Mo., 1964-66; artmobile coordinator Va. Mus., Richmond, 1966-68; exec. dir. Assn. for Pres. Va. Antiquities, Richmond, 1968-70; curator Sydney and Frances Lewis Collection, Richmond, 1970-73; dir. Del. Art Mus., Wilmington, 1973-79, Gibbes Art Gallery, Charleston, S.C., 1980—; art and archtl. critic Richmond newspapers, 1970-73. Author, editor: The 17th Street Market, 1972. Editor: Oystering: A Way of Life (awards 1983, 84), 1983; Charles Fraser of Charleston, 1983; The Miniature Portrait Collection, 1984. Mem. Archtl. Rev. Bd., Richmond, 1969-73, Hist. Zoning Rev. Bd., New Castle County, Del., 1977-79; mem. City Market Adv. Com., Charleston, 1984; chmn. Econs. Amenity Com., Charleston, 1984; mem. Charleston Consortium on Higher Edn., 1982-85. Served to 1st lt. U.S. Army, 1961-63. Recipient 1st place Merit award Va. Press Assn., 1973. Mem. Assn. Art Mus. Dirs., Am. Assn. Museums, Art Mus. Assn. Am., Southeastern Mus. Conf. (council mem.), S.C. Fedn. Museums. Clubs: Vicmead Hunt (Wilmington, Del.); Carolina Yacht, Charleston Tennis, Long Room (Charleston). Avocations: photography; travel. Office: Carolina Art Assn 135 Meeting St Charleston SC 29401

WYSOCKI, JAMES ANTHONY, lawyer; b. Chgo., Oct. 31, 1938; s. Felix B. and Virginia Marie (Konopa) W.; m. M. Cristina Longoria, Dec. 7, 1974; B.B.A. cum laude, U. Notre Dame, 1960, B.Laws (scholar), 1963; J.D., Loyola Sch. Law, New Orleans, 1965. Bar: Ind. 1963, La. 1964, U.S. Dist. Ct. (ea. dist.) La. 1964, U.S. Ct. Appeals (5th cir.) 1966, U.S. Supreme Ct. 1968. U. Notre Dame teaching fellow, 1961-63; law clk. to Frank B. Ellis, U.S. Dist. Judge, Eastern Dist. La., 1963-65; trial atty. Ungar, Dulitz & Martzell, New Orleans, 1965-69; trial atty., sr. ptnr. Heisler & Wysocki and predecessor firms, New Orleans, 1969—; mem. internat. com. to select 100 greatest courses in world Golf mag. Active New Orleans City Ballet, New Orleans Mus. Art, Jr. Opera Com., Preservation Resource Ctr., Lakewood Property Owners Assn., Boy Scouts Am. Contbr. articles to profl. jours. Mem. Fed. Bar Assn. (chpt. pres. 1964-65), New Orleans Acad. Trial Lawyers (pres. 1975-76, co-chmn. legis. com.), Assn. Trial Lawyers Am. (La. state del.), Maritime Law Assn. (1984 conv. com.), Lawyer Pilots Bar Assn. (dir. 1974-82), CAP (squadron comdr. and search pilot), La. Trial Lawyers Assn. (gov. 1973-75, 80-84), ABA, La. Bar Assn. (ho. of dels. 1985—), Greater New Orleans Trial Lawyers Assn., New Orleans Bar Assn., Jefferson Parish Bar Assn., Ind. Bar Assn., Aircraft Owners and Pilots Assn. Roman Catholic. Clubs: Metairie Country, Century, Notre Dame of New Orleans, Freret Carnival. Home: 5638 Evelyn Ct New Orleans LA 70124 Office: 844 Baronne St New Orleans LA 70113-1103

WYSOCZYNSKI, DONALD THOMAS, tool and diemaking company executive; b. Grand Rapids, Mich., Feb. 9, 1931; s. Charles Anthony and Anna Francis (Antoszczak) W.; m. Ruth Marlene Chicklon, Jan. 24, 1953; children—James Allen, Thomas Lee, Gerald Paul. Student Grand Rapids Jr. Coll., 1948-50. Apprentice, Fischer Body div. Gen. Motors Corp., Grand Rapids, 1955-57, Leese Tool and Die, Grand Rapids, 1957-66; tool engr. Grand Rapids Metalcraft, 1966-72; design engr. Slagboom Tool and Die Co., Grand Rapids, 1973-77; div. mgr. Trojan Tool div. Douglas and Lomason Co. Inc., Carrollton, Ga., 1977—. Past bd. dirs. Catholic War Vets. U.S.A.; formerly active Grand Valley council Boy Scouts Am. Served with USN, 1952-54. Recipient Silver Beaver award Boy Scouts Am.; St. George medal for scouting work Grand Rapids Roman Catholic Diocese. Republican. Club: 25. Lodges: Kiwanis, Moose (sec. Carrollton). Elks (chmn. bd. trustees Carrollton). Home: 109 Wilson Circle Carrollton GA 30117 Office: Ave C PO Box 1048 Carrollton GA 30117

XAVER, RICHARD FREDERICK, news photographer, editor; b. South Bend, Ind., Feb. 24, 1956; s. Gerald Edward and Jacqueline Lou (Heeter) X. Student Milton Coll., Wis., 1974-75, Indiana U., 1957-77. Studio supr., tech. dir. assoc. producer, news photographer Sta. WNDU-TV, South Bend, 1971-77; news photographer, editor Sta. WTVN-TV, Columbus, Ohio, 1977-79; news photographer, editor Sta. WWL-TV, New Orleans, 1977—. Co-recipient Emmy award for documentary, Columbus, 1979; awards for photography AP, UPI, 1978-83. Roman Catholic. Office: WWL-TV 1024 N Rampart St New Orleans LA 70124

YAFFE, MICHAEL CHARLES, radio producer, author; b. New Haven, Apr. 29, 1951; s. Goodman and Ruth Y.; m. Gail Beth Sand, June 9, 1974; 1 dau., Emily. B.A. in Music, Clark U., 1973; M.A. in Musicology, U. Toronto, 1975. Asst. dir. ops. Nat. Assn. Schs. Music, Nat. Assn. Schs. Art/Design, Nat. Assn. Schs. Dance, Nat. Assn. Schs. Theatre, Reston, Va., 1976—; producer Sta. WAMU-FM, Washington, 1977-85. Vice-pres., Forest Edge Cluster Assn., Reston. Mem. Am. Musicol. Soc., Greater Washington Soc. Assn. Execs. (mem. edn. Com.), Am. Soc. Assn. Execs., Meeting Planners Internat. Author: Campus Music Programs and Public Radio Stations, 1977; State Arts Agencies and Professional Music Training Institutions, 1978; (with Gail Yaffe) radio programs: The Piano: Black and White and Played All Over, 1980, A Musical Fellowship: The String Quartet, 1981; Conducting: The Mystique of the Maestro, 1980. Office: 11250 Roger Bacon Dr #5 Reston VA 22090

YAMAZAKI, MAKOTO, economics educator; b. Tokyo, Dec. 19, 1948; s. Motoi and Mutsuko (Yamamoto) Y.; m. Abigail Elizabeth Burford, Aug. 4, 1984. B.A. in Law, Keio U., Japan, 1971; B.A. in Econs. and Polit. Sci., Wittenberg U., 1972-74; M.A. in Internat. Relations, Fletcher Sch. of Law and Diplomacy, 1976; Ph.D. in Econs., Duke U., 1984. Instr. Wittenberg U., Springfield, Ohio, 1972-74, asst. to program dir., 1973-75; vis. lectr. Tufts U., Medford, Mass., 1976, teaching asst. 1977-79; teaching asst. Duke U., Durham, N.C., 1982; asst. prof. W.Va. State Coll., Institute, 1984—. Wittenberg U. scholar, 1972; Grad. scholar Duke U., 1980. Mem. Am. Econ. Assn., W.Va. Consortium for Faculty and Course Devel. in Internat. Studies, Omicron Delta Epsilon. Congregationalist. Avocations: running; swimming; tennis; classical music; cooking. Home: 609 Grandview Pointe Dunbar WV 25064

YANARELLA, ERNEST JOHN, political science educator; b. Beacon, N.Y., Apr. 3, 1944; s. Ernest Daniel and Margaret Mary (Kochay) Y.; m. Ann-Marie Decker, July 26, 1969 (dec. June 1983); children—Margaret Elizabeth, John Michael. B.A., Syracuse U., 1966; Ph.D., U. N.C., 1971. Instr. polit. sci. U. N.C.-Chapel Hill, 1969-70; asst. prof. U. Ky., Lexington, 1970-75, assoc. prof., 1975—; vis. lectr. SUNY-Buffalo, summer 1972. Dept. Interior grantee, 1979, 80, 82; Danforth fellow, 1982-85. Mem. Am. Polit. Sci. Assn., Peace Sci. Soc., Council on Peace Research in History, ACLU, Central Ky. Civil Liberties Union, Fellowship of Reconciliation. Mem. Democratic Socialists Am. Episcopalian. Author: The Missile Defense Contro-Versy: Strategy, Technology, and Politics 1955-72, 1977 (Hon. mention Harold Lasswell Award Competition); Energy and the Social Sciences: A Bibliographical Guide to the Literature, 1982; contbr. articles to profl. jours., chpts. to books. Office: U Ky Patterson Office Tower Suite 1659 Lexington KY 40506

YANCEY, CLYDE LAYTON, uranium geologist, uranium consultant; b. Tulsa, July 26, 1953; s. Thomas Spotswood and Mary Jane (Steinberger) Y.; m. Jonalyn Dean Stovall, June 24, 1978; children—Matthew Richard, Charles Layton. B.A. in Geology, Trinity U., 1975; M.S. in Geology, S.D. Sch. of Mines and Tech., 1978. Geologist, U.S. Geol. Survey, Denver, 1978-79; sr. mine geologist Wyo. Mineral Corp., Bruni, Tex., 1979-80; prodn. geologist Caithness Mining Corp., Hebbronville, Tex., 1980-81; geologist Mobil Oil Corp., Corpus Christi, 1981-83; sr. geologist Moore Energy Corp., Corpus Christi, 1983—; pres. Mesquite Energy and Assocs., Corpus Christi, 1982—. Mem., Tuloso-Midway PTA, Corpus Christi, 1982—, Remove Intoxicated Drivers, Corpus Christi, 1984—. Mem. Am. Assn. of Petroleum Geologists, Soc. of Econ. Geologists (assoc. mem.), Soc. of Mining Engrs., South Tex. Minerals Chapter. Republican. Avocations: hunting; woodworking; gun collecting. Office: Moore Energy Corp 4925 Everhart Suite 120 Corpus Christi TX 78411

YANCHAK, DENNIS ALAN, geophysicist, researcher; b. Canonsburg, Pa., Mar. 30, 1955; s. Michael and Helen Josephine (Mathia) Y.; m. Claudia Jo Post, May 29, 1982; 1 child, Ashley Marie. B.S. in Math., Allegheny Coll., 1977, B.S. in Physics with honors, 1977; M.S. in Physics, Carnegie-Mellon U., 1983. Research geophysicist Gulf Research & Devel., Pitts., 1977-84, project geophysicist, Houston, 1984-85; staff geophysicist Amoco Prodn. Co., Houston, 1985—. Contbr. articles to profl. jours. Mem. Soc. Exploration Geophysicists, Am. Assn. Petroleum Geologists. Democrat. Mem. Byzantine Catholic Ch. Office: Amoco Prodn Co PO Box 3092 Houston TX 77253

YANEY, JOSEPH PAUL, management educator; b. Scranton, Pa., May 11, 1939; s. Alexander and Mary (Kuratnick) Y., Jr.; m. Barbara Ann Longon, May 30, 1964; children—Paul Daniel, Monica Lynn. B.A. in Econs., U. Mich., Ann Arbor, 1961, M.B.A., 1964, J.D., 1964, Ph.D., 1969. Bar: Mich. Prof.

mgmt. Ohio State U.-Columbia, 1969-76, Pa. State U.-Middletown, 1976-79, Tex. Tech U., Lubbock, 1979—; cons. in field, 1961—; sole practice law, arbitrator, 1964—. Author: Personnel, 1976; Labor Law, 1977. Leader, South Plains council Boy Scouts Am., 1979—; loaned exec. United Way, 1982. Served to capt. U.S. Army, 1964-66. Mem. Acad. Mgmt. Office: Tex Tech U 3106 42d St Lubbock TX 79413

YANG, SUNG CHUL, political scientist, educator; b. Kok Sung, South Cholla Province, Korea, Nov. 20, 1939; came to U.S., 1965, naturalized, 1978; s. Byung Joo and Hae Ok (Yim) Y.; m. Daisy Lee, Apr. 8, 1967; children—Eugene, Susan. B.A. in Polit. Sci., Seoul Nat. U., 1964; M.A., U. Hawaii, 1967; Ph.D., U. Ky., 1970; postgrad. Columbia U., 1966-67, U. Mich., 1966. Reporter, The Hankook Ilbo and the Korea Times, Seoul, 1963-65; asst. prof. Eastern Ky. U., 1970-75; vis. prof. Northwestern U., Evanston, Ill., 1972, Pembroke State U., N.C., 1975; chmn., prof. social sci. div. and polit. sci. dept. U. Ky. Center, Ft. Knox, 1975-84; prof. polit. sci., mem. Grad. Sch., U. Ky., Lexington, 1984—. Chmn. bd. dirs. Kentuckiana Korean Assn., 1979-81; bd. dirs. Ky. Civil Liberties Union, 1979-82. Recipient Social Sci. Research Council award, 1983; U. Ky. Research Found. grantee, 1982-83. Mem. Am. Polit. Sci. Assn., Assn. Asian Studies, Assn. Korean Polit. Scientists in N.Am. (exec. sec.-treas.). Author: Korea and Two Regimes, 1981.

YANSON, WILLIAM CRAIG, advertising agency executive; b. Cohoes, N.Y., Feb. 20, 1949; s. George and Elizabeth (Craig) Y.; m. Michal Nellans, July 4, 1981. Student U. St. Andrews, Scotland, 1969-70; B.A. in Classics, Union Coll., Schenectady, 1971; postgrad. Harvard U., 1971-73; M.A. in Classics, U. Vt., 1977; M.A. in German, Middlebury Coll., 1977. Coordinator ministry of the arts Cathedral Ch. of St. Paul, Burlington, Vt., 1975-77; tchr. German and classics Wayland (Mass.) High Sch., 1977-79; dir. AdventArts, public info. officer Ch. of Advent, Boston, 1979-81; public relations accounts supr. Pringle Dixon Pringle, Atlanta, 1981—. Mem. Public Relations Soc. Am., German-Am. C. of C., Ga. Soc. Assn. Execs., Am. Soc. Assn. Execs., Phi Beta Kappa. Episcopalian.

YANTIS, JOHN MARSHALL, wholesale trade executive; b. Fort Smith, Ark., Aug. 1, 1918; s. Marshall L. and Eva (Vick) Y.; B.S. in Mech. Engring., U. Mich., 1939; m. Shear L. Southball, May 7, 1976; children—Sarah Welch, Marshall I., John Marshall, Julia Ann. Supr. of stores Atuomotive, Inc., Fort Smith, 1939-40; project engr. Comsel Aircraft Co., San Diego, 1940-41; chief armament engr. Fort Motor Co., Willow Run, Mich., 1941-45, mem. int. research dept., 1945; v.p., gen. mgr. Automotive, Inc., Fort Smith, 1946-57; pres., gen. mgr. Motive Parts Warthorne, Inc., Ft. Smith, 1958-69, pres., chmn. bd. Mid-America Industries, Inc., Fort Smith, 1969—, now chief operating officer; chmn. bd. Wertz Co., 1972—; dir. Mchts. Nat. Bank, Arkansas Best Corp. Pres., Fort Smith Community Chest, 1951-52, Fort Smith United Fund, 1964-65, campaign chmn., 1968; chmn. Sebastian County (Ark.) ARC, 1951-52; chmn. Urban Renewal Authority Ft. Smith, 1973-74, pres. Fort Smith Sch. Bd., 1964-65, Car Case-Council, 1976-77. Mem. Soc. Automotive Engrs., Automotive Acad., Automotive Warehouse Distbr. Assn. (dir. 1969-75, named Automotive Man of Yr. 1974), Automotive Warehouse Distrs. Assn. (1st v.p. 1972-74), Automotive Info. Council (chmn. 1978-79, dir. 1972—), Nat. Standard Parts Assn. (dir. 1955-59, chmn. market research 1951-55), Phi Delta Theta. Episcopalian. Clubs: Thunderbird Country, Rancho Mirage (Calif.); Garden of the Gods (Colorado Springs); Hardscrabble Country, Fianna Hills Country, Town (Fort Smith); O'Donnell Country (Palm Springs, Calif.) Home: 3 Berry Hill St Fort Smith AR 72903 Office: 900 Rogers Bldg Fort Smith AR 72901

YANUCK, MARTIN, social science educator; b. Newark, Mar. 28, 1936; s. Benjamin and Rose (Borsky) Y. B.A., Rutgers U., 1958; M.A., U. Chgo., 1961, Ph.D., 1973. Asst. bibliographer South Asia, U. Chgo. Libraries, 1966-68; asst. prof. U. Ga., Athens, 1968-73; asst. prof. Spelman Coll., Atlanta, 1973-75, assoc. prof., chmn. history dept., 1975—; instr. Peace Corps, Chgo., 1966; dir. South Asia Microform Project, 1968-73. Editor: South Asia Library Resources, 1974. Vice-pres. Response, Inc., Athens, 1969-73; trustee Atlanta Council for Internat. Visitors, 1979-82; mem. council Internat. Magnate High Sch., Atlanta, 1982—; v.p. Congregation Beth Shalom, Atlanta, 1982-84, pres., 1984—. Mem. Assn. Asian Studies (com. South Asia libraries and documentation 1968-73), World History Assn. (steering com. 1982-83, council 1983-84), Am. Hist. Assn., So. Ctr. for Internat. Studies, Ga. Hist. Assn., Atlanta Com. on Fgn. Relations. Avocation: record and book collecting. Home: 6375 Wedgeview Ct Tucker GA 30084 Office: Dept History Spelman Coll Atlanta GA 30314

YARBOROUGH, WILLIAM W., JR., physics educator; b. Tylertown, Miss., Jan. 6, 1945; s. William W. and Katherine E. (Mixon) Y.; m. Cynthia Diane Cox, Sept. 15, 1968. B.A., U. Chattanooga, 1967; Ph.D., Vanderbilt U., 1974. Grad. asst. Vanderbilt U., 1967-73; programmer Werthan Industries, Nashville, 1973-74; mem. faculty Presbyterian Coll., Clinton, S.C., 1974—, chmn. dept. physics, 1981—; pres. Speak Softly, Inc., 1983—. Author computer software. Pres., Community Concert Assn., Clinton, S.C., 1980-82, Laurens County Chorale, 1977—. Recipient Disting. Service award Presbyn. Coll., 1983. Mem. Am. Assn. Physics Tchrs., Am. Phys. Soc., Assn. Computing Machinery, Am. Inst. Physics. Democrat. Baptist. Lodge: Kiwanis (bd. dirs. 1983—). Avocations: golf; boating. Home: 303 Calvert Ave Clinton SC 29325 Office: Dept Physics Presbyterian Coll Clinton SC 29325

YARBRO, CLAUDE LEE, JR., life scientist; b. Jackson, Tenn., Sept. 26, 1922; s. Claude Lee and Laura Belle (Yarbro) Y.; m. Mary Clare Frazier, Mar. 6, 1951; children—Laura Anne, Elizabeth, David. B.A. magna cum laude, Lambuth Co., 1943; postgrad. Vanderbilt U., 1949-51; Ph.D., U. N.C., 1954. Acting prof. math. and physics Lambuth Coll., Jackson, Tenn., 1946-47; instr. Physics Union U. (Tenn.), 1948-49; instr. Vanderbilt U., Nashville, 1949-51; instr., research assoc. biochemistry U. N.C. Sch. Medicine, Chapel Hill, 1954-60; biologist U.S. AEC, Oak Ridge, 1960-75; life scientist U.S. Energy Research and Devel. Adminstrn., Oak Ridge, 1975-77; life scientist U.S. Dept. Energy, Oak Ridge, 1977-84, cons., 1984—; adminstr. ecol., environ. research, edn. and tng. Manpower Research and Devel. Pres. Oak Ridge chpt. St. Andrews Soc., 1980-81; mem. Oak Ridge High Sch. Band Parents Club, 1970-76, Oak Ridge PTA, 1960-76. Served with USNR, 1943-46, 46—. Recipient Coker award Elisha Mitchell Sci. Soc., 1954; Sustained Superior Performance award U.S. AEC, 1968; Superior Job Performance award U.S. Dept. Energy, 1982. Fellow Am. Inst. Chemists; mem. AAAS, Ecol. Soc. Am., Am. Forestry Assn., Sigma Xi. Democrat. Methodist. Contbr. articles to profl. jours. Home: 147 Alger Rd Oak Ridge TN 37830 Office: US Dept Energy PO Box E Oak Ridge TN 37830

YARBROUGH, MARY MORRIS, economics educator, administrator; b. Auburn, Ala., June 3, 1947; d. Bertram C. and Ethel (Key) Morris; m. James E. Yarbrough, Aug. 9, 1969; 1 dau., Susan Elizabeth. B.S., U. Ala., 1969, Ph.D., 1983; M.S., Auburn U., 1973. Math. tchr. Hartselle (Ala.) Jr. High Sch., 1969-71; grad. teaching asst. Auburn U., 1971-73; instr. econs., stats. and data processing Troy State U., 1973-74; instr. econs. and stats. U. Ala.-Huntsville, 1974-75; systems analyst TRW, Huntsville, 1974-75; instr. Calhoun Community Coll., Decatur, Ala., 1975-82, chmn. bus. adminstrn. dept., 1982-85, chmn. bus. div., 1986—; statis. cons. Recipient Outstanding Grad. Student award Auburn U., 1973; Calhoun Found. award Calhoun Community Coll., 1982-83; Outstanding Student award U. Ala., 1983; Title III grantee Fed. Govt., 1982-83. Mem. Ala. Assn. for Higher Edn. in Bus., Am. Statis. Assn., Mid-South Acad. Economists, Ala. Jr. and Community Coll. Assn., Am. Econ. Assn., Calhoun Coll. Found., Alpha Chi Omega Alumni Club, Calhoun Women's Club. Methodist. Contbr. articles to profl. jours. Office: PO Box 2216 Decatur AL 35601

YARIAN, DAVID ARNOLD, clinical psychologist; b. Longview, Tex., Oct. 13, 1947; s. Burton David and Christine (Arnold) Y.; m. Thelma Lee Kidd, May 9, 1971; children—Sarah Elizabeth, Noah David. B.A., Eastern N.Mex. U., 1969; M.A., U. Mich., 1975, Ph.D., 1982. Lic. psychologist, Tenn. Family therapist Ann Arbor Ctr. For Family, Mich., 1976-78; counselor Family & Children's Service, Nashville, 1979-80; psychologist Alive-Hospice of Nashville, 1979—; gen. practice psychology, Nashville, 1980—; cons. in field. Contbr. articles to profl. jours. Mem. Am. Psychol. Assn., Tenn. Psychol. Assn., Nashville Family Therapy Consortium (founding mem., steering com.), Ala. Family Consortium. Avocations: antique collecting; woodworking; reading. Home: 4309 Gray Oaks Dr Nashville TN 37204 Office: 2211 Crestmoor Rd Suite 200 Nashville TN 37215

YARUS, GARY J., real estate investment company executive; b. Cleve., Jan. 9, 1949; s. Leonard and Marilyn S. Yarus; m. Nina Piken, Sept. 20, 1981. B.S., Union Coll., 1971; M.Ed., Harvard U., 1973, M.B.A., 1978. Psychologist, adminstr. Framingham (Mass.) Day Hosp., 1972-76; asst. to pres. beverage div. Gen. Cinema Corp., Miami, Fla., 1978-81; pres. Comml. Real Estate Brokerage, Miami, 1981—. Pres. Snapper Village Homeowners Assn., Miami, 1983-84. Mem. Miami Bd. Real Estate (chmn. nat. speaking com.), Nat. Assn. Securities Dealers. Club: Harvard Bus. Sch. of South Fla. (pres. 1983-85). Home: 330 W 45th St Miami Beach FL 33140 Office: 5046 Biscayne Blvd Miami FL 33137

YASER, BETTY SLADE, economics, finance educator; b. Norfolk, Va., Sept. 23, 1939; d. Frank Moncure and Beatrice Irene (Knighton) Slade; m. Yasar Yaser, Sept. 19, 1964; children—Hoseyin Kenan, Havva Aylin. B.S.F.S., Georgetown Sch. Fgn. Service, 1961; Ph.D., in Econs., Vanderbilt U., 1967. Cons. OEDD, Paris, Ankara, Turkey, 1964-66; sr. econ. cons. U.S. AID, Ankara, 1968-75; free-lance journalist London, 1975-79; dir. bus. studies Schiller U., London, 1981-82; asst. prof. Univ. Houston, 1983—; vis. prof. Vanderbilt U., Nashville, summers 1980-84; advisor Turkish Govt., Ankara, 1967-75. Author: Analysis of Finance System of Turkey, 1967, Fulbright scholar, 1985-86. Mem. Am. Econs. Assn., Southwest Econs. Assn., (v.p. 1984-85), Southwest Fedn. Adminstrv. Disciplines. Democrat. Office: Univ Houston Clearlake 2700 Bay Area Blvd Houston TX 77058

YASREBI, HOSEIN, surgeon; b. Kashan, Iran, Apr. 28, 1939; s. Abulhasan and Tooran (Arbab) Y.; m. Kadijeh Darbani, May 18, 1973; children—Leila, Mona, Sara. M.D., U. Tehran, 1964. Intern, St. Vincent's Med. Ctr., Jacksonville, Fla., 1965; resident JHEP program in gen. surgery Univ. Hosp. of Jacksonville, 1966-70, now mem. staff; practice medicine specializing in gen. surgery, Jacksonville, 1972—; mem. staff Meth. Hosp., Jacksonville, St. Luke's Hosp., Jacksonville; asst. clin. prof. U. Fla. Mem. AMA (Physician Recognition award 1983), Fla. Med. Assn., Southeastern Surg. Congress. Fellow ACS. Past pres. Islamic Center N.E. Fla. Home: 7078 San Fernando Pl Jacksonville FL 32217

YATES, DAVID ANTHONY, civil engineering executive; b. Nashville, July 31, 1953; s. Harvell Eugene and Audrey Ernesteen (Smith) Y.; m. Janet Faye Shipley, Sept. 4, 1976; 1 son, Damon Anthony. B.S., Tenn. Technol. U., 1976. Registered profl. engr., Tenn. Roadway design engr. Tenn. Dept. Transp., Nashville, 1976-82; chief roadway design engr. John Coleman Hayes & Assocs., Nashville, 1982-83; co-owner, v.p. Robbins, Yates & Assocs., Inc., cons. engrs., Lyles, Tenn., 1983—. Dixie Youth Baseball Coll. scholar, 1971. Mem. Order of Engr., ASCE, Civil War Roundtable, Nat. Muzzle Loading Rifle Assn., Lambda Chi Alpha Alumni Assn. Methodist. Home: Route 2 Country Valley Lyles TN 37098 Office: Robbins Yates & Assocs PO Box 27 Lyles TN 37098

YATES, JOE ELTON, real estate developer, state senator; b. Cherokee City, Ark., Aug. 15, 1938; s. Elton Gerald and DovieEsta (Bayley) Y.; m. Anita Joyce Ratcliff, Aug. 28, 1960; children—Christopher Miles, Robyn Keeley, Darien Adam. B.S., U. Ark., 1969, M.A., 1970. Real estate broker, Rogers, Ark., 1976-77; county tax assessor, Bentonville, Ark., 1977-78; owner Landscape Nursery, Gentry, Ark., 1978-82; Benton County collector, Bentonville, 1981-83; asst. dir. land Cooper Communities, Inc., Bentonville, 1983—; land cons., Bentonville, 1976—; cons., researcher State of Ark., Little Rock, 1975-76; mem. Ark. Senate, 1984—; tax collector, Benton County, 1983. Author: Fiscal Analysis of Bellavista, 1983; editor: Atlas of Arkansas, 1973. Mem. Ark. Republican Com., 1983. Served with USAF, 1956-60. Mem. Bentonville C. of C. (dir. 1983-86). Baptist. Home: 711 SW 2d Bentonville AR 72712 Office: Cooper Communities 101 S Main St Bentonville AR 72712

YATES, MARVIN CLARENCE, advertising artist, painter, illustrator; b. Jackson, Tenn., Sept. 22, 1943; s. Marvin Caleb and Mary Louise (Wright) Y.; m. Margaret Sarah Lea, Dec. 6, 1975; children—Wesley, Christen. Student Memphis Acad. Arts, 1962-65. Advt. artist, illustrator Memphis Pub. Co., 1967—. Served to 1st class petty officer USCG, 1966-72. Mem. Am. Watercolor Soc., So. Watercolor Soc. (co-founder), Tenn. Watercolor Soc. (co-founder), Memphis Watercolor Group (co-founder, pres. 1968-84). Avocations: sports; photography. Home: 2261 Montego Dr Cordova TN 38018 Office: Memphis Pub Co 495 Union Memphis TN 38103

YATES, ROBERT DOYLE, anatomy educator; b. Birmingham, Ala., Feb. 28, 1931; s. James William, Jr. and Mildred (Doyle) Y.; m. Jane Congleton, 1955; children—Robert Lee, Pamela C. B.S., U. Ala., 1954, M.S., 1956; Ph.D., U. Ala. Med. Sch., 1959. Student anatomy dept. U. Ala., Birmingham, 1959-60; postdoctoral fellow U. Tex., Galveston, 1961-72; prof. anatomy Tulane Med. Sch., New Orleans, 1972—, chmn. dept., 1972—; adj. prof. Harvard Med. Sch., Boston, 1962-63, Yale Med. Sch., New Haven, 1965-67. Mem. editorial bd. Am. Jour. Anatomy, Anat. Record. Contbr. articles to profl. jours., chpts. to books. Vestryman, Trintity Episc. Ch., Galveston, Tex., 1965-68, Trinity Episc. Ch., New Orleans, 1985—. Served to 1st lt. inf. U.S. Army, 1960-61. Recipient numerous awards NIH, 1965-74; Research Career Devel. award, Golden Apple teaching award AMA Student Assn., 1971. Mem. Am. Assn. Anatomists (chmn. nominating com. 1980), Assn. Anatomy Chairmen (sec.-treas. 1976—), Am. Soc. Cell Biology. Republican. Avocations: tennis; stained glass; beveled glass; hunting. Office: Tulane Med Sch Dept Anatomy 1430 Tulane Ave New Orleans LA 70112

YATES, RUTHERFORD BIRCHARD HAYES, III, printing company executive; b. Houston, Jan. 16, 1951; s. Rutherford B.H. and Genevieve (Batiste) M. A.A., Okla. State Tech. U., 1972. Instr. printing Tex. So. U., 1972; printing foreman Yates Printing & Lithographing Inc., Houston, 1973-78, gen. mgr., 1978-83, pres., 1981—. Recipient Bus. award Houston League Bus. and Profl. Women, 1977; Dale Carnegie award, 1974; Businessman award Forward Times newspaper, 1981. Mem. Mt. Carmel Alumni Assn., Okla. State Tech. Alumni Assn., Tex. So. U. Alumni Assn., Houston Citizens C. of C. (Bus. Achievement award 1976), Printing Industries of Gulf Coast. Democrat. Office: 3514 Wentworth St Houston TX 77004

YAWORSKY, GEORGE MYROSLAW, physicist, technical and management consultant; b. Drohobych, Ukraine, Aug. 4, 1940; s. Myroslaw and Mary (Yaworsky) Y.; m. Zenia Maria Smishkewych, Sept. 9, 1972; 1 dau., Maria Diana. B.S. in Physics, Rensselaer Poly. Inst., 1962, M.B.A., 1977, Ph.D. in Physics, 1979; M.S. in Physics, Carnegie-Mellon U., 1964. Physicist Republic Steel Research Ctr., Independence, Ohio, 1966-68; tech. and mgmt. cons. in ops. research, mktg. analyses, computer modeling, sci. programming and other areas to state govt., pvt. cos., 1972-81; internat. tech. assessment and analysis cons. EG&G, Inc., Rockville, Md., 1981-82; program dir.-computer integrated mfg. Eagle Research Group, Arlington, Va., 1982-83; prin. investigator high volume mfg. Sci. Applications, Inc., McLean, Va., 1983-84; cons. computer integrated mfg., materials sci., tech. transfer and mgmt., 1984—; mem. U.S. del. to Coordinating Com. for Multilateral Export Controls, Paris, 1982. Contbr. articles to profl. jours. Recipient Physics Teaching award Poly. Inst., 1971; John Huntington scholar; Rensselaer Alumni scholar. Mem. N.Y. Acad. Scis., Robotics Internat. of Soc. Mfg. Engrs. (sr.), Computer and Automated Systems Assn. of Soc. Mfg. Engrs. (sr., chmn. Greater Washington chpt. 1985-87), Am. Phys. Soc., Am. Assn. Physics Tchrs., Am. Prodn. and Inventory Control Soc., AAAS, Rensselaer Alumni Assn., Assn. Integrated Mfg. Tech., Robotic Industries Assn., Sigma Xi. Office: 2000 S Eads St Arlington VA 22202

YAX, LAWRENCE DONALD, college administrator; b. Cleve., July 12, 1937; s. Lawrence James and Frances Mae (Meanor) Y.; m. Una Theresa Giroux, Sept. 1, 1961; children—Rachael Lynne, David Lawrence. B.A., Western Res. U., 1960, M.A., 1961, Ph.D., 1971, M.S.L.S., 1973. Info. specialist Brush Wellman Inc., Cleve., 1963-73; instr. English, Cleve. State U., 1969-72; dir. learning resources Pensacola Jr. Coll., Fla., 1973-81, dean instrnl. services, 1981—; chmn. learning resources com. Fla. Dept. Edn., 1984—, bd. dirs. staff and program devel., 1984-85. Bd. dirs. Pensacola Pen Wheels, Inc., 1978—, Pensacola Employment for Handicapped, 1983—; v.p. Epilepsy Soc. NW Fla., 1979—; active Pvt. Indsl. Council, Pensacola, 1984. Recipient Ann. Leadership award Pensacola Pen Wheels, Inc., 1982, Pub. Mention award State Conf. Handicapped Edn., Fla., 1982. Mem. W. Fla. Library Assn., Assn. Ednl. Data System, Phi Delta Kappa. Democrat. Roman Catholic. Avocation: hiking. Home: 4304 Burtonwood Dr Pensacola FL 32514 Office: Pensacola Jr Coll 1000 College Blvd Pensacola FL 32504

YEAGER, PAUL RAY, research executive, aerospace technologist; b. Sherman, Tex., Feb. 7, 1931; s. Paul W. and Clara (Melton) Y.; m. Catherine Cleveland, Feb. 10, 1956; children—Sharon K., David B. B.A. in Physics, Austin Coll., 1952; M.S. in Engring. Mgmt., George Washington U., 1970. Research engr. NASA, Hampton, Va., 1952-58, group leader, 1959-63, head vacuum measurements sect. instrument research div., 1963-68, head environ. measurements sect., 1968-74, head gen. research instrumentation br. 1974—. Patentee (3); contbr. articles to profl. jours. Pres. Dare Sch. PTA, York County, Va., 1973-74; pres., coach Grafton Youth Football, York County, 1972-76; coach Lafayette Jr. Rifle Team, York County, 1977-82; pres. Old Dominion Jr. Rifle League York County, 1979-85. Clubs: Lafayette Gun (coach 1977-82), Va. Rifle (bd. dirs. 1972-75); Nat. Rifle. Home: 201B Paradise Point Rd Grafton VA 23692 Office: NASA Langley Research Ctr Hampton VA 23665

YEARGIN, ROBERT ARNOLD, accounting and financial consultant; b. Nashville, June 27, 1944; s. Arnold E. and Margaret (Dobbs) Y.; B.S., Middle Tenn. State U., 1966; M.B.A., U. Tenn., 1977; m. Mary K. Eskew, July 1, 1978; children—Robert Arnold, Kimberly J. Controller, Anchor Wire Corp., Goodlettsville, Tenn., 1970-73; asst. dir. fiscal services State of Tenn., Nashville, 1973-76; dir. spl. projects-fin. mgmt. Vanderbilt U. Med. Center, Nashville, 1976-77; owner Yeargin & Assoc., Nashville, 1977—; pres. Yeargin Bldg. Corp., 1978—; pres., co-owner A-Team Sports, Inc., 1982—; dir. Nat. Bldg. Corp., Nashville, 1977-78; lectr. in field. Pres., M.B.A. Student Body, U. Tenn., Nashville, 1976-77; chmn. bd. Nat. Hemophilia Found., 1977. Named Jaycee of the Year, 1974-75; numerous other state, regional, nat. awards. Mem. Franklin Rd. Jaycees (v.p. 1975-76), Middle Tenn. State U. Acctg. Soc., Alpha Kappa Psi. Home: 4626 Shy's Hill Rd Nashville TN 37215 Office: 814 19th Ave S Nashville TN 37203

YEARSLEY, ELLIOT NYE, III, petroleum geologist, geological engineer; b. Oakland, Calif., July 21, 1953; s. Elliot Nye and Josephine Elizabeth (Magagnose) Y.; m. Laureen Alyson Kelly, July 30, 1977; 1 child, Adelaide Laureen. B.S. in Geol. Engring., Colo. Sch. Mines, 1981; cert. forestry Coll. Redwoods, 1974. Owner, operator Gardening Service, Chico, Calif., 1975-77; constrn. inspector Cons. Engrs., Yuba City, Calif., 1977; surveyor Calif. Dept. Transp., Marysville, 1978-79; chemist U.S. Geol. Survey, Denver, 1980-81; geol. engr. Tenneco Exploration and Prodn., Lafayette, La., 1982—. Democratic state del., Boulder, Colo., 1980; tchr. Unitarian Ch., Golden, Colo., 1979-81. Mem. Am. Assn. Petroleum Geologists (jr.), Soc. Petroleum Engrs. (assoc.). Democrat. Unitarian. Avocations: gardening; travel; softball. Home: 1000 Kaliste Saloom #18 Lafayette LA 70508 Office: Tenneco Oil Exploration & Prodn PO Box 39300 Lafayette LA 70503

YEH, GEORGE HON CHENG, statistician; b. Chia-Yi, Taiwan, May 10, 1948; came to U.S., 1974, naturalized, 1985; s. Tien Yuan and Shin Kai (Lee) Y.; m. Susan Cingyee Ku, Jan. 9, 1972; children—Jane, James. B.S., Taiwan Normal U., 1971; M.A., SUNY-Buffalo, 1975; M.S., Purdue U., 1978; Ph.D., So. Methodist U., 1981. Teaching asst. SUNY Coll., Buffalo, 1974-75, Purdue U., West Lafayette, Ind., 1975-78; research and teaching asst. So. Meth. U., Dallas, 1978-81, statis. cons., 1979-81; statistician Tex. N.Mex. Power Co., Fort Worth, 1981—. Contbr. articles to profl. jours. Pres. Taiwanese Assn. Am., Dallas-Fort Worth, 1983. Mem. Am. Statis. Assn., Sigma Xi. Home: 3205 Vintage Way Bedford TX 76021 Office: Tex NMex Power Co PO Box 2943 Fort Worth TX 76113

YEH, WALTER HUAI-TEH, composer, educator; b. Shanghai, China, Jan. 7, 1911; came to U.S., 1944, naturalized, 1955; s. Ziang Tsung and Pei-Yu (Huang) Y.; A.B., St. John's U. (China), 1933; grad. summa cum laude Nat. Conservatory of Music (China), 1935; M.A. and Mus.M., Eastman Sch. Music, U. Rochester, 1945; A.M., Harvard, 1948, researcher, 1951-54; Ph.D., U. Rochester, 1949; m. Moong Yue, Aug. 8, 1942; children—Peter Wen-chun, Arthur Cho-chun. Prof. flute Nat. Conservatory of Music, China, 1940-44; prof. music, chmn. joint music dept. Allen U and Benedict Coll., Columbia, S.C., 1954-81; prof. music Allen U., 1954-81, interim pres., 1973, chmn. humanities div., 1957-60, 63-79; chmn. div. fine arts and drama Benedict Coll., 1968-71, 72-74. Composer: Concerto Grosso in F for Oboe, String Quartet and Harp with String Orchestra, 1944; Symphony in D, 1944; Chinese Suite, 1945; Chinese Symphony, 1948; (madrigal) Come Away, Come Away, Death!, 1957; The Cuckoo Chorus, 1958; Hymn for Peace, 1960; And Ruth Said: Intreat Me Not to Leave Thee, 1962; The Solitary Reaper, 1964; She Never Told Her Love, 1965; This Glorious Christmas Night, 1967; Gloria Patri and Kyrie, 1968; The Pattering Rain, 1968; The Lord's Prayer, 1969; We Shall Overcome, 1970; A Tombstone Epitaph, 1971; Alleuia, May Peace Be on Earth, 1972; Farewell for Ever!, 1972; All Glory, Praise and Honor, 1973; Echoes from on the Great Wall, 1974; He Who Loves God Loves All People, 1975; Last Night, 1975; Oh Slide and Stamp!, 1976; For Dust Thou Art, and Unto Dust Shalt Thou Return, 1977; Think! Think! Think!, 1977; Long, Long Ago, 1977; Farewell Alma Mater Dear! God Be With You Till We Meet Again, 1977; Concerto Ecclesiastico, 1979; Orientalia string quartet, 1980; A Song for the Chinese People, 1981; A Japanese Song, 1982; Doxology in Chinese Style, 1983; An Oriental Theme and Variation for String Orchestra, 1985; composer orchestral and choral works, other compositions. Bd. dirs. Columbia Lyric Theatre, 1972-75. Fellow Internat. Inst. Arts and Letters. Lodge: Rotary. Home: 710 Heidt St Columbia SC 29205

YEILDING, FRANK BROOKS, JR., savings and loan executive; b. Birmingham, Ala., Mar. 22, 1904; s. Francis Bee and Morgana (Bland) Y.; m. Augusta Gage Smith, Nov. 18, 1925; children—Augusta Gage Yeilding Hanna, Frank Brooks. B.S., Birmingham-So. Coll., 1925, LL.D. (hon.), 1984. With Jefferson Fed. Savs. and Loan Assn., 1925—, sec., 1927—, sec.-treas., 1929—, pres., 1946—, chmn. bd., chief exec. officer, 1976—; dir., v.p. Internat. Realty Corp.; chmn. bd. Jackson Ins. Agency; v.p., dir. Yeildings Dept. Store; pres. Yeilding Bros. Holding Co.; chmn. bd. Jackson Holding Co. Chmn. bd. dirs., exec. adminstr. Jefferson County War Price and Rationing Bd., 1942-46; Recipient Disting. Alumni award Birmingham-So. Coll., 1968; named to Ala. Acad. Honor, 1983. Mem. Ala. Savs. and Loan League (past pres.), U.S. League Savs. Insts. (past pres.), Newcomen Soc. Am. Methodist. Lodge: Kiwanis (Birmingham). Home: 3015 Brookwood Rd Birmingham AL 35223 Office: Jefferson Savs and Loan Asns 215 N 21st St Birmingham AL 35203

YEISLEY, JOHN CLARKE, army officer; b. Niagara Falls, N.Y., Jan. 16, 1946; s. John Samuel and Phyllis Esther (Van Sickle) Y.; m. Deborah Beth Watcke, July 19, 1969 (div. 1983); children—Michael, Kimberly, David; m. 2d, Mary Jean Yeisley, Aug. 26, 1983. Registered profl. engr., Va. B.S., U.S. Mil. Acad., 1969; M.S.E.E., Ga. Inst. Tech., 1976. Commd. 2d lt. U.S. Army, 1969, advanced through grades to lt. col., 1986; asst. prof. elec. engring. U.S. Mil. Acad., West Point, N.Y., 1976-79; asst. chief scientist U.S. Army OTEA, Falls Church, Va., 1979-83, G3 plans Hdqrs 32d AADCOM, Darmstadt, W. Ger., 1983—. Leader Boy Scouts Am., 1982. Decorated Bronze Star, Army Commendation medal, Meritorious Service medal. Mem. Assn. Grads. U.S. Mil. Acad., Va. Profl. Engrs. Soc. Episcopalian. Home: 1510 N Campbell St El Paso TX 79902 Office: HHB 32D AADCOM CMR 2146 APO New York NY 09175

YELLIN, CAROL LYNN GILMER, editor, author; b. Clinton, Okla., Mar. 3, 1920; d. Thomas Prather and Merry Eulala (Rogers) Gilmer; m. Thomas Orlo Heggen, Aug. 6, 1942 (div.); m. David Gilmer Yellin, Aug. 27, 1950; children—Charles Franklin, Thomas Gilmer, Douglas Simon, Emily Anne. B.S. with honors in History, Northwestern U., 1941, M.S. cum laude in Journalism, 1942. Editorial asst. Readers' Digest, Pleasantville, N.Y., 1942-44, assoc. editor, 1949-64, spl. projects editor Readers' Digest Condensed Books, 1964—; assoc. editor Coronet mag., N.Y.C., 1946-49; freelance writer, editor, editorial cons., Memphis, 1964—; editorial cons. Ctr. So. Folklore, Memphis, 1976—; producer Face to Face, WMC-TV, Memphis, 1981—; adj. prof. journalism dept. Memphis State U., 1975-83; club staff asst. ARC, Hawaii, Guam, Saipan, 1945. Bd. dirs. Memphis YWCA, 1971-78; Tenn. alt. del. Nat. Women's Conf., Houston, 1977. NEH grantee, 1971-74; AAUW Edn. Found. grantee, 1983-84. Mem. Authors Guild, Women in Communications (founding mem.), Women in Cable (dir. Memphis) 1973-75, AAUW, Women's Nat. Book Assn. Democrat. Unitarian. Editor: Tennessee Women, Past and Present, Memphis, 1977; Images of the South, Memphis, 1977; author (with Neil V. Sullivan and Thomas L. Maynard) Bound for Freedom, 1965; contbr. numerous articles to nat. mags.

YELLIN, DAVID GILMER, broadcasting and communication educator, television producer and moderator, author, consultant; b. Phila., Apr. 3, 1916; s. Simon and Freda (Amsterdam) Y.; m. Carol Lynn Gilmer, Aug. 27, 1950; children—Charles Franklin, Thomas Gilmer, Douglas Simon, Emily Anne. B.A., Pa. State Coll., 1937; M.A., Tchrs. Coll., Columbia U., 1963. In theater, network radio and TV, local TV, writer of articles in Esquire, Sat. Evening Post, Harpers, Pageant, Show Mag., Charm, TV Guide, and others; prof. broadcasting and communication Memphis State U., 1964-81, prof. emeritus, 1981—; producer, moderator Face to Face, Sta. WMC-TV, Memphis, 1969—. Served with U.S. Army, 1941-45. Recipient Theater Library Assn. award, 1973. Mem. Author's Guild. Author: Special, 1973; Tomorrow & Tomorrow & Tomorrow, 1985.

YELLMAN, EDWARD KELLER, college official; retired army officer; b. Lexington, Ky., Feb. 22, 1925; s. John Scott and Edna (Keller) Y.; m. Eunice Palmer, June 11, 1955; children—Edward Keller, James P., Gregory S., Michael L., Donna Marie. B.S., U.S. Mil. Acad., 1949; M.S., Lowell U., 1956. Commd. 2d lt. U.S. Army, 1949, advanced through grades to col.; ret., 1979; bus. mgr. No. Va. Community Coll., Woodbridge, 1979—. Decorated Legion of Merit, Bronze Star. Mem. Ret. Officer Assn., Assn. Grads. U.S. Mil. Acad., Riverside Gardens Recreation Assn., Riverside Gardens Civic Assn., Phi Delta Theta. Roman Catholic. Avocations: tennis; swimming; all sports. Home: 8507 Stable Dr Alexandria VA 22308 Office: No Va Community Coll 15200 Neabsco Mills Rd Woodbridge VA 22191

YENAWINE, DAVID LEROY, engineer; b. El Campo, Tex., July 10, 1934; s. George Leroy and Beatrice Maude (Hicks) Y.; B.S. in Ceramic Engring., U. Tex., 1960, Ph.D. in M.E., 1970; M.S. in Metall. Engring., Rensselaer Poly. Inst., 1963; m. Mae Beth Knapp, June 22, 1958; children—Dallas Lee, King Allan, Dean Alden. Sr. metallurgist Pratt & Whitney Aircraft, Middletown, Conn., 1960-64; materials and process engr. Douglas Aircraft Co., Charlotte, N.C., 1964-65; sect. mgr. materials devel. group Tracor, Austin, Tex., 1967-71; mgr. central Q.R.A. labs. Tex. Instruments, Dallas, 1971—. Served with U.S. Army, 1954-56. Registered profl. engr., Tex. Mem. Am. Soc. Metals, Am. Ceramic Soc., Nat. Inst. Ceramic Engrs., AIME, Phi Theta Kappa, Pi Tau Sigma. Contbr. articles to profl. publs. Patentee in field. Home: Rt 3 Box 36 Farmersville TX 75031 Office: PO Box 6015 Dallas TX 75222

YEOMAN, LYNN CHALMERS, pharmacologist, educator; b. Evanston, Ill., May 17, 1943; s. Kenneth Chalmers and Lillian (Warner) Y.; m. Ann Craven, Aug. 20, 1966; children—Caroline, Christopher, Sarah. B.A., DePauw U., 1965; Ph.D., U. Ill., 1970. Teaching asst. U. Ill., Urbana, 1967-68; instr. Baylor Coll. Medicine, Houston, 1972-73, asst. prof. pharmacology, 1973-76, assoc., 1976-84, prof., 1984—; cons. colon cancer working group, sect. gastrointestinal oncology and digestive disease M.D. Anderson Hosp., Houston, 1985—. Author, editor: Methods in Cancer Research, vol. 19, 1982. Editor: Methods in Cancer Research, vol. 20, 1982. Mem. adminstrv. bd. St. Luke's United Meth. Ch., Houston, 1985; parliamentarian Marilyn Estates Civic Assn., Houston, 1985. Recipient Com. of Revision award U.S. Pharmacopeial conv., Inc., 1985. Mem. Am. Soc. Biol. Chemists, Am. Assn. Immunologists, Am. Soc. Cell Biology, Am. Assn. Cancer Research, Soc. for Exptl. Biology and Medicine. Club: Buffalo Field Archery. Avocations: archery; amateur radio. Home: 5434 Rutherglenn Dr Houston TX Office: Baylor Coll Medicine One Baylor Plaza Houston TX 77030

YERGER, IVAN BASS, oil company executive, lawyer; b. Jackson, Miss., Jan. 4, 1934; s. Wirt Adams and Mae Rivers (Applewhite) Y.; m. Jaynne Carr, Nov. 25, 1966 (div. Jan. 1970); m. Sandra Sue Pate, Dec. 30, 1972. B.S. in Petroleum Engring., Okla. U., 1958, B.S. in Geol. Engring., 1958; LL.B., U. Tex., 1964. Bar: Tex. 1964. Assoc. Butler, Binion, Rice, Cook, Houston, 1964-67; stockbroker Smith, Barney & Co., Loeb, Rhodes & Co., Abraham & Co., Dallas, 1969-74; sr. contract adminstr. Enserch Exploration Inc., Dallas, 1974-77; land mgr. Wil-Mac Oil Co., Dallas, 1977-78; v.p. Cimarron Corp., Dallas, 1981—; v.p., dir. Okla. Oil Co., Dallas, 1978—; dir. United Park City Mines Co., Salt Lake City. Served with U.S. Army, 1958-59. Mem. Am. Assn. Petroleum Geologists, Tex. Bar, Dallas Assn. Petroleum Landmen, Dallas Ballet, Dallas Mus. Fine Arts. Republican. Episcopalian. Club: Energy (Dallas). Avocations: swimming; snow skiing; scuba diving; travel. Home: 4048 Hawthorne St Dallas TX 75219 Office: Cimarron Corp 1401 2 Energy Sq Dallas TX 75206

YIELDING, JACKSON MARTIN, JR., architect; b. Kopperston, W. Va., Aug. 24, 1939; s. Jackson Martin and Alma Aliene (Crockett) Y.; m. Wylene Lane, July 24, 1962; children—Beverly Diane, Jackie LaRue. B.A. in Architecture, Auburn U., 1965. Registered architect, Ga., Ala. Architect. intern Hugh Gaston Assoc., Albany, Ga., 1967-69, William Y. McLean, AIA, Tifton, Ga., 1969-70; architect Gaston & Fausett, AIA, Albany, 1970-75; ptnr. Yielding & Wakeford AIA, Albany, 1975—; instr. Albany Jr. Coll., 1984. Mem. Am. Cancer Soc., Dougherty-Lee County, Ga., 1980; bd. dirs. YMCA, Albany, 1983-85. Served to maj. USAR, 1965-67. Recipient Eagle Scout award Black Diamond dist. Boy Scouts Am., Roderfield, W. Va., 1955. Mem. AIA, (bd. dirs. Ga. chpt. 1975, 78, 79, pres. Southwest Ga. 1980), Jaycees. Democrat. Methodist. Club: Hosanna Boosters (pres. 1983-85) (Albany). Lodge: Rotary Internat. (Albany). Avocations: Jogging; coin collecting; hunting; gardening; music. Home: 2309 Sharon Ave Albany GA 31707 Office: 308 3d Ave P O Box 405 Albany GA 31702

YOCHAM, WANDA JUNE BURLESON, seminary administrator; b. Rankin, Tex., Oct. 29, 1934; d. Wesley Hardin and Vivian May Lee (Hickerson) Burleson; student San Angelo Coll., 1953-54, Austin Community Coll., 1974-75, U. Ky. Coll. Bus. Mgmt. Inst., 1977-78, 79; div.; children—James, Kathy. Claims clk. Legal div. Tex. Bd. Hosps. and Schs., Austin Tex., 1959-61; office mgr. George T. Barr Comml. Food Equipment, Orlando, Fla., 1962-64; bus. officer Episcopal Theol. Sem., Austin, Tex., 1964—; treas., dir. Center Hispanic Ministries. Mem. So. Assn. Coll. and Univ. Bus. Officers. Republican. Episcopalian. Address: Episcopal Theol Sem Southwest Box 2247 Austin TX 78767

YOCHMOWITZ, MICHAEL GEORGE, biostatistician, computer educator, consultant; b. Bklyn., Apr. 27, 1948; s. David and Charlotte Dorothy (Haber) Y.; m. Yolanda Maria Pearson, Apr. 1, 1978; 1 child, Samuel Alexander. B.A., Union Coll., 1970, B.S. cum laude, 1970; M.A., U. Rochester, 1972; M.P.H., U. Mich., 1973, Ph.D., 1974. Chief sci. analyst function U.S. Air Force Sch. Aerospace Medicine, Brooks AFB, Tex., 1974-79, chief hazard evaluation function, 1979—; instr. math. San Antonio Coll., 1977-85; dir. Computer Learning Ctr., San Antonio, 1983—; cons. dept. oncology Health Sci. Ctr., San Antonio, 1979-80; abstractor Exec. Scis. Inst., Whippany, N.J., 1979-85. Contbr. articles to profl. jours. and Ency. Statis. Scis. Vice pres. Council for Internat. Relations, San Antonio, 1985—; computer contbr. San Antonio Exec., Real Estate Newsline, San Antonio; bd. dirs. One Elm Place, San Antonio. Grantee NSF, 1970-72; USPHS trainee, 1972-73; UpJohn Gen. fellow, 1973-74. Served to capt. USAF, 1974-79. Mem. Am. Statis. Assn., Biometric Soc., San Antonio N. Side C. of C., Sigma Xi. Jewish. Home: 19919 Encino Royale San Antonio TX 78259 Office: Computer Learning Ctr 11107 Wurzbach Rd Suite 301 San Antonio TX 78230

YODER, DAVID, real estate developer; b. Meyersdale, Pa., Oct. 10, 1931; s. Ernest and Lena (Bender) Y.; B.A. in Music, Goshen (Ind.) Coll., 1957; postgrad. W.Va. U., 1957, 62, 64, U. Vienna, 1962, U. Graz (Austria), 1964; m. Ruby Jeanell Shenk, Sept. 6, 1964; children—Jon, Robert. Exec. v.p. Allegheny Devel. Corp. Inc., Morgantown, W.Va., 1966—; pres. Pineview Realty, Inc., Morgantown, 1969—; sec.-treas. Pineview Supply Corp. 1972—, Allegheny Real Estate Sales, Morgantown, 1975—, also dir.; dir. Allegheny Devel. Corp., Inc., Pineview Realty, Inc.; witness to Com. on Internat. Ops., U.S. Congress, 1977; chmn. Nat. Conf. State Home Builders Assns., 1979; sr. mem. Spl. Task Force on Housing, W.Va. Legislature, 1981; chmn. Interagy. Housing Council of W.Va., 1985—. Chmn., West Run Pub. Service Dist., 1984—; chmn. Com. for Extension of U.S. Route 48, 1985—. Mem. Morgantown Area C. of C., North Central W.Va. Home Builders Assn. (v.p. 1976, pres. 1977-80), Home Builders Assn. of W.Va. (expert witness before U.S. Congress 1979, v.p. 1980-83, pres. 1983-84, life dir.), Nat. Assn. Home Builders (nat. dir. 1979—). Home: Winona Ct Morgantown WV 26505 Office: 1225 Pineview Dr Morgantown WV 26505

YODER, ELMON EUGENE, agricultural engineer; b. Wolford, N.D., Oct. 10, 1921; s. Max Bass and Anna Frances (Guss) Y.; m. Inez Vivian Towle, Oct. 11, 1948; children—Steven, Marilyn, John, Mark. B.S. in Civil Engring., Oreg. State U., 1948, B.S. in Agrl. Engring., 1952, M.S. in Agrl. Engring., 1961. Registered profl. agrl. engr., Ky. Vis. prof. agrl. engring. Kasetsart U.-Bangkok, Thailand, 1954-56; instr. Oreg. State U.-Corvallis, 1956-62; agrl. research engr. U.S. Dept. Agr.-Agrl. Research Service, U. Ky.-Lexington, 1962—. Served with U.S. Army, 1943-46. Mem. Vols. for Internat. Tech. Assistance. Democrat. Methodist. Lodge: Toastmasters. Contbr. over 30 agrl. and engring. articles to profl. publs. Home: 808 Surrey Ln Lexington KY 40503 Office: U Ky Agrl Engring Dept Lexington KY 40546

YODER, LAUREN WAYNE, French educator; b. Newport News, Va., Mar. 9, 1943; s. Lauren Aquilla and Nina Viola (Stemen) Y.; m. Rita Suzanne Frey, June 27, 1964; children—Reinald, Jocelyn. B.A., Eastern Mennonite Coll., 1964; M.A., U. Iowa, 1969, Ph.D., 1973. Tchr. Ecole Secondaire Pedagogique, Kikwit, Zaire, 1966-68; instr. Davidson Coll., N.C., 1973-75, asst. prof. French, 1975-80, assoc. prof., 1980—; Fulbright lectr. U.S. Info. Agy., Paris, 1971-72, Libreville, Gabon, 1980-81; participant NEH summer seminar, Miami, Fla., 1979. Mem. African Lit. Assn., Caribbean Studies Assn., Assn. Caribbean Studies, MLA. Democrat. Mennonite. Avocations: bee-keeping; skiing; gardening. Home: PO Box 1604 Davidson NC 28036 Office: Davidson Coll Davidson NC 28036

YODER, LEON JAY, physician, educator; b. North Canton, Ohio, Dec. 13, 1939; s. Jonas M. and Fannie (Erb) Y.; m. Ina R. Gross, Jan. 30, 1966; children—Seth A., Greta A., Cara L., Sara A. B.A., Bowling Green State U., 1961; D.O., Kansas City Coll. Osteo. Medicine, 1967. Diplomate Am. Bd. Internal Medicine. Chemist Monsanto Research Corp., Miamisburg, Ohio, 1961-63; gen. practice medicine, Tulsa, 1963—; intern Grandview Hosp., Dayton, Ohio, 1967-68; resident in internal medicine VA Med. Ctr., Dayton; assoc. prof. Okla. Coll. of Osteo. Medicine, 1979—; fellow in gastroenterology U. Colo.-Denver, 1976-77. Scoutmaster Indian Nations council Boy Scouts Am., 1977-78; coach St. Mary's Sch., Tulsa, 1977—. Mem. ACP. Republican. Roman Catholic. Avocations: tennis; skiing; classical guitar. Home: 6405 S Erie Ave Tulsa OK 74136 Office: 802 S Jackson St Suite 205 Tulsa OK 74127

YODER, NELSON BRENT, oil company executive; b. N.Y.C., May 31, 1944; s. Nelson James and Doris Anne (Abel) Y.; m. Linda Kay Osborne, Aug. 21, 1965 (div. Oct. 1978); m. Mary Francis Byrnes, Aug. 23, 1980. B.S. in Zoology, Tex. Tech U., 1966, M.S. in Geology, 1968. Paleontologist, Gulf Oil Corp., New Orleans, 1968-71; geologist Gulf Research and Devel. Co., Houston, 1971-74; pres. Integrated Exploration Services, Inc., LaPorte, Tex., 1974—; cons. geologist specializing in carbonate petrography. Mem. Am. Assn. Petroleum Geologists, Soc. Econ. Paleontologists and Mineralogists (treas. Gulf Coast sect. 1983-84), Houston Geol. Soc., Am. Inst. Profl. Geologists, Sigma Gamma Epsilon. Republican. Avocations: sculpture; painting; fishing; photography. Home: 1010 S Country Club Dr PO Box 1546 LaPorte TX 77571 Office: Integrated Exploration Services Inc 3903 Spur 501 LaPorte TX 77571

YOKEL, ROBERT ALLEN, pharmacologist, educator, researcher; b. Rockford, Ill., June 22, 1945; s. Edward Clarence and Lilyann Lucille (Ehlert) Y.; m. Susan Jeanne Brown, Dec. 27, 1969; children—Erich Matthew, Kimberly Allison. B.S. in Pharmacy, U. Wis.-Madison, 1968; Ph.D. in Pharmacology, U. Minn., 1973. Registered pharmacist, Wis., Ohio. Research assoc. Concordia U., Montreal, Que., Can., 1973-75; asst. prof. pharmacology U. Cin., 1975-79; asst. prof., U. Ky., Lexington, 1979-84, assoc. prof. pharmacology, 1984—. Asst. editor: Poisindex, 1979—. Contbr. articles to profl. jours. Named Tchr. of Yr., U. Ky. Alumni Assn., 1985. Mem. Behavioral Pharmacology Soc., Soc. Neurosci., AAAS, Am. Soc. Pharmacology and Exptl. Therapeutics. Avocations: gardening; sailing; woodworking; stamp collecting. Office: U Ky Coll Pharmacy Rose St Lexington KY 40536

YOKELY, RONALD EUGENE, research company executive; b. High Point, N.C., Feb. 7, 1942; s. Clarence Eugene and Grayce (Waddy) Y.; B.S. in Mech. Engring., N.C. State U., Raleigh, 1963; m. E. Joanne Williams, July 6, 1963; children—Rhonda Lynette, Rene Michelle. Test engr. McDonnell Douglas Corp., St. Louis, 1963-67; task leader Simulation Products div. Singer Co., Houston, 1967-68, engring. group supr., 1968-71, engring. sr. supr., sect. mgr. for Skylab.-Command Module simulator, 1971-73; engring. mgr. Philco-Ford Corp., Houston, 1973-75, mgr. earth resources tech. applications studies Aeroneutronic Ford Corp. (formerly Philco-Ford Corp.), Houston, 1975-76; ind. cons. in mgmt. and systems engring., Houston, 1975-76; sr. v.p., dir. mktg. Onyx Corp., Atlanta, 1976-78; pres., treas. Acumenics Research & Tech., Inc., Bethesda, Md., 1978—; corp. v.p. Hadron, Inc., Vienna, Va., 1983—. Registered profl. engr., Tex. Mem. AIAA, Nat. Soc. Profl. Engrs., IEEE, Omega Psi Phi. Episcopalian. Author: A Proposed Aviation Energy Conservation Program for the National Aviation System, 4 vols., 1977; The Impact of Microcomputers on Aviation, 2 vols., 1977; Microcomputers: A Technology Forecast and Assessment to the Year 2000, 1980, Japanese transl., 1981. Home: 11453 Purple Beech Dr Reston VA 22091 Office: 9990 Lee Hwy Fairfax City VA 22030

YOO, CHAI HONG, civil engineering educator; b. Seoul, Korea, Sept. 16, 1939; came to U.S., 1967, naturalized, 1976; s. Chong Ryul Yoo and Kwi Rhe Lim; m. Chum Sook Lee, June 19, 1970; children—Anna, Laura. B.S., Seoul Nat. U., 1962; M.S., U. Md., 1969, Ph.D., 1971. Registered profl. engr., Va., Ala. Structural engr. Pacific Architects and Engrs., Inc., Saigon, Vietnam, 1966-67, McGaughy, Marshall and McMillan Assoc., Norfolk, Va., 1971-72; faculty research assoc. dept. civil engring. U. Md., College Park, 1972-73, vis. asst. prof., 1973-74; asst. prof. civil engring. Marquette U., Milw., 1975-80, assoc. prof., 1980-81; assoc. prof. Auburn U. (Ala.), 1981—; cons. in field. Served to 1st lt. Korean Airforce, 1962-66. NSF grantee, 1979-80, 83—. Mem. ASCE, Am. Soc. for Engring. Edn., Structural Stability Research Council, Sigma Xi, Chi Epsilon, Tau Beta Pi. Contbr. numerous articles to profl. jours. Home: 533 Owens Rd Auburn AL 36830 Office: Harbert Engring Ctr Dept Civil Engring Auburn U Auburn AL 36849

YORK, GUY POLLARD, air force officer, civil engineer, consultant; b. Asheboro, N.C., Nov. 29, 1935; s. Guy Aytch and Evelyn Margaret (Pollard) Y.; m. Virginia Ruth Sumerford, June, 1960; children—George Woltz Pollard, Marjorie Timmerman. B.C.E., Ga. Inst. Tech., 1958, M.S. in Civil Engring., 1963; Ph.D. in Civil Engring., U. Tex., 1970. Registered profl. engr., Ala. Commd. 2d lt. U.S. Air Force, 1958, advanced through grades to col., 1979; asst. base engr. Hahn Air Base, Germany, Brookley AFB, Ala., 1959-65; civil engr. programs Wright-Patterson AFB, Ohio, 1965-66; project engr. constrn. of Tuy Hoa Air Base, Vietnam, 1966-67; chief pavements research Air Force Weapons Lab., N.Mex., 1970-73; sr. civil engring. adviser to Republic of Korea, 1973-75; dir. civil engring. research Civil Engring. Ctr., Panama City, Fla., 1975-79; program mgr. for constrn. Aeropropulsion Systems Test Facility, Arnold Air Force Sta., Tenn., 1979—; instr. soil mechanics Gulf Coast Coll., Fla.; cons., diplomat. Elected lay del. Tenn. Conf. Methodist Ch.; adminstrv. bd. First Meth. Ch., Tullahoma, Tenn. Decorated Bronze Star. Mem. ASCE, Soc. Am. Mil. Engrs. (past post pres., dir.), ASTM, Tollahoma C. of C. (bd. dirs.), Sigma Xi, Chi Epsilon. Republican. Author tech. publs. on creep in concrete, runway hydroplaning, continuously reinforced concrete pavements, bomb damage repair of runways. Home: 5 Vandenberg Dr Tullahoma TN 37388

YORK, JOHN KELLY, management company executive; b. Topeka, Sept. 18, 1921; s. John H. and Ina C. (Smith) Y.; m. Jane Holt, June 16, 1956. B.S. in Edn., A.B., Marion Coll., 1947; M.A. in Edn., Northwestern U., 1948. Tchr. pub. sch., Evanston, Ill., 1949-50; commd. officer U.S. Air Force, 1950, advanced through grades to col.; dir. tng. U.S. Air Force, U.S., Germany, France, China, Philippine Islands, 1950-75; ret., 1975; mgr. tng. European div. Central Tex. Coll., 1975-85; supr. mgmt. systems tng. Southwestern Pub. Services Co., 1978—; vis. instr. Amarillo Coll., Tex., 1980—, Frank Phillips Coll., Borger, Tex., 1980—. Campaign mgr. Republican Com., Amarillo, 1980—; chmn. pub. relations com. Tex. Soc. to Prevent Blindness, Amarillo, 1979; chmn. bd. Polk St. United Methodist Ch., Amarillo, 1984. Named Outstanding Man of Yr. Amarillo C. of C., 1952. Mem. Am. Soc. Tng. Dirs. (bd. dirs. 1981-84), U.S. Air Force Assn. (pres. 1982-83), Ret. Officers Assn. (sec. 1983-84). Lodge: Kiwanis (program chmn. 1981). Avocations: bridge; ping pong; scouting. Home: 4506 Gem Lake Rd Amarillo TX 79106 Office: Southwestern Pub Service Co 6th and Tyler Amarillo TX 79106

YORKER, ALAN MARSHALL, psychologist; b. Hartford, Conn., Nov. 3, 1947; s. Murray Bertram and Helen (Stegall) Y.; m. Beatrice Anne Crofts, Aug. 6, 1978; children—Benjamin Ross, Margaret Anne, Jonathon Merle. B.A., Columbia U., 1969; M.A., Ga. State U., 1974, now postgrad. Lic. marriage, family and child counselor, Ga. Psychology fellow Langley Porter Psychiat. Inst., U. Calif.-San Francisco, 1975-76; staff psychologist Link Counseling Ctr., Atlanta, 1979-84, pvt. practice, Pershing Point Ctr., Atlanta, 1984—; adj. psychologist North Atlanta Mediation Ctr., 1984—. Sexuality cons. Sta. WSB-Channel 2, Atlanta, 1983-84. Co-author curriculum guide, Atlanta pub. sch. system, 1978. Mem. Ga. Psychol. Assn., Atlanta C. of C. (mem. regional devel. council 1985), Am. Psychol. Assn., Am. Assn. Sex Educators, Counselors and Therapists, Columbia U. Alumni Club. Democrat. Jewish. Avocations: railroads. Home: 2116 Heritage Hts Decatur GA 30033 Office: Pershing Point Ctr 1375 Peachtree St Atlanta GA 30309

YORKE-SNEED, KATHRYN, optometrist; b. Pitts., Jan. 12, 1954; d. James M. and Dawn (Disney) Yorke; m. Loyd William Sneed, July 29, 1984; 1 child, Jonathan William. B.A. in Biopsychology, Vassar Coll., 1975; O.D., U. Houston, 1981. Practice optometry, College Station, Tex., 1982—; indsl. vision cons. Westinghouse Electric Corp., College Station, 1982—; dir. vision screening program Brushy Day Care Ctr., Tex., 1983. Troop leader Bluebonnet council Girl Scouts U.S., 1982-83; bd. dirs. Brazos Valley March of Dimes, Bryan, Tex., 1983—. Kuhlman Optometry scholar U. Houston, 1977. Mem. Tex. Assn. Optometrists, Better Vision Inst. (Merit award 1978), Am. Bus. Women's Assn. (recording sec. 1983-84, pres. 1984—, Woman of Yr award 1985), Phi Kappa Phi, Beta Sigma Kappa, Beta Beta Beta. Avocations: music; backpacking; bicycling. Office: 1010A Post Oak Mall College Station TX 77840

YOSHIDA, MAMORU, accounting educator; b. Tokyo, May 24, 1950; s. Suetaro and Thai Yoshida; B.A. in Econs., Keio U., Tokyo, 1973; M.B.A., U. Kans., 1977, postgrad. in acctg., 1978, postgrad. in internat. studies U. Miami, 1981—. C.P.A., N.Y. Acct., Okura Enterprise Co., Ltd., Tokyo, 1973-75; sr. auditor Peat, Marwick, Mitchell & Co., N.Y.C., 1978-81; instr. acctg. Fla. Atlantic U., Boca Raton, 1981—. Recipient Cert. of Merit, SBA, 1976. Mem. Am. Inst. C.P.A.s, N.Y. State Soc. C.P.A.s, Am. Acctg. Assn. (internat. acctg. sect.), Acad. Internat. Bus. Home: 4485 St Andrews Rd Boynton Beach FL 33436 Office: Sch Acctg Fla Atlantic Univ Boca Raton FL 33431

YOSS, MARCI SUE, family physician, emergency physician; b. N.Y.C., Aug. 3, 1954; d. Eugene Joseph and Florence (Sirower) Y.; m. Barry Feingold, Apr. 15, 1984. B.A., Harvard U., 1976, M.D., 1980. Resident in family medicine Duke U., Durham, N.C., 1980-83; family physician Grays Creek Med. Ctr., Fayetteville, N.C., 1983—; emergency physician Nash Gen. Hosp., Rocky Mount, N.C., 1981-83, Highsmith-Rainey Hosp., Fayetteville, 1984—. Recipient award for excellence in teaching med. students Duke U. Med. Ctr., 1983. Mem. Am. Acad. Family Physicians, Am. Soc. Clin. Hypnosis, Nat. Orgn. Women. Home: Rt 12 Box 703-24 Fayetteville NC 28306 Office: Grays Creek Med Ctr Rt 7 Box 279 Fayetteville NC 28306

YOST, FRANK ALBERT, flour milling company executive; b. Louisville, Nov. 25, 1902; s. Frank Kavanaugh and Nell Morton (Bottomley) Y.; m. Ruth Kasey, Oct. 31, 1931; children—(Elizabeth) Ritchey, Anne Wickliffe Yost Harper, Frances Lavinia Yost Knight. B.B.A. cum laude, Emory U., 1925; L.H.D., Ky. Wesleyan Coll., 1969. Pres., mgr., chmn. bd. Hopkinsville Milling Co., Ky., 1925—; mem. wheat flour industry adv. com. U.S. Dept. Agr., 1956; emeritus dir. First City Bank & Trust Co. Supt. ch. sch. Hopkinsville 1st United Meth. Ch., 1935-45, mem. bd. stewards, 1925—, pres. bd., 1954-58, chmn. fin. com., 1960-64, chmn. spl. gifts com. for ret. ministers pension crusade, 1980-81, tchr. men's bible class, part-time 1960—; trustee Ky. Wesleyan Coll., 1951—, chmn., 1965-69; mem. com. 100 Emory U., 1972-85; del. Meth. World Conf., 1966-71, United Meth. Jurisdictional Conf., 1964; chmn. Hopkinsville Sch. Bd. Edn., 1950-65; chmn. Sewerage and Water Works Commn., 1962-70; bd. dirs. Hopkinsville Indsl. Found.; bd. dirs. Pennyroyal Mental Health Ctr., 1965-73, chmn., 1965-73; chmn. bd. dirs. Hopkinsville chpt. ARC, bd. dirs. Hopkinsville Mental Health Bd., 1952-60, chmn., 1952-56; bd. dirs. United Givers Fund; dir. Ky. Gov.'s Adv. Council on Mental Health, 1961-72; bd. dirs. Ky. Mental Health Assn., 1953-85, pres., 1953-55; mem. Ky. Gov.'s Ad Hoc Com. on Edn., 1965-66; active Boston Mus. Fine Arts, 1976—, Christian County Hist. Soc., 1975—; mem. Atheneum Soc., 1942—, pres., 1947-48. Mem. Millers Nat. Fedn. (chmn. 1954-56, exec. com. 1954-85), Nat. Soft Wheat Millers Assn. (bd. dirs., chmn. 1947-48), Am. Corn Millers Fedn. (bd. dirs., chmn. 1961-63), Ky. Millers Assn. (bd. dirs.), NAM (dir. 1976-80), Hopkinsville C. of C., Assoc. Industries Ky. Clubs: Filson, Hopkinsville Hunting and Fishing, Rotary (pres. 1941-42). Home: 506 Deepwood Dr Hopkinsville KY 42240

YOST, RICHARD ALAN, chemistry educator; b. Martins Ferry, Ohio, May 31, 1953; s. Donald Errold and Jessie Lee (Hoover) Y.; m. Katherine Sarah Fitzgerald, June 16, 1979. B.S. in Chemistry, U. Ariz., 1974; Ph.D. in Analytical Chemistry, Mich. State U., 1979. Asst. prof. chemistry U. Fla., Gainesville, 1979-83, assoc. prof. chemistry, 1983—; cons. Lawrence Livermore Nat. Lab., Finnigan MAT Corp., Allied Bendix Environ. Scis. Div. Dist. commr. Boy Scouts Am., 1981-84. Fellow NSF, 1975-79, Am. Chem. Soc. Analytical Div., 1977-78. Mem. Am. Chem. Soc., Am. Soc. Mass Spectrometry, Phi Beta Kappa. Patentee in field. Office: Univ of Fla Chemistry Dept Gainesville FL 32611

YOSTE, CHARLES TODD, lawyer; b. Vicksburg, Miss., Nov. 11, 1948; s. Harry M. and Charlene (Todd) Y. B.S., Miss. State U., 1971; J.D., U. Miss., 1976. Bar: Miss. 1976, U.S. Dist. Ct. Miss. 1976, U.S. Ct. Appeals, 1982. Sole practice, Starkville, Miss., 1976—; city atty. Starkville, Miss., 1979-85, prosecuting atty., 1977-79, city judge, 1981-82. Candidate for Congress 2nd dist. Miss., 1980. Served to capt. U.S. Army, 1971-73. Recipient Outstanding Young Man award Starkville Jaycees, 1980. Mem. ABA, Miss. Bar Assn., Am. Trial Lawyers Assn., Miss. Trial Lawyers Assn., Starkville C. of C. (pres. 1982), Am. Legion. Republican. Roman Catholic. Lodge: Rotary. Home: 902 S Montgomerery St Starkville MS 39759 Office: PO Box 488 Starkville MS 39759

YOUAKIM, MAURICE ISSA, ophthalmologist; b. Jerusalem, July 27, 1939; came to U.S., 1964, naturalized, 1975; s. Issa and Diana (Karmy) Y.; m. Marina Rose Haroutunian, June 17, 1962; children—James, Rima, Samir. B.S., Am. U., Beirut, 1958, M.D., 1962. Diplomate Am. Bd. Ophthalmology. Resident Albany Med. Ctr., N.Y., 1964-67; practice medicine specializing in ophthalmology, Tampa, Fla., 1972—; mem. staff St. Joseph's Hosp., East Pasco, Fla., Tampa Gen. Hosp. Office: 4710 N Habana Tampa FL 33614

YOUNG, ALICE CLARK, university administrator; b. Chattanooga, Dec. 12, 1923; d. B. C. and Ora Lee (McCullough) Clark; m. R. A. Young, Dec. 18, 1948; (div. 1975); children—Kevin Raoul, Cheri Denise, Daryl Clark; m. Henry T. Malone, Feb. 26, 1977 (dec.). B.A. in Sociology, Ga. State U., 1969, M.Ed. in Edn. Adminstrn., 1978. Research interviewer Atlanta Region Met. Planning Commn., 1970-71, Bur. of Census, Dept. Interior, part-time 1972; asst. dean for student services, dir. student ctr. Ga. State U., Atlanta, 1973—. Pres. Pilot Club of Atlanta, 1978-79, bd. dirs. 1979-80, 82-84; active Atlanta Area Pres. Council, 1978-79; pres. Unitarian Universalist Congregation of Atlanta, 1971-73, bd. dirs., 1984—; pres. Mid-South dist. Unitarian Universalist Assn., 1971-73, mem. various coms., 1974-76; active Atlanta Citizens for Clean Air, 1970-71; pres. Fernback Elem. Sch. PTA, 1968-69. Ga. Leadership Insts. grantee, 1979-80. Mem. Am. Personnel and Guidance Assn., Am. Coll. Personnel Assn., So. Coll. Personnel Assn., Ga. Personnel and Guidance Assn., Ga. Assn. of Women Deans, Adminstrs. and Counselors, Ga. Coll. Personnel Assn. (pres. 1982-83), Ga. Assn. for Counseling and Devel. (pres. 1984—), Ga. Leadership Inst. (bd. dirs. 1978—), AAUW, Toastmasters, Mu Rho Sigma, Alpha Lambda Delta (hon.), Omicron Delta Kappa. Avocation: interior design. Home: 1135 Oxford Rd NE Atlanta GA 30306 Office: Ga State U University Plaza Atlanta GA 30303

YOUNG, ANDREW, clergyman, civil rights leader, mayor, former ambassador, former congressman; b. New Orleans, Mar. 12, 1932; s. Andrew J. and Daisy (Fuller) Y.; student Dillard U., 1947-48; B.S., Howard U., 1951; B.D., Hartford Theol. Sem., 1955; D.D. (hon.), Wesleyan U., 1970, United Theol. Sem. Twin Cities, 1970; LL.D. (hon.), Wilberforce U., 1971, Clark Coll., 1973, Yale U., 1973, Swarthmore Coll., Atlanta U., others; m. Jean Childs, June 7, 1954; children—Andrea, Lisa Dow, Paula Jean, Andrew J. III. Ordained to ministry Congregational Ch., 1955; pastor in Thomasville, Ga., 1955-57; asso. dir. dept. youth work Nat. Council Chs., 1957-61; adminstr. Christian edn. program United Ch. Christ, 1961-64; mem. staff So. Christian Leadership Conf., 1961-70, adminstr. citizen edn. program, 1961-64, exec. dir., 1964-70, exec. v.p., 1967-70, now bd. dirs.; mem. 93d-95th Congresses from 5th Ga. Dist., mem. Rules com.; U.S. ambassador to UN, 1977-79; mayor of Atlanta, 1982—. Chmn., Atlanta Community Relations Commn., 1970-72; chmn. bd. Delta Ministry of Miss.; bd. dirs. Martin Luther King, Jr. Center for Social Change, Robert F. Kennedy Meml. Found., Field Found., So. Christian Leadership Conf. Recipient Pax-Christi award St. John's U., 1970; Springarn medal; Presdl. medal of Freedom. Mem. Ams. Dem. Action. Office: Office of Mayor 68 Mitchell St SW Atlanta GA 30303

YOUNG, C. B. FEHRLER, business executive; b. Birmingham, Ala., May 13, 1908; s. Francis D. and Lena Edna (Wells) F.; m. Lois Frances Ellis, Dec. 31, 1934; children—Charles E., Frank B., James T. B.S., Howard Coll., 1930; M.S., Columbia U., 1932, Ph.D., 1935; LL.D., Freed-Hardeman Coll., 1982. Cons., Nat. So. Products Co., Tuscaloosa, Ala., 1935-52, v.p., 1944-51; with Warrior Asphalt Co., Tuscaloosa, 1944-56; founder Auromet Corp., N.Y.C., pres., 1953-56; founder, pres. Ala. So. Warehouse, Inc., Cytho Corp. & M'Lord & M'Lady Cosmetic Co., Douglasville, Ga., 1949—; founder, pres., chmn. bd. Cracker Asphalt Co. (now Young Refining Corp.), Douglasville, Ga., 1955—; chmn. bd. Laketon Refining Corp., Universal Home Products, Inc.; dir. Energy Explorations; chmn. bd., dir. So. Fed. Savs. & Loan, 1974-80; pres. Cinco, Inc., 1977—; chmn. bd. Seminole Refining Corp., St. Marks, Fla., 1985—. Author: Chemistry for Electroplaters, 1947; contbr. tech. articles to profl. jours. Trustee, Freed-Hardeman Coll., Henderson, Tenn., 1978—, Ga. Christian Found., Inc.; hon. bd. dirs. Ga. Engring. Found., Inc., 1975—. Mem. Chemist Club, AAAS, Am. Inst. Chem. Engrs., Ind. Refiners Assn. (pres. 1968-69), Douglas County C. of C. (pres. 1957-59), Epsilon Chi, Sigma Xi, Phi Lambda. Mem. Churches of Christ (elder).

YOUNG, C. W. BILL, congressman; b. Harmarville, Pa., Dec. 16, 1930; m. Marian Ford; children—Pamela Kay, Terry Lee, Kimber. Dist. asst. to Congressman William C. Cramer, 1957-60; senator Fla. Legislature, 1960-70; mem. 92d Congress from 8th Fla. Dist., 93d-99th Congresses from 6th Fla. Dist.; mem. Fla. Constn. Revision Commn., 1965-67; chmn. So. Hwy. Policy Com., 1966-68; Del. Rep. Nat. Conv., 1968; mem. Electoral Coll., 1968. Served to sgt. Fla. N.G., 1948-57. Named Most Valuable Senator, Capitol Press Corps, 1969. Methodist. Office: 2266 Rayburn House Office Bldg Washington DC 20515*

YOUNG, CANDY FRANCES, social worker; b. Nashville, Apr. 1, 1943; d. Nolen D. and Billie Frances (Halbrook) Y. Student U. Tenn., 1961-64, Ray Vogue Sch., 1964-65. Liaison to Gov. of Tenn., Nashville, 1965-67; adminstrv. asst. to Lt. Gov. of Tenn., Nashville, 1967-71; engrossing clk. Tenn. Gen. Assembly, Nashville, 1971-73; sr. counselor Tenn. Dept. Human Services, Nashville, 1973—. Mem. campaign staff Clement for Gov., Nashville, 1978, Sasser for U.S. Senate, Nashville, 1982, Gore for U.S. Senate, Nashville, 1984. Democrat. Mem. First Christian Ch. Avocations: Tenn. history; American antiques; photography. Home: 1004 Vineland Dr Franklin TN 37064 Office: Dept Human Services 901 Murfreesboro Rd Nashville TN 37217

YOUNG, CARL HERMAN, III, architect; b. Miami, Fla., Oct. 25, 1956; s. Carl Herman Jr. and Mary Lynne (Waller) Y. B.Arch., Tulane U., 1979. Project architect Arquitectonica, Miami, 1980—. Mem. AIA. Club: Coconut Grove Sailing. Avocation: sailing. Home: 7300 Mindello St Coral Gables FL 33143 Office: Arquitectonica Internat Corp 4215 Ponce De Leon Blvd Coral Gables FL 33146

YOUNG, DOUGLAS HAMILTON, lawyer, literary agency executive, novelist; b. Kitchener, Ont., Can., Apr. 1, 1938; s. Nelles Douglas and Beatrice (Hamilton) Y.; m. Barbara Jean Pereira, Dec. 11, 1964; 1 dau., Jean. B.A., U. Toronto; Diploma Hague Acad. Internat. Law, Holland, 1962; J.D., Osgood Hall Law Sch. York U., Toronto, Ont., 1962; LL.M., NYU, 1963; LL.M., Harvard U., 1970. With law dept. Celanese Corp. Am., N.Y.C., 1963-64; exec. Exxon, Inc., N.Y.C., 1965-66; asst. sec. Esso Exploration, Inc., N.Y.C., 1965-66; sec. Esso Can., Inc., N.Y.C., 1965-66; sec. Esso Australia, Inc., N.Y.C., 1965-66; sec. Esso Inter-Am., N.Y.C., 1965-66; exec. asst. to sec. Creole Petroleum Corp., Caracas, Venezuela, also sec. to exec. com., 1966-68; asst. prof. law and internat. affairs Carleton U., Ottawa, Ont., 1970-71; atty. Internat. Trade and Investment, Fort Lauderdale, Fla., 1971—; pres. Writer's Lit. Agy., Ft. Lauderdale, 1981—. Mem. Internat. Law Soc., World Federalists, Smithsonian Instn., Christian Children's Fund, Broward Harvard Club. Author: The Tidy Bowl Man Lives, 1982; Jiffy John, 1982; HT-HT, 1986; contbg. author How Peace Come to the World, 1986; also monographs. Home: 615 NE 15 Ct Fort Lauderdale FL 33304

YOUNG, ESTELLE IRENE, dermatologist; b. N.Y.C., Nov. 2, 1945; d. Sidney D. and Blanche (Krosney) Young. B.A. magna cum laude, Mt. Holyoke Coll., 1963; M.D., Downstate Med. Ctr., 1971. Intern, Lenox Hill Hosp., N.Y.C., 1971-72, resident in medicine, 1972-73; resident in dermatology Columbia Presbyn. Hosp., N.Y.C., 1973-74, NYU Med. Ctr., 1974-75, Boston U. Hosp., 1975-76; asst. dermatologist Harvard U. Health Services, Cambridge, Mass., 1975-76; assoc. staff mem. dermatology Boston U. Med. Ctr., 1976-77; practice medicine specializing in dermatology, Petersburg, Va., 1976—; mem. staff Petersburg Gen. Hosp., 1976—, Central State Hosp., 1984—; clin. instr. dept. dermatology Med. Coll. Va., 1976—; sec. med. staff Petersburg Gen. Hosp., 1982—. Fellow Am. Acad. Dermatology; mem. Va. Med. Soc., Va. Dermatology Soc., Tidewater Dermatology Soc. (pres. 1982-83), Southside Va. Med. Soc. Contbr. articles to profl. jours. Home: 2319 Monument Ave Richmond VA 23220 Office: 612 S Sycamore Petersburg VA 23803

YOUNG, FRANCIS BALDWIN, JR., pharmacist; b. Charlotte, N.C., July 24, 1952; s. Francis Baldwin and Martha (Bately) Y. B.S. in Pharmacy, N.D. State U., 1976. Intern pharmacy City Drug Store, Mohall, N.D., 1975-76; pharmacist Ronholm Drug, Jamestown, N.D., 1976-81; pharmacist, mgr. Revco Drug Store Inc., Big Spring, Tex., 1981-83; pharmacist Medicine Shoppe, Big Spring, 1983; pharmacist, owner Medicine Shoppe, Belton, Tex., 1984—; cons. pharmacist Hi Acres Nursing Center, Jamestown, 1978-81, 83—. Named Outstanding Jaycees of Month, 1977, 78, 79, 80, Outstanding project chmn., 1979-80. Mem. N.D. Pharm. Assn., Nat. Assn. Retail Druggist, Am. Soc. Cons. Pharmacists, Am. Topical Assn. (dir. med. subjects unit 1981—), Jamestown Jaycees (Presdl. award of honor 1979; Disting. Service award 1980, chmn. N.D. outstanding projects 1979-80), Tex. Pharm. Assn., Belton Optimists (v.p. 1986-87, Optimist of Month 1986). Roman Catholic. Home: 502 E Central Belton TX 76513-3244 Office: 502 E Central Belton TX 76513

YOUNG, FRANK COLEMAN, JR., ophthalmologist; b. Clinton, S.C., Oct. 24, 1934; s. Frank Coleman and Lois Susan (Adair) Y.; m. JoAnn Marlene Addy, July 1, 1960; children—Frank C. III, Jonelle Susan, Frances Ann. B.A., B.S., Presbyn. Coll., 1956; M.D., Med. Coll. S.C., 1960. Diplomate Am. Bd. Ophthalmology. Intern, Brooke Gen. Hosp., Ft. Sam Houston, Tex., 1960-61, resident, 1963-66; commd. 2d lt. U.S. Army, 1956, advanced through grades to col., 1975, resigned, 1970; practice medicine specializing in ophthalmology, 20/20 Ophthalmic Assocs., P.A., Montgomery, Ala., 1970—; mem. staff Bapt. Med. Ctr., Jackson Hosp., St. Margaret's Hosp. Mem. Am. Acad. Ophthalmology, ACS, AMA. Presbyterian. Home: 3165 Rolling Rd Montgomery AL 36111 Office 20/20 Normandie Dr Montgomery AL 36198

YOUNG, FREDERICK ALBERT, electronics educator; b. St. Petersburg, Fla., Aug. 26, 1934; s. Hollis Edgar and Mabel Miltilda (Greg) Y.; m. Ruth Etsuko Harada, Apr. 24, 1957; children—Mark Allen, Stephen Brian. A.S., in Electronic Tech., Miami-Dade Community Coll., 1974; B.S. in Vocat.-Indsl. Edn., Fla. Internat. U., 1982, M.S. in Adult and Human Resource Edn., 1983. Served with U.S. Navy, 1952-55, with U.S. Air Force, 1955-78; radio-radar analog and digital computer technician, 1952-70; computer system maintenance supt., 1970-73; instr. mgmt. and leadership, 1973-77; dir. profl. mgmt. edn. U.S. Air Force, Homestead AFB, Fla., 1977-78; ret., 1978; field computer engr. Honeywell Corp., 1978-79; tchr. electronics, chmn. dept. Dade County Pub. Schs., Miami, Fla., 1979—. Decorated Meritorious Service medal; named Adult-Vocat. Tchr. of Yr., Dade County Pub. Schs., 1983. Mem. Assn. Supervision and Curriculum Devel., Am. Soc. Tng. and Devel., Am. Vocat. Assn., Fla. Vocat. Assn. (life), Dade County Vocat. Assn. (life), Epsilon Pi Tau, Kappa Delta Pi. Democrat. Lodges: Masons, Shriners. Office: 18180 SW 122nd Ave Room 14-200 Miami FL 33177

YOUNG, GLENN REID, nuclear physicist; b. Kingsport, Tenn., Aug. 22, 1951; s. Howard Seth and Anne Reid (Maven) Y.; m. Katherine Ann Geoffroy, Sept. 28, 1980; children—Meredith Elaine, Lianne Rebecca. B.A., U. Tenn., 1973; Ph.D., MIT, 1977. Research assoc. MIT, Cambridge, 1977-78; research assoc. Oak Ridge (Tenn.) Nat. Lab., 1978-80, staff physicist, 1980—. Mem. Am. Phys. Soc. Phi Beta Kappa, Sigma Xi. Home: 110 A Newell Lane Oak Ridge TN 37830 Office: Oak Ridge Nat Lab Bldg 6003 Oak Ridge TN 37830

YOUNG, JAMES HARVEY, historian, educator, consultant; b. Bklyn., Sept. 8, 1915; s. William Harvey and Blanche (DeBra) Y.; m. Myrna Goode, 1940; 2 children. B.A., Knox Coll., 1937; M.A., U. Ill., Urbana, 1938, Ph.D., 1941; hon. L.H.D., Knox Coll., 1971; hon. D. Sc., Rush U., 1976. Mem. faculty Emory U., Atlanta, 1941—, Charles Howard Candler prof. Am. social history, 1980-84, prof. emeritus, 1984—. Served with U.S. Army, 1943-45. Recipient Edward Kremers award Am. Inst. History Pharmacy, 1962; Fielding H. Garrison lectr. Am. Assn. History Medicine, 1979; Guggenheim fellow, 1966-67; vis. scholar Nat. Library Medicine, 1986. Mem. So. Hist. Assn. (pres. 1982), Am. Hist. Assn., Orgn. Am. Historians, Soc. Am. Historians, Am. Inst. History Pharmacy, Am. Assn. History Medicine (William H. Welch medalist 1982). Author; The Toadstool Millionaires, 1961; The Medical Messiahs, 1967; American Self-Dosage Medicines, 1974. Home: 272 Heaton Park Dr Decatur GA 30030

YOUNG, JAMES MARION, lawyer; b. Winston-Salem, N.C., Nov. 15, 1930; s. William Rector and Celia Marie (Pasley) Y.; m. Barbara Marie Pultz, Feb. 2, 1957; children—Deborah Marie, Rebecca Anne, Catherine Arline, Cynthia Louise. B.A., U. Va., 1953, LL.B., 1957. Bar: Va. Assoc. M.S. McChung, Salem, Va., 1957-58, A. Tracy Loyd, Roanoke, 1958-64, Dodson, Pence & Coulter, Roanoke, 1964-66; ptnr. Dodson Pence Viar Young and Woodrum, Salem, 1966—. Pres. Roanoke County Council PTA, 1970; mem. exec. bd. Blue Ridge Mountains council Boy Scouts Am., 1960—, pres., 1975-77; chmn. City of Salem Electoral Bd., 1968-83. Recipient Disting. Service award Salem Jaycees, 1964; Silver Beaver award Boy Scouts Am., 1976. Mem. ABA, Va. Bar Assn., Roanoke County Bar Assn. (pres. 1970), Salem-Roanoke County C. of C. (pres. 1972). Democrat. Presbyterian. Club: Salem Kiwanis (pres. 1981-82). Office: 25 Library Sq Salem VA 24153

YOUNG, JAMES NOLEN, city fire official; b. Booneville, Miss., Nov. 1, 1924; s. James Alexander and Lu Tishie (Pannell) Y.; m. Elva Marie Dobbins, Dec. 11, 1942; children—Brenda Lanell, Jamie Marie. Student NE Miss. Jr. Coll., 1950. Cert. instr. Miss. Fire Acad. Constrn. worker TVA, Florence, Ala., 1946-61; with Police Dept., Corinth, Miss., 1961-63; with Fire Dept., Corinth, 1964—, chief, 1978—; fire protection coordinator Alcorn County, Corinth, 1978—; instr. Miss. Fire Acad., Pearl, 1983—. Served with USMC, 1943-46. Recipient Fireman of Yr. award VFW, 1978, Outstanding and Dedicated Service award, 1982. Mem. Miss. Fire Fighters Assn., Miss. Fire Chiefs Assn., Miss. Fire Investigators Assn., Internat. Assn. Arson Investigators. Democrat. Mem. Ch. Christ. Clubs: VFW, Am. Legion. Avocations: jewelry making; bird watching; hunting; fishing; camping. Home: 1406 Wenasoga Rd Corinth MS 38834 Office: Corinth Fire Dept 300 Childs St PO Box 352 Corinth MS 28834

YOUNG, JAMES OLIVER, dentist, communication company executive; b. Parris Island, S.C., Apr. 19, 1945; s. William Oliver and Ruth Cherokee (Risner) Y.; m. Virginia Evelyn Koontz; children—Amy Robyn, Jenny Elizabeth, Thomas William. B.S., Southeast State U., Okla., 1967; D.D.S., Baylor U., 1972. Practice dentistry, Ardmore, Okla., 1972—; v.p. Cherokee Telephone Co., Calera, Okla., 1963—; pres. Communication Equipment Co., Calera, 1984—. Trustee Ardmore Devel. Authority, 1980-85; bd. dirs. Ardmore Community Concerts Assn., 1980-85. Fellow Acad. Gen. Dentistry; mem. ADA, Okla. Dental Assn., Okla. C. of C. (bd. dirs. 1984-85). Democrat. Methodist. Lodge: Masons. Avocations: skiing; sailing. Home: 2207 Ridgeway St Ardmore OK 73401 Office: 221 2d Ave NW Ardmore OK 73401

YOUNG, JAMES WADE, electrical engineering consultant; b. Union, Iowa, Aug. 18, 1925; s. Wesley Haden Tucker and Ina Catherin Drake; m. Irene M. Timmerman, June 28, 1985; children—Terry J., Pamela Jo, Wendy Kay. Degree in elec. engring. U.S. Navy, 1945; grad. in Meter Engring., Ft. Wayne Corr. Sch., 1946. Meterman, Iowa Electric Light and Power Co., Eldora, 1942-43, engr., Cedar Rapids, 1946-52, dist. engr., asst. operating mgr., Iowa Falls, 1952-58, system operator, Cedar Rapids, 1958-64, mgr. electric ops., 1964-72, mgr. purchasing and stores, mgr. electric ops., 1972-75; exec. v.p. Challenge Ministries Inc., Dallas, 1975-76, pres., chief exec. officer, bd. dirs., Dallas, 1976—; pres., treas. CSS, Inc., Dallas, 1979—, also dir.; mng. ptnr. CSS Enterprises, Dallas, 1983—; cons. in elec. engring., bus. adminstrn. Bd. dirs. Evangel Coll., Springfield, Mo., 1960-69 1st Assembly God Ch., Cedar Rapids, 1946-75. Served with USN, 1943-46; PTO. Decorated Purple Heart. Republican. Home: 603 NW B St Bentonville AR 72712 Office: CSS Inc 12820 Hillcrest Suite 100 Dallas TX 75230

YOUNG, JESS WOLLETT, lawyer; b. San Antonio, Sept. 16, 1926; s. James and Zetta (Alonso) Y.; student Southwestern U., 1944, U. Tex., 1946-49; B.A., Trinity U., 1956; LL.B., St. Mary's Sch. Law, 1958; m. Mary Alma Keeter, Apr. 17, 1954; children—Zetta, Imogen. Bar: Tex. 1957. Practiced in San Antonio, 1957—; mem. firm, pres., dir. Young & Murray, Inc., 1982-86; sr. ptnr. Young, Murray, Veitch & Davis, 1986—; dir. Dean L. Leeper Co., Dallas; county judge Bexar County (Tex.), 1964; city atty. Olmos Park (Tex.), 1965-70, Poteet (Tex.), 1975-76. Democratic precinct committeeman, San Antonio, 1964-76; state Democratic committeeman, 1970-72; Republican precinct committeeman, San Antonio, 1984—; state Rep. committeeman, 1984—. Served with USNR, 1944-46. Mem. ABA, San Antonio Bar Assn., State Bar Tex., Delta Theta Phi. Club: San Antonio Gun (dir. 1958-63, 80-82). Republican. Home: 321 Thelma Dr San Antonio TX 78212 Office: 4241 Piedras Dr E Suite 115 San Antonio TX 78228

YOUNG, JOE CEAFUS, school system transportation director, educator; b. Jefferson, Tex., Feb. 5, 1926; s. Joe C. and Pinkie M. (Rambo) Y.; m. El Marie McClure, Dec. 29, 1949; children—Rhonda Carol, Marcia Renee. B.S. in Indsl. Edn., Prairie View A&M, 1947, M.S. in Adminstrn., Supervision, 1952. Cert. tchr., counselor, prin., supt. Indsl. arts tchr. Ft. Worth Ind. Sch. Dist., 1947-53, vice prin., 1953-61, prin. successively Guinn Jr. High Sch., Dunbar Jr. High Sch., Dunbar High Sch., 1961-80, dir. transp. Ft. Worth Pub. Schs., 1980—. Dir. North Tex. Lung Assn., 1966-83, pres., 1980-81. Served to col. USAR, 1944-79. Decorated Meritorious Service medal, Legion of Merit; recipient Outstanding Achievement in Indsl. Edn. award Prairie View A&M, 1964. Mem. Tex. Assn. Secondary Sch. Prins., Nat. Assn. Secondary Sch. Prins., Phi Delta Kappa. Presbyterian. Lodge: Masons. Home: 2200 Lucas Dr Fort Worth TX 76112 Office: Fort Worth Sch Dist 215 NE 14th St Fort Worth TX 76106

YOUNG, JOHN HARDIN, lawyer; b. Washington, Apr. 25, 1948; s. John D. and Laura Virginia (Gwathmey) Y. A.B., Colgate U., 1970; J.D., U. Va., 1973; postgrad. Hague (Netherlands) Acad. Internat. Law, 1973; B.C.L., Oxford (Eng.) U., 1976. Bar: Va. 1973, D.C. 1974, Pa. 1979, U.S. Dist. Ct. (ea. dist.) Va. 1974, U.S. Dist. Ct. (ea. dist.) Pa. 1978, U.S. Dist. Ct. D.C. 1974, U.S. Ct. Appeals (3d, 4th, D.C. and fed. cirs.), U.S. Supreme Ct. 1977. Intern U.S. Senator William B. Spong, Jr., Washington, 1968; asst. atty. gen. complex litigation Commonwealth of Va., Richmond, 1976-78; trial counsel U.S. Dept. Labor, Washington, 1981-82; ptnr. Delaney & Young, Washington; dean Nat. Coll. of Advocacy (Comml. Litigation), 1983-85; U.S. rep. UN Internat. Law Seminar, Geneva, 1974; mem. adv. bd. Antitrust Bull., Jour. Reprints for Antitrust Law and Econs.; mem. U.S. Sec. State's Adv. Com. Pvt. Internat. Law, 1982-85; lectr. continuing legal edn. Mem. Am. Law Inst., ABA (chmn. antitrust com. of adminstrv. law sect. 1981—, chmn. continuing legal edn. bd. young lawyers div. 1980-82), Hon. Soc. Middle Temple, Phi Alpha Theta, Phi Delta Phi. Episcopalian. Contbr. articles to legal publs. Home: 5146 Woodmire Ln Alexandria VA 22311 Office: 1629 K St NW Washington DC 20006

YOUNG, JOHN HARLEY, electronics engineer; b. Springfield, Mo., May 10, 1944; s. Louis L. and Clarinda Elizabeth (Kelly) Y.; A.B., Drury Coll., 1966; M.S., Purdue U., 1975; m. Pamela Sue Larkin, Aug. 10, 1965; 1 son, John Edward. Broadcast engr. Ind. Broadcasters, Inc., Springfield, 1964-67; engr. Magnavox Gov. & Indsl. Electronics Co., Ft. Wayne, Ind., 1967-74, sr. engr., 1974-77; sr. engr. LaBarge Electronics, Tulsa, 1977-78; engr. Century Geophys. Corp., Tulsa, 1978-82, prin. engr., 1980-82; cons. Young Systems, 1982—; sr. engr. Telex Computer Products, 1982—; instr. Tulsa Jr. Coll., 1982-83; vis. asst. prof. Oral Roberts U., 1985-86. Music dir. Calvary Ind. Bapt. Ch., Ft. Wayne, 1974-76. Mem. IEEE, ASTM, Internat. Soc. Hybrid Microelectronics, Automatic Test Equipment Assn., Creation Research Soc., Phi Alpha Beta, Phi Eta Sigma. Editor: Okla. Trumpet, 1979—; patentee in field. Office: 6422 E 41st St Tulsa OK 74135

YOUNG, JOYCE LYNOM, counselor educator; b. Memphis, Oct. 25, 1941; d. Lloyd Raymond and Georgia (Carr) Lynom; m. Dr. Josef A. Young, Mar. 26, 1964; 1 son, Jorald Anson (dec.). B.A., LeMoyne Coll., 1963; student George Peabody Coll., 1965; M.Ed., Memphis State U., 1967; Ph.D., So. Ill. U., 1976. Cert. counselor. English tchr. Shelby County Schs., Memphis, 1963-69; English tchr., counselor Memphis City Schs., 1970-74, school counselor, 1976-78; counselor-in-residence So. Ill. U., Carbondale, 1975-76; asst. prof. counseling and personnel services Memphis State U., 1978—; cons. Memphis City Schs., 1979, 82, 85, Shelby State Community Coll., 1979, Freed-Hardeman Coll., Jackson, Tenn., 1979, 80, U.S. Postal Ops., Memphis, 1984, New Memphis Devel. Corp., 1984. Contbr. articles to profl. jours. Bd. dirs. Vol. Ctr. Memphis, 1977—; 1st v.p. Shelby County chpt. Links, Inc., Memphis, 1983—; v.p. Wages of Memphis, 1979-81; mem. Mayor's Council on Drug Abuse, Memphis, 1972-74. Named Outstanding Young Women of Am., 1976, 77; recipient Outstanding Service award Epsilon, Epsilon, Alpha Kappa Alpha Memphis State U., 1979, 80, 84, Beta Epsilon Omega, Alpha Kappa Alpha, 1979, 80, Ednl. Talent Search, 1980, Student Govt. Assn. Memphis State U., 1982. Mem. Am. Assn. for Counseling and Devel. (conv. presenter 1976—), Am. Edn. Research Assn., NEA, Phi Delta Kappa, Alpha Kappa Alpha (undergrad. adv. chpt. 1978-79). Roman Catholic. Avocations: floral designing, tennis. Office: Counseling and Personnel Services Dept Coll Edn Memphis State Univ Patterson #123 Memphis TN 38152

YOUNG, LARRY DALE, medical psychologist; b. Fountain Head, Tenn., Dec. 13, 1948; s. Finley Odell and Hattie Frances (Hickey) Y.; m. Sandra Annette Tice, Dec. 27, 1970; children—Abigail Dawn, Matthew Edward Louis. B.A., David Lipscomb Coll., 1970; M.S., U. Ga., 1972; Ph.D., Harvard U., 1979. Asst. prof. U. Miss., Oxford, 1978-80; asst. prof. med. psychology Bowman Gray Sch. Medicine, Wake Forest U., Winston-Salem, N.C., 1980—; site surveyor Commn. on Accreditation of Rehab. Facilities, Tucson, 1984—. Contbr. articles to profl. jours. Bd. dirs. Piedmont Health Systems Agy., Greensboro, N.C., 1984—. Mem. Am. Psychol. Assn., Assn. for Advancement Behavior Therapy, Soc. for Psychophysiol. Research, Southeastern Psychol. Assn., Biofeedback Soc. N.C. (bd. dirs.), Phi Beta Kappa. Office: Sect on Med Psychology Bowman Gray Sch Medicine Wake Forest U 300 S Hawthorne Rd Winston-Salem NC 27103

YOUNG, LILLIE DEMPSTER, business executive; b. Pitts., May 29, 1947; d. James Garfield and Stephanie (Lockwood) Dempster; B.B.A., Ohio Wesleyan U., 1969; M.B.A., So. Meth. U., 1976; postgrad. U. Tex., Arlington, 1976-77; m. Charles Edward Young, Sept. 19, 1970; children—Christopher Ryan, Erin Leigh, Lindsey Elizabeth. Dir. univ. devel. Transworld Airlines, N.Y.C., 1967; flight attendant Am. Airlines, N.Y.C., 1968, Pan Am. World Airways, N.Y.C., 1969-71; tchr. English, Jacksonville (Fla.) Public Schs., 1971; mgr. acctg. Southwestern Bell Telephone Co., Dallas, 1974-76; asst. dir. univ. devel. So. Meth. U., 1976-77, asso. dir., 1977-78, dir., from 1978; now v.p. corp. services Henry S. Miller Cos. Mem. So. Meth. U. MBA Assn., Exec. Women of Dallas, Council for Advancement and Support of Edn., Delta Delta Delta. Republican. Methodist. Home: 4231 Nashwood St Dallas TX 75234 Office: 2001 Bryan Tower Suite 3000 Dallas TX 75201

YOUNG, MARGARET ALETHA MCMULLEN (MRS. HERBERT WILSON YOUNG), social worker; b. Vossburg, Miss., June 13, 1916; d. Grady Garland and Virgie Aletha (Moore) McMullen; m. Herbert Wilson Young, Aug. 19, 1959. B.A. cum laude, Columbia Bible Coll., 1949; grad. Massey Bus. Coll., 1958; M.S.W., Fla. State U., 1965; postgrad. Jacksonville U., 1961-62, Tulane U., 1967, Miss. U. for Women, 1976. Dir. Christian edn. Eau Claire Presbyn. Ch., Columbia, S.C., 1946-51; tchr. Massey Bus. Coll., Jacksonville, Fla., 1954-57, office mgr., 1957-59; social worker, unit supr. Fla. div. Family Services, St. Petersburg, 1960-66, dist. casework supr., 1966-71; social worker, 1971-77; program supr. Project Playpen, Inc., 1977-82, pres. bd., 1982-83; council mem. Child Devel. Ctr., 1983—; vice chmn. transitional housing com. Religious Housing Com., 1985. Mem. Acad. Cert. Social Workers, Nat. Assn. Social Workers (pres. Tampa Bay chpt. 1973-74, chmn. state nominating com. 1974-76, Nat. Assn. Christians in Social Work. Democrat. Presbyn. Rotary Ann (pres. 1970-71). Home: 330 Roebling Rd N Belleair Clearwater FL 33516

YOUNG, MARJORIE WILLIS, writer, journalist, lectr.; b. Mansfield, Ohio; d. John Edgar and Mary Adelle (Reiter) Willis; student agr. Cornell U., 1924; student Art Students League, 1925-27, Cooper Union, 1925-27, Columbia U., 1927, 43, Sorbonne, 1926-28, U. Paris, 1928-30, Japanese Lang. Sch., Tokyo, 1934-35, N.Y. U., 1944; m. James Russell Young, Oct. 2, 1934; 1 son, Willis Patterson. Columnist in Far East, Internat. News Service, 1938-41; feature writer King Features Syndicate, 1939, Saturday Pictorial Rev., 1941-45; asst. tech. dir. motion picture Behind the Rising Sun, 1943; research dept. Believe It or Not, 1946-48; feature editor and columnist The Sunday Star, Wilmington, Del., 1946-48; promotion dir. David McKay Pub. Co., 1945-48; lectr. Nat. Concert and Artists Corp., 1942-43; feature writer Anderson (S.C.) Independent, 1949-73; feature writer Anderson Daily Mail, 1949-73, asso. editor The New South, ann. spl. edit. of Daily Mail, 1966-73; editor The Safety Jour., Anderson, 1953—; program moderator Decorating for a Holiday, Sta. WAIM-TV, 1953-54, safety program moderator WAIM-TV, 1953-63, program moderator How to Cut and Sew, 1954-55, travel feature program WAIM-WCAC-FM, 1973-82; travel editor Quote mag., 1977-80; editor Vets. of Safety news page, What's What monthly; dir. Capitol City Communications, Inc. Spl. scroll dir. Chinese War Orphans Relief, 1941-45; publicity dir. Crusade for Children, State of Del., 1948; publicity chmn. S.C. Indsl. Nurses Assn., 1953; dir. S.C. 4-H Club TV Safety Program, 1953; coordinator Ann. S.C. State Landmark Conf., 1979. Bd. dirs. Anderson Heritage, Inc. Recipient various awards for safety activities including Disting. Service award S.C. Occupational Safety Council, 1973. Mem. U. S.C. Caroliniana Soc., Writers Assn. Am., Am. Women in Radio and TV, Nat. Recreation Assn., S.C. Recreation Soc. (v.p. and program dir. 1954-56), Anderson County Hist. Soc. (pres. 1978-80), Am. Soc. Safety Engrs., Vets. Safety Internat., (pres. 1979), DAR, Colonial Dames of the XVII Century (S.C. mus. chmn. 1983—). Episcopalian. Clubs: Am. News Women's; Nat. Press Club Washington; Overseas Press of Am.; Cornell Women's (N.Y.C.). Author: Decorating for Joyful Occasions, 1952; It's Time for Christmas Decorations, 1957; Fodor's Tour Guide of South Carolina, 1966-68, Tour Guide of Georgia, 1966-67; Japanese American Cook Book, 1972; The Cateechee Trail, 1975; South Carolina's Women Patriots of the American Revolution, 1975; Mystery of the Ivory Eagle, 1980. Editor: Textile Leaders, 1963. Home: 2003 Laurel Dr Anderson SC 29621 Office: Safety Jour PO Box 4189 Anderson SC 29622

YOUNG, MILTON EARL, oil company executive; b. San Angelo, Tex., Dec. 3, 1929; s. Edward Earl and Annie Mae (North) Y.; m. Clara Louise Sens, June 1, 1957; children—Vanessa Louise, Bradley Earl. A.A., San Angelo Coll., 1950; B.S., U. Tex., 1953. Engr., mgr. Conoco, Tex., Dubai and N.Y.C., 1953-73; v.p. Tesoro Petroleum Corp., San Antonio, 1973-74, sr. v.p. prodn., 1974-85, group v.p. exploration and prodn., 1985—. Pres. bd. dirs. St. Luke's Lutheran Hosp.; mem. devel. bd. Tex. Luth. Coll. Served with USN, 1948-49. Mem. Soc. Petroleum Engrs., Am. Petroleum Inst. (mem. gen. com. prodn.), Ind. Petroleum Assn. Am. Republican. Club: San Antonio Petroleum.

YOUNG, ROBERT ARCHIBALD, III, holding company executive; b. Fort Smith, Ark., Sept. 23, 1940; s. Robert A. and Vivian (Curtis) Y.; m. Mary Carleton McRae, July 20, 1963; children—Tracy Elizabeth, Christiana Carleton, Robert A. IV, Stephen McRae. B.A. in Econs., Washington and Lee U., 1963. Supr. terminal ops. Ark. Best Freight, Fort Smith, 1964-65; pres. Data-Tronics, Inc., Ft. Smith, 1965-67; sr. v.p. Nat. Bank Commerce, Dallas, 1967-70; v.p. fin. Ark. Best Corp., Fort Smith, 1970-73, exec. v.p., 1973, pres., chief operating officer, 1973—; pres. AFB Freight System, Inc., Ft. Smith, 1979—; dir. First Nat. Bank, Ft. Smith. Bd. dirs. ATA Found., Inc.; pres. United Way, Fort Smith, 1981; chmn. bd. Sparks Regional Med. Ctr., Ft. Smith, 1985; trustee Ark. Coll., Batesville. Named Outstanding Young Man of Ark., Ark. Jaycees, 1974; recipient Silver Beaver award Boy Scouts Am., 1974. Mem. Am. Trucking Assn. (v.p.-at-large), Regular Common Carrier Conf. (bd. govs.), Ark. State C. of C. (treas., bd. dirs.), Phi Delta Theta. Presbyterian. Home: 2414 Hendricks Blvd Fort Smith AR 72903 Office: Ark Best Corp 1000 S 21st St Fort Smith AR 72901

YOUNG, ROBERT GEORGE, lawyer; b. Atlanta, Mar. 9, 1923; s. Samuel Rollo and Cidney A. (Young) Y.; m. Martha Latimer, Dec. 10, 1949; children—John Latimer, R. Carlisle, S. Scott. Grad. Ga. Mil. Acad., 1940; A.B., Emory U., 1943; LL.B., U. Ga., 1949. Bar: Ga. 1949. Assoc. Heyman, Howell and Heyman, Atlanta, 1949-51, Heyman and Abram, 1951-53, Marshall, Greene and Neely, Atlanta, 1953-55; ptnr. Heyman, Abram and Young, Atlanta, 1955-63, Edenfield, Heyman and Sizemore, Atlanta, 1963-69, Webb, Parker, Young and Ferguson, Atlanta, 1970-81, Young & Murphy, 1982—; asst. county atty. Fulton County (Ga.), 1966-71, county atty., 1971—. Mem. exec. com. Nat. Assn. R.R. Trial Counsel, 1965-68; treas. Fulton County Republican Exec. Com., 1962-64, bd. dirs. Atlanta Union Mission. Served to lt. (j.g.) USNR, 1944-46; PTO. Mem. ABA, Scotch-Irish Soc. U.S., Alpha Tau Omega. Presbyterian. Clubs: Lawyers of Atlanta, University Yacht, Capital

City, Kiwanis. Home: 3561 Ridgewood Rd Atlanta GA 30327 Office: 229 Peachtree St NE Suite 1902 Atlanta GA 30303

YOUNG, RONALD REX, II, inventor, solar energy institute executive; b. Washington, Dec. 26, 1947; s. Ronald Rex and MaryLou (Richardson) Y.; m. Janie Deborah Ray, May 8, 1973; 1 dau., Wendy Michelle. B.A., U. South Fla., 1976; postgrad. U.S.C., 1977-78. Resident dir. Embery-Riddle Aero. U., Shaw AFB, S.C., 1978-79; editor, pub. weekly TV Shopper, Sumter, S.C., 1979; founder, pres. Solar Energy Inst. S.C., Sumter, 1981—; pres., exec. dir. S.C. Energy Task Force, Inc., 1981—. Served with USAF, 1968-72. Democrat. Baptist. Office: 261 Broad St PO Box 2168 Sumter SC 29151

YOUNG, SAMUEL DOAK, JR., banker; b. El Paso, Mar. 15, 1930; s. Samuel Doak and Elizabeth (Goodman) Y.; m. Marilyn Mays, July 16, 1969; children—Elizabeth Beard Roesler, Emily Beard Williams, M. Allison Beard McGuire, Whitney Blair, Samuel Doak III. B.A. in Econs. cum laude, Stanford U., 1951; cert. with distinction Southwestern Grad. Sch. of Banking, 1960. With 1st State Bank, El Paso, 1953-54; asst. nat. bank examiner Office of Comptroller of Currency, 11th Fed. Res. Dist., 1955-57; v.p. El Paso Nat. Bank, 1957-62, dir., 1957—, exec. v.p., 1962-64, pres., 1964-82, chief exec. officer, 1975-85, chmn. bd., 1982-85; pres., chief exec. officer El Paso Nat. Corp. (formerly Trans Tex. Bancorp.), 1971-85, chmn. bd., chief exec. officer, 1982-85; pres., chief exec. officer La Jolla Village Savs. Bank, 1985—; dir. Tex. Commerce Bancshares, Inc., 1982—, 1st State Bank, El Paso, 1958—; v.p. Trans Tex. Bancorp., Inc., 1967-85; mem. adv. com. Fed. Res. Bank, 1981-84; dir. Hilton Hotels Corp. Trustee El Paso YWCA, also chmn., 1959—; mem. Tex. Research League, 1971-85; bd. dirs. Providence Meml. Hosp., El Paso, 1973—, hon. bd. dirs. Spirit of Love Crisis Nursery, El Paso, 1981—; dirs. Nat. Alliance of Businessmen El Paso, 1969, El Paso Internat. City Assn., 1962-72, El Paso YMCA, 1962-63, El Paso Mcpl. Parking Authority, 1961-64, Tex. United Fund, 1959-66, Better Bus. Bur. El Paso, 1958-61, Blue Cross-Blue Shield, 1977-81, El Paso chpt. Jr. Achievement Program, 1966-79; mem. bus. adminstrn. adv. council U. Tex.-El Paso, 1965—, adv. council found., 1970—; charter mem. Tex. Council on Econ. Edn. 1969—; coordinating bd. Tex. Coll. and Univ. System, 1969-81, mem. Gov.'s Adv. Com. on Edn., 1979-81; vice chmn. Tex. Tchrs. Retirement System, 1961-73. Served with USAF, 1951-53. Mem. Tex. Bankers Assn. (pres. 1980-81, chmn. long range planning com. 1981-82, budget com. 1979-81, mem. exec. com. 1979-81, legis. com. 1981-82, dir. 1977-79, v.p. 1979-80), El Paso Assn. Banks (pres. 1978-79), Southwest Automated Clearing House Assn. (dir. 1980-81), Am. Bankers Assn., Assn. Res. City Bankers (com. on pub. affairs 1981-83), El Paso C. of C., Tex. Mfrs. Assn. (state affairs com. 1969-79), Beta Theta Pi. Episcopalian. Clubs: El Paso Country, La Jolla Beach and Tennis, La Jolla Country, Fairbanks Ranch Country. Lodges: Masons, Shriners.

YOUNG, STANLEY GROUT, materials scientist; b. Colorado Springs, Colo., June 16, 1936; s. Stanley J. and Dorothy G. (Grout) Y.; m. Rose Roldan, June 23, 1962; children—Theodore J., Michael D. Metall. Engr., Colo. Sch. Mines, 1958; M.S. in Metallurgy, Case Inst. Tech., 1968. Program officer U.S. Naval Applied Sci. Labs., Bklyn., 1959-62; research engr. NASA, Lewis Research Center, Alloys Sect., Cleve., 1962-69, Fatigue and Alloys Br., 1969-72; project mgr. Coating Br., 1972-78; materials scientist Lubrication Research, Tribology Br., 1978-82, project mgr. contracts and grants materials for gas turbine engines, 1974-82, sr. materials scientist electron microscopy, Kennedy Space Center, Fla., 1982—; NASA cons. various govt. ags., 1972—. Active Boy Scouts Am. Served to lt. (j.g.) U. S. Navy, 1958-62. Recipient Spl. Achievement award NASA, 1969, 74, 84, KSC safety award, 1985, Tech. Innovation awards, 1968, 71, 74 (3), 81, Invention Disclosure award, 1980; Am. Soc. Metals Scholarship, 1954. Mem. Am. Soc. Metals, ASTM (mem. com. 1964-68), Colo. Sch. Mines Alumni Assn. Lutheran. Contbr. articles to various publs. Patentee in field. Office: NASA Kennedy Space Center DE-MAO-1 FL 32899

YOUNG, WALTER, SR., safety engineer; b. New Orleans, July 13, 1937; s. William F. and Denise (Keys) Y.; m. Amanda McLean, July 2, 1960; children—Regina D. Young Powe, Walter, Rodney A. B.A. in Edn., Northwestern State U., La., 1976; Degree in Computer Programming Spencer Bus. Coll., 1970. Safety supr. Willamette Industries, Inc., Campti, La., 1974—; guest lectr. Northwestern State U., 1975—. Vice-pres. chpt. Gifted and Talented Children, 1972-74; mem. Natchitoches Planning Commn., L., 1984—, Natchitoches Task Force on Industry, 1983—, NAACP Voters and Civil Rights League, 1972—. Served with U.S. Army, 1954-74; Korea, Ger.; Vietnam. Decorated Bronze Star, Air medal, others. Mem. Am. Soc. Ssafety Engrs., Vets. of Safety, Am. Soc. Notaries, Northwestern State U. Alumni Assn., VFW, Omega Psi Phi. Democrat. Methodist. Lodge: Masons (33 degree). Club: Bayou Rod and Gun (program chair 1978-85) (Natchitoches). Avocations: fishing; hunting. Home: 1208 N 5th St Natchitoches LA 71457 Office: PO Box 377 Campti LA 71411

YOUNG, WALTER RICHARD, controller; b. Danville, Ky., Aug. 7, 1947; s. Harold Basil and Dorothy (Devine) Y.; B.S. in Acctg., Western Ky. U., 1969; M.S. (Haggin fellow), U. Ky., 1972; m. Lisette Rowley, June 19, 1971; children—Walter Richard, Ralph Martin, Katharine Elizabeth. With Price Waterhouse & Co., 1972-81, audit mgr., Little Rock, 1977-82; with Fairfield Communities, Inc., 1981—, v.p., corp. controller, 1983—. Treas. Friends Ark. Ednl. TV, 1978-82, chmn. acctg. div. for festival, 1978, 79, 80; active United Way of Pulaski County. Served with USAR, 1969-71. Decorated Army Commendation medal; C.P.A., Ark., Tenn. Mem. Am. Inst. C.P.A.'s, Ark. Soc. C.P.A.'s, Tenn. Soc. C.P.A.'s, Inst. Internal Auditors (past chpt. pres.), Nat. Assn. Accts., Western Ky. U. Alumni Assn., U. Ky. Alumni Assn. Democrat. Baptist. Club: Western Ky. U. Ark. (pres. 1978—). Home: 1014 Chepstow Ln Sherwood AR 72116 Office: 1207 Rebsamen Park Rd Little Rock AR 72202

YOUNG, WILLIAM ALLEN, petroleum geochemist; b. St. Marys, Ohio, May 21, 1930; s. William Raymond and Emma Marie (Steva) Y. B.A., Miami U., Oxford, Ohio, 1952; M.Sc., Ohio State U., 1954, Ph.D., 1957. Geochemist, Carter Oil and Jersey Prodn., Tulsa, 1957-65; research specialist Esso Prodn. Research, Houston, 1965-72; research assoc. Exxon Prodn. Research, Houston, 1972-78, research adviser, 1978—. Contbr. articles to profl. jours. C.E. Kettering fellow, 1954. Mem. Am. Assn. Petroleum Geologists, AAAs, Am. Chem. Soc., (geochemistry div., petroleum div.). Libertarian. Methodist. Office: Exxon Prodn Research Co PO Box 2189 Houston TX 77252

YOUNG, WILLIAM EDGAR, religious organization official; b. Whitesburg, Ga., July 28, 1930; s. Edgar Woodfin and Maude Alva (Duke) Y.; student Warren Wilson Coll., 1951, 54; A.B., Mercer U., 1956; M.R.E., Southwestern Bapt. Theol. Sem., 1958; postgrad. George Peabody Coll. Tchrs., U. Tenn., Nashville, So. Meth. U., U. San Francisco, Lesley Coll.; m. Mary Todd Watts, Mar. 9, 1963; children—William Jefferson, Todd Woodfin. Minister of edn. and music 1st Bapt. Ch., Swainsboro, Ga., 1958-59, Sherman, Tex., 1960-64; tchr. North Cobb High Sch., Marietta, Ga., 1959-60; ch. bus. adminstrn. cons., 1964-65; dir. ch. adminstrn. field services Bapt. Sunday Sch. Bd., Nashville, 1965-70, supr. presch. children's sect. ch. tng. dept., 1970—; adj. prof. Sch. Religious Edn., So. Bapt. Theol. Sem., Louisville; adj. prof. childhood edn. Golden Gate Bapt. Theol. Sem., Mill Valley, Calif., 1980, Sch. Religious Edn., Southwestern Bapt. Theol. Sem., Ft. Worth, 1984; guest lectr. creative writing East Tex. State U., Texarkana. Chmn. Dist. II citizens adv. council Metro Schs., 1975-76; pres. Stanford PTA, 1974-75, Grassland PTA, 1977-78; pres. Franklin High Community Assn.; parent rep. Williamson County curriculum assessment group Middle Sch. Task Force, 1979; mem. adv. council edn. dept. Belmont Coll.; bd. dirs. Tenn. Parents Anonymous. Served with USAF, 1951-54. Recipient Disting. Service award Metro Assn. Religious Edn. Dirs., 1980; Founders award Ga. Ch. Secs. Assn., 1981. Mem. So. Bapt. Religious Edn. Assn. (pres. 1977-78, sec.-treas., bd. dirs. 1984, 85, 86), Assn. Supervision and Curriculum Devel., Assn. Childhood Edn. Internat. (pub. affairs com., early adolescent com.), Nat. Assn. Edn. of Young Children, Am. Soc. Tng. and Devel. Author: Moses, God's Helper, 1976; Jesus, Lord and Savior, 1984; compiler, writer: Developing Your Children's Church Training Program, 1977; contbg. author: The Ministry of Childhood Education, 1985; contbr. chpts. in books; curriculum writer religious publs. Home: 605 Williamsburg Dr Franklin TN 37064 Office: 127 9th Ave N Nashville TN 37234

YOUNG, WILLIAM THOMAS, artist, educator; b. Huntington, W.Va., Oct. 7, 1924; s. William Otterbein and Lenna (Thompson) Y.; m. Bobbye Davis, Aug. 7, 1949 (div. 1954); 1 child, Chris; m. Carolyn McCurdy, 1956; children—Sherry, Steve, Melissa. B.F.A., U. Ala., 1948, M.A. in Fine Arts, 1950; student Hans Hofmann Sch. Art, N.Y.C., 1954-55; Ed.D., Columbia U., 1972. Grad. asst. U. Ala., Tuscaloosa, 1949-50; asst. prof. N. Ala. U., Florence, 1950-52; artist Douglas Aircraft, Inc., Los Angeles, 1952-53; prof. art Wagner Coll., N.Y.C., 1953-69; head prof. art Auburn U., Ala., 1969-70; prof. art U. New Orleans, 1970—. Exhibited paintings and photography in numerous group and one-man shows in U.S., France, Can., Mexico City; represented in exhbns. at Cin. Mus. Art, Bklyn. Mus., Phila. Mus., Canton Mus., Birmingham Mus., Ala., Fort Wayne Mus. Art, Ind., Ind. Curators 10th Anniversary Exhbn., N.Y.C. Art dir. Good Health Mag., 1953-57, Electronic Design Mag., 1954-58. Trustee New Orleans Mus. Art, 1973-79. Served with USAAF, 1943-45. Recipient N.Y.C. Ctr. Gallery award, 1956, 58, Weissglass award Staten Island Mus., 1955; Coll. Liberal Arts U. N.D. grantee, 1973-83. Mem. Coll. Art Assn. Am., AAUP, SE Coll. Art Assn., New Orleans Mus. Art Assn. (trustee 1973-79). Avocations: swimming; bicycling. Home: 5605 W Esplanade Ave Metairie LA 70003 Office: Dept Fine Arts Lake Front New Orleans LA 70148

YOUNG, WILLIAM THOMPSON, soft drink company executive; b. Lexington, Ky., Feb. 15, 1918; s. Willis Samuel and Margaret (Thompson); s. Willis Samuel and Margaret (Young); m. Lucy Hilton Maddox, Apr. 16, 1945; children—William Thompson, Lucy Meade. B.S. in Mech. Engring. with high distinction, U. Ky., 1939. With Bailey Meter Co., Cleve., 1939-41; pres. W.T. Young Foods, Lexington, 1946-55, gen. mgr., 1955-57; chmn. bd. Royal Crown Cos., Inc., Atlanta, W.T. Young Storage Co., Lexington, 1957—; dir. First Security Nat. Bank & Trust Co., Lexington, Ky.-Am. Water Co.; chmn. bd. Transylvania U., Lexington. Bd. dirs. Humana Inc. Served to capt. AUS, 1941-45. Mem. Sigma Alpha Epsilon. Presbyterian. Lodges: Rotary, Optimists (past pres. Lexington chpt.). Office: 2225 Young Dr Lexington KY 40505*

YOUNGBLOOD, RAY WILSON, publishing company executive; b. Tulia, Tex., Feb. 18, 1931; s. Burk Richard and Jenny (Lucile) W.; B.B.A., Tex. Tech. U., 1952; postgrad. U. Tex., 1958; m. Imogene Price, June 7, 1959; children—Michael Ray, Janet Lynn. Auditor, Peat, Marwick, Mitchell & Co., C.P.A.s, Houston, 1958-65; chief acct. Houston Chronicle Pub. Co., 1965-66, controller, asst. treas., 1966-83, treas., 1983—. Served to 1st lt. USAF, 1952-57. Mem. Internat. Newspaper Fin. Execs., (dir. 1971-77), Am. Inst. C.P.A.s, Tex. Soc. C.P.A.s, Planning Execs. Inst., Nat. Assn. Accts., Fin. Execs. Inst. Methodist. Club: Exchange (treas. 1971, 74-75). Office: 801 Texas Ave Houston TX 77002

YOUNGBLOOD, ROBERT SPURGEON, savings and loan association executive; b. Washington, July 10, 1944; s. Richard Andrew and Pauline Mathilde (Rutter) Y.; m. Patricia Hambleton Hall, June 12, 1970; children—Charles Andrew, Todd Richard, Mark Philip. Student Hunter Coll., 1964-65; B.A., SUNY-Plattsburgh, 1968; postgrad. U. Ga. Sch. Exec. Devel., 1975-76, Fla. Internat. U., 1980-81. Mktg. asst. fluorocarbons dept. Union Carbide Corp., N.Y.C., 1964-65; sales supr. Panelfab Internat. Corp., Miami, Fla., 1969-71; sr. sales rep. Victor Comptometer Corp., Hallandale, Fla., 1971-72; asst. v.p., br. mgr. Chase Fed. Savs. and Loan Assn., Margate, Fla., 1972-79, v.p., br. mgr., Hallandale, 1979-83; dir. R.H. Larsen & Assocs., Ft. Lauderdale, Fla., 1984-85; br. mgr. Savs. of Am., Pompano Beach, Fla., 1985—. Active Margate Library Bd., 1974-79, chmn., 1974-78; dep. chmn. Margate Bicentennial Com., 1974-76; mem. Mcpl. Projects Com., 1976; fund raiser United Way, 1975-81; active Jr. Achievement Broward County, 1978-79. Served with AUS, 1967-69. Recipient Margate Jr. C. of C. Spoke award, 1976; certs. of appreciation Margate Kiwanis Club, 1976, Library Bd., 1979; Coconut Creek High Sch. Band award, 1978; WGMA Community Service award, 1978; Broward County Jr. Achievement Rags to Riches award, 1979. Mem. Inst. Fin. Edn., Mall Mchts. Assn. (diplomate; bd. dirs. 1979-81, v.p. 1981-83), Hallandale C. of C. (dir. 1980, chmn. Ambassadors 1980), Theta Kappa Beta. Republican. Christian Scientist. Club: Principia of Broward County (pres. 1981-83). Home: 144 SW 84th Ln Coral Springs FL 33065 Office: Savings of America 225 N Federal Hwy Pompano Beach FL 33062

YOUNGDAHL, PATRICIA LUCY, psychologist, medical school educator; b. Cape Girardeau, Mo., Sept. 8, 1927; d. George B. and Alta Mae (Crites) Lucy; m. James E. Youngdahl, June 13, 1948 (div. Apr. 1974); children—Jay, Kristi, Lincoln, Sara. A.A., Stephens Coll., 1946; B.A., Washington Univ. (Mo.), 1948, M.A., 1950; Ph.D., Fla. Inst. Tech., 1985. Lic. psychological examiner. Assoc. exec. dir. Social Planning Council, St. Louis, 1950-52; instr. psychology U. Ark., Fayetteville, 1958-59, psychological examiner Med. Ctr., Little Rock, 1961-64, asst. prof. Med. Scis. Campus, Little Rock, 1975—. Author: (with others) How to Use Transactional Analysis in the Public Schools, 1974. Mem. exec. com. Pulaski County Dem. Com., Little Rock, 1972—, State Dem. Party, 1980—; chmn. Ark. for Kennedy, 1979-80; del. Nat. Dem. Conv. 1976, 80, 84; chmn. Ark. Women's Polit. Caucus, 1973-83. Named to 100 Ark. Women of Achievement Ark. Press Women's Assn., 1980. Mem. Ark. Psychol. Assn. (legislative chmn. 1982—), Am. Psychol. Assn. (assoc.), Urban League Bd. Mem. Unitarian-Universalist Ch. Home: 7108 Rockwood Rd Little Rock AR 72207 Office: Univ Ark Med Scis 4301 W Markham Little Rock AR 72205

YOUNGER, MARY SUE, statistics educator, consultant, researcher; b. Roanoke, Va., Aug. 28, 1944; d. Douglas Lynch and Sue Menefee (Compton) Y. B.A. in Math., Hollins Coll., 1966; M.S. in Stats., Va. Tech. Inst., 1969, Ph.D. in Stats., 1972. Instr. Va. Tech. Inst., Blacksburg, 1969-72, asst. prof., 1972-74; asst. prof. U. Tenn., Knoxville, 1974-76, assoc. prof., 1976—, asst. dean for grad. bus. programs, 1985—; statis. cons. St. Mary's Hosp., Knoxville, 1982, ELCON, Washington, 1981-82. Author: A Handbook for Linear Regression, 1969; A First Course in Linear Regression, 1985. Manuscript reviewer coll. textbook pubs. Contbr. articles to profl. jours. Mem. Am. Statis. Assn. (v.p. E. Tenn. chpt. 1985), SE Region Am. Inst. for Decision Scis. (pres. 1982). Presbyterian. Avocations: horse trials; equestrian events. Office: Dept Statistics U Tenn Knoxville TN 37996

YOUNGER, ROBERT DALE, psychologist, consultant, researcher; b. Searcy, Ark., Jan. 21, 1954; s. Robert Kelley and Lucy Fern (Dorsey) Y.; m. Sarah Kathryn Saxton, Nov. 29, 1975; children—Jeremy David, Sarah Kathryn. B.A., Harding Coll., Searcy, 1975; M.A., U. N. Ala., 1976; M.S., Auburn U., 1978, Ph.D., 1982. Lic. psychology, Fla., Okla. Psychology intern U. Okla. Health Scis. Ctr., Oklahoma City, 1980-81; clin. psychologist Fed. Prison System, El Reno, Okla., 1981-83; commd. lt. U.S. Navy, 1983; clin. psychologist, Orlando, Fla., 1983—; pvt. practice psychology, Longwood, Fla., 1984—; adj. prof. Ala. Christian Sch. of Religion, Montgomery, 1979-80, Rollins Coll., Winter Park, Fla., 1984—. Author: Sex Differences in Moral Judgement as a Function of Dilemma Content, 1978; Psycho Pathology and the Kinecic Family Drawing, 1982. Contbr. articles to profl. jours. Mem. Am. Psychol. Assn., Southeastern Psychol. Assn., Alpha Chi, Phi Kappa Phi. Republican. Mem. Ch. of Christ. Avocations: speaking at church functions; teaching bible sch. Home: 1330 Pine Sap Ct Orlando FL 32817 Office: Psychiatry Service Naval Hosp Orlando FL 32813

YOUNG-FARMER, JUDITH ANNE, psychological associate; b. Washington, June 28, 1943; d. Frank Leonard and Elizabeth Catherine (Dwyer) Y.; m. Edmund Jerry Higginson, Sept. 4, 1965 (dec. June 1971); children—Kira Anne, Krista Marie; m. Glenn Wayne Farmer, Oct. 12, 1973 (div. Sept. 1983). B.A., Dunbarton Coll. Holy Cross, 1965; M.A., Corpus Christi State U., 1985. Certified psychol. assoc. Research analyst CIA, Washington, 1965-68, U.S. Army Fgn. Scis. and Tech. Ctr., Washington, 1968, Library of Congress, Washington, 1968-70; staff mem. U.S. Senate, Senator Robert Byrd, Washington, 1970; psychol. assoc. Counseling and Psychology Resource Ctr., Corpus Christi, Tex., 1985—. Bd. dirs. Family Counseling Service, Corpus Christi, 1985—; mem. Aux. to Art Mus. S. Tex., Corpus Christi, 1977—. Mem. Am. Psychol. Assn. (assoc.), Am. Assn. Counseling and Devel., Tex. Psychol. Assn. (assoc.). Avocations: jogging; racquetball; travel. Office: Counseling & Psychology Resource Ctr 5440 Everhart St Suite 2 Corpus Christi TX 78411

YOUNGMAN, DARYL CRAIG, industrial engineer; b. Mpls., Feb. 18, 1952; s. Clarence B. and Elinor A. Y.; B.S. in Indsl. Tech., U. Wis., Stout, 1974; m. Catharine Gay Powell, Nov. 4, 1978; 1 son, Christopher Aaron. Auto mechanic Brookdale Pontiac, Mpls., 1970-73; indsl. engr. Electric Machinery Mfg. Co., Mpls., 1974-75; indsl. engr. Donaldson Co., Inc., Chillicothe, Mo., 1976-80; indsl. engr. Sangamo-Weston, Inc., Rabun Gap, Ga., 1980—. Chmn., Richfield (Minn.) chpt. Young Democrats, 1968-70; mem. Richfield Youth Commn., 1968-70; chmn. Mo. Young Dems., 1979. Mem. Am. Inst. Indsl. Engrs., Soc. Mfg. Engrs. (sr.). Home: Route 1 Rabun Gap GA 30568 Office: Box 1171 Clayton GA 30525

YOUNGREN, HARRISON, educator; b. Altona, Ill., Nov. 27; s. David N. and Esther F. (Quick) Y.; A.B., Knox Coll., 1936; M.A., So. Ill. U., 1967, Ph.D., 1975; m. Margaret Rue Stansfield, June 24, 1972. Sales and market researcher Wander Co., 1936-41; commd. 1st lt. U.S. Army, 1941, advanced through grades to lt. col.; ret., 1962; editor Mt. Carmel (Ill.) Daily Republican Register, 1962-64; mem. faculty dept. journalism U. Wis.-Oshkosh, 1969-73; prof. journalism Angelo State U., San Angelo, Tex., 1973—, head dept., 1973-74, 78-79; adviser in mass communications Republic of Korea, 1956-57, Laos, 1958-61; cons. in field. Bd. dirs. Wabash Valley Coll. Found.; mem. Knox Coll. Alumni Adv. Com., 1962—. Mem. Assn. Edn. in Journalism, Tex. Journalism Edn. Council (treas.), San Angelo Press Club (dir.), Kappa Tau Alpha, Sigma Delta Chi (dir. San Angelo chpt.). Democrat. Lutheran. Home: 2425 Lindenwood Ct San Angelo TX 76901 also 614 Cherry St Mount Carmel IL 62863

YOUNKIN, C. GEORGE, archivist; b. Great Bend, Kan., Oct. 13, 1910; s. Charles Franklin and Nannie Sylvia (Wilson) Y.; student Washburn U., 1932-35, Southeastern U., Washington, 1936-37; m. Ruth Ward, Dec. 27, 1939 (dec. 1980); children—Karen (Mrs. John R. Postma), Eleta (Mrs. Stephen B. McElroy), Cheryl (Mrs. Thomas R. Gamble), Chip G. With U.S. Dept. Agr., Washington, 1935-51; with Nat. Archives, Ft. Worth, 1951-75, regional archivist for Ark., La., N.Mex., Okla. and Tex., 1968-75; ret., 1975; pres. S.W. Archives Cons., 1975—; archive cons. Kiowa Hist. and Research Assn., Carnegie, Okla. Mem. council exec. com. and historian Boy Scouts Am., Ft. Worth, 1975—; mem. Gov.'s Adv. Com. on Aged for Tarrant County, 1976-80; mem. Tarrant County Hist. Commn.; trustee Ch. of Good Shepherd, 1980-83. Served with AUS, 1943-45. Recipient Silver Beaver award Boy Scouts Am., 1966, Order of Arrow, Boy Scouts Am., 1966; pub. service award GSA, 1967, spl. service award Fed. Bus. Assn., 1967. Fellow Tex. State Geneal. Soc.; mem. Soc. S.W. Archivists (sec.-treas. 1971-80), Internat. Council Archives, Soc. Am. Archivists (regional activities com.), Nat. Trust Historic Preservation, Kiowa Tia-Piah Soc. Carnegie (Okla.), Westerners Internat., Western History Assn., Tex. Hist. Assn. Dir., Llano Estacado Heritage Quar., 1974-82. Home and Office: 3501 Quail Ln Arlington TX 76016

YOUNT, ROYALL AUSTIN, bishop; b. Hickory, N.C., May 19, 1922; s. Floyd Stephen and Lottie May (Austin) Y.; m. Martha Lee Townsend, June 14, 1945; children—Royall Austin, John Timothy. A.B., Lenoir Rhyne Coll., Hickory, 1942; M.Div., Luth. Theol. So. Sem., Columbia, S.C., 1945; D.D. hon., Newberry Coll., S.C., 1956. Ordained to ministry Lutheran Ch. in Am., 1945, bishop 1980. Pastor St. Paul Luth. Ch., Tampa, Fla., 1945-52; pres. Fla. synod. United Luth. Ch. Am., 1950-62; pres., bishop Fla. synod. Luth. Ch. in Am., Tampa, 1962—; dir. bd. pensions Luth. Ch. in Am., 1978—, com. mem. div. service to mil. personnel, 1976—. Mem. Tampa Selective Service Vd., 1983; trustee Newberry Coll., 1950—. Luth. Theol. So. Sem., 1950—. Democrat.

YOUNT, THOMAS LEO, venture capital executive; b. Birmingham, Ala., Mar. 23, 1928; s. Thomas L. and Hazel Lee (Felts) Y. m. Jane Wilkerson, Sept. 5, 1953; children—Lee Yount Duer, Margaret Yount Polen, Pamela Jane. B.S. in Engring., Vanderbilt U., 1952; postgrad. U. Pitts., 1952-53. Asst. to v.p. purchasing Westinghouse Electric Corp., Pitts., 1952-56; gen. mgr. Internat. Elec. Industries, Nashville, 1956-61; pres. ORTEC, Inc., Oak Ridge, 1961-71; sr. v.p. EG&G, Inc., Wellesley, Mass., 1971-82; commr. Dept. Employment Security, Nashville, 1983-85; pres. Tenn. Innovation Ctr., Inc., Oak Ridge, 1985—; dir. Bank Oak Ridge; mem. adv. panel Office Tech. Assessment, Innovation and Regional Econ. Devel., Washington. Bd. dirs. Tenn. Tech. Corridor, Knoxville Symphony Soc., 1982—. Served with USN, 1946-48. Mem. Beta Gamma Sigma, Omicron Delta Kappa, Tau Beta Pi. Republican. Methodist. Clubs: LeConte (Knoxville); Belle Meade Country (Nashville). Lodge: Rotary. Office: Tenn Innovation Ctr PO Box 607 106 Badger Rd Oak Ridge TN 37830

YOWELL, ROBERT LEE, theatre and dance educator; b. St. Louis, July 16, 1941; s. Walter J. and Edna Mae (Standford) Y.; m. Marsha Adele Reissaus, May 28, 1965; children—Robert Lee, Patrick Edward. A.B., SE Mo. State U., 1966; M.A., St. Louis U., 1968; Ph.D., Bowling Green State U., 1971; postgrad. Northwestern U., 1974. Instr., Florissant Valley Coll., Mo., 1967-68; teaching fellow Bowling Green State U., Ohio, 1968-71; asst. prof. Western Carolina U., Cullowhee, N.C., 1971-73; assoc. prof., chmn. dept. theatre and dance U. Ark.-Little Rock, 1973-80, U. Ala.-Birmingham, 1980—. Editor: Stepping Out: An Introduction to the Arts, 1985. Contbr. articles on theatre children and theatre to profl. jours.; dir. 35 play prodns. Served with U.S. Army, 1959-62. Recipient Obelisk (best direction; mus. comedy) Greater Birmingham Arts Alliance, Ala., 1982, 84. Mem. Ala. Theatre League (treas., v.p., pres.), SW Theatre Conf. (sec., v.p. 1977-80), Ark. Alliance/Arts Edn. (v.p., pres. 1976-77), Conf. on Ark. Theatre (pres. 1975-76), SE Theatre, Am. Theatre Assn. Democrat. Home: 2328 Wexford Ln Vestavia Hills AL 35216 Office: Dept Theatre and Dance U Ala-Birmingham Univ Sta Birmingham AL 35216

YU, EDEN SIU-HUNG, economics educator; b. Shanghai, China, Jan. 28, 1946; came to U.S., 1968, naturalized, 1984; s. Chi Hou and Mee Wo (Sum) Y.; m. Ming-fai Hui, Sept. 1970; children—Pei-hsin Deborah, Ling-hsin Lillian, Guo-hsin Gordon. B.Sc., Chinese U. Hong Kong, 1968; M.S., So. Ill. U., 1970; Ph.D., Washington U., St. Louis, 1976. Assoc. economist Midwest Research Inst., Kansas City, Mo., 1974-76; asst. prof. econs. U. Okla., Norman, 1976-80, assoc. prof., 1980-84; prof. econs. La. State U., Baton Rouge, 1985—; reviewer NSF, 1980—. Author: Air Pollution Damages, 1978; also numerous articles. Asst. editor Missouri Valley Econ. Assn., 1983—. Vice-pres. Chinese Assn. Oklahoma City, 1984. Recipient U. Okla. Regents' award, 1980; grantee in field. Mem. Am. Econ. Assn., Royal Econ. Soc., Regional Sci. Assn., So. Econ. Assn. Office: La State U Baton Rouge LA 70803

YU, SHIRLEY SHIU-FANG, economics educator; b. Taoyuan, Republic of China, b. Mar. 21, 1949; came to U.S., 1971, naturalized, 1983; d. Ching-Tseng and Luan (Tseng) Y. B.A., Nat. Taiwan U., 1971; M.S., Okla. State U., 1973, Ph.D., 1981. Research analyst Merck Sharp & Dohme, West Point, Pa., 1977-79; asst. prof. Tex. Tech. U., Lubbock, 1981—. Contbr. articles to profl. jours. Grantee Pharm. Mfrs. Assn., 1976-77. Mem. Am. Econ. Assn., So. Econ. Assn., Omicron Delta Epsilon. Office: Econs Dept Tex Tech U Lubbock TX 79409

YUDIN, LEE WILLIAM, mental health center administrator, consultant; b. Bklyn., Jan. 26, 1937; s. Irving and Dorothy Y.; m. Jeanne Carter, Apr. 26, 1975; children—Daniel Arthur, Rachel Miriam, John Richard. B.B.A., CCNY, 1958, postgrad., 1958-60; M.S., U. Mass., 1962, Ph.D., 1964. Assoc. dir. research and evaluation West Phila. Community Mental Health Consortium, 1967-69, dir. research and evaluation, 1969-76; dir. research and evaluation Northside Community Mental Health Ctr., Tampa, 1976-77, assoc. dir. community and ctr. services, 1977-78; exec. dir. El Paso Ctr. Mental Health-Mental Retardation, Life Mgmt. Ctr., Tex., 1978—; mgmt. cons. Myers Cons., Clearwater, Fla., 1978, Fla. Mental Health Inst., Tampa, 1978; clin. assoc. prof. U. S. Fla., Tampa, 1977-78; surveyor Joint Commn. on Accreditation of Hosps., Chgo., 1977-81. Mem. Mayor's Com. on Employment of Handicapped, El Paso, 1981-82; state chmn. United Way of El Paso, 1980, govtl. chmn., 1981; chmn. Mayor's Adv. Com./Constrn./Multi-Purpose Bldg. for Handicapped, El Paso, 1979-83. USPHS predoctoral research fellow, 1961-63. Mem. Mental Health Assn. (bd. dirs. 1982-85), Assn. Mental Health Adminstrs. (cert. 1983), Am. Psychol. Assn., Tex. Vol. Consortium (exec. com. 1978—, chmn. mental health com. 1984-85). Avocations: skiing; woodwork. Home: 621 Lakeway Dr El Paso TX 79932 Office: Life Mgmt Ctr PO Box 9997 El Paso TX 79990

YUN, PETER SUBUENG, economics educator; b. Yong-Wol, Korea, June 7, 1936; s. Sea Young and Soon Oak (Kim) Y.; m. Sandy J. Forsythe, June 21, 1970; 1 child, Amy Rebecca. B.A., U. Ga., 1966, Ph.D., 1975; M.A., U. Okla., 1968. Asst. prof. econs. Clinch Valley Coll., Wise, Va., 1974-79, assoc. prof., 1979—, chmn. bus. div., 1979—. Pres., Universal Bus. Services, Wise, 1981—. Invest-in-America grantee, 1979, 80; recipient Outstanding Alumni award Emmanuel Coll., 1984. Mem. Am. Econ. Assn., So. Econ. Assn. Home: PO Box 2620 Wise VA 24293 Office: Clinch Valley Coll PO Box 16 Wise VA 24293

ZABALAOUI, JUDITH, financial planning company executive; b. Gadsden, Ala., Nov. 24, 1937; d. John Gordon and Mary (McKay) Cowan; m. Nash Sadi Zabalaoui, June 5, 1957; children—Michele Anne, Michael Nash. B.S. in Econs., Loyola U., New Orleans, 1968, M.B.A. in Econs., 1970. Cert. fin. planner Coll. for Fin. Planning. Instr. Loyola U., New Orleans, 1968-72; controller/bus. mgr. various non-profit orgns., New Orleans, 1972-75; pres.

Resource Mgmt., Inc., Metairie, La., 1975—, chmn., chief exec. officer, 1978—. Mem. Inst. Cert. Fin. Planners, Internat. Assn. for Fin. Planning (dir.). Author: How To Use Your Business or Profession as a Tax Shelter, 1983. Office: 3510 N Causeway Suite 506 Metairie LA 70002

ZABAN, ERWIN, business executive; b. Atlanta, Aug. 17, 1921; s. Mandle and Sara (Feidelson) Z.; m. Judy Oliver, Apr. 30, 1981; children by previous marriage—Carol Zaban Cooper, Laura Zaban Dinerman, Sara Kay. Vice pres., pres. Zep Mfg. Co., Atlanta, 1937-62, merged into Nat. Service Industries, Inc., Atlanta, 1962, name of Zep Mfg. Co. changed to Nat. Service Industries, Inc., 1963, exec. v.p. Nat. Linen Service, 1962-66, also dir., mem. exec. com., pres. Nat. Service Industries, 1966-79, chief exec. officer, 1972—, chmn. bd., 1975—; dir. First Nat. Bank of Atlanta, 1976—, chmn. audit com. and mem. exec. com., 1981—; dir. Sci. Atlanta Inc., Classic Corp., Engraph Inc. Hon. pres., bd. dirs., mem. exec. com. Atlanta Jewish Community Ctr.; chmn. Atlanta Jewish Welfare Fedn., 1955, hon. trustee for life; former bd. dirs. Jewish Home for Aged, Atlanta; mem. bd. visitors Emory U.; trustee Atlanta U., 1981-82; bd. dirs. Sci. Atlanta, Inc., 1982—, Atlanta Symphony Orch., 1982—. Recipient Man of Year award B'nai B'rith, 1977; Disting. Service award Atlanta Urban League, 1979; Human Relations award Anti-Defamation League, 1981; Father of Year award Father's Day Council, 1982. Mem. Internat. Sanitary Supply Assn. (former v.p. dir.; Disting. Service award 1982). Club: Progressive (past officer, dir.). Home: 3374 Old Plantation Rd NW Atlanta GA 30327 Office: 1180 Peachtree St NE Atlanta GA 30309

ZABLE, NORMAN ARNOLD, lawyer; b. Chgo., July 11, 1934; s. Joseph Irving and Marian (Rosen) Z.; m. Vera Slutzky, June 16, 1963; children—Barak, Brett, Mark. B.B.A., So. Meth. U., 1955, LL.B., 1958. Atty., Dallas, 1958-79; atty. Norman A. Zable P.C., Dallas, 1979—. Democratic precinct chmn., Dallas, 1978-79; assoc. scoutmaster Boy Scouts Am., Dallas, 1978—. Mem. ABA, State Bar Tex., Dallas Bar Assn., Comml. Law League, Mensa. Democrat. Jewish. Home: 16612 Vicarage Ct Dallas TX 75248

ZACCARIA, JAMES AUSTIN, real estate developer, renovation consultant; b. San Antonio, Mar. 25, 1954; s. Michael Angelo and Avalee (Austin) Z. Student San Antonio Coll., 1971-73; B.A., Pratt Inst., 1976; postgrad. Harvard U., 1976; M.A., U. Tex.-San Antonio, 1983. Vice pres. Jack and Jill Schs., San Antonio, 1976—; pres. Cameo Theatre Corp., San Antonio, 1978—; gen. mgr. Catering by Courand, San Antonio, 1980—; pres. James Zaccaria, Environ. Design, San Antonio, 1977—. Bd. dirs. King William Assn., San Antonio, 1978—. Mem. San Antonio Conservation Soc., St. Paul Sq. Assn. Office: 1131 E Commerce #202 San Antonio TX 78210

ZACHARIAS, DONALD WAYNE, university president; b. Salem, Ind., Sept. 28, 1935; s. William Otto and Estelle Mae (Newlon) Z.; B.A., Georgetown (Ky.) Coll., 1957, LL.D. (hon.), 1983; M.A., Ind. U., 1959, Ph.D., 1963; m. Tommie Kline Dekle, Aug. 16, 1959; children—Alan, Eric, Leslie. Asst. prof. communication and theatre Ind. U., 1963-69; assoc. prof. communication U. Tex., Austin, 1969-72, prof., 1972-79, asst. to pres., 1974-77; exec. asst. to chancellor U. Tex. System, 1978-79; pres. Western Ky. U., 1979—; dir. First Fed. Savs. and Loan, Bowling Green, Ky.; cons. savs. and loan leagues. Bd. dirs. Little League, Austin, 1977-78, Greenview Hosp., Bowling Green, 1982-85, United Way, 1983—. Served with U.S. Army, 1959-60. Recipient Teaching award Ind. U. Found., 1963, Cactus Teaching award U. Tex., 1971. Mem. Speech Communication Assn., Internat. Communication Assn., Am. Assn. Higher Edn., Bowling Green-Warren County C. of C. (bd. dirs. 1983—), Phi Kappa Phi (pres. 1978). Democrat. Episcopalian. Author: In Pursuit of Peace: Speeches of the Sixties, 1970. Office: Office of Pres Western Ky U Bowling Green KY 42101

ZACHERT, VIRGINIA, psychologist, educator; b. Jacksonville, Ala., Mar. 1, 1920; d. Rev. R. E. and Cora H. (Massee) Z.; student Norman Jr. Coll., 1937; A.B., Ga. State Woman's Coll. (now Valdosta State Coll.), 1940; M.A., Emory U., 1947; Ph.D., Purdue U., 1949. Statistician, Davison-Paxon Co., Atlanta, 1941-44; research psychologist Mil. Contracts, Auburn Research Found., Ala. Poly. Inst.; indsl. and research psychologist Sturm & O'Brien, cons. engrs., 1958-59; research project dir. Western Design, Biloxi, Miss., 1960-61; self-employed cons. psychologist, Norman Park, Ga., 1961-71, Good Hope, Ga., 1971—; research assoc. med. edn. Med. Coll. Ga. Augusta, 1963-65, assoc. prof., 1965-70, prof., 1970-84, prof. emerita, 1984—, chief learning materials div., 1973-84, chmn. faculty, 1983; mem. Ga. Bd. Examiners of Psychologists, 1974-79, v.p., 1977, pres., 1978. Mem. adv. bd. Comdr. Gen. ATC, USAF, 1967-70; bd. dirs., sec. Health Center Credit Union, 1980-81; cons. Ga. Silver-Haired Legislature, 1980-82; bd. dirs. Sr. Citizens Council, 1980—, mem. exec. com., 1980-83; mem. CSRA Adv. Council on Aging; del. White House Conf. on Aging, 1981. Served as aerologist USN, 1944-46, aviation psychologist USAF, 1949-54. Named Alumna of Yr., Valdosta State Coll., 1980; diplomate Am. Bd. Profl. Psychologists. Fellow Am. Psychol. Assn., AAAS; mem. Am. Statis. Assn., AAUP (chpt. pres. 1978-80), Sigma Xi (chpt. pres. 1979-81). Baptist. Author: (with P. L. Wilds) Essentials of Gynecology-Oncology, 1967, Applications of Gynecology-Oncology, 1967. Home: 1126 Highland Ave Augusta GA 30904 Office: Dept Obstetrics and Gynecology Med Coll Ga Augusta GA 30912

ZACK, GEORGE, orchestra conductor, music director; b. Pine Bluff, Ark., July 8, 1936; s. George Peter and Eugenia (Trianddfilou) Z.; m. Kerry Sheehan, Oct. 4, 1970; children—Katherine Eugenia, Melissa Sheehan. Mus.B. cum laude, Wichita State U., 1958; Mus.M., U. Mich., 1960; Ph.D., Fla. State U., 1960; viola student Robert Courte; postgrd. Yale U., 1970-71. Instr. in music theory U. Mich., 1962-64; assoc. prof. music Hiram Coll., 1964-72; condr., music dir. Wooster Symphony (Ohio), 1965-67, Warren Chamber Orch. (Ohio), 1968—, Lexington Philharm. Orch. (Ky.), 1972—; vis. artist-in-residence Eastern Ky. U., 1976; artist-in-residence James Madison U., 1978; guest condr. Louisville Orch., 1978, Thessaloniki State Orch., Greece, 1981, South Bend Symphony Orch. (Ind.), Youngstown Symphony Orch., (Ohio), Greater Bridgeport Symphony (Conn.), Amarillo Symphony (Tex.), Monterey County Symphony Orch. (Calif.); bd. dirs. Central Ky. Youth Music Soc., 1974—, also acting music dir., condr. symphony orch., leader orch. concert tour to Romania and Soviet Union, 1979; mem. Arts Council, 1972—; conducting student Am. Symphony Orch. League Conducting Inst., summers. grad. asst. Fla. State U., 1960-62; community adv. bd. WEKU-FM, 1979—. Recipient Orpheus award Phi Mu Alpha Sinfonia, 1975. Mem. Am. Fedn. Musicians, Am. Symphony Orch. League, Nat. Assn. Arts and Letters (chmn. membership Ky. chpt.), AHEPA. Greek Orthodox. Author: The Music Dramas of Manolis Kalomiris, 1972. Office: 161 N Mill St Arts Place Lexington KY 40507

ZAEPFEL, GLENN PETER, psychologist; b. N.Y.C., Feb. 15, 1951; s. Walter Henry and Lillian Adair (Kovach) Z.; m. Linda Carrie Grinton, June 1, 1974; children—Peter, Caroline, Christine. B.A., U. S.C., 1973; M.Ed., Ga. State U., 1980, Ph.D., 1985. Milieu therapist Peachtree-Parkwood Hosp., Atlanta, 1978-80; dir. Roswell St. Counseling Ctr., Marietta, Ga., 1980-84; dir. counseling and psychol. services DeKalb Pain Control and Rehab. Ctr., Decatur, Ga., 1981-85; pvt. practice psychology, Columbia, S.C., 1985—; program dir. Bapt. Med. Ctr. Pain Program, Columbia, 1985—, dir. behavioral medicine, 1986—. Mem. Am. Psychol. Assn., Christian Assn. for Psychol. Studies, Am. Rehab. Counseling Assn., Am. Assn. Counseling and Devel. Republican. Presbyterian. Club: Sinfonia Fraternity (Columbia). Avocations: sports; music. Home: 3620 Greenway Dr Columbia SC 29206 Office: Pain Mgmt Program Bapt Med Ctr Taylor at Marion Sts Columbia SC 29220 also 1639 Brabham Ave Columbia SC 29204

ZAGER, LYNNE DONNA, clinical psychologist; b. N.Y.C., Aug. 9, 1954; d. Victor and Muriel (Kagan) Z.; B.A., U. Tenn., 1976; M.S., Fla. State U., 1978, Ph.D., 1981. Lic. psychologist, Tenn. Asst. prof. psychology U. Tenn., Chattanooga, 1981-83; forensic dir. Midtown Mental Health Ctr., Memphis, 1983—; asst. clin. prof. U. Tenn. Ctr. Health Scis., Memphis, 1984—. Mem. Internat. Differential Treatment Assn. (exec. sec. 1982—), Am. Psychol. Assn., Southeastern Psychol. Assn., Soc. Police and Criminal Psychology, Soc. Personality Assessment. Avocations: creative writing; swimming. Office: Midtown Mental Health Ctr 427 Linden Ave Memphis TN 38126

ZAHARIA, ERIC STAFFORD, mental retardation center administrator; b. Pomona, Calif., Aug. 24, 1948; s. Edgar A. and Dorothy (Stafford) Z.; m. Caryle Koentz, Dec. 23, 1967; children—Tye W., Tieg A. B.A., Pomona Coll., 1970; M.Ed., U. Ariz.-Tucson, 1973; Ph.D., George Peabody Coll., 1978; postgrad., Govt. Execs. Inst. U. N.C., Chapel Hill, 1981. Mental retardation worker Ariz. Tng. Program, Tucson, 1970-71, unit dir., 1971-73; dir. residential services Willmar State Hosp., (Minn.), 1973-76; research asst. Inst. on Mental Retardation and Intellectual Devel., Nashville, 1976-78; dir. mental retardation program services Dept. Mental Health/Mental Retardation, State of Tenn., Nashville, 1978-79; dir. Caswell Ctr., Kinston, N.C., 1979—; mem. adj. faculty East Carolina U., Greenville, 1979—. Guest reviewer: Mental Retardation, Jour. Community Psychology. Chmn. Big Bros./Sisters Kinston Inc., 1980-83; bd. dirs. Neuse Enterprises, Inc., Kinston, 1981—; mem. N.C. Coalition for Community Service, Kinston, 1982—. Mem. Am. Assn. Mental Deficiency, Nat. Assn. Supts. Pub. Residential Facilities, Assn. Retarded Citizens, Kinston C. of C. (dir. 1983—). Lodge: Rotary. Office: Caswell Center 2415 W Vernon Ave Kinston NC 28501*

ZAHLER, SANFORD F., physician; b. N.Y.C., June 8, 1933; s. Edward and Byrdie Z.; m. Lois M. Schwardron, Nov. 28, 1959; children—Pamela, Scott, Jonathan; m. Lynne Rosenheim, Dec. 26, 1981. B.S. cum laude, U. S.C., 1952; M.D., Med. U. S.C., 1956. Diplomate Am. Bd. Internal Medicine. Intern, Los Angeles County Gen. Hosp., 1956-57, resident, 1957-58; resident Jackson Meml. Hosp., Miami, Fla., 1960-62; practice medicine specializing in internal medicine, 1962-82; med. dir. inpatient services Miami Gen. Hosp., 1982—; mem. staffs Highland Park Gen. Hosp., Cedars of Lebanon Hosp; dir. utilization mgmt. Internat. Med. Ctrs.-HMO. Served as lt. M.C., USNR, 1957-59. Mem. Fla. Med. Assn., Dade County Med. Assn., Phi Beta Kappa.

ZAHN, DANIEL ALBERT, architect; b. Washington, May 13, 1943; s. Otto and Bess Agnes (Buck) Z.; m. Rosalind Elizabeth Webb, Aug. 30, 1964; children—Michele Metreaud, Jennifer Webb. Registered architect, Va. Draftsman, job capt., project architect, mgr. constrn. adminstrn. and assoc. ptnr. Smithey & Boynton, Architects and Engrs., Roanoke, Va., 1967-81; v.p. S. Lewis Lionberger Co., Roanoke, 1981-85, exec. v.p., 1985—; tchr. adult edn. Roanoke City Schs., 1980-82. Mem. adv. bd. for vocat. edn. Roanoke County Schs., 1978-82; bd. dirs. Roanoke Valley Speech and Hearing Ctr., 1979-82, pres. bd., 1982. Mem. AIA, Va. Soc. AIA. Associated Gen. Contractors Va. (pres. Roanoke dist.). Baptist. Clubs: Hidden Valley Country, Roanoke Valley Square Dancers. Lodge: Kiwanis. Home: 5130 Lynnson Dr Salem VA 24153 Office: 5933 Starkey Rd Roanoke VA 24015

ZAHN, DOUGLAS ALFRED, statistics educator; b. Waverly, Iowa, Aug. 11, 1943; s. Alfred Carl and Odile Marie (Latour) Z.; m. Shirley Jean Bush, June 19, 1965 (div. Apr. 1982); children—Derek, Devin; m. 2d, Andrea Marie Wilson, May 12, 1984. B.A., U. Iowa, 1965; A.M., Harvard U., 1966, Ph.D., 1970. Asst. prof. stats. Fla. State U., Tallahassee, 1969-75, assoc. prof., 1975-84, prof., 1984—; vis. assoc. prof. Harvard U., 1978-79; cons. in field. Recipient Jack Youden prize Am. Soc. for Quality Control, 1975. Mem. Am. Statis. Assn. (Best Paper award Statis. Edn. sect. 1980, 81), Biometric Soc., Phi Beta Kappa, Sigma Xi. Democrat. Presbyterian. Author: The Human Side of Statistical Consulting, 1982; contbr. articles to profl. jours. Home: 249 Timberlane Rd Tallahassee FL 32312 Office: Fla State Univ Statistics Dept Tallahassee FL 32306

ZAHN, LOUIS JENNINGS, educator Spanish, administrator; b. Atlanta, Nov. 24, 1922; s. William Jennings and Rosina Marie (Hunerkopf) Z. A.B., Emory U., 1947, M.A., 1949; Ph.D., U. N.C., 1957. Instr. Armstrong Coll., Savannah, Ga., 1948-49, Emory U., Atlanta, 1950-57; asst. prof. Ga. Inst. Tech., Atlanta, 1957-60, assoc. prof., 1960-64, prof., 1964—, head dept. modern langs., 1976-85, acad. adminstr. intensive courses English for fgn. students, 1958-85, dir. Lang. Inst., 1985—. Author: Vocabulario etimologico documentado del Libro de los exenplos por abc de Sanchez de Vercial, 1961; History of St. John's Lutheran Church, 1869-1969, 1969; Teoria y ejercicios sobre la fonologia y la morfologia de la lengua española, 1974; Juan Ruiz, Libro de buen amor, Part I, Stanzas 1-387, 1975, Part II, 1976. Vice-pres. Circulo Hispanoamericano, Atlanta, 1958-60. Fellow, Emory U. 1947, U. N.C., 1949. Mem. Tchrs. English to Speakers of Other Langs., Nat. Assn. Fgn. Student Affairs, Am. Council Teaching Fgn. Langs., Nat. Assn. Tchrs. Spanish and Portuguese, S. Atlantic Modern Lang. Assn., Phi Sigma Iota. Lutheran. Avocations: antiques; photography; travel. Home: 3131 Queens Walk NE Atlanta GA 30345 Office: Ga Inst Tech Dept Modern Langs Atlanta GA 30332

ZAHORIAN, STEPHEN ANDREW, electrical engineering educator; b. Nov. 20, 1947. B.S. in Elec. Engring., U. Rochester, 1969; M.S. in Elec. Engring., Syracuse U., 1973, PH.D. in Elec. Engring., 1978. Engr., RCA Corp., Burlington, Mass., 1969-71; teaching asst. Syracuse U., N.Y., 1971-75, dissertation researcher, 1976-78, instr. and research engr. elec. and computer engring., 1977-79; asst. prof. Old Dominion U., Norfolk, Va., 1979-84, assoc. prof., 1984—. Served with USAF, 1970-76. Syracuse U. grantee, 1976-77; Gen. Electric Co. grantee, 1978; NSF grantee, 1981-83; Digital Equipment Corp. grantee, 1982-83; Whitaker Found. grantee, 1983-85, 85-86. Recipient Outstanding Instr. award Old Dominion U., 1980. Mem. IEEE, Accoustical Soc. Am., Tau Beta Pi. Contbr. articles to profl. jours. Office: Old Dominion U Norfolk VA 23508

ZAKI, SALEH ABBAS, forensic pathologist; b. Cairo, Oct. 25, 1935; came to U.S., 1969, naturalized, 1976; s. Abbas S. and Hamida M. (Ali) Z.; m. Afaf A. Kassaby, May 18, 1960; children—Maha, Karaz. M.D., Cairo U., 1959; Ph.D., U. Birmingham (Eng.), 1964. Diplomate Am. Bd. Pathology. Rotating intern Cairo U. Teaching Hosp., 1960-61; clin. demonstrator in histopathology Assuit (Egypt) U. Med. Sch., 1961, clin. demonstrator in pathology 1965, lectr. pathology, 1965-68, supr. histopathology labs., 1966-68; research fellow, hon. research fellow dept. pathology U. Birmingham, 1961-65; tutor in pathology dept. pathology, Queen's U. Belfast (No. Ireland), 1968-69; assoc. in pathology Emory U. Sch. Medicine, Atlanta, 1969-70, sr. resident, instr. anatomic pathology dept. pathology, Atlanta, 1972, fellow in cytopathology and clin. instr., 1972, clin. asst. prof. pathology, 1975-77, clin. asst. prof. pediatrics, 1974-77; assoc. prof. div. pathology U. Calgary (Alta., Can.), 1970-71; assoc. med. examiner Fulton County, Atlanta, 1973-77, dir. residency tng. program, 1976-77; assoc. med. staff dept. pathology St. Joseph's Infirmary, Atlanta, 1975-77; assoc. prof. pathology U. Ala.-Birmingham, 1977-78; assoc. coroner/med. examiner Jefferson County, Ala., 1977-78; assoc. med. examiner Fulton County, Atlanta, 1973-77, 78—; assoc. pathologist Hugh Spalding Community Hosp., Atlanta, 1982—. Bd. dirs. Am. Arab Community Ctr., 1982-83; clin. assoc. prof. pathology Morehouse Sch. Medicine, Atlanta, 1983—. Brit. Council scholar, 1961-65. Fellow Am. Acad. Forensic Sci., Coll. Am. Pathologists; mem. Pathol. Soc. Gt. Britain and Ireland, Atlanta Soc. Pathologists, AMA, Coll. Am. Pathologists, Med. Assn. Atlanta, Ga. Med. Assn., Am. Heart Assn., Nat. Assn. Med. Examiners. Republican. Moslem. Contbr. articles to profl. jours. Home: 2716 Cravey Dr NE Atlanta GA 30345 Office: 50 Coca Cola Pl Atlanta GA 30303

ZAKRZEWSKI, SZCZEPAN ED, safety educator, pianist; b. London, Oct. 7, 1949; came to U.S., 1951. A.A., Keene State Coll., 1977, B.A. in Psychology, 1978; M.S. in Transp. Safety, Central Mo. State U., 1979; Ed.D., Tex. A&M U., 1986. Instr. driver edn., 1977-84; safety instr. Lamar U., Beaumont, Tex., 1977—; safety dir. Peerless Products, Inc., Fort Scott, Kans., 1979-80; energy coordinator Mountainland Community Action Agy., Provo, Utah, 1981-83; composer; concert pianist. Served with USN, 1968-70. Mem. Am. Soc. Safety Engrs. Home: PO Box 536 Garrisonville VA 22463

ZAMBELL, RICHARD GEORGE, economist, forecaster; b. Pitts., July 31, 1952; s. Harold George and Rose Jane (Brainard) Z. B.S. in Bus., Fin., Wright State U., 1974, M.S. in Econs., 1979. Research analyst Winters Nat. Bank, Dayton, Ohio, 1972-77; sr. economist BancOhio Nat. Bank, Columbus, 1977-80, chief economist, 1980-83; dir. econ. research Weiss Research, Inc., West Palm Beach, Fla., 1983-85; pres. Weekly Fundamental Forecasts, Inc., Hot Springs Village, Ark., 1985—. Author: Hyperinflation or Depression?, 1984. Named Most Outstanding Fin. Student, Ohio Bankers Assn., 1973. Mem. Am. Econ. Assn., Nat. Assn. Bus. Economists. Avocations: golf; skiing; computer programming.

ZAMBO, RICHARD ALAN, lawyer, energy and regulatory consultant; b. Chgo., July 1, 1945; s. Steven Paul and Anna Jane Zambo; m. Susan Kay Nemeth, Apr. 15, 1972; children—Nicholas Steven, Matthew Joseph. B.S. in Mech. Engring., Purdue U., 1969; J.D., Franklin Pierce Coll., 1980. Bar: Fla. 1980, U.S. Patent Office 1978. Design engr. United Tech., West Palm Beach, Fla., 1969-73; project mgr. Consulting Firm, West Palm Beach, 1973-77; prin. Richard A. Zambo, P.E., Concord, N.H. and West Palm Beach, 1977-80; sole practice, Tampa, Fla., 1980-82, Brandon, Fla., 1982—; energy cons.; lectr. in field. Coach, Youth Soccer League, Brandon, Fla., 1983; chief YMCA Indian Guides, Brandon, 1983; dir. YMCA, Brandon, 1984; chmn. Fla. Internat. Co-generation Soc. Recipient Acad. Achievement award Purdue U., 1969. Mem. Fla. Bar Assn. (chmn. energy com.), Fed. Energy Bar Assn., Fla. Engring. Soc. (energy com.). Roman Catholic. Home: 2214 Wildwood Hollow Dr Valrico FL 33594 Office: 205 N Parsons Ave Brandon FL 33511

ZAMORA, ANTONIO RAFAEL, lawyer; b. Havana, Cuba, Jan. 18, 1941; came to U.S., 1960; s. Juan Clemente and Rosario (Munne) Z.; m. Nelly Reggio, Nov. 28, 1963; children—Maria G., Antonio Rafael. License in Diplomatic and Consular Law, U. Havana, 1960; B.A., U. Fla.-Gainesville, 1965, J.D., 1973; M.A., U. Miami, Fla., 1969. Bar: Fla. 1973. Assoc. Shutts & Bowen, Miami, Fla., 1973-78, ptnr., head internat. dept., 1978-82; ptnr. McDermott, Will & Emery, Miami, 1982-83, mng. ptnr., 1983-84; sr. ptnr. Barnett, Alagia, Zamora & Suarez, Miami, 1984—; pres. Terra Nostrum, Inc., Miami, 1982—; v.p. Corporate Services Inc., Miami, 1984—; dir. Fla. Internat. Bank, Miami, 1983-84; chmn. bd. Commercebank N.A., Miami, 1985—; dir. Internat. Law Conf. for Lawyers of the Americas, 1978, 80. Legal counsel Cuban Am. Nat. Found., Miami, Washington, 1982—; mem. council advisors Hispanic Coalition, Washington, 1984; pres. Hispanic Am. Voters Edn. Inc., Miami, 1984; sec. Brigada 2506, Miami, 1984. Served to lt. USNR, 1963-65. Mem. Interam. Bar Assn., ABA, Cuban Am. Bar Assn. (v.p. 1976-79, disting. service award 1980, dir. emeritus 1982), Fla. Bar. Republican. Roman Catholic. Clubs: Big Five, American (Miami, Fla.); Ocean Reef (Key Largo, Fla.); Miami Rowing. Home: 7500 SW 82d Ct Miami FL 33143 Office: Barnett Alagia Zamora & Suarez 799 Brickell Plaza Suite 606 Miami FL 33131

ZANT, ROBERT FRANKLIN, computer information systems educator, consultant; b. Valdosta, Ga., Sept. 28, 1943; s. John F. and Norma G. (Shadrick) Z.; m. Sue Ann Frazier, Nov. 8, 1961; children—Debra Lynn, Tina Sue. A.A., St. Johns River Jr. Coll., 1963; B.A., U. Fla., 1965, M.A., 1970, Ph.D., 1972. Systems programmer U. Fla., Gainesville, 1966-67; asst. prof. Clemson U., S.C., 1970-74; assoc. prof. N. Tex. State U., Denton, 1974-80, prof. computer information systems, 1980—, chmn. dept., 1982—; cons. Dallas Eye Inst., 1981, Cottingham Bearing Co., Dallas, 1981, Riegel Textile Corp., Greenwood, S.C., 1971-73, Dow-Badashe Co., Anderson, S.C., 1972. Contbr. articles to profl. jours. NDEA fellow, 1967-70. Mem. Am. Inst. for Decision Scis., Inst. Mgmt. Sci., Assn. for Computing Machinery, Denton C. of C. Club: Denton Country. Office: N Tex State U BCIS Dept Denton TX 76203

ZANTZINGER, PAUL TAYLOR, real estate executive; b. N.Y.C., May 24, 1942; s. John S. and Eleanor (Taylor) Z.; m. Gail Lee Keenan, Oct. 19, 1974; children—Shelby, Heather. B.A., U. Pa., 1965, M.B.A., 1967. Lic. real estate broker, Ga. Credit analyst Chem. Bank, N.Y.C., 1969-70; fin. analyst Joseph E. Seagram's & Sons, Inc., N.Y.C., 1970-74; asst. to pres. Ga. Kraft Co., Atlanta, 1974-75; asst. v.p., corp. sec. Kraft Land Services, Inc., Atlanta, 1975-80; v.p. Hooker Barnes, Inc., Atlanta, 1980—; mem. faculty real estate sales and mktg. Farm and Land Inst., 1982-84; dir. World of Frames, Inc. Bd. dirs. Childbirth Edn. Assn., 1979-81, Childhood Autism Diagnostic and Ednl. Found., 1985—; mem. spl. task force Atlanta Regional Commn., 1982-83; mem. adv. task force on environ. impact of waste disposal Fulton County (Ga.), 1983-84. Served to lt. USNR, 1967-70. Named Farm and Land Inst. Realtor of Yr., 1980; Assn. Ga. Realtors and Exchangers Creative Sales award, 1979. Mem. Farm and Land Inst. (past pres.), Assn. Corp. Growth (past chpt. pres.), Fulton Developers Assn. (past pres.), Dekalb Developers Assn., Assn. Ga. Realtors and Exchangers (past v.p.), Navy League U.S. (met. Atlanta council 1975—, dir. 1977-81). Republican. Episcopalian. Lodge: Masons. Home: 3001 Greyfield Trace Marietta GA 30067 Office: 1875 Century Blvd Atlanta GA 30345

ZARKOOB, KHADIJEH SINGH, radiation oncologist, medical educator; b. Tehran, Iran, Oct. 24, 1950; came to U.S., 1978; naturalized, 1983; s. Asadollah and Robabeh (Pazooki) Z.; m. Kanwalcharan Singh Sahni, Feb. 15, 1978. M.D., Pahlavi U., 1976. Diplomate Am. Bd. Radiation Oncology. Intern, Nemazee Hosp., Saadi Hosp., Shiraz, Iran, 1976-77; asst. surgeon Richmond Meml. Hosp., Va., 1979; intern Med. Coll. Va., Va. Commonwealth U. Hosps., Richmond, 1980, resident in radiation oncology, 1980-83, mem. faculty, 1983-84; radiation oncologist Johnston-Willis Hosp., Chippenham Hosp., Petersburg Gen. Hosp.; cancer researcher radiology-radiation therapy, 1984—. Contbr. articles to profl. jours. Mem. Am. Soc. Therapeutic Radiologists, Radiol. Soc. N.Am., Am. Coll. Radiology, Med. Soc. Va., Richmond Acad. Medicine. Home: 1921 Camborne Rd Richmond VA 23298 Office: Johns Radiation Oncology Ctr Johnston-Willis Dr Richmond VA 23235

ZASLAW, JAMES WILLIAM, geologist, geology company executive; b. Chgo., Dec. 1, 1956; s. Stanford Gerard and Shirley Ann (McDowell) Z.; m. Elizabeth Ann Smelser, June 15, 1978 (div. 1981); m. Candace Louise Donaldsen, Jan. 27, 1983; children—Robert Zachary, Dane Erick. B.S. in Geology, U. Mont., 1979. Geologist, Amoco Prodn. Co., Denver, 1979-81; Ward Petroleum Corp., Enid, Okla., 1981-84; ptnr., geologist Z.G. Exploration Inc., Oklahoma City, 1984—. Mem. Am. Assn. Petroleum Geologists (assoc.), Rocky Mountain Assn. Geologists, Internat. Assn. Sedimentologist, Clays and Clay Mineral Soc. Republican. Baptist. Office: ZG Exploration Inc 701 NW 5th Oklahoma City OK 73102

ZAUNER, CHRISTIAN WALTER, exercise physiologist, physical education educator, exercise rehabilitation consultant; b. Phil., July 21, 1930; s. Philip Walter and Margaret Helen (Gilmor) Z.; m. Betty Ann Schwenk, Feb. 1, 1957; children—Beth, Ward, Joe. B.S., West Chester State, 1956; M.S., Syracuse U., 1957; Ph.D., So. Ill. U., 1963. Asst. prof. Temple U., Phila., 1963-65; prof. phys. edn. and medicine U. Fla., Gainesville, 1965-84; dirs. Sports Medicine Inst., Mt. Sinai Med. Ctr., Miami Beach, Fla., 1984—; cons. in exercise rehab. Hosp. Corp. Am.; cons. in sports medicine State of Kuwait, Arab Gulf. Served with USN, 1951-54; China; Korea. Grantee U. Fla., 1971, Am. Scandinavian Found., 1971, Fla. Blue Key, 1978. Fellow Am. Coll. Sports Medicine; mem. Am. Physiol. Soc., N.Y. Acad. Scis., AAHPER, Sigma Chi. Democrat. Roman Catholic. Club: Fla. Track. Contbr. numerous articles to various profl. jours. Home: 39 Camden Dr #7 Bal Harbour FL 33154 Office: Sports Medicine Inst Mt Sinai Med Ctr Miami Beach FL 33140

ZEBROWSKI, RACHEL KATHARINE WILLIAMS, resource company executive, architect; b. Cleve., July 25, 1951; d. David Rogerson, Jr. and Pauline Wilson (Bolton) Williams; m. Joseph Anthony Zebrowski, Jr., Sept. 29, 1984. B.A., Sarah Lawrence Coll., Bronxville, N.Y., 1972; M.Arch., UCLA, 1975. Lic. architect, Calif. Architect in tng. F.P. Lyman, Architect, Malibu, Calif., 1975-77; architect Charles Kober Assoc., Los Angeles, 1977-78, Coy Howard & Co., Venice, Calif., 1978-81, Urban Design Group, Tulsa, 1981-83; v.p. Williams Resources, Inc., Tulsa, 1981—; architect, tchr. City Building Edn., Los Angeles, 1978-81; pres. venture group Williams-McClintock, Tulsa, 1984—. Bd. dirs. Am. Theater Co., Tulsa, 1983-84, Downtown Tulsa Unltd., 1984. Democrat. Episcopalian. Avocations: photography; sports; construction.

ZECHELLA, ALEXANDER PHILIP, oil company executive, former U.S. Navy officer; b. Newport, Ky., 1920; s. Nicholas and Cecila (Rizzi) Z.; m. Jean Bary, June 24, 1942; children—Bary, Pamela, Amy. B.S. in Elec. Engring., U.S. Naval Acad., 1942, Rensselaer Poly Inst., 1947; M.S. in C.E., Rensselaer Poly Inst., 1948. Commd. ensign U.S. Navy, 1942, advanced through grades to comdr., 1953, served, 1939-53, destroyer duty World War II, Korean War; design engr. Nuclear Submarine Bettis Atomic Power Lab., Westinghouse Corp., Pitts., 1953-56, various positions in nuclear power reactors, 1961-71; pres. Offshore Power Systems subs. Westinghouse Corp., Jacksonville, Fla., 1972-79; corp. v.p. Westinghouse Corp, N.Y.C., 1979-80; design. mgr. Shippingport Power Sta., Pitts., 1956-59; constrn. mgr. prototype nuclear aircraft carrier USS Enterprise, Idaho Falls, Idaho, 1959-61; exec. v.p. Charter Co., chmn., pres. Charter Oil Co., Jacksonville, Fla., 1980—. Trustee St. Vincent's Hosp., Jacksonville. Mem. Am. Nuclear Soc., NAM (dir.), Tu Beta Pi, Chi Epsilon. Republican. Episcopalian. Clubs: River, Sawgrass Country. Lodges: Masons; Shriners. Office: Charter Oil Co One Charter Plaza PO Box 2017 Jacksonville FL 32203

ZEDER, JON WOODBRIDGE, lawyer; b. Detroit, Sept. 18, 1942; s. John Frederick and Winifred (Woodbridge) Z.; m. Judith Hainline, Apr. 6 1979; children—Nathan, Evan, Kara. A.B., Brown U., 1963; J.D. with honors, U. Fla., 1966. Assoc., Merson, Sawyer, Miami, Fla., 1966-67; adminstrv. counsel Hydrometals, Inc., Dallas, 1967-70; assoc., then ptnr. Paul & Thomson, Miami, 1970-83; ptnr. Thomson, Zeder, Bohrer, Werth, Adorno & Razook, Miami, 1983—. Mem. exec. com. citizens bd. U. Miami, 1981; patron U. Fla. Law Ctr. Assn., 1967; mem. Pillars Club, United Way, Miami, 1980. Mem. ABA, Dade

County Bar Assn. Democrat. Clubs: Biscayne Bay Yacht, Coral Reef Yacht, University, Brown U. (Miami). Home: 7810 SW 47th Ave Miami FL 33143 Office: 4900 Southeast Fin Ctr 200 S Biscayne Blvd Miami FL 33131

ZEDLER, EMPRESS YOUNG, psychologist; b. Abilene, Tex., Nov. 9, 1908; d. William James and Edith (Deaver) Young; m. Paul Louis Zedler, June 5, 1928. B.A., U. Tex., 1928, M.A., 1948, Ph.D., 1952. Chairperson dept. spl. edn. Southwest Tex. State U., San Marcos, 1960-78; pvt. practice child psychologist, Luling, Tex., 1978—. Fellow Am. Speech Lang. and Hearing Assn., Acad. Cerebral Palsy and Rehabilitative Medicine; mem. Assn. Children's Learning Disabilities (Founders Gold Key award), Am. Psychol. Assn., Tex. Psych. Assn., Tex. Speech Lang. and Hearing Assn. (Internat. award), Acad. Aphasia, Phi Beta Kappa. Episcopalian. Club: Country (Austin). Author: Listening for Speech Sounds, 1955; (with others) Principles of Childhood Learning Disabilities, 1972. Home: PO Box 465 Luling TX 78648

ZEFF, STEPHEN ADDAM, accounting educator; b. Chgo., July 26, 1933; s. Roy David and Hazel (Sex) Z.; B.S., U. Colo., 1955, M.S., 1957; M.B.A., U. Mich., 1960, Ph.D., 1962. Instr. U. Colo., 1955-57; teaching fellow, instr. U. Mich., 1958-61; asst. prof. acctg. Tulane U., New Orleans, 1961-63, assoc. prof., 1963-67, prof., 1967-78; prof. acctg. Rice U., Houston, 1978-79, Herbert S. Autrey prof. acctg., 1979—; vis. assoc. prof. U. Calif., Berkeley, 1964-65, U. Chgo., 1966; vis. prof. Instituto Tecnológico y de Estudios Superiores de Monterrey (Mexico), 1969, Victoria U., Wellington, N.Z., 1976, Harvard U., 1977-78, Northwestern U., 1982, 83, Macquarie U., Australia, 1984; spl. lectr., also hon. sr. Fulbright scholar Monash U., Australia, 1972. Mem. Am. Acctg. Assn., (dir. edn. 1969-71, pres. 1985-86), Am. Econ. Assn., Nat. Assn. Accountants, Fin. Execs. Inst., Accademia Italiana di Economia Aziendale, AAUP. Author: Uses of Accounting for Small Business, 1962, American Accounting Assn. Its First 50 Years, 1966; Forging Accounting Principles in Five Countries: A History and an Analysis of Trends, 1972; Forging Accounting Principles in Australia, 1973; Forging Accounting Principles in New Zealand, 1979. Editor: Business Schools and the Challenge of International Business, 1968; Asset Appreciation, Business Income and Price-Level Accounting: 1918-1935, 1976; The Accounting Postulates and Principles Controversy of the 1960s, 1982. Co-editor: Financial Accounting Theory, Vol. I, 1964, rev., 1973, 85, Vol. II, 1969. Book rev. editor Accounting Rev., 1962-66, editor, 1977-82; founder, editor Boletín Interamericano de Contabilidad, 1968-71. Contbr. articles to profl. jours. Home: 4545 Acacia Bellaire TX 77401

ZEGEL, WILLIAM CASE, professional services corporation executive, consultant; b. Port Jefferson, N.Y., Aug. 4, 1940; s. James William and Helen Alida (Case) Z.; m. Carole Lee Eastman, Aug. 11, 1962; children—Laura Moore, William Eastman. Sc.D. in Chem. Engring., Stevens Inst. Tech., 1965, M.S. in Chem. Engring., 1962, M.E. with high honors, 1961. Registered profl. engr., Fla., Ala., Ga., Tex.; diplomate Am. Acad. Environ. Engrs. Research engr. Allied Chem. Corp., Morristown, N.J., 1964-68; sr. research engr. Scott Research Labs., Plumsteadville, Pa., 1968-72; sr. assoc. Ryckman Edgerly Tomlinson & Assocs., Creve Coeur, Mo., 1972-75; v.p. Environ. Sci. & Engring., Inc., Gainesville, Fla., 1975-79; pres. Water and Air Research, Inc., Gainesville, 1979—; v.p. Spar Group, Gainesville, 1982—; exec. sec. IGWT Ptnrs., Gainesville, 1983—; pres. CTS, Inc., Gainesville, 1983-85; mem. engring. adv. council Coll. Engring., U. Fla., guest lectr. on environ. topics. Contbg. author: Environmental Engineers Handbook, 1972. Patentee air and water pollution control. Contbr. articles to tech. jours. Chmn. Gainesville Salvation Army Adv. Bd., 1981-85; moderator United Ch. Gainesville, 1980-82; chmn. Gainesville Navy League, 1980-83; pres. Alachua County Orgn. Rural Needs, 1977-78; mem. Commn. of Vision 2000 for Alachua County. Mem. Air Pollution Control Assn. (bd. dirs. 1983—, v.p. 1985), Fla. Engring. Soc. (cert. continued profl. devel. 1978—), Am. Inst. Chem. Engrs., Am. Inst. Cons. Engrs., Tau Beta Pi (Disting. Engr. 1981). Lodge: Rotary (bd. dirs. 1979-80). Avocations: sailing; running; camping. Home: 11011 NW 12th Pl Gainesville FL 32606 Office: Water & Air Research Inc 6821 SW Archer Rd Gainesville FL 32608

ZEILLER, WARREN, retired aquarium executive; b. Weehawken, N.J., Nov. 11, 1929; s. Arthur Herman and Ruth (Preusser) Z.; B.Sc. in Animal Husbandry, Colo. A&M Coll., 1955; M.A. in Bus., Mich. State U., 1957; m. Judith Marion Ricciardi, May 27, 1961; children—Dianne Leigh, Todd Kiersted. Mgmt. trainee Grand Union Co., 1956-58; corp. sec., salesman Art Zeiller Co., Inc., Allendale, N.J., 1958-60; salesman Joseph Abraham Ford Co., Miami, Fla, 1960; with Miami Seaquarium, 1960-85, curator, 1962-85, v.p., gen. mgr., 1977-85, ret., 1985; pres. Images of Art, Inc., Coral Gables, Fla.; lectr., cons. in field, TV appearances. Chmn. football com. Jr. Orange Bowl Com., 1975—, treas., 1984-85; adv. bd. Coral Gables War Meml. Youth Center, 1973—, pres., 1981-83; mem. Fla. Hospitality Industry Council, 1983—, Fla. Tourism Adv. Com., 1983—, Met. Dade Beacon Council, 1985; bd. dirs. Dade Marine Inst., Humane Soc. Greater Miami. Served with USN, 1951-55. Fellow Am. Assn. Zool. Parks and Aquariums; mem. Am. Fisheries Soc., Tropical Audubon Soc., Fla. Attractions Assn. (v.p. 1981-82, pres. 1983-84), Mus. and Art Center, Miami Charity Horse Show Assn., Colo. State U. Alumni Assn., Sigma Chi. Republican. Methodist. Club: Rotary (pres. Coral Gables 1978-79). Author: Tropical Marine Invertebrates of Southern Florida and the Bahama Islands, 1974; Tropical Marine Fishes of Southern Florida and the Bahama Islands, 1975; also articles. Patentee surg. cast and cast removal saw. Home: 5016 SW 72nd Ave Miami FL 33155 Office: Miami Seaquarium 4400 Rickenbacker Causeway Miami FL 33149

ZELENY, MARJORIE PFEIFFER (MRS. CHARLES ELLINGSON ZELENY), psychologist; b. Balt., Mar. 31, 1924; d. Lloyd Armitage and Mable (Willian) Pfeiffer; B.A., U. Md., 1947; M.S., U. Ill., 1949, postgrad., 1951-54; m. Charles Ellingson Zeleny, Dec. 11, 1950 (dec.); children—Ann Douglas, Charles Timberlake. Vocat. counseling psychologist VA, Balt., 1947-48; asst. U. Ill., Urbana, 1948-50, research asso. Bur. Research, 1952-53; chief psychologist dept. neurology and psychiatry Ohio State U. Coll. Medicine, Columbus, 1950-51; research psychologist, cons., Tucson and Washington, 1954—. Mem. Am. Psychol. Assn., D.C. Psychol. Assn., AAAS, Soc. Psychol. Study Social Issues, DAR, Mortar Bd., Delta Delta Delta, Sigma Delta Epsilon, Psi Chi, Sigma Tau Epsilon. Roman Catholic. Home: 6825 Wemberly Way McLean VA 22101

ZELEY, JUAN ADELBERTO, steel company executive; b. Budapest, Hungary, Feb. 13, 1921; immigrated to Venezuela, 1953, naturalized, 1956; s. Bela and Elena (Drentea) Z.; Ph.D. in Econs., Tech. U. Budapest, 1944; postgrad. student Hamburg (W.Ger.), Berlin and Paris, 1944-48; m. LaVerna Perley Luce, Nov. 10, 1959. Self-employed in Buenos Aires, 1949-52; sales Hyster Life Truck Co., Caracas, Venezuela, 1952-66; pres., Tanaka de Venezuela C.A., Caracas, 1967—, Incolco, C.A.A., 1975—, Didier de Venezuela, C.A., 1976—, Karrena de Venezuela C.A., 1980—, Didier Equipos Industriales C.A., 1980—, Aviation Maintenance, Inc., Ft. Lauderdale, Fla., 1980—. Mem. Civil Emergency Relief Commn., 1968—. Mem. Aircraft Owners and Pilots Assn. Roman Catholic. Clubs: Aero (Caracas). Office: 1575 W Commercial Blvd Fort Lauderdale Exec Airport Fort Lauderdale FL 33309

ZELL, DOLORES PFAFFENDORF, legislative aide; b. Miami, Fla., July 13, 1944; d. George and Pearl (Watford) Pfaffendorf; B.S. in Edn., William Carey Coll., 1969; M.A. in Coll. Personnel Adminstrn., U. Miami, 1971, postgrad., 1977—. Placement dir. William Carey Coll., Hattiesburg, Miss., 1967-69; asst. dir. Pearson Hall, U. Miami (Fla.), 1969-70; customer service rep. Burdines, Miami, 1970-76; tchr. A.L. Lewis Elem. Sch., Miami Public Schs., 1970-75, area coordinator sch. vol. program, 1975-77, tchr. R.R. Moton Elem. Sch., 1979-80, Coral Reef Elem. Sch., 1979; asst. prin. Opa Locka Elem. Sch. and Bel Aire Elem. Sch., Dade County (Fla.) Public Schs., 1980-81; legis. aide state rep. Dexter Lehtinen, Fla., 1981—; adj. prof. Fla. Internat. U., Miami-Dade Community Coll. Coordinator Lehtinen legis. campaign, 1978, 80. Tchr. Sunday sch. Bapt. Ch.; officer Young Democrats; mem. S. Dade Democratic Club. Mem. Dade County Sch. Adminstrs. Assn., Am. Bus. Women's Assn., Assn. Elem. Sch. Prins., Assn. Supervision and Curriculum Devel., Internat. Reading Assn., Nat. Sch. Vol. Program, Inc., S. Dade Reading Council, Phi Delta Kappa. Club: Briar Bay. Contbr. articles to profl. jours. Home: 13323 SW 103 Pl Miami FL 33176 Office: 18 House Office Bldg The Capitol Tallahassee FL 32301

ZELLERS, CARL FREDRICK, JR., railway executive; b. Wilmington, N.C., Apr. 25, 1932; s. Carl Fredrick and Bessie Jane (Jackson) Z.; m. Betty B. Burroughs, Dec. 8, 1984; children—Patricia, Carl Fredrick, Pamela. Cert. internal auditor. With Atlantic Coast Line R.R. Co., Wilmington, 1950-62, chief clk., 1958-62; sec.-treas. High Point, Thomasville & Denton R.R. Co. (N.C.), 1963-65; with Fla. East Coast Ry., St. Augustine, 1968—, sec., 1974-76, v.p., 1977—, dir., 1982—; pres. Comml. Realty & Devel. Co. div. Fla. East Coast Industries, Inc., 1984—. Mem. Tax Execs. Inst., Fin. Execs. Inst., Inst. Internal Auditors. Republican. Methodist. Home: 22 S Tifton Way Ponte Vedra Beach FL 32082 Office: 1 Malaga St Saint Augustine FL 32084

ZEMEK, MELVILLE MASON, engineer; b. Chgo., June 5, 1919; s. Michael Joseph and Sadie Anna (Olson) Z.; divorced; children—Michael, Karen. B.S. in Elec. Engring., Ga. Inst. Tech., 1940; M.B.A., U. Buffalo, 1948. Registered profl. engr., N.Y., N.J., Tex., Ill. Engr., Factory Mutual, 1940-42; mgr. engr., 1946-77; asst. v.p., engr. Johnson Higgins, Dallas, 1977-82; engr. AID Cons. Engrs., Dallas, 1982—. Contbr. articles to mags. Served as maj. USAF, 1942-46, ETO. Mem. Soc. Fire Protection Engrs., Am. Soc. Safety Engrs., Soc. Wireless Pioneers, Mensa, Intertel, Eta Kappa Nu. Lodges: Masons, Shriners. Avocations: extra class amateur radio operator. Home: 5224 N Peninsula Little Elm TX 75068 Office: AID Cons Engrs 10830 Composite Dr Dallas TX 75220

ZENDELS, DAVID A., financial executive; b. Bklyn., Aug. 28, 1938; s. Morris and Helen (Zelmanow) Z.; m. Norma Gerson, Aug. 30, 1959; children—Michael, Phyllis. B.M.E., Cooper Union, 1959; M.B.A., U. Bridgeport, 1966. Mgr. shop ops. Gen. Electric Co., various locations, 1959-67; various positions Huyck Corp., Wake Forest, N.C., 1967-75, treas., 1975-80; fin. cons., Raleigh, N.C., 1981-82; treas. Peden Steel Co., Raleigh, 1982-85; treas. Peden Devel. Corp., 1985—. Vice pres. Blumenthal Nursing Home, 19—. Lodge: B'nai B'rith (bd. govs.). Office: 1815 N Boulevard Raleigh NC 27604

ZENGER, GEORGE H., nuclear radiologist; b. Cin., Feb. 14, 1929; s. George and Sophie E. (Heitfeld) Z.; m. June Caul, Oct. 7, 1954; children—George Caul, Richard Glen. A.B., Vanderbilt U., 1949; M.D., U. Tenn., 1954. Diplomate Am. Bd. Nuclear Medicine. Resident, Bapt. Med. Ctrs., Birmingham, Ala., 1959-62; pathology U. Tenn., 1953; occupational medicine Lloyd Noland Found., Fairfield, Ala., 1956, 59; instr. radiology residency program Bapt. Med. Ctr., Birmingham, 1962-74; chmn. dept. nuclear medicine Bapt. Med. Ctr., Princeton and Montclair, N.J., 1962-74, Humana Hosp. Audubon, Louisville, 1974—, East End Meml. Hosp., Birmingham, 1962-74; clin. instr. dept. radiology and nuclear medicine U. Ala., 1972-74; clin. instr. dept. radiology U. Louisville, 1979—. Bd. dirs. Jefferson County unit Am. Cancer Soc., 1979-84. Served to capt. M.C., U.S. Army, 1956-58. Mem. Jefferson County Med. Soc., Ky. Med. Assn., Am. Coll. Radiology, Health Physics Soc., Soc. Nuclear Medicine, Greater Louisville Radiol. Assn., Radiol. Soc. N.Am. Republican. Baptist. Clubs: Antique Auto of Am., Rolls Royce of Am., Holstein Assn. Mailing Address: Box 17097 Louisville KY 40217 Home: 5000 Dunvegan Rd Louisville KY 40222 Office: 1 Audubon Plaza Dr Louisville KY 40217

ZENKE, LARRY, educational administrator. Supt. of schs. Tulsa. Office: PO Box 45208 Tulsa OK 74145*

ZENTMEYER, JOHN EDWIN, JR., communication and computer systems co. exec.; b. Winston-Salem, N.C., Sept. 9, 1933; s. John Edwin and Eulalia Francis (Lewis) Z.; B.E.E., U. Va., 1958; m. April Ann Zentmeyer; children—John Edwin, Donald Lansing, James Robert, Deborah Kim, April Elizabeth Anne. With Lee Telephone Co., Martinsville, Va., 1951-56; pres., dir. Electronic Concepts, Charlottesville, Va., 1963-68; pres. ECI div. ATO, Charlottesville, 1967-71; pres., dir. Internat. Communications, Charlottesville, 1971-72; pres., dir. Sound Concepts, Inc., Charlottesville, 1972-76, The Zentmeyer Co., Inc., Tampa, Fla., 1976—; pres. Nat. Telecommunications, Tampa, 1976—, Tampa Airways Inc., 1980—. Mem. IRE, IEEE, NFISB, Tampa C. of C., Tampa Mus., Assn. Christian Athletes. Club: Carrollwood Country. Office: 5312 W Crenshaw St Tampa FL 33614

ZEPKE, BRENT ERIC, lawyer; b. Camden, N.J., Mar. 28, 1943; s. George W. and June E. (Stackhouse) Z.; m. Anne Louise Whitaker, Aug. 26, 1966; children—Chad Eric, Hollie Anne, Grant Austin. B.A., U.N.C., 1967; M.S. in Mgmt., Clemson U., 1969; J.D., U. Tenn., 1973; LL.M. magna cum laude, Temple U., 1977. Bar: Tenn. 1974, D.C. 1975, Pa. 1975, N.J. 1976, Tex. 1981. Instr. indsl. engring. Greenville (S.C.) Inst. Tech., 1968-69; instr. U. Tenn., Knoxville, 1969-74; research contract atty. gen. State of Tenn., 1973; atty. Gulf Oil Corp., Phila., 1974-79; labor counsel Gulf Oil Corp., Houston, 1979-81; mem. firm Pepper, Hamilton & Scheetz, Los Angeles, 1981-83; sr. atty. Coastal Corp., 1983—; adj. prof. mgmt. Temple U., 1976-77; mem. faculty profl. seminars of Practicing Law Inst., N.Y. Law Jour., Exec. Enterprises and Harcourt Brace; participant Nat. Inst. Trial Advocacy, U. Colo., Nat. Coll. Advocacy, Harvard U. Stewart F. Brown fellow Clemson U. Mem. ABA, Tex. Bar Assn., D.C. Bar Assn., Pa. Bar Assn., Tenn. Bar Assn., N.J. Bar Assn., Contemporary Authors, Phi Alpha Delta. Author: Industrial Management, 1972; Mathematical Models for Managers, 1973; Products and the Consumer, 1974; Labor Law, 1977; Business Statistics, 1980; Law for Non-Lawyers, 1983; Personnel Directors Legal Guide, 1984; contbr. articles to profl. jours. Office: Coastal Tower 9 Greenway Plaza Suite 836 Houston TX 77046

ZERFOSS, LESTER FRANK, management consultant, educator; b. Mountaintop, Pa., Nov. 2, 1903; s. Clinton and Mabel (Wilcox) Z.; B.A. cum laude, Pa. State U., 1926, M.Ed., 1934, D.Ed., 1958; m. Harriet Mildred Cary, Dec. 21, 1928 (dec. Dec. 16, 1978); children—Patricia Anne (Mrs. Thomas Sibben), Clinton Cary, Robert Williamson; m. 2d, Irma J. Allen, July 12, 1980. Coll. tchr., pub. sch. adminstr., Pa., 1928-41; supr. design, devel. Gen. Motors Inst., 1942-46; head supervisory devel. Detroit Edison Co., 1946-52; corporate tng. dir. Am. Enka Corp. (N.C.), 1952-59, dir. indsl. relations, mgmt. services, 1952-66, mgmt. cons. for managerial and tech. devel., 1966-68; asso. prof. psychology Asheville-Biltmore Coll., 1966-68; research prof. developmental psychology, dir. mgmt. devel. programs U. N.C. at Asheville, 1968-74, prof. mgmt. and psychology, chmn. dept. mgmt., 1974-76, prof. emeritus, 1976—; pres. L.F. Zerfoss Assos., Inc., 1977—. Mem. bd., head mgmt. devel. com. N.C. Personnel Bd., 1966-70; cons. to gov. for mgmt. devel., 1970-73; mem. Southeastern Regional Manpower Adv. Com., 1966-70, N.C. Adv. Com. for Community Colls. Trustee Brevard Coll., Asheville-Buncombe Tech. Inst. Recipient Distinguished Service award U. N.C., 1976. Mem. Am. Mgmt. Assn. (lectr. mgmt. devel. seminars), Nat. Soc. Advancement Mgmt. (profl. mgr. citation 1962), Am. Soc. Tng. and Devel., N.C. Psychol. Assn., Phi Delta Kappa (Disting. Service award), Kappa Phi Kappa, Kappa Delta Pi, Delta Sigma Phi. Rotarian. Author: Developing Professional Personnel in Business, Industry and Government, 1977. Contbg. author: Training and Development Handbook, 1968; Management Handbook for Plant Engineers, 1978; Psychology in Action, 1978; Personnel Administration in the Collegium, 1982; contbr. articles to profl. jours. Home and Office: Box 386 Liberty SC 29657

ZERMAN, WILLIAM SHERIDAN, fraternal organization administrator; b. Toledo, Ohio; children—Carol Margaret, William Sheridan, Gregory Blackmore. B.S., U. Mich., M.S; L.H.D. (hon.), Athens State Coll. Field sec. Phi Gamma Delta, 1949-51; mem. devel. staff Ohio-Mich. office Nat. Assn. Mfrs., 1951-52; asst. dean of men U. Mich., Ann Arbor, 1952-56; dean of men Ohio Wesleyan U., Delaware, 1956-59; exec. sec. Phi Gamma Delta, 1959-78, exec. dir., 1978—, editor, 1967—. Served with U.S. Army; ETO. Mem. fin. com. So. Hills Methodist Ch.; past chmn. bd. Bluegrass Area Salvation Army; past cabinet mem. United Way; chmn. Lexington Mayor's Com. to Survey City/County Vehicles; mem. student publs. bd. U. Ky. Mem. Am. Personnel and Guidance Assn., Sales and Mktg. Execs. Internat., Lexington C. of C. (bd. dirs.), Am. Soc. Assn. Execs., Sigma Delta Chi (v.p.). Lodges: Rotary, Masons, Shriners (Lexington). Office: 1201 Red Mile Rd Lexington KY 40504

ZERNER, MICHAEL CHARLES, chemistry and physics educator, consultant, researcher; b. Boston, Jan. 31, 1940; s. Maurice Bernard and Blanche (Deutsch) Z.; m. Anna Gunilla Fojerstam, May 5, 1966; children—Erik Mark, Emma Danielle. B.S., Carnegie Mellon Inst., 1961; M.S., Harvard U., 1962, Ph.D., 1966; postdoctoral U. Uppsala, (Sweden), 1968-70. Asst. prof. U. Guelph (Ont., Can.), 1970-74, assoc. prof., 1974-79, prof., 1979-82, adj. prof., 1982—; prof. chemistry and physics U. Fla., Gainesville, 1981—; cons. in theoretical chemistry. Served to capt. U.S. Army, 1966-68. Recipient certificate U.S. Army Materials Command, 1975; NIH fellow, 1968-70; Nat. Sci. and Engring. Research Council of Can., grantee. Fellow AAAS; mem. Am. Chem. Soc. Am. Inst. Physics, N.Y. Acad. Scis., Sigma Xi and others. Patentee in photoconduction and polymer sci.; co-editor Procs. Internat. Conf. Quantum Chemistry, Biology and Pharmacology, 1978; Internat. Congress Quantum Chemistry, 1983, 84. assoc. editor Internat. Jour. Quantum Chemistry; contbr. pubs. to profl. lit. Office: Dept Chemistry U Fla Gainesville FL 32611

ZEROF, HERBERT GODDARD, psychologist; b. N.Y.C., Aug. 18, 1934; s. Albert and Mary Jane (Allen) Z.; m. Aletta Lee McDonald, July 5, 1959; children—Linda Marie, Cheryl Anne. A.B., Stetson U., 1955; B.D., Southeastern Theol. Sem., 1958, Th.M., 1961; Ed.D., U. Pa., 1968. Lic. marital and family therapist, N.C. Assoc. prof. U. N.C., Charlotte, 1971-74; chief psychologist Episcopal Hosp. Community Mental Health Center, Phila., 1969-71; psychologist Swarthmore (Pa.) Coll., 1964-71; sr. instr. dept. psychiatry, Hahnemann Med. Coll., Phila., 1967-69; instr. dept. psychiatry, U. Pa., Phila., 1964-67; assoc. dir. dept. pastoral care Bowman Gray Sch. Medicine, Winston-Salem, 1961-64; dir. Family Therapy Ctr., Charlotte, N.C., 1971—; Eastern regional dir. Family Communication Skills Ctr., San Francisco, 1974-80; cons. U.S. Armed Forces; vis. lectr. Australia and N.Z., Nat. Marriage Guidance Clinics, agys., univs.; cons., dir. community edn. Ctr. for Studies of Suicide Prevention, NIMH, 1968-71. NIMH fellow, 1963-64; recipient Robert L. Dickinson award Am. Assn. Marriage and Family Therapy, 1964. Fellow Am. Orthopsychiat. Assn.; mem. Am. Psychol. Assn., Am. Assn. Marital and Family Therapy, Am. Acad. Polit. and Social Studies, Phi Delta Kappa. Democrat. Baptist. Author: Finding Intimacy, 1978, German edit., 1985; contbr. articles to profl. jours. Home: 3126 Ferncliff Rd Charlotte NC 28211 Office: 2225 Park Rd Charlotte NC 28203

ZICK, LEONARD O., manufacturing executive; b. St. Joseph, Mich., Jan. 16, 1905; s. Otto J. and Hannah (Heyn) Z.; student Western State U., Kalamazoo; m. Anna Essig, June 27, 1925 (dec. May 1976); children—Rowene (Mrs. A. C. Neidow), Arlene (Mrs. Thomas Anton), Constance Mae (Mrs. Hilary Snell), Shirley Ann (Mrs. John Vander Ley) (dec.); m. 2d, Genevieve E. Zick, Nov. 3, 1977. Sr. partner firm Zick, Campbell & Rose, South Bend, Ind., 1928-48; sec.-treas. C. M. Hall Lamp Co., Detroit, 1948-51, pres. 1951-54, chmn. bd., 1954-56; pres., treas., dir. Allen Electric & Equipment Co. (now Allen Group, Inc.), Kalamazoo, 1954-56, The Lithibar Co., Holland, Mich., 1956-61; v.p., treas. Crampton Mfg. Co., 1961-63; mgr. corp. fin. dept. Manley, Bennett, McDonald & Co., Detroit, 1963-68; mgr. Leonard O. Zick & Assos., Holland, 1968—; dir. Eberhard's Foods, Inc. (Grand Rapids), Kandu Industries, Inc. Vice chmn. Army-Navy Munitions Bd., 194-46; asst. to vice chmn. War Prodn. Bd., Washington, 1941-46; former mem. Mich. Republican Central Com. Mem. Nat. Assn. Accts. (past nat. v.p., dir.), Mich. Self Insurers Assn. (past pres.), Fin. Execs. Inst., Stuart Cameron McLeod Soc. (past pres.). Lutheran. Clubs: Detroit Athletic, Rotary (Paul Harris fellow), Renaissance (Detroit); Peninsular (Grand Rapids); Holland (Mich.) Country; Union League (Chgo.); Macawtawa Yacht; East Bay Country (Largo, Fla.). Home: 849 Brook Village Holland MI 49423 also Penthouse Greens 1609F The Fairway 225 Country Club Dr Largo FL 33541

ZIDEK, BERNICE LOUISE (MRS. STEPHEN P. ZIDEK), wire manufacturing company executive; b. Chgo., Oct. 10, 1906; d. Albert and Bessie (Kaberna) Vonder; diploma Englewood (Ill.) Secretarial Coll., 1923; m. Stephen Paul Zidek, July 22, 1925; children—Louise Ann Zidek Pavlin, Charles Edward. Asst. to asst. mgr. Emerson Drug Co., Chgo., 1923-24; office mgr. Van Dyke Industries, Chgo., 1936-38; ptnr. Midland Metal Products Co., Chgo., 1941—. Troop leader to leader trainer Lone Tree Area council Girl Scouts U.S.A., 1938-68. Recipient Thank You award Girl Scouts U.S.A., 1957. Mem. Nat., Fla. State assns. parliamentarians, Am. Guild Flower Arrangers, Floralia, Nat. Council State Garden Clubs (life), Fla. Fedn. Garden Clubs (life), Nat. Council Flower Show Judges (cert. master judge), Freedoms Found. at Valley Forge. Republican. Roman Catholic. Clubs: Bauhinia Garden Circle (pres. 1965-67), Federated Garden Circles of Ft. Lauderdale (pres. 1974-75), Coral Springs Garden, Moraine Valley (Ill.) Parliamentary Unit, Women's Civic Coral Ridge Yacht (Ft. Lauderdale); Country of Coral Springs. Home: 2791 NW 112th Ave Coral Springs FL 33065

ZIEBOLD, JOHN FREDERICK, bank executive; b. Charleston, W.Va., Oct. 12, 1938; s. William Owens and Helen Pearl (Townsend) Z.; m. Page Tucker McFall, Jan. 26, 1962; children—Anne Beury, Mary Townsend, Margaret Tucker. B.S., Yale U., 1962; Nat. Grad. Trust Sch., Northwestern U., 1970-72; Nat. Comml. Lending Sch., U. Okla., 1976. Vice pres. Spartan Gas Co., Charleston, W.Va., 1962-68; asst. trust officer to v.p. Kanawha Valley Bank, Charleston, 1968-74, v.p., 1974—. Mem., Sunrise Found Bd., 1980-85, treas., 1982-84; past bd. dirs. Goodwill Industries of Kanawha Valley. Mem. Robert Morris Assocs. Republican. Episcopalian. Clubs: Rotary (pres., dir.); Edgewood Country (pres., dir.). Office: One Valley Sq Charleston WV 25301

ZIEGLER, AVIS BOSSHART, management and development consultant, writer; b. N.Y.C., Mar. 13, 1931; d. Mark Kenneth and Beatrice (Tepper) Gelber; m. Richard Allan Bosshart (dec. 1965); children—Gail Bosshart Kenmore, Michael Bosshart Ziegler, Catherine Ann Ziegler, John Frederick Ziegler; m. John G. Ziegler, 1969 (div. 1980). Student Purdue U., 1947-48, writer's program State U. Iowa, 1949-50; B. Edn. with honors, Nat. Coll., Edn., Evanston, Ill., 1963; postgrad. Northwestern U., 1964-65. Copywriter Fletcher Richards Advt. Agy., N.Y.C., 1948-49, teaching intern Evanston Pub. Schs., 1963; tchr. pvt. schs., Evanston, 1963-65; staff editor, project dir., sr. in-house author Sci. Research Assocs., subs. IBM, Chgo., 1965-68; cons. mgmt. and devel., writer Profl. Systems Design, Fort Lauderdale, Fla., 1968—; freelance author; owner, operator rental apts., Fort Lauderdale, 1969—. Author: Doctors' Administrative Program, 8 vols., 1977-82; author curriculum materials. Mem. AAAS, Am. Mgmt. Assn., Assn. Ednl. Communications and Tech., Assn. Supervision and Curriculum Devel., Nat. Sci. Tchrs. Assn., Nat. League Am. Pen Women, Am. Mus. Natural History, Fort Lauderdale Mus. Art, Fort Lauderdale Opera Soc., Fort Lauderdale Symphony Soc., Met. Mus. Art. Mem. Ch. of Religious Science. Clubs: Lake Shore (Chgo.); Le Club Internat., Venice of Am. (Fort Lauderdale). Home and Office: 2955 NE 60th St Fort Lauderdale FL 33308

ZIEGLER, JOHN ALAN, political scientist, educator; b. Belleville, Ill., Jan. 28, 1933; s. John Wendell and Georgia Elizabeth (Reppel) Z.; B.S., So. Ill. U., Carbondale, 1955, M.S., 1956; Rotary Found. fellow, St. Andrews (Scotland) U., 1956-57; Ph.D., Syracuse U., N.Y., 1970; m. Carol Ruth Alcorn, June 15, 1963; children—Mimi, Robin. Asst. prof. polit. sci. and social sci. Calif. State U., Hayward, 1966-72; lectr. Am. civilization Calif. State Poly. U., Pomona, 1972-74; prof. polit. sci. Hendrix Coll., Conway, Ark., 1974—, also coordinator Hendrix-Oxford and Hendrix-U. London programs, head social sci. area, 1978-82, chmn. dept. polit. sci. and history, 1974-83. Served with AUS, 1957-60. Mem. Am. Polit. Sci. Assn., AAUP, Friends London Sch. Econs., Friends Churchill Meml., Am. Friends Wilton Park, Center for Study of Presidency, ACLU, London Topographical Soc., Nat Trust Historic Preservation, Soc. Sussex Downsmen (life). Mem. United Ch. Christ. Club: Dundee (Scotland) Curling. Home: 14 Oakdale Dr Conway AR 72032 Office: Hendrix Coll Conway AR 72032

ZIEGLER, KATHRYN WEISS, librarian; b. Wiesbaden, W.Ger., July 29, 1957, came to U.S., 1958; d. Norris Edward and Arla June (Smith) Weiss; m. Mark Hamilton Ziegler, Aug. 18, 1979; 1 child. B.A., Kans. State U., 1978; M.L.S., Emporia State U., 1979. Law librarian Okla. Dept. Libraries, Oklahoma City, 1981; pub. service librarian Met. Library System, Oklahoma City, 1982-83; br. librarian Harris County Pub. Library, Houston, 1983-85; cons. Tech. Evaluation and Cons., Bethany, Okla., 1982. Spanish lang. materials reviewer Lector Jour., 1983—. Mem. Okla. Omniplex, 1982, Harris County Heritage Soc., Houston, 1983-84; vol. Okla. Theater Ctr., Oklahoma City, 1982-83. Home: 3719 Beckett Ridge Humble TX 77338

ZIEGLER, ROBERT GEORGE, chemistry educator; b. The Dalles, Oreg., Apr. 24, 1924; s. Herman and Robbie Beryl (Eslinger) Z.; m. Martha Grace Brindley, July 10, 1953; children—David Carl, Ruth Jeannette, Robbie Ann. B.A., Oreg. State U., 1948, M.S., 1951; Ph.D., U. Tenn., 1969. Control chemist Barium Products, Inc., Modesto, Calif., 1948-49; research chemist Allied Chem. Corp., Hopewell, Va., 1952-57; from assoc. prof. to prof. chemistry Lincoln Meml. U., Harrogate, Tenn., 1957—. Served with inf. U.S. Army, 1944-46. Recipient Sidney Sullivan medallion Lincoln Meml. U., 1981. Fellow Tenn. Acad. Sci.; mem. Am. Chem. Soc., Am. Sci. Affiliation, Am. Assn. Physics Tchrs., Sigma Xi. Baptist. Club: Gideons (pres. 1984—). Avocations: gardening; playing piano and organ; reading. Home: Route 1 Box 19 Harrogate TN 37752 Office: Lincoln Meml U Harrogate TN 37752

ZIEMAN, MICHAEL A., hospital administrator; b. Mobile, Ala., Aug. 23, 1951; s. Stephen A. and Shirley G. (Pohner) Z.; m. Frances Gale Peters, May

1, 1976; children—Michael, Genevieve, Valerie. B.S., Auburn U., 1974; M.P.H., Tulane U., 1976. Cert. mental health adminstr., Ala. Mental health technician Tranquillaire Hosp., Mobile, Ala., 1974-75; adminstrv. trainee Mobile County Bd. Health, 1975-76; adminstrv. asst. Southland Hosp., Mobile, 1976-78, asst. adminstr., 1978; assoc. adminstr. Retreat Hosp., Decatur, Ala., 1978-79; chief exec. officer, adminstr. Charter Woods Hosp., Dothan, Ala., 1979—. Vice chmn. allocations com. Wiregrass United Way, Dothan, 1984. Recipient William Winton Watkins III award Auburn U., 1972; named Outstanding Young Man of Am., U.S. Jr. C. of C., 1979. Mem. Am. Coll. Hosp. Adminstrs. (candidate), Am. Hosp. Assn. (sect. rep.), Am. Pub. Health Assn., Nat. Assn. Pvt. Psychiat. Hosps. (legis. com.), Ala. Assn. Hosp. Execs., Assn. U.S. Army, Dothan C. of C., Omicron Delta Kappa. Roman Catholic. Lodge: Rotary (Dothan). Avocations: boating; deep sea fishing; sailboat racing. Office: Charter Woods Hosp 700 Cottonwood Rd Dothan AL 36302

ZIEMANN, ROBERT LEWIS, accountant; b. Southwick, Idaho, Jan. 23, 1927; s. Gus H. and Wilda (Keeney) Z.; student Oreg. State Coll., 1945-46, U. Idaho, 1948-49; B.B.A., U. Houston, 1952. Accountant, Briscoe, House & Stovall, C.P.A.s, Houston, 1954, Mattison & Riquelmy, C.P.A.s, Houston, 1954-61, Harris, Kerr, Forster & Co., C.P.A.s, Houston, 1961-65; self-employed as C.P.A., Houston, 1965—. Served with USAAF, 1946-47. Elk. Home: 14803 Cypress Meadow Cypress TX also PO Box 66681 Houston TX 77266 Office: 7709 Long Point Houston TX 77055

ZIESCHE, SHIRLEY STEEB, educational administrator; b. Pitts., June 27, 1923; married. B.A. in Sociology, U. Pitts., 1944, M.Ed. in Elem. Edn., 1965. Tchr. presch., 1952-62; tchr., Shady Side Acad., Pitts., 1962-68; tchr. Bd. Public Instrn., Sarasota County, Sarasota, Fla., 1968-71, elem. math. specialist, 1971-74, supr. math. K-12, 1974-85, curriculum supr., 1985—. Judge, clk. Local Election Bd., 1952-53. Cert. in sch. supervision, curriculum and math., elem., jr. coll. Mem. Sarasota Council Tchrs. Math. (v.p. 1972-74), Nat. Council Tchrs. Math., Fla. Council Tchrs. Math., Assn. Supervision and Curriculum Devel., Fla. Assn. Supervision and Curriculum Devel., Fla. Assn. Sch. Adminstrs., Assn. Childhood Edn. Internat. (bd. dirs. Fla. chpt. 1984—), Fla. Assn. Math. Suprs. (sec.-treas. 1976-78, pres.-elect 1979-80, pres. 1980-81), Internat. Council Edn. of Tchrs., Fla. Assn. Instrn. Suprs. and Adminstrs. (bd. dirs. 1981-83), Research Council for Diagnostic and Prescriptive Math., Sch. Sci. and Math. Assn., Math. Assn. Am., Delta Kappa Gamma (v.p. Beta Upsilon chpt.). Author: Birds: Activity Books I and II; Understanding Place Value, A.T., 1970. Home: 5529 Cape Leyte Dr Sarasota FL 34242 Office: Bay Area Basics Plus 2901 W Tamiami Circle Sarasota FL 33580

ZILINSKY, MEL, business executive, consultant; b. N.Y.C., Aug. 8, 1931; s. Irving and Gertrude (Schrader) Z.; m. Myrna Mittler, Mar. 12, 1962; 1 child, Alan Ira. B.B.A., Baruch Coll., 1959. Chief fin. officer various cos., N.Y.C., 1949-72; pres. New Shack Inc., Boca Raton, Fla., 1983—, Mel Zilinsky Sales Co., N.Y.C., 1972—; export mgmt. cons. Nat. Assn. Export Mgmt. Cons., N.Y.C., 1978-82. Served to sgt. USMC, 1952-54. Lodge: KP (dep. grand chancellor 1982). Home: 2406 Lob-Lolly Ln Deerfield Beach FL 33442 Office: Newshack Inc 1375 W Palmetto Pk Rd Boca Raton FL 33432

ZIMMER, CONNIE WHITLOW, librarian; b. Willow Shade, Ky., Nov. 22, 1950; d. Elmer and Carrie Mae (Lester) Whitlow; m. Steven Wilkinson Zimmer, May 29, 1971; 1 dau., Charlotte Melissa. B.A., Western Ky. U., 1972, M.S., 1975. Cert. librarian, Ky. Student asst. dept. geography and geology, Western Ky. U., Bowling Green, 1968-71; ref. librarian Bowling Green Pub. Library, 1971-72; librarian Ohio County Middle Sch., Hartford, Ky., 1972-73; librarian Bowling Green High Sch., 1973-74; night supr. Bowling Green Pub. Library, 1976-77; head librarian Warren East High Sch., Bowling Green, 1974—; video instr. youth camp Western Ky. U., summer 1985. Sponsor trustee scholarship fund Third Dist. Beacon Builders, 1982—; firefighter Barren River Vol. Fire Dept., 1977—. Mem. Warren County Edn. Assn., Third Dist. Edn. Assn., Ky. Edn. Assn., NEA, Ky. Sch. Media Assn., Ky. Library Assn., Third Dist. Sch. Media Assn., ALA, Am. Assn. Sch. Librarians, Gamma Sigma Sigma. Democrat. Baptist. Home: 1421 Halls Chapel Rd Bowling Green KY 42101 Office: 6867 Louisville Rd Warren East High Sch Bowling Green KY 42101

ZIMMER, PAUL HOWARD, manufacturing executive; b. Detroit, Apr. 18, 1929; s. Donald R. and Ora E. (Howie) Z.; student Fla. So. Coll., 1949; m. Rosina Procopio, Dec. 1979; children—Mark Louis, Christina Lee; children by previous marriage—Mallory Zimmer Scholl, Mary J., Robert P. With Zimmer Boat & Trailer Co., Detroit, 1946-50; sec., treas., later pres. Zimmer Industries, Elwood, Ind., 1959-61; founder, chmn. bd., pres., chief exec. officer Zimmer Corp., Pompano Beach, Fla., 1961—. Home: Royal Oak Landing Boca Raton FL Office: 5801 Congress Ave Boca Raton FL 33431

ZIMMERMAN, BILL J., oil company executive; b. Coffeyville, Kans., Aug. 13, 1932; s. Ralph R. and Nellie E. (Brown) Z.; m. Marianne Belt, Nov. 21, 1953 (div. Nov. 1980); children—Kurt R., Julie M. Zimmerman Zorn, Jennifer L. Zimmerman Robbins; m. 2d, Patsy Cantrell, Dec. 8, 1980. B.B.A., So. Meth. U., 1954; J.D., Denver U., 1964. Bar: Colo. 1964, Calif. 1967, N.Y. 1969, Tex. 1974, Okla. 1978. With fin. dept. Seaboard Oil Co., 1953-58; acct. Shell Oil Co., Okla., Colo., Calif., N.Y., Ga., Tex., 1958-76, sr. gas agt., atty., regional atty., 1969-76; sr. group counsel NL Industries, Inc., Houston, 1976-77; assoc. gen. counsel Kerr-McGee Corp., Oklahoma City, 1977-80; v.p., gen. counsel Superior Oil Co., Houston, 1980-83; v.p. and gen. counsel Chapplin Petroleum Co., Ft. Worth, 1983—. Mem. Nat. Republican Com., Tarrant County Rep. Com. Served with U.S. Army, 1955-57. Mem. ABA, Am. Corp. Counsel Assn., Calif. State Bar, Colo. Bar Assn., N.Y. State Bar Assn., Okla. Bar Assn., Tex. Bar (chmn. corp. counsel sect.). Methodist. Clubs: Ft. Worth Petroleum; Shady Oaks Country. Home: 908 Roaring Springs Rd Fort Worth TX 76114 Office: PO Box 7 Fort Worth TX 76101

ZIMMERMAN, CHARLES JOSEPH, JR., aquatic biologist, aquaculturist, businessman; b. Chgo., Apr. 28, 1938; s. Charles J. and Leona (Wesner) Z.; m. Polly Elizabeth Huddleston, June 22, 1963 (div. 1969); m. 2d, Nancy Weaver, Dec. 11, 1976; 1 dau., Jeanne Marie. A.B. in Zoology, Ind. U., 1967, A.M. in Zoology (Fisheries), 1970. Cert. fishery scientist. Profl. biologist, 1967—; environ. assessments Ind. U. Water Resources Research Center, 1968-72; biologist U.S. Fish and Wildlife Service, 1972; project biologist, Dames & Moore, Cons., Atlanta, 1973—; cons. Caolines de Vimianzo, Madrid; aquaculturist, producer rainbow trout, 1978—. Contbr. writings to publs. in field. Served with USN, 1956-62. Mem. So. Appalachian Trout Growers Assn. (pres.), U.S. Trout Farmers Assn. (dir., sec.), Smoky Mountain Trout Growers Coop. (dir., past sec.-treas.), Am. Fisheries Soc., Sigma Xi. Republican. Home: 313 Delmont Dr NE Atlanta GA 30305 Office: 455 E Paces Ferry Rd Suite 200 Atlanta GA 30363

ZIMMERMAN, ELDON RICHARD, insurance company executive; b. Washington, Ill., Dec. 24, 1926; s. Daniel C. and Loella M. (Schantz) Z.; m. Gladys Mae Folks, June 12, 1945 (div. Nov. 1980); children—Carl Delmar, Orville Dean, Louella Mae, Eldon Richard, Daniel Raymond; m. 2d, Linda Belle McClinton, Feb. 28, 1981. B.S. in Bus. Adminstrn., u. Ariz., 1953. C.P.C.U., C.L.U. With Beich's Candies, Bloomington, Ill., 1943-44; file clk. State Farm Mut. Ins. Co., Bloomington, 1946-47, rate clk., 1947-48, rate supr., 1948-49, service supt., 1953-61, dir. internal control, 1962-70, div. mgr., Birmingham, Ala., 1970—. Co-chmn. ins. program Jefferson State Jr. Coll., Birmingham, 1969—. Served with USNR, 1944-46. Mem. C.P.C.U. (edn. chmn. No. Ala. chpt. 1969—, chpt. pres. 1968), C.L.U., Ins. Inst. Am., Assocs. in Mgmt., Assocs. in Risk Mgmt., Alpha Kappa Psi (life). Republican. Lutheran. Clubs: State Farm Toastmasters (pres. Homewood, Ala., 1982); Vocalizers Toastmasters (pres. Vestavia Hills, Ala. 1983). Office: State Farm Mut Auto Ins Co 2100 S 18th St PO Box 26661 Birmingham AL 35297

ZIMMERMAN, EUGENE WALTER, developer, investor, owner motor hotels; b. nr. Jenner Twp., Pa., Mar. 23, 1909; s. Robert and Amanda A. (Walter) Z.; student pub. schs.; m. Eleanor Witt, Apr. 8, 1930 (div. Oct. 1965); children—Doris Joan (Mrs. James H. Mapes), Ronald E., Rosalie Eleanor (Mrs. Ralph C. Johnson); m. Irene Fabian, May 23, 1966. Developer, owner Zimmerman Motor Co., Somerset, Pa., 1938-45, Roof Garden Motor Hotel, 1941-52, Ella-Gene Apts., Ft. Lauderdale, Fla., 1946-49, Motel Harrisburg, Pa., 1950-57 (now known as Holiday Motor Hotel-East), 1957—; developer, owner Holiday Motor Hotel, West, Harrisburg, Pa., 1952—, Holiday Inn Town, 1962—; owner Gene Zimmerman's Automobilorama and Mus., Holiday West, Ft. Lauderdale, Fla., 1965—; ofcl. staff editor Clissold Pub. Co., Chgo. Cons. to motor hotel industry. Recipient Hall of Fame award Am. Motel Mag., Chgo., 1961, Merit Resolution, Pa. Ho. of Reps., 1968. Mem. Am. Hotel Assn., Pa. Motel Assn. (pres. 1953-54, dir. master hosts 1955—, ambassador master hosts 1961, 62), Am. Motor Hotel Assn., (v.p., dir. 1956), Pa., Central Pa. restaurant assns., Nat. Assn. Travel Orgn., Hotel Sales Mgrs. Assn., Hotel Greeters Am., Inter-Am., Internat. hotel assns., Hammond Organ Soc., Tall Cedars Lebanon, Harrisburg C. of C., Am. Airlines (Admiral), Acacia, Antique Automobile Club Am. (sr. judge), Classic Car Club Am., Horseless Carriage Club, Vets. Motor Car Club, Auburn-Cord-Duesenberg Club, Pierce-Arrow Soc., Rolls Royce Owners Club, S.A.R., Am. Soc. Travel Agts., Richard Nixon Assos., Pa. Soc. Republican. Lutheran. Clubs: T.W.A. Ambassador (life), American Airlines Admiral (life) (N.Y.C.); Matson Mariners' (hon. navigator) (San Francisco) Curved Dash Owners (New Hope, Pa.); Executives, Zembo Luncheon (Harrisburg); Le Club International (Fort Lauderdale); Chub Cay (The Bahamas). Lodges: Masons, Shriners, K.T., Rotary. Internat. editor: Am. Motel mag., 1962—. Office: Automobilorama Inc 1500 SE 17th St Fort Lauderdale FL 33316

ZIMMERMAN, RAYMOND, mail order company executive; b. 1933. Owner, Zimmerman's 5 Cent & 10 Cent & 1 Up Stores; with Service Mdse. Co., 1959—, Nashville v.p., 1959-73, pres., 1973-81, 81—, chmn. bd., pres. dir. Address: Service Merchandise Co Inc 2968 Foster Creighton Dr Nashville TN 37204*

ZIMMERMANN, GERDA ANNA MARIA, dancer, educator, choreographer; b. Cuxhaven, Germany, Mar. 26, 1927; came to U.S., 1960; d. Alfred and Irma (Pietsch) Z. Diploma, Gymnastiklehrerinnen Kâté Kühl-Lorenzen, Hamburg, Germany, 1945-47; cert. in modern and ethnic dance Sch. für Theatertanz, Erika Khütz, Hamburg, 1947-50. With Rheinisches Staatstheater, Dusseldorf, Germany, 1950-54; soloist Landestheater Hannover, Germany, 1954-60; soloist Kammertanz Theatre, N.Y., 1964-75; owner dance studio, N.Y.C., 1972-75; assoc. prof. dance U. N.C., Charlotte, 1974—; artistic dir. Kammertanz Theatre, N.C., 1975-76; art dir. New Reflections Dance Theatre, Charlotte, 1976-78; choreographer, performer Gerda Zimmermann Dance Gallery, 1980—. Dancer, choreographer numerous group and solo works. Grantee Wis. Arts Bd. and Nat. Endowment for Arts, 1974, N.C. Arts Council, 1975, 76, 77-78, 81-82, Charlotte Arts & Sci. Council, 1982-83, 83-84, U. N.C., 1984-85. Mem. N.C. Dance Alliance. Avocations: photography; filming; gardening. Office: Dept Performing Arts U NC-Charlotte Charlotte NC 28223

ZIMMERMANN, GERHARDT, conductor; b. Van Wert, Ohio, June 22, 1945; s. Ervin and Ethel Jane (Allen) Z.; m. Sharon Marie Reher, Mar. 17, 1974; children—Anna Marie, Peter Karl Irum. B.Mus., Bowling Green State U.; M.F.A., U. Iowa; student, with James Dixon, Leopold Sipe, Flora Contino, Richard Lert. Tchr. in tng. Genoa (Ohio) Pub. Schs., 1967-70; condr. orch. Augustana Coll., Rock Island, Ill., 1971-72; music dir. Clinton (Iowa) Symphony Orch., 1971-72; asst. prof. music, condr. orchs. Western Ill. U., Macomb, 1972-74; asst. condr. St. Louis Symphony Orch., 1974-78, assoc. condr., 1978-82; music dir., condr. St. Louis Youth Orch., 1975-82, Canton Symphony Orch., 1980—, N.C. Symphony Orch., Raleigh, 1982—; guest condr. Recipient (2d Prize Georg Solti Conducting Competition 1973). Mem. Am. Symphony Orch. League, Nat. Acad. Rec. Arts and Scis., Phi Mu Alpha Sinfonia. Office: NC Symphony Orch Meml Auditorium 2 South St Raleigh NC*

ZINGRONE, NANCY LOUISE, parapsychology researcher; b. Berwyn, Ill., Jan. 9, 1951; d. Anthony Neumann and Janet Harriet (Krug) Z.; m. Michael A. Solomon, Mar. 21, 1973 (div. July 1982). B.A., Mundelein Coll., 1974; M.S. in Edn., No. Ill. U., 1977. Asst. registrar Mundelein Coll., Chgo., 1977-78, adult edn. instr., 1978-80; engaged in family businesses, Chgo. area, 1978-81; lectr. psychology Northeastern Ill. U., Chgo., 1979-82; adminstrv. asst. Chgo. City-Wide Colls., 1981-82; research fellow Inst. for Parapsychology, Durham, N.C., 1982—; founder, dir. edn. Midwest Psi Research Inst., Chgo., 1977-80, pres., 1980-82; adult edn. instr. Field Mus. Natural History, Chgo., 1980-82. Fellow Am. Soc. Psychical Research; assoc. Am. Psychol. Assn., Parapsychology Assn., Am. Assn. Study Mental Imagery, Internat. Imagery Assn.; mem. Ind. Scholars of N.C. Triangle, AAUW. Jewish. Avocations: crafts; history of Am. West; sci. fiction; needlework. Home: 1203 Watts St Apt 1 Durham NC 27701 Office: Inst for Parapsychology 402 N Buchanan Blvd Durham NC 27701

ZINN, BEN T., educator; b. Tel-Aviv, Apr. 21, 1937; came to U.S., 1957, naturalized, 1967; s. Samuel and Fridah (Gelbfish) Cynowicz; m. Rosanne Diamond Zinn; children—Edward R., Leslie H. B.S.M.E., N.Y. U., 1961; M.S.M.E., Stanford U., 1962; M.A., Princeton U., 1963, Ph.D., 1965. Research scientist Am. Standard Research Div., North Brunswick, N.J., summer 1976; asst. research Princeton U., 1964-65; asst. prof. Ga. Inst. Tech., Atlanta, 1965-67, assoc. prof., 1967-70, prof., 1970-73, regents prof., 1973—; cons. Brasilian Space Research Inst., Sao Jose dos Campos, 1978—; mem. bd. visitors Nat. Fire Acad., 1979-83. Editor: AIAA Progress in Astronautics and AE, 1977, 78; assoc. editor AIAA Jour., 1982—. Recipient NASA Certificate of Recognition, 1974; David Orr Mech. Engring. prize, N.Y. U., 1961; Stanford U. fellow, 1961-62; Founder's Day award, N.Y. U., 1961. Mem. AIAA, Combustion Inst., Am. Technion Soc. (v.p.), Sigma Xi, Tau Beta Pi, Pi Tau Sigma. Home: 2006 W Paces Ferry Rd NW Atlanta GA 30327 Office: Ga Inst Tech Aerospace Engring Atlanta GA 30332

ZINN, ELIAS PAUL, electronic, entertainment marketing executive; b. Houston, Nov. 7, 1954; s. Julius and Harriett (Dubinski) Z.; student U. Tex., 1972-74; m. Janis Ann Turboff, Aug. 7, 1977. Salesman, Custom Hi Fi Discount Center, Houston, 1971-72, mgr., 1972-73, v.p. sales, 1974—, v.p. sales and operation, 1974-75, pres., 1975-76, pres., chief exec. officer, chief operating officer, 1976-81; formed Entertainment Mktg. Sales Reps., 1981—, Nu Techmktg. subs., 1983, Easy Electronic Distbn. subs., 1984. Advisor, Better Bus. Bur., Houston, 1976-79. Mem. Electronic Reps. Assn., C. of C., Houston Jaycees. Republican. Jewish. Club: Beth Yeshrun Brotherhood. Home: 1480 Sugar Creek Blvd Sugarland TX 77478 Office: 11231 Southwest Freeway Houston TX 77031

ZINOBER, JOAN WAGNER, industrial psychologist, management consultant; b. Los Angeles, July 30, 1944; d. Leonard Issac and Maida (Prenn) Wagner; m. Peter Wolfson Zinober, June 13, 1971; children—Brett Wagner, Scott Wagner, Bryan Wagner. B.A., Mich. State U., 1965; M.A., U. Conn., 1967, Ph.D., 1970; M.B.A., Fla. Inst. Tech., 1983. Lic. psychologist, Fla. Asst. prof. NYU, 1969-71; research coordinator U.S. Dept. Health and Human Services, Washington, 1971-72; dir. research & evaluation Hillsborough Community Mental Health Ctr., Tampa, 1972-80, dir. Fla. Consortium, Tampa, 1977-80; pres. Zinober Consulting Services, Tampa, 1980—; clin. asst. prof. psychiatry U. South Fla. Med. Sch., 1973-84; chmn. research council Nat. Council of Community Mental Health Ctrs., Washington, 1978-80. Editor: A Trust of Evaluation, 1980; contbr. articles to profl. jours. NIMH grantee, 1977-80, contracts, 1981. Mem. Am. Psychol. Assn., Athena Soc., Am. Soc. for Tng. and Devel.

ZINZOW, JOHN ROBERT, publisher; b. Milw., Nov. 6, 1929; s. John Benjamin and Roselle Barbara (Gerrits) Z.; B.A., U. Chgo., 1952, M.B.A., 1954, M.A. in Econs., 1955. Mem. mfg. mgmt. staff Procter & Gamble, Chgo. and Quincy, Mass., 1957-64; pres. Poole Clarinda Co., Chgo., 1969-71, Programmed Printing Corp., Woodstock, Ill., 1972—, Windward Pub., Inc., Miami, Fla. Active, People for the Am. Way., Washington, 1982-83. Served with U.S. Army, 1955-57. Recipient Spl. Recognition award Burnham Club, 1970. Clubs: Union League, Chgo. Yacht (both Chgo.); Ocean Reef (Key Largo, Fla.). Author: Sportfisherman's Handbook, 1975; Magic of Sea Shells, 1976; Savory Shellfish of North America, 1977; The Shark Book, 1983. Office: 105 NE 25th St Miami FL 33137

ZIPF, ROBERT EUGENE, JR., pathologist; b. Dayton, Ohio, Sept. 18, 1940; s. Robert Eugene and Meriam (Murr) Z.; m. Nancy J. Gaskell, Sept. 11, 1965; children—Karin Lorene, Marjorie Kristine. B.A., DePauw U., 1962; M.D., Ohio State U., 1966. Diplomate Am. Bd. Pathology. Intern, Miami Valley Hosp., Dayton, Ohio, 1966-67; dir. forensic pathology Duke U. Med. Ctr., Durham, N.C., 1967-72; dir. radioisotope pathology Riverside Meth. Hosp., Columbus, 1974-78; dep. cororner, forensic pathologist Franklin County, Columbus, 1974-78; regional forensic pathologist State of N.C., Rocky Mount, 1978—; chmn. pathology Nash Gen. Hosp., Rocky Mount, 1978—; clin. asst. prof. East Carolina U. Med. Sch., Greenville, N.C., 1979—; adj. prof. Atlantic Christian Coll., Wilson, N.C., 1980—, dir. Sch. Med. Tech., 1983—; cons. in field. Contbr. articles to profl. jours. Trustee, United Fund, 1979—. Served to maj. USAF, 1972-74. Fellow Am. Soc. Clin. Pathologist, Am. Acad. Forensic Scientists; mem. Assn. Clin. Scientists, Am. Coll. Nuclear Medicine, N.C. Med. Soc. Home: 120 Newby Ct Rocky Mount NC 27801 Office: Nash Gen Hosp Pathology Lab Rocky Mount NC 27801

ZIRKLE, MICHAEL PERRY, safety executive; b. Clifton, W.Va., Feb. 25, 1949; s. David Perry and Ruth (Henry) Z.; children—Michele Sue, Pamela Lynn. A.A., Hocking Tech. Coll., 1974. Profl. safety mgr. Asst. mgr. Trainee Rizer Oil Co., Pomeroy, Ohio, 1969-71; ptnr. Meigs Tire Ctr., Pomeroy, 1971-73; safety coordinator trainee Babcock & Wilcox Constrn., Pitts., 1973-74; dep. sheriff-lt. Meigs County Sheriff's Dept., Pomeroy, 1974-78; safety coordinator Union Boiler Co., Nitro, W.Va., 1978-80, corp. safety dir., 1980—; bd. dirs. W.Va. Safety Council, Charleston, 1984—. Mem., instr. ARC, Charleston, W.Va., 1981—. Recipient Safety Dir. of Year award, W.Va. Dept. Labor, 1982, Safety Achievement award, 1981, 82, 83, 84. Mem. Am. Soc. Safety Engrs., Assn. Gen. Contractors W.Va. (co-chmn. safety com.). Republican. Lodge: Moose. Avocations: karate; jogging. Home: PO Box 701 Poca WV 25159 Office: Union Boiler Co Route 25 and I64 PO Box 425 Nitro WV 25143

ZITMORE, MILES DAVID, investment broker; b. Harrisburg, Pa., Oct. 17, 1946; s. Albert and Ethel (Loeb) Z.; B.A. in Sociology, Park Coll., 1968; M.S. in Community Devel., U. Mo., Columbia, 1974; m. Esther Levy, Apr. 1, 1976. Cert. fin. planner. Asst. dir. Jewish Community Relations Bur., Kansas City, Mo., 1971-73; asst. dir. S.W. office Am. Jewish Com., Dallas, 1973-81; investment broker A.G. Edwards & Sons, Dallas, 1981—. Sec., organizer Dallas chpt. Com. Econ. Growth of Israel; organizer Dallas Interfaith Task Force for Human Rights and Religious Freedom in the Soviet Union; organizer, Conserve Dallas; mem. Energy Task Force Goals for Dallas; bd. dirs. Hebrew Free Loan Assn. mem. membership com. Mental Health Assn.; chmn. Rotefair Com. Mem. Inst. Cert. Fin. Planners, Internat. Assn. Fin. Planning, Religious Public Relations Council (pres. Dallas chpt.), Am. Soc. Tng. and Devel. (past sec. Dallas chpt.), Public Relations Soc. Internat. Assn. Fin. Planners, Inst. Cert. Fin. Planners, Dallas C. of C. (pub. safety commn.), Leadership Dallas Alumni Assn., Am., Assn. Jewish Community Relations Workers, Dallas C. of C. (grad. Leadership Dallas Program), Shakespeare Guild (dir., membership chmn.). Jewish. Club: Toastmasters. Lodge: Rotary. Home: 7742 Goforth Circle Dallas TX 75238 Office: 411 N Akard St Dallas TX 75201

ZITO, JAMES PROSPER, university medical center administrator; b. Akron, Ohio, Feb. 19, 1948; s. Prosper and Caroline M. (Emmanuele) Z.; m. Joan Larriane Van Zandt, July 31, 1982; children—Christopher, Cassie. B.S. in Pharmacy, U. Cin., 1975; B.S. in Health Mgmt., Southwestern Tex. State U., 1978. Dir. ECG Baylor U. Med. Ctr., Dallas, 1978-80, dir. support services, 1980-81, adminstrv. dir., 1981—; cons. cardiac tng. Squibb & Sons, Dallas, 1983-84; cons. cardiac equipment Buyline M.D., Dallas, 1984. Mem. Med. Group Mgmt. Assn., Tex. Group Mgmt. Assn., Am. Hosp. Assn., Am. Group Practice Assn. Roman Catholic. Avocation: sculptor. Home: 607 Rosedown Mesquite TX 75150 Office: Baylor U Med Ctr 3600 Gaston Ave Dallas TX 75246

ZIVNEY, JAMES RODDIS, JR., chemical company executive; b. Dallas, Aug. 8, 1927; s. James Roddis and Anna Lee (Nechas) Z.; m. Claire Ellen Draper, Feb. 10, 1927; children—Olivia Ann, Cheri Marie, Beverly Jane, Rebecca Dawn. B.S., U. Wyo., 1959. Data analyst The Geotech. Corp., 1949-59; mgr. Martin-Marietta Corp., Denver, 1959-67; corp. pres., chmn. bd. May Chem. Co., Inc., Dallas, 1967—. Served with USAAF, 1945, USN, 1946.

ZOBLE, JERRY EDWIN, geologist; b. Casper, Wyo., Oct. 23, 1930; s. Edwin Joseph and Lois Alycia (Longshore) Z., m. Ruth A. Irvin, Feb. 23, 1952; children—Judith Zoble Gardner, Daniel J., Robin Zoble Ashby. B.S., U. Wyo., 1953, M.A., 1957. Exploration geologist Pan Am. Petroleum Corp., Billings, Mont., Casper, Wyo., and New Orleans, 1957-67; dist. geologist Occidental Petroleum Co., Lafayette, La., 1967-71; cons. geologist, Jackson, Miss., 1971-78; pres. Zoble Exploration, Inc., Jackson, 1978—. Bd. dirs. Capital Found., Miss. Republican. Party, Jackson, 1983—. Mem. Am. Assn. Petroleum Geologists, Ind. Petroleum Assn. Am. (bd. dirs. 1983—), Miss. Geol. Soc. (pres. 1975-76), Mid-Continent Oil and Gas Assn. (sec.-treas. 1984-85), Miss. Landmen's Assn., Nat. C. of C. Clubs: Capital City Petroleum (Jackson), University. Avocations: boating; golf. Home: 133 Cherry Hills Dr Jackson MS 39211 Office: Zoble Exploration Inc 515 Yazoo St Jackson MS 39201

ZOHDI, MAGD ELDIN, educator; b. Cairo, Apr. 18, 1933; came to U.S., 1964, naturalized, 1971; s. Ismail Abdella and Nemat (Rizk) Z.; diploma Cairo U., 1954, B.S., 1962; M.S., U. Kan., 1965; Ph.D., Okla. State U., 1969; m. Omnia Elmenshawy, Sept. 17, 1964; children—Tarek, Mona. With Maintenance Machinery, Cairo, 1954-60; instr. Cairo U., 1962-64; grad. teaching asst. Okla. State U., Stillwater, 1966-69; asso. prof. La. State U., Baton Rouge, 1969-75, prof., 1975—, coordinator engring. mgmt. program, 1976—; pres. Am. Contracting and Trading Corp., Baton Rouge, 1978, Quality Contracting Inc. Fulbright scholar, 1964; recipient Excellence in Undergrad. Teaching award Standard Oil Found., 1971; Presdl. Honor award Okla. State U., 1968. Mem. Soc. Mfg. Engrs., Am. Inst. Indsl. Engrs., Am. Mil. Engrs., Sigma Xi, Tau Beta Pi. Contbr. articles to profl. jours. Home: 5050 S Chalet Ct Baton Rouge LA 70808 Office: 3132 Ceba Bldg La State Univ Baton Rouge LA 70803

ZOLLER, JACK STECKLER, physician; b. New Orleans, June 5, 1928; s. Bernard and Esther Elise (Steckler) Z.; m. Linda Ney Malkin, Apr. 29, 1962; children—Arthur David, Gary Patrick, Glenn Keith, Diana Ruth. B.S., Tulane U., 1946; M.D., La. State U., 1950. Diplomate Am. Bd. Obstetrics and Gynecology. Intern, Phila. Gen. Hosp., 1950-51; resident Charity Hosp., New Orleans, 1951-52, 54-55, Touro Infirmary, New Orleans, 1955-56; practice medicine, specializing in obstetrics and gynecology, Gretna, La., 1956—; pres. Drs. Zoller Lupin Levinson & Cohen, Gretna; pres. med. staff West Jefferson Gen. Hosp., Marreno, La., 1961; vice chmn. bd. Jo Ellen Smith Meml. Hosp., New Orleans. Bd. dirs. Cancer Assn. Greater New Orleans, 1970-78, Meadowcrest Hosp.; pres. Children's Bur., 1979-81; chmn. Jewish Welfare Fund, New Orleans, 1982. Served to capt. M.C., USAF, 1952-54. Mem. AMA, La. Med. Soc., Am. Coll. Obstetricians and Gynecologists, New Orleans Obstet. and Gynecol. Soc. Lodge: Masons. Office: 515 W Bank Expressway Gretna LA 70053

ZONTINE, DAVID HERBERT, neurologist; b. Pitts., Nov. 6, 1938; s. Clarence William and Eleanor Mary (Foley) Z.; B.A., St. Vincent Coll., 1960; M.D., U. Pitts., 1964; m. Patricia Ann Lynch, Aug. 27, 1964; children—Carrie Beth, Matthew David. Intern, Mercy Hosp., Pitts., 1964-65; resident U. Va., Charlottesville, 1968-71, chief resident, 1971; instr. neurology U. Mich. Med. Center, Ann Arbor, 1971-74; asst. chief neurology VA Hosp., Ann Arbor, 1971-74; clin. asst. prof. neurology U. Va. Med. Sch., 1974—; practice medicine specializing in neurology, Winchester, Va., 1974—; mem. staffs Winchester Meml. Hosp., Loudoun Meml. Hosp., King's Daus. Hosp., City Hosp., Martinsburg, W.Va., Warren Meml. Hosp., Front Royal, Va. Served with USNR, 1966-68. Jesse Clark fellow, U. Pitts., 1960-61; diplomate Am. Bd. Psychiatry and Neurology (examiner 1975-77). Mem. Am. Acad. Neurology, Va. Neurol. Assn., No. Va. Med. Soc., Soc. Clin. Neurologists, Winchester-Frederick County Hist. Soc., Preservation of Historic Winchester. Republican. Roman Catholic. Home: 614 Tennyson Ave Winchester VA 22601 Office: 125 Medical Circle Winchester VA 22601

ZOROWSKI, CARL FRANK, engineering educator, university administrator; b. Pitts., July 14, 1930; s. Stanley and Mary Josephine (Kozuch) Z.; m. Sarah Jane Crossley, Aug. 7, 1954 (dec. 1983); children—Kathleen Ann, Karl Alan, Kristine Alaine; m. Louise Parrish Lockwood, Apr. 13, 1985. B.S. in Mech. Engring., Carnegie Inst. Tech., 1952, M.S. in Mech. Engring., 1953, Ph.D., 1956. Instr. Carnegie Inst. Tech., Pitts., 1952-56, asst. prof., 1956-61, assoc. prof., 1961-62; assoc. prof. mech. and aero. engring. dept. N.C. State U., Raleigh, 1964-66, R.J. Reynolds Industries prof., 1966—, assoc. dept. head, 1964-72, dept. head, 1972-79, assoc. dean acad. affairs Sch. Engring., 1979-85; dir. Corp. Cons. Ltd. Served to 2d lt. USAR, 1952-58. Recipient research award Sigma Xi, 1967. Fellow ASME (Richards Meml. award 1975); mem. Am. Soc. Engring. Edn. (Western Electric award 1968), Fiber Soc. (Achievement award 1970). Contbr. pubs. to profl. lit.; patentee in field. Home: 4513 Pitt St Raleigh NC 27609 Office: NC State U Box 7910 Raleigh NC 27695

ZOUKIS, STEPHEN JAMES, lawyer; b. Montpelier, Vt., July 2, 1949; s. Christo S. and Alice Rose (McCormish) Z.; m. Suzan Hardy Moore, Jan. 30, 1971; children—Abigail Moriah, Christopher Hardy. B.S. in M.E. with honors, U. Va., 1971; J.D., Columbia U., 1974. Bar: Ga. 1974. Assoc. atty. Powell, Goldstein, Frazer & Murphy, Atlanta, 1974-76; assoc. atty. Hansell, Post,

Brandon & Dorsey, Atlanta, 1976-79; ptnr. Wildman, Harrold, Allen, Dixon & Masinter, Atlanta, 1979—. Mem. ABA, Atlanta Bar Assn., Ga. Bar Assn. Democrat. Episcopalian. Club: Ansley Golf. Home: 34 Lullwater Estate Rd Atlanta GA 30307 Office: 1200 S Omni International Atlanta GA 30303

ZUBER, RANDOLPH CLARK, urologist; b. Dallas, Apr. 4, 1941; s. Oran H. and Minnie M. (Cuthbertson) Z.; m. Billie Gayle Schumacher, June 20, 1964; children—Randolph Blake, Rustin Kurt. B.A., U. Tex., 1963; M.D., U. Tex. Med. Br., 1967; A.A.P.S., Amarillo Jr. Coll., 1961. Diplomate Am. Bd. Urology. Intern, Kans. U. Med. Ctr., 1967-68, resident in urology, 1969-72; practice medicine, specializing in urology, Kerrville, Tex., 1974—; bishop Ch. of Christ, 1983—. Served to maj. USAF, 1927-74. Decorated Air Force Commendation medal. Fellow ACS; mem. AMA, Am. Urol. Soc., Tex. Urol. Assn. (sec.-treas. 1985—), So. Med. Assn., Tex. Med. Assn. Lodge: Rotary. Office: 710 Water St Suite 300 Kerrville TX 78028

ZUCKER, ALEXANDER, nuclear physicist, research administrator; b. Zagreb, Yugoslavia, Aug. 1, 1924; came to U.S., 1939; s. William and Bertha (Klopfer) Z.; m. Joan-Ellen Jamieson, Nov. 28, 1953; children—Rebecca, Claire, Susannah. B.A., U. Vt., 1947; M.S., Yale U., 1948, Ph.D., 1950. Physicist Oak Ridge Nat. Lab., 1950-60, assoc. dir. electronuclear div., 1960-70, dir. heavy ion project, 1972-74, assoc. dir., 1973—; Ford prof. physics U. Tenn., Knoxville, 1968-72; exec. dir. environ. studies bd. Nat. Acad. Sci./Nat. Acad. Engring., Washington, 1970-72; mem. council on energy engring. research Dept. Energy, 1983—; mem. White House Industry/Nat. Lab. Steel Initiative, 1984—. Editor: Nuclear Science Applications, Sect. B, 1980—. Guggenheim fellow, 1966-67; Fulbright-Hays Research scholar, 1966-67. Fellow Am. Phys. Soc., AAAS, Sigma Xi; mem. Am. Soc. for Metals. Office: Oak Ridge Nat Lab PO Box X Oak Ridge TN 37831

ZUCKER, BENJAMIN, public relations executive; b. Cleve., June 28, 1911; s. Morris Chaim and Rose (Edelman) Z.; m. Edith Faye Roman, Apr. 27, 1941; children—Joan Carol, Lynn Ruth, Claudia Lee. B.A., Case Western Res. U., 1935. Br. mgr. Consol. Radio Artists, 1935-38; treas. Internat. Artists Corp., 1939-52; operating ptnr. Benjamin Zucker & Assocs., Nashville, 1953-58, 70—; mgr. Bank Bus. Devel. div. R.L. Polk & Co., 1960-69; v.p., mktg. dir. The Now Corp., 1970—, cons., 1976—; exec. dir. Endowment Fund, Jewish Fedn. Nashville, 1980—. Author: What About College?, 1965-69; After High School, What?, 1966-69. Served to capt. Adj. Gen. Dept., U.S. Army, 1941-45. Mem. Sales/Mktg. Execs., Bank Mktg. Assn. Jewish. Clubs: Temple Hills Country, B'nai B'rith. Home: 761 Darden Pl Nashville TN 37205 Office: 801 Percy Warner Blvd Nashville TN 37205

ZUCKER, MICHAEL ALAN, real estate executive; b. N.Y.C., Oct. 30, 1953; s. Gerald and Harriet (Rosen) Z.; m. Miriam Yvette Colon, Apr. 25, 1983; 1 child, Ariel Justin. B.S., SUNY-Buffalo, 1975. Lic. real estate broker, Fla. Acct., H.J. Behrman & Co., N.Y.C., 1975-76; asst. v.p. Donald Zucker Co., N.Y.C., 1976-77; asst. v.p. DBL Operating Corp., N.Y.C., 1977-78; v.p. Mortgage Corp. of Am., North Miami Beach, Fla., 1978—. Mem. Internat. Council Shopping Centers. Republican. Avocations: fishing; golfing; art collecting; philately. Office: Mortgage Corp of Am 17071 W Dixie Hwy North Miami Beach FL 33160

ZUCKERMAN, JEROLD JAY, chemistry educator; b. Phila., Feb. 29, 1936; s. Harry Earle and Evlyn Judith (Weisman) Z.; m. Rose Elizabeth Stinson, June 4, 1959; children—Lesley Jeanne, Thomas Abraham, Amanda Joy, Kathryn Jane, Amy Jo Allyn. B.S. (Phila. Bd. Edn. scholar 1953-57, Edgar Fahs Smith scholar 1956-57), U. Pa., 1957; A.M. (NSF fellow 1959, USPHS fellow 1959-60), Harvard U., 1959, Ph.D., 1960; Ph.D. (USPHS fellow), U. Cambridge (Eng.), 1962, Sc.D., 1976; D.h.c., U. Aix-Marseille III (France); Chemist, Smith, Kline & French Labs., Phila., summer 1956, Houdry Process Corp., Marcus Hook, Pa., summer 1957; teaching fellow Harvard U., 1957-60, asst. prof. Summer Sch., 1967, asso. prof., 1970; chemist MIT Lincoln Lab., Lexington, summer 1958; supr. students in chemistry Sidney Sussex Coll., U. Cambridge (Eng.), 1961-62; asst. prof. Cornell U., Ithaca, N.Y., 1962-68; asso. prof. SUNY, Albany, 1968-72, prof. chemistry, 1972-76, dir. research, 1972-73; prof. U. Okla., Norman, 1976—, chmn. dept. chemistry, 1976-80, George Lynn Cross research prof., 1984—; guest prof. Tech. U. Berlin, 1973; prof. associé U. Aix-Marseille III, 1979, 82. Panel chmn. com. NRC-Nat. Acad. Scis., 1970-75; cons. Nat. Inst. Occupational Safety and Health, Bethesda, Md., Walter de Gruyter Co., Berlin, Midwest Research Inst., Kansas City, Life Systems, Inc., ICAIR Systems Div., Cleve., Carstab Corp., Cin., Parkans Internat., Houston, E.I. duPont NEN Med. Products, Billerica, Mass.; panelist NSF. Pres. bd. trustees Brunswick Common Sch. Dist. (N.Y.), 1972-76. NSF research grantee, 1964—; NIH-Nat. Cancer Inst. research grantee, 1963-68; Research Corp. research grantee, 1968-70; Am. Chem. Soc.-Petroleum Research Fund research grantee, 1968-71; NATO grantee, 1977-79, 85—; Office Naval Research grantee, 1977—; Sr. Scientist award Alexander von Humboldt Found., Ger., 1973. Fellow AAAS; mem. AAUP, Am. Chem. Soc., Am. Inst. Chemists, Assn. Harvard Chemists, ASTM, Assn. U. Pa. Chemists, Cambridge Soc., Royal Soc. Chemistry, Sigma Xi, Alpha Chi Sigma, Phi Lambda Upsilon. Office: Dept Chemistry U Okla Norman OK 73019

ZUHDI, MOHAMED NAZIH, physician; b. Beirut, Lebanon, May 19, 1925; s. Omar and Lutfiye (Atef) Z.; came to U.S., 1950; B.A., Am. U., Beirut, Lebanon, 1946, M.D., 1950; children by previous marriage—Omar, Nabil; m. 2d, Annette McMichael; children—Adam, Leyla, Zachariah. Intern St. Vincent's Hosp., N.Y.C., 1950-51, Presbyn.-Columbia Med. Center. N.Y.C., 1951-52; resident Kings County State U. N.Y. Med. Center, N.Y.C., 1952-56; fellow State U. N.Y. Downstate Med. Ctr., Brklyn., 1953-54; resident U. Hosp., Mpls., 1956, Oklahoma City, 1957-58; practice medicine specializing in cardiovascular and thoracic surgery, Oklahoma City, 1958—;; dir. transplantation ctr., chief transplantation surgeon Bapt. Hosp., Oklahoma City; active thoracic and cardiovascular surgery Bapt., Mercy, St. Anthony, South Community, Deaconess, Midwest City hosps.; chmn. Okla. Cardiovascular Inst., Oklahoma City, 1983-84, Okla. Heart Ctr., Oklahoma City, 1984—; dir. transplantation ctr. Bapt. Med. Ctr., Oklahoma City, 1984. Named Hon. Citizen Brazil. Diplomate Am. Bd. Surgery, Am. Bd. Thoracic Surgery. Fellow A.C.S.; mem. Am., Okla. thoracic socs., Am., So., Okla. med. assns., Internat., Coll. Angiology, Am. Coll. Chest Physicians, Oklahoma City C. of C., Oklahoma County Med. Soc., Oklahoma City Clin. Soc., Okla. Surg. Assn., Oklahoma City Surg. Soc., Southwestern Surg. Congress, Am. Coll. Cardiology, Am. Soc. Artificial Internal Organs, Soc. Thoracic Surgeons (founder mem.), Am. Assn. for Thoracic Surgery, Internat. Cardiovascular Soc., Okla. State Heart Assn., Osler Soc., So. Thoracic Surg. Assn., Lillehei Surg. Soc., Internat. Soc. Heart Transplantation, Dwight Harken's Founder's Group Cardiac. Surgery. Contbg. author Cardiac Surgery, 1967, 2d edit., 1972. Contbr. articles to profl. jours.; developer numerous med. devices and techniques. Home: 7305 Lancet Ct Oklahoma City OK 73120 Office: 3400 NW Expressway Oklahoma City OK 73112

ZUKERNICK, HARRY, lawyer; b. N.Y.C., Nov. 25, 1905; s. Jacob and Becky (Meltz) Z.; m. Susan Brower, July 31, 1929; 1 son, Michael. B.B.A., CCNY, 1926; LL.B., Bklyn. Law Sch., 1929. Bar: N.Y. 1930, Fla. 1935, U.S. Ct. Appeals (5th cir.) 1947, U.S. Supreme Ct. 1948. Sole practice, N.Y.C., 1930-35 Miami Beach, Fla., 1935—; chmn. dist. welfare bd. State of Fla. Mem. pres.'s council Brandeis U. Mem. ABA, Fla. Bar (chmn. real property, probate and trust law sect., bd. govs.), Dade County Bar Assn., Miami Beach Bar Assn. (pres. 1950, merit award 1964), Bklyn. Law Sch. Alumni Assn. (pres. Fla. chpt.), Council Bar Assn. Pres. Fla. (Outstanding Past Local Bar Assn. Pres. award 1981), Miami Beach Civic League (pres. 1940), Anti-Defamation League (nat. vice chmn. deferred gifts com.). Author chpts. in law books. Home: 3134 Sheridan Ave Miami Beach FL 33140 Office: 420 Lincoln Rd Suite 329 Miami Beach FL 33139

ZULLO, VICTOR AUGUST, geology educator, paleontologist researcher; b. San Francisco, July 24, 1936; s. Albino John and Marie Leopolda (Gius) Zu. B.A. in Paleontology, U.Calif.-Berkeley, 1958, M.A., 1960, Ph.D., 1963. With Marine Biol. Lab., Woods Hole, Mass., 1962-67, systematics-ecology program, 1962-67, head systematics div., 1963-67, asst. dir., 1964-66; with Calif. Acad. Scis., San Francisco, 1967-70, assoc. curator, 1967-70, chmn. dept. geology, 1968-70; with U. N.C.-Wilmington, 1971—, dir. environ. studies, 1971, prof. geology, 1972—, chmn. earth scis., 1982—; research assoc. Los Angeles County Mus. Natural History. Fellow Calif. Acad. Sci.; mem. Crustacean Soc., Geol. Soc. Am., Paleontol. Soc., Soc. Econ. Paleontologists, Mineralogists, Biol. Soc. Washington, Sigma Xi. Contbr. numerous articles in field to sci. publs. Office: Dept Earth Scis U NC Wilmington NC 28403

ZUNKA, CRAIG A., dentist; b. Front Royal, Va., Sept. 10, 1950; s. John J. and Marie Zunka. B.S. in Biology, Va. Poly. Inst. and State U., 1971; D.D.S., Med. Coll. Va., 1975. Tchr. Ginter Park Elem. Sch., Richmond, Va., 1973-74; clk. Med. Coll. Va., Richmond, 1974-75; asst. prof. U. Fla., Gainesville, 1975-76; dental faculty Homeopathic Med. Sch., Millersville, Pa., 1982—; gen. practice dentistry, Front Royal, 1976—; cons. Warren Meml. Hosp., Front Royal, 1976—. Asst. scoutmaster Boy Scouts Am., Warren County; active Kiwanis Club, Front Royal, 1976—; pres. Shenandoah Area Council chpt. Nat. Eagle Scout Assn., 1980—. Recipient Eagle Scout award Boy Scouts Am., 1965, Woodbadge of Honor award, 1978, Vigil honor award, Order of Arrow award, 1979, Statuette award, 1983; Outstanding Young Man of Yr. award Warren County, 1984. Fellow Am. Acad. Gen. Dentistry; mem. No. Va. Dental Study Group, Am. Acad. Crown and Bridge Prosthodontics, Am. Ctr. Homeopathy, Va. Dental Assn., ADA, Shenandoah Valley Dental Assn., Am. Equilibration Soc., Holistic Dental Assn. (exec. bd. 1982-85), Am. Prosthodontic Soc., Cranial Acad. Am. Acad. Osteopathy, Am. Acad. Functional Prosthodontics. Home: PO Box 1600 Front Royal VA 22630 Office: 197 W 4th St Front Royal VA 22630

ZUREK, MARLA JOY, geologist, dance instructor; b. Uvalde, Tex., Feb. 4, 1954; d. John Samuel and Mary Evelyn (Pike) B.; m. Robert Alan Zurek, Aug. 4, 1973 (div. 1981); 1 child, Laylah. B.S., Sul Ross State U., 1983, postgrad., 1983—. Night office mgr. Western Petroleum Co. N.Am., Carrizo Springs, Tex., 1978; ballet instr., San Angelo, Leakey, Tex., 1979-80; with Tucker Drilling Co., Inc., San Angelo, 1981; research asst. geology dept. Sul Ross State U., Alpine, Tex., 1982—; cons. geol., San Angelo, Brewster County, Tex., 1984—. Ballet instr., Fort Davis, Tex., 1984—. McAnulty scholar Sul Ross State U. 1983. Mem. Am. Assn. Petroleum Geologists, Sul Ross Geology Club. Democrat. Avocations: exploring; ballet; geological photography.

ZURIS, DONALD PAUL, museum administrator, consultant; b. St. Louis, Apr. 26, 1944; s. Paul and Aulene Ardis (Gravelle) Z.; m. Gaye Ann Tabin, May 26, 1979. B.A., Allegheny Coll., 1966; M.A., U. Mo.-Kansas City, 1975. Sales rep. Aluminum Co. of Am., Chgo. and Kansas City, Mo., 1966-73; instr. Longview Community Coll., Lee's Summit, Mo., 1976-80; chief interpreter Watkins Woolen Mill State Hist. Site, Lawson, Mo., 1976-80; curator of edn. Dallas Hist. Soc., 1980-84; exec. dir. Longview Mus. and Arts Ctr., Tex., 1984—; cons. to local sch. dists. Mem. Hist. Landmark Preservation Commn., Plano, Tex., 1983-84; bd. dirs. Longview Arts Council, 1984. Mem. Am. Assn. Museums, Am. Assn. for State and Local History, Art Mus. Assn. Am., Mountain-Plains Mus. Assn., Nat. Trust for Hist. Preservation, Nat. Art Edn. Assn., NE Tex. Mus. Assn., Orgn. Am. Historians, Tex. Assn. Museums. Republican. Lodge: Rotary. Avocations: reading; gardening; model railroading. Home: 2000 Hughey Dr Longview TX 75601 Office: Longview Mus and Arts Ctr 102 W College St Longview TX 75601

ZUSMER, NOEL ROBERT, radiologist, educator; b. Bklyn., N.Y., Oct. 23, 1941; s. Harry and Charlotte (Friedman) Z.; m. Roxanne Hirsch, July 31, 1966; children—Todd, Dean, Lisa. B.S., U. Miami, 1963, M.D., 1967. Diplomate Am. Bd. Radiology. Intern Nassau County Med. Ctr., East Meadow, N.Y., 1967-68; resident in surgery Mt. Sinai Med. Ctr., Miami Beach, Fla., 1968-69, resident in radiobiology, 1971-74, co-dir. ultrasound, 1976-78, dir. ultrasound, 1978—, dir. Sch. Ultrasound Tech., 1978—, also program coordinator Comprehensive Breast Ctr.; chief resident in radiology U. Miami Sch. Medicine, Miami Beach, 1973, instr. radiology, 1973-78, asst. prof. radiology, 1978-83, assoc. prof., 1983—; cons. physician VA Med. Ctr., Miami, 1981—. Served as capt. M.C., USAF, 1969-71; Taiwan. Fellow Am. Coll. Chest Physicians; mem. Dade County Med. Soc., Am. Coll. Radiology, Fla. Radiol. Soc. (program chmn. 1981-82, chmn. com. continuing med. edn. 1981-82), AMA, Am. Inst. Ultrasound in Medicine (reviewer sci. papers 1981—), Phi Delta Epsilon. Club: Mt. Sinai Med. Ctr. Founders. Office: Mt Sinai Med Ct 4300 Alton Rd Miami Beach FL 33140

ZUSSMAN, BERNARD MAURICE, physician; b. N.Y.C., Apr. 26, 1906; s. Julius and Ida (Finkelstein) Z.; B.S., City U. N.Y., 1925; M.A., Columbia U., 1926; M.D., N.Y. U., 1930; m. Jane Erdman, Feb. 10, 1945. Intern, St. Mark's Hosp., N.Y.C., 1930-31, Coney Island Hosp., Bklyn., 1931-32; resident Montefiore Hosp. & Research Center, Bronx, and Mt. Sinai Hosp., N.Y.C., 1932; sr. clin. asst. medicine Beth Israel Hosp. & Research Center, 1932-41, adj. in medicine, 1933-41; practice internal medicine, N.Y.C., 1932-41; practice internal medicine specializing in allergy, Memphis, 1944—; sr. clin. prof. Dept. Medicine, U. Tenn. Center for Health Scis., Memphis; cons. Bapt. Meml. Hosp., USPHS Hosp., LeBonheur Children's Hosp., Meth. Hosp. Bd. dirs. Memphis Arts Council; trustee, regional co-chmn. Nat. Jewish Hosp./Nat. Asthma Center, Denver. Served to 1st lt. M.C., U.S. Army and Med. Reserve Corps, 1939-41, 41-44. Recipient Merit award Am. Coll. Allergists, 1977; Philanthropic Service award Nat. Jewish Hosp. and Research Center/Nat. Asthma Center, 1979; hon. fellow Truman Library Inst. Fellow Am. Acad. Allergy, Am. Coll. Allergists, Am. Geriatrics Assn.; mem. Am. Bd. Internal Medicine (diplomate), Am. Bd. Allergy and Immunology (diplomate), Royal Soc. Health, Internat. Assn. Allergology, N.Y. Acad. Sci., AAAS, Cert. Allergists Assn., N.Y. U. Alumni Assn. (pres. Memphis chpt.). Clubs: Petroleum, Ridgeway Country, Sertoma (dir., spl. award of merit 1981), Pres.'s of U. Tenn., Pres.'s of Memphis State U. Contbr. articles to profl. jours. Home: 321 Greenway Rd Memphis TN 38107 Office: 40 N Pauline St Memphis TN 38105

ZWECK-BRONNER, STANLEY LOUIS, JR., retail merchandising executive; b. Chatham, N.J., Oct. 9, 1936; s. Stanley Louis and Lorraine (Swing) Z-B.; m. Marilyn Ann Lochner, Jan. 30, 1960; children—Michael Swing, Stephen Browning. B.A. in Econs., Cornell U., 1959. Trainee, Lord & Taylor, N.Y.C., 1959-62; buyer Rich's Dept. Store, Atlanta, 1962-65, Selber Bros., Shreveport, La., 1965-67; v.p. gen. mdse. mgr. Hochschild Kohn, Balt., 1967-75, Stewart's Dept. Store, Balt., 1975-76; pres., chief exec. officer, Ivey's Fla. affiliate of BATUS Retail Group, BATUS, Inc., Orlando, Fla., 1976—. Trustee, Arts United Fund, Orlando, 1982—; bd. dirs. Fla. Citrus Sports Assn., Orlando, 1984—; mem. adv. bd. Coll. of Bus. U. Central Fla., Orlando, 1984—. Mem. Orlando Area C. of C. (bd. dirs.). Club: Winter Park Racquet (Fla.). Office: Ivey's Florida PO Box 19113 Orlando FL 32814

ZWEMER, THOMAS JOHN, dental educator; b. Mishawaka, Ind., Mar. 23, 1925; s. John Dewy and Ruth C. (Brooks) Z.; m. Betty Johnson, June 30, 1949; children—John Thomas, Stephen James, Carol Ann. Student Emmanuel Missionary Coll., 1939-43, Atlantic Union Coll., 1946; D.D.S., U. Ill., 1950; M.S., Northwestern U., 1954. Assoc. prof., dir. Marquette U., Milw., 1950-58; prof., chmn. dept. dentistry Loma Linda (Calif.) U., 1958-66; prof. Med. Coll. Ga., Augusta, 1966—, assoc. dean, 1966-84, v.p. for acad. affairs, 1984—; mem. Am. Bd. Orthodontics. Abstract editor Am. Jour. Orthodontics, 1985. Bd. dirs. Health Systems Agy., 1978. Served with U.S. Army, 1943-46. Mem. ADA, Ga. Dental Assn., Eastern Dist. Dental Soc., Am. Coll. Dentists, Internat. Coll. Dentists. Office: Dept Dentistry Med Coll Ga Augusta GA 30912

ZWERNER, ALLAN, department store executive; b. N.Y.C., Aug. 4, 1944; s. Leon and Ruth (Morrison) Z.; m. Renee Rochelle Grosman, June 25, 1967; children—Brian Scott, Michelle Ellen. B.B.A. in Mktg., Pace U., 1968. Trainee, buyer men's outerwear Gimbel's, N.Y.C., 1970-73; buyer Donaldson's, Mpls., 1973-75; buyer Burdine's, Miami, 1975-76, sr. v.p., 1982—; mdse. mgr. Jordan Marsh Co., Boston, 1976-80, v.p., 1980-82. Jewish. Office: Burdine's 22 E Flagler St Miami FL 33101

ZWIBEL, BURTON CHARLES, endodontist; b. Pitts., June 12, 1939; s. George and Harriet Delores (Olender) Z.; m. Lori Evelyn Talenfeld, June 25, 1961; children—Stuart A., Elizabeth A. D.M.D., U. Pitts., 1963. Pvt. practice endodontics, Falls Church and Alexandria, Va., 1965—; clin. assoc. prof. Georgetown U., Washington, 1970-79; mem. staffs Fairfax Hosp., Alexandria Hosp., Commonwealth Drs. Hosp., Potomac Hosp., Jefferson Meml. Hosp. Dep. sheriff Arlington County, Va., 1981—. Served to capt. U.S. Army, 1963-65. Fellow Va. Dental Assn., Am. Coll. Dentists; mem. ADA, Am. Assn. Endodontists, British Endodontic Soc., Va. Acad. Endodontists, Fairfax County Dental Soc., No. Va. Dental Soc. (pres. 1983—), Penick Endodontic Study Club, Alpha Omega, Omicron Kappa Upsilon, Zeta Beta Tau. Republican. Jewish. Lodges: Masons, Shriners. Contbr. articles to profl. jours. Home: 8951 Colesbury Pl Fairfax VA 22031 Office: Seven Corners Profl Bldg Falls Church VA 22044 also 123 S Fayette St Alexandria VA 22314

ZWICK, CHARLES JOHN, banker; b. Plantsville, Conn., July 17, 1926; s. Louis Christian and Mabel (Rich) Z.; B.S. in Agrl. Econs., U. Conn., 1950, M.S., 1951; Ph.D. in Econs., Harvard U., 1954; m. Joan Wallace Cameron, June 21, 1952; children—Robert Louis, Janet Ellen. Instr., U. Conn., 1951, Harvard U., 1954-56; head logistics dept. RAND Corp., 1956-63, mem. research council, 1963-65; asst. dir. U.S. Bur. Budget, 1965-68, dir., 1968-69; pres., dir. SE Banking Corp., Miami, 1969—; trustee Aerospace Corp.; dir. SE Bank N.A., Mastercard Internat., Inc., SE Mortgage Co., So. Bell Tel. & Tel. Co., Manville Corp.; trustee Rand Corp. Chmn., Pres.'s Commn. Mil. Compensation, 1977-78; trustee Com. for Econ. Devel.; mem. Controller Gen.'s Cons. Panel; mem. panel econ. advisors U.S. Congressional Budget Office; mem. council Internat. Exec. Service Corps; mem. Fla. Council 100; trustee Carnegie Endowment Internat. Peace, U. Miami, Brookings Instn.; trustee Eisenhower Found. Served with U.S. Army, 1946-47. Mem. Assn. Res. City Bankers, Conf. Bd., Greater Miami C. of C. Home: 4210 Santa Maria St Coral Gables FL 33146 Office: One Southeast Fin Ctr Miami FL 33131

ZWICK, PETER RONALD, political science educator; b. Bklyn., May 28, 1942; s. Jack Nathan and Anne Helen (Lubin) Z.; m. Shelly Kent Crittendon, July 6, 1963; B.A., Grinnell Coll., 1963; M.A., Duke U., 1967, Ph.D., 1971. Asst. prof. polit. sci. La. State U., Baton Rouge, 1968-80, assoc. prof., 1981—, chmn. dept., 1984—. Author: National Communism, 1983. Mem. Am. Polit. Sci. Assn., So. Polit. Sci. Assn. Home: 10209 Runnymede Ave Baton Rouge LA 70815 Office: Dept Polit Sci La State U Baton Rouge LA 70803

ZYCH, GREGORY, orthopedic surgeon, traumatologist; b. Berwyn, Ill., Feb. 19, 1950; s. Thaddeus F. and Loretta (Stec) Z.; m. Jacqueline M. Lopez, May 27, 1978; 1 child, Gabriela Marie. B.A. in Physiology, So. Ill. U., 1971; D.O., Chgo. Coll. Osteo. Medicine, 1975. Intern Detroit Osteo./Bi-County Hosps., 1975-76; resident in orthopedics and rehab., U. Miami Sch. Medicine, Fla., 1976-79, chief resident, 1979-80; asst. prof. orthopedics and rehab., chief orthopedic trauma, 1980—; instr. U. Colo. Sch. Medicine, Aspen, 1981; lectr. and workshop dir.; vis. prof. numerous univs. in U.S. and Europe. Contbr. articles to profl. jours. Fellow Am. Acad. Orthopedic Surgeons; mem. Miami Orthopedic Soc., Am. Trauma Soc., AAAS. Roman Catholic. Avocations: flying; photography. Office: Dept Orthopedics U Miami PO Box 016960 Miami FL 33101